PATTERSON'S

AMERICAN EDUCATION

2008 Edition

VOLUME CIV

Editorial Staff

Editor Wayne Moody

Assistant Editor Rita Ostdick

Assistant Editor James Thiessen

Assistant Editor Gloria Busch

EDUCATIONAL DIRECTORIES INC.

Educational Directories Inc.
PO Box 68097
Schaumburg IL 60168-0097
(847) 891-1250 or (800) 357-6183
www.ediusa.com

First edition published 1904. One Hundred Fourth edition 2008

ISBN 0-9771602-6-2
ISSN 0079-0230
Library of Congress Catalog Card Number: 04-012953
Printed in the United States of America

CONTENTS

HOW TO USE THIS DIRECTORY

Patterson's AMERICAN EDUCATION (published annually since 1904) is THE standard directory to secondary schools and is the first in a series of school directories published by Educational Directories Inc. Patterson's ELEMENTARY EDUCATION (published annually since 1989) is identical in format to Patterson's AMERICAN EDUCATION but is a directory to elementary schools; and Patterson's SCHOOLS CLASSIFIED (published annually since 1951) is the most comprehensive directory to post-secondary schools available. The three volumes combined fulfill the need for a single, systematized, comprehensive directory to our nation's schools from kindergarten through post-graduate studies.

Patterson's AMERICAN EDUCATION contains 10,904 public school districts, 30,828 public secondary schools, 6,373 private and Catholic secondary schools and more than 7,000 post-secondary schools in an easy-to-use and consistent format. It is an invaluable resource for anyone involved in education or educational research. School registrars, guidance counselors, principals, superintendents, directors of admissions, financial aid officers, schools of education, public libraries, government agencies, armed forces, and business people find it a welcome replacement for the multitude of other directories required for national coverage of our nation's school systems with their variation in size, content, format and publishing date.

One of the primary objectives of this directory is to make available the latest, most comprehensive information about secondary and post-secondary schools in a condensed and easily accessible format. Its general organization is geographical. Entries are arranged alphabetically, by state, then by community (post office) and then by District and School name. Each state begins with a listing of the officials in its Department of Education followed by the head of the State Board of Education. If a state has intermediate superintendents (a level of superintendent between the state superintendent of schools and the superintendents who actually supervise the schools) they appear in a table preceding the community listings. Community listings follow and include the community name, county name, community population, district name, total district student enrollment, the superintendent's name, address, telephone, fax number and website where available followed by a listing of the district schools, showing their enrollment, grade range and the principal's name, address, telephone number and fax number. A district may be responsible for schools in more than one community. To achieve consistency, the district office is listed in the community in which it is located. A cross-reference is provided to and from the schools of the district located in other communities.

A short line may appear at the end of the listing of public secondary schools. This line separates the public secondary schools from the private and Catholic secondary schools and the post-secondary schools located in the community. Private and Catholic school listings include their enrollment, grade range and the principal's name, address, telephone number and fax number. Post-secondary school listings include their name, address and telephone number. Please refer to page vi, "Guide to Editorial Style," for an example of how these elements work together to provide an easy-to-use format.

Schools Listed

Patterson's AMERICAN EDUCATION lists the following types of schools

- **Middle Schools** usually teach any combination of grades five through eight.
- **Junior High Schools** usually teach grades seven through nine.
- **Junior-Senior High Schools** usually teach any combination of grades five through eight and include nine through twelve.
- **High Schools** usually teach grades nine through twelve or ten through twelve.
- **K-12 Schools**
- **Vocational-Technical Schools**

The following are included:

- All graded state approved public secondary schools.
- All graded secondary schools belonging to the National Catholic Education Association.
- All graded, regionally accredited, private secondary schools.
- Private secondary schools belonging to the member associations of the Council of American Private Education.

Non graded, special education schools and other non-traditional secondary schools are not listed.

Patterson's ELEMENTARY EDUCATION lists Kindergarten Schools, Primary Schools, Elementary Schools, Middle Schools and K-12 Schools.

ABBREVIATIONS

AVC. . . Area Vocational Center
AVTS . . Area Vocational Technical School
CCSD . . Community Consolidated School District
CDC . . Child Development Center
CESD . . Consolidated Elementary School District
CISD . . City Independent School District
CSD. . . City School District
CUSD . . Community Unit School District
ECC. . . Early Childhood Center
ECCSD . Elementary Community Consolidated School District
EHSD . . Elementary-High School District
ES . . . Elementary School
ESD. . . Elementary School District
EVD. . . Exempted Village District
HS . . . High School
HSD. . . High School District
IS. . . . Intermediate School
ISD . . . Independent School District
JESD . . Joint Elementary School District
JHS . . . Junior High School
JSD . . . Joint School District
JSHS . . Junior-Senior High School
JUESD . Joint Unified Elementary School District
JUHSD . Joint Unified High School District
JUNESD Joint Union Elementary School District
JUNHSD Joint Union High School District
JUSD . . Joint Unified School District
JVSD . . Joint Vocational School District
K . . . . Kindergarten
MS . . . Middle School
MSHS. . Middle School High School
PS . . . Primary School
RHSD. . Rural High School District
RISD . . Rural Independent School District
ROC . . Regional Occupational Center
ROP . . Regional Occupational Program
RSD. . . Reorganized School District
S . . . . School
SAD. . . School Administrative District
SC . . . School Corporation
SD . . . School District
SHS. . . Senior High School
SSD. . . Separate School District
UESD . . Unified Elementary School District
UFD. . . Union Free District
UHSD. . Unified High School District
UNESD . Union Elementary School District
UNHSD . Union High School District
UNSD. . Union School District
USD. . . Unified School District
Vo/Tech. Vocational/Technical

GUIDE TO EDITORIAL STYLE

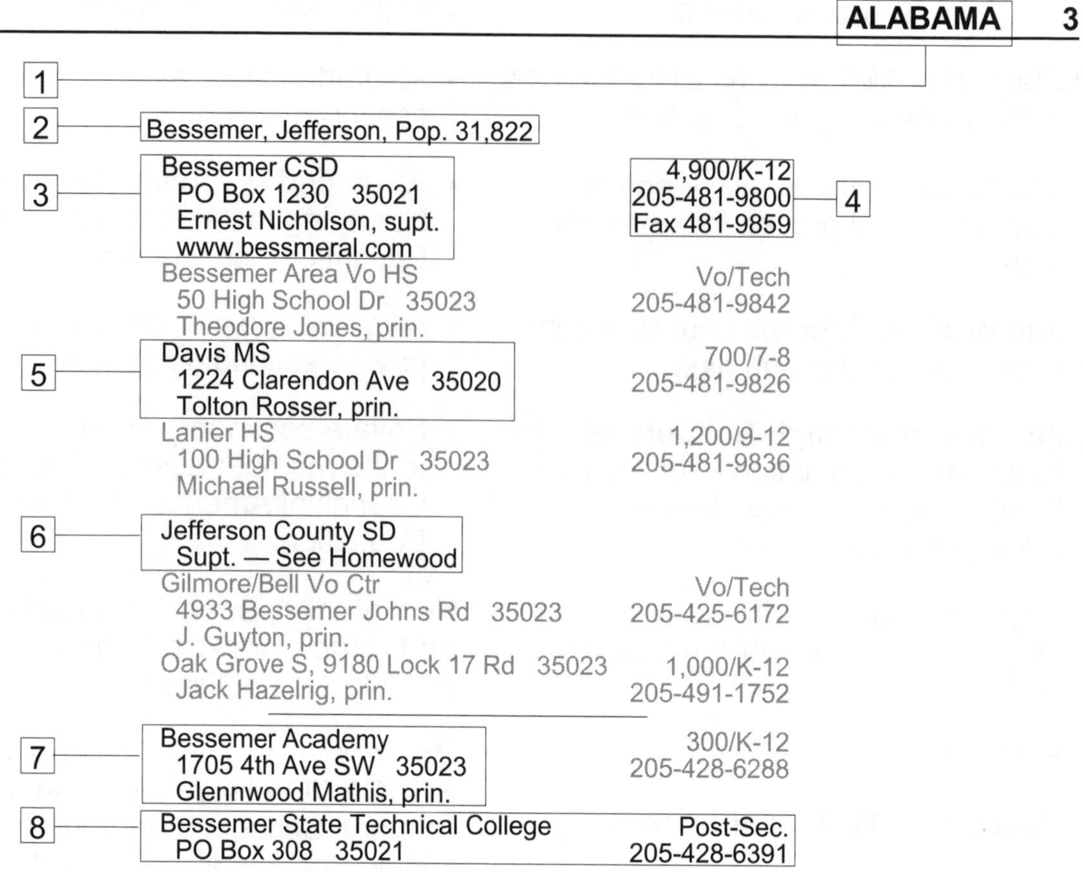

1. State.
2. City, county and city population.
3. Community school districts - school district name (refer to page v for abbreviations), address, superintendent's name and website (please enter as shown to access districts website).
4. Enrollment, grade range and phone number (fax number is included where available).
5. Community schools - school name, address and principal's name.
6. If the school district office is not located in this city, a cross-reference will show office location.
7. Private and Catholic secondary schools appear below a short line in the cities where they are located.
8. Post-secondary schools also appear below the line in the cities where they are located.

SECONDARY SCHOOL COUNTS BY STATE

	Public								
State	Districts	5-9	7-12	9-12	10-12	K-12	Private	Catholic	Total
Alabama	132	223	91	192	8	79	102	10	837
Alaska	54	34	16	35	0	181	15	2	337
Arizona	111	209	8	180	5	4	38	13	568
Arkansas	246	161	139	90	51	2	33	7	729
California	415	1,245	44	934	9	7	623	124	3,401
Colorado	178	264	67	214	4	6	70	10	813
Connecticut	122	170	9	148	1	1	52	26	529
Delaware	16	31	1	23	0	0	34	8	113
District Of Columbia	1	19	0	13	0	0	11	9	53
Florida	67	525	40	353	6	13	457	36	1,497
Georgia	176	441	18	325	6	6	200	12	1,184
Hawaii	1	36	6	33	0	6	37	7	126
Idaho	108	95	36	70	15	12	25	1	362
Illinois	489	706	48	613	21	0	133	81	2,091
Indiana	292	312	102	242	4	4	91	24	1,071
Iowa	342	265	109	239	8	0	27	32	1,022
Kansas	290	229	93	232	8	0	31	19	902
Kentucky	170	224	27	203	1	5	51	28	709
Louisiana	69	207	62	171	4	64	81	53	711
Maine	118	97	14	96	1	9	36	5	376
Maryland	24	234	7	190	2	3	111	38	609
Massachusetts	227	288	42	221	1	2	92	55	928
Michigan	521	563	81	474	22	27	198	53	1,939
Minnesota	328	218	185	162	20	10	59	32	1,014
Mississippi	148	155	56	137	7	42	80	9	634
Missouri	447	336	198	287	13	2	68	48	1,399
Montana	160	214	0	166	1	0	12	6	559
Nebraska	254	107	170	100	4	0	13	30	678
Nevada	16	90	12	65	5	6	22	2	218
New Hampshire	76	84	2	75	0	2	38	7	284
New Jersey	267	393	35	286	10	0	114	70	1,175
New Mexico	89	135	21	89	7	0	41	3	385
New York	646	778	236	706	19	74	359	138	2,956
North Carolina	115	446	12	390	7	5	207	4	1,186
North Dakota	157	37	117	41	4	1	7	5	369
Ohio	611	615	129	597	11	2	122	85	2,172
Oklahoma	430	280	23	379	53	2	36	4	1,207
Oregon	177	200	34	177	3	23	70	11	695
Pennsylvania	498	498	168	385	38	1	256	89	1,933
Rhode Island	32	50	1	48	0	1	19	10	161
South Carolina	85	233	18	168	7	2	99	4	616
South Dakota	158	164	1	159	0	1	11	7	501
Tennessee	119	294	43	233	5	20	94	12	820
Texas	970	1,351	155	969	55	110	278	56	3,944
Utah	40	125	22	32	53	2	48	4	326
Vermont	52	28	21	27	1	10	21	2	162
Virginia	132	328	39	283	15	2	127	15	941
Washington	247	344	46	242	30	23	110	14	1,056
West Virginia	55	123	19	92	5	2	34	8	338
Wisconsin	380	343	64	343	6	11	93	55	1,295
Wyoming	46	56	10	46	6	6	2	2	174
Total	10,904	14,603	2,897	11,975	562	791	4,988	1,385	48,105

Part I

SECONDARY SCHOOLS

ALABAMA

ALABAMA DEPARTMENT OF EDUCATION
50 N Ripley St, Montgomery 36130-1001
Telephone 334-242-9700
Fax 334-242-9708
Website http://www.alsde.edu

State Superintendent of Education Joseph Morton

ALABAMA BOARD OF EDUCATION
50 N Ripley St, Montgomery 36130-1001

President Governor Bob Riley

PUBLIC, PRIVATE AND CATHOLIC SECONDARY SCHOOLS

Abbeville, Henry, Pop. 2,963
Henry County SD 2,700/K-12
PO Box 635 36310 334-585-2206
Dennis Coe, supt. Fax 585-2551
www.henrycountyboe.org/
Abbeville HS 400/9-12
411 Graball Cutoff 36310 334-585-2065
Dale Barnes, prin. Fax 585-6562
Abbeville MS 300/6-8
PO Box 547 36310 334-585-2185
Larry Calloway, prin. Fax 585-1492
Other Schools – See Headland

Abbeville Christian Academy 200/K-12
PO Box 9 36310 334-585-5100
Barbara Lindsey, prin. Fax 585-5100

Adamsville, Jefferson, Pop. 4,845
Jefferson County SD
Supt. — See Birmingham
Bottonfield MS 1,000/6-8
400 Hillcrest Rd 35005 205-379-2550
Dr. Jennifer Maye, prin. Fax 379-2553
Minor HS 1,400/9-12
2285 Minor Pkwy 35005 205-379-4750
David Pike, prin. Fax 379-4795

Addison, Winston, Pop. 713
Winston County SD
Supt. — See Double Springs
Addison HS 300/7-12
PO Box 240 35540 256-747-2286
Olen Bolzle, prin. Fax 747-6410

Akron, Hale, Pop. 514
Hale County SD
Supt. — See Greensboro
Akron Community HS East 200/7-12
PO Box 38 35441 205-372-3787
Fredrica Jimerson, prin. Fax 372-3782

Alabaster, Shelby, Pop. 27,517
Shelby County SD
Supt. — See Columbiana
Thompson HS 1,400/9-12
100 Warrior Dr 35007 205-682-5700
Robin Thomas, prin. Fax 682-5705
Thompson MS 1,300/6-8
1509 Kent Dairy Rd 35007 205-682-5710
Nicke Gaspers, prin. Fax 682-5715

Kingwood Christian S 400/PK-12
1351 Royalty Dr 35007 205-663-3973
Benny Cunningham, hdmstr. Fax 663-7145

Albertville, Marshall, Pop. 18,615
Albertville CSD 3,700/PK-12
107 W Main St 35950 256-891-1183
Smiley Veal, supt. Fax 891-6303
www.albertk12.org
Alabama Avenue MS 600/7-8
600 E Alabama Ave 35950 256-878-2341
Darryl Cooper, prin. Fax 891-6334
Albertville HS 900/9-12
402 E Mccord Ave 35950 256-878-6580
Paul McAbee, prin. Fax 891-6305

Marshall County SD
Supt. — See Guntersville
Asbury S 700/K-12
1990 Asbury Rd 35951 256-878-4068
Susan Collins, prin. Fax 878-5233

Alexander City, Tallapoosa, Pop. 14,957
Alexander City SD 3,500/K-12
375 Lee St 35010 256-234-5074
Dr. Thomas R. Bice, supt. Fax 234-8649
www.alex.k12.al.us
Alexander City MS 600/7-8
359 State St 35010 256-234-8660
Tracy McGhee, prin. Fax 234-8659
Russell HS 1,000/9-12
225 Heard Blvd 35010 256-234-8611
Jim Davidson, prin. Fax 234-8680

Central Alabama Community College Post-Sec.
PO Box 699 35011 256-234-6346

Alexandria, Calhoun
Calhoun County SD
Supt. — See Anniston
Alexandria HS 1,100/6-12
PO Box 180 36250 256-741-4400
Ronald Chambless, prin. Fax 820-7161

Aliceville, Pickens, Pop. 2,465
Pickens County SD
Supt. — See Carrollton
Aliceville JSHS 500/7-12
417 3rd St SE 35442 205-373-6378
Minnie Washington, prin. Fax 373-6730

Alpine, Talladega
Talladega County SD
Supt. — See Talladega
Winterboro HS 400/5-12
22601 AL Highway 21 35014 256-315-5370
Vicky Ozment, prin. Fax 315-5380

Andalusia, Covington, Pop. 8,691
Andalusia CSD 1,600/K-12
122 6th Ave 36420 334-222-3186
Dr. Beverly McAnulty, supt. Fax 222-8631
andalusia.al.schoolwebpages.com
Andalusia HS 500/9-12
701 3rd St 36420 334-222-7569
Dr. Daniel Shakespeare, prin. Fax 222-5834
Andalusia MS 400/6-8
1201 C C Baker Ave, 334-222-6542
Ted Watson, prin. Fax 222-3875

Covington County SD 3,000/K-12
PO Box 460 36420 334-222-7571
Sharon Dye, supt. Fax 222-7573
www.cov.k12.al.us/
Pleasant Home S 600/K-12
12548 Falco Rd 36420 334-222-1315
James Garner, prin. Fax 222-4415
Straughn HS 400/9-12
29448 Straughn School Rd, 334-222-2511
John Thomasson, prin. Fax 222-4010
Straughn MS 100/6-8
29324 Straughn School Rd, 334-222-4090
Shannon Driver, prin. Fax 222-4132
Other Schools – See Florala, Red Level

Lurleen B. Wallace Community College Post-Sec.
PO Box 1418 36420 334-222-6591

Anniston, Calhoun, Pop. 23,741
Anniston CSD 2,600/K-12
PO Box 1500 36202 256-231-5000
Dr. Sammy Felton, supt. Fax 231-5073
www.annistonschools.com/
Anniston HS 600/9-12
1301 Woodstock Ave 36207 256-231-5010
George Jordan, prin. Fax 231-5069
Anniston MS 600/6-8
4800 Mcclellan Blvd 36206 256-231-5020
Lywood Hawkins, prin. Fax 231-5024

Calhoun County SD 8,100/K-12
PO Box 2084 36202 256-741-7400
Judy Stiefel Ed.D., supt. Fax 237-5332
www.calhoun.k12.al.us
Saks HS 600/8-12
4401 Saks Rd 36206 256-741-7000
Jody Whaley, prin. Fax 236-5121
Wellborn HS 700/7-12
135 Pinson Rd 36201 256-741-7600
Charles E. Whatley, prin. Fax 237-7071
White Plains HS 400/7-12
250 White Plains Rd 36207 256-741-7800
Davine Miller, prin. Fax 237-3301
Other Schools – See Alexandria, Jacksonville, Ohatchee, Weaver

---

Donoho S 400/PK-12
2501 Henry Rd 36207 256-237-5477
Janice Hurd, hdmstr. Fax 237-6474
Faith Christian S 300/K-12
4100 Ronnaki Rd 36207 256-236-4499
Dr. Ben Character, hdmstr. Fax 236-4673
Gadsden Business College Post-Sec.
1809 Hillyer Robinson Pky 36207 256-831-3838
Gadsden State Community College Post-Sec.
1801 Coleman Rd 36207 256-835-5400

Sacred Heart S 200/PK-12
16 Morton Rd 36205 256-237-4231
Charlie Maniscalco, prin. Fax 237-2353

Arab, Marshall, Pop. 7,498
Arab CSD 2,600/PK-12
750 Arabian Dr NE 35016 256-586-6011
John Mullins, supt. Fax 586-6013
www.arabcityschools.org
Arab HS 900/9-12
511 Arabian Dr NE 35016 256-586-6026
Patrick Crowder, prin. Fax 586-1948
Arab JHS 600/6-8
911 Old Cullman Rd SW 35016 256-586-6074
John Ingram, prin. Fax 586-1348

Ardmore, Limestone, Pop. 1,106
Limestone County SD
Supt. — See Athens
Ardmore HS 900/6-12
30285 Ardmore Ave 35739 256-423-2685
Mike Owens, prin. Fax 423-4991

Ariton, Dale, Pop. 755
Dale County SD
Supt. — See Ozark
Ariton S 700/K-12
PO Box 750 36311 334-762-2371
Frank Brown, prin. Fax 762-2126

Arley, Winston, Pop. 321
Winston County SD
Supt. — See Double Springs
Meek HS 300/7-12
6615 County Road 41 35541 205-384-5825
Danny Stallings, prin. Fax 384-6825

Ashford, Houston, Pop. 1,932
Houston County SD
Supt. — See Dothan
Ashford JSHS 800/7-12
607 Church St 36312 334-899-5411
James Odom, prin. Fax 899-7450
Houston County AVC Vo/Tech
PO Box 3005 36312 334-899-3308
Glenn Maloy, prin. Fax 899-8854

Ashford Academy 200/K-12
1100 N Broadway St 36312 334-899-3286
David Griggs, prin. Fax 899-7503

Ashland, Clay, Pop. 1,885
Clay County SD 2,100/K-12
PO Box 278 36251 256-354-5414
Ben H. Griffin, supt. Fax 354-5415
Clay County HS 500/7-12
220 3rd St SW 36251 256-354-7510
Anthony Wilkinson, prin. Fax 354-7511
Other Schools – See Lineville

Ashville, Saint Clair, Pop. 2,429
Saint Clair County SD 7,500/PK-12
33205 US Highway 231 35953 205-594-7131
Tom Sanders, supt. Fax 594-4441
www.stclaircountyschools.net
Ashville HS 400/9-12
33215 US Highway 231 35953 205-594-7943
Jody Whaley, prin. Fax 594-4349
Ashville MS 400/5-8
PO Box 340 35953 205-594-7044
Phillip Johnson, prin. Fax 594-2241
Eden Career-Technical Center Vo/Tech
45 County Road 33 35953 205-594-7055
James King, dir. Fax 594-4124
Other Schools – See Moody, Odenville, Ragland, Springville

Athens, Limestone, Pop. 20,972
Athens CSD 2,800/K-12
313 E Washington St 35611 256-233-6600
Dr. Orman Bridges, supt. Fax 233-6640
www.acs-k12.org
Athens HS 800/9-12
PO Box 109 35612 256-233-6613
Chris Bolen, prin. Fax 233-6617
Athens MS 500/7-8
601 S Clinton St 35611 256-233-6620
Joe Jackson, prin. Fax 233-6623

Limestone County SD 8,200/K-12
300 S Jefferson St 35611 256-232-5353
Barry L. Carroll Ed.D., supt. Fax 233-6461
www.lcsk12.org
Clements S 1,100/K-12
7730 US Highway 72 35611 256-729-6564
Donald Wilson, prin. Fax 729-1029
East Limestone S 900/6-12
15641 E Limestone Rd 35613 256-233-6660
Dennis Black, prin. Fax 230-9366
Limestone Co. Career Technical Center Vo/Tech
505 E Sanderfer Rd 35611 256-233-6463
Charlotte Craig, prin. Fax 233-6667
Other Schools – See Ardmore, Elkmont, Lester, Tanner

Athens Bible S 300/K-12
507 Hoffman St 35611 256-232-3525
Joseph Olson, prin. Fax 232-5417
Athens State University Post-Sec.
300 N Beaty St 35611 256-233-8100
Faith Christian Academy 200/PK-12
705 W Sanderfer Rd 35611 256-233-3778
Wayne Forsythe, admin.

Atmore, Escambia, Pop. 7,530
Escambia County SD
Supt. — See Brewton
Escambia County HS 600/9-12
1215 S Presley St 36502 251-368-9181
Fax 368-0674
Escambia County MS 700/5-8
PO Box 1236 36504 251-368-9105
Zickeyous Byrd, prin. Fax 368-0969

Escambia Academy 200/K-12
268 Cowpen Creek Rd 36502 251-368-2080
Leon Hartley, hdmstr. Fax 368-1950
Jefferson Davis Community College Post-Sec.
PO Box 1119 36504 251-368-8118

Attalla, Etowah, Pop. 6,474
Attalla CSD 1,800/PK-12
101 Case Ave SE 35954 256-538-8051
Danny Golden, supt. Fax 538-8388
www.attalla.k12.al.us
Etowah HS 700/9-12
201 Case Ave SE 35954 256-538-8381
John Serafini, prin. Fax 538-2136
Etowah MS 500/6-8
429 4th St SW 35954 256-538-3236
Jerald Cardin, prin. Fax 538-3232

Etowah County SD
Supt. — See Gadsden
Career Technical Center Vo/Tech
105 Burke Ave SE 35954 256-538-3312
Herman McMurtrey, dir. Fax 538-1090

Auburn, Lee, Pop. 49,928
Auburn CSD 5,000/K-12
PO Box 3270 36831 334-887-2100
Dr. J. Terry Jenkins, supt. Fax 887-2107
auburnschools.org
Auburn HS 1,000/10-12
405 S Dean Rd 36830 334-887-4970
Dr. Cathy Long, prin. Fax 887-4177
Auburn JHS 700/8-9
332 E Samford Ave 36830 334-887-1960
Jason Wright, prin. Fax 887-4160

Auburn University 36849 Post-Sec.
334-844-4000
Lee-Scott Academy 700/PK-12
1601 Academy Dr 36830 334-821-2430
Don Roberts, hdmstr. Fax 821-0876

Autaugaville, Autauga, Pop. 865
Autauga County SD
Supt. — See Prattville
Autaugaville S 400/K-12
PO Box 99 36003 334-365-8329
John Clay, prin. Fax 365-8043

Bay Minette, Baldwin, Pop. 7,808
Baldwin County SD 23,800/K-12
2600 Hand Ave 36507 251-937-0306
Faron Hollinger Ed.D., supt. Fax 937-0318
www.bcbe.org
Baldwin County HS 1,200/9-12
1 Tiger Dr 36507 251-937-2341
Eddie Mitchell, prin. Fax 937-2933
Bay Minette MS 600/7-8
1311 W 13th St 36507 251-937-9243
Tammie Fleming, prin. Fax 937-3721
North Baldwin Center for Tech Vo/Tech
505 W Hurricane Rd 36507 251-937-6751
John Cabaniss, prin. Fax 937-4688
Other Schools – See Daphne, Elberta, Fairhope, Foley, Gulf Shores, Robertsdale, Spanish Fort

---

James H. Faulkner State Comm. College Post-Sec.
1900 S US Highway 31 36507 251-580-2100

Bayou La Batre, Mobile, Pop. 2,725
Mobile County SD
Supt. — See Mobile
Alba MS 600/6-8
14180 S Wintzell Ave 36509 251-824-4134
James Gill, prin. Fax 824-1324

Bear Creek, Marion, Pop. 1,021
Marion County SD
Supt. — See Hamilton
Phillips HS 300/7-12
142 School Ave 35543 205-486-3737
Lynda Hall, prin. Fax 486-1716

Beatrice, Monroe, Pop. 403
Monroe County SD
Supt. — See Monroeville
Shields HS 200/7-12
17688 Highway 21 N 36425 251-789-2168
Marion McIntosh, prin. Fax 789-2715

Berry, Fayette, Pop. 1,226
Fayette County SD
Supt. — See Fayette
Berry JSHS 300/7-12
18242 Highway 18 E 35546 205-689-4467
Vic Herren, prin. Fax 689-8819

Bessemer, Jefferson, Pop. 28,641
Bessemer CSD 4,100/K-12
PO Box 1230 35021 205-432-3000
Deborah Horn Ed.D., supt. Fax 432-3085
www.bessk12.org
Bessemer Center for Technology Vo/Tech
50 High School Dr 35022 205-432-3798
Dr. Keith Mahaffey, prin. Fax 432-3811
Davis MS 800/6-8
1224 Clarendon Ave 35020 205-432-3600
Albert Soles, prin. Fax 432-3607
Lanier HS 1,000/9-12
100 High School Dr 35022 205-432-3700
Jerome Cook, prin. Fax 432-3791

Jefferson County SD
Supt. — See Birmingham
Oak Grove HS 900/6-12
9494 Oak Grove Pkwy 35023 205-379-5000
Alan Pruden, prin. Fax 379-5045

Bessemer State Technical College Post-Sec.
PO Box 308 35021 205-426-7389
ITT Technical Institute Post-Sec.
6270 Park South Dr 35022 205-497-5700
Rock Creek Academy 50/PK-12
901 Glaze Dr 35023 205-436-3757
Tammy Hope, admin.

Billingsley, Autauga, Pop. 121
Autauga County SD
Supt. — See Prattville
Billingsley S 800/K-12
PO Box 118 36006 205-755-1629
Van Smith, prin. Fax 755-1633

Birmingham, Jefferson, Pop. 231,483
Alabama Fine Arts SD 300/7-12
1800 8th Ave N 35203 205-252-9241
John Northrop, dir. Fax 251-9541
Alabama Fine Arts JSHS 300/7-12
1800 8th Ave N 35203 205-252-9241
John Northrop, dir. Fax 251-9541

Birmingham CSD 30,900/K-12
PO Box 10007 35202 205-231-4600
Dr. Stan Mims, supt. Fax 231-4761
www.bhm.k12.al.us
Arrington MS 400/6-8
2101 Jefferson Ave SW 35211 205-231-1130
Sherene Carpenter, prin. Fax 231-1133
Banks MS 500/6-8
721 86th St S 35206 205-231-5190
Jessie Daniel, prin. Fax 231-5218
Bush Magnet MS 600/6-8
1112 25th Street Ensley 35218 205-231-6000
Aurlinda Hagler, prin. Fax 231-6007
Carver HS 1,200/9-12
3900 24th St N 35207 205-231-3900
Darrell Hudson, prin. Fax 231-3973
Center Street MS 500/6-8
1832 Center Way S 35205 205-231-7187
Cassandra Fincher Fells, prin. Fax 231-7231
Gaskins MS 500/6-8
200 Dalton Dr 35215 205-231-9200
Millard Hicks, prin. Fax 231-9253
Glenn MS 300/6-8
901 16th St W 35208 205-231-6370
Dr. Cleo Larry, prin. Fax 231-6954
Green Acres MS 500/6-8
1220 67th St W 35228 205-231-1370
Evelyn Baugh, prin. Fax 231-1414
Hayes HS 800/9-11
505 43rd St N 35222 205-231-8440
Fred Stewart, prin. Fax 231-8939
Huffman Magnet HS 1,300/9-12
950 Springville Rd 35215 205-231-5000
Willie Goldsmith, prin. Fax 231-5056
Huffman Magnet MS 400/6-8
517 Huffman Rd 35215 205-231-5370
Milton Hopkins, prin. Fax 231-5426
Jackson-Olin HS 600/9-12
510 12th Street Ensley 35218 205-231-6431
Linda Parson, prin. Fax 231-6527
Kirby MS 300/6-8
1328 28th St N 35234 205-231-3370
Ponzella Fuller, prin. Fax 231-3414
Parker HS 1,100/9-12
900 4th St N 35204 205-231-2370
Joseph Martin, prin. Fax 231-2916
Payne MS 300/6-8
1500 Daniel Payne Dr 35214 205-231-3190
Eddie Cauthen, prin. Fax 231-3236
Putnam Magnet MS 300/6-8
1757 Montclair Rd 35210 205-231-8680
Michael Scott, prin. Fax 231-8685
Smith MS 400/6-8
1124 Five Mile Rd 35215 205-231-5675
Charles Willis, prin. Fax 231-5899
Wenonah HS 800/9-12
2916 Wilson Rd SW 35221 205-231-1675
Regina Carr Hunter, prin. Fax 231-1921
West End HS 800/9-12
1840 Pearson Ave SW 35211 205-231-1740
Allen Lewis, prin. Fax 231-1976
Wilkerson MS 400/6-8
116 11th Ct N 35204 205-231-2740
Constance Burns, prin. Fax 231-2790
Woodlawn Magnet HS 700/9-12
5620 1st Ave N 35212 205-231-8000
Shirley Graham, prin. Fax 231-8084

Hoover CSD
Supt. — See Hoover
Berry MS 1,000/6-8
4500 Jaguar Dr 35242 205-439-2000
Dr. Kathleen Wheaton, prin. Fax 439-2001

Spain Park HS 1,400/9-12
4700 Jaguar Dr 35242 205-439-1400
Billy Broadway, prin. Fax 439-1401

Jefferson County SD 35,400/K-12
2100 18th St S 35209 205-379-2000
Dr. Phil Hammonds, supt. Fax 379-2311
www.jefcoed.com/
Erwin JSHS 1,100/7-12
532 23rd Ave NW 35215 205-379-3400
Van Phillips, prin. Fax 856-6663
Fultondale JSHS 500/7-12
1450 Carson Rd N 35217 205-379-3500
Donna Williamon, prin. Fax 379-3545
Gresham MS 500/6-8
2650 Gresham Dr 35243 205-379-3800
Margaret McCullough, prin. Fax 379-3845
Shades Valley Technical Academy Vo/Tech
5191 Pine Whispers Dr 35210 205-379-3300
Zsolt Batizy, prin. Fax 951-1347
Other Schools – See Adamsville, Bessemer, Gardendale, Hueytown, Irondale, Kimberly, Mc Calla, Morris, Pinson, Pleasant Grove, Trussville, Warrior

Shelby County SD
Supt. — See Columbiana
Oak Mountain HS 1,700/9-12
5476 Caldwell Mill Rd 35242 205-682-5200
Fax 682-5205
Oak Mountain MS 1,200/6-8
5650 Cahaba Valley Rd 35242 205-682-5210
Larry Haynes, prin. Fax 682-5215
Riverchase MS 1,100/6-8
853 Willow Oak Dr 35244 205-682-5510
Charles Smith, prin. Fax 682-5515

Tarrant CSD
Supt. — See Tarrant
Tarrant City MS 500/5-8
1 Wildcat Dr 35217 205-849-0168
Judy Matthews, prin. Fax 849-3728

Alabama State College of Barber Styling Post-Sec.
9480 Parkway E 35215 205-836-2404
Altamont S 400/5-12
PO Box 131429 35213 205-879-2006
Thomas M.S. Wheelock, prin. Fax 871-5666
American Sentinel University Post-Sec.
2101 Magnolia Ave S Ste 200 35205 205-323-6191
Andrew Jackson University Post-Sec.
2919 John Hawkins Pkwy 35244 205-871-9288
Birmingham-Southern College Post-Sec.
900 Arkadelphia Rd 35254 800-523-5793
Briarwood Christian S 1,800/PK-12
2204 Briarwood Way 35243 205-776-5800
Dr. Barrett Mosbacker, supt. Fax 776-5815
Carraway Methodist Medical Center Post-Sec.
1600 Carraway Blvd 35234 205-226-6000
Carroll HS 700/9-12
300 Lakeshore Pkwy 35209 205-940-2400
David Chauvette, prin. Fax 945-7429
Central Park Christian S 200/K-12
1900 43rd St W 35208 205-786-4811
Dr. Levan Parker, hdmstr. Fax 786-0140
Ephesus Junior Academy 200/K-12
829 McMillon Ave SW 35211 205-786-2194
Vernon Norman, prin. Fax 786-0857
Holy Family HS 200/9-12
2001 19th Street Ensley 35218 205-787-9937
Zan Raynor, prin. Fax 787-8530
Jefferson State Community College Post-Sec.
2601 Carson Rd 35215 205-853-1200
Lawson State Community College Post-Sec.
3060 Wilson Rd SW 35221 205-925-2515
Miles College Post-Sec.
PO Box 3800 35208 205-929-1000
Parkway Christian Academy 400/PK-12
959 Huffman Rd 35215 205-833-2410
Rachel Howze, prin. Fax 833-4692
Samford University Post-Sec.
800 Lakeshore Dr 35229 205-726-3673
Southeastern Bible College Post-Sec.
2545 Valleydale Rd 35244 205-970-9200
Strayer University Post-Sec.
3570 Grandview Pkwy 35243 205-453-6300
University of Alabama at Birmingham Post-Sec.
Univ Sta 35294 205-934-4011
University of Alabama Hospital Post-Sec.
619 19th St S 35249 205-934-5490
Virginia College Post-Sec.
65 Bagby Dr 35209 205-802-1200

Blountsville, Blount, Pop. 1,923
Blount County SD
Supt. — See Oneonta
Moore HS 500/7-12
4040 Susan Moore Rd 35031 205-466-7663
Clay Daughtry, prin. Fax 466-7858
Pennington HS 500/7-12
81 College St 35031 205-429-4101
Craig Sosebee, prin. Fax 429-4104

Boaz, Marshall, Pop. 7,893
Boaz CSD 2,100/K-12
PO Box 721 35957 256-593-8180
Leland Dishman, supt. Fax 593-8181
www.boazk12.org/
Boaz HS 500/9-12
907 Brown St 35957 256-593-2401
Lowell Smith, prin. Fax 593-2403
Boaz MS 500/6-8
140 Newt Parker Dr 35957 256-593-0799
Ray Landers, prin. Fax 593-0729

Snead State Community College Post-Sec.
Walnut St 35957 256-593-5120

Brantley, Crenshaw, Pop. 909
Crenshaw County SD
Supt. — See Luverne
Brantley S 600/PK-12
PO Box 86 36009 334-527-8879
Anthony Stallworth, prin. Fax 527-3405

Bremen, Cullman
Cullman County SD
Supt. — See Cullman
Cold Springs HS 400/7-12
PO Box 130 35033 256-287-1787
William Calvert, prin. Fax 287-2841

Brewton, Escambia, Pop. 5,373
Brewton CSD 1,400/K-12
811 Belleville Ave 36426 251-867-8400
Lynn Smith, supt. Fax 867-8403
www.brewtoncityschools.org/
Brewton MS 400/5-8
301 Liles Blvd 36426 251-867-8420
Douglas Prater, prin. Fax 867-8422
Miller HS 400/9-12
1835 Douglas Ave 36426 251-867-8430
Donald Rotch, prin. Fax 867-8432

Escambia County SD 4,500/K-12
PO Box 307 36427 251-867-6251
William Hines, supt. Fax 867-6252
www.escambiak12.net
Escambia-Brewton Area Career/Tech Center Vo/Tech
2824 Pea Ridge Rd 36426 251-867-7829
Jane Henderson, prin. Fax 867-7064
Other Schools – See Atmore, East Brewton, Flomaton

Jefferson Davis Community College Post-Sec.
PO Box 958 36427 251-867-4832

Bridgeport, Jackson, Pop. 2,693
Jackson County SD
Supt. — See Scottsboro
Bridgeport MS 200/5-8
620 Jacobs Ave 35740 256-495-2967
Darrell Kirk, prin. Fax 495-2850

Brilliant, Marion, Pop. 733
Marion County SD
Supt. — See Hamilton
Brilliant HS 200/7-12
PO Box 90 35548 205-465-2322
Jack Hayes, prin. Fax 465-2382

Brookwood, Tuscaloosa, Pop. 1,466
Tuscaloosa County SD
Supt. — See Tuscaloosa
Brookwood HS 800/9-12
15981 Highway 216 35444 205-342-5005
Laura McBride, prin. Fax 556-8972

Brundidge, Pike, Pop. 2,327
Pike County SD
Supt. — See Troy
Pike County JSHS 500/7-12
552 S Main St 36010 334-735-2389
Mike Hall, prin. Fax 735-3176

Bryant, Jackson

Mountain View Christian Academy 100/PK-12
3665 AL Highway 73 35958 256-597-3467
Jonathan Aultman, prin. Fax 597-3467

Butler, Choctaw, Pop. 1,780
Choctaw County SD 2,100/K-12
107 Tom Orr Dr 36904 205-459-3031
William Boggs, supt. Fax 459-3037
choctawboe.k12.al.us/
Choctaw County HS 600/7-12
277 Tom Orr Dr 36904 205-459-2139
Kevin Howard, prin. Fax 459-2277
Orr Career Technical Center Vo/Tech
105 Tom Orr Dr 36904 205-459-3031
B. Smith, prin. Fax 459-3037
Other Schools – See Gilbertown

Patrician Academy 400/K-12
901 S Mulberry Ave 36904 205-459-3605
Marcus Walters Ph.D., prin. Fax 459-4802

Calera, Shelby, Pop. 6,707
Shelby County SD
Supt. — See Columbiana
Calera MSHS 600/6-12
8454 Highway 31 35040 205-682-6100
Ken Mobley, prin. Fax 682-6105

Camden, Wilcox, Pop. 2,228
Wilcox County SD 2,300/PK-12
PO Box 160 36726 334-682-4716
Malcolm Cain, supt. Fax 682-4179
Camden S of Arts & Technology 400/7-8
PO Box 698 36726 334-682-4514
Andre Saulsberry, prin. Fax 682-5934
Wilcox Central HS 700/9-12
PO Box 1089 36726 334-682-9239
James Thomas, prin. Fax 682-5411

Wilcox Academy 300/K-12
PO Box 1149 36726 334-682-9619
Buddy Sumner, prin. Fax 682-2107

Camp Hill, Tallapoosa, Pop. 1,199
Tallapoosa County SD
Supt. — See Dadeville
Bell S 300/K-12
PO Box 490 36850 256-896-2865
Glenda Mennifee, prin. Fax 896-2527

Lyman Ward Military Academy 200/6-12
PO Box 550 36850 800-798-9151
Dr. Chester Carroll, pres. Fax 896-4661

Carbon Hill, Walker, Pop. 2,047
Walker County SD
Supt. — See Jasper
Carbon Hill HS 300/9-12
217 Bulldog Blvd 35549 205-924-8821
Dr. Diane Jones, prin. Fax 924-8877

Carrollton, Pickens, Pop. 956
Pickens County SD 3,100/K-12
PO Box 32 35447 205-367-2080
Dr. Leonard Duff, supt. Fax 367-8404
www.pcboe.org
LaDow Technology Center Vo/Tech
377 Ladow Center Cir 35447 205-367-2080
Mike Maughan, prin. Fax 367-8404
Other Schools – See Aliceville, Gordo, Reform

Pickens Academy 400/PK-12
225 Ray Bass Rd 35447 205-367-8144
Louis McBride, prin. Fax 367-1771

Cedar Bluff, Cherokee, Pop. 1,537
Cherokee County SD
Supt. — See Centre
Cedar Bluff S 600/K-12
3655 Old Highway 9 35959 256-779-6211
Bobby Mintz, prin. Fax 779-8328

Centre, Cherokee, Pop. 3,316
Cherokee County SD 4,200/PK-12
130 E Main St 35960 256-927-3362
Brian Johnson, supt. Fax 927-3399
www.cherokeek12.org/
Centre MS 400/6-8
350 E Main St 35960 256-927-5656
Renee Miller, prin. Fax 927-4656
Cherokee Co. Career & Technology Center Vo/Tech
600 Bay Springs Rd 35960 256-927-5351
Mitchell Guice, prin. Fax 927-3501
Cherokee County HS 500/9-12
910 Warrior Dr 35960 256-927-3625
Doug Davis, prin. Fax 927-6445
Other Schools – See Cedar Bluff, Gaylesville, Leesburg, Spring Garden

Centreville, Bibb, Pop. 2,507
Bibb County SD 3,600/K-12
157 SW Davidson Dr 35042 205-926-9881
Donald McCalla, supt. Fax 926-5075
www.bibbed.org/
Bibb County HS 600/9-12
220 Birmingham Rd 35042 205-926-9071
Dr. Edward Brown, prin. Fax 926-6848
Bibb County JHS 300/7-8
721 Walnut St 35042 205-926-7751
Terry McGee, prin. Fax 926-7786
Other Schools – See West Blocton

Cahawba Christian Academy 100/PK-12
2415 Montevallo Rd 35042 205-926-4676
Diane Thompson, prin. Fax 926-4633

Chatom, Washington, Pop. 1,178
Washington County SD 3,600/K-12
PO Box 1359 36518 251-847-2401
Tim Savage, supt. Fax 847-3611
washingtoncounty.al.schoolwebpages.com
Washington County AVC Vo/Tech
PO Box 1298 36518 251-847-2040
Harold Crouch, prin. Fax 847-3489
Washington County JSHS 600/5-12
PO Box 1329 36518 251-847-2851
Sidney Hinton, prin. Fax 847-2825
Other Schools – See Fruitdale, Leroy, Mc Intosh, Millry

Chelsea, Shelby, Pop. 3,635
Shelby County SD
Supt. — See Columbiana
Chelsea HS 600/9-12
10510 Highway 11 35043 205-682-7200
Pat Grey, prin. Fax 682-7205
Chelsea MS 500/6-8
PO Box 600 35043 205-682-7210
Bill Harper, prin. Fax 682-7215

Cherokee, Colbert, Pop. 1,183
Colbert County SD
Supt. — See Tuscumbia
Cherokee HS 200/9-12
850 High School Dr 35616 256-359-4434
Ricky Willingham, prin. Fax 359-4060
Cherokee MS 200/5-8
4595 Old Lee Hwy 35616 256-359-6432
Larry Grissom, prin. Fax 359-6543

Chickasaw, Mobile, Pop. 6,000
Mobile County SD
Supt. — See Mobile
Clark S of Math & Science 700/4-8
50 12th Ave 36611 251-221-2106
Dianne McWain, prin. Fax 221-2108

Childersburg, Talladega, Pop. 5,000
Talladega County SD
Supt. — See Talladega
Childersburg HS 500/9-12
122 Faye S Perry Dr 35044 256-315-5475
Kevin Maddox, prin. Fax 315-5495
Childersburg MS 600/5-8
800 4th St SE 35044 256-315-5505
Jena Jones, prin. Fax 315-5520

Citronelle, Mobile, Pop. 3,686
Mobile County SD
Supt. — See Mobile
Citronelle HS 700/9-12
19325 Rowe St 36522 251-221-3444
Alex Crane, prin. Fax 221-3448
Lott MS 600/6-8
17740 Celeste Rd 36522 251-221-2240
Randy Campbell, prin. Fax 221-2247

Clanton, Chilton, Pop. 8,336
Chilton County SD 7,200/PK-12
1705 Lay Dam Rd 35045 205-280-3000
Keith Moore, supt. Fax 755-6549
www.chilton.k12.al.us
Chilton County HS 700/9-12
1214 7th St S 35045 205-280-2710
Larry Mahaffey, prin. Fax 755-0618
Clanton MS 700/6-8
835 Temple Rd 35045 205-280-2750
Don Finlayson, prin. Fax 755-2446
LeCroy Career Tech Center Vo/Tech
2829 4th Ave N 35045 205-280-2920
David Conway, prin. Fax 755-2035
Other Schools – See Jemison, Maplesville, Thorsby, Verbena

Grace Community S 50/K-10
PO Box 2644 35046 205-755-4822
Tammie Flanders, admin.

Clayton, Barbour, Pop. 1,402
Barbour County SD 1,300/PK-12
PO Box 429 36016 334-775-3453
Eddie Wright, supt. Fax 775-7301
barbourschools.org
Barbour County HS 400/9-12
PO Box 339 36016 334-775-3545
David Hobdy, prin. Fax 775-8861
Other Schools – See Louisville

Cleveland, Blount, Pop. 1,363
Blount County SD
Supt. — See Oneonta
Blount County Center of Technology Vo/Tech
PO Box 125 35049 205-625-3424
Philip Cleveland, dir. Fax 625-3427
Cleveland HS 400/7-12
71 High School St 35049 205-274-9915
Denise Martin, prin. Fax 274-0201

Coffeeville, Clarke, Pop. 354
Clarke County SD
Supt. — See Grove Hill
Coffeeville JSHS 100/7-12
PO Box 130 36524 251-276-3227
Janice Richardson, prin. Fax 276-0349

Collinsville, DeKalb, Pop. 1,667
De Kalb County SD
Supt. — See Rainsville
Collinsville S 600/K-12
PO Box 269 35961 256-524-2111
Paulette Davis, prin. Fax 524-7526

Columbia, Houston, Pop. 823
Houston County SD
Supt. — See Dothan
Houston County JSHS 400/7-12
PO Box 519 36319 334-696-2221
Scott Stephens, prin. Fax 696-4677

Columbiana, Shelby, Pop. 3,664
Shelby County SD 23,300/K-12
PO Box 1910 35051 205-682-7000
Randy Fuller, supt. Fax 682-7005
www.shelbyed.k12.al.us
Columbiana MS 500/6-8
222 Joiner Town Rd 35051 205-682-6610
Robbie Sauers, prin. Fax 682-6615
School of Technology Vo/Tech
701 Highway 70 35051 205-682-6650
Tim Eliff, prin. Fax 682-6655
Shelby County HS 600/9-12
101 Washington St 35051 205-682-6600
Gene Rogers, prin. Fax 682-6605
Other Schools – See Alabaster, Birmingham, Calera, Chelsea, Montevallo, Pelham, Vincent

---

Cornerstone Christian S 200/PK-12
24975 Highway 25 35051 205-669-7777
Laurie Porter, hdmstr. Fax 669-5283

Cordova, Walker, Pop. 2,336
Walker County SD
Supt. — See Jasper
Bankhead MS 300/5-8
110 School St 35550 205-483-7245
Dr. Gypsy Stovall, prin. Fax 483-7244
Cordova HS 300/9-12
1 Blue Devil Way 35550 205-483-7404
Dr. Jason Adkins, prin. Fax 483-1934

Cottondale, Tuscaloosa
Tuscaloosa CSD
Supt. — See Tuscaloosa
Bryant HS 900/9-12
6315 Mary Harmon Bryant Dr 35453 205-759-3538
Amanda Cassity, prin. Fax 759-8315
Eastwood MS 900/6-8
6314 Mary Harmon Bryant Dr 35453 205-759-3613
Dr. Bruce Prescott, prin. Fax 759-3798

Tuscaloosa County SD
Supt. — See Tuscaloosa
Davis - Emerson MS 500/6-8
1500 Bulldog Blvd 35453 205-342-2750
Dr. Walter Davie, prin. Fax 633-1155

Tuscaloosa Christian S 300/PK-12
PO Box 250 35453 205-553-4303
Dan Lancaster, prin. Fax 553-4259

Cottonwood, Houston, Pop. 1,171
Houston County SD
Supt. — See Dothan
Cottonwood S 800/K-12
663 Houston St 36320 334-691-2587
Judy Fowler, prin. Fax 691-4200

Courtland, Lawrence, Pop. 765
Lawrence County SD
Supt. — See Moulton
Hubbard S 300/K-12
12905 Jessie Jackson Pkwy 35618 256-637-3010
Dr. Denise Stovall, prin. Fax 637-3006

Crossville, DeKalb, Pop. 1,449
De Kalb County SD
Supt. — See Rainsville
Crossville HS 700/6-12
5405 County Road 28 35962 256-528-7858
David Uptain, prin. Fax 528-7840

Cullman, Cullman, Pop. 14,735
Cullman CSD 2,700/K-12
301 1st St NE 35055 256-734-2233
Jan Harris Ed.D., supt. Fax 737-9621
www.cullmancats.net
Cullman City Career Tech S Vo/Tech
800 2nd Ave NE 35055 256-734-7959
Bridgette Chandler, prin. Fax 734-7711
Cullman HS 800/9-12
510 13th St NE 35055 256-734-3923
Patrick Lane Hill, prin. Fax 734-9570
Cullman MS 400/7-8
800 2nd Ave NE 35055 256-734-7959
Jayne Barnett, prin. Fax 734-7711

Cullman County SD 9,700/PK-12
PO Box 1590 35056 256-734-2933
L. Hank Allen, supt. Fax 736-2486
www.ccboe.org/
Cullman Area Career Center Vo/Tech
17640 US Highway 31 35058 256-734-7740
Rebecca Eason, prin. Fax 734-7464
Fairview HS 500/9-12
841 Welcome Rd 35058 256-796-5106
Stanley Burden, prin. Fax 796-9025
Fairview MS 300/6-8
841 Welcome Rd 35058 256-796-0883
Dr. Susan Creel Patterson, prin. Fax 796-0885
Good Hope HS 400/9-12
210 Good Hope School Rd 35057 256-734-3807
Dr. Anita Kilpatrick, prin. Fax 734-3427
Good Hope MS 300/6-8
216 Good Hope School Rd 35057 256-734-9600
Wayne Weissend, prin. Fax 734-9704
West Point HS 600/9-12
4314 County Road 1141 35057 256-734-5375
Darrell Brock, prin. Fax 775-6047
Other Schools – See Bremen, Hanceville, Holly Pond, Vinemont

Cullman Christian S 50/7-8
PO Box 1204 35056 256-739-0505
Allison Siegenthaler, admin.
St. Bernard Prep HS 100/9-12
101 Saint Bernard Ave SE 35055 256-739-6682
Rev. Joel Martin, prin. Fax 734-2925

Dadeville, Tallapoosa, Pop. 3,145
Tallapoosa County SD 3,000/K-12
125 N Broadnax St Rm 113 36853 256-825-1020
Ginger East, supt. Fax 825-1003
tallapoosa.k12.al.us/~bpage/Schools/schools.html
Dadeville HS 600/8-12
227 Weldon St 36853 256-825-7848
Jason Yohn, prin. Fax 825-0697
Other Schools – See Camp Hill, New Site, Notasulga

Daleville, Dale, Pop. 4,545
Daleville CSD 1,400/K-12
626 N Daleville Ave 36322 334-598-2456
Andrew Kelley, supt. Fax 598-9006
www.daleville.k12.al.us
Daleville HS 500/9-12
626 N Daleville Ave 36322 334-598-4461
Mike McDuffie, prin. Fax 598-3850
Daleville MS 500/5-8
626 N Daleville Ave 36322 334-598-4463
Kenneth Seay, prin. Fax 598-9006

Danville, Morgan
Lawrence County SD
Supt. — See Moulton
Speake S 500/K-12
6559 County Road 81 35619 256-974-9201
Dr. Tommy Whitlow, prin. Fax 905-2483

Morgan County SD
Supt. — See Decatur
Danville HS 400/9-12
9235 Danville Rd 35619 256-773-9909
Gilmer Ellis, prin. Fax 773-5622
Danville MS 400/5-8
5933 Highway 36 W 35619 256-773-7723
Gary Walker, prin. Fax 773-7708

Daphne, Baldwin, Pop. 18,581
Baldwin County SD
Supt. — See Bay Minette
Daphne HS 1,700/9-12
9300 Lawson Rd 36526 251-626-8787
Donald Blanchard, prin. Fax 626-3024
Daphne MS 700/7-8
1 Jodie Davis Cir 36526 251-626-2845
Dr. Ernie Rosado, prin. Fax 626-0025

Bayside Academy 700/PK-12
303 Dryer Ave 36526 251-626-2840
Thomas Johnson, prin. Fax 626-2899
United States Sports Academy Post-Sec.
1 Academy Dr 36526 251-626-3303

Deatsville, Elmore, Pop. 361
Elmore County SD
Supt. — See Wetumpka
Holtville HS 400/9-12
10425 Holtville Rd 36022 334-569-3034
Jimmy Hull, prin. Fax 569-1013
Holtville MS 500/5-8
655 Bulldog Ln 36022 334-569-3574
Verna Webb, prin. Fax 569-3258

J. F. Ingram State Technical College Post-Sec.
PO Box 220350 36022 334-285-7870

Decatur, Morgan, Pop. 54,909
Decatur CSD 8,800/PK-12
302 4th Ave NE 35601 256-552-3000
Dr. Samuel L. Houston, supt. Fax 552-3981
www.dcs.edu
Austin HS 1,500/9-12
1625 Danville Rd SW 35601 256-552-3060
Dr. Donald Snow, prin. Fax 350-7802
Brookhaven MS 800/6-8
1302 5th Ave SW 35601 256-552-3045
Dr. Larry Collier, prin. Fax 552-3047
Cedar Ridge MS 800/6-8
2715 Danville Rd SW 35603 256-552-4622
Dr. Elizabeth Lacy, prin. Fax 552-4623
Decatur HS 1,000/9-12
1011 Prospect Dr SE 35601 256-552-3011
Mike Ward, prin. Fax 308-2535
Oak Park MS 700/6-8
1218 16th Ave SE 35601 256-552-3035
Dwight Satterfield, prin. Fax 552-3082

Morgan County SD 7,600/K-12
1325 Point Mallard Pkwy 35601 256-309-2105
Don Murphy, supt. Fax 309-2187
www.morgank12.org
Priceville HS 800/6-12
317 Highway 67 S 35603 256-353-1950
Guy Bowling, prin. Fax 353-2802
Other Schools – See Danville, Falkville, Somerville, Trinity

Calhoun Community College Post-Sec.
PO Box 2216 35609 256-306-2500
Decatur Heritage Christian Academy 400/PK-12
PO Box 5659 35601 256-351-4275
Scott Mayo, hdmstr. Fax 355-4738

Demopolis, Marengo, Pop. 7,555
Demopolis CSD 2,300/PK-12
PO Box 759 36732 334-289-1670
W. Wesley Hill, supt. Fax 289-1689
www.demopolisschools.com/
Demopolis HS 600/9-12
701 US Highway 80 W 36732 334-289-0294
Dr. Isaac Espy, prin. Fax 289-8777
Demopolis MS 600/6-8
300 E Pettus St 36732 334-289-4242
Clarence Jackson, prin. Fax 289-2670

Marengo County SD
Supt. — See Linden
Essex S 200/K-12
70 Hornet Dr 36732 334-289-3504
Loretta McCoy, prin. Fax 289-3591

West Alabama Preparatory S 200/PK-12
1908 Mauvilla Dr 36732 334-289-0452
Lynn Compton, prin. Fax 289-0464

Dixons Mills, Marengo
Marengo County SD
Supt. — See Linden
Marengo S 400/K-12
212 Panther Dr 36736 334-992-2395
George Green, prin. Fax 992-2197

Dora, Walker, Pop. 2,391
Walker County SD
Supt. — See Jasper
Dora HS 500/9-12
330 Glenn C Gant Cir 35062 205-648-6863
Ricky Pate, prin. Fax 648-4709

Dothan, Houston, Pop. 62,713
Dothan CSD 8,700/K-12
500 Dusy St 36301 334-793-1397
Dr. Sam Nichols, supt. Fax 794-1499
www.dothan.k12.al.us
Beverlye MS 500/6-8
1025 S Beverlye Rd 36301 334-794-1432
James Larry Norris, prin. Fax 792-0886
Carver S for Math Science & Technology 600/6-8
1001 Webb Rd 36303 334-794-1440
Dr. James Kelley, prin. Fax 794-1587
Dothan HS 1,500/9-12
1236 S Oates St 36301 334-794-1400
Dr. Georgia Gary, prin. Fax 677-0099
Dothan Technology Center Vo/Tech
3165 Reeves St 36303 334-794-1436
Greg Allen, prin. Fax 794-1439
Girard MS 500/6-8
600 Girard Ave 36303 334-794-1426
Greg Yance, prin. Fax 794-6373
Honeysuckle MS 500/6-8
1665 Honeysuckle Rd 36305 334-794-1420
Patsy Slaughter, prin. Fax 678-6546
Northview HS 1,100/9-12
3209 Reeves St 36303 334-794-1410
Ron Snell, prin. Fax 702-4802

Houston County SD 5,300/K-12
PO Box 1688 36302 334-792-8331
Tim Pitchford, supt. Fax 792-1016
hcboe.us/
Rehobeth HS 600/9-12
373 Malvern Rd 36301 334-677-7002
Matt Swann, prin. Fax 677-2699
Rehobeth MS 500/6-8
5631 County Road 203 36301 334-677-5153
John Dixon, prin. Fax 677-5947
Other Schools – See Ashford, Columbia, Cottonwood, Newton

Emmanuel Christian S 400/K-12
178 Earline Rd 36305 334-792-0935
Mark Redmond, prin. Fax 702-7410
Flowers Hospital Post-Sec.
PO Box 6907 36302 334-793-5000
George C. Wallace State Comm College Post-Sec.
1141 Wallace Dr 36303 334-983-3521
Houston Academy 600/PK-12
901 Buena Vista Dr 36303 334-794-4106
John O'Connell, prin. Fax 793-4053
Providence Christian S 600/1-12
4847 Murphy Mill Rd 36303 334-702-8933
Emory Latta, hdmstr. Fax 702-0700
Southeast Alabama Medical Center Post-Sec.
PO Box 6987 36302 334-793-8100
Troy University Post-Sec.
PO Box 8368 36304 334-983-6556

Double Springs, Winston, Pop. 983
Winston County SD 2,800/PK-12
PO Box 9 35553 205-489-5018
Sue Reed, supt. Fax 489-3203
www.winstonk12.org
Double Springs MS 400/5-8
PO Box 669 35553 205-489-3813
Ben Aderholt, prin. Fax 489-8832
Winston County HS 300/9-12
PO Box 549 35553 205-489-5593
Jeff Cole, prin. Fax 489-8204
Winston Co. Technical Center Vo/Tech
PO Box 1000 35553 205-489-2121
Shandy Porter, prin. Fax 489-2121
Other Schools – See Addison, Arley, Lynn

Douglas, Marshall, Pop. 568
Marshall County SD
Supt. — See Guntersville
Douglas HS 500/9-12
PO Box 300 35964 256-593-2810
Sarah Mitchell, prin. Fax 840-5489
Douglas MS 500/6-8
PO Box 269 35964 256-593-1240
Larry Wilson, prin. Fax 593-1259

East Brewton, Escambia, Pop. 2,424
Escambia County SD
Supt. — See Brewton
Neal HS 400/9-12
801 Andrew Jackson St 36426 251-867-4645
Phillip Ellis, prin. Fax 867-4642
Neal MS 500/5-8
PO Box 2385, 251-867-5035
Dennis Hadaway, prin. Fax 867-5051

Eclectic, Elmore, Pop. 1,112
Elmore County SD
Supt. — See Wetumpka
Eclectic MS 500/5-8
170 S Ann St 36024 334-541-2131
Matt Coker, prin. Fax 541-3556
Elmore County HS 500/9-12
155 N College Ave 36024 334-541-3662
James Adams, prin. Fax 541-4441

Eight Mile, See Prichard
Mobile County SD
Supt. — See Mobile
Blount HS 1,100/9-12
5450 Lott Rd 36613 251-221-3070
Don Mitchell, prin. Fax 221-3075

Elba, Coffee, Pop. 4,181
Coffee County SD 1,900/K-12
400 Reddoch Hill Rd 36323 334-897-5016
Dr. Linda Ingram, supt. Fax 897-6207
www.coffeecountyschools.org
Other Schools – See Jack, Kinston, New Brockton

Elba CSD 900/K-12
131 Tiger Dr 36323 334-897-2801
Danny Weeks, supt. Fax 897-5601
www.elbaed.com
Elba Area Vocational HS Vo/Tech
371 Tiger Dr 36323 334-897-2266
Larry Goodson, prin. Fax 897-5106
Elba HS 400/7-12
371 Tiger Dr 36323 334-897-2266
Johnny Dunn, prin. Fax 897-5106

Elberta, Baldwin, Pop. 583
Baldwin County SD
Supt. — See Bay Minette
Elberta MS 600/4-8
13355 Main St 36530 251-986-8127
Jan Peacock, prin. Fax 986-7472

Elkmont, Limestone, Pop. 493
Limestone County SD
Supt. — See Athens
Elkmont S 1,000/K-12
25630 Evans Ave 35620 256-732-4291
Mickey Glass, prin. Fax 732-3418

Enterprise, Coffee, Pop. 22,892
Enterprise CSD 5,500/K-12
PO Box 311790 36331 334-347-9531
Dr. Jim Reese, supt. Fax 347-5102
www.enterpriseschools.net/
Dauphin JHS 500/8-9
425 Dauphin St 36330 334-347-1141
Aaron Milner, prin. Fax 347-0845
Enterprise JHS 400/8-9
401 W College St 36330 334-347-1733
Greg Faught, prin. Fax 347-1009
Enterprise SHS 1,200/10-12
500 E Watts St 36330 334-347-2640
Rick Rainer, prin. Fax 347-3144

Enterprise-Ozark Community College Post-Sec.
PO Box 1300 36331 334-347-2623

Eufaula, Barbour, Pop. 13,463
Eufaula CSD 2,800/PK-12
420 Sanford Ave 36027 334-687-1100
Barry R. Sadler, supt. Fax 687-1150
www.ecs.k12.al.us
Eufaula HS 800/9-12
530 Lake Dr 36027 334-687-1110
Gary Atkins, prin. Fax 687-1121
Moorer MS 700/6-8
101 Saint Francis Rd 36027 334-687-1130
Barbara Lee, prin. Fax 687-1138

Lakeside S 300/PK-12
1020 Lake Dr 36027 334-687-5748
Patsy Dickert, hdmstr. Fax 687-6306
Wallace Community College Sparks Campus Post-Sec.
PO Box 580 36072 334-687-3543

Eutaw, Greene, Pop. 1,800
Greene County SD 1,600/PK-12
220 Main St 35462 205-372-3114
Dr. Douglas L. Ragland, supt. Fax 372-3247
www.greene.k12.al.us
Carver MS 400/4-8
PO Box 659 35462 205-372-4816
Isaac Atkins, prin. Fax 372-4828
Greene County HS 400/9-12
PO Box 658 35462 205-372-3789
Carolyn Young, prin. Fax 372-3404
Kirksey AVC Vo/Tech
836 County Road 131 35462 205-372-4636
Rhinnie Scott, prin. Fax 372-2358

Warrior Academy 100/K-12
PO Box 920 35462 205-372-3546
John Santoro, prin. Fax 372-9744

Evergreen, Conecuh, Pop. 3,442
Conecuh County SD 1,800/PK-12
100 Jackson St 36401 251-578-1752
Ronnie Brogden, supt. Fax 578-7061
Hillcrest HS 600/8-12
1989 Jaguar Dr 36401 251-578-1126
Preston Fluker, prin. Fax 578-7071

Reid State Technical College Post-Sec.
PO Box 588 36401 251-578-1313
Sparta Academy 300/PK-12
200 Pierce St 36401 251-578-2852
Wayne Hammonds, prin. Fax 578-2878

Excel, Monroe, Pop. 601
Monroe County SD
Supt. — See Monroeville
Excel S 1,000/K-12
PO Box 429 36439 251-765-2351
Kevin York, prin. Fax 765-9153

Fairfield, Jefferson, Pop. 11,696
Fairfield CSD 2,200/K-12
6405 Avenue D 35064 205-783-6850
Dr. Anthony Greene, supt. Fax 783-6805
www.fairfield.k12.al.us
Fairfield Area Vocational HS Vo/Tech
610 Valley Rd 35064 205-785-5176
Dr. Gordon Fears, prin. Fax 783-6748
Fairfield Preparatory HS 800/9-12
610 Valley Rd 35064 205-785-5176
Dr. Gordon Fears, prin. Fax 783-6748
Forest Hills MS 600/6-8
7000 Grasselli Rd 35064 205-783-6841
Ardrene Bishop, prin. Fax 783-6753

Restoration Academy 200/K-12
PO Box 30 35064 205-785-8805
Carl Lynn, admin. Fax 785-8870

Fairhope, Baldwin, Pop. 15,391
Baldwin County SD
Supt. — See Bay Minette
Fairhope HS 1,200/9-12
1 Pirate Dr 36532 251-928-8309
Dr. Beverly Thomas, prin. Fax 990-2053
Fairhope MS 700/6-8
408 N Section St 36532 251-928-2573
Dr. Deadra Powe, prin. Fax 990-0403

Falkville, Morgan, Pop. 1,177
Morgan County SD
Supt. — See Decatur
Falkville JSHS 400/7-12
43 Clark Dr 35622 256-784-5248
Sue Wood, prin. Fax 784-9438

Fayette, Fayette, Pop. 4,761
Fayette County SD 2,600/K-12
PO Box 686 35555 205-932-4611
Reba Anderson, supt. Fax 932-7246
www.fayette.k12.al.us
Fayette County HS 400/9-12
202 14th Ct NE 35555 205-932-6313
Radford Hester, prin. Fax 932-8361
Fayette MS 500/5-8
418 3rd Ave NE 35555 205-932-7660
Debbie Deavours, prin. Fax 932-7661
Hubbertville S 400/K-12
7360 County Road 49 35555 205-487-2845
Tim Dunavant, prin. Fax 487-3375
Other Schools – See Berry

Bevill State Community College Post-Sec.
2631 Temple Ave N 35555 800-526-5755

Flomaton, Escambia, Pop. 1,560
Escambia County SD
Supt. — See Brewton
Flomaton HS 200/9-12
21200 Highway 31 36441 251-296-2627
Scott Hammond, prin. Fax 296-2625

Florala, Covington, Pop. 1,893
Covington County SD
Supt. — See Andalusia
Florala City MS 100/7-8
22975 7th Ave 36442 334-858-3642
Rodney Drish, prin. Fax 858-7181
Florala HS 200/9-12
22114 Begonia St 36442 334-858-3765
Terry Holley, prin. Fax 858-6925

Florence, Lauderdale, Pop. 36,480
Florence CSD 3,900/K-12
541 Riverview Dr 35630 256-768-3015
Dr. Kendy Behrends, supt. Fax 768-3006
www.fcs.k12.al.us/
Florence Career Technical Education Vo/Tech
541 Riverview Dr 35630 256-768-3021
Jeanette Custer, prin. Fax 768-3010
Florence Freshman Center 400/9-9
648 N Cherry St 35630 256-768-2400
Gerald Johnson, prin. Fax 768-2405
Florence HS 1,000/10-12
1201 Bradshaw Dr 35630 256-768-2200
Mike Lewey, prin. Fax 768-2205
Florence MS 700/7-8
648 N Cherry St 35630 256-768-3100
William Griffin, prin. Fax 768-3105

Lauderdale County SD 8,900/K-12
PO Box 278 35631 256-760-1300
Jerry Fulmer, supt. Fax 766-5815
www.lcschools.org
Central S 1,300/K-12
3000 County Road 200 35633 256-764-2903
David Corl, prin. Fax 764-5409
Rogers S 1,300/K-12
300 Rogers Ln 35634 256-757-3106
Timothy Tubbs, prin. Fax 757-9625
Wilson S 1,400/K-12
7601 Highway 17 35634 256-764-8470
Larry Hill, prin. Fax 764-1304
Other Schools – See Killen, Lexington, Rogersville, Waterloo

Heritage Christian University Post-Sec.
PO Box HCU 35630 800-367-3565
Mars Hill Bible S 600/K-12
698 Cox Creek Pkwy 35630 256-767-1203
Dr. Kenny Barfield, hdmstr. Fax 767-6304
Shoals Christian S 300/K-12
301 Heathrow Dr 35633 256-767-7070
Thomas Hughes, hdmstr. Fax 766-5677
University of North Alabama Post-Sec.
Univ Sta 35632 256-765-4100

Foley, Baldwin, Pop. 11,419
Baldwin County SD
Supt. — See Bay Minette
Foley HS 1,200/9-12
1 Pride Pl 36535 251-943-2221
Kenneth Dinges, prin. Fax 943-3538
Foley MS 700/6-8
201 N Pine St 36535 251-943-1255
James Shoots, prin. Fax 943-8221

Fort Deposit, Lowndes, Pop. 1,229
Lowndes County SD
Supt. — See Hayneville
Lowndes County MS 200/6-8
PO Box 393 36032 334-227-4206
Peggy Grant, prin. Fax 227-4125

Fort Payne, DeKalb, Pop. 13,573
Fort Payne CSD 2,500/K-12
PO Box 681029 35968 256-845-0915
James B. Cunningham, supt. Fax 845-4962
www.ftpayk12.org
Fort Payne HS 800/9-12
201 45th St NE 35967 256-845-0535
Ronnie Crabtree, prin. Fax 845-7868
Fort Payne MS 600/6-8
4910 Martin Ave NE 35967 256-845-7501
Shane Byrd, prin. Fax 845-8292

Frisco City, Monroe, Pop. 1,397
Monroe County SD
Supt. — See Monroeville
Frisco City S 200/K-12
PO Box 70 36445 251-267-3261
Kenneth Smith, prin. Fax 267-3728

Fruitdale, Washington
Washington County SD
Supt. — See Chatom
Fruitdale S 500/K-12
PO Box 448 36539 251-827-6655
Dr. Alfred Taylor, prin. Fax 827-6573

Fyffe, DeKalb, Pop. 1,020
De Kalb County SD
Supt. — See Rainsville
Fyffe S 900/K-12
PO Box 7 35971 256-623-2116
Ricky Bryant, prin. Fax 623-4388

Gadsden, Etowah, Pop. 37,405
Etowah County SD 8,700/K-12
3200 W Meighan Blvd 35904 256-549-7578
Michael Bailey, supt. Fax 549-7582
www.ecboe.org/
Gaston S 600/K-12
4550 US Highway 411 35901 256-547-8828
Dr. Miria King-Garner, prin. Fax 543-7124
Hokes Bluff MS 400/5-8
5425 Main St 35903 256-492-1963
Dr. Marguerite W. Early, prin. Fax 492-1950
Southside HS 700/9-12
2150 Highway 77 35907 256-442-2172
Karen Bowlin, prin. Fax 442-2183
Other Schools – See Attalla, Glencoe, Hokes Bluff, Rainbow City, Sardis City, Walnut Grove

Gadsden CSD 3,100/K-12
PO Box 184 35902 256-543-3512
Bob Russell, supt. Fax 549-2950
www.gcs.k12.al.us
Gadsden City HS 9-12
1917 Black Creek Pkwy 35904 256-543-3614
Dr. Ed Miller, prin. Fax 543-4251
Gadsden MS 500/6-8
612 Tracy St 35901 256-547-6341
Joel Gulledge, prin. Fax 547-6323
Litchfield MS 6-8
1109 Hoke St 35903 256-492-6793
Kimberly Smith, prin. Fax 492-4010
Sansom MS 400/6-8
2210 W Meighan Blvd 35904 256-546-4992
Ronald Mayes, prin. Fax 543-1060
Weaver Technical Center Vo/Tech
1515 Campbell Ave 35903 256-439-6843
Tony Reddick, prin. Fax 439-6847

Coosa Christian S 200/K-12
2736 Wills Creek Rd 35904 256-547-1841
C. Michael Davis, prin. Fax 547-0045
Gadsden State Community College Post-Sec.
PO Box 227 35902 256-549-8200

Gardendale, Jefferson, Pop. 12,830
Jefferson County SD
Supt. — See Birmingham
Bragg MS 800/6-8
840 Ash Ave 35071 205-379-2600
Carol Yarborough, prin. Fax 379-2645
Gardendale HS 900/9-12
800 Main St 35071 205-379-3600
Dr. Anna Vacca, prin. Fax 379-3645

Gaylesville, Cherokee, Pop. 142
Cherokee County SD
Supt. — See Centre
Gaylesville S 400/PK-12
760 Trojan Way 35973 256-422-3401
Paul McWhorter, prin. Fax 422-3165

Geneva, Geneva, Pop. 4,379
Geneva CSD 1,200/K-12
511 Panther Dr 36340 334-684-7757
James Bixby, supt. Fax 684-3128
Geneva HS 400/9-12
505 Panther Dr 36340 334-684-9379
Ricky Bennett, prin. Fax 684-3128
Geneva MS 300/6-8
501 Panther Dr 36340 334-684-6431
Elizabeth Mitchell, prin. Fax 684-0476

Geneva County SD 2,700/K-12
PO Box 250 36340 334-684-5690
David Snell, supt. Fax 684-5601
www.genevacounty.schoolinsites.com/
Other Schools – See Hartford, Samson, Slocomb

Georgiana, Butler, Pop. 1,636
Butler County SD
Supt. — See Greenville
Georgiana HS 300/7-12
PO Box 680 36033 334-376-9130
Joseph Dean, prin. Fax 376-2956

Geraldine, DeKalb, Pop. 816
De Kalb County SD
Supt. — See Rainsville
Geraldine S 1,100/K-12
PO Box 157 35974 256-659-2142
Larry Lingerfelt, prin. Fax 659-4296

Gilbertown, Choctaw, Pop. 175
Choctaw County SD
Supt. — See Butler
Southern Choctaw HS 300/7-12
10941 Highway 17 36908 251-843-5645
Betty McBride, prin. Fax 843-5649

Glencoe, Etowah, Pop. 5,265
Etowah County SD
Supt. — See Gadsden
Glencoe HS 300/9-12
803 Lonesome Bend Rd 35905 256-492-2250
Marion Smith, prin. Fax 492-2265
Glencoe MS 300/5-8
809 Lonesome Bend Rd 35905 256-492-5627
Ginger Smith, prin. Fax 492-7076

Gordo, Pickens, Pop. 1,596
Pickens County SD
Supt. — See Carrollton
Gordo JSHS 400/7-12
630 4th St NW 35466 205-364-7353
Jamie Chapman, prin. Fax 364-6160

Goshen, Pike, Pop. 300
Pike County SD
Supt. — See Troy
Goshen JSHS 400/7-12
101 Eagle Cir 36035 334-484-3245
Gene Nelson, prin. Fax 484-3247

Grand Bay, Mobile, Pop. 3,383
Mobile County SD
Supt. — See Mobile
Grand Bay MS 800/6-8
12800 Cunningham Rd 36541 251-865-6511
Suzanne Crist, prin. Fax 865-6182

Grant, Marshall, Pop. 677
Marshall County SD
Supt. — See Guntersville
Smith DAR HS 400/9-12
6077 Main St 35747 256-728-4238
Stacy Anderton, prin. Fax 728-8900
Smith DAR MS 400/5-8
6077 Main St 35747 256-728-5950
Susan Keller, prin. Fax 728-8447

Greensboro, Hale, Pop. 2,616
Hale County SD 3,200/PK-12
1115 Powers St 36744 334-624-8836
Joseph F. Stegall, supt. Fax 624-3415
www.halek12.org
Greensboro East HS 400/7-12
PO Box 460 36744 334-624-9156
Anne Jones, prin. Fax 624-9157
Greensboro West HS 300/7-12
PO Box 40 36744 334-624-7932
Charlene Wiggins, prin. Fax 624-0470
Hale County Technology Center Vo/Tech
PO Box 517 36744 334-624-3691
James Essex, prin. Fax 624-1090
Other Schools – See Akron, Moundville, Newbern

Southern Academy 300/K-12
407 College St 36744 334-624-8111
James Davis, prin. Fax 624-3778

Greenville, Butler, Pop. 7,104
Butler County SD 3,500/K-12
215 Administrative Dr 36037 334-382-2665
Mike Looney, supt. Fax 382-8607
www.butlerco.k12.al.us
Butler County Area Vocational HS Vo/Tech
100 Tiger Dr 36037 334-382-0266
Joseph West, prin. Fax 382-8607

Greenville HS 800/9-12
100 Tiger Dr 36037 334-382-2608
Dr. Kathy Murphy, prin. Fax 382-7202
Greenville MS 800/5-8
300 Overlook Rd 36037 334-382-3450
Jai Hill, prin. Fax 382-0686
Other Schools – See Georgiana, Mc Kenzie

Fort Dale Academy 500/K-12
1100 Gamble St 36037 334-382-2606
David Brantley, prin. Fax 382-0912

Grove Hill, Clarke, Pop. 1,383
Clarke County SD 3,500/PK-12
PO Box 936 36451 251-275-3255
Gerald Stephens, supt. Fax 275-8061
Clarke County HS 400/9-12
PO Box 937 36451 251-275-3368
Debra Dennis, prin. Fax 275-4132
Wilson Hall MS 500/5-8
PO Box 906 36451 251-275-8993
Larry Bagley, prin. Fax 275-4688
Other Schools – See Coffeeville, Jackson

Clarke Preparatory S 400/PK-12
20100 Highway 43 36451 251-275-8576
Teddy Cornelius, prin. Fax 275-8579

Guin, Marion, Pop. 2,246
Marion County SD
Supt. — See Hamilton
Marion County HS 200/7-12
PO Box 549 35563 205-468-3377
Van Nelson, prin. Fax 468-8047

Gulf Shores, Baldwin, Pop. 7,263
Baldwin County SD
Supt. — See Bay Minette
Gulf Shores HS 600/9-12
PO Box 3729 36547 251-968-4747
Eddie Tyler, prin. Fax 968-4770
Gulf Shores MS 500/6-8
450 E 15th Ave 36542 251-968-8719
Sherry Frazier, prin. Fax 967-1577

Guntersville, Marshall, Pop. 7,721
Guntersville CSD 1,800/K-12
PO Box 129 35976 256-582-3159
Andrew Lee, supt. Fax 582-6158
www.guntersvilleboe.com
Guntersville HS 500/9-12
14227 US Highway 431 35976 256-582-2046
Bill Wharton, prin. Fax 582-4742
Guntersville MS 400/6-8
901 Sunset Dr 35976 256-582-5182
Shirl Dollar, prin. Fax 582-4477

Marshall County SD 5,100/PK-12
12380 US Highway 431 35976 256-582-3171
Tim Nabors, supt. Fax 582-3178
www.marshallk12.org
Brindlee Mountain HS 9-12
994 Scant City Rd 35976 256-753-2800
Keith Buchanan, prin. Fax 753-2802
Brindlee Mountain MS 400/6-8
994 Scant City Rd 35976 256-753-2800
Barry Kirkland, prin. Fax 753-2802
Marshall Technical HS Vo/Tech
12312 US Highway 431 35976 256-582-5629
Cindy Wigley, prin. Fax 582-2580
Other Schools – See Albertville, Douglas, Grant

Gurley, Madison, Pop. 854
Madison County SD
Supt. — See Huntsville
Madison County HS 500/9-12
174 Brock Rd 35748 256-776-6247
Freddie Hargett, prin. Fax 776-4302

Hackleburg, Marion, Pop. 1,475
Marion County SD
Supt. — See Hamilton
Hackleburg S 600/K-12
PO Box 310 35564 205-935-3223
Jerry Kuykendall, prin. Fax 935-8092

Haleyville, Winston, Pop. 4,159
Haleyville CSD 1,700/PK-12
2011 20th St 35565 205-486-9231
Dr. Clint A. Baggett, supt. Fax 486-8833
www.havc.k12.al.us
Haleyville Center of Technology Vo/Tech
2007 20th St 35565 205-486-9481
Gary Warren, prin. Fax 486-8735
Haleyville JSHS 700/7-12
2001 20th St 35565 205-486-3122
Roger Satcher, prin. Fax 486-1660

Hamilton, Marion, Pop. 6,496
Marion County SD 3,600/K-12
188 Winchester Dr 35570 205-921-9319
Bravell Jackson, supt. Fax 921-7336
www.mcbe.net
Hamilton HS 400/9-12
211 Aggie Ave 35570 205-921-3281
Ronnie Miller, prin. Fax 921-2333
Hamilton MS 500/5-8
400 Military St S 35570 205-921-7030
Steven Deavours, prin. Fax 921-3821
Other Schools – See Bear Creek, Brilliant, Guin, Hackleburg

Bevill State Community College Post-Sec.
PO Box 9 35570 205-921-3177

Hampton, Tallapoosa
Huntsville CSD
Supt. — See Huntsville
Hampton Cove MS 400/6-8
261 Old Highway 431, 256-428-8380
Dr. Debi Edwards, prin. Fax 428-8383

Hanceville, Cullman, Pop. 3,127
Cullman County SD
Supt. — See Cullman
Hanceville HS 300/9-12
801 Commercial St SE 35077 256-352-6111
Robert Burgess, prin. Fax 352-6491
Hanceville MS 300/6-8
805 Commercial St SE 35077 256-352-6175
Paul Anderson, prin. Fax 352-9741

Wallace State Community College Post-Sec.
PO Box 2000 35077 256-352-8000

Hartford, Geneva, Pop. 2,372
Geneva County SD
Supt. — See Geneva
Geneva County HS 200/9-12
301 Lily St 36344 334-588-2943
Mike Whitaker, prin. Fax 588-3650
Geneva County MS 200/6-8
301 Lily St 36344 334-588-2943
Mike Whitaker, prin. Fax 588-3650

Hartselle, Morgan, Pop. 13,080
Hartselle CSD 3,000/K-12
305 College St NE 35640 256-773-5419
Dr. Mike Reed, supt. Fax 773-5433
www.hartselletigers.org
Hartselle AVC Vo/Tech
904 Sparkman St SW 35640 256-773-5426
Jerry Reeves, prin. Fax 773-5572
Hartselle HS 900/9-12
904 Sparkman St SW 35640 256-773-5426
Jerry Reeves, prin. Fax 773-5572
Hartselle JHS 700/6-8
130 Petain St SW 35640 256-773-6094
Don Pouncey, prin. Fax 773-3499

Harvest, Madison, Pop. 1,922
Madison County SD
Supt. — See Huntsville
Sparkman HS 2,000/9-12
2616 Jeff Rd 35749 256-837-0331
Manuel Wallace, prin. Fax 837-7673

Hayden, Blount, Pop. 520
Blount County SD
Supt. — See Oneonta
Hayden HS 900/7-12
125 Atwood Rd 35079 205-647-0397
Allen Hargett, prin. Fax 647-8633

Hayneville, Lowndes, Pop. 1,141
Lowndes County SD 2,300/K-12
PO Box 755 36040 334-548-2131
Dr. Daniel Boyd, supt. Fax 548-2161
Central HS 400/9-12
145 Main St 36040 334-563-7311
Kenneth Fair, prin. Fax 563-7299
Hayneville MS 300/6-8
PO Box 307 36040 334-548-2184
Harvey Means, prin. Fax 548-5237
Lowndes Co. Career Technical Ctr Vo/Tech
147 Main St 36040 334-563-7389
Donald Dotson, prin. Fax 563-9233
Other Schools – See Fort Deposit, Letohatchee

Hazel Green, Madison, Pop. 2,208
Madison County SD
Supt. — See Huntsville
Hazel Green HS 1,200/9-12
14380 Highway 231 431 N 35750 256-828-0764
John Fanning, prin. Fax 828-6203
Meridianville MS 700/6-8
12975 Highway 231 431 N 35750 256-829-1165
Tom Highfield, prin. Fax 829-1104

Headland, Henry, Pop. 3,714
Henry County SD
Supt. — See Abbeville
Headland HS 400/9-12
8 Sporman St 36345 334-693-2442
Steve Williams, prin. Fax 693-5255
Headland MS 400/6-8
200 Peachtree St 36345 334-693-3764
Rickey Allen, prin. Fax 693-9058

Heflin, Cleburne, Pop. 3,308
Cleburne County SD 2,300/K-12
93 Education St 36264 256-463-5624
Scott Coefield, supt. Fax 463-5709
www.cleburneschools.net
Cleburne County Career Technical S Vo/Tech
11200 Highway 46 36264 256-748-2961
Bill Ayers, prin. Fax 748-3904
Cleburne County HS 600/8-12
520 Evans Bridge Rd 36264 256-463-2012
Dennis Magouirk, prin. Fax 463-5504
Other Schools – See Ranburne

Higdon, Jackson
Jackson County SD
Supt. — See Scottsboro
North Sand Mountain S 700/K-12
PO Box 129 35979 256-597-2111
Chris Davis, prin. Fax 597-2505

Highland Home, Crenshaw
Crenshaw County SD
Supt. — See Luverne
Highland Home S 900/PK-12
18434 Montgomery Hwy 36041 334-537-4369
Joseph Eiland, prin. Fax 537-9805

Hokes Bluff, Etowah, Pop. 4,317
Etowah County SD
Supt. — See Gadsden
Hokes Bluff HS 400/9-12
1865 Appalachian Hwy 35903 256-492-1360
Jeff Lasseter, prin. Fax 492-7502

Holly Pond, Cullman, Pop. 709
Cullman County SD
Supt. — See Cullman
Holly Pond HS 500/7-12
160 New Hope Rd 35083 256-796-5169
Kim Butler, prin. Fax 796-5199

Hollywood, Jackson, Pop. 929
Jackson County SD
Supt. — See Scottsboro
Pruett Center of Technology Vo/Tech
29490 US Highway 72 35752 256-574-6079
Dana Moore, prin. Fax 259-1644

Holt, Tuscaloosa, Pop. 4,125
Tuscaloosa County SD
Supt. — See Tuscaloosa
Holt HS 500/9-12
3801 Alabama Ave NE 35404 205-342-2768
Cliff Booth, prin. Fax 553-8225

Homewood, Jefferson, Pop. 23,963
Homewood CSD 3,200/K-12
PO Box 59366 35259 205-870-4203
Dr. Jodi Newton, supt. Fax 877-4544
www.homewood.k12.al.us
Homewood HS 1,000/9-12
1901 Lakeshore Dr S 35209 205-871-9663
Vic Wilson, prin. Fax 879-0879
Homewood MS 800/6-8
395 Mecca Ave 35209 205-870-0878
Dr. Bill Cleveland, prin. Fax 877-4573

Herzing College Post-Sec.
280 W Valley Ave 35209 205-916-2800

Hoover, Jefferson, Pop. 67,469
Hoover CSD 11,500/K-12
2810 Metropolitan Way 35243 205-439-1015
Andy Craig, supt. Fax 439-1001
www.hoover.k12.al.us
Bumpus MS 800/6-8
1730 Lake Cyrus Club Dr 35244 205-439-2200
Dr. Joy Brown, prin. Fax 439-2201
Hoover HS 2,100/9-12
1000 Buccaneer Dr 35244 205-439-1200
Dr. Sandra Spivey, prin. Fax 439-1201
Simmons JHS 800/6-8
1575 Patton Chapel Rd 35226 205-439-2100
Carol Barber, prin. Fax 439-2101
Other Schools – See Birmingham

Hoover Christian S 100/K-10
2113 Old Rocky Ridge Rd 35216 205-987-3376
Mark Grice, prin. Fax 987-4428
Shades Mountain Christian S 500/PK-12
2290 Old Tyler Rd 35226 205-978-6001
W. Laird Crump, hdmstr. Fax 978-9120

Hope Hull, Montgomery

Hooper Academy 400/K-12
380 Fischer Rd 36043 334-288-5980
Dr. John Niblett, prin. Fax 288-9171

Hueytown, Jefferson, Pop. 15,192
Jefferson County SD
Supt. — See Birmingham
Hueytown HS 1,000/9-12
131 Dabbs Ave 35023 205-379-4150
Randy McCarty, prin. Fax 379-4195
Hueytown MS 800/6-8
701 Sunrise Blvd 35023 205-379-5150
Brett Kirkham, prin. Fax 379-5195

Garywood Christian S 100/K-12
2750 Allson Bonnett Mmrl Dr 35023 205-744-4390
Amanda Kleiser, prin. Fax 332-0225

Huntsville, Madison, Pop. 166,313
Huntsville CSD 22,400/K-12
PO Box 1256 35807 256-428-6800
Dr. Ann Roy Moore, supt. Fax 428-6817
www.hsv.k12.al.us
Butler HS 1,100/9-12
3401 Holmes Ave NW 35816 256-428-7950
Jacqueline Wyse, prin. Fax 428-7951
Challenger MS 700/6-8
13555 Chaney Thompson Rd SE 35803 256-428-7620
Edith Pickens, prin. Fax 428-7621
Chapman MS 400/6-8
2001 Reuben Dr NE 35811 256-428-7640
Dr. James Waters, prin. Fax 428-7641
Columbia HS 9-12
300 Explorer Blvd NW 35806 256-428-7576
Dr. Jennifer Garrett, prin. Fax 428-7579
Davis Hills MS 400/6-8
3221 Mastin Lake Rd NW 35810 256-428-7660
Bryon McGlathery, prin. Fax 428-7661
Grissom HS 1,900/9-12
7901 Bailey Cove Rd SE 35802 256-428-8000
B.T. Drake, prin. Fax 428-8001
Huntsville Center for Technology Vo/Tech
2800 Drake Ave SW 35805 256-428-7810
Eddie Turner, prin. Fax 428-7811
Huntsville HS 1,300/9-12
2304 Billie Watkins St SW 35801 256-428-8050
Leslie Esneault, prin. Fax 428-8051
Huntsville MS 600/6-8
817 Adams St SE 35801 256-428-7700
Jim Caneer, prin. Fax 428-7701
Johnson HS 800/9-12
6201 Pueblo Dr NW 35810 256-428-8100
Dr. Fredonia Williams, prin. Fax 428-8118
Johnson HS International Education 9-12
6201 Pueblo Dr NW 35810 256-428-8100
Dr. Fredonia Williams, prin. Fax 428-8118
Lee Creative & Performing Arts HS 9-12
606 Forrest Cir NE 35811 256-428-8150
Paul Parvin, prin. Fax 428-8151
Lee HS 900/9-12
606 Forrest Cir NE 35811 256-428-8150
Paul Parvin, prin. Fax 428-8151
Lee Pre-Engineering HS 9-12
606 Forrest Cir NE 35811 256-428-8150
Paul Parvin, prin. Fax 428-8151
Mountain Gap MS 500/6-8
821 Mountain Gap Rd SE 35803 256-428-7720
John Timlin, prin. Fax 428-7721

New Century Technology S Vo/Tech
300 Explorer Blvd NW 35806 256-428-7800
Paul Glover, prin. Fax 428-7801
Stone MS 400/6-8
2620 Clinton Ave W 35805 256-428-7740
Peggy Harris, prin. Fax 428-7741
Westlawn MS 400/6-8
4217 9th Ave SW 35805 256-428-7760
Fraizier Barnes, prin. Fax 428-7761
White MS 600/6-8
4800 Sparkman Dr NW 35810 256-428-7680
Annie Savage, prin. Fax 428-7681
Whitesburg MS 600/6-8
107 Sanders Rd SW 35802 256-428-7780
Mike Bible, prin. Fax 428-7781
Other Schools – See Hampton

Madison County SD 17,300/K-12
PO Box 226 35804 256-852-2557
Elam Swaim, supt. Fax 852-2538
www.madison.k12.al.us
Madison County Career Academy Vo/Tech
1275 Jordan Rd 35811 256-852-2170
William Starnes, prin. Fax 851-9790
Monrovia MS 1,000/6-8
1216 Jeff Rd NW 35806 256-430-4499
Derrell Brown, prin. Fax 726-0230
Riverton MS 600/6-8
399 Homer Nance Rd 35811 256-859-3667
Richard Medlen, prin. Fax 851-2610
Other Schools – See Gurley, Harvest, Hazel Green, New Hope, New Market, Toney

---

Catholic HS 200/9-12
4810 Bradford Dr NW 35805 256-430-1760
Vince Aquila, prin. Fax 430-1766
Huntsville Bible College Post-Sec.
904 Oakwood Ave NW 35811 256-539-0834
Huntsville Hospital Post-Sec.
101 Sivley Rd SW 35801 256-533-8123
J. F. Drake State Technical College Post-Sec.
3421 Meridian St N 35811 256-539-8161
Oakwood Adventist Academy 300/K-12
7000 Adventist Blvd 35896 256-726-7010
Olivia Beverly, prin. Fax 726-7016
Oakwood College Post-Sec.
Oakwood Rd NW 35896 256-726-7000
Providence Classical S 100/K-10
4705 Sparkman Dr NW 35810 256-852-8884
Pattie Steward, admin.
Randolph S 700/K-12
1005 Drake Ave SE 35802 256-881-1701
Dr. Byron Hulsey, hdmstr. Fax 881-1784
University of Alabama in Huntsville Post-Sec.
PO Box 1247 35899 256-890-6120
Valley Fellowship Christian Academy 200/PK-12
3616 Holmes Ave NW 35816 256-533-5248
Patti Simon, prin. Fax 533-5253
Virginia College Post-Sec.
2800 Bob Wallace Ave SW #A 35805 256-533-7387
Westminster Christian Academy 500/6-12
1400 Evangel Dr NW 35816 256-705-8000
Robert Illman, hdmstr. Fax 705-8001

Ider, DeKalb, Pop. 688
De Kalb County SD
Supt. — See Rainsville
Ider S 800/K-12
PO Box 127 35981 256-632-2302
Steven Street, prin. Fax 632-3481

Indian Springs, Shelby, Pop. 1,520

Indian Springs S 300/8-12
190 Woodward Dr 35124 205-988-3350
Melville Mackay, dir. Fax 988-3797

Irondale, Jefferson, Pop. 9,531
Jefferson County SD
Supt. — See Birmingham
Shades Valley HS 1,200/9-12
6100 Old Leeds Rd 35210 205-379-5350
Jane Baker, prin. Fax 379-5395

Irvington, Mobile
Mobile County SD
Supt. — See Mobile
Bryant Career Technical S Vo/Tech
8950 Padgett Switch Rd 36544 251-957-2845
Thomas Reed, prin. Fax 957-3170
Bryant HS 1,500/9-12
14001 Hurricane Blvd 36544 251-824-3213
Larry Mouton, prin. Fax 824-3221

Jack, Coffee
Coffee County SD
Supt. — See Elba
Zion Chapel S 700/K-12
29256 Highway 87 36346 334-897-6275
Jerry Barnes, prin. Fax 897-5136

Jackson, Clarke, Pop. 5,285
Clarke County SD
Supt. — See Grove Hill
Jackson HS 500/9-12
321 Stanley Dr 36545 251-246-2571
Robert Hagood, prin. Fax 246-3190
Jackson MS 500/5-8
235 College Ave 36545 251-246-3597
Jessie Taylor, prin. Fax 246-6017

Jackson Academy 200/K-12
PO Box 838 36545 251-246-5552
Lynn Wright, prin. Fax 246-0202

Jacksonville, Calhoun, Pop. 8,862
Calhoun County SD
Supt. — See Anniston
Calhoun Co. Career Technical Center Vo/Tech
1200 Church Ave SE 36265 256-741-4600
David Talley, prin. Fax 435-4221
Pleasant Valley HS 400/7-12
4141 Pleasant Valley Rd 36265 256-741-6700
Charlton Giles, prin. Fax 435-0171

Jacksonville CSD 1,700/K-12
123 College St SW 36265 256-782-5682
Dr. Eric MacKey, supt. Fax 782-5685
www.jacksonville.k12.al.us
Jacksonville HS 800/7-12
1000 George Douthit Dr SW 36265 256-435-4177
Mike Newell, prin. Fax 435-3015

Jacksonville Christian Academy 200/K-12
831 Alexandria Rd SW 36265 256-435-3333
Dr. Tommy Miller, prin. Fax 435-2059
Jacksonville State University Post-Sec.
700 Pelham Rd N 36265 256-782-5000

Jasper, Walker, Pop. 14,088
Jasper CSD 2,600/K-12
PO Box 500 35502 205-384-6880
Dr. Robert Sparkman, supt. Fax 387-5213
www.jasper.k12.al.us/
Maddox MS 600/6-8
1 Panther Trl 35501 205-384-3235
Patsy Stricklin, prin. Fax 387-5208
Walker HS 800/9-12
1601 Highland Ave 35501 205-221-9277
Daniel Gambrell, prin. Fax 387-5228

Walker County SD 8,200/PK-12
PO Box 311 35502 205-387-0555
Dr. Vonda Beaty, supt. Fax 384-0810
www.walkercountyschools.com/
Curry HS 700/9-12
155 Yellow Jacket Dr 35503 205-384-3887
Bobby Gann, prin. Fax 221-7381
Curry MS 400/5-8
115 Yellow Jacket Dr 35503 205-384-3441
David Hendon, prin. Fax 384-1110
Walker County Center for Tech Vo/Tech
1100 Viking Dr 35501 205-387-0561
Debra Ellis, prin. Fax 384-5170
Other Schools – See Carbon Hill, Cordova, Dora, Oakman, Parrish

---

Bevill State Community College Post-Sec.
1411 Indiana Ave 35501 800-777-0372

Jemison, Chilton, Pop. 2,487
Chilton County SD
Supt. — See Clanton
Jemison HS 500/9-12
25195 US Highway 31 35085 205-280-4860
Margo Gibson, prin. Fax 688-4761
Jemison MS 600/5-8
25125 US Highway 31 35085 205-280-4840
Mark Knight, prin. Fax 688-2302

Killen, Lauderdale, Pop. 1,124
Lauderdale County SD
Supt. — See Florence
Brooks JSHS 800/7-12
4300 Highway 72 35645 256-757-2115
Dale Mathis, prin. Fax 757-1136
Thornton Career Technical Center Vo/Tech
7252 Highway 72 35645 256-757-2101
Kenneth Angel, prin. Fax 757-8692

Kimberly, Jefferson, Pop. 2,321
Jefferson County SD
Supt. — See Birmingham
North Jefferson MS 600/6-8
8350 Warrior Kimberly Rd 35091 205-379-5500
Pam Horton, prin. Fax 379-5545

Kinston, Coffee, Pop. 612
Coffee County SD
Supt. — See Elba
Kinston S 500/K-12
201 College St 36453 334-565-3016
Mark Coale, prin. Fax 565-3494

Lafayette, Chambers, Pop. 3,108
Chambers County SD 4,300/PK-12
PO Box 408D 36862 334-864-9343
Leonard Riley, supt. Fax 864-0119
www.chambersk12.org
Chambers County Career Tech Center Vo/Tech
PO Box 318 36862 334-864-8863
Darin Baldwin, prin. Fax 864-9394
Lafayette HS 400/9-12
214 1st Ave SE 36862 334-864-9881
Florence Moore, prin. Fax 864-0650
Powell MS 200/6-8
621 1st St SE 36862 334-864-8876
Terry Reed, prin. Fax 864-8169
Other Schools – See Valley

Chambers Academy 200/K-12
15048 US Highway 431 36862 334-864-9852
Jim Childers, prin. Fax 864-9691

Lanett, Chambers, Pop. 7,590
Lanett CSD 1,000/K-12
105 N Lanier Ave 36863 334-644-5900
Charles Looser, supt. Fax 644-5996
www.lanettcityschools.org
Lanett HS 300/9-12
1301 S 8th Ave 36863 334-644-5965
Sanford Isom, prin. Fax 644-5979
Lanett JHS 200/6-8
1302 Cherry Dr 36863 334-644-5950
Joan Gilbert, prin. Fax 644-5964

Springwood S 400/PK-12
PO Box 1030 36863 334-644-2191
Theresa Williams, hdmstr. Fax 644-2194

Leeds, Jefferson, Pop. 11,053
Leeds CSD 1,300/K-12
PO Box 1083 35094 205-699-5437
Dr. Billy Pack, supt. Fax 699-6629
Leeds HS 400/9-12
8404 Greenwave Dr 35094 205-699-4510
Mark Ford, prin. Fax 699-4515

Leeds MS 300/6-8
1721 Moton St 35094 205-699-4505
Elliot Harris, prin. Fax 699-4509

Leesburg, Cherokee, Pop. 820
Cherokee County SD
Supt. — See Centre
Sand Rock S 1,000/K-12
1950 Sand Rock Ave 35983 256-523-3564
Ben East, prin. Fax 523-3507

Leighton, Colbert, Pop. 835
Colbert County SD
Supt. — See Tuscumbia
Colbert County HS 600/7-12
2200 High School St 35646 256-446-8214
Jackie Hubbard-Witt, prin. Fax 446-8951

Leroy, Washington
Washington County SD
Supt. — See Chatom
Leroy S 800/K-12
PO Box 40 36548 251-246-2000
Larry Massey, prin. Fax 246-2199

Lester, Limestone, Pop. 113
Limestone County SD
Supt. — See Athens
West Limestone S 1,000/K-12
10945 W School House Rd 35647 256-233-6687
Stan Davis, prin. Fax 233-8034

Letohatchee, Lowndes
Lowndes County SD
Supt. — See Hayneville
Calhoun HS 400/9-12
8213 County Road 33 36047 334-227-4515
Robert O. Gardner, prin. Fax 548-5322

Lexington, Lauderdale, Pop. 830
Lauderdale County SD
Supt. — See Florence
Lexington S 900/K-12
101 School St 35648 256-229-6622
Larry Smith, prin. Fax 229-6636

Lincoln, Talladega, Pop. 4,921
Talladega County SD
Supt. — See Talladega
Drew MS 300/7-8
450 Drew Ave 35096 256-315-5280
Dr. Rhonda Lee, prin. Fax 315-5290
Lincoln HS 400/9-12
78989 AL Highway 77 35096 256-315-5295
Terry Roller, prin. Fax 315-5315

Linden, Marengo, Pop. 2,336
Linden CSD 600/K-12
PO Box 480609 36748 334-295-8802
Dr. Walter E. Davis, supt. Fax 295-8801
www.lindencity.org/
Austin JHS 100/6-8
PO Box 480699 36748 334-295-5378
Terry Gosa, prin. Fax 295-5376
Linden HS 200/9-12
PO Box 480729 36748 334-295-4287
Timothy Thurman, prin. Fax 295-0988
Marengo Co. Technology Center Vo/Tech
2450 E Coats Ave 36748 334-295-4237
George Baldwin, prin. Fax 295-1177

Marengo County SD 1,600/K-12
PO Box 480339 36748 334-295-4123
Luke Hallmark, supt. Fax 295-2259
Other Schools – See Demopolis, Dixons Mills, Sweet Water, Thomaston

---

Marengo Academy 400/K-12
PO Box 480639 36748 334-295-4151
H.D. Russell, prin. Fax 295-4159

Lineville, Clay, Pop. 2,389
Clay County SD
Supt. — See Ashland
Lineville JSHS 400/7-12
18 W Main St 36266 256-396-2466
Demita Parson, prin. Fax 396-6935

Livingston, Sumter, Pop. 3,048
Sumter County SD 2,600/K-12
PO Box 10 35470 205-652-9605
Dr. Fred Primm, supt. Fax 652-9641
www.sumter.k12.al.us
Bell-Brown Career Technical Center Vo/Tech
PO Box 1380 35470 205-652-9469
Travis Bailey, prin. Fax 652-9487
Livingston HS 400/9-12
PO Box 40 35470 205-652-2464
Eric Hines, prin. Fax 652-2475
Other Schools – See York

University of West Alabama Post-Sec.
Hwy 11 35470 205-652-3400

Loachapoka, Lee, Pop. 162
Lee County SD
Supt. — See Opelika
Loachapoka HS 300/7-12
PO Box 187 36865 334-887-8038
Jimmy Wilkerson, prin. Fax 887-5228

Locust Fork, Blount, Pop. 1,136
Blount County SD
Supt. — See Oneonta
Locust Fork HS 700/7-12
77 School Rd 35097 205-681-7846
Daniel Smith, prin. Fax 681-6175

Louisville, Barbour, Pop. 580
Barbour County SD
Supt. — See Clayton
Barbour County MS 300/6-8
PO Box 459 36048 334-266-6151
Stacey Turvin, prin. Fax 226-5991

Dixie Academy 100/K-12
PO Box 67 36048 334-266-5311
Glenda Green, prin. Fax 266-5090

Lowndesboro, Lowndes, Pop. 135

Lowndes Academy 300/K-12
PO Box 99 36752 334-278-3366
Randy Skipper, prin. Fax 278-4476

Luverne, Crenshaw, Pop. 2,668
Crenshaw County SD 2,500/PK-12
183 Votec Dr 36049 334-335-6519
Kathi H. Wallace, supt. Fax 335-6510
Crenshaw County AVTS Vo/Tech
183 Votec Dr 36049 334-335-3319
Yvonne Noble, prin. Fax 335-4119
Luverne S 1,000/PK-12
194 First Ave 36049 334-335-3331
Earl Franks, prin. Fax 335-2241
Other Schools – See Brantley, Highland Home

Crenshaw Christian Academy 200/K-12
608 Country Club Dr 36049 334-335-5749
Angela Carpenter, prin. Fax 335-6422

Lynn, Winston, Pop. 719
Winston County SD
Supt. — See Double Springs
Lynn HS 200/8-12
531 E Main St 35575 205-893-5471
Greg Pendley, prin. Fax 893-2484

Mc Calla, Jefferson
Jefferson County SD
Supt. — See Birmingham
McAdory HS 1,500/6-12
4800 McAdory School Rd 35111 205-379-4700
Samuel Staggs, prin. Fax 481-8037

Mc Intosh, Washington, Pop. 252
Washington County SD
Supt. — See Chatom
Mc Intosh HS 300/6-12
PO Box 359 36553 251-944-2441
David Davis, prin. Fax 944-8779

Mc Kenzie, Butler, Pop. 441
Butler County SD
Supt. — See Greenville
Mc Kenzie S 300/K-12
PO Box 158 36456 334-374-2711
J. Randy Williams, prin. Fax 374-8108

Madison, Madison, Pop. 35,893
Madison CSD 7,200/K-12
211 Celtic Dr 35758 256-464-8370
Dr. Steve Nowlin, supt. Fax 774-0404
www.madisoncity.k12.al.us
Discovery MS 1,000/7-9
1304 Hughes Rd 35758 256-837-3735
Sharon Willis, prin. Fax 837-1573
Jones HS 1,600/10-12
650 Hughes Rd 35758 256-772-2547
Robert Parker, prin. Fax 772-6698
Liberty MS 800/7-9
281 Dock Murphy Dr 35758 256-430-0001
Sally Bruer, prin. Fax 430-0282

Madison Academy 800/K-12
325 Slaughter Rd 35758 256-971-1620
Robert Burton, pres. Fax 971-1436

Maplesville, Chilton, Pop. 687
Chilton County SD
Supt. — See Clanton
Isabella S 800/K-12
11338 County Road 15 36750 205-280-2770
Ricky Porter, prin. Fax 755-8549
Maplesville S 500/K-12
PO Box 146 36750 334-366-2991
Maggie Hicks, prin. Fax 366-2531

Marbury, Autauga
Autauga County SD
Supt. — See Prattville
Marbury HS 500/7-12
PO Box A 36051 205-755-2118
Don Hulin, prin. Fax 755-3168

Marion, Perry, Pop. 3,428
Perry County SD 2,100/K-12
PO Box 900 36756 334-683-6528
John Heard, supt. Fax 683-8427
Marion JSHS 500/7-12
PO Box 150 36756 334-683-6741
Bob Coley, prin. Fax 683-8838
Other Schools – See Uniontown

Judson College Post-Sec.
302 Bibb St 36756 800-447-9472
Marion Military Institute Post-Sec.
1101 Washington St 36756 800-664-1842
Marion Military Institute 100/9-12
1101 Washington St 36756 334-683-2303
Col. James Benson, pres. Fax 683-2319

Midfield, Jefferson, Pop. 5,319
Midfield CSD 1,200/K-12
417 Parkwood St 35228 205-923-2262
Donnie Breaseale, supt. Fax 929-0585
www.midfield.k12.al.us/
Midfield Area Vo HS Vo/Tech
1600 High School Rd 35228 205-923-2833
Larry Thornton, prin. Fax 929-0593
Midfield HS 400/9-12
1600 High School Rd 35228 205-923-2833
Charles Anthony, prin. Fax 929-0593
Rutledge MS 400/5-8
1221 8th St 35228 205-780-8647
Nikita Williams, prin. Fax 780-3664

Southeastern School of Cosmetology Post-Sec.
26B Phillips Dr 35228 205-925-0011

Midland City, Dale, Pop. 1,798
Dale County SD
Supt. — See Ozark
Dale County HS 400/9-12
PO Box 1140 36350 334-983-3541
Leavy Boutwell, prin. Fax 983-1549

Millbrook, Elmore, Pop. 14,805
Elmore County SD
Supt. — See Wetumpka
Millbrook MS 1,500/4-8
4228 Chapman Rd 36054 334-285-2100
Dr. Oliver Boone, prin. Fax 285-2102
Stanhope-Elmore HS 1,100/9-12
4300 Main St 36054 334-285-4263
Bruce Fulmer, prin. Fax 285-4575

Millport, Lamar, Pop. 1,062
Lamar County SD
Supt. — See Vernon
South Lamar S 500/K-12
300 Sls Rd 35576 205-662-4411
Garth Moss, prin. Fax 662-4544

Millry, Washington, Pop. 604
Washington County SD
Supt. — See Chatom
Millry S 600/K-12
PO Box 65 36558 251-846-2987
Larry Odom, prin. Fax 846-2986

Mobile, Mobile, Pop. 191,544
Mobile County SD 63,200/PK-12
PO Box 1327 36633 251-221-4000
Dr. Harold Dodge, supt. Fax 221-4399
www.mcpss.com
Baker HS 1,600/9-12
8901 Airport Blvd 36608 251-221-3000
Clem Richardson, prin. Fax 221-3004
Burns MS 1,000/6-8
6175 Girby Rd 36693 251-221-2025
John Adams, prin. Fax 221-2021
Calloway-Smith MS 400/6-8
350 N Lawrence St 36603 251-221-2042
LaTunga Ransom, prin. Fax 221-2041
Causey MS 1,300/6-8
2205 McFarland Rd 36695 251-221-2060
Mary Wood, prin. Fax 221-2062
Chastang MS 800/6-8
2800 Berkley Ave 36617 251-221-2081
Zad Douglas, prin. Fax 221-2080
Davidson HS 1,500/9-12
3900 Pleasant Valley Rd 36609 251-221-3084
Lewis Copeland, prin. Fax 221-3083
Denton MS 600/6-8
3800 Pleasant Valley Rd 36609 251-221-2148
Lori Taylor, prin. Fax 221-2152
Dunbar Magnet S 700/4-8
500 Saint Anthony St 36603 251-221-2160
Rhonda Boone, prin. Fax 221-2162
Eanes MS 800/6-8
1901 Hurtel St 36605 251-221-2189
Douglas July, prin. Fax 221-2191
Hillsdale MS 300/6-8
6301 Biloxi Ave 36608 251-221-2223
Alvin Dailey, prin. Fax 221-2221
Le Flore HS 1,400/9-12
700 Donald St 36617 251-221-3125
Dorothy Robinson, prin. Fax 221-3134
Murphy Area Technical Center Vo/Tech
100 S Carlen St 36606 251-221-3200
Doug Estle, prin. Fax 221-3196
Murphy HS 2,400/9-12
100 S Carlen St 36606 251-221-3186
Doug Estle, prin. Fax 221-3196
Phillips Preparatory S 800/6-8
3255 Old Shell Rd 36607 251-221-2287
Brenda Hartzog, prin. Fax 221-2285
Pillans MS 800/6-8
2051 Gatotkoco Dr 36605 251-221-2300
Gloria Burks, prin. Fax 221-2314
Rain HS 700/9-12
3125 Dauphin Island Pkwy 36605 251-221-3233
Robert Blakely, prin. Fax 470-7759
Scarborough MS 700/6-8
1800 Phillips Ln 36618 251-221-2323
Arnold Tillman, prin. Fax 221-2321
Shaw HS 400/9-12
5960 Arlberg St 36608 251-221-3305
Sylvia Ward, prin. Fax 221-3304
Washington MS 500/6-8
1961 Andrews St 36617 251-221-2361
Rosalyn Dean, prin. Fax 221-2364
Williamson HS 900/9-12
1567 E Dublin St 36605 251-221-3411
Terrence Mixon, prin. Fax 221-3414
Continuous Learning Center Adult
1870 Pleasant Ave 36617 251-221-2122
Grady Gordon, prin. Fax 221-2124
Other Schools – See Bayou La Batre, Chickasaw, Citronelle, Eight Mile, Grand Bay, Irvington, Prichard, Saraland, Satsuma, Semmes, Theodore

Bishop State Community College Post-Sec.
925 Dauphin Island Pkwy 36605 251-479-0003
Bishop State Community College-Carver Post-Sec.
414 Stanton Rd 36617 251-473-8692
Bishop State Community College-Central Post-Sec.
1365 Martin Luther King Ave 36603 251-405-4400
Bishop State Community College-Main Post-Sec.
351 N Broad St 36603 251-690-6419
Blue Cliff School of Therapeutic Massage Post-Sec.
2970 Cottage Hill Rd # 175 36606 251-665-9900
CAPPS College Post-Sec.
3590 Pleasant Valley Rd 36609 251-473-1393
Cottage Hill Christian Academy 200/9-12
7355 Creekwood Dr 36695 251-634-2513
Dr. Charles Lang, supt. Fax 634-2566
Faith Academy 1,800/K-12
8650 Tanner Williams Rd 36608 251-633-7267
Tim Skelton, hdmstr. Fax 633-9133
McGill-Toolen HS 1,100/9-12
1501 Old Shell Rd 36604 251-432-0784
Michelle Haas, prin. Fax 433-8356
Mobile Christian S 700/K-12
5900 Cottage Hill Rd 36609 251-661-1613
James M. Powell, pres. Fax 661-1396
Murray S at Wilmer Hall Childrens Home 50/6-12
3811 Old Shell Rd 36608 251-342-4931
Margie Sumlin, prin. Fax 342-4466
Remington College Post-Sec.
828 Downtowner Loop W 36609 251-343-8200
St. Paul's Episcopal S 1,600/PK-12
161 Dogwood Ln 36608 251-342-6700
Robert Rutledge, hdmstr. Fax 342-1844
Spring Hill College Post-Sec.
4000 Dauphin St 36608 251-380-4000
UMS Wright Prep S 1,300/K-12
65 Mobile St 36607 251-479-6551
Tony Havard, prin. Fax 470-9050
University of Mobile Post-Sec.
5735 College Pkwy 36613 800-946-7267
University of South Alabama Post-Sec.
307 University Blvd N 36688 251-460-6101

Monroeville, Monroe, Pop. 6,690
Monroe County SD 4,300/PK-12
PO Box 967 36461 251-575-2168
Dennis Mixon, supt. Fax 575-5818
www.monroe.k12.al.us/
Monroe County Career Technical Center Vo/Tech
230 Tiger Dr 36460 251-575-4381
Rodney Lord, prin. Fax 575-2017
Monroe County HS 600/9-12
212 Tiger Dr 36460 251-575-3258
Larry Turner, prin. Fax 575-2019
Monroeville JHS 500/6-8
201 York St 36460 251-575-4121
Lana Wilson, prin. Fax 575-2934
Other Schools – See Beatrice, Excel, Frisco City, Uriah

Alabama Southern Community College Post-Sec.
PO Box 2000 36461 251-575-3156
Monroe Academy 600/PK-12
PO Box 927 36461 251-743-3932
Ronnie Williams, hdmstr. Fax 743-4267

Montevallo, Shelby, Pop. 5,092
Shelby County SD
Supt. — See Columbiana
Montevallo HS 400/9-12
980 Oak St 35115 205-682-6400
Judy Simmons, prin. Fax 682-6405
Montevallo MS 300/6-8
235 Samford St 35115 205-682-6410
Vanessa Nason, prin. Fax 682-6415

Shelby Academy 200/PK-12
9178 Highway 22 35115 205-668-2299
DeWayne Kervin, prin. Fax 668-1912
University of Montevallo Post-Sec.
Station 6030 35115 205-665-6000

Montgomery, Montgomery, Pop. 200,127
Montgomery County SD 31,700/PK-12
PO Box 1991 36102 334-223-6700
Linda Robinson, supt. Fax 269-3076
www.mps.k12.al.us
Baldwin Arts & Academics Magnet S 600/6-8
410 S McDonough St 36104 334-269-3870
Jannette Wright, prin. Fax 269-3918
Bellingrath JHS 900/7-9
3488 S Court St 36105 334-269-3623
Rafael Richardson, prin. Fax 269-6173
Brewbaker JHS 1,200/7-9
4425 Brewbaker Dr 36116 334-284-8008
Cheryl Fountain, prin. Fax 284-8052
Brewbaker Technology Magnet HS 500/9-12
4405 Brewbaker Dr 36116 334-284-7100
Mitzi McLaurine, prin. Fax 284-7110
Capitol Heights JHS 800/7-9
116 Federal Dr 36107 334-260-1000
Lorenza Pharrams, prin. Fax 260-1049
Carver HS 1,400/9-12
2001 W Fairview Ave 36108 334-269-3636
Gary Hall, prin. Fax 262-2440
Davis SHS 1,300/10-12
3420 Carter Hill Rd 36111 334-269-3712
Marie Kostick, prin. Fax 269-3715
Floyd MS for Math Science & Technology 500/6-8
3444 Le Bron Rd 36111 334-284-7130
Robert Hunter, prin. Fax 284-7125
Goodwyn JHS 800/7-9
209 Perry Hill Rd 36109 334-260-1021
Vince Johnson, prin. Fax 260-1079
Houston Hill JHS 300/7-9
215 Hall St 36104 334-269-3694
Thomas Cochran, prin. Fax 269-3656
Lanier SHS 900/10-12
1756 S Court St 36104 334-269-3726
Lewis Washington, prin. Fax 269-6180
Lee SHS 1,500/10-12
225 Ann St 36107 334-269-3742
David Sikes, prin. Fax 269-3888
Loveless Academic Magnet HS 400/9-12
921 W Jeff Davis Ave 36108 334-269-3839
Liz Norman, prin. Fax 269-3961
McIntyre MS, 1220 Hugh St 36108 500/6-8
Verna Webb, prin. 334-269-3755
McKee JHS 700/7-9
4017 McInnis Dr 36116 334-284-7528
Bobby Abrams, prin. Fax 241-5308
Southlawn MS 600/6-8
5333 Mobile Hwy 36108 334-284-8086
Tina Minott, prin. Fax 284-8094
Washington Magnet HS 500/9-12
632 S Union St 36104 334-269-3618
Quesha Starks, prin. Fax 269-6140
Other Schools – See Pike Road

Alabama Christian Academy 1,000/K-12
4700 Wares Ferry Rd 36109 334-277-1985
Ronnie Sewell, prin. Fax 279-0604
Alabama State University Post-Sec.
PO Box 271 36101 334-229-4200
Auburn University at Montgomery Post-Sec.
PO Box 244023 36124 334-244-3000

Baptist Medical Center Post-Sec.
301 Brown Springs Rd 36117 334-273-4400
Community College of the Air Force Post-Sec.
130 W Maxwell Blvd 36112 334-953-5033
Eastwood Christian S 300/K-12
1701 E Trinity Blvd 36106 334-272-8195
John Geiger, hdmstr. Fax 386-2399
Evangel Christian Academy 300/K-12
3975 Vaughn Rd 36106 334-272-3882
Rev. Victor Tubbs, prin. Fax 272-5662
Faulkner University Post-Sec.
5345 Atlanta Hwy 36109 334-272-5820
Freedom Life Christian Academy 100/PK-12
221 W Fleming Rd 36105 334-284-1461
Annetta Tate, admin. Fax 281-1912
Huntingdon College Post-Sec.
1500 E Fairview Ave 36106 334-833-4222
Montgomery Academy 600/K-12
3240 Vaughn Rd 36106 334-272-8210
Archibald Douglas, hdmstr. Fax 277-3240
Montgomery Catholic HS 300/9-12
5350 Vaughn Rd 36116 334-272-7220
Susan Vaughn, prin. Fax 272-2440
Montgomery Catholic MS 7-8
5350 Vaughn Rd 36116 334-272-2465
Anne Ceasar, prin. Fax 272-2330
Montgomery Job Corps Center Post-Sec.
1145 Air Base Blvd 36108 334-262-8883
Prince Institute of Professional Studies Post-Sec.
7735 Atlanta Hwy 36117 334-271-1670
St. James S 1,200/PK-12
6010 Vaughn Rd 36116 334-277-8033
Dr. John Lindsell, hdmstr. Fax 277-2542
St. Jude Educational Institute 100/9-12
2048 W Fairview Ave 36108 334-264-5376
John Mitchell, prin. Fax 264-6669
Southern Christian University Post-Sec.
1200 Taylor Rd 36117 800-351-4040
South University Post-Sec.
5355 Vaughn Rd 36116 334-395-8800
The Robert B. Adams/LabCorp CLS Program Post-Sec.
543 S Hull St 36104 334-263-5745
Trenholm State Technical College Post-Sec.
1225 Air Base Blvd 36108 334-832-9000
Trenholm State Technical College Post-Sec.
3920 Troy Hwy 36116 334-420-4200
Trinity Presbyterian S 1,000/K-12
1700 E Trinity Blvd 36106 334-213-2100
Robert Neu, hdmstr. Fax 272-9262
Troy University Montgomery Post-Sec.
PO Box 4419 36103 334-834-1400

Moody, Saint Clair, Pop. 10,764
Saint Clair County SD
Supt. — See Ashville
Moody HS 600/9-12
714 High School Dr 35004 205-640-5127
Ken Storie, prin. Fax 640-2300
Moody JHS 300/7-8
600 High School Dr 35004 205-640-2040
Ronald McFarling, prin. Fax 640-3036

Morris, Jefferson, Pop. 1,868
Jefferson County SD
Supt. — See Birmingham
Jordan JSHS 600/7-12
8601 Old Highway 31 35116 205-379-4850
Dr. Byron Campbell, prin. Fax 379-4895

Moulton, Lawrence, Pop. 3,276
Lawrence County SD 5,700/K-12
14131 Market St 35650 256-905-2400
Dexter Rutherford, supt. Fax 905-2406
www.lawrenceal.org
Lawrence Co. Center of Technology Vo/Tech
PO Box 606 35650 256-974-3751
Wade Fleming, prin. Fax 905-2482
Lawrence County JSHS 700/8-12
102 College St 35650 256-905-2440
Joe Lang, prin. Fax 905-2444
Other Schools – See Courtland, Danville, Mount Hope, Town Creek, Trinity

Moundville, Hale, Pop. 2,188
Hale County SD
Supt. — See Greensboro
Hale County HS 400/7-12
PO Box 188 35474 205-371-2514
Richard McCray, prin. Fax 371-6800

Mountain Brook, Jefferson, Pop. 20,821
Mountain Brook CSD 4,200/K-12
32 Vine St, Birmingham AL 35213 205-871-4608
Charles Mason, supt. Fax 877-8303
www.mtnbrook.k12.al.us
Mountain Brook JHS 1,000/7-9
205 Overbrook Rd, Birmingham AL 35213 205-871-3516
Garry Rickard, prin. Fax 969-8113
Mountain Brook SHS 1,000/10-12
3650 Bethune Dr 35223 205-414-3800
Richard Barlow, prin. Fax 969-8113

Mount Hope, Lawrence
Lawrence County SD
Supt. — See Moulton
Mount Hope S 300/K-12
8455 County Road 23 35651 256-905-2470
Tony Rutherford, prin. Fax 905-2471

Munford, Talladega
Talladega County SD
Supt. — See Talladega
Munford HS 400/7-12
300 Cedars Rd 36268 256-315-5220
Judson Warlick, prin. Fax 315-5240

Muscle Shoals, Colbert, Pop. 12,523
Muscle Shoals CSD 2,600/PK-12
PO Box 2610 35662 256-389-2600
Jeff Wooten, supt. Fax 389-2605
www.mscs.k12.al.us
Muscle Shoals Center for Technology Vo/Tech
PO Box 2186 35662 256-389-2660
Sylvia Coleman, prin. Fax 389-2662
Muscle Shoals HS 700/9-12
1900 Avalon Ave 35661 256-389-2682
H.L. Noah, prin. Fax 389-2689
Muscle Shoals MS 600/6-8
100 Trojan Dr 35661 256-389-2640
Mary Ann Stegall, prin. Fax 389-2647

Northwest-Shoals Community College Post-Sec.
PO Box 2545 35662 256-331-5200

Newbern, Perry, Pop. 228
Hale County SD
Supt. — See Greensboro
Sunshine S 300/K-12
3125 County Road 10 36765 334-624-8747
Herbert Pickens, prin. Fax 624-8781

New Brockton, Coffee, Pop. 1,236
Coffee County SD
Supt. — See Elba
New Brockton HS 400/7-12
210 S Tyler St 36351 334-894-2350
Dale Kelley, prin. Fax 894-5204

New Hope, Madison, Pop. 2,671
Madison County SD
Supt. — See Huntsville
New Hope HS 400/9-12
5216 Main Dr 35760 256-723-4226
Brenda Goodwin, prin. Fax 723-4063

New Market, Madison, Pop. 1,094
Madison County SD
Supt. — See Huntsville
Buckhorn HS 1,000/9-12
4123 Winchester Rd 35761 256-379-2123
Tom Ledbetter, prin. Fax 379-5311

New Site, Tallapoosa, Pop. 828
Tallapoosa County SD
Supt. — See Dadeville
Horseshoe Bend S 800/K-12
10684 Highway 22 E 36256 256-329-9110
Glenn Fuller, prin. Fax 329-9119

Newton, Dale, Pop. 1,679
Houston County SD
Supt. — See Dothan
Wicksburg S 900/K-12
1172 S State Highway 123 36352 334-692-5549
Steve Benton, prin. Fax 692-3184

Normal, Madison

Alabama A & M University Post-Sec.
PO Box 908 35762 256-372-5000

Northport, Tuscaloosa, Pop. 21,216
Tuscaloosa County SD
Supt. — See Tuscaloosa
Collins-Riverside MS 300/6-8
1400 3rd St 35476 205-342-2680
Bryant Williams, prin. Fax 752-8024
Echols MS 500/6-8
2701 Echols Ave 35476 205-342-2884
Nancy Terry, prin. Fax 339-1064
Northside HS 400/9-12
19230 Northside Pkwy 35475 205-342-2755
David W. Patrick, prin. Fax 339-3437
Northside MS 300/6-8
19130 Northside Rd 35475 205-342-2740
June Traweek, prin. Fax 339-4680
Tuscaloosa County HS 1,700/9-12
12500 Wildcat Dr 35475 205-342-2670
Dr. Steve Benson, prin. Fax 339-5086
Wood MS 600/6-8
2300 26th Ave 35476 205-342-2690
Greg Hurst, prin. Fax 339-6642

Notasulga, Macon, Pop. 851
Macon County SD
Supt. — See Tuskegee
Notasulga S 500/K-12
PO Box 10 36866 334-257-3510
Tommy Thompson, prin. Fax 257-4228

Tallapoosa County SD
Supt. — See Dadeville
Reeltown S 800/K-12
4085 AL Highway 120 36866 334-257-3784
Joseph C. Windle, prin. Fax 257-3978

Oakman, Walker, Pop. 948
Walker County SD
Supt. — See Jasper
Oakman JSHS 400/7-12
PO Box 286 35579 205-622-3381
Joel Hagood, prin. Fax 622-3542

Odenville, Saint Clair, Pop. 1,203
Saint Clair County SD
Supt. — See Ashville
Odenville MS 500/5-8
PO Box 610 35120 205-629-2280
Debra Carroll, prin. Fax 620-2282
St. Clair Co. HS 500/9-12
PO Box 550 35120 205-629-6222
Brian Terry, prin. Fax 629-2228

Ohatchee, Calhoun, Pop. 1,211
Calhoun County SD
Supt. — See Anniston
Ohatchee HS 400/7-12
100 Cherokee Trl 36271 256-741-4900
Robin Kines, prin. Fax 892-9181

Oneonta, Blount, Pop. 6,537
Blount County SD 7,800/K-12
PO Box 578 35121 205-625-4102
James E. Carr, supt. Fax 625-4100
www.blountcountyschools.net
Appalachian S 600/K-12
350 County Highway 12 35121 205-274-9712
Steven Love, prin. Fax 274-9706
Other Schools – See Blountsville, Cleveland, Hayden, Locust Fork

Oneonta CSD 1,400/K-12
27605 State Highway 75 35121 205-625-4106
Henry Housch, supt. Fax 274-2910
www.oneontacityschools.com
Oneonta City HS 600/7-12
27605 State Highway 75 35121 205-625-3801
Keith Bender, prin. Fax 625-5015

Opelika, Lee, Pop. 23,804
Lee County SD 9,400/K-12
PO Box 120 36803 334-745-9770
John Painter, supt. Fax 745-9774
www.lee.k12.al.us
Beauregard HS 500/9-12
7343 AL Highway 51 36804 334-745-5916
Richard Brown, prin. Fax 749-6421
Sanford MS 700/5-8
1500 Lee Road 11 36804 334-745-5023
Michelle Rutherford, prin. Fax 745-5685
Other Schools – See Loachapoka, Salem, Smiths Station, Valley

Opelika CSD 4,300/K-12
PO Box 2469 36803 334-745-9700
Fax 745-9706
www.opelikaschools.org
Opelika HS 1,300/9-12
1700 Lafayette Pkwy 36801 334-745-9715
Stan Cox, prin. Fax 745-9721
Opelika MS 1,000/6-8
1206 Denson Dr 36801 334-745-9726
Kenneth Burton, prin. Fax 745-9730

Southern Union State Community College Post-Sec.
1701 Lafayette Pkwy 36801 334-745-6437
Trinity Christian S 200/K-12
PO Box 311 36803 334-745-2464
Sharon Miller, prin. Fax 745-4856

Opp, Covington, Pop. 6,658
Opp CSD 1,400/PK-12
PO Box 840 36467 334-493-3173
Earl Weeks, supt. Fax 493-3060
oppcityschools.com/
Opp HS 500/9-12
502 N Maloy St 36467 334-493-4561
Jeff Rhodes, prin. Fax 493-2146
Opp MS 400/5-8
303 E Stewart Ave 36467 334-493-6332
Aaron Hightower, prin. Fax 493-1120

LBW Community College Post-Sec.
PO Box 910 36467 334-493-3573

Orange Beach, Baldwin, Pop. 5,055

Columbia Southern University Post-Sec.
25326 Canal Rd 36561 251-981-3771

Orrville, Dallas, Pop. 214
Dallas County SD
Supt. — See Selma
Keith MSHS 300/7-12
1166 County Road 115 36767 334-875-4155
Grady Broadnax, prin. Fax 996-8464

Oxford, Calhoun, Pop. 19,981
Oxford CSD 3,400/PK-12
310 E 2nd St 36203 256-241-3140
Dr. Jeff Goodwin, supt. Fax 831-8620
www.oxford.k12.al.us/
Oxford Area Vo HS Vo/Tech
915 Stewart St 36203 256-241-3166
William Holladay, prin. Fax 831-8142
Oxford HS 1,000/9-12
915 Stewart St 36203 256-241-3166
William Holladay, prin. Fax 831-8142
Oxford MS 700/7-8
1750 US Highway 78 W 36203 256-241-3823
Dr. Janice Williams, prin. Fax 835-8813

Ozark, Dale, Pop. 14,833
Dale County SD 2,700/K-12
PO Box 948 36361 334-774-2355
Phillip Parker, supt. Fax 774-3503
www.dalecountyboe.org/
Other Schools – See Ariton, Midland City, Pinckard, Skipperville

Ozark CSD 2,300/K-12
1044 Andrews Ave 36360 334-774-5197
Dr. Daniel C. Payant, supt. Fax 774-2685
ocbecobalt.ocbe.k12.al.us
Carroll HS 900/9-12
455 Forest Ave 36360 334-774-4915
Terry Casey, prin. Fax 774-1865
Carroll HS Career Center Vo/Tech
227 Faust Ave 36360 334-774-4949
Jacqueline Kelley, prin. Fax 774-8314
Smith MS 400/6-8
994 Andrews Ave 36360 334-774-4913
Sylvia Malone, prin. Fax 774-2685

Parrish, Walker, Pop. 1,259
Walker County SD
Supt. — See Jasper
Parrish JSHS 200/7-12
35 Tornado Aly 35580 205-686-7701
Mary Slaughter, prin. Fax 686-9350

Pelham, Shelby, Pop. 19,450
Shelby County SD
Supt. — See Columbiana
Pelham HS 1,200/9-12
2500 Panther Cir 35124 205-682-5500
Bob Lavett, prin. Fax 682-5505

Pell City, Saint Clair, Pop. 11,010
Pell City CSD 4,100/K-12
1000 B Etheredge Pkwy # 201 35128 205-884-4440
Dr. Bobby Hathcock, supt. Fax 814-1010
www.pellcityschools.net
Duran JHS 700/7-8
309 Williamson Dr 35125 205-338-2825
Tony Dowdy, prin. Fax 884-6502

Pell City HS 1,200/9-12
1300 Cogswell Ave 35125 205-338-2250
Helene Bettinger, prin. Fax 338-2838

Victory Christian S 600/PK-12
PO Box 710 35125 205-338-2901
David Weir, prin. Fax 338-3916

Phenix City, Russell, Pop. 29,460
Phenix City SD 4,300/K-12
PO Box 460 36868 334-298-0534
Larry DiChiara, supt. Fax 298-6038
www.pcboe.net
Central HS 1,400/9-12
2400 Dobbs Dr 36870 334-298-3626
Jan Funderburk, prin. Fax 298-7690
South Girard S 400/8-8
521 Fontaine Rd 36869 334-298-2527
Reginald Sparks, prin. Fax 297-8274

Russell County SD 3,400/K-12
PO Box 400 36868 334-298-8791
Lillian Baker, supt. Fax 448-8825
www.russellcountyschools.org
Other Schools – See Seale

Chattahoochee Valley Community College Post-Sec.
2602 College Dr 36869 334-291-4900
Troy University - Phenix City Post-Sec.
1 University Pl 36869 334-297-1007

Phil Campbell, Franklin, Pop. 1,050
Franklin County SD
Supt. — See Russellville
Phil Campbell HS 400/7-12
PO Box 849 35581 205-993-5311
William Smith, prin. Fax 993-5312

Piedmont, Calhoun, Pop. 4,969
Piedmont CSD 1,000/K-12
502 W Hood St 36272 256-447-8831
Matthew Akin, supt. Fax 447-6486
Piedmont HS 300/9-12
750 AL Highway 200 36272 256-447-2829
Hugh McWhorter, prin. Fax 447-8722
Piedmont MS 300/6-8
401 N Main St 36272 256-447-6165
Brenda Formby, prin. Fax 447-8070

Pike Road, Montgomery, Pop. 302
Montgomery County SD
Supt. — See Montgomery
Washington JHS 800/7-9
696 Georgia Washington Rd 36064 334-215-8290
Janet Reese, prin. Fax 215-1304

Pinckard, Dale, Pop. 642
Dale County SD
Supt. — See Ozark
South Dale MS 200/5-8
PO Box D 36371 334-983-3077
David Lee, prin. Fax 983-5882

Pinson, Jefferson, Pop. 10,987
Jefferson County SD
Supt. — See Birmingham
Clay-Chalkville HS 1,500/9-12
6623 Roe Chandler Rd 35126 205-379-3050
Steve Laney, prin. Fax 680-8128
Pinson Valley HS 1,000/9-12
6895 Highway 75 35126 205-379-5100
June Houge, prin. Fax 379-5145
Rudd MS 900/6-8
4526 Rudd School Rd 35126 205-379-5300
Steven Laney, prin. Fax 680-8124

Pisgah, Jackson, Pop. 702
Jackson County SD
Supt. — See Scottsboro
Pisgah S 600/K-12
PO Box 249 35765 256-451-3241
Mark Guffey, prin. Fax 451-3457

Plantersville, Dallas
Dallas County SD
Supt. — See Selma
Dallas County HS 600/9-12
PO Box 145 36758 334-366-2232
Don Ingram, prin. Fax 366-4015

Pleasant Grove, Jefferson, Pop. 10,312
Jefferson County SD
Supt. — See Birmingham
Pleasant Grove JSHS 1,000/7-12
805 7th Ave 35127 205-379-5250
Wayne Byram, prin. Fax 379-5295

Prattville, Autauga, Pop. 30,043
Autauga County SD 9,200/K-12
153 W 4th St 36067 334-365-5706
Larry Butler, supt. Fax 361-3828
www.autaugacountyschool.org
Autauga County Tech Center Vo/Tech
1301 Upper Kingston Rd 36067 334-361-0258
Charles Y. Riddle, prin. Fax 361-3839
Prattville HS 2,100/9-12
1315 Upper Kingston Rd 36067 334-365-8804
Lee Hicks, prin. Fax 358-0011
Prattville JHS 1,100/7-8
1089 Martin Luther King Dr 36067 334-365-6697
Jason Wingate, prin. Fax 361-3870
Other Schools – See Autaugaville, Billingsley, Marbury

Autauga Academy 200/K-12
497 Golson Rd 36067 334-365-4343
Gerald Carter, prin. Fax 365-7713
Prattville Christian Academy 200/PK-12
Old Farm Ln N 36066 334-285-0077
Ron Mitchell, prin. Fax 285-1777

Prichard, Mobile, Pop. 27,963
Mobile County SD
Supt. — See Mobile
Faulkner Career Technical S Vo/Tech
33 W Elm St 36610 251-221-5431
Ronald Coleman, prin. Fax 221-5433
Mobile County Training MS 400/6-8
800 Whitley St 36610 251-221-2267
Aaron Guyton, prin. Fax 221-2269
Vigor HS 900/9-12
838 W Main St 36610 251-221-3045
Leland Whidden, prin. Fax 221-3050

Princeton, Jackson
Jackson County SD
Supt. — See Scottsboro
Paint Rock Valley S 100/K-12
PO Box 150 35766 256-776-2628
Fax 776-0042

Ragland, Saint Clair, Pop. 2,027
Saint Clair County SD
Supt. — See Ashville
Ragland S 600/K-12
1060 Main St 35131 205-472-2123
Hanley Hardy, prin. Fax 472-0086

Rainbow City, Etowah, Pop. 8,880
Etowah County SD
Supt. — See Gadsden
Rainbow MS 600/6-8
454 Lumbley Rd 35906 256-442-1095
Alan Cosby, prin. Fax 442-1028

Gadsden Business College Post-Sec.
3225 Rainbow Dr Ste 246 35906 256-442-2805
Westbrook Christian S 600/PK-12
100 Westminster Dr 35906 256-442-7457
Cynthia Greer, prin. Fax 442-7635

Rainsville, DeKalb, Pop. 4,782
De Kalb County SD 7,500/K-12
PO Box 1668 35986 256-638-6921
Charles D. Warren, supt. Fax 638-9720
www.dekalbk12.org
De Kalb Technology Center Vo/Tech
PO Box 469 35986 256-638-4421
Conner Runyan, prin. Fax 638-4420
Plainview S 1,200/K-12
PO Box 469 35986 256-638-3510
Ronald Bell, prin. Fax 638-6274
Other Schools – See Collinsville, Crossville, Fyffe, Geraldine, Ider, Sylvania, Valley Head

Northeast Alabama Community College Post-Sec.
PO Box 159 35986 256-638-4418

Ranburne, Cleburne, Pop. 471
Cleburne County SD
Supt. — See Heflin
Ranburne HS 400/7-12
21045 Main St 36273 256-568-3402
Fred Lovvorn, prin. Fax 568-2605

Red Bay, Franklin, Pop. 3,282
Franklin County SD
Supt. — See Russellville
Red Bay S 800/K-12
PO Box 1518 35582 256-356-4408
Wesley Thigpen, prin. Fax 356-4418

Red Level, Covington, Pop. 550
Covington County SD
Supt. — See Andalusia
Red Level S 700/K-12
PO Box D 36474 334-469-5315
Johny Odom, prin. Fax 469-6192

Reform, Pickens, Pop. 1,858
Pickens County SD
Supt. — See Carrollton
Pickens County JSHS 400/7-12
PO Box 1239 35481 205-375-2344
Delynn Bouldin, prin. Fax 375-8151

Roanoke, Randolph, Pop. 6,650
Roanoke CSD 1,400/K-12
PO Box 1367 36274 334-863-2628
Chuck Marcum, supt. Fax 863-2849
www.roanokecityschools.org/home.asp
Handley HS 400/9-12
PO Box 1393 36274 334-863-6815
Jim Holley, prin. Fax 863-6284
Handley MS 500/4-8
PO Box 725 36274 334-863-4174
Greg Foster, prin. Fax 863-6129

Robertsdale, Baldwin, Pop. 4,681
Baldwin County SD
Supt. — See Bay Minette
Central Baldwin MS 600/7-8
PO Box 930 36567 251-947-2327
Michael Vivar, prin. Fax 947-1949
Robertsdale HS 1,300/9-12
PO Box 69 36567 251-947-4154
Theresa Bryant, prin. Fax 947-2666
South Baldwin Center for Tech Vo/Tech
PO Box 549 36567 251-947-5041
Kendall Mowdy, prin. Fax 947-4837

Central Christian S 300/PK-12
17395 State Highway 104 36567 251-947-5043
Tim Shelton, admin. Fax 947-2572
Faith Presbyterian Christian S 100/PK-12
PO Box 950 36567 251-947-5012
Marcy Barnhart, prin. Fax 947-5012

Rockford, Coosa, Pop. 405
Coosa County SD 1,500/K-12
PO Box 37 35136 256-377-4913
Todd Wingard, supt. Fax 377-2385
coosaschools.k12.al.us/
Central HS of Coosa County 400/9-12
RR 2 Box 62 35136 256-377-4384
Keith Bullard, prin. Fax 377-4658
Central MS of Coosa County 500/5-8
RR 2 Box 65 35136 256-377-1490
Todd Wingard, prin. Fax 377-1493

Coosa County Science & Technology Ctr Vo/Tech
RR 2 Box 52 35136 256-377-4678
Calvin McKinney, prin. Fax 377-4589

Rogersville, Lauderdale, Pop. 1,186
Lauderdale County SD
Supt. — See Florence
Lauderdale County S 1,000/K-12
PO Box 220 35652 256-247-3414
James Stejskal, prin. Fax 247-3444

Russellville, Franklin, Pop. 8,793
Franklin County SD 3,000/K-12
PO Box 610 35653 256-332-1360
Bill Moss, supt. Fax 331-0069
www.franklin.k12.al.us/
Belgreen S 500/K-12
14220 Highway 187 35653 256-332-1376
Ed Britton, prin. Fax 332-7209
Franklin Co. Career Tech Ctr Vo/Tech
85 Jail Springs Rd 35653 256-332-2127
Orval Seay, prin. Fax 332-2219
Tharptown S 400/K-10
145 Highway 80 35654 256-332-3404
David Riddle, prin. Fax 332-3402
Other Schools – See Phil Campbell, Red Bay, Vina

Russellville CSD 2,400/K-12
1945 Waterloo Rd 35653 256-331-2000
Dr. Wayne Ray, supt. Fax 332-7323
www.rcs.k12.al.us
Russellville HS 700/9-12
1865 Waterloo Rd 35653 256-332-2110
Rex Mayfield, prin. Fax 332-8447
Russellville MS 600/6-8
765 Summit St 35653 256-331-2120
Frankie Hammock, prin. Fax 332-8453

Salem, Lee
Lee County SD
Supt. — See Opelika
Wacoochee JHS 900/7-8
125 Lee Road 254 36874 334-745-3062
Joey Biddle, prin. Fax 745-3565

Samson, Geneva, Pop. 2,025
Geneva County SD
Supt. — See Geneva
Samson HS 200/9-12
209 N Broad St 36477 334-898-2371
Mavis Rials, prin. Fax 898-7576
Samson MS, 209 N Broad St 36477 100/7-8
Mavis Rials, prin. 334-898-1317

Saraland, Mobile, Pop. 12,683
Mobile County SD
Supt. — See Mobile
Adams MS 1,000/6-8
401 Baldwin Rd 36571 251-221-2000
John Powell, prin. Fax 221-2004

Sardis City, DeKalb, Pop. 1,918
Etowah County SD
Supt. — See Gadsden
Sardis JSHS 600/7-12
1420 Church St 35956 256-593-5221
Gerald Beard, prin. Fax 593-5223

Satsuma, Mobile, Pop. 5,951
Mobile County SD
Supt. — See Mobile
Satsuma HS 1,300/9-12
1 Gator Cir 36572 251-221-3269
Deborah Altman, prin. Fax 221-3274

Scottsboro, Jackson, Pop. 14,840
Jackson County SD 6,000/K-12
PO Box 490 35768 256-259-9500
Jerry Jeffery, supt. Fax 259-0076
www.jackson.k12.al.us/
Skyline S 600/K-12
897 County Road 25 35768 256-587-6561
Chad Gorham, prin. Fax 587-6562
Other Schools – See Bridgeport, Higdon, Hollywood, Pisgah, Princeton, Section, Stevenson, Woodville

Scottsboro CSD 2,700/K-12
305 S Scott St 35768 256-218-2100
Dr. Judith Berry, supt. Fax 218-2190
www.scottsboroschools.net
Scottsboro HS 800/9-12
25053 John T Reid Pkwy 35768 256-218-2000
Anthony Ball, prin. Fax 218-2090
Scottsboro JHS 400/7-8
1601 Jefferson St 35768 256-218-2300
Hal Luse, prin. Fax 218-2390

Gaither Beauty College Post-Sec.
414 E Willow St 35768 256-259-1001
Scottsboro Christian Academy 100/PK-12
9545 AL Highway 79 35768 256-259-5398
Debbie Johnson, admin. Fax 574-3639

Seale, Russell
Russell County SD
Supt. — See Phenix City
Russell County HS 1,100/9-12
4699 Highway 431 36875 334-855-4378
Dr. Janet Womack, prin. Fax 855-4334
Russell County MS 600/7-8
4716 Old Seale Hwy 36875 334-855-4453
Larry Screws, prin. Fax 855-4437

Section, Jackson, Pop. 763
Jackson County SD
Supt. — See Scottsboro
Section S 600/K-12
PO Box 10 35771 256-228-6718
Steve Durham, prin. Fax 228-6252

Selma, Dallas, Pop. 19,401
Dallas County SD 4,300/K-12
PO Box 1056 36702 334-875-3440
Dr. Fannie Major-McKenzie, supt. Fax 876-4493
www.dallask12.org

Dallas County Career Technical Center Vo/Tech
1306 Roosevelt St 36701 334-872-8031
Don Willingham, prin. Fax 872-5697
Southside HS 500/9-12
7975 US Highway 80 E 36701 334-872-0518
Bailey Dawson, prin. Fax 872-0295
Tipton MS 300/7-8
2500 Tipton St 36701 334-872-8080
Hattie Shelton, prin. Fax 872-8008
Other Schools – See Orrville, Plantersville, Valley Grande

Selma CSD 4,300/PK-12
PO Box 350 36702 334-874-1600
Verdell Dawson, supt. Fax 874-1604
www.selmacityschools.org
Selma Early College HS 9-12
3000 Earl Goodwin Pkwy 36703 334-876-9395
Irene Smith, prin. Fax 874-9637
Selma HS 1,100/9-12
2180 Broad St 36701 334-874-1680
Roosevelt Wilson, prin. Fax 874-9450
Selma MS CHAT Academy 600/7-8
1701 Summerfield Rd 36701 334-874-1675
Bertram Pickney, prin. Fax 874-1679

Central Christian Academy 200/1-12
1 Bell Rd 36701 334-877-1581
Dayton Dawtins, prin. Fax 877-1586
Concordia College Post-Sec.
PO Box 1329 36702 334-874-5700
George C. Wallace State Comm College Post-Sec.
PO Box 2530 36702 334-876-9227
Meadowview Christian S 400/PK-12
1512 Old Orrville Rd 36701 334-872-8448
Dr. Michael Gaylor, prin. Fax 872-8443
Morgan Academy 600/K-12
PO Box 1587 36702 334-875-4464
Dr. Christopher De Buzna, prin.
Selma University Post-Sec.
1501 Lapsley St 36701 334-872-2533

Semmes, Mobile
Mobile County SD
Supt. — See Mobile
Montgomery HS 1,700/9-12
4275 Snow Rd N 36575 251-221-3153
George Romano, prin. Fax 221-3150
Semmes MS 1,500/6-8
4566 Ed George Rd 36575 251-221-2344
Brenda Shenesey, prin. Fax 221-2347

Sheffield, Colbert, Pop. 9,228
Sheffield CSD 1,200/K-12
300 W 6th St 35660 256-383-0400
Richard L. Gardner, supt. Fax 386-5704
www.scs.k12.al.us/
Sheffield HS 300/9-12
2800 E 19th Ave 35660 256-383-6052
Ronnie Wicks, prin. Fax 386-5707
Sheffield JHS 200/7-8
1803 E 30th St 35660 256-386-5735
Brezofski Anderson, prin. Fax 386-5706

Skipperville, Dale
Dale County SD
Supt. — See Ozark
Long HS 400/7-12
2565 County Road 60 36374 334-774-2380
Jason Steed, prin. Fax 774-3937

Slocomb, Geneva, Pop. 2,033
Geneva County SD
Supt. — See Geneva
Slocomb HS 300/9-12
PO Box 380 36375 334-886-2008
Max Whittaker, prin. Fax 886-9889
Slocomb MS 300/6-8
PO Box 380 36375 334-886-2008
Max Whittaker, prin. Fax 886-9889

Smiths, Lee, Pop. 3,456

Glenwood S 600/K-12
5801 Summerville Rd 36877 334-297-3614
Phillip R. Elder, prin. Fax 214-9027

Smiths Station, Lee, Pop. 4,477
Lee County SD
Supt. — See Opelika
Smiths Station HS 1,600/9-12
1100 Lee Road 298 36877 334-298-0969
Kathie Ledbetter, prin. Fax 298-1304

Somerville, Morgan, Pop. 357
Morgan County SD
Supt. — See Decatur
Brewer HS 800/9-12
59 Eva Rd 35670 256-778-8634
Frances Couey, prin. Fax 778-8012
Brewer Vocational HS Vo/Tech
59 Eva Rd 35670 256-778-8634
Greg Hudson, prin. Fax 778-9119

Spanish Fort, Baldwin, Pop. 5,642
Baldwin County SD
Supt. — See Bay Minette
Spanish Fort JSHS 7-12
PO Box 7504 36577 251-625-3259
Michael Lucci, prin. Fax 615-5648

Chi Alpha Academy 200/PK-12
PO Box 7174 36577 251-626-6801
Tony Harman, prin. Fax 626-6858

Spring Garden, Cherokee
Cherokee County SD
Supt. — See Centre
Spring Garden S 600/K-12
PO Box 31 36275 256-447-7045
Michael Welsh, prin. Fax 447-6947

Springville, Saint Clair, Pop. 3,054
Saint Clair County SD
Supt. — See Ashville
Springville HS 600/9-12
8295 US Highway 11 35146 205-467-7833
Robert Harris, prin. Fax 467-2734
Springville MS 700/4-8
6691 US Highway 11 35146 205-467-2740
Virgil Winslett, prin. Fax 467-2742

Stevenson, Jackson, Pop. 2,138
Jackson County SD
Supt. — See Scottsboro
North Jackson HS 500/9-12
PO Box 848 35772 256-437-2136
Sam Houston, prin. Fax 437-2400
Stevenson MS 300/5-8
701 Kentucky Ave 35772 256-437-2945
Dr. Dianne Brooks, prin. Fax 437-2747

Sulligent, Lamar, Pop. 2,033
Lamar County SD
Supt. — See Vernon
Sulligent S 800/K-12
PO Box 367 35586 205-698-9254
Craig Weeks, prin. Fax 698-8497

Sumiton, Walker, Pop. 2,582

Bevill State Community College Post-Sec.
PO Box 800 35148 205-648-3271

Sweet Water, Marengo, Pop. 231
Marengo County SD
Supt. — See Linden
Sweet Water S 600/K-12
PO Box 127 36782 334-994-4263
Stan Stokley, prin. Fax 994-4686

Sylacauga, Talladega, Pop. 12,956
Sylacauga CSD 1,800/K-12
605 W 4th St 35150 256-245-5256
Dr. Jane Cobia, supt. Fax 245-6665
www.sylacauga.k12.al.us
Nichols-Lawson MS 600/6-8
1550 Talladega Hwy 35150 256-245-4376
Gerald Douglass, prin. Fax 245-4071
Sylacauga HS 700/9-12
701 N Broadway Ave 35150 256-249-8692
Tommy Porch, prin. Fax 245-1026

Talladega County SD
Supt. — See Talladega
Comer Memorial HS 500/7-12
801 Seminole Ave 35150 256-315-5400
Linda McAdam, prin. Fax 315-5420
Fayetteville S 600/K-12
170 WW Averitte Dr 35151 256-315-5550
Joan Doyle, prin. Fax 315-5575

Sylvania, DeKalb, Pop. 1,238
De Kalb County SD
Supt. — See Rainsville
Sylvania S 900/K-12
PO Box 390 35988 256-638-2030
Gary Carlyle, prin. Fax 638-7839

Talladega, Talladega, Pop. 17,149
Talladega CSD 2,800/K-12
501 South St E 35160 256-315-5600
Leonard Messer, supt. Fax 315-5606
www.talladega-cs.net/default.aspx
Ellis JHS 500/7-8
414 Elm St 35160 256-315-5700
Scott Bailey, prin. Fax 315-5704
Talladega Career Tech HS Vo/Tech
110 Piccadilly Dr 35160 256-315-5688
Dr. Trellys Riley, prin. Fax 315-5690
Talladega HS 800/9-12
1177 McMillan St E 35160 256-315-5666
Darren Douthitt, prin. Fax 315-5670

Talladega County SD 7,300/K-12
PO Box 887 35161 256-315-5100
Dr. Cynthia Elsberry, supt. Fax 315-5126
www.tcboe.org
Talladega County Central HS 300/7-12
5104 Howell Cove Rd 35160 256-315-5340
John Galloway, prin. Fax 315-5350
Other Schools – See Alpine, Childersburg, Lincoln, Munford, Sylacauga

---

Alabama Institute for the Deaf and Blind Post-Sec.
PO Box 698 35161
Talladega College Post-Sec.
627 Battle St W 35160 256-362-0206

Tallassee, Elmore, Pop. 5,032
Tallassee CSD 1,800/K-12
308 King St 36078 334-283-6864
Dr. James Jeffers, supt. Fax 283-4338
www.tcschools.com
Southside MS 600/5-8
901 EB Payne Sr Dr 36078 334-283-2151
Ron McDaniel, prin. Fax 283-3577
Tallassee HS 500/9-12
502 Barnett Blvd 36078 334-283-2187
Carl Stewart, prin. Fax 283-6210

Tanner, Limestone
Limestone County SD
Supt. — See Athens
Tanner S 800/K-12
12060 Sommers Rd 35671 256-233-6682
Billy Owens, prin. Fax 233-6449

Tarrant, Jefferson, Pop. 6,691
Tarrant CSD 1,500/PK-12
1318 Alabama St 35217 205-849-3700
Dr. Marti Rizzato, supt. Fax 849-3728
www.tarrant.k12.al.us/
Tarrant City HS 400/9-12
830 Jefferson Blvd 35217 205-849-0172
Andrew Smith, prin. Fax 849-3724
Other Schools – See Birmingham

Theodore, Mobile, Pop. 6,509
Mobile County SD
Supt. — See Mobile
Hankins MS 1,300/6-8
5771 Katherine Hankins Dr 36582 251-221-2200
Cheryl Wittner, prin. Fax 221-2204
Theodore HS 1,700/9-12
6201 Swedetown Rd N 36582 251-221-3351
Ronald Rowell, prin. Fax 221-3355

Magnolia Springs Baptist Academy 200/PK-12
6058 Theodore Dawes Rd 36582 251-653-0251
Bob Ramirez, prin. Fax 653-2668

Thomaston, Marengo, Pop. 375
Marengo County SD
Supt. — See Linden
Johnson S 300/K-12
PO Box 67 36783 334-627-3364
Lepolean Peterson, prin. Fax 627-3396

Thomasville, Clarke, Pop. 4,552
Thomasville CSD 1,700/K-12
PO Box 458 36784 334-636-9955
Dr. Vic Adkison, supt. Fax 636-4096
www.thomasvilleschools.org/
Thomasville HS 400/9-12
777 Gates Dr 36784 334-636-4451
Dr. Brian Clayton, prin. Fax 636-0022
Thomasville MS 500/5-8
781 Gates Dr 36784 334-636-4928
Terry Norton, prin. Fax 636-4924

Alabama Southern Community College Post-Sec.
PO Box 2000 36784 334-636-4429

Thorsby, Chilton, Pop. 1,981
Chilton County SD
Supt. — See Clanton
Thorsby S 900/K-12
54 Opportunity Dr 35171 205-280-4880
Russ Bryan, prin. Fax 646-2197

Toney, Madison
Madison County SD
Supt. — See Huntsville
Sparkman MS 700/6-8
2697 Carters Gin Rd 35773 256-852-0112
Ronnie Blair, prin. Fax 852-4368

Harmony Christian S 50/K-12
PO Box 428 35773 256-852-5607
Liesa Johnston, admin. Fax 420-8301

Town Creek, Lawrence, Pop. 1,209
Lawrence County SD
Supt. — See Moulton
Hatton JSHS 400/7-12
6909 AL Highway 101 35672 256-685-4010
Larry Hancock, prin. Fax 685-4007
Hazlewood JSHS 200/7-12
PO Box 819 35672 256-685-4030
Clyde Goode, prin. Fax 685-4009

Toxey, Choctaw, Pop. 142

South Choctaw Academy 300/K-12
PO Box 160 36921 251-843-2426
M. A. Dempsey, prin. Fax 843-2088

Trinity, Morgan, Pop. 1,842
Lawrence County SD
Supt. — See Moulton
East Lawrence HS 500/8-12
55 County Road 370 35673 256-905-2430
Karen Hitt, prin. Fax 905-2424
East Lawrence MS 700/4-8
99 County Road 370 35673 256-905-2420
Cindy Praytor, prin. Fax 905-2477

Morgan County SD
Supt. — See Decatur
West Morgan HS 700/5-12
261 S Greenway Dr 35673 256-353-5214
Billy Hopkins, prin. Fax 351-0161

Troy, Pike, Pop. 13,935
Pike County SD 2,200/K-12
101 W Love St 36081 334-566-1850
Mark Bazzell, supt. Fax 566-2580
www.pikecountyschools.com
Troy-Pike Regional Center for Technology Vo/Tech
285 Gibbs St 36081 334-566-5395
Al Griffin, prin. Fax 566-1690
Other Schools – See Brundidge, Goshen

Troy CSD 2,400/K-12
PO Box 529 36081 334-566-3741
Dr. Linda Felton-Smith, supt. Fax 566-1425
www.troyschools.net
Henderson HS 700/9-12
PO Box 1006 36081 334-566-3510
David Helms, prin. Fax 566-4940
Henderson MS 600/6-8
PO Box 925 36081 334-566-5770
Chresal Threadgill, prin. Fax 566-3071

Pike Liberal Arts S 300/K-12
PO Box 329 36081 334-566-2023
Cecil Sikes, hdmstr. Fax 566-7091
Troy University 36082 Post-Sec.
334-670-3100

Trussville, Jefferson, Pop. 16,760
Jefferson County SD
Supt. — See Birmingham
Clay-Chalkville MS 1,200/6-8
6700 Trussville Clay Rd 35173 205-379-3100
Maurice Williams, prin. Fax 379-3145

Trussville City SD 4,000/PK-12
113 N Chalkville Rd 35173 205-228-3018
Dr. Suzanne Freeman, supt. Fax 228-3001
trussvillecityschools.com/
Hewitt-Trussville HS 1,200/9-12
5275 Trussville Clay Rd 35173 205-228-3500
Phyllis Montalto, prin. Fax 228-3501

Hewitt-Trussville MS 1,000/6-8
301 Parkway Dr 35173 205-228-3700
Dr. Sunderland Williams, prin. Fax 228-3701

Tuscaloosa, Tuscaloosa, Pop. 81,358
Tuscaloosa CSD 9,500/PK-12
PO Box 038991 35403 205-759-3560
Dr. Joyce Levy, supt. Fax 759-3711
www.tuscaloosacityschools.com
Central HS 600/9-12
905 15th St 35401 205-759-3720
Herbert Ragsdale, prin. Fax 759-3756
Northridge HS 1,000/9-12
2901 Northridge Rd 35406 205-759-3590
Jennifer Box, prin. Fax 759-3605
Tuscaloosa Center for Technology Vo/Tech
1300 37th St E 35405 205-759-3649
James Adkins, coord. Fax 759-3767
Tuscaloosa MS 1,000/6-8
315 McFarland Blvd E 35404 205-759-3652
Eddie Jaynes, prin. Fax 759-3784
Westlawn MS 500/6-8
2800 ML King Jr Blvd 35401 205-759-3673
Zachary Barnes, prin. Fax 759-3770
Night HS Adult
1715 ML King Jr Blvd 35401 205-759-3511
Fax 759-3793
Other Schools – See Cottondale

Tuscaloosa County SD 15,900/PK-12
PO Box 2568 35403 205-758-0411
Dr. Frank Costanzo, supt. Fax 758-2990
www.tcss.net/
Hillcrest HS 1,200/9-12
300 Patriot Pkwy 35405 205-342-2800
Jeffery Hyche, prin. Fax 758-3018
Hillcrest MS 1,000/6-8
401 Hillcrest School Rd 35405 205-342-2820
Wayne Vickers, prin. Fax 752-2467
Other Schools – See Brookwood, Cottondale, Holt, Northport, Vance

---

American Christian Academy 800/PK-12
2300 Veterans Memorial Pkwy 35404 205-553-5963
Dr. Dan Carden, hdmstr. Fax 553-5942
DCH Regional Medical Center Post-Sec.
809 University Blvd E 35401 205-759-7177
Holy Spirit HS 200/7-12
601 37th St E 35405 205-553-5606
Judy Halli, prin. Fax 566-7103
Open Door Christian S 300/PK-12
1785 McFarland Blvd N 35406 205-349-4881
Rebekah Ensor, admin. Fax 349-3246
Shelton State Community College Post-Sec.
9500 Old Greensboro Rd 35405 205-759-1541
Stillman College Post-Sec.
PO Box 1430 35403 205-349-4240
Tuscaloosa Academy 400/PK-12
420 Rice Valley Rd N 35406 205-758-4462
Dr. George B. Elder, hdmstr. Fax 758-4418
University of Alabama Post-Sec.
PO Box 870132 35487 205-348-6010

Tuscumbia, Colbert, Pop. 8,170
Colbert County SD 3,200/K-12
1101 Highway 72 E 35674 256-386-8565
Billy Hudson, supt. Fax 381-9375
colbert.k12.al.us/
Colbert Heights HS 500/7-12
6825 Woodmont Dr 35674 256-383-7875
Leroy Willis, prin. Fax 383-5526
Other Schools – See Cherokee, Leighton

Tuscumbia CSD 1,400/K-12
303 E Commons St S 35674 256-389-2900
Royce Massey, supt. Fax 389-2903
www.tuscumbia.k12.al.us
Deshler Career Technical Center Vo/Tech
200 N Commons St E 35674 256-389-2910
Larry Danley, prin. Fax 389-2915
Deshler HS 500/9-12
200 N Commons St E 35674 256-389-2910
Larry Danley, prin. Fax 389-2915
Northside MS 300/6-8
598 N High St 35674 256-389-2920
Robert Mullen, prin. Fax 389-2921

Covenant Christian S 300/PK-12
1900 Covenant Dr 35674 256-383-4436
Becky Odell, admin. Fax 381-4437

Tuskegee, Macon, Pop. 11,590
Macon County SD 3,000/PK-12
PO Box 830090 36083 334-727-1600
Willie C. Thomas, supt. Fax 724-9990
www.maconk12.org
Washington HS 1,000/9-12
3803 W Mrtn Luther King Hwy 36083 334-727-0073
Dr. Kenneth Oliver, prin. Fax 724-0222
Other Schools – See Notasulga, Tuskegee Institute

Southern Community College Post-Sec.
PO Box 830688 36083 334-727-5220

Tuskegee Institute, See Tuskegee
Macon County SD
Supt. — See Tuskegee
Tuskegee Institute MS 700/6-8
1809 Franklin Rd 36088 334-727-2580
Dr. Dorothy Hooks, prin. Fax 727-5089

Tuskegee University 36088 Post-Sec.
334-727-8011

Union Springs, Bullock, Pop. 3,443
Bullock County SD 1,600/K-12
PO Box 231 36089 334-738-2860
Keith Allen Stewart, supt. Fax 738-2802
bullock.k12.al.us/
Bullock County Career Technical Ctr Vo/Tech
304 Blackmon Ave E 36089 334-738-4370
Charles Cook, prin. Fax 738-4369
Bullock County HS 600/8-12
PO Box 5108 36089 334-738-2198
Robert McDaniel, prin. Fax 738-2606

Uniontown, Perry, Pop. 1,520
Perry County SD
Supt. — See Marion
Hatch JSHS 400/7-12
PO Box 709 36786 334-628-4061
Leslie Turner, prin. Fax 683-4935

Uriah, Monroe
Monroe County SD
Supt. — See Monroeville
Blacksher S 500/PK-12
PO Box 430 36480 251-862-2130
Keith Cardwell, prin. Fax 862-2808

Valley, Chambers, Pop. 9,000
Chambers County SD
Supt. — See Lafayette
Burns MS 800/6-8
292 Johnson St 36854 334-756-3567
Priscilla Holley, prin. Fax 756-7511
Valley HS 800/9-12
501 US Highway 29 36854 334-756-4105
Leon Clark, prin. Fax 756-9602

Lee County SD
Supt. — See Opelika
Beulah HS 600/7-12
4848 Lee Road 270 36854 334-745-5010
Jerry Southwell, prin. Fax 749-1914

Valley Grande, Dallas
Dallas County SD
Supt. — See Selma
Martin MS 400/7-8
2863 County Road 81, 334-872-6417
Finis Sanders, prin. Fax 875-4013

Valley Head, DeKalb, Pop. 639
De Kalb County SD
Supt. — See Rainsville
Valley Head S 500/K-12
PO Box 145 35989 256-635-6228
William Monroe, prin. Fax 635-6229

Vance, Tuscaloosa, Pop. 555
Tuscaloosa County SD
Supt. — See Tuscaloosa
Brookwood MS 700/6-8
17021 Brookwood Pkwy 35490 205-342-2748
Irene Byrd, prin. Fax 553-9910

Verbena, Chilton
Chilton County SD
Supt. — See Clanton
Verbena S 500/K-12
PO Box 128 36091 205-280-2820
Larry Raines, prin. Fax 755-0393

Vernon, Lamar, Pop. 1,984
Lamar County SD 2,400/K-12
PO Box 1379 35592 205-695-7615
Terry Robinson, supt. Fax 695-7678
Lamar County S 700/4-12
8990 Highway 18 35592 205-695-7717
Don Harding, prin. Fax 695-8218
Lamar County School of Technology Vo/Tech
43880 Highway 17 35592 205-695-7129
Jeff Newman, prin. Fax 695-6153
Other Schools – See Millport, Sulligent

Vestavia Hills, Jefferson, Pop. 31,022
Vestavia Hills CSD 5,500/K-12
1204 Montgomery Hwy 35216 205-402-5100
Jamie Blair, supt. Fax 402-5134
www.vestavia.k12.al.us
Pizitz MS 1,200/6-8
2020 Pizitz Dr 35216 205-402-5350
David Miles, prin. Fax 402-5354
Vestavia Hills HS 1,600/9-12
2235 Lime Rock Rd 35216 205-402-5250
Ann C. Jones, prin. Fax 402-5262

Vina, Franklin, Pop. 398
Franklin County SD
Supt. — See Russellville
Vina S 300/K-12
PO Box 36 35593 256-356-4733
James Pharr, prin. Fax 356-4731

Vincent, Shelby, Pop. 1,950
Shelby County SD
Supt. — See Columbiana
Vincent MSHS 500/6-12
42505 Highway 25 35178 205-682-7300
Gary Minnick, prin. Fax 682-7305

Vinemont, Cullman
Cullman County SD
Supt. — See Cullman
Vinemont HS 300/9-12
PO Box 189 35179 256-734-0571
Ronald Barnes, prin. Fax 739-8605
Vinemont MS 300/6-8
PO Box 187 35179 256-739-1943
Michael Grantham, prin. Fax 737-1664

West Point MS 500/6-8
4545 County Road 1141 35179 256-734-5904
Clark Farley, prin. Fax 736-2354

Wadley, Randolph, Pop. 648
Randolph County SD
Supt. — See Wedowee
Wadley S 400/K-12
PO Box 49 36276 256-395-2286
Joe Wilkerson, prin. Fax 395-4488

Southern Union State Community College Post-Sec.
PO Box 1000 36276 256-395-2211

Walnut Grove, Etowah, Pop. 702
Etowah County SD
Supt. — See Gadsden
West End HS 400/7-12
4515 Elm St 35990 205-589-6421
Mark Stancil, prin. Fax 589-4782

Warrior, Jefferson, Pop. 3,037
Jefferson County SD
Supt. — See Birmingham
Corner S 1,000/K-12
10005 Corner School Rd 35180 205-379-3200
Ronald Cooper, prin. Fax 379-3245

Waterloo, Lauderdale, Pop. 207
Lauderdale County SD
Supt. — See Florence
Waterloo S 400/K-12
PO Box 68 35677 256-766-3100
Ronnie Lee, prin. Fax 766-3194

Weaver, Calhoun, Pop. 2,555
Calhoun County SD
Supt. — See Anniston
Weaver HS 500/7-12
917 Clairmont Dr 36277 256-741-7200
Frances Shipp, prin. Fax 820-0811

Wedowee, Randolph, Pop. 824
Randolph County SD 2,300/K-12
PO Box 288 36278 256-357-4611
Wayne Wortham, supt. Fax 357-4844
www.randolph.k12.al.us/
Randolph County S 700/K-12
PO Box 490 36278 256-357-4751
Byron Nix, prin. Fax 357-2310
Randolph-Roanoke Career Tech Vo/Tech
960 Main St S 36278 256-357-2839
Stanley Clarke, prin. Fax 357-4580
Other Schools – See Wadley, Woodland

West Blocton, Bibb, Pop. 1,418
Bibb County SD
Supt. — See Centreville
Bibb County Career/Technical Center Vo/Tech
17191 Highway 5 35184 205-938-7434
Dennis Duncan, prin. Fax 938-2037
West Blocton HS 400/9-12
4734 Truman Aldrich Pkwy 35184 205-938-9002
Suzanne Jones, prin. Fax 938-9546
West Blocton MS 400/5-8
4721 Truman Aldrich Pkwy 35184 205-938-2451
Judson Locke, prin. Fax 938-3261

Wetumpka, Elmore, Pop. 6,905
Elmore County SD 10,300/PK-12
PO Box 817 36092 334-567-1200
Jeffery Langham, supt. Fax 567-1405
www.elmoreco.com
Elmore County Technical Center Vo/Tech
800 Kelly Fitzpatrick Dr 36092 334-567-1219
Carl Thomas, dir. Fax 567-1417
Wetumpka HS 1,000/9-12
1251 Coosa River Pkwy 36092 334-567-5158
Richard Dennis, prin. Fax 567-1178
Wetumpka JHS 600/7-8
409 Alabama St 36092 334-567-1248
Bessie Robinson, prin. Fax 567-1407
Other Schools – See Deatsville, Eclectic, Millbrook

Winfield, Marion, Pop. 4,673
Winfield CSD 1,300/K-12
PO Box 70 35594 205-487-4255
Terrel W. Kirkpatrick, supt. Fax 487-4603
www.winfieldal.org/
Winfield HS 400/9-12
232 Pirate Cv 35594 205-487-6900
Benny Parrish, prin. Fax 487-4257
Winfield MS 400/5-8
481 Apple Ave 35594 205-487-6901
Christopher Cook, prin. Fax 487-4603

Woodland, Randolph, Pop. 208
Randolph County SD
Supt. — See Wedowee
Woodland S 900/K-12
PO Box 157 36280 256-449-2315
Rick Murphy, prin. Fax 449-2316

Woodville, Jackson, Pop. 755
Jackson County SD
Supt. — See Scottsboro
Woodville S 500/K-12
290 County Road 63 35776 256-776-2874
Shane Small, prin. Fax 776-4718

York, Sumter, Pop. 2,625
Sumter County SD
Supt. — See Livingston
Sumter County HS 400/9-12
902 4th Ave 36925 205-392-4771
Ellis Levy, prin. Fax 392-4788

Sumter Academy 300/K-12
181 Sumter Academy Rd 36925 205-392-5238
Paul Kirchharr, hdmstr. Fax 392-5239

ALASKA

ALASKA DEPARTMENT OF EDUCATION
801 W 10th St Ste 200, Juneau 99801-1878
Telephone 907-465-2800
Fax 907-465-4165
Website http://www.eed.state.ak.us/

Commissioner of Education Roger Sampson

ALASKA BOARD OF EDUCATION
801 W 10th St, Juneau 99801-1823

Chairperson Esther Cox

PUBLIC, PRIVATE AND CATHOLIC SECONDARY SCHOOLS

Adak Station, Aleutians West, Pop. 4,633
Aleutian Region SD
Supt. — See Anchorage
Adak S 50/K-12
100 Mechanics Rd, 907-592-3820
Tracy Johnson, prin. Fax 592-2249

Akhiok, Kodiak Island, Pop. 73
Kodiak Island Borough SD
Supt. — See Kodiak
Akhiok S 50/K-12
PO Box 5049 99615 907-836-2223
Bill Watkins, prin. Fax 836-2206

Akiachak, Bethel, Pop. 481
Yupiit SD 500/PK-12
PO Box 51190 99551 907-825-3600
Joseph Slats, supt. Fax 825-3655
www.yupiit.org/
Akiachak S 200/K-12
PO Box 51100 99551 907-825-3616
Eugene Avey, prin. Fax 825-3690
Other Schools – See Akiak, Tuluksak

Akiak, Bethel, Pop. 314
Yupiit SD
Supt. — See Akiachak
Akiak S 100/PK-12
PO Box 52049 99552 907-765-4600
Dan Reum, prin. Fax 765-4642

Akutan, Aleutians East, Pop. 784
Aleutian East Borough SD
Supt. — See Sand Point
Akutan S 50/PK-12
PO Box 25 99553 907-698-2205
Arthur Woodard, prin. Fax 698-2216

Alakanuk, Wade Hampton, Pop. 697
Lower Yukon SD
Supt. — See Mountain Village
Alakanuk S 200/PK-12
PO Box 9 99554 907-238-3312
Russell Grant, prin. Fax 238-3417

Allakaket, Yukon-Koyukuk, Pop. 92
Yukon-Koyukuk SD
Supt. — See Fairbanks
Allakaket S 100/PK-12
PO Box 69 99720 907-968-2205
Nancy Mason, prin. Fax 968-2250

Ambler, Northwest Arctic, Pop. 328
Northwest Arctic Borough SD
Supt. — See Kotzebue
Ambler S 100/PK-12
PO Box 109 99786 907-445-2154
Dr. Elizabeth Balcerek, prin. Fax 445-2159

Anaktuvuk Pass, North Slope, Pop. 262
North Slope Borough SD
Supt. — See Barrow
Nunamiut S 100/PK-12
PO Box 21029 99721 907-661-3226
Robert Meade, prin. Fax 661-3402

Anchorage, Anchorage, Pop. 275,043
Alaska Vocational Technical SD
Supt. — See Seward
AVTEC Allied Health Dept Vo/Tech
1251 Muldoon Rd Ste 11 99504 907-334-2230
Fred Esposito, prin. Fax 334-2287

Aleutian Region SD 50/K-12
PO Box 92230 99509 907-277-2648
Joe Beckford, supt. Fax 277-2649
www.aleutregion.org
Other Schools – See Adak Station, Atka, Nikolski

Anchorage SD 47,900/PK-12
PO Box 196614 99519 907-742-4312
Carol Comeau, supt. Fax 742-4318
www.asdk12.org
AVAIL S Vo/Tech
425 C St 99501 907-742-4930
Catherine Jones, prin. Fax 742-4933
Bartlett HS 1,900/9-12
1101 Muldoon Rd 99506 907-742-1800
Dan Gallego, prin. Fax 742-1825
Central MS of Science 800/7-8
1405 E St 99501 907-742-5100
Johanna Naylor, prin. Fax 742-5125
Clark MS 900/7-8
150 Bragaw St 99508 907-742-4700
Cessilye Williams, prin. Fax 742-4756
Dimond HS 2,000/9-12
2909 W 88th Ave 99502 907-742-7000
Cheryl Guyett, prin. Fax 742-7007
East HS 2,200/9-12
4025 E Northern Lights Blvd 99508 907-742-2100
Michael Graham, prin. Fax 742-2134
Goldenview MS 900/7-8
15800 Golden View Dr 99516 907-348-8626
Julie Maker, prin. Fax 742-8273
Hanshew MS 1,000/7-8
10121 Lake Otis Pkwy 99507 907-349-1561
Sherry Ellers, prin. Fax 349-2835
King Career Center Vo/Tech
2650 E Northern Lights Blvd 99508 907-742-8900
Guy Okada, prin. Fax 742-8907
Mears MS 1,100/7-8
2700 W 100th Ave 99515 907-742-6400
Michael Perkins, prin. Fax 742-6444
Romig MS 800/7-8
2500 Minnesota Dr 99503 907-742-5200
Trudy Genne, prin. Fax 742-5252
Service HS 1,600/9-12
5577 Abbott Rd 99507 907-742-8100
Lou Pondolfino, prin. Fax 742-6615
South Anchorage HS 1,700/9-12
13400 Elmore Rd 99516 907-742-6200
Chuck Fannin, prin. Fax 742-6207
Wendler MS 900/7-8
2905 Lake Otis Pkwy 99508 907-742-7300
Joel Roylance, prin. Fax 742-7307
West HS 1,900/9-12
1700 Hillcrest Dr 99517 907-742-2500
Rick Stone, prin. Fax 742-2525
Other Schools – See Chugiak, Eagle River

Chugach SD 200/PK-12
9312 Vanguard Dr Ste 100 99507 907-522-7400
Bob Crumley, supt. Fax 522-3399
www.chugachschools.com
Other Schools – See Chenega Bay, Tatitlek, Whittier

Alaska Pacific University Post-Sec.
4101 University Dr 99508 800-252-7528
Anchorage Christian S 800/PK-12
6401 E Northern Lights Blvd 99504 907-337-9575
Tom Cobaugh, admin. Fax 338-3903
Career Academy Post-Sec.
1415 E Tudor Rd 99507 907-563-7575
Charter College Post-Sec.
2221 E Northern Lights Blvd 99508 907-277-1000
Gateway S and Learning Center 50/K-12
2511 Sentry Dr 99507 907-522-2240
M. Beverly Lau, hdmstr. Fax 344-0304
Grace Christian S 700/K-12
12407 Pintail St 99516 907-345-4814
Nate Davis, admin. Fax 644-2260
Heritage Christian S 200/PK-12
9251 Lake Otis Pkwy 99507 907-349-8032
Richard Satterfield, prin. Fax 349-8275
Lumen Christi JSHS 100/8-12
8110 Jewel Lake Rd Bldg D 99502 907-245-9231
James Yeargan, prin. Fax 245-9232
University of Alaska Anchorage Post-Sec.
PO Box 141629 99514 907-786-1800

Anchor Point, Kenai Peninsula, Pop. 866
Kenai Peninsula Borough SD
Supt. — See Soldotna
Nikolaevsk S 100/K-12
PO Box 5129 99556 907-235-8972
Mike Sellers, prin. Fax 235-3617

Anderson, Denali, Pop. 324
Denali Borough SD
Supt. — See Healy
Anderson S 100/K-12
PO Box 3120 99744 907-582-2700
Geoff Buerger, prin. Fax 582-2000

Angoon, Skagway-Yakutat-Angoon, Pop. 481
Chatham SD 200/K-12
PO Box 109 99820 907-788-3302
Vance Cortez-Rucker, supt. Fax 788-3252
www.chathamsd.org/
Angoon S 100/K-12
PO Box 209 99820 907-788-3811
Ryan Dorsey, prin. Fax 788-3812
Other Schools – See Gustavus, Haines, Tenakee Springs

Aniak, Bethel, Pop. 581
Kuspuk SD 400/PK-12
PO Box 49 99557 907-675-4250
Dr. Martin Laster, supt. Fax 675-4305
www.kuspuk.org
Aniak JSHS 100/7-12
PO Box 29 99557 907-675-4330
Mac Whyte, prin. Fax 675-4256
Other Schools – See Chuathbaluk, Crooked Creek, Kalskag, Red Devil, Sleetmute, Stony River

Anvik, Yukon-Koyukuk, Pop. 98
Iditarod Area SD
Supt. — See Mc Grath
Blackwell S 50/K-12
PO Box 90 99558 907-663-6348
Kay Holbrook, prin. Fax 663-6349

Arctic Village, Yukon-Koyukuk, Pop. 96
Yukon Flats SD
Supt. — See Fort Yukon
Arctic Village S 50/PK-12
PO Box 22049 99722 907-587-5211
Caroline Tritt-Frank, prin. Fax 587-5210

Atka, Aleutians West, Pop. 81
Aleutian Region SD
Supt. — See Anchorage
Netsvetov S 50/K-12
PO Box 47050 99547 907-839-2210
Lynne Moore, lead tchr. Fax 839-2212

Atmautluak, Bethel, Pop. 258
Lower Kuskokwim SD
Supt. — See Bethel
Alexie Memorial S 100/PK-12
PO Box ATT 99559 907-553-5112
Larry Strunk, prin. Fax 553-5129

Atqasuk, North Slope, Pop. 212
North Slope Borough SD
Supt. — See Barrow
Meade River S 100/PK-12
General Delivery 99791 907-633-6315
Michael Siefert, prin. Fax 633-6215

Barrow, North Slope, Pop. 4,218
North Slope Borough SD 1,900/PK-12
PO Box 169 99723 907-852-5311
Dr. Trent Blankenship, supt. Fax 852-9503
www.nsbsd.org/
Barrow HS 300/9-12
PO Box 960 99723 907-852-8950
Lynda Earring, prin. Fax 852-8969
Hopson Memorial MS 200/6-8
PO Box 509 99723 907-852-3880
Heidi Packer, prin. Fax 852-7794
Other Schools – See Anaktuvuk Pass, Atqasuk, Kaktovik, Nuiqsut, Point Hope, Point Lay, Wainwright

---

Ilisagvik College Post-Sec.
PO Box 749 99723 907-852-3333

Beaver, Yukon-Koyukuk, Pop. 103
Yukon Flats SD
Supt. — See Fort Yukon
Cruikshank S 50/PK-12
PO Box 24050 99724 907-628-6313
Charlene Fisher, prin. Fax 628-6615

Bethel, Bethel, Pop. 6,262
Lower Kuskokwim SD 3,800/PK-12
PO Box 305 99559 907-543-4800
Bill Ferguson, supt. Fax 543-4904
www.lksd.org
Bethel Regional HS 500/6-12
PO Box 700 99559 907-543-3957
Janelle Vanasse, prin. Fax 543-2327
Other Schools – See Atmautluak, Chefornak, Eek, Goodnews Bay, Kasigluk, Kipnuk, Kongiganak, Kwethluk, Kwigillingok, Mekoryuk, Napakiak, Napaskiak, Newtok, Nightmute, Nunapitchuk, Quinhagak, Toksook Bay, Tuntutuliak, Tununak

---

University of Alaska Kuskokwim Campus Post-Sec.
PO Box 368 99559 907-543-4500

Big Lake, Matanuska-Susitna, Pop. 1,477
Matanuska-Susitna Borough SD
Supt. — See Palmer
Houston HS 500/9-12
PO Box 521060 99652 907-892-9400
Mike Vrvilo, prin. Fax 892-9460
Houston MS 400/6-8
PO Box 521060 99652 907-892-9400
Andy Murr, prin. Fax 892-9460

Brevig Mission, Nome, Pop. 278
Bering Strait SD
Supt. — See Unalakleet
Brevig Mission S 100/PK-12
General Delivery 99785 907-642-4021
Robin Gray, prin. Fax 642-4031

Buckland, Northwest Arctic, Pop. 430
Northwest Arctic Borough SD
Supt. — See Kotzebue
Buckland S 200/PK-12
PO Box 91 99727 907-494-2127
Terri Walker, prin. Fax 494-2106

Cantwell, Denali, Pop. 147
Denali Borough SD
Supt. — See Healy
Cantwell S 50/K-12
PO Box 29 99729 907-768-2372
Pete Hauschka, prin. Fax 768-2500

Central, Yukon-Koyukuk, Pop. 52
Yukon Flats SD
Supt. — See Fort Yukon
Far North S 50/K-12
PO Box 30049 99730 907-520-5114
Jack Von Thaer, prin. Fax 520-5151

Chalkyitsik, Yukon-Koyukuk, Pop. 90
Yukon Flats SD
Supt. — See Fort Yukon
Tsuk Taih S 50/PK-12
General Delivery 99788 907-848-8113
Margaret Waldrup, prin. Fax 848-8312

Chefornak, Bethel, Pop. 400
Lower Kuskokwim SD
Supt. — See Bethel
Chaptnquak S 200/PK-12
PO Box 50 99561 907-867-8700
Bruce Sheehan, prin. Fax 867-8727

Chenega Bay, Valdez-Cordova, Pop. 94
Chugach SD
Supt. — See Anchorage
Chenega Bay Community S 50/PK-12
PO Box 8030 99574 907-573-5123
Steve Grajewski, prin. Fax 573-5137

Chevak, Wade Hampton, Pop. 819
Kashunamiut SD 400/K-12
985 KSD Way 99563 907-858-7713
Gary Stevens, supt. Fax 858-7328
Chevak S 400/K-12
985 KSD Way 99563 907-858-7712
Delbert Lantz, prin. Fax 858-7264

Chignik, Lake and Peninsula, Pop. 67
Lake & Peninsula SD
Supt. — See King Salmon
Chignik Bay S 50/PK-12
PO Box 9 99564 907-749-2213
Adam Mokelke, lead tchr. Fax 749-2261

Chignik Lagoon, Lake and Peninsula, Pop. 53
Lake & Peninsula SD
Supt. — See King Salmon
Chignik Lagoon S 50/K-12
PO Box 50 99565 907-840-2210
Adam Mokelke, lead tchr. Fax 840-2265

Chignik Lake, Lake and Peninsula, Pop. 133
Lake & Peninsula SD
Supt. — See King Salmon
Chignik Lake S 50/PK-12
General Delivery 99548 907-845-2210
Mike Flanagan, prin. Fax 845-2254

Chiniak, Kodiak Island, Pop. 69
Kodiak Island Borough SD
Supt. — See Kodiak
Chiniak S 50/K-10
PO Box 5529 99615 907-486-8323
Bill Watkins, prin. Fax 486-3185

Chuathbaluk, Bethel, Pop. 121
Kuspuk SD
Supt. — See Aniak
Crow Village Sam S 50/PK-12
PO Box Chu 99557 907-467-4229
Brad Allen, prin. Fax 467-4122

Chugiak, See Anchorage
Anchorage SD
Supt. — See Anchorage

Chugiak HS 2,000/9-12
16525 Birchwood Loop Rd 99567 907-742-3050
Rick Volk, prin. Fax 742-3148
Mirror Lake MS 700/6-8
22901 Lake Hill Dr 99567 907-742-3500
Scott Batchelder, prin. Fax 742-3545

Circle, Yukon-Koyukuk, Pop. 73
Yukon Flats SD
Supt. — See Fort Yukon
Circle S 50/PK-12
PO Box 49 99733 907-773-1250
Brian Rozell, prin. Fax 773-1259

Coffman Cove, Prince of Wales-Outer Ketchikan, Pop. 180
Southeast Island SD
Supt. — See Thorne Bay
Valentine S 50/K-12
PO Box 18002 99918 907-329-2244
Deedee Jeffreys, lead tchr. Fax 329-2210

Cold Bay, Aleutians East, Pop. 81
Aleutian East Borough SD
Supt. — See Sand Point
Cold Bay S 50/PK-12
PO Box 128 99571 907-532-2409
Ty DeVault, prin. Fax 532-2421

Copper Center, Valdez-Cordova, Pop. 449
Copper River SD
Supt. — See Glennallen
Kenny Lake S 100/1-12
HC 60 Box 224 99573 907-822-3870
Reed Carlson, prin. Fax 822-3794

Sapa Christian S 50/1-12
HC 60 Box 289 99573 907-822-5747
Rev. David Johnson, admin. Fax 822-3764

Cordova, Valdez-Cordova, Pop. 2,327
Cordova CSD 500/PK-12
PO Box 140 99574 907-424-3265
Don Clark, supt. Fax 424-3271
cordovasd.org/
Cordova JSHS 200/7-12
PO Box 140 99574 907-424-3266
Don Clark, prin. Fax 424-5215

Craig, Prince of Wales-Outer Ketchikan, Pop. 1,217
Craig CSD 400/PK-12
PO Box 800 99921 907-826-3274
Ronald Erickson, supt. Fax 826-3322
www.craigschools.com
Craig HS 100/9-12
PO Box 800 99921 907-826-2274
Doug Rhodes, prin. Fax 826-3016
Craig MS 100/6-8
PO Box 800 99921 907-826-3274
Camille Booth, prin. Fax 826-3309

Crooked Creek, Bethel, Pop. 106
Kuspuk SD
Supt. — See Aniak
John S 50/PK-12
General Delivery 99575 907-432-2205
Brad Allen, prin. Fax 432-2206

Deering, Northwest Arctic, Pop. 144
Northwest Arctic Borough SD
Supt. — See Kotzebue
Deering S 100/PK-12
PO Box 36009 99736 907-363-2121
Steve Pile, prin. Fax 363-2128

Delta Junction, Southeast Fairbanks, Pop. 897
Delta-Greely SD 800/PK-12
PO Box 527 99737 907-895-4658
Dan Beck, supt. Fax 895-4246
www.dgsd.k12.ak.us/
Delta Junction HS 200/9-12
PO Box 647 99737 907-895-4460
Rod Schug, prin. Fax 895-4049
Gerstle River S 50/PK-12
PO Box 527 99737 907-895-4655
Laural Jackson, prin. Fax 895-4246
Other Schools – See Fort Greely

Dillingham, Dillingham, Pop. 2,468
Dillingham CSD 500/PK-12
PO Box 170 99576 907-842-5223
Arnold Watland, supt. Fax 842-5634
www.dcsd.k12.ak.us
Dillingham JSHS 300/6-12
PO Box 170 99576 907-842-5221
Brian Midles, prin. Fax 842-4395

Southwest Region SD 700/K-12
PO Box 90 99576 907-842-5287
Jack Foster, supt. Fax 842-5428
dlg.swrsd.org/do/doHomePage.shtml
Other Schools – See Koliganek, Manokotak, New Stuyahok, Togiak

---

University of Alaska Bristol Bay Campus Post-Sec.
PO Box 1070 99576 907-842-5109

Diomede, Nome, Pop. 147
Bering Strait SD
Supt. — See Unalakleet
Diomede S 50/PK-12
PO Box 7099 99762 907-686-3021
Elsie Davis, prin. Fax 686-3022

Dot Lake, Southeast Fairbanks, Pop. 70
Alaska Gateway SD
Supt. — See Tok
Dot Lake S 50/K-12
PO Box 2280 99737 907-882-2663
Gordon Kron, prin. Fax 882-2112

Eagle, Southeast Fairbanks, Pop. 139
Alaska Gateway SD
Supt. — See Tok
Eagle Community S 50/K-12
PO Box 168 99738 907-547-2210
Ann Millard, prin. Fax 547-2302

Eagle River, See Anchorage
Anchorage SD
Supt. — See Anchorage
Eagle River HS 9-12
8701 Yosemite Dr 99577 907-742-2700
Natalie Burnett, prin. Fax 742-2710
Gruening MS 600/7-8
9601 Lee St 99577 907-742-3600
Sven Gustafson, prin. Fax 742-3666

Eagle River Christian S 100/PK-12
10336 E Eagle River Loop Rd 99577 907-694-4602
Denny Archer, admin. Fax 694-4141

Eek, Bethel, Pop. 285
Lower Kuskokwim SD
Supt. — See Bethel
Eek S 100/PK-12
PO Box 50 99578 907-536-5228
Dan Walker, prin. Fax 536-5628

Egegik, Lake and Peninsula, Pop. 99
Lake & Peninsula SD
Supt. — See King Salmon
Egegik S 50/PK-12
PO Box 10 99579 907-233-2210
Lee Webster, lead tchr. Fax 233-2254

Eielson AFB, Fairbanks North Star, Pop. 5,251
Fairbanks-North Star Borough SD
Supt. — See Fairbanks
Eielson JSHS 600/7-12
675 Ravens Way 99702 907-372-3110
Mario Gatto, prin. Fax 372-3202

Elim, Nome, Pop. 316
Bering Strait SD
Supt. — See Unalakleet
Aniguiin S 100/PK-12
PO Box 29 99739 907-890-3021
Steve Sammons, prin. Fax 890-3031

Emmonak, Wade Hampton, Pop. 823
Lower Yukon SD
Supt. — See Mountain Village
Emmonak S 200/PK-12
General Delivery 99581 907-949-1248
William Schildbach, prin. Fax 949-1148

Fairbanks, Fairbanks North Star, Pop. 31,324
Fairbanks-North Star Borough SD 14,200/PK-12
520 5th Ave 99701 907-452-2000
Dr. Ann E. Shortt, supt. Fax 451-0541
www.northstar.k12.ak.us
Hutchison HS Vo/Tech
3750 Geist Rd 99709 907-479-2261
Bill McLeod, prin. Fax 479-8286
Lathrop HS 1,300/9-12
901 Airport Way 99701 907-456-7794
Karen Gaborik, prin. Fax 452-6735
Ryan MS 500/7-8
951 Airport Way 99701 907-452-4751
Carol Digou, prin. Fax 451-8834
Smith MS 500/7-8
1401 Bainbridge Blvd 99701 907-458-7600
Jim Currie, prin. Fax 458-7676
Tanana MS 600/7-8
600 Trainor Gate Rd 99701 907-452-8145
Edwina Strange, prin. Fax 456-2780
West Valley HS 1,300/9-12
3800 Geist Rd 99709 907-479-4221
Marianne Carlson, prin. Fax 474-8901
Other Schools – See Eielson AFB, North Pole

Yukon-Koyukuk SD 400/PK-12
4762 Old Airport Way 99709 907-374-9400
Christopher Simon, supt. Fax 374-9440
www.yksd.com
Other Schools – See Allakaket, Hughes, Huslia, Juneau, Kaltag, Manley Hot Springs, Minto, Nulato, Ruby

---

Fairhill Christian S 200/PK-12
101 City Lights Blvd 99712 907-457-2167
Marilyn Buchanan, prin. Fax 457-4382
Far North Christian S 100/K-12
1110 20th Ave 99701 907-452-7979
Kevin Taylor, admin. Fax 452-5327
Monroe Catholic JSHS 200/7-12
615 Monroe St 99701 907-452-2044
Vince Fantazzi, prin. Fax 456-7481
University of Alaska Fairbanks Post-Sec.
PO Box 757480 99775 907-474-7581
University of Alaska Interior Campus Post-Sec.
PO Box 756720 99775 907-474-7211
University of Alaska Tanana Valley Cmps Post-Sec.
PO Box 758000 99775 907-474-7400

False Pass, Aleutians East, Pop. 59
Aleutian East Borough SD
Supt. — See Sand Point
False Pass S 50/PK-12
PO Box 30 99583 907-548-2224
Ernest McKay, prin. Fax 548-2304

Fort Greely, Southeast Fairbanks, Pop. 1,147
Delta-Greely SD
Supt. — See Delta Junction
Ft. Greely S 200/6-8
Building 725, 907-869-1305
Brian Schaffer, prin. Fax 869-3382

Fort Yukon, Yukon-Koyukuk, Pop. 561
Yukon Flats SD 300/PK-12
PO Box 350 99740 907-662-2515
Linda Evans, supt. Fax 662-3094
www.yukonflats.net
Fort Yukon S 100/PK-12
PO Box 129 99740 907-662-2352
Susan Johnson, prin. Fax 662-2958
Other Schools – See Arctic Village, Beaver, Central, Chalkyitsik, Circle, Stevens Village, Venetie

Fritz Creek, Kenai Peninsula, Pop. 1,426
Kenai Peninsula Borough SD
Supt. — See Soldotna
Kachemak Selo S 100/K-12
PO Box 15007 99603 907-235-5552
Randy Creamer, prin. Fax 235-5644
Voznesenka S 100/K-12
PO Box 15336 99603 907-235-8549
Ray Hillman, prin. Fax 235-6086

Galena, Yukon-Koyukuk, Pop. 641
Galena CSD 100/PK-12
PO Box 299 99741 907-656-1205
Jim Smith, supt. Fax 656-2238
www.galenaalaska.org
Huntington JSHS 100/7-12
PO Box 299 99741 907-656-1205
Chris Reitan, prin. Fax 656-1368

Gambell, Nome, Pop. 653
Bering Strait SD
Supt. — See Unalakleet
Gambell S 200/PK-12
PO Box 169 99742 907-985-5515
Steve Petz, prin. Fax 985-5435

Glennallen, Valdez-Cordova, Pop. 451
Copper River SD 600/K-12
PO Box 108 99588 907-822-3234
Kathy Gearhart, supt. Fax 822-3949
www.crsd.k12.ak.us
Glennallen JSHS 200/7-12
PO Box 108 99588 907-822-5286
Michael Johnson, prin. Fax 822-8501
Other Schools – See Copper Center, Slana

Alaska Bible College Post-Sec.
PO Box 289 99588 907-822-3201

Golovin, Nome, Pop. 145
Bering Strait SD
Supt. — See Unalakleet
Olson S 100/PK-12
PO Box 62040 99762 907-779-3021
Gay Jacobson, prin. Fax 779-3031

Goodnews Bay, Bethel, Pop. 234
Lower Kuskokwim SD
Supt. — See Bethel
Rocky Mountain S 100/PK-12
PO Box 153 99589 907-967-8213
Christopher Carmichael, prin. Fax 967-8228

Grayling, Yukon-Koyukuk, Pop. 184
Iditarod Area SD
Supt. — See Mc Grath
David-Louis Memorial S 50/K-12
PO Box 90 99590 907-453-5135
Marilyn Johnson, prin. Fax 453-5165

Gustavus, Skagway-Yakutat-Angoon, Pop. 380
Chatham SD
Supt. — See Angoon
Gustavus S 50/K-12
PO Box 120 99826 907-697-2248
Robyn Taylor, prin. Fax 697-2378

Haines, Haines, Pop. 1,265
Chatham SD
Supt. — See Angoon
Klukwan S 50/K-12
PO Box 1409 99827 907-767-5551
Ruth Ryan, prin. Fax 767-5573

Haines Borough SD 300/PK-12
PO Box 1289 99827 907-766-2644
Charlie Jones, supt. Fax 766-2508
glacierbears.hbsd.net/
Haines HS 100/9-12
PO Box 1289 99827 907-766-2411
Charlie Jones, prin. Fax 766-2416

Healy, Denali, Pop. 487
Denali Borough SD 300/K-12
PO Box 280 99743 907-683-2278
Kim Langton, supt. Fax 683-2514
denali.ak.schoolwebpages.com/
Tri-Valley S 200/K-12
PO Box 400 99743 907-683-2267
Anne Olson, prin. Fax 683-2632
Other Schools – See Anderson, Cantwell

Holy Cross, Yukon-Koyukuk, Pop. 215
Iditarod Area SD
Supt. — See Mc Grath
Holy Cross S 100/K-12
PO Box 210 99602 907-476-7131
Kay Holbrook, prin. Fax 476-7161

Homer, Kenai Peninsula, Pop. 5,364
Kenai Peninsula Borough SD
Supt. — See Soldotna
Homer HS 500/9-12
600 E Fairview Ave 99603 907-235-4600
Ron Keffer, prin. Fax 235-8933
Homer MS 200/7-8
500 Sterling Hwy 99603 907-235-5700
Dan Beck, prin. Fax 235-5747
Razdolna S 50/K-12
PO Box 15098 99603 907-235-6870
Douglas Waclawski, prin. Fax 235-6485

Hoonah, Skagway-Yakutat-Angoon, Pop. 751
Hoonah CSD 100/K-12
PO Box 157 99829 907-945-3611
Eugene Avey, supt. Fax 945-3492
Hoonah JSHS 100/7-12
PO Box 157 99829 907-945-3613
Deborah Hansen, prin. Fax 945-3607

Hooper Bay, Wade Hampton, Pop. 1,085
Lower Yukon SD
Supt. — See Mountain Village
Hooper Bay S 400/PK-12
General Delivery 99604 907-758-4826
Ken Hagel, prin. Fax 758-4012

Hope, Kenai Peninsula, Pop. 161
Kenai Peninsula Borough SD
Supt. — See Soldotna
Hope S 50/K-12
PO Box 47 99605 907-782-3202
Ken Halverson, admin. Fax 782-3140

Hughes, Yukon-Koyukuk, Pop. 74
Yukon-Koyukuk SD
Supt. — See Fairbanks
Oldman S 50/K-12
PO Box 30 99745 907-889-2204
Joan Jones, prin. Fax 889-2220

Huslia, Yukon-Koyukuk, Pop. 277
Yukon-Koyukuk SD
Supt. — See Fairbanks
Huntington S 100/PK-12
PO Box 110 99746 907-829-2205
Arthur Sosa, prin. Fax 829-2270

Hydaburg, Prince of Wales-Outer Ketchikan, Pop. 351
Hydaburg CSD 100/K-12
PO Box 109 99922 907-285-3491
Don Johnson, supt. Fax 285-3391
www.hydaburg.k12.ak.us
Hydaburg S 100/K-12
PO Box 109 99922 907-285-3591
James Holien, prin. Fax 285-3391

Hyder, Prince of Wales-Outer Ketchikan, Pop. 99
Southeast Island SD
Supt. — See Thorne Bay
Hyder S 50/K-12
PO Box 110 99923 250-636-2100
Kathy Shirley, lead tchr. Fax 636-2112

Igiugig, Bristol Bay, Pop. 33
Lake & Peninsula SD
Supt. — See King Salmon
Igiugig S 50/PK-12
PO Box 4010 99613 907-533-3220
Todd Washburn, lead tchr. Fax 533-3221

Iliamna, Lake and Peninsula, Pop. 94
Lake & Peninsula SD
Supt. — See King Salmon
Newhalen S 100/K-12
PO Box 89 99606 907-571-1211
Reta Doland, prin. Fax 571-1466

Juneau, Juneau, Pop. 30,987
Juneau Borough SD 5,200/PK-12
10014 Crazy Horse Dr 99801 907-463-1700
Peggy Cowan, supt. Fax 463-1768
www.jsd.k12.ak.us
Dryden MS 600/6-8
10014 Crazy Horse Dr 99801 907-463-1850
Tom Milliron, prin. Fax 463-1828
Heeni MS 700/6-8
10014 Crazy Horse Dr 99801 907-463-1899
Barb Mecum, prin. Fax 463-1877
Juneau-Douglas HS 1,700/9-12
10014 Crazy Horse Dr 99801 907-523-1500
Bernie Sorenson, prin. Fax 523-1616

Yukon-Koyukuk SD
Supt. — See Fairbanks
Alyeska Central S K-12
3141 Channel Dr Ste 100 99801 907-586-1566
Patrick Doyle, prin. Fax 586-8106

University of Alaska Southeast Post-Sec.
11120 Glacier Hwy 99801 907-465-6457

Kake, Wrangell-Petersburg, Pop. 667
Kake CSD 200/K-12
PO Box 450 99830 907-785-3741
Eric Gebhart, supt. Fax 785-6439
Kake S K-12
PO Box 450 99830 907-785-3741
Eric Gebhart, prin. Fax 785-6439

Kaktovik, North Slope, Pop. 272
North Slope Borough SD
Supt. — See Barrow
Kaveolook S 100/PK-12
PO Box 20 99747 907-640-6626
Les Kramer, prin. Fax 640-6718

Kalskag, Bethel, Pop. 186
Kuspuk SD
Supt. — See Aniak
Morgan HS 100/7-12
General Delivery 99607 907-471-2288
Bill Gilliland, prin. Fax 471-2242

Kaltag, Yukon-Koyukuk, Pop. 218
Yukon-Koyukuk SD
Supt. — See Fairbanks
Kaltag S 50/PK-12
PO Box 30 99748 907-534-2204
Michael Day, prin. Fax 534-2227

Kasigluk, Bethel, Pop. 425
Lower Kuskokwim SD
Supt. — See Bethel
Akiuk Memorial S 100/PK-12
104 Village Rd 99609 907-477-6829
Carl Williams, prin. Fax 477-6314
Akula Elitnaurvik S 100/K-12
PO Box 79 99609 907-477-6615
Felicia Kleven, prin. Fax 477-6715

Kenai, Kenai Peninsula, Pop. 7,464
Kenai Peninsula Borough SD
Supt. — See Soldotna
Kenai Central HS 500/9-12
9583 Kenai Spur Hwy 99611 907-283-7524
Alan Fields, prin. Fax 283-3230
Kenai MS 400/6-8
201 N Tinker Ln 99611 907-283-4896
Paul Sorenson, prin. Fax 283-3180

Ketchikan, Ketchikan Gateway, Pop. 7,410
Ketchikan Gateway Borough SD 2,000/PK-12
333 Schoenbar Rd 99901 907-247-2142
Harry Martin, supt. Fax 247-3822
www.kgbsd.org
Ketchikan HS 600/9-12
2610 4th Ave 99901 907-225-9815
Larry Eklund, prin. Fax 247-5761
Revilla HS 100/7-12
3131 Baranof Ave 99901 907-225-6681
Doug Gregg, prin. Fax 247-6681
Schoenbar MS 300/7-8
217 Schoenbar Rd 99901 907-225-5138
Bob Hewitt, prin. Fax 225-5761

Southeast Island SD
Supt. — See Thorne Bay
Hollis S 50/K-12
PO Box HYL 99950 907-530-7108
Julie Vasquez, lead tchr. Fax 530-7111
Kasaan S 50/K-12
PO Box Kxa 99950 907-542-2217
David McCourtney, prin. Fax 542-2219
Naukati S 50/K-12
PO Box NKI 99950 907-629-4121
Mark Zintek, lead tchr. Fax 629-4122
Port Protection S 50/K-12
PO Box PPV 99950 907-489-2228
Amy McDonald, lead tchr. Fax 489-2260

Ketchikan Christian Academy 50/1-12
PO Box 7400 99901 907-225-2891
Rev. Bill White, admin. Fax 225-2890
University of Alaska Southeast-Ketchikan Post-Sec.
2600 7th Ave 99901 907-225-6177

Kiana, Northwest Arctic, Pop. 411
Northwest Arctic Borough SD
Supt. — See Kotzebue
Kiana S 100/PK-12
PO Box 190 99749 907-475-2115
Susan Johnson, prin. Fax 475-2120

King Cove, Aleutians East, Pop. 748
Aleutian East Borough SD
Supt. — See Sand Point
King Cove S 100/PK-12
PO Box 69 99612 907-497-2354
Ralph Lindquist, prin. Fax 497-2408

King Salmon, Bristol Bay, Pop. 696
Lake & Peninsula SD 400/PK-12
PO Box 498 99613 907-246-4280
Steve Atwater, supt. Fax 246-4473
www.lpsd.com
Other Schools – See Chignik, Chignik Lagoon, Chignik Lake, Egegik, Igiugig, Iliamna, Kokhanok, Levelock, Nondalton, Pedro Bay, Perryville, Pilot Point, Port Alsworth, Port Heiden

Kipnuk, Bethel, Pop. 470
Lower Kuskokwim SD
Supt. — See Bethel
Chief Paul Memorial S 200/PK-12
PO Box 19 99614 907-896-5011
Jim Marriner, prin. Fax 896-5428

Kivalina, Northwest Arctic, Pop. 399
Northwest Arctic Borough SD
Supt. — See Kotzebue
McQueen S 100/PK-12
General Delivery 99750 907-645-2125
Ken Hagel, prin. Fax 645-2124

Klawock, Prince of Wales-Outer Ketchikan, Pop. 767
Klawock CSD 200/K-12
PO Box 9 99925 907-755-2228
Rich Carlson, supt. Fax 755-2320
www.klawockschool.com/
Klawock S 200/K-12
PO Box 9 99925 907-755-2220
Donald Spink, prin. Fax 755-2913

Kobuk, Northwest Arctic, Pop. 115
Northwest Arctic Borough SD
Supt. — See Kotzebue
Kobuk S 50/PK-12
PO Box 40 99751 907-948-2231
Art Finkenbinder, prin. Fax 948-2225

Kodiak, Kodiak Island, Pop. 6,273
Kodiak Island Borough SD 2,700/K-12
722 Mill Bay Rd 99615 907-481-6200
Betty Walters, supt. Fax 481-6218
www.kodiak.k12.ak.us
Kodiak HS 800/9-12
722 Mill Bay Rd 99615 907-481-2501
Karen Boehler, prin. Fax 481-2505
Kodiak MS 400/7-8
722 Mill Bay Rd 99615 907-486-9213
Steve Doerksen, prin. Fax 486-9061
Other Schools – See Akhiok, Chiniak, Larsen Bay, Old Harbor, Ouzinkie, Port Lions

Kodiak College Post-Sec.
117 Benny Benson Dr 99615 907-486-1235

Kokhanok, Lake and Peninsula, Pop. 152
Lake & Peninsula SD
Supt. — See King Salmon
Kokhanok S 50/K-12
General Delivery 99606 907-282-2210
Todd Washburn, prin. Fax 282-2247

Koliganek, Dillingham, Pop. 181
Southwest Region SD
Supt. — See Dillingham
Koliganek S 100/K-12
PO Box 5052 99576 907-596-3444
Suzan Wiley, prin. Fax 596-3484

Kongiganak, Bethel, Pop. 294
Lower Kuskokwim SD
Supt. — See Bethel
Kiunya Memorial S 100/PK-12
PO Box 5109, 907-557-5126
Daryl Daugaard, prin. Fax 557-5639

Kotlik, Wade Hampton, Pop. 635
Lower Yukon SD
Supt. — See Mountain Village
Kotlik S 200/PK-12
PO Box 20129 99620 907-899-4415
Vic Lewin, prin. Fax 899-4515

Kotzebue, Northwest Arctic, Pop. 3,237
Northwest Arctic Borough SD 2,100/PK-12
PO Box 51 99752 907-442-3472
Norman Eck Ph.D., supt. Fax 442-2246
www.nwarctic.org/
Alaska Technical Center Vo/Tech
PO Box 51 99752 907-442-3733
Cheryl Edenshaw, dir. Fax 442-2764
Kotzebue MSHS 400/6-12
PO Box 264 99752 907-442-3341
David Mason, prin. Fax 442-2141
Other Schools – See Ambler, Buckland, Deering, Kiana, Kivalina, Kobuk, Noatak, Noorvik, Selawik, Shungnak

University of Alaska Chuchi Campus Post-Sec.
PO Box 297 99752 907-442-3400

Koyuk, Nome, Pop. 299
Bering Strait SD
Supt. — See Unalakleet
Koyuk-Malemute S 100/PK-12
PO Box 53009 99753 907-963-3021
Kevin Hunking, prin. Fax 963-2428

Kwethluk, Bethel, Pop. 726
Lower Kuskokwim SD
Supt. — See Bethel
Ket'acik Aap'alluk Memorial S 200/PK-12
PO Box 150 99621 907-757-6014
Doyle Horton, prin. Fax 757-6013

Kwigillingok, Bethel, Pop. 278
Lower Kuskokwim SD
Supt. — See Bethel
Kwigillingok S 100/PK-12
PO Box 109 99622 907-588-8629
Walt Betz, prin. Fax 588-8613

Larsen Bay, Kodiak Island, Pop. 105
Kodiak Island Borough SD
Supt. — See Kodiak
Larsen Bay S 50/K-12
PO Box 70 99624 907-847-2252
Bill Watkins, prin. Fax 847-2260

Levelock, Lake and Peninsula, Pop. 105
Lake & Peninsula SD
Supt. — See King Salmon
Levelock S 50/PK-12
PO Box 89 99625 907-287-3060
Ty Mase, lead tchr. Fax 287-3021

Mc Grath, Yukon-Koyukuk, Pop. 491
Iditarod Area SD 400/PK-12
PO Box 90 99627 907-524-3033
Joe Banghort, supt. Fax 524-3217
www.iditarodsd.org/
Lime Village S 50/K-12
PO Box LVD 99627 907-526-5112
Art Woodard, prin. Fax 526-5225
Mc Grath S 100/K-12
PO Box 290 99627 907-524-3388
Joan O'Neal, prin. Fax 524-3751
Other Schools – See Anvik, Grayling, Holy Cross, Nikolai, Shageluk, Takotna

Manley Hot Springs, Yukon-Koyukuk, Pop. 96
Yukon-Koyukuk SD
Supt. — See Fairbanks
Manley Hart Springs Gladys Dart S 50/PK-12
PO Box 29 99756 907-672-3202
Heidi Wright, prin. Fax 672-3201

Manokotak, Dillingham, Pop. 400
Southwest Region SD
Supt. — See Dillingham
Manokotak S 100/K-12
PO Box 30 99628 907-289-1013
Herman Gerving, prin. Fax 289-2050

Marshall, Wade Hampton, Pop. 374
Lower Yukon SD
Supt. — See Mountain Village
Marshall S 100/PK-12
PO Box 89 99585 907-679-6112
Priscilla Shaw, prin. Fax 679-6637

Mekoryuk, Bethel, Pop. 213
Lower Kuskokwim SD
Supt. — See Bethel
Nuniwaarmiut S 50/PK-12
PO Box 49 99630 907-827-8415
Kevin McCalla, prin. Fax 827-8613

Mentasta Lake, Valdez-Cordova, Pop. 96
Alaska Gateway SD
Supt. — See Tok
Mentasta Lake S 50/K-12
PO Box 6039 99780 907-291-2327
John Cochran, prin. Fax 291-2325

Metlakatla, Prince of Wales-Outer Ketchikan, Pop. 1,407
Annette Islands SD 300/K-12
PO Box 7 99926 907-886-6332
Brett Agenbroad, supt. Fax 886-5130
aisd.k12.ak.us
Leask MS 100/7-8
PO Box 7 99926 907-886-6003
Richard Montgomery, prin. Fax 886-6019
Metlakatla HS 100/9-12
PO Box 7 99926 907-886-6000
Richard Montgomery, prin. Fax 886-5120

Minto, Yukon-Koyukuk, Pop. 218
Yukon-Koyukuk SD
Supt. — See Fairbanks
Minto S 100/PK-12
PO Box 81 99758 907-798-7212
Vicky Charlie, prin. Fax 798-7282

Mountain Village, Wade Hampton, Pop. 808
Lower Yukon SD 2,000/PK-12
PO Box 32089 99632 907-591-2411
John Lamont, supt. Fax 591-2449
do.lysd.k12.ak.us
Beans S 300/PK-12
PO Box 32105 99632 907-591-2819
Nicholas Grubich, prin. Fax 591-2214
Other Schools – See Alakanuk, Emmonak, Hooper Bay, Kotlik, Marshall, Pilot Station, Russian Mission, Saint Marys, Scammon Bay, Sheldon Point

Naknek, Bristol Bay, Pop. 575
Bristol Bay Borough SD 200/K-12
PO Box 169 99633 907-246-4225
Woody Wilson, supt. Fax 246-6857
alaska.ihigh.com/bristolbay/
Bristol Bay MSHS 100/7-12
PO Box 169 99633 907-246-4265
Woody Wilson, prin. Fax 246-4447

Nanwalek, Kenai Peninsula
Kenai Peninsula Borough SD
Supt. — See Soldotna
Nanwalek S 100/K-12
PO Box 8007 99603 907-281-2210
Megan Reinseth, prin. Fax 281-2211

Napakiak, Bethel, Pop. 359
Lower Kuskokwim SD
Supt. — See Bethel
Miller Memorial S 100/PK-12
PO Box 50 99634 907-589-2420
Bruce Kleven, prin. Fax 589-2515

Napaskiak, Bethel, Pop. 397
Lower Kuskokwim SD
Supt. — See Bethel
Qugcuun Memorial S 50/PK-12
PO Box 6199 99559 907-737-7214
Chris Meier, prin. Fax 737-7211
Williams S 100/K-12
PO Box 6089 99559 907-737-7212
Christopher Woodward, prin. Fax 737-7967

Nelson Lagoon, Aleutians East, Pop. 83
Aleutian East Borough SD
Supt. — See Sand Point
Nelson Lagoon S 50/PK-12
PO Box 19 99571 907-989-2225
James Rush, prin. Fax 989-2228

Nenana, Yukon-Koyukuk, Pop. 371
Nenana CSD 800/K-12
PO Box 10 99760 907-832-5464
Robert Thomason, supt. Fax 832-5625
Nenana City S 200/K-12
PO Box 10 99760 907-832-5464
Andy Corbin, prin. Fax 832-5625

New Stuyahok, Dillingham, Pop. 472
Southwest Region SD
Supt. — See Dillingham
Chief Blunka S 200/K-12
PO Box 29 99636 907-693-3144
Gene Anderson, prin. Fax 693-3163

Newtok, Bethel, Pop. 207
Lower Kuskokwim SD
Supt. — See Bethel
Ayaprun S 100/K-12
PO Box WWT 99559 907-237-2505
Grant Kashatok, prin. Fax 237-2506

Nightmute, Bethel, Pop. 211
Lower Kuskokwim SD
Supt. — See Bethel
Nightmute S 100/PK-12
General Delivery 99690 907-647-6313
Mitchell Pioch, prin. Fax 647-6227

Nikiski, Kenai Peninsula, Pop. 2,743
Kenai Peninsula Borough SD
Supt. — See Soldotna
Nikiski MSHS 400/7-12
PO Box 7112 99635 907-776-3456
John O'Brien, prin. Fax 776-3486

Nikolai, Yukon-Koyukuk, Pop. 93
Iditarod Area SD
Supt. — See Mc Grath
Top of the Kuskokwim S 50/K-12
PO Box 9190 99691 907-293-2427
Denis Gardella, prin. Fax 293-2214

Nikolski, Aleutians West, Pop. 35
Aleutian Region SD
Supt. — See Anchorage
Nikolski S 50/K-12
General Delivery 99638 907-576-2200
Tyler Schlung, prin. Fax 576-2230

Ninilchik, Kenai Peninsula, Pop. 456
Kenai Peninsula Borough SD
Supt. — See Soldotna
Ninilchik S 200/K-12
PO Box 39010 99639 907-567-3301
Terry Martin, prin. Fax 567-3504

Noatak, Northwest Arctic, Pop. 333
Northwest Arctic Borough SD
Supt. — See Kotzebue
Napaaqtugmiut S 200/PK-12
PO Box 49 99761 907-485-2153
John Cote, prin. Fax 485-2150

Nome, Nome, Pop. 3,590
Nome SD 700/PK-12
PO Box 131 99762 907-443-2231
Stan Lujan, supt. Fax 443-5144
www.nomeschools.com
Nome-Beltz JSHS 300/7-12
PO Box 131 99762 907-443-5201
Owen Carter, prin. Fax 443-3626

University of Alaska Northwest Campus Post-Sec.
PO Box 400 99762 907-443-2201

Nondalton, Lake and Peninsula, Pop. 188
Lake & Peninsula SD
Supt. — See King Salmon
Nondalton S 100/K-12
100 School Rd 99640 907-294-2210
Ed Cox, prin. Fax 294-2265

Noorvik, Northwest Arctic, Pop. 672
Northwest Arctic Borough SD
Supt. — See Kotzebue
Aqqaluk / Noorvik S 200/PK-12
PO Box 165 99763 907-636-2178
Doyle Horton, prin. Fax 636-2160

North Pole, Fairbanks North Star, Pop. 1,778
Fairbanks-North Star Borough SD
Supt. — See Fairbanks
North Pole HS 900/9-12
601 NPHS Blvd 99705 907-488-3761
A.C. Woolnough, prin. Fax 488-1488
North Pole MS 500/6-8
300 E 8th Ave 99705 907-488-2271
Ernie Manzie, prin. Fax 488-9213

North Pole Christian S 100/PK-12
PO Box 55306 99705 907-488-0133
Ethan Gelineau, prin. Fax 488-8248

Northway, Southeast Fairbanks, Pop. 123
Alaska Gateway SD
Supt. — See Tok
Northway S 100/K-12
PO Box 519 99764 907-778-2287
Donald Hennessey, prin. Fax 778-2221

Nuiqsut, North Slope, Pop. 386
North Slope Borough SD
Supt. — See Barrow
Nuiqsut Trapper S 100/PK-12
3310 3rd Ave 99789 907-480-6712
John Luhrs, prin. Fax 480-6621

Nulato, Yukon-Koyukuk, Pop. 318
Yukon-Koyukuk SD
Supt. — See Fairbanks
Demoski S 100/PK-12
PO Box 65029 99765 907-898-2204
Robert Robertson, prin. Fax 898-2340

Nunapitchuk, Bethel, Pop. 474
Lower Kuskokwim SD
Supt. — See Bethel
Tobeluk Memorial S 200/K-12
PO Box 150 99641 907-527-5325
Charlotte Calhoun, prin. Fax 527-5610

Old Harbor, Kodiak Island, Pop. 217
Kodiak Island Borough SD
Supt. — See Kodiak
Old Harbor S 100/K-12
PO Box 49 99643 907-286-2213
Bill Watkins, prin. Fax 286-2222

Ouzinkie, Kodiak Island, Pop. 206
Kodiak Island Borough SD
Supt. — See Kodiak
Ouzinkie S 100/K-12
PO Box 49 99644 907-680-2204
Bill Watkins, prin. Fax 680-2288

Palmer, Matanuska-Susitna, Pop. 6,920
Matanuska-Susitna Borough SD 14,300/PK-12
501 N Gulkana St 99645 907-746-9255
Robert Doyle, supt. Fax 761-4076
www.matsuk12.us
Beryozava S, 501 N Gulkana St 99645 50/K-12
Laurine Domke, prin. 907-746-9239
Colony HS 1,100/9-12
9550 E Colony Schools Dr 99645 907-746-9500
Cydney Duffin, prin. Fax 746-9572
Colony MS 600/6-8
9250 E Colony Schools Dr 99645 907-761-1500
Jason Mabry, prin. Fax 761-1592

Palmer HS 900/9-12
1170 W Arctic Ave 99645 907-746-8400
Wolfgang Winter, prin. Fax 746-8481
Palmer MS 700/6-8
1159 S Chugach St 99645 907-761-4300
Gene Stone, prin. Fax 761-4372
Valley Pathways HS 200/9-12
PO Box 4897 99645 907-745-2158
James Wanser, prin. Fax 745-1496
Other Schools – See Big Lake, Sutton, Talkeetna, Wasilla

Matanuska Christian S 100/PK-12
248 E Elmwood Ave 99645 907-746-6789
Colleen Hamblen, admin. Fax 746-6788
University of Alaska Matanuska-Susitna Post-Sec.
PO Box 2889 99645 907-745-9774

Pedro Bay, Lake and Peninsula, Pop. 42
Lake & Peninsula SD
Supt. — See King Salmon
Dena'ina S 50/K-12
General Delivery 99647 907-850-2207
Reta Doland, lead tchr. Fax 850-2254

Pelican, Skagway-Yakutat-Angoon, Pop. 139
Pelican CSD 50/PK-12
PO Box 90 99832 907-735-2236
Connie Newman Ph.D., supt. Fax 735-2263
Pelican S 50/PK-12
PO Box 90 99832 907-735-2236
Connie Newman, prin. Fax 735-2263

Perryville, Lake and Peninsula, Pop. 108
Lake & Peninsula SD
Supt. — See King Salmon
Perryville S 50/K-12
PO Box 103 99648 907-853-2210
Adam Mokelke, lead tchr. Fax 853-2267

Petersburg, Wrangell-Petersburg, Pop. 3,010
Petersburg CSD 600/K-12
PO Box 289 99833 907-772-4271
Dr. Gary Jacobasen, supt. Fax 772-4719
www.psgsd.k12.ak.us
Mitkof MS 200/6-8
PO Box 289 99833 907-772-3860
David Morris, prin. Fax 772-3617
Petersburg HS 200/9-12
PO Box 289 99833 907-772-3861
David Morris, prin. Fax 772-4168

Pilot Point, Lake and Peninsula, Pop. 85
Lake & Peninsula SD
Supt. — See King Salmon
Pilot Point S 50/PK-12
PO Box 467 99649 907-797-2210
Mike Flanagan, prin. Fax 797-2267

Pilot Station, Wade Hampton, Pop. 590
Lower Yukon SD
Supt. — See Mountain Village
Pilot Station S 200/PK-12
PO Box 5090 99650 907-549-3212
David Sharstrom, prin. Fax 549-3335

Point Hope, North Slope, Pop. 704
North Slope Borough SD
Supt. — See Barrow
Tikigaq S 200/PK-12
PO Box 148 99766 907-368-2662
Joe Davis, prin. Fax 368-2770

Point Lay, North Slope, Pop. 139
North Slope Borough SD
Supt. — See Barrow
Kali S 100/PK-12
PO Box 59077 99759 907-833-2311
Kitza Durkop, prin. Fax 833-2315

Port Alexander, Wrangell-Petersburg, Pop. 77
Southeast Island SD
Supt. — See Thorne Bay
Port Alexander S 50/K-12
PO Box 8170 99836 907-568-2205
Nick Higson, lead tchr. Fax 568-2261

Port Alsworth, Lake and Peninsula, Pop. 55
Lake & Peninsula SD
Supt. — See King Salmon
Tanalian S 50/PK-12
General Delivery 99653 907-781-2210
Ed Cox, lead tchr. Fax 781-2254

Port Graham, Kenai Peninsula, Pop. 166
Kenai Peninsula Borough SD
Supt. — See Soldotna
Port Graham S 50/K-12
PO Box 5550 99603 907-284-2210
Peggy Arnold-Hoobler, prin. Fax 284-2213

Port Heiden, Lake and Peninsula, Pop. 101
Lake & Peninsula SD
Supt. — See King Salmon
Meshik S 50/K-12
General Delivery 99549 907-837-2210
Mike Flanagan, lead tchr. Fax 837-2265

Port Lions, Kodiak Island, Pop. 234
Kodiak Island Borough SD
Supt. — See Kodiak
Port Lions S 50/K-12
PO Box 109 99550 907-454-2237
Bill Watkins, prin. Fax 454-2377

Quinhagak, Bethel, Pop. 563
Lower Kuskokwim SD
Supt. — See Bethel
Kuinerrarmiut Elitnaurviat S 200/PK-12
General Delivery 99655 907-556-8628
David Bauer, prin. Fax 556-8228

Red Devil, Bethel, Pop. 53
Kuspuk SD
Supt. — See Aniak
Willis S 50/K-12
General Delivery 99656 907-447-3213
Brad Allen, prin. Fax 447-3214

Ruby, Yukon-Koyukuk, Pop. 178
Yukon-Koyukuk SD
Supt. — See Fairbanks
Kangas S 50/PK-12
PO Box 68110 99768 907-468-4465
Bruce Buffmire, prin. Fax 468-4444

Russian Mission, Wade Hampton, Pop. 317
Lower Yukon SD
Supt. — See Mountain Village
Russian Mission S 100/PK-12
PO Box 90 99657 907-584-5615
Jason Moen, prin. Fax 584-5412

Saint George Island, Aleutians West, Pop. 59
Pribilof SD
Supt. — See Saint Paul Island
St. George S 50/PK-12
PO Box 959 99591 907-859-2228
Carol Randall, prin. Fax 859-2229

Saint Marys, Wade Hampton, Pop. 577
Lower Yukon SD
Supt. — See Mountain Village
Pitkas Point S 50/PK-12
PO Box 161 99658 907-438-2571
Larry Johnson, prin. Fax 438-2948

Saint Mary's SD 200/PK-12
PO Box 9 99658 907-438-2411
David Herbert, supt. Fax 438-2735
Saint Mary's S 200/PK-12
PO Box 9 99658 907-438-2411
Dewayne Bahnsen, prin. Fax 438-2735

Saint Michael, Nome, Pop. 366
Bering Strait SD
Supt. — See Unalakleet
Andrews S 100/PK-12
100 Baker St 99659 907-923-3041
Dan Eide, prin. Fax 923-3031

Saint Paul Island, Aleutians West, Pop. 400
Pribilof SD 100/PK-12
PO Box 905 99660 907-546-2221
Jamie Stacks, supt. Fax 546-2327
www.pribilofs.k12.ak.us/
St. Paul S 100/PK-12
PO Box 905 99660 907-546-2221
Jamie Stacks, prin. Fax 546-2356
Other Schools – See Saint George Island

Sand Point, Aleutians East, Pop. 951
Aleutian East Borough SD 300/PK-12
PO Box 429 99661 907-383-5222
Dr. Phil Knight, supt. Fax 383-3496
www.aebsd.org
Sand Point S 100/PK-12
PO Box 269 99661 907-383-2393
Jeanne Perkins, prin. Fax 383-3833
Other Schools – See Akutan, Cold Bay, False Pass, King Cove, Nelson Lagoon

Savoonga, Nome, Pop. 648
Bering Strait SD
Supt. — See Unalakleet
Kingeekuk Memorial S 200/K-12
PO Box 200 99769 907-984-6811
Margaret Koegler, prin. Fax 984-6413

Scammon Bay, Wade Hampton, Pop. 499
Lower Yukon SD
Supt. — See Mountain Village
Scammon Bay S 200/PK-12
General Delivery 99662 907-558-5312
Adrian Reyes, prin. Fax 558-5320

Selawik, Northwest Arctic, Pop. 819
Northwest Arctic Borough SD
Supt. — See Kotzebue
Davis-Ramoth S 300/PK-12
PO Box 29 99770 907-484-2142
Gerald Pickner, prin. Fax 484-2127

Seldovia, Kenai Peninsula, Pop. 300
Kenai Peninsula Borough SD
Supt. — See Soldotna
English S 100/K-12
PO Box 171 99663 907-234-7616
Cheryl Hingley, prin. Fax 234-7617

Seward, Kenai Peninsula, Pop. 3,016
Alaska Vocational Technical SD
PO Box 889 99664 907-224-4140
Fred Esposito, supt. Fax 224-4143
www.avtec.alaska.edu
Alaska Vocational Technical Center Vo/Tech
PO Box 889 99664 907-224-4140
Fred Esposito, prin. Fax 224-4143
Other Schools – See Anchorage

Kenai Peninsula Borough SD
Supt. — See Soldotna
Seward HS 300/9-12
PO Box 1049 99664 907-224-3351
Ginger Blackmon, prin. Fax 224-3306
Seward MS 100/7-8
PO Box 1049 99664 907-224-3351
Trevan Walker, prin. Fax 224-3306

Alaska Vocational Technical School Post-Sec.
PO Box 889 99664 907-224-4159

Shageluk, Yukon-Koyukuk, Pop. 122
Iditarod Area SD
Supt. — See Mc Grath
Innoko River S 50/PK-12
PO Box 53 99665 907-473-8233
Timothy Stathis, prin. Fax 473-8268

Shaktoolik, Nome, Pop. 232
Bering Strait SD
Supt. — See Unalakleet
Shaktoolik S 100/PK-12
PO Box 40 99771 907-955-3021
Linda Goldeski, prin. Fax 955-3031

Sheldon Point, Wade Hampton, Pop. 121
Lower Yukon SD
Supt. — See Mountain Village
Sheldon Point S 100/PK-12
PO Box 32, Nunam Iqua AK 99666 907-498-4112
Lowell Garrett, prin. Fax 498-4235

Shishmaref, Nome, Pop. 565
Bering Strait SD
Supt. — See Unalakleet
Shishmaref S 200/PK-12
1 Seaview Ln 99772 907-649-3021
Joe Braach, prin. Fax 649-3031

Shungnak, Northwest Arctic, Pop. 272
Northwest Arctic Borough SD
Supt. — See Kotzebue
Shungnak S 100/PK-12
PO Box 79 99773 907-437-2151
Kitza Durkop, prin. Fax 437-2177

Sitka, Sitka, Pop. 8,986
Mt. Edgecumbe HSD 400/9-12
1330 Seward Ave 99835 907-966-3200
Bill K. Denkinger, supt. Fax 966-2442
www.mehs.us
Mt. Edgecumbe HS 400/9-12
1330 Seward Ave 99835 907-966-3202
Bernie Gurule, prin. Fax 966-2442

Sitka SD 1,500/PK-12
300 Kostrometinoff St 99835 907-747-8622
Steve Bradshaw, supt. Fax 966-1260
www.ssd.k12.ak.us
Blatchley MS 300/6-8
601 Halibut Point Rd 99835 907-747-8672
Charlie Robison, prin. Fax 966-1460
Sitka HS 400/9-12
1000 Lake St 99835 907-747-3263
Howard Wayne, prin. Fax 747-3229

Sheldon Jackson College Post-Sec.
801 Lincoln St 99835 907-747-5220
University of Alaska Sitka Campus Post-Sec.
1332 Seward Ave 99835 907-747-6653

Skagway, Skagway-Yakutat-Angoon, Pop. 828
Skagway CSD 100/K-12
PO Box 497 99840 907-983-2960
Dr. Michael Dickens, supt. Fax 983-2964
Skagway S 100/K-12
PO Box 497 99840 907-983-2960
Dr. Michael Dickens, prin. Fax 983-2964

Slana, Valdez-Cordova, Pop. 63
Copper River SD
Supt. — See Glennallen
Slana S 50/1-12
PO Box 870 99586 907-822-5868
Bob Snedigar, prin. Fax 822-3850

Sleetmute, Bethel, Pop. 106
Kuspuk SD
Supt. — See Aniak
Egnaty S 50/K-12
General Delivery 99668 907-449-4216
Brad Allen, prin. Fax 449-4217

Soldotna, Kenai Peninsula, Pop. 4,087
Kenai Peninsula Borough SD 9,000/PK-12
148 N Binkley St 99669 907-714-8888
Dr. Donna Peterson, supt. Fax 262-9645
www.kpbsd.k12.ak.us
Peninsula Optional HS 9-12
152 E Park Ave 99669 907-714-8945
Gregg Wilbanks, prin.
Skyview HS 500/9-12
46188 Sterling Hwy 99669 907-260-2300
Randy Neill, prin. Fax 262-6555
Soldotna HS 500/9-12
425 W Marydale Ave 99669 907-260-7000
Todd Syverson, prin. Fax 262-4288
Soldotna MS 600/7-8
426 W Redoubt Ave 99669 907-260-2500
Sharon Moock, prin. Fax 262-7036
Other Schools – See Anchor Point, Fritz Creek, Homer, Hope, Kenai, Nanwalek, Nikiski, Ninilchik, Port Graham, Seldovia, Seward, Tyonek

---

Cook Inlet Academy 200/PK-12
45872 Kalifornsky Beach Rd 99669 907-262-5101
Kevin Spence, prin. Fax 262-1541
Kenai Peninsula College Post-Sec.
34820 College Dr 99669 907-262-0300

Stebbins, Nome, Pop. 552
Bering Strait SD
Supt. — See Unalakleet
Tukurngailnguq S 200/K-12
General Delivery 99671 907-934-3041
Terry Peppers, prin. Fax 934-3031

Sterling, Kenai Peninsula, Pop. 3,802

Academy of Higher Learning 50/K-12
PO Box 682 99672 907-260-7741
Catherine Gibson, prin. Fax 260-7741

Stevens Village, Yukon-Koyukuk, Pop. 102
Yukon Flats SD
Supt. — See Fort Yukon
Stevens Village S 50/PK-12
General Delivery 99774 907-478-7116
Linda Green, prin. Fax 478-7893

Stony River, Bethel, Pop. 51
Kuspuk SD
Supt. — See Aniak
Michael S 50/K-12
General Delivery 99557 907-537-3226
Brad Allen, prin. Fax 537-3237

Sutton, Matanuska-Susitna, Pop. 308
Matanuska-Susitna Borough SD
Supt. — See Palmer
Glacier View S 100/K-12
29170 W Glenn Hwy 99674 907-745-5122
Wendy Taylor, prin. Fax 746-5560

Takotna, Yukon-Koyukuk, Pop. 38
Iditarod Area SD
Supt. — See Mc Grath
Takotna S 50/K-12
PO Box 90 99675 907-298-2115
Robert Absher, prin. Fax 298-2316

Talkeetna, Matanuska-Susitna, Pop. 250
Matanuska-Susitna Borough SD
Supt. — See Palmer
Susitna Valley JSHS 200/7-12
PO Box 807 99676 907-733-2241
Matthew Clark, prin. Fax 733-1363

Tanana, Yukon-Koyukuk, Pop. 290
Tanana CSD 100/K-12
PO Box 89 99777 907-366-7203
Dorothy Jordan, coord. Fax 366-7201
Sommer S 100/K-12
PO Box 89 99777 907-366-7207
Dorothy Jordan, prin. Fax 366-7201

Tatitlek, Valdez-Cordova, Pop. 119
Chugach SD
Supt. — See Anchorage
Tatitlek Community S 50/K-12
PO Box 167 99677 907-325-2252
Jed Palmer, prin. Fax 325-2299

Teller, Nome, Pop. 269
Bering Strait SD
Supt. — See Unalakleet
Isabell S 100/PK-12
100 Airport Ave 99778 907-642-3041
Jay Thomas, prin. Fax 642-3031

Tenakee Springs, Skagway-Yakutat-Angoon, Pop. 98
Chatham SD
Supt. — See Angoon
Tenakee Springs S 50/K-12
PO Box 62 99841 907-736-2204
Diane Zemanek, prin. Fax 736-2204

Thorne Bay, Prince of Wales-Outer Ketchikan, Pop. 503
Southeast Island SD 200/K-12
PO Box 19569 99919 907-828-8254
Jim Nygaard, supt. Fax 828-8257
www.sisd.org
Thorne Bay S 100/K-12
PO Box 5 99919 907-828-3921
Paul Young, lead tchr. Fax 828-3901
Other Schools – See Coffman Cove, Hyder, Ketchikan, Port Alexander

Togiak, Dillingham, Pop. 810
Southwest Region SD
Supt. — See Dillingham
Togiak S 200/K-12
PO Box 50 99678 907-493-5829
David Wick, prin. Fax 493-5933

Tok, Southeast Fairbanks, Pop. 935
Alaska Gateway SD 400/PK-12
PO Box 226 99780 907-883-5151
Al Weinberg, admin. Fax 883-5154
tok.schoolaccess.net/
Tetlin S 50/PK-12
General Delivery 99780 907-324-2104
Margie Grant, prin. Fax 324-2120
Tok S 200/K-12
PO Box 249 99780 907-883-5161
LeAnn Young, prin. Fax 883-5165
Other Schools – See Dot Lake, Eagle, Mentasta Lake, Northway

Toksook Bay, Bethel, Pop. 542
Lower Kuskokwim SD
Supt. — See Bethel
Nelson Island S 200/PK-12
General Delivery 99637 907-427-7815
Talbert Bentley, prin. Fax 427-7612

Tuluksak, Bethel, Pop. 383
Yupiit SD
Supt. — See Akiachak
Tuluksak S 200/PK-12
PO Box 115 99679 907-695-5625
Jeff Ralston, prin. Fax 695-5645

Tuntutuliak, Bethel, Pop. 300
Lower Kuskokwim SD
Supt. — See Bethel
Angapak Memorial S 100/PK-12
General Delivery 99680 907-256-2415
Frank Cook, prin. Fax 256-2527

Tununak, Bethel, Pop. 338
Lower Kuskokwim SD
Supt. — See Bethel
Albert Memorial S 100/K-12
PO Box 49 99681 907-652-6827
Gayle Miller, prin. Fax 652-6028

Tyonek, Kenai Peninsula, Pop. 154
Kenai Peninsula Borough SD
Supt. — See Soldotna
Tebughna S 50/K-12
PO Box 82010 99682 907-583-2291
Sheryl Kaye, prin. Fax 583-2692

Unalakleet, Nome, Pop. 752
Bering Strait SD 1,700/PK-12
PO Box 225 99684 907-624-3611
Jim Hickerson, supt. Fax 624-3099
www.bssd.org
Unalakleet S 200/PK-12
PO Box 130 99684 907-624-3444
Ben Howard, prin. Fax 624-3388
Other Schools – See Brevig Mission, Diomede, Elim, Gambell, Golovin, Koyuk, Saint Michael, Savoonga, Shaktoolik, Shishmaref, Stebbins, Teller, Wales, White Mountain

Unalaska, Aleutians West, Pop. 4,347
Unalaska CSD 400/PK-12
PO Box 570 99685 907-581-3151
John Conwell, supt. Fax 581-3152
www.ucsd.net
Unalaska JSHS 200/5-12
PO Box 570 99685 907-581-1222
John Conwell, prin. Fax 581-2428

Valdez, Valdez-Cordova, Pop. 4,015
Valdez CSD 800/K-12
PO Box 398 99686 907-835-4357
Dr. Lance Bowie, supt. Fax 835-4964
www.valdezcityschools.org/
Gilson JHS 100/7-8
PO Box 827 99686 907-835-2244
Rodney Morrison, prin. Fax 835-2540
Valdez HS 300/9-12
PO Box 1629 99686 907-835-4767
Geary Cantrell, prin. Fax 835-2596

Prince William Sound Community College Post-Sec.
PO Box 97 99686 907-834-1600

Venetie, Yukon-Koyukuk, Pop. 182
Yukon Flats SD
Supt. — See Fort Yukon
Fredson S 50/PK-12
PO Box 39 99781 907-849-8415
Robert Sloyka, prin. Fax 849-8630

Wainwright, North Slope, Pop. 507
North Slope Borough SD
Supt. — See Barrow
Alak S 100/PK-12
PO Box 10 99782 907-763-2541
Dave Lougee, prin. Fax 763-2550

Wales, Nome, Pop. 153
Bering Strait SD
Supt. — See Unalakleet
Wales S 50/PK-12
PO Box 490 99783 907-664-3021
Craig Probst, prin. Fax 664-3031

Wasilla, Matanuska-Susitna, Pop. 8,471
Matanuska-Susitna Borough SD
Supt. — See Palmer
Teeland MS 600/6-8
2788 N Seward Meridian Rd 99654 907-352-7500
Monica Goyette, prin. Fax 352-7585
Wasilla HS 1,200/9-12
701 Bogard Rd 99654 907-352-8200
Dwight Probasco, prin. Fax 352-8280
Wasilla MS 800/6-8
650 Bogard Rd 99654 907-352-5300
Amy Spargo, prin. Fax 352-5380

Cornerstone Christian S 50/K-12
4001 E Darrington Village 99654 907-357-9798
Karen Armstrong, prin. Fax 357-9799
Wasilla Lake Christian S 200/K-12
2001 Palmer Wasilla Hwy 99654 907-373-6439
Christopher Wolfe, admin. Fax 373-5439

White Mountain, Nome, Pop. 205
Bering Strait SD
Supt. — See Unalakleet
White Mountain S 100/PK-12
PO Box 55 99784 907-638-3021
Andy Haviland, prin. Fax 638-3031

Whittier, Valdez-Cordova, Pop. 172
Chugach SD
Supt. — See Anchorage
Whittier Community S 50/PK-12
PO Box 638 99693 907-472-2575
Doug Penn, prin. Fax 472-2409

Wrangell, Wrangell-Petersburg, Pop. 2,117
Wrangell SD 400/K-12
PO Box 2319 99929 907-874-2347
Susan Sciabbarrasi, supt. Fax 874-3137
www.wrangellschools.org
Stikine MS 100/6-8
PO Box 1935 99929 907-874-3393
Monty Buness, prin. Fax 874-3149
Wrangell HS 100/9-12
PO Box 651 99929 907-874-3395
Monty Buness, prin. Fax 874-3143

Yakutat, Skagway-Yakutat-Angoon, Pop. 534
Yakutat SD 100/PK-12
PO Box 429 99689 907-784-3317
Howard Diamond Ph.D., supt. Fax 784-3446
www.yakutatschools.org
Yakutat S 100/PK-12
PO Box 429 99689 907-784-3317
Howard Diamond Ph.D., prin. Fax 784-3446

ARIZONA

ARIZONA DEPARTMENT OF EDUCATION
1535 W Jefferson St, Phoenix 85007-3280
Telephone 602-542-5393
Fax 602-542-5440
Website http://www.ade.az.gov/

Superintendent of Public Instruction Tom Horne

ARIZONA BOARD OF EDUCATION
1535 W Jefferson St Ste 418, Phoenix 85007

Director Vince Yanez

COUNTY SUPERINTENDENTS OF SCHOOLS

Apache County Office of Education
Dr. Pauline Begay, supt. 928-337-7539
PO Box 548, Saint Johns 85936 Fax 337-2033
Cochise County Office of Education
Trudy Berry, supt. 520-432-8950
PO Box 208, Bisbee 85603 Fax 432-7136
www.co.cochise.az.us/ccwebsite/Default.asp
Coconino County Office of Education
Cecilia Owen, supt. 928-779-6591
110 E Cherry Ave, Flagstaff 86001 Fax 779-6571
www.coconino.az.gov/schools.aspx
Gila County Office of Education
Dr. Linda O'Dell, supt. 928-425-3231
1400 E Ash St, Globe 85501 Fax 402-0038
www.gilacountyschools.org
Graham County Office of Education
Donna McGaughey, supt. 928-428-2880
921 W Thatcher Blvd Fax 428-8824
Safford 85546
www.graham.az.gov/county_offices.asp?id=1397§ion=School
Greenlee County Office of Education
Tom Powers, supt. 928-865-2822
PO Box 1595, Clifton 85533 Fax 865-4417
Lapaz County Office of Education
Janice Shelton, supt. 928-669-6183
1112 S Joshua Ave, Parker 85344 Fax 669-4406
www.lapazschools.org
Maricopa County Office of Education
Dr. Sandra Dowling, supt. 602-506-3866
4041 N Central Ave, Phoenix 85012 Fax 506-3753
www.maricopa.gov/Schools/
Mohave County Office of Education
Michael File, supt. 928-753-0747
PO Box 7000, Kingman 86402 Fax 718-4958
www.mcss.k12.az.us/
Navajo County Office of Education
Linda Morrow, supt. 928-524-4204
PO Box 668, Holbrook 86025 Fax 524-4209
www.co.navajo.az.us/
Pima County Office of Education
Dr. Linda Arzoumanian, supt. 520-740-8451
130 W Congress St Fl 4 Fax 623-9308
Tucson 85701
www.schools.pima.gov/
Pinal County Office of Education
Jack Harmon, supt. 520-866-6565
PO Box 769, Florence 85232 Fax 866-4671
www.pinalcounty.org
Santa Cruz County Office of Education
Alfredo Velasquez, supt. 520-375-7940
2150 N Congress Dr Fax 375-7959
Nogales 85621
www.sccedu.org
Yavapai County Office of Education
Tim Carter, supt. 928-771-3326
1015 Fair St Rm 324 Fax 771-3329
Prescott 86305
www.co.yavapai.az.us/
Yuma County Office of Education
Thomas Tyree, supt. 928-373-1006
210 S 1st Ave, Yuma 85364 Fax 329-2008
www.co.yuma.az.us/schsup/

PUBLIC, PRIVATE AND CATHOLIC SECONDARY SCHOOLS

Ajo, Pima, Pop. 2,919
Ajo USD 15 600/PK-12
PO Box 68 85321 520-387-5618
Robert Dooley Ed.D., supt. Fax 387-6545
Ajo HS 9-12
PO Box 68 85321 520-387-7601
Don German, prin. Fax 387-7603

Apache Junction, Pinal, Pop. 32,297
Apache Junction USD 43 5,700/PK-12
1575 W Southern Ave Ste 3 85220 480-982-1110
Gregg Wyman, supt. Fax 982-6474
www.ajusd.org
Apache Junction HS 1,500/9-12
2525 S Ironwood Dr 85220 480-982-1110
Marla Wilson, prin. Fax 982-3787
Desert Shadows MS 600/6-8
801 W Southern Ave 85220 480-982-1110
Robert Pappalardo, prin. Fax 983-4913
Thunder Mountain MS 800/6-8
3700 E 16th Ave 85219 480-982-1110
Russell Sgro, prin. Fax 671-1427

Central Arizona College Post-Sec.
273 E US Highway 60 85219 480-982-7261

Ash Fork, Yavapai
Ash Fork JUSD 31 200/K-12
PO Box 247 86320 928-637-2561
Gary Spiker, supt. Fax 637-2623
Ash Fork HS 50/9-12
PO Box 247 86320 928-637-2561
Gary Spiker, prin. Fax 637-2623
Ash Fork MS 100/6-8
PO Box 247 86320 928-637-2561
Gary Spiker, prin. Fax 637-2623

Avondale, Maricopa, Pop. 66,706
Agua Fria UNHSD 216 3,600/9-12
750 E Riley Dr 85323 623-932-7000
Dudley Butts, supt. Fax 932-2796
www.aguafria.org
Agua Fria HS 1,700/9-12
530 E Riley Dr 85323 623-932-7300
Bryce Anderson, prin. Fax 932-0650
Other Schools – See Buckeye, Goodyear

Littleton ESD 65 2,300/PK-8
1252 S Avondale Blvd 85323 623-478-5600
Roger Freeman Ed.D., supt. Fax 478-5625
www.littletonaz.org
Other Schools – See Cashion

Tolleson UNHSD 214
Supt. — See Tolleson
La Joya Community HS 1,100/9-12
11650 W Whyman Ave 85323 623-478-4400
Cheryl Ingram, prin. Fax 478-7225
Westview HS 2,400/9-12
10850 W Garden Lakes Pkwy, 623-478-4600
Brandi Haskins, prin. Fax 877-4989

Estrella Mountain Community College Post-Sec.
3000 N Dysart Rd, 623-935-8015
Maricopa Beauty College Post-Sec.
515 W Western Ave 85323 623-932-4414
Universal Technical Institute Post-Sec.
10695 W Pierce St 85323 623-245-4600

Bagdad, Yavapai, Pop. 1,858
Bagdad USD 20 300/PK-12
PO Box 427 86321 928-633-4101
Marvin Smith, supt. Fax 633-4345
Bagdad HS 100/9-12
PO Box 427 86321 928-633-2201
Rodney Wilhelm, prin. Fax 633-2541

Benson, Cochise, Pop. 4,934
Benson USD 9 1,000/PK-12
360 S Patagonia St 85602 520-586-2213
David Woodall, supt. Fax 586-2506
www.bensonsd.k12.az.us/
Benson HS 400/9-12
360 S Patagonia St 85602 520-586-2213
Bryan Bullington, prin. Fax 586-2310
Benson MS 300/5-8
360 S Patagonia St 85602 520-586-2213
Jomel Jansson, prin. Fax 586-2253

Bisbee, Cochise, Pop. 6,177
Bisbee USD 2 1,000/PK-12
100 Old Douglas Rd 85603 520-432-5381
Paul McDonald, supt. Fax 432-7622
www.busd.k12.az.us
Bisbee HS 400/9-12
100 Old Douglas Rd 85603 520-432-5714
Jim Gordon, prin. Fax 432-6105
Lowell JHS 200/7-8
100 Old Douglas Rd 85603 520-432-5391
Terri Romo, prin. Fax 432-6106

Bowie, Cochise
Bowie USD 14 100/K-12
PO Box 157 85605 520-847-2545
Bruce Brown, supt. Fax 847-2546
www.bowieusd.k12.az.us
Bowie HS 50/9-12
PO Box 157 85605 520-847-2545
Bruce Brown, prin. Fax 847-2546

Buckeye, Maricopa, Pop. 9,619
Agua Fria UNHSD 216
Supt. — See Avondale
Verrado HS 9-12
20050 W Indian School Rd, 623-932-7400
Thomas Huffman, prin. Fax 853-0369

Buckeye UNHSD 201 1,200/9-12
902 E Eason Ave 85326 623-386-9701
Beverly Hurley, supt. Fax 386-9705
www.buhsd.org
Buckeye Union HS 1,100/9-12
902 E Eason Ave 85326 623-386-9716
Mary Ann Sphar, prin. Fax 386-9711
Youngker HS 9-12
3000 S Apache Rd 85326 623-474-0003
Johnny Ray, prin.
Other Schools – See Goodyear

Bullhead City, Mohave, Pop. 39,101
Bullhead City ESD 15 3,900/K-8
1004 Hancock Rd 86442 928-758-3961
William Allsbrooks, supt. Fax 758-4996
www.bullheadschools.com
Bullhead City JHS 700/6-8
1062 Hancock Rd 86442 928-758-3921
Pat Young, prin. Fax 758-7428
Fox Creek JHS 600/6-8
3101 Desert Sky Dr 86442 928-704-2500
Melinda Sobraske, prin. Fax 704-2504

Colorado River UNHSD 2
Supt. — See Fort Mohave
Mohave HS 1,400/9-12
2251 Highway 95 86442 928-758-3916
Jim Daly, prin. Fax 758-7145

Camp Verde, Yavapai, Pop. 10,155
Camp Verde USD 28 1,500/PK-12
410 Camp Lincoln Rd 86322 928-567-8000
Jeff Van Handel Ph.D., supt. Fax 567-8004
www.cvusd.k12.az.us/
Camp Verde HS 400/9-12
PO Box 728 86322 928-567-8033
Chris Schultz, prin. Fax 567-8045
Camp Verde MS 400/6-8
370 Camp Lincoln Rd 86322 928-567-8014
Dan Brown, prin. Fax 567-8022

Casa Grande, Pinal, Pop. 32,855
Casa Grande ESD 4 5,700/PK-8
1460 N Pinal Ave 85222 520-836-2111
Frank Davidson, supt. Fax 426-3712
www.cgelem.k12.az.us
Cactus MS 900/6-8
1220 E Kortsen Rd 85222 520-421-3330
Jeffrey Lavender, prin. Fax 421-7425

Casa Grande MS 1,000/6-8
300 W McMurray Blvd 85222 520-836-7310
Sylvia Trotter, prin. Fax 836-2399

Casa Grande UNHSD 82 2,500/9-12
1362 N Casa Grande Ave 85222 520-316-3303
Nancy Pifer, supt. Fax 316-3352
cguhs.org
Casa Grande Union HS 2,300/9-12
2730 N Trekell Rd 85222 520-836-8500
Keith Greer, prin. Fax 316-3353

Cashion, See Avondale
Littleton ESD 65
Supt. — See Avondale
Underdown JHS 300/7-8
PO Box 280 85329 623-478-5800
Lenora Owoyemi, prin. Fax 478-5600

Cave Creek, Maricopa, Pop. 4,884
Cave Creek USD 93
Supt. — See Scottsdale
Sonoran Trails MS 600/6-8
PO Box 426 85327 480-272-8600
Dr. Skot Beazley, prin. Fax 272-8699

Chandler, Maricopa, Pop. 234,939
Chandler USD 80 25,500/PK-12
1525 W Frye Rd 85224 480-812-7000
Dr. Camille Casteel, supt. Fax 812-7015
ww2.chandler.k12.az.us/
Andersen JHS 1,200/7-8
1255 N Dobson Rd 85224 480-883-5300
Jim Anderson, prin. Fax 883-5320
Basha HS 1,000/9-12
5990 S Val Vista Dr 85249 480-224-2100
Kristine Marchiando, prin. Fax 224-2120
Bogle JHS 1,000/7-8
1600 W Queen Creek Rd 85248 480-883-5500
Susie Avey, prin. Fax 883-5520
Chandler HS 2,600/9-12
350 N Arizona Ave 85225 480-812-7700
Terry Williams, prin. Fax 812-7720
Hamilton HS 3,200/9-12
3700 S Arizona Ave 85248 480-883-5000
Dr. Fred DePrez, prin. Fax 883-5020
Santan JHS 7-8
1550 E Chandler Heights Rd 85249 480-883-4600
Frank Narducci, prin. Fax 883-4620
Willis JHS 1,100/7-8
401 S McQueen Rd 85225 480-883-5700
Paul Bollard, prin. Fax 883-5720
Other Schools – See Queen Creek

Kyrene ESD 28
Supt. — See Tempe
Kyrene Aprende MS 1,200/6-8
777 N Desert Breeze Blvd E 85226 480-783-2200
Gerri Shaw, prin. Fax 940-0657
Kyrene Del Pueblo MS 1,100/6-8
360 S Twelve Oaks Blvd 85226 480-783-2400
Tom Seiger, prin. Fax 961-4152

Mesa USD 4
Supt. — See Mesa
Hendrix JHS 1,000/7-9
1550 W Summit Pl 85224 480-472-3300
Carlos Alvarado, prin. Fax 472-3320

Artistic Beauty College Post-Sec.
2978 N Alma School Rd Ste 3 85224 480-855-7901
Chandler-Gilbert Community College Post-Sec.
2626 E Pecos Rd 85225 480-732-7000
Golf Academy of Arizona Post-Sec.
670 N Arizona Ave Ste 13 85225 800-342-7342
International Academy of Hair Design Post-Sec.
3350 N Arizona Ave Ste 4 85225 480-820-9422
Quantum Helicopters Post-Sec.
2401 S Heliport Way, 480-814-8118
Seton Catholic HS 600/9-12
1150 N Dobson Rd 85224 480-963-1900
Patricia Collins, prin. Fax 963-1974
Valley Christian HS 400/9-12
6900 W Galveston St 85226 480-705-8888
Clark Stephens, admin. Fax 705-8889

Chinle, Apache, Pop. 5,059
Chinle USD 24 4,000/PK-12
PO Box 587 86503 928-674-9600
Javier Abrego, supt. Fax 674-9608
www.chinleusd.k12.az.us/
Chinle HS 1,100/9-12
PO Box 587 86503 928-674-9507
Douglas Clauschee, prin. Fax 674-9432
Chinle JHS 500/7-8
PO Box 587 86503 928-674-9505
Gloria Grant, prin. Fax 674-9424

Chino Valley, Yavapai, Pop. 9,710
Chino Valley USD 51 2,600/PK-12
PO Box 225 86323 928-636-2458
Allan Grell, supt. Fax 636-1434
www.cvsd.k12.az.us
Chino Valley HS 800/9-12
PO Box 225 86323 928-636-2298
Jeff St. Clair, prin. Fax 636-6219
Heritage MS 700/6-8
PO Box 225 86323 928-636-4464
Harold Tenney, prin. Fax 636-6214

Trinity Christian S 200/PK-12
PO Box 3825 86323 928-636-6306
Kyle Maestri, admin. Fax 636-5131

Clifton, Greenlee, Pop. 2,265
Clifton USD 3 200/PK-12
PO Box 1567 85533 928-865-2752
Sharron Redden, supt. Fax 865-2792
Clifton HS 100/9-12
PO Box 1567 85533 928-865-3262
Sharron Redden, prin. Fax 865-2792

Colorado City, Mohave, Pop. 4,371
Colorado City USD 14 300/PK-12
PO Box 309 86021 928-279-7500
Peter Davis, supt. Fax 279-7510
www.ccusd.net
El Capitan S 300/PK-12
PO Box 309 86021 928-875-9000
Carol Timpson, prin. Fax 875-9098

Coolidge, Pinal, Pop. 8,154
Coolidge USD 21 2,000/K-12
221 W Central Ave 85228 520-723-2042
Dr. Darlene White, supt. Fax 723-2442
www.coolidgeschools.org/
Coolidge HS 600/9-12
800 W Northern Ave 85228 520-723-2305
Tim Hamilton, prin. Fax 723-2306
McCray JHS 8-8
450 N Arizona Blvd 85228 520-723-2102
Susan Price, prin. Fax 723-2104

Central Arizona College Post-Sec.
8470 N Overfield Rd 85228 520-426-4444

Cornville, Yavapai, Pop. 2,089

Oak Creek Ranch S 100/6-12
1165 E Willow Point Rd 86325 928-634-5571
Nadine O'Brien, prin. Fax 634-4915

Corona, Pima
Vail USD 20
Supt. — See Vail
Corona Foothills MS 6-8
16705 S Houghton Rd 85641 520-762-3500
Margaret Steuer, prin. Fax 762-3501

Cottonwood, Yavapai, Pop. 10,894
Cottonwood-Oak Creek ESD 6 1,800/PK-8
1 N Willard St 86326 928-634-2288
Julia Larson, supt. Fax 634-2309
www.cocsd.k12.az.us
Cottonwood MS 700/6-8
1 N Willard St 86326 928-634-2231
Michelle Stadelman, prin. Fax 634-2874

Mingus UNHSD 4 1,200/9-12
1801 E Fir St 86326 928-634-8901
Sharyl Allen, supt. Fax 649-4399
muhs.com
Mingus Union HS 1,200/9-12
1801 E Fir St 86326 928-634-7531
Marc Cooper, prin. Fax 634-0546

Cornerstone Christian Academy 50/7-12
2080 S Highway 260 86326 928-646-9299
Jill Rhoton, prin. Fax 646-8213

Dewey, Yavapai, Pop. 3,640
Humboldt USD 22
Supt. — See Prescott Valley
Bradshaw Mountain MS 400/6-8
12255 E Turquoise Cir 86327 928-759-4900
Brian Buchholtz, prin. Fax 759-4920

Dolan Springs, Mohave, Pop. 1,090
Kingman USD 20
Supt. — See Kingman
Mt. Tipton S 300/K-12
PO Box 248 86441 928-767-3350
Bill Harness, prin. Fax 767-4330

Douglas, Cochise, Pop. 16,791
Douglas USD 27 3,900/PK-12
PO Box 1237 85608 520-364-2447
Gail Zamar, supt. Fax 364-7470
www.dusd.k12.az.us
Borane MS 400/6-8
PO Box 1237 85608 520-364-2461
Diane Drury, prin. Fax 364-5537
Douglas HS 1,100/9-12
PO Box 1237 85608 520-364-3462
Gloria Lopez, prin. Fax 805-4171
Huber JHS 600/6-8
PO Box 1237 85608 520-364-2840
George Watkins, prin. Fax 364-2421

Duncan, Greenlee, Pop. 713
Duncan USD 2 500/K-12
PO Box 710 85534 928-359-2472
John Payne, supt. Fax 359-2807
duncan.k12.az.us
Duncan HS 200/9-12
PO Box 710 85534 928-359-2474
John Payne, prin. Fax 359-1141
Duncan MS 200/4-8
PO Box 710 85534 928-359-2471
Don Smith, prin. Fax 359-1105

Eagar, Apache, Pop. 4,126
Round Valley USD 10
Supt. — See Springerville
Round Valley HS 500/9-12
550 N Butler St 85925 928-333-6800
Renita Kirkham, prin. Fax 333-6820
Round Valley MS 300/6-8
126 W 2nd St 85925 928-333-6700
Alan Bingham, prin. Fax 333-5252

Elfrida, Cochise
Valley UNHSD 22 200/9-12
PO Box 158 85610 520-642-3492
Gary Walker, supt. Fax 642-3523
Valley Union HS 200/9-12
PO Box 158 85610 520-642-3492
Gary Walker, prin. Fax 642-3523

El Mirage, Maricopa, Pop. 22,171
Dysart USD 89
Supt. — See Surprise
Dysart HS 1,300/9-12
11425 N Dysart Rd 85335 623-876-7500
Teddy Irvine, prin. Fax 876-7521

Eloy, Pinal, Pop. 10,855
Eloy ESD 11 1,200/PK-8
1011 N Sunshine Blvd 85231 520-466-2100
Ruby James, supt. Fax 466-2101
Eloy JHS 300/7-8
1011 N Sunshine Blvd 85231 520-466-2140
Danny Rogers, prin. Fax 466-2150

Santa Cruz Valley UNHSD 840 500/9-12
900 N Main St 85231 520-466-2237
Eugene Bichekas, supt. Fax 466-2222
www.santacruzdustdevils.us
Santa Cruz Valley HS 500/9-12
900 N Main St 85231 520-466-2200
Mary Griffith, prin. Fax 466-2222

Toltec ESD 22 900/PK-8
3315 N Toltec Rd 85231 520-466-2360
Dick Lesher, supt. Fax 466-2398
www.toltec.k12.az.us
Toltec MS 400/4-8
3315 N Toltec Rd 85231 520-466-2350
Dave Ascoli, prin. Fax 466-2399

Flagstaff, Coconino, Pop. 57,391
Flagstaff USD 1 11,100/PK-12
3285 E Sparrow Ave 86004 928-527-6000
Dr. Kevin Brown, supt. Fax 527-6015
www.flagstaff.k12.az.us
Coconino HS 1,400/9-12
2801 N Izabel St 86004 928-773-8200
David Roth, prin. Fax 773-8247
Flagstaff HS 1,400/9-12
400 W Elm Ave 86001 928-773-8100
Tony Cullen, prin. Fax 773-8146
Flagstaff MS 700/7-8
755 N Bonito St 86001 928-773-8150
Robert Kuhn, prin. Fax 773-8169
Mount Elden/Renaissance Magnet MS 900/7-8
3223 N 4th St 86004 928-773-8250
Rodney Johnson, prin. Fax 773-8269
Sinagua HS 1,000/9-12
3950 E Butler Ave 86004 928-527-5500
Ute Salisbury, prin. Fax 527-5561

Artistic Beauty College Post-Sec.
1790 E Route 66 86004 928-774-7146
Coconino Community College Post-Sec.
2800 S Lone Tree Rd 86001 928-527-1222
CollegeAmerica Post-Sec.
1800 S Milton Rd 86001 928-526-0763
Montessori S of Flagstaff 50/6-8
2212 E Cedar Ave 86004 928-774-1600
Marlane Spencer, prin. Fax 774-0424
Northern Arizona University Post-Sec.
PO Box 4084 86011 928-523-9011

Florence, Pinal, Pop. 17,053
Florence USD 1 1,200/PK-12
PO Box 2850 85232 520-866-3500
Dr. Richard Sagar, supt. Fax 868-2302
florence.k12.az.us
Florence HS 400/9-12
PO Box 2850 85232 520-866-3560
Nick McVicker, prin. Fax 868-2329

Fort Defiance, Apache, Pop. 4,489
Window Rock USD 8 2,800/K-12
PO Box 559 86504 928-729-6705
Thomas Jackson, supt. Fax 729-5780
www.wrschool.net
Tse Ho Tsoh MS 700/6-8
PO Box 559 86504 928-729-6802
Chuck Foster, prin. Fax 729-7572
Window Rock HS 900/9-12
PO Box 559 86504 928-729-7004
Glenn Haven, prin. Fax 729-7661

Fort Huachuca, See Sierra Vista
Fort Huachuca Accommodation SD 00 900/PK-8
PO Box 12954 85670 520-458-5082
Dr. Ronda Frueauff, supt. Fax 515-5972
www.fthuachuca.k12.az.us
Smith MS 400/6-8
PO Box 12954 85670 520-459-8892
Robert Henderson, prin. Fax 459-8939

Fort Mohave, Mohave
Colorado River UNHSD 2 2,100/9-12
5221 S Highway 95 Ste 5 86426 928-768-1665
Nancy Silk, supt. Fax 768-1702
www.cruhsd.org
Other Schools – See Bullhead City, Mohave Valley

Fort Thomas, Graham
Fort Thomas USD 7 600/K-12
PO Box 28 85536 928-485-9423
Dr. Leon Ben, supt. Fax 485-2058
www.ftthomas.k12.az.us
Fort Thomas JSHS 300/7-12
PO Box 28 85536 928-485-2427
Shane Hawkins, prin. Fax 485-2834

Fountain Hills, Maricopa, Pop. 23,217
Fountain Hills USD 98 2,500/PK-12
16000 E Palisades Blvd 85268 480-664-5011
Dr. Marian Hermie, supt. Fax 664-5099
fhusd.org
Fountain Hills HS 900/9-12
16100 E Palisades Blvd 85268 480-664-5500
Patrick Sweeney, prin. Fax 837-5699
Fountain Hills MS 700/6-8
15414 N McDowell Mountain R 85268 480-664-5400
Tom Brennan, prin. Fax 664-5499

Fredonia, Coconino, Pop. 1,051
Fredonia-Moccasin USD 6 400/PK-12
PO Box 247 86022 928-643-7333
Steve Nielsen, supt. Fax 643-7044
www.fredonia.org/
Fredonia-Moccasin HS 100/9-12
PO Box 247 86022 928-643-7333
Nick Bartlett, prin. Fax 643-7044

Ganado, Apache, Pop. 1,257
Ganado USD 20 2,100/K-12
PO Box 1757 86505 928-755-1099
Deborah Dennison, supt. Fax 755-1005
www.ganado.k12.az.us/
Ganado HS 800/9-12
PO Box 1757 86505 928-755-1402
Emily Arviso, prin. Fax 755-1401
Ganado MS 300/7-8
PO Box 1757 86505 928-755-1220
Lucinda Swedberg, prin. Fax 755-1298

Gila Bend, Maricopa, Pop. 2,055
Gila Bend USD 24 500/PK-12
PO Box V 85337 928-683-2225
James Mosley, supt. Fax 683-2671
gila.az.schoolwebpages.com
Gila Bend HS 100/9-12
PO Box V 85337 928-683-2286
Isaac Perez, prin. Fax 683-6415

Gilbert, Maricopa, Pop. 173,989
Gilbert USD 41 34,800/PK-12
140 S Gilbert Rd 85296 480-497-3300
Brad Barrett Ph.D., supt. Fax 497-3398
www.gilbert.k12.az.us/
Gilbert Classical Academy 7-12
55 N Greenfield Rd 85234 480-497-4034
Brian Rosta, prin. Fax 507-1645
Gilbert HS 3,000/9-12
1101 E Elliot Rd 85234 480-497-0177
Dr. J. Charles Santa Cruz, prin. Fax 497-5673
Gilbert JHS 1,000/7-8
1016 N Burk St 85234 480-892-6908
Kevin Rainey, prin. Fax 813-8240
GPS Technology and Leadership Academy Vo/Tech
55 N Greenfield Rd 85234 480-497-4024
Dr. Edward Fox, prin. Fax 507-1645
Greenfield JHS 1,500/7-8
101 S Greenfield Rd 85296 480-813-1770
Jill Bowers, prin. Fax 813-7279
Highland HS 2,300/9-12
4301 E Guadalupe Rd 85234 480-813-0051
Domonic Salce, prin. Fax 813-0258
Mesquite HS 3,000/9-12
500 S McQueen Rd 85233 480-632-4750
Dominic Marchiando, prin. Fax 632-4777
Mesquite JHS 1,000/7-8
130 W Mesquite St 85233 480-926-1433
Ron Izzett, prin. Fax 813-9002
South Valley JHS 7-8
2034 S Lindsay Rd, 480-855-0015
Marti Farmer, prin. Fax 855-3542
Other Schools – See Mesa

Higley USD 60 4,700/PK-12
2935 S Recker Rd, 480-279-7000
Joyce Lutrey, supt. Fax 279-7005
www.husd.org
Higley HS 1,100/9-12
4068 E Pecos Rd, 480-279-7300
Robert Mileham, prin. Fax 279-7305

Conservatory of Recording Arts/Sciences Post-Sec.
1205 N Fiesta Blvd 85233 480-858-9400
Surrey Garden Christian S 400/K-12
1424 S Promenade Ln 85296 480-279-1366
Tim Ihms, admin. Fax 279-5433

Glendale, Maricopa, Pop. 239,435
Alhambra ESD 68
Supt. — See Phoenix
Barcelona MS 900/4-8
6130 N 44th Ave 85301 623-842-8616
Tyson Kelly, prin. Fax 842-1384

Deer Valley USD 97
Supt. — See Phoenix
Deer Valley HS 2,200/9-12
18424 N 51st Ave 85308 602-467-6700
Barbara Dobbs, prin. Fax 467-6780
Desert Sky MS 1,000/7-8
5130 W Grovers Ave 85308 602-467-6500
Don Morrison, prin. Fax 467-6580
Hillcrest MS 1,000/7-8
22833 N 71st Ave 85310 623-376-3300
Dannene Truett, prin. Fax 376-3380
Mountain Ridge HS 2,700/9-12
22800 N 67th Ave 85310 623-376-3000
Debra Poulson, prin. Fax 376-3080

Glendale ESD 40 12,500/PK-8
7301 N 58th Ave 85301 623-842-8100
Dr. Perry Hill, supt. Fax 842-8198
www.gesd40.org/
Bicentennial North S 600/4-8
7237 W Missouri Ave 85303 623-842-8290
Kenneth Fleming, prin. Fax 848-6133
Challenger MS 1,100/4-8
6905 W Maryland Ave 85303 623-842-8314
Kate Newton, prin. Fax 842-8324
Landmark MS 1,000/6-8
5730 W Myrtle Ave 85301 623-842-8304
John Dalmolin, prin. Fax 842-8330
Mensendick IS 700/4-8
5535 N 67th Ave 85301 623-842-8260
Diane Pesch, prin. Fax 842-8336

Glendale UNHSD 205 14,200/9-12
7650 N 43rd Ave 85301 623-435-6000
Warren Jacobson, supt. Fax 435-6078
guhsdaz.org
Apollo HS 1,700/9-12
8045 N 47th Ave 85302 623-435-6300
Brian Capistran, prin. Fax 435-6369
Glendale HS 1,500/9-12
6216 W Glendale Ave 85301 623-435-6200
Deborah Jordan, prin. Fax 435-6270
Independence HS 1,700/9-12
6602 N 75th Ave 85303 623-435-6100
Mark Farison, prin. Fax 435-6157
Other Schools – See Phoenix

Peoria USD 11 36,200/PK-12
6330 W Thunderbird Rd 85306 623-486-6000
Jack Erb, supt. Fax 486-6009
portal.peoriaud.k12.az.us/default.aspx
Cactus HS 1,800/9-12
6330 W Greenway Rd 85306 623-412-5000
Debbie McKintosh, prin. Fax 412-5020
Ironwood HS 2,100/9-12
6051 W Sweetwater Ave 85304 623-486-6400
Pat Redl, prin. Fax 486-6424
Kellis HS 9-12
8990 W Orangewood Ave 85305 623-412-5425
Shona Miranda, prin. Fax 412-5447
Other Schools – See Peoria

Tolleson UNHSD 214
Supt. — See Tolleson
Copper Canyon HS 9-12
9126 W Camelback Rd 85305 623-478-4800
Sharon Wagner, prin. Fax 478-4802

Washington ESD 6 24,300/PK-8
4650 W Sweetwater Ave 85304 602-347-2600
Dr. Susie Cook, supt. Fax 347-2720
www.wesd.k12.az.us
Other Schools – See Phoenix

Arizona Automotive Institute Post-Sec.
6829 N 46th Ave 85301 623-934-7273
Arizona College of Allied Health Post-Sec.
4425 W Olive Ave Ste 300 85302 602-222-9300
Artistic Beauty College Post-Sec.
10820 N 43rd Ave 85304 623-937-2749
Glendale Community College Post-Sec.
6000 W Olive Ave 85302 623-845-3000
Midwestern University Post-Sec.
19555 N 59th Ave 85308 623-572-3275
Thunderbird The Garvin School Post-Sec.
15249 N 59th Ave 85306 602-978-7011

Globe, Gila, Pop. 7,187
Globe USD 1 1,700/PK-12
501 E Ash St 85501 928-425-3211
Dr. Timothy Trent, supt. Fax 425-8912
www.globeusd.org
Globe HS 700/9-12
501 E Ash St 85501 928-425-3211
John Schreur, prin. Fax 425-8909
High Desert MS 300/5-8
501 E Ash St 85501 928-402-5700
Holly Brown, prin. Fax 402-5788

Goodyear, Maricopa, Pop. 43,941
Agua Fria UNHSD 216
Supt. — See Avondale
Desert Edge HS 300/9-12
15778 W Yuma Rd 85338 623-932-7500
Dr. Bob Rossi, prin. Fax 932-7502
Millennium HS 1,600/9-12
14802 W Wigwam Blvd, 623-932-7500
Dr. Dennis Runyan, prin. Fax 932-7204

Buckeye UNHSD 201
Supt. — See Buckeye
Estrella Foothills HS 100/9-12
13033 S Estrella Pkwy 85338 623-327-2400
Leslie Standerfer, prin. Fax 327-2420

Litchfield ESD 79
Supt. — See Litchfield Park
Western Sky MS 1,000/6-8
4905 N 144th Ave 85338 623-535-6300
Alan Harper, prin. Fax 935-9536

Christ Community Christian Academy 100/K-12
14440 W Indian School Rd, 623-925-8200
Harry McDaniel, prin. Fax 925-0409

Grand Canyon, Coconino
Grand Canyon USD 4 200/K-12
PO Box 519 86023 928-638-2461
Sheila Breen, supt. Fax 638-2461
www.grandcanyonschool.org
Grand Canyon S 200/K-12
PO Box 519 86023 928-638-2461
Robert Kelso, prin. Fax 638-2428

Heber, Navajo, Pop. 1,581
Heber-Overgaard USD 6 500/PK-12
PO Box 547 85928 928-535-4622
Ken VanWinkle, supt. Fax 535-5146
www.heberovergaardschools.org
Capps MS / Mogollon JHS 100/4-8
PO Box 820 85928 928-535-4667
Ron Tenney, prin. Fax 535-9044
Mogollon HS 200/9-12
PO Box 279 85928 928-535-4238
Rick Honsinger, prin. Fax 535-3933

Holbrook, Navajo, Pop. 5,126
Holbrook USD 3 2,000/K-12
PO Box 640 86025 928-524-6144
Mary Koury, supt. Fax 524-3073
www.holbrook.k12.az.us
Holbrook HS 800/9-12
PO Box 640 86025 928-524-2815
Lance Phaturos, prin. Fax 524-3537
Holbrook JHS 400/6-8
PO Box 640 86025 928-524-3959
Linda Crumrine, prin. Fax 524-3766

Holbrook SDA Indian S 100/K-12
PO Box 910 86025 928-524-6845
Paulette Jackson, prin. Fax 524-3190
Northland Pioneer College Post-Sec.
PO Box 610 86025 928-524-7606

Joseph City, Navajo
Joseph City USD 2 400/PK-12
PO Box 8 86032 928-288-3307
Hollis Merrell, supt. Fax 288-3309
myweb.cableone.net/joecity
Joseph City JSHS 200/7-12
PO Box 8 86032 928-288-3361
Bryan Fields, prin. Fax 288-3825

Kayenta, Navajo, Pop. 4,372
Kayenta USD 27 2,600/PK-12
PO Box 337 86033 928-697-2008
Alex Martinez, supt. Fax 697-2160
www.kayenta.k12.az.us
Kayenta MS 600/6-8
PO Box 337 86033 928-697-2297
Marti Gilmore, prin. Fax 697-2308
Monument Valley HS 1,000/9-12
PO Box 337 86033 928-697-2127
Gillian Vormittag, prin. Fax 697-2195

Keams Canyon, Navajo, Pop. 393
Cedar USD 25 400/K-12
PO Box 367 86034 928-738-2366
Damon Clarke, supt. Fax 738-5404
www.cedarusd.org
White Cone HS 9-12
PO Box 367 86034 928-654-3451
Darrel Brinkerhoff, prin. Fax 654-3552

Kearny, Pinal, Pop. 2,765
Ray USD 3 600/PK-12
PO Box 427 85237 520-363-5515
Joseph W. Bullmore, supt. Fax 363-5642
Ray HS 200/9-12
PO Box 427 85237 520-363-5513
Jeffery Duncan, prin. Fax 363-5642
Ray MS 200/5-8
PO Box 427 85237 520-363-5511
Curt Cook, prin. Fax 363-5005

Kingman, Mohave, Pop. 25,547
Kingman USD 20 6,100/PK-12
3033 McDonald Ave 86401 928-753-5678
Dr. Maurice Flores, supt. Fax 753-6910
www.kusd.org
Kingman HS 1,600/9-12
4182 N Bank St, 928-692-6480
Pat Mickelson, prin. Fax 692-6418
Kingman JHS 1,000/6-8
1969 Detroit Ave 86401 928-753-3588
Jerry Arave, prin. Fax 753-1336
White Cliffs MS 6-8
400 Grandview Ave 86401 928-753-6216
John Venenga, prin. Fax 753-4042
Other Schools – See Dolan Springs

Mohave Community College Post-Sec.
1971 E Jagerson Ave, 928-757-0879

Lake Havasu City, Mohave, Pop. 55,338
Lake Havasu USD 1 6,000/PK-12
2200 Havasupai Blvd 86403 928-505-6900
Gail Malay, supt. Fax 505-6999
www.havasu.k12.az.us/
Daytona MS 500/6-8
98 Swanson Plz 86403 928-505-1475
Hector Fimbres, prin. Fax 505-1479
Lake Havasu HS 1,800/9-12
2675 Palo Verde Blvd S 86403 928-854-5001
Kathy Cox, prin. Fax 854-5499
Thunderbolt MS 1,100/6-8
695 Thunderbolt Ave 86406 928-855-4066
Paul Olson, prin. Fax 855-0041

Bethany Christian S 50/1-12
1200 Park Terrace Ave 86404 928-855-2661
Rev. Jerry Adams, prin. Fax 855-0807
Charles of Italy Beauty College Post-Sec.
1987 McCulloch Blvd #205 86403 928-453-6666

Lakeside, Navajo, Pop. 3,492
Blue Ridge USD 32 2,600/PK-12
1200 W White Mountain Blvd 85929 928-368-6126
W. Michael Aylstock, supt. Fax 368-5570
www.brusd.k12.az.us/
Blue Ridge HS 800/9-12
1200 W White Mountain Blvd 85929 928-368-6328
Gerard Ball, prin. Fax 368-8308
Blue Ridge JHS 500/7-8
1200 W White Mountain Blvd 85929 928-368-6377
Greg Schalow, prin. Fax 368-6378

Laveen, Maricopa
Laveen ESD 59 1,800/PK-8
PO Box 29 85339 602-237-9100
Ron Dickson, supt. Fax 237-3376
www.laveeneld.org/
Vista del Sur MS 400/7-8
PO Box 630 85339 602-237-3046
Steve Preis, admin. Fax 237-9139

Phoenix UNHSD 210
Supt. — See Phoenix
Chavez HS 2,400/9-12
3921 W Baseline Rd 85339 602-764-4000
James McElroy, prin. Fax 764-4054

Litchfield Park, Maricopa, Pop. 4,523
Litchfield ESD 79 6,200/PK-8
553 E Plaza Cir 85340 623-935-6000
L. Thomas Heck, supt. Fax 935-1448
www.lesd.k12.az.us/
Wigwam Creek MS 1,100/6-8
553 E Plaza Cir 85340 623-547-1100
David Mayer, prin. Fax 535-8083
Other Schools – See Goodyear

Littlefield, Mohave
Littlefield USD 9 400/PK-12
PO Box 730 86432 928-347-5792
Riley Frei, supt. Fax 347-5795
Beaver Dam HS, PO Box 730 86432 200/6-12
Randon Lawrence, prin. 928-347-5252

Marana, Pima, Pop. 26,098
Marana USD 6 12,600/K-12
11279 W Grier Rd 85653 520-682-3243
Dennis Dearden, supt. Fax 682-2421
www.maranausd.org
Marana Career and Technical HS Vo/Tech
11279 W Grier Rd Ste 128 85653 520-682-4773
Lynne Prouty, dir. Fax 682-4106
Marana MS 1,000/7-8
11279 W Grier Rd Ste 105 85653 520-682-4730
Dr. Allison Murphy, prin. Fax 682-4790
Other Schools – See Tucson

Maricopa, Pinal, Pop. 1,486
Maricopa USD 20 1,200/PK-12
45012 W Honeycutt Ave 85239 520-568-5100
Alma Farrell, supt. Fax 568-5151
www.musd20.org/
Maricopa HS 300/9-12
45012 W Honeycutt Ave 85239 520-568-8102
Burnie Hubbard, prin. Fax 568-7104
Maricopa Wells MS 7-8
45012 W Honeycutt Ave 85239 520-568-7102
Stephanie Sharp, prin. Fax 568-7104

Mayer, Yavapai
Mayer USD 43 600/PK-12
PO Box 1059 86333 928-642-1005
Patrick Dallabetta, supt. Fax 632-4005
www.mayerschools.us
Mayer JSHS 300/7-12
PO Box 1059 86333 928-642-1201
Jim Dean, prin. Fax 632-5714

Orme S 200/7-12
HC 63 Box 3040 86333 928-632-7601
Alyce Brownridge, hdmstr. Fax 632-7605

Mesa, Maricopa, Pop. 442,780
East Valley Institute of Tech. SD 401
1601 W Main St 85201 480-461-4150
Sally Downey Ed.D., supt. Fax 461-4169
evit.com
East Valley Institute of Technology Vo/Tech
1601 W Main St 85201 480-898-6100
Dr. Janet Cox, dir. Fax 461-4169

Gilbert USD 41
Supt. — See Gilbert
Desert Ridge HS 1,500/9-12
10045 E Madero Ave, 480-984-8947
Daniel Coombs, prin. Fax 354-5090
Desert Ridge JHS 800/7-8
10211 E Madero Ave, 480-635-2025
Jean Woods, prin. Fax 635-2044
Highland JHS 1,300/7-8
6915 E Guadalupe Rd 85212 480-632-4739
George Bowers, prin. Fax 632-4729

Mesa USD 4 74,500/PK-12
63 E Main St Ste 101 85201 480-472-0000
Dr. Debra Duvall, supt. Fax 472-0204
www.mpsaz.org
Brimhall JHS 1,400/7-9
4949 E Southern Ave 85206 480-472-2600
Dr. Barbara Remondini, prin. Fax 472-2698
Carson JHS 1,300/7-9
525 N Westwood 85201 480-472-2900
Robert Crispin, prin. Fax 472-2899
Dobson SHS 2,500/10-12
1501 W Guadalupe Rd 85202 480-472-3000
Matthew Gehrman, prin. Fax 472-3075
Fremont JHS 1,500/7-9
1001 N Power Rd 85205 480-472-8300
Patricia Christie, prin. Fax 472-8333
Kino JHS 1,200/7-9
848 N Horne 85203 480-472-2400
Allen Flax, prin. Fax 472-2549
Mesa JHS 1,100/7-9
828 E Broadway Rd 85204 480-472-1300
Catherine McDaniel, prin. Fax 472-1319
Mesa SHS 2,700/10-12
1630 E Southern Ave 85204 480-472-5900
Pete Lesar, prin. Fax 472-5995
Mountain View SHS 2,700/10-12
2700 E Brown Rd 85213 480-472-6900
Craig Luketich, prin. Fax 472-6983
Poston JHS 1,400/7-9
2433 E Adobe St 85213 480-472-2100
Catherine Pletchette, prin. Fax 472-2105
Powell MS 1,300/7-9
855 W 8th Ave 85210 480-472-1000
Nancy Roberts, prin. Fax 472-1110
Red Mountain SHS 2,400/10-12
7301 E Brown Rd 85207 480-472-8000
Gerald Slemmer, prin. Fax 472-8008
Rhodes JHS 1,200/7-9
1860 S Longmore 85202 480-472-2300
Matt Devlin, prin. Fax 472-2299
Shepherd JHS 1,500/7-9
1407 N Alta Mesa Dr 85205 480-472-1800
Eileen Cahoon, prin. Fax 472-1888
Skyline HS 1,700/9-12
845 S Crismon Rd 85208 480-472-9400
Holly Williams, prin. Fax 472-9406
Smith JHS 1,500/7-9
10100 E Adobe Rd 85207 480-472-9900
Bruce Cox, prin. Fax 472-9999
Stapley JHS 1,400/7-9
3250 E Hermosa Vista Dr 85213 480-472-2700
Ken Erickson, prin. Fax 472-2828
Taylor JHS 1,200/7-9
705 S 32nd St 85204 480-472-1500
Greg Fowler, prin. Fax 472-1616
Westwood SHS 2,300/10-12
945 W 8th St 85201 480-472-4400
Helen Riddle, prin. Fax 472-4509
Other Schools – See Chandler

Apollo College Post-Sec.
630 W Southern Ave 85210 480-831-6585
Arizona Sch of Dentistry & Oral Health Post-Sec.
5850 E Still Cir 85206 480-219-6000
Arizona School of Health Sciences Post-Sec.
5850 E Still Cir 85206 480-219-6000
Arizona State University Polytechnic Post-Sec.
7001 E Williams Field Rd 85212 480-727-3278
Earl's Academy of Beauty Post-Sec.
2111 S Alma School Rd #21 85210 480-897-1688
Faith Christian S 100/K-12
PO Box 31300 85275 480-833-1983
Dick Buckingham, admin. Fax 832-1649
International Institute of the Americas Post-Sec.
925 S Gilbert Rd Ste 201 85204 480-545-8755
Keller Graduate School of Management Post-Sec.
1201 S Alma School Rd #5450 85210 480-827-1511
Mesa Community College Post-Sec.
1833 W Southern Ave 85202 480-461-7000
Pima Medical Institute Post-Sec.
957 S Dobson Rd 85202 480-644-0267
Providence Classical S 100/K-12
3426 E University Dr 85213 480-830-7211
Brad Jones, hdmstr. Fax 813-3637
Redeemer Christian S 100/K-12
719 N Stapley Dr 85203 480-962-5003
Denise Monroe Ed.D., prin. Fax 833-7502

Miami, Gila, Pop. 1,841
Miami USD 40 1,100/PK-12
PO Box H 85539 928-425-3271
Don Nelson, supt. Fax 425-7419
miami.az.schoolwebpages.com/education/district/distr
i
Kornegay JHS 200/7-8
PO Box H 85539 928-425-3271
Susan Hocking, prin. Fax 425-5470
Miami HS 300/9-12
PO Box H 85539 928-425-3271
Sherrill Stephens, prin. Fax 425-7027

Mohave Valley, Mohave, Pop. 6,962
Colorado River UNHSD 2
Supt. — See Fort Mohave
River Valley HS 700/9-12
2250 Laguna Rd 86440 928-768-2300
Bud Scully, prin. Fax 768-6156

Mohave Valley ESD 16 1,700/PK-8
PO Box 5070 86446 928-768-2507
Phil Sauceman, supt. Fax 768-2510
www.mvesd16.org
Mohave Valley JHS 500/7-8
6565 Girard Ave 86440 928-768-9196
Whitney Crow, prin. Fax 768-1129

Morenci, Greenlee, Pop. 1,799
Morenci USD 18 1,000/PK-12
PO Box 1060 85540 928-865-2081
Duane Howard, supt. Fax 865-3130
www.morenci.k12.az.us/
Morenci JSHS 400/7-12
PO Box 1060 85540 928-865-3631
Bryan Boling, prin. Fax 865-3614

Nogales, Santa Cruz, Pop. 20,833
Nogales USD 1 5,900/K-12
310 W Plum St 85621 520-287-0800
Dr. Guillermo Zamudio, supt. Fax 287-3586
www.nusd.k12.az.us
Carpenter Middle Academy 700/6-8
595 W Kino St 85621 520-287-0820
Liza Montiel, prin. Fax 287-0817
Desert Shadows MS 800/6-8
340 Boulevard Del Rey David 85621 520-377-2646
Joan Molera, prin. Fax 377-2674
Nogales HS 1,700/9-12
1905 N Apache Blvd 85621 520-377-2021
Mark Valenzuela, prin. Fax 281-4448
Pierson Vocational HS Vo/Tech
451 N Arroyo Blvd 85621 520-287-0915
Joel Kramer, lead tchr. Fax 287-0918

Lourdes HS 100/9-12
555 E Patagonia Hwy 85621 520-287-5659
Sr. Barbara Monsegur, prin. Fax 287-2910

Oro Valley, Pima, Pop. 38,438
Amphitheater USD 10
Supt. — See Tucson
Ironwood Ridge HS 1,700/9-12
2475 W Naranja Dr, 520-696-3900
Sam McClung, prin. Fax 696-3999

Page, Coconino, Pop. 6,794
Page USD 8 3,000/PK-12
PO Box 1927 86040 928-608-4100
Jim Walker, supt. Fax 608-4109
www.pageud.k12.az.us
Page HS 1,100/9-12
PO Box 1927 86040 928-608-4138
Perry Berry, prin. Fax 645-9285
Page MS 800/6-8
PO Box 1927 86040 928-608-4306
Eric Bonniksen, prin. Fax 645-9285

Paradise Valley, Maricopa, Pop. 14,558

Phoenix Country Day S 700/PK-12
3901 E Stanford Dr 85253 602-955-8200
Geoffrey Campbell, hdmstr. Fax 955-1286

Parker, LaPaz, Pop. 3,222
Parker USD 27 1,900/PK-12
PO Box 1090 85344 928-669-9244
Kevin Uden, supt. Fax 669-2515
www.parkerusd.k12.az.us
Parker HS 600/9-12
PO Box 1090 85344 928-669-2202
Le Roy Shontz, prin. Fax 669-2315
Wallace JHS 200/7-8
PO Box 1090 85344 928-669-2141
Jay Sandusky, prin. Fax 669-2515

Patagonia, Santa Cruz, Pop. 825
Patagonia ESD 6 100/PK-8
PO Box 295 85624 520-394-3050
Judy Neal, supt. Fax 394-3051
patagonia.echalk.com
Patagonia MS 50/6-8
PO Box 254 85624 520-394-3000
Judy Neal, prin. Fax 394-3001

Patagonia UNHSD 100/9-12
PO Box 254 85624 520-394-3050
Judy Neal, supt. Fax 394-3051
Patagonia Union HS 100/9-12
PO Box 254 85624 520-394-3000
Judy Neal, prin. Fax 394-3001

Payson, Gila, Pop. 14,729
Payson USD 10 2,700/PK-12
PO Box 919 85547 928-474-2070
Casey O'Brien, supt. Fax 472-2013
www.pusd.k12.az.us/
Payson HS 900/9-12
PO Box 919 85547 928-474-2233
Roy Sandoval, prin. Fax 472-2010
Rim Country MS 600/6-8
PO Box 919 85547 928-474-4511
Monica Nitzsche, prin. Fax 472-2013

Payson Community Christian S 100/PK-12
500 S Mud Springs Rd 85541 928-474-8050
Fax 468-1176

Peach Springs, Mohave, Pop. 787
Peach Springs USD 8 300/K-12
PO Box 360 86434 928-769-2202
Eugene Thomas Ph.D., supt. Fax 769-2676
www.psusd.k12.az.us/
Music Mountain JSHS 100/7-12
PO Box 360 86434 928-769-2202
Dr. Eugene Thomas, prin. Fax 769-2412

Peoria, Maricopa, Pop. 138,200
Peoria USD 11
Supt. — See Glendale
Centennial HS 2,000/9-12
14388 N 79th Ave 85381 623-412-4400
Jim Davis, prin. Fax 412-4420
Liberty HS 9-12
9621 W Speckled Gecko Dr 85383 623-773-6525
Ali Bridgewater, prin. Fax 773-6540
Peoria HS 2,700/9-12
11200 N 83rd Ave 85345 623-486-6300
Dr. Kayla Carter, prin. Fax 486-6330
Sunrise Mountain HS 2,300/9-12
21200 N 83rd Ave 85382 623-487-5125
Jerry Nunez, prin. Fax 487-5140

Southwest Indian S 50/1-12
14202 N 73rd Ave 85381 623-979-6008
Debbie McKelvey, prin. Fax 486-5243

Phoenix, Maricopa, Pop. 1,461,575
Alhambra ESD 68 14,700/PK-8
4510 N 37th Ave 85019 602-336-2920
Dr. Jim Rice, supt. Fax 336-2270
www.alhambra.k12.az.us
Andalucia MS 1,200/4-8
4730 W Campbell Ave 85031 623-848-8646
Kathy Moore, prin. Fax 846-6044
Cordova MS 800/4-8
5631 N 35th Ave 85017 602-841-0704
Barbara Marshall, prin. Fax 973-8416
Granada East MS 1,300/4-8
3022 W Campbell Ave 85017 602-589-0110
Sandra Kennedy, prin. Fax 589-0140
Simpson MS 1,100/4-8
5330 N 23rd Ave 85015 602-246-0699
Cynthia Nicholas, prin. Fax 246-4305
Other Schools – See Glendale

Cartwright ESD 83 17,800/PK-8
3401 N 67th Ave 85033 623-691-4000
Michael Martinez, supt. Fax 691-5920
www.cartwright.k12.az.us
Atkinson MS 1,000/7-8
4315 N Maryvale Pkwy 85031 623-691-1700
Raul Pina, prin. Fax 691-1720

Borman MS 1,000/7-8
3637 N 55th Ave 85031 623-691-5000
Ramona Ramirez, prin. Fax 691-5020
Desert Sands MS 900/7-8
6308 W Campbell Ave 85033 623-691-4900
Bob Mayes, prin. Fax 691-4920
Estrella MS 1,100/7-8
3733 N 75th Ave 85033 623-691-5400
Patricia Heichel, prin. Fax 691-5420

Deer Valley USD 97 31,600/PK-12
20402 N 15th Ave 85027 623-445-5000
Dr. Virginia McElyea, supt. Fax 445-5086
www.dvusd.org
Boulder Creek HS 9-12
40404 N Gavilan Peak Pkwy 85086 623-445-8600
C. Kevin Imes, prin. Fax 445-8680
Deer Valley MS 1,000/7-8
21100 N 27th Ave 85027 623-445-3300
Dr. Dan Courson, prin. Fax 445-3380
Goldwater HS 2,200/9-12
2820 W Rose Garden Ln 85027 623-445-3000
Dr. Mike Anderson, prin. Fax 445-3080
O'Connor HS 1,700/9-12
25250 N 35th Ave, 623-445-7100
Jack Dillard, prin. Fax 445-7180
Other Schools – See Glendale

Fowler ESD 45 3,100/PK-8
1617 S 67th Ave 85043 623-707-4500
Dr. Randall Blecha, supt. Fax 707-4561
www.fesd.org
Santa Maria MS 500/6-8
7250 W Lower Buckeye Rd 85043 623-707-1100
Frank Larby, prin. Fax 707-1110
Western Valley MS 400/6-8
6250 W Durango St 85043 623-707-2200
Louis Daniels, prin. Fax 707-2204

Glendale UNHSD 205
Supt. — See Glendale
Cortez HS 1,200/9-12
8828 N 31st Ave 85051 623-915-8200
Tom Hernandez, prin. Fax 915-8244
Greenway HS 1,700/9-12
3930 W Greenway Rd 85053 623-915-8500
Michael Dellisanti, prin. Fax 915-8560
Moon Valley HS 1,700/9-12
3625 W Cactus Rd 85029 623-915-8000
Michael Fowler, prin. Fax 915-8070
Sunnyslope HS 1,600/9-12
35 W Dunlap Ave 85021 623-915-8760
John Croteau, prin. Fax 915-8762
Thunderbird HS 1,700/9-12
1750 W Thunderbird Rd 85023 623-915-8900
Norman Smalley, prin. Fax 915-8971
Washington HS 1,500/9-12
2217 W Glendale Ave 85021 623-915-8400
Carol Lippert, prin. Fax 915-8437

Isaac ESD 5 8,500/PK-8
3348 W McDowell Rd 85009 602-455-6700
Dr. Kent Paredes Scribner, supt. Fax 455-6701
www.isaacschools.org
Isaac MS 1,000/6-8
3402 W McDowell Rd 85009 602-455-6800
Armando Chavez, prin. Fax 455-6868
Pueblo Del Sol MS 1,000/6-8
3449 N 39th Ave 85019 602-455-6900
Gloria Garino Spencer, prin. Fax 484-4118
Smith MS 6-8
4301 W Fillmore St 85043 602-442-2850
Chad Gestson, prin. Fax 442-2897

Kyrene ESD 28
Supt. — See Tempe
Kyrene Akimel A-al MS 1,100/6-8
2720 E Liberty Ln 85048 480-783-1600
Ernie Broderson, prin. Fax 759-7688
Kyrene Altadena MS 1,200/6-8
14620 S Desert Fthills Pkwy 85048 480-783-1300
Nancy Corner, prin. Fax 460-2094
Kyrene Centennial MS 1,200/6-8
13808 S 36th St 85044 480-783-2500
Kathy Cranson, prin. Fax 496-6110

Madison ESD 38 5,100/PK-8
5601 N 16th St 85016 602-664-7900
Fred Maiocco Ph.D., supt. Fax 664-7999
www.msd38.org
Madison I MS 900/5-8
5525 N 16th St 85016 602-664-7100
Ann Roberts, prin. Fax 664-7199
Madison Meadows MS 700/5-8
225 W Ocotillo Rd 85013 602-664-7600
Boris Morew, prin. Fax 664-7699
Madison Park MS 800/4-8
1431 E Campbell Ave 85014 602-664-7500
Richard Ramos, prin. Fax 664-7599

Osborn ESD 8 3,700/K-8
1226 W Osborn Rd 85013 602-707-2000
Wilma Basnett, supt. Fax 707-2040
www.osbornnet.org
Osborn MS 700/7-8
1102 W Highland Ave 85013 602-707-2400
Marty Makar, prin. Fax 707-2440

Paradise Valley USD 69 34,600/PK-12
15002 N 32nd St 85032 602-867-5100
John Kriekard Ed.D., supt. Fax 867-5251
www.pvschools.net
Explorer MS 600/7-8
22401 N 40th St 85050 480-419-5600
Marianne Bursi, prin. Fax 419-5608
Greenway MS 800/7-8
3002 E Nisbet Rd 85032 602-493-6300
Jesse Acosta, prin. Fax 971-6385

Mountain Trail MS 900/7-8
2323 E Mountain Gate Pass 85024 480-538-7100
Tanya Beckwith, prin. Fax 538-7100
North Canyon HS 2,400/9-12
1700 E Union Hills Dr 85024 623-780-4200
Carol Pollack, prin. Fax 780-4304
Paradise Valley HS 2,000/9-12
3950 E Bell Rd 85032 602-867-5505
Cara Herkamp, prin. Fax 867-5592
Pinnacle HS 1,900/9-12
3535 E Mayo Blvd 85050 480-419-4400
Jason Reynolds, prin. Fax 419-4412
Shadow Mountain HS 1,900/9-12
2902 E Shea Blvd 85028 602-867-5326
Mitch von Gnechten, prin. Fax 867-5317
Shea MS 900/7-8
2728 E Shea Blvd 85028 602-493-6440
Dan Knak, prin. Fax 787-0915
Star Tech Professional Center Vo/Tech
3950 E Bell Rd 85032 602-867-5571
Tony Maldonado, dir. Fax 867-5596
Vista Verde MS 900/7-8
2826 E Grovers Ave 85032 602-493-6013
Elaine Jacobs, prin. Fax 493-7656
Other Schools – See Scottsdale

Pendergast ESD 92 8,500/PK-8
3802 N 91st Ave 85037 623-772-2200
Ron Richards, supt. Fax 877-8188
www.pesd92.org/
Westwind IS 5-8
9040 W Campbell Ave 85037 623-772-2460
Claudio Coria, prin. Fax 872-0327

Phoenix ESD 1 7,700/PK-8
1817 N 7th St 85006 602-257-3755
Dr. Georgina Takemoto, supt. Fax 257-3783
www.phxelem.k12.az.us
Phoenix Preparatory Academy 1,000/5-8
735 E Fillmore St 85006 602-257-4840
John Ewing, prin. Fax 257-4852

Phoenix UNHSD 210 23,900/9-12
4502 N Central Ave 85012 602-271-3100
Raj Chopra Ph.D., supt. Fax 271-3131
www.phxhs.k12.az.us
Alhambra HS 2,600/9-12
3839 W Camelback Rd 85019 602-764-6022
Marty Hoeffel, prin. Fax 271-3497
Browne HS 2,600/9-12
7402 W Catalina Dr 85033 602-764-8500
Virginia Corder, prin. Fax 440-6803
Camelback HS 2,300/9-12
4612 N 28th St 85016 602-764-7001
Pete Garcia, prin. Fax 271-2295
Central HS 2,200/9-12
4525 N Central Ave 85012 602-764-7500
Frank Rasmussen, prin. Fax 271-2385
Hayden HS 2,200/9-12
3333 W Roosevelt St 85009 602-764-3000
Steve Ybarra, prin. Fax 229-8387
Maryvale HS 2,400/9-12
3415 N 59th Ave 85033 602-764-2009
Phillip Verdugo, prin. Fax 271-2597
Metro Tech HS Vo/Tech
1900 W Thomas Rd 85015 602-764-8008
Juvenal Lopez, prin. Fax 452-5302
North HS 2,400/9-12
1101 E Thomas Rd 85014 602-764-6500
Zachary Munoz, prin. Fax 271-2765
Phoenix Union Bioscience HS 9-12
512 E Pierce St 85004 602-764-1526
Dave Silcox, admin. Fax 253-9013
South Mountain HS 2,100/9-12
5401 S 7th St 85040 602-764-5000
Alvin Watson, prin. Fax 271-2880
Other Schools – See Laveen

Riverside ESD 2 300/K-8
1414 S 51st Ave 85043 602-477-8900
Jack Bliss, supt. Fax 272-8378
Kings Ridge MS 5-8
3650 S 64th Ln 85043 602-477-8960
Lee Silver, prin. Fax 936-5531

Roosevelt ESD 66 11,500/K-8
6000 S 7th St 85042 602-243-4800
Dr. Mark Dowling, supt. Fax 243-2637
www.rsd.k12.az.us
Greenfield MS 700/4-8
7009 S 10th St 85042 602-232-4240
Ruben Gonzalez, prin. Fax 243-4973
Julian MS 300/5-8
2149 E Carver Dr 85040 602-232-4950
Patricia Jury, prin. Fax 243-4906

Scottsdale USD 48 26,500/PK-12
3811 N 44th St 85018 480-484-6100
Dr. John Baracy, supt. Fax 484-6287
www.susd.org/
Arcadia HS 1,200/9-12
4703 E Indian School Rd 85018 480-484-6300
Anne-Marie Woolsey, prin. Fax 484-6301
Ingleside MS 800/6-8
5402 E Osborn Rd 85018 480-484-4900
Cindy Hans, prin. Fax 484-4901
Other Schools – See Scottsdale

Tempe UNHSD 213
Supt. — See Tempe
Desert Vista HS 2,800/9-12
16440 S 32nd St 85048 480-706-7900
Anna Battle, prin. Fax 706-7976
Mountain Pointe HS 2,300/9-12
4201 E Knox Rd 85044 480-759-8449
Brenda Mayberry, prin. Fax 759-8458

Washington ESD 6
Supt. — See Glendale
Cholla MS 900/7-8
3120 W Cholla St 85029 602-896-5400
Brenda Case, prin. Fax 896-5420
Desert Foothills JHS 900/7-8
3333 W Banff Ln 85053 602-896-5500
Chris Whitaker, prin. Fax 896-5520
Mountain Sky JHS 900/7-8
16225 N 7th Ave 85023 602-896-6100
Linda Marlar, prin. Fax 896-6120
Palo Verde MS 1,300/7-8
7502 N 39th Ave 85051 602-347-2500
Sheila Shaffer, prin. Fax 347-2520
Royal Palm MS 1,200/7-8
8520 N 19th Ave 85021 602-347-3200
Leonard Hoover, prin. Fax 347-3220

Wilson ESD 7 1,400/PK-8
3025 E Fillmore St 85008 602-681-2200
Antonio Sanchez, supt. Fax 275-7517
www.wsd.k12.az.us
Wilson MS 700/4-8
2929 E Fillmore St 85008 602-683-2400
Cindy Campton, prin. Fax 275-8677

American Indian Coll of Assemblies/God Post-Sec.
10020 N 15th Ave 85021 602-944-3335
American Institute of Technology Post-Sec.
440 S 54th Ave 85043 602-233-2222
Apollo College Post-Sec.
2701 W Bethany Home Rd 85017 602-433-1333
Apollo College Post-Sec.
8503 N 27th Ave 85051 602-864-1571
Argosy University/Phoenix Post-Sec.
2233 W Dunlap Ave 85021 866-216-2777
Arizona Lutheran Academy 200/9-12
6036 S 27th Ave 85041 602-268-8686
Daniel Johnson, prin. Fax 243-1353
Arizona State University West Post-Sec.
PO Box 37110 85069 602-543-5500
Art Institute of Phoenix Post-Sec.
2233 W Dunlap Ave 85021 602-331-7500
Artistic Beauty College Post-Sec.
2727 W Glendale Ave Ste 200 85051 623-939-8364
Bourgade Catholic HS 400/9-12
4602 N 31st Ave 85017 602-973-4000
Sr. Mary McGreevy, prin. Fax 973-5854
Brophy College Prep HS 1,200/9-12
4701 N Central Ave 85012 602-264-5291
Bob Ryan, prin. Fax 234-1669
Bryman School Post-Sec.
2250 W Peoria Ave Ste A100 85029 602-274-4300
CollegeAmerica Post-Sec.
6533 N Black Canyon Hwy 85015 602-246-3041
DeVry University Post-Sec.
2149 W Dunlap Ave 85021 602-870-9220
Everest College Post-Sec.
10400 N 25th Ave Ste 190 85021 602-942-4141
Gateway Community College Post-Sec.
108 N 40th St 85034 602-392-5000
Grand Canyon University Post-Sec.
3300 W Camelback Rd 85017 602-249-3300
High-Tech Institute Post-Sec.
1515 E Indian School Rd 85014 602-279-9700
International Import-Export Institute Post-Sec.
11225 N 28th Dr Ste B201 85029 602-648-5750
International Institute of the Americas Post-Sec.
6049 N 43rd Ave 85019 602-242-6265
Keller Graduate School of Management Post-Sec.
18500 N Allied Way Ste 150 85054 480-657-3223
Long Technical College Post-Sec.
13450 N Black Canyon # 104 85029 602-548-1955
Long Technical College Post-Sec.
4646 E Van Buren St Ste 350 85008 602-252-2171
Motorcycle Mechanics Institute Post-Sec.
2844 W Deer Valley Rd 85027 623-869-9644
91st Psalm Christian S 100/K-12
2020 E Baseline Rd 85042 602-243-1900
Scott Ranney, prin. Fax 243-5919
Northwest Christian S 1,300/PK-12
16401 N 43rd Ave 85053 602-978-5134
Dave Young, supt. Fax 978-5804
Paradise Valley Community College Post-Sec.
18401 N 32nd St 85032 602-787-7411
Phoenix Christian JSHS 500/7-12
1751 W Indian School Rd 85015 602-265-4707
Robert Byrd, supt. Fax 277-7170
Phoenix College Post-Sec.
1202 W Thomas Rd 85013 602-264-2492
Phoenix First Pastors College Post-Sec.
1220 E Rosemonte Dr 85024 602-867-4587
Phoenix Institute of Herbal Medicine Post-Sec.
301 E Bethany Home Rd #A100 85012
602-274-1885
Phoenix Seminary Post-Sec.
4222 E Thomas Rd Ste 400 85018 602-850-8000
Refrigeration School Post-Sec.
4210 E Washington St 85034 602-275-7133
Roberto-Venn Guitar Making School Post-Sec.
4011 S 16th St 85040 602-243-1179
St. Marys Catholic HS 800/9-12
2525 N 3rd St 85004 602-251-2500
Mark Mauro, prin. Fax 251-2595
St. Paul's Preparatory Academy 100/8-12
2645 E Osborn Rd 85016 602-956-9090
Harold Elliott, hdmstr. Fax 956-3018
Scottsdale Christian Academy 1,100/PK-12
14400 N Tatum Blvd 85032 602-992-5100
Dr. Gary Damore, supt. Fax 992-0575
South Mountain Community College Post-Sec.
7050 S 24th St 85042 602-243-8000
Southwestern College Post-Sec.
2625 E Cactus Rd 85032 800-247-2697
The Paralegal Institute Post-Sec.
PO Box 11408 85061 602-212-0501

University of Phoenix Post-Sec.
4615 E Elwood St 85040 480-966-9577
Valley Lutheran HS 200/9-12
5199 N 7th Ave 85013 602-230-1600
Dr. Jay Krause, prin. Fax 230-1602
Western International University Post-Sec.
9215 N Black Canyon Hwy 85021 602-943-2311
Xavier College Prep HS 1,200/9-12
4710 N 5th St 85012 602-277-3772
Sr. Joan Fitzgerald, prin. Fax 279-1346

Pima, Graham, Pop. 1,965
Pima USD 6 600/K-12
PO Box 429 85543 928-485-0529
Troy Thygerson, supt. Fax 485-2343
www.pima.k12.az.us/
Pima HS 200/9-12
PO Box 429 85543 928-485-2221
Joseph Farnsworth, prin. Fax 485-0790
Pima JHS 100/7-8
PO Box 429 85543 928-485-2273
Tony Goodman, prin. Fax 485-2274

Pinon, Navajo, Pop. 468
Pinon USD 4 1,500/PK-12
PO Box 839 86510 928-725-2100
Larry Wallen, supt. Fax 725-2123
www.pusdatsa.org
Pinon Accelerated MS 400/6-8
PO Box 839 86510 928-725-2300
Dorothy Yazzie, prin. Fax 725-2370
Pinon HS 400/9-12
PO Box 839 86510 928-725-2489
James Lesher, prin. Fax 725-2470

Prescott, Yavapai, Pop. 40,360
Prescott USD 1 5,200/K-12
146 S Granite St 86303 928-445-5400
Kevin J. Kapp, supt. Fax 713-3207
www.prescottschools.com
Granite Mountain MS 600/6-8
1800 N Williamson Valley Rd 86305 928-717-3253
Stephanie Hillig, prin. Fax 717-3284
Northpoint Expeditionary Learning Acad 9-12
551 1st St 86301 928-717-3272
Geneva Saint-Amour, prin. Fax 717-2316
Prescott HS 1,800/9-12
1050 Ruth St 86301 928-445-2322
Totsy McCraley, prin. Fax 778-6106
Prescott Mile High MS 600/6-8
300 S Granite St 86303 928-717-3241
Joe Howard, prin. Fax 717-3298

Artistic Beauty College Post-Sec.
410 W Goodwin St 86303 928-778-5064
Embry-Riddle Aeronautical University Post-Sec.
3700 Willow Creek Rd 86301 800-888-3728
Northcentral University Post-Sec.
505 Whipple St 86301 928-541-7777
Prescott College Post-Sec.
220 Grove Ave 86301 928-778-2090
Yavapai College Post-Sec.
1100 E Sheldon St 86301 928-445-7300

Prescott Valley, Yavapai, Pop. 33,068
Humboldt USD 22 5,200/PK-12
8766 E State Route 69 86314 928-759-4000
Dr. Henry E. Schmitt, supt. Fax 759-4020
www.humboldt.k12.az.us
Bradshaw Mountain HS 1,400/9-12
6000 E Long Look Dr 86314 928-759-4100
James Souder, prin. Fax 759-4120
Bradshaw Mountain HS East 9-12
6411 N Robert Rd 86314 928-759-5100
Connie Kudrna, prin. Fax 759-5120
Glassford Hill MS 700/6-8
6901 Panther Path 86314 928-759-4600
Kristen Rex, prin. Fax 759-4620
Other Schools – See Dewey

Queen Creek, Maricopa, Pop. 16,628
Chandler USD 80
Supt. — See Chandler
Payne JHS 7-8
7655 S Higley Rd 85242 480-224-2400
Craig Gilbert, prin. Fax 224-2420

J.O. Combs ESD 44 400/K-8
301 E Combs Rd, 480-987-5300
Jan Langer, supt. Fax 987-3487
www.jocombs.org/
Combs MS 6-8
37327 N Gantzel Rd, 480-987-5320
Eric Samuels, prin. Fax 987-5009

Queen Creek USD 95 2,500/PK-12
20740 S Ellsworth Rd 85242 480-987-5935
Dr. James D. Murlless, supt. Fax 987-9714
www.qcusd.org/
Queen Creek HS 800/9-12
22149 E Ocotillo Rd 85242 480-987-5973
Angela Chomokos, prin. Fax 987-5979
Queen Creek MS 600/6-8
20435 S Ellsworth Rd 85242 480-987-5940
Tom Lindsey, prin. Fax 987-5947

Rio Rico, Santa Cruz, Pop. 100
Santa Cruz Valley USD 35 2,600/PK-12
1374 W Frontage Rd 85648 520-375-8261
Daniel Fontes, supt. Fax 281-7093
www.santacruz.k12.az.us
Calabasas MS 800/6-8
1374 W Frontage Rd 85648 520-375-8600
John Fanning, prin. Fax 375-8690
Rio Rico HS 800/9-12
1374 W Frontage Rd 85648 520-375-8700
Mike Brown, prin. Fax 375-9556

Sacaton, Pinal, Pop. 1,452
Sacaton ESD 18 500/PK-8
PO Box 98 85247 520-562-8600
Dr. James Christensen, supt. Fax 763-4410
Sacaton MS 100/6-8
PO Box 98 85247 520-562-8600
Nicholas DePadre, prin. Fax 763-4410

Safford, Graham, Pop. 8,932
Safford USD 1 2,900/PK-12
734 W 11th St 85546 928-348-7000
Mark Tregaskes, supt. Fax 348-7001
www.saffordusd.k12.az.us
Safford HS 800/9-12
734 W 11th St 85546 928-348-7050
Rich DeRidder, prin. Fax 348-7051
Safford MS 400/7-8
734 W 11th St 85546 928-348-7040
Robert Beeman, prin. Fax 348-7041

Safford College of Beauty Culture Post-Sec.
1550 W Thatcher Blvd 85546 928-428-0331

Sahuarita, Pima, Pop. 9,007
Sahuarita USD 30 2,600/PK-12
350 W Sahuarita Rd 85629 520-625-3502
Jay St. John, supt. Fax 625-4609
sahuarita.k12.az.us
Sahuarita HS 800/9-12
350 W Sahuarita Rd 85629 520-625-3502
Larry McKee, prin. Fax 399-1223
Sahuarita MS 600/6-8
350 W Sahuarita Rd 85629 520-625-3502
Terri Noe, prin. Fax 399-1870

Saint David, Cochise, Pop. 1,468
Saint David USD 21 500/PK-12
PO Box 70 85630 520-720-4781
Kate Mueller, supt. Fax 720-4783
www.stdavidschool.net/
Saint David HS 200/9-12
PO Box 70 85630 520-720-4781
Mark Goodman, dean Fax 720-4783

Saint Johns, Apache, Pop. 3,513
Saint Johns USD 1 1,100/PK-12
PO Box 3030 85936 928-337-2255
Larry Heap, supt. Fax 337-2263
www.sjusd.net
Saint Johns HS 400/9-12
PO Box 429 85936 928-337-2221
Roger Heap, prin. Fax 337-2263
Saint Johns MS 400/4-8
PO Box 3060 85936 928-337-2132
Ed Burgoyne, prin. Fax 337-3147

Saint Michaels, Apache, Pop. 1,119

St. Michael HS 200/9-12
PO Box 650 86511 928-871-4443
Albert Sye, prin. Fax 871-3191

Salome, LaPaz
Bicentennial UNHSD 76 100/9-12
PO Box 519 85348 928-859-3453
Dave Perey, supt. Fax 859-4663
www.salomehs.org
Salome HS 100/9-12
PO Box 519 85348 928-859-3453
Dave Perey, prin. Fax 859-3875

San Carlos, Gila, Pop. 2,918
San Carlos USD 20 1,300/PK-12
PO Box 207 85550 928-475-2315
John Bush, supt. Fax 475-2301
San Carlos HS 300/9-12
PO Box 207 85550 928-475-2378
Dave Pastor, prin. Fax 475-2697
San Carlos JHS 300/6-8
PO Box 207 85550 928-475-2262
Elberta Monroe, prin. Fax 475-2431

Sanders, Apache
Sanders USD 18 1,100/K-12
PO Box 250 86512 928-688-4755
Doug McIntyre, supt. Fax 688-4766
www.susd.k12.az.us
Sanders MS 300/6-8
PO Box 250 86512 928-688-4772
Kalem Norton, prin. Fax 688-4773
Valley HS 300/9-12
PO Box 250 86512 928-688-4200
Rick Lindblad, prin. Fax 688-4202

San Luis, Yuma, Pop. 21,646
Gadsden ESD 32 4,400/PK-8
PO Box 6870 85349 928-627-6540
Raymond Aguilera, supt. Fax 627-3635
www.gesd32.org
San Luis MS 1,100/7-8
PO Box 6870 85349 928-627-6920
Carlos Robles, prin. Fax 627-9339
Southwest JHS 7-8
PO Box 6870 85349 928-627-6580
Richard West, prin. Fax 627-9266

Yuma UNHSD 70
Supt. — See Yuma
San Luis HS 1,300/9-12
1250 N 8th Ave 85349 928-502-6100
Mary Lynn Coleman, prin. Fax 502-6222

San Manuel, Pinal, Pop. 4,009
Mammoth/San Manuel USD 8 1,100/PK-12
PO Box 406 85631 520-385-2337
Dr. Ron Rickel, supt. Fax 385-2621
www.msmusd.k12.az.us
San Manuel JSHS 400/7-12
PO Box 406 85631 520-385-2336
John Ryan, prin. Fax 385-3035

San Simon, Cochise
San Simon USD 18 100/K-12
PO Box 38 85632 520-845-2275
Kathy Moore, supt. Fax 845-2480
www.sansimon.k12.az.us
San Simon S 100/K-12
PO Box 38 85632 520-845-2275
Kathy Moore, prin. Fax 845-2480

Scottsdale, Maricopa, Pop. 226,013
Cave Creek USD 93 5,400/PK-12
33606 N 60th St 85262 480-575-2016
Dr. Tacy Ashby, supt. Fax 488-7055
www.ccusd93.org
Cactus Shadows HS 1,400/9-12
5802 E Dove Valley Rd 85262 480-575-2400
Sid Bailey, prin. Fax 488-6701
Desert Arroyo MS 700/6-8
33401 N 56th St 85262 480-575-2300
Ann Orlando, prin. Fax 488-7059
Other Schools – See Cave Creek

Paradise Valley USD 69
Supt. — See Phoenix
Desert Shadows MS 800/7-8
5858 E Sweetwater Ave 85254 602-493-6000
Carol Kendrick, prin. Fax 494-9266
Horizon HS 2,400/9-12
5601 E Greenway Rd 85254 602-953-4104
Dan Courson, prin. Fax 953-4144
Sunrise MS 800/7-8
4960 E Acoma Dr 85254 602-493-6030
Gregory Martin, prin. Fax 493-6037

Scottsdale USD 48
Supt. — See Phoenix
Chaparral HS 1,800/9-12
6935 E Gold Dust Ave 85253 480-484-6500
Mary Lou Muccino, prin. Fax 484-6501
Cocopah MS 1,100/6-8
6615 E Cholla St 85254 480-484-4400
Dr. Tere Peterson, prin. Fax 484-4401
Copper Ridge Math & Science Academy 9-9
10101 E Thompson Peak Pkwy 85255 480-484-1500
Dr. Michael Wolf, dean Fax 484-1501
Copper Ridge MS 500/6-8
10101 E Thompson Peak Pkwy 85255 480-484-1500
Sheila Burnham, prin. Fax 484-1501
Coronado HS 1,200/9-12
2501 N 74th St 85257 480-484-6800
John Biera, prin. Fax 484-6801
Desert Canyon MS 800/6-8
10203 E McDowell Mntn Ranch 85255 480-484-4600
Tracy Olson, prin. Fax 484-4601
Desert Mountain HS 2,400/9-12
12575 E Via Linda 85259 480-484-7000
Greg Milbrandt, prin. Fax 484-7001
Mohave MS 700/7-8
5520 N 86th St 85250 480-484-5200
Chris Sawyer, prin. Fax 484-5201
Mountainside MS 1,000/6-8
11256 N 128th St 85259 480-484-5500
Chris Asmussen, prin. Fax 484-5501
Saguaro HS 1,700/9-12
6250 N 82nd St 85250 480-484-7200
Tyrus Timbrooks, prin. Fax 484-7201
Supai MS 700/7-8
6720 E Continental Dr 85257 480-484-5800
Daniel Cooper, prin. Fax 484-5801

Artistic Beauty College Post-Sec.
7730 E McDowell Rd 85257 480-949-7557
Devereux-Arizona Treatment Network Post-Sec.
6436 E Sweetwater Ave 85254 480-998-2920
Frank Lloyd Wright Sch of Architecture Post-Sec.
Taliesin West 85261 480-860-2700
Notre Dame Preparatory HS 400/9-12
9701 E Bell Rd 85260 480-634-8200
David Gonsalves, prin. Fax 634-8299
RainStar University Post-Sec.
8370 E Via De Ventura K-100 85258 480-423-0375
Scott Cole Academy Post-Sec.
7201 E Camelback Rd Ste 100 85251 480-994-4222
Scottsdale Community College Post-Sec.
9000 E Chaparral Rd 85256 480-423-6000
Scottsdale Culinary Institute Post-Sec.
8100 E Camelback Rd 85251 480-990-3773
Sonoran Desert Institute Post-Sec.
10245 E Via Linda Ste 102 85258 480-314-2102
Thunderbird Adventist Academy 100/9-12
7410 E Sutton Dr 85260 480-948-3300
Barry Warren, prin. Fax 443-4944

Sedona, Coconino, Pop. 11,220
Sedona-Oak Creek JUSD 9 1,300/PK-12
221 Brewer Rd Ste 100 86336 928-204-6800
Kim Randall, supt. Fax 282-0232
www.sedona.k12.az.us/
Sedona Red Rock HS 400/9-12
995 Upper Red Rock Loop Rd 86336 928-204-6700
Russ Snider, prin. Fax 282-5992

Verde Valley S 100/9-12
3511 Verde Valley School Rd 86351 928-284-2272
Paul Domingue, hdmstr. Fax 284-0432

Seligman, Yavapai
Seligman USD 40 200/K-12
PO Box 650 86337 928-422-3233
Todd Kissick, supt. Fax 422-3642
Seligman HS 100/9-12
PO Box 650 86337 928-422-3233
Patrick Kissick, prin. Fax 422-3642

Sells, Pima, Pop. 2,750
Indian Oasis-Baboquivari USD 40 1,200/K-12
PO Box 248 85634 520-623-1031
Joe Frazier, supt. Fax 383-5441
www.iobusd40.org

Baboquivari HS 300/9-12
PO Box 248 85634 520-383-6800
Paula Hart, prin. Fax 383-4852
Baboquivari MS 200/7-8
PO Box 248 85634 520-383-6800
Paula Hart, prin. Fax 383-4852

Tohono O'odham Community College Post-Sec.
PO Box 3129 85634 520-383-8401

Show Low, Navajo, Pop. 10,000
Show Low USD 10 2,500/PK-12
500 W Old Linden Rd 85901 928-537-6000
Kevin Brackney, supt. Fax 537-6009
www.show-low.k12.az.us
Show Low HS 800/9-12
500 W Old Linden Rd 85901 928-537-6200
Farrell Adams, prin. Fax 537-6299
Show Low JHS 400/7-8
500 W Old Linden Rd 85901 928-537-6100
Connie Lewis, prin. Fax 537-6149

American Indian Christian S 100/K-12
924 Mission Ln Lot 1 85901 928-537-5912
Roger Nosker, dir. Fax 537-5620

Sierra Vista, Cochise, Pop. 41,908
Sierra Vista USD 68 6,600/PK-12
3555 E Fry Blvd 85635 520-515-2714
Renae Humburg, supt. Fax 515-2721
www.sierravistapublicschools.com
Apache MS 700/6-8
3555 E Fry Blvd 85635 520-515-2920
Jeff Spencer, prin. Fax 515-2900
Buena HS 2,600/9-12
3555 E Fry Blvd 85635 520-515-2800
Tad Bloss, prin. Fax 515-2877
Sierra Vista MS 900/6-8
3555 E Fry Blvd 85635 520-515-2930
Jim Sprigg, prin. Fax 515-2941

Cochise College Post-Sec.
901 Colombo Ave 85635 520-515-5412
DeVoe College of Beauty Post-Sec.
750 Bartow Dr 85635 520-458-8660
Shiloh Christian S 100/K-12
200 North Ave 85635 520-459-2869
Angela Tumpkin, prin. Fax 459-7436
Veritas Christian Community S 100/K-12
215 Taylor Dr 85635 520-417-1113
Karen Bolton, hdmstr. Fax 417-0180

Snowflake, Navajo, Pop. 4,958
Snowflake USD 5 2,500/K-12
682 W School Bus Ln 85937 928-536-4156
Monte Silk, supt. Fax 536-2634
www.snowflake.k12.az.us
Snowflake HS 800/9-12
682 W School Bus Ln 85937 928-536-4156
Larry Titus, prin. Fax 536-4240
Snowflake JHS 400/7-8
682 W School Bus Ln 85937 928-536-4156
Edna Jean LaMarca, prin. Fax 536-2634

Somerton, Yuma, Pop. 10,071
Somerton ESD 11 2,500/PK-8
PO Box 3200 85350 928-341-6005
Judith Bobbitt, supt. Fax 341-6090
www.somerton.k12.az.us
Somerton MS 900/6-8
PO Box 3200 85350 928-341-6100
George Brick, prin. Fax 627-6190

Springerville, Apache, Pop. 1,956
Round Valley USD 10 1,400/PK-12
PO Box 610 85938 928-333-6580
Travis Udall, supt. Fax 333-2823
www.elks.net
Other Schools – See Eagar

Sun City, Maricopa, Pop. 38,400

Walter Boswell Memorial Hospital Post-Sec.
10401 W Thunderbird Blvd 85351 623-977-7211

Superior, Pinal, Pop. 3,158
Superior USD 15 600/PK-12
199 N Lobb Ave 85273 520-689-5291
Pete Guzman, supt.
Superior HS 200/9-12
100 W Mary Dr 85273 520-689-3101
Paul Hatch, prin. Fax 689-3197
Superior JHS 100/7-8
100 W Mary Dr 85273 520-689-3101
Paul Hatch, prin. Fax 689-3197

Surprise, Maricopa, Pop. 74,411
Dysart USD 89 10,800/K-12
15802 N Parkview Pl 85374 623-876-7000
Dr. Mark S. Maksimowicz, supt. Fax 876-7042
www.dysart.org
Valley Vista HS 9-10
15550 N Parkview Pl 85374 623-523-8800
Dr. Tammy Hall, prin. Fax 523-8811
Willow Canyon HS 900/9-12
17901 W Lundberg St, 623-876-8000
Kathy Vogt, prin. Fax 523-8011
Other Schools – See El Mirage

Teec Nos Pos, Apache, Pop. 317
Red Mesa USD 27 800/PK-12
HC 61 Box 40 86514 928-656-4100
Peter Belletto, supt. Fax 656-4106
www.rmusd.net
Red Mesa HS 300/9-12
HC 61 Box 40 86514 928-656-4177
Tim Benally, prin. Fax 656-4178

Immanuel Mission S 100/K-12
PO Box 2000 86514 928-674-3616
John Bloom, prin. Fax 826-8120

Tempe, Maricopa, Pop. 161,143
Kyrene ESD 28 18,400/PK-8
8700 S Kyrene Rd 85284 480-783-4000
David Schauer Ed.D., supt. Fax 783-4141
www.kyrene.org
Kyrene MS 1,100/6-8
1050 E Carver Rd 85284 480-783-1000
Susan Poole, prin. Fax 831-0169
Other Schools – See Chandler, Phoenix

Tempe ESD 3 13,700/K-8
PO Box 27708 85285 480-730-7100
Dr. Arthur Tate, supt. Fax 730-7177
www.tempeschools.org
Connolly MS 1,000/6-8
2002 E Concorda Dr 85282 480-967-8933
Kathryn Mullery, prin. Fax 929-9695
Fees MS 1,100/6-8
1600 E Watson Dr 85283 480-897-6063
Reynaldo Cruz, prin. Fax 838-0853
Gililland MS 1,000/6-8
1025 S Beck Ave 85281 480-966-7114
Rick Horvath, prin. Fax 829-6178
McKemy MS 1,000/6-8
2250 S College Ave 85282 480-921-9003
Ardie Sturdivant, prin. Fax 829-6179

Tempe UNHSD 213 13,200/9-12
500 W Guadalupe Rd 85283 480-839-0292
Dr. Shirley Miles, supt. Fax 413-0685
www.tempehighschools.org
Corona Del Sol HS 2,700/9-12
1001 E Knox Rd 85284 480-752-8888
James Denton, prin. Fax 820-3632
Marcos De Niza HS 2,000/9-12
6000 S Lakeshore Dr 85283 480-838-3200
Frank Mirizio, prin. Fax 730-7665
McClintock HS 1,800/9-12
1830 E Del Rio Dr 85282 480-839-4222
Kim Hilgers, prin. Fax 752-8622
Tempe HS 1,400/9-12
1730 S Mill Ave 85281 480-967-1661
Mark Yslas, prin. Fax 736-4096
Other Schools – See Phoenix

Arizona State University Post-Sec.
PO Box 870112 85287 480-965-9011
Carsten Institute of Hair and Beauty Post-Sec.
3345 S Rural Rd 85282 480-491-0449
College of the Humanities and Sciences Post-Sec.
1105 E Broadway Rd 85282 480-317-5955
Collins College School of Design & Tech. Post-Sec.
1140 S Priest Dr 85281 480-966-3000
Conservatory of Recording Arts/Sciences Post-Sec.
2300 E Broadway Rd 85282 480-858-9400
International Academy of Beauty Post-Sec.
4812 S Mill Ave 85282 480-964-8675
International Baptist College Post-Sec.
2150 E Southern Ave 85282 480-838-7070
ITT Technical Institute Post-Sec.
5005 S Wendler Dr 85282 602-437-7500
Lamson College Post-Sec.
1126 N Scottsdale Rd Ste 17 85281 480-898-7000
Remington College Post-Sec.
875 W Elliot Rd 85284 480-834-1000
Rio Salado Community College Post-Sec.
2323 W 14th St 85281 480-517-8000
Southwest Coll of Naturopathic Medicine Post-Sec.
2140 E Broadway Rd 85282 480-858-9100
Southwest Institute of Healing Arts Post-Sec.
1100 E Apache Blvd 85281 480-994-9244
University of Advancing Technology Post-Sec.
2625 W Baseline Rd 85283 800-658-5744

Thatcher, Graham, Pop. 4,121
Thatcher USD 4 1,200/K-12
PO Box 610 85552 928-348-7200
Janice Given, supt. Fax 348-7220
www.thatcherud.k12.az.us
Thatcher HS 400/9-12
601 N 3rd Ave 85552 928-348-7272
Paul Nelson, prin. Fax 348-7273
Thatcher MS 200/7-8
1300 N 4th Ave 85552 928-348-7262
Matt Petersen, prin. Fax 348-7263

Eastern Arizona College Post-Sec.
3714 W Church St 85552 928-428-8233

Tolleson, Maricopa, Pop. 5,974
Tolleson UNHSD 214 5,500/9-12
9801 W Van Buren St 85353 623-478-4000
Kino Flores, supt. Fax 936-5048
www.tuhsd.org
Tolleson Union HS 2,000/9-12
9419 W Van Buren St 85353 623-478-4200
Harold Crenshaw, prin. Fax 936-9366
Other Schools – See Avondale, Glendale

Union ESD 62 100/K-8
3834 S 91st Ave 85353 623-478-5005
Justin Greene, supt. Fax 478-5006
www.uesd.org
Union S 100/6-8
3834 S 91st Ave 85353 623-478-5000
Kendra Stark, prin. Fax 478-5026

Tombstone, Cochise, Pop. 1,569
Tombstone USD 1 1,000/PK-12
PO Box 1000 85638 520-457-2217
Thomas Yarborough, supt. Fax 457-3270
www.tombstone.k12.az.us/
Tombstone HS 400/9-12
PO Box 1000 85638 520-457-2215
Robert Devere, prin. Fax 457-3643

Tonalea, Coconino
San Juan SD
Supt. — See Blanding, UT
Navajo Mountain HS 50/9-12
PO Box 10040 86044 435-678-1287
Fax 678-1289

Tonopah, Maricopa
Saddle Mountain USD 90 700/PK-12
38201 W Indian School Rd 85354 623-386-5688
Roxanne Morris, supt. Fax 386-3364
Tonopah Valley HS 9-12
38201 W Indian School Rd 85354 623-386-5688
John Sigala, prin. Fax 386-3364

Tsaile, Apache, Pop. 1,043

Din College 86556 Post-Sec.
928-724-3311

Tuba City, Coconino, Pop. 7,323
Tuba City USD 15 2,600/PK-12
PO Box 67 86045 928-283-1006
Hector Tahu, supt. Fax 283-5105
www.tcusd.org
Tuba City HS 1,000/9-12
PO Box 67 86045 928-283-1045
Ralph Navarre, prin. Fax 283-1129
Tuba City JHS 600/6-8
PO Box 67 86045 928-283-1055
Lee Tsinigine, prin. Fax 283-1094

Tucson, Pima, Pop. 515,526
Altar Valley ESD 51 800/PK-8
10105 S Sasabe Hwy 85736 520-822-1484
Douglas Roe, supt. Fax 822-1798
Altar Valley MS 400/5-8
10105 S Sasabe Hwy 85736 520-822-9343
John Holt, prin. Fax 822-5801

Amphitheater USD 10 16,800/PK-12
701 W Wetmore Rd 85705 520-696-5000
Vicki Balentine Ph.D., supt. Fax 696-5015
www.amphi.com
Amphitheater HS 1,700/9-12
125 W Yavapai Rd 85705 520-696-5340
Patsy Harris, prin. Fax 696-5410
Amphitheater MS 900/6-8
315 E Prince Rd 85705 520-696-6230
Chuck Bermudez, prin. Fax 696-6236
Canyon Del Oro HS 1,900/9-12
25 W Calle Concordia 85704 520-696-5560
Mike Gemma, prin. Fax 696-5590
Cross MS 1,000/6-8
1000 W Chapala Dr 85704 520-696-5920
Robert Vinyard, prin. Fax 696-5996
La Cima MS 700/6-8
5600 N La Canada Dr 85704 520-696-6730
Gail Gault, prin. Fax 696-6792
Other Schools – See Oro Valley

Catalina Foothills USD 16 5,000/PK-12
2101 E River Rd 85718 520-299-6446
Mary Kamerzell, supt. Fax 577-5307
www.cfsd.k12.az.us
Catalina Foothills HS 1,900/9-12
4300 E Sunrise Dr 85718 520-577-5090
Wagner Van Vlack, prin. Fax 577-5094
Esperero Canyon MS 600/6-8
5801 N Sabino Canyon Rd 85750 520-577-5330
Brian Lorimer, prin. Fax 577-5334
Orange Grove MS 700/6-8
1911 E Orange Grove Rd 85718 520-577-5315
Phil Woodall, prin. Fax 577-5319

Flowing Wells USD 8 5,900/PK-12
1556 W Prince Rd 85705 520-696-8800
Dr. Nicholas Clement, supt. Fax 690-2400
www.flowingwells.k12.az.us
Flowing Wells HS 1,900/9-12
3725 N Flowing Wells Rd 85705 520-696-8000
Jim Brunenkant, prin. Fax 690-2379
Flowing Wells JHS 1,000/7-8
4545 N La Cholla Blvd 85705 520-696-8550
Deborah Schreiner, prin. Fax 690-2420

Marana USD 6
Supt. — See Marana
Marana HS 1,600/9-12
12000 W Emigh Rd 85743 520-616-6400
Jim Doty, prin. Fax 616-6426
Mountain View HS 2,100/9-12
3901 W Linda Vista Blvd 85742 520-579-4400
Jill Atlas, prin. Fax 579-4505
Tortolita MS 1,100/7-8
4101 W Hardy Rd 85742 520-579-4600
Jane D'Amore, prin. Fax 579-4646

Sunnyside USD 12 15,600/PK-12
2238 E Ginter Rd 85706 520-545-2000
Manuel Isquierdo, supt. Fax 545-2120
www.susd12.org
Apollo MS 1,000/6-8
265 W Nebraska St 85706 520-545-4500
Ray Chavez, prin. Fax 545-4516
Challenger MS 1,000/6-8
100 E Elvira Rd 85706 520-545-4600
Wil Arias, prin. Fax 545-4616
Chaparral MS 900/6-8
3700 E Alvord Rd 85706 520-545-4700
Grace Garcia, prin. Fax 545-4716
Desert View HS 1,500/9-12
4101 E Valencia Rd 85706 520-545-5100
Raul Ochoa, prin. Fax 545-5116
Lauffer MS 6-8
5385 E Littletown Rd 85706 520-545-4900
Robert Miranda, prin. Fax 545-4916

Sierra MS 1,100/6-8
5801 S Del Moral Blvd 85706 520-545-4800
Art Menchaca, prin. Fax 545-4816
Sunnyside HS 2,000/9-12
1725 E Bilby Rd 85706 520-545-5300
Raul Nido, prin. Fax 545-5316

Tanque Verde USD 13 1,400/PK-12
11150 E Tanque Verde Rd 85749 520-749-5751
Michael Schwanenberger, supt. Fax 749-5400
www.tanq.org
Gray JHS 400/7-8
4201 N Melpomene Way 85749 520-749-3838
Greg Anderson, prin. Fax 749-9668
Tanque Verde HS 100/9-12
4201 N Melpomene Way 85749 520-749-3838
Greg Anderson, prin. Fax 749-9668

Tucson USD 1 59,300/PK-12
1010 E 10th St 85719 520-225-6000
Roger Pfeuffer, supt. Fax 225-6174
www.tusd.k12.az.us
Carson MS 800/6-8
7777 E Stella Rd 85730 520-584-4700
John Howe, prin. Fax 584-4701
Catalina Magnet HS 1,500/9-12
3645 E Pima St 85716 520-232-8400
W. Daniel Bailey, prin. Fax 232-8401
Cholla Magnet HS 1,600/9-12
2001 W Starr Pass Blvd 85713 520-225-4000
Marcia Volpe Ph.D., prin. Fax 225-4001
Dodge Magnet MS 400/6-8
5831 E Pima St 85712 520-731-4100
Catherine Comstock, prin. Fax 731-4101
Doolen MS 900/6-8
2400 N Country Club Rd 85716 520-232-6900
Charlotte Patterson, prin. Fax 232-6901
Gridley MS 800/6-8
350 S Harrison Rd 85748 520-731-4600
Kathleen Scheppe, prin. Fax 731-4601
Hohokam MS 700/6-8
7400 S Settler Ave 85746 520-908-3700
Ralph Lim, prin. Fax 908-3701
Magee MS 1,000/6-8
8300 E Speedway Blvd 85710 520-731-5000
Jerry Holmes, prin. Fax 731-5001
Mansfeld MS 900/6-8
1300 E 6th St 85719 520-225-1800
Elizabeth Rivera, prin. Fax 225-1801
Maxwell MS 600/6-8
2802 W Anklam Rd 85745 520-225-2000
Javier Fuentes, prin. Fax 225-2001
Naylor MS 800/6-8
1701 S Columbus Blvd 85711 520-584-6800
Don Calhoun, prin. Fax 584-6801
Palo Verde Magnet HS 1,600/9-12
1302 S Avenida Vega 85710 520-584-7400
Tina Isaac, prin. Fax 584-7441
Pistor MS 1,100/6-8
5455 S Cardinal Ave 85746 520-908-5400
Kathryn Manley-Crockett, prin. Fax 908-5411
Pueblo Magnet HS 1,900/9-12
3500 S 12th Ave 85713 520-225-4300
Patricia Dienz, prin. Fax 225-4301
Rincon HS 1,200/9-12
421 N Arcadia Ave 85711 520-232-5600
Angela Julien, prin. Fax 232-5601
Sabino HS 1,700/9-12
5000 N Bowes Rd 85749 520-584-7700
Valerie Payne, prin. Fax 584-7701
Sahuaro HS 2,000/9-12
545 N Camino Seco 85710 520-731-7100
Sam Giangardella, prin. Fax 731-7101
Santa Rita HS 1,300/9-12
3951 S Pantano Rd 85730 520-731-7500
Jonathan Hanson, prin. Fax 731-7501
Secrist MS 600/6-8
3400 S Houghton Rd 85730 520-731-5300
Jim Christ, prin. Fax 731-5301
Townsend MS 600/6-8
2120 N Beverly Ave 85712 520-232-7900
Barbara Kohl, prin. Fax 232-7901
Tucson Magnet HS 2,800/9-12
400 N 2nd Ave 85705 520-225-5000
Dr. Abel Morado, prin. Fax 225-5221
University HS 600/9-12
421 N Arcadia Ave 85711 520-232-5900
Rosy Beetcher, prin. Fax 235-5901
Utterback Magnet MS 1,100/6-8
3233 S Pinal Vis 85713 520-225-3500
Debbie Summers, prin. Fax 225-3501
Vail MS 800/6-8
5350 E 16th St 85711 520-584-5400
David Ross, prin. Fax 584-5401
Valencia MS 800/6-8
4400 W Irvington Rd 85746 520-908-4500
Ray Chavez, prin. Fax 908-4501
Wakefield MS 600/6-8
101 W 44th St 85713 520-225-3800
Wade McRae, prin. Fax 225-3801

Vail USD 20
Supt. — See Vail
Desert Sky MS 700/6-8
9850 E Rankin Loop 85747 520-762-2700
Kevin Carney, prin. Fax 762-2701
Empire HS 9-12
10701 E Mary Ann Cleveland 85747 520-762-3000
Cindy Lee, prin. Fax 762-3001

Apollo College Post-Sec.
3550 N Oracle Rd 85705 520-888-5885
Arizona Academy of Beauty Post-Sec.
5631 E Speedway Blvd 85712 520-885-4120
Arizona Academy of Beauty - North Post-Sec.
4066 N Oracle Rd 85705 520-888-0170
AZ School of Acupuncture & Oriental Med Post-Sec.
4646 E Ft Lowell Rd Ste 105 85712 520-795-0787
AZ State School for the Deaf & Blind Post-Sec.
PO Box 85000 85754 520-770-3719
Artistic Beauty College Post-Sec.
3030 E Speedway Blvd 85716 520-327-6544
Asian Institute of Medical Studies Post-Sec.
3131 N Country Club Rd #100 85716 520-322-6330
Carondelet Saint Marys Hospital Post-Sec.
1601 W Saint Marys Rd 85745 520-622-5833
Chaparral College Post-Sec.
4585 E Speedway Blvd #204 85712 520-327-6866
Desert Christian HS 200/9-12
7525 E Speedway Blvd 85710 520-298-5817
John O'Hair, prin. Fax 298-9312
Desert Christian MS 200/6-8
7525 E Speedway Blvd 85710 520-795-7161
Dennis O'Reilly, prin. Fax 795-3386
Desert Institute of the Healing Arts Post-Sec.
639 N 6th Ave 85705 520-882-0899
Fenster S of Southern Arizona 100/9-12
8500 E Ocotillo Dr 85750 520-749-3340
Don Saffer, hdmstr. Fax 749-3349
Green Fields Country Day S 200/K-12
6000 N Camino De La Tierra 85741 520-297-2288
Deac Etherington M.A., hdmstr. Fax 297-2072
HDS Truck Driving Institute Post-Sec.
PO Box 17600 85731 520-721-5825
Immaculate Heart HS 100/9-12
625 E Magee Rd 85704 520-297-2851
Dan Ethridge, prin. Fax 797-7374
International Institute of the Americas Post-Sec.
5441 E 22nd St 85711 520-748-9799
ITT Technical Institute Post-Sec.
1455 W River Rd 85704 520-408-7488
Pima Community College Post-Sec.
4905 E Broadway Blvd 85709 520-206-4500
Pima Medical Institute Post-Sec.
3350 E Grant Rd 85716 520-326-1600
Pusch Ridge Christian Academy 500/6-12
9500 N Oracle Rd 85704 520-797-0107
Dr. Eric Abrams, prin. Fax 797-0598
River of Life Christian S 100/PK-12
6902 E Golf Links Rd 85730 520-790-7082
Denise Garcia, prin. Fax 790-3891
St. Augustine Catholic HS 9-12
8800 E 22nd St 85710 520-751-8300
Velma Castaneda-Titone, prin. Fax 751-8304
St. Gregory College Preparatory S 300/6-12
3231 N Craycroft Rd 85712 520-327-6395
William Creeden, hdmstr. Fax 327-8276
Salpointe Catholic HS 1,300/9-12
1545 E Copper St 85719 520-327-6581
Jeffrey Mounts, prin. Fax 327-8477
San Miguel HS 9-12
PO Box 22199 85734 520-294-6403
Br. Nick Gonzalez, prin. Fax 294-6417
The Art Center Design College Post-Sec.
2525 N Country Club Rd 85716 520-325-0123
Tucson College Post-Sec.
7310 E 22nd St 85710 520-296-3261
University of Arizona 85721 Post-Sec.
520-621-3237
University of Arizona Medical Center Post-Sec.
1501 N Campbell Ave 85724 520-694-4660

Vail, Pima
Vail USD 20 5,300/K-12
PO Box 800 85641 520-762-2000
Calvin Baker, supt. Fax 762-2001
vail.k12.az.us
Cienega HS 1,300/9-12
12775 Mary Ann Cleveland 85641 520-762-2800
Tricia Pena, prin. Fax 762-2801
Old Vail MS 600/6-8
13299 E Colossal Cave Rd 85641 520-762-2400
Laurie Emery, prin. Fax 762-5840
Pantano HS 50/9-12
12775 E Old Vail Rd 85641 520-762-2000
Heather Pletnick, prin. Fax 762-2930
Other Schools – See Corona, Tucson

Wellton, Yuma, Pop. 1,862
Antelope UNHSD 50 300/9-12
9168 S Avenue 36 E 85356 928-785-4041
Robert Klee, supt. Fax 785-4588
Antelope Union HS 300/9-12
9168 S Avenue 36 E 85356 928-785-3344
Randall O'Donnell, prin. Fax 785-9566

Whiteriver, Navajo, Pop. 3,775
Whiteriver USD 20 2,400/PK-12
PO Box 190 85941 928-338-4842
Earl Pettit, supt. Fax 338-5124
www.wusd.k12.az.us/
Alchesay HS 700/9-12
PO Box 190 85941 928-338-4848
Jeff Fuller, prin. Fax 338-4840
Canyon Day JHS 400/7-8
PO Box 190 85941 928-338-1040
William Stiver, prin. Fax 338-4850

East Fork Lutheran S 50/K-12
PO Box 489 85941 928-338-4455
Richard Carver, prin. Fax 338-1575

Wickenburg, Maricopa, Pop. 6,224
Wickenburg USD 9 1,200/K-12
40 W Yavapai St 85390 928-668-5350
Brett Richards, supt. Fax 668-5390
www.wickenburg.k12.az.us
Vulture Peak MS 300/6-8
920 S Vulture Mine Rd 85390 928-684-6700
Ray Manker, prin. Fax 684-6746
Wickenburg HS 600/9-12
1090 S Vulture Mine Rd 85390 928-684-6600
Thomas Newton, prin. Fax 684-6628

Willcox, Cochise, Pop. 3,769
Willcox USD 13 1,400/PK-12
480 N Bisbee Ave 85643 520-384-4211
Dr. Donald L. Roberts, supt. Fax 384-2025
www.willcox.k12.az.us
Willcox HS 500/9-12
240 N Bisbee Ave 85643 520-384-4214
Joel Todd, prin. Fax 384-5401
Willcox MS 500/4-8
360 N Bisbee Ave 85643 520-384-4218
Doris Jones, prin. Fax 384-6322

Williams, Coconino, Pop. 3,094
Williams USD 2 800/PK-12
PO Box 427 86046 928-635-4473
Thomas McCraley Ed.D., supt. Fax 635-4767
www.wusd2.org
Williams HS 200/9-12
PO Box 427 86046 928-635-4474
Steve Hudgens, prin. Fax 635-2796

Winkelman, Gila, Pop. 444
Hayden/Winkelman USD 41 500/K-12
PO Box 409 85292 520-356-7876
Jeff Gregorich, supt. Fax 356-7303
www.hwusd.k12.az.us/
Hambly MS 200/6-8
PO Box 409 85292 520-356-7876
Jacob Kame, prin. Fax 356-7303
Hayden HS 100/9-12
PO Box 409 85292 520-356-7876
Jacob Kame, prin. Fax 356-7303

Winslow, Navajo, Pop. 9,931
Winslow USD 1 2,600/PK-12
PO Box 580 86047 928-288-8101
Robert Mansell, supt. Fax 288-8292
www.winslowsd.k12.az.us/
Winslow HS 900/9-12
PO Box 580 86047 928-288-8100
Doug Watson, prin. Fax 288-8290
Winslow JHS 400/7-8
PO Box 580 86047 928-288-8300
Jim MacLean, prin. Fax 288-8393

Young, Gila
Young ESD 5 100/PK-12
PO Box 390 85554 928-462-3244
Rick Ullery, supt. Fax 462-3283
Young Teaching HS 50/9-12
PO Box 390 85554 928-462-3244
Rick Ullery, prin. Fax 462-3283

Yuma, Yuma, Pop. 84,688
Crane ESD 13 5,200/PK-8
4250 W 16th St 85364 928-373-3403
Cindy Didway, supt. Fax 782-6831
craneschools.org/
Centennial MS 600/7-8
2650 W 20th St 85364 928-373-3300
Paula Milner, prin. Fax 376-7742
Crane MS 700/7-8
4450 W 32nd St 85364 928-373-3200
Linda Huff, prin. Fax 344-6821

Yuma ESD 1 10,300/K-8
450 W 6th St 85364 928-502-4300
Thomas Rushin, supt. Fax 502-4442
www.yuma.org
Castle Dome MS 1,000/6-8
2353 S Otondo Dr 85365 928-341-1600
Harriet Williams, prin. Fax 341-1700
Fourth Avenue JHS 600/7-8
450 S 4th Ave 85364 928-782-2193
Rob Monson, prin. Fax 783-2195
Gila Vista JHS 700/6-8
2245 S Arizona Ave 85364 928-782-5174
Rusty Tyndall, prin. Fax 782-1483
Woodard JHS 800/6-8
2250 S 8th Ave 85364 928-782-6546
Alan Sullivan, prin. Fax 782-4596

Yuma UNHSD 70 9,100/9-12
3150 S Avenue A 85364 928-502-4600
Tim Foist, supt. Fax 502-4740
www.yumaunion.com
Cibola HS 2,800/9-12
4100 W 20th St 85364 928-502-5700
Tony Steen, prin. Fax 502-6046
Gila Ridge HS, 7150 E 24th St 85365 9-12
Jamie Sheldahl, prin. 928-502-6400
Kofa HS 2,100/9-12
3100 S Avenue A 85364 928-502-5400
Gina Thompson, prin. Fax 502-5693
Yuma HS 2,600/9-12
400 S 6th Ave 85364 928-502-5000
Jeff Magin, prin. Fax 502-5338
Other Schools – See San Luis

Arizona Western College Post-Sec.
PO Box 929 85366 928-317-6000
Yuma Catholic HS 400/9-12
2100 W 28th St 85364 928-317-7900
Sr. Adrianna Schouten, prin. Fax 317-8558

ARKANSAS

ARKANSAS DEPARTMENT OF EDUCATION
4 State Capitol Rm 304A, Little Rock 72201
Telephone 501-682-4475
Fax 501-682-1079
Website arkansased.org/

Commissioner of Education T. Kenneth James

ARKANSAS BOARD OF EDUCATION
4 State Capitol, Little Rock 72201

Chairperson Diane Tatum

EDUCATION SERVICE COOPERATIVES (ESC)

Arch Ford ESC
Phillip Young, dir. 501-354-2269
101 Bulldog Dr, Plumerville 72127 Fax 354-0167
www.afsc.k12.ar.us/
Arkansas River ESC
Carolyn McCoy, dir. 870-534-6129
912 W 6th Ave, Pine Bluff 71601 Fax 534-2847
Crowley's Ridge ESC
John Manning, dir. 870-578-5426
1606 Pine Grove Ln Fax 578-5896
Harrisburg 72432
crowleys.crsc.k12.ar.us/
Dawson ESC
R. Saunders, dir. 870-246-3077
711 Clinton St, Arkadelphia 71923 Fax 246-5892
www.dawson.dsc.k12.ar.us
De Queen/Mena ESC
J. Scott, dir. 870-386-2251
PO Box 110, Gillham 71841 Fax 386-7731
nexus.dmsc.k12.ar.us/
Great Rivers ESC
Suzann McCommon, dir. 870-338-6461
PO Box 2837, West Helena 72390 Fax 338-7905
griver.grsc.k12.ar.us/
Northcentral Arkansas ESC
Dr. Dennis Martin, dir. 870-368-7955
PO Box 739, Melbourne 72556 Fax 368-4920
naesc.k12.ar.us/
Northeast Arkansas ESC
Harrell Austin, dir., 211 W Hickory St 870-886-7717
Walnut Ridge 72476 Fax 886-7719
thor.nesc.k12.ar.us/
Northwest Arkansas ESC
Burton Elliott, dir. 479-267-7450
4 N Double Springs Rd Fax 267-7456
Farmington 72730
starfish.k12.ar.us/
Ozarks Unlimited Resource Cooperative
Rick Nance, dir. 870-743-9100
525 Old Bellefonte Rd Fax 743-9099
Harrison 72601
www.oursc.k12.ar.us/
South Central Service Cooperative
Marsha Daniels, dir. 870-836-2213
400 Maul Rd, Camden 71701 Fax 836-5347
www.scsc.k12.ar.us/
Southeast Arkansas ESC
Bruce Terry, dir. 870-367-6848
1022 Scogin Dr, Monticello 71655 Fax 367-9877
se.sesc.k12.ar.us/
Southwest Arkansas ESC
Lindy Franks, dir. 870-777-3076
500 S Spruce St, Hope 71801 Fax 777-5793
Western Arkansas ESC
Guy Fenter, dir. 479-965-2191
3010 Highway 22 E Ste A Fax 965-2723
Branch 72928
Wilbur D. Mills ESC
Rodger Harlan, dir. 501-882-5467
PO Box 850, Beebe 72012 Fax 882-2155
wdmweb.wmsc.k12.ar.us/

PUBLIC, PRIVATE AND CATHOLIC SECONDARY SCHOOLS

Alma, Crawford, Pop. 4,734
Alma SD 3,100/K-12
PO Box 2359 72921 479-632-4791
Charles Dyer, supt. Fax 632-4793
almasd.net
Alma HS 900/9-12
PO Box 2139 72921 479-632-2162
Jerry Valentine, prin. Fax 632-5070
Alma MS 800/6-8
PO Box 2229 72921 479-632-2168
Pat Whorton, prin. Fax 632-2160

Alpena, Boone, Pop. 387
Alpena SD 500/K-12
PO Box 270 72611 870-437-2220
James Trammell, supt. Fax 437-2133
Alpena JSHS 200/7-12
PO Box 270 72611 870-437-2228
David Bennett, prin. Fax 437-5638

Amity, Clark, Pop. 741
Centerpoint SD 700/PK-12
755 Highway 8 E 71921 870-356-2912
Lewis Diggs, supt. Fax 356-4637
www.centerpoint.dsc.k12.ar.us/
Centerpoint HS 300/9-12
755 Highway 8 E 71921 870-356-3612
Deric Owens, prin. Fax 356-4519
Centerpoint JHS 200/6-8
755 Highway 8 E 71921 870-356-3612
Michael Jackson, prin. Fax 356-4519

Arkadelphia, Clark, Pop. 10,548
Arkadelphia SD 2,200/K-12
235 N 11th St 71923 870-246-5564
Stan Miller, supt. Fax 246-1144
apsd.k12.ar.us/
Arkadelphia HS 700/9-12
401 High School Rd 71923 870-246-7373
Odas Parsons, prin. Fax 246-1154
Goza JHS 500/6-8
1305 Caddo St 71923 870-246-4291
Angela Garner, prin. Fax 246-1153

Arkadelphia Beauty College Post-Sec.
2708 Pine St 71923 870-246-6726
Henderson State University Post-Sec.
1100 Henderson St 71999 870-230-5000
Ouachita Baptist University Post-Sec.
410 Ouachita St 71998 870-245-5000

Armorel, Mississippi
Armorel SD 400/K-12
PO Box 99 72310 870-763-6639
Mike Hunter, supt. Fax 763-0028
armorel.crsc.k12.ar.us
Armorel JSHS 200/7-12
PO Box 99 72310 870-763-7121
Steven Noble, prin. Fax 763-7020

Ashdown, Little River, Pop. 4,592
Ashdown SD 1,700/K-12
511 N 2nd St 71822 870-898-3208
Mike Walker, supt. Fax 898-3709
www.ashdownschools.org
Ashdown JHS 400/7-9
600 S Ellen Dr 71822 870-898-5138
Lin Johnson, prin. Fax 898-4472
Ashdown SHS 400/10-12
751 Rankin St 71822 870-898-3562
John Crowder, prin. Fax 898-4452

Atkins, Pope, Pop. 2,890
Atkins SD 1,100/K-12
307 N Church St 72823 479-641-7871
Boyce Watkins, supt. Fax 641-7569
ahs.afsc.k12.ar.us/
Atkins HS 400/9-12
403 Avenue 3 NW 72823 479-641-7872
Robert Travis, prin. Fax 641-1306
Atkins MS 300/5-8
302 Avenue 2 NW 72823 479-641-1008
Allen D. Wilbanks, prin. Fax 641-5504

Augusta, Woodruff, Pop. 2,456
Augusta SD 500/K-12
320 Sycamore St 72006 870-347-2241
Richard Blevins, supt. Fax 347-5423
Augusta HS 200/9-12
320 Sycamore St 72006 870-347-2515
Kevin Byers, prin. Fax 347-8113

Bald Knob, White, Pop. 3,316
Bald Knob SD 1,300/K-12
103 W Park Ave 72010 501-724-3273
R. Wayne Fawcett, supt. Fax 724-6621
bkps.wmsc.k12.ar.us
ASU Area Career Center Vo/Tech
103 W Park Ave 72010 501-724-3614
Preston Haynie, dir. Fax 724-6865
Bald Knob HS 400/9-12
901 N Hickory St 72010 501-724-3843
Steve Landers, prin. Fax 724-6621
Bald Knob MS 400/5-8
103 W Park Ave 72010 501-724-5652
David Clark, prin. Fax 724-6621

Batesville, Independence, Pop. 9,556
Batesville SD 2,300/K-12
330 E College St 72501 870-793-6831
Ted Hall, supt. Fax 793-6760
www.batesvilleschools.com
Batesville HS 500/10-12
1 Pioneer Dr 72501 870-793-6846
David Campbell, prin. Fax 793-0607
Batesville JHS 500/7-9
2 Pioneer Dr 72501 870-793-7533
Harry Crossett, prin. Fax 793-0626
Southside SD 1,400/K-12
70 Scott Dr 72501 870-251-2341
Danny L. Foley, supt. Fax 251-3316
southside.k12.ar.us/
Southside HS 400/9-12
70 Scott Dr 72501 870-251-2662
Roger Reid, prin. Fax 251-3316
Southside MS 400/5-8
70 Scott Dr 72501 870-251-2332
Joel W. Franks, prin. Fax 251-3316

Bee-Jay's Hairstyling Academy Post-Sec.
130 W Main St 72501 870-793-3898
Lyon College Post-Sec.
PO Box 2317 72503 870-793-9813
University of Arkansas Community College Post-Sec.
PO Box 3350 72503 870-793-7581

Bauxite, Saline, Pop. 442
Bauxite SD 1,100/K-12
800 School St 72011 501-557-5453
Mickey Billingsley, supt. Fax 557-2235
miners.k12.ar.us/default2.htm
Bauxite JSHS 500/7-12
800 School St 72011 501-557-5303
Keith Baker, prin. Fax 557-2274

Bay, Craighead, Pop. 1,953
Bay SD 600/K-12
PO Box 39 72411 870-781-3711
Chip Layne, supt. Fax 781-3712
www.edline.net/pages/bay
Bay JSHS 300/7-12
PO Box 39 72411 870-781-3297
Jodi Cobb, prin. Fax 781-3687

Bearden, Ouachita, Pop. 1,047
Bearden SD 600/K-12
PO Box 195 71720 870-687-2236
Denny Rozenberg, supt. Fax 687-3683
www.scsc.k12.ar.us/bearden/
Bearden HS 200/9-12
PO Box 195 71720 870-687-3670
James Bonsall, prin. Fax 687-2514
Bearden MS 200/5-8
PO Box 195 71720 870-687-3503
Iva Lou Stoker, prin. Fax 687-3683

Beebe, White, Pop. 5,623
Beebe SD 1,800/PK-12
1201 W Center St 72012 501-882-5463
Dr. Belinda Shook, supt. Fax 882-5465
thor.k12.ar.us
Beebe HS 500/9-12
1201 W Center St 72012 501-882-3311
Sheena Williamson, prin. Fax 882-8405
Beebe JHS 200/7-8
1201 W Center St 72012 501-882-8414
Donald Sandlin, prin. Fax 882-8416

Arkansas State University - Beebe Post-Sec.
PO Box 1000 72012 501-882-6452

Bee Branch, Van Buren
South Side SD 500/K-12
334 Southside Rd 72013 501-654-2633
Billy Jackson, supt. Fax 654-2336
ssbb.k12.ar.us/
South Side JSHS 200/7-12
334 Southside Rd 72013 501-654-2242
Travis Love, prin. Fax 654-2331

Benton, Saline, Pop. 25,673
Benton SD 4,300/K-12
PO Box 939 72018 501-778-4861
Dr. Tony Prothro, supt. Fax 776-5777
bentonschooldistrict.dsc.k12.ar.us/
Benton JHS 700/8-9
411 N Border St 72015 501-778-7698
Roger Burton, prin. Fax 776-5744
Benton SHS 900/10-12
211 N Border St 72015 501-778-3288
John Dedman, prin. Fax 776-5783

Harmony Grove SD 800/K-12
2621 N Highway 229 72015 501-778-6271
Daniel Henley, supt. Fax 778-6271
cardinals.dsc.k12.ar.us/default.htm
Harmony Grove HS 200/9-12
2621 N Highway 229 72015 501-776-2337
William Gibbs, prin. Fax 778-6271
Harmony Grove MS 300/5-8
2621 N Highway 229 72015 501-860-6796
Sarah Gober, prin. Fax 778-6271

Bentonville, Benton, Pop. 29,538
Bentonville SD 8,500/K-12
400 NW 2nd St 72712 479-254-5000
Dr. Gary Compton, supt. Fax 271-1159
www.bentonville.k12.ar.us
Bentonville HS 1,700/9-12
1901 SE J St 72712 479-254-5100
Steve Jacoby, prin. Fax 271-1180
Lincoln JHS 700/7-8
1206 Leopard Ln 72712 479-254-5250
Rose Peterson, prin. Fax 464-1128
Washington JHS 700/7-8
1501 NE Wildcat Way 72712 479-254-5345
Kim Garrett, prin. Fax 271-1191

Ambassadors For Christ Academy 200/K-12
PO Box 924 72712 479-273-5635
David Welshenbaugh, admin. Fax 273-0684
Northwest Arkansas Community College Post-Sec.
1 College Dr 72712 479-636-9222

Bergman, Boone, Pop. 438
Bergman SD 800/K-12
PO Box 1 72615 870-741-5213
Joe Couch, supt. Fax 741-6701
bergman.oursc.k12.ar.us/
Bergman HS 300/9-12
PO Box 1 72615 870-741-1414
Bryan Pruitt, prin. Fax 741-6701
Bergman MS 200/5-8
PO Box 1 72615 870-741-8557
Sarah Alexander, prin. Fax 741-6701

Berryville, Carroll, Pop. 4,935
Berryville SD 1,800/K-12
PO Box 408 72616 870-423-7065
Fax 423-6824
bobcat.oursc.k12.ar.us
Berryville HS 500/9-12
PO Box 408 72616 870-423-3312
Ron Harvell, prin. Fax 423-6028
Berryville MS 400/6-8
PO Box 408 72616 870-423-4512
Matt Summers, prin. Fax 423-3195

Bigelow, Perry, Pop. 337
East End SD 700/K-12
PO Box 360 72016 501-759-2808
Mark A. Tyler, supt. Fax 759-2667
bigelow.afsc.k12.ar.us
Bigelow JSHS 300/7-12
PO Box 360 72016 501-759-2602
Paul Gottsponer, prin. Fax 759-3081

Bismarck, Hot Spring
Bismarck SD 1,000/K-12
11636 Highway 84 71929 501-865-4888
David Hopkins, supt. Fax 865-3626
www.bsd-lions.net/
Bismarck HS 300/9-12
11636 Highway 84 71929 501-865-4541
Jarrod Bray, prin. Fax 865-4542
Bismarck MS 300/5-8
11636 Highway 84 71929 501-865-4543
Dan Breshears, prin. Fax 865-4505

Black Rock, Lawrence, Pop. 690
Lawrence County SD
Supt. — See Walnut Ridge
Black Rock JSHS 200/7-12
PO Box 240 72415 870-878-6461
Steve Morris, prin. Fax 878-6051

Blevins, Hempstead, Pop. 364
Blevins SD 500/K-12
PO Box 98 71825 870-874-2801
Donnie Davis, supt. Fax 874-2889
hornet.swsc.k12.ar.us/
Blevins JSHS 200/7-12
PO Box 98 71825 870-874-2281
Billy Lee, prin. Fax 874-2450
Other Schools – See Emmet

Blytheville, Mississippi, Pop. 16,638
Blytheville SD 3,000/K-12
PO Box 1169 72316 870-762-2053
Bruce Daniels, supt. Fax 762-0141
blytheville.k12.ar.us
Blytheville HS 800/9-12
600 N 10th St 72315 870-762-2772
Suzanne Kenner, prin. Fax 762-0175
Blytheville MS 500/7-8
700 Chickasawba St 72315 870-762-2983
Richard Atwill, prin. Fax 762-0174

Arkansas Northeastern College Post-Sec.
2501 S Division St 72315 870-762-1020
Blytheville Academy of Cosmetology Post-Sec.
100 E Main St 72315 870-763-6326
Pathway Christian Academy 100/K-12
PO Box 466 72316 870-763-4561
Kim Brown, prin. Fax 763-7277

Booneville, Logan, Pop. 4,162
Booneville SD 1,100/K-12
381 W 7th St 72927 479-675-3504
Bobby Ashley, supt. Fax 675-3186
www.booneville.k12.ar.us/
Booneville HS 300/10-12
945 N Plum St 72927 479-675-3277
Steve Halter, prin. Fax 675-3214
Booneville JHS 300/7-9
835 E 8th St 72927 479-675-5247
Scotty Pierce, prin. Fax 675-0793

Bradford, White, Pop. 828
Bradford SD 500/K-12
PO Box 60 72020 501-344-2707
Donald Swiney, supt. Fax 344-2707
bradford.wmsc.k12.ar.us/
Bradford JSHS 300/7-12
PO Box 60 72020 501-344-2607
Brad Roberts, prin. Fax 344-2607

Bradley, Lafayette, Pop. 553
Bradley SD 20 400/K-12
521 School Dr 71826 870-894-3313
Oscar Gammye Moore, supt. Fax 894-3344
bradleyweb.swsc.k12.ar.us/
Bradley HS 200/7-12
521 School Dr 71826 870-894-3316
Amanda Brown, prin. Fax 894-3344

Branch, Franklin, Pop. 366
County Line SD 600/K-12
12092 W State Highway 22 72928 479-635-2222
Ashley Whitman, supt. Fax 635-2087
indians.wsc.k12.ar.us/
County Line JSHS 300/7-12
12092 W State Highway 22 72928 479-635-2441
Clint Jones, prin. Fax 635-2452

Briggsville, Yell
Two Rivers SD
Supt. — See Plainview
Fourche Valley JSHS 100/7-12
18148 W Highway 28 72828 479-299-6220
Mary Ballard, prin. Fax 299-6212

Brinkley, Monroe, Pop. 3,520
Brinkley SD 900/K-12
200 Tigers Dr 72021 870-734-5000
Dr. Randy Byrd, supt. Fax 734-5187
www.brinkleyschools.com
Brinkley HS 300/9-12
100 Tigers Dr 72021 870-734-5005
Randy Cannon, prin. Fax 734-1354
Brinkley MS 100/6-8
100 Tigers Dr 72021 870-734-5105
Gloria Conyears, prin. Fax 734-5134

Brockwell, Izard
Izard County Consolidated SD 400/K-12
PO Box 115 72517 870-258-7700
Fred Walker, supt. Fax 258-3140
icc.k12.ar.us/
Izard County Consolidated HS 200/9-12
PO Box 115 72517 870-258-7788
David Harmon, prin. Fax 258-3140
Izard County Consolidated MS 100/5-8
PO Box 115 72517 870-258-7788
Monty McCurley, prin. Fax 258-3140

Brookland, Craighead, Pop. 1,442
Brookland SD 800/K-12
100 W School St 72417 870-932-2080
Kevin McGaughey, supt. Fax 932-2088
brookland.crsc.k12.ar.us/
Brookland JHS 100/7-9
100 W School St 72417 870-932-2080
Keith McDaniel, prin. Fax 932-2088
Brookland SHS 200/10-12
100 W School St 72417 870-932-2080
Steven Hovis, prin. Fax 932-2088

Bryant, Saline, Pop. 13,185
Bryant SD 6,300/K-12
200 NW 4th St 72022 501-847-5600
Dr. Richard Abernathy, supt. Fax 847-5603
www.bryantschools.org
Bethel MS 6-8
200 NW 4th St 72022 501-316-0937
Joe Fisher, prin. Fax 316-0338
Bryant HS 1,800/9-12
200 NW 4th St 72022 501-847-5605
Deborah Bruick, prin. Fax 847-5612
Bryant MS 1,500/6-8
200 NW 4th St 72022 501-847-5651
Sue Reeves, prin. Fax 847-5654

Burdette, Mississippi, Pop. 119

Cotton Boll Technical Institute Post-Sec.
PO Box 36 72321 870-763-1486

Cabot, Lonoke, Pop. 21,039
Cabot SD 7,900/K-12
602 N Lincoln St 72023 501-843-3363
Dr. Frank A. Holman, supt. Fax 843-0576
cabot.k12.ar.us
Cabot HS 1,600/10-12
401 N Lincoln St 72023 501-843-3562
Dr. Tony Thurman, prin. Fax 843-4231
Cabot JHS North 1,000/7-9
38 Spirit Dr 72023 501-605-8470
Georgia Chastain, prin. Fax 605-8472
Cabot JHS South 900/7-9
38 Panther Trl 72023 501-843-2788
Henry Hawkins, prin. Fax 941-7746

Calico Rock, Izard, Pop. 1,025
Calico Rock SD 500/K-12
PO Box 220 72519 870-297-8339
Jerry Skidmore, supt. Fax 297-4233
pirates.k12.ar.us/
Calico Rock JSHS 200/7-12
PO Box 220 72519 870-297-3745
Dewayne Treat, prin. Fax 297-3168

Camden, Ouachita, Pop. 12,204
Camden Fairview SD 2,800/K-12
625 Clifton St 71701 870-836-4193
Dr. Jerry Guess, supt. Fax 836-6039
www.scsc.k12.ar.us/camdenfairview/
Camden Fairview HS 900/9-12
1750 Cash Rd SW 71701 870-837-1300
Peggy Burton, prin. Fax 837-2330
Camden Fairview MS 700/6-8
647 J A Dooley Womack Dr 71701 870-836-9361
Rodney Williams, prin. Fax 836-3717

Harmony Grove SD 800/K-12
401 Ouachita 88 71701 870-574-0971
Harold Davidson, supt. Fax 574-2765
Harmony Grove JSHS 400/7-12
401 Ouachita 88 71701 870-574-0867
Robert A. McAdoo, prin. Fax 574-2765
Other Schools – See Sparkman

Camden Christian Academy 100/K-12
1245 California Ave SW 71701 870-836-3716
Bob Taynor, admin. Fax 836-4511
Professional Cosmetology Education Ctr Post-Sec.
PO Box 429 71711 870-836-5481
Southern Arkansas University Tech Post-Sec.
100 Carr Rd 71701 870-574-4500

Caraway, Craighead, Pop. 1,355
Riverside SD
Supt. — See Lake City
Riverside JHS 200/7-9
PO Box 699 72419 870-482-3327
Polly Owens, prin. Fax 482-3328

Carlisle, Lonoke, Pop. 2,419
Carlisle SD 800/PK-12
520 Center St 72024 870-552-3931
Sherry Holliman, supt. Fax 552-7967
bison.wmsc.k12.ar.us
Carlisle JSHS 300/7-12
716 E 5th St 72024 870-552-3196
Floyd Marshall, prin. Fax 552-3032

Cave City, Sharp, Pop. 1,980
Cave City SD 1,100/K-12
PO Box 600 72521 870-283-5391
Steven Green, supt. Fax 283-6887
www.cavecity.k12.ar.us
Cave City JSHS 500/7-12
PO Box 600 72521 870-283-5392
Marc Walling, prin. Fax 283-6887
Other Schools – See Evening Shade

Cedarville, Crawford, Pop. 1,195
Cedarville SD 900/K-12
PO Box 97 72932 479-474-7220
Dr. Dan Foreman, supt. Fax 410-1804
chs.wsc.k12.ar.us/
Cedarville HS 300/9-12
PO Box 97 72932 479-474-7021
Tommy Thompson, prin. Fax 410-1804
Cedarville MS 300/5-8
PO Box 97 72932 479-474-5847
Curt Ledbetter, prin. Fax 471-7036

Center Ridge, Conway
Nemo Vista SD 500/PK-12
5690 Highway 9 72027 501-893-2925
Cody Beene, supt. Fax 893-2367
nemo.k12.ar.us/
Nemo Vista JSHS 200/7-12
5690 Highway 9 72027 501-893-2811
Jeff Andrews, prin. Fax 893-2367

Charleston, Franklin, Pop. 3,025
Charleston SD 900/K-12
PO Box 188 72933 479-965-7160
Jeff Stubblefield, supt. Fax 965-9989
tigers.wsc.k12.ar.us/
Charleston HS 300/9-12
PO Box 188 72933 479-965-7150
Shane Storey, prin. Fax 965-7140

Charleston MS 200/7-8
PO Box 188 72933 479-965-7170
Melissa Moore, prin. Fax 965-9989

Cherry Valley, Cross, Pop. 702
Cross County SD 7 500/K-12
PO Box 180 72324 870-588-3338
Dr. Matt McClure, supt. Fax 588-3565
crosscountyschooldistrict.com/
Cross County HS 400/7-12
PO Box 180 72324 870-588-3337
Ed Ross, prin. Fax 588-4606

Clarendon, Monroe, Pop. 1,835
Clarendon SD 500/K-12
PO Box 248 72029 870-747-3351
George LaFargue, supt. Fax 747-5963
Clarendon HS 200/7-12
PO Box 248 72029 870-747-3326
Robert Age, prin. Fax 747-5444

Clarksville, Johnson, Pop. 8,311
Clarksville SD 2,300/K-12
1701 W Clark Rd 72830 479-705-3200
Don Johnston, supt. Fax 754-3748
panthernet.wsc.k12.ar.us/
Clarksville JHS 500/7-9
1801 W Clark Rd 72830 479-705-3224
Paul Dean, prin. Fax 754-7431
Clarksville SHS 400/10-12
1703 W Clark Rd 72830 479-705-3212
Steven Wyatt, prin. Fax 754-2492

University of the Ozarks Post-Sec.
415 N College Ave 72830 479-979-1000

Clinton, Van Buren, Pop. 2,475
Clinton SD 1,200/K-12
851 Yellowjacket Ln 72031 501-745-6000
Randal Betts, supt. Fax 745-2475
clinton.k12.ar.us/
Clinton HS 300/10-12
849 Edd St 72031 501-745-6035
Danny Thomas, prin. Fax 745-2450
Clinton JHS 300/7-9
848 Walker St 72031 501-745-6079
Mark Gammill, prin. Fax 745-6065

Coal Hill, Johnson, Pop. 1,040
Westside SD
Supt. — See Hartman
Westside JSHS 300/7-12
PO Box 189 72832 479-497-1171
John H. Burke, prin. Fax 497-1537

Concord, Cleburne, Pop. 266
Concord SD 400/K-12
PO Box 10 72523 870-668-3844
David Burnley, supt. Fax 668-3380
concord.k12.ar.us
Concord JSHS 200/7-12
PO Box 358 72523 870-668-3522
Mike Hopper, prin. Fax 668-3522

Conway, Faulkner, Pop. 51,999
Conway SD 7,100/K-12
2220 Prince St 72034 501-450-4800
Dr. Greg Murry, supt. Fax 450-4898
www.conwayschools.afsc.k12.ar.us
Conway Area Career Center Vo/Tech
2300 Prince St 72034 501-450-4888
Nicholas Stroman, prin. Fax 450-6658
Conway HS East 1,400/9-10
1815 Prince St 72034 501-450-4860
Mickey Siler, prin. Fax 450-6651
Conway HS West 1,100/11-12
2300 Prince St 72034 501-450-4880
Rodney Matheney, prin. Fax 450-4884
Courtway MS 700/7-8
1200 Bob Courtway Dr 72032 501-450-4832
Jerry Whitmore, prin. Fax 450-4839
Stuart MS 700/7-8
2745 Carl Stuart St 72034 501-329-2782
Harvey Benton, prin. Fax 450-4848

Arkansas Beauty School - Conway Post-Sec.
1061 Markham St 72032 501-329-8303
Central Baptist College Post-Sec.
1501 College Ave 72034 501-329-6872
Conway Christian S 400/PK-12
701 Polk St 72032 501-336-9067
Gloria Gwatney-Massey, admin. Fax 336-9251
Hendrix College Post-Sec.
1600 Washington Ave 72032 501-329-6811
St. Joseph HS 200/7-12
502 Front St 72032 501-329-5741
Joe Mallett, prin. Fax 513-6804
University of Central Arkansas Post-Sec.
201 Donaghey Ave 72035 501-450-5000

Corning, Clay, Pop. 3,456
Corning SD 1,000/K-12
PO Box 479 72422 870-857-6818
John Edington, supt. Fax 857-5086
www.corningschools.k12.ar.us/
Corning JSHS 500/7-12
PO Box 479 72422 870-857-3041
Stan Johnson, prin. Fax 857-5086

Cotter, Baxter, Pop. 1,032
Cotter SD 600/K-12
PO Box 70 72626 870-435-6171
Don Sharp, supt. Fax 435-1300
cotter.oursc.k12.ar.us/
Cotter JSHS 300/7-12
PO Box 70 72626 870-435-6323
Dennis Copeland, prin. Fax 435-1300

Cove, Polk, Pop. 383
Van Cove SD 500/K-12
110 S 5th St 71937 870-387-6832
Lyn Graves, supt. Fax 387-2350
vancove.dmsc.k12.ar.us/
Van-Cove JSHS 300/7-12
110 S 5th St 71937 870-387-2744
Terry Thompson, prin. Fax 387-7961

Crossett, Ashley, Pop. 5,802
Crossett SD 2,200/PK-12
219 Main St 71635 870-364-3112
Janice Warren, supt. Fax 364-5499
csd.k12.ar.us
Crossett SHS 500/10-12
219 Main St 71635 870-364-2625
Kelvin Gragg, prin. Fax 364-4792
Norman JHS 600/7-9
219 Main St 71635 870-364-4712
Jim Lucas, prin. Fax 364-3771

Abiding Faith Christian S 100/PK-12
1552 Highway 52 W 71635 870-364-3844
Br. Blaine Beck, dir. Fax 364-6651
Forest Echoes Technical Institute Post-Sec.
1326 Highway 82W 71635 870-364-6414
University of Arkansas - Monticello Post-Sec.
1326 Highway 52 W 71635 870-364-6414

Cushman, Independence, Pop. 467
Cushman SD 400/K-12
PO Box 370 72526 870-793-6321
Gary Anderson, supt. Fax 793-7266
bulldog.k12.ar.us/
Cushman JSHS 200/7-12
PO Box 370 72526 870-793-6321
Dion Stevens, prin. Fax 793-5312

Danville, Yell, Pop. 2,442
Danville SD 900/K-12
PO Box 939 72833 479-495-4800
Jimmy Cunningham, supt. Fax 495-4803
www.dps-littlejohns.net/
Danville JSHS 400/7-12
PO Box 939 72833 479-495-4810
Randy Treat, prin. Fax 495-4832

Dardanelle, Yell, Pop. 4,337
Dardanelle SD 1,800/K-12
209 Cedar St 72834 479-229-4111
John Thompson, supt. Fax 229-1387
lizardlink.afsc.k12.ar.us/
Dardanelle HS 500/9-12
1079 N State Highway 28 72834 479-229-4655
Marcia Lawrence, prin. Fax 229-4687
Dardanelle MS 300/7-8
2032 State Highway 7 N 72834 479-229-4550
Avis Cotton, prin. Fax 229-1697

Decatur, Benton, Pop. 1,352
Decatur SD 500/PK-12
1498 Stadium Ave 72722 479-752-3986
Mike Parrish, supt. Fax 752-2490
decatur.k12.ar.us/
Decatur HS 200/8-12
1498 Stadium Ave 72722 479-752-3983
Dave Smith, prin. Fax 752-2491

Deer, Newton
Deer / Mt. Judea SD 500/K-12
PO Box 56 72628 870-428-5433
Richard Denniston, supt. Fax 428-5901
deer.k12.ar.us
Deer JSHS 100/7-12
PO Box 56 72628 870-428-5288
Junior C. Edgmon, prin. Fax 428-5901
Other Schools – See Mount Judea

Delaplaine, Greene, Pop. 129
Greene County Technical SD
Supt. — See Paragould
Delaplaine JSHS 200/7-12
PO Box 68 72425 870-249-3216
Marilyn Jerome, prin. Fax 249-3898

Delight, Pike, Pop. 303
Delight SD 400/K-12
PO Box 8 71940 870-379-2214
Curtis Turner, supt. Fax 379-2448
Delight JSHS 200/7-12
PO Box 8 71940 870-379-2214
Tanya Wilcher, prin. Fax 379-2448

De Queen, Sevier, Pop. 5,953
De Queen SD 1,900/K-12
PO Box 950 71832 870-584-4312
Bill Blackwood, supt. Fax 642-8881
leopards.k12.ar.us/
De Queen HS 400/10-12
1803 W Coulter Ave 71832 870-642-2426
Judi Jenkins, prin. Fax 642-4931
De Queen MS 500/6-9
1803 W Coulter Ave 71832 870-642-2428
Bob Sikes, prin. Fax 642-5857

Cossatot Community College Univ. of AR Post-Sec.
PO Box 960 71832 870-584-4471

Dermott, Chicot, Pop. 3,463
Dermott SD 500/K-12
PO Box 380 71638 870-538-1000
Alton Newton, supt. Fax 538-1005
dermott.k12.ar.us
Dermott HS 100/10-12
PO Box 380 71638 870-538-1030
Terry Murry, prin. Fax 538-1005
Dermott MS 100/7-9
PO Box 380 71638 870-538-1020
Bobby Brown, prin. Fax 538-1005

Des Arc, Prairie, Pop. 1,821
Des Arc SD 600/K-12
600 Main St 72040 870-256-4164
Rick Green, supt. Fax 256-3701
www.geocities.com/desarceagles/
Des Arc JSHS 300/7-12
600 Main St 72040 870-256-4166
Ricky Burns, prin. Fax 256-3701

De Witt, Arkansas, Pop. 3,414
De Witt SD 1,400/K-12
422 W 1st St 72042 870-946-3576
Tom Wilson, supt. Fax 946-1491
De Witt HS 400/9-12
1614 S Grandview Dr 72042 870-946-4661
Mike Hickey, prin. Fax 946-2746
De Witt MS 300/6-8
301 N Jackson St 72042 870-946-3708
Jeff Rader, prin. Fax 946-1301
Other Schools – See Gillett

Dierks, Howard, Pop. 1,252
Dierks SD 500/K-12
PO Box 124 71833 870-286-2191
Terry Ray, supt. Fax 286-2450
Dierks JSHS 300/7-12
PO Box 124 71833 870-286-3234
Gary Bobo, prin. Fax 286-2450

Donaldson, Hot Spring, Pop. 334
Ouachita SD 400/K-12
166 Schoolhouse Rd 71941 501-384-2318
Ronnie Kissire, supt. Fax 384-5615
Ouachita JSHS 200/7-12
258 Schoolhouse Rd 71941 501-384-2323
Elizabeth Stewart, prin. Fax 384-5614

Dover, Pope, Pop. 1,359
Dover SD 1,400/K-12
PO Box 325 72837 479-331-2916
Danny Lovelady, supt. Fax 331-2205
pirates.afsc.k12.ar.us
Dover HS 400/9-12
PO Box 325 72837 479-331-2120
Jamie Churchill, prin. Fax 331-3286
Dover MS 300/6-8
PO Box 325 72837 479-331-4814
Michael Lee, prin. Fax 331-4965

Dumas, Desha, Pop. 4,862
Dumas SD 1,600/K-12
213 Adams St 71639 870-382-4571
Dr. Tom Cox, supt. Fax 382-4874
dumas.sesc.k12.ar.us/
Dumas JHS 400/7-9
315 S College St 71639 870-382-4476
Edgar Montgomery, prin. Fax 382-2162
Dumas SHS 300/10-12
Dan Gill Dr 71639 870-382-4151
Paul Morara, prin. Fax 382-8904

Earle, Crittenden, Pop. 2,895
Earle SD 500/K-12
PO Box 637 72331 870-792-8486
Jack Crumbly, supt. Fax 792-8897
Dunbar MS 5-8
PO Box 637 72331 870-792-8401
Tagwunda Smith, prin. Fax 792-8403
Earle HS 200/9-12
PO Box 637 72331 870-792-8716
Rickey Nicks, prin. Fax 792-1004

El Dorado, Union, Pop. 20,467
El Dorado SD 4,200/K-12
200 W Oak St 71730 870-864-5001
Bob Watson, supt. Fax 864-5004
www.eldoradopublicschools.com
Barton JHS 700/7-8
400 W Faulkner St 71730 870-864-5051
Sherry Hill, prin. Fax 864-5064
El Dorado HS 1,400/9-12
501 N Timberlane Dr 71730 870-864-5100
Larry Walters, prin. Fax 863-3309

Parkers Chapel SD 700/K-12
401 Parkers Chapel Rd 71730 870-862-4641
John Gross, supt. Fax 881-5092
Parkers Chapel JSHS 400/7-12
401 Parkers Chapel Rd 71730 870-862-2360
Mike LaRue, prin. Fax 881-5095

South Arkansas Community College Post-Sec.
PO Box 7010 71731 870-862-8131

Elkins, Washington, Pop. 1,890
Elkins SD 800/K-12
PO Box 322 72727 479-643-2172
Dr. Robert Allen, supt. Fax 643-3605
elks.k12.ar.us/
Elkins HS 300/9-12
PO Box 322 72727 479-643-3381
Rebecca Martin, prin. Fax 643-2726
Elkins MS 200/7-8
PO Box 322 72727 479-643-2552
Steve Denzer, prin. Fax 643-4272

Emerson, Columbia, Pop. 348
Emerson - Taylor SD 700/K-12
PO Box 129 71740 870-547-2218
James G. Hines, supt. Fax 547-2077
www.scsc.k12.ar.us/emerson/default2.htm
Emerson HS 200/7-12
400 Church St 71740 870-547-2862
Jim L. Deloach, prin. Fax 547-2077
Other Schools – See Taylor

Emmet, Nevada, Pop. 450
Blevins SD
Supt. — See Blevins

Emmet JSHS 7-12
PO Box 330 71835 870-887-2319
Frank Henson, prin. Fax 887-2941

England, Lonoke, Pop. 3,028
England SD 900/K-12
PO Box 410 72046 501-842-2996
Paula Henderson, supt. Fax 842-3698
England HS 300/9-12
501 Pine Bluff Hwy 72046 501-842-2031
Brian Cossey, prin. Fax 842-3263
England MS 300/6-8
1500 NE 1st St 72046 501-842-9606
Ray Scalf, prin. Fax 842-9951

Eureka Springs, Carroll, Pop. 2,350
Eureka Springs SD 700/K-12
42 Greenwood Hollow Rd 72632 479-253-5999
Reck Wallis, supt. Fax 253-5955
eurekaspringsschools.k12.ar.us
Eureka Springs HS 200/9-12
44 Kingshighway 72632 479-253-8875
David Childers, prin. Fax 253-8390
Eureka Springs MS 200/5-8
142 Greenwood Hollow Rd 72632 479-253-7716
Dr. Linda Trice, prin. Fax 253-7809

Clear Spring S 100/PK-12
PO Box 511 72632 479-253-7888
Phyllis Poe, hdmstr. Fax 253-0768

Evening Shade, Sharp, Pop. 480
Cave City SD
Supt. — See Cave City
Evening Shade HS 7-12
200 School Dr 72532 870-266-3391
Jerry Elkins, prin. Fax 266-3657

Everton, Marion, Pop. 177
Ozark Mountain SD
Supt. — See Saint Joe
Bruno-Pyatt JSHS 200/7-12
4754 Highway 125 S 72633 870-427-5227
Kelvin Hudson, prin. Fax 427-5255

Farmington, Washington, Pop. 4,376
Farmington SD 1,500/K-12
42 S Double Springs Rd 72730 479-266-1800
Ron Wright, supt. Fax 267-6030
www.farmcards.org/
Farmington HS 500/9-12
278 W Main St 72730 479-266-1860
Blaine Hipes, prin. Fax 267-6065
Lynch MS 600/5-8
359 Rheas Mill Rd 72730 479-266-1840
Carolyn Odom, prin. Fax 267-6051

Fayetteville, Washington, Pop. 66,655
Fayetteville SD 7,700/K-12
PO Box 849 72702 479-973-8645
Dr. Bobby New, supt. Fax 973-8670
www.fayar.net
Fayetteville SHS 1,700/10-12
1001 W Stone St 72701 479-444-3050
James Price, prin. Fax 444-3056
Ramay JHS 700/8-9
401 S Sang Ave 72701 479-444-3064
Matt Saferite, prin. Fax 444-3013
Woodland JHS 700/8-9
15 E Poplar St 72703 479-444-3067
Dr. Anita Lawson, prin. Fax 444-3039

Arkansas Aviation Technologies Center Post-Sec.
2350 W Old Farmington Rd 72701 479-444-3058
Fayetteville Beauty College Post-Sec.
2167 W 6th St 72701 479-442-5181
Fayetteville Christian S 300/PK-12
2006 E Mission Blvd 72703 479-442-2565
Brad Jones, supt. Fax 444-6156
University of Arkansas at Fayetteville Post-Sec.
1 University Of Arkansas 72701 479-575-2000

Flippin, Marion, Pop. 1,396
Flippin SD 900/K-12
210 Alford St 72634 870-453-2270
Dale Query, supt. Fax 453-5059
flippin.ar.schoolwebpages.com
Flippin HS 300/9-12
103 Alford St 72634 870-453-2233
Dr. John Carey, prin. Fax 453-7380
Flippin MS 200/6-8
308 N 1st St 72634 870-453-6464
Robert Gray, prin. Fax 453-6465

Fordyce, Dallas, Pop. 4,409
Fordyce SD 1,200/PK-12
PO Box 706 71742 870-352-3005
Pam Blake, supt. Fax 352-7187
www.fordyceschools.org/
Fordyce HS 400/9-12
100 Redbug Blvd 71742 870-352-2126
Kirk Nance, prin. Fax 352-7187
Fordyce MS 300/5-8
75 Redbug Blvd 71742 870-352-7121
Crystal Williams, prin. Fax 352-7187

Foreman, Little River, Pop. 1,071
Foreman SD 500/K-12
PO Box 480 71836 870-542-7211
Larry Lairmore, supt. Fax 542-7225
Foreman JSHS 200/7-12
PO Box 480 71836 870-542-7212
James Luther, prin. Fax 542-7227

Forrest City, Saint Francis, Pop. 14,078
Forrest City SD 3,400/K-12
845 N Rosser St 72335 870-633-1485
Lee Vent, supt. Fax 633-1415
mustang.grsc.k12.ar.us/
Forrest City JHS 700/8-9
1133 N Division St 72335 870-633-3230
William Ferguson, prin. Fax 633-6066
Forrest City SHS 700/10-12
467 Victoria St 72335 870-633-1464
Abbie Robinson, prin. Fax 261-1844

Calvary Christian S 200/K-12
1611 N Washington St 72335 870-633-5333
Suzanne Hess, prin. Fax 633-6238
Crowley's Ridge Technical Institute Post-Sec.
1620 New Castle Rd 72335 870-633-5411
East Arkansas Community College Post-Sec.
1700 New Castle Rd 72335 870-633-4480

Fort Smith, Sebastian, Pop. 82,481
Fort Smith SD 12,800/K-12
PO Box 1948 72902 479-785-2501
Ben Gooden Ed.D., supt. Fax 785-1722
www.fssc.k12.ar.us/
Chaffin JHS 700/7-9
3025 Massard Rd 72903 479-452-2226
Dr. Ralph Spencer, prin. Fax 478-3103
Darby JHS 600/7-9
616 N 14th St 72901 479-783-4159
Michael Farrell, prin. Fax 784-8165
Kimmons JHS 700/7-9
2201 N 50th St 72904 479-785-2451
Martin Mahan, prin. Fax 784-8177
Northside SHS 1,400/10-12
2301 N B St 72901 479-783-1171
Ray Martin, prin. Fax 784-8114
Ramsey JHS 900/7-9
3201 Jenny Lind Rd 72901 479-783-5115
Dennis Siebenmorgen, prin. Fax 784-8119
Southside SHS 1,500/10-12
4100 Gary St 72903 479-646-7371
Wayne Haver, prin. Fax 648-8204
Adult Education Adult
501 S 20th St 72901 479-785-1232
Sharon Ellis, dir. Fax 784-8184

Mellie's Beauty College Post-Sec.
311 S 16th St 72901 479-782-5059
Trinity JHS 300/7-9
1205 S Albert Pike Ave 72903 479-782-2451
Ann Finch, prin. Fax 782-7263
Union Christian Academy 700/PK-12
4201 Windsor Dr 72904 479-783-7327
Cheryl Lehman, admin. Fax 783-9342
University of Arkansas at Fort Smith Post-Sec.
PO Box 3649 72913 479-788-7000

Fouke, Miller, Pop. 851
Fouke SD 900/K-12
PO Box 20 71837 870-653-4311
Paulette Smith, supt. Fax 653-2856
Fouke HS 300/9-12
PO Box 20 71837 870-653-4551
Jaye Kay Brown, prin. Fax 653-7823
Fouke MS 200/6-8
PO Box 20 71837 870-653-2304
Ken Endris, prin. Fax 653-7840

Fox, Stone
Mountain View SD
Supt. — See Mountain View
Rural Special HS 7-12
13237 Highway 263 72051 870-363-4202
Brent Howard, prin. Fax 363-4222

Gassville, Baxter, Pop. 1,931

North Central Christian S 100/PK-12
1306 E 9th St 72635 870-424-6622
Debra Bush, prin. Fax 424-6622

Gentry, Benton, Pop. 2,613
Gentry SD 1,400/K-12
201 S Giles Ave 72734 479-736-2253
Dr. Randy Barrett, supt. Fax 736-2245
www.gentrypioneers.com/
Gentry HS 400/9-12
201 S Giles Ave 72734 479-736-2666
Robert King, prin. Fax 736-5202
Gentry MS 300/6-8
201 S Giles Ave 72734 479-736-2251
Larry Cozens, prin. Fax 736-3414

Ozark Adventist Academy 200/9-12
20997 Dawn Hill East Rd 72734 479-736-2221
Perry Pollman, prin. Fax 736-2224

Gillett, Arkansas, Pop. 787
De Witt SD
Supt. — See De Witt
Gillett JSHS 100/7-12
PO Box 179 72055 870-548-2316
Jon Howell, prin. Fax 548-2281

Gosnell, Mississippi, Pop. 3,661
Gosnell SD 1,400/K-12
600 N State Highway 181 72315 870-532-4000
Stan Williams, supt. Fax 532-4002
pirates.crsc.k12.ar.us
Gosnell JSHS 600/7-12
600 N State Highway 181 72315 870-532-4010
Kevin Evans, prin. Fax 532-4031

Gravette, Benton, Pop. 2,275
Gravette SD 1,700/PK-12
609 Birmingham St SE 72736 479-787-4100
Curtis Spann, supt. Fax 787-4108
lions.k12.ar.us/
Gravette HS 500/9-12
325 Lion Dr S 72736 479-787-4180
Jo Ellen Hastings, prin. Fax 787-4188
Gravette JHS 300/7-8
605 Dallas St SE 72736 479-787-4160
Mitchell Wilber, prin. Fax 787-4178

Greenbrier, Faulkner, Pop. 3,615
Greenbrier SD 2,500/K-12
4 School Dr 72058 501-679-4808
Mike Mertens, supt. Fax 679-1024
gps.k12.ar.us/
Greenbrier JHS 400/8-9
10 School Dr 72058 501-679-3433
Aimee Wright, prin. Fax 679-1055
Greenbrier SHS 500/10-12
72 Green Valley Dr 72058 501-679-4236
Steve Lucas, prin. Fax 679-5765

Green Forest, Carroll, Pop. 2,859
Green Forest SD 1,200/K-12
PO Box 1950 72638 870-438-5201
Dr. Larry Bennett, supt. Fax 438-6214
www.gf.k12.ar.us
Green Forest JSHS 400/8-12
PO Box 1950 72638 870-438-5203
Dave Borg, prin. Fax 438-4588

Greenland, Washington, Pop. 1,061
Greenland SD 800/K-12
PO Box 57 72737 479-521-2366
Ronald Brawner, supt. Fax 521-1480
Greenland HS 200/9-12
PO Box 57 72737 479-521-2366
Jay Gardenhire, prin. Fax 521-1350
Greenland MS 300/5-8
PO Box 57 72737 479-521-2366
David Hudgens, prin. Fax 251-1203

Greenwood, Sebastian, Pop. 7,914
Greenwood SD 3,300/K-12
420 N Main St 72936 479-996-4142
Dr. Kay Johnson, supt. Fax 996-4143
www.greenwoodarkansasschools.com
Greenwood SHS 700/10-12
440 E Gary St 72936 479-996-4141
Jerry Efurd, prin. Fax 996-6548
Wells JHS 500/8-9
1211 Raymond E Wells Dr 72936 479-996-7440
Kevin Hesslen, prin. Fax 996-7469

Greers Ferry, Cleburne, Pop. 966
West Side SD 500/K-12
7295 Greers Ferry Rd 72067 501-825-6258
Russell A. Hester, supt. Fax 825-6258
westside.afsc.k12.ar.us/
West Side JSHS 300/7-12
7295 Greers Ferry Rd 72067 501-825-7241
Rick Waters, prin. Fax 825-6258

Gurdon, Clark, Pop. 2,233
Gurdon SD 800/K-12
314 School St 71743 870-353-4454
Bobby Smithson, supt. Fax 353-4455
Cabe MS 300/5-8
7780 Highway 67 S 71743 870-353-4311
Libby White, prin. Fax 353-5149
Gurdon HS 300/9-12
7777 Highway 67 S 71743 870-353-5123
Leonard Gills, prin. Fax 353-5131

Guy, Faulkner, Pop. 551
Guy-Perkins SD 400/K-12
492 Highway 25 N 72061 501-679-7224
Kerry Saylors, supt. Fax 679-3508
thunderbird.k12.ar.us/
Guy-Perkins HS 200/7-12
492 Highway 25 N 72061 501-679-3507
David Westenhover, prin. Fax 679-3508

Hackett, Sebastian, Pop. 726
Hackett SD 600/K-12
102 N Oak St 72937 479-638-8822
William Pittman, supt. Fax 638-7106
hackett.wsc.k12.ar.us/
Hackett JSHS 300/7-12
102 N Oak St 72937 479-638-7003
Neal Perrin, prin. Fax 638-8210

Hamburg, Ashley, Pop. 2,844
Hamburg SD 1,800/PK-12
521 E Lincoln St 71646 870-853-9851
Carlton Lawrence, supt. Fax 853-2842
hamburg.k12.ar.us/
Hamburg JHS 500/7-9
521 E Lincoln St 71646 870-853-2811
John Spradlin, prin. Fax 853-2835
Hamburg SHS 400/10-12
1119 S Main St 71646 870-853-9856
Jeff Senn, prin. Fax 853-2850

Hampton, Calhoun, Pop. 1,512
Hampton SD 700/K-12
PO Box 1176 71744 870-798-2229
Max N. Dyson, supt. Fax 798-2239
hampton.k12.ar.us/
Hampton JSHS 400/7-12
PO Box 1176 71744 870-798-2742
Glenn Johnston, prin. Fax 798-2239

Harrisburg, Poinsett, Pop. 2,165
Harrisburg SD 1,100/K-12
207 W Estes St 72432 870-578-2416
Danny Sample, supt. Fax 578-9366
sting.k12.ar.us
Harrisburg HS 300/9-12
207 W Estes St 72432 870-578-2417
Steve Rorex, prin. Fax 578-2338
Harrisburg MS 400/5-8
207 W Estes St 72432 870-578-2410
Karli Saracini, prin. Fax 578-2338

Harrison, Boone, Pop. 12,764
Harrison SD 2,800/K-12
110 S Cherry St 72601 870-741-7600
Dr. Jerry Moody, supt. Fax 741-4520
harrison.k12.ar.us/
Harrison JHS 700/7-9
515 S Pine St 72601 870-741-3496
Mike Stokes, prin. Fax 741-0101
Harrison SHS 600/10-12
925 Goblin Dr 72601 870-741-8223
Ronny Brown, prin. Fax 741-2606

North Arkansas College Post-Sec.
1515 Pioneer Ridge Dr 72601 870-743-3000

Hartford, Sebastian, Pop. 779
Hartford SD 400/K-12
PO Box 489 72938 479-639-5002
D. Chris Rink, supt. Fax 639-2158
Hartford JSHS 200/7-12
PO Box 489 72938 479-639-2239
Gary Walker, prin. Fax 639-2158

Hartman, Johnson, Pop. 620
Westside SD 600/K-12
122 Thompson St 72840 479-497-1991
Roy L. Hester, supt. Fax 497-9037
westsiderebels.k12.ar.us
Other Schools – See Coal Hill

Hattieville, Conway
Wonderview SD 400/K-12
2436 Highway 95 72063 501-354-0211
Steve Thomas, supt. Fax 354-6071
wonder.k12.ar.us
Wonderview JSHS 200/7-12
2436 Highway 95 72063 501-354-8668
Danny Heard, prin. Fax 354-8602

Havana, Yell, Pop. 393
Western Yell County SD 400/K-12
PO Box 214 72842 479-476-4116
Brad Spikes, supt. Fax 476-4115
wolverines.k12.ar.us
Western Yell County JSHS 200/7-12
PO Box 214 72842 479-476-4100
Barry Fisher, prin. Fax 476-4111

Hazen, Prairie, Pop. 1,562
Hazen SD 600/PK-12
477 N Hazen Ave 72064 870-255-4549
Danny Hazelwood, supt. Fax 255-4508
Hazen JSHS 200/7-12
477 N Hazen Ave 72064 870-255-4546
Roxanne Bradow, prin. Fax 255-4508

Heber Springs, Cleburne, Pop. 7,016
Heber Springs SD 1,700/K-12
800 W Moore St 72543 501-362-6712
Rick Rana, supt. Fax 362-0613
hssdweb.afsc.k12.ar.us/
Heber Springs HS 600/9-12
800 W Moore St 72543 501-362-3141
Charles Nowak, prin. Fax 362-9931
Heber Springs MS 400/6-8
800 W Moore St 72543 501-362-2488
Stanley Wildman, prin. Fax 362-2193

Hector, Pope, Pop. 517
Hector SD 700/K-12
11520 SR 27 72843 479-284-2021
Eric Armour, supt. Fax 284-2350
wildcats.afsc.k12.ar.us/
Hector JSHS 400/7-12
11601 SR 27 72843 479-284-3536
David Waddell, prin. Fax 284-5023

Helena, Phillips, Pop. 5,687
Helena/West Helena SD 3,100/K-12
305 Valley Dr 72342 870-338-4425
Rudolph Howard, supt. Fax 338-4434
hwh.grsc.k12.ar.us/
Other Schools – See West Helena

Phillips Comm. Coll. of the Univ. of AR Post-Sec.
PO Box 785 72342 870-338-6474

Hermitage, Bradley, Pop. 762
Hermitage SD 500/K-12
PO Box 38 71647 870-463-2246
John Jordan, supt. Fax 463-8520
se.sesc.k12.ar.us/hermitage
Hermitage JSHS 300/7-12
PO Box 190 71647 870-463-2235
Neich Robinson, prin. Fax 463-2122

Highland, Sharp, Pop. 1,023
Highland SD 1,600/K-12
Highway 62, 870-856-3275
Ronnie Brogdon, supt. Fax 856-2765
highlandrebels.k12.ar.us/
Highland JSHS 600/8-12
1 Rebel Cir, 870-856-3273
Don Carithers, prin. Fax 856-2765

Hope, Hempstead, Pop. 10,467
Hope SD 2,700/K-12
117 E 2nd St 71801 870-722-2700
Kenneth Muldrew, supt. Fax 777-4087
hope.k12.ar.us
Hope HS 800/9-12
1701 S Main St 71801 870-777-3451
Tommy Morrison, prin. Fax 722-2736
Yerger MS 500/7-8
400 E 9th St 71801 870-722-2770
Larry Muldrew, prin. Fax 722-2707

Spring Hill SD 500/K-12
633 Highway 355 W 71801 870-777-8236
Dickie Williams, supt. Fax 777-9200
springhill.k12.ar.us
Spring Hill JSHS 300/7-12
633 Highway 355 W 71801 870-722-7430
Steve Britton, prin. Fax 722-7425

University of Arkansas Community College Post-Sec.
PO Box 140 71802 870-777-5722

Horatio, Sevier, Pop. 1,025
Horatio SD 900/PK-12
PO Box 435 71842 870-832-2340
Joseph Cornelison, supt. Fax 832-2174
horatio.dmsc.k12.ar.us/
Horatio JSHS 400/7-12
PO Box 435 71842 870-832-2341
James Dobbins, prin. Fax 832-2174

Hot Springs National Park, Garland, Pop. 36,356
Cutter-Morning Star SD 700/K-12
2801 Spring St 71901 501-262-2414
Carl Hughes, supt. Fax 262-0670
eaglesnest.dsc.k12.ar.us/
Cutter-Morning Star JSHS 300/7-12
2801 Spring St 71901 501-262-1220
Charles Ferriter, prin. Fax 262-3771

Fountain Lake SD 1,200/K-12
4207 Park Ave 71901 501-623-5655
Dr. Lowell Hightower, supt. Fax 623-6447
flcobra.k12.ar.us/
Fountain Lake JSHS 600/7-12
4207 Park Ave 71901 501-623-5101
Steve Campbell, prin. Fax 624-4053

Hot Springs SD 3,500/K-12
400 Linwood Ave 71913 501-624-3372
Roy Rowe, supt. Fax 620-7829
hsprings.dsc.k12.ar.us
Hot Springs HS 800/9-12
701 Emory St 71913 501-624-5286
Jim Gentry, prin. Fax 620-7820
Hot Springs MS 700/6-8
700 Main St 71913 501-624-5228
Danny Stanford, prin. Fax 620-7833

Lakeside SD 2,600/K-12
2837 Malvern Ave 71901 501-262-1880
Shawn Cook, supt. Fax 262-2732
lakeside.rams.dsc.k12.ar.us
Lakeside JHS 500/8-9
2865 Malvern Ave 71901 501-262-1316
James Fotioo, prin. Fax 262-6232
Lakeside SHS 600/10-12
2871 Malvern Ave 71901 501-262-1530
Darin Beckwith, prin. Fax 262-6205

Arkansas Career Training Institute Post-Sec.
105 Reserve St 71901 501-624-4411
Christian Ministries Academy 100/K-12
PO Box 8500 71910 501-624-1952
Paul Kern, prin. Fax 318-2624
Crossgate Christian Academy 200/K-12
3102 E Grand Ave 71901 501-262-4222
Bill Vining, supt. Fax 262-9826
Hot Springs Beauty College Post-Sec.
100 Cones Rd 71901 501-624-0203
Lighthouse Christian S 50/PK-12
2535 E Grand Ave 71901 501-617-4310
Dr. Harold Elder, admin.
National Park Community College Post-Sec.
101 College Dr 71913 501-760-4222

Hoxie, Lawrence, Pop. 2,717
Hoxie SD 900/K-12
PO Box 240 72433 870-886-2401
Dennis Truxler, supt. Fax 886-4252
green.nesc.k12.ar.us/
Hoxie JSHS 400/7-12
PO Box 240 72433 870-886-4254
Tim Gardner, prin. Fax 886-4253

Hughes, Saint Francis, Pop. 1,762
Hughes SD 700/K-12
PO Box 9 72348 870-339-2570
Charles Jones, supt. Fax 339-3317
hughes.grsc.k12.ar.us/
Hughes JSHS 300/7-12
PO Box 9 72348 870-339-2580
Sheryl Owens, prin. Fax 339-3317

Huntsville, Madison, Pop. 2,207
Huntsville SD 1,900/K-12
PO Box F 72740 479-738-2011
Dr. Alvin Lievsay, supt. Fax 738-2563
eagle.nwsc.k12.ar.us/
Huntsville HS 700/9-12
PO Box 1377 72740 479-738-2500
Michael Gray, prin. Fax 738-2849
Huntsville MS 300/7-8
PO Box G 72740 479-738-6520
Mike Cain, prin. Fax 738-6259
Other Schools – See Saint Paul

Imboden, Lawrence, Pop. 643
Sloan-Hendrix SD 600/K-12
PO Box 1080 72434 870-869-2384
Michael Holland, supt. Fax 869-2384
shsd.k12.ar.us
Sloan-Hendrix JSHS 300/7-12
PO Box 1080 72434 870-869-2361
Mitch Walton, prin. Fax 869-2361

Jacksonville, Pulaski, Pop. 30,367
Pulaski County Special SD
Supt. — See Little Rock
Jacksonville JHS - Boys 700/8-9
1320 School Dr 72076 501-982-1587
Mike Nellums, prin. Fax 241-2139
Jacksonville MS - Girls 600/6-8
201 Sharp Dr 72076 501-982-9407
Kim Forrest, prin. Fax 241-2108
Jacksonville SHS 800/10-12
2400 Linda Ln 72076 501-982-2128
Ken Clark, prin. Fax 982-1692
North Pulaski HS 900/9-12
718 Harris Rd 72076 501-982-9436
Sonny Bull, prin. Fax 241-2256

Arthur's Beauty College Post-Sec.
2600 John Harden Dr 72076 501-982-8987

Jasper, Newton, Pop. 494
Jasper SD 500/K-12
PO Box 446 72641 870-446-2223
Chuck Archer, supt. Fax 446-2305
jhspirates.k12.ar.us/
Jasper JSHS 300/7-12
PO Box 446 72641 870-446-2223
Charles Emmett, prin. Fax 446-2305
Other Schools – See Kingston, Oark

Jessieville, Garland
Jessieville SD 800/K-12
PO Box 4 71949 501-984-5381
George Foshee, supt. Fax 984-4200
Jessieville JSHS 400/7-12
PO Box 4 71949 501-984-5011
Steve Wright, prin. Fax 984-4200

Jonesboro, Craighead, Pop. 59,358
Jonesboro SD 4,700/PK-12
2506 Southwest Sq 72401 870-933-5800
Dr. Kim Wilbanks, supt. Fax 933-5838
www.jps.k12.ar.us/
Area Technical Center Vo/Tech
1727 S Main St 72401 870-933-5891
Carmack Sanders, prin. Fax 933-5890
Camp JHS 600/7-9
1814 W Nettleton Ave 72401 870-933-5820
William Cheatham, prin. Fax 933-5837
Jonesboro SHS 1,000/10-12
301 Hurricane Dr 72401 870-933-5881
Terry Trotter, prin. Fax 933-5812
MacArthur JHS 600/7-9
1615 Wilkins Ave 72401 870-933-5840
Dr. Brad Faught, prin. Fax 933-5848

Nettleton SD 2,500/K-12
3300 One Pl 72404 870-910-7800
James Dunivan, supt. Fax 910-7854
nettletonschools.net
Nettleton JHS 600/7-9
4208 Chieftan Ln 72401 870-910-7819
Grace Petersen, prin. Fax 910-6984
Nettleton SHS 500/10-12
4201 Chieftan Ln 72401 870-910-7805
Tommy Fowler, prin. Fax 910-7804

Valley View SD 1,700/K-12
2131 Valley View Dr 72404 870-935-6200
Dr. Radius Baker, supt. Fax 972-0373
blazers.k12.ar.us/
Valley View JHS 400/7-9
2118 Valley View Dr Ste A 72404 870-935-4602
Barry Jones, prin. Fax 935-6202
Valley View SHS 300/10-12
2118 Valley View Dr Ste B 72404 870-935-4602
Robert Lindley, prin. Fax 935-6202
Adult Education Center Adult
2311 E Nettleton Ave 72401 870-935-4602
Steve Clayton, prin. Fax 933-5889

Westside Consolidated SD 1,700/K-12
1630 Highway 91 W 72404 870-935-7503
Dr. James Best, supt. Fax 935-2123
warriors.crsc.k12.ar.us/
Westside HS 600/8-12
1630 Highway 91 W 72404 870-935-7501
Pat Lundahl, prin. Fax 268-9119

Ridgefield Christian S 300/PK-12
3824 Casey Springs Rd 72404 870-932-7540
Randy Johnson, admin. Fax 931-9711

Judsonia, White, Pop. 2,087
White County Central SD 700/K-12
3259 Highway 157 72081 501-729-3992
Monty Betts, supt. Fax 729-3992
wccsdweb.wmsc.k12.ar.us/
White County Central JSHS 300/7-12
3259 Highway 157 72081 501-729-3947
Jerry Lacy, prin. Fax 729-3947

Junction City, Union, Pop. 691
Junction City SD 700/K-12
PO Box 790 71749 870-924-4575
Gary Wayman, supt. Fax 924-4565
Junction City JSHS 400/7-12
PO Box 790 71749 870-924-4576
Dale Hux, prin. Fax 924-4565

Kingston, Madison
Jasper SD
Supt. — See Jasper
Kingston JSHS 7-12
PO Box 149 72742 479-665-2995
Earl Rowe, prin. Fax 665-2577

Kirby, Pike
Kirby SD 400/K-12
PO Box 9 71950 870-398-4212
Jeff Alexander, supt. Fax 398-4442
kirby.dsc.k12.ar.us

Kirby JSHS 200/7-12
PO Box 9 71950 870-398-4211
Carla Golden, prin. Fax 398-5413

Lake City, Craighead, Pop. 2,002
Riverside SD 800/K-12
PO Box 178 72437 870-237-4329
Larry Nowlin, supt. Fax 237-4867
Riverside SHS 200/10-12
PO Box 178 72437 870-237-4328
Tommy Knight, prin. Fax 237-4867
Other Schools – See Caraway

Lake Village, Chicot, Pop. 2,608
Lakeside SD 1,200/PK-12
1110 S Lakeshore Dr 71653 870-265-2284
Joyce L. Vaught, supt. Fax 265-5466
lakeside.k12.ar.us/
Lakeside HS 300/9-12
1110 S Lakeshore Dr 71653 870-265-2232
Linda Armour, prin. Fax 265-7302
Lakeside MS 300/6-8
1110 S Lakeshore Dr 71653 870-265-2970
Arthur Gray, prin. Fax 265-7309

Lamar, Johnson, Pop. 1,542
Lamar SD 700/K-12
301 Elberta St 72846 479-885-3907
Dennis Meins, supt. Fax 885-2380
www.serve.com/warriors/
Lamar HS 300/9-12
301 Elberta St 72846 479-885-3344
Mitch Harris, prin. Fax 885-3842
Lamar MS 5-8
301 Elberta St 72846 479-885-6511
Johanna Kenner, prin. Fax 885-2384

Lavaca, Sebastian, Pop. 2,059
Lavaca SD 900/K-12
PO Box 8 72941 479-674-5611
Jared Cleveland, supt. Fax 674-2271
lavacapublicschools.k12.ar.us/
Lavaca HS 300/9-12
PO Box 8 72941 479-674-5612
Eric Saunders, prin. Fax 674-2271
Lavaca MS 300/5-8
PO Box 8 72941 479-674-5618
Marcia Ford, prin. Fax 674-5518

Leachville, Mississippi, Pop. 1,847
Buffalo Island Central SD
Supt. — See Monette
Buffalo Island Central JHS 200/7-9
PO Box 110 72438 870-539-6883
Randy Rose, prin. Fax 539-6696

Lead Hill, Boone, Pop. 295
Lead Hill SD 400/K-12
PO Box 20 72644 870-436-5249
Dr. Shari Marshall, supt. Fax 436-5946
Lead Hill JSHS 200/7-12
PO Box 20 72644 870-436-5677
Alan King, prin. Fax 436-6827

Lepanto, Poinsett, Pop. 2,079
East Poinsett County SD 800/K-12
502 McClellan St 72354 870-475-2472
Michael Pierce, supt. Fax 475-3531
epc.k12.ar.us/
East Poinsett County JSHS 400/7-12
502 McClellan St 72354 870-475-2331
Gary Williams, prin. Fax 475-2206

Leslie, Searcy, Pop. 464
Searcy County SD
Supt. — See Marshall
Leslie MSHS 6-12
800 Elm St 72645 870-447-2431
John Gray, prin. Fax 447-2831
North Central Career Center Vo/Tech
402 Oak St 72645 870-447-6111
Janice Hennessee, prin. Fax 447-2872

Lewisville, Lafayette, Pop. 1,200
Lafayette County SD 300/K-12
PO Box 950 71845 870-921-5500
Jack Broach, supt. Fax 921-4277
lafayette.k12.ar.us/
Other Schools – See Stamps

Lexa, Phillips, Pop. 306
Barton-Lexa SD 800/K-12
9546 Highway 85 72355 870-572-7294
Roy Kirkland, supt. Fax 572-4713
blsd.grsc.k12.ar.us
Barton JSHS 400/7-12
9546 Highway 85 72355 870-572-6867
David Bagley, prin. Fax 572-4713

Lincoln, Washington, Pop. 1,904
Lincoln Consolidated SD 1,100/K-12
PO Box 1127 72744 479-824-3010
Jim Lewis, supt. Fax 824-3045
wolfpride.k12.ar.us
Lincoln HS 300/9-12
201 E School St 72744 479-824-3010
Steven Asp-Schussheim, prin. Fax 824-3042
Lincoln MS 300/6-8
107 E School St 72744 479-824-3010
Elaine King, prin. Fax 824-3042

Little Rock, Pulaski, Pop. 184,564

Little Rock SD 24,700/PK-12
810 W Markham St 72201 501-447-1000
Dr. Roy Brooks, supt. Fax 447-1001
www.lrsd.org/
Central HS 2,200/9-12
1500 S Park St 72202 501-447-1400
Nancy Rousseau, prin. Fax 447-1401
Cloverdale Magnet MS 700/6-8
6300 Hinkson Rd 72209 501-447-2500
Frederick Fields, prin. Fax 447-2501
Dunbar Magnet MS 700/6-8
1100 Wright Ave 72206 501-447-2600
Eunice Thrasher, prin. Fax 447-2601
Fair Magnet HS 1,100/9-12
13420 David O Dodd Rd 72210 501-447-1700
Brenda Allen, prin. Fax 447-1701
Forest Heights MS 700/6-8
5901 Evergreen Dr 72205 501-447-2700
Dr. Deborah Price, prin. Fax 447-2701
Hall HS 1,500/9-12
6700 H St 72205 501-447-1900
John Bacon, prin. Fax 447-1901
Henderson Magnet MS 600/6-8
401 John Barrow Rd 72205 501-447-2800
Marvin Burton, prin. Fax 447-2801
Mann Magnet MS 900/6-8
1000 E Roosevelt Rd 72206 501-447-3100
James Fullerton, prin. Fax 447-3101
McClellan Magnet HS 900/9-12
9417 Geyer Springs Rd 72209 501-447-2100
Dr. Gloria Todd-Hamilton, prin. Fax 447-2101
Metropolitan Career-Tech Center Vo/Tech
7701 Scott Hamilton Dr 72209 501-447-1200
Mike Peterson, prin. Fax 447-1201
Parkview Magnet HS 1,100/9-12
2501 John Barrow Rd 72204 501-447-2300
Dr. Linda Brown, prin. Fax 447-2301
Pulaski Heights MS 700/6-8
401 N Pine St 72205 501-447-3200
Dr. Daniel W. Whitehorn, prin. Fax 447-3201
Adult Education Center Adult
4800 W 26th St 72204 501-447-1850
Paulette Martin, coord. Fax 447-1851
Other Schools – See Mabelvale

Pulaski County Special SD 18,100/PK-12
PO Box 8601 72216 501-490-2000
James Sharpe, supt. Fax 490-0483
www.pcssd.org
Fuller MS 700/6-8
808 E Dixon Rd 72206 501-490-5730
Don Booth, prin. Fax 490-5736
Mills HS 1,000/9-12
1205 E Dixon Rd 72206 501-490-5700
Janice Haynes, prin. Fax 490-5709
Robinson HS 700/9-12
21501 Highway 10 72223 501-868-2400
June Haynie, prin. Fax 868-2405
Robinson MS 400/6-8
21001 Highway 10 72223 501-868-2410
John Pearce, prin. Fax 868-2441
Other Schools – See Jacksonville, Maumelle, North Little Rock, Sherwood

---

Arkansas Baptist College Post-Sec.
1621 Dr Martin Luther King 72202 501-370-4000
Arkansas Baptist JSHS 300/7-12
8400 Ranch Blvd 72223 501-868-5121
Randy Goldsmith, prin. Fax 868-5403
Arkansas Beauty School Post-Sec.
5108 Baseline Rd 72209 501-562-5673
Arkansas School for the Blind Post-Sec.
PO Box 668 72203 501-296-1810
Arkansas School for the Deaf Post-Sec.
PO Box 3811 72203 501-324-9514
Baptist Schools of Allied Health Post-Sec.
11900 Colonel Glenn Rd 72210 501-202-7415
Bee-Jay's Hairstyling Academy Post-Sec.
1907 Hinson Loop Rd 72212 501-224-2442
Catholic HS for Boys 600/9-12
6300 Father Tribou St 72205 501-664-3939
Steve Straessle, prin. Fax 664-6549
Central Arkansas Radiation Therapy Inst. Post-Sec.
PO Box 55050 72215 501-664-8573
Eastern College of Health Vocations Post-Sec.
6423 Forbing Rd 72209 501-568-0211
Eaton Beauty Stylist College Post-Sec.
814 W 7th St 72201 501-375-0211
Episcopal Collegiate S 400/6-12
1701 Cantrell Rd 72201 501-372-1194
Dr. Mercer Neale, hdmstr. Fax 372-2160
ITT Technical Institute Post-Sec.
4520 S University Ave 72204 501-565-5550
Little Rock Christian Academy 1,200/K-12
PO Box 17450 72222 501-868-9822
Dr. Charles Phillips, hdmstr. Fax 868-8766
Lutheran HS 200/9-12
6711 W Markham St 72205 501-663-5117
Mary Kathryn Stein, prin. Fax 663-1017
Mt. St. Mary Academy 9-12
3224 Kavanaugh Blvd 72205 501-664-8006
Sr. Claudia Ward, prin. Fax 666-4382
Philander Smith College Post-Sec.
812 W 13th St 72202 501-375-9845
Pulaski Academy 1,300/PK-12
12701 Hinson Rd 72212 501-604-1915
Ellis Arnold, hdmstr. Fax 225-1974
Remington College Post-Sec.
500 President Clinton # 305 72201 800-829-5488
Remington College Post-Sec.
19 Remington Rd 72204 501-312-0007
St. Vincent Infirmary Medical Center Post-Sec.
2 Saint Vincent Cir 72205 501-660-3910
Southwest Christian Academy 500/PK-12
11301 Geyer Springs Rd 72209 501-565-3276
Sharon Stewart, prin. Fax 565-3567
University of Arkansas at Little Rock Post-Sec.
2801 S University Ave 72204 501-569-3000
University of Arkansas/Medical Sciences Post-Sec.
4301 W Markham St 72205 501-686-5000
Velvatex College of Beauty Culture Post-Sec.
1520 Dr Martin Luther King 72202 501-372-9678
Word of Outreach Christian Academy 100/PK-12
3300 Asher Ave 72204 501-663-0300
Cheryl Washington, admin. Fax 558-0203

Lockesburg, Sevier, Pop. 733
Lockesburg SD 400/K-12
PO Box 88 71846 870-289-5161
Bill Blackwood, supt. Fax 289-5189
Lockesburg JSHS 200/7-12
PO Box 88 71846 870-289-2431
Joe Coulter, prin. Fax 289-3264

Lonoke, Lonoke, Pop. 4,552
Lonoke SD 1,800/K-12
401 W Holly St 72086 501-676-2042
Sharron Havens Ed.D., supt. Fax 676-7074
lonokeschools.org/
Lonoke HS 600/9-12
501 W Academy St 72086 501-676-2476
Phynaus Wilson, prin. Fax 676-3716
Lonoke MS 400/6-8
200 E Locust St 72086 501-676-6670
Jeannie Holt, prin. Fax 676-7013

Lynn, Lawrence, Pop. 305
Hillcrest SD
Supt. — See Strawberry
Hillcrest JHS 100/7-9
PO Box 70 72440 870-528-3462
Gregg Cooper, prin. Fax 528-3766

Mabelvale, Pulaski
Little Rock SD
Supt. — See Little Rock
Mabelvale Magnet MS 600/6-8
10811 Mabelvale West Rd 72103 501-447-3000
Ann Blaylock, prin. Fax 447-3001

Mc Crory, Woodruff, Pop. 1,862
McCrory SD 600/K-12
PO Box 930 72101 870-731-2535
Barry Scott, supt. Fax 731-2536
mccrory.k12.ar.us/
Mc Crory JSHS 300/7-12
PO Box 930 72101 870-731-2851
Lincoln Daniels, prin. Fax 731-2574

Mc Gehee, Desha, Pop. 4,527
McGehee SD 1,200/K-12
PO Box 767 71654 870-222-3670
Dr. Barbara Wood, supt. Fax 222-6957
owls.k12.ar.us/
Mc Gehee JSHS 600/7-12
PO Box 767 71654 870-222-5026
Remmel Grayson, prin. Fax 222-5838

Baptist School of Nursing-SE Post-Sec.
Highway 1 NE 71654

Magazine, Logan, Pop. 910
Magazine SD 500/K-12
485 E Priddy St 72943 479-969-2566
Sandra Beck, supt. Fax 969-8740
magazinerattlers.k12.ar.us
Leftwich HS, 292 E Priddy St 72943 200/7-12
Randy Bryan, prin. 479-969-2640

Magnolia, Columbia, Pop. 10,478
Magnolia SD 2,800/PK-12
PO Box 649 71754 870-234-4933
Dr. John H. Moore, supt. Fax 901-2508
panther.scsc.k12.ar.us/
Magnolia JHS 800/7-9
540 E North St 71753 870-234-2206
Chris Hurley, prin. Fax 234-1293
Magnolia SHS 700/10-12
1400 High School Dr 71753 870-234-2610
Roger Loper, prin. Fax 901-2509

Columbia Christian S 300/K-12
250 Warnock Springs Rd 71753 870-234-2831
John Steelman, prin. Fax 234-1497
Southern Arkansas University Post-Sec.
100 E University 71753 870-235-4000

Malvern, Hot Spring, Pop. 9,068
Glen Rose SD 700/K-12
14334 Highway 67 72104 501-332-6764
Nathan Gills, supt. Fax 332-3031
www.glenrose.k12.ar.us/
Glen Rose HS 300/9-12
14334 Highway 67 72104 501-332-3520
Vic Gandolph, prin. Fax 332-3902
Glen Rose MS 5-8
14334 Highway 67 72104 501-332-3694
Tim Holicer, prin. Fax 332-3902

Magnet Cove SD 800/K-12
472 Magnet School Rd 72104 501-332-5468
Gail McClure, supt. Fax 337-4119
magnetcove.k12.ar.us
Magnet Cove HS 400/7-12
472 Magnet School Rd 72104 501-332-5466
Brad Sullivan, prin. Fax 337-8711

Malvern Special SD 2,000/K-12
1517 S Main St 72104 501-332-7500
Ron Holt, supt. Fax 332-7501
malvern.dsc.k12.ar.us/
Malvern JHS 300/7-8
1910 Roosevelt St 72104 501-332-7530
Danny Lindsey, prin. Fax 332-7532
Malvern SHS 500/9-12
525 E Highland Ave 72104 501-332-6905
Steve Williams, prin. Fax 332-7523

Ouachita Technical College Post-Sec.
1 College Cir 72104 501-332-3658

Mammoth Spring, Fulton, Pop. 1,157
Mammoth Spring SD 400/K-12
410 Goldsmith Ave 72554 870-625-3612
Ronald Taylor, supt. Fax 625-3609
Mammoth Spring JSHS 200/7-12
410 Goldsmith Ave 72554 870-625-7212
Brian Davis, prin. Fax 625-3609

Manila, Mississippi, Pop. 2,813
Manila SD 1,000/K-12
PO Box 670 72442 870-561-4419
Pamela Castor, supt. Fax 561-4410
mps.crsc.k12.ar.us
Manila JSHS 500/7-12
PO Box 670 72442 870-561-4417
Pamela D. Chipman, prin. Fax 561-4243

Mansfield, Scott, Pop. 1,107
Mansfield SD 1,000/K-12
402 Grove St 72944 479-928-4006
Jim Hattabaugh, supt. Fax 928-4482
www.mansfieldtigers.com
Mansfield HS 300/9-12
2500 Highway 71 S 72944 479-928-1105
Tina Smith, prin.
Mansfield MS 300/5-8
400 Grove St 72944 479-928-4451
Kenny Burnett, prin. Fax 928-4323

Marianna, Lee, Pop. 4,792
Lee County SD 1,500/K-12
188 W Chestnut St 72360 870-295-7100
Wayne Thompson, supt. Fax 295-7125
lcsd1.grsc.k12.ar.us/
Lee HS 500/9-12
523 Forest Ave 72360 870-295-7131
Irish Williams, prin. Fax 295-7125
Strong MS 400/6-8
214 S Alabama St 72360 870-295-7140
Carolyn Love, prin. Fax 295-7125

Marion, Crittenden, Pop. 9,792
Marion SD 3,700/K-12
200 Manor St 72364 870-739-5100
Dan Shepherd, supt. Fax 739-5156
marion.crsc.k12.ar.us/
Marion JHS 700/8-9
2 Patriot Dr 72364 870-739-5140
John Heath, prin. Fax 739-5142
Marion SHS 800/10-12
1 Patriot Dr 72364 870-739-5130
John Lowry, prin. Fax 739-5135

Marked Tree, Poinsett, Pop. 2,720
Marked Tree SD 700/K-12
406 Saint Francis St 72365 870-358-2913
Gary Masters, supt. Fax 358-3953
mtree.crsc.k12.ar.us/
Marked Tree JSHS 300/7-12
406 Saint Francis St 72365 870-358-2891
Annesa Thompson, prin. Fax 358-3953

Delta Technical Institute Post-Sec.
PO Box 280 72365 870-358-2117

Marmaduke, Greene, Pop. 1,163
Marmaduke SD 800/K-12
1010 Greyhound Dr 72443 870-597-4693
Debbie Smith, supt. Fax 597-4336
marmaduke.nesc.k12.ar.us/
Marmaduke JSHS 400/7-12
1010 Greyhound Dr 72443 870-597-4693
Keith Richey, prin. Fax 597-4336

Marshall, Searcy, Pop. 1,255
Searcy County SD 800/K-12
PO Box 310 72650 870-448-3011
Andrew Vining, supt. Fax 448-3012
searcycounty.ar.schoolwebpages.com/
Marshall MSHS 400/7-12
PO Box 310 72650 870-448-3331
Jimmy Yarbrough, prin. Fax 448-5306
Other Schools – See Leslie

Marvell, Phillips, Pop. 1,250
Marvell SD 800/PK-12
PO Box 1870 72366 870-829-2101
Ulicious Reed, supt. Fax 829-2044
marvell.grsc.k12.ar.us/
Marvell JSHS 300/7-12
PO Box 1870 72366 870-829-2594
Jimmy Lowery, prin. Fax 829-9700

Maumelle, Pulaski, Pop. 14,318
Pulaski County Special SD
Supt. — See Little Rock
Maumelle MS 6-8
1000 Carnahan Dr 72113 501-851-8990
Kimberly Truslow, prin. Fax 851-8988

Mayflower, Faulkner, Pop. 1,900
Mayflower SD 900/K-12
PO Box 127 72106 501-470-0506
Rhonda Bradford, supt. Fax 470-1343
Mayflower HS 300/9-12
PO Box 127 72106 501-470-0388
Joel Linn, prin. Fax 470-2106
Mayflower MS 200/6-8
PO Box 127 72106 501-470-2111
Dr. Robert Toney, prin. Fax 470-2116

Maynard, Randolph, Pop. 369
Maynard SD 500/K-12
PO Box 499 72444 870-647-2051
Philip Mielke, supt. Fax 647-2301
maynard.nesc.k12.ar.us/
Maynard JSHS 200/7-12
PO Box 499 72444 870-647-2210
Larry Sullinger, prin. Fax 647-8207

Melbourne, Izard, Pop. 1,700
Melbourne SD 500/K-12
PO Box 250 72556 870-368-7070
Gerald Cooper, supt. Fax 368-7071
bearkatz.k12.ar.us/
Melbourne JSHS 200/7-12
PO Box 250 72556 870-368-4345
Kelly Powell, prin. Fax 368-7071
Other Schools – See Mount Pleasant

Ozarka College Post-Sec.
PO Box 10 72556 870-368-7371

Mena, Polk, Pop. 5,608
Mena SD 1,900/K-12
501 Hickory Ave 71953 479-394-1710
John Ponder, supt. Fax 394-1713
170.211.34.2/Mena%20Public%202000/index.htm
Mena HS 600/9-12
700 Morrow St S 71953 479-394-1144
Connie Davis, prin. Fax 394-1145
Mena MS 500/6-8
320r Mena St 71953 479-394-2572
Ken Marshall, prin. Fax 394-0258

Ouachita River SD 600/K-12
143 Polk Road 96 71953 479-394-2348
Marcus O. Willborg, supt. Fax 394-6687
Acorn JSHS 200/7-12
143 Polk Road 96 71953 479-394-5544
Steve Crumpler, prin. Fax 394-6687
Other Schools – See Oden

Rich Mountain Community College Post-Sec.
1100 College Dr 71953 479-394-7622

Mineral Springs, Howard, Pop. 1,293
Mineral Springs SD 500/PK-12
PO Box 189 71851 870-287-4748
Max Adcock, supt. Fax 287-5301
mssd.dmsc.k12.ar.us/
Mineral Springs JSHS 200/7-12
PO Box 189 71851 870-287-4747
Richard Myrick, prin. Fax 287-5300
Other Schools – See Saratoga

Monette, Craighead, Pop. 1,189
Buffalo Island Central SD 800/K-12
PO Box 730 72447 870-486-5411
George Holland, supt. Fax 486-2657
Buffalo Island Central SHS 200/10-12
PO Box 730 72447 870-486-5512
Homer Craig, prin. Fax 486-2657
Other Schools – See Leachville

Monticello, Drew, Pop. 9,327
Drew Central SD 1,000/K-12
440 Highway 83 S 71655 870-367-5369
Michael S. Reeves, supt. Fax 367-1932
www.drewcentral.org/
Drew Central JSHS 500/7-12
440 Highway 83 S 71655 870-460-5501
Frank Ferguson, prin. Fax 367-1932

Monticello SD 2,100/K-12
935 Scogin Dr 71655 870-367-4000
Bobby Harper, supt. Fax 367-1531
www.billies.org
Monticello HS 700/9-12
390 Clyde Ross Dr 71655 870-367-4050
Kenny Pennington, prin. Fax 367-3699
Monticello MS 500/6-8
180 Clyde Ross Dr 71655 870-367-4040
Jay Hughes, prin. Fax 367-5437
Occupational Education Center Vo/Tech
741 Scogin Dr 71655 870-367-4060
Cornelious Branch, prin. Fax 367-1385

University of Arkansas at Monticello Post-Sec.
PO Box 3600 71656 870-367-6811

Morrilton, Conway, Pop. 6,607
South Conway County SD 1,700/K-12
704 E Church St 72110 501-354-9400
Douglas S. Adams, supt. Fax 354-9464
www.sccsd.org
Morrilton HS 800/9-12
701 E Harding St 72110 501-354-9430
Brian Bunch, prin. Fax 354-9468
Morrilton JHS 400/7-8
1400 Poor Farm Rd 72110 501-354-9437
Shawn Halbrook, prin. Fax 354-9429
River Valley Vocational Center Vo/Tech
1905 Poor Farm Rd 72110 501-354-9475
Bruce Bryant, dir. Fax 354-9441

Sacred Heart S 300/K-12
106 N Saint Joseph St 72110 501-354-8113
Brian Bailey, prin. Fax 354-2001
University of Arkansas Community College Post-Sec.
1537 University Blvd 72110 501-354-2465

Mountainburg, Crawford, Pop. 713
Mountainburg SD 800/K-12
129 Highway 71 SW 72946 479-369-2121
Dr. James A. Bridges, supt. Fax 369-2138
dragonsweb.wsc.k12.ar.us/
Mountainburg HS 300/9-12
129 Highway 71 SW 72946 479-369-2146
Barton Hunter, prin. Fax 369-2845
Mountainburg MS 200/5-8
129 Highway 71 SW 72946 479-369-4506
Barton Hunter, prin. Fax 369-4355

Mountain Home, Baxter, Pop. 11,896
Mountain Home SD 3,600/K-12
2465 Rodeo Dr 72653 870-425-1201
Dr. Charles Scriber, supt. Fax 425-1316
bombers.k12.ar.us/
Mountain Home HS 900/9-12
500 Bomber Blvd 72653 870-425-1215
Dana Brown, prin. Fax 508-6097
Mountain Home JHS 300/8-8
2301 Rodeo Dr 72653 870-425-1231
Wesley Henderson, prin. Fax 424-4797

Arkansas State University Mountain Home Post-Sec.
1600 S College St 72653 870-508-6100
Marsha Kay Beauty College Post-Sec.
408 Highway 201 N 72653 870-425-7575

Mountain Pine, Garland, Pop. 827
Mountain Pine SD 700/K-12
PO Box 1 71956 501-767-1540
Ron Looper, supt. Fax 767-1589
Mountain Pine JSHS 300/7-12
PO Box 1 71956 501-767-6917
Doug Booker, prin. Fax 767-0170

Mountain View, Stone, Pop. 2,998
Mountain View SD 1,300/K-12
210 High School Rd 72560 870-269-3443
Al Davidson, supt. Fax 269-3446
mvschools.k12.ar.us
Mountain View JSHS 600/7-12
210 High School Rd 72560 870-269-3943
Mark Mallett, prin. Fax 269-3446
Other Schools – See Fox, Timbo

Mount Ida, Montgomery, Pop. 971
Mount Ida SD 600/K-12
PO Box 1230 71957 870-867-2323
Benny Weston, supt. Fax 867-3734
Mount Ida JSHS 300/7-12
PO Box 1230 71957 870-867-4517
Heath Bennett, prin. Fax 867-3734

Mount Judea, Newton
Deer / Mt. Judea SD
Supt. — See Deer
Mount Judea JSHS 100/7-12
PO Box 56 72655 870-434-5362
Sammie Bye, prin. Fax 434-5359

Mount Pleasant, Izard, Pop. 407
Melbourne SD
Supt. — See Melbourne
Mount Pleasant JSHS 7-12
PO Box 144 72561 870-346-5481
Conny Johnson, prin. Fax 346-5337

Mount Vernon, Faulkner, Pop. 147
Mount Vernon-Enola SD 500/K-12
PO Box 43 72111 501-849-2220
Ronnie Greer, supt. Fax 849-3076
mve.k12.ar.us/
Mount Vernon-Enola JSHS 200/7-12
PO Box 43 72111 501-849-2221
Rudy Beavers, prin. Fax 849-3302

Mulberry, Crawford, Pop. 1,696
Mulberry/Pleasant View Bi-County SD 400/K-12
PO Box D 72947 479-997-1715
Kerry Schneider, supt. Fax 997-1897
www.mulberrypleasantview.homestead.com/
Mulberry JSHS 200/7-12
PO Box D 72947 479-997-1363
Dana Higdon, prin. Fax 997-1897
Other Schools – See Ozark

Murfreesboro, Pike, Pop. 1,713
Murfreesboro SD 500/K-12
PO Box 339 71958 870-285-2201
Dr. Bernie Hellums, supt. Fax 285-2276
Murfreesboro JSHS 300/7-12
PO Box 339 71958 870-285-3678
Roger Featherston, prin. Fax 285-2276

Nashville, Howard, Pop. 4,929
Nashville SD 1,800/K-12
600 N 4th St 71852 870-845-3425
Douglas Graham, supt. Fax 845-7344
scrappers.k12.ar.us/
Nashville JHS 400/7-9
1000 N 8th St 71852 870-845-3418
Deb Tackett, prin. Fax 845-7334
Nashville SHS 400/10-12
1301 Mount Pleasant Dr 71852 870-845-3261
Tate Gordon, prin. Fax 845-7345

Newark, Independence, Pop. 1,233
Cedar Ridge SD 400/K-12
1502 N Hill St 72562 870-799-8691
Dr. Ann Webb, supt. Fax 799-8647
www.cedarridgeschooldistrict.us
Cedar Ridge JSHS 7-12
1500 N Hill St 72562 870-799-8691
Danny Davis, prin. Fax 799-3225

Newport, Jackson, Pop. 7,281
Newport SD 1,700/PK-12
406 Wilkerson Dr 72112 870-523-1311
Ronny Brown, supt. Fax 523-1388
greyhounds.k12.ar.us
Newport HS 400/9-12
406 Wilkerson Dr 72112 870-523-1321
Ronnie Kay Erwin, prin. Fax 523-1383
Newport JHS 300/7-8
406 Wilkerson Dr 72112 870-523-1346
Suzanne Bailey, prin. Fax 523-1388

Arkansas State University - Newport Post-Sec.
7648 Victory Blvd 72112 870-512-7800

Norfork, Baxter, Pop. 521
Norfork SD 500/K-12
44 Fireball Ln 72658 870-499-5228
Mike Seay, supt. Fax 499-5109
panthers.k12.ar.us

Norfork JSHS 200/7-12
136 Mildred Simpson Dr 72658 870-499-7191
Bob Hulse, prin. Fax 499-5659

Norman, Montgomery, Pop. 422
Caddo Hills SD 600/K-12
2268 Highway 8 E 71960 870-356-4495
Donald Henley, supt. Fax 356-3426
caddohills.dsc.k12.ar.us/
Caddo Hills JSHS 300/7-12
2268 Highway 8 E 71960 870-356-3857
James Vines, prin. Fax 356-3426

Norphlet, Union, Pop. 807
Norphlet SD 500/K-12
PO Box 50 71759 870-546-2781
Eddie Miller, supt. Fax 546-2345
www.scsc.k12.ar.us/norphlet/
Norphlet JSHS 300/7-12
PO Box 50 71759 870-546-2781
Keith Coleman, prin. Fax 546-2345

North Little Rock, Pulaski, Pop. 58,803
North Little Rock SD 8,800/PK-12
2700 N Poplar St 72114 501-771-8000
Kenneth Kirspel, supt. Fax 771-8067
www.nlrsd.k12.ar.us
Lakewood MS 700/7-8
2300 Lakeview Rd 72116 501-771-8250
Dr. Ginger Wallace, prin. Fax 771-8268
North Little Rock HS - East Campus 1,400/9-10
2400 Lakeview Rd 72116 501-771-8200
Lee Tackett, prin. Fax 771-8213
North Little Rock HS - West Campus 1,300/6-12
101 W 22nd St 72114 501-771-8100
Anita Cameron, prin. Fax 771-8123
Rose City MS 200/7-8
5500 Lynch Dr 72117 501-955-3600
Penny Elliott, prin. Fax 955-3603

Pulaski County Special SD
Supt. — See Little Rock
Northwood MS 700/6-8
10200 Bamboo Ln 72120 501-833-1170
Thelma Jones-Ramsey, prin. Fax 833-1178
Oak Grove JSHS 800/6-12
10025 Oakland Dr 72118 501-851-5350
Joy Plants, prin. Fax 851-5356

AR College of Barbering & Hair Design Post-Sec.
200 E Washington Ave 72114 501-376-9696
Central Arkansas Christian S 1,100/K-12
1 Windsong Dr 72113 501-758-3160
Dr. Carter Lambert, pres. Fax 791-7975
Lee's School of Cosmetology Post-Sec.
2700 W Pershing Blvd 72114 501-758-2800
New Tyler Barber College Post-Sec.
1221 Bishop Lindsey Ave 72114 501-375-0377
Pulaski Technical College Post-Sec.
3000 W Scenic Dr 72118 501-771-1000

Oark, Johnson
Jasper SD
Supt. — See Jasper
Oark JSHS 7-12
General Delivery 72852 479-292-3353
Anita Cooper, prin. Fax 292-3435

Oden, Montgomery, Pop. 219
Ouachita River SD
Supt. — See Mena
Oden JSHS 100/7-12
PO Box 150 71961 870-326-4311
Doug Carmack, prin. Fax 326-5552

Ola, Yell, Pop. 1,206
Two Rivers SD
Supt. — See Plainview
Ola JSHS 300/7-12
PO Box 279 72853 479-489-4154
Barry Fisher, prin. Fax 489-4167

Omaha, Boone, Pop. 172
Omaha SD 300/K-12
522 College Rd 72662 870-426-3366
Dr. David Land, supt. Fax 426-3360
omaha.k12.ar.us/
Omaha HS 100/7-12
522 College Rd 72662 870-426-3373
Martha Hicks, prin. Fax 426-2926

Osceola, Mississippi, Pop. 8,128
Osceola SD 1,100/PK-12
PO Box 528 72370 870-563-2561
Milton Washington, supt. Fax 563-2181
osceola.ar.schoolwebpages.com
Osceola HS 300/9-12
2800 W Semmes Ave 72370 870-563-2192
Ella Sergeant, prin. Fax 622-1003
Osceola MS 200/6-8
711 W Lee Ave 72370 870-563-2918
Sharon McGee, prin. Fax 622-1030

Ozark, Franklin, Pop. 3,586
Mulberry/Pleasant View Bi-County SD
Supt. — See Mulberry
Pleasant View JSHS 7-12
5750 Hornet Ln 72949 479-997-8469
Rick Young, prin. Fax 997-1667

Ozark SD 1,500/K-12
PO Box 135 72949 479-667-4118
Donald Stone, supt. Fax 667-4092
Ozark JHS 300/8-9
1301 Walden Dr 72949 479-667-4747
Jerrod Burns, prin. Fax 667-0898
Ozark SHS 400/10-12
3500 Jeffers Dr 72949 479-667-4116
Jody Jenkins, prin. Fax 667-5921

Arkansas Valley Technical Institute Post-Sec.
PO Box 506 72949 479-667-2117
Cass Civilian Conservation Job Corps Ctr Post-Sec.
21424 N Highway 23 72949 479-667-3686

Palestine, Saint Francis, Pop. 736
Palestine-Wheatley SD 500/PK-12
PO Box 790 72372 870-581-2646
Donny Collins, supt. Fax 581-4420
www.pwsd.k12.ar.us/
Palestine-Wheatley HS 100/9-12
PO Box 790 72372 870-581-2425
James Williams, prin. Fax 581-4421
Other Schools – See Wheatley

Pangburn, White, Pop. 661
Pangburn SD 700/K-12
1100 Short St 72121 501-728-4511
Ricky Wood, supt. Fax 728-4514
pangburnschools.k12.ar.us/
Pangburn JSHS 400/7-12
1100 Short St 72121 501-728-3513
David Rolland, prin. Fax 728-4514

Paragould, Greene, Pop. 23,775
Greene County Technical SD 3,300/PK-12
5413 W Kingshighway 72450 870-236-2762
Sheila Ford, supt. Fax 236-7333
www.gctsd.k12.ar.us/
Greene County Technical HS 600/10-12
5201 W Kingshighway 72450 870-236-6113
Gene Weeks, prin. Fax 239-6976
Greene County Technical JHS 500/8-9
5207 W Kingshighway 72450 870-239-2147
Michael Todd, prin. Fax 239-2148
Other Schools – See Delaplaine

Paragould SD 2,700/PK-12
1501 W Court St 72450 870-239-2105
Dr. Aaron Hosman, supt. Fax 239-4697
paragould.k12.ar.us/
Paragould HS 800/9-12
1701 W Court St 72450 870-236-7744
Brett Gibson, prin. Fax 239-2934
Paragould JHS 500/7-8
1701 W Court St 72450 870-236-7744
James Brittingham, prin. Fax 239-0185

Crowleys Ridge Academy 300/PK-12
606 Academy Dr 72450 870-236-6909
Dale Horn, pres. Fax 236-6988
Crowley's Ridge College Post-Sec.
100 College Dr 72450 870-236-6901

Paris, Logan, Pop. 3,707
Paris SD 1,000/K-12
602 N 10th St 72855 479-963-3243
Jim Loyd, supt. Fax 963-3620
paris.wsc.k12.ar.us/
Paris HS 300/9-12
2000 E Wood St 72855 479-963-2247
Gary Montgomery, prin. Fax 963-8018
Paris MS 300/5-8
602 N 10th St 72855 479-963-6995
Martha Dodson, prin. Fax 963-8052

Pearcy, Garland
Lake Hamilton SD 3,700/K-12
205 Wolf St 71964 501-767-2306
Steve Anderson, supt. Fax 767-1219
wolves.dsc.k12.ar.us
Lake Hamilton JHS 600/8-9
281 Wolf St 71964 501-767-2731
Jerald Humphries, prin. Fax 767-1711
Lake Hamilton SHS 800/10-12
280 Wolf St 71964 501-767-9311
Vernon Brooks, prin. Fax 767-9318

Pea Ridge, Benton, Pop. 3,344
Pea Ridge SD 1,000/K-12
781 W Pickens Rd 72751 479-451-8181
Michael Van Dyke, supt. Fax 451-8235
www.prs.k12.ar.us/
Pea Ridge JHS 200/7-9
1391 Weston St 72751 479-451-1555
Holly Dayberry, prin. Fax 451-9635
Pea Ridge SHS 300/10-12
781 W Pickens Rd 72751 479-451-8182
Rick Neal, prin. Fax 451-0323

Perryville, Pulaski, Pop. 1,471
Perryville SD 1,000/K-12
823 N Ash St 72126 501-889-2327
Dr. Ron Wilson, supt. Fax 889-5191
mustangs.k12.ar.us/
Perryville JSHS 500/7-12
823 N Ash St 72126 501-889-2326
John Parrish, prin. Fax 889-5006

Piggott, Clay, Pop. 3,661
Piggott SD 1,000/K-12
PO Box 387 72454 870-598-2572
Bruce Evans, supt. Fax 598-5283
piggotths.k12.ar.us/
Piggott HS 500/7-12
PO Box 387 72454 870-598-3815
Barry DeHart, prin. Fax 598-1560

Pine Bluff, Jefferson, Pop. 52,693
Dollarway SD 1,300/PK-12
4900 Dollarway Rd 71602 870-534-7003
Thomas Gathen, supt. Fax 534-7859
www.dollarway.org/
Dollarway HS 300/9-12
4900 Dollarway Rd 71602 870-534-3878
Michael Anthony, prin. Fax 534-1455
Dollarway MS 200/6-8
2602 W Fluker Ave 71601 870-534-5243
Dorothea Hobbs, prin. Fax 535-1215

Pine Bluff SD 5,200/PK-12
PO Box 7678 71611 870-543-4200
Frank Anthony, supt. Fax 543-4208
pbweb.arsc.k12.ar.us/
Pine Bluff SHS 1,100/10-12
711 W 11th Ave 71601 870-543-4300
Rodney Matheney, prin. Fax 543-4302
Robey JHS 1,000/8-9
4101 S Olive St 71603 870-543-4290
Robbie Williams, prin. Fax 850-2027

Watson Chapel SD 3,300/K-12
4100 Camden Rd 71603 870-879-0220
Charles Knight, supt. Fax 879-0588
watson2.arsc.k12.ar.us
Watson Chapel JHS 900/7-9
3900 Camden Rd 71603 870-879-4420
Henry Webb, prin. Fax 879-4426
Watson Chapel SHS 800/10-12
4000 Camden Rd 71603 870-879-3230
Leydel Willis, prin. Fax 879-1842

Jefferson Regional Medical Center Post-Sec.
1515 W 42nd Ave 71603 870-541-7269
St. Joseph JSHS 100/7-12
1501 W 73rd Ave 71603 870-540-0413
Brenda Costello, prin. Fax 540-0345
Southeast Arkansas College Post-Sec.
1900 S Hazel St 71603 870-543-5900
University of Arkansas at Pine Bluff Post-Sec.
1200 University Dr 71601 870-543-8000

Plainview, Yell, Pop. 756
Two Rivers SD 1,100/K-12
PO Box 187 72857 479-272-3113
Earl Jamison, supt. Fax 272-3125
tworivers.k12.ar.us
Plainview-Rover JSHS 100/7-12
PO Box 190 72857 479-272-3111
Lela McChesney, prin. Fax 272-3125
Other Schools – See Briggsville, Ola

Pleasant Plains, Independence, Pop. 271
Midland SD 600/K-12
PO Box 630 72568 501-345-8844
Lynn Roe King, supt. Fax 345-2086
Midland JSHS 300/7-12
PO Box 630 72568 501-345-2610
Vickie Crawford, prin. Fax 345-3355

Pocahontas, Randolph, Pop. 6,765
Pocahontas SD 1,900/K-12
2300 N Park St 72455 870-892-4573
Daryl Blaxton, supt. Fax 892-8857
www.nesc.k12.ar.us/
Pocahontas HS 400/10-12
2312 Stadium Dr 72455 870-892-4573
Ivy Pfeffer, prin. Fax 892-8857
Pocahontas JHS 500/7-9
2405 N Park St 72455 870-892-4573
Byron Busby, prin. Fax 892-8857

Black River Technical College Post-Sec.
PO Box 468 72455 870-892-4565

Pottsville, Pope, Pop. 1,517
Pottsville SD 1,100/K-12
63 W Cedar St 72858 479-968-8101
Larry Dugger, supt. Fax 968-6339
apache.afsc.k12.ar.us
Pottsville HS 200/10-12
500 Apache Dr 72858 479-968-6334
Jonathan Bradley, prin. Fax 968-3442
Pottsville JHS, 250 Apache Dr 72858 200/7-9
Kenneth Bell, prin.

Poyen, Grant, Pop. 281
Poyen SD 500/K-12
PO Box 209 72128 501-332-8884
Jerry Newton, supt. Fax 332-8886
www.poyenschool.com/
Poyen JSHS 200/7-12
PO Box 209 72128 501-332-2939
Bobby Daniel, prin. Fax 332-7800

Prairie Grove, Washington, Pop. 2,996
Prairie Grove SD 1,500/K-12
110 School St 72753 479-846-4213
Chris Webb, supt. Fax 846-2015
tiger.nwsc.k12.ar.us
Prairie Grove HS 400/9-12
500 Cole Dr 72753 479-846-4212
Ron Bond, prin. Fax 846-4207
Prairie Grove MS 500/5-8
807 Catlett St 72753 479-846-4221
Janet Collins, prin. Fax 846-4275

Prescott, Nevada, Pop. 4,285
Prescott SD 1,100/K-12
762 Martin St 71857 870-887-3016
Hyacinth Deon, supt. Fax 887-5021
www.prescott.k12.ar.us/
McRae MS 400/5-8
1030 E 5th St N 71857 870-887-2521
Jamye Barnes, prin. Fax 887-3717
Prescott HS 300/9-12
736 Martin St 71857 870-887-3123
Jeff Fairris, prin. Fax 887-3682

Quitman, Cleburne, Pop. 741
Quitman SD 600/K-12
PO Box 178 72131 501-589-3156
Robert Stewart, supt. Fax 589-3156
quitnet.afsc.k12.ar.us/
Quitman JSHS 300/7-12
PO Box 178 72131 501-589-2554
Larry Freeman, prin. Fax 589-2554

Ravenden Springs, Randolph, Pop. 137
Twin Rivers SD
Supt. — See Williford
Oak Ridge Central JSHS 7-12
5749 Oak Ridge Rd 72460 870-869-2479
David Rutledge, prin. Fax 869-3067

Rector, Clay, Pop. 1,856
Rector SD 700/K-12
PO Box 367 72461 870-595-3151
Robert Louder, supt. Fax 595-9067
Rector HS 300/7-12
PO Box 367 72461 870-595-3553
Wade Williams, prin. Fax 595-9067

Redfield, Jefferson, Pop. 1,173
White Hall SD
Supt. — See White Hall
Redfield JHS 100/7-9
PO Box 350 72132 501-397-2253
James Kight, prin. Fax 397-6534

Rison, Cleveland, Pop. 1,340
Cleveland County SD 800/K-12
PO Box 600 71665 870-325-6344
Scott Holderfield, supt. Fax 325-7094
www.risonschools.org
Rison JSHS 300/7-12
PO Box 600 71665 870-325-6241
Brian Brown, prin. Fax 325-6799

Woodlawn SD 600/K-12
6760 Highway 63 71665 870-357-8108
Billy Williams, supt. Fax 357-8718
bears.k12.ar.us
Woodlawn JSHS 300/7-12
6760 Highway 63 71665 870-357-8171
Jeff Wylie, prin. Fax 357-8718

Rogers, Benton, Pop. 48,353
Rogers SD 12,800/K-12
500 W Walnut St 72756 479-636-3910
Dr. Janie Darr, supt. Fax 631-3504
www.rogers.k12.ar.us
Elmwood JHS 1,000/8-9
1610 S 13th St 72758 479-631-3600
Bob White, prin. Fax 631-3603
Oakdale JHS 1,000/8-9
511 N Dixieland Rd 72756 479-631-3615
James Goodwin, prin. Fax 631-3617
Rogers HS Sophomore Campus 1,000/10-10
2930 S 1st St 72758 479-631-3579
Dr. Larry Ben, prin. Fax 631-3580
Rogers SHS 1,700/11-12
2300 S Dixieland Rd 72758 479-636-2202
Bill Stringer, prin. Fax 631-3554

New Covenant Christian Academy 50/PK-12
2298 S 13th St 72758 479-636-9186
Jody Bricker, prin. Fax 631-1553

Rose Bud, White, Pop. 448
Rose Bud SD 800/K-12
124 School Rd 72137 501-556-5815
Jeff Williams, supt. Fax 556-4201
rbsd.k12.ar.us
Rose Bud JSHS 400/7-12
124 School Rd 72137 501-556-5404
Fred Ramsey, prin. Fax 556-5781

Rosston, Nevada, Pop. 223
Nevada SD 400/K-12
PO Box 50 71858 870-871-2418
Rick McAfee, supt. Fax 871-2419
www.nevadaschooldistrict.net/
Nevada JSHS 200/7-12
PO Box 50 71858 870-871-2478
Frank Bradley, prin. Fax 871-2419

Russellville, Pope, Pop. 25,520
Russellville SD 5,000/K-12
PO Box 928 72811 479-968-1306
Randall Williams, supt. Fax 968-6381
rsdweb.k12.ar.us/
Russellville Area Vo-Technical Center Vo/Tech
2201 S Knoxville Ave 72802 479-968-5422
Jim Franks, prin. Fax 968-7918
Russellville JHS 800/8-9
2000 W Parkway Dr 72802 479-968-1599
Alene Bynum, prin. Fax 890-6419
Russellville SHS 1,200/10-12
2203 S Knoxville Ave 72802 479-968-3151
Wesley White, prin. Fax 968-4264

Arkansas Tech University Post-Sec.
215 W O St 72801 479-968-0389

Saint Joe, Searcy, Pop. 83
Ozark Mountain SD 800/K-12
PO Box 69 72675 870-439-2213
Dr. Delena Gammill, supt. Fax 439-2604
Saint Joe JSHS 100/7-12
PO Box 69 72675 870-439-2213
Ronnie Ruff, prin. Fax 439-2604
Other Schools – See Everton, Western Grove

Saint Paul, Madison, Pop. 162
Huntsville SD
Supt. — See Huntsville
Saint Paul JSHS 7-12
PO Box 125 72760 479-677-2411
Rick Land, prin. Fax 677-2210

Salem, Fulton, Pop. 1,587
Salem SD 700/K-12
313 Highway 62 E Ste 1 72576 870-895-2516
Ken Rich, supt. Fax 895-4062
salem.k12.ar.us/
Salem JSHS 400/7-12
313 Highway 62 E Ste 2 72576 870-895-3293
Wayne Guiltner, prin. Fax 895-4062

Saratoga, Howard, Pop. 200
Mineral Springs SD
Supt. — See Mineral Springs
Saratoga HS 7-12
PO Box 90 71859 870-388-9262
Warren Bane, prin. Fax 388-9205

Scranton, Logan, Pop. 263
Scranton SD 400/K-12
103 N 10th St 72863 479-938-7121
Larry Garland, supt. Fax 938-7564
www.rocketnet.k12.ar.us
Scranton JSHS 200/7-12
103 N 10th St 72863 479-938-7121
Mark Siebenmorgen, prin. Fax 938-7564

Searcy, White, Pop. 20,663
Riverview SD 900/K-12
800 Raider Dr 72143 501-279-0540
Hugh Burge, supt. Fax 279-0737
Riverview-Kensett JHS 100/7-9
820 Raider Dr 72143 501-279-7111
Pat Falcinelli, prin. Fax 279-7166
Riverview SHS 300/10-12
810 Raider Dr 72143 501-279-7700
Kennedy Simmons, prin. Fax 279-2848

Searcy SD 3,700/K-12
801 N Elm St 72143 501-268-3517
James T. Wood, supt. Fax 278-2220
ssweb.wmsc.k12.ar.us/
Ahlf JHS 600/7-8
308 W Vine Ave 72143 501-268-3158
Bill Dunaway, prin. Fax 268-2212
Searcy HS 1,000/9-12
301 N Ella St 72143 501-268-8315
Claude Smith, prin. Fax 268-2249

Arkansas State University Searcy Campus Post-Sec.
PO Box 909 72145 501-268-6191
Harding Academy 600/K-12
PO Box 10775 72149 501-279-7200
Mark Benton M.Ed., hdmstr. Fax 279-7213
Harding University Post-Sec.
900 E Center Ave 72149 501-279-4000
Searcy Beauty College Post-Sec.
1004 S Main St 72143 501-268-6300

Sheridan, Grant, Pop. 4,349
Sheridan SD 4,200/K-12
400 N Rock St 72150 870-942-3135
Scott Spainhour, supt. Fax 942-2931
www.sheridanschools.org/
Sheridan Freshman Academy 400/9-9
510 W Church St 72150 870-942-3232
Dr. Phil Clark, prin. Fax 942-3296
Sheridan MS 900/6-8
500 N Rock St 72150 870-942-3813
Charles Tadlock, prin. Fax 942-3034
Sheridan SHS 900/10-12
700 W Vine St 72150 870-942-3137
Donna Yancey, prin. Fax 942-7546

Sherwood, Pulaski, Pop. 23,149
Pulaski County Special SD
Supt. — See Little Rock
Sylvan Hills HS 1,100/9-12
484 Bear Paw Rd 72120 501-833-1100
Danny Ebbs, prin. Fax 833-1104
Sylvan Hills MS 800/6-8
401 Dee Jay Hudson Dr 72120 501-833-1120
Cherrie Walker, prin. Fax 833-1137

Abundant Life S 500/PK-12
9200 Highway 107 72120 501-835-3120
Dr. Russell Eudy, supt. Fax 835-4428

Shirley, Van Buren, Pop. 342
Shirley SD 500/K-12
154 School Dr 72153 501-723-8191
Jack Robinson, supt. Fax 723-4020
shirley.k12.ar.us/
Shirley JSHS 300/7-12
154 School Dr 72153 501-723-4902
Randy Moore, prin. Fax 723-8114

Siloam Springs, Benton, Pop. 13,604
Siloam Springs SD 2,200/PK-12
PO Box 798 72761 479-524-3191
Kendall Ramey, supt. Fax 524-8002
sssd.k12.ar.us/
Siloam Springs HS 1,000/9-12
1500 W Jefferson St 72761 479-524-5134
Charles D. Abernathy, prin. Fax 524-8211
Siloam Springs MS 800/6-8
1500 N Mount Olive St 72761 479-524-6184
Teresa Morgan, prin. Fax 524-3228

John Brown University Post-Sec.
2000 W University St 72761 479-524-9500

Smackover, Union, Pop. 1,929
Smackover SD 700/K-12
PO Box 109 71762 870-725-3132
Darrell Porter, supt. Fax 725-2385
smackover.k12.ar.us/
Smackover HS 300/7-12
1 Buckaroo Ln 71762 870-725-3101
Jan Henderson, prin. Fax 725-2540

Sparkman, Dallas, Pop. 535
Harmony Grove SD
Supt. — See Camden
Sparkman S K-12
PO Box 37 71763 870-678-2242
Walton Pigott, prin. Fax 678-2917

Springdale, Washington, Pop. 60,096
Springdale SD 14,500/PK-12
PO Box 8 72765 479-750-8800
Dr. Jim Rollins, supt. Fax 750-8812
www.springdaleschools.org
Central JHS 700/8-9
2811 W Huntsville Ave 72762 479-750-8854
Darrell Watts, prin. Fax 750-8700
George JHS 800/8-9
3200 Powell St 72764 479-750-8750
David Nelson, prin. Fax 750-8756
Har-Ber HS 10-12
300 Jones Rd 72762 479-750-8777
Danny Brackett, prin. Fax 306-4250
Southwest JHS 600/8-9
1807 Princeton Ave 72762 479-750-8849
Brice Wagner, prin. Fax 750-8704
Springdale HS 2,700/10-12
1103 W Emma Ave 72764 479-750-8832
Dr. Allen Williams, prin. Fax 750-8811

Baptist School of Nursing-NW Post-Sec.
610 E Emma Ave 72764 479-750-6200
Ecclesia College Post-Sec.
9653 Nations Dr 72762 800-735-9926
Leon's Hair Training Academy Post-Sec.
200 Holcomb St 72764 479-756-6060
Northwest Technical Institute Post-Sec.
PO Box 2000 72765 479-751-8824
Shiloh Christian S 700/PK-12
1707 Johnson Rd 72762 479-756-1140
Ben Mayes, pres. Fax 756-7107

Stamps, Columbia, Pop. 1,984
Lafayette County SD
Supt. — See Lewisville
Lafayette County HS 7-12
1209 Alexander Ln 71860 870-533-4464
Opal Anderson, prin. Fax 533-2367

Star City, Lincoln, Pop. 2,321
Star City SD 1,600/K-12
206 Cleveland St 71667 870-628-4237
Rhonda Mullikin, supt. Fax 628-4228
www.starcityschools.com
Star City HS 500/9-12
206 Cleveland St 71667 870-628-4111
Mike Walker, prin. Fax 628-4228
Star City MS 400/6-8
206 Cleveland St 71667 870-628-5125
Susan White, prin. Fax 628-4228

State University, Craighead

Arkansas State University Post-Sec.
PO Box 1630 72467 870-972-2100

Stephens, Ouachita, Pop. 1,066
Stephens SD 400/K-12
315 W Chert St 71764 870-786-5443
Mark Keith, supt. Fax 786-5095
www.scsc.k12.ar.us/stephens/
Stephens JSHS 300/7-12
315 W Chert St 71764 870-786-5442
Wendell Culen, prin. Fax 786-5095

Strawberry, Lawrence, Pop. 275
Hillcrest SD 300/K-12
PO Box 50 72469 870-528-3856
Greg Crabtree, supt. Fax 528-3383
Hillcrest HS 100/10-12
PO Box 50 72469 870-528-3856
George Green, prin. Fax 528-3383
Other Schools – See Lynn

Strong, Union, Pop. 637
Strong-Huttig SD 500/K-12
PO Box 735 71765 870-797-7322
Saul Lusk, supt. Fax 797-2257
stronghuttig.k12.ar.us/
Huttig JHS 7-8
PO Box 735 71765 870-797-2312
William Neikirk, prin. Fax 797-2257
Strong HS 200/9-12
PO Box 735 71765 870-797-2312
William Neikirk, prin. Fax 797-2257

Stuttgart, Arkansas, Pop. 9,376
Stuttgart SD 1,900/K-12
2501 S Main St 72160 870-674-1303
Dr. Laura Bednar, supt. Fax 673-7337
sps.k12.ar.us
Stuttgart HS 600/9-12
2501 S Main St 72160 870-674-1341
Donnie Boothe, prin. Fax 673-7337
Stuttgart JHS 300/7-8
2501 S Main St 72160 870-674-1368
Howard Larry, prin. Fax 673-7337

Grand Prairie Ev. Methodist Christian S 50/K-12
1104 E 21st St 72160 870-673-2087
Thomas Bormann, prin. Fax 673-4718

Subiaco, Logan, Pop. 448

Subiaco Academy 200/9-12
405 N Subiaco Ave 72865 479-934-1005
Mike Berry, hdmstr. Fax 936-1033

Taylor, Columbia, Pop. 545
Emerson - Taylor SD
Supt. — See Emerson
Taylor JSHS 100/7-12
506 E Pine St 71861 870-694-2251
Mike Lyons, prin. Fax 694-2901

Texarkana, Miller, Pop. 30,006
Genoa Central SD 1,000/PK-12
12472 Highway 196 71854 870-653-4343
Albert Murphy, supt. Fax 653-2624
dragons1.k12.ar.us/dragons/
Cobb MS 300/5-8
11986 Highway 196 71854 870-653-2132
Deloris Coe, prin. Fax 653-6944
Genoa Central HS 300/9-12
12472 Highway 196 71854 870-653-2272
Bobby Hart, prin. Fax 653-6967

Texarkana Arkansas SD 4,300/K-12
3512 Grand Ave 71854 870-772-3371
Dr. Paul Human, supt. Fax 773-2602
txk.k12.ar.us/web/
Arkansas Magnet HS 1,300/9-12
3512 Grand Ave 71854 870-774-7641
Dr. Richard Young, prin. Fax 772-2185
North Heights Magnet JHS 600/7-8
3512 Grand Ave 71854 870-773-1091
Gerald Hatley, prin. Fax 772-2722
Texarkana Area Vocational Center Vo/Tech
3512 Grand Ave 71854 870-772-3662
Dr. Jerry Shipp, dir. Fax 772-3267

Trinity Christian S 300/PK-12
3107 Trinity Blvd 71854 870-779-1009
Ron Fellers, admin. Fax 772-1258

Timbo, Stone
Mountain View SD
Supt. — See Mountain View
Timbo JSHS 7-12
PO Box 6 72680 870-746-4303
Shade Gilbert, prin. Fax 746-4844

Trumann, Poinsett, Pop. 6,922
Trumann SD 1,800/K-12
221 N Pine Ave 72472 870-483-6444
Ronald J. Waleszonia, supt. Fax 483-2602
wildcat.crsc.k12.ar.us/
Trumann JSHS 800/7-12
221 N Pine Ave 72472 870-483-5301
Jimmy Montgomery, prin. Fax 483-2602

Tuckerman, Jackson, Pop. 1,721
Jackson County SD 500/K-12
PO Box 1070 72473 870-349-2232
Chester Shannon, supt. Fax 349-2355
Tuckerman HS 300/8-12
PO Box 1070 72473 870-349-2657
Cathy Tanner, prin. Fax 349-2355

Turrell, Crittenden, Pop. 912
Turrell SD 400/K-12
PO Box 369 72384 870-343-2533
Alfred Hogan, supt. Fax 343-2823
turrell.k12.ar.us
Turrell JSHS 200/7-12
PO Box 369 72384 870-343-2655
Charles Webster, prin. Fax 343-2876

Umpire, Howard
Wickes SD
Supt. — See Wickes
Umpire S K-12
PO Box 60 71971 870-583-2141
DeWayne Taylor, prin. Fax 583-6264

Valley Springs, Boone, Pop. 173
Valley Springs SD 1,000/K-12
PO Box 640 72682 870-429-8371
Mark Sanders, supt. Fax 429-5551
valley.k12.ar.us
Valley Springs HS 300/9-12
PO Box 640 72682 870-429-8120
Charles Trammell, prin. Fax 429-5551
Valley Springs MS 300/5-8
PO Box 640 72682 870-429-8101
Rick Still, prin. Fax 429-8121

Van Buren, Crawford, Pop. 21,249
Van Buren SD 5,500/K-12
2221 E Pointer Trl 72956 479-474-7942
Dr. Merle Dickerson, supt. Fax 471-3146
vbschools.k12.ar.us/
Butterfield JHS 700/7-9
319 N 12th St 72956 479-474-6838
Todd Marshell, prin. Fax 471-3101
Coleman JHS 700/7-9
821 E Pointer Trl 72956 479-471-3160
Becky Guthrie, prin. Fax 471-0249
Van Buren HS 1,200/10-12
2001 E Pointer Trl 72956 479-474-6821
Tom Watkins, prin. Fax 471-3171

Vilonia, Faulkner, Pop. 2,719
Vilonia SD 2,300/K-12
PO Box 160 72173 501-796-3500
Dr. Frank Mitchell, supt. Fax 796-3134
viloniaschools.k12.ar.us/
Vilonia JHS 400/8-9
PO Box 160 72173 501-796-2037
Jim Binan, prin. Fax 796-4326
Vilonia SHS 600/10-12
PO Box 160 72173 501-796-2111
Ed Sellers, prin. Fax 796-8895

Viola, Fulton, Pop. 394
Viola SD 400/K-12
PO Box 380 72583 870-458-2323
Marvin Newton, supt. Fax 458-2214
Viola JSHS 200/7-12
PO Box 380 72583 870-458-2213
John May, prin. Fax 458-2214

Waldron, Scott, Pop. 3,555
Waldron SD 1,700/K-12
1560 W 6th St 72958 479-637-3179
James Floyd, supt. Fax 637-3177
waldron.k12.ar.us
Waldron HS 500/9-12
736 W Highway 80 72958 479-637-3405
Bruce Sikes, prin. Fax 637-5624
Waldron MS 500/5-8
2075 Rice St 72958 479-637-4549
Steve Rose, prin. Fax 637-3165

Walnut Ridge, Lawrence, Pop. 4,724
Lawrence County SD 1,100/K-12
508 E Free St 72476 870-886-6634
Terry Belcher, supt. Fax 886-6635
wrhsbobcats.nesc.k12.ar.us/
Walnut Ridge HS 200/9-12
508 E Free St 72476 870-886-6623
Charles Lee, prin. Fax 886-6624
Other Schools – See Black Rock

Williams Baptist College Post-Sec.
PO Box 3665 72476 870-886-6741

Warren, Bradley, Pop. 6,263
Warren SD 1,600/K-12
PO Box 1210 71671 870-226-8500
Andrew Tolbert, supt. Fax 226-8531
se.sesc.k12.ar.us/warren/
Warren HS 500/9-12
803 N Walnut St 71671 870-226-6736
Jimmy Don Dupuy, prin. Fax 226-8527
Warren MS 400/6-8
PO Box 1210 71671 870-226-2484
Glenetta Burks, prin. Fax 226-8511

Weiner, Poinsett, Pop. 755
Weiner SD 400/K-12
313 N Garfield St 72479 870-684-2253
Betty McGruder, supt. Fax 684-7574
cardinal.k12.ar.us/
Weiner JSHS 200/7-12
313 N Garfield St 72479 870-684-2250
Fax 684-7574

Western Grove, Newton, Pop. 404
Ozark Mountain SD
Supt. — See Saint Joe
Western Grove JSHS 100/7-12
300 School St 72685 870-429-5215
Cynthia Hearn, prin. Fax 429-5276

West Fork, Washington, Pop. 2,195
West Fork SD 1,200/K-12
359 School Ave 72774 479-839-2231
Diane Barrett, supt. Fax 839-8412
www.westforktigers.k12.ar.us
West Fork HS 400/9-12
359 School Ave 72774 479-839-3131
John Karnes, prin. Fax 839-8412
West Fork MS 400/5-8
359 School Ave 72774 479-839-3342
David Skelton, prin. Fax 839-8412

West Helena, Phillips, Pop. 7,876
Helena/West Helena SD
Supt. — See Helena
Central HS 800/9-12
103 School Rd 72390 870-572-4503
Dr. Chris Gelenter, prin. Fax 572-4502
Miller JHS 600/7-8
106 Miller Loop 72390 870-572-3705
Ernest Simpson, prin. Fax 572-4525

De Soto S 300/K-12
PO Box 2807 72390 870-572-6717
E.G. Morris, hdmstr. Fax 572-9531

West Memphis, Crittenden, Pop. 28,181
West Memphis SD 6,100/K-12
PO Box 826 72303 870-735-1915
Bill Kessinger, supt. Fax 732-8643
west.grsc.k12.ar.us
East JHS 400/7-9
1151 Goodwin Ave 72301 870-735-2081
Arther Quarrels, prin. Fax 732-8583
West JHS 500/7-9
331 W Barton Ave 72301 870-735-3161
Jon Collins, prin. Fax 732-8566
West Memphis SHS 1,200/10-12
501 W Broadway St 72301 870-735-3660
Woodrow Burton, prin. Fax 732-8510
Wonder JHS 600/7-9
1401 Madison Ave 72301 870-735-8522
Dan Henderson, prin. Fax 732-8584

American Professional Institute Post-Sec.
103 S Avalon St 72301
Mid-South Community College Post-Sec.
2000 W Broadway St 72301 870-733-6722
Southern Institute of Cosmetology Post-Sec.
103 S Avalon St 72301 870-735-2800
West Memphis Christian S 300/K-12
1101 N Missouri St 72301 870-400-4000
John Armstrong, pres. Fax 400-4001

Wheatley, Saint Francis, Pop. 348
Palestine-Wheatley SD
Supt. — See Palestine
Palestine-Wheatley MS 100/5-8
PO Box 109 72392 870-457-2121
Bobbie Fingers, prin. Fax 457-4840

White Hall, Jefferson, Pop. 5,114
White Hall SD 3,100/K-12
1020 W Holland Ave 71602 870-247-2196
Gary Kees, supt. Fax 247-3707
whsd.arsc.k12.ar.us/
White Hall JHS 600/7-9
8106 Dollarway Rd 71602 870-247-2711
Vicki Scott, prin. Fax 247-4879
White Hall SHS 700/10-12
700 Bulldog Dr 71602 870-247-3255
Bill Mitchell, prin. Fax 247-2756
Other Schools – See Redfield

Wickes, Polk, Pop. 678
Wickes SD 400/K-12
130 School Dr 71973 870-385-7101
Allen Blackwell, supt. Fax 385-2238
warrior.dmsc.k12.ar.us/
Wickes JSHS 200/7-12
130 School Dr 71973 870-385-2366
Andy Curry, prin. Fax 385-7333
Other Schools – See Umpire

Williford, Sharp, Pop. 65
Twin Rivers SD 500/K-12
423 College Ave 72482 870-966-4331
David Gilliland, supt. Fax 966-4490
willifordschool.tripod.com/williford.html
Williford JSHS 7-12
423 College Ave 72482 870-966-4331
Roy Causbie, prin. Fax 966-4490
Other Schools – See Ravenden Springs

Wilson, Mississippi, Pop. 854
South Mississippi County SD 1,400/K-12
22 N Jefferson St 72395 870-655-8633
Rogers Ford, supt. Fax 655-8841
Rivercrest HS 400/9-12
1700 W State Highway 14 72395 870-655-8111
Mitzi S. Smith, prin. Fax 655-8507
Rivercrest JHS 200/7-8
1702 W State Highway 14 72395 870-655-8421
Mike Smith, prin. Fax 655-9980

Wynne, Cross, Pop. 8,569
Wynne SD 2,900/K-12
PO Box 69 72396 870-238-5000
Darrell Smith, supt. Fax 238-5011
wynne.k12.ar.us/
Wynne HS 800/9-12
PO Box 69 72396 870-238-5001
Carl Easley, prin. Fax 238-5009
Wynne JHS 700/6-8
PO Box 69 72396 870-238-5040
David Stepp, prin. Fax 238-5043

Yellville, Marion, Pop. 1,348
Yellville-Summit SD 1,000/K-12
1124 N Panther Ave 72687 870-449-4061
Dr. Jack Leatherman, supt. Fax 449-5003
yspanthers.k12.ar.us/
Yellville-Summit HS 300/9-12
1124 N Panther Ave 72687 870-449-4066
Ralph Bishop, prin. Fax 449-4773
Yellville-Summit MS 300/5-8
1124 N Panther Ave 72687 870-449-6533
Carl Jones, prin. Fax 449-4330

CALIFORNIA

CALIFORNIA DEPARTMENT OF EDUCATION
1430 N St, Sacramento 95814-5901
Telephone 916-319-0800
Fax 916-319-0100
Website http://www.cde.ca.gov

Superintendent of Public Instruction Jack O'Connell

CALIFORNIA BOARD OF EDUCATION
1430 N St, Sacramento 95814-5901

President Kenneth Noonan

COUNTY SUPERINTENDENTS OF SCHOOLS

Alameda County Office of Education
Sheila Jordan, supt. 510-887-0152
313 W Winton Ave, Hayward 94544 Fax 670-4146
www.acoe.org

Alpine County Office of Education
James Parsons, supt. 530-694-2230
43 Hawkside Dr Fax 694-2379
Markleeville 96120
www.alpinecoe.k12.ca.us

Amador County Office of Education
Michael Carey, supt. 209-257-5353
217 Rex Ave, Jackson 95642 Fax 257-5360
www.teachnet.k12.ca.us/

Butte County Office of Education
Don McNelis, supt. 530-532-5650
1859 Bird St, Oroville 95965 Fax 532-5762
www.bcoe.org/

Calaveras County Office of Education
John Brophy, supt. 209-736-4662
PO Box 760, Angels Camp 95222 Fax 736-2138
www.ccoe.k12.ca.us

Colusa County Office of Education
Kay Spurgeon, supt. 530-458-0350
146 7th St, Colusa 95932 Fax 458-8054
www.ccoe.net/

Contra Costa County Office of Education
Joseph Ovick, supt. 925-942-3388
77 Santa Barbara Rd Fax 472-0875
Pleasant Hill 94523
www.cocoschools.org/

Del Norte County Office of Education
Jan Moorehouse, supt. 707-464-0200
301 W Washington Blvd Fax 464-0238
Crescent City 95531
www.delnorte.k12.ca.us

El Dorado County Office of Education
Vicki Barber, supt. 530-622-7130
6767 Green Valley Rd Fax 621-2543
Placerville 95667
www.edcoe.k12.ca.us

Fresno County Office of Education
Larry Powell, supt. 559-265-3000
1111 Van Ness Ave, Fresno 93721 Fax 559-3053
www.fcoe.k12.ca.us

Glenn County Office of Education
Arturo Barrera, supt. 530-934-6575
311 S Villa Ave, Willows 95988 Fax 934-6576
www.glenncoe.org

Humboldt County Office of Education
Garry T. Eagles, supt. 707-445-7000
901 Myrtle Ave, Eureka 95501 Fax 445-7143
www.humboldt.k12.ca.us

Imperial County Office of Education
John Anderson, supt. 760-312-6464
1398 Sperber Rd, El Centro Fax 312-6565
www.icoe.k12.ca.us

Inyo County Office of Education
George Lozito, supt. 760-878-2426
PO Box G, Independence 93526 Fax 878-2279
www.inyo.k12.ca.us/

Kern County Office of Education
Larry Reider, supt. 661-636-4000
1300 17th St, Bakersfield 93301 Fax 636-4130
www.kern.org/

Kings County Office of Education
John Stankovich, supt. 559-584-1441
1144 W Lacey Blvd, Hanford 93230 Fax 589-7000
www.kings.k12.ca.us

Lake County Office of Education
David Geck, supt. 707-262-4101
1152 S Main St, Lakeport 95453 Fax 263-0197
www.lake-coe.k12.ca.us

Lassen County Office of Education
Robert Owens, supt. 530-257-2196
472-013 Johnstonville Rd Fax 257-2518
Susanville 96130
www.lassencoe.org

Los Angeles County Office of Education
Darline P. Robles, supt. 562-922-6111
9300 Imperial Hwy, Downey 90242 Fax 922-6768
www.lacoe.edu

Madera County Office of Education
Sally Frazier Ed.D., supt. 559-673-6051
28123 Avenue 14, Madera 93638 Fax 673-5569
www.maderacoe.k12.ca.us

Marin County Office of Education
Mary Jane Burke, supt. 415-472-4110
PO Box 4925, San Rafael 94913 Fax 491-6625
www.marin.k12.ca.us

Mariposa County Office of Education
Patrick Holland, supt. 209-742-0250
PO Box 8, Mariposa 95338 Fax 966-4549
www.mariposa.k12.ca.us/

Mendocino County Office of Education
Paul Tichinin, supt. 707-467-5000
2240 Old River Rd, Ukiah 95482 Fax 462-0379
www.mcoe.k12.ca.us

Merced County Office of Education
Lee Andersen, supt. 209-381-6600
632 W 13th St, Merced 95341 Fax 381-6767
www.mcoe.org

Modoc County Office of Education
Gary Jones, supt. 530-233-7100
139 Henderson St, Alturas 96101 Fax 233-5531
www.modoccoe.k12.ca.us/

Mono County Office of Education
Catherine Hiatt, supt. 760-932-7311
PO Box 477, Bridgeport 93517 Fax 932-7278
www.monocoe.k12.ca.us

Monterey County Office of Education
Dr. Nancy Kotowski, supt. 831-755-0300
PO Box 80851, Salinas 93912 Fax 755-6473
www.monterey.k12.ca.us

Napa County Office of Education
Barbara Nemko, supt. 707-253-6800
2121 Imola Ave, Napa 94559 Fax 253-6841
www.ncoe.k12.ca.us

Nevada County Office of Education
Terence McAteer, supt. 530-478-6400
112 Nevada City Hwy Fax 478-6410
Nevada City 95959
www.nevco.k12.ca.us/

Orange County Office of Education
William Habermehl, supt. 714-966-4000
PO Box 9050, Costa Mesa 92628 Fax 662-3570
www.ocde.k12.ca.us

Placer County Office of Education
Alfred Nobili, supt. 530-889-8020
360 Nevada St, Auburn 95603 Fax 888-1367
www.placercoe.k12.ca.us

Plumas County Office of Education
Michael Chelotti, supt. 530-283-6500
50 Church St, Quincy 95971 Fax 283-6509
www.pcoe.k12.ca.us

Riverside County Office of Education
David Long, supt. 951-826-6530
PO Box 868, Riverside 92502 Fax 826-6199
www.rcoe.k12.ca.us

Sacramento County Office of Education
David Gordon, supt. 916-228-2500
PO Box 269003 Fax 228-2403
Sacramento 95826
www.scoe.net

San Benito County Office of Education
Tim Foley, supt. 831-637-5393
460 5th St, Hollister 95023 Fax 637-0140
sbcoe.k12.ca.us

San Bernardino Co. Office of Education
Herbert Fischer, supt. 909-386-2400
601 N E St, San Bernardino 92410 Fax 386-2941
www.sbcss.k12.ca.us

San Diego County Office of Education
Randolph Ward Ed.D., supt. 858-292-3500
6401 Linda Vista Rd Fax 268-5864
San Diego 92111
www.sdcoe.k12.ca.us

San Francisco County Office of Education
Gwen Chan, supt., 555 Franklin St 415-241-6000
San Francisco 94102 Fax 241-6012
www.sfusd.edu

San Joaquin County Office of Education
Frederick Wentworth, supt. 209-468-4800
PO Box 213030, Stockton 95213 Fax 468-4975
www.sjcoe.org

San Luis Obispo Co. Office of Education
Julian Crocker, supt. 805-543-7732
3350 Education Dr Fax 541-1105
San Luis Obispo 93405
www.slocs.k12.ca.us

San Mateo County Office of Education
Dr. Jean Holbrook, supt. 650-802-5300
101 Twin Dolphin Dr Fax 802-5564
Redwood City 94065
www.smcoe.k12.ca.us

Santa Barbara County Office of Education
William Cirone, supt. 805-964-4711
PO Box 6307, Santa Barbara 93160 Fax 964-4712
www.sbceo.org

Santa Clara County Office of Education
Colleen Wilcox Ph.D., supt. 408-453-6500
1290 Ridder Park Dr Fax 453-6601
San Jose 95131
www.sccoe.org

Santa Cruz County Office of Education
Michael Watkins, supt. 831-476-7140
809 Bay Ave Ste H, Capitola 95010 Fax 476-5294
www.santacruz.k12.ca.us

Shasta County Office of Education
Tom Armelino, supt. 530-225-0200
1644 Magnolia Ave Fax 225-0329
Redding 96001
www.shastacoe.org/

Sierra County Office of Education
Mary Genasci, supt. 530-994-1044
PO Box 157, Sierraville 96126 Fax 994-1045
www.sierra-coe.k12.ca.us

Siskiyou County Office of Education
Kermith Walters, dir. 530-842-8400
609 S Gold St, Yreka 96097 Fax 842-8436
www.sisnet.ssku.k12.ca.us

Solano County Office of Education
Dee Alarcon, supt. 707-399-4400
5100 Business Center Dr Fax 863-4175
Fairfield
www.solanocoe.k12.ca.us

Sonoma County Office of Education
Dr. Carl Wong, supt. 707-524-2600
5340 Skylane Blvd Fax 578-0220
Santa Rosa 95403
www.sonoma.k12.ca.us

Stanislaus County Office of Education
Martin Petersen, supt. 209-525-4900
1100 H St, Modesto 95354 Fax 525-5147
www.stan-co.k12.ca.us

Sutter County Office of Education
Jeff Holland, supt. 530-822-2900
970 Klamath Ln, Yuba City 95993 Fax 671-3422
www.sutter.k12.ca.us

Tehama County Office of Education
Robert Douglas, supt. 530-527-5811
PO Box 689, Red Bluff 96080 Fax 529-4120
www.tehama.k12.ca.us

Trinity County Office of Education
James French, supt. 530-623-2861
PO Box 1256, Weaverville 96093 Fax 623-4489
www.tcoek12.org/

Tulare County Office of Education
Jim Vidak, supt. 559-733-6300
PO Box 5091, Visalia 93278 Fax 737-4378
www.tcoe.k12.ca.us

Tuolumne County Office of Education
Joseph Silva, supt. 209-536-2000
175 Fairview Ln, Sonora 95370 Fax 536-2003
www.tuolcoe.k12.ca.us

Ventura County Office of Education
Dr. Charles Weis, supt. 805-383-1900
5189 Verdugo Way Fax 383-1908
Camarillo 93012
www.vcss.k12.ca.us

Yolo County Office of Education
Jorge Ayala, supt. 530-668-6700
1280 Santa Anita Ct Ste 100 Fax 668-3848
Woodland 95776
www.ycoe.org

Yuba County Office of Education
Richard Teagarden, supt. 530-749-4900
935 14th St, Marysville 95901 Fax 741-6500
www.yuba.net/

PUBLIC, PRIVATE AND CATHOLIC SECONDARY SCHOOLS

Acampo, San Joaquin

Mokelumne River S — 300/K-12
18950 N Highway 99 95220 — 209-368-7271
Shannon Woodard, supt. — Fax 368-7569

Acton, Los Angeles, Pop. 1,471
Acton-Agua Dulce USD — 2,000/K-12
32248 Crown Valley Rd 93510 — 661-269-0750
Dr. Stan Halperin, supt. — Fax 269-0849
aadusd.k12.ca.us/
High Desert MS — 600/6-8
3620 Antelope Woods Rd 93510 — 661-269-0310
Gerald Watkins, prin. — Fax 269-9336
Vasquez HS — 600/9-12
33630 Red Rover Mine Rd 93510 — 661-269-0410
Martin Young, prin. — Fax 269-5325

Adelanto, San Bernardino, Pop. 24,360
Adelanto ESD — 5,500/K-8
PO Box 70 92301 — 760-246-8691
Chris Van Zee, supt. — Fax 246-4259
www.aesd.net
Columbia MS — 7-8
14409 Aster St 92301 — 760-530-1950
Dr. David Grohosky, prin. — Fax 530-1953
Other Schools – See Victorville

Agoura Hills, Los Angeles, Pop. 22,765
Las Virgenes USD
Supt. — See Calabasas
Agoura HS — 2,200/9-12
28545 Driver Ave 91301 — 818-889-1262
Larry Misel, prin. — Fax 597-0816
Lindero Canyon MS — 1,200/6-8
5844 Larboard Ln 91301 — 818-889-2134
Ronald Kaiser, prin. — Fax 889-9432

Alameda, Alameda, Pop. 70,576
Alameda City USD — 9,400/PK-12
2200 Central Ave 94501 — 510-337-7000
Ardella Dailey, supt. — Fax 522-6926
www.alameda.k12.ca.us
Alameda HS — 1,900/9-12
2201 Encinal Ave 94501 — 510-337-7022
Mike Janvier, prin. — Fax 521-4740
Alameda Science & Technical Institute — Vo/Tech
2200 Central Ave 94501 — 510-337-7059
Sean McPhetridge, prin. — Fax 337-7163
Chipman MS — 600/6-8
401 Pacific Ave 94501 — 510-748-4017
Jud Kempson, prin. — Fax 523-5304
Encinal HS — 1,200/9-12
210 Central Ave 94501 — 510-748-4023
Fax 521-4956
Lincoln MS — 900/6-8
1250 Fernside Blvd 94501 — 510-748-4018
Judith Goodwin, prin. — Fax 523-6217
Wood MS — 800/6-8
420 Grand St 94501 — 510-748-4015
Angela Ehrlich, prin. — Fax 523-8829
Alameda Adult S — Adult
2250 Central Ave 94501 — 510-522-3858
Peggy McCarthy, prin. — Fax 522-0846

Regional Occupational Center & Program
Supt. — None
Oakland-Alameda ROP — Vo/Tech
2200 Central Ave 94501 — 510-337-7094
Sean McPhetridge, dir. — Fax 337-7163

Alameda Beauty College — Post-Sec.
2318 Central Ave 94501 — 510-523-1050
Armstrong University — Post-Sec.
1301 Marina Village Pkwy 94501 — 510-865-1336
College of Alameda — Post-Sec.
555 Atlantic Ave 94501 — 510-522-7221
St. Joseph Notre Dame HS — 500/9-12
1011 Chestnut St 94501 — 510-523-1526
Anthony Aiello, prin. — Fax 523-2181

Alamo, Contra Costa, Pop. 12,277
San Ramon Valley USD
Supt. — See Danville
Stone Valley MS — 700/6-8
3001 Miranda Ave 94507 — 925-552-5640
Shawn McElroy, prin. — Fax 838-5680

Albany, Alameda, Pop. 15,994
Albany City USD — 3,400/K-12
904 Talbot Ave 94706 — 510-558-3750
Dr. William Wong, supt. — Fax 559-6560
www.albany.k12.ca.us
Albany HS — 1,200/9-12
603 Key Route Blvd 94706 — 510-558-2500
Ron Rosenbaum, prin. — Fax 559-6584
Albany MS — 900/6-8
1259 Brighton Ave 94706 — 510-558-3600
Robin Davis, prin. — Fax 559-6547
Albany Adult S — Adult
601 San Gabriel Ave 94706 — 510-559-6580
Barry Shapiro, prin. — Fax 559-6583

Alhambra, Los Angeles, Pop. 87,410
Alhambra City SD — 19,300/K-12
15 W Alhambra Rd 91801 — 626-308-2200
Dr. Julie Hadden, supt. — Fax 281-4020
www.alhambra.k12.ca.us
Alhambra HS — 9-12
101 S 2nd St 91801 — 626-308-2342
Maria Sanchez, prin. — Fax 308-2344
Keppel HS — 9-12
501 E Hellman Ave 91801 — 626-572-2242
Russell Yamanaka, prin. — Fax 572-2258
Alhambra Community Adult S — Adult
101 S 2nd St 91801 — 626-308-2309
Jenny Schulz Mitchell, prin. — Fax 308-2747
Garfield Community Adult S — Adult
217 N Garfield Ave 91801 — 626-308-2247
Ana Escobedo, dir. — Fax 308-2749
Keppel Community Adult S — Adult
501 E Hellman Ave 91801 — 626-572-2209
Other Schools – See Rosemead, San Gabriel

Alhambra Beauty College — Post-Sec.
PO Box 7494 91802 — 626-282-6433
Alliant International University — Post-Sec.
1000 S Fremont Ave 91803 — 626-284-2777
Everest College — Post-Sec.
2215 W Mission Rd 91803 — 626-979-4940
Platt College — Post-Sec.
1000 S Fremont Ave # A9W 91803 — 626-300-5444
Ramona Convent Secondary S — 600/7-12
1701 W Ramona Rd 91803 — 626-282-4151
Kathleen Pillon, prin. — Fax 281-0797

Aliso Viejo, Orange, Pop. 41,541
Capistrano USD
Supt. — See San Juan Capistrano
Aliso Niguel HS — 3,000/9-12
28000 Wolverine Way 92656 — 949-831-5590
Dr. Charles Salter, prin. — Fax 448-9854
Aliso Viejo MS — 1,200/6-8
111 Park Ave 92656 — 949-831-2622
Peggy Swanson, prin. — Fax 643-2784
Avila MS — 1,300/6-8
26278 Wood Canyon Dr 92656 — 949-362-0348
Chris Carter, prin. — Fax 362-9076

Soka University of America — Post-Sec.
1 University Dr 92656 — 949-480-4000

Alpaugh, Tulare
Alpaugh USD — 300/K-12
PO Box 9 93201 — 559-949-8413
Robert Hudson, supt. — Fax 949-8173
Alpaugh JSHS — 100/7-12
PO Box 9 93201 — 559-949-8413
Leonard Cruz, admin. — Fax 949-8173

Alpine, San Diego, Pop. 9,695
Alpine UNESD — 2,300/PK-8
1323 Administration Way 91901 — 619-445-3236
Greg Ryan, supt. — Fax 445-7045
alpineschooldistrict.net/
MacQueen MS — 800/6-8
2001 Tavern Rd 91901 — 619-445-3245
Katy Woodward, prin. — Fax 445-6503

Altadena, Los Angeles, Pop. 44,300
Pasadena USD
Supt. — See Pasadena
Eliot MS — 800/6-8
2184 Lake Ave 91001 — 626-794-7121
Jerry Cradduck, prin. — Fax 794-7238

Sahag-Mesrob Christian S — 300/PK-12
2501 Maiden Ln 91001 — 626-798-5020
Levon Filian, admin. — Fax 798-0036

Alta Loma, San Bernardino
Alta Loma ESD — 7,300/K-8
9390 Baseline Rd 91701 — 909-484-5151
Janet Morey, supt. — Fax 484-5155
www.alsd.k12.ca.us
Alta Loma JHS — 900/7-8
9000 Lemon Ave 91701 — 909-484-5100
Judith Neiuber, prin. — Fax 484-5105
Vineyard JHS — 1,000/7-8
6440 Mayberry Ave 91737 — 909-484-5120
Catherine Perry, prin. — Fax 484-5125

Chaffey JUNHSD
Supt. — See Ontario
Alta Loma HS — 2,900/9-12
8880 Baseline Rd 91701 — 909-989-5511
Jim Woolery, prin. — Fax 987-8321

American Christian Military Academy — 100/PK-12
6331 Haven Ave Ste 13 91737 — 909-988-5966
Pauline Stone, admin. — Fax 984-5277
Chaffey College — Post-Sec.
5885 Haven Ave 91737 — 909-987-1737

Altaville, Calaveras
Bret Harte UNHSD
Supt. — See Angels Camp
Bret Harte Union HS — 900/9-12
PO Box 208 95221 — 209-736-2507
Dean Way, prin. — Fax 736-8383

Alturas, Modoc, Pop. 2,902
Modoc JUSD — 1,000/K-12
906 W 4th St 96101 — 530-233-7201
Douglas Squellati, supt. — Fax 233-4362
www.modoc.k12.ca.us
Modoc HS — 300/9-12
900 N Main St 96101 — 530-233-7501
Tom O'Malley, prin. — Fax 233-7306
Modoc MS — 200/6-8
906 W 4th St 96101 — 530-233-7201
Lane Bates, prin. — Fax 233-7503
Modoc Community Adult S — Adult
802 N East St 96101 — 530-233-7201
Tom O'Malley, prin. — Fax 233-5158

Regional Occupational Center & Program
Supt. — None
Modoc ROP — Vo/Tech
139 Henderson St 96101 — 530-233-7102
Randy Wise, admin. — Fax 233-5561

American Canyon, Napa, Pop. 15,331
Napa Valley USD
Supt. — See Napa
American Canyon MS — 800/6-8
300 Benton Way 94503 — 707-259-8592
Roseann Gasser, prin. — Fax 259-8800

Anaheim, Orange, Pop. 331,804
Anaheim UNHSD — 32,800/7-12
501 N Crescent Way 92801 — 714-999-3511
Joseph Farley Ed.D., supt. — Fax 808-9090
www.auhsd.k12.ca.us/
Anaheim HS — 2,700/9-12
811 W Lincoln Ave 92805 — 714-999-3717
Ben Sanchez, prin. — Fax 772-6537
Ball JHS — 1,500/7-8
1500 W Ball Rd 92802 — 714-999-3663
Jason Allemann, prin. — Fax 563-9214
Brookhurst JHS — 1,400/7-8
601 N Brookhurst St 92801 — 714-999-3613
Russell Earnest, prin. — Fax 999-1764
Dale JHS — 1,400/7-8
900 S Dale Ave 92804 — 714-220-4210
Kirsten Schaefer, prin. — Fax 220-4076
Katella HS — 2,300/9-12
2200 E Wagner Ave 92806 — 714-999-3621
Eamon Kane, prin. — Fax 535-3991
Loara HS — 2,300/9-12
1765 W Cerritos Ave 92804 — 714-999-3677
Pam Krey, prin. — Fax 999-3703
Magnolia HS — 1,800/9-12
2450 W Ball Rd 92804 — 714-220-4221
Ken Fox, prin. — Fax 220-4233
Orangeview JHS — 1,300/7-8
3715 W Orange Ave 92804 — 714-220-4205
Dr. Kevin Astor, prin. — Fax 220-3023
Savanna HS — 2,200/9-12
301 N Gilbert St 92801 — 714-220-4262
Marsha Wagner, prin. — Fax 995-2544
South JHS — 1,600/7-8
2320 E South St 92806 — 714-999-3667
Christian Esperanza, prin. — Fax 999-3721
Sycamore JHS — 1,900/7-8
1801 E Sycamore St 92805 — 714-999-3616
Manuel Colon, prin. — Fax 776-3879
Western HS — 1,800/9-12
501 S Western Ave 92804 — 714-220-4040
Paul Sevillano, prin. — Fax 220-4027
Adult Education — Adult
1800 W Ball Rd 92804 — 714-999-5616
Lynn West, prin. — Fax 999-5650
Other Schools – See Cypress, La Palma

Orange USD
Supt. — See Orange
Canyon HS — 2,200/9-12
220 S Imperial Hwy 92807 — 714-532-8000
Greg Bowden, prin. — Fax 921-0278

Placentia-Yorba Linda USD
Supt. — See Placentia
Esperanza HS — 3,100/9-12
1830 N Kellogg Dr 92807 — 714-779-7870
Dave Flynn, prin. — Fax 693-7527

Regional Occupational Center & Program
Supt. — None
North Orange County ROP — Vo/Tech
385 N Muller St 92801 — 714-502-5800
Patricia Frank, supt. — Fax 535-0891

Acaciawood S — 100/2-12
2530 W La Palma Ave 92801 — 714-995-1800
Michio Miyake, prin.
American Career College — Post-Sec.
1200 N Magnolia Ave 92801 — 714-952-9066
Anaheim Discovery Christian HS — 100/6-12
622 N Gilbert St 92801 — 714-535-2535
Carol Caltharp, admin. — Fax 991-5418
Bethesda Christian University — Post-Sec.
730 N Euclid St 92801 — 714-517-1945
Brownson Technical School — Post-Sec.
1110 S Technology Cir Ste D 92805 — 714-774-9443
California Career School — Post-Sec.
1100 S Technology Cir 92805 — 714-635-6585
Career Academy of Beauty — Post-Sec.
663 N Euclid St 92801 — 714-776-8400
Connelly HS — 200/9-12
2323 W Broadway 92804 — 714-776-1717
Sr. Francine Gunther, prin. — Fax 776-2534
Everest College — Post-Sec.
511 N Brookhurst St Ste 300 92801 — 714-953-6500
Fairmont Preparatory Academy — 800/7-12
2200 W Sequoia Ave 92801 — 714-999-5055
Robert Mendoza, hdmstr. — Fax 999-0150
Integrity Christian S — 100/K-12
4905 E La Palma Ave 92807 — 714-693-2022
Shelly Kitada, admin.
ITT Technical Institute — Post-Sec.
525 N Muller St 92801 — 714-535-3700
Orange County Christian S — 200/PK-12
641 S Western Ave 92804 — 714-821-6227
Elaine Findley, admin. — Fax 952-8823
Saints of Glory S — 50/K-12
1210 W Park Ave 92801 — 714-875-9387
Ichiro Tsuruoka, admin. — Fax 817-0612
Servite HS — 9-12
1952 W La Palma Ave 92801 — 714-774-7575
Michael Brennan, prin. — Fax 774-1404
South Baylo University — Post-Sec.
1126 N Brookhurst St 92801 — 714-533-1495
Southern California Institute of Tech — Post-Sec.
1900 W Crescent Ave 92801 — 714-520-5552
Vineyard Christian S — 400/PK-12
5340 E La Palma Ave 92807 — 714-777-5462
Jim Wilkinson, prin. — Fax 777-5422
Westwood College — Post-Sec.
1551 S Douglass Rd 92806 — 714-704-2727

Anderson, Shasta, Pop. 10,528
Anderson UNHSD — 2,200/9-12
1469 Ferry St 96007 — 530-378-0568
Randy Palomino, supt. — Fax 378-0834
www.anderson.k12.ca.us/
Anderson HS — 800/9-12
1471 Ferry St 96007 — 530-365-2741
Mike Koontz, prin. — Fax 365-5446

Other Schools – See Cottonwood

Cascade UNESD 1,500/K-8
1645 Mill St 96007 530-378-7000
Dr. Wesley Smith, supt. Fax 378-7001
www.shastalink.k12.ca.us/cascade/
Anderson MS 600/6-8
1646 Ferry St 96007 530-378-7060
Carol Koppes, prin. Fax 378-7061

Happy Valley UNESD 600/K-8
16300 Cloverdale Rd 96007 530-357-2134
Lawrence Robins, supt. Fax 357-4143
www.shastalink.k12.ca.us/happyvalley/
Happy Valley MS 300/5-8
17480 Palm Ave 96007 530-357-2111
Steve Westaby, prin. Fax 357-4193

American Christian Academy 1,200/1-12
PO Box 805 96007 530-365-2950
Jim Rose, supt. Fax 365-2950

Angels Camp, Calaveras, Pop. 2,997
Bret Harte UNHSD 1,000/9-12
PO Box 7000 95221 209-736-8340
Michael Chimente, supt. Fax 736-8367
www.bhuhsd.k12.ca.us
Other Schools – See Altaville

Calaveras County Office of Education
PO Box 760 95222 209-736-4662
John Brophy, supt. Fax 736-2138
www.ccoe.k12.ca.us
Calaveras County Adult Education Adult
PO Box 760 95221 209-736-6033
W. Patrick Miller, dir. Fax 736-2138

Regional Occupational Center & Program
Supt. — None
Calaveras County ROP Vo/Tech
PO Box 760 95221 209-736-6033
W. Patrick Miller, dir. Fax 736-2138

Angwin, Napa, Pop. 3,503

Pacific Union College Post-Sec.
1 Angwin Ave 94508 707-965-6311
Pacific Union/College Prep S 100/9-12
1 Angwin Ave 94508 707-965-7272
Larry Aldred, prin. Fax 965-6689

Antelope, Sacramento, Pop. 70
Center JUSD 4,300/K-12
8408 Watt Ave 95843 916-338-6330
Dr. Kevin Jolly, supt. Fax 338-6411
www.centerusd.k12.ca.us
Center HS 1,700/9-12
3111 Center Court Ln 95843 916-338-6420
Ken Gardner, prin. Fax 338-6370
Other Schools – See Roseville

Dry Creek JESD
Supt. — See Roseville
Antelope Crossing MS 1,100/6-8
9200 Palmerson Dr 95843 916-745-2100
Greg O'Meara, prin. Fax 745-2135

Antioch, Contra Costa, Pop. 100,631
Antioch USD 21,200/K-12
PO Box 768 94509 925-706-4100
Dennis Goettsch, supt. Fax 757-2937
www.antioch.k12.ca.us
Antioch HS 2,800/9-12
700 W 18th St 94509 925-706-5300
Jeff Reich, prin. Fax 706-1875
Antioch MS 1,000/6-8
1500 D St 94509 925-706-5316
Stephanie Anello, prin. Fax 706-5430
Black Diamond MS 1,300/6-8
4730 Sterling Hill Dr 94531 925-776-5500
Clarence Isadore, prin. Fax 779-2600
Dallas Ranch MS 1,400/6-8
1401 Mount Hamilton Dr 94531 925-706-4491
Bob Sanchez, prin. Fax 706-1933
Deer Valley HS 3,500/9-12
4700 Lone Tree Way 94531 925-776-5555
Jo Ella Allen, prin. Fax 754-8094
Park MS 1,300/6-8
1 Spartan Way 94509 925-706-5314
Scott Bergerhouse, prin. Fax 706-2376
Antioch Adult & Community Education Ctr. Adult
820 W 2nd St 94509 925-706-5365
Jim Hollingsworth, prin. Fax 778-5843

Antioch Hilltop Christian SDA S 100/K-10
2200 Country Hills Dr 94509 925-778-0214
Monica Greene, prin. Fax 778-7418
Cornerstone Christian S 500/PK-12
1745 E 18th St 94509 925-779-2010
Fax 754-0769
Heritage Baptist Academy 200/K-12
5200 Heidorn Ranch Rd 94531 925-778-2234
Dr. John Mincy, admin.
Western Career College Post-Sec.
2157 Country Hills Dr 94509 925-522-7777

Anza, Riverside
Hemet USD
Supt. — See Hemet
Hamilton HS 500/7-12
57430 Mitchell Rd 92539 951-763-1865
Jim Allured, prin. Fax 763-5420

Apple Valley, San Bernardino, Pop. 65,156
Apple Valley USD 14,200/K-12
22974 Bear Valley Rd 92308 760-247-8001
Robert Seevers, supt. Fax 247-4103
www.avusd.org
Apple Valley HS 2,000/9-12
11837 Navajo Rd 92308 760-247-7206
Judy Jonas, prin. Fax 247-2092

Apple Valley MS 1,600/6-8
12555 Navajo Rd 92308 760-247-7267
Daryl Bell, prin. Fax 247-1226
Granite Hills HS 2,200/9-12
22900 Esaws Ave 92307 760-961-2290
Matt Schulenberg, prin. Fax 961-8755
Sitting Bull MS 6-8
19445 Sitting Bull Rd 92308 760-961-8479
Phyllis Carnahan, prin. Fax 240-8763
Vista Campana MS 1,700/6-8
20700 Thunderbird Rd 92307 760-242-7011
Sonia Waterman, prin. Fax 242-7005

Apple Valley Christian S 300/PK-12
22434 Nisqually Rd 92308 760-247-8412
Jon Watson, admin. Fax 247-6988
Valley Christian S 50/K-12
19923 Bear Valley Rd 92308 760-247-2933
Mary Ann Beaumont, prin. Fax 247-4903

Aptos, Santa Cruz, Pop. 9,061
Pajaro Valley USD
Supt. — See Watsonville
Aptos HS 1,700/9-12
100 Mariner Way 95003 831-688-6565
Diane Burbank, prin. Fax 688-6430
Aptos JHS 700/7-8
1001 Huntington Dr 95003 831-688-3234
Ray Blute, prin. Fax 728-8139

Cabrillo College Post-Sec.
6500 Soquel Dr 95003 831-479-6100

Arbuckle, Colusa, Pop. 1,912
Pierce JUSD 1,300/K-12
PO Box 239 95912 530-476-2892
Patricia Hamilton, supt. Fax 476-2289
www.pierce.k12.ca.us
Johnson JHS 300/6-8
938 Wildwood Rd 95912 530-476-3261
John Ithurburn, prin. Fax 476-2017
Pierce HS 400/9-12
960 Wildwood Rd 95912 530-476-2277
Doug Kaelin, prin. Fax 476-3285

Arcadia, Los Angeles, Pop. 56,153
Arcadia USD 10,100/K-12
234 Campus Dr 91007 626-821-8300
Mimi Hennessy, supt. Fax 821-8647
www.ausd.k12.ca.us
Arcadia HS 3,700/9-12
234 Campus Dr 91007 626-821-8370
David Vannasdall, prin. Fax 821-1712
Dana MS 800/6-8
234 Campus Dr 91007 626-821-8361
Joseph Fox, prin. Fax 447-1965
First Avenue MS 800/6-8
234 Campus Dr 91007 626-821-8362
Beverly Klatt, prin. Fax 446-1660
Foothills MS 800/6-8
234 Campus Dr 91007 626-821-8363
Patricia Hartline, prin. Fax 303-7983

First Presbyterian S 50/9-12
PO Box 2268 91077 626-294-9219
Lily Liu, dir. Fax 294-0362
Rio Hondo Preparatory S 200/6-12
PO Box 662080 91066 626-444-9531
Leslie Orsburn, prin. Fax 442-1113

Arcata, Humboldt, Pop. 16,914
Arcata ESD 500/K-8
1435 Buttermilk Ln 95521 707-822-0351
Douglas White, supt. Fax 822-6589
www.humboldt.k12.ca.us/arcata_sd/index.htm
Sunny Brae MS 300/6-8
1430 Buttermilk Ln 95521 707-822-5988
Lynda Yeoman, prin. Fax 822-7002

Northern Humboldt UNHSD
Supt. — See Mc Kinleyville
Arcata HS 1,000/9-12
1720 M St 95521 707-825-2400
Jay Kirschner, prin. Fax 825-2407
Pacific Coast HS 50/9-12
1720 M St 95521 707-825-2443
David Navarre, prin. Fax 825-2407

Humboldt State University Post-Sec.
1 Harpst St 95521 707-826-3011

Arleta, See Los Angeles
Los Angeles USD
Supt. — See Los Angeles
Arleta HS 9-12
14200 Van Nuys Blvd 91331 818-686-4100
Linda Calvo, prin. Fax 890-1040
New Technology HS @ Arleta 9-12
14200 Van Nuys Blvd 91331 818-686-4100
Fax 890-1040

Armona, Kings, Pop. 3,122
Armona UNESD 900/K-8
PO Box 368 93202 559-583-5000
Steve Bogan, supt. Fax 583-5004
www.kings.k12.ca.us/armona/
Parkview MS 400/5-8
11075 C St 93202 559-583-5020
Phil Holloway, prin. Fax 583-5030

Armona Union Academy 100/K-12
PO Box 397 93202 559-582-4468
Roderick Kerbs, prin. Fax 582-6609

Arroyo Grande, San Luis Obispo, Pop. 16,315
Lucia Mar USD 10,700/K-12
602 Orchard Ave 93420 805-474-3000
Deborah Flores Ph.D., supt. Fax 481-1398
www.lmusd.org/
Arroyo Grande HS 2,200/9-12
495 Valley Rd 93420 805-474-3200
Ryan Pinkerton, prin. Fax 473-4222

Mesa MS 600/7-8
2555 S Halcyon Rd 93420 805-474-3400
Barb LoCoco, prin. Fax 473-4396
Paulding MS 600/7-8
600 Crown Hill St 93420 805-474-3500
Gary Moore, prin. Fax 473-5525
Other Schools – See Nipomo, Pismo Beach

Regional Occupational Center & Program
Supt. — None
Santa Lucia ROP Vo/Tech
602 Orchard Ave 93420 805-474-3000
James Souza, dir. Fax 473-5593

Coastal Christian S 200/K-12
1220 Farroll Ave 93420 805-489-1213
Lance Tullis, admin. Fax 489-5394
Valley View Adventist Academy 100/K-10
230 Vernon St 93420 805-489-2687
Donald Ramey, prin. Fax 489-2704

Artesia, Los Angeles, Pop. 16,672
ABC USD
Supt. — See Cerritos
Ross MS 700/7-8
17707 Elaine Ave 90701 562-924-8331
Cheryl Bodger, prin. Fax 402-6145

Arvin, Kern, Pop. 14,724
Arvin UNESD 3,000/K-8
737 Bear Mountain Blvd 93203 661-854-6500
Ken Bergevin, supt. Fax 854-2362
arvin.k12.ca.us
Haven Drive MS 1,000/6-8
737 Bear Mountain Blvd 93203 661-854-6540
David Bowling, prin. Fax 854-1440

Kern UNHSD
Supt. — See Bakersfield
Arvin HS 2,500/9-12
PO Box 518 93203 661-854-5561
Blanca Cavazos, prin. Fax 854-5943

Atascadero, San Luis Obispo, Pop. 27,130
Atascadero USD 5,300/K-12
5601 West Mall 93422 805-462-4200
John Rogers, supt. Fax 466-2941
www.atas.k12.ca.us
Atascadero Fine Arts Academy 200/4-8
6100 Olmeda Ave 93422 805-460-2500
Cheryl Hockett, prin. Fax 460-2522
Atascadero HS 1,700/9-12
1 High School Hill Rd 93422 805-462-4300
Kimberley Spinks, prin. Fax 462-4387
Atascadero JHS 800/7-8
6501 Lewis Ave 93422 805-462-4360
Kirk Smith, prin. Fax 462-4373

North County Christian S 200/K-12
PO Box 6017 93423 805-466-4457
Rich Jessup, admin. Fax 466-7948

Atherton, San Mateo, Pop. 7,177
Menlo Park City ESD 2,100/K-8
181 Encinal Ave 94027 650-321-7140
Kenneth Ranella, supt. Fax 321-7184
www.mpcsd.org
Other Schools – See Menlo Park

Sequoia UNHSD
Supt. — See Redwood City
Menlo-Atherton HS 2,000/9-12
555 Middlefield Rd 94027 650-322-5311
Denise Plante, prin. Fax 323-1411

Menlo College Post-Sec.
1000 El Camino Real 94027 650-688-3753
Menlo S 800/6-12
50 Valparaiso Ave 94027 650-330-2000
Norman Colb, hdmstr. Fax 330-2002
Sacred Heart Prep S 500/PK-12
150 Valparaiso Ave 94027 650-322-1866
Richard Dioli, prin. Fax 322-7151

Atwater, Merced, Pop. 27,107
Atwater ESD 4,700/K-8
1401 Broadway Ave 95301 209-357-6100
Melinda Hennes, supt. Fax 357-6163
www.aesd.edu
Mitchell Senior ES 1,000/7-8
1753 5th St 95301 209-357-6124
Andrew Kersten, prin. Fax 357-6506

Merced UNHSD 10,200/9-12
3430 A St 95301 209-385-6413
Robert Fore Ph.D., supt. Fax 385-6442
muhsd.k12.ca.us
Atwater HS 1,800/9-12
PO Box 835 95301 209-357-6000
Dr. Linda Lucas, prin. Fax 357-6067
Buhach Colony HS 1,700/9-12
PO Box 753 95301 209-357-6600
Ernest Sopp, prin. Fax 357-6602
Other Schools – See Livingston, Merced

Auburn, Placer, Pop. 12,912
Auburn UNESD 2,600/K-8
255 Epperle Ln 95603 530-885-7242
Michele Schuetz, supt. Fax 885-5170
www.auburn.k12.ca.us/
Cain MS 900/6-8
150 Palm Ave 95603 530-823-6106
Laurie Hockerson, prin. Fax 823-0943

Placer UNHSD 4,700/9-12
PO Box 5048 95604 530-886-4400
Bart O'Brien, supt. Fax 886-4439
www.puhsd.k12.ca.us/
Placer HS 1,600/9-12
275 Orange St 95603 530-885-4581
Dave Horsey, prin. Fax 823-5770

Placer S for Adults Adult
390 Finley St 95603 530-885-8585
Judy McCoy, prin. Fax 823-1406
Other Schools – See Colfax, Foresthill, Loomis

Regional Occupational Center & Program
Supt. — None
Forty-Niner ROP Vo/Tech
360 Nevada St 95603 530-889-5940
Randy Scott, admin. Fax 887-1704

Forest Lake Christian S 700/K-12
12515 Combie Rd 95602 530-269-1535
Jean Schoellerman, dir. Fax 269-1541
Legacy Christian S 50/6-9
3885 Richardson Dr 95602 530-888-7100
Ken Kessenich, dir. Fax 888-7133
Pine Hills Adventist Academy 100/K-12
13500 Richards Ln 95603 530-885-9447
Don Litchfield, prin. Fax 885-5237

Avalon, Los Angeles, Pop. 3,334
Long Beach USD
Supt. — See Long Beach
Avalon S 700/K-12
PO Box 557 90704 310-510-0790
Sally Gregory, prin. Fax 510-2986

Avenal, Kings, Pop. 16,631
Reef-Sunset USD 2,600/K-12
205 N Park Ave 93204 559-386-9083
Dr. Nancy Mellor, supt. Fax 386-5303
www.kings.k12.ca.us/rsusd/
Avenal HS 500/9-12
601 E Mariposa St 93204 559-386-5253
Felipe Meraz, prin. Fax 386-9413
Reef-Sunset MS 600/6-8
608 N 1st Ave 93204 559-386-4128
Cherylin Stoeckmann, prin. Fax 386-4918

Avery, Calaveras, Pop. 900
Vallecito UNSD 900/K-8
PO Box 329 95224 209-795-8000
Glenn Sewell, supt. Fax 795-8005
www.vsd.k12.ca.us
Avery MS 400/6-8
PO Box 329 95224 209-795-8045
Fax 795-8048

Azusa, Los Angeles, Pop. 47,120
Azusa USD 11,800/K-12
PO Box 500 91702 626-967-6211
C. Cervantes McGuire, supt. Fax 858-6123
www.azusausd.k12.ca.us
Azusa HS 1,500/9-12
PO Box 500 91702 626-815-5212
David Williams, prin. Fax 815-5206
Center MS 900/6-8
PO Box 500 91702 626-815-5189
Bob Ware, prin. Fax 815-5534
Foothill MS 1,000/6-8
PO Box 500 91702 626-815-5132
Jackie Littrell, prin. Fax 815-1027
Slauson MS 1,000/6-8
PO Box 500 91702 626-815-5144
Armando Marentes, prin. Fax 815-5147
Other Schools – See Covina, Glendora

Azusa Pacific University Post-Sec.
901 E Alosta Ave 91702 626-969-3434

Baker, San Bernardino
Baker Valley USD 200/K-12
PO Box 460 92309 760-733-4567
Mark Kemp, supt. Fax 733-4605
www.baker.k12.ca.us/
Baker HS 100/9-12
PO Box 460 92309 760-733-4567
Baker JHS 50/7-8
PO Box 460 92309 760-733-4567
Baker Valley Adult S Adult
PO Box 460 92309 760-733-4567

Bakersfield, Kern, Pop. 295,536
Bakersfield CSD 28,200/K-8
1300 Baker St 93305 661-631-4600
Michael Lingo, supt. Fax 326-1485
www.bcsd.com
Chipman JHS 900/7-8
2905 Eissler St 93306 661-631-5210
Russell Taylor, prin. Fax 631-3229
Compton JHS 700/7-8
3211 Pico Ave 93306 661-631-5230
Linda Carbajal, prin. Fax 631-3168
Curran MS 1,000/6-8
1116 Lymric Way 93309 661-631-5240
Kim Edwards, prin. Fax 631-4538
Emerson MS 1,000/6-8
801 4th St 93304 661-631-5260
Kempton Coman, prin. Fax 631-3157
Sequoia MS 1,000/6-8
900 Belle Ter 93304 661-631-5940
Hugh McGowan, prin. Fax 631-3236
Sierra MS 900/6-8
3017 Center St 93306 661-631-5470
Tomas Prieto, prin. Fax 631-4541
Stiern MS 1,400/6-8
2551 Morning Dr 93306 661-631-5480
Warren Ramay, prin. Fax 631-3241
Washington MS 700/6-8
1101 Noble Ave 93305 661-631-5810
Armando Carrillo, prin. Fax 631-3172

Beardsley ESD 1,800/K-8
1001 Roberts Ln 93308 661-393-8550
Dean Bentley, supt. Fax 393-5965
www.beardsleyschool.org/
Beardsley JHS 400/7-8
1001 Roberts Ln 93308 661-392-9254
Rocky Johnson, prin. Fax 399-3925

Edison ESD 1,000/K-8
11518 School St 93307 661-363-5394
Cheri Sanders, supt. Fax 363-4631
www.edisonschooldistrict.org
Edison MS 400/4-8
721 S Edison Rd 93307 661-366-8216
Loreda Clevenger, prin. Fax 366-0922

Fairfax ESD 1,700/K-8
1500 S Fairfax Rd 93307 661-366-7221
Desiree Von Flue, supt. Fax 366-1901
www.fairfax.k12.ca.us/
Fairfax MS 600/6-8
1500 S Fairfax Rd 93307 661-366-4461
Terry Wolfe, prin. Fax 366-5831

Fruitvale ESD 3,300/K-8
7311 Rosedale Hwy 93308 661-589-3830
Dr. Carl Olsen, supt. Fax 589-3674
www.fruitvale.k12.ca.us/
Fruitvale JHS 800/7-8
2114 Calloway Dr 93312 661-589-3933
John Hefner, prin. Fax 588-3259

Greenfield UNESD 8,000/K-8
1624 Fairview Rd 93307 661-837-6000
Gary Rice, supt. Fax 832-2873
www.gfusd.k12.ca.us/
Greenfield MS 1,000/6-8
1109 Pacheco Rd 93307 661-837-6110
Scott McArthur, prin. Fax 832-7431
McKee MS, 205 McKee Rd 93307 600/6-8
Carol Schaefer, prin. 661-837-6060
Ollivier MS 1,000/6-8
7310 Monitor St 93307 661-837-6120
Sheila Johnson, prin. Fax 396-0963

Kern UNHSD 33,400/9-12
5801 Sundale Ave 93309 661-827-3154
Donald Carter, supt. Fax 827-3302
www.kernhigh.org/
Bakersfield HS 2,800/9-12
1241 G St 93301 661-324-9841
David Reese, prin. Fax 324-3401
Centennial HS 2,400/9-12
8601 Hageman Rd 93312 661-588-8601
David Olds, prin. Fax 588-8608
East Bakersfield HS 2,200/9-12
2200 Quincy Dr 93306 661-871-7221
John Gibson, prin. Fax 872-6980
Foothill HS 2,300/9-12
501 Park Dr 93306 661-366-4491
Brenda Lewis, prin. Fax 363-6223
Frontier HS 9-12
6401 Allen Rd, 661-829-1107
Dr. William Bruce, prin. Fax 829-1185
Golden Valley HS 1,800/9-12
801 Hosking Ave 93307 661-827-0800
Dean Juola, prin. Fax 827-0480
Highland HS 2,100/9-12
2900 Royal Scots Way 93306 661-872-2777
Robert Schneider, prin. Fax 871-6052
Liberty HS 2,700/9-12
925 Jewetta Ave 93312 661-587-0925
Pat Preston, prin. Fax 587-1299
North HS 2,300/9-12
300 Galaxy Ave 93308 661-399-3351
Bryon Schaefer, prin. Fax 393-5918
Ridgeview HS 2,300/9-12
8501 Stine Rd 93313 661-398-3100
Steve Holmes, prin. Fax 398-9758
Ruggenberg Career Center Vo/Tech
610 Ansol Ln 93306 661-366-4401
Lu Ellen Fleming, admin. Fax 363-0828
Schuetz Career Center Vo/Tech
8600 Shannon Dr 93307 661-827-4800
Jim Bennett, prin. Fax 827-4804
South HS 2,200/9-12
1101 Planz Rd 93304 661-831-3680
Librado Vasquez, prin. Fax 837-2756
Stockdale HS 2,400/9-12
2800 Buena Vista Rd 93311 661-665-2800
Ramon Hendrix, prin. Fax 665-0914
West HS 2,600/9-12
1200 New Stine Rd 93309 661-832-2822
Dean McGee, prin. Fax 831-5606
Bakersfield Adult HS Adult
501 S Mount Vernon Ave 93307 661-835-1855
Susan Handy, prin. Fax 835-9612
Other Schools – See Arvin, Lake Isabella, Shafter

Norris ESD 2,400/K-8
6940 Calloway Dr 93312 661-387-7000
Wallace McCormick Ph.D., supt. Fax 399-9750
www.norris.k12.ca.us/
Norris MS 800/6-8
6940 Calloway Dr 93312 661-387-7060
Dianne Doremus, prin. Fax 399-9356

Panama-Buena Vista UNSD 14,700/K-8
4200 Ashe Rd 93313 661-831-8331
Kip Hearron, supt. Fax 398-2141
www.pbvusd.k12.ca.us
Actis JHS 600/7-8
2400 Westholme Blvd 93309 661-833-1250
Bill Galloway, prin. Fax 833-9656
Stonecreek JHS 7-8
8000 Akers Rd 93313 661-834-4521
Darryl Johnson, prin. Fax 834-6358
Tevis JHS 900/7-8
3901 Pin Oak Park Blvd 93311 661-664-7211
Robert Machado, prin. Fax 664-9659
Thompson JHS, Fred L. 800/7-8
4200 Planz Rd 93309 661-832-8011
Jon Dean, prin. Fax 832-5165
Warren JHS 1,100/7-8
4615 Mountain Vista Dr 93311 661-665-9210
George Thornburgh, prin. Fax 665-9507

Regional Occupational Center & Program
Supt. — None
Kern County ROP Vo/Tech
1300 17th St 93301 661-824-9313
Armando Vazquez, admin. Fax 824-9316
Kern HSD ROP Vo/Tech
501 S Mount Vernon Ave 93307 661-831-3327
Sandra Banducci, prin. Fax 398-8239

Rio Bravo-Greeley UNESD 800/K-8
6521 Enos Ln, 661-589-2696
Ernie Unruh, supt. Fax 589-2218
www.rbgusd.k12.ca.us
Rio Bravo-Greeley MS 500/4-8
6601 Enos Ln, 661-589-2505
Art Folsom, prin. Fax 588-7204

Rosedale UNESD 4,500/K-8
2553 Old Farm Rd 93312 661-588-6000
Jamie Henderson, supt. Fax 588-6009
www.rosedale.k12.ca.us
Freedom MS 600/7-8
11445 Noriega Rd 93312 661-588-6044
Sue Lemon, prin. Fax 588-6048
Rosedale MS 600/7-8
12463 Rosedale Hwy 93312 661-588-6030
Maria Toretta, prin. Fax 588-6039

Standard ESD 2,700/K-8
1200 N Chester Ave 93308 661-392-2110
Erich Kwek Ed.D., supt. Fax 392-0681
www.standard.k12.ca.us
Standard MS 900/6-8
1222 N Chester Ave 93308 661-392-2130
Tonny Gisbertz, prin. Fax 392-2134

Vineland ESD 900/K-8
14713 Weedpatch Hwy 93307 661-845-3713
Adolph Wirth, supt. Fax 845-8449
www.vinelandschooldistrict.com
Sunset MS 400/5-8
8301 Sunset Blvd 93307 661-845-1320
Mike Gonzalez, prin. Fax 845-3952

Bakersfield Adventist Academy 200/K-12
3333 Bernard St 93306 661-871-1591
Alex Federowski, prin. Fax 871-1594
Bakersfield Christian HS 400/9-12
12775 Stockdale Hwy, 661-410-7000
David Meek, prin. Fax 410-7007
Bakersfield College Post-Sec.
1801 Panorama Dr 93305 661-395-4011
Bethel Apostolic Academy 100/K-12
1418 W Columbus St 93301 661-323-2851
Kevin Bradford, prin.
California State University-Bakersfield Post-Sec.
9001 Stockdale Hwy 93311 661-664-2011
Eternity Preparatory HS 100/9-12
48 Manor St 93308 661-327-5921
Mike Kirkland, hdmstr. Fax 327-5953
Garces Memorial HS 700/9-12
2800 Loma Linda Dr 93305 661-327-2578
Robert Garcia, prin. Fax 327-5427
Lyle's Bakersfield College of Beauty Post-Sec.
2935 F St 93301 661-327-9784
Maric College Post-Sec.
1914 Wible Rd 93304 866-574-5550
Milan Institute Post-Sec.
915 17th St 93301 661-325-8900
San Joaquin Valley College Post-Sec.
201 New Stine Rd 93309 661-834-1026
Santa Barbara Business College Post-Sec.
211 S Real Rd 93309 661-835-1100

Baldwin Park, Los Angeles, Pop. 78,861
Baldwin Park USD 17,500/PK-12
3699 Holly Ave 91706 626-962-3311
Mark Skvarna, supt. Fax 856-4901
www.bpusd.net
Baldwin Park HS 2,400/9-12
3900 Puente Ave 91706 626-960-5431
Luiz Cruz, prin. Fax 856-4059
Holland MS 800/6-8
4733 Landis Ave 91706 626-962-8412
James Rust, prin. Fax 813-6148
Jones JHS 700/7-8
14250 Merced Ave 91706 626-962-8312
Dawn Rust, prin. Fax 856-4291
Olive MS 600/6-8
13701 Olive St 91706 626-962-8416
Richard Novlett, prin. Fax 856-4568
Santa Fe S 400/3-8
4650 Baldwin Park Blvd 91706 626-856-1525
Burke Hamilton, prin. Fax 813-0614
Sierra Vista HS 2,100/9-12
3600 Frazier St 91706 626-962-1300
Jackie White, prin. Fax 856-4577
Sierra Vista JHS 900/7-8
13400 Foster Ave 91706 626-962-1300
Angela Salazar, prin. Fax 856-4577
Baldwin Park Adult & Community Education Adult
4640 Maine Ave 91706 626-939-4456
John Kerr, prin. Fax 856-4384
Baldwin Park Adult S Adult
13307 Francisquito Ave 91706 626-338-5115
John Kerr, prin. Fax 856-4384

Ballico, Merced
Ballico-Cressey ESD 300/K-8
PO Box 49 95303 209-632-5371
Jose Gonzalez, supt. Fax 632-8929
www.ballico.k12.ca.us
Ballico S 200/4-8
PO Box 49 95303 209-632-5371
Jose Gonzalez, prin. Fax 632-8929

Banning, Riverside, Pop. 29,308
Banning USD 4,800/K-12
161 W Williams St 92220 951-922-0200
Kathleen McNamara Ed.D., supt. Fax 922-0227
www.banning.k12.ca.us

Banning HS — 1,200/9-12
100 W Westward Ave 92220 — 951-922-0285
Dr. Jim Broncatello, prin. — Fax 922-2137
Nicolet MS — 800/7-8
101 E Nicolet St 92220 — 951-922-0280
Matt Valdivia, prin. — Fax 922-2748

Calvary Christian S — 200/K-12
PO Box 457 92220 — 951-849-1877
Richard Szydlowski, admin.

Barstow, San Bernardino, Pop. 23,737
Barstow USD — 7,200/K-12
551 S Avenue H 92311 — 760-255-6006
Jerry Bergmans, supt. — Fax 255-6007
www.barstow.k12.ca.us/
Barstow HS — 1,900/9-12
551 S Avenue H 92311 — 760-255-6105
Claire Ellis, prin. — Fax 256-4076
Barstow JHS — 1,100/7-8
551 S Avenue H 92311 — 760-255-6200
Carolyn Norman, prin. — Fax 255-6205

Barstow Community College — Post-Sec.
2700 Barstow Rd 92311 — 760-252-2411

Beaumont, Riverside, Pop. 20,530
Beaumont USD — 5,300/K-12
PO Box 187 92223 — 951-845-1631
Dr. Barry Kayrell, supt. — Fax 845-2319
www.beaumontusd.k12.ca.us/
Beaumont HS — 1,300/9-12
PO Box 187 92223 — 951-845-3171
Marilyn Saucedo, prin. — Fax 769-9289
Mountain View MS — 1,000/6-8
PO Box 187 92223 — 951-845-1627
Victor Kezer, prin. — Fax 845-8679
San Gorgonio MS — 200/6-8
PO Box 187 92223 — 951-769-4391
Brian Wood, prin. — Fax 769-8750

Bell, Los Angeles, Pop. 37,521
Los Angeles USD
Supt. — See Los Angeles
Bell HS — 4,700/9-12
4328 Bell Ave 90201 — 323-560-1800
Onofre DiStefano, prin. — Fax 560-7874

Cynthia's Beauty Academy — Post-Sec.
4130 Gage Ave 90201 — 323-560-2207

Bellflower, Los Angeles, Pop. 74,570
Bellflower USD — 15,400/K-12
16703 Clark Ave 90706 — 562-866-9011
Rick Kemppainen, supt. — Fax 866-7713
www.busd.k12.ca.us/
Bellflower MSHS — 3,300/7-12
15301 Mcnab Ave 90706 — 562-920-1801
Joseph Perry, prin. — Fax 804-2387
Bellflower Adult S — Adult
9242 Laurel St 90706 — 562-461-2218
Pat Dixon, prin. — Fax 461-2221
Other Schools – See Lakewood

American Beauty College — Post-Sec.
16512 Bellflower Blvd 90706 — 562-866-0728
St. John Bosco HS — 1,100/9-12
13640 Bellflower Blvd 90706 — 562-920-1734
Patrick Lee, prin. — Fax 867-5322

Bell Gardens, Los Angeles, Pop. 45,135
Montebello USD
Supt. — See Montebello
Bell Gardens HS — 3,400/9-12
6119 Agra St 90201 — 323-826-5151
Victor Chavez, prin. — Fax 887-7959
Bell Gardens IS — 2,200/5-8
5841 Live Oak St 90201 — 562-927-1319
Michael Rochin, prin. — Fax 806-5131
Suva IS — 1,500/5-8
6660 Suva St 90201 — 562-927-2679
Juan Mendez, prin. — Fax 806-5132
Bell Gardens Adult Education — Adult
6119 Agra St 90201 — 323-887-7955
Kathy Brendzal, prin. — Fax 887-7958
Ford Park Adult — Adult
7800 Scout Ave 90201 — 562-927-7750
Rosemary Grebel, prin. — Fax 806-5133

Faith Christian Academy — 100/K-12
6100 Florence Ave 90201 — 562-806-7540
Ray Marin, prin. — Fax 806-7574

Belmont, San Mateo, Pop. 24,522
Belmont-Redwood Shores ESD — 2,500/K-8
2960 Hallmark Dr 94002 — 650-637-4800
John McIntosh, supt. — Fax 637-4811
www.belmont.k12.ca.us
Ralston IS, 2675 Ralston Ave 94002 — 900/6-8
Maggie O'Reilly, prin. — 650-637-4880

Sequoia UNHSD
Supt. — See Redwood City
Carlmont HS — 2,000/9-12
1400 Alameda De Las Pulgas 94002 — 650-595-0210
Andrea Jenoff, prin. — Fax 591-6067

Notre Dame de Namur University — Post-Sec.
1500 Ralston Ave 94002 — 650-593-1601
Notre Dame HS — 700/9-12
1540 Ralston Ave 94002 — 650-595-1913
Rita Gleason, prin. — Fax 593-9330

Benicia, Solano, Pop. 26,489
Benicia USD — 4,900/PK-12
350 E K St 94510 — 707-747-8300
Shalee Cunningham Ph.D., supt. — Fax 748-0146
www.benicia.k12.ca.us
Benicia HS — 1,800/9-12
1101 Military W 94510 — 707-747-8325
JoAnn Severson, prin. — Fax 745-6769
Benicia MS — 1,300/6-8
1100 Southampton Rd 94510 — 707-747-8340
Susan Hutchinson, prin. — Fax 747-8349

Ben Lomond, Santa Cruz, Pop. 7,884
San Lorenzo Valley USD — 2,600/K-12
325 Marion Ave 95005 — 831-336-5194
Julie Haff, supt. — Fax 336-9531
www.slv.k12.ca.us
Other Schools – See Felton

Benton, Mono
Eastern Sierra USD
Supt. — See Bridgeport
High Desert Academy — 50/9-12
PO Box 956 93512 — 760-933-2315
Nancy Williard, prin. — Fax 933-2316

Berkeley, Alameda, Pop. 100,744
Berkeley USD — 8,900/K-12
2134 Mrtn Lther King Jr Way 94704 — 510-644-6206
Michele Lawrence, supt. — Fax 540-5358
www.berkeley.k12.ca.us
Berkeley HS — 3,100/9-12
2246 Milvia St 94704 — 510-644-6120
Jim Slemp, prin. — Fax 548-4221
King MS — 900/6-8
1781 Rose St 94703 — 510-644-6280
Kit Pappenheimer, prin. — Fax 644-8783
Longfellow Arts & Technology MS — 400/6-8
1500 Derby St 94703 — 510-644-6360
Rebecca Cheung, prin. — Fax 644-8707
Willard MS — 600/6-8
2425 Stuart St 94705 — 510-644-6330
Robert Ithurburn, prin. — Fax 548-4219
Berkeley Adult S — Adult
1701 San Pablo Ave 94702 — 510-644-6130
Margaret Kirkpatrick, prin. — Fax 644-6784

Acupuncture & Integrative Medicine Coll. — Post-Sec.
2550 Shattuck Ave 94704 — 510-666-8248
American Baptist Seminary of the West — Post-Sec.
2606 Dwight Way 94704 — 510-841-1905
Arrowsmith Academy — 100/9-12
2300 Bancroft Way 94704 — 510-540-0440
Saul Drevitch, hdmstr.
Berkeley City College — Post-Sec.
2020 Milvia St 94704 — 510-981-2800
Church Divinity School of the Pacific — Post-Sec.
2451 Ridge Rd 94709 — 510-204-0700
Dominican School of Philosophy/Theology — Post-Sec.
2301 Vine St 94708 — 510-849-2030
Franciscan School of Theology — Post-Sec.
1712 Euclid Ave 94709 — 510-848-5232
Graduate Theological Union — Post-Sec.
2400 Ridge Rd 94709 — 510-649-2400
Jesuit School of Theology at Berkeley — Post-Sec.
1735 Le Roy Ave 94709 — 510-549-5000
Pacific Lutheran Theological Seminary — Post-Sec.
2770 Marin Ave 94708 — 510-524-5264
Pacific School of Religion — Post-Sec.
1798 Scenic Ave 94709 — 510-848-0528
St. Marys College HS — 600/9-12
1294 Albina Ave 94706 — 510-526-9242
Peter Imperial, prin. — Fax 559-6277
Starr King School for the Ministry — Post-Sec.
2441 Le Conte Ave 94709 — 510-845-6232
University of California — Post-Sec.
110 Sproul Hall 94720 — 510-642-6000
Wright Institute — Post-Sec.
2728 Durant Ave 94704 — 510-841-9230

Bermuda Dunes, Riverside, Pop. 4,571

Christian School of the Desert — 500/PK-12
40700 Yucca Ln, — 760-345-2848
David Fulton, prin. — Fax 345-9948

Bethel Island, Contra Costa, Pop. 2,115

Paideia Academy — 50/4-12
3665 Hawthorne Dr # 210 94511 — 925-628-4033
John Crowder, admin.

Beverly Hills, Los Angeles, Pop. 35,078
Beverly Hills USD — 5,100/K-12
255 S Lasky Dr 90212 — 310-551-5100
Kari McVeigh, supt. — Fax 286-2138
www.beverlyhills.k12.ca.us
Beverly Hills HS — 2,200/9-12
241 S Moreno Dr 90212 — 310-229-3685
Joseph Guidetti, prin. — Fax 286-7446
Beverly Hills Adult S — Adult
255 S Lasky Dr 90212 — 310-551-5150
Twila Cook, prin. — Fax 277-6932

West Coast Ultrasound Institute — Post-Sec.
291 S La Cienega Blvd # 500 90211 — 310-289-5123

Bieber, Lassen
Big Valley JUSD — 300/K-12
PO Box 157 96009 — 530-294-5266
Mark Evans, supt. — Fax 294-5396
www.bigvalleyschool.org/
Big Valley HS — 100/9-12
PO Box 157 96009 — 530-294-5231
Mark Evans, prin. — Fax 294-5100
Big Valley IS — 100/4-8
PO Box 157 96009 — 530-294-5214
Ron Shaull, prin. — Fax 294-5109
Big Valley Adult S — Adult
PO Box 157 96009 — 530-294-5231

Big Bear Lake, San Bernardino, Pop. 6,158
Bear Valley USD — 3,200/K-12
PO Box 1529 92315 — 909-866-4631
Allan Pelletier, supt. — Fax 866-2040
www.bigbear.k12.ca.us
Big Bear MS — 600/7-8
PO Box 1607 92315 — 909-866-4634
Julie Chamberlin, prin. — Fax 866-5679
Other Schools – See Sugarloaf

Biggs, Butte, Pop. 1,803
Biggs USD — 800/K-12
300 B St 95917 — 530-868-1281
Lee Funk, supt. — Fax 868-1615
www.biggs.org/
Biggs HS, 300 B St 95917 — 300/9-12
Ralph Vandro, prin. — 530-868-5825
Biggs MS, 300 B St 95917 — 100/7-8
Ralph Vandro, prin. — 530-868-5825

Big Pine, Inyo, Pop. 1,158
Big Pine USD — 200/K-12
PO Box 908 93513 — 760-938-2005
Margaret Dame, supt. — Fax 938-2310
Big Pine HS — 100/9-12
PO Box 908 93513 — 760-938-2222
Margaret Dame, prin. — Fax 938-2310

Regional Occupational Center & Program
Supt. — None
Inyo County ROP — Vo/Tech
PO Box 970 93513 — 760-938-2936
Jim Meadowcroft, dir. — Fax 837-3127

Big Sur, Monterey
Pacific USD — 50/K-12
69325 Highway 1 93920 — 805-927-4507
Raeanna Thomasson, supt. — Fax 927-8123
www.pacificvalleyschool.com
Pacific Valley S — 50/K-12
69325 Highway 1 93920 — 805-927-4507
Raeanna Thomasson, prin. — Fax 927-8123

Bishop, Inyo, Pop. 3,606
Bishop JUNHSD — 800/9-12
301 N Fowler St 93514 — 760-872-3680
Maggie Kingsbury, supt. — Fax 872-6016
www.buhs.k12.ca.us
Bishop Union HS — 800/9-12
301 N Fowler St 93514 — 760-873-4275
Mike Garratt, prin. — Fax 873-3065

Bishop UNESD — 1,400/K-8
800 W Elm St 93514 — 760-872-4352
Richard Anthony, supt. — Fax 872-1063
www.buesd.k12.ca.us
Home Street MS — 500/6-8
201 Home St 93514 — 760-872-1381
Randy Cook, prin. — Fax 872-1877

Bloomington, San Bernardino, Pop. 15,116
Colton JUSD
Supt. — See Colton
Bloomington HS — 2,900/9-12
10750 Laurel Ave 92316 — 909-580-5004
Ignacio Cabrera, prin. — Fax 876-6326
Bloomington MS — 900/7-8
18829 Orange St 92316 — 909-876-4101
Dan Rocha, prin. — Fax 876-4195
Harris MS — 900/7-8
11150 Alder Ave 92316 — 909-876-6300
Sandy Torres, prin. — Fax 820-2238

Bloomington Christian S — 900/PK-12
PO Box 355 92316 — 909-877-2810
Yvonna Williams, admin. — Fax 877-2960

Blythe, Riverside, Pop. 22,130
Palo Verde USD — 3,600/K-12
295 N 1st St 92225 — 760-922-4164
Dr. Alan Jensen, supt. — Fax 922-5942
www.pvusd-bly.k12.ca.us
Blythe MS — 800/6-8
825 N Lovekin Blvd 92225 — 760-922-1300
Ron Chavez, prin. — Fax 922-3748
Palo Verde Valley HS — 900/9-12
667 N Lovekin Blvd 92225 — 760-922-7148
Michael Gilmore, prin. — Fax 922-8916
Twin Palms Continuation & Adult S — Adult
190 N 5th St 92225 — 760-922-4884
Robert Jeppson, prin. — Fax 922-1177

Palo Verde College — Post-Sec.
1 College Dr 92225 — 760-921-5500

Bonsall, San Diego, Pop. 1,881
Bonsall UNESD — 1,600/K-8
31505 Old River Rd 92003 — 760-631-5200
Fax 941-4409
www.sdcoe.k12.ca.us/districts/bonsall/
Sullivan MS — 600/6-8
7350 W Lilac Rd 92003 — 760-631-5210
Lori Cummins, prin. — Fax 631-5230

Boonville, Mendocino
Anderson Valley USD — 600/PK-12
PO Box 457 95415 — 707-895-3774
James Collins, supt. — Fax 895-2665
www.avusd.k12.ca.us
Anderson Valley JSHS — 300/7-12
PO Box 130 95415 — 707-895-3496
James Collins, prin. — Fax 895-3153
Anderson Valley Adult S — Adult
PO Box 457 95415 — 707-895-2953
Donna Pierson-Pugh, prin. — Fax 895-2665

Boron, Kern, Pop. 2,101
Muroc JUSD
Supt. — See North Edwards
Boron JSHS — 300/7-12
26831 Prospect St 93516 — 760-762-5121
Paul Kostopoulos, prin. — Fax 762-5040

Borrego Springs, San Diego, Pop. 2,244
Borrego Springs USD — 500/K-12
1315 Palm Canyon Dr 92004 — 760-767-5357
Consuela Smith, supt. — Fax 767-0494
www.sdcoe.k12.ca.us/districts/borrego/
Borrego Springs HS — 200/9-12
1315 Palm Canyon Dr 92004 — 760-767-5335
Gary Gernandt, prin. — Fax 767-5999
Borrego Springs MS — 100/6-8
1315 Palm Canyon Dr 92004 — 760-767-5335
Gary Gernandt, prin. — Fax 767-5999

Brawley, Imperial, Pop. 22,433
Brawley ESD 3,800/K-8
261 D St 92227 760-344-2330
Terri L. Decker, supt. Fax 344-8928
www.icoe.k12.ca.us/ICOE/Schools/BESD/
Worth JHS 800/7-8
385 D St 92227 760-344-2153
Gerardo Roman, prin. Fax 351-5043

Brawley UNHSD 1,900/9-12
480 N Imperial Ave 92227 760-312-5819
Roberto Moreno, supt. Fax 344-9520
www.brawleyhigh.org
Brawley HS 1,800/9-12
480 N Imperial Ave 92227 760-312-5819
Tony Munguia, prin. Fax 344-9520

Brawley Christian Academy 100/PK-12
430 N 2nd St 92227 760-344-3911
Robert Feist, prin. Fax 344-5864

Brea, Orange, Pop. 38,465
Brea-Olinda USD 6,200/K-12
PO Box 300 92822 714-990-7800
Tim Harvey, supt. Fax 529-2137
bousd.k12.ca.us
Brea JHS 1,100/7-8
400 N Brea Blvd 92821 714-990-7500
Pam Gallarda, prin. Fax 990-7585
Brea-Olinda HS 2,100/9-12
789 Wildcat Way 92821 714-990-7850
Jerry Halpin, prin. Fax 990-7547

Brea School of Exceptional Children Post-Sec.
875 N Brea Blvd 92821
Carbon Canyon Christian S 100/K-12
5600 Carbon Canyon Rd 92823 714-524-5433
Donna Daigle, prin. Fax 524-8710

Brentwood, Contra Costa, Pop. 43,794
Brentwood UNESD 6,500/K-8
255 Guthrie Ln 94513 925-513-6300
J. Douglas Adams, supt. Fax 634-8583
www.brentwood.k12.ca.us
Adams MS 6-8
401 American Ave 94513 925-513-6480
Adam Clark, prin. Fax 513-3470
Bristow MS 1,000/6-8
855 Minnesota Ave 94513 925-513-6460
Sara Branstetter, prin. Fax 516-8725
Hill MS 1,100/6-8
140 Birch St 94513 925-513-6440
Eric Prater, prin. Fax 513-0696

Liberty UNHSD 5,300/9-12
20 Oak St 94513 925-634-2166
Daniel Smith, supt. Fax 634-1687
www.libertyuhsd.k12.ca.us
Liberty HS 2,700/9-12
850 2nd St 94513 925-634-3521
Tim Halloran, prin. Fax 513-2739
Liberty Adult Education S Adult
929 2nd St 94513 925-634-2565
Gene Clare, dir. Fax 634-5317
Other Schools – See Oakley

Gateway Christian S 200/K-12
2401 Shady Willow Ln 94513 925-634-0493
David Stutzman, admin. Fax 634-0402

Bridgeport, Mono
Eastern Sierra USD 500/K-12
PO Box 575 93517 760-932-7443
Larry Plew, supt. Fax 932-7140
www.esusd.org
Eastern Sierra Academy 50/9-12
PO Box 733 93517 760-932-7161
Roger Yost, prin. Fax 932-7162
Other Schools – See Benton, Coleville, Lee Vining

Mono County Office of Education
PO Box 477 93517 760-932-7311
Catherine Hiatt, supt. Fax 932-7278
www.monocoe.k12.ca.us
Other Schools – See Mammoth Lakes

Regional Occupational Center & Program
Supt. — None
Mono County ROP Vo/Tech
PO Box 477 93517 760-932-7311
Edward Inwood, dir. Fax 932-7278

Brisbane, San Mateo, Pop. 3,556
Brisbane ESD 600/K-8
1 Solano St 94005 415-467-0550
Steve Waterman, supt. Fax 467-2914
brisbane.ca.campusgrid.net/home
Lipman MS 200/6-8
1 Solano St 94005 415-467-9541
Pennie Pine, prin. Fax 467-5073

Broderick, See West Sacramento
Washington USD
Supt. — See West Sacramento
Golden State MS 1,000/7-8
1100 Carrie St 95605 916-375-7700
Paul Orlando, prin. Fax 375-7709

Buellton, Santa Barbara, Pop. 4,293
Buellton UNESD 400/K-8
595 2nd St 93427 805-686-2767
Tom Cooper, supt. Fax 686-2719
Jonata MS 200/6-8
301 2nd St 93427 805-688-4222
Patricia Garrett, prin. Fax 688-6611

Buena Park, Orange, Pop. 79,174
Buena Park ESD 6,300/K-8
6885 Orangethorpe Ave 90620 714-522-8412
Lew Becker, supt. Fax 994-1506
www.ocde.k12.ca.us/bpsd
Buena Park JHS 1,300/7-8
6931 Orangethorpe Ave 90620 714-522-8491
Debra Diaz, prin. Fax 523-1602

Fullerton JUNHSD
Supt. — See Fullerton
Buena Park HS 2,100/9-12
8833 Academy Dr 90621 714-992-8600
Ben Wolf, prin. Fax 992-8619

Bethel Baptist Academy 100/K-12
8433 Philodendron Way 90620 714-521-5586
Sharon Wallace, admin.
Speech and Language Development Ctr 300/K-12
8699 Holder St 90620 714-821-3620
Dawn O'Connor, prin.

Burbank, Los Angeles, Pop. 104,108
Burbank USD 15,100/K-12
1900 W Olive Ave 91506 818-729-4400
Dr. Gregory Bowman, supt. Fax 729-4483
www.burbank.k12.ca.us
Burbank HS 2,500/9-12
902 N 3rd St 91502 818-558-4700
Bruce Osgood, prin. Fax 845-6122
Burbank MS 1,100/6-8
3700 W Jeffries Ave 91505 818-558-4646
Anita Schackmann, prin. Fax 842-3727
Burroughs HS 2,500/9-12
1920 W Clark Ave 91506 818-558-4777
Emilio Urioste, prin. Fax 846-9268
Jordan MS 1,100/6-8
420 S Mariposa St 91506 818-558-4622
Sharon Cuseo, prin. Fax 843-3509
Muir MS 1,500/6-8
1111 N Kenneth Rd 91504 818-558-5320
Dr. Daniel Hacking, prin. Fax 841-4637
Burbank Adult S Adult
3811 W Allan Ave 91505 818-558-4611
Dr. Cherise Moore, dir. Fax 558-4620

Bellarmine Jefferson HS 400/9-12
465 E Olive Ave 91501 818-972-1400
Sr. Cheryl Milner, prin. Fax 559-6387
Elegante Beauty College Post-Sec.
200 N San Fernando Blvd 91502 818-954-8894
Holmes Institute Post-Sec.
2600 W Magnolia Blvd 91505 818-556-7757
Intercoast Colleges Post-Sec.
401 S Glenoaks Blvd Ste 211 91502 818-500-8400
Make-up Designory Post-Sec.
129 S San Fernando Blvd 91502 818-729-9420
Providence HS 600/9-12
511 S Buena Vista St 91505 818-846-8141
Michele Schulte, prin. Fax 843-8421
Woodbury University Post-Sec.
7500 N Glenoaks Blvd 91504 818-767-0888

Burlingame, San Mateo, Pop. 27,380
Burlingame ESD 2,400/K-8
1825 Trousdale Dr 94010 650-259-3800
Sonny DaMarto Ed.D., supt. Fax 259-3820
www.burlingameschools.com/
Burlingame IS 800/6-8
1715 Quesada Way 94010 650-259-3830
Ted Barone, prin. Fax 259-3843

San Mateo UNHSD
Supt. — See San Mateo
Burlingame HS 1,400/9-12
400 Carolan Ave 94010 650-558-2899
Matt Biggar, prin. Fax 762-0122

Mercy HS 500/9-12
2750 Adeline Dr 94010 650-343-3631
Laura Held, prin. Fax 343-3358
Mills Peninsula Health Services Post-Sec.
1783 El Camino Real 94010 650-696-5678

Burney, Shasta, Pop. 3,423
Fall River JUSD 1,400/K-12
20375 Tamarack Ave 96013 530-335-4538
Larry Snelling, supt. Fax 335-3115
www.shastalink.k12.ca.us/frjusd/
Burney JSHS 300/7-12
37571 Mountain View Rd 96013 530-335-4576
Larry Hutchinson, prin. Fax 335-3554
Other Schools – See Mc Arthur

Byron, Contra Costa
Byron UNESD 1,500/K-8
14301 Byron Hwy 94514 925-634-6644
Thomas Meyer, supt. Fax 634-9421
www.byron.k12.ca.us
Excelsior MS 500/6-8
14301 Byron Hwy 94514 925-634-2128
Calvin Jones, prin. Fax 634-5120

Calabasas, Los Angeles, Pop. 21,908
Las Virgenes USD 12,100/K-12
4111 Las Virgenes Rd 91302 818-880-4000
Dr. Donald Zimring, supt. Fax 880-4200
www.lvusd.k12.ca.us
Calabasas HS 2,000/9-12
22855 Mulholland Hwy 91302 818-222-7177
Vince Jantz, prin. Fax 223-8477
Stelle MS 1,000/6-8
22450 Mulholland Hwy 91302 818-224-4107
Mary Sistrunk, prin. Fax 224-4989
Wright MS 900/6-8
4029 Las Virgenes Rd 91302 818-880-4614
Steve Rosentsweig, prin. Fax 878-0453
Other Schools – See Agoura Hills

Arbor Academy 200/1-12
26245 Hatmor Dr 91302 818-880-6029
Jill Leibert, admin.
Mesivta of Greater Los Angeles S 50/9-12
25115 Mureau Rd 91302 818-876-0550
Rabbi Shlomo Gottesman, dir. Fax 876-0537
Viewpoint S 1,200/K-12
23620 Mulholland Hwy 91302 818-340-2901
Dr. Robert Dworkoski, hdmstr. Fax 591-0834

Calexico, Imperial, Pop. 36,005
Calexico USD 9,300/K-12
PO Box 792 92232 760-768-3888
David Alvarez, supt. Fax 357-0842
www.calexico.k12.ca.us/
Calexico SHS 2,000/10-12
PO Box 792 92232 760-768-3980
Gilbert Barraza, prin. Fax 357-9640
Camarena JHS 7-9
PO Box 792 92232 760-768-3808
Sergio Pesqueira, prin. Fax 768-3858
De Anza JHS 1,200/7-9
PO Box 792 92232 760-768-3950
Rebecca Ayala-Rodriguez, prin. Fax 357-8251
Moreno JHS 1,200/7-9
PO Box 792 92232 760-768-3960
Kevin Dorward, prin. Fax 768-1905
Morales Adult Education Center Adult
PO Box 792 92232 760-357-7471
Clara Rendon, prin. Fax 357-7246

Calexico Mission S 400/K-12
601 E 1st St 92231 760-357-3711
Susan Smith, prin. Fax 357-3713
Vincent Memorial HS 200/9-12
525 Sheridan St 92231 760-357-3461
Sr. Lilia Barba, prin. Fax 357-0902

California City, Kern, Pop. 11,790
Mojave USD
Supt. — See Mojave
California City MS 400/6-8
9736 Redwood Blvd 93505 760-373-3241
Amy Shermer, prin. Fax 373-1355

Calimesa, Riverside, Pop. 7,491

Mesa Grande Academy 400/K-12
975 Fremont St Ste A 92320 909-795-1112
Alfred Riddle, prin. Fax 795-1653

Calipatria, Imperial, Pop. 7,725
Calipatria USD 1,300/K-12
501 W Main St 92233 760-348-2892
Douglas Kline, supt. Fax 344-8926
calipatria.k12.ca.us/
Calipatria HS 400/9-12
601 W Main St 92233 760-348-2254
Virginia Calsada Medina, prin. Fax 348-2431
Young MS 300/5-8
220 S International Blvd 92233 760-348-2842
Joe Derma, prin. Fax 348-2848

Calistoga, Napa, Pop. 5,190
Calistoga JUSD 900/K-12
1520 Lake St 94515 707-942-4703
Jeff Johnson, supt. Fax 942-6589
www.calistoga.k12.ca.us
Calistoga JSHS 400/7-12
1608 Lake St 94515 707-942-6278
Kevin Eisenberg, prin. Fax 942-6592

Camarillo, Ventura, Pop. 61,576
Oxnard UNHSD
Supt. — See Oxnard
Camarillo HS 2,400/9-12
4660 Mission Oaks Blvd 93012 805-389-6406
Glenn Lipman, prin. Fax 484-8087

Pleasant Valley SD 6,900/PK-8
600 Temple Ave 93010 805-482-2763
Kenneth Moffett, supt. Fax 987-5511
www.pvsd.k12.ca.us
Las Colinas MS 900/6-8
5750 Fieldcrest Dr 93012 805-484-0461
Pat Fitzgerald, prin. Fax 482-2443
Los Altos MS 600/6-8
700 Temple Ave 93010 805-482-4656
Sue Eastman, prin. Fax 388-9059
Monte Vista MS 800/6-8
888 Lantana St 93010 805-482-8891
Sara Davis, prin. Fax 987-8951

Regional Occupational Center & Program
Supt. — None
Ventura County ROP Vo/Tech
465 Horizon Way 93010 805-388-4421
Peggy Velarde, prin. Fax 388-4428

California State University Channel Isle Post-Sec.
1 University Dr 93012 805-437-8400
Cornerstone Christian S 600/PK-12
1777 Arneill Rd 93010 805-987-8621
Lory Selby, supt. Fax 987-8208

Cambria, San Luis Obispo, Pop. 5,382
Coast USD 900/K-12
2950 Santa Rosa Creek Rd 93428 805-927-3880
Pamela Martens, supt. Fax 927-0312
www.cambria.k12.ca.us
Coast Union HS 400/9-12
2950 Santa Rosa Creek Rd 93428 805-927-3889
Karl Dearie, prin. Fax 924-2933
Santa Lucia MS 200/6-8
2850 Schoolhouse Ln 93428 805-927-3693
Denis deClercq, prin. Fax 927-4615

Cameron Park, El Dorado, Pop. 11,897
Buckeye UNESD
Supt. — See Shingle Springs
Camerado Springs MS 700/6-8
2480 Merrychase Dr 95682 530-677-1658
Meg Enns, prin. Fax 677-9537

Campbell, Santa Clara, Pop. 37,042
Campbell UNESD 6,800/K-8
155 N 3rd St 95008 408-364-4200
Dr. Johanna VanderMolen, supt. Fax 341-7280
www.campbellusd.k12.ca.us

Campbell MS 900/5-8
295 Cherry Ln 95008 408-364-4222
Susan Zimmer, prin. Fax 341-7150
Other Schools – See Los Gatos, San Jose

Campbell UNHSD
Supt. — See San Jose
Westmont HS 1,800/9-12
4805 Westmont Ave 95008 408-378-1500
Owen Hege, prin. Fax 379-1720

Pioneer Family Academy 200/K-12
1799 Winchester Blvd 95008 408-313-5113
Kathy Kistler, hdmstr.
Veritas Christian Academy 50/K-12
400 Llewellyn Ave Unit 2 95008 408-984-1255
David Wallace, prin. Fax 871-7929

Canoga Park, See Los Angeles
Los Angeles USD
Supt. — See Los Angeles
Canoga Park HS 2,300/9-12
6850 Topanga Canyon Blvd 91303 818-673-1300
Pamela Hamashita, prin. Fax 702-8942
Columbus MS 1,300/6-8
22250 Elkwood St 91304 818-702-1200
Ann Allocca, prin. Fax 348-2894
Sutter MS 1,500/6-8
7330 Winnetka Ave 91306 818-773-5800
Michael Smith, prin. Fax 341-3039

AGBU Manoogian-Demirdjian S 800/K-12
6844 Oakdale Ave 91306 818-883-2428
Hagop Hagopian, prin. Fax 883-8353
Coutin S 100/5-12
7119 Owensmouth Ave 91303 818-992-0301
Karen Cano, prin. Fax 992-4373
Faith Baptist S 1,300/PK-12
7644 Farralone Ave 91304 818-340-6131
Dr. Roland Rasmussen, dir. Fax 592-0279

Canyon Country, See Santa Clarita
William S. Hart UNHSD
Supt. — See Santa Clarita
Canyon HS 2,800/9-12
19300 Nadal St 91351 661-252-6110
Bob Messina, prin. Fax 251-8512
Sierra Vista JHS 1,400/7-8
19425 Stillmore St 91351 661-252-3113
Randy Parker, prin. Fax 252-2790

Clarita Career College Post-Sec.
27125 Sierra Hwy Ste 329 91351 661-252-1864
Cornerstone Christian S 200/1-12
27945 Oakgale Ave 91351 661-251-9732
Dean Hadfield, prin.
Santa Clarita Christian S 600/K-12
27249 Luther Dr 91351 661-252-7371
Lee Duncan, admin. Fax 252-4354

Canyon Lake, Riverside, Pop. 11,287

Hope Learning Academy 50/7-12
24370 Canyon Lake Dr N # 10 92587 951-244-5038
Rev. Chris Suitt, admin. Fax 244-5038

Capitola, Santa Cruz, Pop. 9,553
Regional Occupational Center & Program
Supt. — None
Santa Cruz County ROP Vo/Tech
809 Bay Ave Ste H 95010 831-479-5335
Robert Rieber, dir. Fax 462-6457

Soquel UNESD 1,900/K-8
620 Monterey Ave 95010 831-464-5630
Kathleen Howard, supt. Fax 475-5196
www.soqueldo.santacruz.k12.ca.us/
New Brighton MS 700/6-8
250 Washburn Ave 95010 831-464-5660
Robert Martin, prin.

Carlsbad, San Diego, Pop. 90,773
Carlsbad USD 9,600/K-12
6225 El Camino Real 92009 760-331-5000
John Roach Ed.D., supt. Fax 331-5094
www.carlsbadusd.k12.ca.us
Aviara Oaks MS 700/6-8
6880 Ambrosia Ln, 760-331-6100
Mare Watson, prin. Fax 438-7894
Calavera Hills MS 300/6-8
4104 Tamarack Ave, 760-331-6400
Erik Trogden, prin. Fax 729-3040
Carlsbad HS 3,000/9-12
3557 Lancer Way 92008 760-331-5100
Maggie Stanchi, prin. Fax 729-6830
Valley MS 900/6-8
1645 Magnolia Ave 92008 760-331-5300
Carolyn Millikin, prin. Fax 720-2326

San Dieguito UNHSD
Supt. — See Encinitas
La Costa Canyon HS 2,700/9-12
3451 Camino de los Coches 92009 760-436-6136
Amy Carlin, prin. Fax 943-3539

Applied Professional Training Post-Sec.
PO Box 131717 92013 800-431-8488
Army and Navy Academy 400/7-12
PO Box 3000 92018 760-729-2385
Stephen Bliss, pres. Fax 720-7121
Gemological Institute of America Post-Sec.
5345 Armada Dr 92008 760-603-4000

Carmel, Monterey, Pop. 4,084
Carmel USD 2,200/K-12
PO Box 222700 93922 831-624-1546
Marvin Biasotti, supt. Fax 626-4052
www.carmelunified.org
Carmel HS 800/9-12
PO Box 222780 93922 831-624-1821
Karl Pallastrini, prin. Fax 626-4313

Carmel MS 600/6-8
PO Box 222740 93922 831-624-2785
Edmund Gross, prin. Fax 624-0839
Carmel Adult Education Adult
PO Box 222700 93922 831-624-1714
Patricia Beebe, prin. Fax 624-8747

Carmichael, Sacramento, Pop. 49,900
San Juan USD 43,500/PK-12
PO Box 477 95609 916-971-7700
Steven Enoch, supt. Fax 971-7758
www.sanjuan.edu
Barrett MS 900/6-8
4243 Barrett Rd 95608 916-971-7842
Lisa Herstrom-Smith, prin. Fax 971-7839
Churchill MS 900/6-8
4900 Whitney Ave 95608 916-971-7324
Dr. Mark Roberts, prin. Fax 971-7856
Other Schools – See Citrus Heights, Fair Oaks, Orangevale, Sacramento

---

College of Career Training Post-Sec.
7220 Fair Oaks Blvd Ste A 95608 916-481-9001
Jesuit HS 1,000/9-12
1200 Jacob Ln 95608 916-482-6060
Rev. Edward Fassett, prin. Fax 480-2119
Sacramento Adventist Academy 200/K-12
5601 Winding Way 95608 916-481-2300
Bettesue Constanzo, prin. Fax 481-7426
Victory Christian HS - Garfield Campus 300/7-12
3045 Garfield Ave 95608 916-488-5601
John Huffman, prin. Fax 488-2589

Carpinteria, Santa Barbara, Pop. 13,549
Carpinteria USD 2,800/K-12
1400 Linden Ave 93013 805-684-4511
Paul Cordeiro, supt. Fax 684-0218
www.cusd.net
Carpinteria HS 900/9-12
4810 Foothill Rd 93013 805-684-4107
Gerardo Cornejo, prin. Fax 566-5952
Carpinteria MS 500/7-8
5351 Carpinteria Ave 93013 805-684-4544
Felicia Sexsmith, prin. Fax 566-3839

Cate S 300/9-12
PO Box 5005 93014 805-684-4127
Benjamin Williams, hdmstr. Fax 684-8940
Pacifica Graduate Institute Post-Sec.
249 Lambert Rd 93013 805-969-3626
Truck Marketing Institute Post-Sec.
1090 Eugenia Pl Ste 101 93013 805-684-4558

Carson, Los Angeles, Pop. 93,955
Long Beach USD
Supt. — See Long Beach
California Academy of Math & Science 600/9-12
1000 E Victoria St 90747 310-243-2025
Kathleen Clark, prin. Fax 516-4041

Los Angeles USD
Supt. — See Los Angeles
Carnegie MS 1,800/6-8
21820 Bonita St 90745 310-952-5700
Patrick Donahoe, prin. Fax 830-9015
Carson HS 3,600/9-12
22328 Main St 90745 310-847-6000
Kenneth Keener, prin. Fax 518-5817
Curtiss MS 1,400/6-8
1254 E Helmick St 90746 310-661-4500
Edna Burems, prin. Fax 537-2115
White MS 1,900/6-8
22102 Figueroa St 90745 310-783-4900
James Noble, prin. Fax 782-8954

California State Univ.-Dominguez Hills Post-Sec.
1000 E Victoria St 90747 310-243-3300
Carson Christian S 100/K-12
21828 Avalon Blvd 90745 310-538-5370
Marian Alexander, prin.
CEI Post-Sec.
20700 Avalon Blvd Ste 210 90746 310-532-6328
Peace & Joy Christian S 100/K-12
21919 Figueroa St 90745 310-898-3121
Wilma Wilson, prin.

Caruthers, Fresno, Pop. 1,603
Caruthers USD 1,500/K-12
PO Box 127 93609 559-864-6500
Dwight Miller, supt. Fax 864-8857
www.caruthers.k12.ca.us
Caruthers HS 600/9-12
PO Box 545 93609 559-864-6500
Jim Sargent, prin. Fax 864-8303

Castaic, Los Angeles
Castaic UNESD
Supt. — See Valencia
Castaic MS 1,400/4-8
28900 Hillcrest Pkwy 91384 661-257-4550
Marcia Dains, prin. Fax 294-9714

Castro Valley, Alameda, Pop. 59,300
Castro Valley USD 8,500/K-12
PO Box 2146 94546 510-537-3000
James Fitzpatrick, supt. Fax 886-8962
www.cv.k12.ca.us
Canyon MS 1,300/6-8
PO Box 2146 94546 510-538-8833
Mark Croghan, prin. Fax 247-9439
Castro Valley HS 2,700/9-12
PO Box 2146 94546 510-537-5910
Debbie Coco, prin. Fax 582-3924
Creekside MS 800/6-8
PO Box 2146 94546 510-247-0665
Mary Ann DeGrazia, prin. Fax 886-0375
Castro Valley Adult S Adult
PO Box 2146 94546 510-886-1000
Jerry Green, dir. Fax 537-8537

Hayward USD
Supt. — See Hayward
Adult Education - Laurel Site Adult
2652 Vergil Ct 94546 510-293-8599
Mahnoush Harirsa, prin.

Castroville, Monterey, Pop. 5,272
North Monterey County USD
Supt. — See Moss Landing
N Monterey Co. Ctr for Independent Study 200/K-12
13998 Castroville Blvd 95012 831-663-7050
Ken Jordan, prin. Fax 633-7095
North Monterey County HS 1,600/9-12
13990 Castroville Blvd 95012 831-633-5221
Steve Hirt, prin. Fax 633-2520
North Montgomery County MS 300/7-8
10301 Seymour St 95012 831-633-3391
David Burke, prin. Fax 633-3680
North Monterey County Adult S Adult
13990 Castroville Blvd 95012 831-633-7050
Ken Jordan, prin. Fax 633-7095

Cathedral City, Riverside, Pop. 51,713
Palm Springs USD
Supt. — See Palm Springs
Cathedral City HS 2,800/9-12
69250 Dinah Shore Dr 92234 760-770-0100
Guillermo Chavez, prin. Fax 770-0149
Coffman MS 1,200/6-8
34603 Plumley Rd 92234 760-770-8617
Terri Simon, prin. Fax 770-8623
Workman MS 1,600/6-8
69300 30th Ave 92234 760-770-8540
Greta Salmi, prin. Fax 770-8545

Coachella Valley Technical Skills Center Post-Sec.
35325 Date Palm Dr Ste 101 92234 760-328-5554
Desert Career College Post-Sec.
67501 E Palm Canyon Dr #C 92234 760-864-1356

Cedarville, Modoc
Surprise Valley JUSD 200/K-12
PO Box 100 96104 530-279-6141
Dr. Michael Sherrod, supt. Fax 279-2210
surprisevalleyhs.org/
Surprise Valley JSHS 100/7-12
PO Box 100 96104 530-279-6146
Dr. Michael Sherrod, prin. Fax 279-2210

Central Valley, Shasta, Pop. 4,340
Gateway USD
Supt. — See Redding
Central Valley HS 1,000/9-12
4066 La Mesa Ave 96019 530-275-7075
Emmett Koerperich, prin. Fax 275-7065

Ceres, Stanislaus, Pop. 40,571
Ceres USD 9,600/K-12
PO Box 307 95307 209-556-1500
Walt Hanline Ed.D., supt. Fax 537-7301
www.ceres.k12.ca.us
Blaker-Kinser JHS 700/7-8
PO Box 307 95307 209-541-0542
Debra Bukko, prin. Fax 541-0174
Central Valley HS 9-12
PO Box 307 95307 209-556-1900
Fred Van Vleck, prin. Fax 531-2748
Ceres HS 2,400/9-12
PO Box 307 95307 209-538-0130
Bob Palous, prin. Fax 538-8978
Hensley JHS 900/7-8
PO Box 307 95307 209-538-0158
Lynda Maben, prin. Fax 538-9428

Central Valley Christian Academy 300/PK-12
2020 Academy Pl 95307 209-537-4521
Donald Krpalek, prin. Fax 538-0706

Cerritos, Los Angeles, Pop. 52,561
ABC USD 21,900/K-12
16700 Norwalk Blvd 90703 562-926-5566
Dr. Gary Smuts, supt. Fax 404-1092
www.abcusd.k12.ca.us
Carmenita MS 700/7-8
13435 166th St 90703 562-926-4405
Valencia Mayfield, prin. Fax 404-7807
Cerritos HS 2,300/9-12
12500 183rd St 90703 562-865-3310
Jeff Green, prin. Fax 924-3187
Gahr HS 1,900/9-12
11111 Artesia Blvd 90703 562-402-4523
George Kambeitz, prin. Fax 924-8136
Haskell MS 600/7-8
11525 Del Amo Blvd 90703 562-860-6529
Susan Hixson Ed.D., prin. Fax 809-7250
Tetzlaff MS 600/7-8
12351 Del Amo Blvd 90703 562-865-9539
Rebecca Caudillo Ed.D., prin. Fax 402-6412
Whitney JSHS 1,000/7-12
16800 Shoemaker Ave 90703 562-229-7745
Patricia Hager, prin. Fax 926-2751
ABC Adult HS Adult
12254 Cuesta Dr 90703 562-926-5566
Augustin Jaramillo, prin. Fax 921-9958
Other Schools – See Artesia, Hawaiian Gardens, Lakewood

Regional Occupational Center & Program
Supt. — None
Southeast LA County ROP Vo/Tech
20122 Cabrillo Ln 90703 562-860-1927
Gilbert Montano, supt. Fax 860-1829

Fremont College Post-Sec.
18000 Studebaker Rd 9th Flr 90703 562-809-5100
Professional Career Institute Post-Sec.
17215 Studebaker Rd Ste 310 90703 562-916-5055
Valley Christian HS 700/9-12
10818 Artesia Blvd 90703 562-865-0281
Scott Edwards, prin. Fax 865-0082
Valley Christian MS 300/7-8
18100 Dumont Ave 90703 562-865-6519
Eric Scholte, prin. Fax 403-3159

Chatsworth, See Los Angeles
Los Angeles USD
Supt. — See Los Angeles
Chatsworth HS 3,000/9-12
10027 Lurline Ave 91311 818-678-3400
Jeffrey Davis, prin. Fax 709-6952
Lawrence MS 2,000/6-8
10100 Variel Ave 91311 818-678-7900
Christopher Rosas, prin. Fax 349-4539

Chaminade MS 600/6-8
19800 Devonshire St 91311 818-363-8127
Christine Hunter, prin. Fax 363-1219

Cherry Valley, Riverside, Pop. 5,945

Cherry Valley Brethren S 100/K-12
39205 Vineland St 92223 951-845-2653
Judy Polman, prin. Fax 845-2026

Chester, Plumas, Pop. 2,082
Plumas USD
Supt. — See Quincy
Chester JSHS 300/7-12
PO Box 797 96020 530-258-2126
Scott Cory, prin. Fax 258-2306

Chico, Butte, Pop. 71,427
Chico USD 12,500/K-12
1163 E 7th St 95928 530-891-3000
Dr. Chet Francisco, supt. Fax 891-3220
www.chicousd.org
Bidwell JHS, 2376 North Ave 95926 700/7-8
Joanne Parsley, prin. 530-891-3080
Chico HS 2,000/9-12
901 Esplanade 95926 530-891-3026
Jim Hanlon, prin. Fax 891-3284
Chico JHS 700/7-8
280 Memorial Way 95926 530-891-3066
Joyce Burdette, prin. Fax 891-3264
Marsh JHS, 2253 Humboldt Rd 95928 600/7-8
Steve Piluso, prin. 530-895-4110
Pleasant Valley HS 1,900/9-12
1475 East Ave 95926 530-879-5100
Michael Rupp, prin. Fax 879-5263

Regional Occupational Center & Program
Supt. — None
Butte County ROP Vo/Tech
2491 Carmichael Dr Ste 100 95928 530-879-7457
Paul Watters, dir. Fax 879-7458

American Christian Academy 100/1-12
13 San Ramon Dr 95973 530-896-1150
Julie Clark, admin.
California State University-Chico Post-Sec.
95929 530-898-6116
Champion Christian JSHS 100/7-12
1184 East Ave 95926 530-345-8008
Rick Stout, prin. Fax 345-5405
Pleasant Valley Baptist S 100/K-12
13539 Garner Ln 95973 530-343-2949
Tim Ruhl, prin.

Chino, San Bernardino, Pop. 77,578
Chino Valley USD 33,100/K-12
5130 Riverside Dr 91710 909-628-1201
Edmond Heatley Ed.D., supt. Fax 590-4911
www.chino.k12.ca.us
Chino HS 2,900/9-12
5472 Park Pl 91710 909-627-7351
Rigoberto Vasquez, prin. Fax 548-6004
Lugo HS 2,300/9-12
13400 Pipeline Ave 91710 909-591-3902
Preston Carr, prin. Fax 548-6020
Magnolia JHS 1,000/7-8
13150 Mountain Ave 91710 909-627-9263
Bonnie Cardinale, prin. Fax 627-2165
Ramona JHS 1,000/7-8
4575 Walnut Ave 91710 909-627-9144
Mike Finkbiner, prin. Fax 517-9258
Chino Community Adult Adult
5130 Riverside Dr 91710 909-628-1201
Richard Meyer, prin. Fax 548-6016
Other Schools – See Chino Hills, Ontario

Chino Valley Christian Academy 100/K-12
12205 Pipeline Ave 91710 909-464-8255
Dennis Leonard, dir.

Chino Hills, San Bernardino, Pop. 75,722
Chino Valley USD
Supt. — See Chino
Ayala HS 2,400/9-12
14255 Peyton Dr 91709 909-627-3584
Fax 464-9239
Canyon Hills JHS 1,300/7-8
2500 Madrugada Dr 91709 909-464-9938
Mike Hunkins, prin. Fax 590-3959
Chino Hills HS 2,500/9-12
16150 Pomona Rincon Rd 91709 909-606-7540
Carl Hampton, prin. Fax 548-6041
Townsend JHS 1,300/7-8
15359 Ilex Dr 91709 909-591-2161
Melody Kohn, prin. Fax 597-4153

Chowchilla, Madera, Pop. 16,525
Alview-Dairyland UNESD 300/K-8
12861 Avenue 18 1/2 93610 559-665-2394
Lori Flanagan, supt. Fax 665-7347
www.adusd.k12.ca.us
Dairyland S 200/4-8
12861 Avenue 18 1/2 93610 559-665-2394
Lori Flanagan, prin. Fax 665-7347

Chowchilla ESD 1,800/K-8
PO Box 910 93610 559-665-8000
Michelle Steagall Ed.D., supt. Fax 665-3036
www.chowchillaelem.k12.ca.us
Wilson MS 600/6-8
PO Box 910 93610 559-665-8070
Paul deAyora Ed.D., prin. Fax 665-8004

Chowchilla UNHSD 900/9-12
805 Humboldt Ave 93610 559-665-1331
Ron Seals, supt. Fax 665-4659
Chowchilla HS 900/9-12
805 Humboldt Ave 93610 559-665-1331
Fred Cogan, prin. Fax 665-1074
Chowchilla Adult/ISP Adult
805 Humboldt Ave 93610 559-665-5683
Rock Smith, prin.

Chula Vista, San Diego, Pop. 210,497
Sweetwater UNHSD 39,800/7-12
1130 5th Ave 91911 619-691-5500
Jesus Gandara Ed.D., supt. Fax 498-1997
www.suhsd.k12.ca.us
Bonita Vista HS 2,600/9-12
751 Otay Lakes Rd 91913 619-216-5000
Bettina Batista, prin. Fax 656-1203
Bonita Vista MS 1,100/7-8
650 Otay Lakes Rd 91910 619-397-2200
Bernard Balanay, prin. Fax 482-9356
Castle Park HS 2,400/9-12
1395 Hilltop Dr 91911 619-691-5600
Earl Wiens, prin. Fax 427-5967
Castle Park MS 1,400/7-8
160 Quintard St 91911 619-691-5490
V. Sandoval-Johnson, prin. Fax 427-8045
Chula Vista MS 1,400/7-9
415 5th Ave 91910 619-498-6800
Doug Jenkins, prin. Fax 427-5723
Chula Vista SHS 2,100/10-12
820 4th Ave 91911 619-691-5765
George Ohnesorgen, prin. Fax 427-5824
Eastlake HS 2,600/9-12
1120 Eastlake Pkwy 91915 619-397-3800
Sebastian Perez, prin. Fax 656-9736
Eastlake MS 1,100/7-8
900 Duncan Ranch Rd 91914 619-591-4000
Victoria Kreiser, prin. Fax 482-0553
Hilltop HS 2,400/9-12
555 Claire Ave 91910 619-691-5640
Susan Williams, prin. Fax 425-3284
Hilltop MS 1,300/7-8
44 E J St 91910 619-498-2700
Linda Stanley, prin. Fax 585-3576
Olympian HS 9-12
1925 Magdalena Ave 91913 619-656-2400
John DeVore, prin. Fax 216-0650
Otay Ranch HS 2,100/9-12
1250 Olympic Pkwy 91913 619-591-5000
Jose Brosz, prin. Fax 591-5010
Rancho del Rey MS 1,300/7-8
1174 E J St 91910 619-216-5077
Tom Rodrigo, prin. Fax 656-3810
Chula Vista Adult S Adult
1034 4th Ave 91911 619-691-5760
Tony Alfaro Ed.D., prin. Fax 425-5447
Other Schools – See Imperial Beach, National City, San Diego, San Ysidro

---

Calvary Christian Academy 500/PK-12
1771 E Palomar St 91913 619-591-2260
Dr. Chapin Marsh, hdmstr. Fax 591-2261
Covenant Christian S 100/K-12
505 E Naples St 91911 619-421-8822
Thomas McManus, prin. Fax 216-9846
Pima Medical Institute Post-Sec.
780 Bay Blvd Ste 101 91910 619-425-3200
Southwestern College Post-Sec.
900 Otay Lakes Rd 91910 619-421-6700

Citrus Heights, Sacramento, Pop. 86,272
San Juan USD
Supt. — See Carmichael
Mesa Verde HS 1,300/9-12
7501 Carriage Dr 95621 916-971-5288
Paul Oropallo, prin. Fax 971-5215
San Juan HS 1,100/9-12
7551 Greenback Ln 95610 916-971-5112
Dave Terwilliger, prin. Fax 971-5111
Sylvan MS 800/7-8
7137 Auburn Blvd 95610 916-971-7873
Jim Shoemake, prin. Fax 971-7896
Sunrise Tech Center Adult
7322 Sunrise Blvd 95610 916-971-5049
Fax 971-7695

American Christian Academy 200/K-12
7412 Hollyhock Ct 95621 916-725-8316
Karen Davis, admin.
National Career Education Post-Sec.
6060 Snrs Vista Dr #3000 95610 916-969-4900
Western Career College Post-Sec.
7301 Greenback Ln Bldg A 95621 916-722-8200

City of Industry, Los Angeles, Pop. 616
Bassett USD
Supt. — See La Puente
Torch Magnet MS 900/6-8
751 Vineland Ave 91746 626-931-2700
Joe Medina, prin. Fax 931-2702

Hacienda La Puente USD 22,700/K-12
PO Box 60002 91716 626-933-1000
Dr. Barbara Nakaoka, supt. Fax 855-3505
www.hlpusd.k12.ca.us/
Workman HS 1,300/9-12
16303 Temple Ave 91744 626-933-8800
Yvette Meneses, prin. Fax 855-3148
Other Schools – See Hacienda Heights, La Puente

Regional Occupational Center & Program
Supt. — None
La Puente Valley ROP Vo/Tech
18501 Gale Ave Ste 100 91748 626-810-3300
Cynthia Parulan-Colfer, supt. Fax 581-9108

Elegante Beauty College Post-Sec.
1600 S Azusa Ave Unit 244 91748 626-965-2532
Everest College Post-Sec.
12801 Crossroads Pkwy S 91746 562-908-2500

Claremont, Los Angeles, Pop. 35,182
Claremont USD 6,900/K-12
2080 N Mountain Ave 91711 909-398-0609
David Cash, supt. Fax 398-0690
www.cusd.claremont.edu
Claremont HS 2,300/9-12
1601 N Indian Hill Blvd 91711 909-624-9053
Fax 624-2128
El Roble IS 1,100/7-8
665 N Mountain Ave 91711 909-398-0343
Kevin Grier, prin. Fax 398-0399
San Antonio HS 50/9-12
125 W San Jose Ave 91711 909-398-0316
Steven Boyd, prin. Fax 398-0384
Claremont Adult S Adult
170 W San Jose Ave Ste 100 91711 909-398-0609
Bill Teague, prin. Fax 626-5109

Claremont Graduate University Post-Sec.
170 E 10th St 91711 909-621-8000
Claremont McKenna College Post-Sec.
500 E 9th St 91711 909-621-8000
Claremont School of Theology Post-Sec.
1325 N College Ave 91711 909-626-3521
Harvey Mudd College Post-Sec.
301 E 12th St 91711 909-621-8000
Keck Graduate Institute Post-Sec.
535 Watson Dr 91711 909-607-7855
Pitzer College Post-Sec.
1050 N Mills Ave 91711 909-621-8219
Pomona College Post-Sec.
333 N College Way 91711 909-621-8000
Scripps College Post-Sec.
1030 Columbia Ave 91711 909-621-8000
Webb S 400/9-12
1175 W Baseline Rd 91711 909-626-3587
Susan Nelson, hdmstr. Fax 621-4582

Clarksburg, Yolo
River Delta USD
Supt. — See Rio Vista
Clarksburg MS 7-9
PO Box 99 95612 916-744-1717
Paul Gengler, prin. Fax 744-5704
Delta HS 300/9-12
PO Box 100 95612 916-744-1714
Paul Gengler, prin. Fax 744-1673

Clayton, Contra Costa, Pop. 11,142
Mount Diablo USD
Supt. — See Concord
Diablo View MS 600/6-8
300 Diablo View Ln 94517 925-672-0898
Michele Cooper, prin. Fax 672-4327

Clearlake, Lake, Pop. 14,728
Konocti USD
Supt. — See Lower Lake
Oak Hill MS 500/6-8
PO Box 7087 95422 707-994-6447
Marie Friedrich, prin. Fax 994-5047

Cloverdale, Sonoma, Pop. 8,016
Cloverdale USD 1,600/K-12
97 School St 95425 707-894-1920
Claudia Rosatti, supt. Fax 894-1922
www.cusd.org/
Cloverdale HS 400/9-12
509 N Cloverdale Blvd 95425 707-894-1900
Gene Lile, prin. Fax 894-4804
Washington MS 600/4-8
129 S Washington St 95425 707-894-1940
Rick Martinez, prin. Fax 894-1946

Clovis, Fresno, Pop. 86,527
Clovis USD 33,100/K-12
1450 Herndon Ave 93611 559-327-9000
Terry Bradley Ed.D., supt. Fax 327-9109
www.clovisusd.k12.ca.us
Alta Sierra IS 1,700/7-8
380 W Teague Ave, 559-327-3500
Devin Blizzard, prin. Fax 327-3590
Buchanan HS 2,900/9-12
1560 Minnewawa Ave 93612 559-327-3000
Don Ulrich, prin. Fax 327-3090
Clark IS 1,300/7-8
902 5th St 93612 559-327-1500
Scott Steele, prin. Fax 327-1556
Clovis East HS 700/9-9
4343 N Leonard Ave, 559-327-4000
Steve Martinez, prin. Fax 327-4190
Clovis HS 2,400/9-12
1055 Fowler Ave 93611 559-327-1000
Norm Anderson, prin. Fax 327-1010
Reyburn IS 1,500/7-8
4300 N DeWolf Ave, 559-327-4500
Barry Jager, prin. Fax 327-4791
Clovis Adult S Adult
1452 David E Cook Way 93611 559-327-2800
John Ballinger, prin. Fax 327-2889
Other Schools – See Fresno

Clovis Christian S 300/PK-12
3105 Locan Ave, 559-291-6302
Phil Laughlin, admin. Fax 291-6278
Institute of Technology - Clovis Campus Post-Sec.
564 W Herndon Ave 93612 559-297-4500
Milan Institute Post-Sec.
731 W Shaw Ave 93612 559-323-2800
San Joaquin College of Law Post-Sec.
901 5th St 93612 559-323-2100
Tower Christian S 300/K-12
8753 Chickadee Ln, 559-298-2772
Ann Raber, admin.

Coachella, Riverside, Pop. 32,432
Coachella Valley USD
Supt. — See Thermal
Cahuilla Desert Academy 1,300/7-8
82489 Avenue 52 92236 760-398-0097
Estella Palacio, prin. Fax 398-0088

Duke MS 7-8
85358 Bagdad Ave 92236 760-398-0139
Erasmo Garcia, prin. Fax 398-5399
Coachella Valley Adult Education Adult
1099 Orchard St 92236 760-398-6302
Guillermo Mendoza, prin. Fax 398-0436

Coalinga, Fresno, Pop. 17,350
Coalinga - Huron JUSD 4,400/K-12
657 Sunset St 93210 559-935-7500
Dr. William McDermott, supt. Fax 935-5329
www.chusd.k12.ca.us
Coalinga HS 1,200/9-12
750 Van Ness St 93210 559-935-7520
Roger Campbell, prin. Fax 935-3571
Coalinga MS 600/6-8
265 Cambridge Ave 93210 559-935-7550
Dawn Contreras-Douglas, prin. Fax 934-1311
Other Schools – See Huron

Faith Christian Academy 100/K-12
450 W Elm Ave 93210 559-935-9209
Tara Davis, prin. Fax 935-0745
West Hills Community College Post-Sec.
300 W Cherry Ln 93210 559-935-0801

Coarsegold, Madera
Chawanakee USD
Supt. — See North Fork
Chawanakee Adult Education Adult
28420 Yosemite Springs Pkwy 93614 559-683-0808
Doug Waltner, prin. Fax 683-8604

Coleville, Mono
Eastern Sierra USD
Supt. — See Bridgeport
Coleville HS 100/9-12
111591 US Highway 395 96107 530-495-2231
Jason Reid, prin. Fax 495-2730

Colfax, Placer, Pop. 1,720
Placer UNHSD
Supt. — See Auburn
Colfax HS 1,000/9-12
24995 Ben Taylor Rd 95713 530-346-2284
Rick Spears, prin. Fax 346-6476

Aviation & Electronic School of America Post-Sec.
PO Box 1810 95713 800-345-2742

Colma, San Mateo, Pop. 1,394
Jefferson ESD
Supt. — See Daly City
Franklin IS 500/7-8
700 Stewart Ave, Daly City CA 94015 650-991-1200
James Parrish, prin. Fax 756-5475

Colton, San Bernardino, Pop. 51,350
Colton JUSD 24,700/PK-12
1212 Valencia Dr 92324 909-580-5000
Dennis Byas Ed.D., supt. Fax 876-6395
www.colton.k12.ca.us
Colton HS 3,300/9-12
777 W Valley Blvd 92324 909-580-5005
John Steven Coke, prin. Fax 876-4093
Colton MS 1,100/7-8
670 W Laurel St 92324 909-580-5009
Chris Marin, prin. Fax 876-4095
Other Schools – See Bloomington, Grand Terrace

Rialto USD
Supt. — See Rialto
Jehue MS 1,600/6-8
1500 N Eucalyptus Ave 92324 909-421-7377
Leonard Buckner, prin. Fax 421-7376

Arrowhead Regional Medical Center Post-Sec.
400 N Pepper Ave 92324 909-580-1000
Four-D College Post-Sec.
1020 E Washington St 92324 909-783-9331

Colusa, Colusa, Pop. 5,826
Colusa USD 1,400/K-12
745 10th St 95932 530-458-7791
Larry Yeghoian, supt. Fax 458-4030
www.colusa.k12.ca.us
Colusa HS 400/9-12
901 Colus Ave 95932 530-458-2156
Steve Peters, prin. Fax 458-5783
Egling MS 500/4-8
813 Webster St 95932 530-458-7631
Ed Conrado, prin. Fax 458-8107

Compton, Los Angeles, Pop. 95,659
Compton USD 30,900/PK-12
501 S Santa Fe Ave 90221 310-639-4321
Dr. Jesse Gonzales, supt. Fax 632-3014
www.compton.k12.ca.us
Bunche MS 1,000/6-8
12338 S Mona Blvd 90222 310-898-6010
Dr. Irella Martinez, prin. Fax 638-4935
Centennial HS 1,300/9-12
2600 N Central Ave 90222 310-635-2715
JaMaiia Bond, prin. Fax 631-9164
Compton HS 2,200/9-12
601 S Acacia Ave 90220 310-635-3881
Jesse Jones, prin. Fax 635-3051
Davis MS 1,500/6-8
621 W Poplar St 90220 310-898-6020
Felix Mendoza, prin. Fax 631-5725
Dominguez HS 2,600/9-12
15301 S San Jose Ave 90221 562-630-0142
Fax 408-2367
Enterprise MS 700/6-8
2600 W Compton Blvd 90220 310-898-6030
Dr. Teodor Brancov, prin. Fax 632-4183
Roosevelt MS 1,400/6-8
1200 E Alondra Blvd 90221 310-898-6040
Rubin White, prin. Fax 631-3298
Walton MS 700/6-8
900 W Greenleaf Blvd 90220 310-898-6060
Gipson Lyles, prin. Fax 631-3409

Whaley MS 1,300/6-8
14401 S Gibson Ave 90221 310-898-6070
Fax 638-7079
Willowbrook MS 600/6-8
2601 N Wilmington Ave 90222 310-898-6080
Stacy Nickleberry, prin. Fax 537-2932
Compton Adult S Adult
1104 E 148th St 90220 310-898-6490
Saundra Bishop, prin. Fax 898-6477
Other Schools – See Los Angeles

Regional Occupational Center & Program
Supt. — None
Compton Unified ROP Vo/Tech
700 N Bullis Rd Ste 12 90221 310-898-6000
Reena Singh, dir. Fax 763-3871

Compton Community College Post-Sec.
1111 E Artesia Blvd 90221 310-900-1600
James Academic Development S 100/K-12
1901 W Reeve St 90220 310-631-6235
Bertha James, prin. Fax 631-9471
Universal College of Beauty Post-Sec.
718 W Compton Blvd 90220 310-635-6969

Concord, Contra Costa, Pop. 123,252
Mount Diablo USD 34,400/K-12
1936 Carlotta Dr 94519 925-682-8000
Gary McHenry, supt. Fax 689-1649
www.mdusd.k12.ca.us
Clayton Valley HS 1,900/9-12
1101 Alberta Way 94521 925-682-7474
Gary Swanson, prin. Fax 825-7859
Concord HS 1,500/9-12
4200 Concord Blvd 94521 925-687-2030
Ronald Miller, prin. Fax 682-4613
El Dorado MS 1,000/6-8
1750 West St 94521 925-682-5700
Barbara Weil, prin. Fax 685-1460
Glenbrook MS 700/6-8
2351 Olivera Rd 94520 925-685-6835
Gary McAdam, prin. Fax 671-9532
Mount Diablo HS 1,500/9-12
2450 Grant St 94520 925-682-4030
Bev Hansen, prin. Fax 687-9658
Oak Grove MS 700/6-8
2050 Minert Rd 94518 925-682-1843
Teresa McCormick, prin. Fax 682-2083
Pine Hollow MS 800/6-8
5522 Pine Hollow Rd 94521 925-672-5444
Karen Gordon, prin. Fax 672-9751
Ygnacio Valley HS 1,400/9-12
755 Oak Grove Rd 94518 925-685-8414
Carolyn Plath, prin. Fax 685-1435
Loma Vista Adult Center Adult
1266 San Carlos Ave 94518 925-685-7340
Joanne Durkee, dir. Fax 687-8217
Other Schools – See Clayton, Pittsburg, Pleasant Hill, Walnut Creek

---

Cameron Academy 100/K-12
PO Box 21383 94521 925-798-2097
Ronald Myers, admin.
Carondelet HS 900/9-12
1133 Winton Dr 94518 925-686-5353
Sr. Marien Dyer, prin. Fax 671-9429
De La Salle HS 1,000/9-12
1130 Winton Dr 94518 925-686-3310
Br. Christopher Brady, prin. Fax 686-3474
Heald College Post-Sec.
5130 Commercial Cir 94520 925-827-1300
Paris Beauty College Post-Sec.
1655 Willow Pass Rd 94520 925-685-7600

Corcoran, Tulare, Pop. 22,456
Corcoran JUSD 3,300/K-12
1520 Patterson Ave 93212 559-992-3104
Rich Merlo, supt. Fax 992-3957
www.corcoran.k12.ca.us
Corcoran HS 900/9-12
1520 Patterson Ave 93212 559-992-5061
Gloria Gravalle, prin. Fax 992-5066
Muir MS 800/6-8
1520 Patterson Ave 93212 559-992-4167
Mike Graville, prin. Fax 992-4423

Corning, Tehama, Pop. 7,140
Corning UNESD 2,000/K-8
1590 South St 96021 530-824-7700
Stephen Kelish, supt. Fax 824-2493
www.cuesd.tehama.k12.ca.us
Maywood MS 700/6-8
1666 Marguerite Ave 96021 530-824-7730
Jeff Harris, prin. Fax 824-7742

Corning UNHSD 1,100/9-12
643 Blackburn Ave 96021 530-824-8000
Bruce Cole, supt. Fax 824-8005
Corning HS 1,000/9-12
643 Blackburn Ave 96021 530-824-8000
Charlie Troughton, prin. Fax 824-8005

Corona, Riverside, Pop. 149,387
Corona-Norco USD
Supt. — See Norco
Auburndale IS 1,100/7-8
1255 River Rd 92880 951-736-3231
Linda Lanyi, prin. Fax 736-3360
Centennial HS 3,000/9-12
1820 Rimpau Ave 92881 951-739-5670
Sam Buenrostro, prin. Fax 739-5693
Citrus Hills IS 1,500/7-8
3211 S Main St 92882 951-736-4600
Michael Ridgway, prin. Fax 736-4623
Corona Fundamental IS 1,000/7-8
1230 S Main St 92882 951-736-3321
Bonnie Paskey, prin. Fax 736-3417
Corona HS 2,900/9-12
1150 W 10th St 92882 951-736-3211
Robert Taylor, prin. Fax 736-3408
El Cerrito MS 900/6-8
7610 El Cerrito Rd 92881 951-736-3216
Lisa Simon, prin. Fax 736-3286

Raney IS 1,600/6-8
1010 W Citron St 92882 951-736-3221
Allen Pietrok, prin. Fax 736-3439
River Heights IS 7-8
7227 Cleveland Ave 92880 951-738-2155
Karen Fisher, prin. Fax 738-2175
Roosevelt HS 9-12
7447 Cleveland Ave 92880 951-738-2100
Dr. Julie Vitale, prin. Fax 738-2104
Santiago HS 3,900/9-12
1395 Foothill Pkwy 92881 951-739-5600
Rupertino Cisneros, prin. Fax 739-5639
Corona-Norco Adult Education Adult
300 S Buena Vista Ave 92882 951-736-3325
JoDee Guerard, prin. Fax 736-7159

Amor Christian Academy 50/1-12
PO Box 2650 92878 951-735-6609
Jesse Reyes, admin. Fax 735-5185
Central CA School of Continuing Educ. Post-Sec.
271 Ott St Ste 23 92882 951-549-0693
Christian Heritage S 400/K-12
PO Box 1780 92878 951-736-3033
Arleen Morris, admin.
Corona Christian S 50/PK-12
1901 W Ontario Ave 92882 951-734-5683
Dr. David Howard, admin. Fax 734-3809

Coronado, San Diego, Pop. 26,424
Coronado USD 2,800/K-12
201 6th St 92118 619-522-8900
Susan Coyle, supt. Fax 437-6570
www.coronado.k12.ca.us
Coronado HS 900/9-12
650 D Ave 92118 619-522-8907
Karl Mueller, prin. Fax 437-0236
Coronado MS 700/6-8
550 F Ave 92118 619-522-8921
Nancy Girvin Ed.D., prin. Fax 522-6948

Costa Mesa, Orange, Pop. 109,830
Newport - Mesa USD 21,800/PK-12
2985 Bear St 92626 714-424-5000
Dr. Jeffrey Hubbard, supt. Fax 424-5018
www.nmusd.us
Costa Mesa JSHS 1,900/7-12
2650 Fairview Rd 92626 714-424-8700
Ed Wong, prin. Fax 424-8770
Early College HS 9-12
390 Monte Vista Ave 92627 949-515-3382
Kathy Slawson, prin. Fax 515-3399
Estancia HS 1,300/9-12
2323 Placentia Ave 92627 949-515-6500
Phil D'Agostino, prin. Fax 515-6571
TeWinkle MS 1,100/6-8
3224 California St 92626 714-424-7965
Kirk Bauermeister, prin. Fax 424-5680
Other Schools – See Newport Beach

Regional Occupational Center & Program
Supt. — None
Coastline ROP Vo/Tech
1001 Presidio Sq 92626 714-979-1955
Dr. Richard Smith, supt. Fax 557-6812

James Albert School of Cosmetology Post-Sec.
281 E 17th St 92627 949-642-0606
Orange Coast College Post-Sec.
PO Box 5005 92628 714-432-0202
Pacific College Post-Sec.
3160 Red Hill Ave 92626 714-662-4402
Paul Mitchell The School Post-Sec.
1534 Adams Ave 92626 714-546-8786
Vanguard University of Southern CA Post-Sec.
55 Fair Dr 92626 714-556-3610
Waldorf S of Orange County 300/PK-10
2350 Canyon Dr 92627 949-574-7775
Holly Derheim, admin. Fax 574-7740
Whittier College School of Law Post-Sec.
3333 Harbor Blvd 92626 714-444-4141

Cottonwood, Shasta, Pop. 1,747
Anderson UNHSD
Supt. — See Anderson
West Valley HS 1,100/9-12
3805 Happy Valley Rd 96022 530-347-7171
Karl Stemmler, prin. Fax 347-0481

Cottonwood UNESD 800/K-8
20512 1st St 96022 530-347-3165
Dale H. Hansen, supt. Fax 347-0247
www.shastalink.k12.ca.us/cotton
West Cottonwood JHS 400/6-8
20512 1st St 96022 530-347-3123
Barry Espil, prin. Fax 347-0247

Evergreen UNSD 900/K-8
19500 Learning Way 96022 530-347-7955
Harley North, supt. Fax 347-7954
www.eusd.tehama.k12.ca.us
Evergreen MS 400/5-8
19500 Learning Way 96022 530-347-7950
Brad Mendenhall, prin. Fax 347-7953

Coulterville, Mariposa
Mariposa County USD
Supt. — See Mariposa
Coulterville HS 50/9-12
PO Box 480 95311 209-878-3955
Dr. Stella Pizelo, prin. Fax 878-3816

Covelo, Mendocino, Pop. 1,057
Round Valley USD 400/K-12
PO Box 276 95428 707-983-6171
Joy Muhleck, supt. Fax 983-6655
Round Valley HS 100/9-12
PO Box 276 95428 707-983-6171
John Nickel, prin. Fax 983-6179

Covina, Los Angeles, Pop. 47,850
Azusa USD
Supt. — See Azusa

Gladstone HS 1,600/9-12
1340 N Enid Ave 91722 626-815-5157
Scott Magnusson, prin. Fax 815-5155

Charter Oak USD 7,200/K-12
PO Box 9 91723 626-966-8331
Norm Kirschenbaum Ed.D., supt. Fax 967-9580
www.cousd.k12.ca.us
Charter Oak HS 2,200/9-12
PO Box 9 91723 626-915-5841
Richard Evers, prin. Fax 915-3398
Royal Oak IS 1,600/6-8
PO Box 9 91723 626-967-6354
Scott Wollam, prin. Fax 331-2074

Covina-Valley USD 14,400/K-12
PO Box 269 91723 626-974-7000
Louis Pappas, supt. Fax 974-7032
www.cvusd.k12.ca.us
Covina HS 1,400/9-12
PO Box 269 91723 626-974-6020
Michael Gautreau, prin. Fax 974-6045
Las Palmas MS 1,100/6-8
PO Box 269 91723 626-974-7200
Josie Paredes, prin. Fax 974-7215
Northview HS 1,400/9-12
PO Box 269 91723 626-974-6120
Fax 974-6145
Sierra Vista MS 1,200/6-8
PO Box 269 91723 626-974-7300
Robert Shivers, prin. Fax 974-7315
Business Center Adult
PO Box 269 91723 626-974-6800
Vincent VanDetta, dir. Fax 974-6814
Tri Community Adult Ed.-Griswold Center Adult
PO Box 269 91723 626-472-7680
Ron Sommer, dir. Fax 472-7681
Other Schools – See West Covina

American Graduate University Post-Sec.
733 N Dodsworth Ave 91724 626-966-4576
Sonrise Christian S 400/4-8
1220 E Ruddock St 91724 626-331-0559
Dr. John Free, prin. Fax 339-8029
Western Christian HS 500/9-12
1115 E Puente St 91724 626-967-0733
Dr. Paul Kienel, supt. Fax 915-8824
Western Christian ISP 500/K-12
124 N Armel Dr 91722 626-332-9981
Marilyn Stephens, dir.

Crescent City, Del Norte, Pop. 7,825
Del Norte County USD 4,100/K-12
301 W Washington Blvd 95531 707-464-6141
Jan Moorehouse, supt. Fax 464-0238
www.delnorte.k12.ca.us
Crescent Elk MS 600/6-8
994 G St 95531 707-464-0320
Billy Hartwick, prin. Fax 464-0326
Del Norte County HS 1,100/9-12
1301 El Dorado St 95531 707-464-0260
Geoff Barney, prin. Fax 465-6923

Regional Occupational Center & Program
Supt. — None
Del Norte County ROP Vo/Tech
1301 El Dorado St 95531 707-464-0274
Jan Moorehouse, dir. Fax 465-6923

Crockett, Contra Costa, Pop. 3,228
John Swett USD 1,800/K-12
400 Parker Ave, 510-245-4300
Michael Roth, supt. Fax 245-4312
www.jsusd.k12.ca.us
Carquinez MS 400/6-8
1099 Pomona St 94525 510-787-1081
Linda Steensrud, prin. Fax 787-2359
Swett HS 700/9-12
1098 Pomona St 94525 510-787-1088
Robert Bass, prin. Fax 787-1930

Cudahy, Los Angeles, Pop. 25,004
Los Angeles USD
Supt. — See Los Angeles
Elizabeth S 2,500/K-12
4811 Elizabeth St 90201 323-562-0175
Barbara Gee, prin. Fax 560-8412

Culver City, Los Angeles, Pop. 39,603
Culver City USD 6,700/K-12
4034 Irving Pl 90232 310-842-4220
Diane Fiello, supt. Fax 842-4205
www.ccusd.k12.ca.us
Culver City HS 2,100/9-12
4401 Elenda St 90230 310-842-4200
Pam Magee, prin. Fax 842-4303
Culver City MS 1,700/6-8
4601 Elenda St 90230 310-842-4200
Jerry Kosch, prin. Fax 842-4304
Culver City Adult S Adult
4909 Overland Ave 90230 310-842-4300
Victor Gallardo, prin. Fax 842-4343

Antioch University Southern California Post-Sec.
400 Corporate Pointe 90230 310-578-1080
Gemological Institute of America Post-Sec.
600 Corporate Point Ste 100 90230 310-670-2100
Kayne ERAS Center 200/K-12
5350 Machado Ln 90230 310-737-9393
Dwight Counsel, prin.
West Los Angeles College Post-Sec.
4800 Freshman Dr 90230 310-287-4200

Cupertino, Santa Clara, Pop. 52,171
Cupertino UNSD 15,100/K-8
10301 Vista Dr 95014 408-252-3000
Phil Quon Ph.D., supt. Fax 255-4450
cupertino.ca.campusgrid.net
Hyde MS 1,000/6-8
19325 Bollinger Rd 95014 408-252-6290
Todd Shimada, prin. Fax 255-3288
Kennedy MS 1,400/6-8
821 Bubb Rd 95014 408-253-1525
Russ Ottey, prin. Fax 257-5777
Lawson MS 6-8
10401 Vista Dr 95014 408-255-7500
Karl Sonntag, prin. Fax 446-4987
Other Schools – See San Jose, Sunnyvale

Fremont UNHSD
Supt. — See Sunnyvale
Cupertino HS 1,500/9-12
10100 Finch Ave 95014 408-366-7300
Bill Richter, prin. Fax 255-8466
Homestead HS 2,000/9-12
21370 Homestead Rd 95014 408-522-2500
Graham Clark, prin. Fax 738-8631
Monta Vista HS 2,400/9-12
21840 McClellan Rd 95014 408-366-7600
April Scott, prin. Fax 252-1519

DeAnza College Post-Sec.
21250 Stevens Creek Blvd 95014 408-864-5678

Cypress, Orange, Pop. 47,383
Anaheim UNHSD
Supt. — See Anaheim
Cypress HS 2,300/9-12
9801 Valley View St 90630 714-220-4144
Ben Carpenter, prin. Fax 220-4174
Lexington JHS 1,200/7-8
4351 Orange Ave 90630 714-220-4201
Jodie Wales, prin. Fax 761-4989
Oxford Academy 1,100/7-12
5172 Orange Ave 90630 714-220-3055
Kathy Scott, prin. Fax 527-7128

Cypress College Post-Sec.
9200 Valley View St 90630 714-484-7000
Touro University International Post-Sec.
5665 Plaza Dr Fl 3 90630 714-816-0366

Daly City, San Mateo, Pop. 100,339
Bayshore ESD 400/K-8
1 Martin St 94014 415-467-5443
Stephen J. Waterman, supt. Fax 467-1542
www.bayshore.k12.ca.us
Robertson IS 200/4-8
1 Martin St 94014 415-467-5443
Norman D. Fobert, prin. Fax 467-1542

Jefferson ESD 6,300/K-8
101 Lincoln Ave 94015 650-991-1000
Barbara B. Wilson Ph.D., supt. Fax 992-2265
www.jsd.k12.ca.us/
Pollicita MS 700/6-8
550 E Market St 94014 650-991-1216
Joseph J. Spaulding, prin. Fax 755-2170
Rivera IS 500/7-8
1255 Southgate Ave 94015 650-991-1225
Jan Hopkins, prin. Fax 755-6273
Other Schools – See Colma

Jefferson UNHSD 5,400/9-12
699 Serramonte Blvd Ste 100 94015 650-550-7900
Michael Crilly, supt. Fax 550-7888
www.juhsd.net
Jefferson HS 1,300/9-12
6996 Mission St 94014 650-550-7700
Alice Campbell, prin. Fax 550-7790
Westmoor HS 1,800/9-12
131 Westmoor Ave 94015 650-550-7400
Richard Morosi, prin. Fax 550-7490
Adult Education Divison Adult
699 Serramonte Blvd Ste 111 94015 650-550-7890
Dana Rumney, prin. Fax 550-7889
Other Schools – See Pacifica

Hilltop Beauty School Post-Sec.
6317 Mission St 94014 650-756-2720

Dana Point, Orange, Pop. 35,867
Capistrano USD
Supt. — See San Juan Capistrano
Dana Hills HS 2,900/9-12
33333 Golden Lantern St 92629 949-496-6666
Rob Nye, prin. Fax 489-8317

Danville, Contra Costa, Pop. 41,852
San Ramon Valley USD 22,800/K-12
699 Old Orchard Dr 94526 925-552-5500
Robert Kessler, supt. Fax 838-3147
www.srvusd.net/
Diablo Vista MS 700/6-8
4100 Camino Tassajara 94506 925-648-8560
Becky Ingram, prin. Fax 648-7167
Los Cerros MS 800/6-8
968 Blemer Rd 94526 925-552-5620
Lisa Ward, prin. Fax 837-3512
Monte Vista HS 2,300/9-12
3131 Stone Valley Rd 94526 925-552-5530
Rebecca Smith, prin. Fax 743-1744
San Ramon Valley HS 2,100/9-12
140 Love Ln 94526 925-552-5580
Joseph Ianora, prin. Fax 838-7802
Wood MS 1,000/6-8
600 El Capitan Dr 94526 925-552-5600
Sandy Budde, prin. Fax 820-1857
Other Schools – See Alamo, San Ramon

Athenian S 400/6-12
2100 Mount Diablo Scenic Bl 94506 925-837-5375
Eleanor Dase, hdmstr. Fax 831-1120

Davis, Yolo, Pop. 60,709
Davis JUSD 8,500/K-12
526 B St 95616 530-757-5300
David Murphy, supt. Fax 757-5423
www.djusd.k12.ca.us
Davis SHS 1,800/10-12
315 W 14th St 95616 530-757-5400
Michael Cawley, prin. Fax 757-5492
Emerson JHS 700/7-9
2121 Calaveras Ave 95616 530-757-5430
Diane Studley, prin. Fax 757-5434
Harper JHS 500/7-9
4000 E Covell Blvd 95616 530-759-2182
David Inns, prin. Fax 759-2321
Holmes JHS 800/7-9
1220 Drexel Dr 95616 530-757-5455
Bev Maul, prin. Fax 757-5435
Davis Adult S Adult
315 W 14th St 95616 530-757-5380
Laurel Clumpner, prin. Fax 757-5381

D-Q University Post-Sec.
PO Box 409 95617 530-758-0470
University of California Post-Sec.
1 Shields Ave 95616 530-752-1011

Delano, Kern, Pop. 45,531
Delano JUNHSD 4,100/9-12
1747 Princeton St 93215 661-725-4000
Sherrill Hufnagel, supt. Fax 721-9390
www.djuhsd.org/
Chavez HS 1,400/9-12
1747 Princeton St 93215 661-720-4502
Saul D. Gonzalez, prin. Fax 725-8875
Delano HS 2,300/9-12
1747 Princeton St 93215 661-720-4121
Richard Smithey, prin. Fax 720-4119
Delano Adult Adult
1747 Princeton St 93215 661-720-4171
Alfred Sanchez, prin. Fax 725-5852

Delano UNESD 7,400/K-8
1405 12th Ave 93215 661-721-5000
Ronald A.Garcia, supt. Fax 725-2446
www.duesd.org
Almond Tree MS 1,000/6-8
1405 12th Ave 93215 661-721-3641
Ken Spencer, prin. Fax 721-3649
Cecil Avenue MS 1,000/6-8
1405 12th Ave 93215 661-721-5030
Martin Bans, prin. Fax 721-5097
La Vina MS 6-8
1405 12th Ave 93215 661-721-3601
Michael Dobrenen, prin. Fax 721-7764

Bakersfield College Post-Sec.
1942 Randolph St 93215 661-725-8020
Sequoia Christian Academy 50/K-12
PO Box 1876 93216 661-721-2721
Roberta Hunter, prin. Fax 721-2721

Delhi, Merced, Pop. 3,280
Delhi USD 2,500/K-12
9716 Hinton Ave 95315 209-656-2000
Bill Baltazar, supt. Fax 668-6133
www.delhi.k12.ca.us
Delhi HS 600/9-12
9716 Hinton Ave 95315 209-669-3178
Mike Horwood, prin. Fax 669-3168
Delhi MS 400/7-8
9716 Hinton Ave 95315 209-669-3178
Dave Woods, prin. Fax 669-3168
Delhi Adult S Adult
9716 Hinton Ave 95315 209-656-2012
Francisca Briones, prin. Fax 669-6165

Denair, Stanislaus, Pop. 3,693
Denair USD 1,200/K-12
3460 Lester Rd 95316 209-632-7514
Edward Parraz, supt. Fax 632-9194
dusd.k12.ca.us
Denair HS 400/9-12
3431 Lester Rd 95316 209-632-9911
Jerry Savelson, prin. Fax 632-8153
Denair MS 300/5-8
3460 Lester Rd 95316 209-632-2510
Darrin Allen, prin. Fax 632-0269

Providence Christian Academy 200/K-12
PO Box 616 95316 209-656-0744
Paulette Applegate, prin.

Desert Hot Springs, Riverside, Pop. 20,492
Palm Springs USD
Supt. — See Palm Springs
Desert Hot Springs HS 1,600/9-12
65850 Pierson Blvd 92240 760-288-7000
Milt Jones, prin. Fax 288-7010
Desert Springs MS 1,500/6-8
66755 Two Bunch Palms Trl 92240 760-251-7200
Ryan Saunders, prin. Fax 251-7206

Image School of Cosmetology Post-Sec.
13070 Palm Dr 92240 760-251-5373
Palm Springs Christian S 50/7-12
66675 Pierson Blvd 92240 760-329-5466
Dr. Alon Barak, hdmstr. Fax 329-9324

Diamond Bar, Los Angeles, Pop. 57,975
Pomona USD
Supt. — See Pomona
Lorbeer MS 1,000/7-8
501 S Diamond Bar Blvd 91765 909-397-4527
Kathrine Morillo-Shone, prin. Fax 396-9022

Walnut Valley USD
Supt. — See Walnut
Chaparral MS 1,300/6-8
1405 Spruce Tree Dr 91765 909-861-6227
Dr. Michael Chavez, prin. Fax 396-0749
Diamond Bar HS 3,200/9-12
21400 Pathfinder Rd 91765 909-594-1405
Denis Paul, prin. Fax 595-8301

Diamond Springs, El Dorado, Pop. 2,872
El Dorado UNHSD
Supt. — See Placerville
El Dorado Adult HS Adult
PO Box 1450 95619 530-622-7073
Don Buchheit, prin. Fax 642-2291

Regional Occupational Center & Program
Supt. — None
Central Sierra ROP Vo/Tech
PO Box 1450 95619 530-295-2296
Dave Soper, dir. Fax 295-1273

Dinuba, Tulare, Pop. 19,308
Dinuba USD 5,600/K-12
1327 E El Monte Way 93618 559-595-7200
Jerry L. Sessions, supt. Fax 591-3334
www.dinubausd.com
Dinuba HS 1,600/9-12
1327 E El Monte Way 93618 559-595-7220
Yolanda Valdez, prin. Fax 591-3655
Washington IS 900/7-8
1327 E El Monte Way 93618 559-595-7252
Nancy Ruble, prin. Fax 595-8158
Dinuba Adult S Adult
1327 E El Monte Way 93618 559-595-7242
Bill Weller, prin. Fax 595-7248

Dinuba Jr. Academy 50/K-10
218 S Crawford Ave 93618 559-591-0194
Emily Villeda, prin. Fax 591-4835

Dixon, Solano, Pop. 17,330
Dixon USD 4,000/K-12
180 S 1st St Ste 6 95620 707-678-5582
Wally Holbrook, supt. Fax 678-0726
www.dixonusd.org
Dixon HS 1,100/9-12
455 E A St 95620 707-678-2391
Tom Herman, prin. Fax 678-9318
Jacobs IS 700/7-8
200 N Lincoln St 95620 707-678-9222
Yolanda Falkenberg, prin. Fax 678-1245

Dorris, Siskiyou, Pop. 875
Butte Valley USD 300/K-12
PO Box 709 96023 530-397-3840
Ed Traverso, supt. Fax 397-3842
www.bvalusd.org/
Butte Valley HS 100/9-12
PO Box 709 96023 530-397-3990
Ed Traverso, prin. Fax 397-3989
Butte Valley Adult S Adult
PO Box 709 96023 530-397-3363
Ed Traverso, prin. Fax 397-3360
Other Schools – See Macdoel

Dos Palos, Merced, Pop. 5,036
Dos Palos Oro Loma JUSD 2,600/K-12
2041 Almond St 93620 209-392-6101
Brian Walker, supt. Fax 392-3347
www.dpol.net
Bryant MS 600/6-8
16695 Bryant Ave 93620 209-392-6186
Katy Miller, prin. Fax 392-2636
Dos Palos HS 700/9-12
1701 E Blossom St 93620 209-392-2131
Terri Gill, prin. Fax 392-2705

Downey, Los Angeles, Pop. 109,718
Downey USD 22,500/K-12
PO Box 7017 90241 562-469-6500
Dr. Wendy Doty, supt. Fax 469-6515
www.dusd.net/
Downey HS 3,800/9-12
11040 Brookshire Ave 90241 562-869-7301
Tom Houts, prin. Fax 469-7340
East MS 1,300/6-8
10301 Woodruff Ave 90241 562-904-3586
Brent Shubin, prin. Fax 469-7240
Griffiths MS 1,400/6-8
9633 Tweedy Ln 90240 562-904-3580
Gregg Stapp, prin. Fax 469-7260
Sussman MS 1,500/6-8
12500 Birchdale Ave 90242 562-904-3572
Gloria Widmann, prin. Fax 469-7280
Warren HS 3,400/9-12
8141 De Palma St 90241 562-869-7306
Eileen Wannett, prin. Fax 469-7360
West MS 1,400/6-8
11985 Old River School Rd 90242 562-904-3565
Craig Bertsch, prin. Fax 469-7300
Downey Adult S Adult
12340 Woodruff Ave 90241 562-940-6200
R. Brossmer, prin. Fax 940-6221

Regional Occupational Center & Program
Supt. — None
Los Angeles County ROP Vo/Tech
9300 Imperial Hwy 90242 562-922-6850
Dr. Nancy Wagner, dir. Fax 928-1672

Calvary Chapel Christian S 1,000/K-12
12808 Woodruff Ave 90242 562-803-4076
Phillip O'Malley, admin. Fax 803-9916
Keystone Academy 200/K-12
8615 Florence Ave Ste 207 90240 562-862-7134
Philip Trout, hdmstr.
Los Amigos Research & Education Inst. Post-Sec.
PO Box 3500 90242 562-401-8111
St. Matthias HS 500/9-12
7851 Gardendale St 90242 562-861-2271
Margaret Meland, prin. Fax 869-8652

Downieville, Sierra
Sierra-Plumas JUSD
Supt. — See Sierraville
Downieville JSHS 50/7-12
PO Box B 95936 530-289-3473
James Berardi, prin. Fax 289-3693

Duarte, Los Angeles, Pop. 22,194
Duarte USD 4,600/K-12
1620 Huntington Dr 91010 626-599-5000
Dr. Dean Conklin, supt. Fax 599-5072
www.duarte.k12.ca.us
Duarte HS 1,200/9-12
1620 Huntington Dr 91010 626-599-5700
Bill Martinez, prin. Fax 599-5784
Northview IS 700/7-8
1620 Huntington Dr 91010 626-599-5600
Miriam Fox, prin. Fax 599-5684

City of Hope Medical Center Post-Sec.
1500 Duarte Rd 91010 626-359-8111

Dublin, Alameda, Pop. 39,328
Dublin USD 4,600/K-12
7471 Larkdale Ave 94568 925-828-2551
Dr. Stephen Hanke, supt. Fax 829-6532
www.dublin.k12.ca.us
Dublin HS 1,300/9-12
8151 Village Pkwy 94568 925-833-3300
Carol Shimizu, prin. Fax 833-3322
Wells MS 1,000/6-8
6800 Penn Dr 94568 925-828-6227
Kathy Rosselle, prin. Fax 829-8851

Valley Christian JSHS 500/7-12
7500 Inspiration Dr 94568 925-560-6200
Jane Kitchen, prin. Fax 828-5623

Dunsmuir, Siskiyou, Pop. 1,870
Dunsmuir JUNHSD 100/9-12
5805 High School Way 96025 530-235-4835
Leonard Foreman, supt. Fax 235-2224
tiger.sisnet.ssku.k12.ca.us/
Dunsmuir HS 100/9-12
5805 High School Way 96025 530-235-4835
Leonard Foreman, prin. Fax 235-2224

Durham, Butte, Pop. 4,784
Durham USD 1,200/K-12
PO Box 300 95938 530-895-4675
Dr. Penny Chennell Carter, supt. Fax 895-4692
www.durhamunified.org/
Durham HS 400/9-12
PO Box 600 95938 530-895-4680
Paul Arnold, prin. Fax 895-4688
Durham IS 300/6-8
PO Box 310 95938 530-895-4690
Rick Desimone, prin. Fax 895-4305

Earlimart, Tulare, Pop. 5,881
Earlimart ESD 1,900/K-8
PO Box 11970 93219 661-849-3386
Dr. Marcella Smith, supt. Fax 849-2352
www.earlimart.org
Earlimart MS 600/6-8
PO Box 11970 93219 661-849-2611
Judith Cunningham, prin. Fax 849-4214

East Palo Alto, San Mateo, Pop. 32,242
Ravenswood City ESD 3,200/PK-8
2160 Euclid Ave 94303 650-329-2800
Maria De La Vega, supt. Fax 323-1072
www.ravenswood.k12.ca.us
Chavez ES 500/4-8
2450 Ralmar Ave 94303 650-329-6700
David Herrera, prin. Fax 326-8902
San Francisco 49er Academy 100/6-8
2086 Clarke Ave 94303 650-614-4300
Phil Duncan, dir. Fax 614-4310

Edwards, Kern
Muroc JUSD
Supt. — See North Edwards
Desert HS 400/9-12
1575 Payne Ave 93523 661-258-4411
Nat Adams, prin. Fax 258-5029
Edwards MS 200/7-8
1575 Payne Ave 93523 661-258-4411
Nat Adams, prin. Fax 258-5029

El Cajon, San Diego, Pop. 92,487
Cajon Valley UNESD 17,200/K-8
PO Box 1007 92022 619-588-3000
Janice L. Cook Ed.D., supt. Fax 588-7653
www.cajonvalley.net/
Cajon Valley MS 900/6-8
395 Ballantyne St 92020 619-588-3092
Rod Girvin, prin. Fax 579-4817
Emerald MS 1,000/6-8
1221 Emerald Ave 92020 619-588-3097
James Raymond, prin. Fax 588-3225
Greenfield MS 900/7-8
1495 Greenfield Dr 92021 619-588-3103
Froylan Villanueva, prin. Fax 588-3648
Hillsdale MS 1,500/6-8
1301 Brabham St 92019 619-441-6156
Don Hohimer, prin. Fax 441-6185
Montgomery MS 1,100/6-8
1570 Melody Ln 92019 619-588-3107
Kelly Madden, prin. Fax 441-6122

Grossmont UNHSD 22,100/9-12
1100 Murray Dr 92020 619-644-8000
Terry Ryan, supt. Fax 465-1349
www.guhsd.net
El Cajon Valley HS 2,200/9-12
1035 E Madison Ave 92021 619-401-4700
Paul Dautremont, prin. Fax 447-3943
Granite Hills HS 2,800/9-12
1719 E Madison Ave 92019 619-593-5500
Georgette Torres, prin. Fax 588-9389
Grossmont HS 2,400/9-12
1100 Murray Dr 92020 619-668-6000
Theresa Kemper, prin. Fax 463-7108
Valhalla HS 1,900/9-12
1725 Hillsdale Rd 92019 619-593-5300
Larry Martinsen, prin. Fax 588-9713
Adult Education-Foothill Adult
1550 Melody Ln 92019 619-401-4200
Colette Fleming, prin. Fax 579-9291
Other Schools – See Lakeside, Santee, Spring Valley

Advanced Training Associates Post-Sec.
1810 Gillespie Way Ste 104 92020 619-596-2766
Christian HS 600/7-12
2100 Greenfield Dr 92019 619-440-1531
Chuck Leslie, supt. Fax 590-1717
Cuyamaca College Post-Sec.
900 Rancho San Diego Pkwy 92019 619-660-4000
Foothills Christian HS 200/9-12
2321 Dryden Rd 92020 619-447-8124
Loren Naffziger, prin. Fax 741-2648
Grossmont College Post-Sec.
8800 Grossmont College Dr 92020 619-644-7000
Je Boutique College of Beauty Post-Sec.
1073 E Main St 92021 619-442-3407
San Diego Christian College Post-Sec.
2100 Greenfield Dr 92019 619-441-2200
Southern California Seminary Post-Sec.
2075 E Madison Ave 92019 888-389-7244

El Centro, Imperial, Pop. 39,636
Central UNHSD 4,100/9-12
351 W Ross Ave, 760-336-4500
C. Thomas Budde Ph.D., supt. Fax 353-3606
www.cuhsd.net
Central Union HS 1,700/9-12
1001 W Brighton Ave, 760-336-4300
Emma Jones, prin. Fax 353-3570
Southwest HS 2,200/9-12
2001 Ocotillo Dr, 760-336-4100
Joe Evangelist, prin. Fax 353-0467
Central Adult Education Adult
1302 S 3rd St, 760-336-4544
Sherry Spencer, dir. Fax 336-4547

El Centro ESD 5,700/K-8
1256 Broadway St, 760-352-5712
Michael Klentschy, supt. Fax 312-9522
www.ecsd.k12.ca.us/
Kennedy MS 800/6-8
900 N 6th St, 760-352-0444
Renato Montano, prin. Fax 353-0325
Wilson JHS 900/7-8
600 S Wilson St, 760-352-5341
Matt Phillips, prin. Fax 337-3800

Regional Occupational Center & Program
Supt. — None
Imperial Valley ROP Vo/Tech
687 W State St, 760-482-2600
Mary Camacho, supt. Fax 482-2751

Christ Community S 100/K-12
585 W Orange Ave, 760-337-9444
Susan Arroyave, prin. Fax 337-1330

El Cerrito, Contra Costa, Pop. 22,868
West Contra Costa USD
Supt. — See Richmond
El Cerrito HS 1,400/9-12
540 Ashbury Ave 94530 510-525-0234
Vince Rhea, prin. Fax 525-1810
Portola MS 700/6-8
1021 Navellier St 94530 510-524-0405
Kal Phan, prin. Fax 559-8784

El Dorado, El Dorado
El Dorado UNHSD
Supt. — See Placerville
Union Mine HS 800/9-10
6530 Koki Ln 95623 530-621-4003
Carl Fickle, prin. Fax 622-6034

El Dorado Hills, El Dorado, Pop. 6,395
Buckeye UNESD
Supt. — See Shingle Springs
Rolling Hills MS 800/6-8
7141 Silva Valley Pkwy 95762 916-933-9290
Gloria Silva, prin. Fax 939-7454

El Dorado UNHSD
Supt. — See Placerville
Oak Ridge HS 1,900/9-12
1120 Harvard Way 95762 916-933-6980
Stephen Wehr, prin. Fax 933-6987

Rescue UNESD
Supt. — See Rescue
Marina Village MS 600/6-8
1901 Francisco Dr 95762 916-933-3993
Colleen Johnson, prin. Fax 933-3995

Elk Creek, Glenn
Stony Creek JUSD 100/K-12
PO Box 68 95939 530-968-5361
Charles Beath, supt. Fax 968-5102
www.glenn-co.k12.ca.us/ech/
Elk Creek JSHS 100/7-12
PO Box 68 95939 530-968-5361
Charles Beath, prin. Fax 968-5102

Elk Grove, Sacramento, Pop. 112,338
Elk Grove USD 58,000/PK-12
9510 Elk Grove Florin Rd 95624 916-686-5085
Steven Ladd Ed.D., supt. Fax 686-7787
www.egusd.k12.ca.us
Albiani MS 7-8
9140 Bradshaw Rd 95624 916-686-5210
Ramona Nelson, prin. Fax 686-5538
Eddy MS 1,100/7-8
9329 Soaring Oaks Dr 95758 916-683-1302
Peter Lambert, prin. Fax 684-6142
Elk Grove HS 2,600/9-12
9800 Elk Grove Florin Rd 95624 916-686-7741
Catherine Guy, prin. Fax 685-5515
Franklin HS 2,600/9-12
6400 Whitelock Pkwy, 916-714-8150
Charlotte Phinizy, prin. Fax 714-8155
Harris MS 1,100/7-8
8691 Power Inn Rd 95624 916-688-0075
Felicia Bessent, prin. Fax 688-0084
Johnson MS 1,500/7-8
10099 Franklin High Rd, 916-714-8181
Patrick McDougall, prin. Fax 714-8177
Kerr MS 1,500/7-8
8865 Elk Grove Blvd 95624 916-686-7728
Patricia Dwairi, prin. Fax 685-2952
Laguna Creek HS 2,100/9-12
9050 Vicino Dr 95758 916-683-1339
Douglas Craig, prin. Fax 683-3128

Monterey Trail HS 900/9-12
8661 Power Inn Rd 95624 916-688-0050
Terry Chapman, prin. Fax 688-0058
Pleasant Grove HS 9-12
9531 Bond Rd 95624 916-686-0230
Frank Lucia, prin. Fax 686-0239
Other Schools – See Sacramento

DeVry University Post-Sec.
2218 Kausen Dr 95758 916-478-2847
Lutheran HS 100/9-12
9270 Bruceville Rd 95758 916-691-2277
Kris Schneider, prin. Fax 691-2292

El Monte, Los Angeles, Pop. 122,513
El Monte City ESD 11,000/K-8
3540 Lexington Ave 91731 626-453-3700
Jeffrey Seymour, supt. Fax 442-1063
www.emcsd.org/
Durfee IS 700/4-8
12233 Star St 91732 626-443-3900
Suzanne Seymour, prin. Fax 579-0451

El Monte UNHSD 10,400/9-12
3537 Johnson Ave 91731 626-444-9005
Kathy M. Furnald, supt. Fax 350-1095
www.emuhsd.k12.ca.us
Arroyo HS 2,300/9-12
4921 Cedar Ave 91732 626-444-9201
Keith Richardson, prin. Fax 443-1175
El Monte HS 2,100/9-12
3048 Tyler Ave 91731 626-444-7701
Joel Kyne, prin. Fax 442-6594
Mountain View HS 1,900/9-12
2900 Parkway Dr 91732 626-443-6181
Sandra Stevens, prin. Fax 442-7284
El Monte/Rosemead Adult Education Adult
10807 Ramona Blvd 91731 626-443-9491
Victor Chavez, prin. Fax 258-5809
Other Schools – See Rosemead, South El Monte

Mountain View ESD 10,000/K-8
3320 Gilman Rd 91732 626-652-4000
Gary Rapkin, supt. Fax 652-4052
www.mtview.k12.ca.us
Kranz IS 1,300/7-8
12460 Fineview St 91732 626-652-4200
Toni Bias, prin. Fax 652-4215
Madrid MS 1,300/6-8
3300 Gilman Rd 91732 626-652-4300
Sylvia Rivera, prin. Fax 652-4315

International Theological Seminary Post-Sec.
3225 Tyler Ave 91731 626-448-0023
Logos Evangelical Seminary Post-Sec.
9358 Telstar Ave 91731 626-571-5110
Palladium Technical Academy Post-Sec.
10507 Valley Blvd Ste 806 91731 626-444-0880
Professional Institute of Beauty Post-Sec.
10801 Valley Mall 91731 626-443-9401

Paso Robles, San Luis Obispo, Pop. 20,187
Paso Robles JUSD 6,700/K-12
PO Box 7010 93447 805-238-2222
Patrick Sayne Ed.D., supt. Fax 237-3324
www.pasoschools.org/
Flamson MS 800/6-8
PO Box 7010 93447 805-237-3350
Frank Galicia, prin. Fax 237-3427
Lewis MS 700/6-8
PO Box 7010 93447 805-237-3450
Rick Oyler, prin. Fax 237-3458
Paso Robles HS 2,100/9-12
PO Box 7010 93447 805-237-3333
Ed Railsback, prin. Fax 237-3424

Advanced Christian Training S 100/K-12
PO Box 97 93447 805-239-0707
William Thompson, admin. Fax 238-1133
Design School of Cosemetology Post-Sec.
715 24th St Ste E 93446 805-237-8575
Solid Rock Christian Academy 50/K-12
4918 Sparrowhawk Ln 93446 805-610-5318
Yasmin Nason, dir.

El Portal, Mariposa
Mariposa County USD
Supt. — See Mariposa
Yosemite Park HS 50/9-12
PO Box 49 95318 209-379-2414
Phyllis Weber, admin. Fax 379-2414

El Segundo, Los Angeles, Pop. 16,517
El Segundo USD 3,300/K-12
641 Sheldon St 90245 310-615-2650
Bruce Auld Ed.D., supt. Fax 640-8272
www.elsegundousd.com
El Segundo HS 1,200/9-12
641 Sheldon St 90245 310-615-2662
Jim Garza, prin. Fax 640-8079
El Segundo MS 800/6-8
641 Sheldon St 90245 310-615-2690
Marian Chiarra, prin. Fax 640-9634

El Sobrante, Contra Costa, Pop. 9,852
West Contra Costa USD
Supt. — See Richmond
Crespi JHS 800/7-8
1121 Allview Ave 94803 510-223-8611
Sherry Bell, prin. Fax 243-2090

Calvary Christian Academy 200/PK-12
4892 San Pablo Dam Rd 94803 510-222-3828
Susan Blankenchip, admin. Fax 222-3702
East Bay Waldorf S 300/K-12
3800 Clark Rd 94803 510-223-3570
Morgan Cleveland, admin. Fax 222-3141
El Sobrante Christian JSHS 200/7-12
5070 Appian Way 94803 510-223-1966
C. Scott Wells, prin. Fax 223-5344

Elverta, Sacramento
Elverta JESD 300/K-8
8920 Elwyn Ave 95626 916-991-4726
Dianna Mangerich Ed.D., supt. Fax 991-5888
www.elverta.k12.ca.us/
Alpha Technology MS 100/6-8
8920 Elwyn Ave 95626 916-991-4726
Dianna Mangerich Ed.D., prin. Fax 991-5888

Emeryville, Alameda, Pop. 8,528
Emery USD 800/K-12
4727 San Pablo Ave 94608 510-601-4000
Anthony Smith Ph.D., supt. Fax 601-4913
www.emeryusd.k12.ca.us
Emery HS 400/7-12
1100 47th St 94608 510-601-4961
Antonio Cediel, prin. Fax 601-4988

Expression College for Digital Arts Post-Sec.
6601 Shellmound St 94608 510-654-2934
Western Career College Post-Sec.
6001 Shellmound St Ste 145 94608 510-601-0133

Empire, Stanislaus
Empire UNESD
Supt. — See Modesto
Teel MS 800/6-8
PO Box 1300 95319 209-526-0684
Nancy Fox, prin. Fax 544-8401

Encinitas, San Diego, Pop. 59,525
San Dieguito UNHSD 11,900/7-12
710 Encinitas Blvd 92024 760-753-6491
Peggy Lynch Ed.D., supt. Fax 943-1542
www.sduhsd.net
Diegueno MS 1,000/7-8
710 Encinitas Blvd 92024 760-944-1892
Marilyn Pugh, prin. Fax 944-3717
Oak Crest MS 1,000/7-8
710 Encinitas Blvd 92024 760-753-6241
Terry Calen, prin. Fax 942-0520
San Dieguito HS Academy 1,500/9-12
710 Encinitas Blvd 92024 760-753-1121
Barbara Gauthier, prin. Fax 753-8142
San Dieguito Adult HS Adult
710 Encinitas Blvd 92024 760-753-7073
Denise Stanley, prin. Fax 436-8376
Other Schools – See Carlsbad, San Diego, Solana Beach

Encino, See Los Angeles

Crespi Carmelite HS 500/9-12
5031 Alonzo Ave 91316 818-345-1672
Fr. Paul Henson, prin. Fax 705-0209
Ferrahian HS 600/6-12
5300 White Oak Ave 91316 818-892-7991
John Kossakian, prin.
Phillips Graduate Institute Post-Sec.
5445 Balboa Blvd 91316 818-386-5600
Westmark S 200/2-12
5461 Louise Ave 91316 818-986-5045
Dr. Leslie Barnebey, hdmstr. Fax 986-2605

Escalon, San Joaquin, Pop. 7,171
Escalon USD 3,100/K-12
1520 Yosemite Ave 95320 209-838-3591
Dave Mantooth, supt. Fax 838-6703
www.escalonusd.org/
El Portal MS 700/6-8
805 1st St 95320 209-838-7095
Pam Collingsworth, prin. Fax 838-3017
Escalon HS 1,000/9-12
1528 Yosemite Ave 95320 209-838-7073
Joel Johannsen, prin. Fax 838-6127

Escondido, San Diego, Pop. 134,085
Escondido UNESD 18,200/PK-8
1330 E Grand Ave 92027 760-432-2400
Jennifer Walters, supt. Fax 735-2874
www.eusd4kids.org/
Bear Valley MS 1,200/6-8
3003 Bear Valley Pkwy S 92025 760-432-4060
Julie Rich, prin. Fax 504-0158
Del Dios MS 1,100/6-8
1400 W 9th Ave 92029 760-432-2439
Darren McDuffie, prin. Fax 432-0728
Hidden Valley MS 1,300/6-8
2700 Reed Rd 92027 760-432-2457
Kyle Ruggles, prin. Fax 480-0845
Mission MS 1,200/6-8
939 E Mission Ave 92025 760-432-2452
Leticia Aroyo, prin. Fax 737-9085
Rincon MS 1,500/6-8
925 Lehner Ave 92026 760-432-2491
Jon Centofranchi, prin. Fax 743-6713

Escondido UNHSD 7,900/9-12
302 N Midway Dr 92027 760-291-3200
Ed Nelson, supt. Fax 480-3163
euhsd.k12.ca.us
Escondido HS 2,600/9-12
1535 N Broadway 92026 760-291-4000
Sue Emerson, prin. Fax 739-7313
Orange Glen HS 2,300/9-12
2200 Glenridge Rd 92027 760-291-5000
Diego Ochoa, prin. Fax 739-7314
San Pasqual HS 2,300/9-12
3300 Bear Valley Pkwy S 92025 760-291-6000
Martin Griffin, prin. Fax 739-7315
Valley HS 400/9-12
410 Hidden Trails Rd 92027 760-291-2240
Saundra Uribe-Silverman, prin. Fax 741-7605
Escondido Adult S Adult
3750 Mary Ln 92025 760-739-7300
Dom Gagliardi, prin. Fax 739-7310

Calvin Christian JSHS 400/6-12
2000 N Broadway 92026 760-489-6430
Frank Steidl, prin. Fax 489-7055
Christian LIFE Academy 200/K-12
PO Box 300038 92030 760-741-7651
Escondido Adventist Academy 300/K-12
1233 W 9th Ave 92029 760-746-1800
Kristine Fuentes, prin. Fax 743-3499
Westminster Seminary California Post-Sec.
1725 Bear Valley Pkwy 92027 760-480-8474

Esparto, Yolo, Pop. 1,487
Esparto USD 900/K-12
26675 Plainfield St 95627 530-787-3446
Dr. Thomas Michaelson, supt. Fax 787-3033
www.espartok12.org
Esparto HS 300/9-12
26675 Plainfield St 95627 530-787-3405
Cheryl Bremer, prin. Fax 787-4850
Esparto MS 200/6-8
26675 Plainfield St 95627 530-787-4151
Chuck Tracy, prin. Fax 787-3890

Etiwanda, See Rancho Cucamonga
Chaffey JUNHSD
Supt. — See Ontario
Etiwanda HS 3,300/9-12
13500 Victoria St 91739 909-899-2531
Lynne Ditfurth, prin. Fax 899-3661

Etiwanda ESD 11,800/K-8
6061 East Ave 91739 909-899-2451
Shawn Judson, supt. Fax 899-1656
www.etiwanda.k12.ca.us
Day Creek IS 900/6-8
12345 Coyote Dr 91739 909-803-3300
Charlayne Sprague, prin. Fax 803-3309
Etiwanda IS 1,200/6-8
6925 Etiwanda Ave 91739 909-899-1701
Janella Cantu-Myricks, prin. Fax 899-5676
Summit IS 900/6-8
5959 East Ave 91739 909-899-1704
Lori Arita, prin. Fax 899-7596
Other Schools – See Fontana

Etna, Siskiyou, Pop. 796
Etna UNHSD
Supt. — See Fort Jones
Etna HS 300/9-12
PO Box 721 96027 530-467-3244
Jim Isbell, prin. Fax 467-5763
Scott River Adult S Adult
PO Box 59 96027 530-467-5279
Ken Fowle, admin. Fax 467-3459

Eureka, Humboldt, Pop. 25,579
Eureka City SD 4,600/K-12
3200 Walford Ave 95503 707-441-2400
Denise Jones, supt. Fax 441-3326
www.eurekacityschools.org
Eureka HS 1,700/9-12
1915 J St 95501 707-441-2508
Bob Steffen, prin. Fax 445-1956
Winship MS 600/6-8
2500 Cypress St 95503 707-441-2487
Paul Gossard, prin. Fax 441-2490
Zane MS 600/6-8
2155 S St 95501 707-441-2470
Teddie Lyons, prin. Fax 441-0286
Eureka Adult Education Adult
674 Allard Ave 95503 707-441-2448
Greg Aslanian, prin. Fax 442-1403

Fortuna UNHSD
Supt. — See Fortuna
Academy of the Redwoods 9-12
7361 Tompkins Hill Rd 95501 707-476-4203
Keri Gelenian, prin.

Regional Occupational Center & Program
Supt. — None
Humboldt County ROP Vo/Tech
901 Myrtle Ave 95501 707-445-7000
Garry Eagles, supt. Fax 445-7143

Frederick and Charles Beauty College Post-Sec.
831 F St 95501 707-443-2733
Gospel Outreach S 50/K-12
PO Box 1022 95502 707-445-1167
David Sczepanski, prin. Fax 445-1562
Redwoods Community College Post-Sec.
7351 Tompkins Hill Rd 95501 707-476-4100
St. Bernard S 300/PK-12
222 Dollison St 95501 707-443-2735
Patrick Daly, pres. Fax 443-4723

Exeter, Tulare, Pop. 9,974
Exeter UNSD 3,100/K-12
134 S E St 93221 559-592-9421
Renee Whitson, supt. Fax 592-9445
www.exeterpublicschools.org/
Exeter Union HS 1,000/9-12
505 Rocky Hill Dr 93221 559-592-2127
Don Brinkman, prin. Fax 592-3539
Wilson MS 700/6-8
265 Albert Ave 93221 559-592-2144
Frank Silveira, prin. Fax 592-5536

Sierra View Junior Academy 100/K-10
19933 Avenue 256 93221 559-592-3689
Gail Cook, prin. Fax 592-5615

Fairfax, Marin, Pop. 7,106
Ross Valley ESD
Supt. — See San Anselmo
White Hill MS 600/6-8
101 Glen Dr 94930 415-454-8390
Michele Patterson, prin. Fax 454-3980

Fairfield, Solano, Pop. 104,476
Fairfield-Suisun USD 23,400/K-12
2490 Hilborn Rd, 707-399-5000
Woodrow Carter Ph.D., supt. Fax 399-1250
www.fsusd.k12.ca.us
Armijo HS 2,400/9-12
824 Washington St 94533 707-438-3378
Steven Peters, prin. Fax 438-3390

Dover MS — 800/6-8
301 E Alaska Ave 94533 — 707-421-4145
Jeff Crane, prin. — Fax 421-4252
Fairfield HS — 2,300/9-12
205 E Atlantic Ave 94533 — 707-438-3000
Patty Barnett, prin. — Fax 421-3977
Grange MS — 700/7-8
1975 Blossom Ave 94533 — 707-421-4175
Eric Tretten, prin. — Fax 422-4004
Green Valley MS — 800/7-8
1350 Gold Hill Rd, — 707-646-7000
Greg Hubbs, prin. — Fax 864-1503
Rodriguez HS — 2,100/9-12
5000 Red Top Rd, — 707-863-7950
Toni Taylor, prin. — Fax 863-7974
Sullivan MS — 900/7-8
2195 Union Ave 94533 — 707-421-4115
Reginald Marsh, prin. — Fax 421-3964
Fairfield-Suisun Adult Education — Adult
1100 Civic Center Dr 94533 — 707-421-4155
Vickie Good, prin. — Fax 421-4158
Other Schools – See Suisun City

Regional Occupational Center & Program
Supt. — None
Solano County ROP — Vo/Tech
2460 Clay Bank Rd 94533 — 707-399-4800
Janet Harden, dir. — Fax 429-1360

Travis USD — 5,300/K-12
2751 De Ronde Dr 94533 — 707-437-4604
Kate Wren Gavlak, supt. — Fax 437-3378
www.travisusd.k12.ca.us
Golden West MS — 900/7-8
2651 De Ronde Dr 94533 — 707-437-8240
Jim Bryan, prin. — Fax 437-3416
Vanden HS — 1,400/9-12
2951 Markeley Ln 94533 — 707-437-8270
Sheila McCabe, prin. — Fax 437-8295

Milan Institute of Cosmetology — Post-Sec.
934 Missouri St 94533 — 707-425-2288
Solano Community College — Post-Sec.
4000 Suisun Valley Rd, — 707-864-7000

Fair Oaks, Sacramento, Pop. 28,300
San Juan USD
Supt. — See Carmichael
Bella Vista HS — 1,900/9-12
8301 Madison Ave 95628 — 916-971-5052
Marlyn Pino-Jones, prin. — Fax 971-5011
Del Campo HS — 1,800/9-12
4925 Dewey Dr 95628 — 916-971-5664
Gail Pierce, prin. — Fax 971-5640
Rogers MS — 900/7-8
4924 Dewey Dr 95628 — 916-971-7889
Monty Muller, prin. — Fax 971-7903

Freedom Christian S — 100/PK-12
7736 Sunset Ave 95628 — 916-962-3247
Annette Coller, admin. — Fax 962-0783
Sacramento Waldorf S — 400/PK-12
3750 Bannister Rd 95628 — 916-961-3900
Elizabeth Beaven, admin. — Fax 961-3970

Fallbrook, San Diego, Pop. 22,095
Fallbrook UNESD — 6,000/K-8
321 Iowa St 92028 — 760-723-7020
Janice Schultz Ed.D., supt. — Fax 723-3895
www.fuesd.k12.ca.us
Potter IS — 1,100/7-8
1743 Reche Rd 92028 — 760-731-4150
Lisa Denham, prin. — Fax 723-5740

Fallbrook UNHSD — 3,200/9-12
2234 S Stagecoach Ln 92028 — 760-723-6332
Thomas Anthony, supt. — Fax 723-1795
www.fuhsd.net
Fallbrook HS — 3,000/9-12
2400 S Stagecoach Ln 92028 — 760-723-6300
Rod King, prin. — Fax 731-6192

Farmersville, Tulare, Pop. 9,918
Farmersville USD — 2,200/K-12
571 E Citrus Dr 93223 — 559-592-2010
Janet Jones, supt. — Fax 592-2203
www.farmersville.k12.ca.us
Farmersville HS — 600/9-12
631 E Walnut Ave 93223 — 559-594-4567
Ernie Flores, prin. — Fax 594-5287
Farmersville JHS — 600/6-8
650 N Virginia Ave 93223 — 559-747-0764
Jenifer Ahlstrand, prin. — Fax 747-2704

Felton, Santa Cruz, Pop. 5,350
San Lorenzo Valley USD
Supt. — See Ben Lomond
San Lorenzo Valley HS — 1,100/9-12
7105 Highway 9 95018 — 831-335-4425
Craig Lewis, prin. — Fax 335-1531
San Lorenzo Valley MS — 400/6-8
7179 Hacienda Way 95018 — 831-335-4452
Chris Mercer, prin. — Fax 335-3812

St. Lawrence Academy — 100/K-12
6184 Highway 9 95018 — 831-335-0328
Wendell Woodthorp, prin. — Fax 335-0353

Ferndale, Humboldt, Pop. 1,394
Ferndale USD — 500/K-12
1231 Main St 95536 — 707-786-5900
Alan Brainerd, supt. — Fax 786-4865
www.ferndalek12.org/
Ferndale HS — 200/9-12
1231 Main St 95536 — 707-786-5900
Alan Brainerd, prin. — Fax 786-4865

Fillmore, Ventura, Pop. 14,895
Fillmore USD — 3,800/K-12
PO Box 697 93016 — 805-524-6000
Jane Kampbell, supt. — Fax 524-6060
www.fillmore.k12.ca.us
Fillmore HS — 1,100/9-12
PO Box 697 93016 — 805-524-6100
Rebecca Larkin, prin. — Fax 524-6121
Fillmore MS — 900/6-8
PO Box 697 93016 — 805-524-6055
Patricia Gradias, prin. — Fax 524-6063

Firebaugh, Madera, Pop. 7,001
Firebaugh-Las Deltas JUSD — 2,500/K-12
1976 Morris Kyle Dr 93622 — 559-659-1476
Wayne Walters Ed.D., supt. — Fax 659-2355
www.fldusd.k12.ca.us/
Firebaugh HS — 700/9-12
1976 Morris Kyle Dr 93622 — 559-659-1415
John Jimenez, prin. — Fax 659-2636
Firebaugh MS — 600/6-8
1976 Morris Kyle Dr 93622 — 559-659-1481
Steve Vollmer, prin. — Fax 659-7106
Firebaugh-Las Deltas Adult S — Adult
1976 Morris Kyle Dr 93622 — 559-659-3899
Sara Soria-Moreno, prin. — Fax 659-1511

Folsom, Sacramento, Pop. 65,611
Folsom-Cordova USD — 18,200/K-12
125 E Bidwell St 95630 — 916-355-1100
Patrick Godwin, supt. — Fax 985-0722
www.fcusd.k12.ca.us
Folsom HS — 2,700/9-12
1655 Iron Point Rd 95630 — 916-355-1115
Paul Richards, prin. — Fax 355-1110
Folsom MS — 1,100/6-8
500 Blue Ravine Rd 95630 — 916-983-4466
Karen Knight, prin. — Fax 983-3462
Sutter MS — 1,000/6-8
715 Riley St 95630 — 916-985-3644
Charles Linebarger, prin. — Fax 985-7044
Other Schools – See Rancho Cordova

Folsom Lake College — Post-Sec.
100 College Pkwy 95630 — 916-608-6500

Fontana, San Bernardino, Pop. 163,860
Etiwanda ESD
Supt. — See Etiwanda
Heritage IS — 1,400/6-8
13766 S Heritage Cir 92336 — 909-357-1345
Laura Rowland, prin. — Fax 357-8945

Fontana USD — 42,000/PK-12
9680 Citrus Ave 92335 — 909-357-5000
Jane Smith, supt. — Fax 357-5012
www.fusd.net/
Alder MS — 1,500/6-8
7555 Alder Ave 92336 — 909-357-5330
Richard Roth, prin. — Fax 357-5348
Almeria MS — 1,100/6-8
7723 Almeria Ave 92336 — 909-357-5350
Gregory Fromm, prin. — Fax 357-5360
Fontana HS — 4,300/9-12
9453 Citrus Ave 92335 — 909-357-5500
Thomas Reasin, prin. — Fax 357-5629
Fontana MS — 1,400/6-8
8425 Mango Ave 92335 — 909-357-5370
Giovanni Annous, prin. — Fax 357-5391
Kaiser HS — 2,600/9-12
11155 Almond Ave 92337 — 909-357-5900
Victor Uribe, prin. — Fax 357-5997
Miller HS — 3,900/9-12
PO Box 5085 92334 — 909-357-5800
Dr. Kenneth Hendershot, prin. — Fax 823-5283
Ruble MS — 1,000/6-8
6762 Juniper Ave 92336 — 909-357-5530
Crystal Whitley, prin. — Fax 357-5539
Sequoia MS — 1,400/7-8
9452 Hemlock Ave 92335 — 909-357-5400
Anne Roth, prin. — Fax 357-5419
Southridge MS — 1,300/6-8
14500 Live Oak Ave 92337 — 909-357-5420
Linda Buck, prin. — Fax 822-4609
Summit HS — 9-12
15551 Summit Ave 92336 — 909-357-5950
Michael Andrus, prin. — Fax 357-5959
Truman MS — 1,200/6-8
16200 Mallory Dr 92335 — 909-357-5190
Paul Pagano, prin. — Fax 357-5199
Fontana Adult S — Adult
9453 Citrus Ave 92335 — 909-357-5555
Pat Meagher, prin. — Fax 357-5556

Agape Christian S — 200/K-12
17777 Merrill Ave 92335 — 909-350-1101
Augustine Smith, prin.

Foresthill, Placer, Pop. 1,409
Foresthill UNESD — 600/K-8
24750 Main St 95631 — 530-367-2966
Jim Roberts, supt. — Fax 367-2470
www.fusd.org
Foresthill Divide MS — 300/5-8
22888 Foresthill Rd 95631 — 530-367-3782
Shannon Jacinto, prin. — Fax 367-4526

Placer UNHSD
Supt. — See Auburn
Foresthill HS — 100/9-12
23319 Foresthill Rd 95631 — 530-367-5244
Sue Lunsford, prin. — Fax 367-4623

Forestville, Sonoma, Pop. 2,443
West Sonoma CUHSD
Supt. — See Sebastopol
El Molino HS — 1,100/9-12
7050 Covey Rd 95436 — 707-824-6570
Frank Anderson, prin. — Fax 887-0448

Fort Bragg, Mendocino, Pop. 6,814
Fort Bragg USD — 2,000/K-12
312 S Lincoln St 95437 — 707-961-2850
Steve Lund, supt. — Fax 964-5002
www.fbusd.org
Fort Bragg HS — 600/9-12
300 Dana St 95437 — 707-961-2880
Allen Urbani, prin. — Fax 961-2884
Fort Bragg MS — 500/6-8
500 N Harold St 95437 — 707-961-2870
Marli Shoop, prin. — Fax 964-9416
Coastal Adult S — Adult
250 S Sanderson Way 95437 — 707-961-2889
Mike Presley, prin. — Fax 964-1017

Fort Irwin, San Bernardino
Silver Valley USD
Supt. — See Yermo
Fort Irwin MS — 300/6-8
1700 Pork Chop Hill St 92310 — 760-386-1133
Joni James, prin. — Fax 386-2448

Fort Jones, Siskiyou, Pop. 669
Etna UNHSD — 400/7-12
PO Box 705 96032 — 530-468-4158
Winifred Walker, supt. — Fax 468-4170
www.sisnet.ssku.k12.ca.us/~ehsdftp/
Scott Valley JHS — 100/7-9
PO Box 607 96032 — 530-468-5565
Winifred Walker, prin. — Fax 468-5658
Other Schools – See Etna

Fortuna, Humboldt, Pop. 11,155
Fortuna UNESD — 800/K-8
843 L St 95540 — 707-725-2293
Charlie Lakin, supt. — Fax 725-2228
www.humboldt.k12.ca.us/fortuna_un/
Fortuna MS — 300/5-8
843 L St 95540 — 707-725-3415
Jim Stewart, prin. — Fax 725-2228

Fortuna UNHSD — 1,200/9-12
379 12th St 95540 — 707-725-4461
Dave Moss, supt. — Fax 725-6085
www.humboldt.k12.ca.us/fortuna_hi/
Fortuna Union HS — 1,100/9-12
379 12th St 95540 — 707-725-4461
Kathy Harrison, prin. — Fax 725-5511
Fortuna Adult Education — Adult
379 12th St 95540 — 707-725-4482
Stephanie Bennett, coord. — Fax 726-0347
Other Schools – See Eureka

Rohnerville ESD — 700/K-8
3850 Rohnerville Rd 95540 — 707-725-7823
Dena McCullough, supt. — Fax 725-4941
www.humboldt.k12.ca.us/rohnerville_sd/index.html
Thomas MS — 400/4-8
2800 Thomas St 95540 — 707-725-5197
Linda Meitner, prin. — Fax 725-8637

New Life Christian S — 100/PK-12
1736 Newburg Rd 95540 — 707-725-9136
Robert Hapgood, prin. — Fax 725-1638

Foster City, San Mateo, Pop. 28,756
San Mateo-Foster City ESD — 10,000/K-8
1170 Chess Dr 94404 — 650-312-7700
Pendery Clark Ed.D., supt. — Fax 312-7779
www.smfc.k12.ca.us
Bowditch MS — 1,000/6-8
1450 Tarpon St 94404 — 650-312-7680
David Holcombe, prin. — Fax 312-7639
Other Schools – See San Mateo

Fountain Valley, Orange, Pop. 55,942
Fountain Valley ESD — 6,300/K-8
10055 Slater Ave 92708 — 714-843-3200
Marc Ecker, supt. — Fax 841-0356
www.fvsd.k12.ca.us
Fulton MS — 700/6-8
8778 El Lago Cir 92708 — 714-375-2816
Chris Christensen, prin. — Fax 375-2825
Masuda MS — 800/6-8
17415 Los Jardines W 92708 — 714-378-4250
Cara Robinson, prin. — Fax 378-4259
Other Schools – See Huntington Beach

Garden Grove USD
Supt. — See Garden Grove
Los Amigos HS — 2,200/9-12
16566 Newhope St 92708 — 714-663-6288
Connie Van Luit, prin. — Fax 663-6518

Huntington Beach UNHSD
Supt. — See Huntington Beach
Fountain Valley HS — 3,000/9-12
17816 Bushard St 92708 — 714-962-3301
Chris Herzfeld, prin. — Fax 964-0491

Ocean View SD
Supt. — See Huntington Beach
Vista View MS — 900/6-8
16250 Hickory St 92708 — 714-842-0626
Robert Miller, prin. — Fax 843-9156

Coastline Community College — Post-Sec.
11460 Warner Ave 92708 — 714-546-7600
Ivory Dental Technology College — Post-Sec.
16600 Harbor Blvd Ste I 92708 — 714-899-8382
Modern Technology School — Post-Sec.
16560 Harbor Blvd Ste K 92708 — 714-418-9100
Sycamore Tree — 100/K-12
17150 Newhope St Ste 701 92708 — 714-668-1343
Sandra Gogel, dir.

Fowler, Fresno, Pop. 4,713
Fowler USD — 2,200/K-12
658 E Adams Ave 93625 — 559-834-2591
John Cruz, supt. — Fax 834-3390
www.fowler.k12.ca.us
Fowler HS — 700/9-12
701 E Main St 93625 — 559-834-2564
Russell Freitas, prin. — Fax 834-3284
Sutter MS — 500/6-8
701 E Walter Ave 93625 — 559-834-6300
Tod Tompkins, prin. — Fax 834-4739

Fremont, Alameda, Pop. 200,468
Fremont USD 31,800/K-12
PO Box 5008 94537 510-657-2350
Douglas Gephart, supt. Fax 659-2597
www.fremont.k12.ca.us
American HS 2,000/9-12
36300 Fremont Blvd 94536 510-796-1776
Mitchell Carter, prin. Fax 791-5331
Centerville JHS 1,100/7-8
37720 Fremont Blvd 94536 510-797-2072
Garo Mirigian, prin. Fax 794-7588
Hopkins JHS 1,000/7-8
600 Driscoll Rd 94539 510-656-3500
Leesa Jack, prin. Fax 656-3731
Horner JHS 900/7-8
41365 Chapel Way 94538 510-656-4000
Sal Herrera, prin. Fax 656-2793
Irvington HS 2,000/9-12
41800 Blacow Rd 94538 510-656-5711
Pete Murchison, prin. Fax 623-9805
Kennedy HS 1,400/9-12
39999 Blacow Rd 94538 510-657-4070
Anthony Kuns, prin. Fax 438-9287
Mission San Jose HS 2,000/9-12
41717 Palm Ave 94539 510-657-3600
Stuart Kew, prin. Fax 657-2302
Thornton JHS 1,100/7-8
4357 Thornton Ave 94536 510-793-9090
Ron Echandia, prin. Fax 793-9756
Walters JHS 900/7-8
39600 Logan Dr 94538 510-656-7211
Khristel Johnson, prin. Fax 656-4056
Washington HS 2,000/9-12
38442 Fremont Blvd 94536 510-505-7300
Linda Fernandez, prin. Fax 794-8437
Fremont Adult S Adult
4700 Calaveras Ave 94538 510-793-6465
Melanie Wade, prin. Fax 793-2271

Regional Occupational Center & Program
Supt. — None
Mission Valley ROC/P Vo/Tech
40230 Laiolo Rd 94538 510-657-1865
Charles Brown, supt. Fax 438-0378

California School for the Blind Post-Sec.
500 Walnut Ave 94536
California School for the Deaf Post-Sec.
39350 Gallaudet Dr 94538 510-794-3684
DeVry University Post-Sec.
6600 Dumbarton Cir 94555 510-574-1100
Fremont Christian S 1,300/PK-12
4760 Thornton Ave 94536 510-744-2249
Rev. C.K. Rankin, supt. Fax 744-2255
Northwestern Polytechnic University Post-Sec.
47671 Westinghouse Dr 94539 510-657-5911
Ohlone College Post-Sec.
PO Box 3909 94539 510-659-6000
Queen of the Holy Rosary College Post-Sec.
43326 Mission Blvd 94539 510-657-2468
Sequoia Institute Post-Sec.
200 Whitney Pl 94539 510-490-6900

Fresno, Fresno, Pop. 461,116
Central USD 11,400/K-12
4605 N Polk Ave 93722 559-274-4700
Marilou Ryder Ed.D., supt. Fax 271-8200
www.centralusd.k12.ca.us
Central HS East Campus 2,200/10-12
3535 N Cornelia Ave 93722 559-276-0280
Robert Griffith, prin. Fax 276-5653
Central HS West Campus 9-12
2045 N Dickenson Ave, 559-276-5276
Edward Robinson, prin. Fax 276-6380
El Capitan MS 800/7-8
4443 W Weldon Ave 93722 559-276-5270
Cheryl Coddington, prin. Fax 276-3121
Rio Vista MS 1,100/7-8
6240 W Palo Alto Ave 93722 559-276-3185
Tim Swain, prin. Fax 276-3199
Central Unified Adult Education Adult
2698 N Brawley Ave 93722 559-276-5230
Fran Bergmann, prin. Fax 276-8204

Clovis USD
Supt. — See Clovis
Clovis West HS 2,800/9-12
1070 E Teague Ave 93720 559-327-2000
Jeanne Hatfield, prin. Fax 327-2490
Kastner IS 1,400/7-8
7676 N 1st St 93720 559-327-2500
Rick Watson, prin. Fax 327-2790

Fresno USD 78,900/PK-12
2309 Tulare St 93721 559-457-3000
Michael Hanson, supt. Fax 457-3786
www.fresno.k12.ca.us/
Ahwahnee MS 800/7-8
1127 E Escalon Ave 93710 559-451-4300
Lisa DeLeon, prin. Fax 439-1808
Baird MS 600/5-8
5500 N Maroa Ave 93704 559-451-4310
Keith Herzog, prin. Fax 432-4075
Bullard HS 2,600/9-12
5445 N Palm Ave 93704 559-451-4320
Tim Belcher, prin. Fax 451-4339
Carver Academy 400/5-8
2463 Martin L King Jr Blvd 93706 559-457-2620
Carolyn Major, prin. Fax 237-2680
Computech MS 700/7-8
555 E Belgravia Ave 93706 559-457-2640
Tanis DeRuosi, prin. Fax 457-2643
Cooper MS 700/7-8
2277 W Bellaire Way 93705 559-248-7050
Scott Lamm, prin. Fax 224-7255
Duncan Polytechnical HS Vo/Tech
4330 E Garland Ave 93726 559-248-7080
Carol Gaab Hansen, prin. Fax 222-6186
Edison HS 2,600/9-12
540 E California Ave 93706 559-457-2650
Richard Lopez, prin. Fax 457-2742

Ft. Miller MS 1,000/7-8
1302 E Dakota Ave 93704 559-248-7100
Debbie Buckman, prin. Fax 221-7548
Fresno HS 3,000/9-12
1839 N Echo Ave 93704 559-457-2780
Bob Reyes, prin. Fax 457-2801
Hoover HS 2,400/9-12
5550 N 1st St 93710 559-451-4000
Toby Wait, prin. Fax 451-4072
Kings Canyon MS 1,000/7-8
5117 E Tulare Ave 93727 559-253-6470
Clark Mello, prin. Fax 253-6474
McLane HS 2,600/9-12
2727 N Cedar Ave 93703 559-248-5100
Frank Silvestro, prin. Fax 226-5232
Roosevelt HS 2,900/9-12
4250 E Tulare St 93702 559-253-5200
Loretta Aragon-Lopez, prin. Fax 253-5319
Scandinavian MS 900/7-8
3216 N Sierra Vista Ave 93726 559-253-6510
Julie Goorabian, prin. Fax 252-7608
Sequoia MS 1,000/7-8
4050 E Hamilton Ave 93702 559-457-3210
Mike Ribera, prin. Fax 497-1745
Sunnyside HS 2,900/9-12
1019 S Peach Ave 93727 559-253-6700
Sheryl Weaver, prin. Fax 253-6799
Tehipite MS 700/7-8
630 N Augusta St 93701 559-457-3420
Richard Pascual, prin. Fax 457-3423
Tenaya MS 1,000/7-8
1239 W Mesa Ave 93711 559-451-4570
Maria Mazzoni, prin. Fax 431-0771
Terronez MS 1,000/7-8
2300 S Willow Ave 93725 559-253-6570
Bryan Wells, prin. Fax 253-6572
Tioga MS 900/7-8
3232 E Fairmont Ave 93726 559-248-7280
Ray Avila, prin. Fax 226-1296
Wawona MS 800/7-8
4524 N Thorne Ave 93704 559-248-7310
Mike Darling, prin. Fax 227-5206
Yosemite MS 800/7-8
1292 N 9th St 93703 559-457-3450
Kathy Chambas, prin. Fax 264-0933
Fresno Adult Education Center Adult
2500 Stanislaus St 93721 559-457-6000
Maria Romero, prin. Fax 457-6033

Regional Occupational Center & Program
Supt. — None
Fresno ROP Vo/Tech
1111 Van Ness Ave Ste 5 93721 559-497-3850
Larry Powell, supt. Fax 497-3806

Washington UNHSD 1,200/9-12
6041 S Elm Ave 93706 559-485-8805
John Pestorich, supt. Fax 485-4435
www.washingtonunion.net
Washington HS 1,100/9-12
6041 S Elm Ave 93706 559-485-8805
Joey Campbell, prin. Fax 485-4435

West Fresno ESD 900/PK-8
2888 S Ivy Ave 93706 559-485-2272
D. Kent Ashworth, admin. Fax 264-0805
West Fresno MS 300/6-8
2888 S Ivy Ave 93706 559-495-5607
Brian Clark, prin. Fax 485-3006

Alliant International University Post-Sec.
5130 E Clinton Way 93727 559-456-2777
California Christian College Post-Sec.
4881 E University Ave 93703 559-251-4215
California State University-Fresno Post-Sec.
93740 559-278-4240
Central Valley Christian Academy 50/K-12
4147 E Dakota Ave 93726 559-226-4644
Timothe Addelsee, prin. Fax 248-2775
Fresno Adventist Academy 200/K-12
5397 E Olive Ave 93727 559-251-5548
Daniel Kittle, prin. Fax 456-1735
Fresno Christian S - Peoples Campus 600/3-12
7280 N Cedar Ave 93720 559-299-1695
Gary Schultz, prin. Fax 299-1051
Fresno City College Post-Sec.
1101 E University Ave 93741 559-442-4600
Fresno Pacific University Post-Sec.
1717 S Chestnut Ave 93702 559-453-2000
Galen College Medical & Dental Assts. Post-Sec.
1325 N Wishon Ave 93728 559-264-9700
Heald College Post-Sec.
255 W Bullard Ave 93704 559-438-4222
Lyle's College of Beauty Post-Sec.
6735 N 1st St Ste 112 93710 559-431-6060
Lyle's Fresno College of Beauty Post-Sec.
3125 W Shaw Ave 93711 559-222-6060
Manchester Beauty College Post-Sec.
3756 N Blackstone Ave 93726 559-224-4242
MCed Career College Post-Sec.
2002 N Gateway Blvd 93727 559-456-0623
Mennonite Brethren Biblical Seminary Post-Sec.
4824 E Butler Ave 93727 559-251-8628
San Joaquin Memorial HS 600/9-12
1406 N Fresno St 93703 559-268-9251
Br. Philip Thez, prin. Fax 268-1351
San Joaquin Valley College Post-Sec.
295 E Sierra Ave 93710 559-448-8282
San Joaquin Valley College Post-Sec.
4985 E Andersen Ave 93727 559-453-0380
Sierra Valley Business College Post-Sec.
4747 N 1st St # D 93726 559-222-0947
Truth Tabernacle Christian S 100/K-12
PO Box 5393 93755 559-225-1027
Diane Estes, prin. Fax 225-0465
Yeshiva Tichon HS 9-12
3585 W Beechwood Ave # 103 93711 800-539-4743
Rabbi Shimon Boyer, admin. Fax 539-4743

Fullerton, Orange, Pop. 132,787
Fullerton ESD 13,900/K-8
1401 W Valencia Dr 92833 714-447-7400
Cameron M. McCune, supt. Fax 447-7414
www.fsd.k12.ca.us
Ladera Vista JHS 1,000/7-8
1700 E Wilshire Ave 92831 714-447-7765
Margy Price, prin. Fax 447-7554
Nicolas JHS 1,200/7-8
1100 W Olive Ave 92833 714-447-7775
Mathew Barnett, prin. Fax 447-7586
Parks JHS 1,000/7-8
1710 Rosecrans Ave 92833 714-447-7785
Sherry Dustin, prin. Fax 447-7753

Fullerton JUNHSD 16,700/9-12
1051 W Bastanchury Rd 92833 714-870-2800
George Giokaris Ed.D., supt. Fax 870-2807
www.fjuhsd.k12.ca.us
Fullerton HS 2,300/9-12
201 E Chapman Ave 92832 714-626-3800
Cathy Gach, prin. Fax 626-3839
Sunny Hills HS 2,400/9-12
1801 Warburton Way 92833 714-626-4200
Ed Atkinson, prin. Fax 738-3728
Troy HS 2,300/9-12
2200 Dorothy Ln 92831 714-626-4400
Maggie Buchan, prin. Fax 626-4492
Other Schools – See Buena Park, La Habra

California State University-Fullerton Post-Sec.
PO Box 34080 92834 714-278-2011
College of Information Technology Post-Sec.
2701 E Chapman Ave Ste 101 92831 714-879-5100
Eastside Christian S 500/PK-12
2505 Yorba Linda Blvd 92831 714-879-2187
David Schoen, supt. Fax 526-5074
Fullerton College Post-Sec.
321 E Chapman Ave 92832 714-992-7000
Fullerton SDA S 50/K-12
2353 W Valencia Dr 92833 714-526-5039
Barbara Irish, prin. Fax 526-7761
Hope International University Post-Sec.
2500 Nutwood Ave 92831 714-879-3901
Rosary HS 700/9-12
1340 N Acacia Ave 92831 714-879-6302
Terry Gonzalez, prin. Fax 879-0853
Southern California College of Optometry Post-Sec.
2575 Yorba Linda Blvd 92831 714-449-7450
Western State University College of Law Post-Sec.
1111 N State College Blvd 92831 714-738-1000

Galt, Sacramento, Pop. 23,173
Galt JUNESD 4,400/K-8
1018 C St Ste 210 95632 209-744-4545
David Dominguez, supt. Fax 744-4553
www.galt.k12.ca.us/
Greer MS 700/6-8
248 W A St 95632 209-745-2641
Robert Nacario, prin. Fax 745-9202
McCaffrey MS 800/6-8
997 Park Terrace Dr 95632 209-745-5462
Ron Rammer, prin. Fax 745-5465

Galt JUNHSD 2,100/9-12
417 C St Ste B 95632 209-745-3061
Thomas Gemma, supt. Fax 744-1560
www.ghsd.k12.ca.us/
Galt HS 2,000/9-12
145 N Lincoln Way 95632 209-745-3081
Bernie Olmos, prin. Fax 745-4786
Adult Education Adult
150 Camellia Way 95632 209-745-5852
Karen Liu, dir. Fax 745-7026

Garberville, Humboldt
Southern Humbolt JUSD 900/K-12
PO Box 129 95542 707-923-2789
Clifton Anderson, supt. Fax 923-2055
www.humboldt.k12.ca.us/sohumb_usd/school/
Other Schools – See Miranda

Gardena, Los Angeles, Pop. 59,891
Los Angeles USD
Supt. — See Los Angeles
Gardena HS 3,300/9-12
1301 W 182nd St 90248 310-354-5000
Russell Thompson, prin. Fax 366-6943
Moneta HS 100/9-12
1230 W 177th St 90248 310-354-4951
Antonio Morreale, prin. Fax 352-4027
Peary MS 2,400/6-8
1415 W Gardena Blvd 90247 310-225-4200
L. Gail Garrett, prin. Fax 329-3957
Gardena-Carson Community Adult S Adult
18120 S Normandie Ave 90248 310-847-6091
Donna Brashear, prin. Fax 323-8981

American College of Medical Technology Post-Sec.
555 W Redondo Bch Blvd #100 90248
310-324-1000
Everest College Post-Sec.
1045 W Rdnd Bch Blvd #275 90247 310-527-7105
Junipero Serra HS 600/9-12
14830 Van Ness Ave 90249 310-324-6675
Rev. Sal Pilato, prin. Fax 352-4953

Garden Grove, Orange, Pop. 166,075
Garden Grove USD 49,900/K-12
10331 Stanford Ave 92840 714-663-6000
Laura Schwalm Ph.D., supt. Fax 663-6100
www.ggusd.k12.ca.us
Alamitos IS 900/7-8
12381 Dale St 92841 714-663-6101
Bill Gates, prin. Fax 663-6277
Bell IS 800/7-8
12345 Springdale St 92845 714-663-6466
Lorraine Rae, prin. Fax 663-6995
Bolsa Grande HS 1,600/9-12
9401 Westminster Ave 92844 714-663-6424
Denise Jay, prin. Fax 663-6029
Doig IS, 12752 Trask Ave 92843 900/7-8
Margaret Feliciani, prin. 714-663-6241

Garden Grove HS 2,200/9-12
11271 Stanford Ave 92840 714-663-6115
Dr. Colleen Cross, prin. Fax 663-6030
Irvine IS 900/7-8
10552 Hazard Ave 92843 714-663-6551
Betsy Arns, prin. Fax 663-6013
Jordan IS 700/7-8
9821 Woodbury Ave 92844 714-663-6124
Steve Osborne, prin. Fax 663-6123
Lake IS 700/7-8
10801 Orangewood Ave 92840 714-663-6506
Dave Biniasz, prin. Fax 663-6065
Pacifica HS 2,000/9-12
6851 Lampson Ave 92845 714-663-6515
Mary Jane Hibbard, prin.
Ralston IS 600/7-8
10851 Lampson Ave 92840 714-663-6366
Jan Cody, prin. Fax 663-7155
Rancho Alamitos HS 1,900/9-12
11351 Dale St 92841 714-663-6415
Frank Mackay, prin.
Santiago HS, 12342 Trask Ave 92843 2,100/9-12
Dr. Lorena Sanchez, prin. 714-663-6215
Walton IS 800/7-8
12181 Buaro St 92840 714-663-6040
Kelly McAmis, prin. Fax 534-4814
Lincoln Education Center Adult
11262 Garden Grove Blvd 92843 714-663-6291
Tracy Gutierrez, dir. Fax 555-2222
Other Schools – See Fountain Valley, Santa Ana, Westminster

Career Academy of Beauty Post-Sec.
12471 Valley View St 92845 714-897-3010
Concorde Career Institute Post-Sec.
12951 Euclid St Ste 101 92840 714-703-1900
Crystal Cathedral Academy 400/PK-12
13280 Chapman Ave 92840 714-971-4158
Sheila Coleman, supt. Fax 971-4028
H.O.P.E. Christian Academy 200/K-12
12211 Magnolia St 92841 714-534-6733
Deborah Haller, dir. Fax 534-6707
Kim Anh Academy of Beauty Post-Sec.
12141 Brookhurst St Ste 101 92840 714-896-9847
Lola Beauty College Post-Sec.
11883 Valley View St 92845 714-894-3366
Orangewood Adventist Academy 300/PK-12
13732 Clinton St 92843 714-534-4694
Ruben Escalante, prin. Fax 534-5931
Thanh Le College School of Cosmetology Post-Sec.
12875 Chapman Ave 92840 714-971-5844
Village Bible Academy 200/1-12
12671 Buaro St 92840 714-537-5344
Chris Zuniga, admin.

Garden Valley, El Dorado
Black Oak Mine USD
Supt. — See Georgetown
Golden Sierra HS 600/9-12
PO Box 175 95633 530-333-8330
Audrey Keebler, prin. Fax 333-8333

Georgetown, El Dorado
Black Oak Mine USD 1,900/K-12
PO Box 4510 95634 530-333-8300
Rob Schamberg, supt. Fax 333-8303
www.bomusd.k12.ca.us
Other Schools – See Garden Valley

Geyserville, Sonoma
Geyserville USD 300/K-12
1300 Moody Ln 95441 707-857-3592
Joseph F. Carnation, supt. Fax 431-8148
www.gusd.com
Geyserville HS 100/9-12
1300 Moody Ln 95441 707-857-3592
Katherine Hadden, prin. Fax 857-3071
Geyserville MS 100/6-8
1300 Moody Ln 95441 707-857-3592
Katherine Hadden, prin. Fax 857-3071

Gilroy, Santa Clara, Pop. 45,718
Gilroy USD 9,700/K-12
7810 Arroyo Cir 95020 408-847-2700
Deborah Flores, supt. Fax 847-4717
www.gusd.k12.ca.us
Brownell MS 900/6-8
7800 Carmel St 95020 408-847-3377
Francisco Fuentes, prin. Fax 846-7521
Gilroy HS 2,500/9-12
750 W 10th St 95020 408-847-2424
James Maxwell, prin. Fax 842-3311
Solorsano MS 500/6-8
7121 Grenache Way 95020 408-848-4121
Sal Tomasello, prin. Fax 848-7121
South Valley MS 900/6-8
385 Ioof Ave 95020 408-847-2828
John Perales, prin. Fax 847-5708

Regional Occupational Center & Program
Supt. — None
Santa Clara County ROP South Vo/Tech
700 W 6th St Ste L 95020 408-842-0361
Dr. David Matuszak, dir. Fax 842-0653

Anchorpoint Christian HS 100/7-12
PO Box 65 95021 408-846-6642
Steve White, pres. Fax 848-4426
Gavilan Community College Post-Sec.
5055 Santa Teresa Blvd 95020 408-847-1400

Glendale, Los Angeles, Pop. 200,065
Glendale USD 28,000/K-12
223 N Jackson St 91206 818-241-3111
Michael Escalante Ed.D., supt. Fax 548-9041
www.gusd.net/
Glendale HS 3,200/9-12
1440 E Broadway 91205 818-242-3161
Kathy Fundukian, prin. Fax 244-6309
Hoover HS 2,600/9-12
651 Glenwood Rd 91202 818-242-6801
Kevin Welsh, prin. Fax 247-8825
Roosevelt MS 1,000/7-8
1017 S Glendale Ave 91205 818-242-6845
Maria Gandera, prin. Fax 552-5188
Toll MS 1,300/7-8
700 Glenwood Rd 91202 818-244-8414
Jan Canfield, prin. Fax 500-1487
Wilson MS 1,200/7-8
1221 Monterey Rd 91206 818-244-8145
Richard Lucas, prin. Fax 244-2050
Other Schools – See La Crescenta

Glendale Adventist Academy 700/K-12
700 Kimlin Dr 91206 818-244-8671
Dr. Glen Baker, prin. Fax 546-1180
Glendale Career College Post-Sec.
1015 Grandview Ave 91201 818-243-1131
Glendale Community College Post-Sec.
1500 N Verdugo Rd 91208 818-240-1000
Holy Family HS 300/9-12
400 E Lomita Ave 91205 818-241-3178
Dr. Michelle Purghart, prin. Fax 241-7753
Moro Beauty College Post-Sec.
124 N Brand Blvd 91203 818-246-7376
Newbridge College Post-Sec.
425 E Colorado St 91205 714-550-8000
North American Computer Consultants Post-Sec.
570 W Stocker St Unit 311 91202 818-500-7227
Northwest College Medical Dental Assts. Post-Sec.
221 N Brand Blvd 91203 818-242-0205
Tobinworld S, 920 E Broadway 91205 300/K-12
Judith Weber, dir. 818-247-7474
Uni Health America/Glendale Mem Hospital Post-Sec.
1420 S Central Ave 91204 818-502-2334

Glendora, Los Angeles, Pop. 50,540
Azusa USD
Supt. — See Azusa
Azusa Adult Educ Center Adult
1134 S Barranca Ave 91740 626-852-8400
Mary Ketza, prin. Fax 852-8407

Glendora USD 7,800/K-12
500 N Loraine Ave 91741 626-963-1611
Catherine Nichols, supt. Fax 335-2196
www.glendora.k12.ca.us
Glendora HS 2,700/9-12
1600 E Foothill Blvd 91741 626-963-5731
Kelly Bruce, prin. Fax 963-2880
Goddard MS 1,000/6-8
859 E Sierra Madre Ave 91741 626-852-4500
Dominic DiGrazia, prin. Fax 852-4520
Sandburg MS 900/6-8
819 W Bennett Ave 91741 626-852-4530
Scott Bell, prin. Fax 852-4521

Citrus College Post-Sec.
1000 W Foothill Blvd 91741 626-963-0323
St. Lucy Priory HS 900/9-12
655 W Sierra Madre Ave 91741 626-335-3322
Fax 335-4373

Gold River, Sacramento

Bryan College Post-Sec.
2317 Gold Meadow Way 95670 866-649-2400

Goleta, Santa Barbara, Pop. 29,367
Santa Barbara SD
Supt. — See Santa Barbara
Dos Pueblos HS 2,300/9-12
7266 Alameda Ave 93117 805-968-2541
Mark Swanitz, prin. Fax 968-2891
Goleta Valley JHS 900/7-8
6100 Stow Canyon Rd 93117 805-967-3486
Veronica Rogers, prin. Fax 967-8176

Gonzales, Monterey, Pop. 8,498
Gonzales USD 2,300/K-12
PO Box G 93926 831-675-0100
Ernest S. Zermeno, supt. Fax 675-2763
www.gusd-district.org
Fairview MS 700/5-8
PO Box G 93926 831-675-3704
Al Velasquez, prin. Fax 675-3274
Gonzales HS 700/9-12
PO Box G 93926 831-675-2495
Liz Modena, prin. Fax 675-8054

Granada Hills, See Los Angeles
Los Angeles USD
Supt. — See Los Angeles
Frost MS 1,700/6-8
12314 Bradford Pl 91344 818-360-2146
Elias De La Torre, prin. Fax 360-9584
Henry MS 1,500/6-8
17340 San Jose St 91344 818-832-3870
Michael Bennett, prin. Fax 368-7333
Kennedy HS 3,200/9-12
11254 Gothic Ave 91344 818-363-6794
Christine Clark, prin. Fax 368-9527
Porter MS 1,700/6-8
15960 Kingsbury St 91344 818-920-2050
Joyce Edelson, prin. Fax 891-7826
Kennedy-San Fernando Adult Education Adult
11254 Gothic Ave 91344 818-368-3702
Carlynn Huddleston, prin. Fax 368-5518

Hillcrest Christian S 800/K-12
17531 Rinaldi St 91344 818-368-7071
David Kendrick, supt. Fax 363-4455
Newberry School of Beauty Post-Sec.
16860 Devonshire St 91344 818-366-3211

Grand Terrace, San Bernardino, Pop. 12,342
Colton JUSD
Supt. — See Colton
Terrace Hills MS 1,100/7-8
22579 De Berry St 92313 909-876-4256
Julia Nichols, prin. Fax 783-3836

Keystone S 700/K-12
11980 Mount Vernon Ave 92313 909-783-8420
Fax 783-8469

Granite Bay, Placer
Eureka UNSD 4,200/K-8
5455 Eureka Rd 95746 916-791-4939
Bob Schultz, supt. Fax 791-5527
www.eureka-usd.k12.ca.us
Cavitt JHS 500/7-8
7200 Fuller Dr 95746 916-791-4152
John Montero, prin. Fax 791-7414
Other Schools – See Roseville

Roseville JUNHSD
Supt. — See Roseville
Granite Bay HS 1,100/9-10
1 Grizzly Way 95746 916-786-8676
Mike McGuire, prin. Fax 786-0766

Grass Valley, Nevada, Pop. 12,449
Grass Valley ESD 1,300/K-8
10840 Gilmore Way 95945 530-273-4483
Jon Byerrum, supt. Fax 273-0248
www.gvsd.k12.ca.us
Gilmore MS 600/6-8
10837 Rough and Ready Hwy 95945 530-273-8479
Brian Buckley, prin. Fax 273-1675

Nevada JUNHSD 4,200/9-12
11645 Ridge Rd 95945 530-273-3351
Maggie Deetz, supt. Fax 273-3372
www.nuhsd.org
Bear River HS 1,100/9-12
11130 Magnolia Rd 95949 530-268-3700
Jim Nieto, prin. Fax 268-8372
Nevada Union HS 2,700/9-12
11761 Ridge Rd 95945 530-273-4431
Marty Mathiesen, prin. Fax 477-9317
Nevada Union Technical HS Vo/Tech
11761 Ridge Rd 95945 530-273-4431
Linda Campbell, admin. Fax 477-9317
Nevada Adult Education Adult
350 Buena Vista St 95945 530-272-2643
Trisha Dellis, prin. Fax 272-3422

Pleasant Ridge UNESD 2,000/K-8
22580 Kingston Ln 95949 530-268-2800
Linda Rooney, supt. Fax 268-2804
www.pleasantridge.k12.ca.us
Magnolia IS 800/6-8
22431 Kingston Ln 95949 530-268-2815
Mark Rodriguez, prin. Fax 268-2819

Christian Encounter HS 50/10-12
PO Box 1022 95945 530-268-0877
Tom Kern, prin. Fax 268-9077

Greenfield, Monterey, Pop. 13,330
Greenfield UNESD 2,400/K-8
493 El Camino Real 93927 831-674-2840
Tom Guajardo, supt. Fax 674-3712
www.greenfield.k12.ca.us/
Vista Verde MS 800/6-8
1199 Elm Ave 93927 831-674-1420
Stella Laurel, prin. Fax 674-1425

King City JUNHSD
Supt. — See King City
Greenfield HS 900/9-12
2025 El Camino Real 93927 831-674-2751
Rudy Garcia, prin. Fax 674-2646
King City Adult Education Adult
2015 El Camino Real 93927 831-674-3275
Cathy Hormann, prin. Fax 674-1187

Greenville, Plumas, Pop. 1,396
Plumas USD
Supt. — See Quincy
Greenville JSHS 200/7-12
117 Grand St 95947 530-284-7197
Kest Porter, prin. Fax 284-6710

Gridley, Butte, Pop. 5,588
Gridley USD 2,100/K-12
429 Magnolia St 95948 530-846-4721
Clark S. Redfield, supt. Fax 846-4595
www.gridley.k12.ca.us/
Gridley HS 700/9-12
300 E Spruce St 95948 530-846-4791
Joan Zappettini, prin. Fax 846-3412
Sycamore MS 500/6-8
1125 Sycamore St 95948 530-846-3636
James Walters, prin. Fax 846-6796

Groveland, Tuolumne, Pop. 2,753
Big Oak Flat-Groveland USD 500/K-12
PO Box 1397 95321 209-962-5765
Philip Yoon, supt. Fax 962-6108
www.bofg.k12.ca.us/
Tioga HS 100/9-12
19304 Ferretti Rd 95321 209-962-4763
Sandra Bradley, prin. Fax 962-4507
Big Oak Flat-Groveland Adult S Adult
PO Box 1397 95321 209-962-5765
Fax 962-6108
Other Schools – See La Grange

Guadalupe, Santa Barbara, Pop. 6,346
Guadalupe UNESD 1,200/K-8
PO Box 788 93434 805-343-2114
Hugo Lara, supt. Fax 343-6155
www.sbceo.org/districts/guadalupeusd/
McKenzie JHS 400/6-8
PO Box 788 93434 805-343-1951
Celia Ramos, prin. Fax 343-6931

Gustine, Merced, Pop. 5,324
Gustine USD 2,000/K-12
1500 Meredith Ave 95322 209-854-3784
Joseph Wilimek, supt. Fax 854-9164
www.gustine.k12.ca.us

Gustine HS 600/9-12
501 North Ave 95322 209-854-6414
Dennis Shaw, prin. Fax 854-1955
Gustine MS 500/6-8
685 Wallis Ave 95322 209-854-6404
Sharon Brown, prin. Fax 854-9575

Hacienda Heights, Los Angeles, Pop. 53,300
Hacienda La Puente USD
Supt. — See City of Industry
Cedarlane MS 500/6-8
16333 Cedarlane Dr 91745 626-933-8000
Janine Ezaki, prin. Fax 855-3819
Los Altos HS 1,900/9-12
15325 Los Robles Ave 91745 626-934-5400
William Roberts, prin. Fax 855-3145
Newton MS 600/6-8
15616 Newton St 91745 626-933-2400
Dr. Stephen Lee, prin. Fax 855-3832
Orange Grove MS 600/6-8
14505 Orange Grove Ave 91745 626-933-7000
Alejandro Rojas, prin. Fax 855-3837
Wilson HS 1,900/9-12
16455 Wedgeworth Dr 91745 626-934-4410
Albert Clegg, prin. Fax 855-3792

Morning Star Christian S 100/K-12
15716 Tetley St 91745 626-333-7784
Marlene Guerrero, admin. Fax 330-8636

Half Moon Bay, San Mateo, Pop. 12,203
Cabrillo USD 3,500/K-12
498 Kelly Ave 94019 650-712-7100
John Bayless, supt. Fax 726-0279
www.cabrillo.k12.ca.us/
Cunha IS 800/6-8
498 Kelly Ave 94019 650-712-7190
Michael Andrews, prin. Fax 712-7195
Half Moon Bay HS 1,100/9-12
498 Kelly Ave 94019 650-712-7200
Susan Milliion, prin. Fax 712-7232
Cabrillo Adult S Adult
498 Kelly Ave 94019 650-712-7224
Michael Bachicha, prin. Fax 712-7225

Hamilton City, Glenn, Pop. 1,811
Hamilton UNHSD 400/9-12
PO Box 488 95951 530-826-3261
Ray Odom, supt. Fax 826-0440
www.glenn-co.k12.ca.us/ham-hs
Hamilton Union HS 300/9-12
PO Box 488 95951 530-826-3261
Ray Odom, prin. Fax 826-0440
Hamilton Adult S Adult
PO Box 488 95951 530-826-3331
Jeannie Robinson, dir. Fax 826-3929

Hanford, Kings, Pop. 47,485
Hanford ESD 4,900/K-8
PO Box 1067 93232 559-585-3601
Rebecca Presley, supt. Fax 584-7833
www.hesd.k12.ca.us/
Kennedy JHS 600/7-8
PO Box 1067 93232 559-585-3850
Jason Strickland, prin. Fax 585-2374
Wilson JHS 600/7-8
PO Box 1067 93232 559-585-3870
Kenneth Eggert, prin. Fax 585-2336

Hanford JUNHSD 3,700/9-12
823 W Lacey Blvd 93230 559-583-5901
William Fishbough, supt. Fax 589-9769
www.kings.k12.ca.us/huhsd
Hanford HS 1,800/9-12
120 E Grangeville Blvd 93230 559-583-5902
Steve France, prin. Fax 582-5229
Hanford West HS 1,700/9-12
1150 W Lacey Blvd 93230 559-583-5903
John Davis, prin. Fax 583-6708
Hanford Adult S Adult
905 Campus Dr 93230 559-583-5905
Mark Dutra, prin. Fax 589-9564

Lakeside UNESD 400/K-8
9100 Jersey Ave 93230 559-582-2868
Dr. Mike Sherrod, supt. Fax 582-7638
www.kings.k12.ca.us/lakeside/
Lakeside ES 200/4-8
9100 Jersey Ave 93230 559-582-2868
Dr. Mike Sherrod, prin. Fax 582-7638

Regional Occupational Center & Program
Supt. — None
Kings County ROP Vo/Tech
1144 W Lacey Blvd 93230 559-589-7026
Tim Bowers, admin. Fax 589-7007

Happy Camp, Siskiyou
Siskiyou UNHSD
Supt. — See Mount Shasta
Happy Camp HS 100/9-12
PO Box 437 96039 530-493-2697
Ernie Micheli, prin. Fax 493-2605

Harbor City, See Los Angeles
Los Angeles USD
Supt. — See Los Angeles
Narbonne HS 3,400/9-12
24300 Western Ave 90710 310-257-7100
Linda Kay, prin. Fax 326-1805

Hawaiian Gardens, Los Angeles, Pop. 15,398
ABC USD
Supt. — See Cerritos
Fedde MS 600/7-8
21409 Elaine Ave 90716 562-924-2309
Paul Gonzales, prin. Fax 809-6895
Adult Education Center Adult
11949 215th St 90716 562-229-7970
Jean Rose, prin.

Turner Christian HS 50/7-12
22427 Norwalk Blvd 90716 562-429-2397
Terryl Bruce, prin. Fax 497-0348

Hawthorne, Los Angeles, Pop. 85,697
Centinela Valley UNHSD
Supt. — See Lawndale
Hawthorne HS 2,900/9-12
4859 W El Segundo Blvd 90250 310-263-4400
Joy Bramlette, prin. Fax 675-7017

Hawthorne SD 9,000/K-8
14120 Hawthorne Blvd 90250 310-676-2276
Donald Carrington, supt. Fax 675-2308
www.hawthorne.k12.ca.us
Carson MS 1,000/6-8
13838 Yukon Ave 90250 310-676-1908
Patricia Jordan, prin. Fax 676-0634
Hawthorne MS 1,000/6-8
4366 W 129th St 90250 310-676-0167
Wendy Ostenson, prin. Fax 675-0924
Prairie Vista MS 1,100/6-8
13600 Prairie Ave 90250 310-679-1003
Christine Fagnano, prin. Fax 679-1142

Wiseburn ESD 2,100/K-8
13530 Aviation Blvd 90250 310-643-3025
Dr. Don Brann, supt. Fax 643-7659
www.wiseburn.k12.ca.us/
Dana MS 800/6-8
13500 Aviation Blvd 90250 310-643-6165
Matthew Wunder, prin. Fax 643-0208

Hawthorne Academy 100/K-12
12500 Ramona Ave 90250 310-644-8841
Dennis Richard, dir.
International School of Cosmetology Post-Sec.
13613 Hawthorne Blvd 90250 310-973-7774
New Journey Christian S 100/PK-12
14204 Prairie Ave 90250 310-676-9042
Colette Arce, prin. Fax 676-9043

Hayfork, Trinity, Pop. 2,605
Mountain Valley USD 400/K-12
PO Box 339 96041 530-628-5265
David Schumaker, supt. Fax 628-5267
www.mvusd.us
Hayfork HS 100/9-12
PO Box 10 96041 530-628-5261
Tom Barnett, prin. Fax 628-3091

Hayfork SDA S 50/1-12
PO Box 580 96041 530-628-1601
Fax 628-4064

Hayward, Alameda, Pop. 140,293
Hayward USD 23,000/PK-12
PO Box 5000 94540 510-784-2600
Janis A. Duran, supt. Fax 784-2641
www.husd.k12.ca.us
Chavez MS 800/7-8
PO Box 5000 94540 510-293-8581
Olga Pineda, prin. Fax 538-8478
Harte MS 600/7-8
PO Box 5000 94540 510-293-8578
Shelly Jones, prin. Fax 886-5926
Hayward HS 2,100/9-12
PO Box 5000 94540 510-293-8586
Mary Ann Heather, prin. Fax 581-3145
King MS 700/7-8
PO Box 5000 94540 510-293-8528
Ricardy Anderson, prin. Fax 786-4139
Mt. Eden HS 2,500/9-12
PO Box 5000 94540 510-293-8539
Fax 786-2269
Ochoa MS 600/7-8
PO Box 5000 94540 510-293-8532
Delores Connors, prin. Fax 786-0559
Tennyson HS 1,800/9-12
PO Box 5000 94540 510-293-8591
Theresa McEwen, prin. Fax 582-0964
Winton MS 800/7-8
PO Box 5000 94540 510-293-8583
Fax 733-9043
Hayward Adult Education Center Adult
PO Box 5000 94540 510-293-8595
Mahnoush Harirsa, prin. Fax 727-1139
Other Schools – See Castro Valley

New Haven USD
Supt. — See Union City
Conley-Caraballo HS 9-12
541 Blanche St 94544 510-471-5126
Mireya Casarez, prin. Fax 475-3949

Regional Occupational Center & Program
Supt. — None
Eden Area ROP Vo/Tech
26316 Hesperian Blvd 94545 510-293-2900
Irene Fujii, dir. Fax 783-2955

San Lorenzo USD
Supt. — See San Lorenzo
East Bay Arts HS 9-12
20450 Royal Ave 94541 510-317-4471
Donn Keith, prin. Fax 317-4495

California State University-East Bay Post-Sec.
25800 Carlos Bee Blvd 94542 510-885-3000
Chabot College Post-Sec.
25555 Hesperian Blvd 94545 510-723-6600
Everest College Post-Sec.
22336 Main St 94541 510-582-9500
Heald College Post-Sec.
25500 Industrial Blvd 94545 510-783-2100
Life Chiropractic College West Post-Sec.
25001 Industrial Blvd 94545 800-788-4476
Moreau HS 1,000/9-12
27170 Mission Blvd 94544 510-881-4300
Terry Lee, prin. Fax 581-5669

Healdsburg, Sonoma, Pop. 11,051
Healdsburg USD 1,800/K-12
1028 Prince Ave 95448 707-431-3117
Robert Carter Ed.D., supt. Fax 433-8403
www.husd.com
Healdsburg HS 1,000/9-12
1024 Prince Ave 95448 707-431-3420
John Curry, prin. Fax 431-3467
Healdsburg JHS 500/6-8
315 Grant St 95448 707-431-3410
Deborah Hall, prin. Fax 431-3593

Rio Lindo Adventist Academy 200/9-12
3200 Rio Lindo Ave 95448 707-431-5100
Doug Schmidt, hdmstr. Fax 431-5115

Helendale, San Bernardino
Helendale ESD 600/K-8
PO Box 249 92342 760-952-1180
Brian Dietz, supt. Fax 952-1178
www.sbcss.k12.ca.us/helendale
Riverview MS 200/6-8
PO Box 249 92342 760-952-1266
Donna Cannon, prin. Fax 952-1180

Hemet, Riverside, Pop. 68,063
Hemet USD 20,700/K-12
2350 W Latham Ave 92545 951-765-5100
Dr. Philip Pendley, supt. Fax 765-5115
www.hemetusd.k12.ca.us
Acacia MS 800/6-8
1200 E Acacia Ave 92543 951-765-1620
Fax 765-5149
Dartmouth MS 1,100/6-8
41535 Mayberry Ave 92544 951-765-2550
Sharleen Rainville, prin. Fax 765-2559
Diamond Valley MS 1,500/6-8
291 W Chambers Ave 92543 951-925-2899
Christine Goennier, prin. Fax 925-6297
Hemet HS 2,500/9-12
41701 Stetson Ave 92544 951-765-5150
Bill Black, prin. Fax 765-5177
Santa Fe MS 1,100/6-8
831 E Devonshire Ave 92543 951-765-6440
Jacqueline Luzak, prin. Fax 765-6444
Tahquitz HS 9-12
4425 W Commonwealth Ave 92545 951-765-6300
Sue Richardson, prin.
West Valley HS 2,900/9-12
3401 Mustang Way 92545 951-765-1600
Mark Lenoir, prin. Fax 765-1607
Hemet Adult Education Adult
26866 San Jacinto St 92543 951-765-5190
Walter Brubaker, prin. Fax 765-5195
Other Schools – See Anza

Baptist Christian S 500/PK-12
26089 Girard St 92544 951-658-3203
Ron Livesay, admin. Fax 658-0723
Image School of Cosmetology Post-Sec.
2627 W Florida Ave 92545 951-766-5759

Hercules, Contra Costa, Pop. 24,109
West Contra Costa USD
Supt. — See Richmond
Hercules MSHS 1,200/6-12
1900 Refugio Valley Rd 94547 510-245-5000
Guy Zakrevsky, prin. Fax 245-1089

Herlong, Lassen
Fort Sage USD 200/K-12
PO Box 6 96113 530-827-2129
Bryan Young, supt. Fax 827-2019
Herlong JSHS 100/7-12
PO Box 97 96113 530-827-2101
Bryan Young, prin. Fax 827-3362

Hermosa Beach, Los Angeles, Pop. 19,500
Hermosa Beach City ESD 1,100/K-8
1645 Valley Dr 90254 310-937-5877
Sharon McClain Ed.D., supt. Fax 376-4974
www.hbcsd.org
Hermosa Valley MS 700/3-8
1645 Valley Dr 90254 310-937-5888
Sylvia Gluck, prin. Fax 798-4365

Hope Chapel Academy 200/K-12
2420 Pacific Coast Hwy 90254 310-374-4673
Rev. Zachary Nazarian, prin.

Hesperia, San Bernardino, Pop. 77,984
Hesperia USD 17,400/K-12
15576 Main St 92345 760-244-4411
Hank Richardson, supt. Fax 244-2806
www.hesperia.org
Cedar MS 7-8
13565 Cedar St, 760-244-6093
David Olney, prin. Fax 244-5439
Hesperia HS 2,600/9-12
9898 Maple Ave 92345 760-244-9898
Larry Porras, prin. Fax 244-0939
Hesperia JHS 1,600/7-8
10275 Cypress Ave 92345 760-244-9386
Robert McCollum, prin. Fax 244-0595
Ranchero MS 1,400/7-8
17607 Ranchero Rd 92345 760-948-0175
Cindy Costa, prin. Fax 948-0381
Sultana HS 2,600/9-12
17311 Sultana St 92345 760-947-6777
Fax 947-6788

Hesperia Christian S 500/PK-12
16775 Olive St 92345 760-244-6164
Sharon Romero, admin. Fax 244-9756

Highland, San Bernardino, Pop. 50,892
Redlands USD
Supt. — See Redlands
Beattie MS, 7800 Boulder Ave 92346 1,200/6-8
Carol Purvine, prin. 909-307-2400

San Bernardino City USD
Supt. — See San Bernardino
Serrano MS 1,200/7-8
3131 Piedmont Dr 92346 909-388-6530
Sandy Simpson, prin. Fax 864-6232

Citrus Valley Christian Academy 100/K-12
7171 Tiara Ave 92346 909-556-7201
Douglas Van Gelder, admin.
Universal Training Center Post-Sec.
3875 Atlantic Ave 92346 909-864-1918

Hillsborough, San Mateo, Pop. 10,615
Hillsborough City ESD 1,400/K-8
300 El Cerrito Ave 94010 650-342-5193
Marilyn Loushin-Miller, supt. Fax 342-6964
www.hcsd.k12.ca.us/
Crocker MS 500/6-8
2600 Ralston Ave 94010 650-342-6331
Janet Chun, prin. Fax 579-5943

Crystal Springs Uplands S 400/6-12
400 Uplands Dr 94010 650-342-4175
Amy Richards, hdmstr. Fax 342-7623

Hilmar, Merced, Pop. 3,392
Hilmar USD 2,400/K-12
7807 Lander Ave 95324 209-667-5701
David Miller Ph.D., supt. Fax 667-1721
www.hilmar.k12.ca.us
Hilmar HS 700/9-12
7807 Lander Ave 95324 209-667-5903
Brett Theodozio, prin. Fax 667-7628
Hilmar MS 600/6-8
7807 Lander Ave 95324 209-632-8847
Andres Zamora, prin. Fax 667-7018

Hollister, San Benito, Pop. 35,941
Hollister SD 6,200/K-8
2690 Cienega Rd 95023 831-630-6300
Ronald Crates Ed.D., supt. Fax 634-2080
www.hesd.org/
Maze MS 1,000/6-8
900 Meridian St 95023 831-636-4480
Bernice Smith, prin. Fax 636-4488
Rancho San Justo MS 1,000/6-8
1201 Rancho Dr 95023 831-636-4450
Don Knapp, prin. Fax 634-4952

San Benito HSD 3,100/9-12
1220 Monterey St 95023 831-637-5831
Stan Rose Ed.D., supt. Fax 637-6524
www.sbhsd.k12.ca.us
San Benito HS 2,900/9-12
1220 Monterey St 95023 831-637-5831
Debbie Padilla, prin. Fax 637-6524

Calvary Christian S 100/K-12
1900 Highland Dr 95023 831-637-2909
Walt Lindquist, prin.
Grace Bible Christian S 50/1-12
634 Monterey St 95023 831-638-1394
Lynn Whiteley, admin. Fax 638-0460

Hollywood, See Los Angeles
Los Angeles USD
Supt. — See Los Angeles
Le Conte MS 2,200/6-8
1316 N Bronson Ave 90028 323-308-1700
Christine Zardeneta, prin. Fax 856-3053

Academy Pacific Travel College Post-Sec.
1777 Vine St # 30 90028 323-462-3211
American Academy of Dramatic Arts Post-Sec.
1336 N La Brea Ave 90028 800-222-2867
Elegance International Post-Sec.
1622 N Highland Ave 90028 323-871-8318
Musicians Institute Post-Sec.
1655 N McCadden Pl 90028 323-462-1384

Holtville, Imperial, Pop. 5,470
Holtville USD 1,800/K-12
621 E 6th St 92250 760-356-2974
Patricia Salcido, supt. Fax 356-4936
www.holtville.k12.ca.us/
Holtville HS 600/9-12
755 Olive Ave 92250 760-356-2926
Jackie Hester, prin. Fax 356-1206
Holtville JHS 400/6-8
800 Beale Ave 92250 760-356-2811
Tish Lyon, prin. Fax 356-5741

Honeydew, Humboldt
Mattole USD 100/K-12
29289 Chambers Rd 95545 707-629-3311
Richard Graey, supt. Fax 629-3575
www.humboldt.k12.ca.us/mattole_usd/
Other Schools – See Petrolia

Hoopa, Humboldt
Klamath-Trinity JUSD 1,100/K-12
PO Box 1308 95546 530-625-4255
Douglas Oliveira, supt. Fax 625-4133
www.humboldt.k12.ca.us/kt_usd/K-T/home.html
Hoopa Valley HS 200/9-12
PO Box 1308 95546 530-625-4218
John Greene, prin. Fax 625-4200

Hughson, Stanislaus, Pop. 5,705
Hughson USD 2,100/K-12
6815 Fox Rd 95326 209-883-4428
Brian Beck, supt. Fax 883-4639
www.hughson.k12.ca.us/
Hughson HS 800/9-12
PO Box 99 95326 209-883-0460
Debra Davis, prin. Fax 883-0870
Ross MS 500/6-8
PO Box 189 95326 209-883-4425
Matthew Shipley, prin. Fax 883-2017

Keyes UNESD
Supt. — See Keyes
Spratling MS 300/6-8
5277 Washington Rd 95326 209-664-3833
Mike Richter, prin. Fax 656-2384

Huntington Beach, Orange, Pop. 194,457
Fountain Valley ESD
Supt. — See Fountain Valley
Talbert MS 600/6-8
9101 Brabham Dr 92646 714-378-4220
Cathie Abdel, prin. Fax 378-4229

Huntington Beach City ESD 6,200/K-8
20451 Craimer Ln 92646 714-964-8888
Roberta DeLuca, supt. Fax 963-9565
www.hbcsd.k12.ca.us
Dwyer MS 1,200/6-8
1502 Palm Ave 92648 714-536-7507
Donald Ruisinger, prin. Fax 960-0955
Sowers MS 1,200/6-8
9300 Indianapolis Ave 92646 714-962-7738
Paul Morrow Ed.D., prin. Fax 968-5580

Huntington Beach UNHSD 15,100/9-12
5832 Bolsa Ave 92649 714-903-7000
Van W. Riley, supt. Fax 892-5750
www.hbuhsd.org
Edison HS 2,200/9-12
21400 Magnolia St 92646 714-962-1356
D'Liese Melendrez, prin. Fax 963-4280
Huntington Beach HS 2,500/9-12
1905 Main St 92648 714-536-2514
David Linzey, prin. Fax 960-7042
Marina HS 2,700/9-12
15871 Springdale St 92649 714-893-6571
Stephen Roderick, prin. Fax 892-7855
Ocean View HS 1,500/9-12
17071 Gothard St 92647 714-848-0656
Karen Gilden, prin. Fax 843-0541
Huntington Beach Adult Education Adult
16666 Tunstall Ln 92647 714-847-2873
Doris Longmead, prin. Fax 841-2283
Other Schools – See Fountain Valley, Westminster

Ocean View SD 10,000/PK-8
17200 Pinehurst Ln 92647 714-847-2551
Karen Colby, supt. Fax 847-1430
www.ovsd.org
Marine View MS 900/6-8
5682 Tilburg Dr 92649 714-846-0624
Carol Parish, prin. Fax 846-2074
Mesa View MS 800/6-8
17601 Avilla Ln 92647 714-842-6608
Leona Olson, prin. Fax 842-8798
Spring View MS 900/6-8
16662 Trudy Ln 92647 714-846-2891
John Drake, prin. Fax 377-9821
Other Schools – See Fountain Valley

Brethren Christian HS 500/7-12
21141 Strathmoor Ln 92646 714-962-6617
Rick Niswonger, admin. Fax 962-3171
Golden West College Post-Sec.
15744 Goldenwest St 92647 714-892-7711
Hebrew Academy 400/PK-12
14401 Willow Ln 92647 714-898-0051
Rabbi Yitzchok Newman, dir. Fax 898-0633
Liberty Christian S 400/K-12
7661 Warner Ave 92647 714-842-5992
Thom Doney, prin. Fax 848-7484
Platt College Post-Sec.
7755 Center Ave Ste 400 92647 714-373-3240

Huntington Park, Los Angeles, Pop. 62,491
Los Angeles USD
Supt. — See Los Angeles
Gage MS 3,800/6-8
2880 E Gage Ave 90255 323-587-5271
Rosa Denny, prin. Fax 589-6925
Huntington Park HS 4,400/9-12
6020 Miles Ave 90255 323-583-3333
Raul Correa, prin. Fax 583-0463
Nimitz MS 3,400/6-8
6021 Carmelita Ave 90255 323-887-5400
Francisco Vasquez, prin. Fax 773-5201
Huntington Park-Bell Community Adult S Adult
2945 Belgrave Ave 90255 323-581-0168
Clifton DeCordoba, prin. Fax 581-5515

California Learning Center Post-Sec.
6812 Pacific Blvd 90255 323-581-0600
ICDC College Post-Sec.
6330 Pacific Blvd Ste 200 90255 323-655-9100

Huron, Fresno, Pop. 7,187
Coalinga - Huron JUSD
Supt. — See Coalinga
Huron MS 300/6-8
PO Box 99 93234 559-945-2926
Irene Fernandez, prin. Fax 945-8482

Idyllwild, Riverside, Pop. 2,853

Idyllwild Arts Academy 300/8-12
PO Box 38 92549 951-659-2171
William Lowman, prin. Fax 659-5463

Imperial, Imperial, Pop. 9,707
Imperial USD 2,700/K-12
219 N E St 92251 760-355-3200
Barbara Layaye, supt. Fax 355-4511
iusd.imperial.k12.ca.us/
Imperial HS 800/9-12
517 W Barioni Blvd 92251 760-355-3220
Lisa Tabarez, prin. Fax 355-0869
Wright IS 500/6-8
885 N Imperial Ave 92251 760-355-3240
Chuck Bush, prin. Fax 355-3256

Imperial Valley College Post-Sec.
PO Box 158 92251 760-352-8320

Imperial Beach, San Diego, Pop. 26,374
Sweetwater UNHSD
Supt. — See Chula Vista
Mar Vista HS 2,200/9-12
505 Elm Ave 91932 619-628-5700
Dr. Louise Phipps, prin. Fax 424-6232

Independence, Inyo
Owens Valley USD 100/K-12
PO Box E 93526 760-878-2405
Joel Hampton, supt. Fax 878-2626
www.ovusd.org
Owens Valley HS 50/9-12
PO Box E 93526 760-878-2405
Joel Hampton, prin. Fax 878-2626

Indio, Riverside, Pop. 70,542
Desert Sands USD
Supt. — See La Quinta
Glenn MS of International Studies 1,400/6-8
79655 Miles Ave 92201 760-200-3700
Jean Carroll, prin. Fax 200-3709
Indio HS 2,600/9-12
81750 Avenue 46 92201 760-775-3550
Rudy Ramirez, prin. Fax 775-3565
Indio MS 1,200/6-8
81195 Miles Ave 92201 760-775-3800
Dan Miller, prin. Fax 775-3807
Jefferson MS 700/6-8
83089 US Highway 111 92201 760-863-3660
Esther Lopez, prin. Fax 775-3597
Wilson MS 500/6-8
83501 Dillon Ave 92201 760-775-3880
Harry Munoz, prin. Fax 775-3885

Milan Institute Post-Sec.
45-691 Monroe St Ste 2 92201 760-347-5000

Inglewood, Los Angeles, Pop. 114,467
Inglewood USD 16,500/K-12
401 S Inglewood Ave 90301 310-419-2700
Dr. Pamela Short-Powell, supt. Fax 680-5128
inglewood.k12.ca.us
City Honors HS 200/9-12
115 W Kelso St 90301 310-680-4880
Thelma Brown, prin. Fax 680-5144
Crozier MS 800/6-8
120 W Regent St 90301 310-680-5280
Beverly Pye, prin. Fax 680-5299
Inglewood HS 2,100/9-12
231 S Grevillea Ave 90301 310-680-5200
Debra Tate, prin. Fax 680-5201
Monroe MS 1,300/6-8
10711 S 10th Ave 90303 310-680-5310
Reginald Sirls, prin. Fax 680-5317
Morningside HS 1,500/9-12
10500 Yukon Ave 90303 310-680-5230
Michael Dennis, prin. Fax 680-5257
Inglewood Adult Education Adult
106 E Manchester Blvd 90301 310-330-5222
Lacy Alexander, prin. Fax 330-5218

Daniel Freeman Mem. Hospital Post-Sec.
333 N Prairie Ave 90301 310-674-7050
Marinello School of Beauty Post-Sec.
240 S Market St 90301 310-674-8100
St. Marys Academy 400/9-12
701 Grace Ave 90301 310-674-8470
Sr. Fay Hagen, prin. Fax 674-6255
South Bay Lutheran HS 100/6-12
3600 W Imperial Hwy 90303 310-672-1101
Judith Tutt-Starr, prin. Fax 672-1115
University of West Los Angeles Post-Sec.
9920 S La Cienega Blvd 90301 310-342-5200
Westwood College of Aviation Technology Post-Sec.
8911 Aviation Blvd 90301 310-337-4444

Ione, Amador, Pop. 7,607
Amador County USD
Supt. — See Jackson
Ione JHS 500/6-8
450 S Mill St 95640 209-257-5500
Bill Murray, prin. Fax 274-0671

Irvine, Orange, Pop. 186,852
Irvine USD 25,000/PK-12
5050 Barranca Pkwy 92604 949-936-5000
Dr. Gwen Gross, supt. Fax 936-5259
www.iusd.org
Creekside HS 200/9-12
311 W Yale Loop 92604 949-936-7400
Paul Mills, prin. Fax 936-7409
Irvine HS 1,800/9-12
4321 Walnut Ave 92604 949-936-7000
Gail Richards, prin. Fax 936-7009
Lakeside MS 700/7-8
3 Lemongrass 92604 949-936-6100
Craig Ritter, prin. Fax 936-6109
Northwood HS 2,100/9-12
4515 Portola Pkwy 92620 949-936-7200
Cassie Parham, prin. Fax 936-7209
Rancho San Joaquin MS 800/7-8
4861 Michelson Dr 92612 949-936-6500
Jeffrey Williamson, prin. Fax 936-6509
Sierra Vista MS 900/7-8
2 Liberty 92620 949-936-6600
Beverly Khalil-White, prin. Fax 936-6609
South Lake MS 600/7-8
655 W Yale Loop 92614 949-936-6700
Bruce Baron, prin. Fax 936-6709
University HS 2,200/9-12
4771 Campus Dr 92612 949-936-7600
John Pehrson, prin. Fax 936-7609
Venado MS 800/7-8
6 Federation Way 92603 949-936-6800
Fran Antenore, prin. Fax 936-6809
Woodbridge HS 2,200/9-12
2 Meadowbrook 92604 949-936-7800
Tom Nelson, prin. Fax 936-7809
Irvine Adult S Adult
311 W Yale Loop 92604 949-936-7450
Karen Bautista, dir. Fax 936-7459

Tustin USD
Supt. — See Tustin
Beckman HS 1,000/9-12
3588 Bryan 92602 714-734-2900
Adele Heuer, prin. Fax 505-9676

Alliant International University Post-Sec.
2500 Michelson Dr Ste 250 92612 949-833-2651
Concordia University Post-Sec.
1530 Concordia 92612 949-854-8002
DeVry University Post-Sec.
430 Exchange Ste 250 92602 714-734-5560
Executive 2000 Post-Sec.
2041 Business Center Dr 92612 949-794-9090
FIDM/The Fashion Institute Post-Sec.
17590 Gillette Ave 92614 949-851-6200
Irvine Valley College Post-Sec.
5500 Irvine Center Dr 92618 949-451-5100
Tarbut V'Torah Day S 600/K-12
5200 Bonita Canyon Dr 92603 949-509-9500
Laura Roth, prin. Fax 856-2400
University of California 92697 Post-Sec.
949-824-5011

Irwindale, Los Angeles, Pop. 1,480

CEI Post-Sec.
4900 Rivergrade Rd Ste E210 91706 626-338-8886
Premiere Career College Post-Sec.
12901 Ramona Blvd Ste D 91706 626-814-2080
Public Health Foundation Enterprises Post-Sec.
12781 Schabarum Ave 91706 626-856-6376

Jackson, Amador, Pop. 4,303
Amador County USD 4,500/K-12
217 Rex Ave 95642 209-257-5353
Mike Carey, supt. Fax 257-5360
www.amadorcoe.org/
Argonaut HS 600/9-12
217 Rex Ave 95642 209-257-7700
Dave Vicari, prin. Fax 223-3149
Jackson JHS 400/6-8
217 Rex Ave 95642 209-257-5700
Janet Pabst, prin. Fax 257-5311
Other Schools – See Ione, Sutter Creek

Regional Occupational Center & Program
Supt. — None
Amador County ROP Vo/Tech
217 Rex Ave 95642 209-267-5274
Elizabeth Chapin-Pinotti, dir. Fax 267-5497

Jamul, San Diego, Pop. 2,258
Jamul-Dulzura UNESD 1,200/K-8
14581 Lyons Valley Rd 91935 619-669-7700
Nadine Bennett, supt. Fax 669-0254
www.jdusd.k12.ca.us/
Oak Grove MS 500/6-8
14344 Olive Vista Dr 91935 619-669-2700
Jeannie Lopez, prin. Fax 669-7632

Joshua Tree, San Bernardino, Pop. 3,898

Boston S, PO Box 708 92252 200/K-12
David Zimmerman, dir. 760-366-8658
Copper Mountain College Post-Sec.
PO Box 1398 92252 760-366-3791

Julian, San Diego, Pop. 1,284
Julian UNESD 400/K-8
PO Box 337 92036 760-765-0661
Kevin Ogden, supt. Fax 765-0220
www.sdcoe.k12.ca.us/districts/julianel/
Julian JHS 100/7-8
PO Box 337 92036 760-765-0575
Brian Duffy, prin. Fax 765-3340

Julian UNHSD 300/9-12
PO Box 417 92036 760-765-3208
Rich Alderson, supt. Fax 765-2926
www.juhsd.org
Julian HS 200/9-12
PO Box 417 92036 760-765-0606
Brian Bristol, prin. Fax 765-2782

Kelseyville, Lake, Pop. 2,861
Kelseyville USD 1,900/K-12
4410 Konocti Rd 95451 707-279-1511
Boyce McClain, supt. Fax 279-9221
www.kusd.lake.k12.ca.us
Kelseyville HS 700/9-12
5480 Main St 95451 707-279-4923
Matt Cockerton, prin. Fax 279-9173
Mountain Vista MS 400/6-8
5081 Konocti Rd 95451 707-279-4060
John Berry, prin. Fax 279-8835

Kentfield, Marin, Pop. 6,030
Kentfield ESD 1,000/K-8
699 Sir Francis Drake Blvd 94904 415-925-2230
Robert Caine, supt. Fax 925-2238
www.kentfieldschools.org/district/
Kent MS 500/5-8
250 Stadium Way 94904 415-458-5970
Skip Kniesche, prin. Fax 458-5973

College of Marin Post-Sec.
835 College Ave 94904 415-457-8811
Marin Catholic HS 700/9-12
675 Sir Francis Drake Blvd 94904 415-464-3800
Don Ritchie, prin. Fax 461-7161

Kerman, Fresno, Pop. 11,223
Kerman USD 3,800/K-12
151 S 1st St 93630 559-846-5383
Roger Halberg, supt. Fax 846-5941
www.kermanusd.k12.ca.us
Kerman HS 1,000/9-12
205 S 1st St 93630 559-842-2500
Jim Volkoff, prin. Fax 846-4229
Kerman MS 600/7-8
601 S 1st St 93630 559-842-3000
Homar Garza, prin. Fax 846-5217
Kerman Adult S Adult
15405 W Sunset Ave 93630 559-842-3500
Nellie Neri, prin. Fax 846-5371

Keyes, Stanislaus, Pop. 2,878
Keyes UNESD 800/K-8
PO Box 310 95328 209-669-2921
Norm Lee, supt. Fax 669-2923
Other Schools – See Hughson

King City, Monterey, Pop. 11,004
King City JUNHSD 2,100/9-12
800 Broadway St 93930 831-385-0606
Jim Schiffman, supt. Fax 385-0695
www.kingcity.k12.ca.us/
King City HS 1,100/9-12
720 Broadway St 93930 831-385-5461
Todd Dearden, prin. Fax 385-0901
Other Schools – See Greenfield

King City UNESD 2,500/K-8
800 Broadway St 93930 831-385-1144
Fax 385-0695
www.kingcity.k12.ca.us/
San Lorenzo MS 900/6-8
415 Pearl St 93930 831-385-5446
Richard Preston, prin. Fax 386-0372

Kingsburg, Fresno, Pop. 11,148
Kingsburg JUNHSD 1,100/9-12
1900 18th Ave 93631 559-897-5156
Linda E. Clark, supt. Fax 897-7759
www.kingsburghigh.k12.ca.us
Kingsburg HS 1,100/9-12
1900 18th Ave 93631 559-897-5156
Linda E. Clark, prin. Fax 897-7759

La Canada Flintridge, Los Angeles, Pop. 20,998
La Canada USD 4,300/K-12
4490 Cornishon Ave 91011 818-952-8300
Jim Stratton, supt. Fax 952-8309
www.lcusd.net
La Canada JSHS 2,300/7-12
4463 Oak Grove Dr 91011 818-952-4200
Dr. Damon Dragos, prin. Fax 952-4214

Flintridge Prep S 500/7-12
4543 Crown Ave 91011 818-790-1178
Peter Bachmann, prin. Fax 952-6247
Flintridge Sacred Heart Academy 9-12
440 Saint Katherine Dr 91011 626-685-8300
Sr. Celeste Botello, prin. Fax 685-8305
Renaissance Academy 100/K-12
4490 Cornishon Ave 91011 818-952-3055
Ann Hazen, prin. Fax 952-3069
St. Francis HS 700/9-12
200 Foothill Blvd 91011 818-790-0325
Thomas Moran, prin. Fax 790-5542

La Crescenta, Los Angeles, Pop. 16,968
Glendale USD
Supt. — See Glendale
Clark Magnet HS 600/9-10
4747 New York Ave 91214 818-248-8324
Douglas Dall, prin. Fax 957-2954
Crescenta Valley HS 2,900/9-12
2900 Community Ave 91214 818-249-5871
Mike Livingston, prin. Fax 541-9531
Rosemont MS 1,400/7-8
4725 Rosemont Ave 91214 818-248-4224
Sally T. Buckley, prin. Fax 248-3790

Ladera Ranch, Orange
Capistrano USD
Supt. — See San Juan Capistrano
Ladera Ranch MS 1,000/6-8
29551 Sienna Pkwy 92694 949-234-5922
Karen Gerhard, prin. Fax 364-1149

Ladera Ranch JHS 100/7-8
26122 ONeill Dr 92694 949-429-3812
Sherry Worel, supt. Fax 429-3820
Pathway S 50/3-8
26162 ONeill Dr 92694 949-218-8948
Susie Wenger, prin. Fax 218-8958

Lafayette, Contra Costa, Pop. 24,767
Acalanes UNHSD 5,900/9-12
1212 Pleasant Hill Rd 94549 925-280-3900
Jim Negri, supt. Fax 932-2336
www.acalanes.k12.ca.us
Acalanes HS 1,300/9-12
1200 Pleasant Hill Rd 94549 925-280-3970
John Nickerson, prin. Fax 280-3971
Other Schools – See Moraga, Orinda, Walnut Creek

Lafayette ESD 3,200/K-8
PO Box 1029 94549 925-299-3502
Bill Levinson, supt. Fax 284-1525
www.lafsd.k12.ca.us
Stanley MS 1,200/6-8
3455 School St 94549 925-283-6282
Sandy Bruketta, prin. Fax 283-1797

Bentley S - Lafayette Campus 300/9-12
1000 Upper Happy Valley Rd 94549 510-843-2512
Richard Fitzgerald, hdmstr. Fax 299-0469

La Grange, Stanislaus
Big Oak Flat-Groveland USD
Supt. — See Groveland
Pedro HS 100/9-12
3090 Merced Falls Rd 95329 209-852-2864
Dr. Lana Rosing, prin. Fax 852-2125

Laguna Beach, Orange, Pop. 24,127
Laguna Beach USD 2,800/K-12
550 Blumont St 92651 949-497-7700
Theresa Daem, supt. Fax 497-6021
www.lagunabeachschools.org
Laguna Beach HS 900/9-12
625 Park Ave 92651 949-497-7750
Donald Austin, prin. Fax 497-7766
Thurston MS 700/6-8
2100 Park Ave 92651 949-497-7785
Joanne Culverhouse, prin. Fax 497-7798

Laguna College of Art and Design Post-Sec.
2222 Laguna Canyon Rd 92651 949-376-6000

Laguna Hills, Orange, Pop. 32,198
Saddleback Valley USD
Supt. — See Mission Viejo
Laguna Hills HS 1,900/9-12
25401 Paseo De Valencia 92653 949-770-5447
Ed Adams, prin. Fax 830-0295

Allied Business School Post-Sec.
22952 Alcalde Dr 92653 949-598-0875

Laguna Niguel, Orange, Pop. 64,664
Capistrano USD
Supt. — See San Juan Capistrano
Niguel Hills MS 1,500/6-8
29070 Paseo De La Escuela 92677 949-234-5360
Jim Hansen, prin. Fax 249-2069

Laguna Niguel Adventist S 50/K-10
29702 Kensington Dr 92677 949-495-0311
Jennie Furness, prin. Fax 363-7006

La Habra, Orange, Pop. 59,326
Fullerton JUNHSD
Supt. — See Fullerton
La Habra HS 2,400/9-12
801 Highlander Ave 90631 562-266-5000
Jennifer Leeman, prin. Fax 691-8280
Sonora HS 2,000/9-12
401 S Palm St 90631 562-266-2000
Rich Peterson, prin. Fax 266-2040

La Habra City ESD 6,400/K-8
PO Box 307 90633 562-690-2300
Richard Hermann, supt. Fax 690-4154
www.lhcsd.k12.ca.us
Imperial MS 1,100/6-8
PO Box 307 90633 562-690-2344
Cathy Seighman, prin. Fax 526-3678
Washington MS 1,100/6-8
PO Box 307 90633 562-690-2374
Gary Mantey, prin. Fax 690-7834

Whittier Christian HS 700/9-12
501 N Beach Blvd 90631 562-694-3803
Robert Brown, prin. Fax 697-1673

La Jolla, See San Diego
San Diego USD
Supt. — See San Diego
La Jolla HS 1,700/9-12
750 Nautilus St 92037 858-454-3081
Dana Shelburne, prin. Fax 459-2188
Muirlands MS 1,100/6-8
1056 Nautilus St 92037 858-459-4211
Christine Hargrave, prin. Fax 459-8075

Bishops S 800/7-12
7607 La Jolla Blvd 92037 858-459-4021
Michael Teitelman, hdmstr. Fax 459-3914
La Jolla Country Day S 1,000/PK-12
9490 Genesee Ave 92037 858-453-3440
Dr. Judith Glickman, prin. Fax 453-8210
National University Post-Sec.
11255 N Torrey Pines Rd 92037 858-642-8000
Scripps Memorial Hospital Post-Sec.
9888 Genesee Ave 92037 858-457-6100
Scripps Research Institute Post-Sec.
10550 N Torrey Pines Rd 92037 858-784-8469
University of California Post-Sec.
9500 Gilman Dr 92093 858-534-2230

Lake Almanor, Plumas

Lake Almanor Christian S 50/K-12
2610 State Route A13 96137 530-596-4100
Gwen Meinhardt, prin. Fax 596-4682

Lake Arrowhead, San Bernardino, Pop. 6,539
Rim of the World USD 5,700/K-12
PO Box 430 92352 909-336-2031
Clint Harwick Ed.D., supt. Fax 337-4527
www.rimsd.k12.ca.us
Henck IS 1,000/7-8
PO Box 430 92352 909-336-0360
Dr. Tom Battle, prin. Fax 336-3449
Rim of the World HS 1,800/9-12
PO Box 430 92352 909-336-2038
Guy Bonanno, prin. Fax 336-0254

Lake Arrowhead Christian S 100/K-12
PO Box 179 92352 909-337-3739
Randall Leonard, prin. Fax 337-4550

Lake Elsinore, Riverside, Pop. 39,258
Lake Elsinore USD 19,800/K-12
545 Chaney St 92530 951-253-7000
Frank Passarella, supt. Fax 253-7084
www.leusd.k12.ca.us
Canyon Lake MS 1,200/6-8
33005 Canyon Hills Rd 92532 951-244-2123
Mike Sepulveda, prin. Fax 244-2103
Elsinore MS 900/6-8
1203 W Graham Ave 92530 951-674-2118
Nori Holland, prin. Fax 674-6302
Lakeland Village MS 6-8
18730 Grand Ave 92530 951-253-7400
Billie DaVolt, prin. Fax 253-7424
Lakeside HS 9-12
32593 Riverside Dr 92530 951-253-7300
Lorie Reitz, prin. Fax 253-7335
Temescal Canyon HS 2,800/9-12
28755 El Toro Rd 92532 951-245-4484
Patrick Kelleher, prin. Fax 245-2974
Terra Cotta MS 1,500/6-8
29291 Lake St 92530 951-674-0641
Ginny Kishbauch, prin. Fax 674-5191

Valley Adult S — Adult
520 Chaney St 92530 — 951-245-2093
Kathy Longe, prin. — Fax 245-1988
Other Schools – See Wildomar

Lake Forest, Orange, Pop. 76,412
Saddleback Valley USD
Supt. — See Mission Viejo
El Toro HS — 2,600/9-12
25255 Toledo Way 92630 — 949-586-6333
Dave Ellick, prin. — Fax 380-9874
Serrano IS — 1,500/7-8
24642 Jeronimo Rd 92630 — 949-586-3221
Linda Garza, prin. — Fax 586-3773

CEI — Post-Sec.
25381 Commercentre Dr #200 92630 — 949-472-4192
Elegante Beauty College — Post-Sec.
23635 El Toro Rd Ste K 92630 — 949-586-4900
Lake Forest Beauty College — Post-Sec.
23600 Rockfield Blvd Ste 3C 92630 — 949-951-8883

Lake Isabella, Kern, Pop. 3,323
Kern UNHSD
Supt. — See Bakersfield
Kern Valley HS — 700/9-12
3340 Erskine Creek Rd 93240 — 760-379-2611
Jeanie Brachear, prin. — Fax 379-8314

Kernville UNESD — 1,000/K-8
PO Box 3077 93240 — 760-379-3651
Mary C. Barlow, supt. — Fax 379-3812
www.kernville.usd.org
Wallace JHS — 300/6-8
PO Box 3077 93240 — 760-379-4646
Todd Farr, prin. — Fax 379-1322

Lakeport, Lake, Pop. 5,241
Lakeport USD — 1,800/K-12
2508 Howard Ave 95453 — 707-262-3000
Erin Smith-Hagberg, supt. — Fax 263-7332
www.lakeport.k12.ca.us
Clear Lake HS — 500/9-12
2508 Howard Ave 95453 — 707-262-3010
Steve Gentry, prin. — Fax 262-3026
Terrace MS — 700/4-8
2508 Howard Ave 95453 — 707-262-3007
Jill Falconer, prin. — Fax 262-5532

Regional Occupational Center & Program
Supt. — None
Lake County ROP — Vo/Tech
1152 S Main St 95453 — 707-262-3498
Dave Geck, dir. — Fax 262-5625

Lakeside, San Diego, Pop. 56,225
Grossmont UNHSD
Supt. — See El Cajon
El Capitan HS — 2,000/9-12
10410 Ashwood St 92040 — 619-443-1081
Bill Sullivan, prin. — Fax 390-8503

Lakeside UNESD — 4,300/K-8
12335 Woodside Ave 92040 — 619-390-2600
Stephen Halfaker, supt. — Fax 561-7929
www.lsschools.k12.ca.us/lakeside/default.htm
Lakeside MS — 700/6-8
11833 Woodside Ave 92040 — 619-390-2636
Steve Mull, prin. — Fax 390-2643
Tierra Del Sol MS — 800/6-8
9611 Petite Ln 92040 — 619-390-2670
Chris McDuffie, prin. — Fax 390-2518

Lakewood, Los Angeles, Pop. 80,467
ABC USD
Supt. — See Cerritos
Artesia HS — 1,800/9-12
12108 Del Amo Blvd 90715 — 562-402-2015
Sergio Garcia, prin. — Fax 809-5604

Bellflower USD
Supt. — See Bellflower
Mayfair MSHS — 3,500/7-12
6000 Woodruff Ave 90713 — 562-925-9981
Lisa Azevedo, prin. — Fax 804-1656

Long Beach USD
Supt. — See Long Beach
Hoover MS — 1,200/6-8
3501 Country Club Dr 90712 — 562-421-1213
Michael Troyer, prin. — Fax 421-8063
Lakewood HS — 4,300/9-12
4400 Briercrest Ave 90713 — 562-425-1281
Allan Taylor, prin. — Fax 421-9616

St. Joseph HS — 800/9-12
5825 Woodruff Ave 90713 — 562-925-5073
Dr. Mary Mendoza, prin. — Fax 925-3315

La Mesa, San Diego, Pop. 53,081
La Mesa-Spring Valley SD — 14,000/K-8
4750 Date Ave 91941 — 619-668-5700
Brian Marshall, supt. — Fax 668-5809
www.lmsvsd.k12.ca.us
La Mesa MS — 1,300/6-8
4200 Parks Ave 91941 — 619-668-5730
Dennis Munden, prin. — Fax 668-8303
Parkway MS — 1,200/6-8
9009 Park Plaza Dr 91942 — 619-668-5810
Cyndi Sutton, prin. — Fax 668-5779
Other Schools – See Spring Valley

California Hair Design Academy — Post-Sec.
8011 University Ave # A-2 91941 — 619-461-8600
La Mesa Christian S — 100/PK-12
9407 Jericho Rd 91942 — 619-463-5591
Phillip Sherwood, admin. — Fax 463-5216

La Mirada, Los Angeles, Pop. 49,640
Norwalk-La Mirada USD
Supt. — See Norwalk
Benton MS — 700/6-8
15709 Olive Branch Dr 90638 — 562-943-1553
Craig Hauke, prin. — Fax 947-3861
Hutchinson MS — 700/6-8
13900 Estero Rd 90638 — 562-944-3268
Bob Easton, prin. — Fax 944-3269
La Mirada HS — 2,400/9-12
13520 Adelfa Dr 90638 — 562-868-0431
Don Jones, prin. — Fax 943-7872
Los Coyotes MS — 600/6-8
14640 Mercado Ave 90638 — 714-523-2051
Dr. Sylvia Begtrup, prin. — Fax 739-2368
Norwalk Adult S — Adult
15920 Barbata Rd 90638 — 562-670-9279
Sharon Renfro, dir. — Fax 670-1654

Biola University — Post-Sec.
13800 Biola Ave 90639 — 562-903-6000
Foundation Christian S — 200/K-12
16450 Phoebe Ave 90638 — 714-865-9211
Jenette Sovilla, admin.
Heights Christian JHS — 300/7-8
12900 Bluefield Ave 90638 — 562-947-3309
Rolland Esslinger, prin. — Fax 947-1001

Lamont, Kern, Pop. 11,517
Lamont ESD — 2,700/K-8
7915 Burgundy Ave 93241 — 661-845-0751
Cheryl McConaughey, supt. — Fax 845-0689
www.lamontschooldistrict.org/
Mountain View MS — 600/7-8
7915 Burgundy Ave 93241 — 661-845-2291
Fred Molina, prin. — Fax 845-1839

Lancaster, Los Angeles, Pop. 134,032
Antelope Valley UNHSD — 22,700/9-12
44811 Sierra Hwy 93534 — 661-948-7655
David Vierra, supt. — Fax 942-8744
www.avdistrict.org
Antelope Valley Union HS — 2,800/9-12
44900 Division St 93535 — 661-948-8552
Trish Lockhart, prin. — Fax 945-8867
Eastside HS — 9-12
3200 E Avenue J8 93535 — 661-948-7655
Tom Grady, prin. — Fax 946-3850
Lancaster HS — 3,500/9-12
44701 Eagle Way 93536 — 661-726-7649
Cheri Kreitz, prin. — Fax 726-7694
Antelope Valley Adult HS — Adult
45110 3rd St E 93535 — 661-942-3042
Terry O'Connor, prin. — Fax 948-0846
Other Schools – See Littlerock, Palmdale, Quartz Hill

Eastside UNSD — 2,800/K-8
45006 30th St E 93535 — 661-952-1200
Gregory Riccio Ph.D., supt. — Fax 952-1220
www.eastside.k12.ca.us
Cole MS — 1,000/6-8
3126 E Avenue I 93535 — 661-946-1041
Yvonne Casillas-Young, prin. — Fax 946-0166

Lancaster ESD — 15,900/K-8
44711 Cedar Ave 93534 — 661-948-4661
Dr. Stephen Gocke, supt. — Fax 948-9398
www.lancaster.k12.ca.us
Amargosa Creek MS — 1,500/6-8
44333 27th St W 93536 — 661-729-6064
Lexy Conte, prin. — Fax 729-6858
Endeavour MS — 200/6-8
831 E Avenue K2 93535 — 661-723-0351
Robert Porter, prin. — Fax 723-1362
New Vista MS — 1,200/6-8
753 E Avenue K2 93535 — 661-726-4271
Deborah Lewis, prin. — Fax 726-4278
Park View MS — 1,300/6-8
808 W Avenue J 93534 — 661-942-0496
Eric George, prin. — Fax 940-5732
Piute MS — 1,300/6-8
425 E Avenue H11 93535 — 661-942-9508
Kathy Lee, prin. — Fax 940-6676

Westside UNESD — 7,000/K-8
41914 50th St W 93536 — 661-722-0716
Regina Rossalli, supt. — Fax 772-5223
www.westside.k12.ca.us
Other Schools – See Palmdale, Quartz Hill

Wilsona ESD
Supt. — See Palmdale
Challenger MS — 700/6-8
41725 170th St E 93535 — 661-264-1790
Bill Perry, prin. — Fax 264-1793

Antelope Valley Christian S — 400/PK-12
3700 W Avenue L 93536 — 661-943-0044
Karen Hester, prin. — Fax 943-6774
Antelope Valley College — Post-Sec.
3041 W Avenue K 93536 — 661-722-6300
Bethel Christian S — 500/PK-12
3100 W Avenue K 93536 — 661-943-2224
Mathias Konnerth, prin. — Fax 943-6574
Calvary Chapel Christian S — 200/1-12
1935 W Avenue L 93534 — 661-942-0404
Tina McMillen, prin.
Country Christian S — 200/1-12
2343 W Avenue K 93536 — 661-729-0142
Rebekah Wilson, prin.
Desert Christian HS — 600/9-12
2340 W Avenue J8 93536 — 661-723-7441
Ronald Johnson, prin. — Fax 723-7437
Desert Christian MS — 400/6-8
44662 15th St W 93534 — 661-723-0665
Brian Roseborough, prin. — Fax 723-6774
Lancaster Baptist S — 500/K-12
4020 E Lancaster Blvd 93535 — 661-946-4668
Ray Cazis, prin. — Fax 946-7374
Lancaster Beauty School — Post-Sec.
44646 10th St W 93534 — 661-948-1672
Paraclete HS — 800/9-12
42145 30th St W 93536 — 661-943-3255
John Anson, prin. — Fax 722-9455
Seton S, 44751 Date Ave 93534 — 700/K-12
Richard Ellis, dir. — 661-948-8881

La Palma, Orange, Pop. 15,805
Anaheim UNHSD
Supt. — See Anaheim
Kennedy HS — 2,400/9-12
8281 Walker St 90623 — 714-220-4101
Kelly Wilson, prin. — Fax 995-1833
Walker JHS — 1,200/7-8
8132 Walker St 90623 — 714-220-4051
Daphne Hammer-Nichols, prin. — Fax 220-2237

La Puente, Los Angeles, Pop. 41,762
Bassett USD — 6,000/K-12
904 Willow Ave 91746 — 626-931-3000
Robert Watanabe, supt. — Fax 918-3105
www.bassett.k12.ca.us
Bassett HS — 1,500/9-12
755 Ardilla Ave 91746 — 626-931-2800
Carolyn Pruitt, prin. — Fax 931-2850
Bassett Adult S Florence Flanner Campus — Adult
1314 Le Borgne Ave 91746 — 626-931-7950
Matthew Smith, dir. — Fax 931-7915
Other Schools – See City of Industry

Hacienda La Puente USD
Supt. — See City of Industry
Grandview MS — 600/6-8
795 Grandview Ln 91744 — 626-934-5801
Mark Chacon, prin. — Fax 855-3824
La Puente HS — 1,800/9-12
15615 Nelson Ave 91744 — 626-934-6700
Ava Smalley, prin. — Fax 855-3798
Sierra Vista MS — 700/6-8
15801 Sierra Vista Ct 91744 — 626-933-4000
Sue Kaiser, prin. — Fax 855-3817
Sparks MS — 1,000/6-8
15100 Giordano St 91744 — 626-933-5000
Sherri Franson, prin. — Fax 855-3848
Hacienda La Puente Valley Adult Ed — Adult
14101 Nelson Ave 91746 — 626-934-2920
Don Carmack, dir. — Fax 934-2900

Rowland USD
Supt. — See Rowland Heights
Nogales HS — 2,500/9-12
401 Nogales St 91744 — 626-965-3437
Nancy Padilla, prin. — Fax 965-4587

Bishop Amat HS — 1,400/9-12
14301 Fairgrove Ave 91746 — 626-962-2495
Dr. Merritt Hemenway, prin. — Fax 960-0994
Hacienda LaPuente Valley Adult Education — Post-Sec.
14101 Nelson Ave 91746 — 626-934-2800

La Quinta, Riverside, Pop. 38,232
Desert Sands USD — 26,400/K-12
47950 Dune Palms Rd 92253 — 760-777-4200
Dr. Doris Wilson, supt. — Fax 771-8505
www.dsusd.us
La Quinta HS — 2,700/9-12
79255 Westward Ho Dr 92253 — 760-772-4150
Donna Salazar, prin. — Fax 772-4166
La Quinta MS — 900/6-8
78900 Avenue 50 92253 — 760-777-4220
Janet Seto, prin. — Fax 777-4216
Paige MS — 6-8
43495 Palm Royale Dr 92253 — 760-238-9710
Derrick Lawson, prin.
Desert Sands Adult S — Adult
47950 Dune Palms Rd 92253 — 760-863-3693
Pam Rutledge, prin. — Fax 863-3696
Other Schools – See Indio, Palm Desert

Larkspur, Marin, Pop. 11,724
Larkspur ESD — 1,000/K-8
230 Doherty Dr 94939 — 415-927-6960
Valerie Pitts, supt. — Fax 927-6964
www.larkspurschools.org
Hall MS — 300/6-8
200 Doherty Dr 94939 — 415-927-6978
Daniel A. Norbutas, prin. — Fax 927-6985

Tamalpais UNHSD — 3,900/9-12
PO Box 605 94977 — 415-945-3720
Bob Ferguson, supt. — Fax 945-3719
www.tamdistrict.org
Redwood HS — 1,500/9-12
395 Doherty Dr 94939 — 415-924-6200
Nancy Neu, prin. — Fax 945-3675
Tamiscal HS — 100/9-12
305 Doherty Dr 94939 — 415-945-3750
Sue Hall, prin. — Fax 945-3752
Other Schools – See Mill Valley, San Anselmo

La Selva Beach, Santa Cruz

Monterey Bay Academy — 200/9-12
783 San Andreas Rd 95076 — 831-728-1481
Tim Kubrock, prin. — Fax 728-1485

Las Flores, Orange
Capistrano USD
Supt. — See San Juan Capistrano
Las Flores MS — 1,700/6-8
25862 Antonio Pkwy, Rcho Sta Marg CA 92688
949-589-6543
Holly Feldt, prin. — Fax 589-9286

Lathrop, San Joaquin, Pop. 13,116

ITT Technical Institute — Post-Sec.
16916 S Harlan Rd 95330 — 209-858-0077

Laton, Fresno, Pop. 1,415
Laton JUSD — 600/PK-12
PO Box 248 93242 — 559-922-4015
Ralph Vandro, supt. — Fax 923-4791
www.laton.k12.ca.us
Laton HS — 200/9-12
PO Box 278 93242 — 559-922-4080
Jim Reed, prin. — Fax 923-4072

La Verne, Los Angeles, Pop. 33,185
Bonita USD
Supt. — See San Dimas

Bonita HS 1,900/9-12
3102 D St 91750 909-971-8220
Robert Ketterling, prin. Fax 971-8229
Ramona MS 1,400/6-8
3490 Ramona Ave 91750 909-971-8260
Mark Rodgers, prin. Fax 971-8269

Calvary Baptist S 200/PK-12
2990 Damien Ave 91750 909-593-4672
Taylora Dial, prin. Fax 392-9533
Damien HS 1,100/9-12
2280 Damien Ave 91750 909-596-1946
Fr. Patrick Travers, prin. Fax 596-6112
Lutheran HS 200/9-12
3960 Fruit St 91750 909-593-4494
Jeremy Lowe, prin. Fax 596-3744
University of La Verne Post-Sec.
1950 3rd St 91750 909-593-3511

Lawndale, Los Angeles, Pop. 32,193
Centinela Valley UNHSD 7,800/9-12
14901 Inglewood Ave 90260 310-263-3200
Dr. Cheryl White, supt. Fax 675-6571
www.centinela.k12.ca.us/
Lawndale HS 1,400/9-12
14901 Inglewood Ave 90260 310-263-3100
Vicente Bravo, prin. Fax 263-3120
Leuzinger HS 3,300/9-12
4118 Rosecrans Ave 90260 310-263-2200
Sonia Miller, prin. Fax 675-7023
Centinela Valley Adult S Adult
4953 Marine Ave 90260 310-263-3155
Dr. Fe Woods, prin. Fax 644-6142
Other Schools – See Hawthorne

Lawndale ESD 5,300/K-8
4161 W 147th St 90260 310-973-1300
Joseph Condon Ed.D., supt. Fax 675-6462
www.lawndale.k12.ca.us
Addams MS, 4161 W 147th St 90260 100/6-8
Frank Noyes, prin. 310-676-8621
Rogers MS 1,300/6-8
4161 W 147th St 90260 310-676-1197
Tina Nielsen, prin. Fax 675-0489

Laytonville, Mendocino, Pop. 1,133
Laytonville USD 500/K-12
PO Box 868 95454 707-984-6414
John Markatos, supt. Fax 984-8223
Laytonville HS 200/9-12
PO Box 868 95454 707-984-6108
Joan Potter, prin. Fax 984-8066

Lebec, Kern
El Tejon USD 1,400/K-12
PO Box 876 93243 661-248-6247
Shelly Mason, supt. Fax 248-6714
www.el-tejon.k12.ca.us
El Tejon MS 600/4-8
PO Box 876 93243 661-248-6680
Shelly Mason, prin. Fax 248-5203
Frazier Mountain HS 500/9-12
PO Box 876 93243 661-248-0310
Dan Penner, prin. Fax 248-0403

Lee Vining, Mono
Eastern Sierra USD
Supt. — See Bridgeport
Lee Vining JSHS 50/7-12
PO Box 268 93541 760-647-6366
Frank Romero, prin. Fax 647-6695

Leggett, Mendocino
Leggett Valley USD 200/K-12
PO Box 186 95585 707-925-6285
Bill Raebe, supt. Fax 925-6396
leggett.k12.ca.us
Leggett Valley HS 50/9-12
PO Box 186 95585 707-925-6230
Katie Sommer, prin. Fax 925-6396
Other Schools – See Whitethorn

Le Grand, Merced, Pop. 1,205
Le Grand UNHSD 600/9-12
12961 Le Grand Rd 95333 209-389-9403
George Hinds, supt. Fax 389-9414
www.lghs.k12.ca.us/
Le Grand Union HS 600/9-12
12961 Le Grand Rd 95333 209-389-9400
Donna Alley, prin. Fax 389-4065

Lemon Grove, San Diego, Pop. 24,124
Lemon Grove ESD 4,300/K-8
8025 Lincoln St 91945 619-825-5600
Ernie Anastos, supt. Fax 462-7959
www.lgsd.k12.ca.us
Lemon Grove MS 900/6-8
7866 Lincoln St 91945 619-825-5628
David Torres, prin. Fax 825-5781
Palm MS 700/6-8
8425 Palm St 91945 619-825-5641
Russell Little, prin. Fax 628-5786

Lemoore, Kings, Pop. 22,699
Lemoore UNESD 3,100/K-8
100 Vine St 93245 559-924-6800
Ronald Meade, supt. Fax 924-6809
www.luesd.k12.ca.us/
Liberty MS 600/7-8
100 Vine St 93245 559-924-6860
Eric Smyers, prin. Fax 924-6869

Lemoore UNHSD 2,100/9-12
5 Powell Ave 93245 559-924-6610
Dr. Paul Terry, supt. Fax 924-9212
www.luhsd.k12.ca.us/
Lemoore HS 2,000/9-12
101 E Bush St 93245 559-924-6600
James Bennett, prin. Fax 924-5086
Lemoore Middle College HS 9-12
351 E Bush St 93245 559-924-6620
Sandi Lowe, prin. Fax 924-6637
Lemoore Adult S Adult
351 E Bush St 93245 559-924-6620
Sandi Lowe, prin. Fax 924-6637

Kings Christian S 300/PK-12
900 E D St 93245 559-924-8301
Duane Daniel, admin. Fax 924-0607

Lennox, Los Angeles, Pop. 22,757
Lennox ESD 6,800/K-8
10319 Firmona Ave 90304 310-330-4950
Dr. Bruce McDaniel, supt. Fax 674-7804
www.lennox.k12.ca.us
Lennox MS 1,500/7-8
10319 Firmona Ave 90304 310-419-1800
Brian Johnson, prin. Fax 677-4635

Lincoln, Placer, Pop. 32,804
Western Placer USD 4,300/K-12
810 J St 95648 916-645-6350
Roger Yohe, supt. Fax 645-6356
www.wpusd.k12.ca.us
Edwards MS 1,000/6-8
204 L St 95648 916-645-6370
Michael Doherty, prin. Fax 645-6379
Lincoln HS 1,100/9-12
790 J St 95648 916-645-6360
David Butler, prin. Fax 645-6349
Twelve Bridges MS 6-8
770 Westview Dr 95648 916-434-5270
Mary Boyle, prin. Fax 434-5240

Linden, San Joaquin, Pop. 1,339
Linden USD 2,500/K-12
18527 Main St 95236 209-887-3894
Ronald Estes, supt. Fax 887-2250
www.sjcoe.net
Linden HS 700/9-12
18527 E Front St 95236 209-887-3073
Stephanie Markle, prin. Fax 887-3815
Other Schools – See Stockton

Lindsay, Tulare, Pop. 10,767
Lindsay USD 3,700/K-12
519 E Honolulu St 93247 559-562-5111
Janet Kliegl, supt. Fax 562-6145
www.lindsay.k12.ca.us
Garvey JHS 600/7-8
340 N Harvard Ave 93247 559-562-1311
Rebecca Mestaz, prin. Fax 562-1411
Lindsay HS 900/9-12
1701 E Tulare Rd 93247 559-562-5911
Lana Weatherly, prin. Fax 562-4291

Littlerock, Los Angeles, Pop. 1,320
Antelope Valley UNHSD
Supt. — See Lancaster
Littlerock HS 2,600/9-12
10833 E Avenue R 93543 661-944-5209
Lisa Oates, prin. Fax 944-5191

Keppel UNESD
Supt. — See Pearblossom
Almondale MS 600/7-8
9330 E Avenue U 93543 661-944-2152
Dawn Evenson, prin. Fax 944-0694

Live Oak, Sutter, Pop. 7,128
Live Oak USD 1,800/K-12
2201 Pennington Rd 95953 530-695-5400
Tom Pritchard, supt. Fax 695-5460
www.lodo.santacruz.k12.ca.us/
Live Oak HS 500/9-12
2351 Pennington Rd 95953 530-695-5415
Bill Cornelius, prin. Fax 695-5422
Live Oak MS 500/5-8
2082 Pennington Rd 95953 530-695-5435
Joanne Bass, prin. Fax 695-5443

Livermore, Alameda, Pop. 78,409
Livermore Valley JUSD 14,100/K-12
685 E Jack London Blvd 94551 925-606-3200
Brenda Miller, supt. Fax 606-3328
www.livermoreschools.com
Christenson MS 700/6-8
5757 Haggin Oaks Ave 94551 925-606-4702
Janet Loughran-Smith, prin. Fax 606-4705
East Avenue MS 800/6-8
3951 East Ave 94550 925-606-4711
Vicki Scudder, prin. Fax 606-4763
Granada HS 2,100/9-12
400 Wall St 94550 925-606-4800
Chris Van Schaack, prin. Fax 606-4808
Junction Avenue MS 800/6-8
298 Junction Ave 94551 925-606-4720
Susan Sambuceti, prin. Fax 606-3318
Livermore HS 2,100/9-12
600 Maple St 94550 925-606-4812
David Chamberlain, prin. Fax 606-4851
Mendenhall MS 900/6-8
1701 El Padro Dr 94550 925-606-4731
Helen Foster, prin. Fax 606-4737
Livermore Adult Community Education Adult
1401 Almond Ave 94550 925-606-4722
Nancy Steele, prin. Fax 606-3389

Regional Occupational Center & Program
Supt. — None
Tri-Valley ROP Vo/Tech
2600 Kitty Hawk Rd Ste 117 94551 925-455-4800
Robert Kreitz, dir. Fax 449-9126

Las Positas College Post-Sec.
3033 Collier Canyon Rd 94551 925-373-5800
Sierra Academy of Aeronautics Post-Sec.
550 Airway Blvd 94551 925-443-6100

Livingston, Merced, Pop. 12,585
Livingston UNESD 2,400/K-8
922 B St 95334 209-394-5400
Henry Escobar, supt. Fax 394-5401
www.lusd.k12.ca.us
Livingston MS 800/6-8
101 F St 95334 209-394-5450
Filomena Sousa, prin. Fax 394-5451

Merced UNHSD
Supt. — See Atwater
Livingston HS 1,100/9-12
1617 Main St 95334 209-394-7961
Nancy Edmiston, prin. Fax 358-1093

Lodi, San Joaquin, Pop. 62,133
Lodi USD 28,100/PK-12
1305 E Vine St 95240 209-331-7000
William Huyett, supt. Fax 331-7256
www.lodiusd.k12.ca.us
Lodi Career Education Vo/Tech
421 S Pleasant Ave 95240 209-331-7642
Steve Colwell, prin. Fax 331-7526
Lodi HS 2,600/9-12
3 S Pacific Ave 95242 209-331-7819
Bill Atterberry, prin. Fax 331-7779
Lodi MS 900/7-8
945 S Ham Ln 95242 209-331-7540
Dawn Vetica, prin. Fax 331-7550
Millswood MS 800/7-8
233 N Mills Ave 95242 209-331-8332
Sheree Flemmer, prin. Fax 331-8347
Tokay HS 2,900/9-12
1111 W Century Blvd 95240 209-331-7990
Erik Sandstrom, prin. Fax 331-7168
Lodi Adult S Adult
542 E Pine St 95240 209-331-7607
Steve Colwell, prin. Fax 331-7167
Other Schools – See Stockton

Elliot Christian HS 200/9-12
2695 W Vine St 95242 209-368-2800
David Couchman, admin. Fax 333-5208
Lodi Academy 100/9-12
1230 S Central Ave 95240 209-368-2781
Doug Brown, prin. Fax 368-6142
Vineyard Christian MS 100/6-8
2301 W Lodi Ave 95242 209-333-8300
Karen Hale, prin. Fax 331-7985

Loma Linda, San Bernardino, Pop. 20,901

Loma Linda Academy 1,500/K-12
10656 Anderson St 92354 909-796-0161
Dr. L. Roo McKenzie, prin. Fax 478-6829
Loma Linda University 92350 Post-Sec.
909-558-1000

Lomita, Los Angeles, Pop. 20,515
Los Angeles USD
Supt. — See Los Angeles
Fleming MS 1,900/6-8
25425 Walnut St 90717 310-257-4500
Janice Hackett, prin. Fax 326-9071

Coastal Academy 200/K-12
25501 Oak St 90717 310-644-0433
M. Grace Di Pasquale, dir.
Nishiyamato Academy 100/K-12
2458 Lomita Blvd 90717 310-325-7040
Masayoshi Nishiura, prin.

Lompoc, Santa Barbara, Pop. 39,985
Lompoc USD 11,300/K-12
PO Box 8000 93438 805-742-3300
Dr. Frank Lynch, supt. Fax 735-8452
www.lusd.org
Cabrillo HS 1,600/9-12
PO Box 8000 93438 805-742-2900
Betty McCallum, prin. Fax 733-4156
El Camino MS 500/6-8
PO Box 8000 93438 805-742-2550
Lore Desmond, prin. Fax 735-1474
Lompoc HS 1,600/9-12
PO Box 8000 93438 805-742-3000
Art Diaz, prin. Fax 735-1411
Lompoc Valley MS 1,100/6-8
PO Box 8000 93438 805-742-2600
Jeff Wagonseller, prin. Fax 737-9480
Vandenberg MS 1,100/6-8
PO Box 8000 93438 805-742-2700
Suszanne Nicastro, prin. Fax 734-1790
Lompoc Adult Education Adult
PO Box 8000 93438 805-742-3100
Susan Williams, prin. Fax 736-3089

Lone Pine, Inyo, Pop. 1,818
Lone Pine USD 400/K-12
PO Box 159 93545 760-876-5579
Fax 876-5438
Lone Pine HS 100/9-12
PO Box 159 93545 760-876-5577
Donna Carson, prin. Fax 876-1037
Lone Pine Adult S Adult
PO Box 159 93545 760-876-5577

Long Beach, Los Angeles, Pop. 474,014
Long Beach USD 94,300/PK-12
1515 Hughes Way 90810 562-997-8000
Christopher Steinhauser, supt. Fax 997-8280
www.lbusd.k12.ca.us
Bancroft MS 1,500/6-8
5301 E Centralia St 90808 562-425-7461
Penelope O'Toole, prin. Fax 425-9741
Cabrillo HS 3,500/9-12
2001 Santa Fe Ave 90810 562-951-7700
Cynthia Terry, prin. Fax 951-7797
DeMille MS 1,300/6-8
7025 E Parkcrest St 90808 562-421-8424
Timothy Spivey, prin. Fax 429-1054
Franklin MS 1,400/6-8
540 Cerritos Ave 90802 562-435-4952
David Taylor, prin. Fax 432-6308
Hamilton MS 1,600/6-8
1060 E 70th St 90805 562-602-0302
Connie Jensen, prin. Fax 602-1354

Hill MS 1,200/6-8
1100 Iroquois Ave 90815 562-598-7611
Peter Davis, prin. Fax 598-6329
Hughes MS 1,500/6-8
3846 California Ave 90807 562-595-0831
Monica Daley, prin. Fax 595-9221
Jefferson MS 1,200/6-8
750 Euclid Ave 90804 562-438-9904
Lori Clark, prin. Fax 439-3718
Jordan 9th Grade Academy 9-9
171 W Bort St 90805 562-984-3710
Rosalind Morgan, prin. Fax 423-0781
Jordan HS 4,400/9-12
6500 Atlantic Ave 90805 562-423-1471
Kelly Hurley, prin. Fax 422-9091
Lindbergh MS 1,300/6-8
1022 E Market St 90805 562-422-2845
Dr. Avery Hall, prin. Fax 423-8176
Long Beach Polytechnic HS Vo/Tech
1600 Atlantic Ave 90813 562-591-0581
Shawn Ashley, prin. Fax 591-0631
Marshall MS 1,400/6-8
5870 E Wardlow Rd 90808 562-429-7013
Sherryl Johnson, prin. Fax 496-1489
Millikan HS 3,900/9-12
2800 Snowden Ave 90815 562-425-7441
Jefferey Cornejo, prin. Fax 425-1151
Renaissance HS for the Arts 500/9-12
235 E 8th St 90813 562-901-0168
Mark Zahn, prin. Fax 435-7147
Rogers MS 900/6-8
365 Monrovia Ave 90803 562-434-7411
Thomas Huff, prin. Fax 434-0581
Stanford MS 1,400/6-8
5871 E Los Arcos St 90815 562-594-9793
Kathleen Cruz, prin. Fax 594-8591
Stephens MS 1,500/6-8
1830 W Columbia St 90810 562-595-0841
Shivaun Williams, prin. Fax 426-5631
Washington MS 1,000/4-8
1450 Cedar Ave 90813 562-591-2434
Constance McKivett, prin. Fax 591-6888
Wilson HS 4,600/9-12
4400 E 10th St 90804 562-433-0481
Diane Brown, prin. Fax 433-2731
Evening HS Adult
1515 Hughes Way 90810 562-989-7872
Matthew Saldana, prin. Fax 997-8650
Long Beach School for Adults Adult
3701 E Willow St 90815 562-595-8893
Fitzgerald Jones, prin. Fax 988-1924
Other Schools – See Avalon, Carson, Lakewood

Regional Occupational Center & Program
Supt. — None
Long Beach USD ROC/P Vo/Tech
3701B E Willow St 90815 562-426-6846
Matt Saldana, prin. Fax 424-8976

American Institute of Health Science Post-Sec.
3501 Atlantic Ave 90807 562-988-2278
Brooks College Post-Sec.
4825 E Pacific Coast Hwy 90804 562-597-6611
California State University-Long Beach Post-Sec.
1250 N Bellflower Blvd 90840 562-985-4111
DeVry University Post-Sec.
3880 Kilroy Airport Way 90806 562-427-0861
First Baptist Church S 200/K-12
1000 Pine Ave 90813 562-432-8447
James Allen, prin. Fax 499-6847
Gethsemane Baptist Christian S 100/K-12
6095 Orange Ave 90805 562-422-4206
Dr. David Smith, prin.
John Wesley Intl. Barber/Beauty Coll Post-Sec.
717 Pine Ave 90813 562-435-7060
Long Beach City College Post-Sec.
4901 E Carson St 90808 562-938-4111
National Institute of Technology Post-Sec.
2161 Technology Pl 90810 562-437-0501
Newbridge College Post-Sec.
3799 E Burnett St 90815 562-498-4500
New Life Christian Academy 100/PK-12
PO Box 5217 90805 562-423-9000
Linda Johnson, prin. Fax 423-4019
Pacific Baptist S 200/K-12
3332 Magnolia Ave 90806 562-426-5214
Dr. Joseph Esposito, prin.
St. Anthony HS 200/9-12
620 Olive Ave 90802 562-435-4496
Gina Rushing, pres. Fax 437-3055
Southwestern Longview Private S 200/K-12
4747 Daisy Ave 90805 562-422-1582
Clarence Horton, dir.

Loomis, Placer, Pop. 6,577
Placer UNHSD
Supt. — See Auburn
Del Oro HS 1,600/9-12
3301 Taylor Rd 95650 916-652-7243
Bob Christiansen, prin. Fax 652-3706

Los Alamitos, Orange, Pop. 11,657
Los Alamitos USD 9,100/PK-12
10293 Bloomfield St 90720 562-799-4700
Carol Hart, supt. Fax 799-4711
www.losalusd.k12.ca.us
Los Alamitos HS 3,000/9-12
3591 Cerritos Ave 90720 562-799-4780
Kelly Godfrey, prin. Fax 799-4798
McAuliffe MS 1,200/6-8
4112 Cerritos Ave 90720 714-816-3320
Dennis Sackett, prin. Fax 816-3362
Oak MS 1,000/6-8
10821 Oak St 90720 562-799-4740
David Downing, prin. Fax 799-4773

Los Altos, Santa Clara, Pop. 27,096
Los Altos ESD 3,900/K-8
201 Covington Rd 94024 650-947-1150
Tim Justus, supt. Fax 947-0118
www.losaltos.k12.ca.us
Blach IS 400/7-8
1120 Covington Rd 94024 650-934-3800
Leslie Crane, prin. Fax 968-3918
Egan IS 500/7-8
100 W Portola Ave 94022 650-917-2200
Brenda Dyckman, prin. Fax 949-3748

Mountain View-Los Altos UNHSD
Supt. — See Mountain View
Los Altos HS 1,700/9-12
201 Almond Ave 94022 650-968-6571
Wynne Satterwhite, prin. Fax 948-8672

Los Altos Hills, Santa Clara, Pop. 8,164

Foothill College Post-Sec.
12345 S El Monte Rd 94022 650-949-7777
Pinewood Private S - Upper Campus 300/7-12
26800 W Fremont Rd 94022 650-941-1532
Scott Riches, pres. Fax 941-4727

Los Angeles, Los Angeles, Pop. 3,844,829
Compton USD
Supt. — See Compton
Vanguard Learning Center 700/6-8
13305 S San Pedro St 90061 310-898-6050
Sonja Bankston-Cullen, prin. Fax 327-7180

Los Angeles USD 671,800/PK-12
333 S Beaudry Ave 90017 213-241-7000
David Brewer, supt. Fax 241-8442
www.lausd.k12.ca.us
Adams MS 2,300/6-8
151 W 30th St 90007 213-744-1502
Joseph Santana, prin. Fax 749-8542
Audubon MS 1,800/6-8
4120 11th Ave 90008 323-290-6300
James Downing, prin. Fax 296-2433
Bancroft MS 1,400/6-8
929 N Las Palmas Ave 90038 323-993-3400
Annie Lykes Webb, prin. Fax 461-8246
Belmont HS 4,900/9-12
1575 W 2nd St 90026 213-250-0244
Gary Yoshinobu, prin. Fax 250-9706
Belvedere MS 2,500/6-8
312 N Record Ave 90063 323-266-5400
Leo Salazar, prin. Fax 269-6769
Berendo MS 3,100/6-8
1157 S Berendo St 90006 213-382-1343
Robert Bilovsky, prin. Fax 382-8599
Bethune MS 2,500/6-8
155 W 69th St 90003 323-541-1800
Daryl Narimatsu, prin. Fax 759-1271
Bravo Medical Magnet HS 1,700/9-12
1200 Cornwell St 90033 323-227-4400
Maria Flores, prin. Fax 342-9139
Burbank MS 2,000/6-8
6460 N Figueroa St 90042 323-255-0108
Fax 257-7420
Burroughs MS 2,200/6-8
600 S Mccadden Pl 90005 323-549-5000
Mirta McKay, prin. Fax 934-9051
Carver MS 2,700/6-8
4410 McKinley Ave 90011 323-233-3261
Evelyn Wesley, prin. Fax 232-5344
Central LA MS 6-8
3500 S Hill St 90007 323-235-7200
Beverley Clarkson, prin. Fax 846-0054
Clay MS 1,800/6-8
12226 S Western Ave 90047 323-600-6000
Pamela Gartrell Jackson, prin. Fax 777-6056
Cochran MS 1,700/6-8
4066 W 17th St 90019 323-730-4300
Scott Schmerelson, prin. Fax 733-9106
Crenshaw HS 2,900/9-12
5010 11th Ave 90043 323-290-7800
Sheilah Sanders, prin. Fax 292-6712
Dorsey HS 2,000/9-12
3537 Farmdale Ave 90016 323-298-8400
George Bartleson, prin. Fax 298-8501
Downtown Business HS 1,100/9-12
1081 W Temple St 90012 213-481-0371
Fax 482-0792
Drew MS 2,600/6-8
8511 Compton Ave 90001 323-583-6961
Barbara Chanaiwa, prin. Fax 583-6030
Eagle Rock JSHS 2,900/7-12
1750 Yosemite Dr 90041 323-340-3500
Salvador Antoni Velasco, prin. Fax 255-3398
Edison MS 2,400/6-8
6500 Hooper Ave 90001 323-587-5108
Coleen Puanani, prin. Fax 581-8389
El Sereno MS 2,400/6-8
2839 N Eastern Ave 90032 323-240-3700
Arthur Duardo, prin. Fax 223-9024
Emerson MS 1,500/6-8
1650 Selby Ave 90024 310-475-8417
Charlotte Lerchenmuller, prin. Fax 474-6517
Fairfax HS 3,000/9-12
7850 Melrose Ave 90046 323-370-1200
Edward Zubiate, prin. Fax 651-5803
Fashion Careers Magnet S Vo/Tech
1081 W Temple St 90012 213-481-0371
Fax 482-0792
Franklin HS 3,300/9-12
820 N Avenue 54 90042 323-550-2000
Luis Manuel Lopez, prin. Fax 258-5940
Fremont HS 4,700/9-12
7676 S San Pedro St 90003 323-565-1200
Larry Higgins, prin. Fax 971-5890
Garfield HS 4,700/9-12
5101 E 6th St 90022 323-268-9361
Omar Del Cueto, prin. Fax 268-4957
Gompers MS 2,000/6-8
234 E 112th St 90061 323-241-4000
David Garcia, prin. Fax 418-0778
Griffith MS 2,200/6-8
4765 E 4th St 90022 323-266-7400
Joseph Caldera, prin. Fax 268-6375
Hamilton HS 3,100/9-12
2955 S Robertson Blvd 90034 310-280-1400
Gary Garcia, prin. Fax 842-8663
Harte Prep MS 1,600/6-8
9301 S Hoover St 90044 323-757-9143
Fax 757-0408
Hollenbeck MS 2,700/6-8
2510 E 6th St 90023 323-780-3000
Jose Torres, prin. Fax 265-0865
Hollywood HS 3,000/9-12
1521 N Highland Ave 90028 323-461-3891
Fonna Bishop, prin. Fax 957-0238
Irving MS 1,700/6-8
3010 Estara Ave 90065 323-259-3700
Kimberly Noble, prin. Fax 254-6447
Jefferson HS 3,500/9-12
1319 E 41st St 90011 323-521-1200
Juan Flecha, prin. Fax 231-4755
Jordan HS 2,500/9-12
2265 E 103rd St 90002 323-568-4100
Stephen Strachan, prin. Fax 249-4709
King-Drew Medical Magnet HS 1,700/9-12
1601 E 120th St 90059 323-566-0420
Juanita Woods, prin. Fax 567-1429
King MS 2,900/6-8
4201 Fountain Ave 90029 323-664-6700
Charlene Hirotsu, prin. Fax 913-3594
LA Center for Enriched Studies 1,600/6-12
5931 W 18th St 90035 323-938-1620
Margaret Kim, prin. Fax 938-8737
Lincoln HS 2,800/9-12
3501 N Broadway 90031 323-441-4600
James Molina, prin. Fax 223-1291
Locke HS 3,200/9-12
325 E 111th St 90061 323-420-2100
Frank Wells, prin. Fax 420-2128
Los Angeles Academy 2,900/6-8
644 E 56th St 90011 323-232-7820
Maria Borges, prin. Fax 231-0136
Los Angeles HS 4,600/9-12
4650 W Olympic Blvd 90019 323-900-2700
Frank Nishimura, prin. Fax 936-8455
Los Angeles Technology Center Vo/Tech
3721 W Washington Blvd 90018 323-732-0153
Maxine Hammond, prin. Fax 731-1568
Mann MS 1,500/6-8
7001 S St Andrews Pl 90047 323-541-1900
Cynthia Arceneaux, prin. Fax 758-8203
Manual Arts HS 3,900/9-12
4131 S Vermont Ave 90037 323-232-1121
Edward Trimis, prin. Fax 232-0837
Marina Del Rey MS 1,300/6-8
12500 Braddock Dr 90066 310-578-2700
Erick Mata, prin. Fax 821-3248
Markham MS 1,900/6-8
1650 E 104th St 90002 323-568-5500
Verna Stroud, prin. Fax 569-6066
Marshall HS 4,700/9-12
3939 Tracy St 90027 323-671-1400
Thomas Abraham, prin. Fax 665-8682
Middle College HS 9-12
11750 S Western Ave 90047 323-820-9343
Wanda Moats, prin. Fax 820-9501
Muir MS 2,300/6-8
5929 S Vermont Ave 90044 323-971-4361
Michael Olivo, prin. Fax 778-9824
New Technology HS @ Central LA 9-12
322 Lucas Ave 90017 213-240-3850
Fax 482-0232
New Technology HS @ Jefferson 9-12
1319 E 41st St 90011 323-521-1290
Fax 521-1294
New Technology HS @ Jordan 9-12
2265 E 103rd St 90002 323-567-0531
Nightingale MS 1,900/6-8
3311 N Figueroa St 90065 323-224-4800
Manuel Diaz, prin. Fax 222-4506
Palms MS 1,900/6-8
10860 Woodbine St 90034 310-253-7600
Bonnie Murrow, prin. Fax 559-0397
Roosevelt HS 4,700/9-12
456 S Mathews St 90033 323-268-7241
Cecilia Quemada, prin. Fax 269-5473
Santee Education Complex 9-12
1921 Maple Ave 90011 213-763-1000
Vince Carbino, prin. Fax 742-9883
Stevenson MS 2,500/6-8
725 S Indiana St 90023 323-780-6400
Teresa Hurtado, prin. Fax 265-3952
Thirty Second Street USC Magnet S 1,000/K-12
822 W 32nd St 90007 213-749-7179
Philip Toyotome, prin. Fax 744-1608
Twain MS 1,200/6-8
2224 Walgrove Ave 90066 310-305-3100
Jeffrey Felz, prin. Fax 398-1627
University HS 2,300/9-12
11800 Texas Ave 90025 310-914-3500
Elois McGehee, prin. Fax 478-6535
Venice HS 3,000/9-12
13000 Venice Blvd 90066 310-577-4200
Janice Davis, prin. Fax 306-3249
Virgil MS 2,600/6-8
152 N Vermont Ave 90004 213-368-2800
Ada Stevens, prin. Fax 389-8973
Washington Prep HS 2,800/9-12
10860 S Denker Ave 90047 323-418-4000
Gail Greer, prin. Fax 754-3517
Webster MS 1,300/6-8
11330 Graham Pl 90064 310-235-4600
Fax 477-0146
Westchester HS 2,600/9-12
7400 W Manchester Ave 90045 310-338-2400
Anita Barner, prin. Fax 410-1067
Wilson HS 2,800/9-12
4500 Multnomah St 90032 323-223-1131
Robert Martinez, prin. Fax 223-7936
Wright MS 1,300/6-8
6550 W 80th St 90045 310-258-6600
Stephen Rochelle, prin. Fax 568-8942
Belmont Community Adult Education Adult
1575 W 2nd St 90026 213-250-9133
Roger Miller, prin. Fax 250-9272
Crenshaw/Washington Adult Education Adult
5010 11th Ave 90043 323-298-8400
Fax 294-8783

East Los Angeles Occupational Center Adult
2100 Marengo St 90033 323-223-1283
Robert Ceja, prin. Fax 223-6365
East Los Angeles Skills Center Adult
3921 Selig Pl 90031 323-224-5970
Pete Fernandez, prin. Fax 222-2351
Evans Community Adult Education Adult
717 N Figueroa St 90012 213-626-7151
Jean Batey, prin. Fax 626-4487
Franklin Adult Education Adult
820 N Avenue 54 90042 323-550-2100
Dianne Baird, prin. Fax 256-2790
Fremont Community Adult S Adult
7676 S San Pedro St 90003 323-565-1300
Michael Wada, prin. Fax 778-8531
Friedman Occupational Center Adult
1646 S Olive St 90015 213-765-2400
Howard Saxe, prin. Fax 748-7406
Garfield Adult Education Adult
5101 E 6th St 90022 323-262-5163
Wanda Chang, prin. Fax 266-3294
Hollywood Community Adult Education Adult
1521 N Highland Ave 90028 323-467-6191
Cynthia Tollette, prin. Fax 467-3382
Jefferson Adult S Adult
1319 E 41st St 90011 323-235-8120
France Wong, prin. Fax 233-9658
Jordan-Locke Adult Education Adult
325 E 111th St 90061 323-420-2065
Fax 757-9416
Los Angeles Adult Education Adult
4650 W Olympic Blvd 90019 323-931-1026
Claudine Ajeti, prin. Fax 936-5496
Manual Arts-Crenshaw Community Adult S Adult
4131 S Vermont Ave 90037 323-234-9177
Maureen Jensen, prin. Fax 234-1310
Metropolitan Skills Center Adult
2801 W 6th St 90057 213-386-7269
James Chacon, prin. Fax 386-4554
Roosevelt Community Adult S Adult
456 S Mathews St 90033 323-263-9388
Christine Furuta, prin. Fax 263-5040
Venice Community Adult S Adult
13000 Venice Blvd 90066 310-577-4230
Philip MacMillan, prin. Fax 577-4238
Waters Employment Preparation Center Adult
10925 S Central Ave 90059 323-564-4451
Janet Clark, prin. Fax 566-0147
Westchester-Emerson Community Adult S Adult
7400 W Manchester Ave 90045 310-258-2000
Patricia Colby, prin. Fax 645-8043
Westside Community Adult S Adult
7850 Melrose Ave 90046 323-370-1040
Paul Hamel, prin. Fax 653-3004
Wilson-Lincoln Adult Education Adult
4500 Multnomah St 90032 323-223-3311
Gertrude Hawkins, prin. Fax 221-0543
Other Schools – See Arleta, Bell, Canoga Park, Carson, Chatsworth, Cudahy, Gardena, Granada Hills, Harbor City, Hollywood, Huntington Park, Lomita, Maywood, Mission Hills, North Hollywood, Northridge, Pacoima, Panorama City, Rancho Palos Verdes, Reseda, San Fernando, San Pedro, Sepulveda, Sherman Oaks, South Gate, Sunland, Sun Valley, Sylmar, Tarzana, Tujunga, Van Nuys, Wilmington, Woodland Hills

Regional Occupational Center & Program
Supt. — None
Los Angeles USD ROC/P Vo/Tech
333 S Beaudry Ave 90017 213-241-3162
Nancy Woodrum, admin. Fax 241-8427

American Career College Post-Sec.
4021 Rosewood Ave 90004 323-383-2862
American Film Institute Post-Sec.
2021 N Western Ave 90027 323-856-7600
American InterContinental University Post-Sec.
12655 W Jefferson Blvd 90066 310-302-2000
Archer S for Girls 500/6-12
11725 W Sunset Blvd 90049 310-873-7000
Arlene Hogan, hdmstr. Fax 873-7070
Arshag Dickranian Armenian S 300/PK-12
1200 N Cahuenga Blvd 90038 323-461-4377
Vartkes Kourouyan, prin. Fax 461-4247
Associated Technical College Post-Sec.
1670 Wilshire Blvd 90017 213-353-1845
Bais Chana Chabad HS 100/9-12
9017 W Pico Blvd 90035 310-278-8995
Batya Lisker, prin. Fax 278-9256
Bais Yaakov S 200/9-12
7353 Beverly Blvd 90036 323-938-3231
Rabbi Yoel Bursztyn, dir. Fax 930-0477
Bishop Conaty-Our Lady Loretta HS 500/9-12
2900 W Pico Blvd 90006 323-737-0012
Sharon Morano, prin. Fax 737-1749
Bishop Mora Salesian HS 300/9-12
960 S Soto St 90023 323-261-7124
Manuel Villarreal, prin. Fax 261-7600
Brentwood S 600/7-12
100 S Barrington Pl 90049 310-476-9633
Dr. Michael Pratt, hdmstr. Fax 476-4087
Bryan College Post-Sec.
2333 Beverly Blvd 90057 213-484-8850
California Design College Post-Sec.
3440 Wilshire Blvd 10th Flr 90010 213-251-3636
California Healing Arts College Post-Sec.
12217 Santa Monica Blvd 90025 310-826-7622
California State University-Los Angeles Post-Sec.
5151 State University Dr 90032 323-343-3000
Cathedral HS 600/9-12
1253 Bishop Rd 90012 323-225-2438
Br. John Montgomery, prin. Fax 222-7223
CEI Post-Sec.
3699 Wilshire Blvd Fl 4 90010 213-351-2000
Charles R. Drew Univ. of Med. & Science Post-Sec.
1621 E 120th St 90059 323-563-4800
Chase College Post-Sec.
3580 Wilshire Blvd Fl 4 90010 213-365-1999
Children's Hospital of Los Angeles Post-Sec.
4650 W Sunset Blvd 90027 323-669-2301
Cleveland Chiropractic College of LA Post-Sec.
590 N Vermont Ave 90004 323-660-6166

Colburn School Post-Sec.
200 S Grand Ave 90012 213-621-2200
Concord Law School Post-Sec.
10866 Wilshire Blvd # 1200 90024 800-439-4794
Dongguk Royal University Post-Sec.
440 Shatto Pl 90020 213-487-0110
East Los Angeles Occupational Center Post-Sec.
2100 Marengo St 90033 323-223-1283
Escuelas Leicester Post-Sec.
1940 S Figueroa St 90007 213-746-7666
Everest College Post-Sec.
3460 Wilshire Blvd Ste 500 90010 213-388-9950
Everest College Post-Sec.
3000 S Robertson Blvd # 300 90034 310-840-5777
FIDM/The Fashion Institute Post-Sec.
919 S Grand Ave 90015 213-624-1200
Golden Day S 400/K-12
4476 Crenshaw Blvd 90043 323-296-6280
Dr. Clark Parker, prin. Fax 290-0190
Harvard-Westlake S 700/7-9
700 N Faring Rd 90077 310-274-7281
Jeanne Huybrechts, hdmstr. Fax 288-3331
Hebrew Union College Post-Sec.
3077 University Ave 90007 213-749-3424
ICDC College Post-Sec.
5422 W Sunset Blvd 90027 323-468-0404
Immaculate Heart HS 500/9-12
5515 Franklin Ave 90028 323-461-3651
Sr. Virginia Hurst, prin. Fax 462-0610
Immaculate Heart MS 200/6-8
5515 Franklin Ave 90028 323-461-3651
Ann Phelps, prin. Fax 462-0610
Institute of Computer Technology Post-Sec.
3200 Wilshire Blvd Fl 4 90010 213-381-3333
International Christian Education Coll. Post-Sec.
3807 Wilshire Blvd Ste 730 90010 213-368-0316
John Tracy Clinic Post-Sec.
806 W Adams Blvd 90007 213-748-5481
Le Lycee Francais de Los Angeles 1,000/PK-12
3261 Overland Ave 90034 310-836-3464
Alain Anselme, dir. Fax 558-8069
Liberty Training Institute Post-Sec.
2706 Wilshire Blvd 90057 213-383-9545
Little Citizens Westside Academy 100/1-12
4256 S Western Ave 90062 323-293-9775
Angela Moore, admin.
Los Angeles Adventist Academy 300/PK-12
846 E El Segundo Blvd 90059 323-321-2585
Dr. Lilly Nelson, prin. Fax 324-3207
Los Angeles City College Post-Sec.
855 N Vermont Ave 90029 323-953-4000
Los Angeles Co. Coll. Nursing/Alld Hlth Post-Sec.
1200 N State St 90033 323-226-4911
Los Angeles Southwest College Post-Sec.
1600 W Imperial Hwy 90047 323-241-5225
Los Angeles Trade-Technical College Post-Sec.
400 W Washington Blvd 90015 213-744-9058
Loyola HS 9-12
1901 Venice Blvd 90006 213-381-5121
Fax 368-3819
Loyola Marymount University Post-Sec.
PO Box 15019 90015 213-736-1180
Loyola Marymount University Post-Sec.
7900 Loyola Blvd 90045 310-338-2700
Lycee International De Los Angeles 500/PK-12
4155 Russell Ave 90027 323-665-4526
John Larner, hdmstr. Fax 665-2607
Marinello School of Beauty Post-Sec.
1241 S Soto St Ste 101 90023 213-627-5561
Marinello School of Beauty Post-Sec.
6111 Wilshire Blvd 90048 323-938-2005
Marinello School of Beauty Post-Sec.
2700 Colorado Blvd Ste 266 90041 323-254-6226
Marlborough HS 500/7-12
250 S Rossmore Ave 90004 323-935-1147
Barbara Wagner, hdmstr. Fax 933-0542
Marymount HS 9-12
10643 W Sunset Blvd 90077 310-472-1205
Mary Gozdecki Ph.D., prin. Fax 476-0910
Medical Institute Post-Sec.
5170 Santa Monica Blvd #300 90029 323-663-2700
Mt. St. Mary's College Post-Sec.
12001 Chalon Rd 90049 310-954-4000
Mt. St. Mary's College - Doheny Campus Post-Sec.
10 Chester Pl 90007 213-746-0450
Murphy Catholic HS 300/9-12
241 S Detroit St 90036 323-935-1161
Denis Munoz, prin. Fax 935-1621
Netan Eli HS 50/9-12
1445 S Robertson Blvd 90035 310-553-7150
Rabbi David Rafi, prin. Fax 553-2199
New Covenant Academy 100/1-12
1111 W Sunset Blvd 90012 213-250-1600
Jason Song, admin. Fax 250-1601
New West Technical Academy 100/5-12
10531 S Vermont Ave 90044 310-241-1850
Dr. Andrew Manley, pres.
Notre Dame Academy for Girls 500/9-12
2851 Overland Ave 90064 310-839-5289
Joan Tyhurst, prin. Fax 839-7957
Occidental College Post-Sec.
1600 Campus Rd 90041 323-259-2500
Ohr Haemet Institute 50/9-12
1030 S Robertson Blvd 90035 310-854-3006
Rabbi David Akhamzadeh, dir. Fax 854-6689
Optimist HS 200/7-12
PO Box 411076 90041 310-443-3100
Alan Eskot, dir. Fax 443-3264
Otis College of Art and Design Post-Sec.
9045 Lincoln Blvd 90045 310-665-6800
Pacific Hills S 300/6-12
8628 Holloway Dr 90069 310-276-3068
Richard Makoff, hdmstr. Fax 657-3831
Pacific States University Post-Sec.
1516 S Western Ave 90006 323-731-2383
Pacific Union College Post-Sec.
1720 E Cesar E Chavez Ave 90033 323-268-5000
Pepperdine University Post-Sec.
6100 Center Dr 90045 310-568-5500
Pilgrim S 400/PK-12
540 S Commonwealth Ave 90020 213-385-7351
Mark Brooks, prin. Fax 386-7264

Pilibos Armenian S 700/K-12
1615 N Alexandria Ave 90027 323-668-2661
Viken Yacoubian, prin. Fax 662-0332
Price S 300/PK-12
7901 S Vermont Ave 90044 323-565-4199
Veon Bradford, prin. Fax 753-6770
Ribet Academy 500/K-12
2911 N San Fernando Rd 90065 323-344-4330
Teresa Ruiz, prin. Fax 344-4339
Sacred Heart of Jesus HS 300/9-12
2111 Griffin Ave 90031 323-225-2209
Sr. Mary Diane Scott, prin. Fax 225-5046
Samra University of Oriental Medicine Post-Sec.
3000 S Robertson Blvd Fl 4 90034 310-202-6444
Shalhevet S, 910 S Fairfax Ave 90036 300/K-12
Ken Milman, dir. 323-930-9333
Southern California Inst. Architecture Post-Sec.
960 E 3rd St 90013 213-613-2200
Southwestern University School of Law Post-Sec.
675 S Westmoreland Ave 90005 213-738-6700
Summit View S - Westside 200/1-12
12101 W Washington Blvd 90066 310-751-1100
SUTECH School of Voc/Tech Training Post-Sec.
PO Box 23098 90023 323-262-3210
UCLA Center for the Health Sciences Post-Sec.
10833 Le Conte Ave 90095 310-825-5654
Universal College of Beauty Post-Sec.
8619 S Vermont Ave 90044 323-750-5750
Universal College of Beauty Post-Sec.
3419 W 43rd Pl 90008 323-298-0045
University of California 90095 Post-Sec.
310-825-4321
University of Judaism Post-Sec.
15600 Mulholland Dr 90077 310-476-9777
University of Southern California Post-Sec.
Health Science Campus 90033 323-226-6501
University of Southern California Post-Sec.
Univ Park 90089 213-740-2311
Verbum Dei HS 300/9-12
11100 S Central Ave 90059 323-564-6651
Susan B. Abelein, prin. Fax 564-9009
Village Glen S - Westside 200/K-12
4160 Grand View Blvd 90066 310-751-1101
Nata Preis, hdmstr.
Virginia School Center Post-Sec.
1033 S Broadway 90015 213-747-8292
Vista S 300/K-12
3200 Motor Ave 90034 310-836-1223
Donna Baker, dir. Fax 836-3506
West Los Angeles Baptist S 100/7-12
1609 S Barrington Ave 90025 310-826-2050
James Lennon, prin. Fax 826-0970
West Los Angeles VA Medical Center Post-Sec.
Wilshire & Sawtelle Blvds 90073 310-824-3132
Westview S, 2000 Stoner Ave 90025 100/6-12
Judith Gordon, prin. 310-478-5544
Westwood College Post-Sec.
3250 Wilshire Blvd Fl 4 90010 213-739-9999
Wildwood Secondary S 400/7-12
11811 W Olympic Blvd 90064 310-478-7189
Hope Boyd, hdmstr. Fax 478-6875
Windward S 500/7-12
11350 Palms Blvd 90066 310-391-7127
Thomas Gilder, hdmstr. Fax 397-5655
Wise Temple S 1,300/K-12
15500 Stephen S Wise Dr 90077 310-889-2282
Metuka Benjamin, dir. Fax 476-2353
World Mission University Post-Sec.
500 Shatto Pl Ste 600 90020 213-385-2322
Yeshiva Gedola of Los Angeles HS 100/9-12
5444 W Olympic Blvd 90036 323-938-2071
Rabbi Yaakov Gross, dir. Fax 938-4650
Yeshiva Ohr Elchonon Chabad Post-Sec.
7215 Waring Ave 90046 323-937-3763
Yeshiva Ohr Elchonon Chabad West Coast 100/9-12
7215 Waring Ave 90046 323-937-3763
Rabbi Ezra Schochet, dean Fax 937-9456
Yeshiva University Boys HS 300/9-12
9760 W Pico Blvd 90035 310-229-0936
Dovid Landesman, prin. Fax 203-3199
Yeshiva University Girls HS 200/9-12
1619 S Robertson Blvd 90035 310-203-0755
Deborah Shrier, prin. Fax 551-0312
Yo San Univ. of Traditional Chinese Med. Post-Sec.
13315 W Washington Blvd 90066 310-577-3000

Los Banos, Merced, Pop. 33,506

Los Banos USD 8,500/K-12
1717 S 11th St 93635 209-826-3801
Paul Alderete, supt. Fax 826-6810
www.losbanosusd.k12.ca.us
Los Banos HS 2,200/9-12
1966 S 11th St 93635 209-826-6033
Dan Martin, prin. Fax 827-4156
Los Banos JHS 1,400/7-8
1750 San Luis St 93635 209-826-0867
Paul Enos, prin. Fax 826-8532

Merced College-Los Banos Campus Post-Sec.
16570 S Mercey Springs Rd 93635 209-826-3431

Los Gatos, Santa Clara, Pop. 28,029

Campbell UNESD
Supt. — See Campbell
Rolling Hills MS 1,000/5-8
1585 More Ave 95032 408-364-4235
Kathleen Gibbs, prin. Fax 341-7070

Loma Prieta JUNESD 700/K-8
23800 Summit Rd 95033 408-353-1101
Henry Castaniada, supt. Fax 353-8051
www.loma.k12.ca.us
English MS 300/6-8
23800 Summit Rd 95033 408-353-1123
Richard Rodriguez, prin. Fax 353-5024

Los Gatos UNESD 2,600/K-8
17010 Roberts Rd 95032 408-335-2000
Suzanne Boxer-Gassman Ed.D., supt. Fax 395-6481
www.lgusd.k12.ca.us
Fisher MS 1,000/6-8
19195 Fisher Ave 95032 408-335-2300
Lisa Fraser, prin. Fax 356-7616

Los Gatos-Saratoga JUNHSD 3,000/9-12
17421 Farley Rd W 95030 408-354-2520
Cary Matsuoka, supt. Fax 354-3375
www.lgsuhsd.org
Los Gatos HS 1,700/9-12
20 High School Ct 95030 408-354-2730
Doug Ramezane, prin. Fax 354-3742
Other Schools – See Saratoga

Los Molinos, Tehama, Pop. 1,709
Los Molinos USD 600/K-12
7851 State Highway 99 E 96055 530-384-7826
Dave Pilger, supt. Fax 384-7832
www.lmusd.tehama.k12.ca.us
Los Molinos HS 200/9-12
PO Box 609 96055 530-384-7900
Dan Curry, prin. Fax 384-1534

Los Nietos, Los Angeles, Pop. 24,164
Los Nietos ESD 2,300/K-8
PO Box 2405 90610 562-692-0271
Lillian Maldonado-French, supt. Fax 699-3395
www.losnietos.k12.ca.us
Los Nietos MS 700/6-8
11425 Rivera Rd 90606 562-695-0637
Marla Duncan, prin. Fax 695-3805

Los Olivos, Santa Barbara

Dunn S 200/6-12
PO Box 98 93441 805-688-6471
James Munger, hdmstr. Fax 686-2078
Midland S 100/9-12
PO Box 8 93441 805-688-5114
William Graham, hdmstr. Fax 686-2470

Los Osos, San Luis Obispo, Pop. 14,377
San Luis Coastal USD
Supt. — See San Luis Obispo
Los Osos MS 500/6-8
1555 El Morro Ave 93402 805-534-2835
Diane Frost, prin. Fax 528-5133

Lost Hills, Kern, Pop. 1,212
Lost Hills Union ESD 600/K-8
PO Box 158 93249 661-797-2626
Jerry Scott, supt. Fax 797-2580
Thomas MS 200/5-8
PO Box 158 93249 661-797-2626
Donna Jackson, prin. Fax 797-3015

Lower Lake, Lake, Pop. 1,217
Konocti USD 3,200/K-12
PO Box 5000 95457 707-994-6475
Louise Nan Ed.D., supt. Fax 994-0210
www.konoctiusd.lake.k12.ca.us/
Lower Lake HS 800/9-12
PO Box 799 95457 707-994-6471
Jeff Dixon, prin. Fax 994-4050
Konocti Adult S Adult
PO Box 5000 95457 707-994-7142
Bill MacDougall, prin. Fax 994-4421
Other Schools – See Clearlake

Loyalton, Sierra, Pop. 817
Sierra-Plumas JUSD
Supt. — See Sierraville
Loyalton HS 200/9-12
PO Box 37 96118 530-993-4454
Clara LaGanga, prin. Fax 993-4667
Loyalton MS 100/6-8
PO Box 5 96118 530-993-4186
Penny Berry, prin. Fax 993-0828

Lucerne Valley, San Bernardino
Lucerne Valley USD 1,000/K-12
8560 Aliento Rd 92356 760-248-6108
Dr. Jim Buckley, supt. Fax 248-6677
www.lvsd.k12.ca.us/
Lucerne Valley HS 300/9-12
10790 Barstow Rd 92356 760-248-2124
Connie McClaine, prin. Fax 248-2162
Lucerne Valley MS 200/7-8
10790 Barstow Rd 92356 760-248-2124
Connie McClaine, prin. Fax 248-2162

Lynwood, Los Angeles, Pop. 71,208
Lynwood USD 16,100/K-12
11321 Bullis Rd 90262 310-886-1600
Dr. Dhyan Lal, supt. Fax 608-7483
www.lynwood.k12.ca.us
Chavez MS, 3898 Abbott Rd 90262 7-8
Dr. Nick Velasquez, prin. 310-886-1600
Firebaugh HS 9-9
5246 Martin Luther King Blv 90262 310-886-1600
Jonas Silverio, prin.
Hosler MS 7-8
11300 Spruce St 90262 310-603-1447
Dr. David Austin, prin. Fax 764-4124
Lynwood HS 3,400/10-12
4050 E Imperial Hwy 90262 310-603-1582
Jose Urias, prin. Fax 638-9253
Lynwood MS 3,000/6-8
12124 Bullis Rd 90262 310-603-1466
Dr. Anim Mener, prin. Fax 638-2156
Lynwood Adult S Adult
4050 E Imperial Hwy 90262 310-604-3096
Jean Jones, prin. Fax 635-9107

St. Francis Career College Post-Sec.
3630 E Imperial Hwy 90262 310-603-1830

Mc Arthur, Shasta
Fall River JUSD
Supt. — See Burney
Fall River JSHS 300/7-12
PO Box 340, 530-336-5515
Greg Hawkins, prin. Fax 336-6256

Mc Cloud, Siskiyou, Pop. 1,555
Siskiyou UNHSD
Supt. — See Mount Shasta
McCloud HS 50/9-12
PO Box 1530, 530-964-2181
James Burger, admin. Fax 964-2011

Macdoel, Siskiyou
Butte Valley USD
Supt. — See Dorris
Butte Valley MS 100/7-9
13001 Old State Hwy 96058 530-398-4415
Ed Traverso, prin. Fax 398-4401

Mc Farland, Kern, Pop. 7,133
McFarland USD 3,100/K-12
601 2nd St 93250 661-792-3081
Tom Valos, supt. Fax 792-2447
www.mcfarlandusd.com
Mc Farland HS 700/9-12
259 W Sherwood Ave 93250 661-792-3126
Sally Hadden, prin. Fax 792-2315
Mc Farland MS 700/6-8
405 Mast Ave 93250 661-792-3340
Lori Schultz, prin. Fax 792-5681

Mc Kinleyville, Humboldt, Pop. 10,749
Mc Kinleyville UNESD 1,300/K-8
2275 Central Ave, 707-839-1549
Alan Jorgensen, supt. Fax 839-1540
www.nohum.k12.ca.us/msd/
Mc Kinleyville MS 400/6-8
2285 Central Ave, 707-839-1508
Anne Hartline, prin. Fax 839-2548

Northern Humboldt UNHSD 1,900/9-12
2755 McKinleyville Ave 95519 707-839-6470
Kenny Richards, supt. Fax 839-6477
www.nohum.k12.ca.us
Mc Kinleyville HS 800/9-12
1300 Murray Rd, 707-839-6400
David Lonn, prin. Fax 839-6407
Northern Humboldt Adult S Adult
2755 McKinleyville Ave, 707-839-6460
Brian Stephens, prin. Fax 839-6457
Other Schools – See Arcata

Madera, Madera, Pop. 52,147
Golden Valley USD 1,700/K-12
37479 Avenue 12, 559-645-7500
Marilyn K. Shepherd, supt. Fax 645-7144
www.gvusd.k12.ca.us
Liberty HS 500/9-12
12220 Road 36, 559-645-3500
Andy Alvarado, prin. Fax 645-4769
Ranchos MS 200/7-8
12220 Road 36, 559-645-3550
Shane Pinkard, prin. Fax 645-3565

Madera USD 17,300/K-12
1902 Howard Rd 93637 559-675-4500
Larry Risinger, supt. Fax 661-7764
www.madera.k12.ca.us
Desmond MS 7-8
26490 Martin St 93638 559-664-1775
Michael Lennemann, prin. Fax 664-1308
Jefferson MS 1,100/7-8
1407 Sunset Ave 93637 559-673-9286
Jesse Carrasco, prin. Fax 673-6930
King MS 1,100/7-8
601 Lilly St 93638 559-674-4681
Daren Miller, prin. Fax 674-4261
Madera HS North Campus 4,200/9-12
200 S L St 93637 559-675-4444
Ron Pisk, prin. Fax 675-4531
Madera HS South Campus 9-12
705 W Pecan Ave 93637 559-675-4450
Mike Rivard, prin. Fax 675-9985
Madera Adult S Adult
955 W Pecan Ave 93637 559-675-4425
Dan Lindstrom, prin. Fax 675-4562

Madera Beauty College Post-Sec.
325 N Gateway Dr 93637 559-673-9201

Mad River, Trinity
Southern Trinity JUSD 200/K-12
680 Van Duzen Rd 95552 707-574-6237
Peggy Canale, supt. Fax 574-6538
Southern Trinity HS 50/9-12
600 Van Duzen Rd 95552 707-574-6239
Peggy Canale, prin. Fax 574-1067

Magalia, Butte, Pop. 8,987
Paradise USD
Supt. — See Paradise
Mountain Ridge MS 400/6-8
13835 W Park Dr 95954 530-873-3864
Steve Harrington, prin. Fax 873-4011

Malibu, Los Angeles, Pop. 13,208
Santa Monica-Malibu USD
Supt. — See Santa Monica
Malibu MSHS 1,300/6-12
30215 Morning View Dr 90265 310-457-6801
Dr. Mark Kelly, prin. Fax 457-4984

Pepperdine University Post-Sec.
24255 Pacific Coast Hwy 90263 310-506-4000

Mammoth Lakes, Mono, Pop. 7,156
Mammoth USD 1,200/K-12
PO Box 3509 93546 760-934-6802
Michael Derisi, supt. Fax 934-6803
Mammoth HS 300/9-12
PO Box 3149 93546 760-934-8541
Beatrice Beyer, prin. Fax 934-3008
Mammoth MS 300/6-8
PO Box 2429 93546 760-934-7072
Gabriel Solorio, prin. Fax 934-7073

Mono County Office of Education
Supt. — See Bridgeport
Mono County Adult S Adult
PO Box 130 93546 760-934-0031
Catherine Hiatt, prin. Fax 934-1443

Manhattan Beach, Los Angeles, Pop. 36,481
Manhattan Beach USD 6,300/K-12
325 S Peck Ave 90266 310-318-7345
Dr. Beverly Rohrer, supt. Fax 303-3822
www.manhattan.k12.ca.us
Manhattan Beach MS 1,300/6-8
325 S Peck Ave 90266 310-545-4878
John Jackson, prin. Fax 303-3829
Mira Costa HS 2,400/9-12
325 S Peck Ave 90266 310-318-7337
Julie Ruisinger, prin. Fax 303-3814

Manteca, San Joaquin, Pop. 62,651
Manteca USD 23,000/K-12
PO Box 32 95336 209-825-3200
Cathy Nichols-Washer Ed.D., supt. Fax 825-3295
www.mantecausd.net/
East Union HS 1,600/9-12
1700 N Union Rd 95336 209-825-3125
John Alba, prin. Fax 825-3148
Manteca HS 1,700/9-12
450 E Yosemite Ave 95336 209-825-3150
Steve Winter, prin. Fax 825-3158
Sierra HS 2,000/9-12
1700 Thomas St 95337 209-825-3175
Rick Arucan, prin. Fax 825-3198
Lindbergh Adult S Adult
311 E North St 95336 209-825-3100
Howard Holtsman, prin. Fax 825-3110
Other Schools – See Stockton

Plumfield Christian Academy 100/K-12
444 Argonaut St 95336 209-823-2655
Douglas Scott, admin. Fax 823-2353

Maricopa, Kern, Pop. 1,160
Maricopa USD 400/K-12
955 Stanislaus St 93252 661-769-8231
Barry Lindaman, supt. Fax 769-8168
www.maricopaschools.org/
Maricopa HS 100/9-12
955 Stanislaus St 93252 661-769-8234
Debra Marker, prin. Fax 769-8168

Marina, Monterey, Pop. 19,006
Monterey Peninsula USD
Supt. — See Monterey
Los Arboles MS 700/6-8
294 Hillcrest Ave 93933 831-384-3550
Shannon Lueken, prin. Fax 384-6353

Mariposa, Mariposa, Pop. 1,152
Mariposa County USD 2,300/K-12
PO Box 8 95338 209-742-0250
Patrick J. Holland Ed.D., supt. Fax 966-4549
mariposa.k12.ca.us
Mariposa County HS 700/9-12
PO Box 127 95338 209-742-0260
Rock Carlson, prin. Fax 742-0264
Mariposa MS 300/7-8
5171 Silva Rd 95338 209-742-0320
Bill Atwood, prin. Fax 742-0382
Other Schools – See Coulterville, El Portal

Markleeville, Alpine
Alpine County Office of Education
43 Hawkside Dr 96120 530-694-2230
James Parsons, supt. Fax 694-2379
www.alpinecoe.k12.ca.us
Alpine County Adult Education Adult
43 Hawkside Dr 96120 530-694-2230
James W. Parsons, prin.

Martinez, Contra Costa, Pop. 35,916
Martinez USD 4,200/K-12
921 Susana St 94553 925-313-0480
John Triolo Ed.D., supt. Fax 313-0476
www.martinez.k12.ca.us/
Alhambra HS 1,300/9-12
150 E St 94553 925-313-0440
Susan Mirkovich, prin. Fax 229-2097
Briones S 100/K-12
614 F St 94553 925-228-9232
Terri Ishmael, prin. Fax 313-9890
Martinez JHS 1,000/6-8
1600 Court St 94553 925-313-0414
Helen Rossi, prin. Fax 370-0143
Martinez Adult Center Adult
600 F St 94553 925-228-3276
Kathy Farwell, dir. Fax 228-6989

Martinez Adult Education Post-Sec.
600 F St 94553 925-228-3276
New Vistas Christian S 50/5-12
68 Morello Ave 94553 925-370-7767
Maria Zablah, admin. Fax 370-6395

Marysville, Yuba, Pop. 12,131
Marysville JUSD 9,400/PK-12
1919 B St 95901 530-741-6000
Gay Todd Ed.D., supt. Fax 742-0573
www.mjusd.k12.ca.us
Alicia IS 600/6-8
1208 Pasado Rd 95901 530-741-6103
Jack Stokes, prin. Fax 741-6129
Foothill IS 300/6-8
5351 Fruitland Rd 95901 530-741-6130
Ken Doglio, prin. Fax 741-6017
Marysville HS 1,000/9-12
12 E 18th St 95901 530-741-6180
Gary Cena, prin. Fax 741-7828
McKenney IS 500/6-8
1904 Huston St 95901 530-741-6187
Charles Ward, prin. Fax 741-6004
Marysville Adult S, 1919 B St 95901 Adult
Carolyn Tindel, prin. 530-741-6005
Other Schools – See Olivehurst

New Life Christian S 200/PK-12
5736 Arboga Rd 95901 530-742-3033
Alison Harrell, admin. Fax 741-8221
Yuba College Post-Sec.
2088 N Beale Rd 95901 530-741-6700

Mather, Sacramento, Pop. 4,885
Regional Occupational Center & Program
Supt. — None
Sacramento County ROP Vo/Tech
10541 Norden Ave 95655 916-228-2721
Linda Mitchell, prin. Fax 228-2505

Institute of Technology - Sacramento Post-Sec.
3695 Bleckely St 95655 916-363-4300
Institute of Technology - Sacramento Post-Sec.
3695 Bleckely St 95655 916-363-4300

Maxwell, Colusa
Maxwell USD 500/K-12
PO Box 788 95955 530-438-2052
Ron Turner, supt. Fax 438-2693
www.maxwell.k12.ca.us
Maxwell HS 100/9-12
PO Box 788 95955 530-438-2291
Ron Turner, prin. Fax 438-2693

Maywood, Los Angeles, Pop. 28,600
Los Angeles USD
Supt. — See Los Angeles
Maywood Academy 9-12
6125 Pine Ave 90270 323-838-6000
Sandra English, prin. Fax 560-9206

Maywood Christian S 100/K-12
3759 E 57th St 90270 323-585-3167
Melvin Valiente, prin.

Meadow Vista, Placer, Pop. 3,067
Placer Hills UNESD 900/K-8
16801 Placer Hills Rd 95722 530-878-2606
Fred Adam, supt. Fax 878-2663
www.phusd.k12.ca.us/
Other Schools – See Weimar

Mendocino, Mendocino
Mendocino USD 700/K-12
PO Box 1154 95460 707-937-5868
Catherine Stone, supt. Fax 937-0714
musd.mcn.org/
Mendocino HS 200/9-12
PO Box 226 95460 707-937-5871
Gail Dickenson, prin. Fax 937-1552
Mendocino MS 200/6-8
PO Box 226 95460 707-937-0564
Bronwyn Rhoades, prin. Fax 937-4753

Mendota, Fresno, Pop. 8,942
Mendota USD 2,400/K-12
115 McCabe Ave 93640 559-655-4942
Gilbert Rossette, supt. Fax 655-4944
www.mendotausd.k12.ca.us/
McCabe JHS 300/7-8
115 McCabe Ave 93640 559-655-4991
Perry Jensen, prin. Fax 655-1229
Mendota HS 600/9-12
115 McCabe Ave 93640 559-655-1993
Victor Villar, prin. Fax 655-0223

Menifee, Riverside, Pop. 100
Menifee UNESD 6,500/K-8
30205 Menifee Rd 92584 951-672-1851
Linda Callaway Ed.D., supt. Fax 672-6447
www.menifeeusd.org
Bell Mountain MS 1,200/6-8
28525 La Piedra Rd 92584 951-301-8496
Paul Drob, prin. Fax 301-5286
Menifee Valley MS 1,100/6-8
26255 Garbani Rd 92584 951-672-6400
Cynthia Deavers, prin. Fax 672-6415

Perris UNHSD
Supt. — See Perris
Paloma Valley HS 2,800/9-12
31375 Bradley Rd 92584 951-672-6030
Jim Smolenski, prin. Fax 672-6037

Revival Christian Academy 100/K-12
29220 Scott Rd 92584 951-672-3157
Diana Miller, dir. Fax 672-9187

Menlo Park, San Mateo, Pop. 29,661
Las Lomitas ESD 1,000/K-8
1011 Altschul Ave 94025 650-854-2880
Dr. Shirley Martin, supt. Fax 854-0882
www.llesd.k12.ca.us
La Entrada MS 600/4-8
2200 Sharon Rd 94025 650-854-3962
Deanna Brummett, prin. Fax 854-5947

Menlo Park City ESD
Supt. — See Atherton
Hillview MS 700/6-8
1100 Elder Ave 94025 650-326-4341
Michael Moore, prin. Fax 325-3861

Sequoia UNHSD
Supt. — See Redwood City
Sequoia District Adult S Adult
3247 Middlefield Rd 94025 650-306-8866
Patricia Cocconi, prin. Fax 365-2420

Mid-Peninsula HS 200/9-12
1340 Willow Rd 94025 650-321-1991
Dr. Douglas Thompson, hdmstr. Fax 321-9921
St. Patrick's Seminary & University Post-Sec.
320 Middlefield Rd 94025 650-325-5621

Merced, Merced, Pop. 73,767
Merced City ESD 10,200/K-8
444 W 23rd St 95340 209-385-6600
Terry Brace, supt. Fax 385-6316
mcsd.k12.ca.us
Cruickshank MS 1,100/6-8
601 Cormorant Dr 95340 209-385-6330
Trisha Wylie, prin. Fax 385-6338
Hoover MS 900/6-8
800 E 26th St 95340 209-385-6631
Tammie Calzadillas, prin. Fax 385-6799
Rivera MS 1,000/6-8
945 Buena Vista Dr 95348 209-385-6680
Joe Havel, prin. Fax 385-6702
Tenaya MS 1,000/6-8
760 W 8th St 95341 209-385-6687
Doug Collins, prin. Fax 385-6365

Merced UNHSD
Supt. — See Atwater
Golden Valley HS 2,400/9-12
PO Box 2188 95344 209-385-8000
Ralf Swenson, prin. Fax 385-8002
Merced HS 2,600/9-12
PO Box 2167 95344 209-385-6465
Thomas Scheidt, prin. Fax 385-6586
Merced Adult S Adult
PO Box 3707 95344 209-385-6524
Carole Roberds, prin. Fax 385-6430

Regional Occupational Center & Program
Supt. — None
Merced County ROP Vo/Tech
632 W 13th St 95341 209-381-6677
Lee Anderson, supt. Fax 381-6766

Weaver UNESD 1,900/K-8
3076 E Childs Ave 95341 209-723-7606
Steve Becker, supt. Fax 725-7128
www.weaverusd.k12.ca.us
Weaver ES 1,100/4-8
3076 E Childs Ave 95341 209-723-2174
Brenda Jones, prin. Fax 725-7116

Merced College Post-Sec.
3600 M St 95348 209-384-6000
Sierra College of Beauty Post-Sec.
1340 W 18th St 95340 209-723-2989
Stone Ridge Christian HS 100/9-12
500 Buena Vista Dr 95348 209-386-0322
Sandra Mobley, prin. Fax 386-0334

Middletown, Lake
Middletown USD 1,800/K-12
20932 Big Canyon Rd 95461 707-987-4100
Korby Olson Ed.D., supt. Fax 987-4105
www.musd.lake.k12.ca.us/
Middletown HS 500/9-12
20932 Big Canyon Rd 95461 707-987-4140
Chris Heller, prin. Fax 987-4146
Middletown MS 300/7-8
20932 Big Canyon Rd 95461 707-987-4160
Tony Limoges, prin. Fax 987-4162
Middletown Adult S Adult
20932 Big Canyon Rd 95461 707-987-4175
Fax 987-4171

Middletown Christian S 100/K-10
PO Box 989 95461 707-987-2556
Melanie Brown, admin. Fax 987-2126

Midway City, Orange, Pop. 4,400

Huntington College of Dental Technology Post-Sec.
14848 Monroe St 92655 - -

Millbrae, San Mateo, Pop. 20,342
Millbrae ESD 2,100/K-8
555 Richmond Dr 94030 650-697-5693
Karen Philip, supt. Fax 697-6865
www.smcoe.k12.ca.us/msd/do/
Taylor MS 900/6-8
850 Taylor Blvd 94030 650-697-4096
Robert Silva, prin. Fax 697-8435

San Mateo UNHSD
Supt. — See San Mateo
Mills HS 1,500/9-12
400 Murchison Dr 94030 650-558-2599
Paul Belzer, prin. Fax 652-1029

Mill Valley, Marin, Pop. 13,286
Mill Valley ESD 2,200/K-8
411 Sycamore Ave 94941 415-389-7700
Ken Benny, supt. Fax 389-7773
Mill Valley MS 700/6-8
425 Sycamore Ave 94941 415-389-7711
Matt Huxley, prin. Fax 389-7780

Tamalpais UNHSD
Supt. — See Larkspur
Tamalpais HS 1,100/9-12
700 Miller Ave 94941 415-388-3292
Chris Holleran, prin. Fax 380-3526

Golden Gate Baptist Theological Seminary Post-Sec.
201 Seminary Dr 94941 415-380-1300

Milpitas, Santa Clara, Pop. 63,383
Milpitas USD 9,600/K-12
1331 E Calaveras Blvd 95035 408-945-2310
Karl Black Ed.D., supt. Fax 945-2421
www.musd.org
Milpitas HS 2,800/9-12
1285 Escuela Pkwy 95035 408-945-5500
Charles Gary, prin. Fax 945-5506
Rancho Milpitas MS 700/7-8
1915 Yellowstone Ave 95035 408-945-5561
Leticia Villa-Gascon, prin. Fax 945-2492
Russell MS 800/7-8
1500 Escuela Pkwy 95035 408-945-2333
Laura Foegal, prin. Fax 945-2491
Milpitas Adult S Adult
1331 E Calaveras Blvd 95035 408-945-2392
Daniel Kreuzer, dir. Fax 945-2378

Heald College Post-Sec.
341 Great Mall Pkwy # A 95035 408-934-4900
Plantation Christian S 100/1-12
PO Box 36073 95036 408-956-1557
Stephen Burns, dir.

Mira Loma, Riverside, Pop. 15,786
Jurupa USD
Supt. — See Riverside
Jurupa Valley HS 3,000/9-12
10551 Bellegrave Ave 91752 951-360-2600
Ilsa Garza-Gonzalez, prin. Fax 360-2612

Miranda, Humboldt
Southern Humboldt JUSD
Supt. — See Garberville
South Fork HS 400/8-12
PO Box 188 95553 707-943-3144
Paula Kelso, prin. Fax 943-3129

Mission Hills, Los Angeles, Pop. 3,112
Los Angeles USD
Supt. — See Los Angeles
North Valley Occupational Center Vo/Tech
11450 Sharp Ave 91345 818-365-9645
Juan Urdiales, prin. Fax 365-2695

Bishop Alemany HS 1,500/9-12
11111 Alemany Dr 91345 818-365-3925
Dr. Jack Monnig, prin. Fax 365-2064

Mission Viejo, Orange, Pop. 94,982
Capistrano USD
Supt. — See San Juan Capistrano
Capistrano Valley HS 2,300/9-12
26301 Via Escolar 92692 949-364-6100
Tom Ressler, prin. Fax 347-0514
Newhart MS 1,700/6-8
25001 Veterans Way 92692 949-855-0162
Tim Reece, prin. Fax 770-1262

Saddleback Valley USD 34,100/K-12
25631 Peter A Hartman Way 92691 949-586-1234
Steven Fish Ed.D., supt. Fax 951-0994
www.svusd.k12.ca.us
La Paz IS 1,300/7-8
25151 Pradera Dr 92691 949-830-1720
Allan Mucerino, prin. Fax 830-3320
Los Alisos IS 1,200/7-8
25171 Moor Ave 92691 949-830-9700
Dr. Jerry Ray, prin. Fax 472-3968
Mission Viejo HS 2,900/9-12
25025 Chrisanta Dr 92691 949-837-7722
Marilyn McDowell, prin. Fax 830-0782
Trabuco Hills HS 2,900/9-12
27501 Mustang Run 92691 949-768-1934
Dan Sullivan, prin. Fax 588-0763
Adult Education Center Adult
25598 Peter A Hartman Way 92691 949-837-8830
Dr. Linda Cistone-Albers, dean Fax 837-1921
Other Schools – See Laguna Hills, Lake Forest, Rancho Santa Margarita

Agape Academy 100/K-12
23632 Via Calzada 92691 949-701-9086
Denise Justiniano, admin.
Grace Academy 100/K-12
24242 Castilla Ln 92691 949-458-0890
Cindy Sheek, admin.
Master's Academy 50/K-12
23052 Alicia Pkwy Ste H107 92692 949-457-1586
Daniel Gammie, admin. Fax 457-1586
Saddleback Christian Academy 300/K-12
26861 Trabuco Rd Ste E76 92691 949-587-9650
Tracey Hodge, hdmstr.
Saddleback College Post-Sec.
28000 Marguerite Pkwy 92692 949-582-4500

Modesto, Stanislaus, Pop. 207,011
Empire UNESD 4,000/K-8
116 N McClure Rd 95357 209-521-2800
Dr. Robert Price, supt. Fax 526-6421
www.empire.k12.ca.us
Glick MS 600/6-8
400 Frazine Rd 95357 209-577-3945
Melva Rush, prin. Fax 577-3975
Other Schools – See Empire

Modesto CSD 32,900/K-12
426 Locust St 95351 209-576-4011
Arturo Flores, supt. Fax 576-4184
www.monet.k12.ca.us
Beyer HS 3,100/9-12
1717 Sylvan Ave 95355 209-576-4311
Randy Fillpot, prin. Fax 576-4352
Davis HS 3,000/9-12
1200 W Rumble Rd 95350 209-576-4500
Jeff Albritton, prin. Fax 576-4028
Downey HS 2,600/9-12
1000 Coffee Rd 95355 209-576-4211
Phil Alfano, prin. Fax 576-4258
Enochs HS 9-12
3201 Sylvan Ave 95355 209-575-8545
Michael Coats, prin. Fax 575-8597
Hanshaw MS 1,100/7-8
1725 Las Vegas St 95358 209-576-4847
Ed Miller, prin. Fax 576-4723
Johansen HS 3,000/9-12
641 Norseman Dr 95357 209-576-4702
Thor Harrison, prin. Fax 576-4752
La Loma JHS 1,000/7-8
1800 Encina Ave 95354 209-576-4627
Mike Henderson, prin. Fax 576-4631
Modesto HS 3,100/9-12
18 H St 95351 209-576-4401
Hugo Ramos, prin. Fax 576-4434
Roosevelt JHS 900/7-8
1330 College Ave 95350 209-576-4871
Dave Kline, prin. Fax 569-2713
Twain JHS 1,000/7-8
707 S Emerald Ave 95351 209-576-4814
Kevin Salaiz, prin. Fax 576-4843

Elliott Adult Education Center — Adult
1440 Sunrise Ave 95350 — 209-576-4621
Barbara Eckerfield, dir. — Fax 576-4863

Regional Occupational Center & Program
Supt. — None
Yosemite ROP — Vo/Tech
1100 H St 95354 — 209-525-5093
Judie Piscitello, dir. — Fax 525-5108

Stanislaus UNESD — 3,300/K-8
3601 Carver Rd 95356 — 209-529-9546
Wayne Brown, supt. — Fax 236-0730
www.stanunion.k12.ca.us
Prescott Sr ES — 700/7-8
2243 W Rumble Rd 95350 — 209-529-9892
Tom Freeman Ed.D., prin. — Fax 529-4406

Sylvan Union ESD — 8,000/K-8
605 Sylvan Ave 95350 — 209-574-5000
Dr. John Halverson, supt. — Fax 524-2672
www.sylvan.k12.ca.us
Savage MS, 3101 Fine Ave 95355 — 6-8
Dave Garcia, prin. — 209-552-3300
Somerset MS — 1,300/6-8
1037 Floyd Ave 95350 — 209-574-5300
Janice Latham, prin. — Fax 529-1110
Ustach MS — 1,600/6-8
2701 Kodiak Dr 95355 — 209-552-3000
Mitch Wood, prin. — Fax 552-3010

Adrian's Beauty College of Turlock — Post-Sec.
2412 McHenry Ave 95350 — 209-632-2233
Big Valley Christian S — 1,100/PK-12
4040 Tully Rd Ste D 95356 — 209-527-3481
Marsha Holbrook, dir. — Fax 569-0138
Brethren Heritage S — 100/K-12
3549 Dakota Ave 95358 — 209-543-7860
Betsy Johns, prin. — Fax 543-7862
California Beauty College — Post-Sec.
1115 15th St 95354 — 209-524-5184
Calvary Temple Christian S — 300/PK-12
1601 Coffee Rd 95355 — 209-529-7154
Jerry Grimshaw, supt. — Fax 529-1129
Central Catholic HS — 400/9-12
200 S Carpenter Rd 95351 — 209-524-9611
Melissa Bengtson, prin. — Fax 524-4913
Community Business College — Post-Sec.
3800 McHenry Ave 95356 — 209-529-3648
Computer Tutor Business & Technical Inst — Post-Sec.
4306 Sisk Rd 95356 — 209-545-5200
Galen College Medical & Dental Assts. — Post-Sec.
1604 Ford Ave Ste 10 95350 — 209-527-5084
Heritage Christian S — 50/K-12
812 Thieman Rd 95356 — 209-545-9009
Kimberly Meyer, prin. — Fax 545-9009
Institute of Technology - Modesto Campus — Post-Sec.
5737 Stoddard Rd 95356 — 209-545-3100
Modesto Christian HS — 300/9-12
5755 Sisk Rd 95356 — 209-529-5510
Cynthia Jewell, prin. — Fax 545-0584
Modesto Christian MS — 200/5-8
5901 Sisk Rd 95356 — 209-529-5510
Rod Lemburg, prin. — Fax 545-1369
Modesto Junior College — Post-Sec.
435 College Ave 95350 — 209-575-6498
North Adrian's Beauty College — Post-Sec.
124 Floyd Ave 95350 — 209-526-2040
San Joaquin Valley College — Post-Sec.
1700 McHenry Village Way #6 95350 — 209-527-7582
Western Pacific Truck School — Post-Sec.
2316 Nickerson Dr 95358 — 209-531-9226
Wood Colony Brethren S — 100/K-12
2524 Finney Rd 95358 — 209-544-9227
Anita Ferrante, admin. — Fax 544-9229

Mojave, Kern, Pop. 3,763
Mojave USD — 2,700/K-12
3500 Douglas Ave 93501 — 661-824-4001
Larry Phelps, supt. — Fax 824-2686
www.mojave.k12.ca.us/
Joshua MS — 400/4-8
3200 Pat Ave 93501 — 661-824-2411
Starletta Darbeau, prin. — Fax 824-5251
Mojave HS — 600/9-12
15732 O St 93501 — 661-824-4088
Cheri Newlander, prin. — Fax 824-3406
Other Schools – See California City

Monrovia, Los Angeles, Pop. 37,954
Monrovia USD — 6,300/PK-12
325 E Huntington Dr 91016 — 626-471-2000
Louise Taylor, supt. — Fax 471-2077
www.monroviaschools.net
Clifton MS — 800/6-8
226 S Ivy Ave 91016 — 626-471-2600
Deb Rinder, prin. — Fax 471-2610
Monrovia HS — 1,800/9-12
845 W Colorado Blvd 91016 — 626-471-2800
Frank Zepeda, prin. — Fax 471-2810
Santa Fe MS — 800/6-8
148 W Duarte Rd 91016 — 626-471-2700
Ron Letourneau, prin. — Fax 471-2710
Monrovia Community Adult Education — Adult
920 S Mountain Ave 91016 — 626-471-3035
Esther McDonald, prin. — Fax 471-3036

Excellence in Education Academy — 500/K-12
2640 S Myrtle Ave 91016 — 626-821-0025
Carolyn Forte, prin. — Fax 821-0216
Mt. Sierra College — Post-Sec.
101 E Huntington Dr 91016 — 626-873-2100

Montclair, San Bernardino, Pop. 35,474
Chaffey JUNHSD
Supt. — See Ontario
Montclair HS — 3,200/9-12
4725 Benito St 91763 — 909-621-6781
Michael Hook, prin. — Fax 621-1882

Ontario-Montclair ESD
Supt. — See Ontario
Serrano MS — 900/7-8
4725 San Jose St 91763 — 909-624-0029
Ellen Lugo, prin. — Fax 445-1687
Vernon MS — 900/6-8
9775 Vernon Ave 91763 — 909-624-5036
Brian Bettger, prin. — Fax 445-1720

Montebello, Los Angeles, Pop. 63,290
Montebello USD — 36,000/K-12
123 S Montebello Blvd 90640 — 323-887-7900
Edward Velasquez, supt. — Fax 887-5890
www.montebello.k12.ca.us
Eastmont IS — 1,800/5-8
400 Bradshawe St 90640 — 323-721-5133
Lorraine Verduzco, prin. — Fax 887-3058
La Merced IS — 2,000/5-8
215 E Avenida De La Merced 90640 — 323-722-7262
Suzette Montano, prin. — Fax 887-5816
Montebello HS — 3,400/9-12
2100 W Cleveland Ave 90640 — 323-728-0121
Jeffrey Schwartz, prin. — Fax 887-7848
Montebello IS — 2,100/5-8
1600 W Whittier Blvd 90640 — 323-721-5111
Susan Donnelly, prin. — Fax 887-3192
Schurr HS — 3,300/9-12
820 N Wilcox Ave 90640 — 323-887-3090
Art Revueltas, prin. — Fax 887-3097
Montebello Adult Education — Adult
149 N 21st St 90640 — 323-887-7844
Robert Martinez, prin. — Fax 724-8175
Schurr Adult Education — Adult
820 N Wilcox Ave 90640 — 323-887-3088
Aracely Ruiz, prin. — Fax 887-3098
Other Schools – See Bell Gardens, Monterey Park

Cantwell Sacred Heart of Mary HS — 600/9-12
329 N Garfield Ave 90640 — 323-887-2066
David Chambers, prin. — Fax 724-4332
Montebello Beauty College — Post-Sec.
2201 W Whittier Blvd 90640 — 323-727-7851
National Polytechnic College — Post-Sec.
2465 W Whittier Blvd # 201 90640 — 323-728-9636

Monterey, Monterey, Pop. 29,217
Monterey Peninsula USD — 10,500/PK-12
PO Box 1031 93942 — 831-645-1200
John Lamb, supt. — Fax 649-4175
www.mpusd.k12.ca.us
Monterey HS — 1,400/9-12
101 Herrmann Dr 93940 — 831-658-1532
Dan Albert, prin. — Fax 649-5149
Del Monte Adult S — Adult
222 Casa Verde Way 93940 — 831-373-4600
Ann Kilty, dir. — Fax 373-1819
Other Schools – See Marina, Seaside

Monterey Institute of Intl. Studies — Post-Sec.
460 Pierce St 93940 — 831-647-4100
Monterey Peninsula College — Post-Sec.
980 Fremont St 93940 — 831-646-4010
Santa Catalina S — PK-12
1500 Mark Thomas Dr 93940 — 831-655-9300
Sr. Claire Barone, hdmstr. — Fax 649-3056
York S — 200/8-12
9501 York Rd 93940 — 831-372-7338
Chuck Harmon, hdmstr. — Fax 372-8055

Monterey Park, Los Angeles, Pop. 62,065
Montebello USD
Supt. — See Montebello
Macy IS — 1,300/5-8
2101 Lupine Ave 91755 — 323-722-0260
Stacey Honda, prin. — Fax 887-3068

East Los Angeles College — Post-Sec.
1301 Avenida Cesar Chavez 91754 — 323-265-8650
Newbridge College — Post-Sec.
583 Monterey Pass Rd 91754 — 626-576-2444

Montgomery Creek, Shasta
Mountain UNESD — 100/K-8
PO Box 368 96065 — 530-337-6214
Michael J. Grady, supt. — Fax 337-6215
www.shastalink.k12.ca.us/muesd/
Montgomery Creek MS — 100/4-8
PO Box 368 96065 — 530-337-6214
Michael J. Grady, prin. — Fax 337-6215

Moorpark, Ventura, Pop. 35,844
Moorpark USD — 7,800/K-12
5297 Maureen Ln 93021 — 805-378-6300
Ellen Smith, supt. — Fax 529-8592
www.mrpk.k12.ca.us
Chaparral MS — 900/6-8
280 Poindexter Ave 93021 — 805-378-6302
Creig Nicks, prin. — Fax 378-6324
Mesa Verde MS — 900/6-8
14000 Peach Hill Rd 93021 — 805-378-6309
Kelli Hays, prin. — Fax 531-6622
Moorpark HS — 2,500/9-12
4500 Tierra Rejada Rd 93021 — 805-378-6305
Kirk Miyashiro, prin. — Fax 531-6498

Moorpark College — Post-Sec.
7075 Campus Rd 93021 — 805-378-1400

Moraga, Contra Costa, Pop. 16,869
Acalanes UNHSD
Supt. — See Lafayette
Campolindo HS — 1,400/9-12
300 Moraga Rd 94556 — 925-280-3950
Carol Kitchens, prin. — Fax 280-3951

Moraga ESD — 1,800/K-8
PO Box 158 94556 — 925-376-5943
Richard Schafer, supt. — Fax 376-8132
www.moraga.k12.ca.us
Moraga IS — 600/6-8
1010 Camino Pablo 94556 — 925-376-7206
Catherine Mikes, prin. — Fax 376-6836

St. Mary's College — Post-Sec.
1928 Saint Marys Rd 94556 — 925-631-4000

Moreno Valley, Riverside, Pop. 178,367
Moreno Valley USD — 35,600/K-12
25634 Alessandro Blvd 92553 — 951-571-7500
Rowena Lagrosa, supt. — Fax 571-7550
www.mvusd.k12.ca.us
Badger Springs MS — 1,600/6-8
24750 Delphinium Ave 92553 — 951-571-4200
Willie Williams, prin. — Fax 571-4205
Canyon Springs HS — 2,900/9-12
23100 Cougar Canyon Dr 92557 — 951-571-4760
Tammy Guzzetta, prin. — Fax 571-4765
Landmark MS — 1,400/6-8
15261 Legendary Dr 92555 — 951-571-4220
Jackie Tafoya, prin. — Fax 571-4225
Moreno Valley HS — 2,200/9-12
23300 Cottonwood Ave 92553 — 951-571-4820
Maribel Mattox, prin. — Fax 571-4825
Mountain View MS — 1,500/6-8
13130 Morrison St 92555 — 951-571-4240
Deborah Fay, prin. — Fax 571-4245
Palm MS — 1,600/6-8
11900 Slawson Ave 92557 — 951-571-4260
Nancy Ross, prin. — Fax 571-4265
Sunnymead MS — 1,000/6-8
23996 Eucalyptus Ave 92553 — 951-571-4280
Chris Schiermeyer, prin. — Fax 571-4285
Valley View HS — 2,400/9-12
13135 Nason St 92555 — 951-571-4850
Kristen Hunter, prin. — Fax 571-4855
Vista Del Lago HS — 2,300/9-12
15150 Lasselle St 92551 — 951-571-4880
Gil Oceguera, prin. — Fax 571-4885
Vista Heights MS — 1,400/6-8
23049 Old Lake Dr 92557 — 951-571-4300
Mike Newcomb, prin. — Fax 571-4305
Moreno Valley Adult HS — Adult
24551 Dracaea Ave 92553 — 951-571-4790
Janine Brauer, admin. — Fax 571-4795

Val Verde USD
Supt. — See Perris
March MS — 6-8
15800 Indian St 92551 — 951-490-0430
Wendy Pospichal, prin. — Fax 490-0435
Rancho Verde HS — 3,200/9-12
17750 Lasselle St 92551 — 951-485-6200
Michael McCormick, prin. — Fax 485-6218
Vista Verde MS — 1,500/6-8
25777 Krameria St 92551 — 951-485-6270
Gary Roughton, prin. — Fax 485-6278

Calvary Chapel Christian S — 600/K-12
11960 Pettit St 92555 — 951-485-6088
John Milhouse, admin. — Fax 485-6718
Elegante Beauty College — Post-Sec.
24741 Alessandro Blvd 92553 — 951-247-2047
Kings Chapel Christian Academy — 100/PK-12
13027 Perris Blvd Ste 110 92553 — 951-242-2210
Kisha Montgomery, admin. — Fax 601-1565
Riverside Community College — Post-Sec.
16130 Lasselle St 92551 — 951-571-6100
Sage College — Post-Sec.
12125 Day St Ste L 92557 — 951-781-2727

Morgan Hill, Santa Clara, Pop. 34,852
Morgan Hill USD — 8,700/K-12
15600 Concord Cir 95037 — 408-201-6023
Dr. Alan Nishino, supt. — Fax 779-2124
www.mhu.k12.ca.us
Britton MS — 800/7-8
80 W Central Ave 95037 — 408-201-6160
Carol Coursey, prin. — Fax 778-2550
Live Oak HS — 1,800/9-12
1505 E Main Ave 95037 — 408-201-6100
Nick Boden, prin. — Fax 776-9097
Sobrato HS — 700/9-12
401 Burnett Ave 95037 — 408-201-6200
Debbie Padilla, prin. — Fax 465-2467
Community Adult Education — Adult
17940 Monterey St 95037 — 408-779-5261
Dennis Browne, prin. — Fax 779-8367
Other Schools – See San Jose

Oakwood Country S — 400/K-10
105 John Wilson Way 95037 — 408-782-7177
Michelle Helvey, prin.
Shadow Mountain Baptist S — 100/K-12
280 Llagas Rd 95037 — 408-782-7806
David Warthan, prin.

Morro Bay, San Luis Obispo, Pop. 10,208
San Luis Coastal USD
Supt. — See San Luis Obispo
Morro Bay HS — 1,000/9-12
235 Atascadero Rd 93442 — 805-771-1845
Peter Zotovich, prin. — Fax 772-5944

Moss Landing, Monterey
North Monterey County USD — 4,400/PK-12
8142 Moss Landing Rd 95039 — 831-633-3343
Carolyn Post, supt. — Fax 633-2937
www.nmcusd.org
Other Schools – See Castroville

Mountain Center, Riverside, Pop. 300

Morning Sky Residential School — Post-Sec.
PO Box 379 92561 — 951-659-4044

Mountain View, Santa Clara, Pop. 69,276
Mountain View-Los Altos UNHSD — 3,600/9-12
1299 Bryant Ave 94040 — 650-940-4668
Dr. Barry Groves, supt. — Fax 961-7008
www.mvla.net/
Mountain View HS — 1,800/9-12
3535 Truman Ave 94040 — 650-940-4600
Keith Moody, prin. — Fax 961-6349

Mountain View/Los Altos Adult Education Adult
333 Moffett Blvd 94043 650-940-1333
Laura Stefanski, dir. Fax 967-4699
Other Schools – See Los Altos

Mountain View-Whisman SD 4,000/K-8
750A San Pierre Way 94043 650-526-3500
Maurice Ghysels, supt. Fax 964-8907
www.mvwsd.org/
Crittenden MS 600/6-8
1701 Rock St 94043 650-903-6945
Karen Robinson, prin. Fax 903-6952
Graham MS 800/6-8
1175 Castro St 94040 650-526-3570
Alicia Henderson, prin. Fax 965-9278

Girls' MS, 180 N Rengstorff Ave 94043 100/6-8
Deborah Hof, hdmstr. 650-968-8338
Mountain View Academy 200/9-12
360 S Shoreline Blvd 94041 650-967-2324
Dan Meidinger, prin. Fax 967-6886
St. Francis HS 1,500/9-12
1885 Miramonte Ave 94040 650-968-1213
Patricia Tennant, prin. Fax 968-1706

Mount Shasta, Siskiyou, Pop. 3,623
Mount Shasta UNSD 700/K-8
595 E Alma St 96067 530-926-6007
Steve Mitrovich, supt. Fax 926-6103
sisnet.ssku.k12.ca.us/~msusdftp/index.html
Sisson S 400/4-8
601 E Alma St 96067 530-926-3846
Karen Snell, prin. Fax 926-2152

Siskiyou UNHSD 800/9-12
624 Everitt Memorial Hwy 96067 530-926-3006
Richard Holmes, supt. Fax 926-3113
siskuhsd2.sisnet.ssku.k12.ca.us/
Mount Shasta HS 500/9-12
710 Everitt Memorial Hwy 96067 530-926-2614
Jim Cox, prin. Fax 926-5162
Siskiyou Adult S Adult
720 Rockfellow Dr 96067 530-926-0425
James Burger, prin. Fax 926-0586
Other Schools – See Happy Camp, Mc Cloud, Weed

Murrieta, Riverside, Pop. 82,778
Murrieta Valley USD 18,700/K-12
41870 Mcalby Ct 92562 951-696-1600
Dr. Stan Scheer, supt. Fax 696-1641
www.murrieta.k12.ca.us
Murrieta Valley HS 3,200/9-12
42200 Nighthawk Way 92562 951-696-1408
Renate Jefferson, prin. Fax 304-1803
Shivela MS 1,600/6-8
24515 Lincoln Ave 92562 951-696-1406
Gary Farmer, prin. Fax 304-1643
Thompson MS 1,700/6-8
24040 Hayes Ave 92562 951-696-1410
Dale Velk, prin. Fax 304-1691
Vista Murrietta HS 2,300/9-12
28251 Clinton Keith Rd 92563 951-894-5750
Darren Daniel, prin. Fax 304-1832
Warm Springs MS 1,400/6-8
39245 Calle de Fortuna 92563 951-696-3503
Timothy Custer, prin. Fax 304-1611

Temecula Valley USD
Supt. — See Temecula
Bella Vista MS 700/6-8
31650 Browning St 92563 951-294-6600
Pam Keller, prin. Fax 294-6624

Calvary Chapel Christian S 1,200/K-12
24225 Monroe Ave 92562 951-834-9190
Desmond Starr, supt. Fax 698-4896
Oak Grove Institute - Jack Weaver 100/K-12
24275 Jefferson Ave 92562 951-677-5599
Dr. Michael Brown, dir.
Sierra Springs Christian S 100/1-12
40960 California Oaks Rd 92562 951-304-3304
Pamela Healey, admin.

Napa, Napa, Pop. 74,782
Napa Valley USD 14,400/K-12
2425 Jefferson St 94558 707-253-3511
John P. Glaser, supt. Fax 253-3855
www.nvusd.k12.ca.us
Harvest MS 900/6-8
2449 Old Sonoma Rd 94558 707-259-8866
Linda Beckstrom, prin. Fax 253-4013
Napa HS 2,400/9-12
2475 Jefferson St 94558 707-253-3711
Barb Franco, prin. Fax 253-3906
New Technology HS Vo/Tech
920 Yount St 94559 707-259-8557
Monica Tipton, prin. Fax 253-8558
Redwood MS 1,100/6-8
3600 Oxford St 94558 707-253-3415
Michael Pearson, prin. Fax 259-0718
Silverado MS 1,000/6-8
1133 Coombsville Rd 94558 707-253-3688
Mike Mansuy, prin. Fax 253-3830
Vintage HS 2,300/9-12
1375 Trower Ave 94558 707-253-3601
Eric Schneider, prin. Fax 253-3604
Napa Adult Education Adult
1600 Lincoln Ave 94558 707-253-3594
Rhonda Slota, prin. Fax 253-3828
Other Schools – See American Canyon

Regional Occupational Center & Program
Supt. — None
Napa County ROP Vo/Tech
2121 Imola Ave 94559 707-253-6830
M.L. Oxford, dir. Fax 253-6917

Justin-Siena HS 700/9-12
4026 Maher St 94558 707-255-0950
Gregory Schmitz, prin. Fax 255-0334
Napa Christian S 300/K-12
2201 Pine St 94559 707-255-5233
Greg Coryell, prin. Fax 255-8530
Napa State Hospital Post-Sec.
2100 Napa Vallejo Hwy 94558 707-253-5428
Napa Valley College Post-Sec.
2277 Napa Vallejo Hwy 94558 707-253-3000
New Life Academy 50/K-12
PO Box 5478 94581 707-255-1062
Clayton Brown, admin. Fax 226-5433

National City, San Diego, Pop. 61,419
Sweetwater UNHSD
Supt. — See Chula Vista
Granger JHS 1,200/7-9
2101 Granger Ave 91950 619-472-6000
Susan Mitchell, prin. Fax 267-4107
National City MS 900/7-8
1701 D Ave 91950 619-336-2600
Lee Romero, prin. Fax 474-1756
Sweetwater HS 2,700/9-12
2900 Highland Ave 91950 619-474-9700
Wes Braddock, prin. Fax 474-7635
National City Adult S Adult
517 Mile Of Cars Way 91950 619-336-9400
Ralph Mora, prin. Fax 336-0641

Bay Vista College of Beauty Post-Sec.
1520 E Plaza Blvd 91950 619-474-6607
Faithful Ambassadors Bible Baptist Acdmy 100/K-12
2432 E 18th St 91950 619-434-2265
Ireneo Austria, admin.
San Diego Academy 300/K-12
2800 E 4th St 91950 619-267-9550
Wayne Longhofer, prin. Fax 267-8662

Needles, San Bernardino, Pop. 5,348
Needles USD 1,200/K-12
1900 Erin Dr 92363 760-326-3891
Dave Renquest, supt. Fax 326-4218
www.needles.k12.ca.us/
Needles HS 300/9-12
1900 Erin Dr 92363 760-326-2191
Mike Kincaid, prin. Fax 326-1212
Needles MS 200/6-8
1900 Erin Dr 92363 760-326-3894
Jim Rolls, prin. Fax 326-4052

Nevada City, Nevada, Pop. 3,032
Nevada City ESD 1,300/K-8
800 Hoover Ln 95959 530-265-1820
Roger Steel, supt. Fax 265-1822
www.ncsd.k12.ca.us
Seven Hills IS 500/6-8
700 Hoover Ln 95959 530-265-1840
Joe Limov, prin. Fax 265-1846

Woolman Semester 50/11-12
13075 Woolman Ln 95959 530-273-3183
Shana Maziarz, hdmstr. Fax 273-9028

Newark, Alameda, Pop. 41,956
Newark USD 7,400/PK-12
5715 Musick Ave 94560 510-818-4112
John C. Bernard, supt. Fax 794-2199
www.nusd.k12.ca.us
Newark JHS 1,200/7-8
6201 Lafayette Ave 94560 510-818-3000
Don Gill, prin. Fax 794-2079
Newark Memorial HS 2,100/9-12
39375 Cedar Blvd 94560 510-818-4300
Bill Morones, prin. Fax 794-2120
Newark Adult S Adult
35777 Cedar Blvd 94560 510-818-3701
Carolyn Scott, prin. Fax 794-2654

Newbury Park, See Thousand Oaks
Conejo Valley USD
Supt. — See Thousand Oaks
Newbury Park HS 2,000/9-12
456 N Reino Rd 91320 805-498-3676
Athol Wong, prin. Fax 499-3549
Sequoia MS 1,100/6-8
2855 Borchard Rd 91320 805-498-3617
Vivian Vina-Hunt, prin. Fax 375-5605

Newbury Park Adventist Academy 100/9-12
180 Academy Dr 91320 805-498-2191
Dr. Harold Crook, prin. Fax 499-1165
Trinity Pacific Christian S 400/K-12
3538 Gerald Dr 91320 805-492-0863
Lorraine Dilworth, admin.

New Cuyama, Santa Barbara
Cuyama JUSD 300/K-12
PO Box 271 93254 661-766-2482
Jan Hensley, supt. Fax 766-2255
Cuyama Valley HS 100/9-12
PO Box 271 93254 661-766-2293
Don Wilson, prin. Fax 766-2593

Newhall, See Santa Clarita
William S. Hart UNHSD
Supt. — See Santa Clarita
Hart HS 2,900/9-12
24825 Newhall Ave 91321 661-259-7575
Gary Fuller, prin. Fax 254-6436
Placerita JHS 1,200/7-8
25015 Newhall Ave 91321 661-259-1551
Rob Gapper, prin. Fax 287-9748

Master's College and Seminary Post-Sec.
21726 Placerita Canyon Rd 91321 661-259-3540

Newman, Stanislaus, Pop. 9,623
Newman-Crows Landing USD 2,400/K-12
890 Main St 95360 209-862-2933
Rick Fauss, supt. Fax 862-0113
www.nclusd.k12.ca.us/
Orestimba HS 700/9-12
707 Hardin Rd 95360 209-862-2916
Joe Terra, prin. Fax 862-0259
Yolo MS 600/6-8
901 Hoyer Rd 95360 209-862-2984
Kathy McWilliams, prin. Fax 862-3734

Newport Beach, Orange, Pop. 79,834
Newport - Mesa USD
Supt. — See Costa Mesa
Corona Del Mar JSHS 2,200/7-12
2101 Eastbluff Dr 92660 949-515-6000
Fal Asrani, prin. Fax 515-6070
Ensign IS 1,200/7-8
2000 Cliff Dr 92663 949-515-6910
Fax 515-3370
Newport Harbor HS 2,400/9-12
600 Irvine Ave 92663 949-515-6300
Michael Vossen, prin. Fax 515-6370

Interior Designers Institute Post-Sec.
1061 Camelback St 92660 949-675-4451

Newport Coast, Orange

Sage Hill 500/9-12
20402 Newport Coast Dr 92657 949-219-0100
Dr. Jacqueline Smethurst, hdmstr.

Nicolaus, Sutter
East Nicolaus JUNHSD 300/9-12
2454 Nicolaus Ave 95659 530-656-2255
Dr. Wayne B. Tierney, supt. Fax 656-1065
www.eastnicolaus.k12.ca.us
East Nicolaus HS 300/9-12
2454 Nicolaus Ave 95659 530-656-2255
Dr. Wayne Tierney, prin. Fax 656-1065

Nipomo, San Luis Obispo, Pop. 7,109
Lucia Mar USD
Supt. — See Arroyo Grande
Nipomo HS 1,200/9-12
525 N Thompson Ave 93444 805-474-3300
Robert Mistele, prin. Fax 929-2551

Highland Preparatory S 100/K-12
PO Box 238 93444 805-929-4059
Kristin Holder, admin. Fax 929-1837

Norco, Riverside, Pop. 26,960
Corona-Norco USD 45,000/K-12
2820 Clark Ave 92860 951-736-5000
Kent Bechler Ph.D., supt. Fax 736-5016
www.cnusd.k12.ca.us
Kennedy HS 10-12
1951 3rd St 92860 951-738-2200
Don Ward, prin. Fax 738-2212
Norco HS 3,000/9-12
2065 Temescal Ave 92860 951-736-3241
John Johnson, prin. Fax 736-3282
Norco IS 1,200/7-8
2711 Temescal Ave 92860 951-736-3206
Teri Dudley, prin. Fax 736-3208
Other Schools – See Corona

North Edwards, Kern, Pop. 1,259
Muroc JUSD 2,200/K-12
17100 Foothill Ave 93523 760-769-4821
Robert Challinor, supt. Fax 769-4241
www.muroc.k12.ca.us
McGowan HS 50/9-12
17100 Lorraine Ave, Edwards CA 93523
760-769-4333
Paul Kostopoulos, prin. Fax 769-1131
Other Schools – See Boron, Edwards

North Fork, Madera
Chawanakee USD 800/K-12
PO Box 400 93643 559-877-6209
Dr. Stephen Foster, supt. Fax 877-4802
www.chawanakee.k12.ca.us
Other Schools – See Coarsegold, O Neals

North Highlands, Sacramento, Pop. 44,600
Grant JUNHSD
Supt. — See Sacramento
Highlands Academy of Art & Design 1,300/7-12
6601 Guthrie St 95660 916-286-1701
Gary Bly, prin. Fax 263-6487
Pacific Careers & Technology HS Vo/Tech
3800 Bolivar Ave 95660 916-286-1970
John Stephens, prin. Fax 263-6404
Campos Verdes Adult Education Center Adult
3701 Stephen Dr 95660 916-263-6505
Hal Steward, dir. Fax 263-6512
Winona Adult Education Adult
3222 Winona Way 95660 916-286-3809
Hal Steward, dir.

North Hills, Los Angeles

Centers of Learning 100/PK-12
PO Box 2037 91393 818-894-3213
Debra Grill, prin. Fax 893-8074
Los Angeles Baptist JSHS 1,000/7-12
9825 Woodley Ave 91343 818-894-5742
Tim Piatt, prin. Fax 892-5018

North Hollywood, See Los Angeles
Los Angeles USD
Supt. — See Los Angeles
East Valley HS 9-12
5525 Vineland Ave 91601 818-753-4400
Marsha Hamm, prin. Fax 487-6922
Madison MS 2,300/6-8
13000 Hart St 91605 818-255-5200
Estelle Baptiste, prin. Fax 765-4692
North Hollywood HS 4,400/9-12
5231 Colfax Ave 91601 818-769-8510
Randall Delling, prin. Fax 508-7124
Reed MS 2,000/6-8
4525 Irvine Ave 91602 818-487-7600
Sally Burford, prin. Fax 766-9069
North Hollywood Adult Education Adult
5231 Colfax Ave 91601 818-252-5627
Kathleen Javaheri, prin. Fax 766-8247

Campbell Hall S 1,000/K-12
PO Box 4036 91617 818-980-7280
Julian Bull, hdmstr. Fax 505-5362
Concorde Career College Post-Sec.
12412 Victory Blvd 91606 818-766-8151
Harvard-Westlake S 900/10-12
3700 Coldwater Canyon Ave 91604 818-980-6692
Jeanne Huybrechts, hdmstr. Fax 487-6631
Maric College Post-Sec.
6180 Laurel Canyon Ste 101 91606 818-763-2563
Marinello School of Beauty Post-Sec.
6219 Laurel Canyon Blvd 91606 818-980-1300
Oakwood S 500/7-12
11600 Magnolia Blvd 91601 818-752-4400
Dr. James Astman, hdmstr. Fax 752-4408
Summit View 200/1-12
6455 Coldwater Canyon Ave 91606 818-623-6300
Nancy Rosenfelt, dir.
Valley Torah Girls' HS 100/9-12
12003 Riverside Dr 91607 818-755-1697
Rachel Grossman, prin. Fax 755-1694

Northridge, See Los Angeles
Los Angeles USD
Supt. — See Los Angeles
Holmes MS 1,500/6-8
9351 Paso Robles Ave 91325 818-678-4100
Valerie Turner, prin. Fax 886-3358
Nobel MS 2,300/6-8
9950 Tampa Ave 91324 818-773-4700
Bob Coburn, prin. Fax 701-9480
Northridge Academy HS 9-12
9601 Zelzah Ave 91325 818-700-2222
Constance Semf, prin. Fax 718-2239
Northridge MS 1,200/6-8
17960 Chase St 91325 818-678-5100
Deborah Wiltz, prin. Fax 885-1461

CA National University Advanced Studies Post-Sec.
8550 Balboa Blvd Ste 210 91325 800-782-2422
California State University-Northridge Post-Sec.
18111 Nordhoff St 91330 818-677-1200
Highland Hall Waldorf S 400/PK-12
17100 Superior St 91325 818-349-1394
Ed Eadon, dir. Fax 349-2390
San Fernando Valley Academy 200/PK-12
17601 Lassen St 91325 818-349-1373
Arsenio Hernandez, prin. Fax 773-6353

Norwalk, Los Angeles, Pop. 105,834
Little Lake City ESD
Supt. — See Santa Fe Springs
Lakeside MS 800/6-8
11000 Kenney St 90650 562-868-9422
Sandra Sanders Ed.D., prin. Fax 863-9252

Norwalk-La Mirada USD 23,600/PK-12
12820 Pioneer Blvd 90650 562-868-0431
Ginger Shattuck, supt. Fax 864-9857
www.nlmusd.k12.ca.us
Corvallis MS 1,000/6-8
11032 Leffingwell Rd 90650 562-868-2678
Matthew Fraijo, prin. Fax 863-4755
Glenn HS 2,100/9-12
13520 Shoemaker Ave 90650 562-868-0431
Linda Granillo, prin. Fax 802-1596
Hargitt MS 800/6-8
12940 Foster Rd 90650 562-864-2593
Dr. Karen Cresswell, prin. Fax 863-8195
Los Alisos MS 1,100/6-8
14800 Jersey Ave 90650 562-868-0865
Ligia Hallstrom, prin. Fax 864-2967
Norwalk HS 2,300/9-12
11356 Leffingwell Rd 90650 562-868-0431
Dina Leslie, prin. Fax 864-0796
Waite MS 900/6-8
14320 Norwalk Blvd 90650 562-921-7981
Dr. Linda Haley, prin. Fax 921-8114
Norwalk Adult S Adult
15711 Pioneer Blvd 90650 562-868-9858
Frances Kusumoto, dir. Fax 863-2159
Other Schools – See La Mirada

Adcon Technical Institute Post-Sec.
12440 Firestone Blvd # 2001 90650 562-864-0506
Cerritos College Post-Sec.
11110 Alondra Blvd 90650 562-860-2451
Grace Christian S 50/PK-12
12722 Woods Ave 90650 562-868-2398
Rev. Robert Rockhill, prin.
New Harvest Christian S 200/PK-12
11364 Imperial Hwy 90650 562-929-0774
Richard Salazar, dir. Fax 484-3260
NTMA Training Center of Southern CA Post-Sec.
14926 Bloomfield Ave 90650 562-921-3722
Pioneer Baptist S 200/K-12
11717 Pioneer Blvd 90650 562-863-5817
Gerald Mitchell, prin. Fax 868-2943

Novato, Marin, Pop. 50,335
Novato USD 7,400/K-12
1015 7th St 94945 415-897-4201
Jan La Torre-Derby, supt. Fax 898-5790
www.nusd.org
Hill MS 600/6-8
720 Diablo Ave 94947 415-893-1557
Louise Koenig, prin. Fax 898-3910
Novato HS 1,100/9-12
625 Arthur St 94947 415-898-2125
Rey Mayoral, prin. Fax 897-4242
San Jose MS 500/6-8
1000 Sunset Pkwy 94949 415-883-7831
Dale Ravazzini, prin. Fax 883-0624
San Marin HS 1,100/9-12
15 San Marin Dr 94945 415-898-2121
Loeta Andersen, prin. Fax 892-8284
Sinaloa MS 700/6-8
2045 Vineyard Rd 94947 415-897-2111
Kit Gabbard, prin. Fax 892-1201

College of Marin Post-Sec.
1800 Ignacio Blvd 94949 415-883-2211
North Bay Christian Academy 100/K-12
6965 Redwood Blvd 94945 415-892-8921
Pam Carraher, prin. Fax 893-1750

Nuevo, Riverside, Pop. 3,010
Nuview UNESD 1,500/K-8
29780 Lakeview Ave 92567 951-928-0066
Jay Hoffman, supt. Fax 928-0324
www.nuview.k12.ca.us
Mountain Shadows MS 600/6-8
30401 Reservoir Ave 92567 951-928-3836
Manuel Peredia, prin. Fax 928-3015

Oakdale, Stanislaus, Pop. 18,561
Oakdale JUSD 4,900/K-12
168 S 3rd Ave 95361 209-848-4884
Wendell Chun, supt. Fax 847-0155
www.oakdale.k12.ca.us
Oakdale HS 1,500/9-12
739 W G St 95361 209-847-3007
Richard Jones, prin. Fax 848-0314
Oakdale JHS 800/7-8
400 S Maag Ave 95361 209-847-2294
Marc Malone, prin. Fax 847-8521
Oakdale Adult Education Adult
200 Hinkley Ave 95361 209-847-9609
Mike Riley, prin. Fax 848-4359

Oakhurst, Madera, Pop. 2,602
Bass Lake JUNESD 1,000/K-8
40096 Indian Springs Rd 93644 559-642-1555
Glenn Reid, supt. Fax 642-1556
www.basslakejuesd.com
Oak Creek IS 300/6-8
40094 Indian Springs Rd 93644 559-642-1570
Dr. Bob Guizar, prin. Fax 683-7279

Yosemite USD 2,500/K-12
50200 Road 427 93644 559-683-8801
Bill McCabe, supt. Fax 683-4160
www.yosemiteusd.com/
Yosemite HS 1,200/9-12
50200 Road 427 93644 559-683-4667
Steve Raupp, prin. Fax 683-8392
Yosemite Adult HS Adult
50200 Road 427 93644 559-683-5544
Roberta Tackett, prin.

Oakland, Alameda, Pop. 395,274
Oakland USD 40,000/PK-12
1025 2nd Ave 94606 510-879-8200
Dr. Kimberly Statham, supt. Fax 879-8800
www.ousd.k12.ca.us/
Best HS 800/9-12
2607 Myrtle St 94607 510-879-3030
James Gray, prin. Fax 879-3039
Brewer JHS 700/6-8
3748 13th Ave 94610 510-879-2100
Jamie Marantz, prin. Fax 879-2109
Business & Information Technology 500/9-12
8601 MacArthur Blvd 94605 510-879-3010
Richard Gaston, prin. Fax 879-3019
Claremont MS 400/6-8
5750 College Ave 94618 510-879-2010
David Chambliss, prin. Fax 879-2019
Cole MS 300/6-8
1011 Union St 94607 510-879-1090
Toby Hopstone, prin. Fax 879-1099
College Prep & Architecture Academy 400/9-12
4610 Foothill Blvd 94601 510-879-1131
Daniel Hurst, prin. Fax 879-8874
East Oakland Community 100/9-12
8251 Fontaine St 94605 510-879-2160
Eric DeMeulenaere, prin. Fax 879-2169
East Oakland School of the Arts 500/9-12
8601 MacArthur Blvd 94605 510-879-3010
Matin Abdel-Qawi, prin. Fax 879-2535
Elmhurst MS 900/6-8
1800 98th Ave 94603 510-879-2026
Matthew Duffy, prin. Fax 879-2024
Excel HS 9-12
2607 Myrtle St 94607 510-879-3030
Yetunde Reeves, prin. Fax 879-3039
Explore MS 6-8
3550 64th Ave 94605 510-879-1040
Asali Waters, prin. Fax 879-1049
Frick MS 700/6-8
2845 64th Ave 94605 510-879-2030
Jerome Gourdine, prin. Fax 879-2039
Harte MS 900/6-8
3700 Coolidge Ave 94602 510-879-2060
Teresa Williams, prin. Fax 879-2069
Havenscourt MS 200/8-8
1390 66th Ave 94621 510-879-8486
David Montes de Oca, prin. Fax 879-2079
KIPP Bridge College Prep S 100/6-8
991 14th St 94607 510-879-2421
David Ling, prin. Fax 879-3182
Kizmet MS 6-8
2607 Myrtle St 94607 510-879-3030
Lynn Dodd, prin. Fax 879-3039
Leadership Preparatory HS 9-12
8601 Macarthur Blvd 94605 510-879-3010
Denise Jeffrey, prin. Fax 879-1997
Life Academy 300/9-12
2111 International Blvd 94606 510-879-4110
Erik Rice, prin. Fax 879-4119
Madison MS 400/6-8
400 Capistrano Dr 94603 510-879-2150
Quiauna Whitfield, prin. Fax 879-2159
Mandela HS 300/9-12
4610 Foothill Blvd 94601 510-879-1141
Robin Bailer-Glover, prin. Fax 879-8876
Media College Prep 400/9-12
4610 Foothill Blvd 94601 510-879-1597
Benjamin Schmoolder, prin. Fax 879-1237
Melrose Leadership Academy 200/6-8
1325 53rd Ave 94601 510-534-1151
Moyra Contreras, prin. Fax 879-1419

Metwest HS 100/9-12
314 E 10th St 94606 510-879-0235
Eve Gordon, prin. Fax 879-0235
Montera JHS 900/6-8
5555 Ascot Dr 94611 510-879-2110
Cheryl Rodby, prin. Fax 879-2119
Oakland HS 2,100/9-12
1023 Macarthur Blvd 94610 510-879-3040
Clement Mok, prin. Fax 879-3049
Oakland Technical HS Vo/Tech
4351 Broadway 94611 510-879-3050
Sheliagh Andujar, prin. Fax 879-3059
Robeson S of Visual & Performing Arts 400/9-12
4610 Foothill Blvd 94601 510-879-1237
Anisa Rasheed, prin. Fax 879-3029
Roosevelt MS 800/6-8
1926 E 19th St 94606 510-879-2120
Theresa Clincy, prin. Fax 879-2129
Simmons MS 200/8-8
2101 35th Ave 94601 510-879-2050
Gregory McNamara, prin. Fax 879-2059
Skyline HS 2,200/9-12
12250 Skyline Blvd 94619 510-879-3060
Fax 879-3069
Westlake MS 600/6-8
2629 Harrison St 94612 510-879-2130
Misha Karigaca, prin. Fax 879-2139
Youth Empowerment S 200/9-12
8251 Fontaine St 94605 510-879-8877
Maureen Benson, prin. Fax 879-7042
Oakland Evening Adult Adult
750 International Blvd 94606 510-879-4020
Brigitte Marshall, prin. Fax 879-4029
Pleasant Valley Adult Adult
920 53rd St 94608 510-879-4090
Dick Stein, prin. Fax 879-1806
Shands Adult S Adult
2455 Church St 94605 510-879-4040
Judy Flores, admin. Fax 879-4044

Regional Occupational Center & Program
Supt. — None
Oakland-Alameda ROP Vo/Tech
1025 2nd Ave 94606 510-879-8474
Garlin Cephas, dir. Fax 879-1845

Academy of Chinese Culture & Health Sci. Post-Sec.
1601 Clay St 94612 510-763-7787
Bentley S 700/K-12
1 Hiller Dr 94618 510-843-2512
Rick Fitzgerald, hdmstr. Fax 843-5162
Bishop O'Dowd HS 1,100/9-12
9500 Stearns Ave 94605 510-577-9100
Joseph Salamack, prin. Fax 638-3259
California College of the Arts Post-Sec.
5212 Broadway 94618 510-594-3600
California School of Podiatric Medicine Post-Sec.
370 Hawthorne Ave 94609 510-869-8727
College Preparatory S 300/9-12
6100 Broadway 94618 510-652-0111
Murray Cohen, prin. Fax 652-7467
Golden Gate Academy 100/K-12
3800 Mountain Blvd 94619 510-531-0110
Fax 531-9434
Head-Royce S 800/K-12
4315 Lincoln Ave 94602 510-531-1300
Paul D. Chapman, hdmstr. Fax 531-2649
Holy Names HS 300/9-12
4660 Harbord Dr 94618 510-450-1110
Sr. Sally Slyngstad, prin. Fax 547-3111
Holy Names University Post-Sec.
3500 Mountain Blvd 94619 510-436-1000
Laney College Post-Sec.
900 Fallon St 94607 510-834-5740
Lincoln University Post-Sec.
401 15th St 94612 510-628-8010
Merritt College Post-Sec.
12500 Campus Dr 94619 510-531-4911
Mills College Post-Sec.
5000 Macarthur Blvd 94613 510-430-2255
Mohammed S 100/K-12
1652 47th Ave 94601 510-436-7755
Faheem Shuaibe, dir. Fax 437-1715
Moler Barber College Post-Sec.
3815 Telegraph Ave 94609 510-652-4177
Morgan S for Girls 200/6-8
PO Box 9966 94613 510-632-6000
Ann Clarke, hdmstr.
Muhammad University of Islam 100/K-12
5277 Foothill Blvd 94601 510-436-0206
Sr. Salamah Muhammad, admin.
Patten Academy of Christian Education 200/K-12
2433 Coolidge Ave 94601 510-533-3121
Sharon Anderson, prin. Fax 535-9381
Patten University Post-Sec.
2433 Coolidge Ave 94601 510-261-8500
St. Andrew Mission Baptist S 200/K-12
PO Box 70378 94612 510-465-8023
Dr. Robeth Lacy, admin. Fax 465-0725
St. Elizabeth HS 300/9-12
1530 34th Ave 94601 510-532-8947
Sr. Liam Brock, prin. Fax 532-9754
St. Martin de Porres S 50/6-8
1630 10th St 94607 510-832-1757
Sr. Barbara Dawson, pres. Fax 832-6481
Samuel Merritt College Post-Sec.
370 Hawthorne Ave 94609 510-869-6511

Oakley, Contra Costa, Pop. 27,177
Liberty UNHSD
Supt. — See Brentwood
Freedom HS 2,100/9-12
1050 Neroly Rd 94561 925-625-5900
Eric Volta, prin. Fax 625-0396

Oakley UNESD 4,500/K-8
91 Mercedes Ln 94561 925-625-0700
Richard K. Rogers Ed.D., supt. Fax 625-1863
www.ouesd.k12.ca.us
Delta Vista MS 900/6-8
4901 Frank Hengel Way 94561 925-625-6840
Greg Hetrick, prin. Fax 625-6850

O'Hara Park MS 800/6-8
1100 OHara Ave 94561 925-625-5060
Roger Macdonald, prin. Fax 625-5096

Faith Christian Learning Center 50/K-12
PO Box 1399 94561 925-625-2161
Karen Lyles, admin. Fax 625-2161

Oak Park, Ventura, Pop. 2,412
Oak Park USD 3,600/PK-12
5801 Conifer St 91377 818-735-3200
Anthony Knight, supt. Fax 879-0372
www.opusd.k12.ca.us
Medea Creek MS 900/6-8
1002 Doubletree Rd 91377 818-707-7922
Laurel Ford, prin. Fax 865-8641
Oak Park HS 1,200/9-12
899 Kanan Rd 91377 818-735-3300
Lynn McCormack, prin. Fax 707-7970

Occidental, Sonoma, Pop. 1,300
Harmony UNESD 300/K-8
1935 Bohemian Hwy 95465 707-874-3280
Fred Adam, supt. Fax 874-1226
www.harmony.k12.ca.us
Salmon Creek MS 200/5-8
1935 Bohemian Hwy 95465 707-874-1205
Brian Burke, prin. Fax 874-1226

Oceanside, San Diego, Pop. 166,108
Oceanside USD 21,300/K-12
2111 Mission Ave 92058 760-757-2560
Kenneth Noonan, supt. Fax 721-9714
www.oside.k12.ca.us
El Camino HS 2,800/9-12
400 Rancho Del Oro Dr 92057 760-757-8550
Dan Daris, prin. Fax 757-5321
Jefferson MS 1,400/6-8
823 Acacia Ave 92058 760-757-6060
Duane Coleman, prin. Fax 757-5791
King MS 1,800/6-8
1290 Ivey Ranch Rd 92057 760-967-1122
Bob Rowe, prin. Fax 967-4154
Lincoln MS 1,400/6-8
2000 California St 92054 760-757-0153
Bob Mueller, prin. Fax 433-2035
Oceanside HS 2,400/9-12
1 Pirates Cove Way 92054 760-722-8201
Kimo Marquardt, prin. Fax 757-2419

Vista USD
Supt. — See Vista
Madison MS 1,300/6-8
4930 Lake Blvd 92056 760-940-0176
Dr. Robert Pack, prin. Fax 940-2081
Roosevelt MS 1,300/6-8
850 Sagewood Dr 92057 760-726-8003
Raif Henry, prin. Fax 726-8596

Futures International High School Post-Sec.
2204 S El Camino Real #312 92054 760-721-0121
Mira Costa College Post-Sec.
1 Barnard Dr 92056 760-757-2121
Oceanside College of Beauty Post-Sec.
1575 S Coast Hwy 92054 760-757-6161
Victory Christian S 50/2-12
PO Box 1760 92051 760-439-6431
Teresa Brugger, prin. Fax 439-6431

Ojai, Ventura, Pop. 7,945
Ojai USD 3,600/K-12
PO Box 878 93024 805-640-4300
Dr. Timothy Baird, supt. Fax 640-4321
www.ojai.k12.ca.us
Matilija JHS 600/7-8
703 El Paseo Rd 93023 805-640-4355
Jackie Law, prin. Fax 640-4398
Nordhoff HS 1,300/9-12
1401 Maricopa Hwy 93023 805-640-4343
Dan Musick, prin. Fax 640-4335

Happy Valley S 100/9-12
PO Box 850 93024 805-646-4343
Paul Amadio, admin. Fax 646-4371
Laurel Springs S 2,500/K-12
PO Box 1440 93024 805-646-2473
Marilyn Mosley-Gordanier, dir. Fax 646-0186
Oak Grove S 200/PK-12
220 W Lomita Ave 93023 805-646-8236
Ellen Hall, dir. Fax 646-6509
Oak Meadow S, PO Box 1626 93024 100/K-12
Rebecca Lowe, admin. 805-646-4510
Ojai Valley S 400/PK-12
723 El Paseo Rd 93023 805-646-1423
Michael Hermes, pres. Fax 646-0362
Thacher S 200/9-12
5025 Thacher Rd 93023 805-646-4377
Michael Mulligan, hdmstr. Fax 640-1322
Villanova Preparatory S 300/9-12
12096 N Ventura Ave 93023 805-646-1464
Anthony Sabatino, hdmstr. Fax 646-4430

Olivehurst, Yuba, Pop. 9,738
Marysville JUSD
Supt. — See Marysville
Lindhurst HS 1,300/9-12
4446 Olive Ave 95961 530-741-6150
Bob Eckardt, prin. Fax 741-6171
Yuba Gardens IS 600/6-8
1964 11th Ave 95961 530-741-6194
Cindy Thomas, prin. Fax 741-7847

Olympic Valley, Placer

Squaw Valley Academy 100/6-12
PO Box 2667 96146 530-583-1558
Donald Rees, hdmstr. Fax 581-1111

O Neals, Madera
Chawanakee USD
Supt. — See North Fork

Mountain Oaks HS 50/9-12
PO Box 210 93645 559-868-4444
Gary Talley, prin. Fax 868-3407

Ontario, San Bernardino, Pop. 172,679
Chaffey JUNHSD 24,400/9-12
211 W 5th St 91762 909-988-8511
Barry Cadwallader, supt. Fax 984-1164
www.cjuhsd.k12.ca.us
Chaffey HS 3,500/9-12
1245 N Euclid Ave 91762 909-988-5560
Tim Ward, prin. Fax 988-0146
Colony HS 2,200/9-12
3850 E Riverside Dr 91761 909-930-2929
Michelle Boyette, prin. Fax 460-5856
Ontario HS 2,600/9-12
901 W Francis St 91762 909-988-7411
Rod Hust, prin. Fax 986-2181
Chaffey Adult S Adult
211 W 5th St 91762 909-988-8511
Gabriel Petrocelli, prin. Fax 983-9916
Other Schools – See Alta Loma, Etiwanda, Montclair, Rancho Cucamonga

Chino Valley USD
Supt. — See Chino
Woodcrest JHS 500/7-8
2725 S Campus Ave 91761 909-923-3455
Diana Yarboi, prin. Fax 923-0851

Mountain View ESD 3,400/K-8
2585 S Archibald Ave 91761 909-947-2205
Dr. Rick Carr, supt. Fax 947-2291
www.mtnview.k12.ca.us
Yokley JHS, 2947 S Turner Ave 91761 1,200/6-8
Bruce Perry, prin. 909-947-6774

Ontario-Montclair ESD 26,100/PK-8
950 W D St 91762 909-459-2500
Dr. Sharon McGehee, supt. Fax 459-2542
www.omsd.k12.ca.us
Danks MS 1,200/6-8
1020 N Vine Ave 91762 909-983-2691
Fax 459-2959
De Anza MS 1,000/6-8
1450 S Sultana Ave 91761 909-986-8577
Leticia Zaragoza, prin. Fax 459-2673
Oaks MS 1,100/7-8
1221 S Oaks Ave 91762 909-988-2050
Jack Young, prin. Fax 988-2081
Wiltsey MS 1,100/7-8
1450 E G St 91764 909-986-5838
Lisa Somerville, prin. Fax 459-2834
Other Schools – See Montclair

Everest College Post-Sec.
1460 S Milliken Ave 91761 909-984-5027
Franklin Career College Post-Sec.
1274 Slater Cir 91761 909-937-9007
Marinello School of Beauty Post-Sec.
940 N Mountain Ave 91762 909-984-5884
Montecito Baptist S 100/K-12
2560 S Archibald Ave 91761 909-923-8455
Luis Lobos, prin.
NTMA Training Center of Southern CA Post-Sec.
1717 S Grove Ave 91761 909-947-9363
Ontario Christian HS 400/9-12
931 W Philadelphia St 91762 909-984-1756
Tim Hoekstra, prin. Fax 460-0176
Platt College Post-Sec.
3700 Inland Empire # 400 91764 909-941-9410
Richard's Beauty College Post-Sec.
200 N Euclid Ave 91762 909-988-7584
San Antonio Christian S 100/K-10
1722 E 8th St 91764 909-982-2301
Shelley Hulin, prin. Fax 982-0921
Westech College Post-Sec.
3491 Concours 91764 909-980-4474

Orange, Orange, Pop. 134,950
Orange USD 29,100/PK-12
PO Box 11022 92856 714-628-4040
Thomas Godley Ed.D., supt. Fax 628-4041
www.orangeusd.k12.ca.us
Career Education Center Vo/Tech
250 S Yorba St 92869 714-997-6066
Teryl Snyder, coord. Fax 997-6035
El Modena HS 2,200/9-12
3920 E Spring St 92869 714-997-6331
John Briquelet, prin. Fax 997-0705
Orange HS 2,400/9-12
525 N Shaffer St 92867 714-997-6211
S.K. Johnson, prin. Fax 633-6460
Portola MS 900/6-8
270 N Palm Dr 92868 714-997-6361
Debra Thompson, prin. Fax 978-0274
Yorba MS 800/7-8
935 N Cambridge St 92867 714-997-6161
Tara Saraye, prin. Fax 532-4759
Other Schools – See Anaheim, Villa Park

Chapman University Post-Sec.
1 University Dr 92866 714-997-6815
COBA Academy Post-Sec.
102 N Glassell St 92866 714-633-5950
Eldorado S for the Gifted Child 200/PK-12
4100 E Walnut Ave 92869 714-633-4774
Dr. Glory Ludwick, dir. Fax 744-3304
Lutheran HS of Orange County 1,200/9-12
2222 N Santiago Blvd 92867 714-998-5151
Gregg Pinick, dir. Fax 998-1371
St. Joseph Hospital Post-Sec.
1100 W Stewart Dr 92868 714-771-8111
Santiago Canyon College Post-Sec.
8045 E Chapman Ave 92869 714-564-4000
South Coast College Post-Sec.
2011 W Chapman Ave 92868 714-635-6464
University of California-Irvine Med. Ctr Post-Sec.
101 The City Dr S 92868 714-456-5678

Orange Cove, Fresno, Pop. 9,578
Kings Canyon JUSD
Supt. — See Reedley

Citrus MS 600/6-8
1400 Anchor Ave 93646 559-626-4194
Rodney Cisneros, prin. Fax 626-7255
Orange Cove HS 9-12
1700 Anchor Ave 93646 559-626-5900
Roger Trujillo, prin. Fax 626-7217

Orangevale, Sacramento, Pop. 26,800
San Juan USD
Supt. — See Carmichael
Carnegie MS 900/7-8
5820 Illinois Ave 95662 916-971-7853
Kent Kern, prin. Fax 971-7849
Casa Roble Fundamental HS 1,800/9-12
9151 Oak Ave 95662 916-971-5452
Vera Vaccaro, prin. Fax 971-5495
Pasteur MS 900/7-8
8935 Elm Ave 95662 916-971-7891
Kamaljit Pannu, prin. Fax 971-7893

Orcutt, Santa Barbara
Orcutt UNESD 4,700/K-8
PO Box 2310 93457 805-938-8900
Dr. Sharon McHolland, supt. Fax 938-8919
www.orcutt-schools.net
Orcutt JHS 600/7-8
608 Pinal Ave 93455 805-938-8700
Alan Majewski, prin. Fax 938-8749
Other Schools – See Santa Maria

Orinda, Contra Costa, Pop. 18,259
Acalanes UNHSD
Supt. — See Lafayette
Miramonte HS 1,400/9-12
750 Moraga Way 94563 925-280-3930
Raul Zamora, prin. Fax 280-3931

Orinda UNESD 2,400/K-8
8 Altarinda Rd 94563 925-254-4901
Frank Brunetti Ph.D., supt. Fax 254-5261
www.orinda.k12.ca.us
Orinda IS 900/6-8
80 Ivy Dr 94563 925-376-4402
Michael Randall, prin. Fax 631-7985

Orinda Academy 100/7-12
19 Altarinda Rd 94563 925-254-7553
Ronald Graydon, dir. Fax 254-4768

Orland, Glenn, Pop. 6,757
Orland JUSD 2,300/K-12
1320 6th St 95963 530-865-1200
Chris von Kleist, supt. Fax 865-1202
www.orlandusd.net
Orland HS 600/9-12
1320 6th St 95963 530-865-1210
Dan Raner Ed.D., prin. Fax 865-1215
Price IS 500/6-8
1320 6th St 95963 530-865-1225
Jeffrey Patch, prin. Fax 865-1227

North Valley Christian S 100/K-12
1148 E Walker St 95963 530-865-4924
Gordon Wiens, supt. Fax 865-4926

Orosi, Tulare, Pop. 5,486
Cutler-Orosi JUSD 4,000/K-12
12623 Avenue 416 93647 559-528-4763
Frank N. Murphy, supt. Fax 528-3132
www.cojusd.org
El Monte JHS 600/7-8
42111 Road 128 93647 559-528-3017
Roel Alvarado, prin. Fax 528-2822
Orosi HS 800/9-12
41815 Road 128 93647 559-528-4731
Gene Etheridge, prin. Fax 528-4930
Cutler-Orosi Adult S Adult
12623 Avenue 416 93647 559-528-6949
Melissa Calvero, prin. Fax 528-3562

Oroville, Butte, Pop. 13,468
Golden Feather UNESD 100/K-8
11679 Nelson Bar Rd 95965 530-533-3833
Lora Haston, supt. Fax 533-3887
www.bcoe.org/home/districts/golden.htm
Concow MS 50/4-8
11679 Nelson Bar Rd 95965 530-533-6033
Lora Haston, prin. Fax 533-3887

Oroville City ESD 3,000/K-8
2795 Yard St 95966 530-532-3000
Donald Remley, supt. Fax 532-3050
www.ocesd.org/
Central MS 800/7-8
2565 Mesa Ave 95966 530-532-3002
Richard Hilliard, prin. Fax 532-3042
Ishi Hills MS 6-8
2255 Foothill Blvd 95966 530-532-3078
Patricia Garrison, prin. Fax 532-3040

Oroville UNHSD 2,900/9-12
2211 Washington Ave 95966 530-538-2300
Oran Roberts, supt. Fax 538-2308
www.ouhsd.org
Las Plumas HS 1,500/9-12
2380 Las Plumas Ave 95966 530-538-2310
Sandy Dovell, prin. Fax 534-5974
Oroville HS 1,200/9-12
1535 Bridge St 95966 530-538-2320
Paul Broughton, prin. Fax 534-6203
Oroville Adult Education Adult
78 Table Mountain Blvd 95965 530-538-5350
Dwayne Robinson, prin. Fax 538-5396

Thermalito UNESD 1,400/K-8
400 Grand Ave 95965 530-538-2900
Gregory Kampf, supt. Fax 538-2909
www.thermalito.org/
Nelson Avenue MS 500/6-8
2255 6th St 95965 530-538-2940
Ken Atterbury, prin. Fax 538-2949

Butte College — Post-Sec.
3536 Butte Campus Dr 95965 — 530-895-2511
Feather River Adventist S — 100/K-10
27 Cox Ln 95965 — 530-533-8848
J. Marvin Whitney, prin. — Fax 533-6496
Northwest Lineman College — Post-Sec.
2009 Challenger Ave 95965 — 530-534-7260

Oxnard, Ventura, Pop. 183,628
Hueneme ESD
Supt. — See Port Hueneme
Blackstock JHS — 1,200/6-8
701 E Bard Rd 93033 — 805-488-3644
Adrian Palazuelos, prin. — Fax 488-1250
Green JHS — 1,100/6-8
3739 S C St 93033 — 805-986-8750
Joel Lovstedt, prin. — Fax 986-8756

Ocean View ESD — 2,600/PK-8
4200 Olds Rd 93033 — 805-488-4441
Dr. Nancy Carroll, supt. — Fax 986-6797
www.ovsd.k12.ca.us
Ocean View JHS — 800/6-8
4300 Olds Rd 93033 — 805-488-6421
Sharon Anderson, prin. — Fax 488-4132

Oxnard ESD — 16,500/K-8
1051 S A St 93030 — 805-487-3918
Rick Miller, supt. — Fax 483-7426
www.oxnardsd.org
Frank IS — 1,400/7-8
1051 S A St 93030 — 805-981-1733
Doug Livingston, prin. — Fax 981-1754
Fremont IS — 1,300/7-8
1051 S A St 93030 — 805-485-5900
Stefan Cvijanovich, prin. — Fax 485-2486
Haydock IS — 1,000/7-8
1051 S A St 93030 — 805-487-6797
Fax 487-7159

Oxnard UNHSD — 15,200/9-12
309 S K St 93030 — 805-385-2500
Judy Dunlap Ed.D., supt. — Fax 483-3069
www.ouhsd.k12.ca.us
Channel Islands HS — 2,700/9-12
1400 Raiders Way 93033 — 805-385-2756
Sylvia Jackson, prin. — Fax 385-2748
Hueneme HS — 2,300/9-12
500 W Bard Rd 93033 — 805-385-2651
John Saunders, prin. — Fax 385-2817
Oxnard HS — 2,900/9-12
3400 W Gonzales Rd, — 805-278-2906
James Edwards, prin. — Fax 278-2912
Pacifica HS — 2,500/9-11
600 E Gonzales Rd, — 805-278-5000
William E. Dabbs, prin. — Fax 278-7187
Rio Mesa HS — 2,100/9-12
545 Central Ave, — 805-278-5500
Rene Rickard, prin. — Fax 278-5525
Oxnard Adult S — Adult
1101 W 2nd St 93030 — 805-385-2584
Wayne Edmonds, prin. — Fax 385-2581
Other Schools – See Camarillo

Rio ESD — 4,000/K-8
3300 Cortez St, — 805-485-3111
Sherianne Cotterell, supt. — Fax 983-0221
www.rio.k12.ca.us
Rio Del Valle MS — 900/7-8
3300 Cortez St, — 805-485-3119
Maria Hernandez, prin. — Fax 981-7737

Academy Education Services — Post-Sec.
3151 W 5th St Ste E101 93030 — 805-984-2511
ITT Technical Institute — Post-Sec.
2051 Solar Dr Ste 150, — 805-988-0143
Modern Beauty Academy — Post-Sec.
699 S C St 93030 — 805-483-4994
Morgan Creek Christian Academy — 100/K-12
723 S D St 93030 — 805-486-4656
Ginger Paschal, admin. — Fax 486-5256
Oxnard College — Post-Sec.
4000 S Rose Ave 93033 — 805-986-5800
St. John's Regional Medical Center — Post-Sec.
1600 N Rose Ave 93030 — 805-988-2500
Santa Clara HS — 300/9-12
2121 Saviers Rd 93033 — 805-483-9502
S. O'Reilly-Hill, prin. — Fax 483-1588

Pacifica, San Mateo, Pop. 37,092
Jefferson UNHSD
Supt. — See Daly City
Oceana HS — 700/9-12
401 Paloma Ave 94044 — 650-550-7300
Samuel Butscher, prin. — Fax 550-7310
Terra Nova HS — 1,400/9-12
1450 Terra Nova Blvd 94044 — 650-550-7600
Sherry Segalas, prin. — Fax 550-7690

Pacifica SD — 3,000/K-8
375 Reina Del Mar Ave 94044 — 650-738-6600
James Lianides, supt. — Fax 557-9672
www.pacificasd.org/
Lacy MS — 600/6-8
1427 Palmetto Ave 94044 — 650-738-6665
Kitty Mindel, prin. — Fax 738-6669

Alma Heights Christian Academy — 300/K-12
1295 Seville Dr 94044 — 650-359-0555
David Welling, dir. — Fax 359-5020

Pacific Grove, Monterey, Pop. 15,091
Pacific Grove USD — 1,800/K-12
555 Sinex Ave 93950 — 831-646-6520
Patrick Perry, supt. — Fax 646-6500
pgusd.org
Pacific Grove HS — 600/9-12
615 Sunset Dr 93950 — 831-646-6590
Stan Dodd, prin. — Fax 646-6660
Pacific Grove MS — 500/6-8
835 Forest Ave 93950 — 831-646-6568
Matt Bell, prin. — Fax 646-6652
Pacific Grove Adult Education — Adult
1025 Lighthouse Ave 93950 — 831-646-6580
Maria Nunez, prin. — Fax 646-6578

Calvary Chapel HS — 100/9-12
1002 David Ave 93950 — 831-656-9434
Skip Joannes, prin. — Fax 656-9670
Stanford University — Post-Sec.
Hopkins Marine Station 93950 — 831-373-0464

Pacoima, See Los Angeles
Los Angeles USD
Supt. — See Los Angeles
MacLay MS — 1,300/6-8
12540 Pierce St 91331 — 818-686-3800
Karen O'Riley, prin. — Fax 834-1012
Pacoima MS — 2,200/6-8
9919 Laurel Canyon Blvd 91331 — 818-686-4200
Paul Rosario, prin. — Fax 834-2021

Palermo, Butte, Pop. 5,260
Palermo UNESD — 1,000/K-8
7390 Bulldog Way 95968 — 530-533-4842
Sam Chimento, supt. — Fax 532-1047
www.palermoschools.org
Palermo MS — 400/6-8
7350 Bulldog Way 95968 — 530-533-4708
Kathleen Coleman, prin. — Fax 532-7801

Palmdale, Los Angeles, Pop. 134,570
Antelope Valley UNHSD
Supt. — See Lancaster
Highland HS — 3,600/9-12
39055 25th St W 93551 — 661-538-0304
Stacy Bryant, prin. — Fax 538-0405
Knight HS — 1,700/9-12
37423 70th St E 93552 — 661-533-9000
Brett Neal, prin. — Fax 533-0111
Palmdale HS — 3,500/9-12
2137 E Avenue R 93550 — 661-273-3181
Eric Riegert, prin. — Fax 273-1093

Palmdale ESD — 22,600/K-8
39139 10th St E 93550 — 661-947-7191
Roger Gallizzi, supt. — Fax 273-5137
www.psd.k12.ca.us
Cactus MS — 1,200/6-8
38060 20th St E 93550 — 661-273-0847
Kate Laferriere, prin. — Fax 273-5514
Desert Willow IS — 500/6-8
36555 Sunny Ln 93550 — 661-285-5866
Thomas Pitts, prin. — Fax 456-1145
Juniper IS — 1,000/7-8
39066 Palm Tree Way 93551 — 661-947-0181
David Ellms, prin. — Fax 456-1576
Mesa IS — 900/6-8
3243 E Avenue R8 93550 — 661-947-0188
Ruth James, prin. — Fax 456-1338
Shadow Hills IS — 900/7-8
37315 60th St E 93552 — 661-533-7400
Suresh Bajnath, prin. — Fax 533-7445

Regional Occupational Center & Program
Supt. — None
Antelope Valley ROP — Vo/Tech
1156 E Avenue S 93550 — 661-575-1025
June Battey, dir. — Fax 575-1037

Westside UNESD
Supt. — See Lancaster
Hillview MS — 900/7-8
40525 Peonza Ln 93551 — 661-722-9993
Joe Andrews, prin. — Fax 722-9483

Wilsona ESD — 2,100/K-8
18050 E Avenue O 93591 — 661-264-1111
Ned McNabb, supt. — Fax 261-3259
Other Schools – See Lancaster

Cornerstone Christian Academy — 100/K-12
17134 E Avenue O 93591 — 661-264-2955
Betty Jo Alford, admin. — Fax 264-2955
Covenant Christian S — 100/1-12
2013 Clearwater Ave 93551 — 661-274-8285
Susan Mitchell, admin.

Palm Desert, Riverside, Pop. 47,058
Desert Sands USD
Supt. — See La Quinta
Palm Desert HS — 2,000/9-12
43570 Phyllis Jackson Ln 92260 — 760-862-4300
Patrick Walsh, prin. — Fax 862-4390
Palm Desert MS — 1,400/6-8
74200 Rutledge Way 92260 — 760-862-4320
Sallie Fraser, prin. — Fax 862-4327

College of the Desert — Post-Sec.
43500 Monterey Ave 92260 — 760-346-8041
Oasis Preparatory S — 50/5-12
39605 Entreprenuer Ln 92211 — 760-772-8255
Susan Roberts, prin. — Fax 772-7446
Xavier College Preparatory S — 9-12
44875 Deep Canyon Rd 92260 — 760-601-3900
Chris Alling, prin. — Fax 346-3871

Palm Springs, Riverside, Pop. 47,082
Palm Springs USD — 23,200/PK-12
980 E Tahquitz Canyon Way 92262 — 760-416-6000
Lorri McCune Ed.D., supt. — Fax 416-6015
www.psusd.k12.ca.us
Cree MS — 1,200/6-8
1011 E Vista Chino 92262 — 760-416-8283
Clarence Nolan, prin. — Fax 416-8287
Palm Springs HS — 1,900/9-12
2401 E Baristo Rd 92262 — 760-778-0400
Ricky Wright, prin. — Fax 778-0481
Palm Springs Adult Education — Adult
333 S Farrell Dr 92262 — 760-416-8450
Virginia Eberhard, prin. — Fax 416-8454
Other Schools – See Cathedral City, Desert Hot Springs

Desert Chapel Christian S — 400/K-12
630 S Sunrise Way 92264 — 760-327-2772
Fred Donaldson, admin. — Fax 322-3674

Palo Alto, Santa Clara, Pop. 56,982
Palo Alto USD — 9,800/K-12
25 Churchill Ave 94306 — 650-329-3737
Mary Frances Callan Ph.D., supt. — Fax 321-3810
www.pausd.org
Gunn HS — 1,700/9-12
780 Arastradero Rd 94306 — 650-354-8200
Noreen Likins, prin. — Fax 493-7801
Jordan MS — 900/6-8
750 N California Ave 94303 — 650-494-8120
Suzanne Barbarasch, prin. — Fax 858-1310
Palo Alto HS — 1,700/9-12
50 Embarcadero Rd 94301 — 650-329-3701
Scott Laurence, prin. — Fax 329-3753
Stanford MS — 800/6-8
480 E Meadow Dr 94306 — 650-856-5188
Don Cox, prin. — Fax 856-3248
Terman MS — 6-8
655 Arastradero Rd 94306 — 650-856-9810
Carmen Giedt, prin. — Fax 856-9878

Castilleja S — 400/6-12
1310 Bryant St 94301 — 650-328-3160
Joan Lonergan, prin. — Fax 326-8036
Eastside College Preparatory S — 200/6-12
1041 Myrtle St 94303 — 650-688-0850
Chris Bischof, prin.
Institute of Transpersonal Psychology — Post-Sec.
1069 E Meadow Cir 94303 — 650-493-4430
Pacific Graduate School of Psychology — Post-Sec.
935 E Meadow Dr 94303 — 650-843-3500

Palo Cedro, Shasta
Junction ESD — 400/K-8
9087 Deschutes Rd 96073 — 530-547-5494
Mary Sakuma, supt. — Fax 547-4829
www.shastalink.k12.ca.us/junction/
Junction IS — 200/6-8
9019 Deschutes Rd 96073 — 530-547-5494
Mary Sakuma, prin. — Fax 547-4829

Shasta UNHSD
Supt. — See Redding
Foothill HS — 1,700/9-12
9733 Deschutes Rd 96073 — 530-547-1700
Kyle Turner, prin. — Fax 245-2700

Bishop Quinn HS — 200/9-12
21893 Old 44 Dr 96073 — 530-547-2900
Karl Hanf, prin. — Fax 547-5349
St. Francis MS — 100/8-8
21945 Old 44 Dr 96073 — 530-547-2900
Karl Hanf, prin. — Fax 547-5349

Palos Verdes Estates, Los Angeles, Pop. 13,812
Palos Verdes Peninsula USD — 11,800/K-12
3801 Via La Selva 90274 — 310-378-9966
Walker Williams, supt. — Fax 378-0732
www.pvpusd.k12.ca.us
Palos Verdes HS — 1,300/9-12
600 Cloyden Rd 90274 — 310-378-8471
Christopher Bowles, prin. — Fax 378-0311
Palos Verdes IS — 1,000/6-8
2161 Via Olivera 90274 — 310-544-4816
Diawn Stanley, prin. — Fax 265-5944
Other Schools – See Rancho Palos Verdes, Rolling Hills

Rolling Hills Prep S — 300/6-12
300 Paseo Del Mar 90274 — 310-791-1101
Peter McCormack, prin. — Fax 373-4931

Palos Verdes Peninsula, See Rolling Hills Estates

Chadwick S — 800/K-12
26800 Academy Dr 90274 — 310-377-1543
Frederick Hill, hdmstr. — Fax 377-0380

Panorama City, See Los Angeles
Los Angeles USD
Supt. — See Los Angeles
Panorama HS — 9-12
8015 Van Nuys Blvd 91402 — 818-909-4500
Susan Lepisto, prin. — Fax 786-6991

Maric College — Post-Sec.
14355 Roscoe Blvd 91402 — 818-672-8907
St. Genevieve HS — 400/9-12
13967 Roscoe Blvd 91402 — 818-894-6417
Daniel Horn, prin. — Fax 892-9853
San Fernando Beauty Academy — Post-Sec.
8700 Van Nuys Blvd 91402 — 818-894-9550

Paradise, Butte, Pop. 26,517
Paradise USD — 4,800/K-12
6696 Clark Rd 95969 — 530-872-6400
Stephen Jennings, supt. — Fax 872-6409
www.paradise.k12.ca.us
Paradise HS — 1,700/9-12
5911 Maxwell Dr 95969 — 530-872-6425
Mike Lerch, prin. — Fax 872-6427
Paradise IS — 500/6-8
5657 Recreation Dr 95969 — 530-872-6465
Michael Ervin, prin. — Fax 876-1852
Other Schools – See Magalia

Lighthouse Christian S — 50/K-12
PO Box 399 95967 — 530-872-9029
Wendy Lightbody, prin. — Fax 877-2246
Paradise Adventist Academy — 200/K-12
PO Box 2169 95967 — 530-877-6540
Ken Preston, prin. — Fax 877-0870

Paramount, Los Angeles, Pop. 56,540
Paramount USD — 15,000/K-12
15110 California Ave 90723 — 562-602-6000
David Verdugo Ed.D., supt. — Fax 602-8111
www.paramount.k12.ca.us

Jackson MS 800/4-8
7220 Jackson St 90723 562-602-8020
Lupe Hernandez, prin. Fax 602-8021
Paramount HS 2,800/10-12
14429 Downey Ave 90723 562-602-6064
Jim Monico, prin. Fax 602-6099
Paramount HS - West Campus 9-9
14708 Paramount Blvd 90723 562-602-8073
Morrie Kosareff, prin. Fax 602-8075
Paramount Adult Education Adult
14507 Paramount Blvd 90723 562-602-8080
Frank Peck, prin. Fax 602-8081

Paramount School of Beauty Post-Sec.
8527 Alondra Blvd Ste 129 90723 714-998-7461

Parlier, Fresno, Pop. 13,025
Parlier USD 3,400/K-12
900 S Newmark Ave 93648 559-646-2731
Rick Rodriguez, supt. Fax 888-0210
www.parlierunified.org/
Parlier HS 800/9-12
601 3rd St 93648 559-646-3573
Elida Padron, prin. Fax 646-2610
Parlier JHS 600/7-8
1200 E Parlier Ave 93648 559-646-1660
Martin Mares, prin. Fax 646-1633

Pasadena, Los Angeles, Pop. 143,731
Pasadena USD 20,000/K-12
351 S Hudson Ave 91101 626-795-6981
Edwin Diaz, supt. Fax 795-5309
www.pusd.us/
Blair HS 1,100/7-12
1201 S Marengo Ave 91106 626-441-2201
Rich Boccia, prin. Fax 441-6148
Marshall Fundamental JSHS 1,800/6-12
990 N Allen Ave 91104 626-798-0713
Steven Miller, prin. Fax 798-0643
Muir HS 1,300/9-12
1905 Lincoln Ave 91103 626-798-7881
Gary Roggenstein, prin. Fax 791-3499
Pasadena HS 2,800/9-12
2925 E Sierra Madre Blvd 91107 626-798-8901
Dr. Derick Evans, prin. Fax 798-1875
Roosevelt S 300/K-12
315 N Pasadena Ave 91103 626-795-9501
Dr. Kathleen Bautista, prin. Fax 795-5180
Washington MS 500/6-8
1505 N Marengo Ave 91103 626-798-6708
Karrone Meeks-Clark, prin. Fax 798-2844
Wilson MS 1,300/6-8
300 Madre St 91107 626-449-7390
Ruth Essln, prin. Fax 584-9895
Other Schools – See Altadena

Art Center College of Design Post-Sec.
1700 Lida St 91103 626-396-2000
California Institute of Technology Post-Sec.
1200 E California Blvd 91125 626-395-6811
California School of Culinary Arts Post-Sec.
521 E Green St 91101 626-403-8490
Emmanuel Bible College Post-Sec.
1605 E Elizabeth St 91104 626-791-2575
Frostig Center 100/1-12
971 N Altadena Dr 91107 626-791-1255
Tobey Shaw, prin.
Fuller Theological Seminary Post-Sec.
135 N Oakland Ave 91182 626-584-5200
Huntington Memorial Hospital Post-Sec.
100 W California Blvd 91105 626-397-5000
Integrated Digital Technologies Post-Sec.
2555 E Colorado Blvd # 200 91107 626-585-6300
La Salle HS 700/9-12
3880 E Sierra Madre Blvd 91107 626-351-8951
Patrick Bonacci, prin. Fax 351-0275
Maranatha HS 600/9-12
169 S Saint John Ave 91105 626-817-4000
Charles E. Crane, prin. Fax 817-4040
Mayfield HS 300/9-12
500 Bellefontaine St 91105 626-799-9121
Rita McBride, prin. Fax 799-8576
Northwest College Medical Dental Assts. Post-Sec.
530 E Union St 91101 626-796-5815
Pacific Oaks College Post-Sec.
5 Westmoreland Pl 91103 626-397-1300
Pasadena City College Post-Sec.
1570 E Colorado Blvd 91106 626-585-7123
Polytechnic S 900/K-12
1030 E California Blvd 91106 626-792-2147
Deborah E. Reed, hdmstr. Fax 796-2249
Westridge S 500/4-12
324 Madeline Dr 91105 626-799-1153
Fran Norris Scoble, hdmstr. Fax 799-9236

Patterson, Stanislaus, Pop. 15,500
Patterson JUSD 4,400/K-12
PO Box 547 95363 209-892-3700
Patrick Sweeney, supt. Fax 892-5803
www.stan-co.k12.ca.us/Patterson/welcome.htm
Creekside MS 1,100/6-8
535 Peregrine Dr 95363 209-892-3600
Shawn Posey, prin. Fax 892-7101
Patterson HS 1,300/9-12
201 N 9th St 95363 209-892-7453
Miguel Guerrero, prin. Fax 892-5935

Patton, San Bernardino, Pop. 1,000

Patton State Hospital Post-Sec.
3102 E Highland Ave 92369 909-425-7297

Pearblossom, Los Angeles
Keppel UNESD 3,000/K-8
PO Box 186 93553 661-944-2155
Dr. Linda Wagner, supt. Fax 944-2933
www.keppel.k12.ca.us
Other Schools – See Littlerock

Pebble Beach, Monterey, Pop. 3,600

Stevenson Upper S 500/9-12
3152 Forest Lake Rd 93953 831-625-8300
Joseph Wandke, pres. Fax 625-5208

Penn Valley, Nevada, Pop. 1,242
Pleasant Valley ESD 700/K-8
14806 Pleasant Valley Rd 95946 530-432-7311
James Voss, supt. Fax 432-7314
www.pvsdnc.k12.ca.us/
Pleasant Valley S 400/4-8
14685 Pleasant Valley Rd 95946 530-432-7333
Clint Johnson, prin. Fax 432-7338

Perris, Riverside, Pop. 45,671
Perris UNHSD 7,600/7-12
155 E 4th St 92570 951-943-6369
Dennis Murray, supt. Fax 940-5378
www.puhsd.org/
Perris HS 2,700/9-12
175 E Nuevo Rd 92571 951-657-2171
Penelope Graham, prin. Fax 940-5717
Pinacate MS 1,300/7-8
1990 S A St 92570 951-943-6441
Dennis Bixler, prin. Fax 940-5344
Other Schools – See Menifee, Sun City

Val Verde USD 15,300/PK-12
975 Morgan St 92571 951-940-6100
C. Fred Workman Ed.D., supt. Fax 940-6121
www.valverde.edu
Citrus Hill HS 9-12
18150 Wood Rd 92570 951-490-0400
John Simonson, prin. Fax 490-0405
Lakeside MS 1,100/6-8
27720 Walnut St 92571 951-443-2440
Robert Block, prin. Fax 443-2445
Rivera MS 1,100/6-8
21675 Martin St 92570 951-940-8570
Ernesto Lizarraga, prin. Fax 940-6133
Other Schools – See Moreno Valley

Pescadero, San Mateo
La Honda-Pescadero USD 400/K-12
PO Box 189 94060 650-879-0286
Timothy Beard, supt. Fax 879-0816
www.lhpusd.net
Pescadero HS 100/9-12
PO Box 730 94060 650-879-0274
Amy Wooliever, prin. Fax 879-0589

Petaluma, Sonoma, Pop. 54,846
Petaluma SD 7,500/K-12
200 Douglas St 94952 707-778-4604
Greta Viguie, supt. Fax 778-4736
www.petalumacityschools.org
Casa Grande HS 1,800/9-12
333 Casa Grande Rd 94954 707-778-4677
Ron Everett, prin. Fax 778-4687
Kenilworth JHS 1,000/7-8
800 Riesling Rd 94954 707-778-4710
Toni Beal, prin. Fax 766-8231
Petaluma HS 1,600/9-12
201 Fair St 94952 707-778-4651
Fax 778-4767
Petaluma JHS 800/7-8
700 Bantam Way 94952 707-778-4724
John Lehmann, prin. Fax 778-4600
Petaluma Adult S Adult
200 Douglas St 94952 707-778-4634
Carol Waxman, prin. Fax 778-4785

St. Vincent de Paul HS 400/9-12
PO Box 517 94953 707-763-1032
John Walker, prin. Fax 763-9448
Santa Rosa Junior College Post-Sec.
680 Sonoma Mountain Pkwy 94954 707-778-2415
Sonoma College Post-Sec.
1304 Southpoint Blvd # 280 94954 707-283-0800

Petrolia, Humboldt
Mattole USD
Supt. — See Honeydew
Mattole Triple Junction HS 50/9-12
PO Box 211 95558 707-629-3250
Gail Dube, prin. Fax 629-3551

Phelan, San Bernardino
Snowline JUSD 7,600/K-12
PO Box 296000 92329 760-868-5817
Arthur Golden, supt. Fax 868-5309
snowline.k12.ca.us
Pinon Mesa MS 1,000/6-8
PO Box 296000 92329 760-868-3126
Michael Murphy, prin. Fax 868-3033
Quail Valley MS 1,000/6-8
PO Box 296000 92329 760-949-4888
Dennis Zimmerman, prin. Fax 949-3663
Serrano HS 2,500/9-12
PO Box 296000 92329 760-868-3222
Sharon Schlegel, prin. Fax 868-3803

Pico Rivera, Los Angeles, Pop. 64,679
El Rancho USD 12,000/PK-12
9333 Loch Lomond Dr 90660 562-942-1500
Norbert Genis, supt. Fax 949-2821
www.erusd.k12.ca.us
Burke MS 800/6-8
8101 Orange Ave 90660 562-801-5059
Mark Matthews, prin. Fax 801-5067
El Rancho HS 3,300/9-12
6501 Passons Blvd 90660 562-801-5355
San Genis, prin. Fax 801-5293
North Park MS 1,100/6-8
4450 Durfee Ave 90660 562-801-5137
John Lopez, prin. Fax 801-5143
Rivera MS 1,000/6-8
7200 Citronell Ave 90660 562-801-5088
Andrew Alvidrez, prin. Fax 801-9158
El Rancho Adult Education Adult
9515 Haney St 90660 562-801-5009
Dwight Jones, prin. Fax 948-2041

Armenian Mesrobian S 300/PK-12
8420 Beverly Rd 90660 323-723-3181
Hilda Saliba, prin.

Piedmont, Alameda, Pop. 10,559
Piedmont City USD 2,600/K-12
760 Magnolia Ave 94611 510-594-2600
Constance Hubbard, supt. Fax 654-7374
www.piedmont.k12.ca.us
Piedmont HS 900/9-12
800 Magnolia Ave 94611 510-594-2626
Randall Booker, prin. Fax 450-0425
Piedmont MS 600/6-8
740 Magnolia Ave 94611 510-594-2660
Jeanne Donovan, prin. Fax 595-3523
Piedmont Adult S Adult
800 Magnolia Ave 94611 510-594-2655
Karen Gnusti, dir. Fax 595-8173

Pine Valley, San Diego, Pop. 1,297
Mountain Empire USD 1,700/K-12
3291 Buckman Springs Rd 91962 619-473-9022
Patrick Judd, supt. Fax 473-9728
www.meusd.net
Mountain Empire HS 500/9-12
3305 Buckman Springs Rd 91962 619-473-8601
Diane Young, prin. Fax 473-8038
Mountain Empire JHS 300/7-8
3305 Buckman Springs Rd 91962 619-473-8601
Steve Gordon, prin. Fax 473-8038

Pinole, Contra Costa, Pop. 19,061
West Contra Costa USD
Supt. — See Richmond
Pinole JHS 800/7-8
1575 Mann Dr 94564 510-724-4042
Harriet Martin, prin. Fax 724-9583
Pinole Valley HS 1,800/9-12
2900 Pinole Valley Rd 94564 510-758-4664
Sue Kahn, prin. Fax 758-6054

Pismo Beach, San Luis Obispo, Pop. 8,419
Lucia Mar USD
Supt. — See Arroyo Grande
Judkins MS 600/7-8
680 Wadsworth Ave 93449 805-474-3600
Bryant Smith, prin. Fax 473-4376

Pittsburg, Contra Costa, Pop. 62,547
Mount Diablo USD
Supt. — See Concord
Riverview MS 900/6-8
205 Pacifica Ave 94565 925-458-3216
Denise Rugani, prin. Fax 458-0875

Pittsburg USD 9,500/PK-12
2000 Railroad Ave 94565 925-473-4000
Reed McLaughlin, supt. Fax 473-4274
www.pittsburg.k12.ca.us
Central JHS 1,100/6-8
1201 Stoneman Ave 94565 925-473-4450
Eric Peyko, prin. Fax 473-4454
Hillview JHS 1,000/6-8
333 Yosemite Dr 94565 925-473-4400
Todd Whitmire, prin. Fax 473-4406
Pittsburg HS 2,400/9-12
250 School St 94565 925-473-4100
Tim Galli, prin. Fax 473-4183
Pittsburg Adult Education Center Adult
1151 Stoneman Ave 94565 925-473-4460
Bob Beck, prin. Fax 473-4470

Christian Center S 300/PK-12
1210 Stoneman Ave 94565 925-439-2552
Ron Matthews, admin. Fax 439-2555
Los Medanos College Post-Sec.
2700 E Leland Rd 94565 925-439-2181

Placentia, Orange, Pop. 49,795
Placentia-Yorba Linda USD 26,000/K-12
1301 E Orangethorpe Ave 92870 714-996-2550
Dennis Smith Ed.D., supt. Fax 524-3034
www.pylusd.org/
El Dorado HS 2,300/9-12
1651 Valencia Ave 92870 714-993-5350
Karen Wilkins, prin. Fax 524-2458
Kraemer MS 1,600/6-8
645 N Angelina Dr 92870 714-996-1551
Minerva Gandara, prin. Fax 996-8407
Tuffree MS 700/7-8
2151 N Kraemer Blvd 92870 714-996-1881
Rosie Baldwin-Shirey, prin. Fax 993-6359
Valencia HS 2,400/9-12
500 N Bradford Ave 92870 714-996-4970
Jim Bell, prin. Fax 996-3159
Other Schools – See Anaheim, Yorba Linda

Placerville, El Dorado, Pop. 10,184
El Dorado UNHSD 6,400/9-12
4675 Missouri Flat Rd 95667 530-622-5081
Sherry Smith, supt. Fax 622-5087
www.eduhsd.k12.ca.us
El Dorado HS 1,300/9-12
561 Canal St 95667 530-622-3634
Jerry Smith, prin. Fax 622-1802
Other Schools – See Diamond Springs, El Dorado, El Dorado Hills, Shingle Springs

Gold Oak UNESD 700/K-8
3171 Pleasant Valley Rd 95667 530-626-3150
Richard Williams, supt. Fax 626-3145
www.gousd.k12.ca.us
Pleasant Valley MS 300/6-8
4120 Pleasant Valley Rd 95667 530-644-9620
Joe Rancatore, prin. Fax 644-9622

Gold Trail UNESD 600/K-8
1575 Old Ranch Rd 95667 530-626-3194
Joe Murchison, supt. Fax 626-3199
www.gtusd.k12.ca.us/
Gold Trail S 400/4-8
889 Cold Springs Rd 95667 530-626-2595
Stephany Rewick, prin. Fax 626-3289

Mother Lode UNESD 1,600/K-8
3783 Forni Rd 95667 530-622-6464
Shanda G. Hahn, supt. Fax 622-6163
www.mlusd.net
Green MS 500/6-8
3781 Forni Rd 95667 530-622-4668
Tim Smith, prin. Fax 622-4680

Placerville UNESD 1,300/K-8
1032 Thompson Way 95667 530-622-7216
John Nordquist, supt. Fax 622-0336
www.pusd.k12.ca.us/
Markham MS 400/6-8
2800 Moulton Dr 95667 530-622-0403
Marc Nigel, prin. Fax 622-5584

Consumnes River College-Eldorado Center Post-Sec.
6699 Campus Dr 95667 530-642-5621
El Dorado Adventist S 200/K-12
1900 Broadway 95667 530-622-3560
Larry Ballew, prin. Fax 622-2604

Planada, Merced, Pop. 3,531
Planada ESD 800/K-8
PO Box 236 95365 209-382-0756
Steve Gomes, supt. Fax 382-1750
www.planada.k12.ca.us/
Chavez MS 300/6-8
PO Box 236 95365 209-382-0768
Ildefonso Nava, prin. Fax 382-0775

Playa Del Rey, See Los Angeles

St. Bernard HS 600/9-12
9100 Falmouth Ave 90293 310-823-4651
Rick Kruska, prin. Fax 827-3365

Pleasant Hill, Contra Costa, Pop. 33,153
Mount Diablo USD
Supt. — See Concord
College Park HS 2,000/9-12
201 Viking Dr 94523 925-682-7670
Barbara Oaks, prin. Fax 676-7892
Pleasant Hill MS 700/6-8
1 Santa Barbara Rd 94523 925-256-0791
Jonathan Roslin, prin. Fax 937-6271
Sequoia MS 900/6-8
265 Boyd Rd 94523 925-934-8174
Hellena Postrik, prin. Fax 946-9063
Valley View MS 800/6-8
181 Viking Dr 94523 925-686-6136
Nadine Rosenzweig, prin. Fax 825-8908

Regional Occupational Center & Program
Supt. — None
Contra Costa County ROP Vo/Tech
77 Santa Barbara Rd 94523 925-942-3368
Marie McClaskey, dir. Fax 934-1057

Diablo Valley College Post-Sec.
321 Golf Club Rd 94523 925-685-1230
John F. Kennedy University Post-Sec.
100 Ellinwood Way 94523 800-696-5358
Pleasant Hill Adventist Academy 300/K-12
796 Grayson Rd 94523 925-934-9261
Alexis Emmerson, prin. Fax 934-5871
Western Career College Post-Sec.
380 Civic Dr Ste 300 94523 925-609-6650

Pleasanton, Alameda, Pop. 65,950
Pleasanton USD 14,200/K-12
4665 Bernal Ave 94566 925-462-5500
John M. Casey, supt. Fax 426-8216
www.pleasanton.k12.ca.us
Amador Valley HS 2,300/9-12
1155 Santa Rita Rd 94566 925-461-6100
Bill Coupe, prin. Fax 461-6133
Foothill HS 2,200/9-12
4375 Foothill Rd 94588 925-461-6650
John Dwyer, prin. Fax 461-6633
Hart MS 1,200/6-8
4433 Willow Rd 94588 925-426-3102
Steve Maher, prin. Fax 460-0799
Harvest Park MS 1,100/6-8
4900 Valley Ave 94566 925-426-4444
Jim Hansen, prin. Fax 426-9613
Pleasanton MS 1,200/6-8
5001 Case Ave 94566 925-426-4390
John Whitney, prin. Fax 426-1382
Amador Valley Adult Ed. & Comm. Services Adult
215 Abbie St 94566 925-461-6150
Glen Sparks, prin. Fax 846-5317

Point Arena, Mendocino, Pop. 475
Point Arena JUNHSD 200/9-12
PO Box 87 95468 707-882-2803
Mark Iacuaniello, supt. Fax 882-2848
Point Arena HS 200/9-12
PO Box 7 95468 707-882-2134
Warren Galletti, prin. Fax 882-3453

Pollock Pines, El Dorado, Pop. 4,291
Pollock Pines ESD 800/K-8
6181A Pine St 95726 530-644-5416
Susan Spencer, supt. Fax 644-5483
www.ppsd.k12.ca.us
Sierra Ridge MS 400/5-8
2700 Amber Trl 95726 530-644-2031
Jeanne Harper, prin. Fax 644-0198

Pomona, Los Angeles, Pop. 153,787
Pomona USD 33,300/K-12
PO Box 2900 91769 909-397-4800
Dr. Thelma Melendez, supt. Fax 397-4881
www.pusd.org
Diamond Ranch HS 1,800/9-12
100 Diamond Ranch Rd 91766 909-397-4715
Monica Principe, prin. Fax 591-9374
Emerson MS 1,000/6-8
635 Lincoln Ave 91767 909-397-4516
Jorge Amancio, prin. Fax 397-5280
Fremont MS 900/7-8
725 W Franklin Ave 91766 909-397-4521
Susan M. Williams, prin. Fax 620-6229
Ganesha HS 1,600/9-12
1151 Fairplex Dr 91768 909-397-4400
Michael Hernandez, prin. Fax 629-4069
Garey HS 2,100/9-12
321 W Lexington Ave 91766 909-397-4451
Curtis Donaldson, prin. Fax 620-1575
Marshall MS 1,100/6-8
1921 Arroyo Ave 91768 909-397-4532
Teresa Mora, prin. Fax 629-8275
Palomares MS 700/6-8
2211 N Orange Grove Ave 91767 909-397-4539
Neville Brown, prin. Fax 625-0337
Pomona HS 1,700/9-12
475 Bangor St 91767 909-397-4498
Marilyn Ghirelli, prin. Fax 629-1410
Simons MS 1,100/6-8
900 E Franklin Ave 91766 909-397-4544
Juaniqua Brimm, prin. Fax 623-4691
Village Academy Vo/Tech
1444 E Holt Ave 91767 909-397-4900
Carol A. Aseltine, prin. Fax 865-9250
Pomona Adult & Career Education Adult
1515 W Mission Blvd Ste 5 91766 909-469-2333
Barbara Thompson, prin. Fax 623-3841
Other Schools – See Diamond Bar

Regional Occupational Center & Program
Supt. — None
San Antonio ROP Vo/Tech
1425 E Holt Ave Ste 101 91767 909-469-2304
Jose Castro, dir. Fax 620-5770

California State Polytechnic University Post-Sec.
3801 W Temple Ave 91768 909-869-2000
CEI Post-Sec.
980 Corporate Center Dr 91768 909-865-9008
City of Knowledge S 200/K-12
3285 N Garey Ave 91767 909-382-0251
Dr. Haleema Shaikley, prin.
DeVry University Post-Sec.
901 Corporate Center Dr 91768 909-622-8866
Northwest College Medical Dental Assts. Post-Sec.
134 W Holt Ave 91768 909-623-1552
Pomona Catholic HS 300/9-12
533 W Holt Ave 91768 909-623-5297
Fax 620-6057
Western University of Health Sciences Post-Sec.
309 E 2nd St 91766 909-623-6116

Porterville, Tulare, Pop. 44,959
Burton ESD 3,100/K-8
264 N Westwood St 93257 559-781-8020
Donald Brown, supt. Fax 781-1403
burton.k12.ca.us
Burton MS 700/7-8
1155 N Elderwood St 93257 559-781-2671
David Huchingson, prin. Fax 788-6424

Porterville USD 13,200/K-12
600 W Grand Ave 93257 559-793-2455
John Snavely Ed.D., supt. Fax 793-1088
www.portervilleschools.org
Bartlett MS 700/7-8
355 N G St 93257 559-782-7100
Lisa Whitworth, prin. Fax 784-3432
Granite Hills HS 1,500/9-12
1701 E Putnam Ave 93257 559-782-7075
Veryl Ann Duncan, prin. Fax 789-9357
Monache HS 2,000/9-12
960 N Newcomb St 93257 559-782-7150
Shirley Houser, prin. Fax 781-3377
Pioneer MS 800/7-8
255 E College Ave 93257 559-782-7200
Isaac Nunez, prin. Fax 784-3507
Porterville HS 1,900/9-12
465 W Olive Ave 93257 559-782-7210
Steve Graybehl, prin. Fax 782-7215
Sequoia MS 7-8
1450 W Castle Ave 93257 559-793-7627
Joe Santos, prin.
Porterville Adult S Adult
900 Pioneer Ave 93257 559-782-7030
Bob Perez, dir. Fax 781-4943
Other Schools – See Strathmore

Landmark Christian Academy 50/K-12
2380 W Olive Ave 93257 559-781-9500
Bertha Hearne, prin. Fax 784-2861
Porterville College Post-Sec.
100 E College Ave 93257 559-791-2200
Porterville Development Center Post-Sec.
PO Box 2000 93258 559-782-2753

Port Hueneme, Ventura, Pop. 22,032
Hueneme ESD 8,100/K-8
205 N Ventura Rd 93041 805-488-3588
Dr. Jerry Dannenberg, supt. Fax 986-8755
www.huensd.k12.ca.us
Other Schools – See Oxnard

Portola, Plumas, Pop. 2,242
Plumas USD
Supt. — See Quincy
Portola JSHS 500/6-12
155 6th Ave 96122 530-832-4284
Kristy Warren, prin. Fax 832-5582

Portola Valley, San Mateo, Pop. 4,417
Portola Valley ESD 700/K-8
4575 Alpine Rd 94028 650-851-1777
Anne Campbell, supt. Fax 851-3700
www.pvsd.net
Corte Madera MS 400/4-8
4575 Alpine Rd 94028 650-851-1777
Joel Willen, prin. Fax 529-8553

Woodside Priory S 100/6-8
302 Portola Rd 94028 650-851-8221
Dora Arrendondo-Marron, prin. Fax 851-2839
Woodside Priory S 200/9-12
302 Portola Rd 94028 650-851-8221
Tim Molak, prin. Fax 851-2839

Potter Valley, Mendocino
Potter Valley Community USD 200/K-12
PO Box 219 95469 707-743-2101
Gary Barr, supt. Fax 743-1930
ntap.k12.ca.us/pvhs/pvcusd.htm
Potter Valley HS 100/7-12
PO Box 219 95469 707-743-1142
Scott Paulin, prin. Fax 743-2879

Poway, San Diego, Pop. 48,476
Poway USD 32,900/K-12
13626 Twin Peaks Rd 92064 858-748-0010
Dr. Donald Phillips, supt. Fax 679-2642
www.powayusd.com
Meadowbrook MS 1,500/6-8
12320 Meadowbrook Ln 92064 858-748-0802
Cathy Brose, prin. Fax 679-0149
Poway HS 3,200/9-12
15500 Espola Rd 92064 858-748-0245
Scott Fisher, prin. Fax 679-6879
Twin Peaks MS 1,600/6-8
14640 Tierra Bonita Rd 92064 858-748-5131
Lyn Antrim, prin. Fax 679-6823
Poway Adult S Adult
13230 Evening Creek Dr S 92064 858-668-4000
Kathleen Porter, dir. Fax 748-7423
Other Schools – See San Diego

Poway Academy of Hair Design Post-Sec.
13266 Poway Rd 92064 858-748-1490

Prather, Fresno, Pop. 30
Sierra USD 2,100/K-12
29143 Auberry Rd 93651 559-855-3662
Dr. Don A. Witzansky, supt. Fax 855-3585
www.sierra.k12.ca.us
Foothill MS 400/6-8
29147 Auberry Rd 93651 559-855-3551
Brent Patten, prin. Fax 855-5350
Other Schools – See Tollhouse

Princeton, Colusa
Princeton JUSD 200/K-12
PO Box 8 95970 530-439-2261
Jess Modesto, supt. Fax 439-2113
www.pjusd.org/
Princeton JSHS 100/7-12
PO Box 8 95970 530-439-2261
Jess Modesto, prin. Fax 439-2113

Prunedale, Monterey, Pop. 7,393

Prunedale Christian Academy 100/PK-12
8145 Prunedale North Rd 93907 831-663-2183
Dr. E.L. Moon, admin. Fax 663-1663

Quartz Hill, Los Angeles, Pop. 9,626
Antelope Valley UNHSD
Supt. — See Lancaster
Quartz Hill HS 3,400/9-12
6040 W Avenue L 93536 661-718-3100
Mark Bryant, prin. Fax 943-8203

Westside UNESD
Supt. — See Lancaster
Walker MS 900/7-8
5632 W Avenue L8 93536 661-943-3258
Robert Garza, prin. Fax 943-2969

Quincy, Plumas, Pop. 4,271
Plumas USD 2,900/K-12
50 Church St 95971 530-283-6500
Mike Chelotti, supt. Fax 283-6509
www.pcoe.k12.ca.us
Quincy JSHS 500/7-12
6 Quincy Junction Rd 95971 530-283-6510
Tim Gallagher, prin. Fax 283-6519
Other Schools – See Chester, Greenville, Portola

Regional Occupational Center & Program
Supt. — None
Plumas County ROP Vo/Tech
50 Church St Ste B 95971 530-283-6500
Terry Oestreich, dir. Fax 283-6509

Feather River Community College Post-Sec.
570 Golden Eagle Ave 95971 530-283-0202
Plumas Christian S 100/K-12
49 S Lindan Ave 95971 530-283-0415
Floren Suetos, admin. Fax 283-2933

Ramona, San Diego, Pop. 13,040
Ramona USD 7,000/K-12
720 9th St 92065 760-787-2000
Pete Schiff, supt. Fax 789-9168
www.ramonausd.net/
Peirce MS 1,100/7-8
1521 Hanson Ln 92065 760-787-2400
Linda Solis, prin. Fax 788-5014
Ramona HS 2,000/9-12
1401 Hanson Ln 92065 760-787-4000
Steve Petsche, prin. Fax 789-4596

Rancho Cordova, Sacramento, Pop. 57,164
Folsom-Cordova USD
Supt. — See Folsom
Cordova HS 2,100/9-12
2239 Chase Dr 95670 916-362-1104
Jacquelyn Levy, prin. Fax 362-1447
Mills MS 1,100/6-8
10439 Coloma Rd 95670 916-363-6544
Dennis Willeford, prin. Fax 361-3744
Mitchell MS 800/6-8
2100 Zinfandel Dr 95670 916-635-8460
DeAnn Kamilos, prin. Fax 635-8979
Folsom-Cordova Adult Education Adult
10850 Gadsten Way 95670 916-635-6810
Dax Bryson, prin. Fax 635-0905

Heald College Post-Sec.
2910 Prospect Park Dr 95670 916-638-1616
IHS Christian S, PO Box 2191 95741 100/K-12
Leanne Kramp, admin. 916-638-7755
ITT Technical Institute Post-Sec.
10863 Gold Center Dr 95670 916-851-3900
San Joaquin Valley College Post-Sec.
11050 Olson Dr 95670

Rancho Cucamonga, San Bernardino, Pop. 169,353

Central ESD 5,100/K-8
10601 Church St Ste 112 91730 909-989-8541
Sharon Nagel, supt. Fax 941-1732
www.csd.k12.ca.us/
Cucamonga MS 1,000/6-8
7611 Hellman Ave 91730 909-987-1788
Jeffrey Koenig, prin. Fax 483-3201
Musser MS 1,100/5-8
10789 Terra Vista Pkwy 91730 909-980-1230
David Soden, prin. Fax 980-3042

Chaffey JUNHSD
Supt. — See Ontario
Los Osos HS 3,000/9-12
6001 Milliken Ave 91737 909-477-6900
Chris Hollister, prin. Fax 460-5872
Rancho Cucamonga HS 2,600/9-12
11801 Lark Dr 91701 909-989-1600
Todd Haag, prin. Fax 945-5355

Cucamonga ESD 2,800/K-8
8776 Archibald Ave 91730 909-987-8942
Claudia Maidenberg, supt. Fax 980-3628
www.cuca.k12.ca.us
Rancho Cucamonga MS 900/6-8
10022 Feron Blvd 91730 909-980-0969
Bruce LaVallee, prin. Fax 481-5381

Regional Occupational Center & Program
Supt. — None
Baldy View ROP Vo/Tech
8265 Aspen St Ste 100 91730 909-980-6490
Jose Castro, supt. Fax 980-8364

San Joaquin Valley College Post-Sec.
10641 Church St 91730 909-948-7582
Universal Technical Institute Post-Sec.
9494 Haven Ave 91730 909-484-1929

Rancho Mirage, Riverside, Pop. 16,514

Eisenhower Memorial Hospital Post-Sec.
39000 Bob Hope Dr 92270 760-340-3911
Marywood Palm Valley S 300/6-12
35525 Da Vall Dr 92270 760-328-0861
Graham Hookey, admin. Fax 770-4541

Rancho Palos Verdes, Los Angeles, Pop. 41,949

Los Angeles USD
Supt. — See Los Angeles
Dodson MS 1,900/6-8
28014 S Montereina Dr 90275 310-241-1900
Elmore Collier, prin. Fax 832-4709

Palos Verdes Peninsula USD
Supt. — See Palos Verdes Estates
Miraleste IS 1,000/6-8
29323 Palos Verdes Dr E 90275 310-732-0900
John Letcher, prin. Fax 521-8915
Ridgecrest IS 900/6-8
28915 Northbay Rd 90275 310-547-2747
Pat Corwin, prin. Fax 265-1716

Marymount College Post-Sec.
30800 Palos Verdes Dr E 90275 310-377-5501

Rancho Santa Fe, San Diego, Pop. 7,000

Rancho Sante Fe ESD 800/K-8
PO Box 809 92067 858-756-1141
Lindy Delaney, supt. Fax 756-0712
www.rsf.k12.ca.us
Rowe MS 200/7-8
PO Box 809 92067 858-756-1141
Blake Isaac, prin. Fax 759-0712

Rancho Santa Margarita, Orange, Pop. 50,682

Capistrano USD
Supt. — See San Juan Capistrano
Tesoro HS 2,900/9-12
1 Tesoro Creek Rd 92688 949-234-5310
Dr. Daniel Burch, prin. Fax 766-3370

Saddleback Valley USD
Supt. — See Mission Viejo
Rancho Santa Margarita IS 1,700/7-8
21931 Alma Aldea 92688 949-459-8253
Dan Graham, prin. Fax 459-8258

Santa Margarita HS 1,600/9-12
22062 Antonio Pkwy 92688 949-766-6000
Br. Lawrence Monroe, prin. Fax 766-6005

Red Bluff, Tehama, Pop. 14,059

Antelope ESD 600/K-8
22630 Antelope Blvd 96080 530-527-1272
Dr. Emily Houck, supt. Fax 527-2931
www.asd.tehama.k12.ca.us/
Berrendos MS 200/6-8
401 Chestnut Ave 96080 530-527-6700
Dr. Emily Houck, prin. Fax 527-2506

Red Bluff JUNHSD 1,900/9-12
PO Box 1507 96080 530-529-8700
Kathleen Wheeler, supt. Fax 529-8709
www.rbuhsd.k12.ca.us/
Red Bluff HS 1,700/9-12
PO Box 1507 96080 530-529-8710
Patrick Gleason, prin. Fax 529-8739

Red Bluff UNESD 2,200/K-8
1755 Airport Blvd 96080 530-527-7200
Charles Allen, supt. Fax 527-9308
www.rbuesd.tehama.k12.ca.us
Vista MS 500/7-8
1770 S Jackson St 96080 530-527-7840
William McCoy, prin. Fax 527-9374

Regional Occupational Center & Program
Supt. — None
Tehama County ROP Vo/Tech
PO Box 689 96080 530-528-7341
Larry Champion, admin. Fax 529-4120

Mercy HS 200/9-12
233 Riverside Way 96080 530-527-8313
Cheryl Ramirez, prin. Fax 527-3058

Redding, Shasta, Pop. 89,641

Columbia ESD 1,000/K-8
10140 Old Oregon Trl 96003 530-223-1915
Frank Adelman, supt. Fax 223-4168
www.columbiasd.com
Mountain View MS 400/6-8
675 Shasta View Dr 96003 530-221-6224
Andrea McClure, prin. Fax 221-5620

Enterprise ESD 3,300/K-8
1155 Mistletoe Ln 96002 530-224-4100
Brian Winstead Ed.D., supt. Fax 224-4101
www.enterprise.k12.ca.us
Parsons MS 700/6-8
750 Hartnell Ave 96002 530-224-4190
Cheryl Kirschman, prin. Fax 224-4191

Gateway USD 2,600/K-12
4411 Mountain Lakes Blvd 96003 530-245-7900
John Strohmayer, supt. Fax 245-7920
www.gateway-schools.org/home.aspx
Buckeye MS 200/6-8
3500 Tamarack Dr 96003 530-225-0456
Laura Kelly, prin. Fax 225-0499
Other Schools – See Central Valley

Pacheco UNESD 700/K-8
7433 Pacheco Rd 96002 530-224-4589
Richard Rhodes, supt. Fax 224-4595
www.pacheco.k12.ca.us
Pacheco S 400/4-8
7430 Pacheco School Rd 96002 530-224-4585
Michael Kurth, prin. Fax 224-4588

Redding ESD 3,600/K-8
PO Box 992418 96099 530-225-0011
Diane Kempley, supt. Fax 225-0015
www.shastalink.k12.ca.us/rsd
Sequoia MS 1,000/6-8
PO Box 992418 96099 530-225-0020
Wendy Pace, prin. Fax 225-0029

Regional Occupational Center & Program
Supt. — None
Shasta-Trinity ROP Vo/Tech
4659 Eastside Rd 96001 530-246-3302
Charlie Hoffman, supt. Fax 246-3306

Shasta UNHSD 5,400/9-12
2200 Eureka Way #B 96001 530-241-3261
Michael Stuart, supt. Fax 225-8499
www.suhsd.net
Enterprise HS 1,400/9-12
3411 Churn Creek Rd 96002 530-222-6601
Eric Peterson, prin. Fax 222-5138
Shasta HS 1,700/9-12
2500 Eureka Way 96001 530-241-4161
Milan Woollard, prin. Fax 241-9571
Other Schools – See Palo Cedro

Grace Baptist S 300/K-12
3782 Churn Creek Rd 96002 530-222-2232
Stephen Roberts, supt. Fax 222-1784
Hope S International 200/K-12
2250 Churn Creek Rd 96002 530-222-2095
Dee Haselhuhn, prin. Fax 222-5819
Lake College Post-Sec.
2655 Bechelli Ln 96002 530-224-7227
Redding Adventist Academy 200/K-12
1356 E Cypress Ave 96002 530-222-1018
Timothy Erich, prin. Fax 222-4260
Redding Christian S 500/K-12
777 Loma Vista Dr 96002 530-223-1226
Dr. Tom Forbes, supt. Fax 223-4755
Shasta Bible College & Graduate School Post-Sec.
2951 Goodwater Ave 96002 530-221-4275
Shasta College Post-Sec.
PO Box 496006 96049 530-225-4600
Simpson University Post-Sec.
2211 College View Dr 96003 530-224-5600

Redlands, San Bernardino, Pop. 69,995

Redlands USD 21,000/K-12
PO Box 3008 92373 909-307-5300
Robert Hodges, supt. Fax 307-5321
www.redlands.k12.ca.us
Clement MS 1,000/6-8
501 E Pennsylvania Ave 92374 909-307-5400
John Massie, prin. Fax 307-5414
Cope MS 1,400/6-8
1000 W Cypress Ave 92373 909-307-5420
Brad Mason, prin. Fax 307-5436
Moore MS 1,300/6-8
1550 E Highland Ave 92374 909-307-5440
Julie Swan, prin. Fax 307-5453
Redlands East Valley HS 3,500/9-12
31000 Colton Ave 92374 909-389-2500
John Maloney, prin. Fax 389-2517
Redlands HS 3,400/9-12
840 E Citrus Ave 92374 909-307-5500
Christina Rivera, prin. Fax 307-5527
Redlands Adult HS Adult
7 W Delaware Ave 92374 909-748-6930
Cheryl Bordelon, prin. Fax 307-5324
Other Schools – See Highland

Regional Occupational Center & Program
Supt. — None
Colton-Redlands-Yucaipa ROP Vo/Tech
1214 Indiana Ct 92374 909-793-3115
Dalene Morris, supt. Fax 793-6901

American College of Health Professions Post-Sec.
700 E Redlands Blvd # U227 92373 909-307-6022
Arrowhead Christian Academy 500/7-12
105 Tennessee St 92373 909-793-0601
Steve Hicok, admin. Fax 792-5691
Community Christian College Post-Sec.
251 Tennessee St 92373 909-335-8863
Packinghouse Christian Academy 300/K-12
9700 Alabama St 92374 909-793-4984
Charles Smith, admin. Fax 307-1852
Redlands Adventist Academy 500/K-12
130 Tennessee St 92373 909-793-1000
Geoff Hayton, prin. Fax 793-9862
University of Redlands Post-Sec.
PO Box 3080 92373 909-793-2121

Redondo Beach, Los Angeles, Pop. 66,824

Redondo Beach Unified SD 7,900/PK-12
1401 Inglewood Ave 90278 310-379-5449
Steven Keller Ed.D., supt. Fax 372-5269
www.rbusd.org/
Adams MS 800/6-8
1401 Inglewood Ave 90278 310-798-8636
Jon Pede, prin. Fax 318-3064
Parras MS 800/6-8
1401 Inglewood Ave 90278 310-798-8616
Sallie Tahajian, prin. Fax 798-8660
Redondo Union HS 2,300/9-12
1401 Inglewood Ave 90278 310-798-8665
Mary Little, prin. Fax 798-4685
South Bay Adult S Adult
1401 Inglewood Ave 90278 310-937-3340
Gerald Striff, prin. Fax 937-3345

South Bay Faith Academy 400/K-12
PO Box 7000 90277 310-379-8242
Roslyn Ballard, prin.

Redwood City, San Mateo, Pop. 73,114

Redwood City ESD 8,000/PK-8
750 Bradford St 94063 650-423-2200
Jan Christensen, supt. Fax 423-2204
www.rcsd.k12.ca.us
Kennedy MS 1,000/6-8
2521 Goodwin Ave 94061 650-365-4611
Warren Sedar, prin. Fax 367-4362
McKinley Institute of Technology 400/6-8
400 Duane St 94062 650-366-3827
Cheryl Bracco, prin. Fax 367-4363
North Star Academy 500/3-8
400 Duane St 94062 650-482-5973
Ray Dawley, prin. Fax 482-5980

Regional Occupational Center & Program
Supt. — None
San Mateo County ROP Vo/Tech
101 Twin Dolphin Dr 94065 650-802-5411
Diane Centoni, dir. Fax 802-5414

Sequoia UNHSD 7,900/9-12
480 James Ave 94062 650-369-1411
Patrick Gemma, supt. Fax 306-8870
www.seq.org
Sequoia HS 1,700/9-12
1201 Brewster Ave 94062 650-367-9780
Morgan Marchbanks, prin. Fax 368-5180
Other Schools – See Atherton, Belmont, Menlo Park, Woodside

Canada College Post-Sec.
4200 Farm Hill Blvd 94061 650-306-3100

Redwood Valley, Mendocino

Ukiah USD
Supt. — See Ukiah
Eagle Peak MS 500/6-8
8601 West Rd 95470 707-485-8154
Carolyn Johnson, prin. Fax 485-9542

Deep Valley Christian S 100/PK-12
PO Box 9 95470 707-485-8778
Jim Burnham, admin. Fax 485-8804

Reedley, Fresno, Pop. 22,368

Kings Canyon JUSD 9,100/K-12
675 W Manning Ave 93654 559-637-1210
Juan Garza, supt. Fax 637-1292
www.kc-usd.k12.ca.us
Grant MS 600/6-8
360 N East Ave 93654 559-637-1266
Bill Wachtel, prin. Fax 638-6772
Navelencia MS 400/6-8
22620 Wahtoke Ave 93654 559-637-1251
Jeremy Brown, prin. Fax 637-1316
Reedley HS 2,100/9-12
740 W North Ave 93654 559-637-1250
Jeff Wiggams, prin. Fax 637-0458
Kings Canyon Adult S Adult
675 W Manning Ave 93654 559-637-1246
Keith Merrihew, dir. Fax 637-9563
Other Schools – See Orange Cove

Immanuel HS 400/7-12
1128 S Reed Ave 93654 559-638-2529
Jerry Meadows, supt. Fax 638-7030
Reedley College Post-Sec.
995 N Reed Ave 93654 559-638-3641

Rescue, El Dorado

Rescue UNESD 3,700/K-8
2390 Bass Lake Rd 95672 530-677-4461
Carol Bly Ed.D., supt. Fax 677-0719
www.rescue.k12.ca.us/
Pleasant Grove MS 700/6-8
2540 Green Valley Rd 95672 530-672-4400
Reid Briggs, prin. Fax 677-5829

Other Schools – See El Dorado Hills

Reseda, See Los Angeles
Los Angeles USD
Supt. — See Los Angeles
Cleveland HS 3,600/9-12
8140 Vanalden Ave 91335 818-885-2300
Robert Marks, prin. Fax 727-0964
Reseda HS 2,700/9-12
18230 Kittridge St 91335 818-758-3600
Alfredo Tarin, prin. Fax 776-0452
Reseda Adult Education Adult
18230 Kittridge St 91335 818-758-3700
Rosario Galvan, prin. Fax 343-2107

Everest College Post-Sec.
18040 Sherman Way # 400 91335 818-774-0550
Marinello School of Beauty Post-Sec.
18442 Sherman Way 91335 818-881-2521
Trinity Lutheran JSHS 100/7-12
18425 Kittridge St 91335 818-342-7855
Jerry Romsa, prin. Fax 342-4491

Rialto, San Bernardino, Pop. 99,513
Rialto USD 28,500/K-12
182 E Walnut Ave 92376 909-820-7700
Edna Herring, supt. Fax 873-0448
www.rialto.k12.ca.us
Carter HS, 2630 N Linden Ave 92377 9-12
Veronica Smith-Iszard, prin. 909-854-4100
Eisenhower HS 2,600/9-12
1321 N Lilac Ave 92376 909-820-7777
Reginald Thompkins, prin. Fax 421-7640
Frisbie MS 1,500/6-8
1442 N Eucalyptus Ave 92376 909-820-7887
Teresa Brown, prin. Fax 820-7885
Kolb MS 1,400/6-8
2351 N Spruce Ave 92377 909-820-7849
John Roach, prin. Fax 875-0374
Kucera MS 1,600/6-8
2140 W Buena Vista Dr 92377 909-421-7662
Monique Conway, prin. Fax 421-7681
Rialto HS 3,500/9-12
595 S Eucalyptus Ave 92376 909-421-7500
Mehran Akhtarkhavari, prin. Fax 421-7584
Rialto MS 1,400/6-8
324 N Palm Ave 92376 909-820-7838
Mark Bline, prin. Fax 820-7940
Rialto Adult S Adult
595 S Eucalyptus Ave 92376 909-820-7785
Peggy Wheeler, prin. Fax 421-7533
Other Schools – See Colton

Lighthouse Christian Academy 100/PK-12
PO Box 520 92377 909-820-2191
Sharon Pierce, prin. Fax 820-2323

Richgrove, Tulare, Pop. 1,899
Richgrove ESD 700/K-8
PO Box 540 93261 661-725-2427
Frank Chavez, supt. Fax 725-5772
www.richgrove.org
Richgrove JHS 200/6-8
20908 Grove Dr 93261 661-725-0315
Frank Chavez, prin.

Richmond, Contra Costa, Pop. 102,186
West Contra Costa USD 31,300/K-12
1108 Bissell Ave 94801 510-231-1100
Bruce Harter, supt. Fax 236-6784
www.wccusd.k12.ca.us
Adams MS 600/6-8
5000 Patterson Cir 94805 510-235-5464
Julian Szot, prin. Fax 233-9450
De Anza HS 1,200/9-12
5000 Valley View Rd 94803 510-223-3811
Vera Rowsey, prin. Fax 223-7984
DeJean MS 900/6-8
3400 Macdonald Ave 94805 510-412-8300
Antoinette Henry-Evans, prin. Fax 236-6680
Kennedy HS 900/9-12
4300 Cutting Blvd 94804 510-235-2291
Julio Franco, prin. Fax 235-1915
Richmond HS 1,800/9-12
1250 23rd St 94804 510-237-8770
Orlando Ramos, prin. Fax 235-0316
Adult Education Adult
5625 Sutter Ave 94804 510-559-2660
Sandy Price, prin. Fax 559-2664
West CC Adult Ed Center Adult
6028 Ralston Ave 94805 510-215-4666
Tim Shaw, prin. Fax 215-0430
Other Schools – See El Cerrito, El Sobrante, Hercules, Pinole, San Pablo

---

Argosy University/San Francisco Campus Post-Sec.
999 Canal Blvd Ste A 94804 510-215-0277
Kaiser Permanente Medical Center Post-Sec.
901 Nevin Ave 94801 510-307-2412
La Cheim S 50/6-12
2853 Groom Dr 94806 510-243-2360
Karen Jackson, dir. Fax 243-2370
Salesian HS 600/9-12
2851 Salesian Ave 94804 510-234-4434
Tim Chambers, prin. Fax 236-4636

Ridgecrest, Kern, Pop. 25,974
Sierra Sands USD 5,500/K-12
113 W Felspar Ave 93555 760-375-3363
Joanna Rummer, supt. Fax 375-3338
www.ssusd.org
Burroughs HS 1,700/9-12
500 E French Ave 93555 760-375-4476
Ernie Bell, prin. Fax 375-1735
Monroe MS 600/6-8
340 W Church Ave 93555 760-375-1301
Dave Ostash, prin. Fax 375-8781
Murray MS 800/6-8
921 E Inyokern Rd 93555 760-446-5525
Kirsti Smith, prin. Fax 446-3838
Sierra Sands Adult S Adult
140 Drummond Ave 93555 760-446-5872
Ingrid Larsen, prin. Fax 499-7053

Calvary Christian S 50/K-12
PO Box 2138 93556 760-375-3133
Glenn Hill, prin. Fax 375-2694
Cerro Coso Community College Post-Sec.
3000 College Heights Blvd 93555 760-384-6100
Immanuel Christian S 200/PK-12
201 W Graaf Ave 93555 760-446-6114
Dr. Wes Johnston, prin. Fax 446-7035

Rio Dell, Humboldt, Pop. 3,158
Rio Dell ESD 300/K-8
95 Center St 95562 707-764-5694
Mary Varner, supt. Fax 764-2656
internet.humboldt.k12.ca.us/riodell_sd/
Monument MS 100/7-8
95 Center St 95562 707-764-3783
Jeff Northern, prin. Fax 764-2656

Rio Linda, Sacramento, Pop. 9,481
Grant JUNHSD
Supt. — See Sacramento
Rio Linda HS 1,900/9-12
6309 Dry Creek Rd 95673 916-286-4500
Rusty Clark, prin. Fax 263-6462
Rio Linda JHS 600/7-8
1101 G St 95673 916-286-1601
Harjinder Mattu, prin. Fax 263-4674

Rio Vista, Solano, Pop. 7,077
River Delta USD 2,000/K-12
445 Montezuma St 94571 707-374-6381
Dr. Alan Newell, supt. Fax 374-2995
www.riverdelta.k12.ca.us/
Rio Vista HS 400/9-12
410 S 4th St 94571 707-374-6336
James Lake, prin. Fax 374-6810
Riverview MS 300/5-8
525 S 2nd St 94571 707-374-2345
James Lake, prin. Fax 374-5623
Wind River Adult S Adult
410 S 4th St 94571 707-374-5610
Robert Hubbell, prin. Fax 374-2944
Other Schools – See Clarksburg

Ripon, San Joaquin, Pop. 13,658
Ripon USD 2,900/K-12
304 N Acacia Ave 95366 209-599-2131
Leo Zuber, supt. Fax 599-6271
www.riponusd.net/
Ripon HS, 301 N Acacia Ave 95366 900/9-12
Jeff Frase, prin. 209-599-4287
Ripon Adult S Adult
304 N Acacia Ave 95366 209-599-2131
Lisa Boje, prin.

Ripon Christian HS 300/9-12
435 Maple Ave 95366 209-599-2155
Mary Ann Sybesma, prin. Fax 599-2170

Riverbank, Stanislaus, Pop. 19,727
Riverbank USD 3,000/K-12
6715 7th St 95367 209-869-2538
Joseph Galindo, supt. Fax 869-1487
www.riverbank.k12.ca.us/home
Cardozo MS 700/6-8
3525 Santa Fe St 95367 209-869-2591
Alice Solis, prin. Fax 869-2714
Riverbank HS 800/9-12
6200 Claus Rd 95367 209-869-1891
Ken Geisick, prin. Fax 869-2116

Riverdale, Fresno, Pop. 1,980
Riverdale JUSD 1,600/K-12
PO Box 1058 93656 559-867-8200
Elaine Cash, supt. Fax 867-6722
www.riverdale.k12.ca.us
Riverdale ES 600/4-8
PO Box 338 93656 559-867-3589
Mark Allein, prin. Fax 867-3393
Riverdale HS 500/9-12
PO Box 726 93656 559-867-3562
Peter Faragia, prin. Fax 867-4750

Riverside, Riverside, Pop. 290,086
Alvord USD 20,000/K-12
10365 Keller Ave 92505 951-509-5070
Kathy Wright, supt. Fax 509-6070
www.alvord.k12.ca.us
Arizona MS 1,300/6-8
10365 Keller Ave 92505 951-351-9343
Chuck Fischer, prin. Fax 351-2187
La Sierra HS 3,000/9-12
10365 Keller Ave 92505 951-351-9238
Robert Cunard, prin. Fax 351-9307
Loma Vista MS 1,100/6-8
10365 Keller Ave 92505 951-351-9216
Fax 351-2153
Norte Vista HS 2,300/9-12
10365 Keller Ave 92505 951-351-9201
Santos Campos, prin. Fax 351-9249
Villegas MS 1,400/6-8
10365 Keller Ave 92505 951-351-6622
Julie Koehler-Mount, prin. Fax 351-7515
Wells MS 1,100/6-8
10365 Keller Ave 92505 951-351-9241
Patricia Nilsen, prin. Fax 351-6606

Jurupa USD 21,200/K-12
4850 Pedley Rd 92509 951-360-4100
Elliott Duchon, supt. Fax 360-4194
www.jusd.k12.ca.us
Jurupa MS 1,100/7-8
8700 Galena St 92509 951-360-2846
Walter Lancaster, prin. Fax 360-8928
Mira Loma MS 1,100/7-8
5051 Steve Ave 92509 951-360-2883
Cindy Freeman, prin. Fax 685-7405
Mission MS 1,100/7-8
5961 Mustang Ln 92509 951-222-7842
Luz Mendez, prin. Fax 369-1407
Patriot HS 9-12
4355 Camino Real 92509 951-361-6500
Jay Trujillo, prin. Fax 361-6526
Rubidoux HS 2,900/9-12
4250 Opal St 92509 951-222-7720
Laurel Fretz, prin. Fax 275-0079
Adult Education Adult
4041 Pacific Ave 92509 951-222-7739
George Monge, prin. Fax 788-8689
Other Schools – See Mira Loma

Regional Occupational Center & Program
Supt. — None
Riverside County ROP Vo/Tech
PO Box 868 92502 951-826-6797
Kevin Rubow, dir. Fax 826-6440

Riverside USD 42,200/K-12
PO Box 2800 92516 951-788-7134
Dr. Susan Rainey, supt. Fax 788-7110
www.rusd.k12.ca.us
Arlington HS 2,200/9-12
2951 Jackson St 92503 951-352-8316
David Hansen, prin. Fax 352-8417
Central MS 700/7-8
4795 Magnolia Ave 92506 951-788-7282
Antonio Garcia, prin. Fax 328-2580
Chemawa MS 1,300/7-8
8830 Magnolia Ave 92503 951-352-8244
Wade Coe, prin. Fax 687-7235
Earhart MS 1,500/7-8
20202 Aptos St 92508 951-697-5700
Judi Paredes, prin. Fax 697-5733
Gage MS 1,200/7-8
6400 Lincoln Ave 92506 951-788-7350
Chuck Hiroto, prin. Fax 787-8067
King HS 2,800/9-12
9301 Wood Rd 92508 951-789-5690
Dan Brooks, prin. Fax 789-5692
North HS 2,600/9-12
1550 3rd St 92507 951-788-7311
Dale Kinnear, prin. Fax 276-2075
Polytechnic HS 2,600/9-12
5450 Victoria Ave 92506 951-788-7203
Frank Paredes, prin. Fax 784-2306
Ramona HS 2,100/9-12
7675 Magnolia Ave 92504 951-352-8429
Maria Armstrong, prin. Fax 352-8446
Sierra MS 1,000/7-8
4950 Central Ave 92504 951-788-7501
Lou Mason, prin. Fax 788-7561
University Heights MS 1,000/7-8
1155 Massachusetts Ave 92507 951-788-7388
Patricia Grice, prin. Fax 276-7649
Riverside Adult S Adult
6735 Magnolia Ave 92506 951-788-7185
James Dawson, prin. Fax 369-4966

Bethel Christian S 400/PK-12
2425 Van Buren Blvd 92503 951-359-1123
Michael Crites, supt. Fax 359-1719
California Baptist University Post-Sec.
8432 Magnolia Ave 92504 951-689-5771
CEI Post-Sec.
1635 Spruce St 92507 951-276-1704
La Sierra Academy 700/K-12
4900 Golden Ave 92505 951-351-1445
Dr. Cyril Connelly, prin. Fax 689-3708
La Sierra University Post-Sec.
4500 Riverwalk Pkwy 92505 951-785-2022
Notre Dame HS 600/9-12
7085 Brockton Ave 92506 951-275-5896
Dr. JoDean Salley, prin. Fax 781-9020
Olive Tree Christian S 400/K-12
4864 Rockingham Pl 92509 951-685-6325
Rebecca Kocsis, admin.
Riverside Christian HS 300/9-12
3532 Monroe St 92504 951-687-0077
Morris Lewis, supt. Fax 687-3340
Riverside Christian MS 100/7-8
8223 California Ave 92504 951-687-4610
Pat VanDyke, prin. Fax 687-4601
Riverside Community College Post-Sec.
4800 Magnolia Ave 92506 951-222-8000
Somerset Educational Services 200/7-12
PO Box 20529 92516 951-789-4405
Cory Darrington, dir.
University of California Post-Sec.
900 University Ave 92521 951-827-1012
Woodcrest Christian S 700/7-12
18401 Van Buren Blvd 92508 951-780-2010
Randy Thompson, supt. Fax 780-2079

Rocklin, Placer, Pop. 49,626
Rocklin USD 9,400/K-12
2615 Sierra Meadows Dr 95677 916-624-2428
Kevin Brown, supt. Fax 630-2229
www.rocklin.k12.ca.us
Granite Oaks MS 800/7-8
2600 Wyckford Blvd 95765 916-315-9009
Mike Melton, prin. Fax 315-9885
Rocklin HS 2,700/9-12
5301 Victory Ln 95765 916-632-1600
Mike Garrison, prin. Fax 632-0305
Spring View MS 700/7-8
5040 5th St 95677 916-624-3381
Marjorie Crawford, prin. Fax 624-5737
Whitney HS 9-12
701 Wildcat Blvd 95765 916-632-6500
Debra Hawkins, prin. Fax 435-2542

Sierra Christian Academy 500/PK-12
6900 Destiny Dr 95677 916-772-1440
Cynthia White, prin. Fax 773-0304
Sierra College Post-Sec.
5000 Rocklin Rd 95677 916-624-3333

Rohnert Park, Sonoma, Pop. 41,101
Cotati-Rohnert Park USD 7,200/K-12
5860 Labath Ave 94928 707-792-4722
Michael Watenpaugh, supt. Fax 792-4537
www.crpusd.org/
Creekside MS 900/6-8
5154 Snyder Ln 94928 707-588-5600
Sandy Kuzma, prin. Fax 588-5607
Mountain Shadows MS 900/6-8
7165 Burton Ave 94928 707-792-4800
Laura Mason, prin. Fax 792-4516
Rancho Cotate HS 2,000/9-12
5450 Snyder Ln 94928 707-792-4750
Joseph Williams, prin. Fax 792-4758
Technology HS Vo/Tech
1801 E Cotati Ave 94928 707-792-4825
Kay Dorner, prin. Fax 792-4727

Sonoma State University Post-Sec.
1801 E Cotati Ave 94928 707-664-2880

Rolling Hills, Los Angeles, Pop. 1,933
Palos Verdes Peninsula USD
Supt. — See Palos Verdes Estates
Palos Verdes Peninsula HS 2,600/9-12
27118 Silver Spur Rd 90274 310-377-4888
Kelly Johnson, prin. Fax 544-4378
PVPUSD Adult Education Adult
38 Crest Rd W 90274 310-541-7626
Rosemary Humphrey, prin. Fax 265-5967

Rosamond, Kern, Pop. 7,430
Southern Kern USD 3,300/K-12
PO Box CC 93560 661-256-5000
Rodney Van Norman, supt. Fax 256-1247
www.skusd.k12.ca.us
Rosamond HS 800/9-12
PO Box CC 93560 661-256-5020
Troy Cox, prin. Fax 256-6880
Tropico MS 800/6-8
PO Box CC 93560 661-256-5040
Leslie Lacey, prin. Fax 256-0630
Southern Kern Adult S Adult
PO Box CC 93560 661-256-5090
Mike Luckenbill, prin. Fax 256-6868

Rosemead, Los Angeles, Pop. 55,119
Alhambra City SD
Supt. — See Alhambra
Southeast Community Adult S Adult
7422 Garvey Ave 91770 626-572-2280
John Kao, prin. Fax 573-4308

El Monte UNHSD
Supt. — See El Monte
Rosemead HS 2,000/9-12
9063 Mission Dr 91770 626-286-3141
Diane Bladen, prin. Fax 286-6396

Garvey ESD 6,100/K-8
2730 Del Mar Ave 91770 626-307-3400
Virginia Peterson Ed.D., supt. Fax 307-1964
www.garvey.k12.ca.us
Garvey IS 800/7-8
2720 Jackson Ave 91770 626-307-3385
Gema Macias Ed.D., prin. Fax 307-3443
Temple IS 500/7-8
8470 Fern Ave 91770 626-307-3360
C.P. Cheung, prin. Fax 307-8162

Rosemead ESD 3,300/K-8
3907 Rosemead Blvd 91770 626-312-2900
Amy Enomoto-Perez Ed.D., supt. Fax 312-2906
www.rosemead.k12.ca.us
Muscatel MS 800/7-8
4201 Ivar Ave 91770 626-287-1139
Dean Wharton, prin. Fax 307-6185

Don Bosco Technical Institute Post-Sec.
1151 San Gabriel Blvd 91770 626-307-6500
Don Bosco Technical Institute 900/9-12
1151 San Gabriel Blvd 91770 626-940-2000
Fr. Michael Gergen, prin. Fax 940-2001
Edgewood College of California Post-Sec.
4930 Earle Ave 91770 626-291-5000
Rosemead Beauty School Post-Sec.
8531 Valley Blvd 91770 626-286-2147
University of the West Post-Sec.
1409 Walnut Grove Ave 91770 626-571-8811

Roseville, Placer, Pop. 105,940
Center JUSD
Supt. — See Antelope
Riles MS 6-8
4747 PFE Rd 95747 916-787-8100
Joyce Duplissea, prin. Fax 773-4131

Dry Creek JESD 7,300/K-8
9707 Cook Riolo Rd 95747 916-771-0646
Mark Geyer, supt. Fax 771-0650
www.drycreek.k12.ca.us
Silverado MS 1,400/6-8
2525 Country Club Dr 95747 916-780-2620
Kevin Kurtz, prin. Fax 780-2635
Other Schools – See Antelope

Eureka UNSD
Supt. — See Granite Bay
Olympus JHS 500/7-8
2625 La Croix Dr 95661 916-782-1667
Kelly Graham, prin. Fax 782-1339

Roseville City ESD 8,000/K-8
1050 Main St 95678 916-771-1600
Richard Pierrucci, supt. Fax 786-5098
www.rcsdk8.org
Buljan MS 1,000/6-8
100 Hallissey Dr 95678 916-771-1720
Greg Gunn, prin. Fax 773-2696
Cooley MS 900/6-8
9300 Prairie Woods Way 95747 916-771-1740
Karen Calkins, prin. Fax 786-3003

Eich IS 600/7-8
1509 Sierra Gardens Dr 95661 916-771-1770
Christine Hudson, prin. Fax 783-7292

Roseville JUNHSD 7,300/9-12
1750 Cirby Way 95661 916-786-2051
Tony Monetti, supt. Fax 786-2681
www.rjuhsd.k12.ca.us
Oakmont HS 1,800/9-12
1710 Cirby Way 95661 916-782-3781
Kathleen Sirovy, prin. Fax 782-4943
Roseville HS 1,900/9-12
1 Tiger Way 95678 916-782-3753
Brad Basham, prin. Fax 786-3846
Woodcreek HS 2,000/9-12
2551 Woodcreek Oaks Blvd 95747 916-771-6565
Jess Borjon, prin. Fax 771-6596
Roseville Adult S Adult
200 Branstetter St 95678 916-782-3952
Joyce Lude, dir. Fax 782-4361
Other Schools – See Granite Bay

Christian Life Academy 50/K-12
628 Royer St 95678 916-956-4662
Peggy Gubitz, prin. Fax 786-7916
Cornerstone Christian S 200/K-12
143 Clinton Ave 95678 916-783-7779
Dr. D. Craig Garbe, hdmstr. Fax 783-1856
Heald College Post-Sec.
7 Sierra Gate Plz 95678 916-789-8600
Valley Christian Academy 300/PK-12
301 W Whyte Ave 95678 916-728-5500
Dr. Brad Gunter, admin. Fax 721-3305

Ross, Marin, Pop. 2,283

Branson HS 300/9-12
PO Box 887 94957 415-454-3612
Peter Esty, hdmstr. Fax 454-2327

Rowland Heights, Los Angeles, Pop. 49,900
Rowland USD 17,800/K-12
1830 Nogales St 91748 626-965-2541
Dr. Maria Ott, supt. Fax 854-8302
www.rowland-unified.org
Alvarado IS 1,100/7-8
1901 Desire Ave 91748 626-964-2358
Ying Tsao, prin. Fax 810-5579
Rowland HS 2,400/9-12
2000 Otterbein Ave 91748 626-965-3448
Robbie Robinson, prin. Fax 810-4859
Rowland Adult & Continuing Education Adult
2100 Lerona Ave 91748 626-965-5975
Rocky Bettar, prin. Fax 854-1191
Other Schools – See La Puente, West Covina

Sacramento, Sacramento, Pop. 456,441
Elk Grove USD
Supt. — See Elk Grove
Florin HS 2,200/9-12
7956 Cottonwood Ln 95828 916-689-8600
Mark Cerutti, prin. Fax 689-7430
Jackman MS 1,300/7-8
7925 Kentwall Dr 95823 916-393-2352
William Del Bonta, prin. Fax 393-4053
Rutter MS 1,200/7-8
7350 Palmer House Dr 95828 916-422-7590
Sara Noguchi, prin. Fax 422-8354
Sheldon HS 3,400/9-12
8333 Kingsbridge Dr 95829 916-681-7500
Paula Duncan, prin. Fax 681-7505
Smedberg MS 1,700/7-8
8239 Kingsbridge Dr 95829 916-681-7525
Keven MacDonald, prin. Fax 681-7530
Valley HS 2,100/9-12
6300 Ehrhardt Ave 95823 916-689-6500
Chris Evans, prin. Fax 682-1528
Adult/Community Education Adult
8401 Gerber Rd 95828 916-686-7717
Kathy Hamilton, dir. Fax 689-5752
Always Learning Adult
8401 Gerber Rd Ste A 95828 916-686-7783
Maureen Sawyer, admin. Fax 689-4372

Grant JUNHSD 11,600/7-12
1333 Grand Ave 95838 916-286-4800
Larry Buchanan Ed.D., supt. Fax 263-6247
www.grant.k12.ca.us
Foothill Farms JHS 900/7-8
5001 Diablo Dr 95842 916-286-1400
Jeff James, prin. Fax 263-3756
Foothill HS 1,500/9-12
5000 McCloud Dr 95842 916-286-1300
Larry Tosta, prin. Fax 263-4685
Grant HS - Main Campus 2,100/9-12
1400 Grand Ave 95838 916-286-1000
Craig Murray, prin. Fax 263-6326
Grant West HS 9-12
1221 South Ave 95838 916-286-1200
Craig Murray, prin. Fax 263-6686
King JHS 1,000/7-8
3051 Fairfield St 95815 916-286-4700
Samuel Harris, prin. Fax 263-6701
Norwood JHS 700/7-8
4601 Norwood Ave 95838 916-649-6600
Roxanne Mitchell, prin. Fax 649-6696
Rio Tierra JHS 700/7-8
3201 Northstead Dr 95833 916-286-1500
Paul Orlando, prin. Fax 263-6971
Vista Nueva Career & Tech HS Vo/Tech
2035 North Ave 95838 916-286-1100
Michael Crossetti, prin. Fax 263-6498
Grant Dist Skills/Adult Center Adult
577 Las Palmas Ave 95815 916-286-7527
Hal Steward, dir.
Other Schools – See North Highlands, Rio Linda

Natomas USD 8,700/K-12
1901 Arena Blvd 95834 916-567-5400
Dr. Steve Farrar, supt. Fax 567-5405
www.natomas.k12.ca.us
Greene MS 900/6-8
2950 W River Dr 95833 916-567-5560
Bob Evans, prin. Fax 567-5569
Inderkum HS 700/9-12
2500 New Market Dr 95835 916-567-5640
Ben Flores, prin. Fax 567-5649
Natomas HS 1,700/9-12
3301 Fong Ranch Rd 95834 916-641-4960
Troy Johnston, prin. Fax 641-5455
Natomas MS 900/6-8
3700 Del Paso Rd 95834 916-567-5540
Carla Najera-Kunsemiller, prin. Fax 567-5549
Sacramento Valley Technical HS Vo/Tech
2500 New Market Dr 95835 916-567-5880
Tanya Parker, dir. Fax 567-5889

Sacramento City USD 46,100/K-12
5735 47th Ave 95824 916-643-7400
Dr. Maggie Mejia, supt. Fax 643-9480
www.scusd.edu
Bacon Basic MS 1,000/6-8
4140 Cuny Ave 95823 916-433-5000
Richard Cvitanov, prin. Fax 433-5166
Benjamin Health Professions HS 9-12
451 McClatchy Way 95818 916-264-3262
Matt Perry, prin. Fax 264-3245
Brannan MS 900/7-8
5301 Elmer Way 95822 916-264-4374
Peter Callas, prin. Fax 264-4481
Burbank HS 2,300/9-12
3500 Florin Rd 95823 916-433-5100
Ted Appel, prin. Fax 433-5199
California MS 700/7-8
1600 Vallejo Way 95818 916-264-4550
Elizabeth Vigil, prin. Fax 264-4477
Carson MS 600/6-8
5301 N St 95819 916-277-6750
Catherine Beckworth, prin. Fax 277-6550
Einstein MS 900/7-8
9325 Mirandy Dr 95826 916-228-5800
Leise Martinez, prin. Fax 228-5813
Goethe MS 800/7-8
2250 68th Ave 95822 916-433-5400
Harriet Young, prin. Fax 433-5518
Johnson HS 2,200/9-12
6879 14th Ave 95820 916-277-6300
Lynne Tafoya, prin. Fax 277-6740
Johnson HS West Campus 800/9-12
5022 58th St 95820 916-277-6400
John Becker, prin. Fax 277-6593
Kennedy HS 2,500/9-12
6715 Gloria Dr 95831 916-433-5200
Mary Shelton, prin. Fax 433-5511
McClatchy HS 2,400/9-12
3066 Freeport Blvd 95818 916-264-4400
Cynthia Clark, prin. Fax 264-4499
Rosemont HS 1,000/9-12
9594 Kiefer Blvd 95827 916-228-5844
Rob Jones, prin. Fax 228-5733
Sutter MS 1,300/7-8
3150 I St 95816 916-264-4150
Greg Purcell, prin. Fax 264-3436
Wood MS 900/7-8
6201 Lemon Hill Ave 95824 916-382-5900
James Wong, prin. Fax 382-5914
Florin Technology Education Center Adult
2401 Florin Rd 95822 916-433-2844
Mary Prather, prin. Fax 433-2847
Fremont S for Adults Adult
2420 N St 95816 916-277-6620
John Miller, prin. Fax 277-6617
Jones Skills Center Adult
5451 Lemon Hill Ave 95824 916-433-2600
Nancy Compton, prin. Fax 433-2640
Old Marshall Adult Education Center Adult
2718 G St 95816 916-264-4113
Mary Prather, prin. Fax 264-4098

San Juan USD
Supt. — See Carmichael
Arcade Fundamental MS 600/6-8
3500 Edison Ave 95821 916-971-7300
Tony Oddo, prin. Fax 971-7821
Arden MS 700/6-8
1640 Watt Ave 95864 916-971-7306
Peggy Picardo, prin. Fax 971-7830
El Camino Fundamental HS 1,700/9-12
4300 El Camino Ave 95821 916-971-7430
Ernie Boone, prin. Fax 971-7429
Encina HS 800/9-12
1400 Bell St 95825 916-971-7538
Myrtle Berry, prin. Fax 971-7555
Mira Loma HS 1,800/9-12
4000 Edison Ave 95821 916-971-7485
Christopher Hoffman, prin. Fax 971-7483
Rio Americano HS 1,800/9-12
4540 American River Dr 95864 916-971-7494
Rob Hollingsworth, prin. Fax 971-7513
Salk MS 500/6-8
2950 Hurley Way 95864 916-971-7312
Jamey Schrey, prin. Fax 971-7694
Winterstein Adult Center Adult
900 Morse Ave 95864 916-971-7419
Bill Bettencourt, prin. Fax 482-8857

Alliant International University Post-Sec.
425 University Ave Ste 211 95825 916-565-2955
American River College Post-Sec.
4700 College Oak Dr 95841 916-484-8011
Bradshaw Christian S 1,000/PK-12
8324 Bradshaw Rd 95829 916-688-0521
Carl Eastvold, supt. Fax 688-0502
California State University-Sacramento Post-Sec.
6000 J St 95819 916-278-6011
Calvary Christian S 100/K-12
5051 47th Ave 95824 916-393-3633
Rodney Barlow, prin. Fax 393-5000

Capital Christian MSHS 600/6-12
9470 Micron Ave 95827 916-856-5611
Todd Jacobs, prin. Fax 856-5950
Christian Brothers HS 1,100/9-12
4315 Mrtn Lthr King Jr Blvd 95820 916-733-3600
Raymond Burnell, prin. Fax 733-3657
Cosumnes River College Post-Sec.
8401 Center Pkwy 95823 916-691-7344
Cristo Rey HS 9-12
6200 McMahon Dr 95824 916-733-2660
Sr. Kathryn Camacho, prin. Fax 739-1310
Elite Progressive School of Cosmetology Post-Sec.
5522 Garfield Ave 95841 916-338-1885
Federico College of Hairstyling Post-Sec.
1515 Sports Dr 95834 916-929-4242
Florin Christian S 200/K-12
8144 Florin Rd 95828 916-386-9792
Rev. Alex Amaro, admin.
High-Tech Institute Post-Sec.
9738 Lincoln Village Dr 95827 866-502-2627
Loretto HS 500/9-12
2360 El Camino Ave 95821 916-482-7793
Sr. Barbara Nelson, prin. Fax 482-3621
Maric College - Sacremento Campus Post-Sec.
4330 Watt Ave Ste 400 95821 916-649-8168
MTI College Post-Sec.
5221 Madison Ave 95841 916-339-1500
My-Le's Beauty College Post-Sec.
5972 Stockton Blvd 95824 916-422-0223
Precision Technical Institute Post-Sec.
9342 Tech Center Dr Ste 600 95826 916-366-3431
Sacramento City College Post-Sec.
3835 Freeport Blvd 95822 916-558-2111
Sacramento Country Day S 600/PK-12
2636 Latham Dr 95864 916-481-8811
Stephen T. Repsher, prin. Fax 481-6016
Sacramento Medical Foundation Blood Bank Post-Sec.
1625 Stockton Blvd 95816 916-456-1500
St. Francis HS 900/9-12
5900 Elvas Ave 95819 916-452-3461
Andreas Agos, prin. Fax 452-1591
Trinity Life Bible College Post-Sec.
5225 Hillsdale Blvd 95842 916-348-4689
Truck Driving Academy Post-Sec.
5711 Florin Perkins Rd 95828 916-381-2285
Universal Technical Institute Post-Sec.
4100 Duckhorn Dr 95834 877-884-2254
University of California-Davis Post-Sec.
2315 Stockton Blvd 95817 916-453-3096
University of the Pacific Post-Sec.
3200 5th Ave 95817 916-739-7105
Western Career College Post-Sec.
8909 Folsom Blvd 95826 916-361-1660
Western Pacific Truck School Post-Sec.
8720 Fruitridge Rd 95826 800-333-1233

Saint Helena, Napa, Pop. 6,028
St. Helena USD 1,400/K-12
465 Main St 94574 707-967-2708
Allan Gordon, supt. Fax 963-1335
www.sthelena.k12.ca.us
St. Helena HS 500/9-12
1401 Grayson Ave 94574 707-967-2740
James Zoll, prin. Fax 967-2735
Stevenson MS 300/6-8
1316 Hillview Pl 94574 707-967-2725
Mary Allen, prin. Fax 967-2734

Culinary Institute of America Greystone Post-Sec.
2555 Main St 94574 800-888-7850

Salida, Stanislaus, Pop. 4,499
Salida UNESD 3,300/K-8
4801 Sisk Rd 95368 209-545-0339
Antonio Borba Ed.D., supt. Fax 545-2682
www.salida.k12.ca.us/
Salida MS - Vella Campus 1,000/6-8
5041 Toomes Rd 95368 209-545-1633
Shannon Kettering, prin. Fax 545-0831

Maric College Post-Sec.
5172 Kiernan Ct 95368 209-543-7000

Salinas, Monterey, Pop. 146,431
Regional Occupational Center & Program
Supt. — None
Mission Trails ROP Vo/Tech
867 E Laurel Dr 93905 831-753-4209
Randy Bangs, dir. Fax 422-5115

Salinas UNHSD 13,800/7-12
431 W Alisal St 93901 831-796-7000
Roger Anton, supt. Fax 796-7005
www.salinas.k12.ca.us
Alisal HS 2,300/9-12
777 Williams Rd 93905 831-796-7610
Dan Burns, prin. Fax 796-7605
El Sausal MS 800/7-8
1155 E Alisal St 93905 831-796-7200
Sylvia Echeverri, prin. Fax 796-7205
Everret Alvarez HS 2,200/9-12
1900 Independence Blvd 93906 831-796-7810
Darren Sylvia, prin. Fax 796-7805
Harden MS 1,200/7-8
1561 McKinnon St 93906 831-796-7310
Abel Valdez, prin. Fax 796-7305
La Paz MS 1,100/7-8
1300 N Sanborn Rd 93905 831-796-7900
Steve Oliver, prin. Fax 796-7905
North Salinas HS 2,100/9-12
55 Kip Dr 93906 831-796-7500
Augie Caresani, prin. Fax 796-7505
Salinas HS 2,700/9-12
726 S Main St 93901 831-796-7400
John Macias, prin. Fax 796-7405
Washington MS 1,300/7-8
560 Iverson St 93901 831-796-7100
Candy McCarthy, prin. Fax 796-7105
Salinas Adult S Adult
20 Sherwood Pl 93906 831-796-6900
Corinne Price, prin. Fax 796-6905

Santa Rita UNESD 3,100/K-8
57 Russell Rd 93906 831-443-7200
James Fontana, supt. Fax 442-1729
www.santaritaschools.org
Gavilan View MS 1,200/6-8
18250 Van Buren Ave 93906 831-443-7212
John Gutierrez, prin. Fax 443-0908

Spreckels UNESD
Supt. — See Spreckels
Buena Vista MS 300/6-8
18250 Tara Dr 93908 831-455-8936
Eric Tarallo, prin. Fax 455-8832

Washington UNESD 1,000/K-8
43 San Benancio Rd 93908 831-484-2166
Dee Baker, supt. Fax 484-2828
schools.monterey.k12.ca.us/~sbenanci/
San Benancio MS 400/6-8
43 San Benancio Rd 93908 831-484-1172
Walt Robison, prin.

Hartnell College Post-Sec.
156 Homestead Ave 93901 831-755-6700
Heald College Post-Sec.
1450 N Main St 93906 831-443-1700
Notre Dame HS 400/9-12
455 Palma Dr 93901 831-751-1850
Sally Donnelly, prin. Fax 757-5749
Palma HS 600/7-12
919 Iverson St 93901 831-422-6391
Br. Patrick Dunne, prin. Fax 422-5065
Soaring Eagles Christian Academy 100/K-12
PO Box 875 93902 831-753-1840
Anna Musumeci, dir. Fax 758-5279

San Andreas, Calaveras, Pop. 2,115
Calaveras USD 3,700/K-12
PO Box 788 95249 209-754-3504
Jim Frost, supt. Fax 754-5361
www.calaveras.k12.ca.us
Calaveras HS 1,100/9-12
PO Box 607 95249 209-754-1811
Mike Merrill, prin. Fax 754-0276
Other Schools – See Valley Springs

San Anselmo, Marin, Pop. 12,018
Ross Valley ESD 1,800/K-8
110 Shaw Dr 94960 415-454-2160
Cheryl Crawley, supt. Fax 454-6840
rvsd.marin.k12.ca.us
Other Schools – See Fairfax

Tamalpais UNHSD
Supt. — See Larkspur
Sir Francis Drake HS 1,100/9-12
1327 Sir Francis Drake Blvd 94960 415-453-8770
Don Drake, prin. Fax 458-3429

San Domenico HS 9-12
1500 Butterfield Rd 94960 415-258-1939
Tekakwitha Wise, prin. Fax 258-1901
San Domenico MS 6-8
1500 Butterfield Rd 94960 415-258-1908
Jay Buckley, prin. Fax 258-1901
San Francisco Theological Seminary Post-Sec.
105 Seminary Rd 94960 415-451-2800

San Bernardino, San Bernardino, Pop. 198,550
Regional Occupational Center & Program
Supt. — None
San Bernardino County ROP Vo/Tech
601 N E St 92410 909-386-2449
Mark Lyons, dir. Fax 386-2479

San Bernardino City USD 57,500/K-12
777 N F St 92410 909-381-1100
Dr. Arturo Delgado, supt. Fax 388-1451
www.sbcusd.k12.ca.us
Arrowview MS 1,600/7-8
2299 N G St 92405 909-881-8109
Arwyn Wild, prin. Fax 881-8119
Arroyo Valley HS 3,200/9-12
1881 W Base Line St 92411 909-381-4295
Karen Craig, prin. Fax 386-2577
Cajon HS 2,700/9-12
1200 W Hill Dr 92407 909-881-8120
Toni Miller, prin. Fax 881-8141
Chavez MS 6-8
6650 Magnolia Ave 92407 909-386-2050
Stephanie Cereceres, prin. Fax 473-8443
Curtis MS 1,400/6-8
1472 E 6th St 92410 909-388-6332
Jim Dilday, prin. Fax 388-6339
Del Vallejo MS 1,700/6-8
1885 E Lynwood Dr 92404 909-881-8280
Charles McWilliams, prin. Fax 881-8285
Golden Valley MS 1,400/6-8
3800 N Waterman Ave 92404 909-881-8168
Steve Perlut, prin. Fax 881-5196
King MS 1,400/6-8
1250 Medical Center Dr 92411 909-388-6350
James Espinoza, prin. Fax 388-6361
Pacific HS 2,500/9-12
1020 Pacific St 92404 909-388-6419
Lorie Jacobson, prin. Fax 388-6427
Richardson Prep JHS 600/6-8
455 S K St 92410 909-388-6438
James Kissinger, prin. Fax 383-0368
San Bernardino HS 2,600/9-12
1850 N E St 92405 909-881-8217
Sandra Rodriguez, prin. Fax 881-8245
San Gorgonio HS 3,100/9-12
2299 Pacific St 92404 909-388-6524
Sandra Robbins, prin. Fax 889-3439
Shandin Hills MS 1,900/6-8
4301 Little Mountain Dr 92407 909-880-6666
Fax 880-6672
San Bernardino Adult S Adult
1200 N E St 92405 909-388-6000
Gary Dehrer, prin. Fax 381-2887
Other Schools – See Highland

Aquinas HS 300/9-12
2772 Sterling Ave 92404 909-886-4659
Daryl Sequeira, prin. Fax 886-7717
Art Institute of CA Inland Empire Post-Sec.
630 E Brier Dr 92408 909-915-2100
California State Univ.-San Bernadino Post-Sec.
5500 University Pkwy 92407 909-880-5000
Concorde Career College Post-Sec.
201 E Airport Dr # A 92408 909-884-8891
Dikaios Christian Academy 200/K-12
PO Box 9067 92427 909-473-0118
Von Sommerville, admin.
Everest College Post-Sec.
217 E Club Center Dr Ste A 92408 909-777-3300
Hair Masters University of Beauty Post-Sec.
208 W Highland Ave 92405 909-882-2987
Inland Technical Skills Center Post-Sec.
320 N E St Ste 513 92401 - -
ITT Technical Institute Post-Sec.
670 Carnegie Dr 92408 909-889-3800
Marinello School of Beauty Post-Sec.
721 W 2nd St Ste E 92410 909-884-8747
San Bernardino Valley College Post-Sec.
701 S Mount Vernon Ave 92410 909-888-6511
Temple Learning Center 100/PK-12
1777 W Base Line St 92411 909-885-4695
Rev. Raymond Turner, admin. Fax 885-5650

San Bruno, San Mateo, Pop. 39,752
San Bruno Park ESD 2,700/K-8
500 Acacia Ave 94066 650-624-3100
David Hutt, supt. Fax 266-9626
sbpsd.k12.ca.us
Parkside IS 600/7-8
1801 Niles Ave 94066 650-624-3180
Angela Addiego, prin. Fax 877-8195

San Mateo UNHSD
Supt. — See San Mateo
Capuchino HS 1,100/9-12
1501 Magnolia Ave 94066 650-558-2799
Edward Marquez, prin. Fax 558-2759

Highlands Christian S 900/PK-12
1900 Monterey Dr 94066 650-266-4339
Vernita Sheley, supt. Fax 742-6228
Skyline College Post-Sec.
3300 College Dr 94066 650-738-4100

San Carlos, San Mateo, Pop. 26,821
San Carlos ESD 500/5-8
826 Chestnut St 94070 650-508-7333
Patty Wool, supt. Fax 508-7340
www.sancarlos.k12.ca.us
Central MS 500/5-8
828 Chestnut St 94070 650-508-7321
Lynette Hovland, prin. Fax 508-7342

San Clemente, Orange, Pop. 60,235
Capistrano USD
Supt. — See San Juan Capistrano
Ayer MS 700/6-8
1271 Calle Sarmentoso 92673 949-366-9607
Dr. Cheryl Baughn, prin. Fax 366-1519
San Clemente HS 3,100/9-12
700 Avenida Pico 92673 949-492-4165
Dr. Charles Hinman, prin. Fax 361-5175
Shorecliffs MS 1,100/6-8
240 Via Socorro 92672 949-498-1660
Kenny Moe, prin. Fax 498-0826
Vista del Mar MS 600/6-8
1130 Avenida Talega 92673 949-234-5955
James Sieger, prin.

St. Michael's Academy 200/K-12
107 W Marquita 92672 949-366-9468
Daniel Sharp, prin. Fax 492-7238

San Diego, San Diego, Pop. 1,255,540
Poway USD
Supt. — See Poway
Bernardo Heights MS 1,700/6-8
12990 Paseo Lucido 92128 858-485-4850
Elaine Johnson, prin. Fax 485-4865
Black Mountain MS 1,500/6-8
9353 Oviedo St 92129 858-484-1300
David Hall, prin. Fax 538-9440
Mesa Verde MS 1,500/6-8
8375 Entreken Way 92129 858-538-5478
Greg Mizel, prin. Fax 538-8636
Mt. Carmel HS 2,200/9-12
9550 Carmel Mountain Rd 92129 858-484-1180
Dr. Tom McCoy, prin. Fax 538-9426
Oak Valley MS 6-8
16055 Wine Creek Rd 92127 858-487-2939
Sonya Wrisley, prin. Fax 457-0991
Rancho Bernardo HS 3,100/9-12
13010 Paseo Lucido 92128 858-485-4800
Paul Robinson, prin. Fax 485-4822
Westview HS 2,000/9-12
13500 Camino del Sur 92129 858-780-2000
Dawn Kastner, prin. Fax 780-2054

Regional Occupational Center & Program
Supt. — None
San Diego County ROP Vo/Tech
6401 Linda Vista Rd Ste 408 92111 858-292-3529
Steve Pinning, dir. Fax 268-9726

San Diego USD 117,600/PK-12
4100 Normal St 92103 619-725-8000
Dr. Carl Cohn, supt. Fax 291-7182
www.sandi.net/
Bell JHS 1,600/7-9
620 Briarwood Rd 92139 619-479-7111
Kristi Dean, prin. Fax 470-6054
Business HS 400/9-12
1405 Park Blvd 92101 619-525-7455
Joseph Austin, prin. Fax 525-7337
Challenger MS 1,200/6-8
10810 Parkdale Ave 92126 858-586-7001
Lamont Jackson, prin. Fax 271-5203

Clairemont HS 1,400/9-12
4150 Ute Dr 92117 858-273-0201
Fax 272-4219
Clark MS 1,600/6-8
4388 Thorn St 92105 619-563-6801
Barbra Balser, prin. Fax 563-9653
Communications Investigations HS 500/9-12
1405 Park Blvd 92101 619-525-7455
Cesar Alcantar, prin. Fax 525-7259
Community Health and Medical Practices 400/9-12
4191 Colts Way 92115 619-583-2500
Kenneth Hurst, prin. Fax 229-9088
Correia JHS 1,000/7-8
4302 Valeta St 92107 619-222-0476
Linda Taggert, prin. Fax 221-0147
Creative Performing & Media Arts S 6-8
5095 Arvinels Ave 92117 858-278-5917
Fred Hilgers, prin. Fax 293-7235
De Portola MS 1,000/6-8
11010 Clairemont Mesa Blvd 92124 858-496-8080
Listy Gillingham, prin. Fax 576-4419
Digital Media and Design HS 400/9-12
7651 Wellington Way 92111 858-496-8370
Cheryl Hibbeln, prin. Fax 278-6349
Farb MS 900/6-8
4880 La Cuenta Dr 92124 858-496-8090
Susan Levy, prin. Fax 576-0931
Foster Construction Tech Academy 300/9-12
7651 Wellington Way 92111 858-496-8370
Glenn Hillegas, dir. Fax 496-4907
Gompers Magnet HS 600/10-12
1110 Carolina Ln 92102 619-527-5138
Donald Mitchell, prin.
Henry HS 2,400/9-12
6702 Wandermere Dr 92120 619-286-7700
Patricia Crowder, prin. Fax 229-0370
Hoover HS 2,200/9-12
4474 El Cajon Blvd 92115 619-283-6281
Douglas Williams, prin. Fax 280-5837
International Business 400/9-12
7651 Wellington Way 92111 858-496-8370
Ana Diaz-Booz, prin. Fax 496-8379
International Studies HS 9-12
1405 Park Blvd 92101 619-525-7455
Karen Wroblewski, prin. Fax 744-7651
Invention & Design Educational Academy 9-12
4191 Colts Way 92115 619-583-2500
John Spiegel, dir. Fax 582-4173
Kroc MS 800/7-8
5050 Conrad Ave 92117 858-496-8150
Susan Manning, prin. Fax 292-5296
Law and Business 400/9-12
4191 Colts Way 92115 619-583-2500
Monique Robertson, prin. Fax 229-2005
Lead Explore Achieve Discover & Serve HS 500/9-12
1405 Park Blvd 92101 619-525-7455
Scott Giusti, prin. Fax 744-7676
Lewis MS 1,100/6-8
5170 Greenbrier Ave 92120 619-583-3233
Dr. Barbara Forcier, prin. Fax 229-1338
Lincoln HS 9-12
140 S 49th St 92113 619-725-8000
Madison HS 1,500/9-12
4833 Doliva Dr 92117 858-496-8410
Carol Whaley, prin. Fax 496-8421
Mann MS 1,200/6-8
4345 54th St 92115 619-582-8990
Valerie Voss, prin. Fax 583-2637
Marshall MS 1,100/6-8
9700 Avenue of Nations 92131
Rick Novak, prin.
Marston MS 1,200/6-8
3799 Clairemont Dr 92117 858-273-2030
Dr. Elizabeth Cook, prin. Fax 272-3460
Media Visual & Performing Arts HS 500/9-12
1405 Park Blvd 92101 619-525-7455
Shirley Rehkopf, prin. Fax 744-7680
Mira Mesa HS 2,600/9-12
10510 Reagan Rd 92126 858-566-2262
Jeff Olivero, prin. Fax 549-9541
Mission Bay HS 1,700/9-12
2475 Grand Ave 92109 858-273-1313
Cheryl Seelos, prin. Fax 270-8294
Montgomery MS 700/6-8
2470 Ulric St 92111 858-496-8330
Jonathan Ton, prin. Fax 292-0125
Morse HS 2,900/9-12
6905 Skyline Dr 92114 619-262-0763
Rocio Weiss, prin. Fax 262-6835
Multimedia and Visual Arts 400/9-12
4191 Colts Way 92115 619-583-2500
Diego Gutierrez, dir. Fax 229-9225
Pacific Beach MS 900/6-8
4676 Ingraham St 92109 858-273-9070
Michelle Irwin, prin. Fax 270-8063
Pershing MS 1,000/6-8
8204 San Carlos Dr 92119 619-465-3234
Sarah Sullivan, prin. Fax 461-5447
Point Loma HS 2,000/9-12
2335 Chatsworth Blvd 92106 619-223-3121
Barbara Samilson, prin. Fax 225-1298
Roosevelt MS 1,000/6-8
3366 Park Blvd 92103 619-293-4450
Dr. Julie Martel, prin. Fax 497-0918
San Diego Met HS Vo/Tech
7250 Mesa College Dr 92111 619-388-2299
Mildred Phillips, prin.
School of Creative & Performing Arts 1,500/6-12
2425 Dusk Dr 92139 619-470-0555
Liz Laughlin, prin. Fax 470-9430
Science Connections & Technology HS 400/9-12
7651 Wellington Way 92111 858-496-8370
Rochelle Dawes, dir. Fax 715-9504
SCITECH HS 500/9-12
1405 Park Blvd 92101 619-525-7455
Dianne Cordero, prin. Fax 744-7677
Scripps Ranch HS 2,300/9-12
10410 Treena St 92131 858-621-9020
Donna Campbell, prin. Fax 621-0646
Serra HS 2,000/9-12
5156 Santo Rd 92124 858-496-8342
Donna Somerville, prin. Fax 571-3457

Standley MS 1,300/6-8
6298 Radcliffe Dr 92122 858-455-0550
Godwin Higa, prin. Fax 546-7627
Taft MS 800/6-8
9191 Gramercy Dr 92123 858-496-8245
Kelly Peacock-Wright, prin. Fax 496-8138
University City HS 1,900/9-12
6949 Genesee Ave 92122 858-457-3040
Ernest Smith, prin. Fax 458-9432
Wangenheim MS 1,400/6-8
9230 Gold Coast Dr 92126 858-578-1400
Robert Grano, prin. Fax 578-9481
Wilson MS 1,100/6-8
3838 Orange Ave 92105 619-280-1661
Bernadette Nguyen, prin. Fax 280-6437
Other Schools – See La Jolla

San Dieguito UNHSD
Supt. — See Encinitas
Canyon Crest Academy 400/9-10
5951 Village Center Loop Rd 92130 858-350-0253
David Jaffe, prin. Fax 350-0280
Carmel Valley MS 1,300/7-8
3800 Mykonos Ln 92130 858-481-8221
Michael Grove, prin. Fax 481-8256
Torrey Pines HS 3,300/9-12
3710 Del Mar Heights Rd 92130 858-755-0125
Brett Killeen, prin. Fax 481-0098

Sweetwater UNHSD
Supt. — See Chula Vista
Mar Vista MS 1,300/7-8
1267 Thermal Ave 92154 619-628-5100
Scott Tanner, prin. Fax 423-8431
Montgomery HS 2,400/9-12
3250 Palm Ave 92154 619-628-3007
Samuel Montes, prin. Fax 424-6473
Montgomery MS 1,100/7-8
1051 Picador Blvd 92154 619-662-4000
Maria Lizarraga, prin. Fax 428-6517
San Ysidro HS 1,800/9-12
5353 Airway Rd 92154 619-710-2300
Hector Espinoza, prin. Fax 710-2318
Southwest HS 2,400/9-12
1685 Hollister St 92154 619-628-3023
Sid Salazar, prin. Fax 423-8253
Southwest MS 900/7-9
2710 Iris Ave 92154 619-628-4000
Steve Lizarraga, prin. Fax 423-1151
Montgomery Adult S Adult
3240 Palm Ave 92154 619-628-3017
Dr. Thomas Teagle, prin. Fax 423-7876

Academy of Our Lady of Peace 800/9-12
4860 Oregon St 92116 619-297-2266
Sr. Dolores Anchondo, prin. Fax 297-2473
Alliant International University Post-Sec.
10455 Pomerado Rd 92131 858-635-4772
Art Institute of California Post-Sec.
7650 Mission Valley Rd 92108 858-598-1200
Associated Technical College Post-Sec.
1445 6th Ave 92101 619-234-2181
Avance Beauty College Post-Sec.
750 Beyer Way Ste B 92154 619-575-1511
Balboa City S, 525 Hawthorn St 92101 100/1-12
Dr. Stephen Parker, dir. 619-298-2990
California College San Diego Post-Sec.
2820 Camino Del Rio S # 300 92108 619-295-5785
California Western School of Law Post-Sec.
225 Cedar St 92101 619-239-0391
Cathedral Catholic HS 9-12
5555 Del Mar Heights Rd 92130 858-523-4000
Michael Deely, prin. Fax 523-4097
Childrens Creative/Performing Arts Acad. 300/K-12
3051 El Cajon Blvd 92104 619-584-2454
Janet Cherif, prin. Fax 584-2422
Coleman College Post-Sec.
8888 Balboa Ave 92123 858-499-0202
Concorde Career Institute Post-Sec.
4393 Imperial Ave Ste 100 92113 619-688-0800
Design Institute of San Diego Post-Sec.
8555 Commerce Ave 92121 858-566-1200
Fashion Careers College Post-Sec.
1923 Morena Blvd 92110 619-275-4700
FIDM/The Fashion Institute Post-Sec.
1010 2nd Ave Ste 200 92101 800-243-3436
Halstrom HS 50/7-12
5333 Mission Center Rd 92108 619-297-5311
Carolyn Lindstrom, dir. Fax 297-5313
Horizon JSHS 600/7-12
5331 Mount Alifan Dr 92111 858-244-0333
Jason Cook, prin. Fax 654-3054
H-Town Christian Academy 50/1-12
6785 Imperial Ave 92114 858-869-3052
Frank Henry, prin. Fax 869-3052
International Prof School of Body Work Post-Sec.
1366 Hornblend St 92109 858-272-4142
ITT Technical Institute Post-Sec.
9680 Granite Ridge Dr 92123 858-571-8500
Keller Graduate School of Management Post-Sec.
2655 Cmno Del Rio N #201 92108 619-683-2446
Lutheran HS of San Diego 100/9-12
2755 55th St 92105 619-262-4444
Hanne Krause, prin. Fax 262-6297
Maranatha Christian S 500/PK-10
9050 Maranatha Dr 92127 858-759-9737
Dennis Frey, prin. Fax 759-4001
Marian Catholic HS 600/9-12
1002 18th St 92154 619-423-2121
George Milke, prin. Fax 423-6910
Maric College Post-Sec.
9055 Balboa Ave 92123 858-279-4500
Maric College East County Post-Sec.
6160 Mission Gorge Rd #108 92120 619-282-9000
Marinello School of Beauty Post-Sec.
7550 Miramar Rd Ste 440 92126 858-547-9260
Midway Baptist S 400/K-12
2460 Palm Ave 92154 619-424-7875
Stephen Johnson, prin. Fax 424-9204
Mueller College of Holistic Studies Post-Sec.
4607 Park Blvd 92116 619-291-9811

National University School of Law Post-Sec.
3580 Aero Ct 92123 619-563-7300
Newschool of Architecture & Design Post-Sec.
1249 F St 92101 619-235-4100
Occupational Training Services Post-Sec.
8799 Balboa Ave Ste 100 92123 858-560-0411
Pacific College of Oriental Medicine Post-Sec.
7445 Mssn Valley Rd #105 92108 619-574-6909
Parker S 700/6-12
6501 Linda Vista Rd 92111 858-569-7900
Dr. Richard Blumenthal, hdmstr. Fax 569-0621
Platt College Post-Sec.
6250 El Cajon Blvd 92115 619-265-0107
Point Loma Nazarene University Post-Sec.
3900 Lomaland Dr 92106 619-849-2200
Remington College Post-Sec.
123 Cmino De La Reina #100N 92108 619-686-8600
St. Augustine HS 700/9-12
3266 Nutmeg St 92104 619-282-2184
Jim Horne, prin. Fax 282-1203
San Diego City College Post-Sec.
1313 Park Blvd 92101 619-230-2400
San Diego Jewish Academy 700/K-12
11860 Carmel Creek Rd 92130 858-704-3700
Larry Acheatel, dir.
San Diego Mesa College Post-Sec.
7250 Mesa College Dr 92111 858-627-2600
San Diego Miramar College Post-Sec.
10440 Black Mountain Rd 92126 619-388-7800
San Diego State University Post-Sec.
5500 Campanile Dr 92182 619-594-5200
Thomas Jefferson School of Law Post-Sec.
2121 San Diego Ave 92110 619-297-9700
Torah HS of San Diego 100/9-12
9001 Towne Centre Dr 92122 858-558-6880
Rabbi Michoel Peikes, prin. Fax 558-6835
Travel University International Post-Sec.
3870 Murphy Canyon Rd #310 92123 858-292-9755
United Truck & Car Driving School Post-Sec.
2425 Camino Del Rio S 92108 619-296-2020
University of California Medical Center Post-Sec.
200 W Arbor Dr # H-910C 92103 619-543-6654
University of San Diego Post-Sec.
5998 Alcala Park 92110 619-260-4600
Veterans Affairs Medical Center Post-Sec.
3350 La Jolla Village Dr 92161 858-552-8585

San Dimas, Los Angeles, Pop. 35,850
Bonita USD 10,200/K-12
115 W Allen Ave 91773 909-971-8200
Dr. Robert C. Otto, supt. Fax 971-8329
www.bonita.k12.ca.us
Lone Hill MS 1,000/6-8
115 W Allen Ave 91773 909-971-8270
Ray Arredondo, prin. Fax 971-8279
San Dimas HS 1,500/9-12
115 W Allen Ave 91773 909-971-8230
Kristine Kulow, prin. Fax 971-8239
Other Schools – See La Verne

ITT Technical Institute Post-Sec.
650 W Cienega Ave 91773 909-971-2300
Life Pacific College Post-Sec.
1100 W Covina Blvd 91773 800-356-0001

San Fernando, Los Angeles, Pop. 24,207
Los Angeles USD
Supt. — See Los Angeles
San Fernando HS 4,400/9-12
11133 Omelveny Ave 91340 818-898-7600
Kenneth Lee, prin. Fax 365-7255
San Fernando MS 2,100/6-8
130 N Brand Blvd 91340 818-837-5400
Rafael Balderas, prin. Fax 365-8911

Calvary Baptist Christian S 100/PK-12
12928 Vaughn St 91340 818-899-8206
Aaron Jackson, prin. Fax 890-0277

San Francisco, San Francisco, Pop. 739,426
Regional Occupational Center & Program
Supt. — None
San Francisco County ROP Vo/Tech
1098 Harrison St 94103 415-355-7711
Marigrace Cohen, coord. Fax 355-7744

San Francisco USD 53,200/PK-12
555 Franklin St 94102 415-241-6000
Gwen Chan, supt. Fax 555-5555
www.sfusd.edu
Academy of Arts & Sciences 9-12
555 Portola Dr 94131 415-695-5700
Donn Harris, prin. Fax 695-5326
Aptos MS 900/6-8
105 Aptos Ave 94127 415-469-4520
Ericka Lovrin, prin. Fax 333-9038
Balboa HS 1,000/9-12
1000 Cayuga Ave 94112 415-469-4090
Patricia Gray, prin. Fax 469-0859
Burton HS 1,800/9-12
400 Mansell St 94134 415-469-4550
Eric Marshall, prin. Fax 239-6806
Davis College Prep Academy 200/7-9
1195 Hudson Ave 94124 415-695-5390
Marcus Blacksher, prin. Fax 920-5067
Denman MS 700/6-8
241 Oneida Ave 94112 415-469-4535
Gary Pacini, prin. Fax 585-8402
Downtown HS 300/9-12
693 Vermont St 94107 415-695-5860
Richard Maggi, prin. Fax 695-5863
Everett MS 500/6-8
450 Church St 94114 415-241-6344
Francisco Duran, prin. Fax 241-6361
Francisco MS 500/6-8
2190 Powell St 94133 415-291-7900
Judith Giampaoli, prin. Fax 291-7910
Galileo Academy of Science & Technology 2,000/9-12
1150 Francisco St 94109 415-749-3430
Vicki Pesek, prin. Fax 771-2322

Giannini MS 1,300/6-8
3151 Ortega St 94122 415-759-2770
Leslie Trook, prin. Fax 664-8541
Hoover MS 1,300/6-8
2290 14th Ave 94116 415-759-2783
Judy Dong, prin. Fax 759-2881
King Academic MS 500/6-8
350 Girard St 94134 415-330-1500
Gil Cho, prin. Fax 468-7295
Lick MS 500/6-8
1220 Noe St 94114 415-695-5675
Carmelo Sgarlato, prin. Fax 695-5360
Lincoln HS 2,500/9-12
2162 24th Ave 94116 415-759-2700
Ron Pang, prin. Fax 566-2224
Lowell HS 2,600/9-12
1101 Eucalyptus Dr 94132 415-759-2730
Amy Hansen, prin. Fax 759-2742
Mann MS 700/6-8
3351 23rd St 94110 415-695-5881
Paul Jacobsen, prin. Fax 282-7868
Marina MS 1,000/6-8
3500 Fillmore St 94123 415-749-3495
Dennis Chew, prin. Fax 921-7539
Marshall HS 900/9-12
45 Conkling St 94124 415-695-5612
Paul Cheng, prin. Fax 285-5283
Mission HS 1,000/9-12
3750 18th St 94114 415-241-6240
Kevin Truitt, prin. Fax 626-1641
Newcomer HS 400/9-12
1350 7th Ave 94122 415-242-2601
Balrai Thiara, prin. Fax 242-2660
O'Connell HS 900/9-12
2355 Folsom St 94110 415-695-5370
Janet Schulze, prin. Fax 695-5379
Presidio MS 1,200/6-8
450 30th Ave 94121 415-750-8435
Alvin Dea, prin. Fax 750-8445
Roosevelt MS 800/6-8
460 Arguello Blvd 94118 415-750-8446
Diane Panagotacos, prin. Fax 750-8455
School of the Arts 600/9-12
555 Portola Dr 94131 415-695-5700
Donn Harris, prin. Fax 695-5326
Small MS for Equity 300/6-8
325 La Grande Ave 94112 415-469-4547
Bill Sanderson, prin. Fax 586-5217
Visitacion Valley MS 500/6-8
450 Raymond Ave 94134 415-469-4590
James Dierke, prin. Fax 469-4703
Wallenberg HS 600/9-12
40 Vega St 94115 415-749-3469
Aileen Murphy, prin. Fax 346-7303
Washington HS 2,300/9-12
600 32nd Ave 94121 415-750-8400
Andrew Ishibashi, prin. Fax 750-8417

Academy of Art University Post-Sec.
79 New Montgomery St 94105 415-274-2200
American College of California Post-Sec.
760 Market St Ste 1009 94102 415-677-9717
American Coll of Traditional Chinese Med Post-Sec.
455 Arkansas St 94107 415-282-7600
American Conservatory Theater Post-Sec.
30 Grant Ave 94108 415-439-2350
Archbishop Riordan HS 800/9-12
175 Phelan Ave 94112 415-586-8200
Gabriel Crotti, prin. Fax 587-1310
Art Institute of California - San Fran Post-Sec.
1170 Market St 94102 888-493-3261
Bay S of San Francisco 100/9-12
35 Keyes Ave 94129 415-561-5800
Rev. Malcolm Manson, hdmstr.
Bridgemont JSHS 100/6-12
777 Brotherhood Way 94132 415-333-7600
Peter Tropper, admin. Fax 333-7603
California College of the Arts Post-Sec.
450 Irwin St 94107 415-703-9500
California Culinary Academy Post-Sec.
625 Polk St 94102 415-771-3536
California Institute of Integral Studies Post-Sec.
1453 Mission St 94103 415-575-6100
City College of San Francisco Post-Sec.
50 Phelan Ave 94112 415-239-3000
Convent of the Sacred Heart HS 200/9-12
2222 Broadway St 94115 415-563-2900
Douglas Grant, prin. Fax 929-0553
Cornerstone Academy 500/6-12
501 Cambridge St 94134 415-585-5183
Derrick Wong, prin. Fax 469-9600
De Marillac Academy 100/4-8
175 Golden Gate Ave 94102 415-552-5220
John Omernik, prin. Fax 621-5632
Drew S 300/9-12
2901 California St 94115 415-409-3739
Samuel Cuddeback, prin. Fax 346-0720
Everest College Post-Sec.
814 Mission St Ste 500 94103 415-777-2500
FIDM/The Fashion Institute Post-Sec.
55 Stockton St 94108 415-433-6691
French-American International S 900/PK-12
150 Oak St 94102 415-558-2000
Jane Camblin, hdmstr. Fax 558-2024
Golden Gate University Post-Sec.
536 Mission St 94105 415-442-7000
Heald College Post-Sec.
350 Mission St 94105 415-808-3000
Hebrew Academy of San Francisco 200/PK-12
645 14th Ave 94118 415-752-7333
Rabbi Pinchas Lipner, dean Fax 752-5851
Immaculate Conception Academy 300/9-12
3625 24th St 94110 415-824-2052
Sr. Janice Wellington, prin. Fax 821-4677
Jewish Community HS of the Bay 200/9-12
1835 Ellis St 94115 415-345-9777
Rabbi Sheldon Dorph, hdmstr. Fax 345-1888
Keller Graduate School of Management Post-Sec.
455 Market St Ste 1650 94105 415-243-8585
Lick-Wilmerding HS 400/9-12
755 Ocean Ave 94112 415-333-4021
Albert Adams, hdmstr. Fax 586-0737

Lycee Francais-Laperouse S 500/K-12
755 Ashbury St 94117 415-661-5232
Alain Cuzin, hdmstr. Fax 661-0246
Mercy HS 600/9-12
3250 19th Ave 94132 415-334-0525
Dorothy McCrea, prin. Fax 334-9726
Miss Marty's Sch. Beauty & Hairstyling Post-Sec.
1087 Mission St 94103 415-227-4240
New College School of Law Post-Sec.
50 Fell St 94102 415-241-1300
Oxman College Post-Sec.
375 3rd Ave 94118 415-751-6461
Sacred Heart Cathedral Prep S 1,200/9-12
1055 Ellis St 94109 415-775-6626
Dr. Ken Hogarty, prin. Fax 931-6941
St. Ignatius College Prep S 1,400/9-12
2001 37th Ave 94116 415-731-7500
Charles Dullea, prin. Fax 731-2227
San Francisco Art Institute Post-Sec.
800 Chestnut St 94133 415-771-7020
San Francisco Christian S 300/K-12
25 Whittier St 94112 415-586-1117
Mark Asire, admin.
San Francisco Conservatory of Music Post-Sec.
50 Oak St 94102 800-899-7326
San Francisco State University Post-Sec.
1600 Holloway Ave 94132 415-338-1111
San Francisco University HS 400/9-12
3065 Jackson St 94115 415-447-3100
Dr. Michael Diamonti, hdmstr. Fax 447-5801
San Francisco Waldorf S 400/PK-12
2938 Washington St 94115 415-931-2750
Joan Caldarera, admin. Fax 931-0590
Saybrook Graduate School Post-Sec.
747 Front St Fl 3 94111 800-825-4480
Sonoma College - San Francisco Post-Sec.
301 Howard St Ste 510 94105 888-649-7801
Stuart Hall HS 200/9-12
1715 Octavia St 94109 415-345-5811
Gordon Sharafinski, hdmstr. Fax 931-9161
University of California Post-Sec.
Parnassus And 3rd Ave 94143 415-476-9000
University of CA Hastings College of Law Post-Sec.
200 McAllister St 94102 415-565-4600
University of San Francisco Post-Sec.
2130 Fulton St 94117 415-422-5555
University of the Pacific Post-Sec.
2155 Webster St 94115 415-929-6400
Urban S of San Francisco 300/9-12
1563 Page St 94117 415-626-2919
Mark Salkind, dir. Fax 626-1125
Voice of Pentecost Academy 200/K-12
1970 Ocean Ave 94127 415-334-0105
Sherwood Jansen, prin.
Woodside International S 100/6-12
1555 Irving St 94122 415-564-1063
John Edwards, hdmstr. Fax 564-2511

San Gabriel, Los Angeles, Pop. 41,056
Alhambra City SD
Supt. — See Alhambra
San Gabriel HS 9-12
801 S Ramona St 91776 626-308-2352
Marsha Gilbert, prin. Fax 308-2332
San Gabriel Community Adult Center Adult
801 S Ramona St 91776 626-308-2319
Fax 308-2748

San Gabriel USD 5,600/K-12
408 Junipero Serra Dr 91776 626-451-5400
Susan Parks Ed.D., supt. Fax 451-5494
www.sgusd.k12.ca.us
Gabrielino HS 1,700/9-12
1327 S San Gabriel Blvd 91776 626-573-2453
Eugene Murphy Ed.D., prin. Fax 573-5089
Jefferson MS 1,200/6-8
1372 E Las Tunas Dr 91776 626-287-5260
John Fox, prin. Fax 285-5387

San Gabriel Mission HS 300/9-12
254 S Santa Anita Ave 91776 626-282-3181
Carolyn Nelson, prin. Fax 282-4209
San Gabriel SDA Academy 700/K-12
8827 E Broadway 91776 626-292-1156
Robert Peeke, prin. Fax 285-4949

Sanger, Fresno, Pop. 22,041
Regional Occupational Center & Program
Supt. — None
Valley ROP Vo/Tech
1305 Q St 93657 559-876-2122
Debbe Marvin-Deeter, dir. Fax 876-2102

Sanger USD 7,200/K-12
1905 7th St 93657 559-875-6521
Marcus Johnson, supt. Fax 875-0311
www.sangerusd.com/
Sanger HS 2,100/9-12
1045 Bethel Ave 93657 559-875-7121
Dan Chacon, prin. Fax 875-5721
Washington Academic MS 1,000/6-8
1705 10th St 93657 559-875-5561
Jon Yost, prin. Fax 875-6365
Sanger Adult S Adult
1045 Bethel Ave 93657 559-875-4235
Jon Taplac, prin. Fax 875-1820

San Jacinto, Riverside, Pop. 30,253
San Jacinto USD 7,200/K-12
2045 S San Jacinto Ave 92583 951-929-7700
Shari Fox Ed.D., supt. Fax 658-3574
www.sanjacinto.k12.ca.us/
Monte Vista MS 800/6-8
181 N Ramona Blvd 92583 951-654-9361
Sharon Raffiee, prin. Fax 654-0173
North Mountain MS 900/6-8
1202 E 7th St 92583 951-487-7797
Garry Packham, prin. Fax 487-7799
San Jacinto HS 1,800/9-12
500 Idyllwild Dr 92583 951-654-7374
Gwen Smith, prin. Fax 654-7702

Alpha Omega Christian S 50/K-12
950 N Ramona Blvd Ste 5 92582 951-487-2079
Susan Hall, prin. Fax 487-0828
Mt. San Jacinto College Post-Sec.
1499 N State St 92583 951-487-6752

San Joaquin, Fresno, Pop. 3,579
Golden Plains USD 1,900/K-12
PO Box 937 93660 559-693-1115
Joann Evans, supt. Fax 693-4366
www.gpusd.k12.ca.us
Golden Plains Adult Educ-San Joaquin Adult
PO Box 937 93660 559-693-2401
Aurora Ramirez, prin. Fax 693-2519
Other Schools – See Tranquillity

San Jose, Santa Clara, Pop. 912,332
Alum Rock UNESD 12,500/PK-8
2930 Gay Ave 95127 408-928-6800
Norma Martinez, supt. Fax 928-6416
www.arusd.org/
Fischer MS 700/6-8
1720 Hopkins Dr 95122 408-928-7500
Nancy Gutierrez, prin. Fax 928-7501
George MS 500/6-8
277 Mahoney Dr 95127 408-928-7600
David Franklin, prin. Fax 928-7601
Mathson MS 500/6-8
2050 Kammerer Ave 95116 408-928-7950
Denise Giacamini, prin. Fax 928-7951
Ocala MS 600/6-8
2800 Ocala Ave 95148 408-928-8350
Oscar Leon, prin. Fax 928-8351
Pala MS 600/6-8
149 N White Rd 95127 408-928-8500
Sid Haro, prin. Fax 928-8501
Renaissance Academy 100/6-8
1720 Hopkins Dr 95122 408-928-1950
Jason Sorich, prin. Fax 928-1951
Sheppard MS 600/6-8
480 Rough and Ready Rd 95133 408-928-8800
Donita Grace, prin. Fax 928-8801

Berryessa UNESD 8,400/K-8
1376 Piedmont Rd 95132 408-923-1800
Marc Liebman Ph.D., supt. Fax 923-0623
www.berryessa.k12.ca.us
Morrill MS 900/6-8
1970 Morrill Ave 95132 408-923-1930
Ron Fairchild, prin. Fax 946-0776
Piedmont MS 1,100/6-8
955 Piedmont Rd 95132 408-923-1945
Joe Amelio, prin. Fax 251-2392
Sierramont MS 1,000/6-8
3155 Kimlee Dr 95132 408-923-1955
Kelly Greelis Green, prin. Fax 729-5840

Campbell UNESD
Supt. — See Campbell
Monroe MS 900/5-8
1055 S Monroe St 95128 408-556-0360
Geertje Bamford, prin. Fax 341-7020

Campbell UNHSD 7,800/9-12
3235 Union Ave 95124 408-371-0960
Rhonda Farber, supt. Fax 558-3006
www.cuhsd.org/
Branham HS 1,500/9-12
1570 Branham Ln 95118 408-267-1020
Tom Utic, prin. Fax 267-2676
Del Mar HS 1,300/9-12
1224 Del Mar Ave Ste A 95128 408-298-0260
Jim Russell, prin. Fax 295-9476
Leigh HS 1,700/9-12
5210 Leigh Ave 95124 408-377-4470
Donna Hope, prin. Fax 265-7525
Other Schools – See Campbell, Saratoga

Cupertino UNSD
Supt. — See Cupertino
Miller MS 800/6-8
6151 Rainbow Dr 95129 408-252-3755
Richard Taylor, prin. Fax 255-5269

East Side UNHSD 24,500/9-12
830 N Capitol Ave 95133 408-347-5000
Bob Nunez, supt. Fax 347-5045
www.esuhsd.org/
Hill HS 2,100/9-12
3200 Senter Rd 95111 408-347-4100
Fax 347-4115
Independence HS 4,000/9-12
1776 Educational Park Dr 95133 408-928-9500
Cec Bell, prin. Fax 928-9515
Lick HS 1,100/9-12
57 N White Rd 95127 408-347-4400
Bill Rice, prin. Fax 347-4415
Mt. Pleasant HS 2,000/9-12
1750 S White Rd 95127 408-937-2800
Grettel Castro-Stanley, prin. Fax 937-2815
Oak Grove HS 2,700/9-12
285 Blossom Hill Rd 95123 408-347-6500
Rich Frias, dir. Fax 347-6515
Overfelt HS 1,500/9-12
1835 Cunningham Ave 95122 408-347-5900
Diego Certa, prin. Fax 347-5915
Piedmont Hills HS 2,100/9-12
1377 Piedmont Rd 95132 408-347-3800
Bruce Shimizu Ed.D., prin. Fax 347-3805
Santa Teresa HS 2,200/9-12
6150 Snell Ave 95123 408-347-6200
John Duran, prin. Fax 347-6215
Silver Creek HS 2,300/9-12
3434 Silver Creek Rd 95121 408-347-5600
Thelma Boac, prin. Fax 347-5615
Yerba Buena HS 1,600/9-12
1855 Lucretia Ave 95122 408-347-4700
Juan Cruz, prin. Fax 347-4715
East Side Adult Center Adult
625 Educational Park Dr 95133 408-928-9300
Cari Vaeth, dir. Fax 928-9309

Evergreen ESD 13,200/K-8
3188 Quimby Rd 95148 408-270-6800
Clif Black, supt. Fax 274-3894
www.eesd.org/
Chaboya MS 1,100/7-8
3276 Fowler Rd 95135 408-270-6900
Bette Samdahl, prin. Fax 270-6916
LeyVa MS 800/7-8
1865 Monrovia Dr 95122 408-270-4992
Dolores Garcia, prin. Fax 270-5462
Quimby Oak MS 1,000/7-8
3190 Quimby Rd 95148 408-270-6735
Phil Bond, prin. Fax 223-4533

Franklin-McKinley ESD 9,800/K-8
645 Wool Creek Dr 95112 408-283-6000
Dr. John Porter, supt. Fax 283-6022
www.fmsd.k12.ca.us
Fair MS 800/7-8
1702 Mclaughlin Ave 95122 408-283-6400
Beverly Hill, prin. Fax 283-6419
Sylvandale JHS 1,000/7-8
653 Sylvandale Ave 95111 408-363-5700
Rafael Cruz, prin. Fax 363-5649

Fremont UNHSD
Supt. — See Sunnyvale
Lynbrook HS 1,900/9-12
1280 Johnson Ave 95129 408-366-7700
Mike White, prin. Fax 257-0551

Moreland ESD 3,100/K-8
4711 Campbell Ave 95130 408-874-2900
Glen Ishiwata, supt. Fax 374-8863
www.moreland.k12.ca.us
Moreland MS 700/6-8
4600 Student Ln 95130 408-874-3300
Norma Jeanne Ready, prin. Fax 379-3622

Morgan Hill USD
Supt. — See Morgan Hill
Murphy MS 600/7-8
141 Avenida Espana 95139 408-281-1500
Barbara Nakasone, prin. Fax 281-0312

Mount Pleasant ESD 2,900/K-8
3434 Marten Ave 95148 408-223-3700
George L. Perez, supt. Fax 223-3715
www.mountpleasant.k12.ca.us
Boeger MS 600/7-8
1944 Flint Ave 95148 408-223-3770
Toni Cook, prin. Fax 223-6959

Oak Grove ESD 11,500/K-8
6578 Santa Teresa Blvd 95119 408-227-8300
Manny Barbara, supt. Fax 227-2719
www.ogsd.k12.ca.us
Bernal IS 900/7-8
6610 San Ignacio Ave 95119 408-578-5731
Katherine Baker, prin. Fax 578-7367
Davis IS 900/7-8
5035 Edenview Dr 95111 408-227-0616
Maria Wetzel, prin. Fax 224-8957
Herman IS 800/7-8
5955 Blossom Ave 95123 408-226-1886
Barry Whittall, prin. Fax 226-1897

Regional Occupational Center & Program
Supt. — None
Metropolitan Education District Vo/Tech
760 Hillsdale Ave 95136 408-723-6464
Paul Hay, supt. Fax 723-6463

San Jose USD 29,900/K-12
855 Lenzen Ave 95126 408-535-6000
Don Iglesias, supt. Fax 535-2362
www.sjusd.org
Burnett MS 800/6-8
850 N 2nd St 95112 408-535-6267
Lisa Aguerria-Lewis, prin. Fax 298-1675
Castillero MS 1,200/6-8
6384 Leyland Park Dr 95120 408-535-6385
Susan Walker, prin. Fax 268-4489
Community Career Academy Vo/Tech
2105 Forest Ave 95128 408-947-2852
Linda Ferdig-Riley, prin.
Gunderson HS 1,100/9-12
622 Gaundabert Ln 95136 408-535-6340
Carrie Catching, prin. Fax 224-2209
Harte MS 1,300/6-8
7050 Bret Harte Dr 95120 408-535-6270
Don McCloskey, prin. Fax 927-0698
Hoover MS 1,100/6-8
1635 Park Ave 95126 408-535-6274
Dorothy Kennedy, prin. Fax 286-4864
Leland HS 1,800/9-12
6677 Camden Ave 95120 408-535-6290
Bob Setterlund, prin. Fax 927-6448
Lincoln HS 1,700/9-12
555 Dana Ave 95126 408-535-6300
Chris Funk, prin. Fax 535-2352
Muir MS 900/6-8
1260 Branham Ln 95118 408-535-6281
Shannon McGee, prin. Fax 535-2319
Pioneer HS 1,500/9-12
1290 Blossom Hill Rd 95118 408-535-6310
Sandy Engel, prin. Fax 535-2357
San Jose HS Academy 1,100/9-12
275 N 24th St 95116 408-535-6320
Dr. Robert Perez, prin. Fax 535-2355
Willow Glen HS 1,300/9-12
2001 Cottle Ave 95125 408-535-6330
Elaine Farace, prin. Fax 535-2353
Willow Glen MS 1,100/6-8
2105 Cottle Ave 95125 408-535-6277
John Tavella, prin. Fax 535-2353

Union ESD 4,400/K-8
5175 Union Ave 95124 408-377-8010
Fax 377-7182
www.unionsd.org
Dartmouth MS 800/6-8
5575 Dartmouth Dr 95118 408-264-1122
Carole Carlson, prin. Fax 264-9332
Union MS 800/6-8
2130 Los Gatos Almaden Rd 95124 408-371-0366
Donna Lewis, prin. Fax 371-1217

Archbishop Mitty HS 1,600/9-12
5000 Mitty Way 95129 408-252-6610
Timothy Brosnan, prin. Fax 252-6967
Bellarmine College Prep S 1,500/9-12
960 W Hedding St 95126 408-294-9224
Mark Pierotti, prin. Fax 297-5585
California College of Communication Post-Sec.
762 Sunset Glen Dr Ste 2 95123 408-374-5066
Center of Employment Training Post-Sec.
701 Vine St 95110 408-287-7924
Everest College Post-Sec.
1245 S Wnchstr Blvd #102 95128 408-246-4171
Evergreen Valley College Post-Sec.
3095 Yerba Buena Rd 95135 408-274-7900
Five Branches Institute Post-Sec.
3031 Tisch Way Ste 605 95128 408-260-0208
Harker S 1,700/K-12
PO Box 9067 95157 408-249-2510
Christopher Nikolo, hdmstr. Fax 984-2325
Liberty Baptist S 300/PK-12
2790 S King Rd 95122 408-274-5613
Russel Barnes, prin. Fax 274-1363
National Hispanic University Post-Sec.
14271 Story Rd 95127 408-273-2680
Nativity S of San Jose 100/6-8
310 Edwards Ave 95110 408-993-1293
Kevin Eagleson, prin. Fax 292-0675
Notre Dame HS 600/9-12
596 S 2nd St 95112 408-294-1113
Mary Beth Riley, prin. Fax 293-9779
Palmer College of Chiropractic West Post-Sec.
90 E Tasman Dr 95134 408-944-6000
Presentation HS 800/9-12
2281 Plummer Ave 95125 408-264-1664
Mary Miller, prin. Fax 266-7333
San Jose City College Post-Sec.
2100 Moorpark Ave 95128 408-298-2181
San Jose State University Post-Sec.
1 Washington Sq 95192 408-924-1000
Valley Christian HS 1,200/9-12
100 Skyway Dr 95111 408-513-2400
Dr. Joel Torode, prin. Fax 513-2424
Valley Christian JHS 500/6-8
100 Skyway Dr Ste 140 95111 408-513-2460
Robert Bridges, prin. Fax 513-2466
Western Career College Post-Sec.
6201 San Ignacio Ave 95119 408-360-0840
White Road Baptist Academy 50/K-12
480 S White Rd 95127 408-272-7713
Chris Dona, admin. Fax 272-7666
William Jessup University Post-Sec.
1190 Saratoga Ave Ste 210 95129 408-278-4343
Willow Vale Christian Children's Center 100/PK-12
1730 Curtner Ave 95125 408-448-0656
Carollyn Ellis, admin. Fax 264-2817

San Juan Bautista, San Benito, Pop. 1,652
Aromas/San Juan USD 1,300/K-12
2300 San Juan Hwy 95045 831-623-4500
Jacquelyn B. Munoz, supt. Fax 623-4907
www.asjusd.k12.ca.us
Anzar HS 400/9-12
2000 San Juan Hwy 95045 831-623-7660
Charlene McKowen, prin. Fax 623-7676
Adult Education Adult
100 Nyland Dr 95045 831-623-9622
Jose Luis Palacios, lead tchr. Fax 623-0614

San Juan Capistrano, Orange, Pop. 34,673
Capistrano USD 50,300/K-12
33122 Valle Rd 92675 949-234-9200
Dr. James Fleming, supt. Fax 489-8646
www.capousd.org/
Forster MS 1,600/6-8
25601 Camino Del Avion 92675 949-234-5907
Carrie Bertini, prin. Fax 234-5926
Capistrano Unified Adult Education Adult
31431 El Camino Real 92675 949-493-0658
Dr. Carol Tomlinson, prin. Fax 489-1421
Other Schools – See Aliso Viejo, Dana Point, Ladera Ranch, Laguna Niguel, Las Flores, Mission Viejo, Rancho Santa Margarita, San Clemente

Regional Occupational Center & Program
Supt. — None
Capistrano-Laguna Beach ROP Vo/Tech
31522 El Camino Real 92675 949-496-3118
Richard Bogart, dir. Fax 496-1850

Capistrano Valley Christian S 500/PK-12
32032 Del Obispo St 92675 949-493-5683
Dr. Dave Baker, supt. Fax 493-6057
Junipero Serra HS 200/9-12
26351 Junipero Serra Rd 92675 949-493-9307
Thomas Waszak, prin. Fax 493-9308
Saddleback Valley Christian S 600/PK-12
26333 Oso Rd 92675 949-443-4050
Edward Carney, admin. Fax 443-3941
St. Margaret Episcopal S 1,200/PK-12
31641 La Novia Ave 92675 949-661-0108
Marcus D. Hurlbut, hdmstr. Fax 489-8042

San Leandro, Alameda, Pop. 78,178
San Leandro USD 8,800/K-12
14735 Juniper St 94579 510-667-3500
Laura Aguayo-Guevara, supt. Fax 667-3569
www.sanleandro.k12.ca.us
Bancroft MS 1,000/6-8
1150 Bancroft Ave 94577 510-667-3560
Mary Ann Valles, prin. Fax 895-4113
Muir MS 1,100/6-8
1444 Williams St 94577 510-667-3571
Belen Magers, prin. Fax 667-3545
San Leandro HS 2,600/9-12
2200 Bancroft Ave 94577 510-667-3540
Amy Furtado, prin. Fax 614-0986
San Leandro Adult S Adult
2255 Bancroft Ave 94577 510-667-6087
Susanne Wong, prin. Fax 352-2183

San Lorenzo USD
Supt. — See San Lorenzo
Washington Manor MS 900/6-8
1170 Fargo Ave 94579 510-317-5500
Jocelyn Lee, prin. Fax 317-5597

Chinese Christian S 700/K-12
750 Fargo Ave 94579 510-351-4959
Robin Hom, supt. Fax 351-1789
Community Christian S 200/K-12
562 Lewelling Blvd 94579 510-351-3684
Susan McCarrie, admin. Fax 351-4906
Western Career College Post-Sec.
15555 E 14th St Ste 500 94578 510-276-3888

San Lorenzo, Alameda, Pop. 19,987
San Lorenzo USD 11,500/K-12
15510 Usher St 94580 510-317-4600
Arnie Glassberg, supt. Fax 278-3048
www.slzusd.org
Arroyo HS 1,900/9-12
15701 Lorenzo Ave 94580 510-317-4000
Richard Lloyd, prin. Fax 278-9067
Bohannon MS 1,000/6-8
800 Bockman Rd 94580 510-317-3800
Gail Yothers, prin. Fax 317-3890
Edendale MS 800/6-8
16160 Ashland Ave 94580 510-317-5100
Janet Clayton, prin. Fax 317-5190
San Lorenzo HS 1,600/9-12
50 E Lewelling Blvd 94580 510-317-3000
Sheryl Cambra, prin. Fax 278-0547
San Lorenzo Adult S Adult
820 Bockman Rd 94580 510-317-4200
Darryl Stucker, prin. Fax 317-4291
Other Schools – See Hayward, San Leandro

Redwood Christian HS 400/7-12
1000 Paseo Grande 94580 510-317-8990
John Bakker, prin. Fax 278-5064

San Luis Obispo, San Luis Obispo, Pop. 43,509
San Luis Coastal USD 7,400/K-12
1500 Lizzie St 93401 805-549-1200
Edward Valentine, supt. Fax 549-9074
www.slcusd.org
Laguna MS 800/7-8
11050 Los Osos Valley Rd 93405 805-596-4055
Steve Anderson, prin. Fax 544-2449
San Luis Obispo HS 1,600/9-12
1499 San Luis Dr 93401 805-596-4040
Will Jones, prin. Fax 542-9075
Adult S Adult
1500 Lizzie St Bldg G 93401 805-549-1222
Greg Halfman, prin. Fax 544-0638
Other Schools – See Los Osos, Morro Bay

California Polytechnic State University Post-Sec.
93407 805-756-1111
Central CA School of Continuing Educ. Post-Sec.
3195 McMillan Ave Ste F 93401 805-543-9123
Cuesta College Post-Sec.
PO Box 8106 93403 805-546-3100
Mission College Preparatory Catholic HS 9-12
682 Palm St 93401 805-543-2131
Rev. Charles Tilley, prin. Fax 543-4359

San Marcos, San Diego, Pop. 73,487
San Marcos USD 15,200/K-12
255 Pico Ave Ste 250 92069 760-752-1299
Kevin Holt, supt. Fax 471-4928
www.smusd.org/
Mission Hills HS 1,900/9-12
1 E Mission Hills Ct 92069 760-290-2700
Brad Lichtman, prin. Fax 290-2680
San Elijo MS 700/6-8
1600 Schoolhouse Way 92078 760-290-2800
Doug Hall, prin. Fax 290-2828
San Marcos HS 1,700/9-12
1615 W San Marcos Blvd 92078 760-290-2200
Julie Mottershaw, prin. Fax 736-8275
San Marcos MS 1,400/6-8
650 W Mission Rd 92069 760-290-2500
Brian Randall, prin. Fax 736-2223
Woodland Park MS 1,400/6-8
1270 Rock Springs Rd 92069 760-290-2455
David Cochrane, prin. Fax 741-6178

California State University-San Marcos Post-Sec.
92096 760-750-4000
CEI Post-Sec.
1050 Los Vallecitos Blvd 92069 760-471-9300
Coleman College Post-Sec.
1284 W San Marcos Blvd #110 92069 760-747-3990
Palomar College Post-Sec.
1140 W Mission Rd 92069 760-744-1150
Palomar Institute of Cosmetology Post-Sec.
355 Via Vera Cruz Ste 3 92078 760-744-7900

San Marino, Los Angeles, Pop. 13,165
San Marino USD 3,300/K-12
1665 West Dr 91108 626-299-7000
Jack R. Rose, supt. Fax 299-7010
www.san-marino.k12.ca.us
Huntington MS 800/6-8
1700 Huntington Dr 91108 626-299-7060
Gary McGuigan, prin. Fax 299-7064
San Marino HS 1,200/9-12
2701 Huntington Dr 91108 626-299-7020
Loren Kleinrock, prin. Fax 299-7037

Southwestern Academy 200/6-12
2800 Monterey Rd 91108 626-799-5010
Kenneth Veronda, prin. Fax 799-0407

San Mateo, San Mateo, Pop. 91,081
San Mateo UNHSD 8,500/9-12
650 N Delaware St 94401 650-558-2299
Samuel Johnson, supt. Fax 762-0249
www.smuhsd.k12.ca.us
Aragon HS 1,500/9-12
900 Alameda De Las Pulgas 94402 650-558-2999
Kirk Black, prin. Fax 558-2952
Hillsdale HS 1,300/9-12
3115 Del Monte St 94403 650-558-2699
Yvonne Shiu, prin. Fax 574-4173
San Mateo HS 1,400/9-12
506 N Delaware St 94401 650-558-2399
Jacqueline McEvoy, prin. Fax 762-0265
San Mateo Adult S Adult
789 E Poplar Ave 94401 650-558-2100
Lawrence Teshara, prin. Fax 762-0232
Other Schools – See Burlingame, Millbrae, San Bruno

San Mateo-Foster City ESD
Supt. — See Foster City
Abbott MS 800/6-8
600 36th Ave 94403 650-312-7600
Cathy Ennon, prin. Fax 312-7605
Bayside MS 700/6-8
2025 Kehoe Ave 94403 650-312-7660
Jeanne Elliot, prin. Fax 312-7634
Borel MS 900/6-8
425 Barneson Ave 94402 650-312-7670
John Cosmos, prin. Fax 312-7644

Alpha Beacon Christian S 200/PK-12
525 42nd Ave 94403 650-212-4222
Dr. Lillian Mark, supt. Fax 212-1026
College of San Mateo Post-Sec.
1700 W Hillsdale Blvd 94402 650-574-6161
Junipero Serra HS 1,000/9-12
451 W 20th Ave 94403 650-345-8207
Lars Lund, prin. Fax 573-6638

San Pablo, Contra Costa, Pop. 31,004
West Contra Costa USD
Supt. — See Richmond
Helms MS 1,200/6-8
2500 Rd 20 94806 510-233-3988
Rachel Bartlett-Preston, prin. Fax 234-5977

Contra Costa College Post-Sec.
2600 Mission Bell Dr 94806 510-235-7800

San Pedro, See Los Angeles
Los Angeles USD
Supt. — See Los Angeles
Cooper Community Day S 100/7-12
2210 N Taper Ave 90731 310-832-0376
Barbara Politz, prin. Fax 832-7914
Dana MS 1,900/6-8
1501 S Cabrillo Ave 90731 310-241-1100
Terry Ball, prin. Fax 514-9925
San Pedro HS 3,400/9-12
1001 W 15th St 90731 310-241-5800
Diana Gelb, prin. Fax 547-3183
Harbor Community Adult S Adult
950 W Santa Cruz St 90731 310-547-4425
Lanny Nelms, prin. Fax 832-3489
Harbor Occupational Center Adult
740 N Pacific Ave 90731 310-547-5551
Anna Madrid, prin. Fax 547-4979

Mary Star of the Sea HS 500/9-12
810 W 8th St 90731 310-547-1138
Rita Dever, prin. Fax 547-1827

San Rafael, Marin, Pop. 55,716
Dixie ESD 1,800/K-8
380 Nova Albion Way 94903 415-492-3700
Thomas Lohwasser, supt. Fax 492-3707
dixiesd.marin.k12.ca.us/
Miller Creek MS 700/6-8
2255 Las Gallinas Ave 94903 415-492-3760
Greg Johnson, prin. Fax 492-3765

Regional Occupational Center & Program
Supt. — None
Marin County ROP Vo/Tech
1111 Las Gallinas Ave 94903 415-499-5860
Gene Abbott, coord. Fax 491-6622

San Rafael CSD 5,600/K-12
310 Nova Albion Way 94903 415-492-3233
Dr. Laura Alvarenga, supt. Fax 492-3245
www.srcs.org
Davidson MS 900/6-8
280 Woodland Ave 94901 415-485-2400
Ed Colucci, prin. Fax 485-2476
San Rafael HS 1,000/9-12
185 Mission Ave 94901 415-485-2330
Judy Colton, prin. Fax 485-2345
Terra Linda HS 1,000/9-12
320 Nova Albion Way 94903 415-492-3100
Carole Ramsey, prin. Fax 492-3105
San Rafael Adult Education Adult
150 Lovell Ave 94901 415-492-3226
Sue Gatlin, prin. Fax 492-3246

Dominican University of California Post-Sec.
50 Acacia Ave 94901 415-457-4440
Marin Academy 400/9-12
1600 Mission Ave 94901 415-453-4550
Bodie Brizendine, prin. Fax 453-8538

San Ramon, Contra Costa, Pop. 49,999
San Ramon Valley USD
Supt. — See Danville
California HS 2,400/9-12
9870 Broadmoor Dr 94583 925-803-7400
Mark Corti, prin. Fax 803-9341
Iron Horse MS 1,000/6-8
12601 Alcosta Blvd 94583 925-824-2820
Kirby Hoy, prin. Fax 824-2830
Pine Valley MS 1,000/6-8
3000 Pine Valley Rd 94583 925-803-7420
Marilyn Nachtman, prin. Fax 828-1972
Windemere Ranch MS 6-8
11611 E Branch Pkwy, 925-479-7400
David Bolin, prin. Fax 479-7469

Santa Ana, Orange, Pop. 340,368
Garden Grove USD
Supt. — See Garden Grove
Fitz IS, 4600 W McFadden Ave 92704 900/7-8
Vicki Braddock, prin. 714-663-6351

Regional Occupational Center & Program
Supt. — None
Central County ROP Vo/Tech
2323 N Broadway Ste 301 92706 714-541-5537
Diana Schneider, dir. Fax 541-5214

Santa Ana USD 58,800/PK-12
1601 E Chestnut Ave 92701 714-558-5501
Jane Russo Ph.D., supt. Fax 558-5610
www.sausd.k12.ca.us
Carr IS 1,800/6-8
2120 W Edinger Ave 92704 714-431-7600
P. Yrarrazaval-Correa, prin. Fax 431-7699
Century HS 2,600/9-12
1401 S Grand Ave 92705 714-568-7000
Greg Rankin, prin. Fax 568-7038
Lathrop IS 1,500/6-8
1111 S Broadway 92707 714-567-3300
Lucinda Clear, prin. Fax 567-3399
MacArthur Fundamental IS 1,300/6-8
600 W Alton Ave 92707 714-513-9800
Marvin Smulowitz, prin. Fax 513-9899
McFadden IS 1,700/6-8
2701 S Raitt St 92704 714-435-3700
Esther Severy, prin. Fax 435-3799
Mendez Fundamental IS 1,500/6-8
2000 N Bristol St 92706 714-972-7800
Cynthia Landsiedel, prin. Fax 972-7899
Saddleback HS 3,200/9-12
2802 S Flower St 92707 714-513-2900
Esther Jones, prin. Fax 513-2911
Santa Ana HS 4,100/9-12
520 W Walnut St 92701 714-567-4900
Dan Salcedo, prin. Fax 567-4952
Segerstrom HS 9-12
2301 W MacArthur Blvd 92704 714-241-5000
Lyn Maher, prin. Fax 241-5999
Sierra IS 1,300/5-8
2021 N Grand Ave 92705 714-567-3500
Brenda McGaffigan, prin. Fax 567-3591
Spurgeon IS 1,800/6-8
2701 W 5th St 92703 714-480-2200
Robert Laxton Ed.D., prin. Fax 480-2215
Valley HS 3,100/9-12
3002 W Centennial Rd 92704 714-433-6600
Antonio Espinosa, prin. Fax 433-6773
Villa Fundamental IS 1,400/6-8
1441 E Chestnut Ave 92701 714-558-5100
Dawn Miller, prin. Fax 558-5103
Willard IS 1,900/5-8
1342 N Ross St 92706 714-480-4800
Jeff Bishop, prin. Fax 480-4899

Tustin USD
Supt. — See Tustin
Foothill HS 2,200/9-12
19251 Dodge Ave 92705 714-730-7464
Al Marzilli, prin. Fax 573-9376
Hewes MS 1,000/6-8
13232 Hewes Ave 92705 714-730-7348
Tracey VanderHayden, prin. Fax 730-7315

Argosy University/Orange County Post-Sec.
3501 W Sunflower Ave 92704 714-338-6200
Art Institute of California Post-Sec.
3601 W Sunflower Ave 92704 714-830-0200
Bethel Baptist S 200/K-12
901 S Euclid St 92704 714-839-3600
Dr. Terry Cantrell, admin. Fax 839-4953
California Coast University Post-Sec.
700 N Main St 92701 714-547-9625
Calvary Chapel S 1,700/K-12
3800 S Fairview St 92704 714-556-0965
Jay Henry, supt. Fax 751-3718
Colleen O'Hara's Beauty Academy Post-Sec.
109 W 4th St Flr 2 92701 714-568-5399
College of Automotive Management Post-Sec.
3000 W MacArthur Blvd Fl 3 92704 714-755-6894
Health Staff Training Institute Post-Sec.
1505 E 17th St Ste 122 92705 714-543-9828
Kensington College Post-Sec.
2428 N Grand Ave Ste D 92705 714-542-8086
Mater Dei HS 2,200/9-12
1202 W Edinger Ave 92707 714-754-7711
Frances Clare, prin. Fax 754-1880
Newbridge College Post-Sec.
1840 E 17th St Ste 140 92705 714-550-8000
Santa Ana College Post-Sec.
1530 W 17th St 92706 714-564-6000
William Howard Taft University Post-Sec.
3700 S Susan St 92704 714-850-4800

Santa Barbara, Santa Barbara, Pop. 85,899
Regional Occupational Center & Program
Supt. — None
Santa Barbara County ROP South Vo/Tech
PO Box 6307 93160 805-964-4711
John Ingram, dir. Fax 569-2507

Santa Barbara SD 15,300/K-12
720 Santa Barbara St 93101 805-963-4331
J. Brian Sarvis, supt. Fax 962-3146
www.sbsdk12.org/
La Colina JHS 1,000/7-8
4025 Foothill Rd 93110 805-967-4506
David Ortiz, prin. Fax 967-3056
La Cumbre JHS 400/7-8
2255 Modoc Rd 93101 805-687-0761
Jo Ann Caines, prin. Fax 563-4636
San Marcos HS 2,200/9-12
4750 Hollister Ave 93110 805-967-4581
Craig Morgan, prin. Fax 967-8358
Santa Barbara HS 2,400/9-12
700 E Anapamu St 93103 805-966-9101
Paul Turnbull, prin. Fax 965-6872
Santa Barbara JHS 1,000/7-8
721 E Cota St 93103 805-963-7751
John Becchio, prin. Fax 962-7196
Other Schools – See Goleta

Anacapa S 100/7-12
814 Santa Barbara St 93101 805-965-0228
Gordon Sichi, hdmstr. Fax 899-2758
Antioch University Post-Sec.
801 Garden St Ste 101 93101 805-962-8179
Avalon Beauty College Post-Sec.
504 N Milpas St 93103 805-966-1931
Bishop Garcia Diego HS 300/9-12
4000 La Colina Rd 93110 805-967-1266
Fr. Tom Elewaut, prin. Fax 964-3178
Brooks Institute of Photography Post-Sec.
801 Alston Rd 93108 805-966-3888
Devereux California Post-Sec.
PO Box 6784 93160 805-968-2525
El Montecito Upper S 100/3-8
630 E Canon Perdido St 93103 805-969-1482
R. Jeannine Morgan, prin. Fax 969-9319
Fielding Graduate University Post-Sec.
2112 Santa Barbara St 93105 805-687-1099
Laguna Blanca S 400/K-12
4125 Paloma Dr 93110 805-687-2461
Douglas W. Jessup, hdmstr. Fax 682-2553
San Roque HS 200/9-12
2300 Garden St 93105 805-687-3717
Santa Barbara Business College Post-Sec.
5266 Hollister Ave 93111 805-967-9677
Santa Barbara City College Post-Sec.
721 Cliff Dr 93109 805-965-0581
Santa Barbara Coll. of Oriental Medicine Post-Sec.
1919 State St 93101 800-549-6299
Santa Barbara Cottage & Gen. Hosp. Post-Sec.
PO Box 689 93102 805-569-7290
University of California 93106 Post-Sec.
805-893-8000
Westmont College Post-Sec.
955 La Paz Rd 93108 805-565-6000

Santa Clara, Santa Clara, Pop. 105,402
Santa Clara USD 14,000/K-12
1889 Lawrence Rd 95051 408-423-2000
Rod Adams, supt. Fax 423-2285
www.scu.k12.ca.us
Buchser MS 1,100/6-8
1111 Bellomy St 95050 408-423-3000
Kyle Eaton, prin. Fax 423-3080
Cabrillo MS 1,000/6-8
2550 Cabrillo Ave 95051 408-423-3700
Stan Garber, prin. Fax 423-3780
Santa Clara HS 1,700/9-12
3000 Benton St 95051 408-423-2600
Brad Syth, prin. Fax 985-2681
Wilcox HS 1,900/9-12
3250 Monroe St 95051 408-423-2400
Tab Taber, prin. Fax 423-2480
Santa Clara Adult Comm Education Center Adult
1840 Benton St 95050 408-423-3500
Daniene Marciano, dir. Fax 423-3580
Other Schools – See Sunnyvale

California Cosmetology College Post-Sec.
955 Monroe St 95050 408-247-2200
Institute for Business and Technology Post-Sec.
2400 Walsh Ave 95051 408-727-1060
Mission College Post-Sec.
3000 Mission College Blvd 95054 408-988-2200
North Valley Baptist S 300/K-12
941 Clyde Ave 95054 408-988-8883
Daniel Azzarello, prin.
St. Lawrence Academy 300/9-12
2000 Lawrence Ct 95051 408-296-3013
Christie Filios, prin. Fax 296-3794
Santa Clara University Post-Sec.
500 El Camino Real 95053 408-554-4000
Sierra S, 220 Blake Ave 95051 100/K-12
Linda Wesley, prin. 408-247-4740

Santa Clarita, Los Angeles, Pop. 168,253
Regional Occupational Center & Program
Supt. — None
Hart ROP Vo/Tech
21515 Centre Pointe Pkwy 91350 661-259-0033
Jan Burns, dir. Fax 254-8653

William S. Hart UNHSD 20,800/7-12
21515 Centre Pointe Pkwy 91350 661-259-0033
Jaime Castellanos, supt. Fax 254-8653
www.hartdistrict.org
Golden Valley HS 1,000/9-12
22501 Robert E Lee Pkwy 91321 661-298-8140
Jacque Snyder, prin. Fax 250-8362
La Mesa JHS 1,200/7-8
26623 May Way 91351 661-250-0022
Pete Fries, prin. Fax 252-3326
Golden Oak Adult S Adult
23201 Dalbey Dr 91355 661-253-0583
Lynda Rick, prin. Fax 260-1371
Other Schools – See Canyon Country, Newhall, Saugus, Stevenson Ranch, Valencia

Advantage Preparatory S 200/K-12
PO Box 802274 91380 661-296-5466
Cynthia Grant, admin.
College of the Canyons Post-Sec.
26455 Rockwell Canyon Rd 91355 661-259-7800

Santa Cruz, Santa Cruz, Pop. 54,760
Live Oak ESD 1,900/K-8
984 Bostwick Ln Ste 1 95062 831-475-6333
Dr. David Paine, supt. Fax 475-2638
www.lodo.santacruz.k12.ca.us

Shoreline MS 600/6-8
855 17th Ave 95062 831-475-6565
Robert Greenlee, prin. Fax 462-1653

Santa Cruz CSD
Supt. — See Soquel
Branciforte MS 500/6-8
315 Poplar Ave 95062 831-429-3883
Kris Munro, prin. Fax 429-3962
Harbor HS 1,200/9-12
300 La Fonda Ave 95062 831-429-3810
Nancy Tocchini, prin. Fax 429-3982
Mission Hill MS 600/6-8
425 King St 95060 831-429-3860
Dona Abrahams-Johnson, prin. Fax 427-4846
Santa Cruz HS 1,200/9-12
415 Walnut Ave 95060 831-429-3960
Karen Edmunds, prin. Fax 429-3944
Santa Cruz Adult Education Adult
2931 Mission St 95060 831-429-3966
Mary Powers, prin. Fax 429-3061

Five Branches Institute Post-Sec.
200 7th Ave 95062 831-476-9424
Kirby Preparatory S 200/6-12
425 Encinal St 95060 831-423-0658
Joshua Karter Ph.D., hdmstr. Fax 423-0679
University of California-Santa Cruz Post-Sec.
95064 831-459-0111

Santa Fe Springs, Los Angeles, Pop. 17,058
Little Lake City ESD 4,900/K-8
10515 Pioneer Blvd 90670 562-868-8241
Phillip Perez Ph.D., supt. Fax 868-1192
www.littlelake.k12.ca.us
Lake Center MS 900/6-8
10503 Pioneer Blvd 90670 562-868-4977
Linda Erdman, prin. Fax 929-4527
Other Schools – See Norwalk

Whittier UNHSD
Supt. — See Whittier
Santa Fe HS 2,700/9-12
10400 Orr and Day Rd 90670 562-698-8121
Monica Oviedo, prin. Fax 868-8277

NTMA Training Center of Southern CA Post-Sec.
13230 Firestone Blvd Ste A 90670 562-404-4295
St. Paul HS 700/9-12
9635 Greenleaf Ave 90670 562-698-6246
Frank Laurenzello, prin. Fax 696-8396

Santa Maria, Santa Barbara, Pop. 84,346
Orcutt UNESD
Supt. — See Orcutt
Lakeview JHS 700/7-8
3700 Orcutt Rd 93455 805-938-8600
Robert Bush, prin. Fax 938-8649

Regional Occupational Center & Program
Supt. — None
Santa Barbara County ROP North Vo/Tech
4893 Bethany Ln 93455 805-937-8427
Ken Main, dir. Fax 937-7489

Santa Maria JUNHSD 7,100/9-12
2560 Skyway Dr 93455 805-922-4573
Jeffrey Hearn Ph.D., supt. Fax 928-9916
www.smjuhsd.k12.ca.us
Pioneer Valley HS 1,300/9-12
675 Panther Dr 93454 805-922-1305
Dee Ringstead, prin. Fax 928-9916
Righetti HS 2,600/9-12
941 E Foster Rd 93455 805-937-2051
Dr. Catherine Ulrich, prin. Fax 934-0819
Santa Maria HS 2,900/9-12
901 S Broadway 93454 805-925-2567
Esther Prieto-Chavez, prin. Fax 922-0215
Santa Maria Adult S Adult
251 E Clark Ave 93455 805-937-6356
Craig Huseth, prin. Fax 934-4743

Santa Maria-Bonita ESD 12,800/K-8
708 S Miller St 93454 805-928-1783
David Francis, supt. Fax 928-7874
www.smbsd.org/
Arellanes JHS 500/7-8
1890 Sandalwood Dr 93455 805-361-6820
Patty Grady, prin. Fax 346-8535
El Camino JHS 600/7-8
219 W El Camino St 93458 805-361-7800
Mark Muller, prin. Fax 346-1851
Fesler JHS 700/7-8
1100 E Fesler St 93454 805-361-7880
Barbara Walker, prin. Fax 346-1849
Kunst JHS 800/7-8
930 Hidden Pines Way 93458 805-361-5800
Ed Cora, prin. Fax 925-8239

Allan Hancock College Post-Sec.
800 S College Dr 93454 805-922-6966
Crossroads Christian JHS 100/7-8
1550 S College Dr 93454 805-922-0237
Susan Pruett, admin. Fax 925-9690
St. Joseph HS 600/9-12
4120 S Bradley Rd 93455 805-937-2038
Joseph Myers, prin. Fax 937-4248
Santa Barbara Business College Post-Sec.
303 Plaza Dr 93454 805-922-8256
Valley Christian Academy 300/K-12
2970 Santa Maria Way 93455 805-937-6317
Charles Mason, prin. Fax 934-2563

Santa Monica, Los Angeles, Pop. 87,800
Santa Monica-Malibu USD 12,500/PK-12
1651 16th St 90404 310-450-8338
John Deasy, supt. Fax 450-1667
www.smmusd.org
Adams MS 1,200/6-8
2425 16th St 90405 310-452-2326
Martha Shaw, prin. Fax 452-5352
Lincoln MS 1,300/6-8
1501 California Ave 90403 310-393-9227
Tristan Komlos, prin. Fax 393-4297
Santa Monica HS 3,400/9-12
601 Pico Blvd 90405 310-395-3204
Hugo Pedroza, prin. Fax 395-5842
Santa Monica-Malibu Adult Education Adult
2510 Lincoln Blvd 90405 310-664-6222
Stephen Martinez, prin. Fax 664-6220
Other Schools – See Malibu

Art Institute of California Post-Sec.
2900 31st St 90405 310-752-4700
Concord HS 100/9-12
1831 Wilshire Blvd Ste B 90403 310-828-9443
Susan Packer Davis, prin.
Crossroads S for Arts & Sciences 1,100/K-12
1714 21st St 90404 310-829-7391
Roger Weaver, prin. Fax 828-5636
Emperor's Coll. of Trad. Oriental Med. Post-Sec.
1807 Wilshire Blvd Ste B 90403 310-453-8300
Lighthouse Christian Academy 100/9-12
1424 Yale St 90404 310-829-2522
George Neos, prin.
Lighthouse S 200/PK-12
1220 20th St 90404 310-829-1741
George Neos, prin. Fax 829-1743
New Roads HS 200/9-12
3131 Olympic Blvd 90404 310-828-5582
David Bryan, hdmstr. Fax 828-2582
New Roads MS 100/6-8
1238 Lincoln Blvd 90401 310-587-2255
David Bryan, hdmstr. Fax 587-2258
Pacifica Christian HS 200/9-12
1730 Wilshire Blvd 90403 310-828-7015
Jim Knight, hdmstr. Fax 829-2063
Pardee RAND Grad Sch of Policy Studies Post-Sec.
PO Box 2138 90407 310-393-0411
St. Monica HS 600/9-12
1030 Lincoln Blvd 90403 310-394-3701
Thom Gasper, prin. Fax 458-1353
Santa Monica College Post-Sec.
1900 Pico Blvd 90405 310-434-4000

Santa Paula, Ventura, Pop. 28,478
Briggs ESD 400/K-8
12465 Foothill Rd 93060 805-525-7540
Mike McLaughlin, supt. Fax 933-1111
www.briggsesd.org/
Briggs MS 200/5-8
14438 W Telegraph Rd 93060 805-525-7151
Deborah Cuevas, prin. Fax 933-3565

Santa Paula ESD 3,900/K-8
201 S Steckel Dr 93060 805-933-8800
Elizabeth Davita Ed.D., supt. Fax 525-0546
www.spesd.org/
Isbell MS 1,300/6-8
221 S 4th St 93060 805-933-8880
Fernando Rivera, prin. Fax 933-5582

Santa Paula UNHSD 1,800/9-12
500 E Santa Barbara St 93060 805-525-0988
David Gomez, supt. Fax 525-6128
www.spuhsd.k12.ca.us
Santa Paula HS 1,600/9-12
404 N 6th St 93060 805-525-4406
J. Antonio Gaitan, prin. Fax 525-1690
Santa Paula Adult Education Adult
325 N Palm Ave 93060 805-525-9502
Lorenzo Moraza, prin. Fax 525-2294

Thomas Aquinas College Post-Sec.
10000 Ojai Rd 93060 800-634-9797

Santa Rosa, Sonoma, Pop. 153,158
Oak Grove UNESD 700/K-8
5285 Hall Rd 95401 707-545-0171
Noel Buehler, supt. Fax 545-0176
www.ogusd.org/
Willowside MS 400/6-8
5285 Hall Rd 95401 707-542-3322
Lisa Saxon, prin. Fax 525-4439

Regional Occupational Center & Program
Supt. — None
Sonoma County ROP Vo/Tech
5340 Skylane Blvd 95403 707-524-2720
Stephen Jackson, dir. Fax 524-2789

Santa Rosa CSD 17,000/K-12
211 Ridgeway Ave 95401 707-528-5373
Sharon Liddell Ed.D., supt. Fax 528-5487
www.srcs.k12.ca.us
Allen HS 1,500/9-12
599 Bellevue Ave 95407 707-528-5020
Mary Gail Stablein, prin. Fax 528-5023
Carillo HS 1,500/9-12
6975 Montecito Blvd 95409 707-528-5790
Mark Klick, prin. Fax 528-5789
Comstock MS 600/7-8
2750 W Steele Ln 95403 707-528-5266
Robert Dahlstet, prin. Fax 528-5480
Cook MS 700/7-8
2480 Sebastopol Rd 95407 707-528-5156
Harriet Gray, prin. Fax 528-5163
Mesa Necessary Small HS 50/9-12
1237 Mendocino Ave 95401 707-528-5227
Peter Giglio, prin. Fax 528-5724
Midrose Necessary Small HS 50/9-12
597 Bellevue Ave 95407 707-528-5041
Martin Cassity, prin. Fax 528-5041
Montgomery HS 1,900/9-12
1250 Hahman Dr 95405 707-528-5191
Laurie Fong, prin. Fax 528-5056
Nueva Vista HS 50/9-12
2230 Lomitas Ave 95404 707-522-3291
Fax 522-3289
Piner HS 1,300/9-12
1700 Fulton Rd 95403 707-528-5245
Janet Olson, prin. Fax 528-5246
Rincon Valley MS 800/7-8
4650 Badger Rd 95409 707-528-5255
Matt Marshall, prin. Fax 528-5644
Santa Rosa HS 2,000/9-12
1235 Mendocino Ave 95401 707-528-5291
Toni Negri, prin. Fax 528-5724
Santa Rosa MS 800/7-8
500 E St 95404 707-528-5281
Kathy Coker, prin. Fax 528-5283
Slater MS 900/7-8
3500 Sonoma Ave 95405 707-528-5241
Jason Lea, prin. Fax 528-5733
Lewis Adult Education Center Adult
2230 Lomitas Ave 95404 707-522-3280
Kathryn Carlsen, prin. Fax 522-3289

Cardinal Newman HS 400/9-12
50 Ursuline Rd 95403 707-546-6470
Grahm Rutherford, prin. Fax 544-8502
Empire College School of Business Post-Sec.
3035 Cleveland Ave 95403 707-546-4000
Lytle's Redwood Empire Beauty College Post-Sec.
186 Wikiup Dr 95403 707-545-8490
Redwood Adventist Academy 200/PK-12
385 Mark West Springs Rd 95404 707-545-1697
Rob Fenderson, prin. Fax 545-8020
Rincon Valley Christian S 400/PK-12
4585 Badger Rd 95409 707-539-1486
Kevin Hofer, admin. Fax 539-1493
Santa Rosa Christian S 300/K-12
950 S Wright Rd 95407 707-542-6414
Dr. Lois Sowers, hdmstr. Fax 542-0421
Santa Rosa Junior College Post-Sec.
1501 Mendocino Ave 95401 707-527-4011
Sonoma Academy 200/9-12
50 Mark West Springs Rd 95403 707-545-1770
Janet Durgin, hdmstr. Fax 636-2474
Summerfield Waldorf S 400/PK-12
655 Willowside Rd 95401 707-575-7194
Fax 575-3217
Ursuline HS 400/9-12
90 Ursuline Rd 95403 707-524-1130
Barbara Johannes, prin. Fax 524-0131

Santa Ynez, Santa Barbara, Pop. 4,200
Santa Ynez Valley UNHSD 1,200/9-12
PO Box 398 93460 805-688-6487
Fred Van Leuven, supt. Fax 686-4454
www.syvuhsd.org
Santa Ynez Valley Union HS 1,200/9-12
PO Box 398 93460 805-688-6487
Norman Clevenger, prin. Fax 688-1913

Santee, San Diego, Pop. 52,306
Grossmont UNHSD
Supt. — See El Cajon
Santana HS 1,800/9-12
9915 N Magnolia Ave 92071 619-448-5500
Kathy Burton, prin. Fax 449-3119
West Hills HS 2,300/9-12
8756 Mast Blvd 92071 619-596-3600
Brian Wilbur, prin. Fax 562-9342

Institute for Creation Research Grad Sch Post-Sec.
10946 Woodside Ave N 92071 619-448-0900

San Ysidro, See San Diego
San Ysidro ESD 5,000/PK-8
4350 Otay Mesa Rd 92173 619-428-4476
Tim Allen, supt. Fax 428-1505
www.sysd.k12.ca.us
San Ysidro MS 1,000/7-8
4345 Otay Mesa Rd 92173 619-428-5551
Carolina Flores, prin. Fax 690-2837

Sweetwater UNHSD
Supt. — See Chula Vista
San Ysidro Adult S Adult
4220 Otay Mesa Rd 92173 619-428-7200
Lenora Neely, prin. Fax 428-0295

Saratoga, Santa Clara, Pop. 29,663
Campbell UNHSD
Supt. — See San Jose
Prospect HS 1,300/9-12
18900 Prospect Rd 95070 408-253-1662
Rita Matthews, prin. Fax 973-1759

Los Gatos-Saratoga JUNHSD
Supt. — See Los Gatos
Saratoga HS 1,300/9-12
20300 Herriman Ave 95070 408-867-3411
Jeff Anderson, prin. Fax 867-3577

Saratoga UNESD 2,400/K-8
20460 Forrest Hills Dr 95070 408-867-3424
Lane Weiss, supt. Fax 867-2312
www.saratogausd.org
Redwood MS 900/6-8
13925 Fruitvale Ave 95070 408-867-3042
Beth Polito, prin. Fax 867-3195

West Valley College Post-Sec.
14000 Fruitvale Ave 95070 408-867-2200

Saugus, See Santa Clarita
William S. Hart UNHSD
Supt. — See Santa Clarita
Saugus HS 2,700/9-12
21900 Centurion Way 91350 661-297-3900
William Bolde, prin. Fax 297-7491

Sausalito, Marin, Pop. 7,184
Sausalito Marin CSD 200/K-8
630 Nevada St 94965 415-332-3190
Debra Bradley Ed.D., supt. Fax 332-9643
www.sausalitomarincityschooldistrict.org/
King Jr Academy 100/7-8
630 Nevada St 94965 415-332-3573
Cherisse Baatin, prin. Fax 332-2492

Scotts Valley, Santa Cruz, Pop. 11,154
Scotts Valley USD 2,800/K-12
4444 Scotts Valley Dr Ste 5 95066 831-438-1820
Dr. Susan Silver, supt. Fax 438-1518
www.svusd.santacruz.k12.ca.us
Scotts Valley HS 900/9-12
555 Glenwood Dr 95066 831-439-9555
Gregg Gunkel, prin. Fax 439-9501
Scotts Valley MS 700/6-8
8 Bean Creek Rd 95066 831-438-0610
Mary Lonhart, prin. Fax 439-8935

Bethany University Post-Sec.
800 Bethany Dr 95066 831-438-3800

Seaside, Monterey, Pop. 34,214
Monterey Peninsula USD
Supt. — See Monterey
Fitch MS 700/6-8
999 Coe Ave 93955 831-899-7080
Ken Harbord, prin. Fax 899-0663
Seaside HS 1,300/9-12
2200 Noche Buena St 93955 831-899-7033
Sheila Keifetz, prin. Fax 899-5781
Cabrillo Adult Education Adult
1295 La Salle Ave 93955 831-899-1615
Ann Kilty, dir.

California State University-Monterey Bay Post-Sec.
100 Campus Ctr 93955 831-582-3000

Sebastopol, Sonoma, Pop. 7,598
Gravenstein UNESD 500/PK-8
3840 Twig Ave 95472 707-823-7008
Linda LaMarre, supt. Fax 823-2108
www.grav.k12.ca.us/
Hillcrest MS 200/6-8
725 Bloomfield Rd 95472 707-823-7653
Linda LaMarre, prin. Fax 823-4630

Sebastopol UNESD 1,000/K-8
7611 Huntley St 95472 707-829-4570
David Wheeler, supt. Fax 829-7427
www.sebusd.org/
Brook Haven MS 400/6-8
7905 Valentine Ave 95472 707-829-4590
David Wheeler, prin. Fax 829-6285

Twin Hills UNESD 600/K-8
700 Watertrough Rd 95472 707-823-0871
Donald Armstrong, supt. Fax 823-5832
www.thusd.k12.ca.us/
Twin Hills MS 300/6-8
1685 Watertrough Rd 95472 707-823-7446
Catherine Bosch, prin. Fax 823-6470

West Sonoma CUHSD 2,600/9-12
462 Johnson St 95472 707-824-6403
Keller McDonald, supt. Fax 824-6490
wscuhsd.k12.ca.us
Analy HS 1,400/9-12
6950 Analy Ave 95472 707-824-2300
Martin Webb, prin. Fax 824-2306
New Vista Adult Education Adult
462 Johnson St 95472 707-824-6485
Ross Bickford, prin. Fax 824-7910
Other Schools – See Forestville

Selma, Fresno, Pop. 22,261
Selma USD 6,300/K-12
3036 Thompson Ave 93662 559-898-6500
Anthony A. Monreal Ed.D., supt. Fax 896-7147
www.selma.k12.ca.us
Lincoln MS 1,000/7-8
1239 Nelson Blvd 93662 559-898-6600
Norma Barajas-Ruiz, prin. Fax 896-0733
Selma HS 1,600/9-12
3125 Wright St 93662 559-898-6550
Mark Babiarz, prin. Fax 891-1110
Selma Adult S Adult
3125 Wright St 93662 559-898-6590
Teresa Wood, coord. Fax 896-4333

Sepulveda, See Los Angeles
Los Angeles USD
Supt. — See Los Angeles
Monroe HS 4,400/9-12
9229 Haskell Ave 91343 818-892-4311
Lynda Schwarz, prin. Fax 892-5622
Sepulveda MS 2,000/6-8
15330 Plummer St 91343 818-892-3151
Barbara Charness, prin. Fax 891-5754

Shafter, Kern, Pop. 14,569
Kern UNHSD
Supt. — See Bakersfield
Shafter HS 1,400/9-12
526 Mannel Ave 93263 661-746-4961
John Davis, prin. Fax 746-6743

Richland UNESD 3,000/K-8
331 N Shafter Ave 93263 661-746-8600
Lyle Mack, supt. Fax 746-8614
www.richland.k12.ca.us
Richland JHS 1,000/6-8
331 N Shafter Ave 93263 661-746-8630
Kathy Mayes, prin. Fax 746-8614

Shandon, San Luis Obispo
Shandon JUSD 300/K-12
PO Box 79 93461 805-238-0286
Chris Crawford, supt. Fax 238-0777
shandon.echalk.com
Shandon HS 100/7-12
PO Box 79 93461 805-238-0286
Chris Crawford, prin. Fax 238-0777

Sherman Oaks, See Los Angeles
Los Angeles USD
Supt. — See Los Angeles
Millikan MS 2,000/6-8
5041 Sunnyslope Ave 91423 818-528-1600
Derek Horowitz, prin. Fax 990-7651

Bridgeport S 100/K-12
13130 Burbank Blvd 91401 818-781-0360
Pamela Clark, prin.
Buckley S 800/K-12
3900 Stansbury Ave 91423 818-783-1610
Dr. Larry Dougherty, hdmstr. Fax 461-6714
DeVry University Post-Sec.
15301 Ventura Blvd Ste 100 91403 888-610-0800
Notre Dame HS 1,200/9-12
13645 Riverside Dr 91423 818-933-3600
Stephanie Connelly, prin.
Village Glen S 200/1-12
13130 Burbank Blvd 91401 818-781-0360
Pamela Clark, prin.

Shingle Springs, El Dorado, Pop. 2,049
Buckeye UNESD 4,400/K-8
PO Box 547 95682 530-677-2261
Teresa Wenig, supt. Fax 677-1015
www.buckeyeusd.org/
Other Schools – See Cameron Park, El Dorado Hills

El Dorado UNHSD
Supt. — See Placerville
Ponderosa HS 2,000/9-12
3661 Ponderosa Rd 95682 530-677-2281
Chris Moore, prin. Fax 676-1401

Latrobe SD 200/K-8
7900 S Shingle Rd 95682 916-677-0260
Jean Pinotti, supt. Fax 672-0463
www.latrobeschool.com/
Millers Hill S 100/4-8
7900 S Shingle Rd 95682 530-677-0260
Jean Pinotti, prin. Fax 672-0463

Shingletown, Shasta
Black Butte UNESD 300/K-8
7752 Ponderosa Way 96088 530-474-3125
Don Aust, supt. Fax 474-3118
www.shastalink.k12.ca.us/bbutte/
Black Butte JHS 100/7-8
7946 Ponderosa Way 96088 530-474-3441
Don Aust, prin. Fax 474-1361

Shoshone, Inyo
Death Valley USD 100/K-12
PO Box 217 92384 760-852-4303
James Copeland, supt. Fax 852-4395
Death Valley Academy 100/7-12
PO Box 217 92384 760-852-4303
James Copeland, prin. Fax 852-4395

Sierra Madre, Los Angeles, Pop. 10,988

Alverno HS 300/9-12
200 N Michillinda Ave 91024 626-355-3463
Fax 355-3153

Sierraville, Sierra
Regional Occupational Center & Program
Supt. — None
Rouse ROP Vo/Tech
PO Box 157 96126 530-994-1044
Mary Genasci, supt. Fax 994-1045

Sierra-Plumas JUSD 500/K-12
PO Box 157 96126 530-994-1044
Gregory Haulk, supt. Fax 994-1045
www.spjusd.org
Other Schools – See Downieville, Loyalton

Signal Hill, Los Angeles, Pop. 10,851

Institute of Network Technology Post-Sec.
2525 Cherry Ave Ste 110, 562-424-9200

Silverado, Orange

St. Michaels Preparatory S 100/9-12
19292 El Toro Rd 92676 949-858-0222
Rev. Gabriel Stack, prin. Fax 858-7365

Simi Valley, Ventura, Pop. 118,687
Simi Valley USD 21,500/K-12
875 Cochran St 93065 805-520-6500
Kathryn Scroggin Ed.D., supt. Fax 520-6504
www.simi.k12.ca.us
Hillside JHS 1,200/6-8
2222 Fitzgerald Rd 93065 805-520-6810
Susanne Wolf, prin. Fax 520-6156
Royal HS 2,900/9-12
1402 Royal Ave 93065 805-306-4875
Daniel Houghton, prin. Fax 520-6644
Santa Susana HS 1,200/9-12
3570 Cochran St 93063 805-520-6800
Pamela Carter, prin. Fax 579-6385
Simi Valley HS 2,500/9-12
5400 Cochran St 93063 805-577-1400
Stephen Pietrolungo, prin. Fax 520-6633
Sinaloa JHS 1,200/6-8
601 Royal Ave 93065 805-520-6830
Leslie Frank, prin. Fax 520-6835
Valley View JHS 1,400/6-8
3347 Tapo St 93063 805-520-6820
Terry Webb, prin. Fax 520-6157
Simi Valley Adult Education Adult
1880 Blackstock Ave 93065 805-579-6200
Marirose Kozak, dir. Fax 522-8902

Grace Brethren JSHS 400/7-12
1350 Cherry Ave 93065 805-522-4667
John Hynes, prin. Fax 522-5617
Heritage Christian Academy 100/K-12
1559 Rosita Dr 93065 805-428-2511
Cheryl Neher, admin.
Simi Valley Adult Education Post-Sec.
1880 Blackstock Ave 93065 805-579-6200
Stoneridge Prep S 50/6-12
1625 Tierra Rejada Rd 93065 805-581-9110
MaLuisa Arnold, dir. Fax 581-2864

Snelling, Merced
Merced River UNESD 200/K-8
2241 Turlock Rd 95369 209-722-4581
Dr. Helio Brasil, supt. Fax 563-1045
www.mercedriver.k12.ca.us
Other Schools – See Winton

Solana Beach, San Diego, Pop. 12,716
San Dieguito UNHSD
Supt. — See Encinitas
Warren MS 600/7-8
155 Stevens Ave 92075 858-755-1558
Anna Pedroza, prin. Fax 755-0891

Santa Fe Christian S 1,100/K-12
838 Academy Dr 92075 858-755-8900
John Murray, hdmstr. Fax 755-2480

Soledad, Monterey, Pop. 27,210
Soledad USD 4,000/K-12
PO Box 186 93960 831-678-3987
Jorge Guzman, supt. Fax 678-2866
www.soledad.monterey.k12.ca.us/
Main Street MS 600/7-8
441 Main St 93960 831-678-6460
Lori Villanueva, prin. Fax 678-0797
Soledad HS 900/9-12
425 Gabilan Dr 93960 831-678-6400
Roberto Nunez, prin. Fax 678-0449

Somerset, El Dorado
Pioneer UNESD 500/K-8
PO Box 8 95684 530-620-3556
Richard Williams, supt. Fax 620-4932
Mountain Creek MS 200/6-8
PO Box 690 95684 530-620-4393
Jeannine Wheeler, prin. Fax 620-6509

Sonoma, Sonoma, Pop. 9,885
Sonoma Valley USD 4,600/K-12
17850 Railroad Ave 95476 707-935-6000
Barbara Young Ed.D., supt. Fax 939-2235
www.sonomavly.k12.ca.us
Altimira MS 600/6-8
17805 Arnold Dr 95476 707-935-6020
Lance Hanson, prin. Fax 935-6027
Harrison MS 500/6-8
1150 Broadway 95476 707-935-6080
Dan Scudero, prin. Fax 935-6083
Sonoma Valley HS 1,600/9-12
20000 Broadway 95476 707-935-4010
Micaela Philpot, prin. Fax 935-4205
Sonoma Valley Adult S Adult
20000 Broadway 95476 707-933-4033
Pam Garramone, prin. Fax 933-4205

New Song S 200/K-12
121 Lichtenberg Ave 95476 707-935-3359
Tenney Singer, admin.

Sonora, Tuolumne, Pop. 4,668
Sonora UNHSD 1,700/9-12
251 Barretta St 95370 209-533-8510
Robert Gaskill, supt. Fax 533-0991
www.sonorahs.k12.ca.us/district
Sonora Union HS 1,600/9-12
430 N Washington St 95370 209-532-5511
Terry Clark, prin. Fax 533-1158

Columbia College Post-Sec.
11600 Columbia College Dr 95370 209-588-5100
Mother Lode Adventist Junior Academy 100/K-10
80 N Forest Rd 95370 209-532-2855
Robert Chinnock, prin. Fax 532-7757

Soquel, Santa Cruz, Pop. 9,188
Santa Cruz CSD 7,400/K-12
405 Old San Jose Rd 95073 831-429-3410
Alan Pagano, supt. Fax 429-3439
www.sccs.santacruz.k12.ca.us
Soquel HS 1,300/9-12
401 Old San Jose Rd 95073 831-429-3909
Jennifer Kollmann, prin. Fax 429-3311
Other Schools – See Santa Cruz

South El Monte, Los Angeles, Pop. 21,666
El Monte UNHSD
Supt. — See El Monte
South El Monte HS 1,400/9-12
1001 Durfee Ave 91733 626-442-0218
Silvia Montero, prin. Fax 442-4794

Valle Lindo ESD 1,300/K-8
1431 Central Ave 91733 626-580-0610
Mary Labrucherie, supt. Fax 575-1534
www.vallelindo.k12.ca.us/
Shively MS 800/4-8
1431 Central Ave 91733 626-580-0610
Lynn Bulgin, prin. Fax 575-1534

South Gate, Los Angeles, Pop. 98,897
Los Angeles USD
Supt. — See Los Angeles
International Studies Learning Center 300/6-11
2560 Tweedy Blvd 90280 323-568-3155
Guillermina Jauregui, prin. Fax 568-3153
Southeast Area MS 1,300/6-8
2560 Tweedy Blvd 90280 323-568-3100
Walter R. Flores, prin. Fax 564-9398
Southeast HS 9-12
2720 Tweedy Blvd 90280 323-568-3400
Jesus Angulo, prin. Fax 566-7918
South Gate HS 4,900/9-12
3351 Firestone Blvd 90280 323-568-5600
Patrick Moretta, prin. Fax 249-0237
South Gate MS 2,700/6-8
4100 Firestone Blvd 90280 323-568-4000
Fax 564-7434
South Gate Adult Education Adult
2525 Firestone Blvd 90280 323-586-3140
Bernadine Gonzalez, prin. Fax 588-1552

Advanced College — Post-Sec.
13180 Paramount Blvd 90280 — 562-408-6969
Career College of America — Post-Sec.
5612 Imperial Hwy 90280 — 562-861-8702

South Lake Tahoe, El Dorado, Pop. 24,016
Lake Tahoe USD — 4,800/K-12
1021 Al Tahoe Blvd 96150 — 530-541-2850
Dr. James Tarwater, supt. — Fax 541-5930
www.ltusd.org/
South Tahoe HS — 1,600/9-12
1735 Lake Tahoe Blvd 96150 — 530-541-4111
Ivone Larson, prin. — Fax 541-4157
South Tahoe MS — 1,100/6-8
2940 Lake Tahoe Blvd 96150 — 530-541-6404
Jackie Nelson, prin. — Fax 541-4624

Lake Tahoe Community College — Post-Sec.
1 College Dr 96150 — 530-541-4660

South Pasadena, Los Angeles, Pop. 24,889
South Pasadena USD — 4,300/K-12
1020 El Centro St 91030 — 626-441-5800
Brian Bristol Ed.D., supt. — Fax 441-5815
www.spusd.net
South Pasadena HS — 1,500/9-12
1401 Fremont Ave 91030 — 626-441-5820
Janet Anderson, prin. — Fax 441-5825
South Pasadena MS — 1,100/6-8
1600 Oak St 91030 — 626-441-5830
Mercedes Metz, prin. — Fax 441-5835

Almansor Center — 100/K-12
1137 Huntington Dr 91030 — 323-257-3006
Dr. Albert Hernandez, prin.

South San Francisco, San Mateo, Pop. 60,735
South San Francisco USD — 9,100/PK-12
398 B St 94080 — 650-877-8700
Barbara Olds, supt. — Fax 583-4717
www.ssfusd.org
Alta Loma MS — 800/6-8
116 Romney Ave 94080 — 650-877-8797
Lou Delorio, prin. — Fax 877-8824
El Camino HS — 1,500/9-12
1320 Mission Rd 94080 — 650-877-8806
Adele Berg, prin. — Fax 589-2343
Parkway Heights MS — 700/6-8
650 Sunset Dr 94080 — 650-877-8788
Jay Rowley, prin. — Fax 225-9427
South San Francisco HS — 1,600/9-12
400 B St 94080 — 650-877-8754
Michael Coyne, prin. — Fax 871-7943
Westborough MS — 700/6-8
2570 Westborough Blvd 94080 — 650-877-8848
Beth Orofino, prin. — Fax 871-5356
South San Francisco Adult — Adult
825 Southwood Dr 94080 — 650-877-8844
Jim Murphy, prin. — Fax 877-8786

Spreckels, Monterey
Spreckels UNESD — 900/K-8
PO Box 7362 93962 — 831-455-2550
Harold Kahn Ed.D., supt. — Fax 455-1871
Other Schools – See Salinas

Spring Valley, San Diego, Pop. 27,100
Grossmont UNHSD
Supt. — See El Cajon
Monte Vista HS — 2,000/9-12
3230 Sweetwater Springs Blv 91977 — 619-660-9902
Paul Wargo, prin. — Fax 670-9749
Mt. Miguel HS — 2,100/9-12
8585 Blossom Ln 91977 — 619-644-8400
Steve Coover, prin. — Fax 589-1143
Steele Canyon HS — 1,900/9-12
12440 Campo Rd 91978 — 619-660-7100
Gary Schwartzwald, prin. — Fax 660-7199

La Mesa-Spring Valley SD
Supt. — See La Mesa
La Presa MS — 1,200/6-8
1001 Leland St 91977 — 619-668-5720
Mike Allmann, prin. — Fax 668-8305
Spring Valley MS — 1,200/6-8
3900 Conrad Dr 91977 — 619-668-5750
Dana Wright, prin. — Fax 668-8302

Heartland Christian S — 100/PK-12
3327 Kenora Dr 91977 — 619-461-7220
Lynda Hansen, prin. — Fax 461-0962

Stanford, Santa Clara, Pop. 18,097

Stanford University — Post-Sec.
520 Lasuen Mall Un 232 94305 — 650-723-2300

Stevenson Ranch, Los Angeles
William S. Hart UNHSD
Supt. — See Santa Clarita
Rancho Pico JHS — 600/7-8
26250 Valencia Blvd 91381 — 661-284-3260
Dave LeBarron, prin. — Fax 255-7523
West Ranch HS — 700/9-12
26255 Valencia Blvd 91381 — 661-222-1220
Bob Vincent, prin. — Fax 255-7261

Stockton, San Joaquin, Pop. 286,926
Lincoln USD — 8,400/PK-12
2010 W Swain Rd 95207 — 209-953-8700
Steve Lowder Ed.D., supt. — Fax 474-7817
www.lusd.net
Lincoln HS — 2,700/9-12
6844 Alexandria Pl 95207 — 209-953-8920
Debbi Holmerud, prin. — Fax 952-4646
Sierra MS — 500/7-8
6768 Alexandria Pl 95207 — 209-953-8749
Terry Asplund, prin. — Fax 953-8747

Linden USD
Supt. — See Linden
Waterloo MS — 500/5-8
7007 Pezzi Rd 95215 — 209-931-0818
Mike McCandless, prin. — Fax 931-2915

Lodi USD
Supt. — See Lodi
Bear Creek HS — 2,600/9-12
10555 Thornton Rd 95209 — 209-953-8234
Daryl Camp, prin. — Fax 953-8247
Delta Sierra MS — 700/7-8
2255 Wagner Heights Rd 95209 — 209-953-8510
Irene Outlaw, prin. — Fax 953-8139
Elkhorn MS — 300/4-8
10505 Davis Rd 95209 — 209-953-8312
Neil Young, prin. — Fax 953-8319
McAuliffe MS — 800/7-8
3838 Iron Canyon Cir 95209 — 209-953-9431
Darla Briggs, prin. — Fax 953-9430
McNair HS — 9-12
9550 Ronald E McNair Way 95210 — 209-953-9245
Jim Davis, prin. — Fax 953-9261
Middle College HS — 200/9-12
5151 Pacific Ave 95207 — 209-954-5790
Sherry Balian, prin. — Fax 954-5875
Morada MS — 800/7-8
5001 Eastview Dr 95212 — 209-953-8490
Steve Takemoto, prin. — Fax 953-8502

Manteca USD
Supt. — See Manteca
New Visions HS — 9-12
4726 McCuen Ave 95206 — 209-938-6225
Katie Peters, prin. — Fax 982-4033
Weston Ranch HS — 1,100/9-12
4606 McCuen Ave 95206 — 209-982-5387
Clara Schmiedt, prin. — Fax 982-5765

Regional Occupational Center & Program
Supt. — None
San Joaquin County ROC/P — Vo/Tech
PO Box 213030 95213 — 209-468-9210
Doug Martin, dir. — Fax 468-4984

Stockton USD — 36,700/K-12
701 N Madison St 95202 — 209-933-7000
Jack McLaughlin, supt. — Fax 933-7071
www.stockton.k12.ca.us
Chavez HS — 9-12
2929 Windflower Ln 95212 — 209-933-7480
William Nelson, prin. — Fax 469-3681
Edison HS — 2,700/9-12
1425 S Center St 95206 — 209-933-7425
Mark Hagemann, prin. — Fax 942-2106
Franklin HS — 3,200/9-12
300 N Gertrude Ave 95215 — 209-933-7435
Scott Luhn, prin. — Fax 464-4708
Merlo Institute of Environmental Tech — 9-12
1670 E 6th St 95206 — 209-933-7190
Pat Hague, prin. — Fax 469-3740
Stagg HS — 3,000/9-12
1621 Brookside Rd 95207 — 209-933-7445
Jessica Anderson, prin. — Fax 954-9037
Weber Institute — Vo/Tech
302 W Weber Ave 95203 — 209-933-7330
Diane Arguijo, dir. — Fax 466-7548
School for Adults — Adult
1525 Pacific Ave 95204 — 209-933-7455
Carol Hirota, prin. — Fax 464-4917

Brookside Christian HS — 100/9-12
915 Rosemarie Ln 95207 — 209-954-7651
Dennis Gibson, admin. — Fax 954-7677
Children's Home of Stockton — 100/K-12
PO Box 201068 95201 — 209-466-0853
Michael Dutra, prin.
Emergency Medical Sciences Training Inst — Post-Sec.
1801 E March Ln Ste 260 95210 — 209-461-5550
Heald College — Post-Sec.
1605 E March Ln 95210 — 209-477-1114
Humphreys College — Post-Sec.
6650 Inglewood Ave 95207 — 209-478-0800
Maric College — Post-Sec.
722 W March Ln 95207 — 209-462-8777
MTI Business College of Stockton — Post-Sec.
6006 N El Dorado St 95207 — 209-957-3030
St. Mary HS — 1,100/9-12
PO Box 7247 95267 — 209-957-3340
Peter Morelli, prin. — Fax 957-0861
San Joaquin Delta College — Post-Sec.
5151 Pacific Ave 95207 — 209-954-5151
San Joaquin General Hospital — Post-Sec.
PO Box 1020 95201 — 209-468-6600
Stockton Christian S — 300/K-12
9021 West Ln 95210 — 209-957-3043
Harry Meeks, admin. — Fax 957-4120
University of the Pacific — Post-Sec.
3601 Pacific Ave 95211 — 209-946-2011
Western Career College — Post-Sec.
1313 W Robinhood Dr Ste B 95207 — 209-956-1240
Western Pacific Truck School — Post-Sec.
1002 N Broadway Ave 95205 — 209-465-1191

Strathmore, Tulare, Pop. 2,353
Porterville USD
Supt. — See Porterville
Strathmore HS — 400/9-12
22568 Avenue 196 93267 — 559-568-1731
Mike Henson, prin. — Fax 568-0091

Strathmore UNESD — 800/K-8
PO Box 247 93267 — 559-568-1283
David DePaoli, supt. — Fax 568-1262
www.suesd.k12.ca.us
Strathmore MS — 300/6-8
PO Box 247 93267 — 559-568-9293
Evelyn Erquhart, prin. — Fax 568-2944

Studio City, See Los Angeles

Bridges Academy — 100/6-12
3921 Laurel Canyon Blvd 91604 — 818-506-1091
Carl Sabatino, hdmstr. — Fax 506-8094

Sugarloaf, San Bernardino
Bear Valley USD
Supt. — See Big Bear Lake
Big Bear HS — 1,000/9-12
351 N Maple Ln 92386 — 909-585-6892
Dr. Rick Jameson, prin. — Fax 585-6809

Suisun City, Solano, Pop. 26,762
Fairfield-Suisun USD
Supt. — See Fairfield
Crystal MS — 800/6-8
400 Whispering Bay Ln 94585 — 707-435-5800
Roxanne Rice, prin. — Fax 435-5806

Sun City, Riverside, Pop. 14,930
Perris UNHSD
Supt. — See Perris
Extended Learning Center — Adult
27070 Sun City Blvd 92586 — 951-679-1535
Kindy Stumpp, prin.

Sunland, See Los Angeles
Los Angeles USD
Supt. — See Los Angeles
Mt. Gleason MS — 1,600/6-8
10965 Mount Gleason Ave 91040 — 818-951-2580
Deborah Acosta, prin. — Fax 352-6209

Fairhaven Christian Academy — 100/K-12
PO Box 4246 91041 — 818-434-7533
Wendy Van der Klomp, prin.

Sunnyvale, Santa Clara, Pop. 128,902
Cupertino UNSD
Supt. — See Cupertino
Cupertino MS — 1,200/6-8
1650 S Bernardo Ave 94087 — 408-245-0303
Kara Butler, prin. — Fax 732-4152

Fremont UNHSD — 9,600/9-12
589 W Fremont Ave 94087 — 408-522-2200
Stephen R. Rowley Ph.D., supt. — Fax 245-5325
www.fuhsd.org
Fremont HS — 1,800/9-12
1279 Sunnyvale Saratoga Rd 94087 — 408-522-2400
Peggy Raun-Linde, prin. — Fax 522-2468
Adult & Community Education — Adult
591 W Fremont Ave 94087 — 408-522-2700
Dennis Frese, dir. — Fax 522-2799
Other Schools – See Cupertino, San Jose

Regional Occupational Center & Program
Supt. — None
Santa Clara County ROP North — Vo/Tech
575 W Fremont Ave 94087 — 408-733-0881
Alyssa Lynch, dir. — Fax 733-0894

Santa Clara USD
Supt. — See Santa Clara
Peterson MS — 1,100/6-8
1380 Rosalia Ave 94087 — 408-423-2800
David Kennedy, prin. — Fax 423-2880

Sunnyvale ESD — 5,900/K-8
PO Box 3217 94088 — 408-522-8200
Joseph Rudnicki, supt. — Fax 522-8338
www.sesd.org
Columbia MS — 1,000/6-8
739 Morse Ave 94085 — 408-522-8247
Jocelyn Lee, prin. — Fax 522-8254
Sunnyvale MS — 1,000/6-8
1080 Mango Ave 94087 — 408-522-8288
Frances Dampier, prin. — Fax 522-8296

Brooks College — Post-Sec.
1120 Kifer Rd 94086 — 408-328-5700
Cogswell College — Post-Sec.
1175 Bordeaux Dr 94089 — 408-541-0100
King's Academy — 800/6-12
562 N Britton Ave 94085 — 408-481-9900
Bob Kellogg, prin. — Fax 481-9932
University of East West Medicine — Post-Sec.
970 W El Camino Real 94087 — 408-733-1878

Sun Valley, See Los Angeles
Los Angeles USD
Supt. — See Los Angeles
Byrd MS — 1,900/6-8
9171 Telfair Ave 91352 — 818-394-4600
Gerald Horowitz, prin. — Fax 767-8125
Francis Polytechnic HS — 4,300/9-12
12431 Roscoe Blvd 91352 — 818-767-4860
Janis Martinez, prin. — Fax 771-0452
Sun Valley MS — 2,800/6-8
7330 Bakman Ave 91352 — 818-765-3010
Antonio Delgado, prin. — Fax 503-9846

Village Christian HS — 600/9-12
8930 Village Ave 91352 — 818-767-8382
Barret Luketic, prin. — Fax 768-2006
Village Christian MS — 500/6-8
8930 Village Ave 91352 — 818-767-8382
Thomas Nare, prin. — Fax 768-2006

Susanville, Lassen, Pop. 18,101
Lassen UNHSD — 1,100/9-12
55 S Weatherlow St 96130 — 530-257-5134
Danny Lewis, supt. — Fax 257-0796
www.lassenhigh.org
Lassen Union HS — 1,000/9-12
1110 Main St 96130 — 530-257-2141
Danny Lewis, prin. — Fax 251-1173
Lassen Adult S — Adult
814 Cottage St 96130 — 530-257-4653

Regional Occupational Center & Program
Supt. — None
Lassen County ROP | Vo/Tech
472-013 Johnstonville Rd 96130 | 530-257-2196
Jud Jensen, dir. | Fax 257-2518

Susanville ESD | 1,300/K-8
109 S Gilman St 96130 | 530-257-8200
David Lutkemeier, supt. | Fax 257-8246
www.susanvillesd.org
Diamond View MS | 300/7-8
850 Richmond Rd 96130 | 530-257-5144
Patricia Gunderson, prin. | Fax 257-7232

Lassen Community College | Post-Sec.
PO Box 3000 96130 | 530-257-6181
New Horizons Christian S | 50/PK-12
995 Paiute Ln 96130 | 530-257-6420
Rebecca Guess, admin. | Fax 257-6423

Sutter, Sutter, Pop. 2,606
Sutter UNHSD | 800/9-12
PO Box 498 95982 | 530-822-5161
Ryan Robison, supt. | Fax 822-5168
www.sutterhigh.k12.ca.us/
Sutter HS | 800/9-12
PO Box 498 95982 | 530-822-5161
Ryan Robison, prin. | Fax 822-5168

Sutter Creek, Amador, Pop. 2,748
Amador County USD
Supt. — See Jackson
Amador HS | 800/9-12
330 Spanish St 95685 | 209-257-7300
Al Van Velzen, prin. | Fax 267-5942

Sylmar, See Los Angeles
Los Angeles USD
Supt. — See Los Angeles
Olive Vista MS | 1,800/6-8
14600 Tyler St 91342 | 818-833-3900
Danford Schar, prin. | Fax 367-8273
Sylmar HS | 3,500/9-12
13050 Borden Ave 91342 | 818-833-3700
Jan Lyons, prin. | Fax 364-1037

Delphi Academy of Los Angeles | 200/K-12
11341 Brainard Ave 91342 | 818-583-1070
Maggie Reinhart, prin.
First Lutheran JSHS | 100/7-12
13361 Glenoaks Blvd 91342 | 818-362-9223
Rick Klein, prin. | Fax 362-9713
ITT Technical Institute | Post-Sec.
12669 Encinitas Ave 91342 | 818-364-5151
Los Angeles Lutheran HS | 300/6-12
13750 Eldridge Ave 91342 | 818-362-5861
Dale Wolfgram, dir. | Fax 367-0043
Los Angeles Mission College | Post-Sec.
13356 Eldridge Ave 91342 | 818-364-7600
Olive View/UCLA Medical Centers | Post-Sec.
14445 Olive View Dr 91342 | 818-364-4224

Taft, Kern, Pop. 9,106
Regional Occupational Center & Program
Supt. — None
West Side ROP | Vo/Tech
PO Box 1337 93268 | 661-765-7185
Dale Countryman, dir. | Fax 765-7187

Taft CSD | 2,200/K-8
820 6th St 93268 | 661-763-1521
Michael Harris, supt. | Fax 763-1495
www.taftcity.k12.ca.us
Lincoln JHS | 700/6-8
810 6th St 93268 | 661-765-2127
Dr. Kathy Orrin, prin. | Fax 763-3970

Taft UNHSD | 1,000/9-12
701 7th St 93268 | 661-763-2300
Curtis T. Dubost Ed.D., supt. | Fax 763-1445
taft.ca.schoolwebpages.com
Taft Union HS | 900/9-12
701 7th St 93268 | 661-763-2300
Marilyn Brown, prin. | Fax 763-4736

Taft College | Post-Sec.
29 Emmons Park Dr 93268 | 661-763-7700

Tahoe City, Placer, Pop. 1,643
Tahoe-Truckee JUSD
Supt. — See Truckee
North Tahoe HS | 500/9-12
PO Box 5099 96145 | 530-581-7000
Bill Frey, prin. | Fax 581-3252
North Tahoe MS | 400/6-8
PO Box 5099 96145 | 530-581-7050
Dave Curry, prin. | Fax 581-1237

Tarzana, See Los Angeles
Los Angeles USD
Supt. — See Los Angeles
Portola MS | 2,200/6-8
18720 Linnet St 91356 | 818-654-3300
Adrienne Shaha, prin. | Fax 996-0292

Assyrian American Christian S | 100/6-12
5955 Lindley Ave 91356 | 818-996-1226
Richard Jensen, prin. | Fax 996-6467
Columbia College Hollywood | Post-Sec.
18618 Oxnard St 91356 | 800-785-0585
Hypnosis Motivation Institute | Post-Sec.
18607 Ventura Blvd Ste 310 91356 | 800-479-9464

Tecate, San Diego

Tecate Christian S | 100/1-12
PO Box 1000 91980 | 619-468-3355
Ronald Hoffman, prin. | Fax 478-5910

Tehachapi, Kern, Pop. 11,752
Tehachapi USD | 4,700/K-12
400 S Snyder Ave 93561 | 661-822-2100
Dr. Marian B. Stephens, supt. | Fax 822-2159
www.teh.k12.ca.us
Jacobsen MS | 1,100/6-8
711 Anita Dr 93561 | 661-822-2150
Eric Triguerio, prin. | Fax 822-2156
Tehachapi HS | 1,400/9-12
801 S Dennison Rd 93561 | 661-822-2130
Michael Arredondo, prin. | Fax 822-1854
Tehachapi Adult S | Adult
20569 Eumatilla Rd 93561 | 661-822-2124
Ria Maaskant, prin. | Fax 822-2188

Heritage Oak S | 100/K-12
20915 Schout Rd 93561 | 661-823-0885
Vanessa Cross, admin. | Fax 823-0863

Temecula, Riverside, Pop. 85,799
Temecula Valley USD | 25,000/K-12
31350 Rancho Vista Rd 92592 | 951-676-2661
David Allmen, supt. | Fax 695-7121
www.tvusd.k12.ca.us
Chaparral HS | 3,000/9-12
27215 Nicolas Rd 92591 | 951-695-4200
Dan Kenley, prin. | Fax 695-4219
Day MS | 1,000/6-8
40775 Camino Campos Verde 92591 | 951-699-8138
Greg Cooke, prin. | Fax 699-4198
Gardner MS | 800/6-8
45125 Via Del Coronado 92592 | 951-699-0080
Jim Flesuras, prin. | Fax 699-0081
Great Oak HS | 1,300/9-12
32555 Deer Hollow Way 92592 | 951-294-6450
Tim Ritter, prin. | Fax 294-6477
Margarita MS | 1,000/6-8
30600 Margarita Rd 92591 | 951-695-7370
Karen Hayes, prin. | Fax 695-7378
Temecula MS | 1,400/6-8
42075 Meadows Pkwy 92592 | 951-302-5151
Rob Sousa, prin. | Fax 302-5160
Temecula Valley HS | 3,000/9-12
31555 Rancho Vista Rd 92592 | 951-695-7300
Scott Schaufele, prin. | Fax 695-7311
Vail Ranch MS | 1,000/6-8
33340 Camino Piedra Rojo 92592 | 951-302-5188
Kevin Groepper, prin. | Fax 302-5195
Temecula Valley Adult S | Adult
31340 Rancho Vista Rd 92592 | 951-506-7996
Juanita Hernandez, prin. | Fax 695-7336
Other Schools – See Murrieta

Linfield Christian S | 900/K-12
31950 Pauba Rd 92592 | 951-676-8111
Karen Raftery, supt. | Fax 695-1291
Mountain View Christian S | 50/K-10
29385 Rancho California Rd 92591 | 951-693-5732
John Wells, admin. | Fax 693-0112
Professional Golfers Career College | Post-Sec.
26109 Ynez Rd 92591 | 800-877-4380
Royale College of Beauty | Post-Sec.
27485 Commerce Center Dr 92590 | 951-676-0833

Temple City, Los Angeles, Pop. 37,363
Temple City USD | 5,600/K-12
9700 Las Tunas Dr 91780 | 626-548-5000
Joan Hillard, supt. | Fax 548-5022
www.templecity.k12.ca.us
Oak Avenue IS | 900/7-8
6623 Oak Ave 91780 | 626-548-5060
David Mintz, prin. | Fax 548-5170
Temple City HS | 2,000/9-12
9501 Lemon Ave 91780 | 626-548-5040
Ray Plutko, prin. | Fax 548-5045
Temple City Adult Education | Adult
9229 Pentland St 91780 | 626-548-5050
Doug Sears, prin. | Fax 548-5118
Temple City Community Learning Center | Adult
9229 Pentland St 91780 | 626-548-5101
Doug Sears, prin. | Fax 548-5118

United Beauty College | Post-Sec.
10229 Lower Azusa Rd 91780 | 626-433-1371

Templeton, San Luis Obispo, Pop. 2,887
Templeton USD | 2,500/K-12
960 Old County Rd 93465 | 805-434-5800
Deborah Bowers Ed.D., supt. | Fax 434-5879
www.tusdnet.k12.ca.us
Eagle Canyon HS | 50/9-12
964 Old County Rd 93465 | 805-434-5833
Gary Duke Ed.D., prin. | Fax 434-3879
Templeton HS | 800/9-12
1200 S Main St 93465 | 805-434-5888
Jim Fotinakes, prin. | Fax 434-0743
Templeton MS | 600/6-8
925 Old County Rd 93465 | 805-434-5813
Jon Lorimer, prin. | Fax 434-5812

Terra Bella, Tulare, Pop. 2,740
Terra Bella UNESD | 900/K-8
9121 Road 240 93270 | 559-535-4451
Frank Betry, supt. | Fax 535-0314
Smith MS | 300/6-8
23825 Avenue 92 93270 | 559-535-4451
Guadalupe Roman, prin. | Fax 535-0829

Thermal, Riverside
Coachella Valley USD | 14,100/K-12
PO Box 847 92274 | 760-399-5137
Foch Pensis, supt. | Fax 399-1008
www.coachella.k12.ca.us
Coachella Valley HS | 2,800/9-12
83800 Airport Blvd 92274 | 760-399-5183
Manuel Arredondo, prin. | Fax 399-0089
Desert Mirage HS | 800/9-12
86150 Avenue 66 92274 | 760-397-2255
Joe Ceja, prin. | Fax 397-8760
Toro Canyon MS | 900/7-8
86150 Avenue 66 92274 | 760-397-2244
| Fax 397-8760
West Shores HS | 100/7-12
2381 Shore Hawk Ave 92274 | 760-394-4331
David Shepard, prin. | Fax 394-0971
Other Schools – See Coachella

Thousand Oaks, Ventura, Pop. 124,359
Conejo Valley USD | 21,900/K-12
1400 E Janss Rd 91362 | 805-497-9511
Mario Contini, supt. | Fax 371-9170
www.conejo.k12.ca.us
Colina MS | 1,200/6-8
1500 E Hillcrest Dr 91362 | 805-495-7429
Michael Waters, prin. | Fax 374-1163
Los Cerritos MS | 1,100/6-8
2100 E Ave De Las Flores 91362 | 805-492-3538
Eleanor Love, prin. | Fax 493-8854
Redwood MS | 1,200/6-8
233 W Gainsborough Rd 91360 | 805-497-7264
Lou Lichtl, prin. | Fax 497-3734
Thousand Oaks HS | 2,600/9-12
2323 N Moorpark Rd 91360 | 805-495-7491
Timothy Carpenter, prin. | Fax 374-1165
Conejo Valley Adult Education | Adult
1025 Old Farm Rd 91360 | 805-497-2761
Bernie Carr, prin. | Fax 374-1167
Other Schools – See Newbury Park, Westlake Village

California Lutheran University | Post-Sec.
60 W Olsen Rd 91360 | 805-492-2411
Hillcrest Christian S | 400/PK-12
384 Erbes Rd 91362 | 805-497-7501
Steve Allen, hdmstr. | Fax 494-9355
La Reina HS | 600/7-12
106 W Janss Rd 91360 | 805-495-6494
Cecilia Coe, prin. | Fax 494-4966

Tiburon, Marin, Pop. 8,671
Reed UNESD | 1,000/K-8
277 Karen Way Ste A 94920 | 415-381-1112
Christine Carter, supt. | Fax 384-0890
www.reedschools.org
Del Mar MS | 400/6-8
105 Avenida Miraflores 94920 | 415-435-1468
Bob Vasser, prin. | Fax 435-6190

Tollhouse, Fresno
Sierra USD
Supt. — See Prather
Sierra HS | 900/9-12
33326 Lodge Rd 93667 | 559-855-8311
Melissa Ireland, prin. | Fax 855-2162

Tomales, Marin
Shoreline USD | 700/K-12
10 John St 94971 | 707-878-2266
Dr. Stephen Rosenthal, supt. | Fax 878-2554
shoreline.marin.k12.ca.us/
Tomales HS | 200/9-12
PO Box 25 94971 | 707-878-2286
Trina Legacy, prin. | Fax 878-2787

Torrance, Los Angeles, Pop. 142,384
Regional Occupational Center & Program
Supt. — None
Southern California ROC | Vo/Tech
2300 Crenshaw Blvd 90501 | 310-224-4200
Christine Hoffman, supt. | Fax 320-1029

Torrance USD | 25,400/K-12
2335 Plaza Del Amo 90501 | 310-972-6500
George Mannon Ed.D., supt. | Fax 972-6012
www.tusd.org
Calle Mayor MS | 900/6-8
4800 Calle Mayor 90505 | 310-533-4548
Chris Sheck, prin. | Fax 972-6389
Casimir MS | 700/6-8
17220 Casimir Ave 90504 | 310-533-4498
Susan Holmes, prin. | Fax 972-6391
Hull MS at Levy | 900/6-8
3420 W 229th Pl 90505 | 310-533-4516
Barry Lafferty, prin. | Fax 972-6397
Jefferson MS | 700/6-8
21717 Talisman St 90503 | 310-533-4794
James Jones, prin. | Fax 972-6398
Lynn MS | 800/6-8
5038 Halison St 90503 | 310-533-4495
Leroy Jackson, prin. | Fax 972-6401
Madrona MS | 800/6-8
21364 Madrona Ave 90503 | 310-533-4562
Ron Richardson, prin. | Fax 972-6402
Magruder MS | 800/6-8
4100 W 185th St 90504 | 310-533-4527
Michael Voight, prin. | Fax 972-6403
North HS | 2,200/9-12
3620 W 182nd St 90504 | 310-533-4412
| Fax 972-6404
Richardson MS | 700/6-8
23751 Nancylee Ln 90505 | 310-533-4790
Matthew Horvath, prin. | Fax 972-6405
South HS | 2,100/9-12
4801 Pacific Coast Hwy 90505 | 310-533-4352
Scott McDowell, prin. | Fax 972-6454
Torrance HS | 2,200/9-12
2200 W Carson St 90501 | 310-533-4396
John O'Brien, prin. | Fax 972-6455
West HS | 2,200/9-12
20401 Victor St 90503 | 310-533-4299
Ben Egan, prin. | Fax 972-6483
Griffith Adult Education Center | Adult
2291 Washington Ave 90501 | 310-533-4454
Christine Vanderleest, prin. | Fax 972-6394
Hamilton Adult Education Center | Adult
2606 W 182nd St 90504 | 310-533-4459
Richard Rose, dir. | Fax 972-6395
Levy Adult Education Center at Hull | Adult
2080 W 231st St 90501 | 310-533-4689
John Black, prin. | Fax 972-6399

Bishop Montgomery HS | 1,200/9-12
5430 Torrance Blvd 90503 | 310-540-2021
Rosemary Libbon, prin. | Fax 543-5102
El Camino College | Post-Sec.
16007 Crenshaw Blvd 90506 | 310-660-3670

International Bilingual S 50/9-12
23800 Hawthorne Blvd 90505 310-373-0430
Nobuhito Suzuki, prin. Fax 376-0670
ITT Technical Institute Post-Sec.
20050 S Vermont Ave 90502 310-380-1555
Los Angeles Co. Harbor UCLA Medical Ctr. Post-Sec.
1000 W Carson St 90502 310-533-2101
Pacific Lutheran HS 100/9-12
PO Box 3295 90510 310-530-1231
Timothy Warneke, prin. Fax 530-1215
South Bay Junior Academy 200/K-10
4400 Del Amo Blvd 90503 310-370-6215
Susan Vlach, prin. Fax 793-8665
Southern CA Regional Occupational Center Post-Sec.
2300 Crenshaw Blvd 90501 310-224-4220
Westwood College - South Bay Campus Post-Sec.
19700 S Vermont Ave Ste 100 90502 310-965-0888

Tracy, San Joaquin, Pop. 79,964
Jefferson ESD 2,100/K-8
7500 W Linne Rd 95304 209-836-3388
Ed Quinn, supt. Fax 836-2930
www.jeffersonschooldistrict.com/
Jefferson S 600/5-8
7500 W Linne Rd 95304 209-835-3053
Jim Bridges, prin. Fax 835-4419

Tracy JUSD 15,500/K-12
1875 W Lowell Ave 95376 209-830-3200
James Franco, supt. Fax 830-3259
www.tracy.k12.ca.us
Monte Vista MS 1,000/6-8
751 W Lowell Ave 95376 209-831-5260
Steve Donahue, prin. Fax 831-5580
Tracy HS 2,400/9-12
315 E 11th St 95376 209-831-5100
Pat Anastasio, prin. Fax 831-5117
West HS 3,200/9-12
1775 W Lowell Ave 95376 209-831-5430
Herman Calad, prin. Fax 831-5433
Williams MS 1,400/6-8
1600 Tennis Ln 95376 209-831-5289
Barbara Montgomery, prin. Fax 831-5294
Tracy Adult S Adult
1902 N Corral Hollow Rd 95376 209-830-3384
Walter Gouveia, prin. Fax 830-3385

Tranquillity, Fresno
Golden Plains USD
Supt. — See San Joaquin
Tranquillity HS 500/9-12
PO Box 457 93668 559-698-7205
Brian Wall, prin. Fax 698-7632

Trona, San Bernardino
Trona JUSD 300/K-12
83600 Trona Rd 93562 760-372-2861
Charles Raff, supt. Fax 372-4534
www.trona.k12.ca.us/
Trona JSHS 200/7-12
83600 Trona Rd 93562 760-372-2865
Charles Raff, prin. Fax 372-4504

Truckee, Nevada, Pop. 15,737
Tahoe-Truckee JUSD 4,400/K-12
11839 Donner Pass Rd 96161 530-582-2500
Dennis Williams, supt. Fax 582-7606
www.ttusd.org
Alder Creek MS 700/6-8
10931 Alder Dr 96161 530-582-2750
Susan Phebus, prin. Fax 582-7640
Tahoe-Truckee HS 900/9-12
11725 Donner Pass Rd 96161 530-582-2600
James Cunningham, prin. Fax 582-7636
Other Schools – See Tahoe City

Tujunga, See Los Angeles
Los Angeles USD
Supt. — See Los Angeles
Verdugo Hills HS 2,300/9-12
10625 Plainview Ave 91042 818-951-5400
Diane Klewitz, prin. Fax 352-3577

Skyward Christian S 200/K-12
7747 Apperson St 91042 818-353-5159
Richard Lowe, hdmstr.
Smart Academy 50/K-12
7754 McGroarty St 91042 818-951-7182
Brendan Moore, prin. Fax 951-7183

Tulare, Tulare, Pop. 50,127
Regional Occupational Center & Program
Supt. — None
Tulare Co. Organization/Vocational Ed. Vo/Tech
4136 N Mooney Blvd 93274 559-688-0571
Ron Johnson, dir. Fax 688-5913

Tulare City ESD 8,200/K-8
600 N Cherry St 93274 559-685-7200
John Beck, supt. Fax 685-7287
www.tcsdk8.org/
Cherry Avenue MS 700/6-8
540 N Cherry St 93274 559-685-7320
Joe Terri, prin. Fax 685-7323
Live Oak MS 700/6-8
980 N Laspina St 93274 559-685-7310
Paula Adair, prin. Fax 685-7313
Los Tules MS 700/6-8
801 W Gail Ave 93274 559-687-3156
Gary Yentes, prin. Fax 685-7374
Mulcahy MS 600/5-8
1001 W Sonora Ave 93274 559-685-7250
John Pendleton, prin. Fax 685-7252

Tulare JUNHSD 4,600/9-12
426 N Blackstone St 93274 559-688-2021
Howard Berger, supt. Fax 687-7317
tulare.k12.ca.us
Countryside HS 50/9-12
1084 S Pratt St 93274 559-687-7384
Janis Lehmann, prin. Fax 687-7388
Tulare Tech Prep S Vo/Tech
737 W Bardsley Ave 93274 559-687-7400
Janis Lehmann, prin. Fax 687-7414
Tulare Union HS 1,900/9-12
755 E Tulare Ave 93274 559-686-4761
Michelle Nunley, prin. Fax 687-7367
Tulare Western HS 2,200/9-12
824 W Maple Ave 93274 559-686-8751
Vern Barlogio, prin. Fax 687-7341
Tulare Adult S Adult
575 W Maple Ave 93274 559-686-0225
Marie Pinto, prin. Fax 687-7447

Tulare Beauty College Post-Sec.
1400 W Inyo Ave 93274 559-688-2901

Tulelake, Siskiyou, Pop. 1,010
Tulelake Basin JUSD 600/K-12
PO Box 640 96134 530-667-2295
William Figgess, supt. Fax 667-4298
www.tulelake.k12.ca.us
Tulelake HS 200/7-12
PO Box 640 96134 530-667-2292
William Figgess, prin. Fax 667-2290

Tuolumne, Tuolumne
Summerville UNHSD 600/9-12
17555 Tuolumne Rd 95379 209-928-4228
John Keiter, supt. Fax 928-1422
www.summbears.k12.ca.us/
Summerville HS 600/9-12
17555 Tuolumne Rd 95379 209-928-4228
David Urquhart, prin. Fax 928-1422

Mother Lode Christian S 200/PK-12
18393 Gardner Ave 95379 209-928-4126
Linda Larson, prin. Fax 928-4613

Turlock, Stanislaus, Pop. 67,669
Chatom UNESD 700/K-8
7201 Clayton Rd 95380 209-664-8505
Fax 664-8508
www.chatom.k12.ca.us
Mountain View MS 200/6-8
10001 Crows Landing Rd 95380 209-664-8515
Cherise Olvera, prin. Fax 669-1733

Turlock USD 100/PK-12
PO Box 819013 95381 209-667-0632
William Gibson Ed.D., supt. Fax 667-6520
www.turlock.k12.ca.us
Dutcher MS 7-8
1441 Colorado Ave 95380 209-667-8817
Kathi Sigona, prin. Fax 667-1332
Pitman HS 9-12
2525 W Christoffersen Pkwy 95382 209-656-1592
Rodney Hollars, prin. Fax 656-1639
Turlock HS 9-12
1600 E Canal Dr 95380 209-667-2055
Dana Trevethan, prin. Fax 634-2698
Turlock JHS 7-8
3951 N Walnut Rd 95382 209-667-0881
Heidi Lawler, prin. Fax 668-3985
Turlock Adult Education Adult
1574 E Canal Dr 95380 209-667-0643
Don Wilkins, prin. Fax 667-0695

California State University-Stanislaus Post-Sec.
801 W Monte Vista Ave 95382 209-667-3122
Turlock Christian HS 300/7-12
PO Box 1540 95381 209-632-2337
Eric Davis, prin. Fax 632-5859

Tustin, Orange, Pop. 69,096
Tustin USD 19,700/K-12
300 S C St 92780 714-730-7305
Richard Bray, supt. Fax 730-7436
www.tustin.k12.ca.us
Columbus Tustin MS 900/6-8
17952 Beneta Way 92780 714-730-7352
James Christensen, prin. Fax 730-7512
Currie MS 900/6-8
1402 Sycamore Ave 92780 714-730-7360
David Mintz, prin. Fax 730-7593
Pioneer MS 1,100/6-8
2700 Pioneer Rd 92782 714-730-7534
Mike Mattos, prin. Fax 730-5405
Tustin HS 2,000/9-12
1171 El Camino Real 92780 714-730-7414
Jonathan Blackmore, prin. Fax 730-7568
Utt MS 900/6-8
13601 Browning Ave 92780 714-730-7573
Christine Matos, prin. Fax 750-7576
Sycamore HS / Tustin Adult S Adult
13780 Orange St 92780 714-730-7395
Betty Sarell, prin. Fax 730-4895
Other Schools – See Irvine, Santa Ana

Adcon Technical Institute Post-Sec.
17821 17th St Ste 120 92780 714-730-7080
Spirit Academy 200/K-12
1372 Irvine Blvd 92780 714-731-2630
Joe Rispoli, admin. Fax 731-2639

Twain Harte, Tuolumne, Pop. 2,170
Twain Harte-Long Barn UESD 500/K-8
18995 Twain Harte Dr 95383 209-586-0999
Mike Brusa, supt. Fax 586-0662
Twain Harte MS 200/6-8
18815 Manzanita Ct 95383 209-586-3266
Mike Woicicki, prin. Fax 586-3975

Twentynine Palms, San Bernardino, Pop. 28,409
Morongo USD 9,600/K-12
PO Box 1209 92277 760-367-9191
James Majchrzak, supt. Fax 367-7189
www.morongo.k12.ca.us
Twentynine Palms HS 1,000/9-12
72750 Wild Cat Way 92277 760-367-9591
Amy Woods, prin. Fax 367-2106
Twentynine Palms JHS 600/7-8
5798 Utah Trl 92277 760-367-9507
Jolie Kelley, prin. Fax 367-0742
Other Schools – See Yucca Valley

Twin Peaks, San Bernardino

Calvary Chapel Christian S 50/1-12
PO Box 1210 92391 909-337-2468
Sandi Balli, admin. Fax 337-9656

Ukiah, Mendocino, Pop. 15,463
Regional Occupational Center & Program
Supt. — None
Mendocino County ROP Vo/Tech
2240 Old River Rd 95482 707-467-5123
Nona Olsen, dir. Fax 468-8212

Ukiah USD 6,300/K-12
925 N State St 95482 707-463-5211
Raymond Chadwick, supt. Fax 463-2120
www.uusd.net/
Pomolita MS 700/6-8
740 N Spring St 95482 707-463-5224
Meredith Rosenberg, prin. Fax 463-5203
Ukiah HS 1,900/9-12
1000 Low Gap Rd 95482 707-463-5253
Ken Montoya, prin. Fax 463-4859
Ukiah Adult Education Adult
1056 N Bush St 95482 707-463-5217
David Gow, prin. Fax 463-0718
Other Schools – See Redwood Valley

Mendocino College Post-Sec.
1000 Hensley Creek Rd 95482 707-468-3000
Ukiah Junior Academy 100/K-10
180 Stipp Ln 95482 707-462-6350
David Schwartz, prin. Fax 462-4026

Union City, Alameda, Pop. 69,176
New Haven USD 11,700/K-12
34200 Alvarado Niles Rd 94587 510-471-1100
Pat Jaurequi, supt. Fax 471-7108
www.nhusd.k12.ca.us
Alvarado MS 1,100/6-8
31604 Alvarado Blvd 94587 510-489-0700
Yvonne Hull, prin. Fax 475-3936
Barnard-White MS 800/6-8
725 Whipple Rd 94587 510-471-5363
Karen Saucedo, prin. Fax 471-8372
Chavez MS 1,100/6-8
2801 Hop Ranch Rd 94587 510-487-1700
Alberto Solorzano, prin. Fax 475-3938
Logan HS 4,200/9-12
1800 H St 94587 510-471-2520
Don Montoya, prin. Fax 471-0514
New Haven Adult S Adult
600 G St 94587 510-489-2185
Nancy George, prin. Fax 471-0554
Other Schools – See Hayward

Upland, San Bernardino, Pop. 73,589
Upland USD 12,300/K-12
390 N Euclid Ave 91786 909-985-1864
Dr. Gary Rutherford, supt. Fax 949-7872
www.upland.k12.ca.us
Pioneer JHS 1,000/7-8
245 W 18th St 91784 909-949-7770
Brett O'Connor, prin. Fax 949-7778
Upland HS 3,600/9-12
565 W 11th St 91786 909-949-7880
Guy Roubian, prin. Fax 949-7895
Upland JHS 1,000/7-8
444 E 11th St 91786 909-949-7810
Brad Cuff, prin. Fax 949-7817

Upland Christian S 700/K-12
100 W 9th St 91786 909-920-5858
Susan Chiappone, prin. Fax 920-5866
Westwood College - Inland Empire Post-Sec.
20 W 7th St 91786 909-931-7500

Upper Lake, Lake
Upper Lake UNESD 600/K-8
PO Box 36 95485 707-275-2357
Kurt Herndon, supt. Fax 275-2205
Upper Lake Union MS 200/6-8
PO Box 36 95485 707-275-0223
Rick Winer, prin. Fax 275-2911

Upper Lake UNHSD 500/9-12
675 Clover Valley Rd 95485 707-275-2338
Patrick Iaccino, supt. Fax 275-9750
www.ulhs.k12.ca.us
Upper Lake Union HS 400/9-12
675 Clover Valley Rd 95485 707-275-2338
Patrick Iaccino, prin. Fax 275-0239

Vacaville, Solano, Pop. 92,985
Vacaville USD 13,800/K-12
751 School St 95688 707-453-6100
John T. Aycock, supt. Fax 453-6999
www.vacavilleusd.org
Jepson MS 1,100/7-8
580 Elder St 95688 707-453-6280
Mark Dietrich, prin. Fax 447-7128
Vaca Pena MS 1,200/7-8
200 Keith Way 95687 707-453-6270
Kristine Golomb, prin. Fax 451-9501
Vacaville HS 2,200/9-12
100 W Monte Vista Ave 95688 707-453-6065
Kari Gibson, prin. Fax 447-5604
Wood HS 2,200/9-12
998 Marshall Rd 95687 707-453-6900
Chris Strong, prin. Fax 451-3656

Vacaville Christian S 1,600/PK-12
1117 Davis St 95687 707-446-1776
Karen Winter, supt. Fax 446-1538

Valencia, See Santa Clarita
Castaic UNESD 3,600/K-8
28131 Livingston Ave 91355 661-257-4500
James Gibson, supt. Fax 257-3596
www.castaic.k12.ca.us/
Other Schools – See Castaic

William S. Hart UNHSD
Supt. — See Santa Clarita
Arroyo Seco JHS 1,300/7-8
27171 Vista Delgado Dr 91354 661-296-0991
Rhondi Durand, prin. Fax 296-3436
Rio Norte JHS 1,100/7-8
28771 Rio Norte Dr 91354 661-295-3700
John Krinkle, prin. Fax 257-1413
Valencia HS 3,200/9-12
27801 Dickason Dr 91355 661-294-1188
Paul Priesz, prin. Fax 294-3828

California Institute of the Arts Post-Sec.
24700 McBean Pkwy 91355 661-255-1050

Vallejo, Solano, Pop. 117,483
Vallejo City USD 17,400/K-12
665 Walnut Ave 94592 707-556-8921
Dr. Richard Damelio, admin. Fax 649-3907
www.vallejo.k12.ca.us
Bethel HS 1,600/9-12
1800 Ascot Pkwy 94591 707-556-5700
Lilli Rollins, prin. Fax 556-5703
Franklin MS 1,000/6-8
501 Starr Ave 94590 707-556-8470
Michael David, prin. Fax 556-8475
Hogan HS 1,800/9-12
850 Rosewood Ave 94591 707-556-8510
Mike Santos, prin. Fax 556-8529
Solano MS 800/6-8
1025 Corcoran Ave 94589 707-556-8600
Sheila Quintana, prin. Fax 556-8615
Springstowne MS 1,100/6-8
2833 Tennessee St 94591 707-556-8620
Fax 556-8624
Vallejo HS 2,000/9-12
840 Nebraska St 94590 707-556-1700
Phillip Saroyan, prin. Fax 556-8729
Vallejo MS 1,000/6-8
1347 Amador St 94590 707-556-8650
Gigi Patrick, prin. Fax 556-8666
Vallejo Adult Education Adult
1140 Capitol St 94590 707-556-8680
Kay Hartley, prin. Fax 556-8686

California Maritime Academy Post-Sec.
200 Maritime Academy Dr 94590 707-654-1000
North Hills Christian S 600/PK-12
200 Admiral Callaghan Ln 94591 707-644-5284
Richard Porter, admin. Fax 644-5295
St. Patrick-St. Vincent HS 600/9-12
1500 Benicia Rd 94591 707-644-4425
Mary Ellen Ryan, prin. Fax 644-3107
Touro Univ. Coll. / Osteopathic Medicine Post-Sec.
1310 Johnson Ln 94592 707-638-5270

Valley Center, San Diego, Pop. 1,711
Valley Center-Pauma USD 4,500/K-12
28751 Cole Grade Rd 92082 760-749-0464
Dr. Lou Obermeyer, supt. Fax 749-1208
www.vcpusd.net/
Valley Center HS 1,500/9-12
28751 Cole Grade Rd 92082 760-751-5500
Lucy Haines, prin. Fax 751-5509
Valley Center MS 700/7-8
28751 Cole Grade Rd 92082 760-751-4295
Chris Sommer, prin. Fax 751-4259

Valley Springs, Calaveras
Calaveras USD
Supt. — See San Andreas
Toyon MS 600/7-8
3412 Double Springs Rd 95252 209-754-2137
John Peckler, prin. Fax 754-5327

Valley Village, See Los Angeles

Valley Torah Boys HS 200/9-12
12517 Chandler Blvd 91607 818-505-7999
Rabbi Avrohām Stulberger, prin. Fax 505-7997

Van Nuys, See Los Angeles
Los Angeles USD
Supt. — See Los Angeles
Birmingham HS 3,600/9-12
17000 Haynes St 91406 818-758-5200
Marsha Coates, prin. Fax 342-5877
Fulton College Prep S 1,600/6-9
7477 Kester Ave 91405 818-785-8624
Robert Garcia, prin. Fax 994-2284
Grant HS 3,000/9-12
13000 Oxnard St 91401 818-756-2700
Linda Ibach, prin. Fax 908-0774
Mulholland MS 1,700/6-8
17120 Vanowen St 91406 818-609-2500
John White, prin. Fax 345-1933
Van Nuys HS 3,500/9-12
6535 Cedros Ave 91411 818-778-6800
Judith Vanderbok, prin. Fax 781-5181
Van Nuys MS 1,500/6-8
5435 Vesper Ave 91411 818-267-5900
Sandra Cruz, prin. Fax 909-7274
Vista MS 1,600/6-8
15040 Roscoe Blvd 91402 818-901-2727
Suzanne Blake, prin. Fax 901-2740
Van Nuys Adult Education Adult
6535 Cedros Ave 91411 818-778-6000
Andres Ameigeiras, prin. Fax 782-8354

California Institute of Locksmithing Post-Sec.
14719 1/2 Oxnard St 91411 818-994-7425
ICDC College Post-Sec.
14434 Sherman Way 91405 818-787-0007
Los Angeles Valley College Post-Sec.
5800 Fulton Ave 91401 818-947-2600
Montclair College Preparatory S 400/6-12
8071 Sepulveda Blvd 91402 818-787-5290
Dr. Vernon Simpson, prin. Fax 786-3382
Nick Harris Detective Academy Post-Sec.
14721 Oxnard St 91411 818-343-6611
The Kings College and Seminary Post-Sec.
14800 Sherman Way 91405 818-779-8040

Ventura, Ventura, Pop. 102,000
Ventura USD 17,700/K-12
255 W Stanley Ave Ste 100 93001 805-641-5000
Dr. Trudy Tuttle Arriaga, supt. Fax 653-7855
www.ventura.k12.ca.us/
Anacapa MS 1,100/6-8
100 S Mills Rd 93003 805-289-7900
Jesus Vaca, prin. Fax 289-7909
Balboa MS 1,400/6-8
247 S Hill Rd 93003 805-289-1800
Fax 289-1806
Buena HS 2,200/9-12
5670 Telegraph Rd 93003 805-289-1826
Kyunghae Schwartz, prin. Fax 289-1854
Cabrillo MS 1,000/6-8
1426 E Santa Clara St 93001 805-641-5155
Glory Page, prin. Fax 641-5377
De Anza MS 700/6-8
2060 Cameron St 93001 805-641-5165
Anne Roundy-Harter, prin. Fax 641-5282
Foothill Technology HS Vo/Tech
100 Day Rd 93003 805-289-0023
Joe Bova, prin. Fax 289-0029
Ventura HS 2,100/9-12
2 N Catalina St 93001 805-641-5116
Val Wyatt, prin. Fax 641-5310
Ventura Adult and Continuing Education Adult
5200 Valentine Rd 93003 805-289-7925
Teresa Johnson, prin. Fax 289-7931

St. Bonaventure HS 700/9-12
3167 Telegraph Rd 93003 805-648-6836
Br. Paulinus Horkan, prin. Fax 648-4903
Ventura College Post-Sec.
4667 Telegraph Rd 93003 805-654-6400
Ventura County Christian S 100/K-12
96 MacMillan Ave 93001 805-641-0187
Lisa Darby, admin. Fax 641-0252

Victorville, San Bernardino, Pop. 91,264
Adelanto ESD
Supt. — See Adelanto
Mesa Linda MS 1,000/7-8
13001 Mesa Linda Ave 92392 760-956-7355
Jeff Youskievicz, prin. Fax 956-7456

Victor Valley UNHSD 8,900/7-12
16350 Mojave Dr, 760-955-3200
Julian Weaver, supt. Fax 245-3128
www.vvuhsd.k12.ca.us/
Cobalt MS 800/7-8
13801 Cobalt Rd 92392 760-955-2530
Greg Johnson, prin. Fax 955-2437
Hook JHS 1,100/7-8
15000 Hook Blvd 92394 760-955-3360
James Nason, prin. Fax 245-5839
Silverado HS 3,400/9-12
14048 Cobalt Rd 92392 760-955-3353
Terry Colvin, prin. Fax 955-3439
Victor Valley HS 2,400/9-12
16500 Mojave Dr, 760-955-3300
Chris Douglass, prin. Fax 955-3319
Victor Valley JHS 700/7-8
16925 Forrest Ave, 760-955-3400
Richard Rojas, prin. Fax 955-1992
Victor Valley Adult Education Adult
15733 1st St, 760-955-3440
Gloria McGee, prin.

Victor Valley Beauty College Post-Sec.
16515 Mojave Dr, 760-245-2522
Victor Valley Christian S 600/PK-12
15260 Nisqually Rd, 760-241-8827
Dr. Linda Byrd, admin. Fax 243-0654
Victor Valley Community College Post-Sec.
18422 Bear Valley Rd, 760-245-4271

Villa Park, Orange, Pop. 6,026
Orange USD
Supt. — See Orange
Cerro Villa MS 1,200/7-8
17852 Serrano Ave 92861 714-997-6251
Aileen Sterling, prin. Fax 921-9331
Villa Park HS 2,300/9-12
18042 Taft Ave 92861 714-532-8020
Ed Howard, prin. Fax 628-4302

Visalia, Tulare, Pop. 108,669
Visalia USD 25,600/K-12
5000 W Cypress Ave 93277 559-730-7300
Stan A. Carrizosa, supt. Fax 730-7508
www.visalia.k12.ca.us
Divisadero MS 900/7-8
1200 S Divisadero St 93277 559-730-7661
Steve Moody, prin. Fax 730-7908
El Diamante HS 1,500/9-12
5100 W Whitendale Ave 93277 559-735-3501
Drew Sorensen, prin. Fax 735-3579
Golden West HS 2,200/9-12
1717 N McAuliff St 93292 559-730-7801
Nancy Powell, prin. Fax 730-7408
Green Acres MS 1,000/7-8
1147 N Mooney Blvd 93291 559-730-7671
Dave Tonini, prin. Fax 730-7918
La Joya MS 1,000/7-8
4711 W La Vida Ave 93277 559-730-7921
Mary Whitfield, prin. Fax 730-7505
Mt. Whitney HS 1,700/9-12
900 S Conyer St 93277 559-730-7602
Jeff Hohne, prin. Fax 730-7679
Redwood HS 2,000/9-12
1001 W Main St 93291 559-730-7367
Todd Oto, prin. Fax 730-7741
Valley Oak MS 1,200/7-8
2000 N Lovers Ln 93292 559-730-7681
Cindy Alonzo, prin. Fax 730-7822
Visalia Adult Education Adult
3110 E Houston Ave 93292 559-730-7655
Jill Rojas, prin. Fax 635-0372

Central Valley Christian S 1,000/PK-12
5600 W Tulare Ave 93277 559-734-9481
John DeLeeuw, supt. Fax 734-7963
College of the Sequoias Post-Sec.
915 S Mooney Blvd 93277 559-730-3700
Estes Inst. Cosmetology Arts & Sciences Post-Sec.
324 E Main St 93291 559-733-3617
Golden State College Post-Sec.
3356 S Fairway St 93277 559-733-4040
Milan Institute of Cosmetology Post-Sec.
3328 S Fairway 93277 559-735-3829
San Joaquin Valley College Post-Sec.
8400 W Mineral King Ave 93291 559-651-2500
Visalia Christian Academy 200/6-12
3737 W Walnut Ave 93277 559-737-9710
Tamara Olson, prin. Fax 737-9714

Vista, San Diego, Pop. 90,402
Vista USD 23,500/K-12
1234 Arcadia Ave 92084 760-726-2170
Dr. Dave Cowles, supt. Fax 630-0196
www.vusd.k12.ca.us
Lincoln MS 1,300/6-8
1234 Arcadia Ave 92084 760-726-5766
Larrie Hall, prin. Fax 945-4273
Rancho Buena Vista HS 3,300/9-12
1234 Arcadia Ave 92084 760-727-7284
Rich Alderson, prin. Fax 598-7062
Vista HS 3,400/9-12
1234 Arcadia Ave 92084 760-726-5611
Larry White, prin. Fax 630-9738
Washington MS 1,200/6-8
1234 Arcadia Ave 92084 760-724-7115
Janet Whiddon, prin. Fax 941-6912
Vista Adult S Adult
1234 Arcadia Ave 92084 760-758-7122
Dick Crane, prin. Fax 726-3277
Other Schools – See Oceanside

Calvary Christian S 300/K-12
885 E Vista Way 92084 760-724-4590
Ronald Barger, admin. Fax 560-0607
Golf Academy of San Diego Post-Sec.
1910 Shadowridge Dr Ste 111, 800-342-7342
Maric College Post-Sec.
2022 University Dr 92083 760-630-1555
Tri City Christian S 1,000/PK-12
302 N Emerald Dr 92083 760-724-3016
Sharon Privett, prin. Fax 724-6643

Walnut, Los Angeles, Pop. 31,424
Walnut Valley USD 15,400/K-12
880 S Lemon Ave 91789 909-595-1261
Fax 444-3435
www.walnutvalley.k12.ca.us
South Pointe MS 1,300/6-8
20671 Larkstone Dr 91789 909-595-8171
Anne Neal, prin. Fax 468-5201
Suzanne MS 1,500/6-8
525 Suzanne Rd 91789 909-594-1657
Jan Keating, prin. Fax 598-6741
Walnut HS 2,700/9-12
400 Pierre Rd 91789 909-594-1333
Russell Lee-Sung, prin. Fax 598-7282
Walnut Valley Adult S Adult
476 S Lemon Ave 91789 909-595-1261
Lisa Raigosa, prin. Fax 594-1272
Other Schools – See Diamond Bar

Mt. San Antonio College Post-Sec.
1100 N Grand Ave 91789 909-594-5611
Southlands Christian S 600/PK-12
1920 Brea Canyon Cut Off Rd 91789 909-598-9733
Glenn Duncan, admin. Fax 468-9943

Walnut Creek, Contra Costa, Pop. 64,196
Acalanes UNHSD
Supt. — See Lafayette
Acalanes Center for Independent Study 50/9-12
1963 Tice Valley Blvd 94595 925-280-3945
Dennis Regalado, prin. Fax 280-3947
Las Lomas HS 1,700/9-12
1460 S Main St 94596 925-280-3920
Patrick Lickiss, prin. Fax 280-3921
Acalanes Adult S & Center Adult
1963 Tice Valley Blvd 94595 925-280-3980
Laura Canciamilla, dir. Fax 395-3981

Mount Diablo USD
Supt. — See Concord
Foothill MS 1,100/6-8
2775 Cedro Ln 94598 925-939-8600
Robert Johnson, prin. Fax 256-4281
Northgate HS 1,600/9-12
425 Castle Rock Rd 94598 925-938-0900
Martha Riley, prin. Fax 945-6429

Walnut Creek ESD 3,300/K-8
960 Ygnacio Valley Rd 94596 925-944-6850
Michael De Sa, supt. Fax 944-1768
www.wcsd.k12.ca.us
Walnut Creek IS 1,200/6-8
2425 Walnut Blvd 94597 925-944-6840
Kevin Collins, prin. Fax 933-1922

Berean Christian HS 400/9-12
245 El Divisadero Ave 94598 925-945-6464
Nelson Noriega, prin. Fax 945-7473
Contra Costa Christian S 400/PK-12
2721 Larkey Ln 94597 925-934-4964
B. J. Huizenga, supt. Fax 934-4966
Legacy Academy 100/1-12
1283 Boulevard Way 94595 925-262-4102
Brad Smith, dir.

Warner Springs, San Diego
Warner USD 300/PK-12
PO Box 8 92086 760-782-3517
Richard Swanson Ph.D., supt. Fax 782-9117
www.sdcoe.k12.ca.us/districts/warner/

Warner HS 200/6-12
PO Box 8 92086 760-782-3517
Ron Koenig Ph.D., prin. Fax 782-0605

Wasco, Kern, Pop. 23,874
Regional Occupational Center & Program
Supt. — None
North Kern Vocational Training Center Vo/Tech
2150 7th St 93280 661-758-3045
Glenda Santillan, dir. Fax 758-5956

Wasco UNESD 3,100/K-8
639 Broadway St 93280 661-758-7100
Gary Bray, supt. Fax 758-7110
www.wuesd.org
Jefferson MS 700/7-8
305 Griffith Ave 93280 661-758-7140
William Elliott, prin. Fax 758-9366

Wasco UNHSD 1,500/9-12
2100 7th St 93280 661-758-8447
Elizabeth McCray, supt. Fax 758-4946
www.wasco.k12.ca.us/
Wasco HS 1,400/9-12
1900 7th St 93280 661-758-7400
Joseph Elwood, prin. Fax 758-9201

Waterford, Stanislaus, Pop. 8,161
Waterford USD 1,800/K-12
219 N Reinway Ave 95386 209-874-1809
Frank Cranley, supt. Fax 874-3109
www.waterford.k12.ca.us
Waterford HS 600/9-12
121 S Reinway Ave 95386 209-874-9060
Don Davis, prin. Fax 874-9065
Waterford MS 400/6-8
12916 Bentley St 95386 209-874-2382
Jose Aldaco, prin. Fax 874-3652

Watsonville, Santa Cruz, Pop. 47,927
Pajaro Valley USD 16,800/K-12
294 Green Valley Rd 95076 831-786-2100
Terry McHenry, supt. Fax 728-4288
www.pvusd.net
Hall MS 900/6-8
201 Brewington Ave 95076 831-728-6270
Artemisa Cortez, prin. Fax 761-6150
Lakeview MS 1,000/6-8
2350 E Lake Ave 95076 831-728-6454
Casey O'Brien, prin. Fax 728-6480
Pajaro MS 500/6-8
250 Salinas Rd 95076 831-728-6238
Stella Moreno, prin. Fax 728-6219
Rolling Hills MS 1,000/6-8
130 Herman Ave 95076 831-728-6341
Rick Ito, prin. Fax 724-7323
Watsonville HS 2,700/9-12
250 E Beach St 95076 831-728-6390
Fax 761-6013
Adult Education Downtown Center Adult
280 Main St 95076 831-728-6330
Bob Harper, coord. Fax 728-6245
Adult Education Green Valley Center Adult
294 Green Valley Rd 95076 831-786-2160
Bob Harper, dir. Fax 786-2193
Other Schools – See Aptos

Green Valley Christian S 400/PK-12
376 S Green Valley Rd 95076 831-724-6505
Sharon Harris, prin. Fax 724-1002
Monte Vista Christian S 800/6-12
2 School Way 95076 831-722-8178
Stephen Sharp, supt. Fax 722-6003
Mt. Madonna S 200/PK-12
491 Summit Rd 95076 408-847-2717
Dr. Sarada Diffenbaugh, prin. Fax 847-5633
St. Francis Central Coast Catholic HS 100/9-12
2400 E Lake Ave 95076 831-724-5933
Keith Mathews, prin. Fax 724-5995

Weaverville, Trinity, Pop. 3,370
Trinity UNHSD 500/9-12
PO Box 1227 96093 530-623-6104
Robert Lowden, supt. Fax 623-3418
www.trinitywolves.org
Trinity HS 400/9-12
PO Box 1060 96093 530-623-6127
Michael McAllister, prin. Fax 623-6661
Trinity Adult S Adult
PO Box 2789 96093 530-623-2541
Lynn Kelly, prin. Fax 623-6026

Weed, Siskiyou, Pop. 3,114
Siskiyou UNHSD
Supt. — See Mount Shasta
Weed HS 200/9-12
909 Hillside Dr 96094 530-938-4774
Michael Matheson, prin. Fax 938-1319

College of the Siskiyous Post-Sec.
800 College Ave 96094 530-938-4461

Weimar, Placer, Pop. 1,300
Placer Hills UNESD
Supt. — See Meadow Vista
Weimar Hills MS 500/4-8
PO Box 255 95736 530-637-4121
Steve Schaumleffel, prin. Fax 637-4054

Weldon, Kern
South Fork UNESD 400/K-8
5225 S Kelso Valley Rd 93283 760-378-4000
Robin Shive, supt. Fax 378-3046
www.southforkschool.org
South Fork MS 100/6-8
5225 S Kelso Valley Rd 93283 760-378-1300
Robin Shive, prin. Fax 378-9113

West Covina, Los Angeles, Pop. 108,185
Covina-Valley USD
Supt. — See Covina
South Hills HS 2,000/9-12
645 S Barranca St 91791 626-974-6220
Judith North, prin. Fax 974-6245
Traweek MS 1,100/6-8
1941 E Rowland Ave 91791 626-974-7400
Jeff Wilson, prin. Fax 974-7415
Tri Community Adult Ed.-Pioneer Center Adult
1651 E Rowland Ave 91791 626-974-6821
Bruce Krall, prin. Fax 974-6830

Regional Occupational Center & Program
Supt. — None
East San Gabriel Valley ROP Vo/Tech
1501 Del Norte St 91790 626-962-5080
Laurel Adler, supt. Fax 472-5145

Rowland USD
Supt. — See Rowland Heights
Giano IS 1,000/7-8
3223 S Giano Ave 91792 626-965-2461
Patricia Cuesta, prin. Fax 854-2212
Rincon IS 700/7-8
2800 E Hollingworth St 91792 626-965-1696
Debi Klotz, prin. Fax 810-4916

West Covina USD 9,300/K-12
1717 W Merced Ave 91790 626-939-4600
Liliam Leis-Castillo, supt. Fax 939-4701
www.wcusd.k12.ca.us
Edgewood MS 1,400/6-8
1625 W Durness St 91790 626-939-4900
James Mandala, prin. Fax 939-4999
Hollencrest MS 800/6-8
2101 E Merced Ave 91791 626-931-1760
Kathy Granger, prin. Fax 931-1762
West Covina HS 2,800/9-12
1609 E Cameron Ave 91791 626-859-2900
Brad Manning, prin. Fax 859-3950

Marinello School of Beauty Post-Sec.
118 Plaza Dr 91790 626-962-1021
Northwest College Medical Dental Assts. Post-Sec.
2121 W Garvey Ave N 91790 626-960-5046

West Hills, Ventura

Chaminade College Prep S 1,100/9-12
7500 Chaminade Ave 91304 818-347-8300
Br. Tom Fahy, prin. Fax 348-8374
New Community Jewish HS 300/9-12
7353 Valley Circle Blvd 91304 818-348-0048
Dr. Bruce Powell, hdmstr.
West Valley Christian S 400/K-12
22450 Sherman Way 91307 818-884-4710
Dr. Robert Lozano, admin. Fax 884-4749

Westlake Village, Los Angeles, Pop. 8,585
Conejo Valley USD
Supt. — See Thousand Oaks
Westlake HS 2,300/9-12
100 N Lakeview Canyon Rd 91362 805-497-6711
Ronald Lipari, prin. Fax 497-2606

Malibu Cove Private S 100/K-12
860 Hampshire Rd 91361 805-267-4818
J. Alfonso, pres.
Oaks Christian S 1,000/6-12
31749 La Tienda Rd 91362 818-575-9900
Jeffrey Woodcock, hdmstr. Fax 575-9951

Westminster, Orange, Pop. 89,523
Garden Grove USD
Supt. — See Garden Grove
La Quinta HS 1,800/9-12
10372 McFadden Ave 92683 714-663-6315
Louise Milner, prin.
McGarvin IS, 9802 Bishop Pl 92683 700/7-8
Jane Jones, prin. 714-663-6218

Huntington Beach UNHSD
Supt. — See Huntington Beach
Westminster HS 2,600/9-12
14325 Goldenwest St 92683 714-893-1381
Shirley Vaughn, prin. Fax 898-4721

Westminster ESD 9,500/PK-8
14121 Cedarwood St 92683 714-894-7311
Roberta Mahler, supt. Fax 899-2781
www.wsd.k12.ca.us
Johnson MS 1,000/6-8
13603 Edwards St 92683 714-894-7244
Heidi DeBritton, prin. Fax 379-0784
Warner MS 900/6-8
14171 Newland St 92683 714-894-7281
Betty DeWolf, prin. Fax 895-2378

Asian American Intl Beauty College Post-Sec.
7871 Westminster Blvd 92683 714-891-0508

West Sacramento, Yolo, Pop. 41,744
Washington USD 6,900/K-12
930 Westacre Rd 95691 916-375-7600
Steven Lawrence Ph.D., supt. Fax 375-7619
www.wusd.k12.ca.us
River City HS 1,600/9-12
1100 Clarendon St 95691 916-375-7800
Stuart MacKay, prin. Fax 375-7809
Washington Adult S Adult
920 Westacre Rd 95691 916-375-7740
Paul Preston, prin. Fax 375-7744
Other Schools – See Broderick

Wyotech Post-Sec.
980 Riverside Pkwy 95605 916-376-8888
Wyotech Post-Sec.
980 Riverside Pkwy 95605 916-376-8888

Westwood, Lassen, Pop. 2,017
Westwood USD 400/K-12
PO Box 1225 96137 530-256-2311
Henry Bietz, supt. Fax 256-3539
Westwood JSHS 200/8-12
PO Box 1510 96137 530-256-3235
Henry Bietz, prin. Fax 256-3693

Wheatland, Yuba, Pop. 3,638
Wheatland ESD 1,300/K-8
PO Box 818 95692 530-633-3130
Debra Pearson, supt. Fax 633-4807
www.wheatland.k12.ca.us/
Bear River MS 500/6-8
100 Wheatland Park Dr 95692 530-633-3135
Julie Tyler, prin. Fax 633-3142

Wheatland UNHSD 700/9-12
1010 Wheatland Rd 95692 530-633-3100
Wayne Gadberry, supt. Fax 633-3109
www.wheatlandhigh.org
Wheatland Union HS 700/9-12
1010 Wheatland Rd 95692 530-633-3100
Wayne Gadberry, prin. Fax 633-3109

Whitethorn, Humboldt
Leggett Valley USD
Supt. — See Leggett
Whale Gulch HS 50/9-12
76811 Usal Rd 95589 707-986-7131
Gordon Piffero, prin. Fax 986-1355

Whittier, Los Angeles, Pop. 84,473
East Whittier City ESD 8,900/K-8
14535 Whittier Blvd 90605 562-698-0351
Dorothy Fagan, supt. Fax 696-9256
www.ewcsd.k12.ca.us
East Whittier MS 1,100/6-8
14421 Whittier Blvd 90605 562-693-3766
Dorka Duron, prin. Fax 945-3542
Granada MS 1,000/6-8
15337 Lemon Dr 90604 562-943-0283
Charles Royce, prin. Fax 943-5413
Hillview MS 1,000/6-8
10931 Stamy Rd 90604 562-946-7446
Toni Eannareno, prin. Fax 946-3066

Lowell JSD 3,300/K-8
11019 Valley Home Ave 90603 562-943-0211
Dr. Patricia Howell, supt. Fax 947-7874
www.ljsd.org
Rancho-Starbuck IS 800/7-8
16430 Woodbrier Dr 90604 562-902-4261
Kim Likert, prin. Fax 947-9911

Regional Occupational Center & Program
Supt. — None
Tri-Cities ROP Vo/Tech
12519 Washington Blvd 90602 562-698-9571
Esperanza Fernandez, supt. Fax 696-5352

South Whittier ESD 4,100/K-8
PO Box 3037 90605 562-944-6231
Richard Graves, supt. Fax 944-9659
www.swhittier.k12.ca.us/
Graves MS 1,000/7-8
13243 Los Nietos Rd 90605 562-944-0135
Kathy Cardiff, prin. Fax 944-9433

Whittier City ESD 7,200/PK-8
7211 Whittier Ave 90602 562-789-3075
Dr. Carmella Franco, supt. Fax 698-6534
www.whittiercity.k12.ca.us
Dexter MS 1,400/6-8
11532 Floral Dr 90601 562-789-3090
Diane Kinnart, prin. Fax 789-3095
Edwards MS 1,100/6-8
6812 Norwalk Blvd 90606 562-789-3115
Monica Sena, prin. Fax 789-3133

Whittier UNHSD 12,700/9-12
9401 Painter Ave 90605 562-698-8121
Sandra Thorstenson, supt. Fax 693-0221
www.wuhsd.k12.ca.us
California HS 2,700/9-12
9800 Mills Ave 90604 562-698-8121
Richard Boline, prin. Fax 946-6094
La Serna HS 2,200/9-12
15301 Youngwood Dr 90605 562-698-8121
Martin Plourde, prin. Fax 698-6918
Pioneer HS 1,700/9-12
10800 Ben Avon St 90606 562-698-8121
Alex Flores, prin. Fax 692-9194
Whittier HS 2,200/9-12
12417 Philadelphia St 90601 562-698-8121
Loring Davies, prin. Fax 698-8925
Adult Education Center Adult
9401 Painter Ave 90605 562-698-8121
Leonard Rivera, prin. Fax 693-5354
Other Schools – See Santa Fe Springs

Marinello School of Beauty Post-Sec.
6538 Greenleaf Ave 90601 562-698-0068
Remnant Christian S 50/K-12
7346 Painter Ave 90602 562-464-2554
James Turnbaugh, admin. Fax 464-2556
Rio Hondo College Post-Sec.
3600 Workman Mill Rd 90601 562-692-0921
Southern CA University of Health Science Post-Sec.
16200 Amber Valley Dr 90604 562-947-8755
Whittier Christian JHS 200/7-8
6548 Newlin Ave 90601 562-698-0527
Robert Sowell, admin. Fax 698-2859
Whittier College Post-Sec.
PO Box 634 90608 562-907-4200

Wildomar, Riverside, Pop. 10,411
Lake Elsinore USD
Supt. — See Lake Elsinore
Brown MS 1,300/6-8
21861 Grand Ave 92595 951-678-8400
Steve Behar, prin. Fax 678-8408
Elsinore HS 2,600/9-12
21800 Canyon Dr 92595 951-253-7200
Jon Hurst, prin. Fax 253-7209

California Lutheran HS 100/9-12
PO Box 1570 92595 951-678-7000
Rev. Gregory Bork, prin. Fax 678-0172

Cornerstone Christian S 300/K-12
34570 Monte Vista Dr 92595 951-674-9381
Jim Phillips, dir. Fax 674-8462
Faith Baptist Academy 200/K-12
PO Box 1030 92595 951-245-8748
Greg Beil, admin.

Williams, Colusa, Pop. 4,755
Williams USD 1,100/K-12
PO Box 7 95987 530-473-2550
Dr. Merrill Grant, supt. Fax 473-5894
www.williamsusd.net
Williams HS 300/9-12
PO Box 7 95987 530-473-5369
Dan Flanigan, prin. Fax 473-5026
Williams MS 500/4-8
PO Box 7 95987 530-473-5304
Arthur Estrada, prin. Fax 473-5928

Willits, Mendocino, Pop. 5,066
Willits USD 2,100/K-12
120 Pearl St 95490 707-459-5314
Steven Jorgensen, supt. Fax 459-7862
www.ctap1.org/wusd/
Baechtel Grove MS 400/6-8
1150 Magnolia St 95490 707-459-2417
Rick Jordan, prin. Fax 459-7881
Willits HS 600/9-12
299 N Main St 95490 707-459-7700
Gordon Oslund, prin. Fax 459-7741
Willits Adult S Adult
120 N Main St 95490 707-459-4801
Catherine Scott, prin. Fax 459-7862

Willow Creek, Humboldt, Pop. 1,576

Willow Creek Christian S 100/K-12
PO Box 1568 95573 530-629-3332
Marie Smith, prin. Fax 629-3332

Willows, Glenn, Pop. 6,296
Glenn County Office of Education
311 S Villa Ave 95988 530-934-6575
Arturo Barrera, supt. Fax 934-6576
www.glenncoe.org
Glenn Adult Program Adult
451 S Villa Ave 95988 530-934-6320
Coleen Parker, dir. Fax 934-6325

Regional Occupational Center & Program
Supt. — None
Glenn County ROP Vo/Tech
525 W Sycamore St 95988 530-934-6575
Coleen Parker, supt. Fax 934-6576

Willows USD 1,800/K-12
334 W Sycamore St 95988 530-934-6600
Steve Olmos, supt. Fax 934-6609
www.willowsunified.org/home.htm
Willows HS 500/9-12
203 N Murdock Ave 95988 530-934-6611
Morton Geivett, prin. Fax 934-6619
Willows IS 500/5-8
1145 W Cedar St 95988 530-934-6633
Steve Sailsbery, prin. Fax 934-6697
Willows Community HS Adult
823 W Laurel St 95988 530-934-6605
Mike Rutherglen, prin. Fax 934-6384

Wilmington, See Los Angeles
Los Angeles USD
Supt. — See Los Angeles
Banning HS 3,300/9-12
1527 Lakme Ave 90744 310-847-3700
Michael Summe, prin. Fax 830-5515
Wilmington MS 2,200/6-8
1700 Gulf Ave 90744 310-847-1500
Veronica Aragon, prin. Fax 549-5307

Los Angeles Harbor College Post-Sec.
1111 Figueroa Pl 90744 310-522-8200
National Polytechnic College Post-Sec.
272 S Fries Ave 90744 310-834-2501
Pacific Harbor Christian S 300/PK-12
1530 N Wilmington Blvd 90744 310-835-5665
Angie Colclasure, supt. Fax 835-6361

Windsor, Sonoma, Pop. 24,968
Windsor USD 3,900/K-12
9291 Old Redwood Hwy 95492 707-837-7700
Steven Herrington Ph.D., supt. Fax 838-4031
www.wusd.org
Windsor HS 1,400/9-12
8695 Windsor Rd 95492 707-837-7767
Patricia Law, prin. Fax 837-7773
Windsor MS 1,000/6-8
9500 Brooks Rd S 95492 707-837-7737
Loren Barker, prin. Fax 837-7743

Windsor Christian Academy 300/PK-12
PO Box 1880 95492 707-838-3757
Tad Theiss, prin. Fax 838-3542

Winterhaven, Imperial
San Pasqual Valley USD 800/PK-12
676 Base Line Rd 92283 760-572-0222
Suzanne Smith, supt. Fax 572-0711
www.sanpasqual.k12.ca.us
San Pasqual Valley HS 200/9-12
676 Base Line Rd 92283 760-572-0222
Lynda Schoonover, prin. Fax 572-0881
San Pasqual Valley MS 200/6-8
676 Base Line Rd 92283 760-572-0222
Rauna Fox, prin. Fax 572-0829

Winters, Yolo, Pop. 6,764
Winters JUSD 1,900/K-12
909 Grant Ave 95694 530-795-6100
Dale J. Mitchell, supt. Fax 795-6114
winters.k12.ca.us
Winters HS 700/9-12
101 Grant Ave 95694 530-795-6140
George Griffin, prin. Fax 795-6147
Winters MS 500/6-8
425 Anderson Ave 95694 530-795-6130
Suzanne Martin, prin. Fax 795-6137

Winton, Merced, Pop. 7,559
Merced River UNESD
Supt. — See Snelling
Washington MS 100/4-8
4402 Oakdale Rd 95388 209-358-5679
Dr. Helio Brasil, prin. Fax 358-2855

Winton ESD 1,800/K-8
PO Box 8 95388 209-357-6175
Michael Crass, supt. Fax 357-1994
www.winton.k12.ca.us
Winton MS 600/6-8
PO Box 1299 95388 209-357-6189
Randall Heller, prin. Fax 358-5889

Woodlake, Tulare, Pop. 7,215
Woodlake UNSD 2,400/K-12
300 W Whitney Ave 93286 559-564-8081
Steve Tietjen, supt. Fax 564-3831
Woodlake Union HS 800/9-12
400 W Whitney Ave 93286 559-564-3307
Tim Hire, prin. Fax 564-3320
Woodlake Valley MS 600/6-8
497 N Palm St 93286 559-564-8061
David East, prin. Fax 564-0702

Woodland, Yolo, Pop. 51,020
Regional Occupational Center & Program
Supt. — None
Yolo County ROP Vo/Tech
1240 Harter Ave 95776 530-668-3710
Gayle McLevich, coord. Fax 668-3850

Woodland JUSD 10,600/K-12
630 Cottonwood St 95695 530-662-0201
Jacki Cottingim Ph.D., supt. Fax 662-6956
www.wjusd.net
Douglass MS 900/7-8
525 Granada Dr 95695 530-666-2191
Jonathan Brunson, prin. Fax 668-9217
Lee MS 800/7-8
520 West St 95695 530-662-0251
Garth Lewis, prin. Fax 662-9423
Pioneer HS 1,200/9-12
1400 Pioneer Ave 95776 530-406-1148
Mark Roberts, prin. Fax 662-3661
Woodland HS 2,000/9-12
21 N West St 95695 530-662-4678
Evelia Genera, prin. Fax 662-7464
Woodland Adult Education Adult
575 Hays St 95695 530-662-0798
Susan Moylan, dir. Fax 662-8039

Woodland Christian S 500/PK-12
1616 West St 95695 530-666-6615
Terry Campbell, admin. Fax 666-3470

Woodland Hills, See Los Angeles
Los Angeles USD
Supt. — See Los Angeles
El Camino Real HS 3,900/9-12
5440 Valley Circle Blvd 91367 818-595-7500
David Fehte, prin. Fax 710-9023
Hale MS 2,200/6-8
23830 Califa St 91367 818-313-7400
Neal Siegel, prin. Fax 346-7517
Taft HS 3,500/9-12
5461 Winnetka Ave 91364 818-227-3600
Sharon Thomas, prin. Fax 592-0877
Woodland Hills Academy 1,200/6-8
20800 Burbank Blvd 91367 818-226-2900
Allan Weiner, prin. Fax 716-0649
El Camino Real Adult Education Adult
5440 Valley Circle Blvd 91367 818-595-8000
Joanna McConaghy, prin. Fax 888-6714
West Valley Occupational Center Adult
6200 Winnetka Ave 91367 818-346-3540
Richard Wormus, prin. Fax 346-3858

Los Angeles Pierce College Post-Sec.
6201 Winnetka Ave 91371 818-347-0551
Louisville HS 500/9-12
22300 Mulholland Dr 91364 818-346-8812
Fax 346-9483
University of West Los Angeles Post-Sec.
6400 Canoga Ave Ste 271 91367 818-883-0529

Woodside, San Mateo, Pop. 5,463
Sequoia UNHSD
Supt. — See Redwood City
Woodside HS 2,000/9-12
199 Churchill Ave 94062 650-367-9750
Linda Common, prin. Fax 367-7263

Yermo, San Bernardino
Silver Valley USD 2,100/PK-12
PO Box 847 92398 760-254-2916
Marc Jackson, supt. Fax 254-2091
www.silvervalley.k12.ca.us
Silver Valley HS 500/9-12
PO Box 847 92398 760-254-2963
Heather Griggs, prin. Fax 254-3043
Silver Valley Adult S Adult
PO Box 847 92398 760-254-2715
Jim Swor, prin. Fax 254-2194

Other Schools – See Fort Irwin

Yorba Linda, Orange, Pop. 64,476
Placentia-Yorba Linda USD
Supt. — See Placentia
Yorba Linda MS 700/6-8
4777 Casa Loma Ave 92886 714-528-7090
Virginia Trapani, prin. Fax 996-2752
Yorba MS 900/7-8
5350 Fairmont Blvd 92886 714-970-0650
Cameron Malotte, prin. Fax 970-1647
Adult Education S Adult
4175 Fairmont Blvd 92886 714-779-6042
Jackie Howland, admin. Fax 779-6825

Friends Christian MS 500/5-8
4231 Rose Dr 92886 714-524-5240
Larry Lewis, prin. Fax 524-5784

Yreka, Siskiyou, Pop. 7,295
Regional Occupational Center & Program
Supt. — None
Siskiyou County ROP Vo/Tech
431 Knapp St 96097 530-842-6151
Kim Greene, dir. Fax 842-1759

Yreka UNESD 1,000/K-8
309 Jackson St 96097 530-842-1168
Dr. Vanston Shaw, supt. Fax 842-4576
sisnet.ssku.k12.ca.us/~yesftp
Jackson Street MS 400/5-8
405 Jackson St 96097 530-842-3561
Paul McCoy, prin. Fax 842-1716

Yreka UNHSD 900/9-12
431 Knapp St 96097 530-842-2521
Mark Greenfield, supt. Fax 842-1759
sisnet.ssku.k12.ca.us/~yuhsdftp/
Discovery HS 100/9-12
431 Knapp St 96097 530-842-1659
Marie Caldwell, prin. Fax 841-1057
Yreka HS 800/9-12
431 Knapp St 96097 530-842-6151
Jennifer McKinnon, prin. Fax 841-0740
Yreka Union HS Adult Education Adult
431 Knapp St 96097 530-842-7829
Maria Rosenlund, dir. Fax 842-1759

Yreka SDA Christian S 100/K-10
346 Payne Ln 96097 530-842-7071
Dr. John Durney, admin. Fax 842-7463

Yuba City, Sutter, Pop. 58,628
Regional Occupational Center & Program
Supt. — None
Tri-County ROP Vo/Tech
970 Klamath Ln 95993 530-822-2952
Randy Page, dir. Fax 822-3003

Yuba City USD 11,600/K-12
750 N Palora Ave 95991 530-822-5200
Nancy Aaberg, supt. Fax 671-2454
www.ycusd.k12.ca.us
Gray Avenue MS 900/6-8
808 Gray Ave 95991 530-822-5240
Brian Gault, prin. Fax 822-5057
Karperos MS 1,200/5-8
1666 Camino De Flores 95993 530-822-5262
Lee McPeak, prin. Fax 671-5356
River Valley HS 9-12
801 El Margarita Rd 95993 530-822-2500
Larry Bonds, prin. Fax 822-2589
Yuba City HS 3,000/9-12
850 B St 95991 530-674-4900
Martin Ramirez, prin. Fax 671-7814

Faith Christian HS 200/7-12
PO Box 1690 95992 530-674-5474
Steve Finlay, prin. Fax 674-0194

Yucaipa, San Bernardino, Pop. 49,100
Yucaipa-Calimesa JUSD 9,200/K-12
12797 3rd St 92399 909-797-0174
Sherry Kendrick, supt. Fax 797-5751
www.yucaipaschools.com
Canyon MS 400/7-8
35948 Susan St 92399 909-790-8580
Melissa Moore, prin. Fax 790-8584
Park View MS 1,100/7-8
34875 Tahoe Dr 92399 909-790-3285
Jeff Litel, prin. Fax 790-3295
Yucaipa HS 2,100/10-12
33000 Yucaipa Blvd 92399 909-797-0106
Bernie Cavanagh, prin. Fax 790-3200
Yucaipa HS Ninth Grade Campus 800/9-9
12358 6th St 92399 909-797-5181
Sherry Smith, prin. Fax 790-6192
Yucaipa Adult S Adult
12787 3rd St 92399 909-797-0121
Eric Vreeman, prin. Fax 790-6115

Crafton Hills College Post-Sec.
11711 Sand Canyon Rd 92399 909-794-2161

Yucca Valley, San Bernardino, Pop. 19,696
Morongo USD
Supt. — See Twentynine Palms
La Contenta JHS 800/7-8
7050 La Contenta Rd 92284 760-228-1802
Jean Johnson, prin. Fax 369-6324
Yucca Valley HS 1,600/9-12
7600 Sage Ave 92284 760-365-3391
Carl Phillips, prin. Fax 365-1845

Joshua Springs Christian S 500/PK-12
57373 Joshua Ln 92284 760-365-3599
Fem Ontiveros, admin. Fax 369-0315

COLORADO

COLORADO DEPARTMENT OF EDUCATION
201 E Colfax Ave, Denver 80203
Telephone 303-866-6600
Fax 303-830-0793
Website http://www.cde.state.co.us

Commissioner of Education Dwight Jones

COLORADO BOARD OF EDUCATION
201 E Colfax Ave, Denver 80203

Chairperson Pamela Jo Suckla

BOARDS OF COOPERATIVE EDUCATIONAL SERVICES (BOCES)

Adams County BOCES
Dave Carroll, dir. 303-286-7294
10290 Huron St, Northglenn 80260 Fax 853-1156
Centennial BOCES
Dale McCall, dir. 303-772-4420
830 S Lincoln St, Longmont 80501 Fax 776-0504
www.cboces.org
Centennial BOCES
Dale McCall, dir., 821 W Platte Ave 970-867-8297
Fort Morgan 80701 Fax 867-6129
www.cboces.org
East Central BOCES
David Van Sant, dir. 719-775-2342
PO Box 910, Limon 80828 Fax 775-9714
www.ecboces.org
Expeditionary BOCES
Robert Stein, dir. 303-759-2076
1700 S Holly St, Denver 80222 Fax 757-7442
www.rmsel.org/
Front Range BOCES
Susan Sparks, dir. 303-556-6028
PO Box 173364, Denver 80217 Fax 556-6060
frontrangeboces.org/
Grand Valley BOCES
Kerry Youngblood, dir. 970-255-2600
2508 Blichman Ave Fax 255-2626
Grand Junction 81505

Larimer BOCES
Jack Hale, dir. 970-613-5173
2880 Monroe Ave, Loveland 80538 Fax 613-5184
Mountain BOCES
Edward Vandertook, dir. 719-486-2603
1713 Mount Lincoln Dr W Fax 486-2109
Leadville 80461
www.mtnboces.org/
Mount Evans BOCES
Joyce Conrey, dir. 303-567-4467
PO Box 3399, Idaho Springs 80452 Fax 567-2208
Northeast Colorado BOCES
Tim Sanger, dir. 970-774-6152
PO Box 98, Haxtun 80731 Fax 774-6157
www.neboces.com
Northwest Colorado BOCES
Jane Toothaker, dir., PO Box 773390 970-879-0391
Steamboat Springs 80477 Fax 879-0442
www.nwboces.k12.co.us
Pikes Peak BOCES
Dr. Corinne Harmon, dir. 719-570-7474
4825 Lorna Pl Fax 380-9685
Colorado Springs 80915
www.ppboces.org
Rio Blanco BOCES
Donna Day, dir. 970-675-2064
234 S Jones Ave, Rangely 81648 Fax 675-5738

San Juan BOCES
Tom Lawson, dir. 970-247-3261
201 E 12th St, Durango 81301 Fax 247-8333
www.sjbocs.org/
San Luis Valley BOCES
John Tillman, dir. 719-589-5851
PO Box 1198, Alamosa 81101 Fax 589-5007
www.slvbocs.org
Santa Fe Trail BOCES
Sandy Malouff, dir. 719-383-2623
PO Box 980, La Junta 81050 Fax 383-2627
South Central BOCES
Cynthia Seidel, dir. 719-647-0023
323 S Purcell Blvd, Pueblo 81007 Fax 647-0136
www.scboces.k12.co.us
Southeastern BOCES
Jo Autrey, dir. 719-336-9046
PO Box 1137, Lamar 81052 Fax 336-9679
www.seboces.k12.co.us/
Southwest BOCES
Victor Bruce, dir. 970-565-8411
PO Box 1420, Cortez 81321 Fax 565-1203
Uncompahgre BOCS
Sharon Davarn, dir. 970-626-2977
PO Box 728, Ridgway 81432 Fax 626-2978
www.unbocs.org/
Ute Pass BOCES
Linda Murray, dir. 719-686-2012
PO Box 99, Woodland Park 80866 Fax 687-8408

PUBLIC, PRIVATE AND CATHOLIC SECONDARY SCHOOLS

Agate, Elbert, Pop. 100
Agate SD 300 100/PK-12
PO Box 118 80101 719-764-2741
Robin Purdy, supt. Fax 764-2751
Agate JSHS 100/6-12
PO Box 118 80101 719-764-2741
Robin Purdy, prin. Fax 764-2751

Aguilar, Las Animas, Pop. 578
Aguilar RSD 6 200/PK-12
PO Box 567 81020 719-941-4188
Jasper Butero, supt. Fax 941-4279
Aguilar JSHS 100/7-12
PO Box 567 81020 719-941-4188
Chris Barela, prin. Fax 941-4279

Akron, Washington, Pop. 1,575
Akron SD R-1 400/K-12
PO Box 429 80720 970-345-2268
Bryce Monasmith, supt. Fax 345-6508
www.akronrams.net/homepage2.htm
Akron HS 100/9-12
600 Elm Ave 80720 970-345-2268
Carl Rice, prin. Fax 345-6508

Alamosa, Alamosa, Pop. 8,682
Alamosa SD RE-11J 2,200/PK-12
209 Victoria Ave 81101 719-587-1600
Henry Herrera, supt. Fax 587-1712
www.alamosa.k12.co.us/
Alamosa HS, 805 Craft Dr 81101 700/9-12
Shelly Swayne, prin. 719-587-6000
Ortega MS, 401 Victoria Ave 81101 600/6-8
Neil Seneff, prin. 719-587-1650

Adams State College Post-Sec.
208 Edgemont Blvd 81101 800-824-6494

Anton, Washington, Pop. 40
Arickaree SD R-2 100/PK-12
12155 County Road NN 80801 970-383-2202
Gena Ramey, supt. Fax 383-2205
Arickaree JSHS 50/7-12
12155 County Road NN 80801 970-383-2202
Gena Ramey, prin. Fax 383-2205

Antonito, Conejos, Pop. 850
South Conejos SD RE-10 300/PK-12
PO Box 398 81120 719-376-5512
Carlos Garcia, supt. Fax 376-5425
scsd.echalk.com/home.asp
Antonito HS 100/9-12
PO Box 398 81120 719-376-5468
Antonio Sandoval, prin. Fax 376-5425
Antonito JHS 50/7-8
PO Box 398 81120 719-376-5468
Antonio Sandoval, prin. Fax 376-5425

Arvada, Jefferson, Pop. 103,966
Jefferson County SD R-1
Supt. — See Golden
Arvada HS 1,600/9-12
7951 W 65th Ave 80004 303-982-0162
Eric Everding, prin. Fax 982-0163
Arvada MS 400/7-8
5751 Balsam St 80002 303-982-1240
Beverly Eidmann, prin. Fax 982-1241
Arvada West HS 1,700/9-12
11325 Allendale Dr 80004 303-982-1303
Rob Bishop, prin. Fax 982-1304
Drake MS 600/7-8
12550 W 52nd Ave 80002 303-982-1510
Linda Rice, prin. Fax 982-1511
Moore MS 800/7-8
8455 W 88th Ave 80005 303-982-0400
John White, prin. Fax 982-0462
North Arvada MS 500/7-8
7285 Pierce St 80003 303-982-0528
Mike Little, prin. Fax 982-0529
Oberon MS 800/7-8
7300 Quail St 80005 303-982-2020
Dana Ellis, prin. Fax 982-2021
Pomona HS 1,700/9-12
8101 W Pomona Dr 80005 303-982-0710
Dan Cohan, prin. Fax 982-0709
Ralston Valley HS 1,400/9-12
13355 W 80th Ave 80005 303-982-5600
Jim Ellis, prin. Fax 982-5601

Faith Christian Academy 300/6-8
6250 Wright St 80004 303-424-7310
Randy Ziemer, prin. Fax 403-2720
Faith Christian Academy 400/9-12
4890 Carr St 80002 303-424-7310
Andrew Hasz, prin. Fax 403-2730
Maranatha Christian Center 900/PK-12
7180 Oak St 80004 303-431-5653
Fax 940-7474

Aspen, Pitkin, Pop. 5,804
Aspen SD 1 1,500/PK-12
235 High School Rd 81611 970-925-3760
Dr. Diana Sirko, supt. Fax 925-5721
www.aspenk12.net/
Aspen HS 500/9-12
235 High School Rd 81611 970-925-3760
Charlie Anastas, prin. Fax 925-1205
Aspen MS 500/5-8
235 High School Rd 81611 970-925-3760
Dr. Paula Canning, prin. Fax 925-8374

Ault, Weld, Pop. 1,425
Ault-Highland SD RE-9 900/K-12
PO Box 68 80610 970-834-1345
Dennis Scheer Ed.D., supt. Fax 834-1347
www.weldre9.k12.co.us
Highland HS 300/9-12
PO Box 68 80610 970-834-2816
Randy Ward, prin. Fax 834-2858
Highland MS 200/6-8
PO Box 68 80610 970-834-2829
Todd Bissell, prin. Fax 834-2663

Aurora, Arapahoe, Pop. 297,235
Aurora SD 31,000/PK-12
1085 Peoria St 80011 303-344-8060
John Barry, supt. Fax 326-1280
www.aps.k12.co.us
Aurora Central HS 2,200/9-12
11700 E 11th Ave 80010 303-340-1600
Dean Stecklein, prin. Fax 326-1270
Aurora Hills MS 1,100/6-8
1009 S Uvalda St 80012 303-341-7450
Jinger Haberer, prin. Fax 326-1250
Columbia MS 1,000/6-8
17600 E Columbia Ave 80013 303-690-6570
James O'Tremba, prin. Fax 326-1251
East MS 1,000/6-8
1275 Fraser St 80011 303-340-0660
Fred Quinonez, prin. Fax 326-1252
Gateway HS 1,800/9-12
1300 S Sable Blvd 80012 303-755-7160
Linda Witulski, prin. Fax 326-1272
Hinkley HS 1,700/9-12
1250 Chambers Rd 80011 303-340-1500
Peter Mosby, prin. Fax 326-1275
Mrachek MS 1,300/6-8
1955 S Telluride St 80013 303-750-2836
Edward Snyder, prin. Fax 326-1254
North MS 800/6-8
12095 Montview Blvd 80010 303-364-7411
Gerardo de la Garza, prin. Fax 326-1256
Pickens Technical Center Vo/Tech
500 Airport Blvd 80011 303-344-4910
Art Bogardus, prin. Fax 326-1277
Rangeview HS 2,100/9-12
17599 E Iliff Ave 80013 303-695-6848
Pamela Turner, prin. Fax 326-1276
South MS 900/6-8
12310 E Parkview Dr 80011 303-364-7623
Kevin Gates, prin. Fax 326-1258
West MS 900/6-8
10100 E 13th Ave 80010 303-366-2671
Dale Krueger, prin. Fax 326-1260

Cherry Creek SD 5
Supt. — See Greenwood Village
Cherokee Trail HS 800/9-12
25901 E Arapahoe Pkwy N 80016 720-886-1900
Dr. Mary Jarvis, prin. Fax 886-1989
Eaglecrest HS 2,600/9-12
5100 S Picadilly St 80015 720-886-1000
Jeanne Piper, prin. Fax 886-1097
Falcon Creek MS 1,200/6-8
6100 S Genoa St 80016 720-886-7700
John Kennedy, prin. Fax 886-7788
Grandview HS 2,600/9-12
20500 E Arapahoe Rd 80016 720-886-6500
Dr. Harry Bull, prin. Fax 886-6698
Horizon Community MS 1,500/6-8
3981 S Reservoir Rd 80013 720-886-6100
Dr. Tony Davis, prin. Fax 886-6253
Laredo MS 1,400/6-8
5000 S Laredo St 80015 720-886-5000
Mark Wahlstrom, prin. Fax 886-5298
Liberty MS 1,100/6-8
21500 E Dry Creek Rd 80016 720-886-2400
Brad Bayer, prin. Fax 886-2688
Overland HS 2,100/9-12
12400 E Jewell Ave 80012 720-747-3700
Jana Frieler, prin. Fax 747-3895
Prairie MS 1,600/6-8
12600 E Jewell Ave 80012 720-747-3000
Dr. Kandy Cassaday, prin. Fax 747-3113
Sky Vista MS 6-8
4500 S Himalaya Cir 80015 720-886-4700
Dr. Tony Poole, prin. Fax 886-4788
Smoky Hill HS 2,700/9-12
16100 E Smoky Hill Rd 80015 720-886-5300
Jeannine Brown, prin. Fax 886-5408
Thunder Ridge MS 1,500/6-8
5250 S Picadilly St 80015 720-886-1500
Mark Sneden, prin. Fax 886-1582

American Health Science University Post-Sec.
1010 S Joliet St Ste 107 80012 303-340-2054
Cambridge College Post-Sec.
350 Blackhawk St 80011 866-502-2627
CedarWood Christian Academy 100/K-12
PO Box 111389 80042 303-361-6456
Gene Oborny, admin. Fax 340-0971
Community College of Aurora Post-Sec.
16000 E Centretech Pkwy 80011 303-360-4700
Concorde Career College Post-Sec.
111 Havana St 80010 303-861-1151
Everest College - Aurora Campus Post-Sec.
14280 E Jewell Ave 80012 303-367-2757
Excelsior HS 200/7-12
15001 E Oxford Ave 80014 303-693-1550
Jann Clevenger, prin. Fax 693-2415
Pickens Technical Center Post-Sec.
500 Airport Blvd 80011 303-344-4910
Platt College Post-Sec.
3100 S Parker Rd 80014 303-369-5151
Regis Jesuit HS for Boys 800/9-12
6400 S Lewiston Way 80016 303-269-8000
Charlie Saulino, prin. Fax 766-2240
Regis Jesuit HS for Girls 9-12
6300 S Lewiston Way 80016 303-269-8100
Gretchen Kessler, prin. Fax 221-4772
Xenon International Post-Sec.
2231 S Peoria St 80014 303-752-1560

Bailey, Park, Pop. 150
Platte Canyon SD 1 1,400/PK-12
57393 US Highway 285 80421 303-838-7666
Jim Walpole Ed.D., supt. Fax 679-7504
Fitzsimmons MS 300/6-8
57093 US Highway 285 80421 303-838-7666
Shannon Clarke, prin. Fax 679-7506
Platte Canyon HS 500/9-12
57243 US Highway 285 80421 303-838-7666
Bryan Krause, prin. Fax 679-7497

Basalt, Pitkin, Pop. 3,007
Roaring Fork SD RE-1
Supt. — See Glenwood Springs
Basalt HS 400/9-12
600 Southside Dr 81621 970-384-5959
Jim Waddick, prin. Fax 384-5955
Basalt MS 500/5-8
51 School St 81621 970-384-5650
Christian Kingsbury, prin. Fax 384-5905

Alpine Christian Academy 100/PK-12
20449 Highway 82 81621 970-927-9106
Mick Bennett, hdmstr. Fax 927-3705

Bayfield, LaPlata, Pop. 1,639
Bayfield SD 10 JT-R 1,200/PK-12
24 S Clover Ln 81122 970-884-2496
Donald Magill, supt. Fax 884-4284
www.bayfield.k12.co.us
Bayfield HS 400/9-12
24 S Clover Ln 81122 970-884-9521
Michael Gearheart, prin. Fax 884-4226
Bayfield MS 300/6-8
24 S Clover Ln 81122 970-884-9592
Michael Lister, prin. Fax 884-4110

Bennett, Adams, Pop. 2,536
Bennett SD 29J 1,100/PK-12
615 7th St 80102 303-644-3234
Richard Coleman, supt. Fax 644-4121
www.bennett29j.k12.co.us
Bennett HS 300/9-12
610 7th St 80102 303-644-3234
Michael Franklin, prin. Fax 644-3894
Bennett MS 300/6-8
455 8th St 80102 303-644-3234
Amy Burns, prin. Fax 644-4398

Berthoud, Larimer, Pop. 5,055
Thompson SD R-2J
Supt. — See Loveland
Berthoud HS 700/9-12
950 Spartan Ave 80513 970-613-7700
Leonard Sherman, prin. Fax 613-7728
Turner MS 500/6-8
950 Massachusetts Ave 80513 970-613-7400
Bill Siebers, prin. Fax 613-7420

Bethune, Kit Carson, Pop. 218
Bethune SD R-5 100/PK-12
PO Box 127 80805 719-346-7513
Janice Thompson, supt. Fax 346-5048
Bethune JSHS, PO Box 127 80805 100/7-12
Shila Adolf, prin. 719-343-7513

Black Hawk, Gilpin, Pop. 107
Gilpin County SD RE-1 400/PK-12
10595 Highway 119 80403 303-582-3444
Ken Ladouceur, supt. Fax 582-3346
gilpin.k12.co.us
Gilpin County JSHS 200/7-12
10595 Highway 119 80403 303-582-3444
Alexis Donaldson, prin. Fax 582-3346

Blanca, Costilla, Pop. 372
Sierra Grande SD R-30 300/K-12
17523 E Highway 160 81123 719-379-3259
Robert Rael, supt. Fax 379-2572
www.sierragrande.k12.co.us
Sierra Grande HS 100/9-12
17523 E Highway 160 81123 719-379-3257
Dennis Lopez, prin. Fax 379-2572
Sierra Grande JHS 100/7-8
17523 E Highway 160 81123 719-379-3257
Dennis Lopez, prin. Fax 379-2572

Boulder, Boulder, Pop. 91,685
Boulder Valley SD RE-2 26,000/PK-12
PO Box 9011 80301 303-447-1010
Dr. George Garcia, supt. Fax 447-5024
www.bvsd.k12.co.us
Arapahoe Ridge HS 300/9-12
6600 Arapahoe Rd 80303 303-447-5284
Dave Krassowski, prin. Fax 447-5149
Boulder HS 2,000/9-12
1604 Arapahoe Ave 80302 303-442-2430
Bud Jenkins, prin. Fax 447-5317
Boulder Technical Education Center Vo/Tech
6600 Arapahoe Rd 80303 303-447-5220
Michael Rask, prin. Fax 447-5258
Casey MS 400/6-8
2410 13th St 80304 303-442-5235
Alison Boggs, prin. Fax 939-9626
Centennial MS 600/6-8
2205 Norwood Ave 80304 303-443-3760
Cheryl Scott, prin. Fax 443-3761
Fairview HS 1,900/9-12
1515 Greenbriar Blvd 80305 303-499-7600
Don Stensrud, prin. Fax 447-5353
Manhattan S of Arts and Academics 500/6-8
290 Manhattan Dr 80303 303-494-0335
Martha Gustafson, prin. Fax 494-0336
New Vista HS 300/9-12
700 20th St 80302 303-494-8037
Rona Wilensky, prin. Fax 447-5094
Platt MS 500/6-8
6096 Baseline Rd 80303 303-499-6800
Alice Lindemann, prin. Fax 499-0628
Southern Hills MS 500/6-8
1500 Knox Dr 80305 303-494-2866
Terry Gillach, prin. Fax 499-9251
Other Schools – See Broomfield, Lafayette, Louisville, Nederland

---

Boulder College of Massage Therapy Post-Sec.
6255 Longbow Dr 80301 303-530-2100
Naropa University Post-Sec.
2130 Arapahoe Ave 80302 303-444-0202
Rolf Institute of Structural Integration Post-Sec.
5055 Chaparral Ct Ste 103 80301 303-449-5903
September S 50/9-12
1902 Walnut St 80302 303-443-9933
Dan Fox, prin. Fax 444-5027
Shining Mountain Waldorf S 300/PK-12
999 Violet Ave 80304 303-444-7697
Agaf Dancy, admin. Fax 444-7701
Tara Performing Arts HS 50/9-12
4180 19th St 80304 303-440-4510
Greg Fisher, admin. Fax 448-0090
University of Colorado 80309 Post-Sec.
303-492-1411

Branson, Las Animas, Pop. 79
Branson RSD 82 1,000/K-12
PO Box 128 81027 719-946-5531
Troy Mayfield, supt. Fax 946-5619
www.bransonschoolonline.com
Branson JSHS 50/7-12
PO Box 128 81027 719-946-5531
Vicki Goebel, prin. Fax 946-5620

Briggsdale, Weld, Pop. 225
Briggsdale SD RE-10 100/K-12
PO Box 125 80611 970-656-3417
Rick Mondt, supt. Fax 656-3479
www.briggsdaleschool.org/
Briggsdale JSHS 100/7-12
PO Box 125 80611 970-656-3417
Rick Mondt, prin. Fax 656-3479

Brighton, Adams, Pop. 28,013
Brighton SD 27J 7,300/PK-12
18551 E 160th Ave 80601 303-655-2900
Rod Blunck Ed.D., supt. Fax 655-2870
www.brightonps27j.k12.co.us
Brighton HS 1,700/9-12
270 S 8th Ave 80601 303-655-4200
Tom Delgado, prin. Fax 655-2883
Overland Trail MS 600/6-8
455 N 19th Ave 80601 303-655-4000
Joseph Libby, prin. Fax 655-2880
Vikan MS 600/6-8
879 Jessup St 80601 303-655-4050
Mary Jones, prin. Fax 655-2881
Other Schools – See Henderson

Brighton Adventist Academy 100/PK-11
820 S 5th Ave 80601 303-659-1223
Fax 558-8837

Broomfield, Boulder, Pop. 43,478
Boulder Valley SD RE-2
Supt. — See Boulder
Broomfield Heights MS 600/6-8
1555 Daphne St 80020 303-466-2387
Gayle Burke, prin. Fax 466-2386

Broomfield HS 1,400/9-12
1 Eagle Way 80020 303-466-7344
Ginger Ramsey, prin. Fax 447-5390

Northglenn-Thornton 12 SD
Supt. — See Thornton
Legacy HS 2,000/9-12
2701 W 136th Ave, 720-972-6700
Cathy Nolan, prin. Fax 972-6897
Westlake MS 900/6-8
2800 W 135th Ave 80020 720-972-5200
Paul Gordon, prin. Fax 972-5239

Cortiva Institute - Colorado Post-Sec.
390 Interlocken Cres # 450 80021 303-996-5050
Holy Family HS 9-12
5195 W 144th Ave 80020 303-410-1411
Sr. Mary Lieb, prin. Fax 466-1935
Westwood College of Aviation Technology Post-Sec.
10851 W 120th Ave 80021 800-888-3995

Brush, Morgan, Pop. 5,186
Brush SD RE-2(J) 1,400/PK-12
PO Box 585 80723 970-842-5176
Bret Miles, supt. Fax 842-4481
www.brushschools.org
Brush HS 500/9-12
PO Box 585 80723 970-842-5171
Tom George, prin. Fax 842-2804
Brush MS 400/6-8
PO Box 585 80723 970-842-5035
Ken Miller, prin. Fax 842-3009

Buena Vista, Chaffee, Pop. 2,174
Buena Vista SD R-31 1,000/PK-12
PO Box 2027 81211 719-395-7000
Tina Goar, supt. Fax 395-7007
Buena Vista HS 300/9-12
PO Box 2027 81211 719-395-7100
Michael Kruger, prin. Fax 395-7106
McGinnis MS 200/6-8
PO Box 2027 81211 719-395-7060
Scott Cope, prin. Fax 395-7090

Mountain BOCES
Supt. — See Leadville
Arrowhead Learning Center 50/5-12
PO Box 1199 81211 719-395-4675
Becky Minnis, prin. Fax 395-4676

Patterson Christian Academy 100/PK-12
PO Box 1243 81211 719-395-6046
Erik Ritschard, admin. Fax 395-2055

Burlington, Kit Carson, Pop. 3,493
Burlington SD RE-6J 800/PK-12
PO Box 369 80807 719-346-8737
Don Anderson, supt. Fax 346-8541
www.burlingtonk12.org/
Burlington HS 200/9-12
380 Mike Lounge Dr 80807 719-346-8455
Duane Arntt, prin. Fax 346-5599
Burlington MS 300/5-8
2600 Rose Ave 80807 719-346-5440
Greg Swiatkowski, prin. Fax 346-7900

Byers, Arapahoe, Pop. 1,065
Byers SD 32J 500/PK-12
444 E Front St 80103 303-822-5292
Tom Turrell, supt. Fax 822-9592
www.byers32j.k12.co.us
Byers HS 200/7-12
444 E Front St 80103 303-822-5292
Terrell Price, prin. Fax 822-8616

Calhan, El Paso, Pop. 876
Calhan SD RJ-1 600/PK-12
PO Box 800 80808 719-347-2541
David Freeman, supt. Fax 347-2144
Calhan HS 200/9-12
PO Box 800 80808 719-347-2766
David MacKenzie, prin. Fax 347-2108
Calhan MS 100/6-8
PO Box 800 80808 719-347-2766
Linda Miller, prin. Fax 347-2108

Campo, Baca, Pop. 135
Campo SD RE-6 100/PK-12
PO Box 70 81029 719-787-2226
Nikki Johnson, supt. Fax 787-0140
Campo JSHS 50/7-12
PO Box 70 81029 719-787-2226
Sharon Kay Maes, prin. Fax 787-0140

Canon City, Fremont, Pop. 16,000
Canon City SD RE-1 3,600/K-12
101 N 14th St 81212 719-276-5700
Dr. Robin Gooldy, supt. Fax 276-5739
www.canoncityschools.org/
Canon City HS 1,300/9-12
1313 College Ave 81212 719-276-5870
Dr. Cindy Compton, prin. Fax 276-5950
Canon City MS 600/6-8
1215 Main St 81212 719-276-5740
Ken Trujillo, prin. Fax 276-5795

Colorado Institute of Taxidermy Post-Sec.
708 Royal Gorge Blvd 81212 719-276-2883

Carbondale, Garfield, Pop. 5,825
Roaring Fork SD RE-1
Supt. — See Glenwood Springs
Carbondale MS 300/6-8
455 S 3rd St 81623 970-384-5700
Cliff Colia, prin. Fax 384-5705
Roaring Fork HS 300/9-12
180 Snowmass Dr 81623 970-384-5757
Dale Parker, prin. Fax 384-5755

Colorado Rocky Mountain S 200/9-12
1493 County Road 106 81623 970-963-2562
Jeff Leahy, prin. Fax 963-9865

Castle Rock, Douglas, Pop. 35,745
Douglas County SD RE-1 40,300/PK-12
620 Wilcox St 80104 303-387-0100
Jim Christensen, supt. Fax 387-0107
www.dcsd.k12.co.us

Castle Rock MS 1,200/7-8
2575 Meadows Pkwy, 303-387-1300
Terry Olson, prin. Fax 387-1301
Castle View HS 9-12
5254 Meadows Dr, 303-387-9000
Lisle Gates, prin. Fax 387-9001
Douglas County HS 2,500/9-12
2842 Front St 80104 303-387-1000
Edna Doherty, prin. Fax 387-1001
Other Schools – See Highlands Ranch, Littleton, Parker

Cedaredge, Delta, Pop. 2,148
Delta County SD 50(J)
Supt. — See Delta
Cedaredge HS 300/9-12
575 SE Deer Creek Dr 81413 970-856-6882
Kathy Perkins, prin. Fax 856-6616
Cedaredge MS 200/6-8
845 SE Deer Creek Dr 81413 970-856-3118
Todd Markley, prin. Fax 856-3235

Centennial, Arapahoe, Pop. 98,243
Littleton SD 6
Supt. — See Littleton
Arapahoe HS 2,200/9-12
2201 E Dry Creek Rd 80122 303-347-6000
Ron Booth, prin. Fax 347-6004
Newton MS 800/6-8
4001 E Arapahoe Rd 80122 303-347-7900
James O'Tremba, prin. Fax 347-7930

Jones International University Post-Sec.
9697 E Mineral Ave 80112 303-784-8045

Center, Rio Grande, Pop. 2,497
Center Consolidated SD 26JT 700/PK-12
500 S Broadway 81125 719-754-3442
George Welsh, supt. Fax 754-3952
www.center.k12.co.us
Center HS, 500 S Broadway 81125 200/9-12
Charleen Schaeffer, prin. 719-754-2232
Skoglund MS, 500 S Broadway 81125 200/6-8
Charleen Schaeffer, prin. 719-754-2232

Cheraw, Otero, Pop. 212
Cheraw SD 31 200/PK-12
PO Box 160 81030 719-853-6655
Rick Lovato, supt. Fax 853-6322
cheraw.k12.co.us
Cheraw HS 100/9-12
PO Box 160 81030 719-853-6655
Kenny Bridges, prin. Fax 853-6322
Cheraw MS 100/6-8
PO Box 160 81030 719-853-6655
Kenny Bridges, prin. Fax 853-6322

Cheyenne Wells, Cheyenne, Pop. 873
Cheyenne County SD RE-5 300/PK-12
PO Box 577 80810 719-767-5866
David Marx, supt. Fax 767-8773
www.cheyennesd.net/
Cheyenne Wells HS 100/9-12
PO Box 577 80810 719-767-5612
Mike Miller, prin.
Cheyenne Wells MS 100/6-8
PO Box 577 80810 719-767-5656
Laurie Kjosness, prin.

Clifton, Mesa, Pop. 12,671
Mesa County Valley SD 51
Supt. — See Grand Junction
Mt. Garfield MS 700/6-8
3475 Front St 81520 970-464-0533
David Spellman, prin. Fax 464-0536

Collbran, Mesa, Pop. 408
Plateau Valley SD 50 500/PK-12
56600 Highway 330 81624 970-487-3547
Gregory Randall, supt. Fax 487-3876
www.plateauvalley.k12.co.us/
Plateau Valley HS 100/9-12
56600 Highway 330 81624 970-487-3547
John Vail, prin. Fax 487-3876
Plateau Valley MS 100/6-8
56600 Highway 330 81624 970-487-3547
John Vail, prin. Fax 487-3876

Colorado City, Pueblo, Pop. 1,149
Pueblo County Rural SD 70
Supt. — See Pueblo
Craver MS 200/6-8
PO Box 19369 81019 719-676-3030
Chuck Scott, prin. Fax 676-3511

Colorado Springs, El Paso, Pop. 369,815
Academy SD 20 16,800/PK-12
1110 Chapel Hills Dr 80920 719-234-1200
Dr. Ken Vedra, supt. Fax 234-1299
www.asd20.org/
Aspen Valley HS 100/9-12
1450 Chapel Hills Dr 80920 719-234-6000
George Stone, prin. Fax 234-6099
Challenger MS 800/6-8
10215 Lexington Dr 80920 719-234-3000
Tony Scott, prin. Fax 234-3199
Eagleview MS 1,100/6-8
1325 Vindicator Dr 80919 719-234-3400
Karon Cofield, prin. Fax 234-3599
Liberty HS 1,400/9-12
8720 Scarborough Dr 80920 719-234-2200
Tom Weston, prin. Fax 234-2399
Mountain Ridge MS 1,200/6-8
9150 Lexington Dr 80920 719-234-3200
Joy Porter, prin. Fax 234-3399
Pine Creek HS 1,500/9-12
10750 Thunder Mountain Ave 80908 719-234-2600
Todd Morse, prin. Fax 234-2799
Rampart HS 1,600/9-12
8250 Lexington Dr 80920 719-234-2000
Gil Bierman, prin. Fax 234-2199
Timberview MS 1,000/6-8
8680 Scarborough Dr 80920 719-234-3600
David Peak, prin. Fax 234-3799
Other Schools – See USAF Academy

Cheyenne Mountain SD 12 4,000/PK-12
1775 LaClede St 80906 719-475-6100
Walter Cooper, supt. Fax 475-6106
www.cmsd.k12.co.us
Cheyenne Mountain HS 1,400/9-12
1200 Cresta Rd 80906 719-475-6110
Paul Martin, prin. Fax 475-6116
Cheyenne Mountain JHS 700/7-8
1200 W Cheyenne Rd 80906 719-475-6120
Lori Smith, prin. Fax 475-6123

Colorado Springs SD 11 29,500/PK-12
1115 N El Paso St 80903 719-520-2000
Dr. Terry Bishop, supt. Fax 577-4546
www.d11.org/
Coronado HS 1,700/9-12
1590 W Fillmore St 80904 719-328-3600
Susan Humphrey, prin. Fax 328-3601
Doherty HS 2,200/9-12
4515 Barnes Rd 80917 719-328-6400
Jill Martin, prin. Fax 328-6401
East MS 400/6-8
1600 N Union Blvd 80909 719-328-2200
Clay Gomez, prin. Fax 448-0498
Holmes MS 700/6-8
2455 Mesa Rd 80904 719-328-3800
Brenda Lebrasse, prin. Fax 448-0358
Irving MS 800/6-8
1702 N Murray Blvd 80915 719-328-6900
Karen Gidley, prin. Fax 573-5094
Jenkins MS 900/6-8
6410 Austin Bluffs Pkwy, 719-328-5300
Jason Ter Horst, prin. Fax 266-5276
Mann MS 700/6-8
1001 E Van Buren St 80907 719-328-2300
Rusty Moomey, prin. Fax 488-0354
Mitchell HS 1,700/9-12
1205 Potter Dr 80909 719-328-6600
Larry Cutter, prin. Fax 328-6601
North MS 600/6-8
612 E Yampa St 80903 719-328-2400
Martha Crisp, prin. Fax 448-0268
Palmer HS 2,000/9-12
301 N Nevada Ave 80903 719-328-5000
Thomas Kelly, prin. Fax 328-5001
Russell MS 800/6-8
3825 Montebello Dr W 80918 719-328-5200
Jeannice Swift, prin. Fax 531-5520
Sabin MS 700/6-8
3605 N Carefree Cir 80917 719-328-7000
Sherry Kalbach, prin. Fax 573-4960
Wasson HS 1,600/9-12
2115 Afton Way 80909 719-328-2000
Robert Slauson, prin. Fax 520-2966
West MS 400/6-8
1920 W Pikes Peak Ave 80904 719-328-3900
Joe Torrez, prin. Fax 448-0141
Adult Education Center Adult
917 E Moreno Ave 80903 719-328-2975
M. Burkhardt-Shields, prin. Fax 578-8757
Doherty Night S Adult
4515 Barnes Rd 80917 719-328-6441
Carol Salaba, prin. Fax 328-6444
Palmer Night S Adult
301 N Nevada Ave 80903 719-328-5040
Larry Bartel, prin. Fax 328-5109

Falcon SD 49
Supt. — See Falcon
Horizon MS 700/6-8
1750 Piros Dr 80915 719-574-7700
Diane Worner, prin. Fax 495-5209
Sand Creek HS 1,700/9-12
7005 N Carefree Cir 80922 719-572-0924
Mike Collins, prin. Fax 495-1196
Skyview MS 900/6-8
6350 Windom Peak Blvd, 719-638-2736
Sandy Rivera, prin. Fax 495-5591

Hanover SD 28 300/K-12
17050 S Peyton Hwy 80928 719-683-2247
Dr. Henry Roman, supt. Fax 683-4602
Hanover JSHS 100/7-12
17050 S Peyton Hwy 80928 719-683-2247
Mike Moore, prin. Fax 683-3805

Harrison SD 2 9,600/PK-12
1060 Harrison Rd 80906 719-579-4880
F. Mike Miles, supt. Fax 579-2014
www.harrison.k12.co.us
Carmel MS 600/6-8
1740 Pepperwood Dr 80910 719-579-3210
Derryck Gowie, prin. Fax 579-2695
Fox Meadow MS 700/6-8
1450 Cheyenne Meadows Rd 80906 719-527-7100
Valerie Garcia, prin. Fax 527-7174
Harrison HS 1,100/9-12
2755 Janitell Rd 80906 719-579-2080
Cheri Martinez, prin. Fax 579-2454
Panorama MS 800/6-8
2145 S Chelton Rd 80916 719-579-3220
Teri Newbold, prin. Fax 579-2756
Sierra HS 1,100/9-12
2250 Jet Wing Dr 80916 719-579-2090
Bryan Wright, prin. Fax 579-2536

Widefield SD 3 8,300/PK-12
1820 Main St 80911 719-391-3000
Dr. Mark Hatchell, supt. Fax 390-4372
wsd3.k12.co.us
Mesa Ridge HS 1,200/9-12
6070 Mesa Ridge Pkwy 80911 719-391-3600
Joe Garrett, prin. Fax 390-9697
Sproul JHS 400/7-8
235 Sumac Dr 80911 719-391-3218
Larry Borchik, prin. Fax 392-3459
Watson JHS 400/7-8
136 Fontaine Blvd 80911 719-391-3255
Kirsten Toy, prin. Fax 392-3419
Widefield HS 1,300/9-12
615 Widefield Dr 80911 719-391-3200
Jim Felice, prin. Fax 391-8072
Other Schools – See Fountain

Blair College Post-Sec.
1815 Jet Wing Dr 80916 719-638-6580

CollegeAmerica - Colorado Springs Post-Sec.
3645 Citadel Dr S 80909 719-637-0600
Colorado College Post-Sec.
14 E Cache La Poudre St 80903 719-389-6000
Colorado Sch. of Professional Psychology Post-Sec.
555 E Pikes Peak Ave # 108 80903 877-442-0505
Colorado School for the Deaf and Blind Post-Sec.
33 N Institute St 80903
Colorado Springs Christian HS 500/9-12
4825 Mallow Rd 80907 719-535-2727
Dr. Roland DeRenzo, supt. Fax 268-2121
Colorado Springs Christian MS 300/6-8
4845 Mallow Rd 80907 719-535-8968
Dr. Roland DeRenzo, supt. Fax 268-2122
Colorado Springs S 500/PK-12
21 Broadmoor Ave 80906 719-475-9747
Charles Landry, prin. Fax 475-9864
Colorado Technical University Post-Sec.
4435 N Chestnut St 80907 719-598-0200
DeVry University Post-Sec.
1175 Kelly Johnson Blvd 80920 719-632-3000
Evangelical Christian Academy 200/7-12
4050 Nonchalant Cir S 80917 719-597-3675
Paul Finch, prin. Fax 597-6983
Fountain Valley S 200/9-12
6155 Fountain Valley School 80911 719-390-7035
Craig Larimer, hdmstr. Fax 392-6138
Hilltop Baptist S 200/K-12
6915 Palmer Park Blvd 80915 719-597-1880
Carl Adams, prin. Fax 597-8168
IntelliTec College Post-Sec.
2315 E Pikes Peak Ave 80909 719-632-7626
International Beauty Academy Post-Sec.
5705 N Academy Blvd 80918 719-597-1413
Memorial Hospital Post-Sec.
1400 E Boulder St 80909 719-365-5000
National American University Post-Sec.
5125 N Academy Blvd 80918 719-277-0588
Nazarene Bible College Post-Sec.
1111 Academy Park Loop 80910 719-596-5110
Penrose-St. Francis Health System Post-Sec.
2215 N Cascade Ave 80907 719-776-5111
Pikes Peak Christian S 600/PK-12
5905 Flintridge Dr 80918 719-598-8610
Ken Preslar, dir. Fax 598-1491
Pikes Peak Community College Post-Sec.
5675 S Academy Blvd 80906 719-576-7711
Remington College Post-Sec.
6050 Erin Park Dr # 250 80918 719-532-1234
St. Mary HS 400/9-12
2501 E Yampa St 80909 719-635-7540
Patty Beckert, prin. Fax 471-7623
Toni & Guy Hairdressing Academy Post-Sec.
332 Main St 80911 719-390-9898
University of Colorado Post-Sec.
1420 Austin Bluffs Pkwy 80918 719-262-3000

Commerce City, Adams, Pop. 34,189
Adams County SD 14 6,500/PK-12
4720 E 69th Ave 80022 303-853-3333
John Lange, supt. Fax 286-9753
www.acsd14.k12.co.us
Adams City HS 1,500/9-12
4625 E 68th Ave 80022 303-289-3111
Wesley Paxton, prin. Fax 288-6113
Adams City MS 700/6-8
4451 E 72nd Ave 80022 303-289-5881
Philip Sorensen, prin. Fax 288-8574
Arnold JSHS 200/7-12
6500 E 72nd Ave 80022 303-289-2983
Allan Hollenbeck, prin. Fax 289-7167
Kearney MS 700/6-8
6160 Kearney St 80022 303-287-0261
Sophia Masewicz, prin. Fax 287-0432

Conifer, Jefferson, Pop. 600
Jefferson County SD R-1
Supt. — See Golden
Conifer HS 1,000/9-12
10441 Highway 73 80433 303-982-5255
Pat Termin, prin. Fax 982-5256
West Jefferson MS 700/6-8
9449 Barnes Ave 80433 303-982-3056
Jean Kelley, prin. Fax 982-3057

Cortez, Montezuma, Pop. 8,244
Montezuma-Cortez SD RE-1 3,100/K-12
PO Box R 81321 970-565-7282
Stacy Houser, supt. Fax 565-2161
www.cortez.k12.co.us
Cortez MS 800/6-8
450 W 2nd St 81321 970-565-7824
Jamie Haukeness, prin. Fax 565-5120
Montezuma-Cortez HS 900/9-12
206 W 7th St 81321 970-565-3722
Ember Conley, prin. Fax 565-5118

San Juan Basin Technical College Post-Sec.
PO Box 970 81321 970-565-8457

Cotopaxi, Fremont, Pop. 130
Cotopaxi SD RE-3 300/PK-12
345 County Road 12 81223 719-942-4131
Geoffrey Gerk, supt. Fax 942-4134
cotopaxire3.org/
Cotopaxi JSHS 200/7-12
345 County Road 12 81223 719-942-4131
Peggy Murphy-Gerk, prin. Fax 942-4134

Craig, Moffat, Pop. 9,143
Moffat County SD RE-1 2,200/K-12
775 Yampa Ave 81625 970-824-3268
Pete Bergmann, supt. Fax 824-6655
moffatsd.org/
Craig MS 400/7-8
915 Yampa Ave 81625 970-824-3289
Bill Toovey, prin. Fax 824-3858
Moffat County HS 800/9-12
900 Finley Ln 81625 970-824-7036
Jane Krogman, prin. Fax 824-3130

Creede, Mineral, Pop. 412
Creede Consolidated SD 1 200/PK-12
PO Box 429 81130 719-658-2220
Buck Stroh, supt. Fax 658-2942
www.creedek12.net
Creede JSHS 100/7-12
PO Box 429 81130 719-658-2220
John Goss, prin. Fax 658-2942

Crested Butte, Gunnison, Pop. 1,546
Gunnison Watershed SD RE 1J
Supt. — See Gunnison
Crested Butte S 400/K-12
PO Box 339 81224 970-641-7720
Stephanie Niemi, prin. Fax 641-7729

Crested Butte Academy 50/9-12
PO Box 1180 81224 970-349-1805
Leon Harris, dir. Fax 349-0997

Cripple Creek, Teller, Pop. 1,065
Cripple Creek-Victor SD RE-1 600/PK-12
PO Box 897 80813 719-689-2685
Susan Holmes, supt. Fax 689-2256
ccvschools.com
Cripple Creek-Victor JSHS 300/7-12
PO Box 897 80813 719-689-2661
Joan Rook, prin. Fax 389-2256

De Beque, Mesa, Pop. 472
De Beque SD 49JT 200/PK-12
PO Box 70 81630 970-283-5418
Doug Pfau, supt. Fax 283-5213
www.debeque.k12.co.us
De Beque JSHS 100/7-12
PO Box 70 81630 970-283-5596
Sue Taylor, prin. Fax 283-5598

Deer Trail, Arapahoe, Pop. 577
Deer Trail SD 26J 200/PK-12
PO Box 129 80105 303-769-4421
Mary Lynch, supt. Fax 769-4600
www.deertrail26j.k12.co.us
Deer Trail JSHS 100/6-12
PO Box 129 80105 303-769-4421
Shannon Hookom, prin. Fax 769-4600

Del Norte, Rio Grande, Pop. 1,569
Del Norte SD C-7 700/K-12
PO Box 159 81132 719-657-4040
Michael Salvato, supt. Fax 657-2546
www.del-norte.k12.co.us/
Del Norte HS 200/9-12
PO Box 159 81132 719-657-4030
Christopher Vance, prin. Fax 657-4024
Del Norte MS 200/6-8
PO Box 159 81132 719-657-4050
Nathan Smith, prin. Fax 657-0329

Delta, Delta, Pop. 8,135
Delta County SD 50(J) 4,400/PK-12
7655 2075 Rd 81416 970-874-4438
Mike McMillan, supt. Fax 874-5744
www.deltaschools.com
Delta HS 600/9-12
1400 Pioneer Rd 81416 970-874-8031
Delaine Hudson, prin. Fax 874-8034
Delta MS 500/6-8
910 Grand Ave 81416 970-874-8046
Kurt Clay, prin. Fax 874-8049
Other Schools – See Cedaredge, Hotchkiss, Paonia

Denver, Denver, Pop. 557,917
Adams County SD 50
Supt. — See Westminster
Carpenter MS 500/6-8
7001 Lipan St 80221 303-428-8583
Kelly Williams, prin. Fax 657-3962
Clear Lake MS 600/6-8
1940 Elmwood Ln 80221 303-428-7526
Carol Peters, prin. Fax 430-6465
Ranum HS 1,500/9-12
2401 W 80th Ave 80221 303-428-9577
Kircher Leday, prin. Fax 657-3952

Denver County SD 1 64,900/PK-12
900 Grant St 80203 720-423-3200
Michael Bennet, supt. Fax 423-3413
www.dpsk12.org/
CEC Middle College of Denver Vo/Tech
2650 Eliot St 80211 720-423-6600
Scott Springer, prin. Fax 423-6604
Denver Center for International Studies 6-12
574 W 6th Ave 80204 720-423-9000
Dan Lutz, prin. Fax 423-9075
Denver S of the Arts 900/6-12
7111 Montview Blvd 80220 720-424-1700
Patricia Bippus, prin. Fax 424-1845
East HS 1,900/9-12
1600 City Park Esplanade 80206 720-423-8300
Kathy Callum, prin. Fax 423-8306
Grant MS 400/6-8
1751 S Washington St 80210 720-423-9360
Greta Martinez, prin. Fax 423-9385
Griffith Opportunity S Vo/Tech
1250 Welton St 80204 720-423-4700
Les Lindauer, dir. Fax 575-4840
Hamilton MS 900/6-8
8600 E Dartmouth Ave 80231 720-423-9500
Reina Gutierrez, prin. Fax 423-9445
Henry MS 800/6-8
3005 S Golden Way 80227 720-423-9560
Wendy Lanier, prin. Fax 423-9585
Hill MS 600/6-8
451 Clermont St 80220 720-423-9680
Don Roy, prin. Fax 423-9705
Jefferson HS 1,100/9-12
3950 S Holly St 80237 720-423-7000
Sandra Just, prin. Fax 423-7047
Kennedy HS 1,600/9-12
2855 S Lamar St 80227 720-423-4300
Jeannie Peppel, prin. Fax 423-4309
Kepner MS 1,000/6-8
911 S Hazel Ct 80219 720-424-0000
Frank Gonzales, prin. Fax 424-0023
King MS 1,100/6-8
19535 E 46th Ave 80249 720-424-0042
Michael Gaither, prin. Fax 424-0557
Kunsmiller MS 900/6-8
2250 S Quitman Way 80219 720-424-0200
Alex Magana, prin. Fax 424-0145
Lake MS 700/6-8
1820 Lowell Blvd 80204 720-424-0260
Hans Keyser, prin. Fax 424-0380
Lincoln HS 1,300/9-12
2285 S Federal Blvd 80219 720-423-5000
Antonio Esquibel, prin. Fax 423-5098
Mann MS 400/6-8
4130 Navajo St 80211 720-423-9800
Jorge Loera, prin. Fax 423-9850
Merrill MS 700/6-8
1551 S Monroe St 80210 720-424-0600
Ann Greenfield, prin. Fax 424-0625
Montbello HS 1,500/9-12
5000 Crown Blvd 80239 720-423-5700
Antwan Wilson, prin. Fax 423-5801
Morey MS 700/6-8
840 E 14th Ave 80218 720-424-0700
Doris Claunch, prin. Fax 424-0727
Noel MS 900/6-8
5290 Kittredge St 80239 720-424-0800
Amanda DeBell, prin. Fax 424-0945
North HS 1,400/9-12
2960 N Speer Blvd 80211 720-423-2700
JoAnn Trujillo-Hays, prin. Fax 423-2708
Place MS 600/6-8
7125 Cherry Creek North Dr 80224 720-424-0960
Keith Mills, prin. Fax 424-0985
Randolph MS 700/6-8
3955 Steele St 80205 720-424-1080
Kristin Waters, prin. Fax 424-1241
Rishel MS 800/6-8
451 S Tejon St 80223 720-424-1260
Sylvia Bookhardt, prin. Fax 424-1350
Roberts MS 4-8
2100 Akron Way 80238 720-424-2640
Patricia Lea, prin. Fax 424-2665
Skinner MS 600/6-8
3435 W 40th Ave 80211 720-424-1420
Nicole Veltze, prin. Fax 424-1446
Smiley MS 500/6-8
2540 Holly St 80207 720-424-1540
Nathaniel Howard, prin. Fax 424-1565
South HS 1,300/9-12
1700 E Louisiana Ave 80210 720-423-6000
William Kohut, prin. Fax 423-6280
Washington HS 1,600/9-12
655 S Monaco Pkwy 80224 720-423-8600
Mario Williams, prin. Fax 423-8614
West HS 1,500/9-12
951 Elati St 80204 720-423-5300
Patrick Sanchez, prin. Fax 423-5410
Night HS, 2211 W 27th Ave 80211 Adult
Darryl Keaton, prin. 303-964-3071

Jefferson County SD R-1
Supt. — See Golden
D'Evelyn JSHS 400/7-12
10359 W Nassau Ave 80235 303-982-2600
Jill Colby, prin. Fax 982-2601

Mapleton SD 1 5,700/PK-12
591 E 80th Ave 80229 303-853-1000
Charlotte Ciancio, supt. Fax 853-1087
www.mapleton.us
Global Leadership Academy 600/K-12
7480 Conifer Rd 80221 303-853-1930
Art Drotar, dir. Fax 853-1956
Mapleton Early College HS 9-12
601 E 64th Ave 80229 303-853-1980
Jeff Park, dir.
Mapleton Preparatory HS 9-12
601 E 64th Ave 80229 303-853-1980
Jeff Park, dir. Fax 853-1996
Welby New Technology HS 9-12
1200 E 78th Ave 80229 303-853-1660
Matt Flores, dir. Fax 853-1670
York International S 600/K-12
9200 York St 80229 303-853-1600
Paul Frank, dir. Fax 853-1656
Other Schools – See Thornton

Northglenn-Thornton 12 SD
Supt. — See Thornton
Niver Creek MS 900/6-8
9450 Pecos St 80260 720-972-5120
Jacque Kerr, prin. Fax 972-5159

Accelerated Schools Foundation 200/K-12
2160 S Cook St 80210 303-758-2003
Jane Queen, admin. Fax 757-4336
American University of Paris Post-Sec.
950 S Cherry St Ste 210 80246 303-757-6333
Arrupe Jesuit HS 9-12
4343 Utica St 80212 303-455-7449
Michael O'Hagan, prin. Fax 455-7453
Art Institute of Colorado Post-Sec.
1200 Lincoln St 80203 800-275-2420
Aspen University Post-Sec.
501 S Cherry St Ste 350 80246 800-441-4746
Bel-Rea Institute of Animal Technology Post-Sec.
1681 S Dayton St, 303-751-8700
Beth Jacob HS of Denver 100/9-12
5100 W 14th Ave 80204 303-893-1333
Esther Melamid, prin. Fax 573-4932
Bishop Machebeuf Catholic HS 500/9-12
458 Uinta Way 80230 303-344-0082
Jessie Skipwith, prin. Fax 344-1582
Centura-St. Anthony Hospital Post-Sec.
4231 W 16th Ave 80204 303-629-4350
CollegeAmerica - Colorado Post-Sec.
1385 S Colorado Blvd Fl 5 80222 303-691-9756
Colorado Academy 900/PK-12
3800 S Pierce St 80235 303-986-1501
Christopher Babbs, hdmstr. Fax 914-2583
Colorado Christian S 200/PK-12
200 S University Blvd 80209 303-777-7723
Rod Hood, admin. Fax 765-2642
Colorado Ctr for Medical Laboratory Sci. Post-Sec.
1719 E 19th Ave 80218 303-839-6485
CO Sch of Traditional Chinese Medicine Post-Sec.
1441 York St Ste 202 80206 303-329-6355
Community College of Denver Post-Sec.
PO Box 173363 80217 303-556-2600
Denver Automotive & Diesel College Post-Sec.
PO Box 9366 80209 303-722-5724
Denver Campus for Jewish Education 400/K-12
2450 S Wabash St 80231 303-369-0663
Philip Kalin, pres. Fax 369-0664
Denver Christian HS 400/9-12
2135 S Pearl St 80210 303-733-2421
Mark Swalley, prin. Fax 733-7734
Denver Health Medical Center Post-Sec.
660 Bannock St 80204 303-436-6611
Denver Lutheran HS 200/9-12
3201 W Arizona Ave 80219 303-934-2345
Dan Gehrke, prin. Fax 934-0455
Denver Waldorf S 300/PK-12
940 Fillmore St 80206 303-777-0531
Fax 744-1216
Emily Griffith Opportunity School Post-Sec.
1250 Welton St 80204 720-423-4700
Heritage College Post-Sec.
12 Lakeside Ln 80212 303-477-7240
Iliff School of Theology Post-Sec.
2201 S University Blvd 80210 303-744-1287
Johnson & Wales University Post-Sec.
7150 Montview Blvd 80220 303-256-9300
Metropolitan State College Post-Sec.
PO Box 173362 80217 303-556-3018
Mile High Adventist Academy 200/PK-12
711 E Yale Ave 80210 303-744-1069
Dennis Dickerson, prin. Fax 744-1060
Mullen HS 1,000/9-12
3601 S Lowell Blvd 80236 303-761-1764
Linda Brady, prin. Fax 761-0502
National American University Post-Sec.
1325 S Colorado Blvd #100 80222 303-758-6700
National Theatre Conservatory Post-Sec.
1050 13th St 80204 303-446-4855
Parks College Post-Sec.
9065 Grant St 80229 303-457-2757
Phlebotomy Learning Center Post-Sec.
1780 S Bellaire St Ste 780 80222 303-584-0575
Pima Medical Institute Post-Sec.
1701 W 72nd Ave Ste 130 80221 303-426-1800
Regis University Post-Sec.
3333 Regis Blvd 80221 303-458-4100
Rocky Mountain College of Art & Design Post-Sec.
1600 Pierce St 80214 800-888-2787
Teikyo Loretto Heights University Post-Sec.
3001 S Federal Blvd 80236 303-936-8441
University of Colorado at Denver Post-Sec.
PO Box 173364 80217 303-556-2400
University of Colorado Health Sciences Post-Sec.
4200 E 9th Ave # C245 80262 303-372-0000
University of Denver Post-Sec.
2199 S University Blvd 80208 303-871-2000
University of Denver University College Post-Sec.
2211 S Josephine St 80208 303-871-3354
Westwood College - Denver North Post-Sec.
7350 Broadway 80221 303-426-7000
Westwood College - Denver South Post-Sec.
3150 S Sheridan Blvd 80227 303-934-2790
Yeshiva Toras Chaim 100/9-12
PO Box 40067 80204 303-629-8200
Dr. Daniel Peckman, prin. Fax 623-5949
Yeshiva Toras Chaim Talmudic Seminary Post-Sec.
1555 Stuart St 80204 303-629-8200

Dolores, Montezuma, Pop. 863
Dolores SD RE-4A 700/PK-12
17631 Highway 145 81323 970-882-7255
Larry Archibeque, supt. Fax 882-7685
www.dolores.k12.co.us
Dolores HS 200/9-12
17631 Highway 145 81323 970-882-7288
Laura Harper, prin. Fax 882-7289
Dolores MS 200/6-8
17631 Highway 145 81323 970-882-7288
Laura Harper, prin. Fax 882-7289

Dove Creek, Dolores, Pop. 683
Dolores County SD RE-2J 300/PK-12
PO Box 459 81324 970-677-2522
Steve Strong, supt. Fax 677-2712
www.dolorescounty.k12.co.us
Dove Creek HS 100/7-12
PO Box 459 81324 970-677-2237
Stephen Baroch, prin. Fax 677-2927

Durango, LaPlata, Pop. 15,501
Durango SD 9-R 4,400/PK-12
201 E 12th St 81301 970-247-5411
Dr. Mary Barter, supt. Fax 247-9581
www.durangoschools.org
Durango HS 1,500/9-12
2390 Main Ave 81301 970-259-1630
Greg Spradling, prin. Fax 385-1493
Escalante MS 500/6-8
141 Baker Ln 81303 970-247-9490
Amy Kendziorski, prin. Fax 385-1194
Miller MS 500/6-8
2608 Junction St 81301 970-247-1418
Bruce Hankins, prin. Fax 385-1191

Colorado Timberline Academy 50/9-12
35554 Highway 550 81301 970-247-5898
Daniel Coye, dir. Fax 259-8067
Durango Air Service Post-Sec.
1340 Airport Rd 81303 970-247-5535
Fort Lewis College Post-Sec.
1000 Rim Dr 81301 970-247-7010
Grace Preparatory Academy of Durango 50/6-12
PO Box 3777 81302 970-385-7544
Catherine Spriggs, admin.

Eads, Kiowa, Pop. 651
Eads SD RE-1 200/PK-12
210 W 10th St 81036 719-438-2218
Glenn Smith, supt. Fax 438-2272
www.eadseagles.com
Eads HS 100/9-12
210 W 10th St 81036 719-438-2214
Betsy Barnett, prin. Fax 438-2272
Eads JHS 50/6-8
900 Maine St 81036 719-438-2216
Glenn Smith, prin. Fax 438-2090

Eagle, Eagle, Pop. 4,276
Eagle County SD RE-50 4,800/PK-12
PO Box 740 81631 970-328-6321
John Brendza, supt. Fax 328-1024
www.eagleschools.net
Battle Mountains HS 700/9-12
750 Eagle Rd 81631 970-328-2930
Brian Hester, prin. Fax 949-1550
Eagle Valley MS 300/6-8
PO Box 1019 81631 970-328-6224
Jerry Santoro, prin. Fax 328-6430
Red Canyon HS 100/9-12
PO Box 4807 81631 970-926-8107
Wade Hill, prin. Fax 926-8133

Other Schools – See Edwards, Gypsum, Minturn

Eaton, Weld, Pop. 3,932
Eaton SD RE-2 1,600/K-12
200 Park Ave 80615 970-454-3402
Randy Miller Ed.D., supt. Fax 454-5193
www.eaton.k12.co.us
Eaton HS 400/9-12
114 Park Ave 80615 970-454-3374
Mark Naill, prin. Fax 454-5190
Eaton MS 500/6-8
225 Juniper Ave 80615 970-454-3358
Kelly Boren, prin. Fax 454-1337

Edgewater, Jefferson, Pop. 5,211
Jefferson County SD R-1
Supt. — See Golden
Jefferson HS 800/9-12
2305 Pierce St 80214 303-982-6056
Jose Martinez, prin. Fax 982-6057

Edwards, Eagle, Pop. 500
Eagle County SD RE-50
Supt. — See Eagle
Berry Creek MS 300/6-8
PO Box 1416 81632 970-328-2960
Robert Cuevas, prin. Fax 926-4137

Vail Christian HS 100/9-12
PO Box 2023 81632 970-926-3015
Gene Hagerman, hdmstr. Fax 926-5682

Elbert, Elbert, Pop. 150
Elbert SD 200 300/PK-12
PO Box 38 80106 303-648-3030
Kelli Loflin, supt. Fax 648-3652
elbertschool.org
Elbert JSHS 100/7-12
PO Box 38 80106 303-648-3030
Bob Beebe, prin. Fax 648-3652

Elizabeth, Elbert, Pop. 1,513
Elizabeth SD C-1 2,500/PK-12
PO Box 610 80107 303-646-4441
Bob Neel, supt. Fax 646-3362
elizabeth.k12.co.us/
Elizabeth HS 800/9-12
PO Box 660 80107 303-646-4616
Jim Trevino, prin. Fax 646-6030
Elizabeth MS 600/6-8
PO Box 369 80107 303-646-4520
Robert McMullen, prin. Fax 646-0980
Frontier HS 100/9-12
PO Box 610 80107 303-646-1798
Robin Gaffney, prin. Fax 646-1329

Ellicott, El Paso
Ellicott SD 22 1,000/K-12
395 S Ellicott Hwy 80808 719-683-2700
Terry Ebert, supt. Fax 683-4442
www.ellicottschools.org
Ellicott HS 300/9-12
375 S Ellicott Hwy 80808 719-683-2700
Jon Rowley, prin. Fax 683-2705
Ellicott MS 300/5-8
350 S Ellicott Hwy 80808 719-683-2700
Chris Smith, prin. Fax 683-5430

Englewood, Arapahoe, Pop. 32,350
Cherry Creek SD 5
Supt. — See Greenwood Village
Campus MS 1,300/6-8
4785 S Dayton St 80111 720-554-2677
Donna McCarl, prin. Fax 554-2782
Career & Technical Education Vo/Tech
9150 E Union Ave 80111 720-554-4553
Fax 554-4531
Cherry Creek HS 3,700/9-12
9300 E Union Ave 80111 720-554-2285
Dr. Kathleen Smith, prin. Fax 554-2239

Englewood SD 1 3,800/PK-12
4101 S Bannock St 80110 303-761-7050
Larry Nisbet, supt. Fax 806-2064
www.englewood.k12.co.us
Englewood HS 900/9-12
3800 S Logan St, 303-806-2266
Linda Torres, prin. Fax 806-2298
Flood MS 400/6-8
3695 S Lincoln St, 303-761-1226
Mandy Braun, prin. Fax 806-2199
Sinclair MS 300/6-8
300 W Chenango Ave 80110 303-781-7817
Randy Johnson, prin. Fax 806-2399

Columbia HealthOne Post-Sec.
501 E Hampden Ave, 303-788-6484
Kent Denver S 700/6-12
4000 E Quincy Ave, 303-770-7660
Todd Horn, hdmstr. Fax 770-7137
Misers Inspection and Training Post-Sec.
2401 S Raritan St 80110 303-761-8860
Misers Inspection and Training Post-Sec.
1825 W Baker Ave 80110 303-922-8821
St. Mary's Academy 200/6-8
4545 S University Blvd, 303-762-8300
Fax 783-6201
St. Mary's Academy 300/9-12
4545 S University Blvd, 303-762-8300
Kathryn McNamee, prin. Fax 783-6201
Tri-County Health Nutrition Services Post-Sec.
7000 E Blleview Ave #301 80111 303-220-9200

Erie, Weld, Pop. 12,351
St. Vrain Valley SD RE-1J
Supt. — See Longmont
Erie HS 300/9-12
3180 County Road 5 80516 303-828-4213
Steven Payne, prin. Fax 494-3873
Erie MS 300/5-8
650 Main St 80516 303-828-3391
Ella Padilla, prin. Fax 828-3817

Vista Ridge Academy 100/K-10
3100 Ridgeview Dr 80516 303-828-4944
Carol Schneider, prin. Fax 828-1525

Estes Park, Larimer, Pop. 5,812
Park SD R-3 1,300/PK-12
1701 Brodie Ave 80517 970-586-2361
Linda Chapman, supt. Fax 586-1108
www.estesschools.org/
Estes Park HS 400/9-12
1600 Manford Ave 80517 970-586-5321
Steve Ramsey, prin. Fax 586-1102
Estes Park MS 300/6-8
1500 Manford Ave 80517 970-586-4439
Tammy Quist, prin. Fax 586-1100

Eagle Rock S 100/9-12
PO Box 1770 80517 970-586-0600
Robert Burkhardt, hdmstr. Fax 586-4805

Evergreen, Jefferson, Pop. 7,582
Clear Creek SD RE-1
Supt. — See Idaho Springs
Clear Creek HS 300/9-12
185 Beaver Brook Canyon Rd 80439 303-679-4600
Frank Reeves, prin. Fax 679-4603

Jefferson County SD R-1
Supt. — See Golden
Evergreen HS 900/9-12
29300 Buffalo Park Rd 80439 303-982-5140
Mike Greek, prin. Fax 982-5141
Evergreen MS 700/6-8
2059 Hiwan Dr 80439 303-982-5020
Roslin Marshall, prin. Fax 982-5021

Fairplay, Park, Pop. 677
Park County SD RE-2 500/PK-12
PO Box 189 80440 719-836-3114
Charles Soper, supt. Fax 836-2275
www.parkcountyschools.org
Silverheels MS 100/6-8
PO Box 189 80440 719-836-4406
Jane Newman, prin. Fax 836-2275
South Park HS 100/9-12
PO Box 189 80440 719-836-2007
Jane Newman, prin. Fax 836-2275

Falcon, El Paso, Pop. 200
Falcon SD 49 9,700/PK-12
10850 E Woodmen Rd 80831 719-495-3601
Dr. Nancy Wright, supt. Fax 495-0832
www.d49.org
Falcon HS 900/9-12
9755 Towner Ave 80831 719-495-2261
John Weishaar, prin. Fax 495-2264
Falcon MS 500/7-8
11990 Swingline Rd 80831 719-495-3661
Don Begier, prin. Fax 495-5237
Other Schools – See Colorado Springs

Federal Heights, Adams, Pop. 11,706

Cornerstone Christian Academy 200/K-12
2300 W 90th Ave 80260 303-451-1421
Larry Zimbelman, admin. Fax 280-0361

Firestone, Weld, Pop. 6,410
St. Vrain Valley SD RE-1J
Supt. — See Longmont
Coal Ridge MS 500/6-8
6201 Booth Dr 80504 303-833-4176
Paul Talafuse, prin. Fax 833-4192

Flagler, Kit Carson, Pop. 590
Arriba-Flagler SD C-20 200/PK-12
PO Box 218 80815 719-765-4684
Thomas Arensdorf, supt. Fax 765-4418
www.arriba-flaglercsd20.net
Flagler HS 100/9-12
PO Box 218 80815 719-765-4684
Tom Arensdorf, prin. Fax 765-4418

Fleming, Logan, Pop. 444
Frenchman SD RE-3 200/PK-12
506 N Fremont Ave 80728 970-265-2111
Jim Copeland, supt. Fax 265-2815
www.flemingschools.org
Fleming HS 100/9-12
506 N Fremont Ave 80728 970-265-2022
Joseph Skerjanec, prin. Fax 265-2029

Florence, Fremont, Pop. 3,685
Florence SD RE-2 1,600/K-12
403 W 5th St 81226 719-784-6312
John Merriam, supt. Fax 784-4140
www.re-2.org/
Florence HS 600/9-12
2006 State Highway 67 81226 719-784-6414
Jim Lucas, prin. Fax 784-3821
Fremont MS 300/6-8
215 Maple St 81226 719-784-4856
Gary Strubel, prin. Fax 784-4060

Florence Christian S 50/PK-12
303 E 3rd St 81226 719-784-6352

Fort Carson, El Paso, Pop. 11,309
Fountain-Fort Carson SD 8
Supt. — See Fountain
Carson MS 500/6-8
6200 Prussman Blvd 80913 719-382-1610
Steve Jerman, prin. Fax 382-8526

Fort Collins, Larimer, Pop. 128,026
Poudre SD R-1 23,300/PK-12
2407 La Porte Ave 80521 970-490-3604
Dr. Jerry Wilson, supt. Fax 490-3514
www.psdschools.org
Blevins JHS 500/7-9
2101 S Taft Hill Rd 80526 970-488-4000
David Linehan, prin. Fax 488-4011
Boltz JHS 900/7-9
720 Boltz Dr 80525 970-472-3700
Dana Calkins, prin. Fax 472-3730
Fort Collins SHS 1,500/10-12
3400 Lambkin Way 80525 970-488-8021
Mark Eversole, prin. Fax 488-8008
Fossil Ridge HS 500/10-12
5400 Ziegler Rd 80528 970-488-6260
Dierdre Cook, prin. Fax 488-6263
Kinard JHS 200/7-9
3002 E Trilby Rd 80528 970-488-5400
Joe Cuddemi, prin. Fax 488-5402
Lesher JHS 600/7-9
1400 Stover St 80524 970-472-3800
Thomas Dodd, prin. Fax 472-3880
Lincoln JHS 600/7-9
1600 Lancer Dr 80521 970-488-5700
Lou Marchesano, prin. Fax 488-5452
Poudre SHS 1,700/10-12
201 S Impala Dr 80521 970-488-6011
Sandra Lundt, prin. Fax 488-6060
Preston JHS 1,000/7-9
4901 Corbett Dr 80528 970-419-7300
Richard Ramirez, prin. Fax 419-7307
Rocky Mountain SHS 1,800/10-12
1300 W Swallow Rd 80526 970-488-7023
Tom Lopez, prin. Fax 488-7001
Webber JHS 800/7-9
4201 Seneca St 80526 970-488-7800
Sandra Bickel, prin. Fax 488-7811
Other Schools – See Laporte, Wellington

Cheeks Intl Academy of Beauty Culture Post-Sec.
2925 S College Ave Unit 9 80525 970-226-1416
CollegeAmerica - Fort Collins Post-Sec.
4601 S Mason St 80525 970-223-6060
Colorado State University Post-Sec.
1062 Campus Delivery 80523 970-491-1101
Front Range Baptist Academy 100/PK-12
625 E Harmony Rd 80525 970-223-2173
Jamison Coppola, prin. Fax 223-5826
Front Range Community College Post-Sec.
4616 S Shields St 80526 970-226-2500
Hair Dynamics Education Center Post-Sec.
6464 S College Ave 80525 970-223-9943
Heritage Christian S 500/K-12
4800 Wheaton Dr 80525 970-482-0868
John Wascom, admin. Fax 482-1501
Institute of Business & Medical Careers Post-Sec.
1609 Oakridge Dr Ste 102 80525 970-223-2669
Weston Distance Learning Post-Sec.
2001 Lowe St 80525 800-347-7899

Fort Lupton, Weld, Pop. 7,121
Weld County SD RE-8 2,600/PK-12
301 Reynolds St 80621 303-857-3200
Mark Payler, supt. Fax 857-3219
www.ftlupton.k12.co.us
Fort Lupton HS 700/9-12
530 Reynolds St 80621 303-857-7100
Michael Campbell, prin. Fax 857-7179
Fort Lupton MS 600/6-8
201 S McKinley Ave 80621 303-857-7200
Carey Sanchez, prin. Fax 857-7287

Fort Morgan, Morgan, Pop. 10,844
Ft. Morgan SD RE-3 3,300/PK-12
715 W Platte Ave 80701 970-867-5633
Dr. Daniel Patterson, supt. Fax 867-0262
www.morgan.k12.co.us
Fort Morgan HS 800/9-12
709 E Riverview Ave 80701 970-867-5648
Ed Raines, prin. Fax 867-3347
Fort Morgan MS 500/7-8
300 Deuel St 80701 970-867-8253
Patrick Haley, prin. Fax 867-4876
Lincoln HS 50/9-12
230 Walnut St 80701 970-867-2924
Vicki Davis, prin. Fax 867-4958

Morgan Community College Post-Sec.
17800 County Road 20 80701 970-542-3100

Fountain, El Paso, Pop. 19,081
Fountain-Fort Carson SD 8 6,000/PK-12
425 W Alabama Ave 80817 719-382-1300
Dwight Jones, supt. Fax 382-7338
www.ffc8.org
Fountain-Fort Carson HS 1,200/9-12
900 Jimmy Camp Rd 80817 719-382-1640
James Calhoun, prin. Fax 382-3228
Fountain MS 800/6-8
515 N Santa Fe Ave 80817 719-382-1580
Debra Keiley, prin. Fax 382-9065
Other Schools – See Fort Carson

Widefield SD 3
Supt. — See Colorado Springs
Janitell JHS 500/7-8
7635 Fountain Mesa Rd 80817 719-391-3295
Aaron Hoffman, prin. Fax 390-7869

Fowler, Otero, Pop. 1,138
Fowler SD R-4J 400/K-12
PO Box 218 81039 719-263-4224
Larry Vibber Ed.D., supt. Fax 263-4625
www.fowler.k12.co.us/
Fowler HS 100/9-12
PO Box 218 81039 719-263-4279
Russell Bates, prin. Fax 263-4625
Fowler JHS 100/7-8
PO Box 218 81039 719-263-4224
Russell Bates, prin. Fax 263-4625

Frederick, Weld, Pop. 6,620
St. Vrain Valley SD RE-1J
Supt. — See Longmont
Frederick HS 600/9-12
600 5th St 80530 303-833-3533
Jim Sundberg, prin. Fax 833-4664

Frisco, Summit, Pop. 2,418
Summit SD RE-1 2,900/PK-12
PO Box 7 80443 970-668-3011
Dr. Millie Hamner, supt. Fax 668-0361
summit.k12.co.us
Summit HS 900/9-12
PO Box 7 80443 970-547-9311
Jim Hesse, prin. Fax 547-1061
Summit MS 600/6-8
PO Box 7 80443 970-668-5037
Iva Katz-Hesse, prin. Fax 668-5038

Fruita, Mesa, Pop. 6,878
Mesa County Valley SD 51
Supt. — See Grand Junction

Fruita MS 700/6-8
239 N Maple St 81521 970-254-6570
Ken Haptonstall, prin. Fax 858-0486
Fruita Monument HS 1,700/9-12
1102 Wildcat Ave 81521 970-254-6600
Jody Mimmack, prin. Fax 254-6668

Gateway, Mesa, Pop. 7,510
Mesa County Valley SD 51
Supt. — See Grand Junction
Gateway S 81522 50/K-12
Jim Hanks, prin. 970-931-2276
Fax 931-2883

Gilcrest, Weld, Pop. 1,149
Weld County SD RE-1 2,000/PK-12
PO Box 157 80623 970-737-2403
Jo Barbie, supt. Fax 737-2516
www.weld-re1.k12.co.us
Valley HS 600/9-12
PO Box 156 80623 970-737-2494
Ben Rainbolt, prin. Fax 737-2203
Other Schools – See La Salle, Platteville

Glenwood Springs, Garfield, Pop. 8,564
Roaring Fork SD RE-1 4,800/PK-12
1405 Grand Ave 81601 970-384-6000
Judy Haptonstall, supt. Fax 384-6005
www.rfsd.k12.co.us
Glenwood Springs HS 700/9-12
1340 Pitkin Ave 81601 970-384-5555
Paul Freeman, prin. Fax 384-5556
Glenwood Springs MS 500/6-8
120 Soccer Field Rd 81601 970-384-5500
Robert Farris, prin. Fax 384-5505
Roaring Fork Career Center Vo/Tech
504A 27th St 81601 970-384-5980
Judy Haptonstall, prin. Fax 384-5985
Other Schools – See Basalt, Carbondale

Colorado Mountain College Post-Sec.
PO Box 10001 81602 800-621-8559
Glenwood Beauty Academy Post-Sec.
51241 Highway 6 Ste 1 81601 970-945-0485

Golden, Jefferson, Pop. 17,366
Jefferson County SD R-1 80,200/PK-12
PO Box 4001 80401 303-982-6500
Dr. Cindy Stevenson, supt. Fax 982-6667
jeffcoweb.jeffco.k12.co.us/
Bell MS 600/7-8
1001 Ulysses St 80401 303-982-4280
Griff Wirth, prin. Fax 982-4281
Golden HS 1,300/9-12
701 24th St 80401 303-982-4200
Mike Murphy, prin. Fax 982-4201
Other Schools – See Arvada, Conifer, Denver, Edgewater, Evergreen, Lakewood, Littleton, Westminster, Wheat Ridge

---

Colorado School of Mines Post-Sec.
1500 Illinois St 80401 303-273-3000

Granada, Prowers, Pop. 611
Granada SD RE-1 300/PK-12
PO Box 259 81041 719-734-5492
Leo Laprarie, supt. Fax 734-5495
Granada JSHS 100/7-12
PO Box 259 81041 719-734-5492
Ty Kemp, prin. Fax 734-5495

Granby, Grand, Pop. 1,685
East Grand SD 2 1,300/PK-12
PO Box 125 80446 970-887-2581
Robb Rankin, supt. Fax 887-2635
www.egsd.org
East Grand MS 300/6-8
PO Box 2210 80446 970-887-3382
Nancy Karas, prin. Fax 887-9234
Middle Park HS 400/9-12
PO Box 130 80446 970-887-2104
Dale Fleming, prin. Fax 887-9454

Grand Junction, Mesa, Pop. 45,299
Mesa County Valley SD 51 20,000/PK-12
2115 Grand Ave 81501 970-254-5100
Dr. J. Tim Mills, supt. Fax 254-5282
www.mesa.k12.co.us
Bookcliff MS 500/6-8
2935 Orchard Ave 81504 970-243-6350
Marty Bassett, prin. Fax 242-8066
Career Center Vo/Tech
2935 North Ave 81504 970-243-3142
Dean Blair, prin. Fax 243-9829
Central HS 1,600/9-12
550 Warrior Way 81504 970-254-6200
Jody Frost, prin. Fax 254-6169
East MS 500/6-8
830 Gunnison Ave 81501 970-242-0512
Leigh Grasso, prin. Fax 242-0513
Grand Junction HS 1,600/9-12
1400 N 5th St 81501 970-254-6900
Kevin Schott, prin. Fax 254-6973
Grand Mesa MS 700/6-8
585 31 1/2 Rd 81504 970-254-6270
Debra Bailey, prin. Fax 254-6307
Orchard Mesa MS 600/6-8
2736 Unaweep Ave 81503 970-254-6320
Brett Livingston, prin. Fax 245-7343
Redlands MS 600/6-8
2200 Broadway 81503 970-245-6084
Kimberly Heutzenroeder, prin. Fax 245-1985
West MS 400/6-8
123 W Orchard Ave 81505 970-254-5090
Vernan Walker, prin. Fax 243-0574
Other Schools – See Clifton, Fruita, Gateway, Palisade

Academy of Beauty Culture Post-Sec.
2992 North Ave 81504 970-245-5570
Cornerstone Christian S 50/6-12
3099 F Rd 81504 970-434-4619
Jeff Brantley, admin. Fax 434-4620
IntelliTec College Post-Sec.
772 Horizon Dr 81506 970-245-8101
Intermountain Adventist Academy 50/PK-10
1704 N 8th St 81501 970-242-5116
David Priest, prin. Fax 242-5659

Mesa State College Post-Sec.
1100 North Ave 81501 970-248-1020
MJM Institute of Cosmetology Post-Sec.
1048 Independent Ave #A113 81505 970-241-9060
Quest Academy 50/9-12
646 29 1/2 Rd 81504 970-245-0913
Cheryl DuCray, admin. Fax 245-1497

Greeley, Weld, Pop. 87,596
Weld County SD 6 16,100/PK-12
1025 9th Ave 80631 970-348-6000
Renae Dreier, supt. Fax 348-6231
www.greeleyschools.org
Brentwood MS 700/6-8
2600 24th Avenue Ct 80634 970-348-3000
John Diebold, prin. Fax 348-3030
Evans MS 800/6-8
2900 15th Ave 80631 970-348-3600
Karen Wangsuick, prin. Fax 348-3630
Franklin MS 700/6-8
818 35th Ave 80634 970-348-3200
Susan Thornbursh, prin. Fax 348-3230
Greeley Central HS 1,400/9-12
1515 14th Ave 80631 970-348-5000
Mary Lauer, prin. Fax 348-5030
Greeley West HS 1,400/9-12
2401 35th Ave 80634 970-348-5400
Bob Harr, prin. Fax 348-5430
Heath MS 900/6-8
2223 16th St 80631 970-348-3400
Mark Rangel, prin. Fax 348-3430
Maplewood MS 600/6-8
1201 21st Ave 80631 970-348-3800
Robert Billings, prin. Fax 348-3830
Northridge HS 1,200/9-12
100 N 71st Ave 80634 970-348-5200
John Borman, prin. Fax 348-5230
Weld Opportunity HS Vo/Tech
2505 1st Ave 80631 970-351-7472
Chris Ingram, prin. Fax 351-7568
Night S, 1401 22nd Ave 80631 Adult
Joan Rhodes, prin. 970-348-3550

Aims Community College Post-Sec.
PO Box 69 80632 970-330-8008
Cheeks Intl Academy of Beauty Culture Post-Sec.
2547 11th Ave Ste B 80631 970-352-4500
Dayspring Christian Academy 300/PK-12
3734 W 20th St 80634 970-330-1151
Del Groen, dir. Fax 330-0565
University of Northern Colorado Post-Sec.
501 20th St 80639 970-351-1890

Greenwood Village, Arapahoe, Pop. 12,817
Cherry Creek SD 5 46,500/PK-12
4700 S Yosemite St 80111 303-773-1184
Dr. Monte Moses, supt. Fax 773-9884
www.ccsd.k12.co.us
Other Schools – See Aurora, Englewood, Littleton

College for Financial Planning Post-Sec.
8000 E Maplewood Ave 80111 303-220-1200
DeVry Institute of Technology Post-Sec.
5775 DTC Blvd 80111 303-694-6600

Grover, Weld, Pop. 155
Pawnee SD RE-12 100/PK-12
PO Box 220 80729 970-895-2222
Phillip Graham, supt. Fax 895-2221
www.pawneeschool.com
Pawnee JSHS 100/7-12
PO Box 220 80729 970-895-2222
Phillip Graham, prin. Fax 895-2221

Gunnison, Gunnison, Pop. 5,298
Gunnison Watershed SD RE 1J 1,500/K-12
800 N Boulevard St 81230 970-641-7760
Bill Chambliss, supt. Fax 641-7777
www.gunnisonschools.net/
Gunnison HS 400/9-12
800 W Ohio Ave 81230 970-641-7700
Mike Adams, prin. Fax 641-7709
Gunnison MS 300/6-8
1099 N 11th St 81230 970-641-7710
Doug Tredway, prin. Fax 641-7739
Gunnison Valley HS 50/9-12
600 N 8th St 81230 970-641-7755
Steven Marantino, prin. Fax 641-7777
Other Schools – See Crested Butte

Western State College of Colorado Post-Sec.
600 N Adams St 81231 970-943-0120

Gypsum, Eagle, Pop. 4,964
Eagle County SD RE-50
Supt. — See Eagle
Eagle Valley HS 600/9-12
PO Box 188 81637 970-328-8960
Mark Strakbein, prin. Fax 524-5607
Gypsum Creek MS 300/6-8
PO Box 5129 81637 970-328-8980
Steve Smith, prin. Fax 524-7393

Haxtun, Phillips, Pop. 995
Haxtun SD RE-2J 300/PK-12
201 W Powell St 80731 970-774-6111
James Poole, supt. Fax 774-7568
www.haxtun.k12.co.us
Haxtun HS 100/9-12
201 W Powell St 80731 970-774-6111
Darcy Garretson, prin. Fax 774-7568

Hayden, Routt, Pop. 1,539
Hayden SD RE-1 500/PK-12
PO Box 70 81639 970-276-3864
Michael Luppes, supt. Fax 276-4217
www.haydensd.org
Hayden HS 200/9-12
PO Box 70 81639 970-276-3761
Troy Zabel, prin. Fax 276-4376
Hayden MS, PO Box 70 81639 100/6-8
Troy Zabel, prin. 970-276-3762

Henderson, Adams, Pop. 500
Brighton SD 27J
Supt. — See Brighton

Prairie View HS 7-12
12909 E 120th Ave 80640 303-688-2900
Chris Rugg, prin.

Highlands Ranch, Douglas, Pop. 10,181
Douglas County SD RE-1
Supt. — See Castle Rock
Cresthill MS 900/7-8
9195 Cresthill Ln 80130 303-387-2800
Sally Stanley, prin. Fax 387-2801
Highlands Ranch HS 1,800/9-12
9375 Cresthill Ln 80130 303-387-2500
Jerry Goings, prin. Fax 387-2501
Mountain Ridge MS 1,000/7-8
10590 Mountain Vista Rdg 80126 303-387-1800
Kara Shepherd, prin. Fax 387-1801
Mountain Vista HS 900/9-10
10585 Mountain Vista Rdg 80126 303-387-1500
Steve Johnson, prin. Fax 387-1501
Ranch View MS 900/7-8
1731 W Wildcat Reserve Pkwy 80129 303-387-2300
Bryan Breuer, prin. Fax 387-2301
Rock Canyon HS 400/9-12
5810 McArthur Ranch Rd 80124 303-387-3000
Dan McMinimee, prin. Fax 387-3001
Thunderridge HS 1,400/9-12
1991 W Wildcat Reserve Pkwy 80129 303-387-2000
Carole Jennings, prin. Fax 387-2001
Eagle Academy Adult
9375 Cresthill Ln 80130 303-387-2700
Doug Seligman, prin. Fax 470-7376

Elliot Christian S 100/6-12
2680 E County Line Rd 80126 303-922-0011
Frank Daugherity, admin. Fax 922-0159

Hoehne, Las Animas, Pop. 150
Hoehne RSD 3 400/PK-12
PO Box 91 81046 719-846-4457
Reid Straabe, supt. Fax 846-4450
www.hoehne.k12.co.us
Hoehne HS, PO Box 91 81046 100/9-12
Chris Whetzel, prin. 719-846-4457
Hoehne JHS, PO Box 91 81046 100/7-8
Chris Whetzel, prin. 719-846-4457

Holly, Prowers, Pop. 997
Holly SD RE-3 300/PK-12
PO Box 608 81047 719-537-6616
Carlyn Yokum, supt. Fax 537-0315
www.holly.k12.co.us
Holly JSHS 200/7-12
PO Box 608 81047 719-537-6512
Ruth Ann Cullen, prin. Fax 537-6519

Holyoke, Phillips, Pop. 2,289
Holyoke SD RE-1J 600/K-12
435 S Morlan Ave 80734 970-854-3634
Stephen Bohrer, supt. Fax 854-4049
www.hcosd.org
Holyoke JSHS 300/7-12
545 E Hale St 80734 970-854-2284
Dave Rice, prin. Fax 854-2441

Hotchkiss, Delta, Pop. 1,043
Delta County SD 50(J)
Supt. — See Delta
Hotchkiss HS 200/9-12
438 Bulldog St 81419 970-872-3882
Mike Beard, prin. Fax 872-2390

Hugo, Lincoln, Pop. 799
Genoa-Hugo SD C113 200/PK-12
PO Box 247 80821 719-743-2428
Robert Ring, supt. Fax 743-2194
Genoa-Hugo HS 100/9-12
PO Box 247 80821 719-743-2428
Charla Hannigan, prin. Fax 743-2194
Genoa-Hugo MS 50/6-8
PO Box 247 80821 719-743-2428
Charla Hannigan, prin. Fax 743-2194

Idaho Springs, Clear Creek, Pop. 1,807
Clear Creek SD RE-1 1,000/PK-12
PO Box 3399 80452 303-567-3850
Dr. Doug Price, supt. Fax 567-3861
www.ccsdre1.org/
Clear Creek Career & Technical S Vo/Tech
PO Box 3399 80452 303-567-3848
Frank Reeves, prin.
Clear Creek MS 200/7-8
PO Box 3369 80452 303-567-4461
Jake Dingman, prin. Fax 567-3856
Other Schools – See Evergreen

Idalia, Yuma, Pop. 100
Idalia SD RJ-3 100/PK-12
PO Box 40 80735 970-354-7298
Tim Gribben, supt. Fax 354-7416
www.idaliaco.us/
Idalia JSHS 100/7-12
PO Box 40 80735 970-354-7298
Tim Gribben, prin. Fax 354-7416

Ignacio, LaPlata, Pop. 679
Ignacio SD 11 JT 700/K-12
PO Box 460 81137 970-563-0500
Juvie Jones, supt. Fax 563-4524
www.ignacio.k12.co.us
Ignacio HS 300/9-12
PO Box 460 81137 970-563-0515
Mark Huffmyer, prin. Fax 563-9465
Ignacio JHS 100/7-8
PO Box 460 81137 970-563-0600
Beverly Lyons, prin. Fax 563-1030

Iliff, Logan, Pop. 218
Valley SD RE-1
Supt. — See Sterling
Caliche JSHS 100/7-12
26308 Buffalo Rd 80736 970-522-8200
Helen Duncan, prin. Fax 522-9400

Joes, Yuma, Pop. 75
Liberty SD J-4 100/PK-12
PO Box 112 80822 970-358-4288
David Eastin, supt. Fax 358-4282
www.libertyschoolj4.com

Liberty JSHS 50/7-12
PO Box 112 80822 970-358-4288
David Eastin, prin. Fax 358-4282

Johnstown, Weld, Pop. 7,250
Weld County SD RE-5J
Supt. — See Milliken
Roosevelt HS 500/9-12
616 N 2nd St 80534 970-587-6000
John Bruce, prin. Fax 587-2608

Julesburg, Sedgwick, Pop. 1,335
Julesburg SD RE-1 300/PK-12
102 W 6th St 80737 970-474-3365
Shawn Ehnes, supt. Fax 474-3742
Julesburg JSHS 100/7-12
102 W 6th St 80737 970-474-3364
Shawn Ehnes, prin. Fax 474-3592

Karval, Lincoln, Pop. 50
Karval SD RE-23 100/PK-12
PO Box 5 80823 719-446-5311
Martin Adams, supt. Fax 446-5332
Karval JSHS 50/7-12
PO Box 5 80823 719-446-5311
Martin Adams, prin. Fax 446-5332

Keenesburg, Weld, Pop. 1,141
Weld County SD RE-3J 1,800/PK-12
PO Box 269 80643 303-536-2000
Dr. Marvin Wade, supt. Fax 536-2010
www.rebel-net.tec.co.us/
Weld Central HS 500/9-12
4715 County Road 59 80643 303-536-2100
Steve Jones, prin. Fax 536-2110
Weld Central JHS 300/7-8
4715 County Road 59 80643 303-536-2100
Monty Talkington, prin. Fax 536-2110

Kersey, Weld, Pop. 1,401
Weld County SD RE-7 1,100/PK-12
PO Box 485 80644 970-336-8500
E. Glenn McClain, supt. Fax 336-8511
www.pvs.k12.co.us/
Platte Valley HS 300/9-12
PO Box 487 80644 970-336-8700
Brad Joens, prin. Fax 336-8794
Platte Valley MS 300/6-8
PO Box 515 80644 970-336-8610
George Clear, prin. Fax 336-8635

Kim, Las Animas, Pop. 67
Kim RSD 88 100/PK-12
PO Box 100 81049 719-643-5295
Art Dowell, supt. Fax 643-5299
www.kim.k12.co.us/
Kim JSHS 50/7-12
PO Box 100 81049 719-643-5295
Art Dowell, prin. Fax 643-5299

Kiowa, Elbert, Pop. 596
Kiowa SD C-2 400/PK-12
PO Box 128 80117 303-621-2220
Bret Robinson, supt. Fax 621-2239
www.kiowaschool.org
Kiowa HS 100/9-12
PO Box 128 80117 303-621-2115
Lance Luitjens, prin. Fax 621-2566
Kiowa MS 100/6-8
PO Box 128 80117 303-621-2785
Lance Luitjens, prin. Fax 621-2566

Kit Carson, Cheyenne, Pop. 225
Kit Carson SD R-1 100/K-12
PO Box 185 80825 719-962-3219
Gerald Keefe, supt. Fax 962-3317
www.kcsdr1.org
Carson JSHS 100/6-12
PO Box 185 80825 719-962-3219
Gerald Keefe, prin. Fax 962-3317

Kremmling, Grand, Pop. 1,554
West Grand SD 1-JT 500/K-12
PO Box 515 80459 970-724-3217
Dr. Jeff Perry, supt. Fax 724-9373
www.westgrand.k12.co.us/
West Grand HS 200/9-12
PO Box 515 80459 970-724-3425
Philip Bonds, prin. Fax 724-3450
West Grand MS 100/6-8
PO Box 515 80459 970-724-3489
Eddy Liddle, prin. Fax 724-9052

Lafayette, Boulder, Pop. 23,884
Boulder Valley SD RE-2
Supt. — See Boulder
Angevine MS 600/6-8
1150 W South Boulder Rd 80026 303-665-5540
Isobel Stevenson, prin. Fax 661-0354
Centaurus HS 1,000/9-12
10300 E South Boulder Rd 80026 303-665-9211
Deirdre Pilch, prin. Fax 447-5368

Dawson S 400/K-12
10455 Dawson Dr 80026 303-665-6679
Brian Johnson, hdmstr. Fax 665-0757

La Jara, Conejos, Pop. 831
North Conejos SD RE-1J 1,200/PK-12
PO Box 72 81140 719-274-5174
John Jordan, supt. Fax 274-5621
north.co.schoolwebpages.com/
Centauri HS 300/9-12
PO Box 72 81140 719-274-5178
Curt Wilson, prin. Fax 274-5637
Centauri MS 300/6-8
PO Box 72 81140 719-274-4301
Tom Salazar, prin. Fax 274-4301

La Junta, Otero, Pop. 7,260
East Otero SD R-1 1,500/K-12
1802 Colorado Ave Ste 200 81050 719-384-6900
Jim Sullivan, supt. Fax 384-6910
www.lajunta.k12.co.us
La Junta HS 500/9-12
1817 Smithland Ave 81050 719-384-4467
Bud Ozzello, prin.
La Junta MS 400/6-8
901 Smithland Ave 81050 719-384-4371
Paul Jebe, prin.

Otero Junior College Post-Sec.
1802 Colorado Ave 81050 719-384-6831

Lake City, Hinsdale, Pop. 359
Hinsdale County SD RE 1 100/PK-12
PO Box 39 81235 970-944-2314
Karen Thormalen, supt. Fax 944-2662
Lake City Community S 100/PK-12
PO Box 39 81235 970-944-2314
Karen Thormalen, prin. Fax 944-2662

Lakewood, Jefferson, Pop. 140,671
Jefferson County SD R-1
Supt. — See Golden
Alameda HS 1,100/9-12
1255 S Wadsworth Blvd 80232 303-982-8160
Shirley Algiene, prin. Fax 982-8161
Bear Creek HS 1,900/9-12
3490 S Kipling St 80227 303-982-8855
Phyllis Emrich, prin. Fax 982-8856
Carmody MS 800/7-8
2050 S Kipling St 80227 303-982-8930
John Schalk, prin. Fax 982-8931
Creighton MS 700/7-8
75 Independence St 80226 303-982-6282
Patty DeLorenzo, prin. Fax 982-6283
Dunstan MS 800/7-8
1855 S Wright St 80228 303-982-9270
Linda Burton, prin. Fax 982-9269
Green Mountain HS 1,600/9-12
13175 W Green Mountain Dr 80228 303-982-9500
Barbara Goings, prin. Fax 982-9501
Jefferson County Open S 300/PK-12
7655 W 10th Ave 80214 303-982-7045
Wendy Wheaton, prin. Fax 982-7046
Lakewood HS 1,800/9-12
9700 W 8th Ave 80215 303-982-7096
Ron Castagna, prin. Fax 982-7097
O'Connell MS 600/7-8
1275 S Teller St 80232 303-982-8370
Pati Montgomery, prin. Fax 982-8371
Warren Occupational Tech Ctr Vo/Tech
13300 W 2nd Pl 80228 303-982-8600
Joe Shaw, prin. Fax 982-8622

Christian Fellowship S 300/PK-12
7700 W Woodard Dr 80227 303-980-6622
Truman Abbott, admin. Fax 980-1337
Colorado Christian University Post-Sec.
8787 W Alameda Ave 80226 303-202-0100
Colorado School of Healing Arts Post-Sec.
7655 W Mississippi #100 80226 303-986-2320
Colorado School of Trades Post-Sec.
1575 Hoyt St 80215 303-233-4697
Mile High Baptist S 100/K-12
8100 W Hampden Ave 80227 303-986-2183
Ohio Center for Broadcasting - Colorado Post-Sec.
1310 Wadsworth Blvd Ste 100 80214 303-937-7070
Red Rocks Community College Post-Sec.
13300 W 6th Ave 80228 303-988-6160

Lamar, Prowers, Pop. 8,414
Lamar SD RE-2 1,600/PK-12
210 W Pearl St 81052 719-336-3251
Wayne Graybeal, supt. Fax 336-2817
www.lamar.k12.co.us
Lamar HS 400/9-12
1900 S 11th St 81052 719-336-3488
Allan Medina, prin. Fax 336-3026
Lamar MS 200/7-8
104 W Park St 81052 719-336-7436
David Tecklenburg, prin. Fax 336-5457

Lamar Community College Post-Sec.
2401 S Main St 81052 719-336-2248

Laporte, Larimer, Pop. 1,500
Poudre SD R-1
Supt. — See Fort Collins
Cache La Poudre JHS 400/7-9
3511 W County Road 54G 80535 970-488-7400
Brian Williams, prin. Fax 488-7433

Larkspur, Douglas, Pop. 306

Griffith Centers for Children 100/6-12
PO Box 95 80118 303-681-2400
Donna Force, dir. Fax 681-2401

La Salle, Weld, Pop. 1,895
Weld County SD RE-1
Supt. — See Gilcrest
North Valley MS 300/6-8
PO Box 248 80645 970-284-5508
Mel Sussman, prin. Fax 284-6595

Las Animas, Bent, Pop. 2,543
Las Animas SD RE-1 600/PK-12
1021 2nd St 81054 719-456-0161
Scott Cuckow, supt. Fax 456-1117
www.lasanimas.k12.co.us
Las Animas HS 100/9-12
300 Grove Ave 81054 719-456-0211
Lorrie Miller, prin. Fax 456-0932
Las Animas MS 100/6-8
1021 2nd St 81054 719-456-0228
Lorrie Miller, prin. Fax 456-0241

La Veta, Huerfano, Pop. 887
La Veta SD RE-2 300/PK-12
PO Box 85 81055 719-742-3562
Dave Seaney, supt. Fax 742-3959
www.laveta.k12.co.us
La Veta JSHS 100/7-12
PO Box 85 81055 719-742-3662
Dave Seaney, prin. Fax 742-5799

Leadville, Lake, Pop. 2,688
Lake County SD R-1 1,200/PK-12
107 Spruce St 80461 719-486-6800
Dr. Bette Bullock, supt. Fax 486-2048
www.lakecountyschools.net/
Lake County HS 300/9-12
1000 W 4th St 80461 719-486-6950
Rhett Parham, prin. Fax 486-3767
Lake County MS 400/5-8
1000 W 6th St 80461 719-486-6830
Deb Forkner, prin. Fax 486-6880

Mountain BOCES 50/
1713 Mount Lincoln Dr W 80461 719-486-2603
Edward Vandertook, dir. Fax 486-2109
www.mtnboces.org/
Other Schools – See Buena Vista

Colorado Mountain College Post-Sec.
901 US Highway 24 80461 800-621-8559

Limon, Lincoln, Pop. 1,879
Limon SD RE-4J 500/K-12
PO Box 249 80828 719-775-2350
Harvey Goodman, supt. Fax 775-9052
www.plains.net/~lps/
Limon JSHS 300/6-12
PO Box 249 80828 719-775-2350
Harvey Goodman, prin. Fax 775-9052

Littleton, Arapahoe, Pop. 40,396
Cherry Creek SD 5
Supt. — See Greenwood Village
West MS 1,300/6-8
5151 S Holly St 80121 720-554-5180
Sheila Graham, prin. Fax 554-5181

Douglas County SD RE-1
Supt. — See Castle Rock
Rocky Heights MS 600/7-8
11033 Monarch Blvd 80124 303-387-3300
Pat Dierberger, prin. Fax 387-3301

Jefferson County SD R-1
Supt. — See Golden
Chatfield HS 2,200/9-12
7227 S Simms St 80127 303-982-3670
Keith Mead, prin. Fax 982-3671
Columbine HS 1,700/9-12
6201 S Pierce St 80123 303-982-4400
Frank DeAngelis, prin. Fax 982-4401
Dakota Ridge HS 1,600/9-12
13399 W Coal Mine Ave 80127 303-982-1970
Jim Jelinek, prin. Fax 982-1971
Deer Creek MS 600/7-8
9201 W Columbine Dr 80128 303-982-3820
Rob Hoover, prin. Fax 982-3821
Falcon Bluffs MS 500/7-8
8449 S Garrison St 80128 303-982-9900
Wendy Rubin, prin. Fax 982-9901
Ken Caryl MS 700/7-8
6509 W Ken Caryl Ave 80128 303-982-4710
Mary Ellen Hansen, prin. Fax 982-4711
Summit Ridge MS 900/7-8
11809 W Coal Mine Dr 80127 303-982-9013
Lisa Myles, prin. Fax 982-8998

Littleton SD 6 15,300/PK-12
5776 S Crocker St 80120 303-347-3300
Scott Murphy, supt. Fax 347-3439
www.littletonpublicschools.net
Euclid MS 900/6-8
777 W Euclid Ave 80120 303-347-7800
Gary Hein, prin. Fax 347-7830
Goddard MS 900/6-8
3800 W Berry Ave 80123 303-347-7850
Dr. Amy Oaks, prin. Fax 347-7880
Heritage HS 1,800/9-12
1401 W Geddes Ave 80120 303-347-7600
Kenneth Moritz, prin. Fax 347-7603
Littleton HS 1,700/9-12
199 E Littleton Blvd 80121 303-347-7700
Kathy Dinmore, prin. Fax 347-7775
Powell MS 900/6-8
8000 S Corona Way 80122 303-347-7850
Becky Friend, prin. Fax 347-3975
Other Schools – See Centennial

Arapahoe Community College Post-Sec.
5900 S Santa Fe Dr 80120 303-797-4222
Denver Seminary Post-Sec.
6399 S Santa Fe Dr 80120 303-762-6982
Front Range Christian HS 300/7-12
6637 W Ottawa Ave 80128 303-979-4582
Rogene Lowe, prin. Fax 979-3591
Rock Solid HS 100/9-12
6570 S Broadway Ste B 80121 303-797-1005
Diann Kidder, prin. Fax 797-1103

Lonetree, See Littleton

University of Phoenix Post-Sec.
10004 Park Meadows Dr 80124 303-755-9090

Longmont, Boulder, Pop. 81,818
St. Vrain Valley SD RE-1J 20,700/PK-12
395 S Pratt Pkwy 80501 303-776-6200
Randy Zila, supt. Fax 682-7343
www.stvrain.k12.co.us
Altoona MS 5-8
4600 Clover Basin Dr 80503 720-494-3730
Joe Mehsling, prin. Fax 494-3989
Heritage MS 800/6-8
233 E Mountain View Ave 80501 303-772-7900
Anne Marie Sanchez, prin. Fax 776-4376
Longmont HS 1,400/9-12
1040 Sunset St 80501 303-776-6014
Rick Olsen, prin. Fax 678-7583
Longs Peak MS 700/6-8
1500 14th Ave 80501 303-776-5611
Matt Buchler, prin. Fax 651-3144
Niwot HS 1,200/9-12
8989 Niwot Rd 80503 303-652-2550
Dennis Daly, prin. Fax 440-9399
Silver Creek HS 800/9-12
4901 Nelson Rd 80503 720-494-3721
Sherri Schumann, prin. Fax 494-1848
Skyline HS 1,400/9-12
600 E Mountain View Ave 80501 720-494-3741
Tom Stumpf, prin. Fax 682-7382
Sunset MS 700/6-8
1300 S Sunset St 80501 303-776-3963
Dawn Macy, prin. Fax 772-2875
Trail Ridge MS 6-8
1000 Button Rock Dr 80501 720-494-3820
Valerie Millert, prin. Fax 494-3829
Westview MS 700/6-8
1651 Airport Rd 80503 303-772-3134
Mark Spencer, prin. Fax 772-0596

Adult Education Lincoln Center — Adult
619 Bowen St 80501 — 303-678-5662
Mary Willoughby, prin. — Fax 776-7426
Other Schools – See Erie, Firestone, Frederick, Lyons, Mead

Faith Baptist S — 300/K-12
833 15th Ave 80501 — 303-776-5677
Randy Peterson, prin. — Fax 682-5359
Longmont Christian S — 400/PK-12
550 Coffman St 80501 — 303-776-3254
Donnie Bennett, prin. — Fax 485-6937

Louisville, Boulder, Pop. 18,358
Boulder Valley SD RE-2
Supt. — See Boulder
Louisville MS — 500/6-8
1341 Main St 80027 — 303-666-6503
Adam Fels, prin. — Fax 665-3703
Monarch HS — 1,700/9-12
329 Campus Dr 80027 — 303-665-5888
Barbara Spelman, prin. — Fax 245-5650

Loveland, Larimer, Pop. 59,563
Thompson SD R-2J — 14,700/K-12
800 S Taft Ave 80537 — 970-613-5000
Dr. Dan Johnson, supt. — Fax 613-5095
www.thompson.k12.co.us
Ball MS — 800/6-8
2660 Monroe Ave 80538 — 970-613-7300
Sheila Pottorff, prin. — Fax 613-7341
Clark MS — 800/6-8
2605 Carlisle Dr 80537 — 970-613-5400
Scott Wallace, prin. — Fax 613-5420
Erwin MS — 800/6-8
4700 Lucerne Ave 80538 — 970-613-7600
David Steward, prin. — Fax 613-7619
Loveland HS — 1,500/9-12
920 W 29th St 80538 — 970-613-5200
Fred Dreier, prin. — Fax 613-7191
Mountain View HS — 1,200/9-12
3500 Mountain Lion Dr 80537 — 970-613-7800
Kevin Aten, prin. — Fax 613-7820
Reed MS — 700/6-8
370 W 4th St 80537 — 970-613-7200
Todd Ball, prin. — Fax 613-7287
Thompson Valley HS — 1,400/9-12
1669 Eagle Dr 80537 — 970-613-7900
Mark Johnson, prin. — Fax 613-7909
Other Schools – See Berthoud

Campion Academy — 200/9-12
300 42nd St SW 80537 — 970-667-5592
John Winslow, prin. — Fax 667-5104
Loveland Christian HS — 50/7-12
3901 14th St SW 80537 — 970-667-6300
Cherylann Dozier, admin. — Fax 593-1961
Resurrection Christian S — 500/K-12
6508 E Crossroads Blvd 80538 — 970-667-1610
Allen Howlett, supt. — Fax 667-1643

Lyons, Boulder, Pop. 1,624
St. Vrain Valley SD RE-1J
Supt. — See Longmont
Lyons MSHS — 400/6-12
PO Box 619 80540 — 303-823-6631
Mark Mills, prin. — Fax 823-5492

Mc Clave, Bent, Pop. 150
McClave SD RE-2 — 300/PK-12
PO Box 1 81057 — 719-829-4517
Terry Webber, supt. — Fax 829-4430
Mc Clave JSHS — 100/7-12
PO Box 1 81057 — 719-829-4517
Terry Webber, prin. — Fax 829-4430

Mancos, Montezuma, Pop. 1,183
Mancos SD RE-6 — 400/PK-12
395 Grand Ave 81328 — 970-533-7748
Michael Canzona, supt. — Fax 533-7954
www.mancosre6.edu
Mancos HS — 100/9-12
355 Grand Ave 81328 — 970-533-7746
Stan Davis, prin. — Fax 533-7537
Mancos MS — 100/6-8
100 S Beech St 81328 — 970-533-9143
Stan Davis, prin. — Fax 533-1463

Manitou Springs, El Paso, Pop. 5,039
Manitou Springs SD 14 — 1,300/PK-12
405 El Monte Pl 80829 — 719-685-2024
Roy G. Crawford, supt. — Fax 685-4536
mssd14.org
Manitou Springs HS — 500/9-12
401 El Monte Pl 80829 — 719-685-2074
Rob Cody, prin. — Fax 685-4755
Manitou Springs MS — 300/6-8
415 El Monte Pl 80829 — 719-685-2127
Keith Elsberry, prin. — Fax 685-4552

Manzanola, Otero, Pop. 496
Manzanola SD 3J — 200/K-12
PO Box 148 81058 — 719-462-5527
Ernie Vigil, supt. — Fax 462-5708
www.manzanola.k12.co.us/
Manzanola JSHS — 100/7-12
PO Box 148 81058 — 719-462-5528
Todd Werner, prin. — Fax 462-5115

Mead, Weld, Pop. 2,663
St. Vrain Valley SD RE-1J
Supt. — See Longmont
Mead MS — 500/6-8
620 Welker Ave 80542 — 970-535-4446
Victoria Teague, prin. — Fax 535-4434

Meeker, Rio Blanco, Pop. 2,222
Meeker SD RE-1 — 600/PK-12
PO Box 1089 81641 — 970-878-9040
Dan Evig, supt. — Fax 878-3682
www.meeker.k12.co.us
Barone MS — 100/6-8
PO Box 690 81641 — 970-878-9060
Pam Stranathan, prin. — Fax 878-4291
Meeker HS — 200/9-12
PO Box 159 81641 — 970-878-9070
Dwayne Newman, prin. — Fax 878-3633

Merino, Logan, Pop. 279
Merino SD RE-4J — 300/K-12
PO Box 198 80741 — 970-522-7424
Dave Kautz, supt. — Fax 522-1541
www.merino.k12.co.us
Merino JSHS — 100/7-12
PO Box 198 80741 — 970-522-7424
Ben Dutton, prin. — Fax 522-1541

Milliken, Weld, Pop. 5,593
Weld County SD RE-5J — 2,200/K-12
110 Centennial Dr Ste A 80543 — 970-587-6050
Dr. Marti Foster, supt. — Fax 587-2607
www.weldre5j.k12.co.us
Milliken MS — 500/6-8
PO Box 339 80543 — 970-587-6300
Trevor Long, prin. — Fax 587-5749
Other Schools – See Johnstown

Minturn, Eagle, Pop. 1,097
Eagle County SD RE-50
Supt. — See Eagle
Minturn MS — 200/6-8
PO Box 280 81645 — 970-328-2920
Toni Boush, prin. — Fax 827-5805

Moffat, Saguache, Pop. 121
Moffat SD 2 — 100/PK-12
PO Box 428 81143 — 719-256-4710
Eli Dokson, supt. — Fax 256-4730
www.moffat.k12.co.us
Moffat HS — 50/9-12
PO Box 428 81143 — 719-256-4710
Michelle Hashbarger, prin. — Fax 256-4730
Moffat MS — 50/6-8
PO Box 428 81143 — 719-256-4710
Michelle Hashbarger, prin. — Fax 256-4730

Monte Vista, Rio Grande, Pop. 4,212
Monte Vista SD C-8 — 1,200/PK-12
345 E Prospect Ave 81144 — 719-852-5996
Don Wilkinson, supt. — Fax 852-6184
www.monte.k12.co.us
Monte Vista HS — 300/9-12
349 E Prospect Ave 81144 — 719-852-3586
James Szoka, prin. — Fax 852-6121
Monte Vista MS — 300/6-8
3720 Sherman Ave 81144 — 719-852-5984
John Wilson, prin. — Fax 852-6199
Byron Syring Delta Center — Adult
345 E Prospect Ave 81144 — 719-852-2212
Pam Bricker, prin. — Fax 852-6184

Sargent SD RE-33J — 400/K-12
7090 N County Road 2 E 81144 — 719-852-4023
Lyle Oliver, supt. — Fax 852-9890
www.sargent.k12.co.us
Sargent JSHS — 200/7-12
7090 N County Road 2 E 81144 — 719-852-4025
James Holmes, prin. — Fax 852-9672

Montrose, Montrose, Pop. 15,479
Montrose County SD RE-1J — 5,600/PK-12
PO Box 10000 81402 — 970-249-7726
Dr. George Voorhis, supt. — Fax 249-7173
www.mcsd.org
Centennial MS — 500/6-8
PO Box 10000 81402 — 970-249-2576
Kirk Henwood, prin. — Fax 240-6461
Columbine MS — 600/6-8
PO Box 10000 81402 — 970-249-2581
Ben Stephenson, prin. — Fax 240-6404
Montrose HS — 1,200/9-12
PO Box 10000 81402 — 970-249-6636
Jill Myers, prin. — Fax 240-6414
Other Schools – See Olathe

Monument, El Paso, Pop. 2,508
Lewis-Palmer SD 38 — 4,900/PK-12
PO Box 40 80132 — 719-488-4700
Dr. Michael Pomarico, supt. — Fax 488-5951
www.lewispalmer.org
Creekside MS — 700/6-8
1330 Creekside Dr 80132 — 719-481-1099
Dianne Kingsland, prin. — Fax 481-0681
Lewis-Palmer HS — 1,800/9-12
1300 Higby Rd 80132 — 719-488-4720
Mark Brewer, prin. — Fax 488-4723
Lewis-Palmer MS — 600/6-8
1776 Woodmoor Dr 80132 — 719-488-4776
Terry Miller, prin. — Fax 488-4780

Morrison, Jefferson, Pop. 410

Silver State Baptist S — 200/PK-12
PO Box 463 80465 — 303-922-8850
Daniel Brock, admin. — Fax 922-4573

Mosca, Alamosa, Pop. 180
Sangre De Cristo SD RE-22J — 300/PK-12
PO Box 145 81146 — 719-378-2321
Lynn Howard, supt. — Fax 378-2327
Sangre De Cristo JSHS — 200/7-12
PO Box 145 81146 — 719-378-2321
Nathan Smith, prin. — Fax 378-2327

Naturita, Montrose, Pop. 665
West End SD RE-2 — 400/PK-12
PO Box 190 81422 — 970-865-2290
Duane Denny, supt. — Fax 865-2573
www.westendschools.org
Other Schools – See Nucla

Nederland, Boulder, Pop. 1,337
Boulder Valley SD RE-2
Supt. — See Boulder
Nederland MSHS — 400/6-12
597 Eldora Rd 80466 — 303-258-3212
Rich Salaz, prin. — Fax 258-8699

New Castle, Garfield, Pop. 3,017
Garfield SD RE-2
Supt. — See Rifle
Coal Ridge HS — 9-12
35947 Highway 6 81647 — 970-625-6710
Jeanie Humble, prin. — Fax 625-6701
Riverside S — 500/5-8
804 Main Dr 81647 — 970-625-7800
Bill Nickell, prin. — Fax 625-7846

New Raymer, Weld, Pop. 109
Prairie SD RE-11 — 100/PK-12
PO Box 68 80742 — 970-437-5351
R. Joe Kimmel, supt. — Fax 437-5732
prairieschool.org
Prairie JSHS — 100/7-12
PO Box 68 80742 — 970-437-5351
Leann Smith, prin. — Fax 437-5732

Northglenn, Adams, Pop. 32,906
Northglenn-Thornton 12 SD
Supt. — See Thornton
Huron MS — 800/6-8
10900 Huron St 80234 — 720-972-5000
Tracy Webber, prin. — Fax 972-5039
Northglenn HS — 2,400/9-12
601 W 100th Pl 80260 — 720-972-4600
Mary Lindimore, prin. — Fax 972-4739
Northglenn MS — 800/6-8
1123 Muriel Dr 80233 — 720-972-5080
Paula Redig, prin. — Fax 972-5119

Community Christian S — 300/K-12
11980 Irma Dr 80233 — 303-452-7514
John Reynolds, admin. — Fax 452-4904
Rocky Mountain Lutheran HS — 100/9-12
11700 Irma Dr 80233 — 303-346-1947
John Barenz, prin. — Fax 451-0817

Norwood, San Miguel, Pop. 460
Norwood SD R-2J — 200/PK-12
PO Box 448 81423 — 970-327-4336
Dr. Larry Ranney, supt. — Fax 327-4116
Norwood HS — 100/9-12
PO Box 448 81423 — 970-327-4336
James Hoffman, prin. — Fax 327-4116

Nucla, Montrose, Pop. 739
West End SD RE-2
Supt. — See Naturita
Nucla JSHS — 200/7-12
PO Box 570 81424 — 970-864-7350
Gordon Shepherd, prin. — Fax 864-7269

Oak Creek, Routt, Pop. 797
South Routt SD RE-3 — 400/PK-12
PO Box 158 80467 — 970-736-2313
Kelly Reed, supt. — Fax 736-2458
www.southroutt.k12.co.us
Soroco HS — 100/9-12
PO Box 158 80467 — 970-736-2531
James Chamberlin, prin. — Fax 736-0211
Soroco MS — 100/6-8
PO Box 158 80467 — 970-736-8531
James Chamberlain, prin. — Fax 736-0182

Olathe, Montrose, Pop. 1,679
Montrose County SD RE-1J
Supt. — See Montrose
Olathe HS — 300/9-12
410 Highway 50 81425 — 970-252-7950
Berry Swenson, prin. — Fax 323-5947
Olathe MS — 300/6-8
410 Highway 50 81425 — 970-252-7950
Berry Swenson, prin. — Fax 323-5947

Ordway, Crowley, Pop. 1,178
Crowley County SD RE-1-J — 600/K-12
PO Box 338 81063 — 719-267-3117
John McCleary, supt. — Fax 267-3130
www.crowley.k12.co.us
Crowley County HS — 200/9-12
PO Box 338 81063 — 719-267-3582
Lisa Bauer, prin. — Fax 267-3585
Crowley County MS — 100/6-8
PO Box 338 81063 — 719-267-9880
Jim Trainor, prin. — Fax 267-9881

Otis, Washington, Pop. 512
Lone Star SD 101 — 100/K-12
44940 County Road 54 80743 — 970-848-2778
Gena Ramey, supt. — Fax 848-0340
www.lonestar.k12.co.us/
Lone Star JSHS — 50/7-12
44940 County Road 54 80743 — 970-848-2778
Jerry Williams, prin. — Fax 848-0340

Otis SD R-3 — 200/PK-12
518 Dungan St 80743 — 970-246-3413
Jeff Durbin, supt. — Fax 246-0518
www.osdco.com
Otis JSHS — 100/7-12
301 Work St 80743 — 970-246-3486
Jim Anderson, prin. — Fax 246-3487

Ouray, Ouray, Pop. 877
Ouray SD R-1 — 300/PK-12
PO Box N 81427 — 970-325-4505
Sandy Kern, supt. — Fax 325-7343
www.ouray.k12.co.us/
Ouray HS — 100/9-12
PO Box N 81427 — 970-325-4218
Nick Schafer, prin. — Fax 325-7343
Ouray MS — 50/7-8
PO Box N 81427 — 970-325-4505
Tim Finkbeiner, prin. — Fax 325-7343

Ovid, Sedgwick, Pop. 316
Platte Valley SD RE-3 — 100/PK-12
PO Box 369 80744 — 970-463-5414
William Pile, supt. — Fax 463-5493
www.plattevsd.k12.co.us/
Revere JSHS — 100/7-12
PO Box 369 80744 — 970-463-5477
Henry Armknecht, prin. — Fax 463-5669

Pagosa Springs, Archuleta, Pop. 1,628
Archuleta County SD 50 JT — 1,600/K-12
PO Box 1498 81147 — 970-264-2228
Duane Noggle, supt. — Fax 264-4631
www.pagosa.k12.co.us
Pagosa Springs HS — 500/9-12
PO Box 1498 81147 — 970-264-2231
David Hamilton, prin. — Fax 264-2239
Pagosa Springs JHS — 300/7-8
PO Box 1498 81147 — 970-264-2794
Chris Hinger, prin. — Fax 264-6112

Palisade, Mesa, Pop. 2,683
Mesa County Valley SD 51
Supt. — See Grand Junction
Palisade HS 900/9-12
3679 G Rd 81526 970-464-5937
Matthew Diers, prin. Fax 464-5102

Paonia, Delta, Pop. 1,584
Delta County SD 50(J)
Supt. — See Delta
Paonia JSHS 300/7-12
846 Grand Ave 81428 970-527-4882
Brent Curtice, prin. Fax 527-4080

Parachute, Garfield, Pop. 1,094
Garfield County SD 16 1,000/PK-12
PO Box 68 81635 970-285-5701
Dr. Steven McKee, supt. Fax 285-5711
www.garcoschools.org
Grand Valley HS 200/9-12
PO Box 68 81635 970-285-5705
Ryan Frink, prin. Fax 285-5715
L.W. St. John MS 200/7-8
PO Box 68 81635 970-285-5704
Scott Pankow, prin. Fax 285-5714

Parker, Douglas, Pop. 38,428
Douglas County SD RE-1
Supt. — See Castle Rock
Chaparral HS 1,900/9-12
15655 Brookstone Dr 80134 303-387-3500
Ron Peterson, prin. Fax 387-3501
Ponderosa HS 1,900/9-12
7007 E Bayou Gulch Rd 80134 303-387-4000
Chuck Puga, prin. Fax 387-4001
Sagewood MS 1,000/7-8
4725 Fox Sparrow Rd 80134 303-387-4300
Ralph Montgomery, prin. Fax 387-4301
Sierra MS 1,100/7-8
6651 E Pine Ln 80138 303-387-3800
Karen Tarbell, prin. Fax 387-3801

Lutheran HS of the Rockies 200/9-12
11249 N Newlin Gulch Blvd 80134 303-841-5551
Juls Clausen, prin. Fax 842-1015

Peetz, Logan, Pop. 225
Plateau SD RE-5 100/PK-12
PO Box 39 80747 970-334-2435
Dean Koester, supt. Fax 334-2360
Peetz HS 100/9-12
PO Box 39 80747 970-334-2361
Dean Koester, prin. Fax 334-2360

Peyton, El Paso, Pop. 200
Peyton SD 23 JT 600/PK-12
13990 Bradshaw Rd 80831 719-749-2330
Rich Campbell, supt. Fax 749-2368
www.peyton.k12.co.us/
Peyton HS 200/9-12
13885 Bradshaw Rd 80831 719-749-2244
Tim Kistler, prin. Fax 749-2567
Peyton MS, 18220 Main St 80831 100/6-8
Tim Kistler, prin. 719-749-2244

Platteville, Weld, Pop. 2,598
Weld County SD RE-1
Supt. — See Gilcrest
South Valley MS 200/6-8
1004 Main St 80651 970-785-2205
Jeff Angus, prin. Fax 785-2180

Pritchett, Baca, Pop. 124
Pritchett SD RE-3 100/PK-12
PO Box 7 81064 719-523-4045
Stephanie Hund, supt. Fax 523-6991
Pritchett HS 50/9-12
PO Box 7 81064 719-523-4045
Stephanie Hund, prin. Fax 523-6991
Pritchett JHS 50/6-8
PO Box 7 81064 719-523-4045
Stephanie Hund, prin. Fax 523-6991

Pueblo, Pueblo, Pop. 103,495
Pueblo CSD 60 16,000/PK-12
315 W 11th St 81003 719-549-7100
Dr. John Covington, supt. Fax 549-7112
www.pueblo60.k12.co.us
Centennial HS 1,100/9-12
2525 Mountview Dr 81008 719-549-7335
Dr. Miguel Elias, prin. Fax 549-7634
Central HS 1,000/9-12
216 E Orman Ave 81004 719-549-7300
Robert Gonzales, prin. Fax 549-7306
Corwin MS 300/6-8
1500 Lakeview Ave 81004 719-549-7400
Dr. Kathy DeNiro, prin. Fax 564-2773
East HS 900/9-12
9 Macneil Rd 81001 719-549-7222
Alan Nelms, prin. Fax 545-0389
Freed MS 600/6-8
715 W 20th St 81003 719-549-7410
Cheryl Madrill-Stringham, prin. Fax 562-0816
Heaton MS 700/6-8
6 Adair Rd 81001 719-549-7420
Denise Garcia-Cooper, prin. Fax 549-7838
Pitts MS 700/6-8
29 Lehigh Ave 81005 719-549-7430
John Huff, prin. Fax 549-7878
Risley MS 400/6-8
625 N Monument Ave 81001 719-549-7440
Rena Jimenez, prin. Fax 549-7926
Roncalli MS 700/6-8
4202 W State Highway 78 81005 719-549-7450
Bradley Farbo, prin. Fax 549-7469
South HS 1,400/9-12
1801 Hollywood Dr 81005 719-549-7255
James Wessely, prin. Fax 549-7759
Keating Education Center Adult
215 E Orman Ave 81004 719-549-7371
Greg Millard, prin. Fax 549-7704

Pueblo County Rural SD 70 7,800/PK-12
24951 E US Highway 50 81006 719-542-0220
Daniel Lere, supt. Fax 542-0225
www.district70.org/
Pleasant View MS 400/6-8
23600 Everett Rd 81006 719-542-7813
Margery Dudley, prin. Fax 542-6291
Pueblo County HS 800/9-12
1050 35th Ln 81006 719-948-3352
John DeLuca, prin. Fax 948-0196
Pueblo Technical Academy Vo/Tech
900 W Orman Ave 81004 719-549-3317
Kent Muckel, prin.
Vineland MS 300/6-8
1132 36th Ln 81006 719-948-3336
Laurie Stratman, prin. Fax 948-2323
Other Schools – See Colorado City, Pueblo West, Rye

Colorado State University - Pueblo Post-Sec.
2200 Bonforte Blvd 81001 719-549-2100
IntelliTec College Post-Sec.
3673 Parker Blvd Ste 250 81008 719-542-3181
Parkview Medical Center Post-Sec.
400 W 16th St 81003 719-584-4573
Pueblo Community College Post-Sec.
900 W Orman Ave 81004 719-549-3200

Pueblo West, Pueblo, Pop. 4,386
Pueblo County Rural SD 70
Supt. — See Pueblo
Pueblo West HS 1,100/9-12
661 W Capistrano Ave 81007 719-547-8050
Martha Nogare, prin.
Pueblo West MS 500/6-8
484 S Maher Dr 81007 719-547-3752
Phillip Compton, prin.
Sky View MS 500/6-8
1047 S Camino De Bravo 81007 719-547-1175
Eric Nielsen, prin.

Rangely, Rio Blanco, Pop. 2,038
Rangely SD RE-4 500/PK-12
550 River Rd 81648 970-675-2207
Jim Day, supt. Fax 675-5143
www.rangelyk12.org/
Rangely HS 200/9-12
234 S Jones Ave 81648 970-675-2253
Patrick Moore, prin. Fax 675-5403
Rangely MS 100/6-8
550 River Rd 81648 970-675-5021
Jim Day, prin. Fax 675-5143

Colorado Northwestern Community College Post-Sec.
500 Kennedy Dr 81648 800-562-1105

Ridgway, Ouray, Pop. 752
Ridgway SD R-2 300/PK-12
1115 Clinton St 81432 970-626-4320
Douglas Bissonette, supt. Fax 626-4337
www.ridgway.k12.co.us/
Ridgway HS 100/9-12
1200 Green St 81432 970-626-5788
Fax 626-3249
Ridgway MS 100/6-8
1200 Green St 81432 970-626-5788
Fax 626-3249

Rifle, Garfield, Pop. 8,038
Garfield SD RE-2 3,900/PK-12
839 Whiteriver Ave 81650 970-625-7600
Dr. Gary Pack, supt. Fax 625-7623
www.garfieldre2.k12.co.us
Rifle HS 900/9-12
1350 Prefontaine Ave 81650 970-625-7725
Todd Ellis, prin. Fax 625-7785
Rifle MS 700/5-8
753 Railroad Ave 81650 970-625-7900
Susan Birdsey, prin. Fax 625-7930
Other Schools – See New Castle

Rocky Ford, Otero, Pop. 4,121
Rocky Ford SD R-2 800/K-12
601 S 8th St 81067 719-254-7423
Nancy Aschermann, supt. Fax 254-7425
www.rockyford.k12.co.us/
Jefferson MS 200/6-8
901 S 11th St 81067 719-254-7669
Monica Johnson, prin. Fax 254-4307
Rocky Ford HS 200/9-12
100 W Washington Ave 81067 719-254-7431
Ryan Nesselhuf, prin. Fax 254-7436

Rush, El Paso, Pop. 100
Miami-Yoder SD 60 JT 300/K-12
420 S Rush Rd 80833 719-478-2186
Rick Walter, supt. Fax 478-5380
Miami-Yoder JSHS 200/7-12
420 S Rush Rd 80833 719-478-2186
Sean Shields, prin. Fax 478-5380

Rye, Pueblo, Pop. 205
Pueblo County Rural SD 70
Supt. — See Pueblo
Rye HS, PO Box 10 81069 300/9-12
Richard Sanchez, prin. 719-489-2271

Saguache, Saguache, Pop. 606
Mountain Valley SD RE-1 200/PK-12
PO Box 127 81149 719-655-0267
Brady Stagner, supt. Fax 655-0269
www.valley.k12.co.us
Mountain Valley HS 100/9-12
PO Box 127 81149 719-655-2578
John Stephens, prin. Fax 655-2875
Mountain Valley MS 50/6-8
PO Box 127 81149 719-655-2578
John Stephens, prin. Fax 655-2875

Salida, Chaffee, Pop. 5,476
Salida SD R-32 1,200/K-12
310 E 9th St 81201 719-530-5252
James Wilson, supt. Fax 539-6220
www.salida.k12.co.us/
Salida HS 400/9-12
905 D St 81201 719-530-5400
Robert Carrick, prin. Fax 539-2407
Salida MS 400/5-8
520 Milford St 81201 719-530-5300
Kirk Banghart, prin. Fax 530-5364

Sanford, Conejos, Pop. 802
Sanford SD 6J 400/PK-12
PO Box 39 81151 719-274-5167
Kevin Edgar, supt. Fax 274-5830
Sanford JSHS 200/7-12
PO Box 39 81151 719-274-5167
David Judd, prin. Fax 274-5830

San Luis, Costilla, Pop. 697
Centennial SD R-1 300/PK-12
PO Box 350 81152 719-672-3322
Diana Cortez, supt. Fax 672-3345
www.centennialschoolsr-1.com
Centennial HS, PO Box 350 81152 100/9-12
David Judd, prin. 719-672-3322
Centennial JHS, PO Box 350 81152 50/7-8
David Judd, prin. 719-672-3322

Seibert, Kit Carson, Pop. 173
Hi-Plains SD R-23
Supt. — See Vona
Hi-Plains JSHS 100/7-12
PO Box 238 80834 970-664-2616
Steven McCracken, prin. Fax 664-2622

Sheridan, Arapahoe, Pop. 5,483
Sheridan SD 2 1,500/PK-12
4000 S Lowell Blvd 80110 720-833-6991
Michael Poore, supt. Fax 833-6649
www.sheridank12.org
Sheridan HS 600/9-12
3201 W Oxford Ave 80110 720-833-6987
Mark Langston, prin. Fax 833-6833
Sheridan MS 400/6-8
4107 S Federal Blvd 80110 720-833-6988
William Wooddell, prin. Fax 833-6903

Sheridan Lake, Kiowa, Pop. 61
Plainview SD RE-2 100/K-12
13997 County Road 71 81071 719-729-3331
Garry Coulter, supt. Fax 727-4471
Plainview JHSH 50/6-12
13997 County Road 71 81071 719-729-3331
Garry Coulter, prin. Fax 727-4471

Silverton, San Juan, Pop. 548
Silverton SD 1 50/K-12
PO Box 128 81433 970-387-5543
Kim White, supt. Fax 387-5791
www.silvertonschool.org
Silverton JSHS 50/6-12
PO Box 128 81433 970-387-5543
Kim White, prin. Fax 387-5791

Simla, Elbert, Pop. 728
Big Sandy SD 100J 200/K-12
PO Box 68 80835 719-541-2292
Steve Wilson, supt. Fax 541-2186
Simla JSHS 100/6-12
PO Box 68 80835 719-541-2291
Rik Dahl, prin. Fax 541-2443

Springfield, Baca, Pop. 1,363
Springfield SD RE-4 300/PK-12
389 Tipton St 81073 719-523-6654
Michael Page, supt. Fax 523-4192
www.springfield.k12.co.us/
Springfield HS 100/9-12
389 Tipton St 81073 719-523-6522
Kyle Hebberd, prin. Fax 523-4361
Springfield JHS 100/7-8
389 Tipton St 81073 719-523-6522
Kyle Hebberd, prin. Fax 523-4361

Steamboat Springs, Routt, Pop. 9,354
Steamboat Springs SD RE-2 1,900/K-12
PO Box 774368 80477 970-879-1530
Donna Howell, supt. Fax 879-3943
www.sssd.k12.co.us
Steamboat Springs HS 700/9-12
PO Box 774368 80477 970-879-1562
Mike Knezevich, prin. Fax 879-8039
Steamboat Springs MS 500/6-8
PO Box 774368 80477 970-879-1058
Tim Bishop, prin. Fax 870-0368

Christian Heritage S 100/K-12
27285 Brandon Cir 80487 970-879-1760
Tim Calkins, prin. Fax 879-5511
Colorado Mountain College Post-Sec.
PO Box 775288 80477 800-621-8559
Whiteman S 100/9-12
42605 County Road 36 80487 970-879-1350
Walt Daub, prin. Fax 879-0506

Sterling, Logan, Pop. 12,589
Valley SD RE-1 1,800/PK-12
415 Beattie St 80751 970-522-0792
Dr. Betty Summers, supt. Fax 522-0525
www.re1valleyschools.org/
Sterling HS 700/9-12
407 W Broadway St 80751 970-522-2944
Doug Stutzman, prin. Fax 522-2900
Sterling MS 500/6-8
1177 Pawnee Ave 80751 970-522-1041
Robert Hall, prin. Fax 522-0306
Other Schools – See Iliff

Northeastern Junior College Post-Sec.
100 College Ave 80751 970-522-6600

Strasburg, Adams, Pop. 1,200
Strasburg SD 31J 900/PK-12
PO Box 207 80136 303-622-9211
Dr. David VanSant, supt. Fax 622-9224
www.strasburg31j.com
Strasburg HS 300/9-12
PO Box 207 80136 303-622-9211
Jeffrey Rasp, prin. Fax 622-9224
Strasburg JHS, PO Box 207 80136 100/7-8
Jeffrey Rasp, prin. 303-622-9211

Stratton, Kit Carson, Pop. 626
Stratton SD R-4 300/PK-12
219 Illinois Ave 80836 719-348-5369
Eric Moser, supt. Fax 348-5555
www.strattonschools.org
Stratton HS 100/9-12
219 Illinois Ave 80836 719-348-5369
Joel Foster, prin. Fax 348-5555
Stratton MS 50/7-8
219 Illinois Ave 80836 719-348-5369
Joel Foster, prin. Fax 348-5555

Swink, Otero, Pop. 683
Swink SD 33 400/K-12
PO Box 487 81077 719-384-8103
Dr. Rocco Fuschetto, supt. Fax 384-5471
www.swink.k12.co.us/
Swink JSHS 200/7-12
PO Box 487 81077 719-384-8103
Randy Bohlander, prin. Fax 384-5471

Tabernash, Grand

Winter Park Christian S 100/1-12
PO Box 518 80478 970-887-9784
Ron Widdifield, prin. Fax 887-9785

Telluride, San Miguel, Pop. 2,303
Telluride SD R-1 400/K-12
725 W Colorado Ave 81435 970-728-6617
Mary Rubadeau, supt. Fax 728-9490
www.tellurideschool.org
Telluride MSHS 100/6-12
725 W Colorado Ave 81435 970-728-4377
Peter Mueller, prin. Fax 728-0257

Thornton, Adams, Pop. 105,182
Mapleton SD 1
Supt. — See Denver
Mapleton Expeditionary S of the Arts 7-12
8990 York St 80229 303-853-1270
Mike Johnston, dir. Fax 853-1296
Skyview Academy HS 1,400/9-12
8990 York St 80229 303-853-1900
Eldon Wire, dir. Fax 853-1926

Northglenn-Thornton 12 SD 31,400/PK-12
1500 E 128th Ave 80241 720-972-4000
Dr. Mike Paskewicz, supt. Fax 972-4169
www.adams12.org
Bollman Technical Education Center Vo/Tech
9451 Washington St 80229 720-972-5820
Dr. Kim Howell, prin. Fax 972-5869
Century MS 900/6-8
13000 Lafayette St 80241 720-972-5240
Larry Pohlit, prin. Fax 972-5279
Horizon HS 2,300/9-12
5321 E 136th Ave 80602 720-972-4400
Joan Watson, prin. Fax 972-4598
Rocky Top MS 700/6-8
14150 York St 80602 720-972-2200
Jami Miller, prin. Fax 972-2303
Shadow Ridge MS 1,400/6-8
12551 Holly St 80241 720-972-5040
Susie Wickham, prin. Fax 972-5079
Thornton HS 2,300/9-12
9351 Washington St 80229 720-972-4800
Janette Walters, prin. Fax 972-4999
Thornton MS 800/6-8
9451 Hoffman Way 80229 720-972-5160
Bobby Ortega, prin. Fax 972-5199
High Plains HS & Extended Education Adult
455 Eppinger Blvd 80229 720-972-5802
Nancy MacDonnell, prin. Fax 972-5819
Other Schools – See Broomfield, Denver, Northglenn, Westminster

---

Artistic Beauty College Post-Sec.
3811 E 120th Ave 80233 303-451-5808
HealthONE North Suburban Medical Center Post-Sec.
9191 Grant St 80229 303-451-7800
ITT Technical Institute Post-Sec.
500 E 84th Ave 80229 303-288-4488
Kaplan College Post-Sec.
500 E 84th Ave Ste W200 80229 800-848-0550

Trinidad, Las Animas, Pop. 9,077
Trinidad SD 1 1,400/K-12
215 S Maple St 81082 719-846-3324
Dr. Jalan Aufderheide, supt. Fax 846-2957
www.trinidad.k12.co.us/
Trinidad HS 500/9-12
816 West St 81082 719-846-2971
Jenifer Mason, prin. Fax 846-7488
Trinidad MS 300/6-8
614 Park St 81082 719-846-4411
Deana Dunford, prin. Fax 846-4740

Trinidad State Junior College Post-Sec.
600 Prospect St 81082 719-846-5621

USAF Academy, El Paso, Pop. 9,062
Academy SD 20
Supt. — See Colorado Springs
Air Academy HS 1,500/9-12
6910 Carlton Dr, 719-234-2400
Dr. Erik Fredell, prin. Fax 234-2599

United States Air Force Academy Post-Sec.
, 719-333-1110

Vail, Eagle, Pop. 4,589

Vail Mountain S 300/K-12
3000 Booth Falls Rd 81657 970-476-3850
Peter Abuisi, prin. Fax 476-3860

Vilas, Baca, Pop. 100
Vilas SD RE-5 400/PK-12
PO Box 727 81087 719-523-6738
Joseph Shields, supt. Fax 523-4818
www.vilashi.com
Vilas Undivided HS 100/7-12
PO Box 727 81087 719-523-6738
Dan Schmidt, prin. Fax 523-4818

Vona, Kit Carson, Pop. 91
Hi-Plains SD R-23 100/PK-12
PO Box 9 80861 970-664-2636
Ronald Conrad, supt. Fax 664-2283
Other Schools – See Seibert

Walden, Jackson, Pop. 646
North Park SD R-1 300/PK-12
PO Box 798 80480 970-723-3300
Lewis Gellett, supt. Fax 723-8486
www.northpark.k12.co.us
North Park JSHS 100/6-12
PO Box 798 80480 970-723-3300
Randy Collins, prin. Fax 723-4702

Walsenburg, Huerfano, Pop. 3,946
Huerfano SD RE-1 600/PK-12
611 W 7th St 81089 719-738-1520
Dr. David Gray, supt. Fax 738-3148
www.huerfano.k12.co.us/
Mall HS 300/7-12
335 W Pine St 81089 719-738-1610
Paul Heesaker, prin. Fax 738-2541

Walsh, Baca, Pop. 682
Walsh SD RE-1 200/PK-12
PO Box 68 81090 719-324-5632
Kyle Hebberd, supt. Fax 324-5426
www.walsheagles.com
Walsh JSHS 100/7-12
PO Box 68 81090 719-324-5221
Tom Meardon, prin. Fax 324-5734

Weldona, Morgan, Pop. 325
Weldon Valley SD RE-20(J) 200/PK-12
911 North Ave 80653 970-645-2411
Robert Petterson, supt. Fax 645-2377
Weldon Valley HS 100/9-12
911 North Ave 80653 970-645-2411
Robert Petterson, prin. Fax 645-2377
Weldon Valley JHS 50/7-8
911 North Ave 80653 970-645-2411
Robert Petterson, prin. Fax 645-2377

Wellington, Larimer, Pop. 3,469
Poudre SD R-1
Supt. — See Fort Collins
Wellington JHS 300/7-9
4001 Wilson Ave 80549 970-568-3944
Alicia Durand, prin. Fax 568-3901

Westcliffe, Custer, Pop. 456
Custer County SD 1 500/PK-12
PO Box 730 81252 719-783-2357
Lance Villers, supt. Fax 783-2334
bobcats.ccs.k12.co.us/district/district.html
Custer County HS 200/9-12
PO Box 730 81252 719-783-2291
Barb Jones, prin. Fax 783-4944
Custer County JHS 100/6-8
PO Box 730 81252 719-783-2291
Barb Jones, prin.

Westminster, Adams, Pop. 105,084
Adams County SD 50 9,300/PK-12
4476 W 68th Ave 80030 303-428-3511
Dr. Roberta Selleck, supt. Fax 428-2810
www.adams50.org
Shaw Heights MS 700/6-8
8780 Circle Dr 80031 303-428-9533
Myla Shepherd, prin. Fax 650-6859
Westminster HS 1,400/9-12
4276 W 68th Ave 80030 303-428-9541
Kevin Braney, prin. Fax 657-3988
Other Schools – See Denver

Jefferson County SD R-1
Supt. — See Golden
Carle MS 7-8
10200 W 100th Ave 80021 303-982-9070
Greg Bushey, prin. Fax 982-9071
Mandalay MS 900/7-8
9651 Pierce St 80021 303-982-9802
Karen Quanbeck, prin. Fax 982-9813
Standley Lake HS 1,700/9-12
9300 W 104th Ave 80021 303-982-3311
Todd Engels, prin. Fax 982-3312

Northglenn-Thornton 12 SD
Supt. — See Thornton
Mountain Range HS 9-12
12500 Huron St 80234 720-972-6300
Julie Enger, prin. Fax 972-6529

Artistic Beauty College Post-Sec.
3049 W 74th Ave Ste A 80030 303-428-5100
Belleview Christian S 300/PK-12
3455 W 83rd Ave 80031 303-427-5459
Gary Dickinson, prin. Fax 426-6768
Denver Academy of Court Reporting Post-Sec.
9051 Harlan St Ste 20 80031 303-427-5292
Devereux Cleo Wallace 100/K-12
8405 Church Ranch Blvd 80021 303-466-7391
Matt Dudek, dir. Fax 466-0904
DeVry University Post-Sec.
1870 W 122nd Ave 80234 303-280-7600
Front Range Community College Post-Sec.
3645 W 112th Ave 80031 303-466-8811
Hyland Christian S 100/K-12
5255 W 98th Ave 80020 303-466-1673
LIFE Christian Academy 200/PK-12
11500 Sheridan Blvd 80020 303-438-1260
Kenneth Walsh, supt. Fax 438-1866

Weston, Las Animas, Pop. 200
Primero RSD RE-2 200/PK-12
20200 State Highway 12 81091 719-868-2715
Gerald Gabbard, supt. Fax 868-2241
www.primeroschool.org/
Primero JSHS 100/6-12
20200 State Highway 12 81091 719-868-2715
Bill Naccarato, prin. Fax 868-2241

Wheat Ridge, Jefferson, Pop. 31,242
Jefferson County SD R-1
Supt. — See Golden
Everitt MS 500/7-8
3900 Kipling St 80033 303-982-1580
Kathleen Norton, prin. Fax 982-1581
Wheat Ridge HS 1,500/9-12
9505 W 32nd Ave 80033 303-982-7695
Pat Harrison, prin. Fax 982-7696
Wheat Ridge MS 400/7-8
7101 W 38th Ave 80033 303-982-2833
B.J. Pell, prin. Fax 982-2834

Beth Eden Baptist S 200/K-12
2600 Wadsworth Blvd 80033 303-232-2313
Steve Curtis M.A., admin. Fax 233-3027
Colorado Catholic Academy 100/K-12
11180 W 44th Ave 80033 303-422-9549
Stephen Doyle, prin. Fax 422-9549
Foothills Academy 200/PK-12
4725 Miller St 80033 303-431-0920
Mary Faddick, prin. Fax 431-9505

Wiggins, Morgan, Pop. 951
Wiggins SD RE-50(J) 600/PK-12
320 Chapman St 80654 970-483-7762
Dr. Sharol Little, supt. Fax 483-6205
www.wiggins50.k12.co.us/
Wiggins HS 300/7-12
320 Chapman St 80654 970-483-7763
Dr. Dean Palmer, prin. Fax 483-7796

Wiley, Prowers, Pop. 476
Wiley SD RE-13 JT 300/PK-12
PO Box 247 81092 719-829-4806
Mike Doyle, supt. Fax 829-4422
www.wiley.k12.co.us
Wiley JSHS 200/7-12
PO Box 247 81092 719-829-4806
Dexter Leach, prin. Fax 829-4805

Windsor, Weld, Pop. 14,874
Weld County SD RE-4 2,900/PK-12
PO Box 609 80550 970-686-8000
Karen Trusler, supt. Fax 686-5280
www.windsor.k12.co.us
Windsor HS 800/9-12
1100 Main St 80550 970-686-8100
Kirk Salmela, prin. Fax 686-0935
Windsor MS 700/6-8
900 Main St 80550 970-686-8200
Douglas Englert, prin. Fax 686-7122

Woodland Park, Teller, Pop. 6,660
Woodland Park SD RE-2 3,100/PK-12
PO Box 99 80866 719-686-2000
Guy Arseneau, supt. Fax 687-8408
www.wpsdk12.org/
Woodland Park HS 1,100/9-12
PO Box 6820 80866 719-686-2067
Jo Spry, prin. Fax 687-3880
Woodland Park MS 800/6-8
PO Box 6790 80866 719-686-2200
John Jamison, prin. Fax 687-8458

Woodrow, Washington, Pop. 20
Woodlin SD R-104 100/PK-12
PO Box 185 80757 970-386-2223
Rose Cronk, supt. Fax 386-2241
www.woodlinschool.com
Woodlin Undivided HS 100/7-12
PO Box 185 80757 970-386-2223
Rose Cronk, prin. Fax 386-2241

Wray, Yuma, Pop. 2,147
Wray SD RD-2 700/PK-12
30222 County Road 35 80758 970-332-5764
Ron Howard, supt. Fax 332-5773
www.wrayschools.org
Buchanan MS 200/5-8
620 W 7th St 80758 970-332-4723
Myra Westfall, prin. Fax 332-3356
Wray HS 200/9-12
30074 County Road 35 80758 970-332-5758
George Purnell, prin. Fax 332-4476

Yoder, El Paso, Pop. 40
Edison SD 54 JT 100/PK-12
14550 Edison Rd 80864 719-478-2125
David Grosche, supt. Fax 478-3000
www.edison54jt.org
Edison JSHS, 14550 Edison Rd 80864 50/6-12
Rachel Paul, prin. 719-478-2125

Yuma, Yuma, Pop. 3,231
Yuma SD 1 900/PK-12
PO Box 327 80759 970-848-5831
Dennis Veal, supt. Fax 848-2256
www.yumaschools.org
Yuma HS 300/9-12
1000 S Albany St 80759 970-848-5488
David Wells, prin. Fax 848-0314
Yuma MS 300/5-8
500 S Elm St 80759 970-848-2000
Donna Fields, prin. Fax 848-4261

CONNECTICUT

CONNECTICUT DEPARTMENT OF EDUCATION
165 Capitol Ave, Hartford 06106
Telephone 860-566-8792
Fax 860-566-8964
Website http://www.state.ct.us/sde

Commissioner of Education Mark McQuillan

CONNECTICUT BOARD OF EDUCATION
165 Capitol Ave, Hartford 06106

Chairperson Allan Taylor

REGIONAL EDUCATIONAL SERVICE CENTERS

Area Coop. Educational Services RESC
Craig Edmondson, dir. 203-498-6800
350 State St, North Haven 06473 Fax 498-6890
www.aces.k12.ct.us

Capitol Region Education Council RESC
Dr. Bruce Douglas, dir. 860-524-4063
111 Charter Oak Ave Fax 548-9924
Hartford 06106
www.crec.org

Cooperative Educational Services RESC
Nancy Cetorelli, dir. 203-365-8803
40 Lindeman Dr, Trumbull 06611 Fax 365-8804
www.ces.k12.ct.us

Eastconn RESC
Paula Colen, dir. 860-455-0707
376 Hartford Tpke, Hampton 06247 Fax 455-8026
www.eastconn.org

Education Connection RESC
Danuta Thibodeau, dir. 860-567-0863
PO Box 909, Litchfield 06759 Fax 567-3381
www.educationconnection.org

Learn RESC
Virginia Seccombe, dir. 860-434-4800
44 Hatchetts Hill Rd Fax 434-4820
Old Lyme 06371
www.learn.k12.ct.us

PUBLIC, PRIVATE AND CATHOLIC SECONDARY SCHOOLS

Ansonia, New Haven, Pop. 18,744
Ansonia SD 2,700/PK-12
42 Grove St 06401 203-736-5095
Dr. Edward Favolise, supt. Fax 736-5098
www.ansonia.org
Ansonia HS 700/9-12
20 Pulaski Hwy 06401 203-736-5060
Wilhemenia Christon, prin. Fax 736-5068
Ansonia MS 700/6-8
115 Howard Ave 06401 203-736-5070
Lynn Bennett-Wallick, prin. Fax 736-1044

Connecticut Technical HS System
Supt. — See Middletown
O'Brien Technical HS Vo/Tech
141 Prindle Ave 06401 203-732-1800
Lisa Hylwa, dir. Fax 735-6236

Avon, Hartford
Avon SD 3,300/PK-12
34 Simsbury Rd 06001 860-404-4700
Richard Kisiel, supt. Fax 404-4702
www.avon.k12.ct.us
Avon HS 900/9-12
510 W Avon Rd 06001 860-404-4740
Lawrence Sparks, prin. Fax 404-4743
Avon MS 600/7-8
375 W Avon Rd 06001 860-404-4770
Jody Goeler, prin. Fax 404-4773

Avon Old Farms S 400/9-12
500 Old Farms Rd 06001 860-404-4100
Kenneth LaRocque, hdmstr. Fax 404-4135

Baltic, New London

Academy of the Holy Family 100/9-12
PO Box 691 06330 860-822-9272
Sr. Loreto Beckstein, prin. Fax 822-1318

Beacon Falls, New Haven
Regional SD 16
Supt. — See Prospect
Woodland Regional HS 800/9-12
135 Back Rimmon Rd 06403 203-881-5551
Dr. Arnold Frank, prin. Fax 881-2015

Berlin, Hartford
Berlin SD 3,300/PK-12
238 Kensington Rd 06037 860-828-6581
Dr. Michael Cicchetti, supt. Fax 829-0832
www.berlinschools.org
Berlin HS 1,100/9-12
139 Patterson Way 06037 860-828-6577
George Synnott, prin. Fax 829-2169
McGee MS 700/6-8
899 Norton Rd 06037 860-828-0323
Brian Benigni, prin. Fax 828-0676

Bethany, New Haven
Regional SD 5
Supt. — See Woodbridge
Amity Regional MS 500/7-8
190 Luke Hill Rd 06524 203-393-3102
Richard Dellinger, prin. Fax 393-0583

Bethel, Fairfield, Pop. 8,835
Bethel SD 3,200/K-12
PO Box 253 06801 203-794-8601
Gary Chesley, supt. Fax 794-8723
www.bethel.k12.ct.us
Bethel HS 1,000/9-12
300 Whittlesey Dr 06801 203-794-8620
Patricia Cosentino, prin. Fax 794-8618
Bethel MS 800/6-8
600 Whittlesey Dr 06801 203-794-8663
Kevin Smith, prin. Fax 794-8718

Bethlehem, Litchfield

Woodhall S 50/9-12
PO Box 550 06751 203-266-7788
Sally Woodhall, hdmstr. Fax 266-5896

Bloomfield, Hartford, Pop. 7,200
Bloomfield SD 2,000/PK-12
1133 Blue Hills Ave 06002 860-769-4200
David G. Title, supt. Fax 769-4215
www.bloomfieldschools.org/
Arace MS 400/7-8
390 Park Ave 06002 860-286-2622
Barbara Maybin, prin. Fax 242-0347
Big Picture HS 9-12
44 Griffin Rd S 06002 860-769-6600
Patricia Hymes, prin. Fax 769-6605
Bloomfield HS 700/9-12
5 Huckleberry Ln 06002 860-286-2630
Irene Zytka, prin. Fax 242-9491

Bolton, Tolland
Bolton SD 900/K-12
108 Notch Rd 06043 860-643-1569
Mark Winzler, supt. Fax 647-8452
Bolton HS 300/9-12
72 Brandy St 06043 860-643-2768
Paul Smith, prin. Fax 645-8374

King's S 100/5-12
PO Box 9175 06043 860-645-6466
James Kirch, prin. Fax 645-1889

Branford, New Haven, Pop. 27,603
Branford SD 3,600/PK-12
1111 Main St 06405 203-488-7276
Dr. Kathleen Halligan, supt. Fax 315-3505
www.branford.k12.ct.us
Branford HS 1,200/9-12
185 E Main St 06405 203-488-7291
Dr. Edmund Higgins, prin. Fax 315-6740
Walsh IS 1,100/5-8
185 Damascus Rd 06405 203-488-8317
Robin Goeler, prin. Fax 481-2785

Branford Hall Career Institute Post-Sec.
1 Summit Pl 06405 203-488-2525
Porter and Chester Institute of Branford Post-Sec.
221 W Main St 06405 203-315-1060

Bridgeport, Fairfield, Pop. 139,008
Bridgeport SD 22,100/PK-12
45 Lyon Ter Rm 203 06604 203-576-7302
John Ramos Ed.D., supt. Fax 337-0150
www.bridgeportedu.com
Bassick HS 1,300/9-12
1181 Fairfield Ave 06605 203-576-7350
Ronald Remey, prin. Fax 576-7736
Central HS 2,300/9-12
1 Lincoln Blvd 06606 203-576-7377
Alejandro Ortiz, prin. Fax 576-7855
Harding HS 1,700/9-12
1734 Central Ave 06610 203-576-7330
Hector Sanchez, prin. Fax 576-7762

Connecticut Technical HS System
Supt. — See Middletown
Bullard-Havens Technical HS Vo/Tech
500 Palisade Ave 06610 203-579-6333
Joseph LaVorgna, dir. Fax 579-6904

Bridgeport Hospital Post-Sec.
267 Grant St 06610 203-384-3464
Bridgeport Hospital School of Nursing Post-Sec.
200 Mill Hill Ave 06610 203-384-3022
Butler Business School Post-Sec.
2710 North Ave 06604 203-333-3601
Housatonic Community College Post-Sec.
900 Lafayette Blvd 06604 203-332-5000
Kolbe Cathedral HS 300/9-12
33 Calhoun Pl 06604 203-335-2554
Jo Anne Jakab, prin. Fax 335-2556
Leon Institute of Hair Design Post-Sec.
111 Wall St 06604 203-333-1465
St. Vincent's College Post-Sec.
2800 Main St 06606 203-576-5235
University of Bridgeport Post-Sec.
126 Park Ave 06604 203-576-4000

Bristol, Hartford, Pop. 61,353
Bristol SD 9,000/PK-12
PO Box 450 06011 860-584-7002
Dr. Michael J. Wasta, supt. Fax 584-7611
www.bristol.k12.ct.us
Bristol Central HS 1,500/9-12
480 Wolcott St 06010 860-584-7732
Dennis Siegmann, prin. Fax 584-7713
Bristol Eastern HS 1,400/9-12
632 King St 06010 860-584-7852
V. Everett Lyons, prin. Fax 584-4886
Chippins Hill MS 1,000/6-8
551 Peacedale St 06010 860-584-3881
Catherine Carbone, prin. Fax 584-4833
Memorial Boulevard MS 500/6-8
70 Memorial Blvd 06010 860-584-7882
Walter Ives, prin. Fax 584-3889
Northeast MS 600/6-8
530 Stevens St 06010 860-584-7839
Rochelle Schwartz, prin. Fax 584-7837

St. Paul HS 300/7-12
1001 Stafford Ave 06010 860-584-0911
Dan Carroll, prin. Fax 585-8815

Broad Brook, Hartford, Pop. 3,585
East Windsor SD
Supt. — See East Windsor
East Windsor MS 500/5-8
38 Main St 06016 860-623-4488
James Slattery, prin. Fax 654-1915

Brookfield, Fairfield
Brookfield SD 3,100/PK-12
PO Box 5194 06804 203-775-7620
John A. Goetz, supt. Fax 740-9008
www.brookfield.k12.ct.us/
Brookfield HS 900/9-12
45 Long Meadow Hill Rd 06804 203-775-7725
Bryan Luizzi, prin. Fax 775-7773

Whisconier MS 1,000/5-8
17 W Whisconier Rd 06804 203-775-7710
Eugenia Slone, prin. Fax 775-7615

Brooklyn, Windham
Brooklyn SD 1,000/PK-8
119 Gorman Rd 06234 860-774-9153
Louise Berry, supt. Fax 774-6938
www.brooklyn.ctschool.net
Brooklyn MS 400/5-8
119 Gorman Rd 06234 860-774-9153
Fax 774-6938

Burlington, Hartford
Regional SD 10 2,700/PK-12
24 Lyon Rd 06013 860-673-2538
Paula Schwartz, supt. Fax 675-4976
www.region10ct.org
Har-Bur MS 700/6-8
26 Lyon Rd 06013 860-673-6163
Kenneth Platz, prin. Fax 673-3481
Mills HS 700/9-12
26 Lyon Rd 06013 860-673-0423
Karissa Niehoff, prin. Fax 673-9128

Canterbury, Windham
Canterbury SD 600/PK-8
45 Westminster Rd 06331 860-546-6950
Sandra Suplicki, supt. Fax 546-6423
Baldwin MS 300/5-8
45 Westminster Rd 06331 860-546-9421
Kathleen Boyhan-Maus, prin. Fax 546-6289

Central Village, Windham
Plainfield SD
Supt. — See Plainfield
Plainfield HS 700/9-12
PO Box 218 06332 860-564-6417
Susan Rourke, prin. Fax 564-2116

Chaplin, Windham
Regional SD 11 300/7-12
304 Parish Hill Rd 06235 860-455-9306
Fax 455-1263
www.parishhill.org/
Parish Hill JSHS 300/7-12
304 Parish Hill Rd 06235 860-455-9584
Dr. Kathryn Walsh, prin. Fax 455-9081

Cheshire, New Haven, Pop. 25,684
Cheshire SD 5,200/PK-12
29 Main St 06410 203-250-2420
Greg Florio, supt. Fax 250-2453
www.cheshire.k12.ct.us/
Cheshire HS 1,600/9-12
525 S Main St 06410 203-250-2511
Judy Gallagher, prin. Fax 250-2563
Dodd MS 800/7-8
100 Park Pl 06410 203-272-3249
Donald Wailonis, prin. Fax 250-7614

Cheshire Academy 400/6-12
10 Main St 06410 203-272-5396
Gerald Larson, hdmstr. Fax 250-7209

Clinton, Middlesex, Pop. 3,439
Clinton SD 2,200/PK-12
137 Glenwood Rd Ste B 06413 860-664-6500
Albert Coviello, supt. Fax 664-6580
www.clintonpublic.org
Eliot MS 500/6-8
69 Fairy Dell Rd 06413 860-664-6503
Linda Tucker, prin. Fax 664-6583
Morgan S 700/9-12
27 Killingworth Tpke 06413 860-664-6504
William Barney, prin. Fax 664-6584

Colchester, New London, Pop. 3,212
Colchester SD 1,900/PK-12
127 Norwich Ave Ste 202 06415 860-537-7260
Karen Loiselle, supt. Fax 537-1252
www.colchesterct.org/
Bacon Academy 900/9-12
611 Norwich Ave 06415 860-537-2378
Jeffry Mathieu, prin. Fax 537-5410
Johnston MS 800/6-8
360 Norwich Ave 06415 860-537-2313
Candace Sullivan, prin. Fax 537-6391

Collinsville, Hartford, Pop. 2,591
Canton SD 1,700/PK-12
4 Market St Ste 100 06019 860-693-7704
Leonard Lanza Ph.D., supt. Fax 693-7706
www.cantonschools.org
Canton HS 500/9-12
76 Simonds Ave 06019 860-693-7707
Gary Gula, prin. Fax 693-7812
Canton MS 300/7-8
76 Simonds Ave 06019 860-693-7712
Joseph Scheideler, prin. Fax 693-7812

Coventry, Tolland, Pop. 10,063
Coventry SD 2,100/K-12
1700 Main St 06238 860-742-7317
Donna Bernard, supt. Fax 742-4567
www.coventrypublicschools.org/
Coventry HS 600/9-12
78 Ripley Hill Rd 06238 860-742-7346
Charles Britton, prin. Fax 742-4591
Hale MS 500/6-8
1776 Main St 06238 860-742-7334
Marie Castle-Good, prin. Fax 742-4565

Cromwell, Middlesex
Cromwell SD 1,500/PK-12
9 Mann Memorial Dr 06416 860-632-4830
Dr. Mark Cohan, supt. Fax 632-4865
www.cromwellschools.org/
Cromwell HS 500/9-12
34 Evergreen Rd 06416 860-632-4841
Barbara Miles, prin. Fax 613-3363
Cromwell MS 500/6-8
6 Mann Memorial Dr 06416 860-632-4853
John Maloney, prin. Fax 632-4863

Holy Apostles College and Seminary Post-Sec.
33 Prospect Hill Rd 06416 860-632-3000

Danbury, Fairfield, Pop. 78,736
Connecticut Technical HS System
Supt. — See Middletown
Abbott Technical HS Vo/Tech
21 Hayestown Ave 06811 203-797-4460
Jerry Salese, dir. Fax 797-4382

Danbury SD 9,500/PK-12
63 Beaver Brook Rd 06810 203-797-4701
Sal Pascavella Ed.D., supt. Fax 830-6560
www.danbury.k12.ct.us
Broadview MS 1,000/6-8
72 Hospital Ave 06810 203-797-4861
Edward Robbs, prin. Fax 790-2856
Danbury HS 2,900/9-12
43 Clapboard Ridge Rd 06811 203-797-4803
Catherine Richard, prin. Fax 797-4730
Rogers Park MS 1,000/6-8
21 Memorial Dr 06810 203-797-4881
Patricia Joaquim, prin. Fax 790-2829

American Academy of Cosmetology Post-Sec.
109 South St 06810 203-744-0900
Danbury Hospital Post-Sec.
24 Hospital Ave 06810 203-797-7210
Hudson Country Montessori S 200/PK-12
44A Shelter Rock Rd 06810 203-744-8088
Mark Meyer, prin. Fax 748-3403
Immaculate HS 400/9-12
73 Southern Blvd 06810 203-744-1510
Richard Stoops Ed.D., prin. Fax 744-1275
Western Connecticut State University Post-Sec.
181 White St 06810 203-837-8200
Wooster S 500/K-12
91 Miry Brook Rd 06810 203-830-3900
George King, hdmstr. Fax 790-7147

Danielson, Windham, Pop. 4,285
Connecticut Technical HS System
Supt. — See Middletown
Ellis Technical HS Vo/Tech
613 Upper Maple St 06239 860-774-8511
Brian Mignault, dir. Fax 779-1563

Killingly SD 3,000/PK-12
PO Box 210 06239 860-779-6600
William Silver, supt. Fax 779-3798
www.killingly.k12.ct.us
Killingly HS 1,000/9-12
79 Westfield Ave 06239 860-779-6620
Mary Christian, prin. Fax 774-0846
Other Schools – See Dayville

Quinebaug Valley Community College Post-Sec.
742 Upper Maple St 06239 860-774-1160

Darien, Fairfield, Pop. 18,130
Darien SD 4,400/PK-12
PO Box 1167 06820 203-656-7412
Donald Fiftal, supt. Fax 656-3052
www.darien.k12.ct.us
Darien HS 900/9-12
80 High School Ln 06820 203-655-3981
Jerome Auclair, prin. Fax 656-3631
Middlesex MS 1,100/6-8
204 Hollow Tree Ridge Rd 06820 203-655-2518
Debi Boccanfuso, prin. Fax 655-1627

Dayville, Windham
Killingly SD
Supt. — See Danielson
Killingly IS 900/5-8
1599 Upper Maple St 06241 860-779-6700
Sheryl Kempain, prin. Fax 779-9639

Deep River, Middlesex, Pop. 2,520
Regional SD 4 900/7-12
PO Box 187 06417 860-526-2417
Kim Caron, supt. Fax 526-5469
www.reg4.k12.ct.us
Valley Regional HS 500/9-12
256 Kelsey Hill Rd 06417 860-526-5328
Donald Gates, prin. Fax 526-8123
Winthrop MS 300/7-8
PO Box 187 06417 860-526-9546
David Russell, prin. Fax 526-3721

Derby, New Haven, Pop. 12,536
Derby SD 1,500/PK-12
PO Box 373 06418 203-736-5027
Janet Robinson, supt. Fax 736-5031
www.derbyps.org/
Derby JSHS 700/7-12
8 Nutmeg Ave 06418 203-736-5032
Michael Novia, prin. Fax 736-5031

Durham, Middlesex, Pop. 2,650
Regional SD 13 2,200/PK-12
135A Pickett Ln 06422 860-349-7200
Susan Viccaro, supt. Fax 349-7203
www.rsd13ct.org/
Coginchaug Regional HS 600/9-12
PO Box 280 06422 860-349-7215
Steven Wysowski, prin. Fax 349-7136
Strong MS 400/7-8
PO Box 435 06422 860-349-7222
Scott Nicol, prin. Fax 349-7225

Lake Grove School at Durham Post-Sec.
459R Wallingford Rd 06422 860-349-3467

East Granby, Hartford
East Granby SD 900/K-12
PO Box 674 06026 860-653-6486
Dr. Christine Mahoney, supt. Fax 413-9075
www.eastgranby.k12.ct.us/
East Granby HS 300/9-12
95 S Main St 06026 860-653-2541
Melissa Bavaro-Grande, prin. Fax 413-9092
East Granby MS 200/6-8
95 S Main St 06026 860-653-2541
Linda Carlson, prin. Fax 413-9092

East Hampton, Middlesex, Pop. 2,167
East Hampton SD 2,100/PK-12
94 Main St 06424 860-365-4000
William Troy, supt. Fax 365-4004
East Hampton HS 500/9-12
50 N Maple St 06424 860-365-4030
Linda Berry, prin. Fax 365-4034
East Hampton MS 500/6-8
19 Childs Rd 06424 860-365-4060
Tracy Barber, prin. Fax 365-4064

East Hartford, Hartford, Pop. 49,400
Capitol Region Education Council RESC
Supt. — See Hartford
Two Rivers Magnet MS 600/6-8
337 E River Dr 06108 860-290-5320
Tom Scarice, prin. Fax 509-3609

East Hartford SD 7,900/PK-12
1110 Main St 06108 860-622-5107
Marion Martinez, supt. Fax 622-5119
www.easthartford.org
CT International Baccalaureate Academy 200/9-12
857 Forbes St 06118 860-622-5560
Art Arpin, prin. Fax 622-5555
East Hartford HS 2,300/9-12
869 Forbes St 06118 860-622-5200
Matt Ryan, prin. Fax 622-5223
East Hartford MS 1,200/7-8
777 Burnside Ave 06108 860-622-5600
Pietro Cerone, prin. Fax 622-5619

Goodwin College Post-Sec.
745 Burnside Ave 06108 860-528-4111
New Testament Baptist Church S 100/PK-12
111 Ash St 06108 860-290-6696
Mark Davis, prin. Fax 290-6698

East Haven, New Haven, Pop. 28,600
East Haven SD 3,900/PK-12
35 Wheelbarrow Ln 06513 203-468-3261
Martin DeFelice, supt. Fax 468-3918
www.east-haven.k12.ct.us/ehsd/
East Haven Academy 200/3-8
200 Tyler St 06512 203-468-3219
Angela Speck, prin. Fax 468-3961
East Haven HS 1,100/9-12
35 Wheelbarrow Ln 06513 203-468-3267
Vanessa Reale, prin. Fax 468-3818
Melillo MS 600/7-8
67 Hudson St 06512 203-468-3227
John Prato, prin. Fax 468-3866

East Lyme, New London
East Lyme SD 3,200/PK-12
PO Box 176 06333 860-739-3966
Paul Smotas, supt. Fax 739-1215
www.eastlymeschools.org
East Lyme HS 1,300/9-12
PO Box 210 06333 860-739-6946
Lawrence Roberts, prin. Fax 739-1241
Other Schools – See Niantic

Easton, Fairfield
Easton SD
Supt. — See Monroe
Keller MS 400/6-8
360 Sport Hill Rd 06612 203-268-8651
Joan Parker, prin. Fax 268-6105

East Windsor, Hartford
East Windsor SD 1,600/PK-12
70 S Main St 06088 860-623-3346
Timothy Howes, supt. Fax 292-6817
www.ewindsor.k12.ct.us/home
East Windsor HS 500/9-12
76 S Main St 06088 860-623-3361
David Chambers, prin. Fax 623-7197
Other Schools – See Broad Brook

Baran Institute of Technology Post-Sec.
PO Box 807 06088 860-627-4300

Ellington, Tolland
Ellington SD 2,400/PK-12
PO Box 179 06029 860-896-2300
Stephen Cullinan, supt. Fax 896-2312
www.ellingtonschools.org
Ellington HS 700/9-12
PO Box 149 06029 860-896-2352
Neil Rinaldi, prin. Fax 896-2366
Ellington MS 400/7-8
46 Middle Butcher Rd 06029 860-896-2339
David Pearson, prin. Fax 896-2351

Enfield, Hartford, Pop. 45,500
Enfield SD 6,600/PK-12
27 Shaker Rd 06082 860-253-6531
John Gallacher, supt. Fax 253-6515
www.enfieldschools.org
Enfield HS 900/9-12
1264 Enfield St 06082 860-253-5540
Thomas Duffy, prin. Fax 253-5555
Fermi HS 1,200/9-12
124 N Maple St 06082 860-763-8800
Paul Newton, prin. Fax 763-8810

Kennedy MS 1,100/7-8
155 Raffia Rd 06082 860-763-8855
Timothy Neville, prin. Fax 763-8888

Asnuntuck Community College Post-Sec.
170 Elm St 06082 860-253-3000
Porter and Chester Institute Post-Sec.
138 Weymouth Rd 06082 860-741-2561

Fairfield, Fairfield, Pop. 54,400
Fairfield SD 9,000/PK-12
PO Box 320189, 203-255-8371
Ann Clark, supt. Fax 255-8245
www.fairfield.k12.ct.us
Fairfield Ludlowe HS 1,000/9-12
785 Unquowa Rd, 203-255-7201
Nancy Larsen, prin. Fax 255-7213
Fairfield Warde HS 1,400/9-12
755 Melville Ave, 203-255-8449
James Coyne, hdmstr. Fax 255-8284
Fairfield Woods MS 600/6-8
1115 Fairfield Woods Rd, 203-255-8334
Lynda Cox, prin. Fax 255-8210
Ludlowe MS 800/6-8
689 Unquowa Rd, 203-255-8345
Glenn Mackno, prin. Fax 255-8214
Tomlinson MS 600/6-8
200 Unquowa Rd, 203-255-8336
Connee Dawson, prin. Fax 255-8211

Fairfield College Prep S 900/9-12
1073 N Benson Rd, 203-254-4000
Dr. Robert A. Perrotta, prin. Fax 254-4108
Fairfield University Post-Sec.
1073 N Benson Rd, 203-254-4000
Notre Dame HS 600/9-12
220 Jefferson St, 203-372-6521
Rev. William Sangiovanni, prin. Fax 374-0387
Sacred Heart University Post-Sec.
5151 Park Ave, 203-371-7999

Falls Village, Litchfield
Regional SD 1 600/9-12
246 Warren Tpke 06031 860-824-0855
Patricia Chamberlain, supt. Fax 824-1271
Housatonic Valley Regional HS 600/9-12
246 Warren Tpke 06031 860-824-5123
Dr. Gretchen Foster-Mosca, prin. Fax 824-5419

Farmington, Hartford, Pop. 2,500
Farmington SD 4,400/PK-12
1 Montieth Dr 06032 860-673-8268
Robert Villanova, supt. Fax 673-8224
www.fpsct.org
Farmington HS 1,400/9-12
10 Montieth Dr 06032 860-673-2514
Kevin Ryan, prin. Fax 673-7284
Robbins MS 700/7-8
20 Wolf Pit Rd 06032 860-677-2683
Kelly Lyman, prin. Fax 676-0697

Miss Porter's S 300/9-12
60 Main St 06032 860-409-3500
M. Burch Tracy Ford, hdmstr. Fax 409-3525
Tunxis Community College Post-Sec.
271 Scott Swamp Rd 06032 860-677-7701
University of Connecticut Health Center Post-Sec.
263 Farmington Ave 06032 860-679-2000

Gales Ferry, New London
Ledyard SD
Supt. — See Ledyard
Ledyard MS 500/7-8
1860 Route 12 06335 860-464-0200
Louis Gabordi, prin. Fax 464-2155

Glastonbury, Hartford, Pop. 27,901
Glastonbury SD 6,400/PK-12
PO Box 191 06033 860-652-7961
Alan Bookman, supt. Fax 652-7979
www.glastonburyus.org
Glastonbury HS 1,900/9-12
330 Hubbard St 06033 860-652-7200
Matthew Dunbar, prin. Fax 652-7267
Smith MS 1,000/7-8
216 Addison Rd 06033 860-652-7040
Donna Schilke, prin. Fax 652-4450

Granby, Hartford
Granby SD 2,000/K-12
15B N Granby Rd 06035 860-844-5250
Gwen Van Dorp, supt. Fax 844-6081
www.granby.k12.ct.us
Granby Memorial HS 700/9-12
315 Salmon Brook St 06035 860-844-3014
Alan Addley, prin. Fax 844-3026
Granby Memorial MS 400/7-8
321 Salmon Brook St 06035 860-844-3029
Shellie Pierce, prin. Fax 844-3039

Greens Farms, Fairfield

Greens Farms Academy 600/K-12
PO Box 998, 203-256-0717
Janet Hartwell, hdmstr. Fax 256-7501

Greenwich, Fairfield, Pop. 57,100
Greenwich SD 9,000/K-12
290 Greenwich Ave 06830 203-625-7400
Larry Leverett Ed.D., supt. Fax 618-9379
www.greenwichschools.org
Central MS 700/6-8
9 Indian Rock Ln 06830 203-661-8500
Carol Walsh, prin. Fax 661-2576
Greenwich HS 2,700/9-12
10 Hillside Rd 06830 203-625-8000
Alan Capasso, prin. Fax 863-8888

Western MS 600/6-8
1 Western Junior Hwy 06830 203-531-5700
Stacey Gross, prin. Fax 531-5220
Other Schools – See Riverside

Brunswick S 800/PK-12
100 Maher Ave 06830 203-625-5800
Thomas Philip, hdmstr. Fax 625-5889
Convent of Sacred Heart S 700/PK-12
1177 King St 06831 203-531-6500
Sr. Joan Magnetti, hdmstr. Fax 531-5206
Greenwich Academy 800/PK-12
200 N Maple Ave 06830 203-625-8900
Molly King, hdmstr. Fax 869-6580

Griswold, See Jewett City
Griswold SD 2,200/PK-12
267 Slater Ave 06351 860-376-7600
Elizabeth Osga, supt. Fax 376-7604
griswold.k12.ct.us
Griswold HS 700/9-12
267 Slater Ave 06351 860-376-7640
Mark Frizzell, prin. Fax 376-7684
Griswold MS 500/6-8
211 Slater Ave 06351 860-376-7630
Preston Shaw, prin. Fax 376-7631

Groton, New London, Pop. 9,493
Connecticut Technical HS System
Supt. — See Middletown
Grasso Technical HS Vo/Tech
189 Fort Hill Rd 06340 860-448-0220
Kerry Bell, dir. Fax 446-9895

Groton SD
Supt. — See Mystic
Fitch HS 1,500/9-12
101 Groton Long Point Rd 06340 860-449-7200
Robert Bacewicz, prin. Fax 449-7255
Fitch MS 500/6-8
61 Fort Hill Rd 06340 860-449-5620
Robert Pendolphi, prin. Fax 449-5623
West Side MS 300/6-8
250 Brandegee Ave 06340 860-449-5630
K. Michael Talbot, prin. Fax 449-5628

Connecticut Center for Massage Therapy Post-Sec.
1154 Poquonnock Rd 06340 877-295-2268
University of Connecticut Post-Sec.
1084 Shennecossett Rd 06340 860-486-4444

Guilford, New Haven, Pop. 19,848
Guilford SD 3,800/PK-12
PO Box 367 06437 203-453-8200
Dr. Thomas Forcella, supt. Fax 453-8211
www.guilford.k12.ct.us/
Adams MS 600/7-8
233 Church St 06437 203-453-2755
Catherine Walker, prin. Fax 453-8446
Guilford HS 1,100/9-12
605 New England Rd 06437 203-453-2741
Bruce Hall, prin. Fax 453-6768

Hamden, New Haven, Pop. 52,600
Connecticut Technical HS System
Supt. — See Middletown
Whitney Technical HS Vo/Tech
71 Jones Rd 06514 203-397-4031
E. Paulett Moore, dir. Fax 397-4129

Hamden SD 6,200/K-12
60 Putnam Ave 06517 203-407-2000
Alida Begina Ed.D., supt. Fax 407-2001
www.hamden.org
Hamden HS 2,200/9-12
2040 Dixwell Ave 06514 203-407-2040
Gary Highsmith, prin. Fax 407-2041
Hamden MS 900/7-8
2623 Dixwell Ave 06518 203-407-3140
Frank Pepe, prin. Fax 407-3141

New Haven SD
Supt. — See New Haven
Fair Haven MS 800/5-8
164 Grand Ave 06517 203-691-2600
Kevin Miller, prin. Fax 691-2697
Hyde Leadership Academy 200/9-12
306 Circular Ave 06514 203-946-8121
John Russell, prin. Fax 946-6161

Eli Whitney Regional Voc. Tech. School Post-Sec.
71 Jones Rd 06514 203-397-4037
Goodwin Institute Post-Sec.
1315 Dixwell Ave 06514 800-889-3282
Hamden Hall Country Day S 600/PK-12
1108 Whitney Ave 06517 203-752-2600
Robert Izzo, hdmstr. Fax 752-2651
New England Technical Institute Post-Sec.
109 Sanford St 06514 203-287-7300
Paier College of Art Post-Sec.
20 Gorham Ave 06514 203-287-3032
Quinnipiac University Post-Sec.
275 Mount Carmel Ave 06518 203-582-8200
Sacred Heart Academy 500/9-12
265 Benham St 06514 203-288-2309
Sr. Ritamary Schulz, prin. Fax 230-9680
St. Martin dePorres Academy 5-8
43 Jones Rd 06514 203-389-1777
Mary Surowiecki, prin. Fax 387-0777
Sawyer School Post-Sec.
1125 Dixwell Ave 06514 203-865-2900
Stone Academy Post-Sec.
1315 Dixwell Ave 06514 203-288-7474
West Woods Christian Academy 200/K-12
2105 State St 06517 203-562-9922
William Kane, admin. Fax 786-4730

Hartford, Hartford, Pop. 124,397
Capitol Region Education Council RESC 2,400/
111 Charter Oak Ave 06106 860-524-4063
Dr. Bruce Douglas, dir. Fax 548-9924
www.crec.org
Greater Hartford Academy of Math/Science 9-12
15 Vernon St 06106 860-757-6305
Howard Thiery, prin. Fax 757-6382
Greater Hartford Academy of the Arts 9-12
15 Vernon St 06106 860-757-6300
Herbert Sheppard, prin.
Metropolitan Learning Center Magnet 700/6-12
1551 Blue Hills Ave, 860-242-0732
Anne McKernan, prin. Fax 242-7836
Other Schools – See East Hartford, Manchester

Connecticut Technical HS System
Supt. — See Middletown
Prince Technical HS Vo/Tech
401 Flatbush Ave 06106 860-951-7112
William Chaffin, dir. Fax 951-1529

Hartford SD 22,100/PK-12
960 Main St 06103 860-695-8401
Steven Adamowski, supt. Fax 722-8502
www.hartfordschools.org
Belizzi MS 700/6-8
215 South St 06114 860-695-2400
Ana Ortiz, prin. Fax 956-9993
Bulkeley HS 1,600/9-12
300 Wethersfield Ave 06114 860-695-1000
Miriam Taylor, prin. Fax 247-3491
Capital Preparatory Magnet S 6-12
960 Main St 06103 860-695-9800
Steven Perry, prin. Fax 722-8520
Fox MS 800/7-8
305 Greenfield St 06112 860-695-6560
Andrew Serrao, prin. Fax 722-8813
Greater Hartford Magnet S 400/6-12
85 Woodland St 06105 860-695-9100
Timothy Sullivan, prin. Fax 722-6449
Hartford HS 1,400/9-12
55 Forest St 06105 860-695-1300
Zandralyn Gordon, prin. Fax 722-8779
Hartford Magnet MS 600/6-8
53 Vernon St 06106 860-757-6200
Cecilia Green, prin. Fax 947-9935
Quirk MS 900/7-8
85 Edwards St 06120 860-695-2140
Amador Mojica, prin. Fax 527-0346
Sports & Medical Science Academy 400/9-12
275 Asylum St 06103 860-695-6900
Eduardo Genao, prin. Fax 722-8017
University HS 100/9-12
30 Elizabeth St 06105 860-695-9020
Elizabeth Colli, prin. Fax 722-6408
Weaver HS 1,200/9-12
415 Granby St 06112 860-695-1640
Paul Stringer, prin. Fax 242-6241
Other Schools – See Windsor

Capital Community College Post-Sec.
950 Main St 06103 860-906-5000
Connecticut Childrens Medical Center Post-Sec.
282 Washington St 06106 860-545-8514
Connecticut Culinary Institute Post-Sec.
85 Sigourney St 06105 860-677-7869
Connecticut Institute for the Blind Post-Sec.
120 Holcomb St 06112
Hartford Area SDA S 100/K-10
474 Woodland St 06112 860-724-5777
Dr. Daniel Amfo, prin. Fax 548-9252
Hartford College for Women Post-Sec.
1265 Asylum Ave 06105 860-236-1215
Hartford Conservatory Post-Sec.
834 Asylum Ave 06105 860-246-2588
Hartford Hospital Post-Sec.
PO Box 5037 06102 860-545-2100
Hartford Seminary Post-Sec.
77 Sherman St 06105 860-509-9500
Institute of Living Schools Post-Sec.
400 Washington St 06106
Prince Regional Vocational Tech School Post-Sec.
500 Brookfield St 06106 860-246-8594
Rensselaer at Hartford Post-Sec.
275 Windsor St 06120 860-548-2400
Sawyer School Post-Sec.
141 Washington St 06106 860-568-1554
Trinity College Post-Sec.
300 Summit St 06106 860-297-2000
Watkinson S 300/6-12
180 Bloomfield Ave 06105 860-236-5618
John Bracker, hdmstr. Fax 233-8295

Hebron, Tolland
Regional SD 8 1,600/7-12
PO Box 1438 06248 860-228-2115
Robert Siminski Ed.D., supt. Fax 228-4346
www.reg8.k12.ct.us/
RHAM HS 1,000/9-12
85 Wall St 06248 860-228-9474
Scott Leslie, prin. Fax 228-9209
RHAM MS 500/7-8
25 RHAM Rd 06248 860-228-9423
Linda Crossman, prin. Fax 228-2471

Allen Inst. Ctr. for Innovative Learning Post-Sec.
PO Box 100 06248 866-666-6910

Higganum, Middlesex, Pop. 1,692
Regional SD 17 2,400/PK-12
PO Box 568 06441 860-345-4534
Gary Mala, supt. Fax 345-2817
rsd17.org
Haddam-Killingworth HS 600/9-12
PO Box 569 06441 860-345-8541
Charles Macunas, prin. Fax 345-8252

Haddam-Killingworth MS — 400/7-8
PO Box 540 06441 — 860-345-8567
Miriam Wagner, prin. — Fax 345-7610

Kensington, Hartford, Pop. 8,306

Mooreland Hill S — 50/5-8
166 Lincoln St 06037 — 860-223-6428
Michael Dooman, hdmstr. — Fax 223-3318

Kent, Litchfield

Kent S — 500/9-12
PO Box 2006 06757 — 860-927-6000
Rev. Richardson Schel, hdmstr. — Fax 927-6014
Marvelwood S — 100/9-12
PO Box 3001 06757 — 860-927-0047
Scott Pottbecker, hdmstr. — Fax 927-5325

Lakeville, Litchfield

Hotchkiss S — 600/9-12
PO Box 800 06039 — 860-435-2591
Robert Mattoon, hdmstr. — Fax 435-8056

Lebanon, New London
Lebanon SD — 1,500/PK-12
891 Exeter Rd 06249 — 860-642-3560
Robert McGray, supt. — Fax 642-4589
www.lebanonct.org/default.htm
Lebanon MS — 400/5-8
891 Exeter Rd 06249 — 860-642-4702
Robert Laskarzweski, prin. — Fax 642-3534
Lyman Memorial HS — 600/9-12
917 Exeter Rd 06249 — 860-642-7567
Stephen Salisbury, prin. — Fax 642-3521

Ledyard, New London
Ledyard SD — 3,000/PK-12
4 Blonder Park Rd 06339 — 860-464-9255
Michael H. Graner, supt. — Fax 464-8589
www.ledyardschools.org
Ledyard HS — 1,100/9-12
24 Gallup Hill Rd 06339 — 860-464-9600
Marcia Griffin, prin. — Fax 464-1990
Other Schools – See Gales Ferry

Litchfield, Litchfield, Pop. 1,340
Litchfield SD — 1,400/PK-12
PO Box 110 06759 — 860-567-7500
Dr. Dominick Vita, supt. — Fax 567-7508
www.litchfieldschools.org
Litchfield JSHS — 700/7-12
PO Box 110 06759 — 860-567-7530
Dr. Timothy Breslin, prin. — Fax 567-7538

Regional SD 6 — 1,100/K-12
98 Wamogo Rd 06759 — 860-567-7400
Anthony J. Bivona, supt. — Fax 567-6652
rsd6.org
Wamogo Regional JSHS — 500/7-12
98 Wamogo Rd 06759 — 860-567-7410
Craig Drezek, prin. — Fax 567-6651

Connecticut Junior Republic — Post-Sec.
PO Box 161 06759
Forman S — 200/9-12
PO Box 80 06759 — 860-567-8712
Mark Perkins, hdmstr. — Fax 567-8317

Madison, New Haven, Pop. 15,485
Madison SD — 3,800/K-12
PO Box 71 06443 — 203-245-6300
Dr. H. Kaye Griffin, supt. — Fax 245-6336
www.madison.k12.ct.us
Hand HS — 1,100/9-12
286 Green Hill Rd 06443 — 203-245-6350
Barbara Britton, prin. — Fax 245-6356
Polson MS — 600/7-8
302 Green Hill Rd 06443 — 203-245-6480
Frank Henderson, prin. — Fax 245-6494

Manchester, Hartford, Pop. 52,500
Capitol Region Education Council RESC
Supt. — See Hartford
Great Path Academy — 100/11-12
PO Box 1046 06045 — 860-512-3561
Thomas Danehy, prin. — Fax 512-6101

Connecticut Technical HS System
Supt. — See Middletown
Cheney Technical HS — Vo/Tech
791 Middle Tpke W 06040 — 860-649-5396
Bruce Sievers, dir. — Fax 649-5263

Manchester SD — 6,600/PK-12
45 N School St, — 860-647-3441
Kathleen Ouellette Ed.D., supt. — Fax 647-5042
boe.townofmanchester.org/
Illing MS — 800/6-8
229 Middle Tpke E 06040 — 860-647-3400
Troy Monroe, prin. — Fax 647-5008
Manchester HS — 2,300/9-12
134 Middle Tpke E 06040 — 860-647-3530
Donald Sierakowski, prin. — Fax 646-3727

Cornerstone Christian S — 200/K-12
236 Main St 06040 — 860-643-0792
Edward Campolongo, hdmstr. — Fax 647-9291
East Catholic HS — 700/9-12
115 New State Rd, — 860-649-5336
Christian Cashman, prin. — Fax 649-7191
Manchester Community College — Post-Sec.
PO Box 1046 06045 — 860-647-6000

Meriden, New Haven, Pop. 59,653
Area Coop. Educational Services RESC
Supt. — See North Haven
Edison MS — 800/6-8
1355 N Broad St 06450 — 203-639-8403
Karen Habegger, prin. — Fax 639-8323

Connecticut Technical HS System
Supt. — See Middletown
Wilcox Technical HS — Vo/Tech
298 Oregon Rd 06451 — 203-238-6260
Richard Cavallaro, dir. — Fax 238-6602

Meriden SD — 8,900/PK-12
22 Liberty St 06450 — 203-630-4171
Mary N. Cortright, supt. — Fax 630-0110
www.meriden.k12.ct.us
Lincoln MS — 700/6-8
164 Centennial Ave 06451 — 203-238-2381
John Lineen, prin. — Fax 238-7258
Maloney HS — 1,400/9-12
121 Gravel St 06450 — 203-238-2334
Robert Angeli, prin. — Fax 630-7011
Platt HS — 1,100/9-12
220 Coe Ave 06451 — 203-235-7963
Timothy Gaffney, prin. — Fax 630-4011
Washington MS — 1,000/6-8
1225 N Broad St 06450 — 203-235-6606
Jean Privitera, prin. — Fax 235-6040

Brio Academy of Cosmetology — Post-Sec.
1231 E Main St 06450 — 203-237-6683

Middlebury, New Haven, Pop. 4,100
Regional SD 15 — 4,500/PK-12
PO Box 395 06762 — 203-758-8258
Dr. Frank Sippy, supt. — Fax 758-1908
www.region15.org
Memorial MS — 600/6-8
PO Box 903 06762 — 203-758-2496
John Sieller, prin. — Fax 758-9594
Other Schools – See Southbury

Westover S — 200/9-12
PO Box 847 06762 — 203-758-2423
Ann Pollina, hdmstr. — Fax 577-4585

Middletown, Middlesex, Pop. 47,438
Connecticut Technical HS System
25 Industrial Park Rd 06457 — 860-807-2200
Abigail Hughes, supt. — Fax 807-2156
www.cttech.org
Vinal Technical HS — Vo/Tech
60 Daniels St 06457 — 860-344-7100
Sheila Fredson, dir. — Fax 344-2162
Other Schools – See Ansonia, Bridgeport, Danbury, Danielson, Groton, Hamden, Hartford, Manchester, Meriden, Milford, New Britain, Norwich, Stamford, Torrington, Waterbury, Willimantic

Middletown SD — 5,200/PK-12
311 Hunting Hill Ave 06457 — 860-638-1401
Michael J. Frechette Ph.D., supt. — Fax 638-1495
www.middletownschools.org
Middletown HS — 1,300/9-12
370 Hunting Hill Ave 06457 — 860-704-4500
Robert Fontaine, prin. — Fax 347-2044
Wilson MS — 700/7-8
1 Wilderman Way 06457 — 860-347-8594
Eugene Nocera, prin. — Fax 347-2158

Mercy HS — 700/9-12
1740 Randolph Rd 06457 — 860-346-6659
Sr. Mary McCarthy, prin. — Fax 344-9887
Middlesex Community College — Post-Sec.
100 Training Hill Rd 06457 — 860-343-5800
Wesleyan University 06459 — Post-Sec.
860-685-2000
Xavier HS — 800/9-12
181 Randolph Rd 06457 — 860-346-7735
Br. William Ciganek, prin. — Fax 346-6859

Milford, New Haven, Pop. 51,734
Connecticut Technical HS System
Supt. — See Middletown
Platt Technical HS — Vo/Tech
600 Orange Ave, — 203-783-5300
Gene LaPorta, dir. — Fax 783-3970

Milford SD — 7,500/PK-12
70 W River St 06460 — 203-783-3402
Gregory A. Firn, supt. — Fax 783-3475
www.milforded.org
East Shore MS — 600/6-8
240 Chapel St 06460 — 203-783-3559
Catherine Williams, prin. — Fax 301-5060
Foran HS — 1,000/9-12
80 Foran Rd 06460 — 203-783-3502
Michael Cummings, prin. — Fax 783-3635
Harborside MS — 700/6-8
175 High St 06460 — 203-783-3523
Raymond Vitali, prin. — Fax 783-3687
Law HS — 1,000/9-12
20 Lansdale Ave 06460 — 203-783-3574
Janet Garagliano, prin. — Fax 783-3586
West Shore MS — 500/6-8
50 Kay Ave 06460 — 203-783-3553
John Barile, prin. — Fax 783-4827

Academy of Our Lady of Mercy — 500/9-12
200 High St 06460 — 203-877-2786
Ann Pratson, prin. — Fax 876-9760

Monroe, Fairfield
Easton SD — 1,000/PK-8
605 Main St 06468 — 203-261-2513
Dr. Allen Fossbender, supt. — Fax 261-4549
www.er9.org
Other Schools – See Easton

Monroe SD — 4,300/PK-12
375 Monroe Tpke 06468 — 203-452-2860
Alan Beitman, supt. — Fax 452-5818
www.monroeps.org
Jockey Hollow S — 700/7-8
365 Fan Hill Rd 06468 — 203-452-2281
John Ceccolini, prin. — Fax 452-2263
Masuk HS — 1,400/9-12
1014 Monroe Tpke 06468 — 203-452-5823
John Battista, prin. — Fax 452-5835

Redding SD — 1,300/K-8
605 Main St 06468 — 203-261-2513
Dr. Allen Fossbender, supt. — Fax 261-4549
www.er9.org
Other Schools – See West Redding

Regional SD 9 — 1,000/9-12
605 Main St 06468 — 203-261-2513
Allen Fossbender, supt. — Fax 261-4549
www.er9.org
Other Schools – See Redding

Moodus, Middlesex, Pop. 1,170
East Haddam SD — 1,400/PK-12
PO Box 401 06469 — 860-873-5090
Steven Durham, supt. — Fax 873-5092
www.easthaddamschools.org
Hale-Ray HS — 300/9-12
PO Box 404 06469 — 860-873-5065
Linda Dadona, prin. — Fax 873-5074
Hale-Ray MS — 500/5-8
PO Box 363 06469 — 860-873-5081
Judy Deleeuw, prin. — Fax 873-5086

Mystic, New London, Pop. 2,618
Groton SD — 5,400/PK-12
1300 Flanders Rd 06355 — 860-572-2100
James Mitchell Ph.D., supt. — Fax 572-2107
www.groton.k12.ct.us
Cutler MS — 500/6-8
160 Fishtown Rd 06355 — 860-572-5830
Monson Lane, prin. — Fax 572-5834
Other Schools – See Groton

Stonington SD
Supt. — See Old Mystic
Mystic MS — 500/5-8
204 Mistuxet Ave 06355 — 860-536-9613
Susan Dumas, prin. — Fax 536-4508

Westlawn Institute of Marine Technology — Post-Sec.
PO Box 6000 06355 — 860-572-7900

Naugatuck, New Haven, Pop. 31,864
Naugatuck SD — 5,200/PK-12
380 Church St 06770 — 203-720-5265
John Tindall-Gibson Ph.D., supt. — Fax 720-5272
www.naugy.net
City Hill MS — 600/7-8
441 City Hill St 06770 — 203-720-5246
Francis Serratore, prin. — Fax 720-5256
Hillside MS — 300/7-8
51 Hillside Ave 06770 — 203-720-5260
Brian Sullivan, prin. — Fax 720-5209
Naugatuck HS — 1,600/9-12
543 Rubber Ave 06770 — 203-720-5400
Lori Ferreira, prin. — Fax 720-5444

New Britain, Hartford, Pop. 71,254
Connecticut Technical HS System
Supt. — See Middletown
Goodwin Regional Technical HS — Vo/Tech
735 Slater Rd 06053 — 860-827-7736
Stephen Anderson, dir. — Fax 827-7862

New Britain SD — 10,900/PK-12
PO Box 1960 06050 — 860-827-2204
Dr. Doris Kurtz, supt. — Fax 612-1533
www.new-britain.k12.ct.us
HALS Academy — 6-8
370 Osgood Ave 06053 — 860-826-1866
Elaine Zottola, prin. — Fax 826-1867
New Britain HS — 3,200/9-12
110 Mill St 06051 — 860-225-6300
Mike Foran, prin. — Fax 225-6350
Pulaski MS — 900/6-8
757 Farmington Ave 06053 — 860-225-7665
Vonetta Romeo-Rivers, prin. — Fax 233-3840
Roosevelt MS — 700/6-8
40 Goodwin St 06051 — 860-612-3334
Brenda Lewis-Collins, prin. — Fax 826-1162
Slade MS — 900/6-8
183 Steele St 06052 — 860-225-6395
Mark Fernandes, prin. — Fax 826-7894

Central Connecticut State University — Post-Sec.
1615 Stanley St 06053 — 860-832-3200
Charter Oak State College — Post-Sec.
55 Paul Manafort Dr 06053 — 860-832-3800
New England Technical Institute — Post-Sec.
200 John Downey Dr 06051 — 860-225-8641

New Canaan, Fairfield, Pop. 17,864
New Canaan SD — 4,100/PK-12
39 Locust Ave 06840 — 203-594-4000
Dr. David E. Abbey, supt. — Fax 594-4035
www.newcanaan.k12.ct.us
New Canaan HS — 1,100/9-12
11 Farm Rd 06840 — 203-594-4600
Tony Pavia, prin. — Fax 594-4619
Saxe MS — 1,300/5-8
468 South Ave 06840 — 203-594-4500
Greg Macedo, prin. — Fax 594-4565

St. Luke's S — 500/5-12
PO Box 1148 06840 — 203-966-5612
Mark Davis, hdmstr. — Fax 972-3450

New Fairfield, Fairfield, Pop. 12,911
New Fairfield SD 3,100/PK-12
3 Brush Hill Rd 06812 203-312-5770
Joseph Castagnola, supt. Fax 312-5609
www.newfairfieldschools.org
New Fairfield HS 900/9-12
54 Gillotti Rd 06812 203-312-5805
Alicia Roy, prin. Fax 312-5803
New Fairfield MS 800/6-8
56 Gillotti Rd 06812 203-312-5886
Diane Hartman-Chesley, prin. Fax 312-5887

New Haven, New Haven, Pop. 124,791
Area Coop. Educational Services RESC
Supt. — See North Haven
Educational Center for the Arts 9-12
55 Audubon St 06510 203-777-5451
Leo Lavallee, prin. Fax 782-3596

New Haven SD 18,100/PK-12
54 Meadow St 06519 203-946-8888
Dr. Reginald Mayo, supt. Fax 946-7300
www.nhps.net
Cooperative Arts & Humanities HS 400/9-12
444 Orange St 06511 203-946-5923
Dr. Dolores Garcia-Blocker, prin. Fax 946-5926
Cross HS 1,700/9-12
181 Mitchell Dr 06511 203-946-8728
Robert Canelli, prin. Fax 946-6932
Cross HS Annex 9-12
45 Nash St 06511 203-946-8635
Fax 946-6487
Hillhouse HS 1,300/9-12
480 Sherman Pkwy 06511 203-946-8484
Lonnie Garris, prin. Fax 946-8487
Hill Regional Career HS Vo/Tech
140 Legion Ave 06519 203-946-5845
Rose Coggins, prin. Fax 946-5949
Hooker MS 200/5-8
804 State St 06511 203-946-6610
Fax 946-6376
Jepson Magnet MS 200/5-8
460 Lexington Ave 06513 203-946-2992
Peggy Pelley, prin. Fax 946-8606
Ross Arts MS 500/5-8
150 Kimberly Ave 06519 203-946-8974
Peggy Moore, prin. Fax 946-5824
Sheridan Academy for Excellence 400/5-8
191 Fountain St 06515 203-946-8828
Fax 946-5661
Troup Magnet Academy of Science 500/5-8
259 Edgewood Ave 06511 203-946-8854
Richard Kaliszewski, prin. Fax 946-7276
Adult & Continuing Education Center Adult
580 Ella T Grasso Blvd 06519 203-946-5884
Alicia Caraballo, prin. Fax 946-6384
Other Schools – See Hamden

Albertus Magnus College Post-Sec.
700 Prospect St 06511 203-773-8550
Berkeley Divinity School Post-Sec.
363 Saint Ronan St 06511 203-764-9300
Gateway Community College Post-Sec.
60 Sargent Dr 06511 203-285-2000
Hopkins S 700/7-12
986 Forest Rd 06515 203-397-1001
Barbara Masters Riley, hdmstr. Fax 389-2249
Southern Connecticut State University Post-Sec.
501 Crescent St 06515 203-392-5200
Yale-New Haven Hospital Post-Sec.
20 York St 06504 203-785-5074
Yale University Post-Sec.
38 Hillhouse Ave 06511 203-432-4771
Yeshiva of New Haven 50/9-12
765 Elm St 06511 203-777-7199
Rabbi Daniel Greer, prin. Fax 777-7198

Newington, Hartford, Pop. 29,300
Newington SD 4,600/PK-12
131 Cedar St 06111 860-665-8610
Ernest Perlini, supt. Fax 665-8616
www.newington-schools.org
Kellogg MS 700/5-8
155 Harding Ave 06111 860-666-5418
Jason Lambert, prin. Fax 667-5925
Newington HS 1,500/9-12
605 Willard Ave 06111 860-666-5611
William Collins, prin. Fax 666-8224
Wallace MS 700/5-8
71 Halleran Dr 06111 860-667-5888
David Milardo, prin. Fax 667-5893

Connecticut Center for Massage Therapy Post-Sec.
75 Kitts Ln 06111 860-667-1886
Hanger Orthopedic Group Post-Sec.
181 Patricia M Genova Dr 06111 860-667-5304

New London, New London, Pop. 26,174
Learn RESC
Supt. — See Old Lyme
Regional Multicultural Magnet S 500/K-12
1 Bulkeley Pl 06320 860-437-7775
Sally Myers, prin. Fax 437-1475

New London SD 2,700/PK-12
134 Williams St 06320 860-447-6000
Christopher Clouet, supt. Fax 447-6016
www.newlondon.org
Jackson MS 700/6-8
36 Waller St 06320 860-437-6480
Jaye Wilson, prin. Fax 437-6494
New London HS 700/9-12
490 Jefferson Ave 06320 860-437-6400
Daniel Sullivan, prin. Fax 271-4036
Science & Technology Magnet HS 9-12
490 Jefferson Ave 06320 860-447-6000
Louis Allen, dir.

New London Adult Education Adult
3 Shaws Cv 06320 860-437-2385
Daniel Gaynor, dir. Fax 437-6460

Connecticut College Post-Sec.
270 Mohegan Ave 06320 860-447-1911
Mitchell College Post-Sec.
437 Pequot Ave 06320 860-701-5000
Ridley-Lowell Business & Technical Inst. Post-Sec.
PO Box 652 06320 860-443-7441
United States Coast Guard Academy Post-Sec.
15 Mohegan Ave 06320 800-883-8724
Williams S 300/7-12
182 Mohegan Ave 06320 860-443-5333
Charlotte Rea, prin. Fax 439-2796

New Milford, Litchfield, Pop. 5,775
New Milford SD 5,200/PK-12
50 East St 06776 860-355-8406
JeanAnn Paddyfote, supt. Fax 210-4132
www.new-milford.k12.ct.us/
New Milford HS 1,600/9-12
388 Danbury Rd 06776 860-350-6647
Greg Shugrue, prin. Fax 210-2256
Schaghticoke MS 800/7-8
23 Hipp Rd 06776 860-354-2204
Dana Ford, prin. Fax 210-2217

Canterbury HS 400/9-12
PO Box 5000 06776 860-210-3800
Thomas Sheehy, hdmstr. Fax 350-4425
Faith Academy 200/PK-12
600 Danbury Rd Ste 2 06776 860-354-7767
Josephine DuBois, prin. Fax 210-3685

Newtown, Fairfield, Pop. 1,835
Newtown SD 5,500/PK-12
31 Pecks Ln 06470 203-426-7621
Evan Pitkoff Ed.D., supt. Fax 270-6199
www.newtown.k12.ct.us
Newtown MS 900/7-8
11 Queen St 06470 203-426-7642
Diane Sherlock, prin. Fax 270-6102
Other Schools – See Sandy Hook

Niantic, New London, Pop. 3,048
East Lyme SD
Supt. — See East Lyme
East Lyme MS 1,000/5-8
31 Society Rd 06357 860-739-4491
Paul Freeman, prin. Fax 739-1219

North Branford, New Haven, Pop. 12,996
North Branford SD
Supt. — See Northford
North Branford HS 700/9-12
49 Caputo Rd 06471 203-484-1465
Michele Saulis, prin. Fax 484-1233
North Branford IS 600/6-8
654 Foxon Rd 06471 203-484-1500
Alan Davis, prin. Fax 484-1505

Northford, New Haven, Pop. 3,200
North Branford SD 2,500/PK-12
PO Box 129 06472 203-484-1440
Dr. Robert Wolfe, supt. Fax 484-1445
www.northbranfordschools.org
Other Schools – See North Branford

North Grosvenordale, Windham, Pop. 1,705
Thompson SD 1,500/PK-12
785 Riverside Dr 06255 860-923-9581
Michael Jolin Ed.D., supt. Fax 923-9638
www.thompson.ctschool.net
Thompson MS 500/5-8
785 Riverside Dr 06255 860-923-9380
Ron Springer, prin. Fax 923-9638
Tourtellotte Memorial HS 400/9-12
785 Riverside Dr 06255 860-923-9303
Stephen Mitchell, prin. Fax 923-3752

North Haven, New Haven, Pop. 22,249
Area Coop. Educational Services RESC 2,000/
350 State St 06473 203-498-6800
Craig Edmondson, dir. Fax 498-6890
www.aces.k12.ct.us
Other Schools – See Meriden, New Haven

North Haven SD 3,800/PK-12
5 Linsley St 06473 203-239-2581
Sara-Jane R. Querfeld, supt. Fax 234-9811
www.north-haven.k12.ct.us/
North Haven HS 1,000/9-12
221 Elm St 06473 203-239-1641
Patricia Brozek, prin. Fax 234-2602
North Haven MS 1,000/6-8
55 Bailey Rd 06473 203-239-1683
Louis Preziosi, prin. Fax 234-2846

Gal Mar Academy of Hairdressing Post-Sec.
97 Washington Ave Ste 8 06473 203-281-4477

North Stonington, New London
North Stonington SD 800/PK-12
297 Norwich Westerly Rd 06359 860-535-2800
Natalie Pukas, supt. Fax 535-1470
www.northstonington.k12.ct.us
Wheeler HS 300/9-12
298 Norwich Westerly Rd 06359 860-535-0377
Stephen Bickford, prin. Fax 535-2536
Wheeler MS 200/6-8
298 Norwich Westerly Rd 06359 860-535-0377
Stephen Bickford, prin. Fax 535-2536

North Stonington Christian Academy 200/PK-12
12 Stillman Rd 06359 860-599-5071
Pamela Wilkinson, dir. Fax 599-2815

Norwalk, Fairfield, Pop. 84,437
Norwalk SD 11,000/PK-12
PO Box 6001 06852 203-854-4000
Dr. Salvatore Corda, supt. Fax 838-3299
www.norwalk.k12.ct.us
Center for Global Studies 9-12
300 Highland Ave 06854 203-852-9488
Roslynne McCarthy, dir. Fax 854-0832
Hale MS 600/6-8
176 Strawberry Hill Ave 06851 203-899-2910
Robert McCain, prin. Fax 899-2914
McMahon HS 1,400/9-12
300 Highland Ave 06854 203-852-9488
Suzanne Koroshetz, prin. Fax 899-2814
Norwalk HS 1,700/9-12
23 Calvin Murphy Dr 06851 203-838-4481
Leonard Mecca, prin. Fax 899-2815
Ponus Ridge MS 700/6-8
21 Hunters Ln 06850 203-847-3557
Linda Sumpter, prin. Fax 899-2924
Roton MS 500/6-8
201 Highland Ave 06853 203-899-2930
Joseph Vellucci, prin. Fax 899-2934
West Rocks MS 800/6-8
81 W Rocks Rd 06851 203-899-2970
Lynne Moore, prin. Fax 899-2974

Gibbs College Post-Sec.
10 Norden Pl 06855 800-845-5333
Norwalk Community College Post-Sec.
188 Richards Ave 06854 203-857-7000
Norwalk Hospital Post-Sec.
24 Stevens St 06850 203-852-2211

Norwich, New London, Pop. 36,598
Connecticut Technical HS System
Supt. — See Middletown
Norwich Technical HS Vo/Tech
590 New London Tpke 06360 860-889-8453
Nikitoula Menounos, dir. Fax 886-4632

Endowed & Incorporated Academies 2,400/9-12
305 Broadway 06360 860-887-2505
Mark Cohan, supt. Fax 887-2004
www.norwichfreeacademy.com
Norwich Free Academy 2,400/9-12
305 Broadway 06360 860-887-2505
Mark Cohan, prin. Fax 887-2004

Norwich SD 4,000/PK-8
90 Town St 06360 860-823-4245
Pamela Aubin, supt. Fax 823-1880
www.norwichpublicschools.org
Kelly MS 700/6-8
25 Mahan Dr 06360 860-823-4211
Fax 892-4302
Teachers Memorial MS 500/6-8
15 Teachers Dr 06360 860-823-4212
William Peckham, prin. Fax 823-4277

Three Rivers Community Technical College Post-Sec.
Mahan Dr 06360 860-886-0177
Three Rivers Community Technical College Post-Sec.
574 New London Tpke 06360 860-823-2845

Oakdale, New London
Montville SD 2,900/PK-12
Old Colchester Rd 06370 860-848-1228
David Erwin, supt. Fax 848-0589
www.montvilleschools.org
Montville HS 800/9-12
800 Old Colchester Rd 06370 860-848-9208
Thomas Amanti, prin. Fax 848-3872
Tyl MS 700/6-8
166 Chesterfield Rd 06370 860-848-2822
Thomas Girard, prin. Fax 848-8854

St. Thomas More S 200/8-12
45 Cottage Rd 06370 860-859-1900
James Hanrahan, hdmstr. Fax 823-3863

Oakville, Litchfield, Pop. 8,741
Watertown SD
Supt. — See Watertown
Swift MS 600/7-8
250 Colonial St 06779 860-945-4830
Marylu Lerz, prin. Fax 945-6449

Old Lyme, New London
Learn RESC 500/
44 Hatchetts Hill Rd 06371 860-434-4800
Virginia Seccombe, dir. Fax 434-4820
www.learn.k12.ct.us
Other Schools – See New London

Regional SD 18 1,600/PK-12
4 Davis Rd W 06371 860-434-7238
David Klein, supt. Fax 434-9959
www.region18.org
Lyme-Old Lyme HS 500/9-12
69 Lyme St 06371 860-434-1651
Jan Guarino-Rhone, prin. Fax 434-8234
Lyme-Old Lyme MS 400/6-8
53 Lyme St 06371 860-434-2568
Jeffrey Ostroff, prin. Fax 434-0717

Lyme Academy College of Fine Arts Post-Sec.
84 Lyme St 06371 860-434-5232

Old Mystic, New London
Stonington SD 2,500/PK-12
PO Box 479 06372 860-572-0506
Michael McKee, supt. Fax 572-1470
www.stoningtonschools.org
Other Schools – See Mystic, Pawcatuck

Old Saybrook, Middlesex, Pop. 9,552
Old Saybrook SD 1,600/PK-12
50 Sheffield St 06475 860-395-3157
Joseph Onofrio, supt. Fax 395-3162
www.oldsaybrook.k12.ct.us
Old Saybrook HS 400/9-12
1111 Boston Post Rd 06475 860-395-3175
Scott Schoonmaker, prin. Fax 395-3179
Old Saybrook MS 600/4-8
60 Sheffield St 06475 860-395-3168
Michael Rafferty, prin. Fax 395-3350

Orange, New Haven, Pop. 12,830
Regional SD 5
Supt. — See Woodbridge
Amity Regional MS 400/7-8
100 Ohman Ave 06477 203-392-3200
Robert Slie, prin. Fax 387-7603

Southern Connecticut Hebrew Academy 200/K-12
261 Derby Ave 06477 203-795-5261
Rabbi Sheya Hecht, prin. Fax 891-9719

Oxford, New Haven
Oxford SD 1,500/PK-8
1 Great Hill Rd 06478 203-888-7754
Judith A. Palmer, supt. Fax 888-2468
www.oxfordpublicschools.org
Great Oak MS 500/6-8
50 Great Oak Rd 06478 203-888-5418
Brian Murphy, prin. Fax 888-7798

Pawcatuck, New London, Pop. 5,289
Stonington SD
Supt. — See Old Mystic
Pawcatuck MS 300/5-8
40 Field St 06379 860-599-5696
Jane Giulini, prin. Fax 599-8948
Stonington HS 700/9-12
176 S Broad St 06379 860-599-5781
Dr. Stephen Murphy, prin. Fax 599-5784

Plainfield, Windham, Pop. 14,363
Plainfield SD 2,600/PK-12
651 Norwich Rd 06374 860-564-6403
Mary Conway, supt. Fax 564-6412
www.plainfieldschools.org/
Plainfield Central MS 600/6-8
75 Canterbury Rd 06374 860-564-6437
Jerry Davis, prin. Fax 564-1147
Other Schools – See Central Village

Plainville, Hartford, Pop. 17,932
Plainville SD 2,600/PK-12
47 Robert Holcomb Way 06062 860-793-3200
Kathleen Binkowski, supt. Fax 747-6790
www.plainvilleschools.org
Plainville HS 900/9-12
47 Robert Holcomb Way 06062 860-793-3220
Gregory Ziogas, prin. Fax 793-3224
MS of Plainville 700/6-8
150 Northwest Dr 06062 860-793-3250
Carole Alvaro, prin. Fax 793-3265

Plantsville, Hartford, Pop. 7,000
Southington SD
Supt. — See Southington
Kennedy MS 800/6-8
1071 S Main St 06479 860-628-3275
Angelo Campagnano, prin. Fax 628-3404

Pomfret, Windham

Pomfret S 300/9-12
PO Box 128 06258 860-963-6100
Bradford Hastings, hdmstr. Fax 963-2086
Rectory S 200/5-9
PO Box 68 06258 860-928-7759
Thomas Army, hdmstr. Fax 963-2355

Portland, Middlesex, Pop. 5,645
Portland SD 1,400/PK-12
33 E Main St 06480 860-342-6790
Dr. Sally Doyen, supt. Fax 342-6791
www.portlandct.org
Portland HS 300/9-12
PO Box 73 06480 860-342-1720
Andrea Lavery, prin. Fax 342-2906
Portland MS 200/7-8
PO Box 686 06480 860-342-1880
Scott Giegerich, prin. Fax 342-3934

Preston, New London
Preston SD 500/PK-8
325 Shetucket Tpke 06365 860-889-6098
Dr. John Welch, supt. Fax 889-8685
www.prestonschools.org/
Preston Plains MS 200/6-8
1 Route 164 06365 860-889-3831
Raymond Bernier, prin. Fax 889-8685

Prospect, New Haven, Pop. 7,775
Regional SD 16 2,700/PK-12
207 New Haven Rd 06712 203-758-6671
Dr. Maggie V. Shook, supt. Fax 758-5797
www.region16ct.org
Long River MS 600/6-8
Columbia Ave 06712 203-758-4421
Kenneth Ross, prin. Fax 758-6948
Other Schools – See Beacon Falls

Putnam, Windham, Pop. 9,031
Putnam SD 1,300/PK-12
126 Church St 06260 860-963-6900
Margo Marvin, supt. Fax 963-6903
www.putnam.k12.ct.us/
Putnam HS 400/9-12
152 Woodstock Ave 06260 860-963-6905
Joseph Fleming, prin. Fax 963-6911
Putnam MS 300/6-8
35 Wicker St 06260 860-963-6920
Joseph Morris, prin. Fax 963-6921

Redding, Fairfield
Regional SD 9
Supt. — See Monroe
Barlow HS 1,000/9-12
100 Black Rock Tpke 06896 203-938-2508
Ross Calabro, prin. Fax 938-0327

Ridgefield, Fairfield, Pop. 6,363
Ridgefield SD 5,500/PK-12
70 Prospect St 06877 203-431-2800
Deborah Low, supt. Fax 431-2810
www.ridgefield.org
East Ridge MS 800/6-8
10 E Ridge Rd 06877 203-438-3744
Martin Fiedler, prin. Fax 431-2843
Ridgefield HS 1,600/9-12
700 N Salem Rd 06877 203-438-3785
Jeff Jaslow, prin. Fax 438-4002
Scotts Ridge MS 600/6-8
750 N Salem Rd 06877 203-894-3400
Marie Doyon, prin. Fax 894-3411

Riverside, Fairfield
Greenwich SD
Supt. — See Greenwich
Eastern MS 700/6-8
51 Hendrie Ave 06878 203-637-1744
Ralph Mayo, prin. Fax 637-3567

Rocky Hill, Hartford, Pop. 16,554
Rocky Hill SD 2,500/PK-12
PO Box 627 06067 860-258-7701
J. A. Camille Vautour Ph.D., supt. Fax 258-7710
www.rockyhillps.us
Griswold MS 600/6-8
144 Bailey Rd 06067 860-258-7741
Richard Watson, prin. Fax 258-7746
Rocky Hill HS 700/9-12
50 Chapin Ave 06067 860-258-7721
Robert Pitocco, prin. Fax 258-7735

Salisbury, Litchfield

Salisbury S 300/9-12
251 Canaan Rd 06068 860-435-5700
Chisholm Chandler, hdmstr. Fax 435-5750

Sandy Hook, Fairfield
Newtown SD
Supt. — See Newtown
Newtown HS 1,600/9-12
12 Berkshire Rd 06482 203-426-7646
Arlene Gottesman, prin. Fax 426-6573

Seymour, New Haven, Pop. 14,288
Seymour SD 2,600/PK-12
98 Bank St 06483 203-888-4565
Thomas Petruny, supt. Fax 888-1704
www.seymourschools.org
Seymour HS 900/9-12
2 Botsford Rd 06483 203-888-2561
Cathy Goodrich, prin. Fax 888-7476
Seymour MS 700/6-8
211 Mountain Rd 06483 203-888-4513
Christine Syriac, prin. Fax 881-7535

Shelton, Fairfield, Pop. 39,477
Shelton SD 5,700/PK-12
382 Long Hill Ave 06484 203-924-1023
Robin Willink, supt. Fax 924-5894
www.sheltonpublicschools.org
Shelton HS 1,800/9-12
120 Meadow St 06484 203-924-9578
Donald Ramia, prin. Fax 924-8236
Shelton IS 900/7-8
675 Constitution Blvd N 06484 203-926-2000
Howard Gura, prin. Fax 926-2017

New England Technical Institute Post-Sec.
8 Progress Dr 06484 203-929-0592

Simsbury, Hartford, Pop. 22,023
Simsbury SD 5,100/PK-12
933 Hopmeadow St 06070 860-651-3361
Diane Ullman, supt. Fax 651-4343
www.simsbury.k12.ct.us
James Memorial MS 900/7-8
155 Firetown Rd 06070 860-651-3341
Erin Murray, prin. Fax 658-3629
Simsbury HS 1,500/9-12
34 Farms Village Rd 06070 860-658-0451
Fax 658-2439

Walker S 200/6-12
230 Bushy Hill Rd 06070 860-658-4467
Susanna Jones, hdmstr. Fax 658-6763
Westminster S 400/9-12
PO Box 337 06070 860-408-3000
W. Graham Cole, hdmstr. Fax 408-3001

Somers, Tolland
Somers SD 1,700/PK-12
55 9th District Rd 06071 860-749-2270
James Chittum, supt. Fax 763-0748
www.somers.k12.ct.us
Avery MS 400/6-8
55 9th District Rd 06071 860-749-2270
Nancy Barry, prin. Fax 763-2073
Somers HS 600/9-12
55 9th District Rd 06071 860-749-2270
Gary Cotzin, prin. Fax 749-9264

New England Tractor Trailer Training Post-Sec.
PO Box 326 06071 860-749-0711

Southbury, New Haven, Pop. 15,818
Regional SD 15
Supt. — See Middlebury
Pomperaug Regional HS 1,300/9-12
234 Judd Rd 06488 203-262-3200
James Agostine, prin. Fax 262-6806
Rochambeau MS 600/6-8
100 Peter Rd 06488 203-264-2711
Anthony Salutari, prin. Fax 264-6638

Southington, Hartford, Pop. 39,200
Southington SD 6,800/PK-12
49 Beecher St 06489 860-628-3202
Fax 628-3205
www.southingtonschools.org
DePaolo MS 800/6-8
385 Pleasant St 06489 860-628-3260
Frank Pepe, prin. Fax 628-3403
Southington HS 2,200/9-12
720 Pleasant St 06489 860-628-3229
Kathleen McGrath, prin. Fax 628-3397
Other Schools – See Plantsville

Branford Hall Career Institute Post-Sec.
35 N Main St 06489 860-276-0600
Briarwood College Post-Sec.
2279 Mount Vernon Rd 06489 860-628-4751

South Kent, Litchfield

South Kent S 100/9-12
40 Bulls Bridge Rd 06785 860-927-3539
Andrew Vadnai, hdmstr. Fax 927-1161

South Windsor, Hartford, Pop. 22,090
South Windsor SD 5,000/K-12
1737 Main St 06074 860-291-1205
Dr. Robert Kozaczka, supt. Fax 291-1291
www.swindsor.k12.ct.us
Edwards MS 1,200/6-8
100 Arnold Way 06074 860-648-5030
Janice Tirinzonie, prin. Fax 648-5029
South Windsor HS 1,600/9-12
161 Nevers Rd 06074 860-648-5000
John Dilorio, prin. Fax 648-5013

Stafford Springs, Tolland, Pop. 4,100
Stafford SD 2,000/PK-12
PO Box 147 06076 860-684-4211
Therese Fishman, supt. Fax 684-5172
www.stafford.ctschool.net/
Stafford HS 600/9-12
PO Box 87 06076 860-684-4233
Francis Kennedy, prin. Fax 684-0424
Stafford MS 500/6-8
PO Box 106 06076 860-684-2785
Kenneth Valentine, prin. Fax 684-4671

Stamford, Fairfield, Pop. 120,045
Connecticut Technical HS System
Supt. — See Middletown
Wright Technical HS Vo/Tech
PO Box 1416 06904 203-324-7363
Sidney Abramowitz, dir. Fax 324-1196

Stamford SD 15,000/PK-12
PO Box 9310 06904 203-977-4543
Dr. Joshua Starr, supt. Fax 977-5964
www.stamfordpublicschools.org/
Academy of Information Technology Vo/Tech
381 High Ridge Rd 06905 203-977-4336
Paul Gross, dir. Fax 977-6638
Cloonan MS 600/6-8
11 W North St 06902 203-977-4544
David Rudolph, prin. Fax 977-4867
Dolan MS 600/6-8
51 Toms Rd 06906 203-977-4441
Charmaine Tourse, prin. Fax 977-4880
Rippowam MS 900/6-8
381 High Ridge Rd 06905 203-977-5255
Janis Rossman, prin. Fax 977-5154
Scofield Magnet MS 600/6-8
641 Scofieldtown Rd 06903 203-977-2750
George Giberti, prin. Fax 977-2766
Stamford HS 2,000/9-12
55 Strawberry Hill Ave 06902 203-977-4227
Suzanne Brown-Koroshclz, prin. Fax 356-1720
Turn of River MS 700/6-8
117 Vine Rd 06905 203-977-4284
Rodney Bass, prin. Fax 977-5037
Westhill HS 2,100/9-12
125 Roxbury Rd 06902 203-977-4838
Camille Figluizzi, prin. Fax 977-4996

Beth Benjamin Academy of Connecticut Post-Sec.
132 Prospect St 06901 203-325-4351
King & Low-Heywood Thomas S 700/PK-12
1450 Newfield Ave 06905 203-322-3496
Thomas B. Main, hdmstr. Fax 329-0291
Stamford Hospital Post-Sec.
PO Box 9317 06904 203-276-7877
Trinity Catholic HS 400/9-12
926 Newfield Ave 06905 203-322-3401
Robert F. D'Aquila, prin. Fax 322-5330
Trinity Catholic MS 200/6-8
948 Newfield Ave 06905 203-322-7383
Rev. Cyprian LaPastina, prin. Fax 324-4435
Yeshiva Bais Binyomin 100/9-12
132 Prospect St 06901 203-325-4351
Rabbi Simcha Schustal, prin. Fax 323-6073

Storrs, Tolland, Pop. 12,198
Mansfield SD 1,400/PK-8
4 S Eagleville Rd 06268 860-429-3350
Gordon Schimmel Ed.D., supt. Fax 429-3379
www.mansfieldct.org
Mansfield MS 700/5-8
205 Spring Hill Rd 06268 860-429-9341
Jeffrey Cryan, prin. Fax 429-1020

Regional SD 19 1,300/9-12
1235 Storrs Rd 06268 860-487-1862
Bruce Silva, supt. Fax 429-0085
www.eosmith.org
Smith HS 1,300/9-12
1235 Storrs Rd 06268 860-487-0877
Louis DeLoreto, prin. Fax 429-7892

University of Connecticut 06269 Post-Sec.
860-486-2000

Stratford, Fairfield, Pop. 50,100
Stratford SD 7,300/PK-12
1000 E Broadway 06615 203-385-4210
Irene Cornish, supt. Fax 381-2012
www.stratford.k12.ct.us
Bunnell HS 1,400/9-12
1 Bulldog Blvd 06614 203-385-4250
Dr. Dudley Orr, prin. Fax 381-2014
Flood MS 700/7-8
490 Chapel St 06614 203-385-4280
Carol Aloi, prin. Fax 381-2033
Stratford HS 1,000/9-12
45 N Parade St 06615 203-385-4230
Margaret Lasek, prin. Fax 381-2021
Wooster MS 600/7-8
150 Lincoln St 06614 203-385-4275
Dr. Linda Paslov, prin. Fax 381-6918

Porter and Chester Institute Post-Sec.
670 Lordship Blvd 06615 203-375-4463

Suffield, Hartford
Suffield SD 2,100/PK-12
350 Mountain Rd 06078 860-668-3800
Jack Reynolds, supt. Fax 668-3805
www.suffield.org
Suffield MS 600/6-8
350 Mountain Rd 06078 860-668-3820
John Warrington, prin. Fax 668-3088
Other Schools – See West Suffield

Connecticut Culinary Institute Post-Sec.
1760 Mapleton Ave 06078 860-668-3500
International Coll. of Hospitality Mgmt. Post-Sec.
1760 Mapleton Ave 06078 860-668-3515
Suffield Academy 400/9-12
PO Box 999 06078 860-668-7315
Charles Cahn, hdmstr. Fax 668-2966

Terryville, Litchfield, Pop. 5,426
Plymouth SD 1,900/PK-12
77 Main St 06786 860-314-8005
Anthony Distasio Ph.D., supt. Fax 314-2766
www.plymouth.k12.ct.us/
Fisher MS 500/6-8
79 N Main St 06786 860-314-2790
Gary Travers, prin. Fax 314-2786
Terryville HS 500/9-12
21 N Main St 06786 860-314-2777
Michael Cerruto, prin. Fax 314-2785

Thomaston, Litchfield, Pop. 6,947
Thomaston SD 1,300/PK-12
PO Box 166 06787 860-283-4796
Lynda Mitchell, supt. Fax 283-6708
www.thomastonschools.net/
Thomaston HS 600/7-12
185 Branch Rd 06787 860-283-3030
James Wenker, prin. Fax 283-3040

Thompson, Windham

Marianapolis Prep S 200/9-12
PO Box 304 06277 860-923-9565
Marilyn Ebbitt, hdmstr. Fax 923-3730

Tolland, Tolland
Tolland SD 2,900/PK-12
51 Tolland Grn 06084 860-870-6850
William D. Guzman, supt. Fax 870-7737
www.tolland.k12.ct.us
Tolland HS 900/9-12
1 Eagle Hill Dr 06084 860-870-6818
Joseph Bacewicz, prin. Fax 870-8168
Tolland MS 1,000/5-8
96 Old Post Rd 06084 860-875-2564
Michael Seroussi, prin. Fax 872-7126

Torrington, Litchfield, Pop. 35,995
Connecticut Technical HS System
Supt. — See Middletown
Wolcott Technical HS Vo/Tech
75 Oliver St 06790 860-496-5300
Daniel Kushman, dir. Fax 496-9022

Torrington SD 4,900/K-12
355 Migeon Ave 06790 860-489-2327
Susan W. O'Brien Ed.D., supt. Fax 489-0726
www.torrington.org
Torrington HS 1,500/9-12
50 Major Besse Dr 06790 860-489-2294
Dr. John Metallo, prin. Fax 489-2853
Torrington MS 1,300/6-8
200 Middle School Dr 06790 860-496-4050
Matthew Harnett, prin. Fax 496-1089

St. Francis of Assisi S 3-8
360 Prospect St 06790 860-489-4177
Jo Anne Gauger, prin. Fax 489-1590

Trumbull, Fairfield, Pop. 34,600
Trumbull SD 6,700/PK-12
6254 Main St 06611 203-452-4301
Ralph Iassogna, supt. Fax 452-4305
www.trumbullps.org
Hillcrest MS 700/6-8
530 Daniels Farm Rd 06611 203-452-4466
Rosemary Seaman, prin. Fax 452-4479

Madison MS 800/6-8
4630 Madison Ave 06611 203-452-4499
Valerie Forshaw, prin. Fax 452-4490
Trumbull HS 2,000/9-12
72 Strobel Rd 06611 203-452-4555
Robert Tremaglio, prin. Fax 452-4593

Christian Heritage S 500/K-12
575 White Plains Rd 06611 203-261-6230
Barry Giller, hdmstr. Fax 452-1531
St. Joseph HS 800/9-12
2320 Huntington Tpke 06611 203-378-9378
Dr. Matthew Kenney, prin. Fax 378-7306

Uncasville, New London, Pop. 2,975

St. Bernard Academy 6-8
1593 Norwich New London Tpk 06382
860-848-3007
Mary Dillman, prin. Fax 848-0261
St. Bernard HS 300/9-12
1593 Norwich New London Tpk 06382
860-848-1271
Br. Robert Daszkiewicz, prin. Fax 848-1274

Vernon Rockville, Tolland, Pop. 28,900
Vernon SD 4,000/PK-12
PO Box 600 06066 860-870-6000
Richard Paskiewicz, supt. Fax 870-6008
www.vernonschools.com
Rockville HS 1,300/9-12
70 Loveland Hill Rd 06066 860-870-6050
Brian Levesque, prin. Fax 870-6314
Vernon Center MS 900/6-8
777 Hartford Tpke 06066 860-870-6070
Dr. Beth Katz, prin. Fax 870-6318

Wallingford, New Haven, Pop. 41,700
Wallingford SD 7,100/PK-12
142 Hope Hill Rd 06492 203-949-6500
Dale Wilson, supt. Fax 949-6550
www.wallingford.k12.ct.us
Hall HS 1,200/9-12
70 Pond Hill Rd 06492 203-294-5350
David Bryant, prin. Fax 294-5353
Hammarskjold MS 800/6-8
106 Pond Hill Rd 06492 203-294-5340
Enrico Buccilli, prin. Fax 294-5322
Moran MS 900/6-8
141 Hope Hill Rd 06492 203-741-2900
Robert Cyr, prin. Fax 741-2939
Sheehan HS 1,000/9-12
142 Hope Hill Rd 06492 203-294-5900
Rosemary Duthie, prin. Fax 294-5980

Choate Rosemary Hall S 900/9-12
333 Christian St 06492 203-697-2000
Edward Shanahan, prin. Fax 697-2720

Washington, Litchfield
Regional SD 12
Supt. — See Washington Depot
Shepaug Valley HS 400/9-12
159 South St 06793 860-868-7326
Eugene Horrigan, prin. Fax 868-0622
Shepaug Valley MS 300/6-8
159 South St 06793 860-868-7326
Lorrie Rodrigue, prin. Fax 868-0622

Devereux Center in Connecticut Post-Sec.
81 Sabbaday Ln 06793 860-868-7377
Devereux Glenholme S 100/4-12
81 Sabbaday Ln 06793 860-868-7377
Gary L. Fitzherbert, hdmstr. Fax 868-7413
Gunnery 300/9-12
99 Green Hill Rd 06793 860-868-7334
Susan Graham, hdmstr. Fax 868-7205

Washington Depot, Litchfield
Regional SD 12 1,200/PK-12
PO Box 386 06794 860-868-6100
Richard E. Carmelich Ph.D., supt. Fax 868-6103
www.region-12.org
Other Schools – See Washington

Waterbury, New Haven, Pop. 107,902
Connecticut Technical HS System
Supt. — See Middletown
Kaynor Technical HS Vo/Tech
43 Tompkins St 06708 203-596-4302
Robert Axon, dir. Fax 596-4308

Waterbury SD 17,500/PK-12
236 Grand St 06702 203-574-8000
Dr. David Snead, supt. Fax 574-8010
www.waterbury.k12.ct.us/
Crosby HS 1,400/9-12
300 Pierpont Rd 06705 203-574-8061
B. Carrington-Lawlor, prin. Fax 574-8072
Kennedy HS 1,300/9-12
422 Highland Ave 06708 203-574-8150
Michael Yamin, prin. Fax 574-8154
North End MS 1,200/6-8
534 Bucks Hill Rd 06704 203-574-8097
Michael LoRusso, prin. Fax 574-8203
Wallace MS 1,300/6-8
3465 E Main St 06705 203-574-8140
Dr. Louis Padua, prin. Fax 574-8141
Waterbury Arts Magnet S 200/6-12
16 S Elm St 06706 203-573-6300
Alan Kramer, prin. Fax 573-6325
West Side MS 1,200/6-8
483 Chase Pkwy 06708 203-574-8120
Charles Nappi, prin. Fax 574-8130
Wilby HS 1,100/9-12
568 Bucks Hill Rd 06704 203-574-8100
Robyn Apicella, prin. Fax 574-6896

Chase Collegiate S 500/PK-12
565 Chase Pkwy 06708 203-236-9560
John Fixx, hdmstr. Fax 236-9494
Goodwin Institute Business School Post-Sec.
101 Pierpont Rd 06705 203-756-5500
Holy Cross HS 800/9-12
587 Oronoke Rd 06708 203-757-9248
Timothy McDonald, prin. Fax 757-3423
Industrial Management and Training Post-Sec.
233 Mill St 06706 203-753-7910
Naugatuck Valley Community College Post-Sec.
750 Chase Pkwy 06708 203-575-8044
Post University Post-Sec.
800 Country Club Rd 06708 203-596-4500
Sacred Heart HS 500/9-12
142 S Elm St 06706 203-753-1605
Jacqueline Jennings, prin. Fax 597-1686
St. Mary's Hospital Post-Sec.
56 Franklin St 06706 203-574-6300
University of Connecticut Post-Sec.
32 Hillside Ave 06710 203-757-1231

Waterford, New London, Pop. 17,930
Waterford SD 2,900/K-12
PO Box 284 06385 860-444-5801
Randall Collins, supt. Fax 444-5870
www.waterfordschools.org
Clark Lane MS 800/6-8
105 Clark Ln 06385 860-443-2837
Michael Lovetere, prin. Fax 437-6985
Waterford HS 1,000/9-12
20 Rope Ferry Rd 06385 860-437-6956
Donald Macrino, prin. Fax 447-7928

Watertown, Litchfield, Pop. 6,000
Watertown SD 3,500/PK-12
10 Deforest St 06795 860-945-4801
Dr. Joseph Erardi, supt. Fax 945-2775
www.watertownctschools.org
Watertown HS 1,000/9-12
324 French St 06795 860-945-4810
Thad Hasbrouck, prin. Fax 945-3348
Other Schools – See Oakville

Porter and Chester Institute Post-Sec.
320 Sylvan Lake Rd 06779 860-274-9294
Taft S 600/9-12
110 Woodbury Rd 06795 860-945-7777
William MacMullen, hdmstr. Fax 945-7858

Westbrook, Middlesex, Pop. 2,060
Westbrook SD 1,000/PK-12
158 McVeagh Rd 06498 860-399-6432
Patricia Charles, supt. Fax 399-8817
www.westbrookctschools.org/
Westbrook HS 300/9-12
156 Mcveagh Rd 06498 860-399-6214
Robert Hale, prin. Fax 399-2007
Westbrook MS 200/6-8
154 McVeagh Rd 06498 860-399-2010
Philip House, prin. Fax 399-2007

Oxford Academy 50/9-12
1393 Boston Post Rd 06498 860-399-6247
Philip Davis, hdmstr. Fax 399-6805

West Hartford, Hartford, Pop. 64,300
West Hartford SD 9,900/PK-12
50 S Main St, 860-561-6600
David Sklarz, supt. Fax 561-6910
www.whps.org
Bristow MS 6-8
34 Highland St, 860-231-2100
Jeanne Camperchioli, prin. Fax 231-2107
Conard HS 1,400/9-12
110 Beechwood Rd, 860-521-1350
Thomas Moore, prin. Fax 521-6699
Hall HS 1,600/9-12
975 N Main St, 860-232-4561
Donald Slater, prin. Fax 236-0366
King Philip MS 1,100/6-8
100 King Philip Dr, 860-233-8236
Mary Hourdequin, prin. Fax 233-0812
Sedgwick MS 1,100/6-8
128 Sedgwick Rd, 860-521-0610
Ben Skaught, prin. Fax 521-7502

American School for the Deaf Post-Sec.
139 N Main St, 860-570-2309
Fox Institute of Business Post-Sec.
99 South St, 860-947-2299
Hartt Community Division Post-Sec.
200 Bloomfield Ave, 860-768-7768
Kingswood-Oxford S 600/6-12
170 Kingswood Rd, 860-233-9631
Dennis Bisgaard, hdmstr. Fax 232-3843
Northwest Catholic HS 600/9-12
29 Wampanoag Dr, 860-236-4221
Margaret Williamson, prin. Fax 586-0911
St. Joseph College Post-Sec.
1678 Asylum Ave, 860-232-4571
St. Timothy MS 200/6-8
225 King Philip Dr, 860-236-0614
Dr. Stephen Balkun, prin. Fax 920-0293
University of Connecticut Post-Sec.
1800 Asylum Ave, 860-241-4700
University of Hartford Post-Sec.
200 Bloomfield Ave, 860-768-4100

West Haven, New Haven, Pop. 52,923
West Haven SD 7,000/PK-12
25 Ogden St 06516 203-937-4310
Dr. JoAnn Andrees, supt. Fax 937-4315
www.whschools.org
Bailey MS 900/6-8
106 Morgan Ln 06516 203-937-4380
Anthony Cordone, prin. Fax 937-4385

Carrigan MS 900/6-8
2 Tetlow St 06516 203-937-4390
Patricia Libero, prin. Fax 937-4393
Stiles Alternative Learning Ctr 9-12
575 Main St 06516 203-931-6860
Lester Hawley, prin. Fax 931-6863
West Haven HS 1,900/9-12
1 McDonough Plz 06516 203-937-4360
Ronald Stancil, prin. Fax 934-4370

Living Word Christian Academy 200/PK-12
225 Meloy Rd 06516 203-931-7750
Lawrence Batza, prin. Fax 931-7540
Notre Dame HS 700/9-12
24 Ricardo St 06516 203-933-1673
Ralph Proto, prin. Fax 933-2474
University of New Haven Post-Sec.
300 Boston Post Rd 06516 203-932-7000

Weston, Fairfield
Weston SD 2,300/PK-12
24 School Rd 06883 203-291-1401
Lynne B. Pierson Ed.D., supt. Fax 291-1415
www.westonk12-ct.org
Weston HS 700/9-12
115 School Rd 06883 203-291-1600
Rose Marie Cipriano, prin. Fax 291-1603
Weston MS 600/6-8
135 School Rd 06883 203-291-1500
Lisa Wolak, prin. Fax 291-1516

Westport, Fairfield, Pop. 24,407
Westport SD 5,200/PK-12
110 Myrtle Ave 06880 203-341-1025
Elliott Landon, supt. Fax 341-1029
www.westport.k12.ct.us/
Bedford MS 800/5-8
88 North Ave 06880 203-341-1510
Angela Wormser, prin. Fax 341-1508
Coleytown MS 500/6-8
255 North Ave 06880 203-341-1610
Kris Biendowski, prin. Fax 341-1603
Staples HS 1,500/9-12
70 North Ave 06880 203-341-1200
John Dodig, prin. Fax 341-1202

Connecticut Center for Massage Therapy Post-Sec.
25 Sylvan Rd S 06880 203-221-7325

West Redding, Fairfield
Redding SD
Supt. — See Monroe
Read MS 600/5-8
Route 53 06896 203-938-2533
Dianne Martin, prin. Fax 938-8667

West Simsbury, Hartford, Pop. 2,149

Master's S 300/PK-12
36 Westledge Rd 06092 860-651-9361
Rick Burslem, hdmstr. Fax 651-9363

West Suffield, Hartford
Suffield SD
Supt. — See Suffield
Suffield HS 800/9-12
1060 Sheldon St 06093 860-668-3810
Thomas Jones, prin. Fax 668-3037

Wethersfield, Hartford, Pop. 26,400
Wethersfield SD 3,700/K-12
127 Hartford Ave 06109 860-571-8110
Patrick Proctor Ed.D., supt. Fax 571-8130
www.wethersfield.k12.ct.us/
Deane MS 600/7-8
551 Silas Deane Hwy 06109 860-571-8300
James Collin, prin. Fax 563-0563
Wethersfield HS 1,200/9-12
411 Wolcott Hill Rd 06109 860-571-8200
Thomas Moore, prin. Fax 571-8240

Connecticut Childrens Medical Center Post-Sec.
170 Ridge Rd 06109 860-545-8551
Porter and Chester Institute Post-Sec.
125 Silas Deane Hwy 06109 860-529-2519

Willimantic, Windham, Pop. 14,746
Connecticut Technical HS System
Supt. — See Middletown
Windham Technical HS Vo/Tech
210 Birch St 06226 860-456-3879
Kirk Murad, dir. Fax 450-0630

Windham SD 3,600/PK-12
322 Prospect St 06226 860-465-2310
Paul K. Perzanoski, supt. Fax 456-2311
www.windham.k12.ct.us
Windham HS 1,000/9-12
355 High St 06226 860-465-2480
Gene Blain, prin. Fax 465-2463
Windham MS 1,100/5-8
123 Quarry St 06226 860-465-2351
Madeline Negron, prin. Fax 465-2353

Eastern Connecticut State University Post-Sec.
83 Windham St 06226 860-456-5000
Windham Community Memorial Hospital Post-Sec.
112 Mansfield Ave 06226 860-456-6800
Windham Regional Vocational Tech School Post-Sec.
210 Birch St 06226 860-456-3789

Willington, Tolland
Willington SD 600/PK-8
40 Old Farms Rd Ste A 06279 860-487-3130
Corinne Berglund, supt. Fax 487-3132
Hall Memorial MS 300/4-8
111 River Rd 06279 860-429-9391
David Harding, prin. Fax 429-5682

Wilton, Fairfield, Pop. 7,200
Wilton SD 4,300/PK-12
PO Box 277 06897 203-762-3381
Gary Richards, supt. Fax 762-2177
www.wilton.k12.ct.us/
Middlebrook MS 1,000/6-8
131 School Rd 06897 203-762-8388
Julia Harris, prin. Fax 762-1716
Wilton HS 1,200/9-12
395 Danbury Rd 06897 203-762-0381
Timothy Canty, prin. Fax 834-0164

Windsor, Hartford, Pop. 27,817
Hartford SD
Supt. — See Hartford
Pathways to Technology Magnet S 200/9-12
184 Windsor Ave 06095 860-695-9450
Christopher Leone, dir. Fax 722-6439

Windsor SD 4,300/PK-12
601 Matianuck Ave 06095 860-687-2000
Elizabeth Feser Ed.D., supt. Fax 687-2009
www.windsorct.org
Sage Park MS 1,000/6-8
25 Sage Park Rd 06095 860-687-2030
Paul Cavaliere, prin. Fax 687-2039
Windsor HS 1,500/9-12
50 Sage Park Rd 06095 860-687-2020
Joseph Arcarese, prin. Fax 687-2029

Branford Hall Career Institute Post-Sec.
995 Day Hill Rd 06095 860-683-4900
Loomis Chaffee S 700/9-12
4 Batchelder Rd 06095 860-687-6000
Russell Weigel, hdmstr. Fax 687-1100
Praise Power & Prayer Christian S 100/K-12
209 Kennedy Rd 06095 860-285-8898

Windsor Locks, Hartford, Pop. 12,358
Windsor Locks SD 1,900/PK-12
58 S Elm St 06096 860-292-5000
Dr. Greg W. Little, supt. Fax 292-5003
www.wlps.org
Windsor Locks HS 600/9-12
58 S Elm St 06096 860-292-5032
Mike Churilla, prin. Fax 292-5039
Windsor Locks MS 500/6-8
7 Center St 06096 860-292-5012
Gregory Blanchfield, prin. Fax 292-5017

Winsted, Litchfield, Pop. 8,254
Endowed & Incorporated Academies 500/9-12
200 Williams Ave 06098 860-379-8521
Dr. David Cressy, supt. Fax 379-6163
gilbertschool.org
Gilbert S 500/9-12
200 Williams Ave 06098 860-379-8521
Daniel Hatch, prin. Fax 379-6163

Regional SD 7 1,100/7-12
PO Box 656 06098 860-379-1084
Dr. Roberta Ohotnicky, supt. Fax 379-0618
www.nwr7.com
Northwestern Regional HS 700/9-12
100 Battistoni Rd 06098 860-379-8525
Wayne Conner, prin. Fax 738-6059
Northwestern Regional MS 400/7-8
100 Battistoni Rd 06098 860-379-7243
Althea Perez, prin. Fax 738-6205

Winchester SD 1,100/PK-8
30 Elm St 06098 860-379-0706
Blaise Salerno, supt. Fax 379-6521
www.winchesterschools.org/
Pearson MS 300/6-8
2 Wetmore Ave 06098 860-379-7588
Clay Krevolin, prin. Fax 379-0406

Northwestern CT Comm. Technical College Post-Sec.
2 Park Pl 06098 860-738-6300

Wolcott, New Haven, Pop. 13,700
Wolcott SD 3,000/PK-12
154 Center St 06716 203-879-8183
Dr. Thomas Smyth, supt. Fax 879-8182
www.wolcottps.org
Tyrrell MS 800/6-8
500 Todd Rd 06716 203-879-8151
Arline Tansley, prin. Fax 879-8419
Wolcott HS 800/9-12
457 Bound Line Rd 06716 203-879-8164
Robert Eberle, prin. Fax 879-8167

Connecticut Institute of Hair Design Post-Sec.
1681 Meriden Rd 06716 203-879-4247

Woodbridge, New Haven, Pop. 7,924
Regional SD 5 2,100/7-12
25 Newton Rd 06525 203-392-2106
Dr. John Brady, supt. Fax 397-4864
www.amityregion5.org
Amity Regional HS 1,200/9-12
25 Newton Rd 06525 203-397-4830
Edward Goldstone, prin. Fax 397-4866
Other Schools – See Bethany, Orange

Woodbury, Litchfield, Pop. 8,131
Regional SD 14 2,300/K-12
PO Box 469 06798 203-263-4330
Robert Cronin Ph.D., supt. Fax 263-0372
Nonnewaug HS 800/9-12
5 Minortown Rd 06798 203-263-2186
John Vecchitto, prin. Fax 263-3570
Woodbury MS 500/6-8
67 Washington Ave 06798 203-263-4306
Ellen Solek, prin. Fax 263-0825

Woodstock, Windham
Endowed & Incorporated Academies 1,100/9-12
57 Academy Rd 06281 860-928-6575
Richard Foye, hdmstr. Fax 963-7222
www.woodstockacademy.org
Woodstock Academy 1,100/9-12
57 Academy Rd 06281 860-928-6575
Richard Foye, hdmstr. Fax 963-7222

Woodstock SD 1,000/PK-8
147A Route 169 06281 860-928-7453
Dr. Francis Baran, supt. Fax 928-0206
www.woodstockschools.net
Woodstock MS 500/5-8
147B Route 169 06281 860-963-6575
Paul Gamache, prin. Fax 963-6577

Hyde S 200/9-12
PO Box 237 06281 860-963-9096
Laura Gauld, hdmstr. Fax 928-0612

DELAWARE

DELAWARE DEPARTMENT OF EDUCATION
401 Federal St Ste 2, Dover 19901-3639
Telephone 302-739-4601
Fax 302-739-4654
Website http://www.doe.k12.de.us

Secretary of Education Valerie Woodruff

DELAWARE BOARD OF EDUCATION
PO Box 1402, Dover 19903-1402

President Jean Allen

PUBLIC, PRIVATE AND CATHOLIC SECONDARY SCHOOLS

Bear, New Castle

Caravel Academy 1,100/PK-12
2801 Del Laws Rd 19701 302-834-8938
Donald C. Keister, hdmstr. Fax 834-3658
Fairwinds Christian S 200/PK-12
801 Seymour Rd 19701 302-328-7404
Greg Shrier, prin. Fax 328-0190
Red Lion Christian Academy 900/PK-12
1390 Red Lion Rd 19701 302-834-2526
Dr. Rob Brown, hdmstr. Fax 836-6346

Bridgeville, Sussex, Pop. 1,578
Woodbridge SD 1,900/PK-12
16359 Sussex Hwy 19933 302-337-7990
Kevin Carson Ed.D., supt. Fax 337-7998
www.wsd.k12.de.us
Wheatley MS 700/5-8
48 Church St 19933 302-337-3469
Delores Tunstall, prin. Fax 337-6016
Woodbridge HS 500/9-12
307 S Laws St 19933 302-337-8289
Gary Rosenthal, prin. Fax 337-0631

Camden Wyoming, Kent, Pop. 1,045
Caesar Rodney SD 6,700/PK-12
PO Box 188 19934 302-697-2173
Harold Roberts Ed.D., supt. Fax 697-3406
www.k12.de.us/caesarrodney/
Fifer MS 800/6-8
109 E Camden Wyoming Ave 19934 302-698-8400
Timothy Nolan, prin. Fax 698-8409
Postlethwait MS 800/6-8
2841 S State St 19934 302-698-8410
Michael Noel, prin. Fax 698-8419
Rodney HS 1,800/9-12
239 Old North Rd 19934 302-697-2161
Kevin Fitzgerald Ed.D., prin. Fax 697-6888
Other Schools – See Dover

Claymont, New Castle, Pop. 9,800
Brandywine SD 10,600/K-12
1000 Pennsylvania Ave 19703 302-793-5000
Dr. James Scanlon, supt. Fax 792-3823
www.bsd.k12.de.us
Other Schools – See Wilmington

Archmere Academy 500/9-12
3600 Philadelphia Pike 19703 302-798-6632
Rev. Joseph McLaughlin, hdmstr. Fax 798-7290

Dagsboro, Sussex, Pop. 555
Indian River SD
Supt. — See Selbyville
Indian River HS 800/9-12
29772 Armory Rd 19939 302-732-1500
Mark Steele, prin. Fax 732-1514

National Massage Therapy Institute Post-Sec.
Route 113 Box 144D 19939 800-264-9835

Delmar, Sussex, Pop. 1,483
Delmar SD 1,100/6-12
200 N 8th St 19940 302-846-9544
Dr. David Ring, supt. Fax 846-2793
www.k12.de.us/delmar
Delmar HS 500/9-12
200 N 8th St 19940 302-846-9544
Cathy Townsend, prin. Fax 846-2793
Delmar MS 500/6-8
200 N 8th St 19940 302-846-9544
Cathy Townsend, prin. Fax 846-2793

Dover, Kent, Pop. 34,288
Caesar Rodney SD
Supt. — See Camden Wyoming
Dover AFB MS 200/6-8
3100 Hawthorne Dr 19901 302-674-3284
Ernestine Adams, prin. Fax 730-4283
Capital SD 5,800/PK-12
945 Forest St 19904 302-672-1500
Michael Thomas Ed.D., supt. Fax 672-1714
www.capital.k12.de.us/
Central MS 1,000/7-8
211 Delaware Ave 19901 302-672-1772
Darren Guido, prin. Fax 672-1733
Dover HS 1,500/9-12
1 Pat Lynn Dr 19904 302-672-1526
Gene Montano, prin. Fax 672-1565

Bayhealth Medical Center Post-Sec.
640 S State St 19901 302-674-7001
Calvary Christian Academy 300/PK-12
1143 E Lebanon Rd 19901 302-697-7860
Aaron Coon, admin. Fax 697-0284
Capitol Baptist S 100/K-12
401 Kesselring Ave 19904 302-678-9190
Thomas Horne, prin. Fax 674-5957
Delaware State University Post-Sec.
1200 N Dupont Hwy 19901 302-857-6060
Delaware Technical & Community College Post-Sec.
100 Campus Dr 19904 302-857-1000
Kent Christian Academy 100/K-12
4462 W Denneys Rd 19904 302-678-3837
Jeanette Berry, prin. Fax 678-5135
Star Technical Institute Post-Sec.
655 S Bay Rd Ste 562 19901 302-736-6111
Wesley College Post-Sec.
120 N State St 19901 302-736-2300

Felton, Kent, Pop. 838
Lake Forest SD 3,600/PK-12
5423 Killens Pond Rd 19943 302-284-3020
Dr. Daniel Curry, supt. Fax 284-4491
www.k12.de.us/lakeforest
Lake Forest HS 800/9-12
5407 Killens Pond Rd 19943 302-284-9291
Dr. Betty Wyatt-Dix, prin. Fax 284-5833
Other Schools – See Harrington

Georgetown, Sussex, Pop. 4,911
Indian River SD
Supt. — See Selbyville
Sussex Central HS 1,100/9-12
26026 Patriots Way 19947 302-934-3166
Dana Goodman, prin. Fax 934-3234
Sussex Central MS 1,000/6-8
301 W Market St 19947 302-856-1900
Vincent Catania, prin. Fax 856-1915

Sussex Technical SD
PO Box 351 19947 302-856-2542
Patrick Savini Ed.D., supt. Fax 856-7078
www.sussexvt.k12.de.us
Sussex Technical HS Vo/Tech
PO Box 351 19947 302-856-0961
Curt Bunting, prin. Fax 856-1760

Delaware Technical & Community College Post-Sec.
PO Box 610 19947 302-856-5400
Delmarva Christian HS 100/9-12
21150 Airport Rd 19947 302-856-4040
William Kemerling, prin. Fax 856-6878

Greenville, New Castle
Red Clay Consolidated SD
Supt. — See Wilmington
DuPont HS 1,300/9-12
50 Hillside Rd 19807 302-651-2626
Samuel Golder, prin. Fax 651-2757
DuPont MS 500/6-8
3130 Kennett Pike 19807 302-651-2690
Theodore Boyer, prin. Fax 425-4585

Greenwood, Sussex, Pop. 883

Greenwood Mennonite S 300/K-12
12802 Mennonite School Rd 19950 302-349-4131
Larry Crossgrove, admin. Fax 349-5076

Harrington, Kent, Pop. 3,236
Lake Forest SD
Supt. — See Felton
Chipman MS 600/7-8
101 W Center St 19952 302-398-8197
James Cave, prin. Fax 398-8375

Hockessin, New Castle
Red Clay Consolidated SD
Supt. — See Wilmington
DuPont MS 900/6-8
735 Meeting House Rd 19707 302-239-3420
John Kennedy, prin. Fax 239-3450

Sanford S 700/PK-12
PO Box 888 19707 302-239-5263
Douglas MacKelcan, hdmstr. Fax 239-5389
Tall Oaks Classical S 100/K-12
1514 Brackenville Rd 19707 302-239-3600
Donald H. Post, hdmstr. Fax 657-8377
Towle Institute 200/K-12
PO Box 580 19707 302-234-4442
Kathleen Todd, prin. Fax 832-3449
Wilmington Christian S 600/PK-12
825 Loveville Rd 19707 302-239-2121
Fax 239-2778

Laurel, Sussex, Pop. 3,822
Laurel SD 2,000/PK-12
1160 S Central Ave 19956 302-875-6100
Keith Duda, supt. Fax 875-6106
www.laurelschooldistrict.org
Laurel HS 500/9-12
1133 S Central Ave 19956 302-875-6120
Dean Ivory, prin. Fax 875-6123
Laurel MS 300/7-8
801 S Central Ave 19956 302-875-6110
Julie Bradley, prin. Fax 875-6148

Lewes, Sussex, Pop. 3,116
Cape Henlopen SD 4,300/K-12
1270 Kings Hwy 19958 302-645-6686
George Stone Ed.D., supt. Fax 645-6684
www.k12.de.us/capehenlopen
Beacon MS 500/6-8
19483 John J Williams Hwy 19958 302-645-6288
T.S. Buckmaster, prin. Fax 644-6118
Cape Henlopen HS 1,200/9-12
1250 Kings Hwy 19958 302-645-7711
John Yore, prin. Fax 645-1356
Other Schools – See Milton

Beebe Medical Center School of Nursing Post-Sec.
424 Savannah Rd 19958 302-645-3251

Lincoln, Sussex

Christian Tabernacle Academy 200/PK-12
PO Box 148 19960 302-422-6471
Ronald Hill, admin. Fax 422-9207

Magnolia, Kent, Pop. 239

St. Thomas More Academy 200/9-12
133 Thomas More Dr 19962 302-697-8100
David McKenzie, prin. Fax 697-8122

Middletown, New Castle, Pop. 9,121
Appoquinimink SD
Supt. — See Odessa
Meredith MS 900/6-8
504 S Broad St 19709 302-378-5001
Dr. Claude McAllister, prin. Fax 378-5008
Middletown HS 1,800/9-12
120 Silver Lake Rd 19709 302-376-4141
Donna Mitchell, prin. Fax 378-5268
Redding MS 700/6-8
201 New St 19709 302-378-5030
James Comegys, prin. Fax 378-5080

New Castle County Voc-Tech SD
Supt. — See Wilmington
St. Georges Technical HS Vo/Tech
555 Hyetts Corner Rd 19709 302-449-3360
Terri Villa, prin.

St. Andrew's S 300/9-12
350 Noxontown Rd 19709 302-378-9511
Daniel Roach, hdmstr. Fax 378-7120

Milford, Sussex, Pop. 7,201
Milford SD 3,700/PK-12
906 Lakeview Ave 19963 302-422-1600
Robert D. Smith Ed.D., supt. Fax 422-1608
www.milfordschooldistrict.org/
Milford HS 1,000/9-12
1019 N Walnut St 19963 302-422-1610
Phyllis Kohel, prin. Fax 424-5463
Milford MS 900/6-8
612 Lakeview Ave 19963 302-422-1620
Kevin Dickerson, prin. Fax 424-5466

Milton, Sussex, Pop. 1,791
Cape Henlopen SD
Supt. — See Lewes
Mariner MS 500/6-8
16391 Harbeson Rd 19968 302-684-8516
Brian Curtis, prin. Fax 684-5606

Newark, New Castle, Pop. 30,060
Christina SD
Supt. — See Wilmington
Christiana HS 1,500/9-12
190 Salem Church Rd 19713 302-454-2123
Noreen Lasorsa, prin. Fax 454-3490
Gauger/Cobbs MS 1,100/7-8
50 Gender Rd 19713 302-454-2358
Amy Levitz, prin. Fax 454-3482
Glasgow HS 1,500/9-12
1901 S College Ave 19702 302-454-2381
Raymond Gravuer, prin. Fax 454-5453
Kirk MS 1,000/7-8
140 Brennen Dr 19713 302-454-2164
Donald Patton, prin. Fax 454-3491
Newark HS 1,800/9-12
750 E Delaware Ave 19711 302-454-2151
Curtis Bedford, prin. Fax 454-2155
Shue-Medill MS 1,200/6-8
1550 Capitol Trl 19711 302-454-2171
Robert Klatzkin, prin. Fax 454-3492

New Castle County Voc-Tech SD
Supt. — See Wilmington
Hodgson Vocational-Technical HS Vo/Tech
2575 Glasgow Ave 19702 302-834-0990
Gerald Allen, prin. Fax 834-0598

Delaware Technical & Community College Post-Sec.
400 Stanton Christiana Rd 19713 302-454-3900
Schilling-Douglas School of Hair Design Post-Sec.
70 Amstel Ave 19711 302-737-5100
University of Delaware 19711 Post-Sec.
302-831-2000

New Castle, New Castle, Pop. 4,836
Colonial SD 9,300/K-12
318 E Basin Rd 19720 302-323-2700
George Meney Ed.D., supt. Fax 323-2748
www.colonial.k12.de.us
Bedford MS 1,200/6-8
801 Coxneck Rd 19720 302-832-6280
Dusty Blakey, prin. Fax 834-6729
McCullough MS 6-8
20 Chase Ave 19720 302-429-4000
Elizabeth Fleetwood, prin. Fax 429-4005
Penn HS 2,400/9-12
713 E Basin Rd 19720 302-323-2800
Jeff Menzer, prin. Fax 323-2955
Read MS 1,100/6-8
314 E Basin Rd 19720 302-323-2760
Paul Walmsley, prin. Fax 323-2763

New Castle Christian Academy 300/PK-12
901 E Basin Rd 19720 302-328-7026
Mark Unruh, admin. Fax 328-7886
Wilmington College Post-Sec.
320 N Dupont Hwy 19720 302-328-9401

Odessa, New Castle, Pop. 322
Appoquinimink SD 6,700/PK-12
PO Box 4010 19730 302-376-4128
Dr. Tony Marchio, supt. Fax 378-5016
apposchooldistrict.com
Other Schools – See Middletown

Seaford, Sussex, Pop. 6,997
Seaford SD 3,300/K-12
390 N Market Street Ext 19973 302-629-4587
Dr. Russell Knorr, supt. Fax 629-2619
www.seaford.k12.de.us
Seaford HS 900/9-12
399 N Market St 19973 302-629-4587
Clarence Davis, prin. Fax 628-4417
Seaford MS 800/6-8
500 E Stein Hwy 19973 302-629-4587
Stephanie Smith, prin. Fax 628-4485

Seaford Christian Academy 300/PK-12
110 Holly St 19973 302-629-7161
David McGown, admin. Fax 629-7726

Selbyville, Sussex, Pop. 1,742
Indian River SD 7,800/PK-12
31 Hoosier St 19975 302-436-1000
Susan Bunting, supt. Fax 436-1007
www.irsd.net/
Selbyville MS 700/6-8
80 Bethany Rd 19975 302-436-1020
Brice Reed, prin. Fax 436-1035
Other Schools – See Dagsboro, Georgetown

Smyrna, Kent, Pop. 7,413
Smyrna SD 3,600/K-12
22 S Main St 19977 302-653-8585
Deborah Wicks, supt. Fax 653-3149
www.smyrna.k12.de.us
Smyrna HS 1,000/9-12
500 Duck Creek Pkwy 19977 302-653-8581
Anthony Soligo, prin. Fax 653-3139
Smyrna MS 700/7-8
700 Duck Creek Pkwy 19977 302-653-8584
Patrik Williams, prin. Fax 653-3424

Wilmington, New Castle, Pop. 72,786
Brandywine SD
Supt. — See Claymont
Brandywine HS 1,300/9-12
1400 Foulk Rd 19803 302-479-1600
Richard Gregg, prin. Fax 479-1604
Concord HS 1,100/9-12
2501 Ebright Rd 19810 302-475-3951
Mark Holodick, prin. Fax 529-3094
Hanby MS 700/7-8
2523 Berwyn Rd 19810 302-479-1631
Ronald Mendenhall, prin. Fax 479-1643
Mt. Pleasant HS 900/9-12
5201 Washington Blvd 19809 302-762-7125
Michael Pullig, prin. Fax 762-7042
Springer MS 600/7-8
2220 Shipley Rd 19803 302-479-1621
Michael Gliniak, prin. Fax 479-1628
Talley MS 500/7-8
1110 Cypress Rd 19810 302-475-3976
Richard Carter, prin. Fax 475-3998

Christina SD 18,700/PK-12
600 N Lombard St 19801 302-552-2600
Lillian Lowery, supt. Fax 429-4109
www.christina.k12.de.us/
Other Schools – See Newark

New Castle County Voc-Tech SD
1417 Newport Rd 19804 302-995-8000
Steven Godowsky Ed.D., supt. Fax 995-8038
www.nccvotech.com/
Delcastle Technical HS Vo/Tech
1417 Newport Rd 19804 302-995-8100
Joseph Jones, prin. Fax 995-8197
Howard HS of Technology Vo/Tech
401 E 12th St 19801 302-571-5400
Evelyn Edney, prin. Fax 571-5843

Delaware Skills Center Adult
13th & Clifford Brown Walk 19801 302-654-5392
Robert Marshall, prin. Fax 654-9418
Other Schools – See Middletown, Newark

Red Clay Consolidated SD 14,800/K-12
4550 New Linden Hill Rd 19808 302-552-3700
Dr. Robert Andrzejewski, supt. Fax 992-7820
www.redclay.k12.de.us
Calloway School of Arts 800/6-12
100 N Dupont Rd 19807 302-651-2700
Julie Rumschlag, prin. Fax 425-4594
Conrad MS 600/6-8
201 Jackson Ave 19804 302-992-5545
Burton Watson, prin. Fax 992-5585
Dickinson HS 1,000/9-12
1801 Milltown Rd 19808 302-992-5500
Chad Carmack, prin. Fax 992-5506
McKean HS 1,100/9-12
301 Mckennans Church Rd 19808 302-992-5520
Sherry Gross, prin. Fax 992-5525
Skyline MS 700/6-8
2900 Skyline Dr 19808 302-454-3410
Janet Basara, prin. Fax 454-3541
Stanton MS 700/6-8
1800 Limestone Rd 19804 302-992-5540
Carolyn Zogby, prin. Fax 992-5586
Groves Adult Education Adult
100 N Dupont Rd 19807 302-651-2709
Les Henry, prin. Fax 658-7137
Other Schools – See Greenville, Hockessin

Christiana Care Health Services Post-Sec.
PO Box 1668 19899 302-428-2571
Concord Christian Academy 200/K-12
2510 Marsh Rd 19810 302-475-3247
Jeffrey Bergey, prin. Fax 475-6462
Dawn Training Centre Post-Sec.
3700 Lancaster Pike 19805 302-633-9075
Deep Muscle Therapy School Post-Sec.
5341 Limestone Rd 19808 302-234-8525
Delaware Technical & Community College Post-Sec.
333 N Shipley St 19801 302-571-5474
Goldey-Beacom College Post-Sec.
4701 Limestone Rd 19808 302-998-8814
Nativity Preparatory S 5-8
1515 Linden St 19805 302-777-1015
Br. Edward Ogden, prin. Fax 777-1225
Padua Academy 600/9-12
905 N Broom St 19806 302-421-3739
Sr. Ann Michele Zwosta, prin. Fax 421-3748
St. Elizabeth HS 400/9-12
1500 Cedar St 19805 302-656-3369
Shirley Bounds, prin. Fax 656-7513
St. Marks HS 9-12
2501 Pike Creek Rd 19808 302-738-3300
Mark Freund, prin. Fax 738-5132
Salesianum S 1,000/9-12
1801 N Broom St 19802 302-654-2495
Rev. William McCandless, prin. Fax 654-7767
Tatnall S 700/PK-12
1501 Barley Mill Rd 19807 302-998-2292
Eric Ruoss, hdmstr. Fax 892-4389
Tower Hill S 700/PK-12
2813 W 17th St 19806 302-575-0550
Dr. Christopher Wheeler, hdmstr. Fax 657-8373
Ursuline Academy 700/PK-12
1106 Pennsylvania Ave 19806 302-658-7158
Elena Bingham, pres. Fax 658-4297
Widener University School of Law Post-Sec.
PO Box 7474 19803 302-477-2100
Wilmington Friends S 800/PK-12
101 School Rd 19803 302-576-2900
Bryan Garman, hdmstr. Fax 576-2939

Woodside, Kent, Pop. 195
Polytech SD
PO Box 22 19980 302-697-2170
Dianne Sole Ed.D., supt. Fax 697-6749
www.polytech.k12.de.us
Polytech HS Vo/Tech
PO Box 97 19980 302-697-3255
Bruce Curry Ed.D., prin. Fax 697-4536

DISTRICT OF COLUMBIA

DISTRICT OF COLUMBIA PUBLIC SCHOOLS
825 N Capitol St NE, Washington 20002
Telephone 202-442-5635
Website http://www.k12.dc.us

Chancellor Michelle Rhee

DISTRICT OF COLUMBIA BOARD OF EDUCATION
825 N Capitol St NE, Washington 20002

President Robert Bobb

PUBLIC, PRIVATE AND CATHOLIC SECONDARY SCHOOLS

Washington, District of Columbia, Pop. 550,521

District of Columbia SD 54,500/PK-12
825 N Capitol St NE 20002 202-724-4222
Clifford Janey Ed.D., supt. Fax 442-5026
www.k12.dc.us/

Anacostia HS 600/9-12
1601 16th St SE 20020 202-698-2155
Ronald Duplessie, prin. Fax 645-3019

Backus MS 300/6-8
5171 S Dakota Ave NE 20017 202-576-6110
Fax 576-6112

Ballou HS 1,000/9-12
3401 4th St SE 20032 202-645-3400
Karen Smith, prin. Fax 767-7297

Banneker HS 400/9-12
800 Euclid St NW 20001 202-673-7322
Anita Berger, prin. Fax 673-2231

Bell Multi-Cultural HS 700/9-12
3101 16th St NW 20010 202-939-7700
Maria Tukeva, prin.

Browne JHS, 850 26th St NE 20002 500/7-9
Keith Stephenson, prin. 202-724-4547

Brown MS, 4800 Meade St NE 20019 300/6-8
Darrin Slade, prin. 202-724-4632

Cardozo HS 800/9-12
1200 Clifton St NW 20009 202-673-7385
Barbara Childs, prin. Fax 673-2232

Coolidge HS 600/9-12
6315 5th St NW 20011 202-576-6143
L. Nelson Burton, prin. Fax 576-6263

Deal JHS 900/7-9
3815 Fort Dr NW 20016 202-282-0100
Melissa Kim, prin. Fax 282-1116

Dunbar HS 900/9-12
1301 New Jersey Ave NW 20001 202-673-7233
Harriett Kargbo, prin. Fax 673-2233

Eastern HS 1,100/9-12
1700 E Capitol St NE 20003 202-698-4500
Fax 724-8744

Eliot JHS 300/7-9
1830 Constitution Ave NE 20002 202-673-8666
Andre Roach, prin. Fax 543-4500

Ellington HS of the Arts 400/9-12
3500 R St NW 20007 202-282-0123
Rory Pullens, prin. Fax 282-1106

Francis JHS 400/7-9
2425 N St NW 20037 202-724-4841
Stephanie Crutchfield, prin. Fax 724-3957

Garnet-Patterson MS 300/5-8
2001 10th St NW 20001 202-673-7329
Veda Usilton, prin. Fax 673-6543

Hardy MS 400/5-8
1401 Brentwood Pkwy NE 20002 202-698-3885
Patrick Pope, prin.

Hart MS 500/6-8
601 Mississippi Ave SE 20032 202-645-3420
Willie Bennett, prin. Fax 645-3426

Hine JHS 600/7-9
335 8th St SE 20003 202-698-3330
Willie Jackson, prin. Fax 724-4775

Jefferson JHS 800/7-9
801 7th St SW 20024 202-724-4881
MenSa Ankh Maa, prin. Fax 724-2459

Johnson JHS 600/7-9
1400 Bruce Pl SE 20020 202-698-1017
Sylvia S. Dark, prin. Fax 645-3693

Kelly Miller MS, 301 49th St NE 20019 500/6-8
Sheena Tuckson, prin. 202-388-6870

Kramer MS 400/6-8
1700 Q St SE 20020 202-698-1188
Kenneth Parker, prin. Fax 645-3553

Lincoln MS, 3101 16th St NW 20010 300/6-8
Lydia Blazquez, prin. 202-939-6680

MacFarland MS 500/6-8
4400 Iowa Ave NW 20011 202-576-6207
Antonia Peters, prin.

McKinley Technology HS Vo/Tech
151 T St NE 20002 – Dan Gohl, prin. 202-281-3950

Roosevelt HS 800/9-12
4301 13th St NW 20011 202-576-6130
Benjamin Hosch, prin. Fax 576-6259

Shaw JHS 500/7-9
925 Rhode Island Ave NW 20001 202-673-7203
Gregory Thomas, prin. Fax 673-2364

Sousa MS 400/6-8
3650 Ely Pl SE 20019 202-645-3170
Fax 582-2953

Spingarn HS 600/9-12
2500 Benning Rd NE 20002 202-724-4525
Reginald Burke, prin. Fax 724-8746

Stuart-Hobson MS 400/5-8
410 E St NE 20002 202-698-4700
Brandon Eatman, prin. Fax 724-4985

Washington Career Development S Vo/Tech
27 O St NW 20001 202-673-7224
William Chiselom, prin. Fax 673-7229

Wilson HS 1,400/9-12
3950 Chesapeake St NW 20016 202-282-0120
Stephen Tarason, prin. Fax 282-0077

Woodson HS 700/9-12
5500 Eads St NE 20019 202-724-4500
Aona Jefferson, prin. Fax 727-9360

Ballou STAY S Adult
3401 4th St SE 20032 202-645-3390
Wilbert Miller, prin. Fax 645-3397

Roosevelt STAY Adult
4301 13th St NW 20011 202-576-8399
Linda Gray, prin.

Spingarn STAY S Adult
2500 Benning Rd NE 20002 202-724-4538
Erline Whitaker, prin.

American University Post-Sec.
4400 Massachusetts Ave NW 20016 202-885-1000

Archbishop Carroll HS 600/9-12
4300 Harewood Rd NE 20017 202-529-0900
Dr. David Stofa, prin. Fax 526-8879

Bennett Beauty Institute Post-Sec.
700 Monroe St NE 20017 202-526-1400

Burke S 300/6-12
4101 Connecticut Ave NW 20008 202-362-8882
David Shapiro, prin. Fax 362-1914

Catholic University of America Post-Sec.
620 Michigan Ave NE 20064 202-319-5000

Corcoran College of Art & Design Post-Sec.
500 17th St NW 20006 202-639-1814

Dominican House of Studies Post-Sec.
487 Michigan Ave NE 20017 202-529-5300

Don Bosco Cristo Rey HS 9-12
PO Box 56481 20040 240-723-6100
Rev. Steve Shafran, pres.

Dudley Beauty College Post-Sec.
2031 Rhode Island Ave NE 20018 202-269-3666

Dupont Park Adventist S 300/PK-10
3942 Alabama Ave SE 20020 202-583-8500
Fax 583-0650

Field S 300/7-12
2301 Foxhall Rd NW 20007 202-295-5800
Dale Johnson, prin. Fax 295-5858

Gallaudet University Post-Sec.
800 Florida Ave NE 20002 202-651-5000

Georgetown Day S 500/9-12
4200 Davenport St NW 20016 202-274-3200
Peter Branch, hdmstr. Fax 364-9603

Georgetown University Post-Sec.
37th And O St NW 20057 202-687-0100

Georgetown Visitation Prep HS 9-12
1524 35th St NW 20007 202-337-3350
Daniel Kerns, hdmstr. Fax 342-5733

George Washington University Post-Sec.
2035 H St NW 20052 202-994-1000

Gonzaga College HS 900/9-12
19 I St NW 20001 202-336-7100
Michael Pakenham, hdmstr. Fax 454-1188

Howard University Post-Sec.
2400 6th St NW 20059 202-806-6100

Howard University School of Divinity Post-Sec.
1400 Shepherd St NE 20017 202-806-0500

Johns Hopkins University Post-Sec.
1740 Massachusetts Ave NW 20036 202-663-5600

Lab S of Washington 300/K-12
4759 Reservoir Rd NW 20007 202-965-6600
Dr. Sally L. Smith, dir. Fax 454-2270

Levine School of Music Post-Sec.
2801 Upton St NW 20008 202-686-8000

Maret S 600/K-12
3000 Cathedral Ave NW 20008 202-939-8800
Marjo Talbott, hdmstr. Fax 939-8884

Model Secondary School for the Deaf Post-Sec.
800 Florida Ave NE 20002 202-651-5466

National Cathedral S 600/4-12
3612 Woodley Rd NW 20016 202-537-6300
Kathleen O. Jamieson, hdmstr. Fax 537-5743

National Conservatory of Dramatic Arts Post-Sec.
1556 Wisconsin Ave NW 20007 202-333-2202

Our Lady of Perpetual Help S 100/5-8
1604 Morris Rd SE 20020 202-678-0211
Charlene Hursey, prin. Fax 610-1519

Parkmont S 100/6-12
4842 16th St NW 20011 202-726-0740
Ron McClain, hdmstr. Fax 726-0748

Potomac College Post-Sec.
4000 Chesapeake St NW 20016 202-686-0876

St. Alban's S 600/4-12
Mount Saint Alban 20016 202-537-6435
Vance Wilson, hdmstr. Fax 537-5613

St. Anselms Abbey S 300/6-12
4501 S Dakota Ave NE 20017 202-269-2350
Rev. Peter Weigand, prin. Fax 269-2373

St. Johns College HS 1,100/9-12
2607 Military Rd NW 20015 202-363-2316
Jeffrey Mancabelli, prin. Fax 686-5162

San Miguel MS 6-8
1525 Newton St NW 20010 202-232-1193
Br. Francis Eells, prin. Fax 232-3987

Sidwell Friends S 1,100/PK-12
3825 Wisconsin Ave NW 20016 202-537-8100
Bruce Stewart, hdmstr. Fax 537-8138

Southeastern University Post-Sec.
501 I St SW 20024 202-488-8162

Strayer University Post-Sec.
1133 15th St NW 20005 202-419-2400

The Institute of World Politics Post-Sec.
1521 16th St NW 20036 202-462-2101

Trinity University Post-Sec.
125 Michigan Ave NE 20017 202-884-9000

University of the D.C. School of Law Post-Sec.
4200 Connecticut Ave NW 20008 202-274-5000

University of the District of Columbia Post-Sec.
4200 Connecticut Ave NW 20008 202-274-5100

Walter Reed Medical Center Post-Sec.
6825 16th St NW 20307 202-782-6104

Washington Hospital Center Post-Sec.
110 Irving St NW 20010 202-877-6101

Washington International S 800/6-12
3100 Macomb St NW 20008 202-243-1800
Richard Hall, hdmstr. Fax 243-1802

Washington Jesuit Academy 50/6-8
800 3rd St NE 20002 202-543-5250
John Hoffman, hdmstr. Fax 543-5901

Washington Theological Union Post-Sec.
6896 Laurel St NW 20012 202-726-8800

Wesley Theological Seminary Post-Sec.
4500 Massachusetts Ave NW 20016 202-885-8600

FLORIDA

FLORIDA DEPARTMENT OF EDUCATION
325 W Gaines St, Tallahassee 32399-0400
Telephone 850-245-0505
Fax 850-245-9667
Website http://www.fldoe.org/

Commissioner of Education Jeanine Blomberg

FLORIDA BOARD OF EDUCATION
325 W Gaines St, Tallahassee 32399-0400

Chairperson T. Willard Fair

PUBLIC, PRIVATE AND CATHOLIC SECONDARY SCHOOLS

Alachua, Alachua, Pop. 7,557
Alachua County SD
Supt. — See Gainesville
Mebane MS 500/6-8
16401 NW 140th St 32615 386-462-1648
Veita Jackson-Carter, prin. Fax 462-9094
Santa Fe HS 1,300/9-12
16213 NW US Highway 441 32615 386-462-1125
Bill Herschleb, prin. Fax 462-1711

Altamonte Springs, Seminole, Pop. 41,057
Seminole County SD
Supt. — See Sanford
Lake Brantley HS 3,300/9-12
991 Sand Lake Rd 32714 407-320-3450
Mary Williams, prin. Fax 320-3600
Teague MS 1,700/6-8
1350 Mcneil Rd 32714 407-320-1550
Adrienne DeRienzo, prin. Fax 320-1545

Altamonte Christian S 300/PK-12
601 Palm Springs Dr 32701 407-831-0950
Rev. Scott Carlson, dir. Fax 831-6840
Champion Preparatory Academy 300/PK-12
721 W Lake Brantley Rd 32714 407-788-0018
Vicki Falco, dir. Fax 788-7625
Everglades University Post-Sec.
887 E Altamonte Dr 32701 866-289-1078
Golf Academy of the South Post-Sec.
1200 E Altamonte Dr #1010 32701 800-342-7342

Altha, Calhoun, Pop. 511
Calhoun County SD
Supt. — See Blountstown
Altha S 700/PK-12
PO Box 67 32421 850-762-3121
Ronnie Hand, prin. Fax 762-9502

Alva, Lee, Pop. 1,036
Lee County SD
Supt. — See Fort Myers
Alva MS 600/6-8
PO Box 128 33920 239-728-2525
Stephen Hutnik, prin. Fax 728-2835

Apalachicola, Franklin, Pop. 2,340
Franklin County SD 1,100/PK-12
155 Avenue E 32320 850-653-8831
Jo Ann Gander, supt. Fax 653-8984
www.franklincountyschools.org/
Apalachicola HS 200/9-12
1 Shark Blvd 32320 850-653-8811
Nick O'Grady, prin. Fax 653-2782
Apalachicola MS 100/6-8
98 12th St 32320 850-653-8857
Nick O'Grady, prin. Fax 653-8420
Franklin County Adult S Adult
155 Avenue E 32320 850-653-8831
Nan Collins, dir. Fax 653-8984
Other Schools – See Carrabelle

Apopka, Orange, Pop. 34,728
Orange County SD
Supt. — See Orlando
Apopka 9th Grade Center 9-9
800 N Wells St 32712 407-905-5500
Scott Sherman, prin.
Apopka HS, 555 Martin St 32712 4,000/9-12
William Floyd, prin. 407-905-5500
Apopka MS 1,600/6-8
425 N Park Ave 32712 407-884-2208
Douglas Guthrie, prin. Fax 884-2217
Piedmont Lakes MS 1,700/6-8
2601 Lakeville Rd 32703 407-884-2265
David Magee, prin. Fax 884-2287
Wolf Lake MS 6-8
1725 W Ponkan Rd 32712 407-464-3317
Dr. Cathy Thornton, prin.

Forest Lake Academy 600/9-12
3909 E Semoran Blvd 32703 407-862-8411
Gloria Becker, prin. Fax 862-7050

Arcadia, DeSoto, Pop. 7,151
De Soto County SD 4,600/PK-12
PO Box 2000 34265 863-494-4222
Adrian Cline, supt. Fax 494-9675
www.desotoschools.com
DeSoto HS 1,300/9-12
1710 E Gibson St 34266 863-494-3434
Daniel Dubbert, prin. Fax 494-7867
DeSoto MS 1,000/6-8
420 E Gibson St 34266 863-494-4133
Dave Bremer, prin. Fax 494-6263
DeSoto County Adult Education Center Adult
310 W Whidden St 34266 863-993-1333
Martha Jo Markey, prin. Fax 993-9181

Atlantic Beach, Duval, Pop. 13,436
Duval County SD
Supt. — See Jacksonville
Marine Science Education Center Vo/Tech
1347 Palmer St 32233 904-247-5973
Karen Davis, prin. Fax 247-5976
Mayport MS 900/6-8
2600 Mayport Rd 32233 904-247-5977
Karen Davis, prin. Fax 247-5987

Auburndale, Polk, Pop. 12,381
Polk County SD
Supt. — See Bartow
Auburndale HS 1,800/9-12
1 Bloodhound Trl 33823 863-965-6200
Ernest Joe, prin. Fax 965-6245
Stambaugh MS 1,000/6-8
226 N Main St 33823 863-965-5494
Allison Kalbfleisch, prin. Fax 965-5496
East Area Adult & Community S Adult
300 E Bridgers Ave 33823 863-965-5475
Sallie Brisbane, prin. Fax 965-5477

Florida Technical College Post-Sec.
298 Havendale Blvd 33823 863-967-8822

Avon Park, Highlands, Pop. 8,872
Highlands County SD
Supt. — See Sebring
Avon Park HS 1,100/9-12
700 E Main St 33825 863-452-4311
Stuart Guthrie, prin. Fax 452-4324
Avon Park MS 700/6-8
401 S Lake Ave 33825 863-452-4333
Dan Johnson, prin. Fax 452-4341

South Florida Community College Post-Sec.
600 W College Dr 33825 863-453-6661
Walker Memorial Academy 200/K-12
1525 W Avon Blvd 33825 863-453-3131
William Farmer, dir. Fax 453-4925

Babson Park, Polk, Pop. 1,125

Webber International University Post-Sec.
PO Box 96 33827 863-638-1431

Baker, Okaloosa
Okaloosa County SD
Supt. — See Fort Walton Beach
Baker S 1,400/PK-12
1369 14th St 32531 850-689-7279
Tom Shipp, prin. Fax 689-7416

Baldwin, Duval, Pop. 1,589
Duval County SD
Supt. — See Jacksonville
Baldwin MSHS 900/6-12
291 Mill St W 32234 904-266-1200
Dr. Donna Richardson, prin. Fax 266-1220

Bartow, Polk, Pop. 16,278
Polk County SD 78,000/PK-12
PO Box 391 33831 863-534-0521
Dr. Gail McKinzie, supt. Fax 519-8231
www.pcsb.k12.fl.us/
Bartow HS 1,200/9-12
1270 S Broadway Ave 33830 863-534-7400
Ron Pritchard, prin. Fax 534-0077
Bartow MS 900/6-8
550 E Clower St 33830 863-534-7415
Harry Williams, prin. Fax 534-7418
Summerlin Academy 9-12
1270 S Broadway Ave 33830 863-534-7287
Mike Butler, prin.
Union Academy MS 400/6-8
1795 E Wabash St 33830 863-534-7435
Steve Petrie, prin. Fax 534-7487
Bartow Adult & Community S Adult
1275 S Broadway Ave 33830 863-534-7450
John Scholler, prin.
Other Schools – See Auburndale, Davenport, Dundee, Eagle Lake, Fort Meade, Frostproof, Haines City, Lake Alfred, Lakeland, Lake Wales, Mulberry, Winter Haven

Bell, Gilchrist, Pop. 390
Gilchrist County SD
Supt. — See Trenton
Bell HS 700/6-12
930 S Main St 32619 352-463-3232
Ronda Parrish, prin. Fax 463-3294

Belle Glade, Palm Beach, Pop. 15,423
Palm Beach County SD
Supt. — See West Palm Beach
Glades Central Community HS 1,300/9-12
1001 SW Avenue M 33430 561-993-4400
Edward Harris, prin. Fax 993-4414
Lake Shore MS 1,200/6-8
425 W Canal St N 33430 561-829-1100
Floyd Henry, prin. Fax 829-1190

Glades Day S 600/PK-12
400 Gator Blvd 33430 561-996-6769
James Teets, hdmstr. Fax 992-9274

Belleview, Marion, Pop. 3,856
Marion County SD
Supt. — See Ocala
Belleview HS 1,800/9-12
10400 SE 36th Ave 34420 352-671-6210
Jim Wohrley, prin. Fax 671-6212
Belleview MS 1,200/6-8
10500 SE 36th Ave 34420 352-671-6235
Lisa Krysalka, prin. Fax 671-6239

Blountstown, Calhoun, Pop. 2,433
Calhoun County SD 2,300/PK-12
20859 Central Ave E Ste G20 32424 850-674-5927
Mary Sue Neves, supt. Fax 674-5814
www.paec.org/calhoun/district/
Blountstown HS 400/9-12
17586 Main St N 32424 850-674-5724
Keith Summers, prin. Fax 674-8865
Blountstown MS 300/6-8
21089 SE Mayhaw Dr 32424 850-674-8234
Mike Johnson, prin. Fax 674-6480
Calhoun County Adult Education Center Adult
17283 NW Charlie Johns St 32424 850-674-8661
Willy Pitts, prin. Fax 237-2355
Other Schools – See Altha

Boca Raton, Palm Beach, Pop. 86,632
Palm Beach County SD
Supt. — See West Palm Beach
Boca Raton Community HS 1,900/9-12
1501 NW 15th Ct 33486 561-338-1400
Geoffrey McKee, prin. Fax 338-1440
Boca Raton Community MS 1,100/6-8
1251 NW 8th St 33486 561-416-8700
Jack Thompson, prin. Fax 416-8777
Eagles Landing MS 1,400/6-8
19500 Coral Ridge Dr 33498 561-470-7000
Ira Margulies, prin. Fax 470-7030
Estridge High Tech MS 6-8
1798 NW Spanish River Blvd 33431 561-989-7800
Debra Johnson, prin. Fax 989-7810
Loggers Run Community MS 1,200/6-8
11584 W Palmetto Park Rd 33428 561-883-8000
Carol Blacharski, prin. Fax 883-8027
Olympic Heights Community HS 2,000/9-12
20101 Lyons Rd 33434 561-852-6900
Peter Licata, prin. Fax 852-6974
Omni MS 1,300/6-8
5775 Jog Rd 33496 561-989-2800
Mark Stenner, prin. Fax 989-2851
Spanish River Community HS 2,600/9-12
5100 Jog Rd 33496 561-241-2200
Constance Tuman-Rugg, prin. Fax 241-2236
West Boca Raton Community HS 1,600/9-12
12811 Glades Rd 33498 561-672-2001
Francis Giblin, prin. Fax 672-2014

Boca Raton Christian S 600/PK-12
315 NW 4th St 33432 561-391-2727
Robert Tennies Ed.D., hdmstr. Fax 367-6808

Boca Raton Preparatory S | 100/PK-12
10333 Diego Dr S 33428 | 561-852-1410
Graham Hurrell, prin. | Fax 470-6124
Claremont Montessori S | 100/PK-12
2450 NW 5th Ave 33431 | 561-394-7674
Harvey Hallenberg, prin. | Fax 394-9792
Everglades University | Post-Sec.
5002 T Rex Ave Ste 100 33431 | 561-912-1211
Florida Atlantic University | Post-Sec.
PO Box 3091 33431 | 561-297-3000
Grandview Preparatory S | 300/PK-12
336 NW Spanish River Blvd 33431 | 561-416-9737
Jacqueline Westerfield, prin. | Fax 416-9739
Klein Jewish Academy | 700/K-12
9701 Donna Klein Blvd 33428 | 561-852-3300
Karen Feller, hdmstr. | Fax 852-3327
Lynn University | Post-Sec.
3601 N Military Trl 33431 | 561-237-7000
Lynn University Conservatory of Music | Post-Sec.
3601 N Military Trl 33431 | 561-237-9001
PC Professor | Post-Sec.
7056 Beracasa Way 33433 | 561-750-7879
Pope John Paul II HS | 900/9-12
4001 N Military Trl 33431 | 561-314-2100
Sr. Eileen Sullivan, prin. | Fax 989-8582
St. Andrew's S | 1,100/PK-12
3900 Jog Rd 33434 | 561-210-2010
Rev. George E. Andrews, hdmstr. | Fax 210-2017
Weinbaum Yeshiva HS | 200/9-12
7902 Montoya Cir N 33433 | 561-417-7422
Shimmie Kaminetsky, dir. | Fax 417-7028
West Boca Medical Center | Post-Sec.
21644 State Road 7 33428 | 561-488-8000

Bonifay, Holmes, Pop. 2,711
Holmes County SD | 3,300/PK-12
701 E Pennsylvania Ave 32425 | 850-547-9341
Steve Griffin, supt. | Fax 547-0381
www.hdsb.org
Bethlehem S | 500/PK-12
2676 Highway 160 32425 | 850-547-3621
T.C. Clemmons, prin. | Fax 547-4856
Bonifay MS | 500/5-8
401 Mclaughlin Ave 32425 | 850-547-2754
Bill Gilley, prin. | Fax 547-3685
Holmes County HS | 500/9-12
825 W Highway 90 32425 | 850-547-9000
Janis Johnson, prin. | Fax 547-6694
Other Schools – See Graceville, Ponce de Leon

Bonita Springs, Lee, Pop. 37,992
Lee County SD
Supt. — See Fort Myers
Bonita Springs MS | 900/6-8
10141 W Terry St 34135 | 239-992-4422
Joe Williams, prin. | Fax 992-9157

Gospel Baptist Christian S | 100/PK-12
24861 Old 41 Rd 34135 | 239-947-2341
William Lytell, admin. | Fax 947-1285
Grace Community S | 100/PK-12
8971 Brighton Ln 34135 | 239-948-7878
Rev. Jeremy Walker, prin. | Fax 949-1597
Lee County Independent Private S | 100/K-12
26801 Pine Ave 34135 | 239-992-6381
Kathleen Sprafka, prin. | Fax 992-6473

Boynton Beach, Palm Beach, Pop. 66,885
Palm Beach County SD
Supt. — See West Palm Beach
Boynton Beach Community HS | 2,000/9-12
4975 Park Ridge Blvd 33426 | 561-752-1200
Kathleen Perry, prin. | Fax 752-1205
Congress MS | 1,100/6-8
101 S Congress Ave 33426 | 561-374-5600
Kathy Harris, prin. | Fax 374-5642
McAuliffe MS | 1,300/6-8
6500 Le Chalet Blvd, | 561-374-6600
Reginald Myers, prin. | Fax 374-6636
Odyssey MS | 1,200/6-8
6161 W Woolbright Rd 33437 | 561-752-1300
Bonnie Fox, prin. | Fax 752-1305

Bethesda Memorial Hospital | Post-Sec.
2815 S Seacrest Blvd 33435 | 561-737-7733
Lake Worth Christian S | 400/PK-12
7592 High Ridge Rd 33426 | 561-586-8216
Robert Hook, admin. | Fax 586-4382
St. Vincent DePaul Regional Seminary | Post-Sec.
10701 S Military Trl 33436 | 561-732-4424

Bradenton, Manatee, Pop. 53,917
Manatee County SD | 38,500/PK-12
PO Box 9069 34206 | 941-708-8770
Dr. Roger Dearing, supt. | Fax 708-8686
www.manatee.k12.fl.us
Bayshore HS | 1,900/9-12
5401 34th St W 34210 | 941-751-7004
David Underhill, prin. | Fax 753-0953
Braden River HS | 9-12
6545 E State Road 70 34203 | 941-751-8230
Jim Pauley, prin. | Fax 751-8250
Braden River MS | 1,100/6-8
6215 River Club Blvd 34202 | 941-751-7080
Randy Petrilla, prin. | Fax 751-7085
Haile MS | 900/6-8
9501 E State Road 64 34212 | 941-714-7240
Janet Kerley, prin. | Fax 714-7245
Harllee MS | 700/6-8
6423 9th St E 34203 | 941-751-7027
James Hird, prin. | Fax 751-7030
Johnson MS | 900/6-8
2121 26th Ave E 34208 | 941-741-3344
Ann McDonald, prin. | Fax 741-3345
King MS | 1,000/6-8
600 75th St NW 34209 | 941-798-6820
Joe Stokes, prin. | Fax 798-6835
Lakewood Ranch HS | 2,600/9-12
5500 Lakewood Ranch Blvd 34211 | 941-727-6100
Mike Wilder, prin. | Fax 727-6099
Lee MS | 1,000/6-8
4000 53rd Ave W 34210 | 941-727-6500
Scot Boice, prin. | Fax 727-6513
Manatee HS | 2,100/9-12
1 Hurricane Ln 34205 | 941-714-7300
Bob Gagnon, prin. | Fax 741-3443
Manatee Technical Institute | Vo/Tech
5603 34th St W 34210 | 941-751-7900
Mary Cantrell, prin. | Fax 751-7927
Manatee Technical Institute East | Vo/Tech
5520 Lakewood Ranch Blvd 34211 | 941-752-8100
Priscilla Haflich, prin. | Fax 727-6254
Nolan MS | 600/6-8
6615 Greenbrook Blvd 34202 | 941-751-8200
Nancy High, prin. | Fax 751-8210
Southeast HS | 2,000/9-12
1200 37th Ave E 34208 | 941-741-3366
Mike Horne, prin. | Fax 741-3372
Sugg MS | 1,000/6-8
3801 59th St W 34209 | 941-741-3157
Willie Clark, prin. | Fax 741-3514
Community HS | Adult
5603 34th St W 34210 | 941-751-7900
Omar Edwards, dir. | Fax 751-7927
Other Schools – See Palmetto

Beauty and Barber Academy | Post-Sec.
5505 Manatee Ave W 34209 | 941-761-4400
Bradenton Christian S | 600/PK-12
3304 43rd St W 34209 | 941-792-5454
Dan van der Kooy, supt. | Fax 795-7190
Bradenton Preparatory Academy | 400/K-12
7900 40th Ave W 34209 | 941-792-7838
Susan Hedgcock, prin. | Fax 798-9920
Community Christian S | 300/PK-12
5500 18th St E 34203 | 941-756-8748
Charles Sartor, prin. | Fax 753-7057
Edison Academic Center | 200/K-12
7431 Manatee Ave W 34209 | 941-794-3630
Barbara Iannarelli, prin. | Fax 794-3955
Florida College of Natural Health | Post-Sec.
616 67th Street Cir E 34208 | 941-954-8999
Gulfcoast Christian Academy | 50/K-12
1700 51st Ave E 34203 | 941-755-1690
Brenda Timms, admin. | Fax 755-0332
Lake Erie College\Osteopathic Medicine | Post-Sec.
5000 Lakewood Ranch Blvd 34211 | 941-756-0690
Manatee Community College | Post-Sec.
5840 26th St W 34207 | 941-752-5000
Manatee Technical Institute | Post-Sec.
5603 34th St W 34210 | 941-751-7900
Manatee Technical Institute East Campus | Post-Sec.
5520 Lakewood Ranch Blvd 34211 | 941-752-8100
Pendleton S | 400/PK-12
5500 34th St W 34210 | 941-739-3964
George Neville, prin. | Fax 739-6483
Providence Community S | 100/PK-12
5512 26th St W 34207 | 941-727-6860
Barry Batson, admin.
St. Stephen's Episcopal S | 800/PK-12
315 41st St W 34209 | 941-746-2121
Jan Pullen, hdmstr. | Fax 746-5699

Brandon, Hillsborough, Pop. 83,200
Hillsborough County SD
Supt. — See Tampa
Brandon HS | 2,100/9-12
1101 Victoria St 33510 | 813-744-8120
Leslie Granich, prin. | Fax 744-8129
Burns MS | 1,500/6-8
615 Brooker Rd 33511 | 813-744-8383
Brenda Nolte, prin. | Fax 740-3623
Mann MS | 800/6-8
409 E Jersey Ave 33510 | 813-744-8400
Nancy Trathowen, prin. | Fax 744-6707
McLane MS | 1,400/6-8
306 N Knights Ave 33510 | 813-744-8100
James Elliott, prin. | Fax 744-8135

Faith Baptist Christian S | 100/PK-12
1118 N Parsons Ave 33510 | 813-654-4936
Dr. Gene Reynolds, prin. | Fax 654-7239

Branford, Suwannee, Pop. 756
Suwannee County SD
Supt. — See Live Oak
Branford HS | 700/6-12
405 Reynolds St NE 32008 | 386-935-1231
Ted Roush, prin. | Fax 935-3867

Bristol, Liberty, Pop. 910
Liberty County SD | 1,200/PK-12
PO Box 429 32321 | 850-643-2275
David H. Summers, supt. | Fax 643-2533
www.firn.edu/schools/liberty/liberty
Liberty County HS | 300/9-12
PO Box 519 32321 | 850-643-2241
Gary Lewis, prin. | Fax 643-4153
Liberty County Adult S | Adult
PO Box 429 32321 | 850-643-2275
Melissa Muza, prin. | Fax 643-2533

Bronson, Levy, Pop. 1,041
Levy County SD | 6,100/PK-12
PO Box 129 32621 | 352-486-5231
Cliff Norris, supt. | Fax 486-5237
www.levy.k12.fl.us
Bronson MSHS | 700/6-12
PO Box 189 32621 | 352-486-5261
Valerie Boughanem, prin. | Fax 486-5263
Other Schools – See Cedar Key, Chiefland, Inglis, Williston

Brooksville, Hernando, Pop. 7,637
Hernando County SD | 20,400/PK-12
919 N Broad St 34601 | 352-797-7000
Wayne Alexander Ed.D., supt. | Fax 797-7101
www.hcsb.k12.fl.us
Central HS | 1,900/9-12
14075 Ken Austin Pkwy 34613 | 352-797-7020
Dennis McGeehan, prin. | Fax 797-7121
Hernando HS | 1,300/9-12
700 Bell Ave 34601 | 352-797-7015
Betty Harper, prin. | Fax 797-7115
Nature Coast Technical HS | Vo/Tech
4057 California St 34604 | 352-797-7088
Margaret Schoelles, prin. | Fax 797-7188
Parrott MS | 1,000/6-8
19220 Youth Dr 34601 | 352-797-7075
Leechele Booker, prin. | Fax 797-7175
Powell MS | 1,400/6-8
4100 Barclay Ave 34609 | 352-797-7095
Earl Deen, prin. | Fax 797-7195
West Hernando MS | 1,300/6-8
14325 Ken Austin Pkwy 34613 | 352-797-7035
Joe Clifford, prin. | Fax 797-7135
Other Schools – See Spring Hill

Hernando Christian Academy | 400/PK-12
7200 Emerson Rd 34601 | 352-796-0616
Ronald Watford, supt. | Fax 799-3400
Pasco-Hernando Community College | Post-Sec.
11415 Ponce De Leon Blvd 34601 | 352-796-6726

Bunnell, Flagler, Pop. 1,479
Flagler County SD | 7,700/PK-12
PO Box 755 32110 | 386-437-7526
Bill Delbrugge, supt. | Fax 437-7577
www.flaglerschools.com
Flagler Palm Coast HS | 2,800/9-12
PO Box 488 32110 | 386-437-7540
Nancy Willis, prin. | Fax 437-7546
Taylor MS | 1,100/6-8
PO Box 815 32110 | 386-446-6700
Winnie Oden, prin. | Fax 446-6711
Other Schools – See Palm Coast

Bushnell, Sumter, Pop. 2,119
Sumter County SD | 5,300/PK-12
2680 W C 476 33513 | 352-793-2315
Richard Shirley, supt. | Fax 793-4180
www.sumter.k12.fl.us
South Sumter HS | 1,100/9-12
706 N Main St 33513 | 352-793-3131
Dr. Preston Morgan, prin. | Fax 793-2992
Other Schools – See Sumterville, Webster, Wildwood

Callahan, Nassau, Pop. 951
Nassau County SD
Supt. — See Fernandina Beach
Callahan MS | 800/6-8
450121 Old Dixie Hwy 32011 | 904-491-7935
Ellen Ryan, prin. | Fax 879-2860
West Nassau County HS | 1,000/9-12
1 Warrior Dr 32011 | 904-491-7942
Ronald Booker, prin. | Fax 879-5843

Cantonment, Escambia, Pop. 4,500
Escambia County SD
Supt. — See Pensacola
Ransom MS | 1,500/6-8
1000 W Kingsfield Rd 32533 | 850-937-2220
Jeff Pomeroy, prin. | Fax 937-2232
Tate HS | 2,000/9-12
PO Box 68 32533 | 850-937-2300
Rick Shackle, prin. | Fax 937-2328

Cape Coral, Lee, Pop. 140,010
Lee County SD
Supt. — See Fort Myers
Baker HS | 600/9-12
3500 Agualinda Blvd 33914 | 239-458-6690
Joe Vetter, prin. | Fax 458-6691
Caloosa MS | 1,200/6-8
610 Del Prado Blvd S 33990 | 239-574-3232
Brian Mangan, prin. | Fax 574-2660
Cape Coral HS | 2,300/9-12
2300 Santa Barbara Blvd 33991 | 239-574-6766
Eric McFee, prin. | Fax 574-7799
Challenger MS | 6-8
380 Santa Barbara Blvd N 33993 | 239-458-6692
Teri Cannady, prin. | Fax 458-3571
Diplomat MS | 1,200/6-8
1039 NE 16th Ter 33909 | 239-574-5257
Angela Roles, prin. | Fax 574-4008
Gulf MS | 1,300/6-8
1809 SW 36th Ter 33914 | 239-549-0606
William Lane, prin. | Fax 549-2806
Lee County HS Tech Center North | Vo/Tech
360 Santa Barbara Blvd 33991 | 239-574-4440
Michael Schiffer, prin. | Fax 458-3721
Mariner HS | 2,200/9-12
701 Chiquita Blvd N 33993 | 239-772-3324
Erik Cioffi, prin. | Fax 772-4880
Mariner MS | 800/6-8
425 Chiquita Blvd N 33993 | 239-772-1848
Richard Hagy, prin.
Trafalgar MS | 1,400/6-8
2120 SW Trafalgar Pkwy 33991 | 239-283-2001
Dr. Angela Pruitt, prin. | Fax 283-5620

Cape Coral Beauty School | Post-Sec.
1214 SE 47th St 33904 | 239-549-1819
Cape Coral Christian S | 200/PK-12
811 Santa Barbara Blvd 33991 | 239-574-3707
Christopher Roy, prin. | Fax 574-0947
Lee County High Tech Center North | Post-Sec.
360 Santa Barbara Blvd N 33993 | 239-574-4440
Radiation Therapy Services | Post-Sec.
1419 SE 8th Ter 33990 | 239-772-3202

Carrabelle, Franklin, Pop. 1,290
Franklin County SD
Supt. — See Apalachicola
Carrabelle S | 500/PK-12
1001 Gray Ave 32322 | 850-697-3815
Richard Key, prin. | Fax 697-4136

Casselberry, Seminole, Pop. 24,298
Seminole County SD
Supt. — See Sanford
South Seminole MS | 1,300/6-8
101 S Winter Park Dr 32707 | 407-320-1350
Robin Dehlinger, prin. | Fax 320-1420

City College | Post-Sec.
853 Semoran Blvd Ste 200 32707 | 407-831-9816
Regent Academy | 100/K-12
910 S Winter Park Dr 32707 | 407-740-0561
Benny Phillips, prin. | Fax 740-5654

Cedar Key, Levy, Pop. 958
Levy County SD
Supt. — See Bronson

Cedar Key S 300/PK-12
951 Whiddon Ave 32625 352-543-5223
Sue Ice, prin. Fax 543-5988

Celebration, Osceola
Osceola County SD
Supt. — See Kissimmee
Celebration HS 1,800/9-12
1809 Celebration Blvd 34747 321-939-6600
Dan White, prin. Fax 939-6652

Century, Escambia, Pop. 1,799
Escambia County SD
Supt. — See Pensacola
Northview HS 500/9-12
4100 W Highway 4 32535 850-327-6681
Gayle Weaver, prin. Fax 327-4015

Chiefland, Levy, Pop. 2,095
Levy County SD
Supt. — See Bronson
Chiefland HS 500/9-12
808 N Main St 32626 352-493-6000
Pam Asbell, prin. Fax 493-6018
Chiefland MS 400/6-8
811 NW 4th Dr 32626 352-493-6025
Bobbie Turnipseed, prin. Fax 493-6048
Adult HS Adult
114 Rodgers Blvd 32626 352-493-9533
Rayanne Giddis, prin. Fax 493-9994

Chipley, Washington, Pop. 3,682
Washington County SD 3,100/PK-12
652 3rd St 32428 850-638-6222
Calvin Stevenson, supt. Fax 638-6226
www.firn.edu/schools/washington/wash/
Chipley HS 600/9-12
1545 Brickyard Rd 32428 850-638-6100
George French, prin. Fax 638-6017
Roulhac MS 500/5-8
1535 Brickyard Rd 32428 850-638-6170
Mike Park, prin. Fax 638-6319
Washington-Holmes Tech Center Vo/Tech
757 Hoyt St 32428 850-638-1180
Olin Gilbert, dir. Fax 638-6177
Other Schools – See Vernon

Washington Holmes Technical Center Post-Sec.
757 Hoyt St 32428 850-638-1180

Citra, Marion
Marion County SD
Supt. — See Ocala
North Marion HS 1,600/9-12
151 W Highway 329 32113 352-671-6010
Kathy Quelland, prin. Fax 671-6011
North Marion MS 900/6-8
2085 W Highway 329 32113 352-671-6035
Jerome Brown, prin. Fax 671-6044

Citrus Springs, Citrus, Pop. 2,213
Citrus County SD
Supt. — See Inverness
Citrus Springs MS 900/6-8
150 W Citrus Springs Blvd 34434 352-344-2244
David Roland, prin. Fax 344-5615

Clearwater, Pinellas, Pop. 108,687
Pinellas County SD
Supt. — See Largo
Clearwater HS 2,100/9-12
540 S Hercules Ave 33764 727-298-1620
Keith Mastorides, prin. Fax 469-5981
Coachman Fundamental MS 600/6-8
2235 NE Coachman Rd 33765 727-669-1190
David Rosenberger, prin. Fax 669-1194
Countryside HS 2,400/9-12
3000 State Road 580 33761 727-725-7956
Gerald Schlereth, prin. Fax 725-7990
Kennedy MS 900/6-8
1660 Palmetto St 33755 727-298-1609
Susan W. Keller, prin. Fax 298-1614
North Pinellas Secondary HS 9-12
1960 Druid Rd E 33764 727-298-3710
Mildred Reed, prin. Fax 298-3714
Oak Grove MS 1,100/6-8
1370 S Belcher Rd 33764 727-524-4430
Dawn Coffin, prin. Fax 524-4416
PTEC Clearwater Vo/Tech
6100 154th Ave N 33760 727-538-7167
Warren Laux, dir. Fax 538-7203
Clearwater Adult Education Center Adult
540 S Hercules Ave 33764 727-469-4190
Christy E. Richards, admin. Fax 469-4193

Allendale Academy Private S 700/K-12
7208 Amhurst Way 33764 727-531-2481
Calvary Christian HS 200/9-12
110A N McMullen Booth Rd 33759 727-449-2247
Thomas J. Cathey, prin. Fax 461-5421
Clearwater Academy International 200/PK-12
801 Drew St 33755 727-446-1722
Jim Zwers, prin. Fax 443-5252
Clearwater Central Catholic HS 600/9-12
2750 Haines Bayshore Rd 33760 727-531-1449
Dulce Roman, prin. Fax 535-7034
Clearwater Christian College Post-Sec.
3400 Gulf To Bay Blvd 33759 727-726-1153
EduTech Centers Post-Sec.
410 Park Place Blvd 33759 727-724-1037
FL Metropolitan Univ. - Pinellas Post-Sec.
2471 N McMullen Booth Rd 33759 727-725-2688
Lakeside Christian S 200/PK-12
1897 Sunset Point Rd 33765 727-461-3311
Jim Jensen, prin. Fax 445-1835
National Aviation Academy Post-Sec.
6225 Ulmerton Rd 33760 727-531-2080
Pinellas Technical Education Center Post-Sec.
6100 154th Ave N 33760 727-538-7167
Sunstate Academy of Hair Design Post-Sec.
2525 Drew St 33765 727-538-3827

Clermont, Lake, Pop. 11,617
Lake County SD
Supt. — See Tavares
Clermont MS 1,000/6-8
301 East Ave 34711 352-243-2460
Dave Coggshall, prin. Fax 243-1407
East Ridge HS 2,700/9-12
13322 Excalibur Rd 34711 352-242-2080
Aurelia Cole, prin. Fax 242-2090
Windy Hill MS 1,400/6-8
3575 Hancock Rd 34711 352-394-2123
David Tucker, prin. Fax 394-7901

Clermont Christian S 50/6-9
PO Box 120992 34712 352-243-6322
Ken Tait, admin. Fax 241-9881

Clewiston, Hendry, Pop. 7,173
Hendry County SD
Supt. — See La Belle
Clewiston HS 1,100/9-12
1501 S Francisco St 33440 863-983-1520
Robert Egley, prin. Fax 983-2168
Clewiston MS 900/6-8
601 W Pasadena Ave 33440 863-983-1530
Garry Ensor, prin. Fax 983-1541
Clewiston Adult S Adult
1501 S Francisco St 33440 863-983-1578
James Way, prin. Fax 983-1595

Cocoa, Brevard, Pop. 16,898
Brevard County SD
Supt. — See Melbourne
Clearlake MS 500/7-8
1225 Clearlake Rd 32922 321-633-3660
Mark Mullins, prin. Fax 617-7731
Cocoa HS 1,400/9-12
2000 Tiger Trl 32926 321-632-5300
Cynthia Van Meter, prin. Fax 636-1218
McNair Magnet MS 400/6-8
1 Challenger Dr 32922 321-633-3630
Rosette Brown, prin. Fax 633-3639
Space Coast JSHS 1,800/7-12
6150 Banyan St 32927 321-638-0750
Robert Spinner, prin. Fax 638-0766

Brevard Community College Post-Sec.
1519 Clearlake Rd 32922 321-632-1111
Brevard Independent Private S 100/PK-12
202 River Heights Dr 32922 321-636-2754
David Amstadt, prin. Fax 636-5981

Cocoa Beach, Brevard, Pop. 12,435
Brevard County SD
Supt. — See Melbourne
Cocoa Beach JSHS 1,500/7-12
1500 Minutemen Cswy 32931 321-783-1776
Tim Cool, prin. Fax 868-6602

Coconut Creek, Broward, Pop. 49,017
Broward County SD
Supt. — See Fort Lauderdale
Atlantic Technical Center Vo/Tech
4700 Coconut Creek Pkwy 33063 754-321-5100
Robert Crawford, prin. Fax 321-5380
Coconut Creek HS 2,600/9-12
1400 NW 44th Ave 33066 754-322-0350
Eugene Butler, prin. Fax 322-0480
Lyons Creek MS 2,100/6-8
4333 Sol Press Blvd 33073 754-322-3700
Washington Collado, prin. Fax 322-3785
Monarch HS 1,700/9-12
5050 Wiles Rd 33073 754-322-1400
Anne Dilgen, prin. Fax 322-1530

Broward Community College-North Campus Post-Sec.
1000 Coconut Creek Blvd 33066 954-972-9100
North Broward Preparatory Schools 1,900/PK-12
7600 Lyons Rd 33073 954-247-0011
David Hicks, hdmstr. Fax 247-0012
Randazzo S 300/PK-12
2251 NW 36th Ave 33066 954-968-1750
Dr. Ronald Simon, hdmstr. Fax 968-1857

Coconut Grove, See Miami
Miami-Dade County SD
Supt. — See Miami
Carver MS 1,000/6-8
4901 Lincoln Dr 33133 305-444-7388
Libia Gonzalez, prin. Fax 529-5148

Carrollton S of the Sacred Heart 700/PK-12
3747 Main Hwy 33133 305-446-5673
Sr. Suzanne Cooke, prin. Fax 446-4160
Ransom Everglades S 600/9-12
3575 Main Hwy 33133 305-460-8800
Ellen Moceri, hdmstr. Fax 854-1846

Cooper City, Broward, Pop. 30,022
Broward County SD
Supt. — See Fort Lauderdale
Cooper City HS 2,500/9-12
9401 Stirling Rd 33328 754-323-0200
Wendy Doll, prin. Fax 323-0330
Pioneer MS 1,800/6-8
5350 SW 90th Ave 33328 754-323-4100
Linda Arnold, prin. Fax 323-4185

Coral Gables, Dade, Pop. 42,871
Miami-Dade County SD
Supt. — See Miami
Coral Gables HS 3,600/8-12
450 Bird Rd 33146 305-443-4871
Jo Anne Gans, prin. Fax 441-8094
Ponce De Leon MS 1,500/6-8
5801 Augusto St 33146 305-661-1611
Anna Rodriguez, prin. Fax 666-3140
Coral Gables SHS Adult Education Center Adult
450 Bird Rd 33146 305-443-4871
Alonzo Kilpatrick, prin. Fax 446-2507

New Professions Technical Institute Post-Sec.
4000 W Flagler St 33134 305-461-2223
University of Miami Post-Sec.
PO Box 248006 33124 305-284-2211

Coral Springs, Broward, Pop. 128,804
Broward County SD
Supt. — See Fort Lauderdale
Coral Glades HS 1,800/9-12
2700 Sportsplex Dr 33065 754-322-1250
David Jones, prin. Fax 322-1380
Coral Springs HS 2,800/9-12
7201 W Sample Rd 33065 754-322-0500
Anne Lynch, prin. Fax 322-0630
Coral Springs MS 1,300/6-8
10300 Wiles Rd 33076 754-322-3000
Victoria Kaufman, prin. Fax 322-3085
Forest Glen MS 1,400/6-8
6501 Turtle Run Blvd 33067 754-322-3400
James McDermott, prin. Fax 322-3485
Ramblewood MS 1,500/6-8
8505 W Atlantic Blvd 33071 754-322-4300
Desmond Blackburn, prin. Fax 322-4385
Sawgrass Springs MS 1,600/6-8
12500 W Sample Rd 33065 754-322-4500
Adeline Andreano, prin. Fax 322-4585
Taravella HS 3,200/9-12
10600 Riverside Dr 33071 754-322-2300
Shawn Cerra, prin. Fax 322-2430

Academy HS - Coral Springs Campus 200/8-12
648 Riverside Dr 33071 954-752-5038
Coral Springs Christian Academy 1,100/PK-12
2251 Riverside Dr 33065 954-752-2870
Robert Clampett, hdmstr. Fax 757-5383

Cottondale, Jackson, Pop. 879
Jackson County SD
Supt. — See Marianna
Cottondale JSHS 500/6-12
2680 Levy St 32431 850-482-9821
Don Wilson, prin. Fax 482-9827

Crawfordville, Wakulla
Wakulla County SD 4,400/K-12
PO Box 100 32326 850-926-0065
David Miller, supt. Fax 926-0123
www.firn.edu/schools/wakulla/wakulla/
Riversprings MS 500/6-8
800 Spring Creek Hwy 32327 850-926-2300
Dod Walker, prin. Fax 926-2111
Wakulla County HS 1,300/9-12
3237 Coastal Hwy 32327 850-926-7125
Mike Crouch, prin. Fax 926-8571
Wakulla MS 600/6-8
22 Jean Dr 32327 850-926-7143
JoAnn Daniels, prin. Fax 926-3752

Crescent City, Putnam, Pop. 1,817
Putnam County SD
Supt. — See Palatka
Crescent City JSHS 900/7-12
2201 S US Highway 17 32112 386-698-1629
Rodney Symonds, prin. Fax 698-3073

Crestview, Okaloosa, Pop. 17,707
Okaloosa County SD
Supt. — See Fort Walton Beach
Crestview HS 1,900/9-12
1250 N Ferdon Blvd 32536 850-689-7177
Andy Johnson, prin. Fax 689-7332
Davidson MS 900/6-8
6261 Old Bethel Rd 32536 850-683-7500
Beth Walthall, prin. Fax 683-7523
Richbourg MS 700/6-8
500 Alabama St 32536 850-689-7229
Bob Jones, prin. Fax 689-7245

Crossroads Christian S 300/K-12
PO Box 295 32536 850-423-1291
Tall Pines Academy 200/PK-12
100 Duggan Ave 32536 850-682-2730
Mike Hinson, dir. Fax 682-0087

Cross City, Dixie, Pop. 1,808
Dixie County SD 2,100/PK-12
PO Box 890 32628 352-498-6131
Dennis Bennett, supt. Fax 498-1308
dixieschools.dixie.k12.fl.us/
Dixie County HS 600/9-12
PO Box 1180 32628 352-498-6410
Charlotte Lord, prin. Fax 498-1287
Rains MS 500/6-8
PO Box 2159 32628 352-498-1346
Beverly Baumer, prin. Fax 498-1283
Dixie County Adult Center Adult
PO Box 890 32628 352-498-6149
Anne Engers, prin. Fax 498-1308

Crystal River, Citrus, Pop. 3,600
Citrus County SD
Supt. — See Inverness
Crystal River HS 1,300/9-12
1205 NE 8th Ave 34428 352-795-4641
Patrick Simon, prin. Fax 795-4519
Crystal River MS 900/6-8
344 NE Crystal St 34428 352-795-2116
Mark McCoy, prin. Fax 795-2378

Westcoast Christian S 50/K-12
718 NW 1st Ave 34428 352-795-2079
R. Marlene Pringle, dir. Fax 795-1104

Cutler Bay, Miami Dade
Miami-Dade County SD
Supt. — See Miami
Centennial MS 1,100/6-8
8601 SW 212th St, 305-235-1581
Elvoyd Fischer, prin. Fax 234-8071

Cutler Ridge, Dade, Pop. 21,268
Miami-Dade County SD
Supt. — See Miami
Cutler Ridge MS 1,400/6-8
19400 Gulfstream Rd 33157 305-235-4761
Thomas Ennis, prin. Fax 254-3746

Dade City, Pasco, Pop. 6,823
Pasco County SD
Supt. — See Land O Lakes

Centennial MS 700/6-8
38505 Centennial Rd 33525 352-524-9700
Thomas Rulison, prin. Fax 524-9791
Pasco Comprehensive HS 1,300/9-12
36850 State Road 52 33525 352-524-5500
Pat Reedy, prin. Fax 524-5591
Pasco MS 800/6-8
13925 14th St 33525 352-524-8400
Jim Lane, prin. Fax 524-8491
Moore-Mickens Education Center Adult
38301 Martin Luther King Bl 33525 352-524-9000
Steve Cox, prin. Fax 524-9091

East Pasco Adventist Academy 100/PK-10
38434 Centennial Rd 33525 352-567-3646
Fax 567-1907
Pasco-Hernando Community College Post-Sec.
34727 Blanton Rd 33523 352-567-6701

Dania, Broward, Pop. 14,456
Broward County SD
Supt. — See Fort Lauderdale
Olsen MS 1,800/6-8
330 SE 11th Ter 33004 754-323-3800
Kim Flynn, prin. Fax 323-3885

Key College Post-Sec.
225 E Dania Beach Blvd 33004 954-923-4440

Davenport, Polk, Pop. 2,017
Polk County SD
Supt. — See Bartow
Ridge Community HS 9-12
500 Orchid Dr 33837 863-419-3315
Sherry Wells, prin. Fax 419-3321

Davie, Broward, Pop. 84,204
Broward County SD
Supt. — See Fort Lauderdale
McFatter Tech Center Vo/Tech
6500 Nova Dr 33317 754-321-5785
Mark Thomas, prin. Fax 321-5980
Nova HS 2,000/9-12
3600 College Ave 33314 754-323-1650
John LaCasse, prin. Fax 323-1780
Nova MS 1,300/6-8
3602 College Ave 33314 754-323-3700
Dr. Ricardo Garcia, prin. Fax 323-3785
Western HS 2,400/9-12
1200 SW 136th Ave 33325 754-323-2400
Scott Fiske, prin. Fax 323-2530

Academy HS - Davie Campus 200/8-12
4850 S Pine Island Rd 33328 954-434-2722
ASM Beauty World Academy Post-Sec.
6423 Stirling Rd 33314 954-321-8411
ITT Technical Institute Post-Sec.
3401 S University Dr 33328 954-476-9300
Kentwood Preparatory S 100/1-12
4650 SW 61st Ave 33314 954-581-8222
Lynette Vanheyzen, prin. Fax 797-0700
Nova Southeastern University Post-Sec.
3301 College Ave 33314 954-262-7300
Nova Southeastern Univ Health Profession Post-Sec.
3200 S University Dr 33328 954-262-1101
Nur Ul-Islam Academy 300/PK-12
10600 SW 59th St 33328 954-434-3288
Kem Hussain, dir. Fax 434-9333
Westlake Preparatory S 100/6-12
4188 S University Dr 33328 954-236-2300
Shirley Gil, hdmstr. Fax 473-0770
William T. McFatter Technical Center Post-Sec.
6500 Nova Dr 33317 954-370-8324

Daytona Beach, Volusia, Pop. 64,421
Volusia County SD
Supt. — See De Land
Campbell MS, 625 S Keech St 32114 1,000/6-8
Vickie Presley, prin. 386-258-4661
Hinson MS 6-8
1860 N Clyde Morris Blvd 32117 386-258-4682
Ted Petrucciani, prin.
Mainland HS 2,100/9-12
1255 W Intl Speedway Blvd 32114 386-258-4665
Patsy Graham, prin.
Seabreeze HS 1,900/9-12
2700 N Oleander Ave 32118 386-258-4674
Bob Wallace, prin. Fax 676-1451

Bethune-Cookman College Post-Sec.
640 Dr Mary Mclod Bthn Blvd 32114 800-448-0228
Daytona Beach Community College Post-Sec.
PO Box 2811 32120 386-255-8131
Embry-Riddle Aeronautical University Post-Sec.
PO Box 11767 32120 800-862-2416
Father Lopez HS 300/9-12
960 Madison Ave 32114 386-253-5213
Linda Dowdy, prin. Fax 252-6101
Halifax Medical Center Post-Sec.
PO Box 2830 32120 386-254-4065
Keiser College Post-Sec.
1800 Business Park Blvd 32114 386-274-5060
Phoenix East Aviation Post-Sec.
561 Pearl Harbor Dr 32114 386-258-0703

Deerfield Beach, Broward, Pop. 76,348
Broward County SD
Supt. — See Fort Lauderdale
Deerfield Beach HS 2,700/9-12
910 SW 15th St 33441 754-322-0650
Kathleen Martinez, prin. Fax 322-0780
Deerfield Beach MS 1,700/6-8
701 SE 6th Ave 33441 754-322-3300
Vincent Alessi, prin. Fax 322-3385

Zion Lutheran Christian S 600/PK-12
959 SE 6th Ave 33441 954-421-3146
Ron Kooy, prin. Fax 421-5465

De Funiak Springs, Walton, Pop. 5,038
Walton County SD 6,000/PK-12
145 S Park St Ste 2 32435 850-892-1100
Carlene Anderson, supt. Fax 892-1191
www.walton.k12.fl.us

Walton Career Development Center Vo/Tech
761 N 20th St 32433 850-892-1240
Gail Cole, dir. Fax 892-1249
Walton HS 700/9-12
555 Walton Rd 32433 850-892-1270
Mike Davis, prin. Fax 892-1279
Walton MS 700/6-8
625 Park Ave 32435 850-892-1280
Russell Hughes, prin. Fax 892-1289
Other Schools – See Freeport, Paxton, Santa Rosa Beach

De Land, Volusia, Pop. 24,375
Volusia County SD 63,600/PK-12
PO Box 2118 32721 386-734-7190
Margaret Smith, supt. Fax 943-3423
www.volusia.k12.fl.us
DeLand HS 3,000/9-12
800 N Hill Ave 32724 386-822-6909
Mitch Moyer, prin. Fax 822-6556
DeLand MS 1,700/6-8
1400 Aquarius Ave 32724 386-822-5678
Matt Krajewski, prin. Fax 822-6583
Southwestern MS 600/6-8
605 W New Hampshire Ave 32720 386-822-6815
Mamie Oatis, prin. Fax 822-6708
Other Schools – See Daytona Beach, Deltona, Holly Hill, New Smyrna Beach, Ormond Beach, Pierson, Port Orange

---

Florida Technical College Post-Sec.
1199 S Woodland Blvd 32720 386-734-3303
Gold Medal Honors Academy 100/K-12
1572 N Woodland Blvd 32720 386-785-0440
Lily Schwarz, prin. Fax 740-8064
Lighthouse Christian Academy 500/PK-12
126 S Ridgewood Ave 32720 386-734-5380
Luke Pearson, prin. Fax 734-5627
Stetson University Post-Sec.
421 N Woodland Boulevard 32720 386-822-7000

Delray Beach, Palm Beach, Pop. 64,757
Palm Beach County SD
Supt. — See West Palm Beach
Atlantic Community HS 2,000/9-12
2455 W Atlantic Ave 33445 561-243-1500
Kathleen Weigel, prin. Fax 243-1532
Carver Community MS 1,400/6-8
101 Barwick Rd 33445 561-638-2100
Lena Roundtree, prin. Fax 638-2181
Delray Full Service Center Adult
301 SW 14th Ave 33444 561-243-1568
Willie Jo Young, prin. Fax 243-1591

American Heritage S of Boca/Delray 1,100/PK-12
6200 Linton Blvd 33484 561-495-7272
Robert Stone, hdmstr. Fax 495-6106
TLC Christian Academy 100/PK-12
111-115 SW 10th Ave 33444 561-278-3115

Deltona, Volusia, Pop. 82,788
Volusia County SD
Supt. — See De Land
Deltona HS 2,900/9-12
100 Wolf Pack Run 32725 386-575-4153
Gary Marks, prin. Fax 789-9843
Deltona MS 1,500/6-8
250 Enterprise Rd 32725 386-575-4150
Tom Russell, prin. Fax 860-3383
Galaxy MS 1,900/6-8
2400 Eustace Ave 32725 386-575-4144
Julian Jones, prin. Fax 789-7058
Heritage MS, 1001 Parnell Ct 32738 1,500/6-8
Dennis Neal, prin. 386-575-4113
Pine Ridge HS 2,600/9-12
926 Howland Blvd 32738 386-575-4195
Dr. Michael Mongelli, prin.

Deltona Christian S 200/PK-12
1200 Providence Blvd 32725 386-574-1971
Byron Herchenroder, admin. Fax 574-1771
Trinity Christian Academy 700/PK-12
875 Elkcam Blvd 32725 386-789-4515
Dennis Robinson, dir. Fax 789-0210

Destin, Okaloosa, Pop. 12,423
Okaloosa County SD
Supt. — See Fort Walton Beach
Destin MS 700/6-8
4608 Legendary Marina Dr 32541 850-833-7655
Sherri Houp, prin. Fax 833-7677

Doral, Dade, Pop. 21,895

ITT Technical Institute Post-Sec.
7955 NW 12th St 33126 305-477-3080
Polytechnic University of the Americas Post-Sec.
8180 NW 36th St 33166 305-418-4220

Dundee, Polk, Pop. 3,064
Polk County SD
Supt. — See Bartow
Dundee Ridge MS 1,000/6-8
5555 Lake Trask Rd 33838 863-419-3088
Kathryn Blackburn, prin. Fax 419-3157

Dunedin, Pinellas, Pop. 36,690
Pinellas County SD
Supt. — See Largo
Dunedin Highland MS 1,200/6-8
70 Patricia Ave 34698 727-469-4112
Margaret Landers, prin. Fax 469-4115
Dunedin HS 2,000/9-12
1651 Pinehurst Rd 34698 727-469-4100
Paul Summa, prin. Fax 469-4143

Dunedin Academy 200/PK-12
1408 County Road 1 34698 727-733-9148
Kathleen Porter, dir. Fax 733-6696

Dunnellon, Marion, Pop. 1,971
Marion County SD
Supt. — See Ocala

Dunnellon HS 1,300/9-12
10055 SW 180th Avenue Rd 34432 352-465-6745
Michelle Lewis, prin. Fax 465-6746
Dunnellon MS 1,000/6-8
21005 Chestnut St 34431 352-465-6720
Jane Ashman, prin. Fax 465-6721

Dunnellon Christian Academy 200/PK-12
20831 Powell Rd 34431 352-489-7716
Rev. Russell Randall, dir. Fax 489-0337

Eagle Lake, Polk, Pop. 2,489
Polk County SD
Supt. — See Bartow
Lake Region HS 2,000/9-12
1995 Thunder Rd 33839 863-297-3099
Joel McGuire, prin. Fax 297-3097

Eagle Lake Christian S 100/PK-12
670 N Eagle Dr 33839 863-294-7259
Sam Diaz, prin. Fax 299-7509

Eastpoint, Franklin, Pop. 1,577

North Tennessee Bible Inst. & Seminary Post-Sec.
556 W Bayshore Dr 32328 850-927-4711

Eatonville, Orange, Pop. 2,390
Orange County SD
Supt. — See Orlando
Hungerford Preparatory HS 500/9-12
100 E Kennedy Blvd 32751 407-622-8200
Thomas Akin, prin. Fax 645-0236

Englewood, Sarasota, Pop. 15,025
Charlotte County SD
Supt. — See Port Charlotte
Lemon Bay HS 1,500/9-12
2201 Placida Rd 34224 941-474-7702
Dan Jeffers, prin. Fax 475-5260

Heritage Christian Academy 100/PK-12
75 Pine St 34223 941-474-5884
Bill Ingham, prin. Fax 473-1797

Estero, Lee, Pop. 3,177
Lee County SD
Supt. — See Fort Myers
Estero HS 2,100/9-12
21900 River Ranch Rd 33928 239-947-9400
George Clover, prin. Fax 947-5017

Eustis, Lake, Pop. 17,683
Lake County SD
Supt. — See Tavares
Eustis HS - Curtright Campus 300/9-9
1801 Bates Ave 32726 352-589-1510
Michael Elchenko, prin. Fax 589-1605
Eustis MS 1,000/6-8
18725 Bates Ave 32736 352-357-3366
Albert Larry, prin. Fax 357-5963
Eustis SHS 800/10-12
1300 E Washington Ave 32726 352-357-4147
Michael Elchenko, prin. Fax 357-7449
Lake Technical Center Vo/Tech
2001 Kurt St 32726 352-589-2250
Terry Miller, dir. Fax 357-4776

Blue Lake Academy 300/PK-12
PO Box 1947 32727 352-357-8655
Fax 357-6956
Lake Technical Center Post-Sec.
2001 Kurt St 32726 352-589-2250

Everglades City, Collier
Collier County SD
Supt. — See Naples
Everglades City S 100/PK-12
PO Box 170 34139 239-377-9800
Bobby Jones, prin. Fax 377-9801

Fernandina Beach, Nassau, Pop. 11,264
Nassau County SD 10,600/PK-12
1201 Atlantic Ave 32034 904-491-9900
John Ruis, supt. Fax 277-9042
www.nassau.k12.fl.us
Fernandina Beach HS 1,700/9-12
435 Citrona Dr 32034 904-491-7937
Jane Arnold, prin. Fax 277-3754
Fernandina Beach MS 700/6-8
315 Citrona Dr 32034 904-491-7938
John Mazzella, prin. Fax 261-8919
Nassau County Adult S Adult
1201 Atlantic Ave 32034 904-491-9899
Brent Lemond, prin. Fax 225-2183
Other Schools – See Callahan, Hilliard, Yulee

Faith Christian Academy 200/PK-12
134 Brady Point Rd 32034 904-321-2137
Wendy Lannon, admin. Fax 321-1707

Fern Park, Seminole, Pop. 8,294

Americare School of Nursing Post-Sec.
7275 Estapona Cir 32730 407-673-7406

Florahome, Putnam
Putnam County SD
Supt. — See Palatka
Roberts MS 400/6-8
901 State Road 100 32140 386-659-1737
Randy Hedstern, prin. Fax 659-1986

Fort Lauderdale, Broward, Pop. 167,380
Broward County SD 253,900/PK-12
600 SE 3rd Ave 33301 754-321-0000
Dr. Frank Till, supt. Fax 321-2701
www.browardschools.com
Ashe MS 1,200/6-8
1701 NW 23rd Ave 33311 754-322-2800
Andrew Luciani, prin. Fax 322-2880
Dandy MS 1,300/6-8
2400 NW 26th St 33311 754-322-3200
Casandra Robinson, prin. Fax 322-3285

Dillard HS 2,300/9-12
2501 NW 11th St 33311 754-322-0800
Merceda Stanley, prin. Fax 322-0930
Fort Lauderdale HS 1,800/9-12
1600 NE 4th Ave 33305 754-322-1100
Dr. Gina Eyerman, prin. Fax 322-1230
New River MS 1,600/6-8
3100 Riverland Rd 33312 754-323-3600
Kathrine Hinden, prin. Fax 323-3685
Parkway MS 1,700/6-8
3600 NW 5th Ct 33311 754-322-4000
David Hall, prin. Fax 322-4085
Stranahan HS 2,200/9-12
1800 SW 5th Pl 33312 754-323-2100
Deborah Owens, prin. Fax 323-2230
Sunrise MS 1,400/6-8
1750 NE 14th St 33304 754-322-4700
Rebecca Dahl, prin. Fax 322-4790
Whiddon-Rodgers Education Center Adult
700 SW 26th St 33315 754-321-7550
Linda Thomas, prin. Fax 321-7590
Whiddon-Rodgers Education Center Annex Adult
1300 SW 32nd Ct 33315 754-321-7600
Linda Thomas, prin. Fax 321-7640
Other Schools – See Coconut Creek, Cooper City, Coral Springs, Dania, Davie, Deerfield Beach, Hallandale, Hollywood, Lauderdale Lakes, Lauderhill, Margate, Miramar, North Lauderdale, Oakland Park, Parkland, Pembroke Pines, Plantation, Pompano Beach, Sunrise, Tamarac, Weston

---

Archbishop Edward McCarthy HS 1,200/9-12
5451 S Flamingo Rd 33330 954-434-8820
Dr. Richard Perhla, prin. Fax 680-4835
Art Institute of Fort Lauderdale Post-Sec.
1799 SE 17th St 33316 954-463-3000
ATI Career Training Center Post-Sec.
2890 W Cypress Creek Rd 33309 954-973-4760
Atlantic Institute of Oriental Medicine Post-Sec.
100 E Broward Blvd Ste 100 33301 954-763-9840
Broward Community College Post-Sec.
225 E Las Olas Blvd 33301 954-475-6500
Calvary Christian Academy 1,300/PK-12
2401 W Cypress Creek Rd 33309 954-556-4447
David Salvatelli, dir. Fax 556-4650
Cardinal Gibbons HS 1,200/9-12
2900 NE 47th St 33308 954-491-2900
Paul Ott, prin. Fax 772-1025
City College Post-Sec.
2000 W Commercial Blvd 33309 954-492-5353
Coral Ridge Nurse's Asst Training School Post-Sec.
2740 E Oakland Park Blvd 33306 954-561-2022
Fort Lauderdale Christian S 300/PK-12
6330 NW 31st Ave 33309 954-972-3444
Gerald A. Mitchell, hdmstr. Fax 977-2681
Fort Lauderdale Preparatory S 200/PK-12
3275 W Oakland Park Blvd 33311 954-485-7500
Anita Lonstein, prin. Fax 485-1732
Keiser University Post-Sec.
1500 NW 49th St 33309 954-776-4456
Knox Theological Seminary Post-Sec.
5554 N Federal Hwy 33308 954-771-0376
Oxford Academy 100/10-12
1919 NE 45th St Ste 115 33308 954-772-4512
Pine Crest S 2,500/PK-12
1501 NE 62nd St 33334 954-492-4100
Lourdes Cowgill, hdmstr. Fax 492-4109
St. Thomas Aquinas HS 2,100/9-12
2801 SW 12th St 33312 954-581-0700
Tina Jones, prin. Fax 581-8263
Sanford Brown Institute Post-Sec.
1201 W Cypress Creek Rd 33309 954-308-7400
University S of Nova Southeastern Univ 1,600/6-12
3301 College Ave 33314 954-262-4400
Dr. Jerome Chermak, hdmstr. Fax 262-3971
Westminster Academy 1,000/PK-12
5601 N Federal Hwy 33308 954-771-4600
Greg Beaupied, hdmstr. Fax 491-3021

Fort Meade, Polk, Pop. 5,742
Polk County SD
Supt. — See Bartow
Fort Meade MSHS 800/6-12
700 Edgewood Dr N 33841 863-285-1180
Tom Ereditario, prin. Fax 285-1186

Fort Myers, Lee, Pop. 58,428
Lee County SD 65,700/PK-12
2055 Central Ave 33901 239-334-1102
Dr. James Browder, supt. Fax 337-8378
www.lee.k12.fl.us/
Cypress Lake HS 2,100/9-12
6750 Panther Ln 33919 239-481-2233
Tracy Perkins, prin. Fax 481-6094
Cypress Lake MS 1,200/6-8
8901 Cypress Lake Dr 33919 239-481-1533
Jeananne Folaros, prin. Fax 481-3121
Dunbar HS 1,100/9-12
3800 Edison Ave 33916 239-461-5322
Carl Burnside, prin. Fax 461-5110
Dunbar MS 1,100/6-8
4750 Winkler Avenue Ext, 239-334-1357
Beth Ellen Bolger, prin. Fax 334-7633
Fort Myers HS 2,300/9-12
2635 Cortez Blvd 33901 239-334-2167
David LaRosa, prin. Fax 334-3095
Fort Myers Middle Academy 800/6-8
3050 Central Ave 33901 239-936-1759
Louise Hollins, prin. Fax 936-4350
Lee County HS Tech Center Central Vo/Tech
3800 Michigan Ave 33916 239-334-4544
Robert Durham, prin. Fax 332-4839
Lee MS 700/6-8
1333 Marsh Ave 33905 239-337-1333
Vivian Smith, prin. Fax 334-4144
Lexington MS 6-8
16351 Summerlin Rd 33908 239-454-6130
Linda Caprarotta, prin. Fax 489-3419
Riverdale HS 2,000/6-12
2600 Buckingham Rd 33905 239-694-4141
Gerald Demming, prin. Fax 694-3527
South Fort Myers HS 9-12
14020 Plantation Rd 33912 239-561-0060
Tommy O'Connell, prin. Fax 561-3612
Three Oaks MS 1,100/6-8
18500 3 Oaks Pkwy, 239-267-5757
Mike Carson, prin. Fax 267-4007
Adult & Community Education Adult
2266 2nd St 33901 239-334-7172
Fax 334-4568
Dunbar Community S Adult
1857 High St 33916 239-334-2941
Dr. Betty Bowers, admin. Fax 334-3519
Other Schools – See Alva, Bonita Springs, Cape Coral, Estero, Lehigh Acres, North Fort Myers

---

Bishop Verot HS 800/9-12
5598 Sunrise Dr 33919 239-274-6700
Rev. Christian Beretta, prin. Fax 274-6798
Canterbury S 700/PK-12
8141 College Pkwy 33919 239-481-4323
Richard Dolvin, hdmstr. Fax 481-8339
Edison College Post-Sec.
PO Box 60210 33906 239-489-9300
Evangelical Christian S 1,200/PK-12
8237 Beacon Blvd 33907 239-936-3319
John Hunte, hdmstr. Fax 939-1445
Florida Christian Institute 200/K-12
940 Tarpon St Bldg E 33916 239-274-5935
Keith Leonardo, dir. Fax 274-5939
Florida Gulf Coast University Post-Sec.
10501 FGCU Blvd 33965 239-590-1000
Heritage Institute Post-Sec.
6811 Palisades Park Ct 33912 239-936-5822
Hodges University Post-Sec.
4501 Colonial Blvd, 239-482-0019
Lee County High Tech Center Central Post-Sec.
3800 Michigan Ave 33916 239-334-4544
Sonshine Christian Academy 200/PK-12
12925 Palm Beach Blvd 33905 239-694-8882
Ken Norvell, prin. Fax 694-8885
Southwest Florida Christian Academy 600/K-12
3750 Colonial Blvd, 239-936-8865
Dr. Phil Tingle, hdmstr. Fax 936-7095
Southwest Florida College Post-Sec.
1685 Medical Ln 33907 239-939-4766
Sunstate Academy of Hair Design Post-Sec.
2418 Colonial Blvd 33907 239-278-1311

Fort Pierce, Saint Lucie, Pop. 38,552
St. Lucie County SD 33,600/PK-12
4204 Okeechobee Rd 34947 772-429-3600
Michael J. Lannon, supt.
www.stlucie.k12.fl.us/index.html
Forest Grove MS 1,300/6-8
3201 S 25th St 34981 772-468-5885
Charles Cuomo, prin. Fax 595-1187
Fort Pierce Central HS 2,200/9-12
1101 Edwards Rd 34982 772-468-5888
John Williams, prin. Fax 468-5761
Fort Pierce Magnet S of the Arts 300/K-12
1100 Delaware Ave 34950 772-467-4278
Dr. David Washington, prin. Fax 460-3094
Fort Pierce Westwood HS 1,700/9-12
1801 Panther Ln 34947 772-468-5400
Linda Bushore, prin. Fax 468-5465
Lincoln Park Academy 1,800/6-12
1806 Avenue I 34950 772-468-5474
Margaret Anderson, prin. Fax 468-5485
McCarty MS 1,200/6-8
1201 Mississippi Ave 34950 772-468-5700
Catherine Smith, prin. Fax 595-1124
Other Schools – See Port Saint Lucie

Ari Ben Aviator Post-Sec.
3800 Saint Lucie Blvd 34946 772-466-4822
Bible Baptist S 200/PK-12
4401 S 25th St 34981 772-461-7215
Faith Baptist S 300/PK-12
3607 Oleander Ave 34982 772-461-3607
Greg Booher, admin. Fax 461-4732
Fort Pierce Beauty Academy Post-Sec.
3028 S US 1 34982 772-464-4885
Golden Rule Academy 100/PK-12
3891 Edwards Rd 34981 772-466-0034
Kim Baumgardner, prin. Fax 466-8102
Indian River Community College Post-Sec.
3209 Virginia Ave 34981 772-462-4700
John Carroll HS 500/9-12
3402 Delaware Ave 34947 772-464-5200
Ben Hopper, prin. Fax 464-5233
Liberty Baptist Academy 400/PK-12
3660 W Midway Rd 34981 772-461-2731
Wallace Cooley, prin. Fax 461-2542
Orange Avenue Baptist S 100/PK-12
100 Cyclone Dr 34945 772-461-1225
Cecil Lane, prin. Fax 461-0605
Palm Vista Christian S 100/PK-12
700 S 33rd St 34947 772-464-1591
Terrell Ray, dir. Fax 464-6861
Sampson Memorial SDA S 50/K-10
3201 Memory Ln 34981 772-465-8386
Fax 468-3447

Fort Walton Beach, Okaloosa, Pop. 19,817
Okaloosa County SD 29,100/PK-12
120 Lowery Pl SE 32548 850-833-3100
Dr. Alexis Tibbetts, supt. Fax 833-3436
www.okaloosaschools.com/
Bruner MS 1,000/6-8
322 Holmes Blvd NW 32548 850-833-3266
John Spolski, prin. Fax 833-3434
Choctawhatchee HS 1,900/9-12
110 Racetrack Rd NW 32547 850-833-3614
Cindy Massarelli, prin. Fax 833-3410
Fort Walton Beach HS 2,000/9-12
400 Hollywood Blvd SW 32548 850-833-3300
Dr. Alexis Tibbetts, prin. Fax 833-3311
Pryor MS 800/6-8
201 Racetrack Rd NW 32547 850-833-3613
Dr. Vivian Green, prin. Fax 833-4276
Other Schools – See Baker, Crestview, Destin, Laurel Hill, Niceville, Shalimar, Valparaiso

---

Calvary Christian Academy 400/PK-12
535 Clifford St 32547 850-862-1414
Jon Gross, admin. Fax 862-9826
Okaloosa Applied Technical Center Post-Sec.
1976 Lewis Turner Blvd 32547 850-833-3500

Fort White, Columbia, Pop. 454
Columbia County SD
Supt. — See Lake City
Fort White HS 1,300/6-12
17828 SW State Road 47 32038 386-497-5952
Keith Hatcher, prin. Fax 497-5951

Freeport, Walton, Pop. 1,474
Walton County SD
Supt. — See De Funiak Springs
Freeport HS 400/9-12
12615 US Highway 331 S 32439 850-892-1200
Michael Murphy, prin. Fax 892-1209
Freeport MS 300/6-8
360 Kylea Laird Dr 32439 850-892-1220
Beth Tucker, prin. Fax 892-1229

Frostproof, Polk, Pop. 2,950
Polk County SD
Supt. — See Bartow
Frostproof MSHS 1,200/6-12
1000 N Palm Ave 33843 863-635-7809
Stephen White, prin. Fax 635-7812

Fruitland Park, Lake, Pop. 3,578

Holy Trinity Episcopal S 50/6-12
2201 Spring Lake Rd 34731 352-787-8855
Thomas J. Boyd, hdmstr. Fax 787-8063

Gainesville, Alachua, Pop. 108,184
Alachua County SD 26,000/PK-12
620 E University Ave 32601 352-955-7300
Dr. W. Daniel Boyd, supt. Fax 955-6700
www.sbac.edu/
Bishop MS 1,000/6-8
1901 NE 9th St 32609 352-955-6701
Mike Thorne, prin. Fax 955-6966
Buchholz HS 2,400/9-12
5510 NW 27th Ave 32606 352-955-6702
Vince Perez, prin. Fax 955-7285
Eastside HS 1,900/9-12
1201 SE 43rd St 32641 352-955-6704
Jeff Charbonnet, prin. Fax 955-7291
Ft. Clarke MS 900/6-8
9301 NW 23rd Ave 32606 352-333-2800
Donna Kidwell, prin. Fax 333-2806
Gainesville HS 2,100/9-12
1900 NW 13th St 32609 352-955-6707
Dr. Wiley Dixon, prin. Fax 955-7283
Kanapaha MS 900/6-8
5005 SW 75th St 32608 352-955-6960
Jennifer Wise, prin. Fax 955-6858
Lincoln MS 900/6-8
1001 SE 12th St 32641 352-955-6711
Don Lewis, prin. Fax 955-7133
Loften HS Vo/Tech
3000 E University Ave 32641 352-955-6839
Dr. Chet Sanders, prin. Fax 955-6999
Westwood MS 1,000/6-8
3215 NW 15th Ave 32605 352-955-6718
James Tenbieg, prin. Fax 955-6897
Other Schools – See Alachua, Hawthorne, Newberry

City College Post-Sec.
2400 SW 13th St 32608 352-335-4000
Cornerstone Academy 300/PK-12
3536 NW 8th Ave 32605 352-378-9337
Leigh Glover, prin. Fax 378-7708
Countryside Christian S 100/PK-12
10926 NW 39th Ave 32606 352-332-9731
Dragon Rises College Oriental Medicine Post-Sec.
901 NW 8th Ave Ste B5 32601 352-371-2833
Florida School of Massage Post-Sec.
6421 SW 13th St 32608 352-378-7891
Oak Hall S 400/6-12
8009 SW 14th Ave 32607 352-332-3609
Richard Gehman, prin. Fax 332-4975
Rock S 200/PK-12
9818 SW 24th Ave 32607 352-331-7625
Bob Carter, prin. Fax 331-9760
St. Francis HS 9-12
11500 NW 39th Ave 32606 352-376-6545
Ernest Herrington, prin. Fax 376-7568
Santa Fe Community College Post-Sec.
3000 NW 83rd St 32606 352-395-5000
University of Florida Post-Sec.
PO Box 114000 32611 352-392-3261
Westwood Hills Christian S 300/PK-12
1520 NW 34th St 32605 352-378-5190
Jay Jethro, prin. Fax 371-6782
Windsor Christian Academy 50/1-12
918 SE County Road 234 32641 352-375-1144
Mike Redmond, admin. Fax 375-7316

Gibsonton, Hillsborough, Pop. 7,706
Hillsborough County SD
Supt. — See Tampa
East Bay HS 2,400/9-12
7710 Big Bend Rd 33534 813-671-5134
Sharon Morris, prin. Fax 671-5139
Eisenhower MS 1,100/6-8
7620 Big Bend Rd 33534 813-671-5121
Dena Collins, prin. Fax 671-5039

Glen Saint Mary, Baker, Pop. 537
Baker County SD
Supt. — See Macclenny
Baker County HS 1,300/9-12
1 Wildcat Dr 32040 904-259-6286
John David Crawford, prin. Fax 259-5617

Gotha, Orange

Central Florida Preparatory S 400/PK-12
PO Box 817 34734 407-290-8073
Rowena Flanders-Ramos, dir. Fax 298-6443

Goulds, Dade, Pop. 7,284
Miami-Dade County SD
Supt. — See Miami
Mays MS 1,000/6-8
11700 SW 216th St 33170 305-233-2300
Kenneth Cooper, prin. Fax 251-5462

Graceville, Jackson, Pop. 2,423
Holmes County SD
Supt. — See Bonifay
Poplar Springs S 300/PK-12
3726 Atomic Dr 32440 850-263-6260
Patty Segrest, prin. Fax 263-1252

Jackson County SD
Supt. — See Marianna
Graceville JSHS 400/6-12
5539 Brown St 32440 850-263-4451
Laurence Pender, prin. Fax 263-3605

The Baptist College of Florida Post-Sec.
5400 College Dr 32440 800-328-2660

Grand Ridge, Jackson, Pop. 802
Jackson County SD
Supt. — See Marianna
Grand Ridge S 500/PK-12
6925 Florida St 32442 850-482-9835
Beth Westmoreland, prin. Fax 482-9834

Greenacres, Palm Beach, Pop. 32,525
Palm Beach County SD
Supt. — See West Palm Beach
Leonard HS 2,300/9-12
4701 10th Ave N 33463 561-641-1200
Terry Costa, prin. Fax 357-1100
Swain MS 6-8
5332 Lake Worth Rd 33463 561-649-6900
Camille Long-Coleman, prin. Fax 649-6910

Greenacres Christian Academy 200/PK-12
4982 Cambridge St 33463 561-965-0363
Tami Donnally, dir. Fax 439-7149
Keiser Career College Post-Sec.
6812 Forest Hill Blvd # D1 33413 561-433-2330

Green Cove Springs, Clay, Pop. 6,085
Clay County SD 32,300/PK-12
900 Walnut St 32043 904-284-6500
David Owens, supt. Fax 284-6525
www.clay.k12.fl.us/
Clay HS 1,100/9-12
2025 State Road 16 W 32043 904-529-2110
Pete McCabe, prin. Fax 529-2112
Green Cove Springs JHS 1,000/7-8
1220 Bonaventure Ave 32043 904-529-2140
Kenneth Francis, prin. Fax 529-2144
Lake Asbury JHS 7-8
2851 Sandridge Rd 32043 904-291-5582
Ed Paulk, prin. Fax 291-5593
Other Schools – See Keystone Heights, Middleburg, Orange Park

Greensboro, Gadsden, Pop. 615
Gadsden County SD
Supt. — See Quincy
West Gadsden HS 500/7-12
PO Box 10 32330 850-442-9500
Rocky Pace, prin. Fax 442-6126

Greenville, Madison, Pop. 829

Greenville Hills Academy 200/6-12
742 SW Greenville Hills Rd 32331 850-948-1200
George Hare, prin. Fax 948-1330

Groveland, Lake, Pop. 5,205
Lake County SD
Supt. — See Tavares
Gray MS 900/6-8
205 E Magnolia St 34736 352-429-3322
Janice Boyd, prin. Fax 429-0133
South Lake HS 1,400/9-12
15600 Silver Eagle Rd 34736 352-394-2100
Dave Bordenkircher, prin. Fax 394-1972

Gulf Breeze, Santa Rosa, Pop. 6,455
Santa Rosa County SD
Supt. — See Milton
Gulf Breeze HS 1,600/9-12
675 Gulf Breeze Pkwy 32561 850-916-4100
Cherry Fitch, prin. Fax 916-4109
Gulf Breeze MS 900/6-8
649 Gulf Breeze Pkwy 32561 850-934-4080
Jennifer Granse, prin. Fax 934-4085
Woodlawn Beach MS 900/6-8
1500 Woodlawn Way 32563 850-934-4010
C.J. Lovallo, prin. Fax 934-4015

Gulfport, Pinellas, Pop. 12,661
Pinellas County SD
Supt. — See Largo
Boca Ciega HS 2,000/9-12
924 58th St S 33707 727-893-2780
Paulagene Nelson, prin. Fax 893-1382

Stetson University Post-Sec.
1401 61st St S 33707 727-345-1121

Haines City, Polk, Pop. 16,371
Polk County SD
Supt. — See Bartow
Boone MS 1,100/6-8
225 S 22nd St 33844 863-421-3302
Pamela Henderson, prin. Fax 421-3305
Haines City HS 2,200/9-12
2800 Hornet Dr 33844 863-421-3281
Duane Collins, prin. Fax 421-3283
International Baccalaureate East HS 9-12
2800 Hornet Dr 33844 863-421-3371
Sue Braiman, prin. Fax 419-3373
Jenkins Academy of Technology Vo/Tech
701 Ledwith Ave 33844 863-421-3267
Eileen Killebrew, prin. Fax 421-3269

Landmark Christian S 300/PK-12
2020 E Hinson Ave 33844 863-422-2037
Wallace Hill, admin. Fax 419-1256
Northridge Christian Academy 300/PK-10
2250 State Road 17 S 33844 863-422-3473
Michael Bartlett, prin. Fax 421-2582

Hallandale, Broward, Pop. 31,163
Broward County SD
Supt. — See Fort Lauderdale
Gulfstream MS 6-8
120 SW 4th Ave 33009 754-323-4700
Debra Patterson, prin. Fax 323-4785
Hallandale HS 1,500/9-12
720 NW 9th Ave 33009 754-323-0900
Rosemary Chambers, prin. Fax 323-1030
Hallandale Adult & Comm Ctr Adult
1000 SW 3rd St 33009 754-321-7050
Dr. Linda Lopez, prin. Fax 321-7135

Academy for Five Element Acupuncture Post-Sec.
1170a E Hllndale Beach Blvd 33009 954-456-6336

Havana, Gadsden, Pop. 1,701
Gadsden County SD
Supt. — See Quincy
East Gadsden HS 1,100/9-12
27001 Blue Star Hwy 32333 850-539-2882
Dr. William Harvey, prin. Fax 539-2863
Havana MS 300/6-8
1210 Kemp Rd 32333 850-539-2822
Dr. Verna Norris, prin. Fax 539-2866

Tallavana Christian S 200/PK-12
5840 Havana Hwy 32333 850-539-5300
Fax 539-8785

Hawthorne, Alachua, Pop. 1,443
Alachua County SD
Supt. — See Gainesville
Hawthorne JSHS 500/6-12
21403 SE 69th Ave 32640 352-481-1900
Dr. Susan Arnold, prin. Fax 481-4859

Hialeah, Dade, Pop. 220,485
Miami-Dade County SD
Supt. — See Miami
American HS 3,000/9-12
18350 NW 67th Ave 33015 305-557-3770
Dr. Louis J. Algaze, prin. Fax 828-7380
Filer MS 1,400/6-8
531 W 29th St 33012 305-822-6601
Luis Diaz, prin. Fax 822-2063
Goleman HS 4,300/8-12
14100 NW 89th Ave 33018 305-362-0676
Carlos Artime, prin. Fax 827-0249
Hialeah HS 4,300/9-12
251 E 47th St 33013 305-822-1500
Lorenzo Ladaga, prin. Fax 828-5513
Hialeah-Miami Lakes HS 3,200/9-12
7977 W 12th Ave 33014 305-823-1330
Karen L. Robinson, prin. Fax 362-4188
Hialeah MS 1,300/6-8
6027 E 7th Ave 33013 305-681-3527
Martha H. Montiel, prin. Fax 681-6225
Marti MS 1,500/6-8
5701 W 24th Ave 33016 305-557-5931
Jose Enriquez, prin. Fax 596-6917
Miami Lakes MS 1,500/6-8
6425 Miami Lakeway N 33014 305-557-3900
Joaquin Hernandez, prin. Fax 828-6753
Palm Springs MS 1,700/6-9
1025 W 56th St 33012 305-821-2460
Melissa Wolin, prin. Fax 828-3987
American SHS Adult Education Adult
18350 NW 67th Ave 33015 305-557-3770
Eddie Colletti, prin. Fax 827-7935
Hialeah-Miami Lakes HS Adult Ed Center Adult
7977 W 12th Ave 33014 305-823-1330
Nilda Diaz, prin. Fax 828-8929
Hialeah SHS Adult Education Center Adult
251 E 47th St 33013 305-822-1500
James Bishop, prin. Fax 821-6018

Advance Science Institute Post-Sec.
3750 W 12th Ave 33012 305-827-5452
Beauty Schools of America Post-Sec.
1060 W 49th St 33012 305-362-9003
Champagnat Catholic S 300/PK-12
369 E 10th St 33010 305-888-3760
Maria Alonso, prin. Fax 883-1174
Compu-Med Vocational Careers Post-Sec.
2900 W 12th Ave Ste 3 33012 305-888-9200
Edison Private S 400/PK-12
3720 E 4th Ave 33013 305-824-0303
Fax 822-4205
First Baptist S 200/PK-12
140 E 7th St 33010 305-888-9776
Florida Christian Academy 50/9-12
551 W 51st Pl 33012 305-822-4666
Ricardo Alfonso, prin.
Florida National College Post-Sec.
4425 W 20th Ave 33012 305-821-3333
Horeb Christian S 300/PK-12
795 W 68th St 33014 305-557-6811
Joseph Socarras, prin. Fax 821-6811
Keiser Career College Post-Sec.
17395 NW 59th Ave 33015 305-820-5003
La Belle Beauty School Post-Sec.
775 W 49th St Ste 5 33012 305-558-0562
Lincoln-Marti S 400/PK-12
1750 E 4th Ave 33010 305-643-4888
Miami Dade Christian Academy 50/9-12
1840 W 49th St Ste 520 33012 305-823-8111
Rodolfo Alfonso, prin. Fax 823-8111
Miami Lakes Educational Center Post-Sec.
5780 NW 158th St 33014 305-557-1100
National School of Technology Post-Sec.
4410 W 16th Ave Ste 52 33012 305-558-9500
Nouvelle Institute Post-Sec.
500 W 49th St Fl 2 33012 305-557-3017
The Praxis Institute Post-Sec.
4162 W 12th Ave 33012 305-556-1424

Hialeah Gardens, Dade, Pop. 19,930

Youth Co-op Training Institute Post-Sec.
12051 W Okeechobee Rd 33018 305-819-8855

Hilliard, Nassau, Pop. 2,913
Nassau County SD
Supt. — See Fernandina Beach
Hilliard MSHS 800/6-12
1 Flashes Ave 32046 904-491-7940
Dale Braddock, prin. Fax 845-7662

Hobe Sound, Martin, Pop. 11,507

Florida Unschoolers 200/K-12
8680 SE Eagle Ave 33455 772-546-0257
Hobe Sound Bible College Post-Sec.
PO Box 1065 33475 772-546-5534
Hobe Sound Christian Academy 200/K-12
PO Box 1065 33475 772-545-1455
William Marshall, dir. Fax 545-1454
Pine S 100/7-12
12350 SE Federal Hwy 33455 772-675-7005
James Cantwell Ed.D., hdmstr. Fax 675-7006

Holiday, Pasco, Pop. 19,360
Pasco County SD
Supt. — See Land O Lakes
Smith MS 6-8
1410 Sweetbriar Dr 34691 727-246-3200
Dr. Chris Dunning, prin. Fax 246-3291

Webster College Post-Sec.
2127 Grand Blvd 34690 727-942-0069

Holly Hill, Volusia, Pop. 12,630
Volusia County SD
Supt. — See De Land
Holly Hill MS 900/6-8
1200 Center Ave 32117 386-258-4663
John Polsinelli, prin. Fax 239-6314

Hollywood, Broward, Pop. 145,629
Broward County SD
Supt. — See Fort Lauderdale
Apollo MS 1,300/6-8
6800 Arthur St 33024 754-323-2900
Aimee Zekofsky, prin. Fax 323-2985
Attucks MS 800/6-8
3500 N 22nd Ave 33020 754-323-3000
Carletha Shaw, prin. Fax 323-3085
Driftwood MS 1,800/6-8
2751 NW 70th Ter 33024 754-323-3100
Jody Perry, prin. Fax 323-3185
Hollywood Hills HS 2,300/9-12
5400 Stirling Rd 33021 754-323-1050
Joyce Ferguson, prin. Fax 323-1180
McArthur HS 2,500/9-12
6501 Hollywood Blvd 33024 754-323-1200
Carol Roland, prin. Fax 323-1330
McNicol MS 1,500/6-8
1602 S 27th Ave 33020 754-323-3400
Kelvin Lee, prin. Fax 323-3485
Sheridan Technical Center Vo/Tech
5400 Sheridan St 33021 754-321-5400
Daniel Boegli, prin. Fax 321-5680
South Broward HS 2,500/9-12
1901 N Federal Hwy 33020 754-323-1800
Alan Strauss, prin. Fax 323-1930

Aukela Christian Military Academy 200/PK-12
2835 Madison St 33020 954-929-7010
Audrey Rodriguez, prin. Fax 927-2523
Chaminade-Madonna College Prep HS 900/9-12
500 E Chaminade Dr 33021 954-989-5150
M. Gloria Ramos, prin. Fax 983-4663
Hollywood Christian S 600/PK-12
1708 N State Road 7 33021 954-966-2350
Dr. Michael Chivalette, hdmstr. Fax 966-0097
Ross Medical Education Center Post-Sec.
6847 Taft St 33024 954-963-0043
Sheridan Hills Christian S 500/PK-12
3751 Sheridan St 33021 954-966-7995
Roy Johnson, hdmstr. Fax 961-1359
Sheridan Technical Center Post-Sec.
5400 Sheridan St 33021 754-321-5400

Homestead, Dade, Pop. 44,494
Miami-Dade County SD
Supt. — See Miami
Campbell Drive MS 1,500/6-8
900 NE 23rd Ave 33033 305-248-7911
Alicia Hidalgo, prin. Fax 248-3518
Homestead HS 3,200/9-12
2351 SE 12th Ave 33034 305-245-7000
Dr. Henry Crawford, prin. Fax 247-5757
Homestead MS 1,300/6-8
650 NW 2nd Ave 33030 305-247-4221
Martin Reid, prin. Fax 247-1098
Redland MS 1,700/6-8
16001 SW 248th St 33031 305-247-6112
Craig DePriest, prin. Fax 248-0628
South Dade HS 2,700/9-12
28401 SW 167th Ave 33030 305-247-4244
L.M. Mijuskovic, prin. Fax 248-3867
South Dade Adult Education Center Adult
109 NE 8th St 33030 305-248-5723
Gilda Santalla, prin. Fax 248-9164

Barrington Academy 200/PK-12
1013 N Redland Rd 33034 305-248-3400
Colonial Christian S 200/PK-12
17105 SW 296th St 33030 305-246-8608
Stephen Hager, prin. Fax 246-1542
First Assembly Christian Academy 100/PK-12
824 W Palm Dr 33034 305-248-0794
Julie Alexander, prin. Fax 246-5030
Redland Christian Academy 200/PK-12
17700 SW 280th St 33031 305-247-7399
Sharon Waldbillig, dir. Fax 247-1147

Hudson, Pasco, Pop. 7,344
Pasco County SD
Supt. — See Land O Lakes
Hudson HS 1,600/9-12
14410 Cobra Way 34669 727-774-4200
Angie Stone, prin. Fax 774-4291
Hudson MS 1,200/6-8
14540 Cobra Way 34669 727-774-8200
Steve Van Gorden, prin. Fax 774-8291

Grace Christian S 200/PK-12
9403 Scot St 34669 727-863-1825
Glenwood Pratt, prin. Fax 862-4484

Immokalee, Collier, Pop. 14,120
Collier County SD
Supt. — See Naples
Immokalee HS 1,300/9-12
701 Immokalee Dr 34142 239-377-1800
Armando Touron, prin. Fax 377-1801
Immokalee MS 1,200/6-8
401 N 9th St 34142 239-377-4200
Lisa Rivera-Scallan, prin. Fax 377-4201

Lorenzo Walker Institute of Technology Post-Sec.
614 S 5th St 34142

Indialantic, Brevard, Pop. 3,076
Brevard County SD
Supt. — See Melbourne
Hoover MS 600/7-8
2000 Hawk Haven Dr 32903 321-727-1611
Barbara Rodrigues, prin. Fax 725-0076

Indiantown, Martin, Pop. 4,794
Martin County SD
Supt. — See Stuart
Indiantown MS 500/5-8
16303 SW Farm Rd 34956 772-597-2146
Debbie Henderson, prin. Fax 597-5854

Inglis, Levy, Pop. 1,611
Levy County SD
Supt. — See Bronson
Forestry Youth Academy Vo/Tech
14251 SE Glass Rd 34449 352-465-8533
Bob King, prin. Fax 489-1201

Interlachen, Putnam, Pop. 1,518
Putnam County SD
Supt. — See Palatka
Interlachen HS 1,000/9-12
126 N County Road 315 32148 386-684-2116
Susan Mathe, prin. Fax 684-3915
Price MS 600/6-8
140 N County Road 315 32148 386-684-2113
Sandra Gilyard, prin. Fax 684-3908

Inverness, Citrus, Pop. 7,295
Citrus County SD 15,500/PK-12
1007 W Main St 34450 352-726-1931
Sandra Himmel, supt. Fax 726-4418
www.citrus.k12.fl.us
Citrus HS 1,600/9-12
600 W Highland Blvd 34452 352-726-2241
Leigh Ann Bradshaw, prin. Fax 726-1368
Inverness MS 1,200/6-8
1950 Highway 41 N 34450 352-726-1471
Bill Farrell, prin. Fax 726-4535
Withlachoochee Technical Institute Vo/Tech
1201 W Main St 34450 352-726-2430
Andrew Buchanan, dir. Fax 726-5842
Other Schools – See Citrus Springs, Crystal River, Lecanto

Inverness Christian Academy 100/PK-12
4222 S Florida Ave 34450 352-726-3759
Dan Riley, prin. Fax 726-0782
Withlacoochee Technical Institute Post-Sec.
1201 W Main St 34450 352-726-2430

Islamorada, Monroe, Pop. 1,220

Island Christian S 200/PK-12
83400 Overseas Hwy 33036 305-664-4933
James Roper, prin. Fax 664-8170

Jacksonville, Duval, Pop. 782,623
Duval County SD 124,000/PK-12
1701 Prudential Dr 32207 904-390-2000
Dr. Joseph Wise, supt. Fax 390-2586
www.educationcentral.org
Anderson HS of the Arts 1,100/9-12
2445 San Diego Rd 32207 904-346-5620
Jackie Cornelius, prin. Fax 346-5636
Arlington MS 900/6-8
8141 Lone Star Rd 32211 904-720-1680
Debbie Smith, prin. Fax 720-1702
Butler MS 600/6-8
900 Acorn St 32209 904-630-6900
Sylvia Johnson, prin. Fax 630-6913
Darnell-Cookman MS 1,300/6-8
1701 N Davis St 32209 904-630-6805
Kelly Coker-Daniels, prin. Fax 630-6811
Davis MS 1,600/6-8
7050 Melvin Rd 32210 904-573-1060
Addison Davis, prin. Fax 573-1066
DuPont MS 1,200/6-8
2710 Dupont Ave 32217 904-739-5200
Gary Finger, prin. Fax 739-5321
Englewood HS 2,000/9-12
4412 Barnes Rd 32207 904-739-5212
Dr. Alvin Brennan, prin. Fax 739-5324
First Coast HS 2,000/9-12
590 Duval Station Rd 32218 904-757-0080
Tony Bellamy, prin. Fax 696-8721
Forrest HS 1,700/9-12
5530 Firestone Rd 32244 904-573-1170
Helene Kirkpatrick, prin. Fax 573-1177
Ft. Caroline MS 1,100/6-8
3787 University Club Blvd 32277 904-745-4927
Kathy Kassees, prin. Fax 745-4937
Gilbert MS 600/6-8
1424 Franklin St 32206 904-630-6700
Jackie Simmons, prin. Fax 630-6713
Grand Park Career Center Vo/Tech
2335 W 18th St 32209 904-630-6894
Marvin McQueen, prin. Fax 630-6898
Highlands MS 1,000/6-8
10913 Pine Estates Rd E 32218 904-696-8771
Catherine Frazier-Wright, prin. Fax 696-8782
Jackson HS 1,500/9-12
3816 N Main St 32206 904-630-6950
Lance Barnett, prin. Fax 630-6955
Johnson MS 1,200/6-8
1840 W 9th St 32209 904-630-6640
Connie Hall, prin. Fax 630-6653
Kernan MS 1,400/6-8
2271 Kernan Blvd S 32246 904-220-1350
David Gilmore, prin. Fax 220-1355
Kirby-Smith MS 900/6-8
2034 Hubbard St 32206 904-630-6600
Dana Krizner, prin. Fax 630-6605
Lake Shore MS 1,200/6-8
2519 Bayview Rd 32210 904-381-7440
Iranetta Wright, prin. Fax 381-7437
Landmark MS 1,600/6-8
101 Kernan Blvd N 32225 904-221-7125
Michael Henry, prin. Fax 221-8847
Landon MS 800/6-8
1819 Thacker Ave 32207 904-346-5650
Mark Ertel, prin. Fax 346-5657
LaVilla S of the Arts 1,100/6-8
501 N Davis St 32202 904-633-6069
Janelle Wagoner, prin. Fax 633-8089
Lee HS 2,000/9-12
1200 McDuff Ave S 32205 904-381-3930
Denise Hall, prin. Fax 381-3945
Mandarin HS 2,900/9-12
4831 Greenland Rd 32258 904-260-3911
Crystal Sisler, prin. Fax 260-5439
Mandarin MS 1,700/6-8
5100 Hood Rd 32257 904-292-0555
Joy Recla, prin. Fax 260-5415
Northwestern MS 900/6-8
2100 W 45th St 32209 904-924-3100
Saryn Hatcher, prin. Fax 924-3284
Oceanway MS 1,300/6-8
143 Oceanway Ave 32218 904-714-4680
John Cochran, prin. Fax 714-4685
Parker HS 2,100/9-12
7301 Parker School Rd 32211 904-720-1650
Scott Flowers, prin. Fax 720-1700
Paxon HS for Advanced Studies 1,500/9-12
3239 Norman E Thagard Blvd 32254 904-693-7583
Carol Daniels, prin. Fax 693-7597
Paxon MS 800/6-8
3276 Norman E Thagard Blvd 32254 904-693-7600
Pam Pierce, prin. Fax 693-7661
Peterson Academy of Technology Vo/Tech
7450 Wilson Blvd 32210 904-573-1150
John Holechek, prin. Fax 573-3206
Raines HS 1,400/9-12
3663 Raines Ave 32209 904-924-3049
Nongongoma Majova-Seane, prin. Fax 924-3058
Randolph Academies of Technology Vo/Tech
1157 Golfair Blvd 32209 904-924-3011
Lorenda Tiscornia, prin. Fax 924-3125
Ribault HS 900/9-12
3701 Winton Dr 32208 904-924-3092
Royce Turner, prin. Fax 924-3154
Ribault MS 600/6-8
3610 Ribault Scenic Dr 32208 904-924-3062
George Maxey, prin. Fax 924-3167
Sandalwood HS 3,300/9-12
2750 John Prom Blvd 32246 904-646-5100
Victoria Schultz, prin. Fax 646-5126
Southside MS 1,100/6-8
2948 Knights Ln E 32216 904-739-5238
LaTanya McNeal, prin. Fax 739-5244
Stanton College Preparatory HS 1,500/9-12
1149 W 13th St 32209 904-630-6760
Debra Lynch, prin. Fax 630-6758
Stilwell MS 1,500/6-8
7840 Burma Rd 32221 904-693-7523
Lawrence Dennis, prin. Fax 693-7539
Stuart MS 1,100/6-8
4815 Wesconnett Blvd 32210 904-573-1000
Dr. Jeanne Ballentine, prin. Fax 573-3213
Twin Lakes Academy 1,700/6-8
8050 Point Meadows Dr 32256 904-538-0825
Don Nelson, prin. Fax 538-0840
White HS 2,100/9-12
1700 Old Middleburg Rd N 32210 904-693-7620
James Clark, prin. Fax 693-7639
Wolfson HS 2,000/9-12
7000 Powers Ave 32217 904-739-5265
Hammond Gracey, prin. Fax 739-5272
Other Schools – See Atlantic Beach, Baldwin, Jacksonville Beach, Neptune Beach

St. Johns County SD
Supt. — See Saint Augustine
Bartram Trail HS 2,300/9-12
2050 Roberts Rd 32259 904-287-6767
Brennan Asplen, prin. Fax 819-8345
Fruit Cove MS 1,000/6-8
3180 Race Track Rd 32259 904-287-2211
Steve McCormick, prin. Fax 819-7885
Switzerland Point MS 1,100/6-8
777 Greenbriar Rd 32259 904-819-8650
Kyle Dresback, prin. Fax 819-8645

Arlington Country Day S 500/K-12
5725 Fort Caroline Rd 32277 904-744-0466
Dr. Fred Lichtward, dir. Fax 744-0859
Baptist Medical Centers Post-Sec.
800 Prudential Dr 32207 904-393-2001
Baptist/St. Vincent's Health System Post-Sec.
1800 Barrs St 32204 904-387-7300
Bishop John J. Snyder HS 200/9-12
5001 Samaritan Way 32210 904-771-1029
David Yazdiya, prin. Fax 908-8988
Bishop Kenny HS 1,500/9-12
PO Box 5544 32247 904-398-7545
Todd Orlando, prin. Fax 398-5728
Broach S - Westside 100/1-12
440 Lenox Sq 32254 904-389-5106
Darrell Lewis, dir. Fax 388-1077
Cedar Creek Christian S 200/PK-12
1372 Lane Ave S 32205 904-781-9151
Jacquelyn Pitts, prin. Fax 781-9182
Concorde Career Institute Post-Sec.
7960 Arlington Expy 32211 904-725-0525
Conservative Christian Academy 50/7-12
12021 Old St Augustine Rd 32258 904-262-7777
Dr. Gene Youngblood, admin. Fax 262-7593
Coral Ridge Baptist S 50/4-12
2967 Huffman Blvd 32246 904-642-2726
Dr. Anthony Fox, prin. Fax 642-3429
Cornerstone Christian S 300/PK-12
4000 Spring Park Rd 32207 904-730-5500
Deborah Wagner, prin. Fax 730-5502
Eagle's View Academy 400/K-12
7788 Ramona Blvd W 32221 904-786-1411
Scott Kinlaw, admin. Fax 786-1445
Edward Waters College Post-Sec.
1658 Kings Rd 32209 904-355-3030
Episcopal HS 900/6-12
4455 Atlantic Blvd 32207 904-396-5751
Dale Reagan, hdmstr. Fax 396-7209
Esprit De Corps Center for Learning 100/PK-12
9840 Wagner Rd 32219 904-924-2000
Betty White, prin. Fax 766-8870
Euro Hair Design Institute Post-Sec.
5995 University Blvd W #3 32216 904-731-4766
First Coast Academy 900/9-12
2725 College St 32205 904-381-1935
Barbara Cornelius, prin. Fax 381-0135
First Coast Christian S 600/PK-12
7587 Blanding Blvd 32244 904-777-3040
Morry Kemple, admin. Fax 777-3045
Florida Coastal School of Law Post-Sec.
8787 Baypine Rd 32256 904-680-7700
Florida Community College Post-Sec.
101 State St W 32202 904-633-8100
Florida Community College Post-Sec.
3939 Roosevelt Blvd 32205 904-381-3400
Florida Community College Post-Sec.
4501 Capper Rd 32218 904-766-6500
Florida Community College Post-Sec.
11901 Beach Blvd 32246 904-646-2111
Florida Technical College Post-Sec.
8711 Lone Star Rd 32211 904-724-2229
Greenwood S 200/2-12
9920 Regency Square Blvd 32225 904-726-5000
Beverly Connell, prin. Fax 726-5056
Heritage Institute Post-Sec.
4130 Salisbury Rd Ste 1100 32216 904-332-0910
ITT Technical Institute Post-Sec.
6600 Youngerman Cir Ste 10 32244 904-573-9100
Jacksonville Adventist Academy 100/PK-12
4298 Livingston Rd 32257 904-268-2433
David Gardner, dir. Fax 268-7770
Jacksonville University Post-Sec.
2800 University Blvd N 32211 904-744-3950
Jones College Post-Sec.
5353 Arlington Expy 32211 904-743-1122
Little Country S 100/PK-12
862 Baisden Rd 32218 904-757-8200
Mandarin Christian S 600/K-12
10850 Old St Augustine Rd 32257 904-268-8667
Pat Stuart, hdmstr. Fax 880-3251
Normandy Beauty School of Jacksonville Post-Sec.
5373 Lenox Ave 32205 904-786-6250
Parsons Academy 200/PK-10
5705 Fort Caroline Rd 32277 904-745-4588
Grace Williams, prin. Fax 762-9819
Potters House Christian Academy 600/PK-12
5732 Normandy Blvd 32205 904-786-0028
Jermall Wright, admin. Fax 695-2954
Providence S 1,500/PK-12
2701 Hodges Blvd 32224 904-223-5270
Don Barfield, hdmstr. Fax 223-4930
Remington College Post-Sec.
7011 A C Sknnr Pky #140 32256 904-296-3435
Riverside Hairstyling Academy Post-Sec.
3530 Beach Blvd 32207 904-398-0502
St. Luke's Hospital/Mayo Clinic Post-Sec.
4201 Belfort Rd 32216 904-296-3733
Sanford-Brown Institute Post-Sec.
10255 Fortune Pkwy Ste 501 32256 904-363-6221
Seacoast Christian Academy 400/PK-12
9570 Regency Square Blvd 32225 904-725-5544
Cynthia Stremmel, admin. Fax 727-6748
Shands Jacksonville Medical Center Post-Sec.
655 W 8th St 32209 904-244-0411
Shekinah Christian Academy 200/K-12
10551 Beach Blvd 32246 904-421-1015
Saundra Armour, prin. Fax 421-1022
Southeastern School of Neuromuscular Post-Sec.
9424 Baymeadows Rd Ste 200 32256 904-448-9499
Stenotype Inst. Court Reporting School Post-Sec.
3986 Blvd Center Dr #200 32207 904-246-7466
Success Academy 100/PK-12
2103 Grand St 32208 904-766-6212
Marian Williams-Johnson, admin. Fax 425-4727
Trinity Baptist College Post-Sec.
800 Hammond Blvd 32221 904-596-2400
Trinity Christian Academy 1,700/PK-12
800 Hammond Blvd 32221 904-596-2400
Clayton Lindstam, admin. Fax 596-2531
Tulsa Welding School Post-Sec.
3500 Southside Blvd 32216 904-646-9353
University Christian S 900/PK-12
5520 University Blvd W 32216 904-737-6330
Duane Sherman, dir. Fax 737-3359
University of North Florida Post-Sec.
4567 Saint Johns Bluff Rd S 32224 904-620-1000
Victory Christian Academy 300/PK-12
10613 Lem Turner Rd 32218 904-764-7781
Jan Van Delinder, dir. Fax 764-7297
West Meadows Baptist Academy 100/K-12
11711 Normandy Blvd 32221 904-786-9308
Dr. Bruce Armstrong, admin. Fax 786-2712

Jacksonville Beach, Duval, Pop. 21,770
Duval County SD
Supt. — See Jacksonville
Fletcher MS 1,400/6-8
2000 3rd St N 32250 904-247-5929
Laurie Flynn, prin. Fax 247-5940

Foundation Academy 200/K-12
107 3rd Ave S 32250 904-241-3515
Nadia Hionides, prin. Fax 241-9857

Jasper, Hamilton, Pop. 1,817
Hamilton County SD 2,000/PK-12
4280 SW County Road 152 32052 386-792-1228
Harry Pennington, supt. Fax 792-3681
www.firn.edu/schools/hamilton/hamilton/
Hamilton County HS 900/7-12
5683 US Highway 129 S 32052 386-792-6540
Gene Starr, prin. Fax 792-6594

Hamilton Vo-Tech Center — Vo/Tech
4280 SW County Road 152 32052 — 386-792-6529
Rex Mitchell, prin. — Fax 792-6623

Jay, Santa Rosa, Pop. 665
Santa Rosa County SD
Supt. — See Milton
Jay JSHS — 500/7-12
13863 Alabama St 32565 — 850-675-4507
Dale Westmoreland, prin. — Fax 675-8573

Jensen Beach, Martin, Pop. 9,884
Martin County SD
Supt. — See Stuart
Jensen Beach HS — 1,100/9-12
2875 NW Goldenrod Rd 34957 — 772-232-3500
Ginger Featherstone, prin. — Fax 232-3699

* * *

Olivet Private S — 200/K-12
4267 NW Federal Hwy # 115 34957 — 772-879-9707
Cathie Mouring, dir.

Juno Beach, Palm Beach, Pop. 3,395

* * *

Batt Private S — 100/PK-12
13205 US Highway 1 Ste 211 33408 — 561-630-9980
Vicki Griswold, dir. — Fax 624-4632

Jupiter, Palm Beach, Pop. 47,909
Palm Beach County SD
Supt. — See West Palm Beach
Independence MS — 1,400/6-8
4001 Greenway Dr 33458 — 561-799-7500
Gwendolyn Johnson, prin. — Fax 799-7505
Jupiter Community HS — 2,700/9-12
500 Military Trl 33458 — 561-744-7900
Paula Nessmith, prin. — Fax 744-7978
Jupiter MS — 1,100/6-8
15245 Military Trl 33458 — 561-745-7200
David Culp, prin. — Fax 745-7246

* * *

Jupiter Christian S — 600/PK-12
1300 Mohawk St 33458 — 561-746-7800
Leslie Downs, pres. — Fax 748-9528

Key Biscayne, Dade, Pop. 10,158
Miami-Dade County SD
Supt. — See Miami
MAST Academy — 500/9-12
3979 Rickenbacker Cswy 33149 — 305-365-6278
Thomas Fisher, prin. — Fax 361-0996

Keystone Heights, Clay, Pop. 1,427
Clay County SD
Supt. — See Green Cove Springs
Keystone Heights JSHS — 1,300/7-12
900 Orchid Ave 32656 — 352-473-2761
Dr. Susan Sailor, prin. — Fax 473-5920

Key West, Monroe, Pop. 23,935
Monroe County SD — 8,300/PK-12
PO Box 1788 33041 — 305-293-1400
Randy Acevedo, supt. — Fax 293-1408
www.keysschools.com
Key West HS — 1,300/9-12
2100 Flagler Ave 33040 — 305-293-1549
John Welsh, prin. — Fax 293-1547
O'Bryant MS — 800/6-8
1105 Leon St 33040 — 305-296-5628
Frank Spoto, prin. — Fax 293-1644
Other Schools – See Marathon, Tavernier

* * *

Florida Keys Community College — Post-Sec.
5901 College Rd 33040 — 305-296-9081

Kissimmee, Osceola, Pop. 59,364
Osceola County SD — 41,800/PK-12
817 Bill Beck Blvd 34744 — 407-870-4600
Blaine Muse, supt. — Fax 870-4010
www.osceola.k12.fl.us
Denn John MS — 1,400/6-8
2001 Denn John Ln 34744 — 407-935-3560
Rob Paswaters, prin. — Fax 935-3572
Discovery IS — 1,500/6-8
5350 San Miguel Rd 34758 — 407-343-7300
Annette Campbell, prin. — Fax 343-7310
Gateway HS — 2,700/9-12
93 Panther Paws Trl 34744 — 407-935-3600
Terry Andrews, prin. — Fax 935-3609
Horizon MS — 1,300/6-8
2020 Ham Brown Rd 34746 — 407-943-7240
Michael Allen, prin. — Fax 943-7250
Kissimmee MS — 1,200/6-8
2410 Dyer Blvd 34741 — 407-870-0857
Paula Evans, prin. — Fax 870-5669
Neptune MS — 1,700/6-8
2727 Neptune Rd 34744 — 407-935-3500
Judy Zieg, prin. — Fax 935-3519
Osceola County S for the Arts — 600/6-12
3151 N Orange Blossom Trl 34744 — 407-931-4803
Michael Vondracek, prin. — Fax 931-3019
Osceola HS — 2,500/9-12
420 S Thacker Ave 34741 — 407-518-5400
Charles Paradiso, prin. — Fax 943-7909
Parkway MS — 1,100/6-8
857 Florida Pkwy 34743 — 407-344-7000
Jeannette Paul-Rivers, prin. — Fax 348-2797
PATHS @ TECO — Vo/Tech
501 Simpson Rd 34744 — 407-344-5080
Laura Rhinehart, dir. — Fax 344-2467
Poinciana HS — 2,500/9-12
2300 S Poinciana Blvd 34758 — 407-870-4860
George Sullivan, prin. — Fax 870-0382
Technical Education Center — Vo/Tech
501 Simpson Rd 34744 — 407-344-5080
Laura Rhinehart, dir. — Fax 344-5089
Adult Learning Center — Adult
705 Simpson Rd 34744 — 407-518-8140
Dave Welty, dir. — Fax 518-8141
Other Schools – See Celebration, Saint Cloud

* * *

Florida Christian College — Post-Sec.
1011 Bill Beck Blvd 34744 — 407-847-8966
Heartland Christian Academy — 300/PK-12
2874 E Irlo Bronson Mem Hwy 34744 — 407-847-5184
Kathy Harkema, prin. — Fax 870-2678
Heritage Christian S — 600/K-12
1500 E Vine St 34744 — 407-847-4087
Karla Beaver, admin. — Fax 932-2806
Hope Christian Academy — 200/K-12
2460 Fortune Rd 34744 — 321-402-0200
Marvin Lane, prin. — Fax 402-0202
Life Academy — 200/K-12
2269 Partin Settlement Rd 34744 — 407-847-8222
Mark Hennesey, prin. — Fax 932-4431
North Kissimmee Christian S — 200/PK-12
425 W Donegan Ave 34741 — 407-847-2877
Yvonne Johnson, prin. — Fax 847-5372
Pleasant Hill Academy — 100/PK-12
PO Box 453536 34745 — 863-427-6760
Carmen Caban-Ruiz, prin. — Fax 427-6763
Technical Education Center - Osceola — Post-Sec.
501 Simpson Rd 34744 — 407-344-5080

La Belle, Hendry, Pop. 3,302
Hendry County SD — 7,400/PK-12
PO Box 1980 33975 — 863-674-4550
Thomas Conner, supt. — Fax 674-4090
www.hendry-schools.org
La Belle HS — 1,100/9-12
4050 E Cowboy Way 33935 — 863-674-4120
Daniel Gilbertson, prin. — Fax 674-4571
La Belle MS — 800/6-8
8000 E Cowboy Way 33935 — 863-674-4646
Gary White, prin. — Fax 674-4645
Labelle Community Adult S — Adult
PO Box 2738, — 863-674-4118
James Way, prin. — Fax 674-4117
Other Schools – See Clewiston

Lake Alfred, Polk, Pop. 3,930
Polk County SD
Supt. — See Bartow
Lake Alfred-Addair MS — 6-8
925 N Buena Vista Dr 33850 — 863-295-5988
Asonja Cross, prin. — Fax 295-5989

Lake Butler, Union, Pop. 1,967
Union County SD — 2,200/PK-12
55 SW 6th St 32054 — 386-496-2045
Carlton Faulk, supt. — Fax 496-2580
www.union.k12.fl.us/
Lake Butler MS — 700/5-8
150 SW 6th St 32054 — 386-496-3046
Mark Bracewell, prin. — Fax 496-4352
Union County HS — 600/9-12
1000 S Lake Ave 32054 — 386-496-3040
Alex Nelson, prin. — Fax 496-4187
Union County Adult HS — Adult
208 SE 6th St 32054 — 386-496-1300
Barry Sams, prin.

Lake City, Columbia, Pop. 10,970
Columbia County SD — 9,800/PK-12
372 W Duval St 32055 — 386-755-8000
Grady D. Markham, supt. — Fax 755-8029
www.columbia.k12.fl.us
Columbia HS — 1,800/9-12
469 SE Fighting Tiger Dr 32025 — 386-755-8080
Terry Huddleston, prin. — Fax 755-8082
Lake City MS — 1,100/6-8
843 SW Arlington Blvd 32025 — 386-758-4800
Tom Dorsett, prin. — Fax 758-4839
Richardson MS — 700/6-8
646 SE Pennsylvania St 32025 — 386-755-8130
Keith Couey, prin. — Fax 755-8154
Vocational Adult & Community Education — Vo/Tech
409 SW Saint Johns St 32025 — 386-755-8190
Melvin Goggins, prin.
Other Schools – See Fort White

* * *

Blake S — 100/PK-12
7443 W US Highway 90 32055 — 386-752-8874
Linnie Jordan, prin. — Fax 752-9453
Lake City Christian Academy — 200/K-12
3035 SW Pinemount Rd 32024 — 386-758-0055
Tana Espenship, prin. — Fax 758-3018
Lake City Community College — Post-Sec.
149 SE College Pl 32025 — 386-752-1822

Lakeland, Polk, Pop. 88,713
Polk County SD
Supt. — See Bartow
Chiles MS Academy — 600/6-8
400 N Florida Ave 33801 — 863-499-2742
Sharon Neuman, prin. — Fax 499-2774
Crystal Lake MS — 900/6-8
2410 N Crystal Lake Dr 33801 — 863-499-2970
Christopher Canning, prin. — Fax 603-6267
Harrison S for the Arts — 400/9-12
750 Hollingsworth Rd 33801 — 863-499-2855
Craig Collins, prin. — Fax 499-2938
Jenkins HS — 2,100/9-12
6000 Lakeland Highlands Rd 33813 — 863-648-3566
Buddy Thomas, prin. — Fax 648-3573
Kathleen HS — 1,600/9-12
2600 Crutchfield Rd 33805 — 863-499-2655
Cecil McClellan, prin. — Fax 499-2726
Kathleen MS — 800/6-8
3627 Kathleen Pnes 33810 — 863-853-6040
Sam Wright, prin. — Fax 853-6037
Lake Gibson HS — 1,900/9-12
7007 N Socrum Loop Rd 33809 — 863-853-6100
Ralph Gilchrest, prin. — Fax 853-6108
Lake Gibson MS — 1,100/6-8
6901 N Socrum Loop Rd 33809 — 863-853-6181
John Barber, prin. — Fax 853-6171
Lakeland Highlands MS — 1,200/6-8
740 Lake Miriam Dr 33813 — 863-648-3500
Robert Hartley, prin. — Fax 648-3580
Lakeland HS — 2,000/9-12
726 Hollingsworth Rd 33801 — 863-499-2900
Mark Thomas, prin. — Fax 499-2917
Sleepy Hill MS — 1,200/6-8
2215 Sleepy Hill Rd 33810 — 863-815-6577
Lee Brackman, prin. — Fax 815-6586
Southwest MS — 1,000/6-8
2815 Eden Pkwy 33803 — 863-499-2840
John Wilson, prin. — Fax 499-2762
Traviss Career Center — Vo/Tech
3225 Winter Lake Rd 33803 — 863-499-2700
Kenneth James, prin. — Fax 499-2706
West Area Adult & Community S — Adult
604 S Central Ave 33815 — 863-499-2835
Loretta Cameron, prin. — Fax 499-2727

* * *

Families of Fairth Cristian Academy — 800/K-12
1248 George Jenkins Blvd 33815 — 863-686-7755
James Lawson, prin. — Fax 686-7086
FL Metropolitan Univ. - Lakeland — Post-Sec.
995 E Memorial Blvd Ste 110 33801 — 863-686-1444
Florida Southern College — Post-Sec.
111 Lake Hollingsworth Dr 33801 — 863-680-4111
Geneva Classical Academy — 100/PK-12
4410 E County Road 540A 33813 — 863-644-1408
Tim Bullock, prin. — Fax 619-5841
Highlands Christian Academy — 100/PK-12
4210 Lakeland Highlands Rd 33813 — 863-646-5031
Mike Odum, admin. — Fax 646-2267
Keiser College — Post-Sec.
2400 Interstate Dr 33805 — 863-682-6020
Lakeland Christian S — 1,000/K-12
1111 Forest Park St 33803 — 863-688-2771
Michael Sligh, hdmstr. — Fax 682-5637
Lakeland Regional Medical Center — Post-Sec.
1324 Lakeland Hills Blvd 33805 — 863-687-1100
Santa Fe Catholic HS — 200/9-12
3110 US Highway 92 E 33801 — 863-665-4188
Gwenda Cote, prin. — Fax 665-4151
Sonrise Christian S — 200/PK-12
3151 Hardin Combee Rd 33801 — 863-665-4187
Donna Ready, dir. — Fax 665-6065
Southeastern University — Post-Sec.
1000 Longfellow Blvd 33801 — 863-667-5000
Traviss Technical Center — Post-Sec.
3225 Winter Lake Rd 33803 — 863-499-2700
Victory Christian Academy — 300/PK-12
PO Box 90489 33804 — 863-858-5614
Lisa Cosicia, prin. — Fax 858-4268

Lake Mary, Seminole, Pop. 14,638
Seminole County SD
Supt. — See Sanford
Greenwood Lakes MS — 1,600/6-8
601 Lake Park Dr 32746 — 407-320-7650
Tom Marcy, prin. — Fax 320-7699
Lake Mary HS — 3,000/9-12
655 Longwood Lake Mary Rd 32746 — 407-320-9550
Boyd Karns, prin. — Fax 320-9512
Markham Woods MS — 6-8
6003 Markham Woods Rd 32746 — 407-871-1750
Roger Gardner, prin.

* * *

ITT Technical Institute — Post-Sec.
1400 S International Pkwy 32746 — 407-660-2900
Lake Mary Preparatory S — 600/PK-12
650 Rantoul Ln 32746 — 407-805-0095
Dr. Pouneh Alcott, prin. — Fax 322-3872

Lake Park, Palm Beach, Pop. 9,039

* * *

Lake Park Baptist S — 400/PK-10
625 Park Ave 33403 — 561-844-2747
Carol Hyatt, prin. — Fax 881-5367

Lake Placid, Highlands, Pop. 1,784
Highlands County SD
Supt. — See Sebring
Lake Placid HS — 800/9-12
202 Green Dragon Dr 33852 — 863-699-5010
Ruth Heckman, prin. — Fax 699-5094
Lake Placid MS — 600/6-8
201 S Tangerine Ave 33852 — 863-699-5030
Derrel Bryan, prin. — Fax 699-5029

Lake Wales, Polk, Pop. 12,964
Polk County SD
Supt. — See Bartow
Lake Wales HS — 1,400/9-12
1 Highlander Way 33853 — 863-678-4222
Clark Berry, prin. — Fax 678-4064
McLaughlin MS — 900/6-8
800 S 4th St 33853 — 863-678-4233
Sharon Kurschner, prin. — Fax 678-4033
Roosevelt Academy — 300/6-12
115 E St 33853 — 863-678-4252
Ron Rizer, prin. — Fax 678-4250

* * *

Vanguard S — 100/5-12
22000 Hwy 27 33859 — 863-676-6091
Cathy Wooley-Brown Ph.D., pres. — Fax 676-8297
Warner Southern College — Post-Sec.
5301 US Highway 27 S 33859 — 863-638-1426

Lake Worth, Palm Beach, Pop. 36,342
Palm Beach County SD
Supt. — See West Palm Beach
Lake Worth Community HS — 3,000/9-12
1701 Lake Worth Rd 33460 — 561-533-6300
Ian Saltzman, prin. — Fax 493-0888
Lake Worth MS — 1,100/6-8
1300 Barnett Dr 33461 — 561-540-5500
Jesus Armas, prin. — Fax 540-5559
Park Vista Community HS — 2,000/9-12
7900 Jog Rd 33467 — 561-491-8400
Nora Rosensweig, prin. — Fax 493-6854
Tradewinds MS — 1,200/6-8
5090 Haverhill Rd 33463 — 561-493-6400
Kathleen Orloff, prin. — Fax 493-6410
Woodlands MS — 1,700/6-8
5200 Lyons Rd 33467 — 561-357-0300
May Gamble, prin. — Fax 357-0307

* * *

Academy of Healing Arts Massage — Post-Sec.
3141 S Military Trl 33463 — 561-965-4686
Cornerstone Academy — 100/PK-12
6863 S Congress Ave 33462 — 561-968-9633
James Brewer, prin. — Fax 968-1110
Medical Career Institute South Florida — Post-Sec.
802 S Dixie Hwy 33460 — 561-493-5022
Palm Beach Community College — Post-Sec.
4200 S Congress Ave 33461 — 561-868-3350

Trinity Christian Academy 700/PK-12
7259 S Military Trl 33463 561-967-1900
Cindy Ansell, prin. Fax 965-4347

Land O Lakes, Pasco, Pop. 7,892
Pasco County SD 58,800/PK-12
7227 Land O Lakes Blvd 34638 813-794-2000
Heather Fiorentino Ph.D., supt. Fax 794-2716
www.pasco.k12.fl.us
Land O'Lakes HS 2,100/9-12
20325 Gator Ln, 813-794-9400
Monica Isle, prin. Fax 794-9491
Pine View MS 1,700/6-8
5334 Parkway Blvd 34639 813-794-4800
David Estabrook, prin. Fax 794-4891
Other Schools – See Dade City, Holiday, Hudson, New Port Richey, Port Richey, Wesley Chapel, Zephyrhills

---

Academy at the Lakes 400/PK-12
2220 Collier Pkwy 34639 813-948-2133
Richard J. Wendlek, hdmstr. Fax 948-2943
Land O'Lakes Christian S 200/PK-12
5105 School Rd, 813-995-9040
Denise Smith, dir. Fax 996-9742

Lantana, Palm Beach, Pop. 10,498
Palm Beach County SD
Supt. — See West Palm Beach
Lantana Community MS 800/6-8
1225 W Drew St 33462 561-540-3400
Ann Clark, prin. Fax 540-3435
Santaluces Community HS 2,400/9-12
6880 Lawrence Rd 33462 561-642-6200
John Stevens, prin. Fax 642-6255

Largo, Pinellas, Pop. 74,473
Pinellas County SD 110,100/PK-12
PO Box 2942 33779 727-588-1818
Dr. Clayton Wilcox, supt. Fax 588-6200
www.pinellas.k12.fl.us
Fitzgerald MS 1,300/6-8
6410 118th Ave 33773 727-547-4526
Bill Corbett, prin. Fax 547-4530
Largo HS 2,300/9-12
410 Missouri Ave N 33770 727-588-3758
Jeffrey Haynes, prin. Fax 588-4037
Largo MS 1,300/6-8
155 8th Ave SE 33771 727-588-4600
Fred Ulrich, prin. Fax 588-3720
Pinellas Park HS 2,300/9-12
6305 118th Ave 33773 727-538-7410
Denise Hart, prin. Fax 507-6174
Other Schools – See Clearwater, Dunedin, Gulfport, Madeira Beach, Palm Harbor, Pinellas Park, Safety Harbor, Saint Petersburg, Seminole, Tarpon Springs

---

Indian Rocks Christian S 1,000/PK-12
12685 Ulmerton Rd 33774 727-596-4321
Don Mayes, supt. Fax 593-5485
Lighthouse Christian Academy 400/K-12
8200 Bryan Dairy Rd 33777 727-319-0700
Remington College Post-Sec.
8550 Ulmerton Rd Ste 100 33771 727-532-1999
Schiller International University Post-Sec.
300 E Bay Dr 33770 727-736-5082
Westside Christian S 100/1-12
11633 137th St N 33774 727-517-2153
Dr. Jerry Forrester, admin. Fax 593-7700

Lauderdale Lakes, Broward, Pop. 31,826
Broward County SD
Supt. — See Fort Lauderdale
Anderson HS 2,700/9-12
3050 NW 41st St 33309 754-322-0200
Kevin Sawyer, prin. Fax 322-0330
Lauderdale Lakes MS 1,000/6-8
3911 NW 30th Ave 33309 754-322-3500
Angela Jackson, prin. Fax 322-3585

Concorde Career Institute Post-Sec.
4000 N State Rd 7 33319 954-731-8880
Hope Career Institute Post-Sec.
3714 W Oakland Park Blvd 33311 954-741-0088
The School of Health Careers Post-Sec.
3190 N State Road 7 33319 954-777-0083

Lauderhill, Broward, Pop. 59,621
Broward County SD
Supt. — See Fort Lauderdale
Lauderhill MS 1,000/6-8
1901 NW 49th Ave 33313 754-322-3600
Leo Nesmith, prin. Fax 322-3685

Laurel Hill, Okaloosa, Pop. 577
Okaloosa County SD
Supt. — See Fort Walton Beach
Laurel Hill S 400/PK-12
8078 4th St 32567 850-652-4111
Rodney Nobles, prin. Fax 652-4659

Lecanto, Citrus, Pop. 1,243
Citrus County SD
Supt. — See Inverness
Lecanto HS 1,600/9-12
3810 W Educational Path 34461 352-746-2334
Kelly Tyler, prin. Fax 746-1675
Lecanto MS 900/6-8
3800 W Educational Path 34461 352-746-2050
James Kusmaul, prin. Fax 746-3639

Seven Rivers Christian S 400/PK-12
4221 W Gulf to Lake Hwy 34461 352-746-5696
Joel Satterly, hdmstr. Fax 746-5520

Leesburg, Lake, Pop. 19,086
Lake County SD
Supt. — See Tavares
Carver MS 800/6-8
1200 Beecher St 34748 352-787-7868
Linda Shepherd, prin. Fax 787-1339
Leesburg HS 1,800/9-12
1401 W Meadows Ave 34748 352-787-5224
Nancy Velez, prin. Fax 787-8892
Oak Park MS 700/6-8
2101 South St 34748 352-787-3232
Letizia Haugabrook, prin. Fax 326-2177

Beacon College Post-Sec.
105 E Main St 34748 352-787-7660
First Academy 400/K-12
219 N 13th St 34748 352-787-7762
Gregory Frescoln, admin. Fax 323-1773
Lake-Sumter Community College Post-Sec.
9501 US Highway 441 34788 352-787-3747

Lehigh Acres, Lee, Pop. 13,611
Lee County SD
Supt. — See Fort Myers
East Lee County HS 9-12
1200 Homestead Rd N 33936 239-369-2932
Merle Winder, prin. Fax 369-3213
Lehigh Acres MS 900/6-8
104 Arthur Ave 33936 239-369-6108
Ray Bowers, prin. Fax 369-8808
Lehigh HS 2,100/9-12
901 Gunnery Rd N 33971 239-693-5353
Peter Bohatch, prin. Fax 693-6702
Varsity Lakes MS 700/6-8
801 Gunnery Rd N 33971 239-694-3464
Ron Davis, prin. Fax 694-7093

Dayspring Independent S 50/K-12
101 Xelda Ave N 33971 239-369-5008
Robert Wiedeman, admin.

Leisure City, Dade, Pop. 19,379
Miami-Dade County SD
Supt. — See Miami
South Dade Skill Ctr Vo/Tech
28300 SW 152nd Ave 33033 305-247-7839
Evelyn Davis, prin. Fax 247-2375

Lithia, Hillsborough
Hillsborough County SD
Supt. — See Tampa
Newsome HS 1,500/9-12
16550 Fishhawk Blvd 33547 813-740-4600
Rebecca Anderson, prin. Fax 740-4604
Randall MS 1,200/6-8
16510 Fishhawk Blvd 33547 813-740-3900
Marcia Elliott, prin. Fax 740-3910

Live Oak, Suwannee, Pop. 6,922
Suwannee County SD 5,200/PK-12
702 2nd St NW 32064 386-364-2601
Walter Boatright, supt. Fax 364-2635
www.suwannee.k12.fl.us
Suwannee-Hamilton Technical Ctr Vo/Tech
415 Pinewood Dr SW 32064 386-364-2750
Dianne Westcott, prin. Fax 364-4698
Suwannee HS 1,300/9-12
1314 Pine Ave SW 32064 386-364-2639
Dawn Lamb, prin. Fax 364-2794
Suwannee MS 1,100/6-8
1730 Walker Ave SW 32064 386-364-2730
Norri Steele, prin. Fax 208-1474
Other Schools – See Branford

Melody Christian Academy 200/PK-12
PO Box 1448 32064 386-364-4800
Suwannee-Hamilton Technical Center Post-Sec.
415 Pinewood Dr SW 32064 386-364-2750

Longwood, Seminole, Pop. 13,580
Seminole County SD
Supt. — See Sanford
Lyman HS 2,500/9-12
865 S Ronald Reagan Blvd 32750 407-320-2050
Frank Casillo, prin. Fax 320-2024
Milwee MS 1,200/6-8
1341 S Ronald Reagan Blvd 32750 407-320-3850
Lois Chavis, prin. Fax 320-3899
Rock Lake MS 1,200/6-8
250 Slade Dr 32750 407-320-9350
M. Walsh, prin. Fax 320-9399

PACE - Brantley Hall S 200/1-12
3221 Sand Lake Rd 32779 407-869-8882
Kathleen Shatlock, prin. Fax 869-8717

Loxahatchee, Palm Beach
Palm Beach County SD
Supt. — See West Palm Beach
Osceola Creek MS 800/6-8
6775 180th Ave N 33470 561-422-2500
Susan Atherley, prin. Fax 422-2510
Seminole Ridge Community HS 9-12
4601 Seminole Pratt Whitney 33470 561-422-2600
Lynne McGee, prin. Fax 422-2623

Lutz, Hillsborough, Pop. 10,552
Hillsborough County SD
Supt. — See Tampa
Martinez MS 1,000/6-8
5601 W Lutz Lake Fern Rd 33558 813-558-1190
Kathleen A. Flanagan, prin. Fax 558-1226

Lynn Haven, Bay, Pop. 15,677
Bay County SD
Supt. — See Panama City
Mosley HS 2,100/9-12
501 Mosley Dr 32444 850-872-4400
Bill Husfelt, prin. Fax 872-4451
Mowat MS 1,000/6-8
1903 W Highway 390 32444 850-271-6140
Shirley Baker, prin. Fax 265-2179

Macclenny, Baker, Pop. 5,186
Baker County SD 4,400/PK-12
392 South Blvd E 32063 904-259-6251
Paula Barton, supt. Fax 259-2825
www.baker.k12.fl.us
Baker County MS 1,100/6-8
211 E Jonathan St 32063 904-259-2226
David Davis, prin. Fax 259-7955
Baker County Adult Center Adult
270 South Blvd E 32063 904-259-6251
Dr. Garlon Webb, prin. Fax 259-0378
Other Schools – See Glen Saint Mary

Madeira Beach, Pinellas, Pop. 4,464
Pinellas County SD
Supt. — See Largo
Madeira Beach MS 1,200/6-8
591 Madeira Beach Cswy 33708 727-547-7697
Brenda Poff, prin. Fax 547-7528

Madison, Madison, Pop. 3,190
Madison County SD 3,000/PK-12
210 NE Duval Ave 32340 850-973-5022
Lou Miller, supt. Fax 973-5027
www.madison.k12.fl.us
Madison County HS 900/9-12
2649 W Us 90 32340 850-973-5061
Ben Killingsworth, prin. Fax 973-5066

North Florida Community College Post-Sec.
1000 Turner Davis Dr 32340 850-973-2288

Maitland, Orange, Pop. 14,125
Orange County SD
Supt. — See Orlando
Maitland MS 1,100/6-8
1901 Choctaw Trl 32751 407-623-1462
Dr. Douglas Ralph, prin. Fax 623-1474

Florida College of Natural Health Post-Sec.
2600 Lake Lucien Dr Ste 140 32751 407-261-0319
Orangewood Christian S 700/PK-12
1221 Trinity Woods Ln 32751 407-339-0223
LuAnne Schendel, hdmstr. Fax 339-4148

Malone, Jackson, Pop. 2,012
Jackson County SD
Supt. — See Marianna
Malone S 600/PK-12
PO Box 68 32445 850-482-9950
Linda Hall, prin. Fax 482-9981

Marathon, Monroe, Pop. 9,822
Monroe County SD
Supt. — See Key West
Marathon HS 600/7-12
350 Sombrero Beach Rd 33050 305-289-2480
Dr. John Pertner, prin. Fax 289-2486

Margate, Broward, Pop. 56,002
Broward County SD
Supt. — See Fort Lauderdale
Margate MS 1,300/6-8
500 NW 65th Ave 33063 754-322-3800
Hudson Thomas, prin. Fax 322-3885

Atlantic Technical Center Post-Sec.
4700 Coconut Creek Pkwy 33063 954-977-2000
Faith Christian S 300/PK-12
6950 Royal Palm Blvd 33063 954-974-2404
Michael Linder, prin. Fax 974-0139
Margate School of Beauty Post-Sec.
5281 Coconut Creek Pkwy 33063 954-972-9630

Marianna, Jackson, Pop. 6,275
Jackson County SD 7,100/PK-12
PO Box 5958 32447 850-482-1200
Daniel Sims, supt. Fax 482-1299
web.jcsb.org
Academy at Marianna HS Vo/Tech
3546 Caverns Rd 32446 850-482-9666
James Sims, prin. Fax 482-9800
Marianna HS 700/9-12
3546 Caverns Rd 32446 850-482-9605
Randy Ward, prin. Fax 482-1247
Marianna MS 700/6-8
4144 South St 32448 850-482-9609
Dr. Gayle Westbrook, prin. Fax 482-9795
Marianna Adult Center Adult
2971 Guyton St 32446 850-482-9617
Durrance Britt, admin. Fax 482-1201
Other Schools – See Cottondale, Graceville, Grand Ridge, Malone, Sneads

---

Chipola College Post-Sec.
3094 Indian Cir 32446 850-526-2761
Masters Academy of NW FL 50/PK-12
PO Box 6302 32447 850-482-3828
Anna Lopez-Wooden, admin. Fax 482-6984

Mayo, Lafayette, Pop. 1,032
LaFayette County SD 1,100/PK-12
363 NE Crawford St 32066 386-294-1351
Fredric Ward, supt. Fax 294-3072
hornet.lafayette.k12.fl.us
LaFayette JSHS 500/6-12
160 NE Hornet Ln 32066 386-294-1701
Gina Hart, prin. Fax 294-4197
Adult Education Adult
363 NE Crawford St 32066 386-294-4120
Debra Land, prin. Fax 294-3072

Melbourne, Brevard, Pop. 76,646
Brevard County SD 70,500/PK-12
2700 Jdge Fran Jamieson Way 32940 321-633-1000
Dr. Richard DiPatri, supt. Fax 633-3432
www.brevard.k12.fl.us
Eau Gallie HS 2,400/9-12
1400 Commodore Blvd 32935 321-242-6400
Thomas Sawyer, prin. Fax 242-6427
Johnson MS 1,000/7-8
2155 Croton Rd 32935 321-242-6430
Robert Fish, prin. Fax 242-6436
Melbourne SHS 1,700/10-12
74 Bulldog Blvd 32901 321-952-5880
James Willcoxon, prin. Fax 952-5898
Palm Bay HS 2,600/9-12
101 Pirate Ln 32901 321-952-5900
John Thomas, prin. Fax 676-2891
Stone MS 700/7-8
1101 E University Blvd 32901 321-723-0741
Andrew Johnson, prin. Fax 951-1497
Viera HS 9-12
6103 Stadium Pkwy 32940 321-632-1770
Mark Tormoen, prin. Fax 433-4338
West Shore JSHS 1,000/7-12
250 Wildcat Aly 32935 321-242-4730
Rick Fleming, prin. Fax 242-4740
South Area Adult/Community Educ. Ctr. Adult
1362 S Babcock St 32901 321-952-5977
Rebecca Camp, prin. Fax 952-5831

Other Schools – See Cocoa, Cocoa Beach, Indialantic, Merritt Island, Palm Bay, Rockledge, Satellite Beach, Titusville, West Melbourne

---

Community Christian S 100/PK-12
1616 Ferndale Ave 32935 321-259-1590
Laurel Earls, prin. Fax 259-5301
Florida Air Academy 500/6-12
1950 Academy Dr 32901 321-723-3211
Antiny White, prin. Fax 676-0422
Florida Institute of Technology Post-Sec.
150 W University Blvd 32901 321-674-8000
FL Metropolitan Univ. - Melbourne Campus Post-Sec.
2401 N Harbor City Blvd 32935 321-253-2929
Holy Trinity Episcopal Academy 900/PK-12
5625 Holy Trinity Dr 32940 321-723-8323
Catherine Ford, hdmstr. Fax 308-9077
Keiser College Post-Sec.
900 S Babcock St 32901 321-255-2255
Melbourne Beauty School Post-Sec.
686 N Wickham Rd 32935 321-259-0001
Melbourne Central Catholic HS 200/9-12
100 E Florida Ave 32901 321-727-0793
Sue Rauch, prin. Fax 727-0798
New Covenant Christian S 100/K-12
1926 S Babcock St 32901 321-724-9603
Sandra Hancock, prin. Fax 724-6932
Wade Christian Academy 100/K-12
4300 N Wickham Rd 32935 321-259-6788
West Melbourne Christian Academy 100/K-12
3150 Milwaukee Ave 32904 321-725-3743
Mark Siler, prin. Fax 725-6661

Merritt Island, Brevard, Pop. 36,800
Brevard County SD
Supt. — See Melbourne
Edgewood JSHS 700/7-12
180 E Merritt Ave 32953 321-454-1030
Kenneth Winn, prin. Fax 452-1176
Jefferson MS 700/7-8
1275 S Courtenay Pkwy 32952 321-453-5154
Sherri Bowman, prin. Fax 459-2854
Merritt Island HS 1,800/9-12
100 Mustang Way 32953 321-454-1000
Gary Shiffrin, prin. Fax 454-1014

Advanced/Basic Hair Design Training Ctr Post-Sec.
2088 N Courtenay Pkwy 32953 321-452-8490
Merritt Island Christian S 700/PK-12
140 Magnolia Ave 32952 321-453-2710
Chris Harmon, hdmstr. Fax 452-6580

Miami, Dade, Pop. 386,417
Miami-Dade County SD 343,200/PK-12
1450 NE 2nd Ave 33132 305-995-1000
Dr. Rudolph Crew, supt. Fax 995-1488
www.dadeschools.net/
Allapattah MS 1,100/6-8
1331 NW 46th St 33142 305-634-9787
Brian Hamilton, prin. Fax 638-8254
Ammons MS 1,100/6-8
17990 SW 142nd Ave 33177 305-971-0158
Irwin Adler, prin. Fax 971-0179
Arvida MS 1,800/6-8
10900 SW 127th Ave 33186 305-385-7144
Nancy Aragon, prin. Fax 383-9472
Baker Aviation S Vo/Tech
3275 NW 42nd Ave 33142 305-871-3143
Ruby B. Jones, prin. Fax 871-5840
Bell MS 1,500/6-8
11800 NW 2nd St 33182 305-220-2075
Ingrid Soto, prin. Fax 229-0798
Braddock HS 4,600/8-12
3601 SW 147th Ave 33185 305-225-9729
Manuel S. Garcia, prin. Fax 221-3312
Brownsville MS 800/7-9
4899 NW 24th Ave 33142 305-633-1481
Regina Lowe-Smith, prin. Fax 635-8702
Chiles MS 2,000/6-8
8190 NW 197th St 33015 305-816-9101
John Messersmith, prin. Fax 816-9248
Citrus Grove MS 1,500/6-8
2153 NW 3rd St 33125 305-642-5055
Emirce Ladaga, prin. Fax 642-9349
Coral Reef HS 2,800/9-12
10101 SW 152nd St 33157 305-232-2044
Adrianne Leal, prin. Fax 252-3454
Country Club MS 6-8
18305 NW 75th Pl 33015 305-820-8800
Jose Bueno, prin. Fax 820-8801
Curry MS 800/6-8
15750 SW 47th St 33185 305-222-2775
Caridad Montano, prin. Fax 229-1521
Dario MS 1,000/6-8
350 NW 97th Ave 33172 305-226-0179
Barbara Mendizabal, prin. Fax 559-0919
Design & Architectural Magnet HS Vo/Tech
4001 NE 2nd Ave 33137 305-573-7135
Dr. Stacy Mancuso, prin. Fax 573-8253
Diego MS 1,200/6-8
3100 NW 5th Ave 33127 305-573-7229
Concepcion Martinez, prin. Fax 573-6415
Doolin MS 1,500/6-8
6401 SW 152nd Ave 33193 305-386-6656
Eduardo Tillet, prin. Fax 408-3068
Doral MS 1,200/6-8
5005 NW 112th Ct 33178 305-592-2822
Tatiana De Miranda, prin. Fax 597-3853
Drew MS 1,000/6-8
1801 NW 60th St 33142 305-633-6057
Charles McLendon, prin. Fax 638-1307
Ferguson HS 1,500/9-12
15900 SW 56th St 33185 305-408-2700
Dr. Donald A. Hoecherl, prin. Fax 408-6487
Glades MS 1,500/6-8
9451 SW 64th Ter 33173 305-271-3342
Elio Falcon, prin. Fax 271-0402
Hammocks MS 2,500/6-8
9889 Hammocks Blvd 33196 305-385-0896
Israel Katz, prin. Fax 382-0861
Hopkins Technical Center Vo/Tech
750 NW 20th St 33127 305-324-6070
James Parker, prin. Fax 545-6397
Jefferson MS 900/7-9
525 NW 147th St 33168 305-681-7481
Maria Garcia, prin. Fax 688-5912
Kinloch Park MS 1,400/6-8
4340 NW 3rd St 33126 305-445-5467
Scott Weiner, prin. Fax 445-3110
Krop HS 3,700/8-12
1410 NE 215th St 33179 305-652-6808
Matthew Welker, prin. Fax 651-8043
Madison MS 1,100/6-8
3400 NW 87th St 33147 305-836-2610
Dr. Tonya Dillard, prin. Fax 696-5249
Mann MS 1,200/6-8
8950 NW 2nd Ave 33150 305-757-9537
Pamela Johnson, prin. Fax 754-0724
McMillan MS 1,500/6-8
13100 SW 59th St 33183 305-385-6877
Dr. Winston Whyte, prin. Fax 387-9641
Miami Central HS 3,000/9-12
1781 NW 95th St 33147 305-696-4161
Robin Atkins, prin. Fax 836-2872
Miami Coral Park HS 4,200/9-12
8865 SW 16th St 33165 305-226-6565
Dr. Nicholas P. Jacangelo, prin. Fax 553-4658
Miami Edison HS 1,500/9-12
6161 NW 5th Ct 33127 305-751-7337
Dr. Jean Teal, prin. Fax 759-4561
Miami Edison MS 900/6-8
6101 NW 2nd Ave 33127 305-754-4683
Richelle Thomas, prin. Fax 757-2219
Miami HS 3,300/9-12
2450 SW 1st St 33135 305-649-9800
Dr. Daniel Tosado, prin. Fax 649-9475
Miami Jackson HS 1,800/9-12
1751 NW 36th St 33142 305-634-2621
Deborah Love, prin. Fax 634-7477
Miami Killian HS 3,800/9-12
10655 SW 97th Ave 33176 305-271-3311
Ricardo Rodriguez, prin. Fax 270-9142
Miami Norland JSHS 2,500/6-12
1050 NW 195th St 33169 305-653-1416
Gale Cunningham, prin. Fax 651-6175
Miami Northwestern HS 2,600/9-12
1100 NW 71st St 33150 305-836-0991
Dr. Dwight Bernard, prin. Fax 691-4955
Miami Palmetto HS 3,500/9-12
7460 SW 118th St 33156 305-235-1360
Howard Weiner, prin. Fax 235-7169
Miami Southridge HS 3,600/9-12
19355 SW 114th Ave 33157 305-238-6110
Carzell Morris, prin. Fax 253-4456
Miami Sunset JSHS 3,300/8-12
13125 SW 72nd St 33183 305-385-4255
Dr. Lucia Cox, prin. Fax 385-6458
Norland MS 1,900/6-8
1235 NW 192nd Ter 33169 305-653-1210
Cheryl Nelson, prin. Fax 654-1237
Palmetto MS 1,200/7-9
7351 SW 128th St 33156 305-238-3911
Lisa Noffo, prin. Fax 233-4849
Reagan/Doral HS 9-12
8600 NW 107th Ave 33178 305-805-1900
Douglas Rodriguez, prin. Fax 805-1901
Richmond Heights MS 1,600/6-8
15015 SW 103rd Ave 33176 305-238-2316
Dr. Mona Jackson, prin. Fax 251-3712
Riviera MS 800/6-8
10301 SW 48th St 33165 305-226-4286
Valerie Carrier, prin. Fax 226-1025
Rockway MS 1,400/6-8
9393 SW 29th Ter 33165 305-221-8212
Maria Cedeno, prin. Fax 221-5940
School for Advanced Studies - North 100/11-12
11380 NW 27th Ave Ste 1111 33167 305-237-1089
Guillermo Munoz, prin. Fax 237-1610
School for Advanced Studies-South 200/11-12
11011 SW 104th St 33176 305-237-0510
Guillermo Munoz, prin. Fax 237-0511
School for Advanced Studies-Wolfson 100/11-12
25 NE 2nd Ave 33132 305-237-7270
Guillermo Munoz, prin.
School for Applied Technology Vo/Tech
225 NE 34th St 33137 305-573-5499
Michael Guthrie, prin. Fax 573-2184
Shenandoah MS 1,400/6-8
1950 SW 19th St 33145 305-856-8282
Lourdes Delgado, prin. Fax 285-4792
South Miami HS 2,900/9-12
6856 SW 53rd St 33155 305-261-8383
Gilberto Bonce, prin. Fax 666-6359
Southwest Miami HS 3,300/9-12
8855 SW 50th Ter 33165 305-274-0181
James Haj, prin. Fax 596-7370
Thomas MS 1,300/6-8
13001 SW 26th St 33175 305-995-3800
Dr. Verona McCarthy, prin. Fax 995-3537
Turner Technical Arts HS Vo/Tech
10151 NW 19th Ave 33147 305-691-8324
Valmarie Rhoden, prin. Fax 693-9463
Varela HS 4,300/9-12
15255 SW 96th St 33196 305-752-7900
Luz Navarro, prin. Fax 386-8987
Washington HS 1,500/9-12
1200 NW 6th Ave 33136 305-324-8900
Dr. Rosann Sidener, prin. Fax 324-4676
West Miami MS 1,400/6-8
7525 SW 24th St 33155 305-261-8383
Jacques Bentolila, prin. Fax 267-8204
Westview MS 1,100/6-8
1901 NW 127th St 33167 305-681-6647
Lavette Hunter, prin. Fax 685-3192
Young Women's Preparatory Academy 6-12
1150 SW 1st St 33130 305-575-1200
Maria Mason, prin.
Dorsey Education Center Adult
7100 NW 17th Ave 33147 305-693-2490
Rose Martin, prin. Fax 691-7492
English Center Adult
3501 SW 28th St 33133 305-445-7731
Rosy Diaz-Duque, prin. Fax 441-2150
Miami Coral Park HS Adult Education Ctr. Adult
8865 SW 16th St 33165 305-226-6565
Robert D. Novak, prin. Fax 559-7415
Miami HS Adult Education Center Adult
2450 SW 1st St 33135 305-649-9800
Eunice Soto, prin. Fax 643-2395
Miami Jackson HS Adult Education Center Adult
1751 NW 36th St 33142 305-634-2621
Judy Hunter, prin. Fax 633-8191
Miami Northwestern HS Adult Ed Center Adult
1100 NW 71st St 33150 305-836-0991
Rose L. Martin, prin. Fax 691-9927
Miami Palmetto HS Adult Education Center Adult
7460 SW 118th St 33156 305-235-1360
Dr. Edward Gehret, prin. Fax 253-3898
Miami Southridge Adult Education Center Adult
19355 SW 114th Ave 33157 305-238-6110
Fax 253-4456
Miami Sunset HS Adult Education Center Adult
13125 SW 72nd St 33183 305-385-4255
Dulce de Villa, prin. Fax 386-9218
Southwest Miami HS Adult Education Ctr. Adult
8855 SW 50th Ter 33165 305-274-0181
Clifton Lewis, prin. Fax 274-3351
Turner Tech Arts Adult Ed Center Adult
10151 NW 19th Ave 33147 305-691-8324
Fax 693-9463

Other Schools – See Coconut Grove, Coral Gables, Cutler Bay, Cutler Ridge, Goulds, Hialeah, Homestead, Key Biscayne, Leisure City, Miami Beach, Miami Gardens, Miami Lakes, Miami Springs, North Miami, North Miami Beach, Opa Locka, Palmetto Bay, Perrine, South Miami

---

Acupuncture & Massage College Post-Sec.
10506 N Kendall Dr 33176 305-595-9500
American Academy 400/9-12
12651 S Dixie Hwy Ste 314 33156 305-233-5723
Robert Kunzler, dir. Fax 233-6225
American HS Academy 400/6-12
10300 SW 72nd St Ste 470-A 33173 305-270-1440
Reinaldo Valentino, prin. Fax 270-1440
Archbishop Coleman Carroll HS 9-12
10300 SW 167th Ave 33196 305-388-6700
Dr. Richard Fenchak, prin. Fax 388-4371
Archbishop Curley-Notre Dame HS 500/9-12
4949 NE 2nd Ave 33137 305-751-8367
Br. Patrick Sean Moffet, prin. Fax 751-3517
ATI Career Training Center Post-Sec.
7265 NW 25th St 33122 305-573-1600
ATI College of Health Post-Sec.
1395 NW 167th St 33169 305-628-1000
Atlantis Academy 200/K-12
9600 SW 107th Ave 33176 305-271-9771
Carlos Aballi, prin. Fax 271-7078
Beauty Schools of America Post-Sec.
1176 SW 67th Ave 33144
Belen Jesuit Prep HS 1,100/6-12
500 SW 127th Ave 33184 305-223-8600
Rev. Marcelino Garcia, prin. Fax 227-2565
Brito Miami Private S 300/PK-12
2732 SW 32nd Ave 33133 305-448-1463
Beatrice Brito-Ferrer, dir. Fax 448-0181
Calusa Preparatory S 300/K-12
12515 SW 72nd St 33183 305-596-3787
Ben Darlington, prin. Fax 596-7589
Carlos Albizu University Post-Sec.
2173 NW 99th Ave 33172 305-593-1223
Champagnat Catholic S 200/PK-12
2609 NW 7th St 33125 305-642-4132
Dr. Reinaldo Alonso, dir. Fax 642-8624
City College Post-Sec.
9300 S Dadeland Blvd Ste PH 33156 305-666-9242
College of Business & Technology Post-Sec.
8991 SW 107th Ave # 200 33176 305-273-4499
Columbus HS 1,300/9-12
3000 SW 87th Ave 33165 305-223-5650
Br. Patrick McNamara, prin. Fax 559-4306
Compu-Med Vocational Careers Post-Sec.
9738 SW 24th St 33165 305-553-2898
Dade Christian S 1,300/PK-12
6601 NW 167th St 33015 305-822-7690
Dr. Mike Hiltibidal, admin. Fax 826-4072
DeVry University Post-Sec.
200 S Biscayne Blvd Ste 500 33131 786-425-1113
Educating Hands School of Massage Post-Sec.
120 SW 8th St 33130 305-285-6991
Florida Career College Post-Sec.
1321 SW 107th Ave Ste 201B 33174 305-553-6065
Florida Christian S 1,400/PK-12
4200 SW 89th Ave 33165 305-226-8152
Dr. Robert Andrews, dir. Fax 226-8166
Florida College of Natural Health Post-Sec.
7925 NW 12th St Ste 201 33126 305-597-9599
Florida International University Post-Sec.
Tamiami Trl 33199 305-348-2000
Florida National College Post-Sec.
11865 SW 26th St 33175 305-266-9999
Florida S of Excellence 100/10-12
2772 SW 137th Ave 33175 305-207-7845
Miguel Fernandez, dir. Fax 207-7854
George T. Baker Aviation School Post-Sec.
3275 NW 42nd Ave 33142 305-871-3143
Greater Miami Academy 200/9-12
500 NW 122nd Ave 33182 305-220-5955
Luis Cortes, prin. Fax 220-5970
Gulliver Prep S 700/9-12
6575 SW 88th St 33156 305-666-7937
Marian Krutulis, dir. Fax 668-3791
Hope Center Post-Sec.
666 SW 4th St 33130 305-545-7572
International Training Careers Post-Sec.
7360 Coral Way 33155 305-263-9696
Jackson Memorial Medical Center Post-Sec.
1611 NW 12th Ave 33136 305-585-6754
Jones College Post-Sec.
11430 N Kendall Dr Ste 200 33176 305-275-9996
Keystone National HS 400/9-12
12840 NW 1st Ct 33168 866-257-6011
Clarence Watson, prin. Fax 257-6013
Killian Oaks Academy 100/PK-12
10545 SW 97th Ave 33176 305-274-2221
La Belle Beauty Academy Post-Sec.
2960 SW 8th St 33135 305-649-4899
Landow Yeshiva/Bais Chana HS 100/PK-12
17330 NW 7th Ave 33169 305-653-8770
Shevy Sossonko, prin. Fax 653-6790

La Progressiva Presbyterian S 300/PK-12
2480 NW 7th St 33125 305-642-8600
Maribel Garcia, admin. Fax 642-2169
La Salle HS 600/9-12
3601 S Miami Ave 33133 305-854-2334
Sr. Patricia Roche, prin. Fax 858-5971
Lincoln-Marti S 700/PK-12
931 SW 1st St 33130 305-643-4888
Lindsey Hopkins Technical Education Ctr Post-Sec.
750 NW 20th St 33127 305-324-6070
Miami Christian S 500/PK-12
200 NW 109th Ave 33172 305-221-7754
Dr. Lorena Morrison, admin. Fax 221-7783
Miami Country Day S 1,000/PK-12
PO Box 380608 33238 305-779-7230
John Davies Ed.D., hdmstr. Fax 758-5107
Miami-Dade College Post-Sec.
300 NE 2nd Ave 33132 305-237-3316
Miami-Dade Community College Post-Sec.
11380 NW 27th Ave 33167 305-237-1245
Miami-Dade Community College Post-Sec.
11011 SW 104th St 33176 305-237-2000
Miami-Dade Community College-Medical Ctr Post-Sec.
950 NW 20th St 33127 305-347-4101
Miami International Univ of Art & Design Post-Sec.
1501 Biscayne Blvd 33132 800-225-9023
National School of Technology Post-Sec.
9020 SW 137th Ave 33186 305-386-9900
National School of Technology Post-Sec.
111 NW 183rd St Ste 200 33169 305-949-9500
New Concept Massage & Beauty School Post-Sec.
2022 SW 1st St 33135 305-642-3020
New World School of the Arts Post-Sec.
300 NE 2nd Ave 33132 305-237-7007
Northwest Christian Academy 400/PK-12
951 NW 136th St 33168 305-685-8734
Susan Nay, admin. Fax 685-5341
Nouvelle Institute Post-Sec.
3271 NW 7th St Ste 106 33125 305-643-3360
Our Lady of Lourdes Academy 800/9-12
5525 SW 84th St 33143 305-667-1623
Sr. Sheila Foy, prin. Fax 663-3121
Professional Training Center Post-Sec.
13926 SW 47th St 33175 305-220-4120
Ransom-Everglades MS 500/6-8
2045 S Bayshore Dr 33133 305-250-6850
Shelly Stamler, dir. Fax 250-4205
Robert Morgan Educational Center Post-Sec.
18180 SW 122nd Ave 33177 305-253-9920
St. Brendan HS 1,200/9-12
2950 SW 87th Ave 33165 305-223-5181
Br. Felix Elardo, prin. Fax 220-7434
St. John Vianney College Seminary Post-Sec.
2900 SW 87th Ave 33165 305-223-4561
School of Virtue and Academic Excellence 50/5-8
8567 Coral Way Ste 144 33155 305-407-3400
Mary Laffitte-Reguera, admin.
Sha'arei Bina Torah Academy for Girls 50/6-12
137 NE 19th St 33132 305-438-1802
Rabbi Elchonon Abramchik, prin. Fax 438-1803
South Florida Institute of Technology Post-Sec.
720 NW 27th Ave 33125 305-649-2050
Technical Career Institute Post-Sec.
7757 W Flagler St Ste 23 33144 305-863-1818
The English Center Post-Sec.
3501 SW 28th St 33133 305-445-7731
The Praxis Institute Post-Sec.
1850 SW 8th St 33135 305-642-4104
TLC Christian Academy #3 100/PK-12
6565 NW 32nd Ave 33147 561-278-3115
Trinity International University Post-Sec.
111 NW 183rd St Ste 500 33169 305-577-4600
Universidad FLET Post-Sec.
14540 SW 136th St Ste 202 33186 305-378-8700
University of Miami Post-Sec.
4600 Rickenbacker Cswy 33149 305-361-4000
US International Christian Academy 50/9-12
5805 Blue Lagoon Dr Ste 136 33126 305-265-5858
Ricardo Alfonso, dir. Fax 244-9355
Westminster Christian HS 400/9-12
6855 SW 152nd St 33157 305-233-2030
David Medder, prin. Fax 238-2259
Westminster Christian MS 300/6-8
6855 SW 152nd St 33157 305-233-2030
John Manoogian, prin. Fax 253-9623
Westwood Christian S 600/6-12
5801 SW 120th Ave 33183 305-274-3380
Edwin Oksanen, hdmstr. Fax 595-7519
World Hope Academy 2,000/9-12
10689 N Kendall Dr Ste 3 33176 305-270-9830
Alan Goldstein, prin. Fax 270-9780

Miami Beach, Dade, Pop. 87,925
Miami-Dade County SD
Supt. — See Miami
Miami Beach HS 2,300/9-12
2231 Prairie Ave 33139 305-532-4515
Dr. Jeanne Friedman, prin. Fax 531-9209
Nautilus MS 1,300/7-8
4301 N Michigan Ave 33140 305-532-3481
Lisa Gonsky, prin. Fax 532-8906
Feinberg-Fisher Community Center Adult
1424 Drexel Ave 33139 305-531-0451
Martha Montaner, prin. Fax 531-2352
Miami Beach Adult Center Adult
1424 Drexel Ave 33139 305-531-0451
Wanda Y. Williams, prin. Fax 531-2352

Landow Yeshiva S/Lubavitch Ed Ctr 400/7-12
1140 Alton Rd 33139 305-653-8770
Rabbi Abraham Korf, dean Fax 653-6790
Mechina HS of South Florida 100/7-12
1965 Alton Rd 33139 305-538-5543
Rabbi Eliyohu Kutoff, prin. Fax 532-3627
Miami Ad School Post-Sec.
955 Alton Rd 33139 305-538-3193
Mt. Sinai Medical Center Post-Sec.
4300 Alton Rd 33140 305-674-2222
RASG Hebrew Academy 600/PK-12
2400 Pine Tree Dr 33140 305-532-6421
Dr. Roni Raab, hdmstr. Fax 535-5670
Talmudic College of Florida Post-Sec.
1910 Alton Rd 33139 305-534-7050
Yeshiva Gedolah Rabbinical College Post-Sec.
1140 Alton Rd 33139 305-673-5664

Miami Gardens, Broward, Pop. 99,438
Miami-Dade County SD
Supt. — See Miami
Carol City MS 1,200/6-8
3737 NW 188th St, 305-624-2652
Dr. Mark Soffian, prin. Fax 623-2955
Lake Stevens MS 1,400/6-8
18484 NW 48th Pl, 305-620-1294
Derick McKoy, prin. Fax 620-1345
Miami Carol City HS 2,500/9-12
3422 NW 187th St, 305-621-5681
Kim Cox, prin. Fax 620-8862
Parkway MS 800/6-8
2349 NW 175th St, 305-624-9613
Paulette Fredrik, prin. Fax 623-9756
Miami Carol City Adult S Adult
3422 NW 187th St, 305-621-5681
Lourdes Garcia, prin. Fax 624-9317

Miami Job Corps Center Post-Sec.
3050 NW 183rd St, 305-626-7800

Miami Lakes, Dade, Pop. 22,321
Miami-Dade County SD
Supt. — See Miami
Miami Lakes Educational Center Vo/Tech
5780 NW 158th St 33014 305-557-1100
James Parker, prin. Fax 364-9279

Goliath Academy 100/10-12
15025 NW 77th Ave Ste 216 33014 305-512-5994
Fax 512-5996
Miami Lake Christian Academy 200/PK-12
6250 Miami Lakes Dr E 33014 305-823-3888

Miami Shores, Dade, Pop. 10,040

Barry University Post-Sec.
11300 NE 2nd Ave 33161 305-899-3000

Miami Springs, Dade, Pop. 13,170
Miami-Dade County SD
Supt. — See Miami
Miami Springs HS 3,500/9-12
751 Dove Ave 33166 305-885-3585
Rafael Villalobos, prin. Fax 884-2632
Miami Springs MS 1,900/6-8
150 S Royal Poinciana Blvd 33166 305-888-6457
Dr. Gail Quigley, prin. Fax 887-5281
Miami Springs HS Adult Education Center Adult
751 Dove Ave 33166 305-885-3585
Robert Hernandez, prin. Fax 884-2632

Middleburg, Clay, Pop. 6,223
Clay County SD
Supt. — See Green Cove Springs
Middleburg HS 1,700/9-12
3750 County Road 220 32068 904-291-5450
David Broskie, prin. Fax 291-5462
Wilkinson JHS 1,200/7-8
5025 County Road 218 32068 904-291-5500
Dr. David McDonald, prin. Fax 291-5510

Calvary Christian Academy 100/K-12
1532 Long Bay Rd 32068 904-282-0407
Dr. Ken Pledger, prin. Fax 282-6212
Madeira Christian Academy 100/K-12
1650 Blanding Blvd 32068 904-291-1875

Milton, Santa Rosa, Pop. 8,131
Santa Rosa County SD 24,600/PK-12
5086 Canal St 32570 850-983-5000
John Rogers, supt. Fax 983-5011
www.santarosa.k12.fl.us/
Avalon MS 800/6-8
5445 King Arthurs Way 32583 850-983-5540
Erma Fillingim, prin. Fax 983-5545
Central JSHS 300/7-12
6180 Central School Rd 32570 850-983-5640
Kenny Owens, prin. Fax 983-5645
Hobbs MS 700/6-8
5317 Glover Ln 32570 850-983-5630
Buddy Powell, prin. Fax 983-5635
King MS 700/6-8
5928 Stewart St 32570 850-983-5660
Charlotte Hatcher, prin. Fax 983-5665
Locklin Technical Center Vo/Tech
5330 Berryhill Rd 32570 850-983-5700
Charles Etheredge, prin. Fax 983-5715
Milton HS 1,800/9-12
5445 Stewart St 32570 850-983-5600
Lewis Lynn, prin. Fax 983-5610
Santa Rosa County Adult HS Adult
5330 Berryhill Rd 32570 850-983-5710
Donna Christopher, prin. Fax 983-5715
Other Schools – See Gulf Breeze, Jay, Navarre, Pace

Radford M. Locklin Technical Center Post-Sec.
5330 Berryhill Rd 32570 850-983-5700
Santa Rosa Christian S 400/PK-12
PO Box 643 32572 850-623-4671
Doris Peppard, prin. Fax 623-9559
West Florida Baptist Academy 300/K-12
5621 Highway 90 32583 850-623-9306
Alan Stewart, dir. Fax 623-8313

Miramar, Broward, Pop. 106,623
Broward County SD
Supt. — See Fort Lauderdale
Everglades HS 3,400/9-12
17100 SW 48th Ct 33027 754-323-0500
Dr. Paul Fetscher, prin. Fax 323-0640
Miramar HS 2,800/9-12
3601 SW 89th Ave 33025 754-323-1350
Deborah Davey, prin. Fax 323-1480
New Renaissance MS 1,700/6-8
10701 Miramar Blvd 33025 754-323-3500
Dr. Shirley McCray, prin. Fax 323-3585
Perry MS 1,400/6-8
3400 Wildcat Way 33023 754-323-3900
Steven Frazier, prin. Fax 323-3985

Continental Academy 1,000/9-12
3241 Executive Way 33025 800-285-3514
Lee Taylor, prin. Fax 820-9230
DeVry University Post-Sec.
2300 SW 145th Ave 33027 954-499-9700
Florida Bible Christian S 700/PK-12
9300 Pembroke Rd 33025 954-431-6770
Robert McCann, prin. Fax 431-5475
Le Cordon Bleu College of Culinary Arts Post-Sec.
3221 Enterprise Way 33025 954-438-8882

Monticello, Jefferson, Pop. 2,546
Jefferson County SD 1,300/PK-12
1490 W Washington St 32344 850-342-0100
Phil Barker, supt. Fax 342-0108
www.firn.edu/schools/jefferson/jefferson/home.html
Howard MS 300/6-8
50 David Rd 32344 850-997-3555
Juliette Fisher-Jackson, prin. Fax 997-4773
Jefferson County HS 400/9-12
50 David Rd 32344 850-997-3555
Juliette Fisher-Jackson, prin. Fax 997-4773
Jefferson County Adult Center Adult
375 S Water St 32344 850-342-0140
Artis Johnson, prin. Fax 342-0402

Aucilla Christian Academy 400/PK-12
7803 Aucilla Rd 32344 850-997-3597
Richard Finlayson, dir. Fax 997-3598

Montverde, Lake, Pop. 956

Montverde Academy 700/PK-12
17235 7th St 34756 407-469-2561
Kasey Kesselring, hdmstr. Fax 469-3711

Moore Haven, Glades, Pop. 1,751
Glades County SD 1,200/K-12
PO Box 459 33471 863-946-2083
Wayne Aldrich, supt. Fax 946-1529
www.firn.edu/schools/glades/glades
Moore Haven JSHS 500/7-12
PO Box 99 33471 863-946-0811
Jean Prowant, prin. Fax 946-1532

Mount Dora, Lake, Pop. 11,474
Lake County SD
Supt. — See Tavares
Mount Dora HS 900/9-12
700 N Highland St 32757 352-383-2177
Claude Pennacchia, prin. Fax 383-6466
Mount Dora MS 600/6-8
1405 Lincoln Ave 32757 352-383-6101
Thomas Sanders, prin. Fax 383-4949

Christian Home & Bible S 800/PK-12
301 W 13th Ave 32757 352-383-2155
David Pahman, prin. Fax 383-3112
Solid Rock Christian S 200/PK-12
21951 US Highway 441 32757 352-735-5777
Diana Bunting, prin.

Mulberry, Polk, Pop. 3,233
Polk County SD
Supt. — See Bartow
Mulberry HS 900/9-12
1 Panther Pl 33860 863-701-1104
George Hatch, prin. Fax 701-1109
Mulberry MS 900/6-8
500 Dr Mlk Jr Ave 33860 863-701-1066
Patricia Barnes, prin. Fax 701-1068

Florida Career Institute Post-Sec.
5925 Imperial Pkwy Ste 200 33860 863-646-1400

Naples, Collier, Pop. 21,709
Collier County SD 39,800/PK-12
5775 Osceola Trl 34109 239-377-0001
Ray Baker, supt. Fax 377-0336
www.collier.k12.fl.us
Collier HS 2,000/9-12
5600 Cougar Dr 34109 239-377-1200
Ronald Miller, prin. Fax 377-1201
Corkscrew MS 1,300/6-8
1165 County Road 858 34120 239-377-3400
Dennis Snider, prin. Fax 377-3401
East Naples MS 1,300/6-8
4100 Estey Ave 34104 239-377-3600
Mike Parrish, prin. Fax 377-3601
Golden Gate HS 1,500/9-12
2925 Magnolia Pond Dr 34116 239-377-1601
Robert Spano, prin. Fax 377-1601
Golden Gate MS 1,000/6-8
2701 48th Ter SW 34116 239-377-3800
Mary Murray, prin. Fax 377-3801
Gulf Coast HS 1,900/9-12
7878 Shark Way 34119 239-377-1400
David Stump, prin. Fax 377-1401
Gulfview MS 700/6-8
255 6th St S 34102 239-377-4000
Kevin Saba, prin. Fax 377-4001
Lely HS 1,700/9-12
1 Lely High School Blvd 34113 239-377-2001
Ken Fairbanks, prin. Fax 377-2001
Manatee MS 600/6-8
1920 Manatee Rd 34114 239-377-4400
Scholastica Choi, prin. Fax 377-4401
Naples HS 1,600/9-12
1100 Golden Eagle Cir 34102 239-377-2200
Dr. Nancy Graham, prin. Fax 377-2201
North Naples MS 900/6-8
16165 Learning Ln 34110 239-377-4600
Frank Zencuch, prin. Fax 377-4601
Oakridge MS 1,100/6-8
14975 Collier Blvd 34119 239-377-4800
John Kasten, prin. Fax 377-4801
Palmetto Ridge HS 1,500/9-12
1655 Victory Ln 34120 239-377-2400
Roy Terry, prin. Fax 377-2401
Pine Ridge MS 1,000/6-8
1515 Pine Ridge Rd 34109 239-377-5000
George Brenco, prin. Fax 377-5001
Walker Institute of Technology Vo/Tech
3710 Estey Ave 34104 239-377-3300
Jeanette Johnson, dir. Fax 377-3301

Other Schools – See Everglades City, Immokalee

Ave Maria University Post-Sec.
1025 Commons Cir 34119 877-283-8648
Community S of Naples 800/PK-12
13275 Livingston Rd 34109 239-597-7575
John Zeller, prin. Fax 598-2973
First Baptist Academy Naples 500/PK-10
3000 Orange Blossom Dr 34109 239-597-2233
Thomas Rider, admin. Fax 597-4187
Hodges University Post-Sec.
2655 Northbrooke Dr 34119 239-513-1122
Lorenzo Walker Institute of Technology Post-Sec.
3702 Estey Ave 34104 239-430-6900
Nicaea Academy 100/PK-12
2200 Santa Barbara Blvd 34116 239-455-9090
Rev. Barton McIntyre, admin. Fax 348-0499
St. John Neumann HS 300/9-12
3000 53rd St SW 34116 239-455-3044
Dr. Laura Campbell, prin. Fax 455-2966
Seacrest Country Day S 500/PK-12
7100 Davis Blvd 34104 239-793-1986
Lynne Powell Ed.D., prin. Fax 793-1460

Navarre, Santa Rosa
Santa Rosa County SD
Supt. — See Milton
Holley-Navarre MS 800/6-8
1976 Williams Creek Dr 32566 850-936-6040
Donald Bowersox, prin. Fax 939-6049
Navarre HS 1,700/9-12
8600 High School Blvd 32566 850-936-6080
Bill Emerson, prin. Fax 936-6088

Neptune Beach, Duval, Pop. 7,018
Duval County SD
Supt. — See Jacksonville
Fletcher HS 2,400/9-12
700 Seagate Ave 32266 904-247-5905
Dane Gilbert, prin. Fax 247-5290

Newberry, Alachua, Pop. 3,804
Alachua County SD
Supt. — See Gainesville
Newberry HS 600/9-12
400 SW 258th St 32669 352-472-1101
Hershel Lyons, prin. Fax 472-1116
Oak View MS 400/6-8
1203 SW 250th St 32669 352-472-1102
Karen Clarke, prin. Fax 472-1131

New Port Richey, Pasco, Pop. 16,928
Pasco County SD
Supt. — See Land O Lakes
Bayonet Point MS 1,100/6-8
11125 Little Rd 34654 727-774-7400
Steve Knobl, prin. Fax 774-7491
Gulf HS 1,600/9-12
5355 School Rd 34652 727-774-3300
Tom Imerson, prin. Fax 774-3391
Gulf MS 1,100/6-8
6419 Louisiana Ave 34653 727-774-8000
Stan Trapp, prin. Fax 774-8091
Marchman Tech Education Center Vo/Tech
7825 Campus Dr 34653 727-774-1700
Sheila Bryan, prin. Fax 774-1791
Mitchell HS 2,400/9-12
2323 Little Rd 34655 727-774-9200
Ric Mellin, prin. Fax 774-9291
Ridgewood HS 2,000/9-12
7650 Orchid Lake Rd 34653 727-774-3900
Randall Koenigsfeld, prin. Fax 774-3991
River Ridge HS 2,000/9-12
11646 Town Center Rd 34654 727-774-7200
Jim Michaels, prin. Fax 774-7291
River Ridge MS 1,600/6-8
11646 Town Center Rd 34654 727-774-7200
Jason Joens, prin. Fax 774-7291
Seven Springs MS 2,000/6-8
2441 Little Rd 34655 727-774-6700
Chris Christoff, prin. Fax 774-6791
Schwettman Adult Education Center Adult
5520 Grand Blvd 34652 727-774-0000
Mimi Foster, prin. Fax 774-0091

Benes International School of Beauty Post-Sec.
7127 US Highway 19 34652 727-848-8415
Elfers Christian S 200/PK-12
5630 Olympia St 34652 727-845-0235
Pasco-Hernando Community College Post-Sec.
10230 Ridge Rd 34654 727-847-2727
Renaissance Academy 100/K-12
8431 Corporate Way 34653 727-845-8150
Dr. Janine Walker Caffrey, prin.
Trinity College of Florida Post-Sec.
2430 Welbilt Blvd 34655 727-376-6911

New Smyrna Beach, Volusia, Pop. 22,356
Volusia County SD
Supt. — See De Land
New Smyrna Beach HS 2,000/9-12
1015 10th St 32168 386-424-2555
Dr. Carole Kelley, prin. Fax 409-5625
New Smyrna Beach MS 1,600/6-8
1200 S Myrtle Ave 32168 386-424-2550
Jim Tager, prin. Fax 426-7476

Niceville, Okaloosa, Pop. 12,582
Okaloosa County SD
Supt. — See Fort Walton Beach
Niceville HS 2,400/9-12
800 John Sims Pkwy E 32578 850-833-4114
Janie Varner, prin. Fax 833-4267
Ruckel MS 900/6-8
201 Partin Dr N 32578 850-833-4142
Janet Hays, prin. Fax 833-3291

Okaloosa-Walton College Post-Sec.
100 College Blvd E 32578 850-678-5111
Rocky Bayou Christian S 700/PK-12
2101 Partin Dr N 32578 850-678-7358
Don Larson, supt. Fax 729-2513

North Fort Myers, Lee, Pop. 42,900
Lee County SD
Supt. — See Fort Myers
North Fort Myers HS 2,200/9-12
5000 Orange Grove Blvd 33903 239-995-2117
Kim Lunger, prin. Fax 995-1243

Temple Christian S 200/PK-12
18841 State Road 31 33917 239-543-3222
Maribeth Singleton, prin. Fax 543-6112

North Lauderdale, Broward, Pop. 42,262
Broward County SD
Supt. — See Fort Lauderdale
Silver Lakes MS 1,300/6-8
7600 Tam Oshanter Blvd 33068 754-322-4600
Jacquelyn Vernon, prin. Fax 322-4685

North Miami, Dade, Pop. 57,654
Miami-Dade County SD
Supt. — See Miami
North Miami HS 3,200/9-12
800 NE 137th St 33161 305-891-6590
Carnell A. White, prin. Fax 895-1788
North Miami MS 1,100/7-9
13105 NE 7th Ave 33161 305-891-5611
Arnold Montgomery, prin. Fax 891-4057
North Miami HS Adult Education Center Adult
800 NE 137th St 33161 305-891-6590
Leslie Prudent, prin. Fax 895-6248

Florida International University Post-Sec.
Biscayne Blvd and 151st St 33181 305-940-5625
Johnson & Wales University Post-Sec.
1701 NE 127th St 33181 305-892-7000
Miami Union Academy 300/PK-12
12600 NW 4th Ave 33168 305-953-9907
Fax 953-3602

North Miami Beach, Dade, Pop. 39,442
Miami-Dade County SD
Supt. — See Miami
Highland Oaks MS 2,600/6-8
2375 NE 203rd St, Miami FL 33180 305-932-3810
Sally J. Alayon, prin. Fax 932-0676
Kennedy MS 2,100/6-8
1075 NE 167th St 33162 305-947-1451
Kay Mikulas, prin. Fax 949-9046
North Miami Beach HS 2,900/9-12
1247 NE 167th St 33162 305-949-8381
Raymond Fontana, prin. Fax 949-0491

Allison Academy 100/6-12
1881 NE 164th St 33162 305-940-3922
Sarah Allison, prin. Fax 940-1820
Bais Yaakov S for Girls 300/6-12
1110 NE 163rd St 33162 305-957-1670
Rabbi Ephraim Leizerson, prin. Fax 957-1677
Hillel Community Day S 1,100/PK-12
19000 NE 25th Ave, Miami FL 33180 305-931-2831
Dr. Richard Barbieri, hdmstr. Fax 932-7463
Rohr MS 100/6-8
1051 N Miami Beach Blvd 33162 305-947-7779
Rabbi Ephraim Palgon, prin. Fax 947-7221
Spirit of Christ Child Development Ctr 100/K-12
18801 W Dixie Hwy, Miami FL 33180 305-935-5001
Camelon Lamb-Pope, prin. Fax 935-5057
Yeshiva Toras Chaim 100/9-12
1025 NE Miami Gardens Dr 33179 305-944-5344
Rabbi David Levine, prin. Fax 947-5021

North Palm Beach, Palm Beach, Pop. 12,633

Benjamin S 1,300/PK-12
11000 Ellison Wilson Rd 33408 561-626-3747
Eugene Gross, hdmstr. Fax 626-8752

North Port, Sarasota, Pop. 42,253
Sarasota County SD
Supt. — See Sarasota
Heron Creek MS 1,700/6-8
6501 W Price Blvd, 941-480-3371
Scott Wilson, prin. Fax 480-3398
North Port HS 1,800/9-12
6400 W Price Blvd, 941-423-8558
Dr. George Kinney, prin. Fax 480-3199

Active Learning Academy 800/PK-12
14503 Tamiami Trl 34287 941-235-2077

Oakland Park, Broward, Pop. 31,713
Broward County SD
Supt. — See Fort Lauderdale
Northeast HS 2,100/9-12
700 NE 56th St 33334 754-322-1550
William Kemp, prin. Fax 322-1680
Rickards MS 1,100/6-8
6000 NE 9th Ave 33334 754-322-4400
Ronald Forsman, prin. Fax 322-4485

ATI Career Training Center Post-Sec.
3501 Powerline Rd 33309 954-563-5899

Ocala, Marion, Pop. 49,745
Marion County SD 39,600/PK-12
PO Box 670 34478 352-671-7700
James Yancey, supt. Fax 671-7581
www.marion.k12.fl.us/
Forest HS 1,900/9-12
5000 SE Maricamp Rd 34480 352-671-4700
Chester Gregory, prin. Fax 671-4702
Fort King MS 1,000/6-8
545 NE 17th Ave 34470 352-671-4725
Wayne Livingston, prin. Fax 671-4726
Horizon Academy - Marion Oak 4-8
365 Marion Oaks Dr 34473 352-236-0530
Juan Cordova, prin. Fax 236-0523
Howard MS 1,200/6-8
1108 NW Martin Luther King 34475 352-671-7225
Kathy Collins, prin. Fax 671-7226
Lake Weir HS 1,800/9-12
10351 SE Maricamp Rd 34472 352-671-4820
Cynthia Saunders, prin. Fax 671-4829
Marion Technical Institute Vo/Tech
1614 E Fort King St 34471 352-671-4765
Mark Vianello, prin. Fax 671-4766
Osceola MS 1,000/6-8
526 SE Tuscawilla Ave 34471 352-671-7100
John McCollum, prin. Fax 671-7101
Vanguard HS 1,800/9-12
7 NW 28th St 34475 352-671-4900
Rick Lankford, prin. Fax 671-4903
West Port HS 1,500/9-12
3733 SW 80th Ave 34481 352-291-4000
Jane Ellspermann, prin. Fax 291-4001
West Port MS 1,200/6-8
3733 SW 80th Ave 34481 352-291-4050
Greg Dudley, prin. Fax 291-4051
Comm Adult Education Center Adult
1014 SW 7th Rd 34471 352-671-7200
Debbie Jenkins, dir. Fax 629-1117
Other Schools – See Belleview, Citra, Dunnellon, Summerfield

Central Florida Community College Post-Sec.
PO Box 1388 34478 352-854-2322
Hale Academy 100/PK-12
3443 SW 20th St 34474 352-854-8835
Peter Trau, hdmstr. Fax 861-8822
Marion Co. School Radiologic Technology Post-Sec.
1014 SW 7th Rd 34471 352-671-7200
Meadowbrook Academy 300/K-12
4741 SW 20th St Ste 1 34474 352-861-0700
James Watts, dir. Fax 861-0533
Ocala Christian Academy 400/PK-12
1714 SE 36th Ave 34471 352-694-4178
Randy Swartz, admin. Fax 694-7192
Oceans S 200/9-12
121 NE 13th Ave 34470 352-236-4406
Ray Cates, prin. Fax 629-1573
St. John Lutheran S 600/PK-12
1915 SE Lake Weir Ave 34471 352-622-7275
Deborah Heath, dir. Fax 622-5564
Shores Christian Academy 200/PK-12
10515 SE 115th Ave 34472 352-687-4454
Rev. Stephen Davison, admin. Fax 687-1462
Trinity Catholic HS 500/9-12
2600 SW 42nd St 34471 352-622-9025
Br. Peter Zawot, prin. Fax 861-8164
Webster College Post-Sec.
2221 SW 19th Avenue Rd 34471 352-629-1941

Ocoee, Orange, Pop. 29,849
Orange County SD
Supt. — See Orlando
Ocoee HS 9-12
1925 Crown Point Pkwy 34761 407-905-3000
Mike Armbruster, prin. Fax 905-3099
Ocoee MS 1,600/6-8
300 S Bluford Ave 34761 407-877-5035
Katherine Clark, prin. Fax 877-5045

Victory Christian Academy 200/PK-12
1601 A D Mims Rd 34761 407-656-1295
Bradley Phillips, dir. Fax 656-6895

Odessa, Hillsborough, Pop. 1,200
Hillsborough County SD
Supt. — See Tampa
Walker MS 1,000/6-8
8282 N Mobley Rd 33556 813-631-4726
Kathleen Hoffman, prin. Fax 631-4738

Okeechobee, Okeechobee, Pop. 5,900
Okeechobee County SD 6,900/PK-12
700 SW 2nd Ave 34974 863-462-5000
Dr. Patricia G. Cooper, supt. Fax 462-5151
www.okee.k12.fl.us/web.nsf
Okeechobee Freshman Campus 500/9-9
610 SW 2nd Ave 34974 863-462-5288
Andy Brewer, prin. Fax 462-5258
Okeechobee HS 1,300/10-12
2800 US Highway 441 N 34972 863-462-5025
Toni Wiersma, prin. Fax 462-5037
Osceola MS 900/6-8
825 SW 28th St 34974 863-462-5070
Theda Bass, prin. Fax 462-5076
Yearling MS 700/6-8
925 NW 23rd Ln 34972 863-462-5056
Brian Greseth, prin. Fax 462-5062

Grace Christian S 100/PK-12
701 S Parrott Ave 34974 863-763-3072
David Ogden, prin. Fax 213-1339

Oldsmar, Pinellas, Pop. 13,552

Oldsmar Christian S 300/PK-12
650 Burbank Rd 34677 813-855-5746

Old Town, Dixie

Dixie County Learning Academy 50/K-12
1357 NE 82 Ave 32680 352-542-3306
Dr. Sylvia Lamenta, prin. Fax 542-7291

Opa Locka, Dade, Pop. 15,081
Miami-Dade County SD
Supt. — See Miami
North Dade MS 900/6-8
1840 NW 157th St 33054 305-624-8415
Eunice Davis, prin. Fax 628-2954

Betesda Christian S 100/PK-12
3300 NW 135th St 33054 305-685-8255
Jose Bello, admin. Fax 685-5338
Florida Memorial University Post-Sec.
15800 NW 42nd Ave 33054 305-626-3600
Monsignor Edward Pace HS 1,300/9-12
15600 NW 32nd Ave 33054 305-624-8534
Ana Garcia, prin. Fax 521-0185
North Dade Academy 100/PK-10
13850 NW 26th Ave 33054 305-725-4755
St. Thomas University Post-Sec.
16401 NW 37th Ave 33054 305-625-6000

Orange Park, Clay, Pop. 9,205
Clay County SD
Supt. — See Green Cove Springs

Fleming Island HS 1,800/9-12
2233 Village Square Pkwy 32003 904-541-2100
Sam Ward, prin. Fax 541-2085
Lakeside JHS 1,400/7-8
2750 Moody Ave 32073 904-213-2980
Randy Oliver, prin. Fax 213-2987
Orange Park HS 2,400/9-12
2300 Kingsley Ave 32073 904-272-8110
Mike Wingate, prin. Fax 272-8181
Orange Park JHS 1,300/7-8
1500 Gano Ave 32073 904-278-2000
James Young, prin. Fax 278-2009
Ridgeview HS 1,700/9-12
466 Madison Ave 32065 904-272-3003
Toni McCabe, prin. Fax 213-3033
Clay Co. Center for Community Education Adult
2306 Kingsley Ave 32073 904-272-8170
John Chappell, admin. Fax 272-8149

Berean Christian Academy 100/PK-12
4459 US Highway 17 32003 904-264-5333
David Wright, prin. Fax 264-9185
Citizen's High School Post-Sec.
PO Box 66089 32065 904-276-1700
Citizens HS 1,000/9-12
188 College Dr 32065 904-276-1700
Larry Lark, prin. Fax 272-6702
Lighthouse Christian S 300/1-12
1542 Kingsley Ave 32073 904-637-0637
Elaine Ludwig, prin. Fax 637-0638
National Heavy Equipment Operator School Post-Sec.
PO Box 65789 32065 904-272-4000
National Training Post-Sec.
PO Box 65789 32065 904-272-4000
North Florida Institute Post-Sec.
560 Wells Rd 32073 904-269-7086
Orange Park Christian Academy 100/K-12
1324 Kingsley Ave 32073 904-269-0096
John Kretas, prin. Fax 269-7445
St. Johns Country Day S 800/PK-12
3100 Doctors Lake Dr 32073 904-264-9572
Gregory Foster, prin. Fax 264-0375

Orlando, Orange, Pop. 213,223
Orange County SD 166,900/PK-12
445 W Amelia St 32801 407-317-3200
Ronald Blocker, supt. Fax 317-3401
www.ocps.k12.fl.us
Avalon MS, 13914 Mailer Blvd 32828 6-8
Judith Frank, prin. 407-207-7839
Boone HS 3,300/9-12
2000 S Mills Ave 32806 407-893-7200
Christopher Bernier, prin. Fax 897-2466
Carver MS 1,100/6-8
4500 Columbia St 32811 407-296-5110
Dawn Ewan, prin. Fax 296-6407
Chain of Lakes MS 1,400/6-8
8700 Conroy Windermere Rd 32835 407-909-5400
Carol Kindt, prin. Fax 909-5410
Colonial 9th Grade Center 9-9
7775 Valencia College Ln 32807 407-249-6369
Robert Allen, prin.
Colonial HS 3,800/9-12
6100 Oleander Dr 32807 407-482-6300
Dr. Paul Mitchell, prin. Fax 737-1450
Conway MS 1,400/6-8
4600 Anderson Rd 32812 407-249-6420
Claudia Vogt, prin. Fax 249-6429
Corner Lake MS 1,600/6-8
1700 Chuluota Rd 32820 407-568-0510
Douglas Loftus, prin. Fax 568-0920
Cypress Creek HS 3,000/9-12
1101 Bear Crossing Dr 32824 407-852-3400
Susan Storch, prin. Fax 850-5160
Discovery MS 2,100/6-8
601 Woodbury Rd 32828 407-384-1555
Dr. Stefanie Shames, prin. Fax 384-1580
Edgewater HS 3,200/9-12
3100 Edgewater Dr 32804 407-835-4900
Arthur Anderson, prin. Fax 245-2758
Evans 9th Grade Center 9-9
2751 Lake Stanley Rd 32818 407-296-6468
Dr. Cap Jadonath, prin.
Evans HS 2,400/9-12
4949 Silver Star Rd 32808 407-522-3400
Karen Wilson, prin. Fax 522-6048
Freedom HS 3,300/9-12
2500 W Taft Vineland Rd 32837 407-816-5600
Mark Brown, prin. Fax 816-5616
Freedom MS 6-8
2850 W Taft Vineland Rd 32837 407-858-6130
Timothy Smith, prin. Fax 858-6132
Glenridge MS 1,300/6-8
2900 Upper Park Rd 32814 407-623-1415
Michele Erickson, prin. Fax 623-1427
Howard MS 900/6-8
800 E Robinson St 32801 407-245-1780
Dr. Carl Cartwright, prin. Fax 245-1785
Hunters Creek MS 2,200/6-8
13400 Town Loop Blvd 32837 407-858-4620
Harold Border, prin. Fax 858-4621
Jackson MS 1,200/6-8
6000 Stonewall Jackson Rd 32807 407-249-6430
Dr. Joseph Miller, prin. Fax 249-6438
Jones HS 1,100/9-12
801 S Rio Grande Ave 32805 407-835-2300
Dr. Bridget Williams, prin. Fax 245-2765
Lee MS 1,000/6-8
1201 Maury Rd 32804 407-245-1800
Tom Pylant, prin. Fax 245-1809
Legacy MS 6-8
11398 Lake Underhill Rd 32825 407-658-5330
Wesley Trimble, prin. Fax 658-5334
Liberty MS 1,300/6-8
3405 S Chickasaw Trl 32829 407-249-6440
Frederick Heid, prin. Fax 249-6449
Lockhart MS 1,100/6-8
3411 Dr Love Rd 32810 407-296-5120
Margaret McMillen, prin. Fax 296-6549
Meadowbrook MS 1,000/6-8
6000 North Ln 32808 407-296-5130
Valeria Maxwell, prin. Fax 296-5139
Meadow Woods MS 1,900/6-8
1800 Rhode Island Woods Cir 32824 407-850-5180
Dr. Isom Rivers, prin. Fax 850-5190
Memorial MS 700/6-8
2220 29th St 32805 407-245-1810
Gail Burke, prin. Fax 245-1820
Mid Florida Tech Vo/Tech
2900 W Oak Ridge Rd 32809 407-855-5880
Dr. Joseph McCoy, prin. Fax 251-6197
Oak Ridge HS 2,100/9-12
6000 Winegard Rd 32809 407-852-3200
Maxine Risper, prin. Fax 850-5152
Odyssey MS 1,500/6-8
9290 Lee Vista Blvd 32829 407-207-3850
Patricia Bowen-Painter, prin. Fax 207-3873
Olympia HS 3,300/9-12
4301 S Apopka Vineland Rd 32835 407-905-6400
Robert Avossa, prin. Fax 905-6465
Orlando Tech Ctr Vo/Tech
301 W Amelia St 32801 407-246-7060
Lynne Voltaggio, prin. Fax 317-3372
Phillips 9th Grade Center 9-9
6500 Turkey Lake Rd 32819 407-355-3200
Steve McKinney, prin. Fax 370-7232
Phillips HS 3,900/9-12
6500 Turkey Lake Rd 32819 407-355-3200
Eugene Trochinski, prin. Fax 370-7232
Robinswood MS 1,300/6-8
6305 Balboa Dr 32818 407-296-5140
Harrison Peters, prin. Fax 296-5148
South Creek MS 6-8
3901 Wetherbee Rd 32837 407-251-2413
Gregory Moody, prin.
Southwest MS 1,400/6-8
6450 Dr Phillips Blvd 32819 407-370-7200
Dr. Anne Carcara, prin. Fax 370-7210
Timber Creek HS 3,300/9-12
1001 Avalon Blvd 32828 321-235-7800
John Wright, prin. Fax 253-7821
Union Park MS 1,400/6-8
1844 Westfall Dr 32817 407-249-6309
Kris Viles, prin. Fax 249-4404
University HS 3,500/9-12
11501 Eastwood Dr 32817 407-482-8700
David Christiansen, prin. Fax 737-1455
Walker MS 1,100/6-8
150 Amidon Ln 32809 407-858-3210
Stephen Frankenstein, prin. Fax 858-3218
Westridge MS 1,300/6-8
3800 W Oak Ridge Rd 32809 407-354-2640
Nelson Pinder, prin. Fax 354-2637
Transition Education ACE Center Adult
3723 Vision Blvd 32839 407-836-3590
Tim Holmes, prin.
Other Schools – See Apopka, Eatonville, Maitland, Ocoee, Windermere, Winter Garden, Winter Park

---

Agape Christian Academy 500/PK-12
2425 N Hiawassee Rd 32818 407-298-1111
Carol Fairweather, prin. Fax 298-0400
Asbury Theological Seminary Post-Sec.
8401 Valencia College Ln 32825 407-482-7500
Audio Recording Technology Institute Post-Sec.
4525 Vineland Rd Ste 201B 32811 407-423-2784
Avalon S 100/K-12
5002 Andrus Ave 32804 407-297-4353
Bishop Moore HS 1,100/9-12
3901 Edgewater Dr 32804 407-293-7561
Maureen Kane, prin. Fax 296-8135
Career Training Institute Post-Sec.
3318 Edgewater Dr 32804 407-884-1816
Central Florida Blood Bank Post-Sec.
8669 Commodity Cir 32819 407-849-6100
Central Florida Christian Academy 500/PK-12
700 Good Homes Rd 32818 407-293-8062
Dave Bess, admin. Fax 290-1579
Christian Victory Academy 100/K-12
PO Box 721436 32872 407-281-6244
Paula Williamson, pres. Fax 281-6244
Devereux-Florida Treatment Network Post-Sec.
5850 T G Lee Blvd Ste 400 32822 407-812-4555
DeVry University Post-Sec.
4000 Millenia Blvd 32839 407-345-2800
DeVry University Post-Sec.
1800 Pembrook Dr Ste 160 32810 407-659-0900
Downey Christian S 300/PK-12
10201 E Colonial Dr 32817 407-275-0340
Dr. Charles Dees, prin. Fax 275-1481
Eastland Christian S 300/PK-12
6000 E Colonial Dr 32807 407-277-5858
Dolores Green, admin. Fax 658-1013
Faith Christian Academy 900/K-12
2008 N Goldenrod Rd 32807 407-275-8031
Chuck Smith, admin. Fax 281-3710
First Academy 900/PK-12
2667 Bruton Blvd 32805 407-206-8600
Dr. Steve Whitaker, hdmstr. Fax 206-8771
Florida College of Integrative Medicine Post-Sec.
7100 Lake Ellenor Dr 32809 407-888-8689
Florida Hospital College of Health Sci Post-Sec.
671 Winyah Dr 32803 407-303-9798
FL Metropolitan Univ. - Orlando College Post-Sec.
5421 Diplomat Cir 32810 407-628-5870
FL Metropolitan Univ. - South Orlando Post-Sec.
9200 S Park Center Loop 32819 407-851-2525
Florida Technical College Post-Sec.
12689 Challenger Pkwy # 130 32826 407-678-5600
Heritage Prep S 300/PK-12
6000 W Colonial Dr 32808 407-293-6000
Dr. Barbara Stewart, hdmstr. Fax 292-7246
High-Tech Institute Post-Sec.
3710 Maguire Blvd 32803 407-893-7400
International Academy of Design & Tech Post-Sec.
5959 Lake Ellenor Dr 32809 407-857-2300
Keiser College Post-Sec.
5600 Lake Underhill Rd 32807 407-273-5800
Lake Highland Prep S 2,000/PK-12
901 Highland Ave 32803 407-206-1900
Warren P. Hudson, pres. Fax 206-1911
Lake Rose Christian Academy 100/K-12
4340 N Hiawassee Rd 32818 407-292-0244
Kathy Jones, prin. Fax 297-7887
Motorcycle Mechanics Institute Post-Sec.
9751 Delegates Dr 32837 407-240-2422
Muslim Academy of Central Florida 200/PK-12
1021 N Goldenrod Rd 32807 407-382-9900
Michael Baker, prin. Fax 277-4190
Orange Technical Educ. Center-Mid FL Post-Sec.
2900 W Oak Ridge Rd 32809 407-855-5880
Orange Technical Educ. Center-Orlando Post-Sec.
301 W Amelia St 32801 407-246-7060
Orlando Christian Prep S 500/PK-12
500 S Semoran Blvd 32807 407-823-9744
Dr. Mike Zobel, admin. Fax 380-1186
Orlando Lutheran Academy 200/6-12
550 N Econlockhatchee Trl 32825 407-275-7750
Dr. Wayne Jensen, prin. Fax 277-1288
Pine Castle Christian Academy 700/PK-12
5933 Randolph Ave 32809 407-438-2737
Dr. Lorne Wenzel, hdmstr. Fax 438-2739
South Orlando Christian Academy 200/PK-12
5815 Makoma Dr 32839 407-859-9511
Elizabeth Campo, prin. Fax 206-0468
Strayer University Post-Sec.
2200 N Alafaya Trl Ste 500 32826 407-926-2000
Teachers Hands Academy 300/PK-12
3001 Curry Ford Rd 32806 407-897-7477
Barbara Serianni, prin. Fax 897-3116
Universal Technical Institute Post-Sec.
2202 W Taft Vineland Rd 32837 321-281-9810
University of Central Florida Post-Sec.
PO Box 25000 32816 407-823-3000
Valencia Community College Post-Sec.
PO Box 3028 32802 407-299-5000
Valencia Community College East Campus Post-Sec.
701 N Econlockhatchee Trl 32825 407-299-5000
West Oaks Academy 100/PK-12
8624 A D Mims Rd 32818 407-292-8481
Thomas Parlier, prin. Fax 292-8838

Ormond Beach, Volusia, Pop. 38,613
Volusia County SD
Supt. — See De Land
Ormond Beach MS 1,700/6-8
151 Domicilio Ave 32174 386-258-4667
Carl Persis, prin. Fax 676-1258

Calvary Christian Academy 300/PK-12
1687 W Granada Blvd 32174 386-672-2081
Anthony Arnett, prin. Fax 615-3736
Harry Wendelstedt Umpire School Post-Sec.
88 S Saint Andrews Dr 32174 386-672-4879

Otter Creek, Levy, Pop. 129

Creekside Christian S 100/PK-12
171 SW 3rd St 32683 352-486-2112

Oviedo, Seminole, Pop. 29,848
Seminole County SD
Supt. — See Sanford
Chiles MS 1,200/6-8
1240 Sanctuary Dr 32766 407-871-7050
Britt Smith, prin. Fax 871-7099
Hagerty HS 9-12
3225 Lockwood Blvd 32765 407-871-0750
Sam Momary, prin. Fax 871-0749
Jackson Heights MS 1,400/6-8
141 Academy Ave 32765 407-320-4550
Winston Bailey, prin. Fax 320-4599
Oviedo HS 3,300/9-12
601 King St 32765 407-320-4050
Robert Lundquist, prin. Fax 320-4000
Tuskawilla MS 1,200/6-8
1801 Tuskawilla Rd 32765 407-320-8550
Michael Mizwicki, prin. Fax 320-8599

Master's Academy 1,000/K-12
1500 Lukas Ln 32765 407-971-2221
Dr. William Harris, supt. Fax 706-0254
Reformed Theological Seminary Post-Sec.
1231 Reformation Dr 32765 407-366-9493

Pace, Santa Rosa, Pop. 6,277
Santa Rosa County SD
Supt. — See Milton
Pace HS 1,900/9-12
4065 Norris Rd 32571 850-995-3600
Frank Lay, prin. Fax 995-3620
Sims MS 900/6-8
5500 Education Dr 32571 850-995-3676
Wanda Knowles, prin. Fax 995-9696

Pahokee, Palm Beach, Pop. 6,554
Palm Beach County SD
Supt. — See West Palm Beach
Pahokee MSHS 900/7-12
900 Larrimore Rd 33476 561-924-6400
Marvin Bain, prin. Fax 924-6457

Palatka, Putnam, Pop. 10,942
Putnam County SD 12,300/PK-12
200 S 7th St 32177 386-329-0510
David Buckles, supt. Fax 329-0520
www.putnamschools.org
Beasley MS 700/6-8
1100 S 18th St 32177 386-329-0569
James Roach, prin. Fax 329-0670
Jenkins MS 700/6-8
1100 N 19th St 32177 386-329-0588
Rick Surrency, prin. Fax 329-0636
Palatka HS 1,700/9-12
302 Mellon Rd 32177 386-329-0579
Karen Hughes, prin. Fax 329-0624
Other Schools – See Crescent City, Florahome, Interlachen

Peniel Baptist Academy 300/PK-12
110 Peniel Church Rd 32177 386-328-1707
Lester Jenkins, prin. Fax 328-0950
St. John's River Community College Post-Sec.
5001 Saint Johns Ave 32177 386-312-4200

Palm Bay, Brevard, Pop. 92,833
Brevard County SD
Supt. — See Melbourne
Bayside HS 2,200/9-12
1901 Degroodt Rd SW 32908 321-956-5000
John Tuttle, prin. Fax 956-5009
Southwest MS 1,400/7-8
451 Eldron Blvd SE 32909 321-952-5800
Robin Novelli, prin. Fax 952-5819

Covenant Christian S 300/K-12
720 Emerson Dr NE 32907 321-727-2661
Steven Barchie, hdmstr. Fax 728-9574
Darlyne McGee's Academy of Cosmetology Post-Sec.
1975 Palm Bay Rd NE #106 32905 321-951-0595

Palm Beach Gardens, Palm Beach, Pop. 48,989
Palm Beach County SD
Supt. — See West Palm Beach
Duncan MS 1,200/6-8
5150 117th Ct N 33418 561-776-3500
Joseph Lee, prin. Fax 776-3550
Dwyer HS 1,900/9-12
13601 N Military Trl 33410 561-625-7800
E. Wayne Gent, prin. Fax 625-7870
Palm Beach Gardens HS 2,700/9-12
4245 Holly Dr 33410 561-694-7300
Jonathan Prince, prin. Fax 691-0515
Watkins MS 900/6-8
9480 MacArthur Blvd 33403 561-776-3600
Ann Wark, prin. Fax 776-3603

Palm City, Martin, Pop. 3,925
Martin County SD
Supt. — See Stuart
Hidden Oaks MS 1,400/6-8
2801 SW Martin Hwy 34990 772-219-1655
Jenny Lambdin, prin. Fax 219-1663

Peace Christian Academy 100/K-12
1484 SW 34th St 34990 772-287-0311
Robert Watts, hdmstr. Fax 287-0321

Palm Coast, Flagler, Pop. 60,952
Flagler County SD
Supt. — See Bunnell
Indian Trails MS 1,000/6-8
5505 Belle Terre Pkwy 32137 386-446-6732
Michele Crosby, prin. Fax 445-7662
Matanzas HS 9-10
3535 Old Kings Rd N 32137 386-447-1575
Chris Pryor, prin. Fax 447-1525
Flagler County Adult & Comm Education S Adult
1 Corporate Plaza Dr 32137 386-446-7612
Mary Gilbert, prin. Fax 446-7620

FAA Center for Management Development Post-Sec.
4500 Palm Coast Pkwy SE 32137 386-446-7136

Palmetto, Manatee, Pop. 13,510
Manatee County SD
Supt. — See Bradenton
Buffalo Creek MS 6-8
7320 69th St E 34221 941-721-2260
Scott Cooper, prin. Fax 721-2277
Lincoln MS 1,200/6-8
305 17th St E 34221 941-721-6840
Reid Wallace, prin. Fax 721-6853
Palmetto HS 1,600/9-12
1200 17th St W 34221 941-723-4848
Debra Valcarcel, prin. Fax 723-4952

Palmetto Bay, Miami Dade
Miami-Dade County SD
Supt. — See Miami
Southwood MS 1,800/6-8
16301 SW 80th Ave, 305-251-5361
Jane Garraux, prin. Fax 251-7464

Palmer Trinity S 600/6-12
7900 SW 176th St, 305-251-2230
Sean Murphy, hdmstr. Fax 254-8812

Palm Harbor, Pinellas, Pop. 61,400
Pinellas County SD
Supt. — See Largo
Carwise MS 1,300/6-8
3301 Bentley Dr 34684 727-724-1442
Garrison T. Linder, prin. Fax 724-1446
Palm Harbor MS 1,500/6-8
1800 Tampa Rd 34683 727-669-1146
Ward Kennedy, prin. Fax 669-1244
Palm Harbor University HS 2,300/9-12
1900 Omaha St 34683 727-669-1131
Dr. Herman Allen, prin. Fax 725-7936
Palm Harbor Community S Adult
1900 Omaha St 34683 727-669-1140
Suzanne B. Wester, admin. Fax 725-7936

Central Florida Institute Post-Sec.
30522 US Highway 19 N 34684 727-786-4707

Palm Springs, Palm Beach, Pop. 15,267

MedVance Institute Post-Sec.
1630 S Congress Ave 33461 561-304-3466

Panama City, Bay, Pop. 37,188
Bay County SD 25,800/PK-12
1311 Balboa Ave 32401 850-872-4100
James McCalister, supt. Fax 872-4367
www.bay.k12.fl.us
Arnold HS 1,400/9-12
550 N Alf Coleman Rd 32407 850-236-3070
Dr. John Haley, prin. Fax 236-3068
Bay HS 1,600/9-12
1200 Harrison Ave 32401 850-872-4600
Mackie Owens, prin. Fax 872-4651
Brown MS 900/6-8
5044 Merritt Brown Way 32404 850-872-4740
Charlotte Marshall, prin. Fax 872-7625
Everitt MS 800/6-8
608 School Ave 32401 850-872-4790
Linda Landen, prin. Fax 872-7721
Haney Technical Center Vo/Tech
3016 Highway 77 32405 850-747-5500
Sandra Davis, prin. Fax 747-5555
Haney Technical HS 200/9-12
3016 Highway 77 32405 850-747-5500
Sandra Davis, prin. Fax 747-5555
Harris HS 300/9-12
819 E 11th St 32401 850-872-4590
Anita Dillard, prin. Fax 747-5799
Jinks MS 700/6-8
600 W 11th St 32401 850-872-4695
Anna McLain, prin. Fax 872-7612
Rosenwald MS 800/6-8
924 Bay Ave 32401 850-872-4580
Mike Riley, prin. Fax 872-7615
Rutherford HS 1,800/9-12
1000 School Ave 32401 850-872-4500
Mike Kennedy, prin. Fax 872-4827
Surfside MS 1,100/6-8
300 Nautilus St 32413 850-233-5180
Sue Harrell, prin. Fax 233-5193
Shaw Adult Center Adult
162 Detroit Ave 32401 850-872-4555
Mike Heptinstall, prin. Fax 872-7587
Other Schools – See Lynn Haven

Bay Medical Center Post-Sec.
615 N Bonita Ave 32401 800-422-2418
Covenant Christian S 400/PK-12
2350 Frankford Ave 32405 850-769-7448
Tom Bingham, admin. Fax 763-2104
Gulf Coast Community College Post-Sec.
5230 W Highway 98 32401 850-769-1551
Panama City Christian S 300/PK-12
1104 Balboa Ave 32401 850-769-6000
Debbie Jones, prin. Fax 785-5212
Tom P. Haney Technical Center Post-Sec.
3016 Highway 77 32405 850-747-5500

Parkland, Broward, Pop. 22,145
Broward County SD
Supt. — See Fort Lauderdale
Stoneman HS 3,200/9-12
5901 Pine Island Rd 33076 754-322-2150
Ann Andersen-Kowalski, prin. Fax 322-2280
Westglades MS 1,600/6-8
11000 Holmberg Rd 33076 754-322-4800
Christine Flynn, prin. Fax 322-4885

Paxton, Walton, Pop. 772
Walton County SD
Supt. — See De Funiak Springs
Paxton S 700/PK-12
PO Box 1168 32538 850-892-1230
Mike Anderson, prin. Fax 892-1239

Pembroke Pines, Broward, Pop. 150,380
Broward County SD
Supt. — See Fort Lauderdale
Flanagan HS 3,300/9-12
12800 Taft St 33028 754-323-0650
Dr. Sharon Shaulis, prin. Fax 323-0780
Glades MS 1,700/6-8
201 SW 172nd Ave 33029 754-323-4600
Krista Herrera, prin. Fax 323-4685
Pines MS 1,500/6-8
200 N Douglas Rd 33024 754-323-4000
Carlton Campbell, prin. Fax 323-4085
Young Resource Center MS 1,900/6-8
901 NW 129th Ave 33028 754-323-4500
Diane Hall, prin. Fax 323-4585

Broward Community College-South Campus Post-Sec.
7200 Pines Blvd 33024 954-963-8835
Florida Career College Post-Sec.
7891 Pines Blvd 33024 954-965-7272
PC Professor Post-Sec.
600 N Hiatus Rd Ste 105 33026 954-704-4444
Pelican Flight Training Center Post-Sec.
1601 SW 75th Ave 33023 954-966-9750

Pensacola, Escambia, Pop. 54,055
Escambia County SD 41,800/PK-12
215 W Garden St 32502 850-469-6121
Jim Paul, supt. Fax 469-6379
www.escambia.k12.fl.us
Bailey MS 1,700/6-8
4110 Bauer Rd 32506 850-492-6136
Judy Pippin, prin. Fax 492-9860
Bellview MS 1,200/6-8
6201 Mobile Hwy 32526 850-941-6080
Vicki Gibowksi, prin. Fax 941-6089
Brentwood MS 800/6-8
201 Hancock Ln 32503 850-494-5640
Marsha Higgins, prin. Fax 494-5699
Brown Barge MS 500/6-8
151 E Fairfield Dr 32503 850-595-6900
Patricia Kerrigan, prin. Fax 595-6920
Brownsville Arts & Science Academy 800/6-8
3700 W Avery St 32505 850-595-6860
Sandra Riley-Rush, prin. Fax 595-6866
Escambia HS 1,800/9-12
1310 N 65th Ave 32506 850-453-3221
Ruth Mims, prin. Fax 453-9381
Ferry Pass MS 1,000/6-8
8355 Yancey Ave 32514 850-494-5650
Ann Bookout, prin. Fax 494-5653
Pensacola HS 1,600/9-12
500 W Maxwell St 32501 850-595-1500
Sara Lewis, prin. Fax 595-1519
Pine Forest HS 1,500/9-12
2500 Longleaf Dr 32526 850-941-6150
Barbara Patterson, prin. Fax 941-6163
Stone Career Center Center Vo/Tech
2400 Longleaf Dr 32526 850-941-6200
Eric Smith, prin. Fax 941-6215
Washington HS 1,600/9-12
6000 College Pkwy 32504 850-475-5257
Steve Marcanio, prin. Fax 494-7297
Wedgewood MS 700/6-8
3420 W Pinestead Rd 32505 850-494-5660
Larry Reid, prin. Fax 494-5672
West Florida HS 1,200/9-12
2400 Longleaf Dr 32526 850-941-6200
Lesa Morgan, prin. Fax 941-6215
Woodham HS 1,300/9-12
150 E Burgess Rd 32503 850-494-7140
Dr. Michael Roberts, prin. Fax 494-7484
Workman MS 900/6-8
6299 Lanier Dr 32504 850-494-5665
Juanita Edwards, prin. Fax 494-5697
Other Schools – See Cantonment, Century, Walnut Hill, Warrington

---

Aletheia Christian Academy 200/PK-12
1700 Woodchuck Ave 32504 850-969-0088
Jeff Caulfield-James, admin. Fax 969-0906
East Hill Christian S 400/PK-12
1301 E Gadsden St 32501 850-432-2321
James Sidbury, admin. Fax 432-7679
Florida Institute of Ultrasound Post-Sec.
8800 University Pkwy Ste A4 32514 850-478-7300
George Stone Vocational Technical Ctr. Post-Sec.
2400 Longleaf Dr 32526 850-941-6200
Jubilee Christian Academy 200/PK-12
PO Box 30269 32503 850-494-2477
Angela Fox, hdmstr. Fax 494-2900
Medical Career Center Post-Sec.
19 W Garden St 32502 850-436-8444
Pensacola Catholic HS 600/9-12
3043 W Scott St 32505 850-436-6400
Sr. Kierstin Martin, prin. Fax 436-6405
Pensacola Christian Academy 2,600/PK-12
10 Brent Ln 32503 850-478-8483
Troy Shoemaker, dir. Fax 479-6572
Pensacola Christian College Post-Sec.
PO Box 18000 32523 850-478-8496
Pensacola Junior College Post-Sec.
1000 College Blvd 32504 850-484-1000
Trinitas Christian S 100/K-12
3301 E Johnson Ave 32514 850-484-3515
Kenneth Trotter, admin. Fax 484-3590
University of West Florida Post-Sec.
11000 University Pkwy 32514 850-474-2000

Perrine, Dade, Pop. 15,576
Miami-Dade County SD
Supt. — See Miami
Morgan Education Center 1,900/9-12
18180 SW 122nd Ave 33177 305-253-9920
Gregory Zawyer, prin. Fax 259-1495

Perry, Taylor, Pop. 6,734
Taylor County SD 3,200/K-12
318 N Clark St 32347 850-838-2500
Oscar Howard, supt. Fax 838-2501
www.taylor.k12.fl.us
Taylor County HS 800/9-12
900 N Johnson Stripling Rd 32347 850-838-2525
Michael Thompson, prin. Fax 838-2521
Taylor County MS 700/6-8
601 E Lafayette St 32347 850-838-2516
Paul Dyal, prin. Fax 838-2559
Taylor Technical Institute Vo/Tech
3233 S Byron Butler Pkwy 32348 850-838-2545
Ken Olsen, prin. Fax 838-2546

Taylor Technical Institute Post-Sec.
3233 S Byron Butler Pkwy 32348 850-838-2545

Pierson, Volusia, Pop. 2,604
Volusia County SD
Supt. — See De Land
Taylor MSHS 1,000/6-12
100 E Washington Ave 32180 386-740-9800
R. Marty Schmidt, prin. Fax 749-6836

Pinellas Park, Pinellas, Pop. 47,352
Pinellas County SD
Supt. — See Largo
Pinellas Park MS 1,200/6-8
6940 70th Ave 33781 727-545-6400
Lori Matway, prin. Fax 547-7894

Center Academy - Pinellas Park 100/5-12
6710 86th Ave 33782 727-541-5716
Patricia Lambert, prin. Fax 544-8186
First Baptist Christian S 200/K-12
5495 Park Blvd 33781 727-544-9465
Humanities Center Inst. of Allied Health Post-Sec.
4045 Park Blvd 33781 727-541-5200
Veritas Preparatory Academy 100/K-12
6565 78th Ave 33781 727-548-6294
Kira Wilson, prin. Fax 541-4540

Plantation, Broward, Pop. 85,989
Broward County SD
Supt. — See Fort Lauderdale
Plantation HS 3,100/9-12
6901 NW 16th St 33313 754-322-1850
Susan Bruining, prin. Fax 322-1980
Plantation MS 1,400/6-8
6600 W Sunrise Blvd 33313 754-322-4100
David Olafson, prin. Fax 322-4185
Seminole MS 1,400/6-8
6200 SW 16th St 33317 754-323-4200
Dr. Kris Black, prin. Fax 323-4285
South Plantation HS 2,600/9-12
1300 SW 54th Ave 33317 754-323-1950
Dr. David Basile, prin. Fax 323-2080

American Academy 500/PK-12
12200 W Broward Blvd 33325 954-472-0022
William Laurie, pres. Fax 472-3088
American Heritage S 2,400/PK-12
12200 W Broward Blvd 33325 954-472-0022
William Laurie, prin. Fax 472-3088
Broward Junior Academy 100/K-10
201 NW 46th Ave 33317 954-316-8301
T. George Aristide, prin. Fax 316-8308
Posnack Hebrew Day S 700/K-12
6511 W Sunrise Blvd 33313 954-583-6100
Geri Stief, prin. Fax 791-5463

Plant City, Hillsborough, Pop. 31,450
Hillsborough County SD
Supt. — See Tampa
Durant HS 2,600/9-12
4748 Cougar Path 33567 813-757-9075
Pamela Bowden, prin. Fax 707-7079
Marshall MS 900/6-8
18 S Maryland Ave, 813-757-9360
Shaylia Hall, prin. Fax 707-7385
Plant City HS 2,500/9-12
1 Raider Pl, 813-757-9370
Dr. David Steele, prin. Fax 757-9135
Simmons Career Center Vo/Tech
1202 W Grant St, 813-707-7430
Leslie Morris, prin. Fax 707-7435

Tomlin MS 1,500/6-8
501 N Woodrow Wilson St, 813-757-9400
Dr. Beverly Carbaugh, prin. Fax 707-7024
Turkey Creek MS 1,100/6-8
5005 Turkey Creek Rd 33567 813-757-9442
Dennis Mayo, prin. Fax 757-9451

Hillsborough Community College Post-Sec.
1206 N Park Rd, 813-757-2100
Hope Christian Academy 100/1-12
1109 W Grant St, 813-752-1000
Michelle Hagel, admin. Fax 752-1367

Pompano Beach, Broward, Pop. 104,179
Broward County SD
Supt. — See Fort Lauderdale
Crystal Lake Community MS 1,700/6-8
3551 NE 3rd Ave 33064 754-322-3100
James Neer, prin. Fax 322-3185
Ely HS 2,500/9-12
1201 NW 6th Ave 33060 754-322-0950
Wade Edmond, prin. Fax 322-1080
Pompano Beach HS 1,000/9-12
600 NE 13th Ave 33060 754-322-2000
David Gordon, prin. Fax 322-2130
Pompano Beach MS 1,200/6-8
310 NE 6th St 33060 754-322-4200
Sonja Braziel, prin. Fax 322-4285

Florida Barber Academy Post-Sec.
3269 N Federal Hwy 33064 954-781-6066
Florida College of Natural Health Post-Sec.
2001 W Sample Rd Ste 100 33064 954-975-6400
FL Metropolitan Univ. Post-Sec.
225 N Federal Hwy 33062 954-568-1600
Highlands Christian Academy 800/PK-12
501 NE 48th St 33064 954-421-1747
Ken Lopez, admin. Fax 421-2429

Ponce de Leon, Holmes, Pop. 469
Holmes County SD
Supt. — See Bonifay
Ponce De Leon JSHS 400/6-12
1477 Ammons Rd 32455 850-836-4242
Buddy Brown, prin. Fax 836-5388

Ponte Vedra Beach, Saint Johns
St. Johns County SD
Supt. — See Saint Augustine
Landrum MS 1,000/6-8
230 Landrum Ln 32082 904-285-9080
Dr. Pherbia Engdahl, prin. Fax 819-8415

Port Charlotte, Charlotte, Pop. 47,600
Charlotte County SD 17,300/PK-12
1445 Education Way 33948 941-255-0808
Dr. David Gayler, supt. Fax 255-0413
www.ccps.k12.fl.us
Charlotte Technical Center Vo/Tech
18200 Cochran Blvd 33948 941-255-7500
Barbara Witte, dir. Fax 255-7509
Murdock MS 1,000/6-8
17325 Mariner Way 33948 941-255-7525
Dr. Christine Dollinger, prin. Fax 255-7533
Port Charlotte HS 2,000/9-12
18200 Cochran Blvd 33948 941-255-7485
Steve Dionisio, prin. Fax 255-7493
Port Charlotte MS 1,000/6-8
23000 Midway Blvd 33952 941-255-7460
Demetrius Revelas, prin. Fax 255-7469
Adult & Community Education Adult
1441 Tamiami Trl Unit 365 33948 941-255-7555
Mike Riley, dir. Fax 255-7433
Other Schools – See Englewood, Punta Gorda, Rotonda West

Charlotte Technical Center Post-Sec.
18150 Murdock Cir 33948 941-255-7500
Community Christian S 300/PK-12
20035 Quesada Ave 33952 941-625-8977
Margaret Adkins, admin. Fax 625-1735
Port Charlotte SDA S 100/K-11
2100 Loveland Blvd 33980 941-625-5237
Marcia Moore, prin. Fax 625-8460

Port Orange, Volusia, Pop. 53,746
Volusia County SD
Supt. — See De Land
Atlantic HS 1,500/9-12
1250 Reed Canal Rd 32129 386-322-6100
Ron Pagano, prin. Fax 322-5649
Creekside MS 1,300/6-8
6801 Airport Rd 32128 386-322-6155
Deborah Drawdy, prin. Fax 304-5508
Silver Sands MS 1,300/6-8
1300 Herbert St 32129 386-322-6175
Dr. Leslie Potter, prin. Fax 322-7574
Spruce Creek HS 2,700/9-12
801 Taylor Rd 32127 386-322-6272
Timothy Egnor, prin. Fax 756-7270

Palmer College of Chiropractic Florida Post-Sec.
4777 City Center Pkwy 32129 386-763-2709

Port Richey, Pasco, Pop. 3,333
Pasco County SD
Supt. — See Land O Lakes
Chasco MS 1,000/6-8
7702 Ridge Rd 34668 727-774-1300
Lawrence Albano, prin. Fax 774-1391

Port Saint Joe, Gulf, Pop. 4,150
Gulf County SD 2,100/PK-12
150 Middle School Rd 32456 850-229-8256
Tim Wilder, supt. Fax 229-6089
www.gulf.k12.fl.us
Port Saint Joe HS 400/9-12
100 Shark Dr 32456 850-229-8251
Duane McFarland, prin. Fax 227-1803
Port Saint Joe MS 300/6-8
191 Middle School Rd 32456 850-227-3211
Juanise Griffin, prin. Fax 229-9078
Gulf County Adult S Adult
2855 Long Ave 32456 850-227-1744
Don Rich, prin. Fax 229-2724
Other Schools – See Wewahitchka

Faith Christian S 100/PK-12
801 20th St 32456 850-229-6707
Dr. William Taylor, chncllr. Fax 227-1307

Port Saint Lucie, Saint Lucie, Pop. 98,538
St. Lucie County SD
Supt. — See Fort Pierce
Northport MS 1,200/6-8
250 NW Floresta Dr 34983 772-340-4700
Eric Seymour, prin. Fax 340-7116
Port Saint Lucie HS 2,200/9-12
1201 SE Jaguar Ln 34952 772-337-6770
Terry Davis, prin. Fax 337-6780
St. Lucie West Centennial HS 2,400/9-12
1485 SW Cashmere Blvd 34986 772-785-6660
Gayle Pike, prin. Fax 785-6679
St. Lucie West MS 1,300/6-8
1001 SW Juliet Ave 34953 772-785-6630
Pam Frederick, prin. Fax 785-6632
Southern Oaks MS 1,200/6-8
5500 NW Saint James Dr 34983 772-785-5640
John Lynch, prin. Fax 785-5660
Southport MS 1,100/6-8
2420 SE Morningside Blvd 34952 772-337-5900
Mary Mosley, prin. Fax 337-5903
Treasure Coast HS 9-12
1000 SW Darwin Blvd 34953 772-807-4300
Helen Roberts, prin.

Keiser Career College Post-Sec.
9468 S US 1 34652 727-398-9990
Morningside Academy 300/6-12
1631 SE Greendon Ave 34952 772-335-2096
William Turner, dir. Fax 335-2095
Port St. Lucie Beauty Academy Post-Sec.
7644 S US 1 34983 772-340-3540
Treasure Coast Christian Academy 200/PK-12
590 NW Peacock Blvd Ste 4 34986 772-343-8088
Cynthia Netwig, prin. Fax 879-6975
Victory Forge Military Academy 50/8-12
638 SW Biltmore St 34983 772-879-7181
Alan Weierman, prin. Fax 878-8160

Princeton, Dade, Pop. 7,073

Princeton Christian S 500/PK-12
PO Box 924916 33092 305-257-3644
Cynthia Stone, prin. Fax 257-5799

Punta Gorda, Charlotte, Pop. 17,111
Charlotte County SD
Supt. — See Port Charlotte
Charlotte HS 2,100/9-12
1250 Cooper St 33950 941-575-5450
Bernard Duffy, prin. Fax 575-5464
Punta Gorda MS 1,000/6-8
825 Carmalita St 33950 941-575-5485
Dr. Donna DiGrazia, prin. Fax 575-5491

IMPAC University Post-Sec.
900 W Marion Ave 33950 941-639-7512

Quincy, Gadsden, Pop. 6,993
Gadsden County SD 6,300/PK-12
35 Martin Luther King Jr Bl 32351 850-627-9651
Reginald James, supt. Fax 627-2760
www.gcps.k12.fl.us
Gadsden Technical Institute Vo/Tech
201 Martin Luther King Jr B 32351 850-875-8324
Debra Rackley, dir. Fax 875-7297
Shanks MS 800/6-8
1400 W King St 32351 850-875-8737
Rosalyn Smith, prin. Fax 875-8775
Gadsden Adult Education Center Adult
201 Martin Luther King Jr B 32351 850-875-8324
Debra Rackley, prin. Fax 875-7269
Other Schools – See Greensboro, Havana

Community Learning Institute 100/PK-12
523 S Pat Thomas Pkwy 32351 850-627-8150
Willie Green, prin. Fax 627-1807
Munroe Day S 300/PK-12
91 Old Mt Pleasant Rd 32352 850-856-5500
Michael Knight, prin. Fax 856-5856

Riverview, Hillsborough, Pop. 6,478
Hillsborough County SD
Supt. — See Tampa
Giunta MS 6-8
4202 Falkenburg Rd S, 813-740-4888
Scott Fritz, prin. Fax 740-4892
Riverview HS 2,700/9-12
11311 Boyette Rd 33569 813-671-5011
Robert Heilmann, prin. Fax 671-5012
Rodgers MS 1,600/6-8
11910 Tucker Rd 33569 813-671-5288
Clara Davis, prin. Fax 671-5245
Spoto HS, 8538 Eagle Palm Dr, 9-12
Clyde Trathowen, prin. 813-672-5405

East Bay Christian S 200/PK-12
10102 Old Big Bend Rd, 813-677-5236
Bruce DuBois, prin. Fax 672-0808
EduTech Centers Post-Sec.
2262 S Falkenburg Rd 33569 800-485-0717
Providence Christian S 400/PK-12
5416 Providence Rd, 813-661-0588
Stephen Weer, dir. Fax 681-3852
Tropical Acres Baptist S 50/K-10
12107 Rhodine Rd, 813-677-8036
L. Jeannette Saxe, dir. Fax 677-8036

Riviera Beach, Palm Beach, Pop. 33,772
Palm Beach County SD
Supt. — See West Palm Beach
Kennedy MS 1,100/6-8
1901 Avenue S 33404 561-845-4500
Donald Greene, prin. Fax 845-4537
Suncoast HS 1,300/9-12
600 W 28th St 33404 561-882-3400
Gloria Crutchfield, prin. Fax 882-3443

Hendley Christian Education Center 400/PK-12
2800 Avenue R 33404 561-881-8015
North Technical Education Center Post-Sec.
7071 Garden Rd 33404 561-881-4600

Rockledge, Brevard, Pop. 24,245
Brevard County SD
Supt. — See Melbourne
Kennedy MS 700/6-8
2100 Fiske Blvd 32955 321-633-3500
Richard Myers, prin. Fax 633-3509
Rockledge HS 1,700/9-12
220 Raider Rd 32955 321-636-3711
Anthony Hines, prin. Fax 632-6064
Central Area Adult Education Adult
1535 Cogswell St 32955 321-633-3575
Dr. Kim Rogers, prin.

Rotonda West, Charlotte
Charlotte County SD
Supt. — See Port Charlotte
Ainger MS 1,100/6-8
245 Cougar Way 33947 941-697-5800
Marcia Louden, prin. Fax 697-5470

Royal Palm Beach, Palm Beach, Pop. 30,886
Palm Beach County SD
Supt. — See West Palm Beach
Crestwood MS 1,400/6-8
64 Sparrow Dr 33411 561-753-5000
Karen Whetsell, prin. Fax 753-5035
Royal Palm Beach HS 3,000/9-12
10600 Okeechobee Blvd 33411 561-753-4000
Jose Garcia, prin. Fax 753-4015

Ruskin, Hillsborough, Pop. 6,046
Hillsborough County SD
Supt. — See Tampa
Lennard HS 9-12
2002 E Shell Point Rd 33570 813-641-5611
Denny Oest, prin.
Shields MS 1,100/6-8
15732 Beth Shields Way 33573 813-672-5338
Fax 672-5342
South County Career Center Vo/Tech
2810 John Sherman Way 33570 813-233-3335
Cleto Chazares, prin. Fax 233-3339

First Baptist/Ruskin Christian S 300/PK-12
820 College Ave W 33570 813-645-6441
Dr. Barry Rumsey, supt. Fax 641-2073

Safety Harbor, Pinellas, Pop. 17,517
Pinellas County SD
Supt. — See Largo
Safety Harbor MS 1,400/6-8
901 1st Ave N 34695 727-724-1400
Alison Kennedy, prin. Fax 724-1407

Saint Augustine, Saint Johns, Pop. 11,915
St. Johns County SD 22,300/PK-12
40 Orange St 32084 904-819-7500
Joseph Joyner Ed.D., supt. Fax 819-7515
www.stjohns.k12.fl.us
Menendez HS 1,600/9-12
600 State Road 206 W 32086 904-819-8660
Dr. Clay Carmichael, prin. Fax 819-8675
Murray MS 800/6-8
150 N Holmes Blvd 32084 904-819-8470
Cathy Mittelstadt, prin. Fax 819-8475
Nease HS 1,800/9-12
10550 Ray Rd, 904-819-8300
Dr. Linda Thomson, prin. Fax 819-8305
Pacetti Bay MS 6-8
245 Meadowlark Ln 32092 904-819-8760
Sue Sparkman, prin.
Rogers MS 1,000/6-8
6250 US Highway 1 S 32086 904-819-8700
Beverly Gordon, prin. Fax 819-8705
Saint Augustine HS 1,600/9-12
3205 Varella Ave 32084 904-819-8530
Tyrone Ramsey, prin. Fax 819-8535
St. Johns Technical HS Vo/Tech
2980 Collins Ave 32084 904-819-8500
Fax 819-8505
Sebastian MS 800/6-8
2955 Lewis Speedway 32084 904-819-3840
Kelly Battel, prin. Fax 819-3845
Webster S 700/PK-12
420 N Orange St 32084 904-819-3860
Fax 819-3865
Other Schools – See Jacksonville, Ponte Vedra Beach

Beacon of Hope Christian S 200/K-10
1230 Kings Estate Rd 32086 904-797-6996
Mary Whitfield, prin. Fax 797-6997
First Coast Technical Institute Post-Sec.
2980 Collins Ave 32084 904-829-1010
Flagler College Post-Sec.
PO Box 1027 32085 904-829-6481
Florida School for the Deaf and Blind Post-Sec.
207 San Marco Ave 32084
Mill Creek Baptist Christian Academy 200/PK-12
6019A State Road 16 32092 904-940-0344
St. John's Academy 100/PK-12
1533 Wildwood Dr 32086 904-824-9224
Wallis Brooks, prin. Fax 823-1145
St. Joseph Academy 300/9-12
155 State Rd 207 32084 904-824-0431
Michael Heubeck, prin. Fax 826-4477
Univ. of St. Augustine for Health Sci. Post-Sec.
1 University Blvd 32086 904-826-0084

Saint Cloud, Osceola, Pop. 21,480
Osceola County SD
Supt. — See Kissimmee
Harmony HS 1,300/9-12
3601 Arthur J Gallagher 34771 407-933-9900
Debra Pace, prin. Fax 933-9901
Saint Cloud HS 1,700/9-12
2000 Bulldog Ln 34769 407-891-3100
Scott Muri, prin. Fax 891-3114
Saint Cloud MS 900/6-8
1975 Michigan Ave 34769 407-891-3200
Robert Studly, prin. Fax 891-3206

Southland Christian S 400/PK-12
2901 17th St 34769 407-891-7723
Rob Ennis, prin. Fax 891-7734

Saint Leo, Pasco, Pop. 782

St. Leo University Post-Sec.
PO Box 6665 33574 352-588-8200

Saint Petersburg, Pinellas, Pop. 247,610
Pinellas County SD
Supt. — See Largo
Azalea MS 1,300/6-8
7855 22nd Ave N 33710 727-893-2606
Teresa Anderson, prin. Fax 893-2624
Bay Point MS 1,200/6-8
2151 62nd Ave S 33712 727-893-1153
Starla Metz, prin. Fax 893-1181
Gibbs HS 2,100/9-12
850 34th St S 33711 727-893-5452
Antelia Campbell, prin. Fax 893-5461
Hollins HS 2,000/9-12
4940 62nd St N 33709 727-547-7876
Michael Bohnet, prin. Fax 547-7727
Hopkins MS 1,300/6-8
701 16th St S 33705 727-893-2400
Maureen Thornton, prin. Fax 893-1600
Lakewood HS 1,800/9-12
1400 54th Ave S 33705 727-893-2916
Dennis Duda, prin. Fax 893-1387
Marshall MS 600/6-8
3901 22nd Ave S 33711 727-552-1737
Dallas Jackson, prin. Fax 552-1741
Meadowlawn MS 1,200/6-8
6050 16th St N 33703 727-570-3097
Gregory Cardone, prin. Fax 570-3396
Northeast HS 2,000/9-12
5500 16th St N 33703 727-570-3138
Patricia Wright, prin. Fax 217-7318
PTEC St. Petersburg Vo/Tech
901 34th St S 33711 727-893-2500
Dorothy Bailey, dir. Fax 893-2776
Riviera MS 1,100/6-8
501 62nd Ave NE 33702 727-570-5150
Philip Wirth, prin. Fax 570-3094
St. Petersburg HS 2,300/9-12
2501 5th Ave N 33713 727-893-1842
Albert Bennett, prin. Fax 893-1399
Southside Fundamental MS 600/6-8
1701 10th St S 33705 727-893-2742
Michael Miller, prin. Fax 893-2129
Tyrone MS 1,100/6-8
6421 22nd Ave N 33710 727-893-1819
Stephanie A. Adkinson, prin. Fax 893-1946
Hollins Evening Adult Education Ctr Adult
4940 62nd St N 33709 727-547-7872
Brenda Vlach, admin. Fax 547-7873
Lakewood Community S Adult
1400 54th Ave S 33705 727-893-2955
Dr. Jane Huber, admin. Fax 893-1375
Northeast Community S Adult
1717 54th Ave N 33714 727-570-3193
Dr. Kathy K. Gregg, admin. Fax 570-3193
Tomlinson Adult Learning Center Adult
296 Mirror Lake Dr N 33701 727-893-2723
Dr. Debby VanderWoude, dir. Fax 893-2782

Admiral Farragut Academy 400/K-12
PO Box 43010 33743 727-384-5500
Robert Fine, hdmstr. Fax 384-5507
Bayfront Medical Center Post-Sec.
701 6th St S 33701 727-893-6604
Broach S 100/1-12
4500 43rd St N 33714 727-526-5700
Felicia Singleton, prin. Fax 525-4322
Canterbury S of Florida 400/PK-12
990 62nd Ave NE 33702 727-525-1419
Mac Hall, hdmstr. Fax 525-2545
Eckerd College Post-Sec.
4200 54th Ave S 33711 727-867-1166
Florida Blood Services Post-Sec.
10100 Dr Mrtn Lthr King St 33716 727-568-5433
Galen Health Institute Post-Sec.
9549 Koger Blvd N Ste 100 33702 727-577-1497
Keswick Christian S 600/PK-12
10101 54th Ave N 33708 727-393-9100
Steven Sinclair, hdmstr. Fax 397-5378
Loraine's Academy Post-Sec.
1012 58th St N 33710 727-347-4247
Northside Christian S 800/PK-12
7777 62nd Ave N 33709 727-541-7593
Mary Brandes, hdmstr. Fax 546-5836
Pinellas Technical Education Center Post-Sec.
901 34th St S 33711 727-893-2500
Poynter Institute for Media Studies Post-Sec.
801 3rd St S 33701 727-821-9494
St. Petersburg Catholic HS 700/9-12
6333 9th Ave N 33710 727-344-4065
Rev. John Serio, prin. Fax 343-9311
St. Petersburg College Post-Sec.
PO Box 13489 33733 727-341-3600
St. Petersburg Theological Seminary Post-Sec.
10830 Navajo Dr 33708 727-399-0276
Shorecrest Preparatory S 1,000/PK-12
5101 1st St NE 33703 727-522-2111
Michael Murphy, hdmstr. Fax 527-4191
University of South Florida Post-Sec.
140 7th Ave S 33701 727-893-9536

Sanford, Seminole, Pop. 47,257
Seminole County SD 65,200/PK-12
400 E Lake Mary Blvd 32773 407-320-0000
Dr. Bill Vogel, supt. Fax 320-0281
www.scps.k12.fl.us
Millennium MS 2,000/6-8
21 Lakeview Ave 32773 407-320-6550
Kate Eglof, prin. Fax 320-6599
Sanford MS 1,400/6-8
1700 S French Ave 32771 407-320-6150
Mark Russi, prin. Fax 320-6265
Seminole HS 2,900/9-12
2701 Ridgewood Ave 32773 407-320-5050
Walt Griffin, prin. Fax 320-5024
Other Schools – See Altamonte Springs, Casselberry, Lake Mary, Longwood, Oviedo, Winter Park, Winter Springs

Delta Connection Academy Post-Sec.
2700 Flightline Ave 32773 407-430-4174
Liberty Christian S 200/K-12
2626 S Palmetto Ave 32773 407-323-1583
Rev. Ron Williams, dir. Fax 323-1588
Seminole Community College Post-Sec.
100 Weldon Blvd 32773 407-328-4722

Santa Rosa Beach, Walton
Walton County SD
Supt. — See De Funiak Springs
Emerald Coast MS 6-8
6694 W County Highway 30A 32459 850-622-5025
John Haro, prin. Fax 622-5027
South Walton HS 500/9-12
645 Greenway Trl 32459 850-622-5020
Mark Ewing, prin. Fax 622-5039

Sarasota, Sarasota, Pop. 53,711
Sarasota County SD 39,000/PK-12
1960 Landings Blvd 34231 941-927-9000
Dr. Gary Norris, supt. Fax 361-6049
www.sarasota.k12.fl.us
Booker HS 1,600/9-12
3201 N Orange Ave 34234 941-355-2967
Jill Dorsett, prin. Fax 359-5757
Booker MS 1,200/6-8
2250 Myrtle St 34234 941-359-5824
Joe Bazenas, prin. Fax 359-5898
Brookside MS 1,200/6-8
3636 S Shade Ave 34239 941-361-6472
Karen Rose, prin. Fax 361-6508
McIntosh MS 1,100/6-8
701 Mcintosh Rd 34232 941-361-6520
Robert Hagemann, prin. Fax 361-6340
Riverview HS 2,700/9-12
1 Ram Way 34231 941-923-1484
Linda Nook, prin. Fax 361-6175
Sarasota County Technical Institute Vo/Tech
4748 Beneva Rd 34233 941-924-1365
Bruce Andersen, dir. Fax 921-7902
Sarasota HS 2,600/9-12
1000 S School Ave 34237 941-955-0181
Jeff Hradek, prin. Fax 361-6380
Sarasota MS 1,400/6-8
4826 Ashton Rd 34233 941-361-6464
Dr. Page Dettmann, prin. Fax 361-6798
Adult & Community Education Center Adult
1086 S Shade Ave 34237 941-361-6590
Jeanne Goble, prin. Fax 361-6382
Other Schools – See North Port, Venice

Argosy University/Sarasota Post-Sec.
5250 17th St 34235 800-331-5995
Cardinal Mooney HS 500/9-12
4171 Fruitville Rd 34232 941-371-4917
Stephen Christie, prin. Fax 371-6924
East West College of Natural Medicine Post-Sec.
3808 N Tamiami Trl 34234 941-355-9080
Everglades University Post-Sec.
6001 Lake Osprey Dr 34240 866-907-2262
Fashion Focus Hair Academy Post-Sec.
2184 Gulf Gate Dr 34231 941-921-4877
Keiser College Post-Sec.
6151 Lake Osprey Dr 34240 941-907-3900
Morningstar Learning Center 100/K-12
PO Box 5502 34277 941-377-6484
Dr. Jacquelin Holland, prin. Fax 377-6484
New College of Florida Post-Sec.
5700 N Tamiami Trl 34243 941-359-4310
New Gate S 300/PK-12
5237 Ashton Rd 34233 941-922-4949
Paul Wenninger, hdmstr. Fax 922-7660
Out of Door Academy-Upper S 100/7-12
5950 Deer Dr 34240 941-907-1159
David Mahler, hdmstr. Fax 907-1251
Potter's Wheel Academy 100/K-12
PO Box 50203 34232 866-335-1098
Reed Palmer, dir. Fax 284-4076
Ringling School of Art & Design Post-Sec.
2700 N Tamiami Trl 34234 941-351-5100
Sarasota Christian S 500/K-12
5415 Bahia Vista St 34232 941-371-6481
Eugene Miller, admin. Fax 371-0898
Sarasota County Technical Institute Post-Sec.
4748 Beneva Rd 34233 941-924-1365
Sarasota Memorial Hospital Post-Sec.
1700 S Tamiami Trl 34239 941-917-1080
Sarasota School of Massage Therapy Post-Sec.
1932 Ringling Blvd 34236 941-957-0577
Sonhaven Preparatory Academy 50/K-12
PO Box 50517 34232 941-360-0033
Dr. Carolyn Hilt, prin. Fax 355-6127
West Florida Christian S 200/PK-12
4311 Wilkinson Rd 34233 941-921-6311
Laurie McGowan, prin. Fax 921-4046

Satellite Beach, Brevard, Pop. 9,811
Brevard County SD
Supt. — See Melbourne
DeLaura MS 800/7-8
300 Jackson Ave 32937 321-773-7581
Jeremy Salmon, prin. Fax 773-0702
Satellite HS 2,100/9-12
300 Scorpion Ct 32937 321-779-2000
Mark Elliott, prin. Fax 773-0703

Satsuma, Putnam

Deseret Academy 200/K-12
304 5th St 32189 386-649-4978
Cinthia Trunk, prin. Fax 649-4479

Sebastian, Indian River, Pop. 19,643
Indian River County SD
Supt. — See Vero Beach
Sebastian River HS 1,900/9-12
9001 90th Ave 32958 772-564-4170
Dr. Margaret Jones, prin. Fax 564-4182
Sebastian River MS 1,300/6-8
9400 County Road 512 32958 772-564-5111
Eileen Shirah, prin. Fax 564-5113

Sebring, Highlands, Pop. 10,431
Highlands County SD 11,900/PK-12
817 Woodlawn Dr 33870 863-471-5555
Wally Cox, supt. Fax 471-5622
www.highlands.k12.fl.us
Hill-Gustat MS 700/6-8
4700 Schumacher Rd 33872 863-471-5437
David Robinson, prin. Fax 314-5245
Sebring HS 1,600/9-12
3514 Kenilworth Blvd 33870 863-471-5500
Toni Stivender, prin. Fax 471-5507
Sebring MS 800/6-8
500 E Center Ave 33870 863-471-5700
Sandi Whidden, prin. Fax 471-5710
Other Schools – See Avon Park, Lake Placid

Heartland Christian S 200/PK-12
1160 Persimmon Ave 33870 863-385-5752
David Noel, hdmstr. Fax 385-6926
Liberty Christian Academy 50/PK-12
420 S Pine St 33870 863-385-0400
Jerry Case, admin. Fax 385-3901

Seffner, Hillsborough, Pop. 5,371
Hillsborough County SD
Supt. — See Tampa
Armwood HS 2,000/9-12
12000 E US Highway 92 33584 813-744-8040
Marc Hutek, prin. Fax 744-8048
Burnett MS 900/6-8
1010 N Kingsway Rd 33584 813-744-6745
Herbert Peeples, prin. Fax 744-8973
Jennings MS 1,400/6-8
9325 Govenors Run Dr 33584 813-740-4575
Joann Johnson, prin. Fax 740-4579

Hillsborough Baptist S 100/PK-12
6021 Williams Rd 33584 813-620-0683
Jim Evans, prin. Fax 663-9776
Seffner Christian Academy 700/PK-12
11605 E US Highway 92 33584 813-626-0001
Roger Duncan, dir. Fax 627-0330

Seminole, Pinellas, Pop. 18,505
Pinellas County SD
Supt. — See Largo
Osceola HS 1,900/9-12
9751 98th St 33777 727-547-7717
Carol Moore, prin. Fax 545-6412
Osceola MS 1,200/6-8
9301 98th St 33777 727-547-7689
Bob Vicari, prin. Fax 547-7667
Seminole HS 2,100/9-12
8401 131st St 33776 727-547-7536
Richard Misenti, prin. Fax 547-7503
Seminole MS 1,200/6-8
8701 131st St 33776 727-547-4520
Judy Leboeuf, prin. Fax 547-7741
Seminole Vocational Education Center Vo/Tech
12611 86th Ave 33776 727-545-6405
Matt Fischer, dir. Fax 545-6408

Shalimar, Okaloosa, Pop. 733
Okaloosa County SD
Supt. — See Fort Walton Beach
Meigs MS 700/6-8
150 Richbourg Ave 32579 850-833-4301
Dr. Lamar White, prin. Fax 833-9392

Sneads, Jackson, Pop. 1,943
Jackson County SD
Supt. — See Marianna
Sneads JSHS 600/6-12
8066 Old Spanish Trl 32460 850-482-9007
Patricia Dickson, prin. Fax 482-9058

Victory Christian Academy 100/PK-12
2271 River Rd 32460 850-593-6699
Rev. David Pipping, admin. Fax 593-3341

South Daytona, Volusia, Pop. 13,733

International Academy Post-Sec.
2550 S Ridgewood Ave 32119 386-767-4600
Warner Christian Academy 600/PK-12
1730 S Ridgewood Ave 32119 386-767-5451
Linda Ashe, hdmstr. Fax 760-6834

South Miami, Dade, Pop. 11,147
Miami-Dade County SD
Supt. — See Miami
South Miami MS 800/7-8
6750 SW 60th St 33143 305-661-3481
Dr. Lisa Robertson, prin. Fax 665-6728

South Miami Christian S 200/PK-12
6767 Sunset Dr 33143 305-666-5171

Spring Hill, Hernando, Pop. 85,900
Hernando County SD
Supt. — See Brooksville
Fox Chapel MS 1,200/6-8
9412 Fox Chapel Ln 34606 352-797-7025
Ray Pinder, prin. Fax 797-7125
Springstead HS 1,700/9-12
3300 Mariner Blvd 34609 352-797-7010
Susan Duval, prin. Fax 797-7110

Bishop McLaughlin HS 9-12
13651 Hays Rd 34610 727-857-2600
Jane Moerschbacher, prin. Fax 857-2610
Spring Hill Christian Academy 300/PK-12
3140 Mariner Blvd 34609 352-683-8485
Charles Gottshall, prin. Fax 683-5087
West Hernando Christian S 200/PK-12
2250 Osowaw Blvd 34607 352-688-9918
Marti Covert, admin. Fax 683-1184
Wider Horizons S 200/PK-12
4060 Castle Ave 34609 352-686-1934

Starke, Bradford, Pop. 5,844
Bradford County SD 3,700/PK-12
501 W Washington St 32091 904-966-6800
Harry M. Hatcher, supt. Fax 966-6030
www.mybradford.us/

Bradford HS 1,000/9-12
581 N Temple Ave 32091 904-966-6091
Randy Whytsell, prin. Fax 966-6020
Bradford MS 800/6-8
527 N Orange St 32091 904-966-6704
Jeff Cable, prin. Fax 966-6714
Bradford Union Vocational Ctr Vo/Tech
609 N Orange St 32091 904-966-6766
Clarence DeSue, dir. Fax 966-6786

Bradford-Union Area Vo-Tech Center Post-Sec.
609 N Orange St 32091 904-966-6760
Hope Christian Academy 100/PK-12
3900 SE State Road 100 32091 352-473-4040
Angie Davis, prin. Fax 473-8176
Northside Christian Academy 200/PK-12
7415 NW County Road 225 32091 904-964-7124
David Coxe, admin. Fax 964-7141

Stuart, Martin, Pop. 15,764
Martin County SD 17,100/PK-12
500 SE Ocean Blvd 34994 772-219-1200
Dr. Sara Wilcox, supt. Fax 219-1231
www.sbmc.org
Anderson MS 6-8
7000 SE Atlantic Ridge Dr 34997 772-221-7100
Dr. Larthenia Howard, prin.
Martin County HS 2,000/9-12
2801 S Kanner Hwy 34994 772-219-1800
Joan Hunt, prin. Fax 219-1821
Murray MS 1,100/6-8
4400 SE Murray St 34997 772-219-1670
Kit Weir, prin. Fax 219-1677
South Fork HS 2,100/9-12
10205 SW Pratt Whitney Rd 34997 772-219-1840
Patricia Schmoyer, prin. Fax 219-1860
Stuart MS 1,300/6-8
575 SE Georgia Ave 34994 772-219-1685
Sigrid George, prin. Fax 219-1690
Adult Education Adult
800 SE Monterey Rd 34994 772-220-7260
William Connolly, coord. Fax 220-7264
Other Schools – See Indiantown, Jensen Beach, Palm City

Chapman School of Seamanship Post-Sec.
4343 SE Saint Lucie Blvd 34997 772-283-8130
Community Christian Academy 300/PK-12
777 SE Salerno Rd 34997 772-288-7227
Paul Humphreys, hdmstr. Fax 600-2727
Star Academy for Pet Stylists Post-Sec.
2201 SE Indian St Unit C6 34997 772-221-9330

Summerfield, Marion
Marion County SD
Supt. — See Ocala
Lake Weir MS 1,300/6-8
10220 SE Sunset Harbor Rd 34491 352-671-6120
Mike Kelly, prin. Fax 671-6121

Sumterville, Sumter
Sumter County SD
Supt. — See Bushnell
Sumter County Adult Center Adult
1425 County Road 526A 33585 352-793-5719
Gloria Croft, prin. Fax 793-6508

Sunrise, Broward, Pop. 90,589
Broward County SD
Supt. — See Fort Lauderdale
Bair MS 1,600/6-8
9100 NW 21st Mnr 33322 754-322-2900
Ellen Etling, prin. Fax 322-2985
Cypress Bay 9th Annex 9-9
270 N New River Cir 33326 754-323-1500
Charles Neely, prin. Fax 323-1535
Piper HS 3,100/9-12
8000 NW 44th St 33351 754-322-1700
Enid Valdez, prin. Fax 322-1830
Westpine MS 1,500/6-8
9393 NW 50th St 33351 754-322-4900
Paula Meadows, prin. Fax 322-4985

Tallahassee, Leon, Pop. 158,500
Leon County SD 30,500/PK-12
2757 W Pensacola St 32304 850-487-7100
Dr. James Croteau, supt. Fax 487-7141
www.leon.k12.fl.us
Belle Vue MS 600/6-8
2214 Bellevue Way 32304 850-488-4467
Reginald Griffin, prin. Fax 922-8494
Chiles HS 1,900/9-12
7200 Lawton Chiles Ln 32312 850-488-1756
Allan Cox, prin. Fax 488-1218
Cobb MS 1,000/6-8
915 Hillcrest St 32308 850-488-3364
Shannon Meeks, prin. Fax 922-2452
Deerlake MS 1,400/6-8
9902 Deer Lk W 32312 850-922-6545
Jackie Pons, prin. Fax 488-3275
Fairview MS 800/6-8
3415 Zillah St 32305 850-488-6880
Roger Pinholster, prin. Fax 922-6326
Godby HS 1,300/9-12
1717 W Tharpe St 32303 850-488-1325
Randy Pridgeon, prin. Fax 922-4162
Griffin MS 700/6-8
800 Alabama St 32304 850-488-8436
Michelle Gayle, prin. Fax 922-4226
Leon HS 1,800/9-12
550 E Tennessee St 32308 850-488-1971
Rocky Hanna, prin. Fax 922-5311
Lincoln HS 1,900/9-12
3838 Trojan Trl 32311 850-487-2110
Martha Bunch, prin. Fax 922-4173
Lively-Technical Center Vo/Tech
500 Appleyard Dr 32304 850-487-7555
Jean Ferguson, prin. Fax 922-3880
Nims MS 500/6-8
723 W Orange Ave 32310 850-488-5960
Pam Hayman, prin. Fax 922-0203
Raa MS 800/6-8
401 W Tharpe St 32303 850-488-6287
Pat Keen, prin. Fax 922-5835
Rickards HS 1,200/9-12
3013 Jim Lee Rd 32301 850-488-1783
Pink Hightower, prin. Fax 922-7104
SAIL HS 300/9-12
725 N Macomb St 32303 850-488-2468
Rosanne Wood, prin. Fax 922-8483
Swift Creek MS 1,000/6-8
2100 Pedrick Rd 32317 850-487-4868
Alice Caswell, prin. Fax 414-2650
Leon Countywide Adult Education Adult
283 Trojan Trl 32311 850-922-5343
Barbara Van Camp, prin. Fax 922-5352

Atlantis Academy of Tallahassee 200/1-12
1500 Miccosukee Rd 32308 850-893-4692
Duwayne Baum, prin. Fax 893-4464
Core Institute Post-Sec.
223 W Carolina St 32301 866-830-0108
Florida A&M University 32307 Post-Sec.
850-599-3000
Florida State University Post-Sec.
600 W College Ave 32306 850-644-2525
John Paul II HS 100/9-12
5100 Terrebonne Dr 32311 850-201-5744
Dr. Randall Felton, prin. Fax 205-3299
Keiser College Post-Sec.
1700 Halstead Blvd 32309 850-906-9494
Lively Area Vocational Technical Center Post-Sec.
3290 Capital Cir SW 32310 850-488-2460
Lively Area Vocational Technical School Post-Sec.
500 Appleyard Dr 32304 850-487-7555
Maclay S 1,000/PK-12
3737 N Meridian Rd 32312 850-893-2138
William Jablon, hdmstr. Fax 893-7434
Maranatha Christian S 200/PK-12
2532 W Tharpe St 32303 850-385-5920
Alan Risk, admin. Fax 386-7785
North Florida Christian S 1,200/PK-12
3000 N Meridian Rd 32312 850-386-6327
Charles Fielding, admin. Fax 385-7188
North Florida Cosmetology Institute Post-Sec.
2424 Allen Rd 32312 850-878-5269
Tallahassee Community College Post-Sec.
444 Appleyard Dr 32304 850-201-8595
Tallahassee Memorial Hospital Post-Sec.
1300 Miccosukee Rd 32308 850-681-5385

Tamarac, Broward, Pop. 59,923
Broward County SD
Supt. — See Fort Lauderdale
Millennium MS 1,500/6-8
5803 NW 94th Ave 33321 754-322-3900
Dr. Cheryl Cendan, prin. Fax 322-3985

Tampa, Hillsborough, Pop. 325,989
Hillsborough County SD 181,100/PK-12
PO Box 3408 33601 813-272-4000
Mary Ellen Elia, supt. Fax 272-4510
www.sdhc.k12.fl.us/
Adams MS 1,200/6-8
10201 N Boulevard 33612 813-975-7665
Odalys Pritchard, prin. Fax 632-6889
Alonso HS 2,600/9-12
8302 Montague St 33635 813-356-1525
Dr. Sandy Bunkin, prin. Fax 356-1529
Bartels MS 6-8
9020 Imperial Oak Blvd 33647 813-907-6801
Maribeth Franklin, prin. Fax 907-6805
Benito MS 1,400/6-8
10101 Cross Creek Blvd 33647 813-631-4694
Bobby Smith, prin. Fax 631-4706
Blake HS 1,800/9-12
1701 N Boulevard 33607 813-272-3422
Jackie Haynes, prin. Fax 272-3715
Bowers/Whitley Career Center Vo/Tech
13609 N 22nd St 33613 813-558-1750
Dr. Anthony Colucci, prin. Fax 558-1761
Buchanan MS 900/6-8
1001 W Bearss Ave 33613 813-975-7600
Dr. Dwight Raines, prin. Fax 975-7610
Chamberlain HS 2,200/9-12
9401 N Boulevard 33612 813-975-7677
Jeff Boldt, prin. Fax 975-7687
Coleman MS 800/6-8
1724 S Manhattan Ave 33629 813-872-5335
Michael Hoskinson, prin. Fax 872-5338
Davidsen MS 1,300/6-8
10501 Montague St 33626 813-558-5300
Michael Miranda, prin. Fax 558-5299
Dowdell MS 1,000/6-8
1208 Wishing Well Way 33619 813-744-8322
Robert Lawson, prin. Fax 740-3616
Erwin Tech Center Vo/Tech
2010 E Hillsborough Ave 33610 813-231-1800
Michael Donohue, prin. Fax 231-1820
Farnell MS 1,400/6-8
13912 Nine Eagles Dr 33626 813-356-1640
John Cobb, prin. Fax 356-1644
Ferrell Magnet MS 700/6-8
4302 N 24th St 33610 813-276-5608
Charles Dixon, prin. Fax 276-5615
Franklin MS 600/6-8
3915 E 21st Ave 33605 813-744-8108
Joe Brown, prin. Fax 744-8579
Gaither HS 2,400/9-12
16200 N Dale Mabry Hwy 33618 813-975-7340
Brenda Grasso, prin. Fax 975-7349
Hill MS 1,100/6-8
5200 Ehrlich Rd 33624 813-975-7325
Barry Davis, prin. Fax 975-4819
Hillsborough HS 2,000/9-12
5000 N Central Ave 33603 813-276-5620
Dr. William Orr, prin. Fax 276-5629
Jefferson HS 1,900/9-12
4401 W Cypress St 33607 813-872-5241
Dan Bonilla, prin. Fax 872-5250
King HS 2,100/9-12
6815 N 56th St 33610 813-744-8333
Carla Bruning, prin. Fax 744-8343
Leto HS 1,800/9-12
4409 W Sligh Ave 33614 813-872-5300
Daniel Bonilla, prin. Fax 872-5314
Liberty MS 1,500/6-8
17400 Commerce Park Blvd 33647 813-558-1180
Debbie Rodgers, prin. Fax 558-1184
Madison MS 700/6-8
4444 W Bay Vista Ave 33611 813-272-3050
John Haley, prin. Fax 233-2796
Memorial MS 1,100/6-8
4702 N Central Ave 33603 813-872-5230
John Copeland, prin. Fax 872-5238
Middleton Magnet HS 2,000/9-12
4801 N 22nd St 33610 813-233-3360
James Gatlin, prin. Fax 233-3364
Monroe MS 700/6-8
4716 W Montgomery Ave 33616 813-272-3020
Juanita Underwood, prin. Fax 272-3027
Orange Grove Magnet MS 600/6-8
3415 N 16th St 33605 813-276-5717
Debra Arias, prin. Fax 276-5857
Pierce MS 1,100/6-8
5511 N Hesperides St 33614 813-872-5344
Victor Fernandez, prin. Fax 871-7978
Plant HS 2,000/9-12
2415 S Himes Ave 33629 813-272-3033
Eric Bergholm, prin. Fax 272-0624
Progress Village MS 900/6-8
8113 Zinnia Dr 33619 813-671-5110
Walt Shaffner, prin. Fax 671-5240
Robinson HS 1,200/9-12
6311 S Lois Ave 33616 813-272-3006
Laura Zavatkay, prin. Fax 272-3014
Sickles HS 2,500/9-12
7950 Gunn Hwy 33626 813-631-4742
Jake Russell, prin. Fax 631-4754
Sligh MS 900/6-8
2011 E Sligh Ave 33610 813-276-5596
Barbara Fillhart, prin. Fax 276-5606
Stewart MS 900/6-8
1125 W Spruce St 33607 813-276-5691
Baretta Wilson, prin. Fax 276-5698
Tampa Bay Technical HS Vo/Tech
6410 Orient Rd 33610 813-744-8360
William Person, prin. Fax 744-8368
Van Buren MS 800/6-8
8715 N 22nd St 33604 813-975-7652
Tony Giancola, prin. Fax 631-4312
Waters Career Center Vo/Tech
2704 N Highland Ave 33602 813-233-2655
Veronica Knight, admin. Fax 233-2659
Webb MS 700/6-8
6035 Hanley Rd 33634 813-872-5351
Carmen Aguero, prin. Fax 872-5359
Wharton HS 2,100/9-12
20150 Bruce B Downs Blvd 33647 813-631-4710
George Gaffney, prin. Fax 631-4722
Williams MS 900/6-8
5020 N 47th St 33610 813-744-8600
Patricia Harrell, prin. Fax 744-8665
Wilson MS 600/6-8
1005 W Swann Ave 33606 813-276-5682
Stephanie Woodford, prin. Fax 233-2540
Young Magnet MS 800/6-8
1807 E Dr Martn Lthr King 33610 813-276-5739
Dr. Angela Oliver, prin. Fax 276-5893
Adult Education Center Adult
2222 N Tampa St 33602 813-276-5654
Shirley Robbins, prin. Fax 276-5662
Aparicio/Levy Adult Technical S Adult
10119 E Ellicott St 33610 813-740-4884
Fax 740-4885
Brewster Tech Center Adult
2222 N Tampa St 33602 813-276-5448
Janice Carter-Collier, prin. Fax 276-5756
Gary Adult S, 5101 N 40th St 33610 Adult
Terry Zartman, prin. 813-740-7660
Learey Technical S Adult
5410 N 20th St 33610 813-231-1907
Paula Clark, prin. Fax 231-1855
Tampa Bay Technical Adult Evening S Adult
6410 Orient Rd 33610 813-744-8360
Candace Odierna, admin. Fax 744-8368
Other Schools – See Brandon, Gibsonton, Lithia, Lutz, Odessa, Plant City, Riverview, Ruskin, Seffner, Temple Terrace, Valrico

Academy of the Holy Names HS 9-12
3319 Bayshore Blvd 33629 813-839-5371
Sarah Regan, prin. Fax 839-1486
American Youth Academy 300/PK-12
5905 E 130th Ave 33617 813-987-9282
Magda Saleh, prin. Fax 987-9262
Argosy University/Tampa Post-Sec.
4401 N Himes Ave Ste 150 33614 813-740-1108
Art Institute of Tampa Post-Sec.
4401 N Himes Ave Ste 150 33614 813-873-2112
Bayshore Christian S 400/PK-12
3909 S MacDill Ave 33611 813-839-4297
Herman Valdes, prin. Fax 835-1404
Berean Academy 200/K-12
10948 N Central Ave 33612 813-932-0552
Bruce Kirby, hdmstr. Fax 930-2134
Berkeley Preparatory S 1,200/PK-12
4811 Kelly Rd 33615 813-885-1673
Joseph Merluzzi, prin. Fax 886-6933
Cambridge S 700/PK-12
6101 N Habana Ave 33614 813-872-6744
Robert Baerwalde, hdmstr. Fax 872-6013
Carrollwood Day S 300/1-12
1515 W Bearss Ave 33613 813-920-2288
Mary Kanter, hdmstr. Fax 920-8237
Citrus Park Christian S 500/PK-12
7705 Gunn Hwy 33625 813-920-3960
Herman Meister, dir. Fax 926-1240
Concorde Career Institute Post-Sec.
4202 W Spruce St 33607 813-874-0094
DeVry University Post-Sec.
3030 N Rocky Point Dr # 100 33607 813-288-8994
D.G. Erwin Technical Center Post-Sec.
2010 E Hillsborough Ave 33610 813-231-1800
Faith Outreach Academy 100/PK-12
7607 Sheldon Rd 33615 813-887-5546
Julie Sierra, prin. Fax 249-6896
FL Metropolitan Univ. - Brandon Post-Sec.
3924 Coconut Palm Dr 33619 813-621-0041
FL Metropolitan Univ. - Tampa Campus Post-Sec.
3319 W Hillsborough Ave 33614 813-879-6000
Gulf Coast College Post-Sec.
3910 N US Highway 301 33619 813-620-1446

Henry W. Brewster Technical Center — Post-Sec.
2222 N Tampa St 33602 — 813-276-5464
Hillsborough Community College — Post-Sec.
1404 Tech Blvd 33619 — 813-253-7000
Hillsborough Community College — Post-Sec.
PO Box 30030 33630 — 813-253-7000
Hillsborough Community College Ybor Camp — Post-Sec.
PO Box 5096 33675 — 813-253-7601
International Academy of Design & Tech — Post-Sec.
5104 Eisenhower Blvd 33634 — 813-881-0007
ITT Technical Institute — Post-Sec.
4809 Memorial Hwy 33634 — 813-885-2244
James Haley Veteran's Hospital — Post-Sec.
13000 Bruce B Downs Blvd 33612 — 813-972-2000
Jesuit HS — 600/9-12
4701 N Himes Ave 33614 — 813-877-5344
Joseph Sabin, prin. — Fax 872-1853
Libertas Academy — 100/K-12
14018 N Boulevard 33613 — 813-964-1779
Hannah Vickery, prin. — Fax 514-1283
Manhattan Beauty School — Post-Sec.
2317 E Fletcher Ave 33612 — 813-264-3535
Manhattan Hairstyling Academy — Post-Sec.
1906 W Platt St 33606 — 813-837-2525
Paideia S of Tampa Bay — 100/K-12
7834 N 56th St 33617 — 813-988-7700
Conrad Bray, hdmstr.
Remington College — Post-Sec.
2410 E Busch Blvd 33612 — 813-935-5700
St. John's Episcopal S — 100/6-8
240 S Plant Ave 33606 — 813-849-4200
Gordon Rode, hdmstr. — Fax 849-1026
Sanford Brown Institute — Post-Sec.
5701 E Hllsbrgh Av #1417 33610 — 813-621-0072
Stepping Stones S — 100/9-12
19046 Bruce B Downs Blvd 33647 — 813-973-0619
Strayer University — Post-Sec.
6302 E M L King Blvd # 450 33619 — 813-663-0100
Strayer University — Post-Sec.
4902 Eisenhower Blvd # 100 33634 — 813-882-0100
Suncoast Center for Natural Health — Post-Sec.
2005 Pan Am Cir Ste 100 33607 — 813-287-1099
Tampa Adventist Academy — 100/PK-10
3205 N Boulevard 33603 — 813-228-7950
David Matthews, prin. — Fax 228-0170
Tampa Baptist Academy — 400/PK-12
300 E Sligh Ave 33604 — 813-238-3229
Dr. Barbara Bode, hdmstr. — Fax 237-3426
Tampa Catholic HS — 700/9-12
4630 N Rome Ave 33603 — 813-870-0860
Patricia Landry, prin. — Fax 877-9136
Tampa General Hospital — Post-Sec.
PO Box 1289 33601 — 813-844-7985
Tampa Preparatory S — 700/6-12
727 W Cass St 33606 — 813-251-8481
D. Gordon MacLeod, prin. — Fax 254-2106
Universal Academy of Florida — 300/PK-12
6801 Orient Rd 33610 — 813-664-0695
Moosa Yahya, dir. — Fax 664-4506
University of South Florida — Post-Sec.
4202 E Fowler Ave 33620 — 813-974-3350
University of Tampa — Post-Sec.
401 W Kennedy Blvd 33606 — 813-253-3333
West Gate Christian S — 400/PK-12
5121 Kelly Rd 33615 — 813-884-5147
Dr. Bruce Turner, admin. — Fax 888-5368

Tarpon Springs, Pinellas, Pop. 22,651
Pinellas County SD
Supt. — See Largo
East Lake HS — 2,300/9-12
1300 Silver Eagle Dr 34688 — 727-942-5419
Clayton Snare, prin. — Fax 942-5441
Tarpon Springs HS — 2,000/9-12
1411 Gulf Rd 34689 — 727-943-4900
Evert Vermeer, prin. — Fax 943-4907
Tarpon Springs MS — 1,500/6-8
501 N Florida Ave 34689 — 727-943-5511
Felita Lott, prin. — Fax 943-5519

St. Petersburg College — Post-Sec.
600 Klosterman Rd W 34689 — 727-791-2400

Tavares, Lake, Pop. 11,621
Lake County SD — 32,300/PK-12
201 W Burleigh Blvd 32778 — 352-253-6500
Anna Cowin, supt. — Fax 343-0198
www.lake.k12.fl.us/
Tavares HS — 1,100/9-12
603 N New Hampshire Ave 32778 — 352-343-3007
Kathy Tatro, prin. — Fax 343-0892
Tavares MS — 1,000/6-8
13032 Lane Park Cutoff 32778 — 352-343-4545
Mike Herring, prin. — Fax 343-7212
Other Schools – See Clermont, Eustis, Groveland, Leesburg, Mount Dora, Umatilla

---

Liberty Christian Academy — 300/PK-12
2451 Dora Ave 32778 — 352-343-0061
Mark Curtis, prin. — Fax 343-2424

Tavernier, Monroe, Pop. 2,433
Monroe County SD
Supt. — See Key West
Coral Shores HS — 800/9-12
89901 Old Hwy 33070 — 305-853-3222
Ron Martin, prin. — Fax 853-3228

Temple Terrace, Hillsborough, Pop. 21,978
Hillsborough County SD
Supt. — See Tampa
Greco MS — 1,100/6-8
6925 E Fowler Ave 33617 — 813-987-6926
Dr. Judith Kennedy, prin. — Fax 987-6863

Florida College — Post-Sec.
119 N Glen Arven Ave 33617 — 813-988-5131

Titusville, Brevard, Pop. 43,767
Brevard County SD
Supt. — See Melbourne
Astronaut HS — 1,600/9-12
800 War Eagle Blvd 32796 — 321-264-3000
Terry Humphrey, prin. — Fax 264-3013
Jackson MS — 700/7-8
1515 Knox Mcrae Dr 32780 — 321-269-1812
James Hickey, prin. — Fax 269-7811
Madison MS — 700/7-8
3375 Dairy Rd 32796 — 321-264-3120
Joan Sparks, prin. — Fax 264-3124
Titusville HS — 1,800/9-12
150 Terrier Trl S 32780 — 321-264-3100
Dr. Lori Hiatt, prin. — Fax 264-3103
North Area Adult Education — Adult
800 Lane Ave 32780 — 321-264-3088
Richard Dobsha, prin.

Helicopter Adventures — Post-Sec.
365 Golden Knights Blvd 32780 — 321-385-2919
Temple Christian S — 200/PK-12
1400 N US Highway 1 32796 — 321-269-2837
Scott Hallock, prin. — Fax 383-9101

Trenton, Gilchrist, Pop. 1,793
Gilchrist County SD — 2,800/PK-12
310 NW 11th Ave 32693 — 352-463-3200
James Vickers, supt. — Fax 463-3276
www.gilchristschools.org
Trenton HS — 700/6-12
1013 N Main St 32693 — 352-463-3210
Lynette Langford, prin. — Fax 463-3264
Other Schools – See Bell

Victory Christian S — 100/7-12
6191 SW County Road 344 32693 — 352-463-1473
Rev. Carl Cornwell, dir. — Fax 796-2687

Umatilla, Lake, Pop. 2,647
Lake County SD
Supt. — See Tavares
Umatilla HS — 900/9-12
320 N Trowell Ave 32784 — 352-669-3131
June Dalton, prin. — Fax 669-5481
Umatilla MS — 800/6-8
305 E Lake St 32784 — 352-669-3171
Bill Miller, prin. — Fax 669-5424

Living Word Academy — 200/PK-12
19624 Quails Nest Run 32784 — 352-669-8966

Valparaiso, Okaloosa, Pop. 6,365
Okaloosa County SD
Supt. — See Fort Walton Beach
Lewis MS — 600/6-8
281 Mississippi Ave 32580 — 850-833-4130
Dr. Linda Smith, prin. — Fax 833-4197

Valrico, See Brandon
Hillsborough County SD
Supt. — See Tampa
Bloomingdale HS — 2,300/9-12
1700 Bloomingdale Ave, — 813-744-8018
Mark West, prin. — Fax 744-8026
Mulrennan MS — 1,300/6-8
4215 Durant Rd, — 813-651-2100
Tim Ducker, prin. — Fax 651-2104

Grace Christian S — 300/K-12
1300 N Valrico Rd 33594 — 813-689-8815
Dr. Robert Gustafson, dir. — Fax 681-7396
Manhattan Hairstyling Academy — Post-Sec.
3244 Lithia Pinecrest #103 33594 — 813-655-4545

Venice, Sarasota, Pop. 20,974
Sarasota County SD
Supt. — See Sarasota
Venice Area MS — 800/6-8
1900 Center Rd 34292 — 941-486-2100
Jack Turgeon, prin. — Fax 486-2108
Venice HS — 2,200/9-12
1 Indian Ave 34285 — 941-488-6726
Candace Millington, prin. — Fax 486-2034

Vernon, Washington, Pop. 766
Washington County SD
Supt. — See Chipley
Vernon HS — 400/9-12
3232 Moss Hill Rd 32462 — 850-535-2046
Bobbie Dawson, prin. — Fax 535-6244
Vernon MS — 200/7-8
3206 Moss Hill Rd 32462 — 850-535-2807
Julia Morales, prin. — Fax 535-1683

Vero Beach, Indian River, Pop. 17,078
Indian River County SD — 15,800/PK-12
1990 25th St 32960 — 772-564-3000
Harry LaCava Ed.D., supt. — Fax 564-3128
www.indian-river.k12.fl.us/
Gifford MS — 1,300/6-8
4530 28th Ct 32967 — 772-564-3550
Dave Kramek, prin. — Fax 564-3561
Oslo MS — 1,200/6-8
480 20th Ave SW 32962 — 772-564-3980
Deborah Long, prin. — Fax 564-4029
Vero Beach Freshman Learning Center — 9-9
1507 19th St 32960 — 772-564-4820
Jane Hudson, prin. — Fax 564-4928
Vero Beach HS — 2,800/9-12
1707 16th St 32960 — 772-564-4620
Jane Hudson, prin. — Fax 564-4720
Indian River Adult Education — Adult
1426 19th St 32960 — 772-564-4955
John Fontana, prin. — Fax 564-4977
Other Schools – See Sebastian

FlightSafety International — Post-Sec.
PO Box 2708 32961 — 772-564-7600
Master's Academy of Vero Beach — 300/PK-12
1105 58th Ave 32966 — 772-794-4655
Dr. H. Grant Powell, hdmstr. — Fax 563-9714
St. Edward's S — 900/PK-12
1895 Saint Edwards Dr 32963 — 772-231-4136
Dr. Charles F. Clark, hdmstr. — Fax 231-6158

Walnut Hill, Escambia
Escambia County SD
Supt. — See Pensacola
Ward MS — 400/6-8
7650 Highway 97 32568 — 850-327-4283
Nancy Gindl, prin. — Fax 327-4991

Warrington, Escambia, Pop. 16,040
Escambia County SD
Supt. — See Pensacola
Warrington MS — 800/6-8
450 S Old Corry Field Rd, Pensacola FL 32507 — 850-453-7440
Christine Nixon, prin. — Fax 453-7572

Wauchula, Hardee, Pop. 4,450
Hardee County SD — 5,000/PK-12
PO Box 1678 33873 — 863-773-9058
Dennis Jones, supt. — Fax 773-0069
www.hardee.k12.fl.us
Hardee HS — 1,200/9-12
830 Altman Rd 33873 — 863-773-3181
Mike Wilkinson, prin. — Fax 773-4390
Hardee JHS — 1,200/6-8
2401 US Highway 17 N 33873 — 863-773-3147
Mae Robinson, prin. — Fax 773-3167
Family Service Center — Adult
901 W Main St 33873 — 863-773-3173
Gerald Kapusta, prin. — Fax 773-3127

Webster, Sumter, Pop. 838
Sumter County SD
Supt. — See Bushnell
South Sumter MS — 900/6-8
773 NW 10th Ave 33597 — 352-793-2232
Kathy Dustin, prin. — Fax 793-3976

Wellington, Palm Beach, Pop. 53,583
Palm Beach County SD
Supt. — See West Palm Beach
Palm Beach Central HS — 2,800/9-12
8499 Forest Hill Blvd, — 561-304-1000
Burley Mondy, prin. — Fax 304-1017
Polo Park MS — 1,600/6-8
11901 Lake Worth Rd 33414 — 561-333-5500
Marcia Andrews, prin. — Fax 333-5505
Wellington Community HS — 3,100/9-12
2101 Greenview Shores Blvd 33414 — 561-795-4900
Cheryl Alligood, prin. — Fax 795-4934
Wellington Landings MS — 1,200/6-8
1100 Aero Club Dr 33414 — 561-792-8100
Mario Crocetti, prin. — Fax 792-8106

Wellington Christian S — 800/PK-12
1000 Wellington Trce 33414 — 561-793-1017
Joseph Austin, prin. — Fax 798-9622

Wesley Chapel, Pasco, Pop. 1,200
Pasco County SD
Supt. — See Land O Lakes
Long MS — 6-8
2025 Mansfield Blvd 33543 — 813-346-6200
Beth Brown, prin. — Fax 346-6291
Weightman MS — 1,800/6-8
30649 Wells Rd, — 813-794-0200
Shae Davis, prin. — Fax 794-0291
Wesley Chapel HS — 2,100/9-12
30651 Wells Rd, — 813-794-8700
Andrew Frelick, prin. — Fax 794-8791
Wiregrass Ranch HS — 9-12
2909 Mansfield Blvd 33543 — 813-346-6000
Ray Bonti, prin. — Fax 346-6091

Faith Baptist Academy — 50/PK-12
6300 Oakley Blvd 33544 — 813-907-9462
Travis Hartsfield, admin. — Fax 907-9986
Saddlebrook Preparatory S — 100/K-12
5700 Saddlebrook Way 33543 — 813-907-4300
Larry Robison, hdmstr. — Fax 991-4713

West Melbourne, Brevard, Pop. 15,054
Brevard County SD
Supt. — See Melbourne
Central MS — 1,200/7-8
2600 Wingate Blvd 32904 — 321-722-4150
Pamela Mitchell, prin. — Fax 722-4165

Brevard Christian S — 200/PK-12
1100 Dorchester Ave 32904 — 321-727-2038
Michael Branch, prin. — Fax 729-4212
Space Coast Health Institute — Post-Sec.
1070 S Wickham Rd 32904 — 321-729-9000

West Miami, Dade, Pop. 5,829

Florida Education Institute — Post-Sec.
5818 SW 8th St 33144 — 305-444-1515

Weston, Broward, Pop. 65,679
Broward County SD
Supt. — See Fort Lauderdale
Cypress Bay HS — 4,700/9-12
18600 Vista Park Blvd 33332 — 754-323-0350
Charles Neely, prin. — Fax 323-0363
Falcon Cove MS — 2,300/6-8
4251 Bonaventure Blvd 33332 — 754-323-3200
Mark Kaplan, prin. — Fax 323-3285
Tequesta Trace MS — 1,700/6-8
1800 Indian Trce 33326 — 754-323-4400
Paul Micensky, prin. — Fax 323-4485

American InterContinental University — Post-Sec.
2250 N Commerce Pkwy 33326 — 888-603-4888
Sagemont S - Upper Campus — 400/6-12
2585 Glades Cir 33327 — 954-389-2454
Brent Goldman, hdmstr. — Fax 389-8106

West Palm Beach, Palm Beach, Pop. 97,498
Palm Beach County SD — 162,300/PK-12
3300 Forest Hill Blvd 33406 — 561-434-8000
Arthur C. Johnson Ph.D., supt. — Fax 434-8571
www.palmbeach.k12.fl.us
Bak MS of the Arts — 1,400/6-8
1725 Echo Lake Dr 33407 — 561-882-3870
Elizabeth Perlman, prin. — Fax 882-3879
Bear Lakes MS — 1,000/6-8
3505 Shenandoah Rd 33409 — 561-615-7700
Anthony Lockhart, prin. — Fax 615-7756

Conniston Community MS 1,000/6-8
673 Conniston Rd 33405 561-802-5400
Mary Stratos, prin. Fax 802-5409
Dreyfoos S of the Arts 1,300/9-12
501 S Sapodilla Ave 33401 561-802-6000
Ellen VanArsdale, prin. Fax 802-6059
Forest Hill Community HS 1,700/9-12
6901 Parker Ave 33405 561-540-2400
Mayra Stafford, prin. Fax 540-2440
Jeaga MS 1,200/6-8
3777 N Jog Rd 33411 561-242-8000
Joseph DePasquale, prin. Fax 242-8005
Okeeheelee MS 1,500/6-8
2200 Pinehurst Dr 33413 561-434-3200
David Samore, prin. Fax 434-3244
Palm Beach Lakes Community HS 2,600/9-12
3505 Shiloh Dr 33407 561-640-5000
Nathan Collins, prin. Fax 688-5340
Palm Springs Community MS 1,900/6-8
1560 Kirk Rd 33406 561-434-3300
Sandra Jinks, prin. Fax 434-3303
Roosevelt Community MS 1,300/6-8
1900 Australian Ave 33404 561-822-0200
George Lockhart, prin. Fax 882-0222
Western Pines MS 1,400/6-8
5949 140th Ave N 33411 561-792-2500
Matthew Shoemaker, prin. Fax 792-2530
Adult Education Center of Palm Beach Adult
2161 N Military Trl 33409 561-640-5074
Cynthia Smith, prin. Fax 688-5209
Other Schools – See Belle Glade, Boca Raton, Boynton Beach, Delray Beach, Greenacres, Jupiter, Lake Worth, Lantana, Loxahatchee, Pahokee, Palm Beach Gardens, Riviera Beach, Royal Palm Beach, Wellington

---

Academy for Practical Nursing/Health Occ Post-Sec.
5154 Okechobee Blvd #201 33417 561-683-1400
Atlantis Academy 200/PK-12
1950 Prairie Rd 33406 561-642-3100
Dennis Kelley, dir. Fax 969-1950
Berean Christian S 900/PK-12
8350 Okeechobee Blvd 33411 561-798-9300
Embree Bolton, hdmstr. Fax 792-3073
Cardinal Newman HS 800/9-12
512 Spencer Dr 33409 561-683-6266
John Clarke, prin. Fax 683-7307
Ephesus Junior Academy 100/K-10
4011 N Shore Dr 33407 561-832-9789
Karen Jones, prin. Fax 832-3567
King's Academy 1,400/PK-12
8401 Belvedere Rd 33411 561-686-4244
Jeffrey Loveland, pres. Fax 686-8017
Lincoln College of Technology Post-Sec.
2410 Metrocentre Blvd 33407 561-842-8324
Northwood University Post-Sec.
2600 N Military Trl 33409 800-458-8325
Palm Beach Atlantic University Post-Sec.
PO Box 24708 33416 561-803-2000
PC Professor Post-Sec.
6080 Okeechobee Blvd 33417 561-684-3333
Ross Medical Education Center Post-Sec.
2601 S Military Trl Ste 29 33415 561-433-1288
South University Post-Sec.
1760 N Congress Ave 33409 561-697-9200
Summit Christian S 900/PK-12
4900 Summit Blvd 33415 561-686-8081
Sam Skelton, hdmstr. Fax 640-7613

Wewahitchka, Gulf, Pop. 1,691
Gulf County SD
Supt. — See Port Saint Joe
Wewahitchka HS 300/9-12
1 Gator Cir 32465 850-639-2228
Larry White, prin. Fax 639-5394
Wewahitchka MS 200/6-8
190 Aligator Aly 32465 850-639-6840
Pam Lister, prin. Fax 639-6929

Wildwood, Sumter, Pop. 3,428
Sumter County SD
Supt. — See Bushnell
Wildwood HS 500/9-12
700 Huey St 34785 352-748-1314
Richard Hampton, prin. Fax 748-7668
Wildwood MS 300/6-8
200 Cleveland Ave 34785 352-748-1510
Chuck Sullivan, prin. Fax 748-7639

Williston, Levy, Pop. 2,508
Levy County SD
Supt. — See Bronson
Williston HS 700/9-12
427 W Noble Ave 32696 352-528-3542
Mike Delucas, prin. Fax 528-2723
Williston MS 600/6-8
20550 NE 42nd Pl 32696 352-528-2941
Ernst Kordgien, prin. Fax 528-2941

Windermere, Orange, Pop. 2,003
Orange County SD
Supt. — See Orlando
Gotha MS 1,800/6-8
9155 Gotha Rd 34786 407-521-2360
Daniel Axtell, prin. Fax 521-2361

Crenshaw S 200/PK-12
PO Box 1159 34786 407-876-9122
Tamie Shuster, prin. Fax 876-9424
Windemere Preparatory S 700/PK-12
6189 State Road 535 34786 407-905-7737
Donna Montague-Russell, prin. Fax 905-7710

Winter Garden, Orange, Pop. 25,500
Orange County SD
Supt. — See Orlando
Lakeview MS 1,600/6-8
1200 W Bay St 34787 407-877-5010
Debra Lucas, prin. Fax 877-5019
West Orange 9th Grade Center 9-9
1625 Beulah Rd 34787 407-905-2400
Edward Jones, prin. Fax 656-4989
West Orange HS 4,100/9-12
1625 Beulah Rd 34787 407-905-2400
Daniel Buckman, prin. Fax 656-4970

Calvary Christian S 200/PK-12
631 S Dillard St 34787 407-656-3001
David Hill, dir. Fax 656-1210
Foundation Academy 600/PK-12
125 E Plant St 34787 407-656-3677
Dr. Russell Richards, admin. Fax 656-0118
Orange Technical Educ. Center-Westside Post-Sec.
955 E Story Rd 34787 407-905-2001

Winter Haven, Polk, Pop. 29,501
Polk County SD
Supt. — See Bartow
Denison MS 1,000/6-8
400 Avenue A SE 33880 863-291-5353
Linda Williams, prin. Fax 291-5347
Jewett Academy 600/6-8
601 Avenue T NE 33881 863-291-5320
Gary McDaniel, prin. Fax 297-3049
Ridge Career Center Vo/Tech
7700 State Road 544 33881 863-419-3060
Lisa Harden, prin. Fax 419-3062
Westwood MS 1,000/6-8
3520 Avenue J NW 33881 863-965-5484
Carolyn Williams, prin. Fax 965-5585
Winter Haven HS 1,800/9-12
600 6th St SE 33880 863-291-5330
Michael Tucker, prin. Fax 297-3024

All Saints' Academy 800/PK-12
5001 State Road 540 W 33880 863-293-5980
Michael Wyman, hdmstr. Fax 294-2819
Haven Christian Academy 200/PK-12
2105 King Rd 33880 863-293-0930
Stace Alcala, prin. Fax 293-0429
Polk Community College Post-Sec.
999 Avenue H NE 33881 863-297-1000
Ridge Vocational-Technical Center Post-Sec.
7700 State Rd 544 33881 863-419-3060

Winter Park, Orange, Pop. 28,179
Orange County SD
Supt. — See Orlando
Winter Park 9th Grade Center 9-9
528 Huntington Ave 32789 407-623-1476
David Stanley, prin. Fax 623-1485
Winter Park HS 3,800/9-12
2100 Summerfield Rd 32792 407-622-3200
Dr. William Gordon, prin. Fax 975-2434
Winter Park Tech Center Vo/Tech
901 W Webster Ave 32789 407-622-2900
Diane Culpepper, prin. Fax 975-2435

Seminole County SD
Supt. — See Sanford
Lake Howell HS 2,000/9-12
4200 Dike Rd 32792 407-320-9050
Dr. Shaune Storch, prin. Fax 320-9025

Central Christian Academy 800/1-12
PO Box 6000 32793 407-332-6988
Leslie Rawle, dir. Fax 332-4413
Central Florida College Post-Sec.
1573 W Fairbanks Ave #100 32789 407-843-3984
Florida Institute of Animal Arts Post-Sec.
3776 Howell Branch Rd 32792 407-657-8088
Full Sail - Real World Education Post-Sec.
3300 University Blvd 32792 407-679-0100
Geneva S 500/PK-12
2025 State Road 436 32792 407-332-6363
Robert Ingram, hdmstr. Fax 332-1664
Herzing College Post-Sec.
1595 S Semoran Blvd #1501 32792 407-478-0500
International Community S 400/PK-12
1021 N New York Ave 32789 407-645-2343
Robyn Terwilleger, prin. Fax 645-2366
Morningstar Academy 900/K-12
1 Purlieu Pl 32792 866-582-2223
Fax 509-7294
Orange Technical Educ. Ctr.-Winter Park Post-Sec.
901 W Webster Ave 32789 407-622-2900
Rollins College Post-Sec.
1000 Holt Ave 32789 407-646-2000
Trinity Prep S 800/6-12
5700 Trinity Prep Ln 32792 407-671-4140
Craig Maughan, hdmstr. Fax 671-6935

Winter Springs, Seminole, Pop. 32,583
Seminole County SD
Supt. — See Sanford
Indian Trails MS 1,500/6-8
415 Tuskawilla Rd 32708 407-320-4350
Eugene Petty, prin. Fax 320-4399
Winter Springs HS 2,600/9-12
130 Tuskawilla Rd 32708 407-320-8750
Michael Blasewitz, prin. Fax 320-8700

Yulee, Nassau, Pop. 6,915
Nassau County SD
Supt. — See Fernandina Beach
Yulee HS 50/9-12
PO Box 160 32041 904-491-7949
Diane Romon, prin. Fax 225-8658
Yulee MS 700/6-8
PO Box 2800 32041 904-491-7944
Deonia Simmons, prin. Fax 225-0104

Zephyrhills, Pasco, Pop. 12,258
Pasco County SD
Supt. — See Land O Lakes
Stewart MS 1,000/6-8
38505 10th Ave, 813-794-6500
Jackson Johnson, prin. Fax 794-6591
Zephyrhills HS 1,500/9-12
6335 12th St, 813-794-6100
Gerri Painter, prin. Fax 794-6191

Zephyrhills Christian Academy 100/PK-12
4781 Allen Rd 33541 813-779-1648
Michael Smith, prin. Fax 799-9829

GEORGIA

GEORGIA DEPARTMENT OF EDUCATION

2054 Twin Towers East, Atlanta 30334
Telephone 404-656-2800
Fax 404-651-6867
Website http://www.doe.k12.ga.us

State Superintendent of Schools Kathy Cox

GEORGIA BOARD OF EDUCATION

2053 Twin Towers East, Atlanta 30334

Chief Executive Officer Kathy Cox

REGIONAL EDUCATIONAL SERVICE AGENCIES (RESA)

Central Savannah River Area RESA
Gene Sullivan, dir. 706-556-6225
PO Box 609, Dearing 30808 Fax 556-8891
www.csraresa.org/resa/

Chattahoochee-Flint RESA
Norman Carter, dir. 229-937-5341
PO Box 1150, Ellaville 31806 Fax 937-5754
www.cfresa.org/

Coastal Plains RESA
Harold Chambers, dir. 229-546-4094
245 N Robinson St, Lenox 31637 Fax 546-4167
www.cpresa.org

First District RESA
Shelly Smith, dir. 912-842-5000
PO Box 780, Brooklet 30415 Fax 842-5161
www.fdresa.org/

Griffin RESA
Dr. Stephanie Gordy, dir. 770-229-3247
PO Box H, Griffin 30224 Fax 228-7316
www.griffinresa.net/

Heart of Georgia RESA
Dr. Charlotte Pipkin, dir. 478-374-2240
1141 Cochran Hwy Fax 374-1524
Eastman 31023
www.hgresa.org/

Metro RESA
Dr. Fran Davis Perkins, dir. 770-432-2404
1870 Teasley Dr SE, Smyrna 30080 Fax 432-6105
www.ciclt.net/mresa

Middle Georgia RESA
Carolyn Williams, dir. 478-475-8630
510 Riley Ave, Fort Valley 31030 Fax 475-8623
www.mgresa.org/

Northeast Georgia RESA
Dr. Russell Cook, dir. 706-742-8292
375 Winter St, Winterville 30683 Fax 742-8928
www.ciclt.net/negaresa/

North Georgia RESA
Larry Harmon, dir. 706-276-1111
4731 Old Highway 5 S Fax 276-1114
Ellijay 30540
www.ngresa.org/

Northwest Georgia RESA
Mona Tucker, dir. 706-295-6189
3167 Cedartown Hwy SE Fax 295-6098
Rome 30161
www.nwgaresa.com/

Oconee RESA
Dr. Mike Walker, dir. 478-552-5178
PO Box 699, Sandersville 31082 Fax 552-6499
www.ga-edtech.org/oconee/

Okefenokee RESA
Dr. Teresa Pack, dir. 912-285-6151
1450 N Augusta Ave Fax 287-6650
Waycross 31503
www.ciclt.net/okresa/

Pioneer RESA
Dr. Sandy Addis, dir. 706-865-2141
PO Box 1789, Cleveland 30528 Fax 865-6748
www.pioneerresa.org/

Southwest Georgia RESA
Kelly Tabb, dir. 229-294-6750
118 McLaughlin St SW Fax 294-6777
Pelham 31779
www.sw-georgia.resa.k12.ga.us

West Georgia RESA
Dr. Ronnie Williams, dir. 770-583-2528
99 Brown School Dr Fax 583-3223
Grantville 30220
www.garesa.org/

PUBLIC, PRIVATE AND CATHOLIC SECONDARY SCHOOLS

Abbeville, Wilcox, Pop. 2,471
Wilcox County SD 1,500/PK-12
103 Broad St N 31001 229-467-2141
Charles Bloodsworth, supt. Fax 467-2302
www.wilcox.k12.ga.us/
Other Schools – See Rochelle

Acworth, Cobb, Pop. 18,428
Cobb County SD
Supt. — See Marietta
Barber MS 6-8
4222 Cantrell Rd NW 30101 770-975-6764
Lisa Williams, prin. Fax 529-0325
Durham MS 1,700/6-8
2891 Mars Hill Rd NW 30101 770-975-6641
Dr. Linda Clark, prin. Fax 975-6643

North Metro Technical College Post-Sec.
5198 Ross Rd SE 30102 770-975-4000

Adairsville, Bartow, Pop. 3,090
Bartow County SD
Supt. — See Cartersville
Adairsville HS 800/9-12
519 Old Highway 41 NW 30103 770-606-5841
Stan Lewis, prin. Fax 773-2722
Adairsville MS 700/6-8
100 College St 30103 770-606-5842
Eddie Chastain, prin. Fax 606-5842

Adel, Cook, Pop. 5,434
Cook County SD 2,500/PK-12
1109 N Parrish Ave 31620 229-896-2294
Dr. Fred Rayfield, supt. Fax 896-3443
www.cook.k12.ga.us/
Cook HS 900/9-12
1200 N Hutchinson Ave 31620 229-896-2213
Charles Bell, prin. Fax 896-3423
Other Schools – See Sparks

Alamo, Wheeler, Pop. 2,451
Wheeler County SD 1,100/PK-12
PO Box 427 30411 912-568-7198
William Clark, supt. Fax 568-1985
www.wheelercountyschools.org
Wheeler County MSHS 600/6-12
RR 1 Box 145 30411 912-568-7166
William Black, prin. Fax 568-7141

Albany, Dougherty, Pop. 75,394
Dougherty County SD 15,700/PK-12
PO Box 1470 31702 229-431-1285
Dr. Sally Whatley, supt. Fax 431-1276
www.docoschools.org
Albany HS 800/9-12
801 W Residence Ave 31701 229-431-3300
Sheila Marshall, prin. Fax 431-3481
Albany MS 600/6-8
1700 Cordell Ave 31705 229-431-3325
Gloria Jones-Baker, prin. Fax 431-3474
Cross MS 600/6-8
324 Lockett Station Rd, 229-431-3362
Dr. Sammie Pringle, prin. Fax 431-3476
Dougherty HS 1,200/9-12
1800 Pearce Ave 31705 229-431-3310
Horace Reid, prin. Fax 431-1302
Dougherty MS 700/6-8
1800 Massey Dr 31705 229-431-3328
Thelma Chunn, prin. Fax 431-3475
Merry Acres MS 800/6-8
1601 Florence Dr 31707 229-431-3338
Dr. Ufot Inyang, prin. Fax 431-1204
Monroe HS 1,000/9-12
900 Lippitt Dr 31701 229-431-3316
Deloris Spears, prin. Fax 431-3380
Radium Springs MS 600/6-8
2600 Radium Springs Rd 31705 229-431-3346
Geraldine Hudley, prin. Fax 431-3552
Southside MS 500/6-8
1615 Newton Rd 31701 229-431-3351
Dr. Johnny Scott, prin. Fax 431-1209
Westover HS 1,300/9-12
2600 Partridge Dr 31707 229-431-3320
Gene Melvin, prin. Fax 431-3349

Albany State University Post-Sec.
504 College Dr 31705 229-430-4600
Albany Technical College Post-Sec.
1704 S Slappey Blvd 31701 229-430-3500
Byne Memorial Baptist Church S 200/PK-12
2832 Ledo Rd 31707 229-436-0173
Jon Davis, hdmstr. Fax 434-0039
Darsey Private S 100/9-12
1201 W Oglethorpe Ave 31707 229-436-5559
C. H. Darsey, prin. Fax 436-0148
Darton College Post-Sec.
2400 Gillionville Rd 31707 229-430-6000
Deerfield-Windsor S 800/PK-12
PO Box 71149 31708 229-435-1301
W.T. Henry, hdmstr. Fax 888-6085
Sherwood Christian Academy 600/PK-12
1418 Old Pretoria Rd, 229-883-5677
Glen Schultz, hdmstr. Fax 883-5794
Turner Job Corps Center Post-Sec.
2000 Schilling Ave 31705 229-883-8500

Alma, Bacon, Pop. 3,361
Bacon County SD 1,900/PK-12
601 N Pierce St 31510 912-632-7363
Richard Wheeler, supt. Fax 632-2454
www.bcraiders.com/
Bacon County HS 500/9-12
901 N Pierce St 31510 912-632-4414
Eddie Mosley, prin. Fax 632-6603
Bacon County MS 400/6-8
901 N Pierce St 31510 912-632-4662
Gavin Vickers, prin. Fax 632-6603

Alpharetta, Fulton, Pop. 40,128
Fulton County SD
Supt. — See Atlanta
Alpharetta HS 1,400/9-12
3595 Webb Bridge Rd 30005 770-521-7640
Bucke Green, prin. Fax 521-7653
Autrey Mill MS 1,000/6-8
4110 Old Alabama Rd 30022 770-521-7622
Dr. Ann Ferrell, prin. Fax 521-7630
Chattahoochee HS 2,000/9-12
5230 Taylor Rd 30022 770-521-7600
Tim Duncan, prin. Fax 521-7659
Haynes Bridge MS 800/6-8
10665 Haynes Bridge Rd 30022 770-740-7030
Debbie Reeves, prin. Fax 667-2842
Holcomb Bridge MS 800/6-8
2700 Holcomb Bridge Rd 30022 770-594-5280
Joy Schroerlucke, prin. Fax 643-3333
Hopewell MS 900/6-8
13060 Cogburn Rd 30004 678-297-3240
Frances Boyd, prin. Fax 297-3250
Milton HS 2,000/9-12
13025 Birmingham Hwy 30004 770-740-7000
Ronald Tesch, prin. Fax 667-2844
Northwestern MS 1,100/6-8
12805 Birmingham Hwy 30004 770-667-2870
Bruce Fraser, prin. Fax 667-2878
Taylor Road MS 900/6-8
5150 Taylor Rd 30022 770-740-7090
Ed Williamson, prin. Fax 619-5609
Webb Bridge MS 1,100/6-8
4455 Webb Bridge Rd 30005 770-667-2940
Elizabeth Fogartie, prin. Fax 667-2948

Bridgeway Christian Academy 400/PK-10
4755 Kimball Bridge Rd 30005 770-751-1972
Linda Miller, hdmstr. Fax 942-1159
DeVry University Post-Sec.
2555 Northwinds Pkwy 30004 770-521-4900
Mill Springs Academy 300/1-12
13660 New Providence Rd 30004 770-360-1336
Robert Moore, pres. Fax 360-1341
Mt. Pisgah Christian S 1,000/PK-12
9820 Nesbit Ferry Rd 30022 678-336-3000
Chris Alexander, hdmstr. Fax 336-3349

Americus, Sumter, Pop. 16,873
Sumter County SD 5,600/PK-12
100 Learning Ln, 229-931-8500
Dr. Dennis McMahon, supt. Fax 931-8555
www.sumterschools.org
Americus Sumpter HS South Campus 1,000/10-12
805 Harrold Ave 31709 229-924-3653
Dr. Larry Moore, prin. Fax 924-1556
Americus Sumter HS North Campus 500/9-9
101 Industrial Blvd, 229-924-5914
Victoria Harris, prin. Fax 928-2827
Staley MS 700/6-8
915 N Lee St, 229-924-3168
Keith Lee, prin. Fax 928-2135
Sumter County MS 600/6-8
439 Bumphead Rd, 229-924-1010
Carolyn Hamilton, prin. Fax 928-5571

Georgia Southwestern State University Post-Sec.
800 Wheatley St 31709 229-928-1279
South Georgia Technical College Post-Sec.
900 S Georgia Tech Pkwy 31709 229-931-2394

Southland Academy 700/PK-12
PO Box 1127 31709 229-924-4406
Adam Smith, prin. Fax 924-2996

Armuchee, Floyd
Floyd County SD
Supt. — See Rome
Armuchee MS 500/6-8
471 Floyd Springs Rd NE 30105 706-378-7924
Bill Gilbert, prin. Fax 378-7983

Ashburn, Turner, Pop. 4,397
Turner County SD 1,800/K-12
PO Box 609 31714 229-567-3338
Ray Jordan, supt. Fax 567-3285
www.turner.k12.ga.us/
Turner County HS 500/9-12
316 Lamar St 31714 229-567-4377
Chad Stone, prin. Fax 567-9243
Turner County MS 400/6-8
316 Lamar St 31714 229-567-4343
Tommy Day, prin. Fax 567-9243

Moultrie Technical College Post-Sec.
222 Rock House Rd 31714

Athens, Clarke, Pop. 102,663
Clarke County SD 11,600/PK-12
PO Box 1708 30603 706-546-7721
James Simms, supt. Fax 369-1804
www.clarke.k12.ga.us
Burney-Harris-Lyons MS 500/6-8
1600 Tallassee Rd 30606 706-548-7208
Robbie Hooker, prin. Fax 357-5263
Cedar Shoals HS 1,600/9-12
1300 Cedar Shoals Dr 30605 706-546-5375
Dr. Tommy Craft, prin. Fax 357-5291
Clarke Central HS 1,500/9-12
350 S Milledge Ave 30605 706-357-5200
Dr. Maxine Easom, prin. Fax 357-5269
Clarke MS 600/6-8
1235 Baxter St 30606 706-543-6547
Dr. Ken Sherman, prin. Fax 548-0257
Coile MS 700/6-8
110 Old Elberton Rd 30601 706-357-5318
Chuck Torbett, prin. Fax 357-5321
Hilsman MS 700/6-8
870 Gaines School Rd 30605 706-548-7281
Dr. Tony Price, prin. Fax 357-5295

Athens Academy 800/PK-12
PO Box 6548 30604 706-549-9225
Robert Chambers, hdmstr. Fax 354-3775
Athens Christian S 800/K-12
1270 Highway 29 N 30601 706-549-7586
Dr. Buhl Cummings, hdmstr. Fax 549-2899
Athens Technical College Post-Sec.
800 Highway 29 N 30601 706-355-5000
Georgia Institute of Cosmetology Post-Sec.
3531 Atlanta Hwy 30606 706-549-6003
Msgr. Walter J. Donovan HS 9-12
590 Lavender Rd 30606 706-433-0223
Geoffray Estes, prin. Fax 433-0229
University of Georgia 30602 Post-Sec.
706-542-3000

Atlanta, Fulton, Pop. 470,688
Atlanta CSD 46,700/PK-12
130 Trinity Ave SW 30303 404-802-2820
Dr. Beverly Hall, supt. Fax 802-1803
www.atlanta.k12.ga.us
Brown MS, 765 Peeples St SW 30310 700/6-8
Dr. Sharon R. Ordu, prin. 404-756-6414
Bunche MS 800/6-8
1925 Niskey Lake Rd SW 30331 404-346-2503
Aaron Fernander, prin. Fax 346-2537
Carson Honors Prep MS 800/6-8
1890 Donald L Hollowell Pky 30318 404-792-5944
Patricia Wells, prin. Fax 792-5924
Coan MS 500/6-8
1550 Hosea L Williams Dr NE 30317 404-371-4854
Dr. Andre Williams, prin. Fax 371-7135
Crim HS 500/9-12
256 Clifton St SE 30317 404-371-4881
Dr. Angelisa Cummings, prin. Fax 371-4889
Douglass HS 2,200/9-12
225 Hamilton E Holmes Dr NW 30318 404-802-3100
J. Austin Brown, prin. Fax 799-8022
Early College HS 500/9-12
55 McDonough Blvd SE 30315 404-802-4405
Marcene Thornton, prin.
Grady HS 1,000/9-12
929 Charles Allen Dr NE 30309 404-802-3001
Dr. Vincent Murray, prin. Fax 853-4099
Harper-Archer MS 6-8
3399 Collier Dr NW 30331 404-699-4794
Michael Milstead, prin. Fax 699-4569
Inman MS 700/6-8
774 Virginia Ave NE 30306 404-802-3200
Dr. Betsy Bockman, prin. Fax 853-4085
Kennedy MS 500/6-8
225 James P Brawley Dr NW 30314 404-802-3600
Linda Cumberlander, prin.
King MS 600/6-8
545 Hill St SE 30312 404-330-4979
Tresa Riney, prin. Fax 330-4196
Long MS 700/6-8
3200 Latona Dr SW 30354 404-802-4800
Dr. Elizabeth Harris, prin. Fax 802-4899
Mays HS 1,800/9-12
3450 Benjamin E Mays Dr SW 30331 404-699-4537
Dr. Tyronne Smith, prin. Fax 699-6781
North Atlanta HS 1,300/9-12
2875 Northside Dr NW 30305 404-351-0895
Scott Bursmith, prin. Fax 351-8763
Parks MS 600/6-8
1090 Windsor St SW 30310 404-752-0742
Christopher Waller, prin. Fax 752-0791
Price MS 900/6-8
1670 Benjamin W Bickers SE 30315 404-624-5128
Sterling Christy, prin. Fax 624-2118
School of Entrepreneurship 9-12
55 McDonough Blvd SE 30315 404-802-4400
Abigail Crawford, prin.
School of Health Sciences & Research 9-12
55 McDonough Blvd SE 30315 404-802-4420
Dr. Darien Jones, prin.
School of Technology 9-12
55 McDonough Blvd SE 30315 404-802-4410
Rodney Ray, prin.
School of the Arts 9-12
55 McDonough Blvd SE 30315 404-802-4415
Dr. Marvin Pryor, prin.
South Atlanta HS 1,300/9-12
2250 Perry Blvd NW 30318 404-362-5057
Esmie Gaynor, prin. Fax 792-5768
Southside HS 1,000/9-12
801 Glenwood Ave SE 30316 404-624-2064
Dr. Shirlene Carter, prin. Fax 624-2111
Sutton MS 700/6-8
4360 Powers Ferry Rd NW 30327 404-256-6920
Mark Mygrant, prin. Fax 705-0100
Sylvan Hills MS 600/6-8
1461 Sylvan Rd SW 30310 404-752-0711
Gwendolyn Atkinson, prin. Fax 756-2290
Therrell HS 1,000/9-12
3099 Panther Trl SW 30311 404-346-2523
Boris Hurst, prin. Fax 346-3097
Turner MS 600/6-8
98 Anderson Ave NW 30314 404-792-5539
Dr. Joyce Clarke, prin.
Walden MS 300/6-8
320 Irwin St NE 30312 404-330-4173
Dr. Flora Goolsby, prin. Fax 521-1596
Washington HS 1,500/9-12
45 Whitehouse Dr SW 30314 404-802-4600
Carter Coleman, prin. Fax 752-6063
Young MS 900/6-8
3116 Benjamin E Mays Dr SW 30311 404-699-4533
Dr. Thomas Kenner, prin. Fax 699-6794
Crim Evening Classes Adult
256 Clifton St SE 30317 404-371-7105
Dr. Angelisa Cummings, prin.
Washington Evening HS Adult
256 Clifton St SE 30317 404-371-7105
Carl Shivers, prin.

DeKalb County SD
Supt. — See Decatur
Chamblee MS 600/7-8
3601 Sexton Woods Dr 30341 678-874-8202
Cynthia Jackson, prin. Fax 874-8210
Cross Keys HS 1,000/9-12
1626 N Druid Hills Rd NE 30319 678-874-6102
Ron Hutcheson, prin. Fax 874-6110
DeKalb S of the Arts 300/8-12
2415 N Druid Hills Rd NE 30329 678-676-2502
Susan McCauley, prin. Fax 676-2510
Lakeside HS 1,400/9-12
3801 Briarcliff Rd NE 30345 678-874-6702
Wayne Chelf, prin. Fax 874-6710
McNair HS 1,200/9-12
1804 Bouldercrest Rd SE 30316 678-874-4902
Chris Beal, prin. Fax 874-4910
Open Campus SHS 800/11-12
2415 N Druid Hills Rd NE 30329 678-676-2602
Mattie Small, prin. Fax 676-2610

Fulton County SD 72,500/PK-12
786 Cleveland Ave SW 30315 404-768-3600
James Wilson, supt. Fax 763-6798
www.fultonschools.org
North Springs HS 1,800/9-12
7447 Roswell Rd NE 30328 770-551-2490
Vicky Ferguson, prin. Fax 551-2498
Ridgeview MS 600/6-8
5340 Trimble Rd NE 30342 404-843-7710
Fax 847-3292
Riverwood HS 1,300/9-12
5900 Heards Dr NW 30328 404-847-1980
Edward Echols, prin. Fax 255-8709
Sandtown MS 1,100/6-8
5400 Campbellton Rd SW 30331 404-346-6500
Kine Geathers, prin. Fax 346-6510
Sandy Springs MS 700/6-8
8750 Colonel Dr 30350 770-552-4970
Kay Walker, prin. Fax 643-3334
Westlake HS 1,300/9-12
2370 Union Rd SW 30331 404-346-6400
Sandra McGary-Ervin, prin. Fax 346-6410
Other Schools – See Alpharetta, College Park, Duluth, East Point, Fairburn, Roswell

---

American InterContinental University Post-Sec.
6600 Peachtree Dunwoody Rd 30328 404-965-6500
American InterContinental University Post-Sec.
3330 Peachtree Rd NE 30326 404-965-5700
Argosy University/Atlanta Post-Sec.
980 Hammond Dr NE Ste 100 30328 770-671-1200
Art Institute of Atlanta Post-Sec.
6600 Peachtree Dunwoody Rd 30328 800-275-4242
Atlanta International S 900/PK-12
2890 N Fulton Dr NE 30305 404-841-3840
Robert Brindley, hdmstr. Fax 841-3873
Atlanta Job Corps Center Post-Sec.
239 W Lake Ave NW 30314 404-794-9512
Atlanta Medical Center Post-Sec.
303 Parkway Dr NE 30312 404-265-4203
Atlanta Metro College Post-Sec.
1630 Metropolitan Pkwy SW 30310 404-756-4000
Atlanta School of Massage Post-Sec.
2 Dunwoody Park 30338 770-454-7167
Atlanta Technical College Post-Sec.
1560 Metropolitan Pkwy SW 30310 404-756-3700
Bauder College Post-Sec.
384 Northyards Blvd NW #190 30313 404-237-7573
Beulah Heights University Post-Sec.
PO Box 18145 30316 404-627-2681
Brandon Hall S 100/4-12
1701 Brandon Hall Dr 30350 770-394-8177
Paul Stockhammer, pres. Fax 804-8821
Brown Coll. of Court Reporting & Med. Post-Sec.
1740 Peachtree St NW 30309 404-876-1227
Brown Mackie College Post-Sec.
6600 Peachtree Dunwoody NE 30328 770-638-0121
Carver Bible College Post-Sec.
3870 Cascade Rd SW 30331 404-527-4520
Clark Atlanta University Post-Sec.
223 James P Brawley Dr SW 30314 404-880-8000
Creative Circus Post-Sec.
812 Lambert Dr NE 30324 404-607-8880
DeVry University Post-Sec.
2 Ravinia Dr Ste 350 30346 770-671-1744
DeVry University Post-Sec.
100 Galleria Pkwy SE #100 30339 678-424-5630
Emory University Post-Sec.
200B Jones Ctr 30322 404-727-6123
Emory University Hospital Post-Sec.
1364 Clifton Rd NE 30322 404-712-4881
Everest Institute Post-Sec.
101 Marietta St NW Ste 600 30303 404-525-1111
Everest Institute Post-Sec.
1706 Northeast Expy NE 30329 404-327-8787
Franklin Academy 100/9-12
1585 Clifton Rd NE 30329 404-633-7404
Wood Smethurst, hdmstr. Fax 321-0610
Galloway S 700/PK-12
215 W Wieuca Rd NW 30342 404-252-8389
Tom Brereton, hdmstr. Fax 252-7770
Georgia Institute of Technology Post-Sec.
225 North Ave NW 30332 404-894-2000
Georgia State University Post-Sec.
PO Box 4009 30302 404-651-2000
Grady Health System Post-Sec.
PO Box 26189 30303 404-616-4252
Greater Atlanta Adventist Academy 100/9-12
401 Hamilton E Holmes Dr NW 30318 404-799-0337
Fax 799-0977
Herzing College Post-Sec.
3393 Peachtree Rd NE # 1003 30326 404-816-4533
Holy Innocents' Episcopal S 1,300/PK-12
805 Mount Vernon Hwy NW 30327 404-255-4026
Kirk Duncan, hdmstr. Fax 250-0815
Holy Spirit Preparatory S PK-12
4449 Northside Dr NW 30327 678-904-2811
Gareth Genner, prin. Fax 904-4983
Howard S 200/PK-12
1192 Foster St NW 30318 404-377-7436
Marifred Cilella, hdmstr. Fax 377-0884
Interdenominational Theological Center Post-Sec.
700 Mrtn Lthr King Jr Dr SW 30314 404-527-7700
International School of Skin/Nailcare Post-Sec.
5600 Roswell Rd NE 30342 404-843-1005
Javelin Technical Training Center Post-Sec.
4501 Circle 75 Ste C-3180 30339 770-859-9779
Lovett S 1,500/K-12
4075 Paces Ferry Rd NW 30327 404-262-3032
Dr. William Peeble, hdmstr. Fax 261-1967
Marist HS 1,000/7-12
3790 Ashford Dunwoody Rd NE 30319
770-457-7201
Fr. Joel Konzen, prin. Fax 457-8402
Mercer University in Atlanta Post-Sec.
3001 Mercer University Dr 30341 678-547-6000
Mohammed Schools of Atlanta 200/PK-12
735 Fayetteville Rd SE 30316 404-378-4219
Safiyyah Shahid, prin. Fax 378-4600
Morehouse College Post-Sec.
830 Westview Dr SW 30314 404-681-2800
Morehouse School of Medicine Post-Sec.
720 Westview Dr SW 30310 404-752-1500
Mt. Vernon Presbyterian S 700/PK-12
471 Mount Vernon Hwy NE 30328 404-252-3448
Dr. Jeff Jackson, hdmstr. Fax 252-6777
Oglethorpe University Post-Sec.
4484 Peachtree Rd NE 30319 404-261-1441
Pace Academy 900/K-12
966 W Paces Ferry Rd NW 30327 404-262-1345
Fred Assaf, hdmstr. Fax 264-9376
Paideia S 900/PK-12
1509 Ponce De Leon Ave NE 30307 404-377-3491
Paul Bianchi, hdmstr. Fax 377-0032
Portfolio Center Post-Sec.
125 Bennett St NW 30309 404-351-5055
Rising Spirit Inst. of Natural Health Post-Sec.
4536 Chamblee Dunwoody Rd 30338 770-457-2021
St. Joseph's Hospital Post-Sec.
5665 Pchtree Dunwoody Rd NE 30342
404-851-7120
St. Pius X HS 1,000/9-12
2674 Johnson Rd NE 30345 404-636-3023
Steven Spellman, prin. Fax 633-8387
Savannah College of Art and Design Post-Sec.
PO Box 77300 30357 404-253-2700
Southwest Atlanta Christian Academy 300/PK-12
PO Box 310750 31131 404-346-2080
Geraldine Thompson, hdmstr. Fax 346-2085
Spelman College Post-Sec.
350 Spelman Ln SW 30314 800-982-2411
Strayer University Post-Sec.
3355 Northeast Expy NE #100 30341 770-454-9270
Strayer University Post-Sec.
3101 TowerCreek Pkwy SE 700 30339 770-612-2170
Temima HS 100/9-12
1985B Lavista Rd NE 30329 404-315-0507
Miriam Feldman, prin. Fax 634-2111
The Psychological Studies Institute Post-Sec.
2055 Mount Paran Rd NW 30327 404-233-3949
Ultrasound Diagnostic School Post-Sec.
1140 Hammond Dr NE # 8-1150 30328
404-248-9070
Weber Jewish Community HS 200/9-12
6751 Roswell Rd NE 30328 404-917-2500
Sim Pearl, hdmstr. Fax 917-2501
Westminster S 1,800/K-12
1424 W Paces Ferry Rd NW 30327 404-355-8673
William Clarkson, pres. Fax 355-6606
Westwood College Post-Sec.
1100 Spring St NW Ste 102 30309 404-745-9096
Westwood College Post-Sec.
2220 Parklake Dr NE 30345 404-962-2999
Yeshiva Atlanta HS 100/9-12
3130 Raymond Dr 30340 770-451-5299
Dewey Holbrook, prin. Fax 451-5571
Yeshiva Ohr Yisroel 50/9-12
1810 Briarcliff Rd NE 30329 404-320-1444
Rabbi Mayer Neuberger, dir. Fax 320-1609

Augusta, Richmond, Pop. 193,101
Richmond County SD 33,300/PK-12
864 Broad St 30901 706-826-1000
Dr. Charles Larke, supt. Fax 826-4613
www.rcboe.org
Academy of Richmond County Comp. HS 1,400/9-12
910 Russell St 30904 706-737-7152
David Robbins, prin. Fax 737-7155
Butler Comprehensive HS 1,200/9-12
2011 Lumpkin Rd 30906 706-796-4959
Walter Reeves, prin. Fax 796-4780
Cross Creek HS 1,300/9-12
3855 Old Waynesboro Rd 30906 706-772-8140
Lynn Warr, prin. Fax 772-8153
Davidson Magnet JSHS 700/6-12
615 12th St 30901 706-823-6924
Vicky Addison, prin. Fax 823-4373
East Augusta MS 500/6-8
320 Kentucky Ave 30901 706-823-6960
Dr. Velma Curtis, prin. Fax 823-6963
Glenn Hills HS 1,200/9-12
2840 Glenn Hills Dr 30906 706-796-4924
Jessie Chambers, prin. Fax 796-4932
Glenn Hills MS 1,100/6-8
2941 Glenn Hills Dr 30906 706-796-4705
Hartley Gibbons, prin. Fax 796-4716

Johnson Health Professions HS 400/9-12
1324 Laney Walker Blvd 30901 706-823-6933
Deborah Walker, prin. Fax 823-6931
Josey Comprehensive HS 1,000/9-12
1701 15th St 30901 706-737-7360
Quentin Motley, prin. Fax 737-7363
Laney Comprehensive HS 600/9-12
1339 Laney Walker Blvd 30901 706-823-6900
Dr. Hawthorne Welcher, prin. Fax 823-6918
Langford MS 700/6-8
3019 Walton Way Ext 30909 706-737-7301
Cheryl Fry, prin. Fax 737-7302
Murphey MS 700/6-8
2610 Milledgeville Rd 30904 706-737-7350
Dorothy James, prin. Fax 737-7353
Sego MS 900/6-8
3420 Julia Ave 30906 706-796-4944
Dr. Ronald Wiggins, prin. Fax 796-4670
Tubman MS 600/6-8
1740 Walton Way 30904 706-737-7250
Rickey Lumpkin, prin. Fax 737-7246
Tutt MS 600/6-8
495 Boy Scout Rd 30909 706-737-7288
Dr. Debbie Alexander, prin. Fax 481-1620
Westside HS 800/9-12
1002 Patriots Way 30907 706-868-4030
Tim Spivey, prin. Fax 868-4005
Evening S Adult
3015 Walton Way Ext 30909 706-731-8805
Winnette Bradley, prin. Fax 737-7271
Other Schools – See Hephzibah

Alleluia Community S 200/K-12
2819 Peach Orchard Rd 30906 706-793-9663
Dan Funsch, prin. Fax 560-2759
Aquinas HS 300/9-12
1920 Highland Ave 30904 706-736-5516
Robert Larcher, prin. Fax 736-2678
Augusta State University Post-Sec.
2500 Walton Way 30904 706-737-1400
Augusta Technical College Post-Sec.
3116 Deans Bridge Rd 30906 706-771-4000
Curtis Baptist S 400/PK-12
1326 Broad St 30901 706-722-5252
Philip Musgrave, hdmstr. Fax 722-1881
Georgia Institute of Cosmetology Post-Sec.
2803 Wrightsboro Rd 30909
Medical College of Georgia Post-Sec.
1120 15th St 30912 706-721-0211
New Life Christian Academy 50/K-12
3336 Wrightsboro Rd Ste 3 30909 706-738-2526
Linda Dunaway, admin.
Paine College Post-Sec.
1235 15th St 30901 800-476-7703
Savannah River College Post-Sec.
2528 Center West Pkwy # A 30909 706-738-5046
University Hospital Health System Post-Sec.
1350 Walton Way 30901 706-722-9011
Westminster S of Augusta 500/PK-12
3067 Wheeler Rd 30909 706-731-7780
Jim Adare, hdmstr. Fax 731-5274

Austell, Cobb, Pop. 6,566
Cobb County SD
Supt. — See Marietta
Cooper MS 1,100/6-8
4605 Ewing Rd 30106 770-819-2438
Peggy Martin, prin. Fax 819-2440
Garrett MS 900/6-8
5235 Powder Springs Rd 30106 770-819-2466
Dr. Phillip Page, prin. Fax 819-2468
South Cobb HS 2,100/9-12
1920 Clay Rd 30106 770-819-2611
Dr. Grant Rivera, prin. Fax 819-2613

Avondale Estates, DeKalb, Pop. 2,623
DeKalb County SD
Supt. — See Decatur
Avondale HS 1,000/9-12
1192 Clarendon Ave 30002 678-874-0402
Mike Worthington, prin. Fax 874-0410
Avondale MS 900/6-8
3131 Old Rockbridge Rd 30002 678-875-0102
Bernetta Jordan, prin. Fax 875-0110

Bainbridge, Decatur, Pop. 11,874
Decatur County SD 5,700/PK-12
100 S West St, 229-248-2200
Ralph Jones, supt. Fax 248-2252
www.dcboe.com
Bainbridge HS 1,600/9-12
1301 E College St, 229-248-2230
Tommie Howell, prin. Fax 248-2260
Hutto MS 700/6-8
1201 Martin Luther King Jr, 229-248-2224
Dr. Marvin Thomas, prin. Fax 243-5303
West Bainbridge MS 700/6-8
1417 Dothan Rd, 229-248-2206
Robert McIntosh, prin. Fax 248-2270

Bainbridge College Post-Sec.
2500 E Shotwell St, 229-248-2500
Grace Christian Academy 300/PK-12
PO Box 1930, 229-243-8851
Dennis Moore, prin. Fax 243-0515

Barnesville, Lamar, Pop. 5,808
Lamar County SD 2,500/PK-12
3 Trojan Way 30204 770-358-5891
Dr. Bill Truby, supt. Fax 358-5897
www.lamar.k12.ga.us
Lamar County Comprehensive HS 800/9-12
1 Trojan Way 30204 770-358-8641
Charles Bonner, prin. Fax 358-8649
Lamar County MS 600/6-8
100 Burnette Rd 30204 770-358-8652
Diane Harvey, prin. Fax 358-8657

Gordon College Post-Sec.
419 College Dr 30204 770-358-5000
Liberty Christian Academy 50/PK-12
619 Old Milner Rd 30204 770-358-7300
Jonathan English, prin.

Baxley, Appling, Pop. 4,402
Appling County SD 3,400/PK-12
249 Blackshear Hwy 31513 912-367-8600
Dr. Charles Webb, supt. Fax 367-1011
www.appling.k12.ga.us
Appling County HS 900/9-12
482 Blackshear Hwy 31513 912-367-8610
Phil Murphy, prin. Fax 366-9877

Appling County MS 800/6-8
2997 Blackshear Hwy 31513 912-367-8630
Dr. Keith Johnson, prin. Fax 367-8803

Bellville, Evans, Pop. 139

Pinewood Christian Academy 600/K-12
PO Box 7 30414 912-739-1272
Dewey Hulsey, hdmstr. Fax 739-2321

Blackshear, Pierce, Pop. 3,421
Pierce County SD 3,400/PK-12
PO Box 349 31516 912-449-2044
Dr. Joy B. Williams, supt. Fax 449-2046
www.pierce.k12.ga.us/
Pierce County HS 900/9-12
4850 County Farm Rd 31516 912-449-2055
Anthony Smith, prin. Fax 449-2061
Pierce County MS 800/6-8
5216 County Farm Rd 31516 912-449-2077
Terri DeLoach, prin. Fax 449-2075

Blairsville, Union, Pop. 683
Towns County SD
Supt. — See Hiawassee
Mountain Education Center Adult
218 School St 30512 706-745-9575
Wade Smith, prin. Fax 745-3588

Union County SD 2,600/K-12
10 Hughes St 30512 706-745-2322
Tommy Stephens, supt. Fax 745-5025
www.union.k12.ga.us
Union County HS 800/9-12
604 Panther Cir 30512 706-745-2216
Ed Rohrbaugh, prin. Fax 745-4122
Union County MS 600/6-8
401 Wellborn Dr 30512 706-745-2483
Karen Roxbury, prin. Fax 745-3920
Other Schools – See Suches

North Georgia Technical College Post-Sec.
434 Meeks Ave 30512 706-781-2300

Blakely, Early, Pop. 5,476
Early County SD 2,600/PK-12
11927 Columbia St, 229-723-4337
Betty Orange, supt. Fax 723-8183
www.early.k12.ga.us
Early County HS 800/9-12
12020 Columbia St, 229-723-3006
Jim Morrell, prin. Fax 723-8690
Early County MS 600/6-8
12053 Columbia St, 229-723-3746
Anthony Yarbrough, prin. Fax 723-3942

Blue Ridge, Fannin, Pop. 1,089
Fannin County SD 3,200/K-12
2290 E First St 30513 706-632-3771
Sandra Mercier, supt. Fax 632-7583
www.fannin.k12.ga.us
Fannin County Career & Technology Center Vo/Tech
2346 E 1st St 30513 706-632-2013
Jeff Wilbanks, dir. Fax 632-6552
Fannin County Comprehensive HS 1,000/9-12
360 Rebels Cir 30513 706-632-2081
Douglas Davenport, prin. Fax 632-4442
Fannin County MS 700/6-8
4560 Old Highway 76 30513 706-632-6100
Angela Berrong, prin. Fax 632-0461

Bogart, Clarke, Pop. 1,094
Oconee County SD
Supt. — See Watkinsville
Malcom Bridge MS 500/6-8
2500 Malcom Bridge Rd 30622 770-725-2319
Tom Odom, prin. Fax 725-0961
North Oconee HS 400/9-12
1081 Rocky Branch Rd 30622 706-769-7760
John Osborne, prin. Fax 769-4766

Prince Avenue Christian S 500/K-12
2201 Ruth Jackson Rd 30622 706-353-1993
Dr. Wendell Murray, hdmstr. Fax 613-7553

Bonaire, Houston
Houston County SD
Supt. — See Perry
Bonaire MS 1,000/6-8
125 GA Highway 96 31005 478-929-6236
Cindy Randall, prin. Fax 929-6245

Bowdon, Carroll, Pop. 1,963
Carroll County SD
Supt. — See Carrollton
Bowdon HS 400/9-12
504 W College St 30108 770-258-5408
Chuck Taylor, prin. Fax 258-7278
Jonesville MS 500/6-8
129 N Jonesville Rd 30108 770-258-1778
Barry Williams, prin. Fax 258-4374
Open Campus HS Adult
225 E College St 30108 770-258-4403
Dot Sayer, prin. Fax 258-8205

Bremen, Haralson, Pop. 5,350
Bremen CSD 1,700/PK-12
504 Laurel St 30110 770-537-5508
Dr. Stanley McCain, supt. Fax 537-0610
www.bremencs.com
Bremen HS 500/9-12
504 Georgia Ave S 30110 770-537-2592
Duane McManus, prin. Fax 537-0714
Sewell MS 400/6-8
515 Laurel St 30110 770-537-4874
Duane McManus, prin. Fax 537-5043

Brooklet, Bulloch, Pop. 1,176
Bulloch County SD
Supt. — See Statesboro
Southeast Bulloch HS 800/9-12
9184 Brooklet Denmark Rd 30415 912-842-2131
Joni Walker-Seier, prin. Fax 842-9411
Southeast Bulloch MS 600/6-8
9124 Brooklet Denmark Rd 30415 912-842-9555
Alan Putz, prin. Fax 842-9559

Brunswick, Glynn, Pop. 15,956
Glynn County SD 12,000/PK-12
PO Box 1677 31521 912-267-4100
Dr. Michael Bull, supt. Fax 265-2011
www.glynn.k12.ga.us

Brunswick HS 1,700/9-12
3920 Habersham St 31520 912-267-4200
Terry Graff, prin. Fax 261-4433
Glynn Academy 1,800/9-12
PO Box 1678 31521 912-267-4210
Baker Davis, prin. Fax 267-4246
Glynn MS 700/6-8
901 George St 31520 912-267-4150
Ricky Rentz, prin. Fax 267-4158
Macon MS 800/6-8
3885 Altama Ave 31520 912-265-3337
Scott Spence, prin. Fax 267-4118
Needwood MS 800/6-8
669 Harry Driggers Blvd 31525 912-261-4488
Dr. Joan Boorman, prin. Fax 261-4491
Performance Learning Center 9-12
1410 I St 31520 912-267-4225
Sheila Spaulding-Wingard, prin. Fax 261-3549
Risley MS 500/6-8
2900 Albany St 31520 912-267-4160
Dr. Valerie Cave, prin. Fax 267-4161

Brunswick Christian Academy 200/PK-12
4231 US Highway 17 N 31525 912-264-4546
Vonda Harrington, prin. Fax 264-0851
Coastal Georgia Community College Post-Sec.
3700 Altama Ave 31520 912-264-7235
Emmanuel Christian S 100/K-12
1010 Old Jesup Rd 31520 912-265-9647
Benny Waldron, prin. Fax 265-9647
Heritage Christian Academy 200/PK-12
4265 Norwich Street Ext 31520 912-264-5491
Cynthia Zangla, admin. Fax 264-0799

Buchanan, Haralson, Pop. 1,018
Haralson County SD 3,800/PK-12
10 Van Wert St 30113 770-646-3882
Larry Ragsdale, supt. Fax 646-8628
www.haralson.k12.ga.us
Other Schools – See Tallapoosa

Buena Vista, Marion, Pop. 1,697
Marion County SD 1,700/PK-12
PO Box 391 31803 229-649-2234
Richard McCorkle, supt. Fax 649-7423
www.marion.k12.ga.us/
Marion County HS 500/9-12
PO Box 177 31803 229-649-7520
Glenn Tidwell, prin. Fax 649-5945
Marion MS 500/5-8
PO Box 16 31803 229-649-2145
Janie Downer, prin. Fax 649-5570

Buford, Gwinnett, Pop. 10,972
Buford CSD 2,400/K-12
70 Wiley Dr Ste 200 30518 770-945-5035
Dr. Geye Hamby, supt. Fax 945-4629
www.bufordcityschools.org
Buford HS 700/9-12
2750 Sawnee Ave 30518 770-945-6768
Steve Miller, prin. Fax 932-7570
Buford MS 600/6-8
2700 Robert Bell Pkwy 30518 770-904-3690
Rachel Adams, prin. Fax 904-3689

Gwinnett County SD
Supt. — See Suwanee
Jones MS 900/6-8
3575 Ridge Rd 30519 770-904-5450
Dr. Richard Holland, prin. Fax 904-5452
Lanier MS 2,100/6-8
918 Buford Hwy 30518 770-945-8419
Jaime Espinosa, prin. Fax 271-5108

Butler, Taylor, Pop. 1,888
Taylor County SD 1,500/PK-12
PO Box 1930 31006 478-862-5224
Wayne Smith, supt. Fax 862-5818
www.taylor.k12.ga.us
Taylor County HS 400/9-12
PO Box 1927 31006 478-862-3314
Clarence Mathise, prin. Fax 862-5818
Taylor County MS 300/6-8
PO Box 580 31006 478-862-5285
Anzy Hardman, prin. Fax 862-5368

Byron, Peach, Pop. 3,251
Peach County SD
Supt. — See Fort Valley
Byron MS 500/6-8
201 Linda Dr 31008 478-956-4999
Ken Banter, prin. Fax 956-3916

Cairo, Grady, Pop. 9,389
Grady County SD 4,500/PK-12
122 N Broad St, 229-377-3701
Steven A. Wooten, supt. Fax 377-3437
www.grady.k12.ga.us
Cairo HS 1,200/9-12
455 5th St SE, 229-377-2222
Tim Helms, prin. Fax 377-2812
Washington MS 700/6-8
1277 Booker Hill Blvd SW, 229-377-2106
Arthur Anderson, prin. Fax 377-7779

Calhoun, Gordon, Pop. 13,570
Calhoun CSD 3,100/PK-12
380 Barrett Rd 30701 706-629-2900
Mike Davis, supt. Fax 629-3235
www.calhounschools.org
Calhoun HS 700/9-12
315 S River St 30701 706-629-9213
Wanda Westmoreland, prin. Fax 602-6652
Calhoun MS 700/6-8
399 S River St 30701 706-629-3340
Bob Orfield, prin. Fax 629-0236

Gordon County SD 6,400/PK-12
PO Box 12001 30703 706-629-7366
Mike Stanton, supt. Fax 625-5671
www.gcbe.org
Ashworth MS 700/6-8
PO Box 12001 30703 706-625-9545
Dr. Chris Richie, prin. Fax 625-0114
Gordon Central HS 1,700/9-12
PO Box 12001 30703 706-629-7391
Clark Maggart, prin. Fax 625-5376
Sonoraville East MS 800/6-8
PO Box 12001 30703 706-629-0793
Theresa Ford, prin. Fax 629-2983
Sonoraville HS 9-12
PO Box 12001 30703 706-602-0320
Bruce Potts, prin. Fax 602-0321

Coosa Valley Technical College — Post-Sec.
1151 Highway 53 Spur SW 30701
Georgia Cumberland Academy — 200/9-12
397 Academy Dr SW 30701 — 706-629-4591
Greg Gerard, prin. — Fax 629-1272

Camilla, Mitchell, Pop. 5,616
Mitchell County SD — 2,300/PK-12
108 S Harney St 31730 — 229-336-2100
Beauford Hicks, supt. — Fax 336-1615
www.mitchell.k12.ga.us
Mitchell County HS — 700/9-12
1000 Newton Rd 31730 — 229-336-0970
Robert Adams, prin. — Fax 336-2171
Mitchell County MS — 500/6-8
55 Griffin Rd 31730 — 229-336-0980
Rodney Bullard, prin. — Fax 336-2139

Westwood S — 400/PK-12
255 Fuller St 31730 — 229-336-7992
Ralph Worsham, hdmstr. — Fax 336-0982

Canton, Cherokee, Pop. 17,685
Cherokee County SD — 29,900/PK-12
PO Box 769, — 770-479-1871
Dr. Frank Petruzielo, supt. — Fax 479-7758
www.cherokee.k12.ga.us
Cherokee HS — 2,100/9-12
930 Marietta Hwy 30114 — 770-479-4112
Pam Biser, prin. — Fax 479-8421
Creekland MS — 900/6-8
1555 Owens Store Rd 30115 — 770-479-3200
Dr. Deborah Wiseman, prin. — Fax 479-3210
Creekview HS — 9-12
1550 Owens Store Rd 30115 — 770-720-7600
Bob Eddy, prin.
Freedom MS — 7-8
10550 Bells Ferry Rd 30114 — 770-345-4100
Dr. Lou Manzella, prin. — Fax 345-4140
Rusk MS — 800/7-8
4695 Hickory Rd 30115 — 770-345-2832
Elaine Daniel, prin. — Fax 345-5073
Sequoyah HS — 2,100/9-12
4485 Hickory Rd 30115 — 770-345-1474
Elliott Berman, prin. — Fax 345-5498
Teasley MS — 1,000/7-8
8871 Knox Bridge Hwy 30114 — 770-479-7077
Lory Hill, prin. — Fax 479-3275
Other Schools – See Woodstock

Carnesville, Franklin, Pop. 617
Franklin County SD — 3,800/K-12
PO Box 99 30521 — 706-384-4554
Dr. Ric Ayer, supt. — Fax 384-7472
www.franklin.k12.ga.us
Franklin County HS — 1,100/9-12
PO Box 543 30521 — 706-384-4525
Diane Toney, prin. — Fax 384-2201
Franklin County MS — 1,000/6-8
PO Box 544 30521 — 706-384-4581
Lucy Floyd, prin. — Fax 384-2284

Carrollton, Carroll, Pop. 21,837
Carroll County SD — 13,600/PK-12
164 Independence Dr 30116 — 770-832-3568
John Zauner, supt. — Fax 834-6399
www.carrollcountyschools.com/
Central HS — 1,200/9-12
113 Central High Rd 30116 — 770-834-3386
Gail Stewart, prin. — Fax 832-0103
Central MS — 1,000/6-8
155 Whooping Creek Rd 30116 — 770-832-8114
Terry Jones, prin. — Fax 836-2782
Technical HS of Carroll Co. — Vo/Tech
1075 Newnan Rd 30116 — 770-832-8380
Cindy Clanton, prin. — Fax 830-5037
Other Schools – See Bowdon, Mount Zion, Temple, Villa Rica

Carrollton CSD — 3,000/K-12
106 Trojan Dr 30117 — 770-832-9633
Thomas Wilson, supt. — Fax 836-2830
www.carrolltoncityschools.net/
Carrollton HS — 1,100/9-12
202 Trojan Dr 30117 — 770-834-7726
Dr. Kent Edwards, prin. — Fax 834-8714
Carrollton JHS — 800/6-8
510 Ben Scott Blvd 30117 — 770-832-6535
David Hicks, prin. — Fax 832-7003

Oak Mountain Academy — 200/K-12
222 Cross Plains Rd 30116 — 770-834-6651
Ricky Parmer, hdmstr. — Fax 834-6785
University of West Georgia 30118 — Post-Sec.
770-836-6500
West Central Technical College — Post-Sec.
997 Newnan Rd 30116 — 770-836-6800

Cartersville, Bartow, Pop. 17,653
Bartow County SD — 9,100/PK-12
PO Box 200007 30120 — 770-606-5800
Dr. Abbe Boring, supt. — Fax 606-5857
www.bartow.k12.ga.us
Cass HS — 1,300/9-12
738 Grassdale Rd NW 30121 — 770-606-5845
Mike Nelson, prin. — Fax 606-3825
Cass MS — 1,000/6-8
195 Fire Tower Rd NW 30120 — 770-606-5846
Kristy Arnold, prin. — Fax 606-3835
Woodland HS — 1,800/8-12
800 Old Alabama Rd SE 30120 — 770-606-5870
Paul Sabin, prin. — Fax 606-2080
Other Schools – See Adairsville, Emerson, Kingston

Cartersville CSD — 3,900/PK-12
PO Box 3310 30120 — 770-382-5880
Dr. J. Howard Hinesley, supt. — Fax 387-7476
www.cartersville.k12.ga.us
Cartersville HS — 1,100/9-12
320 E Church St 30120 — 770-382-3200
Jay Floyd, prin. — Fax 382-0701
Cartersville MS — 900/6-8
825 Douthit Ferry Rd 30120 — 770-382-3666
Jeff Hogan, prin. — Fax 387-7495

Excel Christian Academy — 400/K-12
325 Old Mill Rd 30120 — 770-382-9488
A. Tommy Harris, admin. — Fax 606-9884

Cave Spring, Floyd, Pop. 997

Georgia School for the Deaf — Post-Sec.
232 Perry Farm Rd SW 30124 — 706-777-2200

Cedartown, Polk, Pop. 9,771
Polk County SD — 7,100/PK-12
PO Box 128 30125 — 770-748-3821
Dr. Darrell Sorrells, supt. — Fax 748-5131
www.polk.k12.ga.us/
Cedartown HS — 1,100/9-12
167 Frank Lott Dr 30125 — 770-748-0490
Dr. Ken Prichard, prin. — Fax 749-1872
Cedartown MS — 1,000/6-8
1664 W Syble Brannon Pkwy 30125 — 770-749-8850
Lucy Cromer, prin. — Fax 749-2795
Other Schools – See Rockmart

Vineyard Harvester Christian Academy — 100/K-12
PO Box 687 30125 — 770-748-9320
David Huskins, hdmstr. — Fax 748-5374

Centerville, Houston, Pop. 6,624
Houston County SD
Supt. — See Perry
Thomson MS — 900/6-8
301 Thomson St 31028 — 478-953-0489
Tammy Dunn, prin. — Fax 953-0484

Chamblee, DeKalb, Pop. 9,763
DeKalb County SD
Supt. — See Decatur
Henderson MS — 1,100/6-8
2830 Henderson Mill Rd 30341 — 678-874-2902
Terese Allen, prin. — Fax 874-2910

Interactive College of Technology — Post-Sec.
5303 New Peachtree Rd 30341 — 770-216-2960

Chatsworth, Murray, Pop. 3,924
Murray County SD — 7,600/PK-12
PO Box 40 30705 — 706-695-4531
Dr. Vickie Reed, supt. — Fax 695-8425
www.murray.k12.ga.us
Bagley MS — 1,100/6-8
4600 Highway 225 N 30705 — 706-695-1115
Gina Linder, prin. — Fax 695-7289
Gladden MS — 700/6-8
700 Old Dalton Ellijay Rd 30705 — 706-695-7448
Dr. Maria Bradley, prin. — Fax 517-2479
Murray County HS — 1,900/9-12
1001 Green Rd 30705 — 706-695-1414
Jason Doughty, prin. — Fax 517-2625
Adult Education — Adult
273 Harris St 30705 — 706-695-4641
Joe Jackson, prin. — Fax 695-9103

Chickamauga, Walker, Pop. 2,497
Chickamauga CSD — 1,300/K-12
402 Cove Rd 30707 — 706-382-3100
Melody Day, supt. — Fax 375-5364
www.chickamaugacityschools.org/
Lee HS — 500/9-12
105 Lee Cir 30707 — 706-382-3100
Randall Barker, prin. — Fax 375-4103
Lee MS — 300/6-8
300 Crescent Ave 30707 — 706-382-3100
Kristen Bradley, prin. — Fax 375-7988

Chula, Tift

Tiftarea Academy — 600/PK-12
PO Box 10 31733 — 229-382-0436
Ron Drummonds, prin. — Fax 382-7742

Clarkesville, Habersham, Pop. 1,505
Habersham County SD — 5,200/PK-12
PO Box 70 30523 — 706-754-2118
Dr. Judy C. Forbes, supt. — Fax 754-1549
www.habershamschools.com/
North Habersham MS — 500/7-8
1500 Wall Bridge Rd 30523 — 706-754-2915
Dr. Ben Desper, prin. — Fax 754-8218
Other Schools – See Cornelia, Demorest, Mount Airy

North Georgia Technical College — Post-Sec.
PO Box 65 30523 — 706-754-7700

Clarkston, DeKalb, Pop. 7,078
DeKalb County SD
Supt. — See Decatur
Clarkston HS — 1,200/7-12
618 N Indian Creek Dr 30021 — 678-676-5302
Joe Jenkins, prin. — Fax 676-5310
DeKalb Alternative Night S — Adult
955 N Indian Creek Dr 30021 — 678-676-2876
Tom Willis, prin. — Fax 676-2878

Atlanta Area School for the Deaf — Post-Sec.
890 N Indian Creek Dr 30021 — 404-296-7101
DeKalb Technical College — Post-Sec.
495 N Indian Creek Dr 30021 — 404-297-9522
Georgia Perimeter College — Post-Sec.
555 N Indian Creek Dr 30021 — 404-244-5090

Claxton, Evans, Pop. 2,400
Evans County SD — 1,700/PK-12
613 W Main St 30417 — 912-739-3544
Marion A. Shaw, supt. — Fax 739-2492
www.evans.k12.ga.us
Claxton HS — 500/9-12
102 N Clark St 30417 — 912-739-3993
Glenn Stewart, prin. — Fax 739-2029
Claxton MS — 500/6-8
4 N College St 30417 — 912-739-3646
Diane Holland, prin. — Fax 739-7217

Clayton, Rabun, Pop. 2,100
Rabun County SD — 2,100/PK-12
41 Education St 30525 — 706-746-5376
Robert Arthur, supt. — Fax 746-3084
www.rabun.k12.ga.us
Other Schools – See Tiger

Cleveland, White, Pop. 2,360
White County SD — 3,200/PK-12
113 N Brooks St 30528 — 706-865-2315
Dr. Paul Shaw, supt. — Fax 865-7784
www.white.k12.ga.us
White County HS — 700/10-12
2600 Highway 129 N 30528 — 706-865-2312
Bryan Dorsey, prin. — Fax 865-5981
White County MS — 900/6-8
283 Old Blairsville Rd 30528 — 706-865-4060
Sheila Fussell, prin. — Fax 865-1947
White County Ninth Grade Academy — 300/9-9
328 Old Blairsville Rd 30528 — 706-865-0727
Rodney Green, prin. — Fax 865-0737

Truett McConnell College — Post-Sec.
100 Alumni Dr 30528 — 706-865-2134
White Creek Christian Academy — 100/PK-12
67 Academy Dr 30528 — 706-865-1917
Judy Kinsey, prin. — Fax 865-0862

Cochran, Bleckley, Pop. 4,721
Bleckley County SD — 2,500/PK-12
PO Box 516 31014 — 478-934-2821
Dr. L.C. Evans, supt. — Fax 934-9595
www.bleckley.k12.ga.us
Bleckley County HS — 700/9-12
155 Highway 87 Byp S 31014 — 478-934-6258
W. Richard Smith, prin. — Fax 934-9707
Bleckley County MS — 600/6-8
590 GA Highway 26 E 31014 — 478-934-7270
Anthony Jenkins, prin. — Fax 934-6502

Middle Georgia College — Post-Sec.
1100 2nd St SE 31014 — 478-934-6221

College Park, Fulton, Pop. 20,181
Clayton County SD
Supt. — See Jonesboro
North Clayton HS — 1,500/9-12
1525 Norman Dr, — 770-994-4035
Josette Franklin, prin. — Fax 994-4038
North Clayton MS — 900/6-8
5517 W Fayetteville Rd, — 770-994-4025
Clarence Jackson, prin. — Fax 994-4028

Fulton County SD
Supt. — See Atlanta
Banneker HS — 1,300/9-12
5935 Feldwood Rd, — 770-969-3410
Gregory Middleton, prin. — Fax 969-3418
Camp Creek MS — 700/6-8
4345 Welcome All Rd SW, — 404-669-8030
Minnie Miller, prin. — Fax 669-8228
McNair MS — 700/6-8
2800 Burdett Rd, — 770-991-4160
Ronald Taylor, prin. — Fax 991-4165

Woodward Academy — 2,900/PK-12
1662 Rugby Ave 30337 — 404-765-4000
Dr. Harry Payne, pres. — Fax 765-4009

Collins, Tattnall, Pop. 552
Tattnall County SD
Supt. — See Reidsville
Collins MS — 200/6-8
720 N Main St 30421 — 912-693-2455
Chris Freeman, prin. — Fax 693-9046

Colquitt, Miller, Pop. 1,889
Miller County SD — 1,100/PK-12
PO Box 188, — 229-758-5592
Robert Phillips, supt. — Fax 758-4138
www.miller.k12.ga.us/
Miller County HS — 300/9-12
96 Perry St, — 229-758-4130
Ginger Webster, prin. — Fax 758-3756
Miller County MS — 300/6-8
96 Perry St, — 229-758-4131
Frank Killingsworth, prin. — Fax 758-4152

Columbus, Muscogee, Pop. 185,271
Muscogee County SD — 32,800/PK-12
PO Box 2427 31902 — 706-748-2000
Dr. John Phillips, supt. — Fax 748-2001
www.mcsdga.net/
Arnold Magnet Academy — 800/6-8
2011 51st St 31904 — 706-748-2436
Jose Negron, prin. — Fax 748-2435
Baker MS — 500/6-8
1215 Benning Dr 31903 — 706-683-8721
Dr. JoAnn Brown, prin. — Fax 683-8731
Blackmon Road MS — 900/6-8
7251 Blackmon Rd 31909 — 706-565-2998
Gary Shouppe, prin. — Fax 565-3006
Carver Magnet HS — 1,300/9-12
3100 8th St 31906 — 706-748-2499
Chris Lindsey, prin. — Fax 748-2512
Columbus HS — 1,300/9-12
1700 Cherokee Ave 31906 — 706-748-2534
Susan Bryant, prin. — Fax 748-2546
Double Churches MS — 900/6-8
7611 Whitesville Rd 31904 — 706-748-2678
Dr. Mike Hudson, prin. — Fax 748-2682
East Columbus Magnet Academy — 700/6-8
6100 Georgetown Dr 31907 — 706-565-3026
Dr. Carol Hutcheson, prin. — Fax 565-3031
Eddy MS — 700/6-8
2100 S Lumpkin Rd 31903 — 706-683-8782
Dr. Cleo Griswould, prin. — Fax 683-8789
Fort MS — 600/6-8
2900 Woodruff Farm Rd 31907 — 706-569-3740
Lillia Bernard, prin. — Fax 569-3616
Hardaway HS — 1,300/9-12
2901 College Dr 31906 — 706-748-2766
Matt Bell, prin. — Fax 748-2776
Jordan Vocational HS — Vo/Tech
3200 Howard Ave 31904 — 706-748-2819
Dwain Tovey, prin. — Fax 748-2829
Kendrick HS — 1,200/9-12
6015 Georgetown Dr 31907 — 706-565-2960
Dr. Ed Barnwell, prin. — Fax 565-2971
Marshall MS — 500/6-8
1830 Shepherd Dr 31906 — 706-748-2900
Melvin Blackwell, prin. — Fax 748-2908
Northside HS — 1,300/9-12
2002 American Way 31909 — 706-748-2920
Dr. Renee Mallory, prin. — Fax 748-2931
Richards MS — 800/6-8
2892 Edgewood Rd 31906 — 706-569-3697
Mike Johnson, prin. — Fax 569-3704
Rothschild MS — 700/6-8
1136 Hunt Ave 31907 — 706-569-3709
Chris Cox, prin. — Fax 569-3717
St. Elmo Center for Gifted Education — K-12
2101 18th Ave 31901 — 706-748-3115
Dr. Susan Squiers, prin. — Fax 748-3118

Shaw HS 1,100/9-12
7601 Schomburg Rd 31909 706-569-3638
Dr. Jim Arnold, prin. Fax 569-3648
Spencer HS 1,100/9-12
4340 Victory Dr 31903 706-683-8701
Dr. Issac Neal, prin. Fax 683-8716
Veterans Memorial MS 6-8
2008 Old Guard Rd 31909 706-748-3203
Dr. Gary Shouppe, prin. Fax 748-3211
Muscogee Evening S Adult
1042 Manchester Expy 31904 706-748-2600
Fax 748-2602
Tillinghurst Adult Education Adult
514 Morris Rd 31906 706-683-8741
Karl Roberts, prin. Fax 683-8743
Other Schools – See Midland

Beacon University Post-Sec.
6003 Veterans Pkwy 31909 706-323-5364
Brookstone S 900/PK-12
440 Bradley Park Dr 31904 706-324-1392
Scott Wilson, hdmstr. Fax 571-0178
Calvary Christian S 600/PK-12
7556 Old Moon Rd 31909 706-323-0467
Len McWilliams, hdmstr. Fax 323-1941
Columbus State University Post-Sec.
4225 University Ave 31907 706-568-2001
Columbus Technical College Post-Sec.
928 Manchester Expy 31904 706-649-1800
Grace Christian S 200/PK-12
2915 14th Ave 31904 706-323-9161
Mark Liedtke, prin. Fax 323-8554
Medical Center Post-Sec.
PO Box 951 31902 706-571-1200
Pacelli HS 200/9-12
3556 Trinity Dr 31907 706-561-8243
Monica DesJarlais, prin. Fax 561-3243
Rivertown School of Beauty Post-Sec.
4747 Hamilton Rd Ste B 31904 706-653-9223
Southeastern Beauty School Post-Sec.
PO Box 12483 31917 706-687-1054
Southeastern Beauty School Post-Sec.
PO Box 12483 31917 706-687-1054
Turner S 200/9-12
2917 University Ave 31907 706-561-3518
Robin Eller, prin. Fax 561-4619

Commerce, Jackson, Pop. 5,856
Commerce CSD 1,300/PK-12
PO Box 29 30529 706-335-5500
Dr. James McCoy, supt. Fax 335-5214
www.commerce-city.k12.ga.us
Commerce HS 400/9-12
272 Lakeview Dr 30529 706-335-5942
Donald Drew, prin. Fax 336-6955
Commerce MS 400/5-8
7690 Jefferson Rd 30529 706-335-5594
Mary Evans, prin. Fax 335-6222

Jackson County SD
Supt. — See Jefferson
East Jackson MS 700/6-8
1880 Hoods Mill Rd 30529 706-335-2083
Frank Sarratt, prin. Fax 335-0935

Conyers, Rockdale, Pop. 12,205
Rockdale County SD 14,500/PK-12
PO Box 1199 30012 770-860-4211
Samuel King, supt. Fax 860-4285
www.rockdale.k12.ga.us
Conyers MS 1,100/6-8
400 Sigman Rd NW 30012 770-483-3371
Eugene Baker, prin. Fax 483-9448
Edwards MS 1,300/6-8
2633 Stanton Rd SE 30094 770-483-3255
Tonya Bloodworth, prin. Fax 483-3676
Heritage HS 1,500/9-12
2400 Granade Rd SW 30094 770-483-5428
Greg Fowler, prin. Fax 483-9435
Magnet S for Science/Technology 9-12
1174 Bulldog Cir NE 30012 770-483-8737
Mary Ann Suddeth, dir. Fax 483-7379
Memorial MS 1,400/6-8
3205 Underwood Rd SE 30013 770-922-0139
Emilio Garza, prin. Fax 922-6192
Rockdale Career Academy Vo/Tech
1064 Culpepper Dr SW 30094 770-483-4713
Timothy Melvin, prin. Fax 388-5678
Rockdale County HS 1,500/9-12
1174 Bulldog Cir NE 30012 770-483-8754
Cynthia Hudson, prin. Fax 483-8708
Salem HS 1,600/9-12
3551 Underwood Rd SE 30013 770-929-0176
Robert Cresswell, prin. Fax 922-1292
Evening Academy Adult
3551 Underwood Rd SE 30013 770-929-0176
Robert Cresswell, dir. Fax 483-6164
Other Schools – See Stockbridge

Georgia Career Institute Post-Sec.
1820 Highway 20 SE Ste 200 30013 770-922-7653
Georgia Driving Academy Post-Sec.
1449 V F W Dr SW 30012 770-918-8501
Peachtree Academy 500/PK-12
1801 Ellington Rd SE 30013 770-860-8900
JaNice VanNess, admin. Fax 761-0883
Philadelphia Christian S 300/PK-12
2360 Old Covington Hwy SW 30012 770-483-7789
Keith Scott, prin. Fax 483-4391
Victory Christian S 400/PK-12
1151 Flat Shoals Rd SE 30013 770-929-3758
Phil Wills, hdmstr. Fax 929-8848
Young Americans Christian S 500/PK-12
1701 Honey Creek Rd SE 30013 770-760-7902
Jan Taylor, dir. Fax 760-7981

Cordele, Crisp, Pop. 11,493
Crisp County SD 4,100/PK-12
PO Box 729 31010 229-276-3400
Judy Bean Ed.D., supt. Fax 276-3406
www.crisp.k12.ga.us
Crisp County HS 1,100/9-12
2402 Cougar Aly 31015 229-276-3430
Michael Overstreet, prin. Fax 276-3430
Crisp County MS 1,000/6-8
1116 E 24th Ave 31015 229-276-3460
Michael Lehr, prin. Fax 276-3466

Crisp Academy 300/PK-12
150 Crisp Academy Dr 31015 229-273-6330
Derrel Youngblood, prin. Fax 273-4141

South Georgia Technical College Post-Sec.
402 N Midway Rd 31015 229-271-4040

Cornelia, Habersham, Pop. 3,771
Habersham County SD
Supt. — See Clarkesville
South Habersham MS 600/7-8
237 Old Athens Hwy 30531 706-778-7121
Constance Franklin, prin. Fax 778-2110

Covington, Newton, Pop. 13,856
Newton County SD 15,800/PK-12
PO Box 1469 30015 770-787-1330
Dr. R. Steven Whatley, supt. Fax 784-2950
www.newtoncountyschools.org
Alcovy HS 9-12
14567 Highway 36 30014 770-784-4995
Dave Easterday, prin. Fax 784-4996
Clements MS 1,000/6-8
66 Jack Neely Rd 30016 770-784-2934
Dr. Sylvia Jordan, prin. Fax 784-2992
Cousins MS 700/6-8
8187 Carlton Trl NW 30014 770-786-7311
Scott Sauls, prin. Fax 784-2991
Eastside HS 1,500/9-12
10245 Eagle Dr 30014 770-784-2920
Dr. Robert Daria, prin. Fax 784-2918
Indian Creek MS 1,000/6-8
11051 S By Pass Rd 30014 770-385-6453
Samantha Fuhrey, prin. Fax 385-6456
Newton HS 2,600/9-12
140 Ram Dr 30014 770-787-2250
Joe Gheesling, prin. Fax 784-2957
Veterans Memorial MS 1,100/6-8
13357 Brown Bridge Rd 30016 770-385-6893
Eric Arena, prin. Fax 385-6899

Cumming, Forsyth, Pop. 5,802
Forsyth County SD 23,500/PK-12
1120 Dahlonega Hwy 30040 770-887-2461
Paula Gault, supt. Fax 781-6632
www.forsyth.k12.ga.us
Forsyth Central HS 1,900/9-12
520 Tribble Gap Rd 30040 770-887-8151
Rudy Hampton, prin. Fax 781-2289
Liberty MS 900/6-8
7465 Wallace Tatum Rd 30028 770-781-4889
Dr. Cindy Salloum, prin. Fax 513-3877
North Forsyth HS 1,800/9-12
3635 Coal Mountain Dr 30028 770-781-6637
Nita Giddish, prin. Fax 781-2273
North Forsyth MS 1,000/6-8
3645 Coal Mountain Dr 30028 770-889-0743
Jeff Hunt, prin. Fax 888-1210
Otwell MS 900/6-8
605 Tribble Gap Rd 30040 770-887-5248
Dr. Jeff Zoul, prin. Fax 888-1214
South Forsyth HS 2,300/9-12
585 Peachtree Pkwy 30041 770-781-2264
Gary Davison, prin. Fax 887-1132
South Forsyth MS 800/6-8
2865 Old Atlanta Rd 30041 770-888-3170
Debbie Sarver, prin. Fax 888-3179
Vickery Creek MS 900/6-8
6240 Post Rd 30040 770-667-2580
Connie McCrary, prin. Fax 667-2593
Other Schools – See Suwanee

Covenant Christian Academy 200/PK-12
6905 Post Rd 30040 770-674-2990
Johnathan Arnold, hdmstr. Fax 674-2989
Horizon Christian Academy 200/K-12
PO Box 2715 30028 678-947-3583
Garin Berry, admin. Fax 947-0721
Lanier Technical College Post-Sec.
7745 Majors Rd 30041 770-781-6770
Pinecrest Academy 200/PK-12
955 Peachtree Pkwy 30041 770-888-4477
John Tarpley, pres. Fax 888-0404

Cusseta, Chattahoochee, Pop. 1,258
Chattahoochee County SD 500/PK-12
326 Broad St 31805 706-989-3774
Dalton Oliver, supt. Fax 989-3776
www.chattahoochee.k12.ga.us/
Chattahoochee County MSHS 200/6-12
360 Highway 26 31805 706-989-3678
Dr. James Martin, prin. Fax 989-0649

Cuthbert, Randolph, Pop. 3,491
Randolph County SD 1,600/PK-12
1208 Andrew St, 229-732-3601
Bobby Jenkins, supt. Fax 732-3840
www.sowegak12.org/
Randolph-Clay HS 500/9-12
RR 3 Box 279, 229-732-2101
Lee Byrd, prin. Fax 732-5633
Randolph-Clay MS 300/6-8
RR 3 Box 279, 229-732-2790
Clifford Cooks, prin. Fax 732-5633

Andrew College Post-Sec.
413 College St, 229-732-2171

Dacula, Gwinnett, Pop. 4,425
Gwinnett County SD
Supt. — See Suwanee
Dacula HS 1,800/9-12
123 Broad St 30019 770-963-6664
Donald Nutt, prin. Fax 338-4665
Dacula MS 1,600/6-8
137 Dacula Rd 30019 770-963-1110
Kellye Riggins, prin. Fax 338-4632

Hebron Christian Academy 1,000/K-12
PO Box 1028 30019 770-962-5423
Scott Smith, pres. Fax 339-5683

Dahlonega, Lumpkin, Pop. 4,519
Lumpkin County SD 3,700/PK-12
56 Indian Dr 30533 706-864-3611
Dewey W. Moye, supt. Fax 864-3755
www.lumpkin.k12.ga.us
Lumpkin County HS 1,000/9-12
2001 Indian Dr 30533 706-864-2557
Tracy Sanford, prin. Fax 864-4929
Lumpkin County MS 900/6-8
44 School Dr 30533 706-864-6180
Rick Conner, prin. Fax 864-0199

Hidden Lake Academy 200/7-12
830 Hidden Lake Rd 30533 706-864-4730
Charles Cates, hdmstr. Fax 864-9109
North Georgia College & State University Post-Sec.
30597 706-864-1400

Dallas, Paulding, Pop. 8,667
Paulding County SD 21,700/PK-12
3236 Atlanta Hwy 30132 770-443-8000
Trudy Sowar, supt. Fax 443-8089
www.paulding.k12.ga.us
East Paulding HS 1,700/9-12
3320 E Paulding Dr 30157 770-445-5100
Charles Kuss, prin. Fax 443-6357
East Paulding MS 1,100/6-8
2945 Hiram Acworth Hwy 30157 770-443-7000
Stan Ingram, prin. Fax 443-0116
Jones MS 1,000/6-8
100 Stadium Dr 30132 770-443-8024
David Viness, prin. Fax 443-8026
McClure MS 6-8
315 Bob Grogan Dr 30132
Gail Davis, prin.
Moses MS 1,100/6-8
1066 Old County Farm Rd 30132 770-443-8727
Tracy Bennett, prin. Fax 443-8078
North Paulding HS 9-9
300 N Paulding Dr 30132
Susan Browning, prin.
Paulding County HS 2,000/9-12
1297 Villa Rica Hwy 30157 770-443-8008
Lee Segars, prin. Fax 443-7030
South Paulding MS 1,000/6-8
592 Nebo Rd 30157 770-445-8500
Jim Gottwald, prin. Fax 445-9989
Other Schools – See Douglasville, Hiram, Powder Springs

Dalton, Whitfield, Pop. 32,140
Dalton CSD 6,200/PK-12
PO Box 1408 30722 706-278-8766
Dr. Orval Porter, supt. Fax 226-4583
www.daltonpublicschools.com/
Dalton HS 1,500/9-12
1500 Manly St 30720 706-278-8757
Debbie Freeman, prin. Fax 226-2430
Dalton MS 1,300/6-8
1250 Cross Plains Trl 30721 706-278-3903
Brian Suits, prin. Fax 428-7852

Whitfield County SD 12,500/PK-12
PO Box 2167 30722 706-217-6780
Dr. Katie Brochu, supt. Fax 278-5042
www.whitfield.k12.ga.us
Eastbrook MS 800/6-8
700 Hill Rd 30721 706-278-6135
Brian Satterfield, prin. Fax 226-9859
New Hope MS 6-8
1325 New Hope Rd NW 30720 706-673-2295
George Kopcsak, prin. Fax 673-2086
North Whitfield MS 1,000/6-8
3264 Cleveland Rd 30721 706-259-3381
Andrea Bradley, prin. Fax 259-8168
Southeast Whitfield County HS 1,500/9-12
1954 Riverbend Rd 30721 706-226-2753
Alan Long, prin. Fax 278-3433
Valley Point MS 500/6-8
3796 S Dixie Rd 30721 706-277-9662
Britt Adams, prin. Fax 277-7035
Whitfield County Career Academy Vo/Tech
2300 Maddox Chapel Rd NE 30721 706-876-3600
Phillip Brown, prin. Fax 876-3602
Phoenix HS Adult
2818 Airport Rd 30721 706-272-2206
Fred Toney, prin. Fax 272-2200
Other Schools – See Rocky Face, Tunnel Hill

Christian Heritage S 400/K-12
PO Box 2066 30722 706-277-1198
Renny Scott, hdmstr. Fax 277-2300
Dalton State College Post-Sec.
650 College Dr 30720 706-272-4436
Pathway Christian Academy 100/PK-12
PO Box 4299 30719 706-279-1396
Dr. James Hitte, prin. Fax 529-0957

Damascus, Early, Pop. 265

Southwest Georgia Academy 400/PK-12
14105 State Road 200, 229-725-4792
Doug Dease, prin. Fax 725-5476

Danielsville, Madison, Pop. 508
Madison County SD 4,600/K-12
PO Box 37 30633 706-795-2191
Keith Cowne, supt. Fax 795-5104
www.madison.k12.ga.us
Madison County HS 1,400/9-12
PO Box 7 30633 706-795-2197
Wayne McIntosh, prin. Fax 795-3116
Madison County MS 1,100/6-8
PO Box 690 30633 706-795-3341
Matt Boggs, prin. Fax 795-5753

Darien, McIntosh, Pop. 1,713
McIntosh County SD 1,900/PK-12
200 Pine St 31305 912-437-6645
Dr. William Hunter, supt. Fax 437-2140
www.mcintosh.k12.ga.us/
McIntosh County Academy 500/9-12
1915 Highway 17 N 31305 912-437-6691
Russell Sowell, prin. Fax 437-3077
McIntosh County MS 500/6-8
500 Green St 31305 912-437-6685
Cheryl Peterson, prin. Fax 437-5676

Dawson, Terrell, Pop. 4,859
Terrell County SD 1,700/PK-12
PO Box 151, 229-995-4425
Robert Aaron, supt. Fax 995-4632
www.terrellcountyschools.net/
Terrell County MSHS 800/6-12
PO Box 151, 229-995-2544
Douglas Bell, prin. Fax 995-4523

Terrell Academy 200/K-12
602 Academy Dr SE, 229-995-4242
William Murdock, hdmstr. Fax 995-6149

Dawsonville, Dawson, Pop. 1,066
Dawson County SD 3,100/K-12
PO Box 208 30534 706-265-3246
Nicky Gilleland, supt. Fax 265-1226
www.dawson.k12.ga.us
Dawson County HS 900/9-12
PO Box 129 30534 706-265-6555
Rick Brown, prin. Fax 265-3936
Dawson County MS 700/6-8
PO Box 688 30534 706-265-2714
Bill Zadernak, prin. Fax 265-1426
Riverview MS 6-8
5126 Highway 9 S 30534 706-216-4849
Janice Darnell, prin. Fax 265-1426

Decatur, DeKalb, Pop. 17,884
DeKalb County SD 93,300/PK-12
3770 N Decatur Rd 30032 678-676-1200
Dr. Crawford Lewis, supt. Fax 676-0785
www.dekalb.k12.ga.us
Bethune MS 1,400/6-8
5200 Covington Hwy 30035 678-875-0302
Dr. Terry McMullen, prin. Fax 875-0310
Cedar Grove MS 1,500/6-8
2300 Wildcat Rd 30034 678-874-4202
Agnes Flanagan, prin. Fax 874-4210
Chapel Hill MS 900/6-8
3535 Dogwood Farm Rd 30034 678-676-8502
Carlus Daniel, prin. Fax 676-8510
Columbia HS 1,400/9-12
2106 Columbia Dr 30032 678-874-0802
Dr. Thomas Glanton, prin. Fax 874-0810
Columbia MS 1,200/6-8
3001 Columbia Dr 30034 678-875-0502
Stephanie Amey, prin. Fax 875-0510
DeKalb HS of Technology South Vo/Tech
3303 Panthersville Rd 30034 678-874-4502
Rick Moore, prin. Fax 874-4510
McNair MS 1,100/6-8
2190 Wallingford Dr 30032 678-874-5102
Susan Freeman, prin. Fax 874-5110
Miller Grove MS 1,300/6-8
2215 Miller Rd 30035 678-676-8902
Dr. Triscilla Weaver, prin. Fax 676-8910
Shamrock MS 1,000/6-8
3100 Mount Olive Dr 30033 678-874-7602
Robert Thorpe, prin. Fax 874-7610
Southwest DeKalb HS 1,700/9-12
2863 Kelley Chapel Rd 30034 678-874-1902
John Prince, prin. Fax 874-1910
Towers HS 1,300/9-12
3919 Brookcrest Cir 30032 678-874-2202
Leroy Jenkins, prin. Fax 874-2210
Other Schools – See Atlanta, Avondale Estates, Chamblee, Clarkston, Doraville, Dunwoody, Ellenwood, Lithonia, Stone Mountain, Tucker

Decatur CSD 2,300/PK-12
758 Scott Blvd 30030 404-370-4400
Dr. Phyllis Edwards, supt. Fax 370-4413
www.decatur-city.k12.ga.us
Decatur HS 800/9-12
310 N McDonough St 30030 404-370-4420
Lauri McKain-Fernandez, prin. Fax 370-4434
Renfroe MS 500/6-8
220 W College Ave 30030 404-370-4440
Bruce Roaden, prin. Fax 370-4449

Academe of the Oaks 100/9-12
146 New St 30030 404-405-2173
Fax 377-7178
Agnes Scott College Post-Sec.
141 E College Ave 30030 404-471-6000
Columbia Theological Seminary Post-Sec.
701 S Columbia Dr 30030 404-378-8821
DeKalb Medical Center Post-Sec.
2701 N Decatur Rd 30033 404-501-5206
DeVry University Post-Sec.
250 N Arcadia Ave 30030 404-292-7900
Georgia Perimeter College Post-Sec.
3251 Panthersville Rd 30034 404-244-5090
Greenforest/McCalep Christian Academy 1,100/PK-12
3250 Rainbow Dr 30034 404-486-6737
Albert Walker, hdmstr. Fax 486-1127
Green Pastures Christian S 200/PK-12
5455 Flat Shoals Pkwy 30034 770-987-8121
Gloria Locke, admin. Fax 987-7475
Gupton-Jones College of Funeral Service Post-Sec.
5141 Snapfinger Woods Dr 30035 770-593-2257
Omnitech Institute Post-Sec.
4319 Covington Hwy Ste 202 30035 404-284-8121

Demorest, Habersham, Pop. 1,777
Habersham County SD
Supt. — See Clarkesville
Habersham Ninth Grade Academy 9-9
3115 Demorest Mount Airy 30535 706-778-0830
Pam Dalton, prin. Fax 778-0848

Piedmont College Post-Sec.
PO Box 10 30535 800-277-7020

Donalsonville, Seminole, Pop. 2,702
Seminole County SD 1,700/PK-12
800 S Woolfork Ave, 229-524-2433
Walter L. Pierce, supt. Fax 524-2212
www.seminole.k12.ga.us
Seminole County MSHS 900/6-12
5582 Highway 39 S, 229-524-5135
Monroe Bonner, prin. Fax 524-5178

Doraville, DeKalb, Pop. 9,872
DeKalb County SD
Supt. — See Decatur
Sequoyah MS 1,000/6-8
3456 Aztec Rd 30340 678-676-7902
Trenton Arnold, prin. Fax 676-7910

Douglas, Coffee, Pop. 10,978
Coffee County SD 7,800/PK-12
PO Box 1290 31534 912-384-2086
Billy Smith, supt. Fax 383-5333
coffee.k12.ga.us
Coffee HS 2,000/9-12
159 Trojan Way 31533 912-384-2094
Greg Tanner, prin. Fax 383-5486
East Coffee MS 700/6-8
1020 Gaskin Ave S 31533 912-384-1342
Nelda Flanders, prin. Fax 383-4160
West Coffee MS 1,200/6-8
1303 Peterson Ave S 31533 912-383-4100
Phil Dockery, prin. Fax 383-4124

Citizens Christian Academy 300/PK-12
PO Box 1064 31534 912-384-8862
William Rish, hdmstr. Fax 384-8426
South Georgia College Post-Sec.
100 College Park Dr W 31533 912-389-4231

Douglasville, Douglas, Pop. 27,568
Douglas County SD 20,700/PK-12
PO Box 1077 30133 770-651-2000
Donald Remillard, supt. Fax 920-4159
www.douglas.k12.ga.us
Alexander HS 1,500/9-12
6500 Alexander Pkwy 30135 770-651-6000
Robert Brown, prin. Fax 651-6003
Chapel Hill HS 1,500/9-12
4899 Chapel Hill Rd 30135 770-651-6200
Jason Branch, prin. Fax 651-6205
Chapel Hill MS 700/7-8
3989 Chapel Hill Rd 30135 770-651-5000
William Foster, prin. Fax 920-4242
Chestnut Log MS 800/6-8
2544 Pope Rd 30135 770-651-5100
Kay Davis, prin. Fax 651-5103
Douglas County HS 1,500/9-12
8705 Campbellton St 30134 770-651-6500
Connie Craft, prin. Fax 920-4456
Fairplay MS 800/6-8
8311 Highway 166 30135 770-651-5300
Monte Beaver, prin. Fax 651-5303
Stewart MS 700/6-8
8138 Malone St 30134 770-651-5400
Jay Grimmett, prin. Fax 920-4229
Yeager MS 900/6-8
4000 Kings Hwy 30135 770-651-5600
Jay Grimmett, prin. Fax 651-5603
Other Schools – See Lithia Springs

Paulding County SD
Supt. — See Dallas
Austin MS 6-8
3490 Ridge Rd 30134 770-942-0316
Tammy Allen, prin. Fax 942-0548

Harvester Christian Academy 400/PK-12
4241 Central Church Rd 30135 770-942-1583
Jack North, hdmstr. Fax 942-9332
Heirway Christian Academy 200/PK-12
6758 Spring St 30134 770-489-4392
Phyllis Campbell, prin. Fax 489-4318
Inner Harbour S 200/K-12
4685 Dorsett Shoals Rd 30135 770-942-2391
Dr. Penny Honeycutt, prin. Fax 489-0406
Kings Way Christian S 400/PK-12
6456 The Kings Way 30135 770-949-0812
Ray Conway, admin. Fax 949-1045
West Central Technical College Post-Sec.
4600 Timber Ridge Dr 30135 770-947-7200

Dublin, Laurens, Pop. 16,924
Dublin CSD 2,900/PK-12
207 Shamrock Dr 31021 478-272-3440
Dr. Elaine Connell, supt. Fax 272-1249
echalk.dublinirish.org
Dublin HS 900/9-12
1951 Hillcrest Pkwy 31021 478-272-4727
Dr. Gene Nisbet, prin. Fax 277-9829
Dublin MS 700/6-8
1501 N Jefferson St 31021 478-272-8122
Elgin Dixon, prin. Fax 277-9828

Laurens County SD 6,300/PK-12
467 Firetower Rd 31021 478-272-4767
Jerry Hatcher, supt. Fax 277-2619
www.lcboe.net
East Laurens HS 600/9-12
920 US Highway 80 E 31027 478-272-3144
Kelland Waldrep, prin. Fax 274-1032
East Laurens MS 600/6-8
920 US Highway 80 E 31027 478-272-1201
Dianne Jones, prin. Fax 275-1627
West Laurens HS 1,100/9-12
338 W Laurens School Rd 31021 478-272-1155
Hugh Kight, prin. Fax 275-0643
West Laurens MS 900/6-8
332 W Laurens School Rd 31021 478-272-8452
George Knight, prin. Fax 275-0848

Heart of Georgia Technical Institute Post-Sec.
560 Pinehill Rd 31021 478-275-6590
Trinity Christian S 500/K-12
200 Trinity Rd 31021 478-272-7699
Rick Johnson, prin. Fax 272-7685

Duluth, Gwinnett, Pop. 24,482
Fulton County SD
Supt. — See Atlanta
Northview HS 2,200/9-12
10625 Parsons Rd 30097 770-497-3828
Peter Zervakos, prin. Fax 497-3844
River Trail MS 1,400/6-8
10795 Rogers Cir 30097 770-497-3860
Dawn Melin, prin. Fax 497-3866

Gwinnett County SD
Supt. — See Suwanee
Duluth HS 2,000/9-12
3737 Brock Rd 30096 770-476-5206
Patrick Blenke, prin. Fax 232-3332
Duluth MS 1,700/6-8
3200 Pleasant Hill Rd 30096 770-476-3372
Deborah Fusi, prin. Fax 232-3295
Hull MS 2,000/6-8
1950 Old Peachtree Rd 30097 770-232-3200
Denise Showell, prin. Fax 232-3203
Radloff MS 1,100/6-8
3939 Shackleford Rd 30096 678-245-3400
Dr. Patty Heitmuller, prin. Fax 245-3403

Atlanta Adventist Academy 100/9-12
2959 Duluth Highway 120 30096 404-699-1400
David Denton, prin.
DeVry University Post-Sec.
3505 Koger Blvd Ste 170 30096 678-380-9780

Dunwoody, DeKalb, Pop. 34,400
DeKalb County SD
Supt. — See Decatur
DeKalb HS of Technology North Vo/Tech
1995 Womack Rd 30338 678-874-8400
Delores Washington, prin. Fax 874-8410
Dunwoody HS 1,300/9-12
5035 Vermack Rd 30338 678-874-8502
Stacy Stepney, prin. Fax 874-8510

Empire Beauty School Post-Sec.
4719 Ashford-Dunwoody #205 30338 770-672-2448

Eastman, Dodge, Pop. 5,441
Dodge County SD 3,600/PK-12
720 College St 31023 478-374-3783
Aubrey Corbitt, supt. Fax 374-6697
www.dodge.k12.ga.us
Dodge County HS 1,000/9-12
350 Pearl Bates Ave 31023 478-374-7711
Dr. Susan Long, prin. Fax 374-6987
Dodge County MS 900/6-8
1400 Herman Ave 31023 478-374-6492
Jerome Smith, prin. Fax 374-6484

Georgia Aviation Technical College Post-Sec.
71 Airport Rd 31023 478-374-6402

East Point, Fulton, Pop. 40,680
Fulton County SD
Supt. — See Atlanta
Tri-Cities HS 1,900/9-12
2575 Harris St 30344 404-669-8200
Eldrick Horton, prin. Fax 669-8158
West MS 1,100/6-8
2376 Headland Dr 30344 404-669-8130
Dan Sims, prin. Fax 669-8121
Woodland MS 700/6-8
2816 Briarwood Blvd 30344 404-346-6420
William Bradley, prin. Fax 346-6527

Atlanta Christian College Post-Sec.
2605 Ben Hill Rd 30344 404-761-8861
Pathway Christian S 100/PK-12
1706 Washington Ave 30344 404-763-3216
Jason Nix, prin. Fax 478-0444

Eatonton, Putnam, Pop. 6,758
Putnam County SD 2,700/PK-12
158 Old Glenwood Springs Rd 31024 706-485-5381
Dr. Jim Willis, supt. Fax 485-3820
www.putnam.k12.ga.us/boe/
Putnam County HS 700/9-12
140 Sparta Hwy 31024 706-485-9971
Michael Rowland, prin. Fax 485-3128
Putnam County MS 600/6-8
314 S Washington Ave 31024 706-485-8547
Bessie Brown, prin. Fax 485-7090

Gatewood S 600/PK-12
139 Phillips Dr 31024 706-485-8231
Laura Thompson, hdmstr. Fax 485-2455

Edison, Calhoun, Pop. 1,236
Calhoun County SD
Supt. — See Morgan
Calhoun County MSHS 400/6-12
PO Box 366, 229-835-2435
Willie Williams, prin. Fax 835-3040

Elberton, Elbert, Pop. 4,714
Elbert County SD 2,800/PK-12
50 Laurel Dr 30635 706-213-4000
Samuel Light, supt. Fax 283-6674
www.elbert.k12.ga.us
Elbert County Comprehensive HS 1,100/9-12
600 Abernathy Cir 30635 706-213-4100
Rick Higginbotham, prin. Fax 283-1183
Elbert County MS 6-8
1108 Athens Tech Rd 30635 706-213-4200
Paul Garrett, prin. Fax 283-1117

Ellaville, Schley, Pop. 1,758
Schley County SD 1,100/PK-12
PO Box 66 31806 229-937-2405
William Johnson, supt. Fax 937-5180
www.schleyk12.org/
Schley County MSHS 500/6-12
PO Box 1350 31806 229-937-0560
Larry Stubbs, prin. Fax 937-0565

Ellenwood, Clayton
DeKalb County SD
Supt. — See Decatur
Cedar Grove HS 1,500/9-12
2360 River Rd 30294 678-874-4002
Ron Davis, prin. Fax 874-4010

Annointed Word Christian S International 100/PK-12
3800 Linecrest Rd 30294 404-241-8200
Betty Evans, admin. Fax 328-9801

Ellijay, Gilmer, Pop. 1,519
Gilmer County SD 4,100/PK-12
497 Bobcat Trl 30540 706-276-5000
Dr. Raiford Cantrell, supt. Fax 276-5005
www.gilmerschools.com/
Gilmer HS 1,200/9-12
408 Bobcat Trl 30540 706-276-5080
Randal Parson, prin. Fax 276-5088
Gilmer MS 900/6-8
1860 S Main St 30540 706-276-5030
Nancy Gheesling, prin. Fax 276-5035

Emerson, Bartow, Pop. 1,302
Bartow County SD
Supt. — See Cartersville
South Central MS 700/6-8
224 Old Old Alabama Rd SE 30137 770-606-5865
Gordon Scoggins, prin. Fax 606-3872

Evans, Columbia, Pop. 13,713
Columbia County SD 20,500/PK-12
4781 Hereford Farm Rd 30809 706-541-0650
Thomas Price, supt. Fax 541-2344
www.ccboe.net
Evans HS 1,700/9-12
4550 Cox Rd 30809 706-863-1198
Don Brigdon, prin. Fax 868-3720
Evans MS 900/6-8
4785 Hereford Farm Rd 30809 706-863-2275
Michael Johnson, prin. Fax 868-2190
Greenbrier HS 1,800/9-12
5114 Riverwood Pkwy 30809 706-650-6040
Dr. Margie Hamilton, prin. Fax 650-6045
Greenbrier MS 800/6-8
5120 Riverwood Pkwy 30809 706-650-6080
Jackie Creasy, prin. Fax 650-6085

Lakeside HS 1,500/9-12
533 Blue Ridge Dr 30809 706-863-0027
Dr. Jeff Carney, prin. Fax 868-3721
Lakeside MS 900/6-8
527 Blue Ridge Dr 30809 706-855-6900
Felicia Dumas, prin. Fax 868-2191
Riverside MS 1,000/6-8
1095 Furys Ferry Rd 30809 706-868-3712
Don Putnam, prin. Fax 868-2192
Other Schools – See Grovetown, Harlem

Evans Christian Academy 100/6-12
PO Box 3085 30809 706-364-3565
Freida Lachman, dir. Fax 868-1557

Fairburn, Fulton, Pop. 8,564
Fulton County SD
Supt. — See Atlanta
Bear Creek MS 1,200/6-8
7415 Herndon Rd 30213 770-969-6080
Darron Franklin, prin. Fax 306-3584
Creekside HS 1,700/9-12
7405 Herndon Rd 30213 770-306-4300
Michael Robinson, prin. Fax 306-4313

Arlington Christian S 400/K-12
4500 Ridge Rd 30213 770-964-9871
Chris King, hdmstr. Fax 306-3630
Landmark Christian S 700/K-12
50 SE Broad St 30213 770-306-0647
Matthew Skinner, hdmstr. Fax 969-6551
Our Lady of Mercy Catholic HS 200/9-12
861 Evander Holyfield Hwy 30213 770-461-2202
Daniel Dorsel, prin. Fax 461-9353

Fayetteville, Fayette, Pop. 14,363
Fayette County SD 21,600/PK-12
PO Box 879 30214 770-460-3535
Dr. John DeCotis, supt. Fax 460-8191
www.fcboe.org
Fayette County HS 1,800/9-12
1 Tiger Trl 30214 770-460-3540
Charles Warr, prin. Fax 460-3410
Fayette MS 1,000/6-8
450 Grady Ave 30214 770-460-3550
Sharlene Patterson, prin. Fax 460-3882
Rising Starr MS 1,200/6-8
183 Panther Path 30215 770-486-2721
Len Patton, prin. Fax 486-2727
Starr's Mill HS 1,800/9-12
193 Panther Path 30215 770-486-2710
Audrey Toney, prin. Fax 486-2716
Whitewater HS 800/9-12
100 Wildcat Way 30215 770-460-3935
Greg Stillions, prin. Fax 716-3973
Whitewater MS 1,100/6-8
1533 Highway 85 S 30215 770-460-3450
Sandra Kidd, prin. Fax 460-0362
Fayette Co. Evening HS Adult
205 LaFayette Ave 30214 770-460-3990
Ed Steil, prin. Fax 460-0482
Other Schools – See Peachtree City, Tyrone

Counterpane S 100/PK-12
PO Box 898 30214 770-461-2304
Brenda Erickson, prin. Fax 460-7016
Fayette Beauty Academy Post-Sec.
386 Glynn St N 30214 770-461-4669
Fayette Christian S 200/PK-12
152 Longview Rd 30214 770-461-3538
Henry Sheeley, prin. Fax 460-6013
Grace Christian Academy 200/PK-12
355 McDonough Rd 30214 770-461-0137
Brian Fourman, prin. Fax 461-1190

Fitzgerald, Ben Hill, Pop. 8,920
Ben Hill County SD 3,200/K-12
509 W Palm St 31750 229-409-5500
Dr. John Key, supt. Fax 409-5513
www.ben-hill.k12.ga.us
Ben Hill County MS 700/6-8
134 JC Hunter Rd 31750 229-409-5578
Jackie Hall, prin. Fax 409-5580
Fitzgerald HS 900/9-12
601 W Cypress St 31750 229-409-5530
Dr. Morris Leis, prin. Fax 409-5534

East Central Technical College Post-Sec.
667 Perry House Rd 31750 229-468-2000

Flintstone, Walker
Walker County SD
Supt. — See La Fayette
Chattanooga Valley MS 600/6-8
847 Allgood Rd 30725 706-820-0735
Eugene Ward, prin. Fax 820-0736

Flowery Branch, Hall, Pop. 2,087
Hall County SD
Supt. — See Gainesville
Davis MS 1,000/6-8
4335 Falcon Pkwy 30542 770-965-3020
Eddie Millwood, prin. Fax 965-3025
Flowery Branch HS 1,100/9-12
4450 Hog Mountain Rd 30542 770-967-8000
Dr. Mark Coleman, prin. Fax 967-1218

Heritage Academy 200/6-12
PO Box 398 30542 770-536-6900
Fax 536-4496

Folkston, Charlton, Pop. 3,270
Charlton County SD 2,000/PK-12
500 S 3rd St 31537 912-496-2596
Alexander McQueen, supt. Fax 496-2595
Charlton County JSHS 900/7-12
500 Indian Trl 31537 912-496-2501
Dr. Drew Sauls, prin. Fax 496-3732

Forest Park, Clayton, Pop. 22,201
Clayton County SD
Supt. — See Jonesboro
Babb MS 1,100/6-8
5500 Reynolds Rd 30297 404-362-3880
Felicia Brown, prin. Fax 362-4087
Forest Park HS 1,600/9-12
5452 Phillips Dr 30297 404-362-3890
Delphia Young, prin. Fax 608-7563
Forest Park MS 800/6-8
930 Finley Dr 30297 404-362-3840
Kevin Booker, prin. Fax 362-8899

Arnold/Padrick's Univ of Cosmetology Post-Sec.
4971 Courtney Dr 30297 404-361-5641
Beauty College of America Post-Sec.
1171 Main St 30297 404-361-4098

Forsyth, Monroe, Pop. 4,259
Monroe County SD 2,500/PK-12
PO Box 1308 31029 478-994-2031
Scott Cowart, supt. Fax 994-3364
www.monroe.k12.ga.us
Hubbard MS 6-8
500 Highway 83 S 31029 478-994-6803
Steve Edwards, prin. Fax 994-3061
Persons HS 1,100/9-12
300 Montpelier Ave 31029 478-994-2812
Joe Parlier, prin. Fax 994-7065
Stephens MS 500/6-8
66 Thornton Rd 31029 478-994-6186
Dr. Mike Hickman, prin. Fax 994-7061

Monroe Academy 200/PK-12
433 Highway 41 S 31029 478-994-5986
Ted McMichael, hdmstr. Fax 994-1942

Fort Gaines, Clay, Pop. 1,059
Clay County SD 400/PK-8
PO Box 219, 229-768-2232
Dr. Grady Miles, supt. Fax 768-3654
www.clay.k12.ga.us/
Clay County MS 100/6-8
200 Hobbs Ln, 229-768-2234
Terri Marcus, prin. Fax 768-2363

Fort Oglethorpe, Catoosa, Pop. 8,964
Catoosa County SD
Supt. — See Ringgold
Lakeview-Fort Oglethorpe HS 1,300/9-12
1850 Battlefield Pkwy 30742 706-866-0342
Jerry Ransom, prin. Fax 861-6645

Fort Valley, Peach, Pop. 8,197
Peach County SD 4,000/K-12
PO Box 1018 31030 478-825-5933
Tommy Daniel, supt. Fax 825-9970
www.peachschools.org
Fort Valley MS 500/6-8
712 Peggy Dr 31030 478-825-2413
Dr. Quintin Green, prin. Fax 825-1332
Peach County HS 1,200/9-12
900 Campus Dr 31030 478-825-8258
Claudia Patterson, prin. Fax 825-2290
Other Schools – See Byron

Fort Valley State University Post-Sec.
1005 State University Dr 31030 478-825-6315

Franklin, Heard, Pop. 897
Heard County SD 2,200/PK-12
PO Box 1330 30217 706-675-3320
Benjamin Hyatt, supt. Fax 675-3357
www.heard.k12.ga.us
Heard County Comprehensive HS 500/9-12
545 Main St 30217 706-675-3656
Ronald Furgerson, prin. Fax 675-8729
Heard County MS 500/6-8
269 Old Field Rd 30217 706-675-9247
Marti Robinson, prin. Fax 675-9255

Franklin Springs, Franklin, Pop. 781

Emmanuel College Post-Sec.
PO Box 129 30639 800-860-8800

Gainesville, Hall, Pop. 32,444
Gainesville CSD 5,000/PK-12
508 Oak St 30501 770-536-5275
Dr. Steven E. Ballowe, supt. Fax 287-2004
www.gcssk12.net/
Gainesville HS 1,200/9-12
830 Century Pl 30501 770-536-4441
Michael Kemp, prin. Fax 287-2031
Gainesville MS 1,000/6-8
715 Woodsmill Rd 30501 770-534-4237
Mike Schlabra, prin. Fax 287-2022

Hall County SD 23,200/PK-12
711 Green St NW Ste 100 30501 770-534-1080
Will Schofield, supt. Fax 535-7404
www.hallco.org
Chestatee HS 1,000/9-12
3005 Sardis Rd 30506 770-532-1162
Bill Thompson, prin. Fax 532-2202
Chestatee MS 900/6-8
2740 Fran Mar Dr 30506 770-297-6270
Suzanne Jarrad, prin. Fax 297-6275
East Hall HS 1,000/9-12
3534 E Hall Rd 30507 770-536-9921
Mike Gillum, prin. Fax 535-1184
East Hall MS 900/6-8
4120 E Hall Rd 30507 770-531-9457
Kevin Bales, prin. Fax 531-2327
Johnson HS 1,000/9-12
3305 Poplar Springs Rd 30507 770-536-2394
Dr. Sandra Edwards, prin. Fax 531-3046
Lanier Career Academy Vo/Tech
2723 Tumbling Creek Rd 30504 770-531-2330
Danny Jones, prin.
North Hall HS 1,100/9-12
4885 Mount Vernon Rd 30506 770-983-7331
Gary Brown, prin. Fax 983-7941
North Hall MS 800/6-8
4856 Rilla Rd 30506 770-983-9749
Brad Brown, prin. Fax 983-9993
South Hall MS 900/6-8
3215 Poplar Springs Rd 30507 770-532-4416
Paula Stubbs, prin. Fax 531-2348
Hall Co/Gainesville Evening S Adult
3131 R W Johnson Dr 30507 770-531-2330
Susan Johnson, prin. Fax 450-5978
Other Schools – See Flowery Branch, Oakwood

Brenau Academy 100/9-12
500 Washington St 30501 770-534-6140
Frank Booth, dean Fax 534-6298
Brenau University Post-Sec.
500 Washington St SE 30501 800-252-5119
Gainesville College Post-Sec.
PO Box 1358 30503 770-718-3639
Interactive College of Technology Post-Sec.
2323 Browns Bridge Rd 30504 678-450-0550

Lakeview Academy 600/PK-12
796 Lakeview Dr 30501 770-532-4383
James Curry Robison, hdmstr. Fax 536-6142
Riverside Military Academy 500/7-12
2001 Riverside Dr 30501 800-462-2338
Col. Guy Gardner, hdmstr. Fax 291-3364
Westminster Christian S 200/PK-12
1397 Thompson Bridge Rd 30501 770-534-1081
Ronnie Wallace, prin. Fax 534-1025

Gibson, Glascock, Pop. 741
Glascock County SD 600/PK-12
PO Box 205 30810 706-598-2291
James Holton, supt. Fax 598-2611
Glascock County Consolidated S 600/PK-12
1230 Panther Way 30810 706-598-2121
Sarah Garrett, prin. Fax 598-2621

Glennville, Tattnall, Pop. 5,031
Tattnall County SD
Supt. — See Reidsville
Glennville MS 300/6-8
721 E Barnard St 30427 912-654-1467
Charles Crisp, prin. Fax 654-1300

Glenville Christian Academy 100/K-12
105 Liberty St 30427 912-654-3034
Charles Barnard, prin. Fax 654-3876

Gray, Jones, Pop. 2,109
Jones County SD 4,000/PK-12
PO Box 519 31032 478-986-6580
Jim LeBrun, supt. Fax 986-1624
www.edline.net/pages/Jones_County_BOE
Gray Station MS 6-8
324 GA Highway 18 E 31032 478-986-2090
Alfred Pitts, prin. Fax 986-2099
Jones County Ninth Grade Academy 9-9
110 Maggie Califf St 31032 478-986-3046
Clinton Burston, prin. Fax 986-1504
Jones County SHS 1,000/10-12
339 Railroad St 31032 478-986-5444
Chuck Gibson, prin. Fax 986-1589
Other Schools – See Macon

Greensboro, Greene, Pop. 3,303
Greene County SD 2,100/PK-12
101 E Third St 30642 706-453-7688
Shawn McCollough, supt. Fax 453-9019
www.greene.k12.ga.us
Carson MS 500/6-8
1010 S Main St 30642 706-453-3308
Garrick Askew, prin. Fax 453-4674
Greene County HS 600/9-12
1002 S Main St 30642 706-453-2271
Dr. Michael Ashmore, prin. Fax 453-3311

Greenville, Meriwether, Pop. 938
Meriwether County SD 3,800/PK-12
PO Box 70 30222 706-672-4297
Carol Lane, supt. Fax 672-1618
www.meriwether.k12.ga.us
Greenville HS 500/9-12
PO Box 340 30222 706-672-4930
Brenda Hudson, prin. Fax 672-1424
Greenville MS 400/6-8
PO Box 190 30222 706-672-3115
Robert Johnson, prin. Fax 672-3119
Other Schools – See Manchester

Griffin, Spalding, Pop. 23,286
Griffin-Spalding County SD 9,800/PK-12
PO Box N 30224 770-229-3700
Jesse Bradley, supt. Fax 229-3708
www.spalding.k12.ga.us
Cowan Road MS 700/6-8
1185 Cowan Rd 30223 770-229-3722
Hoby Davenport, prin. Fax 227-8583
Flynt MS 600/6-8
221 Spalding Dr 30223 770-229-3739
Eclan David, prin. Fax 229-3712
Griffin HS 1,700/9-12
1617 W Poplar St 30224 770-229-3752
Dr. Quimby Melton, prin. Fax 229-3752
Kennedy Road MS 6-8
280 Kennedy Rd 30223 770-229-3760
Brenda James, prin. Fax 467-4626
Spalding HS 1,300/9-12
550 Wilson Rd 30224 770-229-3775
Darrell Jeffcoat, prin. Fax 227-6899
Taylor Street MS 800/6-8
234 E Taylor St 30223 770-229-3727
Lindy Pruitt, prin. Fax 229-3770
Griffin Evening S Adult
1617 W Poplar St 30224 770-467-5015
Christina Wiser, prin.

Grace Academy 100/K-12
PO Box 679 30224 770-467-8220
Lynn Fulop, admin. Fax 467-8869
Griffin Technical College Post-Sec.
501 Varsity Rd 30223 770-228-7366

Grovetown, Columbia, Pop. 7,483
Columbia County SD
Supt. — See Evans
Columbia MS 700/6-8
6000 Columbia Rd 30813 706-541-1252
Dr. Donna Anderson, prin. Fax 541-2742
Grovetown MS 500/6-8
5463 Harlem Grovetown Rd 30813 706-855-2514
Carolyn Fries, prin. Fax 868-3734

Guyton, Effingham, Pop. 1,707
Effingham County SD
Supt. — See Springfield
South Effingham HS 1,300/9-12
1220 Noel C Conaway Rd 31312 912-728-7511
W. Lang Brannen, prin. Fax 728-7529
South Effingham MS 900/6-8
1200 Noel C Conaway Rd 31312 912-728-7500
Dr. Mark Winters, prin. Fax 728-7508

Hahira, Lowndes, Pop. 1,915
Lowndes County SD
Supt. — See Valdosta
Hahira MS 1,200/6-8
101 S Nelson St 31632 229-794-2838
Kip McLeod, prin. Fax 794-3564

Valwood S 400/PK-12
4830 US Highway 41 N 31632 229-242-8491
Cobb Atkinson, hdmstr. Fax 245-7894

Hamilton, Harris, Pop. 527
Harris County SD 4,500/PK-12
132 Barnes Mill Rd 31811 706-628-4206
Dr. Susan Andrews, supt. Fax 628-5609
www.harris.k12.ga.us
Harris County - Carver MS 1,100/6-8
PO Box 408 31811 706-628-4951
Arnold Jackson, prin. Fax 628-5737
Harris County HS 1,300/9-12
8281 GA Highway 116 31811 706-628-4278
Roger Couch, prin. Fax 628-4335

Hampton, Henry, Pop. 4,743
Clayton County SD
Supt. — See Jonesboro
Lovejoy HS 1,800/9-12
1587 Mcdonough Rd 30228 770-473-2920
Dr. Sam Jackson, prin. Fax 473-2928
Lovejoy MS 1,100/6-8
1588 Lovejoy Rd 30228 770-473-2933
Keith Colbert, prin. Fax 603-5777

Henry County SD
Supt. — See Mc Donough
Dutchtown HS 600/9-12
149 Mitchell Rd 30228 770-515-7510
Dwala Nobles, prin. Fax 515-7515
Dutchtown MS 1,100/6-8
155 Mitchell Rd 30228 770-515-7500
Susan Downs, prin. Fax 515-7505

Bible Baptist Christian S 200/PK-12
2780 Mount Carmel Rd 30228 770-946-4708
Timothy Lee, prin. Fax 946-4715

Harlem, Columbia, Pop. 1,818
Columbia County SD
Supt. — See Evans
Harlem HS 1,100/9-12
1070 Appling Harlem Rd 30814 706-556-5980
Alan Griffin, prin. Fax 556-5986
Harlem MS 400/6-8
375 W Forrest St 30814 706-556-5990
Walker Davis, prin. Fax 556-5961

Hartwell, Hart, Pop. 4,288
Hart County SD 3,500/K-12
PO Box 696 30643 706-376-5141
Nancy T. Clark, supt. Fax 376-7046
www.hart.k12.ga.us
Hart County HS 1,100/9-12
59 Fifth St 30643 706-376-5461
Dennis Brown, prin. Fax 856-7237
Hart County MS 800/6-8
176 Powell Rd 30643 706-376-5431
Eulin Gibbs, prin. Fax 376-2207

Hawkinsville, Pulaski, Pop. 4,212
Pulaski County SD 1,700/PK-12
206 Mccormick Ave 31036 478-783-7200
Janis Sparrow, supt. Fax 783-7204
www.pulaski.k12.ga.us
Hawkinsville HS 500/9-12
1 Red Devil Dr 31036 478-783-7210
Mary Royal, prin. Fax 783-7251
Pulaski County MS 400/6-8
851 Broad St 31036 478-892-7215
Tony Lester, prin. Fax 783-7297

Hazlehurst, Jeff Davis, Pop. 3,729
Jeff Davis County SD 2,600/K-12
PO Box 1780 31539 912-375-6700
Dr. Lula Mae Perry, supt. Fax 375-6703
www.jeff-davis.k12.ga.us
Davis HS 800/9-12
156 Collins St 31539 912-375-6760
Cecelia McLoon, prin. Fax 375-0945
Davis MS 600/6-8
96 W Jefferson St 31539 912-375-6750
David Stapleton, prin. Fax 375-6756

Hephzibah, Richmond, Pop. 4,210
Richmond County SD
Supt. — See Augusta
Hephzibah Comprehensive HS 1,300/9-12
4558 Brothersville Rd 30815 706-592-2089
Dr. Veta New, prin. Fax 592-3975
Hephzibah MS 1,000/6-8
PO Box 70 30815 706-592-4534
Dr. Deborah Shepherd, prin. Fax 592-3979
Morgan Road MS 800/6-8
3635 Hiers Blvd 30815 706-796-4992
Janie Norris, prin. Fax 560-3947
Spirit Creek MS 900/6-8
115 Dolphin Way 30815 706-592-3987
Sharon McAlevy, prin. Fax 592-3999

Hiawassee, Towns, Pop. 844
Towns County SD 1,100/PK-12
67 Lakeview Cir Ste C 30546 706-896-2279
Dr. Richard Behrens, supt. Fax 896-2632
www.towns.k12.ga.us
Towns County HS 300/9-12
1400 Highway 76 E 30546 706-896-4131
Roy Perren, prin. Fax 896-6628
Towns County MS 300/6-8
1400 Highway 76 E 30546 706-896-4131
Dr. Marian Sumner, prin. Fax 896-6628
Other Schools – See Blairsville

Hinesville, Liberty, Pop. 28,615
Liberty County SD 11,400/PK-12
110 S Gause St 31313 912-876-2161
Steve Wilmoth, supt. Fax 368-6201
www.liberty.k12.ga.us/
Bradwell Institute HS 1,900/9-12
100 Pafford St 31313 912-876-6121
Dr. Vicki Albritton, prin. Fax 876-6914
Frasier MS 800/6-8
910 Long Frasier Dr 31313 912-877-5367
Tom Alexander, prin. Fax 877-3291
Liberty County HS 1,300/9-12
3216 E Oglethorpe Hwy 31313 912-876-4316
Paula Scott, prin. Fax 876-4303
Snelson Golden MS 1,100/6-8
465 Coates Rd 31313 912-877-3112
Dr. Chris Garretson, prin. Fax 368-5342
Other Schools – See Midway

Hiram, Paulding, Pop. 1,762
Paulding County SD
Supt. — See Dallas
Hiram HS 2,000/9-12
702 Ballentine Dr 30141 770-443-1182
Eddie Fincher, prin. Fax 439-5053

Hogansville, Troup, Pop. 2,823
Troup County SD
Supt. — See La Grange
Callaway HS 700/9-12
221 Whitfield Rd 30230 706-845-2070
Kevin Jones, prin. Fax 845-2071

Homer, Banks, Pop. 1,085
Banks County SD 2,200/PK-12
PO Box 248 30547 706-677-2224
Christopher B. Erwin, supt. Fax 677-2223
www.banks.k12.ga.us
Banks County HS 700/9-12
1486 Historic Homer Hwy # A 30547 706-677-2221
Arthur Wheaton, prin. Fax 677-2688
Banks County MS 700/6-8
712 Thompson St 30547 706-677-2277
Matthew Cooper, prin. Fax 677-5227

Homerville, Clinch, Pop. 2,811
Clinch County SD 1,300/K-12
46 S College St 31634 912-487-5321
Dr. Gayle Hughes, supt. Fax 487-5068
www.clinchcounty.com/
Clinch County HS 500/8-12
863 Carswell St 31634 912-487-5366
Alvin Henderson, prin. Fax 487-3272

Hoschton, Jackson, Pop. 1,455
Gwinnett County SD
Supt. — See Suwanee
Mill Creek HS 2,400/9-12
4400 Braselton Hwy 30548 678-714-5850
Jim Markham, prin. Fax 714-5852
Osborne MS 1,700/6-8
4404 Braselton Hwy 30548 770-904-5400
John Campbell, prin. Fax 904-5408

Irwinton, Wilkinson, Pop. 584
Wilkinson County SD 1,700/PK-12
PO Box 206 31042 478-946-5521
Terry Sark, supt. Fax 946-3275
Wilkinson County HS 500/9-12
PO Box 547 31042 478-946-2441
Dr. Harold Johnson, prin. Fax 946-7134
Wilkinson County MS 400/6-8
PO Box 527 31042 478-946-2541
Dr. Aaron Geter, prin. Fax 946-8981

Jackson, Butts, Pop. 4,358
Butts County SD 3,500/K-12
181 N Mulberry St 30233 770-504-2300
Dr. Alan White, supt. Fax 504-2305
www.butts.k12.ga.us
Henderson MS 800/6-8
494 George Tate Dr 30233 770-504-2310
Dr. Mary Jacobs, prin. Fax 504-2315
Jackson HS 1,000/9-12
717 S Harkness St 30233 770-504-2340
Duane Kline, prin. Fax 504-2341

Jasper, Pickens, Pop. 2,837
Pickens County SD 4,200/K-12
159 Stegall Dr 30143 706-253-1700
Michael Ballew, supt. Fax 253-1705
www.pickens.k12.ga.us/
Jasper MS 600/6-8
339 W Church St 30143 706-253-1760
Steven McDaniel, prin. Fax 253-1765
Pickens County MS 500/6-8
1802 Refuge Rd 30143 706-253-1830
Chris LeMieux, prin. Fax 253-1835
Pickens HS 1,300/9-12
500 Dragon Dr 30143 706-253-1800
Tommy Qualls, prin. Fax 253-1815

Appalachian Technical College Post-Sec.
100 Campus Dr 30143 706-253-4500

Jefferson, Jackson, Pop. 5,599
Jackson County SD 6,000/PK-12
1660 Winder Hwy 30549 706-367-5151
Dr. Shannon Adams, supt. Fax 367-9457
www.jackson.k12.ga.us
Jackson County Comprehensive HS 1,600/9-12
1668 Winder Hwy 30549 706-367-5003
Dr. Pat Stueck, prin. Fax 367-2146
West Jackson MS 800/6-8
400 Gum Springs Church Rd 30549 706-367-5267
Dr. Russ Chesser, prin. Fax 367-5068
Regional Evening S Adult
441 Gordon St 30549 706-367-2341
Janice Stowe, prin. Fax 367-1647
Other Schools – See Commerce

Jefferson CSD 1,900/PK-12
575 Washington St 30549 706-367-2880
Dr. John Jackson, supt. Fax 367-2291
www.jeffcityschools.org/
Jefferson HS 500/9-12
575 Washington St 30549 706-367-2881
Dr. Kevin Smith, prin. Fax 367-1884
Jefferson MS 400/6-8
100 Dragon Dr 30549 706-367-2882
Howard McGlennen, prin. Fax 367-5207

Jeffersonville, Twiggs, Pop. 1,219
Twiggs County SD 900/PK-12
PO Box 232 31044 478-945-3127
Dr. Carol Brown, supt. Fax 945-3078
www.twiggs.k12.ga.us
Twiggs County HS 400/9-12
375 Watson Dr 31044 478-945-3112
Walter Stephens, prin. Fax 945-3140
Twiggs County MS 200/5-8
375 Watson Dr 31044 478-945-3113
Fax 945-3140

Twiggs Academy 200/PK-12
961 Hamlin Floyd Rd 31044 478-945-3175
Dediere Fountain, admin. Fax 945-3275

Jesup, Wayne, Pop. 9,851
Wayne County SD 5,100/PK-12
555 Sunset Blvd 31545 912-427-1000
Kendall Keith, supt. Fax 427-1004
www.wayne.k12.ga.us
Puckett MS 700/6-8
475 Durrence Rd 31545 912-427-1061
Denise Voyles, prin. Fax 427-1069
Wayne County HS 1,500/9-12
1 Jacket Dr 31545 912-427-1088
Joe McPipkin, prin. Fax 427-1081
Williams MS 600/6-8
1175 S US Highway 301 31546 912-427-1025
Ronnie Harper, prin. Fax 427-1032

Altamaha Technical College Post-Sec.
1777 W Cherry St 31545 912-427-5800

Jonesboro, Clayton, Pop. 3,922
Clayton County SD 51,300/PK-12
1058 5th Ave 30236 770-473-2700
Dr. Barbara Pulliam, supt. Fax 473-2706
www.clayton.k12.ga.us/
Jonesboro HS 1,700/9-12
7728 Mount Zion Blvd 30236 770-473-2855
Derrick Williams, prin. Fax 603-5177
Jonesboro MS 900/6-8
1308 Arnold St 30236 678-610-4331
Kay Sledge, prin. Fax 610-4347
Kendrick MS 1,500/6-8
7971 Kendrick Rd 30238 770-472-8400
Beverly Garner, prin. Fax 472-8413
Mt. Zion HS 1,800/9-12
2535 Mount Zion Pkwy 30236 770-473-2940
Gary Townsend, prin. Fax 473-2784
Mundy's Mill HS 2,000/9-12
9652 Fayetteville Rd 30238 678-817-3000
Anthony Smith, prin. Fax 817-3007
Mundy's Mill MS 1,000/6-8
1251 Mundys Mill Rd 30238 770-473-2880
Nash Alexander, prin. Fax 603-5779
Pointe South MS 1,100/6-8
8495 Thomas Rd 30238 770-473-2890
Dean Lillard, prin. Fax 477-4603
Roberts MS 1,100/6-8
1905 Walt Stephens Rd 30236 678-479-0100
Darrell Herring, prin. Fax 479-0114
Other Schools – See College Park, Forest Park, Hampton, Morrow, Rex, Riverdale

---

ETI Career Institute Post-Sec.
9500 S Main St 30236 770-477-2799
Everest Institute Post-Sec.
6431 Tara Blvd 30236 770-994-1900
Mt. Zion Christian Academy 500/PK-12
7102 Mount Zion Blvd 30236 770-478-9842
Dr. Pam Adamson, hdmstr. Fax 478-4817

Kathleen, Houston
Houston County SD
Supt. — See Perry
Mossy Creek MS 6-8
200 Danny Carpenter Dr 31047 478-988-6171
Paige Busbee, prin. Fax 218-7538

Kennesaw, Cobb, Pop. 30,522
Cobb County SD
Supt. — See Marietta
Awtrey MS 1,600/6-8
3601 Nowlin Rd NW 30144 770-975-6615
Erin Barnett, prin. Fax 975-6617
Harrison HS 2,300/9-12
4500 Due West Rd NW 30152 678-594-8104
Donald Griggers, prin. Fax 594-8106
Kennesaw Mountain HS 3,000/9-12
1898 Kennesaw Due West Rd 30152 678-594-8190
Sue Gunderman, prin. Fax 594-8192
Lost Mountain MS 1,500/6-8
700 Old Mountain Rd NW 30152 678-594-8224
Dr. Terry Poor, prin. Fax 594-8226
McClure MS 6-8
3660 Old Stilesboro Rd NW 30152 678-331-8131
Susan Wing, prin. Fax 331-8132
North Cobb HS 2,300/9-12
3400 Highway 293 N 30144 770-975-6685
Gary Boling, prin. Fax 975-6687
Palmer MS 1,300/6-8
690 N Booth Rd NW 30144 770-591-5020
Geraldine Ray, prin. Fax 591-5032
Pine Mountain MS 1,200/6-8
2720 Pine Mountain Cir NW 30152 678-594-8252
Dr. Ivia Redmond, prin. Fax 594-8254

Cobb Beauty College Post-Sec.
3096 Cherokee St NW 30144 770-424-6915
Devereux-Georgia Treatment Network Post-Sec.
1291 Stanley Rd NW 30152 800-342-3357
Empire Beauty School Post-Sec.
425 Ernest Barrett Pkwy #H2 30144 770-419-2303
ITT Technical Institute Post-Sec.
1000 Cobb Place Blvd NW 30144 770-426-3000
Kennesaw State University Post-Sec.
1000 Chastain Rd NW 30144 770-423-6000
Mount Paran Christian S 1,100/PK-12
1275 Stanley Rd NW 30152 770-578-0182
Dr. David Tilley, hdmstr. Fax 977-9284
North Cobb Christian S 900/PK-12
4500 Lakeview Dr NW 30144 770-975-0252
Gary Coker, hdmstr. Fax 975-8446
Shiloh Hills Christian S 500/K-12
260 Hawkins Store Rd NE 30144 770-926-7729
John D. Ward, admin. Fax 926-3762

Kingsland, Camden, Pop. 12,063
Camden County SD 9,600/PK-12
311 S East St 31548 912-729-5687
Dr. William Hardin, supt. Fax 729-1489
www.camden.k12.ga.us/
Camden County HS 2,700/9-12
6300 Laurel Island Pkwy 31548 912-729-7318
Dr. John Tucker, prin. Fax 729-7627
Camden MS 1,400/6-8
1300 Middle School Rd 31548 912-729-3113
Mark Durham, prin. Fax 729-7489
Other Schools – See Saint Marys

Kingston, Bartow, Pop. 668
Bartow County SD
Supt. — See Cartersville
Woodland MS at Euharlee 900/6-8
1061 Euharlee Rd 30145 770-606-5871
Lamar Barnes, prin. Fax 606-2092

La Fayette, Walker, Pop. 6,753
Walker County SD 8,900/PK-12
201 S Duke St 30728 706-638-1240
Melissa Mathis, supt. Fax 638-7827
www.walkerschools.org
La Fayette HS 1,000/9-12
5178 Round Pond Rd 30728 706-638-2342
Roger Hibbs, prin. Fax 638-4767
La Fayette MS 1,000/6-8
419 Roadrunner Blvd 30728 706-638-6440
Mike Culberson, prin. Fax 638-7616
Other Schools – See Flintstone, Rossville

La Grange, Troup, Pop. 26,424
Troup County SD 12,100/PK-12
PO Box 1228 30241 706-812-7900
Edwin D. Smith, supt. Fax 812-7904
www.troup.org/
Callaway MS 600/6-8
2244 Hammett Rd, 706-845-2080
Thomas Whatley, prin. Fax 845-2081
Gardner-Newman MS 900/6-8
101 Shannon Dr, 706-883-1535
Dr. Martha Richardson, prin. Fax 883-1562
La Grange HS 1,300/9-12
516 N Greenwood St, 706-883-1590
Steve Cole, prin. Fax 812-7976
Long Cane MS 1,100/6-8
326 Long Cane Rd, 706-845-2085
Kim Warner, prin. Fax 845-2086
Troup County Comprehensive HS 1,300/9-12
1920 Hamilton Rd, 706-812-7957
Bill Parsons, prin. Fax 812-7960
West Side Magnet S 500/3-8
301 Forrest Ave, 706-883-1550
Alane Thompson, prin. Fax 883-1563
Other Schools – See Hogansville

Lafayette Christian S 200/PK-12
PO Box 934, 706-884-6684
John Cipolla, hdmstr. Fax 882-2515
La Grange Academy 200/K-12
1501 Vernon Rd, 706-882-8097
Matt Walsh, hdmstr. Fax 882-8640
La Grange College Post-Sec.
601 Broad St, 706-880-8000
West Georgia Technical College Post-Sec.
303 Fort Dr, 706-845-4323

Lakeland, Lanier, Pop. 2,769
Lanier County SD 1,500/PK-12
PO Box 158 31635 229-482-3966
Dr. Tom Hagler, supt. Fax 482-3020
www.lanier.k12.ga.us/
Lanier County HS 400/9-12
325 W Patten Ave 31635 229-482-3868
Spencer Willis, prin. Fax 482-3368
Lanier County MS 400/6-8
325 W Patten Ave 31635 229-482-8247
Keith Humphrey, prin. Fax 482-8339

Lakeland Adventist S 50/1-12
842 W Thigpen Ave 31635 229-482-2418

Lawrenceville, Gwinnett, Pop. 28,393
Gwinnett County SD
Supt. — See Suwanee
Central Gwinnett HS 2,400/9-12
564 W Crogan St 30045 770-963-8041
Dr. Valerie Clark, prin. Fax 338-4879
Creekland MS 2,800/6-8
170 Russell Rd 30043 770-338-4700
Dr. William Kruskamp, prin. Fax 338-4703
Crews MS 1,300/6-8
1000 Old Snellville Hwy 30044 770-982-6940
Dr. Howard Taylor, prin. Fax 982-6942
Five Forks MS 1,100/6-8
3250 River Dr 30044 770-972-1506
Dr. Mary Hensien, prin. Fax 736-4547
Maxwell HS of Technology Vo/Tech
990 McElvaney Ln 30044 770-963-6838
Donna Powers, prin. Fax 338-4612
Phoenix HS 700/9-12
501 W Pike St 30045 770-513-6862
Dr. Kevin Tashlein, prin. Fax 513-6864
Richards MS 2,300/6-8
3555 Sugarloaf Pkwy 30044 770-995-7133
Judy Stephens, prin. Fax 338-4791
Sweetwater MS 1,700/6-8
3500 Cruse Rd 30044 770-923-4131
Angela Moton, prin. Fax 931-7077

Aviation Institute of Maintenance Post-Sec.
500 Briscoe Blvd 30045 770-377-5600
Branch Christian Academy 100/PK-12
1288 Braselton Hwy 30043 770-277-4722
Janice Sinclair, prin. Fax 277-4365
Empire Beauty College Post-Sec.
1455 Pleasant Hill Rd #105 30044 770-564-0725
Gwinnett Technical College Post-Sec.
5150 Sugarloaf Pkwy 30043 770-962-7580

Leesburg, Lee, Pop. 2,777
Lee County SD 5,500/PK-12
PO Box 399 31763 229-903-2100
Dr. Lawrence T. Walters, supt. Fax 903-2130
www.lee.k12.ga.us
Lee County HS 1,600/9-12
1 Trojan Way 31763 229-903-2260
Kevin Dowling, prin. Fax 903-2291
Lee County MS 1,400/6-8
190 Smithville Rd N 31763 229-903-2140
Gail Melvin, prin. Fax 903-2160

Lexington, Oglethorpe, Pop. 236
Oglethorpe County SD 2,300/PK-12
735 Athens Rd 30648 706-743-8128
Dr. Jeffery C. Welch, supt. Fax 743-3211
www.oglethorpe.k12.ga.us
Oglethorpe County HS 700/9-12
749 Athens Rd 30648 706-743-8124
Phillip Todd, prin. Fax 743-3536
Oglethorpe County MS 600/6-8
757 Athens Rd 30648 706-743-8146
Beverley Levine, prin. Fax 743-3536

Lilburn, Gwinnett, Pop. 11,416
Gwinnett County SD
Supt. — See Suwanee
Berkmar HS 2,800/9-12
405 Pleasant Hill Rd NW 30047 770-921-3636
Kendall Johnson, prin. Fax 806-3715
Berkmar MS 900/6-8
4355 Lawrenceville Hwy NW 30047 770-638-2300
Kenney Wells, prin. Fax 638-2309
Lilburn MS 1,200/6-8
4994 Lawrenceville Hwy NW 30047 770-921-1776
James Rayford, prin. Fax 806-3866
Parkview HS 2,600/9-12
998 Cole Rd SW 30047 770-921-2874
Dr. Charles Buchanan, prin. Fax 806-3797
Trickum MS 1,800/6-8
130 Killian Hill Rd SW 30047 770-921-2705
Lynne Davis, prin. Fax 806-3742

Gwinnett College of Business Post-Sec.
4230 Lwrncvll Hwy NW #11 30047 770-381-7200
Killian Hill Christian S 500/K-12
151 Arcado Rd SW 30047 770-921-3224
Paul Williams, prin. Fax 921-9395
Providence Christian Academy 800/K-12
4575 Lawrenceville Hwy NW 30047 770-279-7200
James Vaught, hdmstr. Fax 279-8258

Lincolnton, Lincoln, Pop. 1,515
Lincoln County SD 1,400/PK-12
PO Box 39 30817 706-359-3742
Dr. G. R. Edmunds, supt. Fax 359-7938
www.lincolncountyschools.org
Lincoln County HS 400/9-12
PO Box 580 30817 706-359-3121
Dr. Becky Barden, prin. Fax 359-3552
Lincoln County MS 400/6-8
PO Box 550 30817 706-359-3069
Pam Carmichael, prin. Fax 359-2200

Lindale, Floyd, Pop. 4,187
Floyd County SD
Supt. — See Rome
Pepperell HS 900/9-12
3 Dragon Dr SE 30147 706-236-1844
Phil Ray, prin. Fax 236-1846
Pepperell MS 800/6-8
200 Hughes Dairy Rd SE 30147 706-236-1849
Frank Pinson, prin. Fax 802-6776

Lithia Springs, Douglas, Pop. 11,403
Douglas County SD
Supt. — See Douglasville
Lithia Springs HS 1,600/9-12
2520 E County Line Rd 30122 770-651-6700
Larry Ruble, prin. Fax 651-6862
Turner MS 800/6-8
7101 Junior High Dr 30122 770-651-5500
Jean Williams, prin. Fax 651-5503

Colonial Hills Christian S 500/PK-12
7131 Mount Vernon Rd 30122 770-941-6342
Westley Smith, admin. Fax 941-2090
Lithia Christian Academy 200/PK-12
2548 Vulcan Dr 30122 770-941-5406
Lanier Motes, admin. Fax 941-9944

Lithonia, DeKalb, Pop. 2,197
DeKalb County SD
Supt. — See Decatur
King HS 2,000/9-12
3991 Snapfinger Rd 30038 678-874-5402
Sylvester Nelloms, prin. Fax 874-5410
Lithonia HS 2,000/9-12
2440 Phillips Rd 30058 678-676-2902
Margie Smith, prin. Fax 676-2910
Lithonia MS 1,600/6-8
2451 Randall Ave 30058 678-875-0702
Patricia May, prin. Fax 875-0710
Miller Grove HS 700/9-12
2645 DeKalb Medical Pkwy 30058 678-875-1102
Dr. Ralph Simpson, prin. Fax 875-1110
Redan MS 1,300/6-8
1775 Young Rd 30058 678-874-7902
Matthew Priester, prin. Fax 874-7910
Salem MS 1,500/6-8
5333 Salem Rd 30038 678-676-9402
Stanley Mons, prin. Fax 676-9410

Lithonia Adventist Academy 50/K-10
3533 Ragsdale Rd 30038 770-482-0294
Fax 482-6224
Luther Rice University Post-Sec.
3038 Evans Mill Rd 30038 770-484-1204
New Birth Christian Academy 200/PK-12
PO Box 610 30058 770-696-9678
Dr. M.O. Clarke, hdmstr. Fax 696-9674

Locust Grove, Henry, Pop. 3,434
Henry County SD
Supt. — See Mc Donough
Luella HS 1,600/9-12
603 Walker Dr 30248 770-898-9822
George Eckerle, prin. Fax 898-9625
Luella MS 1,600/6-8
2075 Hmpton Locust Grove Rd 30248 678-583-8919
Aaryn Schmuhl, prin. Fax 583-8920

Loganville, Walton, Pop. 8,881
Gwinnett County SD
Supt. — See Suwanee
Grayson HS 2,600/9-12
50 Hope Hollow Rd 30052 770-554-1071
Dr. Keith Chaney, prin. Fax 554-1074
McConnell MS 2,100/6-8
550 Ozora Rd 30052 770-554-1000
Dan Hicks, prin. Fax 554-1003

Walton County SD
Supt. — See Monroe
Loganville HS 1,800/9-12
100 Trident Trl 30052 770-466-4892
Gary Hobbs, prin. Fax 466-5334
Loganville MS 900/6-8
152 Clark McCullers Dr 30052 770-466-0713
Eugene Williams, prin. Fax 466-3035
Youth MS 900/6-8
1804 Highway 81 30052 770-466-6849
Jane Burris, prin. Fax 466-8596

Covenant Christian Academy 300/K-12
3425 Loganville Hwy 30052 770-466-7890
Emmaline McKinnon, prin. Fax 466-2833
Faith Academy 1,100/9-12
2571 Highway 78 30052 770-466-7872
Jacquelyn Griggs, prin. Fax 554-0123
Loganville Christian Academy 400/PK-12
2575 Highway 81 30052 770-554-9888
Christy Monda, admin. Fax 554-9881

Lookout Mountain, Walker, Pop. 1,570

Covenant College Post-Sec.
14049 Scenic Hwy 30750 706-820-1560

Louisville, Jefferson, Pop. 2,643
Jefferson County SD 3,300/PK-12
PO Box 449 30434 478-625-7626
Carl Bethune, supt. Fax 625-7459
www.jefferson.k12.ga.us
Hi Tech S Vo/Tech
1200 School St 30434 478-625-7764
Teresa Brooks, prin. Fax 625-3120
Jefferson County HS 1,000/9-12
1157 Warrior Trl 30434 478-625-9991
Dr. Molly Howard, prin. Fax 625-8988
Louisville MS 500/6-8
1200 School St 30434 478-625-7764
Samuel Dasher, prin. Fax 625-3120
Other Schools – See Wrens

Jefferson Academy 300/K-12
2264 US Highway 1 N 30434 478-625-8861
Chuck Wimberley, prin. Fax 625-9196

Ludowici, Long, Pop. 1,558
Long County SD 2,200/PK-12
PO Box 428 31316 912-545-2367
Dr. Edwin Pope, supt. Fax 545-2380
www2.long.k12.ga.us/
Long County HS 500/9-12
PO Box 579 31316 912-545-2135
Dr. Dolores Mallard, prin. Fax 545-2136
Walker MS 900/PK-PK, 4-
PO Box 579 31316 912-545-2069
Vicky Wells, prin. Fax 545-2775

Lumpkin, Stewart, Pop. 1,265
Stewart County SD 700/PK-12
PO Box 547 31815 229-838-4329
Henry Moylan, supt. Fax 838-6984
www.stewart.k12.ga.us/
Stewart County MS 100/6-8
PO Box 706 31815 229-838-4532
Viola Fedd, prin. Fax 838-4352
Stewart-Quitman HS 200/9-12
PO Box 706 31815 229-838-4301
Tommie Dopson, prin. Fax 838-4352

Lyons, Toombs, Pop. 4,384
Toombs County SD 2,800/PK-12
117 E Wesley Ave 30436 912-526-3141
Dr. Kendall Brantley, supt. Fax 526-3291
www.toombs.k12.ga.us/
Toombs County HS 800/9-12
600 Bulldog Rd 30436 912-526-6068
Gail Clark, prin. Fax 526-4612
Toombs County MS 700/6-8
701 Bulldog Rd 30436 912-526-8363
Pam Sears, prin. Fax 526-0240

Toombs Christian Academy 300/PK-12
PO Box 227 30436 912-526-8938
John E. Sharpe, hdmstr. Fax 526-0571

Mableton, Cobb, Pop. 30,600
Cobb County SD
Supt. — See Marietta
Floyd MS 1,000/6-8
4803 Floyd Rd SW 30126 770-819-2453
Dr. Lawrence Bynum, prin. Fax 819-2455
Lindley MS 1,500/6-8
50 Veterans Memorial Hwy SE 30126 770-819-2496
John McCrary, prin. Fax 819-2498
Pebblebrook HS 1,700/9-12
991 Old Alabama Rd SW 30126 770-819-2521
Regina Montgomery, prin. Fax 819-2523

Cumberland Christian Academy 100/6-8
4900 Floyd Rd SW 30126 770-819-6443
Larry Kendrick, hdmstr. Fax 945-0224
Whitefield Academy 600/K-12
1 Whitefield Dr SE 30126 678-305-3000
Timothy Hillen, hdmstr. Fax 305-3010

Mc Donough, Henry, Pop. 3,773
Henry County SD 32,300/PK-12
33 N Zack Hinton Pkwy 30253 770-957-6601
Jack Parish, supt. Fax 914-6178
www.henry.k12.ga.us
Eagle's Landing HS 1,600/9-12
301 Tunis Rd 30253 770-954-9515
Gabriel Crerie, prin. Fax 914-9789
Eagle's Landing MS 900/6-8
295 Tunis Rd 30253 770-914-8189
James Davis, prin. Fax 914-2989
Henry County HS 1,400/9-12
401 Tomlinson St 30253 770-957-3943
Andy Giddens, prin. Fax 957-0368
Henry County MS 1,300/6-8
166 Holly Smith Dr 30253 770-957-3945
Larry Monk, prin. Fax 957-0368
Ola HS 9-12
357 N Ola Rd, 770-288-3222
Ross Iddings, prin. Fax 288-3230
Ola MS 6-8
353 N Ola Rd, 770-288-2108
Louann Jones, prin. Fax 288-2114
Union Grove HS 2,000/9-12
120 E Lake Rd, 678-583-8502
Tom Smith, prin. Fax 583-8850
Union Grove MS 1,600/6-8
210 E Lake Rd, 678-583-8978
Robyn Mullis, prin. Fax 583-8580
Henry County Evening Academy Adult
120 E Lake Rd, 678-583-8856
Vanthony Smith, prin. Fax 583-8850
Other Schools – See Hampton, Locust Grove, Stockbridge

Eagle's Landing Christian Academy 1,300/PK-12
2400 Highway 42 N 30253 770-957-2927
Marshall Chambers, admin. Fax 957-2290

Macon, Bibb, Pop. 94,316
Bibb County SD 22,700/PK-12
484 Mulberry St 31201 478-765-8711
Sharon Patterson, supt. Fax 765-8549
www.bibb.k12.ga.us
Appling MS 600/7-8
1210 Shurling Dr 31211 478-779-2200
Robert Stevenson, prin. Fax 779-2202
Ballard-Hudson MS 7-8
1070 Anthony Rd 31204 478-779-3400
Benjy Morgan, prin. Fax 779-3396
Bloomfield MS 6-8
4375 Bloomfield Drive Ext 31206 478-779-4800
David Dillard, prin. Fax 779-4760
Central Magnet HS 1,300/9-12
2155 Napier Ave 31204 478-779-2300
Dr. Erin Weaver, prin. Fax 779-2307
Howard MS 700/6-8
6600 Forsyth Rd 31210 478-779-3500
Karen Yarbrough, prin. Fax 779-3458
Hutchings HS Vo/Tech
2011 Riverside Dr 31204 478-779-2550
Ron McCall, prin. Fax 779-2540
Miller Magnet MS 800/6-8
751 Hendley St 31204 478-779-4050
Tanzy Kilcrease, prin. Fax 779-4032
Northeast Magnet HS 900/9-12
1646 Upper River Rd 31211 478-779-4100
Dr. Sam Scavella, prin. Fax 779-4136
Rutland HS 900/9-12
6250 Skipper Rd 31216 478-779-3100
Gail Gilbert, prin. Fax 779-3045
Rutland MS 1,100/6-8
6260 Skipper Rd 31216 478-779-4400
Dr. Jerri Hall, prin. Fax 779-4373
Southwest Magnet HS 1,000/9-12
1710 Canterbury Rd 31206 478-779-4500
Tyrone Bacon, prin. Fax 779-4463
Weaver MS 800/7-8
2570 Heath Rd 31206 478-779-4650
Dr. Pam Carswell, prin. Fax 779-4627
Westside Magnet HS 1,700/9-12
2851 Heath Rd 31206 478-779-3800
Laura Perkins, prin. Fax 779-3832

Jones County SD
Supt. — See Gray
Clifton Ridge MS 600/6-8
169 Dusty Ln 31211 478-743-5182
Wes Cavender, prin. Fax 743-8282

American Professional Institute Post-Sec.
1990 Riverside Dr 31201 478-314-4444
Central Fellowship Christian Academy 500/PK-12
8460 Hawkinsville Rd 31216 478-788-6909
Truitt Franklin, admin. Fax 788-1614
Central Georgia Technical College Post-Sec.
3300 Macon Tech Dr 31206 478-757-3501
First Presbyterian Day S 1,000/PK-12
5671 Calvin Dr 31210 478-477-6505
Gregg Thompson, hdmstr. Fax 477-2804
Georgia Academy for the Blind Post-Sec.
2895 Vineville Ave 31204 478-751-6083
Gilead Christian Academy 200/PK-12
1931 Rocky Creek Rd 31206 478-788-0606
Brian Gottschall, prin. Fax 788-4382
Macon State College Post-Sec.
100 College Station Dr 31206 478-471-2700
Medical Center of Central Georgia Post-Sec.
777 Hemlock St 31201 478-633-1234
Mercer University in Macon Post-Sec.
1400 Coleman Ave 31207 800-637-2378
Middle Georgia Christian S 100/PK-10
5859 Thomaston Rd 31220 478-757-9585
Stan Frank, dir. Fax 757-9587
Mt. de Sales Academy 600/7-12
PO Box 6136 31208 478-751-3240
Katy Prebble, prin. Fax 751-3241
Stratford Academy 900/PK-12
6010 Peake Rd 31220 478-477-8073
Michael Collins, hdmstr. Fax 477-0299
Tattnall Square Academy 800/PK-12
111 Trojan Trl 31210 478-477-6760
Barney Hester, hdmstr. Fax 474-7887
Wesleyan College Post-Sec.
4760 Forsyth Rd 31210 800-447-6610
Windsor Academy 300/K-12
4150 Jones Rd 31216 478-781-1621
John Cranford, hdmstr. Fax 781-0757

Mc Rae, Telfair, Pop. 3,041
Telfair County SD 1,700/PK-12
PO Box 240 31055 229-868-5661
Cary Clark, supt. Fax 868-5549
www.telfair.k12.ga.us
Telfair County HS 400/9-12
1900 S 3rd Ave 31055 229-868-6096
Tim Deep, prin. Fax 868-7221
Telfair County MS 400/6-8
101 Highway 280 W 31055 229-868-7465
Coleen McIver, prin. Fax 868-2616

Madison, Morgan, Pop. 3,833
Morgan County SD 3,200/PK-12
1065 East Ave 30650 706-752-4600
Dr. Stan DeJarnett, supt. Fax 752-4601
www.morgan.k12.ga.us
Morgan County HS 1,000/9-12
1231 College Dr 30650 706-342-2336
Dr. Mark Wilson, prin. Fax 342-5046
Morgan County MS 800/6-8
920 Pearl St 30650 706-342-0556
Dr. Joe Hutcheson, prin. Fax 342-5048

Manchester, Meriwether, Pop. 3,719
Meriwether County SD
Supt. — See Greenville
Manchester HS 600/9-12
405 N 5th Ave 31816 706-846-8445
Marlowe Hinson, prin. Fax 846-5081
Manchester MS 500/6-8
700 Martin Luther King Jr D 31816 706-846-2846
Edward Boswell, prin. Fax 846-8111

Manor, Ware
Ware County SD
Supt. — See Waycross
Ware County Magnet S 500/K-12
4650 Manor Millwood Rd S 31550 912-287-2338
Dr. Darlene Tanner, prin. Fax 287-2337

Marietta, Cobb, Pop. 61,261
Cobb County SD 96,200/PK-12
514 Glover St SE 30060 770-426-3300
Fred Sanderson, supt. Fax 426-3329
www.cobb.k12.ga.us
Daniell MS 900/6-8
2900 Scott Rd 30066 678-594-8048
Merilee Heflin, prin. Fax 594-8050
Dickerson MS 1,400/6-8
855 Woodlawn Dr NE 30068 770-578-2710
Dr. Kevin Daniel, prin. Fax 578-2712
Dodgen MS 800/6-8
1725 Bill Murdock Rd 30062 770-578-2726
James Snell, prin. Fax 578-2728
East Cobb MS 1,300/6-8
380 Holt Rd NE 30068 770-578-2740
David Chiprany, prin. Fax 578-2742
Hightower Trail MS 900/6-8
3905 Post Oak Tritt Rd 30062 770-578-7225
Dr. Hilda Wilkins, prin. Fax 578-7227
Kell HS 1,900/9-12
4770 Lee Waters Rd 30066 678-494-7844
Trudie Donovan, prin. Fax 494-7846
Lassiter HS 2,100/9-12
2601 Shallowford Rd 30066 678-494-7863
Chris Shaw, prin. Fax 494-7865
Mabry MS 900/6-8
2700 Jims Rd NE 30066 770-928-5546
Dr. Tim Tyson, prin. Fax 928-5548
McCleskey MS 800/6-8
4080 Maybreeze Rd 30066 770-928-5560
Dr. Jerry Dority, prin. Fax 928-5562
Osborne HS 1,800/9-12
2451 Favor Rd SW 30060 770-437-5900
Steven Miletto, prin. Fax 437-5902
Pope HS 2,000/9-12
3001 Hembree Rd NE 30062 770-578-7900
Dr. Charlotte Stowers, prin. Fax 578-7902
Simpson MS 900/6-8
3340 Trickum Rd NE 30066 770-971-4711
Sharon Jordan, prin. Fax 971-4507
Smitha MS 1,400/6-8
2025 Powder Springs Rd SW 30064 678-594-8267
Sharon Tucker, prin. Fax 594-8269
Sprayberry HS 1,900/9-12
2525 Sandy Plains Rd 30066 770-578-3200
Dr. Susan Galante, prin. Fax 578-3202
Wheeler HS 1,900/9-12
375 Holt Rd NE 30068 770-578-3266
Ed Thayer, prin. Fax 578-3268
Adult Education Center Adult
240 Barber Rd SE 30060 678-594-8011
Tommy Farr, prin. Fax 594-8015
Other Schools – See Acworth, Austell, Kennesaw, Mableton, Powder Springs, Smyrna

Marietta CSD 7,500/K-12
250 Howard St NE 30060 770-422-3500
Dr. Emily Lembeck, supt. Fax 425-4095
www.marietta-city.org
Marietta HS 2,000/9-12
1171 Whitlock Ave SW 30064 770-428-2631
Leigh Colburn, prin. Fax 429-3151
Marietta MS 1,200/7-8
121 Winn St NW 30064 770-422-0311
Tim Jones, prin. Fax 429-3162

Chattahoochee Technical College Post-Sec.
980 S Cobb Dr SE 30060 770-528-4500
Cobb County Christian S 50/PK-12
545 Lorene Dr SW 30060 770-434-1320
Gloria Kelly, admin. Fax 434-1442
Covenant Christian Ministries Academy 200/PK-12
PO Box 4065 30061 770-919-0022
Vanessa Anderson, supt. Fax 919-2098
Cumberland Christian Academy 100/9-12
2115 Pair Rd SW 30008 770-819-9942
Larry Kendrick, hdmstr. Fax 945-0224
Dominion Christian HS 300/9-12
4607 Burnt Hickory Rd NW 30064 770-420-2153
Marc Stout, hdmstr. Fax 420-2510
Everest Institute Post-Sec.
1600 Terrell Rd Ste G 30067 770-303-7997
High-Tech Institute Post-Sec.
1090 Northchase Pky SE #150 30067 770-988-9877
Life University Post-Sec.
1269 Barclay Cir SE 30060 770-426-2600
Roffler Moler Hairstyling College Post-Sec.
1311 Roswell Rd 30062 770-565-3285
Southern Polytech State University Post-Sec.
1100 S Marietta Pkwy SE 30060 770-528-7200
Walker S 1,100/PK-12
700 Cobb Pkwy N 30062 770-427-2689
Donald Robertson, hdmstr. Fax 514-8122

Martinez, Columbia, Pop. 27,700

Augusta Christian S 600/K-12
313 Baston Rd 30907 706-863-2905
Joel Woodcock, hdmstr. Fax 860-6618
Augusta Preparatory Day S 500/PK-12
285 Flowing Wells Rd 30907 706-863-1906
Jack Hall, hdmstr. Fax 863-6198

Metter, Candler, Pop. 4,143
Candler County SD 1,900/PK-12
210 S College St 30439 912-685-5713
Dr. Thomas Bigwood, supt. Fax 685-3068
www.metter.org
Metter HS 500/9-12
34905 GA Highway 129 S 30439 912-685-2134
Michelle Cliett, prin. Fax 685-2897
Metter MS 400/6-8
431 W Vertia St 30439 912-685-5580
Robbie Dollar, prin. Fax 685-4970

Midland, Muscogee
Muscogee County SD
Supt. — See Columbus
Midland MS 1,000/6-8
6990 Warm Springs Rd 31820 706-569-3673
James Wilson, prin. Fax 569-3678

Midway, Liberty, Pop. 1,008
Liberty County SD
Supt. — See Hinesville
Midway MS 900/6-8
425 Edgewater Dr 31320 912-884-6677
Debra Frazier, prin. Fax 884-5944

Milledgeville, Baldwin, Pop. 19,397
Baldwin County SD 6,000/PK-12
PO Box 1188 31059 478-453-4176
C. Trammell, supt. Fax 457-3327
www.baldwin-county-schools.com
Baldwin HS 1,400/9-12
155 GA Highway 49 W 31061 478-453-6429
Lynwood Chandler, prin. Fax 451-3032
Oak Hill MS 1,500/6-8
356 Blandy Rd NW 31061 478-457-3370
Mark Scott, dir. Fax 457-2422
Carver Adult Education Adult
435 E Walton St 31061 478-452-4711
Angela Hudson, prin. Fax 452-7295

Central Georgia Technical College Post-Sec.
54 GA Highway 22 W 31061
Georgia College & State University Post-Sec.
231 W Hancock St 31061 478-445-5350
Georgia Military College Post-Sec.
201 E Greene St 31061 478-445-2700
Milledge Academy 600/PK-12
197 Log Cabin Rd NE 31061 478-452-5570
Larry Prestridge, prin. Fax 452-5000

Millen, Jenkins, Pop. 3,526
Jenkins County SD 1,700/PK-12
PO Box 660 30442 478-982-6000
Joan Blackwood, supt. Fax 982-6002
www.jchs.com/
Jenkins County HS 500/9-12
433 Barney Ave 30442 478-982-4791
Dr. Joseph Kirkland, prin. Fax 982-6015
Jenkins County MS 400/6-8
409 Barney Ave 30442 478-982-1063
Dr. Joseph Kirkland, prin. Fax 982-6015

Monroe, Walton, Pop. 12,329
Walton County SD 11,300/PK-12
200 Double Springs Church R 30656 770-266-4417
Dr. Tim Lull, supt. Fax 266-4420
www.walton.k12.ga.us
Carver MS 900/6-8
1095 Good Hope Rd 30655 770-267-6000
Sean Callahan, prin. Fax 267-4050
Monroe HS 1,200/9-12
300 Double Springs Church 30656 770-266-4599
Seabrook Royal, prin. Fax 266-4598
Other Schools – See Loganville

Walton Academy 900/PK-12
1 Bulldog Dr 30655 770-267-7578
William Nicholson, hdmstr. Fax 267-4023

Montezuma, Macon, Pop. 3,997
Macon County SD
Supt. — See Oglethorpe
Macon County HS 600/9-12
611 Vienna Rd 31063 478-472-8579
Rickey Edmond, prin. Fax 472-6206
Macon County MS 500/6-8
615 Vienna Rd 31063 478-472-7045
Issiah Ross, prin. Fax 472-2549

Monticello, Jasper, Pop. 2,565
Jasper County SD 2,000/PK-12
1125A Fred Smith St 31064 706-468-6350
Jay L. Brinson, supt. Fax 468-0045
www.jasper.k12.ga.us
Jasper County HS 500/9-12
1289 College St 31064 706-468-2227
Howard Fore, prin. Fax 468-4991
Jasper County MS 500/6-8
1289 College St 31064 706-468-2227
Anne Massengale, prin. Fax 468-4991

Piedmont Academy 300/PK-12
PO Box 231 31064 706-468-8818
Dr. Michael Rossi, hdmstr. Fax 468-2409

Morgan, Calhoun, Pop. 1,470
Calhoun County SD 700/PK-12
PO Box 39 39866 229-849-2765
Jewell Howard, supt. Fax 849-2113
www.calhoun.k12.ga.us/
Other Schools – See Edison

Morganton, Union, Pop. 265

Mountain Area Christian Academy 200/PK-12
PO Box 240 30560 706-374-6222
Steven Clagg, admin. Fax 374-4831

Morrow, Clayton, Pop. 5,283
Clayton County SD
Supt. — See Jonesboro
Morrow HS 2,100/9-12
2299 Old Rex Morrow Rd 30260 404-362-3865
Patricia Hill, prin. Fax 362-2044
Morrow MS 800/6-8
5968 Maddox Rd 30260 404-362-3860
Greg Curry, prin. Fax 608-2557

Clayton State University Post-Sec.
5900 Lee St 30260 770-961-3400
Interactive College of Technology Post-Sec.
1580 Southlake Pkwy Ste C 30260 770-960-1298
Javelin Technical Training Center Post-Sec.
1396 Southlake Plaza Dr 30260 770-968-9155

Moultrie, Colquitt, Pop. 14,913
Colquitt County SD 8,500/PK-12
PO Box 2708 31776 229-890-6200
Leonard McCoy, supt. Fax 890-6246
www.colquitt.k12.ga.us/
Colquitt County HS 2,300/9-12
1800 Park Ave SE 31768 229-890-6181
Bob Jones, prin. Fax 890-6166
Gray MS 1,000/6-8
812 11th Ave NW 31768 229-890-6189
Dr. Todd Cason, prin. Fax 890-6123
Williams MS 900/6-8
950 4th St SW 31768 229-890-6183
Doug Howell, prin. Fax 890-6258

Moultrie Technical College Post-Sec.
800 Veterans Pkwy N, 229-891-7000

Mount Airy, Habersham, Pop. 665
Habersham County SD
Supt. — See Clarkesville

Habersham Central SHS 1,100/10-12
171 Raider Cir 30563 706-778-7161
Jim Van Hooser, prin. Fax 778-1258

Central Heights Christian S 100/PK-12
2664 Highway 197 30563 706-778-3360
Danny Young, prin. Fax 776-2723

Mount Berry, Floyd

Berry College Post-Sec.
2277 Martha Berry Hwy NE 30149 706-232-5374

Mount Vernon, Montgomery, Pop. 2,162
Montgomery County SD 1,300/PK-12
PO Box 315 30445 912-583-2301
Dale Clark, supt. Fax 583-4822
www.montgomery.k12.ga.us
Montgomery County HS 400/9-12
701 Dobbins St 30445 912-583-2296
Luke Smith, prin. Fax 583-4469
Montgomery County MS 300/6-8
701 Dobbins St 30445 912-583-2351
Dr. Marvin Howard, prin. Fax 583-4469

Brewton-Parker College Post-Sec.
Highway 280 30445 800-342-1087

Mount Zion, Carroll, Pop. 1,492
Carroll County SD
Supt. — See Carrollton
Mount Zion MSHS 500/6-12
132 Eagle Dr 30150 770-834-6654
Tracey Barrow, prin. Fax 832-9497

Nahunta, Brantley, Pop. 1,044
Brantley County SD 3,400/PK-12
RR 2 Box 22T 31553 912-462-6176
Drew Sauls, supt. Fax 462-6731
www.brantley.k12.ga.us/
Brantley County HS 900/9-12
RR 1 Box 4 31553 912-462-5121
Randy Yonz, prin. Fax 462-5123
Brantley County MS 500/7-8
RR 1 Box 4D 31553 912-462-7092
Shelli Tyre, prin. Fax 462-6785

Nashville, Berrien, Pop. 4,841
Berrien County SD 3,100/PK-12
PO Box 625 31639 229-686-2081
Bobby N. Griffin, supt. Fax 686-9002
www.berrien.k12.ga.us
Berrien HS 900/9-12
500 E Smith Ave 31639 229-686-7428
Mike Parker, prin. Fax 686-6251
Berrien MS 800/6-8
800 Tifton Rd 31639 229-686-2021
Dr. Dennis Proctor, prin. Fax 686-6546

Newnan, Coweta, Pop. 24,654
Coweta County SD 19,700/PK-12
PO Box 280 30264 770-254-2801
Blake Bass, supt. Fax 254-2807
www.cowetaschools.org
Arnall MS 1,100/6-8
700 Lora Smith Rd 30265 770-254-2765
Rick Waggoner, prin. Fax 254-2770
Evans MS 800/6-8
1 Evans Dr 30263 770-254-2780
Walter Drake, prin. Fax 254-2783
Madras MS 900/6-8
240 Edgeworth Rd 30263 770-254-2744
Scott Floyd, prin. Fax 304-5928
Newnan HS 2,000/9-12
190 Lagrange St 30263 770-254-2880
Dr. Steve Barker, prin. Fax 254-2797
Northgate HS 1,400/9-12
3220 Fischer Rd 30265 770-463-5585
Dr. Therese Reddekopp, prin. Fax 463-4982
Smokey Road MS 900/6-8
965 Smokey Rd 30263 770-254-2840
Dr. Laurie Jackson, prin. Fax 304-5933
Other Schools – See Senoia, Sharpsburg

Heritage S 400/PK-12
2093 Highway 29 N 30263 770-253-9898
Judith Griffith, hdmstr. Fax 253-4850
Newnan Christian S 200/PK-12
1608 Highway 29 N 30263 770-253-7175
Doug Anderson, admin. Fax 253-4776
Newnan Classical S 100/K-10
PO Box 71427 30271 770-252-7223
Angie Gruner, prin. Fax 683-7221
West Central Technical College Post-Sec.
160 Martin Luther King Dr 30263 678-423-2000

Newton, Baker, Pop. 867
Baker County SD 400/PK-10
PO Box 40, 229-734-5346
Thomas Rogers, supt. Fax 734-3064
www.baker.k12.ga.us/
Baker County S 400/PK-10
348 GA Highway 37, 229-734-5274
Robert Graper, prin. Fax 734-3071

Norcross, Gwinnett, Pop. 9,887
Gwinnett County SD
Supt. — See Suwanee
Buchanan HS of Technology Vo/Tech
2595 Beaver Ruin Rd 30071 770-326-8000
Meadowcreek HS 2,100/9-12
4455 Steve Reynolds Blvd 30093 770-381-9680
Dr. Angela Pringle, prin. Fax 806-2230
Norcross HS 2,700/9-12
5300 Spalding Dr 30092 770-448-3674
Jonathan Patterson, prin. Fax 447-2664
Pinckneyville MS 1,300/6-8
5440 W Jones Bridge Rd 30092 770-263-0860
Nancy Martin, prin. Fax 447-2617
Summerour MS 1,100/6-8
585 Mitchell Rd 30071 770-448-3045
Dana Pugh, prin. Fax 417-2476

Ashworth College Post-Sec.
430 Technology Pkwy 30092 770-729-8400
Atlanta Institute of Music Post-Sec.
5985 Financial Dr # 200 30071 770-242-7717
Career Education Institute Post-Sec.
5675 Jimmy Carter Blvd #100 30071 678-966-9411
Georgia Medical Institute Post-Sec.
1750 Beaver Ruin Rd Ste 500 30093 770-921-1085
Greater Atlanta Christian S 2,000/PK-12
1575 Indian Trail Rd 30093 770-243-2274
Dr. David Fincher, pres. Fax 243-2213
Hopewell Christian Academy 200/PK-12
182 Hunter St 30071 770-903-3387
Beauty Baldwin, admin. Fax 449-8316
Iverson Business School Post-Sec.
500 Pinnacle Ct 30071 770-446-1333
James Madison High School Post-Sec.
430 Technology Pkwy 30092 770-729-8400
Professional Career Development Inst Post-Sec.
430 Technology Pkwy 30092 770-729-8400
Wesleyan S 1,100/K-12
5405 Spalding Dr 30092 770-448-7640
Zach Young, admin. Fax 448-3699

Oakwood, Hall, Pop. 3,408
Hall County SD
Supt. — See Gainesville
West Hall HS 1,000/9-12
5500 Mcever Rd 30566 770-967-9826
Dr. Jackie Adams, prin. Fax 967-4864
West Hall MS 900/6-8
5470 Mcever Rd 30566 770-967-4871
Dr. Sarah Justus, prin. Fax 967-4874

Lanier Technical College Post-Sec.
2990 Landrum Education Dr 30566 770-531-6300
Maranatha Christian Academy 100/PK-12
PO Box 877 30566 770-536-6334
Dr. Richard Stashevski, admin. Fax 531-9625

Ocilla, Irwin, Pop. 3,417
Irwin County SD 1,800/PK-12
PO Box 225 31774 229-468-7485
Betty Sue Stripling, supt. Fax 468-7220
www.irwin.k12.ga.us/
Irwin County HS 500/9-12
149 Chieftain Cir 31774 229-468-9421
Bobby Conner, prin. Fax 468-9423
Irwin County MS 400/6-8
149 Chieftain Cir 31774 229-468-5517
Brian Chestnutt, prin. Fax 468-3134

Oglethorpe, Macon, Pop. 1,157
Macon County SD 2,100/PK-12
PO Box 488 31068 478-472-8188
Dr. Carolyn Medlock, supt. Fax 472-2042
www.macon.k12.ga.us/
Other Schools – See Montezuma

Oxford, Newton, Pop. 2,214

Oxford College of Emory University Post-Sec.
100 Hamill St 30054 770-784-8888

Peachtree City, Fayette, Pop. 34,524
Fayette County SD
Supt. — See Fayetteville
Booth MS 1,200/6-8
250 S Peachtree Pkwy 30269 770-631-3240
Ted Lombard, prin. Fax 631-3245
McIntosh HS 1,600/9-12
201 Walt Banks Rd 30269 770-631-3232
Tracie Fleming, prin. Fax 631-3278

Pearson, Atkinson, Pop. 1,901
Atkinson County SD 1,700/PK-12
98 Roberts Ave E 31642 912-422-7373
Dr. Paul Jones, supt. Fax 422-7369
www.atkinson.k12.ga.us/
Atkinson County HS 500/8-12
145 Rebel Ln 31642 912-422-3267
Paul Daniel, prin. Fax 422-7889

Pelham, Mitchell, Pop. 3,914
Pelham CSD 1,500/PK-12
188 W Railroad St S 31779 229-294-8715
Dr. Stephen Dunn, supt. Fax 294-2760
Pelham City MS 400/6-8
209 Mathewson Ave SW 31779 229-294-6063
Tom Finland, prin.
Pelham HS 400/9-12
203 Mathewson Ave SW 31779 229-294-8623
Larry Maffit, prin. Fax 294-6069

Pembroke, Bryan, Pop. 2,503
Bryan County SD 6,000/PK-12
66 S Industrial Blvd 31321 912-626-5000
Dr. Sallie Brewer, supt. Fax 653-4386
www.bryan.k12.ga.us/
Bryan County MS 400/6-8
600 Payne Dr 31321 912-626-5050
Deborah Hamm, prin. Fax 653-2705
Byran County HS 500/9-12
1234 Camellia Dr 31321 912-626-5060
Harold Roach, prin. Fax 653-2858
Other Schools – See Richmond Hill

Perry, Houston, Pop. 11,018
Houston County SD 22,900/PK-12
PO Box 1850 31069 478-988-6200
David Carpenter, supt. Fax 988-6259
www.hcbe.net
Perry HS 1,000/9-12
1307 North Ave 31069 478-988-6298
Dr. Darryl Albritton, prin. Fax 988-6381
Perry MS 900/6-8
495 Perry Pkwy 31069 478-988-6285
Thomas Moore, prin. Fax 988-6345
Other Schools – See Bonaire, Centerville, Kathleen, Warner Robins

---

Westfield S 700/PK-12
PO Box 2300 31069 478-987-0547
Clint Humphrey, prin. Fax 987-7379

Pinehurst, Dooly, Pop. 335
Dooly County SD
Supt. — See Vienna
Dooly County MS 300/6-8
11949 Highway 41 31070 229-268-8181
Dr. Daniel Sturdivant, prin. Fax 268-1916

Fullington Academy 300/PK-12
PO Box B 31070 229-645-3383
Robert Mooring, hdmstr. Fax 645-3386

Pooler, Chatham, Pop. 10,019
Savannah-Chatham County SD
Supt. — See Savannah
West Chatham MS 1,000/6-8
800 Pine Barren Rd 31322 912-748-3650
Kerry Coursey, prin. Fax 748-3669

Portal, Bulloch, Pop. 595
Bulloch County SD
Supt. — See Statesboro
Portal MSHS 400/6-12
27245 Highway 80 W 30450 912-865-2640
Jimmy Parrish, prin. Fax 865-5659

Powder Springs, Cobb, Pop. 14,507
Cobb County SD
Supt. — See Marietta
Hillgrove HS 9-12
4165 Luther Ward Rd 30127 678-331-3961
Joseph Boland, prin. Fax 331-8128
Lovinggood MS 6-8
3825 Luther Ward Rd 30127 678-331-3015
Zinta Perkins, prin. Fax 331-3016
McEachern HS 3,500/9-12
2400 New Macland Rd 30127 770-222-3710
Robert Benson, prin. Fax 222-3712
Tapp MS 1,100/6-8
3900 Macedonia Rd 30127 770-222-3758
Denise Magee, prin. Fax 222-3760

Paulding County SD
Supt. — See Dallas
Dobbins MS 1,200/6-8
637 Williams Lake Rd 30127 770-443-4835
Cartess Ross, prin. Fax 439-1672

Powder Springs Beauty College Post-Sec.
4114 Austell Powder Springs 30127 770-439-9432
Total Learning Center Christian S 300/PK-12
PO Box 13 30127 770-943-2484
Georgia White, prin. Fax 943-9458
Youth Christian S 200/PK-12
4967 Brownsville Rd 30127 770-943-1394
Dennis Willis, prin. Fax 943-0756

Quitman, Brooks, Pop. 4,520
Brooks County SD 2,400/PK-12
PO Box 511 31643 229-263-7531
Debra Folsom, supt. Fax 263-5206
www.brooks.k12.ga.us
Brooks County HS 600/9-12
1081 Barwick Rd 31643 229-263-8923
Howard Akers, prin. Fax 263-7049
Brooks County MS 600/6-8
2171 Moultrie Hwy 31643 229-263-7521
Al Williams, prin. Fax 263-9038

Rabun Gap, Rabun

Rabun Gap-Nacoochee S 300/6-12
339 Nacoochee Dr 30568 706-746-7467
John Marshall, hdmstr. Fax 746-2594

Reidsville, Tattnall, Pop. 2,400
Tattnall County SD 3,400/PK-12
146 W Brazell St 30453 912-557-4726
James Turbeville, supt. Fax 557-3036
www.tattnallschools.org/home.asp
Reidsville MS 300/6-8
146 W Brazell St 30453 912-557-3993
Garrett Wilcox, prin. Fax 557-4124
Tattnall County HS 900/9-12
17100 Ga Highway 23 30453 912-557-4374
Bubba Longgrear, prin. Fax 557-4542
Other Schools – See Collins, Glennville

Rex, Clayton
Clayton County SD
Supt. — See Jonesboro
Adamson MS 1,200/6-8
3187 Rex Rd 30273 770-968-2925
Dr. Douglas Hendrix, prin. Fax 968-2949
Rex Mill MS 6-8
6380 Evans Dr 30273 770-515-7614
Susan Patrick, prin. Fax 515-7622

Richmond Hill, Bryan, Pop. 9,187
Bryan County SD
Supt. — See Pembroke
Richmond Hill HS 1,200/9-12
1 Wildcat Dr 31324 912-459-5151
Charles Spann, prin. Fax 756-4958
Richmond Hill MS 1,000/6-8
665 Harris Trail Rd 31324 912-459-5130
Helen Herndon, prin. Fax 756-5369

Rincon, Effingham, Pop. 6,349
Effingham County SD
Supt. — See Springfield
Ebenezer MS 800/6-8
1100 Ebenezer Rd 31326 912-754-7757
Elizabeth Helmly, prin. Fax 754-4012

Effingham Christian S 100/PK-12
PO Box 370 31326 912-826-3327
Scott Bass, admin. Fax 826-6555

Ringgold, Catoosa, Pop. 2,793
Catoosa County SD 10,100/PK-12
PO Box 130 30736 706-965-2297
Denia Reese, supt. Fax 965-8913
www.catoosa.k12.ga.us
Heritage MS 6-8
4005 Poplar Springs Rd 30736 706-937-3568
Chris Lusk, prin. Fax 937-2583
Ringgold HS 1,600/9-12
29 Tiger Trl 30736 706-935-2254
Sharon Vaughn, prin. Fax 965-8910
Ringgold MS 1,300/6-8
217 Tiger Trl 30736 706-935-3381
Lamar Brown, prin. Fax 965-8908
Other Schools – See Fort Oglethorpe, Rossville

Riverdale, Clayton, Pop. 15,475
Clayton County SD
Supt. — See Jonesboro
Riverdale HS 1,800/9-12
160 Roberts Dr 30274 770-473-2905
Dr. Gloria Duncan, prin. Fax 473-2913
Riverdale MS 1,100/6-8
400 Roberts Dr 30274 770-994-4045
Dr. Mildred McCoy, prin. Fax 994-4467
Sequoyah MS 6-8
95 Valley Hill Rd SW 30274 770-515-7524
Shauna Heath, prin. Fax 515-7540

Southern Regional Medical Center Post-Sec.
11 Upper Riverdale Rd SW 30274 770-991-8053

Roberta, Crawford, Pop. 776
Crawford County SD 2,200/PK-12
PO Box 8 31078 478-836-3131
Iwanda Dickey, supt. Fax 836-3114
www.crawford.k12.ga.us
Crawford County Comprehensive HS 600/9-12
PO Box 98 31078 478-836-3126
Mike Campbell, prin. Fax 836-4853
Crawford County MS 500/6-8
PO Box 335 31078 478-836-3181
Anthony English, prin. Fax 836-3795

Rochelle, Wilcox, Pop. 1,418
Wilcox County SD
Supt. — See Abbeville
Wilcox County HS 400/9-12
186 7th Ave 31079 229-365-7231
Arney Bryant, prin. Fax 365-7461
Wilcox County MS 300/6-8
114 7th Ave 31079 229-365-2331
Bland Brooks, prin. Fax 365-2641

Rockmart, Polk, Pop. 4,310
Polk County SD
Supt. — See Cedartown
Elm Street MS 700/6-8
100 Morgan Valley Rd 30153 770-684-3151
Greg Christian, prin. Fax 684-1564
Rockmart HS 800/9-12
990 Cartersville Hwy 30153 770-684-5432
Marvin Williams, prin. Fax 684-4768

Coosa Valley Technical College Post-Sec.
466 Brock Rd 30153

Rock Spring, Walker

Northwestern Technical College Post-Sec.
PO Box 569 30739 706-764-3510

Rocky Face, Whitfield
Whitfield County SD
Supt. — See Dalton
West Side MS 600/6-8
580 Lafayette Rd 30740 706-673-2611
Stan Stewart, prin. Fax 673-5349

Rome, Floyd, Pop. 35,816
Floyd County SD 10,400/PK-12
600 Riverside Pkwy NE 30161 706-234-1031
Kelly C. Henson, supt. Fax 236-1824
www.floydboe.net
Armuchee HS 600/9-12
4203 Martha Berry Hwy NW 30165 706-236-1886
Dr. J.C. Burris, prin. Fax 802-6757
Coosa HS 700/9-12
4454 Alabama Hwy NW 30165 706-236-1870
Sam Sprewell, prin. Fax 290-8142
Coosa MS 600/6-8
212 Eagle Dr NW 30165 706-236-1856
Dr. Lisa Landrum, prin. Fax 802-6766
Floyd County Technical HS Vo/Tech
100 Vocational Dr SW 30161 706-236-1860
Kal Oravet, prin. Fax 236-1862
Model HS 600/9-12
3252 Calhoun Rd NE 30161 706-236-1895
Dr. Glenn White, prin. Fax 802-6750
Model MS 500/6-8
164 Barron Rd NE 30161 706-290-8150
David Tucker, prin. Fax 802-6775
Floyd County Transitional Academy Adult
1910 Morrison Campground Rd 30161
706-236-1884
Melinda Strickland, prin. Fax 802-6780
Other Schools – See Armuchee, Lindale

Rome CSD 5,400/PK-12
508 E 2nd St 30161 706-236-5050
Dr. Gayland Cooper, supt. Fax 802-4311
www.rcs.rome.ga.us
Rome HS 1,500/9-12
1000 Veterans Memorial NE 30161 706-235-9653
Dr. J. Tygar Evans, prin. Fax 236-5078
Rome MS 900/7-8
1020 Veterans Memorial NE 30161 706-235-4695
Robert Costley, prin. Fax 234-5903

Coosa Valley Technical Institute Post-Sec.
1 Maurice Culberson Dr SW 30161 706-295-6927
Darlington S 900/PK-12
1014 Cave Spring Rd SW 30161 706-235-6051
Thomas Whitworth, hdmstr. Fax 232-3600
Georgia Highlands College Post-Sec.
PO Box 1864 30162 706-802-5000
Shorter College Post-Sec.
315 Shorter Ave SW 30165 800-868-6980
Unity Christian S 300/PK-12
2960 New Calhoun Hwy NE 30161 706-292-0700
Glenn Getchell, hdmstr. Fax 292-0772

Rossville, Walker, Pop. 3,416
Catoosa County SD
Supt. — See Ringgold
Lakeview MS 1,100/6-8
416 Cross St 30741 706-866-1040
Bubba Simmons, prin. Fax 861-6644

Walker County SD
Supt. — See La Fayette
Ridgeland HS 1,200/9-12
2478 Happy Valley Rd 30741 706-820-9361
Robert Smith, prin. Fax 820-1342
Rossville MS 600/6-8
1 Bulldog Dr 30741 706-866-2446
Wanda Janeway, prin. Fax 866-1811

Roswell, Fulton, Pop. 85,920
Fulton County SD
Supt. — See Atlanta
Centennial HS 2,000/9-12
9310 Scott Rd 30076 770-650-4230
Scott O'Prey, prin. Fax 650-4250
Crabapple MS 800/6-8
10700 Crabapple Rd 30075 770-552-4520
Dr. Kimothy Jarrett, prin. Fax 552-4524
Elkins Pointe MS 900/6-8
11290 Elkins Rd 30076 770-667-2892
Vivian Bankston, prin. Fax 667-2898
Roswell HS 2,300/9-12
11595 King Rd 30075 770-552-4500
Edward Spurka, prin. Fax 552-4509

Blessed Trinity Catholic HS 800/9-12
11320 Woodstock Rd 30075 678-277-9083
Frank Moore, prin. Fax 277-9756
Fellowship Christian S 600/K-12
480 W Crossville Rd 30075 770-992-4975
Eric Munn, hdmstr. Fax 993-9262

Saint Marys, Camden, Pop. 15,811
Camden County SD
Supt. — See Kingsland
Saint Marys MS 900/6-8
205 Martha Dr 31558 912-882-8626
Dr. Jo Beth Bird, prin. Fax 882-5473

Saint Simons Island, Glynn, Pop. 12,026

Frederica Academy 400/PK-12
200 Hamilton Rd 31522 912-638-9981
Ellen E. Fleming, hdmstr. Fax 638-1442
Whitefield S 100/PK-12
48 Hampton Point Dr 31522 912-634-8177
Renee Shepherd, admin. Fax 634-2900

Sandersville, Washington, Pop. 6,031
Washington County SD 3,700/PK-12
PO Box 716 31082 478-552-3981
Donna Hinton, supt. Fax 552-3128
www.washington.k12.ga.us/
Elder MS 900/6-8
PO Box 816 31082 478-552-2007
Manzie Broxton, prin. Fax 552-7388
Washington County HS 1,100/9-12
PO Box 1057 31082 478-552-2324
Dewey Carey, prin. Fax 552-3140

Brentwood S 400/PK-12
PO Box 955 31082 478-552-5136
Jackie Holton, prin. Fax 552-2947
Sandersville Technical College Post-Sec.
1189 Deepstep Rd 31082 478-553-2060

Savannah, Chatham, Pop. 128,453
Savannah-Chatham County SD 32,400/PK-12
208 Bull St 31401 912-201-5600
Dr. Thomas Lockamy, supt. Fax 201-5628
www.savannah.chatham.k12.ga.us/
Bartlett MS 800/6-8
207 E Montgomery Xrd 31406 912-961-3500
Michael Jones, prin. Fax 961-3515
Beach HS 1,300/9-12
3001 Hopkins St 31405 912-201-5330
Deonn Stone, prin. Fax 201-5335
Coastal MS 800/6-8
170 Whitemarsh Island Rd 31410 912-898-3950
Sherry McClain, prin. Fax 898-3951
DeRenne MS 900/6-8
3609 Hopkins St 31405 912-201-5900
Marsha Tolbert, prin. Fax 201-5903
Groves HS 1,500/9-12
100 Wheathill Rd 31408 912-965-2520
Fax 965-2564
Hubert MS 500/6-8
768 Grant St 31401 912-201-5235
Dr. Toney Jordan, prin. Fax 201-5238
Jenkins HS 1,700/9-12
1800 E De Renne Ave 31406 912-303-6300
William Brannen, prin. Fax 303-6331
Johnson HS 1,200/9-12
3012 Sunset Blvd 31404 912-303-6400
Derrick Muhammad, prin. Fax 303-6418
Myers MS 900/6-8
2025 E 52nd St 31404 912-303-6600
Dora Myles, prin. Fax 303-6604
Savannah Arts Academy 600/9-12
500 Washington Ave 31405 912-201-5000
Odessa Richards, prin. Fax 201-4160
Savannah HS 900/9-12
400 Pennsylvania Ave 31404 912-201-5050
Walter Seabrooks, prin. Fax 201-5054
Shuman MS 800/6-8
415 Goebel Ave 31404 912-201-7500
Robert Lewis, prin. Fax 201-7503
Southwest MS 1,000/6-8
6030 Ogeechee Rd 31419 912-961-3540
Dr. Tangela Madge, prin. Fax 961-3548
Windsor Forest HS 1,700/9-12
12419 Largo Dr 31419 912-961-3400
Barry Lollis, prin. Fax 961-3422
Woodville-Tompkins Career Technical Ctr Vo/Tech
151 Coach Joe Turner St 31408 912-965-6750
Fax 965-6750
Adult Education Center Adult
3609 Hopkins St 31405 912-201-5527
Pat Rossiter, prin. Fax 201-5791
Other Schools – See Pooler

Armstrong Atlantic State University Post-Sec.
11935 Abercorn St 31419 800-633-2349
Benedictine Military S 400/9-12
PO Box 13577 31416 912-644-7000
Fax 356-3527
Bethesda S 100/1-12
9520 Ferguson Ave 31406 912-351-2055
Fax 351-2062
Bible Baptist S 400/PK-12
4700 Skidaway Rd 31404 912-352-3067
Steven Kyle, admin. Fax 352-9830
Calvary Day S 1,000/PK-12
4625 Waters Ave 31404 912-351-2299
Ralph Finnegan, hdmstr. Fax 351-2280
Chatham Academy 100/1-12
4 Oglethorpe Prfssonal Blvd 31406 912-354-4047
Carolyn Hannaford, prin. Fax 354-4633
Memorial Day S 300/PK-12
6500 Habersham St 31405 912-352-4535
Bill Eaves, hdmstr. Fax 352-4536
Providence Christian S 200/PK-12
1950B Chatham Pkwy 31405 912-238-5005
David Osborne, hdmstr. Fax 238-8237
St. Andrew's S on the Marsh 400/PK-12
PO Box 30639 31410 912-897-4941
Emeriel Hubbard, hdmstr. Fax 897-4943
St. Vincent Academy 400/9-12
207 E Liberty St 31401 912-236-5508
Sr. Helen Buttimer, prin. Fax 236-7877
Savannah Christian Preparatory S 1,500/PK-12
PO Box 2848 31402 912-234-1653
Roger Yancey, hdmstr. Fax 234-0491
Savannah College of Art & Design Post-Sec.
PO Box 2072 31402 912-525-5000
Savannah Country Day S 1,000/PK-12
824 Stillwood Dr 31419 912-925-8800
Thomas Bonnell, hdmstr. Fax 920-7800
Savannah State University Post-Sec.
3219 College St 31404 912-356-2187
Savannah Technical College Post-Sec.
5717 White Bluff Rd 31405 912-351-6362
South University Post-Sec.
709 Mall Blvd 31406 912-201-8000

Senoia, Coweta, Pop. 2,719
Coweta County SD
Supt. — See Newnan
East Coweta MS 900/6-8
6291 Highway 16 30276 770-599-6607
Nancy Cook, prin. Fax 599-1051

Sharpsburg, Coweta, Pop. 328
Coweta County SD
Supt. — See Newnan
East Coweta HS 2,000/9-12
400 McCollum-Sharpsburg Rd 30277 770-254-2850
Derek Pitts, prin. Fax 254-2857
Lee MS, 370 Willis Rd 30277 6-8
Dr. Bob Heaberlin, prin. 770-251-1547

Heritage Baptist Educational Ministry 100/K-12
3613 Highway 34 E 30277 770-252-1234
Roy Davis, prin. Fax 304-9576

Shellman, Randolph, Pop. 1,084

Randolph Southern S 300/K-12
PO Box 300, 229-679-5324
Dr. Terry Tedder, prin. Fax 679-5325

Siloam, Greene, Pop. 344

Greene Academy 200/PK-12
PO Box 109 30665 706-467-2147
John Arnold, hdmstr. Fax 467-2147

Smyrna, Cobb, Pop. 47,643
Cobb County SD
Supt. — See Marietta
Campbell HS 2,300/9-12
5265 Ward St SE 30080 678-842-6850
Kehl Arnson, prin. Fax 842-6852
Campbell MS 1,300/6-8
3295 Atlanta Rd SE 30080 678-842-6873
Lynne Hutnik, prin. Fax 842-6875
Griffin MS 1,100/6-8
4010 King Springs Rd SE 30082 678-842-6917
Darryl York, prin. Fax 842-6919

Medix School Post-Sec.
2108 Cobb Pkwy SE 30080 770-980-0002

Snellville, Gwinnett, Pop. 19,238
Gwinnett County SD
Supt. — See Suwanee
Brookwood HS 3,200/9-12
1255 Dogwood Rd 30078 770-972-7642
Jane Stegall, prin. Fax 978-5075
Shiloh HS 2,100/9-12
4210 Shiloh Rd 30039 770-972-8471
Dr. Gwen Tatum, prin. Fax 736-4345
Shiloh MS 1,600/6-8
4285 Shiloh Rd 30039 770-972-3224
Karen Robinson, prin. Fax 736-4563
Snellville MS 1,900/6-8
3155 Pate Rd 30078 770-972-1530
Linda Boyd, prin. Fax 736-4444
South Gwinnett HS 2,200/9-12
2288 Main St E 30078 770-972-4840
Berry Simmons, prin. Fax 736-4329

Snellville Christian Academy 200/PK-12
PO Box 547 30078 770-979-4966
Laurie Duke, prin. Fax 979-3531

Social Circle, Walton, Pop. 4,053
Social Circle CSD 1,500/PK-12
240B W Hightower Trl 30025 770-464-2731
Dr. Bettye J. Ray, supt. Fax 464-0403
www.scboe.org/
Social Circle HS 400/9-12
154 Alcova Dr 30025 770-464-2611
Tony Overstreet, prin. Fax 464-2612
Social Circle MS 300/6-8
154 Alcova Dr 30025 770-464-1932
Dr. Todd McGhee, prin. Fax 464-2612

Soperton, Treutlen, Pop. 2,747
Treutlen County SD 1,200/K-12
202 3rd St S 30457 912-529-4228
Charles Ellington, supt. Fax 529-4226
www.treutlen.net
Treutlen MSHS 600/6-12
1201 Fowler St 30457 912-529-4536
David Avery, prin. Fax 529-6121

Sparks, Cook, Pop. 1,781
Cook County SD
Supt. — See Adel
Cook MS 700/6-8
1000 N Elm St 31647 229-549-5999
Jeff Shealey, prin. Fax 549-5986

Valdosta Technical College Post-Sec.
1001 S Elm St 31647 229-549-7368

Sparta, Hancock, Pop. 1,374
Hancock County SD 1,400/PK-12
PO Box 488 31087 706-444-5775
Dr. Awana Leslie, supt. Fax 444-7026
www.hancock.k12.ga.us
Hancock Central MSHS 800/6-12
1311 Highway 15 N 31087 706-444-7009
Isaac Cleveland, prin. Fax 444-9918

Springfield, Effingham, Pop. 2,034
Effingham County SD 9,800/PK-12
405 N Ash St 31329 912-754-6491
Randy Shearouse, supt. Fax 754-7033
www.effinghamschools.com/

Effingham County HS 1,400/9-12
1589 GA Highway 119 S 31329 912-754-6404
Yancy Ford, prin. Fax 754-6893
Effingham County MS 600/6-8
1290 GA Highway 119 S 31329 912-754-3332
Bobbie Ann Allen, prin. Fax 754-7497
Other Schools – See Guyton, Rincon

Statenville, Echols
Echols County SD 700/PK-12
PO Box 207 31648 229-559-5734
Dr. Michael Akes, supt. Fax 559-0484
www.echols.k12.ga.us/
Echols County S 700/PK-12
PO Box 40 31648 229-559-5413
Tim Ragan, prin. Fax 559-0423

Statesboro, Bulloch, Pop. 24,612
Bulloch County SD 8,500/PK-12
150 Williams Rd Ste A 30458 912-764-6201
Jessie Strickland Ed.D., supt. Fax 764-8436
www.bulloch.k12.ga.us
James MS 500/6-8
18809 US Highway 80 W 30458 912-764-2752
Dr. Daryl Fineran, prin. Fax 489-5916
Langston Chapel MS 700/6-8
156 Langston Chapel Rd 30458 912-681-8779
Elizabeth Williams, prin. Fax 681-6416
Statesboro HS 1,400/9-12
10 Lester Rd 30458 912-489-8751
Marty Waters, prin. Fax 489-5965
Other Schools – See Brooklet, Portal

Bulloch Academy 500/PK-12
873 Westside Rd 30458 912-764-6297
Dr. Brenda Riley, hdmstr. Fax 764-3165
Georgia Southern University Post-Sec.
PO Box 8024 30460 912-681-5611
Ogeechee Technical College Post-Sec.
1 Joseph E Kennedy Blvd 30458 912-681-5500
Trinity Christian S 200/K-12
571 E Main St 30461 912-489-1375
David Lattner, hdmstr. Fax 764-3136

Stillmore, Emanuel, Pop. 755

Emanuel Academy 300/K-12
PO Box 77 30464 912-562-4405
Brian Daughtry, prin. Fax 562-3465

Stockbridge, Henry, Pop. 13,140
Henry County SD
Supt. — See Mc Donough
Austin Road MS 900/6-8
100 Austin Rd 30281 770-507-5407
Janet Brown-Clayton, prin. Fax 507-5413
Stockbridge HS 1,800/9-12
1151 Old Conyers Rd 30281 770-474-8747
Eric Watson, prin. Fax 474-4727
Stockbridge MS 700/6-8
533 Old Conyers Rd 30281 770-474-5710
Vicki Davis, prin. Fax 507-8406
Woodland HS 9-12
800 Moseley Dr 30281 770-389-2784
Bret Cook, prin. Fax 389-2790
Woodland MS 6-8
820 Moseley Dr 30281 770-389-2774
Dr. Terry Oatts, prin. Fax 389-2780

Rockdale County SD
Supt. — See Conyers
Davis MS 6-8
3375 E Fairview Rd SW 30281 770-388-5675
Dr. Wayne Watts, prin. Fax 388-5676

Community Christian S 700/PK-12
2001 Jodeco Rd 30281 678-432-0191
William Gailey, hdmstr. Fax 914-1217
Mt. Vernon Christian S 300/PK-12
1738 Fairview Rd 30281 770-474-1313
John Labor, hdmstr. Fax 474-3010
New Testament Christian Academy 100/PK-12
115 Old Conyers Rd 30281 770-507-5859
Bill Cox, prin. Fax 506-3300

Stone Mountain, DeKalb, Pop. 7,080
DeKalb County SD
Supt. — See Decatur
Champion MS 6-8
5265 Mimosa Dr 30083 678-676-4802
Joanne Doute-Cooper, prin.
Freedom MS 1,100/6-8
505 S Hairston Rd 30088 678-874-8702
Paulette Hammonds, prin. Fax 874-8710
Redan HS 1,500/9-12
5247 Redan Rd 30088 678-676-3602
Andrew Tatum, prin. Fax 676-3610
Stephenson HS 2,400/9-12
701 Stephenson Rd 30087 678-676-4202
Morcease Beasley, prin. Fax 676-4210
Stephenson MS 1,400/6-8
922 Stephenson Rd 30087 678-676-4402
Michael Williamson, prin. Fax 676-4410
Stone Mountain HS 1,600/9-12
4555 Central Dr 30083 678-676-6302
Carolyn D. Williams, prin. Fax 676-6310
Stone Mountain MS 1,100/6-8
4293 Sarr Pkwy 30083 678-676-4802
Dr. Gloria Dodson, prin. Fax 676-4810

Pro Way Hair School Post-Sec.
5684 Memorial Dr 30083 770-879-6673

Suches, Union
Union County SD
Supt. — See Blairsville
Woody Gap S 100/K-12
3736 State Highway 60 30572 706-747-2401
Jinjer Taylor, prin. Fax 747-1419

Summerville, Chattooga, Pop. 4,853
Chattooga County SD 2,500/PK-12
33 Middle School Rd 30747 706-857-3447
Mike Poole, supt. Fax 857-3440
www.chattooga.k12.ga.us
Chattooga HS 800/9-12
989 Highway 114 30747 706-857-2402
Roger Hibbs, prin. Fax 857-2565
Summerville MS 400/6-8
200 Middle School Rd 30747 706-857-2444
Mike Martin, prin. Fax 857-7769

Suwanee, Gwinnett, Pop. 12,553
Forsyth County SD
Supt. — See Cumming
Riverwatch MS 800/6-8
610 James Burgess Rd 30024 678-455-7311
Terri North, prin. Fax 455-7316

Gwinnett County SD 135,000/PK-12
437 Old Peachtree Rd NW 30024 678-301-6000
J. Alvin Wilbanks, supt. Fax 301-6030
www.gwinnett.k12.ga.us/
Collins Hill HS 3,500/9-12
50 Taylor Rd 30024 770-682-4100
Glenn McFall, prin. Fax 682-4105
North Gwinnett HS 2,400/9-12
20 Level Creek Rd 30024 770-945-9558
Dr. John Green, prin. Fax 271-5185
Peachtree Ridge HS 2,400/9-12
1555 Old Peachtree Rd NW 30024 678-957-3100
Dr. Steve Flynt, prin.
Other Schools – See Buford, Dacula, Duluth, Hoschton, Lawrenceville, Lilburn, Loganville, Norcross, Snellville

---

Forsyth Christian S 100/K-12
3149 Old Atlanta Rd 30024 770-777-3279
Christopher Walls, admin. Fax 777-3242

Swainsboro, Emanuel, Pop. 7,162
Emanuel County SD 4,300/PK-12
PO Box 130 30401 478-237-6674
Butch Frye, supt. Fax 237-3404
www.emanuel.k12.ga.us
Swainsboro HS 900/9-12
689 S Main St 30401 478-237-2267
Wayne Greenway, prin. Fax 237-3810
Swainsboro MS 700/6-8
200 Tiger Trl 30401 478-237-8047
Eric Carlyle, prin. Fax 237-4295
Other Schools – See Twin City

East Georgia College Post-Sec.
131 College Cir 30401 478-289-2000
Swainsboro Technical College Post-Sec.
346 Kite Rd 30401 478-289-2200

Sylvania, Screven, Pop. 2,591
Screven County SD 3,000/PK-12
PO Box 1668 30467 912-564-7114
Dr. Whitney Myers, supt. Fax 564-7104
www.screven.k12.ga.us
Screven County HS 900/9-12
110 Halcyondale Rd 30467 912-564-7836
Brett Warren, prin. Fax 564-5521
Screven County MS 800/6-8
126 Friendship Rd 30467 912-564-7468
Edwin Lovett, prin. Fax 564-5505

Sylvester, Worth, Pop. 5,924
Worth County SD 4,100/PK-12
504 E Price St 31791 229-776-8600
Dr. Gary Russell, supt. Fax 776-8603
www.worth.k12.ga.us/
Worth County Comprehensive HS 1,200/9-12
406 W King St 31791 229-776-8625
Dr. Barbara Thomas, prin. Fax 776-8614
Worth County MS 1,000/6-8
1305 N Isabella St 31791 229-776-8620
Paul Zimmer, prin. Fax 776-8624

Talbotton, Talbot, Pop. 1,022
Talbot County SD 800/PK-12
PO Box 515 31827 706-665-8528
Robert W. Patrick, supt. Fax 665-3620
www.talbot.k12.ga.us/
Central HS 200/9-12
PO Box 308 31827 706-665-8577
Edward Tymes, prin. Fax 665-3946
Central MS 200/6-8
PO Box 308 31827 706-665-8578
Edward Tymes, prin. Fax 665-2733

Tallapoosa, Haralson, Pop. 3,031
Haralson County SD
Supt. — See Buchanan
Haralson County Comprehensive HS 1,100/9-12
1655 Georgia Highway 120 30176 770-574-7647
Jim Crocker, prin. Fax 574-7648
Haralson County MS 900/6-8
2633 Georgia Highway 120 30176 770-646-8600
Andy Micacchione, prin. Fax 646-0108

Tallulah Falls, Rabun, Pop. 159

Tallulah Falls S 200/6-12
PO Box 10 30573 706-754-0400
Larry Peevy, hdmstr. Fax 754-3595

Temple, Paulding, Pop. 3,910
Carroll County SD
Supt. — See Carrollton
Temple HS 600/9-12
589 Sage St 30179 770-562-3218
Mike Angresano, prin. Fax 562-1510
Temple MS 600/5-8
275 Rainey Rd 30179 770-562-6001
Charles Johnson, prin. Fax 562-6002
Villa Rica MS 500/6-8
614 Tumlin Lake Rd 30179 770-459-0407
James Stocks, prin. Fax 459-5496

Thomaston, Upson, Pop. 9,265
Thomaston-Upson County SD 4,900/PK-12
205 Civic Center Dr 30286 706-647-9621
Dr. Howard Hendley, supt. Fax 646-9398
www.upson.k12.ga.us
Upson-Lee HS 1,400/9-12
268 Knight Trl 30286 706-647-8171
Cleve Hendrix, prin. Fax 647-3708
Upson-Lee MS 1,300/6-8
101 Holston Dr 30286 706-647-6256
Patsy Dean, prin. Fax 647-3631

Flint River Technical College Post-Sec.
1533 Highway 19 S 30286 706-646-6144

Thomasville, Thomas, Pop. 18,725
Thomas County SD 4,400/PK-12
11343 US Highway 319 N 31757 229-225-4380
Dr. Larry Green, supt. Fax 225-5012
www.thomas.k12.ga.us
Thomas County Central HS 1,500/9-12
4686 US Highway 84 Byp W 31792 229-225-5050
Frank Delaney, prin. Fax 227-2422
Thomas County MS 1,400/5-8
4681 US Highway 84 Byp W 31792 229-225-4394
Debra Knight, prin. Fax 225-4378

Thomasville CSD 3,000/PK-12
915 E Jackson St 31792 229-225-2600
Sabrina Boykins-Everett, supt. Fax 226-6997
www.tcitys.org
MacIntyre Park MS 600/6-8
117 Glenwood Dr 31792 229-225-2628
Gene Christie, prin. Fax 225-3502
Thomasville HS 900/9-12
315 S Hansell St 31792 229-225-2634
Todd Mobley, prin. Fax 225-2663

Brookwood S 500/PK-12
301 Cardinal Ridge Rd 31792 229-226-8070
Mike Notaro, hdmstr. Fax 227-0326
Southwest Georgia Technical College Post-Sec.
15689 US Highway 19 N 31792 229-225-5096
Thomas University Post-Sec.
1501 Millpond Rd 31792 229-226-1621

Thomson, McDuffie, Pop. 6,866
McDuffie County SD 4,200/PK-12
PO Box 957 30824 706-986-4000
Dr. Mark Petersen, supt. Fax 986-4001
www.mcduffie.k12.ga.us
Thomson HS 1,200/9-12
PO Box 1077 30824 706-986-4200
Rudy Falana, prin. Fax 986-4201
Thomson MS 1,100/6-8
PO Box 1140 30824 706-986-4400
Claude Powell, prin. Fax 986-4496

Tifton, Tift, Pop. 16,327
Tift County SD 7,500/PK-12
PO Box 389 31793 229-387-2400
Dr. John Harper, supt. Fax 386-1020
www.tiftschools.com
Eighth Street MS 1,200/7-8
700 8th St W 31794 229-387-2445
Dr. Ryan Gravitt, prin. Fax 386-1036
Tift County HS 1,400/10-12
1 Blue Devil Way 31794 229-387-2475
Mike Duck, prin. Fax 386-1022
Tift County HS Northeast Campus 600/9-9
3021 Fulwood Rd 31794 229-387-2450
Dr. Willie Miles, prin. Fax 386-1038

Abraham Baldwin Agriculture College Post-Sec.
2802 Moore Hwy 31793 229-391-5000
Moultrie Technical College Post-Sec.
52 Tech Dr 31794 229-391-2600

Tiger, Rabun, Pop. 319
Rabun County SD
Supt. — See Clayton
Rabun County HS 600/9-12
230 Wildcat Hill Dr 30576 706-782-4526
Mark Earnest, prin. Fax 782-7550
Rabun County MS 300/7-8
108 Wildcat Hill Dr 30576 706-782-5470
Kent Woerner, prin. Fax 782-4520

Toccoa, Stephens, Pop. 9,103
Stephens County SD 4,300/PK-12
RR 1 Box 1050 30577 706-886-9415
Gary C. Steppe, supt. Fax 886-3882
www.stephenscountyschools.com
Stephens County HS 1,300/9-12
6438 White Pine Rd 30577 706-886-6825
George Sanders, prin. Fax 886-8765
Stephens County MS 1,000/6-8
6270 Roselane 30577 706-886-2880
Tony Crunkleton, prin. Fax 886-2882

North Georgia Technical College Post-Sec.
8989 Highway 17 30577 706-779-8100

Toccoa Falls, Stephens

Toccoa Falls College Post-Sec.
PO Box 800899 30598 800-868-3257

Trenton, Dade, Pop. 2,155
Dade County SD 2,600/PK-12
PO Box 188 30752 706-657-4361
Patty Priest, supt. Fax 657-4572
www.dadecountyschools.org/
Dade County HS 700/9-12
300 Tradition Ln 30752 706-657-7517
Calvin Riddle, prin. Fax 657-4854
Dade MS 600/6-8
250 Pace Dr 30752 706-657-6491
Karen deMarche, prin. Fax 657-3055

Trion, Chattooga, Pop. 2,048
Trion CSD 1,300/PK-12
1255 Pine St 30753 706-734-2363
Dr. Susan Remillard, supt. Fax 734-3397
www.trionschools.org/
Trion HS 300/9-12
919 Allgood St 30753 706-734-7316
Dr. Phil Williams, prin. Fax 734-7692
Trion MS 300/6-8
919 Allgood St 30753 706-734-7433
Cindy Anderson, prin. Fax 734-7517

Tucker, DeKalb, Pop. 26,700
DeKalb County SD
Supt. — See Decatur
Tucker HS 1,300/9-12
5036 Lavista Rd 30084 678-874-3702
James Jackson, prin. Fax 874-3710
Tucker MS 1,000/6-8
2160 Idlewood Rd 30084 678-875-0902
Jerry Hogan, prin. Fax 875-0910

Le Cordon Bleu College of Culinary Arts Post-Sec.
1957 Lakeside Pkwy Ste 515 30084 770-938-4711

Tunnel Hill, Whitfield, Pop. 1,072
Whitfield County SD
Supt. — See Dalton
Northwest Whitfield County HS 1,900/9-12
1651 Tunnel Hill Varnell Rd 30755 706-673-6533
Carolyn Towns, prin. Fax 673-7098

Twin City, Emanuel, Pop. 1,752
Emanuel County SD
Supt. — See Swainsboro
Emanuel County Institute 500/6-12
PO Box 218 30471 478-763-2673
Boyd English, prin. Fax 763-3834

Tyrone, Fayette, Pop. 5,789
Fayette County SD
Supt. — See Fayetteville
Flat Rock MS 900/6-8
325 Jenkins Rd 30290 770-969-2830
Oatha Mann, prin. Fax 969-2835
Sandy Creek HS 1,300/9-12
360 Jenkins Rd 30290 770-969-2840
Roy Rabold, prin. Fax 969-2838

Valdosta, Lowndes, Pop. 45,205
Lowndes County SD 9,300/PK-12
PO Box 1227 31603 229-245-2250
Steve Smith, supt. Fax 245-2255
www.lowndes.k12.ga.us
Lowndes HS 2,700/9-12
1112 N Saint Augustine Rd 31601 229-245-2260
Wes Taylor, prin. Fax 245-2468
Lowndes MS 1,000/6-8
2379 Copeland Rd 31601 229-245-2280
Samuel Clemons, prin. Fax 245-2470
Other Schools – See Hahira

Valdosta CSD 7,200/K-12
PO Box 5407 31603 229-333-8500
Sam Allen, supt. Fax 247-7757
www.gocats.org
Newbern MS 800/6-8
2015 E Park Ave 31602 229-333-8566
Dr. Edward Wilson, prin. Fax 245-5655
Valdosta HS 2,100/9-12
3101 N Forrest St 31602 229-333-8540
Brett Stanton, prin. Fax 333-8584
Valdosta MS 1,000/6-8
110 Burton St 31602 229-333-8555
Martin Roesch, prin. Fax 245-5656

Georgia Christian S 300/PK-12
4359 Dasher Rd 31601 229-559-5131
Marcia Collins, prin. Fax 559-7401
Open Bible Christian S 400/PK-12
3992 N Oak Street Ext 31605 229-244-6694
Peter Smith, prin. Fax 244-1687
Southland Christian S 200/K-12
2206 E Hill Ave 31601 229-245-8111
Jackie Noble, prin. Fax 245-8189
Valdosta State University Post-Sec.
N Patterson St 31698 229-333-5952
Valdosta Technical College Post-Sec.
4089 Val Tech Rd 31602 229-333-2100

Vidalia, Toombs, Pop. 11,037
Vidalia CSD 2,500/PK-12
301 Adams St 30474 912-537-3088
Tim Smith, supt. Fax 538-0938
www.vidalia-city.k12.ga.us
Trippe MS 500/6-8
2200 McIntosh St 30474 912-537-3813
Gwen Warren, prin. Fax 537-3223
Vidalia HS 700/9-12
1001 North St W 30474 912-537-7931
Mitch Harrington, prin. Fax 537-7508

Southeastern Technical College Post-Sec.
3001 E 1st St 30474 912-538-3100

Vienna, Dooly, Pop. 2,952
Dooly County SD 1,500/PK-12
202 E Cotton St 31092 229-268-4761
Dr. John Bembry, supt. Fax 268-6148
www.dooly.k12.ga.us
Dooly County HS 400/9-12
712 N 3rd St 31092 229-268-8181
Randy Ford, prin. Fax 268-1916
Other Schools – See Pinehurst

Villa Rica, Carroll, Pop. 9,897
Carroll County SD
Supt. — See Carrollton
Bay Springs MS 700/6-8
122 Bay Springs Rd 30180 770-459-2098
Bruce Tidaback, prin. Fax 459-2097
Villa Rica HS 1,300/9-12
600 Rocky Branch Rd 30180 770-459-5185
Denzil Rogers, prin. Fax 459-2119

Waco, Haralson, Pop. 506

West Central Technical College Post-Sec.
176 Murphy Campus Blvd 30182 770-537-6000

Waleska, Cherokee, Pop. 816

Reinhardt College Post-Sec.
7300 Reinhardt College Cir 30183 770-720-5600

Warm Springs, Meriwether, Pop. 479

Trinity Christian Academy 100/PK-12
PO Box 882 31830 706-655-2080
Beth Waddell, admin. Fax 655-2099

Warner Robins, Houston, Pop. 57,907
Houston County SD
Supt. — See Perry
Feagin Mill MS 900/6-8
1200 Feagin Mill Rd 31088 478-953-0430
Dr. Jesse Davis, prin. Fax 953-0438
Houston County Career & Technology Ctr. Vo/Tech
1311 Corder Rd 31088 478-322-3280
Michael Parker, prin. Fax 322-3294
Houston County HS 2,100/9-12
920 GA Highway 96 31088 478-988-6360
Sheila Beckham, prin. Fax 988-6341
Huntington MS 6-8
206 Wellborn Rd 31088 478-988-7200
Dr. Gwen Taylor, prin. Fax 542-2247
Northside HS 1,800/9-12
926 Green St 31093 478-929-7858
Dr. J. Robin Hines, prin. Fax 929-7813
Northside MS 700/6-8
500 Johnson Rd 31093 478-929-7845
Ed Mashburn, prin. Fax 929-7124
Warner Robins HS 1,900/9-12
401 S Davis Dr 31088 478-929-7877
Steve Monday, prin. Fax 929-7769
Warner Robins MS 700/6-8
425 Mary Ln 31088 478-929-7832
Dr. Donald Warren, prin. Fax 929-7834

International City Beauty College Post-Sec.
1859 Watson Blvd 31093 478-923-0915
Middle Georgia Technical College Post-Sec.
80 Cohen Walker Dr 31088 478-988-6800

Warrenton, Warren, Pop. 2,012
Warren County SD 900/PK-12
PO Box 228 30828 706-465-3383
Carole Carey, supt. Fax 465-9141
www.warrenschools.com/
Warren County HS 300/9-12
1253 Atlanta Hwy 30828 706-465-3742
Thomas McDonald, prin. Fax 465-0901
Warren County MS 200/6-8
1253 Atlanta Hwy 30828 706-465-3742
Truett Abbott, prin. Fax 465-0901

Briarwood Academy 400/PK-12
4859 Thomson Hwy 30828 706-595-5641
John Hammond, hdmstr. Fax 595-0097

Washington, Wilkes, Pop. 4,150
Wilkes County SD 1,700/K-12
313 N Alexander Ave Ste A 30673 706-678-2718
Joyce Williams, supt. Fax 678-3799
www.wilkes.k12.ga.us
Washington-Wilkes Comprehensive HS 500/9-12
304 Gordon St 30673 706-678-2426
Andrew Jackson, prin. Fax 678-2628
Washington-Wilkes MS 400/6-8
304A Gordon St 30673 706-678-7131
Bill Pendrey, prin. Fax 678-3546

Watkinsville, Oconee, Pop. 2,535
Oconee County SD 5,800/PK-12
PO Box 146 30677 706-769-5130
Dr. Thomas Dohrmann, supt. Fax 769-3500
www.oconee.k12.ga.us
Oconee County HS 1,500/9-12
2721 Hog Mountain Rd 30677 706-769-6655
Mark Channell, prin. Fax 769-9499
Oconee County MS 900/6-8
1101 Mars Hill Rd 30677 706-769-3575
Xerona Thomas, prin. Fax 769-3572
Other Schools – See Bogart

Westminster Christian Academy 300/PK-12
1640 New High Shoals Rd 30677 706-769-9372
Dana James, hdmstr. Fax 769-2050

Waycross, Ware, Pop. 15,112
Ware County SD 6,100/PK-12
1301 Bailey St 31501 912-283-8656
Dr. Joseph Barrow, supt. Fax 283-8698
www.ware.k12.ga.us
Ware County HS 1,600/9-12
700 Victory Dr 31503 912-287-2351
Joe Brasfield, prin. Fax 287-2358
Ware County MS 800/6-8
2301 Cherokee St 31503 912-287-2341
Lee Robertson, prin. Fax 287-2353
Waycross MS 600/6-8
700 Central Ave 31501 912-287-2333
Tim Dixon, prin. Fax 287-2352
Other Schools – See Manor

Okefenokee Technical College Post-Sec.
1701 Carswell Ave 31503 912-287-6584
Waycross College Post-Sec.
2100 S Georgia Pkwy W 31503 912-285-6133

Waynesboro, Burke, Pop. 5,999
Burke County SD 4,600/PK-12
789 Burke Veterans Pkwy 30830 706-554-5101
Linda Bailey, supt. Fax 554-8051
www.burke.k12.ga.us
Burke County HS 1,200/9-12
1057 Burke Veterans Pkwy 30830 706-554-6691
Dr. Wayne Hickman, prin. Fax 554-8070
Burke County MS 1,200/6-8
356 Southside Dr 30830 706-554-3532
Daphney Ivery, prin. Fax 554-8063

Burke Academy 400/K-12
403 GA Highway 56 S 30830 706-554-4479
Brent Cribb, hdmstr. Fax 554-7582
Lord's House of Praise Christian S 100/PK-12
PO Box 1070 30830 706-437-1904
Thomas McKinney, admin. Fax 437-1924

Winder, Barrow, Pop. 12,451
Barrow County SD 9,900/PK-12
179 W Athens St 30680 770-867-4527
Dr. Ron Saunders, supt. Fax 867-4540
www.barrow.k12.ga.us
Apalachee HS 1,300/9-12
940 Haymon Morris Rd 30680 770-586-5111
David McGee, prin. Fax 307-3726
Haymon Morris MS 6-8
1008 Haymon Morris Rd 30680 678-963-0602
Dr. Sheila Kahrs, prin. Fax 867-1854
Russell MS 700/6-8
84 W Midland Ave 30680 770-867-8181
Dr. Russell Claxton, prin. Fax 868-1215
Westside MS 900/6-8
240 Matthews School Rd 30680 770-307-2972
Dr. Eli Welch, prin. Fax 307-2976
Winder-Barrow HS 1,400/9-12
272 N 5th Ave 30680 770-867-4519
Rob Johnson, prin. Fax 867-6412
Winder-Barrow MS 700/6-8
163 King St 30680 770-867-2116
Mary Beth Deaton, prin. Fax 868-1421
Adult Learning Center Adult
89 E Athens St 30680 770-307-1190
Lisa Maloof, dir. Fax 867-8018

Hope Christian Academy 100/PK-12
8 Pleasant Hll Church Rd SE 30680 770-725-2521

Woodbury, Meriwether, Pop. 1,091

Flint River Academy 300/PK-12
PO Box 247 30293 706-553-2541
Connie Strickland, hdmstr. Fax 553-9777

Woodstock, Cherokee, Pop. 19,602
Cherokee County SD
Supt. — See Canton
Booth MS 1,200/7-8
6550 Putnam Ford Dr 30189 770-926-5707
Rick Townsend, prin. Fax 928-2908
Etowah HS 2,000/9-12
6565 Putnam Ford Dr 30189 770-926-4411
Ron Dunnavant, prin. Fax 926-4157
Woodstock HS 2,200/9-12
2010 Towne Lake Hills S Dr 30189 770-592-3500
Bill Sebring, prin. Fax 592-3509
Woodstock MS 1,200/7-8
2000 Twn Lake Hlls South Dr 30189 770-592-3516
Richard Landolt, prin. Fax 591-8054
Polaris Evening S Adult
2010 Towne Lake Hls S Dr 30189 770-926-1662
Dr. Judy Battles, prin. Fax 592-3509

Cherokee Christian S 400/K-12
3075 Trickum Rd 30188 678-494-5464
Michael Lee, hdmstr. Fax 592-4881

Wrens, Jefferson, Pop. 2,261
Jefferson County SD
Supt. — See Louisville
Wrens MS 400/6-8
101 Griffin St 30833 706-547-6580
Julia Wells, prin. Fax 547-6224

Wrightsville, Johnson, Pop. 3,183
Johnson County SD 1,300/PK-12
PO Box 110 31096 478-864-3302
Hayward Cordy, supt. Fax 864-4053
www.johnson.k12.ga.us/
Johnson County HS 400/9-12
210 Trojan Way 31096 478-864-2222
Curtis Dixon, prin. Fax 864-4054
Johnson County MS 300/6-8
210 Trojan Way 31096 478-864-2222
Curtis Dixon, prin. Fax 864-4054

Young Harris, Towns, Pop. 542

Young Harris College Post-Sec.
PO Box 98 30582 706-379-3111

Zebulon, Pike, Pop. 1,194
Pike County SD 3,000/PK-12
PO Box 386 30295 770-567-8489
Dr. Michael Duncan, supt. Fax 567-8349
www.pike.k12.ga.us/
Pike County HS 900/9-12
PO Box 819 30295 770-567-8770
Scott John, prin. Fax 567-1628
Pike County MS 700/6-8
PO Box 405 30295 770-567-3353
Herbert Hodges, prin. Fax 567-3047

HAWAII

HAWAII DEPARTMENT OF EDUCATION
PO Box 2360, Honolulu 96804-2360
Telephone 808-586-3232
Fax 808-586-3234
Website doe.k12.hi.us

Superintendent of Education Patricia Hamamoto

HAWAII BOARD OF EDUCATION
PO Box 2360, Honolulu 96804-2360

Chairperson Karen Knudsen

PUBLIC, PRIVATE AND CATHOLIC SECONDARY SCHOOLS

Aiea, Honolulu, Pop. 8,906
Hawaii SD
Supt. — See Honolulu
Aiea HS 1,300/9-12
98-1276 Ulune St 96701 808-483-7300
John Sosa, prin. Fax 483-7303
Aiea IS 600/7-8
99-600 Kulawea St 96701 808-483-7230
Tom Kurashige, prin. Fax 483-7235

Ewa Beach, Honolulu, Pop. 14,315
Hawaii SD
Supt. — See Honolulu
Campbell HS 2,000/9-12
91-980 North Rd 96706 808-689-1200
Gail Awakuni, prin. Fax 689-1242
Ilima IS 1,200/7-8
91-884 Fort Weaver Rd 96706 808-689-1250
Jon Kitabayashi, prin. Fax 689-1258

Friendship Christian S 300/PK-12
91-1130 Renton Rd 96706 808-687-3638
James Reid, prin. Fax 681-0904
Lanakila Baptist HS 100/7-12
91-1219 Renton Rd 96706 808-681-3146
Rick Denham, prin. Fax 681-0704

Hana, Maui, Pop. 683
Hawaii SD
Supt. — See Honolulu
Hana S 400/K-12
PO Box 128 96713 808-248-4815
Richard Paul, prin. Fax 248-4819

Hilo, Hawaii, Pop. 40,759
Hawaii SD
Supt. — See Honolulu
Hilo HS 1,600/9-12
556 Waianuenue Ave 96720 808-974-4021
Robert Dircks, prin. Fax 974-4036
Hilo IS 600/7-8
587 Waianuenue Ave 96720 808-974-4955
Elaine Christian, prin. Fax 974-6184
Waiakea HS 1,300/9-12
155 W Kawili St 96720 808-974-4888
Dr. Patricia Nekoba, prin. Fax 974-4880
Waiakea IS 900/6-8
200 W Puainako St 96720 808-981-7231
Maureen Duffy, prin. Fax 981-7237
Hilo Community S Adult
450 Waianuenue Ave Ste C 96720 808-974-4100
Leonard Paik, prin. Fax 974-6170

Hawaii Community College Post-Sec.
200 W Kawili St 96720 808-974-7311
St. Joseph JSHS 7-12
1000 Ululani St 96720 808-935-4936
Sr. Marion Kikukawa, prin. Fax 969-9019
University of Hawaii at Hilo Post-Sec.
200 W Kawili St 96720 808-933-3301

Holualoa, Hawaii, Pop. 3,834

Makua Lani Christian S 100/8-12
74-4947 Mamalahoa Hwy 96725 808-329-4898
Thaddea Pitts, prin. Fax 334-0969

Honokaa, Hawaii, Pop. 2,186
Hawaii SD
Supt. — See Honolulu
Honoka'a MSHS 800/7-12
45-527 Pakalana St 96727 808-775-8800
Stanley Hao, prin. Fax 775-8803

Honolulu, Honolulu, Pop. 378,155
Hawaii SD 177,200/PK-12
PO Box 2360 96804 808-586-3230
Patricia Hamamoto, supt. Fax 586-3234
doe.k12.hi.us/
Aliamanu MS 900/7-8
3271 Salt Lake Blvd 96818 808-421-4100
Robert Eggleston, prin. Fax 421-4103
Anuenue S 300/K-12
2528 10th Ave 96816 808-733-8465
Charles Naumu, prin. Fax 733-8467
Central MS 500/6-8
1302 Queen Emma St 96813 808-587-4400
Brian Mizuguchi, prin. Fax 587-4409
Dole MS 800/6-8
1803 Kamehameha IV Rd 96819 808-832-3340
Myron Monte, prin. Fax 832-3349
Farrington HS 2,400/9-12
1564 N King St 96817 808-832-3600
Catherine Payne, prin. Fax 832-3587
Jarrett MS 300/6-8
1903 Palolo Ave 96816 808-733-4888
Gerald Teramae, prin. Fax 733-4894
Kaimuki HS 1,300/9-12
2705 Kaimuki Ave 96816 808-733-4900
Dennis Manalili, prin. Fax 733-4929
Kaimuki MS 700/6-8
631 18th Ave 96816 808-733-4800
Frank Fernandes, prin. Fax 733-4810
Kaiser HS 1,000/9-12
511 Lunalilo Home Rd 96825 808-394-1200
Larry Kaliloa, prin. Fax 394-1245
Kalakaua MS 1,100/6-8
821 Kalihi St 96819 808-832-3130
Randal Tanaka, prin. Fax 832-3140
Kalani HS 1,100/9-12
4680 Kalanianaole Hwy 96821 808-377-7744
Randiann Porras-Tang, prin. Fax 377-2483
Kawananakoa MS 800/6-8
49 Funchal St 96813 808-587-4430
Sandra Ishihara-Shibata, prin. Fax 587-4443
McKinley HS 1,900/9-12
1039 S King St 96814 808-594-0400
Ann Sugabayashi, prin. Fax 594-0407
Moanalua HS 2,000/9-12
2825 Ala Ilima St 96818 808-837-8455
Darrel Galera, prin. Fax 831-7919
Moanalua MS 800/7-8
1289 Mahiole St 96819 808-831-7850
Caroline Wong, prin. Fax 831-7859
Niu Valley MS 500/7-8
310 Halemaumau St 96821 808-377-2440
Justin Mew, prin. Fax 377-2444
Radford HS 1,400/9-12
4361 Salt Lake Blvd 96818 808-421-4200
Robert Stevens, prin. Fax 421-4210
Roosevelt HS 1,600/9-12
1120 Nehoa St 96822 808-587-4600
Dennis Hokama, prin. Fax 587-4637
Stevenson MS 600/6-8
1202 Prospect St 96822 808-587-4520
Gregg Lee, prin. Fax 587-4523
Washington MS 1,000/6-8
1633 S King St 96826 808-973-0177
Michael Harano, prin. Fax 973-0181
Farrington Community S Adult
1101 Kalihi St 96819 808-832-3595
Liberato Viduya, prin. Fax 832-3598
Kaimuki Community S Adult
2705 Kaimuki Ave 96816 808-733-8460
Richard Matsumoto, prin. Fax 733-8463
McKinley Community S Adult
634 Pensacola St Ste 216 96814 808-594-0540
Helen Sanpei, prin. Fax 594-0544
Moanalua/Aiea Community S Adult
2825A Ala Ilima St 96818 808-837-8466
Aileen Hokama, prin. Fax 837-7926
Other Schools – See Aiea, Ewa Beach, Hana, Hilo, Honokaa, Hoolehua, Kahuku, Kahului, Kailua, Kailua Kona, Kaneohe, Kapaa, Kapaau, Kapolei, Keaau, Kealakekua, Kihei, Lahaina, Lanai City, Laupahoehoe, Lihue, Makawao, Mililani, Pahala, Pahoa, Pearl City, Wahiawa, Waialua, Waianae, Wailuku, Waimea, Waipahu

---

Academy of the Pacific 200/6-12
913 Alewa Dr 96817 808-595-6359
Mollie Sperry, hdmstr. Fax 595-4235
Argosy University/Hawaii Post-Sec.
1001 Bishop St Ste 400 96813 808-536-5555
ASSETS S 400/K-12
1 Ohana Nui Way 96818 808-423-1356
Lou Salza, hdmstr. Fax 422-1920
Babel University Professional School Post-Sec.
1720 Ala Moana Blvd Ste A5 96815 808-946-3773
Chaminade University of Honolulu Post-Sec.
3140 Waialae Ave 96816 808-735-4711
Christian Academy 300/PK-12
3400 Moanalua Rd 96819 808-836-0233
Klayton Ko, supt. Fax 836-4415
Damien Memorial S 400/7-12
1401 Houghtailing St 96817 808-841-0195
Michael Weaver, prin. Fax 847-1401
Hawaiian Mission Academy 100/9-12
1438 Pensacola St 96822 808-536-2207
Manuel Rodriguez, prin. Fax 524-3294
Hawaii Baptist Academy 500/7-12
2429 Pali Hwy 96817 808-595-6301
Marsha Hirae, prin. Fax 595-6354
Hawaii Business College Post-Sec.
33 S King St Fl 4 96813 808-524-4014
Hawaii Institute of Hair Design Post-Sec.
71 S Hotel St 96813 808-533-6596
Hawaii Pacific University Post-Sec.
1164 Bishop St 96813 808-544-0200
Hawaii School for the Deaf and the Blind Post-Sec.
3440 Leahi Ave 96815
Hawaii Technology Institute Post-Sec.
629 Pohukaina St 96813 808-522-2700
Hawaii Tokai International College Post-Sec.
2241 Kapiolani Blvd 96826 808-983-4100
Heald College Post-Sec.
1500 Kapiolani Blvd 96814 808-955-1500
Honolulu Community College Post-Sec.
874 Dillingham Blvd 96817 808-845-9211
Honolulu Waldorf High S 100/9-12
1339 Hunakai St 96816 808-735-9311
Connie Starzynski, dir. Fax 735-5292
Institute of Clinical Acupuncture Post-Sec.
100 N Beretania St Ste 203B 96817 808-521-2288
Iolani S 1,800/K-12
563 Kamoku St 96826 808-949-5355
Val Iwashita, hdmstr. Fax 943-2354
Kamehameha S - Kapalama Campus 3,200/K-12
2010 Princess Dr 96817 808-842-8231
Michael Chun, hdmstr. Fax 842-8411
Kapiolani Community College Post-Sec.
4303 Diamond Head Rd 96816 808-734-9111
La Pietra S For Girls 300/6-12
2933 Poni Moi Rd 96815 808-922-2744
Nancy White, hdmstr. Fax 923-4514
Lutheran HS of Hawaii 100/9-12
1404 University Ave 96822 808-949-5302
Arthur Gundell, prin. Fax 947-3701
Maryknoll HS 600/9-12
1526 Alexander St 96822 808-952-7200
Betsey Gunderson, prin. Fax 952-7212
Medical Assisting School of Hawaii Post-Sec.
33 S King St Ste 223 96813 808-524-3363
Mid-Pacific Institute 1,100/6-12
2445 Kaala St 96822 808-973-5000
Joe Rice, prin. Fax 973-5099
New York Technical Institute of Hawaii Post-Sec.
1375 Dillingham Blvd 96817 808-841-5827
Punahou S 3,700/K-12
1601 Punahou St 96822 808-944-5711
Dr. James K. Scott, pres. Fax 944-5779
Remington College Post-Sec.
1111 Bishop St Ste 400 96813 808-942-1000
Sacred Hearts Academy 1,100/PK-12
3253 Waialae Ave 96816 808-734-5058
Betty White, prin. Fax 737-7867
St. Andrew's Priory S 500/K-12
224 Queen Emma Sq 96813 808-536-6102
Marilyn Matsunaga, hdmstr. Fax 538-1035
St. Francis HS 400/6-12
2707 Pamoa Rd 96822 808-988-4111
Sr. Joan of Arc Souza, prin. Fax 988-5497
St. Louis S 700/4-12
3142 Waialae Ave 96816 808-739-7777
Judge Walter Kirimitsu, pres. Fax 739-4853
TransPacific Hawaii College Post-Sec.
5257 Kalanianaole Hwy 96821 808-377-5402
Travel Institute of the Pacific Post-Sec.
1314 S King St Ste 1164 96814 808-591-2708
University of Hawaii at Manoa Post-Sec.
2444 Dole St 96822 808-956-8111
Word of Life Academy 500/PK-12
550 Queen St 96813 808-550-0238
David Sauceda, prin. Fax 550-0253
World Medicine Institute Post-Sec.
1110 University Ave Ste 308 96826 808-949-1050

Hoolehua, Maui
Hawaii SD
Supt. — See Honolulu
Moloka'i HS 400/9-12
PO Box 158 96729 808-567-6950
Linda Puleloa, prin. Fax 567-6960
Moloka'i MS 700/7-8
PO Box 443 96729 808-567-6950
Gary Zukeran, prin. Fax 567-6960

Kahuku, Honolulu, Pop. 2,063
Hawaii SD
Supt. — See Honolulu

Kahuku JSHS 1,900/7-12
56-490 Kamehameha Hwy 96731 808-293-8950
Lisa DeLong, prin. Fax 293-8960

Kahului, Maui, Pop. 16,889
Hawaii SD
Supt. — See Honolulu
Maui HS 1,700/9-12
660 Lono Ave 96732 808-873-3000
Randy Yamanuha, prin. Fax 873-3010
Maui Waena IS 900/6-8
795 Onehee Ave 96732 808-873-3070
Jamie Yap, prin. Fax 873-3066
Maui Community S for Adults Adult
179 W Kaahumanu Ave 96732 808-873-3082
Gwen Ueoka, prin. Fax 873-3046

Ka'ahumanu Hou Christian Schools of Maui 200/PK-12
707 S Puunene Ave 96732 808-871-2477
David Marocco, prin. Fax 871-5668
Maui Community College Post-Sec.
310 W Kaahumanu Ave 96732 808-244-9181

Kailua, Honolulu
Hawaii SD
Supt. — See Honolulu
Kailua HS 1,000/9-12
451 Ulumanu Dr 96734 808-266-7900
Francine Honda, prin. Fax 266-7915
Kailua IS 900/7-8
145 S Kainalu Dr 96734 808-263-1500
Suzanne Mulcahy, prin. Fax 266-7984
Kalaheo HS 1,100/9-12
730 Iliaina St 96734 808-254-7900
James Schlosser, prin. Fax 254-7907
Olomana JSHS 200/7-12
42-471 Kalanianaole Hwy 96734 808-266-7866
August Suehiro, prin. Fax 266-7873
Windward S for Adults Adult
730 Iliaina St 96734 808-254-7955
Gary Takaki, prin. Fax 254-7958

Kailua Christian Academy 50/1-12
1110A Kailua Rd 96734 808-263-9999
Diana Abraham, prin. Fax 263-9902
Le Jardin Academy 800/PK-12
917 Kalanianaole Hwy 96734 808-261-0707
Adrian Allan, prin. Fax 262-9339
Redemption Academy 200/PK-12
355 N Kainalu Dr 96734 808-266-2341
Adrian Yuen Ph.D., admin. Fax 266-2342

Kailua Kona, Hawaii, Pop. 45,944
Hawaii SD
Supt. — See Honolulu
Kealakehe HS 1,500/9-12
74-5000 Puohulihuli St 96740 808-327-4300
Wilfred Murakami, prin. Fax 327-4307
Kealakehe IS 1,100/6-8
74-5062 Onipaa St 96740 808-327-4314
Donald Merwin, prin. Fax 327-4315
Kona Community S Adult
74-5000 Puohulihuli St 96740 808-327-4692
Robert Krueger, prin. Fax 327-4693

Hualalai Academy 200/K-12
74-4966 Kealakaa St 96740 808-326-9866
Felicity Johnson, prin. Fax 329-9542

Kamuela, Hawaii, Pop. 5,972

Hawaii Prep Academy 600/K-12
PO Box 428 96743 808-885-7321
Olaf Jorgenson, hdmstr. Fax 881-4003
Parker S 300/K-12
65-1224 Lindsey Rd 96743 808-885-7933
Carl Sturges, prin. Fax 885-6233
Traditional Chinese Medical College HI Post-Sec.
65-1206 Mamalahoa Hwy 96743 808-885-9226

Kaneohe, Honolulu, Pop. 34,970
Hawaii SD
Supt. — See Honolulu
Castle HS 1,800/9-12
45-386 Kaneohe Bay Dr 96744 808-233-5600
Meredith Maeda, prin. Fax 233-5623
King IS 800/7-8
46-155 Kamehameha Hwy 96744 808-233-5727
Cynthia Chun, prin. Fax 233-5747

Christian Education Institute 50/K-12
45-416 Kamehameha Hwy 96744 808-247-8186
Robin Spencer, admin. Fax 234-5753
Golf Academy of Hawaii Post-Sec.
46-001 Kamehameha Hwy 96744 800-342-7342
Hawaii Pacific University Post-Sec.
45-045 Kamehameha Hwy 96744 808-235-3641
Koolau Baptist Academy 200/PK-12
PO Box 1642 96744 808-233-2900
John Goodale, prin. Fax 233-2903
Windward Community College Post-Sec.
45-720 Keaahala Rd 96744 808-235-7400

Kapaa, Kauai, Pop. 8,149
Hawaii SD
Supt. — See Honolulu
Kapaa HS 1,100/9-12
4695 Mailihuna Rd 96746 808-821-4400
Gilmore Youn, prin. Fax 821-4420
Kapaa MS 700/6-8
4867 Olohena Rd 96746 808-821-4460
Mary Ann Bode, prin. Fax 821-6967

Kapaau, Hawaii, Pop. 1,083
Hawaii SD
Supt. — See Honolulu
Kohala HS 300/9-12
PO Box 279 96755 808-889-7117
Catherine Bratt, prin. Fax 889-7120
Kohala MS 200/6-8
PO Box 777 96755 808-889-7119
Barbara Volhein, prin. Fax 889-7121

Kapolei, Honolulu, Pop. 1,000
Hawaii SD
Supt. — See Honolulu
Kapolei HS 2,200/9-12
91-5007 Kapolei Pkwy 96707 808-692-8200
Alvin Nagasako, prin. Fax 692-8255
Kapolei MS 1,700/6-8
91-5335 Kapolei Pkwy 96707 808-693-7025
Annette Nishikawa, prin. Fax 693-7030

Keaau, Hawaii, Pop. 1,584
Hawaii SD
Supt. — See Honolulu
Kea'au HS 900/9-12
16-725 Keaau Pahoa Rd 96749 808-982-4220
Ann Paulino, prin. Fax 982-4224
Kea'au MS 600/6-8
16-565 Keaau Pahoa Rd 96749 808-982-4200
Jamil Ahmadia, prin. Fax 982-4219

Christian Liberty S 100/PK-12
16-675 Milo St 96749 808-966-8866
Troy Rimel, prin. Fax 966-8866
Kamehameha S - Hawaii Campus 1,000/K-12
16-714 Volcano Rd 96749 808-982-0007
Stan Fortuna, prin. Fax 982-0010

Kealakekua, Hawaii, Pop. 1,453
Hawaii SD
Supt. — See Honolulu
Konawaena HS 900/9-12
81-1043 Konawaena School Rd 96750 808-323-4500
Shawn Suzuki, prin. Fax 323-4515
Konawaena MS 500/6-8
81-1045 Konawaena School Rd 96750 808-323-4566
Nancy Soderberg, prin. Fax 323-4574

Kihei, Maui, Pop. 11,107
Hawaii SD
Supt. — See Honolulu
Lokelani IS 500/6-8
1401 Liloa Dr 96753 808-875-6800
Donna Whitford, prin. Fax 875-6835

Kilauea, Kauai, Pop. 1,685

Kula HS 100/7-12
4551 Kapuna Rd 96754 808-828-0077
David Mireles, hdmstr. Fax 828-0107

Lahaina, Maui, Pop. 9,073
Hawaii SD
Supt. — See Honolulu
Lahaina IS 600/6-8
871 Lahainaluna Rd 96761 808-662-3965
Marsha Nakamura, prin. Fax 662-3968
Lahainaluna HS 1,000/9-12
980 Lahainaluna Rd 96761 808-662-4000
Michael Nakano, prin. Fax 662-3997

Laie, Honolulu, Pop. 5,577

Brigham Young University Post-Sec.
55-220 Kulanui St 96762 808-293-3211

Lanai City, Maui, Pop. 2,400
Hawaii SD
Supt. — See Honolulu
Lanai S 600/K-12
PO Box 630630 96763 808-565-7900
Pierce Myers, prin. Fax 565-7904

Laupahoehoe, Hawaii, Pop. 508
Hawaii SD
Supt. — See Honolulu
Laupahoehoe S 200/K-12
PO Box 189 96764 808-962-2200
Paul McCarty, prin. Fax 962-2202

Lawai, Kauai, Pop. 1,787

Kahili Adventist S 100/K-12
PO Box 480 96765 808-742-9294
Bud Moon Ph.D., prin. Fax 742-6628

Lihue, Kauai, Pop. 5,536
Hawaii SD
Supt. — See Honolulu
Kamakahelei MS 1,000/6-8
4431 Nuhou St 96766 808-241-3200
Debra Badua, prin. Fax 241-3210
Kauai HS 1,300/9-12
3577 Lala Rd 96766 808-274-3160
Linda Tanouye Smith, prin. Fax 274-3170
Kauai Community S for Adults Adult
3607A Lala Rd Ste P-12 96766 808-274-3390
Eugene Uegawa, prin. Fax 274-3393

Island S 300/PK-12
3-1875 Kaumualii Hwy 96766 808-246-0233
Robert Springer, prin. Fax 245-6053
Kauai Community College Post-Sec.
3-1901 Kaumualii Hwy 96766 808-245-8311

Makawao, Maui, Pop. 5,405
Hawaii SD
Supt. — See Honolulu
Kalama IS 1,000/6-8
120 Makani Rd 96768 808-573-8735
John Costales, prin. Fax 573-8748
Kekaulike HS 1,400/9-12
121 Kula Hwy 96768 808-573-8710
Susan Scofield, prin. Fax 573-2231

Kamehemaha S Maui Campus 1,100/K-12
270 Aapueo Pkwy 96768 808-572-3100
Lee Ann DeLima, hdmstr. Fax 573-7062
Seabury Hall S 400/6-12
480 Olinda Rd 96768 808-572-7235
Joseph Schmidt, hdmstr. Fax 572-7196

Mililani, Honolulu, Pop. 28,608
Hawaii SD
Supt. — See Honolulu
Mililani HS 2,400/9-12
95-1200 Meheula Pkwy 96789 808-627-7747
Dr. John Brummel, prin. Fax 627-7375
Mililani MS 1,800/6-8
95-1140 Lehiwa Dr 96789 808-626-7355
Roger Kim, prin. Fax 626-7358

Hanalani S 700/PK-12
94-294 Anania Dr 96789 808-625-0737
Mark Sugimoto, supt. Fax 625-0691

Pahala, Hawaii, Pop. 1,520
Hawaii SD
Supt. — See Honolulu
Ka'u & Pahala S 400/K-12
PO Box 100 96777 808-928-2088
Josephine DeMorales, prin. Fax 928-2092

Pahoa, Hawaii, Pop. 1,027
Hawaii SD
Supt. — See Honolulu
Pahoa JSHS 800/7-12
15-3038 Puna Rd 96778 808-965-2150
Maring Gacusana, prin. Fax 965-2153

Pearl City, Honolulu, Pop. 30,976
Hawaii SD
Supt. — See Honolulu
Highlands IS 1,000/7-8
1460 Hoolaulea St 96782 808-453-6480
Amy Martinson, prin. Fax 453-6484
Pearl City HS 2,000/9-12
2100 Hookiekie St 96782 808-453-6500
Gerald Suyama, prin. Fax 453-6521

Leeward Community College Post-Sec.
96-045 Ala Ike St 96782 808-455-0011
University of Hawaii - West Oahu Post-Sec.
96-129 Ala Ike St 96782 808-454-4700

Wahiawa, Honolulu, Pop. 17,386
Hawaii SD
Supt. — See Honolulu
Leilehua HS 1,800/9-12
1515 California Ave 96786 808-622-6550
Norman Minehira, prin. Fax 622-6554
Wahiawa MS 1,000/6-8
275 Rose St 96786 808-622-6500
Dr. Carol Price, prin. Fax 622-6506
Wheeler MS 600/6-8
2 Wheeler Army Airfield 96786 808-622-6525
Brenda Vierra-Chun, prin. Fax 622-6529
Wahiawa Community S Adult
1515 California Ave 96786 808-622-1634
Leighton Hasegawa, prin. Fax 621-7765

Hawaii Theological Seminary Post-Sec.
PO Box 861754 96786 808-622-4487
Ho'ala S 100/K-12
1067 California Ave Ste A 96786 808-621-1898
Nancy Barry, prin. Fax 622-3615

Waialua, Honolulu, Pop. 3,943
Hawaii SD
Supt. — See Honolulu
Waialua JSHS 700/7-12
67-160 Farrington Hwy 96791 808-637-8200
Valarie Kardash, prin. Fax 637-8209

Waianae, Honolulu, Pop. 8,758
Hawaii SD
Supt. — See Honolulu
Nanakuli JSHS 1,300/7-12
89-980 Nanakuli Ave 96792 808-668-5823
Levi Chang, prin. Fax 668-5828
Waianae HS 2,000/9-12
85-251 Farrington Hwy 96792 808-697-7017
JoAnn Kumasaka, prin. Fax 697-7018
Waianae IS 1,100/7-8
85-626 Farrington Hwy 96792 808-697-7121
John Vannatta, prin. Fax 697-7124

Maili Bible S 100/K-12
87-138 Gilipake St 96792 808-696-3038
Larry Estrella, prin. Fax 696-3060

Wailuku, Maui, Pop. 10,688
Hawaii SD
Supt. — See Honolulu
Baldwin HS 1,700/9-12
1650 Kaahumanu Ave 96793 808-984-5656
Natalie Gonsalves, prin. Fax 984-5674
Iao IS 800/6-8
260 S Market St 96793 808-984-5610
Catherine Kilborn, prin. Fax 984-5617

St. Anthony JSHS 300/7-12
1618 Lower Main St 96793 808-244-4190
Edwina Wilson-Snyder, prin. Fax 242-8081

Waimea, Kauai, Pop. 7,812
Hawaii SD
Supt. — See Honolulu
Niihau S, PO Box 339 96796 50/K-12
William Arakaki, prin. 808-338-6800
Waimea HS 800/9-12
PO Box 339 96796 808-338-6800
William Arakaki, prin. Fax 338-6807

Waipahu, Honolulu, Pop. 33,108
Hawaii SD
Supt. — See Honolulu
Waipahu HS 2,400/9-12
94-1211 Farrington Hwy 96797 808-675-0222
Patricia Pedersen, prin. Fax 675-0257
Waipahu IS 1,400/7-8
94-455 Farrington Hwy 96797 808-675-0177
Randell Dunn, prin. Fax 675-0181
Waipahu Community S Adult
94-1211 Farrington Hwy 96797 808-675-0254
David Stem, prin. Fax 675-0259

IDAHO

IDAHO DEPARTMENT OF EDUCATION
PO Box 83720, Boise 83720-0003
Telephone 208-332-6800
Fax 208-332-6836
Website http://www.sde.state.id.us

Superintendent of Public Instruction Tom Luna

IDAHO BOARD OF EDUCATION
PO Box 83720, Boise 83720-0003

President Milford Terrell

PUBLIC, PRIVATE AND CATHOLIC SECONDARY SCHOOLS

Aberdeen, Bingham, Pop. 1,828
Aberdeen SD 58 600/PK-12
PO Box 610 83210 208-397-4113
Chad Struhs, supt. Fax 397-4114
aberdeen58.org/
Aberdeen HS 300/9-12
PO Box 610 83210 208-397-4152
David Kerns, prin. Fax 397-4439
Aberdeen MS 6-8
PO Box 610 83210 208-397-3280
Joel Wilson, prin. Fax 397-3281

American Falls, Power, Pop. 4,162
American Falls JSD 381 1,600/PK-12
827 Fort Hall Ave 83211 208-226-5173
Dr. Ron Bolinger, supt. Fax 226-5754
www.sd381.k12.id.us
American Falls HS 500/9-12
2966 S Frontage Rd 83211 208-226-2531
Jeff Read, prin. Fax 226-5853
Thomas MS 400/6-8
355 Bannock Ave 83211 208-226-5203
Randy Jensen, prin. Fax 226-5274

Ammon, Bonneville, Pop. 10,925
Bonneville JSD 93
Supt. — See Idaho Falls
Hillcrest HS 1,200/9-12
2800 Owen St 83406 208-525-4429
Scott Miller, prin. Fax 525-4437

Arco, Butte, Pop. 989
Butte County JSD 111 500/PK-12
PO Box 89 83213 208-527-8235
Dr. Amy Pancheri, supt. Fax 527-8950
www.buttecountyschools.org
Butte County HS 200/9-12
PO Box 655 83213 208-527-8237
Brandon Farris, prin. Fax 527-8246
Butte County MS 100/6-8
PO Box 695 83213 208-527-3077
Erik Strom, prin. Fax 527-4950

Arimo, Bannock, Pop. 319
Marsh Valley JSD 21 1,400/PK-12
PO Box 180 83214 208-254-3306
Marvin Hansen, supt. Fax 254-9243
www.marshnet.sd21.k12.id.us
Marsh Valley HS 400/9-12
12655 S Old Highway 91 83214 208-254-3711
Gary Yearsley, prin. Fax 254-9320
Marsh Valley MS 200/7-8
12805 S Old Highway 91 83214 208-254-3260
Linda Reichardt, prin. Fax 254-3631

Ashton, Fremont, Pop. 1,105
Fremont County JSD 215
Supt. — See Saint Anthony
North Fremont JSHS 300/7-12
3581 E 1300 N 83420 208-652-7468
David Risenmay, prin. Fax 652-7784

Bancroft, Caribou, Pop. 363
North Gem SD 149 200/PK-12
PO Box 70 83217 208-648-7848
Kent Stokes, supt. Fax 648-7895
www.sd149.com
North Gem JSHS 100/7-12
PO Box 70 83217 208-648-7848
Kent Stokes, prin. Fax 648-7895

Blackfoot, Bingham, Pop. 10,828
Blackfoot SD 55 4,100/K-12
270 E Bridge St 83221 208-785-8800
Dewane Wren, supt. Fax 785-8809
www.d55.k12.id.us
Blackfoot HS 1,200/9-12
870 S Fisher Ave 83221 208-785-8810
Blaine McInelly, prin. Fax 785-2329
Mountain View MS 600/7-8
645 Mitchell Ln 83221 208-785-8820
Ryan Wilson, prin. Fax 785-8823

Snake River SD 52 1,900/PK-12
103 S 900 W 83221 208-684-3001
Russell Hammond, supt. Fax 684-3003
www.snakeriver.org
Snake River HS 600/9-12
922 W Highway 39 83221 208-684-3061
Dean Bonney, prin. Fax 684-3074
Snake River JHS 300/7-8
918 W Highway 39 83221 208-684-3018
Mark Gabrylczyk, prin. Fax 684-3047

Bliss, Gooding, Pop. 260
Bliss JSD 234 200/K-12
PO Box 115 83314 208-352-4447
Kevin Lancaster, supt. Fax 352-4649
www.bliss.k12.id.us
Bliss S 200/K-12
601 E Highway 30 83314 208-352-4445
Jeff LaCroix, prin. Fax 352-4649

Boise, Ada, Pop. 189,847
ISD of Boise City 25,500/PK-12
8169 W Victory Rd 83709 208-854-4000
Dr. Stan Olson, supt. Fax 854-4003
www.boiseschools.org
Boise SHS 1,200/10-12
1010 W Washington St 83702 208-854-4270
Ken Anderson, prin. Fax 854-4271
Borah SHS 1,500/10-12
6001 Cassia St 83709 208-854-4370
Greg Frederick, prin. Fax 854-4371
Capital SHS 1,600/10-12
8055 Goddard Rd 83704 208-854-4490
Jon Ruzicka, prin. Fax 854-4491
East JHS 700/7-9
415 Warm Springs Ave 83712 208-854-4730
Bonita Hammer, prin. Fax 854-4731
Fairmont JHS 800/7-9
2121 N Cole Rd 83704 208-854-4790
Amy Kohlmeier, prin. Fax 854-4791
Hillside JHS 500/7-9
3536 Hill Rd 83703 208-854-5120
Jeff Farley, prin. Fax 854-5121
Les Bois JHS 900/7-9
4150 E Grand Forest Dr 83716 208-854-5340
Marlys Erickson, prin. Fax 854-5341
North JHS 800/7-9
1105 N 13th St 83702 208-854-5740
Dr. Teri Thaemert, prin. Fax 854-5741
Professional-Technical Education Center Vo/Tech
8201 W Victory Rd 83709 208-854-5810
Jim Marconi, prin. Fax 854-5811
Riverglen JHS 700/7-9
6801 Gary Ln 83714 208-854-5910
David Greene, prin. Fax 854-5914
South JHS 800/7-9
805 Shoshone St 83705 208-854-6110
Dr. Kathleen McCurdy, prin. Fax 854-6111
Timberline SHS 1,100/10-12
701 E Boise Ave 83706 208-854-6230
Betsy Story, prin. Fax 854-6232
Treasure Valley Math & Science Center 7-12
6801 Gary Ln 83714 208-854-6800
Dr. Holly MacLean, prin. Fax 854-6801
West JHS 900/7-9
711 N Curtis Rd 83706 208-854-6450
Richard Webb, prin. Fax 854-6451
Boise Evening S Adult
6001 Cassia St 83709 208-854-6700
Ron Dehlin, prin. Fax 854-4371

Meridian JSD 2
Supt. — See Meridian
Centennial HS 1,900/9-12
12400 W Mcmillan Rd 83713 208-939-1404
Alta Graham, prin. Fax 939-1420
Lake Hazel MS 1,200/6-8
11625 W La Grange St 83709 208-362-3703
Kenton Travis, prin. Fax 362-0258
Scott MS 1,000/6-8
13600 W Mcmillan Rd 83713 208-939-2101
Linda Ventura, prin. Fax 939-1424

Apollo College Boise Post-Sec.
1200 N Liberty St 83704 208-377-8080
Bishop Kelly HS 600/9-12
7009 W Franklin Rd 83709 208-375-6010
Robert Wehde, prin. Fax 375-3626
Boise Bible College Post-Sec.
8695 W Marigold St 83714 800-893-7755
Boise State University Post-Sec.
1910 University Dr 83725 208-426-1011
Covenant Academy 50/K-12
PO Box 532 83701 208-377-2385
David Barrett, admin. Fax 362-8061
Foundations Academy 300/K-12
PO Box 2701 83701 208-323-3888
David Goodwin, hdmstr. Fax 672-0522
ITT Technical Institute Post-Sec.
12302 W Explorer Dr 83713 208-322-8844
Milan Institute Post-Sec.
8590 W Fairview Ave 83704 208-672-9500
Riverstone International School 300/K-12
5493 Warm Springs Ave 83716 208-424-5000
Joe Kennedy, hdmstr. Fax 424-0033
St. Alphonsus Regional Medical Center Post-Sec.
1055 N Curtis Rd 83706 208-378-2000

Bonners Ferry, Boundary, Pop. 2,725
Boundary County SD 101 1,500/PK-12
6577 Main St Ste 101 83805 208-267-3146
Dr. Don Bartling, supt. Fax 267-7217
www.bcsd101.com
Bonners Ferry HS 500/9-12
6485 Tamarack Ln 83805 208-267-3149
Curt-Randall Bayer, prin. Fax 267-5171
Boundary County MS 300/6-8
6577 Main St Ste 100 83805 208-267-5852
Dick Behrens, prin. Fax 267-8099

Bruneau, Owyhee
Bruneau-Grand View JSD 365
Supt. — See Grand View
Rimrock JSHS 200/7-12
39678 State Highway 78 83604 208-834-2260
Phil McCluskey, prin. Fax 834-2516

Buhl, Twin Falls, Pop. 4,015
Buhl JSD 412 1,300/PK-12
920 Main St 83316 208-543-6436
Dr. Richard Hill, supt. Fax 543-6360
www.d412.k12.id.us
Buhl HS 400/9-12
1 Indian Territory 83316 208-543-8262
Mike Gemar, prin. Fax 543-8705
Buhl MS 300/6-8
525 Sawtooth Ave 83316 208-543-8292
Byron Stutzman, prin. Fax 543-6360

Burley, Cassia, Pop. 9,131
Cassia County JSD 151 4,900/PK-12
237 E 19th St 83318 208-878-6600
Gaylen Smyer, supt. Fax 878-4231
www.sd151.k12.id.us
Burley JHS 800/7-9
700 W 16th St 83318 208-878-6613
Steve Copmann, prin. Fax 878-6624
Burley SHS 600/10-12
2100 Park Ave 83318 208-878-6606
Jodie Mills, prin. Fax 878-6647
Other Schools – See Declo, Malta, Oakley

Caldwell, Canyon, Pop. 34,433
Caldwell SD 132 5,900/K-12
1101 Cleveland Blvd 83605 208-455-3300
Dr. Lonnie Barber, supt. Fax 455-3302
www.caldwellschools.org/
Caldwell HS 1,400/9-12
3401 S Indiana Ave 83605 208-455-3304
Mike Farris, prin. Fax 455-3256
Jefferson MS 700/6-8
3311 S 10th Ave 83605 208-455-3309
Randy Schrader, prin. Fax 459-6773
Syringa MS 700/6-8
1100 Willow St 83605 208-455-3305
Louise Daniels, prin. Fax 455-3353

Vallivue SD 139 4,100/PK-12
5207 S Montana Ave 83607 208-454-0445
George Grant, supt. Fax 454-0293
www.vallivue.org
Vallivue HS 1,300/9-12
1407 E Homedale Rd 83607 208-454-9253
Wyatt Tustin, prin. Fax 459-7114
Vallivue MS 700/7-8
16412 S 10th Ave 83607 208-454-1426
Rod Lowe, prin. Fax 454-7846

Albertson College of Idaho Post-Sec.
2112 Cleveland Blvd 83605 208-459-5000
Gem State Academy 100/9-12
16115 S Montana Ave 83607 208-459-1627
Mike Schwartz, prin. Fax 454-9079

Cambridge, Washington, Pop. 354
Cambridge SD 432 200/PK-12
PO Box 39 83610 208-257-3321
Dr. Margaret J. Cox, supt. Fax 257-3323
Cambridge JSHS 100/7-12
PO Box 39 83610 208-257-3311
Angie Lakey-Campbell, prin. Fax 257-3323

Carey, Blaine, Pop. 511
Blaine County SD 61
Supt. — See Hailey
Carey S 200/K-12
PO Box 266 83320 208-823-4391
John Peck, prin. Fax 823-4310

Cascade, Valley, Pop. 1,005
Cascade SD 422 400/PK-12
PO Box 291 83611 208-382-4227
Elsie Krause, supt. Fax 382-3797
www.cascadeschools.org
Cascade JSHS 200/7-12
PO Box 291 83611 208-382-4227
Pal Sartori, dean Fax 382-3797

Castleford, Twin Falls, Pop. 274
Castleford JSD 417 300/PK-12
500 W Main St 83321 208-537-6511
Kelly Murphey, supt. Fax 537-6855
www.castlefordschools.com
Castleford S 300/PK-12
500 W Main St 83321 208-537-6511
Andy Wiseman, prin. Fax 537-6855

Challis, Custer, Pop. 844
Challis JSD 181 500/K-12
PO Box 304 83226 208-879-4231
Rob Campbell, supt. Fax 879-5473
www.d181.k12.id.us/
Challis JSHS 200/7-12
PO Box 304 83226 208-879-2255
Kevin Kemp, prin. Fax 879-5801

Chubbuck, Bannock, Pop. 10,707

The School of Hairstyling Post-Sec.
141 E Chubbuck Rd 83202 208-232-9170

Clark Fork, Bonner, Pop. 578
Lake Pend Oreille SD 84
Supt. — See Ponderay
Clark Fork JSHS 100/7-12
PO Box 129 83811 208-266-1131
Phil Kemink, prin. Fax 266-1692

Coeur d Alene, Kootenai, Pop. 36,259
Coeur D'Alene SD 271 9,300/PK-12
311 N 10th St 83814 208-664-8241
Harry Amend, supt. Fax 664-1748
www.cdaschools.org
Canfield MS 800/6-8
1800 E Dalton Ave 83815 208-664-9188
Jeff Bengtson, prin. Fax 769-2951
Coeur D'Alene HS 1,500/9-12
5530 N 4th St 83815 208-667-4507
Randy Russell, prin. Fax 664-5785
Lake City HS 1,400/9-12
6101 N Ramsey Rd 83815 208-769-0769
John Brumley, prin. Fax 769-2944
Lakes MS 600/6-8
930 N 15th St 83814 208-667-4544
Chris Hammons, prin. Fax 769-2982
Woodland MS 800/6-8
2101 W Saint Michelle 83815 208-667-5996
James Lien, prin. Fax 667-5997
Other Schools – See Post Falls

Lake City Junior Academy 100/PK-10
111 E Locust Ave 83814 208-667-0877
Ron Turner, prin. Fax 665-1462
North Idaho College Post-Sec.
1000 W Garden Ave 83814 208-769-3300
Sage Technical Services Post-Sec.
2845 W Seltice Way 83814 208-765-6346
The Headmasters School of Hair Design Post-Sec.
317 Coeur DAlene Lake Dr 83814 208-664-0541

Cottonwood, Idaho, Pop. 1,070
Cottonwood JSD 242 400/K-12
PO Box 158 83522 208-962-3971
Stan Kress, supt. Fax 962-7780
www.sd242.k12.id.us/District/
Prairie HS 200/9-12
PO Box 540 83522 208-962-3901
David Snodgrass, prin. Fax 962-7702
Prairie MS 100/5-8
PO Box 580 83522 208-962-3521
Rene Forsmann, prin. Fax 962-3319

Council, Adams, Pop. 742
Council SD 13 300/PK-12
PO Box 68 83612 208-253-4217
Murray Dalgleish, supt. Fax 253-4297
www.sd013.k12.id.us
Council JSHS 200/7-12
PO Box 468 83612 208-253-4217
Murray Dalgleish, prin. Fax 253-4297

Craigmont, Lewis, Pop. 548
Highland JSD 305 200/PK-12
PO Box 130 83523 208-924-5211
Clair Garrick, supt. Fax 924-5614
www.sd305.k12.id.us/
Highland JSHS 7-12
PO Box 130 83523 208-924-5452
Clair Garrick, prin. Fax 924-5614

Culdesac, Nez Perce, Pop. 375
Culdesac JSD 342 200/K-12
600 Culdesac Ave 83524 208-843-5413
Darrell Olson, supt. Fax 843-2719
Culdesac S 200/K-12
600 Culdesac Ave 83524 208-843-5413
Darrell Olson, prin. Fax 843-2719

Dayton, Franklin, Pop. 463
West Side JSD 202 600/PK-12
PO Box 39 83232 208-747-3502
Melvin Beutler, supt. Fax 747-3705
www.wssd.k12.id.us
Lee MS 100/6-8
PO Box 140 83232 208-747-3303
Melvin Beutler, prin. Fax 747-3637
West Side HS 200/9-12
PO Box 89 83232 208-747-3411
Stanley Bingham, prin. Fax 747-3990

Deary, Latah, Pop. 515
Whitepine JSD 288
Supt. — See Troy
Deary S 200/4-12
PO Box 9 83823 208-877-1151
Darrah Eggers, prin. Fax 877-1366

Declo, Cassia, Pop. 332
Cassia County JSD 151
Supt. — See Burley
Declo HS 300/9-12
505 E Main St 83323 208-654-2030
Roland Bott, prin. Fax 654-2404
Declo JHS 300/6-8
205 E Main St 83323 208-654-9960
Mark Rose, prin. Fax 654-2070

Dietrich, Lincoln, Pop. 164
Dietrich SD 314 200/PK-12
406 N Park St 83324 208-544-2158
Ed Simons, supt. Fax 544-2832
www.sd314.k12.id.us
Dietrich S 200/PK-12
406 N Park St 83324 208-544-2158
Thomas P. Fenelon, prin. Fax 544-2832

Driggs, Teton, Pop. 1,197
Teton County SD 401 1,400/PK-12
PO Box 775 83422 208-354-2207
Gordon Woolley, supt. Fax 354-2250
www.d401.k12.id.us
Teton HS 500/9-12
555 E Ross Ave 83422 208-354-2952
Chad Williams, prin. Fax 354-2907
Teton MS 300/6-8
PO Box 529 83422 208-354-2971
Monte Woolstenhulme, prin. Fax 354-8685

Dubois, Clark, Pop. 642
Clark County SD 161 200/PK-12
PO Box 237 83423 208-374-5175
Paul Blanford, supt. Fax 374-5178
Clark County JSHS 100/6-12
PO Box 237 83423 208-374-5215
Thomas Monroe, prin. Fax 374-5234

Eagle, Ada, Pop. 17,338
Meridian JSD 2
Supt. — See Meridian
Eagle HS 1,800/9-12
574 Park Ln 83616 208-939-2189
Terry Beck, prin. Fax 939-2453
Eagle MS 1,200/6-8
1000 W Floating Feather Rd 83616 208-939-2216
Tony Nelson, prin. Fax 939-2173

Emmett, Gem, Pop. 6,124
Emmett ISD 221 3,000/PK-12
601 E 3rd St 83617 208-365-6301
Tom Carlsen, supt. Fax 365-2961
www.isd221.net
Emmett HS 700/10-12
721 W 12th St 83617 208-365-6323
Steve Beitia, prin. Fax 365-6100
Emmett JHS 700/7-9
301 E 4th St 83617 208-365-2921
Wade Carter, prin. Fax 365-2427

Fairfield, Camas, Pop. 392
Camas County SD 121 200/K-12
PO Box 370 83327 208-764-2625
Ed Marshall, supt. Fax 764-9218
Camas County HS 100/9-12
PO Box 370 83327 208-764-2472
J.T. Stroder, prin. Fax 764-9218

Filer, Twin Falls, Pop. 1,768
Filer SD 413 1,300/PK-12
700B Stevens St 83328 208-326-5981
John Graham, supt. Fax 326-3350
www.filer.k12.id.us/
Filer HS 500/9-12
3915 Wildcat Way 83328 208-326-5945
Leon Madsen, prin. Fax 326-3419
Filer MS 300/6-8
299 Highway 30 83328 208-326-5906
Gregory Lanting, prin. Fax 326-3385

Firth, Bingham, Pop. 417
Firth SD 59 800/PK-12
PO Box 69 83236 208-346-6815
Sid Tubbs, supt. Fax 346-6814
www.firthschools.org
Firth HS 300/9-12
PO Box 247 83236 208-346-6812
Tana Kellogg, prin. Fax 346-6987
Firth MS 200/5-8
410 Roosevelt St 83236 208-346-6240
Deanne Dye, prin. Fax 346-4306

Fruitland, Payette, Pop. 4,406
Fruitland SD 373 1,600/PK-12
PO Box A 83619 208-452-3595
Alan Felgenhauer, supt. Fax 452-6430
www.fsd.k12.id.us/
Fruitland HS 400/9-12
PO Box A 83619 208-452-4411
Garry Swindell, prin. Fax 452-4485
Fruitland MS 500/5-8
PO Box A 83619 208-452-3350
Diane O'Dell, prin. Fax 452-4063

Garden Valley, Boise
Garden Valley SD 71 50/K-12
PO Box 710 83622 208-462-3756
Vic Koshuta, supt. Fax 462-3570
www.gvsd.net
Garden Valley JSHS 7-12
PO Box 710 83622 208-462-3756
James Buschine, prin. Fax 462-3570

Genesee, Latah, Pop. 879
Genesee JSD 282 300/K-12
PO Box 98 83832 208-285-1161
David Neumann, supt. Fax 285-1495
www.genesee.k12.id.us/
Genesee S 300/K-12
PO Box 98 83832 208-285-1162
Loretta Stowers, prin. Fax 285-1495

Glenns Ferry, Elmore, Pop. 1,451
Glenns Ferry JSD 192 500/PK-12
800 Highway 30 83623 208-366-7436
Wayne Rush, supt. Fax 366-7455
Glenns Ferry HS 200/9-12
639 N Bannock Ave 83623 208-366-7434
Jeremiah Johnston, prin. Fax 366-2056
Glenns Ferry MS 100/6-8
639 N Bannock Ave 83623 208-366-7438
Laron Billingsley, prin. Fax 366-2056

Gooding, Gooding, Pop. 3,320
Gooding JSD 231 1,300/PK-12
507 Idaho St 83330 208-934-4321
T. Robert Stearns, supt. Fax 934-4403
www.gooding.k12.id.us/
Gooding HS 400/9-12
1050 7th Ave W 83330 208-934-4831
Eric Raine, prin. Fax 934-4347
Gooding MS 300/6-8
1045 7th Ave W 83330 208-934-8443
Teresa Jones, prin. Fax 934-4898

Idaho State School for the Deaf/Blind Post-Sec.
1450 Main St 83330 208-934-4457

Grace, Caribou, Pop. 972
Grace JSD 148 500/PK-12
PO Box 347 83241 208-425-3984
Ted Taylor, supt. Fax 425-3809
www.sd148.org/
Grace JSHS 300/7-12
PO Box 348 83241 208-425-3731
Don Yates, prin. Fax 425-3063

Grand View, Owyhee, Pop. 477
Bruneau-Grand View JSD 365 400/PK-12
PO Box 310 83624 208-834-2253
Vickie Chandler, supt. Fax 834-2293
Other Schools – See Bruneau

Grangeville, Idaho, Pop. 3,151
Grangeville JSD 241 1,400/PK-12
714 Jefferson St 83530 208-983-0990
Dr. Wayne Davis, supt. Fax 983-1245
www.jsd241.org/
Grangeville HS 300/9-12
910 S D St 83530 208-983-0580
Gary Stears, prin. Fax 983-3786
Other Schools – See Kooskia, Riggins

Greenleaf, Canyon, Pop. 890

Greenleaf Friends Academy 300/PK-12
PO Box 368 83626 208-459-6346
Kenneth Sheldon, supt. Fax 459-7700

Hagerman, Gooding, Pop. 838
Hagerman JSD 233 400/K-12
324 N 2nd Ave 83332 208-837-4777
Ron Echols, supt. Fax 837-4737
www.hagerman.k12.id.us
Hagerman JSHS 7-12
150 Lake St W 83332 208-837-4572
Mark Kress, prin. Fax 837-6502

Hailey, Blaine, Pop. 7,583
Blaine County SD 61 3,200/K-12
118 W Bullion St 83333 208-578-5000
Jim Lewis, supt. Fax 578-5110
www.blaineschools.org/
Wood River HS 800/9-12
950 Fox Acres Rd 83333 208-578-5020
Graham Hume, prin. Fax 578-5120
Wood River MS 700/6-8
900 N 2nd Ave 83333 208-578-5030
Fritz Peters, prin. Fax 578-5130
Other Schools – See Carey

Hansen, Twin Falls, Pop. 961
Hansen SD 415 — 400/PK-12
550 Main St S 83334 — 208-423-6387
Dennis Coulter, supt. — Fax 423-6808
www.hansen.k12.id.us/
Hansen JSHS — 200/7-12
550 Main St S 83334 — 208-423-5593
Bert Hursh, prin. — Fax 423-6808

Harrison, Kootenai, Pop. 282
Kootenai JSD 274 — 300/K-12
13030 E Ogara Rd 83833 — 208-689-3631
Ron Hill, supt. — Fax 689-3641
Kootenai JSHS — 100/7-12
13030 E Ogara Rd 83833 — 208-689-3311
Rich Lund, prin. — Fax 689-9072

Hayden, Kootenai, Pop. 11,906

North Idaho Christian S — 300/1-12
251 W Miles Ave 83835 — 208-772-7546
Larry Kay, admin. — Fax 762-2749

Hazelton, Jerome, Pop. 720
Valley SD 262 — 700/PK-12
882 Valley Rd 83335 — 208-829-5333
Dr. Laural Nelson, supt. — Fax 829-5548
valley.sd262.k12.id.us
Valley S — 700/PK-12
882 Valley Rd 83335 — 208-829-5961
Brian Hardy, prin. — Fax 829-5548

Homedale, Owyhee, Pop. 2,577
Homedale JSD 370 — 1,300/K-12
116 E Owyhee Ave 83628 — 208-337-4611
Tim Rosandick, supt. — Fax 337-4911
www.homedaleschools.org
Homedale HS — 300/9-12
203 E Idaho Ave 83628 — 208-337-4613
Mike Williams, prin. — Fax 337-4933
Homedale MS — 400/5-8
3437 Johnstone Rd 83628 — 208-337-5780
Keith Field, prin. — Fax 337-5782

Horseshoe Bend, Boise, Pop. 834
Horseshoe Bend SD 73 — 300/K-12
398 School Dr 83629 — 208-793-2225
Scott Mutchie, supt. — Fax 793-2449
www.hsb-73k12.org
Horseshoe Bend MSHS — 200/6-12
398 School Dr 83629 — 208-793-2225
John Cook, prin. — Fax 793-2449

Idaho City, Boise, Pop. 488
Basin SD 72 — 500/PK-12
PO Box 227 83631 — 208-392-4183
Frank Gallant, supt. — Fax 392-9954
Idaho City MSHS — 200/7-12
PO Box 227 83631 — 208-392-4183
John McFarlane, prin. — Fax 392-9954

Idaho Falls, Bonneville, Pop. 52,338
Bonneville JSD 93 — 7,400/PK-12
3497 N Ammon Rd 83401 — 208-525-4400
Dr. Charles Shackett, supt. — Fax 529-0104
www3.d93.k12.id.us/
Bonneville HS — 1,100/9-12
3165 E Iona Rd 83401 — 208-525-4406
John Pymm, prin. — Fax 523-7014
Rocky Mountain MS — 500/7-8
3443 N Ammon Rd 83401 — 208-525-4403
Shalene French, prin. — Fax 525-4469
Sandcreek MS — 700/7-8
2955 Owen St 83406 — 208-525-4416
Lyndon Oswald, prin. — Fax 525-4438
Other Schools – See Ammon

Idaho Falls SD 91 — 10,200/PK-12
690 John Adams Pkwy 83401 — 208-525-7500
George Boland, supt. — Fax 525-7596
www.d91.k12.id.us
Eagle Rock JHS — 900/7-9
2020 Pancheri Dr 83402 — 208-525-7700
Wendy Cavan, prin. — Fax 525-7703
Gale JHS — 700/7-9
955 Garfield St 83401 — 208-525-7720
Jim Shank, prin. — Fax 525-7724
Idaho Falls SHS — 1,200/10-12
601 S Holmes Ave 83401 — 208-525-7740
Randy Hurley, prin. — Fax 525-7768
Skyline SHS — 1,100/10-12
1767 Blue Sky Dr 83402 — 208-525-7770
Trina Caudle, prin. — Fax 525-7778
Taylorview JHS — 900/7-9
350 Castlerock Ln 83404 — 208-524-7850
Roberta Crosser, prin. — Fax 524-7851

Eastern Idaho Technical College — Post-Sec.
1600 S 25th E 83404 — 208-524-3000

Jerome, Jerome, Pop. 8,503
Jerome JSD 261 — 3,000/K-12
107 3rd Ave W 83338 — 208-324-2392
Jim Cobble, supt. — Fax 324-7609
www.d261.k12.id.us
Jerome HS — 900/9-12
104 Tiger Dr 83338 — 208-324-8137
Patti O'Dell, prin. — Fax 324-1266
Jerome MS — 500/7-8
116 3rd Ave W 83338 — 208-324-8134
Eric Anderson, prin. — Fax 324-7458

Kamiah, Lewis, Pop. 1,148
Kamiah JSD 304 — 500/PK-12
RR 1 Box 720 83536 — 208-935-2991
Doug Flaming, supt. — Fax 935-4005
www.kamiah.org/
Kamiah HS — 200/9-12
711 9th St 83536 — 208-935-4067
Steve Higgins, prin. — Fax 935-4068
Kamiah MS — 200/5-8
800 12th St 83536 — 208-935-4040
Carrie Nygaard, prin. — Fax 935-4041

Kellogg, Shoshone, Pop. 2,298
Kellogg JSD 391 — 1,400/K-12
800 Bunker Ave 83837 — 208-784-1348
Sandra Pommerening, supt. — Fax 786-3331
www.sd391.k12.id.us
Kellogg HS — 400/9-12
2 Jacobs Gulch Rd 83837 — 208-784-1371
Ralph Lowe, prin. — Fax 783-0741
Kellogg MS — 400/6-8
810 Bunker Ave 83837 — 208-784-1311
Cal Ketchum, prin. — Fax 784-0134

Silver Valley Christian Academy — 50/PK-12
514 W Brown Ave 83837 — 208-783-3791
Arthur Fleming, admin. — Fax 783-3791

Kendrick, Latah, Pop. 344
Kendrick JSD 283 — 300/PK-12
PO Box 283 83537 — 208-289-4211
Clark Adamson, supt. — Fax 289-4201
Kendrick JSHS — 200/7-12
2001 Highway 3 83537 — 208-289-4202
Jeffrey Cirka, prin. — Fax 289-4213

Kimberly, Twin Falls, Pop. 2,686
Kimberly SD 414 — 1,300/K-12
141 Center St W 83341 — 208-423-4170
John Garner, supt. — Fax 423-6155
www.kimberly.edu/
Kimberly HS — 400/9-12
141 Center St W 83341 — 208-423-4170
Dick Brulotte, prin. — Fax 423-5181
Kimberly MS — 300/6-8
141 Center St W 83341 — 208-423-4170
Jeff Jones, prin. — Fax 423-6155

Kooskia, Idaho, Pop. 665
Grangeville JSD 241
Supt. — See Grangeville
Clearwater Valley JSHS — 200/7-12
PO Box 130 83539 — 208-926-4511
Fred Woods, prin. — Fax 926-4807

Kuna, Ada, Pop. 10,153
Kuna JSD 3 — 3,800/PK-12
1450 Boise St 83634 — 208-922-1000
Jay Hummel, supt. — Fax 922-5646
www.kunaschools.org
Kuna HS — 1,000/9-12
637 E Deer Flat Rd 83634 — 208-955-0200
Scott Hill, prin. — Fax 922-5646
Kuna MS — 900/6-8
1360 Boise St 83634 — 208-922-1002
Deb McGrath, prin. — Fax 922-1030

Lapwai, Nez Perce, Pop. 1,116
Lapwai SD 341 — 500/PK-12
PO Box 247 83540 — 208-843-2622
Harold Ott, supt. — Fax 843-2910
Lapwai JSHS — 200/7-12
PO Box 247 83540 — 208-843-2241
Bryan Samuels, prin. — Fax 843-5289

Leadore, Lemhi, Pop. 89
South Lemhi SD 292 — 100/K-12
PO Box 119 83464 — 208-768-2441
Jim Smith, supt. — Fax 768-2797
www.leadoreschool.org
Leadore S — 100/K-12
PO Box 119 83464 — 208-768-2441
Jim Smith, prin. — Fax 768-2797

Lewiston, Nez Perce, Pop. 31,081
Lewiston ISD 1 — 5,000/PK-12
3317 12th St 83501 — 208-748-3000
Dr. Joy C. Rapp, supt. — Fax 748-3059
www.lewiston.k12.id.us
Jenifer JHS — 600/7-9
1213 16th St 83501 — 208-748-3300
JoAnne Greear, prin. — Fax 748-3349
Lewiston SHS — 1,100/10-12
1114 9th Ave 83501 — 208-748-3100
Dr. Robert Donaldson, prin. — Fax 748-3149
Sacajawea JHS — 700/7-9
3610 12th St 83501 — 208-748-3400
Phil Uhlorn, prin. — Fax 748-3449

Beacon Christian S — 100/K-12
615 Stewart Ave 83501 — 208-743-8361
Richard Rasmussen, prin. — Fax 743-3787
Lewis-Clark State College — Post-Sec.
500 8th Ave 83501 — 208-792-5272
Mr. Leon's School of Hair Design — Post-Sec.
205 10th St 83501 — 208-743-6822
Northwest Childrens Home Education Ctr — 100/K-12
PO Box 1288 83501 — 208-746-8206
Bruce Grimoldby, dir. — Fax 746-7482
The Headmasters School of Hair Design — Post-Sec.
602 Main St 83501 — 208-743-1512

Mc Call, Valley, Pop. 2,876
Mc Call-Donnelly JSD 421 — 1,000/PK-12
120 Idaho St, — 208-634-2161
Dr. Terrell Donicht, supt. — Fax 634-4075
www.mdsd.org
Mc Call-Donnelly HS — 400/9-12
401 N Mission St, — 208-634-2218
Tim Thomas, prin. — Fax 634-7505
Payette Lakes MS — 200/6-8
111 S Samson Trl, — 208-634-5994
Susan Buescher, prin. — Fax 634-5231

Mackay, Custer, Pop. 529
Mackay JSD 182 — 200/PK-12
PO Box 390 83251 — 208-588-2896
Troy Thayne, supt. — Fax 588-2269
Mackay JSHS — 100/7-12
PO Box 390 83251 — 208-588-2262
Troy Thayne, prin. — Fax 588-2549

Malad City, Oneida, Pop. 2,124
Oneida County SD 351 — 900/PK-12
25 E 50 S Ste A 83252 — 208-766-4701
Lynn Schow, supt. — Fax 766-2930
malad.sd351.k12.id.us
Malad HS — 300/9-12
181 Jenkins Ave 83252 — 208-766-4728
John Cockett, prin. — Fax 766-4538
Malad MS — 200/6-8
175 Jenkins Ave 83252 — 208-766-9235
Sheldon Vaughan, prin. — Fax 766-9236

Malta, Cassia, Pop. 174
Cassia County JSD 151
Supt. — See Burley
Raft River JSHS — 200/7-12
PO Box 68 83342 — 208-645-2220
Patrick Manning, prin. — Fax 645-2640

Marsing, Owyhee, Pop. 976
Marsing JSD 363 — 800/K-12
PO Box 340 83639 — 208-896-4111
Harold Schockley, supt. — Fax 896-4790
www.marsingschools.org/
Marsing HS — 200/9-12
PO Box 340 83639 — 208-896-4111
Chuck Stella, prin. — Fax 896-4457
Marsing MS — 200/6-8
PO Box 340 83639 — 208-896-4111
Paul Webster, prin. — Fax 896-5128

Melba, Canyon, Pop. 544
Melba JSD 136 — 300/PK-12
PO Box 185 83641 — 208-495-1141
Robert Larson, supt. — Fax 495-1142
www.melbaschools.org
Melba MSHS — 6-12
PO Box 185 83641 — 208-495-2221
Dick Davis, prin. — Fax 495-2188

Meridian, Ada, Pop. 52,240
Meridian JSD 2 — 27,900/PK-12
1303 E Central Dr 83642 — 208-855-4500
Dr. Linda Clark, supt. — Fax 350-5962
www.meridianschools.org
Heritage MS — 6-8
4990 N Meridian Rd, — 208-350-4130
Susan McInerney, prin.
Lewis & Clark MS — 1,000/6-8
4141 E Pine Ave 83642 — 208-377-1353
Dennis Keogh, prin. — Fax 377-3718
Meridian HS — 1,700/9-12
1900 W Pine Ave 83642 — 208-888-4905
Geoff Stands, prin. — Fax 888-5273
Meridian MS — 1,100/6-8
1507 W 8th St 83642 — 208-855-4225
Lisa Austin, prin. — Fax 855-4249
Mountain View HS — 2,000/9-12
2000 Millenium Way 83642 — 208-855-4050
Aaron Maybon, prin. — Fax 855-4074
Sawtooth MS — 1,000/6-8
3730 N Linder Rd, — 208-855-4200
David Moser, prin. — Fax 855-4224
Other Schools – See Boise, Eagle

Cole Valley Christian HS — 300/7-12
200 E Carlton Ave 83642 — 208-898-9003
Mark Wood, supt. — Fax 898-9016
Northwest Lineman College — Post-Sec.
7600 S Meridian Rd 83642 — 208-888-4817

Middleton, Canyon, Pop. 4,409
Middleton SD 134 — 2,600/PK-12
5 S 3rd Ave W 83644 — 208-585-3027
Dr. Rich Bauscher, supt. — Fax 585-3028
www.msd134.org
Middleton HS — 700/9-12
511 W Main St 83644 — 208-585-6657
Jim Squibb, prin. — Fax 585-3362
Middleton MS — 600/6-8
200 S 4th Ave W 83644 — 208-585-3251
Molly Burger, prin. — Fax 585-2098

Midvale, Washington, Pop. 185
Midvale SD 433 — 100/K-12
PO Box 130 83645 — 208-355-2678
James Warren, supt. — Fax 355-2347
www.midvalerangers.org
Midvale S — K-12
PO Box 130 83645 — 208-355-2234
James Warren, prin. — Fax 355-2347

Montpelier, Bear Lake, Pop. 2,507
Bear Lake County SD 33
Supt. — See Paris
Bear Lake HS — 400/9-12
330 Boise St 83254 — 208-847-0294
Alan Schwab, prin. — Fax 847-0144
Bear Lake MS — 300/6-8
633 Washington St 83254 — 208-847-2255
Bruce Belnap, prin. — Fax 847-3626
Clover Creek HS — 9-12
697 Jackson St 83254 — 208-847-2516
Jill Kunz, prin.

Moscow, Latah, Pop. 21,862
Moscow SD 281 — 2,400/PK-12
650 N Cleveland St 83843 — 208-882-1120
Dr. Candis R. Donicht, supt. — Fax 883-4440
www.sd281.k12.id.us
Moscow JHS — 600/7-9
1410 E D St 83843 — 208-882-3577
Dale Kleinert, prin. — Fax 892-1182
Moscow SHS — 600/10-12
402 E 5th St 83843 — 208-882-2591
Robert Celebrezze, prin. — Fax 892-1136

* * *

Mr. Leon's School of Hair Design — Post-Sec.
618 S Main St 83843 — 208-882-2923
New Saint Andrews College — Post-Sec.
PO Box 9025 83843 — 208-882-1566
University of Idaho — Post-Sec.
PO Box 444264 83844 — 208-885-6111

Mountain Home, Elmore, Pop. 11,565
Mountain Home SD 193 — 4,100/PK-12
PO Box 1390 83647 — 208-587-2580
Tim McMurtrey, supt. — Fax 587-9896
www.mtnhomesd.org
Mountain Home JHS — 600/8-9
1600 E 6th S 83647 — 208-587-2590
Ernest Elliott, prin. — Fax 587-2597
Mountain Home SHS — 800/10-12
300 S 11th E 83647 — 208-587-2570
Jeff Johnson, prin. — Fax 587-2579

* * *

Shiloh Christian S — 50/6-12
PO Box 1012 83647 — 208-587-3828
Michele Ring, lead tchr. — Fax 587-7951

Mullan, Shoshone, Pop. 788
Mullan SD 392 — 100/K-12
PO Box 71 83846 — 208-744-1118
Robin Stanley, supt. — Fax 744-1119
www.sd392.k12.id.us
Mullan JSHS — 100/7-12
PO Box 71 83846 — 208-744-1126
Tom Durbin, prin. — Fax 744-1128

Murtaugh, Twin Falls, Pop. 138
Murtaugh JSD 418 — 200/PK-12
PO Box 117 83344 — 208-432-5451
Dennis Osman, supt. — Fax 432-5477
Murtaugh HS — 100/9-12
PO Box 117 83344 — 208-432-5451
Dennis Osman, prin. — Fax 432-5477
Murtaugh MS — 50/6-8
PO Box 117 83344 — 208-432-5451
Dennis Osman, prin. — Fax 432-5477

Nampa, Canyon, Pop. 71,713
Nampa SD 131 — 12,800/PK-12
619 S Canyon St 83686 — 208-468-4600
Gary Larsen, supt. — Fax 468-4638
www.nsd131.org/
Columbia HS — 9-12
301 S Happy Valley Rd 83687 — 208-468-4763
Heath Thomason, prin.
East Valley MS — 900/6-8
4085 E Greenhurst Rd 83686 — 208-468-4760
Terry Adolfson, prin. — Fax 461-4069
Nampa HS — 1,500/9-12
203 Lake Lowell Ave 83686 — 208-465-2760
Byron Holtry, prin. — Fax 465-2741
Skyview HS — 1,700/9-12
1303 E Greenhurst Rd 83686 — 208-468-7820
Matt Crist, prin. — Fax 468-7822
South MS — 900/6-8
229 W Greenhurst Rd 83686 — 208-468-4740
Stuart Vickers, prin. — Fax 465-2779
West MS — 1,000/6-8
28 S Midland Blvd 83651 — 208-465-2752
Greg Wiles, prin. — Fax 465-2776

* * *

Milan Institute — Post-Sec.
1021 W Hemingway 83651 — 208-461-0616
Nampa Christian S — 700/PK-12
439 W Orchard Ave 83651 — 208-466-8451
David Claar, supt. — Fax 466-8452
Northwest Nazarene University — Post-Sec.
623 Holly St 83686 — 208-467-8011
Razzle Dazzle College of Hair Design — Post-Sec.
120 Holly St 83686 — 208-465-7660

New Meadows, Adams, Pop. 492
Meadows Valley SD 11 — 200/PK-12
PO Box F 83654 — 208-347-2411
Dr. Terrell Donicht, supt. — Fax 347-2624
Meadows Valley S — 200/PK-12
PO Box F 83654 — 208-347-2118
John Preston, prin. — Fax 347-2624

New Plymouth, Payette, Pop. 1,403
New Plymouth SD 372 — 900/PK-12
103 SE Avenue 83655 — 208-278-5740
Ryan Kerby, supt. — Fax 278-3069
New Plymouth HS — 300/9-12
207 S Plymouth Ave 83655 — 208-278-5311
Arlo Decker, prin. — Fax 278-5313
New Plymouth MS — 200/6-8
4400 SW 2nd Ave 83655 — 208-278-5788
Darrell Brown, prin. — Fax 278-3773

Nezperce, Lewis, Pop. 514
Nezperce JSD 302 — 200/PK-12
PO Box 279 83543 — 208-937-2551
Clair Garrick, supt. — Fax 937-2136
www.nezpercesd.us/
Nezperce JSHS — 7-12
PO Box 279 83543 — 208-937-2551
Skip Wilson, prin. — Fax 937-2136

Notus, Canyon, Pop. 540
Notus SD 135 — 300/K-12
PO Box 256 83656 — 208-459-7442
Jim Doramus, supt. — Fax 455-2439
www.notusschools.k12.id.us/
Notus JSHS — 100/7-12
PO Box 256 83656 — 208-459-4633
Brad Frackrell, prin. — Fax 459-6304

Oakley, Cassia, Pop. 663
Cassia County JSD 151
Supt. — See Burley
Oakley JSHS — 200/7-12
PO Box 173 83346 — 208-862-3328
Harold Hatch, prin. — Fax 862-3330

Old Town, Bonner, Pop. 204

* * *

House of the Lord Christian Academy — 200/PK-12
754 Silver Birch Ln, — 208-437-2184
Michael Croston, admin. — Fax 437-0441

Orofino, Clearwater, Pop. 3,145
Orofino JSD 171 — 1,400/PK-12
PO Box 2259 83544 — 208-476-5593
Dale Durkee, supt. — Fax 476-7293
www.sd171.k12.id.us
Orofino HS — 300/9-12
300 Dunlap Rd 83544 — 208-476-5557
Jerry Nelson, prin. — Fax 476-0147
Orofino JHS — 200/7-8
PO Box 706 83544 — 208-476-4613
Shannon Wilson, prin. — Fax 476-3327
Other Schools – See Weippe

Paris, Bear Lake, Pop. 518
Bear Lake County SD 33 — 1,300/PK-12
PO Box 300 83261 — 208-945-2891
Cliff Walters, supt. — Fax 945-2893
Other Schools – See Montpelier

Parma, Canyon, Pop. 1,799
Parma SD 137 — 1,000/K-12
805 E McConnell Ave 83660 — 208-722-5115
Jim Norton, supt. — Fax 722-7937
www.parmaschools.org
Parma HS — 300/9-12
137 Panther Way 83660 — 208-722-5115
Michael Moore, prin. — Fax 722-7153
Parma MS — 300/6-8
905 E McConnell Ave 83660 — 208-722-5115
Peggy Sharkey, prin. — Fax 722-6913

Paul, Minidoka, Pop. 947
Minidoka County JSD 331
Supt. — See Rupert
West Minico MS — 400/6-8
155 S 600 W 83347 — 208-438-5018
Sandra Miller, prin. — Fax 438-8513

Payette, Payette, Pop. 7,560
Payette JSD 371 — 1,800/PK-12
20 N 12th St 83661 — 208-642-9366
Pauline King, supt. — Fax 642-9006
www.payettesd.k12.id.us
McCain MS — 400/6-8
400 N Iowa Ave 83661 — 208-642-4122
Sandy Holloway, prin. — Fax 642-6801
Payette HS — 500/9-12
1500 6th Ave S 83661 — 208-642-3327
Sam Nelson, prin. — Fax 642-3368
Payette Night S — Adult
1215 Center Ave 83661 — 208-642-4705
Patrick Townsend, admin. — Fax 642-9006

* * *

River of Life Christian S — 100/PK-12
800 17th Ave N 83661 — 208-642-4416
Paul Shover, admin. — Fax 642-4413

Plummer, Benewah, Pop. 985
Plummer/Worley JSD 44 — 500/PK-12
PO Box 130 83851 — 208-686-1621
George Olsen, supt. — Fax 686-2108
www.pwsd44.com
Lakeside HS — 100/9-12
PO Box 130 83851 — 208-686-1937
James Phillips, prin. — Fax 686-2201
Lakeside MS — 100/6-8
PO Box 130 83851 — 208-686-1627
Bill Burns, prin. — Fax 686-2201

Pocatello, Bannock, Pop. 53,372
Pocatello/Chubbuck SD 25 — 11,700/PK-12
3115 Pole Line Rd 83201 — 208-232-3563
Mary Vagner, supt. — Fax 235-3280
www.d25.k12.id.us
Century HS — 1,100/9-12
7801 W Diamond Back Dr 83204 — 208-478-6863
Dr. Pat Charlton, prin. — Fax 478-6870
Franklin MS — 700/7-8
2271 E Terry St 83201 — 208-233-5590
Francie Stephens, prin. — Fax 233-1024
Hawthorne MS — 500/7-8
1025 W Eldredge Rd 83201 — 208-237-1680
Doug Reader, prin. — Fax 237-1682
Highland HS — 1,300/9-12
1800 Bench Rd 83201 — 208-237-1300
David Ross, prin. — Fax 237-1350
Irving MS — 500/7-8
911 N Grant Ave 83204 — 208-232-3039
James Harrell, prin. — Fax 232-0379
Pocatello HS — 1,200/9-12
325 N Arthur Ave 83204 — 208-233-2056
Don Cotant, prin. — Fax 232-0365

* * *

Idaho State University — Post-Sec.
PO Box 8270 83209 — 208-282-0211

Ponderay, Bonner, Pop. 697
Lake Pend Oreille SD 84 — 4,000/PK-12
901 N Triangle Dr 83852 — 208-263-2184
Dick Cvitanich, supt. — Fax 263-5053
www.sd84.k12.id.us
Other Schools – See Clark Fork, Sandpoint

Post Falls, Kootenai, Pop. 23,162
Coeur D'Alene SD 271
Supt. — See Coeur d Alene
Riverbend Professional Technical Academy — Vo/Tech
525 W Clearwater Loop Rd 83854 — 208-769-5960
Jason Green, admin.
Post Falls SD 273 — 5,000/K-12
PO Box 40 83877 — 208-773-1658
Jerry Keane, supt. — Fax 773-3218
www.pfsd.com
Post Falls HS — 1,400/9-12
PO Box 40 83877 — 208-773-0581
Steve Smith, prin. — Fax 773-0587
Post Falls MS — 800/6-8
PO Box 40 83877 — 208-773-7554
Debbi Davis, prin. — Fax 773-0884
River City MS — 400/6-8
PO Box 40 83877 — 208-457-0993
Mike Yovetich, prin. — Fax 457-1673

* * *

Classical Christian Academy — 200/K-12
2289 W Seltice Way 83854 — 208-777-4400
Dirk Darrow, hdmstr. — Fax 777-2544
Post Falls Christian Academy — 300/PK-12
PO Box 2306 83877 — 208-777-0457
Jerry Rogers, admin. — Fax 777-0986

Potlatch, Latah, Pop. 735
Potlatch SD 285 — 600/PK-12
130 6th St 83855 — 208-875-0327
Joseph Kren, supt. — Fax 875-1028
www.potlatchidaho.org
Potlatch JSHS — 300/7-12
130 6th St 83855 — 208-875-1231
Gordon Steinbis, prin. — Fax 875-1028

Preston, Franklin, Pop. 5,019
Preston JSD 201 — 2,500/PK-12
120 E 2nd S 83263 — 208-852-0283
Dr. Barbara Taylor, supt. — Fax 852-3976
www.preston.k12.id.us
Preston HS — 700/9-12
151 E 2nd S 83263 — 208-852-0280
Reid Carlson, prin. — Fax 852-3976
Preston JHS — 600/6-8
450 E Valley View Dr 83263 — 208-852-0751
John Anderson, prin. — Fax 852-3976

Priest River, Bonner, Pop. 1,909
West Bonner County SD 83 — 1,500/PK-12
221 Main St 83856 — 208-448-4439
Michael McGuire, supt. — Fax 448-4629
www.sd83.k12.id.us
Priest River JHS — 200/7-8
PO Box 519 83856 — 208-448-1118
Gary Go, prin. — Fax 448-1119
Priest River Lamanna HS — 500/9-12
PO Box 549 83856 — 208-448-1211
Ray Stookey, prin. — Fax 448-1212

Rathdrum, Kootenai, Pop. 5,740
Lakeland JSD 272 — 4,000/PK-12
PO Box 39 83858 — 208-687-0431
Charles Kinsey, supt. — Fax 687-1884
www.lakeland272.org/
Lakeland JHS — 600/7-9
PO Box 98 83858 — 208-687-0661
Laurie Sheffler, prin. — Fax 687-1510
Lakeland SHS — 600/10-12
PO Box 69 83858 — 208-687-0181
Conrad Underdahl, prin. — Fax 687-1313
Other Schools – See Spirit Lake

* * *

Lakes Bible Academy — 50/PK-12
16218 N Westwood Dr 83858 — 208-687-2101
Kelli Uzzi, prin.

Rexburg, Madison, Pop. 26,265
Madison SD 321 — 4,300/K-12
PO Box 830 83440 — 208-359-3300
Dr. Geoffrey Thomas, supt. — Fax 359-3345
www.d321.k12.id.us
Madison JHS — 600/8-9
60 W Main St 83440 — 208-359-3310
Corey Telford, prin. — Fax 359-3352
Madison SHS — 1,000/10-12
134 Madison Ave 83440 — 208-359-3305
Rodger Hampton, prin. — Fax 359-3346

* * *

Brigham Young University - Idaho — Post-Sec.
120 Kimball Building 83460 — 208-356-2011
Career Beauty College — Post-Sec.
57 College Ave 83440 — 208-356-0222

Richfield, Lincoln, Pop. 437
Richfield SD 316 — 200/PK-12
555 N Tiger Dr 83349 — 208-487-2790
Dr. David M. Hocklander, supt. — Fax 487-2055
Richfield S — 200/PK-12
555 N Tiger Dr 83349 — 208-487-2790
Mike Smith, prin. — Fax 487-2055

Rigby, Jefferson, Pop. 3,245
Jefferson County JSD 251 — 3,900/PK-12
201 Idaho Ave 83442 — 208-745-6693
Ron Tolman, supt. — Fax 745-0848
www.d251.k12.id.us
Rigby JHS — 600/8-9
125 N 1st W 83442 — 208-745-6674
Sherry Simmons, prin. — Fax 745-6675
Rigby SHS — 800/10-12
290 N 3800 E 83442 — 208-745-7704
Mark Neish, prin. — Fax 745-7707

Riggins, Idaho, Pop. 404
Grangeville JSD 241
Supt. — See Grangeville
Salmon River JSHS — 100/7-12
PO Box 872 83549 — 208-628-3431
Robin Tellis, prin. — Fax 628-3840

Ririe, Jefferson, Pop. 531
Ririe JSD 252 700/PK-12
PO Box 508 83443 208-538-7482
Ron Perrenoud, supt. Fax 538-7363
www.ririeschools.org
Ririe HS 200/9-12
PO Box 568 83443 208-538-7311
Charles Barber, prin. Fax 538-7860
Ririe MS 200/5-8
PO Box 548 83443 208-538-5175
Ron Perrenoud, prin. Fax 538-7748

Rockland, Power, Pop. 330
Rockland SD 382 100/K-12
PO Box 119 83271 208-548-2221
James Woodworth, supt. Fax 548-2224
www.rbulldogs.org
Rockland S 100/K-12
PO Box 119 83271 208-548-2221
James Woodworth, prin. Fax 548-2224

Rupert, Minidoka, Pop. 5,225
Minidoka County JSD 331 4,000/PK-12
633 Fremont St 83350 208-436-4727
Dr. Scott Rogers, supt. Fax 436-6593
www.sd331.k12.id.us
East Minico MS 600/6-8
1805 H St 83350 208-436-3178
Kevan Vogt, prin. Fax 436-3235
Minico HS 1,200/9-12
292 W 100 S 83350 208-436-4721
Dan Rogers, prin. Fax 436-3266
Other Schools – See Paul

Saint Anthony, Fremont, Pop. 3,375
Fremont County JSD 215 2,400/PK-12
147 N 2nd W 83445 208-624-7542
Dr. Garry Parker, supt. Fax 624-3385
www.sd215.k12.id.us
South Fremont HS 500/9-12
855 N Bridge St 83445 208-624-3416
Larry Bennett, prin. Fax 624-4898
South Fremont JHS 400/6-8
550 N 1st W 83445 208-624-7880
Chester Peterson, prin. Fax 624-4386
Other Schools – See Ashton

Saint Maries, Benewah, Pop. 2,589
Saint Maries JSD 41 1,100/PK-12
PO Box 384 83861 208-245-2579
Dave Cox, supt. Fax 245-3970
www.sd41.k12.id.us/
Saint Maries HS 400/9-12
424 Hells Gulch Rd 83861 208-245-2142
John Cordell, prin. Fax 245-5650
Saint Maries MS 200/6-8
1315 W Jefferson Ave 83861 208-245-3495
Dennis Kachelmier, prin. Fax 245-0506

Salmon, Lemhi, Pop. 3,072
Salmon SD 291 900/PK-12
PO Box 790 83467 208-756-4271
Dan Grabowska, supt. Fax 756-6695
www.salmon.k12.id.us/
Salmon HS 300/9-12
PO Box 790 83467 208-756-2415
John Riddle, prin. Fax 756-3484
Salmon MS 300/5-8
PO Box 790 83467 208-756-2207
Gary Pflueger, prin. Fax 756-2099

Sandpoint, Bonner, Pop. 8,105
Lake Pend Oreille SD 84
Supt. — See Ponderay
Sandpoint HS 1,300/9-12
410 S Division Ave 83864 208-263-3034
Becky Kiebert, prin. Fax 263-5321
Sandpoint MS 500/7-8
310 S Division Ave 83864 208-265-4169
Kim Keaton, prin. Fax 263-5525

Shelley, Bingham, Pop. 4,131
Shelley JSD 60 1,800/PK-12
545 Seminary Ave 83274 208-357-3411
Bryan Jolley, supt. Fax 357-5741
www.shelleyschools.org/
Hobbs MS 500/6-8
350 E Pine St 83274 208-357-7667
Joann Montgomery, prin. Fax 357-3003
Shelley HS 600/9-12
570 W Fir St 83274 208-357-7400
Shon Hocker, prin. Fax 357-5585

Shoshone, Lincoln, Pop. 1,574
Shoshone JSD 312 200/PK-12
409 N Apple St 83352 208-886-2338
Mel Wiseman, supt. Fax 886-2038
www.shoshone.k12.id.us
Shoshone JSHS 7-12
61 E Highway 24 83352 208-886-2381
Joe Hendrickson, prin. Fax 886-2742

Soda Springs, Caribou, Pop. 3,256
Soda Springs JSD 150 900/PK-12
250 E 2nd S 83276 208-547-3371
Dr. Molly Stein, supt. Fax 547-4878
www.sodaschools.org
Soda Springs HS 300/9-12
300 E 1st N 83276 208-547-4308
Michael Button, prin. Fax 547-2629
Tigert MS 200/7-8
250 E 2nd S 83276 208-547-4922
Dr. Molly Stein, prin. Fax 547-2619

Spirit Lake, Kootenai, Pop. 1,500
Lakeland JSD 272
Supt. — See Rathdrum
Timberlake HS 500/9-12
PO Box 909 83869 208-623-6303
Kurt Hoffman, prin. Fax 623-6203
Timberlake JHS, PO Box 1080 83869 7-8
Georgeanne Griffith, prin. 208-623-2582

Sugar City, Madison, Pop. 1,479
Sugar-Salem JSD 322 1,300/PK-12
PO Box 150 83448 208-356-8802
Alan Dunn, supt. Fax 356-7237
www.sd322.k12.id.us/
Sugar-Salem HS 400/9-12
1 S Digger Dr 83448 208-356-0274
Jared Jenks, prin. Fax 359-3167
Sugar-Salem JHS 200/7-8
PO Box 180 83448 208-356-4437
Robert Potter, prin. Fax 358-9717

Sun Valley, Blaine, Pop. 1,444

Community S 300/PK-12
PO Box 2118 83353 208-622-3955
Dr. Jon Maksik, hdmstr. Fax 622-3962

Terreton, Jefferson
West Jefferson SD 253 700/PK-12
1256 E 1500 N 83450 208-663-4542
Steven Lambertsen, supt. Fax 663-4543
wjsd.org
West Jefferson HS 200/9-12
1260 E 1500 N 83450 208-663-4391
Richard Hanson, prin. Fax 663-4390

Troy, Latah, Pop. 744
Troy SD 287 300/K-12
PO Box 280 83871 208-835-3791
Clark Adamson, supt. Fax 835-3790
www.sd287.k12.id.us
Troy JSHS 200/7-12
PO Box 280 83871 208-835-2361
Brad Malm, prin. Fax 835-2441

Whitepine JSD 288 300/K-12
502 First Ave 83871 208-877-1408
Daryl Bertelsen, supt. Fax 877-1570
www.sd288.k12.id.us/
Other Schools – See Deary

Twin Falls, Twin Falls, Pop. 38,630
Twin Falls SD 411 7,000/PK-12
201 Main Ave W 83301 208-733-6900
Wiley Dobbs, supt. Fax 733-6987
www.tfsd.k12.id.us
O'Leary JHS 900/7-9
2350 Elizabeth Blvd 83301 208-733-2155
Ron Withers, prin. Fax 733-8666
Stuart JHS 700/7-9
644 Caswell Ave W 83301 208-733-4875
Steve Smith, prin. Fax 733-4949
Twin Falls SHS 1,400/10-12
1615 Filer Ave E 83301 208-733-6551
Ben Allen, prin. Fax 733-8192

College of Southern Idaho Post-Sec.
PO Box 1238 83303 208-733-9554
Lighthouse Christian S 300/PK-12
259 Main Ave E 83301 208-737-1425
Kevin Newbry, prin. Fax 737-4671
Magic Valley Christian HS 50/7-12
PO Box 5494 83303 208-733-5999
Diane Davis, supt. Fax 735-0141
Mr. Juan's College of Hair Design Post-Sec.
586 Blue Lakes Blvd N 83301 208-733-7777
Twin Falls Christian Academy 100/K-12
798 Eastland Dr N 83301 208-733-1452
Brent Walker, prin. Fax 734-1417

Wallace, Shoshone, Pop. 907
Wallace SD 393 600/PK-12
405 7th St 83873 208-753-4515
Dr. Robert Ranells, supt. Fax 753-4151
www.sd393.k12.id.us
Wallace JSHS 200/7-12
1 Miners Aly 83873 208-753-5315
Matthew Coleman, prin. Fax 753-7105

Weippe, Clearwater, Pop. 390
Orofino JSD 171
Supt. — See Orofino
Timberline JSHS 200/7-12
1150 Highway 11 83553 208-435-4411
Ron Anthony, prin. Fax 435-4846

Weiser, Washington, Pop. 5,420
Weiser SD 431 1,600/PK-12
925 Pioneer Rd 83672 208-414-0616
James Reed, supt. Fax 414-1265
www.sd431.k12.id.us/
Weiser HS 500/9-12
690 W Indianhead Rd 83672 208-414-2595
Dave Davies, prin. Fax 414-1795
Weiser MS 400/6-8
320 E Galloway Ave 83672 208-414-2620
Larry Goto, prin. Fax 414-2094

Wendell, Gooding, Pop. 2,396
Wendell SD 232 1,100/PK-12
PO Box 300 83355 208-536-2418
Greg Lowe, supt. Fax 536-2629
www.sd232.k12.id.us
Wendell HS 300/9-12
750 E Main St 83355 208-536-2100
Jon Goss, prin. Fax 536-2124
Wendell MS 300/5-8
800 E Main St 83355 208-536-5531
Rob Sauer, prin. Fax 536-5957

Wilder, Canyon, Pop. 1,451
Wilder SD 133 500/K-12
PO Box 488 83676 208-482-6228
Daniel B. Arriola, supt. Fax 482-7019
www.sd133.k12.id.us/
Wilder MSHS 200/6-12
PO Box 488 83676 208-482-6229
Joseph Youren, prin. Fax 482-7421

ILLINOIS

ILLINOIS DEPARTMENT OF EDUCATION
100 N 1st St, Springfield 62777-0002
Telephone 866-262-6663
Fax 217-524-8585
Website http://www.isbe.state.il.us

Superintendent of Education Christopher Koch

ILLINOIS BOARD OF EDUCATION
100 N 1st St, Springfield 62777-0002

Chairperson Jesse Ruiz

REGIONAL OFFICES OF EDUCATION (ROE)

Adams/Pike ROE
Raymond Scheiter, supt. 217-277-2080
507 Vermont St, Quincy 62301 Fax 277-2092
www.wc4.org

Alxndr/Jhnsn/Massac/Pulaski/Union ROE
Janet Ulrich, supt. 618-634-2292
17 Rustic Campus Dr, Ullin 62992 Fax 634-2294
www.roe02.k12.il.us/

Bond/Effingham/Fayette ROE
Mark A. Drone, supt. 618-283-5011
300 S 7th St, Vandalia 62471 Fax 283-5013
www.fayette.k12.il.us/roeweb/

Boone/Winnebago ROE
Richard Fairgrieves, supt. 815-636-3060
300 Heart Blvd, Loves Park 61111 Fax 636-3069
www.4roe.org/

Brown/Cass/Morgan/Scott ROE
Stephen Breese, supt. 217-243-1804
110 N West St, Jacksonville 62650 Fax 243-5354
www.roe46.net/

Bureau/Henry/Stark ROE
Bruce Dennison, supt. 309-936-7890
107 S State St, Atkinson 61235 Fax 935-6784
www.bhsroe.k12.il.us

Calhoun/Greene/Jersey/Macoupin ROE
Larry Pfeiffer, supt. 217-854-4016
220 N Broad St, Carlinville 62626 Fax 854-2032
www.roe40.k12.il.us/

Carroll/Jo Daviess/Stephenson ROE
Marie Stiefel, supt. 815-947-3810
500 N Rush St, Stockton 61085 Fax 947-2717
roe8.lth2.k12.il.us/

Champaign/Ford ROE
Judy Pacey, supt. 217-893-3219
200 S Fredrick St, Rantoul 61866 Fax 893-0024
www.roe9.k12.il.us/

Christian/Montgomery ROE
Greg Springer, supt. 217-532-9591
1 Courthouse Sq Rm 202 Fax 824-2464
Hillsboro 62049
www.montgomery.k12.il.us

Clay/Crawford/Jspr/Lwrnce/Rchlnd ROE
Carol S. Steinman, supt. 618-392-4631
103 W Main St Ste 23, Olney 62450 Fax 392-3993

Clinton/Marion/Washington ROE
Keri Jo Garrett, supt. 618-594-2432
930 Fairfax St Ste B, Carlyle 62231 Fax 594-7192
www.roe13.k12.il.us

Clk/Cls/Cumb/Dglas/Edg/Mlt/Shlb ROE
John McNary, supt. 217-348-0151
730 7th St, Charleston 61920 Fax 348-0171
www.roe11.k12.il.us/

DeKalb ROE
Gil Morrison, supt. 815-895-3096
245 W Exchange St Ste 2 Fax 895-4847
Sycamore 60178

DeWitt/Livingston/McLean ROE
G. Lawrence Daghe, supt. 309-888-5120
905 N Main St Ste 1, Normal 61761 Fax 862-0420
www.roe17.k12.il.us/

Dupage ROE
Darlene Ruscitti, supt. 630-407-5800
421 N County Farm Rd Fax 682-7773
Wheaton 60187
www.dupage.k12.il.us/

Edwds/Gtn/Hdn/Pope/Sln/Wbsh/Wyn/Wt ROE
Linda Blackman, supt. 618-253-5581
512 N Main St, Harrisburg 62946 Fax 252-8472
www.roe20.k12.il.us/

Franklin/Williamson ROE
Ronda Baker, supt. 618-438-9711
206 Rushing Dr Ste 1, Herrin 62948 Fax 435-2861
www.roe21.k12.il.us/

Fulton/Schuyler ROE
Alan Coleman, supt. 309-547-3041
PO Box 307, Lewistown 61542 Fax 547-3326
www.fulton.k12.il.us/

Grundy/Kendall ROE
Thomas Centowski, supt. 815-941-3247
1320 Union St, Morris 60450 Fax 942-5384
www.grundy.k12.il.us/

Hamilton/Jefferson ROE
Paul Cross, supt., 1714 Broadway St 618-244-8040
Mount Vernon 62864 Fax 244-8073
www.roe25.com

Hancock/McDonough ROE
Gary Eddington, supt. 309-837-4821
130 S Lafayette St, Macomb 61455 Fax 837-2887
mcdonough.k12.il.us/roe26/

Henderson/Mercer/Warren ROE
Glen W. Braden, supt. 309-734-6822
200 W Broadway, Monmouth 61462 Fax 734-2452
www.hmwroe27.com

Iroquois/Kankakee ROE
Kathleen Pangle, supt. 815-937-2950
189 E Court St Ste 600 Fax 937-2921
Kankakee 60901
www.i-kan.org

Jackson/Perry ROE
Robert L. Koehn, supt. 618-687-7290
1001 Walnut St Fax 687-7296
Murphysboro 62966
www.roe30.k12.il.us/

Kane ROE
Dr. Clem Mejia, supt. 630-232-5955
210 S 6th St, Geneva 60134 Fax 208-5115
www.kaneroe.org/

Knox ROE
Bonnie Harris, supt. 309-345-3828
PO Box 430, Galesburg 61402 Fax 343-2677
www.knox.k12.il.us/knoxcountyroe33/

Lake ROE
Roycealee Wood, supt. 847-543-7833
800 Lancer Ln Ste E128 Fax 543-7832
Grayslake 60030
www.lake.k12.il.us/

LaSalle ROE
William Novotney, supt. 815-434-0780
119 W Madison St, Ottawa 61350 Fax 434-2453
www.roe35.k12.il.us

Lee/Ogle ROE
Amy Jo Clemens, supt. 815-652-2054
7772 Clinton St, Dixon 61021 Fax 652-2053

Logan/Mason/Menard ROE
Jean R. Anderson, supt. 217-732-8388
PO Box 460, Lincoln 62656 Fax 735-1569
logan.k12.il.us/quickanswers38

Macon/Piatt ROE 39
Richard Shelby, supt. 217-872-3721
1690 Huston Dr, Decatur 62526 Fax 872-0239

Madison County ROE
Harry Briggs, supt. 618-692-6200
PO Box 600, Edwardsville 62025 Fax 692-7018
www.madison.k12.il.us/

Marshall/Putnam/Woodford ROE
Rolland D. Marshall, supt. 309-248-8212
PO Box 340, Washburn 61570 Fax 248-7983
www.roe43.k12.il.us/

McHenry ROE
Gene Goeglein, supt. 815-334-4475
2200 N Seminary Ave Fax 338-0475
Woodstock 60098
www.mchenry.k12.il.us/

Monroe-Randolph ROE
Marc Kiehna, supt. 618-939-5650
107 E Mill St, Waterloo 62298 Fax 939-5332
www.monroe.k12.il.us/roe45/

Peoria ROE
Gerald Brookhart, supt. 309-672-6906
324 Main St Ste 401, Peoria 61602 Fax 672-6053
www.peoria.k12.il.us/roe48/

Rock Island ROE
Joseph Vermeire, supt. 309-736-1111
3430 Avenue Of The Cities Fax 736-1127
Moline 61265
www.riroe.com/

Saint Clair ROE
Brad Harriman, supt. 618-397-8930
500 Wilshire Dr, Belleville 62223 Fax 397-8928
www.stclair.k12.il.us/

Sangamon ROE
Helen Tolan, supt. 217-753-6620
200 S 9th St Ste 303 Fax 535-3166
Springfield 62701
www.roe51.org

Suburban Cook ROE
Robert Ingraffia, supt. 708-865-9330
10110 Gladstone St Fax 865-9338
Westchester 60154
www.cook.k12.il.us/

Tazewell ROE
Robin Houchin, supt. 309-477-2290
PO Box 699, Pekin 61555 Fax 347-3735
www.tazewell.k12.il.us/quickanswers53

Vermilion ROE
Michael Metzen, supt. 217-431-2668
200 S College St Ste B Fax 431-2671
Danville 61832
www.roe54.k12.il.us/

Whiteside ROE
Gary Steinert, supt. 815-625-1495
1001 W 23rd St, Sterling 61081 Fax 625-1625
www.wside.k12.il.us/

Will ROE
Richard Duran, supt. 815-740-8360
302 N Chicago St, Joliet 60432 Fax 740-4788
www.will.k12.il.us/

PUBLIC, PRIVATE AND CATHOLIC SECONDARY SCHOOLS

Abingdon, Knox, Pop. 3,379
Abingdon CUSD 217 800/PK-12
401 W Latimer St 61410 309-462-2301
Dr. Magie Stuart, supt. Fax 462-3870
www.abingdon.k12.il.us/
Abingdon HS 200/9-12
600 W Martin St 61410 309-462-2338
Chad Cox, prin. Fax 462-2492
Abingdon MS 200/6-8
202 W Snyder St 61410 309-462-2336
Stan Adcock, prin. Fax 462-2207

Addison, DuPage, Pop. 36,811
Addison SD 4 4,000/PK-8
222 N JF Kennedy Dr Rear 2 60101 630-628-2500
Dr. Donald Hendricks, supt. Fax 628-8829
www.asd4.org
Indian Trail JHS 1,300/6-8
222 N JF Kennedy Dr Frnt 1 60101 630-458-2600
Terry Sliva, prin. Fax 628-2841

DAOES, 301 S Swift Rd 60101
Fred Kane, supt. 630-620-8770
Technology Center of Dupage Vo/Tech
301 S Swift Rd Frnt C 60101 630-620-8770
Fred Kane, prin.

DuPage HSD 88
Supt. — See Villa Park
Addison Trail HS 1,800/9-12
213 N Lombard Rd 60101 630-628-3302
Scott Helton, prin. Fax 628-0177

DeVry University Post-Sec.
1221 N Swift Rd 60101 630-953-1300
Driscoll Catholic HS 500/9-12
555 N Lombard Rd 60101 630-543-6310
Fred Muehleman, prin. Fax 543-2913

Albion, Edwards, Pop. 1,892
Edwards County CUSD 1 1,000/PK-12
37 W Main St 62806 618-445-2814
Robert Brutcher, supt. Fax 445-2272
www.echs.edwrds.k12.il.us/
Edwards County HS 300/9-12
361 W Main St 62806 618-445-2325
Stan Struckmeyer, prin. Fax 445-3154

Aledo, Mercer, Pop. 3,535
Aledo CUSD 201 1,000/PK-12
402 E Main St 61231 309-582-2238
Alan Boucher, supt. Fax 582-7428
www.aledoschools.org
Aledo HS 300/9-12
1500 S College Ave 61231 309-582-2223
Kathy Albert, prin. Fax 582-5920
Aledo JHS 200/6-8
1002 SW 6th St 61231 309-582-2441
Douglas Nelson, prin. Fax 582-2440

Alexander, Morgan
Franklin CUSD 1 400/PK-12
PO Box 140 62601 217-478-3011
Fred Roberts, supt. Fax 478-4921
www.franklinhigh.com
Other Schools – See Franklin

Alexis, Mercer, Pop. 823
United CUSD 304 300/K-12
101 N Holloway St Ofc 2 61412 309-482-3344
Jeffrey Whitsitt, supt. Fax 482-3236
united.k12.il.us/
Other Schools – See Monmouth

Algonquin, McHenry, Pop. 29,022
Community Unit SD 300
Supt. — See Carpentersville
Algonquin MS 500/6-8
520 Longwood Dr 60102 847-658-2545
Peggy Thurow, prin. Fax 658-2547

Jacobs HS 2,100/9-12
2601 Bunker Hill Dr 60102 847-658-2500
Michael Bregy, prin. Fax 658-3203

Consolidated SD 158 4,700/PK-12
650 Academic Dr 60102 847-659-6158
Dr. John Burkey, supt. Fax 659-6122
www.district158.org/
Heineman MS 6-8
725 Academic Dr 60102 847-659-4300
Jim Stotz, prin. Fax 659-4320
Other Schools – See Huntley, Lake in the Hills

Alsip, Cook, Pop. 19,072
Alsip-Hazelgreen-Oaklawn SD 126 1,600/PK-8
11900 S Kostner Ave 60803 708-389-1900
Robert Berger, supt. Fax 396-3793
www.dist126.k12.il.us
Prairie JHS 400/7-8
11910 S Kostner Ave 60803 708-371-3080
Craig Gwaltney, prin. Fax 396-3798

Atwood Heights SD 125 700/PK-8
12150 S Hamlin Ave 60803 708-371-0080
Dr. Thomas Livingston, supt. Fax 371-7847
Hamlin Upper Grade Center 300/6-8
12150 S Hamlin Ave 60803 708-597-1550
Lisa West, prin. Fax 396-0515

Altamont, Effingham, Pop. 2,259
Altamont CUSD 10 800/PK-12
7 S Ewing St 62411 618-483-6195
Jim Littleford, supt. Fax 483-6303
www.altamont.k12.il.us/
Altamont HS 300/9-12
7 S Ewing St 62411 618-483-6194
Jim Strange, prin. Fax 483-5399

Alton, Madison, Pop. 29,433
Alton CUSD 11 4,300/PK-12
PO Box 9028 62002 618-474-2600
David Elson, supt. Fax 463-2126
www.alton.madison.k12.il.us/
Alton HS, 4200 Humbert Rd 62002 2,200/9-12
Philip Trapani, prin. 618-474-2600
Alton MS 6-8
2200 College Ave 62002 618-474-2700
Henrietta Young, prin. Fax 463-2127

CALC Institute of Technology Post-Sec.
235A E Center Dr 62002 618-474-0616
Marquette HS 300/9-12
219 E 4th St 62002 618-465-4029
Michael Slaughter, prin. Fax 463-0582
Mississippi Valley Christian S 200/PK-12
2009 Seminary St 62002 618-462-1071
Jerry Fair, prin. Fax 462-9877
Westminster Christian Academy 100/K-12
1145 College Ave 62002 618-465-1918
Greg Myers, hdmstr. Fax 465-1949

Amboy, Lee, Pop. 2,570
Amboy CUSD 272 1,100/PK-12
11 E Hawley St 61310 815-857-2164
Keith Oates, supt. Fax 857-4434
www.amboy.net/
Amboy HS 300/9-12
11 E Hawley St 61310 815-857-3632
Jeff Thake, prin. Fax 857-3631
Amboy JHS 400/5-8
140 S Appleton Ave 61310 815-857-3528
Joyce Schamberger, prin. Fax 857-4603

Anna, Union, Pop. 5,070
Anna CCSD 37 700/PK-8
301 S Green St 62906 618-833-6812
Bob Odell, supt. Fax 833-3205
www.anna37.union.k12.il.us/
Anna JHS 300/5-8
301 S Green St 62906 618-833-6812
Ronald Cross, prin. Fax 833-6535

Anna-Jonesboro Community HSD 81 600/9-12
608 S Main St 62906 618-833-8421
William Schildknecht, supt. Fax 833-4239
www.ajchs.union.k12.il.us
Anna-Jonesboro HS 600/9-12
608 S Main St 62906 618-833-8502
James Woodward, prin. Fax 833-5931

Annawan, Henry, Pop. 919
Annawan CUSD 226 500/PK-12
501 W South St 61234 309-935-6781
Joe Buresh, supt. Fax 935-6065
Annawan HS 100/9-12
501 W South St 61234 309-935-6781
Linda Rakestraw, prin. Fax 935-6065

Antioch, Lake, Pop. 12,353
Antioch CCSD 34 2,700/PK-8
800 Main St 60002 847-838-8400
Scott Thompson, supt. Fax 838-8404
www.dist34.lake.k12.il.us
Antioch MS 1,000/6-8
800 Highview Dr 60002 847-838-8310
Jim Kallieris, prin. Fax 395-3467

Community HSD 117
Supt. — See Lake Villa
Antioch Community HS 1,700/9-12
1133 Main St 60002 847-395-1421
Michael Nekritz, prin. Fax 395-2435

Arcola, Douglas, Pop. 2,662
Arcola CUSD 306 700/K-12
351 W Washington St 61910 217-268-4963
Reggie Clinton, supt. Fax 268-3809
www.arcola.k12.il.us
Arcola JSHS 300/7-12
351 W Washington St 61910 217-268-4962
Steve Groll, prin. Fax 268-4483

Argenta, Macon, Pop. 852
Argenta-Oreana CUSD 1 800/PK-12
PO Box 440 62501 217-795-2313
Damian Jones, supt. Fax 795-2174
www.argenta-oreana.org/
Argenta-Oreana HS 300/9-12
PO Box 469 62501 217-795-4821
Sean German, prin. Fax 795-4550
Argenta-Oreana MS 100/6-8
PO Box 439 62501 217-795-2163
Steve Johnson, prin. Fax 795-4502

Arlington Heights, Cook, Pop. 74,620
Arlington Heights SD 25 4,800/PK-8
1200 S Dunton Ave 60005 847-758-4900
Dr. Sarah Jerome, supt. Fax 758-4907
www.ahsd25.k12.il.us
South MS 900/6-8
400 S Highland Ave 60005 847-398-4250
Maureen Reilly, prin. Fax 394-6260
Thomas MS 800/6-8
1430 N Belmont Ave 60004 847-398-4260
Thomas O'Rourke, prin. Fax 394-6843

Community Consolidated SD 59 6,200/PK-8
2123 S Arlington Heights Rd 60005 847-593-4300
Dr. Dan Schweers, supt. Fax 593-4409
www.ccsd59.org
Other Schools – See Des Plaines, Elk Grove Village, Mount Prospect

Township HSD 214 12,300/9-12
2121 S Goebbert Rd 60005 847-718-7600
David Schuler, supt. Fax 718-7609
www.d214.org
Hersey HS 1,900/9-12
1900 E Thomas St 60004 847-718-4800
Tina Cantrell, prin. Fax 718-4817
Other Schools – See Buffalo Grove, Elk Grove Village, Mount Prospect, Rolling Meadows, Wheeling

---

Chicago Futabakai Japanese S 700/K-12
2550 N Arlington Heights Rd 60004 847-590-5700
Noboru Hayakawa, prin. Fax 590-9759
Christian Liberty Academy 900/PK-12
502 W Euclid Ave 60004 847-259-4444
Dr. Philip Bennet, prin. Fax 259-9972
Northwest Community Hospital Post-Sec.
800 W Central Rd 60005 847-618-1000
St. Viator HS 1,000/9-12
1213 E Oakton St 60004 847-392-4050
Eileen Manno, prin. Fax 392-4329

Armstrong, Vermilion
Armstrong Twp. HSD 225 200/9-12
PO Box 37 61812 217-569-2122
Bill Mulvaney, supt. Fax 569-2171
Armstrong HS 200/9-12
PO Box 37 61812 217-569-2122
Darren Loschen, prin. Fax 569-2171

Arthur, Douglas, Pop. 2,180
Arthur CUSD 305 500/PK-12
301 E Columbia St 61911 217-543-2511
Travis Wilson, supt. Fax 543-2210
www.arthur.k12.il.us
Arthur HS 100/9-12
301 E Columbia St 61911 217-543-2146
David Vieth, prin. Fax 543-2174
Arthur JHS 100/7-8
301 E Columbia St 61911 217-543-2146
David Vieth, prin. Fax 543-2174

Ashland, Cass, Pop. 1,376
A-C Central CUSD 262 500/PK-12
PO Box 260 62612 217-476-8112
Lyle Rigdon, supt. Fax 476-8100
cass.k12.il.us/ac-central
A-C Central HS 200/9-12
PO Box 260 62612 217-476-3312
Dan Williams, prin. Fax 476-3730
Other Schools – See Chandlerville

Ashton, Lee, Pop. 1,195
Ashton-Franklin Center CUSD 275 700/K-12
611 Western Ave 61006 815-453-7461
John Zick, supt. Fax 453-7462
www.afcschools.net/index.htm
Ashton-Franklin Center HS 200/9-12
611 Western Ave 61006 815-453-7461
Tommy Harvey, prin. Fax 453-7462
Other Schools – See Franklin Grove

Assumption, Christian, Pop. 1,231
Central A & M CUSD 21 1,000/PK-12
105 N College St 62510 217-226-4042
Randall Grigg, supt. Fax 226-4133
www.cam.k12.il.us
Central A & M MS 200/6-8
404 Colegrove St 62510 217-226-4241
Scott Cameron, prin. Fax 226-4442
Other Schools – See Moweaqua

Astoria, Fulton, Pop. 1,160
Astoria CUSD 1 400/PK-12
PO Box 620 61501 309-329-2111
Kirk Abernathy, supt. Fax 329-2214
www.astoria.fulton.k12.il.us
Astoria HS 100/9-12
402 N Jefferson St 61501 309-329-2156
Kirk Abernathy, prin. Fax 329-2246
Astoria JHS 100/6-8
402 N Jefferson St 61501 309-329-2158
Jeannie Goodman, prin. Fax 329-2963

Athens, Menard, Pop. 1,800
Athens CUSD 213 800/PK-12
1 Warrior Way 62613 217-636-8761
Scott Laird, supt. Fax 636-8851
www.athens-213.org
Athens HS 300/9-12
1 Warrior Way 62613 217-636-8314
Dave Root, prin. Fax 636-8851
Athens JHS 200/7-8
1 Warrior Way 62613 217-636-8380
Clay Shoufler, prin. Fax 636-8851

Atwood, Douglas, Pop. 1,250
Atwood-Hammond CUSD 39 400/K-12
PO Box 890 61913 217-578-3111
Kenneth Schwengel, supt. Fax 578-3531
www.ah.k12.il.us
Atwood-Hammond HS 100/9-12
PO Box 890 61913 217-578-2226
Randy Niles, prin. Fax 578-3355

Auburn, Sangamon, Pop. 4,274
Auburn CUSD 10 1,200/PK-12
606 W North St 62615 217-438-6164
Kathryn L. Garrett, supt. Fax 438-6483
sangamon.k12.il.us/auburn/
Auburn HS 300/9-12
511 N 7th St 62615 217-438-6817
Darren Root, prin. Fax 438-6153
Auburn MS 400/5-8
601 N 7th St 62615 217-438-6919
Wayne Jones, prin. Fax 438-3700

Augusta, Hancock, Pop. 625
Southeastern CUSD 337
Supt. — See Bowen
Southeastern HS 200/9-12
PO Box 155 62311 217-392-2125
Todd Fox, prin. Fax 392-2229

Aurora, Kane, Pop. 168,181
Aurora East Unit SD 131 11,800/PK-12
417 5th St 60505 630-299-5550
Jerome Roberts Ed.D., supt. Fax 299-5500
www.d131.kane.k12.il.us/
Aurora East HS 2,500/9-12
500 Tomcat Ln 60505 630-299-8000
Sheila Conrad, prin. Fax 299-8199
Cowherd MS 800/6-8
441 N Farnsworth Ave 60505 630-299-5900
Joan Glotzbach, prin. Fax 299-5901
Simmons MS 900/6-8
1130 Sheffer Rd 60505 630-299-4150
Mechelle Patterson, prin. Fax 299-4151
Waldo MS 900/6-8
56 Jackson St 60505 630-299-8400
Earline Barnes, prin. Fax 299-8401

Aurora West Unit SD 129 12,100/PK-12
80 S River St 60506 630-301-5000
Dr. James Rydland, supt. Fax 844-5710
www.sd129.org/
Herget MS, 1550 Deerpath Rd 60506 6-8
Scott Woods, prin. 630-301-5006
Jefferson MS 900/6-8
1151 Plum St 60506 630-301-5009
Dr. Sandra Kuzniewski, prin. Fax 844-5711
Washington MS 1,000/6-8
231 S Constitution Dr 60506 630-301-5017
Deborah Meyer, prin. Fax 844-5712
West Aurora HS 3,200/9-12
1201 W New York St 60506 630-301-5600
John Glimco, prin. Fax 844-4505
Other Schools – See North Aurora

Illinois Math & Science Academy SD 600/10-12
1500 W Sullivan Rd 60506 630-907-5000
Dr. Stephanie Pace Marshall, pres. Fax 907-5062
www.imsa.edu
Illinois Math & Science Academy 600/10-12
1500 W Sullivan Rd 60506 630-907-5053
Dr. Eric McLaren, prin.

Indian Prairie CUSD 204 27,300/PK-12
780 Shoreline Dr 60504 630-375-3000
Dr. Stephen Daeschner, supt. Fax 375-3009
www.ipsd.org
Granger MS 1,000/6-8
2721 Stonebridge Blvd, 630-375-1010
Mary Kelly, prin. Fax 375-1110
Still MS 1,100/6-8
787 Meadowridge Dr 60504 630-375-3900
Jennifer Nonnemacher, prin. Fax 375-3901
Waubonsie Valley Gold Campus 900/9-9
1305 Long Grove Dr 60504 630-375-3100
Rudy Keller Ed.D., prin. Fax 375-3101
Waubonsie Valley HS 2,400/10-12
2590 Ogden Ave 60504 630-375-3300
James Schmid, prin. Fax 375-3301
Other Schools – See Naperville

Aurora Central Catholic HS 400/9-12
1255 N Edgelawn Dr 60506 630-907-0095
Rev. F. William Etheredge, admin. Fax 907-1076
Aurora Christian HS 500/6-12
2255 W Sullivan Rd 60506 630-892-1551
Paul House, supt. Fax 892-1692
Aurora University Post-Sec.
347 S Gladstone Ave 60506 630-892-6431
Marmion Academy 500/9-12
1000 Butterfield Rd, 630-897-6936
John Milroy, hdmstr. Fax 897-7086
Robert Morris College Post-Sec.
905 Meridian Lake Dr 60504 630-375-8000
Rosary HS 500/9-12
901 N Edgelawn Dr 60506 630-896-0831
Sr. Patricia Burke, prin. Fax 896-8372

Avon, Fulton, Pop. 881
Avon CUSD 176 300/PK-12
320 E Woods St 61415 309-465-3708
Alene Reuschel, supt. Fax 465-9030
www.avonschools.us
Avon HS 100/9-12
320 E Woods St 61415 309-465-3621
Tina Stier, prin. Fax 465-7194
Avon JHS 100/6-8
320 E Woods St 61415 309-465-3621
Alene Reuschel, prin. Fax 465-7194

Barrington, Cook, Pop. 10,179
Barrington CUSD 220 8,900/PK-12
310 James St 60010 847-381-6300
Mary Herrmann, supt. Fax 381-6337
www.cusd220.org
Barrington HS 2,800/9-12
616 W Main St 60010 847-381-1400
Thomas Leonard, prin. Fax 304-1847
Barrington MS Prairie Campus 1,100/6-8
40 E Dundee Rd 60010 847-304-3990
Craig Winkelman, prin. Fax 304-3986
Barrington MS Station Campus 1,000/6-8
215 Eastern Ave 60010 847-381-0464
Donn Mendoza, prin. Fax 842-1343

Barry, Pike, Pop. 1,330
Barry CUSD 1 400/PK-12
401 McDonough St 62312 217-335-2323
Dr. Mark Spaid, supt. Fax 335-2211
www.barryschool.net/
Barry HS 100/9-12
401 McDonough St 62312 217-335-2323
Roy Kirkpatrick, prin. Fax 335-2211
Barry MS 100/6-8
401 McDonough St 62312 217-335-2323
Roy Kirkpatrick, prin. Fax 335-2211

Bartlett, Cook, Pop. 38,479
SD U-46
Supt. — See Elgin
Bartlett HS 3,100/9-12
701 W Schick Rd 60103 630-372-4700
Diane Longfield, prin. Fax 372-4682
Eastview MS 1,100/7-8
321 N Oak Ave 60103 630-213-5550
Donald Donner, prin. Fax 213-5563

Bartonville, Peoria, Pop. 6,146
Limestone Community HSD 310 — 1,100/9-12
4201 Airport Rd 61607 — 309-697-6271
William Beach, supt. — Fax 697-9635
www.limestone.k12.il.us
Limestone HS — 1,100/9-12
4201 Airport Rd 61607 — 309-697-6271
Kelly Funke, admin. — Fax 697-9635

Oak Grove SD 68 — 500/K-8
4812 Pfeiffer Rd 61607 — 309-697-3367
Marc Devore, supt. — Fax 633-2381
www.oakgrove.peoria.k12.il.us/
Oak Grove West JHS — 200/6-8
6018 W Lancaster Rd 61607 — 309-697-0621
Tim Dotson, prin. — Fax 697-0721

Illinois Welding School — Post-Sec.
5901 Washington St 61607 — 309-633-0379

Batavia, Kane, Pop. 27,172
Batavia Unit SD 101 — 6,200/PK-12
335 W Wilson St 60510 — 630-879-4600
Dr. Jack Barshinger, supt. — Fax 345-7896
www.bps101.net
Batavia HS — 1,800/9-12
1200 Main St 60510 — 630-879-4600
Doug Drexler, prin. — Fax 879-4698
Rotolo MS — 1,500/6-8
1501 S Raddant Rd 60510 — 630-879-4620
Donald McKinney, prin. — Fax 879-4624

Beach Park, Lake, Pop. 12,486
Beach Park CCSD 3 — 2,000/PK-8
11315 W Wadsworth Rd 60099 — 847-599-5070
Dr. Robert Di Virgilio, supt. — Fax 263-2133
www.bpd3.lake.k12.il.us/
Beach Park MS — 800/PK-PK, 6-
40667 N Green Bay Rd 60099 — 847-731-6330
Rene Santiago, prin. — Fax 731-2402

Beardstown, Cass, Pop. 5,876
Beardstown CUSD 15 — 1,400/PK-12
101 E 15th St 62618 — 217-323-3099
Robert Bagby, supt. — Fax 323-5190
www.beardstown.com/
Beardstown MSHS — 700/6-12
500 E 15th St 62618 — 217-323-3665
Judy Fitzgerald, prin. — Fax 323-3667

Beecher, Will, Pop. 2,769
Beecher CUSD 200U — 1,000/K-12
PO Box 338 60401 — 708-946-2266
George Obradovich, supt. — Fax 946-3404
www.beecher.will.k12.il.us
Beecher HS — 300/9-12
PO Box 338 60401 — 708-946-2266
Brian Wright, prin. — Fax 946-3403
Beecher JHS — 200/6-8
PO Box 308 60401 — 708-946-2202
John Jennings, prin. — Fax 946-3272

Beecher City, Effingham, Pop. 498
Beecher City CUSD 20 — 500/PK-12
PO Box 98 62414 — 618-487-5100
Dr. Steve Launius, supt. — Fax 487-5242
www.bcity.efingham.k12.il.us/
Beecher City JSHS, PO Box 97 62414 — 200/7-12
Phil Lark, prin. — 618-487-5117

Belleville, Saint Clair, Pop. 41,143
Belle Valley SD 119 — 900/PK-8
1901 Mascoutah Ave 62220 — 618-234-3445
Pamela S. Floit Ph.D., supt. — Fax 234-7730
www.bellevalley.stclair.k12.il.us
Belle Valley MS South — 5-8
1901 Mascoutah Ave 62220 — 618-234-7723
Dr. Tamara Leib, prin. — Fax 234-7980

Belleville SD 118 — 3,400/PK-8
105 W A St 62220 — 618-233-2830
Matt Klosterman, supt. — Fax 233-8355
www.belleville118.stclair.k12.il.us
Central JHS — 400/7-8
1801 Central School Rd 62220 — 618-233-5377
Rocky Horrighs, prin. — Fax 233-5440
West JHS — 400/7-8
840 Royal Heights Rd 62226 — 618-234-8200
Pam Knobeloch, prin. — Fax 234-8220

Belleville Township HSD 201 — 5,000/9-12
2600 W Main St 62226 — 618-222-8241
Greg Moats, supt. — Fax 233-7586
bths201.org/
Belleville HS East — 2,500/9-12
2555 West Blvd 62221 — 618-222-3700
David Kniepkamp, prin. — Fax 222-3799
Belleville HS West — 2,300/9-12
4063 Frank Scott Pkwy W 62223 — 618-222-7500
Robert Dahm, prin. — Fax 235-2484

Harmony Emge SD 175 — 800/PK-8
7401 Westchester Dr 62223 — 618-397-8444
Dr. Gina Segobiano, supt. — Fax 397-8446
www.harmony175.org/
Emge JHS — 400/5-8
7401 Westchester Dr 62223 — 618-397-6557
Andrea Rudanovich, prin. — Fax 397-3011

Whiteside SD 115 — 1,200/PK-8
111 Warrior Way 62221 — 618-239-0000
Peggy Burke, supt. — Fax 239-9240
www.whiteside.stclair.k12.il.us/
Whiteside MS — 5-8
111 Warrior Way 62221 — 618-239-0000
Ron Trelow, prin. — Fax 239-9240

Althoff Catholic HS — 700/9-12
5401 W Main St 62226 — 618-235-1100
David Harris, prin. — Fax 235-9535
Alvareita's College of Cosmetology — Post-Sec.
5400 W Main St 62226 — 618-257-9193
French Academy — 200/PK-12
219 W Main St 62220 — 618-233-7542
Phillip Paeltz, hdmstr. — Fax 233-0541
St. Elizabeth Hospital — Post-Sec.
211 S 3rd St 62220 — 618-234-2120
Southwestern Illinois College — Post-Sec.
2500 Carlyle Ave 62221 — 618-235-2700

Bellwood, Cook, Pop. 19,517
Bellwood SD 88 — 3,300/PK-8
640 Eastern Ave 60104 — 708-344-9344
Dr. Nichelle Rivers, supt. — Fax 344-9416
www.sd88.org
Roosevelt MS — 1,100/6-8
2500 Oak St 60104 — 708-544-3318
Mark Holder, prin. — Fax 544-0192

True Vine Christian Academy — 100/PK-12
400 23rd Ave 60104 — 708-547-8822
Dr. Gloria Lymon, prin.

Belvidere, Boone, Pop. 24,593
Belvidere CUSD 100 — 8,000/PK-12
1201 5th Ave 61008 — 815-544-0301
Fax 544-4260
www.district100.com
Belvidere Central MS — 900/6-8
8787 Beloit Rd 61008 — 815-544-0190
Harry Gries, prin. — Fax 544-1128
Belvidere HS — 2,200/9-12
1500 East Ave 61008 — 815-547-6345
Dr. Chester Pulaski, prin. — Fax 547-7304
Belvidere South MS — 1,000/6-8
919 E 6th St 61008 — 815-544-3175
Peter Sloan, prin. — Fax 544-2780

Bement, Piatt, Pop. 1,739
Bement CUSD 5 — 400/PK-12
201 S Champaign St 61813 — 217-678-4200
Dr. Darrell Stevens, supt. — Fax 678-4251
www.bement.k12.il.us
Bement HS — 100/9-12
201 S Champaign St 61813 — 217-678-4200
Douglas Kepley, prin. — Fax 678-4251
Bement MS — 100/6-8
201 S Champaign St 61813 — 217-678-4200
Elaine Day, prin. — Fax 678-4251

Bensenville, DuPage, Pop. 20,514
Bensenville SD 2 — 2,400/PK-8
210 S Church Rd 60106 — 630-766-5940
Dr. William H. Jordan, supt. — Fax 766-6099
www.bsd2.org
Blackhawk MS — 700/6-8
250 S Church Rd 60106 — 630-766-2601
Michael Robey, prin. — Fax 766-7612

Fenton Community HSD 100 — 1,500/9-12
1000 W Green St 60106 — 630-860-6257
Dr. Alf Logan, supt. — Fax 766-3178
www.fenton100.org
Fenton HS — 1,500/9-12
1000 W Green St 60106 — 630-766-2500
Kathleen Pierce, prin. — Fax 766-3178

Robert Morris College — Post-Sec.
1000 Tower Ln # 200 60106 — 630-787-7800

Benson, Woodford, Pop. 407
Roanoke-Benson CUSD 60
Supt. — See Roanoke
Roanoke-Benson JHS — 200/5-8
PO Box 137 61516 — 309-394-2233
Kris Kahler, prin. — Fax 394-2612

Benton, Franklin, Pop. 6,930
Benton CCSD 47 — 1,000/PK-8
308 E Church St 62812 — 618-439-3136
Richard Cook, supt. — Fax 435-4840
www.benton47.frnkln.k12.il.us/
Benton MS — 400/5-8
1000 Forrest St 62812 — 618-438-4011
Jamie Neal, prin. — Fax 435-2152

Benton Consolidated HSD 103 — 600/9-12
511 E Main St 62812 — 618-439-6415
Kelly Stewart, supt. — Fax 438-8091
www.bentonhighschool.org
Benton Consolidated HS — 600/9-12
511 E Main St 62812 — 618-439-3103
Sue Woodfin, prin. — Fax 438-2915

Berkeley, Cook, Pop. 5,006
Berkeley SD 87 — 2,900/PK-8
1200 N Wolf Rd 60163 — 708-449-3350
Dr. Joseph Palermo, supt. — Fax 547-3341
www.berkeley87.org
MacArthur MS — 500/6-8
1310 N Wolf Rd 60163 — 708-449-3185
Dr. Keith Wood, prin. — Fax 649-3780
Other Schools – See Northlake

Berwyn, Cook, Pop. 51,409
Berwyn North SD 98 — 3,200/K-8
6633 16th St 60402 — 708-484-6200
John Belmont, supt. — Fax 795-2482
www.d98.cook.k12.il.us
Lincoln MS — 1,000/6-8
6432 16th St 60402 — 708-795-2475
Gail Quilty-Feijt, prin. — Fax 795-2880

Berwyn South SD 100 — 3,100/K-8
3401 Gunderson Ave Ste 1 60402 — 708-795-2300
Dr. Patricia Wernet, supt. — Fax 795-2317
www.schooldistrict100.org
Freedom MS — 6-8
3016 Ridgeland Ave 60402 — 708-795-5800
Anthony Cundari, prin. — Fax 795-5806
Heritage MS — 800/6-8
6850 31st St 60402 — 708-749-6110
Leslie Hodes, prin. — Fax 749-6124

J. S. Morton HSD 201
Supt. — See Cicero
Morton West HS — 3,400/9-12
2400 Home Ave 60402 — 708-222-5901
John Lucas, prin. — Fax 222-5903

Bethalto, Madison, Pop. 9,660
Bethalto CUSD 8 — 2,700/PK-12
225 James St 62010 — 618-377-7200
Sandra Wilson, supt. — Fax 377-2845
www.bethalto.org
Civic Memorial HS — 900/9-12
200 School St 62010 — 618-377-7220
Debra Pitts, prin. — Fax 377-7001
Trimpe MS — 700/6-8
910 2nd St 62010 — 618-377-7240
Karen Keener, prin. — Fax 377-7218

Bethany, Moultrie, Pop. 1,261
Okaw Valley CUSD 302 — 400/PK-12
PO Box 97 61914 — 217-665-3232
Marilyn Bayley, supt. — Fax 665-3601
www.okawvalley.org
Okaw Valley HS — 100/9-12
PO Box 249 61914 — 217-665-3631
Paula Duis, prin. — Fax 665-3863
Other Schools – See Findlay

Biggsville, Henderson, Pop. 330
West Central CUSD 235 — 600/PK-12
RR 1 Box 72 61418 — 309-627-2371
Ralph Grimm, supt. — Fax 627-2453
West Central HS — 200/9-12
RR 1 Box 72 61418 — 309-627-2377
Karen Rima, prin. — Fax 627-2120
Other Schools – See Stronghurst

Bismarck, Vermilion, Pop. 551
Bismarck-Henning CUSD 1 — 900/K-12
PO Box 350 61814 — 217-759-7261
Randy Hird, supt. — Fax 759-7942
www.bismarck.k12.il.us
Bismarck-Henning HS — 300/9-12
PO Box 350 61814 — 217-759-7291
Rich Decman, prin. — Fax 759-7815
Bismarck-Henning JHS — 300/5-8
PO Box 350 61814 — 217-759-7301
Scott Watson, prin. — Fax 759-7313

Bloomingdale, DuPage, Pop. 21,924
Bloomingdale SD 13 — 1,500/K-8
164 Euclid Ave 60108 — 630-893-9590
Kim Perkins, supt. — Fax 893-1818
www.sd13.org
Westfield MS — 600/6-8
149 Fairfield Way 60108 — 630-529-6211
Debbie Kling, prin. — Fax 893-9336

Community Consolidated SD 93 — 4,600/PK-8
230 Covington Dr 60108 — 630-893-9393
Henry Gmitro Ed.D., supt. — Fax 539-3450
www.ccsd93.com
Stratford MS — 800/6-8
251 Butterfield Dr 60108 — 630-980-9898
Tom Doyle, prin. — Fax 980-9914
Other Schools – See Carol Stream

Pivot Point Cosmetology Research Center — Post-Sec.
144 E Lake St Ste C 60108 — 847-985-5900

Bloomington, McLean, Pop. 69,749
Bloomington AVC
PO Box 5187 61702 — 309-829-8671
Tom Frazier, dir. — Fax 828-3546
www.bloomingtonavc.org
Bloomington AVC — Vo/Tech
PO Box 5187 61702 — 309-829-8671
Tom Frazier, dir. — Fax 828-3546

Bloomington SD 87 — 5,400/K-12
300 E Monroe St 61701 — 309-827-6031
Robert Nielsen, supt. — Fax 827-5717
www.district87.org
Bloomington HS — 1,500/9-12
1202 E Locust St 61701 — 309-828-5201
Cindy Helmers, prin. — Fax 829-1078
Bloomington JHS — 1,300/6-8
901 Colton Ave 61701 — 309-827-0086
Dr. Susan Silvey, prin. — Fax 829-0084

Central Catholic HS — 300/9-12
1201 Airport Rd 61704 — 309-661-7000
Joy Allen, prin. — Fax 661-7001
Hairmasters Institute of Cosmetology — Post-Sec.
506 S McClun St 61701 — 309-828-1884
Illinois Wesleyan University — Post-Sec.
PO Box 2900 61702 — 309-556-1000

Blue Island, Cook, Pop. 22,788
Community HSD 218
Supt. — See Oak Lawn
Eisenhower HS — 1,700/9-12
12700 Sacramento Ave 60406 — 708-597-6300
Joseph Fowler, prin. — Fax 597-9958

Cook County SD 130 — 3,700/PK-8
12300 Greenwood Ave 60406 — 708-385-6800
Dr. Michael T. Korsak, supt. — Fax 385-8467
www.district130.org/
Kerr MS — 400/6-8
12915 Maple Ave 60406 — 708-385-5959
Gwendolyn DeVries, prin. — Fax 371-6812
Veterans Memorial MS — 400/6-8
12320 Greenwood Ave 60406 — 708-489-6630
Anthony C. Smerz, prin. — Fax 489-3522
Greenbriar S — Adult
12015 Maple Ave 60406 — 708-385-2915
Dr. Carol Crum, prin. — Fax 385-8467
Other Schools – See Crestwood

Cannella School of Hair Design — Post-Sec.
12840 Western Ave 60406 — 708-388-4949
Environmental Technical Institute — Post-Sec.
13010 Division St 60406 — 708-385-0707

Blue Mound, Macon, Pop. 1,056
Meridian CUSD 15
Supt. — See Macon
Meridian MS — 300/6-8
PO Box 320 62513 — 217-692-2148
Andrew Pygott, prin. — Fax 692-2039

Bluffs, Scott, Pop. 729
Scott-Morgan CUSD 2 — 300/PK-12
PO Box 230 62621 — 217-754-3351
Carol Kilver, supt. — Fax 754-3908
bluffs.scott.k12.il.us
Bluffs HS — 100/9-12
PO Box 230 62621 — 217-754-3815
Mekelle Neathery, prin. — Fax 754-3908
Bluffs JHS — 100/6-8
PO Box 230 62621 — 217-754-3815
Mekelle Neathery, prin. — Fax 754-3908

Bluford, Jefferson, Pop. 773
Webber Twp. HSD 204 — 200/9-12
PO Box 110 62814 — 618-732-6121
Roger Pauley, supt. — Fax 732-8784
Webber Twp. HS, PO Box 110 62814 — 200/9-12
Roger Pauley, prin. — 618-732-6121

Bolingbrook, Will, Pop. 68,365
Valley View CUSD 365U
Supt. — See Romeoville
Addams MS 700/6-8
905 Lily Cache Ln 60440 630-759-7200
Chris Schaeflein, prin. Fax 759-6362
Bolingbrook HS 3,100/9-12
365 Raider Way 60440 630-759-6400
James Mitchem, prin. Fax 759-2650
Brooks MS 6-8
350 Blair Ln 60440 630-759-6340
Ronald Krause, prin. Fax 759-6360
Humphrey MS 700/6-8
777 Falconridge Way 60440 630-972-9240
Angelo Armistead, prin. Fax 739-8521

Bourbonnais, Kankakee, Pop. 16,875
Bourbonnais ESD 53 1,900/PK-8
281 W John Casey Rd 60914 815-939-2574
Myron Palomba Ph.D., supt. Fax 939-0481
www.besd53.k12.il.us
Bourbonnais Upper Grade Center 600/7-8
200 W John Casey Rd 60914 815-937-4471
Jon Hodge, prin. Fax 935-7855

Kankakee Area Career Center
PO Box 570 60914 815-939-4971
Donald Fay, supt. Fax 939-7598
www.kacc.k12.il.us
Kankakee Area Career Center Vo/Tech
PO Box 570 60914 815-939-4971
Tom Hahs, prin. Fax 939-7598

Olivet Nazarene University Post-Sec.
1 University Ave 60914 815-939-5011

Bowen, Hancock, Pop. 508
Southeastern CUSD 337 500/PK-12
PO Box 247 62316 217-842-5236
Michael Owen, supt. Fax 842-5248
www.southeastern337.com/
Southeastern JHS 100/5-8
PO Box 247 62316 217-842-5236
Tami Roskamp, prin. Fax 842-5248
Other Schools – See Augusta

Bradford, Stark, Pop. 765
Bradford CUSD 1 200/PK-8
115 High St 61421 309-897-2801
Ellin Lotspeich, supt. Fax 897-4451
Bradford JHS, PO Box 400 61421 100/6-8
Ellin Lotspeich, prin. 309-897-4441

Bradley, Kankakee, Pop. 13,812
Bradley SD 61 1,500/PK-8
111 N Croswell Ave 60915 815-933-3371
Scott Goselin, supt. Fax 939-6601
www.besd61.k12.il.us/
Bradley Central MS 500/6-8
260 N Wabash Ave 60915 815-939-3564
Todd Schweizer, prin. Fax 939-6603

Bradley-Bourbonnais Comm. HSD 307 1,800/9-12
700 W North St 60915 815-937-3707
Michael Hogan, supt. Fax 937-0156
www.bbchs.k12.il.us
Bradley-Bourbonnais Community HS 1,800/9-12
700 W North St 60915 815-937-3707
Bill Gamble, prin. Fax 937-0156

Trend Setters College of Cosmetology Post-Sec.
605 E North St 60915 815-932-5049

Braidwood, Will, Pop. 6,320
Reed-Custer CUSD 255U 1,800/PK-12
255 Comet Dr 60408 815-458-2307
John Asplund, supt. Fax 458-4106
www.rc255.will.k12.il.us/
Reed-Custer HS 600/9-12
249 Comet Dr 60408 815-458-2166
Eric Bernstein, prin. Fax 458-4138
Reed-Custer MS 500/6-8
407 Comet Dr 60408 815-458-2868
Michael Grace, prin. Fax 458-4118

Breese, Clinton, Pop. 4,202
Central Community HSD 71 600/9-12
7740 Old US Highway 50 62230 618-526-4510
Kevin Meyer, supt. Fax 526-2521
www.centralcougars.org/
Central Community HS 600/9-12
7740 Old US Highway 50 62230 618-526-4578
B. Kent Jones, prin. Fax 526-7647

Mater Dei HS 600/9-12
900 Mater Dei Dr 62230 618-526-7216
Dennis Litteken, prin. Fax 526-8310

Bridgeport, Lawrence, Pop. 2,148
Red Hill CUSD 10 1,100/PK-12
1250 Judy Ave 62417 618-945-2061
Michael P. Mauzy, supt. Fax 945-7607
www.red.lawrnc.k12.il.us
Red Hill HS 300/9-12
908 Church St 62417 618-945-8221
Kevin Andersen, prin. Fax 945-7151

Bridgeview, Cook, Pop. 14,933

AQSA S, 7361 W 92nd St 60455 300/PK-12
Khalida Baste, prin. 708-598-2700
Northwestern Business College Post-Sec.
7725 S Harlem Ave 60455 800-682-9113
Universal S 600/PK-12
7350 W 93rd St 60455 708-599-4100
Farhat Siddiqui, prin. Fax 599-1588

Brimfield, Peoria, Pop. 900
Brimfield CUSD 309 700/PK-12
216 E Clinton St 61517 309-446-3378
Dennis McNamara, supt. Fax 446-3716
peoria.k12.il.us/brimfield309/
Brimfield HS 200/9-12
323 E Clinton St 61517 309-446-3349
Robert Larson, prin. Fax 446-3716

Broadlands, Champaign, Pop. 308
Heritage CUSD 8 600/PK-12
PO Box 260 61816 217-834-3393
Andrew Larson, supt. Fax 834-3016
www.heritage.k12.il.us
Heritage HS 200/9-12
PO Box 260 61816 217-834-3392
Andrew Larson, prin. Fax 834-3016
Other Schools – See Homer

Brookfield, Cook, Pop. 18,462
Brookfield Lagrange Park SD 95 900/K-8
3524 Maple Ave 60513 708-485-0606
Thomas Hurlburt, supt. Fax 485-8066
www.district95.org
Gross MS 400/5-8
3524 Maple Ave 60513 708-485-0600
Todd Fitzgerald, prin. Fax 485-0638

Brownstown, Fayette, Pop. 708
Brownstown CUSD 201 500/PK-12
421 S College Ave 62418 618-427-3355
Doug Slover, supt. Fax 427-3704
Brownstown HS 100/9-12
421 S College Ave 62418 618-427-3839
William Wilson, prin. Fax 427-3704
Brownstown JHS 100/7-8
421 S College Ave 62418 618-427-3839
William Wilson, prin. Fax 427-3704

Brussels, Calhoun, Pop. 145
Brussels CUSD 42 100/K-12
PO Box 128 62013 618-883-2131
Tom Knuckles, supt. Fax 883-2514
Brussels HS 100/7-12
PO Box 128 62013 618-883-2131
Jim Roderick, prin. Fax 883-2514

Buckley, Iroquois, Pop. 576

Christ Lutheran HS 50/9-12
PO Box 8 60918 217-394-2547
Dan Cluver, prin. Fax 394-2097

Buda, Bureau, Pop. 581
Bureau Valley CUSD 340
Supt. — See Manlius
Bureau Valley South S 200/3-8
PO Box 337 61314 309-895-2037
Susan Zbrozek, prin. Fax 895-2200

Buffalo, Sangamon, Pop. 463
Tri-City CUSD 1 600/PK-12
PO Box 290 62515 217-364-4811
Dr. Jack Magruder, supt. Fax 364-4812
www.tc.sangamon.k12.il.us
Tri-City HS 200/9-12
PO Box 290 62515 217-364-4530
Randall Dwyer, prin. Fax 364-4812
Tri-City JHS 200/6-8
PO Box 290 62515 217-364-4530
Randall Dwyer, prin. Fax 364-4812

Buffalo Grove, Cook, Pop. 43,115
Aptakisic-Tripp CCSD 102 2,200/PK-8
1231 Weiland Rd 60089 847-353-5660
Dr. John Mink, supt. Fax 634-5334
www.dist102.k12.il.us/
Aptakisic JHS 600/7-8
1231 Weiland Rd 60089 847-353-5500
Mark Kuzniewski, prin. Fax 634-5347

Kildeer Countryside CCSD 96 3,400/PK-8
1050 Ivy Hall Ln 60089 847-459-4260
Dr. Thomas Many, supt. Fax 459-2344
www.district96.k12.il.us
Twin Groves MS 600/6-8
2600 N Buffalo Grove Rd 60089 847-821-8946
Marie Schalke, prin. Fax 821-8949
Other Schools – See Long Grove

Township HSD 214
Supt. — See Arlington Heights
Buffalo Grove HS 2,200/9-12
1100 W Dundee Rd 60089 847-718-4000
Patrice Johannes, prin. Fax 718-4122

Wheeling CCSD 21
Supt. — See Wheeling
Cooper MS 700/6-8
1050 Plum Grove Cir 60089 847-520-2750
Dr. Maureen Reilly, prin. Fax 419-3071

Bunker Hill, Macoupin, Pop. 1,795
Bunker Hill CUSD 8 500/K-12
504 E Warren St 62014 618-585-3116
Marg Rogers, supt. Fax 585-3212
bhschools.org
Bunker Hill HS 200/9-12
314 S Meissner St 62014 618-585-3232
Kevin Blankenship, prin. Fax 585-3241
Meissner JHS 6-8
504 E Warren St 62014 618-585-4464
Brad Skertich, prin. Fax 585-3222

Burbank, Cook, Pop. 27,634
Burbank SD 111 3,300/PK-8
7600 Central Ave 60459 708-496-0500
Dr. Thomas Long, supt. Fax 496-0510
www.burbank.k12.il.us
Liberty JHS 900/7-8
5900 W 81st St 60459 708-952-3255
Dr. Mark Schall, prin. Fax 229-0659

Reavis Township HSD 220 1,700/9-12
6034 W 77th St 60459 708-599-7200
Dr. James Steyskal, supt. Fax 599-8751
www.d220.org
Reavis HS 1,700/9-12
6034 W 77th St 60459 708-599-7200
Daniel Riordan, prin. Fax 599-8751

Queen of Peace HS 900/9-12
7659 Linder Ave 60459 708-458-7600
Dr. Kathleen Hanlon, prin. Fax 458-5734
St. Laurence HS 700/9-12
5556 W 77th St 60459 708-458-6900
James Muting, prin. Fax 458-6908

Burlington, Kane, Pop. 487
Central CUSD 301 2,400/PK-12
PO Box 396 60109 847-464-6005
Dr. Bradley J. Hawk, supt. Fax 464-6021
www.burlington.k12.il.us/
Central HS 800/9-12
PO Box 68 60109 847-464-6030
David Olsen, prin. Fax 464-6039
Central MS 600/6-8
PO Box 397 60109 847-464-6000
Lloyd Stover, prin. Fax 464-1709

Burr Ridge, DuPage, Pop. 10,949
Burr Ridge CCSD 180 700/PK-8
15W451 91st St 60527 630-734-6600
Dr. Frank Rink, supt. Fax 325-6450
www.ccsd180.org
Burr Ridge MS 5-8
15W451 91st St 60527 630-325-5454
Dr. Debra LeBlanc, prin. Fax 325-6450

Gower SD 62
Supt. — See Willowbrook
Gower MS 400/5-8
7941 S Madison St 60527 630-323-8275
Rebecca Laratta, prin. Fax 323-2055

Pleasantdale SD 107 800/PK-8
7450 Wolf Rd 60527 708-784-2013
Dr. Mark Fredisdorf, supt. Fax 246-0161
www.d107.org/
Pleasantdale MS 300/5-8
7450 Wolf Rd 60527 708-246-3210
Meg Pokorny, prin. Fax 352-0092

ITT Technical Institute Post-Sec.
7040 High Grove Blvd 60527 630-455-6470
Olympia College Post-Sec.
6880 N Frontage Rd 60527 630-920-1102

Bushnell, McDonough, Pop. 3,022
Bushnell-Prairie City CUSD 170 800/PK-12
845 Walnut St 61422 309-772-9461
David Messersmith, supt. Fax 772-9462
www.bushnell-pc.k12.il.us/
Bushnell-Prairie City HS 200/9-12
845 Walnut St 61422 309-772-2113
Anita Pyle, prin. Fax 772-2104
Bushnell-Prairie City JHS 200/6-8
847 Walnut St 61422 309-772-3123
Mike Snowden, prin.

Byron, Ogle, Pop. 3,582
Byron CUSD 226 1,400/PK-12
696 N Colfax St 61010 815-234-5491
Dr. Margaret Fostiak, supt. Fax 234-4106
leeogle.org/byron/
Byron HS 600/9-12
696 N Colfax St 61010 815-234-5491
Marty Voiles, prin. Fax 234-4106
Byron MS 400/6-8
325 N Colfax St 61010 815-234-5491
Steve Herkert, prin. Fax 234-4225

Cahokia, Saint Clair, Pop. 15,608
Cahokia CUSD 187 4,800/PK-12
1700 Jerome Ln 62206 618-332-3700
Jana Bechtoldt, supt. Fax 332-3706
www.cahokia.stclair.k12.il.us
Cahokia HS 1,200/9-12
800 Range Ln 62206 618-332-3730
Pam Manning, prin. Fax 332-3747
Sauget Academic Center 200/5-12
1700 Jerome Ln 62206 618-332-3820
Phyllis Jackson, prin. Fax 332-3824
Wirth/Parks MS 1,100/6-8
1900 Mousette Ln 62206 618-332-3722
Tony Brooks, prin. Fax 332-3741

Cairo, Alexander, Pop. 3,342
Cairo Unit SD 1 700/PK-12
2403 Walnut St 62914 618-734-4102
Gary Whitledge, supt. Fax 734-4047
Cairo JSHS 300/7-12
4201 Sycamore St 62914 618-734-2187
Gary Whitledge, prin. Fax 734-2189

Calumet City, Cook, Pop. 37,795
Calumet City SD 155 1,300/K-8
540 Superior Ave 60409 708-862-7665
Dr. Troy Paraday, supt. Fax 868-7555
www.calumetcity155.org/
Wentworth JHS 500/6-8
560 Superior Ave 60409 708-862-0750
Linda Bozeman, prin. Fax 862-1194

Dolton SD 149 3,900/PK-8
292 Torrence Ave 60409 708-868-7861
Traci Brown, supt. Fax 868-7850
www.schooldistrict149.org
Dirksen MS 1,200/6-8
1650 Pulaski Rd 60409 708-868-2340
Ray Warner, prin. Fax 868-7589

Hoover-Schrum Memorial SD 157 900/PK-8
1255 Superior Ave 60409 708-868-7500
Rosemary Hendricks, supt. Fax 868-7511
www.hsdist157.org
Schrum Memorial MS 300/6-8
485 165th St 60409 708-862-4236
Charmyne Taylor, prin. Fax 862-4580

Thornton Fractional Township HSD 215 3,200/9-12
1601 Wentworth Ave 60409 708-585-2309
Dr. Robert K. Wilhite, supt. Fax 585-2318
www.tfd215.org/
Center for Academics & Technology Vo/Tech
1605 Wentworth Ave 60409 708-585-2350
Kent Farlow, prin. Fax 585-2356
Thornton Fractional North HS 1,600/9-12
755 Pulaski Rd 60409 708-585-1000
Dwayne Evans, prin. Fax 585-1010
Other Schools – See Lansing

Westwood College Post-Sec.
80 River Oaks Dr Ste D-49 60409 708-832-1988

Calumet Park, Cook, Pop. 8,124
Calumet Public SD 132 1,300/PK-8
1440 W Vermont Ave 60827 708-388-8920
Dr. Elizabeth Reynolds, supt. Fax 388-2138
Calumet MS 400/6-8
1440 W Vermont Ave 60827 708-388-8820
Dr. Deborah Elliott, prin. Fax 388-8557

Cambridge, Henry, Pop. 2,121
Cambridge CUSD 227 500/PK-12
300 S West St 61238 309-937-2144
Steven J. Fink, supt. Fax 937-5128
Cambridge Community HS 200/9-12
300 S West St 61238 309-937-2051
Robert Reager, prin. Fax 937-5128

Cambridge JHS 100/7-8
300 S West St 61238 309-937-2051
Robert Reager, prin. Fax 937-5128

Campbell Hill, Jackson, Pop. 314
Trico CUSD 176 1,000/K-12
PO Box 220 62916 618-426-1111
Dennis Smith, supt. Fax 426-3625
www.trico176.org
Trico HS 300/9-12
PO Box 336 62916 618-426-1111
Jack Smith, prin. Fax 426-3701
Trico JHS 200/6-8
PO Box 335 62916 618-426-1111
Dennis Smith, prin. Fax 426-3712

Camp Point, Adams, Pop. 1,191
Central CUSD 3 1,000/K-12
2110 Highway 94 N 62320 217-593-7116
Martin Cook, supt. Fax 593-7026
www.cusd3.com/
Central HS 300/9-12
2110 Highway 94 N 62320 217-593-7731
Bill Reed, prin. Fax 593-7025
Central JHS 300/5-8
2110 Highway 94 N 62320 217-593-7741
Donna Veile, prin. Fax 593-7028

Canton, Fulton, Pop. 14,938
Canton Union SD 66 2,700/PK-12
20 W Walnut St 61520 309-647-9411
James Lewis, supt. Fax 649-5036
www.cantonusd.org
Canton HS 800/9-12
1001 N Main St 61520 309-647-1820
Robin Tonkin, prin. Fax 649-5039
Ingersoll MS 800/5-8
1605 E Ash St 61520 309-647-6951
Lan Eberle, prin. Fax 647-6959

Graham Hospital Post-Sec.
210 W Walnut St 61520 309-647-4086
LaMonts Intl School of Cosmetology Post-Sec.
60 E Elm St 61520 309-647-4224
Spoon River College Post-Sec.
23235 N County Road 22 61520 309-647-4645

Carbondale, Jackson, Pop. 24,806
Carbondale Community HSD 165 1,200/9-12
330 S Giant City Rd 62902 618-457-4722
Steven Sabens, supt. Fax 457-3353
www.cchs165.jacksn.k12.il.us/
Carbondale Community HS 1,200/9-12
1301 E Walnut St 62901 618-457-3371
Vicky King, prin. Fax 549-1686

Carbondale ESD 95 1,400/PK-8
PO Box 2048 62902 618-457-3591
David Daum, supt. Fax 457-2043
www.ces95.jacksn.k12.il.us
Carbondale MS 400/6-8
1150 E Grand Ave 62901 618-457-2174
Charles Goforth, prin. Fax 457-2176

Brehm Preparatory S 100/6-12
1245 E Grand Ave 62901 618-457-0371
Dr. Richard Collins, dir. Fax 529-1248
Covenant Christian S 100/PK-12
1218 W Freeman St 62901 618-529-3733
Paul Plunkett, prin. Fax 529-3733
Southern Illinois University 62901 Post-Sec.
618-453-2121

Carlinville, Macoupin, Pop. 5,768
Carlinville CUSD 1 1,600/PK-12
18456 Shipman Rd 62626 217-854-9823
Mike Kelly, supt. Fax 854-2777
www.carlinvilleschools.net/
Carlinville HS 500/9-12
829 W Main St 62626 217-854-3104
Pat Drew, prin. Fax 854-5260
Carlinville MS 300/6-8
110 Illinois Ave 62626 217-854-3106
Pat Drew, prin. Fax 854-4503

Blackburn College Post-Sec.
700 College Ave 62626 217-854-3231

Carlyle, Clinton, Pop. 3,377
Carlyle CUSD 1 1,300/PK-12
1400 13th St 62231 618-594-8283
Joe Novsek, supt. Fax 594-8285
www.carlyle.k12.il.us
Carlyle HS 400/9-12
1461 12th St 62231 618-594-2453
Joe Wilkerson, prin. Fax 594-8286
Carlyle JHS 400/5-8
1631 12th St 62231 618-594-8292
Jim McClaren, prin. Fax 594-8294

Carmi, White, Pop. 5,414
Carmi-White County CUSD 5 1,500/PK-12
301 W Main St 62821 618-382-2341
Dr. Keith Talley, supt. Fax 384-3207
www.carmi.white.k12.il.us
Carmi-White County HS 400/9-12
800 W Main St 62821 618-382-4661
Brad Lee, prin. Fax 382-2453
Carmi-White County MS 300/6-8
205 W Main St 62821 618-382-4631
Terry Gholson, prin. Fax 384-2076

Carol Stream, DuPage, Pop. 40,040
Community Consolidated SD 93
Supt. — See Bloomingdale
Stream MS 800/6-8
283 El Paso Ln 60188 630-462-8940
John Healy, prin. Fax 462-9224

Glenbard Twp. HSD 87
Supt. — See Glen Ellyn
Glenbard North HS 2,800/9-12
990 Kuhn Rd 60188 630-653-7000
Michael Mensik, prin. Fax 653-7259

Carpentersville, Kane, Pop. 37,204
Community Unit SD 300 17,700/PK-12
300 Cleveland Ave 60110 847-426-1300
Dr. Kenneth Arndt, supt. Fax 426-1209
www.d300.org
Carpentersville MS 700/7-8
100 Cleveland Ave 60110 847-426-1380
Stephanie Ramstad, prin. Fax 426-1404

Dundee-Crown HS 2,500/9-12
1500 Kings Rd 60110 847-426-1415
Lynn McCarthy, prin. Fax 426-1245
Other Schools – See Algonquin, Dundee, Hampshire

Carrier Mills, Saline, Pop. 1,841
Carrier Mills-Stonefort CUSD 2 600/PK-12
PO Box 217 62917 618-994-2392
Richard Morgan, supt. Fax 994-2929
www.cmsf.saline.k12.il.us/
Carrier Mills HS 200/9-12
PO Box 217 62917 618-994-2392
Richard Morgan, prin. Fax 994-2929

Carrollton, Greene, Pop. 2,519
Carrollton CUSD 1 700/K-12
702 5th St 62016 217-942-5314
Michael Barry, supt. Fax 942-9259
www.c-hawks.org
Carrollton HS 200/9-12
950 3rd St 62016 217-942-6913
Alan Churchman, prin. Fax 942-6835

Carterville, Williamson, Pop. 5,099
Carterville CUSD 5 1,700/PK-12
306 Virginia Ave 62918 618-985-4826
Tim Bleyer, supt. Fax 985-2041
www.c-ville.wilmsn.k12.il.us/
Carterville HS 500/9-12
816 S Division St 62918 618-985-2940
Don Smith, prin. Fax 985-2741
Carterville IS 500/5-8
300 School St 62918 618-985-6411
Keith Liddell, prin. Fax 985-2492

John A. Logan College Post-Sec.
700 Logan College Dr 62918 618-985-3741

Carthage, Hancock, Pop. 2,548
Carthage CUSD 338 700/PK-12
210 S Adams St 62321 217-357-3922
Vicki Hardy, supt. Fax 357-6793
carthageschools.k12.il.us
Carthage HS 300/9-12
210 S Adams St 62321 217-357-2136
Ray Driskell, prin. Fax 357-3569
Carthage MS 200/5-8
210 S Adams St 62321 217-357-3914
Elizabeth Wujek, prin. Fax 357-3755

Cary, McHenry, Pop. 19,115
Cary CCSD 26 3,500/K-8
400 Haber Rd 60013 847-639-7788
Wayne Schurter Ed.D., supt. Fax 639-3898
mail.cary26.k12.il.us/
Cary JHS 800/7-8
2109 Crystal Lake Rd 60013 847-639-2148
Linda Goeglein, prin. Fax 516-5507

Community HSD 155
Supt. — See Crystal Lake
Cary-Grove HS 1,800/9-12
2208 3 Oaks Rd 60013 847-639-3825
Sue Popp, prin. Fax 639-3873

Casey, Clark, Pop. 2,948
Casey-Westfield CUSD C4 1,200/PK-12
PO Box 100 62420 217-932-2184
Robert Ehlke, supt. Fax 932-5553
www.cw.k12.il.us/
Casey-Westfield HS 400/9-12
306 E Edgar Ave 62420 217-932-2175
Clyde Frankie, prin. Fax 932-2004
Roosevelt JHS 200/7-8
401 E Main St 62420 217-932-2177
Jo Beard, prin. Fax 932-2753

Catlin, Vermilion, Pop. 2,051
Catlin CUSD 5 500/PK-12
701 1/2 W Vermilion St 61817 217-427-2116
Dr. Guy Banicki, supt. Fax 427-2117
www.catlin.k12.il.us
Catlin HS 200/9-12
701 W Vermilion St 61817 217-427-5331
Kevin Thomas, prin. Fax 427-2468

Centralia, Marion, Pop. 13,600
Centralia HSD 200 1,100/9-12
2100 E Calumet St 62801 618-532-7391
Chuck Lane, supt. Fax 532-8952
www.centraliahs.org
Centralia HS 1,100/9-12
2100 E Calumet St 62801 618-532-7391
Steve Ptacek, prin. Fax 532-8952

Centralia SD 135 1,400/PK-8
400 S Elm St 62801 618-532-1907
Thomas W. Hawkins, supt. Fax 532-4986
www.ccs135.com
Centralia JHS, 900 S Pine St 62801 500/6-8
Demetria Rogers, prin. 618-533-7130

Kaskaskia College Post-Sec.
27210 College Rd 62801 618-545-3000

Cerro Gordo, Piatt, Pop. 1,385
Cerro Gordo CUSD 100 600/K-12
PO Box 79 61818 217-763-5221
Brett Robinson, supt. Fax 763-6562
www.cerrogordo.k12.il.us
Cerro Gordo HS 200/9-12
PO Box 79 61818 217-763-2711
Paul Workman, prin. Fax 763-6562
Cerro Gordo MS 100/6-8
PO Box 79 61818 217-763-6411
Paul Workman, prin. Fax 763-6562

Chadwick, Carroll, Pop. 486
Chadwick-Milledgeville CUSD 399 600/PK-12
15 School St 61014 815-684-5191
Roy Webb, supt. Fax 684-5241
www.dist399.net/
Chadwick JHS 100/6-8
PO Box 15 61014 815-684-5191
Roy Webb, prin. Fax 684-5241
Other Schools – See Milledgeville

Champaign, Champaign, Pop. 71,568
Champaign CUSD 4 9,300/PK-12
703 S New St 61820 217-351-3800
Arthur Culver, supt. Fax 352-3590
www.champaignschools.org/
Centennial HS 1,500/9-12
913 Crescent Dr 61821 217-351-3951
Ron Bode, prin. Fax 351-3730

Central HS 1,400/9-12
610 W University Ave 61820 217-351-3914
William Freyman, prin. Fax 351-3919
Edison MS 700/6-8
306 W Green St 61820 217-351-3771
Joe Williams, prin. Fax 355-2564
Franklin MS 600/6-8
817 N Harris Ave 61820 217-351-3819
Angela Smith, prin. Fax 351-3729
Jefferson MS 700/6-8
1115 Crescent Dr 61821 217-351-3790
Dr. Susan Zola, prin. Fax 351-3754

HS of St. Thomas More 200/9-12
3901 N Mattis Ave 61822 217-352-7210
Tim Millage Ph.D., prin. Fax 352-7213
Judah Christian S 500/PK-12
908 N Prospect Ave 61820 217-359-1701
Daniel Cole, prin. Fax 359-0214
Parkland College Post-Sec.
2400 W Bradley Ave 61821 217-351-2200

Chandlerville, Cass, Pop. 716
A-C Central CUSD 262
Supt. — See Ashland
A-C Central JHS 100/6-8
191 S Bluff St 62627 217-458-2224
Sandra Moody, prin. Fax 458-2223

Channahon, Will, Pop. 12,218
Channahon SD 17 1,500/K-8
24920 S Sage St 60410 815-467-4315
Dr. Karin Evans, supt. Fax 467-4343
www.channahon.will.k12.il.us
Channahon JHS 300/7-8
24917 W Sioux Dr 60410 815-467-4314
Matt Swick, prin. Fax 467-2188

Families of Faith Christian Academy 100/PK-12
25124 S Fryer St Ste A 60410 815-521-1381
Rev. Clark Llewellyn, prin. Fax 467-4476

Charleston, Coles, Pop. 20,189
Charleston CUSD 1 2,900/PK-12
410 W Polk Ave 61920 217-639-1000
Dr. Gary Niehaus, supt. Fax 639-1005
www.charleston.k12.il.us
Charleston HS 900/9-12
1603 Lincoln Ave 61920 217-639-5000
Diane Hutchins, prin. Fax 639-5005
Charleston MS 500/7-8
920 Smith Dr 61920 217-639-6000
Sandy Wilson, prin. Fax 639-6005

Charleston Christian Academy 50/K-12
2605 University Dr 61920 217-345-4476
John Best, admin.
Eastern Illinois University Post-Sec.
600 Lincoln Ave 61920 217-581-5000

Chatham, Sangamon, Pop. 9,787
Ball Chatham CUSD 5 4,000/PK-12
201 W Mulberry St 62629 217-483-2416
Dr. Richard Voltz, supt. Fax 483-2940
dist5.bcsd.k12.il.us
Glenwood HS 1,300/9-12
1501 E Plummer Blvd 62629 217-483-2424
Nate Cunningham, prin. Fax 483-5402
Glenwood MS 1,000/6-8
595 Chatham Rd 62629 217-483-2481
Jill Larson, prin. Fax 483-4940

Chester, Randolph, Pop. 7,872
Chester CUSD 139 1,000/PK-12
1940 Swanwick St 62233 618-826-4509
Rebecca Keim, supt. Fax 826-4500
chesteryellowjackets.com
Chester HS 400/9-12
1901 Swanwick St 62233 618-826-2302
Danny Marks, prin. Fax 826-3723

Chicago, Cook, Pop. 2,842,518
City of Chicago SD 299 396,000/PK-12
125 S Clark St 60603 773-553-1000
Arne Duncan, supt. Fax 535-1502
www.cps.k12.il.us/
AASTA 9-12
730 N Pulaski Rd 60624 773-534-6980
Carole Collins Ayanlaja, prin. Fax 534-6805
Academy of Business Entrepreneurship 9-12
6520 S Wood St 60636 773-535-9150
T. Pannell, prin. Fax 535-9090
Academy of Finance 9-12
821 E 103rd St 60628 773-535-5115
Anthony Spivey, prin. Fax 535-5511
A.E.D.F. Equipment Technology Institute 10-12
5630 S Rockwell St 60629 773-535-9230
Wilfredo Ortiz, prin. Fax 535-9411
Albany Park Multicultural Academy 7-8
4929 N Sawyer Ave 60625 773-534-5108
Eileen O'Toole, prin. Fax 534-5178
Allied Health S 9-12
3250 W Monroe St 60624 773-534-6455
Jaquelyn Trainer-Grant, prin. Fax 534-6409
Ames MS 6-8
1920 N Hamlin Ave 60647 773-534-4970
Lorraine Cruz, prin. Fax 534-4975
Amundsen HS 9-12
5110 N Damen Ave 60625 773-534-2320
Carlos Munoz, prin. Fax 534-2330
Arai MS 7-8
900 W Wilson Ave 60640 773-534-2610
Lillie Espinosa-Pappas, prin. Fax 534-2589
Armour S 4-8
950 W 33rd Pl 60608 773-535-4530
Shelley Cordova, prin. Fax 535-4501
Austin Community Academy HS 9-12
231 N Pine Ave 60644 773-534-6300
Dr. Tony Scott, prin. Fax 534-6046
BEST Academy 9-12
2710 E 89th St 60617 773-535-6597
Jo Ann Thomas-Woods Ph.D., prin. Fax 535-6598
Best Practices HS 9-12
2040 W Adams St 60612 773-534-7610
Linda Mims, prin. Fax 534-7601
Big Picture HS - Back of the Yards 9-9
4946 S Paulina St 60609 773-535-9219
Alfredo Nambo, prin. Fax 535-9477
Big Picture HS - Metro 9-9
2710 S Dearborn St 60616 773-534-9160
Kothyn Alexander, prin. Fax 534-9223
Black Magnet S 4-8
9101 S Euclid Ave 60617 773-535-6390
Thomas Little, prin. Fax 535-6047

Bogan Computer Tech HS 9-12
3939 W 79th St 60652 773-535-2180
Robert C. Miller, prin. Fax 535-2165
Bouchet MS 7-8
2001 E 73rd St 60649 773-535-0510
Patricia Williams, prin. Fax 535-0559
Bronzeville Scholastic Institute 9-12
4934 S Wabash Ave 60615 773-535-1150
Dr. Latunja Williams, prin. Fax 535-1228
Brooks College Prep HS 9-12
250 E 111th St 60628 773-535-9930
Dr. Dushon Brown, prin. Fax 535-9939
Burnham ES Anthony Branch 4-8
9800 S Torrence Ave 60617 773-535-6526
Dr. Linda Moore, prin. Fax 535-6568
Business/Finance S 9-12
2100 E 87th St 60617 773-535-6100
Marie Miles, prin. Fax 535-6633
Business Technology HS Vo/Tech
2935 W Polk St 60612 773-534-6900
Obie Laflour, prin. Fax 534-6924
Calumet Career Prep Academy HS Vo/Tech
8131 S May St 60620 773-535-3500
Daya Locke, prin. Fax 535-3526
Canter MS 7-8
4959 S Blackstone Ave 60615 773-535-1410
Carolyn Epps, prin. Fax 535-1047
Career/Theme-Focused SLC 9-12
2245 W Jackson Blvd 60612 773-534-7550
Melver Scott, prin. Fax 534-9330
Carver MS 4-8
801 E 133rd Pl 60827 773-535-5656
Ida Stewart, prin. Fax 535-5020
Carver Military Academy 9-12
13100 S Doty Ave 60827 773-535-5250
John Thomas, prin. Fax 535-5037
Castellanos MS 4-8
2524 S Central Park Ave 60623 773-534-1620
Myriam Romero, prin. Fax 534-1611
C.E.R.T.S. 10-12
6220 S Stony Island Ave 60637 773-535-0880
Dorothy Thomas, prin. Fax 535-0633
Chavez Upper Grade Center 5-8
4831 S Hermitage Ave 60609 773-535-4830
Ariel Correa, prin. Fax 535-4848
Chicago Academy HS 9-9
3400 N Austin Ave 60634 773-534-0146
Brian Sims, prin. Fax 534-0109
Chicago Discovery Academy 9-12
2710 E 89th St 60617 773-535-7947
Lynne Nuzzo, prin. Fax 535-6930
Chicago HS for Agricultural Science 9-12
3857 W 111th St 60655 773-535-2500
David Gilligan, prin. Fax 535-2507
Chicago Military Academy 9-12
3519 S Giles Ave 60653 773-534-9750
Richard Gray, prin. Fax 534-9760
Chicago Vocational Career Academy Vo/Tech
2100 E 87th St 60617 773-535-6100
Maria Miles, prin. Fax 535-6975
Clark Academic Prep HS 6-12
5101 W Harrison St 60644 773-534-6250
Annette Gurley, prin. Fax 534-6292
Clemente Community Academy HS 9-12
1147 N Western Ave 60622 773-534-4000
Leonard Kenebrew, prin. Fax 534-4012
Collins HS 10-12
1313 S Sacramento Dr 60623 773-534-1500
Kenneth McNeal, prin. Fax 534-1399
CoMETS S 9-12
6520 S Wood St 60636 773-535-9150
Audrey Askins, prin. Fax 535-9090
Communications S 9-12
2100 E 87th St 60617 773-535-6100
Marie Miles, prin. Fax 535-6633
Community Links HS 9-12
2401 S Marshall Blvd 60623 773-534-1997
Dr. Carlos Azcoitia, prin. Fax 534-0354
Construction S 9-12
2100 E 87th St 60617 773-535-6099
Marie Miles, prin. Fax 535-6975
Construction Technology Academy 10-12
6520 S Wood St 60636 773-535-9150
Ron Gibbs, prin. Fax 535-9090
Construction Technology HS Vo/Tech
2935 W Polk St 60612 773-534-6900
Michael Dimitroff, prin. Fax 534-6924
Corliss HS 9-12
821 E 103rd St 60628 773-535-5115
Anthony Spivey, prin. Fax 535-5511
Crane HS 9-12
2245 W Jackson Blvd 60612 773-534-7550
Melver Scott, prin. Fax 534-9330
Crane Technical Preparatory Common S 9-12
2245 W Jackson Blvd 60612 773-534-7550
Melver Scott, prin. Fax 534-7557
Culinary Arts HS 9-12
4747 S Union Ave 60609 773-535-1625
Keith Morris, prin. Fax 535-1581
Culinary Arts HS 9-12
3250 W Monroe St 60624 773-534-6455
Kim Minor, prin. Fax 534-6409
Culinary Arts S 10-12
6220 S Stony Island Ave 60637 773-535-0880
Dorothy Thomas, prin. Fax 535-0633
Curie Metro HS 9-12
4959 S Archer Ave 60632 773-535-2100
Jerryelyn Jones, prin. Fax 535-2049
De La Cruz MS 6-8
2317 W 23rd Pl 60608 773-535-4585
Dr. Roy Pletsch, prin. Fax 535-4534
Doolittle MS 5-8
535 E 35th St 60616 773-535-1040
Lori Lennix, prin. Fax 535-1034
Douglass Academy 6-10
543 N Waller Ave 60644 773-534-6176
Dr. Debra Crump, prin. Fax 534-6172
Dunbar Vocational Career Academy Vo/Tech
3000 S King Dr 60616 773-534-9000
Dr. Barbara Hall, prin. Fax 534-9250
Dusable HS 10-12
4934 S Wabash Ave 60615 773-535-1100
Linda Layne, prin. Fax 535-1004
Dyett Academic Center 7-12
555 E 51st St 60615 773-535-1825
Jacquelyn Lemon, prin. Fax 535-1037
Englewood Academy HS 9-12
6201 S Stewart Ave 60621 773-535-3600
Diane Jackson, prin. Fax 535-3586
Evergreen Middle Academy 6-8
3537 S Paulina St 60609 773-535-4836
Elizabeth Elizondo, prin. Fax 535-4853
EXCEL Academy 9-12
730 N Pulaski Rd 60624 773-534-6560
Marva Whaley-Anobah, prin. Fax 534-6556

FACETS S 9-12
6520 S Wood St 60636 773-535-9150
Jennifer Olson, prin. Fax 535-9090
Farragut Career Academy Vo/Tech
2345 S Christiana Ave 60623 773-534-1300
Theresa Plascencia, prin. Fax 534-1336
Fast Trek at Corliss 9-12
821 E 103rd St 60628 773-535-5115
Anthony Spivey, prin. Fax 535-5511
Fenger Academy HS 9-12
11220 S Wallace St 60628 773-535-5430
William Johnson, prin. Fax 535-5450
Field S 4-8
7019 N Ashland Blvd 60626 773-534-2030
Cora Suddoth, prin. Fax 534-2189
Fine and Performing Arts Academy 9-12
1147 N Western Ave 60622 773-534-4000
Fax 534-4012
Foods & Hospitality at Manley 10-12
2935 W Polk St 60612 773-534-6900
Dr. Kathy Flanagan, prin. Fax 534-6924
Foreman HS 9-12
3235 N Leclaire Ave 60641 773-534-3400
Frank Candioto, prin. Fax 534-3684
Freshman Academy 9-9
4747 S Union Ave 60609 773-535-1625
Theresa White, prin. Fax 535-1581
Freshman Academy 9-9
2100 E 87th St 60617 773-535-6100
JoAnn McCriston, prin. Fax 535-6633
Freshman Academy 9-9
5630 S Rockwell St 60629 773-535-9230
Miguel Davis, prin. Fax 535-9411
Gage Park HS 9-12
5630 S Rockwell St 60629 773-535-9230
Anita Andrews, prin. Fax 535-9411
Gallistel Branch MS 6-8
10200 S Avenue J 60617 773-535-6450
Patrick MacMahon, prin. Fax 535-6449
Global Village HS 9-12
5110 N Damen Ave 60625 773-534-2320
Carlos Munoz, prin. Fax 534-2330
Global Visions Academy 9-9
2710 E 89th St 60617 773-535-6905
Sabrena Davis, prin. Fax 535-6492
Gompers Fine Arts Option MS 4-8
12302 S State St 60628 773-535-5475
Melody Seaton, prin. Fax 535-5483
Graphic Design HS 9-12
2935 W Polk St 60612 773-534-6900
Leo Maxie, prin. Fax 534-6924
Grimes S 5-8
5450 W 64th Pl 60638 773-535-2364
David Dalton, prin. Fax 535-2366
Hamline S 4-8
4747 S Bishop St 60609 773-535-4565
Valerie Brown, prin. Fax 535-4546
Hancock College Prep 9-12
4034 W 56th St 60629 773-535-2410
Nancy Apke, prin. Fax 535-2434
Harlan Community Academy HS 9-12
9652 S Michigan Ave 60628 773-535-5400
Reginald Evans, prin. Fax 535-5061
Harper HS 9-12
6520 S Wood St 60636 773-535-9150
Dr. Ron Gibbs, prin. Fax 535-9090
Harvey Academic Preparatory S 8-12
3814 W Iowa St 60651 773-534-6400
Dr. Lona Bibbs, prin. Fax 534-6422
Health S 9-12
2100 E 87th St 60617 773-535-6100
Kinasha Brown, prin. Fax 535-6633
Hirsch Metro HS 9-12
7740 S Ingleside Ave 60619 773-535-3100
Joyce Cooper, prin. Fax 535-3240
Hope College Prep HS 5-12
5515 S Lowe Ave 60621 773-535-3160
Michael Durr, prin. Fax 535-3444
Horticulture HS 9-12
3250 W Adams St 60624 773-534-6455
Carol Williams, prin. Fax 534-6409
Hospitality S 9-12
2100 E 87th St 60617 773-535-6100
Earlene Lee, prin. Fax 535-6633
Hubbard HS 9-12
6200 S Hamlin Ave 60629 773-535-2200
Andrew Manno, prin. Fax 535-2218
Hyde Park Academy HS Vo/Tech
6220 S Stony Island Ave 60637 773-535-0880
Stacey McJunkins, prin. Fax 535-0633
Infinity Math/Science Tech HS 9-12
3120 S Kostner Ave 60623 773-535-4225
Martha Irizarry, prin. Fax 535-4270
International Language & Career Academy 9-12
3535 E 114th St Ste 1 60617 773-535-5725
Ruby Williams, prin. Fax 535-5038
International Language & Career Academy 9-12
6520 S Wood St 60636 773-535-9150
Tresa Cortesi, prin. Fax 535-9090
Irving Park MS 7-8
3815 N Kedvale Ave 60641 773-534-3750
Dr. Carmen Sanchez, prin. Fax 534-3757
Johns Middle Academy 4-8
6936 S Hermitage Ave 60636 773-535-9144
Althea Hammond, prin. Fax 535-9499
Jones College Prep HS 9-12
606 S State St 60605 773-534-8600
Dr. Donald Fraynd, prin. Fax 534-8625
Journalism Communications & Law Academy 9-12
1147 N Western Ave 60622 773-534-4000
Fax 534-4012
JROTC 9-12
2100 E 87th St 60617 773-535-6100
Grover Harper, prin. Fax 535-6633
J.R.O.T.C. Academy 9-12
4747 S Union Ave 60609 773-535-1625
Phyllis Hammond, prin. Fax 535-1581
JROTC Service Corps Academy 9-12
730 N Pulaski Rd 60624 773-534-8960
Ferdinand Wipachit, prin. Fax 534-9866
Juarez Community Academy 9-12
2150 S Laflin St 60608 773-534-7030
Natividad Loredo, prin. Fax 534-7058
Julian HS 9-12
10330 S Elizabeth St 60643 773-535-5170
William Harris, prin. Fax 535-5230
Kelly HS 9-12
4136 S California Ave 60632 773-535-4900
Algrid C. Pretkelis, prin. Fax 535-4841
Kelvyn Park HS 9-12
4343 W Wrightwood Ave 60639 773-534-4200
Dr. Sandra Fontanez-Phelan, prin. Fax 534-4507
Kennedy HS 9-12
6325 W 56th St 60638 773-535-2325
James Gorecki, prin. Fax 535-2485

Kenwood Academy HS 7-12
5015 S Blackstone Ave 60615 773-535-1350
Elizabeth Kirby, prin. Fax 535-1360
King HS 9-12
4445 S Drexel Blvd 60653 773-535-1180
Jeff Wright, prin. Fax 535-1658
KIPP Chicago Youth Village Academy 4-8
2710 S Dearborn St 60616 773-534-9977
Sara Abella, prin. Fax 534-9972
Lake View HS 9-12
4015 N Ashland Ave Ste 1 60613 773-534-5440
Scott Feaman, prin. Fax 534-5585
Lane Tech HS Vo/Tech
2501 W Addison St 60618 773-534-5400
Dr. Antoinette Lobosco, prin. Fax 534-5544
Lincoln Park HS 8-12
2001 N Orchard St 60614 773-534-8130
Bessie Karvelas, prin. Fax 534-8218
Lindblom College Prep HS 8-12
6130 S Wolcott Ave 60636 773-535-9300
Willie Sanders, prin. Fax 535-9314
Lindblom Math/Science Academy 9-12
6130 S Wolcott Ave 60636 773-535-9300
Alan Mather, prin. Fax 535-9314
Logandale MS 6-8
3212 W George St 60618 773-534-5350
Dr. Dennis Sweeney, prin. Fax 534-5349
Lozano Annex 5-8
1501 N Greenview Ave 60622 773-534-4750
Dr. Aurelio Acevedo, prin. Fax 534-4740
Madero MS 6-8
3202 W 28th St 60623 773-535-4466
Dr. Rosa Ramirez, prin. Fax 535-4469
Manley Career Academy Vo/Tech
2935 W Polk St 60612 773-534-6900
Sean Stalling, prin. Fax 534-6924
Manufacturing S 9-12
2100 E 87th St 60617 773-535-6100
Robert Haynes, prin. Fax 535-6633
Marshall Metro HS 9-12
3250 W Adams St 60624 773-534-6455
Ronald Bellamy, prin. Fax 534-6409
Marshall MS 5-8
3900 N Lawndale Ave 60618 773-534-5200
Jose Barillas, prin. Fax 534-5292
Mather HS 9-12
5835 N Lincoln Ave Ste 1 60659 773-534-2350
John Butterfield, prin. Fax 534-2424
Math Scholars 10-12
5015 S Blackstone Ave 60615 773-535-1350
Arthur Slater, prin. Fax 535-1360
Math Science & Tech Academy 9-12
1147 N Western Ave 60622 773-534-4000
Fax 534-4012
Medical & Allied Health at Manley 10-12
2935 W Polk St 60612 773-534-6900
Dr. Kathy Flanagan, prin. Fax 534-6924
Medical Careers Academy 9-12
6631 N Bosworth Ave 60626 773-534-2000
Chadra Lang, prin. Fax 534-2141
Morgan Park JSHS 7-12
1744 W Pryor Ave 60643 773-535-2550
Dr. Beryl Shingles, prin. Fax 535-2706
Moses Vines Prep Academy 9-12
730 N Pulaski Rd 60624 773-534-8808
Patricia Woodson, prin. Fax 534-8945
Multicultural Arts HS 9-12
3120 S Kostner Ave 60623 773-535-4242
Jose Rico, prin. Fax 535-4273
Naval School of Science 9-12
821 E 103rd St 60628 773-535-5115
Fax 535-5511
New Millenium S of Health 9-9
2710 E 89th St 60617 773-535-7650
Dr. Arlana Bedard, prin. Fax 535-6489
Nia MS 4-8
2040 W Adams St 60612 773-534-7494
Michelle Willis, prin. Fax 534-7497
North-Grand HS 9-12
4338 W Wabansia Ave 60639 773-534-8520
Dr. Asuncion Ayala, prin. Fax 534-8535
Northside College Prep HS 9-12
5501 N Kedzie Ave 60625 773-534-3954
Dr. James Lalley, prin. Fax 534-3964
Northwest MS 6-8
5252 W Palmer St 60639 773-534-3250
Marilyn Strojny, prin. Fax 534-3251
Orozco MS 6-8
1940 W 18th St 60608 773-534-7215
Coralia Barraza, prin. Fax 534-7329
Orr Community Academy HS 9-12
730 N Pulaski Rd 60624 773-534-6500
Marva Whaley-Anobah, prin. Fax 534-6570
Paideia Academy 9-9
6631 N Bosworth Ave 60626 773-534-2000
Peggy Miller-Kramer, prin. Fax 534-2141
Payton HS 9-12
1034 N Wells St 60610 773-534-0034
Ellen Estrada, prin. Fax 534-0035
Peace Academy 9-9
6631 N Bosworth Ave 60626 773-534-2000
Margaret Blair, prin. Fax 534-2141
Perez S 3-8
1241 W 19th St 60608 773-534-7650
Sylvia Stamatoglou, prin. Fax 534-7621
Performing and Visual Arts S 10-12
6220 S Stony Island Ave 60637 773-535-0880
Dorothy Thomas, prin. Fax 535-0633
Pershing West MS 4-8
3200 S Calumet Ave 60616 773-534-9240
Cheryl Watkins, prin. Fax 534-9249
Phillips Academy HS 9-12
244 E Pershing Rd 60653 773-535-1603
Euel Bunton, prin. Fax 535-1605
Phoenix Military Academy 9-12
145 S Campbell Ave 60612 773-534-7275
Ferdinand Wipachit, prin. Fax 534-7273
Price S 4-8
4351 S Drexel Blvd 60653 773-535-1300
Dr. Gwendolyn McClinton, prin. Fax 535-1324
PRIDE Institute 10-12
5630 S Rockwell St 60629 773-535-9230
Wilfredo Ortiz, prin. Fax 535-9411
Prosser Career Academy Vo/Tech
2148 N Long Ave 60639 773-534-3200
Kenneth Hunter, prin. Fax 534-3382
Raby S 9-10
3545 W Fulton Blvd 60624 773-534-6755
Janice Jackson, prin. Fax 534-6938
Richards Career Academy Vo/Tech
5009 S Laflin St 60609 773-535-4945
Dr. O. Joyce Smith, prin. Fax 535-4883
Rickover Navy Academy HS 9-12
5900 N Glenwood Ave 60660 773-534-2890
Michael Biela, prin. Fax 534-2895

Rising Starts Academy 7-8
9000 S Exchange Ave 60617 773-535-6360
Ben Perez, prin. Fax 535-6303
Robeson HS 9-12
6835 S Normal Blvd 60621 773-535-3800
James Breashears, prin. Fax 535-3620
Roosevelt HS 9-12
3436 W Wilson Ave 60625 773-534-5000
Dr. Alejandra Alvarez, prin. Fax 534-5044
Schiller MS 4-8
640 W Scott St Ste 1 60610 773-534-8490
Cynthia Fitzpatrick, prin. Fax 534-8016
S.C.O.P.E. 9-12
5015 S Blackstone Ave 60615 773-535-1371
Arthur Slater, prin. Fax 535-1360
School for Social Justice HS 9-12
3120 S Kostner Ave 60623 773-535-4300
Rito Martinez, prin. Fax 535-4271
School of Entrepreneurship 9-11
7627 S Constance Ave 60649 773-535-6190
Bill Gerstein, prin. Fax 535-6960
School of Finance Academy 9-12
4747 S Union Ave 60609 773-535-1625
Joann Scott-Tablo, prin. Fax 535-1581
School of Finance Academy 9-12
3250 W Adams St 60624 773-534-6455
Tierra Buchanan, prin. Fax 534-6409
School of Leadership 9-12
7527 S Constance Ave 60649 773-535-6190
James Patrick, prin. Fax 535-6960
School of Technology HS 9-9
7529 S Constance Ave 60649 773-535-6180
Therese Johnson, prin. Fax 535-6088
School of the Arts 9-12
7529 S Constance Ave 60649 773-535-6180
Doug Maclin, prin. Fax 535-6088
Schurz HS 9-12
3601 N Milwaukee Ave 60641 773-534-3420
Mary Ann Folino, prin. Fax 534-3573
Senn HS 9-12
5900 N Glenwood Ave 60660 773-534-2365
Richard Norman, prin. Fax 534-2369
Simeon Career Academy Vo/Tech
8147 S Vincennes Ave 60620 773-535-3200
Tamara Sterling, prin. Fax 535-3465
South Shore Community Academy 9-12
7529 S Constance Ave 60649 773-535-6180
Bertha Buchanan, prin. Fax 535-6088
Spry Community Links HS 9-12
2400 S Marshall Blvd 60623 773-534-1997
Dr. Carlos Azcoitia, prin. Fax 534-0354
Steinmetz Academic Centre 9-12
3030 N Mobile Ave 60634 773-534-3030
Dr. Eunice Madon, prin. Fax 534-3151
Stevenson MS 6-8
4350 W 79th St 60652 773-535-0215
Pamela Rice, prin. Fax 535-0219
Sullivan HS 9-12
6631 N Bosworth Ave 60626 773-534-2000
Dr. Joseph Atria, prin. Fax 534-2141
Taft HS 7-12
6530 W Bryn Mawr Ave 60631 773-534-1000
Dr. Arthur Tarvardian, prin. Fax 534-1027
Tilden Career Community HS 9-12
4747 S Union Ave 60609 773-535-1625
Phyllis Hammond, prin. Fax 535-1866
Tonti Branch MS 6-8
4950 S Laporte Ave 60638 773-535-2000
Maria Vallejos-Howell, prin. Fax 535-2474
UPLIFT Community S 6-12
900 W Wilson Ave 60640 773-534-2875
Stephanie Moore, prin. Fax 534-2876
Von Steuben Metro HS 9-12
5039 N Kimball Ave 60625 773-534-5100
Pedro Alonso, prin. Fax 534-5210
Washington HS 9-12
3535 E 114th St Ste 1 60617 773-535-5725
Juana Rivera-Vidal, prin. Fax 535-5038
Wells Community Academy HS 9-12
936 N Ashland Ave 60622 773-534-7010
Delores Pidgeon, prin. Fax 534-7078
Westinghouse Career Academy Vo/Tech
3301 W Franklin Blvd 60624 773-534-6400
Dr. Lona Bibbs, prin. Fax 534-6422
Williams Preparatory Academy 6-8
2710 S Dearborn St 60616 773-534-9235
Bernard Murray, prin. Fax 534-9236
Williams Prep S of Medicine 7-12
4934 S Wabash Ave 60615 773-535-1150
Dr. Delores Bedar, prin. Fax 535-1023
World Language/Career Academy 9-12
1147 N Western Ave 60622 773-534-4000
Fax 534-4012
World Language HS 9-12
3120 S Kostner Ave 60623 773-535-4334
Alice Phillips, prin. Fax 535-4272
Young Magnet JSHS 7-12
211 S Laflin St 60607 773-534-7500
Joyce Kenner, prin. Fax 534-7261
Englewood Evening HS Adult
6201 S Stewart Ave 60621 773-535-3600
Diane L. Jackson, prin. Fax 535-3586

Adler School of Professional Psychology Post-Sec.
65 E Wacker Pl 60601 312-201-5900
Advocate Illinois Masonic Post-Sec.
836 W Wellington Ave 60657 773-296-8950
Advocate Trinity Hospital Post-Sec.
2320 E 93rd St 60617 773-978-2000
Agape Love Academy 50/K-10
1150 W 88th St Ste 406 60620 773-881-9717
Carolyn Chambers, admin. Fax 881-9717
American Academy of Art Post-Sec.
332 S Michigan Ave Ste 3 60604 312-461-0600
American Floral Art School Post-Sec.
634 S Wabash Ave # 210 60605 312-922-9328
American Health Information Management Post-Sec.
233 N Michigan Ave Ste 2150 60601 312-233-1184
Archbishop Quigley Preparatory Seminary 200/9-12
103 E Chestnut St 60611 312-787-9343
Rev. Peter Snieg, prin. Fax 787-9167
Argosy University/Chicago Post-Sec.
350 N Orleans St 60654 888-488-7537
Bais Yaakov HS for Girls 100/9-12
3333 W Peterson Ave 60659 773-267-1494
Shulamis Keller, prin. Fax 267-4798
Bnos Rabbeinu HS 9-12
3635 W Devon Ave 60659 773-267-0770
Tsyrl Turen, prin. Fax 267-6107
Brother Rice HS 1,200/9-12
10001 S Pulaski Rd 60655 773-429-4300
James Antos, prin. Fax 779-5239
Cain's Barber College Post-Sec.
365 E 51st St 60615 773-536-4441

Cannella School of Hair Design Post-Sec.
9012 S Commercial Ave 60617 773-221-4700
Cannella School of Hair Design Post-Sec.
5912 W Roosevelt Rd 60644 773-287-3400
Cannella School of Hair Design Post-Sec.
4269 S Archer Ave 60632 773-890-0412
Cannella School of Hair Design Post-Sec.
4217 W North Ave 60639 773-278-4477
Capri Garfield Ridge Sch of Beauty Coll Post-Sec.
2653 W 63rd St 60629 773-778-8161
Cardean University Post-Sec.
111 N Canal St Ste 455 60606 866-948-1289
Catholic Theological Union Post-Sec.
5401 S Cornell Ave 60615 773-324-8000
Chicago Academy for the Arts 200/9-12
1010 W Chicago Ave 60622 312-421-0202
Pamela Jordan, prin. Fax 421-3816
Chicago Hope Academy 100/9-12
2189 W Bowler St 60612 312-491-1600
Tina Muzikowski, dir. Fax 491-1616
Chicago Jesuit Academy 5-8
212 S Francisco Ave 60612 773-638-6103
Matthew Lynch, prin.
Chicago Sch. of Professional Psychology Post-Sec.
325 N Wells St 60610 312-329-6600
Chicago School of Massage Therapy Post-Sec.
17 N State St Fl 5 60602 312-753-7900
Chicago SDA Academy 100/PK-12
7008 S Michigan Ave 60637 773-873-3005
Donaldson Williams, prin.
Chicago State University Post-Sec.
9501 S King Dr 60628 773-995-2000
Chicago Theological Seminary Post-Sec.
5757 S University Ave 60637 773-752-5757
Chicago Waldorf S 400/PK-12
1300 W Loyola Ave 60626 773-465-2662
Sheree Moratto, prin. Fax 465-6648
Chubb Institute Post-Sec.
25 E Washington St 60602 800-248-2237
College of Office Technology Post-Sec.
1520 W Division St 60622 773-278-0042
Columbia College Post-Sec.
600 S Michigan Ave 60605 312-663-1600
Computer Systems Institute Post-Sec.
318 W Adams St Fl 10 60606 312-346-6774
Cook County Hospital Post-Sec.
1825 W Harrison St 60612 312-633-8533
Cooking & Hospitality Inst. of Chicago Post-Sec.
361 W Chestnut St 60610 312-944-0884
Coyne American Institute Post-Sec.
330 N Green St 60607 800-999-5220
Cristo Rey Jesuit HS 500/9-12
1852 W 22nd Pl 60608 773-890-6800
Patricia Garrity, prin. Fax 890-6801
De La Salle Institute Main Campus 1,200/9-12
3434 S Michigan Ave 60616 312-842-7355
James Krygier, prin. Fax 842-5640
De La Salle Institute - West Campus 9-12
1040 W 32nd Pl 60608 773-650-6800
Diane Brown, prin. Fax 650-9722
De Paul University Post-Sec.
1 E Jackson Blvd 60604 312-362-8000
De Paul University Post-Sec.
2323 N Seminary Ave 60614 312-362-8000
DeVry University Post-Sec.
3300 N Campbell Ave 60618 773-929-8500
DeVry University Post-Sec.
225 W Washington St # 100 60606 312-372-4900
Eagles' Wings Urban Academy 100/PK-12
2447 W Granville Ave 60659 773-743-6345
Cynthia Peterson, admin. Fax 743-6068
East-West University Post-Sec.
816 S Michigan Ave 60605 312-939-0111
Erikson Institute Post-Sec.
420 N Wabash Ave 60611 312-755-2250
Gordon Tech HS 600/9-12
3633 N California Ave 60618 773-539-3600
Simon Hess, prin. Fax 539-9158
Greater West Town School Post-Sec.
2021 W Fulton St # 204 60612 312-563-9570
Hales Franciscan HS 200/9-12
4930 S Cottage Grove Ave 60615 773-285-8400
Marilyn Garrison, prin. Fax 285-7025
Hanna Sacks Girls HS 200/9-12
3021 W Devon Ave 60659 773-338-9222
Rabbi Shimon Zehnwirth, prin. Fax 338-2405
Harold S. Washington College Post-Sec.
30 E Lake St 60601 312-553-5600
Harrington College of Design Post-Sec.
200 W Madison St 60606 312-939-4975
Harry S. Truman College Post-Sec.
1145 W Wilson Ave 60640 773-878-1700
Holy Trinity HS 400/9-12
1443 W Division St 60622 773-278-4212
Charlene Szumilas, prin. Fax 278-0144
Ida Crown Jewish Academy 300/9-12
2828 W Pratt Blvd 60645 773-973-1450
Rabbi Leonard Matanky, prin. Fax 973-6131
IIT Chicago-Kent College of Law Post-Sec.
565 W Adams St 60661 312-906-5000
Illinois College of Optometry Post-Sec.
3241 S Michigan Ave 60616 312-225-1700
Illinois Institute of Technology Post-Sec.
3300 S Federal St 60616 312-567-3000
Illinois School of Health Careers Post-Sec.
11 E Adams St Ste 600 60603 312-913-1230
Institute for Clinical Social Work Post-Sec.
200 N Michigan Ave Ste 407 60601 312-726-8480
International Academy of Design & Tech Post-Sec.
1 N State St # 500 60602 312-980-9200
John Marshall Law School Post-Sec.
315 S Plymouth Ct 60604 312-427-2737
Josephinum Academy 200/6-12
1501 N Oakley Blvd 60622 773-276-1261
Sr. Martha Roughan, prin. Fax 292-3963
Keller Graduate School Post-Sec.
8501 W Higgins Rd Ste 410 60631 773-695-1000
Kendall College Post-Sec.
900 N North Branch St 60622 877-588-8860
Kennedy-King College Post-Sec.
6800 S Wentworth Ave 60621 773-602-5000
Lake Forest Graduate Sch. of Management Post-Sec.
230 S LaSalle St Ste 100 60604 312-435-5330
Latin S of Chicago 1,100/PK-12
59 W North Blvd 60610 312-582-6000
Donald Firke, hdmstr. Fax 582-6011
Leo HS 300/9-12
7901 S Sangamon St 60620 773-224-9600
John Kasel, prin. Fax 224-3856
Lexington College Post-Sec.
310 S Peoria St 60607 312-226-6294
Loyola University Post-Sec.
6525 N Sheridan Rd 60626 773-508-2320
Loyola University - Mundelein College Post-Sec.
6525 N Sheridan Rd 60626 773-262-8100

Loyola University of Chicago Post-Sec.
820 N Michigan Ave 60611 312-915-6000
Lubavitch Girls HS 100/9-12
2754 W Rosemont Ave 60659 773-743-7716
Esther Moscowitz, prin. Fax 743-7735
Lubavitch Mesivta of Chicago 100/9-12
2756 W Morse Ave 60645 773-262-0430
Rabbi Moshe Perlstein, dean Fax 338-2209
Lutheran School of Theology at Chicago Post-Sec.
1100 E 55th St 60615 773-256-0700
Luther HS North 300/9-12
5700 W Berteau Ave 60634 773-286-3600
Dr. Jeffrey D. Daley, prin. Fax 286-0304
Luther HS South 300/6-12
3130 W 87th St 60652 773-737-1416
Anthony Rainey, prin. Fax 737-2882
Lycee Francais de Chicago 400/PK-12
613 W Bittersweet Pl 60613 773-665-0066
Dr. Sylvette Nicolini, prin. Fax 665-1725
MacCormac College Post-Sec.
29 E Madison St 60602 312-922-1884
Malcolm X College Post-Sec.
1900 W Van Buren St 60612 312-850-7031
Maranatha Christian Academy 200/K-12
115 W 108th St 60628 773-264-7702
Betty Millsap, prin. Fax 264-8720
Maria HS 500/9-12
6727 S California Ave 60629 773-925-8686
Linda Casey, prin. Fax 925-8885
Marist HS 9-12
4200 W 115th St 60655 773-881-5300
Larry Tucker, prin. Fax 881-0595
McCormick Theological Seminary Post-Sec.
5460 S University Ave 60615 800-228-4687
Meadville/Lombard Theological School Post-Sec.
5701 S Woodlawn Ave 60637 773-256-3000
Medical Careers Institute Post-Sec.
116 S Michigan Ave 60603 312-782-9804
Midwest College of Oriental Medicine Post-Sec.
4334 N Hazel St Ste 206 60613 800-593-2320
Moody Bible Institute Post-Sec.
820 N La Salle Dr 60610 800-967-4624
Morgan Park Academy 500/PK-12
2153 W 111th St 60643 773-881-6700
J. William Adams, hdmstr. Fax 881-8409
Mother McAuley Liberal Arts HS 1,700/9-12
3737 W 99th St 60655 773-881-6500
Sr. Rose Wiorek, prin. Fax 881-6562
Mt. Carmel HS 800/9-12
6410 S Dante Ave 60637 773-324-1020
Rev. Carl Markelz, prin. Fax 324-9235
Northeastern Illinois University Post-Sec.
5500 N Saint Louis Ave 60625 773-583-4050
North Park Coll. & Theological Seminary Post-Sec.
3225 W Foster Ave 60625 773-244-6200
North Shore SDA Jr. Academy 100/PK-10
5220 N California Ave 60625 773-769-0733
Helen Bacchus, prin. Fax 769-0928
Northside Catholic Academy - St. Ita 6-8
5525 N Magnolia Ave 60640 773-271-2008
Sabrina Roy, prin. Fax 271-3101
Northwestern Business College Post-Sec.
4829 N Lipps Ave 60630 773-777-4220
Northwestern Memorial Hospital Post-Sec.
251 E Huron St 60611 312-926-6609
Northwestern University Post-Sec.
303 E Chicago Ave 60611 312-503-6950
Notre Dame HS 400/9-12
3000 N Mango Ave 60634 773-622-9494
Staci Viola, prin. Fax 622-8511
Olive-Harvey College Post-Sec.
10001 S Woodlawn Ave 60628 773-291-6100
Olympia College Post-Sec.
247 S State St Ste 400 60604 312-913-1616
Our Lady of Tepeyac HS 200/9-12
2228 S Whipple St 60623 773-522-0023
Joni Thompson, prin. Fax 522-0508
Parker S 900/PK-12
330 W Webster Ave 60614 773-353-3000
Daniel B. Frank, prin. Fax 549-4669
Providence-St. Mel S 700/K-12
119 S Central Park Blvd 60624 773-722-4600
Jeanette DiBella, prin. Fax 722-9004
Pyramid Career Institute Post-Sec.
3051 N Lincoln Ave 60657 773-975-9898
Resurrection HS 900/9-12
7500 W Talcott Ave 60631 773-775-6616
Jo Marie Yonkus, prin. Fax 775-0611
Richard J. Daley College Post-Sec.
7500 S Pulaski Rd 60652 773-838-7500
Robert Morris College Post-Sec.
401 S State St 60605 312-935-6800
Roosevelt University Post-Sec.
430 S Michigan Ave 60605 312-341-3500
Rosel School of Cosmetology Post-Sec.
2444 W Devon Ave 60659 773-508-5600
Rush University Post-Sec.
600 S Paulina St # 440 60612 312-942-7120
St. Augustine College Post-Sec.
1333 W Argyle St 60640 773-878-8756
St. Benedict HS 400/9-12
3900 N Leavitt St 60618 773-539-0066
Mary Kay Nickels, prin. Fax 539-3397
St. Francis De Sales HS 300/9-12
10155 S Ewing Ave 60617 773-731-7272
Richard Hawkins, prin. Fax 731-7888
St. Gregory the Great HS 200/9-12
1677 W Bryn Mawr Ave 60660 773-907-2100
Erika Mickelburgh, prin. Fax 907-2120
St. Ignatius College Prep HS 1,300/9-12
1076 W Roosevelt Rd 60608 312-421-5900
Dr. Catherine Karl, prin. Fax 421-7124
St. Mary of Providence School Post-Sec.
4200 N Austin Ave 60634
St. Patrick HS 1,000/9-12
5900 W Belmont Ave 60634 773-282-8844
Dr. Joseph Schmidt, prin. Fax 282-2361
St. Rita of Cascia HS 800/9-12
7740 S Western Ave 60620 773-925-6600
Rev. Thomas R. McCarthy, prin. Fax 925-2451
St. Scholastica Academy 200/9-12
7416 N Ridge Blvd 60645 773-764-5715
Anne Matz, prin. Fax 764-0304
St. Xavier University Post-Sec.
3700 W 103rd St 60655 773-298-3000
San Miguel MS 100/6-8
1949 W 48th St 60609 773-890-1481
M. Anderer-McClelland, prin. Fax 254-3382
San Miguel S Gary Comer Campus 5-8
819 N Leamington Ave Ste 1 60651 773-261-8851
Gordon Hannon, prin. Fax 261-8854
School of the Art Institute of Chicago Post-Sec.
37 S Wabash Ave 60603 773-889-5100
SER Business and Technical Institute Post-Sec.
3948 W 26th St Ste 213 60623 773-227-3377

Shimer College Post-Sec.
3424 S State St 60616 312-235-3500
Spanish Coalition for Jobs Post-Sec.
2011 W Pershing Rd 60609 773-247-0707
Spertus College Post-Sec.
618 S Michigan Ave 60605 312-922-9012
Steven Papageorge Hair Academy Post-Sec.
5230 N Clark St 60640 773-561-2376
Taylor Business Institute Post-Sec.
318 W Adams St Fl 5 60606 312-658-5100
Telshe Yeshiva-Chicago Post-Sec.
3535 W Foster Ave 60625 773-463-7738
Telshe Yeshiva HS 100/9-12
3535 W Foster Ave 60625 773-463-7738
Rabbi Shmuel Adler, dir. Fax 463-2849
The Illinois Institute of Art Post-Sec.
350 N Orleans St Lbby 136 60654 312-280-3500
University of Chicago Post-Sec.
5801 S Ellis Ave 60637 773-702-1234
University of Chicago Lab S 1,700/PK-12
1362 E 59th St Ste 1 60637 773-702-9450
Dr. David W. Magill, dir. Fax 702-7455
University of Illinois at Chicago Post-Sec.
PO Box 5220 60680 312-996-3000
Univ. of Chicago Hospital/Roosevelt U. Post-Sec.
5841 S Maryland Ave 60637 773-702-6240
VanderCook College of Music Post-Sec.
3140 S Federal St 60616 800-448-2655
Warde S - Holy Name Cathedral 300/K-K, 5-8
751 N State St 60610 312-466-0700
Mary Reiling, hdmstr. Fax 337-7180
Westwood College Post-Sec.
8501 W Higgins Rd Ste 500 60631 773-380-6800
Westwood College Post-Sec.
17 N State St Fl 3 60602 312-739-0850
Wilbur Wright College North Post-Sec.
4300 N Narragansett Ave 60634 773-777-7900
Yeshivas Meor HaTorah of Chicago 8-12
3050 W Touhy Ave 60645 773-465-0419
Rabbi Eliyahu Millen, dean Fax 465-0520

Chicago Heights, Cook, Pop. 31,373
Bloom Township HSD 206 3,100/9-12
100 W 10th St 60411 708-755-7010
Glen Giannetti, supt. Fax 755-6859
www.bloomdistrict206.org
Bloom HS 1,500/9-12
101 W 10th St 60411 708-755-1122
Dr. Lenell Navarre, prin. Fax 755-1149
Bloom Trail HS 1,500/9-12
22331 Cottage Grove Ave 60411 708-758-7000
Ronald Ray, prin. Fax 758-8372

Chicago Heights SD 170 3,400/PK-8
30 W 16th St 60411 708-756-4165
Thomas Amadio, supt. Fax 756-4164
www.sd170.com/
Washington MS 300/5-8
25 W 16th Pl 60411 708-756-4841
Rhonda Sneed, prin. Fax 756-1008

Flossmoor SD 161 2,600/PK-8
41 E Elmwood Dr 60411 708-647-7000
Dr. Donna C. Joy, supt. Fax 754-2153
www.sd161.org
Other Schools – See Flossmoor

Marian Catholic HS 1,700/9-12
700 Ashland Ave 60411 708-755-7565
Sr. Kathleen Anne Tait, prin. Fax 756-9758
Prairie State College Post-Sec.
202 S Halsted St 60411 708-709-3500

Chicago Ridge, Cook, Pop. 13,668
Chicago Ridge SD 127-5 1,300/PK-8
6135 W 108th St 60415 708-636-2000
Joyce Kleinaitis, supt. Fax 636-0916
www.crsd1275.org
Finley JHS 300/6-8
10835 Lombard Ave 60415 708-636-2005
Mary McDonald, prin. Fax 636-0045

Chillicothe, Peoria, Pop. 5,781
Illinois Valley Central Unit SD 321 2,100/PK-12
1300 W Sycamore St 61523 309-274-5418
Dr. David Kinney, supt. Fax 274-5046
www.ivcschools.com/
Chillicothe Elementary Center 500/3-8
914 W Truitt Ave 61523 309-274-6266
Dianne Pointer, prin. Fax 274-2010
Illinois Valley Central HS 700/9-12
1300 W Sycamore St 61523 309-274-5481
Kenton Bergman, prin. Fax 274-8613

Chrisman, Edgar, Pop. 1,259
Edgar County CUSD 6 400/K-12
23231 IL Highway 1 61924 217-269-2513
Norman Tracy, supt. Fax 269-3231
www.chrisman.k12.il.us
Chrisman HS 100/9-12
23231 IL Highway 1 61924 217-269-2823
Terry Furnish, prin. Fax 269-3231
Chrisman-Scottland JHS 100/6-8
23231 IL Highway 1 61924 217-269-3980
Terry Furnish, prin. Fax 269-3231

Christopher, Franklin, Pop. 2,833
Christopher Unit SD 99 800/PK-12
1 Bearcat Dr 62822 618-724-9461
Mark L. Miller, supt. Fax 724-9400
www.cpher.frnkln.k12.il.us
Christopher HS 200/9-12
1 Bearcat Dr 62822 618-724-9461
Mark Miller, prin. Fax 724-9400

Cicero, Cook, Pop. 82,741
Cicero SD 99 10,600/K-8
5110 W 24th St 60804 708-863-4856
Clyde Senters, supt. Fax 652-8105
cicd99.edu/
Unity JHS West 50/8-8
2115 S 54th Ave 60804 708-863-8268
Denise Boyle, prin. Fax 656-5652

J. S. Morton HSD 201 7,700/9-12
2423 S Austin Blvd 60804 708-222-5702
Dr. Ben Nowakowski, supt. Fax 222-3087
www.jsmortonhs.com
Morton East HS 3,100/10-12
2423 S Austin Blvd 60804 708-222-5751
Frank Zarate, prin. Fax 222-3090
Morton Freshman Center 1,200/9-9
1801 S 55th Ave 60804 708-863-2200
Joseph Gunty, prin. Fax 863-2244
Other Schools – See Berwyn

Morton College Post-Sec.
3801 S Central Ave 60804 708-656-8000

Cisne, Wayne, Pop. 662
North Wayne CUSD 200 500/PK-12
PO Box 235 62823 618-673-2151
Joyce Carson, supt. Fax 673-2152
Cisne HS 200/9-12
PO Box 70 62823 618-673-2154
Penny Arnold, prin. Fax 673-2155
Cisne MS 100/5-8
PO Box 69 62823 618-673-2156
Joyce Carson, prin. Fax 673-2152

Cissna Park, Iroquois, Pop. 774
Cissna Park CUSD 6 400/K-12
511 N 2nd St 60924 815-457-2171
Dr. Daniel Hylbert, supt. Fax 457-3033
www.cissnapark.k12.il.us
Cissna Park HS 100/9-12
511 N 2nd St 60924 815-457-2171
Jeffrey Maurer, prin. Fax 457-3033
Cissna Park JHS 100/6-8
511 N 2nd St 60924 815-457-2171
Jeffrey Maurer, prin. Fax 457-3033

Clarendon Hills, DuPage, Pop. 8,397
CCSD 181
Supt. — See Westmont
Clarendon Hills MS 800/6-8
301 Chicago Ave 60514 630-887-4260
David Bendis, prin. Fax 887-4267

Maercker SD 60 1,400/PK-8
5800 Holmes Ave 60514 630-323-2086
Dr. Catherine Berning, supt. Fax 323-5541
www.maercker.org
Other Schools – See Willowbrook

Clay City, Clay, Pop. 961
Clay City CUSD 10 400/PK-12
PO Box 542 62824 618-676-1431
David Mills, supt. Fax 676-1430
www.claycityschools.org
Clay City HS 100/9-12
PO Box 405 62824 618-676-1522
David Mills, prin. Fax 676-1481
Clay City JHS 100/6-8
PO Box 545 62824 618-676-1521
David Mills, prin. Fax 676-1537

Clifton, Iroquois, Pop. 1,279
Central CUSD 4 1,000/PK-12
PO Box 637 60927 815-694-2231
Tonya Evans, supt. Fax 694-2844
www.clifton-u4.k12.il.us/
Central HS 400/9-12
1134 E 3100 North Rd Ste A 60927 815-694-2321
Shane Schuricht, prin. Fax 694-2709
Nash MS 300/5-8
1134 E 3100 North Rd 60927 815-694-2323
Victoria Marquis, prin. Fax 694-2830

Clinton, DeWitt, Pop. 7,261
Clinton CUSD 15 1,700/PK-12
1210 State Route 54 W 61727 217-935-8321
Dr. Jeff Holmes, supt. Fax 935-2300
www.cusd15.k12.il.us/
Clinton HS 600/9-12
Route 54 W 61727 217-935-8337
Ronald Conner, prin. Fax 935-4029
Clinton JHS 500/6-8
701 Illini Dr 61727 217-935-2103
John Pine, prin. Fax 937-1918

Coal City, Grundy, Pop. 5,170
Coal City CUSD 1 1,900/PK-12
100 S Baima St 60416 815-634-2287
Dr. Kent Bugg, supt. Fax 634-8775
www.coalcity.k12.il.us
Coal City HS 600/9-12
655 W Division St 60416 815-634-2396
Ken Miller, prin. Fax 634-2313
Coal City MS 500/6-8
500 S Carbon Hill Rd 60416 815-634-5039
Frank Perucca, prin. Fax 634-5049

Cobden, Union, Pop. 1,102
Cobden Unit SD 17 700/PK-12
413 N Appleknocker St 62920 618-893-2313
Karl Sweitzer, supt. Fax 893-4772
www.cobdenappleknockers.com/
Cobden HS 200/9-12
413 N Appleknocker St 62920 618-893-4031
Karl Sweitzer, prin. Fax 893-2138
Cobden JHS 100/7-8
413 N Appleknocker St 62920 618-893-4031
Karl Sweitzer, prin. Fax 893-2138

Colchester, McDonough, Pop. 1,394
West Prairie CUSD 103 800/PK-12
204 S Hun St 62326 309-776-3180
Dr. Jonathan Heerboth, supt. Fax 776-3194
www.westprairie.org/
West Prairie MS 200/5-8
600 S Hun St 62326 309-776-3220
Eunice Lutz, prin. Fax 776-3194
Other Schools – See Sciota

Colfax, McLean, Pop. 991
Ridgeview CUSD 19 500/PK-12
309 N Harrison St 61728 309-723-5111
Dr. Larry Dodds, supt. Fax 723-6395
www.ridgeview19.org
Ridgeview JSHS 200/6-12
202 E Wood St 61728 309-723-2951
Jim Campbell, prin. Fax 723-4851

Collinsville, Madison, Pop. 25,487
Collinsville CUSD 10 5,300/PK-12
201 W Clay St 62234 618-346-6350
Dr. Dennis Craft, supt. Fax 343-3673
www.kahoks.org
Collinsville HS 2,000/9-12
2201 S Morrison Ave 62234 618-346-6320
Eric Flohr, prin. Fax 346-6341
Collinsville MS 900/7-8
9801 Collinsville Rd 62234 618-343-2100
Dr. Allen Ellington, prin. Fax 343-2102

Collinsville Chrisitian Academy 100/K-12
1203 Vandalia St 62234 618-345-4224
Debora Legters, prin. Fax 345-6103
Sanford-Brown College Post-Sec.
1101 Eastport Plaza Dr 62234 618-344-5600

Columbia, Monroe, Pop. 8,902
Columbia CUSD 4 1,700/K-12
100 Parkview Dr 62236 618-281-4772
Jack Turner, supt. Fax 281-8081
www.chseagles.com
Columbia HS 500/9-12
100 Parkview Dr 62236 618-281-5001
Sam Keene, prin. Fax 281-8081
Columbia MS 500/5-8
100 Eagle Dr 62236 618-281-4993
Roger Chamberlain, prin. Fax 281-4964

Concord, Morgan, Pop. 174
Triopia CUSD 27 500/PK-12
2204 Concord Arenzville Rd 62631 217-457-2283
Eilzabeth Pressler, supt. Fax 457-2277
www.triopiacusd27.org/education
Triopia JSHS 200/7-12
2204 Concord Arenzville Rd 62631 217-457-2281
Cheri Madson, prin. Fax 457-2277

Coulterville, Randolph, Pop. 1,189
Coulterville Unit SD 1 200/K-12
PO Box 396 62237 618-758-2881
Louis Obernuefemann, supt. Fax 758-2330
www.coulterville1.org/
Coulterville HS 100/9-12
PO Box 396 62237 618-758-2881
Louis Obernuefemann, prin. Fax 758-2330
Coulterville JHS 100/6-8
PO Box 396 62237 618-758-2881
Louis Obernuefemann, prin. Fax 758-2330

Country Club Hills, Cook, Pop. 16,534
Bremen Community HSD 228
Supt. — See Midlothian
Hillcrest HS 1,300/9-12
17401 Crawford Ave 60478 708-799-7000
Patricia Welch, prin. Fax 799-0402

Country Club Hills SD 160 1,500/PK-8
4411 185th St 60478 708-957-6200
Charlie T. Kent, supt. Fax 957-8686
d160.s-cook.k12.il.us/
Southwood MS 500/6-8
18635 Lee St 60478 708-957-6230
Fax 799-4033

Cowden, Shelby, Pop. 593
Cowden-Herrick Community USD 3A 500/K-12
PO Box 188 62422 217-783-2126
Gary Cadwell, supt. Fax 783-2126
www.cowden-herrick.k12.il.us/
Cowden-Herrick HS 200/9-12
PO Box 188 62422 217-783-2125
Jerry Phillips, prin. Fax 783-2124

Crescent City, Iroquois, Pop. 603
Crescent Iroquois CUSD 249 200/K-12
PO Box 190 60928 815-683-2141
Kirt Hendrick, supt. Fax 683-2219
www.crescent.k12.il.us
Crescent-Iroquois HS 100/9-12
PO Box 10 60928 815-683-2161
Rodney Miller, prin. Fax 683-2163

Crest Hill, Will, Pop. 19,438
Chaney-Monge SD 88 500/PK-8
400 Elsie Ave, 815-722-6673
August Tomac, supt. Fax 722-7814
Monge JHS 200/6-8
400 Elsie Ave, 815-722-6673
Cathleen Davis, prin. Fax 722-7814

Crestwood, Cook, Pop. 11,207
Cook County SD 130
Supt. — See Blue Island
Hale MS 400/6-8
5220 135th St 60445 708-385-6690
Linda Battles, prin. Fax 385-2417

Crete, Will, Pop. 8,772
Crete-Monee CUSD 201U 4,700/PK-12
1500 S Sangamon St 60417 708-367-8300
Ronald Patton, supt. Fax 672-2689
www.cm201u.org
Crete-Monee HS 1,500/9-12
760 W Exchange St 60417 708-367-8200
Deb Graham, prin. Fax 672-2888
Other Schools – See University Park

Illinois Lutheran HS 100/7-12
1610 Main St 60417 708-672-3262
Joe Archer, prin. Fax 672-0512

Creve Coeur, Tazewell, Pop. 5,261
Creve Coeur SD 76 700/PK-8
400 N Highland St 61610 309-698-3600
Dr. Jack Wilt, supt. Fax 698-9827
www.cc76.k12.il.us/
Parkview JHS 300/5-8
800 Groveland St 61610 309-698-3610
Kathy Radorich, prin. Fax 698-3902

Crystal Lake, McHenry, Pop. 40,922
Community HSD 155 6,700/9-12
1 Virginia Rd 60014 815-455-8500
Dr. Jill Hawk, supt. Fax 459-5022
www.d155.org
Crystal Lake Central HS 1,400/9-12
45 W Franklin Ave 60014 815-459-2505
Steve Olson, prin. Fax 459-2536
Crystal Lake South HS 1,800/9-12
1200 S McHenry Ave 60014 815-455-3860
Marsha Potthoff, prin. Fax 455-5706
Prairie Ridge HS 1,700/9-12
6000 Dvorak Dr 60012 815-479-0404
Paul Humpa, prin. Fax 459-8993
Other Schools – See Cary

Crystal Lake CCSD 47 9,000/K-8
300 Commerce Dr 60014 815-459-6070
Ronald Miller, supt. Fax 459-0263
www.d47schools.org
Beardsley MS 1,100/6-8
515 E Crystal Lake Ave 60014 815-477-5897
Ron Ludwig, prin. Fax 479-5119
Bernotas MS 1,000/6-8
170 N Oak St 60014 815-459-9210
Lori Sorensen, prin. Fax 479-5116
Lundahl MS 1,000/6-8
560 Nash Rd 60014 815-459-5971
Donn Mendoza, prin. Fax 479-5113

Prairie Grove Consolidated SD 46 — 1,000/K-8
3223 IL Route 176 60014 — 815-459-3023
Dr. Mary Fasbender, supt. — Fax 356-0519
www.dist46.org/
Prairie Grove JHS — 6-8
3225 IL Route 176 60014 — 815-459-3557
Ronald May, prin. — Fax 459-3785

Cosmetology & Spa Institute — Post-Sec.
700 E Terra Cotta Ave 60014 — 815-385-9663
McHenry County College — Post-Sec.
8900 US Highway 14 60012 — 815-455-3700

Cuba, Fulton, Pop. 1,382
Fulton County CUSD 3 — 500/PK-12
PO Box 79 61427 — 309-785-5021
Brad Kenser, supt. — Fax 785-5432
www.cuba.fulton.k12.il.us
Cuba HS — 200/9-12
20325 N State Route 97 61427 — 309-785-5023
Daryle Coleman, prin. — Fax 785-5102
Cuba MS — 100/7-8
20325 N State Route 97 61427 — 309-785-5023
Daryle Coleman, prin. — Fax 785-5102

Cullom, Livingston, Pop. 541
Tri-Point CUSD 6-J
Supt. — See Kempton
Tri-Point HS — 200/9-12
PO Box 316 60929 — 815-689-2110
Todd Bean, prin. — Fax 689-2377

Dakota, Stephenson, Pop. 489
Dakota CUSD 201 — 900/PK-12
400 Campus Dr 61018 — 815-449-2832
Wanda Herrmann, supt. — Fax 449-2459
www.dakota201.com/
Dakota JSHS — 500/7-12
300 Campus Dr 61018 — 815-449-2812
Debra Keith, prin. — Fax 449-2322

Danville, Vermilion, Pop. 32,920
Danville CCSD 118 — 6,400/PK-12
516 N Jackson St 61832 — 217-444-1004
Nanette Mellen, supt. — Fax 444-1021
www.danville.k12.il.us
Danville HS — 1,500/9-12
202 E Fairchild St 61832 — 217-444-1500
Marla Bauerle-Hill, prin. — Fax 444-1529
North Ridge MS — 800/6-8
1619 N Jackson St 61832 — 217-444-3400
Mark Goodwin, prin. — Fax 444-3488
South View MS — 700/6-8
133 E 9th St 61832 — 217-444-1800
Gail Garner, prin. — Fax 431-5874

Oakwood CUSD 76
Supt. — See Fithian
Oakwood JHS — 200/7-8
21600 N 900 East Rd 61834 — 217-443-2883
Debbie Clow, prin. — Fax 776-2228

VOTEC
15009 Catlin Tilton Rd 61834 — 217-442-0461
Kay Smoot, supt. — Fax 431-5861
VOTEC — Vo/Tech
15009 Catlin Tilton Rd 61834 — 217-442-0461
Kay Smoot, prin. — Fax 431-5891

Concept College of Cosmetology — Post-Sec.
2500 Georgetown Rd 61832 — 217-442-9329
Danville Area Community College — Post-Sec.
2000 E Main St 61832 — 217-443-3222
First Baptist Christian S — 300/PK-12
1211 N Vermilion St 61832 — 217-442-2434
Robert Lazzell, prin. — Fax 442-8731
Lakeview College of Nursing — Post-Sec.
903 N Logan Ave 61832 — 217-443-5238
Schlarman HS — 9-12
2112 N Vermilion St 61832 — 217-442-2725
Robert Rice, prin. — Fax 442-0293

Darien, DuPage, Pop. 22,730
Cass SD 63 — 900/PK-8
8502 Bailey Rd 60561 — 630-985-2000
Dr. Kerry Foderaro, supt. — Fax 985-0225
www.cassd63.org
Cass JHS — 400/5-8
8502 Bailey Rd 60561 — 630-985-1900
Mark Enright, prin. — Fax 985-2881

Darien SD 61 — 1,700/PK-8
7414 S Cass Ave 60561 — 630-968-7505
Warren Johnson, supt. — Fax 968-0872
www.darien61.org
Eisenhower JHS — 600/6-8
1410 75th St 60561 — 630-964-5200
Mike Fitzgerald, prin. — Fax 968-8002

Hinsdale Township HSD 86
Supt. — See Hinsdale
Hinsdale South HS — 1,900/9-12
7401 Clarendon Hills Rd 60561 — 630-468-4000
Dr. Claudia Geocaris, prin. — Fax 920-8649

Decatur, Macon, Pop. 77,836
Decatur Area Technical Academy
300 E Eldorado St 62523 — 217-424-3070
Steve Clark, dir.
Decatur Area Technical Academy — Vo/Tech
300 E Eldorado St 62523 — 217-424-3070
Steve Clark, dir.

Decatur SD 61 — 9,200/PK-12
101 W Cerro Gordo St 62523 — 217-424-3011
Gloria Davis, supt. — Fax 424-3009
www.dps61.org/
Decatur MS — 700/7-8
1 Educational Park 62526 — 217-876-8017
Howard Edwards, prin. — Fax 876-8003
Eisenhower HS — 1,200/9-12
1200 S 16th St 62521 — 217-424-3100
April Hicklin, prin. — Fax 424-3050
Jefferson MS — 700/7-8
4735 E Cantrell St 62521 — 217-424-3190
Shannen Ray, prin. — Fax 424-3189
MacArthur HS — 1,300/9-12
1155 N Fairview Ave 62522 — 217-424-3156
Dean Schultz, prin. — Fax 424-3167

Decatur Christian S — 300/PK-12
3475 N Maple Ave 62526 — 217-877-5636
Roger Cox, admin. — Fax 877-7627

Lutheran School Association — 500/K-12
2001 E Mound Rd 62526 — 217-233-2001
Brian Ryherd, supt. — Fax 233-2002
Millikin University — Post-Sec.
1184 W Main St 62522 — 217-424-6211
Mr. John's School of Cosmetology — Post-Sec.
1745 E Eldorado St 62521 — 217-423-8173
Richland Community College — Post-Sec.
1 College Park 62521 — 217-875-7200
St. Teresa HS — 300/9-12
2710 N Water St 62526 — 217-875-2431
Joseph McDaniel, prin. — Fax 875-2436

Deerfield, Lake, Pop. 19,471
Deerfield SD 109 — 3,100/K-8
517 Deerfield Rd 60015 — 847-945-1844
Dr. Renee Goier, supt. — Fax 945-1853
www.dps109.org
Caruso MS — 600/6-8
1801 Montgomery Rd 60015 — 847-945-8430
Andrew Henrikson, prin. — Fax 945-1963
Shepard MS — 500/6-8
440 Grove Ave 60015 — 847-948-0620
Jay Monier, prin. — Fax 948-8589

Township HSD 113
Supt. — See Highland Park
Deerfield HS — 1,700/9-12
1959 Waukegan Rd 60015 — 224-632-3000
Dr. Al Fleming, prin. — Fax 632-3700

Trinity Evangelical Divinity School — Post-Sec.
2065 Half Day Rd 60015 — 800-345-8337
Trinity International University — Post-Sec.
2065 Half Day Rd 60015 — 847-945-8800

DeKalb, DeKalb, Pop. 42,085
De Kalb CUSD 428 — 5,500/PK-12
901 S 4th St 60115 — 815-754-2350
Dr. Paul Beilfuss, supt. — Fax 758-6933
dist428.org
De Kalb HS — 1,600/9-12
1515 S 4th St 60115 — 815-754-2100
Lindsey Hall, prin. — Fax 758-0931
Huntley MS — 600/6-8
821 S 7th St 60115 — 815-754-2241
Roger Scott, prin. — Fax 758-6062
Rosette MS — 700/6-8
650 N 1st St 60115 — 815-754-2226
Craig Bowers, prin. — Fax 758-1097

Northern Illinois University 60115 — Post-Sec.
815-753-1000

De Land, Vermilion, Pop. 473
Deland-Weldon CUSD 57 — 200/PK-12
304 E IL Route 10 61839 — 217-736-2311
Gary Brashear, supt. — Fax 736-2654
www.delwel.k12.il.us/
Deland-Weldon HS — 50/9-12
304 E IL Route 10 61839 — 217-664-3314
Russ Corey, prin. — Fax 736-2654
Other Schools – See Weldon

Delavan, Tazewell, Pop. 1,777
Delavan CUSD 703 — 500/PK-12
907 Locust St 61734 — 309-244-8283
Mary Parker, supt. — Fax 244-7696
Delavan HS — 100/9-12
907 Locust St 61734 — 309-244-8285
Keith Kittell, prin. — Fax 244-8694
Delavan JHS — 100/7-8
907 Locust St 61734 — 309-244-8285
Keith Kittell, prin. — Fax 244-8694

De Pue, Bureau, Pop. 1,791
De Pue Unit SD 103 — 400/PK-12
PO Box 800 61322 — 815-447-2121
R. Thomas Dobrich, supt. — Fax 447-2067
www.bhsroe.k12.il.us/depue/
De Pue HS — 100/9-12
PO Box 800 61322 — 815-447-2121
Steve Sash, prin. — Fax 447-2067

Des Plaines, Cook, Pop. 56,551
CCSD 62 — 4,900/PK-8
777 E Algonquin Rd 60016 — 847-824-1136
Jane Westerhold, supt. — Fax 824-0612
www.d62.org
Algonquin MS — 800/6-8
767 E Algonquin Rd 60016 — 847-824-1205
Martin Wolf, prin. — Fax 824-1270
Chippewa MS — 700/6-8
123 N 8th Ave 60016 — 847-824-1503
Eric Bailey, prin. — Fax 824-1514

Community Consolidated SD 59
Supt. — See Arlington Heights
Friendship JHS — 600/6-8
550 Elizabeth Ln 60018 — 847-593-4350
Jane Paterala, prin. — Fax 593-7182

East Maine SD 63 — 3,500/PK-8
10150 Dee Rd 60016 — 847-299-1900
Dr. Kathleen Williams, supt. — Fax 299-9963
www.emsd63.org
Other Schools – See Niles

Maine Township HSD 207
Supt. — See Park Ridge
Maine West HS — 2,300/9-12
1755 S Wolf Rd 60018 — 847-827-6176
Audrey Haugan, prin. — Fax 296-4916

Oakton Community College — Post-Sec.
1600 E Golf Rd 60016 — 847-635-1600
Willows Academy — 200/6-12
1012 E Thacker St 60016 — 847-824-6900
Mary Keenley, prin. — Fax 824-7089

Dieterich, Effingham, Pop. 597
Dieterich CUSD 30 — 500/K-12
PO Box 187 62424 — 217-925-5249
Bruce Owen, supt. — Fax 925-5447
www.dieterich.k12.il.us/
Dieterich JSHS — 300/7-12
PO Box 187 62424 — 217-925-5247
Daniel Sarver, prin. — Fax 925-5249

Divernon, Sangamon, Pop. 1,145
Divernon CUSD 13 — 300/PK-12
PO Box 20 62530 — 217-628-3414
Kenneth Hendriksen, supt. — Fax 628-3814
www.divy.net

Divernon HS — 100/9-12
PO Box 20 62530 — 217-628-3414
Ronald Ervin, prin. — Fax 628-3814

Dixmoor, Cook, Pop. 3,813
West Harvey-Dixmoor SD 147
Supt. — See Harvey
Parks MS — 500/6-8
14700 Robey Ave 60426 — 708-371-9575
Abigail Phillips, prin. — Fax 371-1412

Dixon, Lee, Pop. 15,372
Dixon Unit SD 170 — 3,000/PK-12
1335 Franklin Grove Rd 61021 — 815-284-7722
James L. Brown, supt. — Fax 284-8576
www.dps.k12.il.us
Dixon HS — 1,100/9-12
300 Lincoln Statue Dr 61021 — 815-284-7723
Michael Grady, prin. — Fax 284-4297
Reagan MS — 900/5-8
620 Division St 61021 — 815-284-7725
Travis McGuire, prin. — Fax 284-1711

Faith Christian S — 100/K-12
7571 S Ridge Rd 61021 — 815-652-4806
Liandro Arellano, supt. — Fax 652-4871
Jack Mabley Development Center — Post-Sec.
1120 Washington Ave 61021 — 815-288-8300
Sauk Valley Community College — Post-Sec.
173 IL Route 2 61021 — 815-288-5511

Dolton, Cook, Pop. 24,504
Dolton SD 148 — 2,900/PK-8
PO Box 160 60419 — 708-841-2290
Dr. Ruby Roberson, supt. — Fax 841-5048
www.district148.net
Roosevelt JHS — 500/7-8
111 W 146th St 60419 — 708-201-2071
Shalonda Randle, prin. — Fax 849-1285

Thornton Twp. HSD 205
Supt. — See South Holland
Thornridge HS — 1,800/9-12
15000 Cottage Grove Ave 60419 — 708-271-4401
Kim Waller, prin. — Fax 271-5028

Dongola, Union, Pop. 803
Dongola Unit SD 66 — 300/K-12
PO Box 190 62926 — 618-827-3841
Nancy Dillow, supt. — Fax 827-4641
www.dongolaschool.com/
Dongola HS — 100/9-12
PO Box 190 62926 — 618-827-3524
Brett Gayer, prin. — Fax 827-4422
Dongola JHS — 100/7-8
PO Box 190 62926 — 618-827-3524
Brett Gayer, prin. — Fax 827-4422

Donovan, Iroquois, Pop. 333
Donovan CUSD 3 — 500/K-12
PO Box 186 60931 — 815-486-7397
Jerome Pankey, supt. — Fax 486-7060
www.donovan.k12.il.us/
Donovan HS — 200/9-12
PO Box 186 60931 — 815-486-7395
Scott Strong, prin. — Fax 486-7060
Donovan JHS — 100/7-8
PO Box 186 60931 — 815-486-7395
Scott Strong, prin. — Fax 486-7060

Downers Grove, DuPage, Pop. 49,094
Center Cass SD 66 — 1,300/PK-8
699 Plainfield Rd 60516 — 630-783-5000
Dr. Jay Tiede, supt. — Fax 910-0980
www.ccsd66.org/
Lakeview JHS — 400/6-8
701 Plainfield Rd 60516 — 630-985-2700
Paul Windsor, prin. — Fax 985-1545

Community HSD 99 — 5,500/9-12
6301 Springside Ave 60516 — 630-795-7100
David Eblen, supt. — Fax 795-7199
www.csd99.org
Downers Grove North HS — 2,300/9-12
4436 Main St 60515 — 630-795-8400
Maria Ward, prin. — Fax 795-8499
Downers Grove South HS — 3,200/9-12
1436 Norfolk St 60516 — 630-795-8500
Mark McDonald, prin. — Fax 795-8599

Downers Grove SD 58 — 4,800/PK-8
1860 63rd St 60516 — 630-719-5800
Dale Martin, supt. — Fax 719-9857
www.dg58.dupage.k12.il.us
Herrick MS — 700/7-8
4435 Middaugh Ave 60515 — 630-719-5810
Dr. Mark Manzi, prin. — Fax 719-1628
O'Neill MS — 600/7-8
635 59th St 60516 — 630-719-5815
Matthew Durbala, prin. — Fax 719-1436

Bridge HS — 50/8-12
2318 Wisconsin Ave 60515 — 630-964-1722
Mary Witt, prin.
Marquette Manor Baptist Academy — 400/PK-12
333 75th St 60516 — 630-964-5363
Steven Tompkins, prin. — Fax 964-5385
Midwestern University — Post-Sec.
555 31st St 60515 — 630-969-4400

Downs, McLean, Pop. 745
Tri-Valley CUSD 3 — 1,100/PK-12
410 E Washington St 61736 — 309-378-2351
Brad Cox, supt. — Fax 378-2223
tri-valley.k12.il.us
Tri-Valley HS — 300/9-12
503 E Washington St 61736 — 309-378-2911
Dave Mouser, prin. — Fax 378-3202
Tri-Valley MS — 400/4-8
505 E Washington St 61736 — 309-378-3414
Jill Lanier, prin. — Fax 378-3214

Cornerstone Christian Acad of McLean Co. — 400/PK-12
22017 E 1200 North Rd 61736 — 309-662-9900
Becky Shamess, admin. — Fax 662-9904

Dundee, Kane, Pop. 4,494
Community Unit SD 300
Supt. — See Carpentersville
Dundee MS — 900/6-8
37W450 IL Route 72 60118 — 847-426-1485
Kara Vicente, prin. — Fax 426-4008

Hair Professionals Academy Post-Sec.
825 Village Quarter Rd # B 60118 847-622-7871

Dunlap, Peoria, Pop. 904
Dunlap CUSD 323 2,700/PK-12
PO Box 395 61525 309-243-7716
Jeanne Williamson, supt. Fax 243-7720
www.dunlapcusd.net
Dunlap HS 800/9-12
PO Box 365 61525 309-243-7751
Michael Miller, prin. Fax 243-9565
Dunlap MS 600/6-8
5200 W Cedar Hills Dr 61525 309-243-7778
Thomas Welsh, prin. Fax 243-1136

Dupo, Saint Clair, Pop. 3,957
Dupo CUSD 196 1,300/PK-12
600 Louisa Ave 62239 618-286-3812
Dr. Michael Koebel, supt. Fax 286-5554
Dupo HS, 600 Louisa Ave 62239 400/9-12
Windy Winfield, prin. 618-286-3214
Dupo JHS, 600 Louisa Ave 62239 200/7-8
Windy Winfield, prin. 618-286-3214

Du Quoin, Perry, Pop. 6,412
Du Quoin CUSD 300 1,500/PK-12
845 E Jackson St 62832 618-542-3856
Gary Kelly, supt. Fax 542-6614
dqud300.perry.k12.il.us
Du Quoin HS 500/9-12
500 E South St 62832 618-542-4744
Lybrand Beard, prin. Fax 542-8822
Du Quoin MS 500/5-8
845 E Jackson St 62832 618-542-2646
Aaron Hill, prin. Fax 542-4373

Christian Fellowship S 100/PK-12
PO Box 227 62832 618-542-6800
Larry Bullock, admin. Fax 542-6806

Durand, Winnebago, Pop. 1,077
Durand CUSD 322 700/K-12
200 W South St 61024 815-248-2171
Douglas DeSchepper Ed.D., supt. Fax 248-2599
www.durandbulldogs.com
Durand HS 200/9-12
200 W South St 61024 815-248-2171
Jeff Pinker, prin. Fax 248-2599
Durand JHS 100/7-8
200 W South St 61024 815-248-2171
Kurt Alberstett, prin. Fax 248-2599

Dwight, Livingston, Pop. 4,360
Dwight Common SD 232 500/PK-8
801 S Columbia St 60420 815-584-6216
Dale Adams, supt. Fax 584-2950
www.dgs.k12.il.us
Dwight Common MS 6-8
801 S Columbia St 60420 815-584-6220
Mark Pagel, prin. Fax 584-3771

Dwight Twp. HSD 230 300/9-12
801 S Franklin St 60420 815-584-6217
Dale Adams, supt. Fax 584-2950
www.dwight.k12.il.us
Dwight Township HS 300/9-12
801 S Franklin St 60420 815-584-6201
Bob Richardson, prin. Fax 584-2950

Earlville, LaSalle, Pop. 1,821
Earlville CUSD 9 500/PK-12
PO Box 539 60518 815-246-8361
Patricia Hahto, supt. Fax 246-8672
Earlville HS 100/9-12
PO Box 539 60518 815-246-8361
Fred Nestler, prin. Fax 246-8672

East Alton, Madison, Pop. 6,609
East Alton SD 13 1,000/PK-8
210 E Saint Louis Ave 62024 618-433-2150
Michael Gray, supt. Fax 254-5048
www.easd13.org/
East Alton MS 300/6-8
1000 3rd St 62024 618-433-2201
Eric Frankford, prin. Fax 433-2203

East Dubuque, Jo Daviess, Pop. 1,985
East Dubuque Unit SD 119 600/PK-12
200 Parklane Dr 61025 815-747-2111
Katherine Bryant, supt. Fax 747-3516
www.edbqhs.org
East Dubuque HS 200/9-12
200 Parklane Dr 61025 815-747-3188
Greg Herbst, prin. Fax 747-3516

East Moline, Rock Island, Pop. 21,250
East Moline SD 37 2,400/PK-8
3555 19 St EM 61244 309-792-2887
Garry Rudish, supt.
www.emsd37.org
Glenview MS 1,000/5-8
3100 7th St 61244 309-755-1919
Jeff Fairweather, prin. Fax 752-2551

United Township AVC
1275 Avenue Of The Cities 61244 309-752-1633
Dr. Barbara Suelter, admin. Fax 752-1608
uths.revealed.net/
United Township Area Career Center Vo/Tech
1275 Avenue Of The Cities 61244 309-752-1691
Larry Shimmin, dir.

United Township HSD 30 1,800/9-12
1275 Avenue of the Cities 61244 309-752-1633
Barbara L. Suelter Ed.D., supt. Fax 752-1608
uths.revealed.net/
United Township HS 1,800/9-12
1275 Avenue of the Cities 61244 309-752-1633
Fred Segura, prin. Fax 752-1608

East Moline Christian S 300/K-12
900 46th Ave 61244 309-796-1485
Rev. James R. Patrick, prin. Fax 796-1152
La' James College of Hairstyling Post-Sec.
485 Avenue of the Cities 61244 309-755-1313

Easton, Mason, Pop. 370
Illini Central CUSD 189
Supt. — See Mason City
Illini Central MS 200/6-8
12544 N State Route 10 62633 309-562-7251
Jeremiah Auble, prin. Fax 562-7256

East Peoria, Tazewell, Pop. 22,536
East Peoria Community HSD 309 1,100/9-12
1401 E Washington St 61611 309-694-8300
Cliff Cobert, supt. Fax 694-8322
www.epchs.k12.il.us/
East Peoria Community HS 1,100/9-12
1401 E Washington St 61611 309-694-8300
Paul Whittington, prin. Fax 694-8322

East Peoria SD 86 1,800/PK-8
601 Taylor St 61611 309-427-5100
Tony Ingold, supt. Fax 698-1364
www.epd86.org
Central JHS 600/6-8
601 Taylor St Ste 1 61611 309-427-5200
Joe Sander, prin. Fax 699-2595

Oehrlein School of Cosmetology Post-Sec.
100 Meadow Ave 61611 309-699-1561

East Saint Louis, Saint Clair, Pop. 30,995
East St. Louis SD 189 8,400/PK-12
1005 State St 62201 618-646-3000
Theresa Saunders Ed.D., supt. Fax 583-7186
www.estlouis.stclair.k12.il.us/
Clark MS 600/6-8
3310 State St 62205 618-646-3750
Roland Coleman, prin. Fax 646-3758
East Saint Louis HS 2,100/9-12
4901 State St 62205 618-646-3700
Terrence Curry, prin. Fax 646-3708
Lincoln MS 800/6-8
12 S 10th St 62201 618-646-3770
Luberta Allen, prin. Fax 646-3778
Younge MS 700/6-8
3939 Caseyville Ave 62204 618-646-3760
Vivian Cockrell, prin. Fax 646-3768

Vee's School of Beauty Culture Post-Sec.
2701 State St 62205 618-274-1751

Edinburg, Christian, Pop. 1,140
Edinburg CUSD 4 400/PK-12
100 E Martin St 62531 217-623-5603
Susan Dudley, supt. Fax 623-5604
www.edinburgschools.net
Edinburg HS 100/9-12
100 E Martin St 62531 217-623-5631
Matt Graham, prin. Fax 623-5604
Edinburg JHS 100/6-8
100 E Martin St 62531 217-623-5733
Matt Graham, prin. Fax 623-5604

Edwardsville, Madison, Pop. 24,047
Edwardsville CUSD 7 7,100/PK-12
708 Saint Louis St 62025 618-656-1182
Dr. Ed Hightower, supt. Fax 692-7423
www.ecusd7.org
Edwardsville HS 2,300/9-12
6161 Center Grove Rd 62025 618-656-7100
Norm Bohnenstiehl, prin. Fax 655-1037
Liberty MS 900/6-8
1 District Dr 62025 618-655-6800
Dennis Cramsey, prin. Fax 655-6801
Lincoln MS 800/6-8
145 West St 62025 618-656-0485
Steve Stuart, prin. Fax 659-1268

Alvareita's College of Cosmetology Post-Sec.
333 S Kansas St 62025 618-656-2593
Metro East Lutheran HS 200/9-12
6305 Center Grove Rd 62025 618-656-0043
Daniel Kostencki, prin. Fax 656-3315
Southern Illinois Univ. Edwardsville Post-Sec.
62026 618-650-2000

Effingham, Effingham, Pop. 12,440
Effingham CUSD 40 3,000/PK-12
PO Box 130 62401 217-540-1500
Daniel Clasby Ph.D., supt. Fax 540-1510
www.effingham.k12.il.us
Effingham HS 900/9-12
1301 W Grove Ave 62401 217-540-1100
Mike McCollum, prin. Fax 540-1102
Effingham JHS 700/6-8
600 S Henrietta St 62401 217-540-1300
Scott Holst, prin. Fax 540-1362

St. Anthony of Padua HS 200/9-12
PO Box 545 62401 217-342-6969
Marianne Larimer, prin. Fax 342-6997

Eldorado, Saline, Pop. 4,416
Eldorado CUSD 4 1,200/PK-12
2200A Illinois Ave 62930 618-273-6394
Gary Siebert, supt. Fax 273-9311
www.eldorado.k12.il.us/
Eldorado HS 400/9-12
2200 Illinois Ave 62930 618-273-2881
Gary Siebert, prin. Fax 273-8153
Eldorado MS 300/6-8
1907 1st St 62930 618-273-8056
Angie Attebury, prin. Fax 273-2943

Elgin, Kane, Pop. 98,645
SD U-46 38,400/PK-12
355 E Chicago St 60120 847-888-5000
Connie L. Neale Ph.D., supt. Fax 608-4173
www.u-46.org/
Abbott MS 600/7-8
949 Van St 60123 847-888-5160
Greg Schneider, prin. Fax 608-2740
Elgin HS 2,300/9-12
1200 Maroon Dr 60120 847-888-5100
David Smiley, prin. Fax 888-6997
Ellis MS 500/7-8
225 S Liberty St 60120 847-888-5151
Perry Hayes, prin. Fax 608-2744
Kimball MS 800/7-8
451 N Mclean Blvd 60123 847-888-5290
Alan Tamburrino, prin. Fax 608-2749
Larkin HS 2,500/9-12
1475 Larkin Ave 60123 847-888-5200
Richard Webb, prin. Fax 888-6996
Larsen MS 500/7-8
665 Dundee Ave 60120 847-888-5250
Dr. Randy Hodges, prin. Fax 888-7172
Other Schools – See Bartlett, South Elgin, Streamwood

Cannella School of Hair Design Post-Sec.
113 W Chicago St 60123 847-742-6611
DeVry University Post-Sec.
385 Airport Rd 60123 847-622-1135

Einstein Academy 100/PK-12
747 Davis Rd 60123 847-697-3836
Cathy Ilani, hdmstr. Fax 697-6085
Elgin Academy 400/K-12
350 Park St 60120 847-695-0300
John Cooper, prin. Fax 695-5017
Elgin Community College Post-Sec.
1700 Spartan Dr 60123 847-697-1000
Fox Valley Lutheran Academy 50/9-12
220 Division St 60120 847-468-8207
Janet Zimdahl, prin. Fax 742-2930
Harvest Christian Academy 600/PK-10
1000 N Randall Rd 60123 847-214-3500
Dr. Jeff Mattner, supt. Fax 214-3501
Institute of Islamic Education 200/6-12
1048 Bluff City Blvd 60120 847-695-4685
Mohammad Saleem, prin. Fax 695-4806
Judson College Post-Sec.
1151 N State St 60123 847-695-2500
St. Edward Central Catholic HS 500/9-12
335 Locust St 60123 847-741-7535
Rev. Edward Seisser, admin. Fax 695-4682
Westminster Christian S 500/PK-12
2700 W Highland Ave, 847-695-0310
Chad Dirkse, admin. Fax 695-0135

Elizabeth, Jo Daviess, Pop. 673
Jo Daviess-Carroll AVC
PO Box 602 61028 815-858-2203
Fax 858-2316
www.jdcavc.org
Jo Daviess-Carroll AVC Vo/Tech
PO Box 602 61028 815-858-2203
Joyce McCready, prin. Fax 858-2316

Elizabethtown, Hardin, Pop. 335
Hardin County CUSD 1 700/PK-12
PO Box 218 62931 618-287-2411
Ernie Fowler, supt. Fax 287-2421
Hardin County HS 200/9-12
RR 2 62931 618-287-2141
Ernie Fowler, prin. Fax 287-8381
Hardin County JHS 100/7-8
RR 2 62931 618-287-2141
Ernie Fowler, prin. Fax 287-8381

Elk Grove Village, Cook, Pop. 34,025
Community Consolidated SD 59
Supt. — See Arlington Heights
Grove JHS 900/6-8
777 W Elk Grove Blvd 60007 847-593-4367
Enza Papeck, prin. Fax 472-3001

Schaumburg CCSD 54
Supt. — See Schaumburg
Mead JHS 700/7-8
1765 Biesterfield Rd 60007 847-357-6000
Steve Pearce, prin. Fax 357-6001

Township HSD 214
Supt. — See Arlington Heights
Elk Grove Village HS 2,000/9-12
500 W Elk Grove Blvd 60007 847-718-4400
Frank DeRosa, prin. Fax 718-4417

Elkville, Jackson, Pop. 939
Elverado CUSD 196 500/PK-12
PO Box 130 62932 618-568-1321
Rebecca Canty, supt. Fax 568-1152
Elverado HS 200/9-12
PO Box 217 62932 618-568-1104
Joy Battagliotti, prin. Fax 568-1551
Other Schools – See Vergennes

Elmhurst, DuPage, Pop. 44,976
Elmhurst SD 205 7,500/PK-12
130 W Madison St 60126 630-834-4530
Dr. Lynn Krizic, supt. Fax 617-2345
www.elmhurst.k12.il.us
Bryan MS 500/6-8
111 W Butterfield Rd 60126 630-617-2350
Rachel Overton, prin. Fax 617-2232
Churchville MS 400/6-8
155 E Victory Pkwy 60126 630-832-8682
Matthew Haug, prin. Fax 617-2387
Sandburg MS 700/6-8
345 E Saint Charles Rd 60126 630-834-4534
Howard Holbrook, prin. Fax 617-2380
York Community HS 2,400/9-12
355 W Saint Charles Rd 60126 630-617-2400
Diana Smith, prin. Fax 617-2399

Cannella School of Hair Design Post-Sec.
191 N York St 60126 630-833-6118
Elmhurst College Post-Sec.
190 S Prospect Ave 60126 630-279-4100
Immaculate Conception HS 200/9-12
217 S Cottage Hill Ave 60126 630-530-3460
Pamela Levar, prin. Fax 530-2290
Timothy Christian HS 400/9-12
1061 S Prospect Ave 60126 630-833-7575
Clyde Rinsema, prin. Fax 833-9821

Elmwood, Peoria, Pop. 1,893
Elmwood CUSD 322 700/PK-12
301 W Butternut St 61529 309-742-8464
Thomas Kahn, supt. Fax 742-8812
www.elmwood.peoria.k12.il.us
Elmwood HS 200/9-12
301 W Butternut St 61529 309-742-2851
Stan Matheny, prin. Fax 742-8093
Elmwood JHS 100/7-8
301 W Butternut St 61529 309-742-2851
Stan Matheny, prin. Fax 742-8093

Elmwood Park, Cook, Pop. 24,499
Elmwood Park CUSD 401 2,800/PK-12
8201 W Fullerton Ave 60707 708-452-7292
Dr. Douglas Rudig, supt. Fax 452-9504
www.sd401.k12.il.us
Elm MS 500/7-8
7607 W Cortland St 60707 708-452-3550
Joan McGarry, prin. Fax 452-0662
Elmwood Park HS 1,000/9-12
8201 W Fullerton Ave 60707 708-583-6211
James Jennings, prin. Fax 452-0732

El Paso, Woodford, Pop. 2,748
El Paso-Gridley CUSD 11 300/PK-12
97 W 5th St 61738 309-527-4410
William James, supt. Fax 527-4040
www.elpaso375.org/
El Paso-Gridley HS 9-12
600 N Elm St 61738 309-527-4415
Karen Krug, prin. Fax 527-4411
Other Schools – See Gridley

Elsah, Jersey, Pop. 640

Principia College 62028 Post-Sec.
618-374-2131

Erie, Whiteside, Pop. 1,573
Erie CUSD 1 700/PK-12
520 5th Ave 61250 309-659-2239
Michael D. Ryan, supt. Fax 659-2230
www.erie1.net
Erie HS 200/9-12
435 6th Ave 61250 309-659-2239
Tim McConnell, prin. Fax 659-2514
Erie MS, 500 5th Ave 61250 200/5-8
Keith Morgan, prin. 309-659-2239

Eureka, Woodford, Pop. 5,084
Eureka CUSD 140 1,600/PK-12
109 W Cruger Ave 61530 309-467-3737
Dr. Randy K. Crump, supt. Fax 467-2377
www.eureka.wodfrd.k12.il.us
Eureka HS 500/9-12
200 W Cruger Ave 61530 309-467-2361
Richard Wherley, prin. Fax 467-2648
Eureka MS 500/5-8
2005 S Main St 61530 309-467-3771
Robert Gold, prin. Fax 467-2052

Eureka College Post-Sec.
300 E College Ave 61530 309-467-3721

Evanston, Cook, Pop. 75,236
Evanston CCSD 65 6,700/PK-8
1500 McDaniel Ave 60201 847-859-8000
Dr. Hardy Murphy, supt. Fax 859-8701
www.district65.net/
Chute MS 600/6-8
1400 Oakton St 60202 847-859-8600
James McHolland, prin. Fax 492-7956
Haven MS 600/6-8
2417 Prairie Ave 60201 847-859-8200
Kathleen Roberson, prin. Fax 492-9983
Nichols MS 600/6-8
800 Greenleaf St 60202 847-859-8660
Gordon Hood, prin. Fax 492-7880

Evanston Township HSD 202 3,100/9-12
1600 Dodge Ave 60201 847-424-7220
Dr. Eric Witherspoon, supt. Fax 492-3872
www.eths.k12.il.us
Evanston Township HS 3,100/9-12
1600 Dodge Ave 60201 847-424-7200
Marilyn Madden, prin. Fax 492-3872

Garrett Evangelical Theological Seminary Post-Sec.
2121 Sheridan Rd 60201 847-866-3900
Northwestern University Post-Sec.
1801 Hinman Ave 60208 847-491-3741
Pivot Point International Post-Sec.
1560 Sherman Ave Ste 700 60201 847-866-0500
Roycemore S 300/PK-12
640 Lincoln St 60201 847-866-6055
Joseph Becker, hdmstr. Fax 866-6545
St. Francis Hospital Post-Sec.
355 Ridge Ave 60202 847-492-4000
Seabury-Western Theological Seminary Post-Sec.
2122 Sheridan Rd 60201 847-328-9300

Evansville, Randolph, Pop. 697

Christ our Savior Lutheran HS 100/9-12
901 Church St 62242 618-853-7300
Sherry L. Prange, prin. Fax 853-7361

Evergreen Park, Cook, Pop. 19,876
Evergreen Park Community HSD 231 900/9-12
9901 S Kedzie Ave 60805 708-424-7400
Dr. James Gallagher, supt. Fax 424-7497
www.evergreenpark.org
Evergreen Park HS 900/9-12
9901 S Kedzie Ave 60805 708-424-7400
Dr. Beth Hart, prin. Fax 424-3045

Evergreen Park ESD 124 2,000/K-8
9400 S Sawyer Ave 60805 708-423-0950
Dr. Craig Fiegel, supt. Fax 423-4292
www.d124.org
Central JHS 500/7-8
9400 S Sawyer Ave 60805 708-424-0148
Kathleen Hatczel, prin. Fax 229-8406

Fairbury, Livingston, Pop. 3,919
Prairie Central CUSD 8 2,100/PK-12
605 N 7th St 61739 815-692-2504
Dr. John Capasso, supt. Fax 692-3195
www.prairiecentral.org
Prairie Central HS 700/9-12
411 N 7th St 61739 815-692-2355
Daniel Schmitt, prin. Fax 692-2438
Other Schools – See Forrest

Fairfield, Wayne, Pop. 5,230
Fairfield Community HSD 225 500/9-12
300 W King St 62837 618-842-2649
David Savage, supt. Fax 842-4465
fchs.wayne.k12.il.us
Fairfield Community HS 500/9-12
300 W King St 62837 618-842-2649
Diana Zurliene, prin. Fax 842-5187

Fairfield SD 112 700/PK-8
806 N 1st St 62837 618-842-6501
Rena Talbert, supt. Fax 842-2932
Center Street S 500/PK-PK, 4-
200 W Center St 62837 618-842-2679
Scott Fuhrhop, prin. Fax 842-4719

Frontier Community College Post-Sec.
RR 1 62837 618-842-3711

Fairview Heights, Saint Clair, Pop. 16,471
Grant CCSD 110 700/PK-8
10110 Old Lincoln Trl 62208 618-398-5577
Dr. Darrel Hardt, supt. Fax 398-5578
www.dist110.com
Grant MS 300/4-8
10110 Old Lincoln Trl 62208 618-397-2764
Matt Stines, prin. Fax 397-7809

Pontiac-William Holliday SD 105 600/PK-8
400 Ashland Dr 62208 618-233-2320
Darrell Sy, supt. Fax 233-0918
www.pontiac.stclair.k12.il.us
Pontiac JHS 200/7-8
400 Ashland Dr 62208 618-233-6004
Paul Holland, prin. Fax 233-0918

Farina, Fayette, Pop. 560
South Central CUSD 401
Supt. — See Kinmundy
South Central HS 9-12
RR 2 Box 91 62838 618-245-3363
David Scott, prin. Fax 245-6165

Farmer City, DeWitt, Pop. 2,005
Blue Ridge CUSD 18 900/PK-12
411 N John St 61842 309-928-9141
Jay Harnack, supt. Fax 928-5478
www.blueridge18.org
Blue Ridge HS 300/9-12
411 N John St 61842 309-928-2622
John Lawrence, prin. Fax 928-5301
Other Schools – See Mansfield

Farmington, Fulton, Pop. 2,514
Farmington Central CUSD 265 1,400/PK-12
212 N Lightfoot Rd 61531 309-245-1000
Mark Doan, supt. Fax 245-9161
www.dist265.com/
Farmington Central JHS 300/6-8
300 N Lightfoot Rd 61531 309-245-1000
Perry Miller, prin. Fax 245-9162
Farmington HS 400/9-12
310 N Lightfoot Rd 61531 309-245-1000
Scott Dearman, prin. Fax 245-9163

Findlay, Shelby, Pop. 685
Okaw Valley CUSD 302
Supt. — See Bethany
Okaw Valley MS 100/6-8
501 W Division 62534 217-756-8521
Joel Hackney, prin. Fax 756-8599

Fisher, Champaign, Pop. 1,654
Fisher CUSD 1 600/K-12
PO Box 700 61843 217-897-6125
Barbara Thompson, supt. Fax 897-6676
www.fisher.k12.il.us
Fisher JSHS 300/7-12
PO Box 670 61843 217-897-1225
Steve Wallick, prin. Fax 897-1708

Fithian, Vermilion, Pop. 552
Oakwood CUSD 76 1,100/PK-12
5834 US Route 150 61844 217-354-4355
Keven Forney, supt. Fax 354-2030
www.ltls.org/jxn.html
Oakwood HS 300/9-12
5870 US Route 150 61844 217-354-2358
Brenda Ludwig, prin. Fax 354-2603
Other Schools – See Danville

Flanagan, Livingston, Pop. 1,061
Flanagan CUSD 4 400/PK-12
PO Box 367 61740 815-796-2233
Roger Mitchell, supt. Fax 796-2856
www.flanagan.k12.il.us/
Flanagan HS 200/9-12
PO Box 367 61740 815-796-2291
Jerry Farris, prin. Fax 796-2856

Flora, Clay, Pop. 4,855
Flora CUSD 35 1,500/PK-12
444 S Locust St 62839 618-662-2412
Gary May, supt. Fax 662-4587
www.florail.us/schools.htm
Flora HS 400/9-12
600 S Locust St 62839 618-662-8316
Darrell Gummert, prin. Fax 662-2725
Henson JHS 300/6-8
609 N Stanford Rd 62839 618-662-8394
Rick Batchelor, prin. Fax 662-8395

Flossmoor, Cook, Pop. 9,390
Flossmoor SD 161
Supt. — See Chicago Heights
Parker JHS 1,000/6-8
2810 School St 60422 708-647-5400
Dr. Vanessa Atkins, prin. Fax 799-9207

Homewood-Flossmoor Community HSD 233 2,900/9-12
999 Kedzie Ave 60422 708-799-3000
Dr. Laura Murray, supt. Fax 799-8552
www.hfhighschool.org
Homewood-Flossmoor HS 2,900/9-12
999 Kedzie Ave 60422 708-799-3000
Dr. Von Mansfield, prin. Fax 335-6995

Ford Heights, Cook, Pop. 3,294
Ford Heights SD 169 600/PK-8
910 Woodlawn Ave 60411 708-758-1370
Gregory Jackson, supt. Fax 758-1372
Beck Upper Grade Center 200/5-8
800 E 14th St 60411 708-758-1400
Stephanie Stephens, prin. Fax 758-0711

Forest Park, Cook, Pop. 15,197
Forest Park SD 91 1,000/K-8
424 Des Plaines Ave 60130 708-366-5700
Dr. Louis Cavallo, supt. Fax 366-5761
www.forestparkschools.org
Forest Park MS 300/6-8
925 Beloit Ave 60130 708-366-5703
Karen Bukowski, prin. Fax 366-2091

Proviso Township HSD 209 4,800/9-12
8601 Roosevelt Rd 60130 708-338-5913
Dr. Stanley Fields, supt.
www.proviso.w-cook.k12.il.us/
Proviso Math & Science Academy 9-12
8601 Roosevelt Rd 60130 708-338-4100
Richard Bryant, prin. Fax 338-4199
Other Schools – See Hillside, Maywood

Forrest, Livingston, Pop. 1,202
Prairie Central CUSD 8
Supt. — See Fairbury
Prairie Central JHS 400/7-8
800 N Wood St 61741 815-657-8660
Danny Vaughan, prin. Fax 657-8677

Forreston, Ogle, Pop. 1,515
Forrestville Valley CUSD 221 1,000/PK-12
PO Box 665 61030 815-938-2036
Lowell Taylor, supt. Fax 938-9028
www.fvdistrict221.org
Forreston HS 300/9-12
PO Box 665 61030 815-938-2175
Christopher Shockey, prin. Fax 938-2546
Forreston MS 300/6-8
PO Box 665 61030 815-938-2195
Craig Mathers, prin. Fax 938-9028

Fox Lake, Lake, Pop. 10,736
Fox Lake Grade SD 114
Supt. — See Spring Grove
Stanton MS 6-8
101 Hawthorne Ln 60020 847-973-4200
William Lomas, prin. Fax 973-4210

Grant Community HSD 124 1,500/9-12
285 E Grand Ave 60020 847-587-2561
Dr. John Benedetti, supt. Fax 587-2991
www.grant.lake.k12.il.us/
Grant Community HS 1,500/9-12
285 E Grand Ave 60020 847-587-2561
Dr. Marilyn Howell, prin. Fax 587-2991

Fox River Grove, McHenry, Pop. 5,084
Fox River Grove SD 3 600/K-8
403 Orchard St 60021 847-516-5100
Jacqueline Krause, supt. Fax 516-9169
www.dist3.org
Fox River Grove MS 5-8
401 Orchard St 60021 847-516-5105
Tim Mahaffy, prin. Fax 516-5104

Frankfort, Will, Pop. 15,819
Frankfort CCSD 157C 1,800/PK-8
10482 Nebraska St 60423 815-469-5922
Dr. Robert J. Madonia, supt. Fax 469-8988
www.fsd157c.org
Hickory Creek MS 700/6-8
22150 S Owens Rd 60423 815-469-4474
Kevin Suchinski, prin. Fax 469-7930

Lincoln-Way Community HSD 210
Supt. — See New Lenox
Lincoln-Way East HS 3,400/9-12
201 Colorado Ave 60423 815-464-4000
Dr. Michael Gardner, prin. Fax 464-4132

Summit Hill SD 161 3,200/PK-8
21133 S 80th Ave 60423 815-469-9103
Keith Pain, supt. Fax 469-9201
Summit Hill JHS 800/7-8
20130 S Rosewood Dr 60423 815-469-4330
Beth Lind, prin. Fax 469-7348

Franklin, Morgan, Pop. 580
Franklin CUSD 1
Supt. — See Alexander
Franklin JSHS 200/6-12
PO Box 199 62638 217-675-2395
David Bruno, prin. Fax 675-2396

Franklin Grove, Lee, Pop. 1,019
Ashton-Franklin Center CUSD 275
Supt. — See Ashton
Ashton-Franklin Center MS 200/5-8
318 E South St, 815-456-2323
Joseph Hilliker, prin. Fax 456-3211

Franklin Park, Cook, Pop. 18,490
Franklin Park SD 84 1,300/PK-8
2915 Maple St 60131 847-455-4230
David Nemec, supt. Fax 455-9094
www.d84.org/
Hester JHS 400/6-8
2836 Gustav St 60131 847-455-2150
John Kosirog, prin. Fax 455-0945

Leyden Community HSD 212 3,500/9-12
3400 Rose St 60131 847-451-3000
Dr. Kathryn Robbins, supt. Fax 671-9079
www.leyden212.org
East Leyden HS 1,900/9-12
3400 Rose St 60131 847-451-3023
Dr. Beth Concannon, prin. Fax 451-3644
Other Schools – See Northlake

Mannheim SD 83 2,800/K-8
10401 Grand Ave 60131 847-455-4413
Bruce A. Lane Ed.D., supt. Fax 451-8290
www.d83.org/
Other Schools – See Melrose Park

Freeburg, Saint Clair, Pop. 4,092
Freeburg CCSD 70 700/PK-8
408 S Belleville St 62243 618-539-3188
Dr. Rob Hawkins, supt. Fax 539-5795
www.frg70.stclair.k12.il.us
Freeburg ES 3-8
408 S Belleville St 62243 618-539-3188
Tomi Diefenbach, prin. Fax 539-6008

Freeburg Community HSD 77 700/9-12
401 S Monroe St 62243 618-539-5533
Andrew Lehman, supt. Fax 539-4887
www.fchs77.stclair.k12.il.us
Freeburg HS 700/9-12
401 S Monroe St 62243 618-539-5533
Benjamin Howes, prin. Fax 539-4887

Freeport, Stephenson, Pop. 25,612
Freeport SD 145 4,400/PK-12
501 E South St 61032 815-232-0300
Dr. Peter Flynn, supt. Fax 232-6717
www.freeport.k12.il.us
Freeport HS 1,300/9-12
701 W Moseley St 61032 815-232-0400
David Thake, prin. Fax 232-0629
Freeport JHS 700/7-8
701 W Empire St 61032 815-232-0500
Scott Wiley, prin. Fax 232-0536

Aquin Central Catholic HS 200/7-12
1419 S Galena Ave 61032 815-235-3154
Kathleen Runte, admin. Fax 235-3185
Highland Community College Post-Sec.
2998 W Pearl City Rd 61032 815-235-6121

Fulton, Whiteside, Pop. 3,853
River Bend CUSD 2 — 1,000/K-12
1110 3rd St 61252 — 815-589-2711
Donald D. Mulch, supt. — Fax 589-4630
www.riverbendschools.org
Fulton HS — 400/9-12
1207 12th St 61252 — 815-589-3511
Kathleen Schipper, prin. — Fax 589-3412
River Bend MS — 200/6-8
415 12th St 61252 — 815-589-2611
James Spielman, prin. — Fax 589-3130

Unity Christian HS — 100/7-12
711 10th St 61252 — 815-589-3912
Dick Ritzema, prin. — Fax 589-4430

Gages Lake, Lake, Pop. 8,349
Warren Township HSD 121 — 1,800/9-12
17962 W Gages Lake Rd 60030 — 847-662-1400
Dr. Philip Sobocinski, supt. — Fax 548-0564
www.wths.net
Other Schools – See Gurnee

Galatia, Saline, Pop. 988
Galatia CUSD 1 — 400/PK-12
200 N Hickory St 62935 — 618-268-6371
Ronald Driemeier, supt. — Fax 268-4949
Galatia HS — 100/9-12
200 N McKinley St 62935 — 618-268-4194
Amy Richey, prin. — Fax 268-4196
Galatia JHS — 100/7-8
200 N McKinley St 62935 — 618-268-4194
Amy Richey, prin. — Fax 268-4196

Galena, Jo Daviess, Pop. 3,405
Galena Unit SD 120 — 800/PK-12
1206 Franklin St 61036 — 815-777-3086
Dr. Dennis Dunton, supt. — Fax 777-0303
www.galenaschools.com
Galena HS — 300/9-12
1206 Franklin St 61036 — 815-777-0917
Elizabeth Murphy, prin. — Fax 777-2089
Galena MS — 200/5-8
1230 Franklin St 61036 — 815-777-2413
Ben Soat, prin. — Fax 777-4259

Tri-State Christian S — 200/PK-12
11084 W US Highway 20 61036 — 815-777-3800
Mary Jane Thorne, prin. — Fax 777-2991

Galesburg, Knox, Pop. 32,017
Galesburg AVC
1135 W Fremont St 61401 — 309-343-3733
Peggy Miller, dir. — Fax 343-1305
Galesburg AVC — Vo/Tech
1135 W Fremont St 61401 — 309-343-3733
Peggy Miller, dir.

Galesburg CUSD 205 — 4,600/PK-12
PO Box 1206 61402 — 309-343-1151
Dr. S. Gene Denisar, supt. — Fax 343-7757
www.galesburg205.org/
Churchill JHS — 600/6-8
905 Maple Ave 61401 — 309-342-3129
Bart Arthur, prin. — Fax 342-6384
Galesburg HS — 1,500/9-12
1135 W Fremont St 61401 — 309-343-4146
Thomas Chiles, prin. — Fax 343-7122
Lombard JHS — 500/6-8
1220 E Knox St 61401 — 309-342-9171
Kim Hanks, prin. — Fax 342-7135

Carl Sandburg College — Post-Sec.
2232 S Lake Storey Rd 61401 — 309-344-2518
Knox College — Post-Sec.
2 E South St 61401 — 309-341-7000

Galt, Whiteside, Pop. 230

Sterling Christian S — 100/PK-12
PO Box 40 61037 — 815-625-0309
Mick Welding, prin. — Fax 625-2658

Galva, Henry, Pop. 2,705
Galva CUSD 224 — 600/PK-12
224 Morgan Rd 61434 — 309-932-2108
James Hochstatter, supt. — Fax 932-8326
cats.k12.il.us
Galva JSHS — 300/7-12
224 Morgan Rd 61434 — 309-932-2151
Richard Kucharz, prin. — Fax 932-2152

Gardner, Grundy, Pop. 1,436
Gardner-South Wilmington Twp. HSD 73 — 200/9-12
PO Box 257 60424 — 815-237-2176
Joseph Ciaccio, supt. — Fax 237-2842
www.gswhs.grundy.k12.il.us
Gardner-South Wilmington Twp. HS — 200/9-12
PO Box 257 60424 — 815-237-2176
Chris Becker, prin. — Fax 237-2842

Geneseo, Henry, Pop. 6,524
Geneseo CUSD 228 — 2,700/PK-12
209 S College Ave 61254 — 309-945-0450
Scott Kuffel, supt. — Fax 945-0445
www.dist228.org
Geneseo HS — 1,000/9-12
700 N State St 61254 — 309-945-0399
Mike Haugse, prin. — Fax 945-0374
Geneseo MS — 600/6-8
333 E Ogden Ave 61254 — 309-945-0599
Tom Domino, prin. — Fax 945-0580

Geneva, Kane, Pop. 23,424
Geneva CUSD 304 — 5,700/PK-12
227 N 4th St 60134 — 630-463-3000
Dr. Kent Mutchler, supt. — Fax 463-3009
www.geneva.k12.il.us/
Geneva Community HS — 1,700/9-12
416 McKinley Ave 60134 — 630-463-3800
Dr. Gregory Fantozzi, prin. — Fax 232-9077
Geneva MS North — 6-8
1357 Viking Dr 60134 — 630-463-3700
Lawrence Bidlack, prin. — Fax 463-3709
Geneva MS South — 1,400/6-8
1415 Viking Dr 60134 — 630-463-3600
Terry Bleau, prin. — Fax 208-7172

Genoa, DeKalb, Pop. 4,671
Genoa-Kingston CUSD 424 — 1,900/PK-12
980 Park Ave 60135 — 815-784-6222
Scott Wakeley, supt. — Fax 784-6059
www.gkschools.org
Genoa-Kingston HS — 500/9-12
980 Park Ave 60135 — 815-784-5111
Don Billington, prin. — Fax 784-3124
Genoa-Kingston MS — 400/6-8
941 W Main St 60135 — 815-784-5222
Angelo Lekkas, prin. — Fax 784-4323

Georgetown, Vermilion, Pop. 3,516
Georgetown-Ridge Farm CUSD 4 — 1,300/PK-12
400 W West St 61846 — 217-662-8488
Kevin Tate, supt. — Fax 662-3402
www.grf.k12.il.us
Georgetown-Ridge Farm HS — 400/9-12
500 W Mulberry St 61846 — 217-662-6716
Steve Sliva, prin. — Fax 662-3404
Miller JHS — 300/6-8
414 W West St 61846 — 217-662-6606
Lisa Gocken, prin. — Fax 662-6345

Gibson City, Ford, Pop. 3,394
Gibson City-Melvin-Sibley CUSD 5 — 1,100/PK-12
217 E 17th St 60936 — 217-784-8296
Charles Aubry, supt. — Fax 784-8558
www.gcms.k12.il.us
GCMS HS — 300/9-12
815 N Church St 60936 — 217-784-4292
Michael J. Lindy, prin. — Fax 784-8293
GCMS MS — 200/6-8
316 E 19th St 60936 — 217-784-8731
Michael Bleich, prin. — Fax 784-8726

Gillespie, Macoupin, Pop. 3,278
Gillespie CUSD 7 — 1,300/PK-12
510 W Elm St 62033 — 217-839-2464
Paul Skeans, supt. — Fax 839-3353
www.gillespie.macoupin.k12.il.us/
Gillespie HS — 400/9-12
612 Broadway St 62033 — 217-839-2114
Joe Tieman, prin. — Fax 839-4302
Gillespie MS, 412 Oregon St 62033 — 300/6-8
Joe Tieman, prin. — 217-839-2116

Gilman, Iroquois, Pop. 1,788
Iroquois West CUSD 10 — 800/PK-12
PO Box 67 60938 — 815-265-4642
Larry Eyre, supt. — Fax 265-7008
www.iwest.k12.il.us/
Iroquois West HS — 300/9-12
PO Box 67 60938 — 815-265-4229
Kim Hawkins, prin. — Fax 265-7008
Other Schools – See Onarga

Girard, Macoupin, Pop. 2,237
Girard CUSD 3 — 700/PK-12
525 N 3rd St 62640 — 217-627-2915
Marlene Brady, supt. — Fax 627-3519
www.girardschools.org/
Girard HS — 200/9-12
525 N 3rd St 62640 — 217-627-2136
Rob Horn, prin. — Fax 627-3519
Girard MS — 200/6-8
525 N 3rd St 62640 — 217-627-2136
Rob Horn, prin. — Fax 627-3519

Glasford, Peoria, Pop. 1,038
Illini Bluffs CUSD 327 — 1,000/PK-12
9611 S Hanna City Glsfrd Rd 61533 — 309-389-2231
Randy Stueve, supt. — Fax 389-2251
www.illinibluffs.com
Illini Bluffs HS — 300/9-12
PO Box 320 61533 — 309-389-5681
John Rumley, prin. — Fax 389-4681
Illini Bluffs MS — 200/6-8
212 N Saylor St 61533 — 309-389-3451
Greg Crider, prin. — Fax 389-3454

Glencoe, Cook, Pop. 8,979
Glencoe SD 35 — 1,400/K-8
620 Greenwood Ave 60022 — 847-835-7800
Cathlene Crawford, supt. — Fax 835-7805
www.glencoeschools.org/
Central S — 600/5-8
620 Greenwood Ave 60022 — 847-835-7600
Ryan Mollet, prin. — Fax 835-7605

Glendale Heights, DuPage, Pop. 32,465
Marquardt SD 15 — 2,600/PK-8
1860 Glen Ellyn Rd 60139 — 630-469-7615
Dr. Loren D. May, supt. — Fax 790-1650
www.d15.us/
Marquardt MS — 800/6-8
1912 Glen Ellyn Rd 60139 — 630-858-3850
Marie Cimaglia, prin. — Fax 790-5042

Queen Bee SD 16 — 2,100/PK-8
1560 Bloomingdale Rd 60139 — 630-260-6100
Dr. James White, supt. — Fax 260-6103
www.queenbee16.org
Glenside MS — 700/6-8
1560 Bloomingdale Rd 60139 — 630-260-6112
Christopher Collins, prin. — Fax 510-8568

Universal Technical Institute — Post-Sec.
601 Regency Dr 60139 — 630-529-2662

Glen Ellyn, DuPage, Pop. 27,193
Glen Ellyn CCSD 89 — 2,300/PK-8
22W600 Butterfield Rd 60137 — 630-469-8900
Dr. John Perdue, supt. — Fax 469-8936
www.ccsd89.org
Glen Crest MS — 900/6-8
725 Sheehan Ave 60137 — 630-469-5220
Dr. Scott Stevens, prin. — Fax 469-5250

Glen Ellyn SD 41 — 3,500/PK-8
793 N Main St 60137 — 630-790-6400
Ann Riebock Ed.D., supt. — Fax 790-1867
www.d41.org
Hadley JHS — 1,100/6-8
240 Hawthorne St 60137 — 630-790-6450
Dr. Christopher Dransoff, prin. — Fax 790-6469

Glenbard Twp. HSD 87 — 9,000/9-12
596 Crescent Blvd 60137 — 630-469-9100
Michael Meissen, supt. — Fax 469-9107
www.glenbard.net
Glenbard South HS — 1,400/9-12
23w200 Butterfield Rd 60137 — 630-469-6500
William Leensvaart, prin. — Fax 469-6572
Glenbard West HS — 2,100/9-12
670 Crescent Blvd 60137 — 630-469-8600
Dr. Jane Thorsen, prin. — Fax 469-8615
Other Schools – See Carol Stream, Lombard

College of DuPage — Post-Sec.
425 Fawell Blvd 60137 — 630-942-2800

Glenview, Cook, Pop. 45,989
Glenview CCSD 34 — 4,000/K-8
1401 Greenwood Rd 60026 — 847-998-5000
Dr. Gerald Hill, supt. — Fax 998-1629
www.glenview34.org
Attea MS — 700/6-8
2500 Chestnut Ave 60026 — 847-486-7700
James Woell, prin. — Fax 729-6251
Springman MS — 700/6-8
2701 Central Rd 60025 — 847-998-5020
Dr. Heather Hopkins, prin. — Fax 998-4032

Northfield Township HSD 225 — 4,800/9-12
1835 Landwehr Rd 60026 — 847-486-4700
Dr. Dave Hales, supt. — Fax 486-4734
www.glenbrook.k12.il.us
Glenbrook South HS — 2,700/9-12
4000 W Lake Ave 60026 — 847-729-2000
Brian Wegley, prin. — Fax 486-4462
Glenbrook Evening HS — Adult
4000 W Lake Ave 60026 — 847-486-4709
Stephen Bournes, prin. — Fax 486-4733
Other Schools – See Northbrook

Glenview New Church S — 100/PK-10
74 Park Dr 60025 — 847-724-0057
Phil Parker, prin. — Fax 724-3042

Glenwood, Cook, Pop. 8,663
Brookwood SD 167 — 1,400/PK-8
201 E Glenwood Dyer Rd 60425 — 708-758-5190
Pamela Hollich, supt. — Fax 757-2104
www.brookwood167.org
Brookwood JHS — 400/7-8
201 E Glenwood Lansing Rd 60425 — 708-758-5252
Bethany Lindsay, prin. — Fax 758-3954

Godfrey, Madison, Pop. 16,996

Alvareita's College of Cosmetology — Post-Sec.
3048 Godfrey Rd 62035 — 618-466-8952
Lewis & Clark Community College — Post-Sec.
5800 Godfrey Rd 62035 — 618-466-3411

Golconda, Pope, Pop. 668
Pope County CUSD 1 — 600/PK-12
RR 2 Box 22 62938 — 618-683-2301
Dr. Alice Sutton, supt. — Fax 683-5181
www.pcusd.com/
Pope County HS — 200/9-12
RR 2 Box 22 62938 — 618-683-3071
Robbie Wright, prin. — Fax 683-9956

Goreville, Johnson, Pop. 970
Goreville CUSD 1 — 600/PK-12
201 S Ferne Clyffe Rd 62939 — 618-995-9831
Steve Webb, supt. — Fax 995-9831
Goreville HS — 9-12
201 S Ferne Clyffe Rd 62939 — 618-995-2142
Barbara Watkins, prin. — Fax 995-1188

Granite City, Madison, Pop. 30,796
Granite City CUSD 9 — 7,300/PK-12
1947 Adams St 62040 — 618-451-5800
Ken Perkins Ed.D., supt. — Fax 451-6135
www.granitecityschools.org
Coolidge MS — 1,000/6-8
3231 Nameoki Rd 62040 — 618-451-5826
Richard Talley, prin. — Fax 876-5154
Granite City HS — 2,300/9-12
3101 Madison Ave 62040 — 618-451-5808
Jerry McKechan, prin. — Fax 451-6296
Grigsby MS — 800/6-8
3801 Cargill Rd 62040 — 618-931-5544
Curt Watters, prin. — Fax 931-5689

Grant Park, Kankakee, Pop. 1,557
Grant Park CUSD 6 — 600/K-12
PO Box 549 60940 — 815-465-6013
Dr. Michael Nicholson, supt. — Fax 465-2505
www.grantpark.k12.il.us/
Grant Park HS — 200/9-12
PO Box 549 60940 — 815-465-2181
Robert Gound, prin. — Fax 465-2505

Granville, Putnam, Pop. 1,388
Putnam County CUSD 535 — 900/K-12
PO Box 607 61326 — 815-339-2238
Mike Struna, supt. — Fax 339-6739
www.pcschools535.org/
Putnam County HS — 300/9-12
PO Box 341 61326 — 815-339-6514
Mike Struna, prin. — Fax 339-2628
Other Schools – See Mc Nabb

Grayslake, Lake, Pop. 21,099
CCSD 46 — 4,000/PK-8
565 Friederick Rd 60030 — 847-223-3650
Ellen L. Correll, supt. — Fax 223-3695
www.d46.k12.il.us
Grayslake MS — 900/7-8
440 Barron Blvd 60030 — 847-223-3680
Marcus Smith, prin. — Fax 223-3526

Grayslake Community HSD 127 — 2,300/9-12
400 N Lake St 60030 — 847-986-3400
Dr. Catherine Finger, supt. — Fax 223-3561
www.d127.org/
Grayslake Community HS - Central Campus — 1,600/9-12
400 N Lake St 60030 — 847-223-8621
Dr. Randy Davis, prin. — Fax 223-3561
Grayslake Community HS - North Campus — 700/9-11
1925 N Route 83 60030 — 847-986-3100
Dr. Kari King, prin. — Fax 986-3023

Lake County HS Technology Campus
19525 W Washington St 60030 — 847-223-6681
Linda Jedlicka, dir. — Fax 223-7363
www.techcampus.org
Lake County HS Technology Campus — Vo/Tech
19525 W Washington St 60030 — 847-223-6681
Linda Jedlicka, dir. — Fax 223-7363

College of Lake County — Post-Sec.
19351 W Washington St 60030 — 847-223-6601
Westlake Christian Academy — 200/PK-12
275 S Lake St 60030 — 847-548-6209
Denise Schlappi, dir. — Fax 548-6481

Grayville, White, Pop. 1,638
Grayville CUSD 1 400/PK-12
728 W North St 62844 618-375-7114
David Jordan, supt. Fax 375-5202
Grayville JSHS 200/6-12
728 W North St 62844 618-375-7114
David Jordan, prin. Fax 375-6521

Greenfield, Greene, Pop. 1,142
Greenfield CUSD 10 500/K-12
311 Mulberry St 62044 217-368-2447
Bill Bishop, supt. Fax 368-2724
Greenfield HS 200/9-12
502 East St 62044 217-368-2219
Mike Dickson, prin. Fax 368-2230

Green Valley, Tazewell, Pop. 702
Midwest Central CUSD 191
Supt. — See Manito
Midwest Central MS 300/6-8
PO Box 219 61534 309-352-2300
J. Douglas Cunningham, prin. Fax 352-2903

Greenview, Menard, Pop. 823
Greenview CUSD 200 300/K-12
PO Box 320 62642 217-968-2295
Gary DePatis, supt. Fax 968-2297
www.menard.k12.il.us/greenviewhs/welcome.htm
Greenview JSHS 100/7-12
PO Box 320 62642 217-968-2295
Phil Sexton, prin. Fax 968-2297

Greenville, Bond, Pop. 7,067
Bond County CUSD 2 1,900/PK-12
1008 N Hena St 62246 618-664-0170
Melanie Allyn, supt. Fax 664-5000
www.bccu2.k12.il.us
Bond City Comm Unit 2 HS 600/9-12
1000 E State Route 140 62246 618-664-1370
Kevin Cochrane, prin. Fax 664-4786
Greenville JHS 300/6-8
1200 Junior High Dr 62246 618-664-1226
Gary Brauns, prin. Fax 664-5071

Greenville Christian Academy 50/K-12
949 Airport Ave 62246 618-664-2175
Darlene Rieder, admin. Fax 664-4350
Greenville College Post-Sec.
315 E College Ave 62246 618-664-2800

Gridley, McLean, Pop. 1,398
El Paso-Gridley CUSD 11
Supt. — See El Paso
El Paso-Gridley JHS 200/7-8
403 McLean St 61744 309-747-2156
Michael Weaver, prin. Fax 747-2475

Griggsville, Pike, Pop. 1,215
Griggsville-Perry CUSD 4 400/PK-12
PO Box 439 62340 217-833-2352
Michael Davies, supt. Fax 833-2354
griggsvilleperry.com
Griggsville-Perry HS 100/9-12
PO Box 439 62340 217-833-2352
Andrea Allen, prin. Fax 833-2354
Other Schools – See Perry

Gurnee, Lake, Pop. 30,772
Gurnee SD 56 2,100/PK-8
900 Kilbourne Rd 60031 847-336-0800
Dr. Ben Martindale, supt. Fax 336-1110
www.d56.lake.k12.il.us/district/
Viking MS 700/6-8
4460 Old Grand Ave 60031 847-336-2108
Patrick Jones, prin. Fax 249-0719

Warren Township HSD 121
Supt. — See Gages Lake
Warren Township HS 9-10
500 N OPlaine Rd 60031 847-662-1400
Steven Isoye, prin. Fax 599-4848
Warren Township HS 11-12
34090 N Almond Rd 60031 847-662-1400
Dr. Doug Domeracki, prin. Fax 599-4489

Woodland CCSD 50 7,000/PK-8
1105 N Hunt Club Rd 60031 847-856-3590
Joy Swoboda, supt. Fax 856-0320
www.dist50.net
Woodland MS 2,300/6-8
7000 Washington St 60031 847-856-3400
Scott Snyder, prin. Fax 856-1306

DeVry University Post-Sec.
1075 Tri State Pkwy Ste 800 60031 847-855-2649

Hamilton, Hancock, Pop. 2,838
Hamilton CCSD 328 700/PK-12
270 N 10th St 62341 217-847-3315
James Jackson, supt. Fax 847-3915
www.hamilton.k12.il.us
Hamilton HS 200/9-12
1100 Keokuk St 62341 217-847-3313
Dan Oakley, prin. Fax 847-3474
Hamilton JHS 100/7-8
270 N 10th St 62341 217-847-3314
Dan Oakley, prin. Fax 847-3915

Hampshire, Kane, Pop. 4,077
Community Unit SD 300
Supt. — See Carpentersville
Hampshire MSHS 400/6-12
560 S State St 60140 847-683-2522
Jim Wallis, prin. Fax 683-1030

Hanover, Jo Daviess, Pop. 797
River Ridge CUSD 210 500/K-12
4141 IL Route 84 S 61041 815-858-9005
Bradley Albrecht, supt. Fax 858-9006
www.riverridge210.org
River Ridge HS 200/9-12
4141 IL Route 84 S 61041 815-858-9005
Thomas Akers, prin. Fax 858-9006
River Ridge MS 100/6-8
4141 IL Route 84 S 61041 815-858-9005
Thomas Akers, prin. Fax 858-9006

Hanover Park, Cook, Pop. 37,229
Keeneyville SD 20 1,700/PK-8
5540 Arlington Dr E 60133 630-894-2250
Dr. Carol Auer, supt. Fax 894-5187
www.esd20.org
Spring Wood MS 600/6-8
5540 Arlington Dr E 60133 630-893-8900
Craig Barringer, prin. Fax 894-9658

Hanover Park College of Beauty Culture Post-Sec.
1166 E Lake St 60133 630-830-6560

Hardin, Calhoun, Pop. 952
Calhoun CUSD 40 600/PK-12
PO Box 387 62047 618-576-2722
Carol Crum, supt. Fax 576-2641
Calhoun HS 200/9-12
PO Box 387 62047 618-576-2229
Chris Diddlebock, prin. Fax 576-8031

Harrisburg, Saline, Pop. 9,628
Harrisburg CUSD 3 2,100/PK-12
40 S Main St 62946 618-253-7637
Dennis Smith, supt. Fax 252-7584
www.hbg.saline.k12.il.us
Harrisburg HS 600/9-12
333 W College St 62946 618-253-7637
Jim Butler, prin. Fax 252-2616
Harrisburg MS 500/6-8
312 Bulldog Blvd 62946 618-253-7107
Karen Crank, prin. Fax 253-4114

Southeastern Illinois College Post-Sec.
3575 College Rd 62946 618-252-6376

Hartsburg, Montgomery, Pop. 343
Hartsburg-Emden CUSD 21 300/PK-12
400 W Front St 62643 217-642-5244
Donald Helm, supt. Fax 642-5333
www.logan.k12.il.us/hartem/
Hartsburg-Emden JSHS 200/5-12
400 W Front St 62643 217-642-5244
Les Stevens, prin. Fax 642-5333

Harvard, McHenry, Pop. 9,104
Harvard CUSD 50 2,300/PK-12
1101 N Jefferson St 60033 815-943-4022
Dr. Richard Crosby, supt. Fax 943-4282
www.d50.mchenry.k12.il.us
Harvard HS 700/9-12
1103 N Jefferson St 60033 815-943-6461
Dr. Michelle McReynolds, prin. Fax 943-8506
Harvard JHS 700/5-8
1301 Garfield St 60033 815-943-6466
Linda Heiden, prin. Fax 943-8521

Harvey, Cook, Pop. 28,771
Harvey SD 152 3,000/PK-8
16001 Lincoln Ave 60426 708-333-0300
Dr. Lela Bridges, supt. Fax 333-0349
www.harvey152.org/
Brooks MS 700/7-8
14741 Wallace St 60426 708-333-6390
Maryann West, prin. Fax 333-3177

Thornton Twp. HSD 205
Supt. — See South Holland
Thornton Twp. HS 2,500/9-12
15001 Broadway Ave 60426 708-225-4101
Angelo Armistead, prin.

West Harvey-Dixmoor SD 147 1,700/PK-8
191 W 155th Pl 60426 708-339-9500
Dr. Alex Boyd, supt. Fax 339-9533
www.whd147.org
Other Schools – See Dixmoor

Ingalls Memorial Hospital Post-Sec.
1 Ingalls Dr 60426 708-333-2300

Havana, Mason, Pop. 3,476
Havana CUSD 126 1,200/PK-12
501 S McKinley St 62644 309-543-3384
Dr. Suellen Girard, supt. Fax 543-3385
mason.k12.il.us/havana126
Havana HS 300/9-12
501 S McKinley St 62644 309-543-3337
Scott Kehrberg, prin. Fax 543-6721
Havana JHS 300/5-8
801 E Laurel Ave 62644 309-543-6677
Jerry Wilson, prin. Fax 543-6678

Hawthorn Woods, Lake, Pop. 7,176
Lake Zurich CUSD 95
Supt. — See Lake Zurich
Lake Zurich MS North Campus 700/6-8
95 Hubbard Ln 60047 847-438-2361
Nate Carter, prin. Fax 438-2381

Hazel Crest, Cook, Pop. 14,415
Hazel Crest SD 152-5 800/PK-8
1910 170th St 60429 708-335-0790
Dr. Sheila Harrison-Williams, supt. Fax 335-3520
www.sd1525.org/
Other Schools – See Markham

Hebron, McHenry, Pop. 1,141
Alden Hebron SD 19 500/PK-12
9604 Illinois St 60034 815-648-2886
Kurt Suhr, supt. Fax 648-2339
www.alden-hebron.org
Alden-Hebron HS 100/9-12
9604 Illinois St 60034 815-648-2442
Janet Fredriksen, prin. Fax 648-2339
Alden-Hebron MS 100/6-8
9604 Illinois St 60034 815-648-2442
Delores Swanson, prin. Fax 648-2339

Henry, Marshall, Pop. 2,530
Henry-Senachwine CUSD 5 600/K-12
1023 College St 61537 309-364-3614
Thomas Urban, supt. Fax 364-2990
www.henrysenachwine.org
Henry-Senachwine Consolidated HS 200/9-12
1023 College St 61537 309-364-2829
Robert Simkins, prin. Fax 364-2990

Herrin, Williamson, Pop. 11,688
Herrin CUSD 4 2,200/K-12
500 N 10th St 62948 618-988-8024
Mark Collins, supt. Fax 942-6998
www.herrinunit.org
Herrin HS 700/9-12
700 N 10th St 62948 618-942-6606
Terry Ryker, prin. Fax 942-7562
Herrin MS 500/6-8
700 S 14th St 62948 618-942-7461
Steve Robinson, prin. Fax 988-8821

Herscher, Kankakee, Pop. 1,554
Herscher CUSD 2 1,900/PK-12
PO Box 504 60941 815-426-2162
William Davison, supt. Fax 426-2872
www.hsd2.k12.il.us
Herscher HS 700/9-12
PO Box 504 60941 815-426-2103
Brian Riegler, prin. Fax 426-2957

Heyworth, McLean, Pop. 2,470
Heyworth CUSD 4 900/PK-12
522 E Main St 61745 309-473-3727
Randall Merker, supt. Fax 473-2220
www.husd4.k12.il.us/
Heyworth HS 400/7-12
308 W Cleveland St 61745 309-473-2322
Jeff Asmus, prin. Fax 473-2323

Hickory Hills, Cook, Pop. 13,542
North Palos SD 117
Supt. — See Palos Hills
Conrady JHS 900/6-8
7950 W 97th St 60457 708-233-4500
Paula Coughlin, prin. Fax 430-8964

Highland, Madison, Pop. 9,200
Highland CUSD 5 2,400/PK-12
PO Box 149 62249 618-654-2106
Marvin Warner, supt. Fax 654-5424
www.highland.madison.k12.il.us/
Highland HS 1,000/9-12
PO Box 149 62249 618-654-7131
Andrew Carmitchel, prin. Fax 654-6548
Highland MS 500/7-8
PO Box 149 62249 618-651-8800
Jeanie Probst, prin. Fax 654-1551

Highland Park, Lake, Pop. 31,380
North Shore SD 112 4,400/PK-8
1936 Green Bay Rd 60035 847-681-6700
Dr. Maureen L. Hager, supt. Fax 266-2379
www.nssd112.org
Edgewood MS 600/6-8
929 Edgewood Rd 60035 847-432-3858
Allison Stein, prin. Fax 432-7326
Elm Place MS 500/6-8
2031 Sheridan Rd 60035 847-432-9217
Eric Olson, prin. Fax 432-9213
Northwood JHS 400/6-8
945 North Ave 60035 847-432-4770
Steven Hamlin, prin. Fax 432-4886

Township HSD 113 3,600/9-12
1040 Park Ave W 60035 224-765-1000
Dr. George Fornero, supt. Fax 765-1060
www.dist113.org
Highland Park HS 1,900/9-12
433 Vine Ave 60035 224-765-2000
John Scornavacco, prin. Fax 765-2700
Other Schools – See Deerfield

Hillsboro, Montgomery, Pop. 4,272
Hillsboro CUSD 3 2,100/PK-12
1311 Vandalia Rd 62049 217-532-2942
Donald Burton, supt. Fax 532-3137
www.hillsboroschools.net
Hillsboro HS 600/9-12
522 E Tremont St 62049 217-532-2841
Kyle Hacke, prin. Fax 532-5179
Hillsboro JHS 500/6-8
909 Rountree St 62049 217-532-3742
David Powell, prin. Fax 532-6211

Hillside, Cook, Pop. 7,771
Proviso Township HSD 209
Supt. — See Forest Park
Proviso West HS 2,700/9-12
4701 Harrison St 60162 708-449-6400
Alexis Wallace, prin. Fax 449-3636

Hinckley, DeKalb, Pop. 2,050
Hinckley-Big Rock CUSD 429 900/K-12
PO Box 1210 60520 815-286-7575
Glen Littlefield, supt. Fax 286-7577
www.hbr429.org
Hinckley-Big Rock HS 300/9-12
PO Box 1210 60520 815-286-7500
Charles Lawson, prin. Fax 286-7505

Hines, Cook

Edward Hines Veterans Admin. Hospital Post-Sec.
PO Box 5000 60141 708-216-2153

Hinsdale, DuPage, Pop. 17,898
CCSD 181
Supt. — See Westmont
Hinsdale MS 600/6-8
100 S Garfield Ave 60521 630-887-1370
Mary Ticknor, prin. Fax 655-9754

Hinsdale Township HSD 86 4,400/9-12
55th And Grant 60521 630-655-6100
Dr. Nicholas Wahl, supt. Fax 325-9153
www.hinsdale86.org
Hinsdale Central HS 2,500/9-12
55th and Grant 60521 630-570-8000
Dr. James Ferguson, prin. Fax 887-1362
Other Schools – See Darien

Hinsdale Adventist Academy 200/PK-12
631 E Hickory St 60521 630-323-9211
Patricia Williams, prin. Fax 323-9237

Hoffman Estates, Cook, Pop. 52,046
Schaumburg CCSD 54
Supt. — See Schaumburg
Eisenhower JHS 700/7-8
800 Hassell Rd, 847-357-5500
Pamela Samson, prin. Fax 357-5501

Township HSD 211
Supt. — See Palatine
Conant HS 2,600/9-12
700 E Cougar Trl, 847-755-3600
Timothy Cannon, prin. Fax 755-3623
Hoffman Estates HS 2,200/9-12
1100 W Higgins Rd, 847-755-5600
Theresa Busch, prin. Fax 755-5623

American Intercontinental Univ Online Post-Sec.
5550 Prairie Stone Pky #400 60192 847-851-5284

Valeo Academy 100/K-10
2500 Beverly Rd 60192 847-645-9300
Lori Jones, prin. Fax 645-9300

Homer, Champaign, Pop. 1,157
Heritage CUSD 8
Supt. — See Broadlands
Heritage JHS 100/6-8
512 W 1st St 61849 217-896-2421
Chris Kerns, prin. Fax 896-2338

Homer Glen, Will
Homer CCSD 33C 2,700/K-8
15733 S Bell Rd, 708-226-7600
William Young, supt. Fax 226-7627
www.homerschools.org
Homer JHS 800/7-8
15711 S Bell Rd, 708-226-7800
Troy Mitchell, prin. Fax 226-7859

Homewood, Cook, Pop. 18,917
Homewood SD 153 2,100/PK-8
18205 Aberdeen St 60430 708-799-5661
Dr. Dale Mitchell, supt. Fax 799-1377
www.homewoodsd153.org/
Hart JHS 600/7-8
18220 Morgan St 60430 708-799-5544
Jeffrey Stawick, prin. Fax 799-8360

Hoopeston, Vermilion, Pop. 5,753
Hoopeston Area CUSD 11 1,300/PK-12
615 E Orange St 60942 217-283-6668
Mark Conolly, supt. Fax 283-5431
www.hoopeston.k12.il.us
Hoopeston Area HS 400/9-12
615 E Orange St 60942 217-283-6662
Hank Hornbeck, prin. Fax 283-5431
Hoopeston Area MS 200/7-8
615 E Orange St 60942 217-283-6664
Hank Hornbeck, prin. Fax 283-7943

Hume, Edgar, Pop. 373
Shiloh CUSD 1 500/PK-12
21751N N 575th St 61932 217-887-2364
James Acklin, supt. Fax 887-2448
www.shiloh.k12.il.us
Shiloh JSHS 200/7-12
21751N N 575th St 61932 217-887-2364
Mark Hettmansberger, prin. Fax 887-2562

Huntley, McHenry, Pop. 17,674
Consolidated SD 158
Supt. — See Algonquin
Huntley HS 1,300/9-12
13719 Harmony Rd 60142 847-659-6600
David Johnson, prin. Fax 659-6620

Hutsonville, Crawford, Pop. 606
Hutsonville CUSD 1 400/PK-12
PO Box 218 62433 618-563-4912
Roger Eddy, supt. Fax 563-9122
Hutsonville HS 100/9-12
PO Box 218 62433 618-563-4913
Monte Newlin, prin. Fax 563-9122

Illiopolis, Sangamon, Pop. 867
Sangamon Valley CUSD 9
Supt. — See Niantic
Sangamon Valley MS 6-8
341 Matilda St 62539 217-486-2241
Bob Meadows, prin. Fax 486-6038

Ina, Jefferson, Pop. 2,430

Rend Lake College Post-Sec.
RR 1 62846 618-437-5321

Ingleside, See Fox Lake
Big Hollow SD 38 1,000/K-8
33315 N Fish Lake Rd 60041 847-587-2632
Ron Pazanin, supt. Fax 587-2663
www.bighollow.us
Taveirne MS 300/6-8
34699 N US Highway 12 60041 847-587-6800
Henny Sands, prin.

Gavin SD 37 800/PK-8
25775 W IL Route 134 60041 847-546-2916
Dr. Donald Coossett, supt. Fax 546-9584
www.gs37.lake.k12.il.us
Gavin South JHS 300/PK-K, 6-8
25775 W IL Route 134 60041 847-546-9336
Ron Banion, prin. Fax 546-9338

Itasca, DuPage, Pop. 8,444
Itasca SD 10 900/PK-8
200 N Maple St 60143 630-773-1232
Dr. Ken Cull, supt. Fax 773-1342
www.itasca.k12.il.us
Peacock MS 300/6-8
301 E North St 60143 630-773-0335
Reinhard Nickisch, prin. Fax 285-7460

Environmental Technical Institute Post-Sec.
1101 W Thorndale Ave 60143 630-285-9100

Jacksonville, Morgan, Pop. 19,470
Jacksonville SD 117 3,700/PK-12
516 Jordan St 62650 217-243-9411
Lee Hovasse, supt. Fax 243-6844
www.morgan.k12.il.us/jvsd117/index.html
Jacksonville HS 1,100/9-12
1211 N Diamond St 62650 217-243-4384
Ed Wainscott, prin. Fax 245-0445
Turner JHS 600/7-8
664 Lincoln Ave 62650 217-243-3383
Beth Brockschmidt, prin. Fax 243-3459

Illinois College Post-Sec.
1101 W College Ave 62650 217-245-3000
Illinois School for the Deaf Post-Sec.
125 S Webster Ave 62650 217-245-5141
Illinois School for Visually Impaired Post-Sec.
658 E State St 62650 217-479-4400
MacMurray College Post-Sec.
447 E College Ave 62650 217-479-7000
Mr. John's School of Cosmetology & Nails Post-Sec.
1429 S Main St 62650 217-243-1744
Routt HS 100/9-12
500 E College Ave 62650 217-243-8563
Randy Verticchio, prin. Fax 243-7497
Westfair Christian Academy 100/K-12
14 Clarke Dr 62650 217-243-7100
Randy Cooper, prin. Fax 243-2386

Jerseyville, Jersey, Pop. 8,187
Jersey CUSD 100 2,900/PK-12
100 Lincoln Ave 62052 618-498-5561
James Whiteside, supt. Fax 498-5265
www.jersey100.k12.il.us/
Illini MS 600/6-8
1101 S Liberty St 62052 618-498-5527
Cynthia Lindsey, prin. Fax 498-7079
Jersey Community HS 1,000/9-12
801 N State St 62052 618-498-5521
Lisa Schuenke, prin. Fax 498-5332

Johnsburg, McHenry, Pop. 6,277
Johnsburg CUSD 12 2,700/PK-12
2222 Church St, 815-385-6916
Dr. Dan Johnson, supt. Fax 385-4715
www.jburgd12.k12.il.us
Johnsburg HS 900/9-12
2002 W Ringwood Rd, 815-385-9233
Kevin Shelton, prin. Fax 344-0451
Johnsburg JHS 900/5-8
2220 Church St, 815-385-6210
Travis Lobbins, prin. Fax 578-2649

Johnston City, Williamson, Pop. 3,476
Johnston City CUSD 1 1,200/PK-12
1103 Monroe Ave 62951 618-983-8021
Gary Schurz, supt. Fax 983-6034
www.jc1.wilmsn.k12.il.us
Johnston City HS 400/9-12
1500 Jefferson Ave 62951 618-983-4700
James Grant, prin. Fax 983-6812

Joliet, Will, Pop. 136,208
Joliet SD 86 10,000/PK-8
420 N Raynor Ave 60435 815-740-3196
Phyllis Wilson Ph.D., supt. Fax 740-6520
www.joliet86.org
Dirksen JHS 500/6-8
203 S Midland Ave 60436 815-729-1566
Kimberly Pfoutz, prin. Fax 744-2346
Gompers JHS 900/6-8
1501 Copperfield Ave 60432 815-727-5276
David Negron, prin. Fax 726-5341
Hufford JHS 1,000/6-8
1125 N Larkin Ave 60435 815-725-3540
Anna White, prin. Fax 744-5974
Washington JHS & Academy 600/6-8
402 Richards St 60433 815-727-5271
Michael Latting, prin. Fax 740-5451

Joliet Township HSD 204 5,200/9-12
201 E Jefferson St 60432 815-727-6970
Paul Swanstrom, supt. Fax 727-1277
www.jths.org/
Joliet Central HS 2,800/9-12
201 E Jefferson St 60432 815-727-6740
John Randich, prin. Fax 727-6824
Joliet West HS 2,400/9-12
401 N Larkin Ave 60435 815-727-6940
Cheryl McCarthy, prin. Fax 744-3070

Plainfield CCSD 202
Supt. — See Plainfield
Aux Sable MS 6-8
2001 Wildspring Pkwy 60431 815-439-7092
Sharon Alexander, prin. Fax 577-9476

Joliet Catholic Academy 1,000/9-12
1200 N Larkin Ave 60435 815-741-0500
Jeffrey Budz, prin. Fax 741-9530
Joliet Junior College Post-Sec.
1216 Houbolt Rd 60431 815-729-9020
Professional Choice Hair Design Academy Post-Sec.
2719 W Jefferson St 60435 815-741-8224
Ridgewood Baptist Academy 300/PK-12
1968 Hillcrest Rd 60433 815-726-3222
Brian Keith, prin. Fax 726-2344
University of St. Francis Post-Sec.
500 Wilcox St 60435 815-740-3360

Joppa, Massac, Pop. 419
Joppa-Maple Grove CUSD 38 300/PK-12
PO Box 10 62953 618-543-9023
Catherine Trampe Ph.D., supt. Fax 543-9264
Joppa JSHS 100/7-12
PO Box 10 62953 618-543-7589
Vickie Artman, prin. Fax 543-9264

Joy, Mercer, Pop. 362
Westmer CUSD 203 500/PK-12
PO Box 436 61260 309-584-4173
Robert Haskell, supt. Fax 584-4115
mercer.k12.il.us/westmer
Westmer HS 200/9-12
PO Box 436 61260 309-584-4174
Paul McMahon, prin. Fax 584-4257
Westmer JHS 100/6-8
PO Box 436 61260 309-584-4174
Paul McMahon, prin. Fax 584-4257

Junction, Gallatin, Pop. 133
Gallatin CUSD 7 900/PK-12
5175 Highway 13 62954 618-272-3821
Les Oyler, supt. Fax 272-4101
Gallatin HS 300/9-12
5175 Highway 13 62954 618-272-5141
Lucinda Schmitt, prin. Fax 272-4101
Gallatin JHS 300/5-8
5175 Highway 13 62954 618-272-7341
Patty Wood, prin. Fax 272-4101

Justice, Cook, Pop. 12,692
Indian Springs SD 109 3,000/PK-8
7540 S 86th Ave 60458 708-496-8700
Dr. Jon Nebor, supt. Fax 496-8641
www.isd109.org
Wilkins JHS 600/7-8
8001 S 82nd Ave 60458 708-496-8708
William Caron, prin. Fax 728-3114

Kankakee, Kankakee, Pop. 26,642
Kankakee SD 111 5,300/PK-12
240 Warren Ave 60901 815-933-0700
Dr. Brian Ali, supt. Fax 933-9981
www.kankakeeschooldistrict.org
Kankakee HS 1,300/9-12
1200 W Jeffery St 60901 815-933-0740
Terrence Martin, prin. Fax 933-9149
Kankakee JHS 800/7-8
2250 E Crestwood St 60901 815-933-0730
Mike Rolinitis, prin. Fax 935-7272

Bishop McNamara HS 400/9-12
550 W Brookmont Blvd 60901 815-932-7413
James Laurenti, prin. Fax 932-0926
Grace Baptist Academy 200/K-12
2499 Waldron Rd 60901 815-939-4579
Dwight Ascher, prin. Fax 939-1334
Kankakee Community College Post-Sec.
100 College Dr 60901 815-802-8100
Kankakee Trinity Academy 200/PK-12
410 S Small Ave 60901 815-935-8080
Brad Prairie, prin. Fax 935-0280

Kansas, Edgar, Pop. 826
Kansas CUSD 3 300/PK-12
PO Box 350 61933 217-948-5174
Chris Long, supt. Fax 948-5577
Kansas HS 100/9-12
PO Box 350 61933 217-948-5175
Dwight Stricklin, prin. Fax 948-5577

Kempton, Ford, Pop. 235
Tri-Point CUSD 6-J 600/PK-12
PO Box 128 60946 815-253-6299
Jeffrey Fritchtnitch, supt. Fax 253-6298
www.tripointschools.org/
Other Schools – See Cullom, Piper City

Kewanee, Henry, Pop. 12,655
Kewanee CUSD 229 1,500/PK-12
210 Lyle St 61443 309-853-3341
Christopher Sullens Ed.D., supt. Fax 852-5504
www.kewaneeschoolsfoundation.org/
Central MS, 215 E Central Blvd 61443 400/4-8
Andy Bullock, prin. 309-853-4290
Kewanee HS 500/9-12
1211 E 3rd St 61443 309-853-3328
Mike Kirkham, prin. Fax 854-0210

Wethersfield CUSD 230 600/PK-12
439 Willard St 61443 309-853-4860
Shane Kazubowski, supt. Fax 856-7976
geese.henry.k12.il.us
Wethersfield JSHS 300/7-12
439 Willard St 61443 309-853-4205
James Peck, prin. Fax 856-7976

Black Hawk College Post-Sec.
1501 State Highway 78 61443 309-852-5671

Kincaid, Christian, Pop. 1,468
South Fork SD 14 400/PK-12
PO Box 20 62540 217-237-4333
Charlotte Davis, supt. Fax 237-4370
South Fork JSHS 200/5-12
PO Box 20 62540 217-237-4333
Charlotte Davis, prin. Fax 237-4370

Kinderhook, Pike, Pop. 241
West Pike CUSD 2 300/PK-12
PO Box 189 62345 217-432-8324
Rodger Hannel, supt. Fax 432-8003
www.westpikeschools.com
West Pike HS 100/9-12
PO Box 189 62345 217-432-8324
Gregory Lesan, prin. Fax 432-8003
West Pike JHS 50/6-8
PO Box 189 62345 217-432-8324
Gregory Lesan, prin. Fax 432-8003

Kinmundy, Marion, Pop. 871
South Central CUSD 401 600/PK-12
PO Box 189 62854 618-547-3414
Judy Cole, supt. Fax 547-7790
South Central MS 5-8
PO Box 40 62854 618-547-7734
Greg Grinestaff, prin. Fax 547-7790
Other Schools – See Farina

Kirkland, DeKalb, Pop. 1,607
Hiawatha CUSD 426 500/K-12
PO Box 428 60146 815-522-6676
Christine Demory, supt. Fax 522-6619
www.hiawatha426.k12.il.us
Hiawatha HS 300/6-12
PO Box 428 60146 815-522-3335
Karen Zinni-Wickline, prin. Fax 522-3312

Knoxville, Knox, Pop. 3,005
Knoxville CUSD 202 1,100/PK-12
600 E Main St 61448 309-289-2328
Lawrence W. Carlton, supt. Fax 289-9614
www.bluebullets.org
Knoxville HS 300/9-12
600 E Main St 61448 309-289-2324
Patrick Callahan, prin. Fax 289-9466
Knoxville JHS 300/5-8
701 E Mill St 61448 309-289-4126
David Summers, prin. Fax 289-4128

Lacon, Marshall, Pop. 1,923
Midland CUSD 7 900/PK-12
206 N High St 61540 309-246-2310
Dean Irlbeck, supt. Fax 246-2311
www.midland-7.org
Other Schools – See Sparland, Varna

Lafox, Kane

Broadview Academy 100/9-12
PO Box 307 60147 630-232-7441
Dr. Randy Siebold, prin. Fax 232-7443

La Grange, Cook, Pop. 15,482
La Grange Highlands SD 106 900/K-8
1750 W Plainfield Rd 60525 708-246-3085
Dr. Arleen Armanetti, supt. Fax 246-0220
www.district106.net
Highlands MS 300/6-8
1850 W Plainfield Rd 60525 708-579-6890
Michael Papierski, prin. Fax 246-0220

La Grange SD 105 1,100/PK-8
1001 S Spring Ave 60525 708-482-2700
Glenn Schlichting Ph.D., supt. Fax 482-2727
www.d105.net
Gurrie MS 300/7-8
1001 S Spring Ave 60525 708-482-2720
Edmond Hood, prin. Fax 482-2724

Lyons Township HSD 204 — 1,800/9-12
100 S Brainard Ave 60525 — 708-579-6451
Dennis Kelly, supt. — Fax 579-6768
www.lths.net
Lyons Township HS North Campus — 1,800/11-12
100 S Brainard Ave 60525 — 708-579-6300
Dave Franson, prin. — Fax 579-3187
Other Schools – See Western Springs

La Grange Park, Cook, Pop. 12,726
La Grange SD 102 — 2,700/PK-8
333 N Park Rd 60526 — 708-482-2400
Dr. Mark Van Clay, supt. — Fax 482-2402
www.dist102.k12.il.us/
Park JHS — 600/7-8
325 N Park Rd 60526 — 708-482-2500
Dr. Laura Schwartz, prin. — Fax 352-1170

Nazareth Academy — 800/9-12
1209 W Ogden Ave 60526 — 708-354-0061
Deborah Vondrasek, prin. — Fax 354-0109

La Harpe, Hancock, Pop. 1,323
La Harpe CUSD 335 — 400/PK-12
404 W Main St 61450 — 217-659-7739
Jo Campbell, supt. — Fax 659-7730
hancock.k12.il.us/laharpe/
La Harpe HS — 100/9-12
404 W Main St 61450 — 217-659-3713
Lila McKeown, prin. — Fax 659-7730
La Harpe JHS — 100/6-8
404 W Main St 61450 — 217-659-3713
Lila McKeown, prin. — Fax 659-7730

Lake Bluff, Lake, Pop. 6,251
Lake Bluff ESD 65 — 1,100/K-8
121 E Sheridan Pl 60044 — 847-234-9400
Dr. David Vick, supt. — Fax 234-6237
www.lbelem.lfc.edu/
Lake Bluff MS — 400/6-8
31 E Sheridan Pl 60044 — 847-234-9407
Michael Donhost, prin. — Fax 615-9144

Lake Forest, Lake, Pop. 21,123
Lake Forest Community HSD 115 — 1,700/9-12
1285 N McKinley Rd 60045 — 847-234-3600
Dr. Harry Griffith, supt. — Fax 582-7797
www.lfhs.org/
Lake Forest HS — 1,700/9-12
1285 N McKinley Rd 60045 — 847-234-3600
Jay Hoffman, prin. — Fax 234-7933

Lake Forest SD 67 — 2,300/PK-8
67 W Deerpath Rd 60045 — 847-234-6010
Dr. Harry Griffith, supt. — Fax 234-2372
www.lfelem.lfc.edu
Deer Path MS - West — 500/7-8
155 W Deerpath Rd 60045 — 847-604-7400
John Steinert, prin. — Fax 234-2389

Lake Forest Academy — 300/9-12
1500 W Kennedy Rd 60045 — 847-234-3210
John Strudwick, hdmstr. — Fax 615-3202
Lake Forest College — Post-Sec.
555 N Sheridan Rd 60045 — 847-234-3100
Lake Forest Graduate Sch. of Management — Post-Sec.
1905 W Field Ct 60045 — 847-234-5005
School of St. Mary MS — 300/4-8
185 E Illinois Rd 60045 — 847-234-0371
Dr. Kevin Zajdel, prin. — Fax 234-9593
Woodlands Academy Sacred Heart — 200/9-12
760 E Westleigh Rd 60045 — 847-234-4300
Madonna Lee Edmunds, prin. — Fax 234-4348

Lake in the Hills, McHenry, Pop. 28,786
Consolidated SD 158
Supt. — See Algonquin
Marlowe MS — 6-8
9625 Haligus Rd, — 847-659-4700
Jake Wakitsch, prin. — Fax 659-4720

Lake Villa, Lake, Pop. 8,492
Community HSD 117 — 2,400/9-12
1625 Deep Lake Rd Ste A 60046 — 847-838-7170
Jay Sabatino Ed.D., supt. — Fax 395-7553
www.d117.org
Lakes Community HS — 600/9-12
1600 Eagle Way 60046 — 847-838-7100
James McKay, prin. — Fax 395-7553
Other Schools – See Antioch

Lake Villa CCSD 41 — 3,300/PK-8
131 McKinley Ave 60046 — 847-356-2385
Dr. John VanPelt, supt. — Fax 356-2670
www.district41.org
Palombi MS — 700/7-8
133 McKinley Ave 60046 — 847-356-2118
Mary Jordan, prin. — Fax 356-0833

Lake Zurich, Lake, Pop. 20,045
Lake Zurich CUSD 95 — 6,500/PK-12
400 S Old Rand Rd 60047 — 847-438-2831
Dr. Brian Knutson, supt. — Fax 438-6702
www.lz95.org
Lake Zurich HS — 2,100/9-12
300 Church St 60047 — 847-438-5155
Mike Egan, prin. — Fax 438-5989
Lake Zurich MS South Campus — 900/6-8
435 W Cuba Rd 60047 — 847-540-7070
Dave Gardner, prin. — Fax 540-9438
Other Schools – See Hawthorn Woods

Quentin Road Christian S — 200/PK-12
60 Quentin Rd 60047 — 847-438-4494
John Fontana, prin.

La Moille, Bureau, Pop. 760
La Moille CUSD 303 — 300/K-12
PO Box 470 61330 — 815-638-2018
Colette Sutton, supt. — Fax 638-2392
Allen JHS — 100/4-8
PO Box 470 61330 — 815-638-2233
James Brandau, prin. — Fax 638-2886
La Moille HS — 100/9-12
PO Box 440 61330 — 815-638-2144
Colette Sutton, prin. — Fax 638-2392

Lanark, Carroll, Pop. 1,483
Eastland CUSD 308 — 700/PK-12
200 S School St 61046 — 815-493-6301
Mark Hansen, supt. — Fax 493-6303
Eastland HS — 200/9-12
500 S School Dr 61046 — 815-493-6341
Jay Ritchie, prin. — Fax 493-6343
Other Schools – See Shannon

Lansing, Cook, Pop. 27,324
Lansing SD 158 — 2,200/PK-8
18300 Greenbay Ave 60438 — 708-474-6700
Veronda Cottle, supt. — Fax 474-9976
www.d158.net
Memorial JHS — 800/6-8
2721 Ridge Rd 60438 — 708-474-2383
Robert Zimbelman, prin. — Fax 474-9976

Sunnybrook SD 171 — 1,100/PK-8
19266 Burnham Ave 60438 — 708-895-0750
Joseph Majchrowicz Ed.D., supt. — Fax 895-8580
www.sd171.org
Heritage MS — 500/5-8
19250 Burnham Ave 60438 — 708-895-0790
Bruce Christensen, prin. — Fax 895-8580

Thornton Fractional Township HSD 215
Supt. — See Calumet City
Thornton Fractional South HS — 1,700/9-12
18500 Burnham Ave 60438 — 708-585-2000
John Hallberg, prin. — Fax 418-0760

American School — Post-Sec.
2200 E 170th St 60438 — 708-418-2800
Illiana Christian HS — 700/9-12
2261 Indiana Ave 60438 — 708-474-0515
Peter Boonstra, prin. — Fax 474-0581
Luther East HS — 100/9-12
2750 Glenwood Lansing Rd 60438 — 708-895-8441
Dale Cooper, prin. — Fax 895-5220

La Salle, LaSalle, Pop. 9,615
La Salle ESD 122 — 800/PK-8
1165 Saint Vincents Ave 61301 — 815-223-0786
Dr. Joan McGuire, supt. — Fax 223-8740
www.lasalleschools.net/
Lincoln JHS — 200/6-8
1165 Saint Vincents Ave 61301 — 815-223-0933
Jerald Carls, prin. — Fax 223-8740

La Salle-Peru Township HSD 120 — 1,200/9-12
541 Chartres St 61301 — 815-223-1721
Dr. Craig Carter, supt. — Fax 223-3444
www.lphs.net/
La Salle-Peru Township HS — 1,200/9-12
541 Chartres St 61301 — 815-223-1721
Deb Nelson, prin. — Fax 223-3444

Lasalle-Peru Area Career Center
6th and Creve Coeur 61301 — 815-223-2454
Mary Stouffer, dir. — Fax 224-5066
Lasalle-Peru Area Career Center — Vo/Tech
6th and Creve Coeur 61301 — 815-223-2454
Mary Stouffer, prin. — Fax 224-5066

Educators of Beauty — Post-Sec.
122 Wright St 61301 — 815-223-7326
Midwest Center Christian Academy — 50/K-10
PO Box 1128 61301 — 815-224-4077
Rev. Karen King, admin. — Fax 224-4447

Lawrenceville, Lawrence, Pop. 4,513
Lawrence County CUSD 20 — 1,300/PK-12
1802 Cedar St 62439 — 618-943-2326
Michael Sutton, supt. — Fax 943-4092
www.cusd20.com
Lawrenceville HS — 400/9-12
503 8th St 62439 — 618-943-3389
Charles Stegall, prin. — Fax 943-4925
Parkview JHS, 1802 Cedar St 62439 — 300/6-8
Corrie Ray, prin. — 618-943-2327

Lebanon, Saint Clair, Pop. 3,749
Lebanon CUSD 9 — 600/PK-12
200 W Schuetz St 62254 — 618-537-4611
Harry Cavanaugh, supt. — Fax 537-9588
www.lebanon.stclair.k12.il.us
Lebanon HS — 200/9-12
200 W Schuetz St 62254 — 618-537-4423
Leigh Jackson, prin. — Fax 537-9588

McKendree College — Post-Sec.
701 College Rd 62254 — 618-537-6830

Leland, LaSalle, Pop. 942
Leland CUSD 1 — 300/K-12
370 N Main St 60531 — 815-495-3821
Ronald Abrell, supt. — Fax 495-4611
www.leland.lasall.k12.il.us
Leland HS — 100/9-12
370 N Main St 60531 — 815-495-3231
Matthew Jokisch, prin. — Fax 495-4611

Lemont, DuPage, Pop. 15,146
Lemont Township HSD 210 — 1,300/9-12
800 Porter St 60439 — 630-257-5838
Dr. Sandra Doebert, supt. — Fax 257-7603
www.lhs210.net
Lemont HS — 1,300/9-12
800 Porter St 60439 — 630-257-5838
Dr. Thomas Trengove, prin. — Fax 243-0310

Lemont-Bromberek Combined SD 113A — 2,600/PK-8
16100 W 127th St 60439 — 630-257-2286
Dr. Tim Ricker, supt. — Fax 243-3005
www.sd113a.org/
Old Quarry MS — 900/6-8
16100 W 127th St 60439 — 630-257-2286
Dawn Pechukas, prin. — Fax 243-3004

Mt. Assisi Academy — 300/9-12
13860 Main St 60439 — 630-257-7844
Sr. Mary Werner, prin. — Fax 257-6362

Lena, Stephenson, Pop. 2,854
Lena Winslow CUSD 202 — 1,100/PK-12
401 Fremont St 61048 — 815-369-3100
John R. Kelley, supt. — Fax 369-3102
www.le-win.net/
Lena-Winslow HS — 400/9-12
516 Fremont St 61048 — 815-369-3115
Dan Todd, prin. — Fax 369-3139
Lena-Winslow JHS — 200/6-8
517 Fremont St 61048 — 815-369-3114
Mark Kuehl, prin. — Fax 369-3162

Le Roy, McLean, Pop. 3,391
Le Roy CUSD 2 — 800/PK-12
600 E Pine St 61752 — 309-962-4211
Edgar Coller, supt. — Fax 962-9312
Le Roy HS — 200/9-12
505 E Center St 61752 — 309-962-2911
Gary Tipsord, prin. — Fax 962-8421
Le Roy JHS — 100/7-8
505 E Center St 61752 — 309-962-2911
Gary Tipsord, prin. — Fax 962-8421

Lewistown, Fulton, Pop. 2,448
Lewistown SD 97 — 800/PK-12
15501 E Avenue L 61542 — 309-547-5826
Bill King, supt. — Fax 547-5235
www.cusd97.fulton.k12.il.us/
Central ES, 15501 E Avenue L 61542 — 300/4-8
Jan Braun, prin. — 309-547-2231
Lewistown Community HS — 200/9-12
15205 N State 100 Hwy 61542 — 309-547-2288
Gavin Sronce, prin. — Fax 547-9870

Lexington, McLean, Pop. 1,866
Lexington CUSD 7 — 600/PK-12
PO Box 67 61753 — 309-365-4141
Dr. Brent McArdle, supt. — Fax 365-7381
www.lexington.k12.il.us
Lexington HS — 200/9-12
PO Box 67 61753 — 309-365-2711
Richard Baker, prin. — Fax 365-5032
Lexington JHS, PO Box 67 61753 — 100/7-8
Richard Baker, prin. — 309-365-2711

Liberty, Adams, Pop. 515
Liberty CUSD 2 — 600/PK-12
505 N Park St 62347 — 217-645-3433
Curtis Simonson, supt. — Fax 645-3241
Liberty HS — 200/9-12
505 N Park St 62347 — 217-645-3433
Jenice Taylor, prin. — Fax 645-3241

Libertyville, Lake, Pop. 21,760
Community HSD 128
Supt. — See Vernon Hills
Libertyville HS — 1,800/9-12
708 W Park Ave 60048 — 847-327-7000
Brad Swanson, prin. — Fax 367-2573

Libertyville SD 70 — 2,600/PK-8
1381 Lake St 60048 — 847-362-9695
Dr. Mark Friedman, supt. — Fax 362-3003
www.d70.k12.il.us
Highland MS — 1,000/6-8
310 W Rockland Rd 60048 — 847-362-9020
Sharon Aspinall, prin. — Fax 362-0870

Lincoln, Logan, Pop. 14,971
Lincoln Community HSD 404 — 900/9-12
1000 Primm Rd 62656 — 217-732-4131
Dean Langdon, supt. — Fax 735-3963
lchs.k12.il.us/
Lincoln Community HS — 900/9-12
1000 Primm Rd 62656 — 217-732-4131
Joyce Hubbard, prin. — Fax 735-3963

Lincoln ESD 27 — 1,100/PK-8
100 S Maple St 62656 — 217-732-2522
Kirby Rodgers, supt. — Fax 732-2198
logan.k12.il.us/les27/
Lincoln JHS — 300/6-8
208 Broadway St 62656 — 217-732-3535
Curtis Nettles, prin. — Fax 732-2685

Lincolnland Technical Education Center
1000 Primm Rd 62656 — 217-732-4131
Cindy Stover, dir. — Fax 735-3963
Lincolnland Technical Education Center — Vo/Tech
1000 Primm Rd 62656 — 217-732-4131
Cindy Stover, dir. — Fax 735-3963

Lincoln Christian College — Post-Sec.
100 Campus View Dr 62656 — 217-732-3168
Lincoln College — Post-Sec.
300 Keokuk St 62656 — 217-732-3155

Lincolnshire, Lake, Pop. 6,841
Adlai E. Stevenson SD 125 — 4,600/9-12
2 Stevenson Dr 60069 — 847-634-4000
Dr. Timothy D. Kanold, supt. — Fax 634-0239
www.district125.k12.il.us
Stevenson HS — 4,600/9-12
1 Stevenson Dr 60069 — 847-634-4000
Janet Gonzalez, prin. — Fax 634-7309

Lincolnshire-Prairieview SD 103 — 1,700/K-8
1370 N Riverwoods Rd 60069 — 847-295-4030
Larry Fleming, supt. — Fax 295-9196
www.district103.k12.il.us
Wright JHS — 800/5-8
1370 N Riverwoods Rd 60069 — 847-295-1560
Joshua Carpenter, prin. — Fax 295-7136

Keller Graduate School of DeVry Univ. — Post-Sec.
25 Tri State Intl Ste 130 60069 — 847-940-7768

Lincolnwood, Cook, Pop. 12,026
Lincolnwood SD 74 — 1,300/PK-8
6950 N East Prairie Rd 60712 — 847-675-8234
Dr. Donald R. Yeoman, supt. — Fax 675-8244
www.sd74.org
Lincoln Hall MS — 400/6-8
6855 N Crawford Ave 60712 — 847-675-8240
Larry Sasso, prin. — Fax 675-8124

Lisle, DuPage, Pop. 23,376
Lisle CUSD 202 — 1,800/PK-12
5211 Center Ave 60532 — 630-493-8000
Dr. J. Peter Lueck, supt. — Fax 971-4054
www.lisle.dupage.k12.il.us/
Lisle HS — 600/9-12
1800 Short St 60532 — 630-493-8300
Ronald Logeman, prin. — Fax 968-0182
Lisle JHS — 400/6-8
5207 Center Ave 60532 — 630-493-8200
Timothy Pociask, prin. — Fax 493-8209

Naperville CUSD 203
Supt. — See Naperville
Kennedy JHS — 1,200/6-8
2929 Green Trails Dr 60532 — 630-420-3220
Donald Perry, prin. — Fax 420-6960

Benedictine University Post-Sec.
5700 College Rd 60532 630-829-6000
Benet Academy 1,300/9-12
2200 Maple Ave 60532 630-719-2782
Stephen A. Marth, prin. Fax 719-2790
DeVry University Post-Sec.
6200 Route 53 Ste G-11 60532 630-969-6624

Litchfield, Montgomery, Pop. 6,771
Litchfield CUSD 12 1,700/PK-12
1702 N State St 62056 217-324-2157
Sharon Johnson, supt. Fax 324-2158
www.litchfield.k12.il.us
Litchfield HS 500/9-12
1705 N State St 62056 217-324-3955
Michael Juenger, prin. Fax 324-5851
Litchfield MS 400/6-8
1701 N State St 62056 217-324-4668
Mark Hunt, prin. Fax 324-5693

Tri-County Beauty Academy Post-Sec.
219 N State St 62056 217-324-9062

Lockport, Will, Pop. 22,161
Lockport SD 91 700/K-8
808 Adams St 60441 815-838-0737
Donna Gray, supt. Fax 834-4339
www.d91.net/index1.htm
Kelvin Grove MS 400/4-8
808 Adams St 60441 815-838-0737
Mary Jo Slingerland, prin. Fax 834-4339

Lockport Township HSD 205 2,600/9-12
1323 E 7th St 60441 815-588-8100
Dr. Garry Raymond, supt. Fax 588-8109
www.lths.org
Lockport Township HS Central Campus 9-9
1222 S Jefferson St 60441 815-588-8200
Dennis Hicks, prin. Fax 588-8209
Lockport Township HS East Campus 2,600/10-12
1333 E 7th St 60441 815-588-8300
K. Brett Gould, prin. Fax 588-8309

Will County SD 92 2,000/PK-8
708 N State St 60441 815-838-8031
Dr. Gary Peck, supt. Fax 838-8034
www.d92.org
Oak Prairie JHS 6-8
15161 S Gougar Rd, 815-836-2724
Mark Murray, prin.

Lombard, DuPage, Pop. 42,816
Glenbard Twp. HSD 87
Supt. — See Glen Ellyn
Glenbard East HS 2,700/9-12
1014 S Main St 60148 630-627-9250
Robert McBride, prin. Fax 627-9264

Lombard SD 44 3,200/PK-8
150 W Madison St 60148 630-827-4400
James Blanche, supt. Fax 620-3798
www.sd44.org/
Glenn Westlake MS 1,100/6-8
1514 S Main St 60148 630-827-4500
Philip Wieczorek, prin. Fax 620-3791

College Preparatory S of America 500/K-12
331 W Madison St 60148 630-889-8000
Saif Qureshi, prin. Fax 889-8012
Illinois Center for Broadcasting Post-Sec.
55 W 22nd St Ste 240 60148 630-916-1700
Montini Catholic HS 600/9-12
19W070 16th St 60148 630-627-6930
Maryann O'Neill, prin. Fax 627-0536
National University of Health Sciences Post-Sec.
200 E Roosevelt Rd 60148 630-629-2000
Northern Baptist Theological Seminary Post-Sec.
660 E Butterfield Rd 60148 630-620-2180

London Mills, Fulton, Pop. 440
Spoon River Valley CUSD 4 500/PK-12
35265 N IL Route 97 61544 309-778-2204
Dave Gilliland, supt. Fax 778-2655
www.spoon-river.k12.il.us
Spoon River Valley HS 100/9-12
35265 N IL Route 97 61544 309-778-2201
Dave Gilliland, prin. Fax 778-2655
Spoon River Valley JHS 100/7-8
35265 N IL Route 97 61544 309-778-2201
Dave Gilliland, prin. Fax 778-2655

Long Grove, Lake, Pop. 7,833
Kildeer Countryside CCSD 96
Supt. — See Buffalo Grove
Woodlawn MS 700/6-8
6362 RFD/Gilmer Rd 60047 847-353-8500
Dr. Christine Jakicic, prin. Fax 949-8237

Louisville, Clay, Pop. 1,256
North Clay CUSD 25 700/PK-12
PO Box C 62858 618-665-3358
Monty Aldrich, supt. Fax 665-3893
North Clay Community HS 200/9-12
PO Box 220 62858 618-665-3102
Carolyn Grahn, prin.

Love Joy, Saint Clair, Pop. 1,099
Brooklyn Unit SD 188 300/PK-12
PO Box 250, 618-271-1028
Dr. Raelynn Parks, supt. Fax 271-9108
www.lovejoy.stclair.k12.il.us
Lovejoy MS 100/6-8
PO Box 250, 618-271-1014
Catherine Calvert, prin. Fax 271-9108
Lovejoy Technology Academy 100/9-12
PO Box 250, 618-271-1014
Catherine Calvert, prin. Fax 271-9108

Loves Park, Winnebago, Pop. 22,983
Harlem Unit SD 122
Supt. — See Machesney Park
Harlem MS 1,200/7-8
735 Windsor Rd 61111 815-654-4510
John Cusimano, prin. Fax 654-4540

Lovington, Moultrie, Pop. 1,196
Lovington CUSD 303 300/PK-12
445 E Church St 61937 217-873-4310
Roy Smith, supt. Fax 873-5311
www.lovington.k12.il.us/
Lovington HS 100/9-12
445 E Church St 61937 217-873-4316
Tracy Garmon, prin. Fax 873-5311

Lyons, Cook, Pop. 10,466
Lyons SD 103 2,200/K-8
4100 Joliet Ave 60534 708-783-4100
Dr. Raymond Lauk, supt. Fax 780-9725
www.sd103.com/
Washington MS 700/6-8
8101 Ogden Ave 60534 708-783-4200
Robert Hildreth, prin. Fax 780-9757

Mc Henry, McHenry, Pop. 19,144
Mc Henry CCSD 15 4,800/PK-8
1011 N Green St, 815-385-7210
R. Alan Hoffman Ed.D., supt. Fax 344-7121
www.d15.org
Mc Henry MS 900/6-8
2120 W Lincoln Rd, 815-385-2522
Lori Miscik, prin. Fax 578-2101
Parkland S 800/6-8
1802 N Ringwood Rd, 815-385-8810
Mike Adams, prin. Fax 363-5023

Mc Henry Community HSD 156 2,300/9-12
4716 W Crystal Lake Rd, 815-385-7900
Dr. Teresa Lane, supt. Fax 344-7153
www.dist156.org
Mc Henry HS - East 900/9-12
1012 N Green St, 815-385-1145
Lynn Schnelker, prin. Fax 363-8435
Mc Henry HS - West 1,300/9-12
4724 W Crystal Lake Rd, 815-385-7077
Dr. Barbara Johnke, prin. Fax 363-8651

Montini MS 300/4-8
1405 N Richmond Rd, 815-385-1022
Sheila Murphy, prin. Fax 363-7536

Machesney Park, Winnebago, Pop. 21,846
Harlem Unit SD 122 7,800/PK-12
8605 N 2nd St 61115 815-654-4500
Pascal V. Deluca, supt. Fax 654-4600
www.harlem.winbgo.k12.il.us
Harlem HS 2,400/9-12
1 Huskie Cir 61115 815-654-4511
Joe Hazen, prin. Fax 654-4525
Other Schools – See Loves Park

Mackinaw, Tazewell, Pop. 1,614
Deer Creek-Mackinaw CUSD 701 1,000/PK-12
PO Box 110 61755 309-359-8965
Steve Yarnall, supt. Fax 359-5291
www.deemack.org/
Deer Creek-Mackinaw HS 300/9-12
PO Box 110 61755 309-359-4421
Bill Lamb, prin. Fax 359-3125

Mc Leansboro, Hamilton, Pop. 2,713
Hamilton County CUSD 10 1,300/PK-12
PO Box 369 62859 618-643-2328
Vince Mitchell, supt. Fax 643-2015
www.unit10.com
Hamilton County JSHS 600/7-12
1 Fox Ln 62859 618-643-2328
Jeff Fetcho, prin. Fax 643-2307

Mc Nabb, Putnam, Pop. 296
Putnam County CUSD 535
Supt. — See Granville
Putnam County JHS 300/5-8
13183 N 350th Ave 61335 815-882-2116
Sandra Micheletti, prin. Fax 882-2118

Macomb, McDonough, Pop. 18,587
Macomb CUSD 185 1,900/PK-12
323 W Washington St 61455 309-833-4161
Dr. Frances Karanovich, supt. Fax 836-2133
district185.macomb.com/
Macomb HS 700/9-12
1525 S Johnson St 61455 309-837-2331
Mark Twomey, prin. Fax 836-1034
Macomb JHS 300/7-8
1525 S Johnson St 61455 309-833-2074
Dana Isackson, prin. Fax 836-1034

McDonough District Hospital Post-Sec.
525 E Grant St 61455 309-833-4101
Western Illinois University Post-Sec.
1 University Cir 61455 309-295-1414

Macon, Macon, Pop. 1,151
Meridian CUSD 15 1,100/PK-12
PO Box 347 62544 217-764-5269
Dr. Frank Meyer, supt. Fax 764-5291
www.meridian.k12.il.us
Meridian HS 300/9-12
PO Box 380 62544 217-764-5233
Jack Blickensderfer, prin. Fax 764-5282
Other Schools – See Blue Mound

Madison, Madison, Pop. 4,558
Madison CUSD 12 1,000/PK-12
1707 4th St 62060 618-877-1712
Dr. Sandra Schroeder, supt. Fax 877-2690
www.schools.lth5.k12.il.us/madison/
Madison HS 200/9-12
600 Farrish St 62060 618-876-7010
Dr. Brian Carey, prin. Fax 877-2694
Madison MS 300/PK-PK, 6-
1003 Farrish St 62060 618-876-6409
Timothy Miller, prin. Fax 877-2693

Mahomet, Champaign, Pop. 5,714
Mahomet-Seymour CUSD 3 2,800/PK-12
PO Box 229 61853 217-586-4995
Keith Oates, supt. Fax 586-5834
www.ms.k12.il.us
Mahomet-Seymour HS 900/9-12
PO Box 1098 61853 217-586-4962
Marty Williams, prin. Fax 586-6844
Mahomet-Seymour JHS 600/6-8
PO Box 560 61853 217-586-4415
Jeff Starwalt, prin. Fax 586-5869

Malta, DeKalb, Pop. 963

Kishwaukee College Post-Sec.
21193 Malta Rd 60150 815-825-2086

Manhattan, Will, Pop. 5,169
Manhattan SD 114 700/PK-PK, 1-
25440 S Gougar Rd 60442 815-478-6093
Howard Butters, supt. Fax 478-7660
www.manhattan114.org
Manhattan JHS 6-8
15606 W Smith Rd 60442 815-478-6090
Ron Pacheco, prin. Fax 478-6094

Christ's Academy 100/PK-12
22811 S Cedar Rd 60442 815-485-2833
Sharon Meiergerd, prin. Fax 485-2833

Manito, Mason, Pop. 1,702
Midwest Central CUSD 191 1,200/PK-12
1010 S Washington St 61546 309-968-6868
Jerry Meyer, supt. Fax 968-7916
www.midwestcentral.org/
Midwest Central HS 300/9-12
910 S Washington St 61546 309-968-6766
Kathryn Cihlar, prin. Fax 968-6340
Other Schools – See Green Valley

Manlius, Bureau, Pop. 348
Bureau Valley CUSD 340 1,100/PK-12
PO Box 289 61338 815-445-3101
Dr. Rick Stoecker, supt. Fax 445-2802
www.bhsroe.k12.il.us/bureauvalley
Bureau Valley HS 500/9-12
PO Box 329 61338 815-445-4004
Terry Gutshall, prin. Fax 445-3017
Other Schools – See Buda

Mansfield, Piatt, Pop. 939
Blue Ridge CUSD 18
Supt. — See Farmer City
Blue Ridge JHS 100/7-8
PO Box 69 61854 217-489-5201
John Weaver, prin. Fax 489-9051

Manteno, Kankakee, Pop. 7,955
Manteno CUSD 5 1,900/K-12
250 N Poplar St 60950 815-928-7000
Michael E. Smith, supt. Fax 468-6439
www.manteno.k12.il.us
Manteno HS 600/9-12
443 N Maple St 60950 815-928-7101
Paul Russert, prin. Fax 468-2344
Manteno MS 500/6-8
250 N Poplar St 60950 815-928-7154
David Conrad, prin. Fax 468-8082

Maple Park, Kane, Pop. 1,132
Fox Valley Career Center
47W326 Keslinger Rd 60151 630-365-5113
Larry Imel, supt. Fax 365-9088
www.kaneland.org
Fox Valley Career Center Vo/Tech
47W326 Keslinger Rd 60151 630-365-5113
Larry Imel, prin. Fax 365-9088

Kaneland CUSD 302 3,600/PK-12
47W326 Keslinger Rd 60151 630-365-5111
Dr. Charles McCormick, supt. Fax 365-9428
www.kaneland.org
Kaneland HS 1,000/9-12
47W326 Keslinger Rd 60151 630-365-5100
Mike Davis, prin. Fax 365-8421
Kaneland MS 800/6-8
1N137 Meredith Rd 60151 630-365-3005
Richard Burchell, prin. Fax 365-5686

Marengo, McHenry, Pop. 7,381
Marengo Community HSD 154 800/9-12
110 Franks Rd 60152 815-568-6511
Dr. Dan Bertrand, supt. Fax 568-6510
www.mchs154.org/
Marengo HS 800/9-12
110 Franks Rd 60152 815-568-6511
Eric Vance, prin. Fax 568-6510

Marengo-Union Consolidated ESD 165 500/PK-8
816 E Grant Hwy 60152 815-568-8323
Dr. Richard Angel, supt. Fax 568-8367
www.marengo.k12.il.us/
Marengo Community MS PK-PK, 5-
816 E Grant Hwy 60152 815-568-5720
Phil Grover, prin. Fax 568-7572

Faith Lutheran HS 50/9-12
1913 Hawthorn Rd 60152 815-338-3547
Robert Schulze, prin. Fax 568-0204

Marion, Williamson, Pop. 17,104
Crab Orchard CUSD 3 400/PK-12
19189 Bailey St 62959 618-982-2181
Derek Hutchins, supt. Fax 982-2080
Crab Orchard HS 100/9-12
19189 Bailey St 62959 618-982-2181
William McSparin, prin. Fax 982-2080

Marion CUSD 2 4,000/PK-12
1700 W Cherry St 62959 618-993-2321
J. Wade Hudgens, supt. Fax 997-0943
www.marionunit2.org/
Marion HS 1,200/9-12
1501 S Carbon St 62959 618-993-8196
Stephen Smith, prin. Fax 997-8749
Marion JHS 900/6-8
1609 W Main St 62959 618-997-1317
Kimberly Brave, prin. Fax 997-0477

Agape Christian HS 100/9-12
5708 Meadowland Pkwy 62959 618-993-9677
Dr. K. Stephen Combs, prin. Fax 993-9665

Marissa, Saint Clair, Pop. 2,044
Marissa CUSD 40 600/PK-12
215 North St 62257 618-295-2313
Kevin Coggdill, supt. Fax 295-2609
Marissa JSHS 300/7-12
300 School View Dr 62257 618-295-2393
Michael Guthrie, prin. Fax 295-2276

Markham, Cook, Pop. 12,304
Hazel Crest SD 152-5
Supt. — See Hazel Crest
Frost MS 300/7-8
2206 W 167th St, 708-210-9929
Maceo Rainey, prin. Fax 210-9582

Prairie-Hills ESD 144 2,900/PK-8
3015 W 163rd St 708-210-2888
Dr. I.V. Foster, supt. Fax 210-9925
phsd144.net/
Prairie-Hills JHS 600/7-8
3035 W 163rd St, 708-210-2860
Tiffany Burnett-Johnson, prin. Fax 210-9208

Maroa, Macon, Pop. 1,563
Maroa-Forsyth CUSD 2 700/PK-12
PO Box 738 61756 217-794-3488
Mike Williams, supt. Fax 794-3878
www.mfschools.org/
Maroa-Forsyth HS 300/9-12
PO Box 738 61756 217-794-3463
Scott Adreon, prin. Fax 794-5459
Maroa-Forsyth MS 6-8
PO Box 738 61756 217-794-5115
Kathy Massey, prin. Fax 794-3351

Marquette Heights, Tazewell, Pop. 2,826
North Pekin & Marquette Hts SD 102 600/PK-8
51 Yates Rd 61554 309-382-2172
Mike Dickson, supt. Fax 382-2122
www.tazewell.k12.il.us/dist102
Georgetowne MS 200/6-8
51 Yates Rd 61554 309-382-3456
Meredith Brooks, prin. Fax 382-2122

Marshall, Clark, Pop. 3,724
Marshall CUSD 2C 1,500/PK-12
503 Pine St 62441 217-826-5912
Rick Manuell, supt. Fax 826-5170
www.marshall.k12.il.us/
Marshall HS 400/9-12
806 N 6th St 62441 217-826-2395
Dale Farr, prin. Fax 826-5511
Marshall JHS 200/7-8
806 N 6th St 62441 217-826-2812
Richard Manuell, prin. Fax 826-6065

Martinsville, Clark, Pop. 1,230
Martinsville CUSD 3C 400/PK-12
PO Box K 62442 217-382-4321
Jill Rogers, supt. Fax 382-4183
www.martinsville.k12.il.us/
Martinsville HS 100/9-12
PO Box K 62442 217-382-4132
Ray Schollenbruch, prin. Fax 382-4761
Martinsville JHS 100/7-8
PO Box K 62442 217-382-4132
Ray Schollenbruch, prin. Fax 382-4761

Mascoutah, Saint Clair, Pop. 5,824
Mascoutah CUSD 19 2,700/PK-12
720 W Harnett St 62258 618-566-7414
Dr. Sam McGowen, supt. Fax 566-4507
www.mascoutah19.k12.il.us
Mascoutah HS 900/9-12
1313 W Main St 62258 618-566-8523
Mike Scholz, prin. Fax 566-8693
Mascoutah MS 400/6-8
846 N 6th St 62258 618-566-2305
Bob G. Stone, prin. Fax 566-2307

Mason City, Mason, Pop. 2,473
Illini Central CUSD 189 900/PK-12
208 N West St 62664 217-482-5180
Chad Allaman, supt. Fax 482-3121
www.mason.k12.il.us/illinicentral189/
Illini Central HS 300/9-12
208 N West St 62664 217-482-3252
Patrick Martin, prin. Fax 482-3323
Other Schools – See Easton

Matteson, Cook, Pop. 15,675
ESD 159 1,100/PK-8
6202 Vollmer Rd 60443 708-720-1300
Dr. Eric King, supt. Fax 720-3218
www.dist159.com
Powell MS 6-8
20600 Matteson Ave 60443 708-283-9600
Pamela Woods, prin. Fax 283-1885

Matteson ESD 162 3,300/PK-8
3625 215th St 60443 708-748-0100
Dr. Blondean Davis, supt. Fax 748-7302
www.sd162.org
Huth MS 700/7-8
3718 213th Pl 60443 708-748-0470
Ronald Jones, prin. Fax 503-1119

Mattoon, Coles, Pop. 17,385
Mattoon CUSD 2 3,200/K-12
1701 Charleston Ave 61938 217-238-8850
Larry Lilly, supt. Fax 238-8855
www.mattoon.k12.il.us
Mattoon HS 1,000/9-12
2521 Walnut Ave 61938 217-238-7800
Ken Reed, prin. Fax 238-7805
Mattoon MS 800/6-8
1200 S 9th St 61938 217-238-5800
Todd Vilardo, prin. Fax 238-5805
Mattoon Area Adult Education Center Adult
1617 Lake Land Blvd 61938 217-235-0361
Mark Nelson, dir. Fax 258-5286

Lake Land College Post-Sec.
5001 Lake Land Blvd 61938 217-234-5253

Maywood, Cook, Pop. 25,777
Proviso Township HSD 209
Supt. — See Forest Park
Proviso East HS 2,100/9-12
807 S 1st Ave 60153 708-344-7000
Milton Patch, prin. Fax 344-5942

Loyola University Post-Sec.
2160 S 1st Ave 60153 708-216-3229
Loyola University Medical Center Post-Sec.
2160 S 1st Ave 60153 708-216-9000

Mazon, Grundy, Pop. 918
Mazon-Verona-Kinsman ESD 2C 300/K-8
1013 North St 60444 815-448-2200
Dr. Lynn Neville, supt. Fax 448-3005
www.mvkmavericks.org
Mazon-Verona-Kinsman MS 200/5-8
1013 North St 60444 815-448-2127
Debra Paulsen, prin. Fax 448-3005

Melrose Park, Cook, Pop. 22,512
Mannheim SD 83
Supt. — See Franklin Park
Mannheim JHS 900/6-8
2600 Hyde Park Ave 60164 847-455-5020
Timothy Daley, prin. Fax 455-2038

Lincoln Technical Institute Post-Sec.
8317 W North Ave 60160 708-344-4700

Walther Lutheran HS 400/9-12
900 Chicago Ave 60160 708-344-0404
Stephen Zielke, prin. Fax 344-0525

Mendon, Adams, Pop. 875
CUSD 4 700/PK-12
PO Box 200 62351 217-936-2111
Diane Robertson, supt. Fax 936-2643
www.cusd4.com
Unity HS 200/9-12
PO Box 200 62351 217-936-2116
William Dorethy, prin. Fax 936-2117
Unity MS 200/6-8
PO Box 200 62351 217-936-2727
Brad Gooding, prin. Fax 936-2730

Mendota, LaSalle, Pop. 7,077
Mendota CCSD 289 1,300/PK-8
1806 Guiles Ave 61342 815-539-7631
Marcia Burress, supt. Fax 538-2927
www.m289.lasall.k12.il.us/
Northbrook S 700/PK-PK, 4-
1804 Guiles Ave 61342 815-539-6237
Cindy Pozzi, prin. Fax 538-3090

Mendota Township HSD 280 600/9-12
2300 W Main St 61342 815-539-7446
Jeff Prusator, supt. Fax 539-3103
mendotahs.org/home.htm
Mendota Township HS 600/9-12
2300 W Main St 61342 815-539-7446
Denise Aughenbaugh, prin. Fax 539-3103

Meredosia, Morgan, Pop. 996
Meredosia-Chambersburg CUSD 11 300/PK-12
PO Box 440 62665 217-584-1744
William Mauser, supt. Fax 584-1129
Meredosia-Chambersburg HS 100/9-12
PO Box 440 62665 217-584-1291
Eugene Link, prin. Fax 584-1741
Meredosia-Chambersburg JHS 100/6-8
PO Box 440 62665 217-584-1291
Eugene Link, prin. Fax 584-1741

Metamora, Woodford, Pop. 3,067
Germantown Hills SD 69 300/PK-8
110 Fandel Rd 61548 309-383-2121
Joe Stieglitz, supt. Fax 383-2123
ghills.metamora.k12.il.us
Germantown Hills MS 3-8
103 Warrior Way 61548 309-383-2121
James B. Dansart, prin. Fax 383-4739

Metamora Twp. HSD 122 900/9-12
PO Box 109 61548 309-367-4151
Kenneth Maurer, supt. Fax 367-4351
mths.metamora.k12.il.us/
Metamora HS 900/9-12
PO Box 109 61548 309-367-4151
Greg Christy, prin. Fax 367-4154

Metropolis, Massac, Pop. 6,468
Massac Unit SD 1 2,400/PK-12
PO Box 530 62960 618-524-9376
William Hatfield, supt. Fax 524-4432
www.unit1.massac.k12.il.us/
Massac County HS 600/9-12
2841 Old Marion Rd 62960 618-524-3440
Danny Stevens, prin. Fax 524-3131
Massac JHS 300/7-8
PO Box 331 62960 618-524-2645
Lynne Lech, prin. Fax 524-2765

Midlothian, Cook, Pop. 13,949
Bremen Community HSD 228 5,000/9-12
15233 Pulaski Rd 60445 708-389-1175
Fax 389-2552
www.bhsd228.com
Bremen HS 1,200/9-12
15203 Pulaski Rd 60445 708-371-3600
Marcia Mendenhall, prin. Fax 371-7194
Other Schools – See Country Club Hills, Oak Forest, Tinley Park

Milford, Iroquois, Pop. 1,310
Milford Township HSD 233 200/9-12
PO Box 304 60953 815-889-5176
Dale Hastings, supt. Fax 889-5221
www.milford.k12.il.us/
Milford Township HS 200/9-12
PO Box 257 60953 815-889-4184
Stephen Totheroit, prin. Fax 889-4871

Millbrook, Kendall, Pop. 303
Newark CCSD 66
Supt. — See Newark
Millbrook JHS 100/5-8
PO Box 214 60536 630-553-5435
Richard Sjolund, prin. Fax 553-1027

Milledgeville, Carroll, Pop. 946
Chadwick-Milledgeville CUSD 399
Supt. — See Chadwick
Milledgeville HS 200/9-12
PO Box 609 61051 815-225-7141
Timothy Schurman, prin. Fax 225-7847

Minonk, Woodford, Pop. 2,158
Fieldcrest CUSD 6 900/PK-12
1 Dornbush Dr 61760 309-432-2177
Randy Vincent, supt. Fax 432-3377
www.fieldcrest.k12.il.us/
Fieldcrest HS 400/9-12
1 Dornbush Dr 61760 309-432-2529
William Lapp, prin. Fax 432-2064
Other Schools – See Wenona

Minooka, Grundy, Pop. 8,403
Minooka CCSD 201 2,300/PK-8
333 McEvilly Rd 60447 815-467-6121
J. Michel Morrow, supt. Fax 467-9544
www.min201.org/
Minooka JHS 700/6-8
333 McEvilly Rd 60447 815-467-2136
Shane Severson, prin. Fax 467-5087

Minooka Community HSD 111 1,700/9-12
PO Box 827 60447 815-467-2557
Dr. David Middleton, supt. Fax 467-9733
www.mchs.net/
Minooka Community HS 1,700/9-12
301 S Wabena Ave 60447 815-467-2140
Robert Williams, prin. Fax 467-2431

Mokena, Will, Pop. 17,396
Mokena SD 159 2,400/PK-8
11244 Willow Crest Ln 60448 708-342-4900
Dr. Gary Bradbury, supt. Fax 479-3143
www.mokena159.com
Mokena JHS 900/6-8
19815 Kirkstone Way 60448 708-342-4870
Julia Wheaton, prin. Fax 479-3122

Trend Setters College of Cosmetology Post-Sec.
19031 Old LaGrange Rd 60448 708-478-6907

Moline, Rock Island, Pop. 42,892
Moline Unit SD 40 7,700/PK-12
1619 11th Ave 61265 309-743-1600
Dr. Cal Lee, supt. Fax 757-3476
www.molineschools.org
Deere MS 600/7-8
2035 11th St 61265 309-743-1622
William Burrus, prin. Fax 757-3668
Moline HS 2,300/9-12
3600 Avenue Of The Cities 61265 309-743-1624
Gary Koeller, prin. Fax 757-3667
Wilson MS 600/7-8
1301 48th St 61265 309-743-1623
Robert Benson, prin. Fax 757-3586

Black Hawk College Post-Sec.
6600 34th Ave 61265 309-796-5000
Brown Mackie College Post-Sec.
1527 47th Ave 61265 309-762-2100
Quad Cities Christian S 50/7-12
1401 16th St 61265 309-762-3800
William Olmstead, prin. Fax 762-8150

Momence, Kankakee, Pop. 3,066
Momence CUSD 1 1,300/PK-12
415 N Dixie Hwy 60954 815-472-3501
Dr. Phillip A. Smith, supt. Fax 472-3516
www.momence.k12.il.us
Momence HS 400/9-12
101 N Franklin St 60954 815-472-6477
Judith Pappas, prin. Fax 472-2055
Momence JHS 400/5-8
801 W 2nd St 60954 815-472-4184
Michele Keiser, prin. Fax 472-3517

Monmouth, Warren, Pop. 9,198
Monmouth-Roseville CUSD 238 1,400/PK-12
401 E 2nd Ave 61462 309-734-4712
Martin Payne, supt. Fax 734-4755
titans.k12.il.us/district/welcome.htm
Monmouth-Roseville HS 400/9-12
325 W 1st Ave 61462 309-734-5118
Jeff Bryan, prin. Fax 734-2918
Other Schools – See Roseville

United CUSD 304
Supt. — See Alexis
United JSHS, 1905 100th St 61462 7-12
Amy Schmitz, prin. 309-734-9411

Yorkwood CUSD 225 400/PK-12
2140 State Highway 135 61462 309-734-8514
Jane Michael, supt. Fax 734-8515
www.yorkwood225.net
Yorkwood HS 100/9-12
2140 State Highway 135 61462 309-734-8511
Kristen Nelson, prin. Fax 734-6094
Yorkwood JHS 100/6-8
2140 State Highway 135 61462 309-734-8511
Kristen Nelson, prin. Fax 734-6094

Monmouth College Post-Sec.
700 E Broadway 61462 309-457-2131

Monticello, Piatt, Pop. 5,275
Monticello CUSD 25 1,600/PK-12
2 Sage Dr 61856 217-762-8511
Dr. Larry McNabb, supt. Fax 762-8534
www.sages.us/
Monticello HS 500/9-12
1 Sage Dr 61856 217-762-8511
Tip Reedy, prin. Fax 762-7421
Monticello MS 400/6-8
2015 E Washington St 61856 217-762-8511
Jeanne Handley, prin. Fax 762-7765

Mooseheart, Kane

Mooseheart S 200/PK-12
255 James J Davis Ave 60539 630-906-3646
Gary Urwiler, supt. Fax 906-3617

Morris, Grundy, Pop. 12,939
Grundy Area Vocational Center
1002 Union St 60450 815-942-4390
David Potts, dir.
gavc.mornet.org/
Grundy AVC, 1002 Union St 60450 Vo/Tech
David Potts, dir. 815-942-4390

Morris Community HSD 101 1,000/9-12
1000 Union St 60450 815-941-5327
Steven Fannin, supt. Fax 941-5407
www.mchs.grundy.k12.il.us
Morris HS 1,000/9-12
1000 Union St 60450 815-941-5326
Kelly Hussey, prin. Fax 941-5405

Morris SD 54 1,300/PK-8
54 White Oak Dr 60450 815-942-0056
Barry Green, supt. Fax 942-0240
dist54.mornet.org
Shabbona MS 400/6-8
725 School St Ste A 60450 815-942-3605
Sheryl Dzuryak, prin. Fax 941-4531

Nettle Creek CCSD 24 C 100/K-8
8820 Scott School Rd 60450 815-942-0511
Ann Chandler, supt. Fax 942-9124
Nettle Creek MS 100/3-8
8820 Scott School Rd 60450 815-942-0511
Ann Chandler, prin. Fax 942-9124

Morrison, Whiteside, Pop. 4,318
Morrison CUSD 6 1,200/PK-12
643 Genesee Ave 61270 815-772-2064
Dr. Jody Ware, supt. Fax 772-4644
www.morrisonschools.org

Morrison HS 400/9-12
643 Genesee Ave 61270 815-772-4071
Janet Ward, prin. Fax 772-4644
Morrison JHS 300/6-8
300 Academic Dr 61270 815-772-7264
Darryl Hogue, prin. Fax 772-2531

Morrison Institute of Technology Post-Sec.
701 Portland Ave 61270 815-772-7218

Morrisonville, Christian, Pop. 1,050
Morrisonville CUSD 1 300/PK-12
PO Box 13 62546 217-526-4431
Wesley Wells, supt. Fax 526-4433
mohawks.net
Morrisonville HS 100/9-12
PO Box 13 62546 217-526-4432
Clay Prigge, prin. Fax 526-4452
Morrisonville JHS 100/7-8
PO Box 13 62546 217-526-4432
Clay Prigge, prin. Fax 526-4452

Morton, Tazewell, Pop. 15,761
Morton CUSD 709 2,600/PK-12
235 E Jackson St 61550 309-263-2581
Dr. R. Scott Russell, supt. Fax 266-6320
www.morton709.org
Morton HS 1,000/9-12
350 N Illinois Ave 61550 309-266-7182
Dennis Johnson, prin. Fax 263-2168
Morton JHS 400/7-8
225 E Jackson St 61550 309-266-6522
Greg Crider, prin. Fax 284-5031

Morton Grove, Cook, Pop. 22,202
Golf ESD 67 500/K-8
9401 Waukegan Rd 60053 847-966-8200
Linda Marks, supt. Fax 966-8290
www.golf67.net
Golf MS 300/5-8
9401 Waukegan Rd 60053 847-965-3740
Keith Westman, prin. Fax 966-9493

Chicagoland Jewish HS 100/9-11
7800 Lyons St Ste 18 60053 847-470-6700
Dr. Ted Schaffner, hdmstr. Fax 324-3701

Mounds, Pulaski, Pop. 1,008
Meridian CUSD 101 700/PK-12
208 Valley Rd 62964 618-342-6776
Dr. Ray Puckett, supt. Fax 342-6856
www.mhs101.pulski.k12.il.us
Meridian HS 200/9-12
1401 Mounds Rd 62964 618-342-6778
Joseph Rains, prin. Fax 342-6856

Mount Carmel, Wabash, Pop. 7,690
Wabash CUSD 348 1,800/K-12
218 W 13th St 62863 618-262-4181
Tim Buss, supt. Fax 262-7912
www.d348.wabash.k12.il.us
Mount Carmel HS 600/9-12
201 N Pear St 62863 618-262-5104
Clyde Leonard, prin. Fax 262-8781
Mount Carmel MS 400/6-8
1520 Poplar St 62863 618-262-5699
Rick Johnston, prin. Fax 263-9096

Wabash Valley College Post-Sec.
2200 College Dr 62863 618-262-8641

Mount Carroll, Carroll, Pop. 1,704
West Carroll CUSD 314
Supt. — See Thomson
West Carroll MS 100/6-8
633 S East St 61053 815-244-2002
Jeanette Ashby, prin. Fax 244-1051

Mount Morris, Ogle, Pop. 3,066
Oregon CUSD 220
Supt. — See Oregon
Rahn JHS 300/7-8
105 W Brayton Rd 61054 815-734-6134
Jeff Fitzpatrick, prin. Fax 734-7129

Mount Olive, Macoupin, Pop. 2,100
Mount Olive CUSD 5 600/PK-12
804 W Main St 62069 217-999-7831
Chad Allison, supt. Fax 999-2150
www.schools.lth5.k12.il.us/mtolive/
Mount Olive HS, 804 W Main St 62069 200/9-12
Ron Ryan, prin. 217-999-4231

Mount Prospect, Cook, Pop. 54,482
Community Consolidated SD 59
Supt. — See Arlington Heights
Holmes JHS 500/6-8
1900 W Lonnquist Blvd 60056 847-593-4390
Robert Bohanek, prin. Fax 593-7386

Mount Prospect SD 57 1,800/PK-8
701 W Gregory St 60056 847-394-7300
Bruce Brown, supt. Fax 394-7311
www.dist57.org
Lincoln JHS 700/6-8
700 W Lincoln St 60056 847-394-7350
Donald Angelaccio, prin. Fax 394-7358

River Trails SD 26 1,600/PK-8
1900 E Kensington Rd 60056 847-297-4120
Edward Tivador, supt. Fax 297-4124
www.rtsd26.org
River Trails MS 600/6-8
1000 N Wolf Rd 60056 847-298-1750
Glenn Purpura, prin. Fax 298-2639

Township HSD 214
Supt. — See Arlington Heights
Prospect HS 2,000/9-12
801 W Kensington Rd 60056 847-718-5200
Karen Rogers, prin. Fax 718-5216

Christian Life College Post-Sec.
400 E Gregory St 60056 847-259-1840
ITT Technical Institute Post-Sec.
1401 Feehanville Dr 60056 847-375-8800

Mount Pulaski, Logan, Pop. 1,632
Mount Pulaski CUSD 23 600/PK-12
119 N Garden St Ste 2 62548 217-792-7222
Philip Shelton, supt. Fax 792-5551
www.mtpulaski.k12.il.us
Mount Pulaski HS 200/9-12
206 S Spring St 62548 217-792-3209
Russ Galusha, prin. Fax 792-3248

Mount Sterling, Brown, Pop. 2,011
Brown County CUSD 1 700/PK-12
503 NW Cross St 62353 217-773-3359
Merle Kenady, supt. Fax 773-2121
www.bcsd1.net
Brown County HS 200/9-12
500 E Main St 62353 217-773-3345
Van Wilson, prin. Fax 773-2128
Brown County MS 200/5-8
504 E Main St 62353 217-773-9152
Marvin Meservey, prin. Fax 773-9121

Mount Vernon, Jefferson, Pop. 16,344
Mount Vernon Area Vocational Center
320 S 7th St 62864 618-246-5602
Robert Knutson, dir. Fax 244-8049
Mount Vernon Area Vocational Center Vo/Tech
320 S 7th St 62864 618-246-5602
Robert Knutson, dir. Fax 244-8049

Mount Vernon CSD 80 1,800/PK-8
1722 Oakland Ave 62864 618-244-8080
Kevin Settle, supt. Fax 244-8082
district.mtv80.org
Casey MS 500/6-8
1829 Broadway St 62864 618-244-8060
Mike Green, prin. Fax 244-8014

Mount Vernon Township HSD 201 1,400/9-12
320 S 7th St 62864 618-244-3700
Terry Milt, supt. Fax 244-8047
www.mvths.org
Mount Vernon HS 1,400/9-12
320 S 7th St 62864 618-244-3700
Jerry Pepple, prin. Fax 244-8047

DuQuoin Beauty College Post-Sec.
212 S 20th St 62864 618-542-9777

Mount Zion, Macon, Pop. 5,032
Mount Zion CUSD 3 2,500/PK-12
455 Elm St 62549 217-864-2366
Darbe Brinkoetter, supt. Fax 864-2020
www.mtzion.k12.il.us
Mount Zion HS 800/9-12
305 S Henderson St 62549 217-864-2363
Greg Bradley, prin. Fax 864-5815
Mount Zion JHS 400/7-8
315 S Henderson St 62549 217-864-2369
Jerry Birkey, prin. Fax 864-6829

Moweaqua, Christian, Pop. 1,845
Central A & M CUSD 21
Supt. — See Assumption
Central A & M HS 300/9-12
229 E Pine St 62550 217-768-3866
Diana Bandy, prin. Fax 768-3797

Mulberry Grove, Bond, Pop. 675
Mulberry Grove CUSD 1 400/K-12
801 W Wall St 62262 618-326-8812
Gregory Irwin, supt. Fax 326-8482
Mulberry Grove HS 100/9-12
801 W Wall St 62262 618-326-8221
Michael Gauch, prin. Fax 326-8482
Mulberry Grove JHS 100/7-8
801 W Wall St 62262 618-326-8221
Michael Gauch, prin. Fax 326-8482

Mundelein, Lake, Pop. 32,774
Diamond Lake SD 76 1,300/PK-8
500 Acorn Ln 60060 847-566-9221
Dr. Roger Prosise, supt. Fax 566-5689
www.d76.lake.k12.il.us/
West Oak MS 600/5-8
500 Acorn Ln 60060 847-566-9220
Christopher Willeford, prin. Fax 970-3534

Fremont SD 79 1,700/PK-8
28855 N Fremont Center Rd 60060 847-566-0169
Dr. Rick Taylor, supt. Fax 566-7280
www.fremont.lake.k12.il.us
Fremont MS 1,000/4-8
28855 N Fremont Center Rd 60060 847-566-9384
Pam Motsenbocker, prin. Fax 566-7805

Mundelein Consolidated HSD 120 2,100/9-12
1350 W Hawley St 60060 847-949-2200
John Barbini, supt. Fax 949-0599
www.mundeleinmustangs.com
Mundelein Consolidated HS 2,100/9-12
1350 W Hawley St 60060 847-949-2200
Dr. John Ahlgrim, prin. Fax 949-0599

Mundelein ESD 75 1,500/PK-8
470 N Lake St 60060 847-949-2700
Cynthia Heidorn Ph.D., supt. Fax 949-2727
www.district75.org
Sandburg MS 800/6-8
855 W Hawley St 60060 847-949-2707
Mark Pilut, prin. Fax 949-2716

Carmel HS 1,400/9-12
1 Carmel Pkwy 60060 847-566-3000
Rev. Robert Carroll, prin. Fax 566-8465
University of St. Mary of the Lake Post-Sec.
1000 E Maple Ave 60060 847-566-6401

Murphysboro, Jackson, Pop. 8,288
Murphysboro CUSD 186 2,100/PK-12
819 Walnut St 62966 618-684-3781
William Riley, supt. Fax 684-2465
www.mboro.jacksn.k12.il.us
Murphysboro HS 700/9-12
50 Blackwood Dr 62966 618-687-2336
Colleen Doyle, prin. Fax 687-3532
Murphysboro MS 500/6-8
2125 Spruce St 62966 618-684-3041
Frank Puttman, prin. Fax 687-1042

Murphysboro Christian Academy 200/PK-12
805 N 16th St 62966 618-684-5083
Gina Noble, prin. Fax 687-5614

Naperville, DuPage, Pop. 141,579
Indian Prairie CUSD 204
Supt. — See Aurora
Crone MS 1,100/6-8
4020 111th St 60564 630-428-5600
Stan Gorbatkin, prin. Fax 428-5601
Gregory MS 1,000/6-8
2621 Springdale Cir 60564 630-428-6300
Stephen Severson, prin. Fax 428-6301
Hill MS 900/6-8
1836 Brookdale Rd 60563 630-428-6200
Allan Davenport, prin. Fax 428-6201
Neuqua Valley Gold Campus 1,000/9-9
3220 Cedar Glade Dr 60564 630-428-6400
Mark Truckenbrod, prin. Fax 428-6401
Neuqua Valley HS 2,700/10-12
2360 95th St 60564 630-428-6000
Dr. Michael Popp, prin. Fax 428-6001
Scullen MS 1,200/6-8
2815 Mistflower Ln 60564 630-428-7000
Kathleen Kosteck, prin. Fax 428-7001

Naperville CUSD 203 18,700/PK-12
203 W Hillside Rd 60540 630-420-6300
Dr. Alan Leis, supt. Fax 420-1066
www.naperville203.org/
Jefferson JHS 900/6-8
1525 N Loomis St 60563 630-420-6307
Mark Pasztor, prin. Fax 420-6930
Lincoln JHS 1,000/6-8
1320 Olympus Dr 60565 630-420-6370
Pam George, prin. Fax 637-4582
Madison JHS 900/6-8
1000 River Oak Dr 60565 630-420-4257
Erin Anderson, prin. Fax 420-6402
Naperville Central HS 3,100/9-12
440 Aurora Ave 60540 630-420-6420
Jim Caudill, prin. Fax 369-6247
Naperville North HS 3,000/9-12
899 N Mill St 60563 630-420-6484
Ross Truemper, prin. Fax 420-4255
Washington JHS 600/6-8
201 N Washington St 60540 630-420-6390
Bob Ross, prin. Fax 420-6474
Other Schools – See Lisle

Keller Graduate School Post-Sec.
2056 Westings Ave Ste 40 60563 630-428-9086
North Central College Post-Sec.
30 N Brainard St 60540 630-637-5100

Nashville, Washington, Pop. 3,083
Nashville Community HSD 99 500/9-12
1300 S Mill St 62263 618-327-8286
Wendy Davis, supt. Fax 327-4512
www.county.washington.k12.il.us
Nashville Comm. HS 500/9-12
1300 S Mill St 62263 618-327-8286
Brad Weathers, prin. Fax 327-4512

Nauvoo, Hancock, Pop. 1,155
Nauvoo-Colusa CUSD 325 400/PK-12
PO Box 308 62354 217-453-6639
Kent Young, supt. Fax 453-6395
www.hancock.k12.il.us/nchs325/
Nauvoo-Colusa HS 200/9-12
PO Box 308 62354 217-453-2231
Kent Young, prin. Fax 453-6395
Nauvoo-Colusa JHS 50/7-8
PO Box 308 62354 217-453-2231
Kent Young, prin. Fax 453-6395

Neoga, Cumberland, Pop. 1,770
Neoga CUSD 3 700/PK-12
PO Box 280 62447 217-895-2201
Dr. Debby Poindexter, supt. Fax 895-3476
www.neoga.k12.il.us
Neoga HS 300/9-12
PO Box 280 62447 217-895-2205
Benjamin Johnson, prin. Fax 895-3957
Neoga JHS 100/7-8
PO Box 280 62447 217-895-2205
Benjamin Johnson, prin. Fax 895-3957

Newark, Kendall, Pop. 1,031
Newark CCSD 66 300/K-8
503 Chicago Rd 60541 815-695-5143
John DeMay, supt. Fax 695-5776
Other Schools – See Millbrook

Newark Community HSD 18 200/9-12
413 Chicago Rd 60541 815-695-5164
Pauline Berggren, supt. Fax 695-5752
www.newarkhs.k12.il.us
Newark Community HS 200/9-12
413 Chicago Rd 60541 815-695-5164
Pauline Berggren, prin. Fax 695-5752

New Athens, Saint Clair, Pop. 2,011
New Athens CUSD 60 600/PK-12
501 Hanft St 62264 618-475-2174
Kyle Freeman, supt. Fax 475-2176
www.newathens.stclair.k12.il.us/
New Athens HS 200/9-12
501 Hanft St 62264 618-475-2173
Dennis Works, prin. Fax 475-2176
New Athens JHS 100/6-8
501 Hanft St 62264 618-475-2172
Jim Marlow, prin. Fax 475-2176

New Berlin, Sangamon, Pop. 1,129
CUSD 16 700/PK-12
PO Box 230 62670 217-488-6111
Valerie Carr, supt. Fax 488-6418
cusd16.k12.il.us
New Berlin HS 200/9-12
PO Box 230 62670 217-488-6012
Doug Furlow, prin. Fax 488-3207
New Berlin JHS 100/7-8
PO Box 230 62670 217-488-6012
Doug Furlow, prin. Fax 488-3207

New Lenox, Will, Pop. 23,197
Lincoln-Way Community HSD 210 6,200/9-12
1801 E Lincoln Hwy 60451 815-462-2100
Dr. Lawrence Wyllie, supt. Fax 485-7648
www.lw210.org
Lincoln-Way Central HS 2,700/9-12
1801 E Lincoln Hwy 60451 815-462-2100
Dr. Monica Schmitt, prin. Fax 485-7648
Other Schools – See Frankfort

New Lenox SD 122 5,300/PK-8
102 S Cedar Rd 60451 815-485-2169
Dr. Michael Sass, supt. Fax 485-2236
www.nlsd122.org
Liberty JHS 600/7-8
151 Lenox St 60451 815-462-7951
Joel Benton, prin. Fax 462-0672
Martino JHS 600/7-8
731 E Joliet Hwy 60451 815-485-7593
Del Bitter, prin. Fax 485-9578

Providence Catholic HS 1,100/9-12
1800 W Lincoln Hwy 60451 815-485-2136
Don Sebestyen, prin. Fax 485-2709

Newton, Jasper, Pop. 3,038
Jasper County CUSD 1 1,100/K-12
609 S Lafayette St 62448 618-783-8459
Ron Alburtus, supt. Fax 783-3679
www.cusd1.jasper.k12.il.us
Newton Community HS 600/9-12
201 West End Ave 62448 618-783-2303
Ruth Kerner, prin. Fax 783-3783

Niantic, Macon, Pop. 690
Sangamon Valley CUSD 9 600/PK-12
PO Box 200 62551 217-668-2338
Wayne Honeycutt, supt. Fax 668-2406
Sangamon Valley HS 9-12
PO Box 200 62551 217-668-2392
Dan Carie, prin. Fax 668-2406
Other Schools – See Illiopolis

Niles, Cook, Pop. 29,330
East Maine SD 63
Supt. — See Des Plaines
Gemini JHS 800/7-8
8955 N Greenwood Ave 60714 847-827-1181
Scott Herrmann, prin. Fax 827-3499

Park Ridge-Niles CCSD 64
Supt. — See Park Ridge
Emerson MS 800/6-8
8101 N Cumberland Ave 60714 847-318-8110
Victoria Mogil, prin. Fax 318-8122

Logos Christian Academy 200/PK-12
7280 N Caldwell Ave 60714 847-647-9456
Larry Murg, prin.
Niles School of Beauty Culture Post-Sec.
8057 N Milwaukee Ave 60714 847-965-8061
Northridge Preparatory S 300/6-12
8320 W Ballard Rd 60714 847-375-0600
Rich Meyer, prin. Fax 375-0606
Notre Dame HS 800/9-12
7655 W Dempster St 60714 847-965-2900
Steven W. Zeier, prin. Fax 965-2975

Noble, Richland, Pop. 713
West Richland CUSD 2 400/PK-12
PO Box 157 62868 618-723-2334
Don Carlyle, supt. Fax 723-2113
www.west.rchlnd.k12.il.us/
West Richland HS 200/9-12
PO Box 157 62868 618-723-2335
Fax 723-2966
West Richland JHS 50/8-8
PO Box 157 62868 618-723-2335
Dick Steinman, prin. Fax 723-2966

Nokomis, Montgomery, Pop. 2,317
Nokomis CUSD 22 800/PK-12
511 Oberle St 62075 217-563-7311
Jean M. Chrostoski, supt. Fax 563-2549
www.nokomis.k12.il.us
Nokomis JSHS 400/7-12
511 Oberle St 62075 217-563-2014
Donald Markey, prin. Fax 563-2671

Normal, McLean, Pop. 49,927
ISU Lab SD 1,100/PK-12
Campus Box 5300 61790 309-438-8542
Robert Dean, supt. Fax 438-3813
www.uhigh.ilstu.edu/labschool/
University HS 600/9-12
Campus Box 7100 61790 309-438-8346
Jeff Hill, prin. Fax 438-5198

McLean Co. Unit SD 5 11,300/PK-12
1809 Hovey Ave 61761 309-452-4476
Dr. Gary Niehaus, supt. Fax 452-7418
www.unit5.org
Chiddix JHS 800/6-8
300 S Walnut St 61761 309-452-1191
Timothy Green, prin. Fax 888-6845
Kingsley JHS 1,000/6-8
303 Kingsley St 61761 309-452-4461
Dr. Lynette Mehall, prin. Fax 454-1845
Normal Community HS 1,700/9-12
3900 E Raab Rd 61761 309-728-5000
Dr. Jeanette Nuckolls, prin. Fax 728-5050
Normal Community West HS 1,500/9-12
501 N Parkside Rd 61761 309-888-6060
Thomas Eder, prin. Fax 451-3012
Parkside JHS 900/6-8
101 N Parkside Rd 61761 309-452-8321
Mary Ahillen, prin. Fax 888-6813

Bloomington-Normal School of Radiography Post-Sec.
900 Franklin Ave 61761 309-452-2834
Calvary Baptist Academy 300/K-12
1017 N School St 61761 309-452-7912
Dr. Ralph Wingate, supt. Fax 451-0033
Heartland Community College Post-Sec.
1500 W Raab Rd 61761 309-827-0500
Illinois State University 61790 Post-Sec.
309-438-2111
Mennonite College of Nursing Post-Sec.
PO Box 5810 61790 309-438-7400

Norridge, Cook, Pop. 14,054
Ridgewood Community HSD 234 900/9-12
7500 W Montrose Ave 60706 708-456-4242
Dr. Robert Lupo, supt. Fax 456-8238
www.ridgenet.org
Ridgewood Community HS 900/9-12
7500 W Montrose Ave 60706 708-456-4242
Kevin Omara, prin. Fax 456-8238

Norris City, White, Pop. 1,059
Norris City-Omaha-Enfield CUSD 3 700/PK-12
PO Box 399 62869 618-378-3222
Michael Phelps, supt. Fax 378-3286
Norris City-Omaha-Enfield HS 200/9-12
PO Box 399 62869 618-378-3312
Cliff Karnes, prin. Fax 378-3364

North Aurora, Kane, Pop. 14,394
Aurora West Unit SD 129
Supt. — See Aurora
Jewel MS 1,000/6-8
1501 Waterford Rd 60542 630-301-5010
Greg Scalia, prin. Fax 907-3161

Northbrook, Cook, Pop. 34,190
Northbrook ESD 27 1,300/K-8
1250 Sanders Rd 60062 847-498-2610
Dr. David Kroeze, supt. Fax 498-5916
www.northbrook27.k12.il.us/
Wood Oaks JHS 500/6-8
1250 Sanders Rd 60062 847-272-1900
Marc Schaffer, prin. Fax 480-4834

Northbrook SD 28 1,800/K-8
1475 Maple Ave 60062 847-498-7900
Julia James Haley Ph.D., supt. Fax 498-7970
www.northbrook28.net
Northbrook JHS 600/6-8
1475 Maple Ave 60062 847-498-7920
Dr. Peggy J. Hoskin, prin. Fax 656-1712

Northbrook/Glenview SD 30 1,100/K-8
2374 Shermer Rd 60062 847-498-4190
Dr. Linda Vieth, supt. Fax 498-8981
www.district30.k12.il.us
Maple JHS 400/6-8
2370 Shermer Rd 60062 847-400-8900
Steven Waitz, prin. Fax 272-0979

Northfield Township HSD 225
Supt. — See Glenview
Glenbrook North HS 2,100/9-12
2300 Shermer Rd 60062 847-272-6400
Dr. Michael Riggle, prin. Fax 509-2411

West Northfield SD 31 900/K-8
3131 Techny Rd 60062 847-272-6880
Debra Hill, supt. Fax 272-4818
www.dist31.k12.il.us
Field MS 300/6-8
2055 Landwehr Rd 60062 847-272-6884
Robert Machak, prin. Fax 272-1050

Sager Soloman Schechter MS 400/6-8
3210 Dundee Rd 60062 847-412-5700
Fax 498-5837

North Chicago, Lake, Pop. 33,376
North Chicago SD 187 4,500/PK-12
2000 Lewis Ave 60064 847-689-8150
Sandra Ellis Ed.D., supt. Fax 689-6328
www.nchi.lfc.edu/
Neal Math Science Academy 600/7-8
1905 Argonne Dr 60064 847-689-6313
Antoinette Weatherspoon, prin. Fax 689-6332
North Chicago Community HS 900/9-12
1717 17th St 60064 847-578-7400
William King, prin. Fax 689-7473

R. Franklin University of Medicine Post-Sec.
3333 Green Bay Rd 60064 847-578-3000

Northfield, Cook, Pop. 5,543
New Trier Twp. HSD 203
Supt. — See Winnetka
New Trier Twp. HS - Northfield Campus 1,000/9-9
7 Happ Rd 60093 847-446-7000
Jan Borja, prin. Fax 446-4759

Sunset Ridge SD 29 500/K-8
525 Sunset Ridge Rd 60093 847-881-9456
Dr. Howard Bultinck, supt.
www.sunset.k12.il.us
Sunset Ridge MS 300/4-8
525 Sunset Ridge Rd 60093 847-881-9400
Dr. Howard Bultinck, prin.

Northlake, Cook, Pop. 11,358
Berkeley SD 87
Supt. — See Berkeley
Northlake MS 500/6-8
202 S Lakewood Ave 60164 708-449-3195
Daniel Sullivan, prin. Fax 547-2548

Leyden Community HSD 212
Supt. — See Franklin Park
West Leyden HS 1,600/9-12
1000 N Wolf Rd 60164 847-451-3154
Wilford Wagner, prin. Fax 451-3180

Oak Brook, DuPage, Pop. 8,835
Butler SD 53 500/K-8
2801 York Rd 60523 630-573-2887
Sandra L. Martin, supt. Fax 573-5374
www.butler53.com
Butler JHS 200/6-8
2801 York Rd 60523 630-573-2760
Edward Condon, prin. Fax 573-1725

Oakbrook Terrace, DuPage, Pop. 2,249

DeVry University Post-Sec.
1 Tower Ln 60181 630-571-1818

Oak Forest, Cook, Pop. 28,116
Arbor Park SD 145 1,400/PK-8
17301 Central Ave 60452 708-687-8040
Allen Jebens, supt. Fax 687-9498
www.arbor145.org/
Arbor Park MS 600/5-8
17303 Central Ave 60452 708-687-5330
Mary Beth Sexton, prin. Fax 535-4527

Bremen Community HSD 228
Supt. — See Midlothian
Oak Forest HS 1,400/9-12
15201 Central Ave 60452 708-687-0500
David Wilson, prin. Fax 687-0594

Forest Ridge SD 142 1,700/PK-8
15000 Laramie Ave 60452 708-687-3334
Dr. Margaret Longo, supt. Fax 687-2970
www.d142.org
Hille MS 600/6-8
5800 151st St 60452 708-687-2860
Courtney Orzel, prin. Fax 687-8569

Capri Oak Forest Coll of Beauty Culture Post-Sec.
15815 Rob Roy Dr 60452 708-687-3020
John Amico's School of Hair Design Post-Sec.
15301 Cicero Ave 60452 708-687-7800

Oakland, Coles, Pop. 943
Oakland CUSD 5 400/K-12
PO Box 200 61943 217-346-2555
Ezra Smithson, supt. Fax 346-2267
www.oak.k12.il.us/
Oakland HS 100/9-12
PO Box 378 61943 217-346-2118
Mike Smith, prin. Fax 346-2267

Oak Lawn, Cook, Pop. 53,991
Community HSD 218 5,200/9-12
10701 Kilpatrick Ave 60453 708-424-2000
Dr. Kevin G. Burns, supt. Fax 424-6389
www.chsd218.org/
Richards HS 1,700/9-12
10601 Central Ave 60453 708-499-2550
Ross Cucio, prin. Fax 499-6941
Other Schools – See Blue Island, Palos Heights

Oak Lawn Community HSD 229 1,700/9-12
9400 Southwest Hwy 60453 708-424-5200
Dr. James J. Briscoe, supt. Fax 424-5297
www.olchs.org
Oak Lawn Community HS 1,700/9-12
9400 Southwest Hwy 60453 708-741-5200
Michael Riordan, prin. Fax 424-5263

Oak Lawn-Hometown SD 123 1,800/PK-8
4201 W 93rd St 60453 708-423-0150
Kathleen McCord, supt. Fax 423-0160
www.d123.org/
Oak Lawn-Hometown MS 6-8
5345 W 99th St 60453 708-499-6400
Andrea Anderson, prin. Fax 499-7684

Ridgeland SD 122 2,300/PK-8
6500 W 95th St 60453 708-599-5550
Kenneth Jandes, supt. Fax 599-5626
www.ridgeland122.com
Simmons MS 500/7-8
6450 W 95th St 60453 708-599-8540
Michael Connolly, prin. Fax 599-8015

Cameo Beauty Academy Post-Sec.
9714 S Cicero Ave 60453 708-636-4660
Fox College Post-Sec.
4201 W 93rd St 60453 708-636-7700
South Side Baptist S 100/K-12
5220 W 105th St 60453 708-425-3435
Robert Burckart, prin. Fax 425-9016

Oak Park, Cook, Pop. 50,757
Oak Park ESD 97 4,900/PK-8
970 Madison St 60302 708-524-3000
Dr. Constance Collins, supt. Fax 524-3019
www.op97.org
Brooks MS 800/6-8
325 S Kenilworth Ave 60302 708-524-3050
Tom Sindelar, prin. Fax 524-3036
Julian MS 800/6-8
416 S Ridgeland Ave 60302 708-524-3040
Victoria Sharts, prin. Fax 524-3035

Oak Park-River Forest SD 200 3,100/9-12
201 N Scoville Ave 60302 708-383-0700
Fax 434-3917
oprfhs.org
Oak Park-River Forest HS 3,100/9-12
201 N Scoville Ave 60302 708-383-0700
Dr. Susan Bridge, prin. Fax 434-3917

Fenwick HS 1,200/9-12
505 Washington Blvd 60302 708-386-0127
Dr. James Quaid, prin. Fax 386-3052
West Suburban College of Nursing Post-Sec.
3 Erie Ct 60302 708-763-6529

Oblong, Crawford, Pop. 1,554
Oblong CUSD 4 700/PK-12
PO Box 40 62449 618-592-3933
Allen Price, supt. Fax 592-3427
Oblong HS 300/9-12
700 S Range St 62449 618-592-4235
Fritz Wheeler, prin. Fax 592-3540

Odin, Marion, Pop. 1,082
Odin Community HSD 700 100/9-12
PO Box 250 62870 618-775-8266
Mike Conlon, supt. Fax 775-8268
Odin HS 100/9-12
PO Box 250 62870 618-775-8266
Fax 775-8268

O Fallon, Saint Clair, Pop. 18,600
O'Fallon CCSD 90 3,300/PK-8
707 N Smiley St 62269 618-632-3666
Dr. Nancy Gibson, supt. Fax 632-7864
www.ofallon90.net/district/
Fulton JHS 800/7-8
307 Kyle Rd 62269 618-628-0090
Dr. Douglas Wood, prin. Fax 624-9390

O'Fallon Township HSD 203 2,300/9-12
600 S Smiley St 62269 618-632-3507
Russell Clover, supt. Fax 632-9730
www.oths.k12.il.us/
O'Fallon HS, 600 S Smiley St 62269 2,300/9-12
Stephen Dirnbeck, prin. 618-632-3507

Shiloh Village SD 85 600/PK-8
125 Diamond Ct 62269 618-632-7434
Jennifer Filyaw, supt. Fax 632-8343
www.shiloh.stclair.k12.il.us
Shiloh MS, 1 Wildcat Xing 62269 5-8
Mark Heuring, prin. 618-632-7434

Oglesby, LaSalle, Pop. 3,621
Oglesby ESD 125 500/PK-8
755 Bennett Ave 61348 815-883-9297
Dr. James Boyle, supt. Fax 883-3568
Washington MS 6-8
212 W Walnut St 61348 815-883-3517
Robert Meehan, prin. Fax 883-3568

Illinois Valley Community College Post-Sec.
815 N Orlando Smith St 61348 815-224-2720

Ohio, Bureau, Pop. 530
Ohio Community HSD 505 100/9-12
PO Box 478 61349 815-376-2934
Dennis Thompson, supt. Fax 376-2102
Ohio Community HS 100/9-12
PO Box 478 61349 815-376-4414
Sharon Flesher, prin. Fax 376-2102

Okawville, Washington, Pop. 1,333
West Washington County CUSD 10 600/K-12
PO Box 27 62271 618-243-6454
Dr. Dennis Fancher, supt. Fax 243-6454
www.okawville-k12.org
Okawville JSHS 300/7-12
400 S Hanover St 62271 618-243-5201
Leon Spinka, prin. Fax 243-6110

Olney, Richland, Pop. 8,470
East Richland CUSD 1 2,100/PK-12
1100 E Laurel St 62450 618-395-2324
Marilyn J. Holt, supt. Fax 392-4147
www.east.rchlnd.k12.il.us
East Richland HS 700/9-12
1200 E Laurel St 62450 618-393-2191
Chris Simpson, prin. Fax 395-1256
East Richland MS 500/6-8
1099 N Van St 62450 618-395-4372
Andy Thomann, prin. Fax 392-3399

Olney Central College Post-Sec.
305 N West St 62450 618-395-7777

Olympia Fields, Cook, Pop. 4,673
Rich Township HSD 227 3,600/9-12
20000 Governors Dr 60461 708-679-5800
Howard Hunigan, supt. Fax 679-5740
www.rich227.org
Rich Central HS 1,300/9-12
3600 W 203rd St 60461 708-675-5600
John Macon, prin. Fax 679-5632
Other Schools – See Park Forest, Richton Park

Onarga, Iroquois, Pop. 1,396
Iroquois West CUSD 10
Supt. — See Gilman
Iroquois West MS 200/6-8
303 N Evergreen St 60955 815-268-4355
Vicki Killus, prin. Fax 265-7008

Oneida, Knox, Pop. 717
ROWVA CUSD 208 800/K-12
PO Box 69 61467 309-483-3711
Gary Buckingham, supt. Fax 483-6123
www.rowva.k12.il.us
ROWVA HS 300/9-12
PO Box 69 61467 309-483-6371
Andy Richmond, prin. Fax 483-8223
ROWVA JHS 100/7-8
PO Box 69 61467 309-483-2803
Chad Wagner, prin. Fax 483-6378

Opdyke, Jefferson
Opdyke-Belle-Rive CCSD 5 200/K-8
PO Box 189 62872 618-756-2492
Brenda Lusby, supt. Fax 756-2792
www.roe25.com/obr/
Opdyke MS 100/5-8
PO Box 189 62872 618-756-2492
Brenda Lusby, prin. Fax 756-2355

Orangeville, Stephenson, Pop. 767
Orangeville CUSD 203 500/PK-12
310 S East St 61060 815-789-4450
Randall Otto, supt. Fax 789-4607
Orangeville HS 200/9-12
201 S Orange 61060 815-789-4289
Loren Beswick, prin. Fax 789-4478
Orangeville JHS 100/7-8
201 S Orange 61060 815-789-4289
Loren Beswick, prin. Fax 789-4478

Oregon, Ogle, Pop. 4,163
Oregon CUSD 220 1,700/PK-12
206 S 10th St 61061 815-732-2186
Dr. William Mattingly, supt. Fax 732-2187
www.ocusd.net
Oregon HS 600/9-12
210 S 10th St 61061 815-732-6241
Jeff Schad, prin. Fax 732-3361
Other Schools – See Mount Morris

Orion, Henry, Pop. 1,703
Orion CUSD 223 1,100/PK-12
PO Box 189 61273 309-526-3388
Donald E. Achelpohl, supt. Fax 526-3711
orionschools.revealed.net/
Orion HS 400/9-12
PO Box 39 61273 309-526-3361
Ron Harris, prin. Fax 526-3854
Orion MS 300/6-8
PO Box 129 61273 309-526-3392
Gary Heard, prin. Fax 526-3872

Orland Park, Cook, Pop. 55,461
Consolidated HSD 230 8,500/9-12
15100 S 94th Ave 60462 708-745-5203
Dr. Patrick McMahon, supt. Fax 349-2105
www.d230.org
Sandburg HS 3,500/9-12
13300 S La Grange Rd 60462 708-671-3100
Debbie Boniface, prin. Fax 361-9714
Other Schools – See Palos Hills, Tinley Park

Orland SD 135 5,900/K-8
15100 S 94th Ave 60462 708-364-3306
Dennis Soustek, supt. Fax 873-6479
www.orland135.org
Century JHS 900/6-8
10801 W 159th St 60467 708-364-3500
Cindy Finley, prin. Fax 349-5840
Jerling JHS 700/6-8
8851 W 151st St 60462 708-364-3700
Steven Cole, prin. Fax 873-6457
Orland JHS 600/6-8
14855 West Ave 60462 708-364-4200
Linda Kane, prin. Fax 349-5843

ITT Technical Institute Post-Sec.
11551 184th Pl 60467 708-326-3200
Robert Morris College Post-Sec.
43 Orland Square Dr 60462 708-226-3800

Oswego, Kendall, Pop. 23,330
Oswego CUSD 308 10,700/PK-12
4175 State Route 71 60543 630-636-3080
Dr. David Behlow, supt. Fax 554-2168
www.oswego308.org
Bednarcick JHS 700/6-8
3025 Heggs Rd 60543 630-636-2500
Janet Stutz, prin. Fax 922-3278
Oswego East HS 700/9-12
1525 Harvey Rd 60543 630-636-2200
Ed Howerton, prin. Fax 554-5830
Oswego HS 2,000/9-12
4250 State Route 71 60543 630-636-2000
Mike Wayne, prin. Fax 554-7160
Thompson JHS 1,000/6-8
440 Boulder Hill Pass 60543 630-636-2600
Tracy Murphy, prin. Fax 554-5193
Traughber JHS 700/6-8
61 Franklin St 60543 630-636-2700
Ralph Kober, prin. Fax 554-5197

Hair Professionals School of Cosmetology Post-Sec.
PO Box 40 60543 630-554-2266

Ottawa, LaSalle, Pop. 18,824
Ottawa ESD 141 2,000/PK-8
320 W Main St 61350 815-433-1133
Craig Doster, supt. Fax 433-1888
www.ottawaelem.lasall.k12.il.us/
Shepherd MS 500/7-8
701 E McKinley Rd 61350 815-434-7925
Michael Bannister, prin. Fax 433-9447

Ottawa Township HSD 140 1,600/9-12
211 E Main St 61350 815-433-1323
Thomas Jobst, supt. Fax 433-1338
www.ottawahigh2.com/
Ottawa Twp. HS 1,600/9-12
211 E Main St 61350 815-433-1323
John Harrison, prin. Fax 433-1338

Marquette HS 200/9-12
1000 Paul St 61350 815-433-0125
Ron Spandet, prin. Fax 433-2632

Palatine, Cook, Pop. 67,232
Palatine CCSD 15 12,300/PK-8
580 N 1st Bank Dr 60067 847-963-3000
Robert A. McKanna, supt. Fax 963-3200
www.ccsd15.net
Sundling JHS 700/7-8
1100 N Smith St 60067 847-963-3700
David Corbett, prin. Fax 963-3706
Winston JHS 700/7-8
900 E Palatine Rd 60074 847-963-7400
Earl Overman, prin. Fax 963-7406
Other Schools – See Rolling Meadows

Township HSD 211 13,000/9-12
1750 S Roselle Rd 60067 847-755-6600
Roger Thornton, supt. Fax 755-6810
www.d211.org
Fremd HS 2,900/9-12
1000 S Quentin Rd 60067 847-755-2600
Marina Scott, prin. Fax 755-2623
Palatine HS 2,600/9-12
1111 N Rohlwing Rd 60074 847-755-1600
Gary Steiger, prin. Fax 755-1623
Other Schools – See Hoffman Estates, Schaumburg

William Rainey Harper College Post-Sec.
1200 W Algonquin Rd 60067 847-925-6000

Palestine, Crawford, Pop. 1,342
Palestine CUSD 3 400/PK-12
PO Box 217 62451 618-586-2713
John Hasten, supt. Fax 586-2905
Palestine HS 100/9-12
102 N Main St 62451 618-586-2712
Arlene Lindsay, prin. Fax 586-5328

Palmyra, Macoupin, Pop. 730
Northwestern CUSD 2 400/PK-12
30953 Route 111 62674 217-436-2210
Gayle Early, supt. Fax 436-2701
northwestern.k12.il.us
Northwestern HS 100/9-12
30889 Route 111 62674 217-436-2011
Charles Barlow, prin. Fax 436-9112
Northwestern JHS 100/7-8
30889 Route 111 62674 217-436-2011
Charles Barlow, prin. Fax 436-9112

Palos Heights, Cook, Pop. 12,561
Community HSD 218
Supt. — See Oak Lawn
Shepard HS 1,800/9-12
13049 S Ridgeland Ave 60463 708-371-1111
Ty Harting, prin. Fax 371-7688

Palos Heights SD 128 800/PK-8
12809 S McVickers Ave 60463 708-597-9040
Dr. Theresa Sak, supt. Fax 597-9089
www.d128.k12.il.us
Independence JHS 300/6-8
6610 W Highland Dr 60463 708-448-0737
Dr. Kathleen Casey, prin.

Chicago Christian HS 400/9-12
12001 S Oak Park Ave 60463 708-388-7650
Robert Payne, prin. Fax 388-0154
Trinity Christian College Post-Sec.
6601 W College Dr 60463 708-597-3000

Palos Hills, Cook, Pop. 17,258
Consolidated HSD 230
Supt. — See Orland Park
Stagg HS 2,500/9-12
8000 W 111th St 60465 708-974-7400
Jeff Leach, prin. Fax 974-0803

North Palos SD 117 2,700/PK-8
7825 W 103rd St 60465 708-598-5500
Dr. Ken Sorrick, supt. Fax 598-5539
www.d117.s-cook.k12.il.us/
Other Schools – See Hickory Hills

Hair Professionals Career College Post-Sec.
10321 S Roberts Rd 60465 708-430-1755
Moraine Valley Community College Post-Sec.
10900 S 88th Ave 60465 708-974-4300

Palos Park, Cook, Pop. 4,757
Palos CCSD 118 1,900/K-8
8800 W 119th St 60464 708-448-4800
Dr. Joseph Dubec, supt. Fax 448-4880
www.palos118.org
Palos South MS 700/6-8
13100 S 82nd Ave 60464 708-448-5971
Donna Clark, prin. Fax 448-0754

Pana, Christian, Pop. 5,529
Pana CUSD 8 1,100/PK-12
PO Box 377 62557 217-562-1500
Dr. David Lett, supt. Fax 562-1501
www.panaschools.com
Pana HS 500/9-12
201 W 8th St 62557 217-562-6600
Gayle McRoberts, prin. Fax 562-6714
Pana JHS 200/7-8
203 W 8th St 62557 217-562-6500
Paul Lauff, prin. Fax 562-6712
Pana Adult Center Adult
PO Box 377 62557 217-562-6695
Don Kroski, prin. Fax 562-4534

First Baptist Christian Academy 100/PK-12
114 Maple St 62557 217-562-5054
Larry Gruis, prin.

Paris, Edgar, Pop. 8,834
Paris CUSD 4 500/PK-8
15601 US Highway 150 61944 217-465-5391
Lorraine Bailey, supt. Fax 466-1225
www.crestwood.k12.il.us
Crestwood JHS 200/6-8
15601 US Highway 150 61944 217-465-5391
Alan Zuber, prin. Fax 466-1225

Paris-Union SD 95 1,700/PK-12
300 S Eads Ave 61944 217-465-8448
Connie Sutton, supt. Fax 463-2243
www.paris95.k12.il.us
Mayo MS 300/6-8
310 E Wood St 61944 217-466-3050
Melanie Ogle, prin. Fax 466-3905
Paris HS 700/9-12
309 S Main St 61944 217-466-1175
Dave Meister, prin. Fax 466-1903

Park Forest, Cook, Pop. 23,036
Park Forest SD 163 2,200/PK-8
242 S Orchard Dr 60466 708-668-9400
Dr. Joyce Carmine, supt. Fax 748-9359
www.sd163.com
Forest Trail MS 800/6-8
215 Wilson St 60466 708-668-9600
Carolyn Stroud, prin. Fax 503-2297

Rich Township HSD 227
Supt. — See Olympia Fields
Rich East Campus HS 1,200/9-12
300 Sauk Trl 60466 708-679-6100
Jeff Craig, prin. Fax 679-7330

Park Ridge, Cook, Pop. 36,983
Maine Township HSD 207 7,000/9-12
1131 S Dee Rd 60068 847-696-3600
Dr. Joel Morris, supt. Fax 696-3254
www.maine207.org
Maine East HS 2,200/9-12
2601 Dempster St 60068 847-825-4484
David Barker, prin. Fax 825-1636
Maine South HS 2,600/9-12
1111 S Dee Rd 60068 847-825-7711
David Claypool, prin. Fax 825-0677
Other Schools – See Des Plaines

Park Ridge-Niles CCSD 64 4,400/PK-8
164 S Prospect Ave 60068 847-318-4300
Dr. Sally Pryor, supt. Fax 318-4351
www.d64.org
Lincoln MS 700/6-8
200 S Lincoln Ave 60068 847-318-4215
Jim Blouch, prin. Fax 318-4210
Other Schools – See Niles

Patoka, Marion, Pop. 618
Patoka CUSD 100 300/K-12
1220 Kinoka Rd 62875 618-432-5440
David Rademacher, supt. Fax 432-5306
www.schools.lth5.k12.il.us/patoka/phs.htm
Patoka HS 100/9-12
1220 Kinoka Rd 62875 618-432-5440
Leslie Venezia, prin. Fax 432-5306
Patoka JHS 100/7-8
1220 Kinoka Rd 62875 618-432-5200
Leslie Venezia, prin. Fax 432-5306

Pawnee, Sangamon, Pop. 2,569
Pawnee CUSD 11 700/PK-12
810 4th St 62558 217-625-2471
Jerry Wesley, supt. Fax 625-2251
www.pawneeschools.org
Pawnee HS 200/9-12
810 4th St 62558 217-625-2471
David Roberts, prin. Fax 625-2251

Paw Paw, Lee, Pop. 857
Paw Paw CUSD 271 300/K-12
PO Box 508 61353 815-627-2841
Robert Priest, supt. Fax 627-2971
www.2paws.net/
Paw Paw JSHS 100/6-12
PO Box 511 61353 815-627-2671
Josh Ebener, prin. Fax 627-8481

Paxton, Ford, Pop. 4,534
Paxton-Buckley-Loda CUSD 10 1,300/K-12
PO Box 50 60957 217-379-3314
Clifford McClure, supt. Fax 379-2862
www.pbl.k12.il.us/
Paxton-Buckley-Loda HS 500/9-12
PO Box 50 60957 217-379-4331
John Rawdin, prin. Fax 379-2491

Paxton-Buckley-Loda JHS 300/6-8
PO Box 50 60957 217-379-9202
Jeff Graham, prin. Fax 379-9169

Payson, Adams, Pop. 1,058
Payson CUSD 1 600/PK-12
404 W State St Ste 1 62360 217-656-3323
Rodger Hannel, supt. Fax 656-4042
adams.k12.il.us/cusd1/
Seymour JSHS 300/7-12
420 W Brainard St 62360 217-656-3355
John Wallace, prin. Fax 656-3584

Pearl City, Stephenson, Pop. 784
Pearl City CUSD 200 500/PK-12
PO Box 9 61062 815-443-2715
Connie Lower, supt. Fax 443-2237
Pearl City HS 100/9-12
PO Box 9 61062 815-443-2715
Tim Thill, prin. Fax 443-2237
Pearl City JHS 100/7-8
PO Box 9 61062 815-443-2715
Tim Thill, prin. Fax 443-2237

Pecatonica, Winnebago, Pop. 2,161
Pecatonica CUSD 321 900/K-12
PO Box 419 61063 815-239-1639
William Faller, supt. Fax 239-2125
www.pecschools.com/
Pecatonica Community MS 300/5-8
PO Box 419 61063 815-239-2612
Francis Fennell, prin. Fax 239-1274
Pecatonica HS 300/9-12
PO Box 419 61063 815-239-2611
Thomas Hoffman, prin. Fax 239-9128

Pekin, Tazewell, Pop. 33,331
Pekin Community HSD 303 2,100/9-12
320 Stadium Dr 61554 309-477-4222
Paula Davis, supt. Fax 477-4376
www.pekinhigh.net
Pekin Community HS 2,100/9-12
1903 Court St 61554 309-477-4331
Craig Smock, prin. Fax 477-4377

Pekin SD 108 3,900/PK-8
501 Washington St Ste B 61554 309-477-4740
Don White, supt. Fax 477-4701
www.pekin.net/pekin108/
Broadmoor JHS 500/7-8
501 Maywood Ave Ste 1 61554 309-477-4731
Marc Fogal, prin.
Edison JHS 400/7-8
1400 Earl St 61554 309-477-4732
Len Ealey, prin. Fax 477-4738

Peoria, Peoria, Pop. 112,685
Norwood ESD 63 500/PK-8
6521 W Farmington Rd 61604 309-676-3523
Dr. Abby Humbles, supt. Fax 676-6099
peoria.k12.il.us/norwood/Tornadoes.html
Norwood MS 5-8
6521 W Farmington Rd 61604 309-676-3523
Becky Jaramillo, prin. Fax 676-6099

Peoria SD 150 14,500/PK-12
3202 N Wisconsin Ave 61603 309-672-6512
Ken Hinton, supt. Fax 672-6820
www.peoria.psd150.org
Bills MS 300/5-8
6001 N Frostwood Pkwy 61615 309-693-4437
Robert Bethel, prin. Fax 693-4438
Columbia MS 300/5-8
2612 N Bootz Ave 61604 309-672-6508
Cindy Janovetz, prin. Fax 685-2238
Coolidge MS 300/5-8
2708 W Rohmann Ave 61604 309-672-6506
Jorge Carballido, prin. Fax 673-7605
Lincoln MS 300/6-8
700 Mary St 61603 309-672-6542
Scott Montgomery, prin. Fax 676-6615
Lindbergh MS 400/5-8
6327 N Sheridan Rd 61614 309-693-4427
Mary Davis, prin. Fax 693-0499
Loucks-Edison MS 500/5-8
2503 N University St 61604 309-685-5677
Gloria Cox, prin.
Manual HS 700/9-12
811 S Griswold St 61605 309-672-6600
William Salzman, prin. Fax 672-6605
Peoria HS 1,000/9-12
1615 N North St 61604 309-672-6630
Randy Simmons, prin. Fax 685-5803
Richwoods HS 1,400/9-12
6301 N University St 61614 309-693-4400
John Meisinger, prin. Fax 693-4414
Rolling Acres-Edison MS 300/5-8
5617 N Merrimac Ave 61614 309-689-1100
Deloris Turner, prin.
Sterling MS 300/5-8
2315 N Sterling Ave 61604 309-672-6557
Tim Delinski, prin. Fax 681-8286
Trewyn MS 300/6-8
1419 S Folkers Ave 61605 309-672-6500
Cheryl Ellis, prin. Fax 673-8537
Von Steuben MS 400/5-8
801 E Forrest Hill Ave 61603 309-672-6561
David Obergfel, prin. Fax 685-7631
Washington MS 200/5-8
3706 N Grand Blvd 61614 309-672-6563
Joan Wojcikewych, prin. Fax 672-6564
Woodruff HS 1,000/9-12
1800 NE Perry Ave 61603 309-672-6665
Teri Dunn, prin. Fax 674-8582
Adult Education Center Adult
839 W Moss Ave 61606 309-672-6702
Colleen Dries, prin.
Adult Education Evening S Adult
839 W Moss Ave 61606 309-672-6703
McKinley Moton, prin.

Pleasant Valley SD 62 500/PK-8
4623 W Red Bud Dr 61604 309-673-6750
Allen Johnson, supt. Fax 674-0165
Pleasant Valley MS 5-8
3314 W Richwoods Blvd 61604 309-679-0634
Sandy Somogyi, prin. Fax 679-0652

Bradley University Post-Sec.
1501 W Bradley Ave 61625 800-447-6460
Illinois Central College Post-Sec.
1 College Dr 61635 309-694-5011
Methodist College of Nursing Post-Sec.
415 NE Saint Mark Ct 61603 309-672-5566
Midstate College Post-Sec.
411 W Northmoor Rd 61614 309-692-4092
Peoria Christian S 1,000/PK-12
3506 N California Ave 61603 309-686-4500
Steve Hutton, admin. Fax 686-2569
Peoria Notre Dame HS 900/9-12
5105 N Sheridan Rd 61614 309-691-8741
Dr. Patricia A. O'Connell, prin. Fax 691-0875
St. Francis Medical Center Post-Sec.
530 NE Glen Oak Ave 61603 309-655-2020
St. Francis Medical Ctr. Coll./Nursing Post-Sec.
511 NE Greenleaf St 61603 309-655-2596
University of Illinois Post-Sec.
PO Box 1649 61656 309-438-2181

Peoria Heights, Peoria, Pop. 6,298
Peoria Heights CUSD 325 800/PK-12
500 E Glen Ave 61616 309-686-8800
Roger Bergia, supt. Fax 686-8801
www.phcusd325.net
Peoria Heights HS 200/9-12
508 E Glen Ave 61616 309-686-8803
Eric Heath, prin. Fax 686-8808

Peoria Christian S - Monroe 300/5-8
3725 N Monroe Ave 61616 309-681-0500
Steve Bowers, prin. Fax 681-9371

Peotone, Will, Pop. 3,981
Peotone CUSD 207U 1,800/K-12
212 W Wilson St 60468 708-258-0991
Kevin Carey, supt. Fax 258-0994
www.peotoneschools.org
Peotone HS 600/9-12
605 W North St 60468 708-258-3236
Doyle Owens, prin. Fax 258-6991
Peotone JHS 500/6-8
1 Blue Devil Dr 60468 708-258-3246
Greg Oliver, prin. Fax 258-6669

Perry, Pike, Pop. 418
Griggsville-Perry CUSD 4
Supt. — See Griggsville
Griggsville-Perry MS 100/5-8
PO Box 98 62362 217-236-9161
Andy Stremlau, prin. Fax 236-7221

Peru, LaSalle, Pop. 9,815
Peru ESD 124 900/PK-8
1325 Park Rd 61354 815-223-0486
Mark Cross, supt. Fax 223-0490
www.perued.net
Peru-Washington JHS 300/6-8
1325 Park Rd 61354 815-223-0301
Lori Madden, prin. Fax 223-0732

St. Bede Academy 300/9-12
Route 6 W 61354 815-223-3140
Michelle Mershon, prin. Fax 223-8580

Petersburg, Menard, Pop. 2,240
PORTA CUSD 202 1,300/PK-12
PO Box 202 62675 217-632-3803
Matthew Brue, supt. Fax 632-3221
www.porta202.org
PORTA HS 400/9-12
PO Box 202 62675 217-632-3216
Darren Hartry, prin. Fax 632-5446
PORTA JHS 200/7-8
PO Box 202 62675 217-632-3219
Jeff Hill, prin. Fax 632-5448

Phoenix, Cook, Pop. 2,069
South Holland SD 151
Supt. — See South Holland
Coolidge MS 500/6-8
15500 7th Ave 60426 708-339-5300
Patricia Payne, prin. Fax 339-5327

New Covenant Christian Academy 100/PK-12
PO Box 1358 60426 708-331-3661
Winston Perkins, prin. Fax 331-2459

Piasa, Macoupin
Southwestern CUSD 9 1,800/PK-12
PO Box 99 62079 618-729-3221
Larry Elsea, supt. Fax 729-3764
www.piasabirds.net
Southwestern HS 600/9-12
PO Box 100 62079 618-729-3211
Bill Wrenn, prin. Fax 729-4276
Southwestern MS 300/7-8
PO Box 70 62079 618-729-3217
Virgil Moore, prin. Fax 729-9231

Pinckneyville, Perry, Pop. 5,452
Pinckneyville Community HSD 101 500/9-12
600 E Water St 62274 618-357-5013
Brent Kreid, supt. Fax 357-6045
www.pchspanthers.com
Pinckneyville HS 500/9-12
600 E Water St 62274 618-357-5013
Jon Green, prin. Fax 357-6045

Pinckneyville SD 50 500/PK-8
301 W Mulberry St 62274 618-357-5161
Tim O'Leary, supt. Fax 357-8731
www.p50.perry.k12.il.us/education/components/sectio
nl
Pinckneyville MS 300/5-8
700 E Water St 62274 618-357-2724
Ryan Swan, prin.

Piper City, Ford, Pop. 749
Tri-Point CUSD 6-J
Supt. — See Kempton
Tri-Point MS 300/PK-K, 4-8
PO Box 158 60959 815-686-2247
Jerry Tkachuk, prin. Fax 686-2663

Pittsfield, Pike, Pop. 4,599
Pikeland CUSD 10 1,400/PK-12
512 S Madison St 62363 217-285-2147
Paula Hawley, supt. Fax 285-5059
Pikeland Community S 600/3-8
601 Piper Ln 62363 217-285-9462
Daniel Brue, prin. Fax 285-9551
Pittsfield HS 400/9-12
201 E Higbee St 62363 217-285-6888
Mark Stuart, prin. Fax 285-9583

Plainfield, Will, Pop. 28,162
Plainfield CCSD 202 21,600/PK-12
15732 S Howard St 60544 815-577-4000
Dr. John R. Harper, supt. Fax 436-7824
www.learningcommunity202.org
Drauden Point MS 1,000/6-8
1911 Drauden Rd, 815-577-4900
Anthony Manville, prin. Fax 439-9385
Heritage Grove MS 1,000/6-8
12425 S Van Dyke Rd, 815-439-4810
Stephen Diveley, prin. Fax 436-4661
Indian Trail MS 800/6-8
14723 S Eastern Ave 60544 815-436-6128
Christian Rivara, prin. Fax 436-7536
Jones MS, 15320 W Wallin Dr 60544 1,000/6-8
Edward Boswell, prin. 815-267-3600
Plainfield HS 2,400/9-12
24120 W Fort Beggs Dr 60544 815-436-3200
Robert Smith, prin. Fax 439-2882
Plainfield North HS 9-12
12005 S 248th Ave, 815-609-8506
Dr. Peter Pasteris, prin. Fax 254-6138
Plainfield South HS 2,800/9-12
7800 Caton Farm Rd, 815-439-5555
Daniel Goggins, prin. Fax 436-5108
Timber Ridge MS 1,100/6-8
2101 S Bronk Rd, 815-439-3410
Glenna Adams, prin. Fax 439-3412
Other Schools – See Joliet

Troy CCSD 30C 2,900/PK-8
5800 Theodore Dr, 815-577-6760
Lawrence Wiers, supt. Fax 577-3795
www.troy30c.org/
Troy MS 800/7-8
5800 Theodore Dr, 815-230-9920
Jeffrey Libowitz, prin. Fax 577-2867

Christ Lutheran Academy 50/9-12
23756 W 127th St, 815-254-8770
Debra Franzen, prin. Fax 487-4143

Plano, Kendall, Pop. 7,338
Plano CUSD 88 1,400/PK-12
800 S Hale St 60545 630-552-8978
William Woody, supt. Fax 552-8548
www.plano88.org/
Plano HS 400/9-12
704 W Abe St 60545 630-552-3178
Bill Johnson, prin. Fax 552-7792
Plano MS 300/6-8
804 S Hale St 60545 630-552-3608
Wayne Czyz, prin. Fax 552-3802

Pleasant Hill, Pike, Pop. 1,012
Pleasant Hill CUSD 3 400/PK-12
PO Box 207 62366 217-734-2311
Michael Dempsey, supt. Fax 734-2629
www.phwolves.com/
Pleasant Hill HS 100/9-12
PO Box 207 62366 217-734-2311
Donna Peebles, prin. Fax 734-2725

Pleasant Plains, Sangamon, Pop. 738
Pleasant Plains CUSD 8 1,300/PK-12
PO Box 20 62677 217-626-1041
Maureen Talbert, supt. Fax 626-1082
ppcusd8.org
Pleasant Plains HS 400/9-12
PO Box 320 62677 217-626-1044
Mike Ward, prin. Fax 626-1667
Pleasant Plains MS 400/5-8
2455 N Farmingdale Rd 62677 217-626-1061
John Marsaglia, prin. Fax 626-2272

Polo, Ogle, Pop. 2,507
Polo CUSD 222 800/PK-12
100 S Union Ave 61064 815-946-3815
Christopher Rademacher, supt. Fax 946-2493
Aplington MS 200/6-8
610 E Mason St 61064 815-946-2519
Andrew Faivre, prin. Fax 946-2537
Polo Community HS 300/9-12
100 S Union Ave 61064 815-946-3314
Andy Siegfried, prin. Fax 946-2493

Pontiac, Livingston, Pop. 11,457
Livingston AVC
1100 E Indiana Ave 61764 815-842-2557
Amy Smith, dir. Fax 842-1005
pontiac.k12.il.us/lavc/lavc.htm
Livingston AVC Vo/Tech
1100 E Indiana Ave 61764 815-842-2557
Amy Smith, dir. Fax 842-1005

Pontiac CCSD 429 1,300/PK-8
117 W Livingston St 61764 815-844-5632
Steve Graham, supt. Fax 844-5773
www.p429.k12.il.us/
Pontiac JHS 500/6-8
600 N Morrow St 61764 815-842-4343
Judy Donze, prin. Fax 844-6230

Pontiac Township HSD 90 900/9-12
1100 E Indiana Ave 61764 815-844-6113
Harlen Cotter, supt. Fax 844-6116
www.pontiac.k12.il.us
Pontiac HS 900/9-12
1100 E Indiana Ave 61764 815-844-6113
James Drengwitz, prin. Fax 844-6116

Poplar Grove, Boone, Pop. 3,077
North Boone CUSD 200 1,500/PK-12
17641 Poplar Grove Rd 61065 815-765-3322
Michael Houselog, supt. Fax 765-2053
www.nbcusd.org
North Boone HS 400/9-12
17823 Poplar Grove Rd 61065 815-765-3311
Christine Troller, prin. Fax 765-3316
North Boone MS 200/7-8
17641 Poplar Grove Rd 61065 815-765-9274
Kristi Crawford, prin. Fax 765-9275

Port Byron, Rock Island, Pop. 1,623
Riverdale CUSD 100 1,100/PK-12
9624 256th St N 61275 309-523-3184
David Bills, supt. Fax 523-3550
www.riroe.k12.il.us/riroe/riverdale/
Riverdale HS 400/9-12
9622 256th St N 61275 309-523-3181
James Boyd, prin. Fax 523-2885
Riverdale MS 200/6-8
9822 256th St N 61275 309-523-3131
Ron Jacobs, prin. Fax 523-3934

Posen, Cook, Pop. 4,929
Posen-Robbins ESD 143-5 1,600/PK-8
14025 S Harrison Ave 60469 708-388-7200
Gregory Wright, supt. Fax 388-3868
Other Schools – See Robbins

Princeton, Bureau, Pop. 7,554
Princeton ESD 115 1,200/PK-8
506 E Dover Rd 61356 815-875-3162
Tim Smith, supt. Fax 875-3101
www.princeton115schools.org
Logan JHS 400/6-8
302 W Central Ave 61356 815-875-6415
J.D. Orwig, prin. Fax 872-0034

Princeton HSD 500 600/9-12
103 S Euclid Ave 61356 815-875-3308
Kirk Haring, supt. Fax 875-8525
www.phs-il.org
Princeton HS 600/9-12
103 S Euclid Ave 61356 815-875-3308
Barb Schmidt, prin. Fax 875-8525

Princeton Christian Academy 100/PK-12
21890 US Highway 34 61356 815-875-2933
Marty Kiser, prin. Fax 875-8113

Princeville, Peoria, Pop. 1,574
Princeville CUSD 326 600/PK-12
302 Cordis Ave 61559 309-385-2213
Kathryn Hanneken, supt. Fax 385-1823
www.princeville326.org/
Princeville HS 200/9-12
302 Cordis Ave 61559 309-385-4660
Jim Colyott, prin. Fax 385-1110

Prophetstown, Whiteside, Pop. 1,960
Prophetstown-Lyndon-Tampico CUSD 3 1,100/PK-12
79 Grove St 61277 815-537-5101
Dave Rogers, supt. Fax 537-5102
wside.k12.il.us/phs/default.htm
Prophetstown HS 300/9-12
310 W Riverside Dr 61277 815-537-5161
Rochelle Streeter, prin. Fax 537-5102
Other Schools – See Tampico

Prospect Heights, Cook, Pop. 16,387
Prospect Heights SD 23 1,500/PK-8
700 N Schoenbeck Rd 60070 847-870-3850
Dr. Gregory P. Guarrine, supt. Fax 870-3896
www.d23.org/
MacArthur MS 500/6-8
700 N Schoenbeck Rd 60070 847-870-3879
Dr. Debra Wilson, prin. Fax 870-3881

Quincy, Adams, Pop. 39,841
Quincy Area Vocational Technical Center
219 Baldwin Dr 62301 217-224-3775
Ron Baugher, dir. Fax 221-4800
www.qps.org/qavtc/
Quincy Area Vocational Technical Center Vo/Tech
219 Baldwin Dr 62301 217-224-3775
Ron Baugher, dir. Fax 221-4800

Quincy SD 172 6,800/PK-12
1444 Maine St 62301 217-223-8700
Thomas Leahy, supt. Fax 228-7162
www.qps.org
Quincy JHS 1,600/7-9
100 S 14th St 62301 217-222-3073
Diane Glaub, prin. Fax 228-7185
Quincy SHS 1,700/10-12
3322 Maine St 62301 217-224-3770
Terry Ellerman, prin. Fax 228-7149

Blessing Hospital Post-Sec.
PO Box 7005 62305 217-223-8400
Blessing-Rieman College of Nursing Post-Sec.
PO Box 7005 62305 217-228-5520
Gem City College Post-Sec.
700 State St 62301 217-222-0391
John Wood Community College Post-Sec.
150 S 48th St 62305 217-224-6500
Quincy Notre Dame HS 500/9-12
1400 S 11th St 62301 217-223-2479
Raymond Heilmann, prin. Fax 223-0023
Quincy University Post-Sec.
1800 College Ave 62301 217-222-8020
Vatterott College Post-Sec.
3609 N Marx Dr 62301 217-224-0600

Ramsey, Fayette, Pop. 1,063
Ramsey CUSD 204 500/PK-12
716 W 6th St 62080 618-423-2335
Charles Stortzum, supt. Fax 423-2314
www.ramsey.fayette.k12.il.us/
Ramsey HS 100/9-12
716 W 6th St 62080 618-423-2333
Nick Casey, prin. Fax 423-2314

Rantoul, Champaign, Pop. 12,483
Rantoul CSD 137 1,700/PK-8
400 E Wabash Ave 61866 217-893-4171
William Trankina, supt. Fax 892-4313
www.rcs.k12.il.us/
Eater JHS, 400 E Wabash Ave 61866 500/6-8
Mike Penicook, prin. 217-892-2115

Rantoul Township HSD 193 800/9-12
200 S Sheldon St 61866 217-892-2151
David Requa, supt. Fax 892-4442
www.rths.k12.il.us
Rantoul Township HS 800/9-12
200 S Sheldon St 61866 217-892-2151
Scott Amerio, prin. Fax 892-4442

Raymond, Montgomery, Pop. 922
Panhandle CUSD 2 500/PK-12
PO Box 49 62560 217-229-4215
Connie Falconer, supt. Fax 229-4216
Lincolnwood HS 200/9-12
PO Box 110 62560 217-229-4237
Robert Wilson, prin. Fax 229-3005
Lincolnwood JHS 100/6-8
PO Box 110 62560 217-229-4237
Robert Wilson, prin. Fax 229-3005

Red Bud, Randolph, Pop. 3,522
Red Bud CUSD 132 1,100/PK-12
815 Locust St 62278 618-282-3507
Steve Harsy, supt. Fax 282-6151
www.redbud.randolph.k12.il.us/
Red Bud HS 400/9-12
815 Locust St 62278 618-282-3826
Bradley Hall, prin. Fax 282-6151

Richmond, McHenry, Pop. 2,215
Nippersink SD 2 1,600/K-8
PO Box 505 60071 815-678-4242
Dr. Paul Hain, supt. Fax 678-2810
www.nippersinkdistrict2.org
Nippersink MS 6-8
10006 N Main St 60071 815-678-7129
Tim Molitor, prin. Fax 678-7210

Richmond-Burton Community HSD 157 700/9-12
PO Box 449 60071 815-678-4525
Dan Oest, supt. Fax 678-4324
www.rbchs.com
Richmond-Burton HS 700/9-12
PO Box 449 60071 815-678-4525
Tom DuBois, prin. Fax 678-4324

Richton Park, Cook, Pop. 12,998
Rich Township HSD 227
Supt. — See Olympia Fields
Rich South Campus HS 1,100/9-12
5000 Sauk Trl 60471 708-679-3000
Roudell Kirkwood, prin. Fax 679-3168

River Forest, Cook, Pop. 11,289
River Forest SD 90 1,400/PK-8
7776 Lake St 60305 708-771-8282
Dr. Marlene Kamm, supt. Fax 771-8291
www.district90.org/
Roosevelt JHS 700/5-8
7560 Oak Ave 60305 708-366-9230
Joanne Trahanas, prin. Fax 771-8291

Concordia University Post-Sec.
7400 Augusta St 60305 708-771-8300
Dominican University Post-Sec.
7900 Division St 60305 708-366-2490
Trinity HS 500/9-12
7574 Division St 60305 708-771-8383
Michele Whitehead, prin. Fax 488-2014

River Grove, Cook, Pop. 10,216

Guerin College Preparatory HS 600/9-12
8001 Belmont Ave 60171 708-453-6233
Elizabeth Brown, prin. Fax 453-6296
Triton College Post-Sec.
2000 5th Ave 60171 708-456-0300

Riverside, Cook, Pop. 8,485
Riverside Brookfield Township HSD 208 1,300/9-12
160 Ridgewood Rd 60546 708-442-7500
Jack Baldermann, supt. Fax 447-5570
www.rbhs208.org
Riverside Brookfield Township HS 1,300/9-12
160 Ridgewood Rd 60546 708-442-7500
Jack Baldermann, prin. Fax 447-5570

Riverside SD 96 1,300/PK-8
63 Woodside Rd 60546 708-447-5007
Dr. Jonathan Lamberson, supt. Fax 447-3252
www.district96.org
Hauser JHS 400/6-8
65 Woodside Rd 60546 708-447-3896
Leslie Berman, prin. Fax 447-5180

Riverton, Sangamon, Pop. 3,043
Riverton CUSD 14 1,500/PK-12
PO Box 1010 62561 217-629-6009
Tom Mulligan, supt. Fax 629-6008
sangamon.k12.il.us/riverton/
Riverton HS 400/9-12
PO Box 560 62561 217-629-6003
Bill Lamkey, prin. Fax 629-6020
Riverton MS 500/5-8
PO Box 530 62561 217-629-6002
Fred Lamkey, prin. Fax 629-6017

Roanoke, Woodford, Pop. 1,988
Roanoke-Benson CUSD 60 600/PK-12
PO Box 320 61561 309-923-8921
Lynn Curtis, supt. Fax 923-7508
www.rb60.com/
Roanoke-Benson HS 200/9-12
PO Box 320 61561 309-923-8401
Mark Zotz, prin. Fax 923-7508
Other Schools – See Benson

Linn Mennonite Christian S 50/K-12
1594 County Road 1700 N 61561 309-923-5641
Carl Kennell, pres.

Robbins, Cook, Pop. 6,375
Posen-Robbins ESD 143-5
Supt. — See Posen
Kellar JHS 500/6-8
14123 S Lydia Ave 60472 708-388-7201
Stacey Hunt, prin. Fax 388-6177

Robinson, Crawford, Pop. 6,471
Robinson CUSD 2 1,700/K-12
PO Box 190 62454 618-544-7511
Earl Williams, supt. Fax 544-9284
www.robinsonschools.com/
Nuttall MS 400/6-8
400 W Rustic St 62454 618-544-8618
Sue Catt, prin. Fax 544-5304
Robinson HS 600/9-12
2000 N Cross St 62454 618-544-9510
Troy Hickey, prin. Fax 544-7921

Lincoln Trail College Post-Sec.
11220 State Highway 1 62454 618-544-8657

Rochelle, Ogle, Pop. 9,712
Rochelle CCSD 231 1,800/PK-8
444 N 8th St 61068 815-562-6363
Todd Prusator, supt. Fax 562-5500
www.d231.rochelle.net/
Rochelle MS 600/6-8
111 School Ave 61068 815-562-7997
Joe Schwartz, prin. Fax 562-8527

Rochelle Township HSD 212 1,100/9-12
1401 Flagg Rd 61068 815-562-4161
Douglas Creason, supt. Fax 562-6693
www.rths.rochelle.net/index.shtml
Rochelle Township HS 1,100/9-12
1401 Flagg Rd 61068 815-562-4161
Richard Craven, prin. Fax 562-6693

Rochester, Sangamon, Pop. 3,004
Rochester CUSD 3A 2,000/PK-12
4 Rocket Dr 62563 217-498-6210
Dr. Thomas Bertrand, supt. Fax 498-8045
www.rochester3a.sangamon.k12.il.us
Rochester HS 600/9-12
1 Rocket Dr 62563 217-498-9761
Dennis Canny, prin. Fax 498-9825
Rochester JHS 300/7-8
3 Rocket Dr 62563 217-498-9761
Scott Riddle, prin. Fax 498-6204

Rock Falls, Whiteside, Pop. 9,470
Rock Falls ESD 13 1,000/PK-8
602 4th Ave 61071 815-626-2604
Jack H. Etnyre, supt. Fax 626-2627
Rock Falls MS 300/6-8
1701 12th Ave 61071 815-626-2626
Jeffrey Brown, prin. Fax 626-3198

Rock Falls Township HSD 301 700/9-12
101 12th Ave 61071 815-625-3886
Dr. Jane Eichman, supt. Fax 625-3889
www.wside.k12.il.us/rfhs
Rock Falls Township HS 700/9-12
101 12th Ave 61071 815-625-3886
Ron McCord, prin. Fax 625-3889

Rockford, Winnebago, Pop. 152,916
Rockford SD 205 28,200/PK-12
201 S Madison St 61104 815-966-3101
Dr. Dennis Thompson, supt. Fax 966-3193
www.rps205.com/
Auburn HS 1,700/9-12
5110 Auburn St 61101 815-966-3300
Richard Jancek, prin. Fax 966-3911
Eisenhower MS 900/6-8
3525 Spring Creek Rd 61107 815-229-2450
Jill Davis, prin. Fax 229-2456
Flinn MS 900/6-8
2525 Ohio Pkwy 61108 815-229-2800
Don Rundall, prin. Fax 229-2894
Guilford HS 2,100/9-12
5620 Spring Creek Rd 61114 815-654-4870
Timothy Kutz, prin. Fax 654-4901
Jefferson HS 1,900/9-12
4145 Samuelson Rd 61109 815-874-9536
Dr. Kenneth Jackson, prin. Fax 874-2800
Kennedy MS 700/6-8
4664 N Rockton Ave 61103 815-654-4880
Theresa Kallstrom, prin. Fax 654-4874
Lincoln MS 1,000/6-8
1500 Charles St 61104 815-229-2400
Michael Valentine, prin. Fax 229-2420
Rockford East HS 1,700/9-12
2929 Charles St 61108 815-229-2100
Todd France, prin. Fax 229-2113
Rockford Environmental Science Academy 1,200/6-8
1800 Ogilby Rd 61102 815-489-5509
Dr. Robert DeLacey, prin. Fax 966-5360
West MS 900/6-8
1900 N Rockton Ave 61103 815-966-3200
Christy Kutz, prin. Fax 966-3216
Wilson MS 300/6-8
520 N Pierpont Ave 61101 815-966-3721
Dr. Thomas Schmitt, prin. Fax 966-8911

Berean Baptist Christian S 300/PK-12
5626 Safford Rd 61101 815-962-4841
Douglas E. Swanson, admin. Fax 962-4851
Boylan Central Catholic HS 1,300/9-12
4000 Saint Francis Dr 61103 815-877-0531
Vince McGuire, admin. Fax 877-2544
Christian Life S 1,100/PK-12
5950 Spring Creek Rd 61114 815-877-5749
Dr. R. Jay Nelson, supt. Fax 877-4358
Educators of Beauty Post-Sec.
128 S 5th St 61104 815-969-7030
Keith S 300/PK-12
1 Jacoby Pl 61107 815-399-8823
Jon Esler, prin. Fax 399-2470
North Love Christian S 200/PK-12
5301 E Riverside Blvd 61114 815-877-6021
Tom Seeley, prin. Fax 877-6076
Rockford Business College Post-Sec.
730 N Church St 61103 815-965-8616
Rockford Christian S 1,200/PK-12
1401 N Bell School Rd 61107 815-399-3465
Randy Taylor, supt. Fax 391-8004
Rockford College Post-Sec.
5050 E State St 61108 815-226-4000
Rockford Lutheran HS 600/7-12
3411 N Alpine Rd 61114 815-877-9551
Don Kortze, supt. Fax 877-4024
Rockford Memorial Hospital Post-Sec.
2400 N Rockton Ave 61103 815-971-5000
Rock Valley College Post-Sec.
3301 N Mulford Rd 61114 815-654-4250
St. Anthony College of Nursing Post-Sec.
5658 E State St 61108 815-395-5100
St. Anthony Medical Center Post-Sec.
5666 E State St 61108 815-226-2000
Swedish-American Hospital Post-Sec.
1401 E State St 61104 815-968-4400

Rock Island, Rock Island, Pop. 38,702
Rock Island SD 41 6,000/PK-12
2101 6th Ave 61201 309-793-5900
Richard Loy, supt. Fax 793-5905
www.risd41.org/
Edison JHS 400/7-8
4141 9th St 61201 309-793-5920
Gary Flecker, prin. Fax 793-5919
Rock Island HS 1,700/9-12
1400 25th Ave 61201 309-793-5950
Dr. Nate Anderson, prin. Fax 793-9866
Washington JHS 500/7-8
3300 18th Ave 61201 309-793-5915
Mark Hepner, prin. Fax 793-5917

Alleman HS 500/9-12
1103 40th St 61201 309-786-7793
Colin Letendre, prin. Fax 786-7834
Augustana College Post-Sec.
639 38th St 61201 309-794-7000

Trinity College of Nursing — Post-Sec.
2122 25th Ave 61201 — 309-779-7700

Rockton, Winnebago, Pop. 5,348
Hononegah Community HSD 207 — 1,900/9-12
307 Salem St 61072 — 815-624-5010
Dr. Randy Gross, supt. — Fax 624-5029
www.hononegah.org
Hononegah Community HS — 1,900/9-12
307 Salem St 61072 — 815-624-5005
Judy Rigby, prin. — Fax 624-5025

Rockton SD 140 — 1,400/PK-8
1050 E Union St 61072 — 815-624-7143
Jean Harezlak, supt. — Fax 624-4640
rockton140.org
Mack MS — 500/6-8
11810 Old River Rd 61072 — 815-624-2611
Jay Larson, prin. — Fax 624-5900

Rolling Meadows, Cook, Pop. 23,909
Palatine CCSD 15
Supt. — See Palatine
Plum Grove JHS — 800/7-8
2600 Plum Grove Rd 60008 — 847-963-7600
Cheryl Quinn, prin. — Fax 963-7606
Sandburg JHS — 600/7-8
2600 Martin Ln 60008 — 847-963-7800
Ed Nelson, prin. — Fax 963-7806

Township HSD 214
Supt. — See Arlington Heights
Rolling Meadows HS — 1,900/9-12
2901 Central Rd 60008 — 847-718-5600
Dr. Charles Johns, prin. — Fax 718-5617

Romeoville, Will, Pop. 36,396
Valley View CUSD 365U — 14,600/PK-12
755 Luther Dr 60446 — 815-886-2700
Dr. Phillip Schoffstall, supt. — Fax 886-7294
www.vvsd.org/
Lukancic MS — 6-8
725 W Normantown Rd 60446 — 815-886-2216
Omar Castillo, prin. — Fax 886-2264
Martinez MS — 1,300/6-8
590 Belmont Dr 60446 — 815-886-6100
Kelly Gilbert, prin. — Fax 886-7264
Romeoville HS — 1,700/9-12
100 N Independence Blvd 60446 — 815-886-1800
John Sparlin, prin. — Fax 886-7272
Other Schools – See Bolingbrook

Wilco Area Career Center
500 Wilco Blvd 60446 — 815-838-6941
Katrina Paddick, dir. — Fax 838-1163
www.wilco.k12.il.us
Wilco Area Career Center — Vo/Tech
500 Wilco Blvd 60446 — 815-838-6941
Elizabeth Kaufman, prin. — Fax 838-1163

Lewis University — Post-Sec.
1 University Pkwy 60446 — 815-838-0500

Roodhouse, Greene, Pop. 2,217
North Greene Unit SD 3
Supt. — See White Hall
North Greene JHS — 200/6-8
403 W North St 62082 — 217-589-4623
Cynthia Carlson, prin. — Fax 589-4028
Roodhouse S — 300/PK-PK, 4-
403 W North St 62082 — 217-589-4623
Cynthia Carlson, prin. — Fax 589-4028

Roscoe, Winnebago, Pop. 6,355
Kinnikinnick CCSD 131 — 1,900/PK-8
5410 Pine Ln 61073 — 815-623-2837
Robert Lauber, supt. — Fax 623-9285
www.kinn131.org
Roscoe MS — 6-8
6121 Elevator Rd 61073 — 815-623-1884
Julie Cropp, prin. — Fax 623-7604

Roselle, DuPage, Pop. 23,240
Lake Park Community HSD 108 — 1,500/9-12
450 Spring Ct 60172 — 630-529-4500
Dr. John Butts, supt. — Fax 295-5414
www.lphs.org
Lake Park HS East — 1,500/9-10
600 Medinah Rd 60172 — 630-529-4500
Dr. Edward Wardzala, prin. — Fax 295-5212
Lake Park HS West — 11-12
500 W Bryn Mawr Ave 60172 — 630-529-4500
Dr. Martin Quinn, prin. — Fax 295-2932

Medinah SD 11 — 800/K-8
700 E Granville Ave 60172 — 630-893-3737
Dr. Joseph Bailey, supt. — Fax 893-4947
www.medinah.dupage.k12.il.us
Medinah MS — 300/6-8
700 E Granville Ave 60172 — 630-893-3838
Dr. Kara Egger, prin. — Fax 893-5198

Roselle SD 12 — 700/K-8
100 E Walnut St 60172 — 630-529-2091
Dr. Steve Epperson, supt. — Fax 529-2467
www.sd12.k12.il.us/
Roselle MS — 300/6-8
500 S Park St 60172 — 630-529-1600
Kathleen Schneiter, prin. — Fax 529-1882

Roseville, McDonough, Pop. 998
Monmouth-Roseville CUSD 238
Supt. — See Monmouth
Monmouth-Roseville JHS — 7-8
200 E Gossett St 61473 — 309-426-2682
Don Farr, prin. — Fax 426-2303

Round Lake, Lake, Pop. 14,803
Round Lake Area SD 116 — 6,400/PK-12
316 S Rosedale Ct 60073 — 847-270-9000
Dr. Janet Elenbogen, supt. — Fax 546-3538
www.rlas-116.org/
Round Lake HS — 1,600/9-12
800 High School Dr 60073 — 847-270-9300
Dr. Jeff Brierton, prin. — Fax 546-5872
Round Lake MS, 2000 Lotus Dr 60073 — 1,000/7-8
Paul Flatley, prin. — 847-270-9400

Roxana, Madison, Pop. 1,504
Roxana CUSD 1 — 1,900/PK-12
401 Chaffer Ave 62084 — 618-254-7544
David Deets, supt. — Fax 254-7547
www.roxana.k12.il.us
Roxana HS — 600/9-12
401 Chaffer Ave 62084 — 618-254-7553
Derek Hacke, prin. — Fax 254-7580
Roxana JHS — 400/6-8
401 Chaffer Ave 62084 — 618-254-7561
Laura Montgomery, prin. — Fax 254-8107

Royal, Champaign, Pop. 273
Prairieview-Ogden CCSD 197 — 200/K-8
PO Box 27 61871 — 217-583-3300
Victor White, supt. — Fax 583-3391
www.prairieview.k12.il.us
Other Schools – See Thomasboro

Rushville, Schuyler, Pop. 3,162
Schuyler-Industry CUSD 5 — 1,200/PK-12
740 Maple Ave 62681 — 217-322-4311
R. Mathew Plater, supt. — Fax 322-4398
www.sid5.com/
Rushville-Industry HS — 300/9-12
730 N Congress St 62681 — 217-322-4316
Donna Sargent, prin. — Fax 322-2844
Schuyler-Industry MS — 400/4-8
750 N Congress St 62681 — 217-322-2773
Cindy Ward, prin. — Fax 322-3938

Saint Anne, Kankakee, Pop. 1,188
Saint Anne Community HSD 302 — 300/9-12
PO Box 630 60964 — 815-427-8141
Kathleen Hickey, supt. — Fax 427-8409
www.sachs.k12.il.us/
Saint Anne Community HS — 300/9-12
PO Box 630 60964 — 815-427-8141
Dan Patterson, prin. — Fax 427-8609

Saint Charles, Kane, Pop. 32,010
Saint Charles CUSD 303 — 13,300/PK-12
201 S 7th St 60174 — 630-513-3030
Dr. Donald Schlomann, supt. — Fax 513-5392
www.d303.org
Haines MS — 1,000/6-8
305 S 9th St 60174 — 630-377-4827
Charlie Kyle, prin. — Fax 377-4830
Saint Charles East HS — 2,000/9-12
1020 Dunham Rd 60174 — 630-584-1100
Bob Miller, prin. — Fax 584-9563
Saint Charles North HS — 2,000/9-12
255 Red Gate Rd 60175 — 630-443-5700
Kim Zupec, prin. — Fax 443-2769
Thompson MS — 1,000/6-8
705 W Main St 60174 — 630-377-4872
Dr. Pamela Kibbons, prin. — Fax 584-9591
Wredling MS — 1,200/6-8
1200 Dunham Rd 60174 — 630-443-3360
Melissa Dockum, prin. — Fax 443-2770

Saint Elmo, Fayette, Pop. 1,408
Saint Elmo CUSD 202 — 500/K-12
1200 N Walnut St 62458 — 618-829-3264
Deborah Philpot, supt. — Fax 829-5161
www.stelmo.org/
Saint Elmo HS — 100/9-12
300 W 12th St 62458 — 618-829-3227
Brian Garrard, prin. — Fax 829-5161
Saint Elmo JHS — 100/7-8
300 W 12th St 62458 — 618-829-3227
Brian Garrard, prin. — Fax 829-5161

Saint Jacob, Madison, Pop. 897
Triad CUSD 2
Supt. — See Troy
Triad MS — 900/6-8
9539 US Highway 40 62281 — 618-644-5511
Dale Sauer, prin. — Fax 644-9435

Saint Joseph, Champaign, Pop. 3,266
Saint Joseph CCSD 169 — 700/PK-8
PO Box 409 61873 — 217-469-2291
Todd Pence, supt. — Fax 469-8906
www.stjoe.k12.il.us
Saint Joseph MS — 300/5-8
PO Box 409 61873 — 217-469-0409
Chris Graham, prin. — Fax 469-2334

Saint Joseph-Ogden Community HSD 305 — 500/9-12
PO Box 890 61873 — 217-469-2586
Dr. Victor E. Zimmerman, supt. — Fax 469-7321
www.sjo.k12.il.us/
Saint Joseph-Ogden HS — 500/9-12
PO Box 890 61873 — 217-469-2332
Chad Uphoff, prin. — Fax 469-8290

Salem, Marion, Pop. 7,574
Salem Community HSD 600 — 800/9-12
1200 N Broadway Ave 62881 — 618-548-0727
Barbara Smith, supt. — Fax 548-8021
www.salemhigh.com
Salem Community HS — 800/9-12
1200 N Broadway Ave 62881 — 618-548-0727
Brad Detering, prin. — Fax 548-8021

Salem SD 111 — 900/K-8
1300 Hawthorn Rd 62881 — 618-548-7702
Mark Cartwright, supt. — Fax 548-7714
www.salem111.com
Salem Franklin Park JHS — 500/4-8
1325 N Franklin St 62881 — 618-548-7704
David Conklin, prin. — Fax 548-7712

Sandoval, Marion, Pop. 1,362
Sandoval CUSD 501 — 600/PK-12
859 W Missouri Ave 62882 — 618-247-3233
Dr. Terry Bethel, supt. — Fax 247-3243
Sandoval HS — 200/9-12
859 W Missouri Ave 62882 — 618-247-3361
Jim Maddox, prin. — Fax 247-3243
Sandoval JHS — 100/7-8
859 W Missouri Ave 62882 — 618-247-3361
Jim Maddox, prin. — Fax 247-3243

Sandwich, DeKalb, Pop. 7,018
Indian Valley Vocational Center
600 Lions Rd 60548 — 815-786-9873
Ron Pieper, dir. — Fax 786-6928
www.indianvalley.org
Indian Valley Vocational Center — Vo/Tech
600 Lions Rd 60548 — 815-786-9873
Ron Pieper, dir. — Fax 786-6928

Sandwich CUSD 430 — 2,500/PK-12
720 Wells St 60548 — 815-786-2187
Rick Schmitt, supt. — Fax 786-6229
www.sandwich430.org
Sandwich Community HS — 800/9-12
515 Lions Rd 60548 — 815-786-2157
Mitchell Nystedt, prin. — Fax 786-2632
Sandwich MS — 600/6-8
600 Wells St 60548 — 815-786-2138
B.J. Richardson, prin. — Fax 786-6606

Sauk Village, Cook, Pop. 10,486
Community Consolidated SD 168 — 1,900/PK-8
21899 Torrence Ave 60411 — 708-758-1610
Rudy Williams, supt. — Fax 758-5929
www.d168.org
Rickover JHS — 600/6-8
22151 Torrence Ave 60411 — 708-758-1900
Julie Iverson, prin. — Fax 758-1601

Savanna, Carroll, Pop. 3,288
West Carroll CUSD 314
Supt. — See Thomson
West Carroll HS — 200/9-12
500 Cragmoor St 61074 — 815-273-7715
Robert Lamb, prin. — Fax 273-7819

Scales Mound, Jo Daviess, Pop. 387
Scales Mound CUSD 211 — 200/PK-12
210 Main St 61075 — 815-845-2215
Dr. Barbara Sloan, supt. — Fax 845-2238
www.scalesmound.net
Scales Mound HS — 100/9-12
210 Main St 61075 — 815-845-2215
Barbara Sloan, prin. — Fax 845-2238
Scales Mound JHS — 100/6-8
210 Main St 61075 — 815-845-2215
Matthew Wiederhott, prin. — Fax 845-2238

Schaumburg, Cook, Pop. 72,805
Schaumburg CCSD 54 — 14,800/PK-8
524 E Schaumburg Rd 60194 — 847-357-5000
Ed Rafferty, supt. — Fax 357-5006
www.sd54.org/
Addams JHS — 800/7-8
700 S Springinsguth Rd 60193 — 847-357-5900
John Schmelzer, prin. — Fax 357-5901
Frost JHS — 700/7-8
320 W Wise Rd 60193 — 847-357-6800
Andrew DuRoss, prin. — Fax 357-6801
Keller JHS — 600/7-8
820 Bode Rd 60194 — 847-357-6500
Stephen Kern, prin. — Fax 357-6501
Other Schools – See Elk Grove Village, Hoffman Estates

Township HSD 211
Supt. — See Palatine
Schaumburg HS — 2,700/9-12
1100 W Schaumburg Rd 60194 — 847-755-4600
Sharon Cross, prin. — Fax 755-4623

Argosy University/Chicago Northwest — Post-Sec.
1000 N Plaza Dr Ste 100 60173 — 847-290-7400
Keller Graduate School — Post-Sec.
1051 Perimeter Dr 60173 — 847-330-0040
Lake Forest Graduate Sch. of Management — Post-Sec.
1295 E Algonquin Rd 60196 — 847-576-1212
Roosevelt University — Post-Sec.
1400 N Roosevelt Blvd 60173 — 847-619-8600
Schaumburg Christian S — 1,300/PK-12
200 N Roselle Rd 60194 — 847-885-3230
James White, prin. — Fax 885-3354
The Illinois Institute of Art — Post-Sec.
1000 N Plaza Dr 60173 — 847-619-3450

Schiller Park, Cook, Pop. 11,597
Schiller Park SD 81 — 1,300/PK-8
4050 Wagner Ave 60176 — 847-671-1816
Dr. Roberta Taylor, supt. — Fax 671-1872
www.sd81.org/
Lincoln MS — 400/6-8
4050 Wagner Ave 60176 — 847-678-2916
Brian Minarcik, prin. — Fax 678-4059

Sciota, McDonough, Pop. 54
West Prairie CUSD 103
Supt. — See Colchester
West Prairie HS — 300/9-12
18575 E 800th St 61475 — 309-456-3750
John Bushmire, prin. — Fax 456-3997

Seneca, LaSalle, Pop. 2,057
Seneca CCSD 170 — 600/PK-8
174 Oak St 61360 — 815-357-8744
Larry Walker, supt. — Fax 357-1516
www.sgs170.org
Seneca MS South Campus — 5-8
410 S Main St 61360 — 815-357-8744
Michael Matteson, prin. — Fax 357-1078

Seneca Township HSD 160 — 500/9-12
PO Box 20 61360 — 815-357-5000
Mark Thurwanger, supt. — Fax 357-5050
www.senecahs.org/
Seneca HS — 500/9-12
PO Box 20 61360 — 815-357-5000
Doug Evans, prin. — Fax 357-1216

Serena, LaSalle
Serena CUSD 2 — 900/K-12
2283 N 3812 Rd 60549 — 815-496-2850
Daniel P. Joyce, supt. — Fax 496-2987
www.unit2.net/
Serena Community HS — 300/9-12
PO Box 107 60549 — 815-496-2361
Patrick Leonard, prin. — Fax 496-2987

Sesser, Franklin, Pop. 2,136
Sesser-Valier CUSD 196 — 800/PK-12
4626 State Highway 154 62884 — 618-625-5105
Jason Henry, supt. — Fax 625-6696
www.s-v.frnkln.k12.il.us/
Sesser-Valier HS — 200/9-12
4626 State Highway 154 62884 — 618-625-5105
Wesley Choate, prin. — Fax 625-6696
Sesser-Valier JHS — 200/6-8
4626 State Highway 154 62884 — 618-625-5105
Judy Logsdon, prin. — Fax 625-3040

Shabbona, DeKalb, Pop. 943
Indian Creek CUSD 425 — 900/K-12
506 S Shabbona Rd 60550 — 815-824-2197
Dr. Bruce Bauer, supt. — Fax 824-2199
www.indiancreekschools.org

Indian Creek HS 300/9-12
506 S Shabbona Rd 60550 815-824-2197
Jim Hammack, prin. Fax 824-2199
Other Schools – See Waterman

Shannon, Carroll, Pop. 799
Eastland CUSD 308
Supt. — See Lanark
Eastland MS 300/4-8
601 S Chestnut St 61078 815-864-2300
Darcie Feltmeyer, prin. Fax 864-2281

Shelbyville, Shelby, Pop. 4,739
Shelbyville CUSD 4 1,300/PK-12
720 W Main St 62565 217-774-4626
Robert Verdun, supt. Fax 774-2521
shelbyville.k12.il.us/
Moulton MS 500/4-8
1001 W North 6th St 62565 217-774-2169
Jacque Eberspacher, prin. Fax 774-3042
Shelbyville HS 400/9-12
1001 W North 6th St 62565 217-774-3926
Kevin Ross, prin. Fax 774-5836

Sparks College Post-Sec.
131 S Morgan St 62565 217-774-5112

Sherrard, Mercer, Pop. 671
Sherrard CUSD 200 1,600/PK-12
PO Box 369 61281 309-593-4075
Robert Cillum, supt. Fax 593-4078
www.sherrard.us
Sherrard HS 500/9-12
4701 176th Ave 61281 309-593-2175
Jim Lee, prin. Fax 593-2775
Sherrard JHS 300/7-8
4701 176th Ave 61281 309-593-2135
Garet Egel, prin. Fax 593-2143

Sidell, Vermilion, Pop. 603
Jamaica CUSD 12 500/PK-12
7087 N 600 East Rd 61876 217-288-9306
Mark Janesky, supt. Fax 288-9306
Jamaica HS 200/9-12
7087 N 600 East Rd 61876 217-288-9392
Mark Janesky, prin.
Jamaica JHS 100/6-8
7087 N 600 East Rd 61876 217-288-9394
Kevin Lipke, prin.

Silvis, Rock Island, Pop. 7,489
Silvis SD 34 700/PK-8
1305 5th Ave 61282 309-792-9325
Ray Bergles, supt. Fax 792-8092
www.silvis34.com
Silvis JHS, 1305 5th Ave 61282 200/6-8
Art Byczynski, prin. 309-792-3511

Skokie, Cook, Pop. 64,678
Niles Township Community HSD 219 4,700/9-12
7700 Gross Point Rd 60077 847-626-3000
Neil Codell, supt. Fax 626-3075
www.niles219.org
Niles North HS 2,200/9-12
9800 Lawler Ave 60077 847-626-2000
Robert Freeman, prin. Fax 626-3340
Niles West HS 2,500/9-12
5701 Oakton St 60077 847-626-2500
Dale Vogler, prin. Fax 626-3700

Skokie SD 68 1,600/K-8
9440 Kenton Ave 60076 847-676-9000
Dr. Frances McTague, supt. Fax 676-9232
www.sd68.k12.il.us
Old Orchard JHS 700/6-8
9310 Kenton Ave 60076 847-676-9010
Margaret Clauson, prin. Fax 676-3827

Skokie SD 69 1,500/PK-8
5050 Madison St 60077 847-675-7666
Dr. Rebecca L. Nelson, supt. Fax 675-7675
www.skokie69.k12.il.us
Lincoln JHS 500/6-8
7839 Lincoln Ave 60077 847-676-3545
James Morrison, prin. Fax 676-3595

Skokie SD 73-5 1,100/PK-8
8000 E Prairie Rd 60076 847-673-1220
Vicki Gunther, supt. Fax 673-1565
www.skokie735.k12.il.us/
McCracken MS 400/6-8
8000 E Prairie Rd 60076 847-673-1220
Kate Donegan, prin. Fax 673-1282

Computer Systems Institute Post-Sec.
8930 Gross Point Rd 60077 847-967-5030
Fasman Yeshiva HS 200/9-12
7135 Carpenter Rd 60077 847-982-2500
Rabbi Moshe Wender, prin. Fax 674-6381
Hebrew Theological College Post-Sec.
7135 Carpenter Rd 60077 847-982-2500
Knowledge Systems Institute Post-Sec.
3420 Main St 60076 847-679-3135
National-Louis University Post-Sec.
5202 Old Orchard Rd Ste 300 60077 224-233-2000
Olympia College Post-Sec.
9811 Woods Dr # 200 60077 847-470-0277
Ort Technical Institute Post-Sec.
5440 Fargo Ave 60077 847-324-5588

Somonauk, DeKalb, Pop. 1,492
Somonauk CUSD 432 1,000/K-12
PO Box 278 60552 815-498-2314
M. Susan Workman, supt. Fax 498-9523
www.somonauk.net/
Somonauk HS 300/9-12
PO Box 278 60552 815-498-2314
David Mantzke, prin. Fax 498-9841
Somonauk MS 300/5-8
PO Box 278 60552 815-498-1866
Jim Prather, prin. Fax 498-1647

South Beloit, Winnebago, Pop. 5,421
South Beloit CUSD 320 1,200/PK-12
850 Hayes Ave 61080 815-389-3478
Michael Duffy, supt. Fax 389-3477
www.southbeloitschooldistrict.org
South Beloit HS 300/9-12
245 Prairie Hill Rd 61080 815-389-9004
Matthew Vosberg, prin. Fax 389-9268
South Beloit JHS 200/7-8
840 Blackhawk Blvd 61080 815-389-1421
Todd Martens, prin. Fax 389-8811

South Elgin, Kane, Pop. 20,758
SD U-46
Supt. — See Elgin
Kenyon Woods MS 800/7-8
1515 Raymond St 60177 847-289-6685
Sue Welu, prin. Fax 628-6166
South Elgin HS 9-12
760 E Main St 60177 847-289-3760
Dr. Jean Bowen, prin. Fax 888-7014

South Holland, Cook, Pop. 21,552
South Holland SD 150 1,100/PK-8
848 E 170th St 60473 708-339-4240
Dr. Jerry Jordan, supt. Fax 339-4244
McKinley JHS 400/6-8
16949 Cottage Grove Ave 60473 708-339-8500
George Harris, prin. Fax 331-5805

South Holland SD 151 1,600/PK-8
320 E 161st Pl 60473 708-339-1516
Dr. Douglas C. Hamilton, supt. Fax 331-7600
www.shsd151.org
Other Schools – See Phoenix

Thornton Twp. HSD 205 6,500/9-12
465 E 170th St 60473 708-225-4000
Dr. J. Kamala Buckner, supt. Fax 225-4004
www.district205.net
Thornwood HS 2,200/9-12
17101 S Park Ave 60473 708-225-4701
Timothy Truesdale, prin. Fax 225-5033
Other Schools – See Dolton, Harvey

Seton Academy 300/9-12
16100 Seton Dr 60473 708-333-6300
Ingia Jackson, prin. Fax 333-1534
South Suburban College of Cook County Post-Sec.
15800 State St 60473 708-596-2000

South Roxana, Madison, Pop. 1,826

Bethel Christian Academy 100/PK-12
PO Box 535 62087 618-254-0188
Ricky Ham, supt. Fax 254-2067

Sparland, Marshall, Pop. 499
Midland CUSD 7
Supt. — See Lacon
Midland MS 300/5-8
901 Hilltop Dr 61565 309-469-3131
Daniel Mair, prin. Fax 469-5701

Sparta, Randolph, Pop. 4,395
Sparta CUSD 140 1,500/PK-12
203B Dean Ave 62286 618-443-5331
Karen Perry, supt. Fax 443-2023
www.sparta.k12.il.us
Sparta HS 500/9-12
205 W Hood St 62286 618-443-4341
Gregory Jones, prin. Fax 443-5059
Sparta-Lincoln MS 500/4-8
203A Dean Ave 62286 618-443-5331
Laura Woodworth, prin. Fax 443-2892

Springfield, Sangamon, Pop. 115,668
Capital Area Career Center
2201 Toronto Rd Ste B, 217-529-5431
John Bailey, supt. Fax 529-7614
Capital Area Career Center Vo/Tech
2201 Toronto Rd Ste B, 217-529-5431
Jim Jones, prin. Fax 529-7861

Springfield SD 186 13,600/PK-12
1900 W Monroe St 62704 217-525-3000
Dr. Diane Rutledge, supt. Fax 525-3005
www.springfield.k12.il.us/
Franklin MS 900/6-8
1200 Outer Park Dr 62704 217-525-3164
Kristine Huddleston, prin. Fax 525-7937
Grant MS 700/6-8
1800 W Monroe St 62704 217-525-3170
Kay Dimon, prin. Fax 525-3390
Jefferson MS 700/6-8
3001 S Allis St 62703 217-525-3176
J. Michael Zimmers, prin. Fax 525-3293
Lanphier HS 1,300/9-12
1300 N 11th St 62702 217-525-3080
Jane Chard, prin. Fax 525-3084
Lincoln Magnet MS 300/6-8
300 S 11th St 62703 217-525-3236
Margaret Kruger, prin. Fax 525-3294
Springfield HS 1,400/9-12
101 S Lewis St 62704 217-525-3100
Chuck Hoots, prin. Fax 525-3122
Springfield Southeast HS 1,300/9-12
2350 E Ash St 62703 217-525-3130
Tammie Bolden, prin. Fax 525-3139
Washington MS 600/6-8
2300 E Jackson St 62703 217-525-3182
Susan Palmer, prin. Fax 525-3319
Lawrence Education Center Adult
101 E Laurel St 62704 217-525-3144
Kathi Lee-Deassuncao, prin. Fax 525-3090

Calvary Academy 400/PK-12
1730 W Jefferson St 62702 217-546-9700
Donna Squires, prin. Fax 546-1926
Lincoln Land Community College Post-Sec.
5250 Shepherd Rd 62703 217-786-2200
Lutheran HS 200/9-12
3500 W Washington St, 217-546-6363
Don Duensing, prin. Fax 546-6489
Midwest Technical Institute Post-Sec.
2731 N Farmers Market Rd 62707 800-504-8882
Robert Morris College Post-Sec.
3101 Montvale Dr 62704 217-793-2500
Sacred Heart-Griffin HS 800/9-12
1200 W Washington St 62702 217-787-1595
Sr. Margaret Joanne Grueter, prin. Fax 787-9856
St. John's College Post-Sec.
421 N 9th St 62702 217-525-5628
St. John's Hospital Post-Sec.
800 E Carpenter St 62769 217-544-6464
Southern Illinois University Post-Sec.
PO Box 19621 62794 217-545-8000
Springfield College in Illinois Post-Sec.
1500 N 5th St 62702 217-525-1420
Undergraduate School of Cosmetology Post-Sec.
PO Box 195 62705 217-753-8990
University of Illinois at Springfield Post-Sec.
PO Box 19243 62794 217-206-6600

Spring Grove, McHenry, Pop. 5,303
Fox Lake Grade SD 114 900/PK-8
29067 W Grass Lake Rd 60081 847-973-4027
John Donnellan, supt. Fax 973-4010
www.flgs.lake.k12.il.us
Other Schools – See Fox Lake

Spring Valley, Bureau, Pop. 5,380
Hall HSD 502 400/9-12
800 W Erie St 61362 815-664-4500
Leo Johnson, supt. Fax 664-2300
Hall HS 400/9-12
800 W Erie St 61362 815-664-2100
Patti Lunn, prin. Fax 664-2300

Stanford, McLean, Pop. 644
Olympia CUSD 16 2,100/PK-12
903 E 800 North Rd 61774 309-379-6011
Donald F. Hahn, supt. Fax 379-2328
www.olympia.org
Olympia HS 700/9-12
7832 N 100 East Rd 61774 309-379-5911
Lance Thurman, prin. Fax 379-2583
Olympia MS 300/7-8
911 E 800 North Rd 61774 309-379-5941
Todd Dugan, prin. Fax 379-5411

Staunton, Macoupin, Pop. 5,109
Staunton CUSD 6 1,400/PK-12
801 N Deneen St 62088 618-635-2962
Kyle Hlafka, supt. Fax 635-2994
www.staunton.macoupin.k12.il.us/
Staunton HS 500/9-12
801 N Deneen St 62088 618-635-3838
Loren Beswick, prin. Fax 635-2834
Staunton JHS 300/6-8
801 N Deneen St 62088 618-635-3831
Mark Skertich, prin. Fax 635-4637

Steeleville, Randolph, Pop. 2,058
Steeleville CUSD 138 400/K-12
701 S Sparta St 62288 618-965-3432
Stephanie Mulholland, supt. Fax 965-3433
Steeleville HS 100/9-12
701 S Sparta St 62288 618-965-3432
Jennifer Hagel, prin. Fax 965-3433

Steger, Cook, Pop. 10,409
Steger SD 194 1,500/PK-8
3753 Park Ave 60475 708-755-0022
Jeanne Domink, supt. Fax 755-9512
www.sd194.org/
Columbia Central MS 400/6-8
94 Richton Rd 60475 708-755-0021
Jeff Nelson, prin. Fax 755-1877

St. Liborius S 100/5-8
3440 Halsted Blvd 60475 708-754-0192
Mary Jane Bartley, prin. Fax 755-3982

Sterling, Whiteside, Pop. 15,381
Sterling CUSD 5 3,500/PK-12
410 E Le Fevre Rd 61081 815-626-5050
Dr. Wil Booker, supt. Fax 622-4113
www.sterlingschools.org
Challand MS 800/6-8
1700 6th Ave 61081 815-626-3300
Suzzette Hesser, prin. Fax 622-4173
Sterling HS 1,100/9-12
1608 4th Ave 61081 815-625-6800
Gerald Binder, prin. Fax 622-4157

Whiteside AVC, 1608 5th Ave 61081
Wilma Hewitt, supt. 815-626-5810
Whiteside AVC, 1608 5th Ave 61081 Vo/Tech
Wilma Hewitt, prin. 815-626-5810

Educators of Beauty Post-Sec.
211 E 3rd St 61081 815-625-0247
Newman Central Catholic HS 200/9-12
1101 W 23rd St 61081 815-625-0500
Rev. Paul Lipinski, admin. Fax 625-8444

Stillman Valley, Ogle, Pop. 1,097
Meridian CUSD 223 1,800/PK-12
207 W Main St 61084 815-645-2606
Robert Prusator, supt. Fax 645-4325
www.meridian223.org
Meridian JHS 400/6-8
207 W Main St 61084 815-645-2277
William Davidson, prin. Fax 645-8181
Stillman Valley HS 600/9-12
425 S Pine St 61084 815-645-2291
Michael Mandzen, prin. Fax 645-8145

Stockton, Jo Daviess, Pop. 1,820
Stockton CUSD 206 600/PK-12
500 N Rush St 61085 815-947-3321
Dr. Kevin Sullivan, supt. Fax 947-2114
www.stocktonschools.com
Stockton HS 200/9-12
540 N Rush St 61085 815-947-3323
Terry Sertle, prin. Fax 947-2673
Stockton MS 100/6-8
500 N Rush St Ste A 61085 815-947-3702
Brad Fox, prin. Fax 947-2114

Strasburg, Shelby, Pop. 582
Stewardson-Strasburg CUSD 5A 500/PK-12
RR 1 Box 67 62465 217-682-3355
Ruth Schneider, supt. Fax 682-3305
www.sscusd.k12.il.us/
Stewardson-Strasburg HS 100/9-12
RR 1 Box 67 62465 217-682-3355
Larry Renshaw, prin. Fax 682-3305

Streamwood, Cook, Pop. 37,312
SD U-46
Supt. — See Elgin
Canton MS 800/7-8
1100 Sunset Cir 60107 630-213-5525
Dr. James Hawkins, prin. Fax 213-5709
Streamwood HS 2,300/9-12
701 W Schaumburg Rd 60107 630-213-5500
Oscar Hawthorne, prin. Fax 483-5909
Tefft MS 800/7-8
1100 Shirley Ave 60107 630-213-5535
Lavonne Smiley, prin. Fax 213-5646

Streator, LaSalle, Pop. 13,899
Streator ESD 44 1,800/PK-8
1520 N Bloomington St 61364 815-672-2926
Dr. Christine Benson, supt. Fax 673-2032
streator44.il.schoolwebpages.com/

Northlawn JHS 600/6-8
202 E 1st St 61364 815-672-4558
Darrick Reiley, prin. Fax 672-8109

Streator Twp. HSD 40 1,000/9-12
600 N Jefferson St 61364 815-672-0545
Dr. Stephan Swanson, supt. Fax 673-3637
Streator Twp. HS 1,000/9-12
600 N Jefferson St 61364 815-672-0545
Amy Mascal, prin. Fax 673-3637

Woodland CUSD 5 500/PK-12
5800 E 3000 North Rd 61364 815-672-5974
Douglas Foster, supt. Fax 673-1630
www.woodland5.org/
Woodland HS 200/9-12
5800 E 3000 North Rd 61364 815-672-2900
Debra Derby, prin.

Rhema Christian Academy 50/PK-12
1634 State Route 23 N 61364 815-672-5751
Kathy Hawthorne, prin. Fax 672-3451

Stronghurst, Henderson, Pop. 846
West Central CUSD 235
Supt. — See Biggsville
West Central MS 100/6-8
PO Box 179 61480 309-924-1531
Jeff Nichols, prin. Fax 924-1122

Sugar Grove, Kane, Pop. 8,416

Waubonsee Community College Post-Sec.
Route 47 at Waubonsee Dr 60554 630-466-7900

Sullivan, Moultrie, Pop. 4,323
Sullivan CUSD 300 1,200/PK-12
725 N Main St 61951 217-728-8341
Terry Pearcy, supt. Fax 728-4139
home.sullivan.k12.il.us/
Sullivan HS 400/9-12
725 N Main St 61951 217-728-8311
Stuart Hott, prin. Fax 728-4139
Sullivan MS 300/6-8
713 N Main St 61951 217-728-8381
Joe Marks, prin. Fax 728-4139

Summit, Cook
Summit SD 104 1,600/PK-8
6021 S 74th Ave 60501 708-458-0505
Kevin Cronin, supt. Fax 458-0532
www.sd104.us
Heritage MS 500/6-8
6021 S 74th Ave 60501 708-458-7590
Dennis Lewis, prin. Fax 728-3111

Summit Argo, Cook, Pop. 9,733
Argo Community HSD 217 1,800/9-12
7329 W 63rd St 60501 708-728-3200
Dr. Frank Stout, supt. Fax 728-3155
www.argo217.k12.il.us/
Argo Community HS 1,800/9-12
7329 W 63rd St 60501 708-728-3200
Thomas Dixey, prin. Fax 728-3155

Swansea, Saint Clair, Pop. 12,274
Wolf Branch SD 113 900/K-8
410 Huntwood Rd 62226 618-277-2100
Bud Martin, supt. Fax 277-5461
www.wolfbranchschooldistrict.org/
Wolf Branch MS 6-8
410 Huntwood Rd 62226 618-277-2100
Jeffrey Burkett, prin. Fax 277-5461

Sycamore, DeKalb, Pop. 14,831
Sycamore CUSD 427 3,300/K-12
245 W Exchange St Ste 1 60178 815-899-8100
Wayne Riesen, supt. Fax 899-8110
www.syc427.org
Sycamore HS 1,100/9-12
Spartan Trail 60178 815-899-8131
Mark Leffler, prin. Fax 899-8166
Sycamore MS 800/6-8
150 Maplewood Dr 60178 815-899-8171
Jane Dargatz, prin. Fax 899-8177

Cornerstone Christian Academy 400/PK-12
355 N Cross St 60178 815-895-8522
Tom Olmstead, hdmstr. Fax 895-8717
Hair Professionals Career College Post-Sec.
2245 Gateway Dr 60178 815-756-3596

Table Grove, Knox, Pop. 389
V I T CUSD 2 400/PK-12
1500 E US Highway 136 61482 309-758-5138
John Marshall, supt. Fax 758-5298
vit.k12.il.us
V I T HS 100/9-12
1502 E US Highway 136 61482 309-758-5136
Phil Snowden, prin. Fax 758-5126
V I T JHS 100/7-8
1502 E US Highway 136 61482 309-758-5136
Phil Snowden, prin. Fax 758-5126

Tamms, Alexander, Pop. 1,150
Egyptian CUSD 5 600/PK-12
20023 Diswood Rd 62988 618-776-5306
Linda Davis, supt. Fax 776-5122
www.egyptianschool.com
Egyptian HS 200/9-12
20023 Diswood Rd 62988 618-776-5251
Larry Houston, prin. Fax 776-5122
Egyptian JHS 200/6-8
20023 Diswood Rd 62988 618-776-5251
Larry Houston, prin. Fax 776-5122

Five County Regional Vocational System
PO Box 70 62988 618-747-2703
Debbie Spomer, supt. Fax 747-2872
Five County Regional Vocational System Vo/Tech
PO Box 70 62988 618-747-2703
Debbie Spomer, prin. Fax 747-2872

Tampico, Whiteside, Pop. 745
Prophetstown-Lyndon-Tampico CUSD 3
Supt. — See Prophetstown
Tampico MS 200/6-8
PO Box 189 61283 815-438-3085
Chad Colmone, prin. Fax 438-3095

Taylor Ridge, Rock Island
Rockridge CUSD 300 1,300/PK-12
14110 134th Ave W 61284 309-795-1167
Jack Bambrick, supt. Fax 795-1719
www.rockridge.k12.il.us
Rockridge HS 400/9-12
14110 134th Ave W 61284 309-795-1736
Clayton Naylor, prin. Fax 795-1763
Rockridge JHS 200/7-8
14110 134th Ave W 61284 309-795-1172
Katherine Hasson, prin. Fax 795-9823

Taylorville, Christian, Pop. 11,240
Taylorville CUSD 3 3,200/PK-12
512 W Spresser St 62568 217-824-4951
Dr. Greggory Fuerstenau, supt. Fax 824-5157
www.taylorvilleschools.com
Taylorville HS 1,000/9-12
815 W Springfield Rd 62568 217-824-2268
Thomas Campbell, prin. Fax 824-3352
Taylorville JHS 800/6-8
120 E Bidwell St 62568 217-824-4924
Kirk Kettelkamp, prin. Fax 824-7180

Teutopolis, Effingham, Pop. 1,634
Teutopolis CUSD 50 1,400/PK-12
PO Box 607 62467 217-857-3535
Fran Thoele, supt. Fax 857-6265
www.teutopolisschools.org/
Teutopolis HS 500/9-12
801 W Main St 62467 217-857-3139
Greg Beck, prin. Fax 857-3473
Teutopolis JHS 200/7-8
904 W Water St 62467 217-857-6678
Bill Fritcher, prin. Fax 857-6678

Thomasboro, Champaign, Pop. 1,222
Prairieview-Ogden CCSD 197
Supt. — See Royal
Prairieview-Ogden JHS 50/7-8
2499 County Road 2100 E 61878 217-694-4122
Jim Morgan, prin. Fax 694-4123

Thompsonville, Franklin, Pop. 593
Thompsonville Community HSD 112 100/9-12
21191 Shawneetown Rd 62890 618-627-2446
Greg Goins, supt. Fax 627-2446
thompsonville.il.schoolwebpages.com/education/distri
c
Thompsonville HS 100/9-12
21135 Shawneetown Rd 62890 618-627-2301
Kim Kaytor, prin. Fax 627-2446

Thompsonville Christian S 50/K-10
PO Box 53 62890 618-627-2065
Nancy O'Brien, prin. Fax 627-2726

Thomson, Carroll, Pop. 536
West Carroll CUSD 314 500/PK-12
801 South St 61285 815-259-2735
Lonny Lemon, supt. Fax 259-3561
Other Schools – See Mount Carroll, Savanna

Tinley Park, Cook, Pop. 57,477
Bremen Community HSD 228
Supt. — See Midlothian
Tinley Park HS 1,100/9-12
6111 175th St 60477 708-532-1900
David Kibelkis, prin. Fax 532-4332

Consolidated HSD 230
Supt. — See Orland Park
Andrew HS 2,500/9-12
9001 171st St, 708-342-5800
Glenn Wood, prin. Fax 532-7383

Kirby SD 140 4,200/PK-8
16931 Grissom Dr 60477 708-532-6462
Dr. Michael Byrne, supt. Fax 532-1512
www.ksd140.org
Grissom MS 800/6-8
17000 80th Ave 60477 708-429-3030
Patricia Dwyer, prin. Fax 532-8529
Prairie View MS 900/6-8
8500 175th St, 708-532-8540
Joel Martin, prin. Fax 532-8544

Tinley Park CCSD 146 2,400/PK-8
6611 171st St 60477 708-614-4500
Dr. Marion Hoyda, supt. Fax 614-8992
www.district146.org
Central MS 800/6-8
18146 Oak Park Ave 60477 708-614-4510
Debra Brennan, prin. Fax 614-7271

Keller Graduate School Post-Sec.
18684 W West Creek Dr 60477 708-342-3300

Toledo, Cumberland, Pop. 1,143
Cumberland CUSD 77 1,000/PK-12
1496 IL Route 121 62468 217-923-3132
Russell Ragon, supt. Fax 923-3132
www.cumberland.k12.il.us/
Cumberland HS 300/9-12
1496 IL Route 121 62468 217-923-3133
Todd Hall, prin. Fax 923-5514
Cumberland JHS 200/6-8
1496 IL Route 121 62468 217-923-3135
Doug Jones, prin. Fax 923-5449

Tolono, Champaign, Pop. 2,776
Tolono CUSD 7 1,300/PK-12
PO Box S 61880 217-485-6510
Michael Shonk, supt. Fax 485-3091
www.roe9.k12.il.us/schools/tolono.htm
Unity HS 500/9-12
1127 County Road 800 N 61880 217-485-6230
Phil Morrison, prin.
Unity JHS 200/6-8
1121 County Road 800 N 61880 217-485-6735
Mary Hettinger, prin.

Toulon, Stark, Pop. 1,368
Stark County CUSD 100
Supt. — See Wyoming
Stark County HS 300/9-12
PO Box 419 61483 309-286-4451
Michael Domico, prin. Fax 286-3321
Stark County JHS, PO Box 659 61483 200/6-8
Michael Domico, prin. 309-286-3451

Tremont, Tazewell, Pop. 2,065
Tremont CUSD 702 1,000/PK-12
400 W Pearl St 61568 309-925-3461
Donald Beard, supt. Fax 925-5817
Tremont HS 300/9-12
400 W Pearl St 61568 309-925-3823
Jeff Hinman, prin. Fax 925-5817
Tremont JHS 200/6-8
400 W Pearl St 61568 309-925-3823
Jeff Hinman, prin. Fax 925-5817

Trenton, Clinton, Pop. 2,651
Wesclin CUSD 3 1,400/PK-12
10003 State Route 160 62293 618-224-7583
Paul Tockstein, supt. Fax 224-9106
wesclin.k12.il.us
Wesclin HS 400/9-12
10003 State Route 160 62293 618-224-7341
John Isenhower, prin. Fax 224-9106
Wesclin JHS 200/7-8
10003 State Route 160 62293 618-224-7355
John Mullett, prin. Fax 224-9106

Troy, Madison, Pop. 9,374
Triad CUSD 2 3,800/PK-12
203 E Throp St 62294 618-667-5400
Dr. Michael Johnson, supt. Fax 667-8854
www.triad.madison.k12.il.us
Triad HS 1,300/9-12
703 E US Highway 40 62294 618-667-5409
Robert Sudhoff, prin. Fax 667-8853
Other Schools – See Saint Jacob

Tuscola, Douglas, Pop. 4,583
Tuscola CUSD 301 1,000/PK-12
409 S Prairie St 61953 217-253-4241
Joe Burgess, supt. Fax 253-4522
www.tuscola.k12.il.us/
East Prairie JHS 300/5-8
409 S Prairie St 61953 217-253-2828
Joseph Yurko, prin. Fax 253-3236
Tuscola HS 300/9-12
500 S Prairie St 61953 217-253-2377
Kyle Ransom, prin. Fax 253-4861

Ullin, Pulaski, Pop. 723
Century CUSD 100 500/PK-12
4721 Shawnee College Rd 62992 618-845-3447
Dr. Paul Franklin, supt. Fax 845-3476
Century HS 100/9-12
4721 Shawnee College Rd 62992 618-845-3518
Terry Moreland, prin. Fax 845-3476
Century MS 100/7-8
4721 Shawnee College Rd 62992 618-845-3518
Melinda Duke, prin. Fax 845-3476

Shawnee Community College Post-Sec.
8364 Shawnee College Rd 62992 618-634-2242

University Park, Will, Pop. 8,102
Crete-Monee CUSD 201U
Supt. — See Crete
Crete-Monee MS 800/7-8
635 Olmstead Ln 60466 708-367-2400
Nehemiah Thomas, prin. Fax 672-2777

Governors State University Post-Sec.
1 University Pkwy 60466 708-534-5000

Urbana, Champaign, Pop. 38,463
Board of Trustees SD 200/9-12
1212 W Springfield Ave 61801 217-333-2870
Kathleen Patton, supt.
University of Illinois HS 200/9-12
1212 W Springfield Ave 61801 217-333-2870
Kathleen Patton, prin.

Urbana SD 116 4,500/PK-12
PO Box 3039 61803 217-384-3636
Dr. Eugene Amberg, supt. Fax 337-4973
www.usd116.org/
Urbana HS 1,300/9-12
1002 S Race St 61801 217-384-3524
Laura Taylor, prin. Fax 384-3532
Urbana MS 1,000/6-8
1201 S Vine St 61801 217-384-3685
Nancy Clinton, prin. Fax 367-3156

Concept College of Cosmetology Post-Sec.
129 N Race St 61801 217-344-7550
Kingswood S 50/K-12
PO Box 834 61803 217-344-5540
Marsh W. Jones, dean Fax 344-5535
Mr. John's School of Cosmetology Post-Sec.
300 S Broadway Ave # 111 61801 217-355-1466
University of Illinois Post-Sec.
901 W Illinois St 61801 217-333-1000

Utica, LaSalle, Pop. 846
Waltham Community CESD 185 100/K-8
946 N 33rd Rd 61373 815-667-4417
Dr. Kristen School, supt. Fax 667-4462
wesd185.org
Waltham North S 3-8
946 N 33rd Rd 61373 815-667-4417
Jason Hamann, prin. Fax 667-4462

Valmeyer, Monroe, Pop. 778
Valmeyer CUSD 3 500/PK-12
300 S Cedar Bluff Dr 62295 618-935-2100
Brian Charron, supt. Fax 935-2108
www.valmeyerk12.org/
Valmeyer HS 100/9-12
300 S Cedar Bluff Dr 62295 618-935-2100
Hattie Doyle, prin.
Valmeyer JHS 100/6-8
300 S Cedar Bluff Dr 62295 618-939-2100
Donna Mueller, prin.

Vandalia, Fayette, Pop. 6,811
Okaw Area Vocational Center
1109 N 8th St 62471 618-283-5150
Darrell Fesser, supt.
Okaw Area Vocational Center Vo/Tech
1109 N 8th St 62471 618-283-5150
Darrell Fesser, prin.

Vandalia CUSD 203 1,800/PK-12
1109 N 8th St 62471 618-283-4525
Rich Well, supt. Fax 283-4107
www.vcs.fayette.k12.il.us/
Vandalia Community HS 500/9-12
1109 N 8th St 62471 618-283-5155
Randy Protz, prin. Fax 283-9855

Vandalia JHS 500/5-8
1011 W Fletcher St 62471 618-283-5151
Rod Grimsley, prin. Fax 283-5165

Varna, Marshall, Pop. 432
Midland CUSD 7
Supt. — See Lacon
Midland HS 300/9-12
1830 State Route 17 61375 309-463-2095
Rolf Sivertsen, prin. Fax 463-2630

Vergennes, Jackson, Pop. 327
Elverado CUSD 196
Supt. — See Elkville
Elverado JHS 100/5-8
PO Box 35 62994 618-684-3527
Belinda Conner, prin. Fax 687-3363

Vernon Hills, Lake, Pop. 23,957
Community HSD 128 3,000/9-12
50 Lakeview Pkwy Ste 101 60061 847-247-4500
Dr. David Clough, supt. Fax 247-4543
www.d128.org/
Vernon Hills HS 1,200/9-12
145 Lakeview Pkwy 60061 847-932-2000
Dr. Ellen Cwick, prin. Fax 932-2049
Other Schools – See Libertyville

Hawthorn CCSD 73 3,200/PK-8
841 W End Ct 60061 847-990-4200
Dr. Youssef Yomtoob, supt. Fax 367-3290
www.hawthorn73.org
Hawthorn MS North 400/6-8
201 W Hawthorn Pkwy 60061 847-990-4400
John Ahlemeyer, prin. Fax 367-8124
Hawthorn MS South 800/6-8
600 Aspen Dr 60061 847-816-8317
Joy Mullaney, prin. Fax 816-9259

Vienna, Johnson, Pop. 1,304
Vienna HSD 133 400/9-12
601 N 1st St 62995 618-658-4461
Dr. Marleis Trover, supt. Fax 658-9727
Vienna HS 400/9-12
601 N 1st St 62995 618-658-3011
Faye Mize, prin. Fax 658-9727

Villa Grove, Douglas, Pop. 2,507
Villa Grove CUSD 302 700/PK-12
400 N Sycamore St 61956 217-832-2261
Dr. Steven N. Poznic, supt. Fax 832-9305
www.vg302.org/education/school/school.php?sectionid=2
Villa Grove HS 300/9-12
400 N Sycamore St 61956 217-832-2321
Mary Pritchard, prin. Fax 832-8450
Villa Grove JHS 100/7-8
400 N Sycamore St 61956 217-832-2261
Sheila Greenwood, prin. Fax 832-9305

Villa Park, DuPage, Pop. 22,616
DuPage County SD 45 3,700/PK-8
255 W Vermont St 60181 630-530-6200
Dr. William Schewe, supt. Fax 530-1624
www.d45.dupage.k12.il.us
Jackson MS 800/6-8
301 W Jackson St 60181 630-530-6240
Tony Palmisano, prin. Fax 530-6271
Jefferson MS 500/6-8
255 W Vermont St 60181 630-530-6230
David Katzin, prin. Fax 993-6348

DuPage HSD 88 4,100/9-12
101 W Highridge Rd 60181 630-530-3980
Dr. Steven K. Humphrey, supt. Fax 832-0198
www.dupage88.net/
Willowbrook HS 2,200/9-12
1250 S Ardmore Ave 60181 630-530-3439
Evelyn Ennsmann, prin. Fax 530-3401
Other Schools – See Addison

Salt Creek SD 48 500/PK-8
1110 S Villa Ave 60181 630-279-8400
Dr. John Correll, supt. Fax 279-6167
www.saltcreek48.com
Albright MS 200/5-8
1110 S Villa Ave 60181 630-279-6160
Linda Stasko, prin. Fax 279-1614

Islamic Foundation S 700/PK-12
300 W Highridge Rd 60181 630-941-8800
Audrey Zahra Williams, prin. Fax 941-8804
Ms. Robert's Academy of Beauty Culture Post-Sec.
17 E Park Blvd 60181 630-941-3880

Virden, Macoupin, Pop. 3,472
Virden CUSD 4 1,000/PK-12
231 W Fortune St 62690 217-965-4226
James Kirbach, supt. Fax 965-3019
www.virdenschools.com/
Virden HS 300/9-12
231 W Fortune St 62690 217-965-4127
Ronald Graham, prin. Fax 965-4006
Virden MS 200/6-8
231 W Fortune St 62690 217-965-3942
Ronald Graham, prin. Fax 965-3124

Virginia, Cass, Pop. 1,730
Virginia CUSD 64 400/PK-12
651 S Morgan St 62691 217-452-3085
Lynn Carter, supt. Fax 452-3088
www.go-redbirds.com
Virginia HS 100/9-12
651 S Morgan St 62691 217-452-3087
Christine Brinkley, prin. Fax 452-3088
Virginia JHS 100/6-8
651 S Morgan St 62691 217-452-3087
Christine Brinkley, prin. Fax 452-3088

Waltonville, Jefferson, Pop. 431
Waltonville CUSD 1 400/PK-12
804 W Knob St 62894 618-279-7211
Ron Daniels, supt. Fax 279-3291
waltonvilleschools.roe25.com/
Waltonville HS 100/9-12
804 W Knob St 62894 618-279-7211
Ron Daniels, prin. Fax 279-7212

Warren, Jo Daviess, Pop. 1,421
Warren CUSD 205 400/PK-12
311 S Water St 61087 815-745-2653
Karen Sirgany Ph.D., supt. Fax 745-2037
www.205warren.net/
Warren JSHS 200/7-12
311 S Water St 61087 815-745-2641
Barb Pohl, prin. Fax 745-2654

Warrensburg, Macon, Pop. 1,209
Warrensburg-Latham CUSD 11 1,100/PK-12
430 W North St 62573 217-672-3514
Emmett Aubry, supt. Fax 672-8468
www.wl.k12.il.us
Warrensburg-Latham HS 300/9-12
425 W North St 62573 217-672-3531
Ken Hatcher, prin. Fax 672-3770

Warrenville, DuPage, Pop. 13,217

Carmel Montessori Academy 100/PK-12
3S238 State Route 59 60555 630-393-2995
Carmen Lafranzo, prin.

Warsaw, Hancock, Pop. 1,648
Warsaw CUSD 316 500/PK-12
340 S 11th St 62379 217-256-4282
Kim Schilson, supt. Fax 256-4282
hancock.k12.il.us/whs/
Warsaw JSHS, 340 S 11th St 62379 300/6-12
Tom Bertucci, prin. 217-256-4281

Washburn, Marshall, Pop. 1,107
Lowpoint-Washburn CUSD 21 400/PK-12
PO Box 580 61570 309-248-7522
Parker Deitrich, supt. Fax 248-7518
Lowpoint-Washburn JSHS 200/7-12
PO Box 580 61570 309-248-7521
Stan Matheny, prin. Fax 248-7410

Washington, Tazewell, Pop. 12,759
District 50 Schools 800/PK-8
304 E Almond Dr 61571 309-745-8914
Roger Stevens, supt. Fax 745-5417
tazewell.k12.il.us/district50/
Manor MS, 1014 School St 61571 400/4-8
James Sharp, prin. 309-745-3921

Washington Community HSD 308 1,100/9-12
115 Bondurant St 61571 309-444-7704
Dr. James Dunnan, supt. Fax 444-7451
www.wacohi.net/
Washington Comm HS 1,100/9-12
115 Bondurant St 61571 309-444-7704
Steve Zimmerman, prin. Fax 444-7451

Washington SD 52 800/PK-8
303 Jackson St 61571 309-444-4182
Dr. Pat Grisham, supt. Fax 444-8538
tazewell.k12.il.us/district52
Washington MS 6-8
105 S Spruce St 61571 309-444-3361
Diane Orr, prin. Fax 444-3941

IL Central Christian S 200/PK-12
22648 Grosenbach Rd 61571 309-698-2000
Keith Thibo, prin.

Waterloo, Monroe, Pop. 9,225
Waterloo CUSD 5 2,600/PK-12
219 Park St 62298 618-939-3453
James Helton, supt. Fax 939-4578
www.wcusd5.net
Waterloo HS 900/9-12
200 Bellefontaine Dr 62298 618-939-3455
Todd Manning, prin. Fax 939-5180
Waterloo JHS 600/6-8
1 Ed Gardner Pl 62298 618-939-3457
Linda Yagge, prin. Fax 939-1383

Gibault Catholic HS 300/9-12
501 Columbia Ave 62298 618-939-3883
Russell Hart, prin. Fax 939-7215

Waterman, DeKalb, Pop. 1,214
Indian Creek CUSD 425
Supt. — See Shabbona
Indian Creek MS 200/6-8
425 S Elm St 60556 815-264-7712
Paula Kennedy, prin. Fax 264-7826

Watseka, Iroquois, Pop. 5,547
Iroquois County CUSD 9 1,200/K-12
109 S 2nd St 60970 815-432-4931
Steve Bianchetta, supt. Fax 432-6889
www.watseka-u9.k12.il.us
Raymond MS 300/6-8
101 W Mulberry St 60970 815-432-2115
James Bunting, prin. Fax 432-6896
Watseka Community HS 400/9-12
138 S Belmont Ave 60970 815-432-2486
Scott Buchanan, prin. Fax 432-5578

Wauconda, Lake, Pop. 10,903
Wauconda CUSD 118 4,100/PK-12
555 N Main St 60084 847-526-7690
Dr. Daniel Coles, supt. Fax 526-1019
www.cusd118.lake.k12.il.us
Wauconda Community HS 1,200/9-12
555 N Main St 60084 847-526-6611
Daniel Klett, prin. Fax 487-3595
Wauconda MS 700/7-8
215 Slocum Lake Rd 60084 847-526-2122
David Wilm, prin. Fax 487-3597

Waukegan, Lake, Pop. 91,396
Waukegan CUSD 60 15,400/PK-12
1201 N Sheridan Rd 60085 847-336-3100
Dr. Donaldo Batiste, supt. Fax 360-5634
www.waukeganschools.org/
Abbott MS 800/6-8
1319 Washington St 60085 847-360-5487
John Samuelian, prin. Fax 360-5394
Benny MS 700/6-8
1401 Montesano Ave 60087 847-360-5460
Samuel Taylor, prin. Fax 360-5395
Jefferson MS 800/6-8
600 S Lewis Ave 60085 847-360-5473
Dr. Bethel Cager, prin. Fax 360-5396
Juarez MS 700/6-8
201 N Butrick St 60085 847-599-4200
Dr. Cathy Watkins, prin. Fax 599-4205
Waukegan HS 2,700/9-12
2325 Brookside Ave 60085 847-360-5621
Edward Guerra, prin. Fax 360-5398
Waukegan Ninth Grade Center 1,100/9-9
1011 Washington St 60085 847-263-4765
Bruce Thezan, prin. Fax 599-4205
Webster MS 800/6-8
930 New York St 60085 847-360-5484
Joan Brixey, prin. Fax 360-5397

Lake County Baptist S 200/PK-12
1550 W Yorkhouse Rd 60087 847-623-7600
Timothy Kowach, prin. Fax 623-2085
St. Martin de Porres HS 9-12
515 S Martin Luther King Jr 60085 847-623-5500
Sr. Judith Murphy, prin. Fax 623-5604

Waverly, Morgan, Pop. 1,272
Waverly CUSD 6 400/PK-12
201 N Miller St 62692 217-435-8121
Debra Rust, supt. Fax 435-3431
www.waverlyscotties.com/
Waverly HS 100/9-12
201 N Miller St 62692 217-435-2211
Debra Rust, prin. Fax 435-3431

Wayne City, Wayne, Pop. 1,075
Wayne City CUSD 100 500/PK-12
PO Box 457 62895 618-895-3103
Dr. Peter Andersen, supt. Fax 895-2331
Wayne City JSHS 200/7-12
PO Box 427 62895 618-895-3103
Myron Caudle, prin. Fax 895-2331

Weldon, DeWitt, Pop. 430
Deland-Weldon CUSD 57
Supt. — See De Land
Deland-Weldon MS 50/7-8
2311 N 300 East Rd 61882 217-736-2401
Russell Corey, prin. Fax 736-2654

Wenona, Marshall, Pop. 1,077
Fieldcrest CUSD 6
Supt. — See Minonk
Fieldcrest MS East 100/7-8
102 W Elm St 61377 815-853-4331
Doug Roberts, prin. Fax 853-4786

Westchester, Cook, Pop. 16,177
Westchester SD 92-5 1,100/K-8
9981 Canterbury St 60154 708-450-2700
Myra Sanders Ph.D., supt. Fax 450-2718
www.sd925.org
Westchester MS 400/6-8
1620 Norfolk Ave 60154 708-450-2735
Mary Leidigh, prin. Fax 450-2752

St. Joseph HS 9-12
1840 Mayfair Ave 60154 708-562-4433
Donna Kiel, prin. Fax 562-4459

West Chicago, DuPage, Pop. 26,554
Benjamin SD 25 900/K-8
28W250 Saint Charles Rd 60185 630-876-7800
Larry Weck, supt. Fax 876-3325
www.bendist25.org
Benjamin MS 400/5-8
28W300 Saint Charles Rd 60185 630-876-7820
Andrea Paterala, prin. Fax 231-3886

Community HSD 94 2,100/9-12
326 Joliet St 60185 630-876-6200
Dr. Lee Rieck, supt. Fax 876-6241
www.d94.org
Community HS 2,100/9-12
326 Joliet St 60185 630-876-6200
John W. Highland, prin. Fax 876-6241

West Chicago ESD 33 3,700/K-8
312 E Forest Ave 60185 630-293-6000
Dr. Ed Leman, supt. Fax 293-6088
www.wegoed33.k12.il.us
West Chicago MS 800/7-8
238 E Hazel St 60185 630-293-6060
Pat Roszowski, prin. Fax 562-2586

Central Medical Education Post-Sec.
550 E Washington St 60185 630-682-1600
Wheaton Academy 600/8-12
900 Prince Crossing Rd 60185 630-562-7500
Jon Keith, prin. Fax 231-0842

Western Springs, Cook, Pop. 12,530
Lyons Township HSD 204
Supt. — See La Grange
Lyons Township HS South Campus 9-10
4900 Willow Springs Rd 60558 708-579-6500
Dave Franson, prin. Fax 579-9573

Western Springs SD 101 1,400/K-8
4335 Howard Ave 60558 708-246-3700
Dr. Brian T. Barnhart, supt. Fax 482-2581
www.d101.org
McClure JHS 500/6-8
4225 Wolf Rd 60558 708-246-7590
F. Daniel Chick, prin. Fax 246-4370

West Frankfort, Franklin, Pop. 8,285
Frankfort CUSD 168 1,800/PK-12
PO Box 425 62896 618-937-2421
George Hopkins, supt. Fax 932-2025
www.wf168.frnkln.k12.il.us/index.htm
Central JHS 300/7-8
1500 E 9th St 62896 618-937-2444
Mark Zahm, prin. Fax 937-2445
Frankfort Community HS 600/9-12
601 E Main St 62896 618-932-3126
John Hixson, prin. Fax 932-6515

Westmont, DuPage, Pop. 24,863
CCSD 181 4,000/PK-8
1010 Executive Dr Ste 100 60559 630-887-1070
Dr. Mary Curley, supt. Fax 887-1079
www.d181.org/
Other Schools – See Clarendon Hills, Hinsdale

Westmont CUSD 201 1,700/PK-12
200 N Linden Ave 60559 630-468-8000
Dr. Steven Baule, supt. Fax 969-9022
www.cusd201.org
Westmont HS 600/9-12
909 Oakwood Dr 60559 630-468-8100
Steven T. Carr, prin. Fax 654-2758
Westmont JHS 400/6-8
944 Oakwood Dr 60559 630-468-8200
Ronald Fiala, prin. Fax 654-2203

Westville, Vermilion, Pop. 3,058
Westville CUSD 2 1,200/K-12
125 W Ellsworth St 61883 217-267-3141
James Owens, supt. Fax 267-3144
www.westville.k12.il.us
Westville HS, 918 N State St 61883 400/9-12
Guy Goodlove, prin. 217-267-2183
Westville JHS, 412 Moses Ave 61883 200/7-8
Greg Lewis, prin. 217-267-2185

Wheaton, DuPage, Pop. 54,700
Community Unit SD 200 14,100/PK-12
130 W Park Ave 60187 630-682-2002
Dr. Richard Drury, supt. Fax 682-2068
www.cusd200.org
Edison MS 800/6-8
1125 S Wheaton Ave 60187 630-682-2050
David Kanne, prin. Fax 682-2337
Franklin MS 600/6-8
211 E Franklin St 60187 630-682-2060
Susan Wolfe, prin. Fax 682-2340
Hubble MS 900/6-8
603 S Main St 60187 630-682-2160
Beth Sullivan, prin. Fax 682-2299
Monroe MS 900/6-8
1855 Manchester Rd 60187 630-682-2285
Wayne Spychala, prin. Fax 682-2331
Wheaton North HS 2,200/9-12
1 Falcon Way 60187 630-784-7300
Jill Bullo, prin. Fax 682-2158
Wheaton/Warrenville South HS 2,400/9-12
1993 Tiger Trl 60187 630-784-7200
Dawn Snyder, prin. Fax 682-2042

Hair Professionals Acad of Cosmetology Post-Sec.
1145 Butterfield Rd 60187 630-653-6630
St. Francis HS 700/9-12
2130 W Roosevelt Rd 60187 630-668-5800
Raeann Huhn, prin. Fax 668-5893
Wheaton College Post-Sec.
501 College Ave 60187 630-752-5000

Wheeling, Cook, Pop. 36,641
Township HSD 214
Supt. — See Arlington Heights
Wheeling HS 2,000/9-12
900 S Elmhurst Rd 60090 847-718-7000
Dorothy Sievert, prin. Fax 718-7007

Wheeling CCSD 21 7,100/PK-8
999 W Dundee Rd 60090 847-537-8270
Dr. Gary Mical, supt. Fax 520-2848
www.ccsd21.org
Holmes MS 800/6-8
221 S Wolf Rd 60090 847-520-2790
Martin Hopkins, prin. Fax 419-3073
London MS 800/6-8
1001 W Dundee Rd 60090 847-520-2745
Jim Parker, prin. Fax 520-2842
Other Schools – See Buffalo Grove

Worsham College of Mortuary Science Post-Sec.
495 Northgate Pkwy 60090 847-808-8444

White Hall, Greene, Pop. 2,609
North Greene Unit SD 3 1,100/PK-12
407 N Main St 62092 217-374-2842
Vicki VanTuyle, supt. Fax 374-2849
www.northgreene.com/
North Greene HS 400/9-12
546 N Main St 62092 217-374-2131
Jim Roesch, prin. Fax 374-2132
Other Schools – See Roodhouse

Williamsfield, Knox, Pop. 593
Williamsfield CUSD 210 300/PK-12
PO Box 179 61489 309-639-2219
Mary Bush, supt. Fax 639-2618
www.billtown.org/
Williamsfield HS, PO Box 179 61489 100/9-12
Mary Bush, prin. 309-639-2216
Williamsfield MS, PO Box 179 61489 100/6-8
Mary Bush, prin. 309-639-2216

Williamsville, Sangamon, Pop. 1,396
Williamsville CUSD 15 1,400/PK-12
800 S Walnut St 62693 217-566-2014
Randy Harhausen, supt. Fax 566-2183
www.wcusd15.org/
Williamsville HS 400/9-12
900 S Walnut St 62693 217-566-3361
Rich Spenn, prin. Fax 566-3792
Williamsville JHS 300/6-8
500 S Walnut St 62693 217-566-3600
Rod McQuality, prin. Fax 566-2475

Willowbrook, DuPage, Pop. 8,893
Gower SD 62 900/PK-8
7700 Clarendon Hills Rd 60527 630-986-5383
Steve Griesbach, supt. Fax 323-3074
www.gower62.com
Other Schools – See Burr Ridge

Maercker SD 60
Supt. — See Clarendon Hills
Westview Hills MS 500/6-8
630 65th St 60527 630-963-1450
Brenda Babinec, prin. Fax 963-0954

Wilmette, Cook, Pop. 26,922
Avoca SD 37 700/K-8
2921 Illinois Rd 60091 847-251-3587
Dr. Joseph M. Porto, supt. Fax 251-7742
www.avoca.k12.il.us
Murphy MS 300/6-8
2921 Illinois Rd 60091 847-251-3617
Dr. Deanna Reed, prin. Fax 251-4179

Wilmette SD 39 3,600/PK-8
615 Locust Rd 60091 847-256-2450
Glenn McGee, supt. Fax 256-1920
wilmette39.org
Wilmette JHS 800/7-8
620 Locust Rd 60091 847-256-7280
David Palzet, prin. Fax 256-0204

Loyola Academy 9-12
1100 Laramie Ave 60091 847-256-1100
David McNulty, prin. Fax 853-4512
Regina Dominican HS 400/9-12
701 Locust Rd 60091 847-256-7660
Kathy Rzany, prin. Fax 256-3726

Wilmington, Will, Pop. 5,957
Wilmington CUSD 209U 1,500/PK-12
715 S Joliet St 60481 815-476-2594
Anthony Jay Plese, supt. Fax 476-3483
www.wilmington.will.k12.il.us
Stevens MS 300/6-8
221 Ryan St 60481 815-476-2189
Marty Felesena, prin. Fax 476-1941
Wilmington HS 500/9-12
715 S Joliet St 60481 815-476-2846
Joseph Hermes, prin. Fax 476-3491

Winchester, Scott, Pop. 1,609
Winchester CUSD 1 700/PK-12
149 S Elm St 62694 217-742-3175
Lawrence Coultas, supt. Fax 742-3312
Winchester HS, 200 W Cross St 62694 200/9-12
Angie Greger, prin. 217-742-3151

Windsor, Shelby, Pop. 1,802
Windsor CUSD 1 400/PK-12
PO Box 200 61957 217-459-2636
Sharon Keck, supt. Fax 459-2661
www.windsor.k12.il.us
Windsor JSHS 200/7-12
1424 Minnesota Ave 61957 217-459-2636
Erik Van Hoveln, prin. Fax 459-2794

Winfield, DuPage, Pop. 9,844
Winfield SD 34 400/PK-8
0S150 Winfield Rd 60190 630-909-4900
Dr. Diane Cody, supt. Fax 260-2382
www.winfield34.org/
Winfield Central S 200/3-8
0S150 Park St 60190 630-909-4960
Patti Palagi, prin. Fax 933-9236

Winnebago, Winnebago, Pop. 3,065
Winnebago CUSD 323 1,700/PK-12
304 E McNair Rd 61088 815-335-2456
Dr. Dennis M. Harezlak, supt. Fax 335-7574
www.winnebagoschools.org/
Winnebago HS 500/9-12
200 E McNair Rd 61088 815-335-2336
Matthew Zickert, prin. Fax 335-7548
Winnebago MS 400/6-8
407 N Elida St 61088 815-335-2364
James Burns, prin. Fax 335-1437

Winnetka, Cook, Pop. 12,452
New Trier Twp. HSD 203 4,000/9-12
385 Winnetka Ave 60093 847-446-7000
Linda Yonke, supt. Fax 446-0874
www.newtrier.k12.il.us
New Trier Twp. HS - Winnetka Campus 2,900/10-12
385 Winnetka Ave 60093 847-446-7000
Debbie Stacey, prin. Fax 446-4759
Other Schools – See Northfield

Winnetka SD 36 2,100/PK-8
1235 Oak St 60093 847-446-9400
Dr. Rebecca Vanderbogert, supt. Fax 446-9408
www.winnetka36.org/
Washburne MS 500/7-8
515 Hibbard Rd 60093 847-446-5892
Daniel Schwartz, prin. Fax 446-1380

Hadley School for the Blind Post-Sec.
700 Elm St 60093 847-446-8111
Music Center of the North Shore Post-Sec.
300 Green Bay Rd 60093 847-446-3822
North Shore Country Day S 400/PK-12
310 Green Bay Rd 60093 847-446-0674
Thomas Doar, prin. Fax 446-0675

Winthrop Harbor, Lake, Pop. 7,090
Winthrop Harbor SD 1 800/K-8
500 North Ave 60096 847-731-3085
Dr. James Tenbusch, supt. Fax 731-3156
www.whsd1.org
North Prairie JHS 300/6-8
500 North Ave 60096 847-731-3089
Theodore Brooks, prin. Fax 731-3152

Wolf Lake, Union
Shawnee CUSD 84 500/K-12
PO Box 128 62998 618-833-5709
Gary Hill, supt. Fax 833-4171
Shawnee HS 100/9-12
PO Box 128 62998 618-833-5307
Brent Boren, prin. Fax 833-5468
Shawnee JHS 100/6-8
PO Box 128 62998 618-833-5307
Brent Boren, prin. Fax 833-5468

Wood Dale, DuPage, Pop. 13,419
Wood Dale SD 7 1,200/PK-8
543 N Wood Dale Rd 60191 630-595-9510
John Corbett, supt. Fax 595-5625
www.wd7.org
Wood Dale JHS 400/6-8
655 N Wood Dale Rd 60191 630-766-6210
Anthony Murray, prin. Fax 766-1839

Woodhull, Henry, Pop. 810
Alwood CUSD 225 500/PK-12
301 E 5th Ave 61490 309-334-2719
Shannon Bumann, supt. Fax 334-2925
www.alwood.net
Alwood MSHS 300/6-12
301 E 5th Ave 61490 309-334-2102
Scott Petrie, prin. Fax 334-2632

Woodlawn, Jefferson, Pop. 644
Woodlawn Community HSD 205 200/9-12
300 N Central St 62898 618-735-2631
Alan Estes, supt. Fax 735-2032
www.roe25.com/woodlawnhs/
Woodlawn Community HS 200/9-12
300 N Central St 62898 618-735-2631
Dave Larkin, prin. Fax 735-2032

Woodridge, DuPage, Pop. 34,058
Woodridge SD 68 3,000/PK-8
7925 Janes Ave 60517 630-985-7925
Jerome Brendel, supt. Fax 910-2060
www.woodridge68.org
Jefferson JHS 700/7-8
7200 Janes Ave 60517 630-852-8010
Ron Freed, prin. Fax 969-7168

Westwood College Post-Sec.
7155 Janes Ave 60517 630-434-8244

Wood River, Madison, Pop. 10,985
East Alton-Wood River Community HSD 14 800/9-12
777 N Wood River Ave 62095 618-254-3151
John Pearson, supt. Fax 254-9113
www.eawr.madison.k12.il.us/
East Alton-Wood River HS 800/9-12
777 N Wood River Ave 62095 618-254-3151
Richard Levek, prin. Fax 254-9113

Wood River-Hartford ESD 15 800/PK-8
501 E Lorena Ave 62095 618-254-0607
Michael Loftus, supt. Fax 254-9048
www.wrh.madison.k12.il.us
Lewis-Clark JHS 200/6-8
501 E Lorena Ave 62095 618-254-4355
Sue Rives, prin. Fax 254-7600

Woodstock, McHenry, Pop. 21,985
Woodstock CUSD 200 6,000/PK-12
227 W Judd St 60098 815-338-8200
Ellyn A. Wrzeski, supt. Fax 338-2005
www.d200.mchenry.k12.il.us
Northwood MS 800/6-8
2121 N Seminary Ave 60098 815-338-4900
Robert Hackbart, prin. Fax 337-2150
Olson MS 600/6-8
720 W Judd St 60098 815-338-0473
Mark Widmer, prin. Fax 338-8142
Woodstock HS 1,900/9-12
501 W South St 60098 815-338-4370
Corey Tafoya, prin. Fax 334-0811

Marian Central Catholic HS 700/9-12
1001 McHenry Ave 60098 815-338-4220
Charles Rakers, prin. Fax 338-4253

Worth, Cook, Pop. 10,652
Worth SD 127 1,100/PK-8
11218 S Ridgeland Ave 60482 708-448-2800
Dr. Rita Wojtylewski, supt. Fax 448-6215
www.worthschools.org
Worth JHS 400/6-8
11151 S New England Ave 60482 708-448-2803
Dr. Peter Yuska, prin. Fax 448-6155

Wyoming, Stark, Pop. 1,390
Stark County CUSD 100 700/PK-12
300 E Van Buren St 61491 309-695-6123
Jerry Klooster, supt.
www.bhsroe.k12.il.us/sccu100/
Other Schools – See Toulon

Yorkville, Kendall, Pop. 10,791
Yorkville CUSD 115 3,100/PK-12
PO Box 579 60560 630-553-4382
Thomas Engler, supt. Fax 553-4398
www.yorkville.k12.il.us
Yorkville HS 900/9-12
797 Game Farm Rd 60560 630-553-4380
Frank Bogner, prin. Fax 553-4397
Yorkville MS 500/7-8
702 Game Farm Rd 60560 630-553-4385
Jeff Szymczak, prin. Fax 553-4592

Zeigler, Franklin, Pop. 1,682
Zeigler-Royalton CUSD 188 700/PK-12
PO Box 38 62999 618-596-5841
George Wilkerson, supt. Fax 596-6789
Zeigler-Royalton HS 200/9-12
PO Box 38 62999 618-596-5841
Quent Hamilton, prin. Fax 596-6789
Zeigler-Royalton JHS 100/7-8
PO Box 87 62999 618-596-2121
Larry Fillingim, prin. Fax 596-2075

Zion, Lake, Pop. 24,303
Zion ESD 6 2,800/PK-8
2200 Bethesda Blvd 60099 847-872-5455
Dr. Ronald Wynn, supt. Fax 746-1280
www.zion6.com
Central JHS 600/7-8
1716 27th St 60099 847-746-1431
Yvonne Brown, prin. Fax 746-9750

Zion-Benton Township HSD 126 2,500/9-12
1 ZB Way 60099 847-731-9300
Dr. Bud Marks, supt. Fax 731-4441
www.zbths.org
Zion-Benton HS 2,500/9-12
1 ZB Way 60099 847-731-9300
Scott Murphy, prin. Fax 731-4408

Zion Christian S 100/K-12
1828 Hebron Ave 60099 847-872-4088
Valerie Burnette, prin. Fax 872-1032

INDIANA

INDIANA DEPARTMENT OF EDUCATION
Room 229, State House, Indianapolis 46204
Telephone 317-232-6610
Fax 317-232-8004
Website http://www.doe.state.in.us

Superintendent of Public Instruction Suellen Reed

INDIANA BOARD OF EDUCATION
200 W Washington St Ste 229, Indianapolis 46204-2798

Chairperson Suellen Reed

EDUCATIONAL SERVICE CENTERS (ESC)

Central Indiana ESC
Tom Pagan, dir., 6321 La Pas Trl — 317-387-7100
Indianapolis 46268 — Fax 328-7298
www.ciesc.k12.in.us/

East Central ESC
Walter Harrison, dir. — 765-825-1247
1601 Indiana Ave — Fax 825-2532
Connersville 47331
www.ecesc.k12.in.us/

Northern Indiana ESC
Jack Davis, dir., 56535 Magnetic Dr — 574-254-0111
Mishawaka 46545 — Fax 254-0148
www.niesc.k12.in.us/

Northwest Indiana ESC
Dr. Charles Costa, dir. — 219-922-0900
2939 41st St, Highland 46322 — Fax 922-1246
www.nwiesc.k12.in.us/

Region 8 ESC
Dr. Roger Smith, dir. — 260-244-9000
PO Box 409, Columbia City 46725 — Fax 244-9001
www.r8esc.k12.in.us/800/intro.htm

Southern Indiana ESC
J. Scott Turney, dir. — 812-482-6641
1102 Tree Lane Dr, Jasper 47546 — Fax 482-6652
www.siec.k12.in.us/

Wabash Valley ESC
Larry Rausch, dir., 3061 Benton St — 765-463-1589
West Lafayette 47906 — Fax 463-1580
www.wvec.k12.in.us/

West Central ESC
David Archer, dir. — 765-653-2727
PO Box 21, Greencastle 46135 — Fax 653-7897
www.wciesc.k12.in.us/

William E. Wilson ESC
Larry Risk, dir., 2101 Grace Ave — 812-256-8000
Charlestown 47111 — Fax 256-8012
www.wesc.k12.in.us/

PUBLIC, PRIVATE AND CATHOLIC SECONDARY SCHOOLS

Akron, Kosciusko, Pop. 1,045
Tippecanoe Valley SC — 2,200/K-12
8343 S State Rd 19 46910 — 574-353-7741
Daniel V. Kramer, supt. — Fax 353-7743
www.tvsc.k12.in.us
Tippecanoe Valley HS — 700/9-12
8345 S State Rd 19 46910 — 574-353-7031
Kirk Doehrmann, prin. — Fax 353-1016
Tippecanoe Valley MS — 600/6-8
11303 W 800 S 46910 — 574-353-7353
Earl Richter, prin. — Fax 353-7189

Albion, Noble, Pop. 2,323
Central Noble Community SC — 1,400/K-12
200 E Main St 46701 — 260-636-2175
Dr. Leo Philbin, supt. — Fax 636-7918
www.centralnoble.k12.in.us/
Central Noble HS — 400/9-12
302 Cougar Ct 46701 — 260-636-2117
Jerry Wellman, prin. — Fax 636-2791
Central Noble MS — 400/6-8
401 E Highland St 46701 — 260-636-2279
Geoff Brose, prin. — Fax 636-2461

Alexandria, Madison, Pop. 5,868
Alexandria Community SC — 1,100/K-12
202 E Washington St 46001 — 765-724-4496
James Willey, supt. — Fax 724-5049
www.alex.k12.in.us
Alexandria-Monroe HS — 500/8-12
1 Burden Ct 46001 — 765-724-4413
Jim Regenold, prin. — Fax 724-5041

Anderson, Madison, Pop. 57,500
Anderson Community SC — 9,500/K-12
1229 Lincoln St 46016 — 765-641-2028
Dr. Timothy D. Long, supt. — Fax 641-2080
www.acsc.net/
Anderson HS — 1,500/9-12
4610 Madison Ave 46013 — 765-641-2037
Philip Nikirk, prin. — Fax 641-2041
East Side MS — 800/6-8
2300 Lindberg Rd 46012 — 765-641-2047
Lucinda McCord, prin. — Fax 641-2050
Ebbertt Education Center — Vo/Tech
325 W 38th St 46013 — 765-641-2121
Timothy Holbert, prin. — Fax 641-2124
Highland HS — 1,500/9-12
2108 E 200 N 46012 — 765-641-2059
Lennon Brown, prin. — Fax 641-2064
North Side MS — 800/6-8
1815 Indiana Ave 46012 — 765-641-2055
Michael Brandon, prin. — Fax 641-2057
South Side MS — 900/6-8
101 W 29th St 46016 — 765-641-2051
Patrick Fassnatcht, prin. — Fax 641-2053

Frankton-Lapel Community SD — 2,300/PK-12
7916 W 300 N 46011 — 765-734-1261
Ned Speicher, supt. — Fax 734-1129
www.frankton-lapel.org
Other Schools – See Frankton, Lapel

Anderson University — Post-Sec.
1100 E 5th St 46012 — 765-649-9071
Apex School of Beauty Culture — Post-Sec.
333 Jackson St 46016 — 765-642-7560
Cross Street Christian S — 50/PK-10
2318 W Cross St 46011 — 765-649-4141
Fax 649-5953
Indiana Business College — Post-Sec.
140 E 53rd St 46013 — 765-644-7514
Indiana Christian Academy — 300/K-12
432 W 300 N 46012 — 765-643-7884
William Newton, prin. — Fax 683-4200
Ivy Tech State College — Post-Sec.
104 W 53rd St 46013 — 765-643-7133
Liberty Christian HS — 200/7-12
2323 Columbus Ave 46016 — 765-644-7774
Dr. Brian Dougherty, supt. — Fax 644-7779

Angola, Steuben, Pop. 7,890
Metro SD of Steuben County — 3,000/K-12
400 S Martha St 46703 — 260-665-2854
Dr. David Goodwin, supt. — Fax 665-9155
www.msdsteuben.k12.in.us
Angola HS — 800/9-12
350 S John McBride Ave 46703 — 260-665-2186
Steve Grill, prin. — Fax 665-7012
Angola MS — 800/6-8
1350 E Maumee St 46703 — 260-665-9581
William Church, prin. — Fax 665-9583

Tri-State University 46703 — Post-Sec.
260-665-4100

Arcadia, Hamilton, Pop. 1,794
Hamilton Heights SC — 2,200/PK-12
410 W Main St 46030 — 317-984-3538
Anthony Cook, supt. — Fax 984-3042
www.hhsc.k12.in.us
Hamilton Heights HS — 700/9-12
PO Box 379 46030 — 317-984-3551
Sterling Boles, prin. — Fax 984-3554
Hamilton Heights MS — 600/6-8
PO Box 609 46030 — 317-984-3588
Chris Walton, prin. — Fax 984-3231

Argos, Marshall, Pop. 1,833
Argos Community SD — 700/K-12
410 N First St 46501 — 574-892-5139
Peter O'Rourke, supt. — Fax 892-6527
www.argos.k12.in.us/
Argos Community JSHS — 300/7-12
500 Yearick St 46501 — 574-892-5137
Peter O'Rourke, prin. — Fax 892-4712

Attica, Fountain, Pop. 3,385
Attica Consolidated SC — 1,000/PK-12
205 E Sycamore St 47918 — 765-762-7000
Dr. Judith Bush, supt. — Fax 762-7007
www.attica.k12.in.us
Attica JSHS — 400/7-12
211 E Sycamore St 47918 — 765-762-7000
Roy Jones, prin. — Fax 762-7017

Auburn, DeKalb, Pop. 12,687

Lakewood Park Christian S — 600/PK-12
5555 County Road 29 46706 — 260-925-1393
Randy Carman, supt. — Fax 925-5010
Reppert School of Auctioneering — Post-Sec.
PO Box 190 46706 — 800-968-4444

Aurora, Dearborn, Pop. 4,064
South Dearborn Community SC — 2,800/PK-12
6109 Squire Pl 47001 — 812-926-2090
Thomas Book, supt. — Fax 926-4216
www.venus.net/~sdearad1/
South Dearborn HS — 1,000/9-12
5770 Highlander Pl 47001 — 812-926-3772
Robert D. Moorhead, prin. — Fax 926-4162
South Dearborn MS — 500/7-8
5850 Squire Pl 47001 — 812-926-6298
Todd Bowers, prin. — Fax 926-2149

Austin, Scott, Pop. 4,694
Scott County SD 1 — 1,500/K-12
PO Box 9 47102 — 812-794-8750
Berley Goodin, supt. — Fax 794-8765
www.scott1.k12.in.us
Austin HS — 400/9-12
401 S Highway 31 47102 — 812-794-8730
Sherman Smith, prin. — Fax 794-8739
Austin MS — 400/6-8
401 S Highway 31 47102 — 812-794-8740
David Deaton, prin. — Fax 794-8739

Avon, Hendricks, Pop. 8,918
Avon Community SC — 6,700/K-12
7203 E US Highway 36 46123 — 317-272-2920
Timothy Ogle, supt. — Fax 272-1704
www.avon.k12.in.us
Avon HS — 1,800/9-12
7575 E County Road 150 S 46123 — 317-272-2586
Rick Adcock, prin. — Fax 272-3100
Avon MS — 1,100/7-8
7199 E US Highway 36 46123 — 317-272-0128
David Leach, prin. — Fax 272-3122

Bainbridge, Putnam, Pop. 785
North Putnam Community SD — 1,900/PK-12
300 N Washington St 46105 — 765-522-6218
Murray Pride, supt. — Fax 522-3562
www.nputnam.k12.in.us
Other Schools – See Roachdale

Batesville, Franklin, Pop. 6,407
Batesville Community SC — 1,900/PK-12
PO Box 121 47006 — 812-934-2194
James Freeland, supt. — Fax 933-0833
www.batesville.k12.in.us/
Batesville HS — 600/9-12
1 Bulldog Blvd 47006 — 812-934-4384
Scott Mills, prin. — Fax 934-5964
Batesville MS — 400/6-8
201 N Mulberry St 47006 — 812-934-5175
Orlando Fontanez, prin. — Fax 933-0834

Battle Ground, Tippecanoe, Pop. 1,356
Tippecanoe SC
Supt. — See Lafayette
Battle Ground MS — 400/6-8
511 Main St 47920 — 765-567-2122
BeAnn Younker, prin. — Fax 567-2325

Bedford, Lawrence, Pop. 13,551
North Lawrence Community SD — 5,600/PK-12
PO Box 729 47421 — 812-279-3521
Dr. Dennis Turner, supt. — Fax 275-1577
www.nlcs.k12.in.us

Bedford MS — 700/6-8
1501 N St 47421 — 812-279-9781
David Schlegel, prin. — Fax 277-3218
Bedford-North Lawrence HS — 1,600/9-12
595 Stars Blvd 47421 — 812-279-9756
Michael Terry, prin. — Fax 279-9304
North Lawrence Vo-Tech Ctr — Vo/Tech
258 BNL Dr 47421 — 812-279-3561
Duane Martin, prin. — Fax 275-1578
Shawswick MS — 200/6-8
71 Shawswick School Rd 47421 — 812-275-6121
Roger Dean, prin. — Fax 275-0543
Other Schools – See Oolitic

Oolitic Christian S — 50/PK-12
270 Erie Church Rd 47421 — 812-279-4060
Dennis Gregory, admin. — Fax 279-3931

Beech Grove, Marion, Pop. 14,069
Beech Grove CSD — 2,400/PK-12
5334 Hornet Ave 46107 — 317-788-4481
Dr. Rex Sager, supt. — Fax 782-4065
www.bgcs.k12.in.us
Beech Grove HS — 700/9-12
5330 Hornet Ave 46107 — 317-786-1447
Harvey Warrner, prin. — Fax 781-2920
Beech Grove MS — 400/7-8
1248 Buffalo St 46107 — 317-784-6649
Thomas Keeley, prin. — Fax 781-2926

St. Francis Hospital Center — Post-Sec.
1600 Albany St 46107 — 317-783-8220

Berne, Adams, Pop. 4,157
South Adams SD — 1,500/K-12
1027 US Highway 27 S 46711 — 260-589-3133
Cathy Egolf, supt. — Fax 589-2065
www.southadams.k12.in.us/
South Adams JSHS — 700/7-12
1000 Parkway St 46711 — 260-589-3131
Brent Lehman, prin. — Fax 589-3042

Bicknell, Knox, Pop. 3,284
North Knox SC — 1,500/K-12
PO Box 187 47512 — 812-735-4434
Joe Adams, supt. — Fax 328-6262
www.nknox.k12.in.us
North Knox HS — 500/9-12
10890 N State Road 159 47512 — 812-735-2990
Tim Grove, prin. — Fax 328-2155

Bloomfield, Greene, Pop. 2,542
Bloomfield SD — 1,100/K-12
500 W South St 47424 — 812-384-4507
Daniel Sichting, supt. — Fax 384-0172
www.bsd.k12.in.us
Bloomfield JSHS — 500/7-12
501 W Spring St 47424 — 812-384-4550
Greg Parsley, prin. — Fax 384-1422

Eastern Greene SD — 1,400/PK-12
RR 4 Box 351 47424 — 812-825-5722
Randy Barrett, supt. — Fax 825-9413
www.egreene.k12.in.us/
Eastern Greene JSHS — 600/7-12
RR 4 Box 623 47424 — 812-825-5621
Kevin Frank, prin. — Fax 825-6661

Bloomington, Monroe, Pop. 69,017
Monroe County Community SC — 10,700/PK-12
315 E North Dr 47401 — 812-330-7700
Dr. John A. Maloy, supt. — Fax 330-7813
www.mccsc.edu
Batchelor MS — 500/7-8
900 W Gordon Pike 47403 — 812-330-7763
Peggy Chambers, prin. — Fax 330-7766
Bloomington HS North — 1,500/9-12
3901 N Kinser Pike 47404 — 812-330-7724
Jeffry Henderson, prin. — Fax 330-7805
Bloomington HS South — 1,900/9-12
1965 S Walnut St 47401 — 812-330-7714
Mark Fletcher, prin. — Fax 330-7810
Hoosier Hills Career Center — Vo/Tech
3070 N Prow Rd 47404 — 812-330-7730
Edward Brown, dir. — Fax 330-7807
Jackson Creek MS — 600/7-8
3980 S Sare Rd 47401 — 812-330-2451
Donna Noble, prin. — Fax 330-2457
Tri-North MS — 500/7-8
1000 W 15th St 47404 — 812-330-7745
Dr. Gale Hill, prin. — Fax 330-7799

Bloomington Hospital — Post-Sec.
PO Box 1149 47402 — 812-336-6821
Hair Arts Academy — Post-Sec.
933 N Walnut St 47404 — 812-339-1117
Harmony S — 200/K-12
PO Box 1787 47402 — 812-334-8349
Steve Bonchek, dir. — Fax 333-3435
HOPE Christian Academy — 50/K-12
4100 N Hartstrait Rd 47404 — 812-876-9008
Stacia Kelly, dir. — Fax 935-8176
Indiana University — Post-Sec.
300 N Jordan Ave 47405 — 812-855-4848
Ivy Tech Community College - Bloomington — Post-Sec.
200 Daniels Way 47404 — 812-332-1559
Lighthouse Christian Academy — 300/PK-12
1201 W That Rd 47403 — 812-824-2000
Rayna Amerine, prin. — Fax 824-2017

Bluffton, Wells, Pop. 9,460
Metro SD of Bluffton-Harrison — 1,500/K-12
805 E Harrison Rd 46714 — 260-824-2620
Dr. Julie Koschnick, supt. — Fax 824-6011
www.bhmsd.k12.in.us
Bluffton-Harrison MS — 500/5-8
1500 Stogdill Rd 46714 — 260-824-3536
Jon Bennett, prin. — Fax 824-6011
Bluffton HS — 500/9-12
1 Tiger Trl 46714 — 260-824-3724
Steve Baker, prin. — Fax 824-6011

Community Christian S — 100/PK-12
1225 W Washington St 46714 — 260-824-1203
Vicki Bell, prin. — Fax 824-9572

Boone Grove, Porter
Porter Township SC
Supt. — See Valparaiso
Boone Grove MS — 400/6-8
325 W 550 S 46302 — 219-464-4828
Paul Schlottman, prin. — Fax 464-4829

Boonville, Warrick, Pop. 6,782
Warrick County SC — 9,300/K-12
300 E Gum St 47601 — 812-897-0400
Brad Schneider, supt. — Fax 897-6033
www.warrick.k12.in.us/
Boonville HS — 900/9-12
300 N 1st St 47601 — 812-897-4701
Mike Whitten, prin. — Fax 897-6061
Boonville JHS — 500/7-8
555 N Yankeetown Rd 47601 — 812-897-1420
William Wilder, prin. — Fax 897-6584
Other Schools – See Lynnville, Newburgh

Borden, Clark, Pop. 832
West Clark Community SC
Supt. — See Sellersburg
Borden JSHS — 300/7-12
301 West St 47106 — 812-967-2087
Lisa Nale, prin. — Fax 967-2086

Bourbon, Marshall, Pop. 1,788
Triton SC — 1,100/K-12
100 Triton Dr 46504 — 574-342-2255
Ted Chittum, supt. — Fax 342-8165
www.triton.k12.in.us/
Triton JSHS — 500/7-12
300 Triton Dr 46504 — 574-342-6505
Michael Chobanov, prin. — Fax 342-8175

Bourbon Christian S — 50/1-12
1325 N Main St 46504 — 574-342-8043
Aaron Yoder, prin. — Fax 342-8145

Brazil, Clay, Pop. 8,214
Clay Community SD
Supt. — See Knightsville
North Clay MS — 1,000/6-8
3 W Knight Dr 47834 — 812-448-1530
Dr. Jeff Allen, prin. — Fax 442-0608
Northview HS — 1,100/9-12
1 W Knight Dr 47834 — 812-448-2661
Tim Rayle, prin. — Fax 446-2647

Bremen, Marshall, Pop. 4,569
Bremen Public SD — 1,500/K-12
512 W Grant St 46506 — 574-546-3929
Russ Mikel, supt. — Fax 546-6303
www.bps.k12.in.us
Bremen HS — 500/9-12
511 W Grant St 46506 — 574-546-3511
Don Harrison, prin. — Fax 546-5477

Bristol, Elkhart, Pop. 1,635

Kessington Christian S — 50/PK-12
19153 County Road 104 46507 — 574-848-4987
Don Dunithan, admin. — Fax 641-2118

Brookville, Franklin, Pop. 2,933
Franklin County Community SC — 3,100/PK-12
1020 Franklin Ave 47012 — 765-647-4128
Dr. William Glentzer, supt. — Fax 647-2417
www.fccsc.k12.in.us
Brookville MS — 500/5-8
9092 Wildcat Ln 47012 — 765-647-6040
Dr. Gary Frost, prin. — Fax 647-4960
Franklin County HS — 1,000/9-12
1 Wildcat Ln 47012 — 765-647-4101
Kim Simonson, prin. — Fax 647-2732

Brownsburg, Hendricks, Pop. 18,290
Brownsburg Community SC — 5,900/K-12
444 E Tilden Dr 46112 — 317-852-5726
Kathleen Corbin, supt. — Fax 852-1015
www.brownsburg.k12.in.us
Brownsburg East MS — 6-8
1250 Airport Rd 46112 — 317-852-2386
Richard Doss, prin. — Fax 852-1023
Brownsburg HS — 1,900/9-12
1000 S Odell St 46112 — 317-852-2258
Bret Daghe, prin. — Fax 852-1490
Brownsburg West MS — 1,000/6-8
1555 S Odell St 46112 — 317-852-3143
Julie Moster, prin. — Fax 858-4100

Bethesda Christian S — 400/K-12
7950 N County Road 650 E 46112 — 317-852-3101
Dee Tidball, prin. — Fax 852-4301

Brownstown, Jackson, Pop. 3,050
Brownstown Central Community SC — 1,700/PK-12
608 W Commerce St 47220 — 812-358-4271
Roger Bane, supt. — Fax 358-5303
www.btownccs.k12.in.us
Brownstown Central HS — 500/9-12
500 N Elm St 47220 — 812-358-3453
Joseph Sheffer, prin. — Fax 358-5318
Brownstown Central MS — 400/6-8
520 W Walnut St 47220 — 812-358-4947
Peggy Cannon, prin. — Fax 358-3940

Bunker Hill, Miami, Pop. 1,017
Maconaquah SC — 2,400/PK-12
7932 S Strawtown Pike 46914 — 765-689-9131
Carmine Gentile, supt. — Fax 689-0995
www.maconaquah.k12.in.us
Maconaquah HS — 700/9-12
256 E 800 S 46914 — 765-689-9131
David Noonan, prin. — Fax 689-9528
Maconaquah MS — 600/6-8
594 E 800 S 46914 — 765-689-9131
James Callane, prin. — Fax 689-9360

Butler, DeKalb, Pop. 2,714
DeKalb County Eastern Community SD — 1,500/K-12
300 E Washington St 46721 — 260-868-2125
Dr. Jeffrey Stephens, supt. — Fax 868-2562
www.eastsideblazers.net
Eastside JSHS — 700/7-12
603 E Green St 46721 — 260-868-2186
Robert Ruch, prin. — Fax 868-5773

Cambridge City, Wayne, Pop. 2,027
Western Wayne SD
Supt. — See Pershing
Lincoln HS — 300/9-12
215 E Parkway Dr 47327 — 765-478-5916
Michael Cerqua, prin. — Fax 478-3262
Lincoln MS — 300/6-8
205 E Parkway Dr 47327 — 765-478-5840
John Engle, prin. — Fax 478-3265

Campbellsburg, Washington, Pop. 585
West Washington SC — 1,000/K-12
9699 W Mount Tabor Rd 47108 — 812-755-4872
Gerald Jackson, supt. — Fax 755-4843
www.wwcs.k12.in.us
West Washington JSHS — 500/7-12
8028 W Batts Rd 47108 — 812-755-4996
Paul Stroud, prin. — Fax 755-4460

Cannelton, Perry, Pop. 1,168
Cannelton CSD — 100/PK-12
125 S 6th St 47520 — 812-547-2637
Marion A. Chapman, supt. — Fax 547-4142
www.cannelton.k12.in.us
Cannelton HS — 100/6-12
119 S 3rd St 47520 — 812-547-3296
Beverly Conrad, prin. — Fax 548-2288

Carmel, Hamilton, Pop. 59,243
Carmel Clay SD — 13,900/PK-12
5201 E 131st St 46033 — 317-844-9961
Dr. Barbara Underwood, supt. — Fax 844-9965
www.ccs.k12.in.us
Carmel HS — 3,800/9-12
520 E Main St 46032 — 317-846-7721
John Williams, prin. — Fax 571-4066
Carmel MS — 1,200/6-8
300 S Guilford Rd 46032 — 317-846-7331
Denise Jacobs, prin. — Fax 571-4067
Clay MS — 1,100/6-8
5150 E 126th St 46033 — 317-844-7251
Kent DeKoninck, prin. — Fax 571-4020
Creekside MS — 1,000/6-8
3525 W 126th St 46032 — 317-733-6420
Tom Harmas, prin. — Fax 733-6422

ITT Technical Institute — Post-Sec.
12650 Hamilton Crossing 46032 — 317-324-9706

Cayuga, Vermillion, Pop. 1,116
North Vermillion Community SC — 800/K-12
5551 N Falcon Dr 47928 — 765-492-4033
Paul Roads, supt. — Fax 492-7001
www.nvc.k12.in.us
North Vermillion JSHS — 400/7-12
5555 N Falcon Dr 47928 — 765-492-3364
Corey Austin, prin. — Fax 492-7006

Cedar Lake, Lake, Pop. 9,901
Hanover Community SC — 1,500/K-12
PO Box 645 46303 — 219-374-3500
Dr. Michael Livovich, supt. — Fax 374-4411
www.hanover.k12.in.us
Hanover Central HS — 500/9-12
10120 W 133rd Ave 46303 — 219-374-3800
Joseph Fetty, prin. — Fax 374-4408
Hanover Central JHS — 200/6-8
10120 W 133rd Ave 46303 — 219-374-3800
Robert McRae, prin. — Fax 374-4408

Centerville, Wayne, Pop. 2,590
Centerville-Abington Community SD — 1,700/PK-12
115 W South St 47330 — 765-855-3475
Philip Stevenson, supt. — Fax 855-2524
www.centerville.k12.in.us
Centerville HS — 600/9-12
507 Willow Grove Rd 47330 — 765-855-3481
Tammy Chavis, prin. — Fax 855-3484
Centerville JHS — 200/7-8
509 Willow Grove Rd 47330 — 765-855-5113
Rick Schauss, prin. — Fax 855-5207

Chalmers, White, Pop. 485
Frontier SC — 800/K-12
PO Box 809 47929 — 219-984-5009
Bernard Graser, supt. — Fax 984-5022
www.frontier.k12.in.us
Frontier JSHS — 400/7-12
1 Falcon Dr 47929 — 219-984-5437
Richard Dehne, prin. — Fax 984-5360

Charlestown, Clark, Pop. 8,052
Greater Clark County SD
Supt. — See Jeffersonville
Charlestown HS — 700/9-12
1 Pirate Pl 47111 — 812-256-3328
Dick Johnson, prin. — Fax 256-7274
Charlestown MS — 500/6-8
8804 High Jackson Rd 47111 — 812-256-6363
Joyce Traub, prin. — Fax 256-7282

Charlottesville, Hancock
Eastern Hancock County Community SC 1,100/PK-12
10370 E County Road 250 N 46117 317-467-0064
Dr. Ellen Welk, supt. Fax 936-5516
www.ehancock.k12.in.us
Eastern Hancock HS 400/9-12
10320 E County Road 250 N 46117 317-936-5595
David Pfaff, prin. Fax 936-5050
Eastern Hancock MS 200/6-8
10380 E County Road 250 N 46117 317-936-5324
David Pfaff, prin. Fax 936-5516

Chesterton, Porter, Pop. 12,032
Duneland SC 5,500/K-12
601 W Morgan Ave 46304 219-983-3605
Dr. Dirk E. Baer, supt. Fax 983-3614
www.duneland.k12.in.us
Chesterton HS 1,800/9-12
2125 S 11th St 46304 219-983-3730
Jim Goetz, prin. Fax 983-3775
Chesterton MS 900/7-8
651 W Morgan Ave 46304 219-983-3776
James Ton, prin. Fax 983-3798

Fairhaven Baptist Academy 200/K-12
86 E Oak Hill Rd 46304 219-926-6636
David Olson, prin. Fax 926-1111

Churubusco, Whitley, Pop. 1,773
Smith-Green Community SD 1,400/PK-12
222 W Tulley St 46723 260-693-2007
Carol Kaiser, supt. Fax 693-6434
www.sgcs.k12.in.us/
Churubusco HS 500/9-12
1 Eagle Dr 46723 260-693-2131
Mark Snyder, prin. Fax 693-3673
Churubusco MS 300/6-8
2 Eagle Dr 46723 260-693-1460
John Davis, prin. Fax 693-1437

Cicero, Hamilton, Pop. 4,368

Indiana Academy 100/9-12
24815 State Road 19 46034 317-984-3575
Peter Cousins, prin. Fax 984-5081

Clarksville, Clark, Pop. 21,060
Clarksville Community SC 1,400/K-12
200 Ettels Ln 47129 812-282-7753
Stephen Fisher, supt. Fax 282-7754
www.ccsc.k12.in.us/
Clarksville HS 500/9-12
800 High School Dr 47129 812-282-8231
Tina Bennett, prin. Fax 282-8234
Clarksville MS 400/6-8
101 Ettels Ln 47129 812-282-8235
Pamela Cooper, prin. Fax 280-5004

Our Lady of Providence HS 600/7-12
707 Providence Way 47129 812-945-2538
Melinda Ernstberger, prin. Fax 981-2538
PJ's College of Cosmetology Post-Sec.
1414 Blackiston Mill Rd 47129 812-282-0459

Clay City, Clay, Pop. 1,036
Clay Community SD
Supt. — See Knightsville
Clay City JSHS 400/7-12
601 Lankford St 47841 812-939-2154
Jeff Bell, prin. Fax 443-2106

Clayton, Hendricks, Pop. 817
Mill Creek Community SC 1,400/PK-12
6631 S County Road 200 W 46118 317-539-9200
Dr. Sherida Brower, supt. Fax 539-9215
www.mccsc.k12.in.us/
Cascade HS 500/9-12
6565 S County Road 200 W 46118 317-539-9315
Todd Gowen, prin. Fax 539-9350
Cascade MS 200/6-8
6423 S County Road 200 W 46118 317-539-9285
Eric Sieferman, prin. Fax 539-9310

Clinton, Vermillion, Pop. 4,906
South Vermillion Community SC 2,100/K-12
PO Box 387 47842 765-832-2426
Steven E. Miller, supt. Fax 832-7391
www.svcs.k12.in.us
South Vermillion HS 600/9-12
770 Wildcat Dr 47842 765-832-3551
Philip Harrison, prin. Fax 832-3510
South Vermillion MS 500/6-8
950 Wildcat Dr 47842 765-832-7727
Angela Harris, prin. Fax 832-5316

Cloverdale, Putnam, Pop. 2,262
Cloverdale Community SD 1,400/PK-12
310 E Logan St 46120 765-795-4664
Carrie Milner, supt. Fax 795-5166
www.cloverdale.k12.in.us
Cloverdale HS 400/9-12
205 E Market St 46120 765-795-4203
Sonny Stoltz, prin. Fax 795-4381
Cloverdale MS 500/5-8
312 E Logan St 46120 765-795-2900
Jeff Brookshire, prin. Fax 795-2901

Columbia City, Whitley, Pop. 8,024
Whitley County Consolidated SD 3,500/PK-12
107 N Walnut St 46725 260-244-5772
Dr. Laura Huffman, supt. Fax 244-4099
www.wccs.k12.in.us
Columbia City HS 1,100/9-12
600 N Whitley St 46725 260-244-6136
Steve Doepker, prin. Fax 244-5610
Indian Springs MS 800/6-8
1692 S State Road 9 46725 260-244-5148
Jan Boylen, prin. Fax 244-4710

Columbus, Bartholomew, Pop. 39,380
Bartholomew Consolidated SC 10,600/PK-12
1200 Central Ave 47201 812-376-4220
Dr. John Quick, supt. Fax 376-4486
www.bcsc.k12.in.us
Central MS 800/7-8
725 7th St 47201 812-376-4287
Randy Gratz, prin. Fax 376-4511
Columbus Area Career Connection Vo/Tech
1400 25th St 47201 812-376-4240
Marilyn Metzler, dir. Fax 376-4699
Columbus East HS 1,400/9-12
230 S Marr Rd 47201 812-376-4369
Gary Goshorn, prin. Fax 376-4358
Columbus North HS 1,900/9-12
1400 25th St 47201 812-376-4432
David Clark, prin. Fax 376-4291
Northside MS 900/7-8
1400 27th St 47201 812-376-4405
Charlie McCoy, prin. Fax 376-4479

Columbus Christian S 200/PK-12
3170 Indiana Ave 47201 812-372-3780
Amy Mathis, admin. Fax 372-3878
Columbus Regional Hospital Post-Sec.
2400 17th St 47201 812-376-5439
Indiana Business College Post-Sec.
2222 Poshard Rd 47203 812-379-9000
Ivy Tech Community College - Columbus Post-Sec.
4475 Central Ave 47203 812-372-9925

Connersville, Fayette, Pop. 14,368
Fayette County SC 3,900/PK-12
1401 Spartan Dr 47331 765-825-2178
Dr. Russell Hodges, supt. Fax 825-8060
www.fayette.k12.in.us
Connersville HS 1,100/9-12
1100 Spartan Dr 47331 765-825-1151
Patricia Flowers, prin. Fax 825-0777
Connersville MS 700/7-8
1900 N Grand Ave 47331 765-825-1139
Beth Denham, prin. Fax 827-4346
Whitewater Technical Career Center Vo/Tech
1300 Spartan Dr 47331 765-825-0521
Milton Eley, prin. Fax 827-0836

Temple Christian S 200/PK-12
1382 E State Road 44 47331 765-825-5198
Jim Tritle, prin.

Converse, Miami, Pop. 1,116
Oak Hill United SC 1,500/PK-12
PO Box 550 46919 765-395-3341
Jim Smith, supt. Fax 395-3343
www.ohusc.k12.in.us
Oak Hill HS 500/9-12
7756 W Delphi Pike Ste 27 46919 765-384-4381
Joel Martin, prin. Fax 384-5414
Oak Hill JHS 300/7-8
7760 W Delphi Pike Ste 27 46919 765-384-4385
Greg Perkins, prin. Fax 384-4386

Corydon, Harrison, Pop. 2,787
South Harrison Community SD 3,200/K-12
315 S Harrison Dr 47112 812-738-2168
Dr. Neyland Clark, supt. Fax 738-2158
www.shcsc.k12.in.us/
Corydon Central HS 700/9-12
375 Country Club Rd 47112 812-738-4181
Carole Apple, prin. Fax 738-1145
Corydon Central JHS 400/7-8
377 Country Club Rd 47112 812-738-4184
Mark Black, prin. Fax 738-5752
Other Schools – See Elizabeth

Covington, Fountain, Pop. 2,465
Covington Community SC 900/PK-12
PO Box 225 47932 765-793-4877
Nate Evans, supt. Fax 793-5209
www.covington.k12.in.us/
Covington Community HS 300/9-12
1017 6th St 47932 765-793-2286
Kirk Booe, prin. Fax 793-5200
Covington MS 200/6-8
514 Railroad St 47932 765-793-4451
Steve Reynolds, prin. Fax 793-5200

Crawfordsville, Montgomery, Pop. 15,155
Crawfordsville Community SD 2,400/PK-12
1000 Fairview Ave 47933 765-362-2342
Kathleen Steele, supt. Fax 364-3237
www.cville.k12.in.us
Crawfordsville HS 700/9-12
1 W Athenian Dr 47933 765-362-2340
Greg Hunt, prin. Fax 364-3200
Tuttle MS 600/6-8
612 S Elm St 47933 765-362-2992
Scott Bowling, prin. Fax 364-3219

North Montgomery Community SC 2,100/K-12
480 W 580 N 47933 765-359-2112
Dr. Robert Brower, supt. Fax 359-2111
www.nm.k12.in.us/
North Montgomery HS 600/9-12
5945 N US Highway 231 47933 765-362-5140
Terry Russell, prin. Fax 362-6710
Northridge MS 600/6-8
482 W 580 N 47933 765-364-1071
Angela Blessing, prin. Fax 362-7985

South Montgomery Community SC
Supt. — See New Market
Southmont HS 600/9-12
6425 S US Highway 231 47933 765-866-0350
Kevin Stewart, prin. Fax 866-2044
Southmont JHS 400/7-8
6425 S US Highway 231 47933 765-866-2023
Mike Sowers, prin. Fax 866-2045

Maranatha Christian S 50/K-12
915 Whitlock Ave 47933 765-362-8881
Gloria Stevens, admin. Fax 362-0151
Wabash College Post-Sec.
301 W Wabash Ave 47933 765-361-6100

Crothersville, Jackson, Pop. 1,544
Crothersville Community SD 600/K-12
201 S Preston St 47229 812-793-2601
Dr. Terry Goodin, supt. Fax 793-3004
Crothersville JSHS 300/6-12
109 S Preston St 47229 812-793-2051
David Schill, prin. Fax 793-3004

Crown Point, Lake, Pop. 22,697
Crown Point Community SC 6,300/PK-12
200 E North St 46307 219-663-3371
Dr. Teresa Eineman, supt. Fax 662-4304
www.cps.k12.in.us
Crown Point HS 2,100/9-12
1500 S Main St 46307 219-663-4885
Ryan Pitcock, prin. Fax 662-5661
Taft MS 1,000/7-8
1000 S Main St 46307 219-663-1507
Michael Hazen, prin. Fax 662-4349

Culver, Marshall, Pop. 1,526
Culver Community SC 1,200/K-12
PO Box 231 46511 574-842-3364
Brad Schuldt, supt. Fax 842-4615
www.culver.k12.in.us
Culver Community HS 300/9-12
701 School St 46511 574-842-3391
Albert Hanselman, prin. Fax 842-3392
Culver Community MS 200/7-8
1 Cavalier Dr 46511 574-842-5690
George Irvin, prin. Fax 842-5691

Culver Academies 700/9-12
1300 Academy Rd Ste 156 46511 574-842-7000
Kathleen Lintner, hdmstr. Fax 842-8161

Daleville, Delaware, Pop. 1,573
Daleville Community SD 700/K-12
8700 S Bronco Dr 47334 765-378-3329
Paul Garrison, supt. Fax 378-3649
www.daleville.k12.in.us
Daleville JSHS 300/7-12
8400 S Bronco Dr 47334 765-378-3371
John Junco, prin. Fax 378-4076

Danville, Hendricks, Pop. 7,425
Danville Community SC 2,400/PK-12
PO Box 469 46122 317-745-2212
Dr. John McKinney, supt. Fax 745-3924
www.danville.k12.in.us
Danville Community HS 700/9-12
100 Warrior Way 46122 317-745-6431
Paul Hamann, prin. Fax 745-3908
Danville MS 400/7-8
49 N Wayne St 46122 317-745-5491
Michael Peters, prin. Fax 745-3949

Decatur, Adams, Pop. 9,547
North Adams Community SD 2,300/K-12
PO Box 670 46733 260-724-7146
James Compton, supt. Fax 724-4777
www.nadams.k12.in.us
Bellmont HS 900/9-12
1000 E North Adams Dr 46733 260-724-7121
Adrian Richie, prin. Fax 724-7826
Bellmont MS 500/6-8
1200 E North Adams Dr 46733 260-724-3137
Craig Anderson, prin. Fax 724-4495

Delphi, Carroll, Pop. 2,980
Delphi Community SC 1,700/K-12
501 Armory Rd 46923 765-564-2100
Ralph Walker, supt. Fax 564-6919
www.delphi.k12.in.us/
Delphi Community HS 500/9-12
501 Armory Rd 46923 765-564-3481
Barry Stone, prin. Fax 564-3260
Delphi Community MS 400/6-8
501 Armory Rd 46923 765-564-3411
Robert DeLaRosa, prin. Fax 564-2135

Demotte, Jasper, Pop. 3,738

Covenant Christian HS 100/9-12
611 15th St SW 46310 219-987-7651
Clarence Oudman, prin. Fax 987-7652

Denver, Miami, Pop. 521
North Miami Community SD 1,200/K-12
PO Box 218 46926 765-985-3891
Brent Kaufman, supt. Fax 985-3904
www.nmcs.k12.in.us/
North Miami MSHS 600/7-12
570 E 900 N 46926 765-985-2931
Chuck Pavey, prin. Fax 985-2056

Donaldson, Marshall

Ancilla Domini College 46513 Post-Sec.
574-936-8898

Dubois, Dubois
Northeast Dubois County SC 900/K-12
5379 E Main St 47527 812-678-2781
Dan Balka, supt. Fax 678-4418
www.nedubois.k12.in.us
Dubois MS 300/5-8
4550 N 4th St 47527 812-678-2181
Bill Hochgesang, prin. Fax 678-2282
Northeast Dubois HS 300/9-12
4711 N Dubois Rd NE 47527 812-678-2251
Rick Gladish, prin. Fax 678-3991

Dugger, Sullivan, Pop. 959
Northeast SC
Supt. — See Hymera
Union JSHS 200/7-12
7356 E County Road 50 S 47848 812-648-2729
Charles Roach, prin. Fax 648-2594

Dunkirk, Jay, Pop. 2,639
Jay SC
Supt. — See Portland
West Jay MS 300/6-8
140 E Highland Ave 47336 765-768-7648
Mike Crull, prin. Fax 768-6152

Dyer, Lake, Pop. 15,071
Lake Central SC
Supt. — See Saint John
Kahler MS 1,200/6-8
600 Joliet St 46311 219-865-3535
Karen Brownell, prin. Fax 865-4428

Mid-America Reformed Seminary Post-Sec.
229 Seminary Dr 46311 219-864-2400

East Chicago, Lake, Pop. 30,946
City of East Chicago SD 6,300/PK-12
210 E Columbus Dr 46312 219-391-4100
Juan Anaya, supt. Fax 391-4126
www.ecps.org
Block JHS 500/7-8
2700 Cardinal Dr 46312 219-391-4084
Michael Milich, prin. Fax 391-4282
East Chicago Central HS 1,400/9-12
1100 W Columbus Dr 46312 219-391-4000
Darnell Adell, prin. Fax 391-4049
West Side JHS 400/7-8
4001 Indianapolis Blvd 46312 219-391-4068
David Allen, prin. Fax 391-4284

Edinburgh, Johnson, Pop. 4,517
Edinburgh Community SC 900/K-12
202 Keeley St 46124 812-526-2681
Dr. Rebecca Sager, supt. Fax 526-0271
www.edinburgh.k12.in.us
Edinburgh Community HS 300/9-12
300 Keeley St 46124 812-526-5501
Kevin Rockey, prin. Fax 526-3439
Edinburgh Community MS 200/6-8
300 Keeley St 46124 812-526-3418
Rich Arkanoff, prin. Fax 526-3430

Elizabeth, Harrison, Pop. 140
South Harrison Community SD
Supt. — See Corydon
South Central JSHS 400/7-12
6675 E Highway 11 SE 47117 812-969-2941
James Crisp, prin. Fax 969-3019

Elkhart, Elkhart, Pop. 52,270
Baugo Community SD 1,800/K-12
29125 County Road 22 46517 574-293-8583
Jerry Cook, supt. Fax 294-2171
www.baugo.com/
Jimtown HS 500/9-12
59021 County Road 3 46517 574-295-2343
Nathan Dean, prin. Fax 294-2171
Jimtown JHS 300/7-8
58903 County Road 3 46517 574-294-6586
Mike Groh, prin. Fax 294-8557

Concord Community SD 4,400/K-12
59040 Minuteman Way 46517 574-875-5161
George Dyer, supt. Fax 875-8762
www.concord.k12.in.us
Concord Community HS 1,500/9-12
59117 Minuteman Way 46517 574-875-6524
Dan Cunningham, prin. Fax 875-8580
Concord JHS 700/7-8
24050 County Road 20 46517 574-875-5122
Kevin Caird, prin. Fax 875-1089

Elkhart Community SD 12,600/PK-12
2720 California Rd 46514 574-262-5516
Mark T. Mow, supt. Fax 262-5733
www.elkhart.k12.in.us
Elkhart Area Career Ctr Vo/Tech
2424 California Rd 46514 574-262-5650
Stephen Barkdull, prin. Fax 262-5801
Elkhart Central HS 1,800/9-12
1 Blazer Blvd 46516 574-295-4700
Frank Serge, prin. Fax 295-4712
Elkhart Memorial HS 1,900/9-12
2608 California Rd 46514 574-262-5600
Mark Tobolski, prin. Fax 262-5625
Moran MS 700/7-8
200 W Lusher Ave 46517 574-295-4805
Levon Johnson, prin. Fax 295-4807
North Side MS 700/7-8
300 Lawrence St 46514 574-262-5570
Sara Jackowiak, prin. Fax 262-5573
West Side MS 700/7-8
101 S Nappanee St 46514 574-295-4815
Kristie Stutsman, prin. Fax 295-4812

Associated Mennonite Biblical Seminaries Post-Sec.
3003 Benham Ave 46517 574-295-3726
Elkhart Christian Academy 600/PK-12
25943 County Road 22 46517 574-293-1609
John Raudenbush, admin. Fax 293-3238
Redeemer Community Christian S 50/K-10
24004 Old US 20 46516 574-264-5739
Valerie Schumacher, prin. Fax 264-5739

Ellettsville, Monroe, Pop. 5,294
Richland-Bean Blossom Community SC 2,800/PK-12
600 Edgewood Dr 47429 812-876-7100
Thomas r. Edington, supt. Fax 876-7020
www.rbbcsc.k12.in.us/
Edgewood HS 900/9-12
601 Edgewood Dr 47429 812-876-2277
Dirk Ackerman, prin. Fax 876-9163
Edgewood JHS 700/6-8
851 W Edgewood Dr 47429 812-876-2005
Larry Sparks, prin. Fax 876-8985

Elnora, Daviess, Pop. 743
North Daviess County Community SD 1,100/K-12
5494 E State Road 58 47529 812-636-8000
Robert W. Bell, supt. Fax 636-7546
www.ndaviess.k12.in.us
North Daviess JSHS 500/7-12
5494 E State Road 58 47529 812-636-8000
Jed Jerrels, prin. Fax 636-7255

Elwood, Madison, Pop. 9,167
Elwood Community SC 1,900/K-12
1306 N Anderson St 46036 765-552-9861
Thomas Austin, supt. Fax 552-8088
www.elwood.k12.in.us
Elwood Community HS 600/9-12
1137 N 19th St 46036 765-552-9854
Nicholas Eccles, prin. Fax 552-1044
Elwood Community MS 500/6-8
1207 N 19th St 46036 765-552-7378
Amy Rauch, prin. Fax 552-2017
Hinds Career Center Vo/Tech
1105 N 19th St 46036 765-552-9881
James Pearson, prin. Fax 552-2021

Eminence, Morgan
Eminence Community SC 500/K-12
PO Box 135 46125 765-528-2101
Dr. Susan Phillips, supt. Fax 528-2262
www.eminence.k12.in.us
Eminence JSHS 300/7-12
PO Box 105 46125 765-528-2221
Max Hoke, prin. Fax 528-2276

Evansville, Vanderburgh, Pop. 115,918
Evansville-Vanderburgh SC 22,000/PK-12
1 SE 9th St 47708 812-435-8477
Dr. Robert Yeager, supt. Fax 435-8421
www.evsc.k12.in.us/
Bosse HS 800/9-12
1300 Washington Ave 47714 812-477-1661
Robert Adams, prin. Fax 474-6976
Central HS 1,400/9-12
5400 N 1st Ave 47710 812-435-8292
John Russell, prin. Fax 435-8515
Evans MS 500/6-8
837 Tulip Ave 47711 812-435-8330
David Smith, prin. Fax 435-8332
Glenwood MS 300/6-8
901 Sweetser Ave 47713 812-435-8242
Sheila Huff, prin. Fax 435-8245
Harrison HS 1,500/9-12
211 Fielding Rd 47715 812-477-1046
Janet Leistner, prin. Fax 474-4118
Harwood MS 400/6-8
3013 N 1st Ave 47710 812-435-8316
Dr. Franzy Fleck, prin. Fax 435-8517
Helfrich Park MS 600/6-8
2603 W Maryland St 47712 812-435-8246
Timothy McIntosh, prin. Fax 435-8249
McGary MS 500/6-8
1535 Joyce Ave 47714 812-476-3035
Don Mosbey, prin. Fax 474-6919
North HS 1,500/9-12
2319 Stringtown Rd 47711 812-435-8283
Brenda Weber, prin. Fax 435-8349
Oak Hill MS 700/6-8
7700 Oak Hill Rd 47725 812-867-6426
Kenneth Wempe, prin. Fax 867-4753
Perry Heights MS 500/6-8
5800 Hogue Rd 47712 812-435-8326
Charles Goodman, prin. Fax 435-8263
Plaza Park MS 600/6-8
7301 Lincoln Ave 47715 812-476-4971
Mary Schweizer, prin. Fax 474-6922
Reitz HS 1,400/9-12
350 Dreier Blvd 47712 812-435-8206
Christine Settle, prin. Fax 435-8217
Thomkins MS 700/6-8
1300 W Mill Rd 47710 812-435-8323
Terry Yunker, prin. Fax 435-8588
Washington MS 500/6-8
1801 Washington Ave 47714 812-477-8983
Rance Ossenberg, prin. Fax 474-6930

Evansville Day S 300/PK-12
3400 N Green River Rd 47715 812-476-3039
Benjamin Hebebrand, hdmstr. Fax 476-4061
Evansville Tri-State Beauty College Post-Sec.
4920 Tippecanoe Dr 47715 812-479-6989
Indiana Business College Post-Sec.
4601 Theatre Dr 47715 812-476-6000
Ivy Tech Community College - Southwest Post-Sec.
3501 N 1st Ave 47710 812-426-2865
Mater Dei HS 600/9-12
1300 Harmony Way 47720 812-426-2258
Marie Williams Ph.D., prin. Fax 421-5717
Reitz Memorial HS 800/9-12
1500 Lincoln Ave 47714 812-476-4973
Gerry Adams, prin. Fax 474-2942
Roger's Academy of Hair Design Post-Sec.
2903 Mount Vernon Ave 47712 812-428-4027
University of Evansville Post-Sec.
1800 Lincoln Ave 47714 800-423-8633
University of Southern Indiana Post-Sec.
8600 University Blvd 47712 812-464-8600
Welborn Baptist Hospital Post-Sec.
401 SE 6th St 47713 812-426-8264
Westside Catholic S St. Boniface Campus 4-8
2031 W Michigan St 47712 812-422-1014
Dan Gilbert, prin. Fax 422-1057

Fairland, Shelby, Pop. 1,348
Northwestern Consolidated SC 1,500/PK-12
4920 W 600 N 46126 317-835-7461
Dr. Larry Moore, supt. Fax 835-4441
www.nwsc.k12.in.us/
Triton Central HS 500/9-12
4774 W 600 N 46126 317-835-3000
Brad Lindsay, prin. Fax 835-3012
Triton MS 500/5-8
4740 W 600 N 46126 317-835-3006
Kern Scott, prin. Fax 835-3008

Fairmount, Grant, Pop. 2,814
Madison-Grant United SC 1,600/PK-12
11580 S E 00 W 46928 765-948-4143
Fred Herron, supt. Fax 948-4150
www.mgargylls.com
Madison-Grant HS 500/9-12
11700 S E 00 W 46928 765-948-4141
Shane Robbins, prin. Fax 948-4874
Madison-Grant JHS 300/7-8
11640 S E 00 W 46928 765-948-5132
Tom Daniel, prin. Fax 948-3671

Farmersburg, Sullivan, Pop. 1,208
Northeast SC
Supt. — See Hymera
North Central JSHS 500/7-12
910 E County Road 975 N 47850 812-397-2132
David Scott, prin. Fax 397-2133

Ferdinand, Dubois, Pop. 2,299
Southeast Dubois County SC 1,100/K-12
432 E 15th St 47532 812-367-1653
Robert Johnson, supt. Fax 367-1075
www.sedubois.k12.in.us
Forest Park JSHS 700/7-12
1440 Michigan St 47532 812-367-1831
Jeffrey Jessee, prin. Fax 367-1172

Fishers, Hamilton, Pop. 57,220
Hamilton Southeastern SD 12,700/PK-12
13485 Cumberland Rd 46038 317-594-4100
Dr. Concetta Raimondi, supt. Fax 594-4109
www.hse.k12.in.us/
Fishers HS 9-12
13000 Promise Rd 46038 317-915-4290
Dr. Scott Syverson, prin. Fax 915-4299
Fishers JHS 1,000/7-8
13257 Cumberland Rd 46038 317-594-4150
Brian Cronk, prin. Fax 594-4159
Hamilton Southeastern HS 3,000/9-12
13910 E 126th St, 317-594-4190
Robert Albano, prin. Fax 594-4199
Hamilton Southeastern JHS 900/7-8
12001 Olio Rd, 317-594-4120
Shari Switzer, prin. Fax 594-4129
Riverside S 5-8
10910 Eller Rd 46038 317-915-4280
Michael Beresford, prin. Fax 915-4289

Flora, Carroll, Pop. 2,161
Carroll Consolidated SC 1,100/K-12
2 S 3rd St 46929 574-967-4113
John Sayers, supt. Fax 967-3831
www.carroll.k12.in.us/
Carroll JSHS 500/7-12
2362 E State Road 18 46929 574-967-4157
Charles Huckstep, prin. Fax 967-4027

Floyds Knobs, Floyd
New Albany-Floyd County Consolidated SD
Supt. — See New Albany
Floyd Central HS 1,500/9-12
6575 Old Vincennes Rd 47119 812-923-8811
John Marsh, prin. Fax 923-4010

Fort Branch, Gibson, Pop. 2,342
South Gibson SC 1,900/K-12
1029 W 650 S 47648 812-753-4230
Stacey Humbaugh, supt. Fax 753-4081
www.sgibson.k12.in.us
Gibson Southern HS 600/9-12
3499 W 800 S 47648 812-753-3011
Jim Isaacs, prin. Fax 753-3021

Fortville, Hancock, Pop. 3,626
Mt. Vernon Community SC 3,200/PK-12
1776 W State Road 234 46040 317-485-3100
Dr. William Riggs, supt. Fax 485-3113
www.mvcsc.k12.in.us
Mt. Vernon HS 900/9-12
8112 N 200 W 46040 317-485-3131
Joseph Loomis, prin. Fax 485-3154
Mt. Vernon MS 600/7-8
1862 W State Road 234 46040 317-485-3160
John Price, prin. Fax 485-3171

Fort Wayne, Allen, Pop. 223,341
East Allen County SD
Supt. — See New Haven
Harding HS 600/9-12
6501 Wayne Trce 46816 260-446-0240
Neal Brown, prin. Fax 446-0249
Prince Chapman Academy 600/6-8
4808 E Paulding Rd 46816 260-446-0270
Deborah Watson, prin. Fax 446-0275

Fort Wayne Community SD 31,500/PK-12
1200 S Clinton St 46802 260-467-1000
Dr. Wendy Robinson, supt. Fax 467-1980
www.fwcs.k12.in.us
Anthis Career Center Vo/Tech
1200 Barr St 46802 260-467-1005
Larry Gerardot, prin. Fax 425-7609
Blackhawk MS 900/6-8
7200 E State Blvd 46815 260-425-7313
Timothy Matthias, prin. Fax 425-7142
Elmhurst HS 1,000/9-12
3829 Sandpoint Rd 46809 260-425-7510
Barbara Gentry, prin. Fax 425-7162

Jefferson MS 700/6-8
5303 Wheelock Rd 46835 260-425-7374
LeeAnn Thompson, prin. Fax 425-7376
Kekionga MS 700/6-8
2929 Engle Rd 46809 260-425-7378
Gary Schafer, prin. Fax 425-7381
Lakeside MS 600/6-8
2100 Lake Ave 46805 260-467-8625
Carlton Mable, prin. Fax 467-8672
Lane MS 600/6-8
4901 Vance Ave 46815 260-425-7386
Jennifer Peckham, prin. Fax 425-7389
Memorial Park MS 600/6-8
2200 Maumee Ave 46803 260-425-7410
Brian Smith, prin. Fax 425-7413
Miami MS 500/6-8
8100 Amherst Dr 46819 260-467-8560
Harold Stevens, prin. Fax 467-8606
Northrop HS 2,100/9-12
7001 Coldwater Rd 46825 260-467-2300
Barbara Ahlersmeyer, prin. Fax 467-2301
North Side HS 1,500/9-12
475 E State Blvd 46805 260-467-2800
Charles DeFord, prin.
Northwood MS 800/6-8
1201 E Washington Center Rd 46825
Matthew Schiebel, prin. 260-467-2930
Portage MS 600/6-8
3521 Taylor St 46802 260-425-7431
Jeff King, prin. Fax 425-7434
Shawnee MS 800/6-8
1000 E Cook Rd 46825 260-425-7447
Linda Johnson, prin. Fax 425-7450
Snider HS 2,100/9-12
4600 Fairlawn Pass 46815 260-425-7570
Steve Simmons, prin. Fax 425-7136
South Side HS 1,500/9-12
3601 S Calhoun St 46807 260-467-2600
Thomas Smith, prin.
Towles IS 500/6-8
420 E Paulding Rd 46816 260-467-4300
Tamara Lake, prin. Fax 467-4364
Wayne HS 1,000/9-12
9100 Winchester Rd 46819 260-425-7630
Joselyn Whitticker, prin. Fax 425-7646

Metro SD of Southwest Allen County 6,200/K-12
4824 Homestead Rd 46814 260-431-2051
Brian Smith, supt. Fax 431-2099
www.sacs.k12.in.us
Homestead HS 1,900/9-12
4310 Homestead Rd 46814 260-431-2251
Dianne Moake, prin. Fax 431-2330
Summit MS 800/6-8
4509 Homestead Rd 46814 260-431-2552
Jim Leinker, prin. Fax 431-2568
Woodside MS 700/6-8
2310 W Hamilton Rd S 46814 260-431-2702
Rick Smith, prin. Fax 431-2723

Northwest Allen County SD 5,500/PK-12
13119 Coldwater Rd 46845 260-637-3155
Dr. Steven Yager, supt. Fax 637-8355
www.nacs.k12.in.us/
Carroll 9th Grade Campus 500/9-9
3905 Carroll Rd 46818 260-637-0064
Kenneth Folks, prin. Fax 637-5868
Carroll HS 1,200/10-12
3701 Carroll Rd 46818 260-637-3161
Deborah Neumeyer, prin. Fax 449-4519
Carroll MS 700/6-8
4027 Hathaway Rd 46818 260-637-5159
John Miller, prin. Fax 637-5478
Maple Creek MS 700/6-8
425 Union Chapel Rd 46845 260-338-0802
Mark Seele, prin. Fax 338-0369

Bishop Dwenger HS 1,000/9-12
1300 E Washington Center Rd 46825 260-496-4700
Fred Tone, prin. Fax 496-4702
Bishop Luers HS 500/9-12
333 E Paulding Rd 46816 260-456-1261
Mary Keefer, prin. Fax 456-1262
Blackhawk Christian S 800/PK-12
7400 E State Blvd 46815 260-493-7470
Dr. Sam Barfell, supt. Fax 493-7258
Brown Mackie College Post-Sec.
3000 E Coliseum Blvd 46805 260-484-4400
Canterbury S 700/PK-12
3210 Smith Rd 46804 260-407-3551
Jonathan Hancock, hdmstr. Fax 436-5137
Concordia Lutheran HS 700/9-12
1601 Saint Joe River Dr 46805 260-483-1102
John Marks, prin. Fax 471-0180
Concordia Theological Seminary Post-Sec.
6600 N Clinton St 46825 260-452-2100
Fort Wayne School of Radiography Post-Sec.
700 Broadway 46802 260-425-3990
Indiana Business College Post-Sec.
6413 N Clinton St 46825 260-471-7667
Indiana Institute of Technology Post-Sec.
1600 E Washington Blvd 46803 260-422-5561
Indiana Univ-Purdue Univ at Fort Wayne Post-Sec.
2101 E Coliseum Blvd 46805 260-481-6100
International Business College Post-Sec.
5699 Coventry Ln 46804 260-459-4500
ITT Technical Institute Post-Sec.
2810 Dupont Commerce Ct 46825 260-497-6200
Ivy Tech Community College - Northeast Post-Sec.
3800 N Anthony Blvd 46805 260-482-9171
Keystone S 200/PK-12
1800 Laverne Ave 46805 260-424-4523
Tammy Henline, dir. Fax 424-4525
Ravenscroft Beauty College Post-Sec.
6110 Stellhorn Rd 46815 260-486-8868
Rudae's School of Beauty Culture Post-Sec.
5317 Coldwater Rd 46825 260-483-2466
Taylor University Post-Sec.
1025 W Rudisill Blvd 46807 260-744-8600
The Masters of Cosmetology College Post-Sec.
1732 Bluffton Rd 46809 260-747-6667
University of St. Francis Post-Sec.
2701 Spring St 46808 260-434-3100

Fountain City, Wayne, Pop. 705
Northeastern Wayne SD 1,100/K-12
PO Box 406 47341 765-847-2821
Stephen Bailey, supt. Fax 847-5355
Northeastern JSHS 600/7-12
7295 N US Highway 27 47341 765-847-2591
Dennis Metzger, prin. Fax 847-5355

Fowler, Benton, Pop. 2,271
Benton Community SC 2,000/K-12
PO Box 512 47944 765-884-0850
Steven R. Wittenauer, supt. Fax 884-1614
www.benton.k12.in.us
Other Schools – See Oxford

Francesville, Pulaski, Pop. 869
West Central SC 900/K-12
117 E Montgomery St 47946 219-567-9161
Charles Mellon, supt. Fax 567-9761
www.west-central.k12.in.us
West Central HS 300/9-12
1852 S US Highway 421 47946 219-567-9119
Don Street, prin. Fax 567-2597
West Central MS 200/6-8
1850 S US Highway 421 47946 219-567-2534
Kay Beasey, prin. Fax 567-9535

Frankfort, Clinton, Pop. 16,432
Clinton Prairie SC 1,000/K-12
4431 W State Road 28 46041 765-659-1339
Charles Fink, supt. Fax 659-5305
www.clintonprairie.com/
Clinton Prairie JSHS 500/7-12
2400 S County Road 450 W 46041 765-659-3305
David Larsh, prin. Fax 659-3205

Frankfort Community SC 3,200/PK-12
50 S Maish Rd 46041 765-654-5585
Dr. Kevin Caress, supt. Fax 659-6220
www.frankfort.k12.in.us
Frankfort HS 900/9-12
1 S Maish Rd 46041 765-654-8545
Kay Antonelli, prin. Fax 654-9224
Frankfort MS 700/6-8
329 N Maish Rd 46041 765-659-3321
Mike McLaughlin, prin. Fax 659-6260

Franklin, Johnson, Pop. 21,747
Franklin Community SC 4,500/K-12
998 Grizzly Cub Dr 46131 317-738-5800
Dr. William Patterson, supt. Fax 738-5812
www.fcsc.k12.in.us
Custer Baker MS 1,100/6-8
101 W State Road 44 46131 317-738-5840
Pam Millikan, prin. Fax 738-5867
Franklin Community HS 1,300/9-12
625 Grizzly Cub Dr 46131 317-738-5700
Jon Milleman, prin. Fax 738-5703

Franklin College Post-Sec.
101 Branigin Blvd 46131 317-738-8000

Frankton, Madison, Pop. 1,864
Frankton-Lapel Community SD
Supt. — See Anderson
Frankton JSHS 600/7-12
610 E Clyde St 46044 765-754-7879
Jerry Hoss, prin. Fax 754-8594

Fremont, Steuben, Pop. 1,659
Fremont Community SD 1,200/K-12
PO Box 665 46737 260-495-5005
Ben Roederer, supt. Fax 495-9798
www.fremonteagles.org/
Fremont HS 400/9-12
PO Box 655 46737 260-495-9876
Rich Cory, prin. Fax 495-1838
Fremont MS 400/5-8
PO Box E 46737 260-495-6100
William Stitt, prin. Fax 495-7301

French Lick, Orange, Pop. 1,923
Springs Valley Community SC 900/K-12
498 S Larry Bird Blvd 47432 812-936-4474
Todd Pritchett, supt. Fax 936-9392
Springs Valley Community JSHS 400/6-12
326 S Larry Bird Blvd 47432 812-936-9984
Gary Boyd, prin. Fax 936-9266

Fulton, Fulton, Pop. 328
Caston SC 800/K-12
PO Box 8 46931 574-857-2035
Robert Huffman, supt. Fax 857-6795
www.caston.k12.in.us/
Caston JSHS 400/7-12
PO Box 128 46931 574-857-3505
Matt Rickett, prin. Fax 857-6795

Garrett, DeKalb, Pop. 5,760
Garrett-Keyser-Butler Community SD 1,700/K-12
900 E Warfield St 46738 260-357-3185
Alan Middleton, supt. Fax 357-4565
Garrett HS 500/9-12
801 E Houston St 46738 260-357-4114
Keeman Lobsiger, prin. Fax 357-5000
Garrett MS 500/5-8
801 E Houston St 46738 260-357-5745
Greg Moe, prin. Fax 357-3575
Other Schools – See Kendallville

Gary, Lake, Pop. 98,715
Gary Community SC 13,300/PK-12
620 E 10th Pl 46402 219-881-5401
Dr. Mary Steele, supt. Fax 881-4102
www.garycsc.k12.in.us/
Bailly MS 800/7-8
4621 Georgia St 46409 219-980-6326
Aurelia Weaver, prin. Fax 981-4463
Emerson Visual Performing Arts JSHS 600/6-12
716 E 7th Ave 46402 219-886-6555
Noah Riley, prin. Fax 881-4125
Gary Career Center Vo/Tech
1800 E 35th Ave 46409 219-962-7571
Jerome Hurt, prin. Fax 962-6269
Pulaski-Dunbar MS 800/7-8
920 E 19th Ave 46407 219-886-6581
Michael Collins, prin. Fax 881-2057
Roosevelt HS 900/9-12
730 W 25th Ave 46407 219-881-1500
Dr. Leotis Swopes, prin. Fax 881-1564
Tolleston MS 900/7-8
2700 W 19th Ave 46404 219-977-2145
Lucille Upshaw, prin. Fax 977-9359
Wallace HS 1,000/9-12
415 W 45th Ave 46408 219-980-6305
Janice Murray-Minor, prin. Fax 981-4462
West Side HS 1,300/9-12
900 Gerry St 46406 219-977-2100
Diane Rouse, prin. Fax 977-2168
Wirt HS 800/9-12
210 N Grand Blvd 46403 219-938-1161
Judy Dunlap, prin. Fax 938-7544

Lake Ridge SC 2,300/K-12
6111 W Ridge Rd 46408 219-838-1819
Dr. Sharon Johnson-Shirley, supt. Fax 989-7801
www.lakeridgeschools.homestead.com
Calumet HS 600/9-12
3900 Calhoun St 46408 219-838-6990
Michael Banham, prin. Fax 989-7849
Lake Ridge MS 500/6-8
3601 W 41st Ave 46408 219-980-0730
Robert Mastej, prin. Fax 980-0731

Indiana University Northwest Post-Sec.
3400 Broadway 46408 219-980-6500
Ivy Tech Community College - Northwest Post-Sec.
1440 E 35th Ave 46409 219-981-1111

Gas City, Grant, Pop. 5,819
Mississinewa Community SC 2,100/PK-12
424 E South A St 46933 765-674-8528
Michael Powell, supt. Fax 674-8529
www.olemiss.k12.in.us/
Baskett MS 500/6-8
125 N Broadway St 46933 765-674-8536
Terry Talbott, prin. Fax 677-4452
Mississinewa HS 600/9-12
1 Indian Trail Dr 46933 765-674-2248
Lezlie Winter, prin. Fax 677-4424

Gaston, Delaware, Pop. 963
Wes-Del Community SD 900/K-12
10290 N County Road 600 W 47342 765-358-4006
Steve McColley, supt. Fax 358-4065
www.wes-del.k12.in.us/
Wes-Del MSHS 500/6-12
10000 N County Road 600 W 47342 765-358-4091
Phillip Gardner, prin. Fax 358-3514

Georgetown, Floyd, Pop. 2,682
New Albany-Floyd County Consolidated SD
Supt. — See New Albany
Highland Hills MS 1,200/6-8
3492 Edwardsville Galena Rd 47122 812-923-4014
Steve Griffin, prin. Fax 923-4031

Goshen, Elkhart, Pop. 31,269
Fairfield Community SD 2,100/K-12
67240 County Road 31 46528 574-831-2188
Thomas Tumey, supt. Fax 831-5698
www.fairfield.k12.in.us
Fairfield JSHS 900/7-12
67530 US Highway 33 46526 574-831-2184
Philip Hoskins, prin. Fax 831-2187

Goshen Community SD 5,900/K-12
613 E Purl St 46526 574-533-8631
Bruce Stahly, supt. Fax 533-2505
www.goshenschools.org/
Goshen HS 1,600/9-12
1 Redskin Rd 46526 574-533-8651
Jim Kirkton, prin. Fax 534-1567
Goshen MS 1,400/6-8
1216 S Indiana Ave 46526 574-533-0391
Ann Eaton, prin. Fax 534-3042

Bethany Christian S 300/6-12
2904 S Main St 46526 574-534-2567
Allan Dueck, prin. Fax 533-0150
Clinton Christian S 100/K-12
61763 County Road 35 46528 574-642-3940
Ben Snyder, prin. Fax 642-3674
Goshen College Post-Sec.
1700 S Main St 46526 574-535-7000
Harrison Christian S 200/1-12
64784 County Road 11 46526 574-862-2515
Ruby Wittmer, prin.

Granger, Saint Joseph, Pop. 20,241
Penn-Harris-Madison SC
Supt. — See Mishawaka
Discovery MS 900/6-8
10050 Brummitt Rd 46530 574-674-6010
Sheryll Harper, prin. Fax 679-4214

Davenport College of Business Post-Sec.
7121 Grape Rd 46530 574-277-8447

Granger Christian S — 200/K-12
52025 Gumwood Rd 46530 — 574-272-5815
Ed Ryan, admin. — Fax 968-2664

Greencastle, Putnam, Pop. 10,065
Area 30 Career Center
1 N Calbert Way Ste A 46135 — 765-653-3515
Michael Walton, supt. — Fax 653-3618
Area 30 Career Center — Vo/Tech
1 N Calbert Way Ste A 46135 — 765-653-3515
Lora Wood, prin. — Fax 653-3618

Greencastle Community SC — 2,000/K-12
PO Box 480 46135 — 765-653-9771
Dr. Robert Green, supt. — Fax 653-1282
www.greencastle.k12.in.us
Greencastle HS — 600/9-12
910 E Washington St 46135 — 765-653-9711
James Church, prin. — Fax 653-4773
Greencastle MS — 400/6-8
400 Percy L Julian Dr 46135 — 765-653-9774
Shawn Gobert, prin. — Fax 653-5381

South Putnam Community SD — 1,400/K-12
3999 S US Highway 231 46135 — 765-653-3119
Bruce Bernhardt, supt. — Fax 653-7476
www.sputnam.k12.in.us
South Putnam JSHS — 700/7-12
1780 E US Highway 40 46135 — 765-653-3148
Keith Puckett, prin. — Fax 653-3149

DePauw University — Post-Sec.
101 E Seminary St 46135 — 765-658-4800

Greenfield, Hancock, Pop. 16,654
Greenfield-Central Community SD — 4,400/PK-12
110 W North St 46140 — 317-462-4434
Dr. Linda Gellert, supt. — Fax 467-4227
www.gcsc.k12.in.us/
Greenfield-Central HS — 1,300/9-12
810 N Broadway St 46140 — 317-462-9211
Steven Bryant, prin. — Fax 467-6723
Greenfield MS — 500/6-8
204 W Park Ave 46140 — 317-462-6827
James Bever, prin. — Fax 467-6730
Other Schools – See Maxwell

Hancock Memorial Hospital — Post-Sec.
801 N State St 46140 — 317-462-0457
PJ's College of Cosmetology — Post-Sec.
1400 W Main St 46140

Greensburg, Decatur, Pop. 10,536
Decatur County Community SD — 2,200/PK-12
1645 W State Road 46 47240 — 812-663-4595
Robert Cupp, supt. — Fax 663-4168
www.decaturco.k12.in.us
North Decatur JSHS — 600/7-12
3172 N State Road 3 47240 — 812-663-4204
Gary Cook, prin. — Fax 663-9606
South Decatur JSHS — 500/7-12
8885 S State Road 3 47240 — 812-591-3330
Bob Hacker, prin. — Fax 591-3331

Greensburg Community SD — 2,100/K-12
504 E Central Ave 47240 — 812-663-4774
Tom Hunter, supt. — Fax 663-5713
www.greensburg.k12.in.us
Greensburg Community HS — 600/9-12
1000 E Central Ave 47240 — 812-663-7176
Phil Chapple, prin. — Fax 663-8911
Greensburg Community JHS — 500/6-8
505 E Central Ave 47240 — 812-663-7523
Garry Moore, prin. — Fax 663-9425

Greentown, Howard, Pop. 2,459
Eastern Howard SC — 1,400/K-12
221 W Main St Ste 1 46936 — 765-628-3391
Dr. Stephen C. Healy, supt. — Fax 628-5017
www.eastern.k12.in.us
Eastern JSHS — 700/7-12
421 S Harrison St 46936 — 765-628-3333
Ronald Matas, prin. — Fax 628-5021

Greenwood, Johnson, Pop. 42,236
Center Grove Community SC — 7,100/K-12
2929 S Morgantown Rd 46143 — 317-881-9326
Dr. Candace Milhon-Baer, supt. — Fax 881-0241
www.centergrove.k12.in.us
Center Grove HS — 2,200/9-12
2717 S Morgantown Rd 46143 — 317-881-0581
Matt Shockley, prin. — Fax 885-4509
Center Grove MS Central — 800/6-8
4900 W Stones Crossing Rd 46143 — 317-882-9391
Jack Parker, prin. — Fax 885-4534
Center Grove MS North — 900/6-8
202 N Morgantown Rd 46142 — 317-885-8800
Jim Snapp, prin. — Fax 885-3388

Central Nine Career Center SD
1999 US Highway 31 S 46143 — 317-888-4401
Timothy Lavery, supt. — Fax 885-8670
www.central9.k12.in.us
Central Nine Career Center — Vo/Tech
1999 US Highway 31 S 46143 — 317-888-4401
John Strader, prin. — Fax 885-8670

Greenwood Community SC — 3,800/K-12
605 W Smith Valley Rd 46142 — 317-889-4060
Dr. David E. Edds, supt. — Fax 889-4068
oak.gws.k12.in.us/
Greenwood Community HS — 1,200/9-12
615 W Smith Valley Rd 46142 — 317-889-4000
James Kaylor, prin. — Fax 889-4039
Greenwood MS — 900/6-8
523 S Madison Ave 46142 — 317-889-4040
Vicki Noblitt, prin. — Fax 889-4044

Greenwood Christian Academy — 300/PK-12
PO Box 387 46142 — 317-859-4150
Bruce Peters, hdmstr. — Fax 859-9072

Griffith, Lake, Pop. 16,666
Griffith Public SD — 2,700/K-12
132 N Broad St 46319 — 219-924-4250
Peter N. Morikis, supt. — Fax 922-5933
www.griffith.k12.in.us
Griffith HS — 800/9-12
600 N Wiggs St 46319 — 219-924-4281
Bonnie Manuel, prin. — Fax 922-5920
Griffith MS — 500/7-8
600 N Raymond St 46319 — 219-924-4280
Terry Mucha, prin. — Fax 922-5927

Hagerstown, Wayne, Pop. 1,673
Nettle Creek SC — 1,300/PK-12
297 E Northmarket St 47346 — 765-489-4543
Joseph Backmeyer, supt. — Fax 489-4914
www.nettlecreek.k12.in.us
Hagerstown JSHS — 600/7-12
701 Baker Rd 47346 — 765-489-4511
Mark Childs, prin. — Fax 489-4333

Hamilton, DeKalb, Pop. 1,504
Hamilton Community SD — 700/K-12
901 S Wayne St 46742 — 260-488-2513
Mark Gould, supt. — Fax 488-2348
www.hamiltoncomm.com/
Hamilton Community JSHS — 300/7-12
903 S Wayne St 46742 — 260-488-2161
Kenneth Webb, prin. — Fax 488-3149

Hamlet, Starke, Pop. 768
Oregon-Davis SC — 700/K-12
5998 N 750 E 46532 — 574-867-2111
William Rentschler, supt. — Fax 867-8191
www.od.k12.in.us
Oregon-Davis JSHS — 300/7-12
5990 N 750 E 46532 — 574-867-4561
Greg Briles, prin. — Fax 867-2481

Hammond, Lake, Pop. 79,217
Hammond CSD — 13,100/PK-12
41 E Williams St 46320 — 219-933-2400
Dr. Walter Watkins, supt. — Fax 933-2495
www.hammond.k12.in.us
Area Career Center — Vo/Tech
5727 S Sohl Ave 46320 — 219-933-2428
Audra Peterson, prin. — Fax 933-1680
Eggers MS — 900/6-8
5825 Blaine Ave 46320 — 219-933-2449
Barbara Fleming, prin. — Fax 933-1675
Gavit MSHS — 1,800/6-12
1670 175th St 46324 — 219-989-7328
Chuck Hall, prin. — Fax 989-7333
Hammond HS — 900/9-12
5926 S Calumet Ave 46320 — 219-933-2442
Otis Watkins, prin. — Fax 933-1688
Morton HS — 900/9-12
6915 Grand Ave 46323 — 219-989-7316
Theresa Mayerik, prin. — Fax 989-7321
Scott MS — 900/6-8
3635 173rd St 46323 — 219-989-7340
Bobbie Escalante, prin. — Fax 989-7342
Other Schools – See Whiting

Bishop Noll Institute — 500/7-12
1519 E Hoffman St 46327 — 219-932-9058
Scott Fech, prin. — Fax 853-1736
Purdue University — Post-Sec.
2200 169th St 46323 — 219-989-2993
St. Margaret Hospital — Post-Sec.
5454 S Hohman Ave 46320 — 219-932-2300
Sawyer College — Post-Sec.
7833 Indianapolis Blvd 46324 — 219-844-0100
Shepherd's Academy — 50/K-12
6518 Grand Ave 46323 — 219-844-8900
Christin Kiesling, prin.

Hanover, Jefferson, Pop. 3,768
Southwestern-Jefferson County Cons SC — 1,400/K-12
239 S Main Cross St 47243 — 812-866-6250
Stephen Telfer, supt. — Fax 866-6256
www.swjcs.k12.in.us/
Southwestern MSHS — 800/6-12
167 S Main Cross St 47243 — 812-866-6230
Mike Costlow, prin. — Fax 866-4680

Hanover College — Post-Sec.
PO Box 108 47243 — 812-866-7000

Hartford City, Blackford, Pop. 6,684
Blackford County SD — 2,300/PK-12
668 W 200 S 47348 — 765-348-7550
Gerald Chabot, supt. — Fax 348-7552
www.bcs.k12.in.us
Blackford HS — 700/9-12
2392 N State Road 3 47348 — 765-348-7560
Dr. Sue Neat, prin. — Fax 348-7568
Hartford City MS — 400/6-8
800 W Van Cleve St 47348 — 765-348-7590
Andrew Glentzer, prin. — Fax 348-7593

Hebron, Porter, Pop. 3,570
Metro SD of Boone Township — 1,000/K-12
307 S Main St 46341 — 219-996-4771
George Letz, supt. — Fax 996-5777
www.hebronschools.k12.in.us/
Hebron HS — 300/9-12
509 S Main St 46341 — 219-996-4771
David Howenstine, prin. — Fax 996-5777
Hebron MS — 200/6-8
307 S Main St 46341 — 219-996-4771
Rick Ankney, prin. — Fax 996-5777

Henryville, Clark
West Clark Community SC
Supt. — See Sellersburg
Henryville JSHS — 400/7-12
215 N Ferguson St 47126 — 812-294-1455
Denise H. Bessler, prin. — Fax 294-4276

Highland, Lake, Pop. 23,172
Highland SC — 3,400/K-12
9145 Kennedy Ave 46322 — 219-924-7400
Renner Ventling, supt. — Fax 922-5637
www.highland.k12.in.us
Highland HS — 1,100/9-12
9135 Erie St 46322 — 219-922-5610
James Conway, prin. — Fax 922-5636
Highland MS — 600/7-8
2941 41st St 46322 — 219-922-5620
Kenneth Winston, prin. — Fax 922-5637

Creative Hair Styling Academy — Post-Sec.
2549 Highway Ave 46322 — 219-838-2004

Hobart, Lake, Pop. 27,768
Hobart CSD — 3,700/K-12
32 E 7th St 46342 — 219-942-8885
Dr. John Leach, supt. — Fax 942-0081
www.hobart.k12.in.us
Hobart HS — 1,100/9-12
36 E 8th St 46342 — 219-942-8521
David Spitzer, prin. — Fax 942-3326
Hobart MS — 900/6-8
705 E 4th St 46342 — 219-942-8541
Mark Lutze, prin. — Fax 947-7194

River Forest Community SC — 1,400/PK-12
3334 Michigan St 46342 — 219-962-2909
Dr. James Rice, supt. — Fax 962-4951
www.rfcsc.k12.in.us
River Forest HS — 300/9-12
3300 Indiana St 46342 — 219-962-7551
Andrew Wielgus, prin. — Fax 962-8338
River Forest JHS — 200/7-8
3250 Indiana St 46342 — 219-962-7811
Christine Cicero, prin. — Fax 962-7554

College of Court Reporting — Post-Sec.
111 W 10th St Ste 111 46342 — 219-942-1459

Hope, Bartholomew, Pop. 2,185
Flat Rock-Hawcreek SC — 1,100/PK-12
PO Box 34 47246 — 812-546-2000
Dr. Phillip Deardorff, supt. — Fax 546-5617
www.flatrock.k12.in.us
Hauser JSHS — 600/7-12
9273 N State Road 9 47246 — 812-546-4421
Tim Stephens, prin. — Fax 546-2005

Howe, Lagrange

Howe Military S — 200/5-12
PO Box 240 46746 — 260-562-2131
James Malerich, hdmstr. — Fax 562-3678

Huntertown, Allen, Pop. 2,136

Heritage Mission S — 50/K-12
1825 W Shoaff Rd 46748 — 260-637-9980
David Mains, dir. — Fax 637-0861

Huntingburg, Dubois, Pop. 5,929
Southwest Dubois County SC — 1,800/PK-12
PO Box 398 47542 — 812-683-3971
Terry Enlow, supt. — Fax 683-2752
www.swdubois.k12.in.us
Southridge HS — 600/9-12
1110 S Main St 47542 — 812-683-2272
Mike Eineman, prin. — Fax 683-2010
Southridge MS — 400/6-8
1112 S Main St 47542 — 812-683-3372
Al Mihajlovits, prin. — Fax 683-2817

Huntington, Huntington, Pop. 17,011
Huntington County Community SC — 5,800/PK-12
1360 Warren Rd 46750 — 260-356-7812
Tracey Shafer, supt. — Fax 358-2216
www.hccsc.k12.in.us
Crestview MS — 600/6-8
1151 W 500 N 46750 — 260-356-6210
Tom Alexander, prin. — Fax 358-2232
Huntington North HS — 2,000/9-12
450 MacGahan St 46750 — 260-356-6104
Ken Kline, prin. — Fax 358-2210
Riverview MS — 600/6-8
2465 Waterworks Rd 46750 — 260-356-0910
Curt Crago, prin. — Fax 358-2243

Huntington College — Post-Sec.
2303 College Ave 46750 — 260-356-6000

Hymera, Sullivan, Pop. 823
Northeast SC — 1,500/PK-12
PO Box 493 47855 — 812-383-5761
Richard Walters, supt. — Fax 383-4591
www.nesc.k12.in.us/
Other Schools – See Dugger, Farmersburg

Indianapolis, Marion, Pop. 783,612
Franklin Twp Community SC — 7,400/PK-12
6141 S Franklin Rd 46259 — 317-862-2411
Walter Bourke, supt. — Fax 862-7238
www.ftcsc.k12.in.us
Franklin Central HS — 1,800/9-12
6215 S Franklin Rd 46259 — 317-862-6646
Kevin Koers, prin. — Fax 862-7262
Franklin Twp. MS — 1,200/7-8
6019 S Franklin Rd 46259 — 317-862-2446
Leland Thompson, prin. — Fax 862-7271

Indianapolis SD 34,400/PK-12
120 E Walnut St 46204 317-226-4000
Dr. Eugene White, supt. Fax 226-4936
www.ips.k12.in.us
Arlington HS 1,600/9-12
4825 N Arlington Ave 46226 317-226-2345
Jacqueline Greenwood, prin. Fax 226-3009
Arsenal Technical HS 2,000/9-12
1500 E Michigan St 46201 317-693-5300
Sarah Bogard, admin. Fax 226-3932
Attucks MS 900/6-9
1140 Dr Mrtn Lthr Kng Jr St 46202 317-226-2800
Robert Faulkens, prin. Fax 226-3495
Broad Ripple HS 1,500/9-12
1115 Broad Ripple Ave 46220 317-693-5700
Greg Allen, admin. Fax 226-3783
Career & Technology Center Vo/Tech
725 N Oriental St 46202 317-693-5430
Luberta Jenkins, prin. Fax 226-3709
Donnan MS 600/7-8
1202 E Troy Ave 46203 317-226-4272
Dexter Suggs, prin. Fax 226-4355
Forest Manor MS 200/7-8
4501 E 32nd St 46218 317-226-4363
Mattie Soloman, prin. Fax 226-4328
Gambold MS 500/7-8
3725 N Kiel Ave 46224 317-226-4108
Yvonne Rambo, prin. Fax 226-3750
Harshman MS 500/7-8
1501 E 10th St 46201 317-226-4101
Linda Casey, prin. Fax 226-3444
Howe Academy 1,200/7-12
4900 Julian Ave 46201 317-693-5590
Robert Berry, prin. Fax 226-4033
Key Learning Community S - River 500/K-12
777 S White River Pkwy W Dr 46221 317-226-4992
Chris Kunkel, prin. Fax 226-3049
Longfellow MS 300/7-8
510 Laurel St 46203 317-226-4228
Phyllis Barnes, prin. Fax 226-3756
Manual HS 1,500/9-12
2405 Madison Ave 46225 317-226-2200
Richard Grismore, prin. Fax 226-3836
Marshall MS 500/7-8
10101 E 38th St 46235 317-693-5460
Jeffrey White, prin. Fax 226-3718
McFarland MS 200/7-8
3200 E Raymond St 46203 317-226-4112
Robert Guffin, prin. Fax 226-3744
Northwest HS 1,300/9-12
5525 W 34th St 46224 317-693-5600
Roy Simpson, prin. Fax 226-3409
Shortridge MS 600/7-8
3401 N Meridian St 46208 317-226-2810
Linda Davis, prin. Fax 226-3725
Sidener MS 200/7-8
2424 Kessler Boulevard E Dr 46220 317-226-4259
James Whisler, prin. Fax 226-3059
Washington Community HS 800/7-12
2215 W Washington St 46222 317-693-5555
Keith Burke, prin. Fax 226-3273
Hope Academy/Day Adult HS Adult
1301 E 16th St 46202 317-226-4116
Vickie Nowland, prin. Fax 226-4524

Metro SD of Decatur Township 4,800/K-12
5275 Kentucky Ave 46221 317-856-5265
Donald Stinson, supt. Fax 856-2156
www.msddecatur.k12.in.us
Decatur Central HS 1,600/9-12
5251 Kentucky Ave 46221 317-856-5288
Joe Preda, prin. Fax 856-2157
Decatur MS 1,000/7-8
5108 S High School Rd 46221 317-856-5274
Mark Anderson, prin. Fax 856-2163

Metro SD of Lawrence Township 15,500/PK-12
7601 E 56th St 46226 317-423-8200
Dr. Michael Copper, supt. Fax 543-3534
www.ltschools.org/
Belzer MS 1,400/6-8
7555 E 56th St 46226 317-545-7411
Ronald Davie, prin. Fax 543-3355
Craig MS 1,300/6-8
6501 Sunnyside Rd 46236 317-823-6805
Troy Knoderer, prin. Fax 823-5223
Fall Creek Valley MS 1,400/6-8
9701 E 63rd St 46236 317-823-5490
James Joiner, prin. Fax 823-5497
Lawrence Central HS 2,200/9-12
7300 E 56th St 46226 317-545-5301
Edward Freije, prin. Fax 543-3348
Lawrence North HS 2,900/9-12
7802 Hague Rd 46256 317-849-9455
Steve Goeglein, prin. Fax 576-6406
McKenzie Career Center Vo/Tech
7250 E 75th St 46256 317-576-6420
Barry Norman, prin. Fax 849-2546

Metro SD of Perry Township 13,700/PK-12
6548 Orinoco Ave 46227 317-789-3700
Dennis Nichols, supt. Fax 789-3709
www.msdpt.k12.in.us
Perry Meridian HS 1,900/9-12
401 W Meridian School Rd 46217 317-789-4400
Joan Ellis, prin. Fax 789-4479
Perry Meridian MS 1,200/7-8
202 W Meridian School Rd 46217 317-789-4100
Scott Johnson, prin. Fax 865-2710
Southport HS 1,800/9-12
971 E Banta Rd 46227 317-789-4800
Barbara Brouwer, prin. Fax 780-4325
Southport MS 1,000/7-8
5715 S Keystone Ave 46227 317-789-4600
Robert Bohannon, prin. Fax 780-4302

Metro SD of Pike Township 10,600/PK-12
6901 Zionsville Rd 46268 317-293-0393
Nathaniel Jones, supt. Fax 297-7896
www.pike.k12.in.us
Guion Creek MS 900/6-8
4401 W 52nd St 46254 317-293-4549
Ms. Kurt Benjamin, prin. Fax 298-2794
Lincoln MS 900/6-8
5353 W 71st St 46268 317-291-9499
Shelly Haley, prin. Fax 297-1673
New Augusta Public Academy North 800/6-8
6450 Rodebaugh Rd 46268 317-387-4328
Stan Hall, prin. Fax 388-7786
Pike Freshman Center 800/9-9
6801 Zionsville Rd 46268 317-347-8600
Shawn Smith, prin. Fax 347-8555
Pike HS 2,000/10-12
5401 W 71st St 46268 317-291-5250
Debra Jacobs, prin. Fax 328-7239

Metro SD of Warren Township 12,000/PK-12
975 N Post Rd 46219 317-869-4300
Dr. Peggy Hinckley, supt. Fax 869-4348
www.warren.k12.in.us
Creston MS 1,200/6-8
10925 Prospect St 46239 317-532-6800
Sheri Marcotte, prin. Fax 532-6899
Raymond Park MS 900/6-8
8575 E Raymond St 46239 317-532-8900
Kathy Deck, prin. Fax 532-8999
Stonybrook MS 1,000/6-8
11300 Stonybrook Dr 46229 317-532-8800
Jimmy Meadows, prin. Fax 532-8899
Walker Career Center Vo/Tech
9651 E 21st St 46229 317-532-6150
Lou Anne Schwenn, prin. Fax 532-6199
Warren Central HS 3,500/9-12
9500 E 16th St 46229 317-532-6200
Rich Shepler, prin. Fax 532-6459

Metro SD of Washington Township 10,200/PK-12
8550 Woodfield Crossing Blv 46240 317-845-9400
Dr. R. Stephen Tegarden, supt. Fax 205-3385
www.msdwt.k12.in.us
Eastwood MS 800/6-8
4401 E 62nd St 46220 317-259-5401
Sylvia Lane, prin. Fax 259-5407
Light Career Center Vo/Tech
1901 E 86th St 46240 317-259-5265
Shawn Wright-Browner, prin. Fax 259-5266
North Central HS 3,300/9-12
1801 E 86th St 46240 317-259-5301
C.E. Quandt, prin. Fax 259-5369
Northview MS 900/6-8
8401 Westfield Rd 46240 317-259-5421
Nikki Tsangaris, prin. Fax 259-5431
Westlane MS 700/6-8
1301 W 73rd St 46260 317-259-5412
Linda Lawrence, prin. Fax 259-5409

Metro SD of Wayne Township 12,400/PK-12
1220 S High School Rd 46241 317-243-8251
Terry Thompson Ed.D., supt. Fax 243-5744
www.wayne.k12.in.us
Chapel Hill 7th & 8th Grade Center 900/7-8
1155 S Girls School Rd 46231 317-241-9285
Jeff Hubble, prin. Fax 243-5728
Davis 9th Grade Center 9-9
1150 N Girls School Rd 46214 317-227-4500
John Taylor, prin. Fax 484-3124
Davis SHS 2,900/10-12
1200 N Girls School Rd 46214 317-244-7691
Joel McKinney, prin. Fax 243-5506
Lynhurst 7th & 8th Grade Center 600/7-8
2805 S Lynhurst Dr 46241 317-247-6265
Dan Wilson, prin. Fax 243-5532

A Cut Above Beauty College Post-Sec.
3810 E Southport Rd 46237 317-781-0959
Art Institute of Indianapolis Post-Sec.
3500 Depauw Blvd 46268 317-613-4800
Aviation Institute of Maintenance Post-Sec.
7251 W McCarty St 46241 317-243-4519
Baptist Academy 300/PK-12
2565 Villa Ave 46203 317-788-1587
Barbara Frye, prin. Fax 781-4759
Bishop Silas Chatard HS 800/9-12
5885 Crittenden Ave 46220 317-251-1451
Al Holok, dean Fax 251-3648
Brebeuf Jesuit Prep S 800/9-12
2801 W 86th St 46268 317-872-7050
Andrew F. Noga, prin. Fax 876-4712
Butler University Post-Sec.
4600 Sunset Ave 46208 317-940-8000
Calvary Christian S 200/PK-12
902 Fletcher Ave 46203 317-262-4034
Charles Barcus, prin. Fax 262-4029
Cardinal Ritter HS 400/7-12
3360 W 30th St 46222 317-924-4333
Jo Hoy, prin. Fax 927-7822
Cathedral HS 1,200/9-12
5225 E 56th St 46226 317-542-1481
David Worland, prin. Fax 543-5050
Christian Theological Seminary Post-Sec.
1000 W 42nd St 46208 317-924-1331
Colonial Christian S 300/PK-12
8140 Union Chapel Rd 46240 317-253-0649
Daniel Nelson, prin. Fax 254-2840
Community Hospital of Indianapolis Post-Sec.
1500 N Ritter Ave 46219 317-355-5529
Covenant Christian HS 400/9-12
7525 W 21st St 46214 317-390-0202
Brian Hudson, prin. Fax 390-6823
Crossroads Bible College Post-Sec.
601 N Shortridge Rd 46219 317-352-8736
DeVry University Post-Sec.
9100 Keystone Xing Ste 350 46240 317-581-8854

Eagledale Christian S 300/K-12
4950 W 34th St 46224 317-291-4783
Galen Fitzsimmons, prin. Fax 291-7568
Heritage Christian S 1,700/K-12
6401 E 75th St 46250 317-849-3441
Ray Casey, supt. Fax 594-5863
Horizon Christian S 300/PK-12
7702 Indian Lake Rd 46236 317-823-4538
Frank Onorio, admin. Fax 826-2438
Indiana Business College Post-Sec.
5460 Victory Dr Ste 100 46203 317-783-5100
Indiana Business College Post-Sec.
550 E Washington St 46204 800-999-9229
Indiana Business College Northwest Post-Sec.
6300 Technology Dr 46278 317-873-6500
Indianapolis Christian S 100/K-12
620 E 10th St 46202 317-636-4560
Betty Speight, prin. Fax 636-1160
Indiana School for the Deaf Post-Sec.
1200 E 42nd St 46205 317-924-4374
Indiana State School for the Blind Post-Sec.
7725 N College Ave 46240 317-253-1481
Indiana University School of Allied Hlth Post-Sec.
1140 W Michigan St 46202 317-274-4702
Indiana Univ-Purdue Univ at Indianapolis Post-Sec.
355 Lansing St 46202 317-274-5555
Indiana Vocational Technical College Post-Sec.
PO Box 1763 46206 317-921-4882
International Business College Post-Sec.
7205 Shadeland Station Way 46256 317-841-6400
ITT Technical Institute Post-Sec.
9511 Angola Ct 46268 317-875-8640
Ivy Tech Community College Central IN Post-Sec.
1 W 26th St 46208 317-921-4882
Kaye Beauty College Post-Sec.
6346 E 82nd St 46250 317-576-8000
Lincoln Technical Institute Post-Sec.
7225 Winton Dr # 128 46268 800-554-4465
Lutheran HS 300/9-12
5555 S Arlington Ave 46237 317-787-5474
Gary St. Clair, dir. Fax 787-2794
Marian College Post-Sec.
3200 Cold Spring Rd 46222 317-955-6000
Martin University Post-Sec.
PO Box 18567 46218 317-543-3235
MedTech College Post-Sec.
6612 E 75th St Ste 300 46250 317-845-0100
Methodist Hosp/Clarian Health Partners Post-Sec.
PO Box 1367 46206 317-929-5900
Park Tudor S 1,000/PK-12
7200 N College Ave 46240 317-415-2700
Douglas S. Jennings, prin. Fax 254-2714
PJ's College of Cosmetology Post-Sec.
5539 Madison Ave 46227
Professional Careers Institute Post-Sec.
7302 Woodland Dr 46278 317-299-6001
Roncalli HS 1,000/9-12
3300 Prague Rd 46227 317-787-8277
Charles Weisenbach, prin. Fax 788-4095
Scecina Memorial HS 400/9-12
5000 Nowland Ave 46201 317-356-6377
Tom Davis, prin. Fax 322-4287
Summit Academy 100/1-12
3600 W 96th St 46268 317-334-9335
Clair Staley, hdmstr. Fax 334-7301
University of Indianapolis Post-Sec.
1400 E Hanna Ave 46227 317-788-3368

Jasonville, Greene, Pop. 2,508
Metro SD Shakamak 900/K-12
RR 2 Box 42 47438 812-665-3550
C.G. Epple, supt. Fax 665-5001
www.shakamak.k12.in.us/
Shakamak JSHS 400/7-12
RR 2 Box 42 47438 812-665-3550
Vanessa Hodge, prin. Fax 665-5001

Jasper, Dubois, Pop. 13,767
Greater Jasper Consolidated SD 3,100/PK-12
1520 Saint Charles St 47546 812-482-1801
Dr. Jerrill Vandeventer, supt. Fax 482-3388
www.gjcs.k12.in.us
Jasper HS 1,100/9-12
1600 Saint Charles St 47546 812-482-6050
Jerald Roberts, prin. Fax 634-3971
Jasper MS 700/6-8
3600 N Portersville Rd 47546 812-482-6454
Matt Day, prin. Fax 482-6457

Jeffersonville, Clark, Pop. 28,621
Greater Clark County SD 10,400/PK-12
2112 Utica Sellersburg Rd 47130 812-283-0701
Dr. Thomas Rohr, supt. Fax 288-4804
www.gcs.k12.in.us
Jeffersonville HS 2,000/9-12
2315 Allison Ln 47130 812-282-6601
Steve Morris, prin. Fax 288-4812
Parkview MS 900/6-8
1600 Brigman Ave 47130 812-288-4844
Mark Laughner, prin. Fax 288-2849
River Valley MS 900/6-8
2220 Veterans Pkwy 47130 812-288-4848
Vicki Lete, prin. Fax 288-4851
Other Schools – See Charlestown, New Washington

Mid-America College of Funeral Service Post-Sec.
3111 Hamburg Pike 47130 812-288-8878

Jonesboro, Grant, Pop. 1,759

King's Academy 100/K-12
1201 S Water St 46938 765-674-1722
Tony Miner, prin. Fax 674-1722

Kendallville, Noble, Pop. 10,018
East Noble SC 3,800/K-12
702 Dowling St 46755 260-347-2502
Dr. H. Steve Sprunger, supt. Fax 347-0111
www.eastnoble.net
East Noble HS 1,200/9-12
901 Garden St 46755 260-347-2032
Ann Linson, prin. Fax 347-2362
Kendallville Central MS 500/6-8
401 E Diamond St 46755 260-347-0100
James Taylor, prin. Fax 347-7168

Garrett-Keyser-Butler Community SD
Supt. — See Garrett
Four County Area Voc Coop Vo/Tech
1607 Dowling St 46755 260-349-0250
Tim Holcomb, prin. Fax 349-0240

Kentland, Newton, Pop. 1,747
South Newton SC 1,000/PK-12
110 N 3rd St 47951 219-474-5184
Ed Corbin, supt. Fax 474-6966
www.newton.k12.in.us/
South Newton HS 300/9-12
13102 S 50 E 47951 219-474-5167
Dan Nelson, prin. Fax 474-6592
South Newton MS 300/6-8
13100 S 50 E 47951 219-474-5167
Dan Nelson, prin. Fax 474-3624

Knightstown, Henry, Pop. 2,026
C.A. Beard Memorial SC 1,400/K-12
345 N Adams St 46148 765-345-5101
David McGuire Ed.D., supt. Fax 345-5103
www.cabeard.k12.in.us
Knightstown HS 400/9-12
8149 W US Highway 40 46148 765-345-5153
James Diagostino, prin. Fax 345-7977
Knightstown IS 400/5-8
1 Panther Trl 46148 765-345-5455
Don Scheumann, prin. Fax 345-5523

Morton Memorial S 100/1-12
10892 N State Road 140 46148 765-345-5141
Patrick Porter, prin. Fax 345-2063

Knightsville, Clay, Pop. 635
Clay Community SD 4,700/PK-12
PO Box 169 47857 812-443-4461
Dr. Dan Schroeder, supt. Fax 442-0849
www.clay.k12.in.us
Other Schools – See Brazil, Clay City

Knox, Starke, Pop. 3,667
Knox Community SC 2,000/K-12
2 Redskin Trl 46534 574-772-1600
Kimberly Knott, supt. Fax 772-1608
www.knox.k12.in.us
Knox Community HS 600/9-12
1 Redskin Trl 46534 574-772-1670
James Condon, prin. Fax 772-1681
Knox Community MS 500/6-8
901 S Main St 46534 574-772-1654
Steve Cronk, prin. Fax 772-1664

Kokomo, Howard, Pop. 46,178
Kokomo-Center Twp Consolidated SC 7,000/PK-12
PO Box 2188 46904 765-455-8000
Dr. Thomas Little, supt. Fax 455-8018
www.kokomoschools.com
Bon Air MS 300/6-8
2796 N Apperson Way 46901 765-454-7035
Chris Lagoni, prin. Fax 454-7039
Central MS 500/6-8
303 E Superior St 46901 765-454-7000
Brian Van Buskirk, prin. Fax 454-7007
Kokomo Area Career Ctr Vo/Tech
2415 S Berkley Rd 46902 765-455-8021
James Little, dir. Fax 455-6850
Kokomo HS 2,000/9-12
2501 S Berkley Rd 46902 765-455-8040
Harold Canady, prin. Fax 455-8060
Lafayette Park MS 500/6-8
923 Korby St 46901 765-454-7065
Doug Arnold, prin. Fax 454-7067
Maple Crest MS 400/6-8
2727 S Washington St 46902 765-455-8085
Dan Hogan, prin. Fax 455-8062

Northwestern SC 1,700/K-12
3075 N Washington St 46901 765-452-3060
Ryan Snoddy, supt. Fax 452-3065
nwsc.k12.in.us
Northwestern HS 500/9-12
3431 N County Road 400 W 46901 765-454-2332
Tim Edsell, prin. Fax 454-2333
Northwestern MS 300/7-8
3431 N County Road 400 W 46901 765-454-2323
Brett Davis, prin. Fax 457-2324

Taylor Community SC 1,600/PK-12
3750 E 300 S 46902 765-453-3035
Dr. Ron Mayes, supt. Fax 455-8531
www.taylor.k12.in.us
Taylor HS 500/9-12
3794 E 300 S 46902 765-453-1101
A.D. Little, prin. Fax 455-5163
Taylor MS 400/6-8
3794 E 300 S 46902 765-455-5186
Derick Bright, prin. Fax 455-5157

Indiana University at Kokomo Post-Sec.
PO Box 9003 46904 765-453-2000
Ivy Tech Community College - Kokomo Post-Sec.
PO Box 1373 46903 765-459-0561
Rudae's School of Beauty Culture Post-Sec.
208 W Jefferson St 46901 765-459-4197
St. Joseph Hospital & Health Center Post-Sec.
1907 W Sycamore St 46901 765-452-5611

Kouts, Porter, Pop. 1,766
East Porter County SC 2,000/K-12
PO Box 370 46347 219-766-2214
Dr. Ron Gardin, supt. Fax 766-2885
www.epcsc.k12.in.us
Kouts MSHS 400/6-12
PO Box 699 46347 219-766-2231
Terry Brownell, prin. Fax 766-3763
Other Schools – See Valparaiso

La Crosse, LaPorte, Pop. 561
Dewey Township SD
Supt. — See La Porte
La Crosse S 100/K-12
PO Box 360 46348 219-754-2461
M. Freeman, prin. Fax 754-2511

Lafayette, Tippecanoe, Pop. 60,459
Lafayette SC 5,600/K-12
2300 Cason St 47904 765-771-6000
Edward Eiler, supt. Fax 771-6049
www.lsc.k12.in.us
Jefferson HS 2,000/9-12
1801 S 18th St 47905 765-772-4700
Glade Montgomery, prin. Fax 772-4713
Tecumseh JHS 700/7-8
2101 S 18th St 47905 765-772-4750
Brett Gruetzmacher, prin. Fax 772-4763

Tippecanoe SC 10,600/K-12
21 Elston Rd 47909 765-474-2481
Richard Wood, supt. Fax 474-0533
www.tsc.k12.in.us
East Tipp MS 400/6-8
7501 E 300 N 47905 765-589-3566
Linda McTaggart, prin. Fax 589-3129
McCutcheon HS 1,500/9-12
4951 US Highway 231 S 47909 765-474-1488
John Beeker, prin. Fax 477-9710
Southwestern MS 300/6-8
2100 W 800 S 47909 765-538-3025
Marilyn Ferguson, prin. Fax 538-2877
Wainwright MS 400/6-8
7501 E 700 S 47905 765-523-2151
Neal McCutcheon, prin. Fax 523-2709
Wea Ridge MS 600/6-8
4410 S 150 E 47909 765-471-2164
Cory Marshall, prin. Fax 474-5347
Other Schools – See Battle Ground, West Lafayette

Central Catholic HS 400/7-12
2410 S 9th St 47909 765-474-2496
Joe Brettnacher, prin. Fax 474-8752
First Assembly Christian Academy 100/PK-12
108 Beck Ln 47909 765-477-5803
Christopher Johns, prin. Fax 474-5845
Indiana Business College Post-Sec.
2 Executive Dr 47905 765-447-9550
Ivy Tech Community College - Lafayette Post-Sec.
PO Box 6299 47903 765-772-9100
Lafayette Beauty Academy Post-Sec.
833 Ferry St 47901 765-742-0068
St. Elizabeth School of Nursing Post-Sec.
1508 Tippecanoe St 47904 765-423-6400

Lagrange, Lagrange, Pop. 2,972
Lakeland SC 2,300/K-12
200 S Cherry St 46761 260-499-2400
Risa Herber, supt. Fax 463-4800
www.lakeland.k12.in.us
Lakeland HS 700/9-12
805 E 075 N 46761 260-499-2470
Patrick Boles, prin. Fax 463-4058
Lakeland MS 600/6-8
1055 E 075 N 46761 260-499-2480
Chris Smith, prin. Fax 463-2648

Prairie Heights Community SC 1,700/K-12
305 S 1150 E 46761 260-351-3214
Paul Thomas, supt. Fax 351-3614
www.ph.k12.in.us/
Prairie Heights HS 500/9-12
245 S 1150 E 46761 260-351-3214
Pat McLaughlin, prin. Fax 351-3048
Prairie Heights MS 600/5-8
395 S 1150 E 46761 260-351-3214
Brenda Rummel, prin. Fax 351-2182

Lake Station, Lake, Pop. 13,565
Lake Station Community SD 1,500/PK-12
2500 Pike St 46405 219-962-1159
Dan DeHaven, supt. Fax 962-4011
www.lakes.k12.in.us
Edison JSHS 600/7-12
3304 Parkside Ave 46405 219-962-8531
Bruce Bush, prin. Fax 962-2064

Lakeville, Saint Joseph, Pop. 557
Union-North United SC 1,300/K-12
22601 Tyler Rd 46536 574-784-8141
Larry Phillips, supt. Fax 784-2181
www.unorth.k12.in.us
Laville JSHS 700/7-12
69969 US Highway 31 46536 574-784-3151
Jeffery Rehlander, prin. Fax 784-8695

Lanesville, Harrison, Pop. 630
Lanesville Community SC 700/K-12
2725 Crestview Ave NE 47136 812-952-2555
Dr. Phil Partenheimer, supt. Fax 952-3762
www.lanesville.k12.in.us/
Lanesville JSHS 300/7-12
2725 Crestview Ave NE 47136 812-952-2555
Janet Page, prin. Fax 952-3762

Lapel, Madison, Pop. 1,846
Frankton-Lapel Community SD
Supt. — See Anderson
Lapel JSHS 400/7-12
2883 S State Rd 13 46051 765-534-3137
Jerry Kemerly, prin. Fax 534-3883

La Porte, LaPorte, Pop. 21,092
Dewey Township SD 100/K-12
809 State St 46350 219-326-6808
Norm Kleist, supt. Fax 362-3313
www.lacrosse.k12.in.us/home.htm
Other Schools – See La Crosse

La Porte Community SC 6,300/PK-12
1921 A St 46350 219-362-7056
Dr. Judith DeMuth, supt. Fax 324-9347
www.lpcsc.k12.in.us
Boston MS 700/6-8
1000 Harrison St 46350 219-326-6930
Dave Birkholz, prin. Fax 324-7108
Kesling MS 800/6-8
306 E 18th St 46350 219-362-7507
Bill Wilmsen, prin. Fax 324-5712
La Porte HS 1,900/9-12
602 F St 46350 219-362-3102
Greg Handel, prin. Fax 324-2142

La Lumiere S 100/9-12
PO Box 5005 46352 219-326-7450
Michael Kennedy, hdmstr. Fax 325-3185

Larwill, Whitley, Pop. 282
Whitko Community SC
Supt. — See Pierceton
Whitko MS 500/6-8
710 N State Road 5 46764 260-327-3603
Jerry Klausing, prin. Fax 327-3805

Lawrenceburg, Dearborn, Pop. 4,750
Lawrenceburg Community SC 1,500/K-12
300 Tiger Blvd 47025 812-537-7200
Dan Kuebler, supt. Fax 537-0759
www.lburg.k12.in.us
Greendale MS 300/6-8
200 Tiger Blvd 47025 812-537-7259
Karl Galey, prin. Fax 537-6385
Lawrenceburg HS 500/9-12
100 Tiger Blvd 47025 812-537-7219
Mark Wayman, prin. Fax 537-7221

Lebanon, Boone, Pop. 14,633
Lebanon Community SC 3,400/K-12
1810 N Grant St 46052 765-482-0380
Dr. Robert Taylor, supt. Fax 483-3053
www.leb.k12.in.us/
Lebanon HS 1,000/9-12
510 Essex Dr 46052 765-482-0400
Stephen Psikula, prin. Fax 483-3040
Lebanon MS 800/6-8
1800 N Grant St 46052 765-482-3400
Michael Brown, prin. Fax 483-3049

Cedars of Lebanon Christian S 50/K-12
PO Box 544 46052 765-485-0650
Cathleen Cryer, admin.

Leo, Allen
East Allen County SD
Supt. — See New Haven
Leo JSHS 1,000/7-12
14600 Amstutz Rd 46765 260-446-0180
Mark Daniel, prin. Fax 446-0189

Leopold, Perry
Perry Central Community SC 1,200/PK-12
18677 Old State Road 37 47551 812-843-5576
Mary Roberson, supt. Fax 843-4746
www.pccs.k12.in.us/
Perry Central JSHS 600/7-12
18677 Old State Road 37 47551 812-843-5121
Jack Wright, prin. Fax 843-4198

Liberty, Union, Pop. 1,940
Union County/College Corner JSD 1,700/K-12
107 S Layman St 47353 765-458-7471
Mark Ransford, supt. Fax 458-5647
www.uc.k12.in.us/
Union County HS 500/9-12
410 Patriot Blvd 47353 765-458-5136
Connie Rosenberger, prin. Fax 458-6315
Union County MS 400/6-8
488 State Route 44 E 47353 765-458-7438
Vicky Snyder, prin. Fax 458-6041

Ligonier, Noble, Pop. 4,423
West Noble SC 2,500/K-12
5050 N US Highway 33 46767 260-894-3191
Dave Speakman, supt. Fax 894-3260
westnoble.k12.in.us/
West Noble HS 700/9-12
5094 N US Highway 33 46767 260-894-3191
Nate Lowe, prin. Fax 894-4708
West Noble MS 800/5-8
5194 N US Highway 33 46767 260-894-3191
William Anders, prin. Fax 894-4703

Lincoln City, Spencer
North Spencer County SC 2,200/PK-12
3720 E State Road 162 47552 812-937-2400
Joan Keller, supt. Fax 937-7187
www.nspencer.k12.in.us
Heritage Hills HS 800/9-12
3644 E County Road 1600 N 47552 812-937-4472
Dan Scherry, prin. Fax 937-4878
Heritage Hills MS 300/7-8
PO Box 1777 47552 812-937-4472
Susan Grundhoefer, prin. Fax 937-4327

Linton, Greene, Pop. 5,808
Linton-Stockton SC 1,400/PK-12
801 1st St NE 47441 812-847-6020
Ronald L. Bush, supt. Fax 847-8659
www.lssc.k12.in.us/

Linton-Stockton HS 400/9-12
10 H St NE 47441 812-847-6024
Nicholas Karazsia, prin. Fax 847-6037
Linton-Stockton JHS 200/7-8
109 I St NE 47441 812-847-6022
Jeff Sparks, prin. Fax 847-6032

Lizton, Hendricks, Pop. 358
North West Hendricks SD 1,600/K-12
PO Box 70 46149 317-994-4100
Larry Rambis, supt. Fax 994-5963
www.hendricks.k12.in.us/
Tri-West HS 500/9-12
7883 N State Rd 39 46149 317-994-4000
Dolores Mueller, prin. Fax 994-5106
Tri-West MS 400/6-8
555 W US Highway 136 46149 317-994-4100
Ronald Ward, prin. Fax 994-4230

Logansport, Cass, Pop. 19,211
Logansport Community SC 4,200/PK-12
2829 George St 46947 574-722-2911
Damon Peigh, supt. Fax 722-7634
www.lcsc.k12.in.us
Century Career Center Vo/Tech
2500 Hopper St 46947 574-722-3811
Stephen Hagen, prin. Fax 753-7649
Columbia MS 400/6-8
1300 N 3rd St 46947 574-753-3797
Kay Scott, prin. Fax 753-6159
Lincoln MS 600/6-8
2901 Usher St 46947 574-753-7115
Susan Swartz, prin. Fax 753-5826
Logansport Community HS 1,300/9-12
1 Berry Ln 46947 574-753-0441
Dr. Terry Sargent, prin. Fax 753-3688
Landmark Adult Learning Center Adult
401 Tanguy St 46947 574-753-6547
Emily Graham, prin. Fax 753-4978

Loogootee, Martin, Pop. 2,680
Loogootee Community SC 1,100/K-12
PO Box 282 47553 812-295-2595
Larry Weitkamp, supt. Fax 295-5595
www.loogootee.k12.in.us/
Loogootee JSHS 500/7-12
201 Brooks Ave 47553 812-295-3254
John Mullen, prin. Fax 295-5595

Lowell, Lake, Pop. 8,039
Tri-Creek SC 3,400/K-12
195 W Oakley Ave 46356 219-696-6661
Dr. Alice A. Neal, supt. Fax 696-2150
www.tricreek.k12.in.us
Lowell HS 1,100/9-12
2051 E Commercial Ave 46356 219-696-7733
James Koger, prin. Fax 696-0042
Lowell MS 800/6-8
200 W Oakley Ave 46356 219-696-7701
John Alessia, prin. Fax 690-2620

Lowell Christian Academy 100/PK-12
PO Box 206 46356 219-696-8094
Deborah Richardson, prin.

Lynn, Randolph, Pop. 1,095
Randolph Southern SC 600/K-12
1 Rebel Dr 47355 765-874-1181
Michael Necessary, supt. Fax 874-1298
Randolph Southern JSHS 300/7-12
2 Rebel Dr 47355 765-874-2541
Michael Manning, prin. Fax 874-1298

Lynnville, Warrick, Pop. 819
Warrick County SC
Supt. — See Boonville
Tecumseh JSHS 400/7-12
5244 W State Route 68 47619 812-922-3237
Richard Lance, prin. Fax 922-3608

Madison, Jefferson, Pop. 12,443
Madison Consolidated SD 3,300/K-12
2421 Wilson Ave 47250 812-273-8511
Thomas G. Patterson, supt. Fax 273-8516
www.madison.k12.in.us/
Madison Consolidated HS 1,000/9-12
743 Clifty Dr 47250 812-265-6672
Jeff Dhonau, prin. Fax 265-5689
Madison Consolidated JHS 800/6-8
701 8th St 47250 812-265-6756
Michael Robinson, prin. Fax 265-5685

Grace Baptist S 100/PK-12
920 Montclair St 47250 812-273-4107
Rev. Joel Almaroad, prin. Fax 265-5151
Ivy Tech Community College - Southeast Post-Sec.
590 Ivy Tech Dr 47250 812-265-2580
King's Daughter's Hospital Post-Sec.
PO Box 447 47250 812-265-5211
Shawe Memorial HS 100/7-12
201 W State St 47250 812-273-2150
Jerry Bomholt, prin. Fax 273-6694

Marengo, Crawford, Pop. 862
Crawford County Community SC 1,700/PK-12
5805 E Administration Rd 47140 812-365-2135
Dr. Mark Eastridge, supt. Fax 365-2783
www.cccs.k12.in.us/
Crawford County JSHS 800/7-12
1130 S State Road 66 47140 812-365-2125
Wayne Apple, prin. Fax 365-2127

Marion, Grant, Pop. 30,644
Eastbrook Community SC 1,600/K-12
560 S 900 E 46953 765-664-0624
Jerry Harshman, supt. Fax 664-0626
www.eastbrookschools.net/index.php
Eastbrook HS 600/9-12
560 S 900 E 46953 765-664-1214
Marjorie Green, prin. Fax 664-1216
Eastbrook JHS 300/7-8
560 S 900 E 46953 765-668-7136
Elizabeth Duckwall, prin. Fax 668-7137

Marion Community SD 5,100/PK-12
PO Box 2020 46952 765-662-2546
Dr. Andrew Nixon, supt. Fax 651-2043
www.marion.k12.in.us/
Marion HS 1,500/9-12
750 W 26th St 46953 765-664-9051
Jack Gardner, prin. Fax 662-0383
Marshall MS 600/6-8
720 N Miller Ave 46952 765-664-0507
James Fox, prin. Fax 651-2086
McCulloch MS 700/6-8
3528 S Washington St 46953 765-674-6917
Dr. Michael Shaffer, prin. Fax 674-8943
Tucker Career & Technology Center Vo/Tech
107 S Pennsylvania St 46952 765-664-9091
Jerry Whitton, prin. Fax 651-2048

Indiana Business College Post-Sec.
830 N Miller Ave 46952 765-662-7497
Indiana Wesleyan University Post-Sec.
4201 S Washington St 46953 765-674-6901
Lakeview Christian S 300/PK-12
5318 S Western Ave 46953 765-677-4266
Kelly Brown, prin. Fax 677-4269
New Horizons Academy 50/9-12
1002 S 350 E 46953 765-668-4009
Brian Baker, supt. Fax 662-1407

Marshall, Parke, Pop. 365
Turkey Run Community SC 700/PK-12
1497 E State Road 47 47859 765-597-2750
Dr. Roberta Bowers, supt. Fax 597-2755
www.tr.k12.in.us
Turkey Run JSHS 300/7-12
1551 E State Road 47 47859 765-597-2700
Pamela Rager, prin. Fax 597-2812

Martinsville, Morgan, Pop. 11,657
Metro SD of Martinsville 5,600/PK-12
460 S Main St 46151 765-342-6641
Ron Furniss, supt. Fax 342-6877
msdadmin.scican.net
Martinsville East MS 700/6-8
1459 E Columbus St 46151 765-342-6675
Eric Bowlen, prin. Fax 349-5236
Martinsville HS 1,600/9-12
1360 E Gray St 46151 765-342-5571
Don Alkire, prin. Fax 349-5256
Martinsville West MS 700/6-8
109 E Garfield Ave 46151 765-342-6628
Suzie O'Neal, prin. Fax 349-5232

Tabernacle Christian S 200/K-12
2189 Burton Ln 46151 765-342-0501
Don Nations, prin. Fax 342-0502

Maxwell, Hancock
Greenfield-Central Community SD
Supt. — See Greenfield
Maxwell MS 500/6-8
102 N Main St 46154 317-326-3121
Harold Olin, prin. Fax 326-4711

Medora, Jackson, Pop. 553
Medora Community SC 300/K-12
PO Box 369 47260 812-966-2210
Dr. Drew Day, supt. Fax 966-2217
www.medorahornets.com
Medora JSHS 100/7-12
82 S George 47260 812-966-2201
Paul White, prin. Fax 966-2217

Merrillville, Lake, Pop. 31,525
Merrillville Community SC 6,700/K-12
6701 Delaware St 46410 219-650-5300
Dr. Tony Lux, supt. Fax 650-5320
www.mvsc.k12.in.us
Merrillville HS 2,200/9-12
276 E 68th Pl 46410 219-650-5307
Mike Krutz, prin. Fax 650-5391
Pierce MS 1,100/7-8
199 E 70th Pl 46410 219-650-5308
Paul McKinney, prin. Fax 650-5483

Andrean HS 700/9-12
5959 Broadway 46410 219-887-5281
Rev. Paul Quanz, prin. Fax 981-5072
Brown Mackie College Post-Sec.
1000 E 80th Pl Ste 101N 46410 219-769-3321
Davenport University Post-Sec.
8200 Georgia St 46410 219-769-5556
DeVry University Post-Sec.
1000 E 80th Pl Ste 609 46410 219-736-7440
Merrillville Beauty College Post-Sec.
48 W 67th Pl 46410 219-769-2232
Olympia College Post-Sec.
707 E 80th Pl Ste 200 46410 219-756-6811
Sawyer College Post-Sec.
3803 E Lincoln Hwy 46410 219-947-4555

Michigan City, LaPorte, Pop. 32,205
Michigan City Area SD 6,900/PK-12
408 S Carroll Ave 46360 219-873-2000
Michael Harding, supt. Fax 873-2072
www.mcas.k12.in.us
Barker MS 400/6-8
319 Barker Rd 46360 219-873-2057
Peggy Scope, prin. Fax 873-3099
Elston MS 800/6-8
317 Detroit St 46360 219-873-2035
Kelly Fargo, prin. Fax 873-2157
Krueger MS 400/6-8
2001 Springland Ave 46360 219-873-2061
Lisa Emshwiller, prin. Fax 873-2063
Michigan City HS 1,900/9-12
8466 W Pahs Rd 46360 219-873-2044
Mark Francesconi, prin. Fax 873-2055
Smith Area Career Center Vo/Tech
817 Lafayette St 46360 219-873-2120
Karen Robinson, dir. Fax 873-2068

Brown Mackie College Post-Sec.
325 E US Highway 20 46360 219-877-3100
Duneland Lutheran HS 50/9-12
1237 E Coolspring Ave 46360 219-874-5103
Laurie Rockenseuss, prin. Fax 842-4870
Lakeshore Medical Lab Training Programs Post-Sec.
402 Franklin St 46360 219-872-7032
Marquette HS 200/9-12
306 W 10th St 46360 219-873-1325
John Albert, prin. Fax 873-1327

Michigantown, Clinton, Pop. 407
Clinton Central SC 1,100/K-12
725 N State Road 29 46057 765-249-2515
Philip Boley, supt. Fax 249-2504
www.clinton.k12.in.us/
Clinton Central JSHS 500/7-12
815 N State Road 29 46057 765-249-2255
Kyle Barrentine, prin. Fax 249-0214

Middlebury, Elkhart, Pop. 3,150
Middlebury Community SD 3,900/K-12
57853 Northridge Dr 46540 574-825-9425
Jim Conner, supt. Fax 825-9426
www.mcsin-k12.org/
Heritage MS 900/6-8
57697 Northridge Dr Bldg 2 46540 574-825-9531
Mitch Miller, prin. Fax 825-9154
Northridge HS 1,200/9-12
57697 Northridge Dr Bldg 1 46540 574-825-2142
Steve Lyng, prin. Fax 825-1473

Middletown, Henry, Pop. 2,384
Shenandoah SC 1,400/K-12
5100 N Raider Rd 47356 765-354-2266
Ronald Green, supt. Fax 354-2274
www.shenandoah.k12.in.us/
Shenandoah HS 400/9-12
7354 W US Highway 36 47356 765-354-6640
Charles Willis, prin. Fax 354-3110
Shenandoah MS 400/6-8
5156 N Raider Rd 47356 765-354-6638
Greg Allen, prin. Fax 354-3120

Milan, Ripley, Pop. 1,806
Milan Community SC 1,300/K-12
412 E Carr St 47031 812-654-2365
Andrew Jackson, supt. Fax 654-2441
www.milan.k12.in.us
Milan HS 400/9-12
609 N Warpath Dr 47031 812-654-3096
Michael Parks, prin. Fax 654-2368
Milan MS 400/5-8
609 N Warpath Dr 47031 812-654-1616
Connie Nobbe, prin. Fax 654-2368

Mishawaka, Saint Joseph, Pop. 48,497
Mishawaka CSD 5,300/K-12
1402 S Main St 46544 574-254-4500
R. Steven Mills, supt. Fax 254-4585
www.mishawaka.k12.in.us
Mishawaka HS 1,600/9-12
1202 Lincoln Way E 46544 574-254-7300
George Marzotto, prin. Fax 254-7481
Young MS 800/7-8
1801 N Main St 46545 574-254-3600
Dave Troyer, prin. Fax 258-3021

Penn-Harris-Madison SC 10,200/K-12
55900 Bittersweet Rd 46545 574-259-7941
Dr. Jerry Thacker, supt. Fax 258-9547
www.phm.k12.in.us
Byrkit HS 9-12
6501 Grape Rd 46545 574-259-2874
Janeen Conway, prin. Fax 259-2876
Grissom MS 600/6-8
13881 Kern Rd 46544 574-633-4061
Gene Hollenberg, prin. Fax 633-2134
Penn HS 3,200/9-12
56100 Bittersweet Rd 46545 574-259-7961
Dr. Dave Tydgat, prin. Fax 258-9543
Schmucker MS 900/6-8
56045 Bittersweet Rd 46545 574-259-5661
Janet Scott, prin. Fax 259-0807
Other Schools – See Granger

Bais Yaakov of Indiana 100/9-12
302 W 8th St 46544 574-257-0689
Miriam Gettinger, prin. Fax 255-7553
Bethel College Post-Sec.
1001 W McKinley Ave 46545 574-259-8511
First Baptist Christian S 200/PK-12
724 N Main St 46545 574-255-3242
Douglas Culp, prin. Fax 258-0397
Marian HS 800/9-12
1311 S Logan St 46544 574-259-5257
Carl Loesch, prin. Fax 258-7668

Mitchell, Lawrence, Pop. 4,626
Mitchell Community SD 2,100/PK-12
441 N 8th St 47446 812-849-4481
John Lantis, supt. Fax 849-2133
www.mitchell.k12.in.us
Mitchell HS 600/9-12
1000 W Bishop Blvd 47446 812-849-3663
Dr. Steve Phillips, prin. Fax 849-5368
Mitchell JHS 500/6-8
1010 W Bishop Blvd 47446 812-849-3747
David Branneman, prin. Fax 849-5841

Modoc, Randolph, Pop. 216
Union SC 500/K-12
PO Box 148 47358 765-853-5464
Philip Dubbs, supt. Fax 853-5070
www.ecesc.k12.in.us/corporations/unionsch/index.htm
Union JSHS 200/7-12
PO Box 148 47358 765-853-5421
Anita Glaze, prin. Fax 853-6057

Monon, White, Pop. 1,654
North White SC 1,000/K-12
121 W State Road 16 47959 219-253-6618
Patrick W. McTaggart, supt. Fax 253-6488
www.nwhite.k12.in.us/
North White HS 300/9-12
310 E Broadway St 47959 219-253-6638
Jeff Jones, prin. Fax 253-7004
North White MS 300/6-8
310 E Broadway St 47959 219-253-7701
Curt Craig, prin. Fax 253-8462

Monroe, Adams, Pop. 778
Adams Central Community SD 1,100/K-12
222 W Washington St 46772 260-692-6193
Michael Pettibone, supt. Fax 692-6198
www.accs.k12.in.us/
Adams Central HS 400/9-12
222 W Washington St 46772 260-692-6151
Bill Hartman, prin. Fax 692-6192
Adams Central MS 300/6-8
222 W Washington St 46772 260-692-6151
Aaron McClure, prin. Fax 692-6192

Monroeville, Allen, Pop. 1,277
East Allen County SD
Supt. — See New Haven
Heritage JSHS 800/7-12
13608 Monroeville Rd 46773 260-446-0140
Chris Hissong, prin. Fax 446-0146

Monrovia, Morgan, Pop. 624
Monroe-Gregg SD 800/PK-12
PO Box 468 46157 317-996-3720
Paul Kaiser, supt. Fax 996-2977
www.scican.net/mgsd
Monrovia HS 400/9-12
PO Box 468 46157 317-996-2259
Jacob Hagist, prin. Fax 996-3519
Monrovia MS 6-8
PO Box 468 46157 317-996-2352
Bobbie Jo Monahan, prin. Fax 996-3429

Montezuma, Parke, Pop. 1,151
Southwest Parke Community SC 1,000/K-12
4851 S Coxville Rd 47862 765-569-2073
Leonard R. Orr, supt. Fax 569-0309
www.swparke.k12.in.us
Riverton Parke JSHS 500/7-12
4907 S Coxville Rd 47862 765-569-2045
Dennis Moody, prin. Fax 569-2047

Montgomery, Daviess, Pop. 381
Barr-Reeve Community SD 700/K-12
PO Box 97 47558 812-486-3220
Brian Harmon, supt. Fax 486-3509
www.barr.k12.in.us/
Barr-Reeve JSHS 300/7-12
PO Box 128 47558 812-486-3265
Travis Madison, prin. Fax 486-2829

Monticello, White, Pop. 5,462
Twin Lakes SC 2,600/PK-12
565 S Main St 47960 574-583-7211
Dr. Thomas Fletcher, supt. Fax 583-8963
www.twinlakes.k12.in.us/
Roosevelt MS 600/6-8
721 W Broadway St 47960 574-583-5552
Scott Clifford, prin. Fax 583-3675
Twin Lakes HS 800/9-12
300 S 3rd St 47960 574-583-7108
Keith Brakel, prin. Fax 583-2861

Mooresville, Morgan, Pop. 11,111
Mooresville Consolidated SC 4,400/PK-12
11 W Carlisle St 46158 317-831-0950
Curtis Freeman, supt. Fax 831-9202
www.mcsc.k12.in.us
Hadley MS 700/7-8
200 W Carlisle St 46158 317-831-9208
Larry Goldsberry, prin. Fax 831-9249
Mooresville HS 1,300/9-12
550 N Indiana St 46158 317-831-9203
Chuck Muston, prin. Fax 831-9206

Morocco, Newton, Pop. 1,159
North Newton SC 1,600/K-12
PO Box 8 47963 219-285-2228
Dr. Terry Barker, supt. Fax 285-2708
www.nn.k12.in.us/
North Newton JSHS 800/7-12
1641 W 250 N 47963 219-285-2252
Mark Gianfermi, prin. Fax 285-2881

Morristown, Shelby, Pop. 1,218
Shelby Eastern SD
Supt. — See Shelbyville
Morristown JSHS 500/6-12
PO Box 260 46161 765-763-1221
Michelle Repar, prin. Fax 763-7170

Mount Summit, Henry, Pop. 297
Blue River Valley SD 800/PK-12
PO Box 217 47361 765-836-4816
Stephen K. Welsh, supt. Fax 836-4817
www.brv.k12.in.us
Other Schools – See New Castle

Mount Vernon, Posey, Pop. 7,238
Metro SD of Mt. Vernon 2,700/PK-12
1000 W 4th St 47620 812-838-4471
Dr. Keith Spurgeon, supt. Fax 833-2078
www.msdmv.k12.in.us
Mount Vernon HS 900/9-12
700 Harriett St 47620 812-838-4356
Steve Riordan, prin. Fax 833-2099
Mount Vernon JHS 700/6-8
701 Tile Factory Rd 47620 812-833-2077
Jerry Funkhouser, prin. Fax 833-2083

Muncie, Delaware, Pop. 66,164
Cowan Community SC 600/K-12
1000 W County Road 600 S 47302 765-289-4866
Larry D. John, supt. Fax 284-0315
www.cowan.k12.in.us
Cowan JSHS 300/7-12
9401 S Nottingham St 47302 765-289-7128
James Suding, prin. Fax 741-5954

Delaware Community SC 2,800/K-12
7821 N State Rd 3 47303 765-284-5074
R. Stephen Gookins, supt. Fax 284-5259
www.delcomschools.org
Delta HS 900/9-12
3400 E State Rd 28 47303 765-288-5597
Gregory Hinshaw, prin. Fax 288-8498
Delta MS 700/6-8
9800 N County Road 200 E 47303 765-747-0869
Don Harman, prin. Fax 213-2131

Muncie Community SD 7,400/K-12
2501 N Oakwood Ave 47304 765-747-5205
Marlin Creasy Ph.D., supt. Fax 747-5341
www.muncie.k12.in.us
Muncie Area Career Center Vo/Tech
2500 N Elgin St 47303 765-747-5250
Jeff Alexander, dir. Fax 747-5455
Muncie Central HS 1,200/9-12
801 N Walnut St 47305 765-747-5260
Dick Daniel, prin. Fax 747-5314
Muncie Southside HS 1,100/9-12
1601 E 26th St 47302 765-747-5320
Rebecca Thompson, prin. Fax 747-5325
Northside MS 900/6-8
2400 W Bethel Ave 47304 765-747-5290
Dr. Maria Sells, prin. Fax 751-0616
Wilson MS 1,000/6-8
3100 S Tillotson Ave 47302 765-747-5370
Dilynn Phelps, prin. Fax 751-0666

University Schools 800/K-12
2000 W University Ave 47306 765-285-8488
Dr. William Sharp, supt. Fax 285-2166
www.bsu.edu
Burris Laboratory S 500/K-12
2000 W University Ave 47306 765-285-8600
Dr. Jay McGee, prin. Fax 285-8620
IN Academy for Science Math & Humanities 300/11-12
2121 W University Ave 47306 765-285-7457
Dr. David Williams, prin. Fax 285-2777

Ball Memorial Hospital Post-Sec.
2401 W University Ave 47303 765-747-3393
Ball State University Post-Sec.
2000 W University Ave 47306 765-289-1241
Heritage Hall Christian S 300/PK-12
6401 W River Rd 47304 765-289-6371
Dennis Ice, prin. Fax 288-9584
Indiana Business College Post-Sec.
411 W Riggin Rd 47303 765-288-8681
Ivy Tech Community College East Central Post-Sec.
4301 S Cowan Rd 47302 765-289-2291
PJ's College of Cosmetology Post-Sec.
2006 N Walnut St 47303

Munster, Lake, Pop. 22,347
Town of Munster SD 3,900/K-12
8616 Columbia Ave 46321 219-836-9111
William Pfister, supt. Fax 836-3215
www.munster.k12.in.us
Munster HS 1,400/9-12
8808 Columbia Ave 46321 219-836-3200
Steven L. Tripenfeldas, prin. Fax 836-3203
Wright MS 1,000/6-8
8650 Columbia Ave 46321 219-836-6260
Randolph Harkabus, prin. Fax 836-0501

Nappanee, Elkhart, Pop. 6,955
Wa-Nee Community SD 3,200/K-12
1300 N Main St 46550 574-773-3131
Joe Sabo, supt. Fax 773-5593
www.wanee.org
Northwood HS 900/9-12
2101 N Main St 46550 574-773-4127
David Maugel, prin. Fax 773-4099
Other Schools – See Wakarusa

South Side Christian S 50/1-12
901 S Main St 46550 574-773-2566
Thomas Mast, admin. Fax 773-4066
United Christian S 100/1-12
29522 County Road 52 46550 574-773-7505
Robert Carroll, prin. Fax 773-7513

Nashville, Brown, Pop. 804
Brown County SC 2,500/PK-12
PO Box 38 47448 812-988-6601
Dr. D. Lynn Reed, supt. Fax 988-5403
www.brownco.k12.in.us
Brown County HS 900/9-12
PO Box 68 47448 812-988-6606
Matthew Stark, prin. Fax 988-5422
Brown County JHS 400/7-8
95 S School House Ln 47448 812-988-6605
Shane Killinger, prin. Fax 988-5415

New Albany, Floyd, Pop. 36,772
New Albany-Floyd County Consolidated SD 11,400/PK-12
PO Box 1087 47151 812-949-4200
Dennis Brooks, supt. Fax 949-6900
www.nafcs.k12.in.us
Hazelwood JHS 800/6-8
1021 Hazelwood Ave 47150 812-949-4280
Jacqueline Apple, prin. Fax 949-6962
New Albany HS 2,000/9-12
1020 Vincennes St 47150 812-949-4272
Stephen Sipes, prin. Fax 949-6910
Prosser S of Technology Vo/Tech
4202 Charlestown Rd 47150 812-949-4266
Alan Taylor, prin. Fax 949-4260
Scribner JHS 800/6-8
910 Old Vincennes Rd 47150 812-949-4283
Rhonda Mull, prin. Fax 949-6974
Other Schools – See Floyds Knobs, Georgetown

Christian Academy of Indiana 700/K-12
1000 Academy Dr 47150 812-944-6200
Kevin Wilson, prin. Fax 944-6902
Indiana University Southeast Post-Sec.
4201 Grant Line Rd 47150 812-941-2000

Newburgh, Warrick, Pop. 3,298
Warrick County SC
Supt. — See Boonville
Castle HS 1,700/9-12
3344 State Route 261 47630 812-853-3331
Phil Delong, prin. Fax 853-9886
Castle JHS 900/7-8
2800 State Route 261 47630 812-853-7347
Robert Hawkins, prin. Fax 858-1089

ITT Technical Institute Post-Sec.
10999 Stahl Rd 47630 812-858-1600
Newburgh Christian S 100/PK-12
7333 Sharon Rd 47630 812-842-0455
Sharon Dunsworth, admin. Fax 853-3511

New Carlisle, Saint Joseph, Pop. 1,629
New Prairie United SC 2,600/K-12
5327 N Cougar Rd 46552 574-654-7273
Duane Wrightson, supt. Fax 654-7274
www.npusc.k12.in.us
New Prairie HS 900/9-12
5333 N Cougar Rd 46552 574-654-7271
Clara Clark, prin. Fax 654-3390
New Prairie JHS 400/7-8
5331 N Cougar Rd 46552 574-654-3070
Jim Holifield, prin. Fax 654-7009

New Castle, Henry, Pop. 18,718
Blue River Valley SD
Supt. — See Mount Summit
Blue River Valley JSHS 400/7-12
4741 N Hillsboro Rd 47362 765-836-4811
Ken Howell, prin. Fax 836-3255

New Castle Community SC 3,800/PK-12
322 Elliott Ave 47362 765-521-7201
Dr. John Newby, supt. Fax 521-7268
www.nccsc.k12.in.us
New Castle Chrysler HS 1,000/9-12
801 Parkview Dr 47362 765-593-6670
Bruce Gaylor, prin. Fax 593-6696
New Castle MS 600/7-8
601 Parkview Dr 47362 765-521-7230
Kellie Stephen, prin. Fax 521-7269

New Harmony, Posey, Pop. 885
New Harmony Town & Twp Cons SD 200/PK-12
PO Box 396 47631 812-682-4401
Fran Thoele, supt. Fax 682-3659
www.harmoniehundred.net/index.html
New Harmony S 200/PK-12
PO Box 396 47631 812-682-4401
Douglas Mills, prin. Fax 682-3659

New Haven, Allen, Pop. 13,676
East Allen County SD 10,100/PK-12
1240 State Road 930 E 46774 260-446-0100
Dr. M. Kay Novotny, supt. Fax 446-0107
www.eacs.k12.in.us
New Haven HS 900/9-12
1300 Green Rd 46774 260-446-0220
Eva Merkel, prin. Fax 446-0228
New Haven MS 700/6-8
900 Prospect Ave 46774 260-446-0230
Thelma Green, prin. Fax 446-0236
Other Schools – See Fort Wayne, Leo, Monroeville, Woodburn

New Market, Montgomery, Pop. 654
South Montgomery Community SC 2,000/K-12
PO Box 8 47965 765-866-0203
Dr. J. Bret Lewis, supt. Fax 866-0736
www.southmont.k12.in.us
Other Schools – See Crawfordsville

New Palestine, Hancock, Pop. 1,826
Southern Hancock County Community SC 3,200/PK-12
PO Box 508 46163 317-861-4463
James Halik, supt. Fax 861-2142
shancock.newpal.k12.in.us/
Doe Creek MS 800/6-8
PO Box 478 46163 317-861-4487
James Voelz, prin. Fax 861-2136
New Palestine HS 900/9-12
PO Box 448 46163 317-861-4417
Janice Bergeson, prin. Fax 861-2125

New Washington, Clark
Greater Clark County SD
Supt. — See Jeffersonville
New Washington MSHS 400/6-12
226 N Highway 62 47162 812-293-3368
Ben Ledbetter, prin. Fax 293-5803

Noblesville, Hamilton, Pop. 38,825
Noblesville SD 7,400/PK-12
1775 Field Dr 46060 317-773-3171
Lynn Lehman, supt. Fax 773-7845
www.noblesvilleschools.org

Noblesville HS 2,000/9-12
18111 Cumberland Rd 46060 317-773-4680
Annetta Petty, prin. Fax 776-6289
Noblesville MS 1,100/7-8
300 N 17th St 46060 317-773-0782
Daniel Chapin, prin. Fax 776-6261

Blessed Theodore Guerin HS 9-12
15300 N Gray Rd, 317-582-0120
Rick Wagner, prin. Fax 582-0140
Kaye Beauty College Post-Sec.
1111 S 10th St 46060 317-773-6189

North Judson, Starke, Pop. 1,867
North Judson-San Pierre SC 1,400/K-12
801 Campbell Dr 46366 574-896-2155
John Heath, supt. Fax 896-2156
www.njsp.k12.in.us
North Judson JHS 400/6-8
950 Campbell Dr 46366 574-896-2167
Annette Zupin, prin. Fax 896-3036
North Judson-San Pierre HS 500/9-12
1 Bluejay Dr 46366 574-896-2158
Kelly Shepherd, prin. Fax 896-3945

North Manchester, Wabash, Pop. 5,980
Manchester Community SD 1,600/K-12
PO Box 308 46962 260-982-7518
Dr. Diana Showalter, supt. Fax 982-4583
www.mcs.k12.in.us
Manchester HS 500/9-12
1 Squire Dr 46962 260-982-2196
Nancy Alspaugh, prin. Fax 982-1034
Manchester JHS 200/7-8
404 W 9th St 46962 260-982-8602
Nancy Alspaugh, prin. Fax 982-1162

Manchester College Post-Sec.
604 E College Ave 46962 260-982-5000

North Vernon, Jennings, Pop. 6,433
Jennings County SC 5,200/K-12
34 W Main St 47265 812-346-4483
Dr. Michael J. Bushong, supt. Fax 346-4490
www.jcsc.org
Jennings County HS 1,300/9-12
800 W Walnut St 47265 812-346-5588
Kendall Wildey, prin. Fax 346-4232
Jennings County MS 900/7-8
820 W Walnut St 47265 812-346-4940
Floyd Bowman, prin. Fax 346-4497

Notre Dame, Saint Joseph, Pop. 10,200

Holy Cross College Post-Sec.
PO Box 308 46556 574-239-8400
St. Mary's College Post-Sec.
46 Madeliva 46556 574-284-4000
University of Notre Dame Post-Sec.
220 Main Building 46556 574-631-5000

Oakland City, Gibson, Pop. 2,596
East Gibson SC 1,000/PK-12
133 E Morton St 47660 812-749-4755
Lynn Blinzinger, supt. Fax 749-3343
Wood Memorial HS 300/9-12
943 S Franklin St 47660 812-749-4757
Roger Benson, prin. Fax 749-3512
Wood Memorial JHS 200/7-8
945A S Franklin St 47660 812-749-4715
Mike Brewster, prin. Fax 749-4988

Oakland City University Post-Sec.
138 N Lucretia St 47660 812-749-4781

Oldenburg, Franklin, Pop. 645

Oldenburg Academy 200/9-12
PO Box 200 47036 812-934-4440
Connie Deardorff, prin. Fax 934-4838

Oolitic, Lawrence, Pop. 1,123
North Lawrence Community SD
Supt. — See Bedford
Oolitic MS 400/6-8
903 Hoosier Ave 47451 812-275-7551
David Dean, prin. Fax 277-3219

Orleans, Orange, Pop. 2,294
Orleans Community SD 900/K-12
173 Marley St 47452 812-865-2688
James Terrell, supt. Fax 865-3428
www.orleans.k12.in.us/
Orleans JSHS 400/7-12
200 W Wilson St 47452 812-865-2688
Gary McClintic, prin. Fax 865-3532

Osgood, Ripley, Pop. 1,655
Jac-Cen-Del Community SC 1,000/K-12
723 N Buckeye St 47037 812-689-4114
Bill Narwold, supt. Fax 689-7423
www.jaccendel.k12.in.us/
Jac-Cen-Del JSHS 400/7-12
4586 N US Highway 421 47037 812-689-4643
Raymond Ratledge, prin. Fax 689-0152

Ossian, Wells, Pop. 2,908
Northern Wells Community SD 2,600/PK-12
PO Box 386 46777 260-622-4125
Gina Berridge, supt. Fax 622-7893
www.nwcs.k12.in.us/
Norwell HS 800/9-12
1100 E US Highway 224 46777 260-543-2213
Greg Mohler, prin. Fax 543-2591
Norwell MS 600/6-8
1100 E US Highway 224 46777 260-543-2218
Robert Hansbarger, prin. Fax 543-2510

Oxford, Benton, Pop. 1,208
Benton Community SC
Supt. — See Fowler
Benton Central JSHS 1,000/7-12
4241 E 300 S 47971 765-884-1600
Howard Feuer, prin. Fax 884-8445

Paoli, Orange, Pop. 3,947
Lost River Career Cooperative SD
610 Elm St 47454 812-723-4818
David Embree, supt. Fax 723-4822
Lost River Career Cooperative S Vo/Tech
610 Elm St 47454 812-723-4818
David Embree, prin. Fax 723-4822

Paoli Community SC 1,600/K-12
501 Elm St 47454 812-723-4717
Alva Sibbitt, supt. Fax 723-5100
www.paoli.k12.in.us
Paoli JSHS 700/7-12
501 Elm St 47454 812-723-3905
Jerry Stroud, prin. Fax 723-4459

Parker City, Randolph, Pop. 1,359
Monroe Central SC 1,000/K-12
1918 N County Road 1000 W 47368 765-468-6868
Dr. Zachary Rozelle, supt. Fax 468-6578
www.monroec.k12.in.us
Monroe Central JSHS 500/7-12
1878 N County Road 1000 W 47368 765-468-7545
Adrian Moulton, prin. Fax 468-8878

Pekin, Washington, Pop. 1,236
East Washington SC 1,800/K-12
1050 N Eastern School Rd 47165 812-967-3926
Gerald Rose, supt. Fax 967-5797
www.ewsc.k12.in.us
Eastern HS 500/9-12
1100 N Eastern School Rd 47165 812-967-3931
David Aly, prin. Fax 967-5767
East Washington MS 600/5-8
1100 N Eastern School Rd 47165 812-967-5000
Linda Luedeman, prin. Fax 967-5737

Pendleton, Madison, Pop. 3,859
South Madison Community SC 3,600/K-12
201 S East St 46064 765-778-2152
Dr. Thomas Warmke, supt. Fax 778-8207
www.smadison.k12.in.us
Pendleton Heights HS 1,100/9-12
1 Arabian Dr 46064 765-778-2161
Glen Nelson, prin. Fax 778-0605
Pendleton Heights MS 600/7-8
301 S East St 46064 765-778-2139
Daniel Joyce, prin. Fax 778-0557

Pershing, Wayne, Pop. 1,531
Western Wayne SD 1,200/K-12
PO Box 217 47370 765-478-5375
Robert Mahon, supt. Fax 478-4577
Other Schools – See Cambridge City

Peru, Miami, Pop. 12,732
Peru Community SD 1,800/PK-12
35 W 3rd St 46970 765-473-3081
Thomas McKaig, supt. Fax 472-5129
www.peru.k12.in.us
Peru HS 800/9-12
401 N Broadway 46970 765-472-3301
Jon Custer, prin. Fax 472-5148
Peru JHS 400/7-8
30 Daniel St 46970 765-473-3084
Sam Watkins, prin. Fax 473-4007

Petersburg, Pike, Pop. 2,501
Pike County SC 2,100/PK-12
907 E Walnut St 47567 812-354-8731
D. Thomas, supt. Fax 354-8733
www.pcsc.k12.in.us
Pike Central HS 600/9-12
1810 E State Road 56 47567 812-354-8478
LeAnne Kelley, prin. Fax 789-2992
Pike Central MS 500/6-8
1814 E State Road 56 47567 812-354-8478
Calvin Biddle, prin. Fax 789-2992

Pierceton, Kosciusko, Pop. 686
Whitko Community SC 2,000/K-12
432 S First St 46562 574-594-2658
Dr. Jeff Hendrix, supt. Fax 594-2326
whitko.org
Other Schools – See Larwill, South Whitley

Plainfield, Hendricks, Pop. 23,532
Plainfield Community SC 4,100/PK-12
985 Longfellow Ln 46168 317-839-2578
Dr. Jerry Holifield, supt. Fax 838-3664
www.plainfield.k12.in.us
Plainfield Community MS 1,000/6-8
401 Elm Dr 46168 317-838-3966
Jerry Goldsberry, prin. Fax 838-3965
Plainfield HS 1,200/9-12
709 Stafford Rd 46168 317-839-7711
Scott Ollinger, prin. Fax 838-3671

PJ's College of Cosmetology Post-Sec.
2026 Stafford Rd 46168

Plymouth, Marshall, Pop. 10,876
Plymouth Community SC 2,800/PK-12
611 Berkley St 46563 574-936-3115
John Hill, supt. Fax 936-3160
www.plymouth.k12.in.us/
Lincoln JHS 500/7-8
220 N Liberty St 46563 574-936-3113
John McNeil, prin. Fax 936-3574
Plymouth HS 1,000/9-12
1 Big Red Dr 46563 574-936-2178
Richard Tobias, prin. Fax 936-4842

Grace Baptist Christian S 100/PK-12
1830 N Michigan St 46563 574-936-3448
Scott Caldwell, prin.

Poneto, Wells, Pop. 235
Southern Wells Community SD 800/K-12
9120 S 300 W 46781 765-728-5537
Neil Potter, supt. Fax 728-8124
www.swraiders.com
Southern Wells JSHS 400/7-12
9120 S 300 W 46781 765-728-5534
Chad Yencer, prin. Fax 728-8124

Portage, Porter, Pop. 35,687
Portage Township SD 8,200/PK-12
6240 US Highway 6 46368 219-762-6511
Michael Berta, supt. Fax 762-3263
www.portage.k12.in.us
Fegely MS 700/6-8
5384 Stone Ave 46368 219-763-8150
Rebecca Lyons, prin. Fax 763-8157
Portage HS 2,500/9-12
6450 US Highway 6 46368 219-764-6026
Caren Swickard, prin. Fax 764-6062
Willowcreek MS 1,300/6-8
5962 Central Ave 46368 219-763-8090
Michelle Stewart, prin. Fax 763-8069

Portage Christian S 300/PK-12
3040 Arlene St 46368 219-762-8962
Tim Rumley, admin. Fax 763-9931

Portland, Jay, Pop. 6,191
Jay SC 3,900/PK-12
404 E Arch St 47371 260-726-9341
Barbara Downing, supt. Fax 726-4959
www.jayschools.k12.in.us
East Jay MS 600/6-8
225 E Water St 47371 260-726-9371
Lee Newman, prin. Fax 726-2383
Jay County HS 1,100/9-12
2072 W State Road 67 47371 260-726-9306
Dr. Woody Barwick, prin. Fax 726-9760
Other Schools – See Dunkirk

Poseyville, Posey, Pop. 1,151
Metro SD of North Posey County 1,500/PK-12
101 N Church St 47633 812-874-2243
John Wood, supt. Fax 874-8806
www.northposey.k12.in.us/
North Posey HS 500/9-12
5900 High School Rd 47633 812-673-4242
Scott Strieter, prin. Fax 673-6616
North Posey JHS 300/7-8
5800 High School Rd 47633 812-673-4244
Linda Crick, prin. Fax 673-6622

Princeton, Gibson, Pop. 8,652
North Gibson SC 2,100/K-12
RR 5 Box 49 47670 812-385-4851
Dr. John A. Cochren, supt. Fax 386-1531
www.ngsc.k12.in.us
Princeton Community HS 600/9-12
RR 5 Box 49 47670 812-385-2591
Jon Abbey, prin. Fax 386-1535
Princeton Community MS 500/6-8
410 E State St 47670 812-385-2020
Dr. Carolyn Cochren, prin. Fax 386-6746

Ramsey, Harrison
North Harrison Community SC 1,900/K-12
1260 Highway 64 NW 47166 812-347-2407
Monty Schneider, supt. Fax 347-2870
www.nhcs.k12.in.us
North Harrison HS 700/9-12
1070 Highway 64 NW 47166 812-347-3148
Kelly Simpson, prin. Fax 347-2875
North Harrison MS 400/6-8
1180 Highway 64 NW 47166 812-347-2421
Jon Howerton, prin. Fax 347-2835

Rensselaer, Jasper, Pop. 6,234
Rensselaer Central SC 1,800/PK-12
605 W Grove St 47978 219-866-7822
Steven York, supt. Fax 866-8360
www.rcsc.k12.in.us/
Rensselaer Central HS 500/9-12
1106 E Grace St 47978 219-866-5175
Edward Habrowski, prin. Fax 866-5135
Rensselaer Central MS 500/6-8
1106 E Bomber Dr 47978 219-866-4661
Kelly Berenda, prin. Fax 866-2103

St. Joseph's College Post-Sec.
PO Box 890 47978 219-866-6000

Richmond, Wayne, Pop. 37,560
Richmond Community SC 5,700/K-12
300 Hub Etchison Pkwy 47374 765-973-3300
Allen Bourff, supt. Fax 973-3417
www.rcs.k12.in.us
Richmond HS 1,700/9-12
380 Hub Etchison Pkwy 47374 765-973-3424
Barbara Bergdoll, prin. Fax 973-3716
Test MS 400/7-8
33 S 22nd St 47374 765-973-3412
Luann Spicer, prin. Fax 973-3712
Worth MS 500/7-8
222 NW 7th St 47374 765-973-3495
Kathy McCarty, prin. Fax 973-3703
Find Center Adult
900 S L St 47374 765-973-3486
Susan Hively, prin. Fax 935-1825

Bethany Theological Seminary Post-Sec.
615 National Rd W 47374 765-983-1800
David Demuth Institute of Cosmetology Post-Sec.
2 SW 5th St 47374 765-935-7964

Earlham Coll. & Earlham Sch. of Religion Post-Sec.
801 National Rd W 47374 765-983-1200
Indiana University East Post-Sec.
2325 Chester Blvd 47374 765-973-8200
Ivy Tech Community College - Richmond Post-Sec.
2325 Chester Blvd 47374 765-966-2656
New Creations Christian S 50/K-12
6400 National Rd E 47374 765-935-2790
Tammy Sealy, admin. Fax 935-3961
PJ's College of Cosmetology Post-Sec.
115 N 9th St 47374 765-962-3005
Reid Hospital & Health Care Services Post-Sec.
1401 Chester Blvd 47374 765-983-3167
Seton Catholic JSHS 100/7-12
233 S 5th St 47374 765-965-6956
Rick Ruhl, prin. Fax 935-9930

Rising Sun, Ohio, Pop. 2,405
Rising Sun-Ohio County Community SD 1,000/K-12
110 S Henrietta St 47040 812-438-2655
Stephen Patz, supt. Fax 438-4636
www.risingsunschools.com/
Rising Sun HS 300/9-12
210 S Henrietta St 47040 812-438-2652
Keith Majewski, prin. Fax 438-2431

Roachdale, Putnam, Pop. 976
North Putnam Community SD
Supt. — See Bainbridge
North Putnam HS 600/9-12
8869 N County Road 250 E 46172 765-522-6282
Alan Zerkel, prin. Fax 522-2862
North Putnam MS 500/6-8
8905 N County Road 250 E 46172 765-522-2900
Mike Wilcox, prin. Fax 522-2863

Rochester, Fulton, Pop. 6,451
Rochester Community SC 2,000/PK-12
PO Box 108 46975 574-223-2159
Dr. Debra Howe, supt. Fax 223-4909
www.rochester.k12.in.us
Rochester Community HS 600/9-12
PO Box 108 46975 574-223-2176
Daniel Ronk, prin. Fax 223-3401
Rochester Community MS 500/6-8
PO Box 108 46975 574-223-2280
Deborah Carter, prin. Fax 223-1531

Rockport, Spencer, Pop. 2,091
South Spencer County SC 1,500/PK-12
PO Box 26 47635 812-649-2591
H. Mike Robinson, supt. Fax 649-4249
www.sspencer.k12.in.us
South Spencer HS 500/9-12
1142 N Orchard Rd 47635 812-649-9157
Robert Combs, prin. Fax 649-2214
South Spencer MS 300/6-8
1298 N Orchard Rd 47635 812-649-2203
Gina Scales, prin. Fax 649-9630

Rockville, Parke, Pop. 2,701
Rockville Community SC 900/K-12
602 Howard Ave 47872 765-569-5582
Gary Storie, supt. Fax 569-6650
www.rockville.k12.in.us
Rockville JSHS 400/7-12
506 N Beadle St 47872 765-569-5686
Dave Mahurin, prin. Fax 569-1047

Rossville, Clinton, Pop. 1,540
Rossville Consolidated SD 1,000/K-12
PO Box 11 46065 765-379-2990
Dr. James Hanna, supt. Fax 379-3014
www.rossville.k12.in.us/
Rossville HS 300/9-12
PO Box 530 46065 765-379-2551
Allen Remaly, prin. Fax 379-2551
Rossville MS 200/6-8
PO Box 530 46065 765-379-2551
Shawn McCracken, prin. Fax 379-2556

Royal Center, Cass, Pop. 817
Pioneer Regional SC 1,000/K-12
PO Box 577 46978 574-643-2605
Dr. David Bess, supt. Fax 643-9977
www.pioneer.k12.in.us/
Pioneer JSHS 500/7-12
PO Box 547 46978 574-643-3145
Robert Brock, prin. Fax 643-2020

Rushville, Rush, Pop. 5,679
Rush County SD 2,700/PK-12
330 W 8th St 46173 765-932-4186
Dr. John Williams, supt. Fax 938-1608
rcs.rushville.k12.in.us/
Rush MS 500/7-8
1601 N Sexton St 46173 765-932-2968
Marla Stevens, prin. Fax 938-2011
Rushville Consolidated HS 800/9-12
1201 Lions Path 46173 765-932-3901
Garry Watson, prin. Fax 932-4051

Russiaville, Howard, Pop. 1,186
Western SC 2,400/K-12
2600 S 600 W 46979 765-883-5576
Ronald Wilson, supt. Fax 883-7946
www.western.k12.in.us
Western HS 700/9-12
2600 S 600 W 46979 765-883-5541
Charles Wolf, prin. Fax 883-4522
Western MS 600/6-8
2600 S 600 W 46979 765-883-5566
Ron Phillips, prin. Fax 883-4531

Saint John, Lake, Pop. 9,545
Lake Central SC 9,000/PK-12
8260 Wicker Ave 46373 219-365-8507
Janet Emerick, supt. Fax 365-6406
www.lakecentral.k12.in.us
Lake Central HS 2,700/9-12
8400 Wicker Ave 46373 219-365-8551
Sandra Platt, prin. Fax 365-7156
Other Schools – See Dyer, Schererville

Saint Leon, Franklin, Pop. 496
Sunman-Dearborn Community SC
Supt. — See Sunman
East Central HS 1,400/9-12
1 Trojan Ln, Brookville IN 47012 812-576-4811
Don Criswell, prin. Fax 576-2047
Sunman-Dearborn MS 700/7-8
8356 Schuman Rd, Brookville IN 47012 812-576-3500
Mark Watkins, prin. Fax 576-3506

Saint Mary of the Woods, Vigo

St. Mary-of-the-Woods College Post-Sec.
1 St Mary of Woods Coll 47876 812-535-5151

Saint Meinrad, Spencer

St. Meinrad School of Theology Post-Sec.
200 Hill Dr 47577 812-357-6611

Salem, Washington, Pop. 6,453
Salem Community SD 2,100/K-12
500 N Harrison St 47167 812-883-4437
Dr. Kim Thurston, supt. Fax 883-1031
www.salemschools.com/
Salem HS 600/9-12
700 N Harrison St 47167 812-883-3904
Jim Ralston, prin. Fax 883-3905
Salem MS, 1001 N Harrison St 47167 500/6-8
Ray Oppel, prin. 812-883-3808

Schererville, Lake, Pop. 28,394
Lake Central SC
Supt. — See Saint John
Grimmer MS 1,000/6-8
225 W 77th Ave 46375 219-865-6985
Janet Zeck, prin. Fax 865-4423

Don Roberts Beauty Academy Post-Sec.
152 E US Highway 30 46375 219-864-1600

Scottsburg, Scott, Pop. 6,060
Scott County SD 2 2,900/K-12
375 E Mcclain Ave 47170 812-752-8946
Robert Hooker, supt. Fax 752-8951
www.scsd2.k12.in.us/
Scottsburg HS 800/9-12
500 S Gardner St 47170 812-752-8927
Derek Marshall, prin. Fax 752-6207
Scottsburg MS 700/6-8
425 S 3rd St 47170 812-752-8926
Kristin Nass, prin. Fax 752-8864

Sellersburg, Clark, Pop. 6,028
West Clark Community SC 3,500/PK-12
601 Renz Ave 47172 812-246-3375
Terry Smith, supt. Fax 246-9731
www.wclark.k12.in.us/IEHome.html
Silver Creek HS 600/9-12
557 Renz Ave 47172 812-246-3391
Michael Crabtree, prin. Fax 246-8184
Silver Creek MS 500/6-8
495 N Indiana Ave 47172 812-246-4421
Reid Bailey, prin. Fax 246-7430
Other Schools – See Borden, Henryville

Ivy Tech Community College - Southern Post-Sec.
8204 Highway 311 47172 812-246-3301
Restoration Christian S 300/PK-12
11515 Highway 31 47172 812-246-9271
Sara Hauselman, prin. Fax 246-0722

Selma, Delaware, Pop. 830
Liberty-Perry Community SC 1,200/K-12
PO Box 337 47383 765-282-5615
James Craig, supt. Fax 281-3733
www.selma.bsu.edu/
Selma MS 300/6-8
10501 E County Road 167 S 47383 765-288-7242
Alice Mehaffey, prin. Fax 281-3727
Wapahani HS 400/9-12
10401 E County Road 167 S 47383 765-289-7323
Bryan Rausch, prin. Fax 281-3724

Seymour, Jackson, Pop. 18,890
Seymour Community SD 3,800/PK-12
1638 S Walnut St 47274 812-522-3340
Dr. Robert Schmielau, supt. Fax 522-8031
www.scsc.k12.in.us
Seymour HS 1,200/9-12
1350 W 2nd St 47274 812-522-4384
James McCormick, prin. Fax 523-2347
Seymour MS 900/6-8
920 N Obrien St 47274 812-522-5453
Barbara Bergdoll, prin. Fax 523-8134

Trinity Lutheran HS 100/9-12
7120 N County Road 875 E 47274 812-524-8547
Daniel Sievert, prin. Fax 524-8523

Sharpsville, Tipton, Pop. 620
Northern Comm Tipton County SD 1,000/K-12
4774 N 200 W 46068 765-963-2585
Dr. Lee Williford, supt. Fax 963-3042
www.ncstc.k12.in.us/
Tri Central JSHS 600/6-12
2115 W 500 N 46068 765-963-2560
Dave Driggs, prin. Fax 963-6844

Shelbyville, Shelby, Pop. 18,063
Blue River Career Programs
801 Saint Joseph St 46176 317-392-4191
William Lyon, supt. Fax 392-5741
www.brcp.net
Blue River Career Ctr Vo/Tech
801 Saint Joseph St 46176 317-392-4191
William Lyon, prin. Fax 392-5741

Shelby Eastern SD 1,600/K-12
2451 N 600 E 46176 765-544-2246
John Jameson, supt. Fax 544-2247
www.ses.k12.in.us/
Other Schools – See Morristown, Waldron

Shelbyville Central SD 3,700/K-12
803 Saint Joseph St 46176 317-392-2505
David Adams, supt. Fax 392-5737
www.shelbycs.org
Shelbyville HS 1,100/9-12
2003 S Miller St 46176 317-398-9731
Tom Zobel, prin. Fax 392-5709
Shelbyville MS 900/6-8
1200 W McKay Rd 46176 317-392-2551
Denny Ramsey, prin. Fax 392-5713

Southwestern Cons Shelby County SC 800/K-12
3406 W 600 S 46176 317-729-5746
Dr. Terry Sargent, supt. Fax 729-5330
www.swshelby.k12.in.us
Southwestern JSHS 400/7-12
3406 W 600 S 46176 317-729-5122
Suzanne Blake, prin. Fax 729-2424

Sheridan, Hamilton, Pop. 2,661
Sheridan Community SD 1,100/PK-12
509 E 4th St 46069 317-758-4172
Derek Arrowood, supt. Fax 758-6248
www.sheridan.org/school/
Sheridan HS 400/9-12
24185 Hinesley Rd 46069 317-758-4431
Ed Baker, prin. Fax 758-2406
Sheridan MS 300/6-8
3030 W 246th St 46069 317-758-6780
Ed Baker, prin. Fax 758-2435

Shoals, Martin, Pop. 817
Shoals Community SC 800/PK-12
11741 Ironton Rd 47581 812-247-2060
Dr. Anthony Nonte, supt. Fax 247-2278
shoals.k12.in.us/
Shoals Community JSHS 300/7-12
7900 US Highway 50 47581 812-247-2090
Stan Mosier, prin. Fax 247-2056

South Bend, Saint Joseph, Pop. 105,262
South Bend Community SC 20,700/PK-12
215 S Saint Joseph St 46601 574-283-8000
Robert Zimmerman, supt. Fax 283-8143
www.sbcsc.k12.in.us
Adams HS 1,500/9-12
808 S Twyckenham Dr 46615 574-283-7700
Todd Wiedemann, prin. Fax 283-7704
Brown IS 700/5-8
737 Beale St 46616 574-287-9680
Margaret Lewis, prin. Fax 283-5581
Clay HS 1,600/9-12
19131 Darden Rd 46637 574-243-7000
Ruth Warren, prin. Fax 243-7005
Clay IS 700/5-8
52900 Lily Rd 46637 574-243-7145
James Knight, prin. Fax 243-7151
Dickinson IS 700/5-8
4404 Elwood Ave 46628 574-283-7625
Dwight Fulce, prin. Fax 283-7633
Edison IS 600/5-8
2701 Eisenhower Ave 46615 574-283-8900
Karla Lee, prin. Fax 283-8903
Greene IS 600/5-8
24702 Roosevelt Rd 46614 574-283-7900
Thomas Fujimura, prin. Fax 283-7903
Jackson IS 700/5-8
5001 Miami St 46614 574-231-5600
Margaret Schaller, prin. Fax 231-5605
Jefferson IS 500/5-8
528 S Eddy St 46617 574-283-8700
James Kapsa, prin. Fax 283-8703
LaSalle Academy 700/5-8
2701 Elwood Ave 46628 574-283-7500
Cynthia Oudghiri, prin. Fax 283-7513
Marshall IS 600/5-8
1433 Byron Dr 46614 574-231-5801
Kristine Simons, prin. Fax 231-5804
Navarre IS 700/5-8
4702 Ford St 46619 574-283-7345
Derrick White, prin. Fax 283-7351
Riley HS 1,500/9-12
1902 Fellows St 46613 574-283-8400
Edward Bradford, prin. Fax 283-8405
Washington HS 1,600/9-12
4747 W Washington St 46619 574-283-7200
George McCullough, prin. Fax 283-7205
Adult Education Adult
3206 Sugar Maple Ln 46628 574-283-7505
Anita Brown, admin. Fax 283-7549

Brown Mackie College Post-Sec.
1030 E Jefferson Blvd 46617 574-237-0774
Community Baptist Christian S 300/K-12
5715 Miami St 46614 574-291-3620
Mark French, prin. Fax 291-3648
Indiana University at South Bend Post-Sec.
PO Box 7111 46634 574-237-4111
Ironwood Christian S 50/K-12
4609 S Ironwood Rd 46614 574-231-8006
Kenneth Mendenhall, admin.
Ivy Tech Community College North Central Post-Sec.
220 Dean Johnson Blvd 46601 574-289-7001

Rabbi Naftali Riff Yeshiva HS 50/9-12
3207 High St 46614 574-291-4239
Louis Sandock, admin. Fax 291-9490
St. Joseph HS 800/9-12
1441 N Michigan St 46617 574-233-6137
Susan Richter, prin. Fax 232-3482
Trinity S at Greenlawn 300/7-12
107 S Greenlawn Ave 46617 574-287-5590
Kerry Koller, prin. Fax 236-6628

South Whitley, Whitley, Pop. 1,847
Whitko Community SC
Supt. — See Pierceton
Whitko HS 600/9-12
1 Big Blue Ave 46787 260-723-5146
Parrish Kruger, prin. Fax 723-4724

Speedway, Marion, Pop. 12,408
School Town of Speedway 1,700/K-12
5335 W 25th St 46224 317-244-0236
N. Andrew Wagner, supt. Fax 486-4843
www.speedway.k12.in.us
Speedway HS 500/9-12
5357 W 25th St 46224 317-244-7238
Ray Lawrence, prin. Fax 486-4838
Speedway JHS 300/7-8
5151 W 14th St 46224 317-244-3359
John Dizney, prin. Fax 486-4845

Spencer, Owen, Pop. 2,549
Spencer-Owen Community SD 3,100/PK-12
205 E Hillside Ave 47460 812-829-2233
Marsha Turner-Shear, supt. Fax 829-6614
www.socs.k12.in.us
Owen Valley HS 900/9-12
622 W State Highway 46 47460 812-829-2266
Kimberly Tucker, prin. Fax 829-6605
Owen Valley MS 600/7-8
626 W State Highway 46 47460 812-829-2249
Amy Elkins, prin. Fax 829-6635

Spiceland, Henry, Pop. 900
South Henry SC 800/K-12
6449 S Cemetery Dr 47385 765-987-7882
Dr. John Magers, supt. Fax 987-7589
www.shenry.k12.in.us/
Other Schools – See Straughn

Straughn, Henry, Pop. 249
South Henry SC
Supt. — See Spiceland
Tri JSHS 400/7-12
6972 S State Road 103 47387 765-987-7988
Scott Seibel, prin. Fax 987-8446

Sullivan, Sullivan, Pop. 4,537
Southwest SC 1,800/PK-12
110 N Main St 47882 812-268-6311
Dr. Rita Brodnax, supt. Fax 268-6312
www.swest.k12.in.us/
Sullivan HS 600/9-12
902 N Section St 47882 812-268-6301
George Bauman, prin. Fax 268-6303
Sullivan JHS 200/7-8
820 N Section St 47882 812-268-4000
Keith Brashear, prin. Fax 268-5368

Sunman, Ripley, Pop. 803
Sunman-Dearborn Community SC 4,300/K-12
PO Box 210 47041 812-623-2291
John Roeder, supt. Fax 623-3341
sunmandearborn.k12.in.us
Other Schools – See Saint Leon

Switz City, Greene, Pop. 311
White River Valley SD 800/K-12
PO Box 1470 47465 812-659-1424
Layton Wall, supt. Fax 659-2278
www.wrv.k12.in.us
White River Valley JSHS 300/7-12
PO Box 1470 47465 812-659-2274
Lee Ann Engelhardt, prin. Fax 659-2278

Syracuse, Kosciusko, Pop. 3,030
Wawasee Community SC 3,500/PK-12
1 Warrior Path Bldg 2 46567 574-457-3188
Dr. Mark Stock, supt. Fax 457-4962
www.wawasee.k12.in.us/
Wawasee HS 1,100/9-12
1 Warrior Path 46567 574-457-3147
Ellen Stevens, prin. Fax 457-4364
Wawasee MS 600/6-8
9850 N State Rd 13 46567 574-457-8839
Anthony Cassel, prin. Fax 457-3575

Tell City, Perry, Pop. 7,690
Tell City-Troy Township SC 1,600/PK-12
837 17th St 47586 812-547-3300
Ronald Etienne, supt. Fax 547-9704
www.tellcity.k12.in.us
Tell City HS 500/9-12
900 12th St 47586 812-547-3131
Dale Stewart, prin. Fax 547-9713
Tell City JHS 400/6-8
3515 Mozart St 47586 812-547-3748
Chad Schenck, prin. Fax 547-9737

Terre Haute, Vigo, Pop. 56,893
Vigo County SC 16,400/PK-12
PO Box 3703 47803 812-462-4216
Daniel Tanoos, supt. Fax 462-4379
www.vigoco.k12.in.us
Honey Creek MS 800/6-8
6601 S Carlisle St 47802 812-462-4372
Patrick Sheehan, prin. Fax 462-4367
Otter Creek MS 800/6-8
4801 N Lafayette St 47805 812-462-4391
Mark Kirby, prin. Fax 462-4388
Rose MS 600/6-8
1275 3rd Ave 47807 812-462-4474
Dr. Tammy Roeschlein, prin. Fax 462-4473
Scott MS 600/6-8
1000 Grant St 47802 812-462-4381
Mark Miller, prin. Fax 462-4370
Terre Haute North Vigo HS 2,100/9-12
3434 Maple Ave 47804 812-462-4312
Mick Newport, prin. Fax 462-4204
Terre Haute South Vigo HS 1,800/9-12
3737 S 7th St 47802 812-462-4252
Troy Fears, prin. Fax 462-4408
Wilson MS 800/6-8
301 S 25th St 47803 812-462-4396
Dr. Sharon Pitts, prin. Fax 232-2217
Other Schools – See West Terre Haute

Holy Cross S 100/5-12
PO Box 2316 47802 812-298-3077
Cary Molinder, prin. Fax 298-3291
Indiana Business College Post-Sec.
3175 S 3rd Pl 47802 812-232-4458
Indiana State University 47809 Post-Sec.
812-237-6311
Ivy Tech Community College Wabash Valley Post-Sec.
8000 S Education Dr 47802 812-299-1121
Rose-Hulman Institute of Technology Post-Sec.
5500 Wabash Ave 47803 812-877-1511
Terre Haute Adventist S 50/K-10
900 S 29th St 47803 812-232-1339
Terre Haute Christian S 100/K-12
2500 Margaret Ave 47802 812-238-2541
Steven Henry, prin. Fax 234-7610

Thorntown, Boone, Pop. 1,573
Western Boone County Community SD 1,900/PK-12
1201 N State Road 75 46071 765-482-6333
Stephen Sailor, supt. Fax 482-0890
www.bccn.boone.in.us/webo
Western Boone JSHS 900/7-12
1205 N State Road 75 46071 765-482-6143
Rob Ramey, prin. Fax 482-6146

Tipton, Tipton, Pop. 5,254
Tipton Community SC 1,900/K-12
221 N Main St 46072 765-675-2147
Robert Schultz, supt. Fax 675-3857
www.tcsc.k12.in.us
Tipton HS 600/9-12
619 S Main St 46072 765-675-7431
Joe Rushton, prin. Fax 675-9519
Tipton MS 500/6-8
817 S Main St 46072 765-675-7521
Shayne Clark, prin. Fax 675-9027

Topeka, Lagrange, Pop. 1,194
Westview SC 2,200/K-12
1545 S 600 W 46571 260-768-4404
Dr. Randall Zimmerly, supt. Fax 768-7368
www.westview.k12.in.us
Westview JSHS 800/7-12
1635 S 600 W 46571 260-768-4146
Troy Albert, prin. Fax 768-7611

Trafalgar, Johnson, Pop. 936
Nineveh-Hensley-Jackson United SD 1,800/K-12
802 S Indian Creek Dr 46181 317-878-2100
Dr. John Reed, supt. Fax 878-5765
www.nhj.k12.in.us
Indian Creek HS 500/9-12
803 W Indian Creek Dr 46181 317-878-2110
Robert Duke, prin. Fax 878-2112
Indian Creek MS 500/6-8
801 W Indian Creek Dr 46181 317-878-2130
Rodney King, prin. Fax 878-2149

Union City, Randolph, Pop. 3,471
Randolph Eastern SC 1,000/K-12
907 N Plum St 47390 765-964-4994
Cathy Stephen, supt. Fax 964-6590
www.resc.k12.in.us/
Union City Community HS 300/9-12
603 N Walnut St 47390 765-964-4840
Mike McDivitt, prin. Fax 964-3775
West Side MS 200/6-8
731 N Plum St 47390 765-964-4830
Janet Caudle, prin. Fax 964-7344

Union Mills, LaPorte
South Central Community SC 800/K-12
9808 S 600 W 46382 219-767-2263
Christopher Smith, supt. Fax 767-2260
www.scentral.k12.in.us/
South Central JSHS 400/7-12
9808 S 600 W 46382 219-767-2266
John Arnett, prin. Fax 767-2260

Upland, Grant, Pop. 3,735

Taylor University Post-Sec.
500 W Reade Ave 46989 765-998-2751

Valparaiso, Porter, Pop. 29,102
East Porter County SC
Supt. — See Kouts
Morgan Twp. MSHS 300/6-12
299 S State Road 49 46383 219-462-5883
Curtis Casbon, prin. Fax 462-4014
Washington Twp. MSHS 400/6-12
381 E State Road 2 46383 219-464-3598
Terry Robbins, prin. Fax 462-3372

Porter Township SC 1,600/K-12
248 S 500 W 46385 219-477-4933
Nicholas Brown, supt. Fax 477-4834
www.ptsc.k12.in.us/
Boone Grove HS 500/9-12
260 S 500 W 46385 219-988-4481
Garry DeRossett, prin. Fax 988-4431
Other Schools – See Boone Grove

Union Township SC 1,600/K-12
599 W 300 N Ste A 46385 219-759-2531
John Hunter, supt. Fax 759-3250
www.union.k12.in.us
Union Township MS 400/6-8
599 W 300 N 46385 219-759-2562
Jerry Lasky, prin. Fax 759-4359
Wheeler HS 500/9-12
587 W 300 N 46385 219-759-2561
Donald Gandy, prin. Fax 759-5602

Valparaiso Community SD 6,200/K-12
3801 Campbell St 46385 219-531-3000
Dr. Michael P. Benway, supt. Fax 531-3009
www.valpo.k12.in.us
Franklin MS 700/6-8
605 Campbell St 46385 219-531-3020
Robert Rarick, prin. Fax 531-3026
Jefferson MS 700/6-8
1600 Roosevelt Rd 46383 219-531-3140
Paul Knauff, prin. Fax 531-3146
Porter County Career Ctr Vo/Tech
1005 Franklin St 46383 219-531-3170
Jon Groth, prin. Fax 531-3173
Valparaiso HS 2,100/9-12
2727 Campbell St 46385 219-531-3070
Patrick Weil, prin. Fax 531-3076

Community College of Indiana-Valparaiso Post-Sec.
3100 Ivy Tech Dr 46383 219-464-8514
Don Roberts Beauty School Post-Sec.
1354 Lincoln Way 46383 219-462-5189
Porter Memorial Hospital Post-Sec.
814 Laporte Ave 46383 219-465-4883
Tall Oaks Christian S 50/K-12
1901 Evans Ave 46383 219-464-9862
Rick Greene, admin.
Valparaiso University 46383 Post-Sec.
219-464-5000
Victory Christian Academy 200/PK-12
3805 LaPorte Ave 46383 219-548-8803
Joyce Folk, admin. Fax 548-8803

Veedersburg, Fountain, Pop. 2,228
Southeast Fountain SC 1,400/K-12
744 E US Highway 136 47987 765-294-2254
Debra Barnes, supt. Fax 294-3200
www.sefschools.org/
Fountain Central JSHS 600/7-12
750 E US Highway 136 47987 765-294-2206
Larry Adams, prin. Fax 294-3204

Versailles, Ripley, Pop. 1,766
South Ripley Community SC 1,300/K-12
207 W Tyson St 47042 812-689-6282
Ted Ahaus, supt. Fax 689-6760
www.sripley.k12.in.us/
South Ripley JSHS 600/7-12
1589 S Benham Rd 47042 812-689-5303
Bill Snyder, prin. Fax 689-6715

Southeastern Career SC
901 W US Highway 50 47042 812-689-5253
Brad Street, supt. Fax 689-6977
Southeastern Career Center Vo/Tech
901 W US Highway 50 47042 812-689-5253
James Rogers, prin. Fax 689-6977

Vevay, Switzerland, Pop. 1,655
Switzerland County SC 1,600/PK-12
305 W Seminary St 47043 812-427-2611
Tracy Caddell, supt. Fax 427-3695
www.switzerland.k12.in.us
Switzerland County HS 500/9-12
1020 W Main St 47043 812-427-2626
Candis Haskell, prin. Fax 427-3445
Switzerland County MS 400/6-8
1004 W Main St 47043 812-427-3809
Nancy Stearns, prin. Fax 427-3807

Vincennes, Knox, Pop. 18,077
South Knox SC 1,100/K-12
6116 E State Rd 61 47591 812-726-4440
Bradley Case, supt. Fax 743-2110
www.sknox.k12.in.us
South Knox MSHS 500/7-12
6136 E State Road 61 47591 812-726-4450
Harry Nolting, prin. Fax 726-4545

Vincennes Community SC 3,000/K-12
300 N 6th St 47591 812-882-4844
Douglas Rose, supt. Fax 885-1427
www.vcsc.k12.in.us
Clark MS 700/6-8
500 Buntin St 47591 812-882-5172
Dennis Query, prin. Fax 885-1419
Lincoln HS 900/9-12
3001 Hart St 47591 812-882-8480
David Chapman, prin. Fax 885-1431

Good Samaritan Hospital Post-Sec.
520 S 7th St 47591 812-885-3195
Rivet MSHS 100/6-12
210 Barnett St 47591 812-882-6215
Dustin Hitt, prin. Fax 886-1939
Vincennes Beauty College Post-Sec.
12 S 2nd St 47591 812-882-1086
Vincennes University Post-Sec.
1002 N 1st St 47591 800-742-9198

Wabash, Wabash, Pop. 11,209
Heartland Career Center SD
79 S 200 W 46992 260-563-7481
Gary Sweet, supt. Fax 563-5544
www.geocities.com/hccin
Heartland Career Ctr Vo/Tech
79 S 200 W 46992 260-563-7481
Mark Hobbs, prin. Fax 563-5544

Metro SD of Wabash County 2,600/K-12
204 N 300 W 46992 260-563-8050
Dr. Scott Hanback, supt. Fax 569-6836
www.msdwc.k12.in.us
Northfield JSHS 600/7-12
154 W 200 N 46992 260-563-8050
William Neale, prin. Fax 569-6839
Southwood JSHS 600/7-12
564 E State Road 124 46992 260-563-8050
Jean Shonkwiler, prin. Fax 569-6843
Whites JSHS 200/6-12
5233 S 50 E 46992 260-563-1158
Sherman Knight, prin. Fax 563-8975

Wabash CSD 1,500/K-12
PO Box 744 46992 260-563-2151
Celia Briggs, supt. Fax 563-2066
www.apaches.k12.in.us
Wabash HS 400/9-12
580 N Miami St 46992 260-563-4131
Stacey Hughes, prin. Fax 563-6806
Wabash MS 400/6-8
150 Colerain St 46992 260-563-4137
Stacey Hughes, prin. Fax 569-9805

Emmanuel Christian S 100/K-12
129 Southwood Dr 46992 260-563-1677
Doug Phillips, prin.

Wakarusa, Elkhart, Pop. 1,666
Wa-Nee Community SD
Supt. — See Nappanee
Northwood MS 800/6-8
301 N Elkhart St 46573 574-862-2710
George Roelandts, prin. Fax 862-2327

Waldron, Shelby
Shelby Eastern SD
Supt. — See Shelbyville
Waldron JSHS 400/6-12
PO Box 369 46182 765-525-6822
Brian Fehribach, prin. Fax 525-9727

Walkerton, Saint Joseph, Pop. 2,200
John Glenn SC 1,800/K-12
101 John Glenn Dr 46574 574-586-3129
Richard Reese, supt. Fax 586-2660
www.jgsc.k12.in.us
Glenn HS 600/9-12
201 John Glenn Dr 46574 574-586-3195
Dan Funston, prin. Fax 586-3905
Urey MS 300/7-8
407 Washington St 46574 574-586-3184
Janet Carey, prin. Fax 586-3714

Walton, Cass, Pop. 1,028
Southeastern SC 1,600/K-12
6422 E State Road 218 46994 574-626-2525
Dr. John Bevan, supt. Fax 626-2751
www.sesc.k12.in.us
Cass JSHS 800/7-12
6422 E State Road 218 46994 574-626-2511
William Isaacs, prin. Fax 626-2172

Warsaw, Kosciusko, Pop. 12,735
Warsaw Community SC 6,500/K-12
PO Box 288 46581 574-371-5098
Robert Haworth, supt. Fax 371-5095
www.warsaw.k12.in.us
Edgewood MS 500/7-8
900 S Union St 46580 574-371-5096
JoElla Smyth, prin. Fax 371-5010
Lakeview MS 600/7-8
848 E Smith St 46580 574-269-7211
Tom Kline, prin. Fax 371-5013
Warsaw Community HS 1,800/9-12
1 Tiger Ln 46580 574-371-5099
Dr. Jennifer Brumfield, prin. Fax 371-5012

Monarch Christian Academy 50/K-12
744 S 325 E 46582 574-268-2869
Debbie Lowe, dir. Fax 269-2307

Washington, Daviess, Pop. 11,357
Twin Rivers Vocational Area SC
301 E South St 47501 812-254-1189
Joyce Memering, supt. Fax 254-8346
Twin Rivers Vocational S Vo/Tech
301 E South St 47501 812-254-1189
Joyce Memering, prin. Fax 254-8346

Washington Community SD 2,500/K-12
301 E South St 47501 812-254-5536
Dr. Bruce Hatton, supt. Fax 254-8346
www.wcs.k12.in.us
Washington HS 800/9-12
608 E Walnut St 47501 812-254-3860
Gary Puckett, prin. Fax 254-8374
Washington JHS 400/7-8
210 NE 6th St 47501 812-254-2682
Gary Twomey, prin. Fax 254-8381

Washington Catholic MSHS 200/6-12
201 NE 2nd St 47501 812-254-2050
Chad Ballengee, prin. Fax 254-8746

Waterloo, DeKalb, Pop. 2,198
DeKalb County Central United SC 4,200/PK-12
3326 County Road 427 46793 260-920-1011
Kenneth Fowble, supt. Fax 837-7767
www.dekalb.k12.in.us
DeKalb HS 1,300/9-12
3424 County Road 427 46793 260-920-1012
David Schnelker, prin. Fax 837-7841
DeKalb MS 1,000/6-8
3338 County Road 427 46793 260-920-1013
Thomas Sanborn, prin. Fax 837-7812

Westfield, Hamilton, Pop. 12,322
Westfield Washington SD 4,900/PK-12
322 W Main St 46074 317-867-8000
Mark Keen, supt. Fax 867-0929
www.wws.k12.in.us
Westfield HS 1,300/9-12
18250 N Union St 46074 317-867-6800
Stacy McGuire, prin. Fax 867-2909
Westfield MS 800/7-8
345 W Hoover St 46074 317-867-6600
Ed Mendoza, prin. Fax 867-1407

West Lafayette, Tippecanoe, Pop. 28,599
Tippecanoe SC
Supt. — See Lafayette
Harrison HS 1,500/9-12
5701 N 50 W 47906 765-463-3511
Doug Lesley, prin. Fax 497-9893
Klondike MS 500/6-8
3307 Klondike Rd 47906 765-463-2544
Christine Cannon, prin. Fax 497-9413

West Lafayette Community SC 2,000/K-12
1130 N Salisbury St 47906 765-746-1641
Iran Floyd, supt. Fax 746-1644
www.wl.k12.in.us/
West Lafayette JSHS 1,000/7-12
1105 N Grant St 47906 765-746-0400
Larry Allen, prin. Fax 746-0422

Purdue University Post-Sec.
475 Stadium Mall Dr 47907 765-494-4600

West Lebanon, Warren, Pop. 789
Metro SD of Warren County
Supt. — See Williamsport
Seeger Memorial JSHS 700/7-12
1222 S State Road 263 47991 765-893-4445
Ralph Shrader, prin. Fax 893-8354

West Terre Haute, Vigo, Pop. 2,255
Vigo County SC
Supt. — See Terre Haute
West Vigo HS 700/9-12
4590 W Sarah Myers Dr 47885 812-462-4282
Tom Balitewicz, prin. Fax 462-4090
West Vigo MS 500/6-8
4750 W Sarah Myers Dr 47885 812-462-4361
Tim Vislosky, prin. Fax 462-4090

Westville, LaPorte, Pop. 5,219
Metro SD of New Durham Township 800/K-12
207 E Valparaiso St 46391 219-785-2239
Robert Harbart, supt. Fax 785-4584
www.westvilleschool.com
Westville JSHS 400/7-12
207 E Valparaiso St 46391 219-785-2531
William Yates, prin. Fax 785-2990

Purdue University Post-Sec.
1401 S US Highway 421 46391 219-785-5200

Wheatfield, Jasper, Pop. 865
Kankakee Valley SC 3,300/K-12
PO Box 278 46392 219-987-4711
Dr. Glenn Krueger, supt. Fax 987-4710
www.kv.k12.in.us
Kankakee Valley HS 1,000/9-12
3923 W State Road 10 46392 219-956-3143
Philip Apple, prin. Fax 956-3143
Kankakee Valley MS 500/7-8
3923 W State Road 10 46392 219-956-3143
William Auker, prin. Fax 956-3143

Whiteland, Johnson, Pop. 4,271
Clark-Pleasant Community SC 4,200/K-12
50 Center St 46184 317-535-7579
Dr. J.T. Coopman, supt. Fax 535-4931
www.cpcsc.k12.in.us
Clark Pleasant MS 600/7-8
222 Tracy St 46184 317-535-7121
Sondra Wooton, prin. Fax 535-2064
Whiteland Community HS 1,100/9-12
300 Main St 46184 317-535-7562
Tom Galovic, prin. Fax 535-7509

Whiting, Lake, Pop. 4,893
Hammond CSD
Supt. — See Hammond
Clark MSHS 1,500/6-12
1921 Davis Ave 46394 219-659-3522
Dr. Juan Anaya, prin. Fax 659-1599

Whiting CSD 800/PK-12
1500 Center St 46394 219-659-0656
Dr. Sandra Martinez, supt. Fax 473-4008
www.whiting.k12.in.us
Whiting HS 200/9-12
1751 Oliver St 46394 219-659-0255
Dirk Flick, prin. Fax 473-1341
Whiting MS 200/6-8
1800 New York Ave 46394 219-473-1344
Jay Harker, prin. Fax 473-1341

Calumet College of St. Joseph Post-Sec.
2400 New York Ave 46394 219-473-7770

Williamsport, Warren, Pop. 1,928
Metro SD of Warren County 1,400/K-12
101 N Monroe St 47993 765-762-3364
Terry Roderick, supt. Fax 762-6623
msdwarco.k12.in.us/
Other Schools – See West Lebanon

Winamac, Pulaski, Pop. 2,436
Eastern Pulaski Community SC 1,400/K-12
711 School Dr 46996 574-946-4010
Fax 946-4510
www.epulaski.k12.in.us/
Winamac Community HS 500/9-12
715 School Dr 46996 574-946-6151
Rick Defries, prin. Fax 946-4219
Winamac Community MS 300/6-8
715 School Dr 46996 574-946-6525
Stan Good, prin. Fax 946-4219

Winchester, Randolph, Pop. 4,845
Randolph Central SC 1,700/K-12
103 N East St 47394 765-584-1401
Philip Wray, supt. Fax 584-1403
www.rc.k12.in.us
Driver MS 400/6-8
130 S 100 E 47394 765-584-4671
Tim Passmore, prin. Fax 584-6271
Winchester Community HS 500/9-12
700 N Union St 47394 765-584-8201
Thomas Osborn, prin. Fax 584-8204

Winona Lake, Kosciusko, Pop. 4,235

Grace College Post-Sec.
200 Seminary Dr 46590 574-372-5100
Grace Theological Seminary Post-Sec.
200 Seminary Dr 46590 574-372-5100
Lakeland Christian Academy 200/7-12
1093 S 250 E 46590 574-267-7265
Joy Lavender, admin. Fax 267-5687

Wolcott, White, Pop. 939
Tri-County SC 800/K-12
105 N 2nd St 47995 219-279-2418
Dr. Gib Crimmins, supt. Fax 279-2242
www.trico.k12.in.us
Tri-County MSHS 500/6-12
11298 W 100 S 47995 219-279-2105
Kathy Goad, prin. Fax 279-2108

Woodburn, Allen, Pop. 1,635
East Allen County SD
Supt. — See New Haven
Woodlan JSHS 700/7-12
17215 Woodburn Rd 46797 260-446-0290
Edwin Yoder, prin. Fax 446-0298

Yorktown, Delaware, Pop. 4,966
Mt. Pleasant Township Community SC 2,200/K-12
8800 W Smith St 47396 765-759-2720
Mary Ann Irwin, supt. Fax 759-7894
www.yorktown.k12.in.us
Yorktown HS 700/9-12
1100 S Tiger Dr 47396 765-759-2550
Kelly Wittman, prin. Fax 759-4040
Yorktown MS 600/6-8
8820 W Smith St 47396 765-759-2660
David Sturgeon, prin. Fax 759-3243

Zionsville, Boone, Pop. 11,853
Zionsville Community SC 4,500/PK-12
900 Mulberry St 46077 317-873-2858
Scott Robison, supt. Fax 873-8003
www.zcs.k12.in.us
Zionsville Community HS 1,300/9-12
1000 Mulberry St 46077 317-873-3355
Jim Eggers, prin. Fax 873-8002
Zionsville MS 1,500/5-8
900 N Ford Rd 46077 317-873-2426
Sean Conner, prin. Fax 733-4001

IOWA DEPARTMENT OF EDUCATION
400 E 14th St, Des Moines 50319-0146
Telephone 515-281-5294
Fax 515-242-5988
Website http://www.state.ia.us/educate

Director of Education Judy Jeffrey

IOWA BOARD OF EDUCATION
400 E 14th St, Des Moines 50319-9000

President Gene Vincent

AREA EDUCATION AGENCIES (AEA)

AEA 267
Dean W. Meier, admin. 319-273-8200
3712 Cedar Heights Dr Fax 273-8229
Cedar Falls 50613
www.aea267.k12.ia.us

Grant Wood AEA 10
Ron Fielder, admin., 4401 6th St SW 319-399-6700
Cedar Rapids 52404 Fax 399-6457
www.aea10.k12.ia.us/

Great River AEA 16
Joe Crozier, admin. 319-753-6561
PO Box 1065, Burlington 52601 Fax 753-1527
www.aea16.k12.ia.us/

Green Valley AEA 14
Connie Maxson, admin. 641-782-8443
1405 N Lincoln St, Creston 50801 Fax 782-4298
www.aea14.k12.ia.us/

Heartland AEA 11
Maxine Kilcrease, admin. 515-270-9030
6500 Corporate Dr Fax 270-5383
Johnston 50131
www.aea11.k12.ia.us/

Keystone AEA 1
Robert Vittengl, admin. 563-245-1480
1400 2nd St NW, Elkader 52043 Fax 245-1484
www.aea1.k12.ia.us

Loess Hills AEA 13
Glenn Grove, admin. 712-366-0503
PO Box 1109, Council Bluffs 51502 Fax 366-3431
www.aea13.org/

Mississippi Bend AEA 9
Glen Pelecky, admin. 563-359-1371
729 21st St, Bettendorf 52722 Fax 359-5967
www.aea9.k12.ia.us/

Northwest AEA 12
Les Douma, admin. 712-274-6000
1520 Morningside Ave Fax 274-6123
Sioux City 51106
www.nwaea.k12.ia.us/

Prairie Lakes AEA 8
Kay Forsythe, admin. 712-335-3588
500 NE 6th St, Pocahontas 50574 Fax 335-4600
www.aea8.k12.ia.us/

Southern Prairie AEA 15
Joe Crozier, admin. 641-682-8591
2814 N Court St, Ottumwa 52501 Fax 682-9083
www.aea15.k12.ia.us./

PUBLIC, PRIVATE AND CATHOLIC SECONDARY SCHOOLS

Ackley, Hardin, Pop. 1,738
AGWSR Community SD 500/K-12
511 State St 50601 641-847-2611
Robert Lehman, supt. Fax 847-2612
www.ackley.k12.ia.us
AGWSR HS 200/9-12
918 4th Ave 50601 641-847-2633
Joel Bagley, prin. Fax 847-3345
Other Schools – See Wellsburg

Adair, Guthrie, Pop. 773
Adair-Casey Community SD 300/K-12
3384 Indigo Ave 50002 641-746-2241
Noel VanDeer, supt. Fax 746-2243
accs.k12.ia.us
Adair-Casey JSHS 200/7-12
3384 Indigo Ave 50002 641-746-2241
William Umbaugh, prin. Fax 746-2243

Adel, Dallas, Pop. 4,046
Adel-De Soto-Minburn Community SD 1,400/PK-12
801 Nile Kinnick Dr S 50003 515-993-4283
Tim Hoffman, supt. Fax 993-4866
www.adel.k12.ia.us
Adel-De Soto-Minburn HS 300/10-12
801 Nile Kinnick Dr S 50003 515-993-4584
Lee Greibel, prin. Fax 993-3025
Adel-De Soto-Minburn MS 100/8-9
801 Nile Kinnick Dr S 50003 515-993-3490
Carole Schlapkohl, prin. Fax 993-1956

Afton, Union, Pop. 886
East Union Community SD 400/K-12
1916 High School Dr 50830 641-347-5215
Steve Clark, supt. Fax 347-5514
www.east-union.k12.ia.us
East Union JSHS 300/6-12
1916 High School Dr 50830 641-347-8421
Mark Weis, prin. Fax 347-5514

Akron, Plymouth, Pop. 1,467
Akron Westfield Community SD 600/PK-12
PO Box 950 51001 712-568-2616
Ron Flynn, supt. Fax 568-2997
www.akron-westfield.k12.ia.us
Akron Westfield HS 200/9-12
PO Box 950 51001 712-568-2020
Derek Briggs, prin. Fax 568-2997
Akron Westfield JHS 100/7-8
PO Box 950 51001 712-568-2020
Cathy Bobier, prin. Fax 568-2997

Albia, Monroe, Pop. 3,679
Albia Community SD 1,200/K-12
120 Benton Ave E 52531 641-932-5165
Kevin Crall, supt. Fax 932-5192
www.albia.k12.ia.us
Albia HS 400/9-12
503 B Ave E 52531 641-932-2161
Linda Hoskins, prin. Fax 932-7069
Albia JHS 200/7-8
505 C Ave E 52531 641-932-2161
Alan Schwarte, prin. Fax 932-7069

Alburnett, Linn, Pop. 539
Alburnett Community SD 600/K-12
PO Box 189 52202 319-842-2261
Mike Harrold, supt. Fax 842-2398
www.alburnett.k12.ia.us
Alburnett JSHS 300/7-12
PO Box 189 52202 319-842-2263
Thomas Stewart, prin. Fax 842-2398

Algona, Kossuth, Pop. 5,505
Algona Community SD 1,300/PK-12
PO Box 717 50511 515-295-3528
Ross Opsal, supt. Fax 295-5166
www.algona.k12.ia.us
Algona HS 400/9-12
600 S Hale St 50511 515-295-7207
Bill Fjetland, prin. Fax 295-9273
Laing MS 300/6-8
213 S Harlan St 50511 515-295-9447
Gregory Stewart, prin. Fax 295-9448

Bishop Garrigan HS 200/9-12
1224 N Mccoy St 50511 515-295-3521
Michael Stence, prin. Fax 295-7739

Alleman, Polk, Pop. 430
North Polk Community SD 1,000/K-12
313 NE 141st Ave 50007 515-685-3014
Dr. Ann Curphey, supt. Fax 685-2002
www.n-polk.k12.ia.us
North Polk JSHS 400/7-12
315 NE 141st Ave 50007 515-685-3528
Gary Fjelland, prin. Fax 685-3520

Allison, Butler, Pop. 981
Allison-Bristow Community SD 300/K-8
PO Box 428 50602 319-267-2205
Warren Davison, supt. Fax 267-2926
www.alli-bris.k12.ia.us/
North Butler MS 200/5-8
PO Box 428 50602 319-267-2552
Dan Huff, prin. Fax 267-2926

Alta, Buena Vista, Pop. 1,874
Alta Community SD 600/PK-12
101 W 5th St 51002 712-200-1010
Dr. Fred Maharry, supt. Fax 200-1602
www.alta.k12.ia.us
Alta HS 200/9-12
101 W 5th St 51002 712-200-1331
Larry Martin, prin. Fax 200-1602
Alta MS 200/5-8
1009 S Main St 51002 712-200-1401
Maxine Lampe, prin. Fax 200-2459

Alton, Sioux, Pop. 1,117
MOC-Floyd Valley Community SD
Supt. — See Orange City
MOC-Floyd Valley MS 300/6-8
1104 5th Ave 51003 712-756-4128
John VandeWeerd, prin. Fax 756-4100

Ames, Story, Pop. 52,263
Ames Community SD 3,600/PK-12
415 Stanton Ave 50014 515-268-6600
W. Ray Richardson, supt. Fax 268-6633
Ames HS 1,500/9-12
1921 Ames High Dr 50010 515-817-0600
Michael McGrory, prin. Fax 817-0601
Ames MS 700/6-8
3915 Mortensen Rd 50014 515-268-2400
Jeff Anderson, prin. Fax 268-2419

Ames Christian S 100/PK-12
925 S 16th St 50010 515-233-0772
Charles Hontz, admin. Fax 232-0005
Iowa State University 50011 Post-Sec.
515-294-4111
Professional Cosmetology Institute Post-Sec.
309 Kitty Hawk Dr 50010 515-232-7250

Anamosa, Jones, Pop. 5,616
Anamosa Community SD 1,300/PK-12
200 S Garnavillo St 52205 319-462-4321
Dr. Dale Monroe, supt. Fax 462-4322
www.anamosa.k12.ia.us
Anamosa HS 400/9-12
209 Sadie St 52205 319-462-3594
Steven Goodall, prin. Fax 462-2332
West MS 300/6-8
200 S Garnavillo St 52205 319-462-3553
Linda Vaughn, prin. Fax 462-4322

Andrew, Jackson, Pop. 452
Andrew Community SD 300/PK-12
PO Box 230 52030 563-672-3221
Kent Hammer, supt. Fax 672-9750
www.andrew.k12.ia.us
Andrew JSHS 200/7-12
PO Box 230 52030 563-672-3221
William Hamilton, prin. Fax 672-9750

Anita, Cass, Pop. 1,166
Anita Community SD 300/K-12
1000 Victory Park Rd 50020 712-762-3238
Dan Crozier, supt. Fax 762-3713
www.anita.k12.ia.us
CAM HS 200/9-12
1000 Victory Park Rd 50020 712-762-3231
Dominic Giegerich, prin. Fax 762-3713

Ankeny, Polk, Pop. 36,681
Ankeny Community SD 6,600/PK-12
PO Box 189 50021 515-965-9600
Dr. Veronica Stalker, supt. Fax 965-4234
www.ankeny.k12.ia.us
Ankeny HS 1,400/10-12
1302 N Ankeny Blvd, 515-965-9630
Brenda Colby, prin. Fax 965-9639
Northview MS 1,000/8-9
1010 NW Prairie Ridge Dr, 515-965-9700
Scott Osborn, prin. Fax 965-9708

Ankeny Christian Academy 200/PK-12
1604 W 1st St, 515-965-8114
Joyce Hansen, admin. Fax 965-8210
Des Moines Area Community College Post-Sec.
2006 S Ankeny Blvd, 515-964-6200
Faith Baptist Bible College Post-Sec.
1900 NW 4th St, 888-324-8448

Anthon, Woodbury, Pop. 634
Anthon-Oto Community SD 300/K-8
PO Box E 51004 712-373-5246
Steve Oberg, supt. Fax 373-5326
www.anthon-oto.k12.ia.us/
Anthon-Oto-Maple Valley MS 200/6-8
PO Box E 51004 712-373-5244
Jane Ellis, prin. Fax 373-5326

Aplington, Butler, Pop. 1,023
Aplington-Parkersburg Community SD
Supt. — See Parkersburg
Aplington-Parkersburg MS 200/6-8
215 10th St 50604 319-347-6621
Jon Thompson, prin. Fax 347-2395

Arlington, Fayette, Pop. 481
Starmont Community SD 800/PK-12
3202 40th St 50606 563-933-4598
Gary Stumberg, supt. Fax 933-2134
www.starmont.k12.ia.us
Starmont HS 300/9-12
3202 40th St 50606 563-933-2218
Fred Kinne, prin. Fax 933-2134
Starmont MS 300/5-8
3202 40th St 50606 563-933-4902
Gerald Hilton, prin. Fax 933-2134

Armstrong, Emmet, Pop. 902
Armstrong-Ringsted Community SD 300/PK-12
PO Box 75 50514 712-868-3550
Randy Collins, supt. Fax 868-3550
www.armstrong.k12.ia.us
Armstrong-Ringsted MSHS 100/6-12
PO Box 75 50514 712-868-3542
Joel Semprini, prin. Fax 868-3550

Arnolds Park, Dickinson, Pop. 1,211
Okoboji Community SD
Supt. — See Milford
Okoboji MS 300/5-8
10 Broadway 51331 712-332-5641
David Dorenkamp, prin. Fax 332-7180

Atlantic, Cass, Pop. 6,959
Atlantic Community SD 1,500/K-12
1100 Linn St 50022 712-243-4252
Dr. Wendy Prigge, supt. Fax 243-8023
www.atlantic.k12.ia.us/
Atlantic HS 500/9-12
1201 E 14th St 50022 712-243-5358
Roger Herring, prin. Fax 243-8007
Atlantic MS 400/6-8
1100 Linn St 50022 712-243-1330
Todd Roecker, prin. Fax 243-8023

Audubon, Audubon, Pop. 2,257
Audubon Community SD 700/PK-12
800 3rd Ave 50025 712-563-2607
Ron Dobson, supt. Fax 563-3607
www.audubon.k12.ia.us/
Audubon JSHS 400/7-12
800 3rd Ave 50025 712-563-2607
Bonnie Lynam, prin. Fax 563-3607

Aurelia, Cherokee, Pop. 973
Aurelia Community SD 300/PK-12
300 Ash St 51005 712-434-2284
Thomas Vint, supt. Fax 434-2053
www.aurelia.k12.ia.us
Aurelia HS 100/9-12
PO Box 367 51005 712-434-5595
David Hickman, prin. Fax 434-2053
Aurelia MS 100/5-8
300 Ash St 51005 712-434-5682
Tom Vint, prin. Fax 434-2053

Avoca, Pottawattamie, Pop. 1,562
A-H-S-T Community SD 600/PK-12
PO Box 158 51521 712-343-6304
Chuck Scott, supt. Fax 343-6915
www.ahst.k12.ia.us
A-H-S-T HS 200/6-12
PO Box 158 51521 712-343-6304
Susie Peterson, prin. Fax 343-6915

Bancroft, Kossuth, Pop. 752
North Kossuth Community SD 300/K-12
PO Box 350 50517 515-885-2464
Mike Landstrum, supt. Fax 885-0041
www.n-kossuth.k12.ia.us
Other Schools – See Swea City

Barnum, Webster, Pop. 196
Manson NW Webster Community SD
Supt. — See Manson
Manson Northwest Webster MS 200/5-8
PO Box 169 50518 515-542-3211
Marlene Johnson, prin. Fax 542-3214

Battle Creek, Ida, Pop. 716
Battle Creek-Ida Grove Community SD
Supt. — See Ida Grove
Battle Creek-Ida Grove MS 200/5-8
600 Chestnut St 51006 712-365-4354
Tony Spradlin, prin. Fax 365-4357

Baxter, Jasper, Pop. 1,063
Baxter Community SD 400/K-12
PO Box 189 50028 641-227-3102
Neil Seales, supt. Fax 227-3217
www.baxter.k12.ia.us
Baxter JSHS 200/7-12
PO Box 189 50028 641-227-3103
Robert Luther, prin. Fax 227-3217

Bedford, Taylor, Pop. 1,525
Bedford Community SD 600/PK-12
PO Box 234 50833 712-523-2656
Joe Drake, supt. Fax 523-3166
www.bedford.k12.ia.us
Bedford MSHS 300/6-12
PO Box 234 50833 712-523-2656
Kim Antisdel-Watson, prin. Fax 523-2308

Belle Plaine, Benton, Pop. 2,919
Belle Plaine Community SD 700/PK-12
1303 2nd Ave 52208 319-444-3611
Mike Milligan, supt. Fax 444-3617
www.belle-plaine.k12.ia.us
Belle Plaine HS 200/9-12
610 13th Ave 52208 319-444-3720
Jodi Bermel, prin. Fax 444-4507
Lincoln JHS 100/7-8
1511 9th Ave 52208 319-444-3631
Christina Jesse, prin. Fax 444-3671

Bellevue, Jackson, Pop. 2,358
Bellevue Community SD 700/PK-12
1601 State St 52031 563-872-4913
Dr. Virgil W. Murray, supt. Fax 872-3216
www.bellevue.k12.ia.us
Bellevue MSHS 400/6-12
1601 State St 52031 563-872-4001
Tom Meyer, prin. Fax 872-3216

Marquette HS 100/9-12
502 Franklin St 52031 563-872-3356
James Squiers, prin. Fax 872-3285

Belmond, Wright, Pop. 2,451
Belmond-Klemme Community SD 700/PK-12
411 10th Ave NE 50421 641-444-4300
Dave Sextro, supt. Fax 444-4524
www.belmond-klemme.k12.ia.us
Belmond-Klemme Community JSHS 300/7-12
411 10th Ave NE 50421 641-444-4300
Larry Frakes, prin. Fax 444-4097

Bettendorf, Scott, Pop. 31,890
Bettendorf Community SD 4,300/K-12
PO Box 1150 52722 563-359-3681
Marty Lucas, supt. Fax 359-3685
www.bettendorf.k12.ia.us
Bettendorf HS 1,500/9-12
3333 18th St 52722 563-332-7001
Jimmy Casas, prin. Fax 332-2326
Bettendorf MS 1,000/6-8
2030 Middle Rd 52722 563-359-3686
Linda Goff, prin. Fax 359-3855

Morning Star Academy 200/PK-12
1426 Tanglefoot Ln 52722 563-359-5700
Cheryl Headley, prin. Fax 359-5737
Rivermont Collegiate 200/PK-12
1821 Sunset Dr 52722 563-359-1366
Rick St. Laurent, hdmstr. Fax 359-7576

Blairsburg, Hamilton, Pop. 227
Northeast Hamilton Community SD 300/K-12
606 Illinois St 50034 515-325-6234
Roark Horn, supt. Fax 325-6235
www.ne-hamilton.k12.ia.us
Northeast Hamilton HS 100/9-12
606 Illinois St 50034 515-325-6234
Patrick Hocking, prin. Fax 325-6235
Northeast Hamilton MS 100/6-8
606 Illinois St 50034 515-325-6234
Patrick Hocking, prin. Fax 325-6235

Blakesburg, Wapello, Pop. 364
Eddyville-Blakesburg Community SD
Supt. — See Eddyville
Eddyville-Blakesburg MS 100/7-8
407 Wilson St 52536 641-938-2203
Dennis Rutledge, prin. Fax 938-2613

Bloomfield, Davis, Pop. 2,597
Davis County Community SD 1,200/PK-12
608 S Washington St 52537 641-664-2200
Anne Morgan, supt. Fax 664-2221
www.dcmustangs.com/
Davis County HS 400/9-12
106 N East St 52537 641-664-2200
Ken McKenna, prin. Fax 664-1763
Davis County MS 400/5-8
500 E North St 52537 641-664-2200
Sam Miller, prin. Fax 664-1767

Bode, Humboldt, Pop. 315
Twin Rivers Community SD 100/PK-12
PO Box 153 50519 515-379-1526
Andrew Woiwood, supt. Fax 379-1645
www.trv.k12.ia.us
Twin Rivers Valley HS 100/9-12
PO Box 153 50519 515-379-1526
Don Hasenkamp, prin. Fax 379-1645

Bonaparte, Van Buren, Pop. 455
Harmony Community SD 400/PK-12
602 8th St 52620 319-592-3600
Dr. Timothy Peterson, supt. Fax 592-3690
www.aea15.k12.ia.us/districts.php
Other Schools – See Farmington

Bondurant, Polk, Pop. 2,203
Bondurant-Farrar Community SD 1,000/PK-12
300 Garfield St SW 50035 515-967-7819
Craig Cochran, supt. Fax 967-7847
www.bondurant.k12.ia.us/
Bondurant-Farrar JSHS 500/7-12
300 Garfield St SW 50035 515-967-3711
Vernon Anderson, prin. Fax 957-9924

Boone, Boone, Pop. 12,831
Boone Community SD 2,300/K-12
500 7th St 50036 515-433-0750
Dr. Theron Schutte, supt. Fax 433-0753
boone.k12.ia.us/
Boone HS 900/9-12
500 7th St 50036 515-433-0890
David Kapfer, prin. Fax 433-0989
Boone MS 400/7-8
1640 1st St 50036 515-433-0020
Nate Heying, prin. Fax 433-0026

Des Moines Area Community College Post-Sec.
1125 Hancock Dr 50036 515-432-7203

Britt, Hancock, Pop. 2,011
West Hancock Community SD 500/PK-12
PO Box 128 50423 641-843-3833
Richard Keith, supt. Fax 843-4717
www.whancock.org/
West Hancock HS 200/9-12
PO Box 278 50423 641-843-3863
Ben Muller, prin. Fax 843-4633
Other Schools – See Kanawha

Brooklyn, Poweshiek, Pop. 1,389
Brooklyn-Guernsey-Malcom Community SD 700/PK-12
1090 Jackson St 52211 641-522-7058
Brad Hohensee, supt. Fax 522-7211
www.brooklyn.k12.ia.us
Brooklyn-Guernsey-Malcom JSHS 300/7-12
1090 Jackson St 52211 641-522-7058
Rick Radcliffe, prin. Fax 522-7211

Buffalo Center, Winnebago, Pop. 897
North Iowa Community SD 600/PK-12
111 3rd Ave NW 50424 641-562-2921
Larry Hill, supt. Fax 562-2921
www.northiowa.org
North Iowa HS 200/9-12
111 3rd Ave NW 50424 641-562-2525
Daniel Dierks, prin. Fax 562-2921
Other Schools – See Thompson

Burlington, Des Moines, Pop. 25,436
Burlington Community SD 3,600/K-12
1429 West Ave 52601 319-753-6791
Dr. Mike Book, supt. Fax 753-6796
www.burlington.k12.ia.us
Burlington Community HS 1,300/9-12
421 Terrace Dr 52601 319-753-2211
Tom Messinger, prin. Fax 753-6634
Madison MS 300/6-8
2132 Madison Ave 52601 319-753-6253
Tim Bolander, prin. Fax 753-6514
Oak Street MS 400/6-8
903 Oak St 52601 319-753-6773
Donita Lynch, prin. Fax 753-0554

Dayton's School of Hair Design Post-Sec.
315 N Main St 52601 319-752-3193
Notre Dame HS 200/7-12
702 S Roosevelt Ave 52601 319-754-8431
Fax 752-8690

Burnside, Webster
Southeast Webster-Grand Community SD 500/PK-12
PO Box 49 50521 515-359-2235
Mike Jorgensen, supt. Fax 359-2236
www.se-webster.k12.ia.us
Southeast Webster-Grand HS 100/9-12
PO Box 49 50521 515-359-2235
Daniel Grandfield, prin. Fax 359-2236
Other Schools – See Dayton

Bussey, Marion, Pop. 456
Twin Cedars Community SD 500/PK-12
2204 Highway G71 50044 641-944-5241
Brian VanderSluis, supt. Fax 944-5824
www.twincedars.k12.ia.us
Twin Cedars JSHS 200/7-12
2204 Highway G71 50044 641-944-5243
Dave Roby, prin. Fax 944-5225

Calmar, Winneshiek, Pop. 1,062
South Winneshiek Community SD 600/PK-12
PO Box 430 52132 563-562-3269
Richard Wede, supt. Fax 562-3260
www.s-winneshiek.k12.ia.us
South Winneshiek HS 300/9-12
PO Box 430 52132 563-562-3226
John Grampovnik, prin. Fax 562-3228
Other Schools – See Ossian

C F S Consolidated S 50/6-8
PO Box 815 52132 563-562-3291
Kathryn Schmitt, prin. Fax 562-3292
Northeast Iowa Community College Post-Sec.
PO Box 400 52132 563-562-3263

Camanche, Clinton, Pop. 4,260
Camanche Community SD 1,000/PK-12
PO Box 170 52730 563-259-3000
Thomas Parker, supt. Fax 259-3005
www.camanche.k12.ia.us
Camanche HS 300/9-12
PO Box 170 52730 563-259-3008
Gary DeLacy, prin. Fax 259-3048
Camanche MS 300/5-8
PO Box 170 52730 563-259-3014
Phil Cochran, prin. Fax 259-3031

Carlisle, Warren, Pop. 3,544
Carlisle Community SD 1,500/PK-12
430 School St 50047 515-989-3589
Tom Lane, supt. Fax 989-3075
www.carlisle.k12.ia.us/

Carlisle HS — 400/9-12
430 School St 50047 — 515-989-0831
Michael Anthony, prin. — Fax 989-3075
Carlisle JHS — 200/7-8
430 School St 50047 — 515-989-0833
Diana Whited, prin. — Fax 989-3075

Carroll, Carroll, Pop. 10,047
Carroll Community SD — 1,800/PK-12
1026 N Adams St 51401 — 712-792-8001
Rob Cordes, supt. — Fax 792-8008
www.carroll.k12.ia.us
Carroll HS — 600/9-12
2809 N Grant Rd 51401 — 712-792-8010
Steve Haluska, prin. — Fax 792-8118
Carroll MS — 400/6-8
3203 N Grant Rd 51401 — 712-792-8020
Jerry Raymond, prin. — Fax 792-8024

Des Moines Area Community College — Post-Sec.
906 N Grant Rd 51401 — 712-792-1755
Kuemper Catholic HS — 400/9-12
109 S Clark St 51401 — 712-792-3596
Penny Miller, prin. — Fax 792-8070
Kuemper Catholic MS — 300/6-8
1519 N West St 51401 — 712-792-2123
Earl Schiltz, prin. — Fax 792-3365

Carson, Pottawattamie, Pop. 706
Riverside Community SD — 700/PK-12
PO Box 218 51525 — 712-484-2212
James Sutton Ed.D., supt. — Fax 484-3957
www.riverside.k12.ia.us
Riverside Community MS — 200/5-8
PO Box 218 51525 — 712-484-2291
Kaylene Kovach, prin. — Fax 484-3957
Other Schools – See Oakland

Cascade, Dubuque, Pop. 2,030
Western Dubuque Community SD
Supt. — See Farley
Cascade JSHS — 400/7-12
505 Johnson St NW 52033 — 563-852-3201
Greg VanderLugt, prin. — Fax 852-7186

Cedar Falls, Black Hawk, Pop. 36,471
Cedar Falls Community SD — 4,400/PK-12
1002 W 1st St 50613 — 319-553-3000
Daniel Smith, supt. — Fax 277-0614
www.cedar-falls.k12.ia.us
Cedar Falls SHS — 1,100/10-12
1015 Division St 50613 — 319-553-2500
Rich Powers, prin. — Fax 277-4604
Holmes JHS — 500/7-9
505 Holmes Dr 50613 — 319-553-2650
David Welter, prin. — Fax 277-0571
Peet JHS — 500/7-9
525 E Seerley Blvd 50613 — 319-553-2710
Mark Farland, prin. — Fax 266-8839

Hamilton College — Post-Sec.
7009 Nordic Dr 50613 — 319-277-0220
La' James College of Hairstyling — Post-Sec.
6322 University Ave 50613 — 319-277-2150
University of Northern Iowa 50614 — Post-Sec.
319-273-2311
Valley Lutheran HS — 50/6-12
4520 Rownd St 50613 — 319-266-4565
Dan Cox, prin. — Fax 266-4054

Cedar Rapids, Linn, Pop. 123,119
Cedar Rapids Community SD — 17,300/PK-12
346 2nd Ave SW 52404 — 319-558-2000
David Markward, supt. — Fax 558-2008
www.cr.k12.ia.us
Franklin MS — 700/6-8
300 20th St NE 52402 — 319-558-2452
Shannon Bucknell, prin. — Fax 398-2454
Harding MS — 900/6-8
4801 Golf St NE 52402 — 319-558-2254
Randy Krejci, prin. — Fax 378-0671
Jefferson HS — 1,500/9-12
1243 20th St SW 52404 — 319-558-2435
Charles McDonnell, prin. — Fax 398-2442
Kennedy HS — 1,800/9-12
4545 Wenig Rd NE 52402 — 319-558-2251
Mary Wilcynski, prin. — Fax 294-1118
McKinley MS — 600/6-8
620 10th St SE 52403 — 319-558-2348
Kristen Rickey, prin. — Fax 398-2347
Metro HS — 500/9-12
1212 7th St SE 52401 — 319-558-2193
Kathy Green, prin. — Fax 398-2117
Roosevelt MS — 700/6-8
300 13th St NW 52405 — 319-558-2153
Steve Hilby, prin. — Fax 398-2424
Taft MS — 700/6-8
5200 E Ave NW 52405 — 319-558-2243
Steve Archibald, prin. — Fax 654-8619
Washington HS — 1,600/9-12
2205 Forest Dr SE 52403 — 319-558-2161
Ralph Plagman, prin. — Fax 398-2016

College Community SD — 3,800/K-12
401 76th Ave SW 52404 — 319-848-5201
Richard Whitehead, supt. — Fax 848-4019
www.prairiepride.org
Prairie HS — 1,100/9-12
401 76th Ave SW 52404 — 319-848-5340
Mark Gronemeyer, prin. — Fax 848-5349
Prairie MS — 900/6-8
401 76th Ave SW 52404 — 319-848-5310
Greg Leytem, prin. — Fax 848-5323

American College of Hairstyling — Post-Sec.
1531 1st Ave SE 52402 — 319-362-1488
Capri College — Post-Sec.
2945 Williams Pkwy SW 52404 — 319-364-1541
Cedar Valley Christian S — 200/PK-12
3636 Cottage Grove Ave SE 52403 — 319-366-7462
Joel DeSousa, prin. — Fax 247-0037
Coe College — Post-Sec.
1220 1st Ave NE 52402 — 319-399-8000
Hamilton College — Post-Sec.
3165 Edgewood Pkwy SW 52404 — 319-363-0481
Holy Family - LaSalle MS — 200/6-8
3700 1st Ave NW 52405 — 319-396-7792
Rick Louk, prin. — Fax 390-6527
Kirkwood Community College — Post-Sec.
PO Box 2068 52406 — 319-398-5411
Mercy-St. Luke's Hospital — Post-Sec.
1026 A Ave NE 52402 — 319-369-7204
Mt. Mercy College — Post-Sec.
1330 Elmhurst Dr NE 52402 — 319-363-8213
Regis MS — 400/6-8
735 Prairie Dr NE 52402 — 319-378-0547
Rick Blackwell, prin. — Fax 247-6099
Xavier HS — 700/9-12
6300 42nd St NE 52411 — 319-294-6635
Tom Keating, prin. — Fax 294-6712

Center Point, Linn, Pop. 2,214
Center Point-Urbana Community SD — 1,200/K-12
PO Box 296 52213 — 319-849-1102
Alan Marshall, supt. — Fax 849-2312
www.cpuschools.org/
Center Point-Urbana HS — 400/9-12
PO Box 296 52213 — 319-849-1102
Jeff Meyerholz, prin. — Fax 849-2068
Urbana-Center Point MS — 400/5-8
PO Box 296 52213 — 319-443-2426
Brent Winterhof, prin. — Fax 443-2764

Centerville, Appanoose, Pop. 5,788
Centerville Community SD — 1,600/K-12
PO Box 370 52544 — 641-856-0601
Richard Turner, supt. — Fax 856-0656
www.centerville.k12.ia.us
Centerville HS — 500/9-12
600 CHS Dr 52544 — 641-856-0813
Bill Messerole, prin. — Fax 856-0809
Howar JHS — 300/7-8
850 S Park Ave 52544 — 641-856-0760
Bruce Karpen, prin. — Fax 856-0761

Indian Hills Community College — Post-Sec.
721 N 1st St 52544 — 641-856-2143

Central City, Linn, Pop. 1,142
Central City Community SD — 500/PK-12
400 Barber St 52214 — 319-438-6183
Bill Mertens, supt. — Fax 438-6110
www.central-city.k12.ia.us
Central City HS — 100/9-12
400 Barber St 52214 — 319-438-6182
David Glynn, prin. — Fax 438-6110
Central City MS — 100/6-8
400 Barber St 52214 — 319-438-6181
Chad Steckel, prin. — Fax 438-6110

Chariton, Lucas, Pop. 4,609
Chariton Community SD — 1,500/PK-12
PO Box 738 50049 — 641-774-5967
Dr. Robert Newsum, supt. — Fax 774-8511
www.chariton.k12.ia.us/
Chariton HS — 500/9-12
501 N Grand St 50049 — 641-774-5066
Keven Seney, prin. — Fax 774-8511
Chariton MS — 400/6-8
1300 N 16th St 50049 — 641-774-5114
Beth Scott-Thomas, prin. — Fax 774-8511

Charles City, Floyd, Pop. 7,606
Charles City Community SD — 1,400/K-12
500 N Grand Ave 50616 — 641-257-6500
David Bradley, supt. — Fax 257-6509
www.charles-city.k12.ia.us
Charles City HS — 600/9-12
1 Comet Dr 50616 — 641-257-6510
Shirley Kelly, prin. — Fax 257-1175
Charles City MS — 400/6-8
500 N Grand Ave 50616 — 641-257-6530
Ron Hoffman, prin. — Fax 228-9842

Charter Oak, Crawford, Pop. 525
Charter Oak-Ute Community SD — 300/PK-12
321 Main St 51439 — 712-678-3325
Rollie Wiebers, supt. — Fax 678-3626
Charter Oak-Ute HS — 100/9-12
321 Main St 51439 — 712-678-3325
Rollie Wiebers, prin. — Fax 678-3626
Charter Oak-Ute JHS — 50/7-8
321 Main St 51439 — 712-678-3325
Rollie Wiebers, prin. — Fax 678-3626

Cherokee, Cherokee, Pop. 5,027
Cherokee Community SD — 1,100/PK-12
PO Box 801 51012 — 712-225-6767
John Chalstrom, supt. — Fax 225-6769
www.cherokee.k12.ia.us/
Cherokee MS — 300/5-8
PO Box 801 51012 — 712-225-6750
Larry Weede, prin. — Fax 225-4841
Washington HS — 400/9-12
PO Box 801 51012 — 712-225-6755
Larry Hunecke, prin. — Fax 225-6765

Western Iowa Tech Community College — Post-Sec.
200 Victory Dr 51012 — 712-225-0238

Churdan, Greene, Pop. 392
Paton-Churdan Community SD — 200/PK-12
PO Box 157 50050 — 515-389-3111
Leonard Griffith, supt. — Fax 389-3113
www.paton-churdan.k12.ia.us
Paton-Churdan JSHS — 100/6-12
PO Box 157 50050 — 515-389-3111
Terry Eisenbarth, prin. — Fax 389-3113

Clarence, Cedar, Pop. 993
North Cedar Community SD
Supt. — See Stanwood
North Cedar MS — 200/6-8
PO Box 310 52216 — 563-452-3179
Greg Fisher, prin. — Fax 452-3972

Clarinda, Page, Pop. 5,523
Clarinda Community SD — 1,200/PK-12
PO Box 59 51632 — 712-542-5165
Paul Honnold, supt. — Fax 542-3802
www.clarinda.k12.ia.us
Clarinda HS — 400/9-12
PO Box 59 51632 — 712-542-5167
Michael Ruffing, prin. — Fax 542-4305
Clarinda MS — 300/5-8
PO Box 59 51632 — 712-542-2132
Margaret Nordland, prin. — Fax 542-5949

Iowa Western Community College — Post-Sec.
923 E Washington St 51632 — 712-542-5117

Clarion, Wright, Pop. 2,873
Clarion-Goldfield Community SD — 900/PK-12
319 3rd Ave NE 50525 — 515-532-3423
Robert Olson, supt. — Fax 532-2628
www.clargold.k12.ia.us
Clarion-Goldfield HS — 300/9-12
1111 Willow Dr 50525 — 515-532-2895
Dennis March, prin. — Fax 532-2897
Clarion-Goldfield MS — 200/6-8
300 3rd Ave NE 50525 — 515-532-2412
Steve Haberman, prin. — Fax 532-2741

Clarksville, Butler, Pop. 1,403
Clarksville Community SD — 400/PK-12
PO Box 689 50619 — 319-278-4008
Robert Longmuir, supt. — Fax 278-4618
www.clarksville.k12.ia.us/
Clarksville JSHS — 200/7-12
PO Box 689 50619 — 319-278-4273
Robert Saathoff, prin. — Fax 278-4981

Clear Lake, Cerro Gordo, Pop. 7,913
Clear Lake Community SD — 1,400/K-12
306 1st Ave N 50428 — 641-357-2181
Mike Wright, supt. — Fax 357-2182
www.clearlake.k12.ia.us
Clear Lake HS — 400/9-12
125 N 20th St 50428 — 641-357-5235
Jay Mathis, prin. — Fax 357-6218
Clear Lake MS — 300/6-8
1601 3rd Ave N 50428 — 641-357-6114
Robert Mondt, prin. — Fax 357-8353

Cleghorn, Cherokee, Pop. 240
Marcus-Meriden-Cleghorn Community SD
Supt. — See Marcus
Marcus-Meriden-Cleghorn MS — 200/4-8
PO Box 97 51014 — 712-436-2244
Bill Sillau, prin. — Fax 436-2695

Clinton, Clinton, Pop. 27,086
Clinton Community SD — 4,300/PK-12
600 S 4th St 52732 — 563-243-9600
Randall Clegg, supt. — Fax 243-2415
www.clinton.k12.ia.us
Clinton HS — 1,200/9-12
817 8th Ave S 52732 — 563-243-7540
Karinne Tharaldson, prin. — Fax 243-9612
Lyons MS — 400/6-8
2810 N 4th St 52732 — 563-242-7858
Dan Boyd, prin. — Fax 242-6168
Washington MS — 600/6-8
751 2nd Ave S 52732 — 563-243-0466
Brian Kenney, prin. — Fax 242-3735

Ashford University — Post-Sec.
400 N Bluff Blvd 52732 — 866-711-1700
Clinton Community College — Post-Sec.
1000 Lincoln Blvd 52732 — 563-244-7000
Prince of Peace Academy College Prep S — 300/K-12
312 S 4th St 52732 — 563-242-1663
Nancy Peart, prin. — Fax 243-8272

Clive, Dallas, Pop. 13,851
West Des Moines Community SD
Supt. — See West Des Moines
Indian Hills JHS — 600/7-8
9401 Indian Hills Dr 50325 — 515-633-4700
Shane Christensen, prin. — Fax 633-4799

Colfax, Jasper, Pop. 2,228
Colfax-Mingo Community SD — 800/K-12
1000 N Walnut St 50054 — 515-674-3646
Ed Ackerman, supt. — Fax 674-3921
www.colfax-mingo.k12.ia.us
Colfax-Mingo HS — 300/9-12
204 N League Rd 50054 — 515-674-4111
Todd Jones, prin. — Fax 674-4940
Other Schools – See Mingo

College Springs, Page, Pop. 241
South Page Community SD — 300/PK-12
PO Box 98 51637 — 712-582-3212
Bill Stattelman, supt. — Fax 582-3217
www.clarinda.heartland.net
South Page JSHS — 100/6-12
PO Box 98 51637 — 712-582-3211
Ron Iles, prin. — Fax 582-3217

Colo, Story, Pop. 808
Colo-Nesco Comm SD
Supt. — See Mc Callsburg
Colo-Nesco HS — 200/9-12
PO Box 215 50056 — 641-377-2282
Steven Buhrow, prin. — Fax 377-2283

Columbus Junction, Louisa, Pop. 1,835
Columbus Community SD 1,000/PK-12
1210 Colton St 52738 319-728-2911
Richard Bridenstine, supt. Fax 728-8750
www.columbus.k12.ia.us
Columbus Community HS 300/9-12
1210 Colton St 52738 319-728-2231
Matt Kingsbury, prin. Fax 728-2205
Columbus Community MS 200/6-8
1210 Colton St 52738 319-728-2233
Matt Kingsbury, prin. Fax 728-2205

Conrad, Grundy, Pop. 1,009
BCLUW Community SD 700/K-12
PO Box 670 50621 641-366-2819
Mike Ashton, supt. Fax 366-2175
www.bcluw.k12.ia.us
BCLUW HS 200/9-12
PO Box 670 50621 641-366-2810
Ben Petty, prin. Fax 366-2951
Other Schools – See Union

Coon Rapids, Carroll, Pop. 1,263
Coon Rapids-Bayard Community SD 500/PK-12
PO Box 297 50058 712-999-2207
Rich Stoffers, supt. Fax 999-7740
www.crbcrusaders.org
Coon Rapids-Bayard JSHS 200/7-12
PO Box 297 50058 712-999-2208
Shawn Zanders, prin. Fax 999-7740

Coralville, Johnson, Pop. 17,811
Iowa City Community SD
Supt. — See Iowa City
Northwest JHS 900/7-8
1507 8th St 52241 319-688-1060
Gregg Shoultz, prin. Fax 339-5728

Corning, Adams, Pop. 1,688
Corning Community SD 600/K-12
904 8th St 50841 641-322-4242
Mike Wells, supt. Fax 322-5149
www.corning.k12.ia.us
Corning HS 200/9-12
904 8th St 50841 641-322-4245
Kent Jorgensen, prin. Fax 322-5149
Corning JHS 100/7-8
10th & Washington 50841 641-322-3213
Patty Morris, prin. Fax 322-4884

Correctionville, Woodbury, Pop. 859
River Valley Community SD 300/PK-12
PO Box 8 51016 712-372-4420
Julie Destiger, supt. Fax 372-4677
River Valley JSHS 200/7-12
PO Box 8 51016 712-372-4656
John Holbrook, prin. Fax 372-4784

Corwith, Hancock, Pop. 330
Corwith-Wesley Community SD 200/K-12
PO Box 220 50430 515-583-2304
Willie Stone, supt. Fax 583-2030
www.corwith-wesley.k12.ia.us
Corwith-Wesley HS 100/9-12
PO Box 220 50430 515-583-2304
Cory Myer, prin. Fax 583-2030

Corydon, Wayne, Pop. 1,521
Wayne Community SD 600/K-12
102 N Dekalb St 50060 641-872-1220
Robert Busch, supt. Fax 872-2091
www.aea15.k12.ia.us./wayne
Wayne Community HS 200/9-12
102 N Dekalb St 50060 641-872-2184
Dave Daughton, prin. Fax 872-2091
Wayne Community JHS 100/7-8
102 N Dekalb St 50060 641-872-2184
Shane Brown, prin. Fax 872-2091

Council Bluffs, Pottawattamie, Pop. 59,568
Council Bluffs Community SD 9,300/PK-12
12 Scott St 51503 712-328-6446
Martha Bruckner, supt. Fax 328-6548
www.cb-schools.org
Jefferson HS 1,100/9-12
2501 W Broadway 51501 712-328-6493
Judy O'Brien, prin. Fax 328-6497
Kirn JHS 700/7-8
100 North Ave 51503 712-328-6454
Dave Schweitzer, prin. Fax 328-6554
Lincoln HS 1,400/9-12
1205 Bonham St 51503 712-328-6481
Melanie Shellberg, prin. Fax 328-6485
Tucker Center for Vocational Education Vo/Tech
815 N 18th St 51501 712-328-6408
Paul Hans, prin. Fax 328-6425
Wilson JHS 700/7-8
715 N 21st St 51501 712-328-6476
Joel Beyenhof, prin. Fax 328-6479

Lewis Central Community SD 2,700/PK-12
1600 E South Omaha Brdge Rd 51503
712-366-8202
Mark Schweer, supt. Fax 366-8315
www.lewiscentral.k12.ia.us
Lewis Central HS 900/9-12
3504 Harry Langdon Blvd 51503 712-366-8222
Chuck Story, prin. Fax 366-8340
Lewis Central MS 600/6-8
3820 Harry Langdon Blvd 51503 712-366-8251
Sean Dunphy, prin. Fax 366-8324

EQ School of Hair Design Post-Sec.
536 W Broadway 51503 712-328-2613
Hamilton College Post-Sec.
1751 Madison Ave Ste 750 51503 712-328-4212
Iowa School for the Deaf Post-Sec.
3501 Harry Langdon Blvd 51503 712-366-0571
Iowa Western Community College Post-Sec.
2700 College Rd 51503 800-432-5852
Jennie Edmundson Memorial Hospital Post-Sec.
933 E Pierce St 51503 712-328-6239
St. Albert HS 400/7-12
400 Gleason Ave 51503 712-328-2316
Jonna Andersen, prin. Fax 328-8316

Cresco, Howard, Pop. 3,774
Howard-Winneshiek Community SD 1,300/K-12
1000 Schroder Dr 52136 563-547-2762
Brian Ney, supt. Fax 547-5973
www.howard-winn.k12.ia.us
Cresco JHS 200/7-8
1000 4th Ave E 52136 563-547-2300
Todd Knobloch, prin. Fax 547-2679
Crestwood HS 500/9-12
1000 Schroder Dr 52136 563-547-2764
Jim Zajicek, prin. Fax 547-4650

Total Look Sch of Cosmetology & Massage Post-Sec.
806 3rd St W 52136 563-547-3624

Creston, Union, Pop. 7,359
Creston Community SD 900/PK-12
619 N Maple St 50801 641-782-7028
Tim Hood, supt. Fax 782-7020
www.creston.k12.ia.us/
Creston HS 500/9-12
601 W Townline St 50801 641-782-2116
Todd Wolverton, prin. Fax 782-9502
Creston MS 300/6-8
805 Academic Ave 50801 641-782-2129
Larry Otten, prin.

Southwestern Community College Post-Sec.
1501 W Townline St 50801 641-782-7081

Crystal Lake, Hancock, Pop. 271
Woden-Crystal Lake Community SD
Supt. — See Woden
Woden-Crystal Lake-Titonka HS 100/9-12
PO Box 135 50432 641-565-3211
Susan Lewerke, prin. Fax 565-3320

Dallas Center, Dallas, Pop. 1,828
Dallas Center-Grimes Community SD 1,600/K-12
PO Box 512 50063 515-992-3866
Gary Sinclair, supt. Fax 992-3079
www.dc-grimes.k12.ia.us
Dallas Center-Grimes MS 400/6-8
PO Box 608 50063 515-992-4343
Lori Phillips, prin. Fax 992-4076
Other Schools – See Grimes

Danville, Des Moines, Pop. 859
Danville Community SD 600/PK-12
419 S Main St 52623 319-392-4223
Stephen McAllister, supt. Fax 392-8390
www.danville.k12.ia.us/
Danville JSHS 300/7-12
419 S Main St 52623 319-392-4222
Paul Giehl, prin. Fax 392-8390

Davenport, Scott, Pop. 98,845
Davenport Community SD 15,500/PK-12
1606 Brady St 52803 563-336-5000
Julio Almanza, supt. Fax 336-5080
www.davenport.k12.ia.us
Central HS 1,500/9-12
1120 N Main St 52803 563-323-9900
Tim Wernentin, prin. Fax 323-3110
North HS 1,100/9-12
626 W 53rd St 52806 563-388-9880
Jane Artman Andrews, prin. Fax 388-9456
Smart IS 600/6-8
1934 W 5th St 52802 563-323-1837
Virginia Weipert, prin. Fax 323-3093
Sudlow IS 700/6-8
1414 E Locust St 52803 563-326-3502
Bruce Potts, prin. Fax 326-2248
West HS 2,100/9-12
3505 W Locust St 52804 563-386-5500
Nancy Jacobsen, prin. Fax 386-5508
Williams IS 800/6-8
3040 N Division St 52804 563-391-6550
Scott McKissick, prin. Fax 391-0149
Wood IS 800/6-8
5701 N Division St 52806 563-391-6350
Rick Herrig, prin. Fax 391-4416
Young IS 400/6-8
1709 N Harrison St 52803 563-326-4432
Marianne Corbin, prin. Fax 326-1165
Other Schools – See Walcott

Assumption HS 400/9-12
1020 W Central Park Ave 52804 563-326-5313
Andy Craig, prin. Fax 326-3510
Capri College Post-Sec.
425 E 59th St 52807 563-388-6642
Christ Lutheran HS 50/9-12
PO Box 1535 52809 563-391-2190
Rev. Steven Anderson, admin.
Davenport Barber-Styling College Post-Sec.
730 E Kimberly Rd 52807 563-391-9950
Hamilton Technical College Post-Sec.
1011 E 53rd St 52807 563-386-3570
Kaplan University Post-Sec.
1801 E Kimberly Rd 52807 563-355-3500
La' James College of Hairstyling Post-Sec.
3802 E 53rd St 52807 563-441-7900
Palmer College of Chiropractic Post-Sec.
1000 Brady St 52803 563-884-5000
St. Ambrose University Post-Sec.
518 W Locust St 52803 563-333-6000

Dayton, Webster, Pop. 837
Southeast Webster-Grand Community SD
Supt. — See Burnside
Southeast Webster-Grand JHS 100/7-8
30850 Paragon Ave 50530 515-359-2235
Daniel Grandfield, prin. Fax 359-2236

Decorah, Winneshiek, Pop. 8,084
Decorah Community SD 1,600/PK-12
510 Winnebago St 52101 563-382-4208
Steven Chambliss, supt. Fax 387-0753
decorah.k12.ia.us/
Decorah HS 700/9-12
100 E Claiborne Dr 52101 563-382-3643
Kim Sheppard, prin. Fax 382-3107
Decorah MS 400/5-8
210 Vernon St 52101 563-382-8427
Leona Hoth, prin. Fax 387-4052

North Wineshiek Community SD 200/PK-8
3495 N Winn Rd 52101 563-735-5411
Tim Dugger, supt. Fax 735-5430
www.n-winn.k12.ia.us/
North Winneshiek MS 100/6-8
3495 N Winn Rd 52101 563-735-5411
Tim Dugger, prin. Fax 735-5430

Luther College Post-Sec.
700 College Dr 52101 563-387-2000

Delhi, Delaware, Pop. 511
Maquoketa Valley Community SD 900/K-12
PO Box 186 52223 563-922-9422
Doug Tuetken, supt. Fax 922-2160
www.maquoketa-v.k12.ia.us
Maquoketa Valley HS 300/9-12
PO Box 186 52223 563-922-2091
Dave Kuehl, prin. Fax 922-2160
Maquoketa Valley MS 200/6-8
PO Box 186 52223 563-922-9411
Thomas Gatto, prin. Fax 922-2160

Denison, Crawford, Pop. 7,374
Denison Community SD 2,000/K-12
819 N 16th St 51442 712-263-2176
Michael Pardun, supt. Fax 263-5233
www.denison.k12.ia.us
Denison HS 700/9-12
819 N 16th St 51442 712-263-3101
Steve Westerberg, prin. Fax 263-6009
Denison MS 400/6-8
1515 Broadway 51442 712-263-9393
Patricia Roush, prin. Fax 263-5418

Denver, Bremer, Pop. 1,642
Denver Community SD 700/PK-12
PO Box 384 50622 319-984-6323
Kathy Gilbert, supt. Fax 984-5345
www.denver.k12.ia.us
Denver HS 200/9-12
PO Box 384 50622 319-984-5639
Paul Gebel, prin. Fax 984-5630
Denver MS 200/6-8
PO Box 384 50622 319-984-6041
Joann Butler, prin. Fax 984-5630

Des Moines, Polk, Pop. 194,163
Des Moines Independent Community SD 29,400/PK-12
1801 16th St 50314 515-242-7911
Dr. Nancy Sebring, supt. Fax 242-7579
www.dmps.k12.ia.us
Brody MS 700/6-8
2501 Park Ave 50321 515-242-8443
Randy Gordon, prin. Fax 244-0927
Callanan MS 600/6-8
3010 Center St 50312 515-242-8101
Kathie Danielson, prin. Fax 242-8103
East HS 2,100/9-12
815 E 13th St 50316 515-242-7788
Mike Zelenovich, prin. Fax 242-7958
Goodrell MS 600/6-8
1421 Walker St 50316 515-242-7365
Dawn Stahly, prin. Fax 262-8967
Harding MS 700/6-8
203 E Euclid Ave 50313 515-242-8445
Donna Christensen, prin. Fax 244-3566
Hiatt MS 600/6-8
1214 E 15th St 50316 515-242-7774
Spence Evans, prin. Fax 242-7789
Hoover HS 1,200/9-12
4800 Aurora Ave 50310 515-242-7300
Connie Cook, prin. Fax 242-7308
Hoyt MS 700/6-8
2700 E 42nd St 50317 515-242-8446
Billy Jean Stone, prin. Fax 265-5059
Lincoln HS 2,200/9-12
2600 SW 9th St 50315 515-242-7500
Albert Graziano, prin. Fax 242-7517
McCombs MS 700/6-8
201 County Line Rd 50320 515-242-8447
Barb Mullahey, prin. Fax 287-2644
Meredith MS 800/6-8
4827 Madison Ave 50310 515-242-7250
Cindy Flesch, prin. Fax 242-8291
Merrill MS 600/6-8
5301 Grand Ave 50312 515-242-8448
Alex Hanna, prin. Fax 274-1844
North HS 1,200/9-12
501 Holcomb Ave 50313 515-242-7200
Vince Lewis, prin. Fax 242-7360
Roosevelt HS 1,600/9-12
4419 Center St 50312 515-242-7272
Anita Micich, prin. Fax 242-7350
Weeks MS 800/6-8
901 E Park Ave 50315 515-242-8449
Susanna Marcucci, prin. Fax 288-8740

Saydel Community SD 1,400/PK-12
5740 NE 14th St 50313 515-264-0866
Dr. Debra VanGorp, supt. Fax 264-0869
www.saydel.k12.ia.us
Saydel HS 500/9-12
5601 NE 7th St 50313 515-262-9325
Tracy Hook, prin. Fax 266-8497
Woodside MS 300/6-8
5810 NE 14th St 50313 515-265-3451
Pam Ewell, prin. Fax 265-0950

AIB College of Business Post-Sec.
2500 Fleur Dr 50321 515-244-4221
American College of Hairstyling Post-Sec.
603 E 6th St 50309 515-244-0971
Des Moines Area Community College Post-Sec.
1100 7th St 50314 515-244-4226
Des Moines Univ. Osteopathic Medical Ctr Post-Sec.
3200 Grand Ave 50312 515-271-1400
Drake University Post-Sec.
2507 University Ave 50311 515-271-2011
Grand View College Post-Sec.
1200 Grandview Ave 50316 515-263-2800
Grandview Park Baptist S 400/PK-12
1701 E 33rd St 50317 515-265-7579
Dick McWilliams, prin. Fax 266-9834
Iowa Methodist Medical Center Post-Sec.
1200 Pleasant St 50309 515-241-6201
Iowa School of Beauty Post-Sec.
3305 70th St 50322 515-278-9939
Mercy College of Health Sciences Post-Sec.
928 6th Ave 50309 515-643-3180
Vatterott College Post-Sec.
6100 Thornton Ave Ste 290 50321 515-309-9000

De Witt, Clinton, Pop. 5,204
Central Clinton Community SD 1,400/K-12
PO Box 110 52742 563-659-0700
Dr. Carol Hansen, supt. Fax 659-0707
www.central-clinton.k12.ia.us
Central HS 600/9-12
PO Box 110 52742 563-659-0715
Brad Oates, prin. Fax 659-0714
Central MS 400/6-8
PO Box 110 52742 563-659-0735
Steve Haines, prin. Fax 659-0766

Diagonal, Ringgold, Pop. 297
Diagonal Community SD 100/PK-12
PO Box 94 50845 641-734-5331
Karlene Stephens, supt. Fax 734-5729
www.diagonal.k12.ia.us
Diagonal JSHS 50/6-12
PO Box 94 50845 641-734-5331
Larry Tepley, prin. Fax 734-5729

Dike, Grundy, Pop. 1,157
Dike-New Hartford Community SD 800/PK-12
PO Box D 50624 319-989-2552
Lindsey Beecher, supt. Fax 989-2735
www.dikenh.k12.ia.us
Dike-New Hartford HS 200/9-12
PO Box D 50624 319-989-2485
Michael Williams, prin. Fax 989-2735
Other Schools – See New Hartford

Donnellson, Lee, Pop. 923
Central Lee Community SD 1,100/K-12
2642 Highway 218 52625 319-835-9510
John Henriksen, supt. Fax 835-3910
www.central-lee.k12.ia.us
Central Lee HS 300/9-12
2642 Highway 218 52625 319-835-9510
Shane Knoche, prin. Fax 835-5709
Central Lee MS 300/6-8
2642 Highway 218 52625 319-835-9510
Kimberly Kirchner, prin. Fax 835-5020

Dubuque, Dubuque, Pop. 57,798
Dubuque Community SD 9,200/PK-12
2300 Chaney Rd 52001 563-552-3012
John Burgart, supt. Fax 552-3014
www.dubuque.k12.ia.us
Dubuque HS 1,600/9-12
1800 Clarke Dr 52001 563-552-5500
Kim Swift, prin. Fax 552-5502
Hempstead HS 1,700/9-12
3715 Pennsylvania Ave 52002 563-552-5200
David Olson, prin. Fax 552-5231
Jefferson MS 800/6-8
1105 Althauser Ave 52001 563-552-4700
Phillip Kramer, prin. Fax 552-4701
Roosevelt MS 6-8
2001 Radford Rd 52002 563-552-5000
Dale Lass, prin. Fax 552-5001
Washington MS 800/6-8
51 N Grandview Ave 52001 563-552-4800
Mark Burns, prin. Fax 552-4801

Capri College Post-Sec.
PO Box 873 52004 563-588-2379
Clarke College Post-Sec.
1550 Clarke Dr 52001 563-588-6300
Emmaus Bible College Post-Sec.
2570 Asbury Rd 52001 563-588-8000
Holy Family MS 100/7-8
1001 Alta Vista St 52001 563-582-7236
Fax 582-7857
Loras College Post-Sec.
1450 Alta Vista St 52001 563-588-7100
Mazzuchelli MS 6-8
2005 Kane St 52001 563-582-7236
Kim Hermsen, prin. Fax 582-7857
University of Dubuque Post-Sec.
2000 University Ave 52001 563-589-3000
University of Dubuque Theological Sem. Post-Sec.
2000 University Ave 52001 800-369-8387

Wahlert HS 700/9-12
2005 Kane St 52001 563-583-9771
Donald Sisler, prin. Fax 583-9775
Wartburg Theological Seminary Post-Sec.
333 Wartburg Pl 52003 563-589-0200

Dunkerton, Black Hawk, Pop. 768
Dunkerton Community SD 500/PK-12
509 S Canfield St 50626 319-822-4295
Robert Cue, supt. Fax 822-9456
www.dunkerton.k12.ia.us
Dunkerton JSHS 200/7-12
509 S Canfield St 50626 319-822-4295
Gregg Eschweiler, prin. Fax 822-9456

Dunlap, Harrison, Pop. 1,117
Boyer Valley Community SD 500/K-12
1102 Iowa Ave 51529 712-643-2251
Debra Johnsen, supt. Fax 643-2279
Boyer Valley MSHS 300/6-12
1102 Iowa Ave 51529 712-643-2258
Chad Straight, prin. Fax 643-2279

Durant, Cedar, Pop. 1,677
Durant Community SD 700/K-12
PO Box 607 52747 563-785-4432
Duane Bark, supt. Fax 785-4611
www.durant.k12.ia.us
Durant HS 200/9-12
PO Box 607 52747 563-785-4431
Monica Rouse, prin. Fax 785-6558
Durant MS 200/5-8
PO Box 607 52747 563-785-4433
Rebecca Stineman, prin. Fax 785-6558

Dyersville, Dubuque, Pop. 4,043

Beckman HS 500/7-12
1325 9th St SE 52040 563-875-7188
Carol Trueg, prin. Fax 875-7242

Dysart, Tama, Pop. 1,289
Union Community SD
Supt. — See La Porte City
Union MS 300/6-8
PO Box 159 52224 319-476-5100
Mark Albertsen, prin. Fax 476-2385

Eagle Grove, Wright, Pop. 3,515
Eagle Grove Community SD 800/PK-12
325 N Commercial Ave 50533 515-448-4749
Rodney Montang, supt. Fax 448-3156
www.eagle-grove.k12.ia.us
Blue MS 300/5-8
1015 NW 2nd St 50533 515-448-4767
Dawn Sievertsen, prin. Fax 448-5527
Eagle Grove HS 300/9-12
415 NW 2nd St 50533 515-448-5143
Iner Joelson, prin. Fax 448-3583

Iowa Central Community College Post-Sec.
316 NW 3rd St 50533 515-448-4723

Earlham, Madison, Pop. 1,332
Earlham Community SD 600/PK-12
PO Box 430 50072 515-758-2235
Douglas Latham, supt. Fax 758-2215
earlham.k12.ia.us/
Earlham HS 200/9-12
PO Box 430 50072 515-758-2214
Jan Fletcher, prin. Fax 758-2215
Earlham MS 100/7-8
PO Box 430 50072 515-758-2213
Jan Fletcher, prin. Fax 758-2215

Early, Sac, Pop. 540
Schaller-Crestland Community SD
Supt. — See Schaller
Schaller-Crestland HS 200/9-12
PO Box 377 50535 712-273-5192
Stuart Fuhs, prin. Fax 273-5120

Eddyville, Mahaska, Pop. 1,072
Eddyville-Blakesburg Community SD 900/PK-12
1301 Berdan Ext 52553 641-969-4226
Dean Cook, supt. Fax 969-4547
www.ebcsd.com/
Eddyville-Blakesburg HS 300/9-12
1301 Berdan Ext 52553 641-969-4288
Scott Williamson, prin. Fax 969-4574
Other Schools – See Blakesburg

Edgewood, Clayton, Pop. 898
Edgewood-Colesburg Community SD 600/PK-12
PO Box 315 52042 563-928-6411
Galen Reinsmoen, supt. Fax 928-6414
www.edge-cole.k12.ia.us
Edgewood-Colesburg JSHS 300/7-12
PO Box 316 52042 563-928-6412
Ed Klamfoth, prin. Fax 928-6414

Eldon, Wapello, Pop. 974
Cardinal Community SD 600/PK-12
4045 Ashland Rd 52554 641-652-7531
Arnie Snook, supt. Fax 652-3143
www.cardinalcomet.org/
Cardinal MSHS 400/6-12
4045 Ashland Rd 52554 641-652-7531
Dennis Augustine, prin. Fax 652-3143

Eldora, Hardin, Pop. 2,847
Eldora-New Providence Community SD 700/K-12
1010 Edgington Ave 50627 641-939-5631
Randall Nichols, supt. Fax 939-3667
www.eldora-np.k12.ia.us
Eldora-New Providence HS 200/9-12
1800 24th St 50627 641-939-3421
Randall Fahr, prin. Fax 939-3423
Eldora-New Providence MS 200/5-8
1100 12th Ave 50627 641-939-2599
John Zimmerman, prin. Fax 939-5057

Eldridge, Scott, Pop. 4,484
North Scott Community SD 3,000/K-12
251 E Iowa St 52748 563-285-4819
Tim Dose, supt. Fax 285-6075
www.north-scott.k12.ia.us
North Scott HS 1,100/9-12
200 S 1st St 52748 563-285-9631
Fax 285-9308
North Scott JHS 500/7-8
502 S 5th St 52748 563-285-8272
David Griffin, prin. Fax 285-6045
Pleasant Valley Community SD 3,200/PK-12
251 E Iowa St 52748 563-332-5550
Jim Spelhaug, supt. Fax 332-4372
www.pleasval.k12.ia.us
Other Schools – See Le Claire, Riverdale

Heritage Christian S 50/K-12
507 Parkview Dr 52748 563-285-9382
Cindy Nees, admin. Fax 285-9343

Elgin, Fayette, Pop. 656
Valley Community SD 600/K-12
23493 Canoe Rd 52141 563-426-5501
Cathleen Molumby, supt. Fax 426-5502
www.valley.k12.ia.us
Valley JSHS 300/7-12
23493 Canoe Rd 52141 563-426-5551
David Fox, prin. Fax 426-5502

Elkader, Clayton, Pop. 1,383
Central Community SD 600/K-12
PO Box 70 52043 563-245-1751
Brian Rodenberg, supt. Fax 245-1763
www.central.k12.ia.us/
Central Community JSHS 300/7-12
PO Box 70 52043 563-245-1750
Dan Yanda, prin. Fax 245-1763

Elk Horn, Shelby, Pop. 613
Elk Horn-Kimballton Community SD 300/PK-12
PO Box 388a 51531 712-764-4616
Casey Berlau, supt. Fax 764-4626
www.elk-horn.k12.ia.us
Elk Horn-Kimballton HS 100/9-12
PO Box 388a 51531 712-764-4606
Casey Berlau, prin. Fax 764-4626

Emmetsburg, Palo Alto, Pop. 3,706
Emmetsburg Community SD 700/PK-12
205 King St 50536 712-852-3201
John Joynt, supt. Fax 852-3338
www.emmetsburg.k12.ia.us
Emmetsburg HS 300/9-12
205 King St 50536 712-852-2966
Jay Jurrens, prin. Fax 852-3317
Emmetsburg MS 200/5-8
1001 Palmer St 50536 712-852-2892
Matt Pugh, prin. Fax 852-3811

Iowa Lakes Community College Post-Sec.
3200 College Dr 50536 712-852-5212

Epworth, Dubuque, Pop. 1,580
Western Dubuque Community SD
Supt. — See Farley
Western Dubuque HS 700/9-12
PO Box 379 52045 563-876-3442
John Hlubek, prin. Fax 876-5512

Divine Word College Seminary Post-Sec.
PO Box 380 52045 563-876-3353

Essex, Page, Pop. 840
Essex Community SD 300/K-12
PO Box 299 51638 712-379-3117
William Crilly, supt. Fax 379-3200
www.ehs-ees.com/
Essex JSHS 100/7-12
PO Box 299 51638 712-379-3115
Allen Stuart, prin. Fax 379-3200

Estherville, Emmet, Pop. 6,347
Estherville Lincoln Central Comm SD 1,300/PK-12
PO Box 118 51334 712-362-2692
Richard J. Magnuson, supt. Fax 362-2410
www.estherville.k12.ia.us
Estherville Lincoln Central HS 400/9-12
1520 Central Ave 51334 712-362-2659
Susan Bish, prin. Fax 362-2406
Estherville Lincoln Central MS 600/3-8
PO Box 118 51334 712-362-2335
Michael Peterson, prin. Fax 362-7822

Iowa Lakes Community College Post-Sec.
300 S 18th St 51334 712-362-7945

Evansdale, Black Hawk, Pop. 4,585
Waterloo Community SD
Supt. — See Waterloo
Bunger MS 500/6-8
157 S Roosevelt Rd 50707 319-433-2550
Brenton Shavers, prin. Fax 433-2564

Everly, Clay, Pop. 645
Clay Central/Everly Community SD
Supt. — See Royal
Clay Central/Everly HS 200/9-12
PO Box 110 51338 712-834-2227
Charles Kuester, prin. Fax 834-2193

Exira, Audubon, Pop. 775
Exira Community SD 300/PK-12
PO Box 335 50076 712-268-5555
Charlie Johnson, supt. Fax 268-2188
www.exira.k12.ia.us
Exira JSHS 100/7-12
PO Box 335 50076 712-268-5318
Larry Kliefoth, prin. Fax 268-5319

Fairbank, Buchanan, Pop. 1,034
Wapsie Valley Community SD — 700/K-12
2535 Viking Ave 50629 — 319-638-6711
Dan Peterson, supt. — Fax 638-7061
www.wapsievalleyschools.com/
Wapsie Valley JSHS — 300/7-12
2535 Viking Ave 50629 — 319-638-6711
Chad Garber, prin. — Fax 638-7061

Fairfield, Jefferson, Pop. 9,404
Fairfield Community SD — 2,000/K-12
607 E Broadway Ave 52556 — 641-472-2655
Steven Triplett, supt. — Fax 472-0269
www.fairfieldsfuture.org
Fairfield HS — 600/9-12
605 E Broadway Ave 52556 — 641-472-2059
Thomas Voorhees, prin. — Fax 472-0269
Fairfield MS — 500/6-8
404 W Fillmore Ave 52556 — 641-472-5019
Gary Henry, prin. — Fax 472-5301

Fairfield Christian S — 50/PK-12
2009 S Main St 52556 — 641-472-4706
Linda McGaffey, admin. — Fax 472-4566
Ideal Girls S — 50/6-12
1661 Highway 1 52556 — 641-472-7224
Maharishi S of the Age of Enlightenment — 200/PK-12
804 Dr Robert Keith Wallace 52556 — 641-472-9400
Ashley Deans Ph.D., hdmstr. — Fax 472-1211
Maharishi University of Management — Post-Sec.
1000 N 4th St 52557 — 641-472-7000

Farley, Dubuque, Pop. 1,363
Western Dubuque Community SD — 2,800/PK-12
PO Box 279 52046 — 563-744-3885
Wayne Drexler, supt. — Fax 744-3093
www.w-dubuque.k12.ia.us
Drexler MS — 500/6-8
PO Box 279 52046 — 563-744-3371
Tim Showalter, prin. — Fax 744-3711
Other Schools – See Cascade, Epworth

Farmington, Van Buren, Pop. 731
Harmony Community SD
Supt. — See Bonaparte
Harmony HS — 100/9-12
33727 Route J40 52626 — 319-592-3192
David Stammeyer, prin. — Fax 592-3135
Harmony MS — 100/6-8
502 N 4th St 52626 — 319-878-3814
Aaron Becker, prin. — Fax 878-3532

Farnhamville, Calhoun, Pop. 399
Prairie Valley Community SD
Supt. — See Gowrie
Prairie Valley MS — 300/5-8
3116 Zearing Ave 50538 — 515-467-5700
Dennis Hammen, prin. — Fax 467-5646

Farragut, Fremont, Pop. 480
Farragut Community SD — 300/PK-12
PO Box 36 51639 — 712-385-8131
Jay Lutt, supt. — Fax 385-8135
www.farragutschools.org
Farragut JSHS — 200/7-12
PO Box 36 51639 — 712-385-8131
Hilding Sandra, prin. — Fax 385-8135

Fayette, Fayette, Pop. 1,341

Upper Iowa University — Post-Sec.
PO Box 1857 52142 — 563-425-5200

Fenton, Kossuth, Pop. 288
Sentral Community SD — 200/K-12
PO Box 109 50539 — 515-889-2261
Arthur Pixler, supt. — Fax 889-2264
Sentral JSHS — 100/6-12
PO Box 109 50539 — 515-889-2261
Mary Recker, prin. — Fax 889-2264

Fonda, Pocahontas, Pop. 588
Newell-Fonda Community SD
Supt. — See Newell
Newell-Fonda MS — 100/6-8
PO Box 503 50540 — 712-288-4445
Randall Nielsen, prin. — Fax 288-5710

Fontanelle, Adair, Pop. 679
Nodaway Valley Community SD
Supt. — See Greenfield
Nodaway Valley MS — 200/6-8
112 S 1st St 50846 — 641-745-2291
Doug Glackin, prin. — Fax 745-3501

Forest City, Winnebago, Pop. 4,250
Forest City Community SD — 1,400/PK-12
810 W K St 50436 — 641-585-2323
Dwight Pierson, supt. — Fax 585-5218
www.forestcity.k12.ia.us
Forest City HS — 500/9-12
206 W School St 50436 — 641-585-2324
Ken Baker, prin. — Fax 585-3034
Forest City MS — 300/6-8
216 W School St 50436 — 641-585-4772
Timothy G. Kuehl, prin. — Fax 585-3432

Forest City Christian S — 50/PK-12
305 Walnut St 50436 — 641-585-3233
Ivon Tokheim, admin. — Fax 585-1390
Waldorf College — Post-Sec.
106 S 6th St 50436 — 800-292-1903

Fort Dodge, Webster, Pop. 25,493
Fort Dodge Community SD — 4,000/K-12
104 S 17th St 50501 — 515-576-1161
Linda Brock, supt. — Fax 576-1988
www.fort-dodge.k12.ia.us
Fort Dodge HS — 1,300/9-12
819 N 25th St 50501 — 515-955-1770
Rick Kuhlman, prin. — Fax 955-3374
Phillips MS — 700/7-8
1015 5th Ave N 50501 — 515-574-5711
Gary Reiners, prin. — Fax 576-3160

Iowa Central Community College — Post-Sec.
330 Avenue M 50501 — 515-576-7201
La' James College of Hairstyling — Post-Sec.
2604 1st Ave S 50501 — 515-576-3119
St. Edmond HS — 500/6-12
501 N 22nd St 50501 — 515-955-5850
Chuck Elbert, prin. — Fax 955-3569

Fort Madison, Lee, Pop. 11,048
Fort Madison Community SD — 2,300/PK-12
PO Box 1423 52627 — 319-372-7252
Kenneth Marang, supt. — Fax 372-7255
www.ft-madison.k12.ia.us
Fort Madison HS — 700/9-12
2001 Avenue B 52627 — 319-372-1862
Bill Maupin, prin. — Fax 372-1325
Fort Madison MS — 500/6-8
1801 Avenue G 52627 — 319-372-4687
Todd Dirth, prin. — Fax 372-0378

Bill Hill's College of Cosmetology — Post-Sec.
910 Avenue G 52627 — 319-372-6248
Holy Trinity HS — 7-12
2600 Avenue A 52627 — 319-372-2486
Doris Turner, prin. — Fax 372-6310

Fredericksburg, Chickasaw, Pop. 903
Sumner-Fredericksburg SD
Supt. — See Sumner
Sumner-Fredericksburg MS — 200/6-8
PO Box 337 50630 — 563-237-5334
James Hotz, prin. — Fax 237-6329

Fremont, Mahaska, Pop. 690
Fremont Community SD — 100/PK-8
PO Box 69 52561 — 641-933-4211
Dean Cook, supt. — Fax 933-4123
Fremont MS — 50/6-8
PO Box 69 52561 — 641-933-4211
Angela Livezey, prin. — Fax 933-4123

Galva, Ida, Pop. 340
Galva-Holstein Community SD
Supt. — See Holstein
Galva-Holstein MS — 100/5-8
207 Noll St 51020 — 712-282-4213
Mike Richard, prin. — Fax 282-4210

Garden Grove, Decatur, Pop. 247
Mormon Trail Community SD
Supt. — See Humeston
Mormon Trail JSHS — 100/7-12
PO Box 177 50103 — 641-443-3425
Francis Newgard, prin. — Fax 443-2644

Garnavillo, Clayton, Pop. 744
Clayton Ridge Community SD
Supt. — See Guttenberg
Clayton Ridge MS — 100/5-8
PO Box 9 52049 — 563-964-2321
Ric Olsen, prin. — Fax 964-2756

Garner, Hancock, Pop. 2,975
Garner-Hayfield Community SD — 900/K-12
PO Box 449 50438 — 641-923-2718
Tyler Williams, supt. — Fax 923-3825
www.garner.k12.ia.us
Garner-Hayfield HS — 300/9-12
PO Box 449 50438 — 641-923-2632
Paul Schoneman, prin. — Fax 923-4005
Garner-Hayfield MS — 200/6-8
PO Box 449 50438 — 641-923-2809
Steve Beecher, prin. — Fax 923-2031

Garwin, Tama, Pop. 549
GMG Community SD — 500/K-12
306 Park St 50632 — 641-499-2239
Michael Ashton, supt. — Fax 499-2159
www.garwin.k12.ia.us
GMG JSHS — 200/7-12
306 Park St 50632 — 641-499-2005
Mark Polich, prin. — Fax 499-2552

George, Lyon, Pop. 1,025
George-Little Rock Community SD — 500/K-12
PO Box 6 51237 — 712-475-3311
Joanne C. Smith, supt. — Fax 475-3574
www.george-lr.k12.ia.us
George-Little Rock HS — 200/9-12
PO Box 6 51237 — 712-475-3311
Scott Guse, prin. — Fax 475-3574
Other Schools – See Little Rock

Gilbert, Story, Pop. 973
Gilbert Community SD — 800/K-12
103 Mathews Dr 50105 — 515-232-3740
John Kinley, supt. — Fax 232-0099
www.gilbert.k12.ia.us
Gilbert HS — 300/9-12
103 Mathews Dr 50105 — 515-232-3738
James Quarnstrom, prin. — Fax 232-0099
Gilbert MS, 201 Mathews Dr 50105 — 100/5-8
Chris Billings, prin. — 515-232-0540

Gilbertville, Black Hawk, Pop. 779

Don Bosco HS — 200/9-12
405 16th Ave 50634 — 319-296-1692
Matt O'Loughlin, prin. — Fax 296-1693

Gilman, Marshall, Pop. 575
East Marshall Community SD — 800/K-12
PO Box 159 50106 — 641-498-7481
Alan Meyer, supt. — Fax 498-2035
www.e-marshall.k12.ia.us
East Marshall MS — 300/5-8
PO Box 159 50106 — 641-498-7483
Robert Schelp, prin. — Fax 498-2180
Other Schools – See Le Grand

Gilmore City, Humboldt, Pop. 515
Gilmore City-Bradgate Community SD — 100/PK-8
402 SE E Ave 50541 — 515-373-6619
Ron Bollmeyer, supt. — Fax 373-6092
www.trv.k12.ia.us
Twin River Valley MS — 100/6-8
402 SE E Ave 50541 — 515-373-6124
Ronald Bollmeyer, prin. — Fax 373-6092

Gladbrook, Tama, Pop. 1,021
Gladbrook-Reinbeck Community SD
Supt. — See Reinbeck
Gladbrook-Reinbeck MS — 200/6-8
PO Box 370 50635 — 641-473-2842
Doran Dahms, prin. — Fax 473-2913

Glenwood, Mills, Pop. 5,650
Glenwood Community SD — 2,100/K-12
103 Central St Ste 300 51534 — 712-527-9034
Dr. Stan Sibley, supt. — Fax 527-4287
www.glenwood.k12.ia.us
Glenwood HS — 600/9-12
400 Sivers Rd 51534 — 712-527-4897
Dave Stickrod, prin. — Fax 527-9554
Glenwood MS — 300/7-8
111 Lacey St 51534 — 712-527-4887
Kerry Newman, prin. — Fax 527-3411

Glidden, Carroll, Pop. 1,228
Glidden-Ralston Community SD — 400/K-12
PO Box 488 51443 — 712-659-3411
Vicki Lowe, supt. — Fax 659-2248
www.glidden-ralston.k12.ia.us
Glidden-Ralston JSHS — 200/7-12
PO Box 488 51443 — 712-659-2205
Kreg Lensch, prin. — Fax 659-2248

Goose Lake, Clinton, Pop. 234
Northeast Community SD — 700/K-12
PO Box 66 52750 — 563-577-2249
James Cox, supt. — Fax 577-2450
www.northeast.k12.ia.us
Northeast MSHS — 300/7-12
PO Box 70 52750 — 563-577-2249
Joe Jarvis, prin. — Fax 577-2248

Gowrie, Webster, Pop. 1,045
Prairie Valley Community SD — 800/PK-12
PO Box 49 50543 — 515-352-3173
James Dick, supt. — Fax 352-5573
www.gowrie.k12.ia.us
Prairie Valley HS — 200/9-12
PO Box 49 50543 — 515-352-3142
Marshall Lewis, prin. — Fax 352-3143
Other Schools – See Farnhamville

Graettinger, Palo Alto, Pop. 866
Graettinger Community SD — 300/K-12
PO Box 58 51342 — 712-859-3286
Dan Mart, supt. — Fax 859-3509
www.graettinger.k12.ia.us
Graettinger/Terril HS — 100/9-12
PO Box 58 51342 — 712-859-3286
Pam Stangeland, prin. — Fax 859-3509

Grand Junction, Greene, Pop. 927
East Greene Community SD — 400/PK-12
PO Box 377 50107 — 515-738-5741
G. Mike Harter, supt. — Fax 738-5719
www.east-greene.k12.ia.us
Grand Junction JSHS — 200/7-12
PO Box 377 50107 — 515-738-5721
Ron McNeill, prin. — Fax 738-5719

Granville, Sioux, Pop. 325

Spalding HS — 100/7-12
PO Box 168 51022 — 712-727-3451
Brad Thiel, prin. — Fax 727-3455

Greene, Butler, Pop. 1,015
Greene Community SD — 400/PK-12
PO Box 190 50636 — 641-816-5523
Steve Ward, supt. — Fax 816-5921
www.greene.k12.ia.us
North Butler HS — 200/9-12
PO Box 190 50636 — 641-816-5631
Thomas Hamrick, prin. — Fax 816-5921

Greenfield, Adair, Pop. 1,984
Nodaway Valley Community SD — 800/K-12
410 NW 2nd St 50849 — 641-743-6127
John Dayton, supt. — Fax 343-7173
www.nod-valley.k12.ia.us
Nodaway Valley HS — 300/9-12
410 NW 2nd St 50849 — 641-743-6141
Roger Raum, prin. — Fax 343-7040
Other Schools – See Fontanelle

Grimes, Polk, Pop. 6,037
Dallas Center-Grimes Community SD
Supt. — See Dallas Center
Dallas Center-Grimes Community HS — 400/9-12
33521 240th St 50111 — 515-986-9747
Mitzi Chizek, prin. — Fax 986-9734

Grinnell, Poweshiek, Pop. 9,332
Grinnell-Newburg Community SD — 1,800/PK-12
927 4th Ave 50112 — 641-236-2700
Edith Eckles, supt. — Fax 236-2699
www.grinnell.k12.ia.us

Grinnell Community HS | 600/9-12
1333 Sunset St 50112 | 641-236-2720
Linda Smoley, prin. | Fax 236-2692
Grinnell Community MS | 500/5-8
132 East St S 50112 | 641-236-2750
Frank Shults, prin. | Fax 236-2732

Grinnell College | Post-Sec.
PO Box 805 50112 | 641-269-4000

Griswold, Cass, Pop. 983
Griswold Community SD | 700/PK-12
PO Box 280 51535 | 712-778-2152
Darwin Lehmann, supt. | Fax 778-4145
www.griswold.k12.ia.us
Griswold MSHS | 400/6-12
PO Box 280 51535 | 712-778-2154
T. J. Dunphy, prin. | Fax 778-2161

Grundy Center, Grundy, Pop. 2,583
Grundy Center Community SD | 700/K-12
1301 12th St 50638 | 319-825-5418
John Stevens, supt. | Fax 825-5419
www.grundy-center.k12.ia.us
Grundy Center HS | 300/9-12
1006 M Ave 50638 | 319-825-5449
Steve Vanderpol, prin. | Fax 825-6415
Grundy Center MS | 200/6-8
1006 M Ave 50638 | 319-825-5464
Philip Laube, prin. | Fax 825-6415

Guthrie Center, Guthrie, Pop. 1,617
Guthrie Center Community SD | 600/PK-12
906 School St 50115 | 641-332-2972
Steve Smith, supt. | Fax 332-2973
www.guthrie.k12.ia.us
Guthrie Center HS | 200/9-12
906 School St 50115 | 641-332-2236
Garold Thomas, prin. | Fax 332-2973
Guthrie Center JHS | 100/7-8
906 School St 50115 | 641-332-2974
Brent Meier, prin. | Fax 332-2973

Guttenberg, Clayton, Pop. 1,943
Clayton Ridge Community SD | 600/K-12
PO Box 520 52052 | 563-252-2341
Allen Nelson, supt. | Fax 252-2656
www.guttenberg.k12.ia.us
Clayton Ridge HS | 300/9-12
PO Box 520 52052 | 563-252-2342
James Whalen, prin. | Fax 252-2656
Other Schools – See Garnavillo

Hamburg, Fremont, Pop. 1,221
Hamburg Community SD | 300/PK-12
105 E St 51640 | 712-382-1063
Dr. Paul Sellon, supt. | Fax 382-1211
www.hamburg.k12.ia.us
Hamburg JSHS | 200/7-12
105 E St 51640 | 712-382-2703
Steve Swartout, prin. | Fax 382-1211

Hampton, Franklin, Pop. 4,224
Hampton-Dumont Community SD | 1,200/PK-12
PO Box 336 50441 | 641-456-2175
Leland Morrison, supt. | Fax 456-5750
www.hampton-dumont.k12.ia.us/
Hampton-Dumont HS | 400/9-12
PO Box 336 50441 | 641-456-4893
Trent Grundmeyer, prin. | Fax 456-4569
Hampton-Dumont MS | 300/6-8
PO Box 336 50441 | 641-456-4735
Dave Wempen, prin. | Fax 456-2023

Harlan, Shelby, Pop. 5,170
Harlan Community SD | 1,600/K-12
2102 Durant St 51537 | 712-755-2152
William Decker, supt. | Fax 755-7312
www.harlan.k12.ia.us
Harlan Community HS | 600/9-12
2102 Durant St 51537 | 712-755-3101
Justin Wagner, prin. | Fax 755-7705
Harlan Community MS | 400/6-8
2108 Durant St 51537 | 712-755-3196
Duane Magee, prin. | Fax 755-3699

Hartley, O'Brien, Pop. 1,565
Hartley-Melvin-Sanborn Community SD | 800/PK-12
173 S Central Ave 51346 | 712-928-2022
Lynn Evans, supt. | Fax 928-3607
www.hartley-ms.k12.ia.us
Hartley-Melvin-Sanborn HS | 300/9-12
PO Box 206 51346 | 712-928-3406
Mark Peterson, prin. | Fax 928-2152
Other Schools – See Sanborn

Hastings, Mills, Pop. 191
Nishna Valley Community SD | 300/K-12
58962 380th St 51540 | 712-624-8696
Russ Finken, supt. | Fax 624-9131
www.nishna-valley.k12.ia.us/
Nishna Valley JSHS | 100/7-12
58962 380th St 51540 | 712-624-8696
Deborah Taylor, prin. | Fax 624-9131

Hawarden, Sioux, Pop. 2,440
West Sioux Community SD | 700/K-12
1300 Avenue P 51023 | 712-551-1461
Paul Olson, supt. | Fax 551-1367
www.westsiouxschools.org/
West Sioux HS | 300/9-12
1300 Avenue P 51023 | 712-551-1181
Kim Buryanek, prin. | Fax 551-1514
West Sioux MS | 200/6-8
1300 Avenue P 51023 | 712-551-1022
Kim Buryanek, prin. | Fax 551-1367

Hinton, Plymouth, Pop. 847
Hinton Community SD | 600/PK-12
PO Box 128 51024 | 712-947-4329
Allen Steen, supt. | Fax 947-4427
www.hintonschool.com/
Hinton HS | 200/9-12
PO Box 128 51024 | 712-947-4328
Susan Martens, prin. | Fax 947-4427
Hinton MS | 100/6-8
PO Box 128 51024 | 712-947-4328
Susan Martens, prin. | Fax 947-4947

Holstein, Ida, Pop. 1,415
Galva-Holstein Community SD | 500/PK-12
PO Box 320 51025 | 712-368-4353
Harold Post, supt. | Fax 368-4843
www.galva-holstein.k12.ia.us/index.htm
Galva-Holstein HS | 200/9-12
PO Box 320 51025 | 712-368-4353
Ken Slater, prin. | Fax 368-4843
Other Schools – See Galva

Holy Cross, Dubuque, Pop. 339

RHCL Catholic S Holy Cross | 100/4-8
PO Box 368 52053 | 563-870-2405
Dennis Rima, prin. | Fax 870-4101

Hubbard, Hardin, Pop. 845
Hubbard-Radcliffe Community SD | 400/PK-12
PO Box 129 50122 | 641-864-2211
Dr. Ron Blakley, supt. | Fax 864-2422
www.hubbard.k12.ia.us
Hubbard-Radcliffe HS | 200/9-12
PO Box 129 50122 | 641-864-2211
Jim Walser, prin. | Fax 864-2422
Radcliffe-Hubbard MS | 100/7-8
PO Box 129 50122 | 641-864-2211
Jim Walser, prin. | Fax 864-2422

Hudson, Black Hawk, Pop. 2,127
Hudson Community SD | 800/K-12
PO Box 240 50643 | 319-988-3233
Ron Crooks, supt. | Fax 988-3235
www.hudson.k12.ia.us
Hudson HS | 200/9-12
PO Box 240 50643 | 319-988-4226
Catherine Hicks, prin. | Fax 988-4174
Hudson MS | 300/5-8
PO Box 240 50643 | 319-988-4137
Mark Schlatter, prin. | Fax 988-4137

Hull, Sioux, Pop. 2,039
Boyden-Hull Community SD | 600/K-12
PO Box 678 51239 | 712-439-2711
Steve Grond, supt. | Fax 439-1419
www.boyden-hull.k12.ia.us
Boyden-Hull JSHS | 300/7-12
PO Box 678 51239 | 712-439-2440
Marjorie Wagner, prin. | Fax 439-1419

Western Christian HS | 400/9-12
PO Box 658 51239 | 712-439-1013
Glenn Schaap, prin. | Fax 439-1407

Humboldt, Humboldt, Pop. 4,366
Humboldt Community SD | 1,300/PK-12
1408 9th Ave N 50548 | 515-332-1330
Joyce Judas, supt. | Fax 332-4478
www.humboldt.k12.ia.us
Humboldt HS | 500/9-12
1500 Wildcat Rd 50548 | 515-332-1430
Lori Westhoff, prin. | Fax 332-7150
Humboldt MS | 300/6-8
210 Taft St N 50548 | 515-332-2812
Bob Pattee, prin. | Fax 332-2023

Humeston, Wayne, Pop. 545
Mormon Trail Community SD | 300/PK-12
PO Box 156 50123 | 641-877-2521
Robert McCurdy, supt. | Fax 877-3400
www.mormontrail.k12.ia.us
Other Schools – See Garden Grove

Huxley, Story, Pop. 2,347
Ballard Community SD | 1,000/K-12
PO Box 307 50124 | 515-597-2811
John Speer, supt. | Fax 597-2965
www.ballard.k12.ia.us/
Ballard Community HS | 400/9-12
PO Box 307 50124 | 515-597-2971
John Ronca, prin. | Fax 597-2964
Ballard Community JHS | 200/7-8
PO Box 307 50124 | 515-597-2971
John Ronca, prin. | Fax 597-2764

Ida Grove, Ida, Pop. 2,218
Battle Creek-Ida Grove Community SD | 700/PK-12
301 Moorehead St 51445 | 712-364-3687
Russ Freeman, supt. | Fax 364-3609
www.bc-ig.k12.ia.us
Battle Creek-Ida Grove HS | 300/9-12
900 John Montgomery Dr 51445 | 712-364-3371
Patrick Miller, prin. | Fax 364-4463
Other Schools – See Battle Creek

Independence, Buchanan, Pop. 6,054
Independence Community SD | 1,400/PK-12
1207 1st St W 50644 | 319-334-7400
Devin Embray, supt. | Fax 334-7404
www.independence.k12.ia.us
Independence HS | 500/9-12
1207 1st St W 50644 | 319-334-7405
Karl Kurt, prin. | Fax 334-6096
Independence MS | 300/6-8
1207 1st St W 50644 | 319-334-7415
Meredith Miller, prin. | Fax 334-7418

Indianola, Warren, Pop. 13,944
Indianola Community SD | 3,200/K-12
1304 E 2nd Ave 50125 | 515-961-9500
Michael Teigland, supt. | Fax 961-9505
www.indianola.k12.ia.us
Indianola HS | 1,000/9-12
1304 E 1st Ave 50125 | 515-961-9510
John Monroe, prin. | Fax 961-9519
Indianola MS | 800/6-8
403 S 15th St 50125 | 515-961-9530
Peggy Fillio, prin. | Fax 961-9535

Simpson College | Post-Sec.
701 N C St 50125 | 515-961-6251

Inwood, Lyon, Pop. 874
West Lyon Community SD | 700/PK-12
1787 182nd St 51240 | 712-753-4917
Ralph Herring, supt. | Fax 753-4928
www.west-lyon.k12.ia.us/
West Lyon HS | 300/9-12
1787 182nd St 51240 | 712-753-4917
Doug Jiskoot, prin. | Fax 753-4928
West Lyon JHS | 100/7-8
1787 182nd St 51240 | 712-753-4917
Doug Jiskoot, prin. | Fax 753-4928

Iowa City, Johnson, Pop. 62,887
Iowa City Community SD | 10,600/PK-12
509 S Dubuque St 52240 | 319-688-1000
Dr. Lane Plugge, supt. | Fax 688-1009
www.iccsd.k12.ia.us/
Iowa City HS | 1,500/9-12
1900 Morningside Dr 52245 | 319-688-1040
Mark Hanson, prin. | Fax 339-5705
Southeast JHS | 700/7-8
2501 Bradford Dr 52240 | 319-688-1070
Deb Wretman, prin. | Fax 339-5735
West HS | 1,700/9-12
2901 Melrose Ave 52246 | 319-688-1050
Jerry Arganbright, prin. | Fax 339-5738
Other Schools – See Coralville, North Liberty

La' James College of Hairstyling | Post-Sec.
227 E Market St 52245 | 319-337-2109
Regina HS | 400/7-12
2150 Rochester Ave 52245 | 319-338-5436
Ray Pechous, prin. | Fax 887-3817
University of Iowa | Post-Sec.
107 Calvin Hall 52242 | 319-335-3500

Iowa Falls, Hardin, Pop. 5,112
Iowa Falls Community SD | 1,100/PK-12
710 North St 50126 | 641-648-6400
John Robbins, supt. | Fax 648-6401
www.iowa-falls.k12.ia.us
Iowa Falls - Alden HS | 400/9-12
1903 Taylor Ave 50126 | 641-648-6440
Frank Schnoes, prin. | Fax 648-3222
Riverbend MS | 200/7-8
1124 Union St 50126 | 641-648-6430
Jeff Burchfield, prin. | Fax 648-6432

Ellsworth Community College | Post-Sec.
1100 College Ave 50126 | 800-322-9235

Janesville, Bremer, Pop. 875
Janesville Consolidated SD | 300/PK-12
PO Box 478 50647 | 319-987-2581
Robert Weber, supt. | Fax 987-2824
www.janesville.k12.ia.us
Janesville JSHS | 100/6-12
PO Box 478 50647 | 319-987-2581
Robert Weber, prin. | Fax 987-2824

Jefferson, Greene, Pop. 4,407
Jefferson-Scranton SD | 1,200/PK-12
204 W Madison St 50129 | 515-386-4168
Michael Haluska, supt. | Fax 386-3591
www.jefferson-scranton.k12.ia.us
Jefferson-Scranton HS | 400/9-12
101 Ram Dr 50129 | 515-386-2188
Karen Younie, prin. | Fax 386-2159
Jefferson-Scranton MS | 300/6-8
203 W Harrison St 50129 | 515-386-8126
Scott Johnson, prin. | Fax 386-2142

Jesup, Buchanan, Pop. 2,413
Jesup Community SD | 800/PK-12
PO Box 287 50648 | 319-827-1700
Sarah Pinion, supt. | Fax 827-3905
www.jesup.k12.ia.us
Jesup HS | 300/9-12
PO Box 287 50648 | 319-827-1700
Rodney Chamberlin, prin. | Fax 827-3905
Jesup MS | 200/5-8
PO Box 287 50648 | 319-827-1700
Lisa Loecher, prin. | Fax 827-3905

Jewell, Hamilton, Pop. 1,090
South Hamilton Community SD | 700/PK-12
PO Box 100 50130 | 515-827-5479
Lyle Schwartz, supt. | Fax 827-5368
www.s-hamilton.k12.ia.us
South Hamilton MSHS | 400/7-12
PO Box 100 50130 | 515-827-5418
Steve Gray, prin. | Fax 827-5368

Johnston, Polk, Pop. 12,931
Johnston Community SD | 4,900/PK-12
PO Box 10 50131 | 515-278-0470
Clay Guthmiller, supt. | Fax 278-5884
www.johnston.k12.ia.us
Johnston MS | 800/8-9
PO Box 10 50131 | 515-278-0476
Brian Carico, prin. | Fax 278-0130
Johnston SHS | 1,000/10-12
PO Box 10 50131 | 515-278-0449
Bruce Hukee, prin. | Fax 276-5795

La' James College of Hairstyling — Post-Sec.
8805 Chambery Blvd 50131 — 515-278-2208

Kalona, Washington, Pop. 2,486
Mid-Prairie Community SD
Supt. — See Wellman
Mid-Prairie MS — 300/6-8
713 F Ave 52247 — 319-656-2241
Nancy Hurd, prin. — Fax 656-2207

Iowa Mennonite HS — 200/9-12
1421 540th St SW 52247 — 319-656-2073
Wilbur Yoder, prin. — Fax 656-2073

Kanawha, Hancock, Pop. 691
West Hancock Community SD
Supt. — See Britt
West Hancock MS — 100/5-8
PO Box 130 50447 — 641-762-3261
Nicole Kooiker, prin. — Fax 762-3263

Keokuk, Lee, Pop. 10,762
Keokuk Community SD — 2,100/K-12
727 Washington St 52632 — 319-524-1402
Jane Babcock, supt. — Fax 524-1114
www.keokuk.k12.ia.us
Keokuk HS — 600/9-12
2285 Middle Rd 52632 — 319-524-2542
Dave Keane, prin. — Fax 524-1784
Keokuk MS — 600/6-8
2002 Orleans Ave 52632 — 319-524-3737
Steven Carman, prin. — Fax 524-1511

Dayton's School of Hair Design — Post-Sec.
23 S 2nd St 52632 — 319-524-6445
Southeastern Community College — Post-Sec.
PO Box 6007 52632 — 319-524-3221

Keosauqua, Van Buren, Pop. 1,076
Van Buren Community SD — 700/PK-12
503 Henry Dr 52565 — 319-293-3334
Karen Stinson, supt. — Fax 293-3301
www.van-buren.k12.ia.us
Van Buren Community JSHS — 400/7-12
405 4th St 52565 — 319-293-3183
Kurt Jirak, prin. — Fax 293-3345

Keota, Washington, Pop. 939
Keota Community SD — 400/PK-12
PO Box 88 52248 — 641-636-2189
Todd Abrahamson, supt. — Fax 636-3009
www.keota.k12.ia.us/
Keota JSHS, PO Box 88 52248 — 200/7-12
Lisa Brenneman, prin. — 641-636-3491

Kingsley, Plymouth, Pop. 1,248
Kingsley-Pierson Community SD — 500/K-12
PO Box 520 51028 — 712-378-2861
Scott Bailey, supt. — Fax 378-3729
www.kingsleypierson.com/
Kingsley-Pierson HS — 200/9-12
PO Box 520 51028 — 712-378-2861
Randy Wiese, prin. — Fax 378-3729
Other Schools – See Pierson

Knoxville, Marion, Pop. 7,512
Knoxville Community SD — 2,000/PK-12
309 W Main St 50138 — 641-842-6552
Randy Flack, supt. — Fax 842-2109
www.knoxville.k12.ia.us
Knoxville HS — 700/9-12
1811 W Madison St 50138 — 641-842-2173
Kevin Crawford, prin. — Fax 842-2066
Knoxville MS — 500/6-8
102 N Lincoln St 50138 — 641-842-3315
Annette Jauron, prin. — Fax 842-5754

Lake City, Calhoun, Pop. 1,693
Southern Cal Community SD — 600/K-12
709 W Main St 51449 — 712-464-7210
Eric Wood, supt. — Fax 464-3724
www.southern-cal.k12.ia.us
Southern Cal MSHS — 300/7-12
709 W Main St 51449 — 712-464-7211
Earl Trachsel, prin. — Fax 464-3724

Lake Mills, Winnebago, Pop. 2,060
Lake Mills Community SD — 700/PK-12
102 S 4th Ave E 50450 — 641-592-0881
Daryl Sherman, supt. — Fax 592-0883
www.lake-mills.k12.ia.us
Lake Mills HS — 200/9-12
102 S 4th Ave E 50450 — 641-592-0893
James Scholbrock, prin. — Fax 592-0883
Lake Mills MS — 200/6-8
102 S 4th Ave E 50450 — 641-592-0894
James Scholbrock, prin. — Fax 592-0883

Lake Park, Dickinson, Pop. 993
Harris-Lake Park Community SD — 300/PK-12
PO Box 8 51347 — 712-832-3809
Tim Christensen, supt. — Fax 832-3812
www.harris-lp.k12.ia.us
Harris-Lake Park MSHS — 200/6-12
PO Box 8 51347 — 712-832-3809
Dennis Peters, prin. — Fax 832-3812

Lake View, Sac, Pop. 1,221
Wall Lake View Auburn SD — 500/PK-12
PO Box 110 51450 — 712-664-5000
Barb Kruthoff, supt. — Fax 664-5021
www.wlva.k12.ia.us
Wall Lake View Auburn HS — 200/9-12
PO Box 110 51450 — 712-664-5001
Kevin Litterer, prin. — Fax 664-5022
Wall Lake View Auburn MS — 100/7-8
PO Box 110 51450 — 712-664-5002
Kevin Litterer, prin. — Fax 664-5022

Lamoni, Decatur, Pop. 2,470
Lamoni Community SD — 400/PK-12
202 N Walnut St 50140 — 641-784-3342
Diane Fine, supt. — Fax 784-6602
lamoni.k12.ia.us
Lamoni HS — 100/9-12
202 N Walnut St 50140 — 641-784-3351
Daniel Day, prin. — Fax 784-6602
Lamoni MS — 100/6-8
202 N Walnut St 50140 — 641-784-7299
Daniel Day, prin. — Fax 784-6602

Graceland University — Post-Sec.
1 University Pl 50140 — 641-784-5000

Lansing, Allamakee, Pop. 987
Eastern Allamakee Community SD — 400/PK-12
696 Main St 52151 — 563-538-4202
Patrick Heiderscheit, supt. — Fax 538-4202
www.e-allamakee.k12.ia.us/
Kee HS — 200/9-12
569 Center St 52151 — 563-538-4201
Patrick Heiderscheit, prin. — Fax 538-4969
Lansing MS — 100/5-8
569 Center St 52151 — 563-538-4118
Cynthia Lapel, prin. — Fax 538-4202

La Porte City, Black Hawk, Pop. 2,301
Union Community SD — 1,200/K-12
200 Adams St 50651 — 319-342-2674
Neil Mullen, supt. — Fax 342-2393
www.union.k12.ia.us/
Union HS — 400/9-12
200 Adams St 50651 — 319-342-2697
Travis Fleshner, prin. — Fax 342-2393
Other Schools – See Dysart

Latimer, Franklin, Pop. 550
CAL Community SD — 200/PK-12
PO Box 459 50452 — 641-579-6087
Steven Lane, supt. — Fax 579-6408
www.cal.k12.ia.us
CAL HS — 100/9-12
PO Box 459 50452 — 641-579-6086
Amy Karg, prin. — Fax 579-6408

Laurens, Pocahontas, Pop. 1,326
Laurens-Marathon Community SD — 400/K-12
300 W Garfield St 50554 — 712-841-5000
Dan Braunschweig, supt. — Fax 841-5010
www.laurens-marathon.k12.ia.us
Laurens-Marathon HS — 200/9-12
300 W Garfield St 50554 — 712-841-5000
Rose Davis, prin. — Fax 841-5010
Laurens-Marathon MS — 100/6-8
300 W Garfield St 50554 — 712-841-5000
Rose Davis, prin. — Fax 841-5010

Lawton, Woodbury, Pop. 729
Lawton-Bronson Community SD — 600/PK-12
PO Box 128 51030 — 712-944-5183
Dr. Robert Morrison, supt. — Fax 944-5568
www.lawton-bronson.k12.ia.us
Lawton JSHS — 400/6-12
PO Box 128 51030 — 712-944-5181
Jeff Thelander, prin. — Fax 944-5568

Le Claire, Scott, Pop. 3,123
Pleasant Valley Community SD
Supt. — See Eldridge
Pleasant Valley JHS — 500/7-8
3501 Wisconsin St 52753 — 563-289-4507
Brian Strusz, prin. — Fax 289-4666

Le Grand, Marshall, Pop. 966
East Marshall Community SD
Supt. — See Gilman
East Marshall HS — 300/9-12
PO Box A 50142 — 641-479-2785
Rex Kozak, prin. — Fax 479-2601

Le Mars, Plymouth, Pop. 9,349
Le Mars Community SD — 2,200/K-12
921 3rd Ave SW 51031 — 712-546-4155
Dr. Todd Wendt, supt. — Fax 546-4157
lemars.k12.ia.us
Le Mars HS — 700/9-12
921 3rd Ave SW 51031 — 712-546-4153
Larry Johnson, prin. — Fax 546-9581
Le Mars MS — 500/6-8
977 3rd Ave SW 51031 — 712-546-7022
Steve Webner, prin. — Fax 546-7024

Gehlen Catholic HS — 200/7-12
709 Plymouth St NE 51031 — 712-546-5126
Jeff Alesch, prin. — Fax 546-9384

Lenox, Taylor, Pop. 1,310
Lenox Community SD — 400/K-12
600 S Locust St 50851 — 641-333-2244
David Henrichs, supt. — Fax 333-2247
www.lenox.k12.ia.us
Lenox JSHS — 200/7-12
600 S Locust St 50851 — 641-333-2244
Ken Myers, prin. — Fax 333-2247

Leon, Decatur, Pop. 1,924
Central Decatur Community SD — 700/PK-12
1201 NE Poplar St 50144 — 641-446-4818
Tom Dannen, supt. — Fax 446-7990
www.central-decatur.k12.ia.us/
Central Decatur JSHS — 400/6-12
1201 NE Poplar St 50144 — 641-446-4816
Rob Meier, prin. — Fax 446-7990

Letts, Louisa, Pop. 390
Louisa-Muscatine Community SD — 900/PK-12
14478 170th St 52754 — 319-726-3541
John Dotson, supt. — Fax 726-3334
www.louisa-muscatine.k12.ia.us
Louisa-Muscatine JSHS — 500/7-12
14354 170th St 52754 — 319-726-3421
Anthony Lohse, prin. — Fax 726-3649

Liberty Center, Warren
Southeast Warren Community SD — 600/PK-12
16331 Tyler St 50145 — 641-466-3510
Harold Hulleman, supt. — Fax 466-3525
www.se-warren.k12.ia.us
Southeast Warren JSHS — 300/7-12
16331 Tyler St 50145 — 641-466-3331
Terry Gladfelter, prin. — Fax 466-3525

Lineville, Wayne, Pop. 238
Lineville-Clio Community SD — 100/PK-12
PO Box 98 50147 — 641-876-5345
Robert McCurdy, supt. — Fax 876-2805
www.aea15.k12.ia.us
Lineville-Clio JSHS — 50/7-12
PO Box 98 50147 — 641-876-5345
Mike Snyder, prin. — Fax 876-2805

Lisbon, Linn, Pop. 1,944
Lisbon Community SD — 600/PK-12
PO Box 839 52253 — 319-455-2075
Vincent Smith, supt. — Fax 455-2733
www.lisbon.k12.ia.us
Lisbon HS — 200/9-12
PO Box 839 52253 — 319-455-2106
Brian Downing, prin. — Fax 455-3208
Lisbon MS — 100/6-8
PO Box 839 52253 — 319-455-2659
Roger Teeling, prin. — Fax 455-3303

Little Rock, Lyon, Pop. 482
George-Little Rock Community SD
Supt. — See George
George-Little Rock MS — 100/6-8
PO Box 247 51243 — 712-479-2771
Janel Guse, prin. — Fax 479-2770

Logan, Harrison, Pop. 1,319
Logan-Magnolia Community SD — 700/PK-12
1200 N 2nd Ave 51546 — 712-644-2250
James Hammrich, supt. — Fax 644-2934
www.logan.k12.ia.us
Logan-Magnolia JSHS — 400/7-12
1200 N 2nd Ave 51546 — 712-644-2250
Katy Sojka, prin. — Fax 644-2934

Lone Tree, Johnson, Pop. 1,081
Lone Tree Community SD — 400/K-12
PO Box 520 52755 — 319-629-4212
Michael Reeves, supt. — Fax 629-4324
www.lone-tree.k12.ia.us
Lone Tree JSHS — 200/6-12
PO Box 520 52755 — 319-629-4610
Mark Hopkins, prin. — Fax 629-4324

Lost Nation, Clinton, Pop. 475
Midland Community SD
Supt. — See Wyoming
Lost Nation MS — 200/5-8
PO Box 217 52254 — 563-678-2142
Lynn Olson, prin. — Fax 678-2135

Lu Verne, Kossuth, Pop. 289
Lu Verne Community SD — 100/PK-PK, 5-
PO Box 69 50560 — 515-882-3357
Willie Stone, supt. — Fax 882-3417
www.luverne.k12.ia.us/
Lu Verne S — 100/PK-PK, 5-
PO Box 69 50560 — 515-882-3357
Willie Stone, prin. — Fax 882-3417

Lytton, Calhoun, Pop. 273
Rockwell City-Lytton Community SD
Supt. — See Rockwell City
Rockwell City-Lytton MS — 100/5-8
PO Box 49 50561 — 712-466-2224
Marc DeMoss, prin. — Fax 466-2658

Mc Callsburg, Story, Pop. 269
Colo-Nesco Comm SD — 500/PK-12
400 Latrobe Ave 50154 — 515-434-2302
Gary Pillman, supt. — Fax 434-2104
www.colo-nesco.k12.ia.us
Other Schools – See Colo, Zearing

Mc Gregor, Clayton, Pop. 789
MFL MarMac Community SD
Supt. — See Monona
MFL MarMac MS — 400/4-8
PO Box D 52157 — 563-873-3463
Dave Meyer, prin. — Fax 873-2371

Madrid, Boone, Pop. 2,420
Madrid Community SD — 600/K-12
201 N Main St 50156 — 515-795-3241
Brian Horn, supt. — Fax 795-2121
madrid.k12.ia.us
Madrid HS — 200/9-12
599 N Kennedy Ave 50156 — 515-795-3240
Mark Cosens, prin. — Fax 795-4408
Madrid JHS — 100/7-8
599 N Kennedy Ave 50156 — 515-795-3240
Mark Cosens, prin. — Fax 795-4408

Mallard, Palo Alto, Pop. 284
West Bend - Mallard Community SD
Supt. — See West Bend
West Bend - Mallard MS — 100/6-8
PO Box 326 50562 — 712-425-3452
Amanda Schmidt, prin. — Fax 425-3413

Malvern, Mills, Pop. 1,342
Malvern Community SD — 400/K-12
422 Main St 51551 — 712-624-8700
Curtis Barclay, supt. — Fax 624-8279
www.malvernschools.org/

Malvern JSHS 200/7-12
1505 E 15th St 51551 712-624-8645
Jim Bonesteel, prin. Fax 624-8124

Manchester, Delaware, Pop. 5,074
West Delaware County Community SD 1,500/PK-12
601 New St 52057 563-927-3515
Rick Hilbert, supt. Fax 927-2785
www.w-delaware.k12.ia.us
West Delaware HS 600/9-12
701 New St 52057 563-927-5002
Jon Nordaas, prin. Fax 927-6222
West Delaware MS 400/5-8
1101 Doctor St 52057 563-927-5004
Randy Stanek, prin. Fax 927-9115

Manilla, Crawford, Pop. 833
IKM Community SD 400/K-12
PO Box 580 51454 712-654-2852
Jeff Kruse, supt. Fax 654-9280
www.ikm.k12.ia.us/
IKM Community HS 100/9-12
PO Box 580 51454 712-654-2852
Denise Philipp, prin. Fax 654-9282
IKM Community JHS 100/5-8
PO Box 580 51454 712-654-9385
Denise Philipp, prin. Fax 654-9282

Manly, Worth, Pop. 1,336
North Central Community SD 500/K-12
PO Box 190 50456 641-454-2211
Bruce Burton, supt. Fax 454-2212
www.northcentral.k12.ia.us
North Central JSHS 300/6-12
PO Box 190 50456 641-454-2208
Ken Estes, prin. Fax 454-2212

Manning, Carroll, Pop. 1,447
Manning Community SD 500/PK-12
209 10th St 51455 712-655-3771
Roger Schmiedeskamp, supt. Fax 655-3311
www.manning.k12.ia.us
Manning JSHS 300/7-12
209 10th St 51455 712-655-3781
Brian Wall, prin. Fax 655-3311

Manson, Calhoun, Pop. 1,760
Manson NW Webster Community SD 700/K-12
1227 16th St 50563 712-469-2202
Mark Egli, supt. Fax 469-2298
www.manson-nw.k12.ia.us
Manson Northwest Webster HS 300/9-12
1601 15th St 50563 712-469-2245
Jeff Anliker, prin. Fax 469-3131
Other Schools – See Barnum

Mapleton, Monona, Pop. 1,230
Maple Valley Community SD 500/PK-12
410 S 6th St 51034 712-881-1319
Steve Oberg, supt. Fax 881-1316
www.maple-valley.k12.ia.us
Maple Valley-Anthon Oto HS 300/9-12
410 S 6th St 51034 712-881-1319
Dan Dougherty, prin. Fax 881-1321

Maquoketa, Jackson, Pop. 6,054
Maquoketa Community SD 1,600/PK-12
612 S Vermont St 52060 563-652-4984
Kim P. Huckstadt, supt. Fax 652-6958
www.maquoketa.k12.ia.us
Maquoketa HS 600/9-12
600 Washington St 52060 563-652-2451
William Walters, prin. Fax 652-5324
Maquoketa MS 400/6-8
200 E Locust St 52060 563-652-4956
Autumn Pino, prin. Fax 652-6885

Marcus, Cherokee, Pop. 1,064
Marcus-Meriden-Cleghorn Community SD 500/PK-12
PO Box 667 51035 712-376-4171
Jan Brandhorst, supt. Fax 376-4302
www.marcus-mer-cleg.k12.ia.us
Marcus-Meriden-Cleghorn Community HS 200/9-12
PO Box 667 51035 712-376-4172
Bill Sillau, prin. Fax 376-4302
Other Schools – See Cleghorn

Marengo, Iowa, Pop. 2,539
Iowa Valley Community SD 600/PK-12
359 E Hilton St 52301 319-642-7714
Laurene Lanich, supt. Fax 642-3023
www.iowa-valley.k12.ia.us
Iowa Valley JSHS 300/7-12
359 E Hilton St 52301 319-642-3332
James Bieschke, prin. Fax 642-3023

Marion, Linn, Pop. 30,233
Linn-Mar Community SD 5,100/PK-12
3333 10th St 52302 319-447-3000
Dr. Kathleen Mulholland, supt. Fax 377-9252
www.linnmar.k12.ia.us/
Excelsior MS 800/6-8
3333 10th St 52302 319-447-3130
Marc McCoy, prin. Fax 373-4930
Linn-Mar HS 1,400/9-12
3111 10th St 52302 319-447-3040
Gerald Van Dyke, prin. Fax 377-0486

Marion ISD 1,900/PK-12
PO Box 606 52302 319-377-4691
Nicholas B. Hobbs, supt. Fax 377-4692
www.marion.k12.ia.us/
Marion HS 600/9-12
675 S 15th St 52302 319-377-9891
Gregory Thomas Ed.D., prin. Fax 377-7621
Vernon MS 500/6-8
1301 5th Ave 52302 319-377-9401
Robert Hoyt, prin. Fax 377-7670

Marshalltown, Marshall, Pop. 25,977
Marshalltown Community SD 3,800/K-12
317 Columbus Dr 50158 641-754-1000
Harrison E. Cass, supt. Fax 754-1003
www.marshalltown.k12.ia.us
Marshalltown HS 1,500/9-12
1602 S 2nd Ave 50158 641-754-1130
Bonnie Lowry, prin. Fax 754-1136
Miller MS 400/7-8
125 S 11th St 50158 641-754-1110
Burton Clement, prin. Fax 754-1115

Iowa School of Beauty Post-Sec.
112 Nicholas Dr 50158 641-752-4223
Marshalltown Community College Post-Sec.
3700 S Center St 50158 641-752-7106

Martensdale, Warren, Pop. 459
Martensdale-St. Mary's Community SD 400/K-12
PO Box 350 50160 641-764-2466
Peggy Huisman, supt. Fax 764-2100
www.m-stmarys.k12.ia.us/
Martensdale-St. Mary's JSHS 200/7-12
PO Box 350 50160 641-764-2486
Gary Friday, prin. Fax 764-2100

Mason City, Cerro Gordo, Pop. 27,909
Mason City Community SD 4,200/PK-12
1515 S Pennsylvania Ave 50401 641-421-4400
Keith Sersland, supt. Fax 421-4448
www.masoncityschools.org
Adams MS 500/6-8
29 S Illinois Ave 50401 641-421-4420
T.J. Jumper, prin. Fax 421-4476
Mason City HS 1,300/9-12
1700 4th St SE 50401 641-421-4431
Douglas Kennedy, prin. Fax 421-4523
Roosevelt MS 500/6-8
1625 S Pennsylvania Ave 50401 641-421-4423
Carol Clayton, prin. Fax 423-3387

Hamilton College Post-Sec.
2570 4th St SW 50401 641-423-2530
La' James College of Hairstyling Post-Sec.
24 2nd St NE 50401 641-424-2161
Newman HS 200/9-12
2445 19th St SW 50401 641-423-6939
Mike Kavars, prin. Fax 423-6653
North Iowa Area Community College Post-Sec.
500 College Dr 50401 641-423-1264
North Iowa Christian S 50/K-12
811 N Kentucky Ave 50401 641-423-6440
Janna Voss, admin. Fax 423-6440
North Iowa Mercy Health Center Post-Sec.
1000 4th St SW 50401 641-422-7722
World Wide College of Auctioneering Post-Sec.
PO Box 949 50402 800-423-5242

Massena, Cass, Pop. 407
C and M Community SD 200/K-8
PO Box 7 50853 712-779-2211
Steve Pelzer, supt. Fax 779-3365
www.candm.k12.ia.us
CAM MS 100/6-8
PO Box 7 50853 712-779-2212
Steve Pelzer, prin. Fax 779-3365

Maxwell, Story, Pop. 764
Collins-Maxwell Community SD 500/K-12
400 Metcalf St 50161 515-387-1115
Doug Miller, supt. Fax 387-8842
www.collins-maxwell.k12.ia.us
Collins-Maxwell MSHS 300/6-12
400 Metcalf St 50161 515-387-1115
Kevin Williams, prin. Fax 387-8842

Maynard, Fayette, Pop. 464
West Central Community SD 300/K-12
PO Box 54 50655 563-637-2283
Jim Patera, supt. Fax 637-2294
www.w-central.k12.ia.us/
West Central JSHS 200/7-12
PO Box 54 50655 563-637-2637
John Johnson, prin. Fax 637-2294

Mediapolis, Des Moines, Pop. 1,587
Mediapolis Community SD 900/K-12
PO Box 358 52637 319-394-3237
Fred Whipple, supt. Fax 394-3021
www.mediapolis.k12.ia.us
Mediapolis HS 300/9-12
725 N Northfield St 52637 319-394-3101
Dennis Heiman, prin. Fax 394-9198
Mediapolis MS 200/6-8
725 N Northfield St 52637 319-394-3101
Dennis Heiman, prin. Fax 394-9198

Melcher, Marion, Pop. 1,310
Melcher-Dallas Community SD 400/PK-12
PO Box 489 50163 641-947-2321
Steve Mitchell, supt. Fax 947-2203
www.melcher-dallas.k12.ia.us
Melcher-Dallas HS 100/9-12
PO Box 158 50163 641-947-3731
Ron Juhler, prin. Fax 947-2203
Melcher-Dallas JHS 100/7-8
PO Box 158 50163 641-947-3731
Ron Juhler, prin. Fax 947-2203

Middle Amana, Iowa, Pop. 350
Clear Creek-Amana Community SD
Supt. — See Oxford
Clear Creek-Amana MS 300/6-8
PO Box 70 52307 319-622-3255
Brad Fox, prin. Fax 622-3108

Miles, Jackson, Pop. 457
East Central Community SD 400/K-12
PO Box 367 52064 563-682-7510
James House, supt. Fax 682-7194
www.east-central.k12.ia.us
East Central Community HS 100/9-12
PO Box 367 52064 563-682-7510
Warren Amman, prin. Fax 682-7194
Other Schools – See Sabula

Milford, Dickinson, Pop. 2,441
Okoboji Community SD 900/PK-12
PO Box 147 51351 712-338-4757
Robert Miller, supt. Fax 338-4758
www.okoboji.k12.ia.us
Okoboji HS 300/9-12
PO Box 147 51351 712-338-2446
Michael Schmitz, prin. Fax 338-2550
Other Schools – See Arnolds Park

Mingo, Jasper, Pop. 275
Colfax-Mingo Community SD
Supt. — See Colfax
Colfax-Mingo MS 200/6-8
307 W Mohawk Dr 50168 641-363-4282
Rebecca Maher, prin. Fax 363-3256

Missouri Valley, Harrison, Pop. 2,932
Missouri Valley Community SD 900/PK-12
109 E Michigan St 51555 712-642-2706
Dr. Tom Micek, supt. Fax 642-2456
www.movalley.k12.ia.us
Missouri Valley HS 300/9-12
605 Lincoln Hwy 51555 712-642-4149
Deidre Drees, prin. Fax 642-4624
Missouri Valley MS 200/6-8
607 Lincoln Hwy 51555 712-642-2707
Frank Smith, prin. Fax 642-3738

Mondamin, Harrison, Pop. 419
West Harrison Community SD 500/K-12
410 Pine St 51557 712-646-2231
Richard Gerking, supt. Fax 646-2891
westharrison.ia.schoolwebpages.com/
West Harrison MSHS 300/6-12
410 Pine St 51557 712-646-2231
Christine Snell, prin. Fax 646-2891

Monona, Clayton, Pop. 1,445
MFL MarMac Community SD 1,000/PK-12
PO Box D 52159 563-539-4795
Dale Crozier, supt. Fax 539-4913
www.mflmarmac.k12.ia.us
MFL MarMac HS 400/9-12
PO Box D 52159 563-539-2031
Ed Berry, prin. Fax 539-4913
Other Schools – See Mc Gregor

Monroe, Jasper, Pop. 1,838
PCM Community SD
Supt. — See Prairie City
PCM HS 300/9-12
PO Box 610 50170 641-259-2315
Lee Griebel, prin. Fax 259-2317

Montezuma, Poweshiek, Pop. 1,419
Montezuma Community SD 600/K-12
PO Box 580 50171 641-623-5121
William Cox, supt. Fax 623-5733
www.montezuma.k12.ia.us
Montezuma HS 200/9-12
PO Box 580 50171 641-623-5121
Rhonna Fiihr, prin. Fax 623-5733
Montezuma JHS 100/7-8
PO Box 580 50171 641-623-5121
Rhonna Fiihr, prin. Fax 623-5733

Monticello, Jones, Pop. 3,701
Monticello Community SD 1,100/PK-12
711 N Maple St 52310 319-465-5963
Randy Achenbach, supt. Fax 465-4092
www.monticello.k12.ia.us/
Monticello HS 400/9-12
850 E Oak St 52310 319-465-6597
Joan Young, prin. Fax 465-4253
Monticello MS 300/5-8
217 S Maple St 52310 319-465-3575
William Gilkerson, prin. Fax 465-6959

Moravia, Appanoose, Pop. 731
Moravia Community SD 400/PK-12
505 N Trussell Ave 52571 641-724-3240
Brad Breon, supt. Fax 724-0629
www.moravia.k12.ia.us
Moravia JSHS 100/7-12
505 N Trussell Ave 52571 641-724-3241
Kathy Carr, prin. Fax 724-0629

Moulton, Appanoose, Pop. 683
Moulton-Udell Community SD 300/PK-12
305 E 8th St 52572 641-642-3665
Richard Turner, supt. Fax 642-3461
Moulton-Udell JSHS 100/7-12
305 E 8th St 52572 641-642-8131
Randy Alger, prin. Fax 642-3461

Mount Ayr, Ringgold, Pop. 1,764
Mount Ayr Community SD 700/PK-12
1001 E Columbus St 50854 641-464-0500
Russ Reiter, supt. Fax 464-2325
www.mtayr.k12.ia.us
Mount Ayr JSHS 300/7-12
1001 E Columbus St 50854 641-464-0510
Matt Patton, prin. Fax 464-2325

Mount Pleasant, Henry, Pop. 8,767
Mount Pleasant Community SD 2,200/PK-12
400 E Madison St 52641 319-385-7750
John Roederer, supt. Fax 385-7788
www.mtpleasantschools.com

Mount Pleasant HS 700/9-12
2104 S Grand Ave 52641 319-385-7700
Todd Liechty, prin. Fax 385-7789
Mount Pleasant MS 500/6-8
400 E Madison St 52641 319-385-7730
Darren Hanna, prin. Fax 385-7735

Iowa Wesleyan College Post-Sec.
601 N Main St 52641 319-385-8021
Mount Pleasant Christian S 100/PK-12
1505 E Washington St 52641 319-385-8613
Michael Peters, admin. Fax 385-8415

Mount Vernon, Linn, Pop. 4,051
Mount Vernon Community SD 1,200/K-12
525 Palisades Rd SW 52314 319-895-8845
Jeff Schwiebert, supt. Fax 895-6185
www.mountvernon.k12.ia.us/
Mount Vernon HS 400/9-12
525 Palisades Rd SW 52314 319-895-8843
Dennis Walsh, prin. Fax 895-6185
Mount Vernon MS 300/6-8
221 1st St NE 52314 319-895-6254
John Krumbholz, prin. Fax 895-8875

Cornell College Post-Sec.
600 1st St SW 52314 319-895-4000

Moville, Woodbury, Pop. 1,480
Woodbury Central Community SD 600/PK-12
PO Box 586 51039 712-873-3128
Thomas Cooper, supt. Fax 873-3162
www.woodbury-central.k12.ia.us
Woodbury Central HS 200/9-12
PO Box 586 51039 712-873-3128
Steve Shanks, prin. Fax 873-3162
Woodbury Central MS 100/6-8
PO Box 586 51039 712-873-3128
Steve Shanks, prin. Fax 873-3162

Murray, Clarke, Pop. 786
Murray Community SD 300/PK-12
PO Box 187 50174 641-447-2517
Dr. Dennis Bishop, supt. Fax 447-2313
www.murray.k12.ia.us/
Murray JSHS 200/7-12
PO Box 187 50174 641-447-2517
Ted Nowakowski, prin. Fax 447-2313

Muscatine, Muscatine, Pop. 22,757
Muscatine Community SD 5,300/PK-12
2900 Mulberry Ave 52761 563-263-7223
Thomas Williams, supt. Fax 263-7729
www.muscatine.k12.ia.us
Central MS 600/6-8
901 Cedar St 52761 563-263-7784
Terry Hogenson, prin. Fax 263-0145
Muscatine HS 1,700/9-12
2705 Cedar St 52761 563-263-6141
Robert Weaton, prin. Fax 264-1794
West MS 700/6-8
600 Kindler Ave 52761 563-263-0411
John Lawrence, prin. Fax 263-6645

Muscatine Community College Post-Sec.
152 Colorado St 52761 563-288-6001

Nashua, Chickasaw, Pop. 1,574
Nashua-Plainfield Community SD 700/PK-12
PO Box 569 50658 641-435-4835
Paul Bisgard, supt. Fax 435-4835
www.nashua-plainfield.k12.ia.us
Nashua-Plainfield HS 200/9-12
PO Box 569 50658 641-435-4166
Randall Strabala, prin. Fax 435-4167
Other Schools – See Plainfield

Neola, Pottawattamie, Pop. 840
Tri-Center Community SD 800/PK-12
33980 310th St 51559 712-485-2257
Brett Nanninga, supt. Fax 485-2411
www.tri-center.k12.ia.us
Tri-Center HS 300/9-12
33980 310th St 51559 712-485-2257
Angela Huseman, prin. Fax 485-2411
Tri-Center MS 200/6-8
33980 310th St 51559 712-485-2211
Brian Wedemeyer, prin. Fax 485-2402

Nevada, Story, Pop. 6,129
Nevada Community SD 1,500/PK-12
1035 15th St 50201 515-382-2783
James S. Walker, supt. Fax 382-2836
www.nevada.k12.ia.us
Nevada HS 500/9-12
1001 15th St 50201 515-382-3521
Raphael Murray, prin. Fax 382-2935
Nevada MS 400/5-8
1035 15th St 50201 515-382-2751
Chris Schmidt, prin. Fax 382-2836

Newell, Buena Vista, Pop. 869
Newell-Fonda Community SD 500/K-12
PO Box 297 50568 712-272-3324
Jeff Dicks, supt. Fax 272-4276
www.newell-fonda.k12.ia.us
Newell-Fonda HS 200/9-12
PO Box 297 50568 712-272-3324
Jeff Dicks, prin. Fax 272-4276
Other Schools – See Fonda

New Hampton, Chickasaw, Pop. 3,528
New Hampton Community SD 1,200/PK-12
710 W Main St 50659 641-394-2134
Karlos McClure, supt. Fax 394-2662
www.new-hampton.k12.ia.us
New Hampton HS 400/9-12
710 W Main St 50659 641-394-2144
Richard Evans, prin. Fax 394-2921
New Hampton MS 300/5-8
206 W Main St 50659 641-394-2259
Donita Landers, prin. Fax 394-2262

New Hartford, Butler, Pop. 640
Dike-New Hartford Community SD
Supt. — See Dike
Dike-New Hartford JHS 100/7-8
508 Beaver 50660 319-983-2206
Jerold Martinek, prin. Fax 983-2207

New London, Henry, Pop. 1,871
New London Community SD 500/K-12
PO Box 97 52645 319-367-0512
Charles Reighard, supt.
www.new-london.k12.ia.us
New London JSHS, PO Box 97 52645 300/6-12
Michael Jones, prin. 319-367-0500

New Sharon, Mahaska, Pop. 1,307
North Mahaska Community SD 600/PK-12
PO Box 89 50207 641-637-2295
Randy Moffit, supt. Fax 637-4559
www.n-mahaska.k12.ia.us
North Mahaska JSHS 300/7-12
PO Box 89 50207 641-637-4187
Douglas Ray, prin. Fax 637-4559

Newton, Jasper, Pop. 15,607
Newton Community SD 3,300/PK-12
807 S 6th Ave W 50208 641-792-5809
Steven McDermott, supt. Fax 792-9159
www.newton.k12.ia.us
Berg MS 500/7-8
1900 N 5th Ave E 50208 641-792-7741
Dave Gallaher, prin. Fax 792-7779
Newton HS 1,000/9-12
800 E 4th St S 50208 641-792-5797
Bill Peters, prin. Fax 792-0005

Des Moines Area Community College Post-Sec.
600 N 2nd Ave W 50208 641-791-3622

Nora Springs, Floyd, Pop. 1,466
Nora Springs-Rock Falls Community SD 500/K-12
PO Box 367 50458 641-749-5301
Todd Lettow, supt. Fax 749-5334
www.ns-rf.com
Nora Springs-Rock Falls MSHS 300/6-12
PO Box 367 50458 641-749-5301
Lynn Baldus, prin. Fax 749-5898

North English, Iowa, Pop. 1,004
English Valleys Community SD 500/PK-12
PO Box 490 52316 319-664-3634
Alan Jensen, supt. Fax 664-3636
www.english-valleys.k12.ia.us
English Valleys JSHS 300/7-12
PO Box 490 52316 319-664-3631
Brad Breon, prin. Fax 664-3670

North Liberty, Johnson, Pop. 8,808
Iowa City Community SD
Supt. — See Iowa City
North Central JHS 7-8
180 Forevergreen Rd E 52317 319-688-1210
Jane Fry, prin. Fax 688-1219

Northwood, Worth, Pop. 2,036
Northwood-Kensett Community SD 500/K-12
PO Box 289 50459 641-324-2021
Thomas Nugent, supt. Fax 324-2092
www.nwood-kensett.k12.ia.us
Northwood-Kensett JSHS 300/7-12
PO Box 289 50459 641-324-2142
Keith Fritz, prin. Fax 324-2174

Norwalk, Warren, Pop. 7,877
Norwalk Community SD 2,200/PK-12
906 School Ave 50211 515-981-0676
Dennis Wulf, supt. Fax 981-0559
www.norwalk.k12.ia.us/
Norwalk HS 700/9-12
1201 North Ave 50211 515-981-4201
Dale Barnhill, prin. Fax 981-9875
Norwalk MS 500/6-8
200 Cherry Pkwy 50211 515-981-0435
Mark Crady, prin. Fax 981-0771

Oakland, Pottawattamie, Pop. 1,460
Riverside Community SD
Supt. — See Carson
Riverside Community HS 200/9-12
PO Box 428 51560 712-482-6464
Murray Fenn, prin. Fax 482-3074

Odebolt, Sac, Pop. 1,045
Odebolt-Arthur Community SD 400/PK-12
PO Box 475 51458 712-668-2289
Russ Freeman, supt. Fax 668-2631
showcase.netins.net/web/oahs/
Odebolt-Arthur HS 100/9-12
PO Box 475 51458 712-668-2827
Chuck Foy, prin. Fax 668-2631
Odebolt-Arthur MS 100/6-8
PO Box 475 51458 712-668-2767
Danielle Trimble, prin. Fax 668-2631

Oelwein, Fayette, Pop. 6,371
Oelwein Community SD 1,300/PK-12
307 8th Ave SE 50662 319-283-3536
Jim Patera, supt. Fax 283-4497
www.oelwein.k12.ia.us
Oelwein HS 500/9-12
315 8th Ave SE 50662 319-283-2731
Frank Christenson, prin. Fax 283-1689
Oelwein MS 300/6-8
300 12th Ave SE 50662 319-283-3015
John Amick, prin. Fax 283-4497

Ogden, Boone, Pop. 2,019
Ogden Community SD 800/K-12
PO Box 250 50212 515-275-2894
Bill Roederer, supt. Fax 275-4537
www.ogdenschools.org/
Ogden HS 300/9-12
PO Box 250 50212 515-275-4034
Jerry Wilson, prin. Fax 275-4972
Ogden MS 300/5-8
PO Box 250 50212 515-275-2912
Mike Van Sickle, prin. Fax 275-2908

Olin, Jones, Pop. 714
Olin Consolidated SD 300/K-12
212 Trilby St 52320 319-484-2155
Charles Liston, supt. Fax 484-2258
www.olin.k12.ia.us
Olin JSHS 100/7-12
212 Trilby St 52320 319-484-2170
Galen Noard, prin. Fax 484-2258

Onawa, Monona, Pop. 2,921
West Monona Community SD 700/PK-12
1314 15th St 51040 712-433-2043
James Simmelink, supt. Fax 433-3803
www.west-monona.k12.ia.us/
West Monona HS 200/9-12
1314 15th St 51040 712-433-2453
Steve Peiffer, prin. Fax 433-3803
West Monona MS 200/6-8
1314 15th St 51040 712-433-9098
Janet Ryan, prin. Fax 433-3803

Orange City, Sioux, Pop. 5,775
MOC-Floyd Valley Community SD 1,300/PK-12
PO Box 257 51041 712-737-4873
Gary Richardson, supt. Fax 737-8789
www.moc-fv.k12.ia.us/
MOC-Floyd Valley HS 400/9-12
615 8th St SE 51041 712-737-4871
Russ Adams, prin. Fax 737-3933
Other Schools – See Alton

Northwestern College Post-Sec.
101 7th St SW 51041 712-737-7000
Unity Christian HS 300/9-12
216 Michigan Ave SW 51041 712-737-4114
Harlan DeVries, prin. Fax 737-2686

Orient, Adair, Pop. 394
Orient-Macksburg Community SD 300/PK-12
PO Box 129 50858 641-337-5061
Gerald D. Waugh, supt. Fax 337-5013
www.orient-macks.k12.ia.us
Orient-Macksburg JSHS 200/7-12
PO Box 129 50858 641-337-5061
Jennifer Sornson, prin. Fax 337-5591

Osage, Mitchell, Pop. 3,462
Osage Community SD 1,000/PK-12
820 Sawyer Dr 50461 641-732-5381
Stephen Williams, supt. Fax 732-5381
www.osage.k12.ia.us
Osage HS 400/9-12
820 Sawyer Dr 50461 641-732-3102
Steve Nicholson, prin. Fax 732-3456
Osage MS 200/6-8
820 Sawyer Dr 50461 641-732-3127
Ross Grafft, prin. Fax 732-5450

Osceola, Clarke, Pop. 4,783
Clarke Community SD 1,400/K-12
PO Box 535 50213 641-342-4969
Ned Cox, supt. Fax 342-6101
www.clarke.k12.ia.us
Clarke Community HS 500/9-12
800 N Jackson St 50213 641-342-6505
David Walkup, prin. Fax 342-2213
Clarke MS 200/7-8
800 N Jackson St 50213 641-342-4221
Steve Seid, prin. Fax 342-2213

Oskaloosa, Mahaska, Pop. 11,026
Oskaloosa Community SD 1,300/K-12
PO Box 710 52577 641-673-8345
Dr. Carolyn McGaughey, supt. Fax 673-8370
www.oskaloosa.k12.ia.us
Oskaloosa HS 700/9-12
1816 N 3rd St 52577 641-673-3407
Andy Pattee, prin. Fax 672-2440
Oskaloosa MS 600/6-8
1704 N 3rd St 52577 641-673-8308
Steve Gray, prin. Fax 673-8308

William Penn University Post-Sec.
201 Trueblood Ave 52577 641-673-1001

Ossian, Winneshiek, Pop. 836
South Winneshiek Community SD
Supt. — See Calmar
South Winneshiek MS 100/6-8
PO Box 298 52161 563-532-9365
Charles Ehler, prin. Fax 532-9855

Ottumwa, Wapello, Pop. 24,798
Ottumwa Community SD 4,700/PK-12
422 Mccarroll Dr 52501 641-684-6596
Jon Sheldahl, supt. Fax 684-6522
www.ottumwa.k12.ia.us
Evans JHS, 812 Chester Ave 52501 700/7-8
Davis Eidahl, prin. 641-684-6511
Ottumwa HS 1,600/9-12
501 E 2nd St 52501 641-683-4444
Steve Hanson, prin. Fax 682-7528

Indian Hills Community College Post-Sec.
525 Grandview Ave 52501 641-683-5111
Iowa School of Beauty Post-Sec.
609 W 2nd St 52501 641-684-6504

Ottumwa Christian S 100/PK-12
458 N Court St 52501 641-683-9119
Pam Eklund, prin. Fax 683-1084

Oxford, Johnson, Pop. 645
Clear Creek-Amana Community SD 1,400/PK-12
PO Box 487 52322 319-828-4510
Paula Vincent, supt. Fax 828-4743
www.cc-amana.k12.ia.us
Other Schools – See Middle Amana, Tiffin

Packwood, Jefferson, Pop. 221
Pekin Community SD 800/PK-12
1062 Birch Ave 52580 319-695-3707
Dr. Roger Macklem, supt. Fax 695-5130
www.pekincsd.org
Pekin HS 200/9-12
1062 Birch Ave 52580 319-695-3705
Art Sathoff, prin. Fax 661-2353
Pekin MS 200/6-8
1062 Birch Ave 52580 319-695-3707
Dan Maeder, prin. Fax 695-5130

Panora, Guthrie, Pop. 1,214
Panorama Community SD 800/PK-12
PO Box 39 50216 641-755-2317
John Millhollin, supt. Fax 755-3008
www.panorama.k12.ia.us/
Panorama HS 200/9-12
PO Box 39 50216 641-755-2317
Dean Schnoes, prin. Fax 755-3008
Panorama MS 200/6-8
PO Box 39 50216 641-755-2317
Mark Johnston, prin. Fax 755-3008

Parkersburg, Butler, Pop. 1,881
Aplington-Parkersburg Community SD 300/PK-12
610 N Johnson St 50665 319-347-2394
Jon Thompson, supt. Fax 347-2395
www.apl-park.k12.ia.us
Aplington-Parkersburg HS 9-12
610 N Johnson St 50665 319-346-1571
Everett Jensen, prin. Fax 346-1012
Other Schools – See Aplington

Paullina, O'Brien, Pop. 1,041
South O'Brien Community SD 700/K-12
PO Box 638 51046 712-949-2115
Dick Nervig, supt. Fax 949-2149
www.s-obrien.k12.ia.us
South O'Brien Secondary S 400/7-12
PO Box 638 51046 712-949-3454
Danial Hoey, prin. Fax 949-3453

Pella, Marion, Pop. 10,291
Pella Community SD 2,100/PK-12
PO Box 468 50219 641-628-1111
Mark Wittmer, supt. Fax 628-1116
www.pella.k12.ia.us
Pella HS 600/9-12
212 E University St 50219 641-628-3870
Mark Lee, prin. Fax 628-7402
Pella MS 500/6-8
613 E 13th St 50219 641-628-4784
David Versteeg, prin. Fax 628-6804

Central College Post-Sec.
812 University St 50219 641-628-9000
Pella Christian HS 300/9-12
604 Jefferson St 50219 641-628-4440
Darryl De Ruiter, prin. Fax 628-3530

Peosta, Dubuque, Pop. 933

Northeast Iowa Community College Post-Sec.
RR 1 52068 563-556-5110

Perry, Dallas, Pop. 8,865
Perry Community SD 1,800/K-12
1219 Warford St 50220 515-465-4656
Randall McCaulley Ed.D., supt. Fax 465-2426
www.perry.k12.ia.us/
Perry HS 500/9-12
1200 18th St 50220 515-465-3503
Dan Marburger, prin. Fax 465-5977
Perry MS 400/6-8
1200 18th St 50220 515-465-3531
Shaun Kruger, prin. Fax 465-8555

Pierson, Woodbury, Pop. 361
Kingsley-Pierson Community SD
Supt. — See Kingsley
Pierson MS 100/6-8
321 4th St 51048 712-375-5939
Randy Wiese, prin. Fax 375-5771

Plainfield, Bremer, Pop. 432
Nashua-Plainfield Community SD
Supt. — See Nashua
Nashua-Plainfield MS 200/5-8
PO Box 38 50666 319-276-4451
Ron Reusche, prin. Fax 276-3541

Pleasant Hill, Polk, Pop. 6,229
Southeast Polk Community SD 4,900/PK-12
8379 NE University Ave 50327 515-967-4294
Thomas J. Downs, supt. Fax 967-4257
www.se-polk.k12.ia.us/
Southeast Polk HS 1,300/9-12
8325 NE University Ave 50327 515-967-6631
Charles Bredlow, prin. Fax 967-6450
Southeast Polk JHS 800/7-8
8031 NE University Ave 50327 515-967-5509
Glenn Dietzenbach, prin. Fax 967-1676

Pleasantville, Marion, Pop. 1,607
Pleasantville Community SD 700/PK-12
415 Jones St 50225 515-848-0555
Dave Isgrig, supt. Fax 848-0561
www.pleasantville.k12.ia.us
Pleasantville HS 200/9-12
415 Jones St 50225 515-848-0541
Gary Niichel, prin. Fax 848-0561
Pleasantville MS 200/6-8
415 Jones St 50225 515-848-0528
Susan Phillips, prin. Fax 848-0561

Pocahontas, Pocahontas, Pop. 1,876
Pocahontas Area Community SD 500/PK-12
202 1st Ave SW 50574 712-335-4311
Joseph Kramer, supt. Fax 335-4206
www.pocahontas.k12.ia.us/
Pocahontas Area JSHS 300/6-12
205 2nd Ave NW 50574 712-335-4848
Roger Francis, prin. Fax 335-3420

Pomeroy, Calhoun, Pop. 658
Pomeroy-Palmer Community SD 200/PK-12
202 E Harrison St 50575 712-468-2268
Larry Kruckenberg, supt. Fax 468-2453
www.pom-palm.k12.ia.us
Pomeroy-Palmer Community HS 100/7-12
202 E Harrison St 50575 712-468-2268
Dan Grandfield, prin. Fax 468-2453

Postville, Allamakee, Pop. 2,322
Postville Community SD 600/K-12
PO Box 717 52162 563-864-7651
David Strudthoff, supt. Fax 864-7659
www.postville.k12.ia.us
Mott HS 200/9-12
PO Box 717 52162 563-864-7651
Michael Mueller, prin. Fax 864-7659

Prairie City, Jasper, Pop. 1,424
PCM Community SD 1,000/PK-12
PO Box 490 50228 515-994-2685
Kirk Nelson, supt. Fax 994-2699
www.pcmonroe.k12.ia.us
PCM MS 200/6-8
PO Box 490 50228 515-994-2686
Ron Young, prin. Fax 994-2686
Other Schools – See Monroe

Preston, Jackson, Pop. 946
Preston Community SD 400/K-12
121 S Mitchell St 52069 563-689-3431
Paul Tobin, supt. Fax 689-5823
www.prestonschools.com/
Preston JSHS 200/7-12
321 W School St 52069 563-689-4221
David Miller, prin. Fax 689-4222

Redfield, Dallas, Pop. 965
West Central Valley SD
Supt. — See Stuart
West Central Valley MS 200/6-8
PO Box B 50233 515-833-2331
P.J. Heinz, prin. Fax 833-2629

Red Oak, Montgomery, Pop. 5,919
Red Oak Community SD 1,300/PK-12
904 N Broad St 51566 712-623-6600
Dr. Kevin Brummer, supt. Fax 623-6603
www.redoakschooldistrict.com
Red Oak HS 400/9-12
2011 N 8th St 51566 712-623-6610
Terry Weber, prin. Fax 623-6613
Red Oak MS 300/6-8
308 E Corning St 51566 712-623-6620
Barbara Sims, prin. Fax 623-6626

Reinbeck, Grundy, Pop. 1,687
Gladbrook-Reinbeck Community SD 700/K-12
300 Cedar St 50669 319-345-2712
Dennis Modlin, supt. Fax 345-2242
www.gladbrook-reinbeck.k12.ia.us
Gladbrook-Reinbeck HS 300/9-12
600 Blackhawk St 50669 319-345-2921
Mike Studt, prin. Fax 345-2242
Other Schools – See Gladbrook

Remsen, Plymouth, Pop. 1,735
Remsen-Union Community SD 400/PK-12
511 Roosevelt Ave 51050 712-786-1101
Kenneth Howard, supt. Fax 786-1104
www.remsen-union.k12.ia.us/
Remsen-Union HS 100/9-12
511 Roosevelt Ave 51050 712-786-1101
Kirk Johnson, prin. Fax 786-1104
Remsen-Union JHS 100/6-8
412 Fulton St 51050 712-786-1192
Kirk Johnson, prin. Fax 786-1194

St. Marys HS 100/9-12
523 Madison St 51050 712-786-1433
Jim Wesselmann, prin. Fax 786-2499

Riceville, Howard, Pop. 834
Riceville Community SD 400/K-12
912 Woodland Ave 50466 641-985-2288
Christopher Anderson, supt. Fax 985-4171
www.riceville.k12.ia.us
Riceville HS 200/9-12
912 Woodland Ave 50466 641-985-2288
Rosemary Cameron, prin. Fax 985-4001

Riverdale, Scott, Pop. 610
Pleasant Valley Community SD
Supt. — See Eldridge
Pleasant Valley HS 1,100/9-12
604 Belmont Rd 52722 563-332-5151
Debbie Menke, prin. Fax 332-8525

Scott Community College Post-Sec.
500 Belmont Rd 52722 563-441-4000

Riverside, Washington, Pop. 961
Highland Community SD 700/PK-12
PO Box B 52327 319-648-3822
Carol Montz, supt. Fax 648-4055
www.highland.k12.ia.us
Highland HS 200/9-12
PO Box B 52327 319-648-2891
Edward Pundt, prin. Fax 648-3310
Highland MS 100/6-8
PO Box B 52327 319-648-5018
Shawn Donovan, prin. Fax 648-4055

Rockford, Floyd, Pop. 899
Rudd-Rockford-Marble Rock Community SD 600/PK-12
PO Box 218 50468 641-756-3610
Steve Ward, supt. Fax 756-2369
www.rockford.k12.ia.us
Rockford JSHS 300/7-12
PO Box 218 50468 641-756-3813
Rick Dosser, prin. Fax 756-2369

Rock Rapids, Lyon, Pop. 2,598
Central Lyon Community SD 600/K-12
PO Box 471 51246 712-472-2664
Dave Ackerman, supt. Fax 472-3543
www.central-lyon.k12.ia.us
Central Lyon HS 200/9-12
PO Box 471 51246 712-472-4051
Curt Busch, prin. Fax 472-2115
Central Lyon MS 200/6-8
PO Box 471 51246 712-472-4041
Dan Kruse, prin. Fax 472-2346

Rock Valley, Sioux, Pop. 2,852
Rock Valley Community SD 600/PK-12
1712 20th Ave 51247 712-476-2125
Dennis Mozer, supt. Fax 476-2125
www.rvcsd.org
Rock Valley JSHS 300/7-12
1712 20th Ave 51247 712-476-2701
David Meylink, prin. Fax 476-2125

Netherlands Reformed Christian S 300/K-12
712 20th Ave SE 51247 712-476-2821
Harold Schelling, prin. Fax 476-5438

Rockwell, Cerro Gordo, Pop. 973
Rockwell-Swaledale Community SD 400/PK-12
PO Box 60 50469 641-822-3236
Tom Fey, supt. Fax 822-4882
www.rsrebels.org
Rockwell-Swaledale MSHS 200/7-12
PO Box 60 50469 641-822-3234
Mark Vervaecke, prin. Fax 822-3273

Rockwell City, Calhoun, Pop. 2,096
Rockwell City-Lytton Community SD 500/PK-12
1000 Tonawanda St 50579 712-297-7341
Dale Black, supt. Fax 297-7320
www.rockwell-city-lytton.k12.ia.us
Rockwell City-Lytton HS 200/9-12
1000 Tonawanda St 50579 712-297-8111
Randy Martin, prin. Fax 297-7320
Other Schools – See Lytton

Roland, Story, Pop. 1,242
Roland-Story Community SD
Supt. — See Story City
Roland-Story MS 300/5-8
206 S Main St 50236 515-388-4348
John Sheahan, prin. Fax 388-4435

Royal, Clay, Pop. 432
Clay Central/Everly Community SD 500/PK-12
PO Box 110 51357 712-933-2242
Monte Montgomery, supt. Fax 933-2243
www.claycentraleverly.com
Clay Central/Everly MS 100/6-8
PO Box 110 51357 712-933-2241
Monte Montgomery, prin. Fax 933-2243
Other Schools – See Everly

Russell, Lucas, Pop. 587
Russell Community SD 100/PK-12
PO Box 487 50238 641-535-2404
Robert McCurdy, supt. Fax 535-4181
Russell JSHS 100/6-12
PO Box 487 50238 641-535-6105
Sally Johnson, prin. Fax 535-4181

Ruthven, Palo Alto, Pop. 716
Ruthven-Ayrshire Community SD 200/PK-12
PO Box 159 51358 712-837-5211
Ervin Rowlands, supt. Fax 837-5210
www.ruthven.k12.ia.us
Ruthven-Ayrshire JSHS 100/7-12
PO Box 159 51358 712-837-5212
Milton Peters, prin. Fax 837-5210

Sabula, Jackson, Pop. 667
East Central Community SD
Supt. — See Miles
Sabula MS 100/6-8
PO Box 307 52070 563-687-2427
David Sievers, prin. Fax 687-2473

Sac City, Sac, Pop. 2,157
Sac Community SD 500/PK-12
400 S 16th St 50583 712-662-7030
Barb Kruthoff, supt. Fax 662-6245
www.sac.k12.ia.us/
Sac Community JSHS 200/7-12
300 S 11th St 50583 712-662-3259
Dennis Olhausen, prin. Fax 662-4323

Saint Ansgar, Mitchell, Pop. 1,022
St. Ansgar Community SD 700/K-12
PO Box 559 50472 641-713-4681
Dwight Widen, supt. Fax 713-4042
www.st-ansgar.k12.ia.us

Saint Ansgar HS 300/9-12
PO Box 559 50472 641-713-4720
Scott Dryer, prin. Fax 713-2449
Saint Ansgar MS 200/5-8
PO Box 559 50472 641-713-4040
Scott Dryer, prin. Fax 713-4042

Sanborn, O'Brien, Pop. 1,309
Hartley-Melvin-Sanborn Community SD
Supt. — See Hartley
Hartley-Melvin-Sanborn MS 200/5-8
PO Box 557 51248 712-930-3281
Dorhout Mark, prin. Fax 930-5414

Schaller, Sac, Pop. 728
Schaller-Crestland Community SD 500/PK-12
PO Box 249 51053 712-275-4267
Dave Kwikkel, supt. Fax 275-4269
www.schaller-crest.k12.ia.us/
Other Schools – See Early

Schleswig, Crawford, Pop. 828
Schleswig Community SD 200/K-8
PO Box 250 51461 712-676-3313
Jack Johnson, supt. Fax 676-3539
www.schleswig.k12.ia.us
Schleswig MS 100/5-8
PO Box 250 51461 712-676-3313
Brian Johnson, prin. Fax 676-3539

Sergeant Bluff, Woodbury, Pop. 3,819
Sergeant Bluff-Luton Community SD 1,500/PK-12
PO Box 97 51054 712-943-4338
Rich Caldwell, supt. Fax 943-1131
www.sergeant-bluff.k12.ia.us
Sergeant Bluff-Luton HS 400/9-12
PO Box 97 51054 712-943-5561
Dan Moore, prin. Fax 943-5887
Sergeant Bluff-Luton MS 300/6-8
PO Box 97 51054 712-943-4235
Rod Earleywine, prin. Fax 943-8780

Seymour, Wayne, Pop. 787
Seymour Community SD 300/PK-12
100 S Park Ave 52590 641-898-2291
Dale Weeks, supt. Fax 898-7500
Seymour JSHS 200/7-12
100 S Park Ave 52590 641-898-2291
Dave Lockridge, prin. Fax 898-7500

Sheffield, Franklin, Pop. 1,002
Sheffield-Chapin Community SD 300/PK-12
PO Box 617 50475 641-892-4160
Cliff Cameron, supt. Fax 892-4379
www.sheffield-chapin.k12.ia.us
Sheffield-Chapin Community HS 200/9-12
PO Box 617 50475 641-892-4461
Randy Buschbaum, prin. Fax 892-4335

Sheldon, O'Brien, Pop. 4,807
Sheldon Community SD 1,000/PK-12
1700 E 4th St 51201 712-324-2504
Robin Spears, supt. Fax 324-5607
www.sheldon.k12.ia.us
Sheldon HS 400/9-12
1700 E 4th St 51201 712-324-2501
Joe Mueting, prin. Fax 324-5607
Sheldon MS 300/5-8
310 23rd Ave 51201 712-324-4346
Cindy Barwick, prin. Fax 324-4347

Northwest Iowa Community College Post-Sec.
603 W Park St 51201 712-324-5061

Shenandoah, Page, Pop. 5,239
Shenandoah Community SD 1,000/PK-12
304 W Nishna Rd 51601 712-246-1581
Dick Profit, supt. Fax 246-3722
www.shenandoah.k12.ia.us
Shenandoah HS 300/9-12
1000 Mustang Dr 51601 712-246-4727
Chris Heslinga, prin. Fax 246-2842
Shenandoah MS 300/5-8
601 Dr Creighton Cir 51601 712-246-2520
Monte Munsinger, prin. Fax 246-6390

Sibley, Osceola, Pop. 2,690
Sibley-Ocheyedan Community SD 900/K-12
120 11th Ave NE 51249 712-754-2533
Jeff Herzberg, supt. Fax 754-2534
www.sibley-ocheyedan.k12.ia.us/
Sibley-Ocheyedan HS 300/9-12
120 11th Ave NE 51249 712-754-3601
Denny Fry, prin. Fax 754-2534
Sibley-Ocheyedan MS 300/5-8
120 11th Ave NE 51249 712-754-2542
Bill Mueller, prin. Fax 754-3651

Sidney, Fremont, Pop. 1,190
Sidney Community SD 400/PK-12
PO Box 609 51652 712-374-2141
Gregg Cruickshank, supt. Fax 374-2013
www.sidney.k12.ia.us
Sidney JSHS 200/7-12
PO Box 609 51652 712-374-2731
Gregg Cruickshank, prin. Fax 374-2013

Sigourney, Keokuk, Pop. 2,168
Sigourney Community SD 700/PK-12
107 W Marion St 52591 641-622-2025
Todd Abrahamson, supt. Fax 622-2319
www.sigourney.k12.ia.us/
Sigourney JSHS 300/7-12
907 E Pleasant Valley St 52591 641-622-2010
Robert Hinrichs, prin. Fax 622-2047

Sioux Center, Sioux, Pop. 6,513
Sioux Center Community SD 1,000/PK-12
550 9th St NE 51250 712-722-2985
Patrick O'Donnell, supt. Fax 722-2986
www.sioux-center.k12.ia.us
Sioux Center HS 300/9-12
550 9th St NE 51250 712-722-2981
Gary McEldowney, prin. Fax 722-2986
Sioux Center MS 300/5-8
550 9th St NE 51250 712-722-3783
Matt Ludwig, prin. Fax 722-2986

Dordt College Post-Sec.
498 4th Ave NE 51250 712-722-6000

Sioux City, Woodbury, Pop. 83,148
Sioux City Community SD 13,400/PK-12
1221 Pierce St 51105 712-279-6667
Larry Williams, supt. Fax 279-6690
www.siouxcityschools.org/
East HS 1,300/9-12
5011 Mayhew Ave 51106 712-274-4000
Jeanene Sampson, prin. Fax 274-4670
East MS 1,000/6-8
5401 Lorraine Ave 51106 712-274-4030
Thomas Peterson, prin. Fax 274-4668
North HS 1,400/9-12
4200 Cheyenne Blvd 51104 712-239-7000
Linda Smoley, prin. Fax 239-8270
North MS 1,200/6-8
2101 Outer Dr N 51108 712-279-6667
Pete Hathaway, prin. Fax 277-5941
West HS 1,200/9-12
2001 Casselman St 51103 712-279-6772
James Vanderloo, prin. Fax 279-6790
West MS 1,000/6-8
3301 W 19th St 51103 712-279-6813
Cynthia Washinowski, prin. Fax 277-6138

Bishop Heelan HS 600/9-12
1021 Douglas St 51105 712-252-0573
Marilyn Blum, prin. Fax 252-4897
Briar Cliff University Post-Sec.
PO Box 2100 51104 712-279-5400
Holy Cross S / Blessed Sacrament Ctr 300/3-8
3030 Jackson St 51104 712-277-4739
Michael Sweeney, prin. Fax 258-3698
Iowa School of Beauty Post-Sec.
2524 Glenn Ave 51106 712-274-9733
Mater Dei S - Nativity Center 100/6-8
4243 Natalia Way 51106 712-274-0268
Carol Happe, prin. Fax 274-0377
Mercy Medical Center - Sioux City Post-Sec.
801 5th St 51101 712-279-2018
Morningside College Post-Sec.
1501 Morningside Ave 51106 712-274-5000
St. Luke's College Post-Sec.
2720 Stone Park Blvd 51104 712-279-3149
Siouxland Community Christian S 200/PK-12
6100 Morningside Ave 51106 712-276-4732
Barbara Blanchard, admin. Fax 276-4752
Western Iowa Tech Community College Post-Sec.
PO Box 5199 51102 712-274-6400

Sioux Rapids, Clay, Pop. 700
Sioux Central Community SD 500/PK-12
4440 US Highway 71 50585 712-283-2571
Dan Frazier, supt. Fax 283-2989
www.sioux-central.k12.ia.us
Sioux Central HS 200/9-12
4440 US Highway 71 50585 712-283-2571
Jeff Scharn, prin. Fax 283-2285
Sioux Central MS 100/6-8
4440 US Highway 71 50585 712-283-2571
Jeff Scharn, prin. Fax 283-2285

Sloan, Woodbury, Pop. 1,022
Westwood Community SD 700/PK-12
1000 Rebel Way 51055 712-428-3355
Kirk Ahrends, supt. Fax 428-3246
www.westwood.k12.ia.us/
Westwood JSHS 300/7-12
1000 Rebel Way 51055 712-428-3303
Gary Schrage, prin. Fax 428-3246

Solon, Johnson, Pop. 1,352
Solon Community SD 1,200/PK-12
301 S Iowa St 52333 319-624-3401
Brad Manard, supt. Fax 624-2518
www.solon.k12.ia.us
Solon HS 300/9-12
600 W 5th St 52333 319-624-3401
Bob Lesan, prin. Fax 624-4091
Solon MS 400/5-8
313 S Iowa St 52333 319-624-3401
Mike Herdliska, prin. Fax 624-2518

Spencer, Clay, Pop. 11,117
Spencer Community SD 2,000/PK-12
PO Box 200 51301 712-262-8950
Greg Ebeling, supt. Fax 262-1116
www.spencer.k12.ia.us
Spencer HS 700/9-12
PO Box 200 51301 712-262-1700
Mike Healy, prin. Fax 262-5704
Spencer MS 400/7-8
PO Box 200 51301 712-262-3345
Steve Barber, prin. Fax 264-3444

Iowa Lakes Community College Post-Sec.
1900 Grand Ave Ste 8 51301 712-262-7141

Spirit Lake, Dickinson, Pop. 4,590
Spirit Lake Community SD 1,300/PK-12
900 20th St 51360 712-336-2820
Tim Grieves, supt. Fax 336-4641
www.spirit-lake.k12.ia.us/
Spirit Lake HS 400/9-12
900 20th St 51360 712-336-3707
Jedd Sherman, prin. Fax 336-3714
Spirit Lake MS 400/5-8
900 20th St 51360 712-336-1370
Steve Ratzlaff, prin. Fax 336-4758

The Faust Institute of Cosmetology Post-Sec.
1543 18th St Ste 15 51360 712-336-3518

Springville, Linn, Pop. 1,001
Springville Community SD 400/K-12
400 Academy St 52336 319-854-6197
Oran Teut, supt. Fax 854-6199
www.springville.k12.ia.us
Springville JSHS 300/6-12
400 Academy St 52336 319-854-6196
Mel Mysak, prin. Fax 854-7891

Stanton, Montgomery, Pop. 710
Stanton Community SD 300/K-12
605 Elliott St 51573 712-829-2162
Judson Ashley, supt. Fax 829-2164
www.stantonschools.com
Stanton JSHS 200/7-12
605 Elliott St 51573 712-829-2162
Jeff Hiser, prin. Fax 829-2164

Stanwood, Cedar, Pop. 651
North Cedar Community SD 900/K-12
PO Box 247 52337 563-942-3358
Mary Jo Hainstock, supt. Fax 942-0014
www.north-cedar.k12.ia.us
North Cedar HS 300/9-12
PO Box 247 52337 563-942-3341
Dain Jeppson, prin. Fax 942-3596
Other Schools – See Clarence

State Center, Marshall, Pop. 1,337
West Marshall Community SD 800/PK-12
PO Box 670 50247 641-483-2660
Ned Sellers, supt. Fax 483-2665
www.w-marshall.k12.ia.us
West Marshall HS 200/9-12
PO Box 670 50247 641-483-2136
James Henrich, prin. Fax 483-2172
West Marshall MS 300/5-8
PO Box 340 50247 641-483-2165
Jeff Barry, prin. Fax 483-9951

Storm Lake, Buena Vista, Pop. 9,963
Storm Lake Community SD 1,900/PK-12
PO Box 638 50588 712-732-8060
Paul Tedesco, supt. Fax 732-8063
www.storm-lake.k12.ia.us
Storm Lake HS 600/9-12
621 Tornado Dr 50588 712-732-8065
Michael Hanna, prin. Fax 732-8068
Storm Lake MS 600/5-8
1811 Hyland Dr 50588 712-732-8080
Ronald Bryan, prin. Fax 732-8084

Buena Vista University Post-Sec.
610 W 4th St 50588 712-749-2235
Iowa Central Community College Post-Sec.
916 Russell St 50588 712-732-2991
St. Mary MSHS 100/5-12
304 Seneca St 50588 712-732-4166
Bev Mach, prin. Fax 732-4590
The Faust Institute of Cosmetology Post-Sec.
1290 Lake Ave 50588 712-732-6571

Story City, Story, Pop. 3,141
Roland-Story Community SD 1,100/PK-12
1009 Story St 50248 515-733-4301
Mike Billings, supt. Fax 733-2131
www.roland-story.k12.ia.us
Roland-Story HS 400/9-12
1009 Story St 50248 515-733-4329
Steve Schlatter, prin. Fax 733-2131
Other Schools – See Roland

Stuart, Guthrie, Pop. 1,750
West Central Valley SD 900/PK-12
PO Box 81 50250 515-523-2187
David Arnold, supt. Fax 523-1166
www.studex.k12.ia.us
West Central Valley HS 300/9-12
PO Box 81 50250 515-523-1313
Deborah Wilson, prin. Fax 523-2765
Other Schools – See Redfield

Sully, Jasper, Pop. 888
Lynnville-Sully Community SD 500/K-12
PO Box 210 50251 641-594-4445
Duane Willhite, supt. Fax 594-2770
www.lynnville-sully.k12.ia.us
Lynnville-Sully HS 200/9-12
PO Box 210 50251 641-594-4445
Preston Kooima, prin. Fax 594-2770
Lynnville-Sully MS 100/6-8
PO Box 310 50251 641-594-3721
Jolene Comer, prin. Fax 594-2770

Sumner, Bremer, Pop. 2,042
Sumner-Fredericksburg SD 900/K-12
PO Box 178 50674 563-578-3341
Rick Pederson, supt. Fax 578-3425
Sumner-Fredericksburg HS 300/9-12
PO Box 178 50674 563-578-3342
Allan Eckelman, prin. Fax 578-3424
Other Schools – See Fredericksburg

Swea City, Kossuth, Pop. 596
North Kossuth Community SD
Supt. — See Bancroft
North Kossuth HS 100/9-12
PO Box 567 50590 515-272-4361
Todd Thompson, prin. Fax 272-4391
North Kossuth MS 100/6-8
PO Box 567 50590 515-272-4361
Todd Thompson, prin. Fax 272-4391

Tabor, Fremont, Pop. 975
Fremont-Mills Community SD 400/PK-12
PO Box 310 51653 712-629-2325
Christopher Herrick, supt. Fax 629-5155
www.fmtabor.k12.ia.us/fm/index.htm
Fremont-Mills MSHS 200/7-12
PO Box 310 51653 712-629-2325
Harva Paul, prin. Fax 629-5155

Tama, Tama, Pop. 2,603
South Tama County Community SD 1,000/PK-12
1702 Harding St 52339 641-484-4811
Larry Molacek, supt. Fax 484-4861
stc.tamatoledo.net/
South Tama County HS 500/9-12
1715 Harding St 52339 641-484-4345
Steve Burr, prin. Fax 484-5152
Other Schools – See Toledo

Terril, Dickinson, Pop. 375
Terril Community SD 100/PK-8
PO Box 128 51364 712-853-6111
Dan Mart, supt. Fax 853-6199
www.terril.k12.ia.us
Terril/Graettinger MS 100/6-8
PO Box 128 51364 712-853-6111
Jared Cecil, prin. Fax 853-6199

Thompson, Winnebago, Pop. 567
North Iowa Community SD
Supt. — See Buffalo Center
North Iowa MS 200/5-8
PO Box 27 50478 641-584-2231
Mike Evans, prin. Fax 584-2230

Thornburg, Keokuk, Pop. 68
Tri-County Community SD 300/PK-12
PO Box 17 50255 641-634-2408
Bill Cox, supt. Fax 634-2145
www.tri-county.k12.ia.us/
Tri-County HS 100/9-12
PO Box 17 50255 641-634-2636
Dennis Phelps, prin. Fax 634-2145
Tri-County JHS 100/7-8
PO Box 17 50255 641-634-2636
Dennis Phelps, prin. Fax 634-2145

Thornton, Cerro Gordo, Pop. 404
Meservey-Thornton Community SD 100/5-8
PO Box 150 50479 641-998-2315
Eldon Pyle, supt. Fax 998-2196
www.meservey-thornton.k12.ia.us/
Meservey-Thornton MS 100/5-8
PO Box 150 50479 641-998-2315
Darrin Praska, prin. Fax 998-2196

Tiffin, Johnson, Pop. 1,473
Clear Creek-Amana Community SD
Supt. — See Oxford
Clear Creek-Amana HS 400/9-12
PO Box 199 52340 319-545-2361
Tom McDonald, prin. Fax 545-2863

Tipton, Cedar, Pop. 3,132
Tipton Community SD 800/K-12
400 E 6th St 52772 563-886-6121
Richard Grimoskas, supt. Fax 886-2341
www.tipton.k12.ia.us
Tipton HS 300/9-12
400 E 6th St 52772 563-886-6027
Chris Habben, prin. Fax 886-2341
Tipton MS 200/6-8
400 E 6th St 52772 563-886-6025
Lori Foley, prin. Fax 886-2555

Titonka, Kossuth, Pop. 543
Titonka Consolidated SD 200/K-8
PO Box 287 50480 515-928-2717
Ron Sadler, supt. Fax 928-2718
Titonka MS 100/6-8
PO Box 287 50480 515-928-2720
Randy Collins, prin. Fax 928-2718

Toledo, Tama, Pop. 2,687
South Tama County Community SD
Supt. — See Tama
South Tama County MS 400/6-8
201 S Green St 52342 641-484-4121
Steve Cose, prin. Fax 484-2699

Traer, Tama, Pop. 1,586
North Tama County Community SD 500/K-12
605 Walnut St 50675 319-478-2265
Thomas McDermott, supt. Fax 478-2917
www.n-tama.k12.ia.us
North Tama JSHS 300/7-12
605 Walnut St 50675 319-478-2911
Irvin Laube, prin. Fax 478-2917

Treynor, Pottawattamie, Pop. 914
Treynor Community SD 600/K-12
PO Box 369 51575 712-487-3414
Kevin Elwood, supt. Fax 487-3332
www.treynor.k12.ia.us
Treynor JSHS 300/7-12
PO Box 369 51575 712-487-3804
Joel Bohlken, prin. Fax 487-3332

Tripoli, Bremer, Pop. 1,269
Tripoli Community SD 500/K-12
209 8th Ave SW 50676 319-882-4201
Robert Longmuir, supt. Fax 882-3103
Tripoli JSHS 300/6-12
209 8th Ave SW 50676 319-882-4202
Troy Heller, prin. Fax 882-3103

Troy Mills, Linn
North Linn Community SD 700/K-12
PO Box 200 52344 319-224-3291
Larry G. Boer, supt. Fax 224-3727
www.northlinn.k12.ia.us
North Linn HS 200/9-12
PO Box 200 52344 319-224-3291
Betty Coleman, prin. Fax 224-3232
North Linn MS 200/6-8
PO Box 200 52344 319-224-3291
Betty Coleman, prin. Fax 224-3232

Truro, Madison, Pop. 480
Interstate 35 Community SD 800/PK-12
PO Box 79 50257 641-765-4291
Bill Maske, supt. Fax 765-4593
www.i-35.k12.ia.us/
Interstate 35 HS 200/9-12
PO Box 79 50257 641-765-4818
Tim Busby, prin. Fax 765-4820
Interstate 35 MS 200/5-8
PO Box 200 50257 641-765-4908
Sharon McKimpson, prin. Fax 765-4905

Underwood, Pottawattamie, Pop. 818
Underwood Community SD 800/PK-12
PO Box 130 51576 712-566-2332
Ed Hawks, supt. Fax 566-2070
www.underwoodeagles.org/
Underwood HS 200/9-12
PO Box 130 51576 712-566-2703
Roger Pearson, prin. Fax 566-2712
Underwood MS 200/6-8
PO Box 130 51576 712-566-2332
J. Lewis Curtis, prin. Fax 566-2070

Union, Hardin, Pop. 402
BCLUW Community SD
Supt. — See Conrad
BCLUW MS 200/5-8
704 Commercial St 50258 641-486-5371
Dirk Borgman, prin. Fax 486-5372

University Park, Mahaska, Pop. 554

Vennard College Post-Sec.
PO Box 29 52595 800-686-8391

Urbandale, Polk, Pop. 34,696
Urbandale Community SD 3,300/PK-12
6200 Aurora Ave Ste 500W 50322 515-457-5000
Dr. Greg Robinson, supt. Fax 457-5018
www.urbandaleschools.com/
Urbandale HS 1,100/9-12
7111 Aurora Ave 50322 515-457-6800
Richard Hutchinson, prin. Fax 457-6801
Urbandale MS 800/6-8
7701 Aurora Ave 50322 515-457-6600
Daniel Meyer, prin. Fax 457-6601

Des Moines Christian S 800/PK-12
13007 Douglas Pkwy 50323 515-252-2480
Dr. Robert Stouffer, admin. Fax 251-6911
Hamilton College Post-Sec.
4655 121st St 50323 515-727-2100

Van Horne, Benton, Pop. 750
Benton Community SD 1,600/PK-12
PO Box 70 52346 319-228-8701
Gary Zittergruen, supt. Fax 228-8254
www.benton.k12.ia.us
Benton Community HS 600/9-12
PO Box 70 52346 319-228-8701
Bruce Johnson, prin. Fax 228-8747
Benton Community MS 200/7-8
PO Box 70 52346 319-228-8701
Jo Prusha, prin. Fax 228-8747

Van Meter, Dallas, Pop. 1,088
Van Meter Community SD 500/K-12
PO Box 257 50261 515-996-9960
Greg DeTimmerman, supt. Fax 996-9954
www.vanmeter.k12.ia.us
Van Meter JSHS 200/7-12
PO Box 257 50261 515-996-2221
John Carver, prin. Fax 996-2488

Ventura, Cerro Gordo, Pop. 676
Ventura Community SD 300/K-12
PO Box 18 50482 641-829-4484
Dan Versteeg, supt. Fax 829-3995
www.ventura.k12.ia.us
Ventura JSHS 200/7-12
PO Box 18 50482 641-829-4484
Lorene Dykstra, prin. Fax 829-3995

Victor, Iowa, Pop. 1,004
H-L-V Community SD 500/PK-12
PO Box B 52347 319-647-2161
William Lynch, supt. Fax 647-2164
www.hlv.k12.ia.us
H-L-V JSHS 200/7-12
PO Box B 52347 319-647-2161
John Long, prin. Fax 647-2164

Villisca, Montgomery, Pop. 1,300
Villisca Community SD 400/K-12
406 E 3rd St 50864 712-826-2552
Teresa Nook, supt. Fax 826-4072
www.villisca.k12.ia.us
Villisca Community JSHS 200/6-12
406 E 3rd St 50864 712-826-2552
Ken Harrison, prin. Fax 826-4072

Vinton, Benton, Pop. 5,219
Vinton-Shellsburg Community SD 1,800/K-12
810 W 9th St 52349 319-436-4728
Dr. Randy L. Braden, supt. Fax 472-3889
www.vinton-shellsburg.k12.ia.us
Tilford MS 500/6-8
308 E 13th St 52349 319-436-4728
Mike Timmermans, prin. Fax 472-4014
Washington HS 600/9-12
212 W 15th St 52349 319-436-4728
Paul Pedersen, prin. Fax 472-5704

Iowa Braille and Sight Saving School Post-Sec.
1002 G Ave 52349 319-472-5221

Walcott, Scott, Pop. 1,530
Davenport Community SD
Supt. — See Davenport
Walcott IS 400/6-8
545 E James St 52773 563-284-6253
Erica Goldstone, prin. Fax 284-5081

Walker, Linn, Pop. 727

Cono Christian S 100/PK-12
3269 Quasqueton Ave 52352 319-448-4395
Andrew Belz, hdmstr. Fax 448-4397

Walnut, Pottawattamie, Pop. 750
Walnut Community SD 300/PK-12
PO Box 528 51577 712-784-2251
Jeff Kruse, supt. Fax 784-2177
www.walnutcs.walnut.iowapages.org
Walnut HS 100/9-12
PO Box 528 51577 712-784-3615
Paul Croghan, prin. Fax 784-2177
Walnut MS 100/6-8
PO Box 528 51577 712-784-3615
Paul Croghan, prin. Fax 784-2177

Wapello, Louisa, Pop. 2,042
Wapello Community SD 800/PK-12
445 N Cedar St 52653 319-523-3641
John Weidner, supt. Fax 523-8151
www.wapello.k12.ia.us
Wapello HS 200/9-12
501 Buchanan Ave 52653 319-523-3241
Steve Bohlen, prin. Fax 523-4408
Wapello JHS 100/7-8
501 Buchanan Ave 52653 319-523-8131
Steve Bohlen, prin. Fax 523-4408

Washington, Washington, Pop. 7,207
Washington Community SD 1,700/K-12
PO Box 926 52353 319-653-6543
Dave Schmitt, supt. Fax 653-5685
www.washington.k12.ia.us/
Washington JHS 400/7-9
1111 S Avenue B 52353 319-653-5414
Curt Mayer, prin. Fax 653-7350
Washington SHS 400/10-12
PO Box 271 52353 319-653-2143
Shane Ehresman, prin. Fax 653-6751

Waterloo, Black Hawk, Pop. 66,483
Waterloo Community SD 9,800/PK-12
1516 Washington St 50702 319-433-1800
Dr. Dewitt Jones, supt. Fax 433-1886
www.waterloo.k12.ia.us
Central MS 800/6-8
1350 Katoski Dr 50701 319-433-2100
Marla Padget, prin. Fax 433-2149
East HS 1,200/9-12
214 High St 50703 319-433-2400
Willie Barney, prin. Fax 433-2498
Hoover MS 700/6-8
630 Hillcrest Rd 50701 319-433-2830
Don Blau, prin. Fax 433-2843
Logan MS 400/6-8
1515 Logan Ave 50703 319-433-2500
Phillip Anderson, prin. Fax 433-2548
West HS 1,900/9-12
425 E Ridgeway Ave 50702 319-433-2700
Dr. Gail Moon, prin. Fax 433-2749
Other Schools – See Evansdale

Allen College Post-Sec.
1825 Logan Ave 50703 319-226-2000
College of Hair Design Post-Sec.
722 Water St Ste 201 50703 319-232-9995
Columbus HS 400/9-12
3231 W 9th St 50702 319-233-3358
Tom Ulses, prin. Fax 235-0733
Covenant Medical Center Post-Sec.
3421 W 9th St 50702 319-272-7296
Hawkeye Community College Post-Sec.
PO Box 8015 50704 319-296-2320
Walnut Ridge Baptist Academy 200/K-12
1307 W Ridgeway Ave 50701 319-235-9309
Kenneth Gould, admin. Fax 833-4780

Waucoma, Fayette, Pop. 252
Turkey Valley Community SD 600/PK-12
3219 Highway 24 52171 563-776-6011
John Rothlisberger, supt. Fax 776-4271
www.turkey-v.k12.ia.us
Turkey Valley JSHS 300/7-12
3219 Highway 24 52171 563-776-6011
Joel Weeks, prin. Fax 776-4271

Waukee, Dallas, Pop. 9,213
Waukee Community SD 4,100/PK-12
560 SE University Ave 50263 515-987-5161
Dr. David Wilkerson, supt. Fax 987-2701
www.waukee.k12.ia.us
Prairieview S 500/8-9
655 SE University Ave 50263 515-987-2770
Juley Murphy-Tiernan, prin. Fax 987-2789
Waukee SHS 700/10-12
555 SE University Ave 50263 515-987-5163
Jody Rarigan, prin. Fax 987-2784

Waukon, Allamakee, Pop. 4,013
Allamakee Community SD 1,400/K-12
1059 3rd Ave NW 52172 563-568-3409
Dave Herold, supt. Fax 568-2677
www.allamakee.k12.ia.us/
Waukon JHS 400/7-9
110 5th St NW 52172 563-568-6321
Joe Griffith, prin. Fax 568-6410

Waukon SHS 400/10-12
1059 3rd Ave NW 52172 563-568-3466
David Ziesmer, prin. Fax 568-2677

Waverly, Bremer, Pop. 9,298
Waverly-Shell Rock Community SD 1,900/K-12
1415 4th Ave SW 50677 319-352-3630
Jere Vyverberg, supt. Fax 352-5676
www.waverly-shellrock.k12.ia.us
Waverly-Shell Rock HS 700/9-12
1405 4th Ave SW 50677 319-352-2087
Ken H. Winter, prin. Fax 352-2098
Waverly-Shell Rock JHS 300/7-8
215 3rd St NW 50677 319-352-3632
Steve Kwikkel, prin. Fax 352-5199

Wartburg College Post-Sec.
PO Box 1003 50677 319-352-8200

Wayland, Henry, Pop. 944
Waco Community SD 500/PK-12
PO Box 158 52654 319-256-6200
Darrell Smith, supt. Fax 256-6213
www.wacohs.com
Waco JSHS 300/7-12
PO Box 158 52654 319-256-6200
Roger Thornburg, prin. Fax 256-6211

Webster City, Hamilton, Pop. 8,077
Webster City Community SD 1,800/PK-12
825 Beach St 50595 515-832-9200
Mike Sherwood, supt. Fax 832-9204
www.webster-city.k12.ia.us
Webster City HS 600/9-12
1001 Lynx Ave 50595 515-832-9210
Larry Hunt, prin. Fax 832-9215
Webster City MS 500/5-8
1101 Des Moines St 50595 515-832-9220
Becky Hacker-Kluver, prin. Fax 832-9225

Iowa Central Community College Post-Sec.
1725 Beach St 50595 515-832-1632

Wellman, Washington, Pop. 1,470
Mid-Prairie Community SD 1,200/PK-12
PO Box 150 52356 319-646-6093
Mark Schneider, supt. Fax 646-2093
www.mid-prairie.k12.ia.us
Mid-Prairie HS 300/9-12
PO Box 150 52356 319-646-6091
Gerry Beeler, prin. Fax 646-6097
Other Schools – See Kalona

Wellsburg, Grundy, Pop. 681
AGWSR Community SD
Supt. — See Ackley
AGWSR MS 200/4-8
PO Box 188 50680 641-869-5121
Robert Hutchcroft, prin. Fax 869-3426

West Bend, Palo Alto, Pop. 817
West Bend - Mallard Community SD 400/PK-12
PO Box 247 50597 515-887-7821
Dr. John Phillips, supt. Fax 887-7785
www.west-bend.k12.ia.us
West Bend - Mallard HS 100/9-12
PO Box 247 50597 515-887-7831
Samuel Swensen, prin. Fax 887-7853
Other Schools – See Mallard

West Branch, Cedar, Pop. 2,269
West Branch Community SD 800/PK-12
PO Box 637 52358 319-643-7213
Craig Artist, supt. Fax 643-7122
www.west-branch.k12.ia.us
West Branch HS 200/9-12
PO Box 637 52358 319-643-7216
Stephen Hennesy, prin. Fax 643-2415
West Branch MS 200/6-8
PO Box 637 52358 319-643-5324
Sara Oswald, prin. Fax 643-5447

Scattergood Friends S 100/9-12
1951 Delta Ave 52358 319-643-7600
Jan Luchini, dir. Fax 643-7485

West Burlington, Des Moines, Pop. 3,231
West Burlington ISD 700/K-12
211 Ramsey St 52655 319-752-8747
James Sleister, supt. Fax 754-9382
www.w-burlington.k12.ia.us/
West Burlington HS 200/9-12
408 W Van Weiss Blvd 52655 319-752-7138
Ron Teater, prin. Fax 754-0075
West Burlington JHS 100/7-8
408 W Van Weiss Blvd 52655 319-752-7138
Ron Teater, prin. Fax 754-0075

Southeastern Community College Post-Sec.
PO Box 180 52655 319-752-2731

West Des Moines, Polk, Pop. 52,768
West Des Moines Community SD 8,500/PK-12
3550 Mills Civic Pkwy 50265 515-633-5000
Thomas Narak, supt. Fax 633-5099
www.wdmcs.org
Stilwell JHS 700/7-8
1601 Vine St 50265 515-633-6000
Tim Miller, prin. Fax 633-6099
Valley HS 1,800/10-12
3650 Woodland Ave 50266 515-633-4000
Vicky Poole, prin. Fax 633-4099
Valley Southwoods Freshman HS 700/9-9
625 S 35th St 50265 515-633-4500
Kent Abrahamson, prin. Fax 633-4599
Other Schools – See Clive

Dowling Catholic HS 1,200/9-12
1400 Buffalo Rd 50265 515-222-1045
Dr. James Dowdle, prin. Fax 222-1056
Iowa Christian Academy 300/PK-12
2501 Vine St 50265 515-221-3999
Donald Beebe, admin. Fax 225-2387

West Liberty, Muscatine, Pop. 3,603
West Liberty Community SD 1,100/PK-12
203 E 7th St 52776 319-627-2116
Rebecca Rodocker, supt. Fax 627-2963
www.wl.k12.ia.us
West Liberty HS 400/9-12
310 W Maxson Ave 52776 319-627-2115
James Hamilton, prin. Fax 627-2038
West Liberty MS 500/3-8
806 N Miller St 52776 319-627-2118
Vicki Vernon, prin. Fax 627-2092

West Point, Lee, Pop. 961

Holy Trinity MS 6-8
PO Box 39 52656 319-837-6131
Daniel Kieler, prin. Fax 837-8112

Westside, Crawford, Pop. 331
Ar-We-Va Community SD 400/PK-12
PO Box 108 51467 712-663-4311
Dana Kunze, supt. Fax 663-4313
www.ar-we-va.k12.ia.us
Westside JSHS 300/6-12
PO Box 108 51467 712-663-4312
Kurt Brosamle, prin. Fax 663-4313

West Union, Fayette, Pop. 2,485
North Fayette Community SD 1,000/PK-12
PO Box 73 52175 563-422-3851
Ron O'Kones, supt. Fax 422-3854
www.n-fayette.k12.ia.us/
North Fayette HS 300/9-12
PO Box 73 52175 563-422-3852
Wayne O'Brien, prin. Fax 422-5798
North Fayette MS 300/6-8
PO Box 73 52175 563-422-3853
Kenneth Haught, prin. Fax 422-3854

Wheatland, Clinton, Pop. 760
Calamus-Wheatland Community SD 600/K-12
PO Box 279 52777 563-374-1292
Charles Freese, supt. Fax 374-1080
www.cal-wheat.k12.ia.us
Calamus-Wheatland JSHS 200/7-12
PO Box 279 52777 563-374-1292
Lonnie Luepker, prin. Fax 374-1080

Whiting, Monona, Pop. 772
Whiting Community SD 200/K-12
PO Box 295 51063 712-455-2468
Myron Ballain, supt. Fax 455-2601
www.whiting.k12.ia.us/
Whiting JSHS 200/6-12
PO Box 295 51063 712-455-2468
William McKelvey, prin. Fax 455-2601

Williamsburg, Iowa, Pop. 2,751
Williamsburg Community SD 1,100/K-12
PO Box 120 52361 319-668-1059
Randy Freeman, supt. Fax 668-9311
www.williamsburg.k12.ia.us
Williamsburg JSHS 600/7-12
PO Box 120 52361 319-668-1050
Steven Johns, prin. Fax 668-9311

Wilton, Muscatine, Pop. 2,866
Wilton Community SD 1,000/PK-12
1002 Cypress St 52778 563-732-2035
Joe Burnett, supt. Fax 732-4121
www.wilton.k12.ia.us
Wilton JSHS 500/7-12
1002 Cypress St 52778 563-732-2629
Ken Crawford, prin. Fax 732-4121

Winfield, Henry, Pop. 1,105
Winfield-Mt. Union Community SD 400/K-12
PO Box E 52659 319-257-7700
M. Lynn Ubben, supt. Fax 257-7714
www.wmu.k12.ia.us/
Winfield-Mt. Union JSHS 200/7-12
PO Box E 52659 319-257-7701
Frederick Probasco, prin. Fax 257-7703

Winterset, Madison, Pop. 4,877
Winterset Community SD 1,600/PK-12
PO Box 30 50273 515-462-2718
Doyle F. Scott Ph.D., supt. Fax 462-2732
www.winterset.k12.ia.us
Winterset HS 500/9-12
624 Husky Dr 50273 515-462-3320
Greg Criswell, prin. Fax 462-2178
Winterset JHS 300/7-8
720 Husky Dr 50273 515-462-3336
Molly Clark, prin. Fax 462-2178

Winthrop, Buchanan, Pop. 769
East Buchanan Community SD 600/PK-12
PO Box 40 50682 319-935-3767
Dale Greimann, supt. Fax 935-3749
www.east-buc.k12.ia.us
East Buchanan HS 200/9-12
PO Box 40 50682 319-935-3367
Tom Mossman, prin. Fax 935-3615
East Buchanan MS 100/6-8
PO Box 40 50682 319-935-3367
Tom Mossman, prin. Fax 935-3615

Woden, Hancock, Pop. 230
Woden-Crystal Lake Community SD 100/K-12
PO Box 135 50484 641-926-5311
Susan Lewerke, supt. Fax 926-5314
Other Schools – See Crystal Lake

Woodbine, Harrison, Pop. 1,624
Woodbine Community SD 500/PK-12
501 Weare St 51579 712-647-2411
Terry Hazard, supt. Fax 647-2526
Woodbine HS 200/7-12
501 Weare St 51579 712-647-2227
Rick Shanks, prin. Fax 647-2279

Woodward, Dallas, Pop. 1,305
Woodward-Granger Community SD 700/K-12
306 W 3rd St 50276 515-438-4333
Jody Gray, supt. Fax 438-4329
www.woodward-granger.k12.ia.us
Woodward-Granger HS 200/9-12
306 W 3rd St 50276 515-438-2115
Delane Galvin, prin. Fax 438-4329
Woodward-Granger MS 100/6-8
306 W 3rd St 50276 515-438-4653
Delane Galvin, prin. Fax 438-4329

Wyoming, Jones, Pop. 623
Midland Community SD 600/PK-12
PO Box 109 52362 563-488-2292
Al Homandberg, supt. Fax 488-2253
www.midland.k12.ia.us
Midland Community HS 200/9-12
PO Box 109 52362 563-488-2292
Nathan Marting, prin. Fax 488-2253
Other Schools – See Lost Nation

Zearing, Story, Pop. 536
Colo-Nesco Comm SD
Supt. — See Mc Callsburg
Colo-Nesco MS 200/5-8
407 S Center St 50278 641-487-7411
Andrew Ward, prin. Fax 487-7414

KANSAS

KANSAS DEPARTMENT OF EDUCATION
120 SE 10th Ave, Topeka 66612-1182
Telephone 785-296-3201
Fax 785-296-7933
Website http://www.ksbe.state.ks.us

Commissioner of Education Dr. Alexa Posny

KANSAS BOARD OF EDUCATION
120 SE 10th Ave, Topeka 66612-1103

Chairperson Dr. Bill Wagnon

PUBLIC, PRIVATE AND CATHOLIC SECONDARY SCHOOLS

Abilene, Dickinson, Pop. 6,409
Abilene USD 435 1,500/PK-12
PO Box 639 67410 785-263-2630
Larry Schmidt, supt. Fax 263-7610
www.usd435.k12.ks.us
Abilene HS 500/9-12
1300 N Cedar St 67410 785-263-1260
Dr. Michael Ford, prin. Fax 263-3327
Abilene MS 400/6-8
500 NW 14th St 67410 785-263-1471
Ron Wilson, prin. Fax 263-4443

Agra, Phillips, Pop. 278
Eastern Heights USD 324
Supt. — See Kirwin
Eastern Heights JSHS 100/6-12
PO Box 209 67621 785-638-2244
Roger Antle, prin. Fax 638-2254

Albert, Barton, Pop. 183
Otis-Bison USD 403 200/K-12
RR 1 Box 76A 67511 620-923-4661
Jake Befort, supt. Fax 923-4224
Other Schools – See Bison, Otis

Allen, Lyon, Pop. 216
North Lyon County USD 251
Supt. — See Americus
Northern Heights HS 200/9-12
1208 Road 345 66833 620-528-3521
Doug Boline, prin. Fax 528-3392

Alma, Wabaunsee, Pop. 764
Mill Creek Valley USD 329 500/PK-12
PO Box 157 66401 785-765-3394
Larry Jackson, supt. Fax 765-3624
www.usd329.org
Wabaunsee HS 200/9-12
PO Box 218 66401 785-765-3315
Dr. Larry Andersen, prin. Fax 765-3523
Other Schools – See Paxico

Almena, Norton, Pop. 454
Northern Valley USD 212 200/PK-12
PO Box 217 67622 785-669-2445
Roger Lowry, supt. Fax 669-2263
www.nvhuskies.org
Northern Valley HS 100/9-12
PO Box 217 67622 785-669-2445
Lonnie Brungardt, prin. Fax 669-2263
Other Schools – See Long Island

Altamont, Labette, Pop. 1,065
Labette County USD 506 1,700/K-12
PO Box 188 67330 620-784-5326
Dennis Wilson, supt. Fax 784-5879
www.usd506.k12.ks.us
Labette County HS 600/9-12
PO Box 407 67330 620-784-5321
Greg Cartwright, prin. Fax 784-2682

Alta Vista, Wabaunsee, Pop. 425
Morris County USD 417
Supt. — See Council Grove
Prairie Heights MS 100/5-8
801 Center St 66834 785-499-6313
Cynthia Schrader, prin. Fax 499-5342

Altoona, Wilson, Pop. 472
Altoona-Midway USD 387
Supt. — See Buffalo
Altoona-Midway MS 50/6-8
PO Box 128 66710 620-568-5725
Lynn Myers, prin. Fax 568-5755

Americus, Lyon, Pop. 932
North Lyon County USD 251 600/PK-12
PO Box 527 66835 620-443-5116
Steven Mollach, supt. Fax 443-5659
www.usd251.org/
Other Schools – See Allen

Andale, Sedgwick, Pop. 808
Renwick USD 267 2,000/PK-12
PO Box 68 67001 316-444-2165
Dr. Dan Peters, supt. Fax 445-2241
www.usd267.com
Andale HS 400/9-12
PO Box 28 67001 316-444-2607
Stan May, prin. Fax 445-2501
Other Schools – See Garden Plain

Andover, Butler, Pop. 9,114
Andover USD 385 3,700/K-12
1432 N Andover Rd 67002 316-733-5017
Mark Evans, supt. Fax 733-3604
www.usd385.org
Andover Central HS 600/9-12
603 E Central Ave 67002 316-266-8800
Mark Templin, prin. Fax 266-8840
Andover Central MS 500/6-8
903 E Central Ave 67002 316-266-8845
Doug Baber, prin. Fax 266-8878
Andover HS 600/9-12
1744 N Andover Rd 67002 316-733-1335
Bob Baier, prin. Fax 733-1945
Andover MS 400/6-8
1628 N Andover Rd 67002 316-733-5061
Brett White, prin. Fax 733-3666

Anthony, Harper, Pop. 2,302
Anthony-Harper USD 361 900/PK-12
PO Box 486 67003 620-842-5183
Keith Custer, supt. Fax 842-5307
www.usd361.org/
Chaparral HS 300/9-12
467 N State Road 14 67003 620-842-5155
Al Petz, prin. Fax 896-2927

Argonia, Sumner, Pop. 500
Argonia USD 359 200/PK-12
504 N Pine St 67004 620-435-6311
Dr. Julie Dolley, supt. Fax 435-6623
www.usd359.k12.ks.us/
Argonia JSHS 100/7-12
504 N Pine St 67004 620-435-6611
Jon Mages, prin. Fax 435-6623

Arkansas City, Cowley, Pop. 11,581
Arkansas City USD 470 2,800/PK-12
PO Box 1028 67005 620-441-2000
Ron Ballard, supt. Fax 441-2009
www.arkcity.com
Arkansas City HS 900/9-12
1200 W Radio Ln 67005 620-441-2010
Marci Shearon, prin. Fax 441-2021
Arkansas City MS 700/6-8
400 E Kansas Ave 67005 620-441-2030
Dr. David Zumwalt, prin. Fax 441-2036

Ark City Christian Academy 100/PK-12
PO Box 1181 67005 620-442-0022
Cynde Fest, prin. Fax 442-0022
Cowley County Community College Post-Sec.
PO Box 1147 67005 620-442-0430

Arma, Crawford, Pop. 1,495
Northeast USD 246 600/K-12
PO Box 669 66712 620-347-4116
Randl Rivers, supt. Fax 347-4087
www.usd246.net
Northeast HS 200/9-12
PO Box 669 66712 620-347-4115
Alan Roberts, prin. Fax 347-4149
Northeast MS 100/6-8
PO Box 669 66712 620-347-8461
Lawrence Hill, prin. Fax 347-4140

Ashland, Clark, Pop. 943
Ashland USD 220 200/PK-12
PO Box 187 67831 620-635-2220
Jerry Cullen, supt. Fax 635-2637
www.ashland.k12.ks.us
Ashland HS 100/9-12
PO Box 187 67831 620-635-2814
Bill Day, prin. Fax 635-2637
Ashland Upper MS 50/7-8
PO Box 187 67831 620-635-2814
Bill Day, prin. Fax 635-2637

Atchison, Atchison, Pop. 10,169
Atchison USD 409 1,600/PK-12
215 N 8th St 66002 913-367-4384
Richard Branstrator, supt. Fax 367-2246
www.usd409.net/
Atchison HS 500/9-12
1500 Riley St 66002 913-367-4162
Forrest Covey, prin. Fax 367-0415
Atchison MS 400/6-8
301 N 5th St 66002 913-367-5363
James Krone, prin. Fax 367-1302

Benedictine College Post-Sec.
1020 N 2nd St 66002 913-367-5340
Maur Hill - Mount Academy 9-12
1000 Green St 66002 913-367-5482
Sharon Pruett, prin. Fax 367-5096
Northeast Kansas Technical College Post-Sec.
1501 Riley St 66002 913-367-6204

Attica, Harper, Pop. 604
Attica USD 511 100/K-12
PO Box 415 67009 620-254-7661
Troy Piper, supt. Fax 254-7872
www.attica.net
Attica JSHS 100/7-12
PO Box 415 67009 620-254-7915
Troy Piper, prin. Fax 254-7872

Atwood, Rawlins, Pop. 1,139
Rawlins County USD 105 400/PK-12
205 N 4th St Ste 1 67730 785-626-3236
Mark Wolters, supt. Fax 626-3083
www.usd105.org
Rawlins County JSHS 200/7-12
100 N 8th St 67730 785-626-3289
Kurt Dillon, prin. Fax 626-1022

Augusta, Butler, Pop. 8,608
Augusta USD 402 2,100/PK-12
2345 Greyhound Dr 67010 316-775-5484
Jim Lentz, supt. Fax 775-5035
www.usd402.com
Augusta HS 700/9-12
2020 Ohio St 67010 316-775-5461
Paul Larkin, prin. Fax 775-3484
Augusta MS 500/6-8
1001 State St 67010 316-775-6383
Eileen Dreiling, prin. Fax 775-3853

Axtell, Marshall, Pop. 433
Axtell USD 488 300/K-12
PO Box N 66403 785-736-2304
Bob Bartkoski, supt. Fax 736-2864
www.usd488.org/
Axtell JSHS 100/7-12
504 Pine St 66403 785-736-2237
Patrick Graham, prin. Fax 736-2295
Other Schools – See Bern

Baileyville, Nemaha
B & B USD 451 200/K-12
PO Box 69 66404 785-336-2326
Jerry Turner, supt. Fax 336-2326
bbh.usd451.k12.ks.us/
Baileyville-St. Benedict JSHS 100/7-12
PO Box 69 66404 785-336-6631
John Vincent, prin. Fax 336-2835

Baldwin City, Douglas, Pop. 3,746
Baldwin City USD 348 1,300/PK-12
PO Box 67 66006 785-594-2721
Paul Dorathy, supt. Fax 594-3408
www.usd348.com/
Baldwin HS 400/9-12
PO Box 67 66006 785-594-2725
Shaun Moseman, prin. Fax 594-2858
Baldwin JHS 300/6-8
PO Box 67 66006 785-594-2448
Connie Wright, prin. Fax 594-2449

Baker University Post-Sec.
PO Box 65 66006 785-594-6451

Barnes, Washington, Pop. 142
Barnes USD 223 500/PK-12
PO Box 188 66933 785-763-4231
Steve Joonas, supt. Fax 763-4461
www.usd223.org
Other Schools – See Hanover, Linn

Basehor, Leavenworth, Pop. 3,287
Basehor-Linwood USD 458 2,000/PK-12
PO Box 282 66007 913-724-1396
Dr. Robert Albers, supt. Fax 724-2709
www.usd458.org
Basehor-Linwood HS 700/9-12
PO Box 255 66007 913-724-2266
Sherry Reeves, prin. Fax 724-2040
Other Schools – See Linwood

Baxter Springs, Cherokee, Pop. 4,246
Baxter Springs USD 508 800/PK-12
1520 Cleveland Ave 66713 620-856-2375
Dennis Burke, supt. Fax 856-3943
www.usd508.org
Baxter Springs HS 200/9-12
100 N Military Ave 66713 620-856-3366
Jamie Carlisle, prin. Fax 856-2918
Baxter Springs MS 200/6-8
1520 Cleveland Ave 66713 620-856-3355
Mike Cook, prin. Fax 856-3943

Belle Plaine, Sumner, Pop. 1,618
Belle Plaine USD 357 800/PK-12
PO Box 760 67013 620-488-2288
Lonn Poage, supt. Fax 488-3517
www.usd357.k12.ks.us
Belle Plaine HS 300/9-12
PO Box 8 67013 620-488-2421
Monte Stewart, prin. Fax 488-3536
Belle Plaine MS 200/6-8
PO Box 457 67013 620-488-2222
Mike Couch, prin. Fax 488-3391

Belleville, Republic, Pop. 1,956
Republic County USD 109 500/K-12
PO Box 469 66935 785-527-5621
James White, supt. Fax 527-5375
www.usd109.org/
Republic County HS 200/9-12
PO Box 469 66935 785-527-2281
Daryl Moore, prin. Fax 527-5505
Republic County MS 100/5-8
PO Box 469 66935 785-527-5669
Mabel Woodman, prin. Fax 527-5375

Beloit, Mitchell, Pop. 3,703
Beloit USD 273 800/PK-12
PO Box 547 67420 785-738-3261
Dr. Joe Harrison, supt. Fax 738-4103
www.usd273.k12.ks.us/
Beloit JSHS 400/7-12
PO Box 606 67420 785-738-3593
Dr. Kelly Arnberger, prin. Fax 738-5566

North Central Kansas Technical College Post-Sec.
PO Box 507 67420 785-738-2276
St. Johns HS 100/7-12
209 S Cherry St 67420 785-738-2942
Martin Hesting, prin. Fax 738-4462

Bennington, Ottawa, Pop. 614
Twin Valley USD 240 600/PK-12
PO Box 38 67422 785-488-3325
Richard Harlan, supt. Fax 488-3326
www.usd240.org
Bennington HS 200/9-12
PO Box 8 67422 785-488-3321
Jay Macy, prin. Fax 488-2939
Other Schools – See Tescott

Benton, Butler, Pop. 817
Circle USD 375
Supt. — See Towanda
Circle MS 200/7-8
14697 SW 20th St 67017 316-778-1470
Nita McLean, prin. Fax 778-1749

Bern, Nemaha, Pop. 200
Axtell USD 488
Supt. — See Axtell
Bern JSHS 100/7-12
PO Box 144 66408 785-336-3031
Jim Struber, prin. Fax 336-2507

Bird City, Cheyenne, Pop. 438
Cheylin USD 103 200/K-12
PO Box 28 67731 785-734-2341
David Zumbahlen, supt. Fax 734-2489
Cheylin West JSHS 100/7-12
PO Box 28 67731 785-734-2341
David Zumbahlen, prin. Fax 734-2489

Bison, Rush, Pop. 220
Otis-Bison USD 403
Supt. — See Albert
Otis-Bison MS 50/6-8
PO Box 297 67520 785-356-2611
Jake Befort, prin. Fax 356-2239

Blue Rapids, Marshall, Pop. 1,048
Valley Heights USD 498
Supt. — See Waterville
Valley Heights JSHS 200/7-12
2274 6th Rd 66411 785-363-2508
Don Potter, prin. Fax 363-2072

Bonner Springs, Wyandotte, Pop. 6,942
Bonner Springs USD 204 2,200/K-12
PO Box 435 66012 913-422-5600
Dr. Robert Van Maren, supt. Fax 422-4193
www.usd204.k12.ks.us
Bonner Springs HS 700/9-12
PO Box 216 66012 913-422-5121
Dr. Jerry Abbott, prin. Fax 422-7284
Clark MS 500/6-8
PO Box 336 66012 913-422-5115
Joe DiPonio, prin. Fax 422-1644

Brewster, Thomas, Pop. 262
Brewster USD 314 100/PK-12
PO Box 220 67732 785-694-2236
Sherri L. Edmundson, supt. Fax 694-2746
www.usd314.k12.ks.us
Brewster HS 100/7-12
PO Box 220 67732 785-694-2236
Sherri L. Edmundson, prin. Fax 694-2746

Brookville, Saline, Pop. 253
Ell-Saline USD 307 500/K-12
412 E Anderson 67425 785-225-6813
Jerry Minneman, supt. Fax 225-6815
www.ellsaline.org
Ell-Saline HS 100/9-12
414 E Anderson 67425 785-225-6633
Paul Alexander, prin. Fax 225-6694
Ell-Saline MS 100/7-8
414 E Anderson 67425 785-225-6633
Paul Alexander, prin. Fax 225-6694

Bucklin, Ford, Pop. 734
Bucklin USD 459 200/K-12
PO Box 8 67834 620-826-3828
Terry Marshall, supt. Fax 826-3377
www.usd459.k12.ks.us/
Bucklin HS 100/9-12
PO Box 8 67834 620-826-3241
Darrel Kohlman, prin. Fax 826-9966

Buffalo, Wilson, Pop. 277
Altoona-Midway USD 387 200/K-12
20584 US 75 Hwy 66717 620-537-7721
Bill Orth, supt. Fax 537-8711
www.altoonamidway.org/
Altoona-Midway HS 100/9-12
20584 US 75 Hwy 66717 620-537-7711
Butch Trabuc, prin. Fax 537-2641
Other Schools – See Altoona

Buhler, Reno, Pop. 1,335
Buhler USD 313 2,200/PK-12
PO Box 320 67522 620-543-2258
David Brax, supt. Fax 543-2510
www.buhlerschools.org
Buhler HS 700/9-12
PO Box 350 67522 620-543-2255
Mike Berblinger, prin. Fax 543-2853
Other Schools – See Hutchinson

Burden, Cowley, Pop. 553
Central USD 462 300/PK-12
PO Box 128 67019 620-438-2218
Marian Hedges, supt. Fax 438-2217
www.usd462.org
Central JSHS 200/7-12
PO Box 128 67019 620-438-2215
Dale Adams, prin. Fax 438-2217

Burlingame, Osage, Pop. 1,015
Burlingame USD 454 300/PK-12
100 Bloomquist Dr Ste A 66413 785-654-3328
Don Blome, supt. Fax 654-3570
www.usd454.net
Burlingame JSHS 100/7-12
100 Bloomquist Dr Ste A 66413 785-654-3315
Tammy Baird, prin. Fax 654-3191

Burlington, Coffey, Pop. 2,707
Burlington USD 244 800/PK-12
200 S 6th St 66839 620-364-8478
Dr. Dale Rawson, supt. Fax 364-8548
www.usd244ks.org
Burlington HS 300/9-12
830 Cross St 66839 620-364-8672
Jim Kuhn, prin. Fax 364-8680
Burlington MS 200/6-8
720 Cross St 66839 620-364-2156
Tim Martin, prin. Fax 364-8560

Burr Oak, Jewell, Pop. 226
Rock Hills USD 107
Supt. — See Mankato
Rock Hills MS 50/5-8
221 N Main St 66936 785-647-6361
Beverly Roemer, prin. Fax 647-5391

Burrton, Harvey, Pop. 913
Burrton USD 369 200/K-12
PO Box 369 67020 620-463-3840
Dale Herl, supt. Fax 463-2636
www.burrton.k12.ks.us/
Burrton HS 100/6-12
PO Box 369 67020 620-463-3820
Eugene Haydock, prin. Fax 463-2096

Victory Village Christian Academy 50/7-12
201 S Victory Rd 67020 620-463-6112
Bill Cowell, prin. Fax 463-2631

Bushton, Rice, Pop. 298
Lorraine USD 328
Supt. — See Lorraine
Quivira Heights HS 100/9-12
500 S Main St 67427 620-562-3597
Lenny Gales, prin. Fax 562-3248

Caldwell, Sumner, Pop. 1,215
Caldwell USD 360 200/PK-12
22 N Webb St 67022 620-845-2585
Jim Reece, supt. Fax 845-2610
www.usd360.com
Caldwell Secondary S 100/6-12
21 N Osage St 67022 620-845-2585
Alan Jamison, prin. Fax 845-2534

Caney, Montgomery, Pop. 1,975
Caney Valley USD 436 800/PK-12
700 E Bullpup Blvd 67333 620-879-9200
Danny Fulton, supt. Fax 879-9209
www.caney.com
Caney Valley JSHS 400/7-12
601 E Bullpup Blvd 67333 620-879-9220
Justin Lockwood, prin. Fax 879-9227

Canton, McPherson, Pop. 812
Canton-Galva USD 419 400/PK-12
PO Box 317 67428 620-628-4901
Bill Seidl, supt. Fax 628-4380
www.canton-galva.k12.ks.us
Canton-Galva HS 100/9-12
PO Box 275 67428 620-628-4401
Jack Koehn, prin. Fax 628-4951
Other Schools – See Galva

Carbondale, Osage, Pop. 1,451
Santa Fe Trail USD 434 1,300/PK-12
PO Box 310 66414 785-665-7168
Terry Schmidt, supt. Fax 665-7164
www.usd434.org
Santa Fe Trail HS 400/9-12
15701 S California Rd 66414 785-665-7161
Brian Kraus, prin. Fax 665-7193

Cawker City, Mitchell, Pop. 474
Waconda USD 272 300/K-12
PO Box 326 67430 785-781-4328
Jeff Teavis, supt. Fax 781-4318
www.usd272.org
Lakeside JHS 100/7-8
PO Box 46 67430 785-781-4911
Robert Green, prin. Fax 781-4861
Other Schools – See Downs

Cedar Vale, Chautauqua, Pop. 669
Cedar Vale USD 285 100/PK-12
PO Box 458 67024 620-758-2265
Kenneth Tarrant, supt. Fax 758-2647
www.cvs285.net
Cedar Vale JSHS 100/6-12
PO Box 458 67024 620-758-2791
Dennis Myers, prin. Fax 758-2704

Centralia, Nemaha, Pop. 504
Vermillion USD 380
Supt. — See Vermillion
Centralia JSHS 100/7-12
PO Box 367 66415 785-857-3324
John Whetzal, prin. Fax 857-3847

Chanute, Neosho, Pop. 9,006
Chanute USD 413 1,700/K-12
315 Chanute 35 Pkwy 66720 620-432-2500
Stephen Parsons, supt. Fax 431-6810
www.usd413.org/
Chanute HS 600/9-12
400 S Highland Ave 66720 620-432-2510
Kent Wire, prin. Fax 431-3020
Royster MS 500/6-8
400 W Main St 66720 620-432-2520
Brad Miner, prin. Fax 431-7841

Neosho County Community College Post-Sec.
800 W 14th St 66720 620-431-2820

Chapman, Dickinson, Pop. 1,243
Chapman USD 473 1,000/K-12
PO Box 249 67431 785-922-6521
Tony Frieze, supt. Fax 922-6446
usd473.net
Chapman HS 400/9-12
PO Box 249 67431 785-922-6561
Richard Hall, prin. Fax 922-7162
Chapman MS 200/6-8
PO Box 249 67431 785-922-6555
Bruce Hurford, prin. Fax 922-6601

Chase, Rice, Pop. 467
Chase-Raymond USD 401 100/K-12
PO Box 366 67524 620-938-2913
David Howard, supt. Fax 938-2622
www.usd401.com/
Chase HS 100/9-12
PO Box 366 67524 620-938-2923
David Howard, prin. Fax 938-2456
Raymond JHS 50/7-8
PO Box 366 67524 620-938-2923
David Howard, prin. Fax 938-2456

Cheney, Sedgwick, Pop. 1,843
Cheney USD 268 800/K-12
100 W 6th Ave 67025 316-542-3512
Brad Neuenswander, supt. Fax 542-0326
www.cheney268.com
Cheney HS 300/9-12
100 W 6th Ave 67025 316-542-3113
Ronald Traxson, prin. Fax 542-3789
Cheney MS 200/6-8
100 W 6th Ave 67025 316-542-0060
Amy Wallace, prin. Fax 542-3789

Cherokee, Crawford, Pop. 718
Cherokee USD 247 800/K-12
PO Box 270 66724 620-457-8350
Tim Burns, supt. Fax 457-8428
www.usd247.com
Southeast HS 300/9-12
PO Box 277 66724 620-457-8365
Greg Gorman, prin. Fax 457-8389

Cherryvale, Montgomery, Pop. 2,266
Cherryvale USD 447 600/PK-12
618 E 4th St 67335 620-336-8130
Randy Wagoner, supt. Fax 336-8133
www.usd447.org
Cherryvale JSHS 300/7-12
700 S Carson St 67335 620-336-8100
George Owens, prin. Fax 336-8110

Chetopa, Labette, Pop. 1,231
Chetopa - St. Paul USD 505 500/PK-12
430 Elm St 67336 620-236-7959
Kim Juenemann, supt. Fax 236-4271
www.usd505.org
Chetopa HS 100/7-12
430 Elm St 67336 620-236-7244
Paul Miller, prin. Fax 236-4271
Other Schools – See Saint Paul

Cimarron, Gray, Pop. 2,029
Cimarron-Ensign USD 102 600/K-12
PO Box 489 67835 620-855-7743
Marc Woofter, supt. Fax 855-7745
www.cimarronschools.net
Cimarron JSHS 300/7-12
PO Box 489 67835 620-855-3323
Bill Brown, prin. Fax 855-3219

Claflin, Barton, Pop. 688
Claflin USD 354 300/K-12
PO Box 346 67525 620-587-3878
Darrell Genereux, supt. Fax 587-2389
www.claflinschools.org
Claflin JSHS 200/7-12
PO Box 348 67525 620-587-3801
Danielle Poland, prin. Fax 587-3677

Clay Center, Clay, Pop. 4,378
Clay Center USD 379 1,300/K-12
PO Box 97 67432 785-632-3176
Michael Folks, supt. Fax 632-5020
www.usd379.org/
Clay Center Community HS 400/9-12
1630 9th St 67432 785-632-2131
Steve Taylor, prin. Fax 632-2076
Clay Center Community MS 300/6-8
935 Prospect St 67432 785-632-3232
Kristen Ryan, prin. Fax 632-6013
Other Schools – See Wakefield

Clearwater, Sedgwick, Pop. 2,214
Clearwater USD 264 1,000/PK-12
PO Box 248 67026 620-584-2091
Mike Roth, supt. Fax 584-6705
www.usd264.org
Clearwater HS 400/9-12
1201 E Ross St 67026 620-584-2361
Steve Meeker, prin. Fax 584-2083
Clearwater MS 200/7-8
140 S 4th St 67026 620-584-2036
Keith Pauly, prin. Fax 584-2199

Clifton, Washington, Pop. 508
Clifton-Clyde USD 224 300/PK-12
PO Box A 66937 785-455-3313
David Roberts, supt. Fax 455-3314
www.usd224.com/
Clifton-Clyde MS 100/4-8
PO Box B 66937 785-455-3323
David Roberts, prin. Fax 455-3524
Other Schools – See Clyde

Clyde, Cloud, Pop. 709
Clifton-Clyde USD 224
Supt. — See Clifton
Clifton-Clyde HS 100/9-12
616 N High St 66938 785-446-3444
Brenda Odgers, prin. Fax 446-3458

Coffeyville, Montgomery, Pop. 10,359
Coffeyville USD 445 1,900/PK-12
615 Ellis St 67337 620-252-6400
Robert Morten, supt. Fax 252-6807
cvilleschools.com
Field Kindley Memorial HS 600/9-12
1110 W 8th St 67337 620-252-6410
Ben Smith, prin. Fax 252-6818
Roosevelt MS 300/7-8
1000 W 8th St 67337 620-252-6420
Alice Morris, prin. Fax 252-6844

Coffeyville Community College Post-Sec.
400 W 11th St 67337 620-251-7700

Colby, Thomas, Pop. 5,030
Colby USD 315 1,100/K-12
600 W 3rd St 67701 785-460-5000
Kirk Nielsen, supt. Fax 460-5050
Colby HS 400/9-12
1890 S Franklin Ave 67701 785-460-5300
Rocky Robbins, prin. Fax 460-5350
Colby MS 300/6-8
750 W 3rd St 67701 785-460-5200
Robb Ross, prin. Fax 460-5250

Colby Community College Post-Sec.
1255 S Range Ave 67701 785-462-4690
Heartland Christian S 100/PK-12
1995 W 4th St 67701 785-460-6419
Jesse Vincent, admin. Fax 460-8337

Coldwater, Comanche, Pop. 774
Comanche County USD 300 300/K-12
PO Box 721 67029 620-582-2181
Michael Baldwin, supt. Fax 582-2540
South Central HS 100/9-12
PO Box 578 67029 620-582-2158
Michael Baldwin, prin. Fax 582-2535
Other Schools – See Protection

Colony, Anderson, Pop. 390
Crest USD 479 100/K-12
PO Box 305 66015 620-852-3540
Doug Spillman, supt. Fax 852-3542
www.usd479.net/
Crest HS 100/6-12
PO Box 325 66015 620-852-3521
Keith Higgins, prin. Fax 852-3357

Columbus, Cherokee, Pop. 3,259
Columbus USD 493 1,100/PK-12
802 S Highschool Ave 66725 620-429-3661
Ken Jones, supt. Fax 429-2673
www.usd493.com
Central S 400/4-8
810 S Highschool Ave 66725 620-429-3943
Bobbi Williams, prin. Fax 429-2882
Columbus HS 400/9-12
124 S Highschool Ave 66725 620-429-3821
Steve Jameson, prin. Fax 429-3657

Concordia, Cloud, Pop. 5,371
Concordia USD 333 1,100/K-12
217 W 7th St 66901 785-243-3518
Beverly Mortimer, supt. Fax 243-8883
www.usd333.com
Concordia JSHS 500/7-12
436 W 10th St 66901 785-243-2452
Cheryl Hochhalter, prin. Fax 243-8805

Cloud County Community College Post-Sec.
PO Box 1002 66901 785-243-1435

Conway Springs, Sumner, Pop. 1,253
Conway Springs USD 356 700/K-12
110 N Monnett St 67031 620-456-2961
Clay Murphy, supt. Fax 456-3173
www.usd356.org
Conway Springs HS 200/9-12
607 W Saint Louis St 67031 620-456-2963
Brent Davis, prin. Fax 456-3314
Conway Springs MS 200/6-8
112 N Cranmer St 67031 620-456-2965
Vance Williams, prin. Fax 456-3313

Copeland, Gray, Pop. 321
Copeland USD 476 100/PK-8
PO Box 156 67837 620-668-5565
Donald Grover, supt. Fax 668-5568
South Gray JHS 50/6-8
PO Box 156 67837 620-668-5565
Dick Bixler, prin. Fax 668-5568

Cottonwood Falls, Chase, Pop. 959
Chase County USD 284 500/K-12
PO Box 569 66845 620-273-6303
Rick Weiss, supt. Fax 273-6717
www.usd284.org/
Chase County HS 200/9-12
PO Box 400 66845 620-273-6354
Stanley Elliott, prin. Fax 273-8337
Other Schools – See Strong City

Council Grove, Morris, Pop. 2,275
Morris County USD 417 900/PK-12
17 Wood St 66846 620-767-5192
Diane Miller, supt. Fax 767-5444
www.cgrove417.org/
Council Grove HS 300/9-12
129 Hockaday St 66846 620-767-5149
Kelly McDiffett, prin. Fax 767-7280
Other Schools – See Alta Vista

Courtland, Republic, Pop. 291
Pike Valley USD 426
Supt. — See Scandia
Pike Valley JHS 100/6-8
PO Box 320 66939 785-374-4221
Chris Vignery, prin. Fax 374-4268

Cunningham, Kingman, Pop. 477
Cunningham USD 332 200/K-12
PO Box 67 67035 620-298-3271
Melvin Ormiston, supt. Fax 298-2562
Cunningham HS 100/9-12
PO Box 98 67035 620-298-2473
Steve Miller, prin. Fax 298-5005

Damar, Rooks, Pop. 150
Palco USD 269
Supt. — See Palco
Damar JHS 50/6-8
PO Box 38 67632 785-839-4265
Lisa Gehring, prin. Fax 839-4278

Deerfield, Kearny, Pop. 892
Deerfield USD 216 300/PK-12
PO Box 274 67838 620-426-8516
Jon Ansley, supt. Fax 426-7890
www.usd216.org/
Deerfield HS 100/9-12
PO Box 274 67838 620-426-8401
Scott Kedrowski, prin. Fax 426-6903
Deerfield MS 100/6-8
PO Box 274 67838 620-426-8401
Scott Kedrowski, prin. Fax 426-6903

Denton, Doniphan, Pop. 178
Midway USD 433 100/K-8
642 Highway 20 E 66017 785-359-6526
Rex Bollinger, supt. Fax 359-6522
www.doniphanwest.org
Doniphan West MS 100/6-8
642 Highway 20 E 66017 785-359-6526
Deanna Scherer, prin. Fax 359-6522

Derby, Sedgwick, Pop. 20,543
Derby USD 260 6,600/PK-12
120 E Washington St 67037 316-788-8400
Craig Wilford, supt. Fax 788-8449
www.derbyschools.com
Derby HS 2,200/9-12
920 N Rock Rd 67037 316-788-8500
Dr. Kristin Sherwood, prin. Fax 788-8593
Derby MS 1,100/7-8
801 E Madison Ave 67037 316-788-8580
Rod Coykendall, prin. Fax 788-8062

De Soto, Johnson, Pop. 5,170
De Soto USD 232 4,800/PK-12
35200 W 91st St 66018 913-583-8300
Sharon Zoellner, supt. Fax 583-8303
www.usd232.org
De Soto HS 400/9-12
35000 W 91st St 66018 913-583-8370
Dave Marford, prin. Fax 583-8376
Lexington Trails MS 400/6-8
8800 Penner Ave 66018 913-583-8360
Mark Schmidt, prin. Fax 583-8366
Other Schools – See Shawnee

Dexter, Cowley, Pop. 350
Dexter USD 471 200/PK-12
PO Box 97 67038 620-876-5415
Jerry Golden, supt. Fax 876-5548
www.usd471.org
Dexter JSHS 100/7-12
PO Box 97 67038 620-876-5415
Robert Holmes, prin. Fax 876-5548

Dighton, Lane, Pop. 1,106
Dighton USD 482 200/PK-12
PO Box 878 67839 620-397-2835
Angela Lawrence, supt. Fax 397-5932
www.usd482.k12.ks.us/
Dighton JSHS 100/7-12
PO Box 939 67839 620-397-5333
Mark Cook, prin. Fax 397-5338

Dodge City, Ford, Pop. 26,104
Dodge City USD 443 5,800/K-12
PO Box 460 67801 620-227-1700
Alan Cunningham, supt. Fax 227-1695
www.usd443.org
Dodge City HS 1,700/9-12
2201 W Ross Blvd 67801 620-227-1611
Jacque Feist, prin. Fax 227-1680
Dodge City MS 800/7-8
2000 6th Ave 67801 620-227-1610
Fax 227-1731

Dodge City Community College Post-Sec.
2501 N 14th Ave 67801 620-225-1321

Douglass, Butler, Pop. 1,799
Douglass USD 396 800/PK-12
PO Box 158 67039 316-747-3300
James Keller, supt. Fax 747-3305
www.usd396.net/
Douglass HS 300/9-12
PO Box 158 67039 316-747-3310
Chad Higgins, prin. Fax 747-3315
Sisk MS 200/6-8
PO Box 158 67039 316-747-3340
Robert Swigart, prin. Fax 747-3346

Downs, Osborne, Pop. 938
Waconda USD 272
Supt. — See Cawker City
Lakeside HS 100/9-12
PO Box 247 67437 785-454-3332
Jim Gierbrecht, prin. Fax 454-3747

Easton, Leavenworth, Pop. 357
Easton USD 449 700/K-12
32502 Easton Rd 66020 913-651-9740
Charles Coblentz, supt. Fax 651-6740
www.easton449.org
Pleasant Ridge HS 300/9-12
32500 Easton Rd 66020 913-651-5556
Andy Metsker, prin. Fax 651-7797
Pleasant Ridge MS 200/6-8
32504 Easton Rd 66020 913-651-5522
Lisa Powers, prin. Fax 651-0049

Effingham, Atchison, Pop. 582
Atchison County Community USD 377 700/PK-12
PO Box 289 66023 913-833-5050
Stephen Wiseman, supt. Fax 833-5210
www.usd377.org/
Atchison County Community HS 300/9-12
PO Box 289 66023 913-833-2240
Mark Preut, prin. Fax 833-2197
Atchison County Community MS 200/5-8
PO Box 289 66023 913-833-4420
Tom Sack, prin. Fax 833-4281

Elbing, Butler, Pop. 208

Berean Academy 300/K-12
PO Box 70 67041 316-799-2211
Terry Tilson, supt. Fax 799-2601

El Dorado, Butler, Pop. 12,659
El Dorado USD 490 2,100/PK-12
124 W Central Ave 67042 316-322-4800
Dr. Tom Biggs, supt. Fax 322-4801
www.eldoradoschools.org
El Dorado HS 600/9-12
401 Mccollum Rd 67042 316-322-4810
Bret McClendon, prin. Fax 322-4811
El Dorado MS 500/6-8
500 W Central Ave 67042 316-322-4820
Stan Ruff, prin. Fax 322-4821

Butler Community College Post-Sec.
901 S Haverhill Rd 67042 316-321-2222

Elkhart, Morton, Pop. 2,036
Elkhart USD 218 700/PK-12
PO Box 999 67950 620-697-2195
Nancy Crowell, supt. Fax 697-2607
www.usd218.org
Elkhart HS 200/9-12
PO Box 999 67950 620-697-2193
Rex Richardson, prin. Fax 697-4415
Elkhart MS 200/5-8
PO Box 999 67950 620-697-2197
Rex Toomey, prin. Fax 697-4828

Ellinwood, Barton, Pop. 2,119
Ellinwood USD 355 600/K-12
300 N Schiller Ave 67526 620-564-3226
Richard Goodschmidt, supt. Fax 564-2206
www.usd355.org/
Ellinwood HS 200/9-12
210 E 2nd St 67526 620-564-3136
Brian Rowley, prin. Fax 564-2816
Ellinwood MS 100/7-8
210 E 2nd St 67526 620-564-3136
Brian Rowley, prin. Fax 564-2816

Ellis, Ellis, Pop. 1,812
Ellis USD 388 400/K-12
PO Box 256 67637 785-726-4281
Kyle Hayden, supt. Fax 726-4677
www.usd388.k12.ks.us
Ellis HS 100/9-12
PO Box 300 67637 785-726-3151
Corey Burton, prin. Fax 726-3169

Ellsworth, Ellsworth, Pop. 2,887
Ellsworth USD 327 600/K-12
PO Box 306 67439 785-472-5561
Doug Moeckel, supt. Fax 472-5563
www.usd327.org
Ellsworth HS 200/9-12
211 W 11th St 67439 785-472-4471
Dale Brungardt, prin. Fax 472-8109
Other Schools – See Kanopolis

Elwood, Doniphan, Pop. 1,153
Elwood USD 486 300/PK-12
PO Box 368 66024 913-365-6735
Michael Newman, supt. Fax 365-3503
www.usd486.org/
Elwood HS 100/9-12
PO Box 368 66024 913-365-6735
Steve Taylor, prin. Fax 365-0012

Emporia, Lyon, Pop. 26,456
Emporia USD 253 4,800/PK-12
PO Box 1008 66801 620-341-2200
John Heim, supt. Fax 341-2205
www.usd253.org
Emporia HS 1,600/9-12
3302 W 18th Ave 66801 620-341-2365
Scott Sheldon, prin. Fax 341-2376
Emporia MS 700/7-8
2300 Graphic Arts Rd 66801 620-341-2335
Steve Ternes, prin. Fax 341-2341

Emporia State University Post-Sec.
1200 Commercial St 66801 620-341-1200
Flint Hills Technical College Post-Sec.
3301 W 18th Ave 66801 620-341-2300

Enterprise, Dickinson, Pop. 811

Enterprise Adventist Academy 50/9-12
PO Box 215 67441 785-263-8211
Stephen Bralley, prin. Fax 263-8368

Erie, Neosho, Pop. 1,167
Erie USD 101 700/K-12
PO Box 137 66733 620-244-3264
Mike Carson, supt. Fax 244-3664
www.cusd101.org/
Erie HS 200/9-12
410 W 3rd St 66733 620-244-3287
Ted Hill, prin. Fax 244-3290

Eskridge, Wabaunsee, Pop. 571
Mission Valley USD 330 500/K-12
PO Box 158 66423 785-449-2282
Jim Markos, supt. Fax 449-2669
www.mv330.org
Mission Valley HS 200/9-12
12685 Mission Valley Rd 66423 785-449-2297
Kimberlee Andersen, prin. Fax 449-2309

Eudora, Douglas, Pop. 5,284
Eudora USD 491 1,300/PK-12
PO Box 500 66025 785-542-4910
Marty Kobza, supt. Fax 542-4909
www.eudoraschools.org/
Eudora HS 400/9-12
PO Box 712 66025 785-542-4980
Dale Sample, prin. Fax 542-4990
Eudora MS 300/6-8
PO Box 701 66025 785-542-4960
Richard Proffitt, prin. Fax 542-4970

Eureka, Greenwood, Pop. 2,739
Eureka USD 389 700/PK-12
216 N Main St 67045 620-583-5588
Randy Corn, supt. Fax 583-8200
www.389ks.org
Eureka JSHS 300/7-12
815 N Jefferson St 67045 620-583-7428
Randy Corns, prin. Fax 583-8222

Everest, Brown, Pop. 304
South Brown County USD 430
Supt. — See Horton
Everest MS 200/5-8
713 S 7th St 66424 785-548-7536
Jackie Wenger, prin. Fax 548-7538

Fort Leavenworth, Leavenworth, Pop. 1,300
Ft. Leavenworth USD 207 1,700/PK-9
207 Education Way 66027 913-651-7373
Deborah Baeuchle, supt. Fax 758-6010
www.ftlvn.com
Patton JHS 400/7-9
1 Patton Cir 66027 913-651-7371
Dr. Martin Gill, prin. Fax 758-6097

Fort Riley, Geary, Pop. 112
Geary County USD 475
Supt. — See Junction City
Fort Riley MS 600/6-8
4020 1st Division Rd 66442 785-717-4500
Joseph Handlos, prin. Fax 717-4501

Fort Scott, Bourbon, Pop. 7,990
Ft. Scott USD 234 2,000/PK-12
424 S Main St 66701 620-223-0800
Dr. Rick Werling, supt. Fax 223-2760
www.usd234.org
Fort Scott HS 700/9-12
1005 S Main St 66701 620-223-0600
Bob Beckham, prin. Fax 223-5368
Fort Scott MS 500/6-8
1105 E 12th St 66701 620-223-3262
Barbara Albright, prin. Fax 223-8946

Fort Scott Community College Post-Sec.
2108 Horton St 66701 620-223-2700

Fowler, Meade, Pop. 578
Fowler USD 225 200/PK-12
PO Box 170 67844 620-646-5661
Sam Seybold, supt. Fax 646-5713
www.usd225.org/
Fowler HS 100/7-12
PO Box 140 67844 620-646-5221
Mark Lackey, prin. Fax 646-5295

Frankfort, Marshall, Pop. 795
Vermillion USD 380
Supt. — See Vermillion
Frankfort JSHS 200/7-12
PO Box 203 66427 785-292-4486
Dean Dalinghaus, prin. Fax 292-4636

Fredonia, Wilson, Pop. 2,455
Fredonia USD 484 800/PK-12
PO Box 539 66736 620-378-4177
Jim Porter, supt. Fax 378-4345
www.fredoniaks.com
Fredonia HS 300/9-12
916 Robinson St 66736 620-378-4172
Jim Lambert, prin. Fax 378-4398
Fredonia MS 200/6-8
203 N 8th St 66736 620-378-4167
Laura Fitzmorris, prin. Fax 378-3635

Frontenac, Crawford, Pop. 3,101
Frontenac USD 249 800/PK-12
208 S Cayuga St 66763 620-231-7551
Destry Brown, supt. Fax 231-2043
www.frontenac249.org
Frontenac JSHS 300/7-12
208 S Cayuga St 66763 620-231-7550
Joe Martin, prin. Fax 231-2043

Galena, Cherokee, Pop. 3,163
Galena USD 499 700/PK-12
702 E 7th St 66739 620-783-4499
Brian Smith, supt. Fax 783-5547
www.usd499.org
Galena HS 200/9-12
702 E 7th St 66739 620-783-4499
Jeff Eberhart, prin. Fax 783-1905
Galena MS 200/6-8
702 E 7th St 66739 620-783-4499
Danny Albright, prin. Fax 783-5214

Galva, McPherson, Pop. 773
Canton-Galva USD 419
Supt. — See Canton
Canton-Galva MS 100/4-8
PO Box 96 67443 620-654-3321
Bob Becker, prin. Fax 654-3335

Garden City, Finney, Pop. 27,098
Garden City USD 457 7,200/PK-12
1205 Fleming St 67846 620-276-5100
Dr. Richard Atha, supt. Fax 276-5220
www.gckschools.com
Garden City HS 1,900/9-12
1412 N Main St 67846 620-276-5170
James Mireles, prin. Fax 276-5176
Henderson MS 600/7-8
2406 Fleming St 67846 620-276-5210
Jessica Bird, prin. Fax 276-5219
Hubert MS 600/7-8
1205 A St 67846 620-276-5200
Gerald Neumann, prin. Fax 276-5287

Garden City Community College Post-Sec.
801 N Campus Dr 67846 620-276-7611

Garden Plain, Sedgwick, Pop. 823
Renwick USD 267
Supt. — See Andale
Garden Plain HS 200/9-12
PO Box 128 67050 316-531-2272
Tracy Bourne, prin. Fax 535-2727

Gardner, Johnson, Pop. 14,317
Gardner Edgerton USD 231 3,500/PK-12
PO Box 97 66030 913-856-2000
Dr. Bill Gilhaus, supt. Fax 856-7330
www.usd231.com
Gardner Edgerton HS 900/9-12
425 N Waverly Rd 66030 913-856-2600
Dave Webb, prin. Fax 856-2690

Pioneer Ridge MS 5-8
16200 Kill Creek Rd 66030 913-856-3850
Tim Brady, prin. Fax 856-3694
Wheatridge MS 500/5-8
318 E Washington St 66030 913-856-2900
G. A. Buie, prin. Fax 856-2980

Garnett, Anderson, Pop. 3,338
Garnett USD 365 1,100/K-12
PO Box 328 66032 785-448-6155
Gordon Myers, supt. Fax 448-6157
www.usd365.k12.ks.us
Anderson County JSHS 500/7-12
1100 W Highway 31 66032 785-448-3115
G.A. Buie, prin. Fax 448-6670

Girard, Crawford, Pop. 2,686
Girard USD 248 1,000/PK-12
415 N Summit St 66743 620-724-4325
Gary Snawder, supt. Fax 724-8446
www.girard248.org/
Girard HS 300/9-12
415 N Summit St 66743 620-724-4326
Blaise Bauer, prin. Fax 724-6136
Girard MS 200/6-8
415 N Summit St 66743 620-724-4114
Randy Heatherly, prin. Fax 724-4610

Glasco, Cloud, Pop. 504
Southern Cloud USD 334 200/K-12
PO Box 427 67445 785-568-2247
Roger Perkins, supt. Fax 568-2298
Glasco HS 50/9-12
PO Box 158 67445 785-568-2291
Tom Lynch, prin. Fax 568-2298
Other Schools – See Miltonvale

Goddard, Sedgwick, Pop. 3,337
Goddard USD 265 4,200/K-12
PO Box 249 67052 316-794-4000
Charles Edmonds, supt. Fax 794-2222
www.goddardusd.com
Eisenhower MS 300/7-8
PO Box 349 67052 316-794-4150
Jerold Longabaugh, prin. Fax 794-4063
Goddard HS 1,300/9-12
PO Box 189 67052 316-794-4100
Cloyce Spradling, prin. Fax 794-4130
Goddard MS 300/7-8
PO Box 279 67052 316-794-4230
Lisa Hogarth, prin. Fax 794-4254

Goessel, Marion, Pop. 547
Goessel USD 411 300/K-12
PO Box 68 67053 620-367-4601
John Fast, supt. Fax 367-4603
www.usd411.org
Goessel JSHS 200/6-12
PO Box 6 67053 620-367-2242
Curt Graves, prin. Fax 367-2571

Goodland, Sherman, Pop. 4,485
Goodland USD 352 900/PK-PK, 1-
PO Box 509 67735 785-899-2397
Shelly Angelos, supt. Fax 899-8504
www.usd352.k12.ks.us
Goodland HS 300/9-12
PO Box 509 67735 785-899-5656
Harvey Swager, prin. Fax 899-8517
Grant JHS 100/7-8
PO Box 509 67735 785-899-7561
Steve Raymer, prin. Fax 899-8525

Northwest Kansas Technical College Post-Sec.
1209 Harrison St 67735 785-899-3641

Grainfield, Gove, Pop. 298
Wheatland USD 292 200/PK-12
PO Box 165 67737 785-673-4213
Gena Stanley, supt. Fax 673-4234
Wheatland MSHS 100/7-12
PO Box 149 67737 785-673-4223
Darrin Herl, prin. Fax 673-4234

Great Bend, Barton, Pop. 15,440
Great Bend USD 428 3,200/PK-12
201 S Patton Rd 67530 620-793-1500
Dr. Thomas W. Vernon, supt. Fax 793-1585
www.usd428.org
Great Bend HS 1,100/9-12
2027 Morton St 67530 620-793-1521
Joyce Carter, prin. Fax 793-1537
Great Bend MS 500/7-8
1919 Harrison St 67530 620-793-1510
David Reiser, prin. Fax 793-1549

Barton County Community College Post-Sec.
245 NE 30 Rd 67530 620-792-2701

Greensburg, Kiowa, Pop. 1,398
Greensburg USD 422 300/PK-12
401 S Oak St 67054 620-723-2145
Darin Headrick, supt. Fax 723-2705
Greensburg HS 100/9-12
420 S Main St 67054 620-723-2164
Randy Fulton, prin. Fax 723-2019

Gridley, Coffey, Pop. 365
Le Roy-Gridley USD 245
Supt. — See Le Roy
Southern Coffey County JHS 100/5-8
PO Box 426 66852 620-836-2151
Gary Haehn, prin. Fax 836-4041

Grinnell, Gove, Pop. 299
Grinnell USD 291 100/K-12
PO Box 68 67738 785-824-3277
Rose Kane, supt. Fax 824-3215
skyways.lib.ks.us/kansas/schools/grinnell/

Grinnell HS 50/9-12
PO Box 68 67738 785-824-3277
Rose Kane, prin. Fax 824-3215
Grinnell MS 50/6-8
PO Box 68 67738 785-824-3277
Rose Kane, prin. Fax 824-3215

Gypsum, Saline, Pop. 399
Southeast of Saline USD 306 700/K-12
5056 E Highway K4 67448 785-536-4291
Robert Goodwin, supt. Fax 536-4247
www.usd306.k12.ks.us
Southeast Saline JSHS 400/7-12
5056 E Highway K4 67448 785-536-4286
Monte Couchman, prin. Fax 536-4292

Halstead, Harvey, Pop. 1,912
Halstead USD 440 700/K-12
520 W 6th St 67056 316-835-2641
Dr. Tom Bishard, supt. Fax 835-2305
www.usd440.com
Halstead HS 200/9-12
520 W 6th St 67056 316-835-2682
David Younger, prin. Fax 835-3673
Halstead MS 300/4-8
221 W 6th St 67056 316-835-2694
David Younger, prin. Fax 835-2469

Hamilton, Greenwood, Pop. 325
Hamilton USD 390 100/K-12
2596 W Rd N 66853 620-678-3244
Richard Stapp, supt. Fax 678-3321
www.hamilton390.net
Hamilton HS 100/7-12
2596 W Rd N 66853 620-678-3651
Richard Barnaby, prin. Fax 678-3321

Hanover, Washington, Pop. 593
Barnes USD 223
Supt. — See Barnes
Hanover HS 100/9-12
209 E North St 66945 785-337-2281
Aaron Birkhofer, prin. Fax 337-2307

Hanston, Hodgeman, Pop. 262
Hanston USD 228 50/6-8
PO Box 219 67849 620-623-2641
Ray Patterson, supt. Fax 623-2096
Hanston JHS 50/6-8
PO Box 219 67849 620-623-2611
Mindy Salmans, prin. Fax 623-4488

Hartford, Lyon, Pop. 505
Southern Lyon County USD 252 500/PK-12
PO Box 278 66854 620-392-5519
Paul Dorathy, supt. Fax 392-5841
www.usd252.org/
Hartford JSHS 100/7-12
PO Box 218 66854 620-392-5515
Curtis Simons, prin. Fax 392-5960
Other Schools – See Olpe

Haven, Reno, Pop. 1,170
Haven USD 312 900/K-12
PO Box 130 67543 620-465-7727
Dr. Patrick Call, supt. Fax 465-3595
www.havenschools.com
Haven HS 300/9-12
PO Box C 67543 620-465-2585
Terry Fehrenbach, prin. Fax 465-7729
Haven MS 100/7-8
PO Box B 67543 620-465-2587
Terry Fehrenback, prin. Fax 465-2588

Haviland, Kiowa, Pop. 574
Haviland USD 474 200/PK-12
PO Box 243 67059 620-862-5256
Mike Waters, supt. Fax 862-5257
Haviland HS 100/9-12
PO Box 243 67059 620-862-5217
Randy VandenHoek, prin. Fax 862-5240

Barclay College Post-Sec.
607 N Kingman St 67059 800-862-0226

Hays, Ellis, Pop. 19,632
Hays USD 489 3,000/K-12
323 W 12th St 67601 785-623-2400
Fred Kaufman, supt. Fax 623-2409
www.usd489.com/
Felten MS 400/6-8
201 E 29th St 67601 785-623-2450
Craig Pallister, prin. Fax 623-2456
Hays HS 1,000/9-12
2300 E 13th St 67601 785-623-2600
Mike Hester, prin. Fax 623-2609
Kennedy MS 200/6-8
1309 Fort St 67601 785-623-2470
Lee Keffer, prin. Fax 623-2476

Fort Hays State University Post-Sec.
600 Park St 67601 785-628-4000
Hays Academy of Hair Design Post-Sec.
1214 E 27th St 67601 785-628-3981
Thomas More Prep-Marion HS 300/9-12
1701 Hall St 67601 785-625-6577
Dennis Coakley, prin. Fax 625-3912

Haysville, Sedgwick, Pop. 9,817
Haysville USD 261 4,400/PK-12
1745 W Grand Ave 67060 316-554-2200
Dr. John Burke, supt. Fax 554-2230
www.usd261.com
Haysville MS 1,100/6-8
900 W Grand Ave 67060 316-554-2251
Dr. Mike Maurer, prin. Fax 554-2258
Other Schools – See Wichita

Healy, Lane
Healy USD 468 100/K-12
5006 N Dodge Rd 67850 620-398-2248
John LaFave, supt. Fax 398-2435
usd468.k12.ks.us
Healy JSHS 100/7-12
5006 N Dodge Rd 67850 620-398-2248
John LaFave, prin. Fax 398-2435

Herington, Dickinson, Pop. 2,468
Herington USD 487 500/PK-12
19 N Broadway 67449 785-258-2263
Scott Carter, supt. Fax 258-2982
www.heringtonschools.org
Herington HS 200/9-12
1401 N D St 67449 785-258-2261
Marlo Klassen, prin. Fax 258-3013
Herington MS 100/6-8
1317 N D St 67449 785-258-2448
Marlo Klassen, prin. Fax 258-3976

Hesston, Harvey, Pop. 3,631
Hesston USD 460 800/K-12
PO Box 2000 67062 620-327-4931
Vern Minor, supt. Fax 327-7157
www.hesstonschools.org
Hesston HS 300/9-12
PO Box 2000 67062 620-327-7122
Larry Thompson, prin. Fax 327-7138
Hesston MS 300/5-8
PO Box 2000 67062 620-327-7111
Randy Linton, prin. Fax 327-7115

Hesston College Post-Sec.
PO Box 3000 67062 620-327-4221

Hiawatha, Brown, Pop. 3,236
Hiawatha USD 415 900/K-12
PO Box 398 66434 785-742-2266
John Severin, supt. Fax 742-2301
www.hiawathaschools.org/
Hiawatha HS 300/9-12
600 Red Hawk Dr 66434 785-742-3312
Rick Johnson, prin. Fax 742-7156
Hiawatha MS 300/5-8
307 S Morrill Ave 66434 785-742-4172
David Coufal, prin. Fax 742-1744

Highland, Doniphan, Pop. 941
Highland USD 425 200/K-12
PO Box 8 66035 785-442-3286
Rex Bollinger, supt. Fax 442-3289
www.doniphanwest.org/
Doniphan West HS 100/9-12
PO Box 8 66035 785-442-3286
Joe Sailors, prin. Fax 442-3289

Highland Community College Post-Sec.
PO Box 68 66035 785-442-6000

Hill City, Graham, Pop. 1,451
Hill City USD 281 400/PK-12
PO Box 309 67642 785-421-2135
Jim Hickel, supt. Fax 421-5657
www.usd281.com/
Hill City HS 100/9-12
PO Box 160 67642 785-421-2117
Bill Goodwin, prin. Fax 421-3029
Longfellow MS 100/5-8
203 N 2nd Ave 67642 785-421-3451
Mike Young, prin. Fax 421-6395

Hillsboro, Marion, Pop. 2,731
Durham-Hillsboro-Lehigh USD 410 700/K-12
812 E A St 67063 620-947-3184
Gordon Mohn, supt. Fax 947-3263
www.usd410.net
Hillsboro HS 300/9-12
500 E Grand Ave 67063 620-947-3991
Dale Honeck, prin. Fax 947-3251
Hillsboro MS 200/6-8
400 E Grand Ave 67063 620-947-3297
Greg Brown, prin. Fax 947-3251

Tabor College Post-Sec.
400 S Jefferson St 67063 620-947-3121

Hoisington, Barton, Pop. 2,996
Hoisington USD 431 600/PK-12
106 N Main St 67544 620-653-4134
Keith Higgins, supt. Fax 653-4073
www.usd431.net/
Hoisington HS 200/9-12
218 E 7th St 67544 620-653-2141
Ben Jacobs, prin. Fax 653-4164
Hoisington MS 100/6-8
360 W 11th St 67544 620-653-4951
Patricia Reinhardt, prin. Fax 653-4483

Holcomb, Finney, Pop. 1,888
Holcomb USD 363 900/PK-12
PO Box 8 67851 620-277-2629
W.S. Landis, supt. Fax 277-2010
users.pld.com/holcomb
Holcomb HS 300/9-12
PO Box 38 67851 620-277-2063
Bill Bierman, prin. Fax 277-0240
Holcomb MS 200/6-8
PO Box 89 67851 620-277-2699
Kristin Ellis, prin. Fax 277-0239

Holton, Jackson, Pop. 3,400
Holton USD 336 1,100/PK-12
PO Box 352 66436 785-364-3650
Dr. Brad Rahe, supt. Fax 364-3975
www.holton.k12.ks.us
Holton HS 300/9-12
901 New York Ave 66436 785-364-2181
Alan Beam, prin. Fax 364-5360
Holton MS 200/6-8
900 Iowa Ave 66436 785-364-2441
Ralph Blevins, prin. Fax 364-5460

North Jackson USD 335 400/PK-12
12692 266th Rd 66436 785-364-2194
Paul Becker, supt. Fax 364-4346
www.jhcobras.net
Jackson Heights HS 100/9-12
12719 266th Rd 66436 785-364-2195
Gary Herman, prin. Fax 364-2487

Hope, Dickinson, Pop. 367
Rural Vista USD 481 400/PK-12
PO Box 217 67451 785-366-7215
Chris Kleidosty, supt. Fax 366-7217
www.usd481.org
Hope HS 100/9-12
PO Box 218 67451 785-366-7221
Ethan Gruen, prin. Fax 366-7115
Other Schools – See White City

Horton, Brown, Pop. 1,843
South Brown County USD 430 700/PK-12
522 Central Ave 66439 785-486-2611
Dr. Steven J. Davies, supt. Fax 486-2496
usd430.k12.ks.us
Horton HS 200/9-12
1120 1st Ave E 66439 785-486-2151
David Norman, prin. Fax 486-2909
Other Schools – See Everest

Howard, Elk, Pop. 764
West Elk USD 282 400/PK-12
PO Box 607 67349 620-374-2113
Bert Moore, supt. Fax 374-2414
Howard West Elk JSHS 200/7-12
PO Box 278 67349 620-374-2147
John Ireland, prin. Fax 374-2414

Hoxie, Sheridan, Pop. 1,149
Hoxie USD 412 300/PK-12
PO Box 348 67740 785-675-3258
Scott Hoyt, supt. Fax 675-2126
www.hoxie.org/
Hoxie JSHS 100/7-12
PO Box 989 67740 785-675-3286
Gary Johnson, prin. Fax 675-2270

Hoyt, Jackson, Pop. 600
Royal Valley USD 337
Supt. — See Mayetta
Royal Valley HS 300/9-12
PO Box 128 66440 785-986-6251
James Holloman, prin. Fax 986-6479

Hugoton, Stevens, Pop. 3,644
Hugoton USD 210 1,100/PK-12
205 E 6th St 67951 620-544-4397
Dr. David Self, supt. Fax 544-7138
www.usd210.org
Hugoton HS 300/9-12
215 W 11th St 67951 620-544-4311
Gardell Schnable, prin. Fax 544-7392
Hugoton MS 200/7-8
115 W 11th St 67951 620-544-4341
Ron Keller, prin. Fax 544-4856

Humboldt, Allen, Pop. 1,921
Humboldt USD 258 500/K-12
801 New York St 66748 620-473-3121
Robert K. Heigele, supt. Fax 473-2023
www.usd258.net
Humboldt HS 200/9-12
1011 Bridge St 66748 620-473-2251
K.B. Criss, prin. Fax 473-2086
Humboldt MS 100/6-8
1105 Bridge St 66748 620-473-3348
K.B. Criss, prin. Fax 473-3141
Humboldt Tech Building Vo/Tech
1116 New York St 66748 620-473-2251
K.B. Criss, prin. Fax 473-2086

Hutchinson, Reno, Pop. 40,961
Buhler USD 313
Supt. — See Buhler
Prairie Hills MS 400/7-8
3200 Lucille Dr 67502 620-662-6052
E. Craig Williams, prin. Fax 694-1002

Hutchinson USD 308 4,700/K-12
PO Box 1908 67504 620-665-4400
Dr. Wynona Winn, supt. Fax 665-4497
www.usd308.com/
Hutchinson HS 1,600/9-12
1401 N Severance St 67501 620-665-4500
Ronn Roehm, prin. Fax 665-4580
Hutchinson MS 8 400/8-8
200 W 14th Ave 67501 620-665-4700
Mike Ellegood, prin. Fax 665-4703

Nickerson USD 309 1,100/K-12
4501 W 4th Ave 67501 620-663-7141
Jerry Burch, supt. Fax 663-7148
www.usd309ks.org
Reno Valley MS 200/7-8
1616 Wilshire Dr 67501 620-662-4573
Julie Wilson, prin. Fax 662-6708
Other Schools – See Nickerson

Central Christian S 300/PK-12
1910 E 30th Ave 67502 620-663-2174
Kenneth Anderson, admin. Fax 663-2176
Hutchinson Community College Post-Sec.
1300 N Plum St 67501 620-665-3500
Sidney's Hairdressing College Post-Sec.
916 E 4th Ave 67501 620-662-5481
Trinity HS 300/7-12
1400 E 17th Ave 67501 620-662-5800
Brian Cordel, prin. Fax 662-1233

Independence, Montgomery, Pop. 9,284
Independence USD 446 2,000/K-12
PO Box 487 67301 620-332-1800
Chuck Schmidt, supt. Fax 332-1811
www.indyschools.com
Independence HS 700/9-12
1301 N 10th St 67301 620-332-1815
Mitch Shaw, prin. Fax 332-1831
Independence MS 400/6-8
300 W Locust St 67301 620-332-1836
Patty Clay, prin. Fax 332-1841

Independence Bible S 100/PK-12
2246 S 10th St 67301 620-331-3780
Matthew Brewer, prin. Fax 331-3780
Independence Community College Post-Sec.
PO Box 708 67301 620-331-4100

Ingalls, Gray, Pop. 312
Ingalls USD 477 300/PK-12
PO Box 99 67853 620-335-5136
Dave Novack, supt. Fax 335-5678
www.ingallsusd477.com/
Ingalls JSHS 100/7-12
PO Box 99 67853 620-335-5135
Jarrod Stoppel, prin. Fax 335-5678

Inman, McPherson, Pop. 1,194
Inman USD 448 400/PK-12
PO Box 129 67546 620-585-6424
Kevin Case, supt. Fax 585-2689
Inman JSHS 200/7-12
PO Box 279 67546 620-585-6441
Scott Friesen, prin. Fax 585-2797

Iola, Allen, Pop. 6,008
Iola USD 257 1,500/PK-12
408 N Cottonwood St 66749 620-365-4700
Dr. Craig Neuenswander, supt. Fax 365-4708
www.usd257.org
Iola HS 500/9-12
300 E Jackson Ave 66749 620-365-4715
David South, prin. Fax 365-4730
Iola MS 300/6-8
600 East St 66749 620-365-4785
Jack Stanley, prin. Fax 365-4770

Allen County Community College Post-Sec.
1801 N Cottonwood St 66749 620-365-5116

Jetmore, Hodgeman, Pop. 914
Jetmore USD 227 300/PK-12
PO Box 100 67854 620-357-8301
Dr. Jim Barrett, supt. Fax 357-6563
www.jetmorek12.org/
Jetmore HS 100/9-12
PO Box 100 67854 620-357-8378
Robert Haug, prin. Fax 357-6563

Jewell, Jewell, Pop. 439
Jewell USD 279
Supt. — See Randall
Jewell HS 100/9-12
PO Box 20 66949 785-428-3233
Robert Turner, prin. Fax 428-3602
Jewell JHS 50/6-8
PO Box 20 66949 785-428-3233
Robert Turner, prin. Fax 428-3602

Johnson, Stanton, Pop. 1,314
Stanton County USD 452 500/PK-12
PO Box C 67855 620-492-6226
Susan Scherling, supt. Fax 492-1326
www.usd452.org
Stanton County HS 200/9-12
PO Box C 67855 620-492-6284
Mark LaTurner, prin. Fax 492-1326
Stanton County MS 100/6-8
PO Box C 67855 620-492-2223
Matt Berens, prin. Fax 492-1375

Junction City, Geary, Pop. 16,402
Geary County USD 475 6,400/PK-12
PO Box 370 66441 785-717-4000
Ronald Walker, supt. Fax 717-4003
www.usd475.org/
Junction City HS 1,600/9-12
900 N Eisenhower Dr 66441 785-717-4200
Stanley Dodds, prin. Fax 717-4201
Junction City MS 800/6-8
300 W 9th St 66441 785-717-4400
Ferrell Miller, prin. Fax 717-4401
Other Schools – See Fort Riley

Barton County Community College Post-Sec.
540 Grant Ave 66441 785-238-8550
St. Xaviers S 100/K-12
200 N Washington St 66441 785-238-2841
Lori Balderrama, prin. Fax 238-5021

Kanopolis, Ellsworth, Pop. 516
Ellsworth USD 327
Supt. — See Ellsworth
Kanopolis MS 100/6-8
PO Box 37 67454 785-472-4477
Ken Cravens, prin. Fax 472-4068

Kansas City, Wyandotte, Pop. 144,210
Kansas City USD 500 19,800/PK-12
625 Minnesota Ave 66101 913-551-3200
Dr. Jill Shackelford, supt. Fax 551-3217
www.kckps.org
Area Technical S Vo/Tech
2220 N 59th St 66104 913-627-4100
Barbara Schilling, prin. Fax 596-5509
Argentine MS 700/6-8
2123 Ruby Ave 66106 913-627-6750
Jereme Brueggeman, prin. Fax 627-6783
Arrowhead MS 400/6-8
1715 N 82nd St 66112 913-627-6600
Laurie Boyd, prin. Fax 627-6654
Central MS 700/6-8
925 Ivandale St 66101 913-627-6150
Kris Ludwig, prin. Fax 627-6152
Coronado MS 400/6-8
1735 N 64th Ter 66102 913-627-6300
Dr. Judi Duff, prin. Fax 627-6358
Eisenhower MS 700/6-8
2901 N 72nd St 66109 913-627-6450
Freda Ogburn, prin. Fax 627-6455
Harmon HS 1,300/9-12
2400 Steele Rd 66106 913-627-7050
Roel Quintanilla, prin. Fax 627-7185
Northwest MS 600/6-8
2400 N 18th St 66104 913-627-4000
Earl Williams, prin. Fax 627-4052
Rosedale MS 600/6-8
3600 Springfield St 66103 913-627-6900
Connie Horner, prin. Fax 627-6957
Schlagle HS 1,000/9-12
2214 N 59th St 66104 913-627-7500
Douglas Bolden, prin. Fax 627-7555
Sumner Academy/Arts & Sciences 1,000/8-12
1610 N 8th St 66101 913-627-7200
Mary Viveros, prin. Fax 627-7205
Washington HS 1,100/9-12
7340 Leavenworth Rd 66109 913-627-7800
Greg Netzer, prin. Fax 627-7850
West MS 500/6-8
2600 N 44th St 66104 913-627-6000
Shelly Beech, prin. Fax 627-6053
Wyandotte HS 1,100/9-12
2501 Minnesota Ave 66102 913-627-7650
Walter Thompson, prin. Fax 627-7700

Piper-Kansas City USD 203 1,400/PK-12
12036 Leavenworth Rd 66109 913-721-2088
Steve Adams, supt. Fax 721-3573
www.piperschools.com/
Piper HS 400/9-12
4400 N 107th St 66109 913-721-2100
Dr. Bob Runnebaum, prin. Fax 721-3867
Piper MS 300/6-8
4420 N 107th St 66109 913-721-1144
Laurence Breedlove, prin. Fax 721-1526

Turner USD 202 3,700/PK-12
800 S 55th St 66106 913-288-4100
Bobby Allen, supt. Fax 288-3401
www.turnerusd202.org/
Turner HS 1,100/9-12
2211 S 55th St 66106 913-288-3300
Michelle Sedler, prin. Fax 288-3301
Turner MS 600/7-8
1312 S 55th St 66106 913-288-4000
William Hatfield, prin. Fax 288-4001

Bishop Ward HS 500/9-12
708 N 18th St 66102 913-371-1201
Dennis Dorr, prin. Fax 371-2145
Cutting Edge Hairstyling Academy Post-Sec.
4327 State Ave 66102 913-321-0214
Donnelly College Post-Sec.
608 N 18th St 66102 913-621-8724
Kansas City Christian MS 100/7-8
5500 Woodend Ave 66106 913-722-9955
Kathy Hirleman, prin. Fax 236-5996
Kansas City Kansas Community College Post-Sec.
7250 State Ave 66112 913-334-1100
Kansas State School for the Blind Post-Sec.
1100 State Ave 66102 913-281-3308
Muncie Christian S 100/K-12
3650 N 67th St 66104 913-299-9884
Rex Vincent, admin. Fax 299-9884
St. John Holy Family MS 6-8
515 Ohio Ave 66101 913-371-3923
Jennifer Sears, prin. Fax 321-5001
University of Kansas Medical Center Post-Sec.
3901 Rainbow Blvd 66160 913-588-5000

Kensington, Smith, Pop. 490
West Smith County USD 238 200/K-12
PO Box 188 66951 785-476-2218
Jeff Yoxall, supt. Fax 476-2258
goldbugcountry.com/
Kensington JSHS 100/7-12
PO Box 188 66951 785-476-2217
Todd Bowman, prin. Fax 476-2210

Kingman, Kingman, Pop. 3,183
Kingman-Norwich USD 331 1,100/PK-12
PO Box 416 67068 620-532-3134
Don L. Mason, supt. Fax 532-3251
www.knusd331.com/
Kingman HS 300/9-12
260 W Kansas Ave 67068 620-532-3136
Rick Henry, prin. Fax 532-3027
Other Schools – See Norwich

Kinsley, Edwards, Pop. 1,547
Kinsley-Offerle USD 347 300/K-12
120 W 8th St 67547 620-659-3646
James Garner, supt. Fax 659-2669
www.kinsleypublicschools.org/
Kinsley-Offerle JSHS 200/7-12
716 Colony Ave 67547 620-659-2126
Kevin Logan, prin. Fax 659-2180

Kiowa, Barber, Pop. 965
South Barber County USD 255 300/K-12
512 Main St 67070 620-825-4115
Bob Hightree, supt. Fax 825-4145
South Barber HS 100/9-12
1220 N 8th St 67070 620-825-4214
Monty Thompson, prin. Fax 825-4250

Kirwin, Phillips, Pop. 214
Eastern Heights USD 324 100/K-12
PO Box 145 67644 785-543-6771
Beth Norris, supt. Fax 543-3023
www.usd324.org
Other Schools – See Agra

Kismet, Seward, Pop. 521
Kismet-Plains USD 483 600/PK-12
RR 1 Box 24A 67859 620-563-7103
Elton Argo, supt. Fax 563-7348
www.usd483.net
Southwestern Heights JSHS 300/6-12
23456 US Highway 54 67859 620-563-7292
Dan Frisby, prin. Fax 563-7383

La Crosse, Rush, Pop. 1,305
La Crosse USD 395 300/K-12
PO Box 778 67548 785-222-2505
Bill Keeley, supt. Fax 222-3240
La Crosse HS 100/9-12
PO Box 810 67548 785-222-2528
Kathy Keeley, prin. Fax 222-3480
La Crosse MS 100/7-8
PO Box 810 67548 785-222-3030
Kathy Keeley, prin. Fax 222-3480

La Cygne, Linn, Pop. 1,146
Prairie View USD 362 1,100/PK-12
13799 KS Highway 152 66040 913-757-2677
Dr. Jim Day, supt. Fax 757-4442
www.pv362.org
Prairie View HS 300/9-12
13731 KS Highway 152 66040 913-757-4447
Alan Jeffery, prin. Fax 757-4443
Prairie View MS 200/6-8
13667 KS Highway 152 66040 913-757-4447
Lee Jones, prin. Fax 757-4443

Lakin, Kearny, Pop. 2,292
Lakin USD 215 700/PK-12
1003 W Kingman Ave 67860 620-355-6761
Randall Steinle, supt. Fax 355-7317
Lakin HS 200/9-12
407 N Campbell St 67860 620-355-6411
Ron Overeem, prin. Fax 355-7250
Lakin MS 200/5-8
1201 W Kingman Ave 67860 620-355-6973
Tammie Huggard, prin. Fax 355-8313

Langdon, Reno, Pop. 72
Fairfield USD 310 400/K-12
16115 S Langdon Rd 67583 620-596-2152
Dr. Fred Marten, supt. Fax 596-2835
www.usd310.org
Fairfield HS 100/9-12
16115 S Langdon Rd 67583 620-596-2481
Thomas Flax, prin. Fax 596-2835
Fairfield MS 100/6-8
16115 S Langdon Rd 67583 620-596-2615
Thomas Flax, prin. Fax 596-2835

Lansing, Leavenworth, Pop. 10,214
Lansing USD 469 2,000/PK-12
613 Holiday Plz 66043 913-727-1100
Dr. Randal Bagby, supt. Fax 727-1619
www.usd469.net/
Lansing HS 700/9-12
220 Lion Ln 66043 913-727-3357
Steve Dike, prin. Fax 727-2001
Lansing MS 500/6-8
509 Ida St 66043 913-727-1197
Kerry Brungardt, prin. Fax 727-1349

Larned, Pawnee, Pop. 3,874
Ft. Larned USD 495 900/PK-12
120 E 6th St 67550 620-285-3185
Jon Flint, supt. Fax 285-2973
www.usd495.net
Larned HS 300/9-12
815 Corse Ave 67550 620-285-2151
Rick Simmoncic, prin. Fax 285-7148
Larned MS 300/5-8
904 Corse Ave 67550 620-285-8430
Jim Krohn, prin. Fax 285-8433

Lawrence, Douglas, Pop. 81,816
Lawrence USD 497 10,000/PK-12
110 McDonald Dr 66044 785-832-5000
Randy Weseman, supt. Fax 832-5016
www.usd497.org
Lawrence Central JHS 500/7-9
1400 Massachusetts St 66044 785-832-5400
Frank Harwood, prin. Fax 832-5403
Lawrence Free State HS 1,200/10-12
4700 Overland Dr 66049 785-832-6050
Joe Snyder, prin. Fax 832-6099
Lawrence HS 1,300/10-12
1901 Louisiana St 66046 785-832-5050
Steven Nilhas, prin. Fax 832-5054
Lawrence South JHS 600/7-9
2734 Louisiana St 66046 785-832-5450
Will Fernandez, prin. Fax 832-5453
Lawrence Southwest JHS 700/7-9
2511 Inverness Dr 66047 785-832-5550
Trish Bransky, prin. Fax 832-5554
Lawrence West JHS 600/7-9
2700 Harvard Rd 66049 785-832-5500
Myron Melton, prin. Fax 832-5504

Bishop Seabury Academy 100/7-12
4120 Clinton Pkwy 66047 785-832-1717
Christopher Carter, hdmstr. Fax 832-1919
Haskell Indian Nations University Post-Sec.
155 Indian Ave Rm 1305 66046 785-749-8404
Pinnacle Career Institute Post-Sec.
1601 W 23rd St Ste 200 66046 800-360-9640
University of Kansas 66045 Post-Sec.
785-864-2700

Veritas Christian S — 100/K-12
256 N Michigan St 66044 — 785-749-0083
Dr. Jeffrey L. Barclay, admin. — Fax 749-0580

Leavenworth, Leavenworth, Pop. 35,213
Leavenworth USD 453 — 4,000/PK-12
PO Box 969 66048 — 913-684-1400
Dr. Mike Aytes, supt. — Fax 684-1407
www.lvksch.org/
Leavenworth HS — 1,500/9-12
2012 10th Ave 66048 — 913-684-1550
John Parker, prin. — Fax 684-1555
Leavenworth West MS — 400/6-8
1901 Spruce St 66048 — 913-684-1520
Deborah Lauxman, prin. — Fax 684-1523
Warren MS — 500/6-8
PO Box 7 66048 — 913-684-1530
Jack Prall, prin. — Fax 684-1539

Crossroads Christian Academy — 50/4-8
PO Box 553 66048 — 913-680-1411
Susy Winfrey, admin. — Fax 680-1411
Immaculata HS — 200/9-12
600 Shawnee St 66048 — 913-682-3900
Mike Connelly, prin. — Fax 682-9036
University of Saint Mary — Post-Sec.
4100 S 4th St 66048 — 913-682-5151
Xavier S — 7-8
721 Osage St 66048 — 913-682-3135
Ann Connor, prin. — Fax 682-5262

Leawood, Johnson, Pop. 30,145
Blue Valley USD 229
Supt. — See Overland Park
Leawood MS — 500/6-8
2410 W 123rd St 66209 — 913-239-5300
Marcia Bone Ed.D., prin. — Fax 345-7418
Prairie Star MS — 500/6-8
14201 Mission Rd 66224 — 913-239-5600
Lyn Rantz Ed.D., prin. — Fax 685-7620

Lebo, Coffey, Pop. 950
Lebo-Waverly USD 243
Supt. — See Waverly
Lebo HS — 200/7-12
PO Box 45 66856 — 620-256-6341
Todd Barker, prin. — Fax 256-6342

Lenexa, Johnson, Pop. 43,434

Brown Mackie College — Post-Sec.
9705 Lenexa Dr 66215 — 913-768-1900
St. James Academy — 9-12
24505 Prairie Star Pkwy 66227 — 913-254-4200
Barbara Burgoon, prin. — Fax 254-4221

Leon, Butler, Pop. 648
Bluestem USD 205 — 700/PK-12
PO Box 8 67074 — 316-742-3261
Dennis Engels, supt. — Fax 742-9265
www.usd205.com
Bluestem HS — 200/9-12
PO Box 338 67074 — 316-742-3281
Neal Weltha, prin. — Fax 742-3813
Bluestem MS — 100/7-8
625 S Mill Rd 67074 — 316-742-3263
David Kohls, prin. — Fax 742-3748

Leoti, Wichita, Pop. 1,440
Leoti USD 467 — 500/PK-12
PO Box 967 67861 — 620-375-4677
Gary Akers, supt. — Fax 375-2304
www.leoti.org/
Wichita County HS — 100/9-12
800 W Broadway 67861 — 620-375-2213
Dan Walker, prin. — Fax 375-4958
Wichita County JHS — 100/6-8
PO Box 908 67861 — 620-375-2219
Dr. Lee Tarrant, prin. — Fax 375-2352

Le Roy, Coffey, Pop. 579
Le Roy-Gridley USD 245 — 300/PK-12
PO Box 278 66857 — 620-964-2212
Mike Kastle, supt. — Fax 964-2413
Southern Coffey County HS — 100/9-12
PO Box 188 66857 — 620-964-2217
Mike Kastle, prin. — Fax 964-2410
Other Schools – See Gridley

Liberal, Seward, Pop. 20,257
Liberal USD 480 — 4,500/PK-12
PO Box 949 67905 — 620-604-1010
Vernon Welch, supt. — Fax 604-1011
www.usd480.net/
Liberal HS — 1,100/9-12
1611 W 2nd St 67901 — 620-604-1200
Keith Adams, prin. — Fax 604-1201
Liberal South MS — 300/7-8
950 S Grant Ave 67901 — 620-604-1300
Brandon Hyde, prin. — Fax 604-1301
Liberal West MS — 300/7-8
500 N Western Ave 67901 — 620-604-1400
Khris Thexton, prin. — Fax 604-1501

Seward County Community College — Post-Sec.
PO Box 1137 67905 — 620-624-1951
Southwest Kansas Technical School — Post-Sec.
PO Box 1599 67905 — 620-626-3819

Lincoln, Lincoln, Pop. 1,289
Lincoln USD 298 — 400/PK-12
PO Box 289 67455 — 785-524-4436
Terry Stratman, supt. — Fax 524-3080
www.usd298.com
Lincoln JSHS — 200/7-12
PO Box 269 67455 — 785-524-4193
S. Allen Konicek, prin. — Fax 524-5114

Lindsborg, McPherson, Pop. 3,305
Smoky Valley USD 400 — 1,000/K-12
126 S Main St 67456 — 785-227-2981
Glen Suppes, supt. — Fax 227-2982
www.smokyvalley.org/
Lindsborg MS — 300/5-8
401 N Cedar St 67456 — 785-227-4249
John Denk, prin. — Fax 227-3650
Smoky Valley HS — 300/9-12
1 Viking Blvd 67456 — 785-227-2909
Marc Williams, prin. — Fax 227-2900

Bethany College — Post-Sec.
421 N 1st St 67456 — 785-227-3311

Linn, Washington, Pop. 388
Barnes USD 223
Supt. — See Barnes
Linn HS — 100/9-12
300 Parkview St 66953 — 785-348-5531
Mike Savage, prin. — Fax 348-5534

Linwood, Leavenworth, Pop. 382
Basehor-Linwood USD 458
Supt. — See Basehor
Basehor-Linwood MS — 300/7-8
PO Box 1 66052 — 913-724-2323
Michael Boyd, prin.

Little River, Rice, Pop. 528
Little River USD 444 — 300/PK-12
PO Box 218 67457 — 620-897-6325
Milt Dougherty, supt. — Fax 897-6788
www.usd444.com/
Little River HS — 100/9-12
PO Box 8 67457 — 620-897-6201
Dawn Johnson, prin. — Fax 897-6203
Little River JHS — 100/6-8
PO Box 8 67457 — 620-897-6201
Dawn Johnson, prin. — Fax 897-6203

Logan, Phillips, Pop. 549
Logan USD 326 — 200/K-12
PO Box 98 67646 — 785-689-7595
Robert Jackson, supt. — Fax 689-7517
www.usd326.k12.ks.us/
Logan HS — 100/7-12
PO Box 98 67646 — 785-689-7574
Robert Jackson, prin. — Fax 689-7543

Long Island, Phillips, Pop. 145
Northern Valley USD 212
Supt. — See Almena
Long Island MS — 100/5-8
PO Box 98 67647 — 785-854-7681
Roger Lowry, prin. — Fax 854-7684

Longton, Elk, Pop. 371
Elk Valley USD 283 — 200/PK-12
PO Box 87 67352 — 620-642-2811
Art Haibon, supt. — Fax 642-6551
www.usd283.org
Elk Valley HS — 100/6-12
PO Box 87 67352 — 620-642-2215
Art Haibon, prin. — Fax 642-3361

Lorraine, Ellsworth, Pop. 133
Lorraine USD 328 — 400/PK-12
PO Box 109 67459 — 785-472-5241
Roger Robinson, supt. — Fax 472-5229
www.usd328.org
Other Schools – See Bushton, Wilson

Lost Springs, Marion, Pop. 68
Centre USD 397 — 300/PK-12
PO Box 38 66859 — 785-983-4304
Robert Kiblinger, supt. — Fax 983-4352
www.centreschools.com
Centre JSHS — 100/7-12
2374 310th St 66859 — 785-983-4321
Robert Kiblinger, prin. — Fax 983-4377

Louisburg, Miami, Pop. 3,313
Louisburg USD 416 — 1,400/PK-12
PO Box 550 66053 — 913-837-2944
Dr. Rick Doll, supt. — Fax 837-5808
www.usd416.org
Louisburg HS — 500/9-12
PO Box 399 66053 — 913-837-2941
Sally Lundblad, prin. — Fax 837-5774
Louisburg MS — 300/6-8
PO Box 308 66053 — 913-837-1351
Charles Golladay, prin. — Fax 837-1361

Lucas, Russell, Pop. 422
Russell County USD 407
Supt. — See Russell
Lucas-Luray HS — 50/9-12
130 N Greeley Ave 67648 — 785-525-6244
Larry Geist, prin. — Fax 525-6245

Lyndon, Osage, Pop. 1,041
Lyndon USD 421 — 400/PK-12
PO Box 488 66451 — 785-828-4413
Brian Spencer, supt. — Fax 828-3686
Lyndon HS — 200/9-12
PO Box 488 66451 — 785-828-4911
Brad Marcotte, prin. — Fax 828-4221

Lyons, Rice, Pop. 3,554
Lyons USD 405 — 800/PK-12
800 S Workman St 67554 — 620-257-5196
Darrel Kellerman, supt. — Fax 257-5197
www.usd405.com
Lyons HS — 300/9-12
601 E American Rd 67554 — 620-257-5114
Gary Sechrist, prin. — Fax 257-3194
Lyons MS — 200/6-8
401 S Douglas Ave 67554 — 620-257-3961
Glenn Fortmayer, prin. — Fax 257-3518

Macksville, Stafford, Pop. 494
Macksville USD 351 — 300/PK-12
PO Box 487 67557 — 620-348-3415
Mike Harvey, supt. — Fax 348-3217
www.usd351.com
Macksville HS — 100/9-12
PO Box 307 67557 — 620-348-2475
Jason May, prin. — Fax 348-2637

Mc Louth, Jefferson, Pop. 785
Mc Louth USD 342 — 600/K-12
PO Box 40 66054 — 913-796-2201
Jean Rush, supt. — Fax 796-6440
www.mclouth.org
Mc Louth HS — 200/9-12
PO Box 40 66054 — 913-796-6122
John Hamon, prin. — Fax 796-6124
Mc Louth MS — 100/6-8
PO Box 40 66054 — 913-796-6122
John Hamon, prin. — Fax 796-6124

Mc Pherson, McPherson, Pop. 12,746
Mc Pherson USD 418 — 2,500/PK-12
514 N Main St 67460 — 620-241-9400
Dr. Randy Watson, supt. — Fax 241-9410
www.mcpherson.com/418
Mc Pherson HS — 900/9-12
801 E 1st St 67460 — 620-241-9500
Lew Faust, prin. — Fax 241-9506
Mc Pherson MS — 500/6-8
700 E Elizabeth St 67460 — 620-241-9450
John Thissen, prin. — Fax 241-9456

Central Christian College of Kansas — Post-Sec.
PO Box 1403 67460 — 620-241-0723
Elyria Christian S — 200/K-12
1644 Comanche Rd 67460 — 620-241-2994
Richard Roberts, admin. — Fax 241-1238
McPherson College — Post-Sec.
PO Box 1402 67460 — 620-241-0731

Madison, Greenwood, Pop. 799
Madison-Virgil USD 386 — 200/PK-12
PO Box 398 66860 — 620-437-2910
Darrel Finch, supt. — Fax 437-2916
www.usd386.org/
Madison HS — 100/7-12
PO Box 398 66860 — 620-437-2912
Darrel Finch, prin. — Fax 437-2911

Maize, Sedgwick, Pop. 2,117
Maize USD 266 — 5,500/PK-12
201 S Park St 67101 — 316-722-0614
Dr. Craig Elliott, supt. — Fax 722-8538
www.usd266.com
Maize HS — 1,800/9-12
11600 W 45th St N 67101 — 316-722-0441
Mike Bonner, prin. — Fax 722-6214
Maize MS — 500/6-8
4600 N Maize Rd 67101 — 316-729-2464
Jeannine Pfannenstiel, prin. — Fax 729-2479
Other Schools – See Wichita

Manhattan, Riley, Pop. 48,668
Manhattan-Ogden USD 383 — 5,000/PK-12
2031 Poyntz Ave 66502 — 785-587-2000
Dr. Robert Shannon, supt. — Fax 587-2006
www.usd383.org
Anthony MS — 400/7-8
2501 Browning Ave 66502 — 785-587-2890
Vickie Kline, prin. — Fax 587-2899
Eisenhower MS — 400/7-8
800 Walters Dr 66502 — 785-587-2880
Greg Hoyt, prin. — Fax 587-2888
Manhattan HS West/East Campus — 1,800/9-12
2100 Poyntz Ave 66502 — 785-587-2100
Terry McCarty, prin. — Fax 587-2132

American Institute of Baking — Post-Sec.
PO Box 3999 66505 — 785-537-4750
Crum's Beauty College — Post-Sec.
512 Poyntz Ave 66502 — 785-776-4794
Flint Hills Christian S — 200/PK-12
3905 Green Valley Rd 66502 — 785-776-2223
Frank Leone, admin. — Fax 776-3016
Kansas State University 66506 — Post-Sec.
785-532-6250
Manhattan Christian College — Post-Sec.
1415 Anderson Ave 66502 — 785-539-3571

Mankato, Jewell, Pop. 843
Rock Hills USD 107 — 200/PK-12
301 N West St 66956 — 785-378-3102
William Walker, supt. — Fax 378-3438
www.usd107.org/
Rock Hills HS — 100/9-12
301 N West St 66956 — 785-378-3126
Allen Walter, prin. — Fax 378-3530
Other Schools – See Burr Oak

Marion, Marion, Pop. 2,028
Marion-Florence USD 408 — 700/K-12
101 N Thorp St 66861 — 620-382-2117
Lee Leiker, supt. — Fax 382-2118
www.usd408.com
Marion HS — 200/9-12
701 E Main St 66861 — 620-382-2168
Ken Arnhold, prin. — Fax 382-6021
Marion MS — 100/7-8
125 S Lincoln St 66861 — 620-382-6070
Tod Gordon, prin. — Fax 382-6073

Marysville, Marshall, Pop. 3,151
Marysville USD 364 — 700/PK-12
211 S 10th St 66508 — 785-562-5308
Doug Powers, supt. — Fax 562-5309
www.marysvilleschools.org

Marysville HS — 300/9-12
1111 Walnut St 66508 — 785-562-5386
John Waugh, prin. — Fax 562-5390
Marysville JHS — 7-8
1005 Walnut St 66508 — 785-562-5356
Cindy Scarbrough, prin. — Fax 562-5390

Mayetta, Jackson, Pop. 359
Royal Valley USD 337 — 900/PK-12
PO Box 219 66509 — 785-966-2246
John Rundle, supt. — Fax 966-2490
www.rv337.com/
Royal Valley MS — 300/5-8
PO Box 189 66509 — 785-966-2251
Dr. Don DeKeyser, prin. — Fax 966-2833
Other Schools – See Hoyt

Meade, Meade, Pop. 1,629
Meade USD 226 — 500/PK-12
PO Box 400 67864 — 620-873-2081
Robert Herbig, supt. — Fax 873-2201
meade.ks.schoolwebpages.com/
Meade HS — 100/9-12
PO Box 400 67864 — 620-873-2981
Jack Pavlovich, prin. — Fax 873-2201

Medicine Lodge, Barber, Pop. 2,028
Barber County North USD 254 — 600/PK-12
PO Box 288 67104 — 620-886-3370
Suzanne Germes, supt. — Fax 886-3640
www.usd254.org/
Medicine Lodge HS — 200/9-12
400 W Eldorado Ave 67104 — 620-886-5667
Mike Hubka, prin. — Fax 886-3053
Medicine Lodge MS — 100/6-8
100 BH Born Blvd 67104 — 620-886-5644
Mark Buck, prin. — Fax 886-3082

Melvern, Osage, Pop. 430
Marais Des Cygnes Valley USD 456 — 200/K-12
PO Box 158 66510 — 785-549-3521
Ted Vannocker, supt. — Fax 549-3659
www.usd456.org
Marais Des Cygnes Valley HS — 100/9-12
PO Box 158 66510 — 785-549-3313
Ted Vannocker, prin. — Fax 549-3576
Marais Des Cygnes Valley MS — 100/6-8
PO Box 158 66510 — 785-549-3313
Steve Burkdoll, prin. — Fax 549-3576

Meriden, Jefferson, Pop. 708
Jefferson West USD 340 — 1,000/PK-12
PO Box 267 66512 — 785-484-3444
Scott Myers, supt. — Fax 484-3148
www.usd340.org
Jefferson West HS — 400/9-12
PO Box 268 66512 — 785-484-3331
Ed West, prin. — Fax 484-2021
Jefferson West MS — 200/6-8
PO Box 410 66512 — 785-484-2900
William Scott, prin. — Fax 484-2904

Miltonvale, Cloud, Pop. 486
Southern Cloud USD 334
Supt. — See Glasco
Miltonvale HS — 100/7-12
PO Box 394 67466 — 785-427-3250
Roger Perkins, prin. — Fax 427-3181

Minneapolis, Ottawa, Pop. 2,015
North Ottawa County USD 239 — 600/K-12
PO Box 257 67467 — 785-392-2167
Dr. Larry Combs, supt. — Fax 392-3038
www.usd239.org/
Minneapolis JSHS — 300/7-12
PO Box 317 67467 — 785-392-2113
Brad Reed, prin. — Fax 392-2275

Minneola, Clark, Pop. 681
Minneola USD 219 — 300/K-12
PO Box 157 67865 — 620-885-4372
Mark Walker, supt. — Fax 885-4509
Minneola HS — 100/9-12
PO Box 157 67865 — 620-885-4611
Steve Meneley, prin. — Fax 885-4509

Montezuma, Gray, Pop. 964
Montezuma USD 371 — 200/PK-12
PO Box 355 67867 — 620-846-2293
Dr. Donald Grover, supt. — Fax 846-2294
sghs.musd371.k12.ks.us/
South Gray HS — 100/9-12
PO Box 355 67867 — 620-846-2281
Tim Skinner, prin. — Fax 846-2181

Moran, Allen, Pop. 541
Marmaton Valley USD 256 — 400/K-12
128 W Oak St 66755 — 620-237-4250
Nancy Meyer, supt. — Fax 237-8872
www.usd256.org
Marmaton Valley HS — 200/7-12
128 W Oak St 66755 — 620-237-4251
Maurice Strecker, prin. — Fax 237-4576

Moscow, Stevens, Pop. 251
Moscow USD 209 — 200/K-12
PO Box 158 67952 — 620-598-2205
Larry Philippi, supt. — Fax 598-2233
moscowschools.us/
Moscow HS — 100/6-12
PO Box 160 67952 — 620-598-2250
Stuart Moore, prin. — Fax 598-2233

Mound City, Linn, Pop. 820
Jayhawk USD 346 — 500/PK-12
PO Box 278 66056 — 913-795-2247
Royce Powelson, supt. — Fax 795-2185
www.usd346.k12.ks.us/
Jayhawk-Linn JSHS — 300/7-12
PO Box D 66056 — 913-795-2224
Danny Brown, prin. — Fax 795-2406

Moundridge, McPherson, Pop. 1,643
Moundridge USD 423 — 400/K-12
PO Box K 67107 — 620-345-8611
Rustin Clark, supt. — Fax 345-8617
www.usd423.org
Moundridge HS — 100/9-12
PO Box 610 67107 — 620-345-2816
Clark Wedel, prin. — Fax 345-5218
Moundridge MS — 100/5-8
PO Box 607 67107 — 620-345-2826
Vance Unrau, prin. — Fax 345-5307

Mullinville, Kiowa, Pop. 258
Mullinville USD 424 — 100/PK-8
PO Box 6 67109 — 620-548-2521
John Jones, supt. — Fax 548-2515
www.mullinville.org
Mullinville JHS — 50/7-8
PO Box 6 67109 — 620-548-2217
John Jones, prin. — Fax 548-2278

Mulvane, Sedgwick, Pop. 5,628
Mulvane USD 263 — 1,600/PK-12
PO Box 130 67110 — 316-777-1102
Donna Augustine-Shaw, supt. — Fax 777-1103
www.usd263.com
Mulvane HS — 600/9-12
1900 N Rock Rd 67110 — 316-777-1183
Steve Rader, prin. — Fax 777-2228
Mulvane MS — 300/6-8
915 Westview Dr 67110 — 316-777-2022
Traci Becker, prin. — Fax 777-4967

Natoma, Osborne, Pop. 329
Paradise USD 399 — 200/PK-12
PO Box 100 67651 — 785-885-4478
Aaron Homburg, supt. — Fax 885-4523
www.usd399.com/
Natoma HS — 100/7-12
PO Box 100 67651 — 785-885-4849
Titus Staples, prin. — Fax 885-4523
Paradise JHS — 7-8
PO Box 10 67651 — 785-885-4849
Titus Staples, prin. — Fax 885-4523

Neodesha, Wilson, Pop. 2,652
Neodesha USD 461 — 800/PK-12
PO Box 88 66757 — 620-325-2610
Daryl Pruter, supt. — Fax 325-2368
www.neodesha.com/neodesha/district.html
Neodesha JSHS — 400/7-12
1000 N 8th St 66757 — 620-325-3015
Terence Wilson, prin. — Fax 325-2382

Ness City, Ness, Pop. 1,326
Ness City USD 303 — 300/PK-12
414 E Chestnut St 67560 — 785-798-2210
Randall Jansonius, supt. — Fax 798-3581
www.nesscityschools.org
Ness City JSHS — 100/7-12
200 N 5th St 67560 — 785-798-3991
George Staten, prin. — Fax 798-3064

Newton, Harvey, Pop. 18,229
Newton USD 373 — 3,600/PK-12
308 E 1st St 67114 — 316-284-6200
Dr. John Morton, supt. — Fax 284-6207
www.newton.k12.ks.us
Chisholm MS — 400/6-8
900 E 1st St 67114 — 316-284-6260
Cesar Pena, prin. — Fax 284-6267
Newton HS — 1,100/9-12
900 W 12th St 67114 — 316-284-6280
Ken Rickard, prin. — Fax 284-6288
Santa Fe MS — 400/6-8
130 W Broadway St 67114 — 316-284-6270
Victoria Adame, prin. — Fax 284-6596

Newton Christian HS — 50/9-12
224 NW 60th St 67114 — 316-283-3858
Roger Ericksten, prin. — Fax 283-3858

Nickerson, Reno, Pop. 1,164
Nickerson USD 309
Supt. — See Hutchinson
Nickerson HS — 300/9-12
305 S Nickerson St 67561 — 620-422-3215
Kevin Abbott, prin. — Fax 422-3229

North Newton, McPherson, Pop. 1,574

Bethel College — Post-Sec.
300 E 27th St 67117 — 316-283-2500

Norton, Norton, Pop. 2,806
Norton USD 211 — 700/PK-12
105 E Waverly St 67654 — 785-877-3386
Greg Mann, supt. — Fax 877-2030
Norton Community HS — 200/9-12
513 W Wilberforce St 67654 — 785-877-3338
Rudy Perez, prin. — Fax 877-6940
Norton JHS — 100/7-8
706 Jones Ave 67654 — 785-877-5851
Larry Mills, prin. — Fax 877-3771

Nortonville, Jefferson, Pop. 598
Jefferson County North USD 339
Supt. — See Winchester
Jefferson County North MS — 100/6-8
100 Charger Ln 66060 — 913-886-3870
Gary Bedigrew, prin. — Fax 886-6280

Norwich, Kingman, Pop. 522
Kingman-Norwich USD 331
Supt. — See Kingman
Norwich HS — 100/9-12
209 Parkway St 67118 — 620-478-2235
Lanny Hower, prin. — Fax 478-2879

Oakley, Logan, Pop. 1,984
Oakley USD 274 — 500/PK-12
208 E 2nd St 67748 — 785-672-4588
Bill Steiner, supt. — Fax 672-3044
Oakley HS — 200/9-12
118 W 7th St 67748 — 785-672-3241
Fred Teeter, prin. — Fax 672-3743
Oakley MS — 100/6-8
611 Center Ave 67748 — 785-672-3820
Robert Sattler, prin. — Fax 672-3010

Oberlin, Decatur, Pop. 1,811
Oberlin USD 294 — 400/PK-12
131 E Commercial St 67749 — 785-475-3805
Kelly Glodt, supt. — Fax 475-3076
www.usd294.org
Decatur Community JSHS — 200/7-12
605 E Commercial St 67749 — 785-475-2231
Charles Haag, prin. — Fax 475-2802

Olathe, Johnson, Pop. 111,334
Olathe USD 233 — 23,200/PK-12
PO Box 2000 66063 — 913-780-7000
Dr. Patricia All, supt. — Fax 780-8007
www.olatheschools.com/
California Trail JHS — 900/7-9
13775 W 133rd St 66062 — 913-780-7220
Larry Katzif, prin. — Fax 780-7229
Chisholm Trail JHS — 700/7-9
16700 W 159th St 66062 — 913-780-7240
Bill Weber, prin. — Fax 780-7249
Frontier Trail JHS — 800/7-9
15300 W 143rd St 66062 — 913-780-7210
Jim McMullen, prin. — Fax 780-7216
Indian Trail JHS — 600/7-9
1440 E 151st St 66062 — 913-780-7230
Tracy Maring, prin. — Fax 780-7234
Olathe East SHS — 1,300/10-12
14545 W 127th St 66062 — 913-780-7120
Dr. Tom Barry, prin. — Fax 780-7137
Olathe North SHS — 1,200/10-12
600 E Prairie St 66061 — 913-780-7140
Dr. Connie Heinen, prin. — Fax 780-7837
Olathe Northwest SHS — 1,100/10-12
21300 College Blvd 66061 — 913-780-7150
Dr. Gwen Poss, prin. — Fax 780-7159
Olathe South SHS — 1,400/10-12
1640 E 151st St 66062 — 913-780-7160
Phil Clark, prin. — Fax 780-7170
Oregon Trail JHS — 600/7-9
1800 W Dennis Ave 66061 — 913-780-7250
Steve Massey, prin. — Fax 780-7256
Pioneer Trail JHS — 600/7-9
15100 W 127th St 66062 — 913-780-7270
Kim Gillespie, prin. — Fax 780-7278
Prairie Trail JHS — 600/7-9
21600 W 107th St 66061 — 913-780-7280
Stacey Yurkovich, prin. — Fax 780-7289
Santa Fe Trail JHS — 600/7-9
1100 N Ridgeview Rd 66061 — 913-780-7290
Kerry Lane, prin. — Fax 780-7296

Kansas School for the Deaf — Post-Sec.
450 E Park St 66061 — 913-791-0573
Metro Academy — 400/K-12
17550 W 159th St 66062 — 913-782-0662
Robin Sullivan, admin.
Mid-America Nazarene University — Post-Sec.
2030 E College Way 66062 — 913-782-3750
Superior School of Hairdressing — Post-Sec.
1215 E Santa Fe St 66061 — 913-782-4004

Olpe, Lyon, Pop. 509
Southern Lyon County USD 252
Supt. — See Hartford
Olpe HS — 200/7-12
PO Box 206 66865 — 620-475-3223
Shari Hatfield, prin. — Fax 475-3951

Onaga, Pottawatomie, Pop. 683
Onaga-Havensville-Wheaton USD 322 — 400/PK-12
PO Box 60 66521 — 785-889-4614
Greg Markowitz, supt. — Fax 889-4662
www.usd322.org
Onaga HS — 100/9-12
PO Box 458 66521 — 785-889-4251
Greg Markowitz, prin. — Fax 889-4944

Osage City, Osage, Pop. 2,987
Osage City USD 420 — 700/K-12
520 Main St 66523 — 785-528-3176
David Carriger, supt. — Fax 528-3932
www.usd420.org
Osage City HS — 200/9-12
515 Ellinwood St 66523 — 785-528-3172
Troy Hutton, prin. — Fax 528-2980

Osawatomie, Miami, Pop. 4,616
Osawatomie USD 367 — 1,200/PK-12
1200 Trojan Dr 66064 — 913-755-4172
Gary French, supt. — Fax 755-2031
Osawatomie HS — 400/9-12
1200 Trojan Dr 66064 — 913-755-2191
Doug Chisam, prin. — Fax 755-2645
Osawatomie MS — 200/6-8
428 Pacific Ave 66064 — 913-755-4155
Dan Welch, prin. — Fax 755-2197

Osborne, Osborne, Pop. 1,440
Osborne County USD 392 — 300/PK-12
234 N 3rd St Ste B 67473 — 785-346-2145
Bill Heinen, supt. — Fax 346-2448
www.usd392.k12.ks.us
Osborne JSHS — 100/7-12
219 N 2nd St 67473 — 785-346-2143
Tom Conway, prin. — Fax 346-2331

Oskaloosa, Jefferson, Pop. 1,149
Oskaloosa USD 341 600/PK-12
404 Park St 66066 785-863-2539
Dr. Harry Austin, supt. Fax 863-3080
www.usd341.org
Oskaloosa HS 200/9-12
404 Park St 66066 785-863-2281
Douglas Beisel, prin. Fax 863-3106
Oskaloosa MS 100/6-8
404 Park St 66066 785-863-3237
Darren Shupe, prin. Fax 863-9247

Oswego, Labette, Pop. 1,996
Oswego USD 504 500/PK-12
PO Box 129 67356 620-795-2126
Terry Karlin, supt. Fax 795-4871
www.usd504.org
Oswego HS 100/9-12
1501 Tomahawk Trl 67356 620-795-2125
Rod Wittmer, prin. Fax 795-2130
Oswego MS 100/6-8
410 Kansas St 67356 620-795-4724
Mikel Ward, prin. Fax 795-4799

Otis, Rush, Pop. 319
Otis-Bison USD 403
Supt. — See Albert
Otis-Bison HS 100/9-12
PO Box 257 67565 785-387-2337
Mark Goodheart, prin. Fax 387-2557

Ottawa, Franklin, Pop. 12,597
Ottawa USD 290 2,300/K-12
123 W 4th St 66067 785-229-8010
Dean Katt, supt. Fax 229-8019
www.usd290.org
Career Technology Educational Coop Vo/Tech
908 W 11th St 66067 785-229-8020
Justin Henry, prin. Fax 229-8029
Ottawa HS 800/9-12
1120 S Ash St 66067 785-229-8020
Justin Henry, prin. Fax 229-8029
Ottawa MS 600/6-8
1230 S Ash St 66067 785-229-8030
Randy Oliver, prin. Fax 229-8039

Bethel Christian Academy 50/PK-12
3755 Nevada Rd 66067 785-242-1226
Donita Callahan, prin. Fax 242-1226
Ottawa University Post-Sec.
1001 S Cedar St 66067 785-242-5200

Overland Park, Johnson, Pop. 164,811
Blue Valley USD 229 19,100/PK-12
PO Box 23901 66283 913-239-4000
Tom Trigg Ed.D., supt. Fax 239-4150
www.bluevalleyk12.org
Blue Valley MS 600/6-8
5001 W 163rd Ter, 913-239-5100
Roxana Rogers, prin. Fax 681-4159
Blue Valley North HS 1,600/9-12
12200 Lamar Ave 66209 913-239-3000
Carter Burns Ed.D., prin. Fax 345-7338
Blue Valley Northwest HS 1,500/9-12
13260 Switzer Rd 66213 913-239-3400
Amy Murphy Ed.D., prin. Fax 681-7035
Blue Valley West HS 1,300/9-12
16200 Antioch Rd, 913-239-3700
Tony Lake, prin. Fax 402-3025
Harmony MS 600/6-8
10101 W 141st St 66221 913-239-5200
Sheila Albers, prin. Fax 681-4811
Lakewood MS 400/6-8
6601 Edgewater Dr 66223 913-239-5800
Scott Currier, prin. Fax 681-4726
Overland Trail MS 600/6-8
6201 W 133rd St 66209 913-239-5400
Jessica Dain Ed.D., prin. Fax 681-4432
Oxford MS 600/6-8
12500 Switzer Rd 66213 913-239-5500
Linda Crosthwait, prin. Fax 681-4502
Other Schools – See Leawood, Stilwell

College of Hair Design Post-Sec.
10324 Mastin St 66212 913-492-4114
Hyman Brand Hebrew Academy 300/K-12
5801 W 115th St 66211 913-327-8150
Marion Gould, hdmstr. Fax 327-8180
Johnson County Community College Post-Sec.
12345 College Blvd 66210 913-469-8500
LaBaron Hairdressing Academy Post-Sec.
8119 Robinson St 66204 913-642-0077
Overland Christian S 100/PK-12
7401 Metcalf Ave 66204 913-722-0272
Greg Blake, prin. Fax 722-2135
St. Thomas Aquinas HS 1,300/9-12
11411 Pflumm Rd 66215 913-345-1411
Dr. Bill Ford, pres. Fax 345-2319
Westminster Christian HS 100/7-12
9333 W 159th St 66221 913-685-9377
William Fischer, prin. Fax 851-8056
Wright Business School Post-Sec.
10975 El Monte St 66211 913-385-7700

Oxford, Sumner, Pop. 1,117
Oxford USD 358 400/PK-12
PO Box 937 67119 620-455-2227
Dr. Deborah Hamm, supt. Fax 455-3680
www.usd358.com
Oxford JSHS 200/7-12
PO Box 970 67119 620-455-2410
Robert Hampton, prin. Fax 455-3741

Palco, Rooks, Pop. 228
Palco USD 269 100/PK-12
PO Box B 67657 785-737-4635
David Miller, supt. Fax 737-4636
www.usd269.k12.ks.us/
Palco HS 50/9-12
PO Box 29 67657 785-737-4645
David Miller, prin. Fax 737-4646
Other Schools – See Damar

Paola, Miami, Pop. 5,292
Paola USD 368 2,000/PK-12
PO Box 268 66071 913-294-8000
Rod Allen, supt. Fax 294-8001
www.usd368.org/
Paola HS 700/9-12
401 Angela Dr 66071 913-294-8070
Jerry Henn, prin. Fax 294-3497
Paola MS 500/6-8
405 N Hospital Dr 66071 913-294-8030
Cynthia Goering, prin. Fax 294-3044

Parsons, Labette, Pop. 11,212
Parsons USD 503 1,500/PK-12
PO Box 1056 67357 620-421-5950
Dr. Deborah Perbeck, supt. Fax 421-5954
www.vikingnet.net
Parsons HS 500/9-12
3030 Morton Ave 67357 620-421-3660
Marty Anderson, prin. Fax 423-8816
Parsons MS 400/6-8
2719 Main St 67357 620-421-4190
Terry Smith, prin. Fax 423-8822

Labette Community College Post-Sec.
200 S 14th St 67357 620-421-6700

Paxico, Wabaunsee, Pop. 212
Mill Creek Valley USD 329
Supt. — See Alma
Mill Creek Valley JHS 100/7-8
PO Box 128 66526 785-636-5353
Daniel Wagner, prin. Fax 636-5116

Peabody, Marion, Pop. 1,302
Peabody-Burns USD 398 400/PK-12
506 N Elm St 66866 620-983-2198
Thomas Alstrom, supt. Fax 983-2247
Peabody-Burns JSHS 200/7-12
810 N Sycamore St 66866 620-983-2196
Mary Brown, prin. Fax 983-2773

Perry, Jefferson, Pop. 883
Perry USD 343 1,000/PK-12
PO Box 729 66073 785-597-5138
Steve Johnston, supt. Fax 597-2254
www.usd343.org/
Perry-Lecompton HS 300/9-12
PO Box 18 66073 785-597-5124
Al Ferrell, prin. Fax 597-5177
Perry-Lecompton MS 200/5-8
PO Box 31 66073 785-597-5159
Armin Landis, prin. Fax 597-5014

Phillipsburg, Phillips, Pop. 2,432
Phillipsburg USD 325 600/PK-12
240 S 7th St 67661 785-543-5281
Kent Otte, supt. Fax 543-2271
www.usd325.com
Phillipsburg HS 200/9-12
410 S 7th St 67661 785-543-5251
Brian Boeve, prin. Fax 543-6305
Phillipsburg MS 200/5-8
647 7th St 67661 785-543-5114
Rick Riffel, prin. Fax 543-2934

Pittsburg, Crawford, Pop. 19,214
Pittsburg USD 250 2,600/K-12
PO Box 75 66762 620-235-3100
Gary Price, supt. Fax 235-3106
www.usd250.org
Pittsburg HS 800/9-12
1978 E 4th St 66762 620-235-3200
Mike Philpot, prin. Fax 235-3210
Pittsburg MS 600/6-8
1310 N Broadway St 66762 620-235-3240
Cory Gibson, prin. Fax 235-3248

Pittsburg State University Post-Sec.
1701 S Broadway St 66762 620-231-7000
St. Mary's Colgan HS 200/7-12
212 E 9th St 66762 620-231-4690
Tom German, prin. Fax 231-0690

Plainville, Rooks, Pop. 1,889
Plainville USD 270 400/PK-12
111 W Mill St 67663 785-434-4678
Beth Reust, supt. Fax 434-7404
Plainville HS 100/9-12
202 SE Cardinal Ave 67663 785-434-4547
Phil Riedel, prin. Fax 434-4689

Pleasanton, Linn, Pop. 1,368
Pleasanton USD 344 400/K-12
PO Box 480 66075 913-352-8534
Tim Conrad, supt. Fax 352-6588
www.usd344.org/
Pleasanton HS 200/7-12
PO Box 480 66075 913-352-8701
David Schmidt, prin. Fax 352-6588

Pomona, Franklin, Pop. 942
West Franklin USD 287 900/PK-12
510 E Franklin St 66076 785-566-3396
Dr. Susan Myers, supt. Fax 566-8325
www.usd287.org
Pomona HS 200/9-12
511 E Franklin St 66076 785-566-3392
Michael Dorst, prin. Fax 566-8454
Other Schools – See Williamsburg

Prairie Village, Johnson, Pop. 21,454

Kansas City Christian HS 200/9-12
4801 W 79th St 66208 913-648-5227
E. Allan Chugg, prin. Fax 648-5269

Pratt, Pratt, Pop. 6,447
Pratt USD 382 1,100/PK-12
401 N Ninnescah St 67124 620-672-4500
Dr. Glen Davis, supt. Fax 672-4509
www.usd382.com
Liberty MS 300/6-8
300 S Iuka St 67124 620-672-4530
Mike McDermeit, prin. Fax 672-4539
Pratt HS 400/9-12
401 S Hamilton St 67124 620-672-4540
Tim Kuhn, prin. Fax 672-4549

Skyline USD 438 400/K-12
20269 W US Highway 54 67124 620-672-5651
Mike Sanders, supt. Fax 672-9377
www.usd438.k12.ks.us
Skyline HS 100/9-12
20269 W US Highway 54 67124 620-672-5651
Herb McPherson, prin. Fax 672-9377

Pratt Community College Post-Sec.
Hwy 61 67124 620-672-5641

Pretty Prairie, Reno, Pop. 600
Pretty Prairie USD 311 300/K-12
PO Box 218 67570 620-459-6241
Brad Wade, supt. Fax 459-6810
www.usd311.com
Pretty Prairie HS 100/9-12
PO Box 326 67570 620-459-6313
Randy Hendrickson, prin. Fax 459-6935
Pretty Prairie MS 100/5-8
PO Box 307 67570 620-459-6911
Randy Hendrickson, prin. Fax 459-6729

Protection, Comanche, Pop. 541
Comanche County USD 300
Supt. — See Coldwater
South Central MS 100/6-8
PO Box 38 67127 620-622-4545
Matt Jellison, prin. Fax 622-4844

Quinter, Gove, Pop. 846
Quinter USD 293 300/PK-12
PO Box 540 67752 785-754-2470
Allaire Homburg, supt. Fax 754-3365
www.quinterhs.org
Quinter JSHS 200/7-12
PO Box 459 67752 785-754-3660
Tucker Woolsey, prin. Fax 754-3905

Randall, Jewell, Pop. 74
Jewell USD 279 200/K-12
PO Box 96 66963 785-739-2216
Ron Kelley, supt. Fax 739-2219
Other Schools – See Jewell

Randolph, Riley, Pop. 135
Blue Valley USD 384 200/K-12
PO Box 98 66554 785-293-5256
Brady Burton, supt. Fax 293-5607
www.usd384.k12.ks.us/home.html
Blue Valley HS 100/9-12
PO Box 68 66554 785-293-5255
Tim Winter, prin. Fax 293-5372
Randolph MS 100/5-8
PO Box 38 66554 785-293-5253
Tim Winter, prin. Fax 293-4405

Ransom, Ness, Pop. 292
Western Plains USD 106 100/PK-12
311 W Ogden St 67572 785-398-2535
James Frank, supt. Fax 398-2492
www.usd106.k12.ks.us/
Western Plains HS 9-12
311 W Ogden St 67572 785-731-2352
Kerry Lacock, prin. Fax 731-2235

Rexford, Thomas, Pop. 151
Golden Plains USD 316
Supt. — See Selden
Golden Plains HS 100/9-12
PO Box 100 67753 785-687-3265
Dr. Roger Baskerville, prin. Fax 687-2285
Golden Plains MS 100/6-8
PO Box 100 67753 785-687-3265
Dr. Roger Baskerville, prin. Fax 687-2285

Richmond, Franklin, Pop. 514
Central Heights USD 288 600/K-12
3521 Ellis Rd 66080 785-869-3455
Deanne Alexander, supt. Fax 869-2675
www.usd288.org/
Central Heights HS 200/9-12
3521 Ellis Rd 66080 785-869-3555
Tom Horstick, prin. Fax 869-2675
Central Heights MS 100/6-8
3521 Ellis Rd 66080 785-869-3809
Buddy Welch, prin.

Riley, Riley, Pop. 692
Riley County USD 378 700/PK-12
PO Box 326 66531 785-485-4000
Brad Starnes, supt. Fax 485-2860
www.usd378.org/
Riley County HS 200/9-12
PO Box 38 66531 785-485-4020
Steve Mies, prin. Fax 485-2426

Riverton, Cherokee
Riverton USD 404 800/K-12
PO Box 290 66770 620-848-3386
David L. Walters, supt. Fax 848-9853
www.usd404.org/

Riverton HS 200/9-12
PO Box 290 66770 620-848-3388
Todd Berry, prin. Fax 848-3609
Riverton MS 200/6-8
PO Box 260 66770 620-848-3355
Becky Murray, prin. Fax 848-3609

Roeland Park, Johnson, Pop. 6,975

Bishop Miege HS 900/9-12
5041 Reinhardt Dr 66205 913-262-2700
Stan Herbic, prin. Fax 262-2752

Rolla, Morton, Pop. 445
Rolla USD 217 200/PK-12
PO Box 167 67954 620-593-4344
Richard Spencer, supt. Fax 593-4250
www.usd217.org
Rolla HS 100/6-12
PO Box 167 67954 620-593-4345
Stuart Sutton, prin. Fax 593-4204

Rosalia, Butler
Flinthills USD 492 300/K-12
PO Box 188 67132 620-476-2237
Dr. Phil Mahan, supt. Fax 476-2253
www.usd492.org/
Flinthills MSHS 200/7-12
PO Box 188 67132 620-476-2215
Larry Gawith, prin. Fax 476-2244

Rose Hill, Butler, Pop. 3,896
Rose Hill USD 394 1,800/PK-12
104 N Rose Hill Rd 67133 316-776-3300
Randal Chickadonz, supt. Fax 776-3309
www.usd394.com
Rose Hill HS 600/9-12
104 N Rose Hill Rd 67133 316-776-3360
John Purvis, prin. Fax 776-3378
Rose Hill MS 400/6-8
104 N Rose Hill Rd 67133 316-776-3320
Kay Walker, prin. Fax 776-3319

Rossville, Shawnee, Pop. 996
Kaw Valley USD 321
Supt. — See Saint Marys
Rossville HS 300/7-12
PO Box 68 66533 785-584-6193
John Johnson, prin. Fax 584-6379

Rozel, Pawnee, Pop. 171
Pawnee Heights USD 496 100/K-12
PO Box 98 67574 620-527-4212
Raymond Patterson, supt. Fax 527-4213
www.usd496.net/
Pawnee Heights HS 100/9-12
PO Box 97 67574 620-527-4211
Dan Binder, prin. Fax 527-4215

Russell, Russell, Pop. 4,342
Russell County USD 407 1,000/K-12
802 N Main St 67665 785-483-2173
David Couch, supt. Fax 483-2175
www.usd407.org/usd/links.html
Ruppenthal MS 200/6-8
400 N Elm St 67665 785-483-3174
Duane Adams, prin. Fax 483-5386
Russell HS 300/9-12
565 E State St 67665 785-483-5631
Larry Bernard, prin. Fax 483-5636
Other Schools – See Lucas

Sabetha, Nemaha, Pop. 2,523
Sabetha USD 441 1,000/PK-12
107 Oregon St 66534 785-284-2175
Dennis Stones, supt. Fax 284-3739
sabetha441.k12.ks.us
Sabetha HS 200/9-12
1011 Blue Jay Blvd 66534 785-284-2155
Todd Evans, prin. Fax 284-2600
Sabetha MS 200/6-8
751 Blue Jay Blvd 66534 785-284-2151
Thomas Palmer, prin. Fax 284-0061
Other Schools – See Wetmore

Saint Francis, Cheyenne, Pop. 1,390
St. Francis Community USD 297 300/K-12
PO Box 1110 67756 785-332-8182
Carl Werner, supt. Fax 332-8177
www.usd297.org/
Saint Francis JSHS 200/7-12
PO Box 1110 67756 785-332-8153
Scott Carmichael, prin. Fax 332-8177

Saint George, Pottawatomie, Pop. 457
Rock Creek USD 323
Supt. — See Westmoreland
Rock Creek JSHS 400/7-12
9355 Flush Rd 66535 785-494-8591
Dennis Post, prin. Fax 494-8595

Saint John, Stafford, Pop. 1,249
St. John-Hudson USD 350 400/K-12
406 N Monroe St 67576 620-549-3564
Dr. James Kenworthy, supt. Fax 549-3964
www.usd350.com/
Saint John JSHS 200/7-12
505 N Broadway St 67576 620-549-3277
Mike Burgan, prin. Fax 549-3279

Saint Marys, Pottawatomie, Pop. 2,253
Kaw Valley USD 321 900/PK-12
411 W Lasley St 66536 785-437-2254
Martin Stessman, supt. Fax 437-3155
www.kawvalley.k12.ks.us/
Saint Marys HS 200/7-12
601 E Lasley St 66536 785-437-6257
Eric Steele, prin. Fax 437-3460
Other Schools – See Rossville

Saint Paul, Neosho, Pop. 657
Chetopa - St. Paul USD 505
Supt. — See Chetopa
Saint Paul HS 100/7-12
1st & Washington 66771 620-449-2245
Felix Diskin, prin. Fax 449-8960

Salina, Saline, Pop. 45,956
Salina USD 305 7,300/PK-12
PO Box 797 67402 785-309-4700
Dr. Robert Winter, supt. Fax 309-4737
www.usd305.com
Lakewood MS 800/6-8
1135 E Lakewood Cir 67401 785-309-4000
Mike Lowers, prin. Fax 309-4001
Salina Area Technical S Vo/Tech
2562 Centennial Rd Ste A 67401 785-309-3100
Duane Custer, dir. Fax 309-3101
Salina Central HS 1,100/9-12
650 E Crawford St 67401 785-309-3500
Stan Vaughn, prin. Fax 309-3501
Salina South HS 1,200/9-12
730 E Magnolia Rd 67401 785-309-3700
Myron Graber, prin. Fax 309-3701
Salina South MS 900/6-8
2040 S 4th St 67401 785-309-3900
Beth Morrison, prin. Fax 309-3901
Salina Adult Education Center Adult
9th & Ash 67401 785-309-4660
Kelly Mobray, dir. Fax 309-4669

Academy of Hair Design Post-Sec.
115 S 5th St 67401 785-825-8155
Brown Mackie College Post-Sec.
2106 S 9th St 67401 785-825-5422
Kansas State University Post-Sec.
2310 Centennial Rd 67401 785-826-2600
Kansas Wesleyan University Post-Sec.
100 E Claflin Ave 67401 785-827-5541
Sacred Heart HS 300/7-12
234 E Cloud St 67401 785-827-4422
John Krajicek, prin. Fax 827-8648
St. Johns Military S 100/7-12
PO Box 5020 67402 785-823-7231
Devon Walter, dean Fax 823-7236
Salina Area Vocational Technical School Post-Sec.
2562 Centennial Rd 67401 785-309-3100

Satanta, Haskell, Pop. 1,179
Satanta USD 507 400/PK-12
PO Box 279 67870 620-649-2234
Ardith Dunn, supt. Fax 649-2668
www.usd507.org
Satanta JSHS 200/7-12
PO Box 69 67870 620-649-2611
Ron Levan, prin. Fax 649-2658

Scandia, Republic, Pop. 374
Pike Valley USD 426 300/PK-12
PO Box 291 66966 785-335-2206
Gary Kraus, supt. Fax 335-2219
www.pikevalley.com/
Pike Valley HS 100/9-12
PO Box 339 66966 785-335-2294
Gary Kraus, prin. Fax 335-2386
Other Schools – See Courtland

Scott City, Scott, Pop. 3,474
Scott County USD 466 900/PK-12
PO Box 288 67871 620-872-7600
Dr. Don Wells, supt. Fax 872-7609
www.usd466.com/
Scott City HS 300/9-12
712 S Main St 67871 620-872-7620
Eric Swanson, prin. Fax 872-7629
Scott City MS 300/5-8
809 W 9th St 67871 620-872-7640
Neal George, prin. Fax 872-7649

Sedan, Chautauqua, Pop. 1,269
Chautauqua County Community USD 286 400/PK-12
302 Sherman St 67361 620-725-3187
Scott Hills, supt. Fax 725-5642
www.usd286-sedan-ks.org
Sedan HS 200/7-12
416 E Elm St 67361 620-725-3186
Mike Todd, prin. Fax 725-3188

Sedgwick, Harvey, Pop. 1,644
Sedgwick USD 439 500/K-12
PO Box K 67135 316-772-5783
Michael Hull, supt. Fax 772-0274
www.usd439.k12.ks.us
Sedgwick HS 100/9-12
PO Box K 67135 316-772-5155
Kevin Stucky, prin. Fax 772-0334

Selden, Sheridan, Pop. 185
Golden Plains USD 316 200/K-12
PO Box 199 67757 785-386-4559
Dr. Roger Baskerville, supt. Fax 386-4562
usd316.k12.ks.us/
Other Schools – See Rexford

Seneca, Nemaha, Pop. 2,068
Nemaha Valley USD 442 500/K-12
318 Main St 66538 785-336-6101
Brian Harris, supt. Fax 336-2268
www.usd442.org
Nemaha Valley HS 200/9-12
214 N 11th St 66538 785-336-3557
Patrick McKernan, prin. Fax 336-3672

Sharon Springs, Wallace, Pop. 733
Wallace County USD 241 200/PK-12
521 N Main St 67758 785-852-4252
Larry Lysell, supt. Fax 852-4603
www.usd241.org/
Wallace County HS 100/9-12
521 N Main St 67758 785-852-4240
Bruce Bolen, prin. Fax 852-4603

Shawnee, Johnson, Pop. 57,628
De Soto USD 232
Supt. — See De Soto
Mill Valley HS 800/9-12
5900 Monticello Rd 66226 913-422-4351
Dr. Joe Novak, prin. Fax 422-4039
Monticello Trails MS 700/6-8
6100 Monticello Rd 66226 913-422-1100
Tobie Waldeck, prin. Fax 422-4990

Central Baptist Theological Seminary Post-Sec.
6601 Monticello Rd 66226 800-677-2287
Cutting Edge Hairstyling Academy Post-Sec.
7377 Quivira Rd 66216 913-962-0076
Maranatha Academy 400/7-12
6826 Lackman Rd 66217 913-631-0637
Dr. Larry Daugherty, supt. Fax 631-0899
Midland Adventist Academy 200/K-12
6915 Maurer Rd 66217 913-268-7400
Gary Kruger, prin. Fax 268-4968

Shawnee Mission, See Merriam
Shawnee Mission USD 512 28,000/PK-12
7235 Antioch Rd 66204 913-993-6200
Marjorie Kaplan Ph.D., supt. Fax 993-6247
www.smsd.org
Antioch MS 500/7-8
8200 W 71st St 66204 913-993-0000
Scott Sherman, prin. Fax 993-0199
Broadmoor Technical Center Vo/Tech
6701 W 83rd St 66204 913-993-9700
Julia Crain, prin. Fax 993-9799
Hocker Grove MS 600/7-8
10400 Johnson Dr 66203 913-993-0200
Debbie Pfortmiller, prin. Fax 993-0399
Indian Hills MS 500/7-8
6400 Mission Rd 66208 913-993-0400
Carla Allen, prin. Fax 993-0599
Indian Woods MS 700/7-8
9700 Woodson Dr 66207 913-993-0600
Jim Wink, prin. Fax 993-0799
Mission Valley MS 600/7-8
8500 Mission Rd 66206 913-993-0800
Dr. Susie Ostmeyer, prin. Fax 993-0999
Shawnee Mission East HS 2,100/9-12
7500 Mission Rd 66208 913-993-6600
Dr. Susan Swift, prin. Fax 993-6899
Shawnee Mission North HS 1,900/9-12
7401 Johnson Dr 66202 913-993-6900
Richard Kramer, prin. Fax 993-7099
Shawnee Mission Northwest HS 1,900/9-12
12701 W 67th St 66216 913-993-7200
Dr. William Harrington, prin. Fax 993-7499
Shawnee Mission South HS 1,800/9-12
5800 W 107th St 66207 913-993-7500
Dr. Joe Gilhaus, prin. Fax 993-7799
Shawnee Mission West HS 2,100/9-12
8800 W 85th St 66212 913-993-7800
Dr. Charles McLean, prin. Fax 993-8099
Trailridge MS 600/7-8
7500 Quivira Rd 66216 913-993-1000
Dr. Larry King, prin. Fax 993-1199
Westridge MS 1,000/7-8
9300 Nieman Rd 66214 913-993-1200
Janice Jackson, prin. Fax 993-1399

Silver Lake, Shawnee, Pop. 1,352
Silver Lake USD 372 700/PK-12
PO Box 39 66539 785-582-4026
Dr. Steven Pegram, supt. Fax 582-5259
www.silverlakeeagles.org
Silver Lake JSHS 400/7-12
PO Box 39 66539 785-582-4639
Larry Winter, prin. Fax 582-4265

Smith Center, Smith, Pop. 1,725
Smith Center USD 237 500/PK-12
PO Box 329 66967 785-282-6665
Ron Meitler, supt. Fax 282-6518
www.usd237.com
Smith Center JSHS 200/7-12
PO Box 329 66967 785-282-6609
Greg Koelsch, prin. Fax 282-5206

Solomon, Dickinson, Pop. 1,056
Solomon USD 393 400/K-12
113 E 7th St 67480 785-655-2541
Jim Runge, supt. Fax 655-2505
www.solomon393.k12.ks.us
Solomon JSHS 200/7-12
409 N Pine St 67480 785-655-2551
Bob Warkentine, prin. Fax 655-3011

South Haven, Sumner, Pop. 368
South Haven USD 509 200/PK-12
PO Box 229 67140 620-892-5216
John Showman, supt. Fax 892-5814
www.usd509.org/
South Haven JSHS 100/6-12
PO Box 229 67140 620-892-5215
Kim White, prin. Fax 892-5814

Spearville, Ford, Pop. 858
Spearville USD 381 300/K-12
PO Box 338 67876 620-385-2676
Mark Littell, supt. Fax 385-2614
Spearville JSHS 200/6-12
PO Box 158 67876 620-385-2631
David Jackson, prin. Fax 385-2641

Spring Hill, Johnson, Pop. 4,494
Spring Hill USD 230 1,500/K-12
101 E South St 66083 913-592-7200
Dr. Barton L. Goering, supt. Fax 592-7270
www.usd230.org

Spring Hill HS 500/9-12
21700 Bronco Blvd 66083 913-592-7299
Dr. Angelo Cocolis, prin. Fax 592-5424
Spring Hill MS 400/6-8
300 E South St 66083 913-592-7288
Stephen Fleer, prin. Fax 592-7225

Stafford, Stafford, Pop. 1,067
Stafford USD 349 300/PK-12
PO Box 400 67578 620-234-5243
Dr. Mary Jo Taylor, supt. Fax 234-6986
www.stafford349.com
Stafford MSHS 200/7-12
PO Box 370 67578 620-234-5248
John Wyrick, prin. Fax 234-6041

Sterling, Rice, Pop. 2,576
Sterling USD 376 500/PK-12
PO Box 188 67579 620-278-3621
Fred Dierksen, supt. Fax 278-3882
www.usd376.com
Sterling HS 200/9-12
308 E Washington Ave 67579 620-278-2171
Gregg Errebo, prin. Fax 278-3237
Sterling JHS 100/7-8
412 N 5th St 67579 620-278-3646
Gregg Errebo, prin. Fax 278-3673

Sterling College Post-Sec.
125 W Cooper St 67579 620-278-2173

Stilwell, Johnson
Blue Valley USD 229
Supt. — See Overland Park
Blue Valley HS 1,300/9-12
6001 W 159th St 66085 913-239-4800
Scott Bacon, prin. Fax 681-4254
Pleasant Ridge MS 700/6-8
9000 W 165th St 66085 913-239-5700
Diana Tate, prin. Fax 681-7111

Stockton, Rooks, Pop. 1,453
Stockton USD 271 400/PK-12
421 Main St 67669 785-425-6367
Casey Robinson, supt. Fax 425-6923
www.usd271.k12.ks.us/
Stockton HS 100/9-12
105 N Cypress St 67669 785-425-6784
Keith Hall, prin. Fax 425-6200

Strong City, Chase, Pop. 583
Chase County USD 284
Supt. — See Cottonwood Falls
Chase County MS 100/5-8
PO Box 279 66869 620-273-6676
Jay Talkington, prin. Fax 273-6690

Sublette, Haskell, Pop. 1,582
Sublette USD 374 400/PK-12
PO Box 670 67877 620-675-2277
Rex Bruce, supt. Fax 675-2652
www.usd374.org/
Sublette MSHS 100/7-12
PO Box 460 67877 620-675-2232
Carey Tresner, prin. Fax 675-8347

Crosswalk Christian S 50/PK-12
PO Box 730 67877 620-675-2283
Kristi Walter, prin. Fax 675-2283

Sylvan Grove, Lincoln, Pop. 301
Sylvan Grove USD 299 200/K-12
504 W 4th St 67481 785-526-7175
Jude Stecklein, supt. Fax 526-7182
www.usd299.k12.ks.us/
Sylvan Unified JSHS 100/7-12
504 W 4th St 67481 785-526-7175
Byron Marshall, prin. Fax 526-7182

Syracuse, Hamilton, Pop. 1,788
Syracuse USD 494 500/PK-12
PO Box 1187 67878 620-384-7872
Joan Friend, supt. Fax 384-7692
www.syracuse.k12.ks.us
Syracuse JSHS 200/7-12
PO Box 1187 67878 620-384-7446
Paul Zuzelski, prin. Fax 384-6686

Tecumseh, Shawnee
Shawnee Heights USD 450 3,400/PK-12
4401 SE Shawnee Heights Rd 66542 785-379-5800
Dr. Martin Stessman, supt. Fax 379-5810
www.snh450.k12.ks.us/
Shawnee Heights HS 1,200/9-12
4201 SE Shawnee Heights Rd 66542 785-379-5880
Warren Watson, prin. Fax 379-5889
Shawnee Heights MS 600/7-8
4335 SE Shawnee Heights Rd 66542 785-379-5830
Tim Hallacy, prin. Fax 379-5848

Tescott, Ottawa, Pop. 331
Twin Valley USD 240
Supt. — See Bennington
Tescott HS 100/9-12
PO Box 196 67484 785-283-4385
David Zlab, prin. Fax 283-4347

Tipton, Mitchell, Pop. 230

Tipton Catholic JSHS 100/7-12
PO Box 146 67485 785-373-5835
Gery Hake, prin. Fax 373-5637

Tonganoxie, Leavenworth, Pop. 3,774
Tonganoxie USD 464 1,600/K-12
PO Box 199 66086 913-845-2153
Dr. Richard Erickson, supt. Fax 845-3629
www.tong464.k12.ks.us
Tonganoxie JHS 400/7-9
PO Box 980 66086 913-845-2627
Steve Woolf, prin. Fax 845-2734
Tonganoxie SHS 400/10-12
PO Box 179 66086 913-845-2654
Tatia Shelton, prin. Fax 845-3716

Topeka, Shawnee, Pop. 121,946
Auburn Washburn USD 437 5,200/PK-12
5928 SW 53rd St 66610 785-339-4000
Dr. Brenda Dietrich, supt. Fax 339-4025
www.usd437.net
Washburn Rural HS 1,600/9-12
5900 SW 61st St 66619 785-339-4100
William Edwards, prin. Fax 339-4125
Washburn Rural MS 800/7-8
5620 SW 61st St 66619 785-339-4300
Gerald Meier, prin. Fax 339-4325

Seaman USD 345 3,400/PK-12
901 NW Lyman Rd 66608 785-575-8600
Mike Mathes, supt. Fax 575-8620
www.usd345.com/
Logan JHS 400/7-9
1124 NW Lyman Rd 66608 785-575-8700
Kathleen Sooter, prin. Fax 575-8703
Northern Hills JHS 500/7-9
5620 NW Topeka Blvd 66617 785-286-8400
Robert Horton, prin. Fax 286-8403
Seaman SHS 800/10-12
4850 NW Rochester Rd 66617 785-286-8300
Ron Vinduska, prin. Fax 286-8320

Topeka USD 501 13,000/PK-12
624 SW 24th St 66611 785-295-3000
Tony Sawyer, supt. Fax 575-6161
www.topeka.k12.ks.us
Chase MS 500/6-8
2250 NE State St 66616 785-295-3840
Teresa Songs, prin. Fax 575-6632
Eisenhower MS 400/6-8
3305 SE Minnesota Ave 66605 785-274-6160
Steven Roberts, prin. Fax 274-4603
French MS 500/6-8
5257 SW 33rd St 66614 785-438-4150
Vicki Weseman, prin. Fax 271-3609
Highland Park HS 900/9-12
2424 SE California Ave 66605 785-274-6000
Dale Cushinberry, prin. Fax 274-4896
Jardine MS 500/6-8
2600 SW 33rd St 66611 785-274-6330
Jeanne Vawter, prin. Fax 274-4768
Kaw Area Technical S Vo/Tech
5724 SW Huntoon St 66604 785-273-7140
Richard Hoffman, dir. Fax 273-7080
Landon MS 400/6-8
731 SW Fairlawn Rd 66606 785-438-4220
Robert Cronkhite, prin. Fax 271-3737
Robinson MS 500/6-8
1125 SW 14th St 66604 785-295-3770
Tammy Austin, prin. Fax 575-6720
Topeka HS 1,700/9-12
800 SW 10th Ave 66612 785-295-3150
Dr. Linda Wiley, prin. Fax 575-6255
Topeka West HS 1,000/9-12
2001 SW Fairlawn Rd 66604 785-438-4000
Dr. Stan Wagstaff, prin. Fax 271-3497
Adult Education Center Adult
5724 SW Huntoon St 66604 785-228-6406
Mary Ann Wittman, coord. Fax 273-7080

American Academy of Hair Design Post-Sec.
901 SW 37th St 66611 785-267-5800
Baker University School of Nursing Post-Sec.
1500 SW 10th Ave 66604 888-866-4242
Bryan Career College Post-Sec.
1527 SW Fairlawn Rd 66604 785-272-0889
Community College of Cosmetology Post-Sec.
3602 SW Topeka Blvd 66611 785-267-7701
Hayden HS 500/9-12
401 SW Gage Blvd 66606 785-272-5210
Mark Madsen, prin. Fax 272-2975
Heritage Christian S 200/PK-12
3102 NW Topeka Blvd 66617 785-286-0427
Aletha Rogers, prin. Fax 286-9898
KAW Area Technical School Post-Sec.
5724 SW Huntoon St 66604 785-273-7140
Mater Dei ES - East Campus 100/6-8
735 SW Jackson St 66603 785-235-0953
Tym Bonilla, prin. Fax 235-5809
Washburn University Post-Sec.
1700 SW College Ave 66621 785-231-1010
WTI Topeka Campus Post-Sec.
3712 SW Burlingame Cir 66609 785-354-4568

Towanda, Butler, Pop. 1,355
Circle USD 375 1,500/K-12
PO Box 9 67144 316-541-2577
Eliese Holt, supt. Fax 536-2249
www.usd375.org
Circle HS 500/9-12
PO Box 158 67144 316-541-2277
Al Sersland, prin. Fax 541-2115
Other Schools – See Benton

Tribune, Greeley, Pop. 722
Greeley County USD 200 200/PK-12
400 W Lawrence St 67879 620-376-4211
Bill Wilson, supt. Fax 376-2465
www.tribuneschools.org
Greeley County HS 100/7-12
400 W Lawrence St 67879 620-376-4265
Ken Bockwinkel, prin. Fax 376-2465

Troy, Doniphan, Pop. 1,017
Troy USD 429 400/PK-12
PO Box 190 66087 785-985-3950
Dr. Doug Huxman, supt. Fax 985-3688
www.troyusd.org/
Troy MSHS 200/7-12
PO Box 160 66087 785-985-3533
Don Cash, prin. Fax 985-3885

Tyro, Montgomery, Pop. 222

Tyro Community Christian S 200/K-12
PO Box 308 67364 620-289-4450
Terry Byrd, prin. Fax 289-4283

Udall, Cowley, Pop. 766
Udall USD 463 300/PK-12
PO Box 386 67146 620-782-3355
Loren Feldkamp, supt. Fax 782-9690
www.usd463.org/
Udall HS 100/9-12
PO Box 356 67146 620-782-3623
Grady Sewell, prin. Fax 782-9689
Udall MS 100/6-8
PO Box 356 67146 620-782-3623
Lyle Pfannenstiel, prin. Fax 782-9689

Ulysses, Grant, Pop. 5,650
Ulysses USD 214 1,700/PK-12
111 S Baughman St 67880 620-356-3655
Bill Hall, supt. Fax 356-5181
www.ulysses.org
Kepley MS 400/6-8
113 N Colorado St 67880 620-356-3025
Juan Perez, prin. Fax 356-3024
Ulysses HS 500/9-12
501 N Mccall St 67880 620-356-1380
Rodger Hilton, prin. Fax 356-5566

Uniontown, Bourbon, Pop. 278
Uniontown USD 235 400/PK-12
401 5th St 66779 620-756-4302
Randy Rockhold, supt. Fax 756-4492
www.usd235.org/
Uniontown HS 200/7-12
601 5th St 66779 620-756-4301
Tracy Smith, prin. Fax 756-4340

Valley Center, Sedgwick, Pop. 5,508
Valley Center USD 262 2,400/PK-12
PO Box 157 67147 316-755-7100
Scott Springston, supt. Fax 755-7102
www.usd262.net
Valley Center HS 800/9-12
800 N Meridian Ave 67147 316-755-7130
Louise Herrington, prin. Fax 755-7134
Valley Center MS 600/6-8
737 N Meridian Ave 67147 316-755-7160
Paul Schultz, prin. Fax 755-7164

Valley Falls, Jefferson, Pop. 1,209
Valley Falls USD 338 400/K-12
700 Oak St 66088 785-945-3214
David Grove, supt. Fax 945-3215
www.usd338.com
Valley Falls HS 100/9-12
601 Elm St 66088 785-945-3229
Robert Davies, prin. Fax 945-3220

Vermillion, Marshall, Pop. 98
Vermillion USD 380 500/PK-12
PO Box 107 66544 785-382-6216
Patrick Meier, supt. Fax 382-6213
www.usd380.com
Other Schools – See Centralia, Frankfort

Victoria, Ellis, Pop. 1,164
Victoria USD 432 300/K-12
PO Box 139 67671 785-735-9212
Linda Kenne, supt. Fax 735-9229
www.usd432.org/
Victoria HS 100/9-12
PO Box 20 67671 785-735-9211
Mike Kreller, prin. Fax 735-9216

Wakeeney, Trego, Pop. 1,800
WaKeeney USD 208 400/PK-12
527 Russell Ave 67672 785-743-2145
Robert Scheib, supt. Fax 743-2071
www.tregoeagles.com/
Trego Community HS 100/9-12
1200 Russell Ave 67672 785-743-2061
Daryl Stegman, prin. Fax 743-2449

Wakefield, Clay, Pop. 874
Clay Center USD 379
Supt. — See Clay Center
Wakefield HS 100/9-12
PO Box 40 67487 785-461-5437
Penny Hargrove, prin. Fax 461-5892

Wamego, Pottawatomie, Pop. 4,243
Wamego USD 320 1,300/PK-12
510 E US Highway 24 66547 785-456-7643
Doug Conwell, supt. Fax 456-8125
www.usd320.com
Wamego HS 500/9-12
801 Lincoln St 66547 785-456-2214
Donna Workman, prin. Fax 456-7382
Wamego MS 300/6-8
1701 Kaw Valley Rd 66547 785-456-7682
Vici Jennings, prin. Fax 456-2944

Washington, Washington, Pop. 1,145
Washington County USD 108 400/PK-12
PO Box 275 66968 785-325-2261
Michael Stegman, supt. Fax 325-2771
www.usd108.org/
Washington JSHS 200/7-12
PO Box 275 66968 785-325-2261
Phil Wilson, prin. Fax 325-2138

Waterville, Marshall, Pop. 628
Valley Heights USD 498 400/K-12
PO Box 89 66548 785-363-2398
John Bergkamp, supt. Fax 363-2269
www.valleyheights.org/

Other Schools – See Blue Rapids

Wathena, Doniphan, Pop. 1,290
Wathena USD 406 400/PK-12
PO Box 38 66090 785-989-4427
Mike Newman, supt. Fax 989-4680
www.wathena406.k12.ks.us
Wathena HS 200/7-12
PO Box 38 66090 785-989-4426
Robert Blair, prin. Fax 989-3317

Waverly, Coffey, Pop. 556
Lebo-Waverly USD 243 600/PK-12
PO Box 457 66871 785-733-2651
Allen Pokorny, supt. Fax 733-2707
www.usd243ks.org/
Waverly HS 100/7-12
PO Box 8 66871 785-733-2561
Karl Hamm, prin. Fax 733-2756
Other Schools – See Lebo

Wellington, Sumner, Pop. 8,098
Wellington USD 353 1,100/K-12
PO Box 648 67152 620-326-4300
Dr. Allen Hillen, supt. Fax 326-4304
www.usd353.com/
Wellington HS 9-12
1700 E 16th St 67152 620-326-4310
Dale Liston, prin. Fax 326-4383
Wellington MS 400/6-8
605 N A St 67152 620-326-4320
Jerry Hodson, prin. Fax 326-4390

Wellsville, Franklin, Pop. 1,631
Wellsville USD 289 800/PK-12
602 Walnut St 66092 785-883-2388
Denise O'Dea, supt. Fax 883-4453
www.wellsville-usd289.org
Wellsville HS 200/9-12
602 Walnut St 66092 785-883-2057
Sheldon Pokorney, prin. Fax 883-2294
Wellsville MS 200/6-8
602 Walnut St 66092 785-883-4350
Mitchell Lubin, prin. Fax 883-2260

Weskan, Wallace
Weskan USD 242 100/PK-12
PO Box 155 67762 785-943-5222
Mike Nulton, supt. Fax 943-5303
www.weskanschools.org/
Weskan JSHS 100/7-12
PO Box 155 67762 785-943-5222
Mike Nulton, prin. Fax 943-5303

Westmoreland, Pottawatomie, Pop. 655
Rock Creek USD 323 700/PK-12
PO Box 70 66549 785-457-3732
Darrel Stufflebeam, supt. Fax 457-3701
www.rockcreekschools.org
Other Schools – See Saint George

Wetmore, Nemaha, Pop. 356
Sabetha USD 441
Supt. — See Sabetha
Wetmore HS 50/9-12
PO Box AB 66550 785-866-2860
Timothy Weis, prin. Fax 866-5450

White City, Morris, Pop. 499
Rural Vista USD 481
Supt. — See Hope
White City HS 100/9-12
PO Box 8 66872 785-349-2211
Adam McDaniel, prin. Fax 349-2138

Whitewater, Butler, Pop. 639
Remington-Whitewater USD 206 500/K-12
PO Box 243 67154 316-799-2115
Jim Johnson, supt. Fax 799-2307
remington.ks.schoolwebpages.com
Remington HS 200/9-12
8850 NW Meadowlark Rd 67154 316-799-2123
James Regier, prin. Fax 799-2943
Remington MS 100/6-8
PO Box 99 67154 316-799-2131
Bruce Krase, prin. Fax 799-2581

Wichita, Sedgwick, Pop. 354,865
Haysville USD 261
Supt. — See Haysville
Haysville Campus HS 1,300/9-12
2100 W 55th St S 67217 316-554-2236
Myron Regier, prin. Fax 554-2241

Maize USD 266
Supt. — See Maize
Maize South MS 1,000/7-8
3701 N Tyler Rd 67205 316-722-0421
John Blazek, prin. Fax 722-4077

Wichita USD 259 45,900/PK-12
201 N Water St 67202 316-973-4000
Winston Brooks, supt. Fax 973-4595
www.usd259.com
Allison Traditional Magnet MS 500/6-8
221 S Seneca St 67213 316-973-4800
Dr. Deborah Laudermilk, prin. Fax 973-4810
Blackbear Bosin Academy 7-9
6123 E 11th St N 67208 316-973-2600
Toby Martin, prin. Fax 973-2610
Brooks Technology & Arts Magnet MS 700/6-8
3802 E 27th St N 67220 316-973-6450
Robert Garner, prin. Fax 973-6581
Coleman MS 600/6-8
1544 N Governeour Rd 67206 316-973-6600
Stephanie Stovall, prin. Fax 973-6699
Curtis MS 700/6-8
1031 S Edgemoor St 67218 316-973-7350
Keith Wilson, prin. Fax 973-7410
Hadley MS 800/6-8
1101 N Dougherty Ave 67212 316-973-7800
Dr. Shelly Martin, prin. Fax 973-7737
Hamilton MS 500/6-8
1407 S Broadway St 67211 316-973-5350
Belinda Whitten, prin. Fax 973-5360
Jardine MS Magnet 700/6-8
3550 E Ross Pkwy 67210 316-973-4300
Judy Rapp, prin. Fax 973-4310
Marshall MS 400/6-8
1510 N Payne Ave 67203 316-973-9000
Mark Jollife, prin. Fax 973-9010
Mayberry Magnet MS 600/6-8
207 S Sheridan St 67213 316-973-5800
Tim Seguine, prin. Fax 973-5808
Mead MS 500/6-8
2601 E Skinner St 67211 316-973-8500
Mike Shaw, prin. Fax 973-8503
Northeast Magnet HS & Downtown Law 700/9-12
1847 N Chautauqua St 67214 316-973-2300
David Wessling, prin. Fax 973-2307
Pleasant Valley MS 600/6-8
2220 W 29th St N 67204 316-973-8000
Charles Wakefield, prin. Fax 973-8008
Robinson MS 700/6-8
328 N Oliver St 67208 316-973-8600
Jennifer Sinclair, prin. Fax 973-8625
Secondary Career Technical Education Vo/Tech
820 S Osage St 67213 316-973-3680
Joel Hudson, dir.
Stucky MS 700/6-8
4545 N Broadview Cir 67220 316-973-8400
Terrell Davis, prin. Fax 973-8410
Truesdell MS 900/6-8
2464 S Glenn Ave 67217 316-973-3900
Fred Lichtenfelt, prin. Fax 973-3904
Wichita East HS 2,300/9-12
2301 E Douglas Ave 67211 316-973-7200
Ken Thiessen, prin. Fax 973-7224
Wichita Heights HS 1,600/9-12
5301 N Hillside St 67219 316-973-1400
Bruce Deterding, prin. Fax 973-1410
Wichita North HS 1,700/9-12
1437 N Rochester St 67203 316-973-6300
Sherman Padgett, prin. Fax 973-6190
Wichita Northwest HS 1,500/9-12
1220 N Tyler Rd 67212 316-973-6000
Jim McNiece, prin. Fax 973-6070
Wichita Southeast HS 1,900/9-12
903 S Edgemoor St 67218 316-973-2700
Leroy Parks, prin. Fax 973-2755
Wichita South HS 1,600/9-12
701 W 33rd St S 67217 316-973-5450
Cara Ledy, prin. Fax 973-5519
Wichita West HS 1,500/9-12
820 S Osage St 67213 316-973-3600
Lori Doyle, prin. Fax 973-3657
Wilbur MS 1,000/6-8
340 N Tyler Rd 67212 316-973-1100
Cherie Crain, prin. Fax 973-1110

Bishop Carroll HS 1,000/9-12
8101 W Central Ave 67212 316-722-2390
Vanessa Harshberger, prin. Fax 722-6670
Classic College of Hair Design Post-Sec.
1675 S Rock Rd Ste 101 67207 316-681-2288
Friends University Post-Sec.
2100 W University Ave 67213 316-295-5000
Independent S 800/K-12
8301 E Douglas Ave 67207 316-686-0152
Chris Ashbrook, hdmstr. Fax 686-3918
Kapaun Mt. Carmel HS 800/9-12
8506 E Central Ave 67206 316-634-0315
Dr. Dennis McGuire, prin. Fax 636-2437
Newman University Post-Sec.
3100 W McCormick St 67213 316-942-4291
Old Town Barber & Beauty College Post-Sec.
1207 E Douglas Ave 67211 316-264-4891
Trinity Academy 200/9-12
12345 E 21st St N 67206 316-634-0909
David Swank, hdmstr. Fax 634-0928
Vatterott College Post-Sec.
3639 N Comotara St 67226 316-634-0066
Vernon's Kansas School of Cosmetology Post-Sec.
2531 S Seneca St 67217 316-265-2629
Wichita Adventist Christian Academy 100/K-10
2725 S Osage Ave 67217 316-267-9472
Sharon Burton, prin.
Wichita Area Technical College Post-Sec.
2021 S Eisenhower St 67209 316-677-1550
Wichita Area Technical College Post-Sec.
324 N Emporia St 67202 316-833-4664
Wichita Area Technical College Post-Sec.
301 S Grove St 67211 316-677-9282
Wichita Collegiate S 1,000/PK-12
9115 E 13th St N 67206 316-634-0433
Tom Davis, hdmstr. Fax 634-0598
Wichita State University Post-Sec.
1845 Fairmount St 67260 316-978-3456
Wichita Technical Institute Post-Sec.
2051 S Meridian Ave 67213 316-943-2241
Xenon International Academy Post-Sec.
3804 W Douglas Ave 67203 316-943-5516

Williamsburg, Franklin, Pop. 359
West Franklin USD 287
Supt. — See Pomona
Williamsburg HS 100/9-12
PO Box 7 66095 785-746-5777
Susan Wildeman, prin. Fax 746-5250

Wilson, Ellsworth, Pop. 767
Lorraine USD 328
Supt. — See Lorraine
Wilson JSHS 100/7-12
PO Box 220 67490 785-658-2202
Brian Smith, prin. Fax 658-2205

Winchester, Jefferson, Pop. 582
Jefferson County North USD 339 500/K-12
310 5th St 66097 913-774-2000
Timothy Marshall, supt. Fax 774-2027
www.usd339.net
Jefferson County North HS 200/9-12
302 5th St 66097 913-774-8515
Michael Hess, prin. Fax 774-8535
Other Schools – See Nortonville

Winfield, Cowley, Pop. 11,861
Winfield USD 465 2,300/PK-12
1407 Wheat Rd 67156 620-221-5100
Marvin Estes, supt. Fax 221-0508
usd465.com/cms/
Winfield HS 800/9-12
300 Viking Blvd 67156 620-221-5160
Greg Rinehart, prin. Fax 221-5165
Winfield MS 400/7-8
130 Viking Blvd 67156 620-221-5130
Dennis Gerber, prin. Fax 221-5147

Southwestern College Post-Sec.
100 College St 67156 620-229-6000

Winona, Logan, Pop. 205
Triplains USD 275 100/PK-12
PO Box 97 67764 785-846-7869
David Porter, supt. Fax 846-7767
www.usd275.k12.ks.us
Winona HS 50/9-12
PO Box 97 67764 785-846-7496
David Porter, prin. Fax 846-7767

Yates Center, Woodson, Pop. 1,493
Woodson USD 366 500/PK-12
PO Box 160 66783 620-625-8804
Rusty Arnold, supt. Fax 625-8806
www.usd366.net
Yates Center HS 200/9-12
PO Box 160 66783 620-625-8820
Noah Francis, prin. Fax 625-8850

KENTUCKY

KENTUCKY DEPARTMENT OF EDUCATION
500 Mero St, Frankfort 40601
Telephone 502-564-4770
Fax 502-564-5680
Website http://www.education.ky.gov

Commissioner of Education Kevin Noland

KENTUCKY BOARD OF EDUCATION
500 Mero St Ste 1, Frankfort 40601-1957

Chairperson Keith Travis

PUBLIC, PRIVATE AND CATHOLIC SECONDARY SCHOOLS

Albany, Clinton, Pop. 2,288
Clinton County SD 1,600/K-12
RR 4 Box 100 42602 606-387-6480
Mickey McFall, supt. Fax 387-5437
www.clinton.k12.ky.us
Clinton County HS 500/9-12
RR 4 Box 35 42602 606-387-5569
David Warinner, prin. Fax 387-8659
Clinton County MS 500/5-8
RR 4 Box 90 42602 606-387-6466
Jimmy Brown, prin. Fax 387-6469

Kentucky Tech System
Supt. — None
Clinton County Area Technology Center Vo/Tech
RR 4 Box 40 42602 606-387-6448
Alfredda Stevens, prin. Fax 387-4035

Alexandria, Campbell, Pop. 7,996
Campbell County SD 4,000/K-12
101 Orchard Ln 41001 859-635-2173
Anthony Strong, supt. Fax 448-2439
www.campbellcountyschools.org/
Campbell County HS 1,500/9-12
909 Camel Xing 41001 859-635-4161
Ginger Webb, prin. Fax 448-4886
Campbell County MS 1,000/6-8
8000 Alexandria Pike 41001 859-635-6077
Dave Sandlin, prin. Fax 448-4863

Kentucky Tech System
Supt. — None
McCormick Area Technology Center Vo/Tech
50 Orchard Ln 41001 859-635-4101
Joseph Amann, prin. Fax 635-2766

Bishop Brossart HS 400/9-12
4 Grove St 41001 859-635-2108
Thomas Seither, prin. Fax 635-2135

Ashland, Boyd, Pop. 21,510
Ashland ISD 3,200/K-12
PO Box 3000 41105 606-327-2706
Phil Eason, supt. Fax 327-2705
www.ashland.k12.ky.us/
Blazer HS 1,000/9-12
1500 Blazer Blvd 41102 606-327-6040
Andy Ballash, prin. Fax 324-0517
Verity MS 500/7-8
2800 Kansas St 41102 606-327-2727
Richard Oppenheimer, prin. Fax 327-2765

Boyd County SD 3,300/PK-12
1104 Bob McCullough Dr 41102 606-928-4141
Howard Osborne, supt. Fax 928-4771
www.boyd.k12.ky.us
Boyd County Career & Technical Center Vo/Tech
12300 Midland Trail Rd 41102 606-928-7120
Loretta Dixon, dir. Fax 928-6432
Boyd County HS 1,000/9-12
12307 Midland Trail Rd 41102 606-928-7100
Rhonda Salisbury, prin. Fax 928-1312
Boyd County MS 700/6-8
1226 Summitt Rd 41102 606-928-9547
Bill Boblett, prin. Fax 928-2067
Other Schools – See Rush

Fairview ISD 800/PK-12
2127 Main St W 41102 606-324-3877
Bill Musick, supt. Fax 324-2288
www.fairview.k12.ky.us
Fairview JSHS 400/7-12
2123 Main St W 41102 606-324-9226
Brad Greene, prin. Fax 325-1486

Ashland Community and Technical College Post-Sec.
1400 College Dr 41101 606-329-2999
Rose Hill Christian S 300/PK-12
1001 Winslow Rd 41102 606-329-1957
Dr. Randy Douglas, admin. Fax 324-6420

Augusta, Bracken, Pop. 1,257
Augusta ISD 300/K-12
307 Bracken St 41002 606-756-2545
John Cordle, supt. Fax 756-2149
www.augusta.k12.ky.us
Augusta JSHS 6-12
207 Bracken St 41002 606-756-2105
Lisa McCane, prin. Fax 756-3000

Barbourville, Knox, Pop. 3,520
Barbourville ISD 300/PK-12
PO Box 520 40906 606-546-3120
Larry Warren, supt. Fax 546-3452
www.barbourvilleind.com
Barbourville S 300/PK-12
PO Box 520 40906 606-546-3129
Paul Middleton, prin. Fax 546-3337

Kentucky Tech System
Supt. — None
Knox County Area Technology Center Vo/Tech
210 Wall St 40906 606-546-5320
Ralph Halcomb, prin. Fax 546-3818

Knox County SD 4,000/PK-12
200 Daniel Boone Dr 40906 606-546-3157
Walter Hulett, supt. Fax 546-2819
www.knox.k12.ky.us/
Knox Central HS 900/9-12
100 Panther Way 40906 606-546-9253
Allen Storie, prin. Fax 546-5684
Knox County MS 7-8
311 N Main St 40906 606-545-5267
Kelly Sprinkles, prin. Fax 546-2161
Other Schools – See Corbin

Union College Post-Sec.
310 College St 40906 606-546-4151

Bardstown, Nelson, Pop. 10,984
Bardstown ISD 1,800/PK-12
308 N 5th St 40004 502-331-8800
Brent Holsclaw, supt. Fax 331-8830
www.btown.k12.ky.us
Bardstown HS 500/9-12
400 N 5th St 40004 502-331-8802
Thomas Hamilton, prin. Fax 331-8832
Bardstown MS 500/6-8
410 N 5th St 40004 502-331-8803
Bob Blackmon, prin. Fax 331-8833

Kentucky Tech System
Supt. — None
Nelson County Area Technology Center Vo/Tech
1060 Bloomfield Rd 40004 502-348-9096
John Sanders, prin. Fax 348-9097

Nelson County SD 4,600/PK-12
PO Box 2277 40004 502-349-7000
Janice Lantz, supt. Fax 349-7004
www.nelson.k12.ky.us
Nelson County HS 1,500/9-12
1070 Bloomfield Rd 40004 502-349-7010
Sara Wilson, prin. Fax 349-7017
Old Kentucky Home MS 600/6-8
301 Wildcat Ln 40004 502-349-7040
Ryan Clark, prin. Fax 349-7042
Other Schools – See Bloomfield

Bethlehem HS 300/9-12
309 W Stephen Foster Ave 40004 502-348-8594
Paul Schum, prin. Fax 349-1247

Bardwell, Carlisle, Pop. 793
Carlisle County SD 800/PK-12
4557 State Route 1377 42023 270-628-3800
Danny Brown, supt. Fax 628-5477
www.carlisle.k12.ky.us/
Carlisle County HS 200/9-12
4557 State Route 1377 42023 270-628-3800
Kelli Edging, prin. Fax 628-3837
Carlisle County MS 200/6-8
4557 State Route 1377 42023 270-628-3800
Jackie Ballard, prin. Fax 628-3974

Barlow, Ballard, Pop. 713
Ballard County SD 1,300/PK-12
3465 Paducah Rd 42024 270-665-8400
Edward Adami, supt. Fax 665-9844
www.ballard.k12.ky.us
Ballard County MS 300/6-8
3561 Paducah Rd 42024 270-665-8400
Casey Allen, prin. Fax 665-5153
Ballard Memorial HS 400/9-12
3561 Paducah Rd 42024 270-665-8400
Donald Shively, prin. Fax 665-5312
Ballard Technical & Career Center Vo/Tech
11 Vocational School Rd 42024 270-665-8400
Dana Rohrer, prin. Fax 665-5006

Beattyville, Lee, Pop. 1,153
Kentucky Tech System
Supt. — None
Lee County Area Technology Center Vo/Tech
PO Box B 41311 606-464-5018
Jerry Hollon, prin. Fax 464-0663

Lee County SD 1,200/K-12
PO Box 668 41311 606-464-5000
Frank Kincaid, supt. Fax 464-5009
www.lee.k12.ky.us
Lee County HS 300/9-12
PO Box J 41311 606-464-5005
James Evans, prin. Fax 464-5014
Lee County MS 300/6-8
PO Box N 41311 606-464-5010
Alice Sipple, prin. Fax 464-5011

Bedford, Trimble, Pop. 740
Trimble County SD 1,600/K-12
PO Box 275 40006 502-255-3201
Marcia Haney-Dunaway, supt. Fax 255-5105
www.trimble.k12.ky.us/
Trimble County HS 500/9-12
1029 Highway 421 N 40006 502-255-7781
Rebecca Moore, prin. Fax 255-5126
Trimble County MS 400/6-8
116 Wentworth Ave 40006 502-255-7361
Mike Genton, prin. Fax 255-5102

Belfry, Pike
Kentucky Tech System
Supt. — None
Belfry Area Technology Center Vo/Tech
PO Box 280 41514 606-353-4951
Annette Harris-Ward, prin. Fax 353-0868

Pike County SD
Supt. — See Pikeville
Belfry HS 700/9-12
PO Box 160 41514 606-237-3900
Rod Varney, prin. Fax 237-5119
Belfry MS 6-8
PO Box 850 41514 606-353-9688
James Hurley, prin. Fax 353-0530

Bellevue, Campbell, Pop. 6,022
Bellevue ISD 800/PK-12
219 Center St 41073 859-261-2108
Wayne Starnes, supt. Fax 261-1708
www.bellevue.k12.ky.us/
Bellevue HS 400/7-12
201 Center St 41073 859-261-2980
Mike Wills, prin. Fax 261-1825

Benton, Marshall, Pop. 4,335
Marshall County SD 4,600/PK-12
86 High School Rd 42025 270-527-8628
Steve Knight, supt. Fax 527-0804
www.marshall.k12.ky.us
Benton MS 300/6-8
906 Joe Creason Dr 42025 270-527-9091
Kem Cothran, prin. Fax 527-9992
Marshall County HS 1,400/9-12
416 High School Rd 42025 270-527-1453
Trent Lovett, prin. Fax 527-0578
Marshall County Technical Center Vo/Tech
341 High School Rd 42025 270-527-8648
Lewis Mathis, prin. Fax 527-1920

South Marshall MS 300/6-8
85 Sid Darnall Rd 42025 270-527-3828
Russell Buchanan, prin. Fax 527-7616
Other Schools – See Calvert City

Christian Fellowship S 200/PK-12
1343 US Highway 68 E 42025 270-527-8377
Donnie Peal, supt. Fax 527-2872

Berea, Madison, Pop. 13,230
Berea ISD 1,100/PK-12
3 Pirate Pkwy 40403 859-986-8446
Gary Conkin, supt. Fax 986-1839
www.berea.k12.ky.us
Berea Community HS 300/9-12
1 Pirate Pkwy 40403 859-986-4911
John Masters, prin. Fax 986-4640
Berea Community MS 200/6-8
1 Pirate Pkwy 40403 859-986-4911
John Masters, prin. Fax 986-4640

Madison County SD
Supt. — See Richmond
Foley MS 800/6-8
211 Glades Rd 40403 859-986-8473
Arno Norwell, prin. Fax 986-3362
Madison Southern HS 900/9-12
213 Glades Rd 40403 859-986-8424
David Gilliam, prin. Fax 986-3092

Berea College 40404 Post-Sec.
859-985-3000

Betsy Layne, Floyd
Floyd County SD
Supt. — See Prestonsburg
Betsy Layne HS 500/9-12
PO Box 437 41605 606-478-9138
Sean Ousley, prin. Fax 478-3805

Beverly, Bell

Red Bird Mission S 200/K-12
15420 S Highway 66 40913 606-598-2416
Robert Ferguson, prin. Fax 598-7314

Bloomfield, Nelson, Pop. 873
Nelson County SD
Supt. — See Bardstown
Bloomfield MS 400/6-8
96 Arnold Ln 40008 502-349-7201
Glenn Spalding, prin. Fax 349-7203

Booneville, Owsley, Pop. 152
Owsley County SD 800/PK-12
PO Box 340 41314 606-593-6363
Stephen Jackson, supt. Fax 593-6368
www.owsley.k12.ky.us
Owsley County JSHS 300/7-12
PO Box 310 41314 606-593-5185
Teresa Barrett, prin. Fax 593-6312

Bowling Green, Warren, Pop. 52,272
Bowling Green ISD 3,500/PK-12
1211 Center St 42101 270-746-2200
Mr. Joseph Tinius, supt. Fax 746-2205
www.b-g.k12.ky.us
Bowling Green HS 1,000/9-12
1801 Rockingham Ave 42104 270-746-2300
Gary Fields, prin. Fax 746-2305
Bowling Green JHS 800/6-8
900 Campbell Ln 42104 270-746-2290
Dr. Penny Masden, prin. Fax 746-2295

Kentucky Tech System
Supt. — None
Warren County Area Technology Center Vo/Tech
365 Technology Way 42101 270-746-7184
Don Evans, prin. Fax 746-7186

Warren County SD 11,400/PK-12
PO Box 51810 42102 270-781-5150
Dale Brown, supt. Fax 781-2392
www.warren.k12.ky.us/
Drakes Creek MS 700/7-8
704 Cypress Wood Ln 42104 270-843-0165
David Hutchison, prin. Fax 782-6138
Greenwood HS 1,400/9-12
5065 Scottsville Rd 42104 270-842-3627
Mark Davis, prin. Fax 842-2037
Moss MS 600/7-8
2565 Russellville Rd 42101 270-843-0166
Tom Renick, prin. Fax 843-8512
Warren Central HS 1,100/9-12
559 Morgantown Rd 42101 270-842-7302
Kathy Goff, prin. Fax 781-5115
Warren East HS 800/9-12
6867 Louisville Rd 42101 270-781-1277
Bailey Norris, prin. Fax 843-2610
Warren East MS 500/7-8
7031 Louisville Rd 42101 270-843-0181
Beverly Dillard, prin. Fax 781-8565

Bowling Green Technical College Post-Sec.
1845 Loop Ave 42101 270-746-7461
Bowling Green Technical College Post-Sec.
1127 Morgantown Rd 42101 270-746-7807
Draughons Junior College Post-Sec.
2421 Industrial Dr 42101 270-843-6750
PJs College of Cosmetology Post-Sec.
1901 Russellville Rd Ste 10 42101 270-846-6444
Western Kentucky University Post-Sec.
1 Big Red Way 42101 270-745-0111

Brandenburg, Meade, Pop. 2,214
Kentucky Tech System
Supt. — None
Meade County Area Technology Center Vo/Tech
110 Greer St 40108 270-422-3955
Faye Campbell, prin. Fax 422-3307

Meade County SD 4,700/PK-12
PO Box 337 40108 270-422-7500
Mitch Crump, supt. Fax 422-5494
www.meade.k12.ky.us
Meade County HS 1,500/9-12
938 Old State Rd 40108 270-422-7515
William Adams, prin. Fax 422-3928
Pepper MS 800/7-8
1055 Old Ekron Rd 40108 270-422-7530
Kellianne Wilson, prin. Fax 422-5515

Brooksville, Bracken, Pop. 609
Bracken County SD 1,200/PK-12
348 W Miami St 41004 606-735-2523
Tony Johnson, supt. Fax 735-3640
www.bracken.k12.ky.us
Bracken County HS 400/9-12
PO Box 128 41004 606-735-3153
Martha Hall, prin. Fax 735-2549
Bracken County MS 400/5-8
167 Parsley Dr 41004 606-735-3425
Leah Jefferson, prin. Fax 735-2057

Brownsville, Edmonson, Pop. 1,039
Edmonson County SD 2,000/K-12
PO Box 129 42210 270-597-2101
Patrick Waddell, supt. Fax 597-2103
www.edmonson.k12.ky.us
Edmonson County HS 600/9-12
220 Wild Cat Way 42210 270-597-2151
Brian Alexander, prin. Fax 597-2962
Edmonson County MS 300/7-8
210 Wild Cat Way 42210 270-597-2932
Ricky Houchin, prin. Fax 597-2182

Buckhorn, Perry, Pop. 149
Perry County SD
Supt. — See Hazard
Buckhorn HS 200/9-12
18392 KY Highway 28 41721 606-398-7176
Harvey Colwell, prin. Fax 398-7930

Buckner, Oldham
Oldham County SD 10,200/PK-12
PO Box 218 40010 502-222-8880
Paul Upchurch, supt. Fax 222-8885
www.oldham.k12.ky.us
Oldham County HS 1,200/9-12
PO Box 187 40010 502-222-9461
Dave Weedman, prin. Fax 222-0558
Oldham County MS 1,000/6-8
PO Box 157 40010 502-222-1451
Chris Kraft, prin. Fax 222-5178
Other Schools – See Crestwood, Goshen

Burgin, Mercer, Pop. 873
Burgin ISD 400/PK-12
PO Box B 40310 859-748-4000
Richard Webb, supt. Fax 748-4010
www.burgin.k12.ky.us
Burgin HS 200/6-12
PO Box B 40310 859-748-5282
Martha Collier, prin. Fax 748-4002

Burkesville, Cumberland, Pop. 1,760
Cumberland County SD 1,100/K-12
PO Box 420 42717 270-864-3377
John Hurt, supt. Fax 864-5803
www.cland.k12.ky.us
Cumberland County HS 300/9-12
PO Box 380 42717 270-864-3451
Kay Graham-Bright, prin. Fax 864-1284
Cumberland County MS 300/6-8
PO Box 70 42717 270-864-5818
Glen Murphy, prin. Fax 864-2590

Burlington, Boone, Pop. 6,070
Boone County SD
Supt. — See Florence
Camp Ernst MS 6-8
6515 Camp Ernst Rd 41005 859-534-4000
Eric McArtor, prin. Fax 534-4001

Burna, Livingston
Livingston County SD
Supt. — See Smithland
Livingston County MS 200/7-8
PO Box 109 42028 270-988-3263
Larry McGregor, prin. Fax 988-2518

Butler, Pendleton, Pop. 634
Pendleton County SD
Supt. — See Falmouth
Sharp MS 700/6-8
35 Wright Rd 41006 859-472-7000
Jeff Aulick, prin. Fax 472-7011

Cadiz, Trigg, Pop. 2,550
Trigg County SD 1,900/K-12
202 Main St 42211 270-522-6075
Tim McGinnis, supt. Fax 522-7782
www.trigg.kyschools.us
Trigg County HS 600/9-12
203 Main St 42211 270-522-2200
Chad Pruitt, prin. Fax 522-2224
Trigg County MS 500/6-8
206 Lafayette St 42211 270-522-2210
James Mangels, prin. Fax 522-2203

Calhoun, McLean, Pop. 813
McLean County SD 1,500/K-12
PO Box 245 42327 270-273-5257
William Melloy, supt. Fax 273-5259
www.mclean.k12.ky.us
McLean County HS 500/9-12
1859 State Route 136 E 42327 270-273-5278
Tommy Burrough, prin. Fax 273-5208
McLean County MS 400/6-8
1901 State Route 136 E 42327 270-273-5191
Tres Settle, prin. Fax 273-9876

Calvert City, Marshall, Pop. 2,749
Marshall County SD
Supt. — See Benton
North Marshall MS 600/6-8
3111 US Highway 95 42029 270-395-7108
Kent Barlow, prin. Fax 395-5449

Campbellsville, Taylor, Pop. 10,906
Campbellsville ISD 1,300/K-12
136 S Columbia Ave 42718 270-465-4162
Diane Woods-Ayers, supt. Fax 465-3918
www.cville.k12.ky.us/
Campbellsville HS 400/9-12
230 W Main St 42718 270-465-8774
Drew Muntz, prin. Fax 789-4007
Campbellsville MS 400/5-8
315 Roberts Rd 42718 270-465-5121
Chris Kidwell, prin. Fax 789-3718

Taylor County SD 2,500/K-12
1209 E Broadway St 42718 270-465-5371
Gary Seaborne, supt. Fax 789-3954
www.taylor.k12.ky.us
Taylor County HS 800/9-12
300 Ingram Ave 42718 270-465-4431
Gaylon Yarberry, prin. Fax 465-5731
Taylor County MS 600/6-8
1207 E Broadway St 42718 270-465-2877
Cherry Harvey, prin. Fax 789-1753

Campbellsville University Post-Sec.
1 University Dr 42718 270-789-5000

Campton, Wolfe, Pop. 410
Wolfe County SD 1,300/PK-12
PO Box 160 41301 606-668-8002
Stephen Butcher, supt. Fax 668-8050
www.wolfe.k12.ky.us
Wolfe County HS 400/9-12
PO Box 790 41301 606-668-8202
Deatrah Barnett, prin. Fax 668-8250
Wolfe County MS 300/6-8
PO Box 460 41301 606-668-8152
Wilma Terrill, prin. Fax 668-8100

Carlisle, Nicholas, Pop. 2,030
Nicholas County SD 1,200/K-12
395 W Main St 40311 859-289-3770
Gregory Reid, supt. Fax 289-3777
www.nicholas.k12.ky.us/
Nicholas County HS 300/9-12
103 School Dr 40311 859-289-3780
Joe Orazen, prin. Fax 289-6429

Carrollton, Carroll, Pop. 3,861
Carroll County SD 1,800/K-12
813 Hawkins St 41008 502-732-7070
Carroll Yager, supt. Fax 732-7073
www.carroll.kyschools.us
Carroll County HS 500/9-12
1706 Highland Ave 41008 502-732-7075
Curt Haun, prin. Fax 732-7012
Carroll County MS 500/6-8
408 5th St 41008 502-732-7080
Bill Hogan, prin. Fax 732-7107

Kentucky Tech System
Supt. — None
Carroll County Area Technology Center Vo/Tech
1704 Highland Ave 41008 502-732-4479
Jennifer Stafford, prin. Fax 732-4837

Christian Academy of Carrollton 200/PK-12
1703 Easterday Rd 41008 502-732-4734
Katie Matson, admin. Fax 732-4732

Catlettsburg, Boyd, Pop. 1,927

Calvary Christian S 100/PK-12
17839 Bear Creek Rd 41129 606-929-5599
Denise Wallace, dir. Fax 928-9219

Cave City, Barren, Pop. 2,054
Caverna ISD 800/PK-12
1102 N Dixie Hwy 42127 270-773-2530
Samuel Dick, supt. Fax 773-2524
www.caverna.k12.ky.us
Other Schools – See Horse Cave

Cecilia, Hardin
Hardin County SD
Supt. — See Elizabethtown
Central Hardin HS 1,500/9-12
3040 Leitchfield Rd 42724 270-737-6800
Ron Ortiz, prin. Fax 765-3889
West Hardin MS 600/6-8
10471 Leitchfield Rd 42724 270-862-3924
James Roe, prin. Fax 862-3647

Clinton, Hickman, Pop. 1,364
Hickman County SD 800/PK-12
416 N Waterfield Dr 42031 270-653-2341
Steve Bayko, supt. Fax 653-6007
www.hickman.k12.ky.us
Hickman County HS 400/7-12
301 Cresap St 42031 270-653-4044
Richard Brazell, prin. Fax 653-3200

Cloverport, Breckinridge, Pop. 1,262
Cloverport ISD 300/PK-12
PO Box 37 40111 270-788-3910
James Skaggs, supt. Fax 788-6290
www.cport.k12.ky.us
Fraize HS 100/9-12
101 4th St 40111 270-788-3388
Josh Powell, prin. Fax 788-6640
Fraize MS 100/6-8
101 4th St 40111 270-788-3388
Josh Powell, prin. Fax 788-6640

Columbia, Adair, Pop. 4,174
Adair County SD 1,800/PK-12
1204 Greensburg St 42728 270-384-2476
Darrell Treece, supt. Fax 384-5841
www.adair.k12.ky.us
Adair County HS 700/9-12
526 Indian Dr 42728 270-384-2751
Troy Young, prin. Fax 384-6900
Adair County MS 300/7-8
322 General John Adair Dr 42728 270-384-5308
Alma Rich, prin. Fax 384-2168

Lindsey Wilson College Post-Sec.
210 Lindsey Wilson St 42728 270-384-8100

Corbin, Whitley, Pop. 8,230
Corbin ISD 2,000/K-12
108 Roy Kidd Ave 40701 606-528-1303
Ed McNeel, supt. Fax 523-1747
www.corbinschools.org
Corbin East S 50/6-12
529 Master St 40701 606-528-4080
Dalene McBurney, prin. Fax 523-3614
Corbin HS 600/9-12
1901 Snyder St 40701 606-528-3902
Joyce Phillips, prin. Fax 523-3627
Corbin MS 500/6-8
706 S Kentucky Ave 40701 606-523-3619
Dave Cox, prin. Fax 523-3621

Kentucky Tech System
Supt. — None
Corbin Area Technology Center Vo/Tech
1909 Snyder St 40701 606-528-5338
Patty Cummins, prin. Fax 528-0532

Knox County SD
Supt. — See Barbourville
Lynn Camp JSHS 500/7-12
100 N KY 830 40701 606-528-5429
Larry Mills, prin. Fax 528-4750

Covington, Kenton, Pop. 42,811
Covington ISD 3,900/PK-12
25 E 7th St 41011 859-392-1000
Jack Moreland, supt. Fax 292-5916
www.covington.k12.ky.us
Holmes JSHS 1,200/8-12
2500 Madison Ave 41014 859-655-9545
Ray Finke, prin. Fax 581-7386
Covington Adult HS Adult
3618 Caroline St 41015 859-292-5937
Marvin Counts, coord. Fax 292-5866

Kenton County SD
Supt. — See Fort Wright
Scott HS 1,200/9-12
5400 Old Taylor Mill Rd 41015 859-356-3146
Clay Dawson, prin. Fax 356-5516

Calvary Christian S 600/PK-12
5955 Taylor Mill Rd 41015 859-356-9201
Donald James, admin. Fax 356-8962
Covington Catholic HS 500/9-12
1600 Dixie Hwy 41011 859-491-2247
Michael Clines, prin. Fax 448-2242
Covington Latin HS 200/8-12
21 E 11th St 41011 859-291-7044
Andrew Barczak, prin. Fax 291-1939
Holy Cross HS 400/9-12
3617 Church St 41015 859-431-1335
Clay Eifert, prin. Fax 655-2184
Notre Dame Academy 600/9-12
1699 Hilton Dr 41011 859-261-4300
Sr. Elaine Marie Winter, prin. Fax 292-7722

Crestview Hills, Kenton, Pop. 3,362

Thomas More College Post-Sec.
333 Thomas More Pkwy 41017 859-341-5800

Crestwood, Oldham, Pop. 2,250
Oldham County SD
Supt. — See Buckner
East Oldham MS 6-8
1201 E Highway 22 40014 502-222-8480
Lynda Redmon, prin. Fax 222-8489
South Oldham HS 1,000/9-12
5901 Veterens Memorial Pkwy 40014 502-241-6681
Dorenda Neihof, prin. Fax 241-0955
South Oldham MS 800/6-8
6403 W Highway 146 40014 502-241-0320
Rob Clayton, prin. Fax 241-1438

Trend Setter's Academy of Beauty Culture Post-Sec.
6539 W Highway 22 40014 502-241-0565

Cumberland, Harlan, Pop. 2,330
Harlan County SD
Supt. — See Harlan
Cumberland HS 300/9-12
600 Redskin Dr 40823 606-589-4625
Ed Clem, prin. Fax 589-2312

Southeast Kentucky Community/Tech Coll Post-Sec.
300 College Rd 40823 606-589-2145

Cynthiana, Harrison, Pop. 6,311
Harrison County SD 3,200/K-12
324 Webster Ave 41031 859-234-7110
Dr. Roy Woodward, supt. Fax 234-8164
www.harrison.k12.ky.us
Harrison County HS 1,000/9-12
320 Webster Ave 41031 859-234-7117
Robert Barr, prin. Fax 234-0115
Harrison County MS 800/6-8
269 Education Dr 41031 859-234-7123
Michael McIntire, prin. Fax 234-8385

Kentucky Tech System
Supt. — None
Harrison County Area Technology Center Vo/Tech
327 Webster Ave 41031 859-234-5286
John Hodge, prin. Fax 234-0658

Danville, Boyle, Pop. 15,409
Boyle County SD 2,700/PK-12
352 N Danville Byp 40422 859-236-6634
Steve Burkich, supt. Fax 236-8624
www.boyle.k12.ky.us
Boyle County HS 900/9-12
1637 Perryville Rd 40422 859-236-5047
Elmer Thomas, prin. Fax 236-7820
Boyle County MS 700/6-8
1651 Perryville Rd 40422 859-236-4212
Mike LaFavers, prin. Fax 236-9596

Danville ISD 1,800/K-12
152 E Martin L King Blvd 40422 859-238-1300
Robert Rowland, supt. Fax 238-1330
www.danville.k12.ky.us
Bate MS 400/6-8
460 Stanford Ave 40422 859-238-1305
Michael Godbey, prin. Fax 238-1343
Danville HS 500/9-12
203 E Lexington Ave 40422 859-238-1308
Joseph Payne, prin. Fax 238-1338

Central Kentucky Technical College Post-Sec.
59 Corporate Dr 40422 859-239-7030
Centre College Post-Sec.
600 W Walnut St 40422 859-238-5200
Kentucky School for the Deaf Post-Sec.
S 2nd St 40422 859-239-7017
National College Post-Sec.
115 E Lexington Ave 40422 859-236-6991

Dawson Springs, Hopkins, Pop. 2,953
Dawson Springs ISD 700/PK-12
118 E Arcadia Ave 42408 270-797-3811
Alexis Seymore, supt. Fax 797-5201
www.dsprings.k12.ky.us/
Dawson Springs HS 200/9-12
317 Eli St 42408 270-797-2957
Renee Miller, prin. Fax 797-5204
Dawson Springs MS 200/5-8
317 Eli St 42408 270-797-2991
Renee Miller, prin. Fax 797-5201

Dayton, Campbell, Pop. 5,556
Dayton ISD 1,000/K-12
200 Clay St 41074 859-491-6565
Gary Rye, supt. Fax 292-3995
www.dayton.k12.ky.us
Dayton HS 500/7-12
200 Greendevil Ln 41074 859-292-7486
Dan Ridder, prin. Fax 261-1606

Dixon, Webster, Pop. 611
Kentucky Tech System
Supt. — None
Webster County Area Technology Center Vo/Tech
PO Box 230 42409 270-639-5035
Tom Sisk, prin. Fax 639-5545

Webster County SD 1,900/PK-12
28 State Route 1340 42409 270-639-5083
James Kemp, supt. Fax 639-0117
www.webster.k12.ky.us
Webster County HS 600/9-12
1922 US Highway 41A S 42409 270-639-5092
Carolyn Sholar, prin. Fax 639-0128

Dry Ridge, Grant, Pop. 2,176
Grant County SD
Supt. — See Williamstown
Grant County HS 1,100/9-12
715 Warsaw Rd 41035 859-824-9739
Tracey Glass-Lamb, prin. Fax 824-9756
Grant County MS 900/6-8
305 School Rd 41035 859-824-7161
James Lacey, prin. Fax 824-7163

Eastern, Floyd
Floyd County SD
Supt. — See Prestonsburg
Allen Central HS 400/9-12
PO Box 139 41622 606-358-9543
Lorena Hall, prin. Fax 358-9247
Allen Central MS 300/6-8
PO Box 193 41622 606-358-0110
Davida Bickford, prin. Fax 358-0112

Eddyville, Lyon, Pop. 2,373
Lyon County SD 1,000/K-12
217 Jenkins Rd 42038 270-388-9715
Dr. Lee Gold, supt. Fax 388-4962
www.lyon.k12.ky.us
Lyon County HS 300/9-12
209 W Fairview Ave 42038 270-388-9715
Carroll Wadlington, prin. Fax 388-2296
Lyon County MS 300/6-8
111 W Fairview Ave 42038 270-388-9715
Victor Zimmerman, prin. Fax 388-0517

Edgewood, Kenton, Pop. 8,913
Kenton County SD
Supt. — See Fort Wright
Dixie Heights HS 1,200/9-12
3010 Dixie Hwy 41017 859-341-7650
Kimberly Banta, prin. Fax 341-2531
Turkey Foot MS 800/6-8
3230 Turkeyfoot Rd 41017 859-341-0216
Tom Arnzen, prin. Fax 341-7217

Gateway Community & Technical College Post-Sec.
790 Thomas More Pkwy 41017 859-442-4150
St. Elizabeth Medical Center Post-Sec.
1 Medical Village Dr 41017 859-301-2170

Edmonton, Metcalfe, Pop. 1,600
Metcalfe County SD 1,600/K-12
1007 W Stockton St 42129 270-432-3171
Patricia Hurt, supt. Fax 432-3170
www.metcalfe.k12.ky.us
Metcalfe County HS 500/9-12
208 Randolph St 42129 270-432-2481
David Nole, prin. Fax 432-2714
Metcalfe County MS 300/7-8
100 Hornet Ave 42129 270-432-3359
Mike Vaught, prin. Fax 432-5828

Elizabethtown, Hardin, Pop. 23,450
Elizabethtown ISD 2,300/K-12
219 Helm St 42701 270-765-6146
Dr. John Millay, supt. Fax 765-2158
www.etown.k12.ky.us
Elizabethtown HS 700/9-12
620 N Mulberry St 42701 270-769-3381
Nathan Huggins, prin. Fax 769-2539
Stone MS 500/6-8
323 Morningside Dr 42701 270-769-6343
Beth Mather, prin. Fax 769-6749

Hardin County SD 12,800/PK-12
65 W A Jenkins Rd 42701 270-769-8800
Nannette Johnston, supt. Fax 769-8888
www.hardin.k12.ky.us
Bluegrass MS 700/6-8
170 W A Jenkins Rd 42701 270-765-2658
Brenda Pirtle, prin. Fax 737-0450
Hardin HS 1,200/9-12
384 W A Jenkins Rd 42701 270-769-8906
Alvin Garrison, prin. Fax 769-8996
Other Schools – See Cecilia, Glendale, Radcliff, Vine Grove

Elizabethtown Beauty School Post-Sec.
308 N Miles St 42701 270-765-2118
Elizabethtown Christian Academy 100/K-10
PO Box 605 42702 270-234-8174
Margaret Atcher, prin. Fax 982-3774
Elizabethtown Community College Post-Sec.
600 College Street Rd 42701 270-769-2371
Elizabethtown Technical College Post-Sec.
620 College Street Rd 42701 270-766-5133
Trend Setter's Academy of Beauty Culture Post-Sec.
622B Westport Rd 42701 270-765-5243

Elkton, Todd, Pop. 1,941
Todd County SD 2,000/PK-12
205 Airport Rd 42220 270-265-2436
David Eakles, supt. Fax 265-5414
www.todd.k12.ky.us
Todd County Central HS 600/9-12
806 S Main St 42220 270-265-2506
Fax 265-9408
Todd County MS 500/6-8
515 W Main St 42220 270-265-2511
Ken Killebrew, prin. Fax 265-9414

Eminence, Henry, Pop. 2,257
Eminence ISD 600/PK-12
291 W Broadway St 40019 502-845-4788
Tina Tipton, supt. Fax 845-2339
www.eminence.k12.ky.us
Eminence JSHS 400/5-12
PO Box 146 40019 502-845-5427
Steve Frommeyer, prin. Fax 845-1310

Erlanger, Kenton, Pop. 16,852
Erlanger-Elsmere ISD 2,300/PK-12
500 Graves Ave 41018 859-727-2009
Michael D. Sander, supt. Fax 727-5653
www.erlanger.k12.ky.us
Lloyd HS 600/9-12
450 Bartlett Ave 41018 859-727-1555
John Riehemann, prin. Fax 727-5912
Tichenor MS 600/6-8
305 Bartlett Ave 41018 859-727-2255
Carl Schwierjohann, prin. Fax 342-2425

St. Henry HS 500/9-12
3755 Scheben Dr 41018 859-525-0255
David Otte, prin. Fax 525-5855

Evarts, Harlan, Pop. 1,052
Harlan County SD
Supt. — See Harlan
Evarts HS 400/9-12
PO Box 9 40828 606-837-2502
Bob Howard, prin. Fax 837-3411

Fairdale, Jefferson, Pop. 6,563
Jefferson County SD
Supt. — See Louisville
Fairdale HS Magnet Career Academy 800/9-12
1001 Fairdale Rd 40118 502-485-8248
Linda Brown, prin. Fax 485-8761

Falmouth, Pendleton, Pop. 2,096
Pendleton County SD 2,700/PK-12
2525 US Highway 27 N 41040 859-654-6911
J. Robert Yost, supt. Fax 654-6143
www.pendleton.k12.ky.us
Pendleton County HS 800/9-12
2359 US Highway 27 N 41040 859-654-3355
Ron Livingood, prin. Fax 654-4235
Other Schools – See Butler

Fern Creek, Jefferson, Pop. 16,406
Jefferson County SD
Supt. — See Louisville
Fern Creek Traditional HS 1,300/9-12
9115 Fern Creek Rd 40291 502-485-8251
Tito Castillo, prin. Fax 485-8032

Flemingsburg, Fleming, Pop. 3,104
Fleming County SD 2,500/K-12
211 W Water St 41041 606-845-5851
Kelley F. Crain, supt. Fax 849-3158
www.fleming.k12.ky.us/
Fleming County HS 800/9-12
1658 Elizaville Rd 41041 606-845-6601
Brad Sorrell, prin. Fax 845-3102
Simons MS 400/7-8
242 W Water St 41041 606-845-9331
Thomas Price, prin. Fax 849-2309

Florence, Boone, Pop. 26,349
Boone County SD 16,000/K-12
8330 US Highway 42 41042 859-283-1003
Bryan Blavatt, supt. Fax 282-3312
www.boone.kyschools.us/
Boone County HS 1,500/9-12
7056 Burlington Pike 41042 859-282-5655
Mark Raleigh, prin. Fax 282-5653
Jones MS 600/6-8
8000 Spruce Dr 41042 859-282-4610
Steve Sorrell, prin. Fax 282-2364
Ockerman MS 800/6-8
8300 US Highway 42 41042 859-282-3240
David Claggett, prin. Fax 282-3242
Other Schools – See Burlington, Hebron, Union

Beckfield College Post-Sec.
16 Spiral Dr 41042 859-371-9393
Hair Design School Post-Sec.
7285 Turfway Rd 41042 859-283-2690
Heritage Academy 300/K-12
7216 US Highway 42 41042 859-525-0213
Howard Davis, admin. Fax 525-0650
Interactive College of Technology Post-Sec.
11 Spiral Dr Ste 8 41042 859-282-8989
National College Post-Sec.
7627 Ewing Blvd 41042 859-525-6510
Southwestern College of Business Post-Sec.
8095 Connector Dr 41042 859-282-9999

Fort Knox, Hardin, Pop. 21,495

Sullivan University Post-Sec.
PO Box 998 40121 502-942-8500

Fort Mitchell, Kenton, Pop. 7,605
Beechwood ISD 1,000/PK-12
50 Beechwood Rd 41017 859-331-3250
Dr. Fred Bassett, supt. Fax 331-7528
www.beechwood.k12.ky.us
Beechwood JSHS 500/7-12
54 Beechwood Rd 41017 859-331-1220
Glen Miller, prin. Fax 426-3744

Kentucky Tech System
Supt. — None
Patton Area Technology Center Vo/Tech
3234 Turkeyfoot Rd 41017 859-341-2266
Ray Stanley, prin. Fax 341-6486

Brown Mackie College Post-Sec.
309 Buttermilk Pike 41017 859-341-5627

Fort Thomas, Campbell, Pop. 15,592
Fort Thomas ISD 2,300/K-12
28 N Fort Thomas Ave 41075 859-781-3333
Larry Stinson, supt. Fax 442-4015
www.fortthomas.kyschools.us/
Highlands HS 800/9-12
2400 Memorial Pkwy 41075 859-781-5900
Elgin Emmons, prin. Fax 442-4221
Highlands MS 600/6-8
2350 Memorial Pkwy 41075 859-441-5222
Mary Adams, prin. Fax 442-4210

Fort Wright, Kenton, Pop. 5,438
Kenton County SD 12,500/PK-12
1055 Eaton Dr 41017 859-344-8888
Tim Hanner, supt. Fax 344-1531
www.kenton.k12.ky.us/
Other Schools – See Covington, Edgewood, Independence, Taylor Mill

Frankfort, Franklin, Pop. 27,210
Frankfort ISD 900/PK-12
309 Shelby St Ste 201 40601 502-875-8661
Dr. Judith M. Lucarelli, supt. Fax 875-8663
www.frankfort.k12.ky.us
Frankfort HS 300/9-12
328 Shelby St 40601 502-875-8655
Beth Crane, prin. Fax 875-8657

Franklin County SD 5,000/PK-12
916 E Main St 40601 502-695-6700
Monte Chance, supt. Fax 695-6708
www.franklin.k12.ky.us/
Bondurant MS 700/6-8
Bondurant Dr 40601 502-875-8440
Greg Gaby, prin. Fax 875-8442
Elkhorn MS 800/6-8
1060 E Main St 40601 502-695-6740
Bob Bell, prin. Fax 695-6745
Franklin Co. Career & Technical Center Vo/Tech
1106 E Main St 40601 502-695-6790
Karen Schneider, prin. Fax 695-6791
Franklin County HS 900/9-12
1100 E Main St 40601 502-695-6750
Sharon Collett, prin. Fax 695-6755
Western Hills HS 700/9-12
100 Doctors Dr 40601 502-875-8400
Dennis Hancock, prin. Fax 227-4568

Frankfort Christian Academy 300/PK-12
1349A US Highway 421 S 40601 502-695-0744
Robert Roach, hdmstr. Fax 695-8725
J & M Academy of Cosmetology Post-Sec.
110A Brighton Park Blvd 40601 502-695-8001
Kentucky State University Post-Sec.
400 E Main St 40601 502-597-6000

Franklin, Simpson, Pop. 8,079
Simpson County SD 2,300/PK-12
PO Box 467 42135 270-586-8877
James Flynn, supt. Fax 586-2011
www.simpson.k12.ky.us
Franklin Simpson HS 900/9-12
PO Box 389 42135 270-586-3273
Lowell Hammers, prin. Fax 586-2021
Franklin Simpson MS 500/6-8
PO Box 637 42135 270-586-4401
Monte Cassady, prin. Fax 586-2048

Frenchburg, Menifee, Pop. 569
Menifee County SD 1,100/K-12
PO Box 110 40322 606-768-8002
Charles Mitchell, supt. Fax 768-8050
www.menifee.k12.ky.us
Menifee County HS 400/9-12
119 Indian Creek Rd 40322 606-768-8102
Elaine Brown, prin. Fax 768-8200
Menifee County MS 200/6-8
59 Indian Creek Rd 40322 606-768-8252
Benny Patrick, prin. Fax 768-8300

Fulton, Fulton, Pop. 2,564
Fulton ISD 400/K-12
313 Main St 42041 270-472-1553
Dianne Owen, supt. Fax 472-6921
www.fultonind.kyschools.us
Fulton City HS 200/7-12
700 Stephen Beale Dr 42041 270-472-1741
Wayne Benningfield, prin. Fax 472-6135

Georgetown, Scott, Pop. 19,988
Scott County SD 6,600/PK-12
PO Box 578 40324 502-863-3663
Dallas Blankenship, supt. Fax 863-5367
www.scott.k12.ky.us
Georgetown MS 500/6-8
730 S Hamilton St 40324 502-863-3805
Tommy Hurt, prin. Fax 867-1372
Ninth Grade Center 500/9-9
1072 Cardinal Dr 40324 502-863-4635
Betty Hughes, prin. Fax 868-0515
Royal Spring MS 6-8
332 Champion Way 40324 502-570-2390
Shannon Gullett, prin. Fax 863-3621
Scott County MS 1,000/6-8
1036 Cardinal Dr 40324 502-863-7202
Jennifer Sutton, prin. Fax 863-7452
Scott County SHS 1,300/10-12
1080 Cardinal Dr 40324 502-863-4131
Chip Southworth, prin. Fax 867-0544

Georgetown College Post-Sec.
400 E College St 40324 502-863-8011

Glasgow, Barren, Pop. 14,062
Barren County SD 4,100/PK-12
202 W Washington St 42141 270-651-3787
Jerry Ralston, supt. Fax 651-8836
www.trojan2000.org
Barren County HS 1,200/9-12
507 Trojan Trl 42141 270-651-6315
Keith Hale, prin. Fax 651-9211
Barren County MS 600/7-8
555 Trojan Trl 42141 270-651-4909
Cortni Crews, prin. Fax 651-5137

Glasgow ISD 1,700/PK-12
PO Box 1239 42142 270-651-6757
Dr. Fred Carter, supt. Fax 651-9791
www.glasgow.kyschools.us/
Glasgow HS 500/9-12
1601 Columbia Ave 42141 270-651-8801
Kelly Bell, prin. Fax 651-5189
Glasgow MS 500/6-8
105 Scottie Dr 42141 270-651-2256
Randy Wilkinson, prin. Fax 651-3090

Kentucky Tech System
Supt. — None
Barren County Area Technology Center Vo/Tech
491 Trojan Trl 42141 270-651-2196
Hal Toms, prin. Fax 651-2197

Bowling Green Technical College Post-Sec.
129 State Ave 42141 270-651-5373
Glasgow Christian Academy 100/PK-12
600 Cavalry Dr 42141 270-651-7729
Tracy Shaw, admin. Fax 651-6811
PJs College of Cosmetology Post-Sec.
124 S Public Sq 42141 270-651-6553

Glendale, Hardin
Hardin County SD
Supt. — See Elizabethtown
East Hardin MS 600/6-8
129 College St 42740 270-369-7370
Paul Connelly, prin. Fax 369-6380

Goshen, Oldham, Pop. 987
Oldham County SD
Supt. — See Buckner
North Oldham HS 700/9-12
1815 S Highway 1793 40026 502-228-0158
Lisa Jarrett, prin. Fax 228-7735
North Oldham MS 900/5-8
1801 S Highway 1793 40026 502-228-9998
Rob Smith, prin. Fax 228-0985

Grayson, Carter, Pop. 3,986
Carter County SD 4,800/PK-12
228 S Carol Malone Blvd 41143 606-474-6696
Larry Prichard, supt. Fax 474-6125
www.carter.k12.ky.us
East Carter County HS 700/9-12
405 Hitchins Rd 41143 606-474-5714
Ada Steele, prin. Fax 475-9200
East Carter MS 600/6-8
520 Robert and Mary St 41143 606-474-5156
Shannon Wilburn, prin. Fax 474-4027
Other Schools – See Olive Hill

Carter Christian Academy 100/PK-12
PO Box 490 41143 606-475-1919
Pat Collier, admin. Fax 475-1433
Kentucky Christian University Post-Sec.
100 Academic Pkwy 41143 606-474-3000

Greensburg, Green, Pop. 2,396
Green County SD 1,600/K-12
PO Box 369 42743 270-932-5231
Marshall Lowe, supt. Fax 932-3624
www.green.k12.ky.us
Green County HS 500/9-12
PO Box 227 42743 270-932-7481
Michael Tucker, prin. Fax 932-3214
Green County MS 400/6-8
PO Box 176 42743 270-932-7773
Timothy Deaton, prin. Fax 932-7617

Kentucky Tech System
Supt. — None
Green County Area Technology Center Vo/Tech
PO Box 167 42743 270-932-4263
Rick Atwell, prin. Fax 932-3072

Greenup, Greenup, Pop. 1,184
Greenup County SD 3,100/K-12
45 Musketeer Dr 41144 606-473-9819
John Younce, supt. Fax 473-5710
www.greenup.k12.ky.us/
Greenup County HS 900/9-12
196 Musketeer Dr 41144 606-473-9812
Matt Baker, prin. Fax 473-7854
Other Schools – See South Shore, Wurtland

Kentucky Tech System
Supt. — None
Greenup County Area Technology Center Vo/Tech
146 Musketeer Dr 41144 606-473-9344
Marsha Martin, prin. Fax 473-9177

Greenville, Muhlenberg, Pop. 4,273
Kentucky Tech System
Supt. — None
Muhlenberg County Area Technology Center Vo/Tech
201 Airport Rd 42345 270-338-1271
Andrew Swansey, prin. Fax 338-6802

Muhlenberg County SD
Supt. — See Powderly
Muhlenberg County Career HS Vo/Tech
3875 St Rt 181 N 42345 270-338-5460
Jim Price, prin. Fax 377-0581
Muhlenberg North HS 800/9-12
501 Robert L Draper Way 42345 270-338-0040
Mark Eades, prin. Fax 338-2442
Muhlenberg North MS 600/6-8
1000 N Main St 42345 270-338-3550
Robby Davis, prin. Fax 338-2911
Muhlenberg South HS 700/9-12
2900 State Route 176 42345 270-338-9409
Randy McCarty, prin. Fax 338-9710
Muhlenberg South MS 500/6-8
200 Pritchett Dr 42345 270-338-4650
Ed McCarraher, prin. Fax 338-0151

Muhlenberg Job Corps Center Post-Sec.
3875 Highway 181 N 42345 270-338-5460

Hardinsburg, Breckinridge, Pop. 2,452
Breckinridge County SD 2,600/PK-12
86 Airport Rd 40143 270-756-3000
Evelyn Neely, supt. Fax 756-6888
www.breck.k12.ky.us/
Other Schools – See Harned

Harlan, Harlan, Pop. 1,912
Harlan County SD 4,600/PK-12
251 Ball Park Rd 40831 606-573-4330
Timothy Saylor, supt. Fax 573-5767
www.harlan.k12.ky.us/
Cawood HS 700/9-12
279 Ball Park Rd 40831 606-573-5029
Michael Ashurst, prin. Fax 573-2424
Other Schools – See Cumberland, Evarts

Harlan ISD 900/K-12
420 E Central St 40831 606-573-8700
David Johnson, supt. Fax 573-8711
www.harlan-ind.k12.ky.us
Harlan MSHS 500/5-12
420 E Central St 40831 606-573-8750
Sheila Smith, prin. Fax 573-8753

Jenny Lea Academy of Cosmetology Post-Sec.
114 N Cumberland Ave 40831 606-573-4276

Harned, Breckinridge
Breckinridge County SD
Supt. — See Hardinsburg
Breckinridge County HS 800/9-12
PO Box 10 40144 270-756-3080
Dale Butler, prin. Fax 756-3081
Breckinridge County MS 600/6-8
PO Box 39 40144 270-756-3060
Kathy Gedling, prin. Fax 756-3061

Kentucky Tech System
Supt. — None
Breckinridge County Area Technology Ctr. Vo/Tech
PO Box 68 40144 270-756-2138
James Carroll, prin. Fax 756-2878

Harrodsburg, Mercer, Pop. 8,126
Kentucky Tech System
Supt. — None
Harrodsburg Area Technology Center Vo/Tech
PO Box 628 40330 859-734-9329
Duane Flora, prin. Fax 734-3613

Mercer County SD 3,000/PK-12
371 E Lexington St 40330 859-734-8400
Bruce Johnson, supt. Fax 734-8404
www.mercer.kyschools.us/
Harrodsburg MS 200/6-8
443 E Lexington St 40330 859-734-8415
Terry Gordon, prin. Fax 734-8425
Hughes Jones Harrodsburg Area Tech Ctr Vo/Tech
661 Tapp Rd 40330 859-734-9329
Duane Flora, prin. Fax 734-3613
King MS 800/5-8
1101 Moberly Rd 40330 859-734-4364
Jennifer Miller, prin. Fax 734-0811
Mercer County HS 700/9-12
937 Moberly Rd 40330 859-734-4364
Terry Yates, prin. Fax 734-6364

Central Kentucky Christian S 100/PK-10
PO Box 207 40330 859-734-9347
Jill Cutler, prin. Fax 734-3717

Hartford, Ohio, Pop. 2,652
Kentucky Tech System
Supt. — None
Ohio County Area Technology Center Vo/Tech
1406 S Main St 42347 270-274-9612
Brad Sisk, prin. Fax 274-9633

Ohio County SD 3,900/PK-12
PO Box 70 42347 270-298-3249
Soretta Ralph, supt. Fax 298-3886
www.ohio.k12.ky.us
Ohio County HS 1,100/9-12
1400 S Main St 42347 270-274-3366
John Stofer, prin. Fax 274-9482
Ohio County MS 600/7-8
1404 S Main St 42347 270-274-7893
Dr. Rebecca Stobaugh, prin. Fax 274-7320

Hawesville, Hancock, Pop. 981
Hancock County SD 1,100/K-12
83 State Route 271 N 42348 270-927-6914
Scott Lewis, supt. Fax 927-6916
www.hancock.k12.ky.us/
Other Schools – See Lewisport

Hazard, Perry, Pop. 4,819
Hazard ISD 800/K-12
325 Broadway St 41701 606-436-3911
Sandra Johnson, supt. Fax 436-2742
www.hazard.k12.ky.us
Eversole MS 300/5-8
601 Broadway St 41701 606-436-4721
John Quillen, prin. Fax 439-3726
Hazard HS 300/9-12
157 Bulldog Ln 41701 606-439-1318
Donald Mobelini, prin. Fax 439-2285

Knott County SD
Supt. — See Hindman
Cordia HS 100/7-12
6060 Lotts Creek Rd 41701 606-785-4457
Dwight Creech, prin. Fax 785-4669

Perry County SD 4,300/K-12
315 Park Ave 41701 606-439-5814
John Paul Amis, supt. Fax 439-2512
www.perry.k12.ky.us/
Perry County Central HS 1,000/9-12
305 Park Ave 41701 606-439-5888
Estill Neace, prin. Fax 439-2825
Other Schools – See Buckhorn

Hazard Community & Technical College Post-Sec.
1 Community College Dr 41701 606-436-5721

Hebron, Boone
Boone County SD
Supt. — See Florence
Conner HS 1,600/9-12
3310 Cougar Path 41048 859-334-4400
Michael Blevins, prin. Fax 334-4406
Conner MS 1,300/6-8
3300 Cougar Path 41048 859-334-4410
Linda Viox, prin. Fax 334-4435

Kentucky Tech System
Supt. — None
Boone County Area Technology Center Vo/Tech
3320 Cougar Path 41048 859-689-7855
Patrick Currin, prin. Fax 689-7828

Henderson, Henderson, Pop. 27,666
Henderson County SD 6,800/K-12
1805 2nd St 42420 270-831-5000
Dr. Thomas Richey, supt. Fax 831-5009
www.hendersonschools.net/
Henderson County Area Technology Center Vo/Tech
2440 Zion Rd 42420 270-831-8850
Victor Doty, prin. Fax 831-8853
Henderson County HS 2,200/9-12
2424 Zion Rd 42420 270-831-8800
Bruce Swanson, prin. Fax 831-8870
Henderson County North MS 800/6-8
1707 2nd St 42420 270-831-5060
Scottie Long, prin. Fax 831-5064
Henderson County South MS 700/6-8
800 S Alves St 42420 270-831-5050
Dane Ferguson, prin. Fax 831-5058

Henderson Community College Post-Sec.
2660 S Green St 42420 270-827-1867
Pat Wilson Beauty College Post-Sec.
326 N Main St 42420 270-826-5195

Hickman, Fulton, Pop. 2,371
Fulton County SD 700/PK-12
2780 Moscow Ave 42050 270-236-3923
Dr. Charles Holliday, supt. Fax 236-2184
www.fulton.k12.ky.us
Fulton County HS 200/9-12
2740 Moscow Ave 42050 270-236-3904
Gary Meredith, prin. Fax 236-9004
Fulton County MS 200/6-8
2770 Moscow Ave 42050 270-236-3923
Julie Jackson, prin. Fax 236-4708

Kentucky Tech System
Supt. — None
Fulton County Area Technology Center Vo/Tech
2720 Moscow Ave 42050 270-236-2517
Tom Pyron, prin. Fax 236-9395

Highland Heights, Campbell, Pop. 5,791

Gateway Community & Technical College Post-Sec.
90 Campbell Dr 41076 859-442-4108

Hi Hat, Floyd
Floyd County SD
Supt. — See Prestonsburg
South Floyd HS 400/9-12
299 Mt Raider Dr Ste 101 41636 606-452-9600
Keith Henry, prin. Fax 452-2155
South Floyd MS 200/7-8
299 Mt Raider Dr Ste 102 41636 606-452-9607
Zenith Hall, prin. Fax 452-4810

Hindman, Knott, Pop. 772
Kentucky Tech System
Supt. — None
Knott County Area Technology Center Vo/Tech
1996 Highway 160 S 41822 606-785-5350
Patrick Goodin, prin. Fax 785-5445

Knott County SD 2,400/PK-12
PO Box 869 41822 606-785-3153
Harold Combs, supt. Fax 785-0800
www.knott.k12.ky.us
Knott County Central HS 700/9-12
PO Box 819 41822 606-785-3166
Bobby Pollard, prin. Fax 785-3169
Other Schools – See Hazard

Hodgenville, Larue, Pop. 2,788
LaRue County SD 2,300/K-12
PO Box 39 42748 270-358-4111
Sam Sanders, supt. Fax 358-3053
www.larue.k12.ky.us
LaRue County HS 700/9-12
925 S Lincoln Blvd 42748 270-358-2210
Paul Mullins, prin. Fax 358-9469
LaRue County MS 400/7-8
911 S Lincoln Blvd 42748 270-358-3196
Lori Indalecio, prin. Fax 358-9088

Hopkinsville, Christian, Pop. 28,821
Christian County SD 8,100/K-12
PO Box 609 42241 270-887-1300
Robert Lovingood, supt. Fax 887-1316
www.christian.k12.ky.us
Career & Technical Center Vo/Tech
705 N Elm St 42240 270-887-1228
Donald Love, prin. Fax 887-1242
Christian County HS 1,300/9-12
220 Glass Ave 42240 270-887-1100
Kathy Hancock, prin. Fax 887-1294
Christian County MS 800/6-8
210 Glass Ave 42240 270-887-1130
Larry Cavanah, prin. Fax 887-1189
Hopkinsville HS 1,000/9-12
430 Koffman Dr 42240 270-887-1200
Jada Mason, prin. Fax 887-1118
Hopkinsville MS 700/6-8
434 Koffman Dr 42240 270-887-1230
Wendy Duvall, prin. Fax 887-1234
North Drive MS 600/6-8
831 North Dr 42240 270-887-1250
Mike Beck, prin. Fax 887-1287

Brown Mackie College Post-Sec.
4001 Fort Campbell Blvd 42240 270-886-1302
Heritage Christian Academy 500/PK-12
8349 Eagle Way Bypass 42240 270-885-2417
Linda Garris, admin. Fax 885-0094
Hopkinsville Community College Post-Sec.
PO Box 2100 42241 270-886-3921
University Heights Academy 300/K-12
1300 Academy Dr 42240 270-886-0254
Pam Nunn, prin. Fax 886-2716

Horse Cave, Hart, Pop. 2,314
Caverna ISD
Supt. — See Cave City
Caverna HS 200/9-12
2276 S Dixie St 42749 270-773-2828
Debbie Lindsey, prin. Fax 773-2825
Caverna MS 200/6-8
2278 S Dixie St 42749 270-773-4665
Barry Nesbitt, prin. Fax 773-2825

Hyden, Leslie, Pop. 196
Kentucky Tech System
Supt. — None
Leslie County Area Technology Center Vo/Tech
PO Box 902 41749 606-672-2859
Dwight Lewis, prin. Fax 672-4943

Leslie County SD 2,000/PK-12
PO Box 949 41749 606-672-2397
Larry Sparks, supt. Fax 672-4224
www.leslie.k12.ky.us
Leslie County HS 600/9-12
PO Box 970 41749 606-672-2337
Patricia Childers, prin. Fax 672-2858
Leslie County MS 300/7-8
PO Box 965 41749 606-672-5580
Dana Coots, prin. Fax 672-5320

Frontier School of Midwifery Post-Sec.
PO Box 528 41749 606-672-2312

Independence, Kenton, Pop. 19,065
Kenton County SD
Supt. — See Fort Wright
Kenton HS 1,400/9-12
11132 Madison Pike 41051 859-363-4100
Richard Culross, prin. Fax 363-4101
Summit View MS 800/6-8
5002 Madison Pike 41051 859-363-4800
David Johnstone, prin. Fax 363-4804
Twenhofel MS 700/6-8
11800 Taylor Mill Rd 41051 859-356-5559
Cheryl Jones, prin. Fax 356-1137

Community Christian Academy 100/PK-12
11875 Taylor Mill Rd 41051 859-356-7990
Tara Bates, prin. Fax 356-7991

Inez, Martin, Pop. 457
Kentucky Tech System
Supt. — None
Martin County Area Technology Center Vo/Tech
HC 68 Box 2177 41224 606-298-3879
Charles Six, prin. Fax 298-7240

Martin County SD 2,300/PK-12
PO Box 366 41224 606-298-3572
Mark Blackburn, supt. Fax 298-4427
www.martin.k12.ky.us
Clark HS 600/9-12
HC 63 Box 810 41224 606-298-3591
Patricia Elliott, prin. Fax 298-5148
Inez MS 400/6-8
PO Box 5001 41224 606-298-3045
Greg Cornette, prin. Fax 298-7314
Other Schools – See Warfield

Irvine, Estill, Pop. 2,714
Estill County SD 2,400/PK-12
PO Box 930 40336 606-723-2181
Bert Hensley, supt. Fax 723-6029
www.estill.k12.ky.us
Estill County HS 700/9-12
2675 Winchester Rd 40336 606-723-3537
Blain Click, prin. Fax 723-4894
Estill County MS 600/6-8
2805 Winchester Rd 40336 606-723-5136
Chesteen Robbins, prin. Fax 723-2041

Jackson, Breathitt, Pop. 2,413
Breathitt County SD 2,200/PK-12
PO Box 750 41339 606-666-2491
Arch Turner, supt. Fax 666-2493
www.breathitt.kyschools.us
Breathitt County HS 700/9-12
2307 Bobcat Ln 41339 606-666-7511
Derek McKnight, prin. Fax 666-7765
Sebastian MS 300/7-8
244 L B J Rd 41339 606-666-8894
Tim Bobrowski, prin. Fax 666-5336

Jackson ISD 600/PK-12
940 Highland Ave 41339 606-666-4979
Timothy Spencer, supt. Fax 666-4350
www.jackson-ind.k12.ky.us
Jackson City S 600/PK-12
940 Highland Ave 41339 606-666-5164
James Yount, prin. Fax 666-2555

Kentucky Tech System
Supt. — None
Breathitt County Area Technology Center Vo/Tech
PO Box 786 41339 606-666-5153
Margaret Gross, prin. Fax 666-5394

Oakdale Christian Academy 100/7-12
5801 Beattyville Rd 41339 606-666-5422
Daniel Fisher, prin. Fax 666-5422

Jamestown, Russell, Pop. 1,711
Russell County SD 2,800/PK-12
PO Box 440 42629 270-343-3191
Scott Pierce, supt. Fax 343-3072
www.russell.k12.ky.us/
Other Schools – See Russell Springs

Jeffersontown, Jefferson, Pop. 26,100
Jefferson County SD
Supt. — See Louisville

Jeffersontown HS Magnet Career Academy 1,000/9-12
9600 Old Six Mile Ln 40299 502-485-8275
Marsha Dohn, prin. Fax 485-8832

Jenkins, Letcher, Pop. 2,297
Jenkins ISD 600/PK-12
PO Box 74 41537 606-832-2183
John Shook, supt. Fax 832-2181
www.jenkins.k12.ky.us
Jenkins MSHS 200/7-12
PO Box 552 41537 606-832-2184
Teresa Bentley, prin. Fax 832-4238

Lancaster, Garrard, Pop. 4,207
Garrard County SD 2,500/PK-12
322 W Maple Ave 40444 859-792-3018
Ray Woolsey, supt. Fax 792-4733
www.garrard.k12.ky.us/
Garrard County HS 700/9-12
304 W Maple Ave 40444 859-792-2146
Kevin Stull, prin. Fax 792-4352
Garrard MS 600/6-8
324 W Maple Ave 40444 859-792-2108
Cindy Rogers, prin. Fax 792-9618

Kentucky Tech System
Supt. — None
Garrard County Area Technology Center Vo/Tech
306 W Maple Ave 40444 859-792-2144
James Alford, prin. Fax 792-4058

Lawrenceburg, Anderson, Pop. 9,403
Anderson County SD 3,700/PK-12
103 N Main St 40342 502-839-3406
Kim Shaw, supt. Fax 839-2501
www.anderson.k12.ky.us/
Anderson County HS 1,100/9-12
1 Bearcat Dr 40342 502-839-5118
Ray Woodyard, prin. Fax 839-3486
Anderson County MS 900/6-8
200 Mustang Trl 40342 502-839-9261
Steve Carmichael, prin. Fax 839-2534

Central Kentucky Technical College Post-Sec.
1500 Bypass N 40342 502-839-8488
Christian Academy of Lawrenceburg 100/PK-12
PO Box 498 40342 502-839-9992
James Everett, admin. Fax 839-3728

Lebanon, Marion, Pop. 5,959
Kentucky Tech System
Supt. — None
Marion County Area Technology Center Vo/Tech
721 E Main St 40033 270-692-3155
Laura Arnold, prin. Fax 692-1357

Marion County SD 3,100/PK-12
755 E Main St 40033 270-692-3721
Roger Marcum, supt. Fax 692-1899
www.marion.k12.ky.us
Lebanon MS 400/6-8
200 Corporate Dr 40033 270-692-3441
Daniel Imes, prin. Fax 692-0266
Marion County HS 900/9-12
735 E Main St 40033 270-692-6066
Taylora Brown, prin. Fax 692-6248
St. Charles MS 300/6-8
1155 Highway 327 40033 270-692-4578
John Brady, prin. Fax 692-1176

Leitchfield, Grayson, Pop. 6,462
Grayson County SD 4,100/PK-12
PO Box 4009 42755 270-259-4011
Barry Anderson, supt. Fax 259-4756
www.graysoncountyschools.com/
Grayson County HS 1,200/9-12
340 School House Rd 42754 270-259-4078
Michael Huffman, prin. Fax 259-6131
Grayson County MS 1,000/6-8
726 John Hill Taylor Dr 42754 270-259-4175
Bill Embry, prin. Fax 259-5875
Grayson County Technology Center Vo/Tech
252 School House Rd 42754 270-259-3195
Cynthia Smith, prin. Fax 259-8082

Leitchfield Christian Academy 100/PK-10
106 E Walnut St 42754 270-259-4076
Jerry Netherland, prin. Fax 259-3240

Lewisport, Hancock, Pop. 1,655
Hancock County SD
Supt. — See Hawesville
Hancock County HS 500/9-12
80 State Route 271 S 42351 270-927-6953
Rick Lasley, prin. Fax 927-8677
Hancock County MS 400/6-8
100 State Route 271 S 42351 270-927-6712
Gina Biever, prin. Fax 927-6712

Lexington, Fayette, Pop. 263,618
Fayette County SD 33,100/PK-12
701 E Main St 40502 859-381-4000
Stu Silberman, supt. Fax 381-4106
www.fcps.net
Beaumont MS 1,100/6-8
2080 Georgian Way 40504 859-381-3094
Kate McAnelly, prin. Fax 381-3109
Bryan Station HS 1,300/9-12
1866 Edgeworth Dr 40505 859-381-3308
Gladys Peoples, prin. Fax 381-3330
Bryan Station Magnet MS 600/6-8
1865 Wickland Dr 40505 859-381-3288
Jim Thomas, prin. Fax 293-3292
Clark MS 800/6-8
3341 Clays Mill Rd 40503 859-381-3036
Lisa Goodin, prin. Fax 381-3037
Clay HS 2,000/9-12
2100 Fontaine Rd 40502 859-381-3423
John Nochta, prin. Fax 381-3430
Crawford MS 500/6-8
1813 Charleston Dr 40505 859-381-3370
Joyce Florence, prin. Fax 381-3378
Dunbar HS 2,200/9-12
1600 Man O War Blvd 40513 859-381-3546
Anthony Orr, prin. Fax 381-3560
Eastside Technical Center Vo/Tech
2208 Liberty Rd 40509 859-381-3740
Joe Norman, prin. Fax 381-3747
Hayes MS, 260 Richardson Pl 40509 900/6-8
Sherri Heise, prin. 859-381-4920
Lafayette HS 2,000/9-12
400 Reed Ln 40503 859-381-3474
Mike McKenzie, prin. Fax 381-3487
Leestown Math Science & Tech MS 600/6-8
2010 Leestown Rd 40511 859-381-3181
Katheryne Kettle, prin. Fax 381-3180
Lexington Traditional Magnet MS 600/6-8
350 N Limestone 40508 859-381-3192
Clay Goode, prin. Fax 381-3199
Morton MS 800/6-8
1225 Tates Creek Rd 40502 859-381-3533
Jock Gum, prin. Fax 381-3536
School for Creative and Performing Arts 300/4-8
400 Lafayette Pkwy 40503 859-381-3332
M. Cunningham-Amos, prin. Fax 381-3334
Southern MS 800/6-8
400 Wilson Downing Rd 40517 859-381-3582
Jane Dreidame, prin. Fax 381-3588
Southside Technical Center Vo/Tech
1784 Harrodsburg Rd 40504 859-381-3603
James Hardin, prin. Fax 381-3807
Tates Creek HS 1,700/9-12
1111 Centre Pkwy 40517 859-381-3620
Sam Meaux, prin. Fax 381-3635
Tates Creek MS 800/6-8
1105 Centre Pkwy 40517 859-381-3052
Greg Quenon, prin. Fax 381-3053
Winburn MS 600/6-8
1060 Winburn Dr 40511 859-381-3967
Tina Stevenson, prin. Fax 381-3971

Blue Grass Baptist S 200/K-12
3743 Red River Dr 40517 859-272-1217
Guy Causey, prin. Fax 273-8658
Bluegrass Community & Technical College Post-Sec.
470 Cooper Dr 40506 859-246-6200
Central Kentucky Technical College Post-Sec.
308 Vo Tech Rd 40511 859-246-2400
Kaufman Beauty School Post-Sec.
701 E High St 40502 859-266-2024
Lexington Beauty College Post-Sec.
90 Southport Dr 40503 859-278-7483
Lexington Catholic HS 900/9-12
2250 Clays Mill Rd 40503 859-277-7183
Sally Stevens, prin. Fax 276-5086
Lexington Christian Academy HS 400/9-12
450 W Reynolds Rd 40503 859-422-5701
Dr. Ollie Gibbs, hdmstr. Fax 224-0456
Lexington Christian Academy JHS 200/7-8
450 W Reynolds Rd 40503 859-477-5702
John Eckelbarger, prin. Fax 422-5792
Lexington Theological Seminary Post-Sec.
631 S Limestone 40508 859-252-0361
National College Post-Sec.
2376 Sir Barton Way 40509 859-253-0621
Pathology and Cytology Laboratories Post-Sec.
290 Big Run Rd 40503 859-278-9513
St. Joseph's Hospital Post-Sec.
1 Saint Joseph Dr 40504 859-278-3436
Sayre S 600/PK-12
194 N Limestone 40507 859-254-1361
Clayton Chambliss, hdmstr. Fax 231-0508
Spencerian College Post-Sec.
1575 Winchester Rd 40505 859-223-9608
Strayer University Post-Sec.
220 Lexington Green Cir 550 40503 859-971-4400
Sullivan University Post-Sec.
2355 Harrodsburg Rd 40504 800-467-6281
Transylvania University Post-Sec.
300 N Broadway 40508 859-233-8300
University of Kentucky 40506 Post-Sec.
859-257-9000
Univ. of Kentucky Chandler Medical Ctr. Post-Sec.
103 Administration Plz A311 40536 859-323-5126

Liberty, Casey, Pop. 1,892
Casey County SD 1,900/PK-12
1922 N US 127 42539 606-787-6941
Linda Hatter, supt. Fax 787-5231
www.casey.k12.ky.us
Casey County HS 700/9-12
1841 E KY 70 42539 606-787-6151
Tim Goodlett, prin. Fax 787-8654
Casey County MS 400/7-8
1673 E KY 70 42539 606-787-6769
Terri Price, prin. Fax 787-5337

Kentucky Tech System
Supt. — None
Casey County Area Technology Center Vo/Tech
1723 E KY 70 42539 606-787-6241
David Horseman, prin. Fax 787-6243

Lick Creek, Pike, Pop. 221
Pike County SD
Supt. — See Pikeville
East Ridge HS 800/9-12
19471 Lick Mountain Rd 41540 606-835-2811
Kevin Justice, prin. Fax 835-2899

Lily, Laurel

Cornerstone Christian S 200/PK-12
420 Lily School Rd 40740 606-526-8893
Matthew Webb, prin. Fax 526-8801

London, Laurel, Pop. 7,787
Laurel County SD 8,700/K-12
275 S Laurel Rd 40744 606-862-4600
David Young, supt. Fax 862-4601
www.laurel.k12.ky.us
North Laurel HS 1,200/9-12
1300 E Hal Rogers Pkwy 40741 606-862-4699
James Durham, prin. Fax 862-4700
North Laurel MS 900/6-8
101 Johnson Rd 40741 606-862-4715
David Hensley, prin. Fax 862-4717
South Laurel HS 1,200/9-12
201 S Laurel Rd 40744 606-862-4727
Jeff Jackson, prin. Fax 862-4728
South Laurel MS 1,100/6-8
223 S Laurel Rd 40744 606-862-4745
Jeff Reed, prin. Fax 862-4746

Lost Creek, Breathitt

Riverside Christian S 100/K-12
General Delivery 41348 606-666-2359
Beverly Burroughs, prin. Fax 666-5211

Louisa, Lawrence, Pop. 2,051
Lawrence County SD 2,600/PK-12
50 Bulldog Ln 41230 606-638-9671
Jeffery May, supt. Fax 638-0128
www.lawrence.k12.ky.us
Lawrence County HS 800/9-12
100 Bulldog Ln 41230 606-638-9676
James Boggs, prin. Fax 638-3227
Louisa MS 500/6-8
9 Bulldog Ln 41230 606-638-4090
Thomas Gibson, prin. Fax 638-4865

Louisville, Jefferson, Pop. 248,762
Jefferson County SD 87,700/PK-12
PO Box 34020 40232 502-485-3011
Stephen Daeschner Ph.D., supt. Fax 485-3991
www.jefferson.k12.ky.us
Atherton HS 900/9-12
3000 Dundee Rd 40205 502-485-8202
John Hudson, prin. Fax 485-8985
Ballard HS 1,700/9-12
6000 Brownsboro Rd 40222 502-485-8206
James Jury, prin. Fax 485-8856
Barret MS 700/6-8
2561 Grinstead Dr 40206 502-485-8207
Tom Wortham, prin. Fax 485-8579
Brown S 300/K-12
546 S 1st St 40202 502-485-8216
Ruth Jarrell, prin. Fax 485-8741
Butler HS 1,600/9-12
2222 Crums Ln 40216 502-485-8220
Stephen Bocko, prin. Fax 485-8517
Carrithers MS 700/6-8
4320 Billtown Rd 40299 502-485-8224
Pat Gausepohl, prin. Fax 485-8394
Central HS Magnet Career Academy 1,000/9-12
1130 W Chestnut St 40203 502-485-8226
Dan Withers, prin. Fax 485-7034
Conway MS 900/6-8
6300 Terry Rd 40258 502-485-8233
Debra Mercer, prin. Fax 485-8076
Doss HS Magnet Career Academy 1,100/9-12
7601 Saint Andrews Church 40214 502-485-8239
Glenn Baete, prin. Fax 485-8080
DuPont Manual HS 1,800/9-12
120 W Lee St 40208 502-485-8241
Beverly Keepers, prin. Fax 485-8035
Farnsley MS 1,000/6-8
3400 Lees Ln 40216 502-485-8242
Rob Stephenson, prin. Fax 485-8663
Highland MS 1,000/6-8
1700 Norris Pl 40205 502-485-8266
Steven Heckman, prin. Fax 485-8831
Iroquois HS Magnet Career Academy 1,100/9-12
4615 Taylor Blvd 40215 502-485-8269
Brian Shumate, prin. Fax 485-8033
Iroquois MS 700/6-8
5650 Southern Pkwy 40214 502-485-8270
Betty Graham, prin. Fax 485-8380
Jefferson County HS 700/9-12
900 S Floyd St 40203 502-485-3173
Buell Snyder, prin. Fax 485-3671
Jefferson County Traditional MS 900/6-8
1418 Morton Ave 40204 502-485-8272
Mark Rose, prin. Fax 485-8635
Jefferson MS 1,100/6-8
1501 Rangeland Rd 40219 502-485-8273
Janice McDowell, prin. Fax 485-8045
Johnson Traditional MS 900/6-8
2509 Wilson Ave 40210 502-485-8277
Beverly Johnson, prin. Fax 485-8679
Kammerer MS 800/6-8
7315 Wesboro Rd 40222 502-485-8279
David Armour, prin. Fax 485-8618
Kennedy Metro MS 100/5-8
4515 Taylorsville Rd 40220 502-485-6950
David Mike, prin. Fax 491-7290
Knight MS 600/6-8
9803 Blue Lick Rd 40229 502-485-8287
Kenneth Black, prin. Fax 485-8073
Lassiter MS 700/6-8
8200 Candleworth Dr 40214 502-485-8288
Dwayne Roberts, prin. Fax 485-8373
Louisville Male HS 1,600/9-12
4409 Preston Hwy 40213 502-485-8292
David Wilson, prin. Fax 485-8770

Meyzeek MS 1,100/6-8
828 S Jackson St 40203 502-485-8299
Keith Look, prin. Fax 485-8641
Moore Traditional HS 700/9-12
6415 Outer Loop 40228 502-485-8304
Edward Weber, prin. Fax 485-8168
Moore Traditional MS 900/6-8
6415 Outer Loop 40228 502-485-8219
Diana Drake-Hicks, prin. Fax 485-8913
Myers MS 900/6-8
3741 Pulliam Dr 40218 502-485-8305
William Bennett, prin. Fax 485-8157
Newburg MS 1,000/6-8
4901 Exeter Ave 40218 502-485-8306
Dianna Drake-Hicks, prin. Fax 485-8883
Noe MS 1,200/6-8
121 W Lee St 40208 502-485-8307
Kathleen Sayre, prin. Fax 485-8056
Pleasure Ridge Park HS Magnet Academy 1,900/9-12
5901 Greenwood Rd 40258 502-485-8311
David Johnson, prin. Fax 485-8093
Seneca HS Magnet Career Academy 1,600/9-12
3510 Goldsmith Ln 40220 502-485-8323
Mary Greenlee, prin. Fax 485-8174
Shawnee HS Magnet Career Academy 600/9-12
4018 W Market St 40212 502-485-8326
Mernia Hill, prin. Fax 485-8738
Southern HS Magnet Career Academy 1,300/9-12
8620 Preston Hwy 40219 502-485-8330
Jerry Keepers, prin. Fax 485-8029
Southern Leadership Academy 700/6-8
4530 Bellevue Ave 40215 502-485-8331
Anita Jones, prin. Fax 485-8381
Waggener Traditional HS 1,100/9-12
330 S Hubbards Ln 40207 502-485-8340
Candace Conway, prin. Fax 485-8140
Western Math Science Tech Magnet HS 800/9-12
2501 Rockford Ln 40216 502-485-8344
Louis Hughley, prin. Fax 485-8969
Western MS 600/6-8
2201 W Main St 40212 502-485-8345
Beth Johnson, prin. Fax 485-8047
Westport MS and Fine Arts Academy 1,000/6-8
8100 Westport Rd 40222 502-485-8346
Devon Woodlee, prin. Fax 485-8590
Youth Performing Arts JSHS 7-12
1517 S 2nd St 40208 502-485-8355
Beverly Keepers, prin. Fax 485-8808
Other Schools – See Fairdale, Fern Creek, Jeffersontown, Middletown, Valley Station

---

Academy of Our Lady of Mercy 400/9-12
1176 E Broadway 40204 502-584-4273
Julie Crone, prin. Fax 584-9651
Assumption HS 1,000/9-12
2170 Tyler Ln 40205 502-458-9551
Mary Ann Steutermann, prin. Fax 454-8411
Bellarmine University Post-Sec.
2001 Newburg Rd 40205 502-452-8000
Beth Haven Christian S 500/PK-12
5515 Johnsontown Rd 40272 502-937-3516
Rick Grice, hdmstr. Fax 937-3364
Brown Cancer Center Post-Sec.
529 S Jackson St 40202 502-588-6905
Brown Mackie College Post-Sec.
3605 Fern Valley Rd 40219 502-968-7191
Christian Academy of Louisville 1,700/K-12
700 S English Station Rd 40245 502-244-3225
David Patterson, supt. Fax 244-1824
Covenant Classical Academy 50/K-12
13902 Factory Ln 40245 502-243-0404
R. Lance Harris, hdmstr. Fax 243-0404
Daymar College Post-Sec.
4400 Brckenridge Ln #415 40218 502-495-1040
DeSales HS 300/9-12
425 W Kenwood Dr 40214 502-368-6519
Tony Medley, prin. Fax 366-6172
Donta School of Beauty Culture Post-Sec.
515 W Oak St 40203 502-583-1018
Eastside Christian Academy 100/K-10
3402 Goose Creek Rd 40241 502-339-0041
C.E. Hydes, prin. Fax 339-0041
Embry-Riddle Aeronautical University Post-Sec.
300 High Rise Dr Ste 392 40213 502-942-0625
Evangel Christian S 300/K-12
5400 Minor Ln 40219 502-968-7744
Roger Hoagland, prin. Fax 968-8414
Galen College of Nursing Post-Sec.
1031 Zorn Ave Ste 400 40207 502-582-2305
Hair Design School Post-Sec.
1049 Bardstown Rd 40204 502-459-8150
Hair Design School Post-Sec.
5314 Bardstown Rd 40291 502-499-0070
Holy Cross HS 300/9-12
5144 Dixie Hwy 40216 502-447-4363
Sr. Maryann Tarquinio, prin. Fax 448-1062
ITT Technical Institute Post-Sec.
10509 Timberwood Cir 40223 502-327-7424
Jefferson Community & Technical College Post-Sec.
109 E Broadway 40202 502-584-0181
Jefferson Technical College Post-Sec.
727 W Chestnut St 40203 502-213-4290
Kentucky Country Day S 800/K-12
4100 Springdale Rd 40241 502-423-0440
Brad Lyman, hdmstr. Fax 423-0445
Kentucky School for the Blind Post-Sec.
1867 Frankfort Ave 40206
Louisville Collegiate S 700/K-12
2427 Glenmary Ave 40204 502-479-0340
Thomas Hobert, hdmstr. Fax 454-8549
Louisville Jr. Academy 50/1-10
2988 Newburg Rd 40205 502-452-2965
Brent Ruckle, prin. Fax 452-2965
Louisville Presbyterian Seminary Post-Sec.
1044 Alta Vista Rd 40205 502-895-3411
Louisville Technical Institute Post-Sec.
3901 Atkinson Square Dr 40218 800-844-6528
More Grace Christian Academy 50/PK-12
100 W Ormsby Ave 40203 502-634-2888
Tori Robertson, admin. Fax 634-2798
National College Post-Sec.
4205 Dixie Hwy 40216 502-447-7634
On Fire Christian Academy 100/K-12
5627 New Cut Rd 40214 502-368-0080
Kristine Salvo, admin. Fax 368-0088
Pitt Academy PK-12
6010 Preston Hwy 40219 502-966-6979
Sherry Downey, prin. Fax 962-8878
Portland Christian JSHS 100/7-12
2500 Portland Ave 40212 502-778-6114
Mary Jodell Seay, dir. Fax 772-7027
Presentation Academy 400/9-12
861 S 4th St 40203 502-583-5935
Barbara Wine, prin. Fax 583-1342
Sacred Heart Academy 800/9-12
3175 Lexington Rd 40206 502-897-6097
Dr. Beverly McAuliffe, prin. Fax 896-3935
St. Francis HS 100/9-12
233 W Broadway 40202 502-736-1000
Alexandra Thurstone, prin. Fax 736-1049
St. Xavier HS 1,400/9-12
1609 Poplar Level Rd 40217 502-637-4712
Nelson Nunn, prin. Fax 634-2171
School of Hair Design Post-Sec.
5120 Dixie Hwy 40216 502-447-0111
Southern Baptist Theological Seminary Post-Sec.
2825 Lexington Rd 40280 502-897-4011
Spalding University Post-Sec.
851 S 4th St 40203 502-585-9911
Spencerian College Post-Sec.
4627 Dixie Hwy 40216 502-447-1000
Sullivan University Post-Sec.
3101 Bardstown Rd 40205 800-844-1354
The Hair Design School Post-Sec.
151 Chenoweth Ln 40207 502-897-9401
Trend Setter's Academy of Beauty Culture Post-Sec.
7283 Dixie Hwy 40258 502-937-6816
Trend Setters' Academy of Beauty Culture Post-Sec.
8111 Preston Hwy 40219 502-962-7710
Trinity HS 1,400/9-12
4011 Shelbyville Rd 40207 502-895-9427
Daniel Zoeller, prin. Fax 895-6837
University of Louisville Post-Sec.
2301 S 3rd St 40208 502-852-5555
Ursuline S for Performing Arts K-12
3105 Lexington Rd 40206 502-897-1816
Lynn Slaughter, dir.
Valor Traditional Academy 100/K-12
11501 Schlatter Rd 40291 502-239-3345
Diane Seel, prin. Fax 239-3344
Walden S 300/K-12
4238 Westport Rd 40207 502-893-0433
Linda VanHouten, prin. Fax 895-8668
Whitefield Academy 700/PK-12
7711 Fegenbush Ln 40228 502-239-2509
Robert Hensley, hdmstr. Fax 239-3144

Ludlow, Kenton, Pop. 4,647
Ludlow ISD 1,000/PK-12
525 Elm St 41016 859-261-8210
Curtis Hall, supt. Fax 291-6811
www.ludlow.k12.ky.us
Ludlow HS 300/9-12
515 Elm St 41016 859-261-8211
Joe Beard, prin. Fax 655-7536
Ludlow MS 200/6-8
150 Adela Ave 41016 859-655-7500
David Rust, prin. Fax 655-7536

Mc Kee, Jackson, Pop. 969
Jackson County SD 2,200/PK-12
PO Box 217 40447 606-287-7181
Ralph Hoskins, supt. Fax 287-8469
www.jackson.k12.ky.us
Jackson County HS 600/9-12
PO Box 427 40447 606-287-7155
Steve Caroll, prin. Fax 287-7123
Jackson County MS 600/6-8
PO Box 1329 40447 606-287-8351
Keith Bingham, prin. Fax 287-8360

Kentucky Tech System
Supt. — None
Jackson Area Technology Center Vo/Tech
PO Box 1509 40447 606-287-2163
Alonzo Moore, prin. Fax 287-7538

Madisonville, Hopkins, Pop. 19,273
Hopkins County SD 7,000/PK-12
320 S Seminary St 42431 270-825-6000
James Stevens, supt. Fax 825-6062
www.hopkins.k12.ky.us
Browning Springs MS 500/6-8
357 W Arch St 42431 270-825-6006
Darrell Wilson, prin. Fax 825-6009
Hopkins County Central HS 1,000/9-12
6625 Hopkinsville Rd 42431 270-825-6133
Susanne Wolford, prin. Fax 825-6135
Madison MS 500/6-8
510 Brown Rd 42431 270-825-6160
Steve Gilliam, prin. Fax 825-6016
Madisonville North Hopkins HS 1,100/9-12
4515 Hanson Rd 42431 270-825-6017
Chad Burgett, prin. Fax 825-6045
Other Schools – See Nortonville

Madisonville Community College Post-Sec.
2000 College Dr 42431 270-821-2250

Manchester, Clay, Pop. 1,968
Clay County SD 3,800/PK-12
128 Richmond Rd 40962 606-598-2168
Douglas Adams, supt. Fax 598-7829
www.clay.k12.ky.us
Clay County HS 1,100/9-12
415 Clay County High Rd 40962 606-598-3737
Michael White, prin. Fax 598-8976
Clay County MS 600/7-8
239 Richmond Rd 40962 606-598-1810
Wayne Napier, prin. Fax 598-1230

Kentucky Tech System
Supt. — None
Clay County Area Technology Center Vo/Tech
1097 N Highway 11 40962 606-598-2194
Eugene Hensley, prin. Fax 598-4201

Southeast School of Cosmetology Post-Sec.
PO Box 493 40962 606-598-7901

Marion, Crittenden, Pop. 3,033
Crittenden County SD 1,300/K-12
601 W Elm St 42064 270-965-3525
John Belt, supt. Fax 965-9064
www.crittenden.k12.ky.us
Crittenden County HS 400/9-12
519 1/2 W Gum St 42064 270-965-2248
Karen Nasseri, prin. Fax 965-2797
Crittenden County MS 300/6-8
519 W Gum St 42064 270-965-5221
Jeremy Suchman, prin. Fax 965-5082

Martin, Floyd, Pop. 636
Kentucky Tech System
Supt. — None
Floyd County Area Technology Center Vo/Tech
HC 79 Box 205 41649 606-285-3088
Lenville Martin, prin. Fax 285-0274

Piarist S 100/9-12
PO Box 870 41649 606-285-3950
Rev. Thomas Carroll, prin. Fax 285-3950

Mayfield, Graves, Pop. 10,288
Graves County SD 4,100/K-12
2290 State Route 121 N 42066 270-328-2656
Brady Link, supt. Fax 328-1561
www.graves.k12.ky.us
Graves County HS 1,300/9-12
1107 W Housman St 42066 270-674-6242
Ward Bushart, prin. Fax 247-8540
Graves County MS 700/7-8
625 Jimtown Rd 42066 270-674-4890
Rim Watson, prin. Fax 251-3693

Kentucky Tech System
Supt. — None
Mayfield/Graves County Area Tech Center Vo/Tech
710 Douthitt St 42066 270-247-4710
Steve Arant, prin. Fax 247-4721

Mayfield ISD 900/PK-12
914 E College St 42066 270-247-3868
Lonnie Burgett, supt. Fax 247-3854
www.mayfield.k12.ky.us
Mayfield HS 400/9-12
700 Douthitt St 42066 270-247-4461
Anthony Hatchell, prin. Fax 247-9624
Mayfield MS 400/6-8
112 W College St 42066 270-247-7521
Lisa Huddleston, prin. Fax 247-8297

Mid-Continent University Post-Sec.
99 E Powell Rd 42066 270-247-8521
Northside Baptist Christian S 100/PK-12
711 N 12th St 42066 270-247-0516
Jan Lewis, prin. Fax 247-7125

Maysville, Mason, Pop. 9,136
Kentucky Tech System
Supt. — None
Mason County Area Technology Center Vo/Tech
646 Kenton Station Rd 41056 606-759-7101
Melanie Jamison, prin. Fax 759-7568

Mason County SD 2,100/PK-12
PO Box 130 41056 606-564-5563
Tim Moore, supt. Fax 564-5392
www.mason.k12.ky.us/
Mason County HS 800/9-12
1320 US Highway 68 41056 606-564-3393
Steven Appelman, prin. Fax 564-5360
Mason County MS 600/6-8
420 Chenault Dr 41056 606-564-6748
Betsy Cook, prin. Fax 564-5958

Maysville Community & Technical College Post-Sec.
1755 US Highway 68 41056 606-759-7141
St. Patrick S 300/1-12
318 Limestone St 41056 606-564-5949
Michael Kirry, prin. Fax 564-8795

Middlesboro, Bell, Pop. 10,858
Middlesboro ISD 1,700/K-12
PO Box 959 40965 606-242-8800
Darryl Wilder, supt. Fax 248-8805
www.mboro.k12.ky.us
Middlesboro HS 500/9-12
4404 Cumberland Ave 40965 606-242-8820
Ed Jones, prin. Fax 242-8825
Middlesboro MS 400/6-8
4400 Cumberland Ave 40965 606-242-8880
Steve Spangler, prin. Fax 242-8885

Collins School of Cosmetology Post-Sec.
111 W Chester Ave 40965 606-248-3602

Middletown, Jefferson, Pop. 6,072
Jefferson County SD
Supt. — See Louisville
Crosby MS 1,100/6-8
303 Gatehouse Ln 40243 502-485-8235
Kirk Lattimore, prin. Fax 485-8424
Eastern HS 1,800/9-12
12400 Old Shelbyville Rd 40243 502-485-8243
James Sexton, prin. Fax 485-3883

Midway, Woodford, Pop. 1,622

Midway College Post-Sec.
512 E Stephens St 40347 800-755-0031

Monticello, Wayne, Pop. 6,062
Kentucky Tech System
Supt. — None
Wayne County Area Technology Center Vo/Tech
150 Cardinal Way 42633 606-348-8424
Danny Guffey, prin. Fax 348-5090

Monticello ISD 800/PK-12
132 College St 42633 606-348-5311
Donnie Robison, supt. Fax 348-3664
www.monticello.k12.ky.us/
Monticello HS 200/9-12
135 Cave St 42633 606-348-5312
Johnny Chaplin, prin. Fax 348-3039
Monticello MS 200/6-8
135 Cave St 42633 606-348-5312
Johnny Chaplin, prin. Fax 348-3039

Wayne County SD 2,200/PK-12
534 Albany Rd 42633 606-348-8484
John Dalton, supt. Fax 348-0734
www.wayne.k12.ky.us
Lloyd MS 400/7-8
200 Cardinal Way 42633 606-348-6691
Robert Wixson, prin. Fax 348-5495
Wayne County HS 700/9-12
2 Kenny Davis Blvd 42633 606-348-5575
Peggy Shearer, prin. Fax 348-3458

Morehead, Rowan, Pop. 7,592
Rowan County SD 3,000/PK-12
121 E 2nd St 40351 606-784-8928
Marvin Moore, supt. Fax 783-1011
www.rowan.k12.ky.us
Rowan County MS 800/6-8
415 W Sun St 40351 606-784-8911
Tresia Swain, prin. Fax 784-5579
Rowan County SHS 900/9-12
499 Viking Dr 40351 606-784-8956
Mark Murray, prin. Fax 784-1067

Lakeside Christian Academy 200/PK-12
2535 US Highway 60 W 40351 606-784-2751
Tammy McKinney, admin. Fax 784-0056
Morehead State University Post-Sec.
100 Admissions Center 40351 606-783-2000
Rowan Technical College Post-Sec.
609 Viking Dr 40351 606-783-1538

Morganfield, Union, Pop. 3,430
Union County SD 2,300/PK-12
510 S Mart St 42437 270-389-1694
Dr. Gerald Novak, supt. Fax 389-9806
www.union.k12.ky.us/
Clements Victory Technical HS Vo/Tech
2302 US Highway 60 E 42437 270-389-2419
Claudia Stocking, prin. Fax 389-9383
Union County HS 700/9-12
4464 US Highway 60 W 42437 270-389-1454
Matt Ciecorka, prin. Fax 389-2715
Union County MS 500/6-8
4465 US Highway 60 W 42437 270-389-0224
Rhonda Callaway, prin. Fax 389-0245

Earle C. Clements Job Corps Center Post-Sec.
2302 US Highway 60 E 42437 270-389-5310

Morgantown, Butler, Pop. 2,552
Butler County SD 1,800/PK-12
PO Box 339 42261 270-526-5624
Larry Woods, supt. Fax 526-5625
www.butler.k12.ky.us/
Butler County HS 700/9-12
PO Box 248 42261 270-526-2204
Mike Elmore, prin. Fax 526-2268
Butler County MS 500/6-8
PO Box 10 42261 270-526-5647
Hazel Short, prin. Fax 526-3238

Kentucky Tech System
Supt. — None
Butler County Area Technology Center Vo/Tech
799 Veterans Way 42261 270-526-2223
Eric Keeling, prin. Fax 526-2273

Mount Olivet, Robertson, Pop. 287
Robertson County SD 400/K-12
PO Box 108 41064 606-724-5431
Charles Brown, supt. Fax 724-5921
school.robertson.k12.ky.us
Deming JSHS 200/7-12
PO Box 168 41064 606-724-5421
Jeremy McCloud, prin. Fax 724-5921

Mount Sterling, Montgomery, Pop. 6,317
Kentucky Tech System
Supt. — None
Montgomery County Area Technology Ctr Vo/Tech
682 Woodford Dr 40353 859-498-1103
Michael Kindred, prin. Fax 498-5960

Montgomery County SD 4,200/PK-12
700 Woodford Dr 40353 859-497-8760
Daniel Freeman, supt. Fax 497-8780
www.montgomery.k12.ky.us
McNabb MS 1,000/6-8
3570 Indian Mound Dr 40353 859-497-8770
Dean Cvit Kovic, prin. Fax 497-9683
Montgomery County HS 1,100/9-12
724 Woodford Dr 40353 859-497-8765
Shannon White, prin. Fax 497-8705

Nu-Tek Academy of Beauty Post-Sec.
153 Evans Dr 40353 859-498-4460

Mount Vernon, Rockcastle, Pop. 2,599
Kentucky Tech System
Supt. — None
Rockcastle County Area Technology Center Vo/Tech
PO Box 275 40456 606-256-4346
Ralph Baker, prin. Fax 256-4337

Rockcastle County SD 2,900/PK-12
245 Richmond St 40456 606-256-2125
Larry Hammond, supt. Fax 256-2126
www.rockcastle.kyschools.us/
Rockcastle County HS 900/9-12
PO Box 1410 40456 606-256-4816
Jennifer Mattingly, prin. Fax 256-3755
Rockcastle County MS 700/6-8
PO Box 1730 40456 606-256-5118
Jason Coguer, prin. Fax 256-2622

Cumberland Technical College Post-Sec.
PO Box 275 40456 606-256-4346

Mount Washington, Bullitt, Pop. 8,624
Bullitt County SD
Supt. — See Shepherdsville
Bullitt East HS 900/9-12
11450 Highway 44 E 40047 502-538-7322
David Marshall, prin. Fax 538-8368
Eastside MS 6-8
6925 Highway 44 E 40047 502-538-3767
Bonita Franklin, prin. Fax 538-0659
Mt. Washington MS 900/6-8
269 Water St 40047 502-538-4227
Denise Allen, prin. Fax 955-9530

Munfordville, Hart, Pop. 1,603
Hart County SD 2,400/PK-12
511 W Union St 42765 270-524-2631
Ricky Line, supt. Fax 524-2634
www.hart.k12.ky.us/
Hart County HS 700/9-12
1014 S Dixie Hwy 42765 270-524-9341
Chris Mueller, prin. Fax 524-3251

Murray, Calloway, Pop. 15,538
Calloway County SD 2,800/PK-12
PO Box 800 42071 270-762-7300
Steve Hoskins, supt. Fax 762-7310
www.calloway.k12.ky.us
Calloway County HS 900/9-12
2108 College Farm Rd 42071 270-762-7375
Yvette Pyle, prin. Fax 762-7380
Calloway County MS 700/6-8
2112 College Farm Rd 42071 270-762-7355
Tawnya Hunter, prin. Fax 762-7360

Kentucky Tech System
Supt. — None
Murray/Calloway County Area Tech Center Vo/Tech
1800 Sycamore St 42071 270-753-1870
Dennis Harper, prin. Fax 759-9656

Murray ISD 1,800/K-12
208 S 13th St 42071 270-753-4363
Bob Rogers, supt. Fax 759-4906
www.murray.kyschools.us
Murray HS 500/9-12
501 Doran Rd 42071 270-753-5202
Teresa Speed, prin. Fax 753-8391
Murray MS 700/4-8
801 Main St 42071 270-753-5125
Lou Carter, prin. Fax 753-9039

Ezell's Cosmetology School Post-Sec.
PO Box 1431 42071 270-753-4723
Murray State University Post-Sec.
PO Box 9 42071 270-762-3011

New Castle, Henry, Pop. 929
Henry County SD 2,100/K-12
326 S Main St 40050 502-845-8600
Tim Abrams, supt. Fax 845-8601
www.henry.k12.ky.us
Henry County HS 600/9-12
1120 Eminence Rd 40050 502-845-8670
Graham Wied, prin. Fax 845-8671
Henry County MS 500/6-8
1124 Eminence Rd 40050 502-845-8660
Steve Swank, prin. Fax 845-8661

Newport, Campbell, Pop. 15,911
Newport ISD 2,200/K-12
301 E 8th St 41071 859-292-3004
Michael Brandt, supt. Fax 292-3073
www.newportwildcats.org/
Newport HS 600/9-12
900 E 6th St 41071 859-292-3023
Scott Draud, prin. Fax 292-8340
Newport MS 500/6-8
30 W 8th St 41071 859-292-3017
David Upchurch, prin. Fax 292-3049

Brighton Center Post-Sec.
601 Washington Ave 41071 859-491-8303
Daymar College - Northern Kentucky Post-Sec.
76 Carothers Rd 41071 859-291-0800
Holy Trinity JHS 6-8
40 Chesapeake Ave 41071 859-292-0487
Sr. Mary Ruth Lubbers, prin. Fax 292-0487
Newport Central Catholic HS 400/9-12
13 Carothers Rd 41071 859-292-0001
Robert Noll, prin. Fax 292-0656
Northern Kentucky University 41099 Post-Sec.
859-572-5100

Nicholasville, Jessamine, Pop. 23,897
Jessamine County SD 6,900/PK-12
871 Wilmore Rd 40356 859-885-4179
Lu Young, supt. Fax 887-4811
www.jessamine.k12.ky.us
East Jessamine HS 900/9-12
815 Sulphur Well Pike 40356 859-885-7240
Janet Granada, prin. Fax 881-0161
East Jessamine MS 900/6-8
851 Wilmore Rd 40356 859-885-5561
Bill Pickett, prin. Fax 887-1797
West Jessamine HS 1,000/9-12
2101 Wilmore Rd 40356 859-887-2421
N. Bart Flener, prin. Fax 887-8854
West Jessamine MS 800/6-8
1400 Wilmore Rd 40356 859-885-2244
Terry Meckstroth, prin. Fax 885-8078
Other Schools – See Wilmore

Barrett & Company School of Hair Design Post-Sec.
973 Kimberly Sq 40356 859-885-9136

Nortonville, Hopkins, Pop. 1,252
Hopkins County SD
Supt. — See Madisonville
South Hopkins MS 500/6-8
9140 Hopkinsville Rd 42442 270-825-6125
Stuart Fitch, prin. Fax 825-6085

Olive Hill, Carter, Pop. 1,823
Carter County SD
Supt. — See Grayson
Carter County Career & Technical Center Vo/Tech
15 Grahn Rd 41164 606-286-4022
Jack Lowe, prin. Fax 286-6333
West Carter County HS 600/9-12
PO Box 1479 41164 606-286-2481
Rebecca Corsetti, prin. Fax 286-8026
West Carter County MS 500/6-8
PO Box 1510 41164 606-286-5354
Sherry Horsley, prin. Fax 286-8556

Oneida, Clay

Oneida Baptist Institute 300/K-12
PO Box 67 40972 606-847-4111
Dan Stockton, prin. Fax 847-4496

Owensboro, Daviess, Pop. 55,459
Daviess County SD 10,600/PK-12
PO Box 21510 42304 270-852-7000
Tom Shelton, supt. Fax 852-7010
www.daviess.k12.ky.us/
Apollo HS 1,400/9-12
2280 Tamarack Rd 42301 270-852-7100
Tom Purcell, prin. Fax 852-7110
Burns MS 800/6-8
4610 Goetz Dr 42301 270-852-7400
Fax 852-7410
College View MS 800/6-8
5061 New Hartford Rd 42303 270-852-7500
Jennifer Crume, prin. Fax 852-7510
Daviess County HS 1,700/9-12
4255 New Hartford Rd 42303 270-852-7300
Matthew Constant, prin. Fax 852-7310
Daviess County MS 800/6-8
1415 E 4th St 42303 270-852-7600
Gates Settle, prin. Fax 852-7610

Owensboro ISD 3,700/PK-12
PO Box 249 42302 270-686-1000
Dr. Larry Vick, supt. Fax 684-5756
www.owensboro.k12.ky.us
Owensboro HS 1,100/9-12
1800 Frederica St 42301 270-686-1110
Anita Burnette, prin. Fax 686-1019
Owensboro MS 600/7-8
1300 Booth Ave 42301 270-686-1130
Janice Eaves, prin. Fax 686-1173

Brescia University Post-Sec.
717 Frederica St 42301 270-685-3131
Daymar College Post-Sec.
3361 Buckland Sq 42301 270-926-4040
Kentucky Wesleyan College Post-Sec.
3000 Frederica St 42301 270-926-3111
Mr. Jim's Beauty College Post-Sec.
1240 Carter Rd 42301 270-684-3505
Owensboro Catholic HS 9-12
1524 W Parrish Ave 42301 270-684-3215
Harold Staples, prin. Fax 684-7050
Owensboro Catholic MS 200/7-8
2540 Christie Pl 42301 270-683-0480
James Duffy, prin. Fax 683-0495
Owensboro Community & Technical College Post-Sec.
1501 Frederica St 42301 270-687-7255
Owensboro Community & Technical College Post-Sec.
4800 New Hartford Rd 42303 270-686-4400
Owensboro Mercy Health System Post-Sec.
811 E Parrish Ave 42303 270-688-2100

Owenton, Owen, Pop. 1,470
Owen County SD 1,700/K-12
1600 Highway 22 E 40359 502-484-3934
Mark Cleveland, supt. Fax 484-9095
www.owen.k12.ky.us

Bowling MS 500/6-8
1960 Highway 22 E 40359 502-484-5701
Jo Ella Wallace, prin. Fax 484-3044
Owen County HS 600/9-12
2340 Highway 22 E 40359 502-484-5509
Tim Hitzfield, prin. Fax 484-0444

Owingsville, Bath, Pop. 1,564
Bath County SD 1,800/PK-12
405 W Main St 40360 606-674-6314
Nancy Hutchinson, supt. Fax 674-2647
www.bath.k12.ky.us
Bath County HS 500/9-12
645 Chenault Dr 40360 606-674-6325
Paul Prater, prin. Fax 674-9188
Bath County MS 500/6-8
432 W Main St 40360 606-674-8165
Lloyd Sartin, prin. Fax 674-2676

Paducah, McCracken, Pop. 25,575
Kentucky Tech System
Supt. — None
Paducah Area Technology Center Vo/Tech
2400 Adams St 42003 270-443-6592
Don Rowlett, prin. Fax 442-6233

McCracken County SD 6,700/PK-12
435 Berger Rd 42003 270-538-4000
M. Tim Heller, supt. Fax 538-4001
www.mccracken.k12.ky.us
Lone Oak HS 800/9-12
225 John E Robinson Dr 42001 270-538-4150
Donna Wear, prin. Fax 538-4151
Lone Oak MS 700/6-8
300 Cumberland Ave 42001 270-538-4130
Larry Hopper, prin. Fax 538-4131
Reidland HS 500/9-12
5349 Old Benton Rd 42003 270-538-4210
Glen Ringstaff, prin. Fax 538-4211
Reidland MS 500/6-8
5347 Benton Rd 42003 270-538-4190
Scott Pullen, prin. Fax 538-4191
Other Schools – See West Paducah

Paducah ISD 2,900/PK-12
PO Box 2550 42002 270-444-5600
R.J. Greene, supt. Fax 444-5607
www.paducah.k12.ky.us
Paducah MS 600/6-8
342 Lone Oak Rd 42001 270-444-5710
Tim Huddleston, prin. Fax 444-5709
Paducah Tilghman HS 800/9-12
2400 Washington St 42003 270-444-5650
Arthur Davis, prin. Fax 444-5659

Community Christian Academy 300/K-12
3230 Buckner Ln 42001 270-575-0025
Clara Downs, admin. Fax 443-2230
Paducah Technical College Post-Sec.
509 S 30th St 42001 800-995-4438
St. Mary HS 200/9-12
1243 Elmdale Rd 42003 270-442-1681
Fax 442-7920
St. Mary MS 200/6-8
1243 Elmdale Rd 42003 270-442-1681
Fax 442-7920
West Kentucky Comm. & Technical College Post-Sec.
PO Box 7380 42002 270-554-9200

Paintsville, Johnson, Pop. 4,141
Johnson County SD 3,700/PK-12
253 N Mayo Trl 41240 606-789-2530
Orville Hamilton, supt. Fax 789-2506
www.johnson.k12.ky.us
Johnson Central HS 1,000/9-12
257 N Mayo Trl 41240 606-789-2500
Steve Whitaker, prin. Fax 789-2547
Johnson County MS 600/7-8
251 N Mayo Trl 41240 606-789-4133
Tim Adams, prin. Fax 789-4135

Paintsville ISD 700/K-12
305 2nd St 41240 606-789-2654
Coy Samons, supt. Fax 789-7412
www.paintsville.k12.ky.us
Paintsville MSHS, 225 2nd St 41240 300/7-12
David Bolen, prin. 606-789-2656

Mayo Technical College Post-Sec.
513 3rd St 41240 606-789-5321

Paris, Bourbon, Pop. 9,334
Bourbon County SD 2,500/PK-12
3343 Lexington Rd 40361 859-987-2180
Lana Fryman, supt. Fax 987-2182
www.bourbon.k12.ky.us/boco/
Bourbon County HS 800/9-12
3343 Lexington Rd 40361 859-987-2185
Travis Huber, prin. Fax 987-5850
Bourbon County MS 600/6-8
3343 Lexington Rd 40361 859-987-2189
Larry Tapp, prin. Fax 987-5854

Paris ISD 700/K-12
310 W 7th St 40361 859-987-2160
Janice Cox-Blackburn, supt. Fax 987-6749
www.paris.k12.ky.us
Paris HS 200/9-12
308 W 7th St 40361 859-987-2168
Vicki Grigson, prin. Fax 987-2132
Paris MS 200/5-8
304 W 7th St 40361 859-987-2163
Travis Earlywine, prin. Fax 987-2164

Park Hills, Kenton, Pop. 2,803

Gateway Community & Technical College Post-Sec.
1025 Amsterdam Rd 41011 859-292-3930

Maysville Community College Post-Sec.
1401 Dixie Hwy 41011

Phelps, Pike, Pop. 1,298
Pike County SD
Supt. — See Pikeville
Phelps HS 500/7-12
PO Box 925 41553 606-456-3482
Mike Hamilton, prin. Fax 456-8988

Pikeville, Pike, Pop. 6,312
Kentucky Tech System
Supt. — None
Millard Area Technology Center Vo/Tech
7925 Millard Hwy 41501 606-437-6059
Jim Bob Hamilton, prin. Fax 437-0502

Pike County SD 9,600/K-12
PO Box 3097 41502 606-433-9200
Roger Wagner, supt. Fax 432-3321
www.pike.k12.ky.us
Millard MS 500/4-8
8015 Millard Hwy 41501 606-432-3380
Tommy Thornsbury, prin. Fax 433-9677
Pike County Central HS 700/9-12
100 Winners Circle Dr 41501 606-432-4352
Eddie McCoy, prin. Fax 432-7733
Shelby Valley HS 600/9-12
125 Douglas Park 41501 606-639-0033
Forrest Dale Johnson, prin. Fax 639-2074
Other Schools – See Belfry, Lick Creek, Phelps, Virgie

Pikeville ISD 1,300/K-12
148 2nd St 41501 606-432-8161
Jerry Green, supt. Fax 432-2119
Pikeville JSHS 600/7-12
120 Championship Dr 41501 606-432-0185
Jon Stratton, prin. Fax 432-2022

East Kentucky Beauty College Post-Sec.
5333 N Mayo Trl 41501 606-432-3627
National College Post-Sec.
50 National College Blvd 41501 606-478-7200
Pikeville College Post-Sec.
147 Sycamore St 41501 606-218-5250
Pikeville Medical Center Post-Sec.
911 S Bypass Rd 41501 606-437-3500

Pine Knot, McCreary, Pop. 1,549
McCreary County SD
Supt. — See Stearns
Pine Knot Career Institute Vo/Tech
PO Box 1990 42635 606-354-2176
David Cothron, coord. Fax 354-2170

Pineville, Bell, Pop. 2,014
Bell County SD 3,000/PK-12
PO Box 340 40977 606-337-7051
George Thompson, supt. Fax 337-1412
www.bellcountyschools.bell.k12.ky.us
Bell County HS 800/9-12
RR 1 Box 88 40977 606-337-7061
Jeff Saylor, prin. Fax 337-0867

Kentucky Tech System
Supt. — None
Bell County Area Technology Center Vo/Tech
RR 7 Box 199A 40977 606-337-3094
Barney Judd, prin. Fax 337-9053

Pineville ISD 600/PK-12
401 W Virginia Ave 40977 606-337-5701
Michael White, supt. Fax 337-9983
www.pineville.k12.ky.us
Pineville JSHS 300/7-12
401 W Virginia Ave 40977 606-337-2361
Paula Goodin, prin. Fax 337-3720

Clear Creek Baptist Bible College Post-Sec.
300 Clear Creek Rd 40977 606-337-3196

Pippa Passes, Knott, Pop. 448

Alice Lloyd College Post-Sec.
100 Purpose Rd 41844 606-368-2101
Buchanan S 200/K-12
100 Purpose Rd 41844 606-368-6108
Yvon Allen, prin. Fax 368-6216

Powderly, Muhlenberg, Pop. 843
Muhlenberg County SD 4,800/K-12
510 W Main St 42367 270-338-2871
Dale Todd, supt. Fax 338-0529
www.mberg.k12.ky.us
Other Schools – See Greenville

Prestonsburg, Floyd, Pop. 3,706
Floyd County SD 6,400/K-12
106 N Front Ave 41653 606-886-2354
Dr. Paul W. Fanning, supt. Fax 886-8862
www.floyd.kyschools.us
Adams MS 400/6-8
2520 S Lake Dr 41653 606-886-2671
Jack Goodman, prin. Fax 886-7026
Prestonsburg HS 600/9-12
825 Blackcat Blvd 41653 606-886-2252
Ted George, prin. Fax 886-1745
Other Schools – See Betsy Layne, Eastern, Hi Hat

Carl D. Perkins Job Corps Center Post-Sec.
478 Meadows Br 41653 606-886-1037
Prestonsburg Community College Post-Sec.
110 Bert T Combs Dr 41653 606-886-3863

Princeton, Caldwell, Pop. 6,447
Caldwell County SD 1,800/PK-12
PO Box 229 42445 270-365-8000
Carrell Boyd, supt. Fax 365-5742
www.caldwell.k12.ky.us/

Caldwell County HS 600/9-12
350 Beckner Ln 42445 270-365-8010
James Schmidt, prin. Fax 365-9742
Caldwell County MS 500/6-8
440 Beckner Ln 42445 270-365-8020
Will Brown, prin. Fax 365-9573

Kentucky Tech System
Supt. — None
Caldwell County Area Technology Center Vo/Tech
130 Vocational School Rd 42445 270-365-5563
Arthur Dunn, prin. Fax 365-5609

Providence, Webster, Pop. 3,549
Providence ISD 400/PK-12
302 W Main St 42450 270-667-7007
Edwina Slack, supt. Fax 667-7606
www.providence.k12.ky.us
Providence HS 100/9-12
301 Cedar St 42450 270-667-7065
Gina Russell, prin. Fax 667-7952

Raceland, Greenup, Pop. 2,477
Raceland-Worthington ISD 1,000/K-12
600 Rams Blvd 41169 606-836-2144
Frank Melvin, supt. Fax 833-5807
www.raceland.k12.ky.us
Raceland-Worthington HS 400/7-12
500 Rams Blvd 41169 606-836-8221
Larry Coldiron, prin. Fax 494-2341

Radcliff, Hardin, Pop. 21,471
Hardin County SD
Supt. — See Elizabethtown
North Hardin HS 1,400/9-12
801 S Logsdon Pkwy 40160 270-351-3167
Bill Dennison, prin. Fax 352-4512
Radcliff MS 500/6-8
1145 S Dixie Blvd 40160 270-351-1171
Laura McGray, prin. Fax 352-5193

North Hardin Christian S 300/PK-12
1298 Rogersville Rd 40160 270-351-7700
A. Paige Hardin, prin. Fax 351-7757

Richmond, Madison, Pop. 30,893
Kentucky Tech System
Supt. — None
Madison County Area Technology Center Vo/Tech
PO Box 809 40476 859-624-4520
Douglas West, prin. Fax 624-9659

Madison County SD 9,700/PK-12
PO Box 768 40476 859-624-4500
Billy Michael Caudill, supt. Fax 624-4508
www.madison.k12.ky.us/
Madison Central HS 1,500/9-12
705 N 2nd St 40475 859-624-4505
Gina Lakes, prin. Fax 623-3925
Madison MS 700/6-8
101 Summit St 40475 859-624-4550
Brad Winkler, prin. Fax 624-4543
Model Laboratory HS 200/9-12
521 Lancaster Ave 40475 859-622-3766
James Dantic, prin. Fax 622-6658
Model Laboratory MS 200/6-8
521 Lancaster Ave 40475 859-622-3766
James Dantic, prin. Fax 622-6658
Moores MS 700/6-8
1143 Berea Rd 40475 859-624-4545
Kevin Combs, prin. Fax 624-4534
Other Schools – See Berea

Eastern Kentucky University Post-Sec.
521 Lancaster Ave 40475 859-622-1000
National College Post-Sec.
125 S Killarney Ln 40475 859-623-8956

Rush, Boyd
Boyd County SD
Supt. — See Ashland
Ramey-Estep HS 200/7-12
2901 Pigeon Roost Rd 41168 606-928-5801
Elizabeth Brewster, prin. Fax 928-5574

Russell, Greenup, Pop. 3,597
Kentucky Tech System
Supt. — None
Russell Area Technology Center Vo/Tech
705 Red Devil Ln 41169 606-836-1256
Keith Parsons, prin. Fax 836-3784

Russell ISD 2,100/PK-12
409 Belfonte St 41169 606-836-9679
Dr. Susan Compton, supt. Fax 836-2865
www.russell-ind.k12.ky.us
Russell HS 700/9-12
709 Red Devil Ln 41169 606-836-9658
Allan Thompson, prin. Fax 836-9650
Russell MS 500/6-8
707 Red Devil Ln 41169 606-836-8135
Sean Horne, prin. Fax 836-0614

Russell Springs, Russell, Pop. 2,537
Kentucky Tech System
Supt. — None
Lake Cumberland Area Technology Center Vo/Tech
PO Box 599 42642 270-866-6175
Jeff Adams, prin. Fax 866-2424

Russell County SD
Supt. — See Jamestown
Russell County HS 900/9-12
2166 S Highway 127 42642 270-866-3341
Darren Gossage, prin. Fax 866-8830
Russell County MS 500/7-8
2258 S Highway 127 42642 270-866-2224
Kenneth Pickett, prin. Fax 866-8679

Russellville, Logan, Pop. 7,271
Kentucky Tech System
Supt. — None
Russellville Area Technology Center — Vo/Tech
1103 W 9th St 42276 — 270-726-8432
Grayson Wells, prin. — Fax 726-6303

Logan County SD — 3,300/PK-12
PO Box 417 42276 — 270-726-2436
Marshall Kemp, supt. — Fax 726-8892
www.logan.k12.ky.us/
Logan County HS — 1,000/9-12
2200 Bowling Green Rd 42276 — 270-726-8454
Bob Nylin, prin. — Fax 726-1108

Russellville ISD — 1,200/PK-12
355 S Summer St 42276 — 270-726-8405
Roger Cook, supt. — Fax 726-4036
www.rville.k12.ky.us/district/
Russellville HS — 400/9-12
1101 W 9th St 42276 — 270-726-8421
Rick Larson, prin. — Fax 726-3685
Russellville MS — 300/5-8
210 E 7th St 42276 — 270-726-8428
Alan Marksberry, prin. — Fax 726-8888

Saint Catharine, Washington

St. Catharine College — Post-Sec.
2375 Bardstown Rd 40061 — 800-599-2000

Salyersville, Magoffin, Pop. 1,604
Magoffin County SD — 2,400/PK-12
PO Box 109 41465 — 606-349-6117
Joe Hunley, supt. — Fax 349-3417
www.magoffin.k12.ky.us/
Magoffin County HS — 700/9-12
201 Hornet Dr 41465 — 606-349-2011
William Helton, prin. — Fax 349-5345
Whitaker MS — 400/7-8
221 Hornet Dr 41465 — 606-349-5190
Johnnie Johnson, prin. — Fax 349-5139

Sandy Hook, Elliott, Pop. 687
Elliott County SD — 1,200/K-12
PO Box 767 41171 — 606-738-8002
John Williams, supt. — Fax 738-8050
www.elliott.k12.ky.us/
Elliott County JSHS — 500/7-12
PO Box 687 41171 — 606-738-8052
Larry Salyer, prin. — Fax 738-8000

Infinite Possibilities Christian Academy — 50/9-12
PO Box 89 41171 — 606-738-6350
Dr. Virginia Cornett, admin. — Fax 738-4788

Scottsville, Allen, Pop. 4,525
Allen County SD — 2,700/PK-12
570 Oliver St 42164 — 270-618-3181
Larry Williams, supt. — Fax 618-3185
www.allen.kyschools.us
Allen County Scottsville HS — 900/9-12
1545 Bowling Green Rd 42164 — 270-622-4119
Greg Dunn, prin. — Fax 622-5882
Allen County Technical Center — Vo/Tech
1501 Bowling Green Rd 42164 — 270-622-4711
Karen Hayes, dir. — Fax 622-7006
Bazzell MS — 500/7-8
201 New Gallatin Rd 42164 — 270-622-7140
Rick Fisher, prin. — Fax 622-4649

Shelbyville, Shelby, Pop. 10,730
Kentucky Tech System
Supt. — None
Shelby County Area Technology Center — Vo/Tech
230 Rocket Ln 40065 — 502-633-6554
Deborah Anderson, prin. — Fax 633-4212

Shelby County SD — 5,600/PK-12
PO Box 159 40066 — 502-633-2375
Elaine Farris, supt. — Fax 633-1988
www.shelby.kyschools.us
Shelby County East MS — 600/6-8
600 Rocket Ln 40065 — 502-633-1478
Anthony Sieg, prin. — Fax 633-6981
Shelby County HS — 1,500/9-12
PO Box 69 40066 — 502-633-2344
Gary Kidwell, prin. — Fax 647-0238
Shelby County West MS — 800/6-8
100 Warriors Way 40065 — 502-633-4869
Kymberly Rice, prin. — Fax 647-4525

Cornerstone Christian Academy — 200/K-12
3850 Frankfort Rd 40065 — 502-633-4070
Matt Maxwell, prin. — Fax 633-4605

Shepherdsville, Bullitt, Pop. 8,874
Bullitt County SD — 11,500/PK-12
1040 Highway 44 E 40165 — 502-543-2271
Keith Davis, supt. — Fax 543-3608
www.bullitt.k12.ky.us
Bernheim MS — 600/6-8
700 Audubon Dr 40165 — 502-543-7614
Roger Hayes, prin. — Fax 543-8295
Bullitt Central HS — 1,300/9-12
1330 Highway 44 E 40165 — 502-543-7021
Jim Beward, prin. — Fax 543-1797
Bullitt Lick MS — 700/6-8
555 W Blue Lick Rd 40165 — 502-543-6806
Scott Hrebicik, prin. — Fax 543-1685
Hebron MS — 800/6-8
3300 E Hebron Ln 40165 — 502-957-3540
Glenn Gray, prin. — Fax 957-6014
North Bullitt HS — 1,000/9-12
3200 E Hebron Ln 40165 — 502-957-2186
Greg Schultz, prin. — Fax 957-6762

Zoneton MS — 6-8
797 Old Preston Hwy N 40165 — 502-955-7067
Rita Muratalla, prin. — Fax 955-7027
Other Schools – See Mount Washington

Kentucky Tech System
Supt. — None
Bullitt County Area Technology Center — Vo/Tech
395 High School Dr 40165 — 502-543-7018
Fax 543-1691

Silver Grove, Campbell, Pop. 1,174
Silver Grove ISD — 300/PK-12
PO Box 400 41085 — 859-441-3894
Danny Montgomery, supt. — Fax 441-4299
www.s-g.k12.ky.us
Silver Grove S — 300/PK-12
PO Box 400 41085 — 859-441-3873
Dennis Bledsoe, prin. — Fax 441-4299

Smithland, Livingston, Pop. 395
Livingston County SD — 900/PK-12
PO Box 219 42081 — 270-928-2111
Jack Monroe, supt. — Fax 928-2112
www.livingston.kyschools.us/
Livingston Central HS — 400/9-12
750 US Highway 60 W 42081 — 270-928-2065
Michael Riley, prin. — Fax 928-2066
Other Schools – See Burna

Somerset, Pulaski, Pop. 12,136
Kentucky Tech System
Supt. — None
Pulaski County Area Technology Center — Vo/Tech
3865 S Highway 27 Ste 101 42501 — 606-678-2998
Beth Hargis, prin. — Fax 678-3032

Pulaski County SD — 7,500/K-12
PO Box 1055 42502 — 606-679-1123
Tim Eaton, supt. — Fax 679-1438
www.pulaski.net
Northern MS — 800/6-8
650 Oak Leaf Ln 42503 — 606-678-5230
Angela Murphy, prin. — Fax 678-2729
Pulaski County HS — 1,000/9-12
511 E University Dr 42503 — 606-679-1574
Robert Bowers, prin. — Fax 677-2771
Southern MS — 1,000/6-8
200 Enterprise Dr 42501 — 606-679-6855
Troy Dotson, prin. — Fax 679-2270
Southwestern HS — 1,200/9-12
1765 WTLO Rd 42503 — 606-678-9000
Boyd Randolph, prin. — Fax 678-9277

Somerset ISD — 1,600/PK-12
305 College St 42501 — 606-679-4451
Wilson Leonard Sears, supt. — Fax 678-0864
www.somerset.k12.ky.us
Meece MS — 500/5-8
210 Barnett St 42501 — 606-678-5821
Nathan Nevels, prin. — Fax 678-2934
Somerset HS — 500/9-12
301 College St 42501 — 606-678-4721
Jeff Perkins, prin. — Fax 677-0087

Somerset Christian S — 200/K-12
PO Box 3330 42564 — 606-451-1600
John Hale, prin. — Fax 677-9850
Somerset Community College — Post-Sec.
808 Monticello St 42501 — 606-679-8501

S Portsmouth, Greenup

Harvest Christian Academy — 100/K-12
PO Box 398 41174 — 606-932-3007
John Bower, prin. — Fax 932-2240

South Shore, Greenup, Pop. 1,243
Greenup County SD
Supt. — See Greenup
McKell MS — 400/6-8
129 Bulldog Ln 41175 — 606-932-3221
Donald Harrison, prin. — Fax 932-9844

Springfield, Washington, Pop. 2,806
Washington County SD — 1,700/PK-12
120 Mackville Hl 40069 — 859-336-5470
Larry Graves, supt. — Fax 336-5480
www.washington.k12.ky.us
Washington County HS — 600/9-12
601 Lincoln Park Rd 40069 — 859-336-5475
Eugene Smith, prin. — Fax 336-5983
Washington County MS — 200/6-8
603 Lincoln Park Rd 40069 — 859-336-5475
Stacy Hall, prin.

Stanford, Lincoln, Pop. 3,452
Kentucky Tech System
Supt. — None
Lincoln County Area Technology Center — Vo/Tech
422 Education Way 40484 — 606-365-8500
Richard Kazsuk, prin. — Fax 365-8504

Lincoln County SD — 3,800/PK-12
PO Box 265 40484 — 606-365-2124
Dr. Teresa Wallace, supt. — Fax 365-1660
www.lincoln.k12.ky.us
Fort Logan HS — 100/9-12
305 Danville Ave 40484 — 606-365-1333
Scott Montgomery, prin. — Fax 365-4020
Lincoln County HS — 1,200/9-12
60 Education Way 40484 — 606-365-9111
Ty Howard, prin. — Fax 365-1750
Lincoln County MS — 700/7-8
285 Education Way 40484 — 606-365-8400
Pam Hart, prin. — Fax 365-8600

Stanton, Powell, Pop. 3,109
Powell County SD — 2,500/PK-12
PO Box 430 40380 — 606-663-3300
Lonnie Morris, supt. — Fax 663-3303
www.powell.k12.ky.us/
Powell County HS — 700/9-12
700 W College Ave 40380 — 606-663-3320
Lance Smith, prin. — Fax 663-3406
Powell County MS — 600/6-8
PO Box 400 40380 — 606-663-3308
Karen Rose, prin. — Fax 663-3307

Stearns, McCreary, Pop. 1,550
McCreary County SD — 2,100/PK-12
120 Raider Way 42647 — 606-376-2591
Ray Ball, supt. — Fax 376-5584
www.mccreary.kyschools.us
McCreary Central HS — 900/9-12
400 Raider Way 42647 — 606-376-5051
David Cothron, prin. — Fax 376-3005
McCreary County MS — 300/7-8
180 Raider Way 42647 — 606-376-5081
Aaron Anderson, prin. — Fax 376-9580
Other Schools – See Pine Knot

Taylor Mill, Kenton, Pop. 6,733
Kenton County SD
Supt. — See Fort Wright
Woodland MS — 700/6-8
5399 Old Taylor Mill Rd 41015 — 859-356-7300
Charles Ladwig, prin. — Fax 356-7595

Taylorsville, Spencer, Pop. 1,173
Spencer County SD — 2,200/PK-12
207 W Main St 40071 — 502-477-3250
R. Larry Holt, supt. — Fax 477-3259
www.spencer.k12.ky.us
Spencer County HS — 700/9-12
520 Taylorsville Rd 40071 — 502-477-3255
Tracy Bale, prin. — Fax 477-3212
Spencer County MS — 600/6-8
PO Box 250 40071 — 502-477-3260
Dena Kent, prin. — Fax 477-6796

Tompkinsville, Monroe, Pop. 2,633
Kentucky Tech System
Supt. — None
Monroe County Area Technology Center — Vo/Tech
PO Box 338 42167 — 270-487-8261
Lee Ann Wall, prin. — Fax 487-0094

Monroe County SD — 2,000/PK-12
309 Emberton St 42167 — 270-487-5456
George Wilson, supt. — Fax 487-5571
www.monroe.k12.ky.us
Monroe County HS — 500/9-12
755 Old Mulkey Rd 42167 — 270-487-6217
Phillip Bartley, prin. — Fax 487-8274
Monroe County MS — 500/6-8
759 Old Mulkey Rd 42167 — 270-487-9624
Kevin Cloyd, prin. — Fax 487-9534

Union, Boone, Pop. 3,379
Boone County SD
Supt. — See Florence
Gray MS — 1,100/6-8
10400 US Highway 42 41091 — 859-384-5333
Tom Hummel, prin. — Fax 384-5318
Ryle HS — 1,400/9-12
10379 US Highway 42 41091 — 859-384-5300
Matthew Turner, prin. — Fax 384-5312

Valley Station, Jefferson, Pop. 22,840
Jefferson County SD
Supt. — See Louisville
Frost MS — 500/6-8
13700 Sandray Blvd 40272 — 502-485-8256
Ursula Wade, prin. — Fax 485-8453
Stuart MS — 1,200/6-8
4601 Valley Station Rd 40272 — 502-485-8334
Jennifer Colley, prin. — Fax 485-8713
Valley Traditional HS — 900/9-12
10200 Dixie Hwy 40272 — 502-485-8339
Greg Sheeley, prin. — Fax 485-8666

Vanceburg, Lewis, Pop. 1,698
Lewis County SD — 2,400/K-12
PO Box 159 41179 — 606-796-2811
Maurice Reeder, supt. — Fax 796-3081
www.lewis.k12.ky.us
Lewis County HS — 700/9-12
PO Box 99 41179 — 606-796-2823
Jamie Weddington, prin. — Fax 796-3066
Lewis County MS — 500/6-8
PO Box 69 41179 — 606-796-6228
Larry Riley, prin. — Fax 796-6255
Meade Vocational Education Center — Vo/Tech
PO Box 130 41179 — 606-796-6106
Stanley Allen, prin. — Fax 796-9739

Vancleve, Breathitt

Kentucky Mountain Bible College — Post-Sec.
PO Box 10 41385 — 800-879-5622
Mt. Carmel HS — 100/8-12
PO Box 2 41385 — 606-666-5008
John Mills, prin. — Fax 666-4612

Versailles, Woodford, Pop. 7,728
Woodford County SD — 3,400/PK-12
330 Pisgah Rd 40383 — 859-873-4701
Paul Stahler, supt. — Fax 873-1614
www.woodford.k12.ky.us
Woodford County HS — 1,200/9-12
180 Frankfort St 40383 — 859-873-5434
Rob Akers, prin. — Fax 873-7731
Woodford County MS — 600/6-8
100 School House Rd 40383 — 859-873-4721
Stephanie Koontz, prin. — Fax 873-4436

Villa Hills, Kenton, Pop. 7,749

Villa Madonna Academy 200/9-12
2500 Amsterdam Rd 41017 859-331-6333
Pamela McQueen, prin. Fax 331-8615

Vine Grove, Hardin, Pop. 3,983
Hardin County SD
Supt. — See Elizabethtown
Alton MS 700/6-8
100 Country Club Rd 40175 270-877-2135
Jama Bennett, prin. Fax 877-6297

Virgie, Pike
Pike County SD
Supt. — See Pikeville
Virgie MS 300/6-8
PO Box 310 41572 606-639-2774
Danny Osborne, prin. Fax 639-4086

Walton, Boone, Pop. 2,856
Walton-Verona ISD 1,200/PK-12
16 School Rd 41094 859-485-4181
Bill Boyle, supt. Fax 485-1810
www.w-v.k12.ky.us
Walton-Verona JSHS 500/7-12
30 School Rd 41094 859-485-7721
Mark Krummen, prin. Fax 485-7739

Warfield, Martin, Pop. 274
Martin County SD
Supt. — See Inez
Warfield MS 200/6-8
PO Box 378 41267 606-395-5900
Robbie Fletcher, prin. Fax 395-5902

Warsaw, Gallatin, Pop. 1,838
Gallatin County SD 1,500/PK-12
PO Box 147 41095 859-567-2828
Dorothy B. Perkins, supt. Fax 567-4528
www.gallatin.k12.ky.us
Gallatin County HS 400/9-12
PO Box 146 41095 859-567-7901
Roxann Booth, prin. Fax 567-8222
Gallatin County MS 400/6-8
PO Box 149 41095 859-567-5791
Amy Sutler, prin. Fax 567-6107

West Liberty, Morgan, Pop. 3,349
Kentucky Tech System
Supt. — None
Morgan County Area Technology Center Vo/Tech
PO Box 249 41472 606-743-8452
Ronnie Woods, prin. Fax 743-8500

Morgan County SD 2,200/K-12
PO Box 489 41472 606-743-8002
Joe Dan Gold, supt. Fax 743-8050
www.morgancountyschools.com/
Morgan County HS 700/9-12
PO Box 606 41472 606-743-8052
Addison Whitt, prin. Fax 743-8100
Morgan County MS 500/6-8
PO Box 580 41472 606-743-8102
Darren Sparkman, prin. Fax 743-8150

West Paducah, McCracken
McCracken County SD
Supt. — See Paducah
Heath HS 600/9-12
4330 Metropolis Lake Rd 42086 270-538-4090
Russ Tilford, prin. Fax 538-4091
Heath MS 500/6-8
4336 Metropolis Lake Rd 42086 270-538-4070
Greg Webb, prin. Fax 538-4071

Whitesburg, Letcher, Pop. 1,512
Kentucky Tech System
Supt. — None
Letcher County Area Technology Center Vo/Tech
185 Circle Dr 41858 606-633-5053
Barbara Ison, prin. Fax 633-8084

Letcher County SD 3,000/PK-12
224 Parks St 41858 606-633-4455
Anna C. Craft, supt. Fax 633-4724
www.letcher.k12.ky.us/
Letcher County Central HS 600/9-12
38 College Dr 41858 606-633-2339
Stephen Boggs, prin. Fax 633-2447
Whitesburg MS 200/6-8
366 Parks St 41858 606-633-2761
Henry Frazier, prin. Fax 633-4137

Jenny Lea Academy of Cosmetology Post-Sec.
74 Parkway Plaza Loop 41858 606-573-4276

Whitesville, Daviess, Pop. 596

Trinity HS 200/9-12
10510 Main Cross St 42378 270-233-5184
Bill Hagan, prin. Fax 233-9293

Williamsburg, Whitley, Pop. 5,162
Whitley County SD 4,600/PK-12
300 Main St 40769 606-549-7000
Lonnie Anderson, supt. Fax 549-7006
www.whitley.k12.ky.us/
Whitley County HS 1,200/9-12
350 Boulevard Of Champions 40769 606-549-7025
Scott Paul, prin. Fax 549-7035
Whitley County MS 700/7-8
351 Boulevard Of Champions 40769 606-549-7050
Rich Prewitt, prin. Fax 549-7055

Williamsburg ISD 700/PK-12
1000 Main St 40769 606-549-6044
Dennis Byrd, supt. Fax 549-6076
www.wburg.k12.ky.us
Williamsburg S 700/PK-12
1000 Main St 40769 606-549-6044
Joy Mack, prin. Fax 549-6076

University of the Cumberlands Post-Sec.
6178 College Station Dr 40769 606-549-2200

Williamstown, Grant, Pop. 3,423
Grant County SD 3,700/K-12
820 Arnie Risen Blvd 41097 859-824-3323
Donald W. Martin, supt. Fax 824-3508
www.grant.k12.ky.us/
Other Schools – See Dry Ridge

Williamstown ISD 900/PK-12
300 Helton St 41097 859-824-7144
Charles Wilson, supt. Fax 824-3237
www.wtown.k12.ky.us
Williamstown JSHS 400/6-12
300 Helton St 41097 859-824-4421
Bob Elliott, prin. Fax 824-4736

Wilmore, Jessamine, Pop. 5,826
Jessamine County SD
Supt. — See Nicholasville
Jessamine Career & Technology Center Vo/Tech
881 Wilmore Rd, 859-881-8324
C. Dexter Knight, prin. Fax 887-9051

Asbury College Post-Sec.
1 Macklem Dr 40390 859-858-3511
Asbury Theological Seminary Post-Sec.
204 N Lexington Ave 40390 800-227-2879

Winchester, Clark, Pop. 16,494
Clark County SD 5,300/K-12
1600 W Lexington Ave 40391 859-744-4545
Ed Musgrove, supt. Fax 745-3935
www.clarkschools.net
Clark HS 1,600/9-12
620 Boone Ave 40391 859-744-6111
Gordon Parido, prin. Fax 745-2418
Clark MS 700/6-8
1 Educational Plz 40391 859-744-0427
Pamela Whitesides, prin. Fax 745-3907
Conkwright MS 500/6-8
360 Mount Sterling Rd 40391 859-744-8433
Becke Cleaver, prin. Fax 745-2027

Kentucky Tech System
Supt. — None
Clark County Area Technology Center Vo/Tech
PO Box 727 40392 859-744-1250
Karen Bothun, prin. Fax 744-9979

Motif Beauty Academy Post-Sec.
23 W Lexington Ave 40391 859-745-5886
Winchester Christian Academy 100/6-12
PO Box 617 40392 859-745-6026
Charlotte Jernigan, prin. Fax 744-5830

Wurtland, Greenup, Pop. 1,046
Greenup County SD
Supt. — See Greenup
Wurtland MS 400/6-8
700 Center St 41144 606-836-1023
Tracy Claxon, prin. Fax 836-3939

LOUISIANA

LOUISIANA DEPARTMENT OF EDUCATION
PO Box 94064, Baton Rouge 70804-9064
Telephone 225-342-3602
Fax 225-342-7316
Website http://www.doe.state.la.us

Superintendent of Education Paul Pastorek

LOUISIANA BOARD OF EDUCATION
PO Box 94064, Baton Rouge 70804-9064

President Linda Johnson

PUBLIC, PRIVATE AND CATHOLIC SECONDARY SCHOOLS

Abbeville, Vermilion, Pop. 11,664
Vermilion Parish SD 8,600/PK-12
PO Box 520 70511 337-893-3973
Randy Schexnayder, supt. Fax 898-0939
www.vrml.k12.la.us
Abbeville HS 800/9-12
1305 Wildcat Dr 70510 337-893-1874
Ralph Thibobeaux, prin. Fax 893-0935
Williams MS 700/6-8
1105 Prairie Ave 70510 337-893-3943
Mikal Stall, prin. Fax 893-5190
Other Schools – See Erath, Gueydan, Kaplan, Maurice

Louisiana Technical College - Gulf Area Post-Sec.
1115 Clover St 70510 337-893-4984
Vermilion Catholic HS 200/9-12
425 Park Ave 70510 337-893-6636
Gerard Richard, prin. Fax 898-0394

Albany, Livingston, Pop. 1,002
Livingston Parish SD
Supt. — See Livingston
Albany HS 500/9-12
PO Box 1090 70711 225-567-9319
Bruce Chaffin, prin. Fax 567-9162
Albany MS 400/6-8
PO Box 1210 70711 225-567-5231
Rachel Jenkins, prin. Fax 567-9177

Alexandria, Rapides, Pop. 45,693
Rapides Parish SD 22,100/PK-12
PO Box 1230 71309 318-487-0888
Gary Jones, supt. Fax 449-3190
www.rapides.k12.la.us
Alexandria HS 1,000/9-12
800 Ola St 71303 318-448-8234
Billy Albritton, prin. Fax 487-9994
Alexandria MS 600/6-8
122 Maryland Ave 71301 318-445-5343
Tim Tharp, prin. Fax 442-8650
Bolton HS 600/9-12
2101 Vance Ave 71301 318-448-3628
William Higgins, prin. Fax 448-4329
Brame MS 800/6-8
4800 Dawn St 71301 318-443-3688
Walter Fall, prin. Fax 442-3966
Peabody Magnet HS 700/9-12
2727 Jones Ave 71302 318-448-3457
Lee Dotson, prin. Fax 487-0771
Smith MS 600/6-8
3100 Jones Ave 71302 318-445-6241
David Brasher, prin. Fax 445-9255
Other Schools – See Ball, Deville, Glenmora, Hineston, Lecompte, Lena, Pineville, Tioga

---

Alexandria Academy of Beauty Post-Sec.
2305 Rapides Ave 71301 318-442-7715
Grace Christian S 400/PK-12
4900 Jackson Street Ext 71303 318-445-8735
Kay Blackburn, prin. Fax 443-1034
Holy Savior Menard HS 600/7-12
4603 Coliseum Blvd 71303 318-445-8233
Ronald Roy, prin. Fax 448-8170
Louisiana State University at Alexandria Post-Sec.
8100 Highway 71 S 71302 318-445-3672
Louisiana Technical College - Alexandria Post-Sec.
PO Box 5698 71307 318-487-5439
Rapides Regional Medical Center Post-Sec.
PO Box 30101 71301 318-473-3150

Amite, Tangipahoa, Pop. 4,390
Tangipahoa Parish SD 18,200/PK-12
59656 Puleston Rd 70422 985-748-7153
Louis Joseph, supt. Fax 748-8587
www.tangischools.org
Amite HS 500/9-12
403 S Laurel St 70422 985-748-9301
Lucille Morris, prin. Fax 748-2814
Northwood HS 100/9-12
202 Robin St 70422 985-748-3989
Rhea Marrs, admin. Fax 748-3990
West Side MS 600/5-8
401 W Oak St 70422 985-748-9073
Jo Fairburn, prin. Fax 748-9225
Other Schools – See Hammond, Independence, Kentwood, Loranger, Ponchatoula, Tickfaw

---

Oak Forest Academy 400/PK-12
600 Walnut St 70422 985-748-4321
Sam Bella, prin. Fax 748-4320

Anacoco, Vernon, Pop. 782
Vernon Parish SD
Supt. — See Leesville
Anacoco JSHS 400/7-12
4740 Port Arthur Ave 71403 337-239-3039
Norman Beason, prin. Fax 238-4228

Angie, Washington, Pop. 236
Washington Parish SD
Supt. — See Franklinton
Angie JHS 200/6-8
64433 Dixon St 70426 985-986-3105
Randy Branch, prin. Fax 986-5515

Arcadia, Bienville, Pop. 2,854
Bienville Parish SD 2,400/PK-12
PO Box 418 71001 318-263-9416
William Britt, supt. Fax 263-3100
www.bienvilleschools.com
Arcadia JSHS 200/7-12
967 Daniel St 71001 318-263-2264
William Wysinger, prin. Fax 263-9703
Other Schools – See Bienville, Castor, Gibsland, Ringgold, Saline

Arnaudville, Saint Landry, Pop. 1,395
St. Landry Parish SD
Supt. — See Opelousas
Beau Chene HS 700/9-12
7076 Highway 93 70512 337-662-5815
Robert Lanclos, prin. Fax 662-3688

Athens, Claiborne, Pop. 254
Claiborne Parish SD
Supt. — See Homer
Athens S 200/PK-12
15520 Highway 9 71003 318-258-3241
Craig Roberson, prin. Fax 258-6160

Mount Olive Christian S 100/PK-12
15349 Highway 9 71003 318-258-5661
Linda Gantt, prin. Fax 258-5662

Atlanta, Winn, Pop. 143
Winn Parish SD
Supt. — See Winnfield
Atlanta S 300/PK-12
118 School Rd 71404 318-628-4613
Susan Horne, prin. Fax 628-4247

Avondale, Jefferson, Pop. 5,813
Jefferson Parish SD
Supt. — See Marrero
Ford MS 500/7-9
435 S Jamie Blvd 70094 504-436-2474
Allen Hayes, prin. Fax 436-0604

Baker, East Baton Rouge, Pop. 13,250
Baker City SD 2,200/PK-12
PO Box 680 70704 225-774-5795
C. Lester Klotz, supt. Fax 774-5797
www.bakerschools.org
Baker HS 600/9-12
3200 Groom Rd 70714 225-775-1259
Earl Langlois, prin. Fax 775-4011
Baker MS 500/6-8
5903 Groom Rd 70714 225-775-9750
Ernest Morris, prin. Fax 775-9753

Bethany Christian S 400/K-12
13855 Plank Rd 70714 225-774-0133
Carolyn DeSalvo, prin. Fax 774-0163
Central Private S 600/PK-12
12801 Centerra Ct 70714 225-261-3341
Kyle Achord, prin. Fax 261-3490

Baldwin, Saint Mary, Pop. 2,603
St. Mary Parish SD
Supt. — See Centerville
Boudreau MS 400/6-8
PO Box 120 70514 337-924-7990
Steven Guillory, prin. Fax 924-7999
West St. Mary HS 500/9-12
PO Box 120 70514 337-924-7990
Steven Guillory, prin. Fax 924-7999

Ball, Rapides, Pop. 3,684
Rapides Parish SD
Supt. — See Alexandria
Tioga JHS 500/7-8
1150 Tioga Rd 71405 318-640-9412
Gerald Crooks, prin. Fax 640-0126

Basile, Evangeline, Pop. 2,382
Evangeline Parish SD
Supt. — See Ville Platte
Basile JSHS 400/5-12
PO Box 666 70515 337-432-5012
Georgeanna Courville, prin. Fax 432-6414

Bastrop, Morehouse, Pop. 12,403
Morehouse Parish SD 4,700/PK-12
PO Box 872 71221 318-281-5784
Richard Hartley, supt. Fax 283-3456
www.mpsb.us/
Bastrop HS 900/9-12
402 Highland Ave 71220 318-281-0194
Thomas Thrower, prin. Fax 281-0457
Career Center 100/9-9
1607 Martin L King S 71220 318-281-1407
Ralph Davenport, prin. Fax 283-3460
Morehouse JHS 500/7-8
1001 W Madison Ave 71220 318-281-0776
Howard Loche, prin. Fax 283-1846

Bastrop Beauty School #1 Post-Sec.
117 S Vine St 71220 318-281-8652
Louisiana Technical College - Bastrop Post-Sec.
PO Box 1120 71221 318-283-0836
Prairie View Academy 300/PK-12
9942 Edwin St 71220 318-281-7044
Edward Bain, prin. Fax 281-4113

Baton Rouge, East Baton Rouge, Pop. 222,064
East Baton Rouge Parish SD 46,500/PK-12
PO Box 2950 70821 225-922-5400
Charlotte D. Placide, supt. Fax 922-5411
www.ebrschools.org/
Baton Rouge Magnet HS 1,300/9-12
2825 Government St 70806 225-383-0520
Nanette Greer, prin. Fax 344-3066
Belaire HS 900/9-12
12121 Tams Dr 70815 225-272-1860
Robert Webb, prin. Fax 272-3782
Broadmoor HS 900/9-12
10100 Goodwood Blvd 70815 225-926-1420
Daryl Glueck, prin. Fax 928-5472
Broadmoor MS 800/6-8
1225 Sharp Rd 70815 225-272-0540
Rebel Ellerbee, prin. Fax 272-0195
Capitol MS 900/6-8
4200 Gus Young Ave 70802 225-231-9292
Lamont Cole, prin. Fax 231-9291
Capitol PreCollege Academy for Boys 9-12
1000 N 23rd St 70802 225-343-0745
Curt Green, prin. Fax 343-0761
Capitol PreCollege Academy for Girls 500/9-12
1000 N 23rd St 70802 225-383-0353
Linda Lewis, prin. Fax 387-1635
Central HS 1,100/9-12
10200 E Brookside Dr 70818 225-261-3438
Ronnie Devall, prin. Fax 261-3501
Central MS 900/6-8
11526 Sullivan Rd 70818 225-261-2237
John Cashio, prin. Fax 261-9973
Crestworth MS 400/7-8
10650 Avenue F 70807 225-775-6845
Angela Thomas, prin. Fax 775-0051
Glasgow MS 600/6-8
1676 Glasgow Ave 70808 225-925-2942
Nellwyn Vordenbaumn-East, prin. Fax 928-3565
Glen Oaks HS 700/9-12
6650 Cedar Grove Dr 70812 225-356-4306
Wilbert August, prin. Fax 359-6782

Glen Oaks MS 800/6-8
5300 Monarch Ave 70811 225-357-3790
Thelemese Porter, prin. Fax 357-1841
Istrouma Magnet HS 700/9-12
3730 Winbourne Ave 70805 225-355-7701
Elisha Jackson, prin. Fax 359-9807
Kenilworth MS 800/6-8
7600 Boone Ave 70808 225-766-8111
Viola Jackson, prin. Fax 767-9061
Lee HS 700/9-12
1105 Lee Dr 70808 225-383-7744
David Phillips, prin. Fax 346-8196
McKinley HS 700/9-12
800 E Mckinley St 70802 225-344-7696
Armond Brown, prin. Fax 387-5435
McKinley Magnet MS 400/6-8
1550 Eddie Robinson Sr Dr 70802 225-388-0089
Joyce Green-Graham, prin. Fax 387-1434
Park Forest MS 800/6-8
3760 Aletha Dr 70814 225-275-6650
Adam Smith, prin. Fax 275-3058
Prescott MS 700/6-8
4055 Prescott Rd 70805 225-357-6481
Elida Bera, prin. Fax 355-2672
Scotlandville Magnet HS 800/9-12
9870 Scotland Ave 70807 225-775-3715
Howard Davis, prin. Fax 774-3767
Scotlandville MS 6-8
9147 Elmgrove Garden Dr 70807 225-774-2510
Clara Whitley-Joseph, prin. Fax 775-6441
Sherwood MS 900/6-8
1020 Marlbrook Dr 70815 225-272-3090
Phyllis Crawford, prin. Fax 273-9459
Southeast MS 800/6-8
15000 S Harrells Ferry Rd 70816 225-753-5930
Milton Hollis, prin. Fax 756-8601
Southern University Lab S 500/PK-12
PO Box 9414 70813 225-771-3490
Sheila Lewis, dir. Fax 771-2782
Tara HS 1,100/9-12
9002 Whitehall Ave 70806 225-927-6100
Luanne Estess, prin. Fax 928-0122
University Lab S 1,000/K-12
Louisiana State Univ 70803 225-578-3221
Dr. Edward Greene, prin. Fax 578-3326
Westdale MS 800/6-8
5650 Claycut Rd 70806 225-924-1308
Sherry Brock, prin. Fax 926-9929
Woodlawn HS 1,100/9-12
15755 Jefferson Hwy 70817 225-753-1200
James Newman, prin. Fax 751-9269
Woodlawn MS 6-8
14939 Tiger Bend Rd 70817 225-751-0436
Shelly Colvin, prin. Fax 753-0159
Rosenwald Adult Education Center Adult
2611 Dayton St 70805 225-355-8678
Bobbie Robertson, prin. Fax 358-4449
Other Schools – See Pride

Recovery SD, PO Box 94064 70804 11,400/PK-12
Leroy Helire, dir. 877-453-2721
www.nolapublicschools.net/
Other Schools – See New Orleans

Baton Rouge Community College Post-Sec.
5310 Florida Blvd 70806 225-216-8040
Baton Rouge General Medical Center Post-Sec.
PO Box 2511 70821 225-387-7767
Baton Rouge School of Computers Post-Sec.
10425 Plaza Americana Dr 70816 225-923-2525
Camelot College Post-Sec.
2618 Wooddale Blvd # A 70805 225-928-3005
Catholic HS 900/8-12
855 Hearthstone Dr 70806 225-383-0397
Br. Barry Landry, prin. Fax 383-0381
Christian Life Academy 600/PK-12
2037 Quail Dr 70808 225-769-6760
Larry Perdue, prin. Fax 769-8068
Court Reporting Institute of Louisiana Post-Sec.
12090 S Harrells Ferry Rd 70816 225-292-1950
Delta College of Arts & Technology Post-Sec.
7380 Exchange Pl 70806 225-928-7770
Desire Street Academy 100/8-12
3852 E Brookstown Dr 70805 225-355-5074
Al Jones, prin. Fax 246-8532
Diesel Driving Academy Post-Sec.
8067 Airline Hwy 70815 225-929-9990
D-Jay's School of Beauty Arts & Sciences Post-Sec.
5131 Government St 70806 225-926-2530
Domestic Health Care Institute Post-Sec.
4826 Jamestown Ave 70808 225-925-5312
Dunham S 600/PK-12
11111 Roy Emerson Dr 70810 225-767-7097
Dr. Bobby Welch, hdmstr. Fax 767-7056
Episcopal S of Baton Rouge 1,000/PK-12
3200 Woodland Ridge Blvd 70816 225-753-3180
Kay Betts, hdmstr. Fax 756-0926
Family Christian Academy 200/K-12
PO Box 262550 70826 225-768-3026
Dave Smith, admin. Fax 768-3213
Gables Academy 100/1-12
15333 Jefferson Hwy 70817 225-752-9231
Susan Kramer, dir. Fax 756-3533
Hosanna Christian Academy 500/PK-12
8850 Goodwood Blvd 70806 225-926-4885
David Hand, admin. Fax 926-8458
ITI Technical College Post-Sec.
13944 Airline Hwy 70817 225-752-4233
Jehovah-Jireh Christian Academy 300/PK-12
1771 N Lobdell Ave 70806 225-932-2357
Glenda Colbert, prin. Fax 932-2360
Jones Creek Adventist Academy 100/K-12
4363 Jones Creek Rd 70817 225-751-8219
Fax 751-3404
Lockworks Academie of Hairdressing Post-Sec.
2834 S Sherwood Forest Blvd 70816 225-295-1435
Louisiana School/Visually Impaired Post-Sec.
PO Box 4328 70821

Louisiana State School for the Deaf Post-Sec.
PO Box 3074 70821
Louisiana State University & A & M Coll. Post-Sec.
Louisiana State Univ 70803 225-388-3202
Louisiana Technical College-Baton Rouge Post-Sec.
3250 N Acadian Thruway E 70805 225-359-9204
Medical Training College Post-Sec.
10525 Plaza Americana Dr 70816 225-926-5820
MedVance Institute Post-Sec.
9255 Interline Ave 70809 225-248-1015
Our Lady of the Lake College Post-Sec.
7434 Perkins Rd 70808 225-768-1700
Our Lady of the Lake Medical Center Post-Sec.
5000 Hennessy Blvd 70808 225-769-7799
Parkview Baptist S 1,600/K-12
5750 Parkview Church Rd 70816 225-291-2500
Kenneth Payne, supt. Fax 293-4135
Redemptorist HS 900/7-12
4000 Saint Gerard Ave 70805 225-357-0936
John Fabre, prin. Fax 357-4555
Remington College Post-Sec.
10551 Coursey Blvd 70816 225-922-3990
Runnels S 800/PK-12
17255 S Harrells Ferry Rd 70816 225-751-5712
Dr. L. K. Runnels, prin. Fax 753-0276
St. Josephs Academy 800/9-12
3015 Broussard St 70808 225-383-7207
Linda Harvison, prin. Fax 344-5714
St. Michael the Archangel HS 800/9-12
PO Box 86110 70879 225-753-9782
Myra Patureau, prin. Fax 753-0605
Southern University A&M College Post-Sec.
Southern University 70813 225-771-4500
Starkey Academy 200/K-12
10510 Joor Rd 70818 225-261-1390
Stephen Whitlow, prin. Fax 261-9399

Bell City, Calcasieu
Calcasieu Parish SD
Supt. — See Lake Charles
Bell City S 500/K-12
PO Box 100 70630 337-622-3210
Reinette Guillory, prin. Fax 622-3595

Belle Chasse, Plaquemines, Pop. 8,512
Plaquemines Parish SD 3,100/PK-12
115 Keating Dr 70037 504-595-6400
Eva Jones, supt. Fax 398-9990
www.ppsb.org/
Belle Chasse HS 800/9-12
8346 Highway 23 70037 504-394-2810
Monica Wertz, prin. Fax 393-1182
Belle Chasse MS 700/5-8
13476 Highway 23 70037 504-656-2315
Joe Williamson, prin. Fax 656-2401
Other Schools – See Braithwaite, Port Sulphur

Belle Rose, Assumption
Assumption Parish SD
Supt. — See Napoleonville
Belle Rose MS 200/5-8
PO Box 229 70341 225-473-8917
Stacy Garrison, prin. Fax 473-8429

Benton, Bossier, Pop. 2,886
Bossier Parish SD 18,600/PK-12
PO Box 2000 71006 318-549-5000
Kenneth Kruithof, supt. Fax 549-5004
www.bossierschools.org
Benton HS 600/9-12
6136 Highway 3 71006 318-549-5240
Scott Smith, prin. Fax 549-5252
Benton MS 700/5-8
6140 Highway 3 71006 318-549-5310
Dwayne Slack, prin. Fax 549-5323
Other Schools – See Bossier City, Elm Grove, Haughton, Plain Dealing, Shreveport

Bernice, Union, Pop. 1,727
Union Parish SD
Supt. — See Farmerville
Bernice S 300/K-12
PO Box 570 71222 318-285-7606
Jackuline Hill, prin. Fax 285-5006

Berwick, Saint Mary, Pop. 4,286
St. Mary Parish SD
Supt. — See Centerville
Berwick HS 500/9-12
700 Pattie Dr 70342 985-384-8450
Buffy Fegenbush, prin. Fax 384-8505
Berwick JHS 400/6-8
3955 Highway 182 70342 985-384-5664
Thomas D. Bourgeois, prin. Fax 384-5663

Bienville, Bienville, Pop. 254
Bienville Parish SD
Supt. — See Arcadia
Bienville S 100/K-12
PO Box 212 71008 318-385-7591
Billy Rogers, prin. Fax 385-7750

Bogalusa, Washington, Pop. 12,964
Bogalusa City SD 2,200/PK-12
PO Box 310 70429 985-281-2100
Jerry Payne, supt. Fax 735-1358
www.bogalusaschools.org/
Bogalusa HS 700/9-12
PO Box 580 70429 985-735-8161
Rodney Brown, prin. Fax 735-9768
Bogalusa MS 400/6-8
1403 North Ave 70427 985-732-3706
Fax 735-6430

Louisiana Technical College - Sullivan Post-Sec.
1710 Sullivan Dr 70427 985-732-6640

Bossier City, Bossier, Pop. 60,505
Bossier Parish SD
Supt. — See Benton

Airline HS 1,400/9-12
2801 Airline Dr 71111 318-549-5080
Kim Gaspard, prin. Fax 549-5093
Bossier HS 700/9-12
777 Bearkat Dr 71111 318-549-6680
David Thrash, prin. Fax 549-6693
Cope MS 600/6-8
4814 Shed Rd 71111 318-549-5380
Judy Grooms, prin. Fax 549-5393
Greenacres MS 700/6-8
2220 Airline Dr 71111 318-549-6210
Kathy Bouck, prin. Fax 549-6223
Parkway HS 1,000/9-12
4301 Panther Dr 71112 318-549-6910
Joe Huffman, prin. Fax 549-6922
Rusheon MS 700/6-8
2401 Old Minden Rd 71112 318-549-6610
Giselle Bryant, prin. Fax 549-6623
Adult Learning Center Adult
415 Monroe St 71111 318-549-6839
Jerry Allen, prin. Fax 549-6842

Bossier Parish Community College Post-Sec.
6220 E Texas St 71111 318-678-6000
Pat Goins Benton Road Beauty School Post-Sec.
1701 Old Minden Rd Ste 36 71111 318-746-7674

Bourg, Terrebonne
Terrebonne Parish SD
Supt. — See Houma
South Terrebone HS 1,100/9-12
3879 Highway 24 70343 985-868-7850
Kenneth Delcambre, prin. Fax 868-7854

Boutte, Saint Charles, Pop. 2,702
St. Charles Parish SD
Supt. — See Luling
Hahnville HS 1,400/9-12
200 Tiger Dr 70039 985-758-7537
Barbara Fuselier, prin. Fax 758-9876

Braithwaite, Plaquemines
Plaquemines Parish SD
Supt. — See Belle Chasse
Phoenix S 400/PK-12
13073 Highway 15 70040 985-333-4573
John Barthelemy, prin. Fax 333-4395

Breaux Bridge, Saint Martin, Pop. 7,902
St. Martin Parish SD
Supt. — See Saint Martinville
Breaux Bridge HS 900/9-12
1015B Breaux Bridge Sr High 70517 337-332-3131
Ronnie Dore, prin. Fax 332-4058
Breaux Bridge JHS 300/7-8
100 Martin St 70517 337-332-2844
Marie Romagosa, prin. Fax 332-4831

Broussard, Lafayette, Pop. 6,754
Lafayette Parish SD
Supt. — See Lafayette
Broussard MS 600/5-8
1325 S Morgan Ave 70518 337-837-9031
Keisha Hawkins, prin. Fax 837-1057

Episcopal S of Acadiana 500/PK-12
1557 Smede Hwy 70518 337-365-1416
Chris Taylor, hdmstr. Fax 367-9841

Brusly, West Baton Rouge, Pop. 2,028
West Baton Rouge Parish SD
Supt. — See Port Allen
Brusly HS 500/9-12
630 Frontage Rd 70719 225-749-2815
Walt Lemoine, prin. Fax 749-8563
Brusly MS 400/6-8
601 N Kirkland St 70719 225-749-3123
Callie Kershaw, prin. Fax 749-8570

Bunkie, Avoyelles, Pop. 4,502
Avoyelles Parish SD
Supt. — See Marksville
Bunkie HS 500/9-12
435 Evergreen St 71322 318-346-6216
Mary Wilson, prin. Fax 346-9611
Bunkie MS 300/7-8
205 S Cottonwood St 71322 318-346-7227
Dexter Compton, prin. Fax 346-6964

Calhoun, Ouachita
Ouachita Parish SD
Supt. — See Monroe
Calhoun MS 500/6-8
191 Highway 80 E 71225 318-644-5840
Don Coker, prin. Fax 644-5418

Calvin, Winn, Pop. 226
Winn Parish SD
Supt. — See Winnfield
Calvin S 300/PK-12
PO Box 80 71410 318-727-8784
Rodney Shelton, prin. Fax 727-9224

Cameron, Cameron, Pop. 2,041
Cameron Parish SD
Supt. — See Lake Charles
Johnson Bayou S 200/K-12
6304 Gulf Beach Hwy 70631 337-569-2138
Gene Reynolds, prin. Fax 569-2673

Campti, Natchitoches, Pop. 1,054
Natchitoches Parish SD
Supt. — See Natchitoches
Lakeview JSHS 600/7-12
PO Box 200 71411 318-476-3360
Terry Williams, prin. Fax 476-2851

Carencro, Lafayette, Pop. 6,097
Lafayette Parish SD
Supt. — See Lafayette

Carencro MS 700/6-8
4301 N University Ave 70520 337-896-6127
Louella Riggs Cook, prin. Fax 896-7620

Castor, Bienville, Pop. 212
Bienville Parish SD
Supt. — See Arcadia
Castor S 400/PK-12
PO Box 69 71016 318-544-7271
Pat Boyd, prin. Fax 544-9077

Cecilia, Saint Martin, Pop. 1,374
St. Martin Parish SD
Supt. — See Saint Martinville
Cecilia HS 600/9-12
PO Box 360 70521 337-667-6221
Anthony Polotzola, prin. Fax 667-6795
Cecilia JHS 400/7-8
PO Box 129 70521 337-667-6226
Fax 667-7352

Centerville, Saint Mary
St. Mary Parish SD 10,100/PK-12
PO Box 170 70522 337-836-9661
Dr. Donald Aguillard, supt. Fax 836-5461
www.stmary.k12.la.us
Centerville S 600/PK-12
PO Box 59 70522 337-836-5103
Mike Galler, prin. Fax 836-9594
Other Schools – See Baldwin, Berwick, Franklin, Morgan City, Patterson

Chalmette, Saint Bernard, Pop. 32,100
St. Bernard Parish SD 900/PK-12
200 E Saint Bernard Hwy 70043 504-301-2000
Doris Voitier, supt. Fax 301-2010
www.stbernard.k12.la.us
Chalmette HS 900/7-12
1100 E Judge Perez Dr 70043 504-301-2600
Wayne Warner, prin. Fax 301-2610

Nunez Community College Post-Sec.
3700 La Fontaine St 70043 504-680-2240

Chauvin, Terrebonne, Pop. 3,375
Terrebonne Parish SD
Supt. — See Houma
Lacache MS 500/5-8
5266 Highway 56 70344 985-594-3945
Kerwin Trosclair, prin. Fax 594-4128

Choudrant, Lincoln, Pop. 580
Lincoln Parish SD
Supt. — See Ruston
Choudrant HS 400/7-12
PO Box 220 71227 318-768-2542
Doug Postel, prin. Fax 768-4182

Church Point, Acadia, Pop. 4,682
Acadia Parish SD
Supt. — See Crowley
Church Point HS 500/9-12
305 E Lougarre St 70525 337-684-5472
Lee Ward Bellard, prin. Fax 684-5137
Church Point MS 300/6-8
340 W Martin Luther King Dr 70525 337-684-6381
Paul Derousselle, prin. Fax 684-0123

Clinton, East Feliciana, Pop. 1,922
East Feliciana Parish SD 2,300/PK-12
PO Box 397 70722 225-683-8277
Glen Brady Ph.D., supt. Fax 683-3320
www.efpsb.k12.la.us
Clinton HS 300/9-12
PO Box 426 70722 225-683-3321
Artis Pinkney, prin. Fax 683-5115
Clinton MS 300/6-8
12126 Liberty St 70722 225-683-5267
Delsia Marshall, prin. Fax 683-9592
Other Schools – See Jackson

Silliman Institute 500/PK-12
PO Box 946 70722 225-683-5383
Marvin Holland, hdmstr. Fax 683-6728

Colfax, Grant, Pop. 1,676
Grant Parish SD 3,600/PK-12
PO Box 208 71417 318-627-3274
Sheila S. Jackson, supt. Fax 627-5931
www.gpsb.org/
Other Schools – See Dry Prong, Georgetown, Montgomery

Columbia, Caldwell, Pop. 467
Caldwell Parish SD 1,900/PK-12
PO Box 1019 71418 318-649-2689
John Sartin, supt. Fax 649-0636
Caldwell Parish HS 500/9-12
163 Spartan Dr 71418 318-649-2750
Sherry Jones, prin. Fax 649-0021
Caldwell Parish JHS 300/7-8
114 Trojan Dr 71418 318-649-2340
Harrell Tucker, prin. Fax 649-2341

Converse, Sabine, Pop. 407
Sabine Parish SD
Supt. — See Many
Converse S 500/K-12
PO Box 10 71419 318-567-2673
Larry Patrick, prin. Fax 567-3400

Cottonport, Avoyelles, Pop. 2,266

Louisiana Technical College - Avoyelles Post-Sec.
508 Choupique Ln 71327 318-876-2401

Cotton Valley, Webster, Pop. 1,169
Webster Parish SD
Supt. — See Minden
Cotton Valley S 300/PK-12
PO Box 457 71018 318-832-4716
Ronnie Rhymes, prin. Fax 832-5273

Coushatta, Red River, Pop. 2,205
Red River Parish SD 1,500/PK-12
PO Box 1369 71019 318-932-4081
Kay Easley, supt. Fax 932-4367
www.rrbulldogs.com/
Red River HS 400/9-12
PO Box 409 71019 318-932-4913
William Edward Wilson, prin. Fax 932-5334
Red River JHS 200/6-8
931 E Carrol St 71019 318-932-5265
Diane L. Newton, prin. Fax 932-9052

Riverdale Academy 300/PK-12
RR 1 Box 104 71019 318-932-5876
John Kerley Ph.D., prin. Fax 932-4355

Covington, Saint Tammany, Pop. 9,347
St. Tammany Parish SD 35,600/PK-12
PO Box 940 70434 985-892-2276
Gayle Sloan, supt. Fax 898-3267
www.stpsb.org
Covington HS 1,500/9-12
73030 Lion Dr 70433 985-892-3422
Danny Guillory, prin. Fax 875-9699
Pitcher JHS 400/7-8
415 S Jefferson Ave 70433 985-892-3021
Jay Gaines, prin. Fax 892-1188
Other Schools – See Folsom, Madisonville, Mandeville, Pearl River, Slidell

---

Aveda Institute Post-Sec.
1355 Polders Ln 70433 985-892-9953
Delta College Post-Sec.
19231 6th Ave 70433 985-892-6651
Northlake Christian S 900/PK-12
70104 Wolverine Dr 70433 985-892-2683
David Diamond, hdmstr. Fax 893-4363
St. Paul's HS 700/8-12
PO Box 928 70434 985-892-3200
Br. Raymond Bulliard, prin. Fax 892-4048
St. Scholastica Academy 700/8-12
PO Box 1210 70434 985-892-2540
Mary Kathryn Villere, prin. Fax 893-5256

Crowley, Acadia, Pop. 13,861
Acadia Parish SD 9,500/PK-12
PO Box 309 70527 337-783-3664
John E. Bourque, supt. Fax 783-3761
www.acadia.k12.la.us/
Crowley HS 600/9-12
263 Hensgens Rd 70526 337-783-5313
Steve Duplechin, prin. Fax 783-7796
Crowley MS 600/6-8
401 W Northern Ave 70526 337-783-5305
Antoinette Pete, prin. Fax 783-5338
Other Schools – See Church Point, Iota, Midland, Rayne

Louisiana Technical College - Acadian Post-Sec.
1933 W Hutchinson Ave 70526 337-788-7521
Northside Christian S 300/K-12
811 E Northern Ave 70526 337-783-3620
Rev. Randy Trahan, prin. Fax 788-3461
Notre Dame HS 500/9-12
910 N Eastern Ave 70526 337-783-3519
Cindy Istre, prin. Fax 788-2115

Cut Off, Lafourche, Pop. 5,325
Lafourche Parish SD
Supt. — See Thibodaux
Larose-Cut Off MS 600/6-8
13356 W Main St 70345 985-693-3273
Matthew Hodson, prin. Fax 693-3270

Delcambre, Vermilion, Pop. 2,146
Iberia Parish SD
Supt. — See New Iberia
Delcambre JSHS 500/6-12
601 W Main St 70528 337-685-2595
Cory Bourque, prin. Fax 685-6099

Delhi, Richland, Pop. 3,055
Richland Parish SD
Supt. — See Rayville
Delhi HS 200/9-12
413 Main St 71232 318-878-2235
Milton Linder, prin. Fax 878-8967
Delhi MS 300/5-8
106 Toombs St 71232 318-878-3748
Sheldon Jones, prin. Fax 878-3749

Denham Springs, Livingston, Pop. 10,206
Livingston Parish SD
Supt. — See Livingston
Denham Springs Freshman HS 500/9-9
940 N Range Ave 70726 225-665-7890
Patty Dumiller, prin. Fax 665-1865
Denham Springs JHS 900/6-8
401 Hatchell Ln 70726 225-665-8898
Jennifer Barclay, prin. Fax 665-8601
Denham Springs SHS 1,300/10-12
1000 N Range Ave 70726 225-665-8851
Harold Wax, prin. Fax 665-4082
Live Oak HS 800/9-12
35086 Hwy 16 70706 225-665-8858
Tracy McRae, prin. Fax 665-8850
Southside JHS 800/6-8
PO Box 907 70727 225-664-4221
Myra Holmes, prin. Fax 664-3307

Community Christian Academy 100/PK-12
400 N River Rd 70726 225-665-5696
Joyce Wilson, prin. Fax 665-3098
Denham Springs Beauty College Post-Sec.
923 Florida Ave SE 70726 225-665-6188

Dequincy, Calcasieu, Pop. 3,310
Calcasieu Parish SD
Supt. — See Lake Charles
Dequincy HS 300/9-12
207 N Overton St 70633 337-786-5251
Craig Neal, prin. Fax 786-7668
Dequincy MS 300/6-8
1603 W 4th St 70633 337-786-3000
Billy Kellogg, prin. Fax 786-5778

Deridder, Beauregard, Pop. 11,103
Beauregard Parish SD 6,000/PK-12
PO Box 938 70634 337-463-5551
Rita Mann, supt. Fax 463-6735
www.beau.k12.la.us/
Beauregard Vocational Center Vo/Tech
PO Box 1090 70634 337-462-2784
Gerald Laughlin, prin.
Deridder HS 800/9-12
PO Box 1090 70634 337-463-3266
Gerald Laughlin, prin. Fax 463-9358
Deridder JHS 700/6-8
415 N Frusha Dr 70634 337-463-9083
Kim Hayes, prin. Fax 463-7696
East Beauregard HS 500/6-12
5364 Highway 113 70634 337-328-7512
Barbara Rutherford, prin. Fax 328-8132
Other Schools – See Fields, Longville, Merryville, Singer

Beckwith Christian S 100/PK-12
5525 Highway 27 70634 337-462-7006

Destrehan, Saint Charles, Pop. 8,031
St. Charles Parish SD
Supt. — See Luling
Destrehan HS 1,400/9-12
1 Wildcat Ln 70047 985-764-9946
Lorel Gonzales, prin. Fax 764-9948
Hurst MS 500/7-8
170 Rd Runner Ln 70047 985-764-6367
Stephen Weber, prin. Fax 764-2678

Deville, Rapides, Pop. 1,113
Rapides Parish SD
Supt. — See Alexandria
Buckeye JSHS 800/7-12
PO Box 439 71328 318-466-5678
Harry Welch, prin. Fax 466-9269

Dodson, Winn, Pop. 341
Winn Parish SD
Supt. — See Winnfield
Dodson S 400/PK-12
PO Box 97 71422 318-628-2172
Crystal Stewart, prin. Fax 628-7515

Donaldsonville, Ascension, Pop. 7,535
Ascension Parish SD 15,600/PK-12
PO Box 189 70346 225-473-7981
Donald Songy, supt. Fax 473-8058
www.apsb.org
Donaldsonville HS 700/7-12
100 Tiger Dr 70346 225-474-2730
Ronald Rabalais, prin. Fax 473-4496
Other Schools – See Geismar, Gonzales, Prairieville, Saint Amant

---

Ascension Catholic HS 200/9-12
311 Saint Vincent St 70346 225-473-9227
Mark Shamburger, prin. Fax 473-9235

Downsville, Union, Pop. 114
Union Parish SD
Supt. — See Farmerville
Downsville S 500/K-12
PO Box 8 71234 318-982-5318
Curtis Williams, prin. Fax 982-5737

Doyline, Webster, Pop. 831
Webster Parish SD
Supt. — See Minden
Doyline JSHS 300/6-12
PO Box 657 71023 318-745-2118
Johnny Rowland, prin. Fax 745-3695

Dry Prong, Grant, Pop. 437
Grant Parish SD
Supt. — See Colfax
Dry Prong JHS 500/7-8
PO Box 147 71423 318-899-5697
Ben LaGrone, prin. Fax 899-7364
Grant HS 700/9-12
17779 Highway 167 71423 318-899-3331
Randy Crawford, prin. Fax 899-5724
Grant Academy Adult
17771 Highway 167 71423 318-899-3999
Norman Garlington, prin. Fax 899-5555

Dubach, Lincoln, Pop. 776
Lincoln Parish SD
Supt. — See Ruston
Dubach HS 100/6-12
7710 Fellowship Rd 71235 318-777-3470
Judy Mabry, prin. Fax 777-8409

Duson, Lafayette, Pop. 1,619
Lafayette Parish SD
Supt. — See Lafayette
Judice MS 500/6-8
2645 S Fieldspan Rd 70529 337-984-1250
Martha P. Broussard, prin. Fax 988-3693

Edgard, Saint John the Baptist, Pop. 2,753
St. John The Baptist Parish SD
Supt. — See Reserve
West St. John HS 200/8-12
PO Box 66 70049 985-497-3271
Elton Oubre, prin. Fax 497-5009

Elizabeth, Allen, Pop. 570
Allen Parish SD
Supt. — See Oberlin
Elizabeth S 300/PK-12
PO Box 580 70638 318-634-5341
Michael Stainback, prin. Fax 634-5218

Elm Grove, Bossier
Bossier Parish SD
Supt. — See Benton
Elm Grove MS 800/6-8
PO Box 108 71051 318-549-6500
Robert Marlow, prin. Fax 549-6513

Elton, Jefferson Davis, Pop. 1,249
Jefferson Davis Parish SD
Supt. — See Jennings
Elton JSHS 300/6-12
902 2nd St 70532 337-584-2991
David Troutman, prin. Fax 584-2244

Epps, West Carroll, Pop. 1,120
West Carroll Parish SD
Supt. — See Oak Grove
Epps S 300/K-12
PO Box 277 71237 318-926-3624
Edwin Guchereau, prin. Fax 926-5655

Erath, Vermilion, Pop. 2,177
Vermilion Parish SD
Supt. — See Abbeville
Erath HS 500/9-12
808 S Broadway St 70533 337-937-8451
Francis Touchet, prin. Fax 937-5109
Erath MS 600/4-8
800 S Broadway St 70533 337-937-4441
Lynn Moss, prin. Fax 937-5125

Eunice, Saint Landry, Pop. 11,527
St. Landry Parish SD
Supt. — See Opelousas
Eunice Career & Technical Education Ctr. Vo/Tech
421 S 10th St 70535 337-457-8686
Mike Corrigan, prin. Fax 457-0307
Eunice HS 800/9-12
301 S Bobcat Dr 70535 337-457-3011
Margaret Leger, prin. Fax 457-3720
Eunice JHS 500/7-8
751 W Oak Ave 70535 337-457-7386
Edward Brown, prin. Fax 457-1764
Eunice Adult Education Adult
PO Box 1486 70535 337-457-7428
George Fisher, prin.

Louisiana Academy of Beauty Post-Sec.
550 E Laurel Ave 70535 337-457-7627
Louisiana State University at Eunice Post-Sec.
PO Box 1129 70535 337-457-7311
St. Edmund HS 300/7-12
351 W Magnolia Ave 70535 337-457-3777
Beth Christ, prin. Fax 457-2510

Evans, Vernon
Vernon Parish SD
Supt. — See Leesville
Evans S 300/PK-12
PO Box 67 70639 337-286-5289
Jimmy Maricle, prin. Fax 286-9298

Farmerville, Union, Pop. 3,662
Union Parish SD 2,600/PK-12
PO Box 308 71241 318-368-9715
Judy Mabry, supt. Fax 368-3311
www.unionparishschools.org/
Farmerville HS 400/9-12
300 Anthony St 71241 318-368-2661
Johnny Mance, prin. Fax 368-2229
Farmerville JHS 300/6-8
606 Bernice St 71241 318-368-9235
Andy Allred, prin. Fax 368-1989
Other Schools – See Bernice, Downsville, Marion, Spearsville

Louisiana Tech. Coll. - North Central Post-Sec.
PO Box 548 71241 318-368-3179
Union Christian Academy 300/PK-10
PO Box 189 71241 318-368-8890
Paul Murray, pres. Fax 368-2920

Ferriday, Concordia, Pop. 3,568
Concordia Parish SD
Supt. — See Vidalia
Ferriday HS 300/9-12
801 Ee Wallace Blvd N 71334 318-757-8626
Michelle Bethea, prin. Fax 757-0763
Ferriday JHS 300/6-8
201 Martin Luther King Blvd 71334 318-757-8695
Dorothy Parker, prin. Fax 757-8696

Huntington S 200/PK-12
300 Lynwood Dr 71334 318-757-4515
Ray King, prin. Fax 757-9348
Louisiana Tech. College - Shelby Jackson Post-Sec.
PO Box 1465 71334 318-757-6501

Fields, Beauregard
Beauregard Parish SD
Supt. — See Deridder
Hyatt S 200/K-12
6249 Highway 109 70653 337-786-6722
Eddie Joslin, prin. Fax 786-8833

Florien, Sabine, Pop. 701
Sabine Parish SD
Supt. — See Many
Florien HS 300/7-12
500 High School Rd 71429 318-586-3681
Eddie Jones, prin. Fax 586-4818

Folsom, Saint Tammany, Pop. 651
St. Tammany Parish SD
Supt. — See Covington
Folsom JHS 200/6-8
83055 Hay Hollow Rd 70437 985-796-3724
Sharon Garrett, prin. Fax 796-3701

Forest, West Carroll, Pop. 264
West Carroll Parish SD
Supt. — See Oak Grove
Forest S 400/K-12
PO Box 368 71242 318-428-3672
Richard M. Strong, prin. Fax 428-8875

Franklin, Saint Mary, Pop. 7,822
St. Mary Parish SD
Supt. — See Centerville
Franklin HS 500/9-12
1401 Cynthia St 70538 337-828-0143
Tybus Burdett, prin. Fax 828-0184
Franklin JHS 500/6-8
525 Morris St 70538 337-828-0855
Jane Bowles, prin. Fax 828-5095
Franklin Adult Education Learning Center Adult
1706 Main St 70538 337-828-0121
Jody Charpentier, prin. Fax 828-0196

Hanson Memorial HS 300/6-12
903 Anderson St 70538 337-828-3487
Kenny Alfred, prin. Fax 828-0787

Franklinton, Washington, Pop. 3,708
Washington Parish SD 4,300/PK-12
PO Box 587 70438 985-839-3436
Darrell Fairburn, supt. Fax 839-5464
www.wpsb.org
Franklinton HS 600/9-12
1 Demon Cir 70438 985-839-6781
Beverly Young, prin. Fax 839-9830
Franklinton JHS 500/6-8
617 Main St 70438 985-839-3501
Pauline Bankston, prin. Fax 839-6912
Pine JSHS 300/6-12
1 Raider Dr 70438 985-848-5243
Geary Mckenzie, prin. Fax 848-9433
Other Schools – See Angie, Mount Hermon, Varnado

Bowling Green S 500/PK-12
700 Varnado St 70438 985-839-5317
Lewis Murray, admin. Fax 839-5668

French Settlement, Livingston, Pop. 1,053
Livingston Parish SD
Supt. — See Livingston
French Settlement JSHS 400/7-12
15875 LA Highway 16 70733 225-698-3561
Lance Hutson, prin. Fax 698-6458

Galliano, Lafourche, Pop. 4,294
Lafourche Parish SD
Supt. — See Thibodaux
South Lafourche HS 1,300/9-12
PO Box 160 70354 985-632-5721
Mary Curole, prin. Fax 632-6723

Geismar, Ascension
Ascension Parish SD
Supt. — See Donaldsonville
Dutchtown HS 1,200/9-12
13165 Highway 73 70734 225-621-8250
David Alexander, prin. Fax 677-8191
Dutchtown MS 800/6-8
13078 Highway 73 70734 225-621-2355
Doug Walker, prin. Fax 621-2351

Georgetown, Grant, Pop. 313
Grant Parish SD
Supt. — See Colfax
Georgetown S 300/PK-12
PO Box 99 71432 318-827-5306
William Norris Ph.D., prin. Fax 827-9481

Gibsland, Bienville, Pop. 1,082
Bienville Parish SD
Supt. — See Arcadia
Gibsland-Coleman S 300/K-12
PO Box 70 71028 318-843-6247
Kenneth Gipson, prin. Fax 843-9804

Glenmora, Rapides, Pop. 1,558
Rapides Parish SD
Supt. — See Alexandria
Glenmora JSHS 300/7-12
PO Box 697 71433 318-748-8145
Brian Parmley, prin. Fax 748-8146
Plainview S 300/PK-12
PO Box 698 71433 318-634-5944
Sonia Rasmussen, prin. Fax 634-5389

Golden Meadow, Lafourche, Pop. 2,145
Lafourche Parish SD
Supt. — See Thibodaux
Golden Meadow MS 500/6-8
630 S Bayou Dr 70357 985-475-7314
Lonnie Rousse, prin. Fax 475-6623

Gonzales, Ascension, Pop. 8,499
Ascension Parish SD
Supt. — See Donaldsonville
East Ascension HS 1,000/9-12
612 E Worthy St 70737 225-621-2400
Randy Watts, prin. Fax 621-2397
Gonzales MS 600/6-8
1502 W Orice Roth Rd 70737 225-621-2505
Charles Barbera, prin. Fax 621-2509

Ascension College Post-Sec.
320 E Ascension St 70737 225-647-6609
Faith Academy 300/PK-12
10469 Airline Hwy 70737 225-644-3110
Kirby Veron, hdmstr. Fax 647-2368

Grambling, Lincoln, Pop. 4,522
Lincoln Parish SD
Supt. — See Ruston
Grambling State University Lab. HS 200/9-12
407 Central Ave 71245 318-274-6153
Dr. Larry Lewis, prin. Fax 274-3215
Grambling State University MS 100/6-8
407 Central Ave 71245 318-274-6531
Dr. Vicki Brown, prin. Fax 274-3360

Grambling State University Post-Sec.
PO Box 864 71245 318-274-3811

Grand Cane, DeSoto, Pop. 197

Central S 200/K-12
PO Box 71 71032 318-858-3319
Greg Womack, prin. Fax 858-6394

Grand Chenier, Cameron
Cameron Parish SD
Supt. — See Lake Charles
South Cameron JSHS 300/8-12
753 Oak Grove Hwy 70643 337-542-4628
Dale Skinner, prin. Fax 542-4419

Grand Coteau, Saint Landry, Pop. 1,035

School of the Sacred Heart 300/PK-12
PO Box 310 70541 337-662-5275
Sr. Claude Demoustier, hdmstr. Fax 662-3011

Grand Isle, Jefferson, Pop. 1,594
Jefferson Parish SD
Supt. — See Marrero
Grand Isle S 200/PK-12
PO Box 995 70358 504-522-8015
Richard Augustin, prin. Fax 787-3878

Grant, Allen
Allen Parish SD
Supt. — See Oberlin
Fairview S 400/PK-12
PO Box 216 70644 318-634-5354
Gary Lockhart, prin. Fax 634-5357

Gray, Terrebonne, Pop. 4,260
Terrebonne Parish SD
Supt. — See Houma
Bourgeois HS 1,000/10-12
1 Reservation Ct 70359 985-872-3277
Nason Authement, prin. Fax 872-3270

Greensburg, Saint Helena, Pop. 615
St. Helena Parish SD 1,400/PK-12
PO Box 540 70441 225-222-4349
Dr. Amy Westbrook, supt. Fax 222-4937
www.sthpk-12.net
St. Helena Central HS 400/9-12
14340 Highway 37 70441 225-222-4402
Gary Porter, prin. Fax 222-6986
St. Helena Central MS 400/5-8
PO Box 1240 70441 225-222-6291
Kathran Randolph, prin. Fax 222-6780

Louisiana Tech. Coll. - Florida Parishes Post-Sec.
PO Box 1300 70441 225-222-4251

Gretna, Jefferson, Pop. 17,161
Jefferson Parish SD
Supt. — See Marrero
Gretna MS 600/7-9
910 Gretna Blvd 70053 504-366-0120
Elizabeth Davis, prin. Fax 366-8807
Jefferson HS 9-12
815 Huey P Long Ave 70053 504-361-8905
Dr. G. LeBlanc, prin. Fax 361-0792
Livaudais MS 700/7-9
925 Lamar Ave 70056 504-393-7544
Debra Cooper, prin. Fax 393-9610

Archbishop Blenk HS 600/8-12
17 Gretna Blvd 70053 504-367-2626
Sr. Maria Colombo, prin. Fax 367-7128
Believer's Life Christian Academy 300/PK-12
501 Lapalco Blvd 70056 504-348-4685
Dr. Wendell Douglas, prin. Fax 340-6611
Gretna Career College Training Institute Post-Sec.
1415 Whitney Ave 70053 504-366-5409
School of Urban Missions Post-Sec.
511 Westbank Expy 70053 504-362-3634

Gueydan, Vermilion, Pop. 1,603
Vermilion Parish SD
Supt. — See Abbeville
Gueydan HS 200/6-12
901 Main St 70542 337-536-6938
Luddy Herpin, prin. Fax 536-7000

Hackberry, Cameron, Pop. 1,664
Cameron Parish SD
Supt. — See Lake Charles
Hackberry S 300/K-12
1390 School St 70645 337-762-3305
Austin Labove, prin. Fax 762-3304

Hammond, Tangipahoa, Pop. 18,096
Tangipahoa Parish SD
Supt. — See Amite
Hammond HS 1,200/9-12
45168 River Rd 70401 985-345-7235
Henry Moore, prin. Fax 345-5252
Hammond JHS 500/7-8
111 J W Davis Dr 70403 985-345-2654
Janice Williams, prin. Fax 542-4215

Tangipahoa Parish Magnet HS 100/9-12
411 E Crystal St 70401 985-542-5634
Dale Brouillette, prin. Fax 542-9987

Louisiana Technical College - Hammond Post-Sec.
PO Box 489 70404 985-543-4120
North Oaks Medical Center Post-Sec.
15790 Medical Arts Dr 70403 985-543-6600
St. Thomas Aquinas HS 9-12
14520 Voss Dr 70401 985-542-7662
Jose Becerra, prin. Fax 542-4010
Southeastern Louisiana University Post-Sec.
PO Box 784 70404 985-549-2000

Harrisonburg, Catahoula, Pop. 728
Catahoula Parish SD 1,700/PK-12
PO Box 290 71340 318-744-5727
Ronald Lofton, supt. Fax 744-9221
cpsbla.org/
Harrisonburg HS 100/9-12
800 Bushley St 71340 318-744-5273
Malcolm Terry, prin. Fax 744-2098
Other Schools – See Jonesville, Sicily Island

Harvey, Jefferson, Pop. 21,222
Jefferson Parish SD
Supt. — See Marrero
Cox HS 500/9-12
2200 Lapalco Blvd 70058 504-367-6388
Darvell Edwards, prin. Fax 367-3176
West Jefferson HS 1,900/9-12
2200 8th St 70058 504-368-6055
Lale Geer, prin. Fax 368-0535

Louisiana Tech. Coll. - West Jefferson Post-Sec.
475 Manhattan Blvd 70058 504-361-6464
St. Rosalie MS 300/6-8
617 2nd Ave 70058 504-348-9330
Mary Wenzel, prin. Fax 348-9331

Haughton, Bossier, Pop. 2,791
Bossier Parish SD
Supt. — See Benton
Haughton HS 1,000/9-12
210 E Mckinley Ave 71037 318-549-5450
Gene Couvillion, prin. Fax 549-5470
Haughton MS 900/6-8
3955 Elm St 71037 318-549-5560
Susan Salter, prin. Fax 549-5573

Haynesville, Claiborne, Pop. 2,540
Claiborne Parish SD
Supt. — See Homer
Haynesville JSHS 400/5-12
9930 Highway 79 71038 318-624-0905
William Kennedy, prin. Fax 624-2488

Claiborne Academy 200/K-12
6741 Highway 79 71038 318-927-2747
Chuck Herrington, prin. Fax 927-4519

Hineston, Rapides
Rapides Parish SD
Supt. — See Alexandria
Oak Hill HS 300/7-12
PO Box 269 71438 318-793-2014
Emily Weatherford, prin. Fax 793-8589

Holden, Livingston
Livingston Parish SD
Supt. — See Livingston
Holden S 600/K-12
30120 LA 441 Hwy 70744 225-567-9367
Linda Pittman, prin. Fax 567-5248

Homer, Claiborne, Pop. 3,552
Claiborne Parish SD 2,500/PK-12
PO Box 600 71040 318-927-3502
James Scriber, supt. Fax 927-9184
Homer HS 300/9-12
1008 N Main St 71040 318-927-2985
Dwight Mitchell, prin. Fax 927-4733
Homer JHS 300/6-8
921 Pelican Dr 71040 318-927-2826
Keith Beard, prin. Fax 927-4376
Other Schools – See Athens, Haynesville, Lisbon, Summerfield

Hornbeck, Vernon, Pop. 403
Vernon Parish SD
Supt. — See Leesville
Hornbeck S 500/PK-12
PO Box 9 71439 318-565-4440
Joey Whiddon, prin. Fax 565-4136

Houma, Terrebonne, Pop. 32,105
Lafourche Parish SD
Supt. — See Thibodaux
Bayou Blue MS 6-8
196 Mazerac St 70364 985-446-5631
Sharon Dugas, prin.

Terrebonne Parish SD 19,000/PK-12
PO Box 5097 70361 985-876-7400
Ed Richard, supt. Fax 872-1411
www.tpsd.org
Ellender Memorial HS 1,100/9-12
3012 Patriot Dr 70363 985-868-7903
Marilyn Schwartz, prin. Fax 868-3503
Evergreen JHS 1,100/7-9
5000 W Main St 70360 985-876-2606
M. Torbert, prin. Fax 868-4395
Grand Caillou MS 500/4-8
3933 Grand Caillou Rd 70363 985-879-3001
Sharon Henry, prin. Fax 879-3009
Houma JHS 1,200/7-9
315 Saint Charles St 70360 985-872-1511
Tom Soudelier, prin. Fax 872-5121
Oaklawn JHS 600/7-8
2215 Acadian Dr 70363 985-872-3904
Demetria Maryland, prin. Fax 917-1917
Terrebonne HS 1,000/10-12
7318 Main St 70360 985-879-3377
Graham Douglas, prin. Fax 223-2270
Terrebonne Vo-Tech HS Vo/Tech
3051 Patriot Dr 70363 985-851-1163
Marcel Fournier, prin. Fax 876-1364
Bayou Cane Adult Education Adult
6484 W Main St 70360 985-876-3180
Fax 876-0411
Other Schools – See Bourg, Chauvin, Gray, Montegut

Houma Christian S 400/K-12
109 Valhi Blvd 70360 985-851-7423
Meco Carlos, prin. Fax 872-4958
L.E. Fletcher Technical Community Coll. Post-Sec.
PO Box 5033 70361 985-857-3655
Omega Institute of Cosmetology Post-Sec.
229 S Hollywood Rd 70360 985-876-9334
South Louisiana Beauty College Post-Sec.
300 Howard Ave 70363 985-873-8978
Vandebilt Catholic HS 900/8-12
209 S Hollywood Rd 70360 985-876-2551
Jim Reiss, prin. Fax 868-9774

Independence, Saint Helena, Pop. 1,718
Tangipahoa Parish SD
Supt. — See Amite
Independence HS 500/9-12
270 Tiger Ave 70443 985-878-9436
Cynthia Williams, prin. Fax 878-4831
Independence MS 300/5-8
PO Box 97 70443 985-878-4376
Malcolm Mizell, prin. Fax 878-4848

Iota, Acadia, Pop. 1,399
Acadia Parish SD
Supt. — See Crowley
Iota HS 400/9-12
456 S 5th St 70543 337-779-2534
Ronald Doguet, prin. Fax 779-2872
Iota MS 200/6-8
426 S 5th St 70543 337-779-2536
Debra Seibert, prin. Fax 779-2594

Iowa, Calcasieu, Pop. 2,591
Calcasieu Parish SD
Supt. — See Lake Charles
Iowa HS 500/9-12
401 W Miller Ave 70647 337-582-3561
David Butler, prin. Fax 582-7477

Jackson, East Feliciana, Pop. 3,774
East Feliciana Parish SD
Supt. — See Clinton
Jackson HS 300/9-12
3501 Highway 10 70748 225-634-5931
Joseph Jones, prin. Fax 634-3207
Jackson MS 200/6-8
3503 Highway 10 70748 225-634-5932
Sharon Jones, prin. Fax 634-5955

Louisiana Technical College - Folkes Post-Sec.
PO Box 808 70748 225-634-2636

Jeanerette, Iberia, Pop. 5,945
Iberia Parish SD
Supt. — See New Iberia
Jeanerette HS 400/9-12
8217 E Old Spanish Trl 70544 337-276-6038
Cynthia Antoine, prin. Fax 276-5016
Jeanerette MS 200/7-8
609 Pellerin Rd 70544 337-276-4320
Cheryl Broussard, prin. Fax 276-7064

Jefferson, Jefferson, Pop. 14,521
Jefferson Parish SD
Supt. — See Marrero
Riverdale HS 1,100/9-12
240 Riverdale Dr 70121 504-833-7288
Connie Tiliakos, prin. Fax 837-5401
Riverdale MS 600/6-8
3900 Jefferson Hwy 70121 504-828-2706
Randy Bennett, prin. Fax 833-5125
Taylor S for Science & Tech 7-12
2012 Jefferson Hwy 70121 504-838-2249
Kristy Philippi, prin. Fax 835-7029

Jena, LaSalle, Pop. 2,872
LaSalle Parish SD 2,700/PK-12
PO Box 90 71342 318-992-2161
Roy Breithaupt, supt. Fax 992-8457
www.lasallepsb.com
Jena HS 500/9-12
PO Box 89 71342 318-992-5195
Scott Windham, prin. Fax 992-4797
Jena JHS 200/7-8
PO Box 920 71342 318-992-5815
June Fowler, prin. Fax 992-6392
Other Schools – See Olla, Urania

Jennings, Jefferson Davis, Pop. 10,652
Jefferson Davis Parish SD 5,300/PK-12
PO Box 640 70546 337-824-1834
Tommy Lee Smith, supt. Fax 824-9737
webserver.jeffersondavis.org/topmain.htm
Hathaway S 500/K-12
4040 Pine Island Hwy 70546 337-824-4452
Mona Miller, prin. Fax 824-2769
Jennings HS 600/9-12
2310 N Sherman St 70546 337-824-0642
James McKeivier, prin. Fax 824-5585
Other Schools – See Elton, Lacassine, Lake Arthur, Roanoke, Welsh

---

Bethel Christian S 200/PK-12
PO Box 729 70546 337-824-0020
Sheila Reed, admin. Fax 824-0579
Louisiana Technical College - M. Smith Post-Sec.
1230 N Main St 70546 337-824-4811

Jonesboro, Jackson, Pop. 3,743
Jackson Parish SD 1,700/PK-12
PO Box 705 71251 318-259-4456
William Gary Black, supt. Fax 259-2527
www.jpsb.us/
Jonesboro-Hodge HS 400/7-12
225 Pershing Hwy 71251 318-259-4138
Bertha Robinson, prin. Fax 259-2701
Weston S 500/PK-12
213 Highway 505 71251 318-259-7313
Wayne Alford, prin. Fax 259-1056
Other Schools – See Quitman

Jonesville, Catahoula, Pop. 2,316
Catahoula Parish SD
Supt. — See Harrisonburg
Block HS 300/8-12
300 Division St 71343 318-339-7996
Donald Money, prin. Fax 339-7901
Central S 100/K-12
244 Larto Bayou Rd 71343 318-339-7574
Andrea Cruse, prin. Fax 339-7925

Kaplan, Vermilion, Pop. 5,131
Vermilion Parish SD
Supt. — See Abbeville
Kaplan HS 500/9-12
200 E Pirate Ln 70548 337-643-6385
Laura LeBeouf, prin. Fax 643-3543
Rost MS 400/5-8
112 W 6th St 70548 337-643-8545
David Dupuis, prin. Fax 643-7013

Kenner, Jefferson, Pop. 69,911
Jefferson Parish SD
Supt. — See Marrero
Bonnabel HS 1,600/9-12
2801 Bruin Dr 70065 504-443-4565
Ray Ferrand, prin. Fax 443-3401
Roosevelt MS 700/6-8
3315 Maine Ave 70065 504-443-1361
Robert Simmons, prin. Fax 443-3425

Herzing College Post-Sec.
2400 Veterans Memorial #410 70062 504-733-0074
John Jay Kenner Academy Post-Sec.
2844 Tennessee Ave 70062 504-467-2951
Moler Beauty College Post-Sec.
1919 Veterans Blvd #100 70062 504-467-1888
Southwest University Post-Sec.
2200 Veterans Blvd 70062 504-468-2900

Kentwood, Tangipahoa, Pop. 2,171
Tangipahoa Parish SD
Supt. — See Amite
Kentwood JSHS 300/7-12
PO Box 88 70444 985-229-2881
Ginger Francois, prin. Fax 229-6031
Sumner JSHS 700/7-12
15841 Highway 440 70444 985-229-8805
John Alston, prin. Fax 229-2043

Kilbourne, West Carroll, Pop. 418
West Carroll Parish SD
Supt. — See Oak Grove
Kilbourne S 400/K-12
PO Box 339 71253 318-428-3721
Shelton Kavalir, prin. Fax 428-3860

Kinder, Allen, Pop. 2,104
Allen Parish SD
Supt. — See Oberlin
Kinder HS 300/9-12
145 Highway 383 70648 337-738-2886
Joseph Kent Reed, prin. Fax 738-5665
Kinder MS 300/6-8
PO Box 610 70648 337-738-3223
Tracey Odom, prin. Fax 738-3425

Labadieville, Assumption, Pop. 1,821
Assumption Parish SD
Supt. — See Napoleonville
Labadieville MS 400/5-8
PO Box 127 70372 985-526-4227
Susan Harrison, prin. Fax 526-4163

Lacassine, Jefferson Davis
Jefferson Davis Parish SD
Supt. — See Jennings
Lacassine S 500/PK-12
PO Box 50 70650 337-588-4206
Brian Lejeune, prin. Fax 588-4283

Lafayette, Lafayette, Pop. 112,030
Lafayette Parish SD 29,500/PK-12
PO Box 2158 70502 337-521-7000
Dr. James Easton, supt. Fax 233-0977
www.lpssonline.com
Acadiana HS 1,800/9-12
315 Rue De Belier 70506 337-984-2646
Janet Hiatt, prin. Fax 984-0769
Acadian MS 500/5-8
4201 Moss St 70507 337-233-2496
Linda Nance, prin. Fax 235-6711
Alleman MS 800/5-8
600 Roselawn Blvd 70503 337-984-7210
Kathy Aloisio, prin. Fax 984-7212
Breaux MS 700/6-8
1400 S Orange St 70501 337-234-2313
Loretta Caldwell, prin. Fax 234-1915
Carencro HS 1,400/9-12
721 W Butcher Switch Rd 70507 337-896-6192
Annette Rath, prin. Fax 896-7592

Comeaux HS 1,900/9-12
100 W Bluebird St 70508 337-984-8395
Joseph Craig, prin. Fax 984-1112
Lafayette HS 2,200/9-12
3000 W Congress St 70506 337-984-5284
Dr. Patrick Leonard, prin. Fax 984-0153
Lafayette MS 400/6-8
1301 W University Ave 70506 337-234-4032
Rick Poulan, prin. Fax 235-4971
Martin MS 800/5-8
401 Broadmoor Blvd 70503 337-984-9796
Bobby Badeaux, prin. Fax 984-9968
Moss MS 600/5-8
805 Teurlings Dr 70501 337-289-1994
Kim Hypolite, prin. Fax 289-1997
Northside HS 1,000/9-12
301 Dunand St 70501 337-232-0681
Carlton Handy, prin. Fax 235-5443
Smith Career Center Vo/Tech
200 18th St 70501 337-233-2026
Carol Vital, prin. Fax 233-2028
Other Schools – See Broussard, Carencro, Duson, Scott, Youngsville

---

Ascension Day S 600/PK-10
1030 Johnston St 70501 337-233-9748
Patrick Dickens, hdmstr. Fax 269-9768
Blue Cliff College Post-Sec.
100 Asma Blvd Ste 350 70508 337-269-0620
Cosmetology Training Center Post-Sec.
2516 Johnston St 70503 337-237-6868
Lafayette General Medical Center Post-Sec.
PO Box 52009 70505 337-261-7381
Lockworks Academie of Hairdressing Post-Sec.
2922 Johnston St 70503 337-233-0511
Louisiana Technical College - Lafayette Post-Sec.
1101 Bertrand Dr 70506 337-262-5962
Remington College Post-Sec.
303 Rue Louis XIV # 8 70508 337-981-4010
Ronnie & Dorman's School of Hair Design Post-Sec.
2002 Johnston St 70503 337-232-1806
St. Genevieve MS 200/6-8
1500 E Willow St 70501 337-266-5553
Julie Champagne, prin. Fax 266-5775
St. Thomas More HS 1,100/9-12
450 E Farrel Rd 70508 337-988-3700
Raymond Simon, prin. Fax 988-2911
South Louisiana Community College Post-Sec.
320 Devalcourt St 70506 337-521-8896
Teurlings Catholic HS 600/9-12
139 Teurlings Dr 70501 337-235-5711
Michael Boyer, prin. Fax 234-8057
Unitech Training Academy Post-Sec.
3605 Ambassador Caffery Pky 70503 337-988-6764
University Medical Center Post-Sec.
2390 W Congress St 70506 337-261-6004
University of Louisiana at Lafayette Post-Sec.
PO Box 44548 70504 337-482-1000

Lafitte, Jefferson, Pop. 1,507
Jefferson Parish SD
Supt. — See Marrero
Fisher MSHS 500/7-12
2529 Jean Lafitte Blvd 70067 504-689-3665
George Hebert, prin. Fax 689-7556

Lake Arthur, Jefferson Davis, Pop. 2,912
Jefferson Davis Parish SD
Supt. — See Jennings
Lake Arthur JSHS 400/7-12
4374 Tiger Ln 70549 337-774-5152
Bridget Thomas, prin. Fax 774-2522

Lake Charles, Calcasieu, Pop. 70,555
Calcasieu Parish SD 32,000/PK-12
PO Box 800 70602 337-491-1600
Wayne Savoy, supt. Fax 437-1293
www.cpsb.org
Barbe HS 1,800/9-12
2200 W Mcneese St 70605 337-478-3626
Charles Adkins, prin. Fax 474-6782
Calcasieu Career Center Vo/Tech
1120 W 18th St 70601 337-491-1720
Kenny Brown, prin. Fax 491-1727
Houston HS 1,000/9-12
880 Sam Houston Jones Pkwy 70611 337-855-3528
Douglas McCullor, prin. Fax 855-3235
LaGrange HS 1,000/9-12
3420 Louisiana Ave 70607 337-477-4571
Bobby Jack Thompson, prin. Fax 477-1565
Lake Charles/Boston HS 500/9-12
1509 Enterprise Blvd 70601 337-436-9594
Solomon Cannon, prin. Fax 436-6532
Molo Magnet MS 400/6-8
2300 Medora St 70601 337-433-6785
James Wilson, prin. Fax 439-0787
Moss Bluff MS 800/6-8
297 Park Rd 70611 337-217-3351
John Duhon, prin. Fax 217-8026
Oak Park MS 500/6-8
2200 Oak Park Blvd 70601 337-478-3310
Martin Guillory, prin. Fax 474-0753
Reynaud MS 300/6-8
745 S Shattuck St 70601 337-436-5729
Ellaweena Woods, prin. Fax 491-0963
T & I Vocational Center Vo/Tech
736 E College St 70607 337-491-1736
George Albers, prin. Fax 474-7553
Washington-Marion Magnet HS 700/9-12
2802 Pineview St 70615 337-433-5892
Merculus Chretien, prin. Fax 436-7829
Welsh MS 1,400/6-8
1500 W Mcneese St 70605 337-477-6611
M.L. Sarver, prin. Fax 474-0519
White MS 700/6-8
1000 E McNeese St 70607 337-477-1648
Christopher Fontenot, prin. Fax 478-7899
Adult & Continuing Education Adult
1015 6th Ave 70601 337-491-1781
Jerry Adams, prin. Fax 437-6164
Other Schools – See Bell City, Dequincy, Iowa, Starks, Sulphur, Vinton, Westlake

Cameron Parish SD 1,800/PK-12
409 E Prien Lake Rd 70601 337-775-5784
Dr. Douglas Chance, supt. Fax 775-5097
www.camsch.org
Grand Lake S 600/K-12
1039 Highway 384 70607 337-598-2231
David Duhon, prin. Fax 598-2961
Other Schools – See Cameron, Grand Chenier, Hackberry

Delta School of Business and Technology Post-Sec.
517 Broad St 70601 337-439-5765
Demmon School of Beauty Post-Sec.
1222 Ryan St 70601 337-439-9265
Hamilton Christian Academy 400/PK-12
1415 8th St 70601 337-439-1178
Dr. Wayne McEntire, prin. Fax 433-1877
Lake Charles Memorial Hospital Post-Sec.
1701 Oak Park Blvd 70601 337-494-3200
Lakewood Christian Academy 100/PK-12
2520 W Sale Rd 70605 337-477-0531
Ray Hoffpauir, prin. Fax 477-4675
McNeese State University Post-Sec.
4100 Ryan St 70605 337-475-5000
St. Louis HS 500/9-12
1620 Bank St 70601 337-436-7275
William Simon, prin. Fax 436-6792
St. Patrick's Hospital Post-Sec.
524 S Ryan St 70601 337-491-7730
Sowela Technical Community College Post-Sec.
PO Box 16950 70616 337-491-2698
Stage One - The Hair School Post-Sec.
209 W College St 70605 337-474-0533

Lake Providence, East Carroll, Pop. 4,584
East Carroll Parish SD 1,600/PK-12
PO Box 792 71254 318-559-2222
Dr. Voleria Millikin, supt. Fax 559-3864
www.e-carrollschools.org
Lake Providence HS 300/9-12
602 Mrtin Luther King Jr Dr 71254 318-559-1984
Rosie Armstrong, prin. Fax 559-5380
Lake Providence JHS 300/6-8
1205 Gould Blvd 71254 318-559-1395
Janice Harris, prin. Fax 559-0679
Monticello S 300/K-12
1046 Highway 577 71254 318-552-6366
Hamilton Brock, prin. Fax 552-7658

Briarfield Academy 200/PK-12
301 Riddle Ln 71254 318-559-2360
Morris Richards, prin. Fax 559-2360
Louisiana Technical College - Tallulah Post-Sec.
PO Box 368 71254 318-559-0239

Laplace, Saint John the Baptist, Pop. 24,194

St. Charles Catholic HS 400/8-12
100 Dominican Rd 70068 985-652-3809
Andrew Cupit, prin. Fax 652-2609

Lecompte, Rapides, Pop. 1,338
Rapides Parish SD
Supt. — See Alexandria
Rapides HS 300/9-12
PO Box 770 71346 318-776-9371
Gene Alford, prin. Fax 776-5844
Raymond MS 200/5-8
PO Box 429 71346 318-776-5489
Clarence Goff, prin. Fax 776-9459

Leesville, Vernon, Pop. 6,160
Vernon Parish SD 9,600/PK-12
201 Belview Rd 71446 337-239-3401
Cynthia Gillespie, supt. Fax 238-5777
www.vpsb.k12.la.us
Hicks S 300/PK-12
1296 Hicks School Rd 71446 337-239-9645
Randy Lansdale, prin. Fax 239-6149
Leesville HS 900/9-12
502 Berry Ave 71446 337-239-3464
James Williams, prin. Fax 239-2485
Leesville JHS 600/7-8
480 Berry Ave 71446 337-239-3874
Roger Rolon, prin. Fax 238-4113
Pickering JSHS 500/7-12
180 Lebleu Rd 71446 337-537-1555
Kevin Lambright, prin. Fax 537-3019
Other Schools – See Anacoco, Evans, Hornbeck, Pitkin, Rosepine, Simpson

---

Faith Training Christian Academy 200/PK-10
603 E Mechanic St 71446 337-239-1055
Richard Reese, prin. Fax 239-6064
Louisiana Technical College-Lamar Salter Post-Sec.
15014 Lake Charles Hwy 71446 337-537-3135

Lena, Rapides
Rapides Parish SD
Supt. — See Alexandria
Northwood S 800/PK-12
8830 Highway 1 N 71447 318-793-8021
Donald Welch, prin. Fax 793-8503

Lisbon, Claiborne, Pop. 156
Claiborne Parish SD
Supt. — See Homer
Pineview S 200/PK-12
430 Hebron Rd 71048 318-353-6334
Sandra Boston, prin. Fax 353-6568

Livingston, Livingston, Pop. 1,577
Livingston Parish SD 21,100/PK-12
PO Box 1130 70754 225-686-7044
Randy Pope, supt. Fax 686-3052
www.lpsb.org
Doyle JSHS 500/7-12
PO Box 160 70754 225-686-2318
Tony Terry, prin. Fax 686-2701
Other Schools – See Albany, Denham Springs, French Settlement, Holden, Maurepas, Springfield, Walker, Watson

Livonia, Pointe Coupee, Pop. 1,336
Pointe Coupee Parish SD
Supt. — See New Roads
Livonia HS 600/7-12
PO Box 549 70755 225-637-2532
Stacey Gueho, prin. Fax 637-3024

Lockport, Lafourche, Pop. 2,596
Lafourche Parish SD
Supt. — See Thibodaux
Lockport MS 400/6-8
720 Main St 70374 985-532-2597
Robert Rome, prin. Fax 532-2833

Logansport, DeSoto, Pop. 1,681
De Soto Parish SD
Supt. — See Mansfield
Logansport HS 300/7-12
PO Box 549 71049 318-697-4338
Lillie Giles, prin. Fax 697-6507
Stanley S 400/PK-12
14323 Highway 84 71049 318-697-2664
Carolyn Phillips, prin. Fax 697-5984

Longville, Beauregard
Beauregard Parish SD
Supt. — See Deridder
South Beauregard JSHS 700/6-12
151 Longville Church Rd 70652 337-725-3536
Marlin Ramsey, prin. Fax 725-6222

Loranger, Tangipahoa
Tangipahoa Parish SD
Supt. — See Amite
Loranger HS 500/9-12
PO Box 560 70446 985-878-6271
Billie J. Theriot, prin. Fax 878-4875
Loranger MS 600/5-8
PO Box 469 70446 985-878-9455
Andre Pellerin, prin. Fax 878-4907

Loreauville, Iberia, Pop. 950
Iberia Parish SD
Supt. — See New Iberia
Loreauville JSHS 400/7-12
PO Box 446 70552 337-229-4701
Carole M. Judice, prin. Fax 229-4275

Luling, Saint Charles, Pop. 2,803
St. Charles Parish SD 9,300/PK-12
13855 River Rd 70070 985-785-6289
Dr. Rodney Lafon, supt. Fax 785-1025
www.stcharles.k12.la.us
Smith MS 6-8
281 Sugarland Pkwy 70070 985-331-1018
Dianne Powell, prin. Fax 331-9385
Other Schools – See Boutte, Destrehan, Paradis, Saint Rose

Lutcher, Saint James, Pop. 3,598
St. James Parish SD 4,000/PK-12
PO Box 338 70071 225-869-5375
Alonzo Luce Ph.D., supt. Fax 869-8845
www.stjames.k12.la.us
Career & Technology Center Vo/Tech
1410 Buddy Whitney St 70071 225-869-3902
Josehine Oubre, prin. Fax 869-7935
Lutcher HS 1,000/7-12
PO Box 489 70071 225-869-5741
Eugene Hoover, prin. Fax 869-8872
Other Schools – See Saint James, Vacherie

Madisonville, Saint Tammany, Pop. 744
St. Tammany Parish SD
Supt. — See Covington
Madisonville JHS 400/4-8
PO Box 850 70447 985-845-3355
Fran Shea, prin. Fax 845-9018

Mamou, Evangeline, Pop. 3,433
Evangeline Parish SD
Supt. — See Ville Platte
Mamou JSHS 800/5-12
1008 7th St 70554 337-468-5793
Charles Hazard, prin. Fax 468-2220

Mandeville, Saint Tammany, Pop. 11,632
St. Tammany Parish SD
Supt. — See Covington
Fontainebleau HS 2,200/9-12
100 Bulldog Dr 70471 985-892-7112
Johnny Vitrano, prin. Fax 892-9894
Fountainebleau JHS 1,200/7-8
100 Hurricane Aly 70471 985-875-7501
Dr. Tim Schneider, prin. Fax 875-7650
Mandeville HS 1,600/9-12
1 Skipper Dr 70471 985-626-5225
Bruce Bundy, prin. Fax 626-5298
Mandeville JHS 700/7-8
639 Carondelet St 70448 985-626-4428
Mary Ann Cucchiara, prin. Fax 674-0401
Monteleone JHS 7-8
63000 Blue Martin Dr 70448 985-951-8088
Donna Addison, prin.

Mangham, Richland, Pop. 563
Richland Parish SD
Supt. — See Rayville

Mangham HS 200/9-12
PO Box 348 71259 318-248-2485
Althan Smith, prin. Fax 248-2406
Mangham JHS 200/6-8
PO Box 428 71259 318-248-2729
Connie Williams, prin. Fax 248-2931

Mansfield, DeSoto, Pop. 5,504
De Soto Parish SD 5,000/PK-12
201 Crosby St 71052 318-872-2836
Walter Lee, supt. Fax 872-1324
www.desoto.k12.la.us
Mansfield HS 400/9-12
401 Kings Hwy 71052 318-872-0793
David Rougeau, prin. Fax 872-2223
Mansfield MS 500/6-8
1915 McArthur Dr 71052 318-872-1309
Clint Fuller, prin. Fax 872-1319
Other Schools – See Logansport, Pelican, Stonewall

Louisiana Technical College - Mansfield Post-Sec.
PO Box 1236 71052 318-872-2243

Mansura, Avoyelles, Pop. 1,564
Avoyelles Parish SD
Supt. — See Marksville
Mansura MS 300/7-8
1869 Saint Jean St 71350 318-964-2332
Allen Wanersdorfer, prin. Fax 964-2110

Many, Sabine, Pop. 2,809
Sabine Parish SD 3,800/PK-12
PO Box 1079 71449 318-256-9228
Dorman Jackson, supt. Fax 256-0105
www.sabine.k12.la.us
Many HS 300/9-12
100 Tiger Dr 71449 318-256-2114
Wayne Chance, prin. Fax 256-0492
Many JHS 400/4-8
1801 Natchitoches Hwy 71449 318-256-3573
Madeline Owens, prin. Fax 256-9619
Other Schools – See Converse, Florien, Negreet, Noble, Pleasant Hill, Zwolle

Louisiana Technical Coll.-Sabine Valley Post-Sec.
PO Box 790 71449 318-256-4101

Marion, Union, Pop. 784
Union Parish SD
Supt. — See Farmerville
Marion S 200/PK-12
PO Box 67 71260 318-292-4410
Nikki Cranford, prin. Fax 292-4422

Marksville, Avoyelles, Pop. 5,707
Avoyelles Parish SD 5,700/PK-12
221 Tunica Dr W 71351 318-253-5982
Dwayne Lemoine, supt. Fax 253-5178
www.avoyellespsb.com
Marksville HS 600/9-12
407 W Bontemps St 71351 318-253-9356
Charles Jones, prin. Fax 253-4256
Marksville MS 400/7-8
152 Schoolhouse Rd 71351 318-253-8952
Mary Speer, prin. Fax 253-9955
Other Schools – See Bunkie, Mansura, Moreauville

Marrero, Jefferson, Pop. 36,100
Jefferson Parish SD 49,300/PK-12
4600 River Rd 70072 504-349-7600
Dr. Diane Roussel, supt. Fax 349-7960
www.jppss.k12.la.us
Cullier Career Center Vo/Tech
1429 Ames Blvd Ste B 70072 504-340-6963
Rita Foster, prin. Fax 341-1022
Ehret HS 2,600/9-12
4300 Patriot St 70072 504-340-7651
Clothilde Cobert, prin. Fax 340-7295
Ellender MS 1,000/6-8
4501 E Ames Blvd 70072 504-341-9469
Frank Rawle, prin. Fax 348-0054
Higgins HS 1,900/9-12
7201 Lapalco Blvd 70072 504-341-2273
Germaine Gilson, prin. Fax 341-8110
Marrero MS 1,000/6-8
4100 7th St 70072 504-341-5842
Earline Bridges, prin. Fax 341-0004
Truman MS 900/6-8
5417 Ehret Rd 70072 504-341-0961
Tommy Ory, prin. Fax 347-4497
Other Schools – See Avondale, Grand Isle, Gretna, Harvey, Jefferson, Kenner, Lafitte, Metairie, Westwego

Archbishop Shaw HS 600/8-12
1000 Barataria Blvd 70072 504-340-6727
Rev. Michael Conway, prin. Fax 340-7899
Immaculata HS 400/8-12
537 Avenue D 70072 504-341-6217
Sr. Marisa DeRose, prin. Fax 341-6229

Maurepas, Livingston
Livingston Parish SD
Supt. — See Livingston
Maurepas S 400/K-12
PO Box 39 70449 225-695-6111
Steve Vampran, prin. Fax 695-3265

Maurice, Vermilion, Pop. 731
Vermilion Parish SD
Supt. — See Abbeville
North Vermilion HS 700/7-12
11609 LA Highway 699 70555 337-898-1491
Michael Guilbeaux, prin. Fax 893-8684

Merryville, Beauregard, Pop. 1,162
Beauregard Parish SD
Supt. — See Deridder
Merryville S 600/K-12
7061 Highway 110 W 70653 337-825-8046
Michael Kay, prin. Fax 825-6443

Metairie, Jefferson, Pop. 145,500
Jefferson Parish SD
Supt. — See Marrero
Adams MS 800/6-8
5525 Henican Pl 70003 504-887-5240
Cheryl Milam, prin. Fax 887-0173
Bunche MS 500/6-8
8101 Simon St 70003 504-737-3132
D. Dumas, prin. Fax 737-7606
East Jefferson HS 1,100/9-12
400 Phlox Ave 70001 504-888-7171
James Kytle, prin. Fax 888-2072
Harris MS 700/6-8
911 Elise Ave 70003 504-733-0867
Otis Guichet, prin. Fax 733-0953
Haynes MS 500/6-8
1416 Metairie Rd 70005 504-837-8300
Jerome Helmstetter, prin. Fax 837-2110
King HS 1,600/9-12
4301 Grace King Pl 70002 504-888-7334
Alfred Johnson, prin. Fax 888-2082
Meisler MS 1,100/6-8
3700 Cleary Ave 70002 504-888-5832
Glenn Fallon, prin. Fax 888-5855

Archbishop Chapelle HS 1,100/8-12
8800 Veterans Memorial Blvd 70003 504-467-3105
Mary Beth Drez, prin. Fax 466-3191
Archbishop Rummel HS 1,300/8-12
PO Box 663 70004 504-834-5592
Michael Scalco, prin. Fax 832-4016
Blue Cliff College Post-Sec.
3200 Cleary Ave 70002 504-456-3141
Crescent City Christian S 500/PK-12
4828 Utica St 70006 504-885-4700
Bill Rigsby, admin. Fax 885-4703
Ecole Classique S 300/PK-12
5236 Glendale St 70006 504-887-3507
Sal Frederico, hdmstr. Fax 887-8140
Heritage Academy 100/6-12
2900 Wytchwood Dr 70003 504-887-7111
Harry DeKay, prin.
Louisiana Technical College - Jefferson Post-Sec.
5200 Blair St 70001 504-736-7074
Lutheran HS 100/9-12
3864 17th St 70002 504-455-4062
Calvin Behrens, prin. Fax 455-4453
Metairie Park Country Day S 500/K-12
300 Park Rd 70005 504-837-5204
Carolyn Chandler, hdmstr. Fax 837-0015
Remington College Post-Sec.
321 Veterans Memorial Blvd 70005 504-831-8889
Ridgewood Prepatatory S 300/PK-12
201 Pasadena Ave 70001 504-835-2545
M. J. Montgomery, hdmstr. Fax 837-1864
St. Martin's Episcopal S 700/PK-12
5309 Airline Dr 70003 504-733-0353
Chris Proctor, hdmstr. Fax 736-8802

Midland, Acadia
Acadia Parish SD
Supt. — See Crowley
Midland JSHS 300/8-12
735 S Crocker St 70559 337-783-3310
John Briley, prin. Fax 783-3332

Minden, Webster, Pop. 13,281
Webster Parish SD 7,200/PK-12
PO Box 520 71058 318-377-7052
Wayne Williams, supt. Fax 377-4114
www.webster.k12.la.us/
Minden HS 800/9-12
PO Box 838 71058 318-377-2766
Morris Busby, prin. Fax 377-9274
Webster JHS 500/7-8
700 E Union St 71055 318-377-3847
Elena Black, prin. Fax 377-1943
Other Schools – See Cotton Valley, Doyline, Sarepta, Shongaloo, Sibley, Springhill

Glenbrook S 300/K-12
1674 Country Club Cir 71055 318-377-2135
Darden Gladney, admin. Fax 377-0578
Louisiana Technical Coll. - NW Louisiana Post-Sec.
PO Box 835 71058 318-371-3035

Monroe, Ouachita, Pop. 51,914
Monroe City SD 9,300/PK-12
PO Box 4180 71211 318-325-0601
Dr. James Dupree, supt. Fax 323-2864
www.monroe.k12.la.us/mcs/
Carroll Magnet HS 700/9-12
PO Box 5040 71211 318-387-8441
Donald Green, prin. Fax 325-6305
Carroll Magnet JHS 500/7-8
2913 Renwick St 71201 318-322-1683
Angela Manning Ph.D., prin. Fax 322-0833
King MS 800/6-8
3716 Nutland Rd 71202 318-387-1825
Debbie Blue, prin. Fax 325-4285
Lee JHS 500/7-8
1600 N 19th St 71201 318-323-1143
Whitney Martin, prin. Fax 325-5236
Neville HS 900/9-12
600 Forsythe Ave 71201 318-323-2237
Brent Vidrine, prin. Fax 387-8774
Wossman HS 700/9-12
1600 Arizona Ave 71202 318-387-2932
Sam Moore, prin. Fax 322-1378
Career Development Center Adult
400 Harrison St 71203 318-343-6179
David Breithaupt, prin. Fax 343-6068
Ouachita Parish SD 17,800/PK-12
PO Box 1642 71212 318-388-2711
Dr. Robert Webber, supt. Fax 338-2221
www.opsb.net
Ouachita JHS 700/7-8
5500 Blanks St 71203 318-345-5100
Marsha Dell Baker, prin. Fax 345-3308
Ouachita Parish HS 1,100/9-12
681 Highway 594 71203 318-343-2769
Todd Guice, prin. Fax 343-9594
Richwood HS 500/9-12
5901 Highway 165 Byp 71202 318-361-0467
Anthony Killian, prin. Fax 361-9810
Richwood JHS 7-8
5901 Highway 165 Byp 71202 318-651-0200
Tereatha Chisley, prin. Fax 398-9825
Sterlington HS 500/7-12
233 Keystone Rd 71203 318-665-2725
Ross Davis, prin. Fax 665-2727
Other Schools – See Calhoun, West Monroe

Career Technical College Post-Sec.
2319 Louisville Ave 71201 318-323-2889
Cloyd's Beauty School #2 Post-Sec.
1311 Winnsboro Rd 71202 318-322-5314
Cloyd's Beauty School #3 Post-Sec.
2514 Ferrand St 71201 318-322-5314
Excelsior Christian S 200/PK-12
3220 Highway 165 S 71202 318-387-7333
Linda Trimble, prin. Fax 387-7330
Ouachita Christian S 800/PK-12
7065 Highway 165 N 71203 318-325-6000
William Stokes, hdmstr. Fax 387-7000
Pat Goins Beauty School Post-Sec.
3138 Louisville Ave 71201 318-322-0796
River Oaks S 300/PK-12
600 Hideaway Rd 71203 318-343-4185
Dr. William Middleton, prin. Fax 343-1107
St. Francis Medical Center Post-Sec.
PO Box 1901 71210 318-327-4141
St. Frederick HS 300/7-12
3300 Westminister Ave 71201 318-323-9636
Jennifer Malone, prin. Fax 323-7456
University of Louisiana at Monroe Post-Sec.
700 University Ave 71209 318-342-1000

Montegut, Terrebonne, Pop. 1,784
Terrebonne Parish SD
Supt. — See Houma
Montegut MS 600/5-8
138 Dolphin St 70377 985-594-5886
Catherine Telford, prin. Fax 594-9666

Monterey, Concordia
Concordia Parish SD
Supt. — See Vidalia
Monterey S 400/PK-12
PO Box 127 71354 318-386-2214
Neeva Sibley, prin. Fax 386-7356

Montgomery, Grant, Pop. 823
Grant Parish SD
Supt. — See Colfax
Montgomery HS 300/7-12
PO Box 428 71454 318-646-2879
Vickey Dubois, prin. Fax 646-3926

Moreauville, Avoyelles, Pop. 934
Avoyelles Parish SD
Supt. — See Marksville
Avoyelles HS 500/9-12
287 Main St 71355 318-985-2361
Brent Whiddon, prin. Fax 985-2786

Morgan City, Saint Mary, Pop. 11,930
St. Mary Parish SD
Supt. — See Centerville
Morgan City HS 800/9-12
2400 Tiger Dr 70380 985-384-1754
Peter Boudreaux, prin. Fax 384-7054
Morgan City JHS 600/6-8
911 Marguerite St 70380 985-384-5922
Kenneth Holmes, prin. Fax 385-4170
Morgan City Adult Education Adult
PO Box 830 70381 985-385-0502
Vincent Holcomb, coord.

Central Catholic HS 200/7-12
2100 Cedar St 70380 985-385-5372
Vic Bonnaffee, prin. Fax 385-3444
Immanuel Christian S 200/PK-12
901 Fig St 70380 985-385-2129
Gwen Ross, admin. Fax 385-3041
Louisiana Tech. Coll. - Young Memorial Post-Sec.
PO Box 2148 70381 985-380-2436

Morganza, Pointe Coupee, Pop. 625
Pointe Coupee Parish SD
Supt. — See New Roads
Pointe Coupee Central HS 600/6-12
8434 Pointe Coupee Rd 70759 225-638-3085
Larry Oliver, prin. Fax 638-9595

Mount Hermon, Washington
Washington Parish SD
Supt. — See Franklinton
Mount Hermon S 500/PK-12
36119 Highway 38 70450 985-877-4642
Ruth Stoudenmier, prin. Fax 877-4710

Napoleonville, Assumption, Pop. 689
Assumption Parish SD 3,800/PK-12
4901 Highway 308 70390 985-369-7251
Earl Martinez, supt. Fax 369-2530
www.assumption.k12.la.us
Assumption HS 1,100/9-12
PO Box 830 70390 985-369-2956
Joey Comeaux, prin. Fax 369-6252

Napoleonville MS 400/5-8
4847 Highway 1 70390 985-369-6587
Craig Stephens, prin. Fax 369-6595
Other Schools – See Belle Rose, Labadieville

Natchitoches, Natchitoches, Pop. 17,701
Natchitoches Parish SD 6,600/PK-12
PO Box 16 71458 318-352-2358
Dr. Elwanda Murphy, supt. Fax 352-8138
www.nat.k12.la.us/
East Natchitoches S 300/4-8
1001 E 5th St 71457 318-352-4516
Carolyn Benefield, prin. Fax 352-4515
Natchitoches Central HS 1,300/9-12
6513 Highway 1 Byp 71457 318-352-2211
David Elkins, prin. Fax 357-8837
NSU Middle Lab S 200/6-8
NSU Campus 71497 318-357-4509
Drew Moore, prin. Fax 357-4260
Other Schools – See Campti

Louisiana Technical College-Natchitoches Post-Sec.
PO Box 657 71458 318-357-3162
Northwestern State University Post-Sec.
College Ave 71497 318-357-6361
St. Mary's S 400/PK-12
PO Box 2070 71457 318-352-8394
Alan Powers, prin. Fax 352-5798

Negreet, Sabine
Sabine Parish SD
Supt. — See Many
Negreet S 400/PK-12
PO Box 14 71460 318-256-2349
Dan Salter, prin. Fax 256-5868

New Iberia, Iberia, Pop. 32,495
Iberia Parish SD 14,000/PK-12
PO Box 200 70562 337-365-2341
E. Baudry, supt. Fax 365-6996
www.iberia.k12.la.us
Anderson Street MS 500/7-8
1059 Anderson St 70560 337-365-3932
James Russell, prin. Fax 367-8285
Belle Place MS 500/7-8
4110 Loreauville Rd 70563 337-364-2141
Bertha Myers, prin. Fax 365-9463
Iberia MS 700/7-8
613 Weeks Island Rd 70560 337-364-3927
Michael Bonin, prin. Fax 365-9681
Iberia Parish Career Center Vo/Tech
618 Recreation Dr 70560 337-365-7231
Nathan Cormier, prin. Fax 367-0875
New Iberia HS 1,600/9-12
1301 E Admiral Doyle Dr 70560 337-369-6412
Curt Landry, prin. Fax 364-6920
Westgate HS 1,100/9-12
2305 Jefferson Island Rd 70560 337-365-2431
James Gray, prin. Fax 364-3487
Other Schools – See Delcambre, Jeanerette, Loreauville

Assembly Christian S 300/K-12
4219 E Admiral Doyle Dr 70560 337-364-4340
Armand Prentiss, prin. Fax 364-8310
Catholic HS 900/4-12
1301 Delasalle Dr 70560 337-364-5116
Dr. Timothy Uhl, prin. Fax 364-5041
Highland Baptist Christian S 400/PK-12
708 Angers St 70563 337-364-2273
Janie Lamothe, admin. Fax 369-6303
Louisiana Technical College - Teche Area Post-Sec.
PO Box 11057 70562 337-373-0011
Neill Institute Post-Sec.
1301A W Saint Peter St 70560 337-365-6570
Vortex Helicopters Post-Sec.
PO Box 9789 70562 228-864-7357

New Orleans, Orleans, Pop. 454,863
Orleans Parish SD 7,500/PK-12
3520 General Degaulle Dr 70114 504-304-5680
Fax 309-2873
www.nops.k12.la.us/
McDonogh 35 HS 1,000/7-12
1331 Kerlerec St 70116 504-942-3593
Philip White, prin.
McMain Magnet JSHS 1,200/7-12
5721 S Claiborne Ave 70125 504-862-5117
Bridgitte Frick, prin. Fax 862-5123
Orleans Parish PM S 7-12
5712 S Claiborne Ave 70125 504-239-3685
Tyrone Casby, prin.

Recovery SD
Supt. — See Baton Rouge
Clark HS 500/9-12
1301 N Derbigny St 70116 504-304-6228
Dr. Charles Michel, prin. Fax 304-6229
Cohen HS, 3510 Dryades St 70115 9-12
Arlene Kennedy, prin. 504-896-4015
Douglass HS 700/9-12
3820 Saint Claude Ave 70117 504-942-2293
Allen Woods, prin.
McDonogh HS 1,100/9-12
2426 Esplanade Ave 70119 504-827-5676
Donald Jackson, prin. Fax 330-0223
Rabouin HS 600/9-12
727 Carondelet St 70130 504-330-0217
Kevin George, prin. Fax 330-0218
Reed HS 1,200/6-12
5316 Michoud Blvd 70129 504-255-9269
Dr. Daniel Hudson, prin. Fax 655-5991

Academy of the Sacred Heart 200/5-8
4521 Saint Charles Ave 70115 504-891-1943
Sr. Cynthia Vives, prin. Fax 891-2755
Academy of the Sacred Heart 300/9-12
4521 Saint Charles Ave 70115 504-891-1943
Sr. Lynne Lieux, prin. Fax 891-9744

Bishop McManus Academy 100/PK-12
8801 Chef Menteur Hwy 70127 504-390-4858
Owen McManus, hdmstr. Fax 324-0268
Brother Martin HS 1,500/8-12
4401 Elysian Fields Ave 70122 504-283-1561
Gregory Rando, prin. Fax 286-8462
Cabrini HS 500/8-12
1400 Moss St 70119 504-482-1193
Yvonne Hrapmann, prin. Fax 483-8671
Cameron College Post-Sec.
PO Box 19288 70179 504-821-5881
Charity-Delgado School of Nursing Post-Sec.
450 S Claiborne Ave 70112 504-568-6483
Culinary Institute of New Orleans Post-Sec.
2100 Saint Charles Ave 70130 504-525-2433
De La Salle HS 700/8-12
5300 Saint Charles Ave 70115 504-895-5717
Gina Hall, prin. Fax 895-1300
Delgado Community College Post-Sec.
615 City Park Ave 70119 504-483-4410
Dillard University Post-Sec.
2601 Gentilly Blvd 70122 504-816-4670
Eastern College of Health Vocations Post-Sec.
201 Evans Rd 70123 504-885-3353
Holy Cross MSHS 1,000/5-12
4950 Dauphine St 70117 504-942-3100
Dr. Joseph H. Murry, prin. Fax 943-7676
Holy Rosary HS 9-12
3368 Esplanade Ave 70119 504-482-7173
Michael Binder, prin. Fax 482-7229
Jesuit HS 1,400/8-12
4133 Banks St 70119 504-483-3817
Michael Giambelluca, prin. Fax 483-3942
Louisiana State University Post-Sec.
1100 Florida Ave 70119 504-948-8530
Louisiana State Univ. Health Sci. Center Post-Sec.
433 Bolivar St 70112 504-568-4808
Loyola University New Orleans Post-Sec.
6363 Saint Charles Ave 70118 504-865-2011
McGehee S 400/PK-12
2343 Prytania St 70130 504-561-1224
Eileen Powers, prin. Fax 525-7910
Medical Center of Louisiana/Charity Cmps Post-Sec.
1541 Tulane Ave 70112 504-568-2311
Moler Beauty College Post-Sec.
3968 Old Gentilly Rd 70126 504-282-2539
Mt. Carmel Academy 1,200/8-12
7027 Milne Blvd 70124 504-288-7626
Sr. Camille Anne Campbell, prin. Fax 288-7629
Newcomb College of Tulane University Post-Sec.
1229 Broadway St 70118 504-865-5594
Newman S 900/PK-12
1903 Jefferson Ave 70115 504-899-5641
Thomas Price, hdmstr. Fax 896-8597
New Orleans Baptist Theological Seminary Post-Sec.
3939 Gentilly Blvd 70126 504-282-4455
New Orleans Job Corps Center Post-Sec.
3052 General Collins Ave #2 70114 504-486-0641
New Orleans School of Urban Missions Post-Sec.
PO Box 53344 70153 800-385-6364
Notre Dame Seminary Post-Sec.
2901 S Carrollton Ave 70118 504-866-7426
Ochsner School of Allied Health Sciences Post-Sec.
1516 Jefferson Hwy 70121 504-842-3267
Our Lady of Holy Cross College Post-Sec.
4123 Woodland Dr 70131 504-394-7744
St. Augustine HS 900/7-12
2600 A P Tureaud Ave 70119 504-944-2424
Rev. John Raphael, prin. Fax 947-7712
St. Marys Academy 600/K-12
3774 Gentilly Blvd 70122 504-948-8886
Sr. Jennie Jones, prin. Fax 948-2120
St. Marys Dominican HS 8-12
7701 Walmsley Ave 70125 504-865-9401
Dr. Nancy Autin, prin. Fax 866-5958
Southern University in New Orleans Post-Sec.
6400 Press Dr 70126 504-286-5000
Touro Infirmary Post-Sec.
1401 Foucher St 70115 504-897-8244
Tulane University Post-Sec.
6823 Saint Charles Ave 70118 504-865-4000
University of New Orleans 70148 Post-Sec.
504-280-6000
Ursuline Academy HS 400/8-12
2635 State St 70118 504-866-2725
Nancy Hernandez, prin. Fax 861-7392
William Carey College Post-Sec.
3939 Gentilly Blvd # 309 70126 504-865-1502
Xavier University Post-Sec.
1 Drexel Dr 70125 504-486-7411
Xavier University Prep HS 500/7-12
5116 Magazine St 70115 504-899-6061
Carolyn Oubre, prin. Fax 891-8766

New Roads, Pointe Coupee, Pop. 4,790
Pointe Coupee Parish SD 2,600/PK-12
PO Box 579 70760 225-638-8674
Dr. Daniel Rawls, supt. Fax 638-3904
Other Schools – See Livonia, Morganza

Catholic HS of Pte. Coupee 300/7-12
504 4th St W 70760 225-638-3469
Dr. Glen Bowman, prin. Fax 638-6471
False River Academy 600/PK-12
201 Major Pkwy 70760 225-638-3783
Kenneth LeBeau, prin. Fax 638-8555
Louisiana Technical College - Jumonville Post-Sec.
605 Hospital Rd 70760 225-342-3070

Noble, Sabine, Pop. 266
Sabine Parish SD
Supt. — See Many
Ebarb S 400/PK-12
5340 Highway 482 71462 318-645-9402
Victor Sepulvado, prin. Fax 645-4689

Oakdale, Allen, Pop. 7,981
Allen Parish SD
Supt. — See Oberlin
Oakdale HS 300/9-12
101 S 13th St 71463 318-335-2338
Danny Hindmon, prin. Fax 335-3257
Oakdale MS 400/5-8
124 S 13th St 71463 318-335-1558
Linda Thompson, prin. Fax 335-4690

Louisiana Technical College - Oakdale Post-Sec.
PO Box EM 71463 318-335-3944

Oak Grove, West Carroll, Pop. 2,044
West Carroll Parish SD 2,300/PK-12
314 E Main St 71263 318-428-2378
Jerry Dosher, supt. Fax 428-3775
www.wcpsb.com
Oak Grove JSHS 400/7-12
501 W Main St 71263 318-428-2308
Mark Bowman, prin. Fax 428-2311
Other Schools – See Epps, Forest, Kilbourne

Oberlin, Allen, Pop. 1,869
Allen Parish SD 4,300/PK-12
PO Box C 70655 337-639-4311
Michael Doucet, supt. Fax 639-2346
www.allen.k12.la.us
Oberlin HS 200/7-12
PO Box D 70655 337-639-4341
Clarice Papillion, prin. Fax 639-2508
Other Schools – See Elizabeth, Grant, Kinder, Oakdale, Reeves

Olla, LaSalle, Pop. 1,359
LaSalle Parish SD
Supt. — See Jena
LaSalle HS 200/9-12
PO Box 458 71465 318-495-5165
Ronda Richardson, prin. Fax 495-5503

Opelousas, Saint Landry, Pop. 22,897
St. Landry Parish SD 14,700/PK-12
PO Box 310 70571 337-948-3657
Lanny Moreau, supt. Fax 942-0204
www.slp.k12.la.us
Northwest HS 500/8-12
3746 Highway 104 70570 337-543-2255
Raymond Cassimere, prin. Fax 543-8796
Opelousas HS 1,100/9-12
PO Box 1269 70571 337-942-5634
Rodney Johnson, prin. Fax 942-6219
Opelousas JHS 800/7-8
PO Box 130 70571 337-942-4957
Ryan Hooks, prin. Fax 942-2659
St. Landry Accelerated Transition S 50/7-8
152 Violet Dr 70570 337-948-4763
Walter Phythian, prin. Fax 948-9792
St. Landry Adult Education Adult
PO Box 660 70571 337-948-8525
Evavattae Green, prin.
Other Schools – See Arnaudville, Eunice, Port Barre, Washington

---

Acadiana Preparatory S 200/PK-12
1592 E Prudhomme St 70570 337-948-6551
David Barham, prin. Fax 948-1006
Louisiana Technical College - T H Harris Post-Sec.
332 E South St 70570 337-948-0239
Opelousas Catholic S 700/K-12
428 E Prudhomme St 70570 337-942-5404
Perry Fontenot, prin. Fax 942-5922
Opelousas School of Cosmetology Post-Sec.
529 E Vine St 70570 337-942-6147
Westminster Christian Academy 500/PK-12
186 Westminster Dr 70570 337-948-8607
William Thompson, supt. Fax 948-8983

Paradis, Saint Charles
St. Charles Parish SD
Supt. — See Luling
Martin MS 500/7-8
434 South St 70080 985-758-7579
Erin Raiford, prin. Fax 758-7570

Parks, Saint Martin, Pop. 540
St. Martin Parish SD
Supt. — See Saint Martinville
Parks MS 400/5-8
1010A Saint Louis Dr 70582 337-845-4753
Roger Wiltz, prin. Fax 845-5532

Patterson, Saint Mary, Pop. 5,152
St. Mary Parish SD
Supt. — See Centerville
Patterson HS 500/9-12
2525 Main St 70392 985-395-2675
Michael Brocato, prin. Fax 395-5453
Patterson JHS 700/4-8
1101 1st St 70392 985-395-6772
Molly Stadalis, prin. Fax 395-6773

Pearl River, Saint Tammany, Pop. 2,044
St. Tammany Parish SD
Supt. — See Covington
Creekside JHS 500/6-8
65434 Highway 41 70452 985-863-5882
Lisa Virga, prin. Fax 863-7658
Pearl River HS 600/9-12
39110 Taylor St 70452 985-863-2591
Michael Winkler, prin. Fax 863-5934

Pelican, DeSoto
De Soto Parish SD
Supt. — See Mansfield
Pelican All Saints S 200/PK-12
200 All Saints Rd 71063 318-755-2318
Toras Hill, prin. Fax 755-2066

Pine Prairie, Evangeline, Pop. 1,211
Evangeline Parish SD
Supt. — See Ville Platte
Pine Prairie S 800/PK-12
PO Box 200 70576 337-599-2300
Marvelyn Harris, prin. Fax 599-2003

Pineville, Rapides, Pop. 14,083
Rapides Parish SD
Supt. — See Alexandria
Pineville HS 1,000/9-12
1511 Line St 71360 318-442-8990
Karl Carpenter, prin. Fax 487-1984
Pineville JHS 600/7-8
501 Edgewood Dr 71360 318-640-0512
Columbus Goodman, prin. Fax 640-9692
Slocum Learning Center Adult
901 Crepe Myrtle St 71360 318-445-7017
Carol Passmore, prin. Fax 445-5690

Louisiana College Post-Sec.
PO Box 566 71359 318-487-7011
Pineville Beauty School Post-Sec.
1008 Main St 71360 318-445-1040

Pitkin, Vernon
Vernon Parish SD
Supt. — See Leesville
Pitkin S 600/PK-12
PO Box 307 70656 318-358-3121
Roger Willis, prin. Fax 358-3580

Plain Dealing, Bossier, Pop. 1,057
Bossier Parish SD
Supt. — See Benton
Plain Dealing HS 100/9-12
300 E Vance St 71064 318-326-7700
Aubrey Sayes, prin. Fax 326-7713
Plain Dealing MS 100/6-8
PO Box 279 71064 318-326-7780
Aubrey Sayes, prin. Fax 326-7788

Plain Dealing Christian Academy 100/PK-12
200 Garrett St 71064 318-326-5823
Barbara Pearson, admin. Fax 326-5907

Plaquemine, Iberville, Pop. 6,717
Iberville Parish SD 4,200/PK-12
PO Box 151 70765 225-687-4341
Martin Bera, supt. Fax 687-5408
www.ipsb.net
Gay MS 500/5-8
PO Box 717 70765 225-687-6845
Dianna Outlaw, prin. Fax 687-6826
Plaquemine HS 600/9-12
59595 Belleview Dr 70764 225-687-6367
Russell Plasczyk, prin. Fax 687-4422
Other Schools – See Rosedale, Saint Gabriel, White Castle

Louisiana Technical College - Westside Post-Sec.
59125 Bayou Rd 70764 225-687-6392
St. John HS 200/9-12
24250 Regina St 70764 225-687-3056
Perry Le Grange, prin. Fax 687-3530

Plaucheville, Avoyelles, Pop. 278

St. Joseph S 300/PK-12
PO Box 59 71362 318-922-3401
Gerard Jeansonne, prin. Fax 922-3776

Pleasant Hill, Sabine, Pop. 719
Sabine Parish SD
Supt. — See Many
Pleasant Hill S 300/PK-12
PO Box 8 71065 318-796-3670
Curt Nix, prin. Fax 796-2644

Ponchatoula, Tangipahoa, Pop. 5,784
Tangipahoa Parish SD
Supt. — See Amite
Ponchatoula HS 1,400/9-12
19452 Highway 22 70454 985-386-3514
Cynthia Foster, prin. Fax 386-0011
Ponchatoula JHS 700/7-8
315 E Oak St 70454 985-370-5322
Gwendolyn Barsley, prin. Fax 370-5327

Port Allen, West Baton Rouge, Pop. 5,062
West Baton Rouge Parish SD 3,400/PK-12
3761 Rosedale Rd 70767 225-343-8309
David Corona, supt. Fax 387-2101
www.wbrschools.net
Devall MS 300/4-8
11851 N River Rd 70767 225-627-4268
John Currier, prin. Fax 627-4278
Port Allen HS 400/9-12
3553 Rosedale Rd 70767 225-383-1107
Warren LeJeune, prin. Fax 344-6312
Port Allen MS 300/5-8
610 Rosedale Rd 70767 225-383-5777
Harry Wright, prin. Fax 346-5030
Other Schools – See Brusly

Port Barre, Saint Landry, Pop. 2,318
St. Landry Parish SD
Supt. — See Opelousas
Port Barre MS 400/5-8
PO Box 69 70577 337-585-7256
William Edgar Duplechain, prin. Fax 585-2290
Port Barre MSHS 400/5-12
PO Box 69 70577 337-585-7256
William Duplechain, prin. Fax 585-2290

Port Sulphur, Plaquemines, Pop. 3,523
Plaquemines Parish SD
Supt. — See Belle Chasse
South Plaquemines HS 7-12
311 Civic Dr 70083 985-564-2743
Stanley Gaudet, prin.

Prairieville, Ascension
Ascension Parish SD
Supt. — See Donaldsonville
Galvez MS 700/5-8
42018 Highway 933 70769 225-621-2424
Linda Embry, prin. Fax 621-2434
Prairieville MS 600/5-8
16200 Highway 930 70769 225-621-2340
Diane Gautreau, prin. Fax 673-4883

Pride, East Baton Rouge
East Baton Rouge Parish SD
Supt. — See Baton Rouge
Northeast JSHS 900/7-12
13700 Pride Port Hudson Rd 70770 225-654-5808
Jessie LeBlanc, prin. Fax 654-5591

Quitman, Jackson, Pop. 165
Jackson Parish SD
Supt. — See Jonesboro
Quitman S 500/PK-12
PO Box 38 71268 318-259-2698
Steve Shovan, prin. Fax 259-1139

Raceland, Lafourche, Pop. 5,564
Lafourche Parish SD
Supt. — See Thibodaux
Central Lafourche HS 1,400/9-12
4820 Highway 1 70394 985-532-3319
Jimmy Ledet, prin. Fax 532-3822
Raceland MS 800/6-8
PO Box C 70394 985-537-5140
Ann Danos, prin. Fax 537-5182
Opportunity Place Adult
196 Johnny Dufrene Dr 70394 985-532-3114
Fax 532-6112

Rayne, Acadia, Pop. 8,516
Acadia Parish SD
Supt. — See Crowley
Armstrong MS 400/6-8
700 Martin Luther King Blvd 70578 337-334-3377
Marshall Thibodeaux, prin. Fax 334-2681
Rayne HS 600/9-12
1016 N Polk St 70578 337-334-3691
Bobby Hamlin, prin. Fax 334-5568

Rayville, Richland, Pop. 4,014
Richland Parish SD 3,400/PK-12
PO Box 599 71269 318-728-5964
Dr. Cathy Stockton, supt. Fax 728-6366
www.richland.k12.la.us
Rayville HS 500/9-12
193 Highway 3048 71269 318-728-3296
Dr. Georgia Ineichen, prin. Fax 728-5652
Rayville JHS 300/6-8
225 Highway 3048 71269 318-728-3618
Tony Guirlando, prin. Fax 728-9374
Other Schools – See Delhi, Mangham

Riverfield Academy 400/PK-12
115 Wood St 71269 318-728-3281
Marie Miller, prin. Fax 728-3285

Reeves, Allen, Pop. 210
Allen Parish SD
Supt. — See Oberlin
Reeves S 300/PK-12
13770 Highway 113 70658 337-666-2414
Cherie Nichols, prin. Fax 666-2812

Reserve, Saint John the Baptist, Pop. 8,847
St. John The Baptist Parish SD 6,300/PK-12
PO Box AL 70084 985-536-1106
Michael K. Coburn, supt. Fax 536-1109
www.stjohn.k12.la.us
East St. John HS 1,400/9-12
1 Wildcat Dr 70084 985-536-4226
Debbie Schum, prin. Fax 536-4286
Other Schools – See Edgard

Louisiana Tech. Coll. - River Parishes Post-Sec.
PO Box AQ 70084 985-536-4418
Reserve Christian S 200/PK-12
PO Box AA 70084 985-536-2418
Rod Aguillard, prin. Fax 479-3135
Riverside Academy 700/PK-12
332 Railroad Ave 70084 985-536-4246
Heidi Tomeny-Duhe, prin. Fax 536-2127

Ringgold, Bienville, Pop. 1,567
Bienville Parish SD
Supt. — See Arcadia
Ringgold JSHS 300/7-12
4044 Bienville Rd Ste B 71068 318-894-2271
William Davis, prin. Fax 894-4444

River Ridge, Jefferson, Pop. 14,800

Curtis Christian S 600/PK-12
10125 Jefferson Hwy 70123 504-737-4621
John Curtis, prin. Fax 737-7326

Roanoke, Jefferson Davis
Jefferson Davis Parish SD
Supt. — See Jennings
Welsh-Roanoke JHS 200/6-8
PO Box 9 70581 337-753-2317
Kenneth Lasserre, prin. Fax 753-2245

Rosedale, Iberville, Pop. 727
Iberville Parish SD
Supt. — See Plaquemine
North Iberville S 500/PK-12
PO Box 200 70772 225-625-2522
Wyvetta Parker, prin. Fax 625-2559

Rosepine, Vernon, Pop. 1,321
Vernon Parish SD
Supt. — See Leesville
Rosepine JSHS 500/7-12
PO Box 369 70659 337-463-6079
Charles Lewis, prin. Fax 462-6132

Ruston, Lincoln, Pop. 20,667
Lincoln Parish SD 6,500/PK-12
410 S Farmerville St 71270 318-255-1430
Danny Bell, supt. Fax 255-3203
www.lincolnschools.org/
Lincoln Parish Career Academy Vo/Tech
1428 Arlington St 71270 318-254-2096
Foster Harris, prin. Fax 254-1247
Ruston HS 1,100/9-12
900 Bearcat Dr 71270 318-255-0807
Mike Milstead, prin. Fax 251-2202
Ruston JHS 600/7-8
481 Tarbutton Rd 71270 318-251-1601
Tim Nutt, prin. Fax 254-5235
Other Schools – See Choudrant, Dubach, Grambling, Simsboro

Bethel Christian S 100/PK-12
2901 Winona Dr 71270 318-255-1112
John Lee, prin. Fax 513-1113
Cedar Creek S 600/PK-12
2400 Cedar Creek Dr 71270 318-255-7707
Connie Bradford, prin. Fax 251-2864
Louisiana Technical College - Ruston Post-Sec.
PO Box 1070 71273 318-251-4145
Louisiana Tech University Post-Sec.
PO Box 3168 71272 318-257-0211
Pat Goins Ruston Beauty School Post-Sec.
213 W Alabama Ave 71270 318-255-2717

Saint Amant, Ascension
Ascension Parish SD
Supt. — See Donaldsonville
Saint Amant HS 1,400/9-12
12035 Highway 431 70774 225-621-2565
Doug Moreau, prin. Fax 621-2573
Saint Amant MS 600/5-8
44317 Highway 429 70774 225-621-2600
Brenda Holmes, prin. Fax 621-2593

Saint Benedict, Saint Tammany

Archbishop Hannan HS 500/8-12
75376 River Rd 70457 985-249-6363
John Serio, prin. Fax 279-6370
St. Joseph Seminary College 70457 Post-Sec.
985-892-1800

Saint Francisville, West Feliciana, Pop. 1,672
West Feliciana Parish SD 2,400/PK-12
PO Box 1910 70775 225-635-3891
Lloyd Lindsey, supt. Fax 635-0108
www.wfpsb.org
West Feliciana HS 700/9-12
PO Box 580 70775 225-635-4561
Michael Thornhill, prin. Fax 635-5588
West Feliciana MS 600/6-8
PO Box 690 70775 225-635-3898
Darryl Powell, prin. Fax 635-6925

Saint Gabriel, Iberville, Pop. 5,527
Iberville Parish SD
Supt. — See Plaquemine
East Iberville S 500/PK-12
3285 Highway 75 70776 225-642-5410
Lionel Johnson, prin. Fax 642-9607

Saint James, Saint James
St. James Parish SD
Supt. — See Lutcher
Saint James HS 700/7-12
PO Box 101 70086 225-265-3911
Harry Francois, prin. Fax 265-2455

Saint Joseph, Tensas, Pop. 1,222
Tensas Parish SD 700/PK-12
PO Box 318 71366 318-766-3269
Carol Johnson, supt. Fax 766-3634
www.tensas.k12.la.us/
Tensas HS 200/7-12
720 Plank Rd 71366 318-766-3585
Noah Johnson, prin. Fax 766-7988

Tensas Academy 200/PK-12
PO Box 555 71366 318-766-4384
Bonnie Adcock, prin. Fax 766-3559

Saint Martinville, Saint Martin, Pop. 6,993
St. Martin Parish SD 8,000/PK-12
PO Box 859 70582 337-394-6261
E.R. Valerie Haaga, supt. Fax 394-6387
www.stmartin.k12.la.us
St. Martinville HS 800/9-12
762 N Main St 70582 337-394-3135
Michael Kreamer, prin. Fax 394-9702
St. Martinville JHS 300/5-8
7190 Main Hwy 70582 337-394-4764
Denise Frederick, prin. Fax 394-9619
Other Schools – See Breaux Bridge, Cecilia, Parks

Louisiana Technical College - Evangeline Post-Sec.
PO Box 68 70582 337-394-6466

Saint Rose, Saint Charles, Pop. 6,259
St. Charles Parish SD
Supt. — See Luling
Cammon MS 300/6-8
234 Pirate Dr 70087 504-467-4536
Sylvia Zeno, prin. Fax 468-3873

ITT Technical Institute Post-Sec.
140 James Dr E 70087 504-463-0338

Saline, Bienville, Pop. 287
Bienville Parish SD
Supt. — See Arcadia
Saline S 300/PK-12
PO Box 129 71070 318-576-3215
Tony Hough, prin. Fax 576-9068

Sarepta, Webster, Pop. 916
Webster Parish SD
Supt. — See Minden
Sarepta S 500/K-12
6041 Highway 2 71071 318-847-4301
William Franklin, prin. Fax 847-4891

Scott, Lafayette, Pop. 8,120
Lafayette Parish SD
Supt. — See Lafayette
Scott MS 900/5-8
PO Box 427 70583 337-235-9698
Ron LeBlanc, prin. Fax 235-9805

Shongaloo, Webster, Pop. 160
Webster Parish SD
Supt. — See Minden
Shongaloo S 300/K-12
229 Highway Alt 2 71072 318-846-2541
Cynthia Hair, prin. Fax 846-2891

Shreveport, Caddo, Pop. 198,874
Bossier Parish SD
Supt. — See Benton
Bossier Parish Technical S Vo/Tech
2010 N Market St 71107 318-676-7811
Carol Johnston, prin. Fax 676-7805

Caddo Parish SD 43,000/PK-12
PO Box 32000 71130 318-603-6300
Ollie Tyler, supt. Fax 631-5241
www.caddo.k12.la.us/
Bethune MS 700/6-8
4331 Henry St 71109 318-636-6336
Perry Daniel, prin. Fax 636-6812
Bickham MS 700/6-8
7240 Old Mooringsport Rd 71107 318-929-4106
James Windham, prin. Fax 929-2416
Broadmoor MS Laboratory 700/6-8
441 Atlantic Ave 71105 318-861-2403
Kimberly Brun, prin. Fax 865-4142
Byrd HS 1,900/9-12
3201 Line Ave 71104 318-869-2567
Jerry Badgley, prin. Fax 869-2253
Caddo Career/Tech Center Vo/Tech
5950 Union Ave 71108 318-636-5150
Bonnie Martinez, prin. Fax 621-9138
Caddo Middle Career & Tech Center Vo/Tech
6310 Clift Ave 71106 318-868-2753
Curtis Hooks, prin. Fax 868-2755
Caddo Parish Magnet HS 1,200/9-12
1601 Viking Dr 71101 318-221-2501
Mary Rounds, prin. Fax 227-1393
Caddo Parish Magnet MS 1,200/6-8
7635 Cornelious Ln 71106 318-868-6588
Kay Robinson, prin. Fax 865-6125
Clark MS 700/6-8
351 Hearne Ave 71103 318-425-8742
Lewis McCulloch, prin. Fax 425-1151
Fair Park HS 700/9-12
3222 Greenwood Rd 71109 318-635-8181
Bruce Daigle, prin. Fax 631-1982
Green Oaks HS 500/9-12
2550 Thomas E Howard Dr 71107 318-425-3411
Cleveland White, prin. Fax 425-3414
Huntington HS 1,200/9-12
6801 Rasberry Ln 71129 318-687-6655
Jerry Davis, prin. Fax 687-0943
Linear MS 500/6-8
1845 Linear St 71107 318-221-1589
Dennis Redden, prin. Fax 221-0130
Linwood MS 800/6-8
401 W 70th St 71106 318-861-2401
Monica Jenkins-Moore, prin. Fax 865-1036
Northwood HS 900/9-12
5939 Old Mooringsport Rd 71107 318-929-3513
Louis Cook, prin. Fax 929-7498
Ridgewood MS 900/6-8
2001 Ridgewood Dr 71118 318-686-0383
Dr. Gerald Burrow, prin. Fax 686-0390
Shreve HS 1,100/9-12
6115 E Kings Hwy 71105 318-865-7137
Dr. Sandra McCalla, prin. Fax 865-5041
Southwood HS 1,600/9-12
9000 Walker Rd 71118 318-686-9512
Kenneth Wood, prin. Fax 687-7588
Washington HS 400/9-12
2104 Milam St 71103 318-222-2186
Dr. Curly White, prin. Fax 226-0628
Woodlawn HS 700/9-12
7340 Wyngate Blvd 71106 318-686-3161
Carter Bedford, prin. Fax 687-6787
Youree Drive MS 1,000/6-8
6008 Youree Dr 71105 318-868-5324
Arleen Hague, prin. Fax 861-5086
Hamilton Terrace Learning Center Adult
1105 Louisiana Ave 71101 318-221-4506
M. Marie Eakin, prin. Fax 424-7864
Other Schools – See Vivian

American School of Business Post-Sec.
702 Professional Dr N 71105 318-798-3333
Ayers Institute Post-Sec.
3010 Knight St Ste 300 71105 318-868-3000
Blue Cliff College Post-Sec.
200 N Thomas Dr # A 71107 318-425-7941
Calvary Baptist Academy 900/PK-12
9333 Linwood Ave 71106 318-687-4923
Rhonda Honea, prin. Fax 687-4925
Centenary College of Louisiana Post-Sec.
PO Box 41188 71134 318-869-5011
Diesel Driving Academy Post-Sec.
PO Box 36949 71133 318-636-6300
Evangel Christian Academy 700/K-12
7425 Broadacres Rd 71129 318-688-7061
Linda Bass, prin. Fax 688-7322
Guy's Shreveport Academy of Cosmetology Post-Sec.
1141 Shreveport Barksdale 71105 318-865-5591
Louisiana State University Post-Sec.
1 University Pl 71115 318-797-5000
Louisiana Tech. Coll.-Shreveport-Bossier Post-Sec.
PO Box 78527 71137 318-676-7811
Loyola College Prep S 400/9-12
921 Jordan St 71101 318-221-2675
G. Frank Israel, prin. Fax 221-2678
Northwestern State University Post-Sec.
1800 Line Ave 71101 318-677-3100
Overton Brooks VA Medical Center Post-Sec.
510 E Stoner Ave 71101 318-424-6037
Pat Goins Shreveport Beauty School Post-Sec.
6363 Hearne Ave Ste 106 71108 318-631-1833
Shreveport Job Corps Center Post-Sec.
2815 Lillian St 71109 318-227-9331
Southern University at Shreveport Post-Sec.
3050 M L King Dr 71107 318-674-3300
University Christian Prep S 100/PK-12
4800 Old Mooringsport Rd 71107 318-221-2697
Carmen Heflen, prin. Fax 221-2790

Sibley, Webster, Pop. 1,087
Webster Parish SD
Supt. — See Minden
Lakeside JSHS 500/7-12
9090 Highway 371 71073 318-377-2133
Beverly Smith, prin. Fax 382-0733

Sicily Island, Catahoula, Pop. 446
Catahoula Parish SD
Supt. — See Harrisonburg
Martin JHS 100/5-8
PO Box 338 71368 318-389-5651
Phyllis Parker, prin. Fax 389-5651
Sicily Island HS 100/9-12
PO Box 128 71368 318-389-5337
Marguerita Krause, prin. Fax 389-5309

Simpson, Vernon, Pop. 522
Vernon Parish SD
Supt. — See Leesville
Simpson S 400/PK-12
PO Box 8 71474 337-383-7810
David Lewis, prin. Fax 383-7655

Simsboro, Lincoln, Pop. 664
Lincoln Parish SD
Supt. — See Ruston
Simsboro S 600/K-12
1 Tiger Dr 71275 318-247-6265
Barbara Kirkland, prin. Fax 247-6276

Singer, Beauregard
Beauregard Parish SD
Supt. — See Deridder
Singer S 300/K-12
153 Highway 110 E 70660 337-463-5908
Dennis Burk, prin. Fax 463-0199

Slidell, Saint Tammany, Pop. 26,840
St. Tammany Parish SD
Supt. — See Covington
Boyet JHS 800/7-8
59295 Rebel Dr 70461 985-643-3775
Mitchell Stubbs, prin. Fax 643-9470
Clearwood JHS 700/4-8
130 Clearwood Dr 70458 985-641-8200
Alan Bennett, prin. Fax 641-7122
Northshore HS 1,600/9-12
100 Panther Dr 70461 985-649-6400
Dr. Michael Peterson, prin. Fax 649-3613
St. Tammany JHS 600/6-8
701 Cleveland Ave 70458 985-643-1592
Hannah Rucker, prin. Fax 643-5873
Salmen HS 900/9-12
300 Spartan Dr 70458 985-643-7359
Byron Williams, prin. Fax 645-8776
Slidell HS 1,900/9-12
1 Tiger Dr 70458 985-643-2992
William Percy, prin. Fax 649-6853
Slidell JHS 1,000/6-8
333 Pennsylvania Ave 70458 985-641-5914
Brennan McCurley, prin. Fax 641-6397

Academy of Creative Hair Design Post-Sec.
740 Oak Harbor Blvd 70458 985-643-2614
First Baptist Christian S 300/1-12
4141 Pontchartrain Dr 70458 985-643-3725
Olive Zenon, admin. Fax 641-9025
Pope John Paul II HS 300/9-12
1901 Jaguar Dr 70461 985-649-0914
Richard Berkowitz, prin. Fax 649-5494

Sorrento, Ascension, Pop. 1,341

Louisiana Technical College - Ascension Post-Sec.
9697 Airline Hwy 70778 225-675-5398
River Parishes Community College Post-Sec.
PO Box 310 70778 225-675-8270

Spearsville, Union, Pop. 149
Union Parish SD
Supt. — See Farmerville
Spearsville S 300/K-12
PO Box 18 71277 318-778-3752
Frankie Futch, prin. Fax 778-3269

Springfield, Livingston, Pop. 406
Livingston Parish SD
Supt. — See Livingston
Springfield HS 300/9-12
PO Box 39 70462 225-294-3256
Edward Foster, prin. Fax 294-4800
Springfield MS 400/4-8
PO Box 40 70462 225-294-3306
Steve Parrill, prin. Fax 294-3307

Springhill, Webster, Pop. 5,237
Webster Parish SD
Supt. — See Minden
Springhill JSHS 400/7-12
507 W Church St 71075 318-539-2563
Melanie Jacobs, prin. Fax 539-2569

Starks, Calcasieu
Calcasieu Parish SD
Supt. — See Lake Charles
Starks S 400/PK-12
PO Box 69 70661 337-743-5341
Vickie Poole, prin. Fax 743-5458

Stonewall, DeSoto, Pop. 1,888
De Soto Parish SD
Supt. — See Mansfield
North DeSoto HS 500/9-12
PO Box 430 71078 318-925-6917
Bart Weaver, prin. Fax 925-1940
North DeSoto MS 500/4-8
PO Box 310 71078 318-925-4520
Keith Simmons, prin. Fax 925-4719

Sulphur, Calcasieu, Pop. 19,608
Calcasieu Parish SD
Supt. — See Lake Charles
LeBlanc MS 400/6-8
1100 N Crocker St 70663 337-527-5296
Thomas Finnie, prin. Fax 527-5297
Lewis MS 800/6-8
1752 Cypress St 70663 337-527-6178
Tony Dougherty, prin. Fax 528-3773
Sulphur 9th Grade Campus 600/9-9
600 Willow Ave 70663 337-527-9100
Charles Hansen, prin. Fax 527-6779
Sulphur SHS 1,300/10-12
100 Sycamore St 70663 337-527-6679
Keith Bonin, prin. Fax 528-3209

Parkview Baptist S 100/K-12
1623 Picard Rd 70663 337-527-7089
Randall Chesson, prin. Fax 528-2291

Summerfield, Claiborne
Claiborne Parish SD
Supt. — See Homer
Summerfield S 300/PK-12
PO Box 158 71079 318-927-3621
D'Arcy Stevens, prin. Fax 927-9160

Tallulah, Madison, Pop. 8,152
Madison Parish SD 1,900/PK-12
PO Box 1620 71284 318-574-3616
Michael Johnson, supt. Fax 574-3667
www.madisonpsb.org/
Madison HS 300/9-12
800 Wyche St 71282 318-574-3529
Will Rogers, prin. Fax 574-5943
Madison MS 300/6-8
900 W Askew St 71282 318-574-0933
Gloria Watkins, prin. Fax 574-9919

Louisiana Technical College - Tallulah Post-Sec.
PO Box 1740 71284 318-574-4820
Tallulah Academy-Delta Christian S 300/K-12
700 Wood St 71282 318-574-2606
Dr. David Bass, prin. Fax 574-3390

Thibodaux, Lafourche, Pop. 14,408
Lafourche Parish SD 14,200/PK-12
PO Box 879 70302 985-446-5631
Jo Ann Matthews, supt. Fax 446-0801
www.lafourche.k12.la.us
East Thibodaux MS 600/6-8
802 E 7th St 70301 985-446-5616
Gerard Lotz, prin. Fax 446-5610
Sixth Ward MS 200/6-8
PO Box 1236 70302 985-633-2449
Marla Tabor, prin. Fax 633-7373
Thibodaux HS 1,500/9-12
1355 Tiger Dr 70301 985-447-4071
Shelba Harlan, prin. Fax 447-3335
West Thiboudaux MS 600/6-8
1111 E 12th St 70301 985-446-6889
Edmond Adams, prin. Fax 447-1777
Other Schools – See Cut Off, Galliano, Golden Meadow, Houma, Lockport, Raceland

---

Louisiana Technical College - LaFourche Post-Sec.
1425 Tiger Dr 70301 985-447-0924
Nicholls State University Post-Sec.
PO Box 2004 70310 985-446-8111
White HS 800/8-12
555 Cardinal Dr 70301 985-446-8486
Myra Luft, prin. Fax 448-1275

Tickfaw, Tangipahoa, Pop. 642
Tangipahoa Parish SD
Supt. — See Amite
Nesom MS 500/6-8
PO Box 280 70466 985-345-2166
Maureen Terese, prin. Fax 345-3731

Tioga, Rapides
Rapides Parish SD
Supt. — See Alexandria
Tioga HS 800/9-12
PO Box 1030 71477 318-640-9661
Kim Hutchinson, prin. Fax 640-9757

Urania, LaSalle, Pop. 685
LaSalle Parish SD
Supt. — See Jena

LaSalle JHS 200/6-8
PO Box 520 71480 318-495-3474
Steve Long, prin. Fax 495-3478

Vacherie, Saint James, Pop. 2,354
St. James Parish SD
Supt. — See Lutcher
Science & Math Academy 7-12
PO Box 482 70090 225-265-3042
Gary Stein, coord. Fax 265-7093

Varnado, Washington, Pop. 347
Washington Parish SD
Supt. — See Franklinton
Varnado HS 200/9-12
25543 Washington St, Angie LA 70426
985-732-2025
Emma Jean Ross, prin. Fax 732-5198

Vidalia, Concordia, Pop. 4,210
Concordia Parish SD 3,800/PK-12
PO Box 950 71373 318-336-4226
Kerry Laster Ph.D., supt. Fax 336-5875
cpsbla.us
Vidalia HS 400/9-12
2201 Murray Dr 71373 318-336-6231
Rick Brown, prin. Fax 336-6233
Vidalia JHS 400/6-8
210 Gillespie St 71373 318-336-6227
Paul Nelson, prin. Fax 336-6229
Other Schools – See Ferriday, Monterey

Vidalia Beauty School Post-Sec.
208 Westside Dr 71373 318-336-2377

Ville Platte, Evangeline, Pop. 8,250
Evangeline Parish SD 6,100/PK-12
1123 Te Mamou Rd 70586 337-363-6651
Toni Hamlin, supt. Fax 363-8086
www.epsb.com
Ville Platte JSHS 800/5-12
210 W Cotton St 70586 337-363-3387
Peggy Edwards, prin. Fax 363-7274
Other Schools – See Basile, Mamou, Pine Prairie

Christian Heritage Academy 200/PK-12
607 Prosper St 70586 337-363-7690
Rev. Jeff Piker, supt. Fax 363-7699
Louisiana Tech. Coll.-Charles B Coreil Post-Sec.
1124 Vocational Dr 70586 337-363-2197
Sacred Heart HS 9-12
114 Trojan Ln 70586 337-363-1475
Andrew Ducote, prin. Fax 363-0348

Vinton, Calcasieu, Pop. 3,173
Calcasieu Parish SD
Supt. — See Lake Charles
Vinton HS 300/9-12
1603 Grace Ave 70668 337-589-7223
Mitch Manuel, prin. Fax 589-7612
Vinton MS 200/6-8
900 Horridge St 70668 337-589-7567
Stephen Hardy, prin. Fax 589-7587

Emmanuel Christian Academy 100/PK-10
PO Box 906 70668 337-589-5354
W.J. Turpin, prin. Fax 589-1222

Vivian, Caddo, Pop. 3,866
Caddo Parish SD
Supt. — See Shreveport
North Caddo HS 400/9-12
201 Airport Dr 71082 318-375-3258
Ken Cochran, prin. Fax 222-8430

Walker, Livingston, Pop. 5,751
Livingston Parish SD
Supt. — See Livingston
Walker HS 1,200/9-12
PO Box 249 70785 225-664-4825
Steve Long, prin. Fax 664-4321
Walker JHS, PO Box 219 70785 400/6-8
Homer Wentzel, prin. 225-665-8970
Westside JHS 600/6-8
12615 Burgess Ave 70785 225-665-8259
Kevin Pope, prin. Fax 665-8283

Washington, Saint Landry, Pop. 1,057
St. Landry Parish SD
Supt. — See Opelousas
North Central HS 200/9-12
6579 Highway 10 70589 337-623-4239
John Murphy, prin. Fax 623-5360
Washington Career & Technical Education Vo/Tech
PO Box 430 70589 337-826-7360
Andrew Leon, prin. Fax 826-5264

Watson, Livingston
Livingston Parish SD
Supt. — See Livingston
Live Oak MS 900/6-8
PO Box 470 70786 225-664-3211
Patricia McCumsey, prin. Fax 664-1551

Welsh, Jefferson Davis, Pop. 3,310
Jefferson Davis Parish SD
Supt. — See Jennings
Welsh HS 300/9-12
306 Bourgeois St 70591 337-734-2361
Patrick Deshotel, prin. Fax 734-4149

Westlake, Calcasieu, Pop. 4,565
Calcasieu Parish SD
Supt. — See Lake Charles
Arnett MS 400/6-8
400 Sulphur Ave 70669 337-436-9657
Vance Richmond, prin. Fax 436-5745
Westlake HS 500/9-12
1000 Garden Dr 70669 337-433-6866
Steve Powers, prin. Fax 433-8088
Westlake HS T & I Vo/Tech
2307 Jones St 70669 337-439-6373
Fax 433-6308

West Monroe, Ouachita, Pop. 13,038
Ouachita Parish SD
Supt. — See Monroe
Good Hope MS 700/6-8
400 Good Hope Rd 71291 318-396-9693
Twainna Calhoun, prin. Fax 397-5110
Riser MS 500/6-8
100 Price Dr 71292 318-387-0567
Donnie Dampier, prin. Fax 387-9072
West Monroe HS 1,900/9-12
201 Riggs St 71291 318-323-3771
Shere Lynne May, prin. Fax 388-4594
West Ouachita HS 1,000/9-12
4061 Caples Rd 71292 318-249-2117
Mickey Merritt, prin. Fax 249-4774
West Ridge MS 600/6-8
6977 Cypress St 71291 318-397-8444
James Aulds, prin. Fax 397-9376
Woodlawn MS 300/6-8
175 Woodlawn School Rd 71292 318-325-1574
Charles Dykes, prin. Fax 325-9858

Claiborne Christian S 300/PK-12
334 Laird St 71291 318-396-7968
Elizabeth Rigdon, prin. Fax 397-0567
Cloyd's Beauty School #1 Post-Sec.
603 Natchitoches St 71291 318-322-5314
Louisiana Tech. Coll. Delta-Ouachita Post-Sec.
609 Vocational Pkwy 71292 318-397-6100
Northeast Baptist S 200/PK-12
5225 I 20 Service Rd 71292 318-325-2077
Anita Watson, prin. Fax 998-0193

Westwego, Jefferson, Pop. 10,489
Jefferson Parish SD
Supt. — See Marrero
Worley MS 700/6-8
801 Spartan Ln 70094 504-348-4964
Hope Alello, prin. Fax 348-7057

White Castle, Iberville, Pop. 1,850
Iberville Parish SD
Supt. — See Plaquemine
White Castle HS 300/7-12
32695 Graham St 70788 225-545-3621
Wayne Rodrigue, prin. Fax 545-2964

Winnfield, Winn, Pop. 5,307
Winn Parish SD 2,800/PK-12
PO Box 430 71483 318-628-6936
Steve Bartlett, supt. Fax 628-2582
www.winnpsb.org
Winnfield HS 500/9-12
PO Box 968 71483 318-628-3506
Karen Griffin, prin. Fax 628-3417
Winnfield MS 400/6-8
685 Thomas Mill Rd 71483 318-628-2765
Kaye Kieffer, prin. Fax 628-1838
Other Schools – See Atlanta, Calvin, Dodson

Louisiana Technical College - Huey Long Post-Sec.
303 S Jones St 71483 318-628-3815

Winnsboro, Franklin, Pop. 4,991
Franklin Parish SD 2,800/PK-12
7293 Prairie Rd 71295 318-435-9046
Dr. Lanny Johnson, supt. Fax 435-3392
www.franklin.k12.la.us
Franklin Parish HS 700/9-12
1600 Glover Dr 71295 318-435-5676
Joseph Bondurant, prin. Fax 435-6493

Franklin Academy 300/K-12
2110 Loop Rd 71295 318-435-9520
Pete Lewis, prin. Fax 435-9508
Louisiana Technical College-NE Louisiana Post-Sec.
1710 Warren St 71295 318-435-2163

Youngsville, Lafayette, Pop. 5,289
Lafayette Parish SD
Supt. — See Lafayette
Youngsville MS 600/5-8
PO Box 1049 70592 337-856-5961
Darrel Combs, prin. Fax 856-9945

Zachary, East Baton Rouge, Pop. 12,258
Zachary Community SD 2,500/PK-12
4656 Main St 70791 225-658-4969
H. Warren Drake, supt. Fax 658-5261
www.zacharyschools.org
Northwestern MS 800/6-8
5200 E Central Ave 70791 225-654-9201
Debby Brian, prin. Fax 658-2025
Zachary HS 1,000/9-12
4100 Bronco Ln 70791 225-654-2776
Kevin Lemoine, prin. Fax 658-0010

Zwolle, Sabine, Pop. 1,768
Sabine Parish SD
Supt. — See Many
Zwolle JSHS 200/7-12
PO Box 188 71486 318-645-6104
Chad Crow, prin. Fax 645-4830

MAINE

MAINE DEPARTMENT OF EDUCATION
23 State House Station, Augusta 04333
Telephone 207-624-6600
Fax 207-624-6700
Website http://www.maine.gov/education/index.shtml

Commissioner of Education Susan A. Gendron

MAINE BOARD OF EDUCATION
23 State House Station, Augusta 04333

Chairperson James Carignan

PUBLIC, PRIVATE AND CATHOLIC SECONDARY SCHOOLS

Ashland, Aroostook
MSAD 32 — 300/K-12
PO Box 289 04732 — 207-435-3661
C. Ann Bridge, supt. — Fax 435-8421
www.sad32.org/
Ashland Community JSHS — 200/6-12
PO Box 369 04732 — 207-435-3481
Robert Hennessey, prin. — Fax 435-6417

Auburn, Androscoggin, Pop. 23,602
Auburn SD — 3,200/K-12
PO Box 800 04212 — 207-784-6431
Barbara Eretzian, supt. — Fax 784-2969
www.auburnschl.edu
Auburn MS — 600/7-8
38 Falcon Dr 04210 — 207-784-1356
Kathleen Fuller-Cutler, prin. — Fax 784-1359
Little HS — 1,100/9-12
77 Harris St 04210 — 207-783-8528
James Miller, prin. — Fax 784-9243

Central Maine Community College — Post-Sec.
1250 Turner St 04210 — 207-755-5100
St. Dominic Regional HS — 400/9-12
121 Gracelawn Rd 04210 — 207-782-6911
Donald Fournier, prin. — Fax 795-6439

Augusta, Kennebec, Pop. 18,626
Augusta SD — 2,600/PK-12
40 Pierce Dr Ste 3 04330 — 207-626-2468
Cornelia Brown, supt. — Fax 626-2444
www.augustaschools.org/
Capitol Area Technical Center — Vo/Tech
40 Pierce Dr 04330 — 207-626-2475
Scott Phair, prin. — Fax 626-2498
Cony HS — 900/9-12
120 Cony St 04330 — 207-626-2460
James Anastasio, prin. — Fax 626-2541
Hodgkins MS, 17 Malta St 04330 — 400/7-8
Jeffrey Boston, prin. — 207-626-2490

University of Maine — Post-Sec.
46 University Dr 04330 — 207-621-3000

Baileyville, Washington
Union SD 107 — 600/PK-12
PO Box 580 04694 — 207-427-6913
Barry McLaughlin, supt. — Fax 427-3166
Woodland JSHS — 300/7-12
14 First Ave 04694 — 207-427-3325
Patricia Metta, prin. — Fax 427-3950

Bangor, Penobscot, Pop. 31,074
Applied Technology Region
Supt. — None
United Technologies Center-Region 4 — Vo/Tech
200 Hogan Rd 04401 — 207-942-5296
Greg Miller, prin. — Fax 942-0776

Bangor SD — 4,000/K-12
73 Harlow St 04401 — 207-992-4150
Robert Ervin, supt. — Fax 992-4163
www.bangorschools.net
Bangor HS — 1,500/9-12
885 Broadway 04401 — 207-992-5500
Norris Nickerson, prin. — Fax 941-6212
Cohen MS — 500/6-8
304 Garland St 04401 — 207-941-6230
Richard Cookson, prin. — Fax 941-6235
Doughty MS — 500/6-8
143 5th St 04401 — 207-941-6220
Robert MacDonald, prin. — Fax 947-7606

All Saints S - St. John Campus — 100/4-8
PO Box 1749 04402 — 207-942-0955
Marcia Diamond, prin. — Fax 942-2398
Bangor Christian S — 300/PK-12
1476 Broadway 04401 — 207-947-7356
Jim Frost, prin. — Fax 262-9528
Bangor Theological Seminary — Post-Sec.
PO Box 411 04402 — 207-942-6781
Bapst Memorial HS — 500/9-12
100 Broadway 04401 — 207-947-0313
Landis Green, hdmstr. — Fax 941-2474
Beal College — Post-Sec.
99 Farm Rd 04401 — 207-947-4591
Eastern Maine Community College — Post-Sec.
354 Hogan Rd 04401 — 207-974-4600
Eastern Maine Medical Center — Post-Sec.
489 State St 04401 — 207-973-7051
Husson College — Post-Sec.
1 College Cir 04401 — 207-941-7000
New England School of Communications — Post-Sec.
1 College Cir 04401 — 207-941-7176
Pierre's School of Cosmetology — Post-Sec.
635 Broadway 04401 — 207-942-0039

Bar Harbor, Hancock, Pop. 2,768

College of the Atlantic — Post-Sec.
105 Eden St 04609 — 207-288-5015

Bar Mills, York
MSAD 6 — 4,000/K-12
PO Box 38 04004 — 207-929-3831
Suzanne Lukas, supt. — Fax 929-5955
www.sad6.k12.me.us
Other Schools – See Buxton, Standish

Bath, Sagadahoc, Pop. 9,257
Bath SD — 1,400/K-12
39 Andrews Rd 04530 — 207-443-6601
Martha Witham, supt. — Fax 443-8295
www.bathpublicschools.com
Bath MS — 400/6-8
6 Old Brunswick Rd 04530 — 207-443-8270
Lawrence Dyer, prin. — Fax 443-8273
Bath Regional Vocational Center — Vo/Tech
800 High St 04530 — 207-443-8257
Merton Dearnley, prin. — Fax 443-8256
Morse HS — 700/9-12
826 High St 04530 — 207-443-8250
Ricque Finucane, prin. — Fax 443-8268

Hyde S — 200/9-12
616 High St 04530 — 207-443-5584
Fax 443-1450

Belfast, Waldo, Pop. 6,872
MSAD 34 — 1,900/K-12
PO Box 363 04915 — 207-338-1960
M. Robbins Young, supt. — Fax 338-4597
www.sad34.net
Belfast Area HS — 600/9-12
98 Waldo Ave 04915 — 207-338-1790
Harris Arthers, prin. — Fax 338-6713
Howard MS — 500/6-8
173 Lincolnville Ave 04915 — 207-338-3320
Kimberly Buckheit, prin. — Fax 338-5588

Berwick, York
MSAD 60
Supt. — See North Berwick
Noble MS — 600/7-8
46 Cranberry Meadow Rd 03901 — 207-698-1320
Daniel Baker, prin. — Fax 698-4400

Bethel, Oxford
MSAD 44 — 1,100/K-12
21 Philbrook St 04217 — 207-824-2185
David W. Murphy Ed.D., supt. — Fax 824-2725
www.sad44.org
Telstar HS — 300/9-12
284 Walkers Mills Rd 04217 — 207-824-2136
Shawn Lambert, prin. — Fax 824-7130
Telstar MS — 300/6-8
284 Walkers Mills Rd 04217 — 207-824-2136
Russell Tornrose, prin. — Fax 824-0496

Gould Academy — 200/9-12
PO Box 860 04217 — 207-824-7700
Fax 824-7728

Biddeford, York, Pop. 22,072
Biddeford SD — 2,100/K-12
PO Box 1865 04005 — 207-282-8280
Sarah-Jane Poli, supt. — Fax 284-7956
www.biddschools.org
Biddeford HS — 900/9-12
20 Maplewood Ave 04005 — 207-282-1596
Bernard Binette, prin. — Fax 282-8275
Biddeford MS — 700/6-8
25 Tiger Way 04005 — 207-282-6400
Charles Lomonte, prin. — Fax 282-7983
Biddeford Regional Center of Tech — Vo/Tech
10 Maplewood Ave 04005 — 207-282-1501
Ronald Gagnon, prin. — Fax 282-7986

University of New England — Post-Sec.
11 Hills Beach Rd 04005 — 207-283-0171

Bingham, Somerset, Pop. 1,071
MSAD 13 — 200/K-12
PO Box 649 04920 — 207-672-5502
N. Kenneth Smith, supt. — Fax 672-5502
www.sad13.k12.me.us/
Quimby MS — 50/5-8
PO Box 649 04920 — 207-672-5500
Fax 672-5502
Upper Kennebec Valley HS — 100/9-12
PO Box 669 04920 — 207-672-3300
Linda MacKenzie, prin. — Fax 672-4485

Blue Hill, Hancock

Stevens Academy — 300/9-12
23 Union St 04614 — 207-374-2808
Jo Ann Douglass, hdmstr. — Fax 374-2982

Boothbay Harbor, Lincoln, Pop. 1,267
Boothbay-Boothbay Harbor Community SD — 800/K-12
51 Emery Ln 04538 — 207-633-2874
Eileen King, supt. — Fax 633-5458
Boothbay Region HS — 300/9-12
236 Townsend Ave 04538 — 207-633-2421
John Tourtillotte, prin. — Fax 633-7129

Brewer, Penobscot, Pop. 9,138
Brewer SD — 1,500/K-12
49 Capri St 04412 — 207-989-3160
Daniel Lee, supt. — Fax 989-8622
www.breweredu.org/
Brewer HS — 900/9-12
79 Parkway S 04412 — 207-989-4140
Rebecca Bubar, prin. — Fax 989-8659
Brewer MS — 300/6-8
5 Somerset St 04412 — 207-989-8640
William Leithiser, prin. — Fax 989-8635

Bridgton, Cumberland, Pop. 2,195
MSAD 61 — 2,200/K-12
900 Portland Rd 04009 — 207-647-3048
Frank Gorham, supt. — Fax 647-5682
www.sad61.k12.me.us/
Other Schools – See Naples

Brunswick, Cumberland, Pop. 14,683
Applied Technology Region
Supt. — None
Maine Vocational Region 10 — Vo/Tech
68 Church Rd 04011 — 207-729-6622
Fax 721-0907

Brunswick SD — 3,400/K-12
35 Union St 04011 — 207-319-1900
James Ashe, supt. — Fax 725-1700
www.brunswick.k12.me.us/
Brunswick HS — 1,200/9-12
116 Maquoit Rd 04011 — 207-319-1910
Bruce Cook, prin. — Fax 798-5515
Brunswick JHS — 800/6-8
65 Columbia Ave 04011 — 207-319-1930
John Paige, prin. — Fax 721-0602

Bowdoin College 04011 — Post-Sec.
207-725-3000

Buckfield, Oxford
MSAD 39 — 600/PK-12
PO Box 190 04220 — 207-336-3456
Richard Colpitts, supt. — Fax 336-2417
www.sad39.k12.me.us

Buckfield JSHS 300/7-12
160 Morrill St 04220 207-336-2151
Donald Reiter, prin. Fax 336-2460

Bucksport, Hancock, Pop. 2,989
Bucksport SD 1,100/K-12
62 Mechanic St 04416 207-469-7311
Marc Curtis, supt. Fax 469-6640
www.bucksportschools.com/
Bucksport HS 500/9-12
102 Broadway 04416 207-469-6650
Thomas Sullivan, prin. Fax 469-2081
Bucksport MS 300/5-8
PO Box 910 04416 207-469-6647
Thomas Jandreau, prin. Fax 469-2068

Buxton, York
MSAD 6
Supt. — See Bar Mills
Bonny Eagle MS 1,000/6-8
92 Sokokis Trl 04093 207-929-3833
Ansel Stevens, prin. Fax 929-9181

Living Waters Christian S 100/PK-12
PO Box 566 04093 207-727-4499
Robert Nelson, prin. Fax 727-4422

Calais, Washington, Pop. 3,308
Union SD 106 800/PK-12
32 Blue Devil Hl 04619 207-454-7561
James Underwood, supt. Fax 454-2516
Calais MSHS 400/7-12
34 Blue Devil Hl Ste 2 04619 207-454-2591
Jeanne Peacock, prin. Fax 454-0306
Saint Croix Regional Tech Center Vo/Tech
34 Blue Devil Hl Ste 1 04619 207-454-2581
Robert Moholland, lead tchr. Fax 454-2597

Washington County Community College Post-Sec.
1 College Dr 04619 207-454-1000

Camden, Knox, Pop. 4,022
Five Towns Community SD 700/9-12
7 Lions Ln 04843 207-236-3358
Patricia Hopkins, supt. Fax 236-7810
www.fivetowns.net
Other Schools – See Rockport

MSAD 28 900/K-8
7 Lions Ln 04843 207-236-3358
Patricia Hopkins, supt. Fax 236-7810
www.fivetowns.net
Camden-Rockport MS 400/5-8
34 Knowlton St 04843 207-236-7805
Brad Fox, prin. Fax 236-7815

Cape Elizabeth, Cumberland, Pop. 8,854
Cape Elizabeth SD 1,900/K-12
PO Box 6267 04107 207-799-2217
Alan Hawkins, supt. Fax 799-2914
www.cape.k12.me.us
Cape Elizabeth HS 600/9-12
345 Ocean House Rd 04107 207-799-3309
Jeffrey Shedd, prin. Fax 767-8050
Cape Elizabeth MS 600/5-8
14 Scott Dyer Rd 04107 207-799-8176
Steven Connolly, prin. Fax 767-0832

Caribou, Aroostook, Pop. 8,308
Caribou SD 1,700/PK-12
628 Main St 04736 207-496-6311
Franklin McElwain, supt. Fax 498-3261
www.cariboschools.org
Caribou HS 600/9-12
308 Sweden St 04736 207-493-4260
Susan Foren-Lamoreau, prin. Fax 493-4244
Caribou MS 500/5-8
21 Glenn St 04736 207-493-4240
Susan White, prin. Fax 493-4243
Caribou Regional Technology Center Vo/Tech
308 Sweden St Ste 1 04736 207-493-4270
Lynn McNeal, prin. Fax 493-4242

Pierre's School of Cosmetology Post-Sec.
30 Skyway Dr 04736 207-498-6067

Carmel, Penobscot
MSAD 23 700/PK-8
44 Plymouth Rd 04419 207-848-5173
John Backus, supt. Fax 848-5196
www.sad23.k12.me.us
Caravel MS 200/6-8
520 Irish Rd 04419 207-848-3615
Rhonda Sperrey, prin. Fax 848-0884

Carabaset Vly, Franklin

Carrabassett Valley Academy 100/8-12
3197 Carrabassett Dr, 207-237-2250
Fax 237-2213

Castine, Hancock

Maine Maritime Academy Post-Sec.
Battle Ave 04420 207-326-4311

Corinth, Penobscot
MSAD 64 1,300/K-12
408 Main St 04427 207-285-3334
Daniel Higgins, supt. Fax 285-4343
msad64.dcix.net
Central HS 400/9-12
PO Box 370 04427 207-285-3326
Garry Spencer, prin. Fax 285-4342
Central MS 300/6-8
PO Box 19 04427 207-285-3177
Martin Gray, prin. Fax 285-4350

Cornish, York

Ossipee Valley Christian S 100/PK-12
1890 North Rd 04020 207-793-4005
Susan Smith, admin. Fax 793-2904

Cumberland Center, Cumberland, Pop. 1,890
MSAD 51 1,400/PK-12
PO Box 6A 04021 207-829-4800
Robert Hasson, supt. Fax 829-4802
www.msad51.org
Greely HS 700/9-12
303 Main St 04021 207-829-4805
Christopher Mosca, prin. Fax 829-2256
Greely MS 6-8
351 Tuttle Rd 04021 207-829-4815
Kim Brandt, prin. Fax 829-4819

Danforth, Washington
MSAD 14 200/PK-12
31A Houlton Rd 04424 207-448-2882
William Dobbins, supt. Fax 448-7235
East Grand S 200/PK-12
31 Houlton Rd 04424 207-448-2260
David Apgar, prin. Fax 448-7880

Deer Isle, Hancock
Deer Isle - Stonington Community SD
Supt. — See Sargentville
Deer Isle - Stonington HS 100/9-12
251 N Deer Isle Rd 04627 207-348-2303
Penny Wendell, prin. Fax 348-2304

Dexter, Penobscot, Pop. 2,650
MSAD 46 1,100/K-12
10 Spring St 04930 207-924-5262
Kevin Jordan, supt. Fax 924-7660
www.msad46.org
Dexter MS 300/5-8
62 Abbott Hill Rd 04930 207-924-5571
Juliana Richard, prin. Fax 924-7668
Dexter Regional HS 400/9-12
12 Abbott Hill Rd 04930 207-924-5536
Stephen Bell, prin. Fax 924-7673
Tri-County Regional Technology Center Vo/Tech
14 Abbott Hill Rd 04930 207-924-7670
Nicholas Vafiades, prin. Fax 924-5539

Dixfield, Oxford, Pop. 1,300
MSAD 21 900/K-12
147 Weld St 04224 207-562-7254
Thomas Ward Ed.D., supt. Fax 562-7059
www.msad21.org
Dirigo HS 400/9-12
145 Weld St 04224 207-562-4251
Daniel Hart, prin. Fax 562-6074
Dirigo MS 200/5-8
45 Middle School Dr 04224 207-562-7552
Celena Ranger, prin. Fax 562-8329

Dover Foxcroft, Piscataquis, Pop. 3,077
MSAD 68 800/K-8
69 High St 04426 207-564-2421
John Dirnbauer, supt. Fax 564-3487
www.sad68.com/
Se Do Mo Cha MS 400/5-8
63 Harrison Ave 04426 207-564-8376
Jay Robinson, prin. Fax 564-6531

Foxcroft Academy 500/9-12
975 W Main St 04426 207-564-8351
Fax 564-8394

Dyer Brook, Aroostook
Southern Aroostook Community SD 400/K-12
922 Dyer Brook Rd, 207-757-8223
Terry Comeau, supt. Fax 757-8257
www.sacs.csd109.k12.me.us/
Southern Aroostook Community S 400/K-12
922 Dyer Brook Rd, 207-757-8206
Jon Porter, prin. Fax 757-8257

East Machias, Washington

Washington Academy 300/9-12
PO Box 190 04630 207-255-8301
Fax 255-8303

East Millinocket, Penobscot, Pop. 2,075
Millinocket SD 700/K-12
45 North St Ste 2 04430 207-746-3500
Sara Alberts, supt. Fax 746-3510
Other Schools – See Millinocket

Union SD 113 600/K-12
45 North St Ste 2 04430 207-746-3500
Sara Alberts, supt. Fax 746-3516
Schenck HS 200/9-12
45 North St 04430 207-746-3511
Pamela Hamilton, prin. Fax 746-3516
Other Schools – See Medway

Easton, Aroostook
Easton SD 200/PK-12
PO Box 126 04740 207-488-7700
Franklin Keenan, supt. Fax 488-2840
Easton JSHS 100/7-12
PO Box 66 04740 207-488-7702
Ralph Conroy, prin. Fax 488-7707

Eastport, Washington, Pop. 1,594
Union SD 104 600/PK-12
102 High St 04631 207-853-2567
Arthur Wittine, supt. Fax 853-6260
Shead HS 200/9-12
89 High St 04631 207-853-6254
Terry Lux, prin. Fax 853-2919

Eliot, York
MSAD 35 2,700/PK-12
180 Depot Rd 03903 207-439-2438
Gerald Clockedile, supt. Fax 439-2531
www.msad35.net/
Marshwood JHS 600/6-8
626 Dow Hwy 03903 207-439-1399
Valerie McKenny, prin. Fax 439-3504
Other Schools – See South Berwick

Ellsworth, Hancock, Pop. 7,021
Ellsworth SD 1,200/K-12
PO Box 4906 04605 207-667-8136
Frank Hackett, supt. Fax 667-6493
www.ellsworthschools.org
Ellsworth HS 500/9-12
299 State St 04605 207-667-4722
William Connors, prin. Fax 667-5027
Ellsworth MS 300/6-8
20 Forrest Ave 04605 207-667-6494
James Newett, prin. Fax 667-6496
Hancock County Tech Center Vo/Tech
112 Boggy Brook Rd 04605 207-667-9729
Katrina Kane, prin. Fax 667-7138

Fairfield, Kennebec, Pop. 2,794
MSAD 49 2,700/PK-12
8 School St 04937 207-453-4200
Dean Baker, supt. Fax 453-4208
www.sad49.k12.me.us/
Lawrence HS 900/9-12
9 School St 04937 207-453-4200
Pamela Swett, prin. Fax 453-4219
Lawrence JHS 400/7-8
7 School St 04937 207-453-4200
Robert Riley, prin. Fax 453-4214

Kennebec Valley Community College Post-Sec.
92 Western Ave 04937 207-453-5000

Falmouth, Cumberland, Pop. 7,610
Falmouth SD 2,100/K-12
51 Woodville Rd 04105 207-781-3200
George Entwistle, supt. Fax 781-5711
www.falmouthschools.org
Falmouth HS 600/9-12
74 Woodville Rd 04105 207-781-7429
Allyn Hutton, prin. Fax 781-3985
Falmouth MS 700/5-8
52 Woodville Rd 04105 207-781-3740
Jeffrey Rodman, prin. Fax 781-7423

Maine Educational Center for the Deaf Post-Sec.
Mackworth Island 04105 207-781-3165

Farmingdale, Kennebec, Pop. 2,070
MSAD 16
Supt. — See Hallowell
Hall-Dale HS 400/9-12
97 Maple St 04344 207-622-6211
Stephen MacDougall, prin. Fax 626-0355
Hall-Dale MS 300/6-8
111 Maple St 04344 207-622-4162
Steven Lavoie, prin. Fax 622-7515

Farmington, Franklin, Pop. 4,197
MSAD 9
Supt. — See New Sharon
Foster Reg Applied Tech Center Vo/Tech
173 Seamon Rd 04938 207-778-3562
Glenn Kapiloff, prin. Fax 778-3562
Mt. Blue HS 900/9-12
129 Seamon Rd 04938 207-778-3561
Joseph Moore, prin. Fax 778-3564
Mt. Blue MS 400/7-8
269 Middle St 04938 207-778-3511
Gary Oswald, prin. Fax 778-5810

University of Maine Post-Sec.
246 Main St 04938 207-778-7000

Fort Fairfield, Aroostook, Pop. 1,729
MSAD 20 600/PK-12
28 High School Dr Ste B 04742 207-473-4455
Jeannette Condon, supt. Fax 473-4095
www.msad20.org/
Fort Fairfield MSHS 400/6-12
28 High School Dr Ste A 04742 207-472-3271
Mark Jenkins, prin. Fax 472-3281

Fort Kent, Aroostook, Pop. 2,123
MSAD 27 1,100/PK-12
23 W Main St Ste 101 04743 207-834-3189
Dr. Patrick O'Neill, supt. Fax 834-3395
Fort Kent Community HS 400/9-12
84 Pleasant St 04743 207-834-5540
Timothy Doak, prin. Fax 834-2723

University of Maine Post-Sec.
23 University Dr 04743 207-834-7500

Freeport, Cumberland, Pop. 1,829
Freeport SD 1,300/PK-12
17 West St 04032 207-865-0928
Elaine Tomaszewski, supt. Fax 865-2855
www.freeportschooldistrict.com/
Freeport HS 500/9-12
30 Holbrook St 04032 207-865-4706
Mark Tinkham, prin. Fax 865-2900
Freeport MS 300/6-8
19 Kendall Ln 04032 207-865-6051
Kathleen Marquis-Girard, prin. Fax 865-2902

Maine Classical S 100/K-12
PO Box 243 04032 207-865-6820
Douglas Carr, hdmstr. Fax 865-6820

Pine Tree Academy — 100/PK-12
67 Pownal Rd 04032 — 207-865-4747
Brendan Krueger, prin. — Fax 865-1768

Frenchville, Aroostook
MSAD 33 — 300/PK-12
PO Box 9 04745 — 207-543-7334
Fern Desjardins, supt. — Fax 543-6242
www.msad33.org
St. John Valley Tech Center — Vo/Tech
PO Box 509 04745 — 207-543-6606
David Morse, prin. — Fax 543-6115
Other Schools – See Saint Agatha

Fryeburg, Oxford, Pop. 1,580
MSAD 72 — 900/K-8
124 Portland St 04037 — 207-935-2600
Gary MacDonald, supt. — Fax 935-3787
www.msad72.k12.me.us/
Ockett MS — 400/6-8
25 Molly Ockett Dr 04037 — 207-935-2401
Sharon Burnell, prin. — Fax 935-4470

Fryeburg Academy — 700/9-12
745 Main St 04037 — 207-935-2001
Daniel Lee, prin. — Fax 935-4292

Gardiner, Kennebec, Pop. 6,237
MSAD 11 — 2,300/PK-12
150 Highland Ave 04345 — 207-582-5346
Paul Knowles, supt. — Fax 582-8305
www.msad11.org
Gardiner Area HS — 800/9-12
40 W Hill Rd 04345 — 207-582-3150
Chad Kempton, prin. — Fax 582-0434
Gardiner Regional MS — 600/6-8
161 Cobbossee Ave 04345 — 207-582-1326
Arthur Warren, prin. — Fax 582-6823

Gorham, Cumberland, Pop. 3,618
Gorham SD — 2,800/K-12
381 Main St Ste 4 04038 — 207-222-1000
Theodore Sharpe, supt. — Fax 839-5003
www.gorhamschools.org/
Gorham HS — 900/9-12
41 Morrill Ave 04038 — 207-222-1100
John Drisko, prin. — Fax 839-7742
Gorham MS — 700/6-8
106 Weeks Rd 04038 — 207-222-1220
Dennis Duquette, prin. — Fax 839-4092

Gray, Cumberland
MSAD 15 — 2,100/K-12
14 Shaker Rd 04039 — 207-657-3335
Victoria Burns, supt. — Fax 657-2040
www.msad15.org/
Gray-New Gloucester HS — 700/9-12
10 Libby Hill Rd 04039 — 207-657-3323
Paul Penna, prin. — Fax 657-3329
Gray-New Gloucester MS — 500/6-8
31 Libby Hill Rd 04039 — 207-657-4994
Peter Cook, prin. — Fax 657-5219

Greenville, Piscataquis, Pop. 1,601
Union SD 60 — 300/K-12
PO Box 100 04441 — 207-695-3708
Heather Perry, supt. — Fax 695-3709
Greenville MSHS — 200/6-12
PO Box 100 04441 — 207-695-2666
Fax 695-4614

Guilford, Piscataquis, Pop. 1,082
MSAD 4 — 900/PK-12
25 Campus Dr Ste 2 04443 — 207-876-3444
Paul Stearns, supt. — Fax 876-3446
www.sad4.com/
Piscataquis Community HS — 300/9-12
9 Campus Dr 04443 — 207-876-4625
Jeffrey Aronson, prin. — Fax 876-4628
Piscataquis Community MS — 300/4-8
25 Campus Dr Ste 1 04443 — 207-876-4301
Gregory Bellemare, prin. — Fax 876-4291

Hallowell, Kennebec, Pop. 2,535
MSAD 16 — 1,000/K-12
7 Reed St 04347 — 207-622-6351
Don Siviski, supt. — Fax 622-7866
www.halldale.org/
Other Schools – See Farmingdale

Hampden, Penobscot, Pop. 3,895
MSAD 22 — 2,300/PK-12
24 Main Rd N 04444 — 207-862-3255
Richard Lyons, supt. — Fax 862-2789
www.sad22.us/
Hampden Academy — 800/9-12
1 Main Rd N 04444 — 207-862-3791
Ruey Yehle, prin. — Fax 862-4577
Reeds Brook MS — 400/6-8
28A Main Rd S 04444 — 207-862-3540
Thomas Ingraham, prin. — Fax 862-3551
Other Schools – See Winterport

Harrington, Washington
MSAD 37 — 800/K-12
PO Box 79 04643 — 207-483-2734
Deborah Stewart, supt. — Fax 483-6051
www.sad37.com
Narraguagus HS — 300/9-12
RR 1 Box 489 04643 — 207-483-2746
Nancy Melhorn, prin. — Fax 483-2771

Hartland, Somerset, Pop. 1,038
MSAD 48
Supt. — See Newport
Somerset Valley MS — 300/5-8
45 Blake St 04943 — 207-938-4770
Don Roux, prin. — Fax 938-2114

Hebron, Oxford

Hebron Academy — 200/6-12
PO Box 309 04238 — 207-966-2100
Fax 966-5291

Hermon, See Bangor
Hermon SD — 1,100/PK-12
31 Billings Rd 04401 — 207-848-4000
Patricia Duran, supt. — Fax 848-5226
www.hermon.net
Hermon HS — 600/9-12
2415 Route 2 04401 — 207-848-4000
Brian Walsh, prin. — Fax 848-5591
Hermon MS — 200/5-8
29 Billings Rd 04401 — 207-848-4000
James Russell, prin. — Fax 848-2163

Hinckley, Somerset

Averill HS / Alfond MS — 100/5-12
PO Box 159 04944 — 207-238-4200
Fax 238-4207

Hiram, Oxford
MSAD 55 — 1,300/K-12
62 Brownfield Rd 04041 — 207-625-8683
Sylvia Pease, supt. — Fax 625-8153
www.sad55.k12.me.us/
Sacopee Valley JSHS — 500/8-12
115 S Hiram Rd 04041 — 207-625-3208
Joseph Findlay, prin. — Fax 625-7869

Holden, Penobscot
MSAD 63 — 600/K-8
202 Kidder Hill Rd 04429 — 207-843-7851
Louise Regan, supt. — Fax 843-7295
www.sad63.net/
Holbrook MS — 300/5-8
202 Kidder Hill Rd 04429 — 207-843-7769
Gary Conyar, prin. — Fax 843-4328

Houlton, Aroostook, Pop. 5,627
Applied Technology Region
Supt. — None
Region 2 School of Applied Tech — Vo/Tech
PO Box 307 04730 — 207-532-9541
Michael Howard, prin. — Fax 532-6975

MSAD 29 — 1,400/PK-12
PO Box 190 04730 — 207-532-6555
Stephen Fitzpatrick, supt. — Fax 532-6481
www.sad29.k12.me.us/
Houlton HS — 400/9-12
7 Bird St 04730 — 207-532-6551
Martin Bouchard, prin. — Fax 532-6282
Houlton JHS — 200/7-8
7 Bird St 04730 — 207-532-6551
Martin Bouchard, prin. — Fax 532-6282

MSAD 70 — 600/PK-12
175 Hodgdon Mills Rd 04730 — 207-532-3015
Robert McDaniel, supt. — Fax 532-2679
www.msad70.net/
Hodgdon HS — 200/9-12
175 Hodgdon Mills Rd 04730 — 207-532-2413
Clark Rafford, prin. — Fax 532-4043

Greater Houlton Christian Academy — 200/PK-12
27 School St 04730 — 207-532-0736
Mark B. Jago, hdmstr. — Fax 532-9553

Howland, Penobscot, Pop. 1,304
MSAD 31 — 700/K-12
23 Cross St 04448 — 207-732-3112
Jerry White, supt. — Fax 732-3390
www.msad31.com/
Hichborn MS — 200/6-8
23 Cross St 04448 — 207-732-3113
Carol Marcinkus, prin. — Fax 732-4085
Penobscot Valley HS — 200/9-12
23 Cross St 04448 — 207-732-3111
Carol Marcinkus, prin. — Fax 732-5500

Islesboro, Waldo
Islesboro SD — 100/K-12
PO Box 118 04848 — 207-734-6723
Donald Kanicki, supt. — Fax 734-8159
www.islesboro-central.islesboro.k12.me.us
Islesboro Central S — 100/K-12
PO Box 118 04848 — 207-734-2251
Michael Wright, prin. — Fax 734-8159

Jackman, Somerset
MSAD 12 — 200/K-12
PO Box 239 04945 — 207-668-7749
Richard Curtis, supt. — Fax 668-4482
www.sad12.com/
Forest Hills Consolidated S — 200/K-12
PO Box 239 04945 — 207-668-5291
Richard Curtis, prin. — Fax 668-4482

Jay, Franklin
Jay SD — 900/K-12
5 Tiger Dr 04239 — 207-897-3936
Robert Wall, supt. — Fax 897-5431
www.jay.k12.me.us
Jay HS — 300/9-12
33 Community Dr 04239 — 207-897-4336
John Robinson, prin. — Fax 897-9313
Jay MS — 300/5-8
23 Community Dr 04239 — 207-897-4319
Scott Albert, prin. — Fax 897-3513

Jonesport, Washington
Moosabec Community SD — 100/9-12
127 Snare Creek Ln 04649 — 207-497-2154
Colleen Haskell, supt. — Fax 497-2703
www.union103.org/
Jonesport-Beals HS — 100/9-12
180 Snare Creek Ln 04649 — 207-497-5454
Colleen Haskell, prin. — Fax 497-3004

Kennebunk, York, Pop. 4,206
MSAD 71 — 2,500/PK-12
87 Fletcher St 04043 — 207-985-1100
Thomas Farrell, supt. — Fax 985-1104
www.msad71.net
Kennebunk HS — 900/9-12
89 Fletcher St 04043 — 207-985-1110
Nelson Beaudoin, prin. — Fax 985-1350
Kennebunk MS — 600/6-8
60 Thompson Rd 04043 — 207-467-8004
Frances Farr, prin. — Fax 467-9059

Heartwood College of Art — Post-Sec.
123 York St 04043 — 207-985-0985

Kennebunkport, York, Pop. 1,100

Landing School of Boatbuilding & Design — Post-Sec.
PO Box 1490 04046 — 207-985-7976

Kents Hill, Kennebec

Kents Hill S — 200/9-12
PO Box 257 04349 — 207-685-4914
George Bonnefond, prin. — Fax 685-9529

Kittery, York, Pop. 5,151
Kittery SD — 1,100/K-12
200 Rogers Rd 03904 — 207-439-6819
Larry Littlefield, supt. — Fax 439-5407
www.kitteryschools.org/
Shapleigh MS — 300/6-8
43 Stevenson Rd 03904 — 207-439-2572
Wanda Avery, prin. — Fax 439-9958
Traip Academy — 300/9-12
12 Williams Ave 03904 — 207-439-1121
Patricia Garnis, prin. — Fax 439-3789

Lee, Penobscot
MSAD 30 — 100/K-8
31 Winn Rd 04455 — 207-738-2665
Frederick Woodman, supt. — Fax 738-2010
www.msad30.org/
Mt. Jefferson JHS — 100/6-8
61 Winn Rd 04455 — 207-738-2866
Fax 738-3817

Lee Academy — 200/9-12
26 Winn Rd 04455 — 207-738-2252
Bruce Lindberg, prin. — Fax 738-3257

Lewiston, Androscoggin, Pop. 36,050
Lewiston SD — 4,500/K-12
36 Oak St 04240 — 207-795-4100
Leon Levesque, supt. — Fax 753-6413
www.lewiston.k12.me.us/
Lewiston HS — 1,400/9-12
156 East Ave 04240 — 207-795-4190
Wilfred LeBlanc, prin. — Fax 795-4119
Lewiston MS — 700/7-8
75 Central Ave 04240 — 207-795-4180
Maureen Lachapelle, prin. — Fax 753-1789
Lewiston Regional Technical Center — Vo/Tech
156 East Ave 04240 — 207-795-4144
Donald Cannan Ed.D., prin. — Fax 795-4147

Andover College — Post-Sec.
475 Lisbon St 04240 — 800-639-3110
Bates College — Post-Sec.
1 Bates College 04240 — 207-786-6000
Central Maine Christian Academy — 100/PK-12
390 Main St 04240 — 207-777-0007
Patricia St. Hilaire, admin. — Fax 777-0007
Central Maine Medical Center — Post-Sec.
70 Middle St 04240 — 207-795-2840
Mr. Bernard's School of Hair Fashion — Post-Sec.
PO Box 1163 04243 — 207-783-7765
Trinity S — 100/6-8
393 Main St 04240 — 207-784-8811
Bonnie Marsh, prin. — Fax 783-9522
Vineyard Christian S — 100/PK-12
9 Foss Rd 04240 — 207-784-9500
Ruth Handler, dir. — Fax 777-3076

Limestone, Aroostook, Pop. 1,245
Limestone SD — 300/K-12
97 High St 04750 — 207-325-4888
Frank McElwain, supt. — Fax 325-4969
Limestone S — 300/K-12
93 High St 04750 — 207-325-4742
Ryan Enman, prin. — Fax 325-4780

Maine School of Science & Mathematics — 100/10-12
95 High St 04750 — 207-325-3303
Walter Warner, supt. — Fax 325-3340
www.mssm.org/
Maine School of Science & Mathematics — 100/10-12
95 High St 04750 — 207-325-3303
Walter Warner, dean — Fax 325-3340

Lincoln, Penobscot, Pop. 3,399
Applied Technology Region
Supt. — None
North Penobscot Tech-Region 3 — Vo/Tech
35 W Broadway 04457 — 207-794-3004
Fax 794-8049

MSAD 67 — 1,300/PK-12
PO Box 250 04457 — 207-794-6500
Michael Marcinkus, supt. — Fax 794-2600
www.sad67.k12.me.us/
Mattanawcook Academy — 400/9-12
33 Reed Dr 04457 — 207-794-6711
James Boothby, prin. — Fax 794-3205

Mattanawcook JHS 400/5-8
41 School St 04457 207-794-8935
Larry Malone, prin. Fax 794-2601

Lisbon, See Lisbon Falls
Union SD 30 1,100/K-12
19 Gartley St 04250 207-353-6711
Shannon Welsh Ed.D., supt. Fax 353-3032
www.union30.org/
Other Schools – See Lisbon Falls

Lisbon Falls, Androscoggin, Pop. 4,674
Union SD 30
Supt. — See Lisbon
Lisbon HS 500/9-12
591 Lisbon St 04252 207-353-3030
Kenneth Healey, prin. Fax 353-7908
Sugg MS 200/7-8
567 Lisbon St 04252 207-353-3055
Richard Green, prin. Fax 353-3053

Litchfield, Kennebec, Pop. 275
Union SD 44
Supt. — See Wales
Ricker MS 300/3-8
573 Richmond Rd 04350 207-268-4136
Christine Lajoie-Cameron, prin. Fax 268-4318

Livermore Falls, Androscoggin, Pop. 1,935
MSAD 36 1,000/K-12
9 Cedar St 04254 207-897-6722
Terry Despres, supt. Fax 897-2362
www.sad36.org/
Livermore Falls HS 300/9-12
25 Cedar St 04254 207-897-3428
Fax 897-2254
Livermore Falls MS 300/6-8
1 Highland Ave 04254 207-897-2121
Ted Finn, prin. Fax 897-9377

Lubec, Washington
MSAD 19 200/K-12
44 South St 04652 207-733-5573
Michael Buckley, supt. Fax 733-2004
Lubec Consolidated S 200/K-12
44 South St 04652 207-733-5591
Peter Doak, prin. Fax 733-2004

Machias, Washington, Pop. 1,773
Union SD 102 500/K-12
RR 1 Box 12A 04654 207-255-6585
Scott Porter, supt. Fax 255-8054
Coastal Washington City Inst of Tech Vo/Tech
110 Court St 04654 207-255-6585
Scott Porter, prin. Fax 255-8054
Machias Memorial HS 100/9-12
109 Court St 04654 207-255-3812
Timothy Reynolds, prin. Fax 255-3093

University of Maine Post-Sec.
9 OBrien Ave 04654 207-255-1200

Madawaska, Aroostook, Pop. 3,653
Madawaska SD 700/PK-12
328 Saint Thomas St Ste 201 04756 207-728-3346
Raymond Freve, supt. Fax 728-7823
www.madhs.mad.k12.me.us/
Madawaska MSHS 400/6-12
135 7th Ave 04756 207-728-3371
Wayne Anderson, prin. Fax 728-3636

Madison, Somerset, Pop. 2,956
MSAD 59 1,000/PK-12
55 Weston Ave 04950 207-696-3323
Sandra MacArthur, supt. Fax 696-5631
www.sad59.k12.me.us/
Madison Area Memorial HS 300/9-12
486 Main St 04950 207-696-3395
Colin Campbell, prin. Fax 696-5644
Madison JHS 300/5-8
205 Main St 04950 207-696-3381
Bonnie Levesque, prin. Fax 696-5640

Mars Hill, Aroostook, Pop. 1,717
MSAD 42 500/PK-12
PO Box 1006 04758 207-425-3771
Roger Shaw, supt. Fax 429-8461
www.cahs.sad42.k12.me.us/
Central Aroostook JSHS 300/7-12
PO Box 310 04758 207-425-2811
Kevin Grass, prin. Fax 429-8460

Medway, Penobscot
Union SD 113
Supt. — See East Millinocket
Medway MS 200/5-8
PO Box 608 04460 207-746-3470
Kevin Towle, prin. Fax 746-5930

Mexico, Oxford, Pop. 2,302
Applied Technology Region
Supt. — None
School of Applied Tech-Region 9 Vo/Tech
377 River Rd 04257 207-364-3764
David Driscoll, prin. Fax 364-2074

MSAD 43 1,500/K-12
3 Recreation Dr 04257 207-364-7896
James Hodgkins, supt. Fax 364-5609
valnet.mtvalleyhs.sad43.k12.me.us
Mountain Valley MS 400/6-8
58 Highland Ter 04257 207-364-7926
Charles Lever, prin. Fax 364-5608
Other Schools – See Rumford

Millinocket, Penobscot, Pop. 6,922
Millinocket SD
Supt. — See East Millinocket
Millinocket MS 200/6-8
199 State St 04462 207-723-6415
Paige Coville, prin. Fax 723-6437

Stearns HS 300/9-12
199 State St 04462 207-723-6430
Brian Jones, prin. Fax 723-6437

Milo, Piscataquis, Pop. 2,129
MSAD 41 800/K-12
37 W Main St 04463 207-943-7317
Shirley Wright, supt. Fax 943-5314
msad41.us/
Penquis Valley HS 400/7-12
48 Penquis Dr 04463 207-943-7346
Scott Gordon, prin. Fax 943-5333

Monmouth, Kennebec
Monmouth SD 800/K-12
PO Box 460 04259 207-933-3062
Stephen Cottrell, supt. Fax 933-3061
www.monmouthschools.org/
Monmouth Academy 200/9-12
96 Academy Rd 04259 207-933-4416
Michael Burnham, prin. Fax 933-7222
Monmouth MS 300/4-8
PO Box 240 04259 207-933-9002
Stephen Philbrook, prin. Fax 933-7252

Mount Desert, Hancock
Mt. Desert Community SD 700/9-12
PO Box 60 04660 207-288-5049
Robert Liebow, supt. Fax 288-5071
www.u98.k12.me.us
Mt. Desert Island HS 700/9-12
PO Box 180 04660 207-288-5011
Sally Leighton, prin. Fax 288-0692

Naples, Cumberland
MSAD 61
Supt. — See Bridgton
Lake Region HS 800/9-12
1877 Roosevelt Trl 04055 207-693-6221
Roger Lowell, prin. Fax 693-4591
Lake Region MS 400/7-8
204 Kansas Rd 04055 207-647-8403
Peter Mortenson, prin. Fax 647-0991
Lake Region Vocational Center Vo/Tech
1879 Roosevelt Trl 04055 207-693-3864
Rosie Schacht, prin. Fax 693-3864

Newcastle, Lincoln

Lincoln Academy 600/9-12
81 Academy Hl 04553 207-563-3596
John Pinkerton, prin. Fax 563-1067

Newport, Penobscot, Pop. 1,843
MSAD 48 2,200/PK-12
PO Box 40 04953 207-368-5091
William Braun, supt. Fax 368-2192
www.msad48.org
Nokomis Regional HS 800/9-12
PO Box 100 04953 207-368-4354
Arnold Shorey, prin. Fax 368-3276
Sebasticook Valley MS 400/5-8
337 Williams Rd 04953 207-368-4592
Fredrick Johnston, prin. Fax 368-4598
Other Schools – See Hartland

New Sharon, Franklin
MSAD 9 2,600/K-12
11 School Ln 04955 207-778-6571
Michael Cormier, supt. Fax 778-4160
www.msad9.com
Other Schools – See Farmington

New Vineyard, Franklin

Open Bible Baptist Christian S 50/PK-12
PO Box 242 04956 207-778-9065
Herman Ellis, prin. Fax 778-9065

Norridgewock, Somerset, Pop. 1,496

Riverview Memorial S 50/K-10
201 Mercer Rd 04957 207-634-2641
Fax 634-5812

North Anson, Somerset
MSAD 74 900/K-12
56 N Main St 04958 207-635-2727
Regina Campbell Ed.D., supt. Fax 635-3599
www.sad74.k12.me.us:16080/district/
Carrabec HS 300/9-12
PO Box 220 04958 207-635-2296
Kenneth Coville, prin. Fax 635-2217

North Berwick, York, Pop. 1,568
MSAD 60 3,000/K-12
PO Box 819 03906 207-676-2234
Paul Andrade, supt. Fax 676-3229
www.sad60.k12.me.us
Noble HS 1,100/9-12
388 Somersworth Rd 03906 207-676-2843
Christian Elkington, prin. Fax 676-2842
Other Schools – See Berwick

North Bridgton, Cumberland

Bridgton Academy 200/12-12
PO Box 292 04057 207-647-3322
Fax 647-8513

North Haven, Knox
MSAD 7 100/PK-12
93 Pulpit Harbor Rd 04853 207-867-4707
Thomas Marx, supt. Fax 867-4438
nhcsxserve.sad7.k12.me.us/
North Haven Community S 100/PK-12
93 Pulpit Harbor Rd 04853 207-867-4707
A. Barney Hallowell, prin. Fax 867-4438

Norway, Oxford, Pop. 3,023
Applied Technology Region
Supt. — None
Oxford Hills Tech-Region 11 Vo/Tech
PO Box 313 04268 207-743-7756
David Mason, prin. Fax 743-0667

Oakland, Kennebec, Pop. 3,510
MSAD 47 2,600/PK-12
41 Heath St 04963 207-465-7384
James Morse Ed.D., supt. Fax 465-9130
www.msad47.org/
Messalonskee HS 900/9-12
131 Messalonskee High Dr 04963 207-465-7381
Lori Putnam, prin. Fax 465-9151
Messalonskee MS 600/6-8
33 School Bus Dr 04963 207-465-2167
Mark Hatch, prin. Fax 465-9683

Old Orchard Beach, York, Pop. 7,789
Old Orchard Beach SD 1,000/PK-12
28 Jameson Hill Rd 04064 207-934-5751
Eric Matthews, supt. Fax 934-1917
Loranger MS 400/4-8
148 Saco Ave 04064 207-934-2361
James Boisvert, prin. Fax 934-3712
Old Orchard Beach HS 300/9-12
40 E Emerson Cummings Blvd 04064 207-934-4461
Richard DiFusco, prin. Fax 934-3705

Old Town, Penobscot, Pop. 7,792
Old Town SD 1,500/K-12
156 Oak St Ste 2 04468 207-827-7171
David Walker, supt. Fax 827-3922
www.otsd.org/
Leonard MS 400/6-8
156 Oak St 04468 207-827-3900
John Keane, prin. Fax 827-3922
Old Town HS 700/9-12
203 Stillwater Ave 04468 207-827-3910
Joseph Gallant, prin. Fax 827-3918

Orono, Penobscot, Pop. 9,789
Union SD 87 1,000/K-12
18 Goodridge Dr 04473 207-866-5521
Kelly Clenchy, supt. Fax 866-7111
www.orono.u87.k12.me.us/
Orono HS 400/9-12
14 Goodridge Dr 04473 207-866-4916
Bruce Bailey, prin. Fax 866-7116
Orono MS 200/6-8
14 Goodridge Dr 04473 207-866-2350
Robert Lucy, prin. Fax 866-7111

University of Maine 04469 Post-Sec.
207-581-1110

Orrington, Penobscot

Calvary Chapel Christian S 200/PK-12
154 River Rd 04474 207-991-9684
Dennis Harvey, prin. Fax 989-0687

Oxford, Oxford, Pop. 1,284
MSAD 17 3,600/K-12
1570 Main St Ste 11 04270 207-743-8972
Mark Eastman Ed.D., supt. Fax 743-2878
www.sad17.k12.me.us/
Other Schools – See South Paris

Phillips, Franklin
MSAD 58 1,000/K-12
1401 Rangeley Rd 04966 207-639-2086
Quenten Clark, supt. Fax 639-5120
www.sad58.k12.me.us/
Other Schools – See Salem

Pittsfield, Somerset, Pop. 3,222
MSAD 53 700/PK-8
73 Hartland Ave 04967 207-487-5107
Michael A. Gallagher, supt. Fax 487-6310
www.msad53.org/
Warsaw MS 400/5-8
167 School St 04967 207-487-5145
George Nevens, prin. Fax 487-4511

Maine Central Institute 500/9-12
295 Main St 04967 207-487-3355
Joanne Szadkowski, hdmstr. Fax 487-3512

Poland, Androscoggin
Union SD 29 1,800/K-12
1146 Maine St 04274 207-998-2753
Nina Schlikin, supt. Fax 998-2727
www.poland-hs.u29.k12.me.us/union29/union29.html
Poland Regional HS 600/9-12
1457 Maine St 04274 207-998-5400
William Doughty, prin. Fax 998-5060
Whittier MS 200/7-8
1457 Maine St 04274 207-998-5400
William Doughty, prin. Fax 998-5060

Portland, Cumberland, Pop. 63,889
Portland SD 7,200/K-12
196 Allen Ave 04103 207-874-8100
Mary Jo O'Connor, supt. Fax 874-8199
www.portlandschools.org
Casco Bay HS 9-12
196 Allen Ave 04103 207-874-8160
Derek Pierce, prin. Fax 797-5437
Deering HS 1,300/9-12
370 Stevens Ave 04103 207-874-8260
Kenneth Kunin, prin. Fax 874-8153
King MS 500/6-8
92 Deering Ave 04102 207-874-8140
Michael McCarthy, prin. Fax 874-8290
Lincoln MS 600/6-8
522 Stevens Ave 04103 207-874-8145
Kathleen Rossi, prin. Fax 874-8288

Moore MS 600/6-8
171 Auburn St 04103 207-874-8150
Lee Crocker, prin. Fax 874-8272
Portland Arts & Technology HS Vo/Tech
196 Allen Ave 04103 207-874-8165
Dana Allen, prin. Fax 874-8170
Portland HS 1,200/9-12
284 Cumberland Ave 04101 207-874-8250
Michael Johnson, prin. Fax 874-8248

Andover College Post-Sec.
901 Washington Ave 04103 800-639-3110
Cheverus HS 500/9-12
267 Ocean Ave 04103 207-774-6238
John Mullen, prin. Fax 828-0207
Headhunter Institute Post-Sec.
1041 Brighton Ave 04102 207-772-2591
Maine College of Art Post-Sec.
97 Spring St 04101 207-775-3052
McAuley HS 300/9-12
631 Stevens Ave 04103 207-797-3802
Sr. Edward Mary Kelleher, prin. Fax 797-3804
Mercy Hospital Post-Sec.
144 State St 04101 207-879-3000
Pierre's School of Cosmetology Post-Sec.
319 Marginal Way 04101 207-774-9413
University of Southern Maine Post-Sec.
PO Box 9300 04104 207-780-4141
Waynflete S 500/PK-12
360 Spring St 04102 207-774-5721
Mark Segar, prin. Fax 772-4782
Westbrook College Post-Sec.
716 Stevens Ave 04103 207-797-7261

Presque Isle, Aroostook, Pop. 9,377
MSAD 1 1,800/PK-12
PO Box 1118 04769 207-764-4101
Gehrig Johnson, supt. Fax 764-4103
www.sad1.org/
Presque Isle HS 600/9-12
16 Griffin St 04769 207-764-0121
Eric Waddell, prin. Fax 764-7720
Presque Isle MS 300/6-8
569 Skyway St 04769 207-764-4474
Anne Blanchard, prin. Fax 764-3078
Presque Isle Regional Tech Center Vo/Tech
79 Blake St 04769 207-764-1356
Gene McLuskey, prin. Fax 764-8107

Northern Maine Community College Post-Sec.
33 Edgemont Dr 04769 207-768-2700
University of Maine at Presque Isle Post-Sec.
181 Main St 04769 207-768-9400

Rangeley, Franklin
Union SD 37 200/K-12
PO Box 97 04970 207-864-3313
Philip Richardson, supt. Fax 864-2451
Rangeley Lakes Regional S 200/K-12
PO Box 97 04970 207-864-3311
Richard Curley, prin. Fax 864-2451

Raymond, Cumberland
Raymond SD 600/K-8
434 Webbs Mills Rd 04071 207-655-8666
Sandra S. Caldwell, supt. Fax 655-8663
www.raymondmaine.org/schools/District/default.htm
Jordan-Small MS 300/5-8
423 Webbs Mills Rd 04071 207-655-4743
Randolph Crockett, prin. Fax 655-6952

Readfield, Kennebec
Maranacook Community SD 900/6-12
45 Millard Harrison Dr 04355 207-685-3336
Richard Abramson, supt. Fax 685-4703
www.maranacook.org
Maranacook Community HS 600/9-12
2250 Millard Harrison Dr 04355 207-685-4923
Carol Fritz, prin. Fax 685-9597
Maranacook Community MS 300/6-8
2100 Millard Harrison Dr 04355 207-685-3128
Mary Callan, prin. Fax 685-9876

Richmond, Sagadahoc, Pop. 1,775
Richmond SD 600/PK-12
PO Box 190 04357 207-737-2221
Martha Witham, supt. Fax 737-8707
www.richmond.k12.me.us/
Richmond HS 200/9-12
132 Main St 04357 207-737-4348
Deborah Smith Fisk, prin. Fax 737-8707
Richmond MS 100/6-8
132 Main St 04357 207-737-8655
Ralph Peterson, prin. Fax 737-8741

Rockland, Knox, Pop. 7,658
Applied Technology Region
Supt. — None
Mid-Coast School of Tech-Region 8 Vo/Tech
1 S Main St 04841 207-594-2161
Fax 594-7506

MSAD 5 1,400/K-12
28 Lincoln St 04841 207-596-6620
Alan Pfeiffer, supt. Fax 596-2004
www.msad5.org
Rockland District HS 500/9-12
400 Broadway 04841 207-596-2010
Michael Gundel, prin. Fax 596-2028
Rockland District MS 300/6-8
30 Broadway 04841 207-596-2020
Deborah Folsom, prin. Fax 596-2026

Rockport, Knox
Five Towns Community SD
Supt. — See Camden
Camden Hills Regional HS 700/9-12
25 Keelson Dr 04856 207-236-7800
Nick Ithomitis, prin. Fax 236-7813

Rumford, Oxford, Pop. 5,419
MSAD 43
Supt. — See Mexico
Mountain Valley HS 600/9-12
799 Hancock St 04276 207-364-4547
Matthew Gilbert, prin. Fax 364-3436

Sabattus, Androscoggin
Oak Hill Community SD 600/9-12
PO Box 220 04280 207-375-4273
Susan Hodgdon, supt. Fax 375-2522
Other Schools – See Wales

Union SD 44
Supt. — See Wales
Sabattus Central S 300/3-8
40 Ball Park Rd 04280 207-375-6961
Beverly Coursey, prin. Fax 375-8871

Saco, York, Pop. 18,230
Union SD 7 2,100/K-8
90 Beach St 04072 207-284-4505
Michael LaFortune, supt. Fax 284-5951
www.saco.org
Saco MS 800/6-8
40 Buxton Rd 04072 207-282-4181
Richard Talbot, prin. Fax 286-1807

Thornton Academy 1,100/6-12
438 Main St 04072 207-282-3361
Fax 282-3508

Saint Agatha, Aroostook
MSAD 33
Supt. — See Frenchville
Wisdom MSHS 100/7-12
PO Box 69 04772 207-543-7717
Tammy LeBlanc, prin. Fax 543-6316

Salem, Franklin
MSAD 58
Supt. — See Phillips
Mt. Abram Regional HS 300/9-12
1513 Salem Rd, 207-678-2701
Jeanne Tucker, prin. Fax 678-2668

Sanford, York, Pop. 10,296
Sanford SD 3,700/K-12
917 Main St Ste 200 04073 207-324-2810
John Turcotte, supt. Fax 324-5742
www.sanford.org
Sanford HS 1,400/9-12
52 Sanford High Blvd 04073 207-324-4050
Allan Young, prin. Fax 490-5152
Sanford JHS 700/7-8
708 Main St 04073 207-324-3114
Becky Brink, prin. Fax 490-5139
Sanford Regional Vocational Center Vo/Tech
52 Sanford High Blvd 04073 207-324-2942
Deborah Guimont, prin. Fax 324-2957

Pierre's School of Cosmetology Post-Sec.
913 Main St 04073 207-490-1274

Sargentville, Hancock
Deer Isle - Stonington Community SD 400/K-12
RR 1 Box 27A 04673 207-359-8400
Robert Webster, supt. Fax 359-8451
Other Schools – See Deer Isle

Scarborough, Cumberland, Pop. 2,586
Scarborough SD 3,300/K-12
PO Box 370 04070 207-730-4100
David Doyle, supt. Fax 730-4104
www.scarborough.k12.me.us
Scarborough HS 1,000/9-12
20 Gorham Rd 04074 207-730-5000
Andrew Dolloff, prin. Fax 730-5007
Scarborough MS 800/6-8
44 Gorham Rd 04074 207-730-4800
Jo Anne Sizemore, prin. Fax 730-4804

Searsport, Waldo, Pop. 1,151
MSAD 56 800/K-12
6 Mortland Rd 04974 207-548-6643
Mary Szwec, supt. Fax 548-2310
www.msad56.org/
Searsport District HS 300/9-12
24 Mortland Rd 04974 207-548-2313
Gregg Palmer, prin. Fax 548-2354
Searsport District MS 200/6-8
26 Mortland Rd 04974 207-548-2311
Brian Corrigan, prin. Fax 548-2352

Skowhegan, Somerset, Pop. 6,990
MSAD 54 2,900/K-12
196 W Front St 04976 207-474-9508
Brent Colbry, supt. Fax 474-7422
www.msad54.org/
Skowhegan Area HS 1,000/9-12
61 Academy Cir 04976 207-474-5511
Richard Wilson, prin. Fax 474-0992
Skowhegan Area MS 500/7-8
155 Academy Cir 04976 207-474-3339
John Krasnavage, prin. Fax 474-9588
Skowhegan Regional Vocational Center Vo/Tech
61 Academy Cir 04976 207-474-2151
Raymond Arbour, prin. Fax 858-4879

South Berwick, York
MSAD 35
Supt. — See Eliot
Marshwood HS 900/9-12
260 Dow Hwy 03908 207-384-4500
Paul Mehlhorn, prin. Fax 384-2151

Berwick Academy 600/K-12
31 Academy St 03908 207-384-2164
Fax 384-3332

South China, Kennebec
Union SD 52
Supt. — See Winslow
China MS 300/5-8
773 Lakeview Dr 04358 207-445-1500
Brenda Beale, prin. Fax 445-3278

Erskine Academy 700/9-12
309 Windsor Rd 04358 207-445-2962
Donald Poulin, hdmstr. Fax 445-5520

South Paris, Oxford, Pop. 2,320
MSAD 17
Supt. — See Oxford
Oxford Hills Comprehensive HS 1,200/9-12
256 Main St 04281 207-743-8914
Theodore Moccia, prin. Fax 743-5326
Oxford Hills MS 600/7-8
100 Pine St 04281 207-743-5946
Harold Small, prin. Fax 743-8048

Oxford Hills Christian Academy 100/K-12
PO Box 318 04281 207-743-5970
Nancy Hanson, admin. Fax 743-9082

South Portland, Cumberland, Pop. 23,742
South Portland SD 3,000/K-12
130 Wescott Rd 04106 207-871-0555
Wendy Houlihan, supt. Fax 871-0559
www.spsd.org
Mahoney MS 300/6-8
240 Ocean St 04106 207-799-7386
Kathy Germani, prin. Fax 767-7731
Memorial MS 400/6-8
120 Wescott Rd 04106 207-773-5629
Megan Welter, prin. Fax 772-4597
South Portland HS 1,000/9-12
637 Highland Ave 04106 207-767-3266
Jeanne Crocker, prin. Fax 767-7713

Greater Portland Christian S 200/K-12
1338 Broadway 04106 207-767-5123
Mary Willink, prin. Fax 767-5124
Maine Medical Center Post-Sec.
SMTC Fort Rd 04106 207-767-9589
Southern Maine Community College Post-Sec.
2 Fort Rd 04106 207-741-5500

Stacyville, Penobscot
MSAD 25 400/K-12
PO Box 20, 207-365-4272
John Doe, supt. Fax 365-4334
www.khs.msad25.k12.me.us/
Katahdin MSHS 200/7-12
PO Box 50, 207-365-4218
Rae Bates, prin. Fax 365-6011

Standish, Cumberland
MSAD 6
Supt. — See Bar Mills
Bonny Eagle HS 1,300/9-12
700 Saco Rd 04084 207-929-3840
Robert Strong, prin. Fax 929-9147

St. Joseph's College of Maine Post-Sec.
278 Whites Bridge Rd 04084 207-892-6766

Sullivan, Hancock
Flanders Bay Community SD 300/9-12
2165 US Hwy 1 Ste 3 04664 207-422-3522
William Webster, supt. Fax 422-9568
Sumner Memorial HS 300/9-12
2456 US Hwy 1 04664 207-422-3510
Michael Eastman, prin. Fax 422-6463

Thomaston, Knox, Pop. 2,445
MSAD 50 1,000/K-12
12 Starr St 04861 207-354-2555
Judith Harvey, supt. Fax 354-2564
www.msad50.org/
Georges Valley HS 300/9-12
47 Valley St 04861 207-354-2502
Robert Beverage, prin. Fax 354-2369
Thomaston MS 200/5-8
65 Watts Ln 04861 207-354-6353
Mary-Alice McLean, prin. Fax 354-6238

Thorndike, Waldo
MSAD 3
Supt. — See Unity
Mt. View HS 500/9-12
577 Mount View Rd 04986 207-568-3255
Lynda Letteney, prin. Fax 568-7550
Mt. View JHS 300/7-8
575 Mount View Rd 04986 207-568-7561
Osmond Crowley, prin. Fax 568-7590

Topsham, Sagadahoc, Pop. 6,147
MSAD 75 3,200/K-12
50 Republic Ave 04086 207-729-9961
J. Michael Wilhelm Ed.D., supt. Fax 725-9354
www.link75.org/
Mt. Ararat HS 1,100/9-12
73 Eagles Way 04086 207-729-2951
Craig King, prin. Fax 729-2953
Mt. Ararat MS 700/6-8
66 Republic Ave 04086 207-729-2950
Brenda Brown, prin. Fax 729-2964

Trenton, Hancock

Life Christian Academy 100/PK-12
171 Bar Harbor Rd 04605 207-667-8622
Renee Clark, admin. Fax 664-0238

Turner, Androscoggin
MSAD 52 — 2,200/PK-12
486 Turner Ctr Rd 04282 — 207-225-3795
Thomas Hanson, supt. — Fax 225-5608
www.msad52.org
Leavitt Area HS — 800/9-12
21 Matthews Way 04282 — 207-225-3533
Patrick Hartnett, prin. — Fax 225-3978
Tripp MS — 400/7-8
65 Matthews Way 04282 — 207-225-3261
Scott Bell, prin. — Fax 225-2102

Unity, Waldo
MSAD 3 — 1,600/K-12
74 School St 04988 — 207-948-6136
Wayne Enman, supt. — Fax 948-2678
www.mvhs.sad3.k12.me.us
Other Schools – See Thorndike

Unity College — Post-Sec.
90 Quaker Hill Rd 04988 — 207-948-3131

Van Buren, Aroostook, Pop. 2,759
MSAD 24 — 400/PK-12
110 School Dr 04785 — 207-868-2746
Clayton Belanger, supt. — Fax 868-5420
Van Buren District HS — 200/7-12
169 Main St 04785 — 207-868-5274
Karla Michaud, prin. — Fax 868-3537
Van Buren Regional Technology Center — Vo/Tech
169 Main St 04785 — 207-868-2746
Clayton Belanger, prin. — Fax 868-5420

Vinalhaven, Knox
MSAD 8 — 200/K-12
22 Arcola Ln 04863 — 207-863-4800
George Joseph, supt. — Fax 863-4572
Vinalhaven S — 200/K-12
22 Arcola Ln 04863 — 207-863-4800
Fax 863-4572

Waldo, See Belfast
Applied Technology Region
Supt. — None
Waldo County Tech Center-Region 7 — Vo/Tech
1022 Waterville Rd 04915 — 207-342-5231
Paul Cochrane, prin. — Fax 342-4070

Waldoboro, Lincoln, Pop. 1,420
MSAD 40
Supt. — See Warren
Gray MS — 200/7-8
PO Box 326 04572 — 207-832-2106
Ben Vail, prin. — Fax 832-2108
Medomak Valley HS — 700/9-12
320 Manktown Rd 04572 — 207-832-5389
Robert Strong, prin. — Fax 832-2280

Wales, Androscoggin
Oak Hill Community SD
Supt. — See Sabattus
Oak Hill HS — 600/9-12
PO Box 400 04280 — 207-375-4950
Patricia Doyle, prin. — Fax 375-4048

Union SD 44 — 1,100/K-8
971 Gardiner Rd 04280 — 207-375-4273
Susan Hodgdon, supt. — Fax 375-2522
www.schoolunion44.org/index.html
Other Schools – See Litchfield, Sabattus

Warren, Knox
MSAD 40 — 2,100/K-12
44 School St 04864 — 207-273-4070
Pamela Carnahan, supt. — Fax 273-4143
shakespeare.mvhs.sad40.k12.me.us
Other Schools – See Waldoboro

Washburn, Aroostook
MSAD 45 — 400/PK-12
33 School St 04786 — 207-455-8301
Brooke Clenchy, supt. — Fax 455-8217
www.msad45.net/
Washburn District HS — 100/9-12
1359 Main St 04786 — 207-455-4501
Robert Doar, prin. — Fax 455-4509

Waterboro, York
MSAD 57 — 3,700/K-12
86 West Rd 04087 — 207-247-3221
Lynda Green, supt. — Fax 247-3477
fc.sad57.k12.me.us/
Massabesic HS — 1,200/9-12
88 West Rd 04087 — 207-247-3141
Deborah Mitchell, prin. — Fax 247-3146
Massabesic JHS — 600/7-8
PO Box 460 04087 — 207-247-6121
Mark Fisher, prin. — Fax 247-8621

Waterville, Kennebec, Pop. 15,621
Waterville SD — 2,000/K-12
25 Messalonskee Ave 04901 — 207-873-4281
Eric Haley, supt. — Fax 872-5531
www.wtvl.k12.me.us
Mid Maine Technical Center — Vo/Tech
3 Brooklyn Ave 04901 — 207-873-0102
Mark Powers, prin. — Fax 873-7057
Waterville HS — 700/9-12
1 Brooklyn Ave 04901 — 207-873-2751
Chris Hollingsworth, prin. — Fax 873-7058
Waterville JHS — 400/6-8
100 W River Rd 04901 — 207-873-2144
Peter Thiboutot, prin. — Fax 873-5752

Colby College — Post-Sec.
150 Mayflower Hill Dr 04901 — 207-872-3000
Pierre's School of Cosmetology — Post-Sec.
251 Kennedy Memorial Dr 04901 — 207-873-0682
Temple Academy — 100/K-12
60 W River Rd 04901 — 207-873-5325
Elise Rossignol, prin. — Fax 692-2659
Thomas College — Post-Sec.
180 W River Rd 04901 — 207-859-1110

Wells, York
Wells-Ogunquit Community SD — 1,500/K-12
PO Box 578 04090 — 207-646-8331
Edward McDonough, supt. — Fax 646-0314
www.wocsd.org/
Wells HS — 500/9-12
PO Box 579 04090 — 207-646-7011
Milton Teguis, prin. — Fax 646-4842
Wells JHS — 500/5-8
PO Box 310 04090 — 207-646-5142
Christopher Chessie, prin. — Fax 646-2899

York County Community College — Post-Sec.
PO Box 529 04090 — 207-646-9282

Westbrook, Cumberland, Pop. 16,108
Westbrook SD — 2,700/K-12
117 Stroudwater St 04092 — 207-854-0800
Stan Sawyer, supt. — Fax 854-0809
www.westbrookschools.org
Wescott JHS — 600/6-8
426 Bridge St 04092 — 207-854-0830
Brian Mazjanis, prin. — Fax 854-0858
Westbrook HS — 900/9-12
125 Stroudwater St 04092 — 207-854-0810
Marc Gousse, prin. — Fax 854-0812
Westbrook Regional Technology Center — Vo/Tech
125 Stroudwater St 04092 — 207-854-0820
Todd Fields, dir. — Fax 854-0822

Windham, Cumberland, Pop. 13,020
Windham SD — 2,800/K-12
228 Windham Center Rd 04062 — 207-892-1800
Sanford Prince, supt. — Fax 892-1805
www.windham.k12.me.us
Windham HS — 900/9-12
406 Gray Rd 04062 — 207-892-1810
Deborah McAfee, prin. — Fax 892-1813
Windham MS — 700/6-8
408 Gray Rd 04062 — 207-892-1820
Harold Shortsleeve, prin. — Fax 892-1826

Windham Christian Academy — 100/PK-12
1051 Roosevelt Trl 04062 — 207-892-2244
Roy Mickelson, prin. — Fax 893-1289

Winslow, Kennebec, Pop. 5,436
Union SD 52 — 2,500/K-12
20 Dean St 04901 — 207-872-1960
Elaine Miller, supt. — Fax 859-2405
www.su52.org/
Winslow HS — 600/9-12
20 Danielson St 04901 — 207-872-1990
Douglas Carville, prin. — Fax 872-1993
Winslow JHS — 300/6-8
6 Danielson St 04901 — 207-872-1973
Hugh Riordan, prin. — Fax 872-1977
Other Schools – See South China

Winterport, Waldo, Pop. 1,274
MSAD 22
Supt. — See Hampden
Wagner MS — 200/6-8
PO Box 739 04496 — 207-223-4309
Dale Williams, prin. — Fax 223-4325

Winthrop, Kennebec, Pop. 2,819
Winthrop SD — 900/PK-12
17A Highland Ave 04364 — 207-377-2296
Mark LaRoach, supt. — Fax 377-3915
www.winthrop.k12.me.us
Winthrop HS — 300/9-12
211 Rambler Rd 04364 — 207-377-2228
Kevin Harrington, prin. — Fax 377-7486
Winthrop MS — 200/6-8
400 Rambler Rd 04364 — 207-377-2249
Karen Criss, prin. — Fax 377-3667

Wiscasset, Lincoln, Pop. 1,233
Wiscasset SD — 800/K-12
214 Gardiner Rd 04578 — 207-882-6303
Jay McIntire, supt. — Fax 882-4077
www.wiscasset.k12.me.us
Wiscasset HS — 400/9-12
272 Gardiner Rd 04578 — 207-882-7722
Susan Poppish, prin. — Fax 882-8251
Wiscasset MS — 200/5-8
83 Federal St 04578 — 207-882-7767
Linda Bleile, prin. — Fax 882-8279

Yarmouth, Cumberland, Pop. 3,338
Yarmouth SD — 1,400/K-12
101 McCartney St 04096 — 207-846-5586
Ken Murphy Ed.D., supt. — Fax 846-2339
www.yarmouth.k12.me.us
Harrison MS — 400/5-8
220 McCartney St 04096 — 207-846-2499
Bruce Brann, prin. — Fax 846-2489
Yarmouth HS — 500/9-12
286 W Elm St 04096 — 207-846-5535
Edward Hall, prin. — Fax 846-2326

North Yarmouth Academy — 300/6-12
148 Main St 04096 — 207-846-9051
Peter Mertz, hdmstr. — Fax 846-8829

York, York, Pop. 9,818
York SD — 2,000/K-12
469 US Route 1 03909 — 207-363-3403
Henry Scipione, supt. — Fax 363-5602
www.yorkschools.org/
York HS — 700/9-12
1 Robert Stevens Dr 03909 — 207-363-3621
Robert Stevens, prin. — Fax 363-1809
York MS — 700/5-8
30 Organug Rd 03909 — 207-363-4214
Stephen Bishop, prin. — Fax 363-1815

MARYLAND

MARYLAND DEPARTMENT OF EDUCATION
200 W Baltimore St, Baltimore 21201
Telephone 410-767-0600
Fax 410-333-6033
Website http://www.marylandpublicschools.org

Superintendent of Schools Nancy Grasmick

MARYLAND BOARD OF EDUCATION
200 W Baltimore St, Baltimore 21201

President Dunbar Brooks

PUBLIC, PRIVATE AND CATHOLIC SECONDARY SCHOOLS

Aberdeen, Harford, Pop. 14,305
Harford County SD
Supt. — See Bel Air
Aberdeen HS 1,400/9-12
251 Paradise Rd 21001 410-273-5500
Thomas M. Szerensits, prin. Fax 273-5587
Aberdeen MS 1,300/6-8
111 Mount Royal Ave 21001 410-273-5510
Chandra Krantz, prin. Fax 273-5542

Abingdon, Harford

New Covenant Christian S 200/K-12
128 Saint Marys Church Rd 21009 443-512-0771
Jason Van Bemmel, admin. Fax 569-3846

Accident, Garrett, Pop. 340
Garrett County SD
Supt. — See Oakland
Northern Garrett County HS 600/9-12
86 Pride Pkwy 21520 301-746-8668
Gary Reichenbecher, prin. Fax 746-8942
Northern MS 500/6-8
371 Pride Pkwy 21520 301-746-8165
William Carlson, prin. Fax 746-8865
Northern Evening HS Adult
86 Pride Pkwy 21520 301-746-8668
Gary Reichenbecher, prin.

Accokeek, Prince George's, Pop. 4,477
Prince George's County SD
Supt. — See Upper Marlboro
Burroughs MS 800/6-8
14400 Berry Rd 20607 301-203-3200
George Covington, prin. Fax 203-3207

Adelphi, Prince George's, Pop. 13,524
Prince George's County SD
Supt. — See Upper Marlboro
Buck Lodge MS 800/7-8
2611 Buck Lodge Rd 20783 301-431-6290
Dr. Constance Gibb, prin. Fax 445-8404

Annapolis, Anne Arundel, Pop. 36,300
Anne Arundel County SD 73,600/PK-12
2644 Riva Rd 21401 410-222-5000
Kevin Maxwell Ph.D., supt. Fax 222-5602
www.aacps.org/
Annapolis HS 1,700/9-12
2700 Riva Rd 21401 410-266-5240
Donald Lilley, prin. Fax 266-5644
Annapolis MS 500/6-8
1399 Forest Dr 21403 410-267-8658
Carolyn Burton-Page, prin. Fax 267-8924
Bates MS 600/6-8
701 Chase St 21401 410-263-0270
Diane Bragdon, prin. Fax 263-0295
Broadneck HS 2,200/9-12
1265 Green Holly Dr, 410-757-1300
Lucinda Hudson, prin. Fax 757-5621
Other Schools – See Arnold, Baltimore, Crofton, Edgewater, Fort Meade, Gambrills, Glen Burnie, Harwood, Linthicum Heights, Lothian, Millersville, Odenton, Pasadena, Severn, Severna Park

---

Annapolis Area Christian S 1,000/PK-12
716 Bestgate Rd 21401 410-266-8251
Larry Kooi, supt. Fax 573-6866
Key S 700/PK-12
534 Hillsmere Dr 21403 410-263-9231
Marcella Yedid, hdmstr. Fax 280-5516
St. John's College Post-Sec.
PO Box 2800 21404 410-263-2371
St. Mary HS 600/9-12
113 Duke Of Gloucester St 21401 410-263-3294
Dr. Charles Reiter, prin. Fax 269-7843
United States Naval Academy Post-Sec.
121 Blake Rd 21402 410-293-1000

Arnold, Anne Arundel, Pop. 20,261
Anne Arundel County SD
Supt. — See Annapolis
Magothy River MS 800/6-8
241 Peninsula Farm Rd Ste 1 21012 410-544-0926
Christopher Mirenzi, prin. Fax 544-1867
Severn River MS 900/6-8
241 Peninsula Farm Rd Ste 2 21012 410-544-0922
Patrick Bathras, prin.

Anne Arundel Community College Post-Sec.
101 College Pkwy 21012 410-647-7100

Baltimore, Baltimore, Pop. 635,815
Anne Arundel County SD
Supt. — See Annapolis
Brooklyn Park MS 600/6-8
200 Hammonds Ln 21225 410-636-2967
Raymond Bibeault, prin.

Baltimore CSD 80,500/PK-12
200 E North Ave 21202 410-396-8700
Charlene Boston Ph.D., admin. Fax 396-8898
www.bcps.k12.md.us
Academy for College & Career Exploration 9-12
1300 W 36th St 21211 410-396-7607
Ivor Mitchell, prin. Fax 426-6750
Acceleration Academy at Gwynn Oak 9-12
5000 Gwynn Oak Ave 21207 410-396-8898
Al Thompson, prin.
Baltimore City College HS 1,500/9-12
3220 The Alameda 21218 410-396-6557
Tim Dawson, prin. Fax 243-0669
Baltimore Freedom Academy 200/9-12
101 S Caroline St 21231 443-984-2737
Tisha Edwards, prin. Fax 675-5205
Baltimore Polytechnic Institute Vo/Tech
1400 W Cold Spring Ln 21209 410-396-7026
Dr. Barney Wilson, prin. Fax 235-5027
Baltimore S for the Arts 300/9-12
712 Cathedral St 21201 410-396-1185
Leslie Shepard, prin. Fax 539-1430
Baltimore Urban League 9-12
520 Orchard St 21201 410-523-8150
Aisha Burgess, prin.
Banks HS 9-12
5000 Truesdale Rd 21206 443-984-1541
Anthony Harold, prin. Fax 254-7455
Calverton MS 1,000/6-8
1100 Whitmore Ave 21216 410-396-0581
Marjorie Miles, prin. Fax 545-7849
Canton MS 400/6-8
801 S Highland Ave 21224 410-396-9172
Tammie Nielsen, prin.
Career Academy Vo/Tech
101 W 24th St 21218 410-396-7454
Callie Green, prin.
Carver Voc-Tech HS Vo/Tech
2201 Pressman St 21216 410-396-0553
Michael Frederick, prin. Fax 396-0059
Central Career Academy at Briscoe Vo/Tech
900 Druid Hill Ave 21201 410-396-0771
Patricia Lowe Gould, prin. Fax 396-0317
Chinquapin MS 900/6-8
900 Woodbourne Ave 21212 410-396-6424
John Wilson, prin. Fax 396-0381
Diggs-Johnson MS 200/8-9
1300 Herkimer St 21223 410-396-1572
Camille Smith, prin. Fax 385-0340
Digital Harbor HS 700/9-12
1100 Covington St 21230 443-984-1256
Brian Eyer, prin. Fax 539-7270
Douglass HS 1,200/9-12
2301 Gwynns Falls Pkwy 21217 410-396-7821
Darline Lyles, prin. Fax 523-7557
Dunbar HS 600/9-12
1400 Orleans St 21231 410-396-9478
Roger Shaw, prin. Fax 545-7526
Dunbar MS 500/6-8
500 N Caroline St 21205 410-396-9296
Crystal Ashe, prin. Fax 396-2954
Edmondson-Westside HS 1,100/9-12
501 N Athol Ave Ste 1 21229 410-396-0685
Delphine Lee, prin. Fax 545-7715
Entrepreneurial Academy 9-12
2000 Edgewood St 21216 410-984-3330
Rose Hamm, prin.
Fallstaff MS 6-8
3801 Fallstaff Rd 21215 410-396-0682
Faith Hibbert, prin. Fax 545-1737
Forest Park HS 800/9-12
3701 Eldorado Ave 21207 410-396-0753
Loretta Breese, prin. Fax 396-0143
Franklin MS 400/6-8
1201 Cambria St 21225 410-396-1373
Paul Llufrio, prin. Fax 396-8434
Garrison MS 900/6-8
3910 Barrington Rd 21207 410-396-0735
Isiah Hemphill, prin. Fax 545-7861
Hamilton MS 900/6-8
5609 Sefton Ave 21214 410-396-6370
Fax 396-6561
Harbor City East HS 300/9-12
2555 Harford Rd 21218 410-396-1513
Magdalen Reyment, prin.
Harford Heights MS 6-8
1919 N Broadway 21213 410-396-9343
Diane Brown, prin.
Harlem Park MS 700/6-8
1500 Harlem Ave 21217 410-396-0612
Teresa Lance, prin. Fax 669-5815
Heritage HS 300/9-12
2801 Saint Lo Dr 21213 410-396-6637
Karen Lawrence, prin. Fax 467-5560
Independence HS 9-12
1250 W 36th St 21211 410-467-1090
Helen Atkinson, prin.
Johnson HS, 2801 Saint Lo Dr 21213 9-12
Tricia Rock, prin. 410-396-6643
Lemmel MS 900/6-8
2801 N Dukeland St 21216 410-396-0664
Quianna Cooke, prin. Fax 225-9457
Lewis HS, 6401 Pioneer Dr 21214 600/9-12
Jean Ragin, prin. 410-545-1746
Lombard MS 600/6-8
1601 E Lombard St 21231 410-396-9261
Valerie Hooper, prin. Fax 396-9039
Maritime Academy 9-12
790 W North Ave 21217 410-396-0242
Marco Clark, prin.
Marshall HS 500/9-12
5000 Truesdale Rd 21206 410-396-5938
Russell Williams, prin.
Marshall MS 700/6-8
5001 Sinclair Ln 21206 410-396-9103
Tony Edwards, prin. Fax 396-6153
Mergenthaler Vo-Tech HS Vo/Tech
3500 Hillen Rd 21218 410-396-6496
Dr. Irby Miller, prin. Fax 243-5354
New Era Academy 100/9-12
2700 Seamon Ave 21225 443-984-2415
John Davis, prin. Fax 355-1130
Northeast MS 700/6-8
5001 Moravia Rd 21206 410-396-9215
Wanda Young, prin. Fax 396-1680
Northwestern HS 1,200/9-12
6900 Park Heights Ave 21215 410-396-0646
Tajah Gross, prin. Fax 396-0866
Paquin S 200/PK-PK, 1-
2200 Sinclair Ln 21213 410-396-9399
Rosetta Stith, prin. Fax 522-2229
Patterson HS 1,800/9-12
100 Kane St 21224 410-396-9276
Laura D'Anna, prin. Fax 633-0179
Pimlico MS 800/6-8
3500 W Northern Pkwy 21215 410-396-0806
Donyall Dickey, prin. Fax 396-0580
Poole MS 400/6-8
1300 W 36th St 21211 410-396-6456
Danielle Lee, prin. Fax 396-7009
Renaissance Academy 9-12
1301 McCulloh St 21217 443-984-3164
Karl Perry, prin.
Savage Institute of Visual Arts 9-12
200 Font Hill Ave 21223 443-984-2833
Angelique Marcus, prin.
Southeast MS 500/6-8
6820 Fait Ave 21224 410-396-9291
Barbara Sparrow, prin. Fax 284-4947
Southwestern HS 900/9-12
200 Font Hill Ave 21223 410-396-1422
Cecelia McDaniel, prin. Fax 396-0209
Stadium S, 1300 Gorsuch Ave 21218 4-8
Ronald Shelly, dir. 443-984-2682

Talent Development S 100/9-12
1500 Harlem Ave 21217 443-984-2744
Jeffrey Robinson, prin.
Thomas Medical Arts Academy 9-12
100 N Calhoun St 21223 410-984-2831
Starletta Jackson, prin.
Upton S 200/K-12
6900 Park Heights Ave 21215 410-396-0775
Fax 225-9005
Walbrook Liberal Arts Academy 200/9-12
2000 Edgewood St 21216 410-396-0723
Lamarge Wyatt, prin.
Washington MS 700/6-8
1301 McCulloh St 21217 410-396-7734
Derek Daniel, prin. Fax 396-0552
W.E.B. Dubois HS 600/9-12
2201 Pinewood Ave 21214 410-396-6435
Delores Berry, prin. Fax 254-5936
West Baltimore MS 1,100/6-8
201 N Bend Rd 21229 410-396-0700
Faye McLean, prin. Fax 396-7700
Western HS 900/9-12
4600 Falls Rd 21209 410-396-7040
Eleanor Matthews, prin. Fax 396-7492
Winston MS 600/6-8
1101 Winston Ave 21212 410-396-6356
Eldon Thomas, prin. Fax 532-6584

Baltimore County SD
Supt. — See Towson
Arbutus MS 900/6-8
5525 Shelbourne Rd 21227 410-887-1402
Kendra Johnson, prin. Fax 536-1164
Carver Center for Arts & Technology 700/9-12
938 York Rd 21204 410-887-2775
Karen Steele, prin. Fax 769-9114
Catonsville HS 1,500/9-12
421 Bloomsbury Ave 21228 410-887-0808
Robert Tomback, prin. Fax 747-9473
Chesapeake HS 1,000/9-12
1801 Turkey Point Rd 21221 410-887-0100
Maria Lowry, prin. Fax 682-3426
Deep Creek MS 800/6-8
1000 S Marlyn Ave 21221 410-887-0112
Anissa Brown-Dennis, prin. Fax 391-6534
Dumbarton MS 900/6-8
300 Dumbarton Rd Ste 1 21212 410-887-3176
Nancy Fink, prin. Fax 887-3176
Dundalk HS 1,400/9-12
1901 Delvale Ave 21222 410-887-7023
Margaret Johnson, prin. Fax 887-7025
Dundalk MS 600/6-8
7400 Dunmanway 21222 410-887-7018
Thomas Shouldice, prin. Fax 887-7284
Eastern Technical HS 1,300/9-12
1100 Mace Ave 21221 410-887-0190
Patrick McCusker, prin. Fax 887-0424
Golden Ring MS 800/6-8
6700 Kenwood Ave 21237 410-887-0130
John Bowden, prin. Fax 682-6750
Holabird MS 700/6-8
1701 Delvale Ave 21222 410-887-7049
Susan Melton, prin. Fax 887-7275
Kenwood HS 1,900/9-12
501 Stemmers Run Rd 21221 410-887-0153
Paul Martin, prin. Fax 887-6382
Lansdowne HS Academy 1,200/9-12
3800 Hollins Ferry Rd 21227 410-887-1415
Lynda Whitlock, prin. Fax 887-1461
Lansdowne MS 800/6-8
2400 Lansdowne Rd 21227 410-887-1411
Barbara Shields, prin. Fax 887-1412
Loch Raven HS 1,100/9-12
1212 Cowpens Ave 21286 410-887-3525
Jacqueline Lamp, prin. Fax 887-5898
Loch Raven Technical Academy 900/6-8
8101 Lasalle Rd 21286 410-887-3518
Linda Wilson, prin. Fax 821-6398
Middle River MS 900/6-8
800 Middle River Rd 21220 410-887-0165
Donna Vlachos, prin. Fax 887-0167
Milford Mill Academy 1,400/9-12
3800 Washington Ave 21244 410-887-0660
Nathaniel Gibson, prin. Fax 887-0681
Old Court MS 1,200/6-8
4627 Old Court Rd 21208 410-887-0742
I. Lynette Woodley, prin. Fax 887-0670
Overlea HS 1,200/9-12
5401 Kenwood Ave 21206 410-887-5241
Elizabeth Parker, prin. Fax 661-0174
Parkville MS 1,100/6-8
8711 Avondale Rd 21234 410-887-5250
Stephen Edgar, prin. Fax 887-5315
Patapsco HS & Center for the Arts 1,600/9-12
8100 Wise Ave 21222 410-887-7060
Edmund Mitzel, prin. Fax 887-7062
Perry Hall HS 2,300/9-12
4601 Ebenezer Rd 21236 410-887-5108
Brian Gonzalez, prin. Fax 887-5116
Perry Hall MS 1,500/6-8
4300 Ebenezer Rd 21236 410-887-5100
Allen Zink, prin. Fax 887-5152
Pikesville HS 1,100/9-12
7621 Labyrinth Rd 21208 410-887-1217
Barbara Walker, prin. Fax 486-8436
Pikesville MS 1,100/6-8
7701 7 Mile Ln 21208 410-887-1207
Maria Talarigo, prin. Fax 887-1259
Pine Grove MS 1,200/6-8
9200 Old Harford Rd 21234 410-887-5270
Laura Newkirk, prin. Fax 668-5237
Sollers Point Technical HS Vo/Tech
325 Sollers Point Rd 21222 410-887-7075
Diane Young, prin. Fax 887-7238
Southwest Academy 1,300/6-8
6200 Johnnycake Rd 21207 410-887-0825
Kevin Roberts, prin. Fax 887-0829
Sparrows Point HS 800/9-12
7400 N Point Rd 21219 410-887-7517
Robert Santa Croce, prin. Fax 887-7533
Sparrows Point MS 600/6-8
7400 N Point Rd 21219 410-887-7524
John Foley, prin. Fax 477-6953
Stemmers Run MS 900/6-8
201 Stemmers Run Rd 21221 410-887-0177
John Ward, prin. Fax 918-1787
Stricker MS 900/6-8
7855 Trappe Rd 21222 410-887-7038
Deborah Klaus, prin. Fax 285-1864
Sudbrook Magnet MS 1,000/6-8
4300 Bedford Rd 21208 410-887-6720
Sharon Robbins, prin. Fax 887-6737
Towson HS 1,500/9-12
69 Cedar Ave 21286 410-887-3608
Dr. Jane Barranger, prin. Fax 583-1375
Western S of Technology 1,100/9-12
100 Kenwood Ave 21228 410-887-0840
Richard Jester, prin. Fax 887-1024
Windsor Mill MS 6-8
8300 Windsor Mill Rd 21244 410-887-0618
Deborah Phelps, prin. Fax 496-1308
Woodlawn HS 2,000/9-12
1801 Woodlawn Dr 21207 410-887-1309
Edward Weglein, prin. Fax 887-1324
Woodlawn MS 900/6-8
3033 Saint Lukes Ln 21207 410-887-1304
Brian Scriven, prin. Fax 298-4352

All-State Career School Post-Sec.
2200 Broening Hwy Ste 160 21224 410-631-1818
Archbishop Curley HS 600/9-12
3701 Sinclair Ln 21213 410-485-5000
Barry Brownlee, prin. Fax 483-2545
Arlington Baptist S 200/K-12
3030 N Rolling Rd 21244 410-655-9300
Dennis Layton, admin. Fax 496-3901
Bais Hamedrash & Mesivta S of Baltimore 100/9-12
6823 Old Pimlico Rd 21209 410-486-0006
Sholom Salfer, prin. Fax 602-9738
Bais Yaakov Eva Winer HS 9-12
6302 Smith Ave 21209 443-548-7700
Rabbi Yechezkel Zweig, prin. Fax 548-6340
Baltimore Actors Theatre Conservatory 50/K-12
300 Dumbarton Rd Ste 2 21212 410-337-8519
Fax 337-8582
Baltimore City Community College Post-Sec.
2901 Liberty Heights Ave 21215 410-462-8000
Baltimore Hebrew University Post-Sec.
5800 Park Heights Ave 21215 410-578-6900
Baltimore International College Post-Sec.
17 Commerce St 21202 410-752-4710
Baltimore School of Massage Post-Sec.
6401 Dogwood Rd 21207 410-944-8855
Baltimore Studio of Hair Design Post-Sec.
318 N Howard St 21201 410-539-1935
Beren HS 200/9-12
400 Mount Wilson Ln 21208 410-484-7200
Jacob Schuchman, prin. Fax 484-3060
Beth Tfiloh Dahan Community S 1,100/PK-12
3300 Old Court Rd 21208 410-486-1905
Zipora Schorr, dir. Fax 415-6348
Boys Latin S of Maryland 600/K-12
822 W Lake Ave 21210 410-377-5192
Dr. H. Mebane Turner, hdmstr. Fax 377-4312
Broadcasting Institute of Maryland Post-Sec.
7200 Harford Rd 21234 410-254-2770
Bryn Mawr S 900/PK-12
109 W Melrose Ave 21210 410-323-8800
Maureen Walsh, hdmstr. Fax 377-8963
Calvert Hall College HS 1,100/9-12
8102 La Salle Rd 21286 410-825-4266
Louis Heidrick, prin. Fax 825-6826
Cardinal Gibbons S 6-12
3225 Wilkens Ave 21229 410-644-1770
Philip Forte, prin. Fax 525-3757
Catholic HS of Baltimore 300/9-12
2800 Edison Hwy 21213 410-732-6200
Keith Harmeyer, prin. Fax 732-7639
College of Notre Dame of Maryland Post-Sec.
4701 N Charles St 21210 410-435-0100
Community College of Baltimore County Post-Sec.
7200 Sollers Point Rd 21222 410-282-6700
Community College of Baltimore County Post-Sec.
7201 Rossville Blvd 21237 410-682-6000
Coppin State University Post-Sec.
2500 W North Ave 21216 410-951-3000
Cristo Rey Jesuit HS 9-12
801 Saint Paul St 21202 410-727-3258
Tom Malone, prin.
Empire Beauty School Post-Sec.
5633 Reisterstown Rd 21215 410-358-4500
Forbush S 300/PK-12
6501 N Charles St 21204 410-938-4400
James Truscello, dir. Fax 938-4421
Friends S of Baltimore 1,000/PK-12
5114 N Charles St 21210 410-649-3200
Matthew Micciche, hdmstr. Fax 649-3213
Gilman S 1,000/PK-12
5407 Roland Ave Ste 1 21210 410-323-3800
Jon McGill, prin. Fax 864-2812
Goucher College Post-Sec.
1021 Dulaney Valley Rd 21204 410-337-6000
Greater Baltimore Medical Center Post-Sec.
6701 N Charles St 21204 410-828-2121
Institute of Notre Dame 400/9-12
901 N Aisquith St 21202 410-522-7800
Anne Seeley, prin. Fax 522-7810
Johns Hopkins University Post-Sec.
600 N Wolfe St 21287 410-955-3182
Johns Hopkins University Post-Sec.
3400 N Charles St 21218 410-516-8000
Kingdom Academy 200/K-12
7000B Rossville Blvd 21237 410-391-8000
Bob McDermott, admin. Fax 391-3090
Loyola College Post-Sec.
4501 N Charles St 21210 410-617-2000
Maryland Beauty Academy of Essex Post-Sec.
505 Eastern Blvd 21221 410-686-4477
Maryland General Hospital Post-Sec.
827 Linden Ave 21201 410-995-8600
Maryland Institute College of Art Post-Sec.
1300 W Mount Royal Ave 21217 410-669-9200
Maryland School for the Blind Post-Sec.
3501 Taylor Ave 21236
Mercy HS 500/9-12
1300 E Northern Pkwy 21239 410-433-8880
Sr. Carol Wheeler, prin. Fax 323-8816
Mercy Hospital Post-Sec.
301 Saint Paul St 21202 410-332-9202
Morgan State University Post-Sec.
1700 E Cold Spring Ln 21251 443-885-3333
Mother Seton Academy 100/6-8
724 S Ann St 21231 410-563-2833
Sr. Eileen Clinton, prin. Fax 563-7353
Mt. St. Joseph HS 1,200/9-12
4403 Frederick Ave 21229 410-644-3300
Barry Fitzpatrick, prin. Fax 646-6221
Mt. Zion Baptist Christian S 300/PK-12
2000 E Belvedere Ave 21239 410-426-2309
Shawn Floyd, prin. Fax 426-5412
National Technological University Post-Sec.
1001 Fleet St 21202 410-843-6401
Ner Israel Rabbinical College Post-Sec.
400 Mount Wilson Ln 21208 410-484-7200
North American Trade Schools Post-Sec.
6901 Security Blvd Ste 16 21244 410-298-4844
Our Lady of Mt. Carmel HS 300/9-12
1706 Old Eastern Ave 21221 410-686-1023
Kathleen Sipes, prin. Fax 686-2361
Peabody Institute Johns Hopkins Univ. Post-Sec.
1 E Mount Vernon Pl 21202 410-659-8150
Purpose & Potential Christian Arts Acad 100/PK-12
5532 Harford Rd 21214 410-444-2899
Patricia Matthews, prin. Fax 444-1434
Rabbi Steinberg MS 300/6-8
6300 Smith Ave 21209 443-548-7700
Rabbi Naftoli Hexter, prin. Fax 548-0347
Roland Park Country S 700/K-12
5204 Roland Ave 21210 410-323-5500
Jean Brune, hdmstr. Fax 323-2164
St. Frances Academy 300/9-12
501 E Chase St 21202 410-539-5794
Sr. Marcia Hall, prin. Fax 685-2650
St. Ignatius Loyola Academy 100/6-8
740 N Calvert St 21202 410-539-8268
Christopher Wilson, prin. Fax 539-4821
St. Mary's Seminary & University Post-Sec.
5400 Roland Ave 21210 410-864-4000
Seton Keough HS 500/9-12
1201 Caton Ave Ste 1 21227 410-646-4444
Dr. Curtis Turner, prin. Fax 573-0107
Sisters Academy of Baltimore 5-8
146 2nd Ave 21227 410-242-1212
Sr. Debra Liesen, prin. Fax 242-5104
Sojourner-Douglass College Post-Sec.
500 N Caroline St 21205 410-276-0306
Talmudical Academy 600/K-12
4445 Old Court Rd 21208 410-484-6600
Rabbi Zvi Teichman, prin. Fax 484-5717
TESST College of Technology Post-Sec.
1520 S Caton Ave 21227 410-644-6400
Union Memorial Hospital Post-Sec.
201 E University Pkwy 21218 410-554-2739
University of Baltimore Post-Sec.
1420 N Charles St 21201 410-837-4200
University of Maryland Post-Sec.
520 W Lombard St 21201 410-706-3100
University of Maryland Post-Sec.
1000 Hilltop Cir 21250 410-455-1000
Yeshivas Lev Shlomo 200/10-12
7201 Park Heights Ave 21208 410-764-6500
Rabbi Aryeh Meister, prin. Fax 764-8871
Yeshivat Rambam/Maimonides Academy 300/PK-12
6300 Park Heights Ave 21215 410-358-6091
Dr. Rita Shloush, hdmstr. Fax 358-4229

Bel Air, Harford, Pop. 10,014

Harford County SD 39,600/PK-12
102 S Hickory Ave 21014 410-838-7300
Jacqueline Haas, supt. Fax 893-2478
www.hcps.org/
Bel Air HS 1,600/9-12
100 Heighe St 21014 410-638-4600
Joseph Voshkuhl, prin. Fax 638-4604
Bel Air MS 1,400/6-8
99 Idlewild St 21014 410-638-4140
Nancy Reynolds, prin. Fax 638-4144
Harford Technical HS Vo/Tech
200 Thomas Run Rd 21015 410-638-3804
Charles Hagan, prin. Fax 638-3820
Patterson Mill MSHS 6-12
85 Patterson Mill Rd 21015 410-809-6078
Wayne Thibeault, prin. Fax 588-5294
Southampton MS 1,500/6-8
1200 Moores Mill Rd 21014 410-638-4150
Barb Canavan, prin. Fax 638-4305
Wright HS 1,900/9-12
1301 N Fountain Green Rd 21015 410-638-4110
William Ekey, prin. Fax 638-4114
Other Schools – See Aberdeen, Edgewood, Fallston, Havre de Grace, Joppa, Pylesville

---

Carroll S 900/9-12
703 E Churchville Rd 21014 410-838-8333
Paul G. Barker, prin. Fax 836-8514
Harford Community College Post-Sec.
401 Thomas Run Rd 21015 410-836-4000
Harford Lutheran S 100/6-10
1515 Emmorton Rd 21014 410-399-9646
David Smith, prin. Fax 399-9645

International Beauty School Post-Sec.
227 Archer St 21014 410-838-0845
John Carroll HS 800/9-12
703 E Churchville Rd 21014 410-879-2480
Paul Barker, prin. Fax 836-8514

Beltsville, Prince George's, Pop. 14,476
Prince George's County SD
Supt. — See Upper Marlboro
High Point HS 2,400/9-12
3601 Powder Mill Rd 20705 301-572-6400
Scott Smith, prin. Fax 572-6481
King MS 1,000/7-8
4545 Ammendale Rd 20705 301-572-0650
Robin Wiltison, prin. Fax 572-0668

TESST Technology Institute Post-Sec.
4600 Powder Mill Rd Ste 500 20705 301-937-8448

Berlin, Worcester, Pop. 3,711
Worcester County SD
Supt. — See Newark
Decatur HS 1,400/9-12
9913 Seahawk Rd 21811 410-641-2171
Louis Taylor, prin. Fax 641-1135
Decatur MS 700/7-8
9815 Seahawk Rd 21811 410-641-2846
Mel Ross, prin. Fax 641-3274

Worcester Preparatory S 600/PK-12
508 S Main St 21811 410-641-3575
Dr. Barry W. Tull, hdmstr. Fax 641-3586
Wor-Wic Community College Post-Sec.
10452 Old Ocean City Blvd 7 21811 410-641-4134

Bethesda, Montgomery, Pop. 55,277
Montgomery County SD
Supt. — See Rockville
Bethesda-Chevy Chase HS 1,700/9-12
4301 E West Hwy 20814 240-497-6300
Sean Bulson, prin. Fax 497-6306
Johnson HS 2,000/9-12
6400 Rock Spring Dr 20814 301-571-6900
Dr. Christopher Garran, prin. Fax 571-6916
North Bethesda MS 700/6-8
8935 Bradmoor Dr 20817 301-571-3883
Alton E. Sumner, prin. Fax 571-3881
Pyle MS 1,300/6-8
6311 Wilson Ln 20817 301-320-6540
Michael Zarchin, prin. Fax 320-6647
Westland MS 900/6-8
5511 Massachusetts Ave 20816 301-320-6515
Daniel Vogelman, prin. Fax 320-7054
Whitman HS 1,900/9-12
7100 Whittier Blvd 20817 301-320-6600
Dr. Alan Goodwin, prin. Fax 320-6594

DeVry University Post-Sec.
4550 Montgomery Ave Ste 100 20814 301-652-8477
Holton-Arms S 700/3-12
7303 River Rd 20817 301-365-5300
Susanna Jones, prin. Fax 365-6085
Landon S 700/3-12
6101 Wilson Ln 20817 301-320-3200
David Armstrong, prin. Fax 320-2787
Lycee Rochambeau 1,100/K-12
9600 Forest Rd 20814 301-530-8260
Martine Quelen, prin. Fax 564-5779
Stone Ridge S of the Sacred Heart 700/PK-12
9101 Rockville Pike 20814 301-657-4322
Dr. Richard Barbieri, hdmstr. Fax 657-2381
Washington Conservatory of Music Post-Sec.
1 Westmoreland Cir 20816 202-320-2770
Washington Waldorf S 300/PK-12
4800 Sangamore Rd 20816 301-229-6107
Fax 229-9379

Bladensburg, Prince George's, Pop. 7,918
Prince George's County SD
Supt. — See Upper Marlboro
Bladensburg HS 1,800/9-12
4200 57th Ave 20710 301-887-6700
Andrea Philips-Hughes, prin. Fax 887-6710

Elizabeth Seton HS 500/9-12
5715 Emerson St 20710 301-864-4532
Sharon Pasterick, prin. Fax 864-8946

Boonsboro, Washington, Pop. 2,982
Washington County SD
Supt. — See Hagerstown
Boonsboro HS 1,000/9-12
10 Campus Ave 21713 301-766-8022
Martin Green, prin. Fax 791-4138
Boonsboro MS 800/6-8
1 J H Wade Dr 21713 301-766-8038
Paul Engle, prin. Fax 432-2644

Bowie, Prince George's, Pop. 53,878
Prince George's County SD
Supt. — See Upper Marlboro
Bowie HS 2,800/9-12
15200 Annapolis Rd 20715 301-805-2600
John Birckhead, prin. Fax 805-2619
Ogle MS 100/6-8
4111 Chelmont Ln 20715 301-805-2641
Kathleen Brady, prin. Fax 805-6674
Tall Oaks Vocational HS Vo/Tech
2112 Church Rd 20721 301-390-0230
Dr. Larry McCray, prin. Fax 390-0228
Tasker MS 1,500/7-8
4901 Collington Rd 20715 301-805-2660
Karen Coley, prin. Fax 805-2663

Belair Baptist Christian Academy 100/K-12
PO Box 796 20718 301-262-0578
Gary Kohl, admin. Fax 262-0578

Bowie State University Post-Sec.
14000 Jericho Park Rd 20715 301-464-3000

Brandywine, Prince George's, Pop. 1,406
Prince George's County SD
Supt. — See Upper Marlboro
Gwynn Park HS 1,500/9-12
13800 Brandywine Rd 20613 301-372-0140
Carletta Marrow, prin. Fax 372-0149
Gwynn Park MS 600/7-8
8000 Dyson Rd 20613 301-372-0120
Warren Tweedy, prin. Fax 372-0119

Brooklandville, Baltimore

Maryvale Prep HS 400/6-12
11300 Falls Rd 21022 410-252-3366
Sr. Shawn Marie Maguire, hdmstr. Fax 252-3740
Park S 900/PK-12
PO Box 8200 21022 410-339-7070
Fax 339-4125
St. Paul's S for Boys 900/PK-12
PO Box 8100 21022 410-825-4400
Thomas J. Reid, hdmstr. Fax 427-0390
St. Paul's S for Girls 500/K-12
PO Box 8100 21022 410-823-6323
Monica M. Gillespie Ph.D., hdmstr. Fax 828-7238

Brunswick, Frederick, Pop. 5,242
Frederick County SD
Supt. — See Frederick
Brunswick HS 900/9-12
101 Cummings Dr 21716 240-236-8600
Kristi Mitchell, prin. Fax 236-8601
Brunswick MS 600/6-8
301 Cummings Dr 21716 240-236-5400
Brian Vasquenza, prin. Fax 236-5401

Burtonsville, Montgomery, Pop. 5,853
Montgomery County SD
Supt. — See Rockville
Banneker MS 900/6-8
14800 Perrywood Dr 20866 301-989-5747
Samuel A. Rivera, prin. Fax 879-1032
Paint Branch HS 1,800/9-12
14121 Old Columbia Pike 20866 301-989-5600
Jeanette E. Dixon, prin. Fax 989-5609

California, Saint Mary's, Pop. 7,626

Blades School of Hair Design Post-Sec.
PO Box 226 20619 301-862-9797

Callaway, Saint Mary's

King's Christian Academy 300/K-12
20738 Point Lookout Rd 20620 301-994-3080
Sarah Patterson, admin. Fax 994-3087

Cambridge, Dorchester, Pop. 11,089
Dorchester County SD 4,800/PK-12
PO Box 619 21613 410-228-4747
Fred Hildenbrand, supt. Fax 228-1847
www.dcps.k12.md.us
Cambridge-South Dorchester HS 1,000/9-12
2475 Cambridge Beltway 21613 410-228-9224
John Wood, prin. Fax 228-0724
Dorchester County School of Technology Vo/Tech
2465 Cambridge Beltway 21613 410-228-3457
John Hurley, prin. Fax 221-9601
Maces Lane MS 600/6-8
1101 Maces Ln 21613 410-228-2111
James Bell, prin. Fax 221-5278
Other Schools – See Hurlock

Countryside Christian S 100/PK-12
5333 Austin Rd 21613 410-228-0574
A. Wayne Burton, prin. Fax 221-8659

Camp Springs, Prince George's, Pop. 16,392

Progressive Christian Academy 300/PK-12
5408 Brinkley Rd 20748 301-449-3160
Rev. Don Massey, admin. Fax 449-0382

Capitol Heights, Prince George's, Pop. 4,313
Prince George's County SD
Supt. — See Upper Marlboro
Central HS 1,100/9-12
200 Cabin Branch Rd 20743 301-499-7080
Fletcher James, prin. Fax 499-7087
Fairmont Heights HS 1,300/9-12
1401 Nye St 20743 301-925-1360
Peggy Nicholson, prin. Fax 925-1371
Walker Mill MS 800/7-8
800 Karen Blvd 20743 301-808-4055
Gorman Brown, prin. Fax 808-4039

Maple Springs Baptist Bible Coll. & Sem. Post-Sec.
4130 Belt Rd 20743 301-736-3631

Catonsville, Baltimore, Pop. 39,820
Baltimore County SD
Supt. — See Towson
Catonsville MS 600/6-8
2301 Edmondson Ave 21228 410-887-0803
Deborah Bittner, prin. Fax 887-1036

Community College of Baltimore County Post-Sec.
800 S Rolling Rd 21228 410-455-6050
Mt. de Sales Academy 500/9-12
700 Academy Rd 21228 410-744-8498
Sr. Elizabeth Allen, prin. Fax 747-5105

Centreville, Queen Anne's, Pop. 2,660
Queen Anne's County SD 7,700/PK-12
202 Chesterfield Ave 21617 410-758-2403
Dr. Bernard Sadusky, supt. Fax 758-8200
www.boe.qacps.k12.md.us

Centreville MS 700/6-8
231 Ruthsburg Rd 21617 410-758-0883
Sue Stein, prin. Fax 758-4447
Queen Anne's County HS 1,100/9-12
125 Ruthsburg Rd 21617 410-758-0500
Richard McNeal, prin. Fax 758-4454
Other Schools – See Stevensville, Sudlersville

Gunston Day S 200/9-12
PO Box 200 21617 410-758-0620
Jeffrey Woodworth, hdmstr. Fax 758-0628

Chesapeake City, Cecil, Pop. 802
Cecil County SD
Supt. — See Elkton
Bohemia Manor HS 700/9-12
2755 Augustine Herman Hwy 21915 410-885-2075
Charles Helm, prin. Fax 885-2485
Bohemia Manor MS 600/6-8
2757 Augustine Herman Hwy 21915 410-885-2095
Berkeley Orr, prin. Fax 885-2485

Chestertown, Kent, Pop. 4,673
Kent County SD 2,500/PK-12
215 Washington Ave 21620 410-778-1595
Anthony Pack, supt. Fax 778-6193
www.kent.k12.md.us
Chestertown MS 400/5-8
402 E Campus Ave 21620 410-778-1771
Gayle Gill, prin. Fax 778-6541
Other Schools – See Galena, Rock Hall, Worton

Washington College Post-Sec.
300 Washington Ave 21620 410-778-2800

Clarksburg, Montgomery
Montgomery County SD
Supt. — See Rockville
Clarksburg HS 9-12
22500 Wims Rd 20871 301-444-3000
James Koutsos, prin. Fax 444-3595
Rocky Hill MS 800/6-8
22401 Brick Haven Way 20871 301-353-8282
Steven Whiting, prin. Fax 601-3197

Clarksville, Howard
Howard County SD
Supt. — See Ellicott City
Clarksville MS 700/6-8
6535 Trotter Rd 21029 410-313-7057
JoAnn Hutchens, prin. Fax 313-7061
River Hill HS 1,500/9-12
12101 Clarksville Pike 21029 410-313-7120
William Ryan, prin. Fax 313-7406

Clear Spring, Washington, Pop. 467
Washington County SD
Supt. — See Hagerstown
Clear Spring HS 500/9-12
12630 Broadfording Rd 21722 301-766-8082
Michael Shockey, prin. Fax 842-0082
Clear Spring MS 400/6-8
12628 Broadfording Rd 21722 301-766-8094
Jeremy Jakoby, prin. Fax 842-3826

Clinton, Prince George's, Pop. 19,987
Prince George's County SD
Supt. — See Upper Marlboro
Decatur MS 900/7-8
8200 Pinewood Dr 20735 301-449-4950
Barry Cyrus, prin. Fax 449-2105
Surrattsville HS 1,400/9-12
6101 Garden Dr 20735 301-599-2453
Alice Swift-Howard, prin. Fax 599-2565

Grace Brethren Christian S 800/PK-12
6501 Surratts Rd 20735 301-868-1600
George Hornickel, dir. Fax 868-9475

Cockeysville, Baltimore, Pop. 18,668
Baltimore County SD
Supt. — See Towson
Cockeysville MS 800/6-8
10401 Greenside Dr 21030 410-887-7626
Philip Taylor, prin. Fax 887-7628

College Park, Prince George's, Pop. 25,171

University of Maryland 20742 Post-Sec.
301-405-1000
University of Maryland Post-Sec.
Univ Blvd And Adelphi Rd 20742 301-985-7000

Colmar Manor, Prince George's, Pop. 1,312

New Covenant Christian Academy 50/PK-12
3805 Lawrence St 20722 301-277-2596
Dr. Cleola Spears, prin. Fax 277-9303

Colora, Cecil

West Nottingham Academy 200/9-12
1079 Firetower Rd 21917 410-658-5556
John Watson, hdmstr. Fax 658-6790

Columbia, Howard, Pop. 88,254
Howard County SD
Supt. — See Ellicott City
Atholton HS 1,300/9-12
6520 Freetown Rd 21044 410-313-7065
Marcia Leonard, prin. Fax 313-7078
Hammond HS 1,300/9-12
8800 Guilford Rd 21046 410-313-7615
Sterlind Burke, prin. Fax 313-7632
Harper's Choice MS 600/6-8
5450 Beaverkill Rd 21044 410-313-6929
C. Stephen Wallis, prin. Fax 313-5612

Long Reach HS 1,500/9-12
6101 Old Dobbin Ln 21045 410-313-7117
Edmund Evans, prin. Fax 313-7422
Oakland Mills HS 1,100/9-12
9410 Kilimanjaro Rd 21045 410-313-6945
Frank Eastham, prin. Fax 313-6948
Oakland Mills MS 500/6-8
9540 Kilimanjaro Rd 21045 410-313-6937
Cynthia Dillon, prin. Fax 313-7447
Wilde Lake HS 1,400/9-12
5460 Trumpeter Rd 21044 410-313-6965
Restia Whitaker, prin. Fax 313-6972
Wilde Lake MS 600/6-8
10481 Cross Fox Ln 21044 410-313-6957
Scott Conroy, prin. Fax 313-6963

Atholton Adventist S 200/K-10
6520 Martin Rd 21044 301-596-5593
Marilynn Peeke, prin. Fax 997-0367
Columbia Center Post-Sec.
6740 Alexander Bell Dr 21046 410-290-1777
Howard Community College Post-Sec.
10901 Little Patuxent Pkwy 21044 410-772-4800
Lincoln Technical Institute Post-Sec.
9325 Snowden River Pkwy 21046 410-290-7100

Cresaptown, Allegany, Pop. 4,586
Allegany County SD
Supt. — See Cumberland
Center for Career & Technical Education Vo/Tech
14211 McMullen Hwy SW 21502 301-729-6486
Deborah Bittinger, prin. Fax 729-0661
Evening HS Adult
14211 McMullen Hwy SW 21502 301-729-6486
Robert Hunter, prin.

Calvary Christian Academy 300/PK-12
PO Box 5154 21505 301-729-0791
Geoff Wheeler, prin. Fax 729-1648

Crisfield, Somerset, Pop. 2,808
Somerset County SD
Supt. — See Westover
Crisfield 8-9 Academy 200/8-9
210 N Somerset Ave 21817 410-968-0150
Monique Ward, prin. Fax 968-1178
Crisfield HS 200/10-12
210 N Somerset Ave 21817 410-968-0150
Debra Josenhans, prin. Fax 968-1178

Crofton, Anne Arundel, Pop. 12,781
Anne Arundel County SD
Supt. — See Annapolis
Crofton MS 900/6-8
2301 Davidsonville Rd 21114 410-793-0280
Sharon Hansen, prin. Fax 793-0295

Crownsville, Anne Arundel, Pop. 1,514

Indian Creek S 600/PK-12
680 Evergreen Rd 21032 410-923-3660
Anne C. Chambers, hdmstr. Fax 923-3884

Cumberland, Allegany, Pop. 20,915
Allegany County SD 9,400/PK-12
PO Box 1724 21501 301-759-2000
Dr. William J. AuMiller, supt. Fax 759-2039
www.boe.allconet.org
Allegany HS 900/9-12
616 Sedgwick St 21502 301-777-8110
Michael S. Calhoun, prin. Fax 759-2534
Braddock MS 700/6-8
909 Holland St 21502 301-777-7990
Danny R. Carter, prin. Fax 777-9741
Ft. Hill HS 1,100/9-12
500 Greenway Ave 21502 301-777-2570
Stephen Lewis, prin. Fax 777-2572
Washington MS 800/6-8
200 N Massachusetts Ave 21502 301-777-5360
Harry Smith, prin. Fax 777-8452
Other Schools – See Cresaptown, Frostburg, Lonaconing, Mount Savage, Westernport

---

Allegany College of Maryland Post-Sec.
12401 Willowbrook Rd 21502 301-784-5000
Bishop Walsh S 600/PK-12
700 Bishop Walsh Rd 21502 301-724-5360
Sr. Phyllis McNally, prin. Fax 722-0555
International Beauty School Post-Sec.
119 N Centre St 21502 301-777-3020

Damascus, Montgomery, Pop. 9,817
Montgomery County SD
Supt. — See Rockville
Baker MS 500/7-8
25400 Oak Dr 20872 301-253-7010
Louise Worthington, prin. Fax 253-7020
Damascus HS 1,900/9-12
25921 Ridge Rd 20872 301-253-7030
Robert G. Domergue, prin. Fax 253-7036

Denton, Caroline, Pop. 3,252
Caroline County SD 5,400/PK-12
204 Franklin St 21629 410-479-1460
Dr. Edward W. Shirley, supt. Fax 479-0108
cl.k12.md.us
Lockerman MS 800/6-8
410 Lockerman St 21629 410-479-2760
Dale Brown, prin. Fax 479-3594
Other Schools – See Federalsburg, Ridgely

Wesleyan Christian S 200/PK-12
PO Box 118 21629 410-479-2292
L.A. Drummond, admin. Fax 479-3294

Easton, Talbot, Pop. 13,447
Talbot County SD 4,500/PK-12
PO Box 1029 21601 410-822-0330
Dr. Karen Salmon, supt. Fax 820-4260
www.tcps.k12.md.us
Easton HS 1,200/9-12
723 Mecklenburg Ave 21601 410-822-4180
Kelly Griffith, prin. Fax 819-5814
Easton MS 900/6-8
201 Peach Blossom Ln 21601 410-822-2910
Marcia Sprankle, prin. Fax 822-7210
Other Schools – See Saint Michaels

Chesapeake Christian S 200/PK-12
1009 N Washington St 21601 410-822-7600
Keith Maxwell, admin. Fax 819-6974
SS. Peter & Paul HS 200/9-12
900 High St 21601 410-822-2275
James Nemeth, prin. Fax 822-1767

Edgewater, Anne Arundel
Anne Arundel County SD
Supt. — See Annapolis
Center of Applied Technology-South Vo/Tech
211 Central Ave E 21037 410-956-5900
Ronald Alberico, prin. Fax 956-5905
Central MS 900/6-8
221 Central Ave E 21037 410-956-5800
Mildred Beall, prin. Fax 956-1266
South River HS 2,000/9-12
201 Central Ave E 21037 410-956-5600
William Myers, prin. Fax 956-5137
South River Evening HS Adult
201 Central Ave E 21037 410-956-0462
Rosaria Jablonski, prin.

Edgewood, Harford, Pop. 23,903
Harford County SD
Supt. — See Bel Air
Edgewood HS 1,400/9-12
2415 Willoughby Beach Rd 21040 410-612-1500
Joseph Schmitz, prin. Fax 612-1585
Edgewood MS 1,300/6-8
2311 Willoughby Beach Rd 21040 410-612-1518
Wayne Perry, prin. Fax 612-1523

Eldersburg, Carroll, Pop. 9,720

St. Stephen's Classical Christian Acad 100/K-12
2275 Liberty Rd 21784 410-795-1249
Rev. Eric Jorgensen, hdmstr. Fax 795-8820

Elkridge, Howard, Pop. 12,953
Howard County SD
Supt. — See Ellicott City
Elkridge Landing MS 700/6-8
7085 Montgomery Rd 21075 410-313-5040
Thomas Saunders, prin. Fax 313-5045
Mayfield Woods MS 600/6-8
7950 Red Barn Way 21075 410-313-5022
Susan Griffith, prin. Fax 313-5029

Elkton, Cecil, Pop. 14,466
Cecil County SD 16,500/PK-12
201 Booth St 21921 410-996-5400
Dr. Carl Roberts, supt. Fax 996-5454
www.ccps.org
Cherry Hill MS 600/6-8
2535 Singerly Rd 21921 410-996-5020
Robert Gerard, prin. Fax 996-5435
Elkton HS 1,100/9-12
110 James St 21921 410-996-5000
Wes Zimmerman, prin. Fax 996-5646
Elkton MS 700/6-8
615 North St 21921 410-996-5010
Elizabeth Cronin, prin. Fax 996-5639
Other Schools – See Chesapeake City, North East, Perryville, Rising Sun

---

Elkton Christian Academy 500/PK-12
144 Appleton Rd 21921 410-398-6444
Dr. Gary Frasier, admin. Fax 392-0397

Ellicott City, Howard, Pop. 56,397
Howard County SD 47,000/PK-12
10910 State Route 108 21042 410-313-6600
Dr. Sydney Cousin, supt. Fax 313-6833
www.hcpss.org
Bonnie Branch MS 700/6-8
4979 Ilchester Rd 21043 410-313-2580
Kathryn McKinley, prin. Fax 313-2586
Burleigh Manor MS 600/6-8
4200 Centennial Ln 21042 410-313-2507
Steve Gibson, prin. Fax 313-2513
Centennial HS 1,600/9-12
4300 Centennial Ln 21042 410-313-2856
Scott Pfeifer, prin. Fax 313-2891
Dunloggin MS 500/6-8
9129 Northfield Rd 21042 410-313-2831
Cher Jones, prin. Fax 313-2530
Ellicott Mills MS 600/6-8
4445 Montgomery Rd 21043 410-313-2839
Michael Goins, prin. Fax 313-2845
Folly Quarter MS 600/6-8
13500 Triadelphia Rd 21042 410-313-1506
Carl Perkins, prin. Fax 313-1509
Howard HS 1,200/9-12
8700 Old Annapolis Rd 21043 410-313-2867
Gina Massella, prin. Fax 313-2870
Mt. Hebron HS 1,600/9-12
9440 Old Frederick Rd 21042 410-313-2880
David Brown, prin. Fax 313-2543
Patapsco MS 700/6-8
8885 Old Frederick Rd 21043 410-313-2848
Jennifer Peduzzi, prin. Fax 313-2852
Other Schools – See Clarksville, Columbia, Elkridge, Fulton, Glenelg, Glenwood, Jessup, Laurel, Marriottsville

---

Glenelg Country S 800/PK-12
12793 Folly Quarter Rd 21042 410-531-8600
Ryland Chapman, hdmstr. Fax 531-1882

Emmitsburg, Frederick, Pop. 2,369

Mt. St. Mary's University Post-Sec.
16300 Old Emmitsburg Rd 21727 301-447-6122

Fallston, Harford, Pop. 5,730
Harford County SD
Supt. — See Bel Air
Fallston HS 1,600/9-12
2301 Carrs Mill Rd 21047 410-638-4120
Kevin Fleming, prin. Fax 638-4125
Fallston MS 1,200/6-8
2303 Carrs Mill Rd 21047 410-638-4129
Mary Blome, prin. Fax 638-4237

James Run Christian Academy 50/9-12
2022 Fallston Rd 21047 410-877-1576
R. Michael Robbins, prin. Fax 877-8738

Federalsburg, Caroline, Pop. 2,637
Caroline County SD
Supt. — See Denton
Richardson HS 600/9-12
25320 Richardson Rd 21632 410-754-5575
Roger Eareckson, prin. Fax 754-3497
Richardson MS 400/6-8
25390 Richardson Rd 21632 410-754-5263
Michael J. Iseman, prin. Fax 754-5695

Forestville, Prince George's, Pop. 16,731
Prince George's County SD
Supt. — See Upper Marlboro
Forestville Military Academy 1,100/9-12
7001 Beltz Dr 20747 301-817-0400
James Smallwood, prin. Fax 817-0416
Jackson MS 1,000/7-8
3500 Regency Pkwy 20747 301-817-0310
Trevor Christopher, prin. Fax 817-0339
Suitland HS 2,600/9-12
5200 Silver Hill Rd 20747 301-817-0500
Mark Fossett, prin. Fax 817-0515

Bishop McNamara HS 800/9-12
6800 Marlboro Pike 20747 301-735-8401
Marco Clark, prin. Fax 735-0934

Fort Meade, Anne Arundel, Pop. 12,509
Anne Arundel County SD
Supt. — See Annapolis
MacArthur MS 1,100/6-8
3500 Rockenbach Rd 20755 410-674-0032
Reginald Farrare, prin. Fax 674-8021
Meade HS 1,800/9-12
1100 Clark Rd 20755 410-674-7710
Joan Valentine, prin. Fax 551-8210
Meade MS 900/6-8
1103 26th St 20755 410-674-2355
Eddie Scott, prin. Fax 674-2612

Fort Washington, Prince George's, Pop. 24,032
Prince George's County SD
Supt. — See Upper Marlboro
Friendly HS 1,700/9-12
10000 Allentown Rd 20744 301-449-4900
Edward Ryans, prin. Fax 449-4911
Gourdine MS 500/7-8
8700 Allentown Rd 20744 301-449-4940
Leatriz Covington, prin. Fax 449-4948
Oxon Hill MS 800/7-8
9570 Fort Foote Rd 20744 301-749-4270
Tricia Hairston, prin. Fax 749-4286

Frederick, Frederick, Pop. 57,907
Frederick County SD 39,100/PK-12
115 E Church St 21701 301-644-5000
Dr. Linda Burgee, supt. Fax 696-6848
www.fcps.org
Ballenger Creek MS 700/6-8
5525 Ballenger Creek Pike 21703 240-236-5700
Mita Badshah, prin. Fax 236-5701
Career and Technology Center Vo/Tech
7922 Opossumtown Pike 21702 240-236-8500
Gregory Solberg, prin. Fax 236-8501
Crestwood MS 500/6-8
7100 Foxcroft Dr 21703 240-566-9000
Kathleen Hartsock, prin. Fax 566-9001
Frederick HS 1,400/9-12
650 Carroll Pkwy 21701 240-236-7000
Denise Fargo-Devine, prin. Fax 236-7015
Johnson HS 2,000/9-12
1501 N Market St 21701 240-236-8200
Marlene Tarr, prin. Fax 236-8201
Johnson MS 700/6-8
1799 Schifferstadt Blvd 21701 240-236-4900
Michelle Concepcion, prin. Fax 236-4901
Linganore HS 1,600/9-12
12013 Old Annapolis Rd 21701 240-236-7800
Margaret Lyburn, prin. Fax 236-7801
Monocacy MS 800/6-8
8009 Opossumtown Pike 21702 240-236-4700
Everett Warren, prin. Fax 236-4701
Tuscarora HS 1,100/9-12
5312 Ballenger Creek Pike 21703 240-236-6400
Jay Berno, prin. Fax 236-6401
West Frederick MS 800/6-8
515 W Patrick St 21701 240-236-4000
Dr. Paulette Shockey, prin. Fax 236-4050
Other Schools – See Brunswick, Ijamsville, Middletown, New Market, Thurmont, Walkersville

---

ABI - AccuTech Business Institute Post-Sec.
550 Highland St Ste 100 21701 301-694-0211
Frederick Community College Post-Sec.
7932 Opossumtown Pike 21702 301-846-2400

Hood College Post-Sec.
401 Rosemont Ave 21701 301-663-3131
Maryland School for the Deaf Post-Sec.
PO Box 250 21705
New Life Christian S 200/K-12
5909 Jefferson Pike 21703 301-663-8418
Paul Kemp, prin. Fax 698-1583
St. John's Catholic Prep S 300/9-12
889 Butterfly Ln 21703 301-662-4210
Chris Cosentino, prin. Fax 662-5166

Frostburg, Allegany, Pop. 7,958
Allegany County SD
Supt. — See Cumberland
Beall JSHS 700/7-12
331 E Main St 21532 301-689-3377
Wayne Nicol, prin. Fax 689-8709

Frostburg State University 21532 Post-Sec.
301-687-4000

Fulton, Howard
Howard County SD
Supt. — See Ellicott City
Lime Kiln MS 600/6-8
11650 Scaggsville Rd 20759 410-880-5988
Brenda Thomas, prin. Fax 880-5996
Reservoir HS 1,300/9-12
11550 Scaggsville Rd 20759 410-888-8850
Adrianne Kaufman, prin. Fax 888-8849

Gaithersburg, Montgomery, Pop. 57,698
Montgomery County SD
Supt. — See Rockville
Forest Oak MS 900/6-8
651 Saybrooke Oaks Blvd 20877 301-670-8242
John Burley, prin. Fax 840-5322
Gaithersburg HS 2,200/9-12
314 S Frederick Ave 20877 301-840-4700
Darryl Williams, prin. Fax 840-4707
Gaithersburg MS 500/7-8
2 Teachers Way 20877 301-840-4554
Carol Goddard, prin. Fax 840-4570
Lakelands Park MS 6-8
1200 Main St 20878 301-670-1400
Joseph Sacco, prin. Fax 670-1418
Montgomery Village MS 800/6-8
19300 Watkins Mill Rd 20886 301-840-4660
Dr. Edgar Malker, prin. Fax 840-6388
Quince Orchard HS 1,900/9-12
15800 Quince Orchard Rd 20878 301-840-4686
Carol Working, prin. Fax 840-4699
Ridgeview MS 700/7-8
16600 Raven Rock Dr 20878 301-840-4770
Dr. Carol Levine, prin. Fax 840-4679
Watkins Mill HS 2,000/9-12
10301 Apple Ridge Rd 20886 301-840-3959
Peter J. Cahall, prin. Fax 840-3980

Aesthetics Institutes of Cosmetology Post-Sec.
15958 Shady Grove Rd Unit C 20877 301-330-9252
Covenant Life S 800/K-12
7501 Muncaster Mill Rd 20877 301-869-4500
Greg Somerville, admin. Fax 948-4920
Ets Chaiyim S 100/K-12
20101 Woodfield Rd 20882 301-216-9592
Dr. Daniel Switzer, prin. Fax 216-9594
Sodexho Marriott Healthcare Mid-Atlantic Post-Sec.
9801 Washingtonian Blvd 20878 301-987-4127

Galena, Kent, Pop. 473
Kent County SD
Supt. — See Chestertown
Galena MS 300/5-8
114 S Main St 21635 410-648-5132
Kenneth Hudock, prin. Fax 648-6881

Gambrills, Anne Arundel
Anne Arundel County SD
Supt. — See Annapolis
Arundel HS 2,000/9-12
1001 Annapolis Rd 21054 410-674-6500
Sharon Stratton, prin. Fax 672-3711

Germantown, Montgomery, Pop. 55,419
Montgomery County SD
Supt. — See Rockville
Clemente MS 1,000/6-8
18808 Waring Station Rd 20874 301-601-0344
Shawn Joseph, prin. Fax 601-0370
King MS 900/6-8
13737 Wisteria Dr 20874 301-353-8080
Marc Cohen, prin. Fax 601-0399
Kingsview MS 1,200/6-8
18909 Kingsview Rd 20874 301-601-4611
Dennis G. Queen, prin. Fax 601-4610
Neelsville MS 800/6-8
11700 Neelsville Church Rd 20876 301-353-8064
Dollye McClain, prin. Fax 353-8094
Northwest HS 1,900/9-12
13501 Richter Farm Rd 20874 301-601-4660
Sylvia K. Morrison, prin. Fax 601-4662
Seneca Valley HS 1,600/9-12
19401 Crystal Rock Dr 20874 301-353-8000
Suzanne Maxey, prin. Fax 353-8004

Montgomery College Post-Sec.
20200 Observation Dr 20876 301-353-7818

Glen Burnie, Anne Arundel, Pop. 38,922
Anne Arundel County SD
Supt. — See Annapolis
Corkran MS 800/6-8
7600 Quarterfield Rd 21061 410-222-6493
Debbie Montgomery, prin.
Glen Burnie HS 2,100/9-12
7550 Baltimore Annapolis Bl 21060 410-761-8950
Sam Salamy, prin. Fax 761-3711
Marley MS 800/6-8
10 Davis Ct 21060 410-761-0934
Susan Cassidy, prin. Fax 761-0736
North County HS 2,200/9-12
10 1st Ave E 21061 410-222-6970
Frank Drazan, prin. Fax 222-6976
Glen Burnie Evening HS Adult
7505 Baltimore Annapolis Bl 21060 410-761-3664
Nelson Horine, prin.

Glencoe, Baltimore

Oldfields S 200/8-12
1500 Glencoe Rd 21152 410-472-4800
George Swope, hdmstr. Fax 472-3141

Glenelg, Howard
Howard County SD
Supt. — See Ellicott City
Glenelg HS 1,300/9-12
14025 Burntwoods Rd 21737 410-313-5528
Karl Schindler, prin. Fax 313-5540

Glenwood, Howard
Howard County SD
Supt. — See Ellicott City
Glenwood MS 600/6-8
2680 State Route 97 21738 410-313-5520
Richard Wilson, prin. Fax 313-5534

Cornerstone Academy of Glenwood 50/1-12
3060 State Route 97 21738 410-489-5775
Carol Parent, admin. Fax 489-5776

Great Mills, Saint Mary's
St. Mary's County SD
Supt. — See Leonardtown
Great Mills HS 1,700/9-12
21130 Great Mills Rd 20634 301-863-4001
Tracey Heibel, prin. Fax 863-4006

Greenbelt, Prince George's, Pop. 22,242
Prince George's County SD
Supt. — See Upper Marlboro
Greenbelt MS 900/7-8
8950 Edmonston Rd 20770 301-513-5040
Judy Austin, prin. Fax 513-5097
Roosevelt HS 2,900/9-12
7601 Hanover Pkwy 20770 301-513-5400
Sylvester Conyers, prin. Fax 614-3446

Hagerstown, Washington, Pop. 38,326
Washington County SD 20,500/PK-12
PO Box 730 21741 301-766-2800
Dr. Elizabeth Morgan, supt. Fax 766-2829
www.wcboe.k12.md.us
Hicks MS 700/6-8
1321 S Potomac St 21740 301-766-8110
Duane McNairn, prin. Fax 766-8116
Northern MS 700/5-8
701 Northern Ave 21742 301-766-8258
Peggy Pugh, prin. Fax 797-5887
North Hagerstown HS 1,300/9-12
1200 Pennsylvania Ave 21742 301-766-8238
Valerie Novak, prin. Fax 733-3158
South Hagerstown HS 1,200/9-12
1101 S Potomac St 21740 301-766-8369
Rick Akers, prin. Fax 766-8474
Washington County Technical HS Vo/Tech
50 W Oak Ridge Dr 21740 301-766-8050
Jeff Stouffer, prin. Fax 797-9743
Western Heights MS 700/5-8
1300 Marshall St 21740 301-766-8403
Dr. Stephen Tarason, prin. Fax 766-8540
Evening HS Adult
1151 S Potomac St 21740 301-766-8460
Fax 766-8471
Other Schools – See Boonsboro, Clear Spring, Hancock, Smithsburg, Williamsport

---

Award Beauty School Post-Sec.
26 E Antietam St 21740 301-733-4520
Broadfording Christian Academy 400/PK-12
13535 Broadfording Church 21740 301-797-8886
Rick Burkett, prin. Fax 797-3155
Grace Academy 400/PK-12
13321 Cearfoss Pike 21740 301-733-2033
Rev. N. Lynn Wakefield, admin. Fax 733-4706
Hagerstown Community College Post-Sec.
11400 Robinwood Dr 21742 301-790-2800
Heritage Academy 300/PK-12
12215 Walnut Point Rd 21740 301-582-2600
Harold Miles, prin. Fax 582-2603
Kaplan College - Hagerstown Campus Post-Sec.
18618 Crestwood Dr 21742 301-739-2670
Paradise Mennonite S 200/1-10
19308 Air View Rd 21742 301-733-1368
St. Maria Goretti HS 200/9-12
1535 Oak Hill Ave 21742 301-739-4266
Christopher Siedor, prin. Fax 739-4261

Halethorpe, Baltimore

Good Shepherd S 100/8-12
4100 Maple Ave 21227 410-247-2770
Lloyd Blumenfeld, dir. Fax 247-1353

Hampstead, Carroll, Pop. 5,451
Carroll County SD
Supt. — See Westminster
North Carroll HS 1,700/9-12
1400 Panther Dr 21074 410-751-3450
Kimberly Dolch, prin. Fax 751-3457
North Carroll MS 700/6-8
2401 Hanover Pike 21074 410-751-3440
Carl Snook, prin. Fax 751-3464
Shiloh MS 800/6-8
3675 Willow St 21074 410-386-4570
James Carver, prin. Fax 386-4579

Hancock, Washington, Pop. 1,736
Washington County SD
Supt. — See Hagerstown
Hancock MSHS 400/6-12
289 W Main St 21750 301-766-8186
Eric Michael, prin. Fax 678-7218

Harwood, Anne Arundel
Anne Arundel County SD
Supt. — See Annapolis
Southern HS 1,200/9-12
4400 Solomons Island Rd 20776 410-867-7100
Jason Dykstra, prin. Fax 867-7100

Havre de Grace, Harford, Pop. 11,884
Harford County SD
Supt. — See Bel Air
Havre De Grace HS 700/9-12
700 Congress Ave 21078 410-939-6600
M. Patricia Walling, prin. Fax 939-6667
Havre De Grace MS 600/6-8
401 Lewis Ln 21078 410-939-6608
Glenn Jensen, prin. Fax 939-6613

Helen, Saint Mary's
St. Mary's County SD
Supt. — See Leonardtown
Brent MS 900/6-8
29675 Point Lookout Rd 20635 301-884-4635
Ryan Hitchman, prin. Fax 884-8937

Huntingtown, Calvert
Calvert County SD
Supt. — See Prince Frederick
Huntington HS 1,400/9-12
4125 Solomons Island Rd 20639 410-414-7036
Rick Webber, prin. Fax 535-4633
Plum Point MS 800/6-8
1475 Plum Point Rd 20639 410-535-7400
Mary Friedman, prin. Fax 535-7413

Calverton S 400/PK-12
300 Calverton School Rd 20639 410-535-0216
Daniel Hildebrand, hdmstr. Fax 535-6934

Hurlock, Dorchester, Pop. 2,003
Dorchester County SD
Supt. — See Cambridge
North Dorchester HS 600/9-12
5875 Cloverdale Rd 21643 410-943-4511
Vaughn Evans, prin. Fax 943-3499
North Dorchester MS 400/6-8
5745 Cloverdale Rd 21643 410-943-3322
Tom Gebert, prin. Fax 943-3797

Hyattsville, Prince George's, Pop. 16,677
Prince George's County SD
Supt. — See Upper Marlboro
Hyattsville MS 800/7-8
6001 42nd Ave 20781 301-209-5830
Gail Golden, prin. Fax 209-5849
Northwestern HS 2,700/9-12
7000 Adelphi Rd 20782 301-985-1820
Jerome Thomas, prin. Fax 985-1833
Orem MS 700/7-8
6100 Editors Park Dr 20782 301-853-0840
Kenneth Calvin, prin. Fax 853-0839
Northwestern Evening HS Adult
7000 Adelphi Rd Ste B220 20782 301-985-1460
Diane Baker, prin. Fax 985-5749

De Matha Catholic HS 1,000/9-12
4313 Madison St 20781 240-764-2200
Dr. Daniel McMahon, prin. Fax 764-2275
Washington United Christian Academy 100/PK-12
PO Box 5417 20782 301-807-9397
Saramma Moses, admin. Fax 772-3999

Ijamsville, Frederick, Pop. 350
Frederick County SD
Supt. — See Frederick
Oakdale MS 600/6-8
9840 Old National Pike 21754 240-236-5500
Neal Case, prin. Fax 236-5501
Urbana HS 1,600/9-12
3471 Campus Dr 21754 240-236-7600
Dr. George Seaton, prin. Fax 236-7601
Urbana MS 6-8
3511 Pontius Ct 21754 240-566-9200
Frank Vetter, prin. Fax 566-9201
Windsor Knolls MS 1,100/6-8
11150 Windsor Rd 21754 240-236-5000
Tracey Lucas, prin. Fax 236-5001

Indian Head, Charles, Pop. 3,642
Charles County SD
Supt. — See La Plata
Henson MS 900/6-8
3535 Livingston Rd 20640 301-375-8550
Ronald Stup, prin. Fax 375-9216
Lackey HS 1,600/9-12
3000 Chicamuxen Rd 20640 301-753-1753
Curry Werkheiser, prin. Fax 743-9076
Smallwood MS 700/6-8
4990 Indian Head Hwy 20640 301-743-5422
Cynthia Warren, prin. Fax 753-8421

Jessup, Howard, Pop. 6,537
Howard County SD
Supt. — See Ellicott City
Patuxent Valley MS 700/6-8
9151 Vollmerhausen Rd 20794 410-880-5840
Robert Motley, prin. Fax 880-5846

Joppa, Harford, Pop. 11,084
Harford County SD
Supt. — See Bel Air
Joppatowne HS 1,100/9-12
555 Joppa Farm Rd 21085 410-612-1510
Macon Tucker, prin. Fax 612-1528

Magnolia MS 900/6-8
299 Fort Hoyle Rd 21085 410-612-1525
Joseph Mascari, prin. Fax 612-1598

Chesapeake Christian S 100/K-12
900 Trimble Rd 21085 410-679-8815
Lisa Gordon, admin. Fax 679-8825

Kensington, Montgomery, Pop. 1,920
Montgomery County SD
Supt. — See Rockville
Einstein HS 1,800/9-12
11135 Newport Mill Rd 20895 301-929-2200
James Fernandez, prin. Fax 649-8279
Newport Mill MS 700/6-8
11311 Newport Mill Rd 20895 301-929-2244
Nelson McLeod, prin. Fax 929-2274

Academy of the Holy Cross 600/9-12
4920 Strathmore Ave 20895 301-942-2100
Sr. Katherine Kase, pres. Fax 929-6440

Kingsville, Baltimore, Pop. 3,550

Open Bible Christian Academy 200/PK-12
13 Open Bible Way 21087 410-593-9940
William Trautman, hdmstr. Fax 593-9942

Landover, Prince George's, Pop. 5,052
Prince George's County SD
Supt. — See Upper Marlboro
Gholson MS 1,000/7-8
900 Nalley Rd 20785 301-883-8390
Teri Hudson, prin. Fax 883-8394
Kenmoor MS 700/7-8
2500 Kenmoor Dr 20785 301-925-2300
Dr. D. Mitchell-Saulsberry, prin. Fax 925-2317

Jericho Christian Academy 300/K-12
8500 Jericho City Dr 20785 301-333-9400
Dr. J. Yvonne Parker, prin. Fax 333-0521
Ultrasound Diagnostic School Post-Sec.
8401 Corporate Dr Ste 500 20785 301-588-0786

Lanham Seabrook, Prince George's, Pop. 16,792
Prince George's County SD
Supt. — See Upper Marlboro
DuVal HS 1,400/9-12
9880 Good Luck Rd 20706 301-918-8600
Anthony Scott, prin. Fax 918-8606
Johnson MS 1,000/7-8
5401 Barker Pl 20706 301-918-8680
Ronald Curtis, prin. Fax 918-8688

Capital Bible Seminary Post-Sec.
6511 Princess Garden Pkwy 20706 301-552-1400
Lanham Christian S 300/K-12
8400 Good Luck Rd 20706 301-552-9102
Gene Pinkard, hdmstr. Fax 552-2021
Lighthouse Christian Academy 50/K-12
PO Box 626 20703 301-552-3179
Sherise Webb, admin.
Washington Bible College Post-Sec.
6511 Princess Garden Pkwy 20706 301-552-1400

La Plata, Charles, Pop. 8,442
Charles County SD 26,000/PK-12
PO Box 2770 20646 301-932-6610
James E. Richmond, supt. Fax 932-6651
www.ccboe.com
La Plata HS 1,700/9-12
6035 Radio Station Rd 20646 301-934-1100
Garth Bowling, prin. Fax 934-5657
Somers MS 1,200/6-8
300 Willow Ln 20646 301-934-4663
Joseph Warfield, prin. Fax 934-2982
Other Schools – See Indian Head, Newburg, Pomfret, Waldorf

College of Southern Maryland Post-Sec.
PO Box 910 20646 301-934-2251

Largo, Prince George's, Pop. 9,475

Prince George's Community College Post-Sec.
301 Largo Rd 20774 301-336-6000

Laurel, Prince George's, Pop. 22,125
Howard County SD
Supt. — See Ellicott City
Hammond MS 600/6-8
8110 Aladdin Dr 20723 410-880-5830
Kerry McGowan, prin. Fax 880-5837
Murray Hill MS 600/6-8
9989 Winter Sun Rd 20723 410-880-5897
Carolyn Jameson, prin. Fax 880-5938

Prince George's County SD
Supt. — See Upper Marlboro
Eisenhower MS 900/7-8
13725 Briarwood Dr 20708 301-497-3620
Charoscar Coleman, prin. Fax 497-3637
Laurel HS 2,100/9-12
8000 Cherry Ln 20707 301-497-2050
Dwayne Jones, prin. Fax 497-2068

Capitol College Post-Sec.
11301 Springfield Rd 20708 800-950-1992
St. Vincent Pallotti HS 500/9-12
113 Saint Marys Pl 20707 301-725-3228
Stephen Edmonds, prin. Fax 776-4343
Tai Sophia Insitute Post-Sec.
7750 Montpelier Rd 20723 800-735-2968

Leonardtown, Saint Mary's, Pop. 2,075
St. Mary's County SD 16,500/PK-12
PO Box 641 20650 301-475-5511
Dr. Michael Martirano, supt. Fax 475-4262
www.smcps.org/
Forrest Career & Technology Center Vo/Tech
24005 Point Lookout Rd 20650 301-475-0242
Robert Taylor, prin. Fax 475-0245
Leonardtown HS 1,800/9-12
23995 Point Lookout Rd 20650 301-475-0200
James Smith, prin. Fax 475-0204
Leonardtown MS 1,000/6-8
24015 Point Lookout Rd 20650 301-475-0230
Charlottis Woodley, prin. Fax 475-0237
Other Schools – See Great Mills, Helen, Lexington Park, Morganza

Leonard Hall Naval Academy 100/6-12
PO Box 507 20650 301-475-8029
Suzanne Wisnieski, prin. Fax 475-8518
St. Mary's Ryken HS 9-12
22600 Camp Calvert Rd 20650 301-475-2814
Mary Jo Hurlburt, pres. Fax 475-7972

Lexington Park, Saint Mary's, Pop. 9,943
St. Mary's County SD
Supt. — See Leonardtown
Esperanza MS 900/6-8
22790 Maple Rd 20653 301-863-4016
Jill Snyder-Mills, prin. Fax 863-4020
Spring Ridge MS 900/6-8
19856 Three Notch Rd 20653 301-863-4031
Maureen Montgomery, prin. Fax 863-4035

Linthicum Heights, Anne Arundel, Pop. 2,980
Anne Arundel County SD
Supt. — See Annapolis
Lindale MS, 415 Andover Rd 21090 1,000/6-8
George Lindley, prin. 410-691-4344

Lonaconing, Allegany, Pop. 1,164
Allegany County SD
Supt. — See Cumberland
Westmar HS 500/9-12
16915 Lwr Georges Crk Rd SW 21539301-463-5751
Gene Morgan, prin. Fax 463-2231

Lothian, Anne Arundel
Anne Arundel County SD
Supt. — See Annapolis
Southern MS 900/6-8
5235 Solomons Island Rd 20711 410-867-2084
Mary Ann Buckley, prin.

Lusby, Calvert
Calvert County SD
Supt. — See Prince Frederick
Mill Creek MS 700/6-8
12200 Margret Taylor Rd 20657 410-535-7824
Darrel Prioleau, prin. Fax 257-7829
Patuxent HS 1,500/9-12
12485 Rousby Hall Rd 20657 410-535-7865
Nancy Highsmith, prin. Fax 535-7875
Southern MS 700/6-8
9615 H G Trueman Rd 20657 410-535-7877
Sylvia Lawson, prin. Fax 535-7879

Lutherville, Baltimore, Pop. 16,442
Baltimore County SD
Supt. — See Towson
Ridgely MS 1,000/6-8
121 E Ridgely Rd 21093 410-887-7650
Susan Evans, prin. Fax 887-7834

Mc Henry, Garrett

Garrett College Post-Sec.
PO Box 151 21541 301-387-3000

Mardela Springs, Wicomico, Pop. 360
Wicomico County SD
Supt. — See Salisbury
Mardela MSHS 700/6-12
24940 Delmar Rd 21837 410-677-5142
Lori Batts, prin. Fax 677-5166

Marriottsville, Howard
Howard County SD
Supt. — See Ellicott City
Marriotts Ridge HS 9-12
12100 Woodford Dr 21104 410-313-5568
Pat Saunderson, prin.
Mount View MS 700/6-8
12101 Woodford Dr 21104 410-313-5545
James Evans, prin. Fax 313-5551

Chapelgate Christian Academy 500/6-12
2600 Marriottsville Rd 21104 410-442-5888
Robin Van Ness, hdmstr. Fax 442-5820

Middletown, Frederick, Pop. 2,860
Frederick County SD
Supt. — See Frederick
Middletown HS 1,300/9-12
200 Schoolhouse Dr 21769 240-236-7400
Kathleen Schlappal, prin. Fax 236-7450
Middletown MS 1,000/6-8
100 Martha Mason St 21769 240-236-4200
Donna Faith, prin. Fax 236-4250

Millersville, Anne Arundel
Anne Arundel County SD
Supt. — See Annapolis
Old Mill HS 2,600/9-12
600 Patriot Ln 21108 410-969-9010
George Kispert, prin. Fax 969-1620
Old Mill MS North 900/6-8
610 Patriot Ln 21108 410-969-5950
Sean McElhaney, prin.
Old Mill MS South 900/6-8
620 Patriot Ln 21108 410-969-7000
William Goodman, prin.

Strayer University Post-Sec.
1520 Jabez Run Ste 100 21108 410-923-4500

Mitchellville, Prince George's, Pop. 12,593
Prince George's County SD
Supt. — See Upper Marlboro
Just MS 1,100/7-8
1300 Campus Way N 20721 301-808-4040
Dr. Marian White-Hood, prin. Fax 808-4567

Woodstream Christian Academy 400/PK-10
9800 Lottsford Rd 20721 301-883-8160
Richard Halloran, admin. Fax 883-8169

Monkton, Baltimore
Baltimore County SD
Supt. — See Towson
Hereford MS 1,000/6-8
712 Corbett Rd 21111 410-887-7902
Cathryn Walrod, prin. Fax 887-7904

Morganza, Saint Mary's
St. Mary's County SD
Supt. — See Leonardtown
Chopticon HS 1,700/9-12
25390 Colton Point Rd 20660 301-475-0215
Joseph North, prin. Fax 475-0222

Mount Airy, Carroll, Pop. 8,375
Carroll County SD
Supt. — See Westminster
Mount Airy MS 600/6-8
102 Watersville Rd 21771 301-751-3554
Virginia Savell, prin. Fax 751-3556

Mount Savage, Allegany
Allegany County SD
Supt. — See Cumberland
Mount Savage S 500/PK-12
13201 New School Rd NW 21545 301-264-3220
Gary Llewellyn, prin. Fax 264-4015

Newark, Worcester
Worcester County SD 6,700/PK-12
6270 Worcester Hwy 21841 410-632-5000
Jon Andes, supt. Fax 632-0364
www.worcester.k12.md.us
Worcester Career & Technology Center Vo/Tech
6268 Worcester Hwy 21841 410-632-5058
Jane Pruitt, prin. Fax 632-5059
Other Schools – See Berlin, Pocomoke City, Snow Hill

Newburg, Charles
Charles County SD
Supt. — See La Plata
Piccowaxen MS 500/6-8
12834 Rock Point Rd 20664 301-934-1977
Kenneth Schroeck, prin. Fax 934-1628

New Carrollton, Prince George's, Pop. 12,818
Prince George's County SD
Supt. — See Upper Marlboro
Carroll MS 900/7-8
6130 Lamont Dr 20784 301-918-8640
Eric Wood, prin. Fax 918-8646

Hair Academy Post-Sec.
8435 Annapolis Rd 20784 301-459-2509

New Market, Frederick, Pop. 463
Frederick County SD
Supt. — See Frederick
New Market MS 900/6-8
125 W Main St 21774 240-236-4600
Daniel Lippy, prin. Fax 236-4650

New Windsor, Carroll, Pop. 1,359
Carroll County SD
Supt. — See Westminster
New Windsor MS 500/6-8
1000 Green Valley Rd 21776 410-751-3355
Donald Bell, prin. Fax 751-3358

North Bethesda, Montgomery, Pop. 38,610

Georgetown Preparatory S 400/9-12
10900 Rockville Pike 20852 301-493-5000
Edward Kowalchick, hdmstr. Fax 493-6128

North East, Cecil, Pop. 2,817
Cecil County SD
Supt. — See Elkton
Cecil County S of Technology Vo/Tech
900 N East Rd 21901 410-996-6250
Lewis Erbe, prin. Fax 996-6256
North East HS 1,100/9-12
300 Irishtown Rd 21901 410-996-6200
Terrill Stammler, prin. Fax 996-6264
North East MS 800/6-8
200 E Cecil Ave 21901 410-996-6210
Kevin Daugherty, prin. Fax 996-6236
Rising Sun HS 1,100/9-12
100 Tiger Dr 21901 410-658-9115
George Larson, prin. Fax 658-9121

Cecil Community College Post-Sec.
1 Seahawk Dr 21901 410-287-6060
Tome S 500/K-12
581 S Maryland Ave 21901 410-287-2050
Dr. F. Darcy Williams, hdmstr. Fax 287-8999

Oakland, Garrett, Pop. 1,896
Garrett County SD 4,700/PK-12
40 S 2nd St 21550 301-334-8900
Wendell Teets, supt. Fax 334-8916
www.ga.k12.md.us/

Southern Garrett County HS 800/9-12
345 Oakland Dr 21550 301-334-9447
Tom Woods, prin. Fax 334-0962
Southern MS 700/6-8
605 Harvey Winters Dr 21550 301-334-8881
John Rickman, prin. Fax 334-2315
Southern Evening HS Adult
345 Oakland Dr 21550 301-334-9447
Thomas Woods, prin.
Other Schools – See Accident

Odenton, Anne Arundel, Pop. 12,833
Anne Arundel County SD
Supt. — See Annapolis
Arundel MS 1,000/6-8
1179 Hammond Ln 21113 410-674-6900
Paul Strickler, prin. Fax 674-6593

Olney, Montgomery, Pop. 23,019
Montgomery County SD
Supt. — See Rockville
Farquhar MS 700/6-8
16915 Batchellors Forest Rd 20832 301-924-3100
Scott Murphy, prin. Fax 924-3152
Parks MS 1,000/6-8
19200 Olney Mill Rd 20832 301-924-3180
Sarah Pinkney-Murkey, prin. Fax 924-3288

Our Lady of Good Counsel HS 1,100/9-12
17301 Old Vic Blvd 20832 301-942-1155
John Graham, prin. Fax 942-3656

Owings, Calvert
Calvert County SD
Supt. — See Prince Frederick
Northern HS 1,600/9-12
2950 Chaneyville Rd 20736 410-257-1519
George Miller, prin. Fax 257-1530
Northern MS 800/6-8
2954 Chaneyville Rd 20736 410-257-1622
Karen Burnett, prin. Fax 257-1623
Windy Hill MS 700/6-8
9560 Boyds Turn Rd 20736 410-257-1560
Ed Cassidy, prin. Fax 257-1556

Owings Mills, Baltimore, Pop. 9,474
Baltimore County SD
Supt. — See Towson
New Town HS 700/9-12
4931 New Town Blvd 21117 410-887-1614
Barbara Cheswick, prin. Fax 654-8897
Owings Mills HS 1,200/9-12
124 S Tollgate Rd 21117 410-887-1700
Diane Garbarino, prin. Fax 581-1713

Empire Beauty School Post-Sec.
9616 Reistertown Rd Ste 105 21117 800-575-5983
Garrison Forest S 600/PK-12
300 Garrison Forest Rd 21117 410-363-1500
G. Peter O'Neill, hdmstr. Fax 363-8441
ITT Technical Institute Post-Sec.
11301 Red Run Blvd 21117 443-394-7115
McDonogh S 1,300/K-12
PO Box 380 21117 410-363-0600
Charles Britton, prin. Fax 581-4777

Oxon Hill, Prince George's, Pop. 35,355
Prince George's County SD
Supt. — See Upper Marlboro
Oxon Hill HS 2,500/9-12
6701 Leyte Dr 20745 301-749-4300
Roney Winn, prin. Fax 749-4320
Potomac HS 1,300/9-12
5211 Boydell Ave 20745 301-702-3900
Donna Daniel, prin. Fax 702-3886

Parkton, Baltimore
Baltimore County SD
Supt. — See Towson
Hereford HS 1,400/9-12
17301 York Rd 21120 410-887-1905
John Bereska, prin. Fax 887-1944

Parkville, Baltimore, Pop. 31,118
Baltimore County SD
Supt. — See Towson
Parkville HS & Center of Technology 2,000/9-12
2600 Putty Hill Ave 21234 410-887-5257
Kevin Harahan, prin. Fax 668-7503

Pasadena, Anne Arundel, Pop. 10,012
Anne Arundel County SD
Supt. — See Annapolis
Chesapeake Bay MS 1,700/6-8
4804 Mountain Rd 21122 410-437-2400
M. Jacques Smith, prin. Fax 437-9920
Chesapeake HS 1,900/9-12
4798 Mountain Rd 21122 410-255-9600
Patricia Plitt, prin. Fax 360-4365
Fox MS, 7922 Outing Ave 21122 800/6-8
Kevin Dennehy, prin. 410-437-5512
Northeast HS 1,500/9-12
1121 Duvall Hwy 21122 410-437-6400
Kathy Kubic, prin. Fax 437-7012

Perry Hall, Baltimore, Pop. 22,723

Perry Hall Christian S 300/K-12
3919 Schroeder Ave 21128 410-256-4886
Cathy Tarbart, admin. Fax 256-5451

Perryville, Cecil, Pop. 3,770
Cecil County SD
Supt. — See Elkton
Perryville HS 1,000/9-12
1696 Perryville Rd 21903 410-996-6000
Peter Callahan, prin. Fax 996-6027
Perryville MS 700/6-8
850 Aiken Ave 21903 410-996-6010
R. Joseph Buckley, prin. Fax 996-6048

Pocomoke City, Worcester, Pop. 3,909
Worcester County SD
Supt. — See Newark
Pocomoke HS 500/9-12
1817 Old Virginia Rd 21851 410-632-5180
Ty Mills, prin. Fax 632-5189
Pocomoke MS 500/4-8
800 8th St 21851 410-632-5150
Caroline Bloxom, prin. Fax 632-5159

Pomfret, Charles
Charles County SD
Supt. — See La Plata
McDonough HS 1,300/9-12
7165 Marshall Corner Rd 20675 301-934-2944
Jervie Petty, prin. Fax 753-8408

Poolesville, Montgomery, Pop. 5,498
Montgomery County SD
Supt. — See Rockville
Poole MS 400/6-8
17014 Tom Fox Ave 20837 301-972-7979
Richard Bishop, prin. Fax 972-7982
Poolesville JSHS 800/7-12
17501 W Willard Rd 20837 301-972-7900
Deena Levine, prin. Fax 972-7943

Port Deposit, Cecil, Pop. 693

Lighthouse Christian Academy 300/PK-12
7 Pleasant View Church Rd 21904 410-378-3279
Fax 658-3004

Potomac, Montgomery, Pop. 44,822
Montgomery County SD
Supt. — See Rockville
Cabin John MS 1,000/6-8
10701 Gainsborough Rd 20854 301-469-1150
Dr. Paulette Smith, prin. Fax 469-1003
Churchill HS 2,100/9-12
11300 Gainsborough Rd 20854 301-469-1200
Dr. Joan Benz, prin. Fax 469-1208

Bullis S 600/3-12
10601 Falls Rd 20854 301-299-8500
Thomas Farquhar, hdmstr. Fax 299-9050
Connelly Holy Child S 400/6-12
9029 Bradley Blvd 20854 301-365-0955
Maureen Appel, hdmstr. Fax 365-0981
German S Washington DC 600/PK-12
8617 Chateau Dr 20854 301-365-4400
Klaus-Dieter Bloch, prin. Fax 365-3905
Heights S 200/9-12
10400 Seven Locks Rd 20854 301-365-4300
Alvaro de Vicente, hdmstr. Fax 365-4303
McLean S of Maryland 500/K-12
8224 Lochinver Ln 20854 301-299-8277
Darlene Pierro, hdmstr. Fax 299-1639
Muslim Community S 100/PK-12
7917 Montrose Rd 20854 301-340-6713
Dr. Mahboobeh Ayat, prin. Fax 340-7339
St. Andrew's Episcopal S 500/6-12
8804 Postoak Rd 20854 301-983-5200
Robert F. Kosasky, hdmstr. Fax 983-4710

Prince Frederick, Calvert, Pop. 1,885
Calvert County SD 17,400/PK-12
1305 Dares Beach Rd 20678 410-535-1700
Jack Smith, supt. Fax 535-7476
www.calvertnet.k12.md.us
Calvert Career Ctr Vo/Tech
330 Dorsey Rd 20678 410-535-7450
Barbara McKimmie, prin. Fax 535-7418
Calvert HS 1,200/9-12
600 Dares Beach Rd 20678 410-535-7333
Susan Johnson, prin. Fax 535-7200
Calvert MS 500/6-8
435 Solomons Island Rd N 20678 410-535-7355
Bruce Hutchinson, prin. Fax 535-7356
Other Schools – See Huntingtown, Lusby, Owings

Princess Anne, Somerset, Pop. 2,800
Somerset County SD
Supt. — See Westover
Washington 8-9 Academy 8-9
10902 Old Princess Anne Rd 21853 410-651-0480
Deborah Dean, prin. Fax 651-0235
Washington HS 400/10-12
10902 Old Princess Anne Rd 21853 410-651-0480
Keith O'Neal, prin. Fax 651-0235

University of Maryland Eastern Shore Post-Sec.
11868 Academic Oval 21853 410-651-2200

Pylesville, Harford
Harford County SD
Supt. — See Bel Air
North Harford HS 1,400/9-12
211 Pylesville Rd 21132 410-638-3650
David Thomas, prin. Fax 638-3666
North Harford MS 1,100/6-8
112 Pylesville Rd 21132 410-638-3658
Dr. Bruce Kovacs, prin. Fax 638-3669

Randallstown, Baltimore, Pop. 30,870
Baltimore County SD
Supt. — See Towson
Deer Park Magnet MS 1,400/6-8
9830 Winands Rd 21133 410-887-0726
Penelope Martin, prin. Fax 887-0704
Randallstown HS 1,300/9-12
4000 Offutt Rd 21133 410-887-0748
Thomas Evans, prin. Fax 887-0759

Reisterstown, Baltimore, Pop. 19,314
Baltimore County SD
Supt. — See Towson
Franklin HS 1,600/9-12
12000 Reisterstown Rd 21136 410-887-1119
Dean Terry, prin. Fax 833-4434
Franklin MS 1,400/6-8
10 Cockeys Mill Rd 21136 410-887-1114
Lynn Wolf, prin. Fax 517-2548

Maryland Beauty Academy Post-Sec.
152 Chartley Dr 21136 410-517-0442
More S 200/6-12
12039 Reisterstown Rd 21136 410-526-5000
Mark Waldman, pres. Fax 526-7631

Ridgely, Caroline, Pop. 1,354
Caroline County SD
Supt. — See Denton
Caroline Career & Technical Ctr Vo/Tech
10855 Central Ave 21660 410-479-0100
Theresa Stafford, prin. Fax 479-1308
North Caroline HS 1,100/9-12
10990 River Rd 21660 410-479-2332
Brian Spiering, prin. Fax 479-2743

Rising Sun, Cecil, Pop. 1,785
Cecil County SD
Supt. — See Elkton
Rising Sun MS 700/6-8
289 Pearl St 21911 410-658-5535
Diana Rudolph, prin. Fax 658-9173

Riverdale, Prince George's, Pop. 5,120
Prince George's County SD
Supt. — See Upper Marlboro
Parkdale HS 2,300/9-12
6001 Good Luck Rd 20737 301-513-5700
David Burton, prin. Fax 513-5209
Wirt MS 700/7-8
62nd Pl & Tuckerman St 20737 301-985-1720
Wendell Coleman, prin. Fax 985-1440

St. Bernard S 100/5-8
5811 Riverdale Rd 20737 301-864-3801
Deborah McFarland, prin. Fax 864-2912

Rock Hall, Kent, Pop. 2,566
Kent County SD
Supt. — See Chestertown
Rock Hall MS 200/5-8
21203 E Sharp St 21661 410-639-2279
Virginia Newlin, prin. Fax 639-2998

Rockville, Montgomery, Pop. 57,402
Montgomery County SD 137,300/PK-12
850 Hungerford Dr 20850 301-279-3000
Jerry Weast Ed.D., supt. Fax 279-3221
www.montgomeryschoolsmd.org
Frost MS 1,200/6-8
9201 Scott Dr 20850 301-279-3949
Dr. Joey N. Jones, prin. Fax 279-3956
Hoover MS 1,100/6-8
8810 Postoak Rd 20854 301-469-1010
Billie Jean Bensen, prin. Fax 469-1013
Magruder HS 2,300/9-12
5939 Muncaster Mill Rd 20855 301-840-4600
Leroy Evans, prin. Fax 840-4617
Montgomery HS 1,900/9-12
250 Richard Montgomery Dr 20852 301-279-8400
E. Moreno Carrasco, prin. Fax 279-8428
Parkland MS 1,200/6-8
6300 Tilden Ln 20852 301-770-8010
Kevin Hobbs, prin. Fax 770-8032
Redland MS 900/6-8
6505 Muncaster Mill Rd 20855 301-840-4680
Carol A. Weiss, prin. Fax 840-4688
Rockville HS 1,200/9-12
2100 Baltimore Rd 20851 301-517-8105
Dr. Debra Munk, prin. Fax 517-8288
Tilden MS 500/7-8
11211 Old Georgetown Rd 20852 301-230-5930
Karen Rabin, prin. Fax 230-5991
West MS 1,100/6-8
651 Great Falls Rd 20850 301-279-3979
Nanette Poirier, prin. Fax 517-8216
Wood MS 1,000/6-8
14615 Bauer Dr 20853 301-460-2150
Dr. Renee Foose, prin. Fax 460-2159
Wootton HS 2,300/9-12
2100 Wootton Pkwy 20850 301-279-8550
Dr. Michael J. Doran, prin. Fax 279-8569
Other Schools – See Bethesda, Burtonsville, Clarksburg, Damascus, Gaithersburg, Germantown, Kensington, Olney, Poolesville, Potomac, Sandy Spring, Silver Spring

---

Berman Hebrew Academy 800/PK-12
13300 Arctic Ave 20853 301-962-9400
Dr. Joshua Levisohn, hdmstr. Fax 962-3991
Montgomery College Post-Sec.
51 Mannakee St 20850 301-279-5000
Montrose Christian S 400/PK-12
5100 Randolph Rd 20852 301-770-5335
Tracy Mohr, hdmstr. Fax 881-7345
Smith Jewish Day S 700/7-12
11710 Hunters Ln 20852 301-881-1400
Jonathan Cannon, hdmstr. Fax 230-1986
Strayer University Post-Sec.
4 Research Pl Ste 100 20850 301-548-5500

Saint James, Washington

St. James S 200/8-12
17641 College Rd 21781 301-733-9330
Rev. D. Stuart Dunnan, hdmstr. Fax 739-1310

Saint Marys City, Saint Mary's, Pop. 3,200

St. Mary's College of Maryland Post-Sec.
18952 E Fisher Rd 20686 301-862-0200

Saint Michaels, Talbot, Pop. 1,139
Talbot County SD
Supt. — See Easton
Saint Michaels MSHS 400/7-12
200 Seymour Ave 21663 410-745-2852
Frank Hagen, prin. Fax 745-9939

Salisbury, Wicomico, Pop. 26,295
Wicomico County SD 14,400/PK-12
PO Box 1538 21802 410-677-4400
Dr. Charlene C. Boston, supt. Fax 677-4444
www.wcboe.org
Bennett HS 1,400/9-12
300 E College Ave 21804 410-677-5141
Clayton J. Belgie, prin. Fax 677-5126
Bennett MS 1,000/6-8
200 E College Ave 21804 410-677-5140
C. Michael Johnson, prin. Fax 677-5133
Parkside HS 1,100/9-12
1015 Beaglin Park Dr 21804 410-677-5143
Steven Grudis, prin. Fax 677-5104
Salisbury MS 900/6-8
607 Morris St 21801 410-677-5149
Michael Cody, prin. Fax 677-5122
Wicomico HS 1,100/9-12
201 Long Ave 21804 410-677-5146
Lorenzo Hughes, prin. Fax 677-5151
Wicomico MS 800/6-8
635 E Main St 21804 410-677-5145
Kimberly D. Miles, prin. Fax 677-5197
Evening HS Adult
PO Box 1538 21802 410-677-4537
Andrew Turner, coord. Fax 677-4418
Other Schools – See Mardela Springs

Agape Christian Academy 50/PK-12
208 Tilghman Rd 21804 410-546-5664
Cynthia Smith, prin. Fax 597-5464
Del-Mar-Va Beauty Academy Post-Sec.
111 Milford St 21804 410-742-7929
Salisbury Christian S 600/PK-12
807 Parker Rd 21804 410-546-0661
Rev. James Fox, hdmstr. Fax 546-4674
Salisbury S 500/PK-12
6279 Hobbs Rd 21804 410-742-4464
Dr. Fred Neill, hdmstr. Fax 546-2310
Salisbury University Post-Sec.
1101 Camden Ave 21801 410-543-6000
Wor-Wic Community College Post-Sec.
32000 Campus Dr 21804 410-334-2800

Sandy Spring, Montgomery, Pop. 3,092
Montgomery County SD
Supt. — See Rockville
Sherwood HS 2,100/9-12
300 Olney Sandy Spring Rd 20860 301-924-3200
William Gregory, prin. Fax 924-3220

Sandy Spring Friends S 500/PK-12
16923 Norwood Rd 20860 301-774-7455
Ken Smith, hdmstr. Fax 924-1115

Severn, Anne Arundel, Pop. 24,499
Anne Arundel County SD
Supt. — See Annapolis
Center of Applied Technology-North Vo/Tech
800 Stevenson Rd 21144 410-969-3100
Dan Schaffhauser, prin. Fax 360-4364

Archbishop Spalding HS 1,000/9-12
8080 New Cut Rd 21144 410-969-9105
Kathleen Mahar, prin. Fax 969-1026
Calvary Chapel Christian Academy 100/PK-12
8064 New Cut Rd 21144 410-969-5101
Barbara Fridy, prin. Fax 969-7729

Severna Park, Anne Arundel, Pop. 28,507
Anne Arundel County SD
Supt. — See Annapolis
Severna Park HS 1,800/9-12
60 Robinson Rd 21146 410-544-0900
James Hamilton, prin. Fax 647-2978
Severna Park MS 1,400/6-8
450 Jumpers Hole Rd 21146 410-647-7900
Sharon Morell, prin. Fax 315-8006
Severna Park Evening HS Adult
60 Robinson Rd 21146 410-544-0182
John France, prin.

Severn S 700/6-12
201 Water St 21146 410-647-7700
Douglas Lagarde, hdmstr. Fax 544-9455

Silver Spring, Montgomery, Pop. 76,540
Montgomery County SD
Supt. — See Rockville
Argyle MS 600/6-8
2400 Bel Pre Rd 20906 301-460-2400
Dr. Debra Mugge, prin. Fax 460-2423
Blair HS 3,300/9-12
51 University Blvd E 20901 301-649-2800
Phillip Gainous, prin. Fax 649-2830
Blake HS 1,900/9-12
300 Norwood Rd 20905 301-879-1300
Carole C. Goodman, prin. Fax 879-1306
Briggs-Chaney MS 900/6-8
1901 Rainbow Dr 20905 301-989-6000
Kimberly Johnson, prin. Fax 989-6020
Eastern MS 900/6-8
300 University Blvd E 20901 301-650-6650
Charlotte C. Boucher, prin. Fax 650-6657
Edison HS of Technology Vo/Tech
12501 Dalewood Dr 20906 301-929-2175
Carlos Hamlin, prin. Fax 929-2177
Kennedy HS 1,500/9-12
1901 Randolph Rd 20902 301-929-2100
Thomas Anderson, prin. Fax 929-2124
Key MS 800/6-8
910 Schindler Dr 20903 301-431-7630
Eric Minus, prin. Fax 431-7639
Lee MS 600/6-8
11800 Monticello Ave 20902 301-649-8100
Mary Beth Waits, prin. Fax 649-8110
Loiederman MS 6-8
12701 Goodhill Rd 20906 301-929-2282
Alison Serino, prin. Fax 962-5993
Northwood HS 400/9-12
919 University Blvd W 20901 301-649-8088
Henry Johnson, prin.
Silver Spring International MS 800/6-8
313 Wayne Ave 20910 301-650-6544
Victoria Parcan, prin. Fax 649-8005
Sligo MS 600/6-8
1401 Dennis Ave 20902 301-649-8121
Richard Rhodes, prin. Fax 649-8145
Springbrook HS 2,000/9-12
201 Valley Brook Dr 20904 301-989-5700
Michael Durso, prin. Fax 622-1875
Takoma Park MS 1,000/6-8
7611 Piney Branch Rd 20910 301-650-6444
Renay Johnson, prin. Fax 230-5924
Wheaton HS 1,500/9-12
12601 Dalewood Dr 20906 301-929-2050
Kevin Lowndes, prin. Fax 929-2081
White Oak MS 900/6-8
12201 New Hampshire Ave 20904 301-989-5780
Dr. Carol Dahlberg, prin. Fax 989-5696

Barrie S 300/PK-12
13500 Layhill Rd 20906 301-576-2800
Tim Trautman, hdmstr. Fax 576-2803
Everest Institute Post-Sec.
8757 Georgia Ave Ste 650 20910 301-495-4400
Forcey Christian MS 100/6-8
12625 Galway Dr 20904 301-572-6607
Ezekiel Wharton, admin. Fax 572-2652
Griggs International Academy Post-Sec.
PO Box 4437 20914 301-680-6570
Griggs University Post-Sec.
PO Box 4437 20914 301-680-6570
Holy Cross Hospital Post-Sec.
1500 Forest Glen Rd 20910 301-905-1216
Montgomery Beauty School Post-Sec.
8736 Arliss St 20901 301-459-2509
National Labor College Post-Sec.
1000 New Hampshire Ave 20903 301-431-6400
Newport S 100/PK-12
12101 Tech Rd 20904 240-645-0145
Rachel Goldfarb, hdmstr. Fax 645-0150
School of Art & Design @ Montgomery Coll Post-Sec.
10500 Georgia Ave 20902 301-649-4454
Thornton Friends S 50/6-8
11612 New Hampshire Ave 20904 301-622-9033
Michael DeHart, hdmstr. Fax 622-4786
Thornton Friends S 100/9-12
13925 New Hampshire Ave 20904 301-384-0320
Michael DeHart, hdmstr. Fax 236-9481
Washington Christian Academy 200/6-12
PO Box 9847 20916 301-649-1070
Larry Danner, hdmstr. Fax 649-9863
Yeshiva College of the Nations Capital Post-Sec.
1216 Arcola Ave 20902 301-593-2534
Yeshiva of Greater Washington - Boys Div 100/7-12
1216 Arcola Ave 20902 301-649-7077
Rabbi Dovid Niman, prin. Fax 649-7053
Yeshiva of Greater Washington - Girls 200/7-12
2010 Linden Ln 20910 301-962-5111
Sima Jacoby, prin. Fax 962-8372

Smithsburg, Washington, Pop. 2,859
Washington County SD
Supt. — See Hagerstown
Smithsburg HS 800/9-12
66 N Main St 21783 301-766-8337
Melvin Whitfield, prin. Fax 824-2617
Smithsburg MS 700/6-8
68 N Main St 21783 301-766-8353
Michael Kuhaneck, prin. Fax 824-5147

Snow Hill, Worcester, Pop. 2,323
Worcester County SD
Supt. — See Newark
Snow Hill HS 400/9-12
305 S Church St 21863 410-632-5270
Tom Davis, prin. Fax 632-5279
Snow Hill MS 400/4-8
522 Coulbourne Ln 21863 410-632-5240
Janet Simpson, prin. Fax 632-5249

Springdale, Prince George's
Prince George's County SD
Supt. — See Upper Marlboro
Flowers HS 2,600/9-12
10001 Ardwick Ardmore Rd 20774 301-636-8000
Helene Nobles-Jones, prin. Fax 636-8008

Stevenson, Baltimore

St. Timothy's S 100/9-12
8400 Greenspring Ave 21153 410-486-7400
Randy Stevens, hdmstr. Fax 486-1167
Villa Julie College Post-Sec.
1525 Greenspring Valley Rd 21153 410-486-7000

Stevensville, Queen Anne's, Pop. 1,862
Queen Anne's County SD
Supt. — See Centreville
Kent Island HS 1,300/9-12
900 Love Point Rd 21666 410-604-2070
Denise Hershberger, prin. Fax 604-2089
Stevensville MS 800/6-8
610 Main St 21666 410-643-3194
Conrad Judy, prin. Fax 643-3046

Sudlersville, Queen Anne's, Pop. 394
Queen Anne's County SD
Supt. — See Centreville
Sudlersville MS 400/6-8
201 N Church St 21668 410-438-3151
Kevin Kintop, prin. Fax 438-3151

Eastern Shore Junior Academy 50/PK-10
407 Dudley Corners Rd 21668 410-438-3288
Lowell Litten, prin. Fax 438-3778

Suitland, Prince George's, Pop. 33,515
Prince George's County SD
Supt. — See Upper Marlboro
Drew-Freeman MS 1,000/7-8
2600 Brooks Dr 20746 301-817-0900
Joyce Edwards, prin. Fax 817-0915

New Creation Academy of Hair Design Post-Sec.
3930 Bexley Pl 20746 301-899-9100

Sykesville, Carroll, Pop. 4,440
Carroll County SD
Supt. — See Westminster
Century HS 1,200/9-12
355 Ronsdale Rd 21784 410-386-4400
Andrew Cockley, prin. Fax 386-4413
Liberty HS 1,100/9-12
5855 Bartholow Rd 21784 410-751-3560
Dwayne Piper, prin. Fax 751-3564
Oklahoma Road MS 900/6-8
6300 Oklahoma Rd 21784 410-751-3600
Catherine Hood, prin. Fax 751-3604
South Carroll HS 1,100/9-12
1300 W Old Liberty Rd 21784 410-751-3575
Eric King, prin. Fax 751-3587
Sykesville MS 900/6-8
7301 Springfield Ave 21784 410-751-3545
Thomas Eckenrode, prin. Fax 751-3573

Takoma Park, Montgomery, Pop. 18,540

Columbia Union College Post-Sec.
7600 Flower Ave 20912 301-891-4000
Montgomery College Post-Sec.
7600 Takoma Ave 20912 301-650-1300
Takoma Academy 300/9-12
8120 Carroll Ave 20912 301-434-4700
C. Dunbar Henri, prin. Fax 434-4814
Washington Adventist Hospital Post-Sec.
7600 Carroll Ave 20912 301-891-7600

Taneytown, Carroll, Pop. 5,453
Carroll County SD
Supt. — See Westminster
Northwest MS 600/6-8
99 Kings Dr 21787 410-751-3270
Steven Johnson, prin. Fax 751-3275

Temple Hills, Prince George's, Pop. 6,865
Prince George's County SD
Supt. — See Upper Marlboro
Crossland HS 1,800/9-12
6901 Temple Hill Rd 20748 301-449-4800
Charles Thomas, prin. Fax 449-4801
Marshall MS 800/7-8
4909 Brinkley Rd 20748 301-702-7540
Ray Adams, prin. Fax 702-7555
Shugart MS 700/6-8
2000 Callaway St 20748 301-702-3950
Ms. Curtis Smalls, prin. Fax 702-3957
Stoddert MS 800/6-8
2501 Olson St 20748 301-702-7500
Rudyard Wallace, prin. Fax 702-7515
Crossland Evening HS Adult
6901 Temple Hill Rd 20748 301-449-4994
Ernest Caldwell, prin. Fax 449-2126

Thurmont, Frederick, Pop. 6,036
Frederick County SD
Supt. — See Frederick
Catoctin HS 1,000/9-12
14745 Sabillasville Rd 21788 240-236-8100
Jack Newkirk, prin. Fax 236-8101
Thurmont MS 700/6-8
408 E Main St 21788 240-236-5100
Barbara Keiling, prin. Fax 236-5101

Timonium, See Lutherville
Baltimore County SD
Supt. — See Towson
Dulaney JSHS 2,000/8-12
255 E Padonia Rd 21093 410-887-7633
Lyle Patzkowsky, prin. Fax 666-8915

R. Paul Academy of Cosmetology Arts/Sci Post-Sec.
1811 York Rd Ste B 21093 410-252-4481

Towson, Baltimore, Pop. 51,793
Baltimore County SD 107,100/PK-12
6901 N Charles St 21204 410-887-4554
Dr. Joe Hairston, supt. Fax 887-4309
www.bcps.org
Other Schools – See Baltimore, Catonsville, Cockeysville, Lutherville, Monkton, Owings Mills, Parkton, Parkville, Randallstown, Reisterstown, Timonium

---

Baltimore Lutheran HS 500/6-12
1145 Concordia Dr 21286 410-825-2323
Randal Gast, hdmstr. Fax 825-2506
Loyola Blakefield HS 1,000/6-12
PO Box 6819 21285 410-823-0601
Rev. Thomas Pesci, pres. Fax 823-5277
Medix School Post-Sec.
700 York Rd 21204 410-337-5155

Notre Dame Preparatory S 700/6-12
815 Hampton Ln 21286 410-825-6202
Clare Pitz, prin. Fax 832-2625
TESST College of Technology Post-Sec.
803 Glen Eagles Ct 21286 410-296-5350
Towson Catholic HS 300/9-12
114 Ware Ave 21204 410-427-4900
Susan Banks, prin. Fax 427-4995
Towson State University Post-Sec.
8000 York Rd 21252 410-830-2000

Union Bridge, Carroll, Pop. 1,085
Carroll County SD
Supt. — See Westminster
Key HS 1,200/9-12
3825 Bark Hill Rd 21791 410-751-3320
Randy Clark, prin. Fax 751-3325

Upper Marlboro, Prince George's, Pop. 683
Prince George's County SD 132,200/PK-12
14201 School Ln 20772 301-952-6000
John Deasy Ph.D., admin. Fax 952-1383
www.pgcps.org
Croom Vocational HS Vo/Tech
8520 Duvall Rd 20772 301-952-7750
Sherrill Lilly, prin. Fax 952-7758
Douglass HS 1,800/9-12
8000 Croom Rd 20772 301-952-2400
Rudolph Saunders, prin. Fax 627-3377
Kettering MS 700/7-8
65 Herrington Dr 20774 301-808-4060
Legaunt Jones, prin. Fax 808-5920
Largo HS 1,900/9-12
505 Largo Rd 20774 301-808-8880
James Wheeler, prin. Fax 808-4066
Madison MS 900/7-8
7300 Woodyard Rd 20772 301-599-2422
Mark King, prin. Fax 599-2562
Wise HS, 12650 Brooke Ln 20772 9-12
Monica Goldson, prin. 301-780-2100
Other Schools – See Accokeek, Adelphi, Beltsville, Bladensburg, Bowie, Brandywine, Capitol Heights, Clinton, Forestville, Fort Washington, Greenbelt, Hyattsville, Landover, Lanham Seabrook, Laurel, Mitchellville, New Carrollton, Oxon Hill, Riverdale, Springdale, Suitland, Temple Hills

---

Capitol Christian Academy 200/PK-12
610 Largo Rd 20774 301-336-2200
Gary O'Neill, admin. Fax 336-6704
Clinton Christian S 700/PK-12
6707 Woodyard Rd 20772 301-599-9600
Travis Crutchfield, admin. Fax 599-9603
Queen Anne S 300/6-12
14111 Oak Grove Rd 20774 301-249-5000
J. Temple Blackwood, hdmstr. Fax 249-3838
Riverdale Baptist S 900/PK-12
1133 Largo Rd 20774 301-249-7000
Terry Zink, admin. Fax 249-3425

Waldorf, Charles, Pop. 15,058
Charles County SD
Supt. — See La Plata
Hanson MS 900/6-8
12350 Vivian Adams Dr 20601 301-645-4520
Stephanie Wesolowski, prin. Fax 870-1182
Mattawoman MS 1,100/6-8
10145 Berry Rd 20603 301-645-7708
William Wise Ed.D., prin. Fax 638-0043
Stoddert MS 800/6-8
2040 Saint Thomas Dr 20602 301-645-1334
Sylvia Lawson, prin. Fax 870-1183
Stone HS 2,100/9-12
3785 Leonardtown Rd 20601 301-645-2601
Heath Morrison, prin. Fax 932-4278
Westlake HS 1,800/9-12
3300 Middletown Rd 20603 301-645-8857
Chrystal Benson, prin. Fax 932-8583

Aaron's Academy of Beauty Post-Sec.
340 Post Office Rd 20602 301-645-3681
Grace Brethren Christian S 500/PK-12
13000 Zekiah Dr 20601 301-645-0406
Lloyd Chadwick, dir. Fax 645-7463

Walkersville, Frederick, Pop. 5,593
Frederick County SD
Supt. — See Frederick
Walkersville HS 1,300/9-12
81 W Frederick St 21793 240-236-7200
Rebecca Koontz, prin. Fax 236-7250
Walkersville MS 900/6-8
55 W Frederick St 21793 240-236-4400
Larkin Hohnke, prin. Fax 236-4401
Evening HS Adult
44 W Frederick St 21793 240-236-8450
Richard Ramsburg, prin. Fax 236-8451

Westernport, Allegany, Pop. 2,020
Allegany County SD
Supt. — See Cumberland
Westmar MS 300/6-8
400 Philos Ave 21562 301-359-3046
Martin E. Crump, prin. Fax 359-8049

Westminster, Carroll, Pop. 17,761
Carroll County SD 28,100/PK-12
125 N Court St 21157 410-751-3000
Charles Ecker, supt. Fax 751-3031
www.carrollk12.org/
Carroll County Career & Tech Center Vo/Tech
1229 Washington Rd 21157 410-751-3669
Catherine Engel, prin. Fax 751-3677
Westminster East MS 800/6-8
121 Longwell Ave 21157 410-751-3656
Jeffrey Alisauckas, prin. Fax 751-3660
Westminster HS 1,800/9-12
1225 Washington Rd 21157 410-751-3630
John Seaman, prin. Fax 751-3640
Westminster West MS 1,100/6-8
60 Monroe St 21157 410-751-3661
Thomas Hill, prin. Fax 751-3667
Winters Mill HS 1,200/9-12
560 Gorsuch Rd 21157 410-386-1500
Kenneth Goncz, prin. Fax 386-1513
Carroll County Evening HS Adult
125 N Court St 21157 410-751-3115
Katy Green, prin. Fax 751-3695
Other Schools – See Hampstead, Mount Airy, New Windsor, Sykesville, Taneytown, Union Bridge

---

Carroll Christian S 300/PK-12
550 Baltimore Blvd 21157 410-876-3838
Fax 876-7766
Carroll Community College Post-Sec.
1601 Washington Rd 21157 410-386-8000
McDaniel College Post-Sec.
2 College Hl 21157 410-848-7000

Westover, Somerset
Somerset County SD 900/PK-12
7982 Crisfield Hwy 21871 410-651-1616
Dr. Karen-Lee Brofee, supt. Fax 651-2931
www.somerset.k12.md.us
Tawes Technology & Career Center Vo/Tech
7982 Crisfield Hwy 21871 410-651-2285
Jim Webster, prin. Fax 651-3154
Other Schools – See Crisfield, Princess Anne

Holly Grove Christian S 500/K-12
7317 Mennonite Church Rd 21871 410-957-0222
Michael Rohrer, prin. Fax 957-4250

Wheaton, Montgomery

American Beauty Academy Post-Sec.
2518 University Blvd W 20902 301-949-3000

White Plains, Charles, Pop. 3,560

Southern Maryland Christian Academy 400/PK-12
PO Box 1668 20695 301-870-2550
Colleen Gaines, prin. Fax 934-2855

Williamsport, Washington, Pop. 2,135
Washington County SD
Supt. — See Hagerstown
Springfield MS 800/6-8
334 Sunset Ave 21795 301-766-8389
Jennifer Ruppenthal, prin. Fax 766-8401
Williamsport HS 900/9-12
5 S Clifton Dr 21795 301-766-8423
Henry Bohlander, prin. Fax 223-9610

Gateway Christian Academy 100/PK-12
PO Box 590 21795 301-582-4595
Greg Prytherch, prin. Fax 223-5972

Worton, Kent
Kent County SD
Supt. — See Chestertown
Kent County HS 800/9-12
25301 Lambs Meadow Rd 21678 410-778-4540
Ed Silver, prin. Fax 778-3802

Wye Mills, Talbot

Chesapeake College Post-Sec.
PO Box 8 21679 410-822-5400

MASSACHUSETTS

MASSACHUSETTS DEPARTMENT OF EDUCATION
350 Main St Ste 28, Malden 02148-5096
Telephone 781-388-3000
Fax 781-388-3392
Website http://www.doe.mass.edu

Commissioner of Education David Driscoll

MASSACHUSETTS BOARD OF EDUCATION
350 Main St, Malden 02148

Chairperson Christopher Anderson

PUBLIC, PRIVATE AND CATHOLIC SECONDARY SCHOOLS

Abington, Plymouth, Pop. 13,817
Abington SD 2,400/PK-12
1 Ralph Hamlin Ln 02351 781-982-2150
John Aherne, supt. Fax 982-2157
www.abington.k12.ma.us
Abington HS 600/9-12
201 Gliniewicz Way 02351 781-982-2160
Teresa Sullivan, prin. Fax 982-0061
Frolio JHS 400/7-8
1071 Washington St 02351 781-982-2170
Felicia Moschella, prin. Fax 982-2173

Acton, Middlesex
Acton-Boxborough Regional SD 2,600/7-12
16 Charter Rd 01720 978-264-4700
William Ryan, supt. Fax 263-8409
ab.mec.edu
Acton-Boxborough Regional HS 1,700/9-12
36 Charter Rd 01720 978-264-4700
Stephen Donovan, prin. Fax 266-2521
Grey JHS 900/7-8
16 Charter Rd 01720 978-264-4700
Craig Hardimon, prin. Fax 266-2535

Acushnet, Bristol, Pop. 3,170
Acushnet SD 1,100/PK-8
708 Middle Rd 02743 508-998-0260
Stephen Donovan, supt. Fax 998-0262
www.acushnetschools.net
Ford MS 500/5-8
708 Middle Rd 02743 508-998-0265
Timothy Plante, prin. Fax 998-7316

Adams, Berkshire, Pop. 6,356
Adams-Cheshire Regional SD
Supt. — See Cheshire
Adams Memorial MS 400/6-8
30 Columbia St 01220 413-743-0554
Kimberly Roberts-Morandi, prin. Fax 743-8424

Agawam, Hampden, Pop. 28,599
Agawam SD
Supt. — See Feeding Hills
Agawam HS 1,200/9-12
760 Cooper St 01001 413-821-0521
Dr. Linda J. Prystupa, prin. Fax 821-0536

Amesbury, Essex, Pop. 12,109
Amesbury SD 2,600/PK-12
10 Congress St 01913 978-388-0507
Charles Chaurette, supt. Fax 388-8315
www.ci.amesbury.ma.us
Amesbury HS 800/9-12
5 Highland St 01913 978-388-4800
Leslie Murray, prin. Fax 388-3393
Amesbury MS 800/5-8
220 Main St 01913 978-388-0515
Michael Curry, prin. Fax 388-1626

Amherst, Hampshire, Pop. 17,824
Amherst-Pelham SD 1,900/7-12
170 Chestnut St 01002 413-362-1810
Jere Hochman, supt. Fax 549-9811
www.arps.org/
Amherst Regional HS 1,300/9-12
21 Matoon St 01002 413-362-1700
Mark Jackson, prin. Fax 549-9704
Amherst Regional MS 600/7-8
170 Chestnut St 01002 413-362-1850
Fran Ziperstein, prin. Fax 549-9812

Amherst College Post-Sec.
PO Box 5000 01002 413-542-2000
Hampshire College Post-Sec.
893 West St 01002 413-549-4600
University of Massachusetts 01003 Post-Sec.
413-545-0111

Andover, Essex, Pop. 8,242
Andover SD 6,000/PK-12
36 Bartlet St 01810 978-623-8501
Claudia Bach Ed.D., supt. Fax 623-8505
www.aps1.net
Andover HS 1,700/9-12
80 Shawsheen Rd 01810 978-623-8632
Peter Anderson, prin. Fax 623-8636
Andover West MS 500/6-8
98 Shawsheen Rd 01810 978-623-8700
Marilyn Holmes, prin. Fax 623-8720
Doherty MS 600/6-8
50 Bartlet St 01810 978-623-8750
Bruce Maki, prin. Fax 623-8770
Wood Hill MS 400/6-8
11 Cross St 01810 978-623-8925
Patrick Bucco, prin. Fax 623-8929

Greater Lawrence SD
57 River Rd 01810 978-686-0194
Dr. Judy Ann Delucia, supt. Fax 687-6209
www.glts.tec.ma.us
Greater Lawrence Technical S Vo/Tech
57 River Rd 01810 978-686-0194
Maureen Busa-Gilbert, prin. Fax 687-6209

Massachusetts School of Law at Andover Post-Sec.
500 Federal St 01810 978-681-0800
Phillips Academy 1,100/9-12
180 Main St 01810 978-749-4000
Barbara Chase, hdmstr. Fax 749-4526

Arlington, Middlesex, Pop. 42,000
Arlington SD 4,400/K-12
869 Massachusetts Ave 02476 781-316-3502
Nate Levenson, supt. Fax 316-3509
www.arlington.k12.ma.us
Arlington HS 1,100/9-12
869 Massachusetts Ave 02476 781-316-3593
Charles Skidmore, prin. Fax 316-3504
Ottoson MS 1,000/6-8
63 Acton St 02476 781-316-3744
Stavroula Bouris, prin. Fax 641-5436

Arlington Catholic HS 800/9-12
16 Medford St 02474 781-646-7770
Stephen Biagioni, prin. Fax 648-8345

Ashburnham, Worcester
Ashburnham-Westminster Regional SD 2,400/PK-12
11 Oakmont Dr 01430 978-827-1434
Mr. Michael Zapantis, supt. Fax 827-5969
www.awrsd.org
Oakmont Regional HS 700/9-12
9 Oakmont Dr 01430 978-827-5907
Donald Lawrence, prin. Fax 827-1413
Overlook MS 600/6-8
10 Oakmont Dr 01430 978-827-1425
Brenda Houle, prin. Fax 827-1423

Cushing Academy 400/9-12
PO Box 8000 01430 978-827-7000
Dr. Jim Tracy, hdmstr. Fax 827-7500

Ashland, Middlesex, Pop. 12,066
Ashland SD 2,200/PK-12
87 W Union St 01721 508-881-0150
Dr. Richard Hoffmann, supt. Fax 881-0161
www.ashland.k12.ma.us
Ashland HS 700/9-12
65 E Union St 01721 508-881-0177
Michael Tempesta, prin. Fax 881-0186
Ashland MS 400/6-8
87 W Union St 01721 508-881-0167
Kevin Carney, prin. Fax 881-0169

Athol, Worcester, Pop. 8,732
Athol-Royalston SD 2,100/PK-12
PO Box 968 01331 978-249-2400
Anthony Polito, supt. Fax 249-2402
www.athol-royalstonschools.org
Athol HS 600/9-12
2363 Main St 01331 978-249-2435
Kent Strong, prin. Fax 249-7217
Athol-Royalston MS 500/6-8
1062 Pleasant St 01331 978-249-2430
John Doty, prin. Fax 249-0055
Bigelow S 100/PK-12
129 Allen St 01331 978-249-2403
Patricia Byrnes, prin. Fax 249-7210

Attleboro, Bristol, Pop. 43,382
Attleboro SD 6,300/PK-12
100 Rathbun Willard Dr 02703 508-222-0012
Pia Durkin Ph.D., supt. Fax 223-1577
www.attleboroschools.com
Attleboro HS 1,900/9-12
100 Rathbun Willard Dr 02703 508-222-5150
Donald Frederick, prin. Fax 223-1579
Brennan MS 600/5-8
320 Rathbun Willard Dr 02703 508-222-6260
Richard L. George, prin. Fax 223-1555
Coelho MS 600/5-8
99 Brown St 02703 508-761-7551
James Rose, prin. Fax 399-6506
Wamsutta MS 700/5-8
300 Locust St 02703 508-223-1540
David Sutherland, prin. Fax 226-2087

Bishop Feehan HS 1,000/9-12
70 Holcott Dr 02703 508-226-6223
William Runey, prin. Fax 226-7696

Auburn, Worcester, Pop. 15,005
Auburn SD 2,300/K-12
5 West St 01501 508-832-7755
Dr. Helene Skrzyniarz, supt. Fax 832-7757
www.auburnpublicschools.com/
Auburn HS 600/9-12
99 Auburn St 01501 508-832-7711
Casey Handfield, prin. Fax 832-7710
Auburn MS 600/6-8
10 Swanson Rd 01501 508-832-7722
Ann O'Leary-Ortiz, prin. Fax 832-8655

Auburndale, See Newton

Lasell College Post-Sec.
1844 Commonwealth Ave 02466 617-243-2225

Avon, Norfolk, Pop. 4,558
Avon SD 700/PK-12
Patrick Clark Dr 02322 508-588-0230
Dr. Margaret Frieswyk, supt. Fax 559-1081
www.avon.k12.ma.us/
Avon MSHS 400/7-12
287 W Main St 02322 508-583-4822
Sharon Hansen, prin. Fax 588-5501

Ayer, Middlesex, Pop. 2,889
Ayer SD 1,400/PK-12
141 Washington St 01432 978-772-8600
Dr. Lore Nielson, supt. Fax 772-7444
www.ayer.k12.ma.us
Ayer HS 400/9-12
141 Washington St 01432 978-772-8600
Don Parker, prin. Fax 772-8615
Ayer MS 400/5-8
141 Washington St 01432 978-772-8600
Lyn Lawrence, prin. Fax 772-8643

Babson Park, Norfolk

Babson College Post-Sec.
PO Box 57310 02457 781-235-1200

Baldwinville, Worcester, Pop. 1,795
Narragansett Regional SD 1,700/PK-12
462 Baldwinville Rd 01436 978-939-5661
Stephen Hemman Ed.D., supt. Fax 939-5179
www.nrsd.org/
Narragansett MS 500/5-8
460 Baldwinville Rd 01436 978-393-5928
Rob Rouleau, prin. Fax 939-8422
Narragansett Regional HS 500/9-12
464 Baldwinville Rd 01436 978-939-5388
John Jasinski, prin. Fax 939-5723

Barnstable, Barnstable, Pop. 48,854

Trinity Christian Academy 100/PK-12
979 Mary Dunn Rd 02630 508-790-0114
Sharon Van Wickle, hdmstr. Fax 790-1293

Barre, Worcester, Pop. 1,094
Quabbin SD 3,300/PK-12
872 South St 01005 978-355-4668
Beverly Brown, supt. Fax 355-6756
www.quabbin.k12.ma.us
Quabbin Regional HS 1,000/9-12
800 South St 01005 978-355-4651
Marilyn Tencza, prin. Fax 355-0163
Quabbin Regional MS 600/7-8
800 South St 01005 978-355-5042
Susanne Musnicki, prin. Fax 355-6104

Bedford, Middlesex, Pop. 12,996
Bedford SD 2,300/K-12
97 McMahon Rd 01730 781-275-7588
Maureen Lacroix, supt. Fax 275-0885
www.bedford.k12.ma.us
Bedford HS 700/9-12
9 Mudge Way 01730 781-275-1700
Jonathon Sills, prin. Fax 275-6664
Glenn MS 500/6-8
99 McMahon Rd 01730 781-275-3201
Phyllis Rotsko, prin. Fax 275-7632

East Coast Aero Tech School Post-Sec.
150 Hanscom Dr 01730 781-274-8448
Middlesex Community College Post-Sec.
210 Springs Rd 01730 781-280-3200

Belchertown, Hampshire, Pop. 2,339
Belchertown SD 1,300/PK-12
PO Box 841 01007 413-323-0456
Richard Pazasis, supt. Fax 323-0448
www.belchertownps.org
Belchertown HS 700/9-12
142 Old Springfield Rd 01007 413-323-9419
Christine Vigneux, prin. Fax 323-9406
Jabish MS 7-8
62 N Washington St 01007 413-323-0433
Thomas Ruscio, prin. Fax 323-0450

Bellingham, Norfolk, Pop. 4,535
Bellingham SD 2,700/PK-12
60 Harpin St 02019 508-883-1706
T.C. Mattock Ed.D., supt. Fax 883-0180
www.bellingham.k12.ma.us
Bellingham HS 800/9-12
60 Blackstone St 02019 508-966-3761
Peter Badalament, prin. Fax 966-4183
Memorial MS 900/5-8
130 Blackstone St 02019 508-883-2330
Elaine D'Alfonso, prin. Fax 883-2037

Belmont, Middlesex, Pop. 24,720
Belmont SD 3,700/K-12
644 Pleasant St 02478 617-993-5401
Peter Holland, supt. Fax 993-5409
www.belmont.k12.ma.us
Belmont HS 1,200/9-12
221 Concord Ave 02478 617-484-5900
Michael Harvey, prin. Fax 484-5909
Chenery MS 1,200/5-8
95 Washington St 02478 617-484-3900
Deborah Alexander, prin. Fax 484-3676

Belmont Hill S 400/7-12
350 Prospect St 02478 617-484-4410
Richard Melvoin, prin. Fax 484-4688
Waldorf HS of Massachusetts Bay 100/9-12
132 Lexington St 02478 617-489-6600
Mara White, admin. Fax 489-6619

Berkley, Bristol
Berkley SD 1,000/K-8
21 N Main St 02779 508-822-5220
Thomas Lynch, supt. Fax 823-1772
Berkley MS 500/5-8
21 N Main St 02779 508-884-9434
T. Ross Edminster, prin. Fax 823-1772

Beverly, Essex, Pop. 39,876
Beverly SD 4,000/PK-12
502 Cabot St 01915 978-921-6100
James Hayes Ed.D., supt. Fax 922-6597
www.beverlyschools.org/index2.shtm
Beverly HS 1,300/9-12
100 Sohier Rd 01915 978-921-6132
Dr. Carla Scuzzarella, prin. Fax 927-9460
Briscoe MS 500/6-8
7 Sohier Rd 01915 978-921-6103
Matthew Poska, prin. Fax 927-7781

Endicott College Post-Sec.
376 Hale St 01915 978-927-0585
Montserrat College of Art Post-Sec.
PO Box 26 01915 800-836-0487
Waring S 100/6-12
35 Standley St 01915 978-927-8793
Peter Smick, hdmstr. Fax 921-2107

Billerica, Middlesex, Pop. 37,609
Billerica SD 6,300/K-12
365 Boston Rd 01821 978-436-9500
Anthony Serio, supt. Fax 436-9595
www.billerica.mec.edu
Billerica Memorial HS 1,500/9-12
35 River St 01821 978-436-9300
Richard Safier, prin. Fax 436-9393
Locke MS 600/6-8
110 Allen Rd 01821 978-436-9420
Alexander Infanger, prin. Fax 436-9424
Marshall MS 900/6-8
15 Floyd St 01821 978-436-9440
Roland Boucher, prin. Fax 439-1242

Shawsheen Valley Vocational Technical SD
100 Cook St 01821 978-667-2111
Charles Lyons, supt. Fax 663-6272
www.shawsheen.tec.ma.us
Shawsheen Valley Technical HS Vo/Tech
100 Cook St 01821 978-667-2111
Robert Cunningham, prin. Fax 663-6272

Blackstone, Worcester, Pop. 8,023
Blackstone-Millville Regional SD 2,200/PK-12
175 Lincoln St 01504 508-883-4400
Everett B. Campbell, supt. Fax 883-9892
www.bmrsd.net
Blackstone-Millville Regional HS 600/9-12
175 Lincoln St 01504 508-876-0117
Richard Porter, prin. Fax 883-9892
Hartnett MS 600/6-8
35 Federal St 01504 508-876-0193
Kimberly Shaver-Hood, prin. Fax 876-0198

Bolton, Worcester
Nashoba Regional SD 3,100/PK-12
50 Mechanic St 01740 978-779-0539
Michael Wood Ed.D., supt. Fax 779-5537
www.nrsd.net
Nashoba Regional HS 900/9-12
12 Green Rd 01740 978-779-2257
John Smith, prin. Fax 779-2854
Other Schools – See Lancaster, Stow

Boston, Suffolk, Pop. 559,034
Boston SD 56,100/PK-12
26 Court St Ste 10 02108 617-635-9000
Michael Contompasis, supt. Fax 635-9059
www.bostonpublicschools.org/
Boston Latin S 2,400/7-12
78 Avenue Louis Pasteur 02115 617-635-8895
Cornelia Kelley, hdmstr. Fax 635-7883
English HS 1,300/9-12
144 McBride St 02130 617-635-8979
Jose Duarte, hdmstr. Fax 635-8988
Quincy Upper S 400/6-12
152 Arlington St 02116 617-635-8940
Bak Fun Wong, prin. Fax 635-8945
Snowden International HS 400/9-12
150 Newbury St 02116 617-635-9989
Gloria Coulter, hdmstr. Fax 635-9996
Other Schools – See Brighton, Charlestown, Dorchester, East Boston, Hyde Park, Jamaica Plain, Mattapan, Roslindale, Roxbury, Roxbury Crossing, South Boston, West Roxbury

Bay State College Post-Sec.
122 Commonwealth Ave 02116 617-217-9000
Benjamin Franklin Inst. of Technology Post-Sec.
41 Berkeley St 02116 617-423-4630
Berklee College of Music Post-Sec.
1140 Boylston St 02215 617-266-1400
Beth Israel Healthcare Post-Sec.
330 Brookline Ave 02215 617-667-2539
Blaine The Beauty Career School Post-Sec.
30 West St 02111 617-266-2661
Boston Architectural Center Post-Sec.
320 Newbury St 02115 617-262-5000
Boston Baptist College Post-Sec.
950 Metropolitan Ave 02136 617-364-3510
Boston Conservatory Post-Sec.
8 Fenway 02215 617-536-6340
Boston Trinity Academy 200/6-12
17 Hale St 02136 617-364-3700
Timothy Wiens, hdmstr. Fax 364-3800
Boston University Post-Sec.
121 Bay State Rd 02215 617-353-2000
Boston University Academy 200/9-12
1 University Rd 02215 617-353-9000
James Berkman, hdmstr. Fax 353-8999
Boston University Medical Center Post-Sec.
100 E Newton St 02118 617-638-5300
Brigham and Women's Hospital Post-Sec.
75 Francis St 02115 617-732-7493
Bunker Hill Community College Post-Sec.
250 Rutherford Ave 02129 617-228-2000
Butera School of Art Post-Sec.
111 Beacon St 02116 617-536-4623
Cathedral HS 300/9-12
74 Union Park St 02118 617-542-2325
Christol Murch, prin. Fax 542-1745
Children's Hospital Post-Sec.
300 Longwood Ave 02115 617-355-6433
Commonwealth S 200/9-12
151 Commonwealth Ave 02116 617-266-7525
William Wharton, hdmstr. Fax 266-5769
Emerson College Post-Sec.
120 Boylston St 02116 617-824-8600
Emmanuel College Post-Sec.
400 Fenway 02115 617-277-9340
Fisher College Post-Sec.
118 Beacon St 02116 617-236-8800
Gibbs College of Boston Post-Sec.
126 Newbury St 02116 617-578-7100
Learning Institute for Beauty Sciences Post-Sec.
867 Boylston St 02116 617-424-6565
Massachusetts College of Art Post-Sec.
621 Huntington Ave 02115 617-232-1555
MA College of Pharmacy & Health Sciences Post-Sec.
179 Longwood Ave 02115 617-732-2800
Massachusetts School Professional Psych. Post-Sec.
221 Rivermoor St 02132 617-327-6777
MGH Institute of Health Professions Post-Sec.
36 1st Ave 02129 617-726-3140
New England College of Finance Post-Sec.
10 High St Ste 204 02110 617-951-2350
New England College of Optometry Post-Sec.
424 Beacon St 02115 800-824-5526
New England Conservatory of Music Post-Sec.
290 Huntington Ave 02115 617-585-1100
New England School of Art & Design Post-Sec.
75 Arlington St 02116 617-573-8785
New England School of Law Post-Sec.
154 Stuart St 02116 617-451-0010
New England School of Photography Post-Sec.
537 Commonwealth Ave 02215 617-437-1868
Newman Preparatory S 300/9-12
247 Marlborough St 02116 617-267-4530
J. Harry Lynch, prin. Fax 267-7070
North Bennet Street School Post-Sec.
39 N Bennet St 02113 617-227-0155
Northeastern University Post-Sec.
360 Huntington Ave 02115 617-373-2000
Richmond University London England Post-Sec.
343 Congress St Ste 3100 02210 617-450-5617
School of the Museum of Fine Arts Post-Sec.
230 Fenway 02115 617-267-6100
Simmons College Post-Sec.
300 Fenway 02115 617-521-2000
Suffolk University Post-Sec.
8 Ashburton Pl 02108 617-573-8460
The Art Inst. of Boston at Lesley Univ. Post-Sec.
700 Beacon St 02215 617-585-6710
Tufts University Post-Sec.
136 Harrison Ave 02111 617-636-7000
University of Massachusetts Boston Post-Sec.
100 William T Mrrissey Blvd 02125 617-287-5000
Urban College of Boston Post-Sec.
178 Tremont St 02111 617-292-4723
Veterans Administration Medical Center Post-Sec.
150 S Huntington Ave 02130 617-232-9500
Wentworth Institute of Technology Post-Sec.
550 Huntington Ave 02115 617-442-9010
Wheelock College Post-Sec.
200 Riverway 02215 617-734-5200
Winsor S 400/5-12
103 Pilgrim Rd 02215 617-735-9500
Rachel Friis Stettler, prin. Fax 739-5519

Bourne, Barnstable, Pop. 1,284
Bourne SD 2,500/PK-12
36 Sandwich Rd 02532 508-759-0660
Edmond LaFleur, supt. Fax 759-1107
www.bourne.k12.ma.us
Bourne HS 600/9-12
75 Waterhouse Rd 02532 508-759-0670
Ronald McCarthy, prin. Fax 759-0677
Bourne MS 800/5-8
77 Waterhouse Rd 02532 508-759-0690
Ernest Frias, prin. Fax 759-0695

Upper Cape Cod Vo-Tech SD
220 Sandwich Rd 02532 508-759-7711
Kevin Farr, supt. Fax 759-7208
Upper Cape Cod Regional Technical S Vo/Tech
220 Sandwich Rd 02532 508-759-7711
Robert Dutch, prin. Fax 759-7208

Boylston, Worcester
Berlin-Boylston SD 500/7-12
215 Main St 01505 508-869-2837
Dr. Marcia Lukon, supt. Fax 869-0023
www.mec.edu/bbps
Tahanto Regional MSHS 500/7-12
1001 Main St 01505 508-869-2333
Carol Bryngelson, prin. Fax 869-0175

Bradford, See Haverhill

Bradford Christian Academy 100/6-12
97 Oxford Ave 01835 978-373-7900
Larry George, hdmstr. Fax 373-7911

Braintree, Norfolk, Pop. 33,800
Braintree SD 5,000/K-12
348 Pond St 02184 781-380-0130
Dr. Peter Kurzberg, supt. Fax 380-0146
www.braintreeschools.org/
Braintree HS 1,400/9-12
128 Town St 02184 781-848-4000
David Swanton, prin. Fax 380-0116
East MS 700/6-8
305 River St 02184 781-380-0170
Kristen St. George, prin. Fax 848-4522
South MS 600/6-8
232 Peach St 02184 781-380-0160
Edward McDonough, prin. Fax 380-0164

Archbishop Williams HS 600/9-12
80 Independence Ave 02184 781-843-3636
Mary Lou Sadowski, prin. Fax 843-3782
Thayer Academy 700/6-12
745 Washington St 02184 781-843-3580
William Koskores, hdmstr. Fax 380-8785

Bridgewater, Plymouth, Pop. 7,242
Bridgewater-Raynham Regional SD
Supt. — See Raynham
Bridgewater-Raynham Regional HS 1,500/9-12
166 Mount Prospect St 02324 508-697-6902
Jeffrey Granatino, prin. Fax 279-2110
Williams MS 1,100/5-8
200 South St 02324 508-697-6968
Howard Gilmore, prin. Fax 697-6775

Bridgewater State College 02325 Post-Sec.
508-697-1237

Brighton, See Boston
Boston SD
Supt. — See Boston
Boston Community Leadership Academy 400/9-12
20 Warren St 02135 617-635-8937
Nicole Bahnam, hdmstr. Fax 635-8942
Brighton HS 1,300/9-12
25 Warren St 02135 617-635-9873
Toby Romer, hdmstr. Fax 635-9892
Edison MS 600/6-8
60 Glenmont Rd 02135 617-635-8436
Eliot Stern, prin. Fax 635-8446

Bryman Institute Post-Sec.
1505 Commonwealth Ave 02135 617-783-9955
Margolis Mesivta of Greater Boston 100/9-12
34 Sparhawk St 02135 617-779-0166
Rabbi Azriel Blumberg, prin. Fax 779-0166
Mt. St. Joseph Academy 300/9-12
617 Cambridge St 02135 617-254-8383
Kathleen Fraser, prin. Fax 254-0240

Brockton, Plymouth, Pop. 94,632
Brockton SD 14,800/PK-12
43 Crescent St 02301 508-580-7511
Basan Nembirkow, supt. Fax 580-7513
www.brocktonpublicschools.com
Brockton HS 4,300/9-12
470 Forest Ave 02301 508-580-7633
Dr. Susan Szachowicz, prin. Fax 580-7600
East JHS 700/7-8
464 Centre St 02302 508-580-7351
Donald Burrell, prin. Fax 580-7090
Gilmore Academy 100/6-8
150 Clinton St 02302 508-580-7274
Terry Starr-Klein, prin. Fax 580-7077
North JHS 700/7-8
108 Oak St 02301 508-580-7371
Fax 580-7088
South MS 700/6-8
105 Keith Avenue Ext 02301 508-580-7311
Kevin Karo, prin. Fax 580-7089

West JHS 700/7-8
271 West St 02301 508-580-7381
Darcy Fernandes, prin. Fax 580-7307
Paine S, 211 Crescent St 02302 Adult
Dr. Linda Faria-Braun, admin. 508-580-7475

Ailano School of Aesthetics Post-Sec.
553 Forest Ave 02301 508-587-3883
Ailano School of Cosmetology Post-Sec.
PO Box 4740 02303 508-583-5433
Brockton Hospital Post-Sec.
680 Centre St 02302 508-941-7044
Cardinal Spellman HS 700/9-12
738 Court St 02302 508-583-6875
Dorothy Lynch, prin. Fax 580-1977
Computer-Ed Business Institute Post-Sec.
375 Westgate Dr 02301 508-941-0730
LaBaron Hairdressing Academy Post-Sec.
240 Liberty St 02301 508-583-1700
Massasoit Community College Post-Sec.
1 Massasoit Blvd 02302 508-588-9100

Brookline, Norfolk, Pop. 57,600
Brookline SD 6,000/PK-12
333 Washington St 02445 617-730-2403
Dr. William Lupini, supt. Fax 730-2108
www.brookline.k12.ma.us/
Brookline HS 1,900/9-12
115 Greenough St 02445 617-713-5000
Robert Weintraub, prin. Fax 713-5005

Boston Graduate Sch for Psychoanalysis Post-Sec.
1583 Beacon St 02446 617-277-3915
Dexter S 400/PK-12
20 Newton St 02445 617-522-5544
William Phinney, prin. Fax 522-8166
Hellenic College/Holy Cross Sch Theology Post-Sec.
50 Goddard Ave 02445 617-731-3500
Maimonides S 700/K-12
34 Philbrick Rd 02445 617-232-4452
Joshua Wolff, dir. Fax 566-2061
Newbury College Post-Sec.
129 Fisher Ave 02445 617-730-7000
New England Hebrew Academy 200/PK-12
PO Box 514 02446 617-731-5330
Rabbi Chaim Ciment, dir. Fax 277-0752
New England Institute of Art Post-Sec.
10 Brookline Pl 02445 617-739-1700
Southfield S 300/PK-12
10 Newton St 02445 617-522-6980
William Phinney, hdmstr. Fax 522-8166

Burlington, Middlesex, Pop. 23,302
Burlington SD 3,500/K-12
123 Cambridge St 01803 781-270-1800
Dr. James Picone, supt. Fax 270-1773
www.burlington.mec.edu
Burlington HS 1,000/9-12
123 Cambridge St 01803 781-270-1800
Linda Hayes, prin. Fax 229-4893
Simonds MS 900/6-8
144 Winn St 01803 781-270-1782
Richard Connors, prin. Fax 270-1654

Open Bible Academy 100/K-12
3 Winn St 01803 781-272-2074
Fred Erwin, prin. Fax 272-7279

Buzzards Bay, Barnstable, Pop. 3,250

Massachusetts Maritime Academy Post-Sec.
101 Academy Dr 02532 508-830-5000

Byfield, Essex
Triton Regional SD 3,500/PK-12
112 Elm St 01922 978-465-2397
Sandra Halloran, supt. Fax 465-8599
www.trsd.net
Triton Regional HS 1,000/9-12
112 Elm St 01922 978-462-8171
Robert C. Manseau, prin. Fax 465-6868
Triton Regional MS 600/7-8
112 Elm St 01922 978-463-5845
Peter Gadd, prin. Fax 465-6868

Governor's Academy 400/9-12
1 Elm St Unit 99 01922 978-465-1763
John Doggett, hdmstr. Fax 463-9896

Cambridge, Middlesex, Pop. 100,135
Cambridge SD 6,200/PK-12
159 Thorndike St 02141 617-349-6494
Dr. Thomas Fowler-Finn, supt. Fax 349-6496
www.cpsd.us
Cambridge Rindge & Latin HS 1,800/9-12
459 Broadway 02138 617-349-6632
Christopher Saheed, prin. Fax 349-6749

Boston Archdiocesan Choir S 5-8
29 Mount Auburn St 02138 617-868-8658
Jennine Zito, prin. Fax 354-7092
Buckingham Browne & Nichols HS 400/9-12
80 Gerrys Landing Rd 02138 617-547-6100
Rebecca Upham, hdmstr. Fax 576-1139
Buckingham Browne & Nichols MS 200/7-8
80 Sparks St 02138 617-800-2336
Rebecca Upham, hdmstr. Fax 491-5159
Cambridge College Post-Sec.
1000 Massachusetts Ave 02138 617-868-1000
Cambridge School of Culinary Arts Post-Sec.
2020 Massachusetts Ave 02140 617-354-2020
Ecole Bilingue S of Boston 500/PK-12
45 Matignon Rd 02140 617-499-1451
John Larner, hdmstr. Fax 499-1454
Episcopal Divinity School Post-Sec.
99 Brattle St 02138 617-868-3450
Harvard University Post-Sec.
8 Garden St 02138 617-495-1000
Hult International Business School Post-Sec.
1 Education St 02141 617-746-1990
Lesley University Post-Sec.
29 Everett St 02138 617-349-8800
Longy School of Music Post-Sec.
1 Follen St 02138 617-876-0956
Massachusetts Institute of Technology Post-Sec.
77 Massachusetts Ave 02139 617-253-1000
Matignon HS 500/9-12
1 Matignon Rd 02140 617-876-1212
Thomas Galligani, prin. Fax 491-0290
North Cambridge Catholic HS 300/9-12
40 Norris St 02140 617-876-6068
Robert McCarthy, prin. Fax 576-1898
Weston Jesuit School of Theology Post-Sec.
3 Phillips Pl 02138 617-492-1960

Canton, Norfolk, Pop. 18,530
Blue Hills Vocational SD
800 Randolph St 02021 781-828-5800
Joseph Ciccolo, supt. Fax 828-0794
www.bluehills.org
Blue Hills Regional Technical S Vo/Tech
800 Randolph St 02021 781-828-5800
Joseph Ciccolo, prin. Fax 828-0794

Canton SD 3,000/PK-12
960 Washington St 02021 781-821-5060
Irene Sherry Kaplan Ed.D., supt. Fax 575-6500
www.cantonma.org
Canton HS 800/9-12
900 Washington St 02021 781-821-5050
Edward Mulvey, prin. Fax 821-5052
Galvin MS 700/6-8
55 Pecunit St 02021 781-821-5070
Thomas LaLiberte, prin. Fax 575-6509

Bay State School of Technology Post-Sec.
225 Turnpike St 02021 781-828-3434

Carver, Plymouth
Carver SD 2,100/PK-12
3 Carver Square Blvd 02330 508-866-6160
Elizabeth Sorrell, supt. Fax 866-2920
www.carver.org
Carver HS 500/9-12
60 S Meadow Rd 02330 508-866-6140
Scott Knief, prin. Fax 866-5639
Carver MS 500/6-8
60 S Meadow Rd 02330 508-866-6130
Daniel Daly, prin. Fax 866-6880

Charlemont, Franklin

Academy at Charlemont 100/7-12
Mohawk Trail 01339 413-339-4912
Todd Sumner, hdmstr. Fax 339-4324

Charlestown, See Boston
Boston SD
Supt. — See Boston
Charlestown HS 1,200/9-12
240 Medford St 02129 617-635-9914
Michael Fung, hdmstr. Fax 635-9928
Edwards MS 500/6-8
28 Walker St 02129 617-635-8516
Michael Sabin, prin. Fax 635-8522

RETS Electronic School Post-Sec.
570 Rutherford Ave 02129 800-739-8700

Charlton, Worcester
Dudley-Charlton Regional SD
Supt. — See Dudley
Charlton MS 900/5-8
2 Oxford Rd 01507 508-248-1423
Kathryn Tucker, prin. Fax 248-1418

Southern Worcester Co. Reg Vocational SD
57 Old Muggett Hill Rd 01507 508-248-5971
David Papagni, supt. Fax 248-4747
www.baypath.tec.ma.us
Bay Path Regional Vo Tech HS Vo/Tech
57 Old Muggett Hill Rd 01507 508-248-5971
Clifford Cloutier, prin. Fax 248-4747

Chatham, Barnstable, Pop. 1,916
Chatham SD 700/PK-12
425 Crowell Rd 02633 508-945-5130
Mary Ann Lanzo, supt. Fax 945-5133
www.chatham.k12.ma.us
Chatham HS 200/9-12
425 Crowell Rd 02633 508-945-5140
Paul Mangelinkx, prin. Fax 945-5110
Chatham MS 200/5-8
425 Crowell Rd 02633 508-945-5148
Marie McKay, prin. Fax 945-5143

Chelmsford, Middlesex, Pop. 33,858
Chelmsford SD 5,700/PK-12
230 North Rd 01824 978-251-5100
Richard Moser Ph.D., supt. Fax 251-5110
www.chelmsford.k12.ma.us/
McCarthy MS 1,000/5-8
250 North Rd 01824 978-251-5122
Frank Tiano, prin. Fax 251-5130
Parker MS 800/5-8
75 Graniteville Rd 01824 978-251-5133
Denise Rainis, prin. Fax 251-5140
Other Schools – See North Chelmsford

Chelsea, Suffolk, Pop. 32,518
Chelsea SD 5,000/PK-12
500 Broadway Ste 200 02150 617-889-8415
Thomas Kingston, supt. Fax 889-8361
chelseaschools.com
Browne S 500/5-8
180 Walnut St 02150 617-889-8652
Cove Davis, prin. Fax 889-8459
Chelsea HS 1,400/9-12
299 Everett Ave 02150 617-889-8418
Morton Orlov, prin. Fax 889-8468
Clark Avenue S 600/5-8
8 Clark Ave 02150 617-889-7540
Linda Breau, prin. Fax 889-7539
Wright S 5-8
180 Walnut St 02150 617-889-8467
Donna Covino, prin. Fax 889-8463

Cheshire, Berkshire
Adams-Cheshire Regional SD 1,800/PK-12
125 Savoy Rd 01225 413-743-2939
Alfred Skrocki, supt. Fax 743-4135
www.acrsd.net
Hoosac Valley HS 500/9-12
125 Savoy Rd 01225 413-743-5200
Henry Duval, prin. Fax 743-8420
Other Schools – See Adams

Chestnut Hill, See Newton

Beaver Country Day S 400/6-12
791 Hammond St 02467 617-738-2700
Peter Hutton, prin. Fax 738-2701
Boston College Post-Sec.
140 Commonwealth Ave 02467 617-552-8000
Brimmer and May S 400/PK-12
69 Middlesex Rd 02467 617-566-7462
Anne Reenstierna, hdmstr. Fax 734-5147
Pine Manor College Post-Sec.
400 Heath St 02467 617-731-7000

Chicopee, Hampden, Pop. 54,680
Chicopee SD 7,500/PK-12
180 Broadway St 01020 413-594-3410
Richard Rege, supt. Fax 594-3552
www.chicopee.mec.edu/
Bellamy MS 1,000/6-8
314 Pendleton Ave 01020 413-594-3527
Matthew Francis, prin. Fax 594-1838
Chicopee Comprehensive HS 1,300/9-12
617 Montgomery St 01020 413-594-3534
Stanley Kozikowski, prin. Fax 594-3492
Chicopee HS 1,100/9-12
820 Front St 01020 413-594-3437
Roland Joyal, prin. Fax 594-3500
Fairview MS 800/6-8
26 Memorial Ave 01020 413-594-3501
Michele Partyka, prin. Fax 594-3509

Elms College Post-Sec.
291 Springfield St 01013 413-594-2761
Porter and Chester Institute Post-Sec.
134 Dulong Cir 01022 413-593-3339

Clinton, Worcester, Pop. 7,943
Clinton SD 1,600/K-12
150 School St 01510 978-365-4200
Gerald M. Gaw, supt. Fax 365-5037
clinton.k12.ma.us
Clinton HS 500/8-12
200 W Boylston St 01510 978-365-4208
James Hastings, prin. Fax 365-4219

Cohasset, Norfolk, Pop. 7,075
Cohasset SD 1,500/PK-12
143 Pond St 02025 781-383-6111
Denise Walsh Ed.D., supt. Fax 383-6507
www.cohassetk12.org
Cohasset MSHS 800/6-12
143 Pond St 02025 781-383-6100
Joel Antolini, prin. Fax 383-6556

Concord, Middlesex, Pop. 4,700
Concord SD 2,000/K-8
120 Meriam Rd 01742 978-318-1500
Brenda Finn Ed.D., supt. Fax 318-1537
www.colonial.net
Concord MS 700/6-8
835 Old Marlboro Rd 01742 978-318-1380
Arthur Unobskey, prin. Fax 318-1392

Concord-Carlisle SD 1,300/9-12
120 Meriam Rd 01742 978-318-1500
Brenda Finn, supt. Fax 318-1537
www.colonial.net
Concord-Carlisle HS 1,300/9-12
500 Walden St 01742 978-318-1400
Arthur Dulong, prin. Fax 318-1435

Concord Academy 300/9-12
166 Main St 01742 978-402-2200
Jacob Dresden, hdmstr. Fax 402-2210
Fenn S 300/4-9
516 Monument St 01742 978-369-5800
Gerard Ward, hdmstr. Fax 371-7520
Middlesex S 400/9-12
PO Box 9122 01742 978-369-2550
Kathleen Carroll Giles, hdmstr. Fax 369-3846

Conway, Franklin

Conway School of Landscape Design Post-Sec.
PO Box 179 01341 413-369-4044

Dalton, Berkshire, Pop. 7,155
Central Berkshire Regional SD 2,200/PK-12
PO Box 299 01227 413-684-0320
Donna Harlan, supt. Fax 684-1520
www.cbrsd.org
Nessacus Regional MS 600/6-8
35 Fox Rd 01226 413-684-0780
Gerard Dery, prin. Fax 684-4214
Wahconah Regional HS 800/9-12
150 Old Windsor Rd 01226 413-684-1330
James Conro, prin. Fax 684-5032

Danvers, Essex, Pop. 24,174
Danvers SD 3,600/K-12
64 Cabot Rd 01923 978-777-4539
Betty G. Allen Ph.D., supt. Fax 777-8931
www.danvers.mec.edu
Danvers HS 1,000/9-12
60 Cabot Rd 01923 978-777-8925
Eileen Erwin, prin. Fax 777-8931
Holten-Richmond MS 900/6-8
57 Conant St 01923 978-774-8590
Michael Cali, prin. Fax 762-8686

North Shore Community College Post-Sec.
1 Ferncroft Rd 01923 978-762-4000

St. Johns Prep S 1,200/9-12
72 Spring St 01923 978-774-1050
Edward Hardiman Ph.D., prin. Fax 774-5767

Dedham, Norfolk, Pop. 23,782
Dedham SD 2,700/PK-12
PO Box 246 02027 781-326-5622
June Doe, supt. Fax 320-0193
www.dedham.k12.ma.us
Dedham HS 800/9-12
140 Whiting Ave 02026 781-326-4773
Alan Winrow, prin. Fax 320-8126
Dedham MS 500/6-8
70 Whiting Ave 02026 781-326-6900
Cynthia Kelly, prin. Fax 461-0354

Noble And Greenough S 500/7-12
10 Campus Dr 02026 781-326-3700
Robert Henderson, hdmstr. Fax 320-8118
Ursuline Academy 7-12
85 Lowder St 02026 781-326-6161
Sr. Mercedes Videira, prin. Fax 326-4898

Deerfield, Franklin

Deerfield Academy 600/9-12
7 Boyden Ln 01342 413-772-0241
Margarita Curtis, prin. Fax 772-1100
Eaglebrook S 300/6-9
Pine Nook Rd 01342 413-774-7411
Andrew Chase, hdmstr. Fax 772-2394

Dighton, Bristol
Bristol County Agricultural SD
135 Center St 02715 508-669-6744
Russell James, supt. Fax 669-6747
www.bristolaggie.mec.edu/
Bristol County Agricultural HS Vo/Tech
135 Center St 02715 508-669-6744
Krista Paynton, prin. Fax 669-6747

Dighton-Rehoboth Regional SD
Supt. — See North Dighton
Dighton MS 400/5-8
1250R Somerset Ave 02715 508-669-4200
Paul Swett, prin. Fax 669-4210

Dorchester, See Boston
Boston SD
Supt. — See Boston
Academy of Public Service 300/9-12
9 Peacevale Rd 02124 617-635-8910
Zachary Robbins, hdmstr. Fax 635-7825
Boston Latin Academy 1,600/7-12
205 Townsend St 02121 617-635-9957
Maria Garcia-Aaronson, hdmstr. Fax 635-6696
Burke HS 800/9-12
77 Lawrence Ave 02121 617-635-9837
Carol Moore, hdmstr. Fax 635-9852
Cleveland MS 500/6-8
11 Charles St 02122 617-635-8631
Andy Tuite, prin. Fax 635-6413
Frederick Pilot MS 700/6-8
270 Columbia Rd 02121 617-635-1650
Debra Socia, prin. Fax 635-1637
Harbor S 300/6-8
294 Bowdoin St 02122 617-635-6365
Amy Marx, prin. Fax 635-6367
King MS 300/6-8
100 Maxwell St 02124 617-635-8212
Audrey Leung-Tat, prin. Fax 635-9356
McCormack MS 800/6-8
315 Mount Vernon St 02125 617-635-8657
Jane King, prin. Fax 635-9788
Noonan Business Academy 300/9-12
9 Peacevale Rd 02124 617-635-9730
John Leonard, hdmstr. Fax 635-7888
TechBoston Academy 200/9-12
9 Peacevale Rd 02124 617-635-1615
Mary Skipper, admin. Fax 635-1621
Wilson MS 500/6-8
18 Croftland Ave 02124 617-635-8827
Claudette Mulligan-Gates, prin. Fax 635-6414

Boston College HS 1,300/9-12
150 William Morrissey Blvd 02125 617-436-3900
Stephen Hughes, prin. Fax 265-3484
Caritas Laboure College Post-Sec.
2120 Dorchester Ave 02124 617-296-8300
Epiphany S 100/5-8
154 Centre St 02124 617-326-0425
John Finley, hdmstr. Fax 326-0424
Seton Academy 9-12
2220 Dorchester Ave 02124 617-296-1087
Maureen White Ed.D., prin. Fax 296-1089

Douglas, Worcester
Douglas SD 1,700/PK-12
21 Davis St 01516 508-476-7901
Nancy Lane, supt. Fax 476-4423
www.douglas.k12.ma.us/
Douglas MSHS 500/8-12
33 Davis St 01516 508-476-4100
Brett Kustigian, prin. Fax 476-7310

Dover, Norfolk, Pop. 2,163
Dover-Sherborn SD 1,100/6-12
157 Farm St 02030 508-785-0036
Perry Davis, supt. Fax 785-2239
www.doversherborn.org
Dover-Sherborn Regional HS 600/9-12
9 Junction St 02030 508-785-0624
Denise Lonergan, prin. Fax 785-8141
Dover-Sherborn Regional MS 500/6-8
155 Farm St 02030 508-785-0635
Frederick Randall, prin. Fax 785-0796

Dracut, Middlesex, Pop. 25,594
Dracut SD 4,200/PK-12
2063 Lakeview Ave 01826 978-957-2660
Elaine Espindle, supt. Fax 957-2682
www.dracut.k12.ma.us
Dracut HS 1,200/9-12
1540 Lakeview Ave 01826 978-957-1500
Patricia Power, prin. Fax 957-9717
Lakeview JHS 700/7-8
1570 Lakeview Ave 01826 978-957-3330
Theresa Rogers, prin. Fax 957-4075

Dudley, Worcester, Pop. 3,700
Dudley-Charlton Regional SD 4,300/PK-12
68 Dudley Oxford Rd 01571 508-943-6888
Sean Gilrein, supt. Fax 943-1077
www.dc-regional.k12.ma.us/
Dudley MS 600/5-8
70 Dudley Oxford Rd 01571 508-943-2224
Gregg Desto, prin. Fax 949-0720
Shepherd Hill Regional HS 1,100/9-12
68 Dudley Oxford Rd 01571 508-943-6700
Timothy M. Schur, prin. Fax 943-5956
Other Schools – See Charlton

Nichols College 01571 Post-Sec.
508-943-1560

Duxbury, Plymouth, Pop. 1,637
Duxbury SD 3,200/K-12
130 Saint George St 02332 781-934-7600
Eileen Williams, supt. Fax 934-7644
www.duxbury.k12.ma.us
Duxbury HS 1,000/9-12
130 Saint George St 02332 781-934-7650
Thomas Kelley, prin. Fax 934-7617
Duxbury MS 700/6-8
130 Saint George St 02332 781-934-7640
Jeffrey Knight, prin. Fax 934-7608

East Boston, See Boston
Boston SD
Supt. — See Boston
East Boston HS 1,400/9-12
86 White St 02128 617-635-9896
Michael Rubin, hdmstr. Fax 635-9726
Umana/Barnes MS 700/6-8
312 Border St 02128 617-635-8481
Dr. Jose Salgado, prin. Fax 635-9595

Savio Prep HS 400/9-12
165 Byron St 02128 617-567-2710
Anders Peterson, hdmstr. Fax 569-6883

East Bridgewater, Plymouth, Pop. 11,104
East Bridgewater SD 2,500/PK-12
11 Plymouth St 02333 508-378-8200
Margaret Strojny Ph.D., supt. Fax 378-8225
www.ebps.net
East Bridgewater HS 700/9-12
11 Plymouth St 02333 508-378-8214
Paul Vieira, prin. Fax 378-8226
Mitchell MS 1,000/4-8
435 Central St 02333 508-378-8209
Stanley Piltch, prin. Fax 378-8228

East Falmouth, Barnstable, Pop. 5,577
Falmouth SD 4,300/PK-12
340 Teaticket Hwy 02536 508-548-0151
Dennis Richards, supt. Fax 457-9032
www.falmouth.k12.ma.us
Other Schools – See Falmouth

Easthampton, Hampshire, Pop. 16,004
Easthampton SD 1,600/PK-12
50 Payson Ave Ste 200 01027 413-529-1500
Deborah Carter, supt. Fax 529-1567
www.easthampton.k12.ma.us
Easthampton HS 400/9-12
70 Williston Ave 01027 413-529-1585
Jeffrey Sealander, prin. Fax 529-1591
White Brook MS 600/5-8
200 Park St 01027 413-529-1530
Julie Salzman, prin. Fax 529-1534

Williston Northampton S 500/7-12
19 Payson Ave 01027 413-529-3000
Brian Wright, hdmstr. Fax 527-9494

East Longmeadow, Hampden, Pop. 13,367
East Longmeadow SD 2,700/K-12
180 Maple St 01028 413-525-5450
Dr. Edward Costa, supt. Fax 525-5456
www.eastlongmeadow.org
Birchland Park MS 700/6-8
50 Hanward Hl 01028 413-525-5480
Kathleen Hill, prin. Fax 525-5320
East Longmeadow HS 900/9-12
180 Maple St 01028 413-525-5460
Richard Freccero, prin. Fax 525-5496

Baptist Village Academy 100/PK-12
50 Parker St 01028 413-525-1153
Timothy Sheranko, admin. Fax 525-9991

East Sandwich, Barnstable, Pop. 3,171
Sandwich SD
Supt. — See Sandwich
Sandwich HS 1,200/9-12
365 Quaker Meeting House Rd 02537 508-888-4900
Ellin Booras, prin. Fax 833-8392

East Taunton, See Taunton
Taunton SD
Supt. — See Taunton
Martin MS 800/5-8
131 Caswell St 02718 508-821-1250
Christopher Baratta, prin. Fax 821-1273

East Walpole, Norfolk, Pop. 3,800
Walpole SD
Supt. — See Walpole
Bird MS 400/6-8
625 Washington St 02032 508-660-7226
Sandra J. Esmond, prin. Fax 660-7229

East Weymouth, Norfolk
Weymouth SD
Supt. — See Weymouth
Adams IS 800/5-8
89 Middle St 02189 781-335-1100
Zeffro Gianetti, prin. Fax 340-2544
Chapman MS 1,300/5-8
1051 Commercial St 02189 781-337-4500
Sheila Fisher, prin. Fax 340-2594

Everett, Middlesex, Pop. 36,837
Everett SD 5,300/PK-12
121 Vine St 02149 617-389-7950
Frederick Foresteire, supt. Fax 394-2408
www.everett.k12.ma.us/
Everett HS 1,700/9-12
548 Broadway 02149 617-394-2490
Janice Gauthier, prin. Fax 389-5841

Pope John XXIII Central HS 500/9-12
888 Broadway 02149 617-389-0240
William Fitzgerald Ph.D., prin. Fax 389-2201

Fairhaven, Bristol, Pop. 16,132
Fairhaven SD 2,300/PK-12
128 Washington St 02719 508-979-4000
Dr. Robert Baldwin, supt. Fax 979-4149
www.fairhavenps.org/
Fairhaven HS 700/9-12
12 Huttleston Ave 02719 508-979-4052
Jean Cote, prin. Fax 979-4140
Hastings MS 600/6-8
30 School St 02719 508-979-4063
Cynthia DeCosta, prin. Fax 979-4068

Fall River, Bristol, Pop. 91,802
Fall River SD 11,300/PK-12
417 Rock St 02720 508-675-8420
Richard D. Pavao, supt. Fax 675-8462
www.fallriver.k12.ma.us/
Durfee HS 2,900/9-12
360 Elsbree St 02720 508-675-8130
Ralph Olsen, prin. Fax 675-8186
Kuss MS 600/6-8
290 Rock St 02720 508-675-8335
Nancy Mullen, prin. Fax 675-1984
Lord MS 700/6-8
151 Amity St 02721 508-675-8208
Debra Decarlo, prin. Fax 675-8253
Morton MS 700/6-8
376 President Ave 02720 508-675-8340
James Murano, prin. Fax 675-8414
Talbot MS 700/6-8
124 Melrose St 02723 508-675-8350
Karol G. Coffin, prin. Fax 675-8356

Greater Fall River Vocational SD
251 Stonehaven Rd 02723 508-678-2891
Rogerio Ramos, supt. Fax 679-6423
www.dimanregional.org/
Diman Regional Vocational Technical HS Vo/Tech
251 Stonehaven Rd 02723 508-678-2891
Brian Bentley, prin. Fax 679-6423

Bishop Connolly HS 400/9-12
373 Elsbree St 02720 508-676-1071
Michael Scanlan, prin. Fax 676-8594
Bristol Community College Post-Sec.
777 Elsbree St 02720 508-678-2811
East Gate Christian Academy 100/PK-12
397 Bay St 02724 508-730-1735
Dr. Ronald Bernier, hdmstr. Fax 674-6166
Rob Roy Academy Fall River Campus Post-Sec.
260 S Main St 02721 508-672-4751

Falmouth, Barnstable, Pop. 4,047
Falmouth SD
Supt. — See East Falmouth
Falmouth HS 1,300/9-12
874 Gifford Street Ext 02540 508-540-2200
Paul Cali, prin. Fax 548-7515
Lawrence MS 700/7-8
113 Lakeview Ave 02540 508-548-0606
Douglas White, prin. Fax 457-9778

Falmouth Academy 200/7-12
7 Highfield Dr 02540 508-457-9696
David Faus, hdmstr. Fax 457-4112
National Grad. Sch. Quality Systems Mgmt Post-Sec.
186 Jones Rd 02540 508-457-1313

Feeding Hills, Hampden, Pop. 5,450
Agawam SD 4,200/K-12
1305 Springfield St Ste 1 01030 413-821-0548
Mary A. Czajkowski Ed.D., supt. Fax 789-1835
www.agawampublicschools.org
Agawam JHS 700/7-8
1305 Springfield St Ste 2 01030 413-821-0561
Kevin Littlefield, prin. Fax 786-4240
Other Schools – See Agawam

Fiskdale, Worcester, Pop. 2,189
Tantasqua SD 1,800/7-12
320 Brookfield Rd 01518 508-347-3077
Daniel Durgin, supt. Fax 347-2697
www.tantasqua.org
Tantasqua Regional HS 900/9-12
319 Brookfield Rd 01518 508-347-9301
Steven Bliss, prin. Fax 347-1049
Tantasqua Regional JHS 600/7-8
320 Brookfield Rd 01518 508-347-7381
Theodore Friend, prin. Fax 347-3994
Tantasqua Regional Tech HS Vo/Tech
319 Brookfield Rd 01518 508-347-3045
Timothy Prouty, prin. Fax 347-1061

Fitchburg, Worcester, Pop. 40,045
Fitchburg SD 5,200/PK-12
376 South St 01420 978-345-3200
Andre Ravenelle, supt. Fax 348-2305
www.fitchburg.k12.ma.us
Academy MS 600/5-8
98 Academy St 01420 978-343-2146
Steven Silverman, prin. Fax 348-2323
Brown Arts Vision S 700/5-8
62 Academy St 01420 978-345-3278
Theresa Mayer, prin. Fax 348-2316

Fitchburg HS 1,500/9-12
140 Arnhow Farm Rd 01420 978-345-3240
Rich Masciarelli, prin. Fax 348-2303
Memorial MS 600/5-8
615 Rollstone St 01420 978-345-3295
Francis Thomas, prin. Fax 343-2121

Montachusett Regional Vo/Tech HSD
1050 Westminster St 01420 978-345-9200
James Culkeen, supt. Fax 345-9165
www.montytech.net
Montachusett Reg Vocational Technical HS Vo/Tech
1050 Westminster St 01420 978-345-9200
Donald Cranson, prin. Fax 348-1176

Fitchburg State College Post-Sec.
160 Pearl St 01420 978-345-2151
Henri's School of Hair Design Post-Sec.
PO Box 2244 01420 978-342-6061
Notre Dame HS 50/7-12
151 South St 01420 978-343-7635
Jeffrey Hammond, prin. Fax 343-6579
St. Bernards HS 500/9-12
45 Harvard St 01420 978-342-3212
James Conry, admin. Fax 345-8067

Florence, See Northampton
Northampton SD
Supt. — See Northampton
Kennedy MS 800/6-8
100 Bridge Rd 01062 413-587-1489
Lesley Wilson, prin. Fax 587-1495

Foxboro, Norfolk, Pop. 5,706
Foxborough SD 2,900/PK-12
60 South St 02035 508-543-1660
Jan Norton, supt. Fax 543-4793
www.foxborough.k12.ma.us
Ahern MS 900/5-8
111 Mechanic St 02035 508-543-1610
Susan Abrams, prin. Fax 543-1613
Foxborough HS 900/9-12
120 South St 02035 508-543-1616
Jeffrey Theodoss, prin. Fax 698-6517

Framingham, Middlesex, Pop. 67,300
Framingham SD 8,100/PK-12
14 Vernon St Ste 201 01701 508-626-9117
Dr. Eugene Thayer, supt. Fax 626-9119
www.framingham.k12.ma.us
Cameron MS 500/6-8
215 Elm St 01701 508-879-2290
Judith Kelly, prin. Fax 788-3560
Framingham HS 2,100/9-12
115 A St 01701 508-620-4963
Michael Welch, prin. Fax 877-6603
Fuller MS 700/6-8
31 Flagg Dr 01702 508-620-4956
Juan Rodriguez, prin. Fax 628-1308
Walsh MS 600/6-8
301 Brook St 01701 508-626-9180
Jay Cummings, prin. Fax 626-9167

South Middlesex Vocational Tech. SD
750 Winter St 01702 508-416-2100
Peter Dewar, supt. Fax 416-2342
www.jpkeefehs.org
Keefe Technical HS Vo/Tech
750 Winter St 01702 508-416-2100
Karl Lord, prin. Fax 416-2342

Blaine The Beauty Career School Post-Sec.
624 Worcester Rd 01702 508-370-3700
Blaine The Beauty Career School Post-Sec.
624 Worcester Rd 01702 580-370-7447
Framingham State College Post-Sec.
PO Box 101 01704 508-620-1220
Marian HS 300/9-12
273 Union Ave 01702 508-875-7646
Sr. Catherine Clifford, prin. Fax 875-0838

Franklin, Norfolk, Pop. 30,893
Franklin SD 6,000/PK-12
355 E Central St 02038 508-541-5243
Wayne Ogden, supt. Fax 533-0321
www.franklin.k12.ma.us
Franklin HS 1,500/9-12
218 Oak St 02038 508-528-5600
Dennis Wilkinson, prin. Fax 541-2107
Mann MS 500/6-8
224 Oak St 02038 508-553-0322
Anne Bergen, prin. Fax 541-7071
Remington MS 400/6-8
628 Washington St 02038 508-541-2130
Timothy Farmer, prin. Fax 541-2124
Sullivan MS 400/6-8
500 Lincoln St 02038 508-553-0322
Beth Wittcoff, prin. Fax 542-2109

Tri-County SD
147 Pond St 02038 508-528-5400
Barbara Renzoni, supt. Fax 528-6074
www.tri-county.tc
Tri-County Regional Vo-Tech HS Vo/Tech
147 Pond St 02038 508-528-5400
Mark Wood, prin. Fax 528-6074

Dean College Post-Sec.
99 Main St 02038 508-541-1900

Gardner, Worcester, Pop. 20,908
Gardner SD 3,200/PK-12
70 Waterford St 01440 978-632-1000
Carol Daring Ph.D., supt. Fax 632-1164
www.gardnerk12.org
Gardner HS 1,000/9-12
200 Catherine St 01440 978-632-1600
Michael Baldassarre, prin. Fax 630-4040
Gardner MS 800/6-8
297 Catherine St 01440 978-632-1603
Michael Hurd, prin. Fax 632-4234

Mt. Wachusett Community College Post-Sec.
444 Green St 01440 978-632-6600

Georgetown, Essex
Georgetown SD 1,700/PK-12
51 North St 01833 978-352-5777
Larry Borin, supt. Fax 352-5778
www.georgetown.k12.ma.us
Georgetown MSHS 800/6-12
11 Winter St 01833 978-352-5790
Peter Lucia, prin. Fax 352-5798

Gloucester, Essex, Pop. 30,713
Gloucester SD 4,000/PK-12
6 School House Rd 01930 978-281-9800
Christopher Farmer, supt. Fax 281-9899
www.gloucesterschools.com
Gloucester HS 1,300/9-12
32 Leslie O Johnson Rd 01930 978-281-9870
Dr. Joseph Sullivan, prin. Fax 281-9733
O'Maley MS 900/6-8
32 Cherry St 01930 978-281-9850
Michael Tracy, prin. Fax 281-9890

Grafton, Worcester
Grafton SD 2,500/PK-12
30 Providence Rd Ste 2 01519 508-839-5421
Joseph Connors Ph.D., supt. Fax 839-7618
www.grafton.k12.ma.us
Grafton Memorial HS 600/9-12
24 Providence Rd 01519 508-839-5425
James Pignataro, prin. Fax 839-8544
Grafton MS 600/6-8
60 North St 01519 508-839-5420
Richard Lind, prin. Fax 839-8528

Granby, Hampshire, Pop. 1,327
Granby SD 1,100/PK-12
387 E State St 01033 413-467-7193
Patricia Stevens, supt. Fax 467-3909
www.granbyschoolsma.org/
Granby JSHS 500/7-12
385 E State St 01033 413-467-7105
Daniel Lynch, prin. Fax 467-3909

Holyoke Catholic HS 400/9-12
66 School St 01033 413-467-2477
Sr. Cornelia Roy, prin. Fax 467-2012

Great Barrington, Berkshire, Pop. 2,810
Berkshire Hills SD
Supt. — See Housatonic
Monument Mountain Regional HS 600/9-12
600 Stockbridge Rd 01230 413-528-3346
Marianne Young, prin. Fax 528-9267
Monument Valley Regional MS 400/5-8
313 Monument Valley Rd 01230 413-644-2300
Jane Furey, prin. Fax 274-2394

Dewey Academy 50/10-12
389 Main St 01230 413-528-9800
Dr. Thomas Bratter, hdmstr. Fax 528-5662
Great Barrington Waldorf HS 50/9-12
454 Main St 01230 413-528-8833
Stephen Sagarin Ph.D., admin. Fax 528-5132
Simon's Rock College of Bard Post-Sec.
80 Alford Rd 01230 413-528-0771

Greenfield, Franklin, Pop. 14,016
Greenfield SD 1,800/PK-12
141 Davis St 01301 413-772-1311
Joseph Ruscio, supt. Fax 774-7940
gpsk12.org
Greenfield HS 500/9-12
1 Lenox Ave 01301 413-772-1350
Nancy Athas, prin. Fax 774-6204
Greenfield MS 500/6-8
195 Federal St 01301 413-772-1360
Chris Collins, prin. Fax 772-1367

Greenfield Community College Post-Sec.
1 College Dr 01301 413-775-1000
Stoneleigh-Burnham S 200/7-12
574 Bernardston Rd 01301 413-774-2711
Paul Bassett, hdmstr. Fax 772-2602

Groton, Middlesex, Pop. 1,044
Groton Dunstable Regional SD
Supt. — See West Groton
Groton Dunstable Regional HS 800/9-12
PO Box 730 01450 978-448-6362
Joseph Dillon, prin. Fax 448-0390
Groton Dunstable Regional MS 900/5-8
PO Box 727 01450 978-448-6155
Beth Raucci, prin. Fax 448-1201

Groton S 400/8-12
PO Box 991 01450 978-448-3363
Richard B. Commons, hdmstr. Fax 448-3100
Lawrence Academy 400/9-12
PO Box 992 01450 978-448-6535
D. Scott Wiggins, hdmstr. Fax 448-9208

Hadley, Hampshire
Hadley SD 600/PK-12
125 Russell St 01035 413-586-0822
Dr. Nicholas Young, supt. Fax 582-6453
www.hadleyschools.org
Hopkins Academy 300/7-12
131 Russell St 01035 413-584-1106
William Mahoney, prin. Fax 582-6455

Hartsbrook S 300/PK-12
193 Bay Rd 01035 413-586-1908
Janine Harrison, admin. Fax 586-9438

Hampden, Hampden
Hampden-Wilbraham SD
Supt. — See Wilbraham
Burgess MS 300/5-8
85 Wilbraham Rd 01036 413-566-8950
Noel Pixley, prin. Fax 566-2163

Hanover, Plymouth, Pop. 11,912
Hanover SD 2,800/PK-12
188 Broadway 02339 781-878-0786
Kristine Nash Ed.D., supt. Fax 871-3374
www.hanoverschools.org
Hanover HS 700/9-12
287 Cedar St 02339 781-878-5450
Edwin Walsh, prin. Fax 871-0590
Hanover MS 900/5-8
45 Whiting St 02339 781-871-1122
Edward Lee, prin. Fax 871-8792

South Shore Regional Vo Tech SD
476 Webster St 02339 781-878-8822
John Kosko, supt. Fax 982-0281
www.ssvotech.org
South Shore Vocational Technical HS Vo/Tech
476 Webster St 02339 781-878-8822
Charles Homer, prin. Fax 982-0281

Hanscom AFB, See Bedford
Lincoln SD
Supt. — See Lincoln
Hanscom MS 300/4-8
Ent Rd 01731 781-274-0050
Mark Kaufman, prin. Fax 274-7329

Hanson, Plymouth, Pop. 2,188
Whitman-Hanson SD
Supt. — See Whitman
Hanson MS 500/6-8
111 Liberty St 02341 781-618-7575
Martin Geoghegan, prin. Fax 618-8815

Hardwick, Worcester

Eagle Hill S 200/8-12
242 Old Petersham Rd 01037 413-477-6000
Peter McDonald, hdmstr. Fax 477-6837

Harvard, Worcester
Harvard SD 1,200/K-12
39 Mass Ave 01451 978-456-4140
Dr. Thomas Jefferson, supt. Fax 456-8592
www.psharvard.org
Bromfield S 700/6-12
14 Mass Ave 01451 978-456-4152
James O'Shea, prin. Fax 456-3013

Harwich, Barnstable
Cape Cod Regional Technical HSD
351 Pleasant Lake Ave 02645 508-432-4500
William Fischer, supt. Fax 432-7916
capetech.us
Cape Cod Regional Technical HS Vo/Tech
351 Pleasant Lake Ave 02645 508-432-4500
Leonard Phelan, prin. Fax 432-7916

Harwich SD 1,300/K-12
81 Oak St 02645 508-430-7200
Dr. Carolyn Cragin, supt. Fax 430-7205
www.harwich.edu
Harwich HS 400/9-12
75 Oak St 02645 508-430-7207
Kevin Turner, prin. Fax 430-7223
Harwich MS 400/6-8
204 Sisson Rd 02645 508-430-7212
Mary Childress, prin. Fax 430-7230

Hatfield, Hampshire, Pop. 1,234
Hatfield SD 500/PK-12
34 School St 01038 413-247-5641
Patrice Dardenne, supt. Fax 247-0201
Smith Academy 200/7-12
34 School St 01038 413-247-5641
Scott A. Goldman, prin. Fax 247-0201

Hathorne, Essex
Essex Agricultural & Technical HSD
PO Box 362 01937 978-774-0050
Helen Hegarty, supt. Fax 774-6530
www.agtech.org
Essex Agricultural & Technical HS Vo/Tech
PO Box 362 01937 978-774-0050
Richard Barbeau, prin. Fax 774-6530

Haverhill, Essex, Pop. 60,242
Haverhill SD 7,700/PK-12
4 Summer St Ste 104 01830 978-374-3400
Raleigh Buchanan Ed.D., supt. Fax 373-1535
www.haverhill-ps.org/
Consentino MS 600/6-8
685 Washington St 01832 978-374-5775
James Scully, prin. Fax 374-3442
Haverhill HS 2,000/9-12
137 Monument St 01832 978-374-5700
Bernard Nangle, prin. Fax 374-5705
Hunking MS 400/6-8
98 Winchester St 01835 978-374-5787
Larry Marino, prin. Fax 372-5890
Nettle MS 500/6-8
150 Boardman St 01830 978-374-5792
Gerald Kayo, prin. Fax 374-3441
Whittier MS 400/6-8
256 Concord St 01830 978-374-5782
Elizabeth Kitsas, prin. Fax 372-5999

Whittier Vocational SD
115 Amesbury Line Rd 01830 978-373-4101
Karen Sarkisian, supt. Fax 521-0260
Whittier Regional Vocational HS Vo/Tech
115 Amesbury Line Rd 01830 978-373-4101
Deborah Depaolo, prin. Fax 521-0260

Northern Essex Community College Post-Sec.
100 Elliott St 01830 978-556-3000

Hingham, Plymouth, Pop. 5,454
Hingham SD 3,700/PK-12
220 Central St 02043 781-741-1500
Dorothy Galo, supt. Fax 749-7457
www.hinghamschools.com/
Hingham HS 1,000/9-12
17 Union St 02043 781-741-1560
Paula Girouard McCann, prin. Fax 741-1515

Hingham MS 800/6-8
1103 Main St 02043 781-741-1550
Roger Boddie, prin. Fax 749-6297

Notre Dame Academy 500/9-12
1073 Main St 02043 781-749-5930
Mary Ellen Cassani, prin. Fax 749-8366

Holbrook, Norfolk, Pop. 11,041
Holbrook SD 1,400/K-12
227 Plymouth St 02343 781-767-1226
Susan E. Martin, supt. Fax 767-1312
www.holbrook.k12.ma.us/
Holbrook JSHS 600/7-12
245 S Franklin St 02343 781-767-4616
Edward Dunn, prin. Fax 767-2697

Holden, Worcester, Pop. 14,628
Wachusett Regional SD
Supt. — See Jefferson
Mountview MS 700/6-8
270 Shrewsbury St 01520 508-829-5577
Preston Shaw, prin. Fax 829-3711
Wachusett Regional HS 1,900/9-12
1401 Main St 01520 508-829-6771
William Beando, prin. Fax 829-4895

Holliston, Middlesex, Pop. 12,926
Holliston SD 3,000/PK-12
370 Hollis St 01746 508-429-0654
Bradford Jackson, supt. Fax 429-0653
www.holliston.mec.edu
Adams MS 700/6-8
323 Woodland St 01746 508-429-0657
Jessica Aran, prin. Fax 429-0690
Holliston HS 900/9-12
370 Hollis St 01746 508-429-0677
Mary Canty, prin. Fax 429-8225

Holyoke, Hampden, Pop. 39,958
Holyoke SD 6,900/PK-12
57 Suffolk St Ste 101 01040 413-534-2005
Dr. Eduardo B. Carballo, supt. Fax 534-2297
www.hps.holyoke.ma.us
Dean Vocational Technical HS Vo/Tech
1045 Main St 01040 413-534-2071
Victor Zwirko, prin. Fax 536-9694
Holyoke HS 1,200/9-12
500 Beech St 01040 413-534-2020
David Dupont, prin. Fax 534-2098
Lynch MS 400/6-8
1575 Northampton St 01040 413-534-2050
Paul Hyry, prin. Fax 532-8443
Peck MS 600/6-8
1916 Northampton St 01040 413-534-2040
Teresa Pudlo, prin. Fax 532-8563

Holyoke Community College Post-Sec.
303 Homestead Ave 01040 413-538-7000

Hopedale, Worcester, Pop. 3,961
Hopedale SD 1,100/PK-12
25 Adin St 01747 508-634-2220
Dr. Patricia C. Ruane, supt. Fax 478-1471
www.hopedale.k12.ma.us
Hopedale JSHS 500/7-12
25 Adin St 01747 508-634-2217
Dennis Breen, prin. Fax 478-5698

Hopkinton, Middlesex, Pop. 2,305
Hopkinton SD 3,300/K-12
89 Hayden Rowe St 01748 508-417-9360
John E. Phelan Ed.D., supt. Fax 497-9833
www.hopkinton.k12.ma.us
Hopkinton HS 900/9-12
90 Hayden Rowe St 01748 508-497-9820
John McCarthy, prin. Fax 497-9829
Hopkinton MS 800/6-8
88 Hayden Rowe St 01748 508-497-9830
William Lynch Ed.D., prin. Fax 497-9803

Housatonic, Berkshire, Pop. 1,184
Berkshire Hills SD 1,400/PK-12
PO Box 596 01236 413-274-6400
Donna Moyer, supt. Fax 274-6407
www.bhrsd.org
Other Schools – See Great Barrington

Hudson, Middlesex, Pop. 14,267
Hudson SD 2,600/K-12
155 Apsley St 01749 978-567-6100
Sheldon Berman, supt. Fax 567-6103
www.hudson.k12.ma.us
Hudson JSHS 1,000/8-12
69 Brigham St 01749 978-567-6250
John Stapelfeld, prin. Fax 567-6285

Hudson Catholic HS 200/9-12
198 Main St 01749 978-562-6701
Caroline Flynn, prin. Fax 567-0755

Hull, Plymouth, Pop. 10,466
Hull SD 1,300/PK-12
7 Hadasah Way 02045 781-925-0771
Dr. Paula DeLaney, supt. Fax 925-0615
www.town.hull.ma.us
Hull HS 400/9-12
180 Main St 02045 781-925-3000
Jonathan Ford, prin. Fax 925-3071
Memorial MS 300/6-8
81 Central Ave 02045 781-925-2040
Andrew Stephens, prin. Fax 925-8002

Huntington, Hampshire
Gateway SD 1,400/PK-12
12 Littleville Rd 01050 413-685-1000
Dr. David B. Hopson, supt. Fax 667-8739
www.grsd.org
Gateway Regional HS 400/9-12
12 Littleville Rd 01050 413-685-1100
Kathleen McSweeney, prin. Fax 667-5593
Gateway Regional MS 400/5-8
12 Littleville Rd 01050 413-685-1200
Peter Curro, prin. Fax 667-5669

Hyannis, Barnstable, Pop. 14,120
Barnstable SD 5,100/PK-12
PO Box 955 02601 508-862-4953
Dr. Patricia Grenier, supt. Fax 790-6454
www.barnstable.k12.ma.us/
Barnstable HS 2,000/9-12
744 W Main St 02601 508-790-6445
Patricia Graves, prin. Fax 790-6430
Barnstable MS 1,000/7-8
895 Falmouth Rd 02601 508-790-6460
Donald Bidgood, prin. Fax 790-6435

Blaine The Beauty Career School Post-Sec.
18 Center St 02601 508-771-1680
Pope John Paul II HS 9-12
120 High School Rd 02601 508-862-6336
Christopher Keavy, pres. Fax 862-6339
St. Francis Xavier Prep S 200/5-8
33 Cross St 02601 508-771-7200
Robert Deburro, hdmstr. Fax 771-7233

Hyde Park, See Boston
Boston SD
Supt. — See Boston
Community Academy of Science & Health 9-12
655 Metropolitan Ave 02136 617-635-8950
Linda Cabral, prin. Fax 635-8948
Engineering S 9-12
655 Metropolitan Ave 02136 617-635-6425
Mweusi Willingham, prin. Fax 635-7698
Rogers MS 600/6-8
15 Everett St 02136 617-635-8700
Andrew Bott, prin. Fax 635-8708
Social Justice Academy 9-12
655 Metropolitan Ave 02136 617-635-6969
Winston Cox, prin. Fax 635-9780

Ipswich, Essex, Pop. 4,132
Ipswich SD 2,100/PK-12
1 Lord Sq 01938 978-356-2935
Richard Korb, supt. Fax 356-0445
www.ipswichschools.org
Ipswich HS 600/9-12
134 High St 01938 978-356-3137
Barry Cahill, prin. Fax 356-3720
Ipswich MS 500/6-8
130 High St 01938 978-356-3535
Cheryl Forster, prin. Fax 412-8169

Jamaica Plain, See Boston
Boston SD
Supt. — See Boston
Curley MS 700/6-8
493 Centre St 02130 617-635-8176
Michelle Madera-Cepeda, prin. Fax 635-8184

Jefferson, Worcester
Wachusett Regional SD 7,000/PK-12
1745 Main St 01522 508-829-1670
Thomas Pandiscio Ed.D., supt. Fax 829-1680
www.wrsd.net
Other Schools – See Holden, Rutland, Sterling

Kingston, Plymouth, Pop. 4,774
Silver Lake Regional SD 1,800/7-12
250 Pembroke St 02364 781-585-4313
Dana Parker, supt. Fax 585-2994
www.silverlake.mec.edu
Silver Lake Regional HS 1,200/9-12
260 Pembroke St 02364 781-585-3844
Richard Kelley, prin. Fax 585-6544
Silver Lake Regional MS 600/7-8
256 Pembroke St 02364 781-582-3555
Dennis Azevedo, prin. Fax 582-3599

Sacred Heart HS 600/7-12
399 Bishops Hwy 02364 781-585-7511
John Enos, prin. Fax 585-7063

Lakeville, Plymouth
Freetown-Lakeville SD 1,900/5-12
98 Howland Rd 02347 508-923-2000
Dr. Stephen Furtado, supt. Fax 923-9960
www.freelake.org/
Apponequet Regional HS 800/9-12
100 Howland Rd 02347 508-947-2660
Gary Lincoln, prin. Fax 946-2350
Freetown-Lakeville MS 800/6-8
96 Howland Rd 02347 508-923-3518
David Patota, prin. Fax 946-2050

Lancaster, Worcester
Nashoba Regional SD
Supt. — See Bolton
Burbank MS 200/6-8
1 Hollywood Dr 01523 978-365-4558
Patrick Perkins, prin. Fax 365-6882

Lawrence, Essex, Pop. 71,314
Lawrence SD 12,200/PK-12
255 Essex St 01840 978-975-5900
Dr. Wilfredo Laboy, supt. Fax 975-5904
www.lawrence.k12.ma.us
Arlington MS 500/5-8
150 Arlington St 01841 978-975-5926
Juan Rodriguez, prin. Fax 975-4004
Lawrence HS 2,600/9-12
233 Haverhill St 01840 978-975-2750
Thomas D. Sharkey Ed.D., prin. Fax 685-0807
Leonard MS 400/6-8
60 Allen St 01840 978-975-5962
Mary Frangipane, prin. Fax 975-7965
South Lawrence East MS 600/5-8
165 Crawford St 01843 978-975-5970
Dina Hickey, prin. Fax 975-2780
Adult Learning Center Adult
243 S Broadway 01843 978-975-5917
Samaria Tavares Hash, admin. Fax 975-6070

Blessed Stephen Bellesini Academy 5-8
94 Bradford St 01840 978-989-0004
Julie DeFillippo, dir. Fax 989-9404

Central Catholic HS 9-12
300 Hampshire St 01841 978-682-0260
David DeFillippo, prin. Fax 685-2707

Lee, Berkshire, Pop. 2,020
Lee SD 900/K-12
310 Greylock St 01238 413-243-0276
Jason P. McCandless, supt. Fax 243-4995
www.lee.k12.ma.us/
Lee MSHS 500/7-12
300 Greylock St 01238 413-243-2787
Kerry Burke, prin. Fax 243-4105

Leicester, Worcester, Pop. 10,191
Leicester SD 1,900/PK-12
1078 Main St 01524 508-892-7040
Michael Dubrule, supt. Fax 892-7043
www.leicester.k12.ma.us/
Leicester HS 500/9-12
174 Paxton St 01524 508-892-7030
Thomas Lauder, prin. Fax 892-7034
Leicester MS 400/6-8
70 Winslow Ave 01524 508-892-7055
Paul Belsito, prin. Fax 892-7047

Lenox, Berkshire, Pop. 1,687
Lenox SD 800/PK-12
6 Walker St Ste 3 01240 413-637-5550
William Coan, supt. Fax 637-5559
www.lenoxps.org
Lenox Memorial HS 500/6-12
197 East St 01240 413-637-5560
Bruce Walker, prin. Fax 637-5564

Leominster, Worcester, Pop. 41,804
Leominster SD 6,200/PK-12
24 Church St 01453 978-534-7700
Marilyn Fratturelli, supt. Fax 534-7775
www.leominster.mec.edu/
Leominster Center Technical Education Vo/Tech
122 Granite St 01453 978-534-7735
George Luoto, prin. Fax 537-7934
Leominster HS 1,200/9-12
122 Granite St 01453 978-534-7715
Dr. William Hart, prin. Fax 537-1765
Samoset MS 600/5-8
100 DeCicco Dr 01453 978-534-7725
Elizabeth Schaper, prin. Fax 466-8603
Sky View MS 700/5-8
500 Kennedy Way 01453 978-534-7780
Donald Lacharite, prin. Fax 840-8600
Southeast MS 600/5-8
95 Viscoloid Ave 01453 978-534-7751
Elizabeth Pratt, prin. Fax 466-8603

Lexington, Middlesex, Pop. 30,600
Lexington SD 6,200/PK-12
1557 Massachusetts Ave 02420 781-861-2550
Paul Ash Ph.D., supt. Fax 863-5829
lps.lexingtonma.org
Clarke MS 700/6-8
17 Stedman Rd 02421 781-861-2450
Steven Flynn, prin. Fax 674-2043
Diamond MS 800/6-8
99 Hancock St 02420 781-861-2460
Joanne Hennessy, prin. Fax 274-0174
Lexington HS 1,900/9-12
251 Waltham St 02421 781-861-2320
Dr. Michael Jones, prin. Fax 861-2440

Minuteman Voc Tech SD
758 Marrett Rd 02421 781-861-6500
William Callahan, supt. Fax 863-1747
www.minuteman.org
Minuteman Regional HS Vo/Tech
758 Marrett Rd 02421 781-861-6500
James Amara, prin. Fax 863-1747

Lexington Christian Academy 300/6-12
48 Bartlett Ave 02420 781-862-7850
Mark Davis, hdmstr. Fax 863-8503

Lincoln, Middlesex, Pop. 2,850
Lincoln SD 1,200/K-8
Ballfield Rd 01773 781-259-9409
Michael Brandmeyer, supt. Fax 259-9246
www.lincnet.org/
Other Schools – See Hanscom AFB

Littleton, Middlesex, Pop. 2,867
Littleton SD 1,500/PK-12
PO Box 1486 01460 978-486-8951
Paul Livingston, supt. Fax 486-9581
www.littletonps.org/
Littleton HS 400/9-12
56 King St 01460 978-952-2555
John Buckey, prin. Fax 486-0758
Littleton MS 300/6-8
55 Russell St 01460 978-486-8938
Kevin Moran, prin. Fax 952-4547

Longmeadow, Hampden, Pop. 15,467
Longmeadow SD 3,400/PK-12
127 Grassy Gutter Rd 01106 413-565-4200
E. Jahn Hart, supt. Fax 565-4215
www.longmeadow.k12.ma.us/
Glenbrook MS 400/6-8
110 Cambridge Cir 01106 413-565-4250
Michael Sullivan, prin. Fax 565-4277
Longmeadow HS 1,100/9-12
95 Grassy Gutter Rd 01106 413-565-4220
Lawrence Berte, prin. Fax 565-4233
Williams MS 400/6-8
410 Williams St 01106 413-565-4260
Mary Sedran, prin. Fax 565-4254

Bay Path College Post-Sec.
588 Longmeadow St 01106 413-565-1000

Lowell, Middlesex, Pop. 103,111
Lowell SD 13,700/PK-12
155 Merrimack St 01852 978-937-7604
Dr. Karla Brooks Baehr, supt. Fax 446-7436
www.lowell.k12.ma.us/

Butler MS 500/5-8
1140 Gorham St 01852 978-937-8973
Eilish A. Connaughton, prin. Fax 937-2819
Daley MS 800/5-8
150 Fleming St 01851 978-937-8981
Liam Skinner, prin. Fax 937-7610
Lowell HS 3,700/9-12
50 Father Morissette Blvd 01852 978-937-8900
William Samaras, hdmstr. Fax 937-8902
Robinson MS 700/5-8
110 June St 01850 978-937-8974
Robert Murphy, prin. Fax 937-8988
Rogers MS 700/5-8
43 Highland St 01852 978-937-7675
Timothy McGillicuddy, prin. Fax 937-7609
Stoklosa MS 5-8
560 Broadway St 01854 978-937-7604
Stephen Gross, prin. Fax 275-6343
Sullivan MS 700/5-8
150 Draper St 01852 978-937-8993
Edith LaBran, prin. Fax 937-3278
Wang MS 700/5-8
365 W Meadow Rd 01854 978-937-7683
Gayle Feeney, prin. Fax 937-7680
Adult Basic Education Program Adult
408 Merrimack St 01854 978-937-8989
Fred Abisi, dir. Fax 458-9007

Blaine The Beauty Career School Post-Sec.
231 Central St 01852 978-459-9959
Community Christian Academy 200/PK-12
105R Princeton Blvd 01851 978-453-4738
Rev. Raffoul Najem, admin. Fax 453-1506
Lowell Academy Hairstyling Institute Post-Sec.
136 Central St 01852 978-453-3235
Lowell Catholic HS 300/9-12
530 Stevens St 01851 978-452-1794
Maryellen DeMarco, prin. Fax 452-5646
Middlesex Community College Post-Sec.
33 Kearney Sq 01852 978-656-3213
University of Massachusetts Lowell Post-Sec.
1 University Ave 01854 978-934-4000

Ludlow, Hampden, Pop. 18,820
Ludlow SD 3,100/PK-12
63 Chestnut St 01056 413-583-8372
Theresa Kane Ed.D., supt. Fax 583-5666
www.ludlowps.org
Baird MS 800/6-8
1 Rooney Rd 01056 413-583-5685
Donna Hogan, prin. Fax 583-5636
Ludlow HS 1,000/9-12
500 Chapin St 01056 413-589-9001
Gordon Smith, prin. Fax 583-5637

Jolie Hair and Beauty Academy Post-Sec.
44 Sewall St 01056 413-589-0747

Lunenburg, Worcester, Pop. 1,694
Lunenburg SD 1,700/PK-12
1033 Massachusetts Ave 01462 978-582-4100
Loxi Jo Calmes, supt. Fax 582-4103
www.lunenburgonline.com/
Lunenburg HS 600/9-12
1079 Massachusetts Ave 01462 978-582-4115
Michael Barney, prin. Fax 582-4153
Turkey Hill MS 400/6-8
129 Northfield Rd 01462 978-582-4110
Keith Hochstein, prin. Fax 582-4109

Twin City Christian S 300/PK-12
194 Electric Ave 01462 978-582-4901
Gregory Arnold, admin. Fax 582-4978

Lynn, Essex, Pop. 88,792
Lynn SD 13,600/PK-12
90 Commercial St 01905 781-593-1680
Nicholas Kostan, supt. Fax 477-7487
www.lynnschools.org/
Breed MS 1,000/6-8
90 OCallaghan Way 01905 781-477-7330
James Ridley, prin. Fax 581-6985
Career Development Center Vo/Tech
33 N Common St 01902 781-268-3000
Rhonda Cormier, prin.
Classical HS 1,500/9-12
235 OCallaghan Way 01905 781-477-7404
Warren White, prin. Fax 477-7212
English HS 1,500/9-12
50 Goodridge St 01902 781-477-7366
Andrew M. Fila, prin. Fax 477-7365
Lynn Vocational Technical Institute Vo/Tech
80 Neptune Blvd 01902 781-477-7420
Brian Coughlin, prin. Fax 477-7415
Marshall MS 900/6-8
19 Porter St 01902 781-477-7360
Anita Rassias, prin. Fax 477-7355
Pickering MS 700/6-8
70 Conomo Ave 01904 781-477-7440
Patricia A. Barton, prin. Fax 477-7202

St. Mary JSHS 600/7-12
35 Tremont St 01902 781-595-7885
Dr. Raymond Bastarache, prin. Fax 599-8707

Lynnfield, Essex, Pop. 11,274
Lynnfield SD 2,100/PK-12
55 Summer St 01940 781-334-5800
Richard Palermo, supt. Fax 334-5802
www.lynnfield.k12.ma.us/
Lynnfield HS 600/9-12
275 Essex St 01940 781-334-5820
Robert Hassett, prin. Fax 334-7207
Lynnfield MS 700/5-8
505 Main St 01940 781-334-5810
Stephen Ralston, prin. Fax 334-7203

Malden, Middlesex, Pop. 55,871
Malden SD 6,200/PK-12
200 Pleasant St 02148 781-397-7204
Joan Connolly, supt. Fax 397-7276
www.malden.mec.edu
Malden HS 1,600/9-12
77 Salem St 02148 781-397-7223
Dana Brown, prin. Fax 397-7224

Blaine The Beauty Career School Post-Sec.
347 Pleasant St 02148 781-397-7400
Learning Institute for Beauty Sciences Post-Sec.
384 Main St 02148 781-324-3400
Malden Catholic HS 700/9-12
99 Crystal St 02148 781-322-3098
Thomas Arria, hdmstr. Fax 397-0573
New England Hair Academy Post-Sec.
110 Florence St Ste 203 02148 781-324-6799

Manchester, Essex, Pop. 5,286
Manchester Essex Regional SD 1,300/K-12
36 Lincoln St 01944 978-526-4919
Robert Shaps, supt. Fax 526-7585
www.mersd.org
Manchester Essex Regional MSHS 600/7-12
36 Lincoln St 01944 978-526-4412
Jim Lee, prin. Fax 526-2044

Mansfield, Bristol, Pop. 7,170
Mansfield SD 4,800/K-12
2 Park Row 02048 508-261-7500
John Moretti, supt. Fax 261-7509
www.mansfieldschools.com
Mansfield HS 1,200/9-12
250 East St 02048 508-261-7540
William Farrington, prin. Fax 339-0259
Qualters MS 1,200/6-8
240 East St 02048 508-261-7530
David Thomson, prin. Fax 261-7535

Marblehead, Essex, Pop. 19,971
Marblehead SD 3,100/PK-12
9 Widger Rd 01945 781-639-3141
Dr. Philip Devaux, supt. Fax 639-3149
www.marblehead.com/schools
Marblehead HS 1,000/9-12
2 Humphrey St 01945 781-639-3100
John Ziergiebel, prin. Fax 639-3105
Marblehead Veterans MS 400/7-8
217 Pleasant St 01945 781-639-3120
Libby Moore, prin. Fax 639-3130

Marion, Plymouth, Pop. 1,426

Tabor Academy 500/9-12
66 Spring St 02738 508-748-2000
Jay Stroud, hdmstr. Fax 291-6666

Marlborough, Middlesex, Pop. 37,444
Assabet Valley SD
215 Fitchburg St 01752 508-485-9430
Eugene Carlo, supt. Fax 460-3472
www.assabettech.com
Assabet Valley Regional Technicall HS Vo/Tech
215 Fitchburg St 01752 508-485-9430
Mary Jo Nawrocki, prin. Fax 460-3472

Marlborough SD 4,800/PK-12
17 Washington St 01752 508-460-3509
Barbara McGann, supt. Fax 485-1142
www.marlborough.k12.ma.us
Marlborough HS 1,600/8-12
431 Bolton St 01752 508-460-3500
Mary Carlson, prin. Fax 460-3501

Hillside S 100/5-9
404 Robin Hill St 01752 508-485-2824
David Beecher, hdmstr. Fax 485-4420

Marshfield, Plymouth, Pop. 4,002
Marshfield SD 4,600/PK-12
76 S River St 02050 781-834-5000
Middleton McGoodwin Ed.D., supt. Fax 834-5070
marshfield.ma.schoolwebpages.com/
Furnace Brook MS 1,000/6-8
500 Furnace St 02050 781-834-5020
Alfred Makein, prin. Fax 834-5899
Marshfield HS 1,200/9-12
167 Forest St 02050 781-834-5050
Robert Keuther, prin. Fax 834-5040

Mashpee, Barnstable
Mashpee SD 2,000/K-12
150A Old Barnstable Rd 02649 508-539-1500
Ann Bradshaw, supt. Fax 477-5805
www.mashpee.k12.ma.us
Mashpee HS 1,000/7-12
500 Old Barnstable Rd 02649 508-539-3600
Lou Ann St. Cyr, prin. Fax 539-3607

Mattapan, See Boston
Boston SD
Supt. — See Boston
Lewenberg MS 400/6-8
20 Outlook Rd 02126 617-635-8623
Myrtlene Mayfield, prin. Fax 635-9947
Mildred Avenue MS 600/6-8
5 Mildred Ave 02126 617-635-1645
Kennietha Jones, prin. Fax 635-1641

Mattapoisett, Plymouth, Pop. 2,949
Old Rochester Regional SD 1,200/7-12
135 Marion Rd 02739 508-758-2772
Dr. William Cooper, supt. Fax 758-2802
www.oldrochester.org
Old Rochester Regional HS 800/9-12
135 Marion Rd 02739 508-758-3745
Bruce Clarke, prin. Fax 758-3167
Old Rochester Regional JHS 500/7-8
133 Marion Rd 02739 508-758-4928
Simonne J. Conlon, prin. Fax 758-6021

Maynard, Middlesex, Pop. 10,325
Maynard SD 1,400/PK-12
12 Bancroft St 01754 978-897-2222
Dr. Mark R. Masterson, supt. Fax 897-4610
web.maynard.ma.us/schools/
Fowler MS 600/4-8
3 Tiger Dr 01754 978-897-6700
Robert Brooks, prin. Fax 897-5737
Maynard HS 300/9-12
1 Tiger Dr 01754 978-897-8891
John Lent, prin. Fax 897-6089

Medfield, Norfolk, Pop. 5,985
Medfield SD 3,100/PK-12
459 Main St Fl 3 02052 508-359-2302
Robert Maguire, supt. Fax 359-9829
www.medfield.net
Blake MS 700/6-8
24 Pound St 02052 508-359-2396
Margaret Mongiello, prin. Fax 359-0134
Medfield HS 900/9-12
88R South St 02052 508-359-8385
Andrew Keough, prin. Fax 359-2963

Montrose S 100/6-12
29 North St 02052 508-359-2423
Dr. Karen Bohlin, prin. Fax 359-2597

Medford, Middlesex, Pop. 53,523
Medford SD 4,700/PK-12
489 Winthrop St 02155 781-393-2442
Roy Belson, supt. Fax 393-2322
www.medford.k12.ma.us
Andrews MS 600/6-8
3000 Mystic Valley Pkwy 02155 781-393-2228
Alan Levy, prin. Fax 395-8128
McGlynn MS 600/6-8
3004 Mystic Valley Pkwy 02155 781-393-2333
James Deveney, prin. Fax 393-5462
Medford HS 1,300/9-12
489 Winthrop St 02155 781-393-2301
Paul Krueger, prin. Fax 395-1468
Medford Vo-Tech HS Vo/Tech
489 Winthrop St 02155 781-393-2260
William Mahoney, prin. Fax 395-1468

Lawrence Memorial/Regis College Post-Sec.
170 Governors Ave 02155 781-306-6600
St. Clement S 200/K-12
579 Boston Ave 02155 617-395-9170
Robert Chevrier, prin. Fax 396-3254
The Elizabeth Grady School of Esthetics Post-Sec.
222 Boston Ave 02155 781-391-9380
Tufts University Post-Sec.
520 Boston Ave 02155 617-628-5000

Medway, Norfolk, Pop. 9,931
Medway SD 2,900/PK-12
45 Holliston St 02053 508-533-3222
Dr. Richard Grandmont, supt. Fax 533-3226
www.medwayschools.org
Medway HS 700/9-12
88 Summer St 02053 508-533-6643
Richard Pearson, prin. Fax 533-3246
Medway MS 1,000/5-8
45 Holliston St 02053 508-533-3230
Joanne Senier-LaBarre, prin. Fax 533-3257

Melrose, Middlesex, Pop. 26,365
Melrose SD 3,500/PK-12
360 Lynn Fells Pkwy 02176 781-662-2000
Joseph Casey, supt. Fax 979-2149
www.melroseschools.com
Melrose HS 900/9-12
360 Lynn Fells Pkwy 02176 781-979-2202
Dan Burke, prin. Fax 979-2205
Melrose MS 800/6-8
350 Lynn Fells Pkwy 02176 781-979-2102
Thomas Brow, prin. Fax 979-2104

Mendon, Worcester
Mendon-Upton Regional SD 2,700/PK-12
PO Box 5 01756 508-634-1585
Antonio Fernandes, supt. Fax 634-1582
mu-regional.k12.ma.us
Other Schools – See Upton

Methuen, Essex, Pop. 44,609
Methuen SD 7,300/PK-12
10 Ditson Pl 01844 978-681-1317
Jeanne Whitten Ed.D., supt. Fax 794-4749
www.methuen.k12.ma.us
Methuen HS 1,900/9-12
1 Ranger Rd 01844 978-681-1360
Arthur Nicholson, prin. Fax 681-1397

Fellowship Christian Academy 100/PK-12
1 Fellowship Way 01844 978-686-9373
Christopher Dyer, prin. Fax 685-7466
Presentation of Mary Academy 300/9-12
209 Lawrence St 01844 978-682-9391
Rose Maria Redman, prin. Fax 975-3595

Middleboro, Plymouth, Pop. 6,837
Middleborough SD 3,600/PK-12
30 Forest St 02346 508-946-2000
Robert Sullivan, supt. Fax 946-2004
www.middleboro.k12.ma.us
Middleboro HS 900/9-12
71 E Grove St 02346 508-946-2010
Katherine Flaherty, prin. Fax 946-8852
Nichols MS 900/6-8
112 Tiger Dr 02346 508-946-2020
Scott Kellett, prin. Fax 946-2019

Bay State College Post-Sec.
71 E Grove St 02346 508-946-5559

Middleton, Essex, Pop. 4,921
North Shore Regional Vocational SD
PO Box 806 01949 978-762-0001
Amelia O'Malley, supt. Fax 777-8403
www.nsths.mec.edu
North Shore Regional Vocational HS Vo/Tech
PO Box 806 01949 978-762-0001
Richard McLaughlin, prin. Fax 762-4589

Milford, Worcester, Pop. 23,339
Milford SD 4,200/PK-12
31 W Fountain St 01757 508-478-1100
Thomas J. Davoren, supt. Fax 478-1459
www.milford.ma.us/schools.htm

Milford HS 1,100/9-12
31 W Fountain St 01757 508-478-1110
John Brucato, prin. Fax 478-1460
Milford MS East 300/8-8
45 Main St 01757 508-478-1170
Joseph Pfeil, prin. Fax 634-2381

Millbury, Worcester, Pop. 12,228
Millbury SD 2,000/PK-12
12 Martin St 01527 508-865-9501
David Roach, supt. Fax 865-0888
www.millbury.k12.ma.us
Millbury JSHS 900/7-12
12 Martin St 01527 508-865-5841
Linda Swenson, prin. Fax 865-0888

Millis, Norfolk, Pop. 4,081
Millis SD 1,300/PK-12
245 Plain St 02054 508-376-7000
Peter Sanchioni, supt. Fax 376-7020
www.millis.k12.ma.us/
Millis HS 300/9-12
245 Plain St 02054 508-376-7010
Linda McCann, prin. Fax 376-7020
Millis MS 400/5-8
245 Plain St 02054 508-376-7014
Andrew Zitoli, prin. Fax 376-7020

Milton, Norfolk, Pop. 27,000
Milton SD 3,600/PK-12
25 Gile Rd 02186 617-696-4808
Magdalene Giffune, supt. Fax 696-5099
www.edline.net/pages/Milton_Public_Schools
Milton HS 1,000/9-12
25 Gile Rd 02186 617-696-4470
John Drottar, prin. Fax 696-5038
Pierce MS 900/6-8
451 Central Ave 02186 617-696-4568
John Phelan, prin. Fax 698-2238

Curry College Post-Sec.
1071 Blue Hill Ave 02186 617-333-0500
Fontbonne Academy 600/9-12
930 Brook Rd 02186 617-696-3241
Mary Ellen Barnes, prin. Fax 696-7688
Milton Academy 1,000/K-12
170 Centre St 02186 617-898-1798
Robin Robertson, hdmstr. Fax 898-1700

Monson, Hampden, Pop. 2,101
Monson SD 1,600/PK-12
PO Box 159 01057 413-267-4150
Richard Nabel, supt. Fax 267-9168
www.monsonschools.com
Granite Valley MS 500/5-8
21 Thompson St 01057 413-267-4155
Patricia Clem, prin. Fax 267-4624
Monson HS 400/9-12
55 Margaret St 01057 413-267-4589
James Peters, prin. Fax 267-4157

Montague, Franklin
Gill-Montague SD
Supt. — See Turners Falls
Great Falls MS 200/7-8
224 Turnpike Rd 01351 413-863-3188
Jeffrey Kenney, prin. Fax 863-3189
Turners Falls HS 400/9-12
222 Turnpike Rd 01351 413-863-9341
Jeffrey Kenney, prin. Fax 863-3189

Nantucket, Nantucket, Pop. 3,069
Nantucket SD 1,200/K-12
10 Surfside Rd 02554 508-228-7285
Robert Pellicone, supt. Fax 325-5318
www.npsk.org
Nantucket HS 400/9-12
10 Surfside Rd 02554 508-228-7280
George Kelly, prin. Fax 325-5318
Peirce MS 300/6-8
10 Surfside Rd 02554 508-228-7283
Lyndell Kalman, prin. Fax 325-7597

Natick, Middlesex, Pop. 30,700
Natick SD 4,600/PK-12
13 E Central St 01760 508-647-6500
James Connolly, supt. Fax 647-6506
www.natick.k12.ma.us
Kennedy MS 500/5-8
165 Mill St 01760 508-647-6650
Rosemary Vickery, prin. Fax 647-6658
Natick HS 1,200/9-12
15 West St 01760 508-647-6600
John Hughes, prin. Fax 651-7372
Wilson MS 800/5-8
22 Rutledge Rd 01760 508-647-6670
Ruth Evans, prin. Fax 647-6678

Walnut Hill S 300/9-12
12 Highland St 01760 508-650-5020
Stephanie Perrin, hdmstr. Fax 655-3726

Needham, Norfolk, Pop. 29,200
Needham SD 4,900/PK-12
1330 Highland Ave 02492 781-455-0400
Daniel Gutekanst, supt. Fax 455-0417
www.needham.k12.ma.us/
Pollard MS 1,100/6-8
200 Harris Ave 02492 781-455-0480
Glenn Brand, prin. Fax 455-0413
Other Schools – See Needham Heights

Franklin W. Olin College of Engineering Post-Sec.
Olin Way 02492 781-292-2300
Haddad MS 200/6-8
110 May St 02492 781-449-0133
Jane Abel, prin. Fax 449-8096
St. Sebastians Country Day S 300/7-12
1191 Greendale Ave 02492 781-449-5200
William Burke, hdmstr. Fax 449-5630

Needham Heights, Norfolk
Needham SD
Supt. — See Needham

Needham HS 1,400/9-12
609 Webster St 02494 781-455-0800
Paul Richards, prin. Fax 449-5111

New Bedford, Bristol, Pop. 93,102
Greater New Bedford Reg Vo/Tech HSD
1121 Ashley Blvd 02745 508-998-3321
Michael Shea, supt. Fax 995-7268
www.gnbvt.edu
Greater New Bedford Reg. Vo Tech HS Vo/Tech
1121 Ashley Blvd 02745 508-998-3321
Luis Lopes, prin. Fax 995-7268

New Bedford SD 14,000/PK-12
455 County St 02740 508-997-4511
Michael Longo, supt. Fax 997-0298
www.newbedford.k12.ma.us/
Keith MS, 225 Hathaway Blvd 02740 700/7-8
Joaquim Costa, prin. 508-997-4511
New Bedford HS 3,300/9-12
230 Hathaway Blvd 02740 508-997-4511
Donald Vasconcelles, prin. Fax 991-7483
Normandin MS 1,300/6-8
81 Felton St 02745 508-997-4511
Jeanne Bonneau, prin. Fax 995-6975
Roosevelt MS 900/6-8
119 Frederick St 02744 508-997-4511
Brian Abdallah, prin. Fax 997-1198

LaBaron Hairdressing Academy Post-Sec.
281 Union St 02740 508-996-6611
Nazarene Christian Academy 200/PK-12
764 Hathaway Rd 02740 508-992-7944
Susan Helm, prin. Fax 994-1457
Rob Roy Academy Post-Sec.
1872 Acushnet Ave 02746 508-995-8711
St. Luke's Hospital Post-Sec.
101 Page St 02740 508-997-1525

Newburyport, Essex, Pop. 17,414
Newburyport SD 2,300/K-12
70 Low St 01950 978-465-4457
Dr. Kevin Lyons, supt. Fax 462-3495
www.newburyport.k12.ma.us/
Newburyport HS 800/9-12
241 High St 01950 978-465-4440
Dee Gould, prin. Fax 465-2198
Nock MS 700/5-8
70 Low St 01950 978-465-4447
Barry Hopping, prin. Fax 465-4074

Newton, Middlesex, Pop. 83,158
Newton SD
Supt. — See Newtonville
Bigelow MS 500/6-8
42 Vernon St 02458 617-552-7800
Todd Harrison, prin. Fax 552-7752
Oak Hill MS 600/6-8
130 Wheeler Rd 02459 617-559-9200
Henry Van Putten, prin. Fax 552-5547

Boston College Post-Sec.
885 Centre St 02459 617-552-4350
Hebrew College Post-Sec.
160 Herrick Rd 02459 617-559-8610
Mt. Alvernia HS 200/7-12
790 Centre St 02458 617-969-2260
Kathleen Kent, prin. Fax 969-4246
New England School of Acupuncture Post-Sec.
150 California St 02458 617-558-1788
Newton Country Day S 400/5-12
785 Centre St 02458 617-244-4246
Sr. Barbara Rogers, prin. Fax 965-5313
Trinity Catholic HS 200/9-12
575 Washington St 02458 617-244-1841
Kelly Surapaneni, prin. Fax 796-9175

Newton Center, See Newton
Newton SD
Supt. — See Newtonville
Brown MS 800/6-8
125 Meadowbrook Rd 02459 617-552-7409
John Jordan, prin. Fax 552-7729
Newton South HS 1,600/9-12
140 Brandeis Rd 02459 617-559-6700
Brian Salzer, prin. Fax 559-6701

Andover Newton Theological School Post-Sec.
210 Herrick Rd 02459 800-864-2687
Bais Yaakov of Boston HS 50/9-12
561 Ward St 02459 617-965-7547
Rabbi Tsvi Yehuda Levin, prin. Fax 965-0345
Mt. Ida College Post-Sec.
777 Dedham St 02459 617-969-7000
Solomon Schechter Day S Greater Boston 300/4-8
125 Wells Ave 02459 617-928-9100
Arnold Zar-Kessler, hdmstr. Fax 964-9401

Newtonville, See Newton
Newton SD 11,400/PK-12
100 Walnut St 02460 617-559-6100
Dr. Jeffrey Young, supt. Fax 559-6101
www.newton.mec.edu/
Day MS 800/6-8
21 Minot Pl 02460 617-559-9100
Gina Healy, prin. Fax 559-9103
Newton North HS 2,100/9-12
360 Lowell Ave 02460 617-559-6200
Jennifer Price, prin. Fax 559-6204
Other Schools – See Newton, Newton Center

Norfolk, Norfolk
King Philip SD 2,000/7-12
18 King St 02056 508-520-7991
Richard J. Robbat, supt. Fax 520-2044
www.kingphilip.org
King Philip Regional MS North 800/7-8
18 King St 02056 508-541-7324
Dr. Susan Gilson, prin. Fax 541-3467
Other Schools – See Wrentham

North Adams, Berkshire, Pop. 14,010
North Adams SD 2,000/PK-12
191 E Main St Ste 1 01247 413-662-3225
James Montepare, supt. Fax 662-3212
www.napsk12.org/
Conte MS 500/6-8
24 N Church St 01247 413-662-3200
Diane Ryczek, prin. Fax 662-3212
Drury HS 600/9-12
1130 S Church St 01247 413-662-3240
Amy Meehan, prin. Fax 662-3239

Northern Berkshire Vocational SD
70 Hodges Crossroads 01247 413-663-5383
James Brosnan, supt. Fax 664-9424
www.mccanntech.org
McCann Technical S Vo/Tech
70 Hodges Crossroads 01247 413-663-5383
Gary Rivers, prin. Fax 664-9424

C.H. McCann Technical School Post-Sec.
70 Hodges Crossroads 01247 413-663-5383
Massachusetts College of Liberal Arts Post-Sec.
375 Church St 01247 413-662-5000

Northampton, Hampshire, Pop. 28,715
Northampton SD 3,000/PK-12
212 Main St Rm 200 01060 413-587-1331
Isabelina Babcock, supt. Fax 587-1318
www.nps.northampton.ma.us
Northampton HS 900/9-12
380 Elm St 01060 413-587-1346
Beth Singer, prin. Fax 587-1374
Other Schools – See Florence

Northampton-Smith SD
80 Locust St 01060 413-587-1414
Frank Llamas, supt. Fax 587-1405
Smith Vocational & Agricultural HS Vo/Tech
80 Locust St 01060 413-587-1414
Veronica Carroll, prin. Fax 587-1406

Smith College 01063 Post-Sec.
413-584-2700

North Andover, Essex, Pop. 22,792
North Andover SD 4,200/PK-12
43 High St 01845 978-794-1503
Daniel O'Connor, supt. Fax 794-0231
www.nandover.mec.edu
North Andover HS 1,300/9-12
430 Osgood St 01845 978-794-1711
Susan Nicholson, prin. Fax 688-3536
North Andover MS 1,100/6-8
495 Main St 01845 978-794-1870
Joan McQuade, prin. Fax 794-3619

Brooks S 400/9-12
1160 Great Pond Rd 01845 978-686-6101
Lawrence Becker, prin. Fax 725-6215
Merrimack College Post-Sec.
315 Turnpike St 01845 978-683-7111

North Attleboro, Bristol, Pop. 16,178
North Attleborough SD 4,700/PK-12
6 Morse St 02760 508-643-2100
Richard Smith, supt. Fax 643-2110
www.naschools.net
North Attleboro HS 1,200/9-12
1 Wilson W Whitty Way 02760 508-643-2115
Robert Gay, prin. Fax 643-2173
North Attleboro MS 1,200/6-8
564 Landry Ave 02760 508-643-2130
Victoria Ekk, prin. Fax 643-2134

Northborough, Worcester, Pop. 5,761
Northborough-Southborough SD 4,800/PK-12
44 Bearfoot Rd Ste 1A 01532 508-351-7000
Rosemary Joseph, supt. Fax 351-7049
www.nsboro.k12.ma.us/
Algonquin Regional HS 1,300/9-12
79 Bartlett St 01532 508-351-7010
Edward Gallagher, prin. Fax 393-9226
Melican MS 700/6-8
145 Lincoln St 01532 508-351-7020
Patricia Montimurro, prin. Fax 351-7006
Other Schools – See Southborough

North Brookfield, Worcester, Pop. 2,635
North Brookfield SD 800/K-12
10 High School Dr 01535 508-867-9821
Erin Nosek, supt. Fax 867-8148
www.northbrookfield.k12.ma.us
North Brookfield JSHS 400/7-12
10 High School Dr 01535 508-867-7131
Raymond LeMay, prin. Fax 867-3496

North Chelmsford, Middlesex
Chelmsford SD
Supt. — See Chelmsford
Chelmsford HS 1,800/9-12
200 Richardson Rd 01863 978-251-5111
W. Allen Thomas, prin. Fax 251-5117

North Dartmouth, Bristol, Pop. 8,000
Dartmouth SD
Supt. — See South Dartmouth
Dartmouth MS 1,100/6-8
366 Slocum Rd 02747 508-997-9333
Stephen Pettey, prin. Fax 999-7720

Bishop Stang HS 800/9-12
500 Slocum Rd 02747 508-996-5602
Theresa Dougall, pres. Fax 994-6756
Southern New England School of Law Post-Sec.
333 Faunce Corner Rd 02747 508-998-9600
University of Massachusetts Dartmouth Post-Sec.
285 Old Westport Rd 02747 508-999-8000

North Dighton, Bristol
Dighton-Rehoboth Regional SD 3,400/PK-12
2700 Regional Rd 02764 508-252-5000
Dr. Francis Connor, supt. Fax 252-5024
www.drregional.org/

Dighton-Rehoboth Regional HS 1,000/9-12
2700 Regional Rd 02764 508-252-5025
Gail Van Buren, prin. Fax 252-5079
Other Schools – See Dighton, Rehoboth

North Eastham, Barnstable, Pop. 1,570
Nauset SD
Supt. — See Orleans
Nauset Regional HS 1,100/9-12
100 Cable Rd 02651 508-255-1505
Thomas Conrad, prin. Fax 255-9701

North Easton, Bristol, Pop. 4,400
Easton SD 3,800/PK-12
PO Box 359 02356 508-230-3200
Dr. William Simmons, supt. Fax 238-3563
www.easton.k12.ma.us/
Ames HS 800/10-12
100 Lothrop St 02356 508-230-3210
Wesley Paul, prin. Fax 238-7325
Easton JHS 900/7-9
98 Columbus Ave 02356 508-230-3222
John Giuggio, prin. Fax 230-0198

Stonehill College Post-Sec.
320 Washington St 02357 508-565-1373

Northfield, Franklin, Pop. 1,322
Pioneer Valley SD 1,100/PK-12
97 F Sumner Turner Rd 01360 413-498-2911
Kevin Courtney, supt. Fax 498-0045
www.pioneervalley.k12.ma.us
Pioneer Valley Regional JSHS 500/7-12
97 F Sumner Turner Rd 01360 413-498-2931
Cheri McDaniel-Thomas, prin. Fax 498-0184

Northfield Mt. Hermon S 700/9-12
206 Main St 01360 413-498-3000
Thomas Sturtevant, hdmstr. Fax 498-3152

North Quincy, See Quincy
Quincy SD
Supt. — See Quincy
Atlantic MS 500/6-8
86 Hollis Ave 02171 617-984-8727
Laura Bogan, prin. Fax 984-8646
North Quincy HS 1,600/9-12
316 Hancock St 02171 617-984-8744
Louis Ioanilli, prin. Fax 984-8647

North Reading, Middlesex, Pop. 12,002
North Reading SD 2,700/K-12
19 Sherman Rd 01864 978-664-7810
David Troughton, supt. Fax 664-0252
ps.north-reading.k12.ma.us/
North Reading HS 700/9-12
191 Park St 01864 978-664-7800
Jon Bernard, prin. Fax 664-7826
North Reading MS 700/6-8
19 Sherman Rd 01864 978-664-7806
Richard C. Hodges, prin. Fax 276-0679

Norton, Bristol, Pop. 1,899
Norton SD 3,200/PK-12
64 W Main St 02766 508-285-0100
Patricia Ansay, supt. Fax 285-0199
www.edline.net/pages/Norton_Public_Schools
Norton HS 700/9-12
66 W Main St 02766 508-285-0160
Raymond Dewar, prin. Fax 285-0164
Norton MS 800/6-8
215 W Main St 02766 508-285-0140
Roger Parent, prin. Fax 286-9457

New Testament Christian S 200/PK-12
PO Box AJ 02766 508-285-9771
Lynne Brennan, prin. Fax 285-6775
Wheaton College Post-Sec.
26 E Main St 02766 800-394-6003

Norwell, Plymouth
Norwell SD 2,100/PK-12
322 Main St 02061 781-659-8800
Donald J. Beaudette Ed.D., supt. Fax 659-8805
www.norwellschools.org
Norwell HS 600/9-12
18 South St 02061 781-659-8810
Matthew Keegan, prin. Fax 659-1824
Norwell MS 500/6-8
328 Main St 02061 781-659-8814
Rodrigo Borgueta, prin. Fax 659-8822

Norwood, Norfolk, Pop. 28,500
Norwood SD 3,700/PK-12
PO Box 67 02062 781-762-6804
Dr. Edward P. Quigley, supt. Fax 762-0229
www.norwood.k12.ma.us/
Coakley MS 900/6-8
PO Box 67 02062 781-762-7880
Margery Tessier, prin. Fax 255-5630
Norwood HS 1,100/9-12
PO Box 67 02062 781-769-2333
George Usevich, prin. Fax 762-0826

FINE Mortuary College Post-Sec.
150 Kerry Pl 02062 781-762-1211
ITT Technical Institute Post-Sec.
333 Boston Providence Tpke 02062 781-278-0708
Universal Technical Institute Post-Sec.
1 Upland Rd 02062 781-948-2030

Oak Bluffs, Dukes
Martha's Vineyard SD
Supt. — See Vineyard Haven
Martha's Vineyard Regional HS 800/9-12
PO Box 1385 02557 508-693-1033
Margaret Regan, prin. Fax 693-1891

Orange, Franklin, Pop. 3,791
Ralph C. Mahar Regional SD 700/7-12
PO Box 680 01364 978-544-2920
Gholamreza Namin, supt. Fax 544-8383
www.rcmahar.org
Mahar Regional HS 700/7-12
PO Box 680 01364 978-544-2542
Francis Zak, prin. Fax 544-8383

Orleans, Barnstable, Pop. 1,699
Nauset SD 1,700/6-12
78 Eldridge Park Way 02653 508-255-8800
Michael Gradone, supt. Fax 240-2351
www.nausetschools.org
Nauset Regional MS 600/6-8
70 S Orleans Rd 02653 508-255-0016
Greg Baecker, prin. Fax 240-1105
Other Schools – See North Eastham

Osterville, Barnstable, Pop. 2,911

Cape Cod Academy 400/K-12
PO Box 469 02655 508-428-5400
Clark Daggett, prin. Fax 428-0701

Oxford, Worcester, Pop. 5,969
Oxford SD 2,200/PK-12
5 Sigourney St 01540 508-987-6050
Ernest Boss, supt. Fax 987-6054
www.oxps.org
Oxford HS 600/9-12
495 Main St 01540 508-987-6081
David Grenier, prin. Fax 987-6083
Oxford MS 700/5-8
497 Main St 01540 508-987-6074
Katherine Hackett, prin. Fax 987-2588

Palmer, Hampden, Pop. 4,069
Palmer SD 2,000/PK-12
24 Converse St Ste 1 01069 413-283-2650
Dr. Gerald Fournier, supt. Fax 283-2655
www.palmerschools.org
Palmer HS 700/8-12
4105 Main St 01069 413-283-6511
Bonny Rathbone, prin. Fax 283-3476

Pathfinder Vocational-Technical SD
240 Sykes St 01069 413-283-9701
Gerald Paist, supt. Fax 284-0032
www.pathfindertech.org/
Pathfinder Reg Vocational Technical HS Vo/Tech
240 Sykes St 01069 413-283-9701
Mark Condon, prin. Fax 284-0032

Paxton, Worcester

Anna Maria College Post-Sec.
50 Sunset Ln 01612 508-849-3360

Peabody, Essex, Pop. 51,239
Peabody SD 6,600/PK-12
21 Johnson St 01960 978-536-6500
Nadine Binkley, supt. Fax 536-6504
www.peabody.k12.ma.us/
Higgins MS 1,600/6-8
1 King St 01960 978-536-4800
Melissa Matarazzo, prin. Fax 536-4810
Peabody Veterans Memorial HS 1,900/9-12
485 Lowell St 01960 978-536-4500
Patrick Larkin, prin. Fax 535-9578

Bishop Fenwick HS 900/9-12
99 Margin St 01960 978-531-8200
Sr. Catherine Fleming, admin. Fax 538-0333

Pembroke, Plymouth
Pembroke SD 3,200/PK-12
72 Pilgrim Rd 02359 781-829-1178
Dr. Patricia Randall, supt. Fax 826-1182
www.pembroke.mec.edu
Pembroke Community MS 500/7-8
559 School St 02359 781-294-0911
Steven LaMarche, prin. Fax 294-0916
Pembroke HS 700/9-12
80 Learning Ln 02359 781-293-9281
Ruth Lynch, prin. Fax 293-2812

Pepperell, Middlesex, Pop. 2,350
North Middlesex SD
Supt. — See Townsend
Nissitissit MS 600/6-8
33 Chase Ave 01463 978-433-0114
Michael Tikonoff, prin. Fax 433-0118

Pittsfield, Berkshire, Pop. 43,860
Pittsfield SD 6,500/PK-12
269 1st St 01201 413-499-9512
Dr. Katherine Darlington, supt. Fax 448-2643
www.pittsfield.net/
Herberg MS 800/6-8
501 Pomeroy Ave 01201 413-448-9640
Christopher Jacoby, prin. Fax 448-9644
Pittsfield HS 900/9-12
300 East St 01201 413-499-9535
Howard Eberwein, prin. Fax 443-7216
Reid MS 700/6-8
950 North St 01201 413-448-9620
Beth Narvaez, prin. Fax 443-1587
Taconic HS 1,000/9-12
96 Valentine Rd 01201 413-448-9600
Douglas McNally, prin. Fax 499-4835

Berkshire Community College Post-Sec.
1350 West St 01201 413-499-4660
Berkshire Medical Center Post-Sec.
725 North St 01201 413-447-2144
Mildred Elley Business School Post-Sec.
505 East St 01201 413-499-8618
Miss Hall's S 200/9-12
PO Box 1166 01202 413-443-6401
Jeannie Norris, hdmstr. Fax 448-2994
St. Joseph Central HS 8-12
22 Maplewood Ave 01201 413-447-9121
Donna Quallen, prin. Fax 443-7020

Plymouth, Plymouth, Pop. 7,258
Plymouth SD 8,600/PK-12
253 S Meadow Rd 02360 508-830-4300
Barry Haskell, supt. Fax 746-1873
www.plymouthschools.com
Plymouth Community IS 1,400/5-8
117 Long Pond Rd 02360 508-830-4450
Dr. Fred Sarke, prin. Fax 830-4464
Plymouth North HS 1,000/9-12
41 Obery St 02360 508-830-4400
John Siever, prin. Fax 830-4405
Plymouth South HS 900/9-12
490 Long Pond Rd 02360 508-224-7512
Patricia Connors, prin. Fax 224-6765
Plymouth South MS 900/5-8
488 Long Pond Rd 02360 508-224-2725
Anna Stompleski, prin. Fax 224-5660
Plymouth South Technical S Vo/Tech
490 Long Pond Rd 02360 508-224-7512
Patricia Connors, prin. Fax 224-9532

Prides Crossing, See Beverly

Landmark S 500/2-12
PO Box 227 01965 978-236-3010
Robert Broudo, hdmstr. Fax 921-0361

Provincetown, Barnstable, Pop. 3,374
Provincetown SD 200/PK-12
2 Mayflower Ln 02657 508-487-5000
Jessica Waugh, supt. Fax 487-5098
www.provincetown.k12.ma.us
Provincetown JSHS 100/7-12
12 Winslow St 02657 508-487-5040
Dr. Floriano Pavao, prin. Fax 487-5089

Quincy, Norfolk, Pop. 90,250
Quincy SD 8,700/PK-12
70 Coddington St 02169 617-984-8700
Dr. Richard DeCristofaro, supt. Fax 984-8806
www.quincypublicschools.com
Broad Meadows MS 400/6-8
50 Calvin Rd 02169 617-984-8723
Lawrence Taglieri, prin. Fax 984-8834
Central MS 600/6-8
1012 Hancock St 02169 617-984-8725
Stephen Sylvia, prin. Fax 984-8661
Point Webster MS 300/5-8
60 Lancaster St 02169 617-984-6600
James McGuire, prin. Fax 984-6609
Quincy HS 1,400/9-12
52 Coddington St 02169 617-984-8751
Frank Santoro, prin. Fax 984-8643
Sterling MS 300/6-8
444 Granite St 02169 617-984-8729
Earl Metzler, prin. Fax 984-8640
Other Schools – See North Quincy

Eastern Nazarene College Post-Sec.
23 E Elm Ave 02170 617-773-6350
Mansfield Beauty School Post-Sec.
200 Parkingway St 02169 617-479-1090
MA Sch. of Barbering & Mens Hairstyling Post-Sec.
1585 Hancock St 02169 617-770-4444
Quincy College Post-Sec.
34 Coddington St 02169 617-984-1600
Rhodec International Post-Sec.
59 Coddington St Ste 104 02169 617-472-4942
Woodward S for Girls 100/6-12
1102 Hancock St 02169 617-773-5610
Carol Andrews, prin. Fax 770-1551

Randolph, Norfolk, Pop. 31,200
Randolph SD 3,100/PK-12
40 Highland Ave 02368 781-961-6205
Dr. Richard H. Silverman, supt. Fax 961-6295
www.randolph.mec.edu/
Randolph Community MS 700/7-8
225 High St 02368 781-961-6243
John Sheehan, prin. Fax 961-6286
Randolph HS 1,000/9-12
70 Memorial Pkwy 02368 781-961-6220
William Conard, prin. Fax 961-6235

Raynham, Bristol, Pop. 2,100
Bridgewater-Raynham Regional SD 6,000/PK-12
777 Pleasant St 02767 508-824-2730
Robert McIntyre, supt. Fax 824-2746
www.bridge-rayn.org
Raynham MS 700/5-8
420 Titicut Rd 02767 508-997-0504
Paul Grueter, prin. Fax 977-0659
Other Schools – See Bridgewater

Reading, Middlesex, Pop. 22,539
Reading SD 4,200/K-12
82 Oakland Rd 01867 781-944-5800
Patrick Schettini J.D., supt. Fax 942-9149
www.reading.k12.ma.us/
Coolidge MS 500/6-8
89 Birch Meadow Dr 01867 781-942-9158
Craig Martin, prin. Fax 942-9118
Parker MS 500/6-8
45 Temple St 01867 781-944-1236
Linda Darisse, prin. Fax 942-9008
Reading Memorial HS 1,200/9-12
62 Oakland Rd 01867 781-944-8200
Joseph Finigan, prin. Fax 942-5435

Austin Preparatory S 700/6-12
101 Willow St 01867 781-944-4900
Paul Moran, prin. Fax 944-7530

Rehoboth, Bristol
Dighton-Rehoboth Regional SD
Supt. — See North Dighton
Beckwith MS 600/5-8
330R Winthrop St 02769 508-252-5080
Debra Pincince, prin. Fax 252-5082

Revere, Suffolk, Pop. 45,807
Revere SD 5,400/PK-12
101 School St 02151 781-286-8226
Dr. Paul Dakin, supt. Fax 286-8221
www.revereps.mec.edu
Anthony MS 6-8
107 Newhall St 02151 781-388-7520
Christopher Malone, prin. Fax 388-7521
Garfield Magnet MS 600/6-8
176 Garfield Ave 02151 781-286-8298
Patricia Massa, prin. Fax 286-8128
Revere HS 1,400/9-12
101 School St 02151 781-286-8222
David Deruosi, prin. Fax 286-8378
Seacoast MSHS 200/7-12
101 School St 02151 781-485-2715
Thomas Misci, prin. Fax 485-2718

Rochester, Plymouth
Old Colony Reg Vocational Technical HSD
476 North Ave 02770 508-763-8011
David Ferreira, supt. Fax 763-9821
www.oldcolony.tec.ma.us
Old Colony Reg Vocational Tech HS Vo/Tech
476 North Ave 02770 508-763-8011
Gary Brown, prin. Fax 763-9821

Rockland, Plymouth, Pop. 16,123
Rockland SD 2,000/K-12
34 Mackinlay Way 02370 781-878-3893
James A. Kerrigan, supt. Fax 982-1483
www.rockland.mec.edu/
Rockland HS 800/9-12
52 Mackinlay Way 02370 781-871-0541
Stephen Sangster, prin. Fax 878-0158
Rogers MS 400/6-8
100 Taunton Ave 02370 781-878-4341
Paul Stanish, prin. Fax 871-8448

Master's Academy 100/K-12
525 Beech St 02370 781-871-8214
David McGee, prin. Fax 871-8721

Rockport, Essex, Pop. 5,448
Rockport SD 1,000/K-12
24 Jerdens Ln 01966 978-546-1200
Rosemary A. Ditullio Ph.D., supt. Fax 546-1205
rockport.k12.ma.us
Rockport HS 300/9-12
24 Jerdens Ln 01966 978-546-1234
Charles Symonds, prin. Fax 546-1205
Rockport MS 300/6-8
26 Jerdens Ln 01966 978-546-1250
Charles Symonds, prin. Fax 546-1205

Roslindale, See Boston
Boston SD
Supt. — See Boston
Irving MS 700/6-8
105 Cummins Hwy 02131 617-635-8072
James Watson, prin. Fax 635-9363

Roxbury, See Boston
Boston SD
Supt. — See Boston
Dearborn MS 500/6-8
35 Greenville St 02119 617-635-8412
Teresa Soares-Pena, prin. Fax 635-8419
Lewis MS 300/6-8
131 Walnut Ave 02119 617-635-8137
Ronald Spratling, prin. Fax 635-6341
O'Bryant HS of Mathematics & Science 900/9-12
55 Malcolm X Blvd 02120 617-635-9932
Joel Stembridge, hdmstr. Fax 635-7769
Timilty MS 700/6-8
205 Roxbury St 02119 617-635-8109
Valeria Lowe-Barehmi, prin. Fax 635-8115
Boston Adult Technical Academy Adult
75 Malcolm X Blvd 02120 617-635-1542
Rachel Bonkovsky, dir. Fax 635-6362

Roxbury Crossing, See Boston
Boston SD
Supt. — See Boston
Madison Park Technical Vocational HS Vo/Tech
75 Malcolm X Blvd 02120 617-635-8970
Charles McAfee, hdmstr. Fax 635-9831

Roxbury Community College Post-Sec.
1234 Columbus Ave 02120 617-427-0060

Rutland, Worcester, Pop. 2,145
Wachusett Regional SD
Supt. — See Jefferson
Central Tree MS 500/5-8
281 Main St 01543 508-886-0073
C. Erik Githmark, prin. Fax 886-0141

Devereux Center in Massachusetts Post-Sec.
PO Box 219 01543 508-886-4746

Salem, Essex, Pop. 41,756
Salem SD 4,700/PK-12
29 Highland Ave 01970 978-740-1212
Dr. Lawrence Callahan, supt. Fax 740-3083
www.salem.k12.ma.us/
Collins MS 900/6-8
29 Highland Ave 01970 978-740-1191
Mary Manning, prin. Fax 740-1183
Salem HS 1,400/9-12
77 Wilson St 01970 978-740-1123
David Angeramo, prin. Fax 740-1110

Salem State College Post-Sec.
352 Lafayette St 01970 978-741-6000

Sandwich, Barnstable, Pop. 2,998
Sandwich SD 4,100/PK-12
16 Dewey Ave 02563 508-888-1054
Nancy Young, supt. Fax 888-9505
www.sandwich.k12.ma.us
Other Schools – See East Sandwich

Saugus, Essex, Pop. 26,200
Saugus SD 3,100/PK-12
23 Main St 01906 781-231-5000
Keith Manville, supt. Fax 233-9424
www.mec.edu/saugus/
Belmonte MS 800/6-8
25 Dow St 01906 781-231-5052
Charles Naso, prin. Fax 233-5665
Saugus HS 800/9-12
1 Pierce Memorial Dr 01906 781-231-5027
Joseph Diorio, prin. Fax 231-5030

Scituate, Plymouth, Pop. 5,180
Scituate SD 3,100/K-12
606 Chief Justice Cushing 02066 781-545-8759
Mark Mason, supt. Fax 545-6291
www.scituate.k12.ma.us/
Gates IS 500/7-8
327 First Parish Rd 02066 781-545-8760
Richard Blake, prin. Fax 545-8767
Scituate HS 900/9-12
606 Chief Justice Cushing 02066 781-545-8750
Donna Nuzzo-Mueller, prin. Fax 545-8758

Seekonk, Bristol, Pop. 13,046
Seekonk SD 2,000/PK-12
69 School St 02771 508-336-7711
Dr. Emile Chevrette, supt. Fax 336-2264
seekonkschools.lucasproject.com/
Hurley MS 600/6-8
650 Newman Ave 02771 508-761-7570
Frederick Nelson, prin. Fax 336-9630
Seekonk HS 700/9-12
261 Arcade Ave 02771 508-336-7272
Marcia McGovern, prin. Fax 336-8535

Sharon, Norfolk, Pop. 5,893
Sharon SD 3,500/PK-12
1 School St 02067 781-784-1570
Claire Jackson Ph.D., supt. Fax 784-1573
www.sharon.k12.ma.us
Sharon HS 1,100/9-12
181 Pond St 02067 781-784-1554
Jose Libano, prin. Fax 784-1550
Sharon MS 800/6-8
75 Mountain St 02067 781-784-1560
Kevin O'Rourke, prin. Fax 784-8432

Chabad Day S 100/PK-12
162 N Main St 02067 781-784-4269
Sara Wolosow, prin. Fax 634-0485

Sheffield, Berkshire
Southern Berkshire Regional SD 1,000/PK-12
PO Box 339 01257 413-229-8778
Valerie Spriggs, supt. Fax 229-2913
sbrsd.org
Mount Everett Regional HS 400/7-12
PO Box 326 01257 413-229-8734
Glenn Devoti, prin. Fax 229-2044

Berkshire S 400/9-12
245 N Undermountain Rd 01257 413-229-8511
Michael Maher, hdmstr. Fax 229-1010

Shelburne Falls, Franklin, Pop. 1,996
Mohawk Trail SD 1,400/PK-12
24 Ashfield Rd 01370 413-625-0192
Michael Buoniconti, supt. Fax 625-0196
www.mohawkschools.org
Mohawk Trail Regional HS 800/7-12
26 Ashfield Rd 01370 413-625-9811
Brian Beck, prin. Fax 625-6652

Shirley, Middlesex, Pop. 1,559
Shirley SD 700/PK-8
34 Lancaster Rd 01464 978-425-2630
Malcolm Reid, supt. Fax 425-2639
Shirley MS 300/5-8
1 Hospital Rd 01464 978-425-2630
Ruthann Petruno-Goguen, prin. Fax 425-0474

Shrewsbury, Worcester, Pop. 25,900
Shrewsbury SD 5,600/K-12
100 Maple Ave 01545 508-841-8400
Dr. Anthony Bent, supt. Fax 841-8490
www.shrewsbury-ma.gov/schools/index.asp
Oak MS 900/7-8
45 Oak St 01545 508-841-1200
Joseph Sawyer, prin. Fax 841-1223
Shrewsbury HS 1,400/9-12
64 Holden St 01545 508-841-8800
Brian Reagan, prin. Fax 841-8858

St. John's HS 1,100/9-12
378 Main St 01545 508-842-8934
Michael W. Welch, admin. Fax 842-3670

Somerset, Bristol, Pop. 17,655
Somerset SD 2,800/K-12
580 Whetstone Hill Rd 02726 508-324-3100
Richard Medeiros, supt. Fax 324-3107
www.musictown.mec.edu
Somerset HS 1,000/9-12
270 Grandview Ave 02726 508-324-3115
Robert Pineault, prin. Fax 324-3118
Somerset MS 600/6-8
1141 Brayton Ave 02726 508-324-3140
Elizabeth Ponte, prin. Fax 324-3145

Somerville, Middlesex, Pop. 74,963
Somerville SD 4,700/PK-12
181 Washington St 02143 617-625-6600
Anthony Pierantozzi, supt. Fax 625-4731
www.somerville.k12.ma.us
Somerville HS 1,600/9-12
81 Highland Ave 02143 617-625-6600
Anthony Ciccariello, prin. Fax 629-4763

Computer-Ed Business Institute Post-Sec.
5 Middlesex Ave 02145 781-933-7681

Southborough, Worcester
Northborough-Southborough SD
Supt. — See Northborough
Trottier MS 500/6-8
49 Parkerville Rd 01772 508-485-2400
Linda Murdock, prin. Fax 481-1506

St. Marks S 300/9-12
PO Box 9105 01772 508-786-6000
John Warren, hdmstr. Fax 786-6109

South Boston, See Boston
Boston SD
Supt. — See Boston
Excel HS 400/9-12
95 G St 02127 617-635-9870
Ligia Noriega, hdmstr. Fax 635-9711
Gavin MS 600/6-8
215 Dorchester St 02127 617-635-8817
Alexander Mathews, prin. Fax 635-8826
Monument HS 400/9-12
95 G St 02127 617-635-9865
Jonathan Pizzi, hdmstr. Fax 635-9857

Southbridge, Worcester, Pop. 13,631
Southbridge SD 2,400/K-12
41 Elm St Ste 11 01550 508-764-5414
Dale Hanley, supt. Fax 764-8325
www.southbridge.k12.ma.us/
Southbridge HS 600/9-12
25 Cole Ave 01550 508-764-5450
Sheila Haskins, prin. Fax 764-5479
Wells JHS 600/6-8
82 Marcy St 01550 508-764-5440
Jason DeFalco, prin. Fax 764-5496

South Dartmouth, Bristol, Pop. 9,850
Dartmouth SD 4,300/PK-12
8 Bush St 02748 508-997-3391
Stephen Russell, supt. Fax 991-4184
www.dartmouth.k12.ma.us/
Dartmouth HS 1,300/9-12
555 Bakerville Rd 02748 508-961-2700
Donna Dimery, prin. Fax 910-1410
Other Schools – See North Dartmouth

South Deerfield, Franklin, Pop. 1,906
Frontier Regional SD 700/7-12
219 Christian Ln 01373 413-665-1155
Regina H. Nash Ed.D., supt. Fax 665-8506
Frontier Regional JSHS 700/7-12
113 N Main St 01373 413-665-2118
Donald Skroski, prin. Fax 665-1518

South Dennis, Barnstable, Pop. 3,559
Dennis-Yarmouth SD
Supt. — See South Yarmouth
Wixon MS 600/4-8
901 Route 134 02660 508-398-7695
Lisa McMahon, prin. Fax 398-7608

South Easton, Bristol
Southeastern Regional Voc Tech SD
250 Foundry St 02375 508-238-4374
James Hager, supt. Fax 230-3779
www.sersd.org
Southeastern Regional Vo-Tech HS Vo/Tech
250 Foundry St 02375 508-238-4371
Jerome Burke, prin. Fax 230-8352

Southeastern Technical Institute Post-Sec.
250 Foundry St 02375 508-238-1860

South Hadley, Hampshire, Pop. 5,400
South Hadley SD 2,300/PK-12
116 Main St Ste 202 01075 413-538-5060
Gus Sayer, supt. Fax 532-6284
www.shschools.com
Smith MS 800/5-8
100 Mosier St 01075 413-538-5074
Erica Faginski, prin. Fax 538-5003
South Hadley HS 700/9-12
153 Newton St 01075 413-538-5063
Daniel Smith, prin. Fax 532-6538

Mt. Holyoke College Post-Sec.
50 College St 01075 413-538-2000
Valley Christian S 100/PK-12
36 Hadley St 01075 413-533-8545
Janet Goss, prin. Fax 533-8544

South Hamilton, Essex, Pop. 2,750
Hamilton-Wenham SD
Supt. — See Wenham
Hamilton-Wenham Regional HS 700/9-12
775 Bay Rd 01982 978-468-5300
Robert Krol, prin. Fax 468-0241
Miles River MS 500/6-8
787 Bay Rd 01982 978-468-5320
Janice Desantis, prin. Fax 468-8454

Gordon-Conwell Theological Seminary Post-Sec.
130 Essex St 01982 978-468-7111
Pingree S 300/9-12
537 Highland St 01982 978-468-4415
Peter M. Cowen, hdmstr. Fax 468-3758

South Lancaster, Worcester, Pop. 1,772

Atlantic Union College Post-Sec.
PO Box 1000 01561 978-368-2000
South Lancaster Academy 100/9-12
PO Box 1129 01561 978-368-8544
Allyson Cram, prin. Fax 365-2244

Southwick, Hampden
Southwick-Tolland SD 1,900/PK-12
86 Powder Mill Rd 01077 413-569-5391
Thomas Witham, supt. Fax 569-1711
www.strsd.southwick.ma.us/
Powder Mill MS 600/5-8
94 Powder Mill Rd 01077 413-569-5951
Ronald Peloquin, prin. Fax 569-1710

Southwick HS 600/9-12
93 Feeding Hills Rd 01077 413-569-6171
Michael J. Camerota, prin. Fax 569-1723

South Yarmouth, Barnstable, Pop. 10,358
Dennis-Yarmouth SD 3,400/K-12
296 Station Ave 02664 508-398-7600
Dan Cabral, supt. Fax 398-7622
www.dy-regional.k12.ma.us/
Dennis-Yarmouth Regional HS 1,100/9-12
210 Station Ave 02664 508-398-7630
Kenneth Jenks, prin. Fax 398-7602
Other Schools – See South Dennis, West Yarmouth

Spencer, Worcester, Pop. 6,306
Spencer-East Brookfield SD 2,200/PK-12
306 Main St 01562 508-885-8500
Ralph Hicks Ed.D., supt. Fax 885-8504
www.ultranet.com/~seb
Knox Trail JHS 400/7-8
73 Ash St 01562 508-885-8550
John Williams, prin. Fax 885-8557
Prouty HS 600/9-12
302 Main St 01562 508-885-8505
Kevin Wells, prin. Fax 885-8511

Springfield, Hampden, Pop. 151,732
Springfield SD 25,800/PK-12
195 State St 01103 413-787-7100
Dr. Joseph Burke, supt. Fax 787-7211
www.sps.springfield.ma.us
Chestnut Accelerated MS 1,200/6-8
355 Plainfield St 01107 413-750-2333
Lydia Martinez, prin. Fax 750-2351
Duggan MS 900/6-8
1015 Wilbraham Rd 01109 413-787-7410
Jonathan Swan, prin. Fax 750-2209
Forest Park MS 900/6-8
46 Oakland St 01108 413-787-7420
Bonnie Osgood, prin. Fax 787-7419
Kennedy MS 700/6-8
1385 Berkshire Ave 01151 413-787-7510
Frances Cameron, prin. Fax 787-7561
Kiley MS 1,000/6-8
180 Cooley St 01128 413-787-7240
Catherine McCarthy, prin. Fax 787-7247
Putnam Vocational Technical HS Vo/Tech
1300 State St 01109 413-787-7424
Kevin McCaskill, prin. Fax 787-7330
Springfield Central HS 2,000/9-12
1840 Roosevelt Ave 01109 413-787-7085
Richard Stoddard, prin. Fax 787-7040
Springfield Expeditionary Learning S 200/6-12
1170 Carew St 01104 413-750-2929
Stephen Mahoney, prin. Fax 750-2978
HS of Commerce 1,700/9-12
415 State St 01105 413-787-7220
Robert Fernandes, prin. Fax 787-7041
Springfield HS of Science-Tech 1,800/9-12
1250 State St 01109 413-750-2000
Karen Lott, prin. Fax 750-2047
Van Sickle MS 1,100/6-8
1170 Carew St 01104 413-750-2887
Cheryl DeSpirt-Lambert, prin. Fax 750-2972

American International College Post-Sec.
1000 State St 01109 413-737-7000
Cathedral HS 800/9-12
260 Surrey Rd 01118 413-782-5285
John Miller, prin. Fax 782-5065
MacDuffie S 200/6-12
1 Ames Hill Dr 01105 413-734-4971
Kathryn Gibson, prin. Fax 734-6693
Mansfield Beauty School Post-Sec.
266 Bridge St 01103 413-788-7575
Pioneer Valley Christian S 300/PK-12
965 Plumtree Rd 01119 413-782-8031
Timothy Duff, hdmstr. Fax 782-8033
Springfield College Post-Sec.
263 Alden St 01109 413-748-3000
Springfield Technical Community College Post-Sec.
1 Armory Sq 01105 413-781-7822
Ultrasound Diagnostic School Post-Sec.
365 Cadwell Dr 01104 413-739-4700
Western New England College Post-Sec.
1215 Wilbraham Rd 01119 413-782-3111

Sterling, Worcester
Wachusett Regional SD
Supt. — See Jefferson
Chocksett MS 400/5-8
40 Boutelle Rd 01564 978-422-6552
Marguerite Snow, prin. Fax 422-7720

Stoneham, Middlesex, Pop. 22,203
Stoneham SD 3,000/PK-12
149 Franklin St 02180 781-279-3826
Joseph Connelly, supt. Fax 279-3818
www.stonehamschools.net/
Stoneham HS 900/9-12
149 Franklin St 02180 781-279-3810
Thomas Ryan, prin. Fax 279-2070
Stoneham MS 700/6-8
101 Central St 02180 781-279-3840
Christine McMenimen, prin. Fax 279-3843

Edgewood/Greater Boston Academy 100/PK-12
108 Pond St 02180 781-665-9053
Rondi Aastrup, prin. Fax 665-3264

Stoughton, Norfolk, Pop. 27,500
Stoughton SD 4,000/PK-12
232 Pearl St 02072 781-344-4000
Claire McCarthy, supt. Fax 344-6417
www.stoughtonschools.org/
O'Donnell MS 1,000/6-8
211 Cushing St 02072 781-344-7002
Wayne R. Hester, prin. Fax 297-5263
Stoughton HS 1,200/9-12
232 Pearl St 02072 781-344-7001
Philip Iacobacci, prin. Fax 341-6041

Stow, Middlesex
Nashoba Regional SD
Supt. — See Bolton

Hale MS 300/6-8
55 Hartley Rd 01775 978-897-4788
Margaret Morgan, prin. Fax 897-3631

Sudbury, Middlesex
Lincoln-Sudbury SD 1,500/9-12
390 Lincoln Rd 01776 978-443-9961
John Ritchie, supt. Fax 443-8824
www.lsrhs.net/
Lincoln-Sudbury Regional HS 1,500/9-12
390 Lincoln Rd 01776 978-443-9961
John Ritchie, prin. Fax 443-8824

Sudbury SD 3,100/K-8
40 Fairbank Rd Ste C 01776 978-443-1058
John Brackett, supt. Fax 443-9001
www.sudbury.k12.ma.us
Curtis MS 1,000/6-8
22 Pratts Mill Rd 01776 978-443-1071
Kathryn J. Codianne, prin. Fax 443-1098

Sutton, Worcester
Sutton SD 1,500/PK-12
383 Boston Rd 01590 508-581-1600
Cecilia DiBella, supt. Fax 865-6463
www.suttonschools.net/
Sutton HS 400/9-12
383 Boston Rd 01590 508-581-1640
Paul Daigle, prin. Fax 917-0063
Sutton MS 400/6-8
409 Boston Rd 01590 508-581-1630
Deborah Cimo, prin. Fax 865-6463

Swampscott, Essex, Pop. 13,650
Swampscott SD 2,400/K-12
207 Forest Ave 01907 781-596-8800
Matthew Malone Ed.D., supt. Fax 598-4379
swampscottk12ma.us/
Swampscott HS 800/9-12
207 Forest Ave 01907 781-596-8830
Lawrence Murphy Ed.D., prin. Fax 598-4379
Swampscott MS 600/6-8
71 Greenwood Ave 01907 781-596-8820
Ralph Watson Ed.D., prin. Fax 593-2126

Marian Court College Post-Sec.
35 Littles Point Rd 01907 781-595-6768

Swansea, Bristol
Swansea SD 2,000/K-12
1 Gardners Neck Rd 02777 508-675-1195
Stephen C. Flanagan, supt. Fax 672-1040
www.swanseaschools.org
Case HS 600/9-12
70 School St 02777 508-675-7483
Brian McCann, prin. Fax 646-4405
Case JHS 500/6-8
195 Main St 02777 508-675-0116
Robert Monteiro, prin. Fax 646-4413

Cornerstone Christian Academy 50/PK-12
1436 G A R Hwy 02777 508-675-0644
Thomas Sullivan, prin. Fax 675-0607
New England Christian Academy 200/PK-12
271 Sharps Lot Rd 02777 508-676-3011
Dr. Gary Morris, prin. Fax 646-0392

Taunton, Bristol, Pop. 56,251
Bristol-Plymouth Regional-Tech SD
940 County St 02780 508-823-5151
Richard Gross Ed.D., supt. Fax 880-7287
www.bptech.org
Bristol-Plymouth Regional Technical S Vo/Tech
940 County St 02780 508-823-5151
Carolyn Pearson, prin. Fax 822-2687

Taunton SD 8,400/PK-12
50 Williams St 02780 508-821-1100
Dr. Arthur Stellar, supt. Fax 821-1177
www.tauntonschools.org
Friedman MS 900/5-8
500 Norton Ave 02780 508-821-1493
John Cabral, prin. Fax 821-3185
Mulcahey MS 600/5-8
28 Clifford St 02780 508-821-1255
Dr. Anthony Azar, prin. Fax 821-1360
Parker MS 500/5-8
50 Williams St 02780 508-821-1111
Manuel Fernandez, prin. Fax 821-1361
Taunton HS 2,000/9-12
50 Williams St 02780 508-821-1101
Matt Mattos, prin. Fax 821-1362
Other Schools – See East Taunton

Coyle & Cassidy HS 9-12
2 Hamilton St 02780 508-823-6164
Dr. Mary Pat Tranter, prin. Fax 823-2530
Rob Roy Academy Taunton Campus Post-Sec.
1 School St 02780 508-822-1405
Taunton Catholic MS 300/5-8
61 Summer St 02780 508-822-0491
Margaret Menear, prin. Fax 824-0469

Tewksbury, Middlesex, Pop. 11,000
Tewksbury SD 4,800/PK-12
139 Pleasant St 01876 978-640-7800
Christine McGrath, supt. Fax 640-7804
www.mec.edu/tewksbury/
Tewksbury Memorial HS 1,200/9-12
320 Pleasant St 01876 978-640-7825
Gerald Ferris, prin. Fax 640-7829
Wynn MS 800/7-8
1 Griffin Way 01876 978-640-7846
John Donoghue, prin. Fax 640-7850

Electrology Institute of New England Post-Sec.
1501 Main St Ste 50 01876 800-548-6339

Topsfield, Essex, Pop. 2,711
Masconomet SD 2,100/7-12
20 Endicott Rd 01983 978-887-2323
Claire Sheff Kohn, supt. Fax 887-3573
www.masconomet.org

Masconomet Regional HS 1,300/9-12
20 Endicott Rd 01983 978-887-2323
Pamela Culver, prin. Fax 887-7243
Masconomet Regional MS 800/7-8
20 Endicott Rd 01983 978-887-2323
Catherine Cullinane, prin. Fax 887-1991

Townsend, Middlesex, Pop. 1,164
North Middlesex SD 4,700/PK-12
23 Main St 01469 978-597-8713
Maureen Marshall, supt. Fax 597-6534
nmiddlesex.mec.edu
Hawthorne Brook MS 600/6-8
64 Brookline St 01469 978-597-6914
Pamela Miller, prin. Fax 597-5261
North Middlesex Regional HS 1,200/9-12
19 Main St 01469 978-597-8721
Richard Manley, prin. Fax 597-0350
Other Schools – See Pepperell

Turners Falls, Franklin, Pop. 4,731
Franklin County Technical SD
82 Industrial Blvd 01376 413-863-9561
Dr. Steven Johnson, supt. Fax 863-2816
www.fcts.org
Franklin County Technical HS Vo/Tech
82 Industrial Blvd 01376 413-863-9561
Paul Cohen, prin. Fax 863-2816

Gill-Montague SD 1,200/PK-12
35 Crocker Ave 01376 413-863-9324
Sue Gee, supt. Fax 863-4560
www.gmrsd.org
Other Schools – See Montague

Edwards Academy 100/K-12
251 Millers Falls Rd 01376 413-863-3700
Alfred Popp, hdmstr. Fax 863-8170
Hallmark Institute of Photography Post-Sec.
PO Box 308 01376 413-863-2478

Tyngsboro, Middlesex
Greater Lowell Technical HSD
250 Pawtucket Blvd 01879 978-441-4800
James M. Cassin, supt. Fax 441-5353
www.gltech.org
Greater Lowell Technical HS Vo/Tech
250 Pawtucket Blvd 01879 978-441-4807
Mary Jo Santoro, prin. Fax 441-5353

Tyngsborough SD 2,300/PK-12
50 Norris Rd 01879 978-649-7488
David Hawkins, supt. Fax 649-7199
www.tyngsboroughps.org/
Tyngsboro HS 700/9-12
36 Norris Rd 01879 978-649-7571
Donald Ciampa, prin. Fax 649-4210
Tyngsboro MS 500/6-8
50 Norris Rd 01879 978-649-3115
Stephen Coughlan, prin. Fax 649-8673

Academy of Notre Dame HS 200/9-12
180 Middlesex Rd 01879 978-649-7611
Sr. Mary Farren, prin. Fax 649-2909

Upton, Worcester, Pop. 2,347
Blackstone Valley Regional Vo/Tech SD
65 Pleasant St 01568 508-529-7758
Michael Fitzpatrick, supt. Fax 529-3079
www.valleytech.k12.ma.us
Blackstone Valley Regional Vo-Tech HS Vo/Tech
65 Pleasant St 01568 508-529-7758
Richard Brennan, prin. Fax 839-2403

Mendon-Upton Regional SD
Supt. — See Mendon
Nipmuc Regional HS 900/8-12
90 Pleasant St 01568 508-529-2130
Joan Scribner, prin. Fax 529-2129

Uxbridge, Worcester, Pop. 3,400
Uxbridge SD 2,000/K-12
21 S Main St 01569 508-278-8648
Daniel J. Stefanilo, supt. Fax 278-8612
uxbridgeschools.com
Uxbridge HS 500/9-12
62 Capron St 01569 508-278-8636
George Zini, prin. Fax 278-8627
Whitin MS 700/5-8
120 Granite St 01569 508-278-8640
Howard Boyaj, prin. Fax 278-8639

Vineyard Haven, Dukes, Pop. 1,762
Martha's Vineyard SD 800/9-12
4 Pine St 02568 508-693-2007
James Weiss Ed.D., supt. Fax 693-3190
www.mv.k12.ma.us
Other Schools – See Oak Bluffs

Wakefield, Middlesex, Pop. 24,825
Northeast Metro Vocational SD
100 Hemlock Rd 01880 781-246-0810
Patricia Cronin, supt. Fax 246-4919
northeastmetrotech.com
Northeast Metro Regional Vocational HS Vo/Tech
100 Hemlock Rd 01880 781-246-0810
John Crowley, prin. Fax 246-4919

Wakefield SD 3,400/K-12
60 Farm St 01880 781-246-6400
Dr. Maynard Suffredini, supt. Fax 245-9164
www.wakefield.k12.ma.us/
Galvin JHS 1,100/5-8
525 Main St 01880 781-246-6410
Paula Mullen, prin. Fax 224-5009
Wakefield Memorial HS 1,000/9-12
60 Farm St 01880 781-246-6440
Elinor Freedman, prin. Fax 246-4714

Our Lady of Nazareth Academy 200/9-12
14 Winship Dr 01880 781-245-5210
Sr. Joanne Forker, prin. Fax 245-6648

Walpole, Norfolk, Pop. 5,495
Norfolk County Agricultural SD
400 Main St 02081 508-668-0268
Angela Avery, supt. Fax 668-0612
www.norfolkaggie.org
Norfolk County Agricultural HS Vo/Tech
400 Main St 02081 508-668-0268
Gail Murphy, prin. Fax 668-0612

Walpole SD 3,800/PK-12
135 School St 02081 508-660-7200
Kathleen A. Smith, supt. Fax 668-1167
www.walpole.ma.us
Johnson MS 500/6-8
111 Robbins Rd 02081 508-660-7242
Sheryl Biss, prin. Fax 660-7240
Walpole HS 1,000/9-12
275 Common St 02081 508-660-7257
Alan Bernstein, prin. Fax 850-7958
Other Schools – See East Walpole

Waltham, Middlesex, Pop. 59,556
Waltham SD 4,700/PK-12
617 Lexington St 02452 781-314-5440
Dr. Susan Parrella, supt. Fax 314-5411
www.city.waltham.ma.us/SCHOOL/WebPAge/tofc.htm
Kennedy MS 500/6-8
655 Lexington St 02452 781-314-5560
John Cawley, prin. Fax 314-5571
McDevitt MS 600/6-8
75 Church St 02452 781-314-5590
Brad Morgan, prin. Fax 314-5601
Waltham HS 1,400/9-12
617 Lexington St 02452 781-314-5440
John Graceffa, prin. Fax 647-0309

Bentley College Post-Sec.
175 Forest St 02452 781-891-2000
Blaine The Beauty Career School Post-Sec.
314 Moody St 02453 781-899-1500
Brandeis University Post-Sec.
415 South St 02453 781-736-3500
Center for Digital Imaging Arts at BU Post-Sec.
282 Moody St 02453 800-808-2342
Chapel Hill-Chauncy Hall S 200/9-12
785 Beaver St 02452 781-894-2644
Siri Akal Khalsa, hdmstr. Fax 894-8768
Sodexho Marriott Services Post-Sec.
200 5th Ave 02451 800-926-7429

Ware, Hampshire, Pop. 6,533
Ware SD 1,200/K-12
PO Box 240 01082 413-967-4271
Dr. Mary-Elizabeth Beach, supt. Fax 967-9580
www.ware.k12.ma.us
Ware JSHS 400/8-12
237 West St 01082 413-967-6234
Lucille Brindisi, prin. Fax 967-9053

Wareham, Plymouth, Pop. 19,232
Wareham SD 3,400/PK-12
54 Marion Rd Ste 1 02571 508-291-3500
James D. Collins, supt. Fax 291-3578
www.warehamps.org/district/index.htm
Wareham HS 1,000/9-12
7 Viking Dr 02571 508-291-3510
John Amaral, prin. Fax 291-3577
Wareham MS 800/6-8
4 Viking Dr 02571 508-291-3550
John Amaral, prin. Fax 291-3580

Warren, Worcester, Pop. 1,516
Quaboag Regional SD 1,500/PK-12
PO Box 1538 01083 413-436-9256
Carol Jacobs, supt. Fax 436-9738
www.quaboag.org
Quaboag Regional MSHS 600/7-12
PO Box 909 01083 413-436-5991
Michael Rooney, prin. Fax 436-9636

Watertown, Middlesex, Pop. 32,303
Watertown SD 2,300/K-12
30 Common St 02472 617-926-7700
Dr. Steven A. Hiersche, supt. Fax 923-1234
www.watertown.k12.ma.us
Watertown HS 700/9-12
50 Columbia St 02472 617-926-7760
Michael Noftsker, prin. Fax 926-7723
Watertown MS 500/6-8
68 Waverley Ave 02472 617-926-7783
James Carter, prin. Fax 926-5407

Perkins School for the Blind Post-Sec.
175 N Beacon St 02472 617-972-7285

Wayland, Middlesex, Pop. 2,500
Wayland SD 2,900/K-12
PO Box 408 01778 508-358-3774
Gary Burton, supt. Fax 358-7708
www.wayland.k12.ma.us
Wayland HS 900/9-12
264 Old Connecticut Path 01778 508-358-3705
Charles Ruopp, prin. Fax 358-8082
Wayland MS 700/6-8
201 Main St 01778 508-655-6670
Charlie Schlegel, prin. Fax 655-2548

Webster, Worcester, Pop. 11,849
Webster SD 1,800/K-12
PO Box 430 01570 508-943-0104
Gregory Ciardi Ph.D., supt. Fax 949-2364
www.webster-schools.org
Bartlett JSHS 800/7-12
52 Lake Pkwy 01570 508-943-8552
Michael Hackenson, prin. Fax 949-8274

Wellesley, Norfolk, Pop. 26,600
Wellesley SD 4,300/K-12
40 Kingsbury St 02481 781-446-6210
Matthew King, supt. Fax 446-6207
www.wellesley.mec.edu/
Wellesley HS 1,100/9-12
50 Rice St 02481 781-446-6290
Rena Mirkin, prin. Fax 237-6004
Wellesley MS 1,000/6-8
50 Kingsbury St 02481 781-446-6235
John D'Auria, prin. Fax 239-1206

Dana Hall S 500/6-12
45 Dana Rd 02482 781-235-3010
Blair Jenkins, prin. Fax 235-6491
Massachusetts Bay Community College Post-Sec.
50 Oakland St 02481 781-239-3000
Wellesley College Post-Sec.
106 Central St 02481 781-235-0320

Wendell, Franklin

Lake Grove School-Maple Valley Post-Sec.
PO Box 767 01379 888-585-9007

Wenham, Essex, Pop. 4,212
Hamilton-Wenham SD 2,200/K-12
5 School St 01984 978-468-5310
Dr. Marinel D. McGrath, supt. Fax 468-7889
www.hw-regional.k12.ma.us
Other Schools – See South Hamilton

Gordon College Post-Sec.
255 Grapevine Rd 01984 978-927-2300

West Barnstable, Barnstable, Pop. 1,508

Cape Cod Community College Post-Sec.
2240 Iyannough Rd 02668 508-362-2131

Westborough, Worcester, Pop. 3,917
Westborough SD 3,500/PK-12
PO Box 1152 01581 508-836-7700
Dr. Anne Towle, supt. Fax 836-7704
www.westborough.org
Gibbons MS 600/7-8
20 Fisher St 01581 508-836-7740
Dr. David Fredette, prin. Fax 836-7744
Westborough HS 1,100/9-12
90 W Main St 01581 508-836-7720
John Pierce, prin. Fax 836-7723

West Boylston, Worcester, Pop. 6,611
West Boylston SD 1,100/K-12
125 Crescent St 01583 508-835-2917
Thomas J. Kane, supt. Fax 835-8992
www.wbschools.com
West Boylston S 700/6-12
125 Crescent St 01583 508-835-4475
Francine Bullock, prin. Fax 835-8992

Salter School Post-Sec.
184 W Boylston St Ste 1 01583 508-853-1074

West Bridgewater, Plymouth
West Bridgewater SD 1,100/PK-12
2 Spring St 02379 508-894-1230
Dr. Patricia Oakley, supt. Fax 894-1232
wbridgewaterschools.com
West Bridgewater JSHS 500/7-12
155 W Center St 02379 508-894-1220
Jeffrey Szymaniak, prin. Fax 894-1226

New England Baptist Academy 100/PK-12
560 N Main St 02379 508-584-5188
Rev. Joseph Coppola, prin. Fax 584-7555

Westfield, Hampden, Pop. 40,525
Westfield SD 6,600/PK-12
22 Ashley St 01085 413-572-6403
Shirley Alvira, supt. Fax 572-6518
www.k12.westfield.ma.us/
North MS 800/6-8
350 Southampton Rd 01085 413-572-6441
Ronald Rix, prin. Fax 572-1669
South MS 700/6-8
30 W Silver St 01085 413-568-1900
Anne Marie Nicolai, prin. Fax 572-4892
Westfield HS 1,700/9-12
177 Montgomery Rd 01085 413-572-6466
Raymond Broderick, prin. Fax 572-6346
Westfield Vocational Technical HS Vo/Tech
33 Smith Ave 01085 413-572-6533
Hilary Weisgerber, dir. Fax 572-6542

St. Marys HS 100/9-12
27 Bartlett St 01085 413-568-5692
Paul Romani, prin. Fax 562-3501
Westfield State College Post-Sec.
PO Box 1630 01086 413-572-5300

Westford, Middlesex
Nashoba Valley Technical SD
100 Littleton Rd 01886 978-692-4711
Judith Klimkiewicz, supt. Fax 392-0570
Nashoba Valley Technical HS Vo/Tech
100 Littleton Rd 01886 978-692-4711
Victor Kiloski, prin. Fax 392-0570

Westford SD 5,100/K-12
23 Depot St 01886 978-692-5560
Everett Olsen, supt. Fax 692-4842
www.westford.mec.edu/schools
Blanchard MS 600/6-8
14 West St 01886 978-692-5582
Suzanne McGrail, prin. Fax 692-5598
Stony Brook S 600/6-8
9 Farmers Way 01886 978-692-2708
Peter Cohen, prin. Fax 692-5391
Westford Academy 1,400/9-12
30 Patten Rd 01886 978-692-5570
Ellen Parker, prin. Fax 692-5567

West Groton, Middlesex
Groton Dunstable Regional SD 2,900/PK-12
73 Pepperell Rd 01472 978-448-5505
Alan Genovese, supt. Fax 448-9402
www.gdrsd.org
Other Schools – See Groton

Westhampton, Hampshire
Hampshire SD 900/7-12
19 Stage Rd 01027 413-527-7200
Dr. Barbara Ripa, supt. Fax 529-9497
Hampshire Regional JSHS 900/7-12
19 Stage Rd 01027 413-527-7680
James Connolly, prin. Fax 527-1831

West Newbury, Essex
Pentucket SD 3,400/PK-12
22 Main St 01985 978-363-2280
Paul Livingston Ed.D., supt. Fax 363-1165
www.prsd.org
Pentucket Regional HS 1,000/9-12
24 Main St 01985 978-363-5507
Arlene Townes, prin. Fax 363-2730
Pentucket Regional MS 500/7-8
20 Main St 01985 978-363-2957
Renzo Binaghi, prin. Fax 363-2720

Weston, Middlesex, Pop. 10,200
Weston SD 2,400/PK-12
89 Wellesley St 02493 781-529-8080
Alan Oliff, supt. Fax 529-8097
www.westonschools.org/
Weston HS 700/9-12
444 Wellesley St 02493 781-529-8030
Anthony Parker, prin. Fax 529-8043
Weston MS 600/6-8
456 Wellesley St 02493 781-529-8060
John Gibbons, prin. Fax 529-8072

Blessed John XXIII National Seminary Post-Sec.
558 South Ave 02493 781-899-5500
Cambridge S of Weston 300/9-12
45 Georgian Rd 02493 781-642-8600
Jane Moulding, hdmstr. Fax 398-8344
Regis College Post-Sec.
235 Wellesley St 02493 781-768-2000
Rivers S 400/6-12
333 Winter St 02493 781-235-9300
Thomas Olverson, hdmstr. Fax 239-3614

Westport, Bristol, Pop. 13,852
Westport Community SD 1,900/PK-12
17 Main Rd 02790 508-636-1137
Dr. Linda Galton, supt. Fax 636-1146
www.westportschools.org
Westport HS 500/9-12
19 Main Rd 02790 508-636-1050
Cheryl Tutalo, prin. Fax 636-1053
Westport MS 700/5-8
400 Old County Rd 02790 508-636-1090
James Gibney, prin. Fax 636-7413

West Roxbury, See Boston
Boston SD
Supt. — See Boston
Brook Farm Business & Service Academy 9-12
1205 VFW Pkwy 02132 617-635-6956
Edmund Donnelly, prin. Fax 635-7894
Media Communications Technology HS 9-12
1205 VFW Pkwy 02132 617-635-8935
Sung-Joon Pai, prin. Fax 635-7912
Parkway Academy of Technology & Health 9-12
1205 VFW Pkwy 02132 617-635-6732
Barbara Ferrer, prin. Fax 635-8927
Urban Science Academy 9-12
1205 VFW Pkwy 02132 617-635-8930
Rasheed Meadows, prin. Fax 635-7895
West Roxbury Education Complex 1,400/9-12
1205 VFW Pkwy 02132 617-635-8917
Donald Pellegrini, hdmstr. Fax 635-7997

Catholic Memorial HS 900/7-12
235 Baker St 02132 617-469-8000
Richard Chisholm, prin. Fax 325-0888
Roxbury Latin S 300/7-12
101 Saint Theresa Ave 02132 617-325-4920
Kerry Brennan, hdmstr. Fax 325-3585

West Springfield, Hampden, Pop. 27,989
West Springfield SD 3,900/PK-12
26 Central St Ste 33 01089 413-263-3290
Dr. Suzanne Marotta, supt. Fax 739-8748
www.wsps.org
West Springfield HS 1,200/9-12
425 Piper Rd 01089 413-263-3400
Peter Dufresne, prin. Fax 781-4836
West Springfield MS 1,000/6-8
31 Middle School Dr 01089 413-263-3406
Thomas McNulty, prin. Fax 781-0965

Kay Harvey Hairdressing Academy Post-Sec.
11 Central St 01089 413-732-7117

Westwood, Norfolk, Pop. 12,557
Westwood SD 2,700/PK-12
220 Nahatan St 02090 781-326-7500
John Antonucci, supt. Fax 326-8154
www.westwood.k12.ma.us
Thurston MS 700/6-8
850 High St 02090 781-326-7500
Victor Palladino, prin. Fax 326-2709
Westwood HS 800/9-12
200 Nahatan St 02090 781-326-7500
Emily Parks, prin. Fax 461-8561

Xaverian Brothers HS 1,100/9-12
800 Clapboardtree St 02090 781-326-6392
Br. Daniel Skala, hdmstr. Fax 320-0458

West Yarmouth, Barnstable, Pop. 5,409
Dennis-Yarmouth SD
Supt. — See South Yarmouth
Mattacheese MS 600/6-8
440 Higgins Crowell Rd 02673 508-778-7979
Emily Mezzetti, prin. Fax 778-7987

Weymouth, Norfolk, Pop. 53,900
Weymouth SD 6,600/K-12
111 Middle St 02189 781-335-1460
Joseph Rull, supt. Fax 335-8777
www.weymouth.ma.us/schools/index.asp

Weymouth HS 2,000/9-12
1 Wildcat Way 02190 781-337-7500
Marilyn Slattery, prin. Fax 340-2568
Other Schools – See East Weymouth

South Shore Christian Academy 300/PK-12
45 Broad St 02188 781-331-4340
Theodore Chamberlain, hdmstr. Fax 331-9956

Whitinsville, Worcester, Pop. 5,639
Northbridge SD 2,600/PK-12
87 Linwood Ave 01588 508-234-8156
Paul Soojian, supt. Fax 234-8469
www.nps.org/
Northbridge HS 700/9-12
427 Linwood Ave 01588 508-234-6221
Christine Johnson, prin. Fax 234-0802
Northbridge MS 800/5-8
171 Linwood Ave 01588 508-234-8718
Michael Gauthier, prin. Fax 234-9718

Whitinsville Christian S 700/PK-12
279 Linwood Ave 01588 508-234-8211
Lance Engbers, hdmstr. Fax 234-8212

Whitman, Plymouth, Pop. 13,240
Whitman-Hanson SD 4,400/PK-12
600 Franklin St 02382 781-618-7411
John McEwan Ed.D., supt. Fax 618-7498
www.whrsd.k12.ma.us
Whitman-Hanson Regional HS 1,200/9-12
600 Franklin St 02382 781-618-7020
Pamela A. Gould, prin. Fax 618-7099
Whitman MS 600/6-8
101 Corthell Ave 02382 781-781-7035
George Ferro, prin. Fax 781-7091
Other Schools – See Hanson

Wilbraham, Hampden, Pop. 3,352
Hampden-Wilbraham SD 3,700/PK-12
621 Main St 01095 413-596-3884
Dr. Paul Gagliarducci, supt. Fax 599-1328
www.hwrsd.org
Minnechaug Regional HS 1,400/9-12
621 Main St 01095 413-596-9011
Martin O'Shea, prin. Fax 596-8907
Wilbraham MS 500/7-8
466 Stony Hill Rd 01095 413-596-9061
Stephen Hale, prin. Fax 596-9382
Other Schools – See Hampden

Wilbraham & Monson Academy 300/6-12
423 Main St 01095 413-596-6811
Rodney LaBrecque, hdmstr. Fax 596-2448

Williamstown, Berkshire, Pop. 4,791
Mount Greylock Regional SD 700/7-12
1781 Cold Spring Rd 01267 413-458-9582
Dr. William Travis, supt. Fax 458-2856
www.mgrhs.org
Mount Greylock Regional JSHS 700/7-12
1781 Cold Spring Rd 01267 413-458-9582
Timothy Payne, prin. Fax 458-2856

Buxton S 100/9-12
291 South St 01267 413-458-3919
C. William Bennett, dir. Fax 458-9427
Williams College 01267 Post-Sec.
413-597-3131

Wilmington, Middlesex, Pop. 17,654
Wilmington SD 3,800/PK-12
161 Church St 01887 978-694-6000
William H. McAlduff, supt. Fax 694-6005
www.wilmington.k12.ma.us
Wilmington HS 900/9-12
159 Church St 01887 978-694-6060
Eric Tracy, prin. Fax 694-6074
Wilmington MS 1,000/6-8
25 Carter Ln 01887 978-694-6080
Frank Orlando, prin. Fax 694-6085

Winchendon, Worcester, Pop. 4,316
Winchendon SD 1,700/PK-12
175 Grove St 01475 978-297-0031
Peter Azar Ed.D., supt. Fax 297-5250
www.winchendonk12.org
Murdock MSHS 700/7-12
3 Memorial Dr 01475 978-297-1256
William Waight, prin. Fax 297-0509

Winchendon S 200/8-12
172 Ash St 01475 978-297-1223
J. William Labelle, hdmstr. Fax 297-0911

Winchester, Middlesex, Pop. 20,267
Winchester SD 3,700/PK-12
154 Horn Pond Brook Rd 01890 781-721-7004
V. James Marini, supt. Fax 721-0016
www.winchester.k12.ma.us
McCall MS 800/6-8
458 Main St 01890 781-721-7026
Evander French, prin. Fax 721-0886
Winchester HS 1,000/9-12
80 Skillings Rd 01890 781-721-7020
Thomas Gwin, prin. Fax 721-7042

Winthrop, Suffolk, Pop. 18,127
Winthrop SD 2,100/PK-12
45 Pauline St 02152 617-846-5500
Dr. Steven Jenkins, supt. Fax 539-0891
www.winthrop.k12.ma.us
Winthrop HS 600/9-12
400 Main St 02152 617-846-5500
Gail Conlon, prin. Fax 539-0535
Winthrop MS 500/6-8
151 Pauline St 02152 617-846-5507
Zoe Haskell, prin. Fax 539-1115

Woburn, Middlesex, Pop. 37,147
Woburn SD 4,500/K-12
55 Locust St 01801 781-937-8233
Carl Batchelder Ed.D., supt. Fax 937-3805
woburnpublicschools.com/
Joyce JHS 500/6-8
55 Locust St 01801 781-937-8233
W. Spencer Mullin Ph.D., prin. Fax 932-0668
Kennedy JHS 600/6-8
33 Middle St 01801 781-937-8230
Carl Nelson, prin. Fax 937-8223
Woburn HS 1,400/9-12
88 Montvale Ave 01801 781-937-8210
Robert Norton, prin. Fax 937-8216

Catherine Hinds Institute of Esthetics Post-Sec.
300 Wildwood Ave 01801 781-935-3344
ITT Technical Institute Post-Sec.
10 Forbes Rd 01801 781-937-8324

Woods Hole, Barnstable

Woods Hole Oceanographic Institution Post-Sec.
86 Water St 02543 508-457-2000

Worcester, Worcester, Pop. 175,898
Worcester SD 23,900/PK-12
20 Irving St 01609 508-799-3116
James Caradonio Ed.D., supt. Fax 799-3119
www.wpsweb.com/default2.asp
Accelerated Learning Lab S 800/PK-12
15 Claremont St 01610 508-799-3077
June Eressy, prin. Fax 799-8202
Burncoat HS 1,400/9-12
179 Burncoat St 01606 508-799-3300
John Bierfeldt, prin. Fax 799-8206
Burncoat MS 700/7-8
135 Burncoat St 01606 508-799-3390
Lisa A. Houlihan, prin. Fax 799-8207
Doherty Memorial HS 1,500/9-12
299 Highland St 01602 508-799-3270
Sally Maloney, prin. Fax 799-3276
Forest Grove MS 1,000/7-8
495 Grove St 01605 508-799-3420
Maureen McCullough, prin. Fax 799-8218
North HS 1,300/9-12
150 Harrington Way 01604 508-799-3370
David Elworthy, prin. Fax 799-8252
South Community HS 1,500/9-12
170 Apricot St 01603 508-799-3325
Maureen R. Ciccone, prin. Fax 799-8242
Sullivan MS 1,000/7-8
140 Apricot St 01603 508-799-3350
Robert Jennings, prin. Fax 799-8244
University Park Campus S 200/7-12
12 Freeland St 01603 508-799-3591
June Eressy, coord. Fax 799-8159
Worcester East MS 800/7-8
420 Grafton St 01604 508-799-3430
Rose M. Dawkins, prin. Fax 799-8251
Worcester Technical HS Vo/Tech
1 Skyline Dr 01605 508-799-1940
Sheila Frias, prin. Fax 799-1933

Assumption College Post-Sec.
500 Salisbury St 01609 508-767-7000
Bancroft S 600/K-12
110 Shore Dr 01605 508-853-2640
Scott Reisinger, hdmstr. Fax 853-7824
Bancroft School of Massage Therapy Post-Sec.
333 Shrewsbury St 01604 508-757-7923
Becker College Post-Sec.
61 Sever St 01609 508-791-9241
Clark University Post-Sec.
950 Main St 01610 508-793-7711
College of the Holy Cross Post-Sec.
1 College St 01610 508-793-2011
First Assembly Christian Academy 100/PK-12
30 Tyler Prentice Rd 01605 508-853-8641
April Graziano, prin. Fax 853-2169
Hair in Motion Beauty Academy Post-Sec.
73 Hamilton St 01604 508-756-6060
Holy Name Central Catholic HS 900/7-12
144 Granite St 01604 508-753-6371
Edward Reynolds, admin. Fax 831-1287
Notre Dame Academy 300/9-12
425 Salisbury St 01609 508-757-6200
Sr. Ann Morrison, prin. Fax 757-7200
Quinsigamond Community College Post-Sec.
670 W Boylston St 01606 508-853-2300
Rob Roy Academy Post-Sec.
150 Pleasant St 01609 508-799-2111
St. Mary HS 200/7-12
50 Richland St 01610 508-753-1170
Rev. Thaddeus Stachura, prin. Fax 795-0560
St. Peter-Marian Central HS 1,100/7-12
781 Grove St 01605 508-852-5555
Matthew Sturgis, prin. Fax 852-7238
University of Massachusetts at Worcester Post-Sec.
55 Lake Ave N 01655 508-856-8989
Worcester Academy 600/6-12
81 Providence St 01604 508-754-5302
Dexter Morse, hdmstr. Fax 752-2382
Worcester Polytechnic Institute Post-Sec.
100 Institute Rd 01609 508-831-5000
Worcester State College Post-Sec.
486 Chandler St 01602 508-929-8000
Yeshiva Achei Tmimim Academy 100/PK-12
22 Newton Ave 01602 508-752-0904
Rabbi Hershel Fogelman, dean Fax 799-7413

Wrentham, Norfolk
King Philip SD
Supt. — See Norfolk
King Philip Regional HS 1,200/9-12
201 Franklin St 02093 508-384-1000
Elaine Hanson, prin. Fax 384-1006

MICHIGAN

MICHIGAN DEPARTMENT OF EDUCATION
608 W Allegan St, Lansing 48933-1524
Telephone 517-373-3324
Fax 517-335-4565
Website http://www.michigan.gov/mde

Superintendent of Public Instruction Michael Flanagan

MICHIGAN BOARD OF EDUCATION
608 W Allegan St, Lansing 48933-1524

President Kathleen N. Straus

INTERMEDIATE SCHOOL DISTRICTS (ISD)

Allegan Area ESA
Ronald Fuller, supt. 269-673-2161
310 Thomas St, Allegan 49010 Fax 673-2361
www.alleganaesa.org/

Alpena-Montmorency-Alcona ESD
Thomas Lanway, supt. 989-354-3101
2118 US Highway 23 S Fax 356-3385
Alpena 49707
www.amaesd.k12.mi.us

Barry ISD
James A. Hund, supt. 269-945-9545
535 W Woodlawn Ave Fax 945-2575
Hastings 49058
www.barryisd.org

Bay-Arenac ISD
Michael R. Dewey, supt. 989-686-4410
4228 2 Mile Rd, Bay City 48706 Fax 667-3286
www.baisd.net

Berrien County ISD
Jeffrey Siegel, supt. 269-471-7725
711 Saint Joseph Ave Fax 471-2941
Berrien Springs 49103
www.remc11.k12.mi.us/bcisd

Branch ISD
Michael Beckwith, supt. 517-279-5730
370 Morse St, Coldwater 49036 Fax 279-5766
www.branch-isd.org

Calhoun ISD
Christopher Wigent, supt. 269-781-5141
17111 G Dr N, Marshall 49068 Fax 781-7071
www.calhounisd.org

Charlevoix-Emmet ISD
Mark Eckhardt, supt. 231-547-9947
8568 Mercer Rd, Charlevoix 49720 Fax 547-5621
www.charemisd.org

Cheboygan-Otsego-Presque Isle ISD
Mary Vratanina, supt. 231-238-9394
6065 Learning Ln Fax 238-8551
Indian River 49749
www.copesd.k12.mi.us

Clare-Gladwin RESD
Doug Dodge, supt. 989-386-3851
4041 E Mannsiding Rd Fax 386-3238
Clare 48617
www.cgresd.net/

Clinton County RESA
Lawrence Lloyd, supt. 989-224-6831
1013 S US Highway 27 Ste A Fax 224-9574
Saint Johns 48879
www.ccresa.org

C.O.O.R. ISD
Robert Jones, supt. 989-275-9555
PO Box 827, Roscommon 48653 Fax 275-5881
www.coorisd.k12.mi.us

Copper Country ISD
Dennis Harbour, supt. 906-482-4250
PO Box 270, Hancock 49930 Fax 482-1931
www.copperisd.org

Delta-Schoolcraft ISD
Michael Koster, supt. 906-786-9300
2525 3rd Ave S, Escanaba 49829 Fax 786-9318
www.dsisd.k12.mi.us

Dickinson-Iron ISD
Johanna Ostwald, supt. 906-779-2690
1074 Pyle Dr, Kingsford 49802 Fax 779-2669
www.diisd.org

Eastern Upper Peninsula ISD
Peter Everson, supt., PO Box 883 906-632-3373
Sault Sainte Marie 49783 Fax 632-1125
www.eupisd.com/

Eaton ISD
Albert Widner, supt. 517-543-5500
1790 Packard Hwy Fax 543-6633
Charlotte 48813
www.eaton.k12.mi.us/

Genesee ISD
Thomas Svitkovich Ed.D., supt. 810-591-4400
2413 W Maple Ave, Flint 48507 Fax 591-7570
www.geneseeisd.org

Gogebic-Ontonagon ISD
Bruce Mayle, supt. 906-575-3438
PO Box 218, Bergland 49910 Fax 575-3373
www.goisd.org/

Gratiot-Isabella RESD
Michael Matlosz, supt. 989-875-5101
PO Box 310, Ithaca 48847 Fax 875-7531
www.edzone.net/giresd/

Hillsdale ISD
Robert W. Henthorne, supt. 517-437-0990
310 W Bacon St, Hillsdale 49242 Fax 439-4388
www.hillsdale-isd.org

Huron ISD
Robert Colby, supt. 989-269-6406
711 E Soper Rd, Bad Axe 48413 Fax 269-9218
www.hisd.k12.mi.us

Ingham ISD
Stanley Kogut, supt. 517-676-1051
2630 W Howell Rd, Mason 48854 Fax 676-1277
www.inghamisd.org

Ionia County ISD
George Hubbard, supt. 616-527-4900
2191 Harwood Rd, Ionia 48846 Fax 527-4731
www.ionia-isd.k12.mi.us

Iosco RESA
Thomas Caldwell, supt. 989-362-3006
27 N Rempert Rd Fax 362-9076
Tawas City 48763
www.iresa.k12.mi.us

Jackson County ISD
John Graves, supt. 517-768-5200
6700 Browns Lake Rd Fax 787-2026
Jackson 49201
www.jcisd.org

Kalamazoo RESA
W. Craig Misner, supt. 269-385-1500
1819 E Milham Ave Fax 381-9423
Kalamazoo 49002
www.kresa.org

Kent ISD
Michael Weiler, supt. 616-364-1333
2930 Knapp St NE Fax 364-1488
Grand Rapids 49525
www.kentisd.org

Lapeer County ISD
Joseph Keena, supt. 810-664-5917
1996 W Oregon St, Lapeer 48446 Fax 664-1011
www.lcisd.k12.mi.us

Lenawee ISD
Stephen Krusich, supt. 517-265-2119
4107 N Adrian Hwy, Adrian 49221 Fax 265-7405
www.lisd.us/

Lewis Cass ISD
John Ostrowski, supt. 269-445-6204
61682 Dailey Rd, Cassopolis 49031 Fax 445-2981
www.lewcass.k12.mi.us

Livingston ESA
Sally Vaughn, supt. 517-546-5550
1425 W Grand River Ave Fax 546-7047
Howell 48843
www.lesa.k12.mi.us

Macomb ISD
Michael DeVault, supt. 586-228-3300
44001 Garfield Rd Fax 286-1523
Clinton Township 48038
www.misd.net

Manistee ISD
Charlene Myers, supt. 231-723-4264
1710 Merkey Rd W Fax 723-1690
Manistee 49660
www.manistee.org

Marquette-Alger RESA
June Schaefer, supt. 906-226-5100
321 E Ohio St, Marquette 49855 Fax 226-5134
www.maresa.org

Mason-Lake ISD
Jeanne Oakes, supt. 231-757-3716
2130 W US Highway 10 Fax 757-2406
Ludington 49431
www.mlisd.k12.mi.us

Mecosta-Osceola ISD
Curtis Finch, supt., 15760 190th Ave 231-796-3543
Big Rapids 49307 Fax 796-3300
www.moisd.org

Menominee ISD
Lawrence Godwin, supt. 906-863-5665
1201 41st Ave, Menominee 49858 Fax 863-7776
www.mc-isd.org

Midland County ESA
Clark Volz, supt. 989-631-5890
3917 Jefferson Ave, Midland 48640 Fax 631-4361
www.mcesa.k12.mi.us

Monroe County ISD
Donald Spencer, supt. 734-242-5799
1101 S Raisinville Rd Fax 242-0567
Monroe 48161
misd.k12.mi.us/

Montcalm Area ISD
George Stamas, supt. 989-831-5261
PO Box 367, Stanton 48888 Fax 831-8727
www.maisd.com

Muskegon Area ISD
Susan Meston, supt. 231-777-2637
630 Harvey St, Muskegon 49442 Fax 773-3498
www.muskegonisd.org

Newaygo County RESA
Robert E. DeVries, supt. 231-924-0381
4747 W 48th St, Fremont 49412 Fax 924-8910
www.ncresa.org/

Oakland ISD
Vickie Markavitch, supt. 248-209-2000
2111 Pontiac Lake Rd Fax 209-2206
Waterford 48328
www.oakland.k12.mi.us

Oceana ISD
Jeanne Oakes, supt. 231-873-5651
844 S Griswold St, Hart 49420 Fax 873-5779
oceanaisd.com

Ottawa Area ISD
Karen McPhee, supt. 616-738-8940
13565 Port Sheldon St Fax 738-8946
Holland 49424
www.oaisd.org

Saginaw ISD
Richard Lane, supt. 989-399-7473
6235 Gratiot Rd, Saginaw Fax 793-1571
www.sisd.cc/

St. Clair County RESA
Dan DeGrow, supt. 810-364-8990
PO Box 1500, Marysville 48040 Fax 364-7474
www.sccresa.org/

St. Joseph County ISD
Barbara Marshall, supt. 269-467-5400
62445 Shimmel Rd Fax 467-4309
Centreville 49032
www.sjcisd.org

Sanilac ISD
Timothy Edwards Ph.D., supt. 810-648-4700
175 E Aitken Rd, Peck 48466 Fax 648-5784
www.sanilac.k12.mi.us

Shiawassee RESD
John Hagel, supt. 989-743-3471
1025 N Shiawassee St Fax 743-6477
Corunna 48817
www.sresd.org/

Traverse Bay Area ISD
Michael Kenney, supt. 231-922-6200
PO Box 6020, Traverse City 49696 Fax 922-6270
www.tbaisd.k12.mi.us

Tuscola ISD
Carol Socha, supt. 989-673-2144
1385 Cleaver Rd, Caro 48723 Fax 673-5366
www.tisd.k12.mi.us

Van Buren ISD
Jeffrey Mills, supt. 269-674-8091
490 S Paw Paw St Fax 674-8030
Lawrence 49064
www.vbisd.org/

Washtenaw ISD
William Miller, supt. 734-994-8100
PO Box 1406, Ann Arbor 48106 Fax 994-2203
www.wash.k12.mi.us/

Wayne RESA
Marlene Davis, supt. 734-334-1300
PO Box 807, Wayne 48184 Fax 334-1760
www.resa.net

Wexford-Missaukee ISD
Scott Crosby, supt. 231-876-2260
9907 E 13th St, Cadillac 49601 Fax 876-2272
www.wmisd.org

PUBLIC, PRIVATE AND CATHOLIC SECONDARY SCHOOLS

Ada, Kent
Forest Hills SD
Supt. — See Grand Rapids
Central MS 700/7-8
5810 Ada Dr SE 49301 616-493-8750
Nancy Flink, prin. Fax 493-8764
Eastern HS 500/9-12
2200 Pettis Ave NE 49301 616-493-8830
Linda LaBerteaux, prin. Fax 493-8839
Eastern MS 500/7-8
2200 Pettis Ave NE 49301 616-493-8850
Ted Curro, prin. Fax 493-8859

Addison, Lenawee, Pop. 611
Addison Community SD 1,200/K-12
219 N Comstock St 49220 517-547-6123
Richard Naughton, supt. Fax 547-3838
scnc.addison.k12.mi.us
Addison HS 400/9-12
219 N Comstock St 49220 517-547-6121
Gayle Dodson, prin. Fax 547-3838
Addison MS 300/6-8
219 N Comstock St 49220 517-547-6125
Kevin Ohrman, prin. Fax 547-3838

Adrian, Lenawee, Pop. 21,784
Adrian SD 3,300/K-12
785 Riverside Ave Ste 1 49221 517-263-2115
Lindle Cochran, supt. Fax 265-5381
www.adrian.k12.mi.us
Adrian HS 1,200/9-12
785 Riverside Ave 49221 517-263-2181
Gerald Burg, prin. Fax 263-0814
Adrian MS 7-8 600/7-8
615 Springbrook Ave 49221 517-263-0543
Mike Perez, prin. Fax 265-5984

Lenawee ISD
4107 N Adrian Hwy 49221 517-265-2119
Stephen Krusich, supt. Fax 265-7405
www.lisd.us/
LISD Vocational-Technical Center Vo/Tech
1372 N Main St 49221 517-263-2108
Larry Schroeder, prin. Fax 263-9433

Madison SD 1,100/PK-12
3498 Treat Hwy 49221 517-263-0741
James Hartley, supt. Fax 265-5635
www.madison.k12.mi.us
Madison HS 300/9-12
3498 Treat Hwy 49221 517-263-0742
Connie Ries, prin. Fax 265-1848
Madison MS 6-8
3498 Treat Hwy 49221 517-263-0743
Brad Anschuetz, prin. Fax 265-5635

Adrian College Post-Sec.
110 S Madison St 49221 517-265-5161
Berean Baptist Academy 100/K-12
751 W Maumee St 49221 517-263-5050
Justin Raymond, prin. Fax 266-2491
Fiser's College of Cosmetology Post-Sec.
329 1/2 E Maumee St 49221 517-264-2199
Jackson Community College Post-Sec.
1376 N Main St 49221 517-265-5515
Jackson Community College Post-Sec.
2651 W Cadmus Rd 49221 517-263-1351
Lenawee Christian S 500/PK-12
111 Wolf Creek Hwy 49221 517-265-7590
Peggy Thompson, supt. Fax 265-6558
Siena Heights University Post-Sec.
1247 E Siena Heights Dr 49221 517-263-0731

Alanson, Emmet, Pop. 811
Littlefield SD 400/K-12
7400 North St 49706 231-548-2261
Bently Laser, supt. Fax 548-2132
www.alansonvikings.net/
Littlefield S 400/K-12
7400 North St 49706 231-548-2261
Edward Cole, prin. Fax 548-2132

Alba, Antrim
Alba SD 200/PK-12
PO Box 10 49611 231-584-2000
Jeffery DiRosa, supt. Fax 584-2001
www.torchlake.com/albaschool/
Alba S 200/PK-12
PO Box 10 49611 231-584-2000
Jeffrey DiRosa, prin. Fax 584-2001

Albion, Calhoun, Pop. 9,348
Albion SD 1,600/PK-12
1418 Cooper St 49224 517-629-9166
Larry Ley, supt. Fax 629-8209
www.albion.k12.mi.us
Albion HS 500/9-12
225 E Watson St 49224 517-629-9421
Debra Swartz, prin. Fax 630-3305
Washington Gardner MS 400/6-8
401 E Michigan Ave 49224 517-629-9448
Julie Cummins, prin. Fax 629-8257

Albion College Post-Sec.
611 E Porter St 49224 517-629-1000

Algonac, Saint Clair, Pop. 4,598
Algonac Community SD 2,400/K-12
1216 Saint Clair Blvd 48001 810-794-9364
Dennis Guiser, supt. Fax 794-0040
www.algonac.k12.mi.us
Algonac HS 700/9-12
5200 Taft Rd 48001 810-794-4911
Michael Sharrow, prin. Fax 794-8876
Algonquin MS 600/6-8
9185 Marsh Rd 48001 810-794-9317
Andrew Rogers, prin. Fax 794-8872

Allegan, Allegan, Pop. 4,963
Allegan SD 3,000/PK-12
550 5th St 49010 269-673-5431
Kevin Harness, supt. Fax 673-5463
www.alleganpublicschools.org/
Allegan HS 900/9-12
1560 Lincoln Rd 49010 269-673-7002
Jim Mallard, prin. Fax 686-2486
White MS 700/6-8
3300 115th Ave 49010 269-673-2241
George Mohr, prin. Fax 686-0309

Allendale, Ottawa, Pop. 6,950
Allendale SD 2,100/PK-12
6561 Lake Michigan Dr 49401 616-892-5570
Catherine Ceglarek, supt. Fax 895-6690
www.allendale.k12.mi.us
Allendale HS 600/9-12
10760 68th Ave 49401 616-892-5585
Steve Scholten, prin. Fax 895-4280
Allendale MS 600/5-8
6561 Lake Michigan Dr 49401 616-892-5595
Rocky Thompson, prin. Fax 895-9111

Grand Valley State University Post-Sec.
1 Campus Dr 49401 616-895-6611

Allen Park, Wayne, Pop. 28,083
Allen Park SD 3,500/K-12
9601 Vine Ave 48101 313-827-2150
John Sturock, supt. Fax 827-2151
www.apps.k12.mi.us
Allen Park HS 1,100/9-12
18401 Champaign Rd 48101 313-827-1200
Janet McBurney, prin. Fax 827-1231
Allen Park MS 800/6-8
8401 Vine Ave 48101 313-827-2200
Michael Dawson, prin. Fax 827-2251

Cabrini HS 200/9-12
15305 Wick Rd 48101 313-388-0110
Cheryl Szczodrowski, prin. Fax 388-1876
Inter City Baptist S 300/K-12
4700 Allen Rd 48101 313-928-6900
James Hubbard, prin. Fax 928-7310

Alma, Gratiot, Pop. 9,260
Alma SD 2,400/PK-12
1500 Pine Ave 48801 989-463-3111
Don Pavlik, supt. Fax 466-2943
www.almaschools.net
Alma HS 800/9-12
1500 Pine Ave 48801 989-463-3111
Donald Everhart, prin. Fax 463-2176
Alma MS 600/6-8
1700 Pine Ave 48801 989-463-3111
Carolyn Studley, prin. Fax 466-7612
Alma Adult Education Adult
300 Republic Ave 48801 989-463-3111
Kathy Johnston, prin. Fax 466-6814

Gratiot-Isabella RESD
Supt. — See Ithaca
Gratiot Technical Education Center Vo/Tech
327 E Center St 48801 989-466-4832
Fax 466-9734

Alma College Post-Sec.
614 W Superior St 48801 989-463-7111

Almont, Lapeer, Pop. 2,874
Almont Community SD 1,400/K-12
401 Church St 48003 810-798-8561
Steven Zott, supt. Fax 798-2367
www.almont.k12.mi.us
Almont HS 600/9-12
4701 Howland Rd 48003 810-798-8595
R. Robert Watt, prin. Fax 798-7011
Almont MS 6-8
4624 Kidder Rd 48003 810-798-3578
Thomas English, prin. Fax 798-3549

Alpena, Alpena, Pop. 10,792
Alpena SD 4,700/K-12
2373 Gordon Rd 49707 989-358-5040
David J. Werner, supt. Fax 358-5041
www.alpenaschools.com
Alpena HS 1,700/9-12
3303 S 3rd Ave 49707 989-358-5200
Claudia Werner, prin. Fax 358-5205
Thunder Bay JHS 800/7-8
3500 S 3rd Ave 49707 989-358-5400
Joyce McCoy, prin. Fax 358-5499
ACES/Oxbow Adult/Alternative/Comm Educ Adult
700 Pinecrest St 49707 989-358-5170
Patrick Timmons, prin. Fax 358-5175

Alpena Community College Post-Sec.
666 Johnson St 49707 989-356-9021

Ann Arbor, Washtenaw, Pop. 113,271
Ann Arbor SD 17,100/PK-12
PO Box 1188 48106 734-994-2200
Dr. Todd Roberts, supt. Fax 994-2414
www.aaps.k12.mi.us/
Clague JHS 800/6-8
2616 Nixon Rd 48105 734-994-1976
Michael Hecker, prin. Fax 994-1645
Community HS 500/9-12
401 N Division St 48104 734-994-2025
Peter Ways, dean Fax 994-0042
Forsyth JHS 700/6-8
1655 Newport Rd 48103 734-994-1985
Janet Schwamb, prin. Fax 994-5749
Huron HS 2,100/9-12
2727 Fuller Rd 48105 734-994-2043
Arthur Williams, prin. Fax 994-2048
Pioneer HS 2,900/9-12
601 W Stadium Blvd 48103 734-994-2126
Louis Young, prin. Fax 994-2198
Scarlett JHS 600/6-8
3300 Lorraine St 48108 734-971-1694
Benjamin Edmondson, prin. Fax 971-1274
Slauson JHS 800/6-8
1019 W Washington St 48103 734-994-2005
Patricia Rose, prin. Fax 994-1681
Tappan JHS 800/6-8
2251 E Stadium Blvd 48104 734-994-2016
Gary Court, prin. Fax 997-1873
Stone S Adult
2800 Stone School Rd 48104 734-971-2665
Gayl Dybdahl, prin. Fax 971-7759

Cleary University - Washtenaw Campus Post-Sec.
3601 Plymouth Rd 48105 734-332-4477
Concordia University Post-Sec.
4090 Geddes Rd 48105 734-995-7300
Father Gabriel Richard HS 400/9-12
4333 Whitehall Dr 48105 734-662-0496
Brian P. Wolcott, prin. Fax 662-4133
Greenhills S 500/6-12
850 Greenhills Dr 48105 734-769-4010
Peter Fayroian, prin. Fax 769-5029
Michigan Islamic Academy 100/PK-12
2301 Plymouth Rd 48105 734-665-8882
Nebila Gomaa, prin. Fax 665-9058
Ross Medical Education Center Post-Sec.
4741 Washtenaw Ave 48108 734-434-7320
Steiner S of Ann Arbor 100/9-12
2230 Pontiac Trl 48105 734-669-9394
Kirk Williams, admin. Fax 669-9396
University of Michigan-Ann Arbor Post-Sec.
1220 Student Activities Bld 48109 734-764-1817
University of Michigan-Ann Arbor Post-Sec.
400 N Ingalls St 48109 734-764-7188
Washtenaw Community College Post-Sec.
PO Box D-1 48106 734-973-3300

Armada, Macomb, Pop. 1,650
Armada Area SD 2,200/PK-12
74500 Burk St 48005 586-784-4512
Arnold Kummerow, supt. Fax 784-4268
www.macomb.k12.mi.us/armada
Armada HS 600/9-12
23655 Armada Center Rd 48005 586-784-2400
Lillian Demas, prin. Fax 784-9592
Armada MS 500/6-8
23550 Armada Center Rd 48005 586-784-2500
William Zebelian, prin. Fax 784-8650
Macomb Academy of Arts & Sciences 200/9-12
23211 Prospect Ave 48005 586-784-2150
Elsie Ritzenhein, prin. Fax 784-8688

Ashley, Gratiot, Pop. 521
Ashley Community SD 400/K-12
PO Box 6 48806 989-847-4000
Kyle Mayer, supt. Fax 847-3500
www.bearnet.net
Ashley JSHS 200/7-12
PO Box 6 48806 989-847-2514
Tom Saylor, prin. Fax 847-4204

Athens, Calhoun, Pop. 1,075
Athens Area SD 800/K-12
300 E Holcomb St 49011 269-729-5427
Dr. Randall Davis, supt. Fax 729-9610
www.athensk12.org
Athens HS 300/9-12
300 E Holcomb St 49011 269-729-5414
Joseph Chambers, prin. Fax 729-9616
Athens MS 200/5-8
515 E Williams St 49011 269-729-5421
Richard Franklin, prin. Fax 729-9613

Factoryville Christian S 50/PK-12
33650 Factoryville Rd 49011 269-729-4203
Paul DeVall, admin. Fax 729-4182

Atlanta, Montmorency
Atlanta Community SD 400/K-12
PO Box 619 49709 989-785-4877
James Mouch, supt. Fax 785-2611
www.atlanta.k12.mi.us

Atlanta JSHS — 200/7-12
PO Box 619 49709 — 989-785-4842
Derrel Kent, prin. — Fax 785-2617

Attica, Lapeer
Lapeer County ISD
Supt. — See Lapeer
Lapeer County ISD Education Center — Vo/Tech
690 N Lake Pleasant Rd 48412 — 810-664-1124
Dorothy Oppenheiser, prin. — Fax 724-7600

Auburn, Bay, Pop. 2,057
Bay City SD
Supt. — See Bay City
Western HS — 1,400/9-12
500 W Midland Rd 48611 — 989-662-4481
Oren Lusher, prin. — Fax 662-4413
Western MS — 900/6-8
500 W Midland Rd 48611 — 989-662-4489
Paula Weiss, prin. — Fax 662-0185

Auburn Hills, Oakland, Pop. 21,011
Avondale SD — 3,800/PK-12
2940 Waukegan St 48326 — 248-537-6000
George Heitsch, supt. — Fax 537-6005
www.avondale.k12.mi.us
Avondale HS — 1,100/9-12
2800 Waukegan St 48326 — 248-537-6100
Fred Cromie, prin. — Fax 537-6105
Other Schools – See Rochester Hills

Auburn Hills Christian S — 200/K-12
PO Box 4386 48321 — 248-373-3399
Scott Wickson, prin. — Fax 373-2001
Baker College of Auburn Hills — Post-Sec.
1500 University Dr 48326 — 248-340-0600
Oakland Christian S — 600/K-12
3075 Shimmons Rd 48326 — 248-373-2700
Randall Speck, admin. — Fax 373-9255

Au Gres, Arenac, Pop. 982
Au Gres-Sims SD — 500/K-12
PO Box 648 48703 — 989-876-7150
Gary Marchel, supt. — Fax 876-6752
www.ags-schools.org
Au Gres-Sims JSHS — 300/6-12
PO Box 648 48703 — 989-876-7157
Pamela Morris, prin. — Fax 876-6860

Augusta, Kalamazoo, Pop. 852
Galesburg-Augusta Community SD
Supt. — See Galesburg
Galesburg-Augusta MS — 300/6-8
750 W Van Buren St 49012 — 269-484-2020
Christopher Hurley, prin. — Fax 484-2021

Bad Axe, Huron, Pop. 3,246
Bad Axe SD — 1,300/K-12
760 S Van Dyke Rd 48413 — 989-269-9938
James Wencel, supt. — Fax 269-2739
hatchet.badaxe.k12.mi.us/newsite/
Bad Axe HS — 400/9-12
200 N Barrie Rd 48413 — 989-269-9593
Wayne Brady, prin. — Fax 269-6947
Bad Axe JHS — 300/6-8
750 S Van Dyke Rd 48413 — 989-269-2735
Virginia Lounsbury, prin. — Fax 269-9001

Huron ISD
711 E Soper Rd 48413 — 989-269-6406
Robert Colby, supt. — Fax 269-9218
www.hisd.k12.mi.us
Huron Area Technical Center — Vo/Tech
1160 S Van Dyke Rd 48413 — 989-269-9284
Darlene Bailey, prin. — Fax 269-2844

Great Lakes College — Post-Sec.
150 Nugent Rd 48413 — 989-755-3444

Baldwin, Lake, Pop. 1,157
Baldwin Community SD — 600/K-12
525 4th St 49304 — 231-745-4791
Randall Howes, supt. — Fax 745-3240
www.baldwin.k12.mi.us
Baldwin JSHS — 200/7-12
525 4th St 49304 — 231-745-4683
Faith Thomas-Jones, prin. — Fax 745-2898

Bangor, Van Buren, Pop. 1,882
Bangor SD — 1,500/K-12
801 W Arlington St 49013 — 269-427-6800
Ronald Davis, supt. — Fax 427-8274
www.bangorvikings.org
Bangor HS — 500/9-12
801 W Arlington St 49013 — 269-427-6844
Jeff Melvin, prin. — Fax 427-8274
Bangor MS — 400/6-8
803 W Arlington St 49013 — 269-427-6824
Jim Greydanus, prin. — Fax 427-8274

Baraga, Baraga, Pop. 1,252
Baraga Area SD — 500/K-12
PO Box 428 49908 — 906-353-6664
Norman McKindles, supt. — Fax 353-7454
www.baragaschools.org
Baraga JSHS — 300/7-12
PO Box 428 49908 — 906-353-6661
Dennis Ruuspakka, prin. — Fax 353-6662

Bath, Clinton
Bath Community SD — 1,000/K-12
PO Box 310 48808 — 517-641-6721
Dennis Furton, supt. — Fax 641-6958
www.bath.k12.mi.us
Bath HS — 300/9-12
PO Box 310 48808 — 517-641-6724
Bart Rypstra, prin. — Fax 641-7046
Bath MS — 300/6-8
PO Box 310 48808 — 517-641-6781
Lorenda Jonas, prin. — Fax 641-4996

Battle Creek, Calhoun, Pop. 53,202
Battle Creek SD — 6,500/PK-12
3 Van Buren St W 49017 — 269-965-9500
Dr. Charles Coleman, supt. — Fax 965-9474
www.battlecreekpublicschools.org
Battle Creek Central HS — 1,700/9-12
100 Van Buren St W 49017 — 269-965-9526
Bruce Barney, prin. — Fax 660-5864
Calhoun Area Technology Center — Vo/Tech
475 Roosevelt Ave E 49017 — 269-968-2271
Gene Niedzwiecki, prin. — Fax 968-4344
Kellogg MS — 600/6-8
60 Van Buren St W 49017 — 269-965-9655
Bobbi Morehead, prin. — Fax 965-9789
Northwestern MS — 400/6-8
176 Limit St 49017 — 269-965-9607
Scott Millin, prin. — Fax 965-9525
South Hill Academy — 300/6-12
50 Spencer St 49014 — 269-965-9671
Maurice Ware, prin. — Fax 965-9682
Adult Education Center — Adult
77 Capital Ave NE 49017 — 269-965-9515
Sharlie Jones, prin. — Fax 965-9545
Other Schools – See Springfield

Harper Creek Community SD — 2,300/K-12
7454 B Dr N 49014 — 269-979-1136
John Severson, supt. — Fax 660-1190
www.harpercreek.net
Harper Creek HS — 900/9-12
12677 Beadle Lake Rd 49014 — 269-979-1121
Steve Guerra, prin. — Fax 441-2206
Harper Creek MS — 500/5-8
7290 B Dr N 49014 — 269-979-1131
Gary Garland, prin. — Fax 979-4613

Lakeview SD — 2,900/K-12
15 Arbor St 49015 — 269-565-2400
Cindy S. Ruble, supt. — Fax 565-2428
www.lakeviewspartans.org
Lakeview HS — 1,100/9-12
15060 Helmer Rd S 49015 — 269-565-3700
Steve Skalka, prin. — Fax 565-3708
Lakeview MS — 500/5-8
300 28th St S 49015 — 269-565-3900
Jim Owen, prin. — Fax 565-3908

Pennfield SD — 1,900/K-12
8587 Pennfield Rd 49017 — 269-961-9781
Dale Kimball, supt. — Fax 961-9799
www.pennfield.k12.mi.us
Pennfield Dunlap MS — 500/6-8
8587 Pennfield Rd 49017 — 269-961-9784
Don Hepner, prin. — Fax 961-9799
Pennfield HS — 600/9-12
8587 Pennfield Rd 49017 — 269-961-9770
Barry Duckham, prin. — Fax 961-9799

Battle Creek SDA Academy — 200/PK-12
480 Parkway Dr, — 269-965-1278
Kevin Kossick, prin. — Fax 965-3250
Calhoun Christian S — 100/PK-12
PO Box 872 49016 — 269-979-4166
Carrie Krontz, admin. — Fax 979-4166
Davenport College of Business — Post-Sec.
200 Van Buren St W 49017 — 269-968-6105
Kambly School/Developmentally Impaired — Post-Sec.
1003 North Ave 49017
Kellogg Community College — Post-Sec.
450 North Ave 49017 — 269-965-3931
St. Philip Catholic Central HS — 100/9-12
20 Cherry St 49017 — 269-963-4503
Marcy Arnson, prin. — Fax 963-5590
St. Philip MS — 6-8
20 Cherry St 49017 — 269-963-4935
Marcy Arnson, prin. — Fax 963-5590
Wright Beauty Academy — Post-Sec.
492 Capital Ave SW 49015 — 269-964-4016

Bay City, Bay, Pop. 34,879
Bangor Township SD — 2,400/K-12
3520 Old Kawkawlin Rd 48706 — 989-684-8121
Michael Andress, supt. — Fax 684-6000
www.bangorschools.org
Glenn HS — 900/9-12
3201 Kiesel Rd 48706 — 989-684-7510
Patti Smith, prin. — Fax 684-1545
McAuliffe MS — 600/6-8
3281 Kiesel Rd 48706 — 989-686-7640
Barbara Bibbee, prin. — Fax 684-7633

Bay City SD — 9,100/K-12
910 N Walnut St 48706 — 989-686-9700
Carolyn Wierda, supt. — Fax 686-1047
www.bcschools.net
Central HS — 1,700/9-12
1624 Columbus Ave 48708 — 989-893-9541
Tim Marciniak, prin. — Fax 893-0333
Handy MS — 1,100/6-8
601 Blend St 48706 — 989-684-1723
Carla Derocher, prin. — Fax 684-1960
Other Schools – See Auburn

All Saints HS — 200/9-12
217 S Monroe St 48708 — 989-892-2533
J.B. Watters, prin. — Fax 892-7188
Bayshire Beauty Academy — Post-Sec.
917 Saginaw St 48708 — 989-894-2431
Great Lakes College — Post-Sec.
3930 Traxler Ct 48706 — 989-686-1572
Holy Family MS — 100/6-8
2307 S Monroe St Ste 200 48708 — 989-892-8332
Fax 892-8727

Bear Lake, Manistee, Pop. 331
Bear Lake SD — 300/K-12
PO Box 188 49614 — 231-864-3133
Gregory Webster, supt. — Fax 864-3434
www.bearlake.k12.mi.us
Bear Lake Secondary S — 200/6-12
PO Box 188 49614 — 231-864-3133
Michael Matesich, prin. — Fax 864-3434

Beaver Island, Charlevoix
Beaver Island Community SD — 100/K-12
PO Box 235 49782 — 231-448-2744
Kathleen McNamara, supt. — Fax 448-2919
www.beaverisland.k12.mi.us
Beaver Island Community S — 100/K-12
PO Box 235 49782 — 231-448-2744
Kathleen McNamara, prin. — Fax 448-2919

Beaverton, Gladwin, Pop. 1,118
Beaverton Rural SD — 1,400/K-12
PO Box 529 48612 — 989-246-3000
Joan Cashin, supt. — Fax 435-7631
www.brs.cgresd.net
Beaverton HS — 600/9-12
3090 Crockett Rd 48612 — 989-246-3010
Jeffrey Budge, prin. — Fax 246-3366
Beaverton MS — 500/4-8
440 S Ross St 48612 — 989-246-3020
Gregory Paxton, prin. — Fax 246-3420

Belding, Ionia, Pop. 5,895
Belding Area SD — 2,400/PK-12
1975 Orchard St 48809 — 616-794-4700
Charles Barker, supt. — Fax 794-4730
www.bas-k12.org/
Belding HS — 700/9-12
850 Hall St 48809 — 616-794-4900
Aaron West, prin. — Fax 794-4956
Belding MS — 600/6-8
410 Ionia St 48809 — 616-794-4400
John Deiter, prin. — Fax 794-4420

Bellaire, Antrim, Pop. 1,146
Bellaire SD — 500/K-12
204 W Forrest Home Ave 49615 — 231-533-8141
James Emery, supt. — Fax 533-6797
www.bellairepublicschools.com/
Bellaire HS — 200/9-12
204 W Forrest Home Ave 49615 — 231-533-8015
James Emery, prin. — Fax 533-8244

Belleville, Wayne, Pop. 3,853
Van Buren SD — 6,000/K-12
555 W Columbia Ave 48111 — 734-697-9123
Pete L. Lazaroff, supt. — Fax 697-6385
www.resa.net/vanburen
Belleville HS — 1,900/9-12
501 W Columbia Ave 48111 — 734-697-9133
Sheila Brown, prin. — Fax 697-6551
North MS — 800/6-8
47097 McBride Ave 48111 — 734-697-9171
Dianne Tilson, prin. — Fax 697-6573
South MS — 700/6-8
45201 Owen St 48111 — 734-697-8711
Michelle Herring, prin. — Fax 697-6576

Michigan Institute of Aeronautics — Post-Sec.
47884 D St 48111 — 734-483-3758

Bellevue, Eaton, Pop. 1,375
Bellevue Community SD — 800/K-12
201 West St 49021 — 269-763-9432
David Blossom, supt. — Fax 763-3101
www.bellevue-schools.com/
Bellevue HS — 300/9-12
575 Love Hwy 49021 — 269-763-9413
Monica Burger, prin. — Fax 763-3955
Bellevue MS — 300/5-8
904 W Capital Ave 49021 — 269-763-9401
Karyn Hall, prin. — Fax 763-3266

Benton Harbor, Berrien, Pop. 10,749
Benton Harbor Area SD — 3,500/PK-12
PO Box 1107 49023 — 269-605-1000
Carole Schmidt, supt. — Fax 605-1010
www.bhas.org
Benton Harbor HS — 1,300/9-12
870 Colfax Ave 49022 — 269-605-1200
Carole Fetke, prin. — Fax 605-0761
Fair Plain Renaissance MS — 400/6-8
120 E Napier Ave 49022 — 269-605-0658
Mary Meeks, prin. — Fax 605-1403
Hull MS — 400/6-8
1716 Territorial Rd 49022 — 269-605-1500
Eric Williams, prin. — Fax 605-1503
M. L. K. Freshman Academy — 9-9
750 E Britain Ave 49022 — 269-605-2400
Louretta Powell, prin. — Fax 605-2403

Lake Michigan College — Post-Sec.
2755 E Napier Ave 49022 — 269-927-8100

Benzonia, Benzie, Pop. 476
Benzie County Central SD — 2,000/K-12
9222 Homestead Rd 49616 — 231-882-9654
David Micinski, supt. — Fax 882-9121
www.benzie.k12.mi.us
Benzie Central HS — 600/9-12
PO Box 240 49616 — 231-882-4497
Peter Olson, prin. — Fax 882-5699
Benzie Central JHS — 300/7-8
930 Homestead Rd 49616 — 231-882-4498
David Clasen, prin. — Fax 882-7627

Berkley, Oakland, Pop. 15,089
Berkley SD
Supt. — See Oak Park
Anderson MS — 600/6-8
3205 Catalpa Dr 48072 — 248-837-8200
Steve Frank, prin. — Fax 546-0696
Berkley HS — 1,400/9-12
2325 Catalpa Dr 48072 — 248-837-8100
Derrick Lopez, prin. — Fax 544-5860

Berrien Springs, Berrien, Pop. 1,951
Berrien Springs SD 1,600/PK-12
1 Sylvester Ave 49103 269-471-2891
James Bermingham, supt. Fax 471-2590
www.homeoftheshamrocks.org
Berrien Springs HS 500/9-12
1 Sylvester Ave 49103 269-471-1748
Patrick Weckel, prin. Fax 471-1511
Berrien Springs MS 400/6-8
1 Sylvester Ave 49103 269-471-2796
Ryan Pesce, prin. Fax 471-2590

Andrews Academy 300/9-12
8833 Garland Ave 49104 269-471-3138
Allan Chase, prin. Fax 471-6368
Andrews University 49104 Post-Sec.
269-471-7771

Bessemer, Gogebic, Pop. 1,957
Bessemer City SD 400/PK-12
301 E Sellar St 49911 906-667-0802
Al Gaiss, supt. Fax 667-0318
www.bessemerareaschools.org
Johnston JSHS 300/7-12
100 W Lead St 49911 906-667-0413
Mark Johnson, prin. Fax 667-0320

Beverly Hills, Oakland, Pop. 10,086
Birmingham SD
Supt. — See Birmingham
Berkshire MS 800/6-8
21707 W 14 Mile Rd 48025 248-203-4702
Jim Moll, prin. Fax 203-4802
Groves HS 1,400/9-12
20500 W 13 Mile Rd 48025 248-203-3530
Fred Procter, prin. Fax 203-3636

Detroit Country Day MS Hillview Campus 400/6-8
22400 Hillview Ln 48025 248-646-7985
Gerald Hanson, hdmstr. Fax 646-3459
Detroit Country Day S 13 Mile Campus 1,500/9-12
22305 W 13 Mile Rd 48025 248-646-7717
Gerald Hanson, hdmstr. Fax 646-2458

Big Rapids, Mecosta, Pop. 10,704
Big Rapids SD 2,100/PK-12
21034 15 Mile Rd 49307 231-796-2627
Thomas Langdon, supt. Fax 592-0639
www.brps.k12.mi.us
Big Rapids HS 700/9-12
21175 15 Mile Rd 49307 231-796-7651
Tim Haist, prin. Fax 592-8505
Big Rapids MS 400/6-8
500 N Warren Ave 49307 231-796-9965
Russ Greenleaf, prin. Fax 592-3494

Mecosta-Osceola ISD
15760 190th Ave 49307 231-796-3543
Curtis Finch, supt. Fax 796-3300
www.moisd.org
Mecosta-Osceola Career Center Vo/Tech
15830 190th Ave 49307 231-796-5805
Tim Rigling, prin. Fax 796-0262

Ferris State University Post-Sec.
901 S State St 49307 231-591-2000

Birch Run, Saginaw, Pop. 1,719
Birch Run Area SD 1,900/K-12
12400 Church St 48415 989-624-9307
Wayne S. Wright, supt. Fax 624-5081
www.birchrun.k12.mi.us
Birch Run HS 600/9-12
12450 Church St 48415 989-624-9392
Tricia Murphy-Alderman, prin. Fax 624-8502
Greene MS 600/5-8
8225 Main St 48415 989-624-5821
Doug Rowley, prin. Fax 624-8507

Birmingham, Oakland, Pop. 19,081
Birmingham SD 8,000/PK-12
550 W Merrill St 48009 248-203-3000
Richard Perry, supt. Fax 203-3007
www.birmingham.k12.mi.us
Derby MS 700/6-8
1300 Derby Rd 48009 248-203-5003
Deborah Hubbell, prin. Fax 203-4948
Seaholm HS 1,200/9-12
2436 W Lincoln St 48009 248-203-3707
Terry Piper, prin. Fax 203-3706
Other Schools – See Beverly Hills, Bloomfield Hls

Eton Academy 200/1-12
1755 E Melton Rd 48009 248-642-1150
Peter Pullen, hdmstr. Fax 642-3670
Roeper S 200/6-8
1051 Oakland Ave 48009 248-203-7402
Randall Dunn, hdmstr. Fax 642-8619
Roeper S 200/9-12
1051 Oakland Ave 48009 248-203-7448
Randall Dunn, hdmstr. Fax 642-8619

Blanchard, Isabella
Montabella Community SD
Supt. — See Edmore
Montabella HS 300/9-12
1456 N County Line Rd 49310 989-427-5175
Shane Riley, prin. Fax 427-5107
Montabella MS 300/5-8
1324 N County Line Rd 49310 989-427-5414
Mark Prout, prin. Fax 427-5602

Blissfield, Lenawee, Pop. 3,256
Blissfield Community SD 1,400/K-12
630 S Lane St 49228 517-486-2205
Paul Palka, supt. Fax 486-5701
www.blissfield.k12.mi.us
Blissfield HS 500/9-12
630 S Lane St 49228 517-486-2148
Jerry Johnson, prin. Fax 486-4749
Blissfield MS 300/6-8
1305 Beamer Rd 49228 517-486-4420
Mark Willson, prin. Fax 486-4758

Bloomfield Hls, Oakland, Pop. 3,851
Birmingham SD
Supt. — See Birmingham
Birmingham Covington S 600/3-8
1525 Covington Rd, 248-203-4425
Dale Truding, prin. Fax 203-4433

Bloomfield Hills SD 5,900/K-12
PO Box 816, 248-341-5400
Steven Gaynor, supt. Fax 341-5449
www.bloomfield.org
Andover HS 1,000/9-12
4200 Andover Rd, 248-341-5500
Heidi Kattula, prin. Fax 341-5699
Bloomfield Hills MS 500/6-8
4200 Quarton Rd, 248-341-6000
Kaarin Averill, prin. Fax 341-6099
East Hills MS 500/6-8
2800 Kensington Rd, 248-341-6200
Arnold Jahnke, prin. Fax 341-6299
International Academy 100/9-12
1020 E Square Lake Rd, 248-341-5900
Bert Okma, prin. Fax 341-5959
Lahser HS 1,000/9-12
3456 Lahser Rd, 248-341-5700
Charlie Hollerith, prin. Fax 341-5899
Other Schools – See West Bloomfield

Academy of the Sacred Heart 500/PK-12
1250 Kensington Rd, 248-646-8900
Sr. Bridget Bearss, prin. Fax 646-4143
Brother Rice HS 700/9-12
7101 Lahser Rd, 248-647-2526
David Kozlowski, prin. Fax 647-8170
Cranbrook Academy of Art Post-Sec.
PO Box 801 48303 248-645-3300
Cranbrook S 1,600/PK-12
PO Box 801, 248-645-3602
Arlyce Seibert, prin. Fax 645-3524
Marian HS 600/9-12
7225 Lahser Rd, 248-644-1750
Sr. Kathleen Budesky, prin. Fax 644-6107
Oakland Community College Post-Sec.
2480 Opdyke Rd 48304 248-341-2000

Bloomingdale, Van Buren, Pop. 511
Bloomingdale SD 1,500/K-12
PO Box 217 49026 269-521-3900
Brett Geier, supt. Fax 521-3907
www.bdalecards.org/
Bloomingdale HS 400/9-12
PO Box 217 49026 269-521-3910
Rick Reo, prin. Fax 521-3915
Bloomingdale MS 400/6-8
PO Box 217 49026 269-521-3950
Kevin Simmons, prin. Fax 521-3958

Boyne City, Charlevoix, Pop. 3,292
Boyne City SD 1,200/K-12
321 S Park St Ste 1 49712 231-439-8190
Robert Alger, supt. Fax 439-8195
www.boyne.k12.mi.us
Boyne City HS 400/9-12
1035 Boyne Ave 49712 231-439-8100
Karen Jarema, prin. Fax 439-8194
Boyne City MS 400/5-8
1025 Boyne Ave 49712 231-439-8200
Mindy Porter, prin. Fax 439-8233

Boyne Falls, Charlevoix, Pop. 347
Boyne Falls SD 300/K-12
PO Box 356 49713 231-549-2211
Gary Urman, supt. Fax 549-2922
www.boynefalls.org
Boyne Falls S 300/K-12
PO Box 356 49713 231-549-2212
Paul Zagata, prin. Fax 549-2922

Breckenridge, Gratiot, Pop. 1,318
Breckenridge Community SD 1,000/K-12
PO Box 217 48615 989-842-3182
Jeff Jennette, supt. Fax 842-3625
breck.edzone.net/
Breckenridge HS 300/9-12
PO Box 217 48615 989-842-3182
Sheila Pilmore, prin. Fax 842-3186
Breckenridge MS 200/6-8
PO Box 217 48615 989-842-3182
Sheila Pilmore, prin. Fax 842-3186

Brethren, Manistee
Kaleva Norman Dickson SD 900/K-12
PO Box 36 49619 231-477-5353
Gregory Webster, supt. Fax 477-5240
www.knd.k12.mi.us
Brethren HS 300/9-12
PO Box 36 49619 231-477-5355
Wayne Bernier, prin. Fax 477-5242
Brethren MS 200/7-8
PO Box 36 49619 231-477-5354
Wayne Bernier, prin. Fax 477-5351

Bridgeport, Saginaw, Pop. 8,569
Bridgeport-Spaulding Community SD 1,400/PK-12
PO Box 657 48722 989-777-1770
Desmon Daniel, supt. Fax 777-4720
www.bscs.k12.mi.us
Bridgeport HS 600/9-12
4691 Bearcat Blvd 48722 989-777-3100
Andrew Kowalczyk, prin. Fax 777-6910
Bridgeport-Spaulding MS 400/7-8
4221 Bearcat Blvd 48722 989-777-0440
David Hurst, prin. Fax 777-2284

Bridgeport Baptist Academy 100/K-12
PO Box 249 48722 989-777-6811
John Howell, prin. Fax 777-7376

Bridgman, Berrien, Pop. 2,449
Bridgman SD 1,000/K-12
9964 Gast Rd 49106 269-466-0271
Kevin Ivers, supt. Fax 466-0221
www.bridgmanschools.com
Bridgman HS 400/9-12
9964 Gast Rd 49106 269-465-6848
Jim Hutfilz, prin. Fax 466-0355
Reed MS 300/5-8
10254 California 49106 269-465-5410
Patrick Weckel, prin. Fax 466-0393

Brighton, Livingston, Pop. 7,139
Brighton Area SD 7,100/K-12
125 S Church St 48116 810-299-4000
James Craig, supt. Fax 299-4045
bas.k12.mi.us/
Brighton HS 2,200/9-12
7878 Brighton Rd 48116 810-299-4100
Ken Hamman, prin. Fax 299-4111
Maltby MS 800/6-8
4740 Bauer Rd 48116 810-299-3600
Marcia Tomasko, prin. Fax 299-3610
Scranton MS 900/6-8
8415 Maltby Rd 48116 810-299-3700
Henry Vecchioni, prin. Fax 299-3710

Ross Medical Education Center Post-Sec.
8110 Murphy Dr 48116 810-227-0160

Brimley, Chippewa
Brimley Area SD 500/K-12
7134 S M 221 49715 906-248-3219
Alan Kantola, supt. Fax 248-3220
www.eup.k12.mi.us/brimley/
Brimley HS 200/7-12
7134 S M 221 49715 906-248-3218
Brian Reattoir, prin. Fax 248-5339

Bay Mills Community College Post-Sec.
12214 W Lakeshore Dr 49715 906-248-3354

Britton, Lenawee, Pop. 678
Britton-Macon Area SD 600/K-12
201 College Ave 49229 517-451-4581
Robert Tebo, supt. Fax 451-8595
Britton-Macon S 600/K-12
201 College Ave 49229 517-451-4581
Randy Salisbury, prin. Fax 451-8595

Bronson, Branch, Pop. 2,346
Bronson Community SD 1,400/K-12
215 W Chicago St 49028 517-369-3257
Bob Walter, supt. Fax 369-2802
www.bronson.k12.mi.us
Bronson JSHS 700/7-12
450 E Grant St 49028 517-369-3230
Sean McNatt, prin. Fax 369-3506

Brooklyn, Jackson, Pop. 1,363
Columbia SD 1,700/K-12
11775 Hewitt Rd 49230 517-592-6641
Brent Beamish, supt. Fax 592-8090
columbiaschooldistrict.org
Columbia Central HS 600/9-12
11775 Hewitt Rd 49230 517-592-6634
David Slusher, prin. Fax 592-8909
Columbia MS 500/6-8
321 School St 49230 517-592-2181
Greg Meschke, prin. Fax 592-3447

Brown City, Sanilac, Pop. 1,310
Brown City Community SD 1,100/K-12
PO Box 160 48416 810-346-2781
Jerry Steigerwald, supt. Fax 346-3762
www.bc.k12.mi.us
Brown City JSHS 500/7-12
PO Box 160 48416 810-346-2781
Scott Roper, prin. Fax 346-2381

Brownstown, See Flat Rock
Woodhaven-Brownstown SD 5,100/K-12
24975 Van Horn Rd 48134 734-783-3300
Barbara Lott, supt. Fax 783-3316
www.woodhaven.k12.mi.us
Woodhaven HS 1,100/10-12
24787 Van Horn Rd 48134 734-783-3333
Michael Vogel, prin. Fax 783-3342
Other Schools – See Woodhaven

Buchanan, Berrien, Pop. 4,531
Buchanan Community SD 1,800/PK-12
401 W Chicago St 49107 269-695-8401
Diana Davis, supt. Fax 695-8450
www.buchananschools.com
Buchanan HS 500/9-12
401 W Chicago St 49107 269-695-8403
Richard Gregg, prin. Fax 695-8414
Buchanan MS 400/6-8
610 W 4th St 49107 269-695-8406
Joseph Malbouef, prin. Fax 695-8459

Buckley, Wexford, Pop. 565
Buckley Community SD 400/K-12
PO Box 38 49620 231-269-3325
Chet Janik, supt. Fax 269-3833
www.buckleyschools.com
Buckley Community S 400/K-12
PO Box 38 49620 231-269-3325
Chet Janik, prin. Fax 269-3833

Burr Oak, Saint Joseph, Pop. 771
Burr Oak Community SD 300/K-12
PO Box 337 49030 269-489-2213
Terry Conklin, supt. Fax 489-5198
www.remc12.k12.mi.us/burr-oak/

Burr Oak HS 200/7-12
PO Box 337 49030 269-489-5534
Terry Conklin, prin. Fax 489-5198

Burton, Genesee, Pop. 30,916
Atherton Community SD 1,000/K-12
3354 S Genesee Rd 48519 810-591-9182
Mark Madden, supt. Fax 591-1926
www.athertonschools.com
Atherton HS 400/9-12
3354 S Genesee Rd 48519 810-591-9184
Robert Belous, prin. Fax 591-9180
Atherton MS 400/4-8
3444 S Genesee Rd 48519 810-591-0604
Trevor Alward, prin. Fax 591-9456

Bendle SD 1,200/PK-12
2283 E Scottwood Ave 48529 810-591-2501
John Angle, supt. Fax 591-2210
www.bendleschools.org
Bendle HS 400/9-12
2294 E Bristol Rd 48529 810-591-5103
William Parish, prin. Fax 591-2510
Bendle MS 300/6-8
4093 Barnes Ave 48529 810-591-3385
Scott Williams, prin. Fax 591-2540

Bentley Community SD 1,000/K-12
1170 N Belsay Rd 48509 810-591-9100
John Schantz, supt. Fax 591-9102
www.bentleyschools.org/bentleycs/site/default.asp
Bentley HS 300/9-12
1150 N Belsay Rd 48509 810-591-5811
Richard Cunningham, prin. Fax 591-9158
Bentley MS 300/5-8
1180 N Belsay Rd 48509 810-591-9040
Folke Boman, prin. Fax 591-9166

Faithway Christian S 300/PK-12
1225 S Center Rd 48509 810-743-0055
Jude Barlage, admin. Fax 743-0033
Genesee Christian S 400/PK-12
1223 S Belsay Rd 48509 810-743-3108
Jerry Kramer, prin. Fax 743-3230
St. Thomas More Academy 100/K-12
6456 E Bristol Rd 48519 810-742-2411
Dan Le Blanc, prin. Fax 742-4803
Valley Christian Academy 200/PK-12
3266 S Genesee Rd 48519 810-742-4500
Karen Kennamer, prin. Fax 742-4537

Byron, Shiawassee, Pop. 582
Byron Area SD 1,300/K-12
312 W Maple St 48418 810-266-4881
Dr. Mark E. Miller, supt. Fax 266-5723
www.byron.k12.mi.us
Byron HS 400/9-12
312 W Maple St 48418 810-266-4620
Tom Dykstra, prin. Fax 266-5010
Byron MS 300/6-8
312 W Maple St 48418 810-266-4422
Terry Evanish, prin. Fax 266-4151

Byron Center, Kent
Byron Center SD 3,000/K-12
8542 Byron Center Ave SW 49315 616-878-6100
Howard Napp, supt. Fax 878-6120
www.bcpsk12.net
Byron Center HS 900/9-12
8500 Burlingame Ave SW 49315 616-878-6600
Karl Nelson, prin. Fax 878-6620
Byron Center West MS 500/7-8
8654 Homerich Ave SW 49315 616-878-6500
Mike Spahr, prin. Fax 878-6520

Wayland UNSD 3,200/K-12
500 100th St SW 49315 269-792-2181
Eivor Swan, supt. Fax 877-0520
www.wayland.k12.mi.us
Other Schools – See Wayland

Zion Christian S 100/PK-12
7555 Byron Center Ave SW 49315 616-878-9472
Tom Kwekel, prin. Fax 878-9473

Cadillac, Wexford, Pop. 10,167
Cadillac Area SD 3,300/K-12
421 S Mitchell St 49601 231-876-5000
Paul Liabenow, supt. Fax 876-5021
www.vikingnet.org
Cadillac JHS 600/8-9
500 Chestnut St 49601 231-876-5700
Dave Champion, prin. Fax 876-5721
Cadillac SHS 800/10-12
400 Linden St 49601 231-876-5800
William Chilman, prin. Fax 876-5821

Wexford-Missaukee ISD
9907 E 13th St 49601 231-876-2260
Scott Crosby, supt. Fax 876-2272
www.wmisd.org
Wexford-Missaukee Area Career Tech Vo/Tech
9901 E 13th St 49601 231-876-2200
Fax 876-2212

Baker College of Cadillac Post-Sec.
9600 E 13th St 49601 231-876-3100
Cadillac Heritage Christian S 100/PK-12
1706 Wright St 49601 231-775-4272
William Goodwill, admin. Fax 775-2999

Caledonia, Kent, Pop. 1,278
Caledonia Community SD 3,500/PK-12
9753 Duncan Lake Ave SE 49316 616-891-8185
Jerry Phillips, supt. Fax 891-9253
www.caledonia.k12.mi.us
Caledonia HS 1,100/9-12
9050 Kraft Ave SE 49316 616-891-8129
Jim Glazier, prin. Fax 891-7038
Duncan Lake MS 400/6-8
9757 Duncan Lake Ave SE 49316 616-891-1380
Cheryl Davis, prin. Fax 891-0833
Kraft Meadows MS 400/6-8
9230 Kraft Ave SE 49316 616-891-8649
Brian Leatherman, prin. Fax 891-7013

Dutton Christian MS 100/6-8
6729 Hanna Lake Ave SE 49316 616-698-8660
Daniel Netz, admin. Fax 698-2281

Calumet, Houghton, Pop. 812
Calumet-Laurium-Keweenaw SD 1,600/K-12
57070 Mine St 49913 906-337-0311
Darryl Pierce, supt. Fax 337-1406
www.clk.k12.mi.us
Calumet HS 500/9-12
57070 Mine St 49913 906-337-0311
Robert Barrette, prin. Fax 337-5405
Washington MS 400/6-8
57070 Mine St 49913 906-337-0311
Michael Steber, prin. Fax 337-5406

Camden, Hillsdale, Pop. 542
Camden-Frontier SD 600/K-12
4971 W Montgomery Rd 49232 517-368-5991
Wendy Moore, supt. Fax 368-5959
Camden Frontier HS 200/9-12
4971 W Montgomery Rd 49232 517-368-5255
Reed Kimball, prin. Fax 368-5950
Camden Frontier MS 100/6-8
4971 W Montgomery Rd 49232 517-368-5255
Reed Kimball, prin. Fax 368-5950

Canton, Wayne, Pop. 81,500
Plymouth-Canton Community SD
Supt. — See Plymouth
Canton HS 2,000/9-12
8415 N Canton Center Rd 48187 734-416-2850
Dr. Cassandra Smith, prin. Fax 416-7531
Discovery MS 900/6-8
45083 Hanford Rd 48187 734-416-2880
Roche LaVictor, prin. Fax 416-2895
Plymouth HS 1,400/9-12
8400 N Beck Rd 48187 734-582-5500
Dr. Michael Bee, prin. Fax 582-5555
Salem HS 2,000/9-12
46181 Joy Rd 48187 734-416-7800
Gerald Ostoin, prin. Fax 416-7791

Agape Christian Academy 200/PK-12
PO Box 87770 48187 734-394-0357
Rev. Mark Moore, prin. Fax 394-0206
Plymouth Christian Academy 700/PK-12
43065 Joy Rd 48187 734-459-3505
Dr. Marilyn Meell, hdmstr. Fax 459-9997

Capac, Saint Clair, Pop. 2,233
Capac Community SD 1,800/PK-12
403 N Glassford St 48014 810-395-4321
Jerry Jennex, supt. Fax 395-4858
www.capac.k12.mi.us
Capac JSHS 700/8-12
541 N Glassford St 48014 810-395-3800
Michael Mrozinski, prin. Fax 395-2427

Carleton, Monroe, Pop. 2,874
Airport Community SD 3,300/PK-12
11270 Grafton Rd 48117 734-654-2414
Larry Audet, supt. Fax 654-3424
www.airport.k12.mi.us
Airport HS 1,100/9-12
11330 Grafton Rd 48117 734-654-6208
Robert Matkovic, prin. Fax 654-3005
Wagar MS 800/6-8
11200 Grafton Rd 48117 734-654-6205
Mark Arnold, prin. Fax 654-0057

Carney, Menominee, Pop. 220
Carney-Nadeau SD 300/K-12
PO Box 68 49812 906-639-2000
Steven Martin, supt. Fax 639-2176
www.cnps.us
Carney-Nadeau S 300/K-12
PO Box 68 49812 906-639-2171
Steven Martin, prin. Fax 639-2176

Caro, Tuscola, Pop. 4,193
Caro Community SD 2,100/K-12
301 N Hooper St 48723 989-673-3166
Neil Beckwith, supt. Fax 673-6248
caro.mi.schoolwebpages.com
Caro HS 700/9-12
301 N Hooper St 48723 989-673-3165
George Rierson, prin. Fax 673-8707
Caro MS 500/6-8
301 N Hooper St 48723 989-673-3167
JoAnn Nordstrom, prin. Fax 673-1225

Tuscola ISD
1385 Cleaver Rd 48723 989-673-2144
Carol Socha, supt. Fax 673-5366
www.tisd.k12.mi.us
Tuscola Technology Center Vo/Tech
1401 Cleaver Rd 48723 989-673-5300
Steve Ley, prin. Fax 673-4228

Great Lakes College Post-Sec.
1231 Cleaver Rd 48723 989-673-5857

Carrollton, Saginaw, Pop. 6,521
Carrollton SD
Supt. — See Saginaw
Carrollton HS 400/9-12
PO Box 548 48724 989-753-3433
Traci Smith, prin. Fax 754-1041
Carrollton MS 400/6-8
PO Box 517 48724 989-753-9704
Tiffany Peterson, prin. Fax 754-1470

Carson City, Montcalm, Pop. 1,197
Carson City-Crystal Area SD 1,200/K-12
PO Box 780 48811 989-584-3138
Robert Swanson, supt. Fax 584-3539
www.carsoncity.k12.mi.us
Carson City HS 400/9-12
PO Box 780 48811 989-584-3175
Beth Robb, prin. Fax 584-3043
Carson City MS 300/6-8
PO Box 780 48811 989-584-3903
Charles Larkins, prin. Fax 584-3259

Fellowship Baptist Academy 100/PK-12
8070 S Bloomer St 48811 989-584-6430
Kevin McAlvey, prin. Fax 584-6716

Carsonville, Sanilac, Pop. 493
Carsonville-Port Sanilac SD 600/K-12
100 N Goetze Rd 48419 810-657-9393
Harold Titus, supt. Fax 657-9060
www.carsport.k12.mi.us
Carsonville-Port Sanilac JSHS 300/7-12
100 N Goetze Rd 48419 810-657-9394
Ann Binienda, prin. Fax 657-9431

Casco, Saint Clair
Anchor Bay SD 6,600/K-12
5201 County Line Rd Ste 100 48064 586-725-2861
Leonard Woodside, supt. Fax 725-0290
www.anchorbay.misd.net
Other Schools – See Fair Haven, New Baltimore

Caseville, Huron, Pop. 887
Caseville SD 100/K-12
PO Box 1068 48725 989-856-2940
Dr. Dan Tighe, supt. Fax 856-3095
www.caseville.k12.mi.us
Caseville S 100/K-12
PO Box 1068 48725 989-856-7192
Ken Ewald, prin. Fax 856-8641

Cass City, Tuscola, Pop. 2,606
Cass City SD 1,500/PK-12
4868 Seeger St 48726 989-872-2200
Ronald Wilson, supt. Fax 872-5015
www.casscity.k12.mi.us
Cass City HS 500/9-12
4868 Seeger St 48726 989-872-2148
Chad Daniels, prin. Fax 872-5015
Cass City MS 500/5-8
4805 Ale St 48726 989-872-4397
Jeff Hartel, prin. Fax 872-2990

Cassopolis, Cass, Pop. 1,840
Cassopolis SD 1,200/K-12
63700 Brick Church Rd 49031 269-445-0500
Gregory Weatherspoon, supt. Fax 445-0505
www.cassopolis.k12.mi.us
Beatty JSHS 500/7-12
22721 Diamond Cove St 49031 269-445-0540
Anthony Habra, prin. Fax 445-3112

Cedar Lake, Montcalm

Great Lakes Adventist Academy 200/9-12
PO Box 68 48812 989-427-5181
Raymond Davis, prin. Fax 427-5027

Cedar Springs, Kent, Pop. 3,234
Cedar Springs SD 2,300/PK-12
204 E Muskegon St 49319 616-696-1204
Andrew Booth, supt. Fax 696-3755
www.csredhawks.org
Cedar Springs HS 1,000/9-12
204 E Muskegon St 49319 616-696-1200
Karl Pilar, prin. Fax 696-4016
Cedar Springs MS 600/7-8
204 E Muskegon St 49319 616-696-9100
Bill VanHorn, prin. Fax 696-3109

Cedarville, Mackinac
Les Cheneaux Community SD 300/K-12
PO Box 366 49719 906-484-2256
Rod Goehmann, supt. Fax 484-2072
eup.k12.mi.us/les_cheneaux
Cedarville MSHS 100/6-12
PO Box 366 49719 906-484-2256
Randy Schaedig, prin. Fax 484-2403

Center Line, Macomb, Pop. 8,308
Center Line SD 3,000/PK-12
26400 Arsenal 48015 586-510-2000
Judith P. Pritchett, supt. Fax 510-2019
www.clps.org
Center Line HS 900/9-12
26300 Arsenal 48015 586-510-2100
Michael Dodge, prin. Fax 510-2119
Wolfe MS 700/6-8
8640 McKinley 48015 586-510-2300
Amy Maruca, prin. Fax 510-2319

Central Lake, Antrim, Pop. 988
Central Lake SD 500/K-12
PO Box 128 49622 231-544-3141
Michael Linton, supt. Fax 544-2903
clps.k12.mi.us
Central Lake JSHS 300/6-12
PO Box 128 49622 231-544-3341
Todd Derenzy, prin. Fax 544-2903

Centreville, Saint Joseph, Pop. 1,555
Centreville SD 1,000/K-12
PO Box 158 49032 269-467-5220
William Miller, supt. Fax 467-5226
cpschools.org
Centreville HS 300/9-12
PO Box 158 49032 269-467-5210
Mike Morris, prin. Fax 467-5214
Centreville MS 100/7-8
PO Box 158 49032 269-467-5205
Barbara Lester, prin. Fax 467-4864

Glen Oaks Community College — Post-Sec.
62249 Shimmel Rd 49032 — 269-467-9945

Charlevoix, Charlevoix, Pop. 2,776
Charlevoix SD — 1,400/K-12
208 W Clinton St 49720 — 231-547-3200
James Cooper, supt. — Fax 547-0556
www.rayder.net
Charlevoix HS — 500/9-12
05200 Marion Center Rd 49720 — 231-547-3222
Gary Grundman, prin. — Fax 547-3245
Charlevoix MS — 400/5-8
108 E Garfield Ave 49720 — 231-547-3206
Keith Haske, prin. — Fax 547-3244

Charlotte, Eaton, Pop. 9,069
Charlotte SD — 3,300/K-12
378 State St 48813 — 517-541-5100
Carl Ellinger, supt. — Fax 541-5105
www.charlottenet.org
Charlotte HS — 1,000/9-12
378 State St 48813 — 517-541-5600
Leland Wheaton, prin. — Fax 541-5605
Charlotte MS — 1,100/5-8
1068 Carlisle Hwy 48813 — 517-541-5700
Christopher Rugh, prin. — Fax 541-5705

Chassell, Houghton
Chassell Township SD — 300/K-12
PO Box 140 49916 — 906-523-4691
Michael Gaunt, supt. — Fax 523-4969
www.cts.k12.mi.us/
Chassell Township S — 300/K-12
PO Box 140 49916 — 906-523-4491
George Stockero, prin. — Fax 523-4969

Cheboygan, Cheboygan, Pop. 5,191
Cheboygan Area SD — 1,800/K-12
905 W Lincoln Ave 49721 — 231-627-4436
Paul L. Ellinger, supt. — Fax 627-9105
cheboygan.k12.mi.us/
Cheboygan HS — 800/9-12
801 W Lincoln Ave 49721 — 231-627-7191
Randy Johnson, prin. — Fax 627-2430
Cheboygan MS — 600/6-8
905 W Lincoln Ave 49721 — 231-627-7103
Mark Dombroski, prin. — Fax 627-4151

Chelsea, Washtenaw, Pop. 4,801
Chelsea SD — 2,800/K-12
500 Washington St 48118 — 734-433-2200
David Killips, supt. — Fax 433-2218
www.chelsea.k12.mi.us
Beach MS — 500/7-8
445 Mayer Dr 48118 — 734-433-2202
Patrick Little, prin. — Fax 433-2212
Chelsea HS — 1,000/9-12
740 N Freer Rd 48118 — 734-433-2201
Ronald Mead, prin. — Fax 433-2211

Chesaning, Saginaw, Pop. 2,463
Chesaning UNSD — 2,000/K-12
PO Box 95 48616 — 989-845-7020
Kathy Stewart, supt. — Fax 845-3722
www.chesaningschools.net
Chesaning MS — 600/5-8
431 N 4th St 48616 — 989-845-7040
Michael McGough, prin. — Fax 845-5335
Chesaning Union HS — 600/9-12
850 N 4th St 48616 — 989-845-2040
Duane Ellis, prin. — Fax 845-2117

Chesterfield, Macomb
L'Anse Creuse SD
Supt. — See Harrison Township
L'Anse Creuse MS East — 700/6-8
30300 Hickey Rd 48051 — 586-493-5200
Mike VanCamp, prin. — Fax 493-5205

Clare, Clare, Pop. 3,233
Clare SD — 1,500/PK-12
201 E State St 48617 — 989-386-9945
Greg McMillan, supt. — Fax 386-6055
www.clare.k12.mi.us/
Clare HS — 500/9-12
306 Schoolcrest Ave 48617 — 989-386-7789
Lee Turner, prin. — Fax 386-1236
Clare MS — 500/5-8
209 E State St 48617 — 989-386-9979
Steve Newkirk, prin. — Fax 386-4008

Clarkston, Oakland, Pop. 980
Clarkston Community SD — 6,200/PK-12
6389 Clarkston Rd 48346 — 248-623-5400
Albert Roberts, supt. — Fax 623-5450
ww2.clarkston.k12.mi.us/
Clarkston HS — 1,800/10-12
6093 Flemings Lake Rd 48346 — 248-623-3600
Jan Meagher, prin. — Fax 623-3535
Clarkston JHS — 400/8-9
6595 Waldon Rd 48346 — 248-623-5600
Shawn Ryan, prin. — Fax 623-5680

Oakland ISD
Supt. — See Waterford
Oakland Technical Campus NW — Vo/Tech
8211 Big Lake Rd 48346 — 248-922-5800
Chuck Locklear, prin. — Fax 922-5805

Springfield Christian Academy — 100/K-12
8585 Dixie Hwy 48348 — 248-625-9760
Patrick Wagner, dir. — Fax 625-9640

Clawson, Oakland, Pop. 12,337
Clawson SD — 1,400/K-12
626 Phillips Ave 48017 — 248-655-4400
James Nolan, supt. — Fax 655-4425
www.clawson.k12.mi.us
Clawson HS — 500/9-12
101 John M Ave 48017 — 248-655-4200
Daveda Colbert, prin. — Fax 655-4205
Clawson MS — 300/6-8
150 John M Ave 48017 — 248-655-4250
John Dickinson, prin. — Fax 655-4251

Academy of Court Reporting — Post-Sec.
1330 W 14 Mile Rd 48017 — 248-353-4880

Climax, Kalamazoo, Pop. 748
Climax-Scotts Community SD — 600/K-12
372 S Main St 49034 — 269-746-2400
Dr. Geoffrey Balkam, supt. — Fax 746-4374
www.remc12.k12.mi.us/climax-scotts/
Climax-Scotts JSHS — 300/7-12
372 S Main St 49034 — 269-746-2300
Ron Ehlers, prin. — Fax 746-4142

Clinton, Lenawee, Pop. 2,354
Clinton Community SD — 1,200/K-12
341 E Michigan Ave 49236 — 517-456-6501
David Pray, supt. — Fax 456-4324
www.clinton.k12.mi.us/
Clinton HS — 400/9-12
340 E Michigan Ave 49236 — 517-456-6511
Timothy Wilson, prin. — Fax 456-2042
Clinton MS — 300/6-8
100 E Franklin St 49236 — 517-456-6507
Donald Dunham, prin. — Fax 456-4997

Clinton Township, Macomb, Pop. 95,648
Chippewa Valley SD — 14,200/K-12
19120 Cass Ave 48038 — 586-723-2000
Mark Deldin, supt. — Fax 723-2001
www.chippewavalleyschools.org
Algonquin MS — 600/6-8
19150 Briarwood Ln 48036 — 586-723-3500
Dan Martini, prin. — Fax 723-3501
Chippewa Valley HS — 2,100/9-12
18300 19 Mile Rd 48038 — 586-723-2300
Dr. Jerry Davisson, prin. — Fax 723-2301
Seneca MS — 1,200/6-8
42755 Romeo Plank Rd 48038 — 586-723-3900
Todd Distelrath, prin. — Fax 723-3901
Wyandot MS — 600/6-8
39490 Garfield Rd 48038 — 586-723-4200
Darleen Sims, prin. — Fax 723-4201
Other Schools – See Macomb

Clintondale Community SD — 2,500/PK-12
35100 Little Mack Ave 48035 — 586-791-6300
George Sassin, supt. — Fax 790-7643
www.clintondale.k12.mi.us
Clintondale HS — 800/9-12
35200 Little Mack Ave 48035 — 586-791-6300
Gregory Green, prin. — Fax 790-7645
Clintondale MS — 600/6-8
35300 Little Mack Ave 48035 — 586-791-6300
Michael Gray, prin. — Fax 790-7642

L'Anse Creuse SD
Supt. — See Harrison Township
Pankow Center — Vo/Tech
24600 Fredrick Pankow Blvd 48036 — 586-783-6570
Gerald Hope, prin. — Fax 783-6577

Baker College of Clinton Township — Post-Sec.
34950 Little Mack Ave 48035 — 586-791-6610
Faith Christian S — 200/K-12
23130 Remick Dr 48036 — 586-783-9630
Matt Fenton, prin. — Fax 783-9628
Macomb Community College — Post-Sec.
44575 Garfield Rd 48038 — 586-445-7999

Clio, Genesee, Pop. 2,619
Clio Area SD — 3,500/PK-12
430 N Mill St 48420 — 810-591-0500
Fay Latture, supt. — Fax 591-0140
www.clioschools.org
Carter MS — 1,100/5-8
300 Upland Dr 48420 — 810-591-0503
Carole Chapman, prin. — Fax 591-8148
Clio HS — 1,100/9-12
1 Mustang Dr 48420 — 810-591-1359
Keith Smith, prin. — Fax 591-8169

Coldwater, Branch, Pop. 10,783
Branch ISD
370 Morse St 49036 — 517-279-5730
Michael Beckwith, supt. — Fax 279-5766
www.branch-isd.org
Branch Area Career Center — Vo/Tech
366 Morse St 49036 — 517-279-5721
Michael Hoffner, prin. — Fax 279-5777

Coldwater Community SD — 3,200/PK-12
401 Sauk River Dr 49036 — 517-279-5910
Milli Haug, supt. — Fax 279-7651
www.coldwater.k12.mi.us/
Coldwater HS — 1,000/9-12
275 N Fremont St 49036 — 517-279-5930
John Heistan, prin. — Fax 278-2475
Legg MS — 800/6-8
175 Green St 49036 — 517-279-5940
Ron Drzewicki, prin. — Fax 279-5945

School of Creative Hair Design — Post-Sec.
470 Marshall St 49036 — 517-279-2355

Coleman, Midland, Pop. 1,266
Coleman Community SD — 1,000/K-12
PO Box 522 48618 — 989-465-6060
Al Roeseler, supt. — Fax 465-9853
www.colemanschools.net
Coleman HS — 300/9-12
PO Box 522 48618 — 989-465-6171
Mary Pitchford, prin. — Fax 465-9222
Coleman MS — 300/6-8
991 E Railway St 48618 — 989-465-6177
Loren Partlo, prin. — Fax 465-9855

Coloma, Berrien, Pop. 1,524
Coloma Community SD — 2,200/PK-12
PO Box 550 49038 — 269-468-2424
Terry Ann Boguth, supt. — Fax 468-2440
www.ccs.coloma.org
Coloma JHS — 400/8-9
PO Box 550 49038 — 269-468-2405
Peter Olsen, prin. — Fax 468-2428
Coloma SHS — 500/10-12
PO Box 550 49038 — 269-468-2400
John Brown, prin. — Fax 468-2423

Colon, Saint Joseph, Pop. 1,189
Colon Community SD — 900/K-12
400 Dallas St 49040 — 269-432-3442
Lloyd Kirby, supt. — Fax 432-2577
www.colonschools.org
Colon JSHS — 400/7-12
400 Dallas St 49040 — 269-432-3231
Jill Groenendyk, prin. — Fax 432-9851

Commerce Township, Oakland, Pop. 26,955
Huron Valley SD
Supt. — See Highland
Oak Valley MS — 700/6-8
4200 White Oak Trl 48382 — 248-684-8101
Scott Lindberg, prin. — Fax 684-8105

Walled Lake Consolidated SD
Supt. — See Walled Lake
Central HS — 1,200/9-12
1600 E Oakley Park Rd 48390 — 248-956-4700
Dr. David Barry, prin. — Fax 956-4705
Northern HS — 1,600/9-12
6000 Bogie Lake Rd 48382 — 248-956-5300
Greg Diamond, prin. — Fax 956-5305
Smart MS — 1,000/6-8
8500 Commerce Rd 48382 — 248-956-3500
Mindy MoeKouris, prin. — Fax 956-3505

Comstock Park, Kent, Pop. 6,530
Comstock Park SD — 2,400/PK-12
PO Box 800 49321 — 616-254-5001
Dwight Anderson, supt. — Fax 784-5404
www.cppschools.com
Comstock Park HS — 700/9-12
PO Box 900 49321 — 616-254-5200
John Kraus, prin. — Fax 785-9835
Mill Creek MS — 500/6-8
PO Box 850 49321 — 616-254-5100
August Harju, prin. — Fax 785-2464

Concord, Jackson, Pop. 1,112
Concord Community SD — 1,000/K-12
PO Box 338 49237 — 517-524-8850
Robert Bada, supt. — Fax 524-8613
www.ccs.k12.mi.us
Concord HS — 300/9-12
PO Box 338 49237 — 517-524-8384
Michael Corey, prin. — Fax 524-6196
Concord MS — 300/6-8
PO Box 338 49237 — 517-524-8854
Michael Corey, prin. — Fax 524-7324

Constantine, Saint Joseph, Pop. 2,161
Constantine SD — 1,500/K-12
664 Canaris St 49042 — 269-435-8900
Norman Taylor, supt. — Fax 435-8980
www.constps.org
Constantine HS — 500/9-12
1 Falcon Dr 49042 — 269-435-8920
Tim Staffen, prin. — Fax 435-8981
Constantine MS — 400/6-8
260 W 6th St 49042 — 269-435-8940
Seth Parker, prin. — Fax 435-8982

Cooks, Schoolcraft
Big Bay de Noc SD — 300/K-12
8928 00.25 Rd 49817 — 906-644-2773
John Peterson, supt. — Fax 644-2615
www.bigbayschool.com
Big Bay de Noc S — 300/K-12
8928 00.25 Rd 49817 — 906-644-2773
Julie Peterson, prin. — Fax 644-2615

Coopersville, Ottawa, Pop. 4,222
Coopersville Area SD — 2,400/K-12
198 East St 49404 — 616-997-3200
Kevin O'Neill, supt. — Fax 997-3214
www.coopersvillebroncos.org/
Coopersville JHS — 600/6-8
198 East St 49404 — 616-997-3400
Tom Fox, prin. — Fax 997-3414
Coopersville SHS — 800/9-12
198 East St 49404 — 616-997-3500
Ron Veldman, prin. — Fax 997-3514

Corunna, Shiawassee, Pop. 3,377
Corunna SD — 2,300/K-12
124 N Shiawassee St 48817 — 989-743-6338
John Smith, supt. — Fax 743-4474
corunna.k12.mi.us
Corunna HS — 700/9-12
417 E King St 48817 — 989-743-3441
Kelly Smith, prin. — Fax 743-5901
Corunna MS — 500/6-8
400 N Comstock St 48817 — 989-743-5641
John Fattal, prin. — Fax 743-8761

Covert, Van Buren
Covert SD — 600/K-12
35323 M 140 Hwy 49043 — 269-764-3701
Dr. Stephanie Burrage, supt. — Fax 764-8598
www.covertps.org
Covert HS — 200/9-12
35323 M 140 Hwy 49043 — 269-764-3730
Ricky Jones, prin. — Fax 764-8598

Covert MS 100/6-8
35323 M 140 Hwy 49043 269-764-3740
Craig LeSuer, prin. Fax 764-8598

Croswell, Sanilac, Pop. 2,548
Croswell-Lexington SD 2,500/PK-12
5407 Peck Rd 48422 810-679-1000
Charles Smith, supt. Fax 679-1005
www.cros-lex.k12.mi.us
Croswell-Lexington HS 800/9-12
5461 Peck Rd 48422 810-679-1500
Theo Kerhoulas, prin. Fax 679-1505
Croswell-Lexington MS 600/6-8
5485 Peck Rd 48422 810-679-1400
Dale Ann Ogden, prin. Fax 679-1405

Crystal Falls, Iron, Pop. 1,649
Forest Park SD 600/K-12
801 Forest Pkwy 49920 906-875-6761
Tom Jayne, supt. Fax 875-4660
www.fptrojans.org
Forest Park JSHS 300/7-12
801 Forest Pkwy 49920 906-875-6869
Daniel Seder, prin. Fax 875-4660

Custer, Mason, Pop. 322
Mason County Eastern SD 600/K-12
18 S Main St 49405 231-757-3733
Ellen Bonter, supt. Fax 757-9671
mceschools.com
Mason County Eastern JSHS 400/6-12
18 S Main St 49405 231-757-3733
Shane Peters, prin. Fax 757-9671

Dansville, Ingham, Pop. 437
Dansville SD 900/K-12
PO Box 187 48819 517-623-6120
Michael V. Simeck, supt. Fax 623-6719
www.dansville.org
Dansville HS 300/9-12
PO Box 187 48819 517-623-6120
Amy Hodgson, prin. Fax 623-0127
Dansville MS 200/6-8
PO Box 187 48819 517-623-6120
David O. Sheathelm, prin. Fax 623-6719

Davison, Genesee, Pop. 5,372
Davison Community SD 5,400/K-12
PO Box 319 48423 810-591-0801
R. Clay Perkins, supt. Fax 591-7813
www.davison.k12.mi.us
Davison HS 1,500/9-12
1250 N Oak Rd 48423 810-591-3531
Kevin Brown, prin. Fax 591-3555
Davison MS 900/7-8
600 S Dayton St 48423 810-591-0848
Shelly Fenner-Krasny, prin. Fax 591-2754

Faith Baptist S 400/K-12
7306 E Atherton Rd 48423 810-653-9661
Larry Nagengast, prin. Fax 658-0087

Dearborn, Wayne, Pop. 94,090
Dearborn SD 16,300/PK-12
18700 Audette St 48124 313-827-3020
Dr. John Artis, supt. Fax 827-3137
www.dearbornschools.org
Bryant MS 700/6-8
460 N Vernon St 48128 313-827-2900
Lawrence Dockham, prin. Fax 827-2905
Dearborn HS 1,700/9-12
19501 Outer Dr 48124 313-827-1600
Gail Shenkman, prin. Fax 827-1605
Ford HS 1,400/9-12
20601 Rotunda Dr 48124 313-827-1500
Gerald Dodd, prin. Fax 827-1505
Fordson HS 2,300/9-12
13800 Ford Rd 48126 313-827-1400
Imad Fadlallah, prin. Fax 827-1405
Salina IS 500/4-8
2623 Salina St 48120 313-827-6600
Glenn Maleyko, prin. Fax 827-6605
Smith MS 600/6-8
23851 Yale St 48124 313-827-2800
Hassane Jaafar, prin. Fax 827-2805
Stout MS 700/6-8
18500 Oakwood Blvd 48124 313-827-4600
Julia Maconochie, prin. Fax 827-4605
Woodworth MS 700/6-8
4951 Ternes St 48126 313-827-7100
Troy Patterson, prin. Fax 827-7105

Davenport University - Eastern Region Post-Sec.
4801 Oakman Blvd 48126 313-581-4400
Divine Child HS 900/9-12
1001 N Silvery Ln 48128 313-562-1990
Margaret Knuth, prin. Fax 562-9361
Everest Institute Post-Sec.
23400 Michigan Ave Ste 200 48124 313-562-4228
Henry Ford Community College Post-Sec.
5101 Evergreen Rd 48128 313-845-9615
University of Michigan-Dearborn Post-Sec.
4901 Evergreen Rd 48128 313-593-5000

Dearborn Heights, Wayne, Pop. 56,176
Crestwood SD 3,500/PK-12
1501 N Beech Daly Rd 48127 313-278-0903
Joseph Pius, supt. Fax 278-4774
www.csdm.k12.mi.us/
Crestwood HS 1,100/9-12
1501 N Beech Daly Rd 48127 313-278-7475
James Baker, prin. Fax 792-0205
Riverside MS 1,100/5-8
25900 W Warren St 48127 313-792-0201
Mary Kerwin, prin. Fax 792-0201

Dearborn Heights SD 7 2,900/K-12
20629 Annapolis St 48125 313-278-1900
Jeffrey Bartold, supt. Fax 278-1413
www.resa.net/district7
Annapolis HS 900/9-12
4650 Clippert St 48125 313-278-9870
Dan Scott, prin. Fax 278-1238
Best JHS 700/6-8
22201 Powers Ave 48125 313-278-6200
Jon Znamierowski, prin. Fax 278-2470

Westwood Community SD 2,300/K-12
3335 S Beech Daly St 48125 313-565-1900
Dr. Ernando F. Minghine, supt. Fax 565-3162
www.westwood.k12.mi.us
Robichaud JSHS 1,100/7-12
3601 Janet St 48125 313-565-8850
Pamela Harris, prin. Fax 565-0304

Decatur, Van Buren, Pop. 1,890
Decatur SD 1,200/PK-12
110 Cedar St 49045 269-423-6800
Dr. Elizabeth Godwin, supt. Fax 423-6849
www.raiderpride.org/
Decatur HS 300/9-12
110 Cedar St 49045 269-423-6850
Rick Bushon, prin. Fax 423-6899
Decatur MS 400/5-8
405 N Phelps St 49045 269-423-6900
Larry Smith, prin. Fax 423-6949

Deckerville, Sanilac, Pop. 928
Deckerville Community SD 800/K-12
2633 Black River St 48427 810-376-3615
Alan Broughton, supt. Fax 376-3115
www.deckerville.k12.mi.us
Deckerville JSHS 400/7-12
2633 Black River St 48427 810-376-3875
Donald Schelke, prin. Fax 376-3115

Deerfield, Lenawee, Pop. 968
Deerfield SD 400/K-12
PO Box 217 49238 517-447-3215
Larry Shilling, supt. Fax 447-3282
deerfield.schoolwebpages.com
Deerfield S 400/K-12
PO Box 217 49238 517-447-3015
Dr. Lana Callihan, prin. Fax 447-3282

Delton, Barry
Delton Kellogg SD 1,900/K-12
327 N Grove St 49046 269-623-9200
Cynthia Vujea, supt. Fax 623-9269
www.dkschools.org/
Delton Kellogg HS 600/9-12
327 N Grove St 49046 269-623-9226
Rick Arnett, prin. Fax 623-9292
Delton Kellogg MS 600/5-8
6325 Delton Rd 49046 269-623-9229
Brooke Ballee, prin. Fax 623-9259

De Tour Village, Chippewa, Pop. 416
De Tour Area SD 200/K-12
PO Box 429 49725 906-297-2421
Rod Goehmann, supt. Fax 297-3403
eup.k12.mi.us/detour/index.html
De Tour JSHS 100/6-12
PO Box 429 49725 906-297-2011
Angela Reed, prin. Fax 297-3403

Detroit, Wayne, Pop. 886,671
Detroit SD 127,700/PK-12
7321 2nd Ave 48202 313-873-7450
William Coleman, supt. Fax 873-7433
www.detroitk12.org
Barbour Magnet MS 900/6-8
4209 Seneca St 48214 313-866-2300
Randall Moody, prin. Fax 866-2262
Beaubien MS 700/7-9
19701 Wyoming St 48221 313-494-7250
Dr. Karyn Brantley-Johnson, prin. Fax 494-7241
Breithaupt Vocational Education Vo/Tech
9300 Hubbell St 48228 313-866-9550
Vanessa Spencer, prin. Fax 866-9605
Cass Technical HS Vo/Tech
2501 2nd Ave 48201 313-263-2000
Lenora Ashford, prin. Fax 263-2001
Central HS 1,200/9-12
2425 Tuxedo St 48206 313-252-3000
Anthony Womack, prin. Fax 866-0969
Cerveny MS 600/6-8
15850 Strathmoor St 48227 313-866-9600
Gladys Stoner, prin. Fax 866-9626
Chadsey HS 900/9-12
5335 Martin St 48210 313-596-3690
Shirley Hightower, prin. Fax 596-7686
Cleveland MS 1,000/6-8
13322 Conant St 48212 313-866-3500
Donna Thornton, prin. Fax 866-3592
Clippert Academy 400/5-8
1981 McKinstry St 48209 313-849-5009
Kim Gonzalez, prin. Fax 849-5740
Cody HS 1,900/9-12
18445 Cathedral St 48228 313-866-9200
Belinda Raines, prin. Fax 866-9266
Columbus MS 700/6-8
18025 Brock St 48205 313-866-2070
Alvin Wood, prin. Fax 866-2098
Communications & Media Arts HS 500/9-12
14771 Mansfield St 48227 313-866-9300
Kim Gray, prin. Fax 866-9304
Cooley HS 1,400/9-12
15055 Hubbell St 48227 313-866-9400
Thomas Woodhouse, prin. Fax 866-9422
Crockett HS, 8950 Saint Cyril St 48213 9-12
Brenda Belcher, prin. 313-866-7399
Crockett Tech S Vo/Tech
571 Mack Ave 48201 313-494-1805
Barbara Eason, prin. Fax 494-0992

Davis Aerospace Technical HS Vo/Tech
10200 Erwin St 48234 313-866-5401
Nina Graves-Hicks, prin. Fax 866-5408
Denby Technical & Preparatory HS Vo/Tech
12800 Kelly Rd 48224 313-866-7200
Beth Cole, prin. Fax 866-2038
Detriot School of Arts 500/9-12
123 Selden St 48201 313-494-6000
Dr. Denise Davis-Cotton, prin. Fax 494-2129
Detroit HS of Technology Vo/Tech
18875 Ryan Rd 48234 313-866-4068
Dr. Deborah Jenkins, prin. Fax 866-4067
Detroit International Academy 9-12
8401 Woodward Ave 48202 313-873-3050
Beverly Hibbler, prin. Fax 873-3088
Drew MS 800/6-8
9600 Wyoming St 48204 313-873-6880
Gerlma Johnson, prin. Fax 873-0114
Earhart MS 700/6-8
1000 Scotten St 48209 313-849-3945
Gerald Vasquez, prin. Fax 849-4746
Farwell MS 700/6-8
19955 Fenelon St 48234 313-866-3702
Laverne Jordan, prin. Fax 866-3632
Finney HS 1,600/9-12
17200 Southampton St 48224 313-417-8800
Alvin Ward, prin. Fax 417-8816
Ford HS 1,700/9-12
20000 Evergreen Rd 48219 313-494-7567
Terry Truvillion, prin. Fax 494-7565
Golightly Career and Technical Center Vo/Tech
900 Dickerson St 48215 313-822-8820
Dr. Laura Royster, prin. Fax 822-8980
Hally Magnet MS 700/6-8
2585 Grove St 48221 313-494-3939
Rita Davis, prin. Fax 494-7089
Heilmann Park MS 900/6-8
19035 Crusade St 48205 313-866-7233
Cheryl Harshaw, prin. Fax 866-7329
Henderson S 5-8
16101 W Chicago St 48228 313-852-0512
Clara Flowers, prin. Fax 852-0523
Hutchins MS 500/5-8
8820 Woodrow Wilson St 48206 313-873-2777
Dr. Virginia Clay, prin. Fax 873-1068
Joy MS 700/6-8
4611 Fairview St 48214 313-866-9900
Deborah Hurst, prin. Fax 866-9898
Kettering HS 1,400/9-12
6101 Van Dyke St 48213 313-866-5336
Ms. Willie Howard, prin. Fax 852-9615
King HS 2,000/9-12
3200 E Lafayette St 48207 313-494-7373
Paul Gray, prin. Fax 494-7359
Lessenger MS 700/6-8
8401 Trinity St 48228 313-945-1330
Eric George, prin. Fax 945-1557
Longfellow MS 500/6-8
13141 Rosa Parks Blvd 48238 313-852-1575
Bettie Ried, prin. Fax 852-1599
Ludington Magnet MS 600/5-8
19355 Edinborough Rd 48219 313-494-7549
Jennifer Shelton, prin. Fax 494-7707
MacKenzie HS 1,600/9-12
9275 Wyoming St 48204 313-873-9900
Bernard Bonam, prin. Fax 873-9930
McNair MS 700/6-8
4180 Marlborough St 48215 313-417-8790
John White, prin. Fax 417-8796
Miller MS 700/6-9
2322 Dubois St 48207 313-494-2642
Sharon Dennis, prin. Fax 494-7351
Mumford HS 2,100/9-12
17525 Wyoming St 48221 313-494-7064
Linda S. Spight, prin. Fax 494-7124
Munger MS 700/6-8
5525 Martin St 48210 313-596-3565
Sharon Robinson, prin. Fax 596-3561
Murray-Wright HS 1,400/9-12
2001 W Warren Ave 48208 313-596-3555
Grady Jones, prin. Fax 596-3552
Nolan MS 700/6-8
1150 E Lantz St 48203 313-866-7730
Daryl McDuffie, prin. Fax 866-7725
Northern HS 1,100/9-12
9026 Woodward Ave 48202 313-873-1250
Dr. Marvin Youmans, prin. Fax 873-1290
Northwestern HS 1,300/9-12
2200 W Grand Blvd 48208 313-596-0700
Patricia Pickett, prin. Fax 596-0710
Osborn HS 2,000/9-12
11600 E 7 Mile Rd 48205 313-866-0343
Matthew Dixon, prin. Fax 866-0356
Pershing HS 2,000/9-12
18875 Ryan Rd 48234 313-866-7700
Dr. Deborah Jenkins, prin. Fax 866-3296
Phoenix Multicultural Academy 500/6-8
7735 Lane St 48209 313-849-2419
Anna Rodriguez, prin. Fax 849-1170
Randolph Career and Technical Center Vo/Tech
17101 Hubbell St 48235 313-494-7100
Joseph W. Smith, prin. Fax 494-7114
Redford HS 1,700/9-12
21431 Grand River Ave 48219 313-494-7500
Garnet Green, prin. Fax 494-7511
Renaissance HS 900/9-12
6565 W Outer Dr 48235 313-416-4600
Deborah Harley, prin. Fax 416-4620
Robinson MS 600/6-8
13000 Essex Ave 48215 313-866-5500
Sharon Lee, prin. Fax 866-5580
Ruddiman MS 500/6-8
7350 Southfield Fwy 48228 313-271-0120
Anthony Huston, prin. Fax 271-0979
Scott MS 900/6-8
18400 Hoover St 48205 313-866-6700
Beverly Butler, prin. Fax 866-2693

Southeastern HS 1,900/9-12
2962 Fairview St 48214 313-866-4500
Brenda Gatlin, prin. Fax 866-5555
Southwestern HS 900/9-12
6921 W Fort St 48209 313-849-4521
Robert Hodge, prin. Fax 849-4734
Taft MS 700/6-8
19501 Berg Rd 48219 313-494-7577
Naomi Lewis, prin. Fax 494-7538
Western International HS 1,400/9-12
1500 Scotten St 48209 313-849-4758
Rebecca Luna, prin. Fax 849-4695
Other Schools – See Redford

Al-Ikhlas Training Academy 200/K-12
1201 E Grand Blvd 48211 313-925-0880
Nadir Ahmad, prin. Fax 925-8032
College for Creative Studies Post-Sec.
201 E Kirby St 48202 313-664-7400
Cornerstone S - Nevada MS 200/6-8
6861 E Nevada St 48234 313-892-1860
Dennis Wrosch, prin. Fax 892-1861
Detroit Health Department Post-Sec.
1151 Taylor St 48202 313-876-4090
Detroit Urban Lutheran S 300/K-12
8181 Greenfield Rd 48228 313-582-9900
R. David Siefker, prin. Fax 582-0817
DMC University Laboratories Post-Sec.
4201 Saint Antoine St 48201 313-745-3053
Everest Institute Post-Sec.
300 River Place Dr Ste 1000 48207 313-567-5350
Grace Hospital Post-Sec.
6071 W Outer Dr 48235 313-966-3525
Harper Hospital Post-Sec.
3990 John R St 48201 313-745-9375
Henry Ford Hospital Post-Sec.
2799 W Grand Blvd 48202 313-876-1257
Lewis College of Business Post-Sec.
17370 Meyers Rd 48235 313-862-6300
Loyola HS 200/9-12
15325 Pinehurst St 48238 313-861-2407
DeLisa Jones, prin. Fax 861-4718
Marygrove College Post-Sec.
8425 W McNichols Rd 48221 313-927-1200
Michigan Barber School Post-Sec.
8988 Grand River Ave # 90 48204 313-894-2300
Sacred Heart Major Seminary Post-Sec.
2701 W Chicago 48206 313-883-8500
St. John's Hospital Post-Sec.
22101 Moross Rd 48236 313-343-7531
SER Business and Technical Institute Post-Sec.
9301 Michigan Ave 48210 313-846-2240
University of Detroit/Jesuit HS 900/7-12
8400 S Cambridge Ave 48221 313-862-5400
Susan Rowe, prin. Fax 862-3299
University of Detroit-Mercy Post-Sec.
4001 W McNichols Rd 48221 313-993-1000
Wayne County Community College Post-Sec.
801 W Fort St 48226 313-496-2500
Wayne State University Post-Sec.
5980 Cass Ave 48202 313-577-2424
Westside Christian Academy 100/PK-12
9540 Bramell 48239 313-255-5760
Daryl Ounanian, prin. Fax 255-0809

De Witt, Clinton, Pop. 4,499
DeWitt SD 2,800/K-12
PO Box 800, 517-668-3000
Tina Templin, supt. Fax 668-3018
www.dewitt.edzone.net
DeWitt JHS 400/7-8
PO Box 800, 517-668-3200
Neil Hufnagel, prin. Fax 668-3255
Other Schools – See Lansing

Dexter, Washtenaw, Pop. 3,198
Dexter Community SD 3,500/K-12
7714 Ann Arbor St 48130 734-424-4100
Evelynn Shirk, supt. Fax 424-4112
www.dexter.k12.mi.us
Dexter HS 1,100/9-12
2200 N Parker Rd 48130 734-424-4240
Kit Moran, prin. Fax 424-2747
Mill Creek MS 600/7-8
7305 Dexter Ann Arbor Rd 48130 734-424-4150
Jami Bronson, prin. Fax 424-4159

Dollar Bay, Houghton
Dollar Bay-Tamarack City SD 300/K-12
PO Box 371 49922 906-482-5800
Jan Quarless, supt. Fax 487-5931
www.dollarbay.k12.mi.us
Dollar Bay JSHS 100/7-12
PO Box 371 49922 906-482-5812
William Tarbox, prin. Fax 487-5940

Douglas, Allegan, Pop. 1,196
Saugatuck SD 700/PK-12
PO Box 818 49406 269-857-1444
Timothy Wood, supt. Fax 857-1448
www.saugatuck.k12.mi.us
Other Schools – See Saugatuck

Dowagiac, Cass, Pop. 5,955
Dowagiac UNSD 2,700/PK-12
206 Main St 49047 269-782-4400
Peg Stowers, supt. Fax 782-3152
www.dowagiacschools.org
Dowagiac MS 400/7-8
57072 Riverside Dr 49047 269-782-4440
Michael Frazier, prin. Fax 782-4449
Union HS 700/9-12
701 W Prairie Ronde St 49047 269-782-4420
Paul Hartsig, prin. Fax 782-9518

Southwestern Michigan College Post-Sec.
58900 Cherry Grove Rd 49047 269-782-1000

Dryden, Lapeer, Pop. 813
Dryden Community SD 800/K-12
3866 Rochester Rd 48428 810-796-9534
Thomas J. Goulette, supt. Fax 796-3698
www.dryden.k12.mi.us
Dryden JSHS 400/7-12
3866 Rochester Rd 48428 810-796-2266
Ruth Fox, prin. Fax 796-2510

Dundee, Monroe, Pop. 3,892
Dundee Community SD 1,700/PK-12
420 Ypsilanti St 48131 734-529-2350
John Raab, supt. Fax 529-5606
www.dundee.k12.mi.us
Dundee HS 500/9-12
130 Viking Dr 48131 734-529-7008
Jacqueline Schultz, prin. Fax 529-7053
Dundee MS 500/5-8
420 Ypsilanti St 48131 734-529-2350
John Krimmel, prin. Fax 529-5606

Durand, Shiawassee, Pop. 3,868
Durand Area SD 1,700/PK-12
310 N Saginaw St 48429 989-288-2681
Dr. Jan Amsterburg, supt. Fax 288-3553
durand.k12.mi.us/
Durand Area HS 600/9-12
9575 E Monroe Rd 48429 989-288-2684
Lyle Thomas, prin. Fax 288-2986
Durand MS 500/6-8
9550 E Lansing Rd 48429 989-288-3435
Adam Neisler, prin. Fax 288-5563

East China, Saint Clair, Pop. 3,216
East China SD 5,400/K-12
1585 Meisner Rd 48054 810-676-1018
Rodney Green, supt. Fax 676-1037
www.ecsd.us
Other Schools – See Marine City, Saint Clair

East Jordan, Charlevoix, Pop. 2,338
East Jordan SD 1,300/K-12
PO Box 399 49727 231-536-0053
Robert Hansen, supt. Fax 536-3310
www.ejps.org/
East Jordan HS 400/9-12
PO Box 399 49727 231-536-2259
Tammy Jackson, prin. Fax 536-3536
East Jordan MS 300/6-8
PO Box 399 49727 231-536-2823
Michael Haynes, prin. Fax 536-0051

East Lansing, Ingham, Pop. 46,419
East Lansing SD 3,500/K-12
841 Timberlane St Ste A 48823 517-333-7420
David Chapin, supt. Fax 333-7470
www.elps.k12.mi.us
East Lansing HS 1,100/9-12
509 Burcham Dr 48823 517-333-7539
Paula Steele, prin. Fax 333-7513
MacDonald MS 600/7-8
1601 Burcham Dr 48823 517-333-7600
Debra Auge, prin. Fax 333-5098

Career Quest Learning Center Post-Sec.
5000 Northwind Dr Ste 120 48823 517-318-3330
Douglas J Educational Center Post-Sec.
333 Albert Ave Ste 110 48823 517-333-9656
Lakeside Christian S 100/PK-12
7868 E M 78 48823 517-339-1037
Treila Jill Friar, dir. Fax 339-0103
MI State Univ. - Detroit College of Law Post-Sec.
230 Law College Bldg 48824 517-432-0222
Michigan State University Post-Sec.
250 Administration Bldg 48824 517-355-1855

Eastpointe, Macomb, Pop. 33,180
East Detroit SD 5,800/K-12
15115 Deerfield Ave 48021 586-445-4400
Bruce Kefgen, supt. Fax 445-4427
www.eastdetroit.org
East Detroit HS 1,700/9-12
15501 Couzens Ave 48021 586-445-4455
Paul Szymanski, prin. Fax 445-4522
Kelly MS 800/6-8
24701 Kelly Rd 48021 586-445-4570
Ira Hamden, prin. Fax 445-4582
Oakwood MS 700/6-8
14825 Nehls Ave 48021 586-445-4600
Sam Ellis, prin. Fax 445-4612
Kellwood S Adult
19200 Stephens Dr 48021 586-445-4451
Robin White, admin. Fax 445-4450

Eaton Rapids, Eaton, Pop. 5,266
Eaton Rapids SD 3,000/K-12
501 King St 48827 517-663-8155
William DeFrance, supt. Fax 663-2236
www.erps.k12.mi.us
Eaton Rapids HS 1,000/9-12
800 State St 48827 517-663-2231
David Johnson, prin. Fax 663-0616
Eaton Rapids MS 500/7-8
815 Greyhound Dr 48827 517-663-8151
Stephen Dembowski, prin. Fax 663-0625

Eau Claire, Berrien, Pop. 643
Eau Claire SD 800/K-12
PO Box 398 49111 269-461-6947
D. Stefan Jaggi, supt. Fax 461-0089
www.eauclairepublicschools.com/
Eau Claire HS 300/9-12
7450 Hochberger Rd 49111 269-461-6997
Mark Costello, prin. Fax 461-0065
Eau Claire MS 100/6-8
7450 Hochberger Rd 49111 269-461-0083
Chris Porter, prin. Fax 461-0065

Eben Junction, Alger
Superior Central SD 400/K-12
PO Box 148 49825 906-439-5531
Mary Kay Wanska, supt. Fax 439-5734
superiorcentralschools.org/
Superior Central S 400/K-12
PO Box 148 49825 906-439-5532
William Saunders, prin. Fax 439-5234

Ecorse, Wayne, Pop. 10,757
Ecorse SD 900/PK-12
4024 W Jefferson Ave 48229 313-294-4750
Emma Epps, supt. Fax 294-4769
www.resa.net/ecorse/
Ecorse Community HS 500/8-12
27385 W Outer Dr 48229 313-294-4700
Stan Childress, prin. Fax 294-4709

Edmore, Montcalm, Pop. 1,258
Montabella Community SD 900/PK-12
PO Box 349 48829 989-427-5148
Ronald Farrell, supt. Fax 427-3828
www.montabella.com
Other Schools – See Blanchard

Edwardsburg, Cass, Pop. 1,114
Edwardsburg SD 2,300/K-12
69410 Section St 49112 269-663-3055
Sherman Ostrander, supt. Fax 663-6485
www.edwardsburgpublicschools.org/
Edwardsburg HS 700/9-12
69410 Section St 49112 269-663-1044
David Zech, prin. Fax 663-8915
Edwardsburg MS 600/6-8
69410 Section St 49112 269-663-1031
Anthony Koontz, prin. Fax 663-8638

Elk Rapids, Antrim, Pop. 1,710
Elk Rapids SD 1,500/K-12
707 E 3rd St 49629 231-264-8692
Jon Hoover, supt. Fax 264-6538
www.erschools.com
Cherryland MS 300/6-8
707 E 3rd St 49629 231-264-8991
Terry Morris, prin. Fax 264-9370
Elk Rapids HS 500/9-12
308 Meguzee Pt 49629 231-264-8108
Steven Gallagher, prin. Fax 264-0895

Ellsworth, Antrim, Pop. 466
Ellsworth Community SD 200/K-12
9467 Park St 49729 231-588-2544
Patrick Bootz, supt. Fax 588-6183
www.ellsworth.k12.mi.us/
Ellsworth Community S 200/K-12
9467 Park St 49729 231-588-2544
Patrick Bootz, prin. Fax 588-6183

Elsie, Clinton, Pop. 1,005
Ovid-Elsie Area SD 1,800/K-12
8989 E Colony Rd 48831 989-834-2271
Wayne Petroelje, supt. Fax 862-5887
www.oe.k12.mi.us/
Ovid-Elsie HS 500/9-12
8989 E Colony Rd 48831 989-834-2271
Kirk Baese, prin. Fax 862-4463
Ovid-Elsie MS 300/7-8
8989 E Colony Rd 48831 989-834-2271
Jerry Goosen, prin. Fax 862-4463

Engadine, Mackinac
Engadine Consolidated SD 300/K-12
W13920 Melville St 49827 906-477-6313
Stu Hobbs, supt. Fax 477-6643
www.eup.k12.mi.us/engadine
Engadine JSHS 100/7-12
W13920 Melville St 49827 906-477-6449
Stu Hobbs, prin. Fax 477-6643

Erie, Monroe
Mason Consolidated SD 1,400/PK-12
2400 Mason Eagle Dr 48133 734-848-5475
Marlene Mills, supt. Fax 848-2516
scnc.eriemason.k12.mi.us/
Mason HS 500/9-12
2400 Mason Eagle Dr 48133 734-848-5755
Thomas McGarry, prin. Fax 848-5425
Mason MS 400/6-8
2260 Samaria Rd 48133 734-848-4944
Tom McGarry, prin. Fax 848-0035

Escanaba, Delta, Pop. 12,679
Escanaba Area SD 2,900/K-12
1500 Ludington St 49829 906-786-5411
Thomas Smith, supt. Fax 786-0106
www.escanabaschool.com
Escanaba HS 1,100/9-12
500 S Lincoln Rd 49829 906-786-6521
Gerald Kulbertis, prin. Fax 786-2166
Escanaba MS 500/7-8
1500 Ludington St 49829 906-786-7462
Catherine Johnson, prin. Fax 786-5958

Bay de Noc Community College Post-Sec.
2001 N Lincoln Rd 49829 906-786-5802
U.P. Academy of Hair Design Post-Sec.
1625 Sheridan Rd 49829 906-786-5750

Essexville, Bay, Pop. 3,590
Essexville-Hampton SD 1,400/K-12
303 Pine St 48732 989-894-9700
Corinne Netzley, supt. Fax 894-9705
www.e-hps.net
Cramer JHS 500/6-8
313 Pine St 48732 989-894-9740
James Glasgow, prin. Fax 894-9720
Garber HS 600/9-12
213 Pine St 48732 989-894-9710
Doug Trombley, prin. Fax 894-9730

Evart, Osceola, Pop. 1,734
Evart SD 1,200/K-12
PO Box 917 49631 231-734-5594
Howard Hyde, supt. Fax 734-2931
www.evart.k12.mi.us/
Evart HS 400/9-12
6221 95th Ave 49631 231-734-5551
Alan Kullman, prin. Fax 734-4156
Evart MS 400/5-8
321 N Hemlock St 49631 231-734-4222
Sue Lenahan, prin. Fax 734-2931

Ewen, Ontonagon
Ewen-Trout Creek SD 300/K-12
14312 Airport Rd 49925 906-988-2350
Catherine Shamion, supt. Fax 988-2549
www.etc.k12.mi.us/
Ewen-Trout Creek JSHS 200/7-12
14312 Airport Rd 49925 906-988-2365
Lee Lindberg, prin. Fax 988-2864

Fairgrove, Tuscola, Pop. 619
Akron-Fairgrove SD 400/K-12
PO Box 217 48733 989-693-6163
Joe Candela, supt. Fax 693-6560
www.a-f.k12.mi.us
Akron-Fairgrove JSHS 200/7-12
PO Box 217 48733 989-693-6112
John Amend, prin. Fax 693-6160

Fair Haven, Saint Clair, Pop. 1,505
Anchor Bay SD
Supt. — See Casco
Anchor Bay HS 1,900/9-12
6319 County Line Rd 48023 586-648-2525
Judy Stefanac, prin. Fax 716-8306

Fairview, Oscoda
Fairview Area SD 300/K-12
1879 E Miller Rd 48621 989-848-7000
Bruce Nelson, supt. Fax 848-7070
www.fairview.k12.mi.us
Fairview JSHS 100/7-12
1879 E Miller Rd 48621 989-848-7050
Raymond Poellet, prin. Fax 848-7073

Farmington, Oakland, Pop. 10,035
Farmington SD 11,600/PK-12
32500 Shiawassee Rd 48336 248-489-3349
Susan Zurralec, supt. Fax 489-3348
www.farmington.k12.mi.us
Farmington HS 1,400/9-12
32000 Shiawassee Rd 48336 248-489-3455
John Barrett, prin. Fax 489-3474
Other Schools – See Farmington Hills

Mercy HS 800/9-12
29300 W 11 Mile Rd 48336 248-476-8020
Caroline Witte, prin. Fax 476-3691

Farmington Hills, Oakland, Pop. 80,223
Farmington SD
Supt. — See Farmington
Dunckel MS 700/6-8
32800 W 12 Mile Rd 48334 248-489-3577
Allen Archer, prin. Fax 489-3590
East MS 800/6-8
25000 Middlebelt Rd 48336 248-489-3601
Ken Sanders, prin. Fax 489-3606
Harrison HS 1,200/9-12
29995 W 12 Mile Rd 48334 248-489-3499
Jim Myers, prin. Fax 489-3514
North Farmington HS 1,400/9-12
32900 W 13 Mile Rd 48334 248-785-2005
Richard Jones, prin. Fax 855-2060
Power MS 700/6-8
34740 Rhonswood St 48335 248-489-3622
Robert Kovar, prin. Fax 489-3628
Warner MS 600/6-8
30303 W 14 Mile Rd 48334 248-785-2030
Mildred Crawley Taylor, prin. Fax 855-2831
Farmington Community S Adult
30415 Shiawassee Rd 48336 248-489-3333
Pat Karas, prin. Fax 489-3380

Michigan Sch of Professional Psychology Post-Sec.
26811 Orchard Lake Rd 48334 248-476-1122
Oakland Community College Post-Sec.
27055 Orchard Lake Rd 48334 248-522-3400

Farwell, Clare, Pop. 850
Farwell Area SD 1,600/K-12
371 E Main St 48622 989-588-9917
David Peterson, supt. Fax 588-6440
Farwell HS 500/9-12
399 E Michigan St 48622 989-588-9913
Phyllis Hall, prin. Fax 588-6041
Farwell MS 500/5-8
500 E Ohio St 48622 989-588-9915
Catheryn Gross, prin. Fax 588-3337

Felch, Dickinson
North Dickinson County SD 400/K-12
W6588 State Highway M69 49831 906-542-9281
Claude Siders, supt. Fax 542-6950
www.go-nordics.com
North Dickinson S 400/K-12
W6588 State Highway M69 49831 906-542-9281
Dan Nurmi, prin. Fax 542-6950

Fennville, Allegan, Pop. 1,446
Fennville SD 1,400/K-12
5 Memorial Dr 49408 269-561-7331
Mark Dobias, supt. Fax 561-5792
www.fennvilleschools.org/
Fennville HS 400/9-12
4 Memorial Dr 49408 269-561-7241
Amber Lugten, prin. Fax 561-6901
Fennville MS 300/6-8
1 Memorial Dr 49408 269-561-7341
Jody Martin, prin. Fax 561-2143
Pearl Alternative & Adult Education Ctr Adult
5 Memorial Dr 49408 269-561-2343
Dave Coffindaffer, dir. Fax 561-8630

Fenton, Genesee, Pop. 11,946
Fenton Area SD 3,700/K-12
3100 Owen Rd 48430 810-591-4701
Peggy Yates, supt. Fax 591-4705
www.fenton.k12.mi.us
Fenton HS 1,200/9-12
3200 W Shiawassee Ave 48430 810-591-2600
Mark Suchowski, prin. Fax 591-2605
Schmidt MS 600/7-8
3255 Donaldson Dr 48430 810-591-7700
Kevin Cornell, prin. Fax 591-7705

Lake Fenton Community SD 1,000/K-12
11425 Torrey Rd 48430 810-591-2532
Ralph Coaster, supt. Fax 591-9866
lake-fenton.k12.mi.us
Lake Fenton MS 6-8
11425 Torrey Rd 48430 810-591-2209
Nancy Harrison, prin. Fax 591-8475
Other Schools – See Linden

Charles Stewart Mott Community College Post-Sec.
2100 W Thompson Rd 48430 810-762-0200

Ferndale, Oakland, Pop. 21,460
Ferndale SD 2,700/PK-12
2920 Burdette St 48220 248-586-8652
Gary Meier, supt. Fax 586-8655
www.ferndaleschools.org
Ferndale HS 1,100/9-12
881 Pinecrest Dr 48220 248-548-8621
Herb Ivory, prin. Fax 586-8620
Ferndale MS 600/7-8
725 Pinecrest Dr 48220 248-586-8830
Dawn Warren, prin. Fax 586-8834
University HS Vo/Tech
1244 Paxton St 48220 248-586-8846
George Tomey, prin. Fax 586-8857
Taft Education Center Adult
427 Allen St 48220 248-586-8916
Fran Foote, dir. Fax 586-8909
Other Schools – See Oak Park

Virginia Farrell Beauty School Post-Sec.
22925 Woodward Ave 48220 248-398-4647

Fife Lake, Grand Traverse, Pop. 466
Forest Area Community SD 900/K-12
7741 Shippy Rd SW 49633 231-369-4191
Matthew Cairy, supt. Fax 369-4153
www.forestarea.k12.mi.us
Forest Area HS 300/9-12
7661 W Shippy Rd SW 49633 231-369-2884
M.J. Grajewski, prin. Fax 369-3646
Forest Area MS 200/6-8
7661 W Shippy Rd SW 49633 231-369-2867
M.J. Grajewski, prin. Fax 369-3618

Flat Rock, Wayne, Pop. 9,560
Flat Rock Community SD 1,800/K-12
28639 Division St 48134 734-782-2451
John Dardzinski, supt. Fax 782-9665
www.flatrockschools.org
Flat Rock HS 500/9-12
25600 Seneca St 48134 734-782-1270
Mary Ann Perttunen, prin. Fax 782-2509
Simpson MS 400/6-8
24900 Meadows Ave 48134 734-782-2453
Blaine Armstrong, prin. Fax 782-0812

Flint, Genesee, Pop. 118,551
Beecher Community SD 1,700/PK-12
1020 W Coldwater Rd 48505 810-591-9200
Forrest Gunderson, supt. Fax 591-5755
www.beecherschools.org/
Other Schools – See Mount Morris

Carman-Ainsworth Community SD 4,800/K-12
G3475 W Court St 48532 810-591-3700
William Haley, supt. Fax 591-3323
www.carman.k12.mi.us
Carman-Ainsworth HS 1,600/9-12
1300 N Linden Rd 48532 810-591-3240
Steve Tunnicliff, prin. Fax 591-3215
Carman-Ainsworth JHS 1,000/6-8
1409 W Maple Ave 48507 810-591-3500
Kevin Summey, prin. Fax 591-3594

Flint Community SD 14,100/PK-12
923 E Kearsley St 48503 810-760-1000
Dr. Walter Milton, supt. Fax 760-6790
www.flintschools.org
Central Academy 800/10-12
601 Crapo St 48503 810-760-1042
Maria Boyd-Springer, prin. Fax 760-7671
Flint Northern HS 700/10-12
G3284 Mackin Rd 48504 810-760-1740
Fred White, prin. Fax 760-5009
Genessee Area Skill Ctr Vo/Tech
G5081 Torrey Rd 48507 810-760-1444
Doug Weir, prin. Fax 760-7759
Holmes Gender Based Academy 500/7-9
6602 Oxley Dr 48504 810-760-1620
Cheryl Adkins, prin. Fax 760-5346
Northwestern Academy 300/10-12
G2138 W Carpenter Rd 48505 810-760-1780
Cheryl Tate, prin. Fax 760-6809
Southwestern Academy 600/10-12
1420 W 12th St 48507 810-760-1400
Corinne Archie-Edwards, prin. Fax 760-7772
Whittier Classical Academy 700/7-9
701 Crapo St 48503 810-760-1175
Sandra Morgan-Jones, prin. Fax 760-5175
Mott Adult HS Adult
2421 Corunna Rd 48503 810-760-7723
George Barker, prin. Fax 760-1945

Kearsley Community SD 3,700/PK-12
4396 Underhill Dr 48506 810-591-8000
Jeffry Morgan, supt. Fax 591-8421
www.kearsley.k12.mi.us
Armstrong MS 900/6-8
6161 Hopkins Rd 48506 810-591-9929
Patti Yorks, prin. Fax 591-9944
Kearsley HS 1,200/9-12
4302 Underhill Dr 48506 810-591-8000
Kevin Walworth, prin. Fax 591-9883

Westwood Heights SD 1,200/PK-12
3484 N Jennings Rd 48504 810-591-0870
John McEwan, supt. Fax 591-0898
www.hamadyhawks.net
Hamady HS 400/9-12
3223 W Carpenter Rd 48504 810-591-0890
Keely Mounger, prin. Fax 591-5140
Hamady MS 200/6-8
3223 W Carpenter Rd 48504 810-591-0895
Keely Mounger, prin. Fax 591-5140

Baker College of Flint Post-Sec.
1050 W Bristol Rd 48507 810-767-4000
Charles Stewart Mott Community College Post-Sec.
1401 E Court St 48503 810-762-0200
Flint Institute of Barbering Post-Sec.
3214 Flushing Rd 48504 810-232-4711
Hurley Medical Center Post-Sec.
701 W 8th Ave 48503 810-257-9237
Kettering University Post-Sec.
1700 W 3rd Ave 48504 810-762-9500
Michigan School for the Blind Post-Sec.
1301 W Court St 48503 810-257-1400
Mr. David's School of Cosmetolgy Post-Sec.
3600 S Dort Hwy 48507 810-742-9010
Powers HS 700/9-12
G2040 W Carpenter Rd 48505 810-591-4741
Thomas Furnas, prin. Fax 591-0383
Ross Medical Education Center Post-Sec.
1036 Gilbert St 48532 810-230-1100
University of Michigan-Flint Post-Sec.
303 E Kearsley St 48502 810-762-3000

Flushing, Genesee, Pop. 8,110
Flushing Community SD 4,500/PK-12
522 N McKinley Rd 48433 810-591-1180
Barbara Goebel, supt. Fax 591-0656
www.flushing.k12.mi.us
Flushing HS 1,400/9-12
5039 Deland Rd 48433 810-591-3770
Gary Whitmire, prin. Fax 591-0693
Flushing MS 800/7-8
8100 Carpenter Rd 48433 810-591-2800
Rita Brust, prin. Fax 591-0148

Fort Gratiot, Saint Clair, Pop. 8,968
Port Huron Area SD
Supt. — See Port Huron
Fort Gratiot MS 700/6-8
3985 Keewahdin Rd 48059 810-984-6544
Debra Ladensack, prin. Fax 385-1624

Fowler, Clinton, Pop. 1,081
Fowler SD 500/PK-12
PO Box 408 48835 989-593-2296
Scott Koenigsknecht, supt. Fax 593-2125
www.fps.k12.mi.us
Fowler HS 200/9-12
PO Box 407 48835 989-593-2250
Daymond Grifka, prin. Fax 593-2358

Most Holy Trinity MS 100/4-8
11144 W Kent St 48835 989-593-2616
Anne Hufnagel, prin. Fax 593-2801

Fowlerville, Livingston, Pop. 3,132
Fowlerville Community SD 2,900/K-12
PO Box 769 48836 517-223-6000
Ed Alverson, supt. Fax 223-6022
www.fvl.k12.mi.us
Fowlerville HS 700/9-12
700 N Grand Ave 48836 517-223-6002
Wayne Roedel, prin. Fax 223-6065
Fowlerville JHS 500/7-8
7677 W Sharpe Rd 48836 517-223-6003
Tom Tannar, prin. Fax 223-6199

Frankenmuth, Saginaw, Pop. 4,803
Frankenmuth SD 1,300/K-12
941 E Genesee St 48734 989-652-9958
Mary Anne Ackerman, supt. Fax 652-9780
www.frankenmuth.k12.mi.us/
Frankenmuth HS 600/9-12
525 E Genesee St 48734 989-652-9955
Donald Zoller, prin. Fax 652-7253
Rittmueller MS 300/5-8
965 E Genesee St 48734 989-652-6119
Martin Mattlin, prin. Fax 652-2921

Frankfort, Benzie, Pop. 1,493
Frankfort-Elberta Area SD 600/K-12
534 11th St 49635 231-352-4641
Thomas Stobie, supt. Fax 352-5066
www.frankfort.k12.mi.us
Frankfort JSHS 300/7-12
534 11th St 49635 231-352-4781
Matt Stapleton, prin. Fax 352-6501

Fraser, Macomb, Pop. 15,095
Fraser SD 5,100/PK-12
33466 Garfield Rd 48026 586-293-5100
Richard Repicky, supt. Fax 293-0480
www.macomb.k12.mi.us/fraser/schfras.htm
Fraser HS 1,600/9-12
34270 Garfield Rd 48026 586-879-2000
Dr. David Richards, prin. Fax 293-1953
Richards MS 800/7-8
33500 Garfield Rd 48026 586-294-5720
Jeffrey Wood, prin. Fax 294-1678

Freeland, Saginaw, Pop. 1,421
Freeland Community SD 1,700/K-12
710 Powley Dr 48623 989-695-5527
Allen Veenkant, supt. Fax 695-5789
www.freeland.k12.mi.us
Freeland HS 500/9-12
8250 Webster Rd 48623 989-695-2586
Jon Good, prin. Fax 695-8022
Freeland MS 300/7-8
8250 Webster Rd 48623 989-692-4032
Christopher Arrington, prin. Fax 692-4034

Free Soil, Mason, Pop. 180
Freesoil Community SD 100/K-12
8480 N Democrat St 49411 231-464-5651
Ronald Nurnberger, supt. Fax 464-5337
Freesoil Community JSHS 100/7-12
8480 N Democrat St 49411 231-464-5651
Ronald Nurnberger, prin. Fax 464-5337

Fremont, Newaygo, Pop. 4,256
Fremont SD 2,500/K-12
220 W Pine St 49412 231-924-2350
John D. Kingsnorth Ph.D., supt. Fax 924-5264
www.fremont.net
Fremont HS 800/9-12
204 E Main St 49412 231-924-5300
Thomas Palmer, prin. Fax 924-9262
Fremont MS 600/6-8
500 Woodrow St 49412 231-924-0230
Carolyn Hummel, prin. Fax 924-9149

Newaygo County RESA 100/
4747 W 48th St 49412 231-924-0381
Robert E. DeVries, supt. Fax 924-8910
www.ncresa.org/
Newaygo County Career-Tech Center Vo/Tech
4645 W 48th St 49412 231-924-0380
Kirk Wyers, dir.

Providence Christian HS 100/9-12
5479 W 72nd St 49412 231-924-9780
Louis Meeuenberg, admin. Fax 924-1676

Fruitport, Muskegon, Pop. 1,087
Fruitport Community SD 3,100/PK-12
3255 Pontaluna Rd 49415 231-865-4100
Nicholas Ceglarek, supt. Fax 865-3393
www.fruitportschools.net
Fruitport HS 1,000/9-12
357 N 6th Ave 49415 231-865-3101
Jeffery Haase, prin. Fax 865-6351
Fruitport MS 700/6-8
3113 Pontaluna Rd 49415 231-865-3128
James Reinhart, prin. Fax 865-4086

Calvary Christian S 300/PK-12
5873 Kendra Rd 49415 231-865-2141
Tom Kapanka, admin. Fax 865-8730

Galesburg, Kalamazoo, Pop. 1,926
Galesburg-Augusta Community SD 1,300/PK-12
1076 N 37th St 49053 269-484-2000
Eric Palmu, supt. Fax 484-2001
www.gacsnet.org
Galesburg-Augusta HS 400/9-12
1076 N 37th St 49053 269-484-2010
Todd Reynolds, prin. Fax 484-2011
Other Schools – See Augusta

Galien, Berrien, Pop. 578
Galien Township SD 200/PK-8
PO Box 248 49113 269-545-3364
Marilyn Tilmann, supt. Fax 545-2483
www.remc11.k12.mi.us./galien
Galien MS 50/6-8
PO Box 248 49113 269-545-3365
Marilyn Tilmann, prin. Fax 545-2483

Garden City, Wayne, Pop. 28,960
Garden City SD 4,600/K-12
1333 Radcliff St 48135 734-762-8300
Richard Witkowski, supt. Fax 762-8530
www.resa.net/gardencity/
Garden City HS 1,500/9-12
6500 Middlebelt Rd 48135 734-762-8350
Jerry Perttunen, prin. Fax 762-8531
Garden City MS 800/7-8
1851 Radcliff St 48135 734-762-8400
Brian Sumner, prin. Fax 762-8532
Cambridge Center Adult
28901 Cambridge St 48135 734-762-8430
Jack Pelon, prin. Fax 762-8534

United Christian S 100/PK-12
29205 Florence St 48135 734-522-6487
Roger Stombaugh, prin. Fax 522-3020

Gaylord, Otsego, Pop. 3,730
Gaylord Community SD 3,300/K-12
615 S Elm Ave 49735 989-705-3080
Cheryl Wojtas, supt. Fax 732-6029
www.gaylordschools.com
Gaylord HS 1,100/9-12
90 Livingston Blvd 49735 989-731-0969
Lori Pearson, prin. Fax 731-2585
Gaylord MS 600/7-8
600 E 5th St 49735 989-731-0848
Gerald Belanger, prin. Fax 732-2632

Grace Baptist Christian S 100/PK-12
PO Box 177 49734 989-731-1221
Robert Perrotti, prin. Fax 731-1122
St. Mary Cathedral S 400/PK-12
321 N Otsego Ave 49735 989-732-5801
Tom Saporito, prin. Fax 732-2085

Genesee, Genesee
Genesee SD 1,000/PK-12
PO Box 220 48437 810-591-1650
Mark Hilt, supt. Fax 591-1646
www.genesee.k12.mi.us
Genesee JSHS 500/7-12
7347 N Genesee Rd 48437 810-591-1450
Richard Carsten, prin. Fax 591-0302

Gibraltar, Wayne, Pop. 5,191
Gibraltar SD
Supt. — See Woodhaven
Carlson HS 900/9-12
30550 W Jefferson Ave 48173 734-379-7100
William Stevenson, prin. Fax 379-5444
Shumate MS 900/6-8
30550 W Jefferson Ave 48173 734-379-7600
Brad Coon, prin. Fax 379-2370

Gladstone, Delta, Pop. 5,255
Gladstone Area SD 1,700/K-12
400 S 10th St 49837 906-428-2417
Thomas Watson, supt. Fax 789-8457
www.gladstoneschools.com
Gladstone HS 600/9-12
2100 State Highway M35 49837 906-428-9200
Brady Downey, prin. Fax 789-8312
Gladstone MS 400/6-8
300 S 10th St 49837 906-428-2295
Dave Ballard, prin. Fax 789-8404

Gladwin, Gladwin, Pop. 3,018
Gladwin Community SD 2,000/K-12
1206 N Spring St 48624 989-426-9255
Rick W. Seebeck, supt. Fax 426-5981
www.gcsnet.org
Gladwin HS 700/9-12
1400 N Spring St 48624 989-426-7341
Patrick Dillon, prin. Fax 426-6031
Gladwin JHS 500/6-8
401 N Bowery Ave 48624 989-426-3808
Clair Wetmore, prin. Fax 426-6038

Skeels Christian S 100/PK-12
3956 N M 18 48624 989-426-2054
Rick Lopez, admin. Fax 426-2054

Glen Arbor, Leelanau

Leelanau S 100/9-12
1 Old Homestead Rd 49636 231-334-5800
Richard Odell, pres. Fax 334-5898

Gobles, Van Buren, Pop. 807
Gobles SD 1,100/K-12
PO Box 412 49055 269-628-5618
Scott Dunsmore, supt. Fax 628-5306
www.gobles.org/
Gobles HS 400/9-12
PO Box 412 49055 269-628-2113
Corey Harbaugh, prin. Fax 628-2748
Gobles MS 200/7-8
PO Box 412 49055 269-628-5680
Chris Miller, prin. Fax 628-5768

Gobles Jr. Academy 50/1-10
32110 6th Ave 49055 269-628-2704
Thomas Coffee, prin. Fax 628-7314

Goodrich, Genesee, Pop. 1,567
Goodrich Area SD 2,100/K-12
8029 Gale Rd 48438 810-591-2250
Kimberley A. Hart, supt. Fax 591-2550
www.goodrich.k12.mi.us/
Goodrich HS 700/9-12
8029 Gale Rd 48438 810-591-2251
David St. Aubin, prin. Fax 591-2234
Goodrich MS 500/6-8
7480 Gale Rd 48438 810-591-4210
Jerry Lawrason Ph.D., prin. Fax 636-7879

Grand Blanc, Genesee, Pop. 7,898
Grand Blanc Community SD 5,100/PK-12
11920 S Saginaw St 48439 810-591-6000
Dr. Michael Newton, supt. Fax 591-6018
www.grandblancschools.org
Grand Blanc HS 1,600/10-12
12500 Holly Rd 48439 810-591-6638
Jennifer Hammond, prin. Fax 591-6693
Grand Blanc HS West 9-9
1 Jewett Trl 48439 810-591-6350
Fax 591-6400
Grand Blanc MS East 6-8
6100 Perry Rd 48439 810-591-9632
Clarence Garner, prin. Fax 591-0242
Grand Blanc MS West 6-8
1515 E Reid Rd 48439 810-591-0556
Jeff Neall, prin. Fax 591-0182

Sharps Academy of Hairstyling Post-Sec.
8166 Holly Rd 48439 810-695-6742

Grand Haven, Ottawa, Pop. 10,586
Grand Haven Area SD 5,800/PK-12
1415 S Beechtree St 49417 616-850-5015
Keith Konarska, supt. Fax 850-5010
www.ghaps.org
Grand Haven HS 2,000/9-12
17001 Ferris St 49417 616-850-6000
Scott Grimes, prin. Fax 850-6010
Lakeshore MS 600/6-8
900 Cutler St 49417 616-850-6500
Julia Houle, prin. Fax 850-6510
White Pines MS 800/6-8
1400 S Griffin St 49417 616-850-6300
Mike Shelton, prin. Fax 850-6310

Grand Ledge, Eaton, Pop. 7,768
Grand Ledge SD 5,400/PK-12
220 Lamson St 48837 517-627-3241
Marsha Wells, supt. Fax 627-1767
www.glps.k12.mi.us/
Beagle MS 500/6-8
600 W South St 48837 517-627-4274
Charles Phillips, prin. Fax 622-1752
Grand Ledge HS 1,800/9-12
820 Spring St 48837 517-627-5194
Richard Pochert, prin. Fax 627-2591
Hayes MS 700/6-8
12620 Nixon Rd 48837 517-627-5080
Jill Mangrum, prin. Fax 622-1922

Grand Marais, Alger
Burt Township SD 100/K-12
PO Box 338 49839 906-494-2543
Thomas Scaife, supt. Fax 494-2522
Burt Township S 100/K-12
PO Box 338 49839 906-494-2521
Thomas Scaife, prin. Fax 494-2522

Grand Rapids, Kent, Pop. 193,780
East Grand Rapids SD 2,900/K-12
2915 Hall St SE 49506 616-235-3535
Dr. Sara Shubel, supt. Fax 235-6730
www.egrps.org/
East Grand Rapids HS 1,000/9-12
2211 Lake Dr SE 49506 616-235-7555
Patrick Cwayna, prin. Fax 235-7592
East Grand Rapids MS 700/6-8
2425 Lake Dr SE 49506 616-235-7551
J. Peter Stuursma, prin. Fax 235-7587

Forest Hills SD 9,400/K-12
6590 Cascade Rd SE 49546 616-493-8800
Daniel Behm, supt. Fax 493-8560
www.fhps.k12.mi.us
Forest Hills Central HS 1,300/9-12
5901 Hall St SE 49546 616-493-8700
Terry Urquhart, prin. Fax 493-8721
Forest Hills Northern HS 1,100/9-12
3801 Leonard St NE 49525 616-493-8600
Jon Gregory, prin. Fax 493-8644
Northern Hills MS 400/7-8
3775 Leonard St NE 49525 616-493-8650
Nancy Susterka, prin. Fax 493-8686
Other Schools – See Ada

Grand Rapids SD 19,600/PK-12
PO Box 117 49501 616-819-2000
Bernard Taylor Ed.D., supt. Fax 819-3480
www.grps.k12.mi.us
Alger MS 6-8
921 Alger St SE 49507 616-819-6200
Michael Ghareeb, prin. Fax 819-6201
Burton MS 600/6-8
2133 Buchanan Ave SW 49507 616-819-2269
Jesus Solis, prin. Fax 819-2282
Central HS 900/9-12
421 Fountain St NE 49503 616-819-2310
Ed Shalhoup, prin. Fax 819-2369
Creston HS 1,000/9-12
1720 Plainfield Ave NE 49505 616-819-2424
Kurt Johnson, prin. Fax 819-2427
Harrison MS 400/6-8
1440 Davis Ave NW 49504 616-819-2570
Gary Barton, prin. Fax 819-2571
Kent Vocational Options Vo/Tech
864 Crahen Ave NE 49525 616-819-2740
Karen Truax, prin. Fax 819-2747
Madison MS 6-8
1050 Iroquois Dr SE 49506 616-819-2640
Jackie Bell, prin. Fax 819-2660
Northwest Career Pathways Vo/Tech
1138 Pine Ave NW 49504 616-819-2702
Claude Presley, prin. Fax 819-2700
Ottawa Hills HS 1,200/9-12
2055 Rosewood Ave SE 49506 616-819-2900
Martha Williams, prin. Fax 819-2877
Riverside MS 400/7-8
265 Eleanor St NE 49505 616-819-2969
Michelle Ghareeb, prin. Fax 819-2981
Union HS 1,200/9-12
1800 Tremont Blvd NW 49504 616-819-3160
Janice Johnson, prin. Fax 819-3205
Westwood MS 600/6-8
1524 Mount Mercy Dr NW 49504 616-819-3322
Raul Ysasi, prin. Fax 819-3301
Adult Education - Vandenberg Adult
409 Lafayette Ave SE 49503 616-819-2734
Esther Kuiper, prin. Fax 819-3272

Kelloggsville SD 2,000/PK-12
242 52nd St SE 49548 616-538-7460
Samuel Wright, supt. Fax 530-8194
www.kelloggsville.k12.mi.us
Kelloggsville HS 500/9-12
23 Jean St SW 49548 616-532-1570
Mike Fine, prin. Fax 532-7780
Kelloggsville MS 500/6-8
4650 Division Ave S 49548 616-532-1575
Scott Gunn, prin. Fax 532-1579

Kenowa Hills SD 3,600/K-12
2325 4 Mile Rd NW 49544 616-784-2511
James Gillette, supt. Fax 784-8323
khps.org
Kenowa Hills HS 1,200/9-12
3825 Hendershot Ave NW 49544 616-784-2400
Peggy Mathis, prin. Fax 647-0149
Kenowa Hills MS 600/7-8
3950 Hendershot Ave NW 49544 616-785-3225
Ruth Posthumus, prin. Fax 784-2404

Northview SD 3,200/PK-12
4365 Hunsberger Ave NE 49525 616-363-6861
Michael Stearns, supt. Fax 363-9609
www.nvps.net
Crossroads MS 500/7-8
4400 Ambrose Ave NE 49525 616-361-3430
F. Andrew Scogg, prin. Fax 363-7868
Northview HS 1,200/9-12
4451 Hunsberger Ave NE 49525 616-363-4857
Mark Thomas, prin. Fax 361-3494

Aquinas College Post-Sec.
1607 Robinson Rd SE 49506 800-678-9593
Calvin College Post-Sec.
3201 Burton St SE 49546 616-957-6000
Calvin Theological Seminary Post-Sec.
3233 Burton St SE 49546 616-957-6036
Catholic Central HS 900/9-12
319 Sheldon Blvd SE 49503 616-233-5801
Steve Passinault, prin. Fax 459-0257
Chic University of Cosmetology Post-Sec.
1735 4 Mile Rd NE 49525 616-363-9853
Chic University of Cosmetology Post-Sec.
455 Standale Plz NW, 616-735-9680
Cornerstone University Post-Sec.
1001 E Beltline Ave NE 49525 616-949-5300
Covenant Christian HS 300/10-12
1401 Ferndale Ave SW, 616-453-5048
Richard Noorman, prin. Fax 453-4277
Davenport University Post-Sec.
6191 Kraft Ave SE 49512 866-383-3548
Grace Bible College Post-Sec.
PO Box 910 49509 800-968-1887
Grand Rapids Christian HS 1,100/9-12
2300 Plymouth Ave SE 49506 616-574-5500
Jim Primus, prin. Fax 241-3141
Grand Rapids Christian MS 300/6-8
1875 Rosewood Ave SE 49506 616-574-6350
Mary Broene, prin. Fax 574-6316
Grand Rapids Community College Post-Sec.
143 Bostwick Ave NE 49503 616-234-4000
Grand Rapids SDA Academy 200/K-12
1151 Oakleigh Rd NW 49504 616-791-9797
Debra Barr, prin. Fax 791-7242
ITT Technical Institute Post-Sec.
4020 Sparks Dr SE 49546 616-956-1060
Kendall College of Art & Design Post-Sec.
17 Fountain St NW 49503 616-451-2787
Kent Career/Technical Center Post-Sec.
1655 E Beltline Ave NE 49525 616-364-8421
Legacy Christian MS 200/6-8
67 68th St SW 49548 616-455-3860
Vince Bonnema, prin. Fax 455-1960
North Hills Classical Academy 100/K-12
2777 Knapp St NE 49525 616-365-0525
Peter VandeBrake, hdmstr. Fax 365-3683
NorthPointe Christian HS 400/7-12
3101 Leonard St NE 49525 616-942-0350
Bob Hoffman, prin. Fax 942-4647
Olympia Career Training Institute Post-Sec.
1750 Woodworth St NE 49525 616-364-8464
Plymouth Christian HS 200/7-12
965 Plymouth Ave NE 49505 616-454-9481
Laura Ash, prin. Fax 454-7243
Reformed Bible College Post-Sec.
3333 E Beltline Ave NE 49525 616-222-3000
Ross Medical Education Center Post-Sec.
2035 28th St SE Ste O 49508 616-243-3070
South Christian HS 800/9-12
160 68th St SW 49548 616-455-3210
Larry Plaisier, prin. Fax 455-8840
Spectrum Health Post-Sec.
100 Michigan St NE 49503 616-391-1605
Taratuta School of Truck Driving Post-Sec.
2215 Oak Indstrl Dr NE #212 49505 616-742-9000
West Catholic HS 600/9-12
1801 Bristol Ave NW 49504 616-233-5900
Stan Spetoskey, prin. Fax 453-4320

Grandville, Kent, Pop. 16,711
Grandville SD 5,700/K-12
3131 Barrett Ave SW 49418 616-254-6550
Ronald Caniff, supt. Fax 254-6557
www.grandville.k12.mi.us
Grandville HS 1,900/9-12
4700 Canal Ave SW 49418 616-254-6430
Randy Morris, prin. Fax 254-6462
Grandville MS 900/7-8
3535 Wilson Ave SW 49418 616-254-6610
Theresa Waterbury, prin. Fax 254-6613

Calvin Christian HS 500/9-12
3750 Ivanrest Ave SW 49418 616-538-0990
Barbara Engbers, prin. Fax 538-9930
Calvin Christian MS 200/7-8
3740 Ivanrest Ave SW 49418 616-531-7400
John Kramer, prin. Fax 531-7402

Grant, Newaygo, Pop. 885
Grant SD 2,300/PK-12
148 Elder St 49327 231-834-5621
Scott Bogner, supt. Fax 834-7146
www.grantps.net
Grant HS 700/9-12
331 E State Rd 49327 231-834-5622
Tom Szocinski, prin. Fax 834-8043
Grant MS 700/5-8
96 E 120th St 49327 231-834-5910
Lance Jones, prin. Fax 834-9029

Grass Lake, Jackson, Pop. 1,171
Grass Lake Community SD 1,200/K-12
990 Grass Lake Rd 49240 517-522-5540
Brad Hamilton, supt. Fax 522-8195
www.grasslakeschools.com
Grass Lake HS 400/9-12
11500 Warrior Trl 49240 517-522-5570
Brian Thompson, prin. Fax 522-5490
Grass Lake MS 400/5-8
1000 Grass Lake Rd 49240 517-522-5550
Douglas Moeckel, prin. Fax 522-4775

Grayling, Crawford, Pop. 1,943
Crawford AuSable SD 2,000/PK-12
1135 N Old 27 49738 989-344-3500
Joseph Powers, supt. Fax 348-6822
www.casdk12.net/
Grayling HS 700/9-12
1135 N Old 27 49738 989-344-3532
Doniel Pummell, prin. Fax 348-7799
Grayling MS 500/6-8
500 Spruce St 49738 989-344-3550
Jeffrey Branch, prin. Fax 348-7045

Greenville, Montcalm, Pop. 8,306
Greenville SD 3,800/K-12
1414 Chase St 48838 616-754-3686
Terance Lunger, supt. Fax 754-5374
www.greenville.k12.mi.us
Greenville HS 1,200/9-12
111 N Hillcrest St 48838 616-754-3681
Harold Deines, prin. Fax 754-1994
Greenville MS 1,000/6-8
1321 Chase St 48838 616-754-9361
Diane Brissette, prin. Fax 754-2901

Grosse Ile, Wayne, Pop. 9,781
Grosse Ile Township SD 2,000/K-12
23276 E River Rd 48138 734-362-2555
Dena Dardzinski, supt. Fax 362-2594
www.gischools.org/
Grosse Ile HS 700/9-12
7800 Grays Dr 48138 734-362-2400
Delores Elswick, prin. Fax 362-2496
Grosse Ile MS 500/6-8
23270 E River Rd 48138 734-362-2500
Cynthia Taylor, prin. Fax 362-2596

Grosse Pointe, Wayne, Pop. 5,426
Grosse Pointe SD 8,900/K-12
389 Saint Clair St 48230 313-432-3000
Dr. C. Suzanne Klein, supt. Fax 432-3002
www.gpschools.org
Brownell MS 700/6-8
260 Chalfonte Ave 48236 313-432-3900
Dr. Michael Dib, prin. Fax 432-3902
Grosse Pointe North HS 1,600/9-12
707 Vernier Rd 48236 313-432-3200
Tim Bearden, prin. Fax 432-3202
Grosse Pointe South HS 1,700/9-12
11 Grosse Pointe Blvd 48236 313-432-3500
Al Diver, prin. Fax 432-3502
Parcells MS 800/6-8
20600 Mack Ave 48236 313-432-4600
Mark Mulholland, prin. Fax 432-4602
Pierce MS 600/6-8
15430 Kercheval Ave 48230 313-432-4700
Gary Buslepp, prin. Fax 432-4702

University Liggett S 700/PK-12
1045 Cook Rd 48236 313-884-4444
Matthew H. Hanley, prin. Fax 884-1775
University Liggett S 200/6-8
850 Briar Cliff Dr 48236 313-886-4220
Lynne Myavec, prin. Fax 417-8002

Gwinn, Marquette, Pop. 2,370
Gwinn Area Community SD 1,400/K-12
50 W State Highway M35 49841 906-346-9283
Steven Peffers, supt. Fax 346-3616
www.gwinn.k12.mi.us
Gwinn HS 400/9-12
50 W State Highway M35 49841 906-346-9247
Kevin Luokkala, prin. Fax 346-0300
Gwinn MS 200/7-8
135 W Granite St 49841 906-346-5914
Kimberly Van Drese, prin. Fax 346-6213

Hale, Iosco
Hale Area SD 800/K-12
200 W Main St 48739 989-728-7661
Rhonda Provoast, supt. Fax 728-2406
Hale HS 300/9-12
415 E Main St 48739 989-728-2861
Susan Gillings, prin. Fax 728-7101
Hale MS 300/5-8
311 N Washington St 48739 989-728-3551
Denis Fitzgerald, prin. Fax 728-9551

Hamilton, Allegan
Hamilton Community SD 2,600/K-12
4815 136th Ave 49419 269-751-5148
James Kos, supt. Fax 751-7116
www.hamiltonschools.us
Hamilton HS 800/9-12
4911 136th Ave 49419 269-751-5185
Doug Braschler, prin. Fax 751-7670
Hamilton MS 600/6-8
4845 136th Ave 49419 269-751-4436
Scott Smith, prin. Fax 751-8560

Hamtramck, Wayne, Pop. 21,994
Hamtramck SD 3,000/PK-12
PO Box 12012 48212 313-872-9270
Felix Chow, supt. Fax 872-8679
www.hamtramck.k12.mi.us
Hamtramck HS 900/9-12
11410 Charest St 48212 313-892-7505
Patrick Victor, prin. Fax 892-1990
Kosciuszko MS 800/6-8
2333 Burger St 48212 313-365-4625
Dennis Kemp, prin. Fax 365-4760

Hancock, Houghton, Pop. 4,223
Hancock SD 1,000/K-12
417 Quincy St 49930 906-487-5925
John Vaara, supt. Fax 487-5216
www.hancock.k12.mi.us
Hancock Central HS 300/9-12
501 Campus Dr 49930 906-483-2540
John Sanregret, prin. Fax 483-2539
Hancock MS 200/6-8
417 Quincy St 49930 906-487-5923
Monica Healy, prin. Fax 487-5924

Finlandia University Post-Sec.
601 Quincy St 49930 906-482-5300

Harbor Beach, Huron, Pop. 1,719
Harbor Beach Community SD 700/K-12
402 S 5th St 48441 989-479-3261
Ron Kraft, supt. Fax 479-9881
www.harborbeach.k12.mi.us/
Harbor Beach HS 300/9-12
402 S 5th St 48441 989-479-3261
Doug Hassler, prin. Fax 479-9881
Harbor Beach MS 200/5-8
402 S 5th St 48441 989-479-3261
Denise Kish, prin. Fax 479-9881

Harbor Springs, Emmet, Pop. 1,594
Harbor Springs SD 1,100/K-12
800 S State Rd 49740 231-526-4545
Dr. David Larson, supt. Fax 526-4544
www.harborps.org
Harbor Springs HS 400/9-12
327 E Bluff Dr 49740 231-526-4800
Susan Jacobs, prin. Fax 526-4833
Harbor Springs MS 300/6-8
800 S State Rd 49740 231-526-4700
Wil Cwikiel, prin. Fax 526-4760

Harbor Light Christian S 100/PK-12
8333 Clayton Rd 49740 231-347-7859
Loren Vannest, admin. Fax 347-7703

Harper Woods, Wayne, Pop. 13,621
Harper Woods SD 1,200/K-12
20225 Beaconsfield St 48225 313-839-1296
Dr. Terri Spencer, supt. Fax 839-1249
www.hwschools.org
Harper Woods HS 400/9-12
20225 Beaconsfield St 48225 313-839-7400
Peter Newman, prin. Fax 839-4360
Harper Woods MS 200/7-8
20225 Beaconsfield St 48225 313-839-7400
Peter Newman, prin. Fax 839-4360

Regina HS 500/9-12
20200 Kelly Rd 48225 313-526-0220
Sr. M. Leanne Leszczynski, prin. Fax 526-5850

Harris, Menominee
Bark River-Harris SD 700/K-12
PO Box 350 49845 906-466-9981
Russell Pirlot, supt. Fax 466-2925
www.dsisd.k12.mi.us/barkriver
Bark River-Harris JSHS 300/7-12
PO Box 350 49845 906-466-5321
Mary Brayak, prin. Fax 466-2925

Harrison, Clare, Pop. 2,083
Harrison Community SD 1,800/K-12
PO Box 529 48625 989-539-7871
Christopher L. Rundle, supt. Fax 539-7491
www.cgresd.net/hcs
Harrison HS 700/9-12
PO Box 529 48625 989-539-7417
Thomas House, prin. Fax 539-4319
Harrison MS 500/6-8
PO Box 529 48625 989-539-7194
Kathy McAndrew, prin. Fax 539-0460

Mid-Michigan Community College Post-Sec.
1375 S Clare Ave 48625 989-386-6622

Harrison Township, Macomb, Pop. 24,685
L'Anse Creuse SD 11,300/PK-12
36727 Jefferson Ave 48045 586-783-6300
Dr. DiAnne Pellerin, supt. Fax 783-6310
www.lc-ps.org
L'Anse Creuse HS 1,800/9-12
38495 LAnse Creuse St 48045 586-783-6400
Patrick Mulcahy, prin. Fax 783-6408
L'Anse Creuse MS Central 600/6-8
38000 Reimold St 48045 586-783-6430
Patricia Rabenburg, prin. Fax 783-6437
L'Anse Creuse MS South 600/6-8
34641 Jefferson Ave 48045 586-493-5620
Greg Dixon, prin. Fax 493-5625
Other Schools – See Chesterfield, Clinton Township, Macomb, Mount Clemens

Hart, Oceana, Pop. 1,996
Hart SD 1,200/PK-12
301 Johnson St W 49420 231-873-6214
Peter Moss, supt. Fax 873-6244
www.hart.k12.mi.us
Hart HS 400/9-12
300 Johnson St W 49420 231-873-5691
Randy Nesbit, prin. Fax 873-0586
Hart MS 300/6-8
308 Johnson St W 49420 231-873-6320
Phillip Espinoza, prin. Fax 873-0245

Hartford, Van Buren, Pop. 2,433
Hartford SD 1,400/K-12
115 School St 49057 269-621-7000
David Levstek, supt. Fax 621-3887
www.hartford-schools.org
Hartford HS 400/9-12
121 School St 49057 269-621-7100
Kenneth Kent, prin. Fax 621-7160
Hartford MS 300/6-8
141 School St 49057 269-621-7200
John Visser, prin. Fax 621-7260

Hartland, Livingston
Hartland Consolidated SD
Supt. — See Howell
Hartland HS 1,600/9-12
10635 Dunham Rd 48353 810-746-2200
Chuck Hughes, prin. Fax 746-2201
Hartland MS 900/7-8
3250 Hartland Rd 48353 810-746-2400
Steve Livingway, prin. Fax 746-2401

Haslett, Ingham, Pop. 10,230
Haslett SD 2,900/K-12
5593 Franklin St 48840 517-339-8242
Michael Duda, supt. Fax 339-1360
www.haslett.k12.mi.us/
Haslett HS 900/9-12
5450 Marsh Rd 48840 517-339-8249
Bart Wegenke, prin. Fax 339-7353
Haslett MS 700/6-8
1535 Franklin St 48840 517-339-8233
Andy Pridgeon, prin. Fax 339-4837

Hastings, Barry, Pop. 7,166
Hastings Area SD 3,400/PK-12
232 W Grand St 49058 269-948-4400
Christopher Cooley, supt. Fax 948-4425
www.hassk12.org
Hastings HS 1,000/9-12
520 W South St 49058 269-948-4409
Timothy Johnston, prin. Fax 948-8081
Hastings MS 800/6-8
232 W Grand St 49058 269-948-4404
Michael Karasinski, prin. Fax 945-6101

Barry County Christian S 100/PK-12
2999 McKeown Rd 49058 269-948-2151
Ken Oosterhouse, admin. Fax 948-2795

Hazel Park, Oakland, Pop. 18,391
Hazel Park SD 4,000/PK-12
23136 Hughes Ave 48030 248-542-3910
Victor C. Mayo Ed.D., supt. Fax 544-5443
www.hazelpark.k12.mi.us/
Hazel Park HS 1,200/9-12
23400 Hughes Ave 48030 248-544-5216
Don Vogt, prin. Fax 544-5389
Hazel Park JHS 700/7-8
22770 Highland Ave 48030 248-658-2300
Douglas Esler, prin.
Hazel Park Adult S Adult
420 W 9 Mile Rd 48030 248-544-5388
Gary Tweddle, prin.

Hemlock, Saginaw, Pop. 1,601
Hemlock SD 1,500/K-12
PO Box 260 48626 989-642-5282
Rudy Godefroidt, supt. Fax 642-2773
www.hemlock.k12.mi.us
Hemlock HS, PO Box 260 48626 500/9-12
Rudy Godefroidt, prin. 989-642-5287
Hemlock MS, PO Box 260 48626 400/6-8
Terry Keyser, prin. 989-642-5253

Hermansville, Menominee
North Central Area SD 400/PK-12
PO Box 159 49847 906-498-7737
Donald Palmer, supt. Fax 498-2235
www.ncajets.org
Other Schools – See Powers

Hesperia, Oceana, Pop. 987
Hesperia Community SD 1,100/K-12
PO Box 338 49421 231-854-6185
Dean Havelka, supt. Fax 854-1586
www.hesp.net
Hesperia HS 300/9-12
PO Box 338 49421 231-854-6385
Dennis Love, prin. Fax 854-6070
Hesperia MS 400/5-8
PO Box 338 49421 231-854-6475
David Bukala, prin. Fax 854-6096

Hickory Corners, Kalamazoo
Gull Lake Community SD
Supt. — See Richland
Gull Lake MS 500/7-8
9500 N 40th St 49060 269-671-5135
Craig Bartholomew, prin. Fax 671-4077

Highland, Oakland
Huron Valley SD 10,700/PK-12
2390 S Milford Rd 48357 248-684-8000
Jackie Johnston, supt. Fax 684-8235
www.huronvalley.k12.mi.us
Highland MS 700/6-8
305 N John St 48357 248-684-8080
Martin Lindberg, prin. Fax 684-8186
Milford HS 1,900/9-12
2380 S Milford Rd 48357 248-684-8091
Michael Krystyniak, prin. Fax 684-8094
Other Schools – See Commerce Township, Milford, White Lake

Highland Park, Wayne, Pop. 15,430
Highland Park SD 2,200/PK-12
20 Bartlett St 48203 313-957-3000
Arthur Carter Ed.D., supt. Fax 868-4950
www.resa.net/highlandpark/index.htm
Highland Park Career Acad/Adult Ed Vo/Tech
Glendale at 2nd Ave 48203 313-957-3007
Belvin Liles, dir. Fax 852-0206
Highland Park Community HS 800/9-12
15900 Woodward Ave 48203 313-957-3002
Jared Davis, prin. Fax 868-0483

Hillman, Montmorency, Pop. 679
Hillman Community SD 600/K-12
PO Box 518 49746 989-742-2908
Jack Richards, supt. Fax 742-3376
hillman.amaesd.k12.mi.us
Hillman JSHS 300/7-12
PO Box 518 49746 989-742-4538
Jack Richards, prin. Fax 742-4536

Hillsdale, Hillsdale, Pop. 7,904
Hillsdale Community SD 1,800/PK-12
30 S Norwood Ave 49242 517-437-4401
Richard Ames, supt. Fax 439-4194
www.hillsdaleschools.org
Davis MS 400/6-8
30 N West St 49242 517-439-4326
Jackie Wickham, prin. Fax 437-1195
Hillsdale HS 600/9-12
30 S Norwood Ave 49242 517-439-4320
Douglas Willer, prin. Fax 437-0377

Hillsdale ISD 100/
310 W Bacon St 49242 517-437-0990
Robert W. Henthorne, supt. Fax 439-4388
www.hillsdale-isd.org
Workforce Development & Tech Center Vo/Tech
279 Industrial Dr 49242 517-437-3729
Kevin Leonard, dir. Fax 437-3743

Hillsdale Academy 200/K-12
1 Academy Ln 49242 517-439-8644
Kenneth Calvert, prin. Fax 607-2794
Hillsdale Beauty College Post-Sec.
64 Waldron St 49242 517-437-4670
Hillsdale College Post-Sec.
33 E College St 49242 517-437-7341
Jackson Community College Post-Sec.
PO Box 712 49242 517-437-3343

Holland, Ottawa, Pop. 34,429
Holland SD 3,800/PK-12
156 W 11th St 49423 616-494-2000
Frank Garcia, supt. Fax 392-8225
www.hollandpublicschools.org/
Holland HS 1,600/9-12
600 Van Raalte Ave 49423 616-494-2200
William Trujillo, prin. Fax 393-7534
West MS 500/6-8
500 W 24th St 49423 616-494-2350
Kathryn Curry, prin. Fax 393-7544

Ottawa Area ISD
13565 Port Sheldon St 49424 616-738-8940
Karen McPhee, supt. Fax 738-8946
www.oaisd.org
Careerline Tech Center Vo/Tech
13663 Port Sheldon St 49424 616-738-8950
Dale Henderson, dir.

West Ottawa SD 7,500/K-12
1138 136th Ave 49424 616-738-5700
Dr. Patricia Koeze, supt. Fax 738-5792
www.westottawa.net
Harbor Lights S 1,200/6-8
1024 136th Ave 49424 616-738-6700
Jeri Start, prin. Fax 738-6791
Macatawa Bay MS 600/6-8
3700 140th Ave 49424 616-786-2000
Greg Wieman, prin. Fax 786-2091
West Ottawa HS 1,900/9-12
3685 Butternut Dr 49424 616-786-1000
Kent Henson, prin. Fax 786-1091

Calvary S of Holland 200/PK-12
518 Plasman Ave 49423 616-396-4494
Paul Davis, admin. Fax 396-0326
Holland Christian HS 900/9-12
950 Ottawa Ave 49423 616-820-2905
Troy Stahl, prin. Fax 820-2910
Hope College Post-Sec.
PO Box 9000 49422 616-395-7000
North Shore Christian MS 200/6-8
556 Butternut Dr 49424 616-820-4055
Gary Dewey, lead tchr. Fax 820-4060
South Shore Christian MS 200/6-8
850 Ottawa Ave 49423 616-820-3205
Mark Van Dyke, prin. Fax 820-3210
Western Theological Seminary Post-Sec.
101 E 13th St 49423 616-392-8555

Holly, Oakland, Pop. 6,375
Holly Area SD 4,200/K-12
111 College St 48442 248-328-3100
R. Kent Barnes, supt. Fax 328-3145
www.hollyareaschools.com
Holly HS 1,400/9-12
6161 E Holly Rd 48442 248-328-3200
David Nuss, prin. Fax 328-3204
Sherman MS 700/7-8
14470 N Holly Rd 48442 248-328-3400
Anne Doriean, prin. Fax 328-3404

Adelphian Jr. Academy 50/1-10
PO Box 208 48442 248-634-9481
Diane Barlow, prin. Fax 634-9222

Holt, Ingham, Pop. 11,744
Holt SD 5,700/K-12
5780 Holt Rd 48842 517-694-0401
Thomas Davis, supt. Fax 694-1335
www.hpsk12.net/
Holt JHS 1,000/7-8
1784 Aurelius Rd 48842 517-694-7117
Johnny Scott, prin. Fax 694-3535
Holt SHS 1,300/10-12
5885 Holt Rd 48842 517-694-2162
Brian Templin, prin. Fax 699-3451
9th Grade Campus 500/9-9
5780 Holt Rd 48842 517-694-4370
Nick Johnson, prin. Fax 694-8362

Capitol City Baptist S 200/PK-12
5100 Willoughby Rd 48842 517-694-6122
Brian Ogle, prin. Fax 694-3344
Central Lutheran HS 50/9-12
2418 Aurelius Rd 48842 517-694-3182
Janice Poellet, prin. Fax 694-6371

Holton, Muskegon
Holton SD 1,100/K-12
PO Box 159 49425 231-821-1700
John Fazer, supt. Fax 821-1724
www.remc4.k12.mi.us/holton/
Holton HS 300/9-12
PO Box 159 49425 231-821-1725
Troycie Nichols, prin. Fax 821-1774
Holton MS 400/5-8
PO Box 159 49425 231-821-1775
Ken Haggart, prin. Fax 821-1824

Homer, Calhoun, Pop. 1,819
Homer Community SD 1,000/K-12
403 S Hillsdale St 49245 517-568-4461
Brent Holcomb, supt. Fax 568-4468
www.homer.k12.mi.us/
Homer HS 300/9-12
403 S Hillsdale St 49245 517-568-4464
Tom Salow, prin. Fax 568-7125
Homer MS 300/5-8
403 S Hillsdale St 49245 517-568-4456
Scott Salow, prin. Fax 568-4468

Hopkins, Allegan, Pop. 572
Hopkins SD 1,500/K-12
PO Box 278 49328 269-793-7261
Thomas Martin, supt. Fax 793-3154
www.hpsvikings.org
Hopkins HS 500/9-12
333 S Clark St 49328 269-793-7616
Bruce Vanderwall, prin. Fax 793-7085
Hopkins MS 300/6-8
215 S Clark St 49328 269-793-7407
Ken Szczepanski, prin. Fax 793-4086

Horton, Jackson
Hanover-Horton SD 1,400/K-12
PO Box 60 49246 517-563-0100
Linda Brian, supt. Fax 563-0150
hhsd.k12.mi.us
Hanover-Horton HS 500/9-12
10000 Moscow Rd 49246 517-563-0101
Rod Hardy, prin. Fax 563-0155
Hanover-Horton MS 300/6-8
10000 Moscow Rd 49246 517-563-0102
Denise Dennison, prin. Fax 563-9140

Houghton, Houghton, Pop. 7,076
Houghton-Portage Township SD 1,300/K-12
1603 Gundlach Rd 49931 906-482-0451
William Polkinghorne, supt. Fax 487-9764
www.houghton.k12.mi.us/
Houghton Central HS 500/9-12
1603 Gundlach Rd 49931 906-482-0450
Kathryn Simila, prin. Fax 487-5218
Houghton MS 300/6-8
1603 Gundlach Rd 49931 906-482-4871
James Luoma, prin. Fax 483-2566

Michigan Technological University Post-Sec.
1400 Townsend Dr 49931 906-487-1885

Houghton Lake, Roscommon, Pop. 3,353
Houghton Lake Community SD 1,300/K-12
6001 W Houghton Lake Dr 48629 989-366-2000
Peter Injasoulian, supt. Fax 366-2070
www.hlcs.k12.mi.us
Houghton Lake HS 600/8-12
4433 W Houghton Lake Dr 48629 989-366-2006
Jack Kramer, prin. Fax 366-2071

Houghton Lake Institute of Cosmetology Post-Sec.
PO Box 669 48629 - -

Howard City, Montcalm, Pop. 1,617
Tri County Area SD
Supt. — See Sand Lake
Tri County HS 700/9-12
21338 Kendaville Rd 49329 231-937-4338
Mark Simons, prin. Fax 937-5684
Tri County MS 600/6-8
21350 Kendaville Rd 49329 231-937-4318
Kurt Mabie, prin. Fax 937-6319

Howell, Livingston, Pop. 9,757
Hartland Consolidated SD 5,300/K-12
9525 E Highland Rd 48843 810-746-2100
Janet Sifferman, supt. Fax 746-2101
Other Schools – See Hartland

Howell SD 8,400/K-12
411 N Highlander Way 48843 517-548-6234
W. Charles Breiner, supt. Fax 548-6229
www.howellschools.com
Highlander Way MS 900/6-8
511 N Highlander Way 48843 517-548-6252
Sandra Moore, prin. Fax 545-1455
Howell HS 1,900/10-12
1200 W Grand River Ave 48843 517-548-6206
Fax 545-1496

Howell HS Freshman Campus 700/9-9
1400 W Grand River Ave 48843 517-548-6267
Larry Cowger, prin. Fax 545-1439
Three Fires MS 1,000/6-8
4125 Crooked Lake Rd 48843 517-548-6387
Sue Muntz, prin. Fax 548-7524

Cleary University - Livingston Campus Post-Sec.
3750 Cleary Dr 48843 517-548-3670
Howell College of Cosmetology Post-Sec.
1800 Dorr Rd 48843 517-546-4155

Hudson, Lenawee, Pop. 2,415
Hudson Area SD 1,100/K-12
781 N Maple Grove Ave 49247 517-448-8912
Kathryn Malnar Ed.D., supt. Fax 448-8570
www.hudson.k12.mi.us
Hudson Area HS 400/9-12
771 N Maple Grove Ave 49247 517-448-8912
Mike Osborne, prin. Fax 448-8975
Hudson MS 300/6-8
771 N Maple Grove Ave 49247 517-445-8912
Mike Osborne, prin. Fax 448-5702

Hudsonville, Ottawa, Pop. 7,052
Hudsonville SD 5,000/PK-12
3886 Van Buren St 49426 616-669-1740
Roxanne DeWeerd, supt. Fax 669-4878
www.hudsonville.k12.mi.us
Baldwin Street MS 700/6-8
3835 Baldwin St 49426 616-669-7750
David Powers, prin. Fax 669-7755
Hudsonville Freshman Campus S 400/9-9
5535 School Ave 49426 616-669-1510
Curt McDowell, prin. Fax 669-4895
Hudsonville SHS 1,100/10-12
5037 32nd Ave 49426 616-669-1500
Dave Feenstra, prin. Fax 669-4891
Riley Street MS 400/6-8
2745 Riley St 49426 616-669-1740
Mike Cooke, prin. Fax 896-1925

Freedom Baptist S 400/PK-12
6340 Autumn Dr 49426 616-669-2270
Philip B. Hayes, prin. Fax 669-2410
Hudsonville Christian MS 400/6-8
3925 Van Buren St 49426 616-669-7487
Dan Pott, prin. Fax 669-2031
Unity Christian HS 800/9-12
3487 Oak St 49426 616-669-1820
Jack Postma, prin. Fax 669-5760

Ida, Monroe
Ida SD 1,700/K-12
3145 Prairie St 48140 734-269-3110
Marv Dick, supt. Fax 269-2294
www.idaschools.org
Ida HS 600/9-12
3145 Prairie St 48140 734-269-3485
Cathy Griffith, prin. Fax 269-3495
Ida MS 500/5-8
3145 Prairie St 48140 734-269-2220
Sheldon Wiens, prin. Fax 269-2576

Imlay City, Lapeer, Pop. 3,850
Imlay City Community SD 2,400/PK-12
PO Box 128 48444 810-724-9861
Gary Richards, supt. Fax 724-4307
www.imlay.k12.mi.us/
Imlay City HS 700/9-12
1001 Norlin Dr 48444 810-724-9810
Stuart Cameron, prin. Fax 724-9897
Imlay City MS 600/6-8
495 W 1st St 48444 810-724-9811
Erik Mason, prin. Fax 724-9896

Indian River, Cheboygan
Inland Lakes SD 1,100/K-12
4363 S Straits Hwy 49749 231-238-6868
Mary Jo Dismang, supt. Fax 238-4181
www.inlandlakes.org
Inland Lakes HS 400/9-12
4363 S Straits Hwy 49749 231-238-6868
Donald Killingbeck, prin. Fax 238-7240
Inland Lakes MS 300/5-8
4363 S Straits Hwy 49749 231-238-6868
Matthew Hirsh, prin. Fax 238-4872

Inkster, Wayne, Pop. 28,870
Inkster SD 1,200/PK-12
29115 Carlysle St 48141 734-722-5310
Thomas Maridada, admin. Fax 722-2150
www.inksterschools.org/
Blanchette MS 300/6-8
1771 Henry Ruff Rd 48141 734-326-7041
Maurice Washington, prin. Fax 722-5402
Inkster HS 300/9-12
3250 Middlebelt Rd 48141 734-326-8519
Nick Edwards, prin. Fax 467-9698

Peterson-Warren Academy 100/K-12
PO Box 888 48141 313-565-5808
Juanita Martin, prin. Fax 565-7784

Interlochen, Grand Traverse

Interlochen Arts Academy 500/9-12
PO Box 199 49643 231-276-7200
Timothy Wade, prin. Fax 276-7885

Ionia, Ionia, Pop. 12,336
Ionia SD 3,200/K-12
250 E Tuttle Rd 48846 616-527-9280
Patricia Batista, supt. Fax 527-8846
www.ionia.k12.mi.us
Heartlands Institute of Technology Vo/Tech
250 E Tuttle Rd 48846 616-527-6540
Anne Sharkey-Scott, prin. Fax 527-6670
Ionia HS 1,000/9-12
250 E Tuttle Rd 48846 616-527-0600
Benjamin Kirby, prin. Fax 527-8057
Ionia MS 800/6-8
438 Union St 48846 616-527-0040
Cheri Meier, prin. Fax 527-3380

Iron Mountain, Dickinson, Pop. 8,173
Iron Mountain SD 1,300/PK-12
Prospect & A St 49801 906-779-2600
Dennis Chartier, supt. Fax 779-2676
www.imschools.org
Central MS 300/6-8
301 E Hughitt St 49801 906-779-2620
Robert Strang, prin. Fax 779-2634
Iron Mountain HS 400/9-12
300 W B St 49801 906-779-2610
Maryann Boddy, prin. Fax 779-2638

Iron River, Iron, Pop. 3,112
West Iron County SD 1,100/PK-12
601 Garfield Ave 49935 906-265-9218
Timothy Peruzzi, supt. Fax 265-9736
www.westiron.org
West Iron County HS 400/9-12
701 Garfield Ave 49935 906-265-5184
Christopher Thomson, prin. Fax 265-2294
West Iron County MS 300/5-8
612 W Adams St 49935 906-265-0016
Michael Berutti, prin. Fax 265-3402

Ironwood, Gogebic, Pop. 5,728
Ironwood Area SD 1,100/PK-12
650 E Ayer St 49938 906-932-0200
James Rayner, supt. Fax 932-9915
www.ironwood.k12.mi.us/
Wright MSHS 700/6-12
650 E Ayer St 49938 906-932-0932
Tim Kolesar, prin. Fax 932-9915

Gogebic Community College Post-Sec.
E4946 Jackson Rd 49938 906-932-4231

Ishpeming, Marquette, Pop. 6,507
Ishpeming SD 1 900/PK-12
319 E Division St 49849 906-485-5501
Stephen Piereson, supt. Fax 485-1422
www.ishpemingschools.com
Ishpeming HS 300/9-12
319 E Division St 49849 906-485-1066
Brian Sarvello, prin.
Phelps IS, 700 E North St 49849 300/5-8
Charleen Willey, prin. 906-486-4438

NICE Community SD 1,300/K-12
300 S Westwood Dr 49849 906-485-1021
Henry Bothwell, supt. Fax 485-4095
www.nice.k12.mi.us/
Aspen Ridge MS 300/6-8
350 Aspen Ridge School Rd 49849 906-485-3176
Dennis Tasson, prin. Fax 485-3182
Westwood HS 400/9-12
300 S Westwood Dr 49849 906-485-1023
David Boase, prin. Fax 485-1530

Ithaca, Gratiot, Pop. 3,101
Gratiot-Isabella RESD
PO Box 310 48847 989-875-5101
Michael Matlosz, supt. Fax 875-7531
www.edzone.net/giresd/
Other Schools – See Alma

Ithaca SD 1,500/K-12
710 N Union St 48847 989-875-3700
Charles Schnetzler, supt. Fax 875-4538
www.ithacaschools.net
Ithaca HS 400/9-12
710 N Union St 48847 989-875-3373
Steven Netzley, prin. Fax 875-2500
Ithaca MS 200/7-8
710 N Union St 48847 989-875-3373
Steven Netzley, prin. Fax 875-2500

Jackson, Jackson, Pop. 34,879
East Jackson Community SD 1,600/K-12
1404 N Sutton Rd 49202 517-764-2090
Bruce Van Eyck, supt. Fax 764-6033
scnc.ejs.k12.mi.us/
East Jackson HS 500/9-12
1566 N Sutton Rd 49202 517-764-1700
Kevin Herendeen, prin. Fax 764-6083
East Jackson MS 400/6-8
4340 Walz Rd 49201 517-764-6010
Heather Jacobs, prin. Fax 764-6081

Jackson County ISD 50/
6700 Browns Lake Rd 49201 517-768-5200
John Graves, supt. Fax 787-2026
www.jcisd.org
Jackson Area Career Center Vo/Tech
6800 Browns Lake Rd 49201 517-768-5200
Denise Belt, prin. Fax 787-2844

Jackson SD 6,200/PK-12
522 Wildwood Ave 49201 517-841-2200
Daniel Evans, supt. Fax 789-8056
jps.k12.mi.us/~jps/
Firth MS 6-9
205 Seymour Ave 49202 517-841-3870
Robert Smoots, prin. Fax 768-5904
Jackson HS 1,800/9-12
544 Wildwood Ave 49201 517-841-3700
Pam Fitzgerald, prin. Fax 768-5910
MS at Parkside 1,000/7-8
2400 4th St 49203 517-841-2300
David Kiesel, prin. Fax 768-5968

Northwest Community SD 3,600/PK-12
4000 Van Horn Rd 49201 517-569-2247
Emily Kress, supt. Fax 569-2395
www.nsd.k12.mi.us
Kidder MS 900/6-8
6700 Rives Junction Rd 49201 517-569-2247
Dan Brooks, prin. Fax 569-2931
Northwest HS 1,100/9-12
4200 Van Horn Rd 49201 517-569-2247
Erik Bergh, prin. Fax 569-2398

Vandercook Lake SD 1,300/K-12
1000 E Golf Ave 49203 517-782-9044
Anthony Hollow, supt. Fax 788-3690
scnc.vandy.k12.mi.us
Vandercook Lake JSHS 700/6-12
1000 E Golf Ave 49203 517-782-8167
Mark Schonhard, prin. Fax 782-3730

Western SD
Supt. — See Parma
Western Options Ctr & Adult & Comm Educ Adult
3950 Catherine St 49203 517-841-8700
Deborah Batchelder, prin. Fax 841-8807

Baker College of Jackson Post-Sec.
2800 Springport Rd 49202 517-789-6123
Jackson Catholic MS 300/7-8
915 Cooper St 49202 517-784-3385
Anthony Shaughnessy, prin. Fax 782-7883
Jackson Christian HS 100/9-12
4200 Lowe Rd 49203 517-783-2658
Bob Stanton, prin. Fax 783-4235
Jackson Christian MS 100/6-8
4200 Lowe Rd 49203 517-783-2658
Todd Barney, prin. Fax 783-4235
Jackson Community College Post-Sec.
2111 Emmons Rd 49201 517-787-0800
Jackson Community College Post-Sec.
3610 Wildwood Ave 49202 517-787-7012
Lumen Christi HS 700/9-12
3483 Spring Arbor Rd 49203 517-787-0630
Patrick Kalahar, prin. Fax 787-1066

Jenison, Ottawa, Pop. 17,882
Jenison SD 4,600/PK-12
8375 20th Ave 49428 616-457-8890
Thomas TenBrink, supt. Fax 457-8898
www.jpsonline.org/
Jenison HS 1,600/9-12
2140 Bauer Rd 49428 616-457-3400
Mark Dievendorf, prin. Fax 457-4070
Jenison JHS 800/7-8
8295 20th Ave 49428 616-457-1402
Donna Bergeon, prin. Fax 457-8090

Johannesburg, Otsego
Johannesburg-Lewiston Area SD 900/K-12
10854 M 32 E 49751 989-732-1773
James Hilgendorf, supt. Fax 732-6556
www.jlas.org
Johannesburg-Lewiston HS 300/9-12
10854 M 32 E 49751 989-731-4420
Will Kearney, prin. Fax 732-6556

Jonesville, Hillsdale, Pop. 2,293
Jonesville Community SD 1,300/PK-12
202 Wright St 49250 517-849-9075
Michael Potts, supt. Fax 849-2434
www.jonesvilleschools.org
Jonesville HS 300/9-12
460 Adrian Rd 49250 517-849-9934
Chellie Broesamle, prin. Fax 849-2755
Jonesville MS 300/6-8
401 E Chicago St 49250 517-849-3210
Penny Snyder, prin. Fax 849-3213

Kalamazoo, Kalamazoo, Pop. 72,700
Comstock SD 2,500/K-12
3010 Gull Rd 49048 269-388-9461
Dr. David Hutton, supt. Fax 388-9481
www.comstockps.org
Comstock HS 900/9-12
2107 N 26th St 49048 269-388-9400
Donald Eastman, prin. Fax 388-9454
Comstock Northeast MS 700/6-8
1423 N 28th St 49048 269-388-9433
Jay Birchmeier, prin. Fax 388-9664
Adult Education Adult
3010 Gull Rd 49048 269-388-9477
Steve Symons, prin. Fax 388-9491

Kalamazoo RESA
1819 E Milham Ave 49002 269-385-1500
W. Craig Misner, supt. Fax 381-9423
www.kresa.org
Young Adult Program Adult
422 E South St Ste A 49007 269-488-9601
Jane Bilicki, prin. Fax 488-9613

Kalamazoo SD 9,800/K-12
1220 Howard St 49008 269-337-0100
Michael Rice, supt. Fax 337-0149
www.kalamazoopublicschools.com
Central HS 1,400/9-12
2432 N Drake Rd 49006 269-337-0300
Von Washington, prin. Fax 337-0391
Hillside MS 500/7-8
1941 Alamo Ave 49006 269-337-0570
Fax 337-1618
Maple Magnet MS 600/7-8
922 W Maple St 49008 269-337-0730
Fax 337-1633
Milwood Magnet MS 400/6-8
2916 Konkle St 49001 269-337-0670
Kevin Campbell, prin. Fax 337-1628
Norrix HS 1,400/9-12
606 E Kilgore Rd 49001 269-337-0200
David LaPrairie, prin. Fax 337-1617

Community Education Center Adult
714 S Westnedge Ave 49007 269-337-0446
Theresa Jacobson, admin. Fax 337-0490

Parchment SD
Supt. — See Parchment
Barclay Hills Education Center Adult
1125 E Mosel Ave 49004 269-488-1470
April Goodwin, prin. Fax 488-1480

Davenport University Post-Sec.
4123 W Main St 49006 269-552-3308
Everest Institute Post-Sec.
5177 W Main St 49009 269-381-9616
Heritage Christian Academy 300/K-12
6312 Quail Run Dr 49009 269-372-1400
James Wessing, admin. Fax 372-6018
Kalamazoo Christian HS 500/9-12
2121 Stadium Dr 49008 269-381-2250
Thomas Kamp, prin. Fax 381-0319
Kalamazoo Christian MS 200/6-8
3333 S Westnedge Ave 49008 269-343-3645
Jeff Blamer, prin. Fax 343-4649
Kalamazoo College Post-Sec.
1200 Academy St 49006 269-337-7000
Kalamazoo Jr. Academy 50/K-10
1601 Nichols Rd 49006 269-342-8943
Donelle O'Connor, prin. Fax 342-1892
Kalamazoo Valley Community College Post-Sec.
PO Box 4070 49003 269-372-5000
Msgr. Hackett HS 500/9-12
1000 W Kilgore Rd 49008 269-381-2646
Tim Eastman, prin. Fax 381-3919
Reformed Heritage Christian S 100/K-12
700 Fletcher Ave 49006 269-383-0505
James Haveman, admin. Fax 383-2381
Western Michigan University 49008 Post-Sec.
269-387-1000
West Michigan Coll of Barbering & Beauty Post-Sec.
3026 Lovers Ln 49001 269-381-4424

Kalkaska, Kalkaska, Pop. 2,205
Kalkaska SD 1,800/K-12
PO Box 580 49646 231-258-9109
Lee Sandy, supt. Fax 258-4474
www.kpschools.com/
Kalkaska HS 600/9-12
PO Box 580 49646 231-258-9167
Dale Kasza, prin. Fax 258-5188
Kalkaska MS 400/6-8
PO Box 580 49646 231-258-4040
Diane Swoverland, prin. Fax 258-3576

Kent City, Kent, Pop. 1,074
Kent City Community SD 1,000/K-12
200 N Clover St 49330 616-678-7714
Julius Koenigsknecht, supt. Fax 678-4320
www.kent-city.k12.mi.us
Kent City HS 400/9-12
351 N Main St 49330 616-678-4210
Fred Groenke, prin. Fax 678-4371
Kent City MS 6-8
285 N Main St 49330 616-678-4214
Greg Apkarian, prin. Fax 678-5099

Algoma Christian S 300/PK-12
PO Box 220 49330 616-678-7480
Daniel Beach, admin. Fax 678-7484

Kentwood, Kent, Pop. 46,491
Kentwood SD 8,800/PK-12
5820 Eastern Ave SE 49508 616-455-4400
Dr. Mary Leiker, supt. Fax 455-4476
www.kentwoodps.org
Crestwood MS 600/6-8
2674 44th St SE 49512 616-455-1200
John Keenoy, prin. Fax 455-2338
East Kentwood Freshman Campus HS 800/9-9
6170 Valley Lane Dr SE 49508 616-698-9292
Michele Siderman, prin. Fax 698-0313
East Kentwood HS 2,000/10-12
6230 Kalamazoo Ave SE 49508 616-698-6700
Joe Beel, prin. Fax 698-2384
Pinewood MS 800/6-8
2100 60th St SE 49508 616-455-1224
Dave Chesney, prin. Fax 455-2054
Valleywood MS 600/6-8
1110 50th St SE 49508 616-538-7670
Michael Zoerhoff, prin. Fax 538-9301
Kentwood Community Education Adult
28 60th St SE 49548 616-261-6166
Brian O'Hara, prin. Fax 261-6170

West Michigan Lutheran HS 100/9-12
1934 52nd St SE 49508 616-455-2200
John Engelbrecht, prin. Fax 455-2211

Kimball, Saint Clair, Pop. 7,247

New Life Christian Academy 200/PK-12
5517 Griswold Rd 48074 810-367-3770
Lee Ann Shimmel, admin. Fax 367-2249

Kinde, Huron, Pop. 503
North Huron SD 600/K-12
21 Main St 48445 989-874-4100
Maryann Thompson, supt. Fax 874-4109
www.nhuron.org
North Huron JSHS 300/7-12
21 Main St 48445 989-874-4101
Elizabeth Loegel, prin. Fax 874-4129

Kingsford, Dickinson, Pop. 5,565
Breitung Township SD 2,000/K-12
2000 W Pyle Dr 49802 906-779-2650
Craig Allen, supt. Fax 779-9017
www.kingsford.org
Kingsford HS 700/9-12
431 Hamilton Ave 49802 906-779-2670
Robert Usitalo, prin. Fax 779-2883
Kingsford MS 500/6-8
445 Hamilton Ave 49802 906-779-2680
David Holmes, prin. Fax 774-1354

Dickinson-Iron ISD
1074 Pyle Dr 49802 906-779-2690
Johanna Ostwald, supt. Fax 779-2669
www.diisd.org
Dickinson-Iron Tech Educ Center Vo/Tech
300 North Blvd 49802 906-779-2697
Paul Bonsall, prin. Fax 779-2087

Kingsley, Grand Traverse, Pop. 1,524
Kingsley Area SD 1,500/K-12
402 Fenton Rd 49649 231-263-5262
Lynn Gullekson, supt. Fax 263-5282
www.kingsley.k12.mi.us/
Kingsley Area HS 500/9-12
402 Fenton Rd 49649 231-263-5262
Terry Street, prin. Fax 263-2630
Kingsley Area MS 500/5-8
402 Fenton Rd 49649 231-263-5262
Ken Knudsen, prin. Fax 263-4623

Kingston, Tuscola, Pop. 442
Kingston Community SD 700/PK-12
5790 State St 48741 989-683-2294
George Bednorek, supt. Fax 683-2644
www.kingston.k12.mi.us
Kingston JSHS 300/7-12
5790 State St 48741 989-683-2550
Joseph Murphy, prin. Fax 683-2644

Kinross, Chippewa

Maplewood Baptist Academy 100/K-12
3255 W M 80 49752 906-495-1572
Joshua Rader, prin. Fax 495-7433

Laingsburg, Shiawassee, Pop. 1,270
Laingsburg Community SD 1,200/PK-12
205 S Woodhull Rd 48848 517-651-2705
Richard Dunham, supt. Fax 651-9075
laingsburg.k12.mi.us
Laingsburg HS 400/9-12
8008 Woodbury Rd 48848 517-651-5091
Denny Fulk, prin. Fax 651-9621
Laingsburg MS 300/6-8
112 High St 48848 517-651-5034
Gregory Kingdon, prin. Fax 651-6213

Lake City, Missaukee, Pop. 940
Lake City Area SD 1,200/K-12
PO Box 900 49651 231-839-4333
Harry E. Ashton, supt. Fax 839-5219
www.lakecityschools.net
Lake City HS 400/9-12
PO Box 900 49651 231-839-4331
Judy Baase, prin. Fax 839-6031
Lake City MS 300/6-8
PO Box 900 49651 231-839-7163
Dave Swanson, prin. Fax 839-6042

Lake Leelanau, Leelanau

St. Mary S 200/PK-12
PO Box 340 49653 231-256-9636
Fax 256-7239

Lake Linden, Houghton, Pop. 1,044
Lake Linden-Hubbell SD 600/K-12
601 Calumet St 49945 906-296-6211
Randall Roberts, supt. Fax 296-0943
www.lakelinden.k12.mi.us
Lake Linden Hubbell JSHS 300/7-12
601 Calumet St 49945 906-296-6681
Craig Sundblad, prin. Fax 296-0219

Lake Odessa, Ionia, Pop. 2,288
Lakewood SD 2,500/K-12
639 Jordan Lake St 48849 616-374-8043
Michael O'Mara, supt. Fax 374-8858
www.lakewood.k12.mi.us
Lakewood HS 800/9-12
7223 Velte Rd 48849 616-374-8868
Brian Williams, prin. Fax 374-1468
Other Schools – See Woodland

Lake Orion, Oakland, Pop. 2,756
Lake Orion Community SD 7,700/PK-12
315 N Lapeer St 48362 248-693-5413
Christine Lehman, supt. Fax 693-5466
www.lakeorion.k12.mi.us/
Lake Orion Community HS 2,300/9-12
495 E Scripps Rd 48360 248-693-5420
Todd Dunckley, prin. Fax 693-5459
Scripps MS 600/6-8
385 E Scripps Rd 48360 248-693-5440
Dan Haas, prin. Fax 693-5301
Waldon MS 600/6-8
2509 Waldon Rd 48360 248-391-1100
Heidi Kast, prin. Fax 391-5452
Other Schools – See Oakland

Lake Orion Baptist S 100/K-12
255 E Scripps Rd 48360 248-693-6203
Dennis Quattlebaum, prin. Fax 693-6177

Lakeview, Montcalm, Pop. 1,122
Lakeview Community SD 1,700/PK-12
123 5th St 48850 989-352-6226
J. Mark Parsons, supt. Fax 352-8245
www.lakeviewschools.net
Lakeview HS 600/9-12
9800 Youngman Rd 48850 989-352-7221
Michael Travis, prin. Fax 352-6320
Lakeview MS 400/6-8
516 Washington St 48850 989-352-8016
Robert Ivan, prin. Fax 352-6710

L Anse, Baraga, Pop. 2,147
L'Anse Area SD 800/K-12
201 N 4th St 49946 906-524-6121
Ray Pasquali, supt. Fax 524-6001
www.laschools.k12.mi.us
L'Anse HS 200/9-12
201 N 4th St 49946 906-524-6122
Henry Moore, prin. Fax 524-6231
L'Anse MS 200/6-8
201 N 4th St 49946 906-524-5390
Robert Willman, prin. Fax 524-0345

Lansing, Ingham, Pop. 115,518
DeWitt SD
Supt. — See De Witt
DeWitt HS 900/9-12
3100 W Clark Rd 48906 517-668-3100
Michael Foster, prin. Fax 668-3155

Lansing SD 14,500/PK-12
519 W Kalamazoo St 48933 517-755-1000
Dr. E. Sharon Banks, supt. Fax 755-1019
www.lansingschools.net/
Eastern HS 1,500/9-12
220 N Pennsylvania Ave 48912 517-755-1050
Pam Backus-Diggs, prin. Fax 755-1059
Everett HS 1,700/9-12
3900 Stabler St 48910 517-755-1080
Susan Land, prin. Fax 755-1089
Gardner MS 1,000/6-8
333 Dahlia Dr 48911 517-755-1120
Norm Gear, prin. Fax 755-1129
Hill Vocational Center Vo/Tech
5815 Wise Rd 48911 517-755-1060
Cordell Henderson, prin. Fax 755-1069
Otto MS 900/6-8
500 E Thomas St 48906 517-755-1150
Rod Doig, prin. Fax 755-1159
Pattengill MS 700/6-8
1017 Jerome St 48912 517-755-1130
Synthia Taylor, prin. Fax 755-1139
Rich MS 700/6-8
2600 Hampden Dr 48911 517-755-1160
Sandra Noecker, prin. Fax 755-1169
Sexton HS 1,100/9-12
102 Mcpherson Ave 48915 517-755-1070
Bersheril Bailey, prin. Fax 755-1079

Waverly Community SD 3,200/PK-12
515 Snow Rd 48917 517-321-7265
Thomas J. Pillar, supt. Fax 321-8577
web.waverly.k12.mi.us/index.cfm
Waverly HS 1,100/9-12
160 Snow Rd 48917 517-323-3831
David Percival, prin. Fax 323-7714
Waverly MS 500/7-8
620 Snow Rd 48917 517-321-7240
Vincent Perkins, prin. Fax 321-5789

Davenport College of Business Post-Sec.
220 E Kalamazoo St 48933 517-484-2600
Educational Inst./American Hotel-Lodging Post-Sec.
2113 N High St 48906 800-344-3320
Greater Lansing Adventist S 100/K-10
5330 W St Joe Hwy 48917 517-321-5565
Chad Bernard, prin. Fax 321-5580
Great Lakes Christian College Post-Sec.
6211 W Willow Hwy 48917 517-321-0242
Lansing Catholic Central HS 9-12
501 Marshall St 48912 517-267-2100
Thomas Maloney, prin. Fax 267-2135
Lansing Christian S 600/PK-12
3405 Belle Chase Way 48911 517-882-5779
James Koan, supt. Fax 882-5849
Lansing Community College Post-Sec.
419 N Capitol Ave 48933 517-483-1620
New Covenant Christian S 100/K-12
PO Box 80707 48908 517-323-8903
Jim Ryckman, prin. Fax 323-0421
Ross Medical Education Center Post-Sec.
913 W Holmes Rd Ste 260 48910 517-887-0180
Thomas M. Cooley Law School Post-Sec.
PO Box 13038 48901 517-371-5140

Lapeer, Lapeer, Pop. 9,370
Lapeer Community SD 6,700/PK-12
1025 W Nepessing St 48446 810-667-2401
Debbie Thompson, supt. Fax 667-2411
www.lapeerschools.org
Lapeer East HS 1,500/8-12
933 S Saginaw St 48446 810-667-2418
Kelly Paige, prin. Fax 667-2422
Lapeer West HS 1,500/8-12
170 Millville Rd 48446 810-667-2423
Kevin Walters, prin. Fax 667-2428

Lapeer County ISD
1996 W Oregon St 48446 810-664-5917
Joseph Keena, supt. Fax 664-1011
www.lcisd.k12.mi.us
Other Schools – See Attica

Health Enrichment Center Post-Sec.
204 E Nepessing St 48446 810-667-9453

Lathrup Village, Oakland, Pop. 4,157
Southfield SD
Supt. — See Southfield
Lathrup HS 1,700/9-12
19301 W 12 Mile Rd 48076 248-746-7204
Marcia Williams, prin. Fax 746-7488

Lawrence, Van Buren, Pop. 1,030
Lawrence SD 800/PK-12
650 W Saint Joseph St 49064 269-674-8233
Richard Stoll, supt. Fax 674-8206
www.lawrenceschools.cc
Lawrence JSHS 400/7-12
650 W Saint Joseph St 49064 269-674-8232
John Overley, prin. Fax 674-8206

Van Buren ISD
490 S Paw Paw St 49064 269-674-8091
Jeffrey Mills, supt. Fax 674-8030
www.vbisd.org/
Van Buren Technology Center Vo/Tech
250 South St 49064 269-674-8091
Fax 674-8954

Lawton, Van Buren, Pop. 1,852
Lawton Community SD 1,100/PK-12
101 Primary Way 49065 269-624-7900
Joseph Trimboli, supt. Fax 624-6489
www.lawtoncs.org
Lawton HS 300/9-12
880 E 2nd St 49065 269-624-7800
Tammy Wilson, prin. Fax 624-6554
Lawton MS 300/6-8
100 Blue Pride Dr 49065 269-624-7600
Tim Cerven, prin. Fax 624-5206

Leland, Leelanau
Leland SD 500/K-12
PO Box 498 49654 231-256-9857
Michael Hartigan, supt. Fax 256-9844
mail.leland.k12.mi.us
Leland S 500/K-12
PO Box 498 49654 231-256-9857
Terry Breen, prin. Fax 256-9844

Le Roy, Osceola, Pop. 266
Pine River Area SD 1,100/K-12
17445 Pine River Rd 49655 231-829-3141
Jim Ganger, supt. Fax 829-4410
www.pineriver.org/
Pine River Area HS 500/9-12
17445 Pine River Rd 49655 231-829-3841
Barb Parmenter, prin. Fax 829-4410
Pine River MS 300/6-8
17445 Pine River Rd 49655 231-829-4064
Darrell Holmes, prin. Fax 829-4410

Leslie, Ingham, Pop. 2,268
Leslie SD 1,400/K-12
432 N Main St 49251 517-589-8200
Robert Howe, supt. Fax 589-5340
www.lesliek12.net/
Leslie HS 500/9-12
4141 Hull Rd 49251 517-589-8294
Jeff Manthei, prin. Fax 589-5720
Leslie MS 400/5-8
400 Kimball St 49251 517-589-8218
Rick Samulak, prin. Fax 589-5714

Lincoln, Alcona, Pop. 352
Alcona Community SD 1,000/K-12
PO Box 249 48742 989-736-6212
Shawn Thornton, supt. Fax 736-6261
Alcona HS 300/9-12
PO Box 249 48742 989-736-8534
Jim Watts, prin. Fax 736-8495
Alcona MS 200/6-8
PO Box 249 48742 989-736-8534
Terrence Allison, prin. Fax 736-3184

Lincoln Park, Wayne, Pop. 38,237
Lincoln Park SD 5,100/K-12
1650 Champaign Rd 48146 313-389-0200
Randall H. Kite, supt. Fax 389-1322
www.resa.net/lincolnpark
Lincoln Park HS 1,400/9-12
1701 Champaign Rd 48146 313-389-0234
Dr. Kathy Evans, prin. Fax 383-5738
Lincoln Park MS 900/7-8
2800 Lafayette Blvd 48146 313-389-0757
Betty Diener, prin. Fax 389-0761

Linden, Genesee, Pop. 3,452
Lake Fenton Community SD
Supt. — See Fenton
Lake Fenton HS 500/9-12
4070 Lahring Rd 48451 810-591-9405
Julie Williams, prin. Fax 591-9495

Linden Community SD 2,900/PK-12
7205 Silver Lake Rd 48451 810-591-0980
Elizabeth Leonard, supt. Fax 591-5587
www.lindenschools.org
Linden HS 900/9-12
7201 Silver Lake Rd 48451 810-591-0410
Brian Boudreau, prin. Fax 591-8014
Linden MS 700/6-8
15425 Lobdell Rd 48451 810-591-0712
Julie Brown, prin. Fax 591-0155

Litchfield, Hillsdale, Pop. 1,429
Litchfield Community SD 500/K-12
210 Williams St 49252 517-542-2388
Clair Dean, supt. Fax 542-2580
www.litchfieldschools.com/
Litchfield JSHS 300/6-12
210 Williams St 49252 517-542-2386
Craig Lehrke, prin. Fax 542-2649

Livonia, Wayne, Pop. 97,977
Clarenceville SD 2,000/PK-12
20210 Middlebelt Rd 48152 248-919-0400
Cheryl M. Leach, supt. Fax 919-0430
www.clarenceville.k12.mi.us
Clarenceville HS 700/9-12
20155 Middlebelt Rd 48152 248-919-0408
Paul Shepich, prin. Fax 919-0438
Clarenceville MS 500/6-8
20210 Middlebelt Rd 48152 248-919-0406
Kathleen Guntzviller, prin. Fax 919-0436

Livonia SD 12,000/PK-12
15125 Farmington Rd 48154 734-744-2500
Randy A. Liepa, supt. Fax 744-2569
www.livonia.k12.mi.us
Churchill HS 2,300/9-12
8900 Newburgh Rd 48150 734-744-2650
R. Joseph Anderson, prin. Fax 744-2652
Emerson MS 700/7-8
29100 W Chicago St 48150 734-744-2665
Thomas Tobe, prin. Fax 744-2667
Franklin HS 1,700/9-12
31000 Joy Rd 48150 734-744-2655
Daniel Willenborg, prin. Fax 744-2657
Frost MS 800/7-8
14041 Stark Rd 48154 734-744-2670
Christina Berry, prin. Fax 744-2672
Holmes MS 600/7-8
16200 Newburgh Rd 48154 734-744-2675
Eric Stromberg, prin. Fax 744-2677
Livonia Career/Technical Center Vo/Tech
8985 Newburgh Rd 48150 734-744-2816
Dr. Janet Haas, prin. Fax 744-2817
Stevenson HS 2,200/9-12
33500 6 Mile Rd 48152 734-744-2660
Steven Archibald, prin. Fax 744-2662
Other Schools – See Westland

Ladywood HS 500/9-12
14680 Newburgh Rd 48154 734-591-1544
Sr. Mary Smith, prin. Fax 591-4214
Madonna University Post-Sec.
36600 Schoolcraft Rd 48150 734-432-5300
Schoolcraft College Post-Sec.
18600 Haggerty Rd 48152 734-462-4400
Virginia Farrell Beauty School Post-Sec.
33425 5 Mile Rd 48154 734-427-3970

Lowell, Kent, Pop. 4,140
Lowell Area SD 3,900/K-12
300 High St 49331 616-987-2500
Gregory Pratt, supt. Fax 987-2511
www.lowellschools.com/
Lowell HS 1,200/9-12
11700 Vergennes St 49331 616-987-2900
Scott Vashaw, prin. Fax 987-2911
Lowell MS 900/6-8
750 Foreman St 49331 616-987-2800
Linda Warren, prin. Fax 987-2811

Ludington, Mason, Pop. 8,292
Ludington Area SD 2,500/K-12
809 E Tinkham Ave 49431 231-845-7303
Cal DeKuiper, supt. Fax 843-4930
www.lasd.net
DeJonge JHS 400/7-8
706 E Tinkham Ave 49431 231-845-3810
Mark Boon, prin. Fax 845-3814
Ludington HS 800/9-12
508 N Washington Ave 49431 231-845-3880
Mark Boon, prin. Fax 845-3881

Mason-Lake ISD
2130 W US Highway 10 49431 231-757-3716
Jeanne Oakes, supt. Fax 757-2406
www.mlisd.k12.mi.us
Other Schools – See Scottville

Mc Bain, Missaukee, Pop. 747
McBain Rural Agricultural SD 1,100/PK-12
107 E Maple St 49657 231-825-2165
Daniel Bachman, supt. Fax 825-2119
www.mcbain.k12.mi.us
Mc Bain HS 400/9-12
107 E Maple St 49657 231-825-2412
Phillip Christensen, prin. Fax 825-2119
Mc Bain MS 200/6-8
107 E Maple St 49657 231-825-8041
Gail Loeks, prin. Fax 825-2119

Northern Michigan Christian S 400/PK-12
128 S Martin St 49657 231-825-2492
Marilyn Visser, prin. Fax 825-2371

Mackinac Island, Mackinac, Pop. 491
Mackinac Island SD 100/K-12
PO Box 340 49757 906-847-3377
Roger Schrock, supt. Fax 847-3773
mackinac.eup.k12.mi.us
Mackinac Island S 100/K-12
PO Box 340 49757 906-847-3377
Roger Schrock, prin. Fax 847-3773

Mackinaw City, Cheboygan, Pop. 862
Mackinaw City SD 200/K-12
609 W Central Ave 49701 231-436-8211
Jeffrey Curth, supt. Fax 436-5434
www.mackcity.k12.mi.us
Mackinaw City JSHS 100/7-12
609 W Central Ave 49701 231-436-8211
Vince LaCavera, prin.

Macomb, Macomb, Pop. 22,714
Chippewa Valley SD
Supt. — See Clinton Township
Dakota HS 2,200/9-12
21051 21 Mile Rd 48044 586-723-2702
Tom Heethius, prin. Fax 723-2701
Iroquois MS 900/6-8
48301 Romeo Plank Rd 48044 586-723-3700
James Capoferi, prin. Fax 723-3701

L'Anse Creuse SD
Supt. — See Harrison Township
L'Anse Creuse HS - North 1,800/9-12
23700 21 Mile Rd 48042 586-493-5270
David Jackson, prin. Fax 493-5275
L'Anse Creuse MS North 600/6-8
46201 Fairchild Rd 48042 586-493-5260
John Da Via, prin. Fax 493-5265

Lutheran HS North 600/9-12
16825 24 Mile Rd 48042 586-781-9151
Steven Buuck, prin. Fax 781-8673

Madison Heights, Oakland, Pop. 30,251
Lamphere SD 2,400/K-12
31201 Dorchester Ave 48071 248-589-1990
Marsha Pando, supt. Fax 589-2618
www.lamphere.k12.mi.us
Lamphere HS 800/9-12
610 W 13 Mile Rd 48071 248-589-3943
Ed Okuniewski, prin. Fax 589-0240
Page MS 600/6-8
29615 Tawas St 48071 248-589-3428
Douglas Kelley, prin. Fax 545-1870

Madison SD 1,100/PK-12
25421 Alger St 48071 248-399-7800
Dr. William Harrison, supt. Fax 399-2229
www.madisonschools.k12.mi.us/
Madison HS 600/9-12
915 E 11 Mile Rd 48071 248-548-1800
Robert Crowell, prin. Fax 548-9758
Wilkinson MS 300/7-8
26524 John R Rd 48071 248-399-0455
Fred Agemy, prin. Fax 399-1965

Bishop Foley HS 500/9-12
32000 Campbell Rd 48071 248-585-1210
Joanne Molnar, prin. Fax 585-3667
Dorsey Business School Post-Sec.
30821 Barrington St 48071 248-588-9660

Mancelona, Antrim, Pop. 1,386
Mancelona SD 1,200/K-12
PO Box 739 49659 231-587-9764
Matthew J. Miller, supt. Fax 587-9500
mancelonaschools.org/
Mancelona HS 400/9-12
PO Box 739 49659 231-587-8551
John Smith, prin. Fax 587-5401
Mancelona MS 400/5-8
PO Box 739 49659 231-587-9869
Jennifer Sabsook, prin. Fax 587-0615

Manchester, Washtenaw, Pop. 2,240
Manchester Community SD 1,300/K-12
410 City Rd 48158 734-428-9711
David Oegema Ph.D., supt. Fax 428-9188
www.mcs.k12.mi.us
Manchester HS 400/9-12
20500 Dutch Dr 48158 734-428-7333
Kevin Mowrer, prin. Fax 428-0178
Manchester MS 400/5-8
710 City Rd 48158 734-428-7442
Shanna Spickard, prin. Fax 428-9264

Manistee, Manistee, Pop. 6,656
Manistee Area SD 1,500/K-12
550 Maple St Ste 2 49660 231-723-3521
Robert Olsen, supt. Fax 723-1507
www.honoredstudents.org
Manistee HS 600/9-12
525 12th St 49660 231-723-2547
Andy Huber, prin. Fax 398-9277
Manistee MS 300/6-8
550 Maple St 49660 231-723-3271
Matt Kieffer, prin. Fax 723-5879

Manistee ISD
1710 Merkey Rd W 49660 231-723-4264
Charlene Myers, supt. Fax 723-1690
www.manistee.org
Shoreline Career Education Center Vo/Tech
772 E Parkdale Ave 49660 231-723-4264
Daniel Long, prin. Fax 723-1520

Manistee Catholic Central S 300/PK-12
1200 US Highway 31 S 49660 231-723-2529
Bryan Burns, prin. Fax 723-0669

Manistique, Schoolcraft, Pop. 3,460
Manistique Area SD 800/K-12
100 N Cedar St 49854 906-341-4300
Esther Mudge, supt. Fax 341-2374
www.manistique.k12.mi.us
Manistique HS 400/9-12
100 N Cedar St 49854 906-341-4300
Butch Yurk, prin. Fax 341-8473
Manistique MS 300/6-8
100 N Cedar St 49854 906-341-4300
Jason Lockwood, prin. Fax 341-8473

Manton, Wexford, Pop. 1,219
Manton Consolidated SD 1,100/K-12
105 5th St 49663 231-824-6411
Lon D. Schneider, supt. Fax 824-4101
www.manton.k12.mi.us
Manton HS 300/9-12
105 5th St 49663 231-824-6411
Fax 824-6114
Manton MS 400/5-8
105 5th St 49663 231-824-6401
Sue Murchie, prin. Fax 824-4121

Maple City, Leelanau
Glen Lake Community SD 900/K-12
3375 W Burdickville Rd 49664 231-334-3061
Joan Groening, supt. Fax 334-6255
www.glenlake.k12.mi.us
Glen Lake JSHS 500/6-12
3375 W Burdickville Rd 49664 231-334-3061
Kevin Kelly, prin. Fax 334-6295

Marcellus, Cass, Pop. 1,111
Marcellus Community SD 1,000/K-12
PO Box 48 49067 269-646-7655
Mary Cooper, supt. Fax 646-2700
www.marcelluscs.org/
Marcellus HS 300/9-12
PO Box 48 49067 269-646-5081
William Markovich, prin. Fax 646-5021
Marcellus MS 300/5-8
PO Box 48 49067 269-646-3158
Mary McCrumb, prin. Fax 646-2438

Howardsville Christian S 200/K-12
53441 Bent Rd 49067 269-646-9367
Dick Masse, admin. Fax 646-7006

Marine City, Saint Clair, Pop. 4,475
East China SD
Supt. — See East China
Marine City HS 800/9-12
1085 Ward St 48039 810-676-1900
William Jedele, prin. Fax 676-1925
Marine City MS 600/6-8
6373 King Rd 48039 810-676-1201
Michael Alley, prin. Fax 676-1225

Cardinal Mooney College Prep S 9-12
660 S Water St 48039 810-765-8825
Sr. Karen Lietz, prin. Fax 765-7164

Marion, Osceola, Pop. 837
Marion SD 700/K-12
PO Box O 49665 231-743-2486
Charles Chase, supt. Fax 743-2890
marion.k12.mi.us
Marion JSHS 400/7-12
PO Box O 49665 231-743-2836
Larry Johnson, prin. Fax 743-9622

Marlette, Sanilac, Pop. 2,070
Marlette Community SD 1,300/K-12
6230 Euclid St 48453 989-635-7425
Duane Lange, supt. Fax 635-7103
www.marlette.k12.mi.us
Marlette HS 400/9-12
3051 Moore St 48453 989-635-4930
Dale Moore, prin. Fax 635-5300
Marlette MS 500/4-8
6230 Euclid St 48453 989-635-7427
Michael Distelrath, prin. Fax 635-7103

Marquette, Marquette, Pop. 20,581
Marquette Area SD 3,400/K-12
1201 W Fair Ave 49855 906-225-5320
Jon Harrwig, supt. Fax 225-5340
www.mapsnet.org
Bothwell MS 800/6-8
1200 Tierney St 49855 906-225-4262
Sara Norton, prin. Fax 225-4229
Marquette HS 1,300/9-12
1203 W Fair Ave 49855 906-225-4254
Robert Anthony, prin. Fax 225-5370

Father Marquette MS 100/5-8
414 W College Ave 49855 906-226-7912
Karen Ogles, prin. Fax 225-9962
Marquette General Hospital Post-Sec.
420 W Magnetic St 49855 906-225-3434
Northern Michigan University Post-Sec.
1401 Presque Isle Ave 49855 906-227-1000

Marshall, Calhoun, Pop. 7,363
Marshall SD 2,500/K-12
100 E Green St 49068 269-781-1250
Dr. Joyce K. Phillips, supt. Fax 789-1813
www.marshall.k12.mi.us/
Marshall HS 800/9-12
701 N Marshall Ave 49068 269-781-1252
Ronald Behrenwald, prin. Fax 781-5304
Marshall MS 800/5-8
100 E Green St 49068 269-781-1250
David Turner, prin. Fax 781-7757

Martin, Allegan, Pop. 421
Martin SD 700/K-12
PO Box 241 49070 269-672-7194
D.G. Alexander, supt. Fax 672-7116
www.martin.k12.mi.us
Martin MSHS 400/6-12
PO Box 241 49070 269-672-5555
Dirk Weeldreyer, prin. Fax 672-9263

East Martin Christian HS 50/9-12
518 118th Ave 49070 269-672-7673
George Fennema, prin. Fax 672-7826

Marysville, Saint Clair, Pop. 10,042
Marysville SD 2,700/K-12
1111 Delaware Ave 48040 810-364-7731
John Silveri, supt. Fax 364-3150
www.marysville.k12.mi.us/mps/
Marysville HS 900/9-12
1325 Michigan Ave 48040 810-364-7161
Bill Farnsworth, prin. Fax 364-8878
Marysville IS 600/6-8
400 Collard Dr 48040 810-364-6336
John Sazehn, prin. Fax 364-4456

St. Clair County RESA 500/
PO Box 1500 48040 810-364-8990
Dan DeGrow, supt. Fax 364-7474
www.sccresa.org/
Career Technical Center Vo/Tech
PO Box 1500 48040 810-364-8990
Fax 364-8139

Mason, Ingham, Pop. 7,985
Ingham ISD
2630 W Howell Rd 48854 517-676-1051
Stanley Kogut, supt. Fax 676-1277
www.inghamisd.org
Capital Area Career Center Vo/Tech
611 Hagadorn Rd 48854 517-244-1330
Jim Menapace, prin. Fax 676-3602

Mason SD 3,100/K-12
118 W Oak St 48854 517-676-2484
James C. Harvey, supt. Fax 676-6058
scnc.mason.k12.mi.us
Mason HS 1,100/9-12
1001 S Barnes St 48854 517-676-9055
Lance Delbridge, prin. Fax 244-6412
Mason MS 700/6-8
235 Temple St 48854 517-676-6514
Daniel McConeghy, prin. Fax 676-0287

Mattawan, Van Buren, Pop. 2,838
Mattawan Consolidated SD 3,500/K-12
56720 Murray St 49071 269-668-3361
James Weeldreyer, supt. Fax 668-2372
www.mattawan.k12.mi.us
Mattawan HS 1,100/9-12
56720 Murray St 49071 269-668-3361
Colin Ripmaster, prin. Fax 668-8245
Mattawan MS 800/6-8
56720 Murray St 49071 269-668-3361
Jan Hall, prin. Fax 668-3188

Mayville, Tuscola, Pop. 1,034
Mayville Community SD 1,100/PK-12
6250 Fulton St 48744 989-843-6115
Bob Smith, supt. Fax 843-6988
www.mayville.k12.mi.us
Mayville HS 400/9-12
6250 Fulton St 48744 989-843-6115
Rhonda Blackburn, prin. Fax 843-7208
Mayville MS 300/6-8
6210 Fulton St 48744 989-843-6115
John LaGraff, prin. Fax 843-7209

Melvindale, Wayne, Pop. 10,612
Melvindale-Northern Allen Park SD 1,900/K-12
18530 Prospect St 48122 313-389-3300
Cora Kelly, supt. Fax 389-3312
www.melnap.k12.mi.us
Melvindale HS 800/9-12
18656 Prospect St 48122 313-389-3320
Russell Pickell, prin. Fax 389-2072
Strong MS 700/6-8
3303 Oakwood Blvd 48122 313-389-3330
Dr. Kim Soranno-Bond, prin. Fax 389-2077

Mendon, Saint Joseph, Pop. 933
Mendon Community SD 800/K-12
148 Kirby Rd 49072 269-496-8491
Charles Frisbie, supt. Fax 496-8234
www.mendonschools.org
Mendon HS 200/9-12
148 Kirby Rd 49072 269-496-8491
Jay Peterson, prin. Fax 496-8234
Mendon MS 200/6-8
148 Kirby Rd 49072 269-496-8491
Jay Peterson, prin. Fax 496-8234

Menominee, Menominee, Pop. 8,753
Menominee Area SD 1,400/PK-12
1230 13th St 49858 906-863-9951
Dr. Carol Swingle, supt. Fax 863-1171
www.menominee.k12.mi.us/
Menominee HS 600/9-12
2101 18th St 49858 906-863-7814
Paul Schneider, prin. Fax 863-8883
Menominee JHS 300/7-8
2101 18th St 49858 906-863-9929
Randy Verkerke, prin. Fax 863-8883

Merrill, Saginaw, Pop. 758
Merrill Community SD 900/PK-12
PO Box 488 48637 989-643-7261
John Searles, supt. Fax 643-5570
www.astihosted.com/mcsddcp/
Merrill HS 300/9-12
PO Box 488 48637 989-643-7231
Gary Smith, prin. Fax 643-7942
Merrill MS 200/6-8
PO Box 488 48637 989-643-7247
Gary Smith, prin. Fax 643-5971

Mesick, Wexford, Pop. 463
Mesick Consolidated SD 900/K-12
PO Box 275 49668 231-885-1200
Dennis Stratton, supt. Fax 885-1234
www.mesick.org
Mesick HS 300/9-12
PO Box 275 49668 231-885-1201
Fred Boss, prin. Fax 885-2554
Mesick MS 300/5-8
PO Box 275 49668 231-885-1207
Deann Jenkins, prin. Fax 885-2544

Michigan Center, Jackson, Pop. 4,863
Michigan Center SD 1,400/PK-12
400 S State St 49254 517-764-5778
Mark Haag, supt. Fax 764-5790
scnc.mcps.k12.mi.us
Michigan Center JSHS 700/7-12
400 S State St 49254 517-764-1440
Tom Claus, prin. Fax 764-3346

Middleton, Gratiot
Fulton SD 800/PK-12
8060 Ely Hwy 48856 989-236-7300
Charles Seguna, supt. Fax 236-7660
www.fulton.edzone.net
Fulton HS 300/9-12
8060 Ely Hwy 48856 989-236-7232
Chuck Mungall, prin. Fax 236-7628
Fulton MS 100/7-8
8060 Ely Hwy 48856 989-236-7232
Terry Maier, prin. Fax 236-7628

Middleville, Barry, Pop. 2,790
Thornapple-Kellogg SD 2,900/PK-12
10051 Green Lake Rd 49333 269-795-3313
Kevin Konarska, supt. Fax 795-5401
www.tk.k12.mi.us
Thornapple-Kellogg HS 1,000/9-12
3885 Bender Rd 49333 269-795-3394
Tony Koski, prin. Fax 795-5492
Thornapple-Kellogg MS 600/6-8
10375 Green Lake Rd 49333 269-795-3349
Jon Washburn, prin. Fax 795-5455

Midland, Midland, Pop. 41,760
Bullock Creek SD 2,000/K-12
1420 S Badour Rd 48640 989-631-9022
John M. Hill, supt. Fax 631-2882
www.bcreek.k12.mi.us
Bullock Creek HS 700/9-12
1420 S Badour Rd 48640 989-631-2340
Charles Schwedler, prin. Fax 631-2882
Bullock Creek MS 500/6-8
644 S Badour Rd 48640 989-631-9260
Craig Carmoney, prin. Fax 832-4018

Midland SD 9,500/K-12
600 E Carpenter St 48640 989-923-5001
Carl Ellinger, supt. Fax 923-5003
www.mps.k12.mi.us
Central MS 600/6-8
305 E Reardon St 48640 989-923-5571
Paula Geller, prin. Fax 923-5518
Dow HS 1,500/9-12
3901 N Saginaw Rd 48640 989-923-5382
Janice Goodall, prin. Fax 923-5301
Jefferson MS 900/6-8
800 W Chapel Ln 48640 989-923-5873
Michael Decker, prin. Fax 923-5800
Midland HS 1,800/9-12
1301 Eastlawn Dr 48642 989-923-5181
Michael Frazee, prin. Fax 923-5100
Northeast MS 900/6-8
1305 E Sugnet Rd 48642 989-923-5772
Margaret Lee, prin. Fax 923-5780

Calvary Baptist Academy 400/PK-12
6100 Perrine Rd 48640 989-832-3341
Michael Reece, prin. Fax 832-7443
Davenport University - Central Region Post-Sec.
3555 E Patrick Rd 48642 989-835-5588
Midland Christian S 100/PK-12
4417 W Wackerly St 48640 989-835-9881
William Spicer, prin. Fax 835-5201
Northwood University Post-Sec.
4000 Whiting Dr 48640 800-457-7878

Milan, Monroe, Pop. 5,376
Milan Area SD 2,200/K-12
100 Big Red Dr 48160 734-439-5050
Dennis McComb, supt. Fax 439-5083
www.milanareaschools.org/
Milan HS 700/9-12
200 Big Red Dr 48160 734-439-5000
Ron Reed, prin. Fax 439-5084
Milan MS 500/6-8
920 North St 48160 734-439-5200
William Brown, prin. Fax 439-5288

Milford, Oakland, Pop. 6,587
Huron Valley SD
Supt. — See Highland
Muir MS 600/6-8
425 George St 48381 248-684-8060
Gayle Lizzet, prin. Fax 684-8068

West Highland Christian Academy 100/K-12
1116 S Hickory Ridge Rd 48380 248-887-6698
Eunice Sanford, admin. Fax 887-4645

Millington, Tuscola, Pop. 1,115
Millington Community SD 1,300/K-12
8780 Dean Dr 48746 989-871-5227
Lawrence R. Kroswek, supt. Fax 871-5260
www.mcsdistrict.com
Meachum JHS 500/5-8
8537 Gleason St 48746 989-871-5269
Gary Iwinski, prin. Fax 871-5249
Millington HS 500/9-12
8780 Dean Dr 48746 989-871-5221
Thomas Frampton, prin. Fax 871-5244

Mio, Oscoda, Pop. 1,886
Mio-AuSable SD 800/K-12
1110 W 8th St 48647 989-826-2400
Christina Siwik, supt. Fax 826-2415
www.mio.k12.mi.us
Mio-AuSable HS 300/9-12
1110 W 8th St 48647 989-826-2481
James Gendernalik, prin. Fax 826-2416
Mio-AuSable MS 100/7-8
1110 W 8th St 48647 989-826-2481
James Gendernalik, prin. Fax 826-2416

Monroe, Monroe, Pop. 21,791
Jefferson SD 2,500/PK-12
2400 N Dixie Hwy 48162 734-289-5550
Timothy Fitzpatrick, supt. Fax 289-5574
www.jefferson.k12.mi.us/
Jefferson HS 800/9-12
5707 Williams Rd 48162 734-289-5555
David Vensel, prin. Fax 289-5595
Jefferson MS 400/PK-PK, 7-
5102 N Stoney Creek Rd 48162 734-289-5565
Stephen Kinsland, prin. Fax 289-5596

Monroe SD 6,800/K-12
PO Box 733 48161 734-265-3000
David Taylor, supt. Fax 265-3001
www.monroe.k12.mi.us

Cantrick MS 600/6-8
1008 Riverview Ave 48162 734-265-3800
Jeffrey LaRoux, prin. Fax 265-3801

Monroe HS 2,200/9-12
901 Herr Rd 48161 734-265-3400
Ralph Carducci, prin. Fax 265-3401

Monroe MS 1,000/6-8
503 Washington St 48161 734-265-4000
Ryan McLeod, prin. Fax 265-4001

Meadow Montessori S 200/PK-12
1670 S Raisinville Rd 48161 734-241-9496
Catharine Calder, hdmstr. Fax 241-0829

Michigan College of Beauty Post-Sec.
15232 1/2 S Dixie Hwy 48161 734-241-8877

Monroe County Community College Post-Sec.
1555 S Raisinville Rd 48161 734-242-7300

St. Mary HS 400/9-12
108 W Elm Ave 48162 734-241-0663
Matthew Saxer, prin. Fax 241-9042

Montague, Muskegon, Pop. 2,339

Montague Area SD 1,500/PK-12
4882 Stanton Blvd 49437 231-893-1515
James Booth, supt. Fax 894-6586
www.montague.k12.mi.us

Chisholm MS 400/6-8
4700 Stanton Blvd 49437 231-894-5617
Gary Beaudoin, prin. Fax 894-5728

Montague HS 500/9-12
4900 Stanton Blvd 49437 231-894-2661
Kevin Kruger, prin. Fax 893-0609

Montrose, Genesee, Pop. 1,552

Montrose Community SD 1,800/PK-12
PO Box 3129 48457 810-591-7267
Mark Kleinhans, supt. Fax 591-7268
www.montrose.k12.mi.us

Hill-McCloy HS 500/9-12
PO Box 3129 48457 810-591-8822
James Ply, prin. Fax 591-7281

Kuehn-Haven MS 500/5-8
PO Box 3129 48457 810-591-8832
Edward Graham, prin. Fax 591-7282

Morenci, Lenawee, Pop. 2,352

Morenci Area SD 900/PK-12
500 Page St 49256 517-458-7501
Kyle Griffith, supt. Fax 458-7821
www.morenci.k12.mi.us

Morenci HS 300/9-12
788 Coomer St 49256 517-458-7502
Nate Parker, prin. Fax 458-7146

Morenci MS 300/5-8
304 Page St 49256 517-458-7506
Kay Johnson, prin. Fax 458-3379

Morley, Mecosta, Pop. 501

Morley Stanwood Community SD 1,600/K-12
4700 Northland Dr 49336 231-856-4392
Linda L.H. Myers, supt. Fax 856-4180
morleystanwood.org

Morley-Stanwood HS 500/9-12
4700 Northland Dr 49336 231-856-4444
Dennis Szczerowski, prin. Fax 856-7012

Morley-Stanwood MS 500/5-8
4808 Northland Dr 49336 231-856-4550
Terry Baker, prin. Fax 856-0136

Morrice, Shiawassee, Pop. 888

Morrice Area SD 700/K-12
691 Purdy Ln 48857 517-625-3142
Bruce Burger, supt. Fax 625-3866
www.morrice.k12.mi.us

Morrice JSHS 300/7-12
691 Purdy Ln 48857 517-625-3143
Samuel Manino, prin. Fax 625-8935

Mount Clemens, Macomb, Pop. 17,053

L'Anse Creuse SD
Supt. — See Harrison Township

L'Anse Creuse/Mt Clemens Adult Educ Ctr. Adult
33 N River Rd 48043 586-783-6420
Michelle Irwin, prin. Fax 783-6423

Mount Clemens Community SD 2,700/PK-12
167 Cass Ave 48043 586-469-6100
Dr. T.C. Wallace, supt. Fax 469-5569
www.mtcps.org

Mount Clemens HS 700/9-12
155 Cass Ave 48043 586-461-3400
Nelson Jackson, prin. Fax 469-7058

Mount Clemens MS 400/7-8
161 Cass Ave 48043 586-461-3300
Paul Reeves, prin. Fax 469-7066

Mount Morris, Genesee, Pop. 3,321

Beecher Community SD
Supt. — See Flint

Beecher HS 500/9-12
6255 Neff Rd 48458 810-591-9220
Jerri Lynn Williams, admin. Fax 591-6911

Beecher MS 300/7-8
6255 Neff Rd 48458 810-591-9220
Jerri Lynn Williams, admin. Fax 591-6911

Riley Adult Education Adult
1149 W Klein St 48458 810-591-9219
D. Cassidy, coord. Fax 591-5617

Mount Morris Consolidated SD 3,200/K-12
12356 Walter St 48458 810-591-8760
Lisa Hagel, supt. Fax 591-7469
www.mtmorrisschools.org

Johnson HS 800/9-12
8041 Neff Rd 48458 810-591-2370
John Ploof, prin. Fax 591-3410

Mount Morris JHS 500/7-8
12356 Walter St 48458 810-591-7100
Matthew Olson, prin. Fax 591-7105

Mount Pleasant, Isabella, Pop. 26,253

Beal City SD 700/PK-12
3117 Elias Rd 48858 989-644-3901
Robert J. Kjolhede, supt. Fax 644-5847
www.edzone.net/bealcity/

Beal City JSHS 300/7-12
3117 Elias Rd 48858 989-644-3944
Jeffrey Jackson, prin. Fax 644-5847

Mount Pleasant SD 3,500/K-12
720 N Kinney Ave 48858 989-775-2300
Gary Allen, supt. Fax 775-2309
www.mtpleasant.edzone.net

Mount Pleasant HS 1,200/9-12
1155 S Elizabeth St 48858 989-775-2200
Jeffrey Thoenes, prin. Fax 773-0631

Mt. Pleasant Vocational Education Ctr Vo/Tech
1155 S Elizabeth St 48858 989-775-2210
Michael Pung, prin. Fax 775-2215

West IS 600/7-8
440 S Bradley St 48858 989-775-2220
Luke Stefanovsky, prin. Fax 775-2229

Mount Pleasant Comm. & Adult Ed. Adult
1651 S Bamber Rd 48858 989-775-2370
Mary Murphy, prin. Fax 773-7840

Central Michigan University Post-Sec.
100 Warriner Hall 48859 989-774-4000

M.J. Murphy Beauty College Post-Sec.
201 W Broadway St 48858 989-772-2339

Mt. Pleasant Christian Academy 50/K-12
1802 E High St 48858 989-773-9082
Michael Hoge, admin. Fax 772-7468

Sacred Heart Academy 200/7-12
316 E Michigan St 48858 989-772-1457
Denny Starnes, prin. Fax 772-1707

Saginaw Chippewa Tribal College Post-Sec.
2274 Enterprise Dr 48858 989-775-4123

Munising, Alger, Pop. 2,386

Munising SD 700/K-12
411 Elm Ave 49862 906-387-2251
Barbara Hase, supt. Fax 387-5416
www.mps-up.com

Munising MSHS 300/7-12
810 State Highway M28 W 49862 906-387-2103
Peter Kelto, prin. Fax 387-5686

Muskegon, Muskegon, Pop. 39,919

Muskegon Area ISD
630 Harvey St 49442 231-777-2637
Susan Meston, supt. Fax 773-3498
www.muskegonisd.org

Muskegon Area Career Tech Center Vo/Tech
200 Harvey St 49442 231-767-3600
Mike Carpenter, prin. Fax 767-2692

Muskegon SD 6,400/PK-12
349 W Webster Ave 49440 231-720-2000
Colin Armstrong, supt. Fax 720-2050
www.muskegon.k12.mi.us/

Bunker JHS 700/6-8
2312 Denmark St 49441 231-720-2300
Bradley Perkins, prin. Fax 720-2325

Muskegon HS 1,600/9-12
80 W Southern Ave 49441 231-720-2800
David Lewis, prin. Fax 720-2811

Steele JHS 600/6-8
1150 Amity Ave 49442 231-720-3000
Arthur Duren, prin. Fax 720-3025

Oakridge SD 2,000/PK-12
275 S Wolf Lake Rd 49442 231-788-7100
Thomas Paniucki, supt. Fax 788-7114
www.oakridgeschools.org

Oakridge HS 600/9-12
5493 Hall Rd 49442 231-788-7300
Dave Mieras, prin. Fax 788-7314

Oakridge MS 300/7-8
251 S Wolf Lake Rd 49442 231-788-7400
Jason Kennedy, prin. Fax 788-7414

Orchard View SD 2,600/PK-12
35 S Sheridan Dr 49442 231-760-1300
B. Jack VanderWall, supt. Fax 760-1323
www.orchardview.org

Orchard View HS 800/9-12
2310 Marquette Ave 49442 231-760-1400
Jerry Walter, prin. Fax 760-1407

Orchard View MS 700/6-8
35 S Sheridan Dr 49442 231-760-1500
Jim Nielsen, prin. Fax 760-1506

Reeths-Puffer SD
Supt. — See North Muskegon

Reeths-Puffer HS 1,400/9-12
1545 Roberts Rd 49445 231-744-1647
Daniel Beckeman, prin. Fax 744-4796

Baker College of Muskegon Post-Sec.
1903 Marquette Ave 49442 231-777-5200

Muskegon Catholic Central HS 300/9-12
1145 W Laketon Ave 49441 231-755-2201
Robert Bridges, prin. Fax 755-8615

Muskegon Catholic Central MS 200/5-8
1145 W Laketon Ave 49441 231-759-0180
Michael Devitt, prin. Fax 755-2415

Muskegon Community College Post-Sec.
221 S Quarterline Rd 49442 231-773-9131

Ross Medical Education Center Post-Sec.
950 W Norton Ave 49441 231-730-9531

Western Michigan Christian HS 200/9-12
455 E Ellis Rd 49441 231-799-9644
David VerMerris, prin. Fax 798-9018

Muskegon Heights, Muskegon, Pop. 11,821

Muskegon Heights SD 1,900/PK-12
2603 Leahy St 49444 231-830-3200
Dana Bryant, supt. Fax 830-3560
www.remc4.k12.mi.us/muskegon-hts/

Muskegon Heights HS 600/9-12
2441 Sanford St 49444 231-830-3700
Danny Smith, prin. Fax 830-3534

Muskegon Heights MS 300/7-8
55 E Sherman Blvd 49444 231-830-3600
Reedell Holmes, prin. Fax 830-3572

Napoleon, Jackson, Pop. 1,332

Napoleon Community SD 1,600/K-12
PO Box 308 49261 517-536-8667
James Graham, supt. Fax 536-8006
www.napoleonschools.org

Napoleon HS 500/9-12
PO Box 308 49261 517-536-8667
Barb Nugent, prin. Fax 536-8007

Napoleon MS 400/6-8
PO Box 308 49261 517-536-8667
Shelley Jusick, prin. Fax 536-8005

Negaunee, Marquette, Pop. 4,471

Negaunee SD 1,500/K-12
101 S Pioneer Ave 49866 906-475-4157
Jim Derocher, supt. Fax 475-5107
www.negaunee.k12.mi.us/

Negaunee HS 500/9-12
500 W Arch St 49866 906-475-7861
Robert Bonetti, prin. Fax 475-7989

Negaunee MS 400/6-8
102 W Case St 49866 906-475-7866
Dan Skewis, prin. Fax 475-6408

Newaygo, Newaygo, Pop. 1,685

Newaygo SD 1,900/K-12
PO Box 820 49337 231-652-6984
Larry Lethorn, supt. Fax 652-6505
www.newaygo.net

Newaygo HS 600/9-12
PO Box 820 49337 231-652-1646
Joel Lantz, prin. Fax 652-3500

Newaygo MS 500/6-8
PO Box 820 49337 231-652-1285
Troy Lindley, prin. Fax 652-9704

New Baltimore, Macomb, Pop. 11,165

Anchor Bay SD
Supt. — See Casco

Anchor Bay MS North 800/6-8
52805 Ashley Dr 48047 586-725-7373
Tim Brisbois, prin. Fax 725-6760

Anchor Bay MS South 800/6-8
48650 Sugarbush Rd 48047 586-949-4510
Douglas Glassford, prin. Fax 949-4739

Newberry, Luce, Pop. 1,598

Tahquamenon Area SD 1,100/PK-12
700 Newberry Ave 49868 906-293-3226
Alice Walker, supt. Fax 293-3709
eup.k12.mi.us/tahquamenon

Newberry HS 300/9-12
700 Newberry Ave 49868 906-293-3243
Tonya Perry, prin.

Newberry MS 300/6-8
700 Newberry Ave 49868 906-293-5197
Dennis Peacock, prin.

New Boston, Wayne

Huron SD 2,300/K-12
32044 Huron River Dr 48164 734-782-2441
Thomas Hosler, supt. Fax 783-0338
www.huronschools.org

Huron HS 800/9-12
32044 Huron River Dr 48164 734-782-1436
Rod Hopper, prin. Fax 783-1534

Renton JHS 500/6-8
31578 Huron River Dr 48164 734-782-2483
Kurt Mrocko, prin. Fax 783-0327

New Buffalo, Berrien, Pop. 2,274

New Buffalo Area SD 700/K-12
1112 E Clay St 49117 269-469-6010
Michael Lindley, supt. Fax 469-3315
www.nbas.org/

New Buffalo HS 300/9-12
1112 E Clay St 49117 269-469-6001
Ronald Hart, prin. Fax 469-6017

New Buffalo MS 200/6-8
1112 E Clay St 49117 269-469-6003
William Welling, prin. Fax 469-6017

New Haven, Macomb, Pop. 4,708

New Haven Community SD 600/PK-12
PO Box 482000 48048 586-749-5123
Dr. James Avery, supt. Fax 749-6307
newhaven.misd.net/

New Haven HS 300/9-12
PO Box 482000 48048 586-749-5104
Denise Robbins, prin. Fax 749-8460

Other Schools – See Ray

New Lothrop, Shiawassee, Pop. 598

New Lothrop Area SD 800/PK-12
PO Box 339 48460 810-638-5091
John Strycker, supt. Fax 638-7277
www.newlothrop.k12.mi.us

New Lothrop JSHS 400/7-12
PO Box 339 48460 810-638-5054
Michael Carmean, prin. Fax 638-5057

Newport, Monroe

Lutheran HS South 50/9-12
8290 N Telegraph Rd 48166 734-586-8832
Steven Garrabrandt, prin. Fax 586-2478

Niles, Berrien, Pop. 11,738
Brandywine Community SD 1,200/K-12
1830 S 3rd St 49120 269-684-7150
Gary Rider, supt. Fax 684-8998
www.remc11.k12.mi.us/brandy/
Brandywine MSHS 400/7-12
1700 Bell Rd 49120 269-683-4800
Greg Jones, prin. Fax 683-1186

Niles Community SD 3,600/PK-12
111 Spruce St 49120 269-683-0732
Douglas Law, supt. Fax 684-6337
www.nilesschools.org
Niles HS 1,100/9-12
1441 Eagle St 49120 269-683-2894
James Knoll, prin. Fax 684-9516
Ring Lardner MS 600/7-8
801 N 17th St 49120 269-683-6610
Douglas Langmeyer, prin. Fax 684-9524
Niles Adult Education Adult
111 Spruce St 49120 269-684-4480
Richard Klemm, dir. Fax 684-9548

North Adams, Hillsdale, Pop. 500
North Adams-Jerome SD 600/K-12
4555 Knowles Rd 49262 517-287-4214
Christopher Voisin, supt. Fax 287-4722
www.najps.org
North Adams-Jerome JSHS 300/7-12
4555 Knowles Rd 49262 517-287-4214
Carl Christenson, prin. Fax 287-4722

North Branch, Lapeer, Pop. 1,008
North Branch Area SD 2,700/K-12
PO Box 3620 48461 810-688-3570
Alan Piwinski, supt. Fax 688-4344
northbranchschools.lapeer.org/
North Branch HS 800/9-12
PO Box 3620 48461 810-688-3001
Mark Hiltunen, prin. Fax 688-8057
North Branch MS 400/7-8
PO Box 3620 48461 810-688-4431
John Sherman, prin. Fax 688-4344

North Muskegon, Muskegon, Pop. 4,012
North Muskegon SD 900/K-12
1600 Mills Ave 49445 231-719-4100
Mr. John L. Weaver, supt. Fax 744-0739
www.nmps.k12.mi.us
North Muskegon HS 300/9-12
1507 Mills Ave 49445 231-719-4110
James VanBergen, prin. Fax 744-0739
North Muskegon MS 200/6-8
1507 Mills Ave 49445 231-719-4110
James VanBergen, prin. Fax 744-0739

Reeths-Puffer SD 4,100/PK-12
991 W Giles Rd 49445 231-744-4736
Stephen Cousins, supt. Fax 744-9497
www.reeths-puffer.org/
Reeths-Puffer MS 700/7-8
1911 W Giles Rd 49445 231-744-4721
Steve Edwards, prin. Fax 744-6049
Other Schools – See Muskegon

Northport, Leelanau, Pop. 651
Northport SD 200/K-12
PO Box 188 49670 231-386-5153
Ty Wessell, supt. Fax 386-9838
Northport S 200/K-12
PO Box 188 49670 231-386-5154
Ty Wessell, prin. Fax 386-9838

Northville, Oakland, Pop. 6,311
Northville SD 6,400/K-12
501 W Main St 48167 248-349-3400
Leonard Rezmierski, supt. Fax 347-6928
www.northville.k12.mi.us/
Hillside MS 800/6-8
775 N Center St 48167 248-344-8493
James Cracraft, prin. Fax 334-8480
Meads Mill MS 800/6-8
16700 Franklin Rd, 248-344-8435
Sue Meyer, prin. Fax 334-1830
Northville HS 1,900/9-12
45700 6 Mile Rd, 248-344-8420
Rob Watson, prin. Fax 344-8497

Norton Shores, Muskegon, Pop. 23,479
Mona Shores SD 4,200/K-12
3374 Mccracken St 49441 231-780-4751
Terry Babbitt, supt. Fax 780-2099
www.monashores.net
Mona Shores HS 1,400/9-12
1121 Seminole Rd 49441 231-780-4711
Dennis Vanderstelt, prin. Fax 780-3634
Mona Shores MS 1,000/6-8
1700 Woodside Rd 49441 231-759-8506
Scott Levandoski, prin. Fax 755-0514

Norway, Dickinson, Pop. 2,973
Norway-Vulcan Area SD 900/PK-12
300 Section St 49870 906-563-9552
Randall Van Gasse, supt. Fax 563-5169
www.norway.k12.mi.us
Norway HS 300/9-12
300 Section St 49870 906-563-9542
Donald Byczek, prin. Fax 563-8708
Vulcan MS, 300 Section St 49870 300/5-8
Andrew Hongisto, prin. 906-563-9563

Novi, Oakland, Pop. 53,115
Novi Community SD 6,200/K-12
25345 Taft Rd 48374 248-449-1200
Peter Dion, supt. Fax 449-1219
www.novi.k12.mi.us
Novi HS 1,900/9-12
24062 Taft Rd 48375 248-449-1500
John Lawrence, prin. Fax 449-1519
Novi MS 1,000/7-8
49000 W 11 Mile Rd 48374 248-449-1600
Milan Obrenovich, prin. Fax 449-1619

Catholic Central HS 9-12
27225 Wixom Rd 48374 248-596-3810
Rev. Richard Ranalletti, prin. Fax 596-3839
Franklin Road Christian S 300/K-12
40800 W 13 Mile Rd 48377 248-668-7100
Rev. Timothy Gambino, supt. Fax 668-7101
Novi Christian S 200/1-12
45301 W 11 Mile Rd 48375 248-349-9441
Dr. Gary Elfner, admin. Fax 349-3481

Oakland, Oakland
Lake Orion Community SD
Supt. — See Lake Orion
Oakview MS 600/6-8
917 Lake George Rd 48363 248-693-0321
Alice Seppanen, prin. Fax 693-5419

Oak Park, Oakland, Pop. 31,194
Berkley SD 4,300/PK-12
14700 Lincoln St 48237 248-837-8000
Tresa Zumsteg Ph.D., supt. Fax 544-5835
www.berkley.k12.mi.us
Other Schools – See Berkley

Ferndale SD
Supt. — See Ferndale
Center for Advanced Studies & the Arts 11-12
23561 Rosewood St 48237 248-586-8860
Bill James, prin. Fax 548-8863
Ferndale Adult & Community Education Adult
22001 Republic Ave 48237 248-586-8900
Fran Foote Ph.D., dir. Fax 586-8882

Oak Park SD 3,500/PK-12
13900 Granzon St 48237 248-336-7700
Sandra Harris, supt. Fax 336-7738
www.oakparkschools.org
Oak Park HS 1,400/9-12
13701 Oak Park Blvd 48237 248-336-7740
Lisa Phillips, prin. Fax 336-7758
Roosevelt MS 800/6-8
23261 Scotia Rd 48237 248-336-7620
William Washington, prin. Fax 336-7638

Beth Jacob School for Girls 400/K-12
14390 W 10 Mile Rd 48237 248-544-9070
Shulamis Rubinfeld, prin. Fax 544-4662
Michigan Jewish Institute Post-Sec.
25401 Coolidge Hwy 48237 248-414-6900
Oholei Yosef Yitzchak Lubavich S 100/K-12
14100 W 9 Mile Rd 48237 248-541-5441
Rabbi B. Stein, prin. Fax 541-6022
Yeshiva Gedolah HS 100/9-12
24600 Greenfield Rd 48237 248-968-3360
David Wayntraub, prin. Fax 968-8613
Yeshiva Gedolah Rabbinical College Post-Sec.
24600 Greenfield Rd 48237 248-968-3360

Okemos, Ingham, Pop. 20,216
Okemos SD 4,000/K-12
4406 Okemos Rd 48864 517-349-1418
Lee Gerard Ph.D., supt. Fax 349-6235
okemos.k12.mi.us/
Chippewa MS 500/6-8
4000 Okemos Rd 48864 517-349-4460
Thomas Tweedy, prin. Fax 347-9824
Kinawa MS 500/6-8
1900 Kinawa Dr 48864 517-349-9220
Barbara Hoevel, prin. Fax 347-4189
Okemos HS 1,400/9-12
2800 Jolly Rd 48864 517-351-7900
John Lanzetta, prin. Fax 351-2850

Olivet, Eaton, Pop. 1,789
Olivet Community SD 1,300/K-12
255 1st St 49076 269-749-9129
David Campbell, supt. Fax 749-9701
www.olivetschools.org
Olivet HS 400/9-12
255 1st St 49076 269-749-3671
Randall VanDyke, prin. Fax 749-4560
Olivet MS 500/4-8
255 1st St 49076 269-749-9953
M. Bensinger, prin. Fax 749-9701

Olivet College Post-Sec.
300 S Main St 49076 269-749-7000

Onaway, Presque Isle, Pop. 961
Onaway Area SD 800/K-12
4549 M 33 49765 989-733-4970
Bob Szymoniak, supt. Fax 733-8612
www.onawayschools.com/
Onaway HS 300/9-12
4549 M 33 49765 989-733-4800
Bob Szymoniak, prin. Fax 733-4889
Onaway MS 200/6-8
4549 M 33 49765 989-733-4850
Bob Szymoniak, prin. Fax 733-4899

Onekama, Manistee, Pop. 634
Onekama Consolidated SD 500/K-12
5016 Main St 49675 231-889-4251
Kevin Hughes, supt. Fax 889-3720
www.onekama.k12.mi.us
Onekama MSHS 300/6-12
5016 Main St 49675 231-889-5521
Gina Hagen, prin. Fax 889-9567

Onsted, Lenawee, Pop. 1,021
Onsted Community SD 1,000/K-12
PO Box 220 49265 517-467-2174
Max Baxter, supt. Fax 467-2026
www.onsted.k12.mi.us
Onsted HS 600/9-12
PO Box 220 49265 517-467-2171
Dave Lauer, prin. Fax 467-6910
Onsted MS 500/6-8
PO Box 220 49265 517-467-2168
Ryan Rowe, prin. Fax 467-6907

Ontonagon, Ontonagon, Pop. 1,637
Ontonagon Area SD 600/K-12
301 Greenland Rd 49953 906-884-4963
Matthew Lukshaitis, supt. Fax 884-2057
www.oasd.k12.mi.us
Ontonagon JSHS 300/7-12
701 Parker Ave 49953 906-884-4433
John Shiner, prin. Fax 884-2742

Orchard Lake, Oakland

St. Marys Preparatory HS 500/9-12
3535 Indian Trl 48324 248-683-0530
James Glowacki, prin. Fax 683-1740
SS. Cyril and Methodius Seminary Post-Sec.
3535 Indian Trl 48324 248-683-0310

Ortonville, Oakland, Pop. 1,509
Brandon SD 3,600/K-12
1025 S Ortonville Rd 48462 248-627-1800
Thomas Miller, supt. Fax 627-4533
www.brandon.k12.mi.us
Brandon HS 1,200/9-12
1025 S Ortonville Rd 48462 248-627-1820
Dr. Michael Ferguson, prin. Fax 627-5628
Brandon MS 600/7-8
609 S Ortonville Rd 48462 248-627-1830
Dr. William Snyder, prin. Fax 627-7201

Oscoda, Iosco, Pop. 1,061
Oscoda Area SD 1,400/PK-12
3550 E River Rd 48750 989-739-2033
Christine Beardsley, supt. Fax 739-2325
www.oscodaschools.org
Oscoda Area HS 600/9-12
3550 E River Rd 48750 989-739-9121
Rexford G. Hart, prin. Fax 739-1688
Richardson S 400/3-8
3630 E River Rd 48750 989-739-9173
Charles Negro, prin. Fax 739-2510

Otisville, Genesee, Pop. 845
LakeVille Community SD 1,800/K-12
11107 Washburn Rd 48463 810-591-6525
Theodora Gardella, supt. Fax 591-6538
www.lakeville.k12.mi.us/
Lakeville HS 700/9-12
11107 Washburn Rd 48463 810-591-4051
Dennis Grunden, prin. Fax 591-6522
Lakeville MS 500/6-8
11107 Washburn Rd 48463 810-591-3945
Aaron Moran, prin. Fax 591-6632

Otsego, Allegan, Pop. 3,941
Otsego SD 2,200/PK-12
313 W Allegan St 49078 269-692-6066
Dennis M. Patzer, supt. Fax 692-6074
www.otsegops.org/
Otsego HS 700/9-12
540 Washington St 49078 269-692-6166
Herve Dardis, prin. Fax 692-6188
Otsego MS 500/6-8
538 Washington St 49078 269-692-6199
Bill Houseman, prin. Fax 692-6203

Ottawa Lake, Monroe
Whiteford Agricultural SD 800/PK-12
6655 Consear Rd 49267 734-856-1443
Craig Haugen, supt. Fax 854-6463
scnc.whiteford.k12.mi.us
Whiteford HS 300/9-12
6655 Consear Rd 49267 734-856-1443
Jeff Humason, prin. Fax 856-2564
Whiteford MS 200/6-8
6655 Consear Rd 49267 734-856-1443
Jeff Humason, prin. Fax 856-2564

Owendale, Huron, Pop. 279
Owendale-Gagetown Area SD 200/K-12
7166 E Main St 48754 989-678-4261
Dana Compton, supt. Fax 678-4284
www.owengage.org/
Owendale-Gagetown JSHS 100/6-12
7166 E Main St 48754 989-678-4141
Dana Compton, prin. Fax 678-0920

Owosso, Shiawassee, Pop. 15,422
Owosso SD 4,000/K-12
PO Box 340 48867 989-723-8131
Greg Gray, supt. Fax 723-7777
www.owosso.k12.mi.us
Owosso HS 1,300/9-12
765 E North St 48867 989-723-8231
Marci Williams, prin. Fax 729-5600
Owosso MS 600/7-8
219 N Water St 48867 989-723-3460
Rich Collins, prin. Fax 729-5760

Baker College of Owosso Post-Sec.
1020 S Washington St 48867 989-729-3300

Oxford, Oakland, Pop. 3,564
Oxford Area Community SD 4,100/K-12
105 Pontiac St 48371 248-969-5000
Virginia Brennan-Kyro, supt. Fax 969-5016
www.oxford.k12.mi.us
Oxford HS 1,200/9-12
745 N Oxford Rd 48371 248-969-5100
Mike Schweig, prin. Fax 969-5145
Oxford MS 900/6-8
1420 E Lakeville Rd 48371 248-969-1800
Kenneth Weaver, prin. Fax 969-1840

Painesdale, Houghton
Adams Township SD 400/K-12
PO Box 37 49955 906-482-0599
Patrick Rozich, supt. Fax 487-5999
www.adams.k12.mi.us
Jeffers JSHS 200/7-12
PO Box 37 49955 906-482-0580
Janice Maierle, prin. Fax 487-5999

Paradise, Chippewa
Whitefish Township Community SD 100/K-12
PO Box 58 49768 906-492-3353
Patrick Rowley, supt. Fax 492-3254
www.eup.k12.mi.us/whitefish
Whitefish Township S 100/K-12
PO Box 58 49768 906-492-3353
Patrick Rowley, prin. Fax 492-3254

Parchment, Kalamazoo, Pop. 1,813
Parchment SD 1,800/K-12
520 N Orient St 49004 269-488-1050
Michael O'Connor, supt. Fax 488-1060
www.parchmentschools.org
Parchment HS 600/9-12
1916 E G Ave 49004 269-488-1100
Scott Karaptian, prin. Fax 488-1110
Parchment MS 400/6-8
307 N Riverview Dr 49004 269-488-1200
George Stamas, prin. Fax 488-1210
Other Schools – See Kalamazoo

Parma, Jackson, Pop. 879
Western SD 2,800/K-12
1400 S Dearing Rd 49269 517-841-8100
William Coale Ph.D., supt. Fax 841-8801
www.westernschools.org/
Western HS 800/9-12
1400 S Dearing Rd 49269 517-841-8200
Brent Cryderman, prin. Fax 841-8802
Western MS 700/6-8
1400 S Dearing Rd 49269 517-841-8300
Amy Potts, prin. Fax 841-8803
Other Schools – See Jackson

Paw Paw, Van Buren, Pop. 3,328
Paw Paw SD 2,200/K-12
119 Johnson Rd 49079 269-657-8800
Mark Bielang, supt. Fax 657-7292
www.ppps.org
Paw Paw HS 700/9-12
30609 E Red Arrow Hwy 49079 269-657-8840
Michael Dahlinger, prin. Fax 655-0009
Paw Paw MS 500/6-8
313 W Michigan Ave 49079 269-657-8870
Donald Barnhouse, prin. Fax 657-5011

Peck, Sanilac, Pop. 587
Peck Community SD 600/K-12
222 E Lapeer St 48466 810-378-5171
David M. Bush, supt. Fax 378-5116
www.peck.k12.mi.us
Peck JSHS, 222 E Lapeer St 48466 300/7-12
Willard Roles, prin. 810-378-5501

Sanilac ISD
175 E Aitken Rd 48466 810-648-4700
Timothy Edwards Ph.D., supt. Fax 648-5784
www.sanilac.k12.mi.us
Sanilac Career Center Vo/Tech
175 E Aitken Rd 48466 810-648-4700
Deborah Wild, dir. Fax 648-4834

Pellston, Emmet, Pop. 798
Pellston SD 800/K-12
172 Park St 49769 231-539-8682
William Tebbe, supt. Fax 539-8838
www.pellstonschools.org/
Pellston HS 200/9-12
172 Park St 49769 231-539-8801
Teresa Emery, prin. Fax 539-8110
Pellston MS 200/6-8
172 Park St 49769 231-539-8801
Anthony Basanese, prin. Fax 539-8110

Pentwater, Oceana, Pop. 984
Pentwater SD 300/K-12
600 Park St 49449 231-869-4100
Jake Huffman, supt. Fax 869-4535
www.pentwater.k12.mi.us
Pentwater S 300/K-12
600 Park St 49449 231-869-4100
Jake Huffman, prin. Fax 869-4535

Perry, Shiawassee, Pop. 2,052
Perry SD 2,000/PK-12
PO Box 900 48872 517-625-3108
Jacklyn Hurd, supt. Fax 625-6256
www.perry.k12.mi.us
Perry HS 600/9-12
2555 W Britton Rd 48872 517-625-3104
Steven Liestenfeltz, prin. Fax 625-0012
Perry MS 500/6-8
2775 W Britton Rd 48872 517-625-6196
Dan Hare, prin. Fax 625-0120

Petersburg, Monroe, Pop. 1,138
Summerfield SD 800/K-12
17555 Ida West Rd 49270 734-279-1035
John Hewitt, supt. Fax 279-1448
www.summerfield.k12.mi.us
Summerfield HS 300/9-12
17555 Ida West Rd 49270 734-279-1012
Scott Leach, prin. Fax 279-1018
Summerfield MS 100/7-8
232 E Elm St 49270 734-279-1013
Jodi Bucher, prin. Fax 279-1017

Petoskey, Emmet, Pop. 6,198
Petoskey SD 3,100/K-12
PO Box 247 49770 231-348-2100
John Scholten, supt. Fax 348-2342
www.petoskeyschools.org
Petoskey HS 1,100/9-12
1500 Hill St 49770 231-348-2160
David Snyder, prin. Fax 348-2214
Petoskey MS 700/6-8
801 Northmen Dr 49770 231-348-2150
David Gracy, prin. Fax 348-2234

North Central Michigan College Post-Sec.
1515 Howard St 49770 231-348-6600

Pickford, Chippewa
Pickford SD 400/K-12
PO Box 278 49774 906-647-6285
Keith Krahnke, supt. Fax 647-3706
pickford.eup.k12.mi.us/
Pickford HS 100/9-12
PO Box 278 49774 906-647-4028
Neil Harrison, prin. Fax 647-3706

Pigeon, Huron, Pop. 1,130
Elkton-Pigeon-Bay Port Laker SD 1,100/K-12
6136 Pigeon Rd 48755 989-453-4600
Robert Drury, supt. Fax 453-4609
www.lakerschools.org/
Laker HS 400/9-12
6136 Pigeon Rd 48755 989-453-4600
Lisa Dicamillo, prin. Fax 453-4615
Laker MS 300/6-8
6136 Pigeon Rd 48755 989-453-4600
Lisa DiCamillo, prin. Fax 453-4609

Pinckney, Livingston, Pop. 2,435
Pinckney Community SD 5,000/K-12
2130 E MI 36 48169 810-225-3900
Daniel Danosky, supt. Fax 225-3905
www.pcs.k12.mi.us
Pathfinder S 800/7-8
2100 E MI 36 48169 810-225-5200
Richard Todd, prin. Fax 225-5205
Pinckney Community HS 1,600/9-12
10255 Dexter Pinckney Rd 48169 810-225-5500
James Darga, prin. Fax 225-5505

Livingston Christian S 100/PK-12
550 E Hamburg St 48169 734-878-9818
Theodore Nast, admin. Fax 878-9830

Pinconning, Bay, Pop. 1,349
Pinconning Area SD 1,800/K-12
605 W 5th St 48650 989-879-4556
Darren Kroczaleski, supt. Fax 879-4705
www.pasd.org/
Pinconning Area HS 700/9-12
605 W 5th St 48650 989-879-2311
Mike Vieau, prin. Fax 879-7258
Pinconning Area MS 300/7-8
605 W 5th St 48650 989-879-2311
Keith Wetters, prin. Fax 879-7258

Pittsford, Hillsdale
Pittsford Area SD 700/K-12
9304 Hamilton Rd 49271 517-523-3481
Richard S. Satterlee, supt. Fax 523-3467
www.pas.k12.mi.us/
Pittsford JSHS 300/7-12
9304 Hamilton Rd 49271 517-523-3481
Charles Pelham, prin. Fax 523-2059

Freedom Farm Christian S 100/K-12
9400 E Beecher Rd 49271 517-523-3426
Timothy Neinas, prin. Fax 523-3427

Plainwell, Allegan, Pop. 3,996
Plainwell Community SD 2,800/PK-12
600 School Dr 49080 269-685-5823
Susan Wakefield, supt. Fax 685-1108
www.plainwellschools.org
Plainwell HS 900/9-12
684 Starr Rd 49080 269-685-9554
Ron Faurot, prin. Fax 685-9064
Plainwell MS 700/6-8
720 Brigham St 49080 269-685-5813
William Willett, prin. Fax 685-2099

Plymouth, Wayne, Pop. 9,100
Plymouth-Canton Community SD 17,800/K-12
454 S Harvey St 48170 734-416-2700
Dr. James Ryan, supt. Fax 416-4932
www.pccs.k12.mi.us
Central MS 800/6-8
650 Church St 48170 734-416-2990
Joyce Johnson, prin. Fax 416-7699
East MS 800/6-8
1042 S Mill St 48170 734-416-4950
Marsha Hoff, prin. Fax 416-4949
Pioneer MS 800/6-8
46081 Ann Arbor Rd W 48170 734-416-2770
Philip Freeman, prin. Fax 416-7569
West MS 800/6-8
44401 W Ann Arbor Trl 48170 734-416-7550
Ellison Franklin, prin. Fax 416-7648
Other Schools – See Canton

Metropolitan SDA Jr Academy 50/K-10
15585 N Haggerty Rd 48170 734-420-4044
David Tripp, prin. Fax 420-3710
Michigan Theological Seminary Post-Sec.
41550 E Ann Arbor Trl 48170 734-207-9581

Pontiac, Oakland, Pop. 67,331
Oakland ISD
Supt. — See Waterford
Joblink Career Center Vo/Tech
1847 N Perry St 48340 248-276-9470
Roland Hill, dir. Fax 276-9471
Oakland Technical Campus NE Vo/Tech
1371 N Perry St 48340 248-451-2700
Scott Harris, dean Fax 451-2720

Pontiac SD 8,800/K-12
47200 Woodward Ave 48342 248-451-6800
Mildred Mason Ph.D., supt. Fax 451-6890
www.pontiac.k12.mi.us
Jefferson MS 500/6-8
600 Motor St 48341 248-451-7620
Wendy Fitzpatrick, prin. Fax 451-7631
Lincoln MS 500/6-8
131 Hillside Dr 48342 248-451-7650
Gloria Hill, prin. Fax 451-7670
Madison MS 800/6-8
1275 N Perry St 48340 248-451-8010
Arlee Ewing, prin. Fax 451-8034
Pontiac Central HS 1,400/9-12
300 W Huron St 48341 248-451-7100
Tommaleta Hughes, prin. Fax 451-7181
Pontiac Northern HS 1,500/9-12
1051 Arlene Ave 48340 248-451-7300
Tommie Hicks, prin. Fax 451-7321
Bethune South Campus Adult
154 Lake St 48341 248-451-8060
Janice Hill, prin. Fax 451-8063

Marist Academy 300/6-8
1300 Giddings Rd 48340 248-373-5371
Sandra Favrow, prin. Fax 373-4707
Notre Dame Preparatory HS 800/9-12
1300 Giddings Rd 48340 248-373-5300
Rev. Joseph Hindelang, prin. Fax 373-8024
Oakland County Health Division Post-Sec.
1200 N Telegraph Rd 48341 248-858-1832

Portage, Kalamazoo, Pop. 45,277
Portage SD 8,800/K-12
8111 S Westnedge Ave 49002 269-323-5000
Marsha Wells, supt. Fax 323-5001
www.portageps.org
Northern HS 1,300/9-12
1000 Idaho Ave 49024 269-323-5400
Jim French, prin. Fax 323-5490
North MS 600/6-8
5808 Oregon Ave 49024 269-323-5700
Celeste Shelton-Harris, prin. Fax 323-5790
Portage Central HS 1,500/9-12
8135 S Westnedge Ave 49002 269-323-5200
Eric Alburtus, prin. Fax 323-5290
Portage Central MS 700/6-8
8305 S Westnedge Ave 49002 269-323-5600
David Babcock, prin. Fax 323-5690
West MS 700/6-8
7145 Moorsbridge Rd 49024 269-323-5800
Larry Killips, prin. Fax 323-5890

Chic University of Cosmetology Post-Sec.
6091 Constitution Blvd 49024 269-329-3333
Wright Beauty Academy Post-Sec.
6666 Lovers Ln 49002 269-321-8708

Port Hope, Huron, Pop. 288
Port Hope Community SD 100/K-12
7840 Portland Rd 48468 989-428-4151
Scott Belt, supt. Fax 428-4153
Port Hope S 100/K-12
7840 Portland Rd 48468 989-428-4151
Michael Bowman, prin. Fax 428-4153

Port Huron, Saint Clair, Pop. 31,501
Port Huron Area SD 11,200/PK-12
PO Box 5013 48061 810-984-3101
Thomas Shorkey, supt. Fax 984-6606
www.port-huron.k12.mi.us
Central MS 700/6-8
200 32nd St 48060 810-984-6533
Terry Stoneburner, prin. Fax 989-2709
Chippewa MS 700/6-8
2800 Chippewa Trl 48060 810-984-6539
Lisa Duman, prin. Fax 989-2712
Holland Woods MS 500/6-8
1617 Holland Ave 48060 810-984-6548
Cheryl Rogers, prin. Fax 989-2713
Port Huron HS 1,900/9-12
2215 Court St 48060 810-984-2611
Ken Semelsberger, prin. Fax 984-6559
Port Huron Northern HS 1,600/9-12
1799 Krafft Rd 48060 810-984-2671
Craig Dahlke, prin. Fax 984-2747
Port Huron Adult Ed Programs Adult
1320 Washington Ave 48060 810-984-6552
Gloria Henry, prin. Fax 984-6624
Other Schools – See Fort Gratiot

Baker College of Port Huron Post-Sec.
3403 Lapeer Rd 48060 810-985-7000
McCormick Catholic Academy 100/6-8
2865 Henry St 48060 810-985-9599
Deborah Krueger, prin. Fax 985-9686
Port Huron Hospital Post-Sec.
1001 Kearney St 48060 810-987-5000
Ross Medical Education Center Post-Sec.
3568 Pine Grove Ave 48060 810-982-0454
St. Clair County Community College Post-Sec.
323 Erie St 48060 810-984-3881

Portland, Ionia, Pop. 3,822
Portland SD 2,000/K-12
1100 Ionia Rd 48875 517-647-4161
Charles Dumas, supt. Fax 647-2975
www.portlandk12.org
Portland HS 600/9-12
1100 Ionia Rd 48875 517-647-2981
David Bouck, prin. Fax 647-1791

Portland MS 500/6-8
745 Storz St 48875 517-647-2985
Bill Carlton, prin. Fax 647-2820

St. Patrick HS 100/9-12
122 N West St 48875 517-647-7551
Sr. Patricia Kidder, prin. Fax 647-4545

Posen, Presque Isle, Pop. 282
Posen Consolidated SD 9 300/K-12
PO Box 187 49776 989-766-2573
John Palmer, supt. Fax 766-2519
www.posen.k12.mi.us
Posen Consolidated JSHS 200/7-12
PO Box 187 49776 989-766-2471
Dru Milliron, prin. Fax 766-2519

Potterville, Eaton, Pop. 2,205
Potterville SD 900/K-12
420 N High St 48876 517-645-2662
William Eis, supt. Fax 645-0092
www.pps.k12.mi.us/
Potterville HS 300/9-12
422 N High St 48876 517-645-7609
Linda Wigginton, prin. Fax 645-0177
Potterville MS 300/5-8
424 N High St 48876 517-645-4777
Scott Martin, prin. Fax 645-0091

Powers, Menominee, Pop. 424
North Central Area SD
Supt. — See Hermansville
North Central JSHS 200/7-12
PO Box 601 49874 906-497-5226
Randall Platti, prin. Fax 497-5066

Prescott, Ogemaw, Pop. 285
Whittemore-Prescott Area SD
Supt. — See Whittemore
Whittemore-Prescott JHS 200/7-8
PO Box 100 48756 989-873-4986
Dorothy Miller, prin. Fax 873-6096

Quincy, Branch, Pop. 1,657
Quincy Community SD 1,500/PK-12
1 Educational Pkwy 49082 517-639-7141
Joseph Lopez, supt. Fax 639-4273
www.quincyschools.org
Quincy HS 500/9-12
18 Colfax St 49082 517-639-9245
William Milnes, prin. Fax 639-3701
Quincy MS 400/6-8
32 Fulton St 49082 517-639-4201
David Spalding, prin. Fax 639-3701

Rapid River, Delta
Rapid River SD 500/K-12
PO Box 68 49878 906-474-6411
Terri Mileski, supt. Fax 474-9903
Rapid River JSHS 300/6-12
PO Box 68 49878 906-474-6411
Karen Lundquist, prin. Fax 474-9883

Ravenna, Muskegon, Pop. 1,238
Ravenna SD 1,200/K-12
12322 Stafford St 49451 231-853-2231
Jeanette Magsig, supt. Fax 853-2193
www.ravenna.k12.mi.us
Ravenna HS 400/9-12
2766 S Ravenna Rd 49451 231-853-2218
Scott Sherman, prin. Fax 853-6981
Ravenna MS 300/6-8
2700 S Ravenna Rd 49451 231-853-2268
Dale Overbeek, prin. Fax 853-2629

Ray, Macomb
New Haven Community SD
Supt. — See New Haven
New Haven MS 300/5-8
24125 26 Mile Rd 48096 586-749-3401
David Rayes, prin. Fax 749-8338

Reading, Hillsdale, Pop. 1,104
Reading Community SD 900/K-12
519 W Elm St 49274 517-283-2166
Robert Luchenbill, supt. Fax 283-3519
www.rcsk12.org
Owens JSHS 400/7-12
301 Chestnut St 49274 517-283-2142
Rick Bailey, prin. Fax 283-3758

Redford, Wayne, Pop. 51,100
Detroit SD
Supt. — See Detroit
Ann Arbor Trail MS 400/6-8
7635 Chatham 48239 313-274-8560
Deborah Ferguson, prin. Fax 274-8074

Redford Union SD 4,300/PK-12
18499 Beech Daly Rd 48240 313-242-6000
Donna Rhodes, supt. Fax 242-6025
www.redfordu.k12.mi.us
Hilbert MS 900/6-8
26440 Puritan 48239 313-242-4000
Susan Shelton, prin. Fax 242-4005
Redford Union HS 1,200/9-12
17711 Kinloch 48240 313-242-4200
Karen Moran, prin. Fax 242-4205
Pearson Education Center Adult
19990 Beech Daly Rd 48240 313-242-6100
Patrick Duffy, dir. Fax 242-6105

South Redford SD 3,300/K-12
26141 Schoolcraft 48239 313-535-4000
William F. Weber Ph.D., supt. Fax 535-6121
southredford.net
Pierce MS 800/6-8
25605 Orangelawn 48239 313-937-8880
Michael White, prin. Fax 937-9486

Thurston HS 1,100/9-12
26255 Schoolcraft 48239 313-535-4000
William Zolkowski, prin. Fax 592-0740

Ross Medical Education Center Post-Sec.
9327 Telegraph Rd 48239 313-794-6448

Reed City, Osceola, Pop. 2,418
Reed City Area SD 1,500/K-12
829 S Chestnut St Ste A 49677 231-832-2201
Steven Westhoff, supt. Fax 832-2202
Reed City HS 600/9-12
225 W Church Ave 49677 231-832-2224
Tom Antioho, prin. Fax 832-2501
Reed City MS 500/6-8
233 W Church Ave 49677 231-832-6174
Tim Webster, prin. Fax 832-6180

Reese, Tuscola, Pop. 1,365
Reese SD 1,100/PK-12
PO Box 389 48757 989-868-9864
Storm Lairson, supt. Fax 868-9570
www.reese.k12.mi.us/
Reese HS 400/9-12
PO Box 389 48757 989-868-4191
Ryle Kiser, prin. Fax 868-4091
Reese MS 300/5-8
PO Box 389 48757 989-868-4157
Jan Jones, prin. Fax 868-1609

Remus, Mecosta
Chippewa Hills SD 2,700/PK-12
3226 Arthur Rd 49340 989-967-2000
Cheryl Hahnenberg, supt. Fax 967-2009
www.chsd.us
Chippewa Hills HS 800/9-12
3226 Arthur Rd 49340 989-967-2100
John Zolynsky, prin. Fax 967-2109
Chippewa Hills IS 600/6-8
3102 Arthur Rd 49340 989-967-2200
Bob Grover, prin. Fax 967-2209

Republic, Marquette
Republic-Michigamme SD 100/K-12
227 Maple St 49879 906-376-2277
Vicki Holsworth, supt. Fax 376-8299
www.republicmichigamme.maisd.k12.mi.us
Republic-Michigamme S 100/K-12
227 Maple St 49879 906-376-2277
Vicki Holsworth, prin. Fax 376-8299

Richland, Kalamazoo, Pop. 707
Gull Lake Community SD 3,000/K-12
11775 E D Ave 49083 269-629-5880
Rich Ramsey, supt. Fax 629-5527
www.gulllakecs.org
Gull Lake HS 1,000/9-12
9550 M 89 49083 269-629-5803
James Corstange, prin. Fax 629-3077
Other Schools – See Hickory Corners

Richmond, Macomb, Pop. 5,607
Richmond Community SD 2,100/PK-12
68931 S Main St 48062 586-727-3565
Patrick Bird, supt. Fax 727-2098
www.richmond.misd.net/
Richmond HS 700/9-12
35320 Division Rd 48062 586-727-3225
Patrick Olsen, prin. Fax 727-9072
Richmond MS 700/5-8
35250 Division Rd 48062 586-727-7552
Timm Kelly, prin. Fax 727-2545

Riley, Saint Clair
Memphis Community SD 1,100/K-12
34110 Bordman Rd 48041 810-392-2151
Dr. David Symington, supt. Fax 392-3614
www.memphis.k12.mi.us
Memphis HS 400/9-12
34130 Bordman Rd 48041 810-392-2186
Sharon Manthey, prin. Fax 392-2083
Memphis JHS 300/6-8
34130 Bordman Rd 48041 810-392-2131
Kenneth Reygaert, prin. Fax 392-2513

River Rouge, Wayne, Pop. 9,202
River Rouge SD 1,500/PK-12
1460 Coolidge Hwy 48218 313-297-9600
Marie Miller, supt. Fax 842-8790
www.resa.net/riverrouge/index.htm
River Rouge HS 800/8-12
1460 Coolidge Hwy 48218 313-297-9600
Rosa Benford, prin. Fax 297-7322

Riverview, Wayne, Pop. 12,744
Riverview Community SD 2,600/K-12
13425 Colvin St Ste 1 734-285-9660
Dennis Desmarais, supt. Fax 285-9822
www.riverviewschools.com
Riverview HS 900/9-12
12431 Longsdorf St, 734-285-7361
Charles Pike, prin. Fax 785-6598
Seitz MS 600/6-8
17800 Kennebec St, 734-285-2043
Fred Keier, prin. Fax 285-6649

Detroit Business Institute Post-Sec.
19100 Fort St, 734-479-0660
Richard HS 400/9-12
15325 Pennsylvania Rd, 734-284-1875
Br. James Rottenbucher, prin. Fax 284-9304

Rochester, Oakland, Pop. 11,209
Rochester Community SD 14,400/K-12
501 W University Dr 48307 248-726-3000
Dave Pruneau, supt. Fax 726-3105
www.rochester.k12.mi.us/
Hart MS 1,000/6-8
6500 Sheldon Rd 48306 248-726-4500
Cheryl Tocco, prin. Fax 726-4505
Reuther JHS 700/6-8
1430 E Auburn Rd 48307 248-726-4700
Dave Hurst, prin. Fax 726-4705
Van Hoosen JHS 800/6-8
1339 N Adams Rd 48306 248-726-4900
Stephen Cook, prin. Fax 726-4905
Other Schools – See Rochester Hills

Rochester Hills, Oakland, Pop. 69,995
Avondale SD
Supt. — See Auburn Hills
Avondale MS 600/7-8
1445 W Auburn Rd 48309 248-537-6300
Todd Robinson, prin. Fax 537-6305

Rochester Community SD
Supt. — See Rochester
Adams HS 1,400/9-12
3200 W Tienken Rd 48306 248-726-5200
Diann Flack, prin. Fax 726-5205
Rochester HS 1,800/9-12
180 S Livernois Rd 48307 248-726-5400
Wendy Shepard, prin. Fax 726-5405
Stony Creek HS 1,400/9-12
575 E Tienken Rd 48306 248-726-5700
Dan Hickey, prin. Fax 726-5705
West JHS 800/6-8
500 Old Perch Rd 48309 248-726-5000
Mike Dillon, prin. Fax 726-5005

Holy Family Regional S - South Campus 500/4-8
2633 John R Rd 48307 248-299-3798
Sr. Karen Hawver, prin. Fax 299-3843
Lutheran HS Northwest 300/9-12
1000 Bagley Dr 48309 248-852-6677
Paul Looker, prin. Fax 852-2667
Oakland University Post-Sec.
2200 N Squirrel Rd 48309 248-370-2100
Rochester College Post-Sec.
800 W Avon Rd 48307 248-218-2000
Rochester Hills Christian S 300/PK-12
3300 S Livernois Rd 48307 248-852-0585
Karen Patton, prin. Fax 852-4757

Rock, Delta
Mid Peninsula SD 300/K-12
5055 Saint Nicholas 31st Rd 49880 906-359-4387
Mike Loy, supt. Fax 359-4167
midpen.dsisd.net/
Mid Peninsula S 300/K-12
5055 Saint Nicholas 31st Rd 49880 906-359-4390
Bethney Bergh, prin. Fax 359-4113

Rockford, Kent, Pop. 5,062
Rockford SD 7,600/PK-12
350 N Main St 49341 616-863-6320
Michael Shibler Ph.D., supt. Fax 866-1911
www.rockfordschools.org
East Rockford MS 900/6-8
8615 9 Mile Rd NE 49341 616-863-6140
Dan Warren, prin. Fax 863-6565
North Rockford MS 900/6-8
397 E Division St 49341 616-863-6300
Lisa Weidenfeller, prin. Fax 866-5998
Rockford Freshman Center 600/9-9
4500 Kroes St NE 49341 616-863-6348
Douglas VanderJagt, prin. Fax 866-7134
Rockford HS 1,800/10-12
4100 Kroes St NE 49341 616-863-6030
Daniel Zang, prin. Fax 866-5997

Rogers City, Presque Isle, Pop. 3,201
Rogers City Area SD 600/K-12
251 W Huron Ave 49779 989-734-9100
Paul Mancine, supt. Fax 734-7428
www.rcas.k12.mi.us
Rogers City JSHS 400/6-12
1033 W Huron Ave 49779 989-734-9170
Deborah Jones, prin. Fax 734-2969

Romeo, Macomb, Pop. 3,815
Romeo Community SD 5,500/K-12
316 N Main St 48065 586-752-0200
Joseph Beck, supt. Fax 752-0228
www.romeo.k12.mi.us
Romeo HS 1,800/9-12
11091 32 Mile Rd 48065 586-752-0300
Gavin Johnson, prin. Fax 752-0402
Romeo MS 700/6-8
297 Prospect St 48065 586-752-0240
Sam Argiri, prin. Fax 752-0256
Other Schools – See Washington

Romulus, Wayne, Pop. 23,853
Romulus Community SD 4,000/PK-12
36540 Grant St 48174 734-532-1600
Carl Weiss, supt. Fax 532-1611
www.romulus.net/
Romulus HS 1,200/9-12
9650 Wayne Rd 48174 734-532-1000
Daniel Hurst, prin. Fax 532-1001
Romulus JHS 700/7-8
37300 Wick Rd 48174 734-532-1700
Phyllis Adkins, prin. Fax 532-1701

Roscommon, Roscommon, Pop. 1,105
Gerrish-Higgins SD 1,800/K-12
PO Box 825 48653 989-275-6600
Donald Mick, supt. Fax 275-6608
www.ghsd.k12.mi.us/
Roscommon HS 600/9-12
PO Box 825 48653 989-275-6675
Daniel Scow, prin. Fax 275-6681
Roscommon MS 600/5-8
PO Box 825 48653 989-275-6640
Ron Alden, prin. Fax 275-6609

Kirtland Community College Post-Sec.
10775 N Saint Helen Rd 48653 989-275-5000

Rose City, Ogemaw, Pop. 715
West Branch-Rose City Area SD
Supt. — See West Branch
Rose City MS 200/5-8
PO Box 407 48654 989-343-2250
Shelly Fales, prin. Fax 343-2299

Roseville, Macomb, Pop. 47,708
Roseville Community SD 6,400/K-12
18975 Church St 48066 586-445-5505
John Kment, supt. Fax 771-1772
www.rcs.misd.net
Eastland JHS 600/7-9
18700 Frank St 48066 586-445-5702
Mark Blaszkowski, prin. Fax 445-5721
Roseville HS 1,400/10-12
17855 Common Rd 48066 586-445-5542
Peter Hedemark, prin. Fax 445-5654
Roseville JHS 1,000/7-9
16250 Martin Rd 48066 586-445-5605
Paul Schummer, prin. Fax 445-5620

Dorsey Business School Post-Sec.
31542 Gratiot Ave 48066 586-296-3225

Royal Oak, Oakland, Pop. 58,299
Oakland ISD
Supt. — See Waterford
Oakland Technical Campus SE Vo/Tech
5055 Delemere Ave 48073 248-288-4020
Bonnie Crowson, dean Fax 288-4071

Royal Oak SD 5,100/PK-12
1123 Lexington Blvd 48073 248-435-8400
Thomas Moline, supt. Fax 435-6170
www.royaloakschools.com
Addams MS 700/6-8
2222 W Webster Rd 48073 248-288-3100
Cecilia Boyer, prin. Fax 288-3144
Keller MS 700/6-8
1505 N Campbell Rd 48067 248-542-6500
George Guzzio, prin. Fax 542-9227
Royal Oak HS 1,200/9-12
1500 Lexington Blvd 48073 248-435-8500
Thomas Neville, prin. Fax 288-8733

David Pressley School of Cosmetology Post-Sec.
1127 S Washington Ave 48067 248-548-5090
Oakland Community College Post-Sec.
739 S Washington Ave 48067 248-246-2400
Shrine Academy 7-8
3500 W 13 Mile Rd 48073 248-549-2928
Gabrielle Erken, prin. Fax 549-2953
Shrine HS 300/9-12
3500 W 13 Mile Rd 48073 248-549-2925
Gabrielle Erken, prin. Fax 549-2953
William Beaumont Hospital Post-Sec.
3601 W 13 Mile Rd 48073 248-551-0681

Rudyard, Chippewa
Rudyard Area SD 1,000/K-12
PO Box 246 49780 906-478-3771
Gary Davis, supt. Fax 478-3912
eup.k12.mi.us/rudyard/index.html
Rudyard HS 300/9-12
PO Box 246 49780 906-478-3471
Richard Guimond, prin. Fax 478-4101
Rudyard MS, PO Box 246 49780 300/6-8
Richard Smith, prin. 906-478-3710

Saginaw, Saginaw, Pop. 58,361
Buena Vista SD 1,200/PK-12
PO Box 14829 48601 989-755-2184
Deborah T. Clarke, supt. Fax 755-0286
www.bvsd.us
Buena Vista HS 300/9-12
PO Box 14829 48601 989-754-1493
Fax 758-0915
Ricker MS 500/5-8
PO Box 14829 48601 989-753-6438
Theresa Doyle, prin. Fax 753-4953

Carrollton SD 1,300/K-12
3211 Carla Dr 48604 989-754-1475
Craig Douglas, supt. Fax 754-1470
www2.carrollton.k12.mi.us/
Carrollton Omni Adult Education Adult
479 Shattuck Rd 48604 989-753-3478
Mary Beth Handeyside, prin. Fax 754-1470
Other Schools – See Carrollton

Saginaw SD 10,200/PK-12
550 Millard St 48607 989-399-6500
Gerald Dawkins, supt. Fax 399-6635
www.spsd.net
Central MS 600/6-8
1010 Hoyt Ave 48607 989-399-5300
Nathaniel McClain, prin. Fax 399-5315
Hill HS 1,400/9-12
3115 Mackinaw St 48602 989-399-5800
Kathleen Andros, prin. Fax 399-5815
Saginaw Arts & Sciences Academy 400/6-12
200 Congress Ave 48602 989-399-5500
Janet Nash, prin. Fax 399-5515
Saginaw Career Complex Vo/Tech
2102 Weiss St 48602 989-399-6150
Julie Walker, prin. Fax 399-6165
Saginaw HS 1,200/9-12
3100 Webber St 48601 989-399-6000
Clifford Davis, prin. Fax 399-6015
South MS 700/6-8
224 N Elm St 48602 989-399-5600
Craig McCane, prin. Fax 399-5615
Webber MS 600/6-8
2600 Prescott Ave 48601 989-399-5700
Billy Erwin, prin. Fax 399-5715

Saginaw Township Community SD 5,200/PK-12
PO Box 6278 48608 989-399-8044
Jerry Seese Ed.D., supt. Fax 797-1801
stcs.org
Heritage HS 1,700/9-12
3465 N Center Rd 48603 989-799-5790
Michael Newman, prin. Fax 799-5159
White Pine MS 1,100/6-8
505 N Center Rd, 989-797-1814
Bonnie Eaves, prin. Fax 797-1859

Swan Valley SD 1,700/PK-12
8380 OHern Rd 48609 989-921-3701
Richard Syrek, supt. Fax 921-3705
www.swanvalley.k12.mi.us
Swan Valley HS 600/9-12
8400 OHern Rd 48609 989-921-2401
Mat McRae, prin. Fax 921-2405
Swan Valley MS 400/6-8
453 Van Wormer Rd 48609 989-921-2601
Karsten Schlenter, prin. Fax 921-2605

Community Baptist Christian S 200/PK-12
8331 Gratiot Rd 48609 989-781-2340
Vicki Torrey, prin. Fax 781-1344
Davenport University Post-Sec.
5300 Bay Rd 48604 989-799-7800
Grace Christian S 100/PK-12
4619 Mackinaw Rd 48603 989-793-2129
Deanne Beson, prin. Fax 793-2125
Michigan Lutheran Seminary 300/9-12
2777 Hardin St 48602 989-793-1041
Paul Prange, pres. Fax 793-4213
Nouvel Catholic Central HS 500/9-12
2555 Wieneke Rd 48603 989-791-4330
Paul Fallon, prin. Fax 797-6610
Ross Medical Education Center Post-Sec.
4054 Bay Rd 48603 989-793-9800
St. Mary's Medical Center Post-Sec.
800 S Washington Ave 48601 989-776-8176
Valley Lutheran HS 300/9-12
3560 McCarty Rd 48603 989-790-1676
John Brandt, prin. Fax 790-1680

Saint Charles, Saginaw, Pop. 2,169
St. Charles Community SD 1,000/K-12
891 W Walnut St 48655 989-865-9961
Michael Wallace, supt. Fax 865-6185
www.stccs.org
Saint Charles HS 400/9-12
881 W Walnut St 48655 989-865-9991
Heather Ballien, prin. Fax 865-8185
Thurston MS 300/6-8
893 W Walnut St 48655 989-865-9927
Patricia Sowle, prin. Fax 865-2429

Saint Clair, Saint Clair, Pop. 5,881
East China SD
Supt. — See East China
Saint Clair HS 1,000/9-12
2200 Clinton Ave 48079 810-676-1700
Ronald Miller, prin. Fax 676-1725
Saint Clair MS 700/6-8
4335 Yankee Rd 48079 810-676-1800
Kevin Miller, prin. Fax 676-1825

Saint Clair Shores, Macomb, Pop. 61,896
Lake Shore SD 3,200/K-12
28850 Harper Ave 48081 586-285-8480
Brian Annable, supt. Fax 285-8463
www.lakeshoreschools.org
Kennedy MS 800/6-8
23101 Masonic Blvd 48082 586-285-8800
Gordon Kennedy, prin. Fax 285-8804
Lake Shore HS 1,100/9-12
22980 E 13 Mile Rd 48082 586-285-8900
Lara Erickson, prin. Fax 285-8904

Lakeview SD 3,000/K-12
20300 Statler St 48081 586-445-4000
Sandra Feeley Myrand, supt. Fax 445-4029
www.lakeview.misd.net
Jefferson MS 700/6-8
27900 Rockwood St 48081 586-445-4130
Fred Zielke, prin. Fax 445-4041
Lakeview HS 1,100/9-12
21100 E 11 Mile Rd 48081 586-445-4045
Robert duBois, prin. Fax 445-4072

South Lake SD 2,500/K-12
23101 Stadium Dr 48080 586-435-1600
William C. Putney, supt. Fax 445-4202
www.solake.org
South Lake HS 900/9-12
21900 E 9 Mile Rd 48080 586-435-1400
Louis Steigerwald, prin. Fax 445-4243
South Lake MS 400/7-8
21621 California St 48080 586-435-1300
Richard Norsigian, prin. Fax 778-3151

Virginia Farrell Beauty School Post-Sec.
23620 Harper Ave 48080 586-775-6640

Saint Ignace, Mackinac, Pop. 2,535
St. Ignace Area SD 700/K-12
429 W Portage St 49781 906-643-8145
Mike Springsteen, supt. Fax 643-0247
stignace.eup.k12.mi.us/
Lasalle HS 300/8-12
443 W Portage St 49781 906-643-8800
Donald Gustafson, prin. Fax 643-7696

Saint Johns, Clinton, Pop. 7,513
Saint Johns SD 3,400/K-12
PO Box 230 48879 989-227-4050
Robert Kudwa, supt. Fax 227-4099
www.stjohns.edzone.net
Saint Johns HS 1,100/9-12
501 W Sickles St 48879 989-227-4000
Mark Palmer, prin. Fax 227-4199
Saint Johns MS 800/6-8
900 W Townsend Rd 48879 989-227-4300
Dennis Toth, prin. Fax 227-4399

Saint Joseph, Berrien, Pop. 8,656
St. Joseph SD 2,600/K-12
3275 Lincoln Ave 49085 269-926-3100
Carole Schmidt Ph.D., supt. Fax 926-3103
www.remc11.k12.mi.us/stjoe/
St. Joseph HS 1,000/9-12
2521 Stadium Dr 49085 269-926-3200
Jeffrey Runser, prin. Fax 926-3203
Upton MS 700/6-8
800 Maiden Ln 49085 269-926-3400
Allen Skibbe, prin. Fax 926-3403

Lake Michigan Catholic HS 200/9-12
915 Pleasant St 49085 269-983-2511
John Berlin, prin. Fax 983-0883
Lake Michigan Catholic MS 100/6-8
915 Pleasant St 49085 269-983-2511
John Berlin, prin. Fax 983-0883
Michigan Lutheran HS 100/9-12
615 E Marquette Woods Rd 49085 269-429-7861
Michael Butzow, prin. Fax 429-4428
Twin City Beauty College Post-Sec.
2600 Lincoln Ave 49085 269-428-2900

Saint Louis, Gratiot, Pop. 5,445
St. Louis SD 1,200/PK-12
113 E Saginaw St 48880 989-681-2545
Robert Lange, supt. Fax 681-5894
www.edzone.net/~stlouis
Nurnberger MS 300/6-8
312 Union St 48880 989-681-5155
George Herrington, prin. Fax 681-4658
St. Louis HS 400/9-12
113 E Saginaw St 48880 989-681-2500
Tom Steere, prin. Fax 681-4535

Saline, Washtenaw, Pop. 8,826
Saline Area SD 5,300/PK-12
200 N Ann Arbor St 48176 734-429-8000
Dr. Beverley Geltner, supt. Fax 429-8010
www.salineschools.com
Saline HS 1,700/9-12
1300 Campus Pkwy 48176 734-429-8030
Jean Durst, prin. Fax 429-8036
Saline MS 900/7-8
7190 N Maple Rd 48176 734-429-8070
Nic Cooper, prin. Fax 429-8076

Washtenaw Christian Academy 300/PK-12
7200 Moon Rd 48176 734-429-7733
Amy Houpt, prin. Fax 944-8343

Sand Creek, Lenawee
Sand Creek Community SD 900/K-12
6850 Sand Creek Hwy 49279 517-436-3108
John Hackett, supt. Fax 436-3143
scnc.sandcreek.k12.mi.us
Sand Creek JSHS 500/7-12
6518 Sand Creek Hwy 49279 517-436-3124
Steven Laundra, prin. Fax 436-3193

Sand Lake, Montcalm, Pop. 512
Tri County Area SD 2,300/K-12
PO Box 79 49343 616-636-5454
James K. Scholten M.A., supt. Fax 636-5677
www.tricountyschools.com
Other Schools – See Howard City

Sandusky, Sanilac, Pop. 2,694
Sandusky Community SD 1,300/K-12
191 E Pinetree Ln 48471 810-648-3400
Timothy A. Lentz, supt. Fax 648-5113
www.sandusky.k12.mi.us
Sandusky HS 400/9-12
191 E Pinetree Ln 48471 810-648-3401
Fred Hicks, prin. Fax 648-3148
Sandusky MS 400/5-8
395 S Sandusky Rd 48471 810-648-3300
Mary Lou Ruggles, prin. Fax 648-5221

Sanford, Midland, Pop. 930
Meridian SD 1,300/PK-12
3361 N Meridian Rd 48657 989-687-3200
William Newkirk, supt. Fax 687-3222
www.merps.k12.mi.us
Meridian HS 500/9-12
3303 N Meridian Rd 48657 989-687-3300
Dennis Stine, prin. Fax 687-3309
Meridian JHS 400/6-8
3475 N Meridian Rd 48657 989-687-3360
William Chilman, prin. Fax 687-3364

Saranac, Ionia, Pop. 1,332
Saranac Community SD 1,200/K-12
88 Pleasant St 48881 616-642-1400
Dan Bauer, supt. Fax 642-1405
www.saranac.k12.mi.us
Harker MS 300/6-8
234 Weeks Rd 48881 616-642-1300
Randy Masterson, prin. Fax 642-1305
Saranac HS 400/9-12
150 Pleasant St 48881 616-642-1100
Brad Jacobs, prin. Fax 642-1105

Saugatuck, Allegan, Pop. 1,040
Saugatuck SD
Supt. — See Douglas
Saugatuck MSHS 300/6-12
401 Elizabeth St 49453 269-857-2133
Timothy Travis, prin. Fax 857-6145

Sault Sainte Marie, Chippewa, Pop. 15,300
Sault Sainte Marie Area SD 2,700/PK-12
876 Marquette Ave 49783 906-635-6609
Daniel Reattoir Ed.D., supt. Fax 635-6642
www.eup.k12.mi.us/sault/
Sault Area Career Center Vo/Tech
904 Marquette Ave 49783 906-635-6652
Gary Deuman, prin. Fax 635-6641
Sault Sainte Marie Area HS 1,000/9-12
904 Marquette Ave 49783 906-635-6605
John Sherry, prin. Fax 635-6641
Sault Sainte Marie MS 700/6-8
684 Marquette Ave 49783 906-635-6604
Tom Stabile, prin. Fax 635-3841

Lake Superior State University Post-Sec.
650 W Easterday Ave 49783 888-800-5778

Schoolcraft, Kalamazoo, Pop. 1,504
Schoolcraft Community SD 1,200/K-12
629 E Clay St 49087 269-488-7390
Douglas Knobloch, supt. Fax 488-7391
www.schoolcraftschools.org
Schoolcraft HS 400/9-12
629 E Clay St 49087 269-488-7350
John Kolassa, prin. Fax 488-7364
Schoolcraft MS 200/7-8
629 E Clay St 49087 269-488-7300
Douglas Maltby, prin. Fax 488-7303

Scottville, Mason, Pop. 1,273
Mason County Central SD 1,600/PK-12
300 W Broadway Ave 49454 231-757-3713
Jeff Mount, supt. Fax 757-5716
www.mccschools.com
Mason County Central HS 500/9-12
210 W Broadway Ave 49454 231-757-4748
Jack Murchie, prin. Fax 757-9084
Mason County Central MS 500/5-8
310 W Beryl St 49454 231-757-3724
Kevin Kimes, prin. Fax 757-4820
Community Education Consortium Adult
300 W Broadway Ave 49454 231-757-3471
Christy Christmas, prin. Fax 757-5716

Mason-Lake ISD
Supt. — See Ludington
Mason-Lake ISD Tech Prep Partnership Vo/Tech
3000 N Stiles Rd 49454 231-845-6211
Michael Robinson, admin. Fax 845-8661

West Shore Community College Post-Sec.
PO Box 277 49454 231-845-6211

Sebewaing, Huron, Pop. 1,861
Unionville-Sebewaing SD 1,000/K-12
2203 Wildner Rd 48759 989-883-2360
John Walker, supt. Fax 883-9021
www.usa.k12.mi.us
Unionville-Sebewaing HS 400/9-12
2203 Wildner Rd 48759 989-883-2534
Michael Harris, prin. Fax 883-9739
Unionville-Sebewaing MS 300/5-8
2203 Wildner Rd 48759 989-883-3140
Mark Gainforth, prin. Fax 883-9469

Shelby, Oceana, Pop. 1,971
Shelby SD 1,800/PK-12
525 N State St 49455 231-861-5211
Dana McGrew, supt. Fax 861-5416
hs.shelby.k12.mi.us/
Shelby HS 500/9-12
641 N State St 49455 231-861-4452
Fran Schamber, prin. Fax 861-6867
Shelby MS 400/6-8
525 N State St 49455 231-861-4521
Vaughn White, prin. Fax 861-0415

Shelby Township, Macomb, Pop. 69,500
Utica Community SD
Supt. — See Sterling Heights
Eisenhower SHS 2,000/10-12
6500 25 Mile Rd 48316 586-797-1300
Gloria Bawol, prin. Fax 797-1301
Malow JHS 1,300/7-9
6400 25 Mile Rd 48316 586-797-3500
Robert Hock, prin. Fax 797-3501
Shelby JHS 1,200/7-9
51700 Van Dyke Ave 48316 586-797-3700
Patricia Gonser, prin. Fax 797-3701

Shepherd, Isabella, Pop. 1,379
Shepherd SD 1,700/K-12
PO Box 219 48883 989-828-5520
Fax 828-5679
www.edzone.net/~shepherd
Shepherd HS 600/9-12
100 E Hall St 48883 989-828-6601
Nate Bootz, prin. Fax 828-5452
Shepherd MS 400/6-8
150 E Hall St 48883 989-828-6605
Claire Bunker, prin. Fax 828-6578

Sidney, Montcalm
Montcalm Area ISD
Supt. — See Stanton
Montcalm Area Career Center Vo/Tech
1550 W Sidney Rd 48885 989-328-6621
Paula Fortino, prin. Fax 328-2000

Montcalm Community College Post-Sec.
2800 College Dr 48885 989-328-2111

Southfield, Oakland, Pop. 76,818
Southfield SD 9,900/PK-12
24661 Lahser Rd 48033 248-746-8500
Wanda Cook-Robinson Ph.D., supt. Fax 746-8540
www.southfield.k12.mi.us
Birney MS 900/6-8
27225 Evergreen Rd 48076 248-746-8800
Sterling Russell, prin. Fax 352-0709
Levey MS 800/6-8
25300 W 9 Mile Rd, 248-746-8740
Kelly Dean, prin. Fax 746-8718
Southfield HS 1,700/9-12
24675 Lahser Rd, 248-746-8601
Michael Horn, prin. Fax 746-8773
Thompson MS 600/6-8
16300 Lincoln Dr 48076 248-746-7400
Josha Talison, prin. Fax 746-7493
Other Schools – See Lathrup Village

Akiva Hebrew Day S 300/PK-12
21100 W 12 Mile Rd 48076 248-386-1625
Teri Giannetti, prin. Fax 386-1632
Detroit Business Institute Post-Sec.
23077 Greenfield Rd #LL28 48075 248-552-6300
Everest Institute Post-Sec.
26111 Evergreen Rd Ste 201 48076 248-799-9933
Lawrence Technological University Post-Sec.
21000 W 10 Mile Rd 48075 248-204-4000
Lawton School Post-Sec.
20755 Greenfield Rd Ste 300 48075 248-569-7787
Northwestern Technological Institute Post-Sec.
24567 Northwestern Hwy #200 48075 248-358-4006
Oakland Community College Post-Sec.
22322 Rutland Ave 48075 248-233-2700
Providence Hospital Post-Sec.
16001 W 9 Mile Rd 48075 248-424-3000
Southfield Christian S 700/K-12
28650 Lahser Rd 48034 248-357-3660
Phil Ackley, prin. Fax 357-5271
Specs Howard School of Broadcast Arts Post-Sec.
19900 W 9 Mile Rd 48075 248-358-9000
Yeshivas Darchei Torah S 300/K-12
21550 W 12 Mile Rd 48076 248-948-1080
Sara Kahn, prin. Fax 948-1825

Southgate, Wayne, Pop. 29,572
Southgate Community SD 5,000/K-12
13201 Trenton Rd 48195 734-246-4600
David Peden, supt. Fax 283-6791
www.southgateschools.com
Anderson HS 1,100/10-12
15475 Leroy St 48195 734-246-4611
Michael Kell, prin. Fax 246-7840
Davidson MS 800/8-9
15800 Trenton Rd 48195 734-246-4628
Marilyn Svaluto, prin. Fax 246-7280
Asher Adult & Community Education Adult
14101 Leroy St 48195 734-246-4633
Judy Cock, dir. Fax 246-7244

Dorsey Business School Post-Sec.
15755 Northline Rd 48195 734-285-5400

South Haven, Van Buren, Pop. 5,157
South Haven SD 2,100/PK-12
554 Green St 49090 269-637-0520
Robert Black, supt. Fax 637-3025
www.shps.org
Baseline MS 500/6-8
7357 Baseline Rd 49090 269-637-0530
John Weiss, prin. Fax 639-8009
Mohr HS 800/9-12
600 Elkenburg St 49090 269-637-0500
Dene Hadden, prin. Fax 637-0516

South Lyon, Oakland, Pop. 11,040
South Lyon Community SD 6,800/K-12
345 S Warren St 48178 248-573-8127
William Pearson, supt. Fax 437-8686
www.slcs.us
Centennial MS 700/6-8
62500 9 Mile Rd 48178 248-573-8600
David Phillips, prin. Fax 573-8611
Millennium MS 900/6-8
61526 9 Mile Rd 48178 248-573-8200
Ronald Webber, prin. Fax 573-8231
South Lyon HS 2,000/9-12
1000 N Lafayette St 48178 248-573-8150
Larry Jackson, prin. Fax 437-0233

Sparta, Kent, Pop. 4,046
Sparta Area SD 2,700/PK-12
465 S Union St 49345 616-887-8253
Kent Swinson, supt. Fax 887-9958
www.spartaschools.org
Sparta HS 800/9-12
480 S State St 49345 616-887-8213
Ron Pincumbe, prin. Fax 887-1264
Sparta MS 900/5-8
240 Glenn St 49345 616-887-8211
Joel Stoner, prin. Fax 887-1080

Spring Arbor, Jackson, Pop. 2,010

Spring Arbor University Post-Sec.
106 E Main St 49283 517-750-1200

Springfield, Calhoun, Pop. 5,203
Battle Creek SD
Supt. — See Battle Creek
Springfield MS 400/5-8
1023 Avenue A, 269-965-9640
Jane Berger, prin. Fax 962-2486

Spring Lake, Ottawa, Pop. 2,383
Spring Lake SD 2,300/PK-12
345 Hammond St 49456 616-846-5500
Larry Mason, supt. Fax 846-9830
www.spring-lake.k12.mi.us
Spring Lake HS 800/9-12
16140 148th Ave 49456 616-846-5501
Mike Gilchrist, prin. Fax 847-5855
Spring Lake MS 300/7-8
345 Hammond St 49456 616-846-5502
Ron Schneider, prin. Fax 847-7913

Springport, Jackson, Pop. 682
Springport SD 1,000/K-12
PO Box 100 49284 517-857-3495
Roland Pakonen, supt. Fax 857-4179
scnc.sps.k12.mi.us/
Springport HS 300/9-12
PO Box 100 49284 517-857-3475
Chris Kregal, prin. Fax 857-3251
Springport MS 300/6-8
PO Box 100 49284 517-857-3445
Tanya Overweg, prin. Fax 857-3453

Standish, Arenac, Pop. 2,036
Standish-Sterling Community SD 1,900/PK-12
3789 Wyatt Rd 48658 989-846-3670
Claude Inch, supt. Fax 846-7890
www.standish-sterling.org
Standish-Sterling Central HS 600/9-12
2401 Grove Street Rd 48658 989-846-3660
Mark Williams, prin. Fax 846-3666
Standish-Sterling MS 600/5-8
3789 Wyatt Rd 48658 989-846-4526
Beverly Skinner, prin. Fax 846-4529

Stanton, Montcalm, Pop. 1,527
Central Montcalm SD 2,100/PK-12
PO Box 9 48888 989-831-5243
Roger Thelen, supt. Fax 831-5580
www.qualityschool.org
Central Montcalm HS 700/9-12
1480 S Sheridan Rd 48888 989-831-2100
Jerry Winkler, prin. Fax 831-2110
Central Montcalm MS 300/7-8
1480 S Sheridan Rd 48888 989-831-2200
Sandy SanMiguel, prin. Fax 831-2210
Central Montcalm Adult/Community Educ Adult
618 W Main St 48888 989-831-7902
Kathryn Betts, prin. Fax 831-7862

Montcalm Area ISD 50/
PO Box 367 48888 989-831-5261
George Stamas, supt. Fax 831-8727
www.maisd.com
Other Schools – See Sidney

Stephenson, Menominee, Pop. 835
Stephenson Area SD 700/K-12
PO Box 509 49887 906-753-2221
Roger Cole, supt. Fax 753-4676
www.stephenson.k12.mi.us
Stephenson JSHS 400/6-12
PO Box 529 49887 906-753-2222
Michael Harrington, prin. Fax 753-2326

Sterling Heights, Macomb, Pop. 128,034
Utica Community SD 29,100/PK-12
11303 Greendale Dr 48312 586-797-1000
Christine Johns Ed.D., supt. Fax 797-1001
www.astihosted.com/ucsdcp/DesktopDefault.aspx
Bemis JHS 1,000/7-8
12500 19 Mile Rd 48313 586-797-2500
Joyce Spade, prin. Fax 797-2501
Davis JHS 900/7-9
11311 Plumbrook Rd 48312 586-797-2700
Robert McBroom, prin. Fax 797-2701
Ford HS 1,900/9-12
11911 Clinton River Rd 48313 586-797-1600
Robert Monroe, prin. Fax 797-1601
Heritage JHS 600/7-9
37400 Dodge Park Rd 48312 586-797-3100
Linda Hall, prin. Fax 797-3101
Jeanette JHS 1,000/7-9
40400 Gulliver Dr 48310 586-797-3300
Robyn Thompson, prin. Fax 797-3301
Stevenson SHS 1,800/10-12
39701 Dodge Park Rd 48313 586-797-1900
Jerry Willis, prin. Fax 797-1901
Other Schools – See Shelby Township, Utica

Warren Consolidated SD
Supt. — See Warren
Career Prep Center Vo/Tech
12200 15 Mile Rd 48312 586-825-2800
Frank Antonucci, prin. Fax 698-4519
Carleton JHS 600/6-8
8900 15 Mile Rd 48312 586-825-2590
Stephen Bigelow, prin. Fax 698-4286
Flynn JHS 600/6-8
2899 Fox Hill Dr 48310 586-825-2900
Thomas Cassidy, prin. Fax 698-4304
Grissom JHS 800/6-8
35701 Ryan Rd 48310 586-825-2560
Shaun Greene-Beebe, prin. Fax 698-4313
Sterling Heights HS 1,500/9-12
12901 15 Mile Rd 48312 586-825-2700
Robert Shaner, prin. Fax 698-4253

Parkway Christian S 500/PK-12
14500 Metropolitan Pkwy 48312 586-446-9900
Sandra Ondra, prin. Fax 446-9904
Sterling Christian S 100/PK-12
33380 Ryan Rd 48310 586-268-5420
Tony Bryson, prin. Fax 795-0929

Stevensville, Berrien, Pop. 1,164
Lakeshore SD 2,900/PK-12
5771 Cleveland Ave 49127 269-428-1400
Donald Frank, supt. Fax 428-1574
www.lakeshoreschools.k12.mi.us
Lakeshore HS 1,000/9-12
5771 Cleveland Ave 49127 269-428-1402
William Scaletta, prin. Fax 428-1572
Lakeshore MS 600/6-8
1459 W John Beers Rd 49127 269-428-1408
William Shepard, prin. Fax 428-1571

Stockbridge, Ingham, Pop. 1,279
Stockbridge Community SD 1,800/K-12
305 W Elizabeth St 49285 517-851-7188
Bruce Brown, supt. Fax 851-8334
panthernet.net
Stockbridge HS 600/9-12
416 N Clinton St 49285 517-851-7770
Karl Heidrich, prin. Fax 851-9446
Stockbridge MS 400/6-8
305 W Elizabeth St 49285 517-851-8149
Sean Williams, prin. Fax 851-8334

Sturgis, Saint Joseph, Pop. 11,134
Sturgis SD 3,100/K-12
107 W West St 49091 269-659-1500
Robert Olsen, supt. Fax 659-1584
sturgis.k12.mi.us
Sturgis HS 900/9-12
216 Vinewood Ave 49091 269-659-1515
Wayne Stitt, prin. Fax 659-1532
Sturgis MS 700/6-8
1400 E Lafayette St 49091 269-659-1550
Eric Anderson, prin. Fax 659-1553
Community/Adullt S Adult
107 W West St 49091 269-659-1540
Cheryl Locey, prin. Fax 659-1584

Heartwood Renaissance Academy 50/7-12
705 E West St 49091 269-651-3383
Gretchen Andersen, dir. Fax 659-8443
Lake Area Christian S 100/PK-12
63590 Borgert Rd 49091 269-651-5135
Dean Miller, admin. Fax 651-8648

Suttons Bay, Leelanau, Pop. 590
Suttons Bay SD 900/PK-12
PO Box 367 49682 231-271-8604
James Leyndyke, supt. Fax 271-8691
www.suttonsbay.k12.mi.us
Suttons Bay HS 300/9-12
PO Box 367 49682 231-271-8603
Susan Rummel, prin. Fax 271-8690
Suttons Bay MS 200/7-8
PO Box 367 49682 231-271-8602
Cody Inglis, prin. Fax 271-8689

Swartz Creek, Genesee, Pop. 5,341
Swartz Creek Community SD 4,200/PK-12
8354 Cappy Ln 48473 810-591-2381
Dr. Jeff Pratt, supt. Fax 591-2784
www.swartzcreek.org
Swartz Creek HS 1,300/9-12
1 Dragon Dr 48473 810-591-1801
Michael Vanderlip, prin. Fax 591-1895
Swartz Creek MS 1,000/6-8
8230 Crapo St 48473 810-591-1705
Kevin Klaeren, prin. Fax 591-1712

Tawas City, Iosco, Pop. 1,952
Iosco RESA
27 N Rempert Rd 48763 989-362-3006
Thomas Caldwell, supt. Fax 362-9076
www.iresa.k12.mi.us
Career & Technical Education Center Vo/Tech
27 N Rempert Rd 48763 989-362-3006
James O'Farrell, dir. Fax 362-6905

Tawas Area SD 1,500/K-12
245 W M 55 48763 989-984-2250
Donald Thwing, supt. Fax 984-2253
www.tawas.net
Tawas Area HS 500/9-12
255 W M 55 48763 989-984-2100
James Kiblinger, prin. Fax 984-2106
Tawas Area MS 300/7-8
255 W M 55 48763 989-984-2150
William Grusecki, prin. Fax 984-2165

Taylor, Wayne, Pop. 64,962
Taylor SD 8,900/PK-12
23033 Northline Rd 48180 734-374-1200
Lee Lewis, supt. Fax 287-6083
www.taylorschools.net/
Career Center HS Vo/Tech
9601 Westlake St 48180 313-295-5757
Edward Buchynski, prin.
Hoover MS 600/7-8
27101 Beverly Rd 48180 313-295-5775
Teresa Winnie, prin. Fax 295-8354
Kennedy HS 1,500/9-12
13505 Kennedy Dr 48180 734-374-1229
Tom Bluhm, prin. Fax 374-1676
Truman HS 1,800/9-12
11211 Beech Daly Rd 48180 734-946-6551
Fax 946-6590
West MS 800/7-8
10575 William St 48180 313-295-5783
Michael Wiltse, prin. Fax 291-2203

Baptist Park S 200/PK-12
12501 Telegraph Rd 48180 734-287-2720
Roger Cook, admin. Fax 287-2184
Light and Life Christian S 200/PK-12
8900 Pardee Rd 48180 313-292-1660
Rev. George Kennedy, admin. Fax 292-0489
Oakwood Jr. Academy 100/K-10
26300 Goddard Rd 48180 313-291-6790
Lynnette Jefferson, prin. Fax 291-3713
Taylortown School of Beauty Post-Sec.
23129 Ecorse Rd 48180 313-291-2177

Tecumseh, Lenawee, Pop. 8,863
Tecumseh SD 3,400/K-12
212 N Ottawa St 49286 517-424-7318
Michael McAran, supt. Fax 423-3847
tps.k12.mi.us
Tecumseh HS 1,100/9-12
760 Brown St 49286 517-423-6008
Robert Scheick, prin. Fax 423-9644
Tecumseh MS 1,000/5-8
307 N Maumee St 49286 517-423-1105
Rick Hilderley, prin. Fax 423-1300

Tekonsha, Calhoun, Pop. 706
Tekonsha Community SD 300/K-12
245 S Elm St 49092 517-767-4121
Donald Vernon, supt. Fax 767-3465
www.tekonsha.k12.mi.us
Tekonsha MSHS 100/6-12
245 S Elm St 49092 517-767-4121
Joe Huepenbecker, prin. Fax 767-3465

Temperance, Monroe, Pop. 6,542
Bedford SD 5,400/K-12
1623 W Sterns Rd 48182 734-850-6000
Jon White, supt. Fax 850-6099
www.bedford.k12.mi.us
Bedford HS 1,800/9-12
8285 Jackman Rd 48182 734-850-6100
Dennis Caldwell, prin. Fax 850-6199
Bedford JHS 900/7-8
8405 Jackman Rd 48182 734-850-6200
Mary L. Zaums, prin. Fax 850-6299

State Line Christian S 400/K-12
6320 Lewis Ave 48182 734-847-6774
John Morrissey, prin. Fax 847-4968

Three Oaks, Berrien, Pop. 1,768
River Valley SD 800/K-12
15480 Three Oaks Rd 49128 269-756-9541
Robert Schroeder, supt. Fax 756-6631
www.rivervalleyschools.org/
River Valley HS 400/7-12
15480 Three Oaks Rd 49128 269-756-9541
Jose Vera, prin. Fax 756-3007

Three Rivers, Saint Joseph, Pop. 7,342
Three Rivers Community SD 2,700/K-12
851 6th Avenue Rd 49093 269-279-1100
Roger Rathburn, supt. Fax 279-5584
www.trschools.org
Three Rivers HS 900/9-12
700 6th Ave 49093 269-279-1120
Dan Ryan, prin. Fax 273-8014
Three Rivers MS 700/6-8
1101 Jefferson St 49093 269-279-1130
Gloria Wimbley, prin. Fax 279-1139
Three Rivers Adult & Community Education Adult
416 Washington St 49093 269-279-9581
Lois Millet, dir. Fax 279-1160

Traverse City, Grand Traverse, Pop. 14,513
Traverse Bay Area ISD
PO Box 6020 49696 231-922-6200
Michael Kenney, supt. Fax 922-6270
www.tbaisd.k12.mi.us
TBA Career Tech Center Vo/Tech
880 Parsons Rd 49686 231-922-6273
Fax 922-6364

Traverse City Area SD 10,700/PK-12
PO Box 32 49685 231-933-1725
Jim Feil, supt. Fax 933-1726
www.tcaps.net
Traverse City Central HS 1,300/10-12
PO Box 32 49685 231-933-3500
Michael Murray, prin. Fax 933-3506
Traverse City East JHS 1,200/6-9
PO Box 32 49685 231-933-7300
Glenn Solowiej, prin. Fax 933-6998
Traverse City West JHS 1,500/7-9
PO Box 32 49685 231-933-8200
Pam Alfieri, prin. Fax 933-8205
Traverse City West SHS 1,400/10-12
PO Box 32 49685 231-933-7500
Joe Tibaldi, prin. Fax 933-7506

Munson Medical Center Post-Sec.
1105 6th St 49684 231-935-6501
Northwestern Michigan College Post-Sec.
1701 E Front St 49686 231-922-1000
St. Elizabeth Ann Seton MS 300/6-8
1601 3 Mile Rd N 49686 231-932-4810
Janet Troppman, prin. Fax 932-4814
St. Francis HS 300/9-12
123 E 11th St 49684 231-946-8038
Charles Taylor, prin. Fax 946-1878
Traverse City Christian S 100/7-12
753 Emerson Rd 49686 231-929-1747
K. Patrick Rode Ph.D., prin. Fax 929-1831

Trenton, Wayne, Pop. 19,311
Trenton SD 2,800/K-12
2603 Charlton Rd 48183 734-676-8600
Dr. John Savel, supt. Fax 676-4851
www.resa.net/trenton/
Arthurs MS 700/6-8
4000 Marian Dr 48183 734-676-8700
Stephanie Spurr, prin. Fax 676-7364
Trenton HS 1,100/9-12
2601 Charlton Rd 48183 734-692-4530
Michael Doyle, prin. Fax 692-4615

Troy, Oakland, Pop. 81,168
Troy SD 11,900/PK-12
4400 Livernois Rd 48098 248-823-4000
Dr. Barbara Fowler, supt. Fax 823-4013
www.troy.k12.mi.us
Athens HS 2,000/9-12
4333 John R Rd 48085 248-823-2900
Fax 823-2913
Baker MS 600/6-8
1291 Torpey Dr 48083 248-823-4600
Larry Hahn, prin. Fax 823-4613
Boulan Park MS 800/6-8
3570 Northfield Pkwy 48084 248-823-4900
Jo Kwasny, prin. Fax 823-4913
Larson MS 800/6-8
2222 E Long Lake Rd 48085 248-823-4800
Dennis Seppanen, prin. Fax 823-4813
Smith MS 700/6-8
5835 Donaldson Dr 48085 248-823-4700
Joseph Hosang, prin. Fax 823-4713
Troy HS 1,900/9-12
4777 Northfield Pkwy 48098 248-823-2700
Mark Dziatczak, prin. Fax 823-2713

Bethany Christian S 300/PK-12
2601 John R Rd 48083 248-689-4821
Robert McIlwaine, prin. Fax 689-3441
Carnegie Institute Post-Sec.
550 Stephenson Hwy Ste 100 48083 248-589-1078
Christian Leadership Academy 100/K-12
3668B Livernois Rd 48083 248-457-1510
George Kelly, hdmstr. Fax 457-1520
ITT Technical Institute Post-Sec.
1522 E Big Beaver Rd 48083 248-524-1800
Michigan College of Beauty Post-Sec.
3498 Rochester Rd 48083 248-528-0303
Walsh Coll. Accountancy & Bus. Admin. Post-Sec.
PO Box 7006 48007 248-689-8282

Twining, Arenac, Pop. 183
Arenac Eastern SD 200/PK-12
PO Box 98 48766 989-867-4234
Rocky Aldrich, supt. Fax 867-4241
www.arenaceastern.org
Arenac Eastern S 200/PK-12
PO Box 98 48766 989-867-4234
Jonathan Fitzpatrick, prin. Fax 867-4241

Ubly, Sanilac, Pop. 819
Ubly Community SD 900/K-12
2020 Union St 48475 989-658-8202
Hal Hooks, supt. Fax 658-2361
bearcat.ubly.k12.mi.us/
Ubly HS 300/9-12
2020 Union St 48475 989-658-8554
Frederick Ligrow, prin. Fax 658-2072

Union City, Branch, Pop. 1,776
Union City Community SD 1,200/K-12
430 Saint Joseph St 49094 517-741-8091
Martin Chard, supt. Fax 741-5205
www.ucschools.net/
Union City HS 400/9-12
430 Saint Joseph St 49094 517-741-8561
Michael Furnas, prin. Fax 741-3772
Union City MS 400/5-8
435 Saint Joseph St 49094 517-741-5381
Ronna Steel, prin. Fax 741-8513

University Center, Bay

Delta College 48710 Post-Sec.
989-686-9093
Saginaw Valley State University Post-Sec.
7400 Bay Rd 48710 989-790-4000

Utica, Macomb, Pop. 4,913
Utica Community SD
Supt. — See Sterling Heights
Eppler JHS 700/7-9
45461 Brownell St 48317 586-797-2900
Juliet Patterson, prin. Fax 797-2901
Utica SHS 1,600/10-12
47255 Shelby Rd 48317 586-797-2200
Janet Jones, prin. Fax 797-2201

Vanderbilt, Otsego, Pop. 597
Vanderbilt Area SD 200/K-12
947 Donovan St 49795 989-983-4121
Jeffrey Liedel, supt. Fax 983-4571
www.vanderbilt.k12.mi.us
Vanderbilt Area S 200/K-12
947 Donovan St 49795 989-983-2561
Jeffrey Liedel, prin. Fax 983-3051

Vassar, Tuscola, Pop. 2,776
Vassar SD 1,900/K-12
220 Athletic St 48768 989-823-8535
R. Middlin, supt. Fax 823-7823
www.vassar.k12.mi.us
Vassar HS, 220 Athletic St 48768 500/9-12
Paul Wojno, prin. 989-823-8534
Vassar MS, 220 Athletic St 48768 300/7-8
Phil Marcy, prin. 989-823-8533

Juniata Christian S 200/K-12
5656 Washburn Rd 48768 989-843-5326
Dean Bryan, prin.

Vermontville, Eaton, Pop. 797
Maple Valley SD 1,700/PK-12
11090 Nashville Hwy 49096 517-852-9699
Kim L. Kramer, supt. Fax 852-5076
mvs.k12.mi.us
Maple Valley JSHS 800/7-12
11090 Nashville Hwy 49096 517-852-9275
Todd Gonser, prin. Fax 852-2283

Vestaburg, Montcalm
Vestaburg Community SD 800/K-12
7188 Avenue B 48891 989-268-5353
Donald Myers, supt. Fax 268-5852
www.vcs-k12.net
Vestaburg HS 200/9-12
7188 Avenue B 48891 989-268-5343
Michael Joslyn, prin. Fax 268-5246
Vestaburg MS 200/6-8
7188 Avenue B 48891 989-268-5883
Judy Shimunek, prin. Fax 268-5898

Vicksburg, Kalamazoo, Pop. 2,189
Vicksburg Community SD 2,800/PK-12
PO Box 158 49097 269-321-1000
Charles Glaes, supt. Fax 321-1055
www.vicksburg-community-schools.org
Vicksburg HS 900/9-12
501 E Highway St 49097 269-321-1100
Rob Kuhlman, prin. Fax 321-1155
Vicksburg MS 700/6-8
348 E Prairie St 49097 269-321-1300
Greg Tibbetts, prin. Fax 321-1355

Wakefield, Gogebic, Pop. 1,956
Wakefield-Marenisco SD 300/K-12
715 Putnam St 49968 906-224-9421
Lawrence Kapugia, supt. Fax 224-1771
www.wakefield.k12.mi.us
Wakefield-Marenisco S 300/K-12
715 Putnam St 49968 906-224-7211
Carrie Nyman, prin. Fax 224-1771

Waldron, Hillsdale, Pop. 577
Waldron Area SD 400/K-12
13380 Waldron Rd 49288 517-286-6251
John McGonigle, supt. Fax 286-6254
www.waldron.k12.mi.us/
Waldron HS 100/9-12
13380 Waldron Rd 49288 517-286-6251
Steve Philipp, prin. Fax 286-6254
Waldron MS 100/6-8
13380 Waldron Rd 49288 517-286-6251
Steve Philipp, prin. Fax 286-6254

Walkerville, Oceana, Pop. 265
Walkerville SD 400/PK-12
PO Box 68 49459 231-873-4850
Ronald Stoneman, supt. Fax 873-5861
www.walkerville.k12.mi.us
Walkerville JSHS 200/7-12
PO Box 68 49459 231-873-3652
Jeffrey Forner, prin. Fax 873-5615

Walled Lake, Oakland, Pop. 6,919
Walled Lake Consolidated SD 15,000/PK-12
850 Ladd Rd Bldg D 48390 248-956-2000
William Hamilton Ed.D., supt. Fax 956-2123
www.walledlake.k12.mi.us
Geisler MS 900/6-8
46720 W Pontiac Trl 48390 248-956-2900
Karen Jacobson, prin. Fax 956-2905
Western HS 1,600/9-12
600 Beck Rd 48390 248-956-4400
Leit Jones, prin. Fax 956-4405
Other Schools – See Commerce Township, West Bloomfield, Wixom

Warren, Macomb, Pop. 135,311
Fitzgerald SD 3,200/PK-12
23200 Ryan Rd 48091 586-757-1750
Janette Brill, supt. Fax 758-0991
www.fitz.k12.mi.us
Chatterton MS 700/6-8
24333 Ryan Rd 48091 586-757-6650
Marcia Keast, prin. Fax 758-0928
Fitzgerald HS 1,100/9-12
23200 Ryan Rd 48091 586-757-7070
Laurie Fournier, prin. Fax 757-5536

Van Dyke SD 4,000/K-12
23500 Mac Arthur Blvd 48089 586-758-8333
Kathleen Spaulding, supt. Fax 758-8332
www.macomb.k12.mi.us/vandyke
Lincoln HS 1,100/9-12
22900 Federal Ave 48089 586-758-8306
Robert Blair, prin. Fax 758-8304
Lincoln MS 700/7-8
22500 Federal Ave 48089 586-758-8320
Alena Zachery, prin. Fax 758-8322

Warren Consolidated SD 15,800/K-12
31300 Anita Dr 48093 586-825-2400
Dr. James Clor, supt. Fax 698-4095
www.wcs.k12.mi.us/
Beer MS 700/6-8
3200 Martin Rd 48092 586-574-3175
Annette Lauria, prin. Fax 698-4277
Carter MS 800/6-8
12000 Masonic Blvd 48093 586-825-2620
Doug Babcock, prin. Fax 698-4295
Cousino HS 1,800/9-12
30333 Hoover Rd 48093 586-574-3100
Gregory Bishop, prin. Fax 698-4204
Warren-Mott HS 1,700/9-12
3131 E 12 Mile Rd 48092 586-574-3250
Brad Martin, prin. Fax 698-4226
Other Schools – See Sterling Heights

Warren Woods SD 3,100/K-12
12900 Frazho Rd 48089 586-439-4400
Robert Livernois Ph.D., supt. Fax 445-4004
warrenwoods.misd.net
Warren Woods MS 800/6-8
13400 E 12 Mile Rd 48088 586-439-4403
Jennifer McFarlane, prin. Fax 574-9830
Warren Woods Tower HS 1,000/9-12
27900 Bunert Rd 48088 586-439-4402
Stacey Denewith-Fici, prin. Fax 445-8013

Davenport University - Warren Post-Sec.
27650 Dequindre Rd 48092 586-558-8700
De La Salle Collegiate HS 700/9-12
14600 Common Rd 48088 586-778-2207
Patrick Adams, prin. Fax 778-5118
Immaculate Conception Ukranian HS 100/9-12
29400 Westbrook Ave 48092 586-574-0510
Michaeline Weigle, prin. Fax 574-2723
Macomb Christian S 200/PK-12
28501 Lorraine Ave 48093 586-751-8980
Beverly Edwards, prin. Fax 751-7946
Macomb Community College Post-Sec.
14500 E 12 Mile Rd 48088 586-445-7000
Ross Medical Education Center Post-Sec.
27120 Dequindre Rd 48092 586-574-0830

Washington, Macomb
Romeo Community SD
Supt. — See Romeo
Powell MS 700/6-8
62100 Jewell Rd 48094 586-752-0270
Jeffrey LaPerriere, prin. Fax 752-0276

Waterford, Oakland, Pop. 74,500
Oakland ISD
2111 Pontiac Lake Rd 48328 248-209-2000
Vickie Markavitch, supt. Fax 209-2206
www.oakland.k12.mi.us
Oakland Science Math & Technology Ctr Vo/Tech
1480 Scott Lake Rd 48328 248-209-2399
Fax 209-2390
Other Schools – See Clarkston, Pontiac, Royal Oak, Wixom

Waterford SD 10,800/PK-12
1150 Scott Lake Rd 48328 248-682-7800
Robert Neu, supt. Fax 706-4888
www.waterford.k12.mi.us
Crary MS 800/6-8
501 N Cass Lake Rd 48328 248-682-9300
Craig Blomquist, prin. Fax 682-0220
Kettering HS 1,500/9-12
2800 Kettering Dr 48329 248-673-1261
Josh Wenning, prin. Fax 673-1778
Mason MS 900/6-8
3835 W Walton Blvd 48329 248-674-2281
Cheryl Ellsworth, prin. Fax 673-3718
Mott HS 1,800/9-12
1151 Scott Lake Rd 48328 248-674-4134
Raymond Nester, prin. Fax 674-2825
Pierce MS 900/6-8
5145 Hatchery Rd 48329 248-674-0331
Yvonne Dixon, prin. Fax 674-4222

Michigan College of Beauty Post-Sec.
5620 Dixie Hwy 48329 248-623-9494
Mt. Zion Christian S 100/K-12
3200 Beacham Dr 48329 248-334-0488
Thomas Kocik, prin. Fax 334-0465
Oakland Community College Post-Sec.
7350 Cooley Lake Rd 48327 248-942-3100
Our Lady of the Lakes HS 200/9-12
5495 Dixie Hwy 48329 248-623-0340
Thomas Oppat, prin. Fax 623-7536
Our Lady of the Lakes MS 200/6-8
5501 Dixie Hwy 48329 248-623-2201
Kathleen Lewis, prin. Fax 623-6550
Waterford Christian Academy 200/PK-12
220 N Cass Lake Rd 48328 248-682-8112
Vonda Morga, admin. Fax 682-3414

Watersmeet, Gogebic
Watersmeet Township SD 200/K-12
PO Box 217 49969 906-358-4504
George R. Peterson, supt. Fax 358-4713
www.watersmeet.k12.mi.us/
Watersmeet Township S 200/K-12
PO Box 217 49969 906-358-4555
George R. Peterson, prin. Fax 358-3036

Watervliet, Berrien, Pop. 1,801
Watervliet SD 1,400/K-12
450 E Red Arrow Hwy 49098 269-463-5566
Robert Gabel, supt. Fax 463-6809
www.watervliet.k12.mi.us/
Watervliet HS 500/9-12
450 E Red Arrow Hwy 49098 269-463-4221
Greg Chisek, prin. Fax 463-6809
Watervliet MS 300/6-8
450 E Red Arrow Hwy 49098 269-463-0342
Dave Armstrong, prin. Fax 463-0325

Grace Christian S 200/K-12
325 N M 140 49098 269-463-5545
Jonathan Kohns Ed.D., admin. Fax 463-5739

Wayland, Allegan, Pop. 3,948
Wayland UNSD
Supt. — See Byron Center
Wayland HS 1,100/9-12
870 E Superior St 49348 269-792-2254
Thomas Cutler, prin. Fax 792-1101
Wayland Union MS 500/7-8
701 Wildcat Dr 49348 269-792-2306
Carolyn Whyte, prin. Fax 792-1102

Wayne, Wayne, Pop. 18,589
Wayne-Westland Community SD
Supt. — See Westland
Franklin MS 800/6-8
33555 Annapolis St 48184 734-419-2400
Darlene Scott, prin. Fax 595-2401
Wayne Memorial HS 2,000/9-12
3001 4th St 48184 734-419-2200
John Albrecht, prin. Fax 595-2227

Dorsey Business School Post-Sec.
34841 Veterans Plz 48184 734-595-1540
Oakwood - Hospital Annapolis Center Post-Sec.
33155 Annapolis St 48184 734-467-4000

Webberville, Ingham, Pop. 1,497
Webberville Community SD 600/K-12
309 E Grand River Rd 48892 517-521-3422
William Skilling, supt. Fax 521-4139
www.webbervilleschools.org
Webberville JSHS 300/7-12
309 E Grand River Rd 48892 517-521-3447
Brian Friddle, prin. Fax 521-4740

West Bloomfield, Oakland, Pop. 67,200
Bloomfield Hills SD
Supt. — See Bloomfield Hls
West Hills MS 400/6-8
2601 Lone Pine Rd 48323 248-341-6100
Edward Bretzlaff, prin. Fax 341-6199

Walled Lake Consolidated SD
Supt. — See Walled Lake
Walnut Creek MS 800/6-8
7601 Walnut Lake Rd 48323 248-956-2400
Joan Heinz, prin. Fax 956-2405

West Bloomfield SD 6,900/K-12
5810 Commerce Rd 48324 248-865-6420
Dr. Gary Faber, supt. Fax 865-6481
www.westbloomfield.k12.mi.us/
Abbott MS 800/6-8
3380 Orchard Lake Rd 48324 248-865-3670
Amy Hughes, prin. Fax 865-3671
Orchard Lake MS 800/6-8
6000 Orchard Lake Rd 48322 248-865-4480
Sonja James, prin. Fax 865-4481
West Bloomfield HS 2,100/9-12
4925 Orchard Lake Rd 48323 248-865-6720
Bob Pyles, prin. Fax 865-6721

Jewish Academy of Metropolitan Detroit 200/9-12
6600 W Maple Rd 48322 248-592-5263
Rabbi Lee Buckman, prin. Fax 592-0022

West Branch, Ogemaw, Pop. 1,905
West Branch-Rose City Area SD 2,500/K-12
PO Box 308 48661 989-343-2000
David L. Marston, supt. Fax 343-2006
www.wbrc.k12.mi.us/
Ogemaw Heights HS 900/9-12
PO Box 308 48661 989-343-2020
David Walby, prin. Fax 343-2130
Surline MS 600/5-8
PO Box 308 48661 989-343-2140
Patsy Marchel, prin. Fax 343-2239
Other Schools – See Rose City

Ogemaw Hills Christian S 100/K-12
2106 S Gray Rd 48661 989-345-2084
LeAnne Gormong, admin. Fax 345-2094

Westland, Wayne, Pop. 85,623
Livonia SD
Supt. — See Livonia
Western Wayne Skill Center - Ford Vo/Tech
8075 Ritz Ave 48185 734-744-2810
Alphonse DiPaolo, prin. Fax 744-2811

Wayne-Westland Community SD 13,500/PK-12
36745 Marquette St 48185 734-419-2000
Dr. Gregory Baracy, supt. Fax 595-2123
www.wwcsd.net/
Adams MS 700/6-8
33475 Palmer Rd 48186 734-419-2380
David Ingham, prin. Fax 595-2374
Ford Career-Technical Center Vo/Tech
36455 Marquette St 48185 734-419-2100
Ginny Kowalski, prin. Fax 595-2127
Glenn HS 2,200/9-12
36105 Marquette St 48185 734-419-2300
Joan Sedik, prin. Fax 595-2338
Marshall MS 900/6-8
35100 Bay View St 48186 734-419-2277
Paul Salah Ph.D., prin. Fax 595-2588
Stevenson MS 900/6-8
38501 Palmer Rd 48186 734-419-2350
Ginny O'Brien, prin. Fax 595-2692
Tinkham Adult and Community Education Adult
450 S Venoy Rd 48186 734-419-2427
Tim Dziobak, prin. Fax 595-2439
Other Schools – See Wayne

Huron Valley Lutheran HS 100/9-12
33740 Cowan Rd 48185 734-525-0160
Daniel Schultz, prin. Fax 525-6717
Lutheran HS Westland 200/9-12
33300 Cowan Rd 48185 734-422-2090
Steven Schwecke, prin. Fax 422-8566
Virginia Farrell Beauty School Post-Sec.
34580 Ford Rd 48185 734-729-9220
Westland Christian Academy 500/K-12
34033 Palmer Rd 48186 734-326-3581
Carol Enersen, admin. Fax 326-3352

Westphalia, Clinton, Pop. 835
Pewamo-Westphalia SD 400/K-12
5101 S Clintonia Rd 48894 989-587-5100
Ronald Simon, supt. Fax 587-5120
www.pw.k12.mi.us
Pewamo-Westphalia JSHS 300/7-12
5101 S Clintonia Rd 48894 989-587-5100
Jody McKean, prin. Fax 587-3550

White Cloud, Newaygo, Pop. 1,432
White Cloud SD 1,100/PK-12
PO Box 1003 49349 231-689-6820
Ethan Ebenstein, supt. Fax 689-3210
www.whitecloud.net
White Cloud HS 500/9-12
PO Box 1000 49349 231-689-1707
Barry Seabrook, prin. Fax 689-3349
White Cloud MS 200/6-8
PO Box 1001 49349 231-689-2181
Tom Cameron, prin. Fax 689-3339

Whitehall, Muskegon, Pop. 2,839
Whitehall SD 2,200/PK-12
541 E Slocum St 49461 231-893-1005
Darlene Dongvillo, supt. Fax 894-6450
www.whitehall.k12.mi.us

Whitehall HS — 700/9-12
3100 White Lake Dr 49461 — 231-893-1020
John VanLoon, prin. — Fax 893-2923
Whitehall MS — 500/6-8
401 S Elizabeth St 49461 — 231-893-1030
Dale McKenzie, prin. — Fax 894-6844

White Lake, Oakland, Pop. 22,608
Huron Valley SD
Supt. — See Highland
International Academy West HS — 9-12
1630 Bogie Lake Rd 48383 — 248-676-2735
Bert Okma, prin. — Fax 676-2734
Lakeland HS — 1,400/9-12
1630 Bogie Lake Rd 48383 — 248-676-8320
Bob Behnke, prin. — Fax 676-8381
White Lake MS — 700/6-8
1450 Bogie Lake Rd 48383 — 248-684-8004
Paul Gmelin, prin. — Fax 676-8437

White Pigeon, Saint Joseph, Pop. 1,599
White Pigeon Community SD — 900/K-12
410 Prairie Ave 49099 — 269-483-7676
Marvin Schneider, supt. — Fax 483-2256
www.wpcschools.org
White Pigeon HS — 300/9-12
410 Prairie Ave 49099 — 269-483-7679
Patrick West, prin. — Fax 483-8742
White Pigeon MS — 200/7-8
410 Prairie Ave 49099 — 269-483-7679
Patrick West, prin. — Fax 483-2256

Whitmore Lake, Washtenaw, Pop. 3,251
Whitmore Lake SD — 1,300/K-12
8845 Main St 48189 — 734-449-4464
Scott Menzel, supt. — Fax 449-5336
www.wlps.net/
Whitmore Lake HS — 400/9-12
7430 Whitmore Lake Rd 48189 — 734-449-4461
Tom DeKeyser, prin. — Fax 449-5576
Whitmore Lake MS — 400/5-8
8877 Main St 48189 — 734-449-4715
Michael Benczarski, prin. — Fax 449-1042

Whittemore, Iosco, Pop. 462
Whittemore-Prescott Area SD — 1,300/K-12
PO Box 250 48770 — 989-756-2500
Ted Matuszak, supt. — Fax 756-2278
www.wpas.net/
Whittemore-Prescott Area HS — 400/9-12
PO Box 280 48770 — 989-756-2501
Scott Reynolds, prin. — Fax 756-3363
Other Schools – See Prescott

Williamston, Ingham, Pop. 3,790
Williamston Community SD — 2,000/PK-12
418 Highland St 48895 — 517-655-4361
Joel Raddatz, supt. — Fax 655-7500
www.wmston.k12.mi.us
Williamston HS — 700/9-12
3939 Vanneter Rd 48895 — 517-655-2142
Randal Bowles, prin. — Fax 655-7501
Williamston MS — 500/6-8
3845 Vanneter Rd 48895 — 517-655-4668
Christine Sermak, prin. — Fax 655-7502

Wilson, Menominee, Pop. 1,391

Wilson Jr. Academy — 50/1-10
N13925 County Road 551 49896 — 906-639-2566
Vanessa Gust, prin. — Fax 639-2566

Wixom, Oakland, Pop. 13,384
Oakland ISD
Supt. — See Waterford
Oakland Technical Campus SW — Vo/Tech
1000 Beck Rd 48393 — 248-668-5600
Allen Beckner, dean — Fax 668-5670

Walled Lake Consolidated SD
Supt. — See Walled Lake
Banks MS — 900/6-8
1760 Charms Rd 48393 — 248-956-2200
Mark Hess, prin. — Fax 956-2205

Wolverine, Cheboygan, Pop. 352
Wolverine Community SD — 300/K-12
PO Box 219 49799 — 231-525-8201
Susan Denise, supt. — Fax 525-8591
www.wolverine.k12.mi.us
Wolverine HS — 100/7-12
PO Box 219 49799 — 231-525-9050
Gary Phillips, prin. — Fax 525-8251

Woodhaven, Wayne, Pop. 13,354
Gibraltar SD — 3,400/PK-12
19370 Vreeland Rd 48183 — 734-692-4000
Eric Federico, supt. — Fax 692-7577
resa.net/gibraltar
Other Schools – See Gibraltar

Woodhaven-Brownstown SD
Supt. — See Brownstown
Henry MS — 900/8-9
24825 Hall Rd 48183 — 734-362-6100
Molly Mazei, prin. — Fax 362-3045

Woodland, Barry, Pop. 501
Lakewood SD
Supt. — See Lake Odessa
Lakewood MS — 600/6-8
8699 Brown Rd 48897 — 616-374-2400
David Nisbet, prin. — Fax 374-2424

Wyandotte, Wayne, Pop. 26,940
Wyandotte SD — 4,300/K-12
639 Oak St 48192 — 734-759-5000
Dr. Patricia Cole, supt. — Fax 759-5009
www.wyandotte.org
Roosevelt HS — 1,400/9-12
540 Eureka Rd 48192 — 734-759-5000
Mary McFarlane, prin. — Fax 759-5009
Wilson MS — 700/7-8
1275 15th St 48192 — 734-759-5300
Thomas Kell, prin. — Fax 759-5309

Our Lady of Mt. Carmel HS — 100/9-12
2609 10th St 48192 — 734-284-7311
Sr. Mary Van Camp, prin. — Fax 284-8566

Wyoming, Kent, Pop. 70,122
Godfrey-Lee SD — 1,500/K-12
1324 Burton St SW 49509 — 616-241-4722
Jack Wallington, supt. — Fax 241-4707
www.godfrey-lee.k12.mi.us
Lee HS — 400/9-12
1335 Lee St SW 49509 — 616-452-3296
David Britten, prin. — Fax 241-4677
Lee MS — 300/6-8
1335 Lee St SW 49509 — 616-452-3296
David Britten, prin. — Fax 241-4677

Godwin Heights SD — 2,100/PK-12
15 36th St SW 49548 — 616-252-2090
Valdis Gailitis, supt. — Fax 252-2232
www.godwinschools.org
Godwin Heights HS — 600/9-12
50 35th St SW 49548 — 616-252-2050
Jonathan Whan, prin. — Fax 252-2067
Godwin Heights MS — 500/6-8
111 36th St SE 49548 — 616-252-2070
Nkenge Bergan, prin. — Fax 252-2075

Wyoming SD — 5,300/K-12
3575 Gladiola Ave SW, — 616-530-7550
Jon A. Felske, supt. — Fax 530-7557
www.wyoming.k12.mi.us
Jackson Park MS — 600/6-8
1331 33rd St SW 49509 — 616-530-7540
Kirk Bloomquist, prin. — Fax 249-7659
Newhall MS — 700/6-8
1840 38th St SW, — 616-530-7590
Adrian Lamar, prin. — Fax 249-7673
Rogers HS — 900/9-12
1350 Prairie Pkwy SW 49509 — 616-530-7580
Gary Karasinski, prin. — Fax 530-7589
Wyoming Park HS — 800/9-12
2125 Wrenwood St SW, — 616-530-7560
Stewart Schofield, prin. — Fax 249-7649

Potter's House HS — 100/9-12
2500 Newport St SW, — 616-249-8050
John Walcott, admin. — Fax 249-8555
Tri-Unity Christian HS — 200/7-12
2104 44th St SW, — 616-532-6766
Tom Aldrich, prin. — Fax 532-8701

Yale, Saint Clair, Pop. 1,993
Yale SD — 2,300/K-12
198 School Dr 48097 — 810-387-4274
Frank Johnson, supt. — Fax 387-4418
www.yale.k12.mi.us
Yale HS — 700/9-12
247 School Dr 48097 — 810-387-3231
Kenneth Nicholl, prin. — Fax 387-9108
Yale JHS — 600/6-8
198 School Dr 48097 — 810-387-3231
Joseph Haynes, prin. — Fax 387-9207

Ypsilanti, Washtenaw, Pop. 21,832
Lincoln Consolidated SD — 4,800/PK-12
8970 Whittaker Rd 48197 — 734-484-7000
Fred Williams, supt. — Fax 484-1212
lincoln.k12.mi.us
Lincoln HS — 1,500/9-12
7425 Willis Rd 48197 — 734-484-7004
Derrick Coleman, prin. — Fax 484-7012
Lincoln MS — 1,300/6-8
8744 Whittaker Rd 48197 — 734-484-7033
Lynn Cleary, prin. — Fax 484-7088

Willow Run Community SD — 2,000/K-12
235 Spencer Ln 48198 — 734-481-8200
Dr. Doris Hope-Jackson, supt. — Fax 481-8151
www.wrcs.k12.mi.us/
Willow Run HS — 700/9-12
235 Spencer Ln 48198 — 734-961-6015
Fax 481-8185
Willow Run MS — 6-8
235 Spencer Ln 48198 — 734-961-6162
Fax 481-8170
Adult Education — Adult
181 Oregon St 48198 — 734-961-6454
Karyn Goven, prin. — Fax 482-3550

Ypsilanti SD — 3,900/PK-12
1885 Packard Rd 48197 — 734-714-1218
Dr. James Hawkins, supt. — Fax 714-1220
www.ypsd.org
East MS — 500/6-8
510 Emerick St 48198 — 734-714-1400
Janice Sturdivant, prin. — Fax 714-1423
Regional Career Technical Center — Vo/Tech
2095 Packard Rd 48197 — 734-714-1276
Bob Wilkinson, prin. — Fax 714-1274
West MS — 600/6-8
105 N Mansfield St 48197 — 734-714-1300
Monica Merritt, prin. — Fax 714-1303
Ypsilanti HS — 1,200/9-12
2095 Packard Rd 48197 — 734-714-1000
Layne Hunt, prin. — Fax 714-1029

Ave Maria College — Post-Sec.
PO Box 373 48106 — 734-337-4545
Calvary Christian Academy — 200/K-12
1007 Ecorse Rd 48198 — 734-482-1990
Cathy White, prin. — Fax 484-5118
Eastern Michigan University 48197 — Post-Sec.
734-487-1849

Zeeland, Ottawa, Pop. 5,532
Zeeland SD — 5,100/PK-12
PO Box 110 49464 — 616-748-3000
Gary L. Feenstra, supt. — Fax 748-3035
www.zeeland.k12.mi.us
Cityside MS — 700/6-8
320 E Main Ave 49464 — 616-748-3200
Jon Voss, prin. — Fax 748-3210
Creekside MS — 500/6-8
179 W Roosevelt Ave 49464 — 616-748-3300
Greg Eding, prin. — Fax 748-3325
Zeeland East HS — 1,600/9-12
3333 96th Ave 49464 — 616-748-3100
Nate Robrahn, prin. — Fax 748-3198
Zeeland West HS — 9-12
3390 100th Ave 49464 — 616-748-4500
Colleen Johnson, prin. — Fax 748-4505

MINNESOTA

MN DEPARTMENT OF EDUCATION
1500 Highway 36 W, Roseville 55113-4035
Telephone 651-582-8200
Website cfl.state.mn.us

Commissioner of Education Alice Seagren

PUBLIC, PRIVATE AND CATHOLIC SECONDARY SCHOOLS

Ada, Norman, Pop. 1,555
Ada-Borup SD 2854 500/PK-12
604 W Thorpe Ave 56510 218-784-5300
Ollen Church, supt. Fax 784-3475
www.ada.k12.mn.us
Ada-Borup JSHS 300/7-12
604 W Thorpe Ave 56510 218-784-5300
Michael Kolness, prin. Fax 784-3475

Adams, Mower, Pop. 782
Southland SD 500 700/K-12
PO Box 351 55909 507-582-3283
Gary Kuphal, supt. Fax 582-7813
www.isd500.k12.mn.us
Southland HS 300/9-12
PO Box 351 55909 507-582-3568
Jon Ellerbusch, prin. Fax 582-7813
Southland MS 200/6-8
PO Box 351 55909 507-582-3568
Jon Ellerbusch, prin. Fax 582-7813

Adrian, Nobles, Pop. 1,231
Adrian SD 511 600/PK-12
PO Box 40 56110 507-483-2266
Roger Graff, supt. Fax 483-2342
www.adrianschool.net
Adrian HS 200/9-12
PO Box 40 56110 507-483-2232
Roger Graff, prin. Fax 483-2375
Adrian MS 200/6-8
PO Box 40 56110 507-483-2232
Roger Graff, prin. Fax 483-2375

Aitkin, Aitkin, Pop. 1,997
Aitkin SD 1 1,300/PK-12
306 2nd St NW 56431 218-927-2115
Bernie Novak, supt. Fax 927-4234
www.aitkin.k12.mn.us
Aitkin HS 600/7-12
306 2nd St NW 56431 218-927-2115
Steven Wilkowski, prin. Fax 927-4234

Albany, Stearns, Pop. 2,007
Albany SD 745 1,700/PK-12
PO Box 330 56307 320-845-2171
Dr. Scott Thielman, supt. Fax 845-4017
www.albany.k12.mn.us
Albany HS 600/9-12
PO Box 330 56307 320-845-2171
Tim Wege, prin. Fax 845-4017
Albany JHS 200/7-8
PO Box 330 56307 320-845-2171
Charles Griffith, prin. Fax 845-4017

Albert Lea, Freeborn, Pop. 17,915
Albert Lea SD 241 3,500/K-12
211 W Richway Dr 56007 507-379-4800
David Prescott, supt. Fax 379-4898
albertlea.k12.mn.us
Albert Lea HS 1,200/9-12
2000 Tiger Ln 56007 507-379-5340
Alan Root, prin. Fax 379-5498
Southwest MS 600/7-8
1601 W Front St 56007 507-379-5240
Marsha Langseth, prin. Fax 379-5338

Riverland Community College Post-Sec.
2200 Riverland Dr 56007 507-373-0656

Albertville, Wright, Pop. 5,733
Saint Michael-Albertville SD 885 3,900/PK-12
11343 50th St NE 55301 763-497-3180
Dr. Marcia Ziegler, supt. Fax 497-6588
www.stma.k12.mn.us
Saint Michael-Albertville HS 1,000/9-12
11343 50th St NE 55301 763-497-2192
Dale Carlson, prin. Fax 497-6590
Other Schools – See Saint Michael

Alden, Freeborn, Pop. 634
Alden-Conger ISD 242 400/K-12
PO Box 99 56009 507-874-3240
Joe Guanella, supt. Fax 874-2747
www.alden-conger.org
Alden-Conger HS 200/6-12
PO Box 99 56009 507-874-3240
Paul Ragatz, dean Fax 874-2747

Alexandria, Douglas, Pop. 10,603
Alexandria SD 206 4,100/K-12
PO Box 308 56308 320-762-2141
Dr. Terry Quist, supt. Fax 762-2765
www.alexandria.k12.mn.us
Discovery JHS 1,000/7-9
510 McKay Ave N 56308 320-762-7900
Chad Duwenhoegger, prin. Fax 762-8347
Jefferson SHS 1,100/10-12
1401 Jefferson St 56308 320-762-2142
Joseph Hill, prin. Fax 762-7749

Alexandria Technical College Post-Sec.
1601 Jefferson St 56308 320-762-0221

Amboy, Blue Earth, Pop. 534
Maple River SD 2135
Supt. — See Mapleton
Maple River West MS 100/6-8
PO Box 70 56010 507-674-3046
Michelle Schrantz, prin. Fax 674-3079

Andover, Anoka, Pop. 29,745
Anoka-Hennepin SD 11
Supt. — See Coon Rapids
Andover HS 1,600/9-12
2115 Andover Blvd NW 55304 763-506-8400
Dan Dehnicke, prin. Fax 767-3575
Oak View MS 1,200/6-8
15400 Hanson Blvd NW 55304 763-506-5600
Jinger Gustafson, prin. Fax 506-5603

Meadow Creek Christian S 700/PK-12
3037 Bunker Lake Blvd NW 55304 763-427-4595
Wendall Harris, supt. Fax 427-3398

Annandale, Wright, Pop. 2,996
Annandale SD 876 1,800/K-12
PO Box 190 55302 320-274-5602
Steve Niklaus, supt. Fax 274-5978
www.annandale.k12.mn.us
Annandale HS 600/9-12
PO Box 190 55302 320-274-8208
Richard Ofstedal, prin. Fax 274-2316
Annandale MS 600/5-8
PO Box 190 55302 320-274-8226
Dean Jennissen, prin. Fax 274-5978

Anoka, Anoka, Pop. 17,608
Anoka-Hennepin SD 11
Supt. — See Coon Rapids
Anoka HS 2,500/9-12
3939 7th Ave 55303 763-506-6200
Terry Abram, prin. Fax 506-6203
Moore MS 1,000/6-8
1523 5th Ave 55303 763-506-5000
Kathy Baufield, prin. Fax 506-5003
Sandburg MS 1,000/6-8
1902 2nd Ave 55303 763-506-6000
Mary Wolverton, prin. Fax 506-6003
Secondary Technical Education Program Vo/Tech
1355 W Highway 10 55303 763-433-3401
Ginny Karbowski, dir.

Anoka Technical College Post-Sec.
1355 W Highway 10 55303 763-576-4700

Apple Valley, Dakota, Pop. 49,856
Rosemount-Apple Valley-Eagan ISD 196
Supt. — See Rosemount
Apple Valley HS 2,400/9-12
14450 Hayes Rd 55124 952-431-8200
Steve Degenaar, prin. Fax 431-8744
Eastview HS 2,300/9-12
6200 140th St W 55124 952-431-8900
Randall Peterson, prin. Fax 431-8911
Falcon Ridge MS 1,200/6-8
12900 Johnny Cake Ridge Rd 55124 952-431-8760
Noel Mehus, prin. Fax 431-8770
School of Enviromental Studies 11-12
12155 Johnny Cake Ridge Rd 55124 952-431-8750
Dan Bodette, prin. Fax 431-8755
Scott Highlands MS 800/6-8
14011 Pilot Knob Rd 55124 952-423-7581
Daniel Wilharber, prin. Fax 423-7601
Valley MS 1,100/6-8
900 Garden View Dr 55124 952-431-8300
Dave McKeag, prin. Fax 431-8313

Glory Academy 50/K-10
16108 Harmony Path 55124 952-898-3079
Dean Engelman, prin.

Arden Hills, Ramsey, Pop. 9,780
Mounds View SD 621
Supt. — See Shoreview
Mounds View HS 1,900/9-12
1900 Lake Valentine Rd 55112 651-633-4031
Julie Wikelius, prin. Fax 639-6063

Arlington, Sibley, Pop. 2,063
Sibley East SD 2310 1,300/PK-12
PO Box 1000 55307 507-964-2292
John Langenbrunner, supt. Fax 964-8245
www.sibleyeast.org/
Sibley East SHS 300/10-12
PO Box 1000 55307 507-964-8235
James Swanson, prin. Fax 964-8245
Other Schools – See Gaylord

Ashby, Grant, Pop. 449
Ashby SD 261 300/K-12
PO Box 30 56309 218-747-2257
Allan Jensen, supt. Fax 747-2289
www.ashby.k12.mn.us
Ashby JSHS 200/7-12
PO Box 30 56309 218-747-2257
Roger Jansen, prin. Fax 747-2289

Country Bible Christian Academy 50/PK-12
27871 140th Ave 56309 218-685-4026
Thomas Aul, admin. Fax 685-6712

Aurora, Saint Louis, Pop. 1,751
Mesabi East SD 2711 900/PK-12
601 N 1st St W 55705 218-229-3321
Gene Paulson, supt. Fax 229-3736
www.mesabieast.k12.mn.us/
Mesabi East JSHS 400/7-12
601 N 1st St W 55705 218-229-3321
Jorma Rahkola, prin. Fax 229-3736

Austin, Mower, Pop. 23,469
Austin SD 492 3,600/K-12
401 3rd Ave NW 55912 507-433-0966
Dr. Candace Raskin, supt. Fax 433-0950
www.austin.k12.mn.us
Austin HS 1,200/9-12
301 3rd St NW 55912 507-433-0401
Bradley Bergstrom, prin. Fax 433-0403
Ellis MS 900/6-8
1700 4th Ave SE 55912 507-433-8800
Katie Berglund, prin. Fax 433-7330

Pacelli HS 100/9-12
311 4th St NW 55912 507-437-3278
Norm Blaser, prin. Fax 433-5693
Riverland Community College Post-Sec.
1900 8th Ave NW 55912 507-433-0600

Babbitt, Saint Louis, Pop. 1,616
Saint Louis County SD 2142
Supt. — See Virginia
Babbitt JSHS 200/7-12
30 South Dr 55706 218-827-3101
Steve Reznicek, prin. Fax 827-3103

Badger, Roseau, Pop. 476
Badger SD 676 200/PK-12
PO Box 68 56714 218-528-3201
Gwen Borgen, supt. Fax 528-3366
www.badger.k12.mn.us
Badger JSHS 100/7-12
PO Box 68 56714 218-528-3201
Gwen Borgen, prin. Fax 528-3366

Bagley, Clearwater, Pop. 1,205
Bagley SD 162 1,100/PK-12
202 Bagley Ave NW 56621 218-694-6184
Gary Bratvold, supt. Fax 694-3221
www.bagley.k12.mn.us/
Bagley JSHS 500/7-12
1130 Main Ave N 56621 218-694-3120
Steve Cairns, prin. Fax 694-3225

Barnesville, Clay, Pop. 2,295
Barnesville SD 146 800/K-12
PO Box 189 56514 218-354-2217
Phil Jensen, supt. Fax 354-7260
www.barnesville.k12.mn.us/
Barnesville JSHS 400/7-12
PO Box 189 56514 218-354-2228
Bryan Strand, prin. Fax 354-2305

Barnum, Carlton, Pop. 614
Barnum SD 91 700/PK-12
3675 County Road 140 55707 218-389-6978
David Bottem, supt. Fax 389-3259
www.barnum.k12.mn.us
Barnum JSHS 300/7-12
3675 County Road 140 55707 218-389-3273
Billie Jo Steen, prin. Fax 389-3259

Barrett, Grant, Pop. 346
West Central Area SD 2342 — 800/PK-12
301 County Road 2 56311 — 320-528-2650
Fax 528-2279
www.westcentralareaschools.net
West Central Area Secondary S — 400/7-12
301 County Road 2 56311 — 320-528-2520
Nels Onstad, prin. — Fax 528-2609

Battle Lake, Otter Tail, Pop. 778
Battle Lake SD 542 — 500/K-12
402 Summit St W 56515 — 218-864-5215
Rick Bleichner, supt. — Fax 864-8651
Battle Lake JSHS — 300/7-12
402 Summit St W 56515 — 218-864-5215
Jeff Drake, prin. — Fax 864-8651

Baudette, Lake of the Woods, Pop. 1,029
Lake of the Woods SD 390 — 700/PK-12
PO Box 310 56623 — 218-634-2735
Connie Nelson, supt. — Fax 634-2467
www.blw.k12.mn.us/
Lake of the Woods JSHS — 400/7-12
PO Box 310 56623 — 218-634-2510
Mark Nohner, prin. — Fax 634-2750

Baxter, Crow Wing, Pop. 7,400
Brainerd SD 181
Supt. — See Brainerd
Forestview MS — 5-8
12149 Knollwood Dr 56425 — 218-454-6000
Carol Pasanen, prin. — Fax 822-6238

Lake Region Christian S — 200/PK-12
7398 Fairview Rd 56425 — 218-828-1226
Steve Ogren, prin. — Fax 828-1643

Becker, Sherburne, Pop. 3,868
Becker SD 726 — 2,500/PK-12
12000 Hancock St SE 55308 — 763-261-4502
Steven Dooley, supt. — Fax 261-4559
www.becker.k12.mn.us
Becker HS — 700/9-12
12000 Hancock St SE 55308 — 763-261-4501
David Lund, prin. — Fax 261-4559
Becker MS — 600/6-8
12000 Hancock St SE 55308 — 763-261-6300
Nancy Helmer, prin. — Fax 261-6306

Belgrade, Stearns, Pop. 718
Belgrade-Brooten-Elrosa SD 2364
Supt. — See Brooten
Belgrade-Brooton-Elrosa JSHS — 400/7-12
PO Box 339 56312 — 320-254-8211
Matt Bullard, prin. — Fax 254-3784

Belle Plaine, Scott, Pop. 4,546
Belle Plaine SD 716 — 1,400/PK-12
220 S Market St 56011 — 952-873-2400
Kelly Smith, supt. — Fax 873-6909
www.belleplaine.k12.mn.us/
Belle Plaine HS — 400/9-12
220 S Market St 56011 — 952-873-2403
Lowell Hoffman, prin. — Fax 873-6909
Belle Plaine JHS — 200/7-8
130 S Willow St 56011 — 952-873-2402
Matthew Hillman, dean — Fax 873-3314

Bellingham, Lac qui Parle, Pop. 190
Bellingham SD 371 — 100/K-12
522 1st St 56212 — 320-568-2118
Ray Seiler, supt. — Fax 568-2230
Bellingham HS — 50/7-12
522 1st St 56212 — 320-588-2118
Ray Seiler, prin. — Fax 588-2230

Bemidji, Beltrami, Pop. 13,296
Bemidji SD 31 — 4,500/K-12
3300 Gillett Dr NW 56601 — 218-333-3100
Dr. James Hess, supt. — Fax 333-3129
www.bemidji.k12.mn.us
Bemidji HS — 1,400/9-12
3300 Gillett Dr NW 56601 — 218-444-1600
Richard Anderson, prin. — Fax 444-1630
Bemidji MS — 1,000/6-8
3300 Gillett Dr NW 56601 — 218-333-3215
James Wheeler, prin. — Fax 333-3333

Bemidji State University — Post-Sec.
1500 Birchmont Dr NE 56601 — 218-755-2000
Northwest Technical College — Post-Sec.
905 Grant Ave SE 56601 — 218-755-4270
Oak Hills Christian College — Post-Sec.
1600 Oak Hills Rd SW 56601 — 888-751-8670

Benson, Swift, Pop. 3,189
Benson SD 777 — 1,100/PK-12
1400 Montana Ave 56215 — 320-843-2710
Shelly Johnson, supt. — Fax 843-2262
www.benson.k12.mn.us
Benson JSHS — 500/7-12
1400 Montana Ave 56215 — 320-843-2710
Lee Westrum, prin. — Fax 843-2262

Bertha, Todd, Pop. 448
Bertha-Hewitt SD 786 — 500/K-12
PO Box 8 56437 — 218-924-2500
Robert Sieling, supt. — Fax 924-3252
Bertha JSHS — 200/7-12
PO Box 8 56437 — 218-924-2500
Mary Merchant, prin. — Fax 924-3252

Bigfork, Itasca, Pop. 455
Grand Rapids SD 318
Supt. — See Grand Rapids
Bigfork JSHS — 100/7-12
PO Box 228 56628 — 218-743-3444
Scott Patrow, prin. — Fax 743-3443

Big Lake, Sherburne, Pop. 8,804
Big Lake SD 727 — 3,300/PK-12
501 Minnesota Ave 55309 — 763-262-5218
Jonathan Miller, supt. — Fax 262-5144
www.biglake.k12.mn.us
Big Lake HS — 800/9-12
501 Minnesota Ave 55309 — 763-262-2547
Mark Canton, prin. — Fax 262-2543
Big Lake MS — 800/6-8
601 Minnesota Ave 55309 — 763-262-2567
Glenn Evans, prin. — Fax 262-2563

Birchdale, Koochiching
South Koochiching-Rainy River SD 363
Supt. — See Northome
Indus JSHS — 100/7-12
8560 Highway 11 56629 — 218-634-2425
Wade Pilloud, prin. — Fax 634-1334

Blackduck, Beltrami, Pop. 755
Blackduck SD 32 — 800/PK-12
PO Box 550 56630 — 218-835-5200
Robert G. Doetsch, supt. — Fax 835-4491
www.blackduck.k12.mn.us
Blackduck HS — 400/7-12
PO Box 550 56630 — 218-835-5210
Wendy Templin, prin. — Fax 835-4491

Blaine, Anoka, Pop. 54,084
Anoka-Hennepin SD 11
Supt. — See Coon Rapids
Blaine HS — 2,900/9-12
12555 University Ave NE 55434 — 763-506-6500
Norm Hande, prin. — Fax 506-6503
Roosevelt MS — 1,200/6-8
650 125th Ave NE 55434 — 763-506-5800
Greg Blodgett, prin. — Fax 506-5803

Spring Lake Park SD 16
Supt. — See Spring Lake Park
Westwood MS — 1,000/6-8
711 91st Ave NE 55434 — 763-784-8625
Paula Hoff, prin. — Fax 786-7815

Regency Beauty Academy — Post-Sec.
40 County Road 10 NE 55434 — 763-784-9102

Blooming Prairie, Steele, Pop. 1,962
Blooming Prairie SD 756 — 800/PK-12
202 4th Ave NW 55917 — 507-583-4426
Barry Olson, supt. — Fax 583-7952
www.blossoms.k12.mn.us
Blooming Prairie JSHS — 400/7-12
202 4th Ave NW 55917 — 507-583-4426
Barry Olson, prin. — Fax 583-7952

Bloomington, Hennepin, Pop. 81,164
Bloomington SD 271 — 10,400/K-12
1350 W 106th St 55431 — 952-681-6400
Les Fujitake, supt. — Fax 681-6401
www.bloomingtonschools.info/
Jefferson HS — 1,700/9-12
4001 W 102nd St 55437 — 952-806-7600
Steve Hill, prin. — Fax 806-7601
Kennedy HS — 1,700/9-12
9701 Nicollet Ave S 55420 — 952-681-5000
Ron Simmons, prin. — Fax 681-5001
Oak Grove MS — 800/6-8
1300 W 106th St 55431 — 952-681-6600
Ray Knoss, prin. — Fax 681-6601
Olson MS — 800/6-8
4551 W 102nd St 55437 — 952-806-8600
Thomas Lee, prin. — Fax 806-8601
Valley View MS — 700/6-8
8900 Portland Ave S 55420 — 952-681-5800
Andrew Kubas, prin. — Fax 681-5801

Academy College — Post-Sec.
1101 E 78th St 55420 — 952-851-0066
Bethany Academy — 300/K-12
4300 W 98th St 55437 — 952-831-8686
Jesse Hinrichs, supt. — Fax 831-9568
Concordia Academy - Bloomington — 100/7-12
8201 Park Ave S 55420 — 952-854-0224
Lynn Henry, prin. — Fax 854-8527
National American University — Post-Sec.
112 W Market 55425 — 952-883-0439
Normandale Community College — Post-Sec.
9700 France Ave S 55431 — 952-832-6000
Northwestern Health Sciences University — Post-Sec.
2501 W 84th St 55431 — 952-888-4777
Scot Lewis School of Cosmetology — Post-Sec.
9749 Lyndale Ave S 55420 — 952-881-8662

Blue Earth, Faribault, Pop. 3,452
Blue Earth Area ISD 2860 — 1,200/K-12
315 E 6th St 56013 — 507-526-3188
Dale Brandsoy, supt. — Fax 526-2432
www.blueearth.k12.mn.us
Blue Earth Area MS — 200/6-8
315 E 6th St 56013 — 507-526-3115
Melissa McGuire, prin. — Fax 526-2432
Blue Earth HS — 400/9-12
1125 N Grove St 56013 — 507-526-3201
Jack Eustice, prin. — Fax 526-3260

Bovey, Itasca, Pop. 661
Greenway SD 316
Supt. — See Coleraine
Connor-Jasper MS — 400/5-8
PO Box 40 55709 — 218-245-2661
Dennis Perreault, prin. — Fax 245-3483

Braham, Isanti, Pop. 1,574
Braham SD 314 — 900/K-12
PO Box 488 55006 — 320-396-3313
Craig Schultz, supt. — Fax 396-3068
www.braham.k12.mn.us
Braham Area JSHS — 400/7-12
PO Box 488 55006 — 320-396-4444
Kurt Kahlenbeck, prin. — Fax 396-3068

Brainerd, Crow Wing, Pop. 13,684
Brainerd SD 181 — 4,300/PK-12
804 Oak St 56401 — 218-454-6900
Gerald Walseth, supt. — Fax 822-6901
www.isd181.org/
Brainerd HS South Campus — 9-9
400 Quince St 56401 — 218-454-5200
William Severson, prin. — Fax 828-5201
Brainerd SHS — 1,600/10-12
702 S 5th St 56401 — 218-454-6200
Erich Heise, prin. — Fax 824-6325
Other Schools – See Baxter

Central Lakes College — Post-Sec.
501 W College Dr 56401 — 218-855-8000

Brandon, Douglas, Pop. 419
Brandon SD 207 — 300/PK-12
PO Box 185 56315 — 320-524-2263
Mark Westby, supt. — Fax 524-2228
www.brandon.k12.mn.us
Brandon HS — 200/7-12
PO Box 185 56315 — 320-524-2263
Tom Trisko, prin. — Fax 524-2228

Breckenridge, Wilkin, Pop. 3,373
Breckenridge SD 846 — 900/PK-12
810 Beede Ave 56520 — 218-643-6822
David Pace, supt. — Fax 641-4035
www.breckenridge.k12.mn.us
Breckenridge HS — 300/9-12
710 13th St N 56520 — 218-643-2694
Daniel Bettin, prin. — Fax 643-5229
Breckenridge MS — 200/6-8
810 Beede Ave 56520 — 218-643-6681
Donald Schill, prin. — Fax 643-5021

Brooklyn Center, Hennepin, Pop. 27,551
Brooklyn Center SD 286 — 1,700/PK-12
6500 Humboldt Ave N 55430 — 763-561-2120
Fax 560-2647
www.brookcntr.k12.mn.us/
Brooklyn Center JSHS — 800/7-12
6500 Humboldt Ave N 55430 — 763-561-2120
Bryan Bass, prin. — Fax 561-1062

Brown College — Post-Sec.
6860 Shingle Creek Pkwy 55430 — 763-566-2279
Minnesota School of Business — Post-Sec.
5910 Shingle Creek Pky #200 55430 — 763-566-7777
National American University — Post-Sec.
6120 Earle Brown Dr Ste 100 55430 — 763-560-8377

Brooklyn Park, Hennepin, Pop. 68,550
Osseo SD 279
Supt. — See Maple Grove
Brooklyn JHS — 1,100/7-9
7377 Noble Ave N 55443 — 763-569-7700
Rob Mendolia, prin. — Fax 569-7707
North View JHS — 1,300/7-9
5869 69th Ave N 55429 — 763-585-7200
Peg Vickerman, prin. — Fax 585-7210
Park Center SHS — 1,500/10-12
7300 Brooklyn Blvd 55443 — 763-569-7600
Kelli Parpart, prin. — Fax 569-7606

Hennepin Technical College — Post-Sec.
9000 Brooklyn Blvd 55445 — 763-488-2500
North Hennepin Community College — Post-Sec.
7411 85th Ave N 55445 — 763-424-0702

Brooten, Stearns, Pop. 623
Belgrade-Brooten-Elrosa SD 2364 — 800/PK-12
PO Box 39 56316 — 320-346-2278
Warren Schmidt, supt. — Fax 346-2589
Other Schools – See Belgrade

Browerville, Todd, Pop. 721
Browerville SD 787 — 500/PK-12
PO Box 185 56438 — 320-594-2272
Larry Werder, supt. — Fax 594-8105
www.browerville.k12.mn.us/
Browerville JSHS — 300/7-12
PO Box 185 56438 — 320-594-2272
Robert Schaefer, prin. — Fax 594-8105

Browns Valley, Traverse, Pop. 631
Browns Valley SD 801 — 200/PK-8
PO Box N 56219 — 320-695-2103
Brenda Reed, supt. — Fax 695-2868
Browns Valley MS — 100/5-8
PO Box N 56219 — 320-695-2103
Brenda Reed, prin. — Fax 695-2868

Brownton, McLeod, Pop. 792
McLeod West SD 2887 — 300/K-12
PO Box 99 55312 — 320-328-5214
Thomas Hiebert, supt. — Fax 328-5216
mcleod.k12.mn.us
McLeod West HS — 100/7-12
PO Box 99 55312 — 320-328-5214
Fax 328-5216

Buffalo, Wright, Pop. 13,290
Buffalo SD 877 — 5,400/K-12
214 1st Ave NE 55313 — 763-682-5200
Jim Bauck, supt. — Fax 682-8785
www.buffalo.k12.mn.us
Buffalo Community MS — 1,200/6-8
1300 Highway 25 N 55313 — 763-682-8200
Julie Swaggert, prin. — Fax 682-8209
Buffalo HS — 1,700/9-12
877 Bison Blvd 55313 — 763-682-8100
Nicholas Miller, prin. — Fax 682-8118

Burnsville, Dakota, Pop. 59,159
Burnsville-Eagan-Savage ISD 191 — 10,600/K-12
100 River Ridge Ct 55337 — 952-707-2000
Benjamin Kanninen, supt. — Fax 707-2002
www.isd191.org
Burnsville SHS — 2,400/10-12
600 Highway 13 E 55337 — 952-707-2100
Kay Joyce, prin. — Fax 707-2102
Metcalf JHS — 800/7-9
2250 Diffley Rd 55337 — 952-707-2400
Kelly Ronn, prin. — Fax 707-2402
Nicollet JHS — 800/7-9
400 E 134th St 55337 — 952-707-2600
Sue Slater, prin. — Fax 707-2602
Other Schools – See Savage

Oliver Thein Beauty College — Post-Sec.
150 Cobblestone Ln 55337 — 612-435-3882

Butterfield, Watonwan, Pop. 526
Butterfield SD 836 — 200/K-12
PO Box 189 56120 — 507-956-2771
Lisa Shellum, supt. — Fax 956-3431
Butterfield JSHS — 100/7-12
PO Box 189 56120 — 507-956-2771
Lisa Shellum, prin. — Fax 956-3431

Byron, Olmsted, Pop. 4,509
Byron SD 531 — 1,600/PK-12
1887 2nd Ave NW 55920 — 507-775-2383
Wendy Shannon Ph.D., supt. — Fax 775-2385
bears.byron.k12.mn.us
Byron HS — 600/8-12
1887 2nd Ave NW 55920 — 507-775-2301
Michael Duffy, prin. — Fax 775-2303

Caledonia, Houston, Pop. 2,939
Caledonia SD 299 — 900/PK-12
511 W Main St 55921 — 507-725-3389
Michael Moriarty, supt. — Fax 725-3558
www.cps.k12.mn.us/
Caledonia Area HS — 400/9-12
825 N Warrior Ave 55921 — 507-725-3316
Ronald Helmers, prin. — Fax 725-3319
Caledonia Area MS — 200/6-8
825 N Warrior Ave 55921 — 507-725-3316
Brian Doty, prin. — Fax 725-3319

Cambridge, Isanti, Pop. 7,198
Cambridge-Isanti SD 911 — 4,800/PK-12
315 7th Ln NE 55008 — 763-689-6188
Bruce Novak, supt. — Fax 689-6200
www.cambridge.k12.mn.us
Cambridge-Isanti HS — 1,600/9-12
430 8th Ave NW 55008 — 763-689-6066
Mitchell Clausen, prin. — Fax 689-6060
Cambridge MS — 800/5-8
31374 Xylite St NE 55008 — 763-552-6300
Charlie Burroughs, prin. — Fax 552-6399
Other Schools – See Isanti

Anoka-Ramsey Community College — Post-Sec.
300 Polk St S 55008 — 763-689-7000
Cambridge Christian S — 200/K-12
2211 Main St S 55008 — 763-689-3806
Sarah Newton, admin. — Fax 689-3807

Campbell, Wilkin, Pop. 232
Campbell-Tintah SD 852 — 100/PK-12
PO Box 8 56522 — 218-630-5311
Lee Kulland, supt. — Fax 630-5881
www.angelfire.com/home/ctschool
Campbell-Tintah S — 100/PK-12
PO Box 8 56522 — 218-630-5311
Lee Kulland, prin. — Fax 630-5881

Canby, Yellow Medicine, Pop. 1,784
Canby SD 891 — 600/PK-12
307 1st St W 56220 — 507-223-2001
Loren Hacker, supt. — Fax 223-2011
www.canbymn.org/
Canby JSHS — 400/7-12
307 1st St W 56220 — 507-223-2002
Robert Slaba, prin. — Fax 223-2012

Minnesota West Community & Tech College — Post-Sec.
1011 1st St W 56220 — 800-658-2535

Cannon Falls, Goodhue, Pop. 3,914
Cannon Falls SD 252 — 1,300/PK-12
820 Minnesota St E 55009 — 507-263-6800
Todd Sesker, supt. — Fax 263-2555
www.cannonfallsschools.com
Cannon Falls HS — 700/7-12
820 Minnesota St E 55009 — 507-263-6800
Steve Fredrickson, prin. — Fax 263-2515

Carlton, Carlton, Pop. 795
Carlton SD 93 — 600/PK-12
PO Box 310 55718 — 218-384-4225
Scott Hoch, supt. — Fax 384-3543
www.carlton.k12.mn.us
Carlton JSHS — 300/7-12
PO Box 310 55718 — 218-384-4226
Dave Battaglia, prin. — Fax 384-3607

Cass Lake, Cass, Pop. 867
Cass Lake-Bena SD 115 — 1,100/PK-12
208 Central Ave NW 56633 — 218-335-2204
Carl Remmers, supt. — Fax 335-2614
www.clbs.k12.mn.us
Cass Lake-Bena HS — 200/9-12
15308 State Highway 371 NW 56633 — 218-335-2203
Pernell Knutson, prin. — Fax 335-7649
Cass Lake-Bena MS — 400/5-8
15314 State Highway 371 NW 56633 — 218-335-7851
Steve Novak, prin. — Fax 335-1194

Center City, Chisago, Pop. 597

Hazelden Graduate School — Post-Sec.
PO Box 11 55012 — 651-213-4175

Champlin, Hennepin, Pop. 23,302
Anoka-Hennepin SD 11
Supt. — See Coon Rapids
Champlin Park HS — 3,100/9-12
6025 109th Ave N 55316 — 763-506-6800
Rhoda Mhirpiri, prin. — Fax 506-6803
Jackson MS — 2,300/6-8
6000 109th Ave N 55316 — 763-506-5200
Tom Sullivan, prin. — Fax 506-5203

Chaska, Carver, Pop. 22,820
Chaska SD 112 — 8,100/K-12
11 Peavey Rd 55318 — 952-556-6100
David Jennings, supt. — Fax 556-6109
www.district112.org
Chaska MS East — 1,000/6-8
1600 Park Ridge Dr 55318 — 952-556-7600
James Bach, prin. — Fax 556-7609
Chaska MS West — 900/6-8
140 Engler Blvd 55318 — 952-556-7400
Sheryl Hough, prin. — Fax 556-7409
Chaska SHS — 1,800/10-12
545 Pioneer Trl 55318 — 952-556-7100
Paul McMahan, prin. — Fax 556-7109
Pioneer Ridge Freshman Center — 700/9-9
1085 Pioneer Trl 55318 — 952-556-7800
Dennis Baldus, prin. — Fax 556-7809

Southwest Christian HS — 200/9-12
103 Peavey Rd 55318 — 952-556-0040
Dr. Paul Norby, admin. — Fax 556-5567

Chatfield, Fillmore, Pop. 2,462
Chatfield SD 227 — 900/PK-12
205 Union St NE 55923 — 507-867-4210
Philip Minkkinen, supt. — Fax 867-3147
www.chatfield.k12.mn.us/
Chosen Valley JSHS — 400/7-12
205 Union St NE 55923 — 507-867-4210
Randy Paulson, prin. — Fax 867-3147

Chisago City, Chisago, Pop. 3,071

Chisago Lakes Baptist S — 100/K-12
9387 Wyoming Trl 55013 — 651-257-4587
Alan Hodak, prin.

Chisholm, Saint Louis, Pop. 4,701
Chisholm SD 695 — 800/PK-12
300 3rd Ave SW 55719 — 218-254-5726
James Varichak, supt. — Fax 254-3741
www.chisholm.k12.mn.us
Chisholm HS — 400/7-12
301 4th St SW 55719 — 218-254-5726
Jerry Lawrence, prin. — Fax 254-3741

Chokio, Stevens, Pop. 441
Chokio-Alberta SD 771 — 100/K-12
PO Box 68 56221 — 320-324-7131
Paul Brownlow, supt. — Fax 324-2731
Chokio-Alberta S — 100/K-12
PO Box 68 56221 — 320-324-7131
Paul Brownlow, prin. — Fax 324-2731

Circle Pines, Anoka, Pop. 5,356
Centennial SD 12 — 6,900/K-12
4707 North Rd 55014 — 763-792-6000
Dr. Roger Worner, supt. — Fax 792-6050
www.isd12.org
Centennial HS — 2,100/9-12
4757 North Rd 55014 — 763-792-5000
Tom Breuning, prin. — Fax 792-5050
Other Schools – See Lino Lakes

Clara City, Chippewa, Pop. 1,353
MACCRAY SD 2180 — 800/K-12
PO Box 690 56222 — 320-847-2154
Greg Schmidt, supt. — Fax 847-3239
www.maccray.k12.mn.us/
MACCRAY HS — 300/9-12
PO Box 690 56222 — 320-847-2478
Gary Sims, prin. — Fax 847-3239
MACCRAY JHS — 100/7-8
PO Box 690 56222 — 320-847-3525
Gary Sims, prin. — Fax 847-5220

Clearbrook, Clearwater, Pop. 536
Clearbrook-Gonvick ISD 2311 — 500/K-12
16770 Clearwater Lake Rd 56634 — 218-776-3112
Diane Lehse, supt. — Fax 776-3117
www.cgbearzone.com
Clearbrook-Gonvick JSHS — 300/7-12
16770 Clearwater Lake Rd 56634 — 218-776-3112
Lon Burgess, prin. — Fax 776-3117

Cleveland, LeSueur, Pop. 707
Cleveland SD 391 — 200/PK-12
PO Box 310 56017 — 507-931-5953
Brian Phillips, supt. — Fax 931-9088
cleveland.k12.mn.us/
Cleveland S — 200/PK-12
PO Box 310 56017 — 507-931-5953
Brian Phillips, prin. — Fax 931-9088

Climax, Polk, Pop. 243
Climax SD 592 — 200/PK-12
PO Box 67 56523 — 218-857-2385
Norman Baumgarn, supt. — Fax 857-3544
www.climax.k12.mn.us
Climax HS — 100/7-12
PO Box 67 56523 — 218-857-2395
Shirley Moger, prin. — Fax 857-3544

Clinton, Big Stone, Pop. 415
Clinton-Graceville-Beardsley SD 2888 — 400/K-12
PO Box 361 56225 — 320-325-5282
Mary Smidt, supt. — Fax 325-5509
www.graceville.k12.mn.us
Other Schools – See Graceville

Cloquet, Carlton, Pop. 11,476
Cloquet SD 94 — 2,200/PK-12
302 14th St 55720 — 218-879-6721
Kenneth Scarbrough, supt. — Fax 879-6724
www.cloquet.k12.mn.us
Cloquet HS — 700/9-12
1000 18th St 55720 — 218-879-3393
Warren Peterson, prin. — Fax 879-6494
Cloquet MS — 500/6-8
509 Carlton Ave 55720 — 218-879-3328
Tom Brenner, prin. — Fax 879-4175

Cloquet Christian Academy — 100/PK-12
1705 Wilson Ave 55720 — 218-879-2536
Jason Peterson, admin. — Fax 879-8889
Fond du Lac Tribal Community College — Post-Sec.
2101 14th St 55720 — 218-879-0800

Cokato, Wright, Pop. 2,700
Dassel-Cokato SD 466 — 2,300/PK-12
PO Box 1700 55321 — 320-286-4100
Jeff Powers, supt. — Fax 286-4101
www.dc.k12.mn.us
Dassel-Cokato HS — 700/9-12
PO Box 1600 55321 — 320-286-4100
Mark Herman, prin. — Fax 286-4201
Dassel-Cokato MS — 700/5-8
PO Box 1500 55321 — 320-286-4100
Gary Johnson, prin. — Fax 286-4176

Cold Spring, Stearns, Pop. 3,646
Rocori SD 750 — 2,300/PK-12
534 5th Ave N 56320 — 320-685-4901
Scott R. Staska, supt. — Fax 685-4906
www.rocori.k12.mn.us/
Rocori HS — 800/9-12
534 5th Ave N 56320 — 320-685-8683
Terry Bizal, prin. — Fax 685-4968
Rocori MS — 400/7-8
533 Main St 56320 — 320-685-3296
Cheryl Schmidt, prin. — Fax 685-3474

Coleraine, Itasca, Pop. 1,041
Greenway SD 316 — 1,200/PK-12
PO Box 195 55722 — 218-245-6500
Rochelle Van Den Heuvel, supt. — Fax 245-6507
www.greenway.k12.mn.us/
Greenway HS — 400/9-12
PO Box 520 55722 — 218-245-1287
Dan Adams, prin. — Fax 245-2397
Other Schools – See Bovey

Collegeville, Stearns

St. Johns Preparatory S — 300/7-12
PO Box 4000 56321 — 320-363-3321
Kathy Kockler, prin. — Fax 525-7737
St. John's University — Post-Sec.
PO Box 7155 56321 — 320-363-2011

Columbia Heights, Anoka, Pop. 18,110
Columbia Heights SD 13 — 3,000/K-12
1440 49th Ave NE 55421 — 763-528-4500
Dr. Nancy Kaldor, supt. — Fax 571-9203
www.colheights.k12.mn.us
Central MS — 700/6-8
900 49th Ave NE 55421 — 763-586-4701
Brian Espe, prin. — Fax 528-4707
Columbia Heights HS — 1,000/9-12
1400 49th Ave NE 55421 — 763-528-4600
Matt Schoen, prin. — Fax 571-9267

Comfrey, Brown, Pop. 354
Comfrey SD 81 — 200/K-12
305 Ochre St W 56019 — 507-877-3491
Wayne Olson, supt. — Fax 877-3492
comfreyed.org
Comfrey JSHS — 100/7-12
305 Ochre St W 56019 — 507-877-3491
Wayne Olson, prin. — Fax 877-3492

Cook, Saint Louis, Pop. 622
Saint Louis County SD 2142
Supt. — See Virginia
Cook JSHS — 200/7-12
306 E Vermilion Blvd 55723 — 218-666-5221
Kevin Abrahamson, prin. — Fax 666-5223

Coon Rapids, Anoka, Pop. 62,417
Anoka-Hennepin SD 11 — 40,500/PK-12
11299 Hanson Blvd NW 55433 — 763-506-1000
Dr. Roger Giroux, supt. — Fax 506-1003
www.anoka.k12.mn.us
Coon Rapids HS — 2,800/9-12
2340 Northdale Blvd NW 55433 — 763-506-7100
Jeffrey McGonigal, prin. — Fax 506-7103
Coon Rapids MS — 1,600/6-8
11600 Raven St NW 55433 — 763-506-4800
Michelle Langenfeld, prin. — Fax 506-4803
Northdale MS — 1,500/6-8
11301 Dogwood St NW 55448 — 763-506-5400
Laurie Jacklitch, prin. — Fax 506-5403
Other Schools – See Andover, Anoka, Blaine, Champlin

Anoka-Ramsey Community College — Post-Sec.
11200 Mississippi Blvd NW 55433 — 763-427-2600

Cottage Grove, Washington, Pop. 32,553
South Washington County SD 833 — 15,700/K-12
7362 E Point Douglas Rd S 55016 — 651-458-6300
Tom Nelson, supt. — Fax 458-6318
www.sowashco.k12.mn.us

Cottage Grove JHS 1,100/7-9
9775 Indian Blvd S 55016 651-768-6800
Elise Block, prin. Fax 768-6828
Park SHS 1,700/10-12
8040 80th St S 55016 651-768-3700
Efe Agbamu, prin. Fax 768-3705
Other Schools – See Saint Paul Park, Woodbury

Cotton, Saint Louis
Saint Louis County SD 2142
Supt. — See Virginia
Cotton JSHS 100/7-12
PO Box 187 55724 218-482-3232
Sidney Simonson, prin. Fax 482-3233

Cottonwood, Lyon, Pop. 1,123
Lakeview SD 2167 600/K-12
PO Box 107 56229 507-423-5164
Wayne Kazmierczak, supt. Fax 423-5568
www.lakeview2167.com
Lakeview HS 300/7-12
PO Box 107 56229 507-423-5166

Cromwell, Carlton, Pop. 201
Cromwell-Wright SD 95 300/PK-12
PO Box 7 55726 218-644-3737
Herbert Hilinski, supt. Fax 644-3992
www.cromwellwright.k12.mn.us
Cromwell-Wright JSHS 200/7-12
PO Box 7 55726 218-644-3716
Tom Cawcutt, prin. Fax 644-3992

Crookston, Polk, Pop. 7,929
Crookston SD 593 1,500/K-12
402 Fisher Ave Ste 593 56716 218-281-5313
Wayne Gilman, supt. Fax 281-3505
www.crookston.k12.mn.us
Crookston HS 600/8-12
402 Fisher Ave 56716 218-281-2144
Richard Koop, prin. Fax 281-4709

University of Minnesota Post-Sec.
2900 University Ave 56716 218-281-6510

Crosby, Crow Wing, Pop. 2,222
Crosby-Ironton SD 182 1,300/PK-12
711 Poplar St 56441 218-545-8801
Jamie Skjeveland, supt. Fax 545-8836
www.ci.k12.mn.us
Crosby-Ironton JSHS 600/7-12
711 Poplar St 56441 218-545-8802
Jim Christenson, prin. Fax 545-8835

Crystal, Hennepin, Pop. 21,645

Calvin Christian HS 9-12
3415 Louisiana Ave N 55427 763-531-1732
Steven Ahrenholz, prin. Fax 531-8075

Dawson, Lac qui Parle, Pop. 1,448
Dawson-Boyd SD 378 600/PK-12
848 Chestnut St 56232 320-769-2955
Brad Madsen, supt. Fax 769-4502
dawsonboydschools.org/
Dawson-Boyd JSHS 300/7-12
848 Chestnut St 56232 320-769-2955
Keri Bergson, prin. Fax 769-4502

Deer River, Itasca, Pop. 924
Deer River SD 317 1,000/PK-12
PO Box 307 56636 218-246-2420
Matt Grose, supt. Fax 246-8948
www.isd317.org
Deer River JSHS 500/7-12
PO Box 307 56636 218-246-8241
Matthew Grose, prin. Fax 246-8717

Delano, Wright, Pop. 4,551
Delano SD 879 2,000/PK-12
700 Elm Ave E Ste 2 55328 763-972-3365
John Sweet, supt. Fax 972-6706
www.delano.k12.mn.us
Delano HS 600/9-12
700 Elm Ave E Ste 2 55328 763-972-3365
Dr. Bruce Locklear, prin. Fax 972-6706
Delano MS 600/5-8
700 Elm Ave E Ste 2 55328 763-972-3365
Richard Rominski, prin. Fax 972-6706

Detroit Lakes, Becker, Pop. 7,914
Detroit Lakes SD 22 2,600/PK-12
PO Box 766 56502 218-847-9271
Mark Adams, supt. Fax 847-9273
www.detroitlakes.com
Detroit Lakes HS 900/9-12
1301 Roosevelt Ave 56501 218-847-4491
Steven Morben, prin. Fax 846-1797
Detroit Lakes MS 600/6-8
510 11th Ave 56501 218-847-9228
Michael Suckert, prin. Fax 847-0057

MN State Community & Technical College Post-Sec.
900 Highway 34 E 56501 800-492-4836

Dilworth, Clay, Pop. 3,452
Dilworth-Glyndon-Felton SD 2164 1,400/PK-12
PO Box 188 56529 218-287-2371
Bernie Lipp, supt. Fax 287-2709
www.dgf.k12.mn.us
Dilworth-Glyndon-Felton JHS 200/7-8
PO Box 188 56529 218-287-2148
Colleen Houglum, prin. Fax 287-2709
Other Schools – See Glyndon

Dodge Center, Dodge, Pop. 2,524
Triton SD 2125 1,100/K-12
813 W Highway St 55927 507-374-2192
Robert Kelly, supt. Fax 374-6524
www.triton.k12.mn.us/
Triton HS 400/9-12
813 W Highway St 55927 507-374-6305
Brett Joyce, prin. Fax 374-2447
Other Schools – See West Concord

Duluth, Saint Louis, Pop. 84,896
Duluth SD 709 10,100/PK-12
215 N 1st Ave E 55802 218-336-8752
Keith Dixon, supt. Fax 336-8773
www.duluth.k12.mn.us
Central HS 1,000/9-12
800 E Central Entrance 55811 218-733-2130
Lisa Mitchell-Krocak, prin. Fax 733-2153
Denfeld HS 1,200/9-12
4405 W 4th St 55807 218-628-4863
Ed Crawford, prin. Fax 628-4870
East HS 1,400/9-12
2900 E 4th St 55812 218-728-7426
Laurie Knapp, prin. Fax 728-7439
Morgan Park MS 500/6-8
1243 88th Ave W 55808 218-626-4512
Denise Clairmont, prin. Fax 626-4520
Ordean MS 800/6-8
301 N 40th Ave E 55804 218-525-0810
Jerry Maki, prin. Fax 525-0815
Secondary Technical S Vo/Tech
802 E Central Entrance 55811 218-336-8975
Jim Arndt, admin. Fax 336-8979
Woodland MS 800/6-8
201 Clover St 55812 218-728-7456
Bonnie Wolden, prin. Fax 728-7460
Area Learning Center Adult
215 N 1st Ave E 55802 218-336-8790
Beth Tamminen, admin. Fax 336-8791

College of Saint Scholastica Post-Sec.
1200 Kenwood Ave 55811 218-723-6000
Cosmetology Careers Unlimited - Duluth Post-Sec.
121 W Superior St 55802 218-722-7484
Duluth Business University Post-Sec.
4724 Mike Colalillo Dr 55807 218-722-3361
Lake Superior College Post-Sec.
2101 Trinity Rd 55811 218-733-7600
Lakeview Christian Academy 300/PK-12
155 W Central Entrance 55811 218-723-8844
Don Chamberlain, admin. Fax 722-7850
Marshall S 500/5-12
1215 Rice Lake Rd 55811 218-727-7266
Barbara Brueggmann, hdmstr. Fax 727-1569
University of Minnesota Post-Sec.
10 University Dr 55812 218-726-8000

Eagan, Dakota, Pop. 63,665
Rosemount-Apple Valley-Eagan ISD 196
Supt. — See Rosemount
Black Hawk MS 1,000/6-8
1540 Deerwood Dr 55122 651-683-8521
Richard Wendorff, prin. Fax 683-8527
Dakota Hills MS 1,400/6-8
4183 Braddock Trl Ste 1 55123 651-683-6800
Steven Troen, prin. Fax 683-6858
Eagan HS 2,300/9-12
4185 Braddock Trl 55123 651-683-6900
Polly Reikowski, prin. Fax 683-6910

Argosy University/Twin Cities Post-Sec.
1515 Central Pkwy 55121 651-846-2882
Rasmussen College Post-Sec.
3500 Federal Dr 55122 651-687-9000
Trinity S at River Ridge 400/7-12
601 River Ridge Pkwy 55121 952-854-0008
William Wacker, prin. Fax 854-3232

Eagle Bend, Todd, Pop. 590
Eagle Valley SD 2759 300/PK-12
PO Box 299 56446 218-738-6442
Stephen Twitchell, supt. Fax 738-6493
www.evps.k12.mn.us
Eagle Valley JSHS 200/7-12
PO Box 299 56446 218-738-6442
Deanna Mattson-Millar, prin. Fax 738-6493

East Grand Forks, Polk, Pop. 7,734
East Grand Forks SD 595 1,800/PK-12
PO Box 151 56721 218-773-3494
Walt Aanenson, supt. Fax 773-7408
www.egf.k12.mn.us/
Central MS 400/6-8
PO Box 151 56721 218-773-1141
Robert Simonson, prin. Fax 773-9112
East Grand Forks HS 600/9-12
PO Box 151 56721 218-773-2405
Steven Heyd, prin. Fax 773-3070

Northland Community & Technical College Post-Sec.
2022 Central Ave NE 56721 800-451-3441
Sacred Heart HS 200/7-12
122 3rd St NW 56721 218-773-0230
Phillip Meyer, prin. Fax 773-7042

Eden Prairie, Hennepin, Pop. 60,649
Eden Prairie SD 272 10,000/K-12
8100 School Rd 55344 952-975-7000
Melissa Krull Ph.D., supt. Fax 975-7012
www.edenpr.org
Central MS 1,500/7-8
8025 School Rd 55344 952-975-7300
Joe Epping, prin. Fax 975-7320
Eden Prairie HS 3,300/9-12
17185 Valley View Rd 55346 952-975-8000
Conn McCartan, prin. Fax 975-8020

International School of Minnesota 600/PK-12
6385 Beach Rd 55344 952-918-1800
Susan Berg, dir. Fax 918-1801
Rasmussen College Post-Sec.
7905 Golden Triangle # 100 55344 952-545-2000

Eden Valley, Meeker, Pop. 925
Eden Valley-Watkins SD 463 800/PK-12
298 Brooks St N 55329 320-453-2900
Larry Peterson, supt. Fax 453-5600
www.evw.k12.mn.us
Eden Valley Secondary S 400/7-12
298 Brooks St N 55329 320-453-2900
Bruce Kiehn, prin. Fax 453-5600

Edgerton, Pipestone, Pop. 976
Edgerton SD 581 300/PK-12
PO Box 28 56128 507-442-7881
Leroy Domagala, supt. Fax 442-8541
edgertonpublic.com
Edgerton JSHS 200/7-12
PO Box 28 56128 507-442-7881
Gene Miller, prin. Fax 442-8541

Southwest Minnesota Christian HS 100/9-12
550 W Elizabeth St 56128 507-442-4471
Paul Bootsma, prin. Fax 442-5801

Edina, Hennepin, Pop. 45,567
Edina SD 273 7,300/K-12
5701 Normandale Rd Ste 1 55424 952-848-3900
Ric Dressen, supt. Fax 848-3901
www.edina.k12.mn.us
Edina SHS 1,700/10-12
6754 Valley View Rd 55439 952-848-3800
Aldo Sicoli, prin. Fax 848-3801
South View MS 1,100/6-9
4725 S View Ln 55424 952-848-3700
Trevor Johnson, prin. Fax 848-3701
Valley View MS 1,200/6-9
6750 Valley View Rd 55439 952-848-3500
Shawn Dudley, prin. Fax 848-3501

Elgin, Wabasha, Pop. 938
Plainview-Elgin-Millville ISD 2899
Supt. — See Plainview
Plainview-Elgin-Millville JHS 100/7-8
70 1st St SE 55932 507-876-2521
Clark Olstad, prin. Fax 876-2110

Elk River, Sherburne, Pop. 21,329
Elk River Area SD 728 9,700/PK-12
815 Highway 10 55330 763-241-3400
Mark Bezek, supt. Fax 241-3407
www.elkriver.k12.mn.us
Elk River Area HS 1,800/9-12
900 School St NW 55330 763-241-3434
Terry Bizal, prin. Fax 241-3421
Salk JHS 600/6-8
11970 Highland Rd NW 55330 763-241-3455
Julie Athman, prin. Fax 241-3456
Vandenberg JHS 600/6-8
948 Proctor Ave NW 55330 763-241-3450
Clair Olson, prin. Fax 241-3451
Other Schools – See Rogers, Zimmerman

Rivers Christian Academy 100/K-12
829 School St NW 55330 763-441-6594
Kenneth Mitchell, prin. Fax 441-2150

Ellsworth, Nobles, Pop. 521
Ellsworth SD 514 100/PK-12
PO Box 8 56129 507-967-2242
George Berndt, supt. Fax 967-2588
Ellsworth S 100/PK-12
PO Box 8 56129 507-967-2151
George Berndt, prin. Fax 967-2588

Ely, Saint Louis, Pop. 3,633
Ely SD 696 700/PK-12
600 E Harvey St 55731 218-365-6166
Thomas W. Bruels, supt. Fax 365-6138
www.ely.k12.mn.us
Memorial JSHS 400/7-12
600 E Harvey St 55731 218-365-6166
Joselyn Murphy, prin. Fax 365-6138

Vermillion Community College Post-Sec.
1900 E Camp St 55731 800-475-6666

Erskine, Polk, Pop. 416
Win-E-Mac SD 2609 500/K-12
23130 345th St SE 56535 218-687-2236
Dan Parent, supt. Fax 563-2902
www.win-e-mac.k12.mn.us
Win-E-Mac JSHS 300/7-12
23130 345th St SE 56535 218-687-2236
Kevin McKeever, prin. Fax 563-2902

Esko, Carlton
Esko SD 99 1,100/PK-12
PO Box 10 55733 218-879-2969
Aaron Fischer, supt. Fax 879-7490
www.esko.k12.mn.us/
Lincoln JSHS 600/7-12
PO Box 10 55733 218-879-4673
Randy Bowen, prin. Fax 879-7490

Evansville, Douglas, Pop. 554
Evansville SD 208 200/PK-12
PO Box 40 56326 218-948-2241
Allan Jensen, supt. Fax 948-2441
www.evansville.k12.mn.us/
Evansville JSHS 100/7-12
PO Box 40 56326 218-948-2241
Allen Jensen, prin. Fax 948-2441

Eveleth, Saint Louis, Pop. 3,661
Eveleth-Gilbert SD 2154 1,400/PK-12
801 Jones St 55734 218-744-7701
Michael Lang, supt. Fax 744-4381
isd2154.k12.mn.us
Eveleth-Gilbert SHS 300/10-12
801 Jones St 55734 218-744-7707
Deborah Hilde, prin. Fax 744-4381
Other Schools – See Gilbert

Mesabi Range Community & Technical Coll. Post-Sec.
PO Box 648 55734 218-744-3302

Excelsior, Hennepin, Pop. 2,294
Minnetonka SD 276
Supt. — See Minnetonka
Minnetonka West MS 1,000/6-8
6421 Hazeltine Blvd 55331 952-401-5300
Bill Jacobson, prin. Fax 401-5350

Eyota, Olmsted, Pop. 1,708
Dover-Eyota SD 533 1,100/PK-12
615 South Ave SE 55934 507-545-2125
Bruce Klaehn, supt. Fax 545-2349
www.desch.org
Dover-Eyota JSHS 500/7-12
615 South Ave SE 55934 507-545-2631
Todd Rowekamp, prin. Fax 545-2218

Fairfax, Renville, Pop. 1,279
GFW SD 2365
Supt. — See Gibbon
GFW MS 300/5-8
PO Box 489 55332 507-426-7251
Ralph Fairchild, prin. Fax 426-7425

Prairie Lutheran MS 50/5-8
PO Box 412 55332 507-426-7755
Macord Johnson, prin. Fax 426-8372

Fairmont, Martin, Pop. 10,505
Fairmont Area SD 2752 1,800/K-12
115 S Park St 56031 507-238-4234
Harlow Hanson, supt. Fax 235-4050
fairmont.k12.mn.us
Fairmont JSHS 900/7-12
900 Johnson St 56031 507-238-4411
Lynn Manske, prin. Fax 238-4070

Faribault, Rice, Pop. 22,047
Faribault SD 656 4,000/PK-12
PO Box 618 55021 507-333-6016
Gwendolyn Jackson, supt. Fax 333-6077
www.faribault.k12.mn.us/
Faribault HS 1,300/9-12
330 9th Ave SW 55021 507-333-6100
Lyle Turtle, prin. Fax 333-6248
Faribault MS 1,000/6-8
704 17th St SW 55021 507-333-6300
Jill Louters, prin. Fax 333-6400

Bethlehem Academy 200/7-12
105 3rd Ave SW 55021 507-334-3948
Bette Blaisdell, prin. Fax 334-3949
Minnesota School for the Deaf Post-Sec.
PO Box 308 55021
Riverland Technical College Post-Sec.
1225 3rd St SW 55021 800-422-0391
Shattuck/St. Marys S 300/6-12
PO Box 218 55021 507-333-1500
Nick Stoneman, hdmstr. Fax 333-1627

Farmington, Dakota, Pop. 17,740
Farmington SD 192 5,300/K-12
421 Walnut St 55024 651-463-5000
Dr. Bradley Meeks, supt. Fax 463-5010
www.farmington.k12.mn.us
Farmington MS West 800/8-9
4200 208th St W 55024 651-460-1500
Christine Weymouth, prin. Fax 460-1510
Farmington SHS 1,000/10-12
800 Denmark Ave 55024 651-460-1400
Monica Kittock-Sargent, prin. Fax 460-1410

Christian Life S 200/PK-12
6300 212th St W 55024 651-463-4545
Pastor Darin Kindle, admin. Fax 463-8353

Fergus Falls, Otter Tail, Pop. 13,722
Fergus Falls SD 544 2,700/PK-12
1519 Pebble Lake Rd 56537 218-998-0544
Gerald Ness, supt. Fax 998-3952
www.fergusfalls.k12.mn.us
Fergus Falls HS 900/9-12
518 Friberg Ave 56537 218-736-6971
Greg Winter, prin. Fax 998-3946
Fergus Falls MS 900/5-8
601 Randolph Ave 56537 218-998-0544
Dean Monke, prin. Fax 998-3943

Hillcrest Lutheran Academy 200/7-12
610 Hillcrest Dr 56537 218-739-3371
Jeff Isaac, prin. Fax 739-3372
MN State Community & Technical College Post-Sec.
1414 College Way 56537 218-739-7500

Fertile, Polk, Pop. 866
Fertile-Beltrami SD 599 500/PK-12
PO Box 648 56540 218-945-6933
Don Blaeser, supt. Fax 945-6934
fertilebeltrami.k12.mn.us/FBSchool/Home/home.htm
Fertile-Beltrami JSHS 300/7-12
PO Box 648 56540 218-945-6953
Brian Clarke, prin. Fax 945-6934

Finlayson, Pine, Pop. 323
East Central SD 2580 700/PK-12
61085 State Highway 23 55735 320-245-2289
Jeffrey Peura, supt. Fax 245-5453
www.eastcentral.k12.mn.us
Other Schools – See Sandstone

Fisher, Polk, Pop. 417
Fisher SD 600 300/K-12
313 Park Ave 56723 218-891-4105
Randy Bruer, supt. Fax 891-4251
www.fisher.k12.mn.us
Fisher JSHS 200/7-12
313 Park Ave 56723 218-891-4905
Erik Erie, prin. Fax 891-4251

Floodwood, Saint Louis, Pop. 503
Floodwood SD 698 400/PK-12
PO Box 287 55736 218-476-2285
Palmer Anderson, supt. Fax 476-2813
www.floodwood.k12.mn.us/
Floodwood JSHS 200/7-12
PO Box 287 55736 218-476-2285
Theresa Sorenson, prin. Fax 476-2813

Foley, Benton, Pop. 2,373
Foley SD 51 1,700/PK-12
PO Box 297 56329 320-968-7175
Dr. Fred Nolan, supt. Fax 968-8608
foley.k12.mn.us
Foley HS 600/9-12
PO Box 397 56329 320-968-7246
Alan Niemann, prin. Fax 968-8456
Foley MS 600/4-8
PO Box 297 56329 320-968-6251
Brad Kelvington, prin. Fax 968-8608

Forest Lake, Washington, Pop. 17,353
Forest Lake SD 831 7,400/K-12
6100 210th St N 55025 651-982-8100
Lynn Steenblock, supt. Fax 982-8114
www.forestlake.k12.mn.us
Century JHS 1,000/7-9
21395 Goodview Ave N 55025 651-982-8600
Dr. Benjamin Lewis, prin. Fax 982-8690
Forest Lake SHS 1,800/10-12
6101 Scandia Trl N 55025 651-982-8400
Dr. Steve Massey, prin. Fax 982-8428
Southwest JHS 700/7-9
943 9th Ave SW 55025 651-982-8700
Marc Peterson, prin. Fax 982-8798

Foreston, Mille Lacs, Pop. 507

Faith Christian S 100/K-12
11818 160th Ave 56330 320-294-5501
Randy Peterson, admin. Fax 294-5197

Fosston, Polk, Pop. 1,515
Fosston SD 601 600/PK-12
301 1st St E 56542 218-435-6335
Dale Salberg, supt. Fax 435-1663
www.fosston.k12.mn.us
Fosston JSHS 300/7-12
301 1st St E 56542 218-435-1909
John Strom, prin. Fax 435-6340

Frazee, Becker, Pop. 1,396
Frazee-Vergas SD 23 1,100/PK-12
305 N Lake St 56544 218-334-3181
Deron Stender, supt. Fax 334-3182
www.frazee.k12.mn.us/
Frazee JSHS 600/7-12
305 N Lake St 56544 218-334-3181
Terry Karger, prin. Fax 334-4696

Fridley, Anoka, Pop. 26,515
Fridley SD 14 2,500/K-12
6000 Moore Lake Dr W 55432 763-502-5000
Mark Robertson, supt. Fax 502-5040
www.fridley.k12.mn.us
Fridley HS 800/9-12
6000 Moore Lake Dr W 55432 763-502-5600
Dr. Dave Webb, prin. Fax 502-5640
Fridley MS 800/5-8
6100 Moore Lake Dr W 55432 763-502-5400
Margaret Leibfried, prin. Fax 502-5440

Totino-Grace HS 1,100/9-12
1350 Gardena Ave NE 55432 763-571-9116
Julie Michels, prin. Fax 571-9118

Fulda, Murray, Pop. 1,272
Fulda SD 505 500/PK-12
410 N College Ave 56131 507-425-2514
Luther Onken, supt. Fax 425-2001
www.fps.mntm.org
Fulda JSHS 300/7-12
410 N College Ave 56131 507-425-2516
Luther Onken, prin. Fax 425-2001

Gaylord, Sibley, Pop. 2,194
Sibley East SD 2310
Supt. — See Arlington
Sibley East JHS 300/7-9
PO Box 356 55334 507-237-3315
Steve Harter, prin. Fax 237-3300

Gibbon, Sibley, Pop. 764
GFW SD 2365 900/PK-12
323 E 11th St 55335 507-834-9813
Stephen Malone, supt. Fax 834-6264
www.gfw.k12.mn.us
Other Schools – See Fairfax, Winthrop

Gilbert, Saint Louis, Pop. 1,772
Eveleth-Gilbert SD 2154
Supt. — See Eveleth
Eveleth-Gilbert JHS 300/7-9
Summit St 55741 218-741-7773
Jan Mesich, prin. Fax 741-7504

Glencoe, McLeod, Pop. 5,553
Glencoe-Silver Lake SD 2859 1,100/PK-12
1621 16th St E 55336 320-864-2455
John Hornung, supt. Fax 864-6320
www.gsl.k12.mn.us
Glencoe-Silver Lake HS 50/9-12
1621 16th St E 55336 320-864-2400
Scot Kerbaugh, prin. Fax 864-6475
Lincoln JHS 300/7-8
1621 16th St E 55336 320-864-2455
Chris Sonju, prin. Fax 864-2475

Glenville, Freeborn, Pop. 701
Glenville-Emmons SD 2886 400/K-12
PO Box 38 56036 507-448-2889
David Vik, supt. Fax 448-2836
www.geschools.com
Glenville-Emmons JSHS 200/7-12
230 5th St SE 56036 507-448-2889
David Vik, prin. Fax 448-2836

Glenwood, Pope, Pop. 2,564
Minnewaska SD 2149 1,200/PK-12
25122 State Highway 28 56334 320-239-4800
Gregory Ohl, supt. Fax 239-1362
www.minnewaska.k12.mn.us
Minnewaska Area HS 500/9-12
25122 State Highway 28 56334 320-239-4800
Lyle Katzenmeyer, prin. Fax 239-1362
Minnewaska Area MS 200/5-8
25122 State Highway 28 56334 320-239-4800
Pat Falk, prin. Fax 239-1362

Glyndon, Clay, Pop. 1,168
Dilworth-Glyndon-Felton SD 2164
Supt. — See Dilworth
Dilworth-Glyndon-Felton HS 400/9-12
513 Parke Ave S 56547 218-498-2263
Tom Gravel, prin. Fax 498-2488

Golden Valley, Hennepin, Pop. 20,003
Robbinsdale SD 281
Supt. — See New Hope
Sandburg MS 1,300/6-8
2400 Sandburg Ln 55427 763-504-8200
Tom Henderlite, prin. Fax 504-8231

Goodhue, Goodhue, Pop. 929
Goodhue SD 253 600/PK-12
PO Box 128 55027 651-923-4447
Robert Bangston, supt. Fax 923-4083
www.goodhue.net
Goodhue JSHS 300/7-12
PO Box 128 55027 651-923-4447
Mark Roubinek, prin. Fax 923-4083

Goodridge, Pennington, Pop. 107
Goodridge SD 561 200/K-12
PO Box 195 56725 218-378-4133
Galen Clow, supt. Fax 378-4142
www.goodridge.k12.mn.us
Goodridge JSHS 100/7-12
PO Box 195 56725 218-378-4133
Timothy Lutz, prin. Fax 378-4142

Graceville, Big Stone, Pop. 574
Clinton-Graceville-Beardsley SD 2888
Supt. — See Clinton
Clinton-Graceville-Beardsley HS 200/7-12
PO Box 398 56240 320-748-7233
Larry Mischke, prin. Fax 748-7159

Granada, Martin, Pop. 305
Granada - Huntley - East Chain SD 2536 300/PK-12
PO Box 17 56039 507-447-2211
Randy Grupe, supt. Fax 447-2214
www.ghec.k12.mn.us
Granada - Huntley - East Chain JSHS 200/7-12
PO Box 17 56039 507-447-2211
Robert Grant, prin. Fax 447-2214

Grand Marais, Cook, Pop. 1,426
Cook County SD 166 500/K-12
101 W 5th St 55604 218-387-2271
Charles Futterer, supt. Fax 387-1093
www.cookcountyschools.org/
Cook County MSHS 200/6-12
101 W 5th St 55604 218-387-2273
John Engelking, prin. Fax 387-9746

Grand Meadow, Mower, Pop. 946
Grand Meadow SD 495 400/K-12
PO Box 68 55936 507-754-5318
Joseph Brown, supt. Fax 754-5608
www.gm.k12.mn.us/
Grand Meadow HS 100/9-12
PO Box 68 55936 507-754-5310
David Stadum, prin. Fax 754-5608
Grand Meadow MS 100/5-8
PO Box 68 55936 507-754-5310
David Stadum, prin. Fax 754-5608

Grand Rapids, Itasca, Pop. 8,277
Grand Rapids SD 318 3,700/K-12
820 NW 1st Ave 55744 218-327-5700
Joe Silko, supt. Fax 327-5702
www.isd318.org
Elkington MS 800/6-8
1000 NE 8th Ave 55744 218-327-5800
Len Rothlisberger, prin. Fax 327-5801
Grand Rapids HS 1,200/9-12
800 NW Conifer Dr 55744 218-327-5760
Jim Smokrovich, prin. Fax 327-5761
Other Schools – See Bigfork

Itasca Community College Post-Sec.
1851 E US Highway 169 55744 218-327-4460

Granite Falls, Yellow Medicine, Pop. 2,988
Yellow Medicine East SD 2190 900/K-12
450 9th Ave 56241 320-564-4081
Dwayne Strand, supt. Fax 564-4781
www.yme.k12.mn.us
Yellow Medicine East JSHS 400/7-12
450 9th Ave 56241 320-564-4083
Karen Norell, prin. Fax 564-4782

Minnesota West Community & Tech College Post-Sec.
1593 11th Ave 56241 800-657-3247

Greenbush, Roseau, Pop. 770
Greenbush-Middle River SD 2683 500/PK-12
PO Box 70 56726 218-782-2231
Ron Ruud, supt. Fax 782-3141
www.middleriver.k12.mn.us/
Greenbush-Middle River HS 100/9-12
PO Box 70 56726 218-782-2232
Eldon Sparby, prin. Fax 782-2165
Other Schools – See Middle River

Grove City, Meeker, Pop. 600
ACGC SD 2396 700/PK-12
27250 Minnesota Highway 4 56243 320-857-2271
Pamela Kyllingstad, supt. Fax 857-2989
acgc.k12.mn.us
ACGC JSHS 400/5-12
27250 Minnesota Highway 4 56243 320-857-2276
Sherri Broderius, prin. Fax 857-2937

Grygla, Marshall, Pop. 233
Grygla SD 447 200/PK-12
PO Box 18 56727 218-294-6155
Galen Clow, supt. Fax 294-6766
Grygla JSHS 100/7-12
PO Box 18 56727 218-294-6155
Patti Johnson, prin. Fax 294-6766

Hallock, Kittson, Pop. 1,087
Kittson Central SD 2171 400/PK-12
PO Box 670 56728 218-843-3682
Bruce Jensen, supt. Fax 843-2856
kittson.k12.mn.us
Kittson Central HS 200/7-12
PO Box 670 56728 218-843-3682
Terry Ogorek, prin. Fax 843-2856

Halstad, Norman, Pop. 575
Norman County West SD 2527
Supt. — See Hendrum
Norman County West JSHS 200/7-12
PO Box 328 56548 218-456-2151
Caline Olson, prin. Fax 456-2193

Hancock, Stevens, Pop. 694
Hancock SD 768 200/K-12
PO Box 367 56244 320-392-5622
Jerry Martinson, supt. Fax 392-5156
Hancock JSHS 100/7-12
PO Box 367 56244 320-392-5622
Jerry Martinson, prin. Fax 392-5156

Harmony, Fillmore, Pop. 1,119
Fillmore Central SD 2198 700/PK-12
PO Box 599 55939 507-886-6464
Myrna Luehmann, supt. Fax 886-6642
www.fillmorecentral.k12.mn.us/
Fillmore Central HS 200/9-12
PO Box 599 55939 507-886-6464
Heath Olstad, prin. Fax 886-6642
Other Schools – See Preston

Hastings, Dakota, Pop. 20,910
Hastings SD 200 5,100/K-12
1000 11th St W 55033 651-437-6111
Tim Collins, supt. Fax 437-1928
www.hastings.k12.mn.us
Hastings HS 1,800/9-12
200 General Sieben Dr 55033 651-480-0205
Mike Johnson, prin. Fax 480-8128
Hastings MS 1,200/6-8
1000 11th St W 55033 651-438-0705
Mark Zuzek, prin. Fax 438-0707

Hawley, Clay, Pop. 1,892
Hawley SD 150 900/K-12
PO Box 608 56549 218-483-4647
Phil Jensen, supt. Fax 483-4802
www.hawley.k12.mn.us/
Hawley JSHS 400/7-12
PO Box 608 56549 218-483-3555
Mike Martin, prin. Fax 483-4802
Spring Prairie S 50/K-12
PO Box 608 56549 218-483-3316
Wayne LePard, prin. Fax 483-4638

Hayfield, Dodge, Pop. 1,370
Hayfield SD 203 900/PK-12
9 6th Ave SE 55940 507-477-3235
Ron Evjen, supt. Fax 477-3230
www.hayfield.k12.mn.us/
Hayfield JSHS 400/7-12
9 6th Ave SE 55940 507-477-3235
Brandon Macrafic, prin. Fax 477-3230

Hector, Renville, Pop. 1,140
Buffalo Lake-Hector SD 2159 600/PK-12
PO Box 307 55342 320-848-2233
Dr. Rick Clark, supt. Fax 848-2401
blh.k12.mn.us
Buffalo Lake-Hector JSHS 300/6-12
PO Box 307 55342 320-848-2233
Cory Klabunde, prin. Fax 848-2401

Hendrum, Norman, Pop. 304
Norman County West SD 2527 300/PK-12
PO Box 39 56550 218-861-5800
Caline Olson, supt. Fax 861-6223
www.ncw.k12.mn.us
Other Schools – See Halstad

Henning, Otter Tail, Pop. 812
Henning SD 545 400/PK-12
500 School Ave 56551 218-583-2927
Deborah Wanek, supt. Fax 583-2312
www.henning.k12.mn.us
Henning JSHS 200/7-12
500 School Ave 56551 218-583-2927
Chris Ellingson, prin. Fax 583-2312

Herman, Grant, Pop. 425
Herman-Norcross SD 264 100/K-12
PO Box 288 56248 320-677-2291
Tom Knoll, supt. Fax 677-2412
herman.mn.schoolwebpages.com
Herman JSHS 100/7-12
PO Box 288 56248 320-677-2291
Steve Wymore, prin. Fax 677-2412

Hermantown, Saint Louis, Pop. 8,861
Hermantown SD 700 2,000/K-12
4307 Ugstad Rd 55811 218-729-9313
Brad Johnson, supt. Fax 729-9315
www.hermantown.k12.mn.us
Hermantown HS 700/9-12
4335 Hawk Circle Dr 55811 218-729-8874
Lois Backscheider, prin. Fax 729-0180
Hermantown MS 800/4-8
4289 Ugstad Rd 55811 218-729-6690
David Radovich, prin. Fax 729-9890

Hibbing, Saint Louis, Pop. 16,509
Hibbing SD 701 2,400/K-12
800 E 21st St 55746 218-263-4850
Robert Belluzzo, supt. Fax 262-0494
www.hibbing.k12.mn.us
Hibbing HS 1,300/7-12
800 E 21st St 55746 218-263-0400
Mike Finco, prin. Fax 262-5137

Cosmetology Careers Unlimited - Hibbing Post-Sec.
110 E Howard St 55746 218-263-8354
Hibbing Community College Post-Sec.
1515 E 25th St 55746 218-262-7200

Hill City, Aitkin, Pop. 462
Hill City SD 2 400/PK-12
500 Ione Ave 55748 218-697-2394
Scott Vedbraaten, supt. Fax 697-2594
www.hillcity.k12.mn.us/
Hill City JSHS 200/7-12
500 Ione Ave 55748 218-697-2394
Dean Yocum, prin. Fax 697-2594

Hills, Rock, Pop. 595
Hills-Beaver Creek SD 671 300/PK-12
PO Box 547 56138 507-962-3240
David Deragisch, supt. Fax 962-3238
www.hbcpatriots.com
Hills-Beaver Creek JSHS 200/7-12
PO Box 547 56138 507-962-3240
David Deragisch, prin. Fax 962-3238

Hinckley, Pine, Pop. 1,440
Hinckley-Finlayson SD 2165 1,100/PK-12
PO Box 308 55037 320-384-6277
Jack Almos, supt. Fax 384-6135
www.hf.k12.mn.us/
Hinckley-Finlayson HS 500/7-12
PO Box 308 55037 320-384-6132
Rob Prater, prin. Fax 384-6135

Holdingford, Stearns, Pop. 710
Holdingford SD 738 1,100/PK-12
PO Box 250 56340 320-746-2196
John Haas, supt. Fax 746-2274
www.holdingford.k12.mn.us
Holdingford JSHS 500/7-12
PO Box 250 56340 320-746-2221
Patrick Vandrovec, prin. Fax 746-9959

Hopkins, Hennepin, Pop. 16,825
Hopkins SD 270 7,600/K-12
1001 Highway 7 55305 952-988-4000
John Schultz, supt. Fax 988-4020
www.hopkins.k12.mn.us
Other Schools – See Minnetonka

Blake S 1,400/PK-12
110 Blake Rd S 55343 952-988-3400
John Gulla, hdmstr. Fax 988-3455

Houston, Winona, Pop. 1,001
Houston SD 294 900/PK-12
306 W Elm St 55943 507-896-5323
Kim Ross, supt. Fax 896-3452
www.houston.k12.mn.us
Houston JSHS 200/7-12
306 W Elm St 55943 507-896-5323
Todd Lundberg, prin. Fax 896-4665

Howard Lake, Wright, Pop. 1,957
Howard Lake-Waverly-Winsted SD 2687 800/PK-12
PO Box 708 55349 320-543-3521
George Ladd, supt. Fax 543-3590
www.hlww.k12.mn.us
Howard Lake MS 6-8
PO Box 708 55349 320-543-3501
Brad Sellner, prin. Fax 543-3590
Howard Lake-Waverly-Winsted HS 400/9-12
PO Box 708 55349 320-543-3471
Michael Day, prin. Fax 543-3590

Hutchinson, McLeod, Pop. 13,722
Hutchinson SD 423 3,000/PK-12
30 Glen St NW 55350 320-587-2860
Dan Vanoverbeke, supt. Fax 587-4590
www.hutch.k12.mn.us
Hutchinson HS 1,000/9-12
1200 Roberts Rd SW 55350 320-587-2151
Ron Johnson, prin. Fax 587-8217
Hutchinson MS 700/6-8
1365 S Grade Rd SW 55350 320-587-2854
Todd Grina, prin. Fax 587-2857

Maplewood Academy 100/9-12
700 Main St N 55350 320-587-2830
Steve Sherman, prin. Fax 587-5649
Ridgewater College-Hutchinson Campus Post-Sec.
2 Century Ave SE 55350 320-587-3636

International Falls, Koochiching, Pop. 6,332
International Falls SD 361 1,100/1-12
1515 11th St 56649 218-283-8468
Don Langan, supt. Fax 283-8104
www.isd361.k12.mn.us
Falls HS 700/7-12
1515 11th St 56649 218-283-2571
Tim Everson, prin. Fax 283-2384

Rainy River Community College Post-Sec.
1501 Highway 71 56649 218-285-7722

Inver Grove Heights, Dakota, Pop. 33,182
Inver Grove Heights Community SD 199 3,600/PK-12
2990 80th St E 55076 651-306-7800
Dr. Deirdre Wells, supt. Fax 306-7295
www.invergrove.k12.mn.us
Inver Grove Heights MS 900/6-8
8167 Cahill Ave 55076 651-306-7200
Joshua Alexander, prin. Fax 306-7152
Simley HS 1,200/9-12
2920 80th St E 55076 651-306-7000
Richard Ehlers, prin. Fax 306-7016

Inver Hills Community College Post-Sec.
2500 80th St E 55076 651-450-8500

Iron, Saint Louis, Pop. 135
Saint Louis County SD 2142
Supt. — See Virginia
Cherry JSHS 200/7-12
3943 Tamminen Rd 55751 218-258-8991
John Metsa, prin. Fax 258-8993

Isanti, Isanti, Pop. 5,167
Cambridge-Isanti SD 911
Supt. — See Cambridge
Isanti MS 500/6-8
201 Centennial Dr 55040 763-691-8661
Timothy Truebenbach, prin. Fax 691-8662
Minnesota Center S 100/6-8
201 Centennial Dr 55040 763-691-8661
Timothy Truebenbach, prin. Fax 691-8677

Isle, Mille Lacs, Pop. 873
Isle SD 473 600/K-12
PO Box 25 56342 320-676-3146
Allen Ralston, supt. Fax 676-3966
www.isle.k12.mn.us
Isle JSHS 300/7-12
PO Box 25 56342 320-676-3101
Jeff Searles, dean Fax 676-3966

Ivanhoe, Lincoln, Pop. 621
Ivanhoe SD 403 200/7-12
PO Box 9 56142 507-694-1540
Cornelius Smit, supt. Fax 694-1125
www.lincolnhi.org
Lincoln HS 200/7-12
PO Box 9 56142 507-694-1540
Cornelius Smit, prin. Fax 694-1125

Jackson, Jackson, Pop. 3,454
Jackson County Central SD 2895 1,200/PK-12
PO Box 119 56143 507-847-3608
Gery Arndt, supt. Fax 847-3078
www.jccschools.com/
Jackson County Central HS 400/9-12
PO Box 119 56143 507-847-5310
Jim Hirman, prin. Fax 847-3078
Other Schools – See Lakefield

Minnesota West Community & Tech College Post-Sec.
PO Box 269 56143 800-658-2522

Janesville, Waseca, Pop. 2,148
Janesville-Waldorf-Pemberton SD 2835 600/PK-12
PO Box 389 56048 507-234-5478
Tami Sens, supt. Fax 234-5796
Janesville-Waldorf-Pemberton HS 300/7-12
PO Box 389 56048 507-234-5796
Michael Meihak, prin. Fax 234-5135

Jordan, Scott, Pop. 5,120
Jordan SD 717 1,500/PK-12
500 Sunset Dr 55352 952-492-6200
Larry Kauzlarich, supt. Fax 492-4445
www.jordan.k12.mn.us
Jordan HS 400/9-12
600 Sunset Dr 55352 952-492-4400
Mark Ruggeberg, prin. Fax 492-4425
Jordan MS 500/5-8
500 Sunset Dr 55352 952-492-2332
Lance Chambers, prin. Fax 492-4450

Karlstad, Kittson, Pop. 722
Tri-County SD 2358 300/PK-12
PO Box 178 56732 218-436-2261
Ron Ruud, supt. Fax 436-2263
www.tricounty.k12.mn.us
Tri-County HS 100/7-12
PO Box 178 56732 218-436-2374
Dave Sorgaard, prin. Fax 436-3422

Kasson, Dodge, Pop. 5,333
Kasson-Mantorville SD 204 2,000/PK-12
101 16th St NE 55944 507-634-1100
Peter Grant, supt. Fax 634-6661
www.komets.k12.mn.us
Kasson-Mantorville HS 500/9-12
101 16th St NE 55944 507-634-2961
Jerry Reker, prin. Fax 634-4745
Kasson-Mantorville MS 300/7-8
105 16th St NE 55944 507-634-4030
Alan Hodge, prin. Fax 634-6485

Kelliher, Beltrami, Pop. 302
Kelliher SD 36 — 300/PK-12
PO Box 259 56650 — 218-647-8286
Terry Bartness, supt. — Fax 647-8660
www.kelliher.k12.mn.us
Kelliher JSHS — 200/6-12
PO Box 259 56650 — 218-647-8286
Shelly DeJean, dean — Fax 647-8660

Kenyon, Goodhue, Pop. 1,665
Kenyon-Wanamingo SD 2172
Supt. — See Wanamingo
Kenyon-Wanamingo HS — 300/9-12
400 6th St 55946 — 507-789-6186
Donna Judson, prin. — Fax 789-6188
Kenyon-Wanamingo MS — 300/5-8
400 6th St 55946 — 507-789-6186
Patrick Walsh, prin. — Fax 789-6188

Kerkhoven, Kandiyohi, Pop. 711
Kerkhoven-Murdock-Sunburg SD 775 — 600/PK-12
PO Box 168 56252 — 320-264-1411
Martin Heidelberger, supt. — Fax 264-1410
www.kms.k12.mn.us
Kerkhoven JSHS — 300/7-12
PO Box 168 56252 — 320-264-1412
Michael Coquyt, prin. — Fax 264-1410

Kiester, Faribault, Pop. 510
United South Central SD 2134
Supt. — See Wells
United South Central MS — 300/5-8
PO Box 300 56051 — 507-294-3206
Tracy Frank, prin. — Fax 294-3215

Kimball, Stearns, Pop. 687
Kimball SD 739 — 800/PK-12
PO Box 368 55353 — 320-398-5585
John Tritabaugh, supt. — Fax 398-5595
www.kimball.k12.mn.us/
Kimball JSHS — 400/7-12
PO Box 368 55353 — 320-398-7700
Eric Widvey, prin. — Fax 398-7733

La Crescent, Houston, Pop. 5,095
La Crescent-Hokah SD 300 — 1,500/PK-12
703 S 11th St 55947 — 507-895-4484
David Krenz, supt. — Fax 895-8560
www.isd300.k12.mn.us
La Crescent HS — 500/9-12
1301 Lancer Dr 55947 — 507-895-4481
Rick Wolter, prin. — Fax 895-4490
La Crescent MS — 400/6-8
1301 Lancer Dr 55947 — 507-895-4474
Ben Barton, prin. — Fax 895-8597

Lake Benton, Lincoln, Pop. 667
Lake Benton SD 404 — 200/K-12
PO Box 158 56149 — 507-368-4236
Stephen Kjorness, supt. — Fax 368-4347
www.lakebentonschool.org/
Lake Benton JSHS — 100/7-12
PO Box 158 56149 — 507-368-4236
Joan Ratzloff, prin. — Fax 368-4347

Lake City, Wabasha, Pop. 5,282
Lake City SD 813 — 1,400/PK-12
PO Box 454 55041 — 651-345-2198
Jerry Jensen, supt. — Fax 345-3709
www.lake-city.k12.mn.us
Lincoln JSHS — 700/7-12
PO Box 454 55041 — 651-345-4553
Thomas Boe, prin. — Fax 345-3709

Lake Crystal, Blue Earth, Pop. 2,516
Lake Crystal Wellcome Memorial SD 2071 — 800/PK-12
PO Box 160 56055 — 507-726-2323
Les Norman, supt. — Fax 726-2334
www.isd2071.k12.mn.us
Lake Crystal Wellcome Memorial JSHS — 400/7-12
PO Box 160 56055 — 507-726-2110
Linda Isebrand, prin. — Fax 726-2283

Lake Elmo, Washington, Pop. 7,615
Stillwater Area SD 834
Supt. — See Stillwater
Oak-Land JHS — 1,000/7-9
820 Manning Ave N 55042 — 651-351-8500
Derek Berg, prin. — Fax 351-8505

Lakefield, Jackson, Pop. 1,698
Jackson County Central SD 2895
Supt. — See Jackson
Jackson County Central MS — 300/6-8
PO Box 338 56150 — 507-662-6625
Kari Wilkinson, prin. — Fax 662-5083

Sioux Valley Lutheran HS — 50/9-12
72957 400th Ave 56150 — 507-839-3517
Fax 839-3516

Lake Park, Becker, Pop. 830
Lake Park-Audubon ISD 2889 — 600/K-12
PO Box 479 56554 — 218-238-5914
Dale Hogie, supt. — Fax 238-5643
www.lakeparkaudubon.org
Lake Park-Audubon JSHS — 300/7-12
PO Box 479 56554 — 218-238-5916
Kevin Ricke, prin. — Fax 238-6828

Lakeville, Dakota, Pop. 51,484
Lakeville Area SD 194 — 9,000/K-12
8670 210th St W 55044 — 952-232-2000
Gary Amoroso, supt. — Fax 469-6054
www.isd194.k12.mn.us
Century MS — 500/6-8
18610 Ipava Ave 55044 — 952-232-2300
Catherine Gillach, prin. — Fax 469-6103
Kenwood Trail JHS — 600/6-8
19455 Kenwood Trl 55044 — 952-232-3800
Jerry Pederson, prin. — Fax 469-3508
Lakeville North HS — 2,300/9-12
19600 Ipava Ave 55044 — 952-232-3600
Marne Berkvam, prin. — Fax 469-3367
Lakeville South HS — 9-12
21135 Jacquard Ave 55044 — 952-232-3300
Scott Douglas, prin. — Fax 469-8383
McGuire JHS — 600/6-8
21220 Holyoke Ave 55044 — 952-232-2200
Craig Menozzi, prin. — Fax 469-7224

Lamberton, Redwood, Pop. 805
Red Rock Central SD 2884 — 500/PK-12
PO Box 278 56152 — 507-752-7361
Dr. John Brennan, supt. — Fax 752-6133
www.rrcnet.org
Red Rock Central HS — 300/6-12
PO Box 278 56152 — 507-752-7361
Bruce Olson, prin. — Fax 752-6133

Lancaster, Kittson, Pop. 328
Lancaster SD 356 — 200/PK-12
PO Box 217 56735 — 218-762-5400
Bradley Homstad, supt. — Fax 762-5512
www.lancaster.k12.mn.us/
Lancaster JSHS — 100/7-12
PO Box 217 56735 — 218-762-5400
Bradley Homstad, prin. — Fax 762-5512

Lanesboro, Fillmore, Pop. 767
Lanesboro SD 229 — 400/PK-12
100 Kirkwood St E 55949 — 507-467-2229
Jeff Boggs, supt. — Fax 467-3026
Lanesboro JSHS — 200/7-12
100 Kirkwood St E 55949 — 507-467-2229
Brett Clarke, prin. — Fax 467-3026

Laporte, Hubbard, Pop. 150
Laporte SD 306 — 300/PK-12
315 Main St W 56461 — 218-224-2288
Harvey Johnson, supt. — Fax 224-2905
laporte.k12.mn.us
Laporte JSHS — 200/7-12
315 Main St W 56461 — 218-224-2288
Clyde Hadrava, prin. — Fax 224-2905

Le Center, LeSueur, Pop. 2,308
Le Center SD 392 — 700/K-12
150 W Tyrone St 56057 — 507-357-6802
Tony Boyer, supt. — Fax 357-4825
lc.k12.mn.us
Le Center JSHS — 300/7-12
150 W Tyrone St 56057 — 507-357-6802
Matt Helgerson, prin. — Fax 357-4825

Le Roy, Mower, Pop. 917
Le Roy SD 499 — 400/PK-12
PO Box 1000 55951 — 507-324-5743
Arnold Prince, supt. — Fax 324-5149
www.leroy.k12.mn.us
Le Roy-Ostrander JSHS — 200/7-12
PO Box 1000 55951 — 507-324-5741
Steven Sallee, prin. — Fax 324-5149

Lester Prairie, McLeod, Pop. 1,601
Lester Prairie SD 424 — 400/K-12
PO Box 158 55354 — 320-395-2521
Joseph Miller, supt. — Fax 395-4204
www.lp.k12.mn.us
Lester Prairie JSHS — 200/7-12
PO Box 158 55354 — 320-395-3001
Joe Miller, prin. — Fax 395-4204

Le Sueur, LeSueur, Pop. 4,257
Le Sueur-Henderson SD 2397 — 1,300/PK-12
115 1/2 N 5th St Ste 200 56058 — 507-665-8828
David Johnson, supt. — Fax 665-6858
www.isd2397.k12.mn.us
Le Sueur-Henderson MSHS — 700/7-12
901 Ferry St 56058 — 507-665-3305
Kevin Enerson, prin. — Fax 665-6012

Lewiston, Winona, Pop. 1,485
Lewiston-Altura SD 857 — 800/PK-12
PO Box 741 55952 — 507-523-2191
Bruce Montplaisir, supt. — Fax 523-3460
www.lewalt.k12.mn.us
Lewiston-Altura JSHS — 400/7-12
PO Box 741 55952 — 507-523-2191
Lance Zellmann, prin. — Fax 523-3460

Lindstrom, Chisago, Pop. 3,934
Chisago Lakes SD 2144 — 3,500/PK-12
13750 Lake Blvd 55045 — 651-213-2000
Michael McLoughlin, supt. — Fax 213-2050
www.chisagolakes.k12.mn.us
Chisago Lakes HS — 1,100/9-12
13750 Lake Blvd 55045 — 651-213-2500
Dave Ertl, prin. — Fax 213-2550
Chisago Lakes MS — 800/6-8
13750 Lake Blvd 55045 — 651-213-2400
John Menard, prin. — Fax 213-2051

Lino Lakes, Anoka, Pop. 19,424
Centennial SD 12
Supt. — See Circle Pines
Centennial MS — 1,700/6-8
399 Elm St 55014 — 763-792-5400
Jerry Meschke, prin. — Fax 792-5450

Litchfield, Meeker, Pop. 6,658
Litchfield SD 465 — 1,900/PK-12
114 N Holcombe Ave Ste 100 55355 — 320-693-2444
William Wold, supt. — Fax 593-6528
www.litchfield.k12.mn.us
Litchfield HS — 600/9-12
901 N Gilman Ave 55355 — 320-693-2424
Mike Goodrum, prin. — Fax 593-3308
Litchfield MS — 400/6-8
340 E 10th St 55355 — 320-693-2441
Patrick Devine, prin. — Fax 593-3485

Little Canada, Ramsey, Pop. 9,543
Roseville Area SD 623
Supt. — See Roseville
Roseville Area MS — 900/7-8
15 County Road B2 E 55117 — 651-482-5280
Juanita Hoskins, prin. — Fax 482-5299

Little Falls, Morrison, Pop. 8,139
Little Falls SD 482 — 2,700/K-12
1001 5th Ave SE 56345 — 320-632-2002
Curt Tryggestad, supt. — Fax 632-2010
www.lfalls.k12.mn.us
Little Falls Community HS — 1,100/9-12
1001 5th Ave SE 56345 — 320-616-2200
Bob Just, prin. — Fax 616-2210
Little Falls Community MS — 600/6-8
1000 1st Ave NE 56345 — 320-616-4200
Maxine Strege, prin. — Fax 616-4210

Mary of Lourdes MS — 100/5-8
205 3rd St NW 56345 — 320-632-6742
Paul Scheiffert, prin. — Fax 632-3556

Littlefork, Koochiching, Pop. 714
Littlefork-Big Falls SD 362 — 200/PK-12
700 Main St 56653 — 218-278-6614
Fred Seybert, supt. — Fax 278-6615
www.isd362.k12.mn.us
Littlefork-Big Falls S — 200/PK-12
700 Main St 56653 — 218-278-6614
Fred Seybert, prin. — Fax 278-6615

Long Lake, Hennepin, Pop. 1,827
Orono SD 278 — 2,500/K-12
PO Box 46 55356 — 952-449-8300
Dr. Karen Orcutt, supt. — Fax 449-8399
www.orono.k12.mn.us
Orono HS — 800/9-12
PO Box 26 55356 — 952-449-8400
Dave Benson, prin. — Fax 449-8449
Orono MS — 600/6-8
PO Box 16 55356 — 952-449-8450
Pat Wroten, prin. — Fax 449-8453

Long Prairie, Todd, Pop. 2,944
Long Prairie-Grey Eagle SD 2753 — 1,400/PK-12
205 2nd St S 56347 — 320-732-2194
Donald Hansen, supt. — Fax 732-3791
www.lpge.k12.mn.us/
Long Prairie-Grey Eagle HS — 500/9-12
510 9th St NE 56347 — 320-732-2194
Karrie Boser, prin. — Fax 732-6470
Long Prairie MS — 300/6-8
205 2nd St S 56347 — 320-732-2194
Paul Weinzierl, prin. — Fax 732-2844

Luverne, Rock, Pop. 4,466
Luverne SD 2184 — 1,300/PK-12
709 N Kniss Ave 56156 — 507-283-8088
Gary Fisher, supt. — Fax 283-9681
www.isd2184.net/
Luverne HS — 400/9-12
709 N Kniss Ave 56156 — 507-283-4491
Donna Judson, prin. — Fax 283-9681
Luverne MS — 300/6-8
709 N Kniss Ave 56156 — 507-283-4491
Donna Judson, prin. — Fax 283-9681

Lyle, Mower, Pop. 576
Lyle SD 497 — 200/K-12
700 E 2nd St 55953 — 507-325-4146
Jerry Reshetar, supt. — Fax 325-4611
www.lyle.k12.mn.us
Lyle HS — 100/7-12
700 E 2nd St 55953 — 507-325-2201
Royce Helmbrecht, prin. — Fax 325-4611

Mabel, Fillmore, Pop. 743
Mabel-Canton SD 238 — 300/PK-12
PO Box 337 55954 — 507-493-5423
Marcia Love, supt. — Fax 493-5425
www.mabelcanton.k12.mn.us/
Mabel-Canton JSHS — 100/7-12
PO Box 337 55954 — 507-493-5422
Kay Dahle, prin. — Fax 493-5425

Mc Gregor, Aitkin, Pop. 405
Mc Gregor ISD 4 — 500/PK-12
PO Box 160, — 218-768-2111
Rick Herman, supt. — Fax 768-3901
www.mcgregor.k12.mn.us
Mc Gregor JSHS — 300/7-12
PO Box 160, — 218-768-2111
Paul Grams, prin. — Fax 768-3802

Madelia, Watonwan, Pop. 2,218
Madelia SD 837 — 600/PK-12
320 Buck Ave SE 56062 — 507-642-3232
Brian Grenell, supt. — Fax 642-3622
Madelia JSHS — 300/7-12
320 Buck Ave SE 56062 — 507-642-3232
Allan Beyer, prin. — Fax 642-3622

Madison, Lac qui Parle, Pop. 1,654
Lac Qui Parle Valley SD 2853 — 1,000/PK-12
2860 291st Ave 56256 — 320-752-4200
Robert Munsterman, supt. — Fax 752-4401
www.lqpv.org/
Lac Qui Parle Valley JSHS — 600/7-12
2860 291st Ave 56256 — 320-752-4200
Jon Fulton, prin. — Fax 752-4401

Mahnomen, Mahnomen, Pop. 1,176
Mahnomen SD 432 — 700/PK-12
PO Box 319 56557 — 218-935-2211
John Kringen, supt. — Fax 935-5921
Mahnomen JSHS — 400/7-12
PO Box 319 56557 — 218-935-2213
Jack Stronstad, prin. — Fax 935-5921

Mahtomedi, Washington, Pop. 8,017
Mahtomedi SD 832 3,000/K-12
1520 Mahtomedi Ave 55115 651-407-2000
Dr. Mark Wolak, supt. Fax 407-2025
www.mahtomedi.k12.mn.us
Mahtomedi HS 1,100/9-12
8000 75th St N 55115 651-407-2100
John Deir, prin. Fax 407-2125
Mahtomedi MS 800/6-8
8100 75th St N 55115 651-407-2200
Dr. Sharon Zweber, prin. Fax 407-2225

Mankato, Blue Earth, Pop. 34,976
Mankato SD 77 6,800/K-12
PO Box 8741 56002 507-387-1868
E.R. Waltman, supt. Fax 387-4257
www.isd77.k12.mn.us
Mankato East HS 1,000/9-12
2600 Hoffman Rd 56001 507-387-5671
Donald Poplau, prin. Fax 387-7927
Mankato East JHS 500/7-8
2600 Hoffman Rd 56001 507-345-6625
Rich Dahman, prin. Fax 387-2890
Mankato West HS 1,200/9-12
1351 S Riverfront Dr 56001 507-387-3461
Bruce Borchers, prin. Fax 345-1502
Other Schools – See North Mankato

Bethany Lutheran College Post-Sec.
700 Luther Dr 56001 507-344-7000
Fitzgerald MS 200/6-8
110 N 5th St 56001 507-388-9344
Kim Meyer, prin. Fax 388-2750
Immanuel Lutheran S 100/K-12
421 N 2nd St 56001 507-345-3027
Karl Olmanson, prin. Fax 345-1562
Loyola HS 9-12
145 Good Counsel Dr 56001 507-388-2997
Shelley Schultz, prin. Fax 388-3081
Minnesota State University Mankato Post-Sec.
PO Box 8400 56002 507-389-2463
Rasmussen College Post-Sec.
501 Holly Ln 56001 507-625-6556
Sr. Rosalind Gefre School of Massage Post-Sec.
416 S Front St 56001 507-344-0220

Maple Grove, Hennepin, Pop. 59,756
Osseo SD 279 21,300/PK-12
11200 93rd Ave N 55369 763-391-7000
Susan Hintz, supt. Fax 391-7070
www.district279.org
Maple Grove JHS 1,600/7-9
7000 Hemlock Ln N 55369 763-315-7600
Laurel Anderson, prin. Fax 315-7601
Maple Grove SHS 1,800/10-12
9800 Fernbrook Ln N 55369 763-391-8700
Wendy Loberg, prin. Fax 391-8701
Other Schools – See Brooklyn Park, Osseo

Heritage Christian Academy 600/PK-12
15655 Bass Lake Rd 55311 763-463-2200
Rodney Nelson, pres. Fax 463-2299

Maple Lake, Wright, Pop. 1,878
Maple Lake SD 881 900/PK-12
PO Box 760 55358 320-963-3171
Mark Redemske, supt. Fax 963-3170
www.maplelake.k12.mn.us
Maple Lake JSHS 500/7-12
PO Box 820 55358 320-963-3171
Mary James, prin. Fax 963-3170

Mapleton, Blue Earth, Pop. 1,653
Maple River SD 2135 1,200/PK-12
PO Box 515 56065 507-524-3918
Willis Schoeb, supt. Fax 524-4882
www.isd2135.k12.mn.us/
Maple River HS 400/9-12
PO Box 515 56065 507-524-3918
Dan Anderson, prin. Fax 524-4919
Other Schools – See Amboy, Minnesota Lake

Maplewood, Ramsey, Pop. 35,085
North St. Paul-Maplewood-Oakdale SD 622
Supt. — See North Saint Paul
Glenn MS 900/6-8
1560 County Road B E 55109 651-748-6300
Nancy Weinand, prin. Fax 748-6391
Maplewood MS 900/6-8
2410 Holloway Ave E 55109 651-748-6500
Ruthanne Strohn, prin. Fax 748-6591

Hill-Murray HS 900/7-12
2625 Larpenteur Ave E 55109 651-777-1376
Dr. Susan Paul, prin. Fax 748-2444

Marshall, Lyon, Pop. 12,291
Marshall SD 413 1,500/K-12
401 S Saratoga St 56258 507-537-6924
Klint Willert, supt. Fax 537-6931
www.swmn.org
Marshall HS 800/9-12
400 Tiger Dr 56258 507-537-6920
Brian Jones, prin. Fax 537-6933
Marshall MS 300/5-8
207 N 4th St 56258 507-537-6938
Mary Kay Thomas, prin. Fax 537-6942

Southwest Minnesota State University Post-Sec.
1501 State St 56258 507-537-7678

Mayer, Carver, Pop. 1,139

Mayer Lutheran HS 300/9-12
305 5th St NE 55360 952-657-2251
Kevin Wilaby, prin. Fax 657-2344

Mazeppa, Wabasha, Pop. 784
Zumbrota-Mazeppa SD 2805 1,200/PK-12
PO Box 222 55956 507-843-4080
Roger Rueckert, supt. Fax 843-4086
www.zmschools.us/
Zumbrota-Mazeppa MS 400/5-8
343 3rd Ave NE 55956 507-843-2165
Richard Meyerhofer, prin. Fax 843-5853
Other Schools – See Zumbrota

Medford, Steele, Pop. 1,164
Medford ISD 763 700/PK-12
750 2nd Ave SE 55049 507-451-5250
Gary Hanson, supt. Fax 451-6474
www.medford.k12.mn.us/
Medford JSHS 300/7-12
750 2nd Ave SE 55049 507-451-5250
Keith Kottke, prin. Fax 451-6474

Melrose, Stearns, Pop. 3,145
Melrose SD 740 1,100/PK-12
546 N 5th Ave E 56352 320-256-4224
Howard Caldwell, supt. Fax 256-4311
www.melrose.k12.mn.us
Melrose HS 600/9-12
546 N 5th Ave E 56352 320-256-4224
Chad Doetkott, prin. Fax 256-4311
Melrose MS 6-8
546 N 5th Ave E 56352 320-256-4224
Randy Bergquist, prin. Fax 256-4311

Menahga, Wadena, Pop. 1,197
Menahga SD 821 700/PK-12
PO Box 160 56464 218-564-4141
Fred Seybert, supt. Fax 564-5401
www.menahga.k12.mn.us
Menahga JSHS 300/7-12
PO Box 160 56464 218-564-4141
Mary Merchant, prin. Fax 564-5401

Mendota Heights, Dakota, Pop. 11,338
West St. Paul-Mendota Hts-Eagan SD 197 4,700/K-12
1897 Delaware Ave 55118 651-681-2300
Jay Haugen, supt. Fax 681-9102
isd197.org
Friendly Hills MS 700/5-8
701 Mendota Heights Rd 55120 651-905-4100
Susan Larkin, prin. Fax 905-4101
Sibley HS 1,500/9-12
1897 Delaware Ave 55118 651-681-2350
Helen Fisk, prin. Fax 405-2461
Other Schools – See West Saint Paul

Brown College Post-Sec.
1440 Northland Dr 55120 651-905-3400
Convent of the Visitation S 600/PK-12
2455 Visitation Dr 55120 651-683-1700
Dawn Nichols, hdmstr. Fax 454-7144
Le Cordon Bleu College of Culinary Arts Post-Sec.
1315 Mendota Heights Rd 55120 651-675-4700
St. Thomas Academy 700/7-12
949 Mendota Heights Rd 55120 651-454-4570
Thomas Mich Ph.D., hdmstr. Fax 454-4574

Middle River, Marshall, Pop. 314
Greenbush-Middle River SD 2683
Supt. — See Greenbush
Greenbush-Middle River JHS 100/6-8
PO Box 130 56737 218-222-3310
Sharon Schultz, prin. Fax 222-3314

Milaca, Mille Lacs, Pop. 2,954
Milaca SD 912 1,900/PK-12
500 Highway 23 W 56353 320-982-7210
Dr. Barbra Zakrajsek, supt. Fax 982-7179
www.milaca.k12.mn.us/
Milaca HS 1,000/7-12
500 Highway 23 W 56353 320-982-7206
Richard Rhoades, prin. Fax 983-3566

Minneapolis, Hennepin, Pop. 372,811
Minneapolis SD 1 34,500/PK-12
807 Broadway St NE 55413 612-668-0000
William Green Ph.D., supt. Fax 668-0195
www.mpls.k12.mn.us
Afrocentric Academy 400/6-8
1501 Aldrich Ave N 55411 612-668-2600
Tiffanie Brooks, admin. Fax 668-2610
Anthony MS 600/6-8
5757 Irving Ave S 55419 612-668-3240
Jackie Hanson, prin. Fax 668-3250
Anwatin MS 600/6-8
256 Upton Ave S 55405 612-668-2450
Beth Russell, prin. Fax 668-2460
Edison HS 1,200/9-12
700 22nd Ave NE 55418 612-668-1300
Larry Lucio, prin. Fax 668-1320
Field MS 500/5-8
4645 4th Ave S 55419 612-668-3640
Erin Glynn, prin. Fax 668-3661
Folwell MS 500/6-8
3611 20th Ave S 55407 612-668-4550
Carla Steinbach, prin. Fax 668-4560
Henry HS 1,400/9-12
4320 Newton Ave N 55412 612-668-2000
Gary Kociemba, prin. Fax 668-1993
Lake Harriet Upper ES 600/3-8
4912 Vincent Ave S 55410 612-668-3310
Marsha Seltz, prin. Fax 668-3320
Northeast MS 500/6-8
2955 Hayes St NE 55418 612-668-1500
Ben Perry, prin. Fax 668-1510
North HS 1,100/9-12
1500 James Ave N 55411 612-668-1700
Michael Favor, prin. Fax 668-1770
Olson MS 600/6-8
1601 51st Ave N 55430 612-668-1640
Barbara Muir, prin. Fax 668-1650
Roosevelt HS 1,300/9-12
4029 28th Ave S 55406 612-668-4800
Bruce Gilman, prin. Fax 668-4810
Sanford MS 400/6-8
3524 42nd Ave S 55406 612-668-4900
Meredith Davis, prin. Fax 668-4910
South HS 1,800/9-12
3131 19th Ave S 55407 612-668-4300
Linda Nelson, prin. Fax 668-4310
Southwest HS 1,600/9-12
3414 W 47th St 55410 612-668-3030
Bill Smith, prin. Fax 668-3080
Washburn HS 1,300/9-12
201 W 49th St 55419 612-668-3400
Steve Couture, prin. Fax 668-3410

Wayzata SD 284 9,700/PK-12
210 County Road 101 N 55447 952-745-5000
Bob Ostlund, supt. Fax 745-5091
www.wayzata.k12.mn.us
Other Schools – See Plymouth, Wayzata

Art Institutes International Minnesota Post-Sec.
15 S 9th St 55402 612-332-3361
Art Instruction Schools Post-Sec.
3400 Technology Dr 55418 612-362-5000
Augsburg College Post-Sec.
2211 Riverside Ave 55454 612-330-1000
Aveda Institute Post-Sec.
400 Central Ave SE 55414 612-378-7404
Bais Yaakov HS of the Twin Cities 50/9-12
4221 Sunset Blvd 55416 952-915-9117
Sarah Gibber, prin. Fax 915-9116
Blake S - Northrup Campus 400/9-12
511 Kenwood Pkwy 55403 952-988-3700
Marc Bogursky, prin. Fax 988-3705
Breck S 1,200/PK-12
123 Ottawa Ave N 55422 763-381-8100
Fax 381-8288
Capella University Post-Sec.
225 S 6th St Fl 9 55402 888-227-3552
Carondelet Catholic S Upper Campus 300/3-8
3210 W 51st St 55410 612-927-8673
Sr. Katherine Rossini, prin. Fax 927-7426
Cristo Rey Jesuit HS 9-12
3041 4th Ave S 55408 612-276-0140
Kristine Melloy Ph.D., prin.
De La Salle HS 600/9-12
1 De La Salle Dr 55401 612-676-7600
Barry Lieske, prin. Fax 362-9641
Dunwoody College of Technology Post-Sec.
818 Dunwoody Blvd 55403 612-374-5800
Hennepin County Medical Center Post-Sec.
701 Park Ave 55415 612-347-2352
Herzing College Post-Sec.
5700 W Broadway Ave 55428 763-535-3000
Maranatha Christian Academy 800/PK-12
4021 Thomas Ave N 55412 612-588-2850
Brian Sullivan, admin. Fax 588-7854
Minneapolis College of Art & Design Post-Sec.
2501 Stevens Ave 55404 612-874-3700
Minneapolis Community and Tech College Post-Sec.
1501 Hennepin Ave 55403 612-341-7000
Minneapolis VA Medical Center Post-Sec.
1 Veterans Dr 55417 612-725-2000
Minnehaha Academy 500/9-12
3100 W River Pkwy 55406 612-729-8321
Nancy Johnson, prin. Fax 728-7787
North Central University Post-Sec.
910 Elliot Ave 55404 612-332-3491
North Memorial Medical Center Post-Sec.
3300 Oakdale Ave N 55422 763-520-5200
St. Mary's Campus Coll. of St. Catherine Post-Sec.
2500 S 6th St 55454 612-332-5521
St. Mary's University of Minnesota Post-Sec.
2500 Park Ave 55404 866-437-2788
San Miguel MS 50/6-8
3800 Pleasant Ave 55409 612-870-1109
Sr. Mary Willette, prin. Fax 870-1224
Summit Academy OIC Post-Sec.
935 Olson Memorial Hwy 55405 612-377-0150
University of Minnesota Post-Sec.
231 Pillsbury Dr SE 55455 612-625-5000
Walden University Post-Sec.
155 5th Ave S Ste 100 55401 612-338-7224
Woodcrest Baptist Academy 200/K-12
6875 University Ave NE 55432 763-571-6409
Loren Isaacs, prin. Fax 571-3978

Minneota, Lyon, Pop. 1,377
Minneota SD 414 500/K-12
PO Box 98 56264 507-872-6532
John Kraker, supt. Fax 872-5172
www.minneotaschools.org/
Minneota JSHS 200/7-12
PO Box 98 56264 507-872-6175
Fax 872-6494

Minnesota Lake, Faribault, Pop. 659
Maple River SD 2135
Supt. — See Mapleton
Maple River East MS 100/6-8
PO Box 218 56068 507-462-3348
James Bisel, prin. Fax 462-3219

Minnetonka, Hennepin, Pop. 50,045
Hopkins SD 270
Supt. — See Hopkins
Hopkins HS 2,000/10-12
2400 Lindbergh Dr 55305 952-988-4500
Willie Jett, prin. Fax 988-4716
Hopkins North JHS 1,000/7-9
10700 Cedar Lake Rd 55305 952-988-4800
Patrice Schmidt, prin. Fax 988-4869
Hopkins West JHS 900/7-9
3830 Baker Rd 55305 952-988-4400
Terry Wolfson, prin. Fax 988-4477

Minnetonka SD 276 7,500/K-12
5621 County Rd 101 55345 952-401-5000
Dennis Peterson, supt. Fax 401-5083
www.minnetonka.k12.mn.us
Minnetonka East MS 900/6-8
17000 Lake Street Ext 55345 952-401-5200
Pete Dymit, prin. Fax 401-5268
Minnetonka HS 2,500/9-12
18301 Highway 7 55345 952-401-5700
David Adney, prin. Fax 401-5709
Other Schools – See Excelsior

Minnetonka Christian Academy 200/K-12
3500 Williston Rd 55345 952-935-4497
Fax 935-4498

Minnetrista, Hennepin, Pop. 5,501
Westonka SD 277 2,200/K-12
5901 Sunnyfield Rd E 55364 952-491-8000
Kevin Borg, supt. Fax 491-8012
www.westonka.k12.mn.us
Other Schools – See Mound

Montevideo, Chippewa, Pop. 5,365
Montevideo SD 129 1,500/PK-12
2001 Williams Ave 56265 320-269-8833
David Baukol, supt. Fax 269-8834
www.montevideoschools.com
Montevideo HS 500/9-12
1501 Williams Ave 56265 320-269-6446
Bruce Bergeson, prin. Fax 269-6446
Montevideo MS 500/5-8
2001 Williams Ave 56265 320-269-6431
Chad Pederson, prin. Fax 269-8834

Montgomery, LeSueur, Pop. 3,076
Montgomery-Lonsdale SD 394 1,000/PK-12
101 2nd St NE 56069 507-364-8100
Ray Farwell, supt. Fax 364-8103
www.montlonsdale.k12.mn.us
Montgomery-Lonsdale HS 500/7-12
101 2nd St NE 56069 507-364-8111
Alan Fitterer, prin. Fax 364-8103

Monticello, Wright, Pop. 10,882
Monticello SD 882 3,800/PK-12
302 Washington St 55362 763-271-0300
James Johnson, supt. Fax 271-0313
www.monticello.k12.mn.us
Monticello HS 1,100/9-12
5225 School Blvd 55362 763-271-0350
Doug Standke, prin. Fax 271-0359
Monticello MS 900/6-8
800 E Broadway St 55362 763-271-0500
Jeff Scherber, prin. Fax 271-0510

Moorhead, Clay, Pop. 34,081
Moorhead SD 152 3,300/K-12
2410 14th St S 56560 218-284-3330
Dr. Larry Nybladh, supt. Fax 284-3332
www.moorhead.k12.mn.us
Horizon MS 6-8
3601 12th Ave S 56560 218-284-7300
Colleen Tupper, prin. Fax 284-7333
Moorhead HS 1,700/9-12
2300 4th Ave S 56560 218-284-2300
Eugene Boyle, prin. Fax 284-2333

Concordia College Post-Sec.
901 8th St S 56562 218-299-4000
MN State Community & Technical College Post-Sec.
1900 28th Ave S 56560 800-426-5603
Minnesota State University Moorhead Post-Sec.
1104 7th Ave S 56563 218-236-2011
Park Christian S 500/PK-12
300 17th St N 56560 218-236-0500
Terinne Berg, admin. Fax 236-7301
Rita's Moorhead Beauty College Post-Sec.
1024 Center Ave 56560 218-236-7201

Moose Lake, Carlton, Pop. 2,551
Moose Lake SD 97 800/PK-12
PO Box 489 55767 218-485-4435
Timothy Caroline, supt. Fax 485-8110
Moose Lake JSHS 400/7-12
PO Box 489 55767 218-485-4622
Robert Indihar, prin. Fax 485-8681

Mora, Kanabec, Pop. 3,449
Mora SD 332 1,900/PK-12
400 Maple Ave E 55051 320-679-6200
Douglas Conboy, supt. Fax 679-6209
www.mora.k12.mn.us
Mora HS 900/7-12
400 Maple Ave E 55051 320-679-6220
Mark Antonson, prin. Fax 679-6238

Morgan, Redwood, Pop. 846
Cedar Mountain SD 2754 400/K-12
PO Box 188 56266 507-249-5990
Robert Tews, supt. Fax 249-3149
Cedar Mountain JSHS 200/7-12
PO Box 188 56266 507-249-5888
Stephanie Perry, prin. Fax 249-3149

Morris, Stevens, Pop. 5,091
Morris SD 769 1,000/PK-12
201 S Columbia Ave 56267 320-589-4840
Scott Monson, supt. Fax 589-3203
www.morris.k12.mn.us
Morris Area JSHS 500/7-12
201 S Columbia Ave 56267 320-589-4400
Scott Wolf, prin. Fax 589-3203

University of Minnesota Post-Sec.
600 E 4th St 56267 320-589-2211

Morristown, Rice, Pop. 1,021
Waterville-Elysian-Morristown SD 2143
Supt. — See Waterville
Waterville-Elysian-Morristown JHS 200/7-8
PO Box 278 55052 507-685-4222
Bernardine Sauter, prin. Fax 685-2420

Cannon Valley Lutheran HS 50/9-12
PO Box 346 55052 507-685-2636
Douglas Mierow, admin. Fax 685-4502

Motley, Morrison, Pop. 667
Staples-Motley ISD 2170
Supt. — See Staples
Motley-Staples MS 400/6-8
PO Box 68 56466 218-352-6170
Dean Ogg, prin. Fax 352-6508

Mound, Hennepin, Pop. 9,416
Westonka SD 277
Supt. — See Minnetrista
Mound-Westonka HS 1,000/8-12
5905 Sunnyfield Rd E 55364 952-491-8100
Keith Randklev, prin. Fax 491-8103

Mounds View, Ramsey, Pop. 12,106
Mounds View SD 621
Supt. — See Shoreview
Edgewood MS 500/6-8
5100 Edgewood Dr 55112 763-784-2010
Penny Howard, prin. Fax 639-6253

Mountain Iron, Saint Louis, Pop. 2,945
Mountain Iron-Buhl SD 712 600/PK-12
5529 Emerald Ave 55768 218-735-8271
Loren Sauter, supt. Fax 735-8244
Mountain Iron-Buhl JSHS 300/7-12
5529 Emerald Ave 55768 218-735-8217
Don Stahl, prin. Fax 735-8217

Mountain Lake, Cottonwood, Pop. 2,008
Mountain Lake SD 173 500/PK-12
PO Box 400 56159 507-427-2325
William Strom, supt. Fax 427-3047
www.mountainlake.k12.mn.us
Mountain Lake JSHS 200/7-12
PO Box 400 56159 507-427-2325
William Strom, prin. Fax 427-3047

Mountain Lake Christian S 100/PK-12
710 11th Ave 56159 507-427-2010
John Newton, admin. Fax 427-3123

Nashwauk, Itasca, Pop. 897
Nashwauk-Keewatin SD 319 700/PK-12
400 2nd St 55769 218-885-2705
John Klarich, supt. Fax 885-2905
Nashwauk JSHS 400/7-12
400 2nd St 55769 218-885-1280
Robert Bestul, prin. Fax 885-2910

Nevis, Hubbard, Pop. 376
Nevis SD 308 500/PK-12
PO Box 138 56467 218-652-3500
Steven Rassier, supt. Fax 652-3505
www.nevis.k12.mn.us
Nevis JSHS 300/7-12
PO Box 138 56467 218-652-3500
Jodi Sandmeyer, prin. Fax 652-3505

New Brighton, Ramsey, Pop. 20,738
Mounds View SD 621
Supt. — See Shoreview
Highview MS 800/6-8
2300 7th St NW 55112 651-633-8144
Mona Fadness, prin. Fax 639-6273
Irondale HS 1,600/9-12
2425 Long Lake Rd 55112 651-786-5200
Colleen Wambach, prin. Fax 639-6043

United Theological Seminary/Twin Cities Post-Sec.
3000 5th St NW 55112 651-255-6107

Newfolden, Marshall, Pop. 344
Marshall County Central SD 441 400/K-12
PO Box 189 56738 218-874-8530
Ronald Paggen, supt. Fax 874-8581
www.newfolden.k12.mn.us/
Marshall County Central HS 200/7-12
PO Box 189 56738 218-874-7225
Bryan Thygeson, prin. Fax 874-8581

New Hope, Hennepin, Pop. 20,296
Robbinsdale SD 281 12,800/K-12
4148 Winnetka Ave N 55427 763-504-8000
Stan F. Mack, supt. Fax 504-8979
www.rdale.k12.mn.us
Robbinsdale Cooper HS 2,000/9-12
8230 47th Ave N 55428 763-504-8500
Jeff McGonigal, prin. Fax 504-8531
Other Schools – See Golden Valley, Plymouth, Robbinsdale

New London, Kandiyohi, Pop. 1,196
New London-Spicer SD 345 1,600/K-12
PO Box 430 56273 320-354-2252
Paul Carlson, supt. Fax 354-9001
nls.k12.mn.us
New London-Spicer HS 600/9-12
PO Box 430 56273 320-354-2252
Kevin Acquard, prin. Fax 354-9001
New London-Spicer MS 500/5-8
PO Box 430 56273 320-354-2252
Rick Swenson, prin. Fax 354-4244

New Prague, Scott, Pop. 6,439
New Prague Area SD 721 2,400/K-12
410 Central Ave N 56071 952-758-1700
Dr. Steve Bruchman, supt. Fax 758-1799
www.np.k12.mn.us
New Prague HS 1,000/9-12
221 12th St NE 56071 952-758-1200
Tom Doig, prin. Fax 758-1299
New Prague MS 700/6-8
721 Central Ave N 56071 952-758-1400
Tim Dittberner, prin. Fax 758-1499

New Richland, Waseca, Pop. 1,159
NRHEG SD 2168 1,000/PK-12
PO Box 427 56072 507-465-3205
Kevin Wellen, supt. Fax 465-8633
NRHEG HS 300/9-12
PO Box 427 56072 507-465-3205
Paul Sparby, prin. Fax 465-8633

New Ulm, Brown, Pop. 13,619
New Ulm SD 88 2,300/PK-12
400 S Payne St 56073 507-359-8401
Harold Remme, supt. Fax 359-8406
www.newulm.k12.mn.us/
New Ulm HS 900/9-12
414 S Payne St 56073 507-359-8420
Mark Bergmann, prin. Fax 359-8432
New Ulm MS 400/7-8
15 N State St 56073 507-359-8480
Steve Weber, prin. Fax 359-7012

Cathedral HS 9-12
600 N Washington St 56073 507-354-4511
Jason Olson, prin. Fax 354-5711
Holy Trinity MS 200/5-8
515 N State St 56073 507-354-4311
Shelly Bauer, prin. Fax 354-7071
Martin Luther College Post-Sec.
1995 Luther Ct 56073 507-354-8221
Minnesota Valley Lutheran HS 300/9-12
45638 561st Ave 56073 507-354-6851
Tim Plath, prin. Fax 354-6854

New York Mills, Otter Tail, Pop. 1,186
New York Mills SD 553 800/PK-12
PO Box 218 56567 218-385-4201
Todd Cameron, supt. Fax 385-2551
www.nymills.k12.mn.us
New York Mills JSHS 400/7-12
PO Box 218 56567 218-385-4211
Matthew Aker, prin. Fax 385-2551

Nicollet, Nicollet, Pop. 991
Nicollet SD 507 200/K-12
PO Box 108 56074 507-232-3411
Todd Meyer, supt. Fax 232-3536
isd507.k12.mn.us
Nicollet S 200/K-12
PO Box 108 56074 507-232-3448
Todd Meyer, prin. Fax 232-3536

North Branch, Chisago, Pop. 10,234
North Branch SD 138 2,800/PK-12
PO Box 370 55056 651-674-1000
Rodney Reisnouer, supt. Fax 674-1010
www.northbranch.k12.mn.us
North Branch HS 1,100/9-12
38175 Grand Ave 55056 651-674-1500
Brad Windschill, prin. Fax 674-1510
North Branch MS 1,000/6-8
38431 Lincoln Trl 55056 651-674-1300
Todd Tetzlaff, prin. Fax 674-1310

Northfield, Rice, Pop. 18,671
Northfield SD 659 3,700/PK-12
1400 Division St S 55057 507-663-0629
L. Chris Richardson Ph.D., supt. Fax 663-0611
www.nfld.k12.mn.us
Northfield HS 1,300/9-12
1400 Division St S 55057 507-663-0630
Joel Leer, prin. Fax 645-3455
Northfield MS 900/6-8
2200 Division St S 55057 507-663-0650
Burt Bemmels, prin. Fax 663-0660

Carleton College Post-Sec.
1 N College St 55057 507-646-4000
Laura Baker School Post-Sec.
211 Oak St 55057 507-645-8866
St. Olaf College Post-Sec.
1500 Saint Olaf Ave 55057 507-646-2222

North Mankato, Nicollet, Pop. 12,078
Mankato SD 77
Supt. — See Mankato
Dakota Meadows JHS 600/7-8
1900 Howard Dr 56003 507-387-5077
Shane Baier, prin. Fax 387-1119

South Central College Post-Sec.
1920 Lee Blvd 56003 507-389-7200

North Oaks, Ramsey, Pop. 4,141
Mounds View SD 621
Supt. — See Shoreview
Chippewa MS 1,100/6-8
5000 Hodgson Rd, 651-483-6635
Fax 639-6233

Northome, Koochiching, Pop. 220
South Koochiching-Rainy River SD 363 400/K-12
PO Box 465 56661 218-897-5275
Dr. Jerry Struss, supt. Fax 897-5280
www.northome.k12.mn.us
Northome JSHS 100/7-12
PO Box 465 56661 218-897-5275
Shannon Avenson, prin. Fax 897-5280
Other Schools – See Birchdale

Northrop, Martin, Pop. 247

Martin Luther HS 100/9-12
PO Box 228 56075 507-436-5249
Robert Patrick, prin. Fax 436-5240

North Saint Paul, Ramsey, Pop. 12,568
North St. Paul-Maplewood-Oakdale SD 622 11,100/K-12
2520 12th Ave E 55109 651-748-7410
Patricia Phillips, supt. Fax 748-7413
www.isd622.org/
North HS 2,100/9-12
2416 11th Ave E 55109 651-748-6000
Greg Nelson, prin. Fax 748-6091
Other Schools – See Maplewood, Oakdale

Norwood Young America, Carver, Pop. 3,317
Central ISD 108 1,000/PK-12
PO Box 247 55368 952-467-7000
Brian Corlett, supt. Fax 467-7003
www.central.k12.mn.us
Central HS 400/9-12
PO Box 247 55368 952-467-7100
Ron Brand, prin. Fax 467-7103
Central MS 200/6-8
PO Box 247 55368 952-467-7200
Kevin Starr, prin. Fax 467-7203

Oakdale, Washington, Pop. 27,389
North St. Paul-Maplewood-Oakdale SD 622
Supt. — See North Saint Paul
Skyview Community MS 900/6-8
1100 Heron Ave N 55128 651-702-8000
Thomas Harrold, prin. Fax 702-8091
Tartan HS 1,700/9-12
828 Greenway Ave N 55128 651-702-8600
John Bezek, prin. Fax 702-8799

Globe College Post-Sec.
7166 10th St N 55128 651-730-5100

Ogilvie, Kanabec, Pop. 477
Ogilvie SD 333 600/K-12
333 School Dr 56358 320-272-5000
Tom Rich, supt. Fax 272-5072
www.ogilvie.k12.mn.us
Ogilvie HS 300/7-12
333 School Dr 56358 320-272-5000
Jeffrey Ehlenz, prin. Fax 272-5072

Okabena, Jackson, Pop. 179
Heron Lake-Okabena SD 330 300/PK-12
PO Box 97 56161 507-853-4507
Becky Cselovszki, supt. Fax 853-4642
www.ssc.mntm.org
Southwest Star Concept S 200/7-12
PO Box 97 56161 507-853-4507
Becky Cselovszki, prin. Fax 853-4642

Oklee, Red Lake, Pop. 382
Oklee SD 627 100/7-12
PO Box 100 56742 218-796-5136
James Guetter, supt. Fax 796-5139
Red Lake County Central HS 100/7-12
PO Box 100 56742 218-796-5136
Michael Bergevin, prin. Fax 796-5139

Olivia, Renville, Pop. 2,504
BOLD SD 2534 900/K-12
701 9th St S 56277 320-523-1031
Dr. Michael Funk, supt. Fax 523-2399
www.bold.k12.mn.us
BOLD JSHS 500/7-12
701 9th St S 56277 320-523-1031
John Double, dean Fax 523-5410

Onamia, Mille Lacs, Pop. 916
Onamia SD 480 800/K-12
35465 125th Ave 56359 320-532-4174
John Varner, supt. Fax 532-4658
www.onamia.k12.mn.us
Onamia JSHS 400/7-12
35465 125th Ave Ste 1 56359 320-532-4174
Dennis Hitzemann, prin. Fax 532-4658

Orr, Saint Louis, Pop. 247
Saint Louis County SD 2142
Supt. — See Virginia
Orr JSHS 100/7-12
PO Box 307 55771 218-757-3225
Sidney Simonson, prin. Fax 757-3666

Ortonville, Big Stone, Pop. 2,011
Ortonville SD 62 300/PK-12
200 Trojan Dr 56278 320-839-6181
Jeffrey Taylor, supt. Fax 839-3708
www.ortonville.k12.mn.us
Ortonville S 300/PK-12
200 Trojan Dr 56278 320-839-6183
Joel Stattelman, prin. Fax 839-2499

Osakis, Douglas, Pop. 1,568
Osakis SD 213 700/PK-12
PO Box X 56360 320-859-2191
Gregg Allen, supt. Fax 859-2835
Osakis JSHS 400/7-12
PO Box X 56360 320-859-2192
Tim Roggenbuck, prin. Fax 859-2835

Osseo, Hennepin, Pop. 2,551
Osseo SD 279
Supt. — See Maple Grove
Osseo JHS 1,200/7-9
10223 93rd Ave N 55369 763-391-8800
Willie Johnson, prin. Fax 391-8801
Osseo SHS 1,700/10-12
317 2nd Ave NW 55369 763-391-8500
Bob Perdaems, prin. Fax 391-8501

Owatonna, Steele, Pop. 24,133
Owatonna SD 761 4,900/K-12
515 W Bridge St 55060 507-444-8600
Tom Tapper, supt. Fax 444-8688
www.owatonna.k12.mn.us/
Owatonna HS 1,700/9-12
333 E School St 55060 507-444-8810
Don Johnson, prin. Fax 444-8999
Owatonna JHS 800/7-8
500 15th St NE 55060 507-444-8710
Kyle DeKam, prin. Fax 444-8799

Owatonna Christian S 100/PK-12
265 26th St NE 55060 507-451-3495
Eric Fjetland, prin. Fax 451-3762
Pillsbury Baptist Bible College Post-Sec.
315 S Grove Ave 55060 507-451-2710

Parkers Prairie, Otter Tail, Pop. 998
Parkers Prairie ISD 547 600/PK-12
PO Box 46 56361 218-338-6011
Russ Johnson, supt. Fax 338-4077
Parkers Prairie JSHS 300/7-12
PO Box 46 56361 218-338-6011
Connie Wenker, prin. Fax 338-4077

Park Rapids, Hubbard, Pop. 3,445
Park Rapids SD 309 1,700/PK-12
301 Huntsinger Ave 56470 218-237-6500
Glenn Chiodo, supt. Fax 237-6519
www.parkrapids.k12.mn.us
Century MS 500/5-8
501 Helten Ave 56470 218-237-6300
Bruce Gravalin, prin. Fax 237-6349
Park Rapids Area HS 600/9-12
401 Huntsinger Ave 56470 218-237-6400
Al Judson, prin. Fax 237-6401

Paynesville, Stearns, Pop. 2,243
Paynesville SD 741 900/PK-12
217 W Mill St 56362 320-243-3410
Todd Burlingame, supt. Fax 243-7525
www.paynesvilleschools.com/
Paynesville MSHS 400/6-12
795 W Highway 23 56362 320-243-3761
Lorie Floura, prin. Fax 243-4534

Pelican Rapids, Otter Tail, Pop. 2,357
Pelican Rapids SD 548 1,100/PK-12
PO Box 642 56572 218-863-5910
Kent Baldry, supt. Fax 863-5915
Pelican Rapids JSHS 600/7-12
PO Box 642 56572 218-863-5910
Glenn Moerke, prin. Fax 863-5915

Pequot Lakes, Crow Wing, Pop. 1,874
Pequot Lakes SD 186 1,400/PK-12
30805 Olson St 56472 218-568-4996
Rick Linnell, supt. Fax 568-5259
pequotlakes.k12.mn.us/
Pequot Lakes HS 500/9-12
30805 Olson St 56472 218-568-9210
John McDonald, prin. Fax 568-9250
Pequot Lakes MS 400/6-8
30805 Olson St 56472 218-568-9357
Randy Hansen, prin. Fax 568-9202

Perham, Otter Tail, Pop. 2,711
Perham-Dent SD 549 1,600/PK-12
200 5th St SE 56573 218-346-4501
Tamara Uselman, supt. Fax 346-4506
www.perham.k12.mn.us
Perham HS 600/9-12
200 5th St SE 56573 218-346-6500
John Rutten, prin. Fax 346-6504
Prairie Wind MS 500/5-8
480 Coney St W 56573 218-346-1700
Kitty Krueger, prin. Fax 346-1704

Peterson, Fillmore, Pop. 220
Rushford-Peterson SD 239
Supt. — See Rushford
Rushford-Peterson MS 200/6-8
PO Box 8 55962 507-875-2238
Jeffrey Miller, prin. Fax 875-2316

Pierz, Morrison, Pop. 1,316
Pierz SD 484 1,000/PK-12
112 Kamnic St 56364 320-468-6458
George Weber, supt. Fax 468-6408
www.pierz.k12.mn.us
Healy JSHS 600/7-12
112 Kamnic St 56364 320-468-6458
Paul Demorett, prin. Fax 468-6577

Pillager, Cass, Pop. 480
Pillager SD 116 700/PK-12
323 E 2nd St 56473 218-746-3772
Chuck Arns, supt. Fax 746-4236
www.pillager.k12.mn.us/
Pillager JSHS 400/7-12
323 E 2nd St 56473 218-746-3557
Scott Doss, prin. Fax 746-3406

Pine City, Pine, Pop. 3,323
Pine City SD 578 1,700/K-12
1400 Main St S 55063 320-629-4000
Darwin Bostic, supt. Fax 629-4070
www.pinecity.k12.mn.us
Pine City JSHS 800/7-12
1400 Main St S 55063 320-629-4112
George Johnson, prin. Fax 629-4105

Pine Technical College Post-Sec.
900 4th St SE 55063 320-629-5100

Pine Island, Goodhue, Pop. 3,170
Pine Island SD 255 1,200/K-12
PO Box 398 55963 507-356-8326
Chris Bates, supt. Fax 356-8827
www.pineisland.k12.mn.us
Pine Island HS 400/9-12
PO Box 398 55963 507-356-8326
Kevin Cardille, prin. Fax 356-8827
Pine Island MS 400/5-8
PO Box 398 55963 507-356-2488
Darren Overton, prin. Fax 356-8827

Pine River, Cass, Pop. 958
Pine River-Backus SD 2174 900/PK-12
PO Box 610 56474 218-587-4720
Catherine Bettino, supt. Fax 587-4120
www.prbackus.k12.mn.us
Pine River-Backus HS 500/7-12
PO Box 610 56474 218-587-4425
Kristil McDonald, prin. Fax 587-3108

Pipestone, Pipestone, Pop. 4,161
Pipestone Area SD 2689 1,200/PK-12
1401 7th St SW 56164 507-825-5861
Jim Lentz, supt. Fax 825-6718
pas.k12.mn.us
Pipestone HS 400/9-12
1401 7th St SW 56164 507-825-5861
Ray Staatz, prin. Fax 825-6729
Pipestone MS 400/5-8
1401 7th St SW 56164 507-825-5861
Ray Staatz, prin. Fax 825-6729

Minnesota West Community & Tech College Post-Sec.
1314 N Hiawatha Ave 56164 507-825-5471

Plainview, Wabasha, Pop. 3,296
Plainview-Elgin-Millville ISD 2899 900/PK-12
500 W Broadway 55964 507-534-3651
Eric Bartleson, supt. Fax 534-3907
www.pem.k12.mn.us/
Plainview-Elgin-Millville HS 400/9-12
500 W Broadway 55964 507-534-3128
Bill Ihrke, prin. Fax 534-3907
Other Schools – See Elgin

Plymouth, Hennepin, Pop. 69,701
Robbinsdale SD 281
Supt. — See New Hope
Plymouth MS 1,100/6-8
10011 36th Ave N 55441 763-504-7100
Susan Manikowski, prin. Fax 504-7131
Robbinsdale Armstrong HS 2,300/9-12
10635 36th Ave N 55441 763-504-8800
David Dahl, prin. Fax 504-8831

Wayzata SD 284
Supt. — See Minneapolis
Wayzata Central MS 900/6-8
305 Vicksburg Ln N 55447 763-745-6000
Steven Root, prin. Fax 745-6091
Wayzata East MS 700/6-8
12000 Ridgemount Ave W 55441 763-745-6200
Michael Trewick, prin. Fax 745-6291
Wayzata HS 3,100/9-12
4955 Peony Ln N, 763-745-6600
Craig Paul, prin. Fax 745-6691

Providence Academy 500/PK-12
15100 Schmidt Lake Rd, 763-258-2500
Dr. Todd Flanders, hdmstr. Fax 258-2501
Scot Lewis Beauty School Post-Sec.
4124 Lancaster Ln N 55441 763-551-0562
West Lutheran HS 200/9-12
3350 Harbor Ln N 55447 763-509-9378
Merlin Meitner, prin. Fax 509-0861

Preston, Fillmore, Pop. 1,377
Fillmore Central SD 2198
Supt. — See Harmony
Fillmore Central MS 200/5-8
PO Box 50 55965 507-765-3843
Brenda Lentz, prin. Fax 765-3636

Princeton, Mille Lacs, Pop. 4,694
Princeton SD 477 3,400/PK-12
706 1st St 55371 763-389-2422
Mark Sleeper, supt. Fax 389-9142
www.princeton.k12.mn.us
Princeton HS 1,100/9-12
807 8th Ave S 55371 763-389-4101
Peter Olson, prin. Fax 389-5816
Princeton MS 800/6-8
1100 4th Ave N 55371 763-389-6705
Richard Lahn, prin. Fax 389-6737

Prinsburg, Kandiyohi, Pop. 446

Central Minnesota Christian S 300/PK-12
PO Box 98 56281 320-978-8700
Rodney DeBoer, supt. Fax 978-6797

Prior Lake, Scott, Pop. 22,168
Prior Lake - Savage Area SD 719 5,000/K-12
PO Box 539 55372 952-226-0000
Dr. Tom Westerhaus, supt. Fax 226-0049
www.priorlake-savage.k12.mn.us
Hidden Oaks MS 900/6-8
PO Box 539 55372 952-226-0700
Sasha Kuznetsov, prin. Fax 226-0749
Twin Oaks MS 6-8
PO Box 539 55372 952-226-0500
Dr. Corey Lunn, prin. Fax 226-0549
Other Schools – See Savage

Proctor, Saint Louis, Pop. 2,779
Proctor SD 704 1,800/PK-12
131 9th Ave 55810 218-628-4934
Diane Rauschenfels, supt. Fax 628-4937
www.proctor.k12.mn.us
Jedlicka MS 400/6-8
131 9th Ave 55810 218-628-4926
Kim Juntunen, prin. Fax 628-4932
Proctor HS 600/9-12
131 9th Ave 55810 218-628-4926
Nancy Olson, prin. Fax 628-4931

Randolph, Dakota, Pop. 341
Randolph SD 195 500/PK-12
PO Box 38 55065 507-263-2151
Donald Pressnall, supt. Fax 645-5950
www.randolph.k12.mn.us

Randolph JSHS 200/7-12
PO Box 38 55065 507-263-2151
Michael Kelley, prin. Fax 645-5950

Redlake, Beltrami, Pop. 1,068
Red Lake SD 38 1,300/PK-12
PO Box 499 56671 218-679-3353
Stuart Desjarlait, supt. Fax 679-2321
Red Lake HS 300/9-12
PO Box 499 56671 218-679-3733
Everett Arnold, prin. Fax 679-2717
Red Lake MS 300/6-8
PO Box 499 56671 218-679-2700
Gregory Ferrin, prin. Fax 679-2733

Red Lake Falls, Red Lake, Pop. 1,590
Red Lake Falls SD 630 400/PK-12
PO Box 399 56750 218-253-2139
Alan Foley, supt. Fax 253-2135
LaFayette JSHS 200/7-12
PO Box 399 56750 218-253-2163
Mike Verdun, prin. Fax 253-4480

Red Wing, Goodhue, Pop. 15,799
Red Wing SD 256 2,800/K-12
2451 Eagle Ridge Dr 55066 651-385-4500
Stan Slessor, supt. Fax 385-4510
www.redwing.k12.mn.us
Red Wing HS 1,000/9-12
2451 Eagle Ridge Dr 55066 651-385-4600
Beth Borgen, prin. Fax 385-4610
Twin Bluff MS 700/6-8
2120 Twin Bluff Rd 55066 651-385-4530
Nancy Glasenapp, prin. Fax 385-4540

Minnesota State College Southeast Tech. Post-Sec.
308 Pioneer Rd 55066 800-657-4849

Redwood Falls, Redwood, Pop. 5,272
Redwood Area SD 2897 1,400/PK-12
100 George Ramseth Dr 56283 507-644-3531
Rick Ellingworth, supt. Fax 644-3057
redwood.mntm.org
Redwood Valley HS 500/9-12
100 George Ramseth Dr 56283 507-644-3511
Don Yrjo, prin. Fax 644-3057
Redwood Valley MS 500/5-8
100 George Ramseth Dr 56283 507-644-3521
Wade Mathers, prin. Fax 644-3057

Remer, Cass, Pop. 385
Northland Community SD 118 500/PK-12
316 Main St E Rm 200 56672 218-566-2351
Mike Doro, supt. Fax 566-3199
www.isd118.k12.mn.us
Northland HS 300/7-12
316 Main St E Rm 300 56672 218-566-2352
Joe Akre, prin. Fax 566-3199

Renville, Renville, Pop. 1,282
Renville County West SD 2890 500/K-12
PO Box 338 56284 320-329-8362
John Widvey, supt. Fax 329-3271
www.rcw.k12.mn.us
Renville County West HS 300/7-12
PO Box 338 56284 320-329-8368
Lance Bagstad, prin. Fax 329-8191

Richfield, Hennepin, Pop. 33,497
Richfield SD 280 4,000/K-12
7001 Harriet Ave 55423 612-798-6000
Barbara Devlin, supt. Fax 798-6057
www.richfield.k12.mn.us
Richfield HS 1,400/9-12
7001 Harriet Ave 55423 612-798-6100
Dr. Jill Johnson, prin. Fax 798-6127
Richfield JHS 900/6-8
7461 Oliver Ave S 55423 612-798-6400
Stephen West, prin. Fax 798-6427

Academy of Holy Angels 900/9-12
6600 Nicollet Ave 55423 612-798-2600
Heidi Foley, prin. Fax 798-2610
Adler Graduate School Post-Sec.
1550 E 78th St 55423 612-861-7554
Blessed Trinity S 200/4-8
6720 Nicollet Ave 55423 612-869-5200
Kim Doyle, prin. Fax 767-2191
Minnesota School of Business Post-Sec.
1401 W 76th St Ste 500 55423 612-861-2000

Robbinsdale, Hennepin, Pop. 13,331
Robbinsdale SD 281
Supt. — See New Hope
Robbinsdale MS 700/6-8
3730 Toledo Ave N 55422 763-504-4800
Christopher Holden, prin. Fax 504-4831

Rochester, Olmsted, Pop. 94,950
Rochester ISD 535 15,400/PK-12
615 7th St SW 55902 507-328-3000
Romain Dallemand, supt. Fax 328-4212
www.rochester.k12.mn.us
Adams MS, 1525 31st St NW 55901 1,000/6-8
Richard Jones, prin. 507-328-5700
Century HS, 2525 Viola Rd NE 55906 1,800/9-12
Chuck Briscoe, prin. 507-328-5100
Friedell MS, 1200 S Broadway 55904 400/6-8
Monica Bowler, prin. 507-328-5650
Kellogg MS, 503 17th St NE 55906 1,100/6-8
Dwight Jennings, prin. 507-328-5800
Marshall HS, 1510 14th St NW 55901 1,600/9-12
Richard Stirn, prin. 507-328-5400
Mayo HS, 1420 11th Ave SE 55904 1,700/9-12
Tim Dorway, prin. 507-328-5500
Willow Creek MS 1,000/6-8
2425 11th Ave SE 55904 507-328-5900
Jeffrey Elstad, prin.

Hawthorne Adult Literacy Center Adult
700 4th Ave SE 55904 507-328-4440
Julie Nigon, admin.

Crossroads College Post-Sec.
920 Mayowood Rd SW 55902 507-288-4563
Lourdes HS 600/9-12
621 W Center St 55902 507-289-3991
Dennis Nigon, prin. Fax 289-4008
Mayo School of Health Sciences Post-Sec.
200 1st Ave SW 55905 507-284-3678
Rochester Community & Technical College Post-Sec.
851 30th Ave SE 55904 507-285-7210
Rochester Community & Technical College Post-Sec.
1926 Collegeview Rd E 55904 800-247-1296
St. Mary's Hospital/Mayo Medical Center Post-Sec.
1216 2nd St NW 55901 507-255-5221
Schaeffer Academy 400/K-12
2700 Schaeffer Ln NE 55906 507-286-1050
Keith Phillips, hdmstr. Fax 282-3823
Sr. Rosalind Gefre School of Massage Post-Sec.
300 Elton Hills Dr NW 55901 507-286-8608
University of Minnesota Rochester Post-Sec.
855 30th Ave SE 55904 507-280-2838

Rockford, Wright, Pop. 3,808
Rockford SD 883 1,700/PK-12
PO Box 9 55373 763-477-9165
Michael Smith, supt. Fax 477-5833
www.rockford.k12.mn.us
Rockford HS 600/9-12
PO Box 70 55373 763-477-5846
Eric Williams, prin. Fax 477-6123
Rockford MS 400/6-8
PO Box 189 55373 763-477-5831
Marie Flanary, prin. Fax 477-5832

Rogers, Hennepin, Pop. 6,042
Elk River Area SD 728
Supt. — See Elk River
Rogers HS 900/9-12
21000 141st Ave N 55374 763-274-3140
Roman Pierskalla, prin. Fax 274-3141
Rogers JHS 800/6-8
20855 141st Ave N 55374 763-241-3550
Gary Bachmann, prin. Fax 241-3518

Roseau, Roseau, Pop. 2,814
Roseau SD 682 1,400/PK-12
509 3rd St NE 56751 218-463-1471
Larry Guggisberg, supt. Fax 463-3243
www.roseau.k12.mn.us/
Roseau JSHS 700/7-12
509 3rd St NE 56751 218-463-2770
Terry Gotziaman, prin. Fax 463-3658

Rosemount, Dakota, Pop. 19,311
Rosemount-Apple Valley-Eagan ISD 196 27,800/K-12
14445 Diamond Path W 55068 651-423-7700
John D. Currie, supt. Fax 423-7633
www.district196.org
Rosemount HS 2,100/9-12
3335 142nd St W 55068 651-423-7501
Gregory Clausen, prin. Fax 423-7511
Rosemount MS 1,000/6-8
3135 143rd St W 55068 651-423-7570
Mary Thompson, prin. Fax 423-7664
Other Schools – See Apple Valley, Eagan

Dakota Co. Technical College Post-Sec.
1300 145th St E 55068 651-423-8000
First Baptist Secondary S 100/7-12
14400 Diamond Path W 55068 651-423-2271
Charlies Graves, prin. Fax 423-8844

Roseville, Ramsey, Pop. 32,079
Roseville Area SD 623 6,300/K-12
1251 County Road B2 W 55113 651-635-1600
John Thein, supt. Fax 635-1659
www.isd623.org
Roseville Area HS 2,100/9-12
1240 County Road B2 W 55113 651-635-1660
Connie Nicholson, prin. Fax 635-1699
Other Schools – See Little Canada

American Academy of Acupuncture Post-Sec.
1925 County Road B2 W 55113 651-631-0204
Concordia Academy 500/9-12
2400 Dale St N 55113 651-484-8429
Tim Berner, admin. Fax 484-0594
Minneapolis Business College Post-Sec.
1711 County Road B W 55113 651-636-7406
National American University Post-Sec.
1550 Highway 36 W 55113 651-644-1265
North Heights Christian Academy 300/K-12
2701 Rice St 55113 651-484-7825
Jeffrey Taylor, prin. Fax 484-8636

Rothsay, Wilkin, Pop. 508
Rothsay SD 850 100/K-12
123 2nd St NW 56579 218-867-2117
Mary Donohue Stetz, supt. Fax 867-2376
www.rothsay.k12.mn.us
Rothsay S 100/K-12
123 2nd St NW 56579 218-867-2116
Mary Donohue Stetz, prin. Fax 867-2376

Round Lake, Nobles, Pop. 409
Round Lake SD 516 200/7-12
445 Harrison St 56167 507-945-8123
John Cselovszki, supt. Fax 945-8124
www.svrlb.mntm.org
Round Lake JSHS 200/7-12
445 Harrison St 56167 507-945-8123
John Cselovszki, prin. Fax 945-8124

Royalton, Morrison, Pop. 919
Royalton SD 485 700/PK-12
PO Box 5 56373 320-584-5531
John Franzoia, supt. Fax 584-5218
www.royalton.k12.mn.us
Royalton JSHS 400/7-12
PO Box 5 56373 320-584-5531
Lee Obermiller, prin. Fax 584-5218

Rush City, Chisago, Pop. 2,986
Rush City SD 139 1,000/K-12
PO Box 566 55069 320-358-4855
Vern Koepp, supt. Fax 358-1351
www.rushcity.k12.mn.us
Rush City HS 500/7-12
PO Box 566 55069 320-358-4795
Mark Saari, prin. Fax 358-1261

Rushford, Fillmore, Pop. 1,786
Rushford-Peterson SD 239 700/PK-12
PO Box 627 55971 507-864-7785
Jeffrey Miller, supt. Fax 864-2085
www.r-pschools.com
Rushford-Peterson HS 200/9-12
PO Box 627 55971 507-864-7786
Brad Johnson, prin. Fax 864-2085
Other Schools – See Peterson

Russell, Lyon, Pop. 342
R T R ISD 2902
Supt. — See Tyler
R T R MS 100/6-8
3rd & Prairie 56169 507-823-4371
Fax 823-4657

Saginaw, Saint Louis
Saint Louis County SD 2142
Supt. — See Virginia
Albrook JSHS 200/7-12
7427 Seville Rd 55779 218-729-8322
Gary Friedlieb, prin. Fax 729-8808

Saint Anthony, Hennepin, Pop. 7,915
Saint Anthony-New Brighton SD 282 1,700/PK-12
3303 33rd Ave NE 55418 612-706-1000
Rod Thompson, supt. Fax 706-1020
www.stanthony.k12.mn.us
Saint Anthony MS 400/6-8
3303 33rd Ave NE 55418 612-706-1030
Shirley Gregoire, prin. Fax 706-1040
Saint Anthony Village HS 600/9-12
3303 33rd Ave NE 55418 612-706-1100
Thomas Keith, prin. Fax 706-1020

Saint Bonifacius, Hennepin, Pop. 2,310

Crown College Post-Sec.
8700 College View Dr 55375 952-446-4100

Saint Charles, Winona, Pop. 3,393
Saint Charles SD 858 1,100/PK-12
600 E 6th St 55972 507-932-4423
Thomas Ames, supt. Fax 932-4700
www.scschools.net
Saint Charles HS 500/7-12
600 E 6th St 55972 507-932-4420
Henry Welle, prin. Fax 932-4700

Saint Clair, Blue Earth, Pop. 813
Saint Clair SD 75 700/PK-12
PO Box 99 56080 507-245-3501
Keith Klein, supt. Fax 245-3517
www.isd75.k12.mn.us/
Saint Clair JSHS 300/7-12
PO Box 99 56080 507-245-3027
Dustin Bosshart, prin. Fax 245-3690

Saint Cloud, Stearns, Pop. 59,458
Saint Cloud Area SD 742 9,600/PK-12
1000 44th Ave N 56303 320-253-9333
Bruce Watkins, supt. Fax 529-4343
www.isd742.org
Apollo HS 1,400/9-12
1000 44th Ave N 56303 320-253-1600
Charles Eisenreich, prin. Fax 253-8475
North JHS 600/7-8
1212 29th Ave N 56303 320-251-2159
Robert Huot, prin. Fax 251-7350
South JHS 800/7-8
1120 15th Ave S 56301 320-251-1322
Eric Williams, prin. Fax 251-2911
Technical HS 1,600/9-12
233 12th Ave S 56301 320-252-2231
Roger Ziemann, prin. Fax 252-0257

Cathedral HS & John XXIII MS 800/7-12
PO Box 1579 56302 320-251-3421
Lynn Grewing, prin. Fax 253-5576
Model College of Hair Design Post-Sec.
201 8th Ave S 56301 320-253-4222
Rasmussen College Post-Sec.
226 Park Ave S 56301 320-251-5600
Saint Cloud Christian S 300/K-12
PO Box 1002 56302 320-252-8182
MaryJo Froemming, admin. Fax 656-9678
St. Cloud Hospital Post-Sec.
1406 6th Ave N 56303 320-255-5666
St. Cloud State University Post-Sec.
720 4th Ave S 56301 877-654-7278
St. Cloud Technical College Post-Sec.
1540 Northway Dr 56303 320-252-0101
SS. Peter Paul & Michael MS 300/5-8
1215 11th Ave N 56303 320-251-5295
Sharon Bichler, prin. Fax 251-5295

Saint Francis, Anoka, Pop. 6,449
Saint Francis SD 15 5,100/K-12
4115 Ambassador Blvd NW 55070 763-753-7040
Edward Saxton, supt. Fax 753-4693
www.stfrancis.k12.mn.us

Saint Francis HS 1,800/9-12
3325 Bridge St NW 55070 763-213-1500
Paul Neubauer, prin. Fax 213-1693
Saint Francis MS 900/6-8
23026 Ambassador Blvd NW 55070 763-213-8500
Dale Johnson, prin. Fax 753-3821

Trinity Lutheran S 100/K-12
3812 229th Ave NW 55070 763-753-1234
William Dunk, prin. Fax 753-1774

Saint James, Watonwan, Pop. 4,592
Saint James SD 840 1,200/PK-12
500 8th Ave S 56081 507-375-5974
Nordy Nelson, supt. Fax 375-7143
www.stjames.k12.mn.us
Saint James JSHS 500/8-12
500 8th Ave S 56081 507-375-3381
Bruce Aamot, prin. Fax 375-4371

Saint Joseph, Stearns, Pop. 5,089

College of Saint Benedict Post-Sec.
37 College Ave S 56374 320-363-5011

Saint Louis Park, Hennepin, Pop. 44,114
Saint Louis Park SD 283 4,200/K-12
6425 W 33rd St 55426 952-928-6000
Debra Bowers, supt. Fax 928-6020
www.slpschools.org
Saint Louis Park HS 1,300/9-12
6425 W 33rd St 55426 952-928-6100
Robert Laney, prin. Fax 928-6113
Saint Louis Park JHS 700/7-8
2025 Texas Ave S 55426 952-928-6300
Les Bork, prin. Fax 928-6383

Benilde-St. Margarets HS 1,100/7-12
2501 Highway 100 S 55416 952-927-4176
Stacy Furness, prin. Fax 920-8889
Groves Academy 200/1-12
3200 Highway 100 S 55416 952-920-6377
John Alexander, hdmstr. Fax 920-2068
Health System Minnesota/Methodist Hosp. Post-Sec.
6500 Excelsior Blvd 55426 952-993-3601
High-Tech Institute Post-Sec.
5100 Gamble Dr Ste 200 55416 763-560-9700

Saint Michael, Wright, Pop. 12,850
Saint Michael-Albertville SD 885
Supt. — See Albertville
Saint Michael-Albertville MS 900/6-8
4862 Naber Ave NE 55376 763-497-2655
Jennifer Kelly, prin. Fax 497-6591

Saint Paul, Ramsey, Pop. 280,404
Saint Paul SD 625 38,800/PK-12
360 Colborne St 55102 651-293-8100
Dr. Meria Carstarphen, supt. Fax 290-8331
www.spps.org
Arlington HS 1,900/9-12
1495 Rice St 55117 651-293-6900
Patty Murphy, prin. Fax 293-6904
Battle Creek MS 700/7-8
2121 N Park Dr 55119 651-293-8960
Peter Christensen, prin. Fax 293-8866
Central HS 2,100/9-12
275 Lexington Pkwy N 55104 651-632-6000
Mary Mackbee, prin. Fax 293-5433
Cleveland JHS 400/7-8
1000 Walsh St 55106 651-293-8880
Jill Gebeke, prin. Fax 293-8888
Como Park HS 1,400/9-12
740 Rose Ave W 55117 651-293-8800
Dan Mesick, prin. Fax 293-8806
Harding HS 2,100/9-12
1540 6th St E 55106 651-793-4700
Todd Hochman, prin. Fax 293-8912
Hazel Park MS 800/7-8
1140 White Bear Ave N 55106 651-293-8920
Nadya Parker, prin. Fax 228-3609
Highland Park HS 1,400/9-12
1015 Snelling Ave S 55116 651-293-8940
Omoyefe Agbamu, prin. Fax 293-8939
Highland Park JHS 800/7-8
975 Snelling Ave S 55116 651-293-8950
Theresa Battle, prin. Fax 293-8953
Humboldt HS 800/9-12
30 Baker St E 55107 651-293-8600
Mike Sodomka, prin. Fax 293-8605
Humboldt JHS 500/7-8
640 Humboldt Ave 55107 651-293-8630
Tim Williams, prin. Fax 293-6660
International Academy / LEAP 300/7-12
631 Albert St N 55104 651-228-7706
Rose Santos, prin. Fax 228-7711
Johnson HS 1,600/9-12
1349 Arcade St 55106 651-293-8890
Kay Arndt, prin. Fax 293-8895
Murray JHS 800/7-8
2200 Buford Ave 55108 651-293-8740
Winston Tucker, prin. Fax 293-8742
Ramsey JHS 800/7-8
1700 Summit Ave 55105 651-293-8860
Bruce Maeda, prin. Fax 298-1587
Saint Paul Open S 400/K-12
90 Western Ave S 55102 651-293-8670
Todd Bartholomy, prin. Fax 293-5308
Washington Technology Magnet MS 800/6-8
1041 Marion St 55117 651-293-8830
Mike McCollor, prin. Fax 228-4331
Evening HS Adult
275 Lexington Pkwy N 55104 651-632-6015
Peter Atakpu, prin. Fax 632-6036
Hubbs Center for Lifelong Learning Adult
1030 University Ave W 55104 651-290-4822
Fax 290-4785
Other Schools – See Woodbury

Bethel College Post-Sec.
3900 Bethel Dr 55112 651-638-6400
Bethel Seminary Post-Sec.
3949 Bethel Dr 55112 651-638-6180
Christ's Household of Faith S 200/K-12
355 Marshall Ave 55102 651-265-3400
Ed Cavin, prin. Fax 227-9813
College of Saint Catherine Post-Sec.
2004 Randolph Ave 55105 651-690-6000
College of Saint Scholastica Post-Sec.
340 Cedar St 55101 651-298-1015
College of Visual Arts Post-Sec.
344 Summit Ave 55102 800-224-1536
Concordia University-St. Paul Post-Sec.
275 Syndicate St N 55104 651-641-8278
Cretin-Derham Hall HS 1,300/9-12
550 Albert St S 55116 651-690-2443
Richard Engler, prin. Fax 696-3394
E Metro Opportunities Industrialization Post-Sec.
1919 University Ave W # 500 55104 651-291-5088
Faith Baptist Christian S 100/K-12
1365 Westminster St, 651-771-5568
Rod Golightly, admin. Fax 771-1680
Hamline University Post-Sec.
1536 Hewitt Ave 55104 651-523-2800
Luther Seminary Post-Sec.
2481 Como Ave 55108 800-588-4373
Macalester College Post-Sec.
1600 Grand Ave 55105 651-696-6000
McNally Smith College of Music Post-Sec.
19 Exchange St E 55101 651-291-0177
Metropolitan State University Post-Sec.
700 7th St E 55106 651-793-1300
Mounds Park Academy 700/PK-12
2051 Larpenteur Ave E 55109 651-777-2555
Michael Downs, hdmstr. Fax 777-8633
Northwestern College Post-Sec.
3003 Snelling Ave N 55113 651-631-5100
NTI-School of CAD Technology Post-Sec.
950 Blue Gentian Rd Ste 500 55121 952-944-0080
St. Agnes HS 200/9-12
530 Lafond Ave 55103 651-228-1161
Jeff Brengman, hdmstr. Fax 228-1158
St. Bernard S 400/PK-12
170 Rose Ave W 55117 651-489-1338
Jeffrey Lenzmeier, prin. Fax 488-9466
St. Paul Academy & Summit S 1,000/6-12
1712 Randolph Ave 55105 651-698-2451
Bryn Roberts, hdmstr. Fax 698-6787
St. Paul College Post-Sec.
235 Marshall Ave 55102 651-846-1600
Scot Lewis School Post-Sec.
1905 Suburban Ave 55119 651-209-6930
University of St. Thomas Post-Sec.
2115 Summit Ave 55105 651-962-5000
William Mitchell College of Law Post-Sec.
875 Summit Ave 55105 651-227-9171

Saint Paul Park, Washington, Pop. 5,028
South Washington County SD 833
Supt. — See Cottage Grove
Oltman JHS 800/7-9
1020 3rd St 55071 651-768-3500
Becky Schroeder, prin. Fax 768-3555

Hope Christian Academy 100/K-12
920 Holley Ave Ste 2 55071 651-459-6438
Randy Krussow, prin. Fax 769-2108

Saint Peter, Nicollet, Pop. 10,162
Saint Peter SD 508 1,800/K-12
100 Lincoln Dr 56082 507-934-5703
Jeffrey Olson, supt. Fax 934-2805
www.stpeterschools.org
Saint Peter HS 600/9-12
100 Lincoln Dr 56082 507-934-4210
Paul Peterson, prin. Fax 934-4783
Saint Peter MS 300/7-8
100 Lincoln Dr 56082 507-934-4210
Joe Nicklay, prin. Fax 934-4783

Gustavus Adolphus College Post-Sec.
800 W College Ave 56082 507-933-8000

Sandstone, Pine, Pop. 2,519
East Central SD 2580
Supt. — See Finlayson
East Central Secondary S 300/6-12
214 Eagle Dr 55072 320-245-2216
F. Joseph Giesen, prin. Fax 245-2448

Sartell, Stearns, Pop. 12,668
Sartell-St Stephen SD 748 2,300/PK-12
212 3rd Ave N 56377 320-656-3715
Dr. Dale Gasser, supt. Fax 656-3765
www.sartell.k12.mn.us
Sartell HS 900/9-12
748 7th St N 56377 320-656-0748
Brenda Steve, prin. Fax 656-5296
Sartell MS 900/5-8
627 3rd Ave N 56377 320-253-2200
Michael Spanier, prin. Fax 253-1403

Sauk Centre, Stearns, Pop. 3,915
Sauk Centre SD 743 1,100/PK-12
903 State Rd 56378 320-352-2284
Dan Brooks, supt. Fax 352-3404
www.isd743.k12.mn.us/
Sauk Centre JHS 300/7-9
903 State Rd 56378 320-352-2258
Belinda Selfors, prin. Fax 352-3404
Sauk Centre SHS 300/10-12
903 State Rd 56378 320-352-2258
Cory Larson, prin. Fax 352-3404

Sauk Rapids, Benton, Pop. 11,523
Sauk Rapids-Rice SD 47 3,600/PK-12
1833 Osauka Rd 56379 320-253-4703
Greg Vandal, supt. Fax 255-1914
www.isd47.org
Sauk Rapids-Rice HS 1,200/9-12
1835 Osauka Rd 56379 320-253-4700
Erich Martens, prin. Fax 258-1717
Sauk Rapids-Rice MS 800/6-8
901 1st St S 56379 320-654-9073
Larry Stracke, prin. Fax 259-8909
Hillside ECFE & ABE Adult
30 4th Ave S 56379 320-255-8910
Deborah Campbell, dir. Fax 258-1197

Sr. Rosalind Gefre School of Massage Post-Sec.
1007 Industrial Dr S 56379 320-259-6185

Savage, Scott, Pop. 26,581
Burnsville-Eagan-Savage ISD 191
Supt. — See Burnsville
Eagle Ridge JHS 900/7-9
13955 Glendale Rd 55378 952-707-2800
David Helke, prin. Fax 707-2802

Prior Lake - Savage Area SD 719
Supt. — See Prior Lake
Prior Lake HS 1,700/9-12
7575 150th St W 55378 952-226-8600
Dr. Craig Olson, prin. Fax 226-8649

Sebeka, Wadena, Pop. 680
Sebeka SD 820 600/PK-12
PO Box 249 56477 218-837-5101
Dave Fjeldheim, supt. Fax 837-5967
www.sebeka.com
Sebeka JSHS 300/7-12
PO Box 249 56477 218-837-5101
Dave Fjeldheim, prin. Fax 837-5967

Shakopee, Scott, Pop. 31,233
Shakopee SD 720 5,100/K-12
505 Holmes St S 55379 952-496-5006
Jon McBroom, supt. Fax 445-8446
www.shakopee.k12.mn.us
Shakopee JHS 1,200/7-9
1137 Marschall Rd 55379 952-496-5752
Chris Lindholm, prin. Fax 496-5792
Shakopee SHS 1,000/10-12
200 10th Ave E 55379 952-496-5152
James Murphy, prin. Fax 445-3268

Sherburn, Martin, Pop. 1,060
Martin County West SD 2448
Supt. — See Welcome
Martin County West HS 300/9-12
16 W 5th St 56171 507-764-4671
David Traetow, prin. Fax 764-4691

Shoreview, Ramsey, Pop. 26,855
Mounds View SD 621 9,400/K-12
350 Highway 96 W 55126 651-636-3650
Dan Hoverman, supt. Fax 639-6204
www.moundsviewschools.org
Other Schools – See Arden Hills, Mounds View, New Brighton, North Oaks

Silver Bay, Lake, Pop. 1,982
Lake Superior SD 381
Supt. — See Two Harbors
Kelly JSHS, 137 Banks Blvd 55614 300/7-12
George Starkovich, prin. 218-226-4437

Slayton, Murray, Pop. 1,953
Murray County Central SD 2169 800/PK-12
2420 28th St 56172 507-836-6183
Steve Jones, supt. Fax 836-6375
Murray County Central JSHS 400/7-12
2420 28th St 56172 507-836-6184
Steve Jones, prin. Fax 836-6375

Sleepy Eye, Brown, Pop. 3,478
Sleepy Eye SD 84 700/PK-12
400 4th Ave SW 56085 507-794-7903
Arla Dockter, supt. Fax 794-5404
Sleepy Eye JSHS 300/7-12
400 4th Ave SW 56085 507-794-7904
Shane Laffen, prin. Fax 794-5404

St. Mary JSHS 300/7-12
104 Saint Marys St NW 56085 507-794-4121
Jerry Neubauer, prin. Fax 794-4841

South Saint Paul, Dakota, Pop. 19,787
South St. Paul SD 6 3,200/PK-12
104 5th Ave S 55075 651-457-9400
Dr. Dana Babbitt, supt. Fax 457-9485
www.sspps.org
South Saint Paul HS 1,600/7-12
700 2nd St N 55075 651-457-9408
H. Butch Moening, prin. Fax 457-9455

Springfield, Brown, Pop. 2,135
Springfield SD 85 700/PK-12
12 Burns Ave 56087 507-723-4283
Luther Heller, supt. Fax 723-6407
www.springfield.mntm.org/
Springfield JSHS 300/7-12
12 Burns Ave 56087 507-723-4288
Karen Strasser, prin. Fax 723-4447

Spring Grove, Houston, Pop. 1,281
Spring Grove SD 297 400/K-12
PO Box 626 55974 507-498-3221
James Busta, supt. Fax 498-3470
Spring Grove JSHS 200/7-12
PO Box 626 55974 507-498-3223
Nancy Gulbranson, prin. Fax 498-3470

Spring Lake Park, Anoka, Pop. 6,699
Spring Lake Park SD 16 — 3,300/K-12
8000 Highway 65 NE 55432 — 763-786-5570
Don Helmstetter, supt. — Fax 784-7838
www.springlakeparkschools.org
Spring Lake Park HS — 1,300/9-12
8001 Able St NE 55432 — 763-786-5571
Frank Herman, prin. — Fax 786-2661
Other Schools – See Blaine

Spring Valley, Fillmore, Pop. 2,480
Kingsland SD 2137
Supt. — See Wykoff
Kingsland HS — 300/9-12
705 N Section Ave 55975 — 507-346-7276
Darrin Strosahl, prin. — Fax 346-7278

Staples, Todd, Pop. 3,121
Staples-Motley ISD 2170 — 1,500/PK-12
202 Pleasant Ave NE 56479 — 218-894-2430
Mark Schmitz, supt. — Fax 894-1828
www.isd2170.k12.mn.us/
Staples-Motley HS — 500/9-12
401 Centennial Ln 56479 — 218-894-2431
Jim Hofer, prin. — Fax 894-2434
Other Schools – See Motley

Central Lakes College — Post-Sec.
1830 Airport Rd 56479 — 218-894-5100

Stephen, Marshall, Pop. 672
Stephen-Argyle Central SD 2856 — 200/PK-12
PO Box 68 56757 — 218-478-3315
Chris Mills, supt. — Fax 478-3537
www.sac.k12.mn.us/
Stephen JSHS — 200/7-12
PO Box 68 56757 — 218-478-3314
Mark Kroulik, prin. — Fax 478-3537

Stewartville, Olmsted, Pop. 5,494
Stewartville SD 534 — 1,800/PK-12
500 4th St SW 55976 — 507-533-1438
Dr. David Thompson, supt. — Fax 533-4012
ssd.k12.mn.us
Stewartville HS — 600/9-12
500 4th St SW 55976 — 507-533-1600
Bruce Hoff, prin. — Fax 533-4143
Stewartville MS — 400/6-8
500 4th St SW 55976 — 507-533-1666
Joseph Jezierski, prin. — Fax 533-1021

Stillwater, Washington, Pop. 17,378
Stillwater Area SD 834 — 8,700/K-12
1875 Greeley St S 55082 — 651-351-8301
Keith Ryskoski, supt. — Fax 351-8380
www.stillwater.k12.mn.us
Stillwater Area SHS — 2,200/10-12
5701 Stillwater Blvd N 55082 — 651-351-8040
Chris Lennox, prin. — Fax 351-8049
Stillwater JHS — 1,100/7-9
523 Marsh St W 55082 — 651-351-6905
Richard Wippler, prin. — Fax 351-6999
Other Schools – See Lake Elmo

Swanville, Morrison, Pop. 344
Swanville SD 486 — 400/PK-12
PO Box 98 56382 — 320-547-2431
Gene Harthan, supt. — Fax 547-2576
www.swanville.k12.mn.us
Swanville JSHS — 100/7-12
PO Box 98 56382 — 320-547-2431
Dennis Saurer, prin. — Fax 547-2576

Thief River Falls, Pennington, Pop. 8,377
Thief River Falls SD 564 — 2,000/PK-12
230 Labree Ave S 56701 — 218-681-8711
Irv Peterson, supt. — Fax 681-3252
trf.k12.mn.us
Franklin MS — 500/6-8
300 Spruce Ave S 56701 — 218-681-8813
Bob Wayne, prin. — Fax 681-4771
Lincoln HS — 700/9-12
101 Knight Ave S 56701 — 218-681-7432
Tom Hunt, prin. — Fax 681-4510

Northland Community & Technical College — Post-Sec.
Highway 1 E 56701 — 800-628-9918

Tower, Saint Louis, Pop. 469
Saint Louis County SD 2142
Supt. — See Virginia
Tower-Soudan JSHS — 100/7-12
PO Box 469 55790 — 218-753-4040
Sidney Simonson, prin. — Fax 753-6461

Tracy, Lyon, Pop. 2,089
Tracy SD 417 — 800/PK-12
934 Pine St 56175 — 507-629-5500
David A. Marlette, supt. — Fax 629-5507
tracy.k12.mn.us
Tracy JSHS — 500/7-12
934 Pine St 56175 — 507-629-5500
Chad Anderson, prin. — Fax 629-5507

Trimont, Martin, Pop. 712
Martin County West SD 2448
Supt. — See Welcome
Martin County West JHS — 200/7-8
PO Box 408 56176 — 507-639-2081
Allison Schmidt, prin. — Fax 639-2091

Truman, Martin, Pop. 1,201
Truman SD 458 — 400/K-12
PO Box 276 56088 — 507-776-2111
John Larson, supt. — Fax 776-3379
www.truman.k12.mn.us
Truman JSHS — 200/7-12
PO Box 276 56088 — 507-776-2111
Dan Kunkel, prin. — Fax 776-3379

Twin Valley, Norman, Pop. 822
Norman County East SD 2215 — 400/PK-12
PO Box 420 56584 — 218-584-5151
Larry Swanson, supt. — Fax 584-5170
nce.k12.mn.us/
Norman County East HS — 200/7-12
PO Box 420 56584 — 218-584-5151
Gregory Lund, prin. — Fax 584-5170

Two Harbors, Lake, Pop. 3,533
Lake Superior SD 381 — 1,300/PK-12
1640 Highway 2 55616 — 218-834-8201
Phil Minkkinen, supt. — Fax 834-8239
www.isd381.k12.mn.us/
Two Harbors JSHS — 600/6-12
1640 Highway 2 Ste 100 55616 — 218-834-8201
Robert Nyberg, prin. — Fax 834-5513
Other Schools – See Silver Bay

Tyler, Lincoln, Pop. 1,118
R T R ISD 2902 — 600/PK-12
PO Box 659 56178 — 507-247-5913
Bruce Houck, supt. — Fax 247-3876
www.rtrschools.org
R T R HS — 200/9-12
PO Box 659 56178 — 507-247-5911
Tim Christensen, prin. — Fax 247-3876
Other Schools – See Russell

Ulen, Clay, Pop. 561
Ulen-Hitterdal SD 914 — 300/K-12
PO Box 389 56585 — 218-596-8853
Allen H. Zenor, supt. — Fax 596-8610
www.ulenhitterdal.k12.mn.us
Ulen-Hitterdal JSHS — 100/7-12
PO Box 389 56585 — 218-596-8853
Kent Henrickson, prin. — Fax 596-8610

Underwood, Otter Tail, Pop. 325
Underwood SD 550 — 500/K-12
100 Southern Ave E 56586 — 218-826-6101
Gary Sletten, supt. — Fax 826-6310
www.underwood.k12.mn.us
Underwood JSHS — 200/7-12
100 Southern Ave E 56586 — 218-826-6102
John Hamann, prin. — Fax 826-6310

Upsala, Morrison, Pop. 413
Upsala SD 487 — 400/PK-12
PO Box 190 56384 — 320-573-2174
Gene Harthan, supt. — Fax 573-2173
Upsala JSHS — 200/7-12
PO Box 190 56384 — 320-573-2176
Tim Pahl, prin. — Fax 573-2173

Verndale, Wadena, Pop. 554
Verndale SD 818 — 500/PK-12
411 SW Brown St 56481 — 218-445-5184
James Madsen, supt. — Fax 445-5185
www.verndale.k12.mn.us
Verndale JSHS — 200/7-12
411 SW Brown St 56481 — 218-445-5184
Dean Krogstad, prin. — Fax 445-5185

Vesta, Redwood, Pop. 322
Wabasso SD 640
Supt. — See Wabasso
Vesta JSHS — 50/7-12
320 Centre St W 56292 — 507-342-7111
Ted Suss, prin. — Fax 347-7111

Victoria, Carver, Pop. 5,702

Holy Family HS — 400/9-12
8101 Kochia Ln 55386 — 952-443-4659
Kathie Brown, prin. — Fax 443-1822

Virginia, Saint Louis, Pop. 8,666
Saint Louis County SD 2142 — 2,300/PK-12
1701 N 9th Ave 55792 — 218-749-8130
Charles Rick, supt. — Fax 749-8133
www.isd2142.k12.mn.us/
Other Schools – See Babbitt, Cook, Cotton, Iron, Orr, Saginaw, Tower

Virginia SD 706 — 1,700/PK-12
411 S 5th Ave 55792 — 218-742-3901
Phillip Johnson, supt. — Fax 742-3960
www.virginia.k12.mn.us/
Virginia Secondary S — 800/7-12
411 S 5th Ave 55792 — 218-742-3916
Laverne Hakly, prin.

Mesabi Range Community & Technical Coll. — Post-Sec.
1001 Chestnut St W 55792 — 218-749-7700

Wabasha, Wabasha, Pop. 2,553
Wabasha-Kellogg SD 811 — 700/PK-12
2113 Hiawatha Dr E 55981 — 651-565-3559
Jim Freihammer, supt. — Fax 565-2769
www.wabasha-kellogg.k12.mn.us/
Wabasha-Kellogg JSHS — 400/7-12
2113 Hiawatha Dr E 55981 — 651-565-3559
Jon Stern, prin. — Fax 565-2769

Wabasso, Redwood, Pop. 656
Wabasso SD 640 — 400/PK-12
PO Box 69 56293 — 507-342-5114
Ted Suss, supt. — Fax 342-5203
www.wabassoschool.com
Wabasso JSHS — 200/7-12
PO Box 69 56293 — 507-342-5114
Ted Suss, prin. — Fax 342-5203
Other Schools – See Vesta

Waconia, Carver, Pop. 8,692
Waconia SD 110 — 2,600/PK-12
512 Industrial Blvd 55387 — 952-442-0600
Jerry Kjergaard, supt. — Fax 442-0639
www.waconia.k12.mn.us

Clearwater MS — 800/5-8
1650 Community Dr 55387 — 952-442-0650
Peter Gustafson, prin. — Fax 442-0659
Waconia HS — 800/9-12
1400 Community Dr 55387 — 952-442-0670
Mark Fredericksen, prin. — Fax 442-0679

Wadena, Wadena, Pop. 4,107
Wadena-Deer Creek SD 2155 — 1,300/PK-12
PO Box 151 56482 — 218-632-2155
Jerome Enget, supt. — Fax 632-2199
www.wdc2155.k12.mn.us
Wadena-Deer Creek HS — 700/7-12
PO Box 151 56482 — 218-632-2300
Tim Bjorge, prin. — Fax 632-2399

MN State Community & Technical College — Post-Sec.
PO Box 566 56482 — 800-247-2007

Waite Park, Stearns, Pop. 6,832

St. Cloud Regency Beauty Academy — Post-Sec.
110 2nd St S 56387 — 320-251-0500

Walker, Cass, Pop. 1,170
Walker-Hackensack-Akeley SD 113 — 900/PK-12
PO Box 4000 56484 — 218-547-1311
Jeff Lindstrom, supt. — Fax 547-4298
www.wha.k12.mn.us
Walker-Hackensack-Akeley HS — 300/9-12
PO Box 4000 56484 — 218-547-4210
Peggy Novak, prin. — Fax 547-4297
Walker-Hackensack-Akeley MS — 300/6-8
PO Box 4000 56484 — 218-547-5321
Peggy Novak, prin. — Fax 547-5333

Walnut Grove, Redwood, Pop. 561
Westbrook-Walnut Grove SD 2898
Supt. — See Westbrook
Westbrook-Walnut Grove MS — 200/5-8
PO Box 278 56180 — 507-859-2141
Paul Olson, prin. — Fax 859-2329

Wanamingo, Goodhue, Pop. 1,043
Kenyon-Wanamingo SD 2172 — 900/PK-12
225 3rd Ave 55983 — 507-824-2211
Jeff Evert, supt. — Fax 824-2212
Other Schools – See Kenyon

Warren, Marshall, Pop. 1,630
Warren-Alvarado-Oslo SD 2176 — 500/PK-12
224 E Bridge Ave 56762 — 218-745-5393
Dr. Ken Henry, supt. — Fax 745-5886
www.wao.k12.mn.us
Warren-Alvarado-Oslo JSHS — 300/7-12
224 E Bridge Ave 56762 — 218-745-4646
Seann Dikkers, prin. — Fax 745-7658

Warroad, Roseau, Pop. 1,699
Warroad SD 690 — 1,200/PK-12
510 Cedar Ave NW 56763 — 218-386-1472
Craig Oftedahl, supt. — Fax 386-1909
www.warroad.k12.mn.us
Warroad HS — 500/9-12
510 Cedar Ave NW 56763 — 218-386-1820
William Kirkeby, prin. — Fax 386-1909
Warroad MS — 400/4-8
510 Cedar Ave NW 56763 — 218-386-1877
Craig Oftedahl, prin. — Fax 386-2179

Waseca, Waseca, Pop. 9,445
Waseca SD 829 — 2,000/PK-12
501 Elm Ave E 56093 — 507-835-2500
James Schmitt, supt. — Fax 835-1161
www.waseca.k12.mn.us
Waseca HS — 700/9-12
1717 2nd St NW 56093 — 507-835-5470
Jeanne Swanson, prin. — Fax 835-1724
Waseca JHS — 400/7-8
400 19th Ave NW 56093 — 507-835-1048
Bill Bunkers, prin. — Fax 835-1063

Watertown, Carver, Pop. 3,932
Watertown-Mayer SD 111 — 1,500/PK-12
1001 Highway 25 Shls NW 55388 — 952-955-0200
Karsten Anderson, supt. — Fax 955-0215
www.wm.k12.mn.us/
Watertown-Mayer HS — 500/9-12
1001 Highway 25 Shls NW 55388 — 952-955-0240
Scott Gengler, prin. — Fax 955-0251
Watertown-Mayer MS — 500/5-8
1001 Highway 25 Shls NW 55388 — 952-955-0210
Scott Alger, dean — Fax 955-0215

Waterville, LeSueur, Pop. 1,881
Waterville-Elysian-Morristown SD 2143 — 1,000/PK-12
500 Paquin St E 56096 — 507-362-4432
Joel Whitehurst, supt. — Fax 362-4561
www.wem.k12.mn.us/
Waterville-Elysian-Morristown HS — 300/9-12
500 Paquin St E 56096 — 507-362-4431
John Kaplan, prin. — Fax 362-4561
Other Schools – See Morristown

Waubun, Mahnomen, Pop. 392
Waubun SD 435 — 600/PK-12
PO Box 98 56589 — 218-473-6171
Boyd Bradbury, supt. — Fax 473-6191
Waubun JSHS — 300/7-12
PO Box 98 56589 — 218-473-6173
Helen Kennedy, prin. — Fax 473-6190

Wayzata, Hennepin, Pop. 3,941
Wayzata SD 284
Supt. — See Minneapolis
Wayzata West MS — 700/6-8
149 Barry Ave N 55391 — 952-745-6400
Susan Sommerfed, prin. — Fax 745-6491

Welcome, Martin, Pop. 681
Martin County West SD 2448 900/K-12
PO Box 268 56181 507-728-8276
Randy Grupe, supt. Fax 728-8278
www.martin.k12.mn.us
Other Schools – See Sherburn, Trimont

Wells, Faribault, Pop. 2,485
United South Central SD 2134 1,000/PK-12
250 2nd Ave SW 56097 507-553-3134
Robert Stuerman, supt. Fax 553-5929
www.usc.k12.mn.us
United South Central HS 400/9-12
250 2nd Ave SW 56097 507-553-5819
Kelly Schlaak, prin. Fax 553-5929
Other Schools – See Kiester

Westbrook, Cottonwood, Pop. 762
Westbrook-Walnut Grove SD 2898 500/PK-12
PO Box 129 56183 507-274-5450
Loy Woelber, supt. Fax 274-6113
Westbrook-Walnut Grove HS 200/9-12
PO Box 128 56183 507-274-5450
William Richards, prin. Fax 858-2329
Other Schools – See Walnut Grove

West Concord, Dodge, Pop. 826
Triton SD 2125
Supt. — See Dodge Center
Triton MS 300/6-8
PO Box 38 55985 507-527-2211
Craig Schlichting, prin. Fax 527-2213

West Saint Paul, Dakota, Pop. 19,070
West St. Paul-Mendota Hts-Eagan SD 197
Supt. — See Mendota Heights
Heritage MS 800/5-8
121 Butler Ave W 55118 651-905-4000
Chris Hiti, prin. Fax 905-4001

St. Croix Lutheran HS 300/9-12
1200 Oakdale Ave 55118 651-455-1521
Richard Gibson, prin. Fax 451-3968
Sr. Rosalind Gefre School of Massage Post-Sec.
149 Thompson Ave Ste 150 55118 651-554-3013

Wheaton, Traverse, Pop. 1,488
Wheaton Area SD 803 400/PK-12
1700 3rd Ave S 56296 320-563-8283
Daniel Posthumus, supt. Fax 563-4218
www.wheaton.k12.mn.us
Wheaton JSHS 200/6-12
1700 3rd Ave S 56296 320-563-8282
Russ Armstrong, prin. Fax 563-4218

White Bear Lake, Ramsey, Pop. 23,733
White Bear Lake Area SD 624 7,700/PK-12
4855 Bloom Ave 55110 651-407-7500
Dr. Theodore Blaesing, supt. Fax 407-7566
www.whitebear.k12.mn.us
Central MS 1,000/6-8
4857 Bloom Ave 55110 651-653-2888
Noel Schmidt, prin. Fax 653-2885
Sunrise Park MS 50/6-8
2399 Cedar Ave 55110 651-653-2700
David Law, prin. Fax 653-2716
White Bear Lake Area HS North Campus 1,500/9-10
5040 Bald Eagle Ave 55110 651-653-2920
William Soltys, prin. Fax 653-2630
White Bear Lake Area HS South Campus 1,300/11-12
3551 McKnight Rd N 55110 651-773-6200
Timothy Wald, prin. Fax 773-6215

Century College Post-Sec.
3300 Century Ave N 55110 651-779-3200

Willmar, Kandiyohi, Pop. 18,183
Willmar SD 347 4,100/K-12
611 5th St SW 56201 320-231-8500
Kathryn Leedom, supt. Fax 231-1061
www.willmar.k12.mn.us
Willmar HS 1,300/9-12
2701 30th St NE 56201 320-231-8300
Rob Anderson, prin. Fax 231-8460
Willmar JHS 600/7-8
201 Willmar Ave SE 56201 320-214-6000
Mike Prunty, prin. Fax 235-1254

Rice Memorial Hospital Post-Sec.
301 Becker Ave SW 56201 320-231-4530
Ridgewater College-Willmar Campus Post-Sec.
PO Box 1097 56201 320-235-5114

Willow River, Pine, Pop. 379
Willow River SD 577 500/PK-12
PO Box 66 55795 218-372-3131
Steve Wymore, supt. Fax 372-3132
Willow River JSHS 200/7-12
PO Box 66 55795 218-372-3131
Steve Wymore, prin. Fax 372-3132

Windom, Cottonwood, Pop. 4,416
Windom SD 177 1,000/K-12
PO Box C177 56101 507-831-6901
Douglas Froke, supt. Fax 831-6919
www.windom.k12.mn.us
Windom Area HS 300/9-12
PO Box C177 56101 507-831-6910
Mark Roubinek, prin. Fax 831-6909
Windom MS 300/5-8
PO Box C177 56101 507-831-6910
Tom Farrell, prin. Fax 831-6909

Winona, Winona, Pop. 26,587
Winona Area SD 861 3,800/K-12
903 Gilmore Ave 55987 507-494-0861
Paul Durand, supt. Fax 494-0863
www.winona.k12.mn.us
Winona HS 1,400/9-12
901 Gilmore Ave 55987 507-494-1504
Nancy Wondrasch, prin. Fax 494-1501
Winona MS 1,200/5-8
1570 Homer Rd 55987 507-494-1000
Sharon Suchla, prin. Fax 494-1002

Cotter HS 300/9-12
1115 W Broadway St 55987 507-453-5802
Sandra Blank, prin. Fax 453-5006
Cotter JHS 100/7-8
101 E Wabasha St 55987 507-453-5366
Dave Forney, prin. Fax 453-5806
Hope Lutheran HS 50/9-12
253 Liberty St 55987 507-474-7799
Tammy O'Laughlin, admin. Fax 452-8992
Minnesota State College Southeast Tech. Post-Sec.
PO Box 409 55987 507-453-2700
St. Mary's University of Minnesota Post-Sec.
700 Terrace Hts Ste 2 55987 507-452-4430
Winona State University Post-Sec.
PO Box 5838 55987 507-457-5000

Winsted, McLeod, Pop. 2,367

Holy Trinity S 300/PK-12
PO Box 38 55395 320-485-2182
Bill Tschida, prin. Fax 485-4283

Winthrop, Sibley, Pop. 1,290
GFW SD 2365
Supt. — See Gibbon
GFW HS 300/9-12
PO Box 1001 55396 507-647-5382
Jeff Bertrang, prin. Fax 647-4329

Woodbury, Washington, Pop. 52,479
Saint Paul SD 625
Supt. — See Saint Paul
Crosswinds Arts & Science S 500/6-10
600 Weir Dr 55125 651-379-2600
Roger Kocinskis, prin. Fax 379-2690

South Washington County SD 833
Supt. — See Cottage Grove
Lake JHS 1,000/7-9
3133 Pioneer Dr 55125 651-768-6400
Todd Hochman, prin. Fax 768-6428
Woodbury JHS 800/7-9
1425 School Dr 55125 651-768-4500
Dennis Roos, prin. Fax 768-4567
Woodbury SHS 1,800/10-12
2665 Woodlane Dr 55125 651-768-4400
Linda Plante, prin. Fax 768-4412

New Life Academy 600/PK-12
6758 Bailey Rd 55129 651-459-4121
Dr. Aaron Gonzalez, admin. Fax 459-6194

Worthington, Nobles, Pop. 11,092
Worthington SD 518 2,300/K-12
1117 Marine Ave 56187 507-372-2172
John Landgaard, supt. Fax 372-2174
www.isd518.net
Worthington HS 700/9-12
1211 Clary St 56187 507-376-6121
Scott Backer, prin. Fax 372-4304
Worthington MS 500/6-8
1401 Crailsheim Dr 56187 507-376-4174
Jeff Britten, prin. Fax 372-1424

Minnesota West Community & Tech College Post-Sec.
1450 Collegeway 56187 507-372-2107

Wrenshall, Carlton, Pop. 349
Wrenshall SD 100 400/PK-12
PO Box 68 55797 218-384-4274
Shawn Northey, supt. Fax 384-4293
Wrenshall JSHS 200/7-12
PO Box 68 55797 218-384-4274
Sue Frank, prin. Fax 384-4293

Wykoff, Fillmore, Pop. 448
Kingsland SD 2137 800/PK-12
201 Bartlett St W 55990 507-352-4341
Larry Tompkins, supt. Fax 352-6071
www.kingsland.k12.mn.us
Kingsland MS 200/6-8
PO Box 96 55990 507-352-2731
Jim Hecimovich, prin. Fax 352-6071
Other Schools – See Spring Valley

Zimmerman, Sherburne, Pop. 4,724
Elk River Area SD 728
Supt. — See Elk River
Zimmerman JSHS 6-12
25900 4th St W 55398 763-241-3505
Marco Voce, prin. Fax 241-3506

Zumbrota, Goodhue, Pop. 2,966
Zumbrota-Mazeppa SD 2805
Supt. — See Mazeppa
Zumbrota-Mazeppa HS 400/9-12
705 Mill St 55992 507-732-7395
Erick Enger, prin. Fax 732-4511

MISSISSIPPI

MISSISSIPPI DEPARTMENT OF EDUCATION
PO Box 771, Jackson 39205-0771
Telephone 601-359-3513
Fax 601-359-3242
Website http://www.mde.k12.ms.us

Superintendent of Education Hank Bounds

MISSISSIPPI BOARD OF EDUCATION
PO Box 771, Jackson 39205-0771

Chairperson Claude Hartley

PUBLIC, PRIVATE AND CATHOLIC SECONDARY SCHOOLS

Aberdeen, Monroe, Pop. 6,227
Aberdeen SD 1,700/PK-12
PO Box 607 39730 662-369-4682
Lavon Reed, supt. Fax 369-0987
www.aberdeen.k12.ms.us
Aberdeen HS 500/9-12
PO Box 607 39730 662-369-8933
Natoya Jones, prin. Fax 369-6004
Shivers JHS 200/7-8
PO Box 607 39730 662-369-6241
James Swindell, prin. Fax 369-3207

Monroe County SD
Supt. — See Amory
Monroe County Technical Center Vo/Tech
50057 Airport Rd 39730 662-369-7845
Billy Loague, dir. Fax 369-9607

Ackerman, Choctaw, Pop. 1,631
Choctaw County SD 1,800/PK-12
PO Box 398 39735 662-285-4022
Dr. Arlene Amos, supt. Fax 285-4049
www.choctaw.k12.ms.us/
Ackerman JSHS 500/7-12
PO Box 296 39735 662-285-4101
Ronda Huffman, prin. Fax 285-4099
Choctaw County Career & Technology Ctr Vo/Tech
PO Box 775 39735 662-285-4152
Freddie King, prin. Fax 285-4199
Other Schools – See Weir

Amory, Monroe, Pop. 7,415
Amory SD 1,800/K-12
PO Box 330 38821 662-256-5991
Jim Sappington, supt. Fax 256-6302
www.amoryschools.com/
Amory HS 500/9-12
PO Box 330 38821 662-256-5753
David Poss, prin. Fax 256-5754
Amory MS 500/6-8
700 2nd Ave N 38821 662-256-5658
Cheryl Moore, prin. Fax 256-6304
Amory Vocational Center Vo/Tech
PO Box 330 38821 662-256-7601
Andy Cantrell, prin. Fax 256-1649

Monroe County SD 2,400/K-12
PO Box 209 38821 662-257-2176
Jimmy Dahlem, supt. Fax 257-2181
www.monroe.k12.ms.us
Advanced Learning Center 10-12
52251 Highway 25 S 38821 662-256-2495
Tim Dickerson, prin. Fax 256-2731
Hatley S 1,000/K-12
60186 Hatley Rd 38821 662-256-4563
Van Pearson, prin. Fax 256-5626
Other Schools – See Aberdeen, Hamilton, Smithville

Anguilla, Sharkey, Pop. 813
South Delta SD
Supt. — See Rolling Fork
South Delta MS 300/6-8
PO Box 487 38721 662-873-6535
James Tankson, prin. Fax 873-6073

Arcola, Washington, Pop. 525
Hollandale SD
Supt. — See Hollandale
Chambers MS 100/7-8
PO Box 396 38722 662-827-2438
Angela Johnson, prin. Fax 827-7168

Deer Creek S 200/K-12
PO Box 376 38722 662-827-5165
F. E. Allegrezza, admin. Fax 827-5128

Ashland, Benton, Pop. 564
Benton County SD 1,300/K-12
PO Box 247 38603 662-224-6252
Ron Wilkerson, supt. Fax 224-3607
www.benton.k12.ms.us
Ashland HS 200/9-12
PO Box 187 38603 662-224-6247
John Bostick, prin. Fax 224-3614
Ashland JHS 200/6-8
PO Box 368 38603 662-224-6485
Walker Tucker, prin. Fax 224-3609
Benton Co. Regional Vocational Center Vo/Tech
PO Box 754 38603 662-224-3108
Belinda Massengill, prin. Fax 224-3629
Other Schools – See Hickory Flat

Avon, Washington
Western Line SD 1,800/K-12
PO Box 50 38723 662-335-7186
Larry Green, supt. Fax 378-2285
www.westernline.k12.ms.us/
Riverside HS 500/7-12
PO Box 80 38723 662-335-4527
Michael Mcneece, prin. Fax 334-1797
Other Schools – See Greenville

Baldwyn, Lee, Pop. 3,352
Baldwyn SD 1,000/K-12
107 W Main St 38824 662-365-1000
Harvey G. Brooks, supt. Fax 365-1003
baldwyn.ms.schoolwebpages.com/
Baldwyn HS 200/9-12
512 N Fourth St 38824 662-365-1020
Ronnie Hill, prin. Fax 365-1028
Baldwyn MS 300/5-8
452 N Fourth St 38824 662-365-1015
Ronnie Hill, prin. Fax 365-1029

Bassfield, Jefferson Davis, Pop. 287
Jefferson Davis County SD
Supt. — See Prentiss
Bassfield JSHS 400/7-12
PO Box 370 39421 601-943-5391
Dr. L.C. Firle, prin. Fax 943-5790

Batesville, Panola, Pop. 7,708
South Panola SD 4,500/K-12
209 Boothe St 38606 662-563-9361
Dr. Keith Shaffer, supt. Fax 563-6077
www.southpanola.k12.ms.us
Batesville JHS 1,000/6-8
507 Tiger Dr 38606 662-563-4503
Darrell Tucker, prin. Fax 563-6038
South Panola HS 1,200/9-12
601 Tiger Dr 38606 662-563-4756
Dr. Gearl Loden, prin. Fax 563-8993

Batesville Job Corps Center Post-Sec.
821 Highway 51 S 38606 662-563-4656
North Delta S 500/PK-12
330 Green Wave Ln 38606 662-563-4536
John Howell, admin. Fax 563-5690

Bay Saint Louis, Hancock, Pop. 9,433
Bay St. Louis-Waveland SD 2,300/K-12
201 Carroll Ave 39520 228-467-6621
Kim Stasny, supt. Fax 466-4895
www.bwsd.org/
Bay HS 700/9-12
750 Blue Meadow Rd 39520 228-467-6611
Marca Alexander, prin. Fax 466-0883
Bay-Waveland MS 600/6-8
600 Pine St 39520 228-463-0315
Carolyn Barcelona, prin. Fax 467-5872

Our Lady Academy 300/7-12
222 S Beach Blvd 39520 228-467-7048
Sr. Jackie Howard, prin. Fax 467-1666
St. Stanislaus College Prep S 500/6-12
304 S Beach Blvd 39520 228-467-9057
Paul Verlander, prin. Fax 466-2972

Bay Springs, Jasper, Pop. 2,194
West Jasper Consolidated SD 1,700/K-12
PO Box 610 39422 601-764-2280
Kaye Patrick, supt. Fax 764-4490
www.westjasper.k12.ms.us/
Bay Springs HS 300/9-12
PO Box 389 39422 601-764-4151
Bryan Hoda, prin. Fax 764-6445
Bay Springs MS 300/5-8
PO Box 587 39422 601-764-3378
George Duke, prin. Fax 764-2329
Other Schools – See Heidelberg, Stringer

Sylva-Bay Academy 300/K-12
PO Box J 39422 601-764-2157
Dr. Lavahn Moss, hdmstr. Fax 764-6755

Belden, Lee

Tupelo Christian Preparatory S 400/PK-10
PO Box 367 38826 662-844-8604
Steve Orr, hdmstr. Fax 844-8620

Belmont, Tishomingo, Pop. 1,965
Tishomingo County Special Municipal SSD
Supt. — See Iuka
Belmont S 1,000/K-12
PO Box 250 38827 662-454-7924
Andy Chumbley, prin. Fax 454-7611

Belzoni, Humphreys, Pop. 2,541
Humphreys County SD 1,900/K-12
PO Box 678 39038 662-247-6000
Joyce McNair, supt. Fax 247-6004
www.humphreyscsd.com
Humphreys County HS 500/9-12
PO Box 658 39038 662-247-6040
Jimmie Washington, prin. Fax 247-6044
Humphreys County Vocational Center Vo/Tech
PO Box 672 39038 662-247-6030
Jimmy Hurst, prin. Fax 247-6034
Humphreys JHS 300/7-8
610 Cohn St 39038 662-247-6050
Barbara Williams, prin. Fax 247-6054

Humphreys Academy 200/1-12
PO Box 179 39038 662-247-1572
Mac W. Abernathy, admin. Fax 247-2776

Benoit, Bolivar, Pop. 584
Benoit SD 300/PK-12
PO Box 189 38725 662-742-3287
Dr. Beverly Culley, supt. Fax 742-3149
www.benoit.k12.ms.us/
Brooks S 300/PK-12
PO Box 8 38725 662-742-3257
Brenda Hopson, prin. Fax 742-3498

Benton, Yazoo

Benton Academy 500/K-12
PO Box 308 39039 662-673-9722
Cindy Shipp, prin. Fax 673-9090

Biloxi, Harrison, Pop. 50,209
Biloxi Public SD 6,200/K-12
PO Box 168 39533 228-374-1810
Paul Tisdale, supt. Fax 436-5171
www.biloxischools.net
Biloxi JHS 1,000/8-9
1424 Father Ryan Ave 39530 228-435-1421
Murray Killebrew, prin. Fax 435-1426
Biloxi SHS 1,100/10-12
1845 Richard Dr 39532 228-435-6105
Pamela Manners, prin. Fax 435-6353
Career Technology Center Vo/Tech
1845 Richard Dr 39532 228-435-6318
Glenn Dedeaux, prin. Fax 435-6318

St. Patrick HS 7-12
18300 Highway 67 39532 228-702-0500
Bobby Trosclair, prin. Fax 702-0511

Blue Mountain, Tippah, Pop. 713
South Tippah SD
Supt. — See Ripley
Blue Mountain S 300/K-12
408 W Mill St 38610 662-685-4706
Eddie Conner, prin. Fax 685-4706

Blue Mountain College Post-Sec.
PO Box 160 38610 662-685-4771

Blue Springs, Union, Pop. 153
Union County SD
Supt. — See New Albany
East Union S 800/K-12
1548 Highway 9 S 38828 662-534-6920
Walter Moore, prin. Fax 534-6542

Bogue Chitto, Lincoln, Pop. 689
Lincoln County SD
Supt. — See Brookhaven
Bogue Chitto S 600/K-12
385 Monticello St 39629 601-734-2723
Bill McGehee, prin. Fax 734-6020

Booneville, Prentiss, Pop. 8,585
Booneville SD 1,400/K-12
PO Box 358 38829 662-728-2171
Larry Morgan, supt. Fax 728-4940
www.booneville.k12.ms.us

Booneville HS 400/9-12
300B W George E Allen Dr 38829 662-728-5445
Rickey J. Neaves, prin. Fax 728-2953
Booneville MS 500/5-8
300A W George E Allen Dr 38829 662-728-5843
Rickey J. Neaves, prin. Fax 728-2427

Prentiss County SD 2,100/K-12
PO Box 179 38829 662-728-4911
Kenneth Chism, supt. Fax 728-2000
www2.mde.k12.ms.us/5900/index.html
Jumpertown S 300/K-12
717 Highway 4 W 38829 662-728-6378
Anthony Michael, prin. Fax 728-9420
Prentiss County Vocational Technical S Vo/Tech
302 W George E Allen Dr 38829 662-728-9259
Linda Sweeney, dir. Fax 728-9259
Thrasher S 400/K-12
167 County Road 1040 38829 662-728-5233
Cathy Trimble, prin. Fax 728-8107
Other Schools – See New Site, Wheeler

Northeast Mississippi Community College Post-Sec.
101 Cunningham Blvd 38829 662-728-7751

Brandon, Rankin, Pop. 19,390
Rankin County SD 14,900/K-12
PO Box 1359 39043 601-825-5590
Dr. Lynn Weathersby, supt. Fax 825-2618
www.rcsd.ms/
Brandon HS 1,200/9-12
3090 Highway 18 39042 601-825-2261
George Gilreath, prin. Fax 591-1037
Brandon MS 1,000/6-8
408 S College St 39042 601-825-5998
Buddy Bailey, prin. Fax 825-8402
Other Schools – See Florence, Flowood, Pelahatchie, Puckett, Richland, Sandhill

Brookhaven, Lincoln, Pop. 9,907
Brookhaven SD 2,900/PK-12
326 E Court St 39601 601-833-6661
Lea Barrett Ed.D., supt. Fax 833-4154
www.telapex.com/~bschool/index.html
Alexander JHS 500/7-8
713 Beauregard St 39601 601-833-7549
Johnny Waller, prin. Fax 835-5467
Brookhaven HS 800/9-12
443 E Monticello St 39601 601-833-4498
Susan Chapman, prin. Fax 823-3792
Brookhaven Technical Center Vo/Tech
325 E Court St 39601 601-833-8335
Don Coleman, dir. Fax 835-3985

Lincoln County SD 2,900/K-12
PO Box 826 39602 601-835-0011
Terry M. Brister, supt. Fax 833-3030
lcsd.k12.ms.us/
Enterprise S 700/K-12
1601 Highway 583 SE 39601 601-833-7284
Shannon Eubanks, prin. Fax 835-1261
Star S 1,000/K-12
1880 Highway 550 NW 39601 601-833-3473
Wayne Rogers, prin. Fax 835-1261
West Lincoln S 600/K-12
948 Jackson Liberty Dr SW 39601 601-833-4600
Jason Case, prin. Fax 833-9909
Other Schools – See Bogue Chitto

Brookhaven Academy 500/K-12
PO Box 3339 39603 601-833-4041
Dr. Miller Hammill, hdmstr. Fax 833-1846

Brooklyn, Forrest
Forrest County Agricultural HSD
215 Old Highway 49 E 39425 601-582-4102
Kyle Nobles, supt. Fax 545-9483
forrest.schoolspan.com
Forrest County Agricultural HS Vo/Tech
215 Old Highway 49 E 39425 601-582-4741
Karen Norwood, prin. Fax 582-9031

Bruce, Calhoun, Pop. 2,032
Calhoun County SD
Supt. — See Pittsboro
Bruce HS 400/7-12
PO Box 248 38915 662-983-3350
Rickie Vaughn, prin. Fax 983-3356

Byhalia, Marshall, Pop. 716
Marshall County SD
Supt. — See Holly Springs
Byhalia HS 500/9-12
278 Highway 309 S 38611 662-838-2206
Don Jackson, prin. Fax 838-2218
Byhalia MS 300/6-8
172 Highway 309 N 38611 662-838-2591
Kerry Reid, prin. Fax 838-5141

Caledonia, Monroe, Pop. 974
Lowndes County SD
Supt. — See Columbus
Caledonia HS 500/9-12
111 Confederate Dr 39740 662-356-2001
Mike Putnam, prin. Fax 356-2036
Caledonia MS 500/6-8
105 Confederate Dr 39740 662-356-2042
Karen Pittman, prin. Fax 356-2045

Calhoun City, Calhoun, Pop. 1,815
Calhoun County SD
Supt. — See Pittsboro
Calhoun City HS 400/6-12
PO Box 559 38916 662-628-5112
Dale Hays, prin. Fax 628-6240

Calhoun Academy 200/PK-12
PO Box C 38916 662-412-2087
Cameron Wright, hdmstr. Fax 412-2081

Camden, Madison
Madison County SD
Supt. — See Flora
Jackson HS 400/9-12
2000 Loring Rd 39045 662-468-2531
Reginal Barnes, prin. Fax 468-3430

Canton, Madison, Pop. 12,507
Canton SD 2,700/K-12
403 Lincoln St 39046 601-859-4110
Dwight Luckett, supt. Fax 859-4023
www.cantonpublicschooldistrict.com/
Canton Career Center Vo/Tech
487 N Union Street Ext 39046 601-859-3984
Michael Myrick, prin. Fax 859-1115
Canton HS 800/9-12
634 Finney Rd 39046 601-859-5325
Cleveland Anderson, prin. Fax 859-2554
Nichols MS 800/6-8
529 Mace St 39046 601-859-3741
Roosevelt Greenwood, prin. Fax 859-6561

Madison County SD
Supt. — See Flora
Madison Career & Tech Center Vo/Tech
1633 W Peace St 39046 601-859-6847
Mike Thomas, dir. Fax 859-0372
Madison Crossing MS 6-8
300 Yandell Rd 39046 601-898-7702
Brad Peets, prin. Fax 898-7709
Northeast Madison MS 300/6-8
820 Sulphur Springs Rd 39046 601-855-2406
Dr. Earnest Ward, prin. Fax 859-7615

Canton Academy 300/K-12
PO Box 116 39046 601-859-5231
David Glasgow, prin. Fax 859-5232

Carriere, Pearl River
Pearl River County SD 2,500/K-12
7441 Highway 11 39426 601-798-7744
Dennis Penton, supt. Fax 798-3527
www.prc.k12.ms.us/
Pearl River Central HS 700/9-12
7407 Highway 11 39426 601-798-1986
Loren Harris, prin. Fax 799-0068
Pearl River Central JHS 500/6-8
7391 Highway 11 39426 601-798-5654
Nileve Quave, prin. Fax 798-2822

Carrollton, Carroll, Pop. 397
Carroll County SD 1,100/K-12
PO Box 256 38917 662-237-9276
Billy Joe Ferguson, supt. Fax 237-9703
www.ccs.k12.ms.us/
Other Schools – See North Carrollton

Carroll Academy 400/K-12
PO Box 226 38917 662-237-6858
Carl Blaylock, hdmstr. Fax 237-9231

Carson, Jefferson Davis
Jefferson Davis County SD
Supt. — See Prentiss
Davis County Voc-Tech Center Vo/Tech
PO Box 70 39427 601-792-5005
Dr. Thomas Johnson, dir. Fax 792-2511

Carthage, Leake, Pop. 4,771
Leake County SD 3,200/K-12
PO Box 478 39051 601-267-4579
Melanie H. Hartley, supt. Fax 267-5283
www.leakesd.k12.ms.us
Carthage HS 400/9-12
704 N Jordan St 39051 601-267-7713
J.B. Norwood, prin. Fax 267-3738
Carthage JHS 400/6-8
801 Martin Luther King Dr 39051 601-267-8909
Haywood Hannah, prin. Fax 267-5902
Edinburg S 500/K-12
673 Mars Hill Rd 39051 601-267-7137
Steven Parrish, prin. Fax 267-3007
Leake County Vo-Tech Ctr Vo/Tech
703 N West St 39051 601-267-8442
Monte Ladner, prin. Fax 267-5150
Thomastown S 400/K-12
7100 Highway 429 39051 601-267-7896
Calvin Melton, prin. Fax 298-1295
Other Schools – See Walnut Grove

Academy of Hair Design #7 Post-Sec.
215 Highway 35 N 39051 601-267-8031
J & J Hair Design College Post-Sec.
116 E Franklin St 39051 601-267-3678

Centreville, Wilkinson, Pop. 1,591
Wilkinson County SD
Supt. — See Woodville
Winans MS 400/6-8
PO Box 610 39631 601-645-0008
Robert Williams, prin. Fax 645-0170

Centreville Academy 300/K-12
PO Box 70 39631 601-645-5912
Lea E. Hurst, prin. Fax 645-5940

Charleston, Tallahatchie, Pop. 2,054
East Tallahatchie Consolidated SD 1,600/K-12
411 E Chestnut St 38921 662-647-5524
William Tribble, supt. Fax 647-3720
www2.mde.k12.ms.us/6811/
Charleston HS 400/9-12
411 E Chestnut St 38921 662-647-5359
Ellis Smith, prin. Fax 647-3724
Charleston MS 700/4-8
411 E Chestnut St 38921 662-647-5486
Glinda Hardy, prin. Fax 647-2396
East Tallahatchie Vocational Ctr Vo/Tech
411 E Chestnut St 38921 662-647-5359
Barbara Herod-Hence, prin. Fax 647-3724

Strider Academy 200/K-12
3698 MS Highway 32 Central 38921 662-647-5833
Joe Bradshaw, prin. Fax 647-5702

Clarksdale, Coahoma, Pop. 19,297
Clarksdale Municipal SD 3,400/K-12
PO Box 1088 38614 662-627-8500
Dr. Wilma Wade, supt. Fax 627-8542
www.cdps.k12.ms.us/
Clarksdale HS 700/9-12
PO Box 1088 38614 662-627-8530
Olenza McBride, prin. Fax 627-8549
Higgins MS 400/6-8
PO Box 1088 38614 662-627-8550
Reginald Griffin, prin. Fax 627-8543
Keen Vocational Center Vo/Tech
PO Box 1088 38614 662-627-8580
Jim Cobbs, prin. Fax 627-8582
Oakhurst MS 400/6-8
PO Box 1088 38614 662-627-8560
Linda Downing, prin. Fax 627-8512

Coahoma County Agricultural HSD
3240 Friars Point Rd 38614 662-624-9424
Dr. Vivian Presley, supt. Fax 624-4315
www2.mde.k12.ms.us/1402
Coahoma Agricultural HS Vo/Tech
3240 Friars Point Rd 38614 662-621-4160
John Brown, prin. Fax 624-8045

Coahoma County SD 1,400/K-12
PO Box 820 38614 662-624-5448
Pauline Rhoads, supt. Fax 624-5512
www.coahoma.k12.ms.us
Coahoma County JSHS 300/7-12
1535 Lee Dr 38614 662-627-7378
James Bryant, prin. Fax 627-9731

Coahoma Community College Post-Sec.
3240 Friars Point Rd 38614 662-627-2571
Lee Academy 500/PK-12
415 Lee Dr 38614 662-627-7891
Ricky Weiss, prin. Fax 627-7896

Cleveland, Bolivar, Pop. 12,818
Cleveland SD 3,100/PK-12
305 Merritt Dr 38732 662-843-3529
Montrell Greene Ph.D., supt. Fax 843-9731
www.cleveland.k12.ms.us/
Cleveland Career Development & Tech Ctr. Vo/Tech
601 3rd St 38732 662-843-8818
Judy Stevenson, dir. Fax 843-0308
Cleveland HS 500/9-12
300 W Sunflower Rd 38732 662-843-2460
Arthur Holbrook, prin. Fax 843-2455
East Side HS 500/9-12
601 Lucy Seaberry Blvd 38732 662-843-2338
Richard Gray, prin. Fax 843-1900
Green JHS 300/7-8
205 N Bolivar Ave 38732 662-843-2456
Robert Montesi, prin. Fax 843-6820
Smith MS 300/7-8
715 S Martin Luther King Dr 38732 662-843-4355
Sylvester Cannon, prin. Fax 843-7334

Bayou Academy 400/PK-12
PO Box 417 38732 662-843-3708
Robert Foust, admin. Fax 843-9618
Delta State University Post-Sec.
Hwy 8 W 38733 662-846-3000

Clinton, Hinds, Pop. 26,017
Clinton SD 4,800/K-12
PO Box 300 39060 601-924-7533
Tommye Henderson, supt. Fax 924-6345
www.clintonpublicschools.com
Clinton Career Complex Vo/Tech
713 Lakeview Dr 39056 601-924-0247
Margera Harris, prin. Fax 924-1168
Clinton HS 1,000/10-12
401 Arrow Dr 39056 601-924-5656
James Reeves, prin. Fax 924-4622
Clinton JHS 800/7-8
711 Lakeview Dr 39056 601-924-0619
Anthony Goins, prin. Fax 924-7703
Sumner Hill JHS 400/9-9
400 W Northside Dr 39056 601-924-5510
Willie McInnis, prin. Fax 924-4182

Mississippi College Post-Sec.
PO Box 4086 39058 601-925-3000
Mount Salus Christian S 300/PK-12
PO Box 240 39060 601-924-6652
Phyllis Hurley, admin. Fax 924-3377

Coffeeville, Yalobusha, Pop. 947
Coffeeville SD 700/K-12
16849 Okahoma St 38922 662-675-8941
Eddie Anderson, supt. Fax 675-5004
www2.mde.k12.ms.us/8111/index.htm
Coffeeville HS 200/8-12
16849 Okahoma St 38922 662-675-8904
Michael Moore, prin. Fax 675-8905

Coldwater, Tate, Pop. 1,649
Tate County SD
Supt. — See Senatobia
Coldwater HS 300/9-12
671 West St 38618 662-622-5511
Lakimberly Gallagher, prin. Fax 622-7601
Senatobia/Tate Vocational-Technical Ctr Vo/Tech
165 W Central Ave 38618 662-622-5149
Richard Hartley, prin. Fax 622-7005

Collins, Covington, Pop. 2,761
Covington County SD 3,300/K-12
PO Box 1269 39428 601-765-4457
Isaac Sanford, supt. Fax 765-4102
www.cov.k12.ms.us/
Collins HS 500/9-12
PO Box 1479 39428 601-765-3203
Nick Hillman, prin. Fax 765-4116
Collins MS 500/5-8
PO Box 757 39428 601-765-4908
Kevin Jackson, prin. Fax 765-4100
Covington County Vocational Ctr Vo/Tech
PO Box 1268 39428 601-765-8253
Cecil Easterling, prin. Fax 765-6360
Other Schools – See Mount Olive, Seminary

Collinsville, Lauderdale, Pop. 1,364
Lauderdale County SD
Supt. — See Meridian
West Lauderdale S 1,200/5-12
9916 W Lauderdale Rd 39325 601-737-2277
Mike Ethridge, prin. Fax 737-2377

Columbia, Marion, Pop. 6,408
Columbia SD 1,800/K-12
613 Bryan Ave 39429 601-736-2366
Dr. Marietta James, supt. Fax 736-2653
www.columbiaschools.org
Columbia HS 500/9-12
1009 Broad St 39429 601-736-5334
Sheila Burbridge, prin. Fax 731-1068
Jefferson MS 400/6-8
611 Owens St 39429 601-736-2786
Raymond Powell, prin. Fax 731-3762

Marion County SD 2,000/PK-12
600 Broad St 39429 601-736-7193
Craig Robbins, supt. Fax 736-6274
East Marion JSHS 300/7-12
527 E Marion School Rd 39429 601-736-5100
Karl Mann, prin. Fax 736-8215
Loftin Career and Technology Ctr Vo/Tech
1140 Highway 13 S 39429 601-736-6095
Ron Fortenberry, prin. Fax 731-2077
Other Schools – See Foxworth

Columbia Academy 500/K-12
1548 Highway 98 E 39429 601-736-6418
H. Tom Porter, hdmstr. Fax 736-0098

Columbus, Lowndes, Pop. 24,425
Columbus Municipal SD 4,800/PK-12
PO Box 1308 39703 662-241-7400
Dr. Del Phillips, supt. Fax 241-7453
www.columbuscityschools.org/
Columbus HS 1,400/9-12
215 Hemlock St 39702 662-241-7200
Peirce McIntosh, prin. Fax 241-7205
Lee MS 800/7-8
1815 Military Rd 39701 662-241-7300
Cindy Wamble, prin. Fax 241-7305
McKellar Technology Center Vo/Tech
810 N Browder St 39702 662-241-7290
Cathy Kemp, prin. Fax 241-7293

Lowndes County SD 5,400/K-12
1053 Highway 45 S 39701 662-244-5000
Michael Halford, supt. Fax 244-5043
www.lowndes.k12.ms.us/
New Hope HS 800/9-12
3419 New Hope Rd 39702 662-244-4701
Bobby Eiland, prin. Fax 244-4725
New Hope MS 800/6-8
462 Center Rd 39702 662-244-4740
Joe York, prin. Fax 244-4758
West Lowndes HS 200/9-12
644 S Frontage Rd 39701 662-328-1369
Roosevelt Bridges, prin. Fax 327-3353
West Lowndes MS 200/6-8
1380 Motley Rd 39701 662-244-5060
Robert Smith, prin. Fax 327-4857
Other Schools – See Caledonia

Heritage Academy 700/K-12
625 Magnolia Ln 39705 662-327-5272
Tommy Gunn, admin. Fax 327-2226
Mississippi University for Women Post-Sec.
1100 College St Unit W1613 39701 662-329-7106

Como, Panola, Pop. 1,321
North Panola SD
Supt. — See Sardis
North Panola Career & Technical Center Vo/Tech
601 Railroad St 38619 662-526-5804
Dr. Jessie Edwards, prin. Fax 526-0160

Corinth, Alcorn, Pop. 14,256
Alcorn SD 3,700/K-12
PO Box 1420 38835 662-286-5591
Mike Wamsley, supt. Fax 286-7713
www.alcorn.k12.ms.us
Alcorn Career & Technology Center Vo/Tech
2101 Norman Rd 38834 662-286-7727
Edward M. Settle, prin. Fax 286-5674
Biggersville JSHS 200/7-12
571 Highway 45 38834 662-286-3542
Gary Johnson, prin. Fax 286-3023
Kossuth HS 400/9-12
15 County Road 604 38834 662-286-3653
Bo Seago, prin. Fax 286-3507
Kossuth MS 500/5-8
17 County Road 604 38834 662-286-7093
Fred Jackson, prin. Fax 286-6837
Other Schools – See Glen

Corinth SD 1,800/K-12
1204 N Harper Rd 38834 662-287-2425
Edward Lee Childress, supt. Fax 286-1885
www.corinth.k12.ms.us
Corinth HS 500/9-12
1310 N Harper Rd 38834 662-286-1000
Wayne Henry, prin. Fax 286-1003
Corinth JHS 300/7-8
1000 E 5th St 38834 662-286-1261
Brian Knippers, prin. Fax 287-0296

ICS The Wright Beauty College Post-Sec.
2077 Highway 72 E Anx 38834 662-287-0944

Crawford, Oktibbeha, Pop. 634
Oktibbeha County SD
Supt. — See Starkville
East Oktibbeha County HS 200/7-12
1780 Moor High Rd 39743 662-272-5660
Clifford Reynolds, prin. Fax 272-5231

Crystal Springs, Copiah, Pop. 5,913
Copiah County SD
Supt. — See Hazlehurst
Crystal Springs HS 500/9-12
201 Newton St 39059 601-892-4791
Angela Jones, prin. Fax 892-2071
Crystal Springs MS 800/4-8
2092 S Pat Harrison Dr 39059 601-892-2722
Adren McCoy, prin. Fax 892-9949

Mississippi Job Corps Center Post-Sec.
PO Box 817 39059 601-892-3348

Decatur, Newton, Pop. 1,426
Newton County SD 1,800/K-12
PO Box 97 39327 601-635-2317
Billy Pierce, supt. Fax 635-4025
www.newton.k12.ms.us
Newton Co. Career and Technical Center Vo/Tech
PO Box 742 39327 601-635-4138
Wayne McDill, prin. Fax 635-4024
Newton County HS 900/6-12
PO Box 278 39327 601-635-2718
Ken Stringer, prin. Fax 635-4045

East Central Community College Post-Sec.
PO Box 129 39327 601-635-2111
Newton County Academy 200/PK-12
PO Box 25 39327 601-635-2756
Mike Tucker, admin. Fax 635-3525

De Kalb, Kemper, Pop. 923
Kemper County SD 1,300/PK-12
PO Box 219 39328 601-743-2657
June Wright, supt. Fax 743-9297
kemper.k12.ms.us/
Kemper County HS 500/7-12
PO Box 429 39328 601-743-5292
Wayne Benn, prin. Fax 743-5952
Stennis Vocational Complex Vo/Tech
PO Box 88 39328 601-743-5226
Jacqueline Pollock, prin. Fax 743-2351

Kemper Academy 300/K-12
PO Box 459 39328 601-743-2232

D Iberville, Harrison, Pop. 7,868
Harrison County SD
Supt. — See Gulfport
D'Iberville HS 900/9-12
3320 Warrior Dr, 228-392-2678
Elmer Mullins, prin. Fax 392-7807
D'Iberville MS 600/5-8
10000 Gorenflo Rd, 228-392-1746
Wanda Morra, prin. Fax 392-9948

Drew, Sunflower, Pop. 2,215
Drew SD 700/K-12
286 W Park Ave 38737 662-745-6657
Dennis Silas, supt. Fax 745-6630
www2.mde.k12.ms.us/6720
Drew HS 200/9-12
288 Green Ave 38737 662-745-8586
Sammie Armstrong, prin. Fax 745-6630
Hunter MS 200/5-8
10 Swoope Rd 38737 662-745-8940
Sam Evans, prin. Fax 745-6630

North Sunflower Academy 200/K-12
148 Academy Rd 38737 662-756-2547
Charlie Francis, admin. Fax 756-2580

Durant, Holmes, Pop. 2,845
Durant SD 600/K-12
PO Box 669 39063 662-653-3175
Glennie Carlisle, supt. Fax 653-6151
Durant HS 200/7-12
PO Box 669 39063 662-653-3429
Willie Dale, prin. Fax 653-3472

Holmes County SD
Supt. — See Lexington
Williams-Sullivan S 500/K-12
14494 Highway 51 39063 662-653-6262
Sandra Winston, prin. Fax 653-6519

Ecru, Pontotoc, Pop. 1,015
Pontotoc County SD
Supt. — See Pontotoc
North Pontotoc HS 400/9-12
8324 Highway 15 N 38841 662-489-5612
Roger Smith, prin. Fax 489-7068
North Pontotoc MS 400/6-8
8324 Highway 15 N 38841 662-489-2479
Libby Young, prin. Fax 489-2985

Ellisville, Jones, Pop. 3,735
Jones County SD 7,700/K-12
5204 Highway 11 N 39437 601-649-5201
Thomas Prine, supt. Fax 649-1613
www.jones.k12.ms.us/
South Jones JSHS 1,000/7-12
313 Anderson St 39437 601-477-8452
Richard Shoemake, prin. Fax 477-3505
Other Schools – See Laurel

Jones County Junior College Post-Sec.
900 S Court St 39437 601-477-4000

Enterprise, Clarke, Pop. 454
Enterprise SD 800/K-12
503 S River Rd 39330 601-659-7965
Arthur McMillan, supt. Fax 659-3254
www.esd.k12.ms.us/
Enterprise HS 200/9-12
501 S River Rd 39330 601-659-4435
Mike Weathers, prin. Fax 659-3274
Enterprise MS 300/4-8
105 Short St 39330 601-659-7722
Pamela Jones, prin. Fax 659-7722

Ethel, Attala, Pop. 458
Attala County SD
Supt. — See Kosciusko
Ethel JSHS 300/7-12
PO Box 340 39067 662-674-5673
Roger Hill, prin. Fax 674-5817

Eupora, Webster, Pop. 2,265
Webster County SD 1,800/PK-12
212 W Clark Ave 39744 662-258-5921
Jimmy Pittman, supt. Fax 258-3134
www.webster.k12.ms.us/
Career & Technology Center Vo/Tech
102 Hall Rd 39744 662-258-8206
Jack Treloar, prin. Fax 258-6769
Eupora HS 500/7-12
404 W Fox Ave 39744 662-258-4041
James Mason, prin. Fax 258-4716
Other Schools – See Maben

Falkner, Tippah, Pop. 208
North Tippah SD
Supt. — See Tiplersville
Falkner JSHS 300/7-12
PO Box 139 38629 662-837-7892
Kurt Kutrip, prin. Fax 837-8800

Fayette, Jefferson, Pop. 2,133
Jefferson County SD 1,200/K-12
PO Box 157 39069 601-786-3721
John E. Dickey, supt. Fax 786-8441
Jefferson County HS 400/9-12
2277 Main St 39069 601-786-3919
Barbara Lewis, prin. Fax 786-6002
Jefferson County JHS 300/7-8
468 Highway 33 39069 601-786-3900
Michael Brown, prin. Fax 786-2273
Jefferson County Vocational Center Vo/Tech
205 Industrial Park Rd 39069 601-786-3642
David Perry, prin. Fax 786-2271

Flora, Madison, Pop. 1,478
Madison County SD 10,100/K-12
PO Box 159 39071 601-879-3000
Michael Kent, supt. Fax 879-3039
www.madison.k12.ms.us
East Flora MS 100/6-8
PO Box J 39071 601-879-3809
William Carter, prin. Fax 879-3158
Other Schools – See Camden, Canton, Madison, Ridgeland

Tri-County Academy 200/K-12
PO Box K 39071 601-879-8517
Keith Lockhart, prin. Fax 879-3373

Florence, Rankin, Pop. 3,063
Rankin County SD
Supt. — See Brandon
Florence HS 600/9-12
232 Highway 469 N 39073 601-845-2205
Tony Martin, prin. Fax 845-3752
Florence MS 500/6-8
123 Beverly Dr 39073 601-845-2862
Beverly Weathersby, prin. Fax 845-2114
McLaurin JSHS 500/7-12
130 Tiger Dr 39073 601-845-2247
Bill Lenington, prin. Fax 845-1170

Wesley College Post-Sec.
PO Box 1070 39073 800-748-9972

Flowood, Rankin, Pop. 6,762
Rankin County SD
Supt. — See Brandon
Northwest HS 1,300/9-12
5805 Highway 25 39232 601-992-2242
Jean Massey, prin. Fax 992-6005
Northwest MS 1,100/6-8
1 Paw Print Pl 39232 601-992-1329
Jacob McEwen, prin. Fax 992-1347

University Christian S 300/K-12
1240 Luckney Rd 39232 601-992-5333
Pam Ulrich, admin. Fax 992-5320

Forest, Scott, Pop. 6,029
Forest Municipal SD 1,600/K-12
325 Cleveland St 39074 601-469-3250
Skip Lathem, supt. Fax 469-3101
www2.mde.k12.ms.us/6220/
Forest HS 400/9-12
511 Cleveland St 39074 601-469-3255
Billy Wilbanks, prin. Fax 469-8250
Hawkins MS 500/5-8
803 E Oak St 39074 601-469-1474
Phylis Campbell, prin. Fax 469-8251

Scott County SD 3,700/K-12
100 E First St 39074 601-469-3861
Frank McCurdy, supt. Fax 469-3874
www.scott.k12.ms.us
Forest/Scott County Career & Tech Ctr Vo/Tech
521 Cleveland St 39074 601-469-2913
Chuck Wade, prin. Fax 469-2917
Scott Central S 900/K-12
2415 Old Jackson Rd 39074 601-469-4883
Dr. Janet McLin, prin. Fax 469-3746
Other Schools – See Lake, Morton, Sebastopol

Foxworth, Marion
Marion County SD
Supt. — See Columbia
West Marion JSHS 300/7-12
2 W Marion St 39483 601-736-6381
Craig Wise, prin. Fax 731-7937

French Camp, Choctaw, Pop. 389

French Camp Academy 200/9-12
1 Fine Pl 39745 662-547-6113
Daniel Martin, prin. Fax 547-6302

Fulton, Itawamba, Pop. 4,102
Itawamba County SD 3,700/PK-12
605 S Cummings St 38843 662-862-2159
F. G. Wiygul, supt. Fax 862-4713
www.itawamba.k12.ms.us/
Itawamba Agricultural HS 600/9-12
11900 Highway 25 S 38843 662-862-3104
Michael Nanney, prin. Fax 862-5494
Itawamba County Vocational Center Vo/Tech
PO Box 548 38843 662-862-3137
Gary Hamm, prin. Fax 862-3138
Other Schools – See Mantachie, Tremont

Itawamba Community College Post-Sec.
602 W Hill St 38843 662-862-8000

Gallman, Copiah

Copiah Academy 500/K-12
PO Box 125 39077 601-892-3770
Carol Rigby, prin. Fax 892-6222

Gautier, Jackson, Pop. 16,846
Pascagoula SD
Supt. — See Pascagoula
Gautier HS 800/9-12
4307 Gautier Vancleave Rd 39553 228-522-8783
Myrick Nicks, prin. Fax 522-8788
Gautier MS 800/6-8
1920 Graveline Rd 39553 228-522-8806
Emily Sims, prin. Fax 522-8813

Mississippi Gulf Coast Community College Post-Sec.
39553 228-497-9602

Glen, Alcorn, Pop. 294
Alcorn SD
Supt. — See Corinth
Alcorn Central HS 500/9-12
8 County Road 254 38846 662-286-8720
Tim Cannon, prin. Fax 286-8720
Alcorn Central MS 500/5-8
8A County Road 254 38846 662-286-3674
Dan Burcham, prin. Fax 286-6712

Goodman, Madison, Pop. 1,220

Holmes Community College Post-Sec.
PO Box 369 39079 662-472-2312

Greenville, Washington, Pop. 38,724
Greenville SD 7,200/PK-12
PO Box 1619 38702 662-334-7000
Fax 334-7021
www.gvillepublicschools.com/
Coleman MS 600/7-8
400 Highway 1 N 38701 662-334-7036
Linda Felton, prin. Fax 334-7040
Greenville Technical Center Vo/Tech
PO Box 4620 38704 662-334-7171
Sherry E. Jackson, prin. Fax 334-2848
Greenville-Weston HS - Greenville Campus 1,700/9-12
419 E Robertshaw St 38701 662-334-7062
Carey Spears, prin. Fax 334-7060
Greenville-Weston HS Weston Campus 9-12
901 Archer St 38701 662-334-7080
Carey Spears, prin. Fax 334-7091
Solomon MS 600/7-8
556 Bowman Blvd 38701 662-334-7050
Michael McNeece, prin. Fax 334-7053

Western Line SD
Supt. — See Avon
O'Bannon HS 400/7-12
PO Box 5816 38704 662-335-2637
Willie Goins, prin. Fax 334-1689

Delta Beauty College Post-Sec.
697 Delta Pl 38701 662-332-0587
Greenville Christian S 400/K-12
PO Box 4398 38704 662-332-0946
Ricky White, hdmstr. Fax 332-0948
St. Joseph HS 200/7-12
700 Golf St 38701 662-378-9711
Paul Artman, prin. Fax 378-3496
Washington S 800/K-12
1605 E Reed Rd 38703 662-334-4096
Rodney Brown, hdmstr. Fax 332-0434

Greenwood, LeFlore, Pop. 17,344
Greenwood SD 3,200/PK-12
401 Howard St 38930 662-453-4231
Dr. Leslie Daniels, supt. Fax 455-7409
www.greenwood.k12.ms.us/
Greenwood Career and Technical Ctr Vo/Tech
616 Sycamore Ave 38930 662-455-7414
Kirby Love, prin. Fax 455-8979
Greenwood HS 700/9-12
1209 Garrard Ave 38930 662-455-7450
Percy Powell, prin. Fax 455-7468
Greenwood MS 500/7-8
1200 Garrard Ave 38930 662-455-3661
Lorita Harris, prin. Fax 455-5559

Leflore County SD 3,000/K-12
1901 Highway 82 W 38930 662-453-8566
Cedell Pulley, supt. Fax 459-7265
www.leflorecountyschools.org
East MS 400/4-8
208 Meadowbrook Rd 38930 662-453-9182
Annie Johnson, prin. Fax 451-7734
Elzy HS 700/7-12
604 Elzy Ave 38930 662-453-3394
Byron Haynes, prin. Fax 459-7266
Leflore County Vocational Center Vo/Tech
PO Box 1158 38935 662-453-7706
Charles Streeter, prin. Fax 453-7733
Other Schools – See Itta Bena

Pillow Academy 900/K-12
69601 Highway 82 W 38930 662-453-1266
Termie Land, hdmstr. Fax 455-6484

Grenada, Grenada, Pop. 14,569
Grenada SD 4,400/K-12
PO Box 1940 38902 662-226-1606
Dr. Buddy Pender, supt. Fax 226-7994
www.gsd.k12.ms.us/
Grenada HS 1,100/9-12
1875 Fairground Rd 38901 662-226-8844
Robert Wade, prin. Fax 227-6109
Grenada MS 1,200/6-8
28 Jones Rd 38901 662-226-5135
Sean Brewer, prin. Fax 227-6106
Grenada Vocational Complex Vo/Tech
2035 Jackson Ave 38901 662-226-5969
Cliff Craven, prin. Fax 226-5992

Academy of Hair Design #1 Post-Sec.
2003B Commerce St 38901 662-226-2462
Kirk Academy 400/PK-12
PO Box 1008 38902 662-226-2791
Allen Smithers Ph.D., hdmstr. Fax 226-2791

Gulfport, Harrison, Pop. 72,464
Gulfport SD 6,100/K-12
2001 Pass Rd 39501 228-865-4600
Glen East, supt. Fax 865-4718
www.gulfportschools.k12.ms.us/
Bayou View MS 800/6-8
212 43rd St 39507 228-865-4633
Jerry Morgan, prin. Fax 867-1967
Gulfport Central MS 700/6-8
1310 42nd Ave 39501 228-870-1035
Eddie Peasant, prin. Fax 870-1041
Gulfport HS 1,600/9-12
100 Perry St 39507 228-896-7525
Michael Lindsey, prin. Fax 896-6867
Gulfport Vocational Annex S Vo/Tech
100 Perry St 39507 228-896-6011
David Fava, prin. Fax 896-7686

Harrison County SD 12,600/K-12
11072 Highway 49 39503 228-539-6500
Henry Arledge, supt. Fax 539-6507
www.harrison.k12.ms.us/
Harrison Central 9th Grade S 700/9-9
10453 Klein Rd 39503 228-832-6711
Becki Moore, prin. Fax 832-0940
Harrison Central HS 1,500/10-12
15600 School Rd 39503 228-832-2610
Russell Clark, prin. Fax 832-7433
Harrison County Vocational Complex Vo/Tech
15600 School Rd 39503 228-832-6652
Lary Thrash, prin. Fax 539-5965
North Gulfport MS 1,000/7-8
4715 Illinois Ave 39501 228-864-8944
Charles Dubra, prin. Fax 863-7326
Other Schools – See D Iberville

Blue Cliff College Post-Sec.
12251 Bernard Pkwy 39503 228-896-9727
Chris' Beauty College Post-Sec.
1265 Pass Rd 39501 228-864-2920
Gulfport Job Corps Center Post-Sec.
3300 20th St 39501 228-864-9691
Mississippi Gulf Coast Community College Post-Sec.
39507 228-896-3355
William Carey College Post-Sec.
1856 Beach Dr 39507 228-867-9201

Guntown, Lee, Pop. 1,311
Lee County SD
Supt. — See Tupelo
Guntown MS 700/6-8
PO Box 8 38849 662-348-8801
Phil Ferguson, prin. Fax 348-8810

Hamilton, Monroe
Monroe County SD
Supt. — See Amory
Hamilton S 700/K-12
40201 Hamilton Rd 39746 662-343-8307
Mark Howell, prin. Fax 343-5813

Hattiesburg, Forrest, Pop. 47,176
Forrest County SD 2,300/K-12
PO Box 1977 39403 601-545-6055
Kay H. Clay Ed.D., supt. Fax 545-6054
www.forrest.k12.ms.us/
North Forrest JSHS 400/7-12
693 Eatonville Rd 39401 601-545-9304
Jon Will, prin. Fax 545-9318

Hattiesburg SD 4,600/K-12
PO Box 1569 39403 601-582-5078
Annie Wimbish Ed.D., supt. Fax 582-6666
www.hpsd.k12.ms.us/
Burger MS 700/7-8
174 W S F Tatum Blvd 39401 601-582-0536
Joann Wynn, prin. Fax 582-0572
Hattiesburg HS 900/10-12
301 Hutchinson Ave 39401 601-544-0811
Yvonne Bryant, prin. Fax 582-2524
9th Grade Academy 300/9-9
301 Hutchinson Ave 39401 601-544-0811
Yvonne Bryant, prin. Fax 583-7325

Lamar County SD
Supt. — See Purvis
Oak Grove HS 1,200/9-12
5198 Old Highway 11 39402 601-264-7232
Wayne Folks, prin.
Oak Grove MS 1,000/6-8
2543 Old Highway 24 39402 601-264-4634
Ben Burnett, prin. Fax 264-0160

Academy of Hair Design #6 Post-Sec.
5912 US Highway 49 39401 601-583-1290
Alpha Christian S 200/K-10
PO Box 1361 39403 601-583-3144
Tonyia Fairley-Benton, admin. Fax 544-4090
Antonelli College Post-Sec.
1500 N 31st Ave 39401 601-583-4100
Forrest General Hospital Post-Sec.
6051 U S Highway 49 39401 601-288-4201
Hattiesburg Radiology Group Post-Sec.
5000 W 4th St 39402 601-288-4241
Presbyterian Christian HS 400/7-12
221 Bonhomie Rd 39401 601-582-4956
Chip Jones, prin. Fax 582-4960
Sacred Heart S 300/PK-12
608 Southern Ave 39401 601-583-8683
Dr. Maribeth Andereck, prin. Fax 583-8684
University of Southern Mississippi Post-Sec.
PO Box 5165 39406 601-266-5000
William Carey College Post-Sec.
498 Tuscan Ave 39401 800-962-5991

Hazlehurst, Copiah, Pop. 4,372
Copiah County SD 2,900/PK-12
254 W Gallatin St 39083 601-894-1341
Rickey Clopton, supt. Fax 894-2634
www.copiahcounty.org/School%20District.htm
Other Schools – See Crystal Springs, Wesson

Hazlehurst CSD 1,700/PK-12
119 Robert McDaniel Dr 39083 601-894-1152
Jay Norals, supt. Fax 894-3170
Hazlehurst HS 500/9-12
101 S Haley St 39083 601-894-2489
Marvin Davis, prin. Fax 894-2033
Hazlehurst MS 500/5-8
112 School Dr 39083 601-894-3463
James Holloway, prin. Fax 894-2629

Heidelberg, Jasper, Pop. 810
East Jasper SD 1,100/K-12
PO Box E 39439 601-787-3281
Dr. Beverly Bullard, supt. Fax 787-3410
www.eastjasper.k12.ms.us
Heidelberg JSHS 500/7-12
PO Box M 39439 601-787-3414
Dr. Odessa Borten, prin. Fax 787-3416

West Jasper Consolidated SD
Supt. — See Bay Springs
Jasper County Career Development Ctr Vo/Tech
2419 Highway 528 39439 601-787-4753
Stephen Sullivan, prin. Fax 787-2060

Heidelberg Academy 200/K-12
PO Box Q 39439 601-787-4589
Jack Thompson, hdmstr. Fax 787-3371

Hernando, DeSoto, Pop. 9,890
DeSoto County SD 24,000/K-12
5 E South St 38632 662-429-5271
Milton Kuykendall, supt. Fax 429-4198
www.desoto.k12.ms.us/
Hernando HS 1,000/9-12
805 Dilworth Ln 38632 662-429-4170
Freddie Joseph, prin. Fax 449-1100
Hernando MS 900/6-8
700 Dilworth Ln 38632 662-429-4154
Jerry Darnell, prin. Fax 429-4189
Other Schools – See Horn Lake, Lake Cormorant, Olive Branch, Southaven

Hickory Flat, Benton, Pop. 542
Benton County SD
Supt. — See Ashland
Hickory Flat S 600/K-12
1005 Spruce St 38633 662-333-7731
Gerald Clark, prin. Fax 333-4127

Hollandale, Washington, Pop. 3,189
Hollandale SD 900/K-12
PO Box 128 38748 662-827-2276
Willie Amos, supt. Fax 827-5261
www2.mde.k12.ms.us/7611/
Simmons HS 200/9-12
PO Box 428 38748 662-827-2228
Roger Liddell, prin. Fax 827-2231
Other Schools – See Arcola

Holly Springs, Marshall, Pop. 8,014
Holly Springs SD 1,700/K-12
840 Highway 178 E 38635 662-252-2183
Irene Walton, supt. Fax 252-7718
www.hssd.k12.ms.us
Holly Springs HS 500/9-12
165 N Walthall St 38635 662-252-4371
John Chase, prin. Fax 252-7720
Holly Springs JHS 300/7-8
325 E Falconer Ave 38635 662-252-7737
Lonnie Williams, prin.
Holly Springs Vocational S Vo/Tech
410 E Falconer Ave 38635 662-252-2071
Bob Bigham, prin. Fax 252-7719

Marshall County SD 3,400/K-12
158 E College Ave 38635 662-252-4271
Dan Ranolph, supt. Fax 252-5129
www.mcs.k12.ms.us/
Byers S 900/K-12
4178 Highway 72 38635 662-851-7826
Gary Hannah, prin. Fax 851-4027
Other Schools – See Byhalia, Potts Camp

Marshall Academy 400/PK-12
100 Academy Dr 38635 662-252-3449
Jane Hubbard, admin. Fax 252-4510
Rust College Post-Sec.
150 Rust Ave 38635 662-252-8000

Horn Lake, DeSoto, Pop. 22,151
DeSoto County SD
Supt. — See Hernando
Horn Lake HS 1,500/9-12
3360 Church Rd 38637 662-393-5273
Jim Ferguson, prin. Fax 393-5275
Horn Lake MS 1,500/6-8
6125 Hurt Rd 38637 662-393-7443
Van Alexander, prin. Fax 342-5039

Houlka, Chickasaw, Pop. 553
Chickasaw County SD 500/PK-12
PO Box 480 38850 662-568-3333
Kathy Davis, supt. Fax 568-2993
chickasaw.k12.ms.us/
Houlka S 500/PK-12
PO Box 277 38850 662-568-2772
William W. Cotton, prin. Fax 568-7931

Houston, Chickasaw, Pop. 3,980
Houston SD 1,900/K-12
PO Box 351 38851 662-456-3332
Dr. Steve Coker, supt. Fax 456-5259
www.houston.k12.ms.us
Houston HS 500/9-12
PO Box 568 38851 662-456-3320
Rick Allen, prin. Fax 456-3527
Houston MS 400/6-8
PO Box 192 38851 662-456-5174
Burnell McDonald, prin. Fax 456-2254
Houston Vocational Center Vo/Tech
PO Box 608 38851 662-456-3748
Beverly James, prin. Fax 456-5172

Independence, Tate
Tate County SD
Supt. — See Senatobia
Independence HS 500/9-12
3184 Highway 305, 662-233-4691
Mike Neyman, prin. Fax 233-2214
Independence MS 300/5-8
505 Sycamore Rd, 662-233-0250
Malinda White, prin. Fax 233-0253

Indianola, Sunflower, Pop. 11,321
Indianola SD 2,600/K-12
702 Highway 82 E 38751 662-887-2654
Dr. King Rush, supt. Fax 887-7042
www.indianolaschools.org/

Gentry HS 600/10-12
801 BB King Rd 38751 662-887-2433
Mario Kirsey, prin. Fax 887-7410
Merritt MS 500/6-8
705 Kinlock Rd 38751 662-887-1449
Dr. Valerie Simpson, prin. Fax 887-5247
Pennington JHS 200/9-9
701 Chapman St 38751 662-887-1852
Sam Brock, prin. Fax 887-5453

Sunflower County SD 1,800/K-12
PO Box 70 38751 662-887-4919
Thomas Edwards, supt. Fax 887-7051
www2.mde.k12.ms.us/6700/scsd.html
Other Schools – See Moorhead, Ruleville

Indianola Academy 500/PK-12
PO Box 967 38751 662-887-2025
Dr. Sammy Henderson, hdmstr. Fax 887-3117

Itta Bena, LeFlore, Pop. 2,019
Leflore County SD
Supt. — See Greenwood
Leflore County HS 500/7-12
PO Box 564 38941 662-254-7762
Charles Ollie, prin. Fax 254-7530

Mississippi Valley State University Post-Sec.
14000 Highway 82 W # 7222 38941 662-254-9041

Iuka, Tishomingo, Pop. 2,987
Tishomingo County Special Municipal SSD 3,200/K-12
1620 Paul Edmondson Dr 38852 662-423-3206
John Moore, supt. Fax 423-7313
www.tishomingo.k12.ms.us
Iuka MS 400/5-8
507 W Quitman St 38852 662-423-3316
Jimmy Smith, prin. Fax 423-2426
Tishomingo County HS 600/9-12
701 Highway 72 38852 662-423-7300
Terry King, prin. Fax 423-7307
Other Schools – See Belmont, Tishomingo

Jackson, Hinds, Pop. 177,977
Jackson SD 29,800/PK-12
PO Box 2338 39225 601-960-8700
Earl Watkins Ph.D., supt. Fax 960-8713
www.jackson.k12.ms.us
Bailey Magnet HS 500/9-12
1900 N State St 39202 601-960-5343
Calvin Lockett, prin. Fax 592-2496
Blackburn MS 500/6-8
1311 W Pearl St 39203 601-960-5329
Bobby Brown, prin. Fax 360-2601
Brinkley MS 500/6-8
3535 Albermarle Rd 39213 601-987-3573
Dr. Leroy Pope, prin. Fax 987-3746
Callaway HS 900/9-12
601 Beasley Rd 39206 601-987-3535
Clinton Johnson, prin. Fax 987-3729
Chastain MS 1,000/6-8
4650 Manhattan Rd 39206 601-987-3550
Dr. Michael Ellis, prin. Fax 987-4930
Forest Hill HS 1,000/9-12
2607 Raymond Rd 39212 601-371-4313
Norm Chappell, prin. Fax 371-4379
Hardy MS 600/6-8
545 Ellis Ave 39209 601-960-5362
Nehru Brown, prin. Fax 360-2686
Hill HS 1,100/9-12
2185 Fortune St 39204 601-960-5354
Lydia Haynes, prin. Fax 360-2625
Jackson Career Development Center Vo/Tech
2703 First Ave 39209 601-960-5322
Isaac Norwood, prin. Fax 960-5411
Lanier HS 800/9-12
833 Maple St 39203 601-960-5369
Stanley Blackmon, prin. Fax 960-4047
Murrah HS 1,100/9-12
1400 Murrah Dr 39202 601-960-5380
Dr. Roy Brookshire, prin. Fax 360-2622
Northwest Jackson MS 600/6-8
7020 Medgar Evers Blvd 39213 601-987-3609
Dr. Edward Buck, prin. Fax 987-4975
Peeples MS 1,000/6-8
290 Treehaven Dr 39212 601-371-4345
Sam Kursar, prin. Fax 371-4722
Powell MS 900/6-8
3655 Livingston Rd 39213 601-987-3580
Dr. Freddrick Murray, prin. Fax 987-3583
Provine HS 1,000/9-12
2400 Robinson St 39209 601-960-5393
Tex Red, prin. Fax 360-2606
Rowan MS 300/6-8
136 E Ash St 39202 601-960-5349
Tony Winters, prin. Fax 960-4046
Siwell Road MS 700/6-8
1983 N Siwell Rd 39209 601-923-2550
Dr. Josephine Kelly, prin. Fax 923-2570
Whitten MS 800/6-8
210 Daniel Lake Blvd 39212 601-371-4309
Marvin Grayer, prin. Fax 371-4728
Wingfield HS 1,000/9-12
1985 Scanlon Dr 39204 601-371-4350
Robert Mack, prin. Fax 371-4734

Academy of Hair Design #3 Post-Sec.
1815 Terry Rd 39204 601-372-9800
Antonelli College Post-Sec.
2323 Lakeland Dr 39232 601-362-9991
Belhaven College Post-Sec.
1500 Peachtree St 39202 601-968-5927
Christ Missionary & Industrial S 200/PK-12
3910 Main St 39213 601-366-6413
Mary Seay, hdmstr. Fax 366-5152
Education Center S 200/1-12
4080 Old Canton Rd 39216 601-982-2812
Lynn Macon, prin. Fax 982-2827
Hillcrest Christian S 700/K-12
4060 S Siwell Rd 39212 601-372-0149
Tom Prather, hdmstr. Fax 371-8061
Hinds Community College Post-Sec.
1750 Chadwick Dr 39204 601-372-6507
Jackson Academy 1,500/PK-12
PO Box 14978 39236 601-362-9676
Pat Taylor, hdmstr. Fax 364-5722
Jackson Preparatory S 800/6-12
PO Box 4940 39296 601-939-8611
Susan Lindsay, hdmstr. Fax 936-4068
Jackson State University Post-Sec.
1440 J R Lynch St 39217 601-979-2100
Magnolia College of Cosmetology Post-Sec.
4725 I-55 N 39206 601-362-6940
Millsaps College Post-Sec.
PO Box 15495 39210 601-974-1000
Mississippi Baptist Medical Center Post-Sec.
1225 N State St 39202 601-968-5130
Mississippi College Post-Sec.
151 E Griffith St 39201 601-353-3907
Mississippi School for the Blind Post-Sec.
1252 Eastover Dr 39211 601-984-8000
Mississippi School for the Deaf Post-Sec.
1253 Eastover Dr 39211 601-984-8001
Reformed Theological Seminary Post-Sec.
5422 Clinton Blvd 39209 601-923-1600
St. Dominic-Jackson Memorial Hospital Post-Sec.
969 Lakeland Dr 39216 601-364-6935
Traxler School of Hair Post-Sec.
2845 Suncrest Dr 39212 601-371-3253
University of Mississippi Medical Center Post-Sec.
2500 N State St 39216 601-984-1010
Virginia College Post-Sec.
5360 I 55 N 39211 601-977-0960
Wesley Biblical Seminary Post-Sec.
PO Box 9938 39286 601-957-1314

Kilmichael, Montgomery, Pop. 735
Montgomery County SD
Supt. — See Winona
Montgomery County HS 200/7-12
PO Box 278 39747 662-262-5535
Lewis Zeigler, prin. Fax 262-4218

Kiln, Hancock, Pop. 1,262
Hancock County SD 4,200/K-12
17304 Highway 603 39556 228-255-0376
David Kopf, supt. Fax 255-0378
www.hancock.k12.ms.us
Hancock HS 1,100/9-12
7084 Stennis Airport Rd 39556 228-467-2251
Joel Myrick, prin. Fax 467-2689
Hancock MS 1,000/6-8
7070 Stennis Airport Rd 39556 228-467-1889
Denise Wilkinson, prin. Fax 467-2812
Hancock Vocational Technical Center Vo/Tech
7180 Stennis Airport Rd 39556 228-467-3568
Rick Saucier, prin. Fax 466-4944

Kosciusko, Attala, Pop. 7,334
Attala County SD 1,300/PK-12
100 Courthouse Ste 3 39090 662-289-2801
Curtis Burrell, supt. Fax 289-2804
www2.mde.k12.ms.us/0400/
Kosciusko-Attala County Voc Complex Vo/Tech
450 Highway 12 E 39090 662-289-2689
Tony Holder, prin. Fax 289-2701
Other Schools – See Ethel, Mc Adams

Kosciusko SSD 2,100/K-12
206 S Huntington St 39090 662-289-4771
Dr. David Sistrunk, supt. Fax 289-1177
Kosciusko HS 600/9-12
206 S Huntington St 39090 662-289-2424
Jonathan Carnes, prin. Fax 289-8767
Kosciusko JHS 500/6-8
206 S Huntington St 39090 662-289-3737
Tony McGee, prin. Fax 289-5388

Magnolia Bible College Post-Sec.
PO Box 1109 39090 662-289-2896

Lake, Newton, Pop. 404
Scott County SD
Supt. — See Forest
Lake Attendance Center 500/K-12
24442 Highway 80 39092 601-775-3248
Randy Martin, prin. Fax 775-3861
Lake MS 300/5-8
1770 E Scott Rd 39092 601-775-3614
Kathy Myers, prin. Fax 775-8830

Lake Cormorant, DeSoto
DeSoto County SD
Supt. — See Hernando
Lake Cormorant MS 5-8
3203 Wilson Mill Rd 38641 662-781-0778
Rhonda Guice, prin.

Laurel, Jones, Pop. 18,298
Jones County SD
Supt. — See Ellisville
Fatherree Voc-Tech Center Vo/Tech
2409 Moose Dr 39440 601-425-2378
Bruce Strickland, prin. Fax 425-2349
Northeast Jones JSHS 1,100/7-12
68 Northeast Dr 39443 601-425-2347
A. Dwain Strickland, prin. Fax 649-1736
West Jones JSHS 1,300/7-12
254 Springhill Rd 39443 601-729-8144
Mark Herrington, prin. Fax 729-8148

Laurel SD 2,900/PK-12
PO Box 288 39441 601-649-6391
Dr. Glenn McGee, supt. Fax 649-6398
www.laurelschools.com
Jones MS 500/7-8
1125 N 5th Ave 39440 601-428-5312
Carl Michael Day, prin. Fax 426-6775
Laurel HS 700/9-12
1100 W 12th St 39440 601-649-4145
Carolyn Stone, prin. Fax 426-2347
Laurel Vocational Technical Center Vo/Tech
1100 W 11th St 39440 601-649-4144
Lydia Sanders, prin. Fax 428-1390

Laurel Christian S 400/PK-12
PO Box 8425 39441 601-649-3999
Rick Bartley, hdmstr. Fax 649-1027
Mississippi College of Beauty Culture Post-Sec.
732 Sawmill Rd 39440 601-428-7127
Southeastern Baptist College Post-Sec.
4229 Highway 15 N 39440 601-426-6346

Leakesville, Greene, Pop. 1,007
Greene County SD 2,000/K-12
PO Box 1329 39451 601-394-2364
Richard Fleming, supt. Fax 394-5542
www.greene.k12.ms.us/
Greene County HS 500/9-12
4336 High School Rd 39451 601-394-5290
Mike Chatham, prin. Fax 394-4878
Greene County Vo-Tech Complex Vo/Tech
173 Vo Tech Rd 39451 601-394-2973
Mike Mizell, prin. Fax 394-5953
Leakesville JHS 400/5-8
PO Box 1479 39451 601-394-2495
Debbie McLeod, prin. Fax 394-5690

Learned, Hinds, Pop. 47

Rebul Academy 300/PK-12
5257 Learned Rd 39154 601-885-6802
Jack Rice, hdmstr. Fax 885-6843

Leland, Washington, Pop. 5,157
Leland SD 900/K-12
408 4th St 38756 662-686-5000
Johnnye Breland, supt. Fax 686-5029
www2.mde.k12.ms.us/7612/
Leland HS 300/9-12
403 E 3rd St 38756 662-686-5020
Glenda Jackson, prin. Fax 686-5027
Leland School Park MS 300/6-8
200 Milam St 38756 662-686-5017
Connie Bowman, prin. Fax 686-5042
Leland Vo Complex Vo/Tech
S Deer Creek Dr 38756 662-686-5025
Allen Clark, prin. Fax 686-5024

Lexington, Holmes, Pop. 1,941
Holmes County SD 3,500/K-12
PO Box 630 39095 662-834-2175
Stephen Bailey, supt. Fax 834-9060
holmes.k12.ms.us/
Holmes County Vocational Center Vo/Tech
PO Box 390 39095 662-834-3052
Frank Kimes, prin. Fax 834-3053
Marshall S 1,000/K-12
12572 Highway 12 39095 662-235-5113
George Jackson, prin. Fax 235-5551
McClain HS 800/6-12
PO Box 270 39095 662-834-2172
Dr. Percy Washington, prin. Fax 834-2709
Other Schools – See Durant

Central Holmes Christian S 300/PK-12
130 Robert E Lee Dr 39095 662-834-3011
Terry Cox, hdmstr. Fax 834-1011

Liberty, Amite, Pop. 686
Amite County SD 1,300/K-12
PO Box 378 39645 601-657-4361
Charles E. Kirkfield, supt. Fax 657-4291
www.amite.k12.ms.us/
Amite County HS 300/9-12
PO Box 328 39645 601-657-8920
David Terrell, prin. Fax 657-4044
Amite County Vocational Educational S Vo/Tech
PO Box 770 39645 601-657-8081
Augustus Russ, prin. Fax 657-8098

Amite School Center 300/K-12
PO Box 354 39645 601-657-8896

Long Beach, Harrison, Pop. 17,283
Long Beach SD 3,200/K-12
19148 Commission Rd 39560 228-864-1146
Carrolyn Hamilton, supt. Fax 863-3196
www.lbsd.k12.ms.us
Long Beach HS 1,000/9-12
300 E Old Pass Rd 39560 228-863-6945
Susan Whiten, prin. Fax 864-8961
Long Beach MS 800/6-8
204 N Cleveland Ave 39560 228-864-3370
Mary Jean Harvey, prin. Fax 867-1789

New Life Academy 50/K-12
20201 28th St 39560 228-865-0034
Larry Ficklin, supt. Fax 863-2885
University of Southern Mississippi Post-Sec.
730 E Beach Blvd 39560 228-865-4500

Lorman, Jefferson

Alcorn State University Post-Sec.
PO Box 359 39096 601-877-6147

Louisville, Winston, Pop. 6,797
Louisville Municipal SD 2,800/K-12
PO Box 909 39339 662-773-3411
Harry Kemp, supt. Fax 773-4013
louisville.k12.ms.us/
Eiland MS 300/7-8
508 Camille Ave 39339 662-773-9001
Penny Hill, prin. Fax 773-4016
Louisville HS 500/9-12
200 Ivy Ave 39339 662-773-3431
Ken McMullan, prin. Fax 773-4017
Waiya S 500/K-12
13937 Highway 397 39339 662-773-6770
Janie Hailey-Tarlton, prin. Fax 773-6764
Winston-Louisville Vocational Center Vo/Tech
204 Ivy Ave 39339 662-773-6152
James Webb, dir. Fax 773-9572
Other Schools – See Noxapater

Grace Christian S 200/PK-12
173 McLeod Rd 39339 662-773-8524
Thomas Dickson, hdmstr. Fax 773-4308
Winston Academy 400/PK-12
PO Box 545 39339 662-773-3569
Farrell Rigby, prin. Fax 773-8373

Lucedale, George, Pop. 2,890
George County SD 4,100/K-12
5152 Main St 39452 601-947-6993
Donnie Howell, supt. Fax 947-8805
www.george.k12.ms.us

George County HS 1,100/9-12
9284 Highway 63 S 39452 601-947-3116
Paul Wallace, prin. Fax 947-1076
George County MS 1,000/6-8
330 Church St 39452 601-947-3106
Patsy Horn, prin. Fax 947-6004

Lumberton, Lamar, Pop. 2,476
Lumberton SD 800/K-12
PO Box 551 39455 601-796-2441
Dr. Robert Walker, supt. Fax 796-2051
www.lumberton.k12.ms.us/
Lumberton HS 200/9-12
PO Box 551 39455 601-796-2451
Dennis Holder, prin. Fax 796-7907

Bass Memorial Academy 100/9-12
6433 U S Highway 11 39455 601-794-8561
Fax 794-8881

Maben, Webster, Pop. 765
Oktibbeha County SD
Supt. — See Starkville
West Oktibbeha County HS 200/7-12
PO Box 506 39750 662-263-8106
Helen Kennard, prin. Fax 263-5440

Webster County SD
Supt. — See Eupora
East Webster HS 300/7-12
RR 2 Box 468 39750 662-263-5321
Bill Brand, prin. Fax 263-4518

Mc Adams, Attala
Attala County SD
Supt. — See Kosciusko
Mc Adams JSHS 300/7-12
PO Box 127 39107 662-289-3838
Bryan Weaver, prin. Fax 289-7181

Mc Comb, Pike, Pop. 11,957
McComb SD 2,800/K-12
PO Box 868, 601-684-4661
Pat Cooper, supt. Fax 249-4732
www.mccomb.k12.ms.us
Business & Technology Complex Vo/Tech
1003 Virginia Ave, 601-684-5288
Betty Wilson, prin. Fax 249-2454
Denman JHS 500/7-8
1211 Louisiana Ave, 601-684-2387
Tom Catchings, prin. Fax 249-3564
Mc Comb HS 700/9-12
310 7th St, 601-684-5678
Levander German, prin. Fax 249-4737
Other Schools – See Summit

Parklane Academy 900/K-12
1115 Parklane Dr, 601-684-7841
Billy Swindle, admin. Fax 684-4166
SW Mississippi Regional Medical Center Post-Sec.
PO Box 1307, 601-249-1807

Macon, Noxubee, Pop. 2,353
Noxubee County SD 2,100/PK-12
PO Box 540 39341 662-726-4527
Kevin Jones Ed.D., supt. Fax 726-2809
www.noxcnty.k12.ms.us
Liddell MS 500/5-8
PO Box 229 39341 662-726-4880
Louise Tate, prin. Fax 726-5044
Noxubee County HS 600/9-12
PO Box 590 39341 662-726-4428
Royce Stephens, prin. Fax 726-5048
Noxubee County Vocational Center Vo/Tech
PO Box 266 39341 662-726-4225
Annie Snow, dir. Fax 726-2804

Central Academy 300/K-12
PO Box 231 39341 662-726-4817

Madden, Leake

Leake Academy 500/PK-12
PO Box 128 39109 601-267-4461
Jerry Crowe, hdmstr. Fax 267-6933

Madison, Madison, Pop. 16,737
Madison County SD
Supt. — See Flora
Madison Central HS 1,300/9-12
1417 Highland Colony Pkwy 39110 601-856-7121
Edith Mitchell, prin. Fax 853-2712
Madison MS 1,400/6-8
1365 Mannsdale Rd 39110 601-605-4171
Ron Morrison, prin. Fax 853-2254
Scott S 500/9-9
200 Crawford St 39110 601-605-0054
Ted Poore, prin. Fax 898-5017

Madison-Ridgeland Academy 900/K-12
7601 Old Canton Rd 39110 601-856-4455
Tommy Thompson, hdmstr. Fax 853-3835
St. Joseph Catholic HS 400/7-12
PO Box 2027 39130 601-898-4800
William Heller, prin. Fax 898-4689

Magee, Simpson, Pop. 4,294
Simpson County SD
Supt. — See Mendenhall
Magee HS 500/9-12
501 Choctaw St E 39111 601-849-2263
George Huffman, prin. Fax 849-2144
Magee MS 600/5-8
300 1st St NE 39111 601-849-3334
Terrell Luckey, prin. Fax 849-6130

Magnolia, Pike, Pop. 2,079
South Pike SD 2,000/K-12
250 W Bay St 39652 601-783-3742
Dr. Bill Gunnell, supt. Fax 783-6733
www.southpike.org
South Pike HS 500/9-12
205 W Myrtle St 39652 601-783-2312
Alonzell Dillon, prin. Fax 783-4179
South Pike JHS 300/7-8
275 W Myrtle St 39652 601-783-2574
Joe Leavy, prin. Fax 783-2272
South Pike Vo Ctr Vo/Tech
252 W Bay St 39652 601-783-5832
Brenda Jackson, prin. Fax 783-3491

Mantachie, Itawamba, Pop. 1,134
Itawamba County SD
Supt. — See Fulton
Mantachie HS 500/7-12
PO Box 38 38855 662-282-4276
Scott Blackley, prin. Fax 282-4270

Marks, Quitman, Pop. 1,893
Quitman County SD 1,600/K-12
PO Box E 38646 662-326-5451
Valmadge Towner, supt. Fax 326-3694
www2.mde.k12.ms.us/6000/
Palmer JSHS 500/8-12
PO Box 350 38646 662-326-5191
Edgar Holman, prin. Fax 326-8918
Quitman County Vocational S Vo/Tech
PO Box 117 38646 662-326-8427
Charles Phipps, prin. Fax 326-8430

Delta Academy 300/PK-12
PO Box 70 38646 662-326-8164
Shirley Morris, admin. Fax 326-3201

Meadville, Franklin, Pop. 508
Franklin County SD 1,500/PK-12
PO Box 605 39653 601-384-2340
Lona Thomas, supt. Fax 384-2393
www2.mde.k12.ms.us/1900/index.htm
Franklin County Vo-Tech Ctr Vo/Tech
PO Box 155 39653 601-384-5889
Jack Hollingsworth, prin. Fax 384-5578
Franklin HS 400/9-12
PO Box 666 39653 601-384-2965
Marion Bilbo, prin. Fax 384-2498
Franklin JHS 300/6-8
236 Edison St S 39653 601-384-2441
Marshall Bankston, prin. Fax 384-2085

Mendenhall, Simpson, Pop. 2,544
Simpson County SD 4,200/K-12
111 Education Ln 39114 601-847-1562
Jack McAlpin, supt. Fax 847-8003
www2.mde.k12.ms.us/6400/index.htm
Mendenhall HS 700/9-12
207 Circle Dr 39114 601-847-2411
Roosevelt Oatis, prin. Fax 847-8002
Mendenhall JHS 500/5-8
733 Dixie Ave 39114 601-847-2296
Onnie Sue Lee, prin. Fax 847-7175
Simpson County Technical Center Vo/Tech
3415 Simpson Highway 49 39114 601-847-4000
Dr. Kay Berry, prin. Fax 847-8011
Other Schools – See Magee

Simpson County Academy 600/K-12
124 Academy Cir 39114 601-847-1395
Ilene Floyd, prin. Fax 847-1338

Meridian, Lauderdale, Pop. 38,605
Lauderdale County SD 6,300/K-12
PO Box 5498 39302 601-693-1683
David Little, supt. Fax 485-1748
www.lauderdale.k12.ms.us
Clarkdale S 900/K-12
7000 Highway 145 39301 601-693-4463
Jan Miller, prin. Fax 483-6329
Northeast Lauderdale HS 600/9-12
702 Briarwood Rd 39305 601-679-8523
Rob Calcote, prin. Fax 679-7515
Northeast MS 700/5-8
7763 Highway 39 39305 601-483-3532
Richard Kelly, prin. Fax 485-0846
Southeast HS 400/9-12
2362 Long Creek Rd 39301 601-483-5501
Billy Burnham, prin. Fax 483-6347
Southeast MS 500/5-8
2535 Old Highway 19 SE 39301 601-485-5751
Kenny Neal, prin. Fax 485-2302
Other Schools – See Collinsville

Meridian SD 6,100/K-12
PO Box 31 39302 601-483-6271
Sylvia Autry, supt. Fax 484-4917
www.mpsd.k12.ms.us
Collins Vocational Center Vo/Tech
PO Box 31 39302 601-483-3331
Lisa Barfield, prin. Fax 484-5173
Griffin JHS 400/8-9
2814 Davis St 39301 601-484-4073
Derricka Thomas, prin. Fax 484-4090
Meridian SHS 1,100/10-12
2320 32nd St 39305 601-482-3191
Vicky Hood, prin. Fax 483-5502
Northwest JHS 500/8-9
4400 32nd St 39307 601-484-4094
Wanda Kendrick, prin. Fax 484-5180

Calvary Christian S 200/PK-12
3917 7th St 39307 601-483-2305
Ann Schroeder, hdmstr. Fax 482-5376
Final Touch Beauty School Post-Sec.
5700 N Hills St 39307 601-485-7733
Lamar S 600/K-12
544 Lindley Rd 39305 601-482-1345
John Stephens, admin. Fax 482-7202
Meridian Community College Post-Sec.
910 Highway 19 N 39307 601-483-8241
Pentecostal Christian Academy 50/PK-12
PO Box 1390 39302 601-693-7375
Fred Summerville, supt. Fax 693-7347

Mississippi State, Oktibbeha, Pop. 12,400

Mississippi State University Post-Sec.
PO Box J 39762 662-325-2323

Mize, Smith, Pop. 283
Smith County SD
Supt. — See Raleigh
Mize S 800/K-12
PO Box 187 39116 601-733-2242
David Burris, prin. Fax 733-2243

Monticello, Lawrence, Pop. 1,724
Lawrence County SD 2,300/K-12
346 Thomas E Jolly Dr W 39654 601-587-2506
Russell Caudill, supt. Fax 587-2221
www.lawrence.k12.ms.us
Lawrence County HS 700/9-12
PO Box 488 39654 601-587-4910
Daryl Scoggin, prin. Fax 587-5001
Lawrence County Vo-Tech Ctr Vo/Tech
PO Box 578 39654 601-587-9346
P. Darrell Turner, prin. Fax 587-2980
Paige MS 400/5-8
PO Box 489 39654 601-587-2128
Tamm Fairburn, prin. Fax 587-7178

Mooreville, Lee
Lee County SD
Supt. — See Tupelo
Mooreville HS 400/9-12
PO Box 60 38857 662-842-6859
Robert Smith, prin. Fax 841-5988
Mooreville MS 300/6-8
PO Box 60 38857 662-680-4894
Craig Cherry, prin. Fax 680-4896

Moorhead, Sunflower, Pop. 2,472
Sunflower County SD
Supt. — See Indianola
Moorhead MS 100/6-8
PO Box 749 38761 662-246-5680
Verna Ransom, prin. Fax 246-5080

Mississippi Delta Community College Post-Sec.
PO Box 668 38761 662-246-6322

Morton, Scott, Pop. 3,441
Scott County SD
Supt. — See Forest
Jack Upper MS 500/5-8
PO Box 500 39117 601-732-6977
Tanya Walker, prin. Fax 732-2242
Morton HS 400/9-12
238 E Fourth Ave 39117 601-732-6210
Sarah Richardson, prin. Fax 732-8086

Moss Point, Jackson, Pop. 15,125
Jackson County SD
Supt. — See Vancleave
East Central HS 800/9-12
21700 Slider Rd 39562 228-588-7000
Tim Anderson, prin. Fax 588-7045
East Central MS 700/6-8
5404 Hurley Wade Rd 39562 228-588-7009
R. L. Watson, prin. Fax 588-7043

Moss Point SD 3,800/PK-12
4924 Church St 39563 228-475-0691
Dr. Rachel Carpenter, supt. Fax 474-3302
www.mp.k12.ms.us/
Magnolia JHS 600/7-8
4924 Church St 39563 228-475-1429
Kim Staley, prin. Fax 474-3397
Moss Point HS 1,100/9-12
4924 Church St 39563 228-475-5721
Tommy Molden, prin. Fax 474-3305
Moss Point Vocational Center Vo/Tech
4924 Church St 39563 228-474-1455
B.P. Johnson, prin. Fax 474-1458

Mound Bayou, Bolivar, Pop. 2,018
Mound Bayou SD 700/K-12
201 Green St 38762 662-741-2555
William Crockett, supt. Fax 741-2726
Kennedy Memorial HS 300/7-12
204 N Edwards Ave 38762 662-741-2510
Dr. I.D. Thompson, prin. Fax 741-2246

Mount Olive, Covington, Pop. 900
Covington County SD
Supt. — See Collins
Mt. Olive S 500/K-12
PO Box 309 39119 601-797-3914
Clay Anglin, prin. Fax 797-3980

Myrtle, Union, Pop. 558
Union County SD
Supt. — See New Albany
Myrtle S 700/K-12
1008 Hawk Ave 38650 662-988-2416
Vince Jordan, prin. Fax 988-2001
West Union S 500/K-12
1610 State Road 30 W 38650 662-534-4982
Paul Correro, prin. Fax 534-6716

Natchez, Adams, Pop. 16,966
Natchez-Adams SD 2,900/PK-12
10 Homochitto St 39120 601-445-2800
Dr. Anthony L. Morris, supt. Fax 445-2818
www.natchez.k12.ms.us/
Fallin Career & Technology Center Vo/Tech
315 Sgt Prentiss Dr 39120 601-445-2902
Linda Grafton, prin. Fax 445-2967
Lewis MS 800/7-8
1221 N Dr ML King Jr St 39120 601-445-2927
Bettye Bell, prin. Fax 445-2966
Natchez HS 1,100/9-12
319 Sgt Prentiss Dr 39120 601-445-2863
James Loftin, prin. Fax 445-3014

Adams County Christian S 500/PK-12
300 Chinquapin Ln 39120 601-442-1422
John R. Gray, admin. Fax 442-1477
Cathedral Unit S 600/PK-12
701 N Dr ML King Jr St 39120 601-442-2531
Patrick Sanguinetti, prin. Fax 442-0960
Copiah-Lincoln Community College Post-Sec.
11 Copiah Lincoln Circle 39120 601-442-9111
Trinity Episcopal Day S 400/PK-12
1 Mallan G Morgan Dr 39120 601-442-5424
Dr. Delecia Seay Carey, hdmstr. Fax 442-3216

Nettleton, Itawamba, Pop. 2,019
Nettleton SD 1,000/K-12
165 Mullen Ave 38858 662-963-2151
James Malone, supt. Fax 963-7407
www.nettletonschools.com/
Nettleton HS 400/9-12
165 Mullen Ave 38858 662-963-2306
Vince McLemore, prin. Fax 963-7407

Nettleton MS — 200/4-8
1532 Maple Rd 38858 — 662-963-7406
Van Ross, prin. — Fax 963-7407

New Albany, Union, Pop. 8,009
New Albany SD — 2,000/K-12
301 State Highway 15 N 38652 — 662-534-1800
Charles E. Garrett Ed.D., supt. — Fax 534-3608
www.newalbany.k12.ms.us
New Albany HS — 500/9-12
201 State Highway 15 N 38652 — 662-534-1805
Jay Foster, prin. — Fax 534-1817
New Albany MS — 500/6-8
400 Apple St 38652 — 662-534-1820
Robert Merritt, prin. — Fax 534-1819
New Albany Vocational Complex — Vo/Tech
203 State Highway 15 N 38652 — 662-534-1810
Earl Richard, prin. — Fax 534-1811

Union County SD — 2,700/K-12
PO Box 939 38652 — 662-534-1960
John Weeden, supt. — Fax 534-1961
www.union.k12.ms.us
Ingomar S — 600/K-12
1384 County Road 101 38652 — 662-534-2680
Kenny Roberts, prin. — Fax 534-3624
Other Schools – See Blue Springs, Myrtle

New Augusta, Perry, Pop. 696
Perry County SD — 1,300/K-12
PO Box 137 39462 — 601-964-3211
Gregory S. Dearman, supt. — Fax 964-8204
www.perry.k12.ms.us/
Perry Central HS — 300/9-12
PO Box 139 39462 — 601-964-3235
Rhett Ladner, prin. — Fax 964-8273
Perry County Vocational Tech Center — Vo/Tech
PO Box 138 39462 — 601-964-8282
Rex Buckhaults, prin. — Fax 964-8562

New Site, Prentiss
Prentiss County SD
Supt. — See Booneville
New Site HS — 200/9-12
1020 Highway 4 E 38859 — 662-728-5205
Luke Ledbetter, prin. — Fax 728-1965

Newton, Newton, Pop. 3,700
Newton Municipal SD — 1,000/K-12
205 School St 39345 — 601-683-2451
Raymond Clark, supt. — Fax 683-7131
www.nmsd.k12.ms.us
Newton HS — 200/9-12
201 W First St 39345 — 601-683-2232
Dr. Bill Shaw, prin. — Fax 683-6808
Newton Municipal Career Center — Vo/Tech
203 W First St 39345 — 601-683-6338
Aimee Brown, prin. — Fax 683-2283
Pilate MS — 400/5-8
531 E Church St 39345 — 601-683-3926
Dr. Virginia Young, prin. — Fax 683-7139

North Carrollton, Carroll, Pop. 475
Carroll County SD
Supt. — See Carrollton
George JSHS — 500/7-12
PO Box 398 38947 — 662-237-4701
Cory Blaylock, prin. — Fax 237-4522

Noxapater, Winston, Pop. 415
Louisville Municipal SD
Supt. — See Louisville
Noxapater S — 400/K-12
220 W Alice St 39346 — 662-724-4241
James Brooks, prin. — Fax 724-4240

Ocean Springs, Jackson, Pop. 17,783
Jackson County SD
Supt. — See Vancleave
St. Martin HS — 1,300/7-12
10800 Yellow Jacket Rd 39564 — 228-875-8418
Toriano Holloway, prin. — Fax 875-8426

Ocean Springs SD — 5,400/K-12
PO Box 7002 39566 — 228-875-7706
Robert Hirsch, supt. — Fax 875-7708
www.ossd.k12.ms.us
Keys Technology Center — Vo/Tech
PO Box 7002 39566 — 228-872-3411
Jan Griffin, dir. — Fax 872-0011
Ocean Springs HS — 1,700/9-12
PO Box 7002 39566 — 228-875-0333
David Baggett, prin. — Fax 872-0023
Ocean Springs MS — 1,400/6-8
PO Box 7002 39566 — 228-872-6210
Dr. Scherrine Davenport, prin. — Fax 872-9850

Day Spa Career College — Post-Sec.
3900 Bienville Blvd 39564 — 228-875-4809

Okolona, Chickasaw, Pop. 2,955
Okolona SSD — 800/K-12
PO Box 510 38860 — 662-447-2353
Hansell Gunn, supt. — Fax 447-9955
okolona.k12.ms.us/
Okolona JSHS — 400/7-12
404 Winter St 38860 — 662-447-2362
Paul Dobbs, prin. — Fax 447-3306
Okolona Vocational Complex — Vo/Tech
605 N Church St 38860 — 662-447-3331
Amy Anderson, prin. — Fax 447-2721

Olive Branch, DeSoto, Pop. 27,964
DeSoto County SD
Supt. — See Hernando
Center Hill MSHS — 6-10
13250 Kirk Rd 38654 — 662-890-2490
George Loper, prin. — Fax 890-2458
Lewisburg MSHS — 6-10
1755 Craft Rd 38654 — 662-890-6708
James Brady, prin. — Fax 890-6202
Olive Branch HS — 1,800/9-12
9366 E Sandidge Rd 38654 — 662-893-3344
Kyle Brigance, prin. — Fax 895-3353
Olive Branch MS — 1,500/6-8
6530 Blocker St 38654 — 662-895-4610
Danny Freeze, prin. — Fax 895-7358

Oxford, Lafayette, Pop. 13,618
Lafayette County SD — 2,000/PK-12
100 Commodore Dr 38655 — 662-234-3271
W. Michael Foster, supt. — Fax 236-3019
www.lafayette.k12.ms.us
Lafayette HS — 500/9-12
160 Commodore Dr 38655 — 662-234-3614
Adam Pugh, prin. — Fax 234-3856
Lafayette MS — 500/6-8
102 Commodore Dr 38655 — 662-234-1664
Rodney Flowers, prin. — Fax 232-8736
Oxford/Lafayette School of Applied Tech — Vo/Tech
1904 Highway 7 S 38655 — 662-234-9469
Mary Beth Lowrey, prin. — Fax 236-2496

Oxford SD — 3,100/PK-12
224 Bramlett Blvd 38655 — 662-234-3541
Jerry Webb Ed.D., supt. — Fax 232-2862
www.oxford.k12.ms.us
Oxford HS — 800/9-12
222 Bramlett Blvd 38655 — 662-234-1562
William Hovious, prin. — Fax 236-7941
Oxford MS — 500/7-8
501 Mrtin Luther King Jr Dr 38655 — 662-234-2288
Martha Shotts, prin. — Fax 234-0235

Pascagoula, Jackson, Pop. 25,173
Pascagoula SD — 7,400/K-12
PO Box 250 39568 — 228-938-6491
Wayne Rodolfich, supt. — Fax 938-6528
www.psd.k12.ms.us
Applied Technology Center — Vo/Tech
2602 Market St 39567 — 228-938-6579
Ms. Pat Taylor, dir. — Fax 938-6597
Colmer MS — 600/6-8
3112 Eden St 39581 — 228-938-6473
Nick Overby, prin. — Fax 938-6593
Lott MS — 500/6-8
2234 Pascagoula St 39567 — 228-938-6465
Shannon Vincent, prin. — Fax 938-6463
Pascagoula HS — 1,200/9-12
1716 Tucker Ave 39567 — 228-938-6443
Cindy Jackson, prin. — Fax 938-6445
Other Schools – See Gautier

Resurrection Catholic MSHS — 100/7-12
520 Watts Ave 39567 — 228-762-3353
Darnell Cuevas, prin. — Fax 769-1226

Pass Christian, Harrison, Pop. 6,851
Pass Christian SD — 1,500/K-12
6303 W Wittman Rd 39571 — 228-255-6200
Sue Matheson Ed.D., supt. — Fax 255-6204
www.pc.k12.ms.us/
Pass Christian HS — 600/9-12
720 W North St 39571 — 228-255-6211
Cathy Broadway, prin. — Fax 452-7340
Pass Christian MS — 500/6-8
6303 W Wittman Rd 39571 — 228-255-6219
Joe Nelson, prin.

Pearl, Rankin, Pop. 23,111
Pearl SD — 3,700/K-12
PO Box 5750 39288 — 601-932-7921
Dr. John Ladner, supt. — Fax 932-7929
www.pearl.k12.ms.us/
Pearl HS — 1,000/9-12
500 Pirates Cv 39208 — 601-932-7931
Raymond Morgigno, prin. — Fax 932-7992
Pearl JHS — 900/6-8
200 Mary Ann Dr 39208 — 601-932-7952
Karen Wilson, prin. — Fax 932-7998

Academy of Hair Design #4 — Post-Sec.
3167 Highway 80 E 39208 — 601-939-4441

Pelahatchie, Rankin, Pop. 1,490
Rankin County SD
Supt. — See Brandon
Pelahatchie JSHS — 300/7-12
PO Box 569 39145 — 601-854-8135
Brad Peets, prin. — Fax 854-8638

East Rankin Academy — 700/PK-12
PO Box 509 39145 — 601-854-5691
Robert Gates, hdmstr. — Fax 854-5893

Perkinston, Stone

Mississippi Gulf Coast Community College — Post-Sec.
PO Box 609 39573 — 601-928-5211

Petal, Forrest, Pop. 10,088
Petal SSD — 3,600/K-12
PO Box 523 39465 — 601-545-3002
James Hutto, supt. — Fax 584-4700
www.petalschools.com
Petal HS — 1,000/9-12
1145 Highway 42 39465 — 601-583-3538
Jack Linton, prin. — Fax 545-1229
Petal MS — 900/6-8
203 Highway 42 39465 — 601-584-6301
Michael Hogan, prin. — Fax 584-4716

Pheba, Clay

Hebron Christian S — 200/K-12
6230 Henryville Rd 39755 — 662-494-7513
Sam Pearson, prin. — Fax 494-1002

Philadelphia, Neshoba, Pop. 7,618
Neshoba County SD — 3,000/K-12
PO Box 338 39350 — 601-656-3752
V.C. Manning, supt. — Fax 656-3789
www.neshoba.k12.ms.us/
Neshoba Central HS — 700/9-12
1125 Golf Course Rd 39350 — 601-656-6004
Joey Blount, prin. — Fax 656-6004
Neshoba Central MS — 700/6-8
1000 Saint Francis Dr 39350 — 601-656-4636
Jimmy Buchanan, prin. — Fax 389-2989

Philadelphia SD — 1,100/K-12
248 Byrd Ave N 39350 — 601-656-2955
Dr. Joseph White, supt. — Fax 656-3141
www.philadelphia.k12.ms.us/
Philadelphia HS — 300/9-12
248 Byrd Ave N 39350 — 601-656-2672
Bobby Luke, prin. — Fax 656-0015
Philadelphia MS — 200/7-8
248 Byrd Ave N 39350 — 601-656-6439
Ben Johnson, prin. — Fax 656-5328

Picayune, Pearl River, Pop. 10,830
Picayune SD — 3,600/K-12
706 Goodyear Blvd 39466 — 601-798-3230
Brent Harrell, supt. — Fax 798-1742
www.pcu.k12.ms.us/
Picayune JHS — 600/7-8
702 Goodyear Blvd 39466 — 601-798-5449
Dean Shaw, prin. — Fax 799-4715
Picayune Memorial HS — 1,000/9-12
800 Fifth Ave 39466 — 601-798-1380
Kent Kirkland, prin. — Fax 798-4705
PMHS Career & Technology Center — Vo/Tech
600 Goodyear Blvd 39466 — 601-798-7601
Dean Shaw, prin. — Fax 799-4711

Piney Woods, Rankin

Piney Woods S — 200/9-12
PO Box 100 39148 — 601-845-2214
Sekufele Lewanika, hdmstr. — Fax 845-2604

Pittsboro, Calhoun, Pop. 207
Calhoun County SD — 2,500/PK-12
119 W Main St 38951 — 662-412-3152
Beth Hardin, supt. — Fax 412-3157
www.calhoun.k12.ms.us/
Other Schools – See Bruce, Calhoun City, Vardaman

Plantersville, Lee, Pop. 1,318
Lee County SD
Supt. — See Tupelo
Plantersville MS — 100/5-8
PO Box 129 38862 — 662-842-4690
Kenneth Jones, prin. — Fax 791-0491

Pontotoc, Pontotoc, Pop. 5,784
Pontotoc CSD — 2,300/K-12
140 Education Dr 38863 — 662-489-3336
Conwell Duke, supt. — Fax 489-7932
www.pontotoc.k12.ms.us
Pontotoc HS — 600/9-12
123 N Main St 38863 — 662-489-1275
Al Sparkman, prin. — Fax 489-5255
Pontotoc JHS — 700/5-8
132 N Main St 38863 — 662-489-8360
Cristie Hooker, prin. — Fax 489-8947

Pontotoc County SD — 3,000/K-12
285 Highway 15 S 38863 — 662-489-3932
John Simmons, supt. — Fax 489-3922
www.pcsd.k12.ms.us/
Pontotoc Ridge Career & Tech Center — Vo/Tech
354 Ridge Dr 38863 — 662-489-1826
Phil Ryan, prin. — Fax 489-0704
South Pontotoc HS — 400/9-12
1523 S Pontotoc Rd 38863 — 662-489-5925
Tim West, prin. — Fax 489-8598
South Pontotoc MS — 300/6-8
1523 S Pontotoc Rd 38863 — 662-489-3476
Scotty Collins, prin. — Fax 489-6252
Other Schools – See Ecru

Poplarville, Pearl River, Pop. 2,663
Poplarville SSD — 2,000/PK-12
302 S Julia St 39470 — 601-795-8477
Gylde Fitzpatrick, supt. — Fax 795-0712
poplarvilleschools.org/
Poplarville Career Development Center — Vo/Tech
9 Career Center Cir 39470 — 601-795-8343
Marlene Cole, prin. — Fax 795-1353
Poplarville HS — 500/9-12
1 Hornet Dr 39470 — 601-795-8424
Ilene Davis, prin. — Fax 795-1345
Poplarville MS — 500/6-8
6 Spirit Dr 39470 — 601-795-1350
Leah Stevens, prin. — Fax 795-1351

Pearl River Community College — Post-Sec.
Station A 39470 — 601-795-6801

Port Gibson, Claiborne, Pop. 1,765
Claiborne County SD — 1,700/K-12
404 Market St 39150 — 601-437-4232
Annie Kilcrease Ph.D., supt. — Fax 437-4409
Claiborne Co. Voc Educational Complex — Vo/Tech
PO Box 47 39150 — 601-437-3800
Nathaniel Martin, dir. — Fax 437-3801
Port Gibson HS — 500/9-12
159 Old Highway 18 39150 — 601-437-4190
Nathaniel Martin, prin. — Fax 437-4409
Port Gibson MS — 400/6-8
161 Ramsey Dr 39150 — 601-437-4251
Earl Taylor, prin. — Fax 437-3099

Chamberlain-Hunt Academy — 200/7-12
124 McComb Ave 39150 — 601-437-4291
A. Shane Blanton, pres. — Fax 437-4313

Potts Camp, Marshall, Pop. 509
Marshall County SD
Supt. — See Holly Springs
Potts Camp S — 500/4-12
PO Box 697 38659 — 662-333-6354
Ken Basil, prin. — Fax 333-7023

Prentiss, Jefferson Davis, Pop. 1,061
Jefferson Davis County SD — 2,100/K-12
PO Box 1197 39474 — 601-792-4267
Wayne Fortenberry, supt. — Fax 792-2251
www.jeffersondavis.k12.ms.us
Prentiss JHS — 600/6-12
PO Box 1168 39474 — 601-792-4646
Audie Reese McCormick, prin. — Fax 792-8149
Other Schools – See Bassfield, Carson

Prentiss Christian S 400/K-12
PO Box 1287 39474 601-792-8549
Danny Quick, prin. Fax 792-2560

Puckett, Rankin, Pop. 354
Rankin County SD
Supt. — See Brandon
Puckett Attendance Center 300/7-12
PO Box 40 39151 601-825-5742
Scott Parham, prin. Fax 825-9838

Purvis, Lamar, Pop. 2,445
Lamar County SD 7,000/K-12
PO Box 609 39475 601-794-1030
Glenn Swan, supt. Fax 794-1012
www.lamar.k12.ms.us
Lamar County Vo-Tech Ctr Vo/Tech
41 College Dr 39475 601-794-8298
Rita Bush, prin. Fax 794-1026
Purvis HS 500/9-12
PO Box 1089 39475 601-794-2708
C.H. Bryant, prin. Fax 794-2150
Purvis MS 400/6-8
PO Box 1089 39475 601-794-2708
Linda Greer, prin. Fax 794-2150
Other Schools – See Hattiesburg, Sumrall

Lamar Christian S 400/PK-12
PO Box 880 39475 601-794-0016
Louis Nicolosi, admin. Fax 794-3726

Quitman, Clarke, Pop. 2,388
Quitman SD 2,300/K-12
104 E Franklin St 39355 601-776-2186
Suzanne Hawley, supt. Fax 776-1051
www.qsd.k12.ms.us/
Clarke County Vocational Center Vo/Tech
910 N Archusa Ave 39355 601-776-5219
Willie Plummer, dir. Fax 776-5219
Quitman HS 600/9-12
210 S Jackson Ave 39355 601-776-3341
Charlie Parkerson, prin. Fax 776-6136
Quitman JHS 600/6-8
501 W Lynda St 39355 601-776-6243
Shannon Sudbury, prin. Fax 776-1288

Raleigh, Smith, Pop. 1,257
Smith County SD 3,000/K-12
PO Box 308 39153 601-782-4296
Warren Woodrow, supt. Fax 782-9895
www.smith.k12.ms.us/
Raleigh HS 600/7-12
RR 1 Box 500 39153 601-782-4261
Jay Gilbert, prin. Fax 782-4359
Smith County Vocational Complex Vo/Tech
PO Box 37 39153 601-782-4211
Fax 782-9842

Other Schools – See Mize, Taylorsville

Raymond, Hinds, Pop. 1,681
Hinds County SD 5,800/K-12
13192 Highway 18 39154 601-857-5222
Dr. Stephen Handley, supt. Fax 857-8548
www.hinds.k12.ms.us/
Carver MS 6-8
417 Palestine St 39154 601-857-5006
Lana Clark, prin. Fax 857-4935
Hinds County Career Center Vo/Tech
PO Box 789 39154 601-857-5536
Sammy White, prin. Fax 857-2212
Raymond HS 500/9-12
14050 Highway 18 39154 601-857-8016
John Neal, prin. Fax 857-2007
Other Schools – See Terry

Central Hinds Academy 400/K-12
2894 Raymond Bolton Rd 39154 601-857-5568
Steven Harrell, hdmstr. Fax 857-5082
Hinds Community College Post-Sec.
PO Box 1100 39154 601-857-5261

Richland, Rankin, Pop. 7,051
Rankin County SD
Supt. — See Brandon
Richland HS 400/7-12
1202 Highway 49 S 39218 601-939-5144
Stanley Shows, prin. Fax 939-7631

Richton, Greene, Pop. 1,008
Richton SD 700/K-12
PO Box 568 39476 601-788-6581
Bruce Weigle, supt. Fax 788-9391
Richton JSHS 300/7-12
PO Box 568 39476 601-788-9608
Lana McIlwain, prin. Fax 788-6390

Ridgeland, Madison, Pop. 21,236
Madison County SD
Supt. — See Flora
Olde Towne MS 700/6-8
210 Sunnybrook Rd 39157 601-898-8730
Allen Lawrence, prin. Fax 853-8108
Ridgeland HS 800/9-12
586 Sunnybrook Rd 39157 601-898-5023
Lee Boozer, prin. Fax 853-7822

St. Andrew's Episcopal S 1,200/PK-12
370 Old Agency Rd 39157 601-853-6000
Robert Rutledge, hdmstr. Fax 853-6001

Ripley, Tippah, Pop. 5,633
South Tippah SD 2,700/K-12
PO Box 439 38663 662-837-7156
Dr. Wardell Herring, supt. Fax 837-1362
www.stippah.k12.ms.us/
North South Tippah County Vo-Tech Ctr Vo/Tech
PO Box 533 38663 662-837-9798
Howard Newby, prin. Fax 837-8833
Pine Grove S 600/K-12
3510A County Road 600 38663 662-837-7789
William Witt, prin. Fax 837-8179
Ripley HS 500/9-12
720 S Clayton St 38663 662-837-7583
Lynn McGee, prin. Fax 837-0118
Ripley MS 600/5-8
718 S Clayton St 38663 662-837-7959
James Storey, prin. Fax 837-0251
Other Schools – See Blue Mountain

Foster's Cosmetology College Post-Sec.
PO Box 66 38663 662-837-9334

Rolling Fork, Sharkey, Pop. 2,237
South Delta SD 1,300/PK-12
PO Box 219 39159 662-873-4302
Katherine Tankson, supt. Fax 873-4198
South Delta HS 400/9-12
303 Parkway Ave 39159 662-873-4308
Spurgeon Banyard, prin. Fax 873-6106
South Delta Vocational S Vo/Tech
285 Maple St 39159 662-873-2029
Beverly Wilson, prin. Fax 873-4194
Other Schools – See Anguilla

Sharkey Issaquena Academy 300/K-12
272 Academy Dr 39159 662-873-4241

Rosedale, Bolivar, Pop. 2,421
West Bolivar SD 1,100/K-12
PO Box 189 38769 662-759-3525
Henry Phillips, supt. Fax 759-6795
www.wbsd.k12.ms.us/
Barnes Vocational Center Vo/Tech
PO Box 160 38769 662-759-3791
Arthur Holmes, prin. Fax 759-6795
West Bolivar HS 300/9-12
PO Box 398 38769 662-759-3346
Simon Carter, prin. Fax 759-6795
West Bolivar MS 300/5-8
PO Box 159 38769 662-759-3743
Larry Johnson, prin. Fax 759-6795

Ruleville, Sunflower, Pop. 2,935
Sunflower County SD
Supt. — See Indianola
Ruleville Central HS 300/9-12
360 L F Packer Dr 38771 662-756-4757
James Johnson, prin. Fax 756-0052
Ruleville MS 300/6-8
PO Box 129 38771 662-756-4698
Robert Latham, prin. Fax 756-4902

Saltillo, Lee, Pop. 3,789
Lee County SD
Supt. — See Tupelo
Saltillo HS 700/9-12
PO Box 460 38866 662-869-5466
Keith Steele, prin. Fax 869-7229

Sandhill, Rankin
Rankin County SD
Supt. — See Brandon
Pisgah HS 300/7-12
PO Box 70 39161 601-829-1138
Norman Session, prin. Fax 829-1753

Sarah, Tate
Tate County SD
Supt. — See Senatobia
Strayhorn HS 9-12
86 Mustang Dr 38665 662-562-9246
Lee Darnell, prin. Fax 562-9249

Sardis, Panola, Pop. 2,033
North Panola SD 1,500/K-12
470 Highway 51 S 38666 662-487-2305
Glendora Dugger, supt. Fax 487-2050
npanola.k12.ms.us/
North Panola HS 500/9-12
PO Box 278 38666 662-487-1070
Anthony Barnes, prin. Fax 487-2052
Other Schools – See Como

Scooba, Kemper, Pop. 597

East Mississippi Community College Post-Sec.
PO Box 158 39358 662-476-8442

Sebastopol, Scott, Pop. 232
Scott County SD
Supt. — See Forest
Sebastopol Attendance Center 600/K-12
PO Box 86 39359 601-625-8654
Charles Brown, prin. Fax 625-9426

Seminary, Covington, Pop. 349
Covington County SD
Supt. — See Collins
Seminary S 1,100/K-12
PO Box 34 39479 601-722-3220
Larry Kinslow, prin. Fax 722-3972

Senatobia, Tate, Pop. 6,869
Senatobia Municipal SD 1,800/K-12
104 McKie St 38668 662-562-4897
Mike Flynn, supt. Fax 562-4996
www.senatobia.k12.ms.us/
Senatobia JSHS 800/7-12
221 Warrior Dr 38668 662-562-4230
Jerry Barrett, prin. Fax 562-6659

Tate County SD 2,400/K-12
107 Court St 38668 662-562-5861
Gary Walker, supt. Fax 562-8516
www.tcsd.k12.ms.us/
Other Schools – See Coldwater, Independence, Sarah

J & J Hair Design College Post-Sec.
562 W Main St Ste B 38668 662-562-8010
Magnolia Heights S 700/K-12
1 Chiefs Dr 38668 662-562-4491
Dr. Marvin Lishman, admin. Fax 562-0386
Northwest Mississippi Community College Post-Sec.
4975 Highway 51 N 38668 662-562-3200

Shannon, Lee, Pop. 1,704
Lee County SD
Supt. — See Tupelo
Shannon JSHS 900/7-12
PO Box 8 38868 662-767-9566
Mike Scott, prin. Fax 767-2847

Shaw, Bolivar, Pop. 2,236
Shaw SD 700/K-12
PO Box 510 38773 662-754-2611
Charles Barron, supt. Fax 754-2612
www2.mde.k12.ms.us/0615/shdhot.htm
Shaw HS 300/8-12
PO Box 510 38773 662-754-2611
John Sullivan, prin. Fax 754-4418

Shelby, Bolivar, Pop. 2,701
North Bolivar SD 900/K-12
PO Box 28 38774 662-398-4000
Ronzy Humphrey, supt. Fax 398-7884
www.nbsd.k12.ms.us/
Broad Street HS 300/8-12
PO Box 149 38774 662-398-4040
Frederick Ford, prin. Fax 398-5900

Smithville, Monroe, Pop. 879
Monroe County SD
Supt. — See Amory
Smithville S 700/K-12
60017 Highway 23 38870 662-651-4276
Sam Wilson, prin. Fax 651-4163

Southaven, DeSoto, Pop. 38,840
DeSoto County SD
Supt. — See Hernando
Desoto Central HS 700/9-12
2911 Central Pkwy 38672 662-536-3612
Charlie Tipton, prin. Fax 536-3623
Desoto Central MS 900/6-8
2611 Central Pkwy 38672 662-349-6660
Chad White, prin. Fax 349-1045
DeSoto County Vocational Complex Vo/Tech
847 Rasco Rd W 38671 662-393-6211
Phillip Sublett, prin. Fax 393-5708
Southaven HS 1,400/9-12
755 Rasco Rd 38671 662-393-9300
Jeff Gilder, prin. Fax 342-1393
Southaven MS 1,300/6-8
175 Rasco Rd E 38671 662-280-0422
Mike McCoy, prin. Fax 280-3613

Northwest Mississippi Community College Post-Sec.
5197 WE Ross Pkwy 38671 662-342-1570
Southern Baptist Educational Center 1,200/PK-12
7400 Getwell Rd 38672 662-349-3096
David Manley, pres. Fax 349-4962

Starkville, Oktibbeha, Pop. 22,131
Oktibbeha County SD 900/K-12
105 Dr Douglas L Conner Dr 39759 662-323-1472
Walter Conley, supt. Fax 323-9614
www.oktibbeha.k12.ms.us
Other Schools – See Crawford, Maben

Starkville SD 3,900/PK-12
401 Greensboro St 39759 662-324-4050
Dr. Phillip Burchfield, supt. Fax 324-4068
www.starkville.k12.ms.us
Armstrong JHS 600/7-8
303 McKee St 39759 662-324-4070
Bob Fuller, prin. Fax 324-4075
Millsaps Career & Tech Center Vo/Tech
803 Louisville St 39759 662-324-4170
James Stidham, prin. Fax 324-4103
Starkville HS 1,100/9-12
603 Yellow Jacket Dr 39759 662-324-4130
Kathi Wilson, prin. Fax 324-4128

Starkville Academy 800/K-12
505 Academy Rd 39759 662-323-7814
Bobby Eiland, hdmstr. Fax 323-5480
Starkville Christian S 100/PK-12
303 Lynn Ln 39759 662-323-7453
Rev. Randall Witbeck, prin. Fax 323-7571

Steens, Lowndes

Immanuel Center for Christian Education 300/PK-12
6405 Military Rd 39766 662-328-7888
Bob Williford, admin. Fax 328-7750

Stringer, Jasper
West Jasper Consolidated SD
Supt. — See Bay Springs
Stringer S 700/K-12
PO Box 68 39481 601-428-5508
Margaret Pollard, prin. Fax 426-6760

Summit, Pike, Pop. 1,603
McComb SD
Supt. — See Mc Comb
Summit Learning Center Adult
1201 Baldwin St 39666 601-276-2254
Alvin Hogan, prin. Fax 276-2820

North Pike SD 1,800/K-12
1036 Jaguar Trl 39666 601-276-2216
Dr. Ben Cox, supt. Fax 276-3666
North Pike HS 500/9-12
1022 Jaguar Trl 39666 601-276-2175
Darryl Brock, prin. Fax 276-2720
North Pike MS 600/5-8
2034 Highway 44 NE 39666 601-684-3283
Danny Rushing, prin. Fax 684-3269

Southwest Mississippi Community College Post-Sec.
39666 601-276-2001

Sumrall, Lamar, Pop. 1,163
Lamar County SD
Supt. — See Purvis
Sumrall HS 400/9-12
PO Box 187 39482 601-758-4730
Jennifer Ward, prin. Fax 758-0512
Sumrall MS, Highway 42 39482 300/6-8
Larry Easterling, prin. 601-794-1030

Taylorsville, Smith, Pop. 1,297
Smith County SD
Supt. — See Raleigh
Taylorsville S 900/K-12
PO Box 8 39168 601-785-6942
Jeff Duvall, prin. Fax 785-9711

Terry, Hinds, Pop. 701
Hinds County SD
Supt. — See Raymond
Byram MS 1,000/6-8
2009 Byram Bulldog Blvd 39170 601-372-4597
David Campbell, prin. Fax 346-2383

Terry HS 1,000/9-12
235 W Beasley St 39170 601-878-5905
Dr. Bill Sellers, prin. Fax 878-2782

Tiplersville, Tippah
North Tippah SD 1,300/K-12
PO Box 65 38674 662-223-4384
Junior Wooten, supt. Fax 223-5379
Other Schools – See Falkner, Walnut

Tishomingo, Tishomingo, Pop. 317
Tishomingo County Special Municipal SSD
Supt. — See Iuka
Tishomingo County Vocational Center Vo/Tech
PO Box 890 38873 662-438-6689
Gary Taylor, dir. Fax 438-6777

Tougaloo, Hinds

Tougaloo College Post-Sec.
500 W County Line Rd 39174 601-977-7700

Tremont, Itawamba, Pop. 396
Itawamba County SD
Supt. — See Fulton
Tremont Attendance Center 300/K-12
PO Box 9 38876 662-652-3391
Jerry Wiygul, prin. Fax 652-3994

Tunica, Tunica, Pop. 1,089
Tunica County SD 2,200/PK-12
PO Box 758 38676 662-363-2811
Jerry Gentry, supt. Fax 363-3061
www.tunica.k12.ms.us/
Rosa Fort HS 500/9-12
PO Box 997 38676 662-363-1343
Larry Ball, prin. Fax 363-4222
Tunica MS 500/6-8
PO Box 967 38676 662-363-4224
Glenn Rogers, prin. Fax 357-1058
Tunica Vo-Tech Center Vo/Tech
2400 Old Highway 61 N 38676 662-363-2051
Dorothy Dunn, prin. Fax 363-2052

Tunica Institute of Learning S 200/K-12
PO Box 966 38676 662-363-1051
Walt Gaston, prin. Fax 363-2037

Tupelo, Lee, Pop. 35,673
Lee County SD 5,900/K-12
1280 College View St 38804 662-841-9144
Johnny Green, supt. Fax 680-6012
www.leecountyschools.us/
Other Schools – See Guntown, Mooreville, Plantersville, Saltillo, Shannon

Tupelo SD 7,000/PK-12
PO Box 557 38802 662-841-8850
Dr. Randy McCoy, supt. Fax 841-8887
www.tupeloschools.com/
Tupelo HS 1,800/9-12
4125 Cliff Gookin Blvd 38801 662-841-8970
John Curlee, prin. Fax 841-8987
Tupelo HS Career Center Vo/Tech
4125 Cliff Gookin Blvd 38801 662-841-8990
M.D. Cameron, prin. Fax 840-8799
Tupelo MS 1,100/7-8
1009 Varsity Dr 38801 662-840-8780
Linda Clifton, prin. Fax 840-1831

Creations College of Cosmetology Post-Sec.
PO Box 2635 38803 662-844-9264
Mississippi University for Women-Tupelo Post-Sec.
1918 Briar Ridge Rd 38804 662-844-0284
North Mississippi Medical Center Post-Sec.
830 S Gloster St 38801 662-841-3136
Tupelo Christian Academy 100/PK-12
PO Box 167 38802 662-791-7731

Tylertown, Walthall, Pop. 1,898
Walthall County SD 2,600/K-12
814A Morse Ave 39667 601-876-3401
Greg Ellzey, supt. Fax 876-6982
www.wcsd.k12.ms.us/
Dexter S 300/K-12
927 Highway 48 E 39667 601-876-3985
Jerry Pigott, prin. Fax 876-5410
Salem S 600/K-12
881 Highway 27 N 39667 601-876-2580
Charles Boyd, prin. Fax 876-4155
Tylertown JSHS 700/7-12
204 High School Rd 39667 601-876-3370
Cynthia Magee, prin. Fax 876-3122
Walthall County Career & Tech Center Vo/Tech
803 Ball Ave 39667 601-222-1500
Wade Carney, prin. Fax 222-1506

Union, Newton, Pop. 2,102
Union SD 800/K-12
PO Box 445 39365 601-774-9579
Don Brantley, supt. Fax 774-0600
www.unioncity.k12.ms.us/
Union HS 200/9-12
101 Forest St 39365 601-774-8257
Joey Ezelle, prin. Fax 774-9600
Union MS 300/5-8
115 James St 39365 601-774-5303
Brett Rigby, prin. Fax 774-9607

University, See Oxford

University of Mississippi 38677 Post-Sec.
662-232-7226

Utica, Hinds, Pop. 922
Hinds County Agricultural HSD
PO Box 1089 39175 601-885-7047
Dr. Clyde Muse, supt. Fax 885-2676
Hinds County Agricultural HS Vo/Tech
PO Box 1089 39175 601-885-7083
Robert Strong, prin. Fax 885-2676

Vancleave, Jackson, Pop. 3,214
Jackson County SD 8,300/K-12
12210 Colonel Vickrey Rd 39565 228-826-1757
Rucks H. Robinson Ed.D., supt. Fax 826-3393
www.jcsd.k12.ms.us/
Jackson County Technology Center Vo/Tech
12425 Highway 57 39565 228-826-5944
Dino Vecchio, prin. Fax 826-4209
Vancleave HS 700/9-12
12424 Highway 57 39565 228-826-4701
Todd Knight, prin. Fax 826-5066
Vancleave MS 600/6-8
4725 Bull Dog Ln 39565 228-826-5902
Joe Hubal, prin. Fax 826-1421
Other Schools – See Moss Point, Ocean Springs

Vardaman, Calhoun, Pop. 1,019
Calhoun County SD
Supt. — See Pittsboro
Vardaman HS 300/7-12
PO Box 193 38878 662-682-7574
Gregg Pepper, prin. Fax 682-7743

Vicksburg, Warren, Pop. 25,752
Vicksburg Warren SD 8,400/K-12
1500 Mission 66 39180 601-638-5122
Dr. James Price, supt. Fax 631-2819
www.vwsd.k12.ms.us
Vicksburg HS 1,000/9-12
3701 Drummond St 39180 601-636-2914
Derrick Reed, prin. Fax 631-2885
Vicksburg JHS 700/7-8
1533 Baldwin Ferry Rd 39180 601-636-1966
Michael Winters, prin. Fax 631-2830
Warren Central HS 1,100/9-12
1000 Highway 27 39180 601-638-3372
Pam Wilbanks, prin. Fax 631-2937
Warren Central JHS 800/7-8
1630 Baldwin Ferry Rd 39180 601-638-3981
Cedric Magee, prin. Fax 631-2839

Campus Preparatory Christian S 200/K-12
219 Baptist Dr 39180 601-631-0014
Hinds Community College Post-Sec.
755 Highway 27 39180 601-638-0600
Porters Chapel Academy 200/K-12
3460 Porters Chapel Rd 39180 601-638-3733
Lynn Baker M.Ed., hdmstr. Fax 638-6311
St. Aloysius MSHS 300/7-12
1900 Grove St 39183 601-636-2256
Michele Townsend, prin. Fax 631-0430

Walnut, Tippah, Pop. 759
North Tippah SD
Supt. — See Tiplersville
Walnut S 500/K-12
PO Box 240 38683 662-223-6471
Jay McCoy, prin. Fax 223-5275

Walnut Grove, Leake, Pop. 1,260
Leake County SD
Supt. — See Carthage
South Leake HS 300/7-12
PO Box 159 39189 601-253-2393
James Chambers, prin. Fax 253-0100

Water Valley, Yalobusha, Pop. 3,822
Water Valley SD 1,300/K-12
PO Box 788 38965 662-473-1203
Sammy Higdon, supt. Fax 473-1225
www.wvsd.k12.ms.us/
Water Valley JSHS 500/7-12
PO Box 647 38965 662-473-2468
Glenn Kitchens, prin. Fax 473-1444

Waynesboro, Wayne, Pop. 5,719
Wayne County SD 3,800/K-12
810 Chickasawhay St 39367 601-735-4871
R.P. Staten, supt. Fax 735-4872
www.mde.k12.ms.us/districts/wayne.htm
Wayne County HS 1,000/9-12
1325 Azalea Dr 39367 601-735-2851
Al Smith, prin. Fax 735-1389
Wayne County Vocational Center Vo/Tech
800 Collins St 39367 601-735-5036
Bobby Jones, prin. Fax 735-6326
Waynesboro MS 700/5-8
155 Wayne St 39367 601-735-3159
DeJuan Walley, prin. Fax 735-6316

Wayne Academy 200/K-12
PO Box 308 39367 601-735-2921
Allen Stevens, admin. Fax 735-2117

Webb, Tallahatchie, Pop. 540
West Tallahatchie SD 1,100/K-12
PO Box 129 38966 662-375-9291
Howard Hollins, supt. Fax 375-9294
www2.mde.k12.ms.us/6812/index.htm
West Tallahatchie HS 600/7-12
PO Box 130 38966 662-375-8829
Iva Houston, prin. Fax 375-7402

Weir, Choctaw, Pop. 530
Choctaw County SD
Supt. — See Ackerman
Weir S 500/PK-12
PO Box 98 39772 662-547-7062
Glen Beard, prin. Fax 547-7074

Wesson, Copiah, Pop. 1,692
Copiah County SD
Supt. — See Hazlehurst
Wesson S 1,000/K-12
1048 Grove St 39191 601-643-2221
Billy Britt, prin. Fax 643-2458

Copiah-Lincoln Community College Post-Sec.
PO Box 457 39191 601-643-5101

West Point, Clay, Pop. 11,582
West Point SD 3,400/PK-12
PO Box 656 39773 662-494-4242
Steve Montgomery, supt. Fax 494-8605
www.westpoint.k12.ms.us/
Fifth Street JHS 600/7-8
PO Box 776 39773 662-494-2191
Alvin Taylor, prin. Fax 494-2432
West Point Career and Technology Center Vo/Tech
PO Box 1136 39773 662-494-6176
Rob Smith, prin. Fax 495-2426
West Point HS 1,000/9-12
PO Box 616 39773 662-494-5083
Tim Fowler, prin. Fax 494-0969

Gibson's Barber & Beauty College Post-Sec.
PO Box 990 39773 662-494-5444
Oak Hill Academy 600/PK-12
800 N Eshman Ave 39773 662-494-5043
Jack Henderson, hdmstr. Fax 494-0487

Wheeler, Prentiss
Prentiss County SD
Supt. — See Booneville
Wheeler S 400/K-12
PO Box 98 38880 662-365-2629
Todd Swinney, prin. Fax 365-2535

Wiggins, Stone, Pop. 4,463
Stone County SD 2,500/K-12
214 Critz St N 39577 601-928-7247
James Morrison, supt. Fax 928-5122
stoneweb.stone.k12.ms.us
Stone HS 700/9-12
400 Border Ave E 39577 601-928-5492
David Ledner, prin. Fax 928-6874
Stone MS 700/6-8
532 Central Ave E 39577 601-928-4876
Mike Gavin, prin. Fax 928-6440

Winona, Montgomery, Pop. 4,934
Montgomery County SD 500/K-12
PO Box 687 38967 662-283-4533
Sammie McCaskill, supt. Fax 283-4584
www.mcsd.k12.ms.us
Other Schools – See Kilmichael

Winona SD 1,300/K-12
218 Fairground St 38967 662-283-3731
John Buchanan, supt. Fax 283-1003
www2.mde.k12.ms.us/4920/wps.html
Dulin Career and Technical Ctr Vo/Tech
300 N Applegate St 38967 662-283-3601
Dwight Lollar, prin. Fax 283-9807
Winona HS 600/7-12
301 Fairground St 38967 662-283-1244
Dr. Tom Taylor, prin. Fax 283-4267

Winona Christian S 200/PK-12
1014 S Applegate St 38967 662-283-1169
Rick Hammarstrom, admin. Fax 283-3333

Woodville, Wilkinson, Pop. 1,162
Wilkinson County SD 1,500/PK-12
PO Box 785 39669 601-888-3582
Mildred McGhee, supt. Fax 888-3133
www2.mde.k12.ms.us/7900
King Vocational Complex Vo/Tech
PO Box 1193 39669 601-888-4394
Gwendolyn Vanderson, prin. Fax 888-4740
Wilkinson County HS 400/9-12
522 Pinckneyville Rd 39669 601-888-4228
Melvin Craige, prin. Fax 888-4736
Other Schools – See Centreville

Wilkinson County Christian Academy 300/K-12
PO Box 977 39669 601-888-4313
Carrie Cupit, admin. Fax 888-3588

Yazoo City, Yazoo, Pop. 11,879
Yazoo City Municipal SD 2,800/PK-12
1133 Calhoun Ave 39194 662-746-2125
Rebecca Turner-Berry, supt. Fax 746-9210
www.yazoocity.k12.ms.us/
Woolfolk MS 1,100/5-8
209 E Fifth St 39194 662-746-2904
Elease Lee, prin. Fax 746-8609
Yazoo City HS 600/9-12
1825 Dr Mrtn Lthr Kng Jr Dr 39194 662-746-2378
John Wallace, prin. Fax 746-3779
Yazoo City Vocational Center Vo/Tech
1825 Dr Mrtn Lthr Kng Jr Dr 39194 662-746-7642
Patricia Hall, prin. Fax 746-0991

Yazoo County SD 1,800/K-12
PO Box 1088 39194 662-746-4672
Dr. Jack Nicholson, supt. Fax 746-9270
www.yazoo.k12.ms.us
Yazoo County HS 500/9-12
6789 Highway 49 Frontage Rd 39194 662-746-1492
Phillip Chisolm, prin. Fax 746-1593
Yazoo County JHS 300/7-8
6781 Highway 49 Frontage Rd 39194 662-746-1596
Ray Mathis, prin. Fax 746-1616

Manchester Academy 400/PK-12
2132 Gordon Ave 39194 662-746-5913
Bryan Dendy, hdmstr. Fax 746-5108

MISSOURI

MISSOURI DEPARTMENT OF EDUCATION
PO Box 480, Jefferson City 65102-0480
Telephone 573-751-4212
Fax 573-751-1179
Website http://www.dese.mo.gov

Commissioner of Education D. Kent King

MISSOURI BOARD OF EDUCATION
PO Box 480, Jefferson City 65102-0480

President Peter Herschend

PUBLIC, PRIVATE AND CATHOLIC SECONDARY SCHOOLS

Adrian, Bates, Pop. 1,839
Adrian R-III SD 700/K-12
PO Box 98 64720 816-297-2710
Doug Hedrick, supt. Fax 297-2980
www.adrian.k12.mo.us/
Adrian JSHS 300/7-12
PO Box 98 64720 816-297-4460
Chris Shanks, prin. Fax 297-2980

Advance, Stoddard, Pop. 1,216
Advance R-IV SD 400/K-12
PO Box 370 63730 573-722-3581
Michael Redman, supt. Fax 722-9886
www.advance.k12.mo.us/default.asp
Advance JSHS 200/7-12
PO Box 370 63730 573-722-3584
C.A. Counts, prin. Fax 722-5479

Albany, Gentry, Pop. 1,832
Albany R-III SD 500/PK-12
101 W Jefferson St 64402 660-726-3911
Dwayne Cross, supt. Fax 726-5841
www.albany.k12.mo.us
Albany HS 200/9-12
101 W Jefferson St 64402 660-726-3912
Michael Adkins, prin. Fax 726-5841
Albany MS 100/6-8
101 W Jefferson St 64402 660-726-3912
Michael Adkins, prin. Fax 726-5841

Alma, Lafayette, Pop. 378
Santa Fe R-X SD 400/K-12
PO Box 197 64001 660-674-2238
Dr. Douglas Wright, supt. Fax 674-2239
schoolweb.missouri.edu/santafe.k12.mo.us/
Santa Fe HS 200/7-12
PO Box 197 64001 660-674-2236
Tom Burton, prin. Fax 674-2760

Alton, Oregon, Pop. 648
Alton R-IV SD 700/K-12
RR 2 Box 2180 65606 417-778-7216
Sheila Wheeler, supt. Fax 778-6394
schoolweb.missouri.edu/alton.k12.mo.us
Alton HS 400/7-12
RR 2 Box 2180 65606 417-778-7215
Dave McQuerter, prin. Fax 778-7851

Amoret, Bates, Pop. 217
Miami R-I SD 200/K-12
RR 1 Box 418 64722 660-267-3480
Verlin Tyler, supt. Fax 267-3630
www.miami-eagles.k12.mo.us/
Miami JSHS 100/7-12
RR 1 Box 418 64722 660-267-3484
Garry Dunn, prin. Fax 267-3630

Anderson, McDonald, Pop. 1,902
McDonald County R-I SD 3,600/PK-12
100 Mustang Dr 64831 417-845-3321
Randall Smith, supt. Fax 845-6972
www.mcdonaldco.k12.mo.us/
Anderson JHS 200/7-8
100 Red Bird Ln 64831 417-845-3488
Ted Snodgrass, prin. Fax 845-7406
McDonald County HS 1,000/9-12
100 Mustang Dr 64831 417-845-3322
Stephen Buckingham, prin. Fax 845-8467

Annapolis, Iron, Pop. 298
South Iron County R-I SD 500/PK-12
PO Box 218 63620 573-598-4241
Brad Crocker, supt. Fax 598-4210
www.schoolweb.missouri.edu/southiron.k12.mo.us/
South Iron JSHS 200/7-12
PO Box 218 63620 573-598-4241
David Haug, prin. Fax 598-4210

Appleton City, Saint Clair, Pop. 1,318
Appleton City R-II SD 400/K-12
PO Box 126 64724 660-476-2161
Bob Elder, supt. Fax 476-5564
appletoncity.k12.mo.us/
Appleton City HS 200/7-12
PO Box 126 64724 660-476-2118
Jaret Tomlinson, prin. Fax 476-5564

Archie, Cass, Pop. 958
Archie R-V SD 600/PK-12
PO Box 106 64725 816-293-5312
Dr. Forrest Bollow, supt. Fax 293-5712
Archie JSHS 300/6-12
PO Box 106 64725 816-293-5312
Rick Stark, prin. Fax 293-5712

Arnold, Jefferson, Pop. 20,413
Fox C-6 SD 11,400/PK-12
745 Jeffco Blvd 63010 636-296-8000
Dr. Dianne Brown, supt. Fax 282-5170
www.fox.k12.mo.us
Fox HS 1,800/9-12
751 Jeffco Blvd 63010 636-296-5210
Dr. Kevin Rossiter, prin. Fax 282-6980
Fox MS 600/7-8
743 Jeffco Blvd 63010 636-296-5077
Laura Gabler, prin. Fax 282-5171
Ridgewood MS 500/7-8
1401 Ridgewood School Rd 63010 636-282-1459
Kristen Pelster, prin. Fax 282-5193
Other Schools – See Imperial

Holy Child MS 100/6-8
2322 Tenbrook Rd 63010 636-296-1544
Joann Coyle, prin. Fax 296-7823
ITT Technical Institute Post-Sec.
1930 Meyer Drury Dr 63010 636-464-6600

Ash Grove, Greene, Pop. 1,491
Ash Grove R-IV SD 900/K-12
100 N Maple Ln 65604 417-751-2534
Richard Harris, supt. Fax 751-2283
www.ashgrove.k12.mo.us/
Ash Grove JSHS 400/7-12
100 N Maple Ln 65604 417-751-2330
Don Christensen, prin. Fax 751-2889

Ashland, Boone, Pop. 2,175
Southern Boone County R-I SD 1,300/K-12
PO Box 168 65010 573-657-2147
Susan Gauzy, supt. Fax 657-5513
schoolweb.missouri.edu/ashland.k12.mo.us/
Southern Boone County HS 400/9-12
PO Box 168 65010 573-657-2144
Johnny Thompson, prin. Fax 657-9035
Southern Boone County MS 300/6-8
PO Box 168 65010 573-657-2146
Robert Simpson, prin. Fax 657-5519

Atlanta, Macon, Pop. 453
Atlanta C-3 SD 200/K-12
PO Box 367 63530 660-239-4212
William Perkins, supt. Fax 239-4205
www.atlanta.k12.mo.us/
Atlanta JSHS 100/7-12
PO Box 367 63530 660-239-4211
Steve Coulson, prin. Fax 239-4205

Aurora, Lawrence, Pop. 7,307
Aurora R-VIII SD 2,100/PK-12
409 W Locust St 65605 417-678-3373
Dr. Dale Slagle, supt. Fax 678-4043
www.hdnet.k12.mo.us
Aurora HS 600/9-12
101 S Roosevelt Ave 65605 417-678-3355
Alana Pharis, prin. Fax 678-2905
Robinson JHS 300/7-8
1044 S Lincoln Ave 65605 417-678-3630
Bill Kirby, prin. Fax 678-2487

Ava, Douglas, Pop. 3,078
Ava R-I SD 1,600/PK-12
PO Box 338 65608 417-683-4717
Dr. Andrew Underwood, supt. Fax 683-6329
www.avaschools.k12.mo.us/
Ava HS 500/9-12
PO Box 338 65608 417-683-5747
David Rickner, prin. Fax 683-2306
Ava MS 500/5-8
PO Box 338 65608 417-683-3835
Brad Plackemeier, prin. Fax 683-9101

Ava Victory Academy 100/PK-12
PO Box 608 65608 417-683-6630
Daniel Letzinger, admin. Fax 683-1402
Teen Harvest 50/5-12
HC 71 Box 352 65608 417-683-1080
Paul Neighbour, admin. Fax 683-1080

Bakersfield, Ozark, Pop. 286
Bakersfield R-IV SD 400/PK-12
PO Box 38 65609 417-284-7333
Jackie Estes, supt. Fax 284-7335
Bakersfield JSHS 200/6-12
PO Box 38 65609 417-284-3744
Greg Jackson, prin. Fax 284-7335

Ballwin, Saint Louis, Pop. 30,481
Parkway C-2 SD
Supt. — See Chesterfield
Parkway South HS 2,100/9-12
801 Hanna Rd 63021 314-415-7700
Gary Mazzola, prin. Fax 415-7712
Parkway Southwest MS 800/6-8
701 Wren Ave 63021 314-415-7300
Chelsea Watson, prin. Fax 415-7334
Parkway West HS 1,500/9-12
14653 Clayton Rd 63011 314-415-7500
Beth Plunkett, prin. Fax 415-7534

Rockwood R-VI SD
Supt. — See Eureka
Crestview MS 1,200/6-8
16025 Clayton Rd 63011 636-207-2520
James Wipke, prin. Fax 207-2529
Lafayette HS 2,100/9-12
17050 Clayton Rd 63011 636-458-7200
John Shaughnessy, prin. Fax 458-7219
Selvidge MS 700/6-8
235 New Ballwin Rd 63021 636-207-2622
Sean Stryhal, prin. Fax 207-2632

Grabber School of Hair Design Post-Sec.
14557 Manchester Rd 63011 636-227-4440

Barnard, Nodaway, Pop. 250
South Nodaway County R-IV SD 200/PK-12
209 Morehouse St 64423 660-652-3221
Terry Hutchings, supt. Fax 652-3413
missouri.ihigh.com/southnodaway
South Nodaway JSHS 100/7-12
209 Morehouse St 64423 660-652-3727
Kyle Collins, prin. Fax 652-3411

Bell City, Stoddard, Pop. 453
Bell City R-II SD 300/K-12
25254 Walnut St 63735 573-733-4444
Rhonda Niemczyk, supt. Fax 733-4114
Bell City JSHS 200/7-12
25254 Walnut St 63735 573-733-4444
Matthew Asher, prin. Fax 733-4114

Belle, Maries, Pop. 1,348
Maries County R-II SD 800/PK-12
PO Box 819 65013 573-859-3800
Dr. Ted Spessard, supt. Fax 859-3883
Belle HS 200/9-12
PO Box 819 65013 573-859-6114
Thomas Keller, prin. Fax 859-3883
Other Schools – See Bland

Belton, Cass, Pop. 24,140
Belton SD 124 4,800/PK-12
110 W Walnut St 64012 816-348-1000
Dr. Kenneth Southwick, supt. Fax 348-1068
www.beltonschools.org
Belton HS Freshman Center 400/9-9
801 W North Ave 64012 816-348-1726
Bob Poisal, prin. Fax 348-1727
Belton SHS 1,000/10-12
107 Pirate Pkwy 64012 816-348-1036
Virgil Poisal, prin. Fax 348-1516
Yeokum MS 700/7-8
613 Mill St 64012 816-348-1042
Jeff Mehlenbacher, prin. Fax 348-1534

Heartland Family S 200/PK-12
810 S Cedar St 64012 816-331-1000
Brian Baker, hdmstr. Fax 322-2782

Benton, Scott, Pop. 729
Scott County R-IV SD 1,000/K-12
4035 State Highway 77 63736 573-545-3887
Don Moore, supt. Fax 545-3929
kelly.k12.mo.us/
Kelly HS 300/9-12
4035 State Highway 77 63736 573-545-3541
Tom Hulshof, prin. Fax 545-4485
Scott County MS 300/6-8
4035 State Highway 77 63736 573-545-3541
Mark Kiehne, prin. Fax 545-4386

Stage One The Hair Academy Post-Sec.
547 County Highway 250 63736 573-335-5078

Berkeley, Saint Louis, Pop. 9,631
Ferguson-Florissant R-II SD
Supt. — See Florissant
Berkeley MS 400/7-8
8300 Frost Ave 63134 314-524-3883
Winston Rogers, prin. Fax 521-4826

Bernie, Stoddard, Pop. 1,801
Bernie R-XIII SD 600/PK-12
516 W Main Ave 63822 573-293-5333
Robin Ritchie, supt. Fax 293-5731
www.bernie.k12.mo.us
Bernie JSHS 300/7-12
516 W Main Ave 63822 573-293-5334
Scott Mercer, prin. Fax 293-5731

Bethany, Harrison, Pop. 3,060
South Harrison County R-II SD 900/PK-12
PO Box 445 64424 660-425-8044
Richard Smith, supt. Fax 425-7050
www.shr2.k12.mo.us
North Central Career Center Vo/Tech
PO Box 445 64424 660-425-2196
Larry Linthacum, dir. Fax 425-2197
South Harrison County R-II HS 400/7-12
PO Box 445 64424 660-425-8051
Dennis Eastin, prin. Fax 425-7447

Bevier, Macon, Pop. 729
Bevier C-4 SD 200/K-12
400 Bloomington St 63532 660-773-6611
Joan Patrick, supt. Fax 773-6964
Bevier HS 100/9-12
400 Bloomington St 63532 660-773-5213
Kenneth Kelso, prin. Fax 773-6964

Billings, Christian, Pop. 1,142
Billings R-IV SD 400/K-12
118 W Mount Vernon Rd 65610 417-744-2623
Cynthia Brandt, supt. Fax 744-4545
www.billings.k12.mo.us
Billings HS 200/7-12
118 W Mount Vernon Rd 65610 417-744-2551
Jim Millsap, prin. Fax 744-2720

Bismarck, Saint Francois, Pop. 1,558
Bismarck R-V SD 600/K-12
PO Box 257 63624 573-734-6111
Dr. Damon Gamble, supt. Fax 734-2957
schoolweb.missouri.edu/bismarck.k12.mo.us
Bismarck JSHS 300/7-12
PO Box 257 63624 573-734-6111
James Bell, prin. Fax 734-2957

Black, Reynolds
Lesterville R-IV SD
Supt. — See Lesterville
Lesterville Ranch Campus 100/K-12
RR 1 Box 127 63625 573-269-4207
Mary T. Balderas, prin. Fax 269-4277

Bland, Gasconade, Pop. 571
Maries County R-II SD
Supt. — See Belle
Maries County MS 200/6-8
PO Box 10 65014 573-646-3912
Dwane Smith, prin. Fax 646-3148

Bloomfield, Stoddard, Pop. 1,888
Bloomfield R-XIV SD 800/PK-12
PO Box 650 63825 573-568-4564
Dr. Sheila Perry, supt. Fax 568-4565
bloomfield.k12.mo.us/
Bloomfield HS 200/9-12
PO Box 650 63825 573-568-2146
Eric Boles, prin. Fax 568-2147

Blue Eye, Stone, Pop. 97
Blue Eye R-V SD 700/PK-12
PO Box 105 65611 417-779-5332
Dan Ray, supt. Fax 779-2151
www.blueeye.k12.mo.us
Blue Eye HS 200/9-12
PO Box 105 65611 417-779-5331
Ben Johnson, prin. Fax 779-2151
Blue Eye MS 300/5-8
PO Box 38 65611 417-779-4299
Craig Linson, prin. Fax 779-4526

Blue Springs, Jackson, Pop. 53,099
Blue Springs R-IV SD 13,300/K-12
1801 NW Vesper St 64015 816-224-1300
Dr. Paul Kinder, supt. Fax 224-1310
www.bluesprings-schools.net
Blue Springs Freshman Center 1,100/9-9
2103 NW Vesper St 64015 816-224-1325
Dan Anderson, prin. Fax 224-1344
Blue Springs HS 1,600/10-12
2000 NW Ashton Dr 64015 816-229-3459
David Adams, prin. Fax 229-1025
Blue Springs South HS 1,400/10-12
1200 SE Adams Dairy Pkwy 64014 816-224-1315
Keith Maxey, prin. Fax 224-1324
Brittany Hill MS 800/6-8
2701 NW 1st St 64014 816-224-1700
Lee Holstrom, prin. Fax 224-1704
Moreland Ridge MS 900/6-8
900 SW Bishop Dr 64015 816-224-1800
Kevin Grover, prin. Fax 224-1805
Sunny Vale MS 700/6-8
3930 S R D Mize Rd 64015 816-224-1330
Beverly Leonard, prin. Fax 224-1309
Other Schools – See Lees Summit

House of Heavilin Beauty College Post-Sec.
2000 SW State Route 7 64014 816-229-9000
Plaza Heights Christian Academy 200/PK-12
1500 SW Clark Rd 64015 816-228-0670
Michael Hart, admin. Fax 229-4092

Bolivar, Polk, Pop. 10,179
Bolivar R-I SD 2,400/PK-12
524 W Madison St 65613 417-326-5291
Leonard Zanatta, supt. Fax 326-3562
www.bolivar.k12.mo.us/
Bolivar HS 700/9-12
1401 Highway D 65613 417-326-5228
J. Collins, prin. Fax 326-4325
Bolivar MS 600/6-8
604 W Jackson St 65613 417-326-3811
Shane Dublin, prin. Fax 326-8277

Southwest Baptist University Post-Sec.
1600 University Ave 65613 417-328-5281

Bonne Terre, Saint Francois, Pop. 6,520
North St. Francois County R-I SD 3,100/PK-12
300 Berry Rd 63628 573-358-2247
Yancy Poorman, supt. Fax 358-2377
www.ncsd.k12.mo.us/
North St. Francois County HS 1,000/9-12
7151 Raider Rd 63628 573-358-8890
Ron McCutchen, prin. Fax 358-0021
Unitec Career Center Vo/Tech
7163 Raider Rd 63628 573-358-2271
Steve Noble, prin. Fax 358-3577
Other Schools – See Desloge

Boonville, Cooper, Pop. 8,669
Boonville R-I SD 1,500/PK-12
736 Main St 65233 660-882-7474
Mark Ficken, supt. Fax 882-5721
www.boonville.k12.mo.us/
Boonslick Technical Education Center Vo/Tech
1694 W Ashley Rd 65233 660-882-5306
Joyce Schuster, dir. Fax 882-3269
Boonville HS 500/9-12
1690A W Ashley Rd 65233 660-882-7426
Jay M. Webster, prin. Fax 882-3368
Elliott MS 400/6-8
700 Main St 65233 660-882-6649
Ono Monachino, prin. Fax 882-8646

Bosworth, Carroll, Pop. 388
Bosworth R-V SD 200/PK-12
102 E Eldridge St 64623 660-534-7311
Linda Specie, supt. Fax 534-7409
Bosworth JSHS 100/7-12
102 E Eldridge St 64623 660-534-7311
Linda Specie, prin. Fax 534-7409

Bourbon, Crawford, Pop. 1,408
Crawford County R-I SD 1,100/PK-12
1444 S Old Highway 66 65441 573-732-4426
Christopher Gaines, supt. Fax 732-4545
warhawks.k12.mo.us/
Bourbon HS 300/9-12
1500 S Old Highway 66 65441 573-732-5615
Tami Bobbitt, prin. Fax 732-4407
Bourbon MS 400/5-8
363 Jost St 65441 573-732-4424
James Hale, prin. Fax 732-4424

Bowling Green, Pike, Pop. 5,185
Bowling Green R-I SD 1,500/K-12
700 W Adams St 63334 573-324-5441
Frank Berlin, supt. Fax 324-2439
www.bgschools.k12.mo.us
Bowling Green HS 500/9-12
700 W Adams St 63334 573-324-5341
Kent Hufty, prin. Fax 324-3011
Bowling Green MS 400/6-8
700 W Adams St 63334 573-324-2181
Jeff Swartz, prin. Fax 324-2439

Bradleyville, Taney, Pop. 84
Bradleyville R-I SD 200/K-12
PO Box 20 65614 417-796-2288
Joe Combs, supt. Fax 796-2289
Bradleyville JSHS 100/7-12
PO Box 20 65614 417-796-2288
Robert Comer, prin. Fax 796-2289

Branson, Taney, Pop. 7,010
Branson R-IV SD 3,400/K-12
400 Cedar Ridge Dr 65616 417-334-6541
Dr. Doug Hayter, supt. Fax 334-6619
www.branson.k12.mo.us
Branson HS 1,100/9-12
935 Buchanan Rd 65616 417-334-6511
Chip Arnette, prin. Fax 332-3212
Branson JHS 500/7-8
263 Buccaneer Dr 65616 417-334-3087
Brad Swofford, prin. Fax 336-3913

Faith Christian Academy 100/PK-12
627 Skyview Dr 65616 417-337-5605
Frances Hatten, prin. Fax 337-5625

Brashear, Adair, Pop. 272
Adair County R-II SD 300/K-12
205 W Dewey St 63533 660-323-5272
Diane Bradley, supt. Fax 323-5250
brashear.k12.mo.us
Adair County R-II JSHS 100/7-12
205 W Dewey St 63533 660-323-5272
Jeff McHenry, prin. Fax 323-5250

Braymer, Caldwell, Pop. 962
Braymer C-4 SD 400/PK-12
400 Bobcat Ave 64624 660-645-2284
Dr. Dorothy Benson, supt. Fax 645-2780
www.brayc4.k12.mo.us/
Braymer JSHS 200/7-12
400 Bobcat Ave 64624 660-645-2284
Gwenda Barton, prin. Fax 645-2780

Breckenridge, Caldwell, Pop. 462
Breckenridge R-I SD 100/K-12
400 W Colfax St 64625 660-644-5715
Roger Blakely, supt. Fax 644-5710
www.breckenridgeschool.org/
Breckenridge JSHS 50/7-12
400 W Colfax St 64625 660-644-5715
John Dunham, prin. Fax 644-5710

Brentwood, Saint Louis, Pop. 7,365
Brentwood SD 800/K-12
90 Yorkshire Lane Ct 63144 314-962-4507
Charles Penberthy, supt. Fax 962-7302
www.brentwood.k12.mo.us
Brentwood HS 200/9-12
2221 High School Dr 63144 314-962-3837
David Faulkner, prin. Fax 963-3166
Brentwood MS 200/6-8
9127 White Ave 63144 314-962-8238
Julie Sperry, prin. Fax 968-8724

Brighton, Polk
Pleasant Hope R-VI SD
Supt. — See Pleasant Hope
Pleasant Hope Ranch S 100/6-12
5545 N Highway 13 65617 417-376-3000
Vera Ker, prin. Fax 376-3575

Bronaugh, Vernon, Pop. 248
Bronaugh R-VII SD 200/PK-12
527 E 6th St 64728 417-922-3211
Patricia Phillips, supt. Fax 922-3308
www.bronaugh.k12.mo.us/
Bronaugh JSHS 100/7-12
527 E 6th St 64728 417-922-3211
Tim Judd, prin. Fax 922-3308

Brookfield, Linn, Pop. 4,506
Brookfield R-III SD 1,200/PK-12
124A N Pershing Dr 64628 660-258-7443
Dr. Paul Barger, supt. Fax 258-4711
www.brookfield.k12.mo.us
Brookfield Area Career Center Vo/Tech
122 N Pershing Dr 64628 660-258-2682
Carey Smith, prin. Fax 258-3875
Brookfield HS 300/9-12
124 N Pershing Dr 64628 660-258-7242
Bob Brinkley, prin. Fax 258-2871
Brookfield MS 300/6-8
126 N Pershing Dr 64628 660-258-7335
Melinda Wilbeck, prin. Fax 258-2190

Broseley, Butler
Twin Rivers R-X SD 1,000/K-12
PO Box 146 63932 573-328-4321
Andy Arbeitman, supt. Fax 328-1070
www.semo.net/schools/TwinRivers/
Twin Rivers HS 300/9-12
PO Box 146 63932 573-328-4730
Jerry Stockton, prin. Fax 328-1511

Brunswick, Chariton, Pop. 895
Brunswick R-II SD 300/PK-12
1008 County Rd 65236 660-548-3550
Dr. Bill Page, supt. Fax 548-3029
schoolweb.missouri.edu/brunswick.k12.mo.us/
Brunswick JSHS 100/7-12
1008 County Rd 65236 660-548-3771
David Figg, prin. Fax 548-3072

Bucklin, Linn, Pop. 496
Bucklin R-II SD 100/K-12
26832 Highway 129 64631 660-695-3555
Rick Roberts, supt. Fax 695-3345
www.bucklin.k12.mo.us/
Bucklin R-II S 100/K-12
26832 Highway 129 64631 660-695-3225
Rick Roberts, prin. Fax 695-3345

Buffalo, Dallas, Pop. 3,006
Dallas County R-I SD 1,900/PK-12
309 W Commercial St 65622 417-345-2222
Gary Arthaud, supt. Fax 345-8446
www.dallasr1.k12.mo.us/
Buffalo HS 600/9-12
500 W Main St 65622 417-345-2223
Shawn Randles, prin. Fax 345-8495
Buffalo MS 600/5-8
1001 Truman 65622 417-345-2335
Sandra Goss, prin. Fax 345-5968
Other Schools – See Louisburg

Bunceton, Cooper, Pop. 357
Cooper County R-IV SD 200/K-12
PO Box 110 65237 660-427-5347
Mary Battles, supt. Fax 427-5348
bunceton.k12.mo.us
Bunceton JSHS 100/7-12
PO Box 110 65237 660-427-5415
Connie Kunze, prin. Fax 427-5348

Bunker, Reynolds, Pop. 437
Bunker R-III SD 300/K-12
PO Box 365 63629 573-689-2507
Glenda Milner, supt. Fax 689-2011
Bunker JSHS 100/7-12
PO Box 365 63629 573-689-2211
Ken Cook, prin. Fax 689-2011

Burlington Junction, Nodaway, Pop. 613
West Nodaway R-I SD 400/PK-12
PO Box 260 64428 660-725-4613
Terry Buholt, supt. Fax 725-4300
West Nodaway JSHS 200/7-12
PO Box 260 64428 660-725-3317
Jim Cassity, prin. Fax 725-4300

Butler, Bates, Pop. 4,249
Ballard R-II SD 100/K-12
RR 1 Box 497 64730 816-297-2656
Gary Layton, supt. Fax 297-4002
Ballard JSHS 100/7-12
RR 1 Box 497 64730 816-297-2656
John Siebeneck, prin. Fax 297-4002

Butler R-V SD 1,100/PK-12
420 S Fulton St 64730 660-679-0653
Sterling Green, supt. Fax 679-6626
butler.k12.mo.us
Butler JSHS 500/7-12
420 S Fulton St 64730 660-679-6121
Greg Sewell, prin. Fax 679-6626

Cabool, Texas, Pop. 2,140
Cabool R-IV SD 900/PK-12
PO Box 613 65689 417-962-3153
Wesley Davis, supt. Fax 962-5043
www.cabool.k12.mo.us/index.html
Cabool HS 300/9-12
PO Box 613 65689 417-962-3153
Dan Chappell, prin. Fax 962-5663
Cabool MS 300/5-8
PO Box 613 65689 417-962-3153
Gary Flippin, prin. Fax 962-0078

Cadet, Washington
Kingston SD K-14 800/K-12
10047 Diamond Rd 63630 573-438-4982
Gary Milner, supt. Fax 438-8813
www.kingston.k12.mo.us/
Kingston HS 300/9-12
10047 Diamond Rd 63630 573-438-4982
Dale Van Deven, prin. Fax 438-1212
Kingston MS 200/6-8
10047 Diamond Rd 63630 573-438-4982
Dale Van Deven, prin. Fax 438-1212

Cainsville, Harrison, Pop. 373
Cainsville R-I SD 100/PK-12
PO Box 108 64632 660-893-5213
Donald Wilburn, supt. Fax 893-5713
Cainsville JSHS 100/7-12
PO Box 108 64632 660-893-5214
Donald Wilburn, prin. Fax 893-5713

Cairo, Randolph, Pop. 304
Northeast Randolph County R-IV SD 400/K-12
301 W Martin St 65239 660-263-2788
Marge Gibson, supt. Fax 263-5735
Northeast JSHS 200/6-12
301 W Martin St 65239 660-263-2788
Greg Taylor, prin. Fax 263-5735

Caledonia, Washington, Pop. 163
Valley R-VI SD 500/K-12
1 Viking Dr 63631 573-779-3446
John Yount, supt. Fax 779-3505
www.valley.k12.mo.us/
Valley JSHS 200/7-12
1 Viking Dr 63631 573-779-3515
Ray Politte, prin. Fax 779-3346

Calhoun, Henry, Pop. 508
Calhoun R-VIII SD 200/PK-12
409 S College St 65323 660-694-3422
John Crane, supt. Fax 694-3501
Calhoun JSHS 100/7-12
200 W 7th St 65323 660-694-3412
Brian Wishard, prin. Fax 694-3333

California, Moniteau, Pop. 4,137
Moniteau County R-I SD 1,300/K-12
211 S Owen St Ste B 65018 573-796-2145
Mary Wood, supt. Fax 796-6123
www.californiak12.org/
California HS 500/9-12
1501 W Buchanan St 65018 573-796-4911
Scott Jarvis, prin. Fax 796-4503
California MS 300/6-8
211 S Owen St 65018 573-796-2146
Amy Ramsdell, prin. Fax 796-8257

Camdenton, Camden, Pop. 3,061
Camdenton R-III SD 4,000/PK-12
PO Box 1409 65020 573-346-9213
Ronald Hendricks, supt. Fax 346-9211
camdenton.k12.mo.us/
Camdenton HS 1,400/9-12
PO Box 1409 65020 573-346-9232
Dr. Brian Henry, prin. Fax 346-9238
Camdenton MS 700/7-8
PO Box 1409 65020 573-346-9257
Sean Kirksey, prin. Fax 346-9288
Lake Career & Technical Center Vo/Tech
PO Box 1409 65020 573-346-9260
Dr. Gail White, dir. Fax 346-9284

Cameron, Clinton, Pop. 9,141
Cameron R-I SD 1,500/PK-12
423 N Chestnut St 64429 816-632-2170
Dr. Ronald White, supt. Fax 632-2612
www.cameron.k12.mo.us
Cameron HS 500/9-12
1022 S Chestnut St 64429 816-632-2129
Don Gerber, prin. Fax 632-1634
Cameron MS 500/5-8
915 Park Ave 64429 816-632-2185
Dwight Sanders, prin. Fax 632-3752

Campbell, Dunklin, Pop. 1,872
Campbell R-II SD 700/PK-12
801 S State Route 53 63933 573-246-2133
Darrell Wilburn, supt. Fax 246-3212
www.campbell.k12.mo.us
Campbell JSHS 300/7-12
801 S State Route 53 63933 573-246-2576
Jay Thornton, prin. Fax 246-2890

Canton, Lewis, Pop. 2,502
Canton R-V SD 600/PK-12
200 S 4th St 63435 573-288-5216
David Tramel, supt. Fax 288-5442
canton.k12.mo.us/
Canton JSHS 300/7-12
200 S 4th St 63435 573-288-5216
Andy Turgeon, prin. Fax 288-5442

Culver-Stockton College Post-Sec.
1 College Hl 63435 573-288-5221

Cape Girardeau, Cape Girardeau, Pop. 36,204
Cape Girardeau SD 63 4,000/PK-12
301 N Clark St 63701 573-335-1867
Mark Bowles, supt. Fax 335-1820
cape.k12.mo.us
Cape Girardeau Career & Technology Ctr. Vo/Tech
1080 S Silver Springs Rd 63703 573-334-0826
Rich Payne, dir. Fax 334-5930
Central HS 1,400/9-12
1000 S Silver Springs Rd 63703 573-335-8228
Dr. Mike Cowan, prin. Fax 334-1114
Central JHS 700/7-8
205 Caruthers St 63701 573-334-2923
Roy Merideth, prin. Fax 335-7173

Cape Girardeau Career & Technical School Post-Sec.
1080 S Silver Springs Rd 63703 573-334-0826
Eagle Ridge Christian S 200/PK-12
4210 State Highway K 63701 573-339-1335
Janice Margrabe, admin. Fax 339-1390
Metro Business College Post-Sec.
1732 N Kingshighway St 63701 573-334-9181
Notre Dame Regional HS 500/9-12
265 Notre Dame Dr 63701 573-335-6772
Br. David Migliorino, prin. Fax 335-3458
Southeast MO Hospital College of Nursing Post-Sec.
2001 William St # 2 63703 573-334-6825
Southeast Missouri State University Post-Sec.
1 University Plz 63701 573-651-2000

Cardwell, Dunklin, Pop. 751
Southland C-9 SD 400/PK-12
500 S Main St 63829 573-654-3574
Raymond Lasley, supt. Fax 654-3575
Southland JSHS 200/7-12
500 S Main St 63829 573-654-3531
Ted Wilkerson, prin. Fax 654-3534

Carl Junction, Jasper, Pop. 6,483
Carl Junction R-I SD 2,900/K-12
PO Box 4 64834 417-649-7026
Phillip Cook, supt. Fax 649-6594
www.cj.k12.mo.us
Carl Junction HS 800/9-12
PO Box 4 64834 417-649-7081
Georgiana McGriff, prin. Fax 649-5791
Carl Junction JHS 500/7-8
PO Box 4 64834 417-649-7246
Debra Elbrader, prin. Fax 649-0022

Carrollton, Carroll, Pop. 4,012
Carrollton R-VII SD 1,000/PK-12
300 E 9th St 64633 660-542-2769
Fax 542-3416
Carrollton Area Career Center Vo/Tech
305 E 10th St 64633 660-542-0000
George Eiserer, dir. Fax 542-0600
Carrollton HS 300/9-12
300 E 9th St 64633 660-542-1276
Robert O. Kottman, prin. Fax 542-1903
Carrollton JHS 200/7-8
300 E 9th St 64633 660-542-3472
Brent Dobbins, prin. Fax 542-3169

Carthage, Jasper, Pop. 13,096
Carthage R-IX SD 3,700/PK-12
710 Lyon St 64836 417-359-7000
Gary Reed, supt. Fax 359-7004
www.carthage.k12.mo.us
Carthage JHS 900/7-9
827 E Centennial Ave 64836 417-359-7050
Ron Wallace, prin. Fax 359-7057
Carthage SHS 800/10-12
714 S Main St 64836 417-359-7020
Phil Lewis, prin. Fax 359-7037
Carthage Technical Center Vo/Tech
609 S River St 64836 417-359-7026
Eddie Stephens, prin. Fax 359-7098

Caruthersville, Pemiscot, Pop. 6,450
Caruthersville SD 18 1,600/PK-12
1711 Ward Ave 63830 573-333-6100
Dr. Nick Thiele, supt. Fax 333-6108
www.caruthersville.k12.mo.us/
Caruthersville HS 400/9-12
1708 Ward Ave 63830 573-333-6110
Mike Wallace, prin. Fax 333-6117
Caruthersville MS 400/6-8
1705 Ward Ave 63830 573-333-6120
Jimmie Jean Bullington, prin. Fax 333-1835

Cassville, Barry, Pop. 3,095
Cassville R-IV SD 2,100/PK-12
1501 Main St 65625 417-847-2221
Jim Orrell, supt. Fax 847-4009
wildcats.cassville.k12.mo.us/
Cassville HS 700/9-12
1501 Main St 65625 417-847-3137
Brad F. Hanson, prin. Fax 847-5111
Cassville MS 500/6-8
1501 Main St 65625 417-847-3136
Eric White, prin. Fax 847-3156

Cedar Hill, Jefferson, Pop. 1,966
Northwest R-I SD
Supt. — See High Ridge
Northwest HS 2,300/9-12
6005 Cedar Hill Rd 63016 636-274-0555
James Knirr, prin. Fax 274-2076

Center, Ralls, Pop. 637
Ralls County R-II SD 800/PK-12
21622 Highway 19 63436 573-267-3397
Deanette Jarman, supt. Fax 267-3538
rallsr2.k12.mo.us/
Twain HS 300/9-12
21622 Highway 19 63436 573-267-3397
Paul Mensching, prin. Fax 267-3538
Twain JHS 200/6-8
21622 Highway 19 63436 573-267-3397
Cheryl Mack, prin. Fax 267-3538

Centerview, Johnson, Pop. 258
Johnson County R-VII SD 700/PK-12
92 NW State Route 58 64019 660-656-3316
Dr. Craig Eaton, supt. Fax 656-3633
crs.k12.mo.us
Crest Ridge HS 200/9-12
92 NW State Route 58 64019 660-656-3391
Rebecca Gudde, prin. Fax 656-3633
Crest Ridge MS 200/6-8
92 NW State Route 58 64019 660-656-3843
Rebecca Gudde, prin. Fax 656-3633

Johnson County Christian Academy 100/PK-12
401 S Walnut St 64019 660-656-3307
Rick Deno, admin. Fax 656-3320

Centralia, Boone, Pop. 3,657
Centralia R-VI SD 1,400/PK-12
635 S Jefferson St 65240 573-682-3561
Darin Ford, supt. Fax 682-2181
www.centralia.k12.mo.us
Boren MS 400/5-8
110 N Jefferson St 65240 573-682-2617
Vincent Matlick, prin. Fax 682-1500
Centralia HS 400/9-12
849 S Jefferson St 65240 573-682-3508
John Rinehart, prin. Fax 682-2749

Sunnydale Adventist Academy 100/9-12
6818 Audrain Road 9139 65240 573-682-2164
Gary Russell, prin. Fax 682-3136

Chadwick, Christian
Chadwick R-I SD 200/K-12
7090 State Highway 125 S 65629 417-634-3588
Dr. William Wheeler, supt. Fax 634-2668
Chadwick JSHS 100/7-12
7090 State Highway 125 S 65629 417-634-3588
Jesse Blevins, prin. Fax 634-2668

Chaffee, Scott, Pop. 3,006
Chaffee R-II SD 600/PK-12
517 W Yoakum Ave 63740 573-887-3532
Ken Latham, supt. Fax 887-3926
schoolweb.missouri.edu/chaffeeRII.k12.mo.us
Chaffee JSHS 300/7-12
517 W Yoakum Ave 63740 573-887-3226
Neil Glass, prin. Fax 887-3926

Chamois, Osage, Pop. 473
Osage County R-I SD 200/K-12
614 S Poplar St 65024 573-763-5666
Thomas Allen, supt. Fax 763-5686
www.chamois.k12.mo.us
Chamois JSHS 100/7-12
614 S Poplar St 65024 573-763-5393
Brad Strobel, prin. Fax 763-5686

Charleston, Mississippi, Pop. 5,129
Charleston R-I SD 1,200/K-12
PO Box 39 63834 573-683-3776
Kevin Miller, supt. Fax 683-2909
charleston.k12.mo.us/
Charleston HS 300/9-12
PO Box 39 63834 573-683-3761
David Wilson, prin. Fax 683-2909
Charleston MS 300/6-8
PO Box 39 63834 573-683-3346
Pamela Ferrell, prin. Fax 683-2909

Chesterfield, Saint Louis, Pop. 47,020
Parkway C-2 SD 19,000/PK-12
455 N Woods Mill Rd 63017 314-415-8100
Robert Malito Ph.D., supt. Fax 415-8009
www.pkwy.k12.mo.us/index.cfm
Parkway Central HS 1,400/9-12
369 N Woods Mill Rd 63017 314-415-7900
Tim Gannon, prin. Fax 415-7913
Parkway Central MS 1,000/6-8
471 N Woods Mill Rd 63017 314-415-7800
Lauretta Holloway, prin. Fax 415-7834
Parkway West MS 1,100/6-8
2312 Baxter Rd 63017 314-415-7400
Linda Lelonek, prin. Fax 415-7409
Other Schools – See Ballwin, Creve Coeur, Manchester

Rockwood R-VI SD
Supt. — See Eureka
Marquette HS 2,100/9-12
2351 Clarkson Rd 63017 636-537-4300
Dr. Paige Muench, prin. Fax 537-4319

Chesterfield Day S 500/PK-12
1100 White Rd 63017 314-469-6622
Marianne Kearney, prin. Fax 469-7889
Gateway Academy PK-12
17815 Wild Horse Creek Rd 63005 636-519-9099
Larry Hofstetter, dir. Fax 519-1621
Logan College of Chiropractic Post-Sec.
1851 Schoettler Rd 63017 636-227-2100
St. Joseph's Institute for the Deaf Post-Sec.
1809 Clarkson Rd 63017 636-532-3211
Westwood Jr. Academy 50/PK-10
16601 Wild Horse Creek Rd 63005 636-519-8222
Fax 519-8221

Chilhowee, Johnson, Pop. 340
Chilhowee R-IV SD 100/K-12
101 Highway 2 64733 660-678-2511
Andy Henley, supt. Fax 678-5711
www.chilhowee.k12.mo.us
Chilhowee JSHS 100/7-12
101 Highway 2 64733 660-678-4511
Renee Gregory, prin. Fax 678-5711

Chillicothe, Livingston, Pop. 8,686
Chillicothe R-II SD 2,000/K-12
PO Box 530 64601 660-646-4566
Dale Wallace, supt. Fax 646-6508
www.chillicotheschools.org/
Chillicothe HS 600/9-12
2801 Hornet Rd 64601 660-646-0700
Thomas Anderson, prin. Fax 646-7106
Chillicothe MS 500/6-8
1529 Calhoun St 64601 660-646-1916
Bryan Prewitt, prin. Fax 646-5065
Grand River Tech S Vo/Tech
1200 Fair St 64601 660-646-3414
Ron Wolf, prin. Fax 646-3568

Chillicothe Beauty Academy Post-Sec.
505 Elm St 64601 660-646-4198

Clarksville, Pike, Pop. 512
Pike County R-III SD 600/PK-12
28176 Highway WW 63336 573-242-3546
Paul Terpening, supt. Fax 485-2393
www.clopton.k12.mo.us
Clopton JSHS 300/7-12
28176 Highway WW 63336 573-242-3546
Larry Lagemann, prin. Fax 485-2393
Other Schools – See Eolia

Clarkton, Dunklin, Pop. 1,280
Clarkton C-4 SD 400/PK-12
PO Box 637 63837 573-448-3712
Philip Harrison, supt. Fax 448-5182
www.clarkton.k12.mo.us
Clarkton JSHS 200/7-12
PO Box 637 63837 573-448-3712
Merlyn Johnson, prin. Fax 448-3226

Clayton, Saint Louis, Pop. 16,061
Clayton SD 2,600/PK-12
2 Mark Twain Cir 63105 314-854-6000
Dr. Don Senti, supt. Fax 854-6094
www.clayton.k12.mo.us
Clayton HS 900/9-12
1 Mark Twain Cir 63105 314-854-6600
Dr. Louise Losos, prin. Fax 854-6793
Wydown MS 600/6-8
6500 Wydown Blvd 63105 314-854-6400
Mary Ann Goldberg, prin. Fax 854-6491

Cleveland, Cass, Pop. 674
Midway R-I SD 600/K-12
5801 State Route 2 64734 816-250-2994
Paul Fregeau, supt. Fax 899-2823
www.midway.k12.mo.us
Midway JSHS 300/7-12
5801 State Route 2 64734 816-250-2994
Doug Dahman, prin. Fax 899-2823

Clever, Christian, Pop. 1,242
Clever R-V SD 700/K-12
103 S Public Ave 65631 417-743-4800
Richard Henson, supt. Fax 743-4802
www.clever.k12.mo.us
Clever HS 200/9-12
401 Inman St 65631 417-743-4830
Robert Parker, prin. Fax 743-4832
Clever MS 200/5-8
103 S Public Ave 65631 417-743-4820
Benjy Fenske, prin. Fax 743-4802

Clifton Hill, Randolph, Pop. 129
Westran R-I SD
Supt. — See Huntsville
Westran MS 200/6-8
622 Harlan St 65244 660-261-4511
Carl Brown, prin. Fax 261-4292

Climax Springs, Camden, Pop. 85
Climax Springs R-IV SD 200/PK-12
119 Nort Dr 65324 573-347-3905
Daniel Slack, supt. Fax 347-9931
csprings.k12.mo.us/
Climax Springs JSHS 100/7-12
119 Nort Dr 65324 573-347-2351
Mary Ann Gerriets, prin. Fax 347-2394

Clinton, Henry, Pop. 9,414
Clinton SD 124 1,700/PK-12
701 S 8th St 64735 660-885-2237
William Biggerstaff, supt. Fax 885-7033
clinton.k12.mo.us
Clinton HS 700/9-12
701 S 8th St 64735 660-885-2247
Frank Dahman, prin. Fax 885-2012
Clinton MS 500/6-8
701 S 8th St 64735 660-885-3353
Andy Ford, prin. Fax 885-4826
Clinton Technical S Vo/Tech
701 S 8th St 64735 660-885-6101
Richard Wells, dir. Fax 885-6789

Cole Camp, Benton, Pop. 1,160
Cole Camp R-I SD 800/K-12
500 S Keeney St 65325 660-668-4427
Dr. Jerry Cochran, supt. Fax 668-4703
Cole Camp HS 300/9-12
500 S Keeney St 65325 660-668-3751
Perry Gorrell, prin. Fax 668-4703
Cole Camp MS 200/6-8
500 S Keeney St 65325 660-668-3502
Tyler Clark, prin. Fax 668-4703

Columbia, Boone, Pop. 91,814
Columbia SD 93 16,300/PK-12
1818 W Worley St 65203 573-214-3400
Dr. Phyllis Chase, supt. Fax 214-3401
www.columbia.k12.mo.us/
Columbia Area Career Ctr Vo/Tech
4203 S Providence Rd 65203 573-214-3800
Dr. Arden Boyer-Stephens, dir. Fax 214-3801
Hickman SHS 2,000/10-12
1104 N Providence Rd 65203 573-214-3000
Michael Jeffers, prin. Fax 214-3057
Jefferson JHS 900/8-9
713 Rogers St 65201 573-214-3210
Nyle Klinginsmith, prin. Fax 214-3211
Oakland JHS 800/8-9
3405 Oakland Pl 65202 573-214-3220
Dr. Kimberly Presko, prin. Fax 214-3221
Rock Bridge SHS 1,600/10-12
4303 S Providence Rd 65203 573-214-3100
Andy Kohl, prin. Fax 214-3109
West JHS 1,000/8-9
401 Clinkscales Rd 65203 573-214-3230
Dr. Sandra Logan, prin. Fax 214-3231

Christian Fellowship S 300/PK-12
4600 Christian Fellowshp Rd 65203 573-445-8565
Dr. Rick Mueller, admin. Fax 445-8564
Columbia Beauty Academy Post-Sec.
503 E Nifong Blvd 65201 573-445-6611
Columbia College Post-Sec.
1001 Rogers St 65201 800-231-2391
Jerry's School of Hairstyling Post-Sec.
1001 Royal Birkdale Dr 65203 573-449-7527
Stephens College Post-Sec.
PO Box 2121 65215 573-442-2211
University of Missouri Post-Sec.
228 Jesse Hall 65211 573-882-2121

Conception, Nodaway

Conception Seminary College 64433 Post-Sec.
660-944-2886

Conception Junction, Nodaway, Pop. 197
Jefferson C-123 SD 200/PK-12
37614 US Highway 136 64434 660-944-2316
Rob Dowis, supt. Fax 944-2315
www.jc123.k12.mo.us/
Jefferson JSHS 100/7-12
37614 US Highway 136 64434 660-944-2316
Tim Jermain, prin. Fax 944-2315

Concordia, Lafayette, Pop. 2,413
Concordia R-II SD 500/PK-12
PO Box 879 64020 660-463-7235
Mary Beth Scherer, supt. Fax 463-1326
www.concordia.k12.mo.us
Concordia JSHS 200/7-12
PO Box 879 64020 660-463-2246
Mike Trautman, prin. Fax 463-4081

St. Paul Lutheran HS 200/9-12
PO Box 719 64020 660-463-2238
Bill Lemmons, prin. Fax 463-7621

Conway, Laclede, Pop. 774
Laclede County R-I SD 800/PK-12
726 W Jefferson Ave 65632 417-589-2951
Larry Clinefelter, supt. Fax 589-3202
www.conwayschooldistrict.com
Conway HS 300/9-12
726 W Jefferson Ave 65632 417-589-2941
Sondra Caffey, prin. Fax 589-2500
Conway JHS 100/7-8
726 W Jefferson Ave 65632 417-589-8247
Cindy Hawkins, prin. Fax 589-2500

Cooter, Pemiscot, Pop. 437
Cooter R-IV SD 300/K-12
PO Box 218 63839 573-695-3312
William Crowder, supt. Fax 695-3073
Cooter JSHS 200/7-12
PO Box 218 63839 573-695-4972
Frank Killian, prin. Fax 695-3073

Cottleville, Saint Charles, Pop. 2,333

St. Charles Community College Post-Sec.
4601 Mid Rivers Mall Dr 63376 636-922-8000

Craig, Holt, Pop. 297
Craig R-III SD 100/K-12
402 N Ward St 64437 660-683-5351
Hershel Ferguson, supt. Fax 683-5769
www.schoolweb.missouri.edu/craigr3.k12.mo.us
Craig JSHS 100/7-12
402 N Ward St 64437 660-683-5431
Terry Petersen, prin. Fax 683-5769

Crane, Stone, Pop. 1,442
Crane R-III SD 700/K-12
PO Box 405 65633 417-723-5300
Tyler Laney, supt. Fax 723-5551
www.crane.k12.mo.us
Crane HS 200/9-12
PO Box 405 65633 417-723-5383
Bill Redus, prin. Fax 723-5551
Crane MS 200/5-8
PO Box 405 65633 417-723-8177
Karla Edwards, prin. Fax 723-5551

Creighton, Cass, Pop. 350
Sherwood Cass R-VIII SD 900/PK-12
PO Box 98 64739 660-499-2834
Freddie Doherty, supt. Fax 499-2624
sherwood.k12.mo.us
Sherwood HS 300/9-12
PO Box 98 64739 660-499-2239
Stephen Fox, prin. Fax 499-2258
Sherwood MS 200/6-8
PO Box 98 64739 660-499-2203
Tim Komer, prin. Fax 499-2585

Creve Coeur, Saint Louis, Pop. 16,975
Parkway C-2 SD
Supt. — See Chesterfield
Parkway Northeast MS 1,000/6-8
181 Coeur De Ville Dr 63141 314-415-7100
Kim Brandon, prin. Fax 415-7113
Parkway North HS 1,400/9-12
12860 Fee Fee Rd, Saint Louis MO 63146
314-415-7600
Jenny Marquart, prin. Fax 415-7634

Crocker, Pulaski, Pop. 1,010
Crocker R-II SD 600/PK-12
PO Box 488 65452 573-736-5000
Dr. Jim Bogle, supt. Fax 736-5924
www.crocker.k12.mo.us/
Crocker JSHS 300/7-12
PO Box 488 65452 573-736-5000
Monica Davis, prin. Fax 736-2801

Crystal City, Jefferson, Pop. 4,508
Crystal City SD 47 600/K-12
1100 Mississippi Ave 63019 636-937-4411
Ronald Swafford, supt. Fax 937-2512
www.crystal.k12.mo.us/
Crystal City HS 300/9-12
1100 Mississippi Ave 63019 636-937-2005
Tammy Ridgeway, prin. Fax 937-2512

Cuba, Crawford, Pop. 3,447
Crawford County R-II SD 1,400/K-12
1 Wildcat Pride Dr 65453 573-885-2534
Waymon W. Boast, supt. Fax 885-3900
www.cuba.k12.mo.us/
Cuba HS 400/9-12
1 Wildcat Pride Dr 65453 573-885-2534
Ben Yocom, prin. Fax 885-7726
Cuba MS 400/5-8
1 Wildcat Pride Dr 65453 573-885-2534
J.W. Brandt, prin. Fax 885-6278

Dadeville, Dade, Pop. 224
Dadeville R-II SD 200/K-12
PO Box 188 65635 417-995-2201
Nancy Brannon, supt. Fax 995-2110
Dadeville JSHS 100/7-12
PO Box 188 65635 417-995-2201
Matt Bushey, prin. Fax 995-2110

Dearborn, Platte, Pop. 531
North Platte County R-I SD 700/PK-12
212 W 6th St 64439 816-450-3511
Dr. Francis Moran, supt. Fax 992-8727
www.nplatte.k12.mo.us/
North Platte HS 200/9-12
212 W 6th St 64439 816-450-3344
John Green, prin. Fax 992-8955
North Platte JHS 100/7-8
212 W 6th St 64439 816-450-3350
Roger Giger, prin. Fax 992-3665

Deepwater, Saint Clair, Pop. 505
Lakeland R-III SD 500/PK-12
12530 Lakeland School Dr 64740 417-644-2223
Ryan Huff, supt. Fax 644-2316
www.lakelandschools.com/index.html
Lakeland JSHS 200/7-12
12530 Lakeland School Dr 64740 417-644-2223
Jeff Osner, prin. Fax 644-2316

Deering, Pemiscot, Pop. 130
Delta C-7 SD 300/K-12
PO Box 297 63840 573-757-6648
James Williams, supt. Fax 757-9691
www.schoolweb.missouri.edu/deltac7.k12.mo.us/
Delta C-7 JSHS 100/7-12
PO Box 297 63840 573-757-6611
Kenny Copley, prin. Fax 757-9691

De Kalb, Buchanan, Pop. 258
Buchanan County R-IV SD 400/K-12
702 Main St 64440 816-685-3160
Lane Novinger, supt. Fax 685-3203
De Kalb JSHS 200/7-12
702 Main St 64440 816-685-3211
Travis A. Dittemore, prin. Fax 685-3156

Delta, Cape Girardeau, Pop. 536
Delta R-V SD 300/PK-12
PO Box 787 63744 573-794-2500
Nate Crowden, supt. Fax 794-2504
Delta JSHS 200/7-12
PO Box 787 63744 573-794-2511
James Gloth, prin. Fax 794-2504

Desloge, Saint Francois, Pop. 5,143
North St. Francois County R-I SD
Supt. — See Bonne Terre

North County MS 500/7-8
406 E Chestnut St 63601 573-431-6700
Larry Kekec, prin. Fax 431-5203

Mineral Area College Post-Sec.
PO Box 1000 63601 573-431-4593

De Soto, Jefferson, Pop. 6,552
Desoto SD 73 2,800/K-12
610 Vineland School Rd 63020 636-586-1000
Terry Noble, supt. Fax 586-1009
www.desoto.k12.mo.us
De Soto HS 900/9-12
815 Amvets Dr 63020 636-586-1050
Brent Norton, prin. Fax 586-1059
De Soto JHS 500/7-8
731 Amvets Dr 63020 636-586-1030
Brian Tharp, prin. Fax 586-1039

Dexter, Stoddard, Pop. 7,596
Dexter R-XI SD 2,000/PK-12
1031 Brown Pilot Ln 63841 573-614-1000
Dr. Kenneth Jackson, supt. Fax 614-1002
dexter.k12.mo.us/
Dexter HS 600/9-12
1101 W Grant St 63841 573-614-1030
Bryce Matthews, prin. Fax 614-1032
Hill MS 500/6-8
1107 Brown Pilot Ln 63841 573-614-1010
Dr. Roger Alsup, prin. Fax 614-1012

Diamond, Newton, Pop. 846
Diamond R-IV SD 900/K-12
PO Box 68 64840 417-325-5186
Mark Mayo, supt. Fax 325-5338
www.diamondwildcats.org/
Diamond HS 300/9-12
PO Box 68 64840 417-325-5188
Patricia Wilson, prin. Fax 325-5331
Diamond MS 300/5-8
PO Box 68 64840 417-325-5336
Danny DeWitt, prin. Fax 325-5333

Dixon, Pulaski, Pop. 1,548
Dixon R-I SD 1,100/PK-12
PO Box A 65459 573-759-7163
Dawna Burrow, supt. Fax 759-2506
www.dixonr1.yhti.net/
Dixon HS 300/9-12
PO Box A 65459 573-759-7119
Paulette Crouthers, prin. Fax 759-3625
Dixon MS 300/6-8
PO Box A 65459 573-759-7139
Jim Brown, prin. Fax 759-6627

Doniphan, Ripley, Pop. 1,924
Doniphan R-I SD 1,700/PK-12
309 Pine St 63935 573-996-3819
Kevin Sandlin, supt. Fax 996-5865
www.doniphanr1.k12.mo.us
Current River Vocational S Vo/Tech
301 E Spring St 63935 573-996-2915
John Wesemann, prin. Fax 996-7838
Doniphan HS 500/9-12
5 Ball Park Rd 63935 573-996-3312
Rhoda Barnett, prin. Fax 996-3739
Doniphan MS 400/6-8
651 E Summit St 63935 573-996-3614
Donald Sanders, prin. Fax 996-4525

Dora, Ozark
Dora R-III SD 300/PK-12
PO Box 14 65637 417-261-2346
Dr. Chris Berger, supt. Fax 261-2673
www.dora.org
Dora JSHS 200/7-12
PO Box 14 65637 417-261-2263
Rick Luna, prin. Fax 261-2673

Drexel, Bates, Pop. 1,115
Drexel R-IV SD 400/K-12
PO Box 860 64742 816-657-4715
Patricia Yocum, supt. Fax 657-4798
Drexel HS 200/7-12
PO Box 860 64742 816-619-2287
Gerald D. Whalen, prin. Fax 657-4798

Eagleville, Harrison, Pop. 326
North Harrison R-III SD 200/PK-12
12023 Fir St 64442 660-867-5222
Nancy Parman, supt. Fax 867-5263
North Harrison County JSHS 100/7-12
12023 Fir St 64442 660-867-5221
Mark Fletcher, prin. Fax 867-5263

Earth City, Saint Louis

ITT Technical Institute Post-Sec.
3640 Corporate Trail Dr 63045 314-298-7800
Midwest Institute - Earth City Post-Sec.
4260 Shoreline Dr 63045 314-344-3334

Easton, Buchanan, Pop. 253
East Buchanan County C-1 SD
Supt. — See Gower
East Buchanan MS 200/6-8
301 N County Park Rd 64443 816-473-2451
Douglas Miller, prin. Fax 473-2604

East Prairie, Mississippi, Pop. 3,117
East Prairie R-II SD 1,100/PK-12
304 E Walnut St 63845 573-649-3562
Scott Downing, supt. Fax 649-5455
www.eprairie.k12.mo.us
East Prairie HS 300/9-12
304 E Walnut St 63845 573-649-3564
Steve Douglas, prin. Fax 649-3208
East Prairie JHS 200/7-8
210 E Washington St 63845 573-649-9368
Eva Hinshaw, prin. Fax 649-9370

Edina, Knox, Pop. 1,162
Knox County R-I SD 600/PK-12
RR 3 Box 59 63537 660-397-2228
Terry Robertson, supt. Fax 397-3998
www.knox.k12.mo.us/
Knox County JSHS 300/7-12
RR 3 Box 59 63537 660-397-2231
D.J. Leverton, prin. Fax 397-3282

Eldon, Miller, Pop. 4,934
Eldon R-I SD 2,000/PK-12
112 S Pine St 65026 573-392-8000
Dr. C.J. Huff, supt. Fax 392-8080
www.eldon.k12.mo.us/
Eldon Career Center Vo/Tech
112 S Pine St 65026 573-392-8060
Matt Davis, dir. Fax 392-9154
Eldon HS 600/9-12
101 S Pine St 65026 573-392-8010
Leane McNay, prin. Fax 392-5057
Eldon MS 300/7-8
1400 N Grand Ave 65026 573-392-8020
Chris Miller, prin. Fax 392-9151

El Dorado Springs, Cedar, Pop. 3,849
El Dorado Springs R-II SD 1,300/PK-12
901 S Grand Ave 64744 417-876-3112
Greg Koetting, supt. Fax 876-2128
El Dorado Springs HS 400/9-12
901 S Grand Ave 64744 417-876-3112
David Copeland, prin. Fax 876-2128
El Dorado Springs MS 300/6-8
901 S Grand Ave 64744 417-876-3112
David Hedrick, prin. Fax 876-2128

El Dorado Christian S 200/PK-12
1600 S Ohio St 64744 417-876-2201
Jeanne Mark, prin. Fax 876-4913

Ellington, Reynolds, Pop. 1,013
Southern Reynolds County R-II SD 600/PK-12
1 School St 63638 573-663-3591
Clay Whitener, supt. Fax 663-2412
www.ellington.k12.mo.us/
Southern Reynolds County HS 300/7-12
1 School St 63638 573-663-2291
Armand Spurgin, prin. Fax 663-2155

Ellsinore, Carter, Pop. 363
East Carter County R-II SD 800/PK-12
24 S Herren Ave 63937 573-322-5625
Dr. Tim Hager, supt. Fax 322-8586
www.ecarter.k12.mo.us
East Carter County R-II HS 300/9-12
24 S Herren Ave 63937 573-322-5653
Barry Stahl, prin. Fax 322-5720
East Carter County R-II MS 100/6-8
24 S Herren Ave 63937 573-322-5420
Eric Allen, prin. Fax 322-5420

Elsberry, Lincoln, Pop. 2,417
Elsberry R-II SD 900/K-12
PO Box 106 63343 573-898-5554
Larry Flanagan, supt. Fax 898-3140
schoolweb.missouri.edu/elsberry.k12.mo.us/
Cannon MS 300/5-8
PO Box 106 63343 573-898-5554
Ken Youmans, prin. Fax 898-5825
Elsberry HS 300/9-12
PO Box 106 63343 573-898-5554
Errol Spratt, prin. Fax 898-9132

Eminence, Shannon, Pop. 550
Eminence R-I SD 300/PK-12
PO Box 730 65466 573-226-3251
Donna Depee, supt. Fax 226-3250
eminence.echalk.com/
Eminence JSHS 100/7-12
PO Box 730 65466 573-226-3252
Garry Cutts, prin. Fax 226-3211

Eolia, Pike, Pop. 455
Pike County R-III SD
Supt. — See Clarksville
Pike-Lincoln Technical Center Vo/Tech
PO Box 38 63344 573-485-2900
Krista Flowers, dir. Fax 485-2388

Essex, Stoddard, Pop. 530
Richland R-I SD 400/K-12
24456 State Highway 114 63846 573-283-5332
Michael Kiehne, supt. Fax 283-5798
www.richland.k12.mo.us/
Richland JSHS 200/7-12
24456 State Highway 114 63846 573-283-5332
Brian Hukel, prin. Fax 283-5798

Eugene, Cole, Pop. 159
Cole County R-V SD 800/K-12
PO Box 78 65032 573-498-4000
Mark Blythe, supt. Fax 498-4090
www.coler-v.k12.mo.us/
Eugene JSHS 400/7-12
PO Box 78 65032 573-498-4001
Rob Ferguson, prin. Fax 498-4091

Eureka, Saint Louis, Pop. 8,957
Rockwood R-VI SD 22,200/PK-12
111 E North St 63025 636-938-2200
Dr. Craig Larson, supt. Fax 938-2251
www.rockwood.k12.mo.us
Eureka HS 1,500/9-12
4525 Highway 109 63025 636-938-2400
Dr. Kevin Keltner, prin. Fax 938-2411
Other Schools – See Ballwin, Chesterfield, Fenton, Glencoe

Everton, Dade, Pop. 322
Everton R-III SD 200/K-12
211 E School St 65646 417-535-2221
Chuck Adams, supt. Fax 535-4105
www.evertontigers.org
Everton JSHS 100/7-12
211 E School St 65646 417-535-2221
Terry Winton, prin. Fax 535-4105

Ewing, Lewis, Pop. 453
Lewis County C-1 SD 800/PK-12
PO Box 366 63440 573-209-3217
Jacqueline Ebeling, supt. Fax 209-3318
www.lewis.k12.mo.us
Highland JSHS 500/7-12
PO Box 366 63440 573-209-3215
Paul Sulser, prin. Fax 209-3469

Excelsior Springs, Clay, Pop. 11,472
Excelsior Springs SD 40 3,300/PK-12
PO Box 248 64024 816-630-9200
James Horton, supt. Fax 630-9203
tigernet.estigers.k12.mo.us/
Excelsior Springs Career Ctr Vo/Tech
PO Box 248 64024 816-630-9240
Don Roberts, dir. Fax 630-9245
Excelsior Springs HS 900/9-12
PO Box 248 64024 816-630-9210
Alan Bunch, prin. Fax 630-9227
Excelsior Springs MS 700/6-8
PO Box 248 64024 816-630-9230
William Bielefeld, prin. Fax 630-9236
Excelsior Springs Technical HS Vo/Tech
PO Box 248 64024 816-630-5501
Tom Mayfield, prin. Fax 637-1806

Martinez School of Cosmetology Post-Sec.
248 1/2 E Broadway St 64024 816-630-3900

Exeter, Barry, Pop. 737
Exeter R-VI SD 300/K-12
RR 1 Box 509 65647 417-835-2922
Tina Nolan, supt. Fax 835-3201
www.exeter.k12.mo.us/
Exeter HS 100/9-12
RR 1 Box 509 65647 417-835-3745
Robert Taylor, prin. Fax 835-3201

Fairfax, Atchison, Pop. 622
Fairfax R-III SD 200/PK-12
500 E Main St 64446 660-686-2421
Ed Defenbaugh, supt. Fax 686-2848
www.fairfaxk12mo.us/
Fairfax JSHS 100/7-12
500 E Main St 64446 660-686-2851
Dustin Barnes, prin. Fax 686-3436

Fair Grove, Greene, Pop. 1,283
Fair Grove R-X SD 1,100/K-12
PO Box 367 65648 417-759-2233
John Link, supt. Fax 759-7150
www.fairgrove.k12.mo.us
Fair Grove HS 300/9-12
PO Box 367 65648 417-759-2554
David Hunter, prin. Fax 759-7685
Fair Grove MS 300/6-8
PO Box 367 65648 417-759-2556
Charity Rael, prin. Fax 759-9053

Fair Play, Polk, Pop. 439
Fair Play R-II SD 400/K-12
PO Box 1020 65649 417-654-2231
Renee Sagaser, supt. Fax 654-5028
www.fairplay.k12.mo.us/
Fair Play JSHS 200/7-12
PO Box 1020 65649 417-654-2232
Danny Cantrell, prin. Fax 654-3503

Farmington, Saint Francois, Pop. 15,176
Farmington R-VII SD 3,700/PK-12
PO Box 570 63640 573-701-1300
Dr. W. L. Sanders, supt. Fax 701-1309
www.farmington.k12.mo.us
Farmington HS 1,100/9-12
1 Black Knight Dr 63640 573-701-1310
Matt Ruble, prin. Fax 701-1329
Farmington MS 600/7-8
506 S Fleming St 63640 573-701-1330
Dorothy Winslow, prin. Fax 701-1339

Mineral Area Regional Medical Center Post-Sec.
1212 Weber Rd 63640 573-756-4581
Missouri Beauty Academy Post-Sec.
222 E Columbia St 63640 573-756-2730

Faucett, Buchanan
Mid-Buchanan County R-V SD 700/K-12
3221 State Route H SE 64448 816-238-1646
John James, supt. Fax 238-4150
www.midbuchanan.k12.mo.us
Mid-Buchanan JSHS 300/7-12
3221 State Route H SE 64448 816-238-1646
Bob Pierce, prin. Fax 238-2484

Fayette, Howard, Pop. 2,701
Fayette R-III SD 700/PK-12
705 Lucky St 65248 660-248-2153
Russ Brock, supt. Fax 248-3702
www.fayette.k12.mo.us/
Clark MS 200/6-8
704 Lucky St 65248 660-248-3800
Kevin Beeler, prin. Fax 248-2610
Fayette HS 200/9-12
510 N Cleveland St 65248 660-248-2124
Darren Rapert, prin. Fax 248-2120

Central Methodist University Post-Sec.
411 Central Methodist Sq 65248 660-248-3391

Fenton, Saint Louis, Pop. 4,376
Rockwood R-VI SD
Supt. — See Eureka
Rockwood South MS 1,000/6-8
1628 Hawkins Rd 63026 636-861-7723
Dr. Karen Seiber, prin. Fax 861-7730
Rockwood Summit HS 1,300/9-12
1780 Hawkins Rd 63026 636-861-7700
Dale Menke, prin. Fax 861-7717

Allied College - South Post-Sec.
645 Gravois Bluffs Blvd 63026 800-502-2627
St. Louis College of Health Careers Post-Sec.
1297 N Highway Dr 63026 636-529-0000
Sanford-Brown College Post-Sec.
1345 Smizer Mill Rd 63026 636-651-1600

Festus, Jefferson, Pop. 10,905
Festus R-VI SD 2,900/K-12
1515 Midmeadow Ln 63028 636-937-4920
Dr. Randy Sheriff, supt. Fax 937-8525
www.csd.org/festus
Festus HS 900/9-12
501 Westwind Dr 63028 636-937-5410
Karen Biehle, prin. Fax 937-8048
Festus MS 500/7-8
1717 W Main St 63028 636-937-5417
Thomas Gotsch, prin. Fax 937-4171

Jefferson County R-VII SD 700/PK-8
1250 Dooling Hollow Rd 63028 636-937-9188
Dr. J. Thomas Guenzler, supt. Fax 937-9189
Danby-Rush Tower MS 200/6-8
1250 Dooling Hollow Rd 63028 636-937-9188
Kim Weik, prin. Fax 937-9189

St. Pius X HS 400/9-12
1030 Saint Pius Dr 63028 636-931-7488
Norma Overberg, prin. Fax 931-7487

Florissant, Saint Louis, Pop. 51,812
Ferguson-Florissant R-II SD 12,700/PK-12
1005 Waterford Dr 63033 314-506-9000
Jeffrey Spiegel, supt. Fax 506-9010
www.fergflor.org/
Cross Keys MS 900/7-8
14205 Cougar Dr 63033 314-506-9700
David Watkins, prin. Fax 506-9701
McCluer HS 1,600/9-12
1896 S New Florissant Rd 63031 314-506-9400
Nicole Whitesell, prin. Fax 506-9401
McCluer North HS 1,600/9-12
705 Waterford Dr 63033 314-506-9200
Dr. Hopper, prin. Fax 506-9201
Other Schools – See Berkeley, Saint Louis

Hazelwood SD 19,100/K-12
15955 New Halls Ferry Rd 63031 314-953-5000
Chris L. Wright Ph.D., supt. Fax 953-5085
www.hazelwoodschools.org/
Hazelwood Central HS 2,600/9-12
15875 New Halls Ferry Rd 63031 314-953-5400
Frank Smith, prin. Fax 953-5413
Hazelwood MS 1,300/7-8
1605 Shackelford Rd 63031 314-953-5500
Darrell Strong, prin. Fax 953-5513
Other Schools – See Hazelwood, Saint Louis

Special SD of St. Louis County
Supt. — See Saint Louis
North County Technical S Vo/Tech
1700 Derhake Rd 63033 314-989-7600
Mike Powers, prin. Fax 989-7665

Missouri Sch. of Barbering & Hairstyling Post-Sec.
1125 N US Highway 67 63031 314-839-0310
North County Christian S 500/PK-12
845 Dunn Rd 63031 314-972-6227
Ken Rankin, admin. Fax 972-6220
St. Louis Christian College Post-Sec.
1360 Grandview Dr 63033 314-837-6777

Fordland, Webster, Pop. 746
Fordland R-III SD 600/PK-12
1230 School St 65652 417-738-2296
Brian Wilson, supt. Fax 767-4483
www.fordland.k12.mo.us
Fordland HS 200/9-12
1248 School St 65652 417-738-2212
Eric Kurre, prin. Fax 767-2240
Fordland MS 200/6-8
1230 School St 65652 417-738-2119
Judy Kindall, prin. Fax 767-4483

Forsyth, Taney, Pop. 1,706
Forsyth R-III SD 1,200/PK-12
PO Box 187 65653 417-546-6384
Dr. Tom Darnell, supt. Fax 546-2204
www.forsythr3.k12.mo.us/
Forsyth HS 400/9-12
PO Box 187 65653 417-546-6383
Bruce Simpson, prin. Fax 546-5987
Forsyth MS 300/5-8
PO Box 187 65653 417-546-6382
Ben Bilyeu, prin. Fax 546-6943

Fort Leonard Wood, Pulaski, Pop. 15,863

Lincoln University Post-Sec.
Truman Educ Center Bldg 499 65473 573-681-5421

Fredericktown, Madison, Pop. 4,035
Fredericktown R-I SD 1,900/PK-12
704 E Highway 72 63645 573-783-2570
Dr. Kelly Burlison, supt. Fax 783-7045
Fredericktown HS 600/9-12
805 E Highway 72 63645 573-783-3628
John K. Gibbs, prin. Fax 783-8224
Fredericktown MS 500/6-8
501 Park Dr 63645 573-783-6555
Chadd Starkey, prin. Fax 783-8079

Fulton, Callaway, Pop. 12,101
Fulton SD 58 2,300/PK-12
2 Hornet Dr 65251 573-642-2206
Dr. Mark Enderle, supt. Fax 642-1444
www.fulton.k12.mo.us/
Fulton HS 800/9-12
1 Hornet Dr 65251 573-642-2023
Teresa Arms, prin. Fax 592-7401
Fulton MS 600/6-8
403 E 10th St 65251 573-642-7221
Jeffrey Wright, prin. Fax 642-6282

Missouri School for the Deaf Post-Sec.
505 E 5th St 65251 573-592-4000
Westminister College Post-Sec.
501 Westminster Ave 65251 573-642-3361
William Woods University Post-Sec.
1 University Ave 65251 573-642-2251

Gainesville, Ozark, Pop. 607
Gainesville R-V SD 700/PK-12
HC 3 Box 170 65655 417-679-4260
Bill Looney, supt. Fax 679-4270
gainesville.mo.schoolwebpages.com
Gainesville HS 300/7-12
160 Bulldog Dr 65655 417-679-4200
Joe Donley, prin. Fax 679-4270

Galena, Stone, Pop. 528
Galena R-II SD 500/PK-12
PO Box 286 65656 417-357-6027
Cynthia Allen, supt. Fax 357-8444
Galena JSHS 200/7-12
PO Box 286 65656 417-357-6618
Shane Stocks, prin. Fax 357-8444

Gallatin, Daviess, Pop. 1,776
Gallatin R-V SD 600/PK-12
602 S Olive St 64640 660-663-2171
James Ruse, supt. Fax 663-2559
gallatin.k12.mo.us
Gallatin JSHS 300/7-12
602 S Olive St 64640 660-663-2171
Charles Burrell, prin. Fax 663-2559

Galt, Grundy, Pop. 275
Grundy County R-V SD 200/K-12
PO Box 6 64641 660-673-6511
Robert Deaver, supt. Fax 673-6523
Grundy County JSHS 100/7-12
PO Box 6 64641 660-673-6511
Randy Huffman, prin. Fax 673-6523

Garden City, Cass, Pop. 1,667

Training Center Christian S 100/PK-12
PO Box 200 64747 816-773-8367
Judy Williams, admin. Fax 862-6052

Gideon, New Madrid, Pop. 1,019
Gideon SD 37 400/K-12
PO Box 227 63848 573-448-3911
Dr. David Hollingshead, supt. Fax 448-5197
gideon.k12.mo.us/
Gideon JSHS 200/7-12
PO Box 227 63848 573-448-3471
Keenan Buchanan, prin. Fax 448-3868

Gilman City, Daviess, Pop. 383
Gilman City R-IV SD 200/PK-12
PO Box 45 64642 660-876-5221
David Cross, supt. Fax 876-5553
Gilman City JSHS 100/7-12
PO Box 45 64642 660-876-5221
Roger Alley, prin. Fax 876-5553

Gladstone, Clay, Pop. 27,306
North Kansas City SD 74
Supt. — See North Kansas City
Antioch MS 900/6-8
2100 NE 65th St 64118 816-413-6200
Robert Russell, prin. Fax 413-6205

Paris II Educational Center Post-Sec.
6840 N Oak Trfy 64118 816-468-6666

Glasgow, Howard, Pop. 1,205
Howard County R-II SD 300/PK-12
860 Randolph St 65254 660-338-2012
Michael Reynolds, supt. Fax 338-2610
www.glasgow.k12.mo.us/
Glasgow JSHS 200/7-12
860 Randolph St 65254 660-338-2012
Michael Reynolds, prin. Fax 338-2610

Glencoe, Saint Louis
Rockwood R-VI SD
Supt. — See Eureka
LaSalle Springs MS 800/6-8
3300 Highway 109 63038 636-938-2425
Scott Francin, prin. Fax 938-2434
Rockwood Valley MS 900/6-8
1220 Babler Park Dr 63038 636-458-7324
Dr. Katie Reboulet, prin. Fax 458-7325
Wildwood MS 800/6-8
17401 Manchester Rd 63038 636-458-7360
Dr. Gregory Batenhorst, prin. Fax 458-7372

Golden City, Barton, Pop. 918
Golden City R-III SD 300/PK-12
1208 Walnut St 64748 417-537-4900
Susan Whittle, supt. Fax 537-8717
Golden City JSHS 100/7-12
1208 Walnut St 64748 417-537-8311
Larry Malle, prin. Fax 537-8717

Gower, Buchanan, Pop. 1,433
East Buchanan County C-1 SD 700/K-12
100 Smith St 64454 816-424-6466
Charles Nance, supt. Fax 424-3511
www.ebsk12.com/
East Buchanan HS 200/9-12
100 Smith St 64454 816-424-6460
Scott Antle, prin. Fax 424-6410
Other Schools – See Easton

Graham, Nodaway, Pop. 186
Nodaway-Holt R-VII SD 300/PK-12
318 S Taylor St 64455 660-939-2137
Bruce Skoglund, supt. Fax 939-2200
www.asde.com/~nodholt/
Nodaway-Holt HS 100/7-12
318 S Taylor St 64455 660-939-2135
Jenny Saunders, prin. Fax 939-2201

Grain Valley, Jackson, Pop. 8,644
Grain Valley R-V SD 2,300/K-12
PO Box 304 64029 816-847-5006
Dr. Chris Small, supt. Fax 229-4831
www.grainvalley.k12.mo.us
Grain Valley HS 600/9-12
PO Box 304 64029 816-847-5000
Mike Witt, prin. Fax 847-5002
Grain Valley MS 600/6-8
PO Box 304 64029 816-229-3499
Theresa Nelson, prin. Fax 847-5017

Granby, Newton, Pop. 2,230
East Newton County R-VI SD 1,600/K-12
22808 E Highway 86 64844 417-472-6231
Tanya Vest, supt. Fax 472-3500
www.enr6.k12.mo.us
East Newton HS 400/9-12
22876 E Highway 86 64844 417-472-6238
Todd McCrackin, prin. Fax 472-7129

Grandview, Jackson, Pop. 24,549
Grandview C-4 SD 4,200/PK-12
13015 10th St 64030 816-316-5000
Dr. Ralph Teran, supt. Fax 316-5050
www.csd4.k12.mo.us
Grandview HS 1,300/9-12
2300 High Grove Rd 64030 816-316-5800
Ted Vernon, prin. Fax 316-5898
Grandview MS 700/6-8
12650 Manchester Ave 64030 816-316-5600
Cynthia Johnson, prin. Fax 316-5699

Grandview Christian S 200/K-12
12340 Grandview Rd 64030 816-767-8630
Krista Sharpe, admin. Fax 763-5029
House of Heavilin Beauty College Post-Sec.
12020 Blue Ridge Ext 64030 816-767-8000

Grant City, Worth, Pop. 826
Worth County R-III SD 400/K-12
RR 3 Box 107 64456 660-564-3389
Dr. Linda Gray Smith, supt. Fax 564-2193
wc.k12.mo.us/index.html
Worth County JSHS 200/7-12
RR 3 Box 107 64456 660-564-2218
Dale Healy, prin. Fax 564-2193

Green City, Sullivan, Pop. 650
Green City R-I SD 300/PK-12
301 Northeast St 63545 660-874-4128
Charlotte Baker, supt. Fax 874-4515
www.greencity.k12.mo.us/
Green City JSHS 100/7-12
301 Northeast St 63545 660-874-4127
Donnie Campbell, prin. Fax 874-5010

Greenfield, Dade, Pop. 1,299
Greenfield R-IV SD 500/K-12
410 College St 65661 417-637-5321
David Hardage, supt. Fax 637-5805
greenfield.k12.mo.us/
Greenfield JSHS 200/7-12
410 College St 65661 417-637-5328
Michael Redlich, prin. Fax 637-5805

Green Ridge, Pettis, Pop. 455
Green Ridge R-VIII SD 400/K-12
PO Box 70 65332 660-527-3315
Tim Lenz, supt. Fax 527-3299
greenridge.k12.mo.us
Green Ridge JSHS 200/7-12
PO Box 70 65332 660-527-3315
Ty Payne, prin. Fax 527-3299

Greenville, Wayne, Pop. 446
Greenville R-II SD 900/PK-12
PO Box 320 63944 573-224-3844
Jim Morrison, supt. Fax 224-3412
Greenville HS 300/9-12
PO Box 320 63944 573-224-3618
Todd Porter, prin. Fax 224-3580
Greenville JHS 200/7-8
PO Box 320 63944 573-224-3833
Rick Rainwater, prin. Fax 224-3580

Hale, Carroll, Pop. 478
Hale R-I SD 200/PK-12
PO Box 248 64643 660-565-2417
Michael Spears, supt. Fax 565-2418
Hale JSHS 100/7-12
PO Box 248 64643 660-565-2417
Michael Spears, prin. Fax 565-2418

Half Way, Polk, Pop. 188
Halfway R-III SD 300/K-12
2150 Highway 32 65663 417-445-2351
Tim Boatwright, supt. Fax 445-2026
www.halfwayschools.org
Halfway JSHS 100/7-12
2150 Highway 32 65663 417-445-2211
Tammy Highley, prin. Fax 445-2026

Hallsville, Boone, Pop. 955
Hallsville R-IV SD — 1,200/PK-12
421 E Highway 124 65255 — 573-696-5512
Thomas Baugh, supt. — Fax 696-3606
www.hallsville.org/
Hallsville HS — 300/9-12
421 E Highway 124 65255 — 573-696-5512
Paul Dodson, prin. — Fax 696-1482
Hallsville MS — 400/5-8
421 E Highway 124 65255 — 573-696-5512
Christopher Crane, prin. — Fax 696-7238

Hamilton, Caldwell, Pop. 1,811
Hamilton R-II SD — 700/PK-12
PO Box 128 64644 — 816-583-2134
Stephen Yost, supt. — Fax 583-2139
Hamilton MS — 200/5-8
PO Box 128 64644 — 816-583-2173
Troy Ford, prin. — Fax 583-2686
Penney HS — 200/9-12
PO Box 128 64644 — 816-583-2136
Tim Schieber, prin. — Fax 583-2319

Hannibal, Marion, Pop. 17,649
Hannibal SD 60 — 3,600/PK-12
4650 McMasters Ave 63401 — 573-221-1258
Dr. Jill Janes, supt. — Fax 221-2994
www.hannibal.k12.mo.us
Hannibal Career & Technical Center — Vo/Tech
4550 McMasters Ave 63401 — 573-221-4430
Roger McGregor, dir. — Fax 221-7971
Hannibal HS — 1,200/9-12
4500 Mcmasters Ave 63401 — 573-221-2733
Darin Powell, prin. — Fax 221-9511
Hannibal MS — 900/6-8
4700 Mcmasters Ave 63401 — 573-221-5840
Kenneth Treaster, prin. — Fax 221-7779

Hannibal Area Voc. Technical School — Post-Sec.
4550 McMasters Ave 63401 — 573-221-4430
Hannibal-LaGrange College — Post-Sec.
2800 Palmyra Rd 63401 — 573-221-3675

Hardin, Ray, Pop. 590
Hardin-Central C-2 SD — 200/K-12
PO Box 548 64035 — 660-398-4394
Steven Andes, supt. — Fax 398-4396
www.hardincentral.k12.mo.us/phpnuke/
Hardin-Central JSHS — 100/7-12
PO Box 548 64035 — 660-398-4394
Dean Hays, prin. — Fax 398-4396

Harrisburg, Boone, Pop. 182
Harrisburg R-VIII SD — 600/K-12
1000 S Harris St 65256 — 573-875-5604
Richard K. Davis, supt. — Fax 875-8877
www.harrisburg.k12.mo.us
Harrisburg HS — 200/9-12
801 S Harris St 65256 — 573-875-5602
Lesa Rapert, prin. — Fax 443-1559
Harrisburg MS — 100/7-8
233 S Harris St 65256 — 573-817-5857
Steve Combs, prin. — Fax 875-8936

Harrisonville, Cass, Pop. 9,790
Harrisonville R-IX SD — 2,600/PK-12
503 S Lexington St 64701 — 816-380-2727
Todd White, supt. — Fax 380-3134
www.harrisonvilleschools.org/
Cass Career Center — Vo/Tech
1600 E Elm St 64701 — 816-380-3253
James Spencer, dir. — Fax 884-3179
Harrisonville HS — 800/9-12
1504 E Elm St 64701 — 816-380-3273
Timothy Quinn, prin. — Fax 380-5853
Harrisonville MS — 600/6-8
601 S Highland Dr 64701 — 816-380-7654
Debra Schuler, prin. — Fax 884-5733

Harrisonville Christian S West Campus — 100/5-8
1202 S Commercial St 64701 — 816-884-6499
Al Sancken, admin. — Fax 884-6479

Hartville, Wright, Pop. 603
Hartville R-II SD — 800/PK-12
PO Box 460 65667 — 417-741-7676
Dr. Sharon Hayden, supt. — Fax 741-7746
schoolweb.missouri.edu/hartville.k12.mo.us/
Hartville JSHS — 400/7-12
PO Box 460 65667 — 417-741-7676
Jennifer Sanders, prin. — Fax 741-7746

Hayti, Pemiscot, Pop. 3,066
Hayti R-II SD — 800/K-12
PO Box 469 63851 — 573-359-6500
Thomas Tucker, supt. — Fax 359-6502
www.edline.net/pages/hhs
Hayti HS — 400/7-12
PO Box 469 63851 — 573-359-6503
David Gilmore, prin. — Fax 359-6504

Pemiscot County Special SD
1317 State Highway 84 63851 — 573-359-0021
Sandra Manley, supt. — Fax 359-6525
Pemiscot County Vocational S — Vo/Tech
1317 State Highway 84 63851 — 573-359-2601
James White, dir. — Fax 359-1317

Hazelwood, Saint Louis, Pop. 25,535
Hazelwood SD
Supt. — See Florissant
Hazelwood West HS — 1,700/9-12
1 Wildcat Ln 63042 — 314-953-5800
Ingrid Clark-Jackson, prin. — Fax 953-5813
Hazelwood West MS — 1,100/7-8
1 Wildcat Ln 63042 — 314-953-5800
Ingrid Clark-Jackson, prin. — Fax 953-5813

Sanford-Brown College — Post-Sec.
75 Village Square Shop Ctr 63042 — 314-731-5200

Herculaneum, Jefferson, Pop. 3,172
Dunklin R-V SD — 1,300/PK-12
PO Box 306 63048 — 636-479-5200
Dr. Victor Buehler, supt. — Fax 479-6208
www.dunklin.k12.mo.us/
Herculaneum HS — 500/9-12
1 Blackcat Dr 63048 — 636-479-5200
Andy Runzi, prin. — Fax 479-4479
Senn-Thomas MS — 400/5-8
200 Senn Tomas Dr 63048 — 636-479-5200
Tom Okruch, prin. — Fax 479-7219

Hermann, Gasconade, Pop. 2,735
Gasconade County R-I SD — 1,100/K-12
164 State Highway 100 W 65041 — 573-486-2116
Chris Neale, supt. — Fax 486-3032
www.hermann.k12.mo.us
Hermann HS — 400/9-12
164 State Highway 100 W 65041 — 573-486-5425
Gary Menke, prin. — Fax 486-3058
Hermann MS — 400/4-8
164 State Highway 100 W 65041 — 573-486-3121
Mark Brooks, prin. — Fax 486-5106

Hermitage, Hickory, Pop. 509
Hermitage R-IV SD — 300/K-12
PO Box 327 65668 — 417-745-6418
Shelly Aubuchon, supt. — Fax 745-6475
Hermitage HS — 100/9-12
PO Box 327 65668 — 417-745-6417
Ed Vest, prin. — Fax 745-6475
Hermitage MS — 50/7-8
PO Box 327 65668 — 417-745-6417
Ed Vest, prin. — Fax 745-6475

Higbee, Randolph, Pop. 652
Higbee R-VIII SD — 200/K-12
PO Box 128 65257 — 660-456-7277
Ted Rathburn, supt. — Fax 456-7278
Higbee JSHS — 100/7-12
PO Box 128 65257 — 660-456-7206
Karl Janson, prin. — Fax 456-7207

Higginsville, Lafayette, Pop. 4,660
Lafayette County C-1 SD — 1,000/PK-12
805 W 31st St 64037 — 660-584-3631
Donald Quick, supt. — Fax 584-2622
huskers.k12.mo.us
Lafayette County HS — 300/9-12
807a W 31st St 64037 — 660-584-3661
Joseph Mintner, prin. — Fax 584-8666
Lafayette County MS — 300/6-8
807b W 31st St 64037 — 660-584-7161
Jerry Hocker, prin. — Fax 584-8666

Highlandville, Christian, Pop. 921
Spokane R-VII SD — 700/PK-12
167 Kentling Ave 65669 — 417-443-2200
Dr. Mickie Harris, supt. — Fax 443-2205
www.spokane.k12.mo.us
Other Schools – See Spokane

High Ridge, Jefferson, Pop. 4,423
Northwest R-I SD — 7,200/K-12
2843 Community Ln 63049 — 636-677-3473
Dr. John Urkevich, supt. — Fax 677-5480
www.nwr1.k12.mo.us/
Other Schools – See Cedar Hill, House Springs

Hillsboro, Jefferson, Pop. 1,784
Grandview R-II SD — 900/K-12
11470 Highway C 63050 — 636-944-3941
Dr. Michael Brown, supt. — Fax 944-5239
schoolweb.missouri.edu/grandviewr2
Grandview HS — 300/9-12
11470 Highway C 63050 — 636-944-3390
Maurice Creason, prin. — Fax 944-3515
Grandview MS — 200/6-8
11470 Highway C 63050 — 636-944-3931
James Keeling, prin. — Fax 944-5239

Hillsboro R-III SD — 3,600/K-12
20 Hawk Dr 63050 — 636-789-0060
Randal Charles, supt. — Fax 789-3216
www.hillsboro.k12.mo.us/
Hillsboro HS — 1,200/9-12
123 Leon Hall Pkwy 63050 — 636-789-0010
Cheryl Aylesworth, prin. — Fax 789-3211
Hillsboro JHS — 600/7-8
12 Hawk Dr 63050 — 636-789-0020
Terry Edwards, prin. — Fax 789-3212

Christian Outreach S — 100/PK-12
4450 Outreach Dr 63050 — 636-789-3411
John Speropoulos, prin. — Fax 789-2585
Jefferson College — Post-Sec.
1000 Viking Dr 63050 — 636-797-3000

Holcomb, Dunklin, Pop. 697
Holcomb R-III SD — 600/PK-12
PO Box 190 63852 — 573-792-3113
Jeff Bullock, supt. — Fax 792-3118
holcomb.k12.mo.us/
Holcomb JSHS — 200/7-12
PO Box 190 63852 — 573-792-3362
Scottie Blackburn, prin. — Fax 792-3631

Holden, Johnson, Pop. 2,543
Holden R-III SD — 1,400/PK-12
1612 S Main St 64040 — 816-732-5568
Scott Slava, supt. — Fax 732-4336
schoolweb.missouri.edu/holden.k12.mo.us/
Holden HS — 500/9-12
1901 S Main St 64040 — 816-732-5523
Matt Lindsey, prin. — Fax 732-4142
Holden MS — 400/6-8
301 Eagle Dr 64040 — 816-732-4125
Greg Montgomery, prin. — Fax 732-2009

Hollister, Taney, Pop. 3,835
Hollister R-V SD — 1,100/PK-12
1798 State Highway BB 65672 — 417-243-4005
Dr. Timothy Taylor, supt. — Fax 334-2663
www.hollister.k12.mo.us/
Hollister HS — 300/9-12
2112 State Highway BB 65672 — 417-243-4045
Chris Ford, prin. — Fax 336-2240
Hollister JHS — 200/7-8
1798 State Highway BB 65672 — 417-243-4055
Travis Shaw, prin.

Trinity Christian Academy — 100/PK-12
119 Myrtle Ave 65672 — 417-334-7084
Holly Gregory, prin. — Fax 334-1794

Hopkins, Nodaway, Pop. 561
North Nodaway County R-VI SD — 300/PK-12
PO Box 260 64461 — 660-778-3411
Joan Bolon, supt. — Fax 778-3210
www.nnr6.k12.mo.us/
North Nodaway County JSHS — 100/6-12
PO Box 260 64461 — 660-778-3315
Charles McKee, prin. — Fax 778-3210

Hornersville, Dunklin, Pop. 681
Senath-Hornersville C-8 SD
Supt. — See Senath
Senath-Hornersville MS — 300/5-8
601 School St 63855 — 573-737-2455
Lee Gattis, prin. — Fax 737-2456

House Springs, Jefferson
Northwest R-I SD
Supt. — See High Ridge
Northwest Valley MS — 1,200/7-8
PO Box 500 63051 — 636-671-3470
Kevin Carl, prin. — Fax 671-1535

Houston, Texas, Pop. 2,005
Houston R-I SD — 1,000/PK-12
423 W Pine St 65483 — 417-967-3024
Clinton Waters, supt. — Fax 967-4887
www.houston.k12.mo.us
Houston HS — 400/9-12
423 W Pine St 65483 — 417-967-3024
Audrey Kell, prin. — Fax 967-3669
Houston MS — 200/6-8
423 W Pine St 65483 — 417-967-3024
Charlie Malam, prin. — Fax 967-5481

Hughesville, Pettis, Pop. 181
Pettis County R-V SD — 400/K-12
16215 Highway H 65334 — 660-827-0772
Amy Fagg, supt. — Fax 827-7162
www.northwest.k12.mo.us
Northwest JSHS — 200/7-12
16215 Highway H 65334 — 660-827-0774
Brett Hieronymus, prin. — Fax 827-7162

Humansville, Polk, Pop. 986
Humansville R-IV SD — 400/K-12
300 N Oak St 65674 — 417-754-2535
Leonard Tourtillott, supt. — Fax 754-8565
www.humansville.k12.mo.us/
Humansville HS — 200/7-12
300 N Oak St 65674 — 417-754-2219
Mark Koca, prin. — Fax 754-8565

Hume, Bates, Pop. 346
Hume R-VIII SD — 100/K-12
PO Box 402 64752 — 660-643-7411
David Quick, supt. — Fax 643-7506
Hume JSHS — 100/6-12
PO Box 402 64752 — 660-643-7411
Cindy Pirch, prin. — Fax 643-7506

Huntsville, Randolph, Pop. 1,625
Westran R-I SD — 700/PK-12
210 W Depot St 65259 — 660-277-4429
Kelly Shelby, supt. — Fax 277-4420
westran.k12.mo.us/
Westran HS — 200/9-12
601 Hornet Ln 65259 — 660-277-4415
Mike Nagel, prin. — Fax 277-4644
Other Schools – See Clifton Hill

Hurley, Stone, Pop. 160
Hurley R-I SD — 200/K-12
PO Box 248 65675 — 417-369-3271
Doug Arnold, supt. — Fax 369-2212
schoolweb.missouri.edu/hurley.k12.mo.us/
Hurley JSHS — 100/7-12
PO Box 248 65675 — 417-369-3271
Lisa May, prin. — Fax 369-2212

Iberia, Miller, Pop. 673
Iberia R-V SD — 800/PK-12
PO Box 156 65486 — 573-793-6818
James McLeod, supt. — Fax 793-6821
www.iberia.k12.mo.us/
Iberia HS — 300/7-12
PO Box 156 65486 — 573-793-2228
Don Fields, prin. — Fax 793-2946

Imperial, Jefferson, Pop. 4,156
Fox C-6 SD
Supt. — See Arnold
Seckman HS — 1,600/9-12
2800 Seckman Rd 63052 — 636-282-1485
Don Grimshaw, prin. — Fax 282-5177
Seckman MS — 800/7-8
2840 Seckman Rd 63052 — 636-296-5707
David R. Black, prin. — Fax 296-5707

Windsor C-1 SD 3,000/K-12
6208 US Highway 61/67 63052 636-464-4400
Dr. Rudy Duran, supt. Fax 464-4454
www.windsor.k12.mo.us/district/

Windsor HS 900/9-12
6208 US Highway 61/67 63052 636-464-4429
Michael Steinkamp, prin. Fax 464-4456

Windsor MS 700/6-8
6208 US Highway 61/67 63052 636-464-4417
Ernie Perkins, prin. Fax 464-4473

Independence, Jackson, Pop. 110,208

Fort Osage R-I SD 4,800/K-12
2101 N Twyman Rd 64058 816-650-7000
Larry E. Ewing, supt. Fax 650-3888
www.fortosage.net

Career & Technology Center Vo/Tech
2101 N Twyman Rd 64058 816-650-7180
Mike Pantleo, prin. Fax 650-7195

Ft. Osage HS 1,500/9-12
2101 N Twyman Rd 64058 816-650-7030
Gail Horn, prin. Fax 650-7088

Osage Trail MS 800/7-8
2101 N Twyman Rd 64058 816-650-7151
James Morrill, prin. Fax 650-7152

Independence SD 30 10,900/PK-12
218 N Pleasant St 64050 816-521-2700
Dr. Jim Hinson, supt. Fax 521-2999
www.indep.k12.mo.us

Bingham MS 900/6-8
1716 S Speck Rd 64057 816-796-4850
Charles Garner, prin. Fax 796-4880

Bridger MS 900/6-8
18200 E State Route 78 64057 816-796-4800
Belinda Woodson, prin. Fax 796-4812

Chrisman HS 1,700/9-12
1223 N Noland Rd 64050 816-521-2720
Jason Dial, prin. Fax 521-2729

Pioneer MS 800/6-8
1656 S Speck Rd 64057 816-796-4885
Elizabeth Savidge, prin. Fax 796-4899

Truman HS 1,700/9-12
3301 S Noland Rd 64055 816-521-2710
Kristel Barr, prin. Fax 521-2913

Kansas City SD 33
Supt. — See Kansas City

Nowlin MS 800/6-8
2800 S Hardy Ave 64052 816-418-4125
Dr. Sheila Dannar, prin. Fax 418-4145

Van Horn HS 1,100/9-12
1109 S Arlington Ave 64053 816-418-4000
Dr. Mary Long, prin. Fax 418-4021

Englewood Christian Academy 300/PK-12
10628 E Winner Rd 64052 816-254-8313
Brian Ross, admin. Fax 254-7065

Graceland University Post-Sec.
1401 W Truman Rd 64050 816-833-0524

Independence College of Cosmetology Post-Sec.
815 W 23rd St 64055 816-252-4247

Metropolitan Community College Post-Sec.
20301 E State Route 78 64057 816-220-6577

National American University Post-Sec.
3620 Arrowhead Ave 64057 816-353-4554

St. Mary Bundschu Memorial HS 200/9-12
622 N Main St 64050 816-252-8733
Judy Warren, prin. Fax 252-2780

Ironton, Iron, Pop. 1,362

Arcadia Valley R-II SD 1,200/PK-12
750 Park Dr 63650 573-546-9700
Clifford Carver, supt. Fax 546-7314
www.av.k12.mo.us

Arcadia Valley Career Tech Vo/Tech
650 Park Dr 63650 573-546-9700
Dave Ruhman, prin. Fax 546-6956

Arcadia Valley HS 400/9-12
520 Park Dr 63650 573-546-9700
Lance Sprenkel, prin. Fax 546-3934

Arcadia Valley MS 400/5-8
550 Park Dr 63650 573-546-9700
Kent Huddleston, prin. Fax 546-7304

Jackson, Cape Girardeau, Pop. 12,982

Jackson R-II SD 4,400/K-12
614 E Adams St 63755 573-243-9501
Ron Anderson, supt. Fax 243-9503
www.jackson.k12.mo.us

Hawkins JHS 800/8-9
210 N West Ln 63755 573-243-9533
Cory Crosnoe, prin. Fax 243-9584

Jackson SHS 1,200/10-12
315 S Missouri St 63755 573-243-9513
Richard McClard, prin. Fax 243-9524

Saxony Lutheran HS 100/9-12
2004 Saxony Ln 63755 573-204-7555
Craig Ernstmeyer, prin. Fax 204-7445

Jameson, Daviess, Pop. 123

North Daviess R-III SD 100/PK-12
413 E 2nd St 64647 660-828-4123
Julie Kirby, supt. Fax 828-4122
www.ndaviess.k12.mo.us

North Daviess JSHS 50/7-12
413 E 2nd St 64647 660-828-4123
Kristi Critten, prin. Fax 828-4122

Jamesport, Daviess, Pop. 516

Tri-County R-VII SD 200/PK-12
904 W Auberry Grv 64648 660-684-6118
Fax 684-6218

Tri-County JSHS 100/7-12
904 W Auberry Grv 64648 660-684-6116
Dennis Croy, prin. Fax 684-6218

Jamestown, Moniteau, Pop. 397

Jamestown C-1 SD 200/K-12
222 School St 65046 660-849-2141
James Deeken, supt. Fax 849-2600

Jamestown C-I JSHS 100/7-12
222 School St 65046 660-849-2141
Kevin Kohler, prin. Fax 849-2600

Jasper, Jasper, Pop. 1,037

Jasper County R-V SD 500/K-12
201 W Mercer St 64755 417-394-2416
Kathy Fall, supt. Fax 394-2394
www.jasper.k12.mo.us/

Jasper County JSHS 300/7-12
201 W Mercer St 64755 417-394-2511
Bill Hodge, prin. Fax 394-2394

Jefferson City, Cole, Pop. 39,062

Blair Oaks R-II SD 700/K-12
6124 Falcon Ln 65101 573-636-2020
Dr. James Jones, supt. Fax 636-2202
www.blairoaks.k12.mo.us

Blair Oaks JSHS 400/7-12
6124 Falcon Ln 65101 573-635-8514
Gary Verslues, prin. Fax 635-6327

Jefferson City SD 8,200/PK-12
315 E Dunklin St 65101 573-659-3000
Bert Kimble, supt. Fax 659-3044
www.jcps.k12.mo.us

Jefferson City HS 1,800/10-12
609 Union St 65101 573-659-3050
Richard Pemberton, prin. Fax 659-3153

Jefferson MS 1,000/6-8
1201 Fairgrounds Rd 65109 573-659-3250
Roberta Hubbs, prin. Fax 659-3259

Lewis and Clark MS 1,000/6-8
325 Lewis and Clark Dr 65101 573-659-3200
Robert Steffes, prin. Fax 659-3209

Nichols Career Center Vo/Tech
605 Union St 65101 573-659-3100
Mike Kriegshauser, prin. Fax 659-3154

Simonsen Ninth Grade Center 700/9-9
501 E Miller St 65101 573-659-3125
Ron Fritz, prin. Fax 659-7362

Helias HS 900/9-12
1305 Swifts Hwy 65109 573-635-6139
Sr. Jean Dietrich, prin. Fax 635-5615

Lincoln University Post-Sec.
820 Chestnut St 65101 573-681-5000

Merrell Univ of Beauty Arts & Science Post-Sec.
1101R Southwest Boulevard 65109 573-635-4433

Metro Business College Post-Sec.
1407 Southwest Blvd 65109 573-635-6600

Nichols Career Center Post-Sec.
605 Union St 65101 573-659-3100

Jennings, Saint Louis, Pop. 14,926

Jennings SD 3,200/PK-12
2559 Dorwood Dr 63136 314-653-8000
Dr. Terry Stewart, supt. Fax 653-8030
www.jenningsk12.net/index.html

Jennings HS 800/9-12
8850 Cozens Ave 63136 314-653-8100
Clarence Holman, prin. Fax 653-8102

Jennings JHS 600/7-8
8831 Cozens Ave 63136 314-653-8150
Sam Gilkey, prin. Fax 653-8168

Joplin, Jasper, Pop. 47,183

Joplin R-VIII SD 7,300/PK-12
PO Box 128 64802 417-625-5200
Dr. Jim Simpson, supt. Fax 625-5210
www.joplin.k12.mo.us

Franklin Tech S Vo/Tech
PO Box 128 64802 417-625-5260
David Rockers, dir. Fax 625-5266

Joplin HS 2,000/9-12
PO Box 128 64802 417-625-5230
Dr. Kerry Sachetta, prin. Fax 625-5238

Memorial MS 700/6-8
PO Box 128 64802 417-625-5250
Stephen Gilbreth, prin. Fax 625-5256

North MS 400/6-8
PO Box 128 64802 417-625-5270
Barbara D. Cox, prin. Fax 625-5273

South MS 600/6-8
PO Box 128 64802 417-625-5280
Ron Mitchell, prin. Fax 625-5284

Franklin Technology Ctr - MSSU Campus Adult
PO Box 128 64802 417-695-4400
Dr. Richard Saporito, prin.

Class Act I School of Cosmetology Post-Sec.
512 Main St 64801 417-781-7070

College Heights Christian S 600/PK-12
4311 Newman Rd 64801 417-782-4114
Daniel Lewis, prin. Fax 659-9092

Franklin Technology - MSSU Post-Sec.
3950 Newman Rd 64801 417-659-4400

Jefferson Independent Day S 300/PK-12
3401 Newman Rd 64801 417-781-5124
Bill Carter, hdmstr. Fax 781-1949

McAuley Catholic HS 200/9-12
930 S Pearl Ave 64801 417-624-9320
Gene Koester, prin. Fax 626-8334

Messenger College Post-Sec.
300 E 50th St 64804 417-624-7070

Missouri Southern State University Post-Sec.
3950 Newman Rd 64801 417-625-9300

New Dimensions School of Hair Design Post-Sec.
705 Illinois Ave Ste 12 64801 417-782-2875

Ozark Christian College Post-Sec.
1111 N Main St 64801 417-624-2518

St. John's Regional Medical Center Post-Sec.
2727 Mc Clelland Blvd 64804 417-781-2727

St. Peter MS 100/6-8
802 Byers Ave 64801 417-624-5605
Greg Emory, prin. Fax 624-6254

Vatterott College Post-Sec.
809 Illinois Ave 64801 417-781-5633

Wichita Technical Institute Post-Sec.
1531 E 32nd St 64804 417-206-9115

Kahoka, Clark, Pop. 2,193

Clark County R-I SD 1,100/PK-12
427 W Chestnut St 63445 660-727-2377
Ritchie Kracht, supt. Fax 727-2035

Clark County HS 400/9-12
680 E Main St 63445 660-727-2205
Jason Harper, prin. Fax 727-2245

Clark County MS 200/6-8
384 N Jefferson St 63445 660-727-3319
Jason Church, prin. Fax 727-2035

Shiloh Christian S 50/K-12
RR 1 Box 68A 63445 573-853-4337
Ken Penfield, admin. Fax 853-4505

Kansas City, Jackson, Pop. 444,965

Center SD 58 2,500/PK-12
8701 Holmes Rd 64131 816-349-3300
Dr. Robert Bartman, supt. Fax 349-3431
www.center.k12.mo.us

Center HS 800/9-12
8715 Holmes Rd 64131 816-349-3330
Harold Hawkins, prin. Fax 349-3427

Center MS 600/6-8
326 E 103rd St 64114 816-612-4000
Linda Williams, prin. Fax 612-4053

Hickman Mills C-I SD 7,100/K-12
9000 Old Santa Fe Rd 64138 816-316-7000
Dr. Marge Williams, supt. Fax 316-7020
www.hickmanmills.org

Ervin JHS 900/6-8
10530 Greenwood Rd 64134 816-316-7600
Angie McConico, prin. Fax 316-7601

Hickman Mills HS 1,200/9-12
9010 Old Santa Fe Rd 64138 816-316-7300
Bill Sculley, prin. Fax 316-8009

Ruskin HS 900/9-12
7000 E 111th St Ste 46 64134 816-316-7400
Jim Tinsley, prin. Fax 316-7475

Smith-Hale JHS 900/6-8
8925 Longview Rd 64134 816-316-7700
Jan Davis, prin. Fax 316-7704

Kansas City SD 33 27,000/PK-12
1211 McGee St 64106 816-418-7000
Anthony Amato, supt. Fax 418-7631
www.kcmsd.net

Central HS 1,000/9-12
3221 Indiana Ave 64128 816-418-2000
William McClendon, prin. Fax 418-2027

Central Magnet MS 600/6-8
3611 E Linwood Blvd 64128 816-418-2100
Jeanette Pointer-Shelby, prin. Fax 418-2115

Kansas City MS of the Arts 600/6-8
4848 Woodland Ave 64110 816-418-2400
Dr. Juanita Hempstead, prin. Fax 418-2415

King MS 500/6-8
4201 Indiana Ave 64130 816-418-2475
Archie Brown, prin. Fax 418-2480

Lincoln College Prep HS 600/9-12
2111 Woodland Ave 64108 816-418-3000
Regina Ellis, prin. Fax 418-3015

Lincoln College Prep MS 6-8
2012 E 23rd St 64127 816-418-3525
Kenneth Holstine, prin. Fax 418-3530

Manual Career & Tech Center Vo/Tech
1215 E Truman Rd 64106 816-418-5207
Tom Levin, prin. Fax 418-5215

Manual East Campus Career & Tech Center Vo/Tech
1924 Van Brunt Blvd 64127 816-418-3131
Fax 418-1389

Northeast HS 1,100/9-12
415 Van Brunt Blvd 64124 816-418-3300
Vicki Murillo, prin. Fax 418-3310

Northeast MS 700/6-8
4904 Independence Ave 64124 816-418-3400
T. Allen McClain, prin. Fax 418-3410

Paseo Academy of Performing Arts 700/9-12
4747 Flora Ave 64110 816-418-2275
Dr. Juanita Hempstead, prin. Fax 418-2300

Rogers MS 600/6-8
6400 E 23rd St 64129 816-418-4770
Arlene Penner, prin. Fax 418-4803

Southeast HS 800/9-12
3500 E Meyer Blvd 64132 816-418-1075
Dr. Mark Harrison, prin. Fax 418-1080

Westport HS 9-12
315 E 39th St 64111 816-418-6100
Connie Espinoza, prin. Fax 418-6185

Westport MS 400/6-8
300 E 39th St 64111 816-418-6200
Derald Davis, prin. Fax 418-6262

Other Schools – See Independence

North Kansas City SD 74
Supt. — See North Kansas City

Career & Technical Education Vo/Tech
1950 NE 46th St 64116 816-413-5056
Leigh Anne Knight, dir. Fax 413-5215

Eastgate MS 800/6-8
4700 NE Parvin Rd 64117 816-413-5800
Daniel Clemens, prin. Fax 413-5805

Maple Park MS 800/6-8
5300 N Bennington Ave 64119 816-413-5700
Charlotte Sands, prin. Fax 413-5705

New Mark MS 1,000/6-8
515 NE 106th St 64155 816-413-6300
Terri Stirlen, prin. Fax 413-6305

Northgate MS 700/6-8
2117 NE 48th St 64118 816-413-6100
Steve St. Louis, prin. Fax 413-6105
Oak Park HS 2,000/9-12
825 NE 79th Ter 64118 816-413-5300
Fred Skretta, prin. Fax 413-5305
Staley HS 9-12
2800 NE Shoal Creek Pkwy 64155 816-413-4100
Clark Mershon, prin. Fax 413-4105
Winnetonka HS 1,700/9-12
5815 NE 48th St 64119 816-413-5500
Matt Lindsey, prin. Fax 413-5505

Park Hill SD 9,400/K-12
7703 NW Barry Rd 64153 816-359-4000
Dr. Dennis Fisher, supt. Fax 359-4049
www.parkhill.k12.mo.us
Congress MS 800/7-8
8150 N Congress Ave 64152 816-359-4230
Dr. Timothy Todd, prin. Fax 359-4219
Lakeview MS 800/7-8
6720 NW 64th St 64151 816-359-4220
Jim Dunn, prin. Fax 359-4229
Park Hill HS 1,500/9-12
7701 NW Barry Rd 64153 816-359-4110
J. Bradford Kincheloe, prin. Fax 359-4119
Park Hill South HS 1,500/9-12
4500 NW River Park Dr 64150 816-359-4120
Dale Longenecker, prin. Fax 359-4129

Raytown C-2 SD
Supt. — See Raytown
Raytown MS 1,100/6-8
4900 Pittman Rd 64133 816-268-7360
Dr. Georgetta May, prin. Fax 268-7365

ARAMARK Healthcare Support Services SW Post-Sec.
1000 Carondelet Dr 64114 816-943-2146
Archbishop O'Hara HS 500/9-12
9001 James A Reed Rd 64138 816-763-4800
Walter Bowman, prin. Fax 763-0156
Aviation Institute of Maintenance Post-Sec.
3130 Terrace St 64111 816-753-9920
Avila University Post-Sec.
11901 Wornall Rd 64145 816-942-8400
Barstow S 600/PK-12
11511 State Line Rd 64114 816-942-3255
Art Atkison, hdmstr. Fax 942-3227
Blue Ridge Christian S 300/K-12
8524 Blue Ridge Blvd 64138 816-358-0950
Gary Rogers, prin. Fax 358-1138
Calvary Bible College & Theological Sem Post-Sec.
15800 Calvary Rd 64147 816-322-0110
Cleveland Chiropractic College Post-Sec.
6401 Rockhill Rd 64131 816-501-0100
Concorde Career College Post-Sec.
3239 Broadway St 64111 816-531-5223
Cristos Academy 50/7-12
11000 Ruskin Way 64134 816-966-8877
Eric Smith, admin. Fax 966-2018
DeVry University Post-Sec.
11224 Holmes Rd 64131 816-941-0430
DeVry University Post-Sec.
1100 Main St Ste 118 64105 816-221-1300
Faith Academy 200/PK-10
4300 N Corrington Ave 64117 816-455-2847
Donna Houpe, admin. Fax 455-8041
Grantham University Post-Sec.
7200 NW 86th St 64153 800-955-2527
Heritage College Post-Sec.
1200 E 104th St Ste 300 64131 816-942-5474
High-Tech Institute Post-Sec.
9001 State Line Rd 64114 816-444-4300
House of Heavilin Beauty College Post-Sec.
5720 Troost Ave 64110 816-523-2471
ITT Technical Institute Post-Sec.
9150 E 41st Ter 64133 816-276-1400
Kansas City Academy 100/6-12
7933 Main St 64114 816-444-5225
Mary Statz, prin. Fax 444-8354
Kansas City Art Institute Post-Sec.
4415 Warwick Blvd 64111 800-522-5224
KC Univ. of Medicine and Biosciences Post-Sec.
1750 Independence Ave 64106 816-283-2000
Keller Graduate School Post-Sec.
11224 Holmes Rd 64131 816-941-0367
Lutheran HS 100/9-12
12411 Wornall Rd 64145 816-241-5478
Chris Domsch, prin. Fax 876-2069
Maple Woods Community College Post-Sec.
2601 NE Barry Rd 64156 816-437-3000
Midwestern Baptist Theological Seminary Post-Sec.
5001 N Oak Trfy 64118 816-414-3700
Milestone Academy 50/9-12
PO Box 266555 64126 816-665-9770
Peter Flournoy, hdmstr. Fax 241-0880
Nazarene Theological Seminary Post-Sec.
1700 E Meyer Blvd 64131 816-333-6254
Notre Dame De Sion HS 400/9-12
10631 Wornall Rd 64114 816-942-3282
Michelle Olson, prin. Fax 942-4052
Pembroke Hill S 1,200/PK-12
400 W 51st St 64112 816-936-1200
Steve Bellis, hdmstr. Fax 936-1208
Pembroke Hill S - Ward Pkwy Campus 700/6-12
5121 State Line Rd 64112 816-936-1500
Steve Bellis, hdmstr. Fax 936-1509
Penn Valley Community College Post-Sec.
3201 Southwest Traffic Way 64111 816-759-4000
Pinnacle Career Institute Post-Sec.
1001 E 101st Ter Ste 325 64131 800-614-0900
Research College of Nursing Post-Sec.
2525 E Meyer Blvd 64132 816-995-2800
Research Medical Center Post-Sec.
2316 E Meyer Blvd 64132 816-276-4101
Rockhurst HS 1,000/9-12
9301 State Line Rd 64114 816-363-2036
Larry Ruby, prin. Fax 363-3764
Rockhurst University Post-Sec.
1100 Rockhurst Rd 64110 816-501-4000
St. Luke's College Post-Sec.
8320 Ward Pkwy Ste 300 64114 816-932-2367
St. Paul School of Theology Post-Sec.
5123 E Truman Rd 64127 816-483-9600
St. Pius X HS 400/9-12
1500 NE 42nd Ter 64116 816-453-3450
Joseph Monachino, prin. Fax 452-7099
St. Teresa Academy 500/9-12
5600 Main St 64113 816-501-0011
Nancy Hand, prin. Fax 523-0232
Truman Medical Center Post-Sec.
2301 Holmes St 64108 816-556-3153
University of Missouri Post-Sec.
5100 Rockhill Rd 64110 816-235-1000
Vatterott College Post-Sec.
8955 E 38th Ter 64129 816-861-1000

Kearney, Clay, Pop. 7,399
Kearney R-I SD 2,800/K-12
1002 S Jefferson St 64060 816-628-4116
Dr. Chris Belcher, supt. Fax 628-4074
www.kearney.k12.mo.us
Kearney HS 1,000/9-12
715 E 19th St 64060 816-628-4585
Daryl Rinne, prin. Fax 628-3383
Summit Ridge MS 500/6-8
2215 S Campus St 64060 816-628-2650
Randy Wepler, prin. Fax 628-1938

Kennett, Dunklin, Pop. 11,028
Kennett SD 39 2,200/PK-12
510 College Ave 63857 573-717-1100
Jerry Noble, supt. Fax 717-1016
www.kennett.k12.mo.us
Kennett Career & Technology Center Vo/Tech
1400 W Washington St 63857 573-717-1123
Doug Irvin, dir. Fax 717-1386
Kennett HS 500/9-12
1400 W Washington St 63857 573-717-1120
Edward Siebenhuener, prin. Fax 717-1128
Kennett MS 500/6-8
510 College Ave 63857 573-717-1105
Ward Billings, prin. Fax 717-1106

Keytesville, Chariton, Pop. 516
Keytesville R-III SD 200/PK-12
27247 Highway 5 65261 660-288-3767
Paul Vossler, supt. Fax 288-3110
schoolweb.missouri.edu/keytesville.k-12.mo.us
Keytesville JSHS 100/7-12
27247 Highway 5 65261 660-288-3767
Rena Roth, prin. Fax 288-3110

King City, Gentry, Pop. 944
King City R-I SD 400/PK-12
PO Box 189 64463 660-535-4319
Kendall Ebersold, supt. Fax 535-4765
www.kingcity.k12.mo.us
King City JSHS 200/7-12
PO Box 189 64463 660-535-4319
John Silkett, prin. Fax 535-4765

Kingdom City, Callaway, Pop. 137
North Callaway County R-I SD 1,300/K-12
2690 US Highway 54 65262 573-386-2214
Dr. Roy Moss, supt. Fax 386-2169
northcallaway.k12.mo.us/
North Callaway HS 500/9-12
2700 US Highway 54 65262 573-386-2211
Carol Green, prin. Fax 386-2403

Kingsville, Johnson, Pop. 260
Kingsville R-I SD 300/K-12
PO Box 7 64061 816-597-3422
Kevin Coleman, supt. Fax 597-3702
www.kingsville.k12.mo.us/
Kingsville JSHS 100/7-12
PO Box 7 64061 816-597-3422
Lorna Warren, prin. Fax 597-3702

Kirbyville, Taney, Pop. 143
Kirbyville R-VI SD 300/K-8
6225 E State Highway 76 65679 417-337-8913
Jerry Parrett, supt. Fax 348-0794
www.kirbyville.k12.mo.us/
Kirbyville MS 200/4-8
6225 E State Highway 76 65679 417-348-0444
Addie Gaines, prin. Fax 348-0525

Kirksville, Adair, Pop. 16,986
Kirksville R-III SD 2,500/PK-12
1901 E Hamilton St 63501 660-665-7774
Patrick Williams, supt. Fax 665-3281
www.kirksville.k12.mo.us
Kirksville Area Technical Center Vo/Tech
1103 Cottage Grove Ave 63501 660-665-2865
Teresa Jones, prin. Fax 626-1477
Kirksville HS 800/9-12
1300 Cottage Grove Ave 63501 660-665-4631
Randy Mikel, prin. Fax 626-1439
Kirksville MS 600/6-8
1515 Cottage Grove Ave 63501 660-665-3793
Mike Bartig, prin. Fax 626-1418

Kirksville Coll. of Osteopathic Medicine Post-Sec.
800 W Jefferson St 63501 660-626-2237
School of Health Management Post-Sec.
800 W Jefferson St 63501 660-626-2237
Truman State University Post-Sec.
100 E Normal St 63501 660-785-4000

Kirkwood, Saint Louis, Pop. 27,038
Kirkwood R-VII SD 5,000/K-12
11289 Manchester Rd 63122 314-213-6101
David Damerall, supt. Fax 984-0002
www.kirkwood.k12.mo.us
Kirkwood HS 1,700/9-12
801 W Essex Ave 63122 314-213-6110
David Holley, prin. Fax 984-4412
Nipher MS 600/6-8
700 S Kirkwood Rd 63122 314-213-6180
Carol Migneron, prin. Fax 213-6178
North Kirkwood MS 600/6-8
11287 Manchester Rd 63122 314-213-6170
Jeanette Tendai, prin. Fax 213-6177

St. Louis Community College Post-Sec.
11333 Big Bend Rd 63122 314-984-7500
Ursuline Academy 600/9-12
341 S Sappington Rd 63122 314-966-4556
Dr. Patricia Hensley, prin. Fax 966-4662

Knob Noster, Johnson, Pop. 2,734
Knob Noster R-VIII SD 1,700/PK-12
401 E Wimer St 65336 660-563-3186
Dr. Margret Anderson, supt. Fax 563-3026
knobnoster.k12.mo.us/
Knob Noster HS 500/9-12
504 S Washington Ave 65336 660-563-2283
Richard Miller, prin. Fax 563-3384
Knob Noster MS 400/6-8
211 E Wimer St 65336 660-563-2260
Peter Greene, prin. Fax 563-3274

Koshkonong, Oregon, Pop. 208
Oregon-Howell R-III SD 300/K-12
PO Box 398 65692 417-867-5601
Dr. Steve Morgan, supt. Fax 867-3757
koshkonong.k12.mo.us/
Koshkonong JSHS 200/7-12
PO Box 398 65692 417-867-5601
Jeanie White, prin. Fax 867-3757

Laddonia, Audrain, Pop. 600
Community R-VI SD 300/K-12
35063 Highway BB 63352 573-492-6223
Dr. Carrie Eidson, supt. Fax 492-6268
www.cr6.net/
Community HS 100/6-12
35063 Highway BB 63352 573-492-6222
Jacob Moss, prin. Fax 492-6407

Lake Ozark, Camden, Pop. 1,915
School of the Osage R-II SD 1,700/PK-12
PO Box 1960 65049 573-365-4091
Dr. Mary Ann Johnson, supt. Fax 365-5748
www.osage.k12.mo.us
Osage JHS 300/7-8
1501 School Rd 65049 573-365-5343
Tony Slack, prin. Fax 365-3761
Other Schools – See Osage Beach

Lamar, Barton, Pop. 4,602
Lamar R-I SD 1,300/PK-12
202 W 7th St 64759 417-682-3527
Mike Resa, supt. Fax 682-6013
www.lamar.k12.mo.us
Lamar Area Voc-Tech S Vo/Tech
202 W 7th St 64759 417-682-3384
Karl Morey, dir. Fax 682-3420
Lamar HS 400/9-12
202 W 7th St 64759 417-682-5571
Kevin Baldwin, prin. Fax 681-0328
Lamar MS 300/6-8
202 W 7th St 64759 417-682-3548
Alan Ray, prin. Fax 682-3420

La Monte, Pettis, Pop. 1,062
La Monte R-IV SD 400/PK-12
301 S Washington St 65337 660-347-5439
Joan Twidwell, supt. Fax 347-5467
La Monte JSHS 200/7-12
301 S Washington St 65337 660-347-5439
Kevin Kultgen, prin. Fax 347-5467

La Plata, Macon, Pop. 1,442
La Plata R-II SD 400/K-12
201 W Moore St 63549 660-332-7001
Thomas Ward, supt. Fax 332-7929
laplata.k12.mo.us
La Plata JSHS 200/7-12
201 W Moore St 63549 660-332-7001
Steve Safley, prin. Fax 332-7656

Laquey, Pulaski
Laquey R-V SD 800/PK-12
PO Box 130 65534 573-765-3716
Bob Boulware, supt. Fax 765-4052
www.laquey.k12.mo.us/
Laquey R-V HS 200/9-12
PO Box 130 65534 573-765-4051
Gary Houchens, prin. Fax 765-5608
Laquey R-V MS 200/5-8
PO Box 130 65534 573-765-3129
Jerry Stenson, prin. Fax 765-3129

Lathrop, Clinton, Pop. 2,328
Lathrop R-II SD 900/K-12
700 East St 64465 816-528-7500
Dr. Chris Blackburn, supt. Fax 528-7514
schoolweb.missouri.edu/lathrop.k12.mo.us
Lathrop HS 300/9-12
612 Center St 64465 816-528-7600
Tod Winterboer, prin. Fax 528-7637
Lathrop MS 200/6-8
700 Center St 64465 816-528-7700
Chris Fine, prin. Fax 528-7759

Lawson, Ray, Pop. 2,406
Lawson R-XIV SD 1,300/PK-12
PO Box 157 64062 816-580-7277
S. Craig Barker, supt. Fax 296-7723
schoolweb.missouri.edu/lawson.k12.mo.us/
Lawson HS 400/9-12
PO Box 157 64062 816-580-7270
Don Edwards, prin. Fax 296-3048

Lawson MS 400/5-8
PO Box 157 64062 816-580-7279
Pat Penning, prin. Fax 296-3164

Leadwood, Saint Francois, Pop. 1,173
West St. Francois County R-IV SD 1,000/PK-12
1124 Main St 63653 573-562-7535
Stacy Stevens, supt. Fax 562-7510
westco.k12.mo.us/
West County MS 300/6-8
1124 Main St 63653 573-562-7544
Kevin Coffman, prin. Fax 562-7510
Other Schools – See Park Hills

Lebanon, Laclede, Pop. 13,336
Lebanon R-III SD 4,600/PK-12
321 S Jefferson Ave 65536 417-532-9141
Dr. Duane Widhalm, supt. Fax 532-9492
www.lebanon.k12.mo.us
Lebanon HS 1,500/9-12
777 Brice St 65536 417-532-9144
Robert Smith, prin. Fax 532-3386
Lebanon JHS 800/7-8
500 N Adams Ave 65536 417-532-9121
Matt Searson, prin. Fax 533-3805
Lebanon Tech & Career Center Vo/Tech
Hwy 64 Bypass 65536 417-532-5494
Gail Holcomb, prin. Fax 532-4510

Lees Summit, Jackson, Pop. 74,948
Blue Springs R-IV SD
Supt. — See Blue Springs
Delta Woods MS 600/6-8
4401 NE Lakewood Way 64064 816-795-5830
Steve Cook, prin. Fax 795-5839

Lee's Summit R-VII SD 16,100/PK-12
600 SE Miller St 64063 816-986-1000
Dr. David McGehee, supt. Fax 986-1170
www.leesummit.k12.mo.us
Campbell MS 1,000/7-8
1201 NE Colbern Rd 64086 816-986-3175
Dr. Vicki Porter, prin. Fax 986-3245
Lee's Summit HS 1,900/9-12
400 SE Blue Pkwy 64063 816-986-2000
John Faulkenberry, prin. Fax 986-2095
Lee's Summit North HS 2,200/9-12
901 NE Douglas St 64086 816-986-3000
Dr. Dave Ulrich, prin. Fax 986-3170
Lee's Summit West HS 900/9-12
2600 SW Ward Rd 64082 816-986-4000
Dr. Cindy Bateman, prin. Fax 986-4115
Pleasant Lea MS 900/7-8
630 SW Persels Rd 64081 816-986-1175
Janette Cooley, prin. Fax 986-1225
Summit Lakes MS 700/7-8
3500 SW Windemere Dr 64082 816-986-1375
Dr. Don Andrews, prin. Fax 986-1435
Summit Technical Academy Vo/Tech
777 NW Blue Pkwy 64086 816-524-3366
Bob White, prin. Fax 524-1436

Lee's Summit Community Christian S 700/PK-12
1450 SW Jefferson St 64081 816-524-0185
Linda Harrelson, admin. Fax 524-4105
Longview Community College Post-Sec.
500 SW Longview Rd 64081 816-672-2000

Leeton, Johnson, Pop. 626
Leeton R-X SD 400/PK-12
500 N Main St 64761 660-653-2301
Dr. William Nicely, supt. Fax 653-4315
www.leeton.k12.mo.us/
Leeton HS 100/9-12
500 N Main St 64761 660-653-4314
Jeff Curley, prin. Fax 653-4315
Leeton MS 100/6-8
500 N Main St 64761 660-653-4314
Jeff Curley, prin. Fax 653-4315

Leopold, Bollinger
Leopold R-III SD 200/K-12
PO Box 39 63760 573-238-2211
Derek Urhahn, supt. Fax 238-9868
schoolweb.missouri.edu/leopold.k12.mo.us/
Leopold JSHS 100/7-12
PO Box 39 63760 573-238-2211
Keenan Kinder, prin. Fax 283-9868

Lesterville, Reynolds
Lesterville R-IV SD 300/PK-12
PO Box 120 63654 573-637-2201
Earlene Fox, supt. Fax 637-2279
Lesterville JSHS 100/7-12
PO Box 120 63654 573-637-2201
Susan Myers, prin. Fax 637-2279
Other Schools – See Black

Lexington, Lafayette, Pop. 4,632
Lexington R-V SD 1,000/PK-12
100 S 13th St 64067 660-259-4369
James F. Judd, supt. Fax 259-4992
www.lexington.k12.mo.us
Lexington HS 300/9-12
2309 Aull Ln 64067 660-259-4391
Jerry Mitchell, prin. Fax 259-2166
Lexington MS 300/5-8
1111 S 24th St 64067 660-259-4611
Al Voelker, prin. Fax 259-2538
Lex La-Ray Tech Ctr Vo/Tech
2323 High School Dr 64067 660-259-2264
Brandon Russell, prin. Fax 259-6262

Wentworth Military Academy Post-Sec.
1880 Washington Ave 64067 660-259-2221
Wentworth Military Academy 300/9-12
1880 Washington Ave 64067 660-259-2221
Maj. Gen. John Little, supt. Fax 259-2677

Liberal, Barton, Pop. 811
Liberal R-II SD 500/PK-12
PO Box 38 64762 417-843-5115
William Harvey, supt. Fax 843-6698
Liberal HS 200/9-12
PO Box 38 64762 417-843-2125
Mark Drake, prin. Fax 843-2403
Liberal MS 100/6-8
PO Box 38 64762 417-843-6033
Margaret Gillard, hdmstr. Fax 843-2403

Liberty, Clay, Pop. 29,042
Liberty SD 53 8,100/PK-12
650 Conistor Ln 64068 816-736-5300
Dr. W. Scott Taveau, supt. Fax 736-5306
www.liberty.k12.mo.us
Liberty JHS 700/8-9
600 W Kansas St 64068 816-736-5380
Scott Carr, prin. Fax 736-5384
Liberty SHS 1,700/10-12
200 Blue Jay Dr 64068 816-736-5340
Dr. Martin Jacobs, prin. Fax 736-5345
South Valley JHS 500/8-9
800 Midjay Dr 64068 816-736-7300
Dr. Brad Armstrong, prin. Fax 736-7301

William Jewell College Post-Sec.
500 College Hl 64068 816-781-7700

Licking, Texas, Pop. 1,500
Licking R-VIII SD 900/PK-12
PO Box 179 65542 573-674-2911
Dr. John Hood, supt. Fax 674-4064
Licking JSHS 500/7-12
PO Box 149 65542 573-674-2711
Stephen Denbow, prin. Fax 674-2142

Lincoln, Benton, Pop. 1,103
Lincoln R-II SD 600/K-12
PO Box 39 65338 660-547-3514
Michael Ringen, supt. Fax 547-3729
Lincoln JSHS 300/7-12
PO Box 39 65338 660-547-3514
Alan Bancroft, prin. Fax 547-3729

Linn, Osage, Pop. 1,424
Osage County R-II SD 700/PK-12
1212 E Main St 65051 573-897-4200
Nancy Gillespie, supt. Fax 897-3768
www.linn.k12.mo.us
Linn JSHS 400/7-12
1212 E Main St 65051 573-897-4216
Jo Ellen Hicks, prin. Fax 897-4570

Linn State Technical College Post-Sec.
1 Technology Dr 65051 573-897-3603

Lockwood, Dade, Pop. 962
Lockwood R-I SD 400/K-12
400 W 4th St 65682 417-232-4513
Bill Rogers, supt. Fax 232-4187
www.lockwood.k12.mo.us/
Lockwood HS 100/9-12
400 W 4th St 65682 417-232-4513
Dennis Cornish, prin. Fax 232-4187

Lone Jack, Jackson, Pop. 697
Lone Jack C-6 SD 500/K-12
201 W Lne Jack Lees Smmt Rd 64070816-697-3539
Ronald Davies, supt. Fax 697-8869
www.lonejackc6.net
Lone Jack JSHS 300/7-12
313 S Bynum Rd 64070 816-697-2215
Scott Stewart, prin. Fax 566-3128

Louisburg, Dallas, Pop. 154
Dallas County R-I SD
Supt. — See Buffalo
Dallas County Career Center Vo/Tech
PO Box 100 65685 417-752-3491
Alex Kyser, prin. Fax 752-3493

Louisiana, Pike, Pop. 3,881
Louisiana R-II SD 800/PK-12
3321 Georgia St 63353 573-754-4261
Dan Jones, supt. Fax 754-4319
www.schoolweb.missouri.edu/louisiana.k12.mo.us
Louisiana HS 300/9-12
3321 Georgia St 63353 573-754-6181
James York, prin. Fax 754-5964
Louisiana MS 200/6-8
3321 Georgia St 63353 573-754-5340
Chuck Tophinke, prin. Fax 754-5377

Ludlow, Livingston, Pop. 198
Southwest Livingston County R-I SD 200/K-12
4944 Highway DD 64656 660-738-4433
John Locker, supt. Fax 738-4441
www.southwestr1.org/
Southwest Livingston County JSHS 100/7-12
4944 Highway DD 64656 660-738-4433
Butch Fore, prin. Fax 738-4441

Macks Creek, Camden, Pop. 284
Macks Creek R-V SD 400/PK-12
245 State Rd N 65786 573-363-5909
Alan Stauffacher, supt. Fax 363-0127
mcreek.k12.mo.us/
Macks Creek JSHS 200/7-12
245 State Rd N 65786 573-363-5911
Donna Herman, prin. Fax 363-5981

Macon, Macon, Pop. 5,428
Macon County R-I SD 1,300/PK-12
702 N Missouri St 63552 660-385-5719
Debbie Livingston, supt. Fax 385-7179
www.macon.k12.mo.us/
Macon Area Vocational Technical S Vo/Tech
702 N Missouri St 63552 660-385-2158
Mickey E. Briscoe, dir. Fax 385-3667
Macon County HS 400/9-12
702 N Missouri St 63552 660-385-5748
Dwight E. Tietsort, prin. Fax 385-2746
Macon County MS 300/6-8
702 N Missouri St 63552 660-385-2189
Dustin Fanning, prin. Fax 385-7230

Madison, Monroe, Pop. 562
Madison C-3 SD 300/PK-12
309 S Thomas St 65263 660-291-5115
Fred Weibling, supt. Fax 291-5006
www.schoolweb.missouri.edu/madisonc3.k12.mo.us/
Madison JSHS 200/7-12
309 S Thomas St 65263 660-291-4515
Warren Salmons, prin. Fax 291-5006

Malden, Dunklin, Pop. 4,635
Malden R-I SD 1,100/K-12
505 Burkhart St 63863 573-276-5794
Kenneth Cook, supt. Fax 276-5796
www.malden.k12.mo.us/
Malden JSHS 500/7-12
505 Burkhart St 63863 573-276-4546
Robert Wilson, prin. Fax 276-4548

Malta Bend, Saline, Pop. 243
Malta Bend R-V SD 100/K-12
PO Box 10 65339 660-595-2371
Ryan Nowlin, supt. Fax 595-2430
Malta Bend JSHS 100/6-12
PO Box 10 65339 660-595-2371
Roger Feagan, prin. Fax 595-2430

Manchester, Saint Louis, Pop. 18,970
Parkway C-2 SD
Supt. — See Chesterfield
Parkway South MS 700/6-8
760 Woods Mill Rd 63011 314-415-7200
Craig Fenner, prin. Fax 415-7213

Kennedy HS 9-12
500 Woods Mill Rd 63011 636-227-5900
Christine Bolesta, prin. Fax 227-0298

Mansfield, Wright, Pop. 1,352
Mansfield R-IV SD 700/PK-12
316 W Ohio St 65704 417-924-8458
Arlene Magnin, supt. Fax 924-3427
www.mansfieldschool.net/
Mansfield HS 200/9-12
315 W Ohio St 65704 417-924-3236
Randy Short, prin. Fax 924-8789
Mansfield JHS 100/7-8
316 W Ohio St 65704 417-924-8625
Randy Short, prin. Fax 924-8789

Maplewood, Saint Louis, Pop. 8,808
Maplewood-Richmond Heights SD 600/PK-12
7539 Manchester Rd 63143 314-644-4400
Dr. Linda Henke, supt. Fax 781-3160
Maplewood Richmond Heights HS 300/9-12
7539 Manchester Rd 63143 314-644-4401
S. Patrick McEvoy, prin. Fax 644-3681
Other Schools – See Saint Louis

Marble Hill, Bollinger, Pop. 1,512
Woodland R-IV SD 900/K-12
RR 3 Box 3210 63764 573-238-3343
Dennis Parham, supt. Fax 238-2153
www.woodland.k12.mo.us/
Woodland JSHS 400/7-12
RR 3 Box 3210 63764 573-238-2663
Jennings Wilkinson, prin. Fax 238-0186

New Salem Baptist Academy 100/PK-12
HC 64 Box 4220 63764 573-238-2643
Rodney DaVault, admin. Fax 238-1107

Marceline, Linn, Pop. 2,405
Marceline R-V SD 700/K-12
400 E Santa Fe Ave 64658 660-376-3371
Ed Schoenfelt, supt. Fax 376-6001
www.marceline.k12.mo.us
Marceline HS 200/9-12
314 E Santa Fe Ave 64658 660-376-2411
Gabe Edgar, prin. Fax 376-6016
Marceline MS 200/6-8
314 E Santa Fe Ave 64658 660-376-2411
Gabe Edgar, prin. Fax 376-6016

Marionville, Lawrence, Pop. 2,161
Marionville R-IX SD 800/K-12
PO Box 409 65705 417-258-7755
Larry Brown, supt. Fax 258-2564
www.marionville.us/
Marionville JSHS 300/7-12
PO Box 409 65705 417-258-2521
Mark Marler, prin. Fax 258-5625

Marquand, Madison, Pop. 266
Marquand-Zion R-VI SD 200/K-12
PO Box A 63655 573-783-3388
Duane Schindler, supt. Fax 783-3067
Marquand-Zion JSHS 100/7-12
PO Box A 63655 573-783-3388
Pamela Moyers, prin. Fax 783-3067

Marshall, Saline, Pop. 12,403
Marshall SD 2,500/K-12
860 W Vest St 65340 660-886-7414
Dr. Robert Gordon, supt. Fax 886-5641
www.marshallschools.com/
Bueker MS 800/5-8
565 S Odell Ave 65340 660-886-6833
Lance Tobin, prin. Fax 886-7529
Marshall HS 900/9-12
805 S Miami Ave 65340 660-886-2244
Carol Smith, prin. Fax 886-2669
Saline County Career Ctr Vo/Tech
900 W Vest St 65340 660-886-6958
Dr. Greg Nolting, dir. Fax 886-3092

Missouri Valley College Post-Sec.
500 E College St 65340 660-831-4000

Marshfield, Webster, Pop. 6,763
Marshfield R-I SD 2,900/PK-12
170 State Highway DD 65706 417-859-2120
Michael Wutke, supt. Fax 859-2193
www.mr1.k12.mo.us/
Marshfield HS 900/9-12
370 State Highway DD 65706 417-859-2120
Jan Hibbs, prin. Fax 859-7756
Marshfield JHS 700/6-8
660 N Locust St 65706 417-859-2120
Alan Thomas, prin. Fax 859-4970

Maryland Heights, Saint Louis, Pop. 26,544
Pattonville R-III SD
Supt. — See Saint Ann
Pattonville HS 1,900/9-12
2497 Creve Coeur Mill Rd 63043 314-213-8051
Jeff Marion, prin. Fax 213-8651
Pattonville Hts MS 600/6-8
195 Fee Fee Rd 63043 314-213-8033
Scot Mosher, prin. Fax 213-8633

Allied College - North Post-Sec.
13723 Riverport Dr Ste 103 63043 866-501-1291

Maryville, Nodaway, Pop. 10,567
Maryville R-II SD 1,300/PK-12
1429 S Munn Ave 64468 660-562-3255
Vickie Miller, supt. Fax 562-4113
www.maryville.k12.mo.us/
Maryville HS 500/9-12
1503 S Munn Ave 64468 660-562-3511
Ronald Landherr, prin. Fax 562-4822
Maryville MS 400/5-8
525 W South Hills Dr 64468 660-562-3244
Kevin Pitts, prin. Fax 562-4130
Northwest Technical S Vo/Tech
1515 S Munn Ave 64468 660-562-3022
Mike Jordan, dir. Fax 562-2010

Northwest Missouri State University Post-Sec.
800 University Dr 64468 660-562-1212

Maysville, DeKalb, Pop. 1,165
Maysville R-I SD 700/K-12
PO Box 68 64469 816-449-2308
Ronald McElwain, supt. Fax 449-5678
maysville.k12.mo.us/
Maysville JSHS 300/7-12
PO Box 68 64469 816-449-2154
Paul Niece, prin. Fax 449-5610

Meadville, Linn, Pop. 443
Meadville R-IV SD 300/PK-12
PO Box 217 64659 660-938-4111
Kenneth Dudley, supt. Fax 938-4100
Meadville JSHS 100/7-12
PO Box 217 64659 660-938-4112
Ron Holcer, prin. Fax 938-4100

Memphis, Scotland, Pop. 2,003
Scotland County R-I SD 700/PK-12
RR 3 Box 19A 63555 660-465-8531
David Shalley, supt. Fax 465-8636
scotland.k12.mo.us/
Scotland County JSHS 300/7-12
RR 3 Box 19A 63555 660-465-8901
Kenneth Cross, prin. Fax 465-7715

Mendon, Chariton, Pop. 201
Northwestern R-I SD 200/PK-12
PO Box 43 64660 660-272-3201
William Jones, supt. Fax 272-3419
Northwestern HS 100/9-12
PO Box 43 64660 660-272-3201
Ron Garber, prin. Fax 272-3738
Northwestern MS 100/5-8
PO Box 43 64660 660-272-3201
Ron Garber, prin. Fax 272-3738

Mercer, Mercer, Pop. 330
North Mercer County R-III SD 200/PK-12
PO Box 648 64661 660-382-4214
Dan Owens, supt. Fax 382-4236
www.northmercer.k12.mo.us
Mercer JSHS 100/7-12
PO Box 648 64661 660-382-4214
Stacy Snyder, prin. Fax 382-4239

Mexico, Audrain, Pop. 11,018
Mexico SD 59 2,400/K-12
920 S Jefferson St 65265 573-581-3773
T. Lloyd Little, supt. Fax 581-4410
www.mexicoschools.net/
Hart Mexico Area Vo Tech S Vo/Tech
905 N Wade St 65265 573-581-5684
Duane Bennett, dir. Fax 581-7084
Mexico HS 800/9-12
639 N Wade St 65265 573-581-4296
Gregory Baber, prin. Fax 581-3788
Mexico JHS 600/6-8
1200 W Boulevard St 65265 573-581-4664
Nancy A. Goedeke, prin. Fax 581-8440

Missouri Military Academy 300/6-12
204 Grand Ave 65265 573-581-1776
Ronald Kelly, hdmstr. Fax 581-0081

Milan, Sullivan, Pop. 1,849
Milan C-2 SD 600/PK-12
373 S Market St 63556 660-265-4414
Bill Lewis, supt. Fax 265-4315
Milan HS 200/9-12
373 S Market St 63556 660-265-4415
Mark Forster, prin. Fax 265-4315
Milan MS 100/5-8
373 S Market St 63556 660-265-4421
Tennille Banner, prin. Fax 265-4315

Miller, Lawrence, Pop. 792
Miller R-II SD 600/K-12
110 W 6th St 65707 417-452-3515
Dr. Anthony Rossetti, supt. Fax 452-2709
Miller JSHS 300/7-12
110 W 6th St 65707 417-452-3271
David Geurin, prin. Fax 452-3936

Moberly, Randolph, Pop. 13,921
Moberly SD 2,300/PK-12
926 Kwix Rd 65270 660-269-2600
Robert Bach, supt. Fax 269-2611
moberly.k12.mo.us/
Moberly Area Technical Center Vo/Tech
1625 Gratz Brown St 65270 660-269-2690
Mike Barner, dir. Fax 269-2692
Moberly HS 700/9-12
1625 Gratz Brown St 65270 660-269-2660
Gena McCluskey, prin. Fax 263-5977
Moberly MS 500/6-8
920 Kwix Rd 65270 660-269-2680
Aaron Vitt, prin. Fax 269-8519

Central Christian College of the Bible Post-Sec.
911 E Urbandale Dr 65270 888-263-3900
Maranatha SDA S 50/5-8
1400 E McKinsey St 65270 660-263-8600
Moberly Area Community College Post-Sec.
101 College Ave 65270 660-263-4110

Mokane, Callaway, Pop. 196
South Callaway County R-II SD 1,000/PK-12
10135 State Road C 65059 573-676-5225
Dr. Nick Boren, supt. Fax 676-5134
www.sc.k12.mo.us/
South Callaway HS 300/9-12
10135 State Road C 65059 573-676-5211
Troy Clawson, prin. Fax 676-5132
South Callaway MS 300/5-8
10135 State Road C 65059 573-676-5216
Michael R. Auer, prin. Fax 676-5347

Monett, Barry, Pop. 8,349
Monett R-I SD 2,000/PK-12
800 E Scott St 65708 417-235-7422
Dr. Charles Cudney, supt. Fax 235-1415
hs1.monett.k12.mo.us/
Monett HS 600/9-12
1 David Sippy Dr 65708 417-235-5445
David Steward, prin. Fax 235-7884
Monett MS 300/7-8
700 9th St 65708 417-235-6228
John Jungmann, prin. Fax 235-3278
Southwest Area Career Center Vo/Tech
711 9th St 65708 417-235-7022
Ted Dorton, dir. Fax 235-8270

Monroe City, Monroe, Pop. 2,556
Monroe City R-I SD 800/PK-12
401 US Highway 24/36 E 63456 573-735-4631
Dr. Kirk Eidson, supt. Fax 735-2413
www.monroe.k12.mo.us/
Monroe City MS 200/5-8
430 N Washington St 63456 573-735-4742
Fred Cochrane, prin. Fax 735-2413
Monroe City R-I HS 300/9-12
401 US Highway 24/36 E 63456 573-735-4626
James Redmon, prin. Fax 735-2413

Montgomery City, Montgomery, Pop. 2,513
Montgomery County R-II SD 1,400/PK-12
418 N Highway 19 63361 573-564-2278
Donald Francis, supt. Fax 564-6182
www.mc-wildcats.org/
Montgomery County MS 300/6-8
418 N Highway 19 63361 573-564-2253
Lyndel Whittle, prin. Fax 564-6182
Montomery County HS 500/9-12
394 N Highway 19 63361 573-564-2213
Lisa Bethel, prin. Fax 564-3516

Montrose, Henry, Pop. 431
Montrose R-XIV SD 100/K-12
307 E 2nd St 64770 660-693-4812
Kevin Gwaltney, supt. Fax 693-4594
Montrose HS 50/9-12
307 E 2nd St 64770 660-693-4812
Kevin Gwaltney, prin. Fax 693-4594

Morrisville, Polk, Pop. 362
Marion C. Early R-V SD 700/K-12
PO Box 96 65710 417-376-2255
Dr. Ron McIntire, supt. Fax 376-3243
mcearly.k12.mo.us
Early JSHS 400/6-12
PO Box 96 65710 417-376-2216
Mark Summers, prin. Fax 376-3243

Mound City, Holt, Pop. 1,110
Mound City R-II SD 300/PK-12
PO Box 247 64470 660-442-3737
Ken Eaton, supt. Fax 442-5941
Mound City HS 100/7-12
PO Box 247 64470 660-442-5429
Jason Eggers, prin. Fax 442-5941

Mountain Grove, Wright, Pop. 4,594
Mountain Grove R-III SD 1,400/K-12
PO Box 806 65711 417-926-3177
Bridget Williams, supt. Fax 926-3177
www.mgr3.k12.mo.us
Mountain Grove HS 500/9-12
PO Box 806 65711 417-926-3177
Marcie Stumpff, prin. Fax 926-1702
Mountain Grove MS 400/5-8
PO Box 806 65711 417-926-3177
J.T. Hale, prin. Fax 926-1673
Ozark Mountain Technical Center Vo/Tech
PO Box 806 65711 417-926-3177
Earl Crofford, dir. Fax 926-6858

Mountain View, Howell, Pop. 2,546
Mountain View-Birch Tree R-III SD 1,400/PK-12
PO Box 464 65548 417-934-2020
Jerry Nicholson, supt. Fax 934-5404
mvbt.k12.mo.us/
Liberty HS 400/9-12
PO Box 464 65548 417-934-2020
Steven Richards, prin. Fax 934-5404
Liberty MS 300/7-8
PO Box 464 65548 417-934-2020
Walt Belcher, prin. Fax 934-5404

Mount Vernon, Lawrence, Pop. 4,402
Mt. Vernon R-V SD 1,600/K-12
731 S Landrum St 65712 417-466-7573
Dan Breeden, supt. Fax 466-7058
Mount Vernon HS 500/9-12
400 W Highway 174 65712 417-466-7526
Russ Cruzan, prin. Fax 466-4307
Mount Vernon MS 500/5-8
731 S Landrum St 65712 417-466-3137
Robert Senninger, prin. Fax 466-7058

Myrtle, Oregon
Couch R-I SD 300/PK-12
RR 1 Box 1187 65778 417-938-4211
Tom Bull, supt. Fax 938-4267
Couch JSHS 200/7-12
RR 1 Box 1187 65778 417-938-4212
Randall Eagleman, prin. Fax 938-4267

Naylor, Ripley, Pop. 614
Naylor R-II SD 400/K-12
RR 2 Box 512 63953 573-399-2505
Stephen Cookson, supt. Fax 399-2874
schoolweb.missouri.edu/naylor.k12.mo.us/
Naylor JSHS 200/7-12
RR 2 Box 512 63953 573-399-2506
Terry Arnold, prin. Fax 399-2388

Neelyville, Butler, Pop. 503
Neelyville R-IV SD 700/PK-12
PO Box 8 63954 573-989-3813
Larry Graves, supt. Fax 989-3434
neelyville.k12.mo.us/
Neelyville JSHS 300/7-12
PO Box 8 63954 573-989-3815
Brad Hagood, prin. Fax 989-6322

Neosho, Newton, Pop. 11,130
Neosho R-V SD 4,400/PK-12
511 S Neosho Blvd 64850 417-451-8600
Dr. Richard Page, supt. Fax 451-8604
www.neosho.k12.mo.us
Neosho HS 1,200/9-12
511 S Neosho Blvd 64850 417-451-8670
Charles Blaney, prin. Fax 451-8605
Neosho JHS 300/8-8
511 S Neosho Blvd 64850 417-451-8660
Jennifer Cryer, prin. Fax 451-8687

Crowder College Post-Sec.
601 Laclede Ave 64850 417-451-3223
Neosho Beauty College Post-Sec.
116 N Wood St 64850 417-451-7216
Ozark Christian Academy 100/K-12
PO Box 786 64850 417-451-1100
Joyce Prihoda, prin. Fax 451-9902

Nevada, Vernon, Pop. 8,457
Nevada R-V SD 2,600/PK-12
800 W Hickory St 64772 417-448-2000
Craig Noah, supt. Fax 448-2006
www.nevada.k12.mo.us
Nevada HS 800/9-12
800 W Hickory St 64772 417-448-2020
Bryan Thomsen, prin. Fax 448-2039
Nevada MS 600/6-8
900 N Olive St 64772 417-448-2040
Steve Beckett, prin. Fax 448-2048
Nevada Regional Tech-Center Vo/Tech
900 W Ashland St 64772 417-448-2090
Sean Smith, dir. Fax 448-2092

Calvary Christian S 50/K-12
113 W Arch St 64772 417-667-4200
Betty Morris, prin. Fax 667-2503
Cottey College Post-Sec.
1000 W Austin Blvd 64772 417-667-8181

New Bloomfield, Callaway, Pop. 688
New Bloomfield R-III SD 600/K-12
PO Box 188 65063 573-491-3700
Michael Parnell, supt. Fax 491-3772
www.callaway.k12.mo.us
New Bloomfield JSHS 200/7-12
PO Box 188 65063 573-491-3700
Julie Trammell, prin. Fax 491-3696

Newburg, Phelps, Pop. 479
Newburg R-II SD 500/PK-12
PO Box C 65550 573-762-2211
Jane Reeves, supt. Fax 762-2512
www.newburg.k12.mo.us
Newburg JSHS 200/7-12
PO Box C 65550 573-762-2331
Steve Guffey, prin. Fax 762-2512

New Cambria, Macon, Pop. 223
Macon County R-IV SD 200/K-12
PO Box 70 63558 660-226-5615
Ron Garber, supt. Fax 226-5618
schoolweb.missouri.edu/maconr4.k12.mo.us/
Macon County JSHS 100/7-12
PO Box 70 63558 660-226-5615
Carol Burstert, prin. Fax 226-5618

New Franklin, Howard, Pop. 1,113
New Franklin R-I SD — 400/PK-12
412 W Broadway 65274 — 660-848-2141
Dr. Jeanie Gordon, supt. — Fax 848-2226
www.nfranklin.k12.mo.us/
New Franklin MSHS — 200/6-12
412 W Broadway 65274 — 660-848-2314
David Haggard, prin. — Fax 848-3071

New Haven, Franklin, Pop. 1,950
New Haven SD — 400/K-12
100 Park Dr 63068 — 573-237-3231
Kyle Kruse, supt. — Fax 237-5959
New Haven HS — 200/9-12
100 Park Dr 63068 — 573-237-2629
Timothy Strobel, prin. — Fax 237-5959
New Haven MS — 50/7-8
100 Park Dr 63068 — 573-237-2900
Dennis Carey, prin. — Fax 237-5959

New Madrid, New Madrid, Pop. 3,131
New Madrid County R-I SD — 1,800/PK-12
310 US Highway 61 63869 — 573-688-2161
Bill Nance, supt. — Fax 688-2169
Central HS — 500/9-12
310 US Highway 61 63869 — 573-688-2165
John Garner, prin. — Fax 688-2169
Central MS — 400/6-8
308 US Highway 61 63869 — 573-688-2176
Thomas Drummond, prin. — Fax 688-2245
New Madrid R-I Tech Skills Center — Vo/Tech
310 US Highway 61 63869 — 573-688-2161
Lance Tollison, dir. — Fax 688-2169

Newtown, Sullivan, Pop. 197
Newtown-Harris R-III SD — 100/K-12
PO Box 128 64667 — 660-794-2245
W. Anderson, supt. — Fax 794-2730
www.nhtigers.k12.mo.us/
Newtown-Harris JSHS — 100/7-12
PO Box 128 64667 — 660-794-2245
Misty Foster, prin. — Fax 794-2730

Niangua, Webster, Pop. 484
Niangua R-V SD — 200/PK-12
301 Rumsey St 65713 — 417-473-6101
Andy Adams, supt. — Fax 473-6124
schoolweb.missouri.edu/niangua.k12.mo.us
Niangua JSHS — 100/7-12
301 Rumsey St 65713 — 417-473-6101
Richard Wylie, prin. — Fax 473-6124

Nixa, Christian, Pop. 15,925
Nixa R-II SD — 4,500/PK-12
205 North St 65714 — 417-875-5400
Dr. Stephen Kleinsmith, supt. — Fax 725-7405
www.nixa.k12.mo.us
Nixa HS — 1,200/9-12
514 S Nicholas Rd 65714 — 417-724-3500
Mark Overstreet, prin. — Fax 724-3515
Nixa JHS — 700/7-8
205 North St 65714 — 417-875-5430
Mark McGehee, prin. — Fax 875-5426

Norborne, Carroll, Pop. 792
Norborne R-VIII SD — 200/K-12
PO Box 192 64668 — 660-593-3319
Douglas Carpenter, supt. — Fax 593-3657
www.schoolweb.missouri.edu/norborne.k12.mo.us/index.html
Norborne HS — 100/7-12
PO Box 192 64668 — 660-593-3319
Wade Schroeder, prin. — Fax 593-3657

Normandy, Saint Louis, Pop. 5,032
Normandy SD
Supt. — See Saint Louis
Normandy MS — 900/7-8
7855 Natural Bridge Rd 63121 — 314-493-0500
Todd Williams, prin. — Fax 493-0560

North Kansas City, Clay, Pop. 5,388
North Kansas City SD 74 — 17,200/PK-12
2000 NE 46th St 64116 — 816-413-5000
Dr. Thomas Cummings, supt. — Fax 413-5005
www.nkcsd.k12.mo.us
North Kansas City HS — 1,800/9-12
620 E 23rd Ave 64116 — 816-413-5900
Dr. Dan Wartick, prin. — Fax 413-5905
Other Schools – See Gladstone, Kansas City

Colorado Technical University — Post-Sec.
520 E 19th Ave 64116 — 816-472-7400
North Kansas City Hospital — Post-Sec.
2800 Clay Edwards Dr 64116 — 816-691-2000

Norwood, Wright, Pop. 576
Norwood R-I SD — 500/K-12
675 N Hawk St 65717 — 417-746-4101
Don Forrest, supt. — Fax 746-9950
www.norwood.k12.mo.us/
Norwood HS — 200/9-12
675 N Hawk St 65717 — 417-746-4101
Marcella Swatosh, prin. — Fax 746-9950
Norwood MS — 100/5-8
675 N Hawk St 65717 — 417-746-4101
Fred Vanbibber, prin. — Fax 746-4804

Novinger, Adair, Pop. 524
Adair County R-I SD — 300/PK-12
600 Rombauer Ave 63559 — 660-488-6411
William Lake, supt. — Fax 488-5400
www.novinger.k12.mo.us
Adair County JSHS — 200/7-12
600 Rombauer Ave 63559 — 660-488-6411
Richard Johnson, prin. — Fax 488-5400

Oak Grove, Jackson, Pop. 6,763
Oak Grove R-VI SD — 2,100/PK-12
1305 Salem St 64075 — 816-690-4156
Dr. James Haley, supt. — Fax 690-3031
www.oakgrove.k12.mo.us
Oak Grove HS — 600/9-12
605 SE 12th St 64075 — 816-690-4152
Randall McClain, prin. — Fax 690-5666
Oak Grove MS — 500/6-8
401 SE 12th St 64075 — 816-690-4154
Keith Roskens, prin. — Fax 690-3976

Oak Ridge, Cape Girardeau, Pop. 208
Oak Ridge R-VI SD — 400/K-12
PO Box 10 63769 — 573-266-3218
Dr. Gerald Landewee, supt. — Fax 266-0133
www.showme.net/ork/
Oak Ridge JSHS — 200/7-12
PO Box 10 63769 — 573-266-3630
Allan Horrell, prin. — Fax 266-0133

Odessa, Lafayette, Pop. 4,841
Odessa R-VII SD — 2,300/K-12
701 S 3rd St 64076 — 816-633-5316
Sandra Sloan, supt. — Fax 633-8582
www.odessa.k12.mo.us/
Odessa HS — 700/9-12
713 S 3rd St 64076 — 816-633-5533
Brenda VanGilder, prin. — Fax 633-7506
Odessa MS — 700/5-8
607 S 5th St 64076 — 816-633-1500
Sherry Billings, prin. — Fax 633-7101

O Fallon, Saint Charles, Pop. 59,678
Ft. Zumwalt R-II SD — 18,500/K-12
110 Virgil St 63366 — 636-272-6620
Dr. Bernard DuBray, supt. — Fax 980-1946
www.fzschools.org
Ft. Zumwalt North HS — 1,300/9-12
1230 Tom Ginnever Ave 63366 — 636-272-4447
Joe Sutton, prin. — Fax 272-6124
Ft. Zumwalt North MS — 1,200/6-8
210 Virgil St 63366 — 636-281-2356
Tim Jamieson, prin. — Fax 281-0005
Ft. Zumwalt West HS — 2,400/9-12
1251 Turtle Creek Dr 63366 — 636-281-4030
Neil Berry, prin. — Fax 281-0202
Ft. Zumwalt West MS — 1,200/6-8
150 Waterford Crossing Dr, — 636-272-6690
Lori Jessen, prin. — Fax 272-6361
Other Schools – See Saint Peters

Christian HS — 300/7-12
1145 Tom Ginnever Ave 63366 — 636-978-1680
H. Eric Pipkin, prin. — Fax 978-5024
St. Dominic HS — 700/9-12
31 Saint Dominic Dr 63366 — 636-240-8303
Cathy Fetter, prin. — Fax 240-9884

Oran, Scott, Pop. 1,259
Oran R-III SD — 300/K-12
PO Box 250 63771 — 573-262-2330
Mitchell Wood, supt. — Fax 262-2330
www.oran.k12.mo.us
Oran JSHS — 200/7-12
PO Box 250 63771 — 573-262-3345
Travis Spane, prin. — Fax 262-2289

Oregon, Holt, Pop. 901
South Holt County R-I SD — 300/K-12
201 S Barbour St 64473 — 660-446-2282
Bob Ottman, supt. — Fax 446-2312
www.southholtr1.com
South Holt County JSHS — 200/7-12
201 S Barbour St 64473 — 660-446-3454
Mike Leach, prin. — Fax 446-2312

Orrick, Ray, Pop. 867
Orrick R-XI SD — 500/PK-12
100 Kirkham St 64077 — 816-770-0094
Marcus Stucker, supt. — Fax 496-2306
www.orrick.k12.mo.us
Orrick JSHS — 200/7-12
100 Kirkham St 64077 — 816-770-3327
Rick Wrisinger, prin. — Fax 496-3829

Osage Beach, Camden, Pop. 4,259
School of the Osage R-II SD
Supt. — See Lake Ozark
Osage HS — 500/9-12
636 Highway 42 65065 — 573-348-0115
Tony Hermann, prin. — Fax 348-9774

Osborn, DeKalb, Pop. 448
Osborn R-0 SD — 100/K-12
275 Clinton Ave 64474 — 816-675-2217
Gaylon Whitmer, supt. — Fax 675-2222
schoolweb.missouri.edu/osborn.k12.mo.us/
Osborn JSHS — 100/7-12
275 Clinton Ave 64474 — 816-675-2217
Mike Trosper, prin. — Fax 675-2222

Osceola, Saint Clair, Pop. 818
Osceola SD — 600/PK-12
76 SE Highway WW 64776 — 417-646-8143
Aron Bennett, supt. — Fax 646-8075
www.osceola.k12.mo.us
Osceola JSHS — 300/7-12
76 SE Highway WW 64776 — 417-646-8144
Herb Collins, prin. — Fax 646-8549

Otterville, Cooper, Pop. 486
Otterville R-VI SD — 300/K-12
PO Box 177 65348 — 660-366-4391
Rhonda Meyer, supt. — Fax 366-4293
Otterville JSHS — 100/7-12
PO Box 177 65348 — 660-366-4621
Jean Carton, prin. — Fax 366-4293

Overland, Saint Louis, Pop. 16,082
Ritenour SD
Supt. — See Saint Louis
Ritenour HS — 1,800/9-12
9100 Saint Charles Rock Rd 63114 — 314-493-6105
Rhonda Haniford, prin. — Fax 429-6725
Ritenour MS — 700/6-8
2500 Marshall Ave 63114 — 314-493-6250
Suzanne Johnson, prin. — Fax 429-6726

Owensville, Gasconade, Pop. 2,544
Gasconade County R-II SD — 2,000/K-12
PO Box 536 65066 — 573-437-2177
Dr. Sally Knight, supt. — Fax 437-5808
owensville.k12.mo.us
Owensville HS — 600/9-12
PO Box 536 65066 — 573-437-2174
Kurt Keller, prin. — Fax 437-7174
Owensville MS — 500/6-8
PO Box 536 65066 — 573-437-2172
Teresa Ragan, prin. — Fax 437-6704

Ozark, Christian, Pop. 15,265
Ozark R-VI SD — 4,400/K-12
PO Box 166 65721 — 417-582-5900
Dr. Gordon Pace, supt. — Fax 582-5960
www.ozark.k12.mo.us
Ozark HS — 1,200/9-12
PO Box 166 65721 — 417-582-5901
Mark Wheeler, prin. — Fax 582-5944
Ozark JHS — 700/7-8
PO Box 166 65721 — 417-582-4701
Jeff Simpson, prin. — Fax 582-4714

Pacific, Franklin, Pop. 7,098
Meramec Valley R-III SD — 3,500/PK-12
126 N Payne St 63069 — 636-271-1400
Randy George, supt. — Fax 271-1406
www.mvr3.k12.mo.us/
Pacific HS — 1,100/9-12
425 Indian Warpath Dr 63069 — 636-627-1414
Tom Sauvage, prin. — Fax 257-8340
Riverbend MS — 8-8
2085 Highway N 63069 — 636-271-1481
Gary Peck, prin. — Fax 271-8080

Palmyra, Marion, Pop. 3,443
Palmyra R-I SD — 1,100/K-12
PO Box 151 63461 — 573-769-2066
Eric Churchwell, supt. — Fax 769-4218
schoolweb.missouri.edu/palmyra.k12.mo.us
Palmyra HS — 400/9-12
PO Box 151 63461 — 573-769-2067
Kevin Hillman, prin. — Fax 769-4218
Palmyra MS — 300/5-8
PO Box 151 63461 — 573-769-2174
Mary Scholl, prin. — Fax 769-4227

Paris, Monroe, Pop. 1,468
Paris R-II SD — 500/PK-12
740 Cleveland St 65275 — 660-327-4112
Jim Masters, supt. — Fax 327-4290
paris.k12.mo.us/site/
Paris HS — 200/9-12
25686 Business Highway 24 65275 — 660-327-4111
Sally Eales, prin. — Fax 327-6220
Paris JHS — 100/7-8
25678 Business Highway 24 65275 — 660-327-4563
Sally Eales, prin. — Fax 327-4782

Park Hills, Saint Francois, Pop. 8,525
Central R-III SD — 1,900/PK-12
200 High St 63601 — 573-431-2616
Dr. David Stevens, supt. — Fax 431-2107
www.centralr3.org
Central HS — 500/9-12
116 Rebel Dr 63601 — 573-431-1211
Brad Coleman, prin. — Fax 431-0700
Central MS — 500/6-8
801 Columbia St 63601 — 573-431-1322
Mike Harlow, prin. — Fax 431-5393

West St. Francois County R-IV SD
Supt. — See Leadwood
West County HS — 300/9-12
768 Highway M 63601 — 573-562-7521
Eric Moyers, prin. — Fax 562-7510

Parkville, Platte, Pop. 5,116

Park University — Post-Sec.
8700 NW River Park Dr 64152 — 816-741-2000

Patton, Bollinger
Meadow Heights R-II SD — 600/K-12
RR 1 Box 2365 63662 — 573-866-0060
Ron Huff, supt. — Fax 866-3240
Meadow Heights JSHS — 300/7-12
RR 1 Box 2365 63662 — 573-866-2924
Mitchell Nanney, prin. — Fax 866-2219

Pattonsburg, Daviess, Pop. 243
Pattonsburg R-II SD — 200/PK-12
PO Box 200 64670 — 660-367-2111
Wendell Burns, supt. — Fax 367-4205
Pattonsburg JSHS — 100/7-12
PO Box 200 64670 — 660-367-2111
Chris Gannan, prin. — Fax 367-4205

Peculiar, Cass, Pop. 3,832
Raymore-Peculiar R-II SD — 4,800/PK-12
PO Box 366 64078 — 816-892-1300
Jeff Kyle, supt. — Fax 892-1380
www.raypec.k12.mo.us
Raymore-Peculiar Freshman Center — 400/9-9
PO Box 366 64078 — 816-892-1500
Eric Arnold, prin. — Fax 892-1501
Raymore-Peculiar MS — 900/7-8
PO Box 366 64078 — 816-892-1550
David Mitchell, prin. — Fax 892-1551

Raymore-Peculiar SHS 1,100/10-12
PO Box 366 64078 816-892-1400
Sherri Miller, prin. Fax 892-1401

Perryville, Perry, Pop. 7,935
Perry County SD 32 2,200/K-12
326 College St 63775 573-547-7500
Beverly Schonhoff, supt. Fax 547-8572
www.perryville.k12.mo.us
Perry County MS 600/5-8
326 College St 63775 573-547-7500
Velda Haertling, prin. Fax 547-1962
Perryville Area Career Center Vo/Tech
326 College St 63775 573-547-7500
David Toney, dir. Fax 517-0396
Perryville HS 800/9-12
326 College St 63775 573-547-7500
Dr. Steven E. Wolf, prin. Fax 517-0592

St. Vincent JSHS 300/7-12
210 S Waters St 63775 573-547-2560
Lisa Best, prin. Fax 547-4145

Philadelphia, Marion
Marion County R-II SD 200/PK-12
PO Box 100 63463 573-439-5913
Dianna Hoenes, supt. Fax 439-5914
Marion County JSHS 100/7-12
PO Box 100 63463 573-439-5913
Eric Spratt, prin. Fax 439-5914

Piedmont, Wayne, Pop. 1,975
Clearwater R-I SD 1,100/PK-12
RR 4 Box 1004 63957 573-223-7426
Blane Keel, supt. Fax 223-2932
Clearwater HS 400/9-12
RR 4 Box 1004 63957 573-223-4524
Paul D'Amico, prin. Fax 223-3208
Clearwater MS 400/5-8
RR 4 Box 1004 63957 573-223-7724
Samuel Holmes, prin. Fax 223-3117

Pierce City, Lawrence, Pop. 1,442
Pierce City R-VI SD 800/PK-12
300 N Myrtle St 65723 417-476-2555
Russell Moreland, supt. Fax 476-5213
schoolweb.missouri.edu/piercecity.k12.mo.us/
Pierce City HS 300/9-12
300 N Myrtle St 65723 417-476-2515
Shawn Johnson, prin. Fax 476-3516
Pierce City MS 200/6-8
300 N Myrtle St 65723 417-476-2842
Gayla DeGraffenreid, prin. Fax 476-5405

Pilot Grove, Cooper, Pop. 739
Pilot Grove C-4 SD 300/PK-12
107 School St 65276 660-834-6915
Mark Pottorff, supt. Fax 834-6925
www.schoolweb.missouri.edu/pilotgrovec4.k12.mo.us/
Pilot Grove HS 100/9-12
107 School St 65276 660-834-4415
Mike Scott, prin. Fax 834-4401
Pilot Grove MS 100/6-8
107 School St 65276 660-834-4415
Mike Scott, prin. Fax 834-4401

Plato, Texas, Pop. 65
Plato R-V SD 500/PK-12
PO Box A 65552 417-458-3333
V. Leon Slape, supt. Fax 458-4706
www.plato.k12.mo.us/
Plato JSHS 300/6-12
PO Box A 65552 417-458-4980
Charles Crain, prin. Fax 458-4706

Platte City, Platte, Pop. 4,907
Platte County R-III SD 2,600/PK-12
PO Box 1400 64079 816-858-5420
Dr. Mark Harpst, supt. Fax 858-5593
pcr3pirates.org
Northland Career Center Vo/Tech
PO Box 1400 64079 816-858-5505
Cheryl Hill, dir. Fax 858-3278
Platte City MS 500/6-8
PO Box 1400 64079 816-858-2036
Terry Hart, prin. Fax 858-3748
Platte County HS 700/9-12
PO Box 1400 64079 816-858-2822
Craig Robinson, prin. Fax 858-5140

Plattsburg, Clinton, Pop. 2,442
Clinton County R-III SD 800/K-12
PO Box 287 64477 816-539-2183
W. M. Lord, supt. Fax 539-2412
ccr3.k12.mo.us
Clinton County R-III MS 200/6-8
PO Box 287 64477 816-539-3920
Gene Hay, prin. Fax 539-2412
Plattsburg HS 300/9-12
PO Box 287 64477 816-539-2184
Kenneth Tongue, prin. Fax 539-3315

Pleasant Hill, Cass, Pop. 6,747
Pleasant Hill R-III SD 2,000/PK-12
318 Cedar St 64080 816-540-3161
Dr. Wesley Townsend, supt. Fax 540-5135
www.pleasanthillschools.com
Pleasant Hill HS 700/9-12
1 Rooster Way 64080 816-540-3111
Tim Ryan, prin. Fax 987-6084
Pleasant Hill MS 300/7-8
1301 E Myrtle St 64080 816-540-2149
Jenny Bell, prin. Fax 987-2017

Pleasant Hope, Polk, Pop. 575
Pleasant Hope R-VI SD 900/K-12
PO Box 387 65725 417-267-2850
Bob Biggs, supt. Fax 267-4373
Pleasant Hope HS 300/9-12
PO Box 387 65725 417-267-2271
Gary Jenkins, prin. Fax 267-5007
Pleasant Hope MS 300/5-8
PO Box 387 65725 417-267-7701
Bill Redinger, prin. Fax 267-9221
Other Schools – See Brighton

Point Lookout, Taney

College of the Ozarks 65726 Post-Sec.
417-334-6411

Polo, Caldwell, Pop. 602
Polo R-VII SD 400/K-12
300 W School St 64671 660-354-2326
Robert Newhart, supt. Fax 354-2910
polo.k12.mo.us/
Polo HS 100/9-12
300 W School St 64671 660-354-2524
Jason Snodgrass, prin. Fax 354-2738
Polo MS 100/5-8
300 W School St 64671 660-354-2200
Beverly Deis, prin. Fax 354-3162

Poplar Bluff, Butler, Pop. 16,912
Poplar Bluff R-I SD 4,800/PK-12
1110 N Westwood Blvd 63901 573-785-7751
Ernie Lawson, supt. Fax 785-0336
www.r1schools.org
Poplar Bluff HS 1,300/9-12
1300 Victory Ln 63901 573-785-6471
Scot Young, prin. Fax 785-6471
Poplar Bluff JHS 800/7-8
550 N Westwood Blvd 63901 573-785-5602
Bob Case, prin. Fax 785-5602
Technical Career Center Vo/Tech
3203 Oak Grove Rd 63901 573-785-2248
Jean Winston, prin. Fax 785-4168

Three Rivers Community College Post-Sec.
2080 Three Rivers Blvd 63901 573-840-9600

Portageville, New Madrid, Pop. 3,071
Portageville SD 800/PK-12
904 King Ave 63873 573-379-3855
Kerwin Urhahn, supt. Fax 379-5817
portageville.k12.mo.us
Portageville HS 200/9-12
904 King Ave 63873 573-379-3819
Jason Aycock, prin. Fax 379-3159
Portageville MS 300/5-8
902 King Ave 63873 573-379-3853
Judy Scherer, prin. Fax 379-3159

Potosi, Washington, Pop. 2,709
Potosi R-III SD 2,500/PK-12
400 N Mine St 63664 573-438-5485
Randy Davis, supt. Fax 438-5487
www.potosi.k12.mo.us
Evans MS 400/7-8
303 S Lead St 63664 573-438-2101
Don Young, prin. Fax 438-4635
Potosi HS 700/9-12
1 Trojan Dr 63664 573-438-2156
Rhonda Phares, prin. Fax 438-2269

Prairie Home, Cooper, Pop. 225
Prairie Home R-V SD 200/K-12
PO Box 105 65068 660-841-5296
Dr. Larry Davis, supt. Fax 841-5513
Prairie Home JSHS 100/7-12
PO Box 105 65068 660-841-5296
Robert Glenn, prin. Fax 841-5513

Princeton, Mercer, Pop. 969
Princeton R-V SD 400/K-12
1008 E Coleman St 64673 660-748-3211
Alan Hamilton, supt. Fax 748-3212
www.tigertown.k12.mo.us/
Princeton JSHS 200/7-12
1008 E Coleman St 64673 660-748-3490
George Scurlock, prin. Fax 748-3212

Purdin, Linn, Pop. 215
Linn County R-I SD 300/PK-12
PO Box 130 64674 660-244-5035
John Brinkley, supt. Fax 244-5025
www.linnr1.k12.mo.us
Linn County JSHS 100/7-12
PO Box 130 64674 660-244-5035
Ryan Livingston, prin. Fax 244-5242

Purdy, Barry, Pop. 1,146
Purdy R-II SD 700/K-12
PO Box 248 65734 417-442-3216
Jerry Lingo, supt. Fax 442-3963
purdy.k12.mo.us/
Purdy HS 200/9-12
PO Box 248 65734 417-442-3215
Robert Vice, prin. Fax 442-3963
Purdy MS 200/6-8
PO Box 248 65734 417-442-7066
Janet McComick, prin. Fax 442-3963

Puxico, Stoddard, Pop. 1,150
Puxico R-VIII SD 900/PK-12
481 N Bedford St 63960 573-222-3762
Jerry Hobbs, supt. Fax 222-3137
www.puxico.k12.mo.us
Mingo/Puxico Technical HS Vo/Tech
481 N Bedford St 63960 573-222-2675
William Pogue, prin. Fax 222-3137
Puxico HS 300/9-12
451 N Hickman St 63960 573-222-3542
Kyle Dare, prin. Fax 222-2441
Puxico JHS 100/6-8
481 N Bedford St 63960 573-222-3542
Stanley Crisel, prin. Fax 222-2441

Queen City, Schuyler, Pop. 646
Schuyler County R-I SD 700/PK-12
PO Box 339 63561 660-766-2204
Marty Albertson, supt. Fax 766-2400
www.schuyler.k12.mo.us
Schuyler County R-I HS 200/9-12
PO Box 100 63561 660-766-2424
Mike Rennells, prin. Fax 766-2646
Schuyler County R-I MS 100/7-8
PO Box 248 63561 660-766-2296
Kirk Cohagan, prin. Fax 766-2400

Ravenwood, Nodaway, Pop. 439
Northeast Nodaway County R-V SD 200/PK-12
PO Box 206 64479 660-937-3112
James Farmer, supt. Fax 937-3110
www.nen.k12.mo.us
Northeast Nodaway HS 100/7-12
PO Box 206 64479 660-937-3125
Sandy Seipel, prin. Fax 937-3110

Raytown, Jackson, Pop. 28,923
Raytown C-2 SD 8,800/PK-12
6608 Raytown Rd 64133 816-268-7000
Dr. Dale Houck, supt. Fax 268-7019
www.raytownschools.org/
Herndon Career Center Vo/Tech
11501 E State Route 350 64138 816-268-7140
Dr. Brian Mann, dir. Fax 268-7149
Raytown HS 1,500/9-12
6019 Blue Ridge Blvd 64133 816-268-7300
Dr. Brian Huff, prin. Fax 268-7315
Raytown South HS 1,400/9-12
8211 Sterling Ave 64138 816-268-7330
Dr. Kevin Overfelt, prin. Fax 268-7345
Raytown South MS 1,000/6-8
8401 E 83rd St 64138 816-268-7380
Randy Thomas, prin. Fax 268-7385
Other Schools – See Kansas City

Cedarvale Junior Academy 50/PK-10
9933 E 56th St 64133 816-353-4828
S. Smith, prin. Fax 737-3111

Reeds Spring, Stone, Pop. 672
Reeds Spring R-IV SD 2,100/PK-12
22595 Main St 65737 417-272-8173
Angie Besendorfer, supt. Fax 272-8656
www.wolves.k12.mo.us
Gibson Technical Center Vo/Tech
386 W State Highway 76 65737 417-272-3271
Don York, prin. Fax 272-1529
Reeds Spring HS 600/9-12
20277 State Highway 413 65737 417-272-8171
Jim Chandler, prin. Fax 272-1481
Reeds Spring MS 400/7-8
21016 Main St 65737 417-272-8245
Mendy Moss, prin. Fax 272-8490

Republic, Greene, Pop. 10,637
Republic R-III SD 3,400/PK-12
518 N Hampton Ave 65738 417-732-3605
Dr. Pam Hedgpeth, supt. Fax 732-3609
www.republic.k12.mo.us/
Republic HS 900/9-12
1 Tiger Dr 65738 417-732-3650
Vickie Neal, prin. Fax 732-3659
Republic MS 500/7-8
518 N Hampton Ave 65738 417-732-3640
Pat Mithelavage, prin. Fax 732-3649

Rich Hill, Bates, Pop. 1,500
Rich Hill R-IV SD 500/K-12
703 N 3rd St 64779 417-395-2418
Garry Pirch, supt. Fax 395-2407
www.richhill.k12.mo.us/
Rich Hill HS 200/7-12
703 N 3rd St 64779 417-395-4191
Terry Mayfield, prin. Fax 395-2407

Richland, Pulaski, Pop. 1,776
Richland R-IV SD 700/PK-12
714 E Jefferson Ave 65556 573-765-3241
Joe Ridgeway, supt. Fax 765-5552
schoolweb.missouri.edu/richlandr4.k12.mo.us/
Richland HS 200/9-12
714 E Jefferson Ave 65556 573-765-3711
Doug Smith, prin. Fax 765-5552
Richland JHS 100/7-8
714 E Jefferson Ave 65556 573-765-3711
Michele Hedges, prin. Fax 765-5552

Richmond, Ray, Pop. 6,075
Richmond R-XVI SD 1,600/PK-12
749 Driskill Dr 64085 816-776-6912
Jim Robins, supt. Fax 776-5554
richmond.k12.mo.us
Richmond HS 500/9-12
451 E South St 64085 816-776-2226
Karen Southwick, prin. Fax 776-8748
Richmond MS 400/6-8
715 S Wellington St 64085 816-776-5841
Damon Kizzire, prin. Fax 776-2788

Ridgeway, Harrison, Pop. 536
Ridgeway R-V SD 100/PK-12
305 Main St 64481 660-872-6813
Troy Gregory, supt. Fax 872-6230
Ridgeway JSHS 100/7-12
305 Main St 64481 660-872-6813
Joe Shelton, prin. Fax 872-6230

Risco, New Madrid, Pop. 364
Risco R-II SD 200/K-12
PO Box 17 63874 573-396-5568
Stan Templeton, supt. Fax 396-5503
www.risco.k12.mo.us/
Risco JSHS 100/7-12
PO Box 17 63874 573-396-5568
Jeanie Johnston, prin. Fax 396-5503

Rock Port, Atchison, Pop. 1,343
Rock Port R-II SD 400/K-12
600 S Nebraska St 64482 660-744-6298
Richard Baldwin, supt. Fax 744-5539
rockport.k12.mo.us
Rock Port JSHS 200/7-12
600 S Nebraska St 64482 660-744-6296
Brian Lee, prin. Fax 744-5539

Rogersville, Greene, Pop. 2,239
Logan-Rogersville R-VIII SD 1,800/PK-12
100 E Front St 65742 417-753-2891
Dr. Richard A. Markley, supt. Fax 753-3063
logrog.net/
Logan-Rogersville HS 600/9-12
4700 S State Highway 125 65742 417-753-2813
Jeremy Tucker, prin. Fax 753-3960
Logan-Rogersville MS 500/6-8
8225 E Farm Road 174 65742 417-753-2896
Richard McPheeters, prin. Fax 753-3182

Rolla, Phelps, Pop. 17,717
Rolla SD 31 4,100/PK-12
500A Forum Dr 65401 573-458-0100
Jerry Giger, supt. Fax 458-0105
rolla.k12.mo.us
Rolla JHS 700/8-9
1360 Soest Rd 65401 573-458-0130
Craig Hounsom, prin. Fax 458-0135
Rolla SHS 1,100/10-12
900 Bulldog Run 65401 573-458-0140
Roger Berkbuegler, prin. Fax 458-0145
Rolla Technical Center Vo/Tech
500 Forum Dr 65401 573-458-0160
Janece Martin, dir. Fax 458-0164
Rolla Technical Institute Vo/Tech
1304 E 10th St 65401 573-458-0150
Floyd Baker, dir. Fax 458-0155

Metro Business College Post-Sec.
1202 E State Route 72 65401 573-364-8464
Salem College of Hairstyling Post-Sec.
1051 Kingshighway St Ste 1 65401 573-368-3136
University of Missouri Post-Sec.
102 Parker 65409 573-341-4164

Rosendale, Andrew, Pop. 184
North Andrew County R-VI SD 400/K-12
9120 Highway 48 64483 816-567-2965
Jim Shultz, supt. Fax 567-2096
schoolweb.missouri.edu/nandrew.k12.mo.us/
North Andrew HS 100/9-12
9120 Highway 48 64483 816-567-2525
Shannon Nolte, prin. Fax 567-2096
North Andrew MS 100/6-8
9120 Highway 48 64483 816-567-2527
Shannon Nolte, prin. Fax 567-2096

Russellville, Cole, Pop. 735
Cole County R-I SD 800/PK-12
PO Box 427 65074 573-782-3534
Richard Morelock, supt. Fax 782-3545
www.cole.k12.mo.us
Cole County R-I MS 200/6-8
PO Box 430 65074 573-782-4915
Matt Abernathy, prin. Fax 782-3775
Russellville HS 200/9-12
PO Box 427 65074 573-782-3973
Zach Templeton, prin. Fax 782-3262

Saint Albans, Franklin

Chesterfield Day S 100/PK-12
PO Box 78 63073 636-458-6688
Marianne Kearney, hdmstr. Fax 458-6660

Saint Ann, Saint Louis, Pop. 13,408
Pattonville R-III SD 5,700/K-12
11097 Saint Charles Rock Rd 63074 314-213-8500
Hugh Kinney, supt. Fax 213-8601
www.psdr3.org
Holman MS 700/6-8
11055 Saint Charles Rock Rd 63074 314-213-8032
Jim Schwab, prin. Fax 213-8632
Other Schools – See Maryland Heights

Ritenour SD
Supt. — See Saint Louis
Hoech MS 800/6-8
3312 Ashby Rd 63074 314-493-6200
Tim Streicher, prin. Fax 426-3837

Patsy & Rob's Academy of Beauty Post-Sec.
18 Northwest Plz 63074 314-298-8808
Vatterott College Post-Sec.
3925 Industrial Dr 63074 800-345-6018

Saint Charles, Saint Charles, Pop. 61,253
Francis Howell R-III SD 18,300/PK-12
4545 Central School Rd 63304 636-851-4000
Dr. Renee Schuster, supt. Fax 851-4093
www.fhsdschools.org
Barnwell MS 900/6-8
1035 Jungs Station Rd 63303 636-851-4100
David Eckhoff, prin. Fax 851-4095
Hollenbeck MS 800/6-8
4555 Central School Rd 63304 636-851-5400
Woody Borgschulte, prin. Fax 851-4132
Howell Central HS 2,200/9-12
5199 Highway N 63304 636-851-4600
Sonny Arnel, prin. Fax 851-4111
Howell HS 1,800/9-12
7001 S Highway 94 63304 636-851-4700
Chris Greiner, prin. Fax 851-4116
Howell North HS 2,100/9-12
2549 Hackmann Rd 63303 636-851-4900
Darlene Jones, prin. Fax 851-4123
Howell Union HS 9-12
1405 Highway D 63304 636-851-5000
Shelley Kelley, prin. Fax 851-4127
Saeger MS 800/6-8
5201 Highway N 63304 636-851-5600
Brian Schick, prin. Fax 851-4138
Other Schools – See Weldon Spring

Orchard Farm R-V SD 1,200/K-12
2165 Highway V 63301 636-250-5000
Dr. Daniel G. Dozier, supt. Fax 250-5444
www.ofsd.k12.mo.us
Orchard Farm HS 400/9-12
2165 Highway V 63301 636-250-5400
Tim McInnis, prin. Fax 250-5425
Orchard Farm MS 300/6-8
2165 Highway V 63301 636-250-5300
Marcia Cummins, prin. Fax 250-5306

St. Charles R-VI SD 5,900/K-12
1025 Country Club Rd 63303 636-443-4000
Dr. Kim Harding, supt. Fax 443-4001
www.stcharles.k12.mo.us
Hardin MS 700/6-8
1950 Elm St 63301 636-443-4300
Michael Ebert, prin. Fax 443-4301
Jefferson MS 700/6-8
2660 Zumbehl Rd 63301 636-443-4400
Gerry Kettenbach, prin. Fax 443-4401
Lewis & Clark Career Center Vo/Tech
2400 Zumbehl Rd 63301 636-443-4950
Kathy Frederking, prin. Fax 443-4951
St. Charles HS 1,000/9-12
725 N Kingshighway St 63301 636-443-4100
Dr. Mark Eggers, prin. Fax 443-4101
St. Charles West HS 1,000/9-12
3601 Droste Rd 63301 636-443-4200
Kim Fitterling, prin. Fax 443-4201

Duchesne HS 700/9-12
2550 Elm St 63301 636-946-6767
Rev. Kenneth Brown, prin. Fax 946-6267
Lewis & Clark Career Center Post-Sec.
2400 Zumbehl Rd 63301 636-443-4950
Lindenwood University Post-Sec.
209 S Kingshighway St 63301 636-949-2000

Saint Clair, Franklin, Pop. 4,420
St. Clair R-XIII SD 2,400/K-12
905 Bardot St 63077 636-629-3500
Michael D. Murphy, supt. Fax 629-4466
stclair.k12.mo.us/
Saint Clair HS 900/9-12
1015 School Dr 63077 636-629-3500
Vicki Enyart, prin. Fax 629-1979
Saint Clair JHS, 925 School Dr 63077 600/6-8
Steven Weinhold, prin. 636-629-3500

Sainte Genevieve, Sainte Genevieve, Pop. 4,666
St. Genevieve County R-II SD 2,100/K-12
375 N 5th St 63670 573-883-4500
Mikel Stewart, supt. Fax 883-5957
www.stegen.k12.mo.us
Sainte Genevieve HS 700/9-12
715 Washington St 63670 573-883-4500
Charles Crouther, prin. Fax 883-5957
Sainte Genevieve MS 500/6-8
211 N 5th St 63670 573-883-4500
John Boyd, prin. Fax 883-5957

Valle Catholic HS 200/9-12
40 N 4th St 63670 573-883-7496
Sara Menard, prin. Fax 883-9142

Saint Elizabeth, Miller, Pop. 300
St. Elizabeth R-IV SD 200/PK-12
PO Box 68 65075 573-493-2246
Sid Doerhoff, supt. Fax 493-2380
www.schoolweb.missouri.edu/st.elizabeth.k12.mo.us
Saint Elizabeth JSHS 100/7-12
PO Box 68 65075 573-493-2246
Leroy Heckemeyer, prin. Fax 493-2380

Saint James, Phelps, Pop. 3,941
St. James R-I SD 1,800/PK-12
122 E Scioto St 65559 573-265-2300
Joy Tucker, supt. Fax 265-6126
St. James HS 700/9-12
101 E Scioto St 65559 573-265-2300
Christopher Jackson, prin. Fax 265-3652
St. James MS 400/6-8
1 Tiger Dr 65559 573-265-2300
Keith McCarthy, prin. Fax 265-6302

Saint Joseph, Buchanan, Pop. 72,663
St. Joseph SD 11,300/PK-12
925 Felix St 64501 816-671-4000
Melody Smith, supt. Fax 671-4470
www.sjsd.k12.mo.us
Benton HS 900/9-12
5655 S 4th St 64504 816-671-4030
Jeffery Modis, prin. Fax 671-4036
Bode MS 500/7-8
720 N Noyes Blvd 64506 816-671-4050
Roberta Dias, prin. Fax 671-4473
Central HS 1,600/9-12
2602 Edmond St 64501 816-671-4080
Marlie Williams, prin. Fax 671-4474
Hillyard Technical Center Vo/Tech
3434 Faraon St 64506 816-671-4170
Regenia Briggs, dir. Fax 671-4479
Lafayette HS 800/9-12
412 E Highland Ave 64505 816-671-4220
Dr. Tyran Sumy, prin. Fax 671-4480
Robidoux MS 400/7-8
4212 Saint Joseph Ave 64505 816-671-4350
Krista Sly, prin. Fax 671-4487
Spring Garden MS 400/7-8
5802 S 22nd St 64503 816-671-4380
Lara Gilpin, prin. Fax 671-4489
Truman MS 500/7-8
3227 Olive St Ste 45 64507 816-671-4400
Beery Johnson, prin. Fax 671-4491

Bishop Le Blond HS 200/9-12
3529 Frederick Ave 64506 816-279-1629
Janet Wilcox, prin. Fax 279-5488
Missouri Western State College Post-Sec.
4525 Downs Dr 64507 816-271-4200
St. Joseph Christian S 300/PK-12
5401B Gene Field Rd 64506 816-279-3760
Lydia Zuidema, supt. Fax 279-3836
Vatterott College Post-Sec.
3131 Frederick Ave 64506 816-364-5399

Saint Louis, Saint Louis, Pop. 332,223
Affton SD 101 2,500/K-12
8701 Mackenzie Rd 63123 314-638-8770
Dr. Don Francis, supt. Fax 631-2548
www.affton.k12.mo.us
Affton HS 800/9-12
8309 Mackenzie Rd 63123 314-638-6330
Jeff Morris, prin. Fax 633-5990
Rogers MS 600/6-8
7550 Mackenzie Rd 63123 314-351-9679
Jeff Remelius, prin. Fax 351-6381

Bayless SD 1,600/PK-12
4530 Weber Rd 63123 314-631-2244
Maureen Clancy-May, supt. Fax 544-6315
csd.org/schools/bayless/baylesshome.html#bsd
Bayless HS 500/9-12
4532 Weber Rd 63123 314-544-6342
Denise Swanger, prin. Fax 544-6315
Bayless JHS 300/7-8
4530 Weber Rd 63123 314-544-6306
Ron Tucker, prin. Fax 544-6315

Ferguson-Florissant R-II SD
Supt. — See Florissant
Ferguson MS 900/7-8
70 January Ave 63135 314-506-9600
Susan Kelly, prin. Fax 506-9601
McCluer South - Berkeley HS 600/9-12
201 Brotherton Ln 63135 314-506-9800
Ellis Shaw, prin. Fax 506-9801

Hancock Place SD 1,900/PK-12
9101 S Broadway 63125 314-544-1300
Dr. Ed Stewart, supt. Fax 631-3752
hancock.k12.mo.us
Hancock HS 500/9-12
229 W Ripa Ave 63125 314-544-1200
Jason Naucke, prin. Fax 544-6427
Hancock Place MS 500/6-8
243 W Ripa Ave 63125 314-544-6423
Scott Wilkerson, prin. Fax 544-6470

Hazelwood SD
Supt. — See Florissant
Hazelwood East HS 1,900/9-12
11300 Dunn Rd 63138 314-953-5600
Mark Martin, prin. Fax 953-5613
Kirby MS 1,100/7-8
1865 Dunn Rd 63138 314-953-5700
Dr. Richard Bass, prin. Fax 953-5713

Ladue SD 3,300/PK-12
9703 Conway Rd 63124 314-994-7080
David Benson, supt. Fax 994-0441
www.ladue.k12.mo.us
Ladue MS 800/6-8
9701 Conway Rd 63124 314-993-3900
Cathy Richter, prin. Fax 997-8736
Watkins HS 1,100/9-12
1201 S Warson Rd 63124 314-993-6447
Joseph Powers, prin. Fax 994-1467

Lindbergh R-VIII SD 5,500/K-12
4900 S Lindbergh Blvd 63126 314-729-2480
Dr. James Sandfort, supt. Fax 729-2482
www.lindbergh.k12.mo.us
Lindbergh HS 1,800/9-12
4900 S Lindbergh Blvd 63126 314-729-2410
Dr. Ron Helms, prin. Fax 729-2412
Sperreng MS 1,300/6-8
12111 Tesson Ferry Rd 63128 314-729-2420
Dr. Jennifer Tiller, prin. Fax 729-2422

Maplewood-Richmond Heights SD
Supt. — See Maplewood
Maplewood Richmond Heights MS 200/7-8
7539 Manchester Rd 63143 314-644-4406
C. Denean Vaughn, prin. Fax 781-4629

Mehlville R-IX SD 11,600/K-12
3120 Lemay Ferry Rd 63125 314-467-5000
Terry Noble, supt. Fax 467-5099
www.mehlvilleschooldistrict.com/
Bernard MS 800/6-8
1054 Forder Rd 63129 314-467-6600
Michele Condon, prin. Fax 467-6699
Buerkle MS 700/6-8
623 Buckley Rd 63125 314-467-6800
Scott Hayes, prin. Fax 467-6899
Mehlville HS 2,000/9-12
3200 Lemay Ferry Rd 63125 314-467-6000
Vincent Viviano, prin. Fax 467-6099
Oakville HS 2,100/9-12
5557 Milburn Rd 63129 314-467-7000
William Scheffler, prin. Fax 467-7099
Oakville MS 700/6-8
5950 Telegraph Rd 63129 314-467-7400
Mike Salsman, prin. Fax 467-7499
Washington MS 600/6-8
5165 Ambs Rd 63128 314-467-7600
Robert Linderer, prin. Fax 467-7699

Normandy SD 5,400/PK-12
3855 Lucas and Hunt Rd 63121 314-493-0400
Connie Calloway, supt. Fax 493-0475
www.normandy.k12.mo.us
Normandy HS 1,300/9-12
6701 Saint Charles Rock Rd 63133 314-493-0600
Carl Hudson, prin. Fax 493-0668
Other Schools – See Normandy

Ritenour SD 6,100/K-12
2420 Woodson Rd 63114 314-493-6010
Paul Doerrer, supt. Fax 426-7144
www.ritenour.k12.mo.us
Other Schools – See Overland, Saint Ann

Riverview Gardens SD 7,500/K-12
1370 Northumberland Dr 63137 314-869-2505
Dr. Henry P. Williams, supt. Fax 869-6354
www.rgsd.org
Central MS 900/7-8
9800 Patricia Barkalow Dr 63137 314-869-2505
Yolander Pittman, prin. Fax 388-6028
Riverview Gardens HS 2,000/9-12
1218 Shepley Dr 63137 314-869-4700
Marshall Peeples, prin. Fax 388-6020
Westview MS 7-8
1950 Nemnich Rd 63136 314-867-0410
Christopher Petty, prin. Fax 388-6055

Special SD of St. Louis County 600/10-12
12110 Clayton Rd 63131 314-989-8100
Dr. Peter Kachris, supt. Fax 989-8440
ssd.k12.mo.us
South County Technical HS Vo/Tech
12721 W Watson Rd 63127 314-989-7400
Dave Baker, prin. Fax 989-7503
Other Schools – See Florissant

St. Louis City SD 31,200/PK-12
801 N 11th St 63101 314-231-3720
Dr. Diana Bourisaw, supt. Fax 345-2661
www.slps.org/
Beaumont HS 1,200/9-12
3836 Natural Bridge Ave 63107 314-533-2410
Travis Brown, prin. Fax 535-0786
Blewett MS 400/6-8
1927 Cass Ave 63106 314-231-7738
Annie Chambers, prin. Fax 231-0073
Blow Preparatory JHS 200/7-9
516 Loughborough Ave 63111 314-353-1349
Gregory Cosby, prin. Fax 353-9048
Bunche International Studies MS 400/6-8
3125 S Kingshighway Blvd 63139 314-772-1779
Carol Howard, prin. Fax 772-1715
Busch/Academic-Athletic Academy 300/6-8
5910 Clifton Ave 63109 314-352-1043
Calvin Starks, prin. Fax 352-3685
Carnahan HS 200/8-9
4041 S Broadway 63118 314-457-0582
Dr. Alice Roach, prin. Fax 457-9741
Carr Lane Visual & Performing Art MS 600/6-8
1004 N Jefferson Ave 63106 314-231-0413
Melba Davis, prin. Fax 241-1213
Central Visual and Performing Arts HS 500/9-12
3125 S Kingshighway Blvd 63139 314-771-2772
Dr. Stanley Engram, prin. Fax 771-0135
Cleveland NJROTC Academy 800/9-12
1212 N 22nd St 63106 314-231-1443
Sherman Curtis, prin. Fax 231-4895
Community Access Job Training Vo/Tech
4915 Donovan Ave 63109 314-481-4095
Dr. Roland Werner, prin. Fax 481-4220
Compton-Drew ILC MS 500/6-8
5130 Oakland Ave 63110 314-652-9282
Andrea Walker, prin. Fax 652-9371
Fanning MS Community Education Center 300/6-8
3417 Grace Ave 63116 314-772-1038
Verona Bowers, prin. Fax 772-0437
Gateway HS 1,300/9-12
5101 McRee Ave 63110 314-776-3300
Kathryn Piller, prin. Fax 776-8267
Gateway Preparatory JHS 400/7-9
1200 N Jefferson Ave 63106 314-241-2295
Vickie Rogers, prin. Fax 241-7698
Humboldt MS 400/6-8
2516 S 9th St 63104 314-772-5566
Georgia L. Calhoun, prin. Fax 772-3180
Lafayette 9th Grade Center 9-9
815 Ann Ave 63104 314-762-0252
Sylvia Shead, prin. Fax 771-1688
Langston MS 500/6-8
5511 Wabada Ave 63112 314-383-2908
Carol Barnes, prin. Fax 385-4632
Long MS Community Education Center 500/6-8
5028 Morganford Rd 63116 314-481-3440
Alva Blue, prin. Fax 481-7329
L'Ouverture MS 300/6-8
3021 Hickory St 63104 314-664-3579
Juanita Jones, prin. Fax 664-7955
McKinley Classical Jr. Academy 400/6-8
2156 Russell Blvd 63104 314-773-0027
Brenda Smith, prin. Fax 771-9749
Metro HS 300/9-12
4015 McPherson Ave 63108 314-534-3894
Wilfred D. Moore, prin. Fax 531-4894
Miller Career Academy Vo/Tech
1000 N Grand Blvd 63106 314-371-0394
Stephen Warmack, prin. Fax 371-1311
Northwest MS 400/7-8
5140 Riverview Blvd 63120 314-385-4774
Valerie Carter, prin. Fax 385-3651
Roosevelt HS 1,400/9-12
3230 Hartford St 63118 314-776-6040
Shepard Pittman, prin. Fax 776-0152
Soldan International Studies HS 800/9-12
918 Union Blvd 63108 314-367-9222
Thomas Cason, prin. Fax 367-1898
Stevens MS Community Education Center 300/6-8
1033 Whittier St 63113 314-533-8550
Larry Schleicher, prin. Fax 533-0306
Stowe Preparatory JHS 300/7-9
5750 Lotus Ave 63112 314-382-7310
Vernice Hicks, prin. Fax 382-4277
Sumner Magnet HS 1,100/9-12
4248 Cottage Ave 63113 314-371-1048
Randolph Spencer, prin. Fax 531-9852
Transportation & Law Academy 9-9
5140 Riverview Blvd 63120 314-385-4774
Valerie Carter-Thomas, prin. Fax 385-3651
Turner 9th Grade Center 9-9
2615 Billups Ave 63113 314-535-8482
Kacy Seals, prin. Fax 535-0196
Vashon HS 1,400/9-12
3035 Cass Ave 63106 314-533-9487
Barbara Sharp, prin. Fax 533-7540
Webster MS 300/7-8
2127 N 11th St 63106 314-231-9196
Rose Mary Johnson, prin. Fax 231-3927
Williams 9th Grade Academy 9-9
3955 Saint Ferdinand Ave 63113 314-533-0201
Amy Phillips, prin. Fax 531-1789
Yeatman-Liddell Preparatory JHS 300/7-9
4265 Athlone Ave 63115 314-261-8132
Valerie Taylor, prin. Fax 389-4613
Washington Education Center Adult
2030 S Vandeventer Ave 63110 314-771-4041
Annette Hayes, prin. Fax 771-4053

University City SD 3,600/PK-12
8136 Groby Rd 63130 314-290-4000
Dr. James Victory, supt. Fax 725-7692
www.ucityschools.org
Other Schools – See University City

Webster Groves SD
Supt. — See Webster Groves
Hixson MS 700/7-8
630 S Elm Ave 63119 314-963-6450
Dr. Mary Stefanus, prin. Fax 918-4624

Wellston SD 600/PK-12
6574 Saint Louis Ave 63121 314-290-7900
Dr. Charles Brown, supt. Fax 290-7905
www.wellston.k12.mo.us
Bishop MS 200/5-8
6310 Wellsmar Ave 63133 314-290-7600
Robert Hudson, prin. Fax 290-7605
Eskridge HS 100/9-12
1200 Sutter Ave 63133 314-290-7800
Lonnie Cole, prin. Fax 290-7810

Aquinas Institute of Theology Post-Sec.
23 S Spring Ave 63108 314-256-8800
Bais Yaakov HS of St. Louis 50/9-12
700 N and South Rd 63130 314-863-9230
Dr. William H. Solomon, prin. Fax 863-3856
Barnes-Jewish College of Nursing Post-Sec.
306 S Kingshighway Blvd 63110 314-454-7055
Bishop DuBourg HS 700/9-12
5850 Eichelberger St 63109 314-832-3030
Bridget Timoney, prin. Fax 832-0529
Block Yeshiva HS 100/9-12
1146 N Warson Rd 63132 314-872-8701
Rabbi Gabriel Munk, prin. Fax 872-8703
Burroughs S 500/7-12
755 S Price Rd 63124 314-993-4040
Keith Shahan, hdmstr. Fax 993-6458
Cardinal Ritter College Prep HS 300/9-12
701 N Spring Ave 63108 314-446-5500
Carmele Hall, prin. Fax 446-5571
Central Institute for the Deaf Post-Sec.
818 S Euclid Ave 63110 314-652-3200
Chaminade College Preparatory S 1,000/6-12
425 S Lindbergh Blvd 63131 314-993-4400
Rev. Ralph Siefert, pres. Fax 993-4403
Christian Brothers College HS 9-12
1850 De La Salle Dr 63141 314-985-6100
Br. David Poos, prin. Fax 985-6115
Churchill S 100/2-10
1035 Price School Ln 63124 314-997-4343
Sandra Gilligan, dir. Fax 997-2760
Clayton University Post-Sec.
11939 Manchester Rd # 123 63131 636-825-6305
Concordia Seminary Post-Sec.
801 De Mun Ave 63105 314-721-5934
Cor Jesu Academy 500/9-12
10230 Gravois Rd 63123 314-842-1546
Sr. Kathleen Coonan, prin. Fax 842-6061
Covenant Theological Seminary Post-Sec.
12330 Conway Rd 63141 800-264-8064
Crossroads S 200/7-12
500 De Baliviere Ave 63112 314-367-8085
William Handmaker, hdmstr. Fax 367-9711
Deaconess College of Nursing Post-Sec.
6150 Oakland Ave 63139 314-768-3044
De LaSalle MS 6-8
4145 Kennerly Ave 63113 314-531-9820
Robert Sweeny, prin. Fax 531-4820
De Smet Jesuit HS 1,200/9-12
233 N New Ballas Rd 63141 314-567-3500
Dr. Gregory Densberger, prin. Fax 567-1519
DeVry University Post-Sec.
1801 Park 270 Dr Ste 260 63146 314-542-4222
DVA Medical Center Post-Sec.
1 Jefferson Barracks Rd 63125 314-894-6631
Elaine Steven Beauty College Post-Sec.
10420 W Florissant Ave 63136 314-868-8196
Fontbonne University Post-Sec.
6800 Wydown Blvd 63105 314-889-1419
Harris-Stowe State University Post-Sec.
3026 Laclede Ave 63103 314-340-3300
Hickey College Post-Sec.
940 Westport Plz 63146 314-434-2212
IHM Health Studies Center Post-Sec.
2500 Abbott Pl 63143 314-768-1234
IHM Health Studies Center Post-Sec.
3663 Lindell Blvd 63108 314-768-1000
Incarnate Word Academy 500/9-12
2788 Normandy Dr 63121 314-725-5850
Dr. Randy Mikolas, prin. Fax 725-2308
Jefferson S 100/7-12
4100 S Lindbergh Blvd 63127 314-843-4151
William Rowe, hdmstr. Fax 843-3527
Kenrick School of Theology Post-Sec.
5200 Glennon Dr 63119 314-792-6100
Life Christian S 200/PK-12
13001 Gravois Rd 63127 314-842-1781
Amy Goodberlet, prin. Fax 843-2731
Logos S 100/7-12
9137 Old Bonhomme Rd 63132 314-997-7002
Kathy Boyd, prin. Fax 997-6848
Loyola Academy 100/6-8
3854 Washington Blvd 63108 314-531-9091
Kevin Lee, prin. Fax 531-3603
Lutheran HS North 400/9-12
5401 Lucas and Hunt Rd 63121 314-389-3100
Tim Hipenbecker, prin. Fax 389-3103
Lutheran HS South 500/9-12
9515 Tesson Ferry Rd 63123 314-631-1400
Paul Crisler, prin. Fax 631-7762
Lutheran School of Nursing Post-Sec.
3547 S Jefferson Ave 63118 314-577-5850
Marian MS 50/5-8
4130 Wyoming St 63116 314-771-7674
Sr. Rosalie Wisniewski, prin. Fax 351-5496
Mary Institute/St. Louis Country Day S 1,200/PK-12
101 N Warson Rd 63124 314-993-5100
Lisa Lyle, hdmstr. Fax 995-7470
Maryville University of St. Louis Post-Sec.
650 Maryville University Dr 63141 314-529-9300
Midwest Institute for Medical Assistants Post-Sec.
10910 Manchester Rd 63122 314-965-8363
Missouri Baptist University Post-Sec.
1 College Park Dr 63141 314-434-1115
Missouri College Post-Sec.
10121 Manchester Rd 63122 314-821-7700
Missouri School for the Blind Post-Sec.
3815 Magnolia Ave 63110 314-776-4320
Missouri Tech Post-Sec.
1167 Corporate Lake Dr 63132 314-569-3600
National Academy of Beauty Arts Post-Sec.
157 Concord Plz 63128 314-842-3616
Nerinx Hall HS 600/9-12
530 E Lockwood Ave 63119 314-968-1505
Jane Kosash, prin. Fax 968-0604
Notre Dame HS 500/9-12
320 E Ripa Ave 63125 314-544-1015
Sr. Michelle Emmerich, prin. Fax 544-8003
Parks College of St. Louis University Post-Sec.
221 N Grand Blvd # 119 63103 314-977-2500
Patricia Stevens College Post-Sec.
330 N 4th St Ste 306 63102 314-421-0949
Principia S 600/PK-12
13201 Clayton Rd 63131 314-434-2100
Peter Stevens, hdmstr. Fax 275-3583
Ranken Technical College Post-Sec.
4431 Finney Ave 63113 314-371-0236
Rosati-Kain HS 400/9-12
4389 Lindell Blvd 63108 314-533-8513
Sr. Joan Andert, prin. Fax 533-1618
St. Elizabeth Academy 200/9-12
3401 Arsenal St 63118 314-771-5134
Susan Geldmacher, prin. Fax 771-3528
St. John's Mercy Medical Center Post-Sec.
615 S New Ballas Rd 63141 314-569-6182
St. John the Baptist Prep HS 200/9-12
5021 Adkins Ave 63116 314-351-5604
Dr. John Kosash, prin. Fax 351-3050
St. John Vianney HS 800/9-12
1311 S Kirkwood Rd 63122 314-965-4853
Larry Keller, prin. Fax 965-1950
St. Joseph Academy 600/9-12
2307 S Lindbergh Blvd 63131 314-965-7205
Nancy Repking, prin. Fax 965-9114
St. Louis College of Health Careers Post-Sec.
909 S Taylor Ave 63110 314-652-0300
St. Louis College of Pharmacy Post-Sec.
4588 Parkview Pl 63110 314-367-8700
St. Louis Community College Post-Sec.
3400 Pershall Rd 63135 314-595-4200
St. Louis Community College Post-Sec.
5600 Oakland Ave 63110 314-644-9100
St. Louis Hair Academy Post-Sec.
3701 Kossuth Ave 63107 314-533-3125
St. Louis Priory S 400/7-12
500 S Mason Rd 63141 314-434-3690
Rev. Michael Brunner, hdmstr. Fax 576-7088
St. Louis University Post-Sec.
221 N Grand Blvd 63103 314-977-2222
St. Louis University HS 1,100/9-12
4970 Oakland Ave 63110 314-531-0330
Dr. Mary Schenkenberg, prin. Fax 531-8446
St. Mary's HS 500/9-12
4701 S Grand Blvd 63111 314-481-8400
Kevin Hacker, prin. Fax 481-3670
Tower Grove Christian S 300/K-12
4257 Magnolia Ave 63110 314-776-6473
Jim Kerr, prin. Fax 776-4867
Trinity Catholic HS 600/9-12
1720 Redman Rd 63138 314-741-1333
Mary Hey, prin. Fax 741-1335
University of Missouri Post-Sec.
1 University Blvd 63121 314-516-5000
Vatterott College Post-Sec.
12970 Maurer Industrial Dr 63127 314-843-4200
Villa Duchesne HS 300/9-12
801 S Spoede Rd 63131 314-432-2021
Dr. Patty Fagin, prin. Fax 432-7713
Villa Duchesne JHS 100/7-8
801 S Spoede Rd 63131 314-810-3552
Dr. Patty Fagin, prin. Fax 432-7713

Visitation Academy 200/7-8
3020 N Ballas Rd 63131 314-625-9123
Mary Ellen Schraeder, prin. Fax 432-7210
Visitation Academy 300/9-12
3020 N Ballas Rd 63131 314-625-9100
Rosalie Henry, hdmstr. Fax 432-7210
Washington University in St. Louis Post-Sec.
1 Brookings Dr 63130 314-935-5000
Webster University Post-Sec.
470 E Lockwood Ave 63119 314-968-6900
Westminster Christian Academy 800/7-12
10900 Ladue Rd 63141 314-997-2900
James Marsh, hdmstr. Fax 997-2903
Whitfield S 500/6-12
175 S Mason Rd 63141 314-434-5141
Ruth Greathouse, prin. Fax 434-6193

Saint Peters, Saint Charles, Pop. 53,397
Ft. Zumwalt R-II SD
Supt. — See O Fallon
DuBray MS 1,000/6-8
100 DuBray Dr 63376 636-279-7979
Mike Anderson, prin. Fax 278-4749
Ft. Zumwalt East HS 9-12
600 1st Executive Ave 63376 636-477-2400
Henry St. Pierre, prin. Fax 477-2495
Ft. Zumwalt South HS 2,100/9-12
8050 Mexico Rd 63376 636-978-1212
Dr. Graham Weir, prin. Fax 980-1745
Ft. Zumwalt South MS 1,200/6-8
300 Knaust Rd 63376 636-281-0776
Paul Myers, prin. Fax 281-0006

Abbott Acad of Cosmetology Arts/Sciences Post-Sec.
2101 Parkway Dr 63376 636-447-0100
Lutheran HS of St. Charles County 400/9-12
5100 Mexico Rd 63376 636-928-5100
Larry Marty, prin. Fax 928-8451
Sanford-Brown College Post-Sec.
100 Richmond Center Blvd 63376 888-793-2433

Salem, Dent, Pop. 4,789
Salem R-80 SD 1,500/K-12
1400 Tiger Pride Dr 65560 573-729-6642
Steve Bryant, supt. Fax 729-8493
www.salem.k12.mo.us/
Salem JHS 400/7-9
1400 Tiger Pride Dr 65560 573-729-4261
Larry Maxwell, prin. Fax 729-2720
Salem SHS 500/10-12
1400 Tiger Pride Dr 65560 573-729-2222
John Smith, prin. Fax 729-7408

Salisbury, Chariton, Pop. 1,635
Salisbury R-IV SD 500/K-12
PO Box 314 65281 660-388-6699
Todd Willhite, supt. Fax 388-6753
Salisbury JSHS 300/7-12
PO Box 314 65281 660-388-6442
Carole Pearson, prin. Fax 388-5651

Sarcoxie, Jasper, Pop. 1,340
Sarcoxie R-II SD 800/K-12
PO Box 310 64862 417-548-3134
Charles Price, supt. Fax 548-6165
Sarcoxie JSHS 400/6-12
PO Box 310 64862 417-548-2153
John Ihm, prin. Fax 548-6165

Savannah, Andrew, Pop. 4,925
Savannah R-III SD 2,400/K-12
PO Box 151 64485 816-324-3144
Donald Lawrence, supt. Fax 324-5594
www.savannah.k12.mo.us
Savannah HS 700/9-12
701 State Rte E 64485 816-324-3128
Steve Kellepouris, prin. Fax 324-6536
Savannah MS 500/6-8
701 W Chestnut St 64485 816-324-3126
Leisa Blair, prin. Fax 324-6397

Scott City, Scott, Pop. 4,584
Scott City R-I SD 1,000/K-12
3000 Main St 63780 573-264-2381
Diann Bradshaw-Ulmer, supt. Fax 264-2206
scschools.k12.mo.us/
Scott City HS 300/9-12
3000 Main St 63780 573-264-2138
Kerry Thompson, prin. Fax 264-2206
Scott City MS 200/6-8
3000 Main St 63780 573-264-2139
Michael Umfleet, prin. Fax 264-2206

Sedalia, Pettis, Pop. 20,430
Sedalia SD 200 4,400/PK-12
2806 Matthew Dr 65301 660-829-6450
Marvin Ebersold, supt. Fax 827-8938
www.sedalia200.com
Sedalia MS 1,000/6-8
2205 S Ingram Ave 65301 660-829-6500
Martin White, prin. Fax 827-6112
Smith-Cotton HS 1,300/9-12
312 E Broadway Blvd 65301 660-829-6300
Todd Whitney, prin. Fax 829-6409

American College of Hair Design Post-Sec.
125 Duke Rd 65301 660-827-3295
Applewood Christian S 100/K-12
25396 Highway O 65301 660-827-4700
Pamela Young, prin.
Sacred Heart HS 100/9-12
416 W 3rd St 65301 660-827-3800
Dr. Mark Register, admin. Fax 827-3806
State Fair Community College Post-Sec.
3201 W 16th St 65301 660-530-5800

Senath, Dunklin, Pop. 1,641
Senath-Hornersville C-8 SD 800/K-12
PO Box 370 63876 573-738-2669
Larry Wood, supt. Fax 738-9845
www.shs.k12.mo.us/
Senath-Hornersville HS 200/9-12
PO Box 370 63876 573-738-2661
Kim Campbell, prin. Fax 738-3481
Other Schools – See Hornersville

Seneca, Newton, Pop. 2,237
Seneca R-VII SD 1,600/K-12
PO Box 469 64865 417-776-3426
Joe Layton, supt. Fax 776-2177
schoolweb.missouri.edu/seneca.k12.mo.us/
Seneca HS 600/9-12
PO Box 469 64865 417-776-3926
Tosha Fax, prin. Fax 776-1878
Wells MS 400/6-8
PO Box 469 64865 417-776-3911
Tracey Welch, prin. Fax 776-2673

Seymour, Webster, Pop. 1,960
Seymour R-II SD 1,000/PK-12
416 E Clinton Ave 65746 417-935-2287
Frank Rowles, supt. Fax 935-4060
schoolweb.missouri.edu/seymour.k12.mo.us/
Seymour HS 300/9-12
625 E Clinton Ave 65746 417-935-4508
Bruce Denney, prin. Fax 935-4539
Seymour MS 200/6-8
501 E Clinton Ave 65746 417-935-4626
Brian Bell, prin. Fax 935-2848

Shelbina, Shelby, Pop. 1,886
Shelby County R-IV SD 800/PK-12
4154 Highway 36 63468 573-588-4961
Timothy Hadfield, supt. Fax 588-2490
www.cardinals.k12.mo.us
South Shelby MSHS 400/6-12
4154 Highway 36 63468 573-588-4163
Brett Thompson, prin. Fax 588-2490

Shelbyville, Shelby, Pop. 686
North Shelby SD 400/PK-12
3071 Highway 15 63469 573-633-2410
Larry Smoot, supt. Fax 633-2138
www.nshelby.k12.mo.us
North Shelby JSHS 200/7-12
3071 Highway 15 63469 573-633-2410
Kimala Gaines, prin. Fax 633-2138

Sheldon, Vernon, Pop. 534
Sheldon R-VIII SD 200/K-12
PO Box 68 64784 417-884-5113
Phyllis Sprenkle, supt. Fax 884-5331
www.sheldon.k12.mo.us
Sheldon JSHS 100/7-12
PO Box 68 64784 417-884-5111
Connie Estes, prin. Fax 884-5331

Sikeston, Scott, Pop. 17,180
Scott County Central SD 400/PK-12
20794 US Highway 61 63801 573-471-2686
Dr. Joel Holland, supt. Fax 471-2686
scottcentral.k12.mo.us
Scott County Central JSHS 200/7-12
20794 US Highway 61 63801 573-471-2001
Lennies McFerren, prin. Fax 471-2004

Sikeston R-6 SD 3,800/K-12
1002 Virginia St 63801 573-472-2581
Stephen Borgsmiller, supt. Fax 472-2584
www.sikeston.k12.mo.us
Sikeston Career & Technology Center Vo/Tech
1002 Virginia St 63801 573-471-5442
Laura Hendley, dir. Fax 472-8861
Sikeston JHS 600/8-9
1002 Virginia St 63801 573-471-0792
Andy Comstock, prin. Fax 471-0793
Sikeston SHS 800/10-12
1002 Virginia St 63801 573-472-8850
Tom Williams, prin. Fax 472-8857

Silex, Lincoln, Pop. 232
Silex R-I SD 300/K-12
PO Box 46 63377 573-384-5227
Glenn Niffen, supt. Fax 384-5996
schoolweb.missouri.edu/silex.k12.mo.us/
Silex JSHS 200/7-12
PO Box 46 63377 573-384-5227
Bruce Werkmeister, prin. Fax 384-5996

Slater, Saline, Pop. 1,954
Slater SD 400/PK-12
515 Elm St 65349 660-529-2278
Paul Vaillancourt, supt. Fax 529-2279
Slater HS 200/9-12
515 Elm St 65349 660-529-3133
Paul Crews, prin. Fax 529-2279

Smithton, Pettis, Pop. 502
Smithton R-VI SD 600/K-12
505 S Myrtle Ave 65350 660-343-5316
Bill Hadlow, supt. Fax 343-5389
smithton.k12.mo.us
Smithton JSHS 300/7-12
505 S Myrtle Ave 65350 660-343-5318
Barbara Bancroft, prin. Fax 343-5389

Smithville, Clay, Pop. 7,118
Smithville R-II SD 2,000/PK-12
645 S Commercial Ave 64089 816-532-0406
Dr. Robert Leachman, supt. Fax 532-4192
www.smithville.k12.mo.us/
Smithville HS 600/9-12
645 S Commercial Ave 64089 816-532-0405
Todd Hinnenkamp, prin. Fax 532-4193
Smithville MS 500/6-8
675 S Commercial Ave 64089 816-532-1122
Susan Hurst, prin. Fax 532-3210

Sparta, Christian, Pop. 1,226
Sparta R-III SD 700/PK-12
PO Box 160 65753 417-634-4284
Jeff Hyatt, supt. Fax 634-3156
www.sparta.k12.mo.us/
Sparta HS 200/9-12
PO Box 160 65753 417-634-3224
Teresa McKenzie, prin. Fax 634-3156
Sparta MS 200/6-8
PO Box 160 65753 417-634-5518
Joy Finney, prin. Fax 634-3156

Spokane, Christian
Spokane R-VII SD
Supt. — See Highlandville
Spokane HS 200/9-12
PO Box 218 65754 417-443-3502
Daryl Bernskoetter, prin. Fax 443-7714
Spokane MS 200/6-8
PO Box 220 65754 417-443-3506
Pamila Rowe, prin. Fax 443-2069

Springfield, Greene, Pop. 150,298
Springfield R-XII SD 23,800/PK-12
940 N Jefferson Ave 65802 417-523-0000
Dr. Norman Ridder, supt. Fax 523-0196
springfieldpublicschoolsmo.org
Carver MS 800/6-8
3325 W Battlefield St 65807 417-523-6800
Dr. Dan O'Reilly, prin. Fax 523-6800
Central HS 1,400/6-12
423 E Central St 65802 417-523-9600
Everett Isaacs, prin. Fax 523-9695
Cherokee MS 1,000/6-8
420 E Farm Rd 182 65810 417-523-7200
Matt Pearce, prin. Fax 523-7295
Glendale HS 1,500/9-12
2727 S Ingram Mill Rd 65804 417-523-8900
Gary Prouty, prin. Fax 523-8995
Hickory Hills MS 500/6-8
3429 E Trafficway St 65802 417-523-7100
Kelly Allison, prin. Fax 523-7195
Hillcrest HS 1,300/9-12
3319 N Grant Ave 65803 417-523-8000
Justin Herrell, prin. Fax 523-8095
Jarrett MS 600/6-8
840 S Jefferson Ave 65806 417-523-6600
Dr. Nathaniel Quinn, prin. Fax 523-2163
Kickapoo HS 1,700/9-12
3710 S Jefferson Ave 65807 417-523-8500
David Schmitz, prin. Fax 523-8595
Parkview HS 1,500/9-12
516 W Meadowmere St 65807 417-523-9200
Chance Wistrom, prin. Fax 523-2337
Pershing MS 800/6-8
2120 S Ventura Ave 65804 417-523-2400
Dr. Kim Finch, prin. Fax 523-2495
Pipkin MS 600/6-8
1215 N Boonville Ave 65802 417-523-6000
Dr. Sharri Harwick, prin. Fax 523-6195
Pleasant View MS 400/6-8
2210 E State Highway AA 65803 417-523-2100
Dr. Ronald Snodgrass, prin. Fax 523-2395
Reed MS 600/6-8
2000 N Lyon Ave 65803 417-523-6300
Leslie Ford, prin. Fax 523-6395
Study MS 500/6-8
2343 W Olive St 65802 417-523-6510
James T. Rush, prin. Fax 523-6495

Assemblies of God Theological Seminary Post-Sec.
1435 N Glenstone Ave 65802 417-268-1000
Baptist Bible College Post-Sec.
628 E Kearney St 65803 800-228-5754
Bryan College Post-Sec.
237 S Florence Ave 65806 417-862-5700
Central Bible College Post-Sec.
3000 N Grant Ave 65803 800-831-4222
Cox College of Nursing & Health Sciences Post-Sec.
1423 N Jefferson Ave 65802 417-269-3401
Drury University Post-Sec.
900 N Benton Ave 65802 417-873-7879
Evangel University Post-Sec.
1111 N Glenstone Ave 65802 417-865-2811
Everest College Post-Sec.
1010 W Sunshine St 65807 417-864-7220
Forest Inst./Professional Psychology Post-Sec.
1322 S Campbell Ave 65807 417-831-7902
Global University Post-Sec.
1211 S Glenstone Ave 65804 417-862-9533
Greenwood Laboratory S 400/K-12
901 S National Ave, 417-836-5124
Dr. Janice Duncan, dir. Fax 836-8449
Missouri College of Cosmetology North Post-Sec.
2555 W Kearney St 65803 417-866-2786
Missouri State University Post-Sec.
901 S National Ave, 417-836-5000
New Covenant Academy 400/PK-12
3304 S Cox Ave 65807 417-887-9848
Cynthia Evans, supt. Fax 887-2419
Ozarks Technical Community College Post-Sec.
1001 E Chestnut Expy 65802 417-447-7500
Professional Massage Training Center Post-Sec.
229 E Commercial St 65803 417-863-7682
St. John's Regional Health Center Post-Sec.
1235 E Cherokee St 65804 417-885-2845
St. John's School of Nursing Post-Sec.
4431 S Fremont Ave 65804 417-885-2098
Southwest Baptist University Post-Sec.
4431 S Fremont Ave 65804 417-841-5046
Springfield Catholic HS 300/9-12
2340 S Eastgate Ave 65809 417-887-8817
Dean Crayton, prin. Fax 885-1165
Springfield SDA S 50/5-8
704 S Belview Ave 65802 417-862-0833
Vatterott College Post-Sec.
3850 S Campbell Ave 65807 417-831-8116

Stanberry, Gentry, Pop. 1,192
Stanberry R-II SD 400/PK-12
610 N Park St 64489 660-783-2136
Dr. Bruce Johnson, supt. Fax 783-2177
www.sr2.k12.mo.us/
Stanberry JSHS 200/7-12
610 N Park St 64489 660-783-2163
Gregory Dias, prin. Fax 783-2177

Steele, Pemiscot, Pop. 2,169
South Pemiscot County R-V SD 800/K-12
611 Beasley Rd 63877 573-695-4426
Mitchell Fisher, supt. Fax 695-4427
South Pemiscot HS 300/7-12
611 Beasley Rd 63877 573-695-3342
Brandon Jones, prin. Fax 695-7461

Steelville, Crawford, Pop. 1,454
Steelville R-III SD 1,000/PK-12
PO Box 339 65565 573-775-2175
Harvey Richards, supt. Fax 775-2179
steelville.k12.mo.us
Steelville HS 300/9-12
PO Box 339 65565 573-775-2144
Mike Whittaker, prin. Fax 775-5050
Steelville MS 300/5-8
PO Box 339 65565 573-775-2176
Nancy Obermiller, prin. Fax 775-2591

Stet, Carroll
Stet R-XV SD 100/K-12
18760 Cardinal Rd 64680 660-484-3122
Lachrissa Smith, supt. Fax 484-3124
Stet JSHS 100/7-12
18760 Cardinal Rd 64680 660-484-3122
Steven Street, prin. Fax 484-3124

Stewartsville, DeKalb, Pop. 746
Stewartsville C-2 SD 300/K-12
902 Buchanan St 64490 816-669-3792
Alan Kerr, supt. Fax 669-8125
www.geocities.com/stewartsvillec2/index.html
Stewartsville JSHS 200/7-12
902 Buchanan St 64490 816-669-3258
John Reed, prin. Fax 669-8125

Stockton, Cedar, Pop. 2,004
Stockton R-I SD 1,100/K-12
PO Box 190 65785 417-276-5143
Dr. Vicki Sandberg, supt. Fax 276-3765
www.schoolweb.missouri.edu/stockton.k12.mo.us/
Stockton HS 300/9-12
PO Box 190 65785 417-276-5141
John French, prin. Fax 276-6389
Stockton MS 400/5-8
PO Box 190 65785 417-276-6161
Bill Crabtree, prin. Fax 276-4909

Stoutland, Camden, Pop. 186
Stoutland R-II SD 500/PK-12
7584 State Road T 65567 417-286-3984
Geanine Bloch, supt. Fax 286-3153
www.schoolweb.missouri.edu/stoutland/
Stoutland JSHS 300/7-12
7584 State Road T 65567 417-286-3711
B. Steven Burns, prin. Fax 286-3981

Stover, Morgan, Pop. 1,022
Morgan County R-I SD 800/PK-12
701 N Oak St 65078 573-377-2217
Jackie Wilkerson, supt. Fax 377-2211
schoolweb.missouri.edu/stover.k12.mo.us/
Morgan County R-I HS 200/9-12
701 N Oak St 65078 573-377-2218
Thomas Wales, prin. Fax 377-2211
Morgan County R-I MS 300/5-8
701 N Oak St 65078 573-377-4284
Timothy Beydler, prin. Fax 377-4441

Strafford, Greene, Pop. 1,909
Strafford R-VI SD 1,000/K-12
201 W McCabe St 65757 417-736-7000
John Collins, supt. Fax 736-7016
straffordschools.net
Strafford HS 300/9-12
201 W McCabe St 65757 417-736-7000
Brett Soden, prin. Fax 736-7020
Strafford MS 300/5-8
211 W McCabe St 65757 417-736-7000
Shane Pierce, prin. Fax 736-7019

Sturgeon, Boone, Pop. 913
Sturgeon R-V SD 500/K-12
210 W Patton St 65284 573-687-3515
Stan Ingraham, supt. Fax 687-2116
www.sturgeon.k12.mo.us/
Sturgeon HS 200/9-12
210 W Patton St 65284 573-687-3512
Gina Mills, prin. Fax 687-3441
Sturgeon MS 200/5-8
210 W Patton St 65284 573-687-2155
Jeff Carr, prin. Fax 687-1226

Sullivan, Franklin, Pop. 6,613
Sullivan SD 2,200/PK-12
138 Taylor St 63080 573-468-5171
Dr. James Thornsberry, supt. Fax 468-7720
www.eagles.k12.mo.us
Sullivan HS 700/9-12
1073 E Vine St 63080 573-468-5181
Jennifer Schmidt, prin. Fax 860-3524
Sullivan MS 500/6-8
1156 Elmont Rd 63080 573-468-5191
Terri Parks, prin. Fax 860-2326

Summersville, Texas, Pop. 555
Summersville R-II SD 500/K-12
PO Box 198 65571 417-932-4045
Marc Hampton, supt. Fax 932-5360
www.summersville.k12.mo.us/
Summersville JSHS 200/7-12
PO Box 198 65571 417-932-4929
Keith McGee, prin. Fax 932-5360

Sweet Springs, Saline, Pop. 1,551
Sweet Springs R-VII SD 400/K-12
105 Main St 65351 660-335-4860
Boyd Jones, supt. Fax 335-4378
sweetsprings.k12.mo.us/
Sweet Springs JSHS 200/7-12
105 Main St 65351 660-335-6341
Rex Roberts, prin. Fax 335-6379

Tarkio, Atchison, Pop. 1,866
Tarkio R-I SD 400/K-12
312 S 11th St 64491 660-736-4161
Linda Blum, supt. Fax 736-4546
www.tarkio.k12.mo.us
Tarkio JSHS 200/7-12
312 S 11th St 64491 660-736-4118
Jason Tolen, prin. Fax 736-4546

Thayer, Oregon, Pop. 2,171
Thayer R-II SD 700/PK-12
401 E Walnut St 65791 417-264-7261
Bill Garrison, supt. Fax 264-4608
thayer.k12.mo.us/
Thayer JSHS 300/7-12
401 E Walnut St 65791 417-264-7261
Kevin Hedden, prin. Fax 264-4608

Theodosia, Ozark, Pop. 253
Lutie R-VI SD 200/K-12
HC 4 Box 4775 65761 417-273-4274
Christopher Felmlee, supt. Fax 273-4171
www.schoolweb.missouri.edu/lutie.k12.mo.us
Lutie JSHS 100/7-12
HC 4 Box 4775 65761 417-273-4150
Tammy Shrable, prin. Fax 273-4171

Tina, Carroll, Pop. 196
Tina-Avalon R-II SD 200/PK-12
11896 Highway 65 64682 660-622-4211
David Garber, supt. Fax 622-4210
tinaavalon.k12.mo.us/
Tina-Avalon JSHS 100/7-12
11896 Highway 65 64682 660-622-4212
Jason Whitt, prin. Fax 622-4210

Tipton, Moniteau, Pop. 3,142
Tipton R-VI SD 600/K-12
305 US Highway 50 E 65081 660-433-5520
Paul Wootten, supt. Fax 433-5241
tipton.k12.mo.us/
Tipton HS 300/7-12
305 US Highway 50 E 65081 660-433-5529
Alfred Norman, prin. Fax 433-2419

Trenton, Grundy, Pop. 6,121
Trenton R-IX SD 1,200/K-12
1607 Normal St 64683 660-359-3994
Becky Albrecht, supt. Fax 359-3995
www.trentonr9.k12.mo.us/
Trenton HS 400/9-12
1415 Oklahoma Ave 64683 660-359-2291
Dan Wiebers, prin. Fax 359-4073
Trenton MS 400/5-8
1417 Oklahoma Ave 64683 660-359-4328
Toni Cox, prin. Fax 359-6554

North Central Missouri College Post-Sec.
1301 Main St 64683 660-359-3948

Troy, Lincoln, Pop. 9,862
Troy R-III SD 5,300/K-12
951 W College St 63379 636-462-6098
Terry Morrow, supt. Fax 528-2411
www.troy.k12.mo.us
Buchanan HS 1,600/9-12
1190 Old Cap Au Gris Rd 63379 636-528-4618
Stephen Hunter, prin. Fax 528-5164
Troy MS 900/7-8
713 W College St 63379 636-528-7057
Mary Ingmire, prin. Fax 528-2199

Tuscumbia, Miller, Pop. 223
Miller County R-III SD 300/K-12
PO Box 1 65082 573-369-2375
Nancy Henke, supt. Fax 369-2833
www.tuscumbialions.com/
Tuscumbia HS 100/9-12
PO Box 1 65082 573-369-2375
Doug Kempker, prin. Fax 369-2833

Union, Franklin, Pop. 8,897
Union R-XI SD 2,900/K-12
PO Box 440 63084 636-583-8626
Dr. VeAnn Tilson, supt. Fax 583-2403
union.k12.mo.us
Union HS 900/9-12
PO Box 440 63084 636-583-2513
Dennis Lottman, prin. Fax 583-4203
Union MS 500/7-8
PO Box 440 63084 636-583-5855
Nathan Bailey, prin. Fax 583-6156

East Central College Post-Sec.
1964 Prairie Dell Rd 63084 636-583-5193

Union Star, DeKalb, Pop. 412
Union Star R-II SD 100/K-12
6132 NW State Route Z 64494 816-593-2294
Steve Thompson, supt. Fax 593-4427
Union Star JSHS 100/7-12
6132 NW State Route Z 64494 816-593-2294
Clinton Fine, prin. Fax 593-4427

Unionville, Putnam, Pop. 1,981
Putnam County R-I SD 800/K-12
803 S 20th St 63565 660-947-3361
Heath Halley, supt. Fax 947-2912
www.nemr.net/~midgets
Putnam County HS 200/9-12
803 S 20th St 63565 660-947-2481
Jeremy Watt, prin. Fax 947-2912
Putnam County MS 200/6-8
802 S 18th St 63565 660-947-3237
Barbara Hodges, prin. Fax 947-2912

University City, Saint Louis, Pop. 37,170
University City SD
Supt. — See Saint Louis
Brittany Woods MS 600/7-8
8125 Groby Rd 63130 314-290-4280
Bernadette White, prin. Fax 997-1786
University City HS 1,100/9-12
7401 Balson Ave 63130 314-290-4100
Dr. Elizabeth Bender, prin. Fax 290-4120

Urbana, Hickory, Pop. 426
Hickory County R-I SD 800/K-12
RR 1 Box 838 65767 417-993-4241
Mark Beem, supt. Fax 993-4269
hickorycountyschools.net/
Skyline HS 200/9-12
RR 1 Box 838 65767 417-993-4226
Randall Dougherty, prin. Fax 993-5947
Skyline MS 300/5-8
RR 1 Box 838 65767 417-993-4254
Daniel Roberts, prin. Fax 993-5948

Valley Park, Saint Louis, Pop. 6,405
Valley Park SD 1,100/PK-12
1 Main St 63088 636-923-3500
Laura Kinder, supt. Fax 861-1002
www.vp.k12.mo.us
Valley Park HS 200/9-12
1 Main St 63088 636-923-3500
Randall Fidler, prin. Fax 225-0542
Valley Park MS 200/6-8
1 Main St 63088 636-923-3500
Tad Savage, prin. Fax 225-1529

Van Buren, Carter, Pop. 817
Van Buren R-I SD 500/PK-12
PO Box 550 63965 573-323-4281
Dr. Jeffrey Lindsey, supt. Fax 323-4297
schoolweb.missouri.edu/vanburen.k12.mo.us
Van Buren JSHS 300/6-12
PO Box 550 63965 573-323-4295
Mark Wood, prin. Fax 323-4295

Vandalia, Audrain, Pop. 4,067
Van-Far R-I SD 600/K-12
2200 W US Highway 54 63382 573-594-6111
Kevin Freeman, supt. Fax 594-2878
www.vf.k12.mo.us
Van-Far JSHS 300/7-12
2200 W US Highway 54 63382 573-594-6442
Bob Evans, prin. Fax 594-3054

Verona, Lawrence, Pop. 720
Verona R-VII SD 400/K-12
PO Box 7 65769 417-498-2274
William Sweet, supt. Fax 498-6590
schoolweb.missouri.edu/verona.k12.mo.us/
Verona JSHS 100/7-12
PO Box 7 65769 417-498-6775
David Knight, prin. Fax 498-6590

Versailles, Morgan, Pop. 2,662
Morgan County R-II SD 1,500/PK-12
913 W Newton St 65084 573-378-4231
Jeffery Carter, supt. Fax 378-5714
www.mcr2.k12.mo.us/
Morgan County HS 500/9-12
913 W Newton St 65084 573-378-4697
Tom Andreas, prin. Fax 378-2704
Morgan County MS 400/6-8
913 W Newton St 65084 573-378-5432
Matt Unger, prin. Fax 378-6610

Viburnum, Iron, Pop. 811
Iron County C-4 SD 500/K-12
PO Box 368 65566 573-244-5422
Perry Dobson, supt. Fax 244-3410
www.ironc4.k12.mo.us
Viburnum JSHS 200/7-12
PO Box 368 65566 573-244-5521
Doug Ruck, prin. Fax 244-3410

Vienna, Maries, Pop. 635
Maries County R-I SD 600/K-12
PO Box 218 65582 573-422-3304
Richard Spacek, supt. Fax 422-3185
Vienna HS 300/7-12
PO Box 218 65582 573-422-3363
Warren Ripley, prin. Fax 422-3185

Villa Ridge, Franklin, Pop. 1,865

Crosspoint Christian S 100/K-12
PO Box 100 63089 636-742-5380
Diane Beumer, prin. Fax 742-5917

Walker, Vernon, Pop. 279
Northeast Vernon County R-I SD 200/PK-12
216 E Leslie Ave 64790 417-465-2221
Charles Naas, supt. Fax 465-2388
Northeast Vernon County R-I HS 100/7-12
216 E Leslie Ave 64790 417-465-2221
Brad Landoll, prin. Fax 465-2388

Walnut Grove, Greene, Pop. 626
Walnut Grove R-V SD 300/K-12
PO Box 187 65770 417-788-2543
Marty Witt, supt. Fax 788-1254

Walnut Grove JSHS 200/7-12
PO Box 187 65770 417-788-2544
Darin Meinders, prin. Fax 788-1254

Wardell, Pemiscot, Pop. 262
North Pemiscot County R-I SD 400/K-12
PO Box 38 63879 573-628-3471
Keith Henke, supt. Fax 628-3472
North Pemiscot County JSHS 200/6-12
PO Box 38 63879 573-628-3465
Terry Hamilton, prin. Fax 628-3418

Warrensburg, Johnson, Pop. 17,769
Warrensburg R-VI SD 3,100/K-12
PO Box 638 64093 660-747-7823
Deborah Orr, supt. Fax 747-9615
warrensburg.k12.mo.us
Warrensburg Area Career Center Vo/Tech
205 S Ridgeview Dr 64093 660-747-2283
Dan Gordon, prin. Fax 747-3778
Warrensburg HS 1,000/9-12
1411 S Ridgeview Dr 64093 660-747-2262
Simone Dillingham, prin. Fax 747-8731
Warrensburg MS 800/6-8
640 E Gay St 64093 660-747-5612
Jim Elliott, prin. Fax 747-8779

Central Missouri State University Post-Sec.
64093 660-543-4111

Warrenton, Warren, Pop. 6,612
Warren County R-III SD 2,800/K-12
302 Kuhl Ave 63383 636-456-6901
Dr. John Long, supt. Fax 456-7687
www.warrencor3.org
Black Hawk MS 700/6-8
302 Kuhl Ave 63383 636-456-6903
Barbara Crowell, prin. Fax 456-1445
Warren County R-III HS 900/9-12
803 Pinckney St 63383 636-456-6902
David Buck, prin. Fax 456-5771

Warsaw, Benton, Pop. 2,268
Warsaw R-IX SD 1,500/PK-12
PO Box 248 65355 660-438-7120
Brett Reese, supt. Fax 438-3749
www.warsaw.k12.mo.us/
Boise MS 300/6-8
PO Box 1750 65355 660-438-9079
Brent Depee, prin. Fax 438-3749
Warsaw HS 500/9-12
PO Box 248 65355 660-438-7351
Dan Decker, prin. Fax 438-3749

Washburn, Barry, Pop. 468
Southwest R-V SD 800/PK-12
PO Box 297 65772 417-826-5410
Richard Asbill, supt. Fax 826-5603
www.swr5.k12.mo.us
Southwest HS 200/9-12
PO Box 297 65772 417-826-5413
Larry Sorrells, prin. Fax 826-5603
Southwest MS 300/5-8
PO Box 297 65772 417-826-5050
Ben Abramovitz, prin. Fax 826-5603

Washington, Franklin, Pop. 14,136
Washington SD 4,100/PK-12
PO Box 357 63090 636-239-2727
Dr. Scott Huddleston, supt. Fax 239-3315
www.washington.k12.mo.us
Four Rivers Career Center Vo/Tech
550 Blue Jay Dr 63090 636-239-7777
Steve Matyas, prin. Fax 239-0791
Washington HS 1,400/9-12
600 Blue Jay Dr 63090 636-239-4717
Richard Riggs, prin. Fax 390-4157
Washington MS 600/7-8
401 E 14th St 63090 636-239-4783
Dr. Richard Martin, prin. Fax 239-4252

St. Francis Borgia Regional HS 600/9-12
1000 Borgia Dr 63090 636-239-7871
George Wingbermuehle, prin. Fax 239-1198

Waynesville, Pulaski, Pop. 3,511
Waynesville R-VI SD 3,400/K-12
200 Fleetwood Dr 65583 573-774-6497
Dr. Judene Blackburn, supt. Fax 774-6491
waynesville.k12.mo.us
Waynesville HS 1,500/9-12
200 GW Ln 65583 573-774-6401
Allen Voth, prin. Fax 774-2393
Waynesville MS 500/7-8
1001 Historic 66 W 65583 573-774-6198
Jess Grizzell, prin. Fax 774-6089
Waynesville Technical Academy Vo/Tech
810 Roosevelt St 65583 573-774-6106
Dr. Bob Chapman, dir. Fax 774-3355

Central College of Cosmetology Post-Sec.
PO Box 463 65583 573-336-3888

Weaubleau, Hickory, Pop. 536
Weaubleau R-III SD 500/PK-12
509 N Center St 65774 417-428-3317
Jason Buckner, supt. Fax 428-3521
www.weaubleau.k12.mo.us/
Weaubleau HS 200/7-12
509 N Center St 65774 417-428-3368
Rodney Delmont, prin. Fax 428-3004

Webb City, Jasper, Pop. 10,764
Webb City R-VII SD 3,900/PK-12
411 N Madison St 64870 417-673-6000
Ronald Lankford, supt. Fax 673-6007
www.wccards.k12.mo.us/
Webb City HS 1,100/9-12
621 N Madison St 64870 417-673-6010
Stephen Gollhofer, prin. Fax 673-6017
Webb City JHS 600/7-8
807 W 1st St 64870 417-673-6030
Trey Moeller, prin. Fax 673-6037

Webster Groves, Saint Louis, Pop. 22,896
Webster Groves SD 4,100/K-12
400 E Lockwood Ave 63119 314-961-1233
Dr. Brent Underwood, supt. Fax 918-4023
www.webster.k12.mo.us
Webster Groves HS 1,300/9-12
100 Selma Ave 63119 314-963-6400
Dr. Jon D. Clark, prin. Fax 963-6483
Other Schools – See Saint Louis

Eden Theological Seminary Post-Sec.
475 E Lockwood Ave 63119 314-961-3627

Weldon Spring, Saint Charles, Pop. 5,361
Francis Howell R-III SD
Supt. — See Saint Charles
Bryan MS 1,100/6-8
605 Independence Rd 63304 636-477-3060
Sue Hartman, prin. Fax 477-3075
Howell MS 800/6-8
825 OFallon Rd 63304 636-851-4800
Amy Johnston, prin. Fax 851-4121

Wellington, Lafayette, Pop. 783
Wellington-Napoleon R-IX SD 400/K-12
PO Box 280 64097 816-934-2531
Jeffrey Sumy, supt. Fax 934-8649
www.well-nap.k12.mo.us/
Wellington-Napoleon JSHS 200/7-12
PO Box 280 64097 816-240-2621
Kenneth Holland, prin. Fax 934-8649

Wellsville, Montgomery, Pop. 1,398
Wellsville Middletown R-I SD 500/PK-12
900 Burlington St 63384 573-684-2428
Kerry Hesse, supt. Fax 684-2018
wmr1.k12.mo.us/
Wellsville JSHS 300/6-12
900 Burlington St 63384 573-684-2017
Connie Hesse, prin. Fax 684-2018

Wentzville, Saint Charles, Pop. 17,988
Wentzville R-IV SD 8,700/K-12
1 Campus Dr 63385 636-327-3800
Dr. Terry Adams, supt. Fax 327-8611
www.wentzville.k12.mo.us
Holt HS 1,300/9-12
600 Campus Dr 63385 636-327-3876
John Waters, prin. Fax 327-3953
Timberland HS 1,100/9-12
559 E Highway N 63385 636-327-3988
David Waters, prin. Fax 327-3922
Wentzville MS 1,000/6-8
405 Campus Dr 63385 636-327-3815
Nathan Tyson, prin. Fax 327-3954
Wentzville South MS 1,000/6-8
561 E Highway N 63385 636-327-3928
Jennifer Waters, prin. Fax 327-3955

Midwest University Post-Sec.
851 Parr Rd 63385 636-327-4645

Weston, Platte, Pop. 1,644
West Platte County R-II SD 700/K-12
1103 Washington St 64098 816-640-2236
Kyle B. Stephenson, supt. Fax 386-2104
schoolweb.missouri.edu/wprii.k12.mo.us/index.htm
West Platte County JSHS 300/7-12
1103 Washington St 64098 816-640-2292
Stanley Coulson, prin. Fax 386-2293

Westphalia, Osage, Pop. 331
Osage County R-III SD 800/PK-12
PO Box 37 65085 573-455-2375
Archie Derboven, supt. Fax 455-9884
www.fatima.k12.mo.us/
Fatima JSHS 400/7-12
PO Box 37 65085 573-455-2550
Daniel Ramsey, prin. Fax 455-9884

West Plains, Howell, Pop. 11,348
Richards R-V SD 400/K-8
3461 County Road 1710 65775 417-256-5239
Jerry Premer, supt. Fax 256-3314
Richards MS 100/6-8
3461 County Road 1710 65775 417-256-5239
Reta House, prin. Fax 256-3314

West Plains R-VII SD 2,500/K-12
613 W 1st St 65775 417-256-6150
Karla Eslinger, supt. Fax 256-8616
wphs.k12.mo.us/
South Central Career Center Vo/Tech
610 E Olden St 65775 417-256-6150
Rodney Wood, dir. Fax 256-5786
West Plains HS 1,200/9-12
602 E Olden St 65775 417-256-6150
Ronald Estes, prin. Fax 256-8908
West Plains MS 600/5-8
730 E Olden St 65775 417-256-6150
Dr. Fred Czerwonka, prin. Fax 256-8907

Faith Assembly Christian S 100/PK-12
PO Box 748 65775 417-256-1817
Roberta Jacobs, admin. Fax 257-2838
Missouri State University - West Plains Post-Sec.
128 Garfield Ave 65775 417-255-7255

Wheatland, Hickory, Pop. 402
Wheatland R-II SD 300/K-12
PO Box 68 65779 417-282-6433
Eric Cooley, supt. Fax 282-5733
www.wheatlandschool.com/
Wheatland JSHS 200/7-12
PO Box 68 65779 417-282-5833
Matt Gunter, prin. Fax 282-5733

Wheaton, Barry, Pop. 732
Wheaton R-III SD 400/K-12
PO Box 249 64874 417-652-3914
Jim Cummins, supt. Fax 652-7355
Wheaton JSHS 200/7-12
PO Box 249 64874 417-652-7249
Lance Massey, prin. Fax 652-7355

Willard, Greene, Pop. 3,330
Willard R-II SD 3,200/K-12
460 Kime St 65781 417-742-2584
Dr. Kent Medlin, supt. Fax 742-2586
www.willard.k12.mo.us/
Willard HS 1,000/9-12
515 E Jackson St 65781 417-742-3524
Don Tuck, prin. Fax 742-3667
Willard MS 600/7-8
205 S Miller Rd 65781 417-742-2588
Amy Sims, prin. Fax 742-3505

Willow Springs, Howell, Pop. 2,116
Willow Springs R-IV SD 1,300/PK-12
215 W 4th St 65793 417-469-3260
Derrick Hutsell, supt. Fax 469-5127
www.willowspringsschool.com/
Willow Springs HS 400/9-12
215 W 4th St 65793 417-469-2114
Jimalee James, prin. Fax 469-2507
Willow Springs MS 400/5-8
215 W 4th St 65793 417-469-3211
Malcolm Gum, prin. Fax 469-1229

Windsor, Henry, Pop. 3,265
Henry County R-I SD 700/PK-12
210 North St 65360 660-647-3533
Mary Elsensohn, supt. Fax 647-2711
henrycountyr1.k12.mo.us
Windsor JSHS 300/7-12
210 North St 65360 660-647-3106
Kyle Powell, prin. Fax 647-3218

Winfield, Lincoln, Pop. 850
Winfield R-IV SD 1,600/K-12
701 W Elm St 63389 636-668-8188
Dr. Arnold Bell, supt. Fax 668-8641
schoolweb.missouri.edu/winfield.k12.mo.us/
Winfield HS 500/9-12
701 W Elm St 63389 636-668-8130
Tim Reller, prin. Fax 566-6455
Winfield MS 400/6-8
701 W Elm St 63389 636-668-8001
Jeff Haug, prin. Fax 668-6044

Winona, Shannon, Pop. 1,317
Winona R-III SD 600/PK-12
PO Box 248 65588 573-325-8101
Scott Lindsey, supt. Fax 325-8447
Winona HS 200/9-12
PO Box 248 65588 573-325-8101
Donald Wakefield, prin. Fax 325-4700

Winston, Daviess, Pop. 253
Winston R-VI SD 200/PK-12
PO Box 38 64689 660-749-5456
Lisa Bielby, supt. Fax 749-5432
Winston JSHS 100/7-12
PO Box 38 64689 660-749-5456
Jeremy Covey, prin. Fax 749-5432

Wright City, Warren, Pop. 2,440
Wright City R-II SD 1,500/PK-12
PO Box 198 63390 636-745-7200
Dr. Mark Porter, supt. Fax 745-3613
www.wrightcity.k12.mo.us/
Wright City HS 400/9-12
PO Box 198 63390 636-745-7500
Mike Dorband, prin. Fax 745-7518
Wright City MS 500/5-8
PO Box 198 63390 636-745-7300
Kip Dickinson, prin. Fax 745-7304

Zalma, Bollinger, Pop. 97
Zalma R-V SD 200/K-12
HC 2 Box 184 63787 573-722-5504
Darryl Sauer, supt. Fax 722-9870
Zalma JSHS 100/7-12
HC 2 Box 184 63787 573-722-3320
Gerard Vandeven, prin. Fax 722-9870

MONTANA

MONTANA OFFICE OF PUBLIC INSTRUCTION
PO Box 202501, Helena 59620-2501
Telephone 406-444-3095
Fax 406-444-2893
Website http://www.opi.state.mt.us

State Superintendent of Public Instruction Linda McCulloch

MONTANA BOARD OF EDUCATION
PO Box 202501, Helena 59620-2501

Chairperson Diane Fladmo

COUNTY SUPERINTENDENTS OF SCHOOLS

Beaverhead County Office of Education
Dorothy Donovan, supt. 406-683-3737
2 S Pacific St, Dillon 59725 Fax 683-3769
Big Horn County Office of Education
Gary Hickey, supt. 406-665-9820
PO Box 908, Hardin 59034 Fax 665-9738
Blaine County Office of Education
Carol Elliot, supt. 406-357-3270
PO Box 819, Chinook 59523 Fax 357-2199
Broadwater County Office of Education
Judy Gillespie, supt. 406-266-9215
515 Broadway St, Townsend 59644 Fax 266-3674
Carbon County Office of Education
Jerry Scott, supt. 406-446-1301
PO Box 116, Red Lodge 59068 Fax 446-9155
Carter County Office of Education
Carole Carey, supt. 406-775-8721
PO Box 352, Ekalaka 59324 Fax 775-8703
Cascade County Office of Education
Jess Anderson, supt. 406-454-6776
325 2nd Ave N, Great Falls 59401 Fax 454-6778
Chouteau County Office of Education
Larry Stollfuss, supt. 406-622-3242
PO Box 459, Fort Benton 59442 Fax 622-3028
Custer County Office of Education
Ellen Zook, supt. 406-874-3421
1010 Main St, Miles City 59301 Fax 874-3452
Daniels County Office of Education
Patricia McDonnell, supt. 406-487-2651
PO Box 67, Scobey 59263 Fax 487-5432
Dawson County Office of Education
Steve Engebretson, supt. 406-377-3963
207 W Bell St, Glendive 59330 Fax 377-2022
Deer Lodge County Office of Education
Michael O'Rourke, supt. 406-563-4178
800 Main St, Anaconda 59711 Fax 563-5476
Fallon County Office of Education
Marlene Ferrell, supt. 406-778-7127
PO Box 1117, Baker 59313 Fax 778-3431
Fergus County Office of Education
Shirley Barrick, supt. 406-538-3136
712 W Main St, Lewistown 59457 Fax 538-2819
Flathead County Office of Education
Marcia Sheffels, supt. 406-758-5720
800 S Main St, Kalispell 59901 Fax 758-5850
Gallatin County Office of Education
Mary Ellen Fitzgerald, supt. 406-582-3090
311 W Main St Rm 107 Fax 582-3093
Bozeman 59715
Garfield County Office of Education
Karla Christensen, supt. 406-557-6115
PO Box 28, Jordan 59337 Fax 557-2625
Glacier County Office of Education
Jetta Johnson, supt. 406-873-2295
1210 E Main St, Cut Bank 59427 Fax 873-9103
Golden Valley County Office of Education
Jennae Mitchell, supt. 406-568-2342
107 Kemp St, Ryegate 59074 Fax 568-2498

Granite County Office of Education
Jo Ann Husbyn, supt. 406-859-3831
PO Box 520, Philipsburg 59858 Fax 859-3817
Hill County Office of Education
Shirley Isbell, supt. 406-265-5481
315 4th St, Havre 59501 Fax 265-5487
Jefferson County Office of Education
Garry Pace, supt. 406-225-4114
PO Box H, Boulder 59632 Fax 225-4149
Judith Basin County Office of Education
Julie Peevey, supt. 406-566-2277
PO Box 307, Stanford 59479 Fax 566-2211
Lake County Office of Education
Gale Decker, supt. 406-883-7262
106 4th Ave E, Polson 59860 Fax 883-7283
www.lakecounty-mt.org/schools
Lewis & Clark County Office of Education
Marsha Davis, supt. 406-447-8344
316 N Park Ave Ste 301 Fax 447-8370
Helena 59623
Liberty County Office of Education
Rachel Ghekiere, supt. 406-759-5216
PO Box 684, Chester 59522 Fax 759-5996
Lincoln County Office of Education
Ron Higgins, supt. 406-293-7781
418 Mineral Ave, Libby 59923 Fax 293-9794
Madison County Office of Education
Judi Osborn, supt. 406-843-4217
PO Box 247, Virginia City 59755 Fax 843-5261
McCone County Office of Education
Jackie Becker, supt. 406-485-3590
PO Box 180, Circle 59215 Fax 485-2689
Meagher County Office of Education
Bonnie Lower, supt., PO Box 354 406-547-1112
White Sulphur Springs 59645 Fax 547-3388
Mineral County Office of Education
Billye Ann Bricker, supt. 406-822-3534
PO Box 100, Superior 59872 Fax 822-3579
Missoula County Office of Education
Rachel Vielleux, supt. 406-258-4860
438 W Spruce St, Missoula 59802 Fax 258-3973
Musselshell County Office of Education
Kathryn Pfister, supt. 406-323-1470
506 Main St, Roundup 59072 Fax 323-3303
Park County Office of Education
Rodney Olson, supt. 406-222-4148
414 E Callender St Fax 222-4199
Livingston 59047
Petroleum County Office of Education
Lisa Solf, supt. 406-429-5551
PO Box 226, Winnett 59087 Fax 429-6328
Phillips County Office of Education
Vivian Taylor, supt. 406-654-2010
PO Box 138, Malta 59538 Fax 654-1213
Pondera County Office of Education
Jo Stone, supt. 406-271-4055
20 4th Ave SW Ste 307 Fax 271-4070
Conrad 59425

Powder River County Office of Education
Charlotte Miller, supt. 406-436-2488
PO Box 300, Broadus 59317 Fax 436-2151
Powell County Office of Education
Jules Waber, supt. 406-846-3680
409 Missouri Ave Fax 846-2784
Deer Lodge 59722
Prairie County Office of Education
Cindy Bond, supt. 406-635-5577
PO Box 566, Terry 59349 Fax 635-5576
Ravalli County Office of Education
Ernie Jean, supt. 406-375-6522
215 S 4th St Ste B, Hamilton 59840 Fax 375-6523
Richland County Office of Education
Gail Anne Staffanson, supt. 406-433-1608
201 W Main St, Sidney 59270 Fax 433-3731
Roosevelt County Office of Education
Pat Stennes, supt. 406-653-6266
400 2nd Ave S, Wolf Point 59201 Fax 653-6203
Rosebud County Office of Education
Sharyn Thomas, supt. 406-346-2537
PO Box 407, Forsyth 59327 Fax 346-2537
Sanders County Office of Education
Kathy McEldery, supt. 406-826-4288
PO Box 519, Plains 59859 Fax 826-4288
Sheridan County Office of Education
June Johnson, supt. 406-765-3403
100 W Laurel Ave Fax 765-2609
Plentywood 59254
Silver Bow County Office of Education
Edward Heard, supt. 406-497-6215
155 W Granite St, Butte 59701 Fax 497-6328
Stillwater County Office of Education
Barbara Campbell, supt. 406-322-8057
PO Box 1139, Columbus 59019 Fax 322-8007
Sweet Grass County Office of Education
Linda DeCock, supt. 406-932-5147
PO Box 1310, Big Timber 59011 Fax 932-5112
Teton County Office of Education
Diane Inbody, supt. 406-466-2907
PO Box 610, Choteau 59422 Fax 466-2138
Toole County Office of Education
Boyd Jackson, supt. 406-424-8329
226 1st St S, Shelby 59474 Fax 424-8321
Treasure County Office of Education
Kathleen Thomas, supt. 406-342-5545
PO Box 429, Hysham 59038 Fax 342-5445
Valley County Office of Education
Lynne Nyquist, supt. 406-228-6226
501 Court Sq Ste 2 Fax 228-9027
Glasgow 59230
Wheatland County Office of Education
Susan Beley, supt. 406-632-4816
PO Box 637, Harlowton 59036 Fax 632-4880
Wibaux County Office of Education
Patricia Zinda, supt. 406-796-2481
PO Box 199, Wibaux 59353 Fax 796-2625
Yellowstone County Office of Education
A.J. Micheletti, supt. 406-256-6933
PO Box 35022, Billings 59107 Fax 256-6930
www.co.yellowstone.mt.us

PUBLIC, PRIVATE AND CATHOLIC SECONDARY SCHOOLS

Absarokee, Stillwater, Pop. 1,067
Absarokee SD 300/K-12
327 S Woodard Ave 59001 406-328-4583
David Huether, supt. Fax 328-4077
www.absarokee.k12.mt.us/
Absarokee HS 100/9-12
327 S Woodard Ave 59001 406-328-4583
Kevin Smith, prin. Fax 328-4077
Absarokee MS 100/7-8
327 S Woodard Ave 59001 406-328-4583
Kevin Smith, prin. Fax 328-4077

Alberton, Mineral, Pop. 422
Alberton SD 2 200/K-12
PO Box 330 59820 406-722-4413
James Baldwin, supt. Fax 722-3040
Alberton HS 100/9-12
PO Box 330 59820 406-722-3381
Art Walsh, prin. Fax 722-3040
Alberton MS 50/7-8
PO Box 330 59820 406-722-4413
Art Walsh, prin. Fax 722-3040

Anaconda, Deer Lodge, Pop. 10,093
Anaconda SD 10 1,100/PK-12
400 Main St 59711 406-563-6361
James Whealon, supt. Fax 563-6333
Anaconda HS 500/9-12
515 Main St 59711 406-563-5269
Walt Hansen, prin. Fax 563-5260
Moodry JHS 200/6-8
3rd & Cherry 59711 406-563-6242
Sue Meredith, prin. Fax 563-5093

Arlee, Lake, Pop. 489
Arlee SD JT & 8 500/PK-12
PO Box 37 59821 406-726-3216
Gordon Friberg, supt. Fax 726-3940
www.arlee.k12.mt.us/
Arlee HS 100/9-12
PO Box 37 59821 406-726-3216
Richard Bachmeier, prin. Fax 726-3940
Arlee JHS 100/7-8
PO Box 37 59821 406-726-3216
Lisa Miller, prin. Fax 726-3940

Ashland, Rosebud, Pop. 484
Ashland ESD 32J 100/PK-8
PO Box 17 59003 406-784-2568
Dale Bernard, supt. Fax 784-6138

Ashland MS — 50/7-8
PO Box 17 59003 — 406-784-2568
Dale Bernard, prin. — Fax 784-6138

St. Labre Indian S — 300/6-12
1000 Tongue River Rd 59004 — 406-784-4500
Scott Gion, prin. — Fax 784-4565

Augusta, Lewis and Clark
Augusta SD 45 — 100/PK-12
PO Box 307 59410 — 406-562-3384
Russ Bean, supt. — Fax 562-3898
Augusta HS — 50/9-12
PO Box 307 59410 — 406-562-3384
Russ Bean, prin. — Fax 562-3898
Augusta MS — 50/7-8
PO Box 307 59410 — 406-562-3384
Russ Bean, prin. — Fax 562-3898

Bainville, Roosevelt, Pop. 151
Bainville SD — 100/PK-12
PO Box 177 59212 — 406-769-2321
Dennis Maasjo, supt. — Fax 769-3291
Bainville HS — 50/9-12
PO Box 177 59212 — 406-769-2321
Paula Schledewitz, prin. — Fax 769-3291
Bainville MS — 50/7-8
PO Box 177 59212 — 406-769-2321
Paula Schledewitz, prin. — Fax 769-3291

Baker, Fallon, Pop. 1,628
Baker SD 12 — 400/PK-12
PO Box 659 59313 — 406-778-3574
Donald Schillinger, supt. — Fax 778-2785
www.baker.k12.mt.us/
Baker HS — 100/9-12
PO Box 659 59313 — 406-778-3329
David Breitbach, prin. — Fax 778-2785
Baker JHS — 100/7-8
PO Box 659 59313 — 406-778-3329
David Breitbach, prin. — Fax 778-2785

Belfry, Carbon
Belfry SD 3 — 100/PK-12
PO Box 210 59008 — 406-664-3319
Martha Young, supt. — Fax 664-3274
Belfry HS — 50/9-12
PO Box 210 59008 — 406-664-3319
Martha Young, prin. — Fax 664-3274
Belfry MS — 50/7-8
PO Box 210 59008 — 406-664-3319
Martha Young, prin. — Fax 664-3274

Belgrade, Gallatin, Pop. 7,033
Belgrade SD 44 — 2,700/PK-12
PO Box 166 59714 — 406-388-6951
Herbert Benz, supt. — Fax 388-0122
www.belgrade.k12.mt.us
Belgrade HS — 800/9-12
303 N Hoffman St 59714 — 406-388-4224
Craig Cummings, prin. — Fax 388-4633
Belgrade MS — 400/7-8
410 Triple Crown St 59714 — 406-388-1309
Kevin McNelis, prin. — Fax 388-8894

Belt, Cascade, Pop. 610
Belt SD 29 — 300/PK-12
PO Box 197 59412 — 406-277-3351
Calvin Johnson, supt. — Fax 277-4466
Belt HS — 100/9-12
PO Box 197 59412 — 406-277-3351
Craig Cummings, prin. — Fax 277-4466
Belt MS — 100/7-8
PO Box 197 59412 — 406-277-3351
William Edwards, prin. — Fax 277-4466

Bigfork, Flathead
Bigfork SD 38 — 900/PK-12
PO Box 188 59911 — 406-837-7400
Russell Kinzer, supt. — Fax 837-7407
Bigfork HS — 400/9-12
PO Box 188 59911 — 406-837-7420
Thom Peck, prin. — Fax 837-7245
Bigfork MS — 200/7-8
PO Box 188 59911 — 406-837-7412
Wayne Loeffler, prin. — Fax 837-7438

Swan River ESD 4 — 200/PK-8
1205 Swan Hwy 59911 — 406-837-4528
Fax 837-4055
Swan River MS — 50/7-8
1205 Swan Hwy 59911 — 406-837-4528
Peter Loyda, prin. — Fax 837-4055

Big Sandy, Chouteau, Pop. 643
Big Sandy SD 11 — 200/PK-12
PO Box 570 59520 — 406-378-2501
Edward Ray, supt. — Fax 378-2275
Big Sandy HS — 100/9-12
PO Box 570 59520 — 406-378-2502
Edward Ray, prin. — Fax 378-2275
Big Sandy JHS — 50/7-8
PO Box 570 59520 — 406-378-2502
Edward Ray, prin. — Fax 378-2275

Big Timber, Sweet Grass, Pop. 1,725
Big Timber ESD 1 — 400/PK-8
PO Box 887 59011 — 406-932-5939
Gary Harkness, supt. — Fax 932-4069
www.bigtimber-gs.k12.mt.us
Big Timber MS — 100/7-8
PO Box 887 59011 — 406-932-5939
Mark Ketcham, prin. — Fax 932-4069

Sweet Grass County HSD — 200/9-12
PO Box 886 59011 — 406-932-5993
Alvin Buerkle, supt. — Fax 932-5982
Sweet Grass County HS — 200/9-12
PO Box 886 59011 — 406-932-5993
Kip Ryan, prin. — Fax 932-5982

Billings, Yellowstone, Pop. 98,721
Billings SD 2 — 15,700/PK-12
415 N 30th St 59101 — 406-247-3780
Jack Copps, supt. — Fax 247-3882
www.billings.k12.mt.us
Billings HS — 1,900/9-12
425 Grand Ave 59101 — 406-247-2100
Dennis Holmes, prin. — Fax 255-3521
Billings West HS — 2,100/9-12
2201 Saint Johns Ave 59102 — 406-655-1400
Dennis Sulser, prin. — Fax 655-3100
Career Center — Vo/Tech
3723 Central Ave 59102 — 406-655-3070
Stan Barr, prin. — Fax 655-3096
Castle Rock MS — 700/7-8
1441 Governors Blvd 59105 — 406-237-6600
Shaun Harrington, prin. — Fax 254-1116
James MS — 600/7-8
1200 30th St W 59102 — 406-655-3124
Kip Farnum, prin. — Fax 655-3129
Lewis & Clark MS — 600/7-8
1315 Lewis Ave 59102 — 406-237-6700
Steve Pomroy, prin. — Fax 237-6762
Riverside MS — 600/7-8
3700 Madison Ave 59101 — 406-255-3740
Lewis Anderson, prin. — Fax 255-3534
Skyview HS — 1,600/9-12
1775 High Sierra Blvd 59105 — 406-247-2300
Bob Whalen, prin. — Fax 255-3507
Adult & Basic Education — Adult
415 N 30th St 59101 — 406-247-3703
Woodrow Jensen, prin. — Fax 247-3799

Canyon Creek ESD 4 — 200/PK-8
3139 Duck Creek Rd 59101 — 406-656-4471
Stephanie Long, supt. — Fax 655-1031
www.canyoncreek.k12.mt.us/
Canyon Creek MS — 100/7-8
3139 Duck Creek Rd 59101 — 406-656-4471
Stephanie Long, prin. — Fax 655-1031

Elder Grove ESD 8 — 300/K-8
1532 S 64th St W 59106 — 406-656-2893
Rob McDonald, supt. — Fax 651-4346
Elder Grove MS — 100/7-8
1532 S 64th St W 59106 — 406-656-2893
Monica Pugh, prin. — Fax 651-1987

Elysian ESD 23 — 100/PK-8
6416 Elysian Rd 59101 — 406-656-4101
Fax 656-9941
Elysian MS — 50/7-8
6416 Elysian Rd 59101 — 406-656-4101
Brenda Koch, prin. — Fax 656-9941

Lockwood ESD 26 — 1,200/PK-8
1932 US Highway 87 E 59101 — 406-252-6022
Eileen Johnson, supt. — Fax 259-2502
www.lockwood.k12.mt.us/
Lockwood MS — 400/6-8
1932 US Highway 87 E 59101 — 406-259-0154
Mike Sullivan, prin. — Fax 259-2502

Adelphi Christian Academy — 50/7-12
PO Box 502 59103 — 406-294-9144
Wes Watkins, admin.
Billings Central Catholic HS — 300/9-12
3 Broadwater Ave 59101 — 406-245-6651
Sheldon Hanser, prin. — Fax 259-3124
Billings Christian S — 100/K-12
4525 Grand Ave 59106 — 406-656-9484
Paul Waggoner, prin. — Fax 655-4880
College of Coiffure Art — Post-Sec.
1423 Wyoming Ave 59102 — 406-656-9114
Montana State University - Billings — Post-Sec.
1500 University Dr 59101 — 406-657-2011
MSU Billings College of Technology — Post-Sec.
3803 Central Ave 59102 — 406-656-4445
Rocky Mountain College — Post-Sec.
1511 Poly Dr 59102 — 406-657-1000
Sage Technical Commerical Driving School — Post-Sec.
3044 Hesper Rd 59102 — 800-545-4546
St. Francis Upper S — 200/6-8
205 N 32nd St 59101 — 406-259-5037
Jim Stanton, prin. — Fax 259-7981
St. Vincent's Hospital & Health Center — Post-Sec.
PO Box 35200 59107 — 406-657-7102

Bonner, Missoula, Pop. 1,669
Potomac ESD 11 — 100/PK-8
29750 Potomac Rd 59823 — 406-244-5581
Fax 244-5840
Potomac MS — 50/7-8
29750 Potomac Rd 59823 — 406-244-5581
Roland Dierken, lead tchr. — Fax 244-5840

Boulder, Jefferson, Pop. 1,436
Boulder ESD 7 — 200/PK-8
PO Box 838 59632 — 406-225-3740
Robert Klein, supt. — Fax 225-3289
Boulder MS — 100/7-8
PO Box 838 59632 — 406-225-3316
Steve Schwartz, prin. — Fax 225-9218

Jefferson HSD 1 — 300/9-12
PO Box 838 59632 — 406-225-3740
Robert Klein, supt. — Fax 225-3289
Jefferson HS — 300/9-12
PO Box 838 59632 — 406-225-3317
T.J. Eyer, prin. — Fax 225-3289

Box Elder, Hill
Box Elder SD — 300/PK-12
PO Box 205 59521 — 406-352-4195
Robert Heppner, supt. — Fax 352-3830
Box Elder HS — 100/9-12
PO Box 205 59521 — 406-352-4195
Mark Irvin, prin. — Fax 352-3830
Box Elder MS — 100/7-8
PO Box 205 59521 — 406-352-4195
Mark Irvin, prin. — Fax 352-3830

Rocky Boy SD 87 — 500/PK-12
RR 1 Box 620 59521 — 406-395-4291
Voyd St. Pierre, supt. — Fax 395-4829
Rocky Boy HS — 100/9-12
RR 1 Box 620 59521 — 406-395-4270
Voyd St. Pierre, prin. — Fax 395-4829
Rocky Boy MS — 100/7-8
RR 1 Box 620 59521 — 406-395-4270
Josephine Corcoran, prin. — Fax 395-4829

Stone Child College — Post-Sec.
PO Box 1082 59521 — 406-395-4313

Bozeman, Gallatin, Pop. 33,535
Anderson ESD 41 — 200/PK-8
10040 Cottonwood Rd 59718 — 406-587-1305
Terry Vanderpan, supt. — Fax 587-2501
www.theandersonschool.org/
Anderson MS — 100/7-8
10040 Cottonwood Rd 59718 — 406-587-1305
Terry Vanderpan, prin. — Fax 587-2501

Bozeman SD 7 — 5,200/PK-12
PO Box 520 59771 — 406-522-6001
Dr. Michael Redburn, supt. — Fax 522-6065
www.bozeman.k12.mt.us/
Bozeman HS — 2,000/9-12
205 N 11th Ave 59715 — 406-522-6200
Godfrey Saunders, prin. — Fax 522-6222
Chief Joseph MS — 500/6-8
309 N 11th Ave 59715 — 406-522-6300
Diane Cashell, prin. — Fax 522-6306
Sacajawea MS — 600/6-8
3525 S 3rd Rd 59715 — 406-522-6470
Diana McDonough, prin. — Fax 522-6474

LaMotte ESD 43 — 100/PK-8
841 Bear Canyon Rd 59715 — 406-586-2838
Fax 586-8626
www.lamotteschool.com
LaMotte MS — 50/7-8
841 Bear Canyon Rd 59715 — 406-586-2838
LeeAnn Burke, prin. — Fax 585-8626

Monforton ESD 27 — 100/PK-8
6001 Monforton School Rd 59718 — 406-586-1557
Lynne Scalia, supt. — Fax 587-5049
Monforton MS — 50/7-8
6001 Monforton School Rd 59718 — 406-586-1557
Lynne Scalia, prin. — Fax 587-5049

Academy of Cosmetology — Post-Sec.
133 W Mendenhall St 59715 — 406-587-1265
Headwaters Academy — 50/6-8
418 W Garfield St 59715 — 406-585-9997
Tim McWilliams, hdmstr. — Fax 585-9992
Heritage Christian S — 300/PK-12
4310 Durston Rd 59718 — 406-587-9311
Mathew Henry, admin. — Fax 587-1838
Montana State University - Bozeman — Post-Sec.
103 Culbertson Hall 59715 — 406-994-2452
Mt. Ellis Academy — 100/9-12
3641 Bozeman Trail Rd 59715 — 406-587-5178
Fax 587-5170
Petra Academy — 100/K-12
100 S Discovery Dr Ste 101 59718 — 406-582-8165
Louise Turner, prin. — Fax 556-8777

Brady, Pondera
Dutton/Brady SD 28
Supt. — See Dutton
Dutton/Brady MS — 50/5-8
309 2nd Ave NE 59416 — 406-753-2522
James Mepham, prin. — Fax 753-2270

Bridger, Carbon, Pop. 752
Bridger SD 2 — 200/PK-12
PO Box 467 59014 — 406-662-3533
John Ballard, supt. — Fax 662-3076
www.bridger.k12.mt.us
Bridger HS — 100/9-12
PO Box 467 59014 — 406-662-3533
John Ballard, prin. — Fax 662-3076
Bridger MS — 50/7-8
PO Box 467 59014 — 406-662-3588
John Ballard, prin. — Fax 662-3520

Broadus, Powder River, Pop. 445
Broadus SD 79J — 300/PK-12
PO Box 500 59317 — 406-436-2658
Richard Cameron, supt. — Fax 436-2660
Broadus MS — 100/7-8
PO Box 500 59317 — 406-436-2658
Jim Hansen, prin. — Fax 436-2660
Powder River County District HS — 100/9-12
PO Box 500 59317 — 406-436-2658
Jim Hansen, prin. — Fax 436-2660

Broadview, Yellowstone, Pop. 150
Broadview SD 21-J — 200/PK-12
PO Box 147 59015 — 406-667-2337
Rey Busch, supt. — Fax 667-2195
Broadview HS — 50/9-12
PO Box 147 59015 — 406-667-2337
Rey Busch, prin. — Fax 667-2195
Broadview MS — 50/7-8
PO Box 147 59015 — 406-667-2337
Rey Busch, prin. — Fax 667-2195

Brockton, Roosevelt, Pop. 243
Brockton SD 55 — 200/PK-12
PO Box 198 59213 — 406-786-3195
Dr. Robert Smith, supt. — Fax 786-3121
www.brockton.k12.mt.us/

Brockton HS 100/9-12
PO Box 198 59213 406-786-3311
Dr. Robert Smith, prin. Fax 786-3377
Gilligan MS 50/7-8
PO Box 198 59213 406-786-3311
Dr. Robert Smith, prin. Fax 786-3377

Browning, Glacier, Pop. 1,078
Browning SD 9 1,900/PK-12
PO Box 610 59417 406-338-2715
Mary Johnson, supt. Fax 338-3200
www.bps.k12.mt.us/
Browning HS 600/9-12
PO Box 610 59417 406-338-2745
Janet Guardipee, prin. Fax 338-2844
Other Schools – See Cut Bank

Blackfeet Community College Post-Sec.
PO Box 819 59417 406-338-5441

Butte, Silver Bow, Pop. 32,716
Butte SD 1 4,600/PK-12
111 N Montana St 59701 406-533-2500
Chuck Uggetti, supt. Fax 533-2525
www.butte.k12.mt.us
Butte HS 1,500/9-12
401 S Wyoming St 59701 406-533-2200
John Metz, prin. Fax 533-2220
East MS 800/7-8
2600 Grand Ave 59701 406-533-2600
Larry Driscoll, prin. Fax 496-2670

Butte Academy of Beauty Culture Post-Sec.
303 W Park St 59701 406-723-8565
Butte Central Catholic HS 200/9-12
9 S Idaho St 59701 406-782-6761
Tim Norbeck, prin. Fax 723-3873
Montana Tech College of Technology Post-Sec.
25 Basin Creek Rd 59701 406-496-3701
Montana Tech of the University of MT Post-Sec.
1300 W Park St 59701 406-496-4101

Cascade, Cascade, Pop. 798
Cascade SD 400/PK-12
PO Box 529 59421 406-468-9383
June Sprout, supt. Fax 468-2212
www.cascade.k12.mt.us
Cascade HS 100/9-12
PO Box 529 59421 406-468-2267
Dave Marzolf, prin. Fax 468-2212
Cascade MS 100/7-8
PO Box 529 59421 406-468-2267
Dave Marzolf, prin. Fax 468-2212

Charlo, Lake, Pop. 358
Charlo SD 7-J 400/PK-12
PO Box 10 59824 406-644-2207
Wes Young, supt. Fax 644-2400
www.charlo.k12.mt.us/
Charlo HS 100/9-12
PO Box 10 59824 406-644-2206
Steve Love, prin. Fax 644-2400
Charlo MS 100/7-8
PO Box 10 59824 406-644-2206
Clair Rasmussen, prin. Fax 644-2401

Chester, Liberty, Pop. 811
Chester-Joplin-Inverness SD 300/PK-12
PO Box 550 59522 406-759-5108
Glen Johnson, supt. Fax 759-5867
Chester-Joplin-Inverness HS 100/9-12
PO Box 550 59522 406-759-5108
Pam Graff, prin. Fax 759-5867
Chester-Joplin-Inverness MS 50/7-8
PO Box 550 59522 406-759-5108
Pam Graff, prin. Fax 759-5867

Chinook, Blaine, Pop. 1,299
Chinook SD 10 400/PK-12
PO Box 1059 59523 406-357-2628
Jay Eslick, supt. Fax 357-2238
Chinook HS 100/9-12
PO Box 1059 59523 406-357-2236
Matt Molyneaux, prin. Fax 357-2238
Chinook MS 100/7-8
PO Box 1059 59523 406-357-2237
Matt Molyneaux, prin. Fax 357-2238

Choteau, Teton, Pop. 1,738
Choteau SD 1 500/PK-12
204 7th Ave NW 59422 406-466-5303
Kent Kultgen, supt. Fax 466-5305
Choteau HS 200/9-12
204 7th Ave NW 59422 406-466-5303
Neal Wedum, prin. Fax 466-5305
Choteau MS 100/7-8
204 7th Ave NW 59422 406-466-5303
Neal Wedum, prin. Fax 466-5305

Circle, McCone, Pop. 584
Circle SD 1 200/K-12
PO Box 99 59215 406-485-2545
Mike Radakovich, supt. Fax 485-2332
Circle HS 100/9-12
PO Box 99 59215 406-485-3600
Ken Larson, prin. Fax 485-2332
Redwater MS 50/7-8
PO Box 99 59215 406-485-2140
Ken Larson, prin. Fax 485-2332

Clancy, Jefferson
Clancy ESD 1 300/PK-8
PO Box 209 59634 406-933-5575
Robert Klein, supt. Fax 933-5715
www.clancy.k12.mt.us/
Clancy MS 100/7-8
PO Box 209 59634 406-933-5575
Bruce Dunkle, prin. Fax 933-5715

Montana City ESD 27 400/PK-8
11 McClellan Creek Rd 59634 406-442-6779
Tony Kloker, supt. Fax 443-8875
Montana City MS 100/6-8
11 McClellan Creek Rd 59634 406-442-6779
Kathy Kidder, prin. Fax 443-8875

Clinton, Missoula
Clinton ESD 32 200/K-8
PO Box 250 59825 406-825-3113
Mark Latrielle, supt. Fax 825-3114
Clinton MS 50/7-8
PO Box 250 59825 406-825-3113
Eric McBride, prin. Fax 825-3114

Clyde Park, Park, Pop. 348
Shields Valley SD
Supt. — See Wilsall
Shields Valley HS 100/9-12
405 1st St E 59018 406-686-4621
Michael Todryk, prin. Fax 686-4937

Colstrip, Rosebud, Pop. 2,331
Colstrip SD 19 700/PK-12
PO Box 159 59323 406-748-4699
Harry Cheff, supt. Fax 748-2268
www.colstrip.k12.mt.us/
Brattin MS 200/6-8
PO Box 159 59323 406-748-4699
Dinny Bennett, prin. Fax 748-3143
Colstrip HS 200/9-12
PO Box 159 59323 406-748-4699
Dennis Davenport, prin. Fax 748-2517

Columbia Falls, Flathead, Pop. 4,440
Columbia Falls SD 6 2,500/PK-12
PO Box 1259 59912 406-892-6550
Michael Nicosia, supt. Fax 892-6552
www.sd6.k12.mt.us
Columbia Falls HS 900/9-12
PO Box 1259 59912 406-892-6500
Terri Burghardt, prin. Fax 892-6583
Columbia Falls JHS 400/7-8
PO Box 1259 59912 406-892-6530
Dave Wick, prin. Fax 892-6528

Deer Park ESD 2 100/PK-8
2105 Middle Rd 59912 406-892-5388
Fax 892-3504
Deer Park MS 50/7-8
2105 Middle Rd 59912 406-892-5388
Dennis Haverlandt, prin. Fax 892-3504

Columbus, Stillwater, Pop. 1,897
Columbus SD 6 600/PK-12
433 N 3rd St 59019 406-322-5373
Allan Sipes, supt. Fax 322-5028
www.columbus.k12.mt.us/
Columbus HS 200/9-12
433 N 3rd St 59019 406-322-5373
George McKay, prin. Fax 322-5028
Columbus MS 200/6-8
415 N 3rd St 59019 406-322-5375
Ron Osborne, prin. Fax 322-5376

Condon, Missoula
Swan Valley ESD 33 50/PK-8
6423 MT Highway 83 59826 406-754-2320
Fax 754-2627
Swan Valley MS 50/7-8
6423 MT Highway 83 59826 406-754-2320
Shirley Webb, prin. Fax 754-2627

Conrad, Pondera, Pop. 2,600
Conrad SD 10 600/PK-12
215 S Maryland St 59425 406-278-5521
Lynn Utterback, supt. Fax 278-3630
www.montana.com/conrad/
Conrad HS 200/9-12
308 S Illinois St 59425 406-278-3285
Paul Stenerson, prin. Fax 278-3806
Utterback MS 100/7-8
24 2nd Ave SW 59425 406-278-3227
Craig Barringer, prin. Fax 271-2680

Corvallis, Ravalli
Corvallis SD 1 1,400/PK-12
PO Box 700 59828 406-961-4211
Daniel Sybrant, supt. Fax 961-5144
www.corvallis.k12.mt.us
Corvallis HS 500/9-12
PO Box 700 59828 406-961-3201
Trevor Laboski, prin. Fax 961-4894
Corvallis JHS 300/7-8
PO Box 700 59828 406-961-3007
Thomas Miller, prin. Fax 961-5144

Crow Agency, Big Horn, Pop. 1,446

Little Big Horn College 59022 Post-Sec.
406-638-3104

Culbertson, Roosevelt, Pop. 714
Culbertson SD 200/PK-12
PO Box 459 59218 406-787-6246
Larry Crowder, supt. Fax 787-6244
culbertsonschool.k12.mt.us
Culbertson HS 100/9-12
PO Box 459 59218 406-787-6241
Jerry Waagen, prin. Fax 787-6244
Culbertson MS 50/7-8
PO Box 459 59218 406-787-6241
Jerry Waagen, prin. Fax 787-6244

Custer, Yellowstone
Custer SD 15 100/K-12
PO Box 69 59024 406-856-4117
Andrew Veis, supt. Fax 856-4206
Custer HS 50/9-12
PO Box 69 59024 406-856-4117
Garret Franks, prin. Fax 856-4206

Custer MS 50/7-8
PO Box 69 59024 406-856-4117
Andrew Veis, prin. Fax 856-4206

Cut Bank, Glacier, Pop. 3,167
Browning SD 9
Supt. — See Browning
Browning MS 300/7-8
DelBonita Rd 59427 406-338-2725
Julie Hayes, prin. Fax 338-5320

Cut Bank SD 15 800/PK-12
101 3rd Ave SE 59427 406-873-2229
Wade Johnson, supt. Fax 873-4691
www.cutbank.k12.mt.us
Cut Bank HS 300/9-12
101 3rd Ave SE 59427 406-873-5629
Eric Christanot, prin. Fax 873-4691
Cut Bank JHS 100/7-8
101 3rd Ave SE 59427 406-873-4421
Don Paulson, prin. Fax 873-4691

Darby, Ravalli, Pop. 835
Darby SD 9 500/PK-12
209 School Dr 59829 406-821-3841
Bruce Wallace, supt. Fax 821-4977
www.darby.k12.mt.us/
Darby HS 200/9-12
209 School Dr 59829 406-821-3252
Dan Peters, prin. Fax 821-4904
Darby MS 100/7-8
209 School Dr 59829 406-821-3252
Dan Peters, prin. Fax 821-4904

Deer Lodge, Powell, Pop. 3,313
Deer Lodge ESD 1 500/PK-8
444 Montana Ave 59722 406-846-1553
Tom Cotton, supt. Fax 846-1599
Duvall MS 100/7-8
444 Montana Ave 59722 406-846-1684
Rick Chrisman, prin. Fax 846-1599

Powell County HSD 300/9-12
709 Missouri Ave 59722 406-846-2757
Rick Duncan, supt. Fax 846-2759
pchs.dl.k12.mt.us
Powell County HS 300/9-12
709 Missouri Ave 59722 406-846-2757
Terry Mosier, prin. Fax 846-2759

Denton, Fergus, Pop. 288
Denton SD 84 100/PK-12
PO Box 1048 59430 406-567-2370
Bill Phillips, supt. Fax 567-2559
Denton HS 100/9-12
PO Box 1048 59430 406-567-2370
Bill Phillips, prin. Fax 567-2559
Denton JHS 50/7-8
PO Box 1048 59430 406-567-2370
Bill Phillips, prin. 406-567-2559

Dillon, Beaverhead, Pop. 3,988
Beaverhead County HSD 400/9-12
104 N Pacific St 59725 406-683-2361
Fred Chouinard, supt. Fax 683-5263
Beaverhead County HS 400/9-12
104 N Pacific St 59725 406-683-2361
Gary Haverfield, prin. Fax 683-5263

Dillon ESD 10 700/PK-8
225 E Reeder St 59725 406-683-4311
Melinda Berkram, supt. Fax 683-4312
www.dillonelem.k12.mt.us/
Dillon MS 200/6-8
14 Cottom Dr 59725 406-683-2368
Randy Shipman, prin. Fax 683-2369

University of Montana - Western Post-Sec.
710 S Atlantic St 59725 406-683-7011

Dixon, Sanders
Dixon ESD 9 100/PK-8
PO Box 10 59831 406-246-3566
Fax 246-3379
Dixon MS 50/7-8
PO Box 10 59831 406-246-3566
Mark Faroni, prin. Fax 246-3379

Dodson, Phillips, Pop. 110
Dodson SD 100/PK-12
PO Box 278 59524 406-383-4362
Les Wells, supt. Fax 383-4489
Dodson HS 50/9-12
PO Box 278 59524 406-383-4362
Les Wells, prin. Fax 383-4489
Dodson MS 50/7-8
PO Box 278 59524 406-383-4362
Les Wells, prin. Fax 383-4489

Drummond, Granite, Pop. 332
Drummond SD 200/PK-12
PO Box 349 59832 406-288-3281
Paula Johnston, supt. Fax 288-3299
Drummond HS 100/9-12
PO Box 349 59832 406-288-3281
Kitty Logan, prin. Fax 288-3299
Drummond MS 50/7-8
PO Box 349 59832 406-288-3283
Kitty Logan, prin. Fax 288-3299

Dutton, Teton, Pop. 372
Dutton/Brady SD 28 100/PK-12
101 2nd St NE 59433 406-476-3424
Tim Tharp, supt. Fax 476-3342
Dutton/Brady HS 50/9-12
101 2nd St NE 59433 406-476-3424
Tim Tharp, prin. Fax 476-3342
Other Schools – See Brady

East Helena, Lewis and Clark, Pop. 1,848
East Helena ESD 9 — 1,100/PK-8
PO Box 1280 59635 — 406-227-7700
Ron Whitmoyer, supt. — Fax 227-5534
www.ehps.k12.mt.us
East Valley MS — 400/6-8
PO Box 1280 59635 — 406-227-7740
Dan Rispens, prin. — Fax 227-9730

Ekalaka, Carter, Pop. 395
Carter County HSD — 100/9-12
PO Box 458 59324 — 406-775-8767
Wade Northrop, supt. — Fax 775-8766
Carter County HS — 100/9-12
PO Box 458 59324 — 406-775-8767
Wade Northrop, prin. — Fax 775-8766

Ekalaka ESD 15 — 100/PK-8
PO Box 458 59324 — 406-775-8767
Wade Northrop, supt. — Fax 775-8766
Ekalaka MS — 50/7-8
PO Box 458 59324 — 406-775-8767
Wade Northrop, prin. — Fax 775-8766

Ennis, Madison, Pop. 973
Ennis SD 52 — 400/PK-12
PO Box 517 59729 — 406-682-4258
Douglas Walsh, supt. — Fax 682-7751
Ennis HS — 100/9-12
PO Box 517 59729 — 406-682-4258
Greg Fitzgerald, prin. — Fax 682-7751
Ennis MS — 50/7-8
PO Box 517 59729 — 406-682-4237
Brian Hilton, prin. — Fax 682-7751

Eureka, Lincoln, Pop. 1,028
Eureka SD — 900/PK-12
PO Box 2000 59917 — 406-297-5637
Gary Blaz, supt. — Fax 297-2644
www.eureka.k12.mt.us/
Eureka MS — 100/7-8
PO Box 2000 59917 — 406-297-5600
Trevor Utter, prin. — Fax 297-5653
Lincoln County HS — 400/9-12
PO Box 2000 59917 — 406-297-5700
Alan Robbins, prin. — Fax 297-5714

Fairfield, Teton, Pop. 635
Fairfield SD 21 — 400/PK-12
PO Box 399 59436 — 406-467-2103
Dennis Davis, supt. — Fax 467-2554
www.fairfield.k12.mt.us/
Fairfield HS — 200/9-12
PO Box 399 59436 — 406-467-2528
Les Meyer, prin. — Fax 467-2554
Fairfield MS — 50/7-8
PO Box 399 59436 — 406-467-2425
Les Meyer, prin. — Fax 467-2554

Greenfield ESD 75 — 100/PK-8
590 Mt Highway 431 59436 — 406-467-2433
Fax 467-3138
Greenfield MS — 50/7-8
590 Mt Highway 431 59436 — 406-467-2433
Loren Sasser, prin. — Fax 467-3138

Fairview, Richland, Pop. 666
Fairview SD — 200/PK-12
PO Box 467 59221 — 406-742-5265
Matt Schriver, supt. — Fax 742-3336
www.fairview.k12.mt.us/
Fairview HS — 100/9-12
PO Box 467 59221 — 406-742-5265
Luke Kloker, prin. — Fax 742-8265
Fairview MS — 50/7-8
PO Box 467 59221 — 406-742-5265
Luke Kloker, prin. — Fax 742-8265

Florence, Ravalli
Florence-Carlton SD 15-6 — 900/PK-12
5602 Old US Highway 93 59833 — 406-273-6751
John McGee, supt. — Fax 273-2802
www.florence.k12.mt.us
Florence-Carlton HS — 300/9-12
5602 Old US Highway 93 59833 — 406-273-6301
Rebecca Stapert, prin. — Fax 273-2643
Florence-Carlton MS — 200/7-8
5602 Old US Highway 93 59833 — 406-273-0587
Ed Norman, prin. — Fax 273-0545

Forsyth, Rosebud, Pop. 1,888
Forsyth SD 4 — 400/PK-12
PO Box 319 59327 — 406-346-2796
David Shreeve, supt. — Fax 346-7455
Forsyth HS — 100/9-12
PO Box 319 59327 — 406-346-2796
Doug Roberts, prin. — Fax 346-9219
Forsyth MS — 100/7-8
PO Box 319 59327 — 406-346-2796
Doug Roberts, prin. — Fax 346-9219

Fort Benton, Chouteau, Pop. 1,475
Ft. Benton SD 1 — 400/PK-12
PO Box 399 59442 — 406-622-5691
Robert Anderson, supt. — Fax 622-5691
www.fortbenton.k12.mt.us/
Fort Benton HS — 100/9-12
PO Box 399 59442 — 406-622-3213
Jim Howard, prin. — Fax 622-5691
Fort Benton JHS — 100/7-8
PO Box 399 59442 — 406-622-3213
Jim Howard, prin. — Fax 622-5691

Frazer, Valley, Pop. 403
Frazer SD 2 — 100/K-12
PO Box 488 59225 — 406-695-2241
Richard Whitesell, supt. — Fax 695-2243
Frazer HS — 100/9-12
PO Box 488 59225 — 406-695-2241
Richard Whitesell, prin. — Fax 695-2243
Frazer MS — 50/7-8
PO Box 488 59225 — 406-695-2241
Richard Whitesell, prin. — Fax 695-2243

Lustre Christian HS — 50/9-12
HC 66 Box 57 59225 — 406-392-5735
Al Leland, lead tchr. — Fax 392-5765

Frenchtown, Missoula
Frenchtown SD 40 — 1,200/PK-12
PO Box 117 59834 — 406-626-2600
Randy Cline, supt. — Fax 626-2605
www.frenchtown.k12.mt.us
Frenchtown HS — 400/9-12
PO Box 117 59834 — 406-626-2670
Rory Weishaar, prin. — Fax 626-2676
Frenchtown MS — 200/7-8
PO Box 117 59834 — 406-626-2650
Jon Fimmel, prin. — Fax 626-2605

Froid, Roosevelt, Pop. 191
Froid SD — 100/K-12
PO Box 218 59226 — 406-766-2343
Roger Britton, supt. — Fax 766-2206
Froid HS — 50/9-12
PO Box 218 59226 — 406-766-2342
Roger Britton, prin. — Fax 766-2206
Froid MS — 50/7-8
PO Box 218 59226 — 406-766-2342
Roger Britton, prin. — Fax 766-2206

Fromberg, Carbon, Pop. 492
Fromberg SD 30 — 200/PK-12
PO Box 189 59029 — 406-668-7611
Randy Durr, supt. — Fax 668-7669
Fromberg HS — 100/9-12
PO Box 189 59029 — 406-668-7315
Randy Durr, prin. — Fax 668-7669
Fromberg MS — 50/7-8
PO Box 189 59029 — 406-668-7315
Randy Durr, prin. — Fax 668-7669

Gallatin Gateway, Gallatin
Gallatin Gateway ESD 35 — 100/PK-8
PO Box 265 59730 — 406-763-4415
Kim DeBruycker, supt. — Fax 763-4886
Gallatin Gateway MS — 50/7-8
PO Box 265 59730 — 406-763-4415
Kim DeBruycker, prin. — Fax 763-4886

Ophir ESD 72 — 100/PK-8
45465 Gallatin Rd 59730 — 406-995-4281
AnneMarie Mistretta, supt. — Fax 995-2161
Ophir MS — 50/7-8
45465 Gallatin Rd 59730 — 406-995-4281
AnneMarie Mistretta, prin. — Fax 995-2161

Gardiner, Park
Gardiner SD — 200/PK-12
510 Stone St 59030 — 406-848-7261
Leland Stocker, supt. — Fax 848-9489
Gardiner HS — 100/9-12
510 Stone St 59030 — 406-848-7261
Ken Ballagh, prin. — Fax 848-9489
Gardiner MS — 50/7-8
510 Stone St 59030 — 406-848-7563
Ken Ballagh, prin. — Fax 848-9489

Geraldine, Chouteau, Pop. 258
Geraldine SD — 100/PK-12
PO Box 347 59446 — 406-737-4311
Rodney Simpson, supt. — Fax 737-4478
Geraldine HS — 50/9-12
PO Box 347 59446 — 406-737-4371
Rodney Simpson, prin. — Fax 737-4478
Geraldine MS — 50/7-8
PO Box 347 59446 — 406-737-4371
Rodney Simpson, prin. — Fax 737-4478

Geyser, Judith Basin
Geyser SD 58 — 100/PK-12
PO Box 70 59447 — 406-735-4368
Tobin Novasio, supt. — Fax 735-4452
Geyser HS — 50/9-12
PO Box 70 59447 — 406-735-4368
Tobin Novasio, prin. — Fax 735-4452
Geyser MS — 50/7-8
PO Box 70 59447 — 406-735-4368
Tobin Novasio, prin. — Fax 735-4452

Glasgow, Valley, Pop. 3,018
Glasgow SD 1-A — 800/PK-12
PO Box 28 59230 — 406-228-2406
Glenn Hageman, supt. — Fax 228-2407
www.glasgow.k12.mt.us/
Glasgow HS — 200/9-12
PO Box 28 59230 — 406-228-2485
Margaret Markle, prin. — Fax 228-4061
Glasgow MS — 100/7-8
PO Box 28 59230 — 406-228-2485
Margaret Markle, prin. — Fax 228-4061

Glendive, Dawson, Pop. 4,670
Glendive SD — 1,200/PK-12
PO Box 701 59330 — 406-377-5293
Jim Germann, supt. — Fax 377-6212
Dawson County HS — 400/9-12
PO Box 701 59330 — 406-377-5265
Bruce Clausen, prin. — Fax 377-8206
Washington MS — 400/5-8
PO Box 701 59330 — 406-377-2356
Ross Farber, prin. — Fax 377-2357

Dawson Community College — Post-Sec.
PO Box 421 59330 — 406-377-3396

Grass Range, Fergus, Pop. 145
Grass Range SD 27 — 100/PK-12
PO Box 58 59032 — 406-428-2122
Debbie Combs, supt. — Fax 428-2235
Grass Range HS — 50/9-12
PO Box 58 59032 — 406-428-2341
Debbie Combs, prin. — Fax 428-2235
Grass Range MS — 50/7-8
PO Box 58 59032 — 406-428-2122
Debbie Combs, prin. — Fax 428-2235

Great Falls, Cascade, Pop. 56,338
Great Falls SD 1 — 9,400/PK-12
PO Box 2429 59403 — 406-268-6001
Dr. W. Bryan Dunn, supt. — Fax 268-6002
www.gfps.k12.mt.us
East MS — 600/7-8
4040 Central Ave 59405 — 406-268-6500
Shelly Fagenstrom, prin. — Fax 268-6524
Great Falls HS — 1,900/9-12
1900 2nd Ave S 59405 — 406-268-6250
Fred Anderson, prin. — Fax 268-6256
North MS — 600/7-8
2601 8th St NE 59404 — 406-268-6525
Tom Maguire, prin. — Fax 268-6575
Russell HS — 1,600/9-12
228 17th Ave NW 59404 — 406-268-6100
Dick Kloppel, prin. — Fax 268-6109

Benefits Health Care-West Campus — Post-Sec.
PO Box 5013 59403 — 406-727-3333
Dahl's College of Beauty — Post-Sec.
718 Central Ave 59401 — 406-454-3453
Foothills Community Christian S — 200/PK-12
2210 5th Ave N 59401 — 406-452-5276
Ted Clark, admin. — Fax 452-8606
Great Falls Central Catholic HS — 100/9-12
121 23rd St S 59401 — 406-791-5940
Hugh Smith, prin. — Fax 454-5942
Montana School for the Deaf and Blind — Post-Sec.
3911 Central Ave 59405 — 406-771-6000
Montana State Univ Great Falls College — Post-Sec.
2100 16th Ave S 59405 — 406-771-4300
University of Great Falls — Post-Sec.
1301 20th St S 59405 — 406-761-8210

Hamilton, Ravalli, Pop. 4,443
Hamilton SD 3 — 1,600/PK-12
217 Daly Ave 59840 — 406-363-2280
John Matt, supt. — Fax 363-1843
www.hsd3.org
Hamilton HS — 500/9-12
327 Fairgrounds Rd 59840 — 406-375-6060
Kevin Conwell, prin. — Fax 375-6076
Hamilton MS — 400/6-8
209 S 5th St 59840 — 406-363-2121
Barbara Solomon, prin. — Fax 363-7032

Hardin, Big Horn, Pop. 3,510
Hardin SD 17-H — 1,600/PK-12
RR 1 Box 1001 59034 — 406-665-1304
Albert Peterson, supt. — Fax 665-2784
www.hardin.k12.mt.us
Hardin HS — 500/9-12
702 N Terry Ave 59034 — 406-665-6300
Keith Campbell, prin. — Fax 665-1909
Hardin MS — 400/6-8
611 5th St W 59034 — 406-665-6350
Don Gilbertson, prin. — Fax 665-1409

Harlem, Blaine, Pop. 806
Harlem SD 12 — 600/PK-12
PO Box 339 59526 — 406-353-2289
Neil Terhune, supt. — Fax 353-2674
Harlem HS — 200/9-12
PO Box 339 59526 — 406-353-2287
Terry Bolen, prin. — Fax 353-2339
Harlem MS — 100/7-8
PO Box 339 59526 — 406-353-2287
Terry Bolen, prin. — Fax 353-2339

Fort Belknap College — Post-Sec.
PO Box 159 59526 — 406-353-2607

Harlowton, Wheatland, Pop. 941
Harlowton SD 16 — 300/PK-12
PO Box 288 59036 — 406-632-4822
Andrew Begger, supt. — Fax 632-4416
Harlowton HS — 100/9-12
PO Box 288 59036 — 406-632-4324
Gregg Wasson, prin. — Fax 632-4416
Hillcrest MS — 50/7-8
PO Box 288 59036 — 406-632-4361
Gregg Wasson, prin. — Fax 632-4416

Harrison, Madison
Harrison SD 23 — 100/PK-12
PO Box 7 59735 — 406-685-3471
Darren Strauch, supt. — Fax 685-3430
Harrison HS — 50/9-12
PO Box 7 59735 — 406-685-3471
Darren Strauch, prin. — Fax 685-3430
Harrison MS — 50/7-8
PO Box 7 59735 — 406-685-3471
Darren Strauch, prin. — Fax 685-3430

Havre, Hill, Pop. 9,390
Havre SD — 1,900/PK-12
PO Box 7791 59501 — 406-265-4356
Kirk Miller, supt. — Fax 265-8460
www.havre.k12.mt.us/
Havre HS — 700/9-12
PO Box 7791 59501 — 406-265-6731
Jim Donovan, prin. — Fax 265-3217
Havre MS — 400/6-8
1441 11th St W 59501 — 406-265-9613
Vance Blatter, prin. — Fax 265-4414

Montana State University Northern — Post-Sec.
PO Box 7751 59501 — 406-265-3700

Hays, Blaine, Pop. 333
Hays-Lodge Pole SD 50 200/PK-12
PO Box 110 59527 406-673-3120
Dwain Haggard, supt. Fax 673-3294
Hays-Lodge Pole HS 100/9-12
PO Box 110 59527 406-673-3120
Amy Snow, prin. Fax 673-3415
Hays-Lodge Pole MS 100/7-8
PO Box 110 59527 406-673-3120
Norma King, prin. Fax 673-3415

Heart Butte, Pondera, Pop. 499
Heart Butte SD 1 200/PK-12
PO Box 259 59448 406-338-3344
Richard Richardson, supt. Fax 338-2088
Heart Butte HS 100/9-12
PO Box 259 59448 406-338-3344
Lori Falcon, prin. Fax 338-5832
Heart Butte MS 50/7-8
PO Box 259 59448 406-338-2200
Lori Falcon, prin. Fax 338-5832

Helena, Lewis and Clark, Pop. 27,383
Helena SD 1 8,000/K-12
55 S Rodney St 59601 406-324-2001
Dr. Bruce Messinger, supt. Fax 324-2035
www.helena.k12.mt.us/
Anderson MS 1,000/6-8
1200 Knight St 59601 406-324-2800
Bruce Campbell, prin. Fax 324-2801
Capital HS 1,400/9-12
100 Valley Dr 59601 406-324-2500
Randy Carlson, prin. Fax 324-2501
Helena HS 1,600/9-12
1300 Billings Ave 59601 406-324-2200
Greg Upham, prin. Fax 324-2201
Helena MS 800/6-8
1025 N Rodney St 59601 406-324-1000
Tom Lipp, prin. Fax 324-1001

Carroll College Post-Sec.
1601 N Benton Ave 59625 406-447-4300
Helena Christian S 100/K-12
1421 N Roberts St 59601 406-442-3821
Ray Fuller, supt. Fax 442-3821
Helena College of Tech of the Univ of MT Post-Sec.
1115 N Roberts St 59601 406-444-6800

Highwood, Chouteau
Highwood SD 100/PK-12
160 West St S 59450 406-733-2081
Tim Bronk, supt. Fax 733-2671
Highwood HS 50/9-12
160 West St S 59450 406-733-2081
Tim Bronk, prin. Fax 733-2671
Highwood MS 50/6-8
160 West St S 59450 406-733-2081
Tim Bronk, prin. Fax 733-2671

Hinsdale, Valley
Hinsdale SD 100/PK-12
PO Box 398 59241 406-364-2314
Stephen Henderson, supt. Fax 364-2205
Hinsdale HS 50/9-12
PO Box 398 59241 406-364-2314
Stephen Henderson, prin. Fax 364-2205
Hinsdale MS 50/7-8
PO Box 398 59241 406-364-2314
Don Johnson, prin. Fax 364-2205

Hobson, Judith Basin, Pop. 231
Hobson SD 25 100/PK-12
PO Box 410 59452 406-423-5483
Wesley Coy, supt. Fax 423-5260
www.hobson.k12.mt.us/
Hobson HS 50/9-12
PO Box 410 59452 406-423-5483
Linda Deegan, prin. Fax 423-5260
Hobson MS 50/7-8
PO Box 410 59452 406-423-5483
Linda Deegan, prin. Fax 423-5260

Hot Springs, Sanders, Pop. 565
Hot Springs SD 14J 200/PK-12
PO Box 1005 59845 406-741-3285
Larry Markuson, supt. Fax 741-3287
Hot Springs HS 100/9-12
PO Box 1005 59845 406-741-2962
Larry Markuson, prin. Fax 741-3287
Hot Springs MS 50/7-8
PO Box 1005 59845 406-741-2962
Larry Markuson, prin. Fax 741-3287

Hysham, Treasure, Pop. 262
Hysham SD 1 100/PK-12
PO Box 272 59038 406-342-5237
Larry Fink, supt. Fax 342-5257
www.hysham.k12.mt.us/
Hysham HS 50/9-12
PO Box 272 59038 406-342-5237
Larry Fink, prin. Fax 342-5257
Hysham MS 50/7-8
PO Box 272 59038 406-342-5237
Larry Fink, prin. Fax 342-5257

Joliet, Carbon, Pop. 601
Joliet SD 7 400/PK-12
PO Box 590 59041 406-962-2200
Les Cabot, supt. Fax 962-3958
Joliet HS 100/9-12
PO Box 590 59041 406-962-3541
Marilyn Vukonich, prin. Fax 962-3958
Joliet MS 100/7-8
PO Box 590 59041 406-962-3541
Marilyn Vukonich, prin. Fax 962-3958

Jordan, Garfield, Pop. 339
Jordan SD 1 200/PK-12
PO Box 409 59337 406-557-2259
Jennifer O'Connor, supt. Fax 557-2778
Garfield County HS 100/9-12
PO Box 409 59337 406-557-2259
Jennifer O'Connor, prin. Fax 557-2778
Jordan MS 50/7-8
PO Box 409 59337 406-557-2259
Jennifer O'Connor, prin. Fax 557-2778

Judith Gap, Wheatland, Pop. 145
Judith Gap SD 21J 100/PK-12
PO Box 67 59453 406-473-2211
Don Amundson, supt. Fax 473-2250
Judith Gap HS 50/9-12
PO Box 67 59453 406-473-2211
Don Amundson, prin. Fax 473-2250
Judith Gap MS 50/7-8
PO Box 67 59453 406-473-2211
Don Amundson, prin. Fax 473-2250

Kalispell, Flathead, Pop. 18,480
Cayuse Prairie ESD 10 200/K-8
897 Lake Blaine Rd 59901 406-756-4560
Fax 756-4570
Cayuse Prairie MS 50/7-8
897 Lake Blaine Rd 59901 406-756-4560
Rick Nadeau, prin. Fax 756-4570
Evergreen ESD 50 800/PK-8
18 W Evergreen Dr 59901 406-751-1111
Joel Voytoski, supt. Fax 752-2307
Evergreen JHS 200/7-8
20 W Evergreen Dr 59901 406-751-1131
Kim Anderson, prin. Fax 751-1134
Fair-Mont-Egan ESD 3 100/PK-8
797 Fairmont Rd 59901 406-755-7072
Fax 755-7077
Fair-Mont-Egan MS 50/7-8
797 Fairmont Rd 59901 406-755-7072
Christine Anthony, prin. Fax 755-7077
Helena Flats ESD 15 200/K-8
1000 Helena Flats Rd 59901 406-257-2301
Paul Jenkins, supt. Fax 257-2304
Helena Flats MS 50/7-8
1000 Helena Flats Rd 59901 406-257-2301
Paul Jenkins, prin. Fax 257-2304
Kalispell SD 5 4,400/PK-12
233 1st Ave E 59901 406-751-3434
Dr. Darlene Schottle, supt. Fax 751-3416
www.sd5.k12.mt.us
Flathead SHS 1,800/10-12
644 4th Ave W 59901 406-751-3500
Callie Langohr, prin. Fax 751-3505
Kalispell JHS 300/8-9
205 Northwest Ln 59901 406-751-3800
Barry Grace, prin. Fax 751-3805
Smith Valley ESD 89 200/PK-8
2901 US Highway 2 W 59901 406-756-4535
Fax 756-4534
Smith Valley MS 50/7-8
2901 US Highway 2 W 59901 406-756-4535
Harold Welling, prin. Fax 756-4534
West Valley ESD 1 400/PK-8
2290 Farm To Market Rd 59901 406-755-7239
Todd Fiske, supt. Fax 755-7300
West Valley MS 100/6-8
2290 Farm to Market Rd 59901 406-755-7239
Todd Fiske, prin. Fax 755-7300

Flathead Valley Community College Post-Sec.
777 Grandview Dr 59901 406-756-3822
Stillwater Christian S 300/K-12
255 FFA Dr 59901 406-752-4400
Daniel Makowski, supt. Fax 755-4061

Kila, Flathead
Kila ESD 20 100/PK-8
PO Box 40 59920 406-257-2428
Fax 755-6663
Kila MS 50/7-8
PO Box 40 59920 406-257-2428
Renee Boisseau, prin. Fax 755-6663

Lambert, Richland
Lambert SD 100/PK-12
PO Box 260 59243 406-774-3333
Connie Newman, supt. Fax 774-3335
www.midrivers.com/~ihs/
Lambert HS 50/9-12
PO Box 260 59243 406-774-3333
Connie Newman, prin. Fax 774-3335
Lambert MS 50/7-8
PO Box 260 59243 406-774-3333
Connie Newman, prin. Fax 774-3335

Lame Deer, Rosebud, Pop. 1,918
Lame Deer SD 6 500/PK-12
PO Box 96 59043 406-477-6305
Gary Scott, supt. Fax 477-6535
www.lamedeer.k12.mt.us/
Lame Deer HS 100/9-12
PO Box 96 59043 406-477-8900
Larry Ketcham, prin. Fax 477-8906
Lame Deer MS 100/7-8
PO Box 96 59043 406-477-8900
Verna Ivey, prin. Fax 477-8906

Chief Dull Knife College Post-Sec.
PO Box 98 59043 406-477-6215

Laurel, Yellowstone, Pop. 6,342
Laurel SD 7 1,700/PK-12
410 Colorado Ave 59044 406-628-8623
Josh Middleton, supt. Fax 628-8625
www.laurel.k12.mt.us
Laurel HS 600/9-12
203 E 8th St 59044 406-628-7911
Karen Underwood, prin. Fax 628-3558
Laurel MS 400/6-8
410 Colorado Ave 59044 406-628-6919
Linda Filpula, prin. Fax 628-3350

Lavina, Golden Valley, Pop. 236
Lavina SD 2 100/PK-12
PO Box 290 59046 406-636-2143
Loren Osler, supt. Fax 636-4911
Lavina HS 50/9-12
PO Box 290 59046 406-636-2143
Loren Osler, prin. Fax 636-4911
Lavina MS 50/7-8
PO Box 290 59046 406-636-2143
Loren Osler, prin. Fax 636-4911

Lewistown, Fergus, Pop. 6,099
Lewistown SD 1 1,400/PK-12
215 7th Ave S 59457 406-538-8777
Charles Brown, supt. Fax 538-7292
www.lewistown.k12.mt.us
Fergus HS 500/9-12
1001 Casino Creek Dr 59457 406-538-2321
Scott Dubbs, prin. Fax 538-3835
Lewistown MS 200/7-8
914 W Main St 59457 406-538-5419
Pat Hould, prin. Fax 538-2300

Libby, Lincoln, Pop. 2,648
Libby SD 4 1,400/PK-12
724 Louisiana Ave 59923 406-293-8811
K. Maki, supt. Fax 293-8812
www.libby.org/plummer/lps/
Libby HS 600/9-12
150 Education Way 59923 406-293-8802
Rik Rewerts, prin. Fax 293-3927
Libby MS 500/4-8
101 Ski Rd 59923 406-293-2763
Ron Goodman, prin. Fax 293-2862

Kootenai Valley Christian S 100/PK-12
1024 Montana Ave 59923 406-293-2303
Myresa Boulware, admin. Fax 293-2303

Lima, Beaverhead, Pop. 227
Lima SD 12 100/PK-12
PO Box 186 59739 406-276-3571
Tim Dehl, supt. Fax 276-3495
Lima HS 50/9-12
PO Box 186 59739 406-276-3571
Tim Dehl, prin. Fax 276-3495
Lima MS 50/7-8
PO Box 186 59739 406-276-3571
Tim Dehl, prin. Fax 276-3495

Lincoln, Lewis and Clark
Lincoln SD 38 200/PK-12
PO Box 39 59639 406-362-4201
Kathy Heisler, supt. Fax 362-4030
Lincoln HS 100/9-12
PO Box 39 59639 406-362-4201
Carla Anderson, prin. Fax 362-4030
Lincoln MS 50/7-8
PO Box 39 59639 406-362-4201
Carla Anderson, prin. Fax 362-4030

Livingston, Park, Pop. 7,146
Livingston SD 1,500/PK-12
132 S B St 59047 406-222-0861
Andrew Anderson, supt. Fax 222-7323
www.livingston.k12.mt.us
Park HS 600/9-12
102 View Vista Dr 59047 406-222-0448
Eric Messerli, prin. Fax 222-9404
Sleeping Giant MS 300/6-8
301 View Vista Dr 59047 406-222-3292
Tena Versland, prin. Fax 222-3512
Pine Creek ESD 19 50/K-8
2575 E River Rd 59047 406-222-0059
Fax 222-0059
Pine Creek MS 50/7-8
2575 E River Rd 59047 406-222-0059
Leah Shannon-Beye, lead tchr. Fax 222-0059

Lodge Grass, Big Horn, Pop. 522
Lodge Grass SD 27 400/PK-12
PO Box 810 59050 406-639-2304
Doug Woods, supt. Fax 639-2388
www.lodgegrass.k12.mt.us/
Lodge Grass HS 200/9-12
PO Box 810 59050 406-639-2385
John Small, prin. Fax 639-2066
Lodge Grass MS 100/7-8
PO Box 810 59050 406-639-2333
Kenneth Deputee, prin. Fax 639-2388

Lolo, Missoula, Pop. 2,746
Lolo ESD 7 600/PK-8
11395 US Highway 93 S 59847 406-273-0451
Michael Magone, supt. Fax 273-2628
www.lolo.k12.mt.us/
Lolo MS 200/6-8
11395 US Highway 93 S 59847 406-273-6141
Dave Hansen, prin. Fax 273-2628
Woodman ESD 18 50/K-8
18470 Highway 12 W 59847 406-273-6770
Fax 273-6659
Woodman MS 50/7-8
18470 Highway 12 W 59847 406-273-6770
Louise Rhode, prin. Fax 273-6659

Malta, Phillips, Pop. 1,922
Malta SD 600/PK-12
PO Box 670 59538 406-654-1871
Kris Kuehn, supt. Fax 654-2226
www.montanavision.net/~maltahs
Malta HS 200/9-12
South 9th St W 59538 406-654-2002
John Roberts, prin. Fax 654-2226

Malta JHS 100/7-8
South 9th St W 59538 406-654-2225
John Roberts, prin. Fax 654-2226

Manhattan, Gallatin, Pop. 1,465
Manhattan SD 3 600/PK-12
PO Box 425 59741 406-284-6460
Jerry Pease, supt. Fax 284-6853
Manhattan HS 200/9-12
PO Box 425 59741 406-284-3341
Bob Moore, prin. Fax 284-3104
Manhattan MS 100/7-8
PO Box 425 59741 406-284-3250
Scott Schumacher, prin. Fax 284-4122

Manhattan Christian S 400/PK-12
8000 Churchill Rd 59741 406-282-7261
Randall VanDyk, admin. Fax 282-7701

Marion, Flathead
Marion ESD 54 100/PK-8
205 Gopher Ln 59925 406-854-2333
Fax 854-2690
Marion MS 50/7-8
205 Gopher Ln 59925 406-854-2333
Kris Queen, prin. Fax 854-2690

Medicine Lake, Sheridan, Pop. 228
Medicine Lake SD 7 100/PK-12
PO Box 265 59247 406-789-2211
David Kloker, supt. Fax 789-2213
Medicine Lake HS 50/9-12
PO Box 265 59247 406-789-2211
David Kloker, prin. Fax 789-2213
Medicine Lake MS 50/7-8
PO Box 265 59247 406-789-2211
David Kloker, prin. Fax 789-2213

Melstone, Musselshell, Pop. 137
Melstone SD 100/PK-12
PO Box 97 59054 406-358-2352
Chad Johnson, supt. Fax 358-2346
Melstone HS 50/9-12
PO Box 97 59054 406-358-2352
Chad Johnson, prin. Fax 358-2346
Melstone MS 50/7-8
PO Box 97 59054 406-358-2352
Chad Johnson, prin. Fax 358-2346

Miles City, Custer, Pop. 8,162
Miles City SD 1 1,700/PK-12
1604 Main St 59301 406-234-3840
Jack Regan, supt. Fax 234-3147
garfieldweb.com/milescity/
Custer County District HS 600/9-12
20 S Center Ave 59301 406-234-4920
Rick Powell, prin. Fax 234-4923
Washington MS 300/7-8
210 N 9th St 59301 406-234-2084
Jon Plowman, prin. Fax 234-7403

Miles Community College Post-Sec.
2715 Dickinson St 59301 406-234-3031

Missoula, Missoula, Pop. 62,923
Bonner ESD 14 400/PK-8
9045 Highway 200 59802 406-258-6151
Doug Ardiana, supt. Fax 258-6153
www.bonner.k12.mt.us
Bonner MS 100/7-8
9045 Highway 200 59802 406-258-6151
Doug Ardiana, prin. Fax 258-6153

DeSmet ESD 20 100/PK-8
6355 Padre Ln 59808 406-549-4994
Fax 549-4994
DeSmet MS 50/7-8
6355 Padre Ln 59808 406-549-4994
Rose Woodford, prin. Fax 549-4994

Hellgate ESD 4 1,200/PK-8
2385 Flynn Ln 59808 406-728-5626
Dr. Doug Reisig, supt. Fax 728-5636
www.hellgate.k12.mt.us
Hellgate MS 400/6-8
2385 Flynn Ln 59808 406-721-2452
Nancy Singleton, prin. Fax 728-0967

Missoula SD 1 8,900/PK-12
215 S 6th St W 59801 406-728-2400
Jim Clark, supt. Fax 542-4009
www.mcps.k12.mt.us
Big Sky HS 1,400/9-12
3100 South Ave W 59804 406-728-2401
Paul Johnson, prin. Fax 549-4616
Hellgate HS 1,300/9-12
900 S Higgins Ave 59801 406-728-2402
Jane Bennett, prin. Fax 728-2496
Meadow Hill MS 500/6-8
4210 S Reserve St 59803 406-542-4045
Nick Carter, prin. Fax 721-4418
Porter MS 600/6-8
2510 W Central Ave 59804 406-542-4060
Gail Chandler, prin. Fax 542-4098
Sentinel HS 1,100/9-12
901 South Ave W 59801 406-728-2403
Rob Watson, prin. Fax 329-5959
Washington MS 600/6-8
645 W Central Ave 59801 406-542-4085
Robert Gearheart, prin. Fax 721-7346
Other Schools – See Seeley Lake

Target Range ESD 23 400/PK-8
4095 South Ave W 59804 406-549-9239
Bill Coulter, supt. Fax 728-8841
www.target.k12.mt.us
Target Range MS 100/7-8
4095 South Ave W 59804 406-549-9239
Bill Coulter, prin. Fax 728-8841

Loyola Sacred Heart HS 200/9-12
320 Edith St 59801 406-549-6101
Jeremy Beck, prin. Fax 542-1432
Modern Beauty School Post-Sec.
2700 Paxson St Ste G 59801 406-721-1800
St. Patrick Hospital Post-Sec.
PO Box 4587 59806 406-543-7271
University of Montana 59812 Post-Sec.
406-243-0211
Univ of Montana Missoula College of Tech Post-Sec.
909 South Ave W 59801 406-243-7882

Moore, Fergus, Pop. 188
Moore SD 44 100/PK-12
509 Highland Ave 59464 406-374-2231
David Lloyd, supt. Fax 374-2490
Moore HS 50/9-12
509 Highland Ave 59464 406-374-2231
David Lloyd, prin. Fax 374-2490
Moore MS 50/7-8
509 Highland Ave 59464 406-374-2231
David Lloyd, prin. Fax 374-2490

Nashua, Valley, Pop. 303
Nashua SD 13E 200/PK-12
PO Box 170 59248 406-746-3411
Gary Fisher, supt. Fax 746-3458
Nashua HS 50/9-12
PO Box 170 59248 406-746-3411
Gary Fisher, prin. Fax 746-3458
Nashua MS 50/7-8
PO Box 170 59248 406-746-3411
Gary Fisher, prin. Fax 746-3458

Noxon, Sanders
Noxon SD 10 200/K-12
300 Noxon Ave 59853 406-847-2442
Jackie Veto, supt. Fax 847-2232
Noxon HS 100/9-12
300 Noxon Ave 59853 406-847-2442
Kelly Moore, prin. Fax 847-2232
Noxon MS 50/7-8
300 Noxon Ave 59853 406-847-2442
Kelly Moore, prin. Fax 847-2232

Opheim, Valley, Pop. 103
Opheim SD 9D 100/PK-12
PO Box 108 59250 406-762-3214
Leroy Nelson, supt. Fax 762-3348
Opheim HS 50/9-12
PO Box 108 59250 406-762-3214
Leroy Nelson, prin. Fax 762-3348
Opheim MS 50/7-8
PO Box 108 59250 406-762-3214
Leroy Nelson, prin. Fax 762-3348

Pablo, Lake, Pop. 1,298

Salish Kootenai College Post-Sec.
PO Box 70 59855 406-675-4800

Park City, Stillwater
Park City SD 5 300/PK-12
PO Box 278 59063 406-633-2406
Dick Webb, supt. Fax 633-2913
Park City HS 100/9-12
PO Box 278 59063 406-633-2350
Thomas Gauthier, prin. Fax 633-2913
Park City MS 100/7-8
PO Box 278 59063 406-633-2350
Thomas Gauthier, prin. Fax 633-2913

Peerless, Daniels
Peerless SD 2 50/PK-12
PO Box 475 59253 406-893-4377
Terry Puckett, supt. Fax 893-4399
Peerless HS 50/9-12
PO Box 475 59253 406-893-4377
Terry Puckett, prin. Fax 893-4399
Peerless MS 50/7-8
PO Box 475 59253 406-893-4377
Terry Puckett, prin. Fax 893-4399

Philipsburg, Granite, Pop. 959
Philipsburg SD 1 200/PK-12
PO Box 400 59858 406-859-3232
Mike Cutler, supt. Fax 859-3674
Granite HS 100/9-12
PO Box 400 59858 406-859-3232
Mike Cutler, prin. Fax 859-3674
Philipsburg MS 50/7-8
PO Box 400 59858 406-859-3232
Sue Johnson, prin. Fax 859-3674

Plains, Sanders, Pop. 1,247
Plains SD 1 500/PK-12
PO Box 549 59859 406-826-3666
Richard Magera, supt. Fax 826-4439
Plains HS 200/9-12
PO Box 549 59859 406-826-3666
Larry McDonald, prin. Fax 826-4439
Plains MS 100/7-8
PO Box 549 59859 406-826-3666
Larry McDonald, prin. Fax 826-4439

Plentywood, Sheridan, Pop. 1,774
Plentywood SD 20 400/PK-12
100 E Laurel Ave 59254 406-765-1803
Joe Bennett, supt. Fax 765-1195
www.plentywood.k12.mt.us/
Plentywood HS 100/9-12
100 E Laurel Ave 59254 406-765-1803
Rob Pedersen, prin. Fax 765-1195
Plentywood MS 100/7-8
100 E Laurel Ave 59254 406-765-1803
Rob Pedersen, prin. Fax 765-1195

Plevna, Fallon, Pop. 131
Plevna SD 55 100/K-12
PO Box 158 59344 406-772-5666
Jule Walker, supt. Fax 772-5548
Plevna HS 50/9-12
PO Box 158 59344 406-772-5666
Jule Walker, prin. Fax 772-5548
Plevna MS 50/7-8
PO Box 158 59344 406-772-5666
Jule Walker, prin. Fax 772-5548

Polson, Lake, Pop. 4,828
Polson SD 23 1,600/PK-12
111 4th Ave E 59860 406-883-6355
Sue McCormick, supt. Fax 883-6345
www.polson.k12.mt.us
Polson HS 600/9-12
111 4th Ave E 59860 406-883-6351
Rixon Rafter, prin. Fax 883-6330
Polson MS 300/7-8
111 4th Ave E 59860 406-883-6335
Brian Adams, prin. Fax 883-6334

Poplar, Roosevelt, Pop. 904
Poplar SD 9 900/PK-12
PO Box 458 59255 406-768-3409
Ivan Small, supt. Fax 768-5510
www.poplar.k12.mt.us/
Poplar HS 200/9-12
PO Box 458 59255 406-768-5603
Julanne Gauger, prin. Fax 768-5617
Poplar JHS 100/7-8
PO Box 458 59255 406-768-5602
Diana Knudson, prin. Fax 768-5604

Fort Peck Community College Post-Sec.
PO Box 398 59255 406-768-5551

Power, Teton
Power SD 30 200/PK-12
PO Box 155 59468 406-463-2251
Ward Fifield, supt. Fax 463-2360
www.power.k12.mt.us/
Power HS 100/9-12
PO Box 155 59468 406-463-2251
Jon Konen, prin. Fax 463-2360
Power MS 50/7-8
PO Box 155 59468 406-463-2251
Jon Konen, prin. Fax 463-2360

Pray, Park
Arrowhead ESD 75 200/PK-8
PO Box 37 59065 406-333-4359
Adam Galvin, supt. Fax 333-4975
www.arrowheadschool.net
Arrowhead MS 50/7-8
PO Box 37 59065 406-333-4359
Adam Galvin, prin. Fax 333-4975

Pryor, Big Horn, Pop. 654
Pryor SD 100/K-12
PO Box 229 59066 406-259-7329
Luke Enemy Hunter, supt. Fax 245-8938
Plenty Coups HS 100/9-12
PO Box 229 59066 406-259-7329
Dell Fritzler, prin. Fax 245-8938
Pryor MS 50/7-8
PO Box 229 59066 406-259-7329
Dell Fritzler, prin. Fax 245-8938

Ramsay, Silver Bow
Ramsay ESD 3 100/K-8
PO Box 105 59748 406-782-5470
Fax 723-8905
Ramsay MS 50/7-8
PO Box 105 59748 406-782-5470
Rosemary Garvey, prin. Fax 723-8905

Rapelje, Stillwater
Rapelje SD 32 100/K-12
PO Box 89 59067 406-663-2215
Jerry Thompson, supt. Fax 663-2299
Rapelje HS 50/9-12
PO Box 89 59067 406-663-2215
Jerry Thompson, prin. Fax 663-2299
Rapelje MS 50/7-8
PO Box 89 59067 406-663-2215
Jerry Thompson, prin. Fax 663-2299

Red Lodge, Carbon, Pop. 2,401
Red Lodge SD 1 500/PK-12
PO Box 1090 59068 406-446-1804
Mark Brajcich, supt. Fax 446-2037
Red Lodge HS 200/9-12
PO Box 1090 59068 406-446-1903
Rex Ternan, prin. Fax 446-3953
Red Lodge MS 100/7-8
PO Box 1090 59068 406-446-2110
Tina Lynch, prin. Fax 446-3975

Reedpoint, Stillwater
Reed Point SD 9-9 100/PK-12
PO Box 338, 406-326-2245
Tim Dolphay, supt. Fax 326-2339
www.reedpoint.k12.mt.us/
Reed Point HS 50/9-12
PO Box 338, 406-326-2245
Tim Dolphay, prin. Fax 326-2339
Reed Point MS 50/7-8
PO Box 338, 406-326-2225
Tim Dolphay, prin. Fax 326-2339

Richey, Dawson, Pop. 179
Richey SD 100/K-12
PO Box 60 59259 406-773-5680
Brad Moore, supt. Fax 773-5554
Richey HS 50/9-12
PO Box 60 59259 406-773-5523
Brad Moore, prin. Fax 773-5554

Richey MS — 50/7-8
PO Box 60 59259 — 406-773-5680
Brad Moore, prin. — Fax 773-5554

Roberts, Carbon
Roberts SD 5 — 100/K-12
PO Box 78 59070 — 406-445-2421
Jeff Bermes, supt. — Fax 445-2506
Roberts HS — 100/9-12
PO Box 78 59070 — 406-445-2421
Jeff Bermes, prin. — Fax 445-2506
Roberts MS — 50/7-8
PO Box 78 59070 — 406-445-2421
Jeff Bermes, prin. — Fax 445-2506

Ronan, Lake, Pop. 1,968
Ronan SD 30 — 1,300/PK-12
PO Box R 59864 — 406-676-3390
Andrew Holmlund, supt. — Fax 676-3392
www.ronank12.edu/
Ronan HS — 400/9-12
PO Box R 59864 — 406-676-3390
Tom Stack, prin. — Fax 676-3330
Ronan MS — 300/6-8
PO Box R 59864 — 406-676-3390
Andrea Johnson, prin. — Fax 676-2852

Rosebud, Rosebud
Rosebud SD 12 — 100/PK-12
PO Box 38 59347 — 406-347-5353
Dan Lantis, supt. — Fax 347-5544
Rosebud HS — 50/9-12
PO Box 38 59347 — 406-347-5353
Dan Lantis, prin. — Fax 347-5544
Rosebud MS — 50/7-8
PO Box 38 59347 — 406-347-5353
Dan Lantis, prin. — Fax 347-5544

Roundup, Musselshell, Pop. 1,916
Roundup SD 55 — 600/K-12
700 3rd St W 59072 — 406-323-1507
William Schlepp, supt. — Fax 323-1927
Roundup HS — 200/9-12
525 6th Ave W 59072 — 406-323-2402
Chad Sealey, prin. — Fax 323-1583
Roundup MS — 100/7-8
525 6th Ave W 59072 — 406-323-2402
Chad Sealey, prin. — Fax 323-1583

Roy, Fergus
Roy SD 74 — 100/K-12
PO Box 9 59471 — 406-464-2511
Dustin Sturm, supt. — Fax 464-2561
Roy HS — 50/9-12
PO Box 9 59471 — 406-464-2511
Dustin Sturm, prin. — Fax 464-2561
Roy MS — 50/7-8
PO Box 9 59471 — 406-464-2511
Dustin Sturm, prin. — Fax 464-2561

Rudyard, Hill
North Star SD — 100/PK-12
PO Box 129 59540 — 406-355-4481
Terry Grant, supt. — Fax 355-4532
North Star HS — 100/9-12
PO Box 129 59540 — 406-355-4481
Terry Grant, prin. — Fax 355-4532
North Star MS — 50/7-8
PO Box 129 59540 — 406-355-4481
Terry Grant, prin. — Fax 355-4532

Ryegate, Golden Valley, Pop. 304
Ryegate SD 1 — 100/K-12
PO Box 129 59074 — 406-568-2211
Robert Rooley, supt. — Fax 568-2528
Ryegate HS — 50/9-12
PO Box 129 59074 — 406-568-2211
Robert Rooley, prin. — Fax 568-2528
Ryegate MS — 50/7-8
PO Box 129 59074 — 406-568-2211
Robert Rooley, prin. — Fax 568-2528

Saco, Phillips, Pop. 203
Saco SD — 100/PK-12
PO Box 298 59261 — 406-527-3531
Glen Monson, supt. — Fax 527-3479
Saco HS — 50/9-12
PO Box 298 59261 — 406-527-3531
Tanya Funk, prin. — Fax 527-3479
Saco MS — 50/7-8
PO Box 298 59261 — 406-527-3531
Tanya Funk, prin. — Fax 527-3479

Saint Ignatius, Lake, Pop. 796
St. Ignatius SD 28 — 500/PK-12
PO Box 1540 59865 — 406-745-4420
Dr. Tim Skinner, supt. — Fax 745-4421
St. Ignatius HS — 200/9-12
PO Box 1540 59865 — 406-745-3811
Jason Sargent, prin. — Fax 745-4060
St. Ignatius MS — 100/6-8
PO Box 1540 59865 — 406-745-3811
Jason Sargent, prin. — Fax 745-4060

Saint Regis, Mineral
Saint Regis SD 1 — 200/PK-12
PO Box K 59866 — 406-649-2427
Becky Aaring, supt. — Fax 649-2788
www.stregis.k12.mt.us/
Saint Regis HS — 100/9-12
PO Box K 59866 — 406-649-2311
Don Almquist, prin. — Fax 649-2788
Saint Regis MS — 50/7-8
PO Box K 59866 — 406-649-2311
Don Almquist, prin. — Fax 649-2788

Sand Coulee, Cascade
Centerville SD 5 — 300/PK-12
PO Box 100 59472 — 406-736-5167
Mike Meyer, supt. — Fax 736-5210
www.centerville.k12.mt.us/
Centerville HS — 100/9-12
PO Box 100 59472 — 406-736-5167
Matthew McCale, prin. — Fax 736-5210
Centerville MS — 100/7-8
PO Box 100 59472 — 406-736-5167
Matthew McCale, prin. — Fax 736-5210

Savage, Richland
Savage SD — 100/PK-12
PO Box 110 59262 — 406-776-2317
Loren Dunk, supt. — Fax 776-2260
Savage HS — 50/9-12
PO Box 110 59262 — 406-776-2317
John McNeil, prin. — Fax 776-2419
Savage MS — 50/7-8
PO Box 110 59262 — 406-776-2317
John McNeil, prin. — Fax 776-2419

Scobey, Daniels, Pop. 991
Scobey SD 1 — 200/PK-12
PO Box 10 59263 — 406-487-2202
Dave Selvig, supt. — Fax 487-2204
Scobey HS — 100/9-12
PO Box 10 59263 — 406-487-2202
George Rider, prin. — Fax 487-2204
Scobey MS — 50/7-8
PO Box 10 59263 — 406-487-2202
George Rider, prin. — Fax 487-2204

Seeley Lake, Missoula
Missoula SD 1
Supt. — See Missoula
Seeley-Swan HS — 200/9-12
PO Box 416 59868 — 406-677-2224
Tom Korst, prin. — Fax 677-2949

Seeley Lake ESD 34 — 200/PK-8
PO Box 840 59868 — 406-677-2265
Suzanne Dobb, supt. — Fax 677-2264
Seeley MS — 50/7-8
PO Box 840 59868 — 406-677-2265
Suzanne Dobb, prin. — Fax 677-2264

Shelby, Toole, Pop. 3,304
Shelby SD 14 — 300/PK-12
1010 Oilfield Ave 59474 — 406-434-2622
Tom Rogers, supt. — Fax 434-2959
www.shelby.k12.mt.us/
Shelby HS — 200/9-12
1001 Valley St 59474 — 406-424-8910
Shawn Clark, prin. — Fax 434-7273
Shelby MS — 100/7-8
1001 Valley St 59474 — 406-424-8910
Shawn Clark, prin. — Fax 434-7273

Shepherd, Yellowstone
Shepherd SD 37 — 900/PK-12
PO Box 8 59079 — 406-373-5461
Robert Barnes, supt. — Fax 373-5284
www.shepherd.k12.mt.us/
Shepherd HS — 300/9-12
PO Box 8 59079 — 406-373-5300
Kenneth Poepping, prin. — Fax 373-5342
Shepherd MS — 100/7-8
PO Box 8 59079 — 406-373-5873
Matt Torix, prin. — Fax 373-5648

Sheridan, Madison, Pop. 689
Sheridan SD 5 — 200/PK-12
PO Box 586 59749 — 406-842-5302
Dr. J. Michael Bundy, supt. — Fax 842-5391
www.sheridan.k12.mt.us/
Sheridan HS — 100/9-12
PO Box 586 59749 — 406-842-5401
Jory Thompson, prin. — Fax 842-5856
Sheridan MS — 50/7-8
PO Box 586 59749 — 406-842-5302
Dr. J. Michael Bundy, prin. — Fax 842-5391

Sidney, Richland, Pop. 4,470
Sidney SD — 1,100/PK-12
200 3rd Ave SE 59270 — 406-433-4080
Doug Sullivan, supt. — Fax 433-4358
www.sidneyps.com
Sidney HS — 500/9-12
1012 4th Ave SE 59270 — 406-433-2330
Dan Farr, prin. — Fax 433-2481
Sidney MS — 200/6-8
415 S Central Ave 59270 — 406-433-4050
Rollie Sullivan, prin. — Fax 433-4052

Simms, Cascade
Sun River Valley SD — 300/PK-12
PO Box 380 59477 — 406-264-5111
Elaine Forrest, supt. — Fax 264-5188
www.tigers.3rivers.net/
Simms HS — 100/9-12
PO Box 380 59477 — 406-264-5110
Steve Jones, prin. — Fax 264-5189
Other Schools – See Sun River

Somers, Flathead
Somers ESD 29 — 500/PK-8
PO Box 159 59932 — 406-857-3661
Teri Wing, supt. — Fax 857-3144
www.somersdist29.org
Somers MS — 200/6-8
PO Box 159 59932 — 406-857-3661
Lori Schieffer, prin. — Fax 857-3144

Stanford, Judith Basin, Pop. 428
Stanford SD 12 — 100/PK-12
PO Box 506 59479 — 406-566-2265
Scott Chauvet, supt. — Fax 566-2772
Stanford HS — 50/9-12
PO Box 506 59479 — 406-566-2265
Scott Chauvet, prin. — Fax 566-2772
Stanford MS — 50/7-8
PO Box 506 59479 — 406-566-2265
Scott Chauvet, prin. — Fax 566-2772

Stevensville, Ravalli, Pop. 1,855
Lone Rock ESD 13 — 300/PK-8
1112 Three Mile Creek Rd 59870 — 406-777-3314
John Miller, supt. — Fax 777-2770
Lone Rock MS — 100/7-8
1112 Three Mile Creek Rd 59870 — 406-777-3314
Marjorie Johnson, prin. — Fax 777-2770

Stevensville SD 2 — 1,100/PK-12
300 Park St 59870 — 406-777-5481
Dennis Kimzey, supt. — Fax 777-1381
www.stevensville.k12.mt.us/
Stevensville HS — 500/9-12
300 Park St 59870 — 406-777-5481
Jim Notaro, prin. — Fax 777-5291
Stevensville JHS — 200/7-8
300 Park St 59870 — 406-777-5533
Bob Connors, prin. — Fax 777-5291

Sunburst, Toole, Pop. 346
Sunburst SD 2 — 300/PK-12
PO Box 710 59482 — 406-937-2811
John Hvidsten, supt. — Fax 937-2828
Sunburst HS — 100/9-12
PO Box 710 59482 — 406-937-2811
John Hvidsten, prin. — Fax 937-2828
Sunburst MS — 50/7-8
PO Box 710 59482 — 406-937-2816
Brian Barrows, prin. — Fax 937-4444

Sun River, Cascade
Sun River Valley SD
Supt. — See Simms
Sun River MS — 100/6-8
301 Largent St 59483 — 406-264-5330
Rick Danelson, prin. — Fax 264-5333

Superior, Mineral, Pop. 910
Superior SD 3 — 400/K-12
PO Box 400 59872 — 406-822-3600
Bill Woodford, supt. — Fax 822-3601
www.sd3.k12.mt.us/
Superior HS — 100/9-12
PO Box 400 59872 — 406-822-4851
Allan Labbe, prin. — Fax 822-4396
Superior MS — 100/7-8
PO Box 400 59872 — 406-822-4851
Allan Labbe, prin. — Fax 822-4396

Terry, Prairie, Pop. 563
Terry SD 5 — 200/PK-12
PO Box 187 59349 — 406-635-5533
Dale Kimmet, supt. — Fax 635-5705
www.terry.k12.mt.us/
Terry HS — 100/9-12
PO Box 187 59349 — 406-635-5533
Dale Kimmet, prin. — Fax 635-5705
Terry MS — 50/7-8
PO Box 187 59349 — 406-635-5595
Dale Kimmet, prin. — Fax 635-5705

Thompson Falls, Sanders, Pop. 1,392
Thompson Falls SD 2 — 500/K-12
PO Box 129 59873 — 406-827-3323
Jerry Pauli, supt. — Fax 827-3020
Thompson Falls HS — 200/9-12
PO Box 129 59873 — 406-827-3561
Don Jensen, prin. — Fax 827-9463
Thompson Falls MS — 100/7-8
PO Box 129 59873 — 406-827-3593
Tom Holleran, prin. — Fax 827-0306

Three Forks, Gallatin, Pop. 1,845
Three Forks SD J-24 — 600/PK-12
212 E Neal St 59752 — 406-285-3216
John Overstreet, supt. — Fax 285-3216
Three Forks HS — 200/9-12
210 E Neal St 59752 — 406-285-3503
Tom Blakely, prin. — Fax 285-3503
Three Forks MS — 100/7-8
210 E Neal St 59752 — 406-285-3503
Tom Blakely, prin. — Fax 285-3503

Townsend, Broadwater, Pop. 1,950
Townsend SD 1 — 700/PK-12
201 N Spruce St 59644 — 406-266-5512
Brian Patrick, supt. — Fax 266-4957
Broadwater HS — 200/9-12
201 N Spruce St 59644 — 406-266-3455
Rob Hankins, prin. — Fax 266-3448
Townsend MS — 100/7-8
201 N Spruce St 59644 — 406-266-4983
Brad Racht, prin. — Fax 266-4966

Trout Creek, Sanders
Trout Creek ESD 6 — 100/PK-8
4 School Ln 59874 — 406-827-3629
Fax 827-4185
Trout MS — 50/7-8
4 School Ln 59874 — 406-827-3629
Daisy Nikola, lead tchr. — Fax 827-4185

Troy, Lincoln, Pop. 982
Troy SD 1 — 500/PK-12
PO Box 867 59935 — 406-295-4606
Brady Selle, supt. — Fax 295-4802
Troy HS — 200/9-12
PO Box 867 59935 — 406-295-4520
Rodney Smith, prin. — Fax 295-5371
Troy MS — 100/7-8
PO Box 867 59935 — 406-295-4520
Rodney Smith, prin. — Fax 295-5371

Turner, Blaine
Turner SD 43 — 100/PK-12
PO Box 40 59542 — 406-379-2315
Gordon Hahn, supt. — Fax 379-2398
Turner HS — 50/9-12
PO Box 40 59542 — 406-379-2219
Gordon Hahn, prin. — Fax 379-2398

Turner MS 50/7-8
PO Box 40 59542 406-379-2219
Gordon Hahn, prin. Fax 379-2398

Twin Bridges, Madison, Pop. 418
Twin Bridges SD 7 200/PK-12
PO Box 419 59754 406-684-5657
David Whitesell, supt. Fax 684-5458
www.twinbridges.k12.mt.us
Twin Bridges HS 100/9-12
PO Box 419 59754 406-684-5657
David Whitesell, prin. Fax 684-5458
Twin Bridges MS 50/7-8
PO Box 419 59754 406-684-5613
Douglas Denson, prin. Fax 684-5458

Ulm, Cascade
Ulm ESD 85 100/PK-8
PO Box 189 59485 406-866-3313
Fax 866-3209
Ulm MS 50/7-8
PO Box 189 59485 406-866-3313
Lauri Ingebritson, prin. Fax 866-3209

Valier, Pondera, Pop. 472
Valier SD 18 200/PK-12
PO Box 528 59486 406-279-3613
Matt Genger, supt. Fax 279-3764
Valier HS 100/9-12
PO Box 528 59486 406-279-3613
Matt Genger, prin. Fax 279-3764
Valier MS 50/7-8
PO Box 528 59486 406-279-3314
Matt Genger, prin. Fax 279-3510

Vaughn, Cascade
Vaughn ESD 74 100/PK-8
480 Central Ave 59487 406-965-2231
Fax 965-3703
Vaughn MS 50/7-8
480 Central Ave 59487 406-965-2231
Jack O'Connor, prin. Fax 965-3703

Victor, Ravalli
Victor SD 7 300/PK-12
425 4th Ave 59875 406-642-3221
Orville Getz, supt. Fax 642-3446
www.victor.k12.mt.us/
Victor HS 100/9-12
425 4th Ave 59875 406-642-3221
Danny Johnston, prin. Fax 642-3446
Victor MS 100/6-8
425 4th Ave 59875 406-642-3221
Danny Johnston, prin. Fax 642-3446

Westby, Sheridan, Pop. 148
Westby SD 3 50/PK-12
PO Box 109 59275 406-385-2258
Wayne Koterba, supt. Fax 385-2430
www.westbyschool.k12.mt.us/
Westby HS 50/9-12
PO Box 109 59275 406-385-2258
Wayne Koterba, prin. Fax 385-2430
Westby MS 50/7-8
PO Box 109 59275 406-385-2225
Wayne Koterba, prin. Fax 385-2430

West Yellowstone, Gallatin, Pop. 1,223
West Yellowstone SD 69 200/PK-12
PO Box 460 59758 406-646-7617
Brian Bagley, supt. Fax 646-7232
West Yellowstone HS 100/9-12
PO Box 460 59758 406-646-7617
Brian Bagley, prin. Fax 646-7232
West Yellowstone MS 50/7-8
PO Box 460 59758 406-646-7617
Brian Bagley, prin. Fax 646-7232

Whitefish, Flathead, Pop. 7,067
Olney-Bissell ESD 58 100/PK-8
5955 Farm To Market Rd 59937 406-862-2828
Fax 862-2838
Bissell MS 50/7-8
5955 Farm to Market Rd 59937 406-862-2828
Lona Everett, prin. Fax 862-2838

Whitefish SD 44 1,900/PK-12
600 2nd St E 59937 406-862-8640
Jerry House, supt. Fax 862-1507
www.wfps.k12.mt.us
Whitefish Central JHS 300/7-8
600 2nd St E 59937 406-862-8650
Kim Anderson, prin. Fax 862-8664
Whitefish HS 700/9-12
600 2nd St E 59937 406-862-8600
Kent Paulson, prin. Fax 862-2586

Whitehall, Jefferson, Pop. 1,156
Whitehall SD 500/PK-12
PO Box 1109 59759 406-287-3455
Pat Audet, supt. Fax 287-3843
Whitehall HS 200/9-12
PO Box 1109 59759 406-287-3862
Doug Richards, prin. Fax 287-3843
Whitehall JHS 100/7-8
PO Box 1109 59759 406-287-3882
Luann Metcalf, prin. Fax 287-5508

White Sulphur Springs, Meagher, Pop. 1,017
White Sulphur Springs SD 8 100/PK-12
PO Box C 59645 406-547-3751
Cal Moore, supt. Fax 547-3922
www.whitesulphur.k12.mt.us/
White Sulphur Springs HS 100/9-12
PO Box C 59645 406-547-3351
Andy Lind, prin. Fax 547-2407
White Sulphur Springs MS 50/7-8
PO Box C 59645 406-547-3351
Andy Lind, prin. Fax 547-2407

Whitewater, Phillips
Whitewater SD 100/PK-12
PO Box 46 59544 406-674-5418
Darin Cummings, supt. Fax 674-5460
Whitewater HS 50/9-12
PO Box 46 59544 406-674-5417
Darin Cummings, prin. Fax 674-5460
Whitewater MS 50/7-8
PO Box 46 59544 406-674-5417
Darin Cummings, prin. Fax 674-5460

Wibaux, Wibaux, Pop. 505
Wibaux SD 6 200/PK-12
121 F St N 59353 406-796-2474
Renee Rasmussen, supt. Fax 796-2259
Wibaux HS 100/9-12
121 F St N 59353 406-795-2474
Fax 795-2259
Wibaux JHS 50/7-8
121 F St N 59353 406-796-2474
Janet Huisman, prin. Fax 796-2259

Willow Creek, Gallatin
Willow Creek SD 100/PK-12
PO Box 189 59760 406-285-6991
D.K. Brooks, supt. Fax 285-6923
www.willowcreek.k12.mt.us/
Willow Creek HS 50/9-12
PO Box 189 59760 406-285-6991
D.K. Brooks, prin. Fax 285-6923
Willow Creek MS 50/7-8
PO Box 189 59760 406-285-6991
D.K. Brooks, prin. Fax 285-6923

Wilsall, Park
Shields Valley SD 300/PK-12
PO Box 131 59086 406-578-2535
Jason Butcher, supt. Fax 578-2176
Shields Valley MS 50/7-8
PO Box 131 59086 406-578-2535
Michael Todryk, prin. Fax 578-2176
Other Schools – See Clyde Park

Winifred, Fergus, Pop. 151
Winifred SD 115 100/PK-12
PO Box 109 59489 406-462-5349
Stephanie Wooderchak, supt. Fax 462-5477
Winifred HS 100/9-12
PO Box 109 59489 406-462-5420
Stephanie Wooderchak, prin. Fax 462-5477
Winifred MS 50/7-8
PO Box 109 59489 406-462-5349
Stephanie Wooderchak, prin. Fax 462-5477

Winnett, Petroleum, Pop. 176
Winnett SD 100/PK-12
PO Box 167 59087 406-429-2251
Dr. Clay Dunlap, supt. Fax 429-7631
Winnett HS 50/9-12
PO Box 167 59087 406-429-2251
Dr. Clay Dunlap, prin. Fax 429-7631
Winnett MS 50/7-8
PO Box 167 59087 406-429-2251
Dr. Clay Dunlap, prin. Fax 429-7631

Wolf Point, Roosevelt, Pop. 2,623
Frontier ESD 3 100/PK-8
6996 Roy St 59201 406-653-2501
Justin Jimison, supt. Fax 653-2508
Frontier MS 50/7-8
6996 Roy St 59201 406-653-2501
Justin Jimison, prin. Fax 653-2508

Wolf Point SD 45 900/PK-12
220 4th Ave S 59201 406-653-2361
Paul Huber, supt. Fax 653-1881
wolfpoint.k12.mt.us/
Wolf Point HS 300/9-12
213 6th Ave S 59201 406-653-1200
Joseph Paine, prin. Fax 653-3104
Wolf Point JHS 100/7-8
213 6th Ave S 59201 406-653-1200
Lester McCormick, prin. Fax 653-3104

Worden, Yellowstone
Huntley Project SD 24 800/PK-12
1477 Ash St 59088 406-967-2540
David Mahon, supt. Fax 967-2547
www.huntley.k12.mt.us/
Huntley Project HS 300/9-12
2436 N 15th Rd 59088 406-967-2540
Tynie Mader, prin. Fax 967-2589
Huntley Project MS 100/7-8
2427 N 15th Rd 59088 406-967-2540
Frank Hollowell, prin. Fax 967-3054

Wyola, Big Horn
Wyola ESD 29 100/PK-8
PO Box 66 59089 406-343-2722
Dr. Linda Brown, supt. Fax 343-5901
Wyola MS 50/7-8
PO Box 66 59089 406-343-2722
Fax 343-5901

NEBRASKA

NEBRASKA DEPARTMENT OF EDUCATION
PO Box 94987, Lincoln 68509-4987
Telephone 402-471-2295
Fax 402-471-0117
Website http://www.nde.state.ne.us

Commissioner of Education Doug Christensen

NEBRASKA BOARD OF EDUCATION
PO Box 94987, Lincoln 68509-4987

President Fred Meyer

EDUCATIONAL SERVICE UNITS (ESU)

ESU 1
Robert H. Uhing, admin. 402-287-2061
211 10th St, Wakefield 68784 Fax 287-2065
www.esu1.org/

ESU 2
Michael Ough, admin. 402-721-7710
PO Box 649, Fremont 68026 Fax 721-7712
www.esu2.org/

ESU 3
Gil Kettlehut, admin. 402-597-4800
6949 S 110th St, La Vista 68128 Fax 597-4811
www2.esu3.org/esu3/

ESU 4
Jon Fisher, admin. 402-274-4354
PO Box 310, Auburn 68305 Fax 274-4356
www.esu4.org/

ESU 5
Al Schneider, admin. 402-223-5277
900 W Court St, Beatrice 68310 Fax 223-5279
www.esu5.org/

ESU 6
Dr. Dan Shoemake, admin. 402-761-3341
PO Box 748, Milford 68405 Fax 761-3279
www.esu6.org/

ESU 7
Norman Ronell, admin. 402-564-5753
2657 44th Ave, Columbus 68601 Fax 563-1121
gilligan.esu7.org/

ESU 8
Randall Peck, admin. 402-887-5041
PO Box 89, Neligh 68756 Fax 887-4604
www.esu8.org/

ESU 9
Calvin Loughran, admin. 402-463-5611
PO Box 2047, Hastings 68902 Fax 463-9555
www.esu9.org/

ESU 10
Wayne Bell, admin. 308-237-5927
PO Box 850, Kearney 68848 Fax 237-5920
www.esu10.org/

ESU 11
Ron Karr, admin. 308-995-6585
PO Box 858, Holdrege 68949 Fax 995-6587
www.esu11.org/

ESU 13
Terry Miller, admin. 308-635-3696
4215 Avenue I, Scottsbluff 69361 Fax 635-0680
www.esu13.org/

ESU 15
Brent McMurtrey, admin. 308-334-5160
PO Box 398, Trenton 69044 Fax 334-5581
www.esu15.org

ESU 16
Margene Beatty, admin. 308-284-8481
PO Box 915, Ogallala 69153 Fax 284-8483
www.esu16.org/

ESU 17
Dennis Radford, admin. 402-387-1420
207 N Main St, Ainsworth 69210 Fax 387-1028
www.esu17.org/

ESU 18
David Myers, admin. 402-436-1610
PO Box 82889, Lincoln 68501 Fax 436-1620
www.lps.org/

ESU 19 402-557-2002
, 3215 Cuming St, Omaha 68131 Fax 557-2019
www.ops.org/

PUBLIC, PRIVATE AND CATHOLIC SECONDARY SCHOOLS

Adams, Gage, Pop. 486
Freeman SD 300/K-12
PO Box 259 68301 402-988-2525
John Brazell, supt. Fax 988-3475
www.freemanpublicschools.org/
Freeman JSHS 100/7-12
PO Box 259 68301 402-988-2525
Bob Michl, prin. Fax 988-3475

Ainsworth, Brown, Pop. 1,717
Ainsworth SD 500/K-12
PO Box 65 69210 402-387-2333
Darrell Peterson, supt. Fax 387-0525
www.ainsworthschools.org/
Ainsworth HS 200/9-12
PO Box 65 69210 402-387-2082
Harvey Wewel, prin. Fax 387-0525
Ainsworth MS 100/6-8
PO Box 65 69210 402-387-2082
Harvey Wewel, prin. Fax 387-0525

Albion, Boone, Pop. 1,672
Boone Central SD 600/K-12
PO Box 391 68620 402-395-2134
Larry Lambert, supt. Fax 395-2137
www.boonecentral.esu7.org/
Boone Central HS 300/9-12
PO Box 391 68620 402-395-2134
Darrell Barnes, prin. Fax 395-2137
Other Schools – See Petersburg

Allen, Dixon, Pop. 400
Allen Consolidated SD 200/K-12
PO Box 190 68710 402-635-2484
Don Schmidt, supt. Fax 635-2331
allenweb.esu1.org/
Allen JSHS 100/7-12
PO Box 190 68710 402-635-2484
Monty Miller, prin. Fax 635-2331

Alliance, Box Butte, Pop. 8,331
Alliance SD 1,800/K-12
1604 Sweetwater Ave 69301 308-762-5475
Larry Ross, supt. Fax 762-8249
www.allianceps.org/
Alliance HS 600/9-12
100 W 14th St 69301 308-762-3359
Deron Dolfi, prin. Fax 762-3359
Alliance MS 500/5-8
1100 Laramie Ave 69301 308-762-3079
Rita Moravek, prin. Fax 762-7302

Alma, Harlan, Pop. 1,110
Alma SD 300/K-12
PO Box 170 68920 308-928-2131
Donald A. Ferguson, supt. Fax 928-2763
www.esu11.k12.ne.us/alma/home
Alma JSHS 200/7-12
PO Box 170 68920 308-928-2131
Paul Joseph, prin. Fax 928-2763

Amherst, Buffalo, Pop. 269
Amherst SD 300/K-12
PO Box 8 68812 308-826-3131
Ted Classen, supt. Fax 826-4865
sites.amherst.k12.ne.us/
Amherst JSHS 200/7-12
PO Box 8 68812 308-826-3131
Roger Thomsen, prin. Fax 826-4865

Ansley, Custer, Pop. 493
Ansley SD 200/K-12
PO Box 370 68814 308-935-1121
Michael McCabe, supt. Fax 935-9103
Ansley JSHS 100/7-12
PO Box 370 68814 308-935-1121
Lance C. Bristol, prin. Fax 935-9103

Arapahoe, Furnas, Pop. 954
Arapahoe SD 300/K-12
PO Box 360 68922 308-962-5458
Damon McDonald, supt. Fax 962-7481
www.esu11.org/arapahoe/fp.html
Arapahoe HS 100/7-12
PO Box 360 68922 308-962-5458
Daren Hatch, prin. Fax 962-7481

Arcadia, Valley, Pop. 337
Arcadia SD 100/K-12
PO Box 248 68815 308-789-6522
Michael McCabe, supt. Fax 789-6214
sites.arcadia.k12.ne.us/arcadia/
Arcadia JSHS 100/7-12
PO Box 248 68815 308-789-6522
Donald Jacobs, prin. Fax 789-6214

Arlington, Washington, Pop. 1,192
Arlington SD 600/K-12
PO Box 580 68002 402-478-4173
Nathan Stineman, supt. Fax 478-4176
www.apseagles.org/
Arlington JSHS 300/7-12
PO Box 580 68002 402-478-4171
Lynn Johnson, prin. Fax 478-4176

Arnold, Custer, Pop. 618
Arnold SD 200/K-12
PO Box 399 69120 308-848-2226
Robert Brown, supt. Fax 848-2201
sites.arnold.k12.ne.us/arnoldhome/
Arnold JSHS 100/7-12
PO Box 399 69120 308-848-2226
Michael Harvey, prin. Fax 848-2201

Arthur, Arthur, Pop. 123
Arthur County SD 100/K-12
PO Box 145 69121 308-764-2253
John Frates, supt. Fax 764-2206
Arthur County JSHS 50/7-12
PO Box 145 69121 308-764-2253
Scott Trimble, prin. Fax 764-2206

Ashland, Saunders, Pop. 2,493
Ashland-Greenwood SD 800/PK-12
1200 Boyd St 68003 402-944-2128
Craig Pease, supt. Fax 944-3310
www.agps.org/
Ashland-Greenwood HS 300/9-12
1200 Boyd St 68003 402-944-2114
Ray Bentzen, prin. Fax 944-2116
Ashland-Greenwood MS 100/7-8
1200 Boyd St 68003 402-944-2114
Ray Bentzen, prin. Fax 944-2116

Atkinson, Holt, Pop. 1,151
West Holt SD 400/K-12
PO Box 457 68713 402-925-2890
William McAllister, supt. Fax 925-2177
West Holt Rural HS 200/9-12
PO Box 457 68713 402-925-2890
Kevin L. Young, prin. Fax 925-2177

Auburn, Nemaha, Pop. 3,076
Auburn SD 900/K-12
820 Central Ave Ste 1 68305 402-274-4830
Steve Schneider, supt. Fax 274-5227
www.auburnpublicschools.org/
Auburn JSHS 400/7-12
1829 Central Ave 68305 402-274-4328
Kevin Reiman, prin. Fax 274-5434

Aurora, Hamilton, Pop. 4,282
Aurora SD 1,300/K-12
300 L St 68818 402-694-6923
Larry Ramaekers, supt. Fax 694-5097
www.aurora.k12.ne.us/
Aurora MS 300/7-9
300 L St 68818 402-694-6915
Kenneth Thiele, prin. Fax 694-3815
Aurora SHS 300/10-12
300 L St 68818 402-694-6968
Douglas Kittle, prin. Fax 694-2573

Axtell, Kearney, Pop. 708
Axtell Community SD 300/K-12
PO Box 97 68924 308-743-2414
Thomas Sandberg, supt. Fax 743-2417
www.esu11.org/axtell/INDEX.HTM
Axtell JSHS 200/7-12
PO Box 97 68924 308-743-2415
Douglas Hinze, prin. Fax 743-2417

Bancroft, Cuming, Pop. 490
Bancroft-Rosalie SD 300/K-12
PO Box 129 68004 402-648-3337
Jon Cerny, supt. Fax 648-3338
www.bancroft-rosalie.org/
Bancroft HS 100/9-12
PO Box 129 68004 402-648-3336
Mike Sjuts, prin. Fax 648-3338
Bancroft JHS 50/7-8
PO Box 129 68004 402-648-3336
Mike Sjuts, prin. Fax 648-3338

Bartlett, Wheeler, Pop. 115
Wheeler Central SD 100/K-12
PO Box 68 68622 308-654-3273
Dan Hoesly, supt. Fax 654-3237
teachers.esu8.org/WheelerCentral/
Wheeler Central JSHS 100/7-12
PO Box 68 68622 308-654-3273
Dan Hoesly, prin. Fax 654-3237

Bartley, Red Willow, Pop. 348
Southwest SD 179 400/K-12
PO Box 187 69020 308-692-3223
David Hendricks, supt. Fax 692-3221
www.southwest.k12.ne.us/home
Southwest MS 100/6-8
PO Box 187 69020 308-692-3223
Don Hosick, prin. Fax 692-3221
Other Schools – See Indianola

Bassett, Rock, Pop. 660
Rock County SD 200/K-12
PO Box 448 68714 402-684-3411
David Wade, supt. Fax 684-3671
cumulus.rchs.esu17.k12.ne.us/
Rock County HS 100/9-12
PO Box 448 68714 402-684-3411
Steve Camp, prin. Fax 684-3671

Battle Creek, Madison, Pop. 1,178
Battle Creek SD 500/K-12
PO Box 100 68715 402-675-6905
Jay Bellar, supt. Fax 675-1038
bcps.esu8.org/
Battle Creek JSHS 300/7-12
PO Box 100 68715 402-675-3705
Mark Lenihan, prin. Fax 675-1038

Bayard, Morrill, Pop. 1,155
Bayard SD 400/K-12
PO Box 607 69334 308-586-1700
Allen D. Gross, supt. Fax 586-1638
Bayard JSHS 200/7-12
PO Box 607 69334 308-586-1700
Robert C. Gregory, prin. Fax 586-1638

Beatrice, Gage, Pop. 12,890
Beatrice SD 2,300/PK-12
320 N 5th St 68310 402-223-1500
Dale Kruse, supt. Fax 223-1509
www.beatricepublicschools.org/
Beatrice HS 800/9-12
600 Orange Blvd 68310 402-223-1515
Jason Sutter, prin. Fax 223-1510
Beatrice MS 500/6-8
215 N 5th St 68310 402-223-1545
Randy Schlueter, prin. Fax 223-1547

Joseph's College of Beauty Post-Sec.
618 Court St 68310 402-223-3588
Southeast Community College Post-Sec.
4771 W Scott Rd 68310 402-228-3468

Bellevue, Sarpy, Pop. 47,334
Bellevue SD 9,000/PK-12
1600 Highway 370 68005 402-293-4000
Dr. John Deegan, supt. Fax 293-5002
www.bellevuepublicschools.org
Bellevue East HS 1,400/9-12
1401 High School Dr 68005 402-293-4150
Brad Stueve, prin. Fax 293-4259
Bellevue West HS 1,500/9-12
1501 Thurston Ave 68123 402-293-4040
Kevin Rohlfs, prin. Fax 293-4149
Fontenelle MS 700/7-8
701 Kayleen Dr 68005 402-293-4360
Doug Schaefer, prin. Fax 293-4450
Lewis & Clark MS 7-8
13502 S 38th St 68123 402-898-8760
Dr. Mike Smith, prin.
Mission MS 700/7-8
2202 Washington St 68005 402-293-4260
Laurie Hanna, prin. Fax 293-4350

Bellevue University Post-Sec.
1000 Galvin Rd S 68005 402-293-3700

Benedict, York, Pop. 276
Cross County Community SD
Supt. — See Stromsburg
Cross County MS - Benedict 100/5-8
PO Box 135 68316 402-732-6677
Ron Nickel, prin. Fax 732-6678

Benkelman, Dundy, Pop. 914
Dundy County SD 300/PK-12
PO Box 586 69021 308-423-2738
Dr. Dallas Watkins, supt. Fax 423-2711
www.dctigers.net/
Dundy County HS 100/9-12
PO Box 586 69021 308-423-2738
Jim Kent, prin. Fax 423-2711

Bennington, Douglas, Pop. 913
Bennington SD 600/K-12
11620 N 156th St 68007 402-238-3044
Terry Haack, supt. Fax 238-2185
www.benningtonschools.org/
Bennington JSHS 300/7-12
16610 Bennington Rd 68007 402-238-2447
Stan Turner, prin. Fax 238-2950

Bertrand, Phelps, Pop. 791
Bertrand SD 200/K-12
PO Box 278 68927 308-472-3427
Dr. Greg Barnes, supt. Fax 472-3429
www.esu11.org/bertrand/home.html
Bertrand JSHS 100/7-12
PO Box 278 68927 308-472-3427
Michael Williams, prin. Fax 472-3429

Big Springs, Deuel, Pop. 399
South Platte SD 100/K-12
PO Box 457 69122 308-889-3622
David Spencer, supt. Fax 889-3523
southplatte.ne.schoolwebpages.com/
South Platte HS 100/7-12
PO Box 457 69122 308-889-3622
Jane Brown, prin. Fax 889-3523

Blair, Washington, Pop. 7,765
Blair Community SD 2,300/PK-12
PO Box 288 68008 402-426-2610
Steven Shanahan, supt. Fax 426-3110
www.blairschools.org/
Blair HS 700/9-12
PO Box 288 68008 402-426-4941
Thomas Anderson, prin. Fax 426-4949
Otte Blair MS 500/6-8
PO Box 288 68008 402-426-3678
James Sides, prin. Fax 426-1788

Dana College Post-Sec.
2848 College Dr 68008 402-426-9000

Bloomfield, Knox, Pop. 1,049
Bloomfield SD 200/PK-12
PO Box 308 68718 402-373-4800
John Post, supt. Fax 373-2712
bloomfield.esu1.org/
Bloomfield JSHS 100/7-12
PO Box 308 68718 402-373-4800
John Post, prin. Fax 373-2712

Blue Hill, Webster, Pop. 798
Blue Hill SD 400/K-12
PO Box 217 68930 402-756-2085
Glen Larsen, supt. Fax 756-2086
www.bluehillschools.org/
Blue Hill JSHS 200/7-12
PO Box 217 68930 402-756-3043
Rodney Olson, prin. Fax 756-3044

Boys Town, Douglas, Pop. 891

Boys Town HS 400/9-12
13803 Flanagan Blvd 68010 402-498-1800
Robert Gehringer, prin. Fax 498-3246

Bradshaw, York, Pop. 326
Heartland Community SD
Supt. — See Henderson
Heartland Community JHS 100/7-8
PO Box 98 68319 402-736-4353
Blaine Friesen, prin. Fax 736-4602

Brady, Lincoln, Pop. 379
Brady SD 200/K-12
PO Box 68 69123 308-584-3317
Patrick W. Cullen, supt. Fax 584-3725
athena.esu16.org/bradyschool/index.htm
Brady JSHS 100/7-12
PO Box 68 69123 308-584-3317
Patrick W. Cullen, prin. Fax 584-3725

Brainard, Butler, Pop. 346
East Butler SD 300/K-12
PO Box 36 68626 402-545-2081
James Koontz, supt. Fax 545-2023
www.ebutler.esu7.org/eastbutler.html
Brainard JSHS 200/7-12
PO Box 36 68626 402-545-2081
Gerald Reinsch, prin. Fax 545-2023

Bridgeport, Morrill, Pop. 1,493
Bridgeport SD 63 500/K-12
PO Box 430 69336 308-262-1470
Randall R. Butcher, supt. Fax 262-1470
www.bridgeportschools.org/
Bridgeport JSHS 200/7-12
PO Box 430 69336 308-262-0346
Michael Mitchell, prin. Fax 262-0444

Broken Bow, Custer, Pop. 3,311
Broken Bow SD 800/PK-12
323 N 7th Ave 68822 308-872-6821
Timothy Shafer, supt. Fax 872-2751
www.bbps.org/
Broken Bow HS 300/9-12
323 N 7th Ave 68822 308-872-2475
Ken Kujath, prin. Fax 872-2528
Broken Bow MS 200/6-8
322 N 9th Ave 68822 308-872-6441
Edward Lowe, prin. Fax 872-2751

Bruning, Thayer, Pop. 262
Bruning-Davenport USD
Supt. — See Davenport
Bruning-Davenport HS 100/9-12
PO Box 70 68322 402-353-4445
Trudy Clark, prin. Fax 353-4445

Burwell, Garfield, Pop. 1,063
Burwell SD 400/PK-12
PO Box 670 68823 308-346-4150
Daniel Bird, supt. Fax 346-5430
Burwell JSHS 200/7-12
PO Box 670 68823 308-346-4150
David Owen, prin. Fax 346-5430

Cairo, Hall, Pop. 787
Centura SD 600/PK-12
PO Box 430 68824 308-485-4258
David Schley, supt. Fax 485-4780
www.centura.k12.ne.us/
Centura JSHS 300/7-12
PO Box 430 68824 308-485-4258
Gary Monter, prin. Fax 485-4780

Callaway, Custer, Pop. 625
Callaway SD 200/K-12
PO Box 188 68825 308-836-2272
Patrick Osmond, supt. Fax 836-2771
sites.callaway.k12.ne.us/
Callaway JSHS 100/7-12
PO Box 188 68825 308-836-2272
Rodney Ready, prin. Fax 836-2771

Cambridge, Furnas, Pop. 971
Cambridge SD 300/K-12
PO Box 100 69022 308-697-3322
Ronald Streit, supt. Fax 697-4880
www.esu11.org/cambridge/
Cambridge HS 100/9-12
PO Box 100 69022 308-697-3322
Don Keyser, prin. Fax 697-4880

Cedar Bluffs, Saunders, Pop. 617
Cedar Bluffs SD 300/PK-12
PO Box 66 68015 402-628-2060
Jeffrey Walburn, supt. Fax 628-2005
www.cedarbluffsschools.org/
Cedar Bluffs JSHS 100/7-12
PO Box 66 68015 402-628-2080
Daniel Cleveland, prin. Fax 628-2108

Cedar Rapids, Boone, Pop. 371
Cedar Rapids SD 200/K-12
408 W Dayton St 68627 308-358-0640
Amy Malander, supt. Fax 358-0211
www.cedar.esu7.org/
Cedar Rapids JSHS 100/7-12
408 W Dayton St 68627 308-358-0640
Matthew Asche, prin. Fax 358-0211

Central City, Merrick, Pop. 2,891
Central City SD 800/PK-12
PO Box 57 68826 308-946-3055
Jeffrey D. West, supt. Fax 946-3149
home.centralcityps.org/
Central City HS 200/9-12
PO Box 57 68826 308-946-3086
Shawn McDiffett, prin. Fax 946-2954
Central City MS 200/5-8
PO Box 57 68826 308-946-3056
Thomas McGuire, prin. Fax 946-2124

Nebraska Christian S 200/PK-12
1847 Inskip Ave 68826 308-946-3836
Daniel Woods, admin. Fax 946-3837

Chadron, Dawes, Pop. 5,320
Chadron SD 1,000/K-12
602 E 10th St 69337 308-432-0700
Sherlock V. Hirning, supt. Fax 432-0702
www.chadronschools.org/
Chadron HS 300/9-12
901 Cedar St 69337 308-432-0707
Stephen Osborn, prin. Fax 432-0723
Chadron MS 300/5-8
551 E 6th St 69337 308-432-0708
Richard Moore, prin. Fax 432-0720

Pine Ridge Job Corps
Supt. — None
Pine Ridge Job Corps Vo/Tech
15710 Highway 385 69337 308-432-3316
Brian Kizer, prin. Fax 432-4145

Chadron State College Post-Sec.
1000 Main St 69337 308-432-6000

Chambers, Holt, Pop. 312
Chambers SD 200/K-12
PO Box 218 68725 402-482-5233
Robert Hanger, supt. Fax 482-5234
chambers.esu8.org/
Chambers JSHS 100/7-12
PO Box 218 68725 402-482-5233
Robert Hanger, prin. Fax 482-5234

Chappell, Deuel, Pop. 935
Creek Valley SD 300/K-12
PO Box 608 69129 308-874-2911
Dennis O'Connor, supt. Fax 874-2602
creekvalleystorm.com/
Creek Valley HS 100/7-12
PO Box 608 69129 308-874-3310
Brent Christensen, prin. Fax 874-2604
Other Schools – See Lodgepole

Clarks, Merrick, Pop. 341
High Plains Community SD
Supt. — See Polk
High Plains MS 100/6-8
PO Box 205 68628 308-548-2216
Karyee LeSuer, prin. Fax 548-2120

Clarkson, Colfax, Pop. 680
Clarkson SD 200/K-12
PO Box 140 68629 402-892-3454
Daniel C. Polk, supt. Fax 892-3455
teachers.esu7.org/clarkson/
Clarkson JSHS 200/7-12
PO Box 140 68629 402-892-3454
Rich Lemburg, prin. Fax 892-3455

Clay Center, Clay, Pop. 813
Clay Center SD 200/PK-12
PO Box 125 68933 402-762-3561
Lee Sayer, supt. Fax 762-3200
www.esu9.org/%7Ecc/home.html
Clay Center JSHS 100/7-12
PO Box 125 68933 402-762-3561
Jim Bovee, prin. Fax 762-3200

Clearwater, Antelope, Pop. 357
Nebraska USD 1
Supt. — See Royal
Clearwater JSHS 100/7-12
PO Box 38 68726 402-485-2505
Jeff Hoesing, prin. Fax 485-2634

Cody, Cherry, Pop. 148
Cody-Kilgore SD 200/K-12
PO Box 216 69211 402-823-4190
Larry Sweley, supt. Fax 823-4275
Cody-Kilgore JSHS 100/7-12
PO Box 216 69211 402-823-4190
Kathleen Fullerton, prin. Fax 823-4275

Coleridge, Cedar, Pop. 501
Coleridge Community SD 200/K-12
PO Box 37 68727 402-283-4844
Dr. Daniel Hoesing, supt. Fax 283-4230
coleridge.esu1.org/
Coleridge JSHS 100/7-12
PO Box 37 68727 402-283-4844
Craig Frerichs, prin. Fax 283-4230

Columbus, Platte, Pop. 20,909
Columbus SD 3,500/K-12
PO Box 947 68602 402-563-7000
Dr. Paul Hillyer, supt. Fax 563-7005
www.columbuspublicschools.org
Columbus HS 1,100/9-12
PO Box 947 68602 402-563-7050
Amy Romshek, prin. Fax 563-7058
Columbus MS 800/6-8
PO Box 947 68602 402-563-7060
Douglas Kluth, prin. Fax 563-7068

Lakeview CSD 700/K-12
3744 83rd St 68601 402-563-2345
Paul Calvert, supt. Fax 564-5209
www.lakeview.esu7.org/
Lakeview HS 300/9-12
3744 83rd St 68601 402-563-2345
Robert Arp, prin. Fax 564-5209

Central Community College Post-Sec.
PO Box 1027 68602 402-564-7132
Scotus Central Catholic JSHS 300/7-12
1554 18th Ave 68601 402-564-7165
Wayne Morfeld, prin. Fax 564-6004

Cook, Johnson, Pop. 309
Nemaha Valley SD 200/K-12
PO Box 255 68329 402-864-4171
Jack Moles, supt. Fax 864-2074
www.nemahavalley.org/
Cook JSHS 100/7-12
PO Box 255 68329 402-864-4171
Kirk Gottschalk, prin. Fax 864-2074

Cozad, Dawson, Pop. 4,222
Cozad CSD 1,000/K-12
PO Box 15 69130 308-784-2745
John Grinde, supt. Fax 784-2728
Cozad HS 300/9-12
PO Box 268 69130 308-784-2744
Phill Parker, prin. Fax 784-2728
Cozad MS 200/6-8
1810 Meridian Ave 69130 308-784-2746
Todd Hilyard, prin. Fax 784-2606

Crawford, Dawes, Pop. 1,035
Crawford SD 300/PK-12
908 5th St 69339 308-665-1537
Merrell Nelsen, supt. Fax 665-1483
www.cpsrams.org/
Crawford JSHS 100/7-12
908 5th St 69339 308-665-1531
Merrell Nelsen, prin. Fax 665-1483

Creighton, Knox, Pop. 1,187
Creighton SD 400/K-12
PO Box 10 68729 402-358-3663
Fred Boelter, supt. Fax 358-3804
creighton.esu1.org/
Creighton Community JSHS 300/7-12
PO Box 10 68729 402-358-3663
Jeff Jensen, prin. Fax 358-3804

Crete, Saline, Pop. 6,308
Crete SD 1,600/PK-12
920 Linden Ave 68333 402-826-5855
Kyle McGowan, supt. Fax 826-5120
www.creteschools.com
Crete HS 500/9-12
1500 E 15th St 68333 402-826-5811
Tim Conway, prin. Fax 826-2701
Crete MS 400/6-8
1700 Glenwood Ave 68333 402-826-5844
Kim Jacobson, prin. Fax 826-7789

Doane College Post-Sec.
1014 Boswell Ave 68333 402-826-2161

Crofton, Knox, Pop. 710
Crofton Community SD 400/K-12
PO Box 429 68730 402-388-2440
Randall Anderson, supt. Fax 388-4265
www.croftonschools.com/
Crofton JSHS 200/7-12
PO Box 429 68730 402-388-2440
Todd Strom, prin. Fax 388-4265

Curtis, Frontier, Pop. 736
Medicine Valley SD 200/K-12
PO Box 9 69025 308-367-4106
Barry Limoges, supt. Fax 367-4108
www.mvraiders.org/
Medicine Valley JSHS 100/7-12
PO Box 9 69025 308-367-4106
Alan Garey, prin. Fax 367-4108

Nebraska Coll of Technical Agriculture Post-Sec.
404 E 7th St 69025 308-367-4124

Dalton, Cheyenne, Pop. 322
Leyton SD 300/PK-12
PO Box 297 69131 308-377-2303
James M. Calder, supt. Fax 377-2304
Leyton HS 100/9-12
PO Box 297 69131 308-377-2303
Sue Kandel, prin. Fax 377-2304

Davenport, Thayer, Pop. 296
Bruning-Davenport USD 200/K-12
PO Box 190 68335 402-364-2225
Candace Conradt, supt. Fax 364-2477
www.bruning.esu6.org/Homepage.htm
Bruning-Davenport MS 50/7-8
PO Box 190 68335 402-364-2225
Candace Conradt, prin. Fax 364-2477
Other Schools – See Bruning

David City, Butler, Pop. 2,558
David City SD 700/PK-12
750 D St 68632 402-367-4590
Jerry Phillips, supt. Fax 367-3479
www.davidcitypublicschools.org/
David City JSHS 300/7-12
750 D St 68632 402-367-3187
Tom Jahde, prin. Fax 367-3479

Aquinas HS 300/6-12
PO Box 149 68632 402-367-3175
David McMahon, prin. Fax 367-3176

Daykin, Jefferson, Pop. 167
Meridian SD 200/K-12
PO Box 190 68338 402-446-7265
Stephen Deger, supt. Fax 446-7246
www.meridian.esu6.k12.ne.us/
Meridian JSHS 100/7-12
PO Box 190 68338 402-446-7265
Kenneth Stauss, prin. Fax 446-7246

Deshler, Thayer, Pop. 790
Deshler SD 300/K-12
PO Box 547 68340 402-365-7272
Larry Wilbeck, supt. Fax 365-7560
www.deshler.esu6.k12.ne.us/
Deshler JSHS 200/7-12
PO Box 547 68340 402-365-7272
Jack Waite, prin. Fax 365-7560

De Witt, Saline, Pop. 577
Tri County SD 400/K-12
72520 Highway 103 68341 402-683-2015
Timothy Dewaard, supt. Fax 683-2116
www.tricountyschools.org/
Tri County JSHS 200/7-12
72520 Highway 103 68341 402-683-2015
Dennis Shipp, prin. Fax 683-2116

Dodge, Dodge, Pop. 683
Dodge SD 200/K-12
209 N Ash St 68633 402-693-2207
Thomas Reeser, supt. Fax 693-2209
www.dodgepublicschools.org/
Dodge JSHS 100/7-12
209 N Ash St 68633 402-693-2207
Patty Novicki, prin. Fax 693-2209

Doniphan, Hall, Pop. 762
Doniphan-Trumbull SD 500/K-12
PO Box 300 68832 402-845-2282
Del Prindle, supt. Fax 845-6688
sites.esu9.org/doniphantrumbull/
Doniphan-Trumbull JSHS 200/7-12
PO Box 300 68832 402-845-6531
Alois Meier, prin. Fax 845-6688

Dorchester, Saline, Pop. 630
Dorchester SD 200/K-12
PO Box 7 68343 402-946-2781
Alan Ehlers, supt. Fax 946-6271
www.dorchester.esu6.k12.ne.us/
Dorchester JSHS 100/7-12
PO Box 7 68343 402-946-2781
Brian Redinger, prin. Fax 946-6271

Dunning, Blaine, Pop. 90
Sandhills SD 100/K-12
PO Box 29 68833 308-538-2224
Alberta Moore, supt. Fax 538-2228
sites.sandhills.k12.ne.us/sandhillspanthers/
Dunning JSHS 100/7-12
PO Box 29 68833 308-538-2224
Alberta Moore, prin. Fax 538-2228

Elba, Howard, Pop. 239
Elba SD 100/K-12
PO Box 100 68835 308-863-2228
Michael Gillming, supt. Fax 863-2329
userweb.esu10.org/~elba@esu10.org/
Elba JSHS 100/7-12
PO Box 100 68835 308-863-2228
Theresa Petska, prin. Fax 863-2329

Elgin, Antelope, Pop. 681
Elgin SD 100/K-12
PO Box 399 68636 402-843-2455
Gayla Fredrickson, supt. Fax 843-2475
elgineagles.org/
Elgin HS 100/9-12
PO Box 399 68636 402-843-2457
Corey Fisher, prin. Fax 843-2475

Pope John XXIII Central Catholic HS 100/7-12
PO Box 179 68636 402-843-5325
Jason Heitz, prin. Fax 843-2297

Elkhorn, Douglas, Pop. 8,192
Elkhorn SD 3,700/PK-12
502 Glenn St 68022 402-289-2579
Roger Breed Ed.D., supt. Fax 289-2585
www.elkhornweb.org/
Elkhorn HS 1,000/9-12
711 Veterans Dr 68022 402-289-4239
Bary Habrock, prin. Fax 289-4383
Elkhorn MS 400/6-8
500 Hillcrest St 68022 402-289-2428
Michael Tomjack, prin. Fax 289-1639
Other Schools – See Omaha

Mt. Michael Benedictine HS 200/9-12
22520 Mount Michael Rd 68022 402-289-2541
Tom Ridder, prin. Fax 289-4539

Elm Creek, Buffalo, Pop. 867
Elm Creek SD 300/K-12
PO Box 490 68836 308-856-4300
Larry Babcock, supt. Fax 856-4907
www.elmcreek.k12.ne.us/
Elm Creek JSHS 200/7-12
PO Box 490 68836 308-856-4300
Gary Brouillette, prin. Fax 856-4907

Elwood, Gosper, Pop. 712
Elwood SD 300/K-12
PO Box 107 68937 308-785-2491
Richard D. Einspahr, supt. Fax 785-2322
www.esu11.org/elwood/elwhome.html
Elwood JSHS 100/7-12
PO Box 107 68937 308-785-2491
Jon Davis, prin. Fax 785-2322

Emerson, Dakota, Pop. 816
Emerson-Hubbard SD 300/K-12
PO Box 9 68733 402-695-2621
Thomas Becker, supt. Fax 695-2622
emersonhubbardschools.org/
Emerson-Hubbard JSHS 200/7-12
PO Box 9 68733 402-695-2636
Ed Stansberry, prin. Fax 695-2622

Eustis, Frontier, Pop. 410
Eustis-Farnham SD 200/K-12
PO Box 9 69028 308-486-3991
Carl Dietz, supt. Fax 486-5350
www.esu11.org/eustis/home.htm
Eustis-Farnham HS 100/7-12
PO Box 9 69028 308-486-3991
Kyle Hemmerling, prin. Fax 486-5350

Ewing, Holt, Pop. 414
Ewing SD 100/K-12
PO Box 98 68735 402-626-7235
Dr. Gayla Fredrickson, supt. Fax 626-7236
www.esu8.org/~ewing/homepage.html
Ewing JSHS 100/7-12
PO Box 98 68735 402-626-7235
Greg A. Appleby, prin. Fax 626-7236

Exeter, Fillmore, Pop. 679
Exeter-Milligan SD 300/PK-12
PO Box 139 68351 402-266-5911
Thomas Sharp, supt. Fax 266-4811
Exeter-Milligan JSHS 200/7-12
PO Box 139 68351 402-266-5911
Lindley Schlueter, prin. Fax 266-4811

Fairbury, Jefferson, Pop. 4,020
Fairbury SD 1,000/PK-12
703 K St 68352 402-729-6104
Frederick J. Helmink, supt. Fax 729-6392
www.fairburyjeffs.org/
Fairbury JSHS 500/7-12
1501 9th St 68352 402-729-6116
Jeff Vetter, prin. Fax 729-6275

Fairfield, Clay, Pop. 441
South Central Nebraska Unified SD 1,100/PK-12
30671 Highway 14 68938 402-726-2151
Kent Miller, supt. Fax 726-2208
162.127.9.3:8080/scnud5/
Sandy Creek JSHS 200/7-12
30671 Highway 14 68938 402-726-2151
Jason Searle, prin. Fax 726-2208
Other Schools – See Nelson, Superior

Fairmont, Fillmore, Pop. 659
Fillmore Central SD
Supt. — See Geneva
Fillmore Central MS 200/5-8
PO Box 157 68354 402-268-3411
Jeremy Klein, prin. Fax 268-3491

Falls City, Richardson, Pop. 4,218
Falls City SD 900/PK-12
PO Box 129 68355 402-245-2825
Dr. Jon Habben, supt. Fax 245-2022
www.fctigers.org/
Falls City HS 300/9-12
1400 Fulton St 68355 402-245-2116
Arlan Andreesen, prin. Fax 245-5050
Falls City MS 200/6-8
PO Box 129 68355 402-245-3455
Rick Johnson, prin. Fax 245-2022

Sacred Heart S 200/K-12
1820 Fulton St 68355 402-245-4151
Doug Goltz, prin. Fax 462-2106

Firth, Lancaster, Pop. 687
Norris SD 160 1,700/PK-12
25211 S 68th St 68358 402-791-0000
Roy Baker, supt. Fax 791-0025
www.norris160.org
Norris HS 500/9-12
25211 S 68th St 68358 402-791-0010
John Skretta, prin. Fax 791-0025

Norris MS 400/6-8
25211 S 68th St 68358 402-791-0020
Barry Stark, prin. Fax 791-0025

Fort Calhoun, Washington, Pop. 917
Fort Calhoun SD 600/K-12
PO Box 430 68023 402-468-5592
Gerald Beach, supt. Fax 468-5593
www.fortcalhounschools.org/
Fort Calhoun JSHS 300/7-12
PO Box 430 68023 402-468-5591
Donald Johnson, prin. Fax 468-5593

Franklin, Franklin, Pop. 980
Franklin SD 300/K-12
1001 M St 68939 308-425-6283
Mike Lucas, supt. Fax 425-6553
www.esu11.org/franklin/franklin.home.html
Franklin JSHS 200/7-12
1001 M St 68939 308-425-6283
Fax 425-6553

Fremont, Dodge, Pop. 25,314
Fremont SD 4,600/PK-12
130 E 9th St 68025 402-727-3000
Dr. Stephen Sexton, supt. Fax 727-3002
www.fpsweb.org
Fremont HS 1,300/9-12
1750 N Lincoln Ave 68025 402-727-3050
Joe Sajevic, prin. Fax 727-3033
Fremont MS 1,000/6-8
540 Johnson Rd 68025 402-727-3100
Gale Hamilton, prin. Fax 727-3963

Archbishop Bergan JSHS 200/6-12
545 E 4th St 68025 402-721-9683
Ron Beacom, prin. Fax 721-5366
Bahner College of Hairstyling Post-Sec.
1660 N Grant St 68025 402-721-6500
Midland Lutheran College Post-Sec.
900 N Clarkson St 68025 402-721-5480

Friend, Saline, Pop. 1,204
Friend SD 300/K-12
PO Box 67 68359 402-947-2781
Chris Effken, supt. Fax 947-2026
www.friend.esu6.org/
Friend JSHS 200/7-12
PO Box 67 68359 402-947-2781
James Moore, prin. Fax 947-2026

Fullerton, Nance, Pop. 1,259
Fullerton SD 400/K-12
PO Box 520 68638 308-536-2431
Jeffrey Anderson, supt. Fax 536-2432
teachers.esu7.org/fps/
Fullerton HS 100/9-12
PO Box 520 68638 308-536-2431
Pat Larsen, prin. Fax 536-2432

Geneva, Fillmore, Pop. 2,149
Fillmore Central SD 600/K-12
1410 L St 68361 402-759-4955
Mark Norvell, supt. Fax 759-4038
www.fcps.esu6.org/
Fillmore Central HS 200/9-12
1410 L St 68361 402-759-3141
James Rose, prin. Fax 759-4038
Other Schools – See Fairmont

Genoa, Nance, Pop. 883
Twin River SD 400/K-12
PO Box 640 68640 402-993-2274
Donald Graff, supt. Fax 993-7718
www.esu7.org/~trweb/
Twin River JSHS at Genoa 200/7-12
PO Box 640 68640 402-993-2911
Tod Heier, prin. Fax 993-7718

Gering, Scotts Bluff, Pop. 7,767
Gering SD 2,100/PK-12
1800 8th St 69341 308-436-3125
Don Hague, supt. Fax 436-4301
www.geringschools.net
Gering JHS 500/7-9
800 Q St 69341 308-436-3123
Maurie Deines, prin. Fax 436-6010
Gering SHS 500/10-12
1500 U St 69341 308-436-3121
Eldon Hubbard, prin. Fax 436-4214

Gibbon, Buffalo, Pop. 1,753
Gibbon SD 600/K-12
PO Box 790 68840 308-468-6555
Larry Witt, supt. Fax 468-5164
www.gibbon.k12.ne.us/
Gibbon JSHS 300/7-12
PO Box 790 68840 308-468-5721
Julie Schnitzler, prin. Fax 468-5164

Giltner, Hamilton, Pop. 400
Giltner SD 200/K-12
PO Box 160 68841 402-849-2238
Kenneth Mahlin, supt. Fax 849-2440
www.esu9.org/~giltner@esu9.org/
Giltner JSHS 100/7-12
PO Box 160 68841 402-849-2238
John Poppert, prin. Fax 849-2440

Gordon, Sheridan, Pop. 1,589
Gordon-Rushville SD 600/K-12
PO Box 530 69343 308-282-1322
William Tuma, supt. Fax 282-2207
www.grmustangs.org
Gordon-Rushville HS 200/9-12
PO Box 530 69343 308-282-1322
Lori Liggett, prin. Fax 282-2207
Other Schools – See Rushville

Gothenburg, Dawson, Pop. 3,692
Gothenburg SD 800/K-12
1322 Avenue I 69138 308-537-3651
Michael Teahon, supt. Fax 537-3965
userweb.esu10.org/~gothenbu@esu10.org/
Gothenburg JSHS 400/7-12
1322 Avenue I 69138 308-537-3651
Randy Evans, prin. Fax 537-3965

Grand Island, Hall, Pop. 44,546
Grand Island SD 8,000/PK-12
PO Box 4904 68802 308-385-5900
Dr. Stephen Joel, supt. Fax 385-5949
www.gips.org/
Barr MS 700/6-8
602 W Stolley Park Rd 68801 308-385-5875
Jeff Gilbertson, prin. Fax 385-5880
Grand Island HS 1,900/9-12
2124 N Lafayette Ave 68803 308-385-5950
Dr. Kenton Mann, prin. Fax 385-5966
Walnut MS 800/6-8
1600 N Custer Ave 68803 308-385-5990
Vikki Deuel, prin. Fax 385-5992
Westridge MS 300/6-8
1812 Mansfield Rd 68803 308-385-5886
Dr. Dan Brosz, prin. Fax 385-5003

Northwest SD 1,400/K-12
2710 N North Rd 68803 308-385-6398
Bill L. Mowinkel, supt. Fax 385-6393
Northwest HS 700/9-12
2710 N North Rd 68803 308-385-6398
Doyle Denney, prin. Fax 385-6393

Central Catholic HS 300/6-12
1200 Ruby Ave 68803 308-384-2440
Gregory Logston, prin. Fax 389-3274
Central Community College Post-Sec.
PO Box 4903 68802 308-398-4222
Heartland Lutheran HS 100/9-12
3900 W Husker Hwy 68803 308-385-3900
Fred Chandler, dir. Fax 381-7415
Joseph's College of Beauty Post-Sec.
305 W 3rd St 68801 308-381-8848

Grant, Perkins, Pop. 1,145
Perkins County SD 300/K-12
PO Box 829 69140 308-352-4735
Kirk Russell, supt. Fax 352-4769
www.pcs.k12.ne.us/
Perkins County HS 100/9-12
PO Box 829 69140 308-352-4735
Dean Friedel, prin. Fax 352-4769
Other Schools – See Madrid

Greeley, Greeley, Pop. 511
Greeley-Wolbach SD 200/PK-12
PO Box 160 68842 308-428-3145
Gene Haddix, supt. Fax 428-5395
teachers.esu10.org/gwtitans/
Greeley-Wolbach HS 100/9-12
PO Box 160 68842 308-428-3145
Todd Beck, prin. Fax 428-5395
Other Schools – See Wolbach

Gretna, Sarpy, Pop. 4,860
Gretna SD 2,000/K-12
11717 S 216th St 68028 402-332-3265
Kevin Riley, supt. Fax 332-5833
gretna.esu3.org/
Gretna HS 600/9-12
11335 S 204th St 68028 402-332-3936
Kirk Eledge, prin. Fax 332-4119
Gretna MS 500/6-8
11705 S 216th St 68028 402-332-3048
Harvey Birky, prin. Fax 332-2931

Hampton, Hamilton, Pop. 439
Hampton SD 200/K-12
458 5th St 68843 402-725-3117
Holly Herzberg, supt. Fax 725-3334
www.esu9.org/~hampton@esu9.org/
Hampton JSHS 100/7-12
458 5th St 68843 402-725-3116
Gerald Eickhoff, prin. Fax 725-3334

Harrisburg, Banner
Banner County SD 200/K-12
PO Box 5 69345 308-436-5263
Lana Sides, supt. Fax 436-5252
schools.esu13.org/bannercounty/
Banner County JSHS 100/7-12
PO Box 5 69345 308-436-5263
Gerald Wallace, prin. Fax 436-5252

Harrison, Sioux, Pop. 277
Sioux County SD 100/K-12
PO Box 38 69346 308-668-2415
William Porter, supt. Fax 668-2260
Sioux County HS 50/9-12
PO Box 38 69346 308-668-2415
Matthew Stetson, prin. Fax 668-2260

Hartington, Cedar, Pop. 1,587
Hartington SD 300/K-12
PO Box 75 68739 402-254-3947
Scott Swisher, supt. Fax 254-3945
hartington.esu1.org/
Hartington JSHS 200/7-12
PO Box 75 68739 402-254-3947
Russell Flamig, prin. Fax 254-3945

Cedar Catholic HS 200/7-12
PO Box 15 68739 402-254-3906
Robert Bengston, prin. Fax 254-3976

Harvard, Clay, Pop. 943
Harvard SD 300/K-12
PO Box 100 68944 402-772-2171
Larry Turnquist, supt. Fax 772-2204
www.harvard.esu9.org/
Harvard JSHS 100/7-12
PO Box 100 68944 402-772-2171
Brent Williamson, prin. Fax 772-2204

Hastings, Adams, Pop. 25,437
Adams Central SD 800/K-12
PO Box 1088 68902 402-463-3285
Melvin Crowe, supt. Fax 463-6344
Adams Central JSHS 500/7-12
PO Box 1088 68902 402-463-3285
David Barrett, prin. Fax 463-6344

Hastings SD 3,200/PK-12
714 W 5th St 68901 402-461-7500
Gene Cosby, supt. Fax 461-7509
www1.hastings.esu9.k12.ne.us/
Hastings HS 1,000/9-12
1100 W 14th St 68901 402-461-7550
Jay Opperman, prin. Fax 461-7535
Hastings MS 500/7-8
505 N Hastings Ave 68901 402-461-7520
Jeffrey Schneider, prin. Fax 461-7650

Central Community College Post-Sec.
PO Box 1024 68902 402-463-9811
Hastings College Post-Sec.
PO Box 269 68902 402-463-2402
Joseph's College of Beauty Post-Sec.
828 W 2nd St 68901 402-463-1357
Mary Lanning Memorial Hospital Post-Sec.
715 N Saint Joseph Ave 68901 402-463-4521
St. Cecilia MSHS 400/6-12
521 N Kansas Ave 68901 402-462-2105
Marie Butler, prin. Fax 462-2106

Hayes Center, Hayes, Pop. 226
Hayes Center SD 200/K-12
PO Box 8 69032 308-286-3341
Thomas McMahon, supt. Fax 286-3330
Hayes Center JSHS 100/7-12
PO Box 8 69032 308-286-3341
Kathryn Repass, prin. Fax 286-3330

Hay Springs, Sheridan, Pop. 585
Hay Springs SD 200/PK-12
PO Box 280 69347 308-638-4434
Ernest Griffiths, supt. Fax 638-7500
www.hshawks.com/
Hay Springs HS 100/9-12
PO Box 280 69347 308-638-4434
Ernest Griffiths, prin. Fax 638-7500
Hay Springs MS 50/6-8
PO Box 280 69347 308-638-4434
Mikal Shalikow, prin. Fax 638-7500

Hebron, Thayer, Pop. 1,410
Thayer Central Community SD 300/K-12
PO Box 9 68370 402-768-6117
Drew Harris, supt. Fax 768-6110
www.thayercentral.org/
Thayer Central HS 100/7-12
PO Box 9 68370 402-768-6117
Tom Kiburz, prin. Fax 768-6110

Hemingford, Box Butte, Pop. 916
Hemingford SD 400/PK-12
PO Box 217 69348 308-487-3328
Casper Ningen, supt. Fax 487-5215
www.hemingfordschools.org/
Hemingford JSHS 200/7-12
PO Box 217 69348 308-487-3328
Peggy Thayer, prin. Fax 487-5215

Henderson, York, Pop. 999
Heartland Community SD 300/K-12
PO Box 626 68371 402-723-4434
Norman Yoder, supt. Fax 723-4431
www.heartlandschools.org/
Heartland Community HS 100/9-12
PO Box 626 68371 402-723-4434
Blaine Friesen, prin. Fax 723-4431
Other Schools – See Bradshaw

Hershey, Lincoln, Pop. 568
Hershey SD 500/K-12
PO Box 369 69143 308-368-5574
Dr. Michael Cunning, supt. Fax 368-5570
webquests.esu16.org:8080/hershey/
Hershey JSHS 300/7-12
PO Box 369 69143 308-368-5573
Richard Elsasser, prin. Fax 368-5570

Hildreth, Franklin, Pop. 352
Wilcox-Hildreth SD
Supt. — See Wilcox
Wilcox-Hildreth MS 100/6-8
PO Box 157 68947 308-938-3825
Roger Boyer, prin. Fax 938-5335

Holdrege, Phelps, Pop. 5,349
Holdrege SD 1,200/K-12
PO Box 2002 68949 308-995-8663
Cynthia Wendell, supt. Fax 995-6956
www.thedusters.org/
Holdrege HS 400/9-12
PO Box 2002 68949 308-995-6558
Bob Drews, prin. Fax 995-8662
Holdrege MS 300/5-8
PO Box 2002 68949 308-995-5421
Russell Baker, prin. Fax 995-4970

Homer, Dakota, Pop. 603
Homer Community SD 400/PK-12
PO Box 340 68030 402-698-2377
Bruce Johnson, supt. Fax 698-2379
homerweb.esu1.org/
Homer JSHS 200/7-12
PO Box 340 68030 402-698-2377
Randy Pirner, prin. Fax 698-2379

Hooper, Dodge, Pop. 798
Logan View SD 500/K-12
2163 County Road G 68031 402-654-3317
Dr. Jeffrey Edwards, supt. Fax 654-3699
www.loganview.org/
Logan View JSHS 300/7-12
2163 County Road G 68031 402-654-3317
Kolin Haecker, prin. Fax 654-3699

Howells, Colfax, Pop. 635
Howells SD 200/K-12
PO Box 159 68641 402-986-1621
Thomas Reeser, supt. Fax 986-1261
Howells JSHS 200/7-12
PO Box 159 68641 402-986-1621
Dan Martin, prin. Fax 986-1261

Humboldt, Richardson, Pop. 852
Humboldt & Table Rock Steinauer USD 2007 400/PK-12
PO Box 31 68376 402-862-2235
Clinton Kimbrough, supt. Fax 862-3135
www.humboldt.esu6.org
Humboldt & Table Rock Steinauer HS 100/9-12
PO Box 31 68376 402-862-2235
Laurie Kimbrough, prin. Fax 862-3135
Other Schools – See Table Rock

Humphrey, Platte, Pop. 768
Humphrey SD 200/PK-12
PO Box 278 68642 402-923-1230
Greg Sjuts, supt. Fax 923-1235
www.humphrey.esu7.org/
Humphrey JSHS 100/7-12
PO Box 278 68642 402-923-1230
Marty Moser, prin. Fax 923-1235

St. Francis S 300/K-12
300 S 7th St Ste 277 68642 402-923-0818
Darron Arlt, prin. Fax 923-1590

Hyannis, Grant, Pop. 257
District 11 Area Schools 200/K-12
PO Box 286 69350 308-458-2202
Raymond Davis, supt. Fax 458-2227
Hyannis JSHS 100/7-12
PO Box 286 69350 308-458-2202
Dennis R. Wilbur, prin. Fax 458-2227

Imperial, Chase, Pop. 1,876
Chase County SD 600/K-12
PO Box 577 69033 308-882-4304
Matthew Fisher, supt. Fax 882-5629
www.ccschools.cc/schools/
Chase County HS 200/9-12
PO Box 577 69033 308-882-4304
Michael Sorensen, prin. Fax 882-5629

Indianola, Red Willow, Pop. 611
Southwest SD 179
Supt. — See Bartley
Southwest HS 100/9-12
39145 Road 718 69034 308-364-2202
Matt Springer, prin. Fax 364-2508

Johnson, Nemaha, Pop. 253
Johnson-Brock SD 300/K-12
PO Box 186 68378 402-868-5235
Warren Barnell, supt. Fax 868-4785
manila.esu4.org/JohnsonBrock/
Johnson JSHS 100/7-12
PO Box 186 68378 402-868-5235
Jacquelyn Kelsay, prin. Fax 868-4785

Kearney, Buffalo, Pop. 28,958
Kearney SD 5,000/PK-12
310 W 24th St 68845 308-698-8000
Dr. Brian Maher, supt. Fax 698-8001
www.kearneypublicschools.org/
Horizon MS 500/6-8
915 W 35th St 68845 308-698-8120
Kipp Petersen, prin. Fax 698-8143
Kearney HS 1,400/9-12
3610 6th Ave 68845 308-698-8060
Steve Wickham, prin. Fax 698-8061
Kearney West HS 200/7-12
2802 30th Ave 68845 308-338-2011
Anthony Kleidosty, prin. Fax 865-5323
Sunrise MS 500/6-8
4611 Avenue N 68847 308-698-8150
Lance Fuller, prin. Fax 698-8152

Joseph's of Kearney Sch of Hair Design Post-Sec.
2213 Central Ave 68847 308-234-6594
Kearney Catholic HS 300/6-12
PO Box 1866 68848 308-234-2610
Terrence Torson, prin. Fax 234-4986
University of Nebraska at Kearney Post-Sec.
905 W 25th St 68845 308-865-8526

Kenesaw, Adams, Pop. 913
Kenesaw SD 200/K-12
PO Box 129 68956 402-752-3215
William Troshynski, supt. Fax 752-3579
www.esu9.org/~kenesaw/
Kenesaw JSHS 100/7-12
PO Box 129 68956 402-752-3215
Robby Thompson, prin. Fax 752-3579

Kimball, Kimball, Pop. 2,341
Kimball SD 600/K-12
816 E 3rd St 69145 308-235-2188
Troy Unzicker, supt. Fax 235-3269
kimball.k12.ne.us/
Kimball JSHS 300/7-12
901 S Nadine St 69145 308-235-4861
Chad L. Denker, prin. Fax 235-4128

Laurel, Cedar, Pop. 924
Laurel-Concord SD 400/K-12
PO Box 8 68745 402-256-3133
Daniel Hoesing, supt. Fax 256-9465
www.laurel.esu1.org
Laurel-Concord JSHS 200/7-12
PO Box 8 68745 402-256-3731
Leslie Owen, prin. Fax 256-9465

La Vista, Sarpy, Pop. 15,692
Papillion-La Vista SD
Supt. — See Papillion
La Vista JHS 700/7-8
7900 Edgewood Blvd 68128 402-898-0436
Thomas Furby, prin. Fax 898-0442

Leigh, Colfax, Pop. 432
Leigh Community SD 200/K-12
PO Box 98 68643 402-487-2228
Grant Norgaard, supt. Fax 487-2607
www.esu7.org/~leiweb/leigh.html
Leigh JSHS 100/7-12
PO Box 98 68643 402-487-2228
Steven Borer, prin. Fax 487-2607

Lewellen, Garden, Pop. 244
Garden County SD
Supt. — See Oshkosh
Garden County JHS 100/5-8
PO Box 268 69147 308-778-5561
Greg Stanfield, prin. Fax 778-5568

Lewiston, Pawnee, Pop. 81
Lewiston SD 200/K-12
306 Tiger Ave 68380 402-865-4675
Dr. Bruce McCoy, supt. Fax 865-4875
www.lewistonschools.org/
Lewiston JSHS 100/7-12
306 Tiger Ave 68380 402-865-4675
Dan Parks, prin. Fax 865-4875

Lexington, Dawson, Pop. 10,085
Lexington SD 2,800/PK-12
PO Box 890 68850 308-324-4681
Clarence Chessmore Ed.D., supt. Fax 324-2528
www.lex.esu10.org/
Lexington HS 700/9-12
705 W 13th St 68850 308-324-4691
David Gordon, prin. Fax 324-7224
Lexington MS 600/6-8
1100 N Washington St 68850 308-324-2349
Dean Tickle, prin. Fax 324-6612

Lincoln, Lancaster, Pop. 239,213
Lincoln SD 31,900/PK-12
PO Box 82889 68501 402-436-1000
E. Susan Gourley Ph.D., supt. Fax 436-1620
www.lps.org/
Culler MS 500/6-8
5201 Vine St 68504 402-436-1210
Dan Larson, prin. Fax 458-3210
Dawes MS 400/6-8
5130 Colfax Ave 68504 402-436-1211
Dave Knudsen, prin. Fax 458-3211
Goodrich MS 700/6-8
4600 Lewis Ave 68521 402-436-1213
Michael Henninger, prin. Fax 458-3213
Irving MS 800/6-8
2745 S 22nd St 68502 402-436-1214
Hugh McDermott, prin. Fax 458-3214
Lefler MS 600/6-8
1100 S 48th St 68510 402-436-1215
Kelly Schrad, prin. Fax 458-3215
Lincoln East HS 1,600/9-12
1000 S 70th St 68510 402-436-1302
Dr. Mary Lehmanowsky, prin. Fax 436-1325
Lincoln HS 1,800/9-12
2229 J St 68510 402-436-1301
Dr. Michael Wortman, prin. Fax 458-1540
Lincoln Northeast HS 1,600/9-12
2635 N 63rd St 68507 402-436-1303
Kurt Glathar, prin. Fax 436-1345
Lincoln Northstar HS 1,500/9-12
5801 N 33rd St 68504 402-436-1305
Dr. Nancy Becker, prin. Fax 436-1054
Lincoln Southeast HS 1,600/9-12
2930 S 37th St 68506 402-436-1304
Dr. Patrick Hunter-Pirtle, prin. Fax 436-1357
Lincoln Southwest HS 1,700/9-12
7001 S 14th St 68512 402-436-1306
Jerry Wilks, prin. Fax 436-1085
Lux MS 900/6-8
7800 High St 68506 402-436-1220
William Bucher, prin. Fax 458-3292
Mickle MS 700/6-8
2500 N 67th St 68507 402-436-1216
John Neal, prin. Fax 458-3216
North Star MS 200/6-8
5801 N 33rd St 68504 402-436-1305
Dr. Nancy Becker, prin. Fax 436-1054
Park MS 700/6-8
855 S 8th St 68508 402-436-1212
Dr. Terry Neddenriep, prin. Fax 458-3212
Pound MS 700/6-8
4740 S 45th St 68516 402-436-1217
Dr. Christopher Deibler, prin. Fax 458-3217
Scott MS 900/6-8
2200 Pine Lake Rd 68512 402-436-1218
Dr. Linda Hix, prin. Fax 458-3218

Bryan LGH College of Health Science Post-Sec.
5035 Everett St 68506 402-481-8697
College of Hair Design Post-Sec.
304 S 11th St 68508 402-477-4040
College View Academy 100/K-12
5240 Calvert St 68506 402-483-1181
David Branum, prin. Fax 483-5574
Hamilton College - Lincoln Campus Post-Sec.
PO Box 82826 68501 402-474-5315
Joseph's College of Beauty Post-Sec.
2637 O St 68510 402-435-2333
Lincoln Christian S 500/PK-12
5801 S 84th St 68516 402-488-8888
Mark Wilson, supt. Fax 488-6617
Lincoln Lutheran JSHS 400/6-12
1100 N 56th St 68504 402-467-5404
Scott Ernstmeyer, prin. Fax 467-5405
Lincoln Pius X HS 1,000/9-12
6000 A St 68510 402-488-0931
Thomas Korta, prin. Fax 488-1061
Myotherapy Institute Post-Sec.
6020 S 58th St 68516 402-421-7410
Nebraska Wesleyan University Post-Sec.
5000 Saint Paul Ave 68504 402-466-2371
Parkview Christian S 100/PK-12
4400 N 1st St 68521 402-474-5820
Larry Frost, supt. Fax 474-5830
Southeast Community College Post-Sec.
8800 O St 68520 402-437-2500
Union College Post-Sec.
3800 S 48th St 68506 402-488-2331
University of Nebraska Post-Sec.
14th & R Sts 68588 402-472-7211

Lindsay, Platte, Pop. 270

Holy Family S 200/1-12
PO Box 158 68644 402-428-3455
Nathan Vitosh, prin. Fax 428-3231

Litchfield, Sherman, Pop. 260
Litchfield SD 100/K-12
PO Box 167 68852 308-446-2244
Michael Gillming, supt. Fax 446-2244
sites.litchfield.k12.ne.us/
Litchfield JSHS 100/7-12
PO Box 167 68852 308-446-2244
Brad Stithem, prin. Fax 446-2244

Lodgepole, Cheyenne, Pop. 359
Creek Valley SD
Supt. — See Chappell
Creek Valley MS 100/5-8
PO Box 158 69149 308-483-5252
Katherine Urbanek, prin. Fax 483-5251

Loomis, Phelps, Pop. 375
Loomis SD 200/K-12
PO Box 250 68958 308-876-2111
Keith Fagot, supt. Fax 876-2372
teachers.esu11.org/loomis/
Loomis JSHS 100/7-12
PO Box 250 68958 308-876-2111
Keith Fagot, prin. Fax 876-2372

Louisville, Cass, Pop. 1,073
Louisville SD 500/K-12
PO Box 489 68037 402-234-3585
Edward Kasl, supt. Fax 234-2141
www.louisvillepublicschools.org/
Louisville HS 200/9-12
PO Box 489 68037 402-234-3585
Cindy Osterloh, prin. Fax 234-2141
Louisville MS 100/6-8
PO Box 489 68037 402-234-3585
Cindy Osterloh, prin. Fax 234-2141

Loup City, Sherman, Pop. 924
Loup City SD 300/K-12
PO Box 628 68853 308-745-0120
Caroline Winchester, supt. Fax 745-0130
www.loupcity.k12.ne.us/
Loup City HS 100/9-12
PO Box 628 68853 308-745-0548
Nicholas Hodge, prin. Fax 745-0130

Lynch, Boyd, Pop. 239
Lynch SD 100/K-12
PO Box 98 68746 402-569-2081
Nelson Dahl, supt. Fax 569-2091
lynch.esu8.org/
Lynch JSHS 100/7-12
PO Box 98 68746 402-569-2081
Nelson Dahl, prin. Fax 569-2091

Lyons, Burt, Pop. 912
Lyons-Decatur Northeast SD 300/K-12
PO Box 526 68038 402-687-2363
Fred Hansen, supt. Fax 687-2472
www.lyonsdecaturschools.org/
Northeast JSHS 200/7-12
PO Box 526 68038 402-687-2349
Douglas Smith, prin. Fax 687-2472

Mc Cook, Red Willow, Pop. 7,926
Mc Cook SD 1,100/K-12
700 W 7th St 69001 308-345-2510
Donald Marchant, supt. Fax 345-2511
www.mccookbison.org/
Mc Cook JHS 200/7-9
800 W 7th St 69001 308-345-6940
Dennis Berry, prin. Fax 345-6941
Mc Cook SHS 400/10-12
600 W 7th St 69001 308-345-5422
Jerome Smith, prin. Fax 345-5477

Mid-Plains Community College Post-Sec.
1205 E 3rd St 69001 800-658-4348

Mc Cool Junction, York, Pop. 388
Mc Cool Junction SD 200/K-12
PO Box 278 68401 402-724-2231
Curtis Cogswell, supt. Fax 724-2232
www.mccool.esu6.org/
Mc Cool Junction JSHS 100/7-12
PO Box 278 68401 402-724-2231
Grant Fisher, prin. Fax 724-2232

Macy, Thurston, Pop. 836
UMO N HO N Nation SD 300/PK-12
PO Box 280 68039 402-837-5622
Morris Bates, supt. Fax 837-5245
macyweb.esu1.org/
UMO N HO N Nation HS 100/9-12
PO Box 280 68039 402-837-5622
David Friedli, prin. Fax 837-5245

UMO N HO N Nation MS 100/6-8
PO Box 280 68039 402-837-5622
Mary Wilson, prin. Fax 837-5245

Nebraska Indian Community College Post-Sec.
PO Box 428 68039 402-837-5078

Madison, Madison, Pop. 2,309
Madison SD 600/K-12
PO Box 450 68748 402-454-3336
David Melick, supt. Fax 454-2238
madison.esu8.org/
Madison HS 200/9-12
PO Box 450 68748 402-454-3336
Steve Borer, prin. Fax 454-2238
Madison MS 100/6-8
PO Box 450 68748 402-454-3336
Steve Borer, prin. Fax 454-2238

Madrid, Perkins, Pop. 256
Perkins County SD
Supt. — See Grant
Perkins County MS 50/6-8
PO Box 501 69150 308-326-4201
Terry Prante, prin. Fax 326-4231

Malcolm, Lancaster, Pop. 441
Malcolm SD 500/K-12
10004 NW 112th St 68402 402-796-2151
Gene Neddenriep, supt. Fax 796-2178
www.malcolmschools.esu6.org/
Malcolm JSHS 200/7-12
10002 NW 112th St 68402 402-796-2151
Earl Nannen, prin. Fax 796-2189

Maxwell, Lincoln, Pop. 323
Maxwell SD 300/PK-12
PO Box 188 69151 308-582-4585
Charles Hervert, supt. Fax 582-4584
userweb.esu16.org/~maxwell/home.html
Maxwell JSHS 100/7-12
PO Box 188 69151 308-582-4585
Aubrey Boucher, prin. Fax 582-4584

Maywood, Frontier, Pop. 294
Maywood SD 200/K-12
PO Box 46 69038 308-362-4223
Barry Limoges, supt. Fax 362-4454
webquests.esu16.org:8080/Maywood/
Maywood JSHS 100/7-12
PO Box 46 69038 308-362-4223
Jeffrey Koehler, prin. Fax 362-4454

Mead, Saunders, Pop. 623
Mead SD 300/K-12
PO Box 158 68041 402-624-2745
George Robertson, supt. Fax 624-2001
www.meadpublicschools.org/
Mead JSHS 200/7-12
PO Box 158 68041 402-624-3435
Cliff Owen, prin. Fax 624-2001

Merna, Custer, Pop. 384
Anselmo-Merna SD 200/K-12
PO Box 68 68856 308-643-2224
Richard Schlesselman, supt. Fax 643-2243
sites.esu10.org/anselmomerna/
Anselmo-Merna JSHS 100/7-12
PO Box 68 68856 308-643-2224
Susan McNeil, prin. Fax 643-2243

Milford, Seward, Pop. 2,053
Milford SD 700/PK-12
PO Box C 68405 402-761-3321
Kevin Wingard, supt. Fax 761-3322
www.milfordpublicschools.org/
Milford JSHS 300/7-12
PO Box C 68405 402-761-2525
Tod Meyer, prin. Fax 761-2663

Southeast Community College Post-Sec.
600 State St 68405 402-761-2131

Minatare, Scotts Bluff, Pop. 784
Minatare SD 200/K-12
PO Box 425 69356 308-783-1232
Charles Bunner, supt. Fax 783-2982
www.minatareschools.com/
Minatare JSHS 100/7-12
PO Box 425 69356 308-783-1733
Michael W. Halley, prin. Fax 783-2982

Minden, Kearney, Pop. 2,913
Minden SD 800/PK-12
PO Box 301 68959 308-832-2440
Scott Maline, supt. Fax 832-2567
Jones MS 300/4-8
PO Box 301 68959 308-832-2338
John Osgood, prin. Fax 832-3236
Minden HS 300/9-12
PO Box 301 68959 308-832-2254
Steve Sampy, prin. Fax 832-1892

Mitchell, Scotts Bluff, Pop. 1,796
Mitchell SD 600/K-12
1819 19th Ave 69357 308-623-1707
Kent Halley, supt. Fax 623-1330
www.mpstigers.com
Mitchell JSHS 300/7-12
1819 19th Ave 69357 308-623-1707
Heath Peters, prin. Fax 623-1330

Morrill, Scotts Bluff, Pop. 941
Morrill SD 500/K-12
PO Box 486 69358 308-247-3414
Roy Ingram, supt. Fax 247-2196
schools.esu13.org/morrill/
Morrill JSHS 200/7-12
PO Box 486 69358 308-247-2149
Dr. Kenton McLellan, prin. Fax 247-2196

Mullen, Hooker, Pop. 497
Mullen SD 200/K-12
PO Box 127 69152 308-546-2223
Jeffery Hoesing, supt. Fax 546-2209
Mullen JSHS 100/7-12
PO Box 127 69152 308-546-2223
Joel Ruybalid, prin. Fax 546-2209

Murdock, Cass, Pop. 273
Elmwood-Murdock SD 400/K-12
PO Box 407 68407 402-867-2341
Daniel Novak, supt. Fax 867-2009
www.elm.esu3.org/index.htm
Elmwood-Murdock JSHS 200/7-12
PO Box 407 68407 402-867-2341
Tim Allemang, prin. Fax 867-2009

Murray, Cass, Pop. 494
Conestoga SD 600/PK-12
PO Box 184 68409 402-235-2992
Mark Sievering, supt. Fax 227-2992
www.conestogacougars.org/
Conestoga JSHS 300/7-12
PO Box 40 68409 402-235-2271
Angela Leifeld, prin. Fax 235-2421

Nebraska City, Otoe, Pop. 7,035
Nebraska City SD 1,300/PK-12
215 N 12th St 68410 402-873-6033
Keith Rohwer, supt. Fax 873-6030
www.nebcity.esu6.org
Nebraska City HS 500/9-12
141 Steinhart Park Rd 68410 402-873-3360
Mark Adler, prin. Fax 873-3831
Nebraska City MS 300/6-8
909 1st Corso 68410 402-873-5591
Jenny Powell, prin. Fax 873-5641

Lourdes Central S 200/6-12
412 2nd Ave 68410 402-873-6154
Jeremy Hazuka, prin. Fax 873-3154
Nebraska School for Visually Handicapped Post-Sec.
10th St & 10th Ave 68410

Neligh, Antelope, Pop. 1,542
Neligh-Oakdale SD 400/K-12
PO Box 149 68756 402-887-4166
Glen Morgan, supt. Fax 887-5322
teachers.esu8.org/nohs/
Neligh-Oakdale JSHS 200/7-12
PO Box 149 68756 402-887-4166
George Loofe, prin. Fax 887-5322

Nelson, Nuckolls, Pop. 539
South Central Nebraska Unified SD
Supt. — See Fairfield
Lawrence/Nelson JSHS 100/7-12
PO Box 368 68961 402-225-3371
Clayton Waddle, prin. Fax 225-5431

Newcastle, Dixon, Pop. 285
Newcastle SD 200/K-12
PO Box 187 68757 402-355-2231
Dan Hoesing, supt. Fax 355-2635
newcastle.esu1.org/
Newcastle JSHS 100/7-12
PO Box 187 68757 402-355-2231
Scott Cole, prin. Fax 355-2635

Newman Grove, Madison, Pop. 774
Newman Grove SD 300/K-12
PO Box 370 68758 402-447-2721
Loren Pokorny, supt. Fax 447-2445
newman.esu8.org/
Newman Grove JSHS 200/7-12
PO Box 370 68758 402-447-6294
Beth Nelson, prin. Fax 447-2445

Niobrara, Knox, Pop. 358
Niobrara SD 100/K-12
247 N Highway 12 68760 402-857-3323
Margaret Sandoz, supt. Fax 857-3877
www.esu1.org/niobrara/niobrara.html
Niobrara JSHS 100/5-12
247 N Highway 12 68760 402-857-3322
Craig Marshall, prin. Fax 857-3716

Santee SD 100/K-12
206 Frazier Ave E 68760 402-857-2741
Bruce Blanchard, supt. Fax 857-2743
santeeweb.esu1.org/
Santee HS 50/9-12
206 Frazier Ave E 68760 402-857-2741
Vincent Hurley, prin. Fax 857-2743

Norfolk, Madison, Pop. 23,946
Norfolk SD 4,000/PK-12
PO Box 139 68702 402-644-2500
Randy Nelson Ed.D., supt. Fax 644-2506
www.norfolkpublicschools.org/
Norfolk JHS 700/8-9
PO Box 139 68702 402-644-2516
David Wright, prin. Fax 644-2519
Norfolk SHS 1,000/10-12
PO Box 139 68702 402-644-2529
Stephen Morton, prin. Fax 644-2538

Joseph's College of Beauty Post-Sec.
202 W Madison Ave 68701 402-371-3358
Lutheran HS Northeast 100/9-12
PO Box 2454 68702 402-379-3040
Paul Leckband, prin. Fax 379-8340
Norfolk Catholic JSHS 300/7-12
2300 W Madison Ave 68701 402-371-2784
Jeff Bellar, prin. Fax 379-2929
Northeast Community College Post-Sec.
PO Box 469 68702 402-371-2020

North Bend, Dodge, Pop. 1,211
North Bend Central SD 500/K-12
PO Box 160 68649 402-652-3268
James Havelka, supt. Fax 652-8348
northbend.esu2.org/
North Bend Central JSHS 300/7-12
PO Box 160 68649 402-652-3268
Randall McIntyre, prin. Fax 652-8348

North Platte, Lincoln, Pop. 24,324
North Platte SD 4,100/K-12
PO Box 1557 69103 308-535-7100
Dr. Paul Brochtrup, supt. Fax 535-5300
www.nppsd.org
Adams MS 700/6-8
1200 Mcdonald Rd 69101 308-535-7112
Todd Rhodes, prin. Fax 535-5309
Madison MS 200/6-8
1400 N Madison Ave 69101 308-535-7126
Tim Vanderheiden, prin. Fax 535-5303
North Platte HS 1,200/9-12
1220 W 2nd St 69101 308-535-7105
Jim Whitney, prin. Fax 535-7111

Mid-Plains Community College Post-Sec.
601 W State Farm Rd 69101 800-658-4308
Mid-Plains Community College Post-Sec.
1101 Halligan Dr 69101 800-658-4308
North Platte Beauty Academy Post-Sec.
107 W 6th St 69101 308-532-4664
St. Patrick HS 200/7-12
PO Box 970 69103 308-532-1874
Mark Stillstead, admin. Fax 532-8015

Oakland, Burt, Pop. 1,298
Oakland Craig SD 500/K-12
309 N Davis Ave 68045 402-685-5661
David Jones, supt. Fax 685-5697
ocknights.esu2.org/
Oakland Craig HS 200/9-12
309 N Davis Ave 68045 402-685-5661
Michael Apple, prin. Fax 685-5697
Oakland Craig JHS 100/7-8
309 N Davis Ave 68045 402-685-5661
Michael Apple, prin. Fax 685-5697

Odell, Gage, Pop. 336
Diller-Odell SD 300/K-12
PO Box 188 68415 402-766-4171
David Schindler, supt. Fax 766-4211
www.dillerodell.org/
Diller-Odell JSHS 200/7-12
PO Box 188 68415 402-766-4171
Darrell Vitosh, prin. Fax 766-4211

Ogallala, Keith, Pop. 4,696
Ogallala SD 1,000/PK-12
205 E 6th St 69153 308-284-4060
Tucker Lillis, supt. Fax 284-3981
www.opsd.org/
Ogallala HS 400/9-12
602 E G St 69153 308-284-4029
Dan Hadden, prin. Fax 284-3869
Ogallala MS 300/6-8
205 E 6th St 69153 308-284-4478
Dave Carpenter, prin. Fax 284-8129

Omaha, Douglas, Pop. 414,521
Elkhorn SD
Supt. — See Elkhorn
Elkhorn Ridge MS 500/6-8
17880 Marcy St 68118 402-334-9302
Kevin Riggert, prin. Fax 334-9378

Millard SD 20,000/PK-12
5606 S 147th St 68137 402-715-8200
Dr. Keith Lutz, supt. Fax 715-8409
www.mpsomaha.org
Andersen MS 700/6-8
15404 Adams St 68137 402-715-8440
Jeff Alfrey, prin. Fax 715-8410
Beadle MS 700/6-8
18201 Jefferson St 68135 402-715-6100
John Southworth, prin. Fax 715-6140
Kiewit MS 1,000/6-8
15650 Howard St 68118 402-715-1470
Lori Jasa, prin. Fax 715-1490
Millard Central MS 800/6-8
12801 L St 68137 402-715-8225
Beth Balkus, prin. Fax 715-8574
Millard North HS 2,400/9-12
1010 S 144th St 68154 402-715-1365
Brian Begley, prin. Fax 715-1336
Millard North MS 600/6-8
2828 S 139th St 68144 402-715-1280
Joan Wilson, prin. Fax 715-1275
Millard South HS 2,000/9-12
14905 Q St 68137 402-715-8268
Curtis Case, prin. Fax 715-6160
Millard West HS 1,900/9-12
5710 S 176th Ave 68135 402-715-6000
Dr. Richard Kolowski, prin. Fax 715-6060
Russell MS 800/6-8
5304 S 172nd St 68135 402-715-8500
Mitch Mollring, prin. Fax 715-8368

Omaha SD 44,700/PK-12
3215 Cuming St 68131 402-557-2222
John Mackiel, supt. Fax 557-2019
www.ops.org
Benson HS 1,500/9-12
5120 Maple St 68104 402-557-3000
Lisa Dale, prin. Fax 557-3039
Beveridge Magnet MS 800/7-8
1616 S 120th St 68144 402-557-4000
Cara Riggs, prin. Fax 557-4009
Bryan HS 1,600/9-12
4700 Giles Rd 68157 402-557-3100
Dave Collins, prin. Fax 557-3139

Bryan MS 900/7-8
8210 S 42nd St 68147 402-557-4100
Susan Colvin, prin. Fax 557-4129
Buffet Magnet MS 300/5-8
14101 Larimore Ave 68164 402-561-6160
Dr. ReNae Kehrberg, prin. Fax 561-6170
Burke HS 2,000/9-12
12200 Burke St 68154 402-557-3200
Dr. Connie Eichhorn, prin. Fax 557-3239
Career Center Vo/Tech
3230 Burt St 68131 402-557-3700
Bob Whitehouse, prin. Fax 557-2629
Central HS 2,500/9-12
124 N 20th St 68102 402-557-3300
Greg Emmel, prin. Fax 557-3339
Hale MS 400/7-8
6143 Whitmore St 68152 402-557-4200
M. Patricia Nedley, prin. Fax 557-4229
King Science Magnet MS 400/5-8
3720 Florence Blvd 68110 402-557-3720
Dr. Deborah Frison, prin. Fax 557-4459
Lewis & Clark MS 700/7-8
6901 Burt St 68132 402-557-4300
Dr. Lisa Sterba, prin. Fax 557-4309
Marrs Magnet MS 400/5-8
5619 S 19th St 68107 402-557-4400
Pamela Cohn, prin. Fax 557-4429
McMillan Magnet MS 800/7-8
3802 Redick Ave 68112 402-557-4500
Dr. Keith Bigsby, prin. Fax 557-4509
Monroe MS 800/7-8
5105 Bedford Ave 68104 402-557-4600
Herman Colvin, prin. Fax 557-4609
Morton MS 600/7-8
4606 Terrace Dr 68134 402-557-4700
Matt Brandl, prin. Fax 557-4709
Norris MS 1,000/7-8
2235 S 46th St 68106 402-557-4800
Burrell Williams, prin. Fax 557-4809
Omaha North HS 1,900/9-12
4410 N 36th St 68111 402-557-3400
Gene Haynes, prin. Fax 557-3439
Omaha Northwest HS 2,000/9-12
8204 Crown Point Ave 68134 402-557-3500
Bernice Nared, prin. Fax 557-3539
Omaha South HS 1,800/9-12
4519 S 24th St 68107 402-557-3600
Nancy Faber, prin. Fax 557-3639

Westside Community SD 5,600/PK-12
909 S 76th St 68114 402-390-2100
Kenneth Bird Ed.D., supt. Fax 390-2136
www.westside66.org/
Westside HS 1,900/9-12
8701 Pacific St 68114 402-343-2600
Pat Hutchings, prin. Fax 343-2608
Westside MS 1,000/7-8
8601 Arbor St 68124 402-390-6464
Eric Weber, prin. Fax 390-6454

Assumption/Guadalupe S 100/3-8
5602 S 22nd St 68107 402-734-4504
Cheryl Castle, prin. Fax 734-4505
Bishop Clarkson Memorial Hospital Post-Sec.
4350 Dewey Ave 68105 402-552-3203
Brownell-Talbot S 500/PK-12
400 N Happy Hollow Blvd 68132 402-556-3772
Diane Desler, hdmstr. Fax 553-2994
Capitol School of Hairstyling - West Post-Sec.
2819 S 125th Ave Ste 268 68144 402-333-3329
Clarkson College Post-Sec.
101 S 42nd St 68131 800-647-5500
College of Saint Mary Post-Sec.
7000 Mercy Rd 68106 402-399-2400
Concordia Lutheran JSHS 200/7-12
15656 Fort St 68116 402-445-4000
Matthew Korte, prin. Fax 965-9310
Creighton Preparatory S 1,000/9-12
7400 Western Ave 68114 402-393-1190
John Naatz, prin. Fax 343-1889
Creighton University Post-Sec.
2500 California Plz 68178 402-280-2700
Duchesne Academy 300/9-12
3601 Burt St 68131 402-558-3800
Laura Hickman, prin. Fax 558-0051
Grace University Post-Sec.
1311 S 9th St 68108 402-449-2800
Gross HS 600/9-12
7700 S 43rd St 68147 402-734-2000
Dr. Dorothy Ostrowski, prin. Fax 734-4270
Hamilton College Post-Sec.
3350 N 90th St 68134 402-572-8500
Immanuel Medical Center Post-Sec.
6901 N 72nd St 68122 402-572-2270
ITT Technical Institute Post-Sec.
9814 M St 68127 402-331-2900
Jesuit MS 100/4-8
2311 N 22nd St 68110 402-346-4464
Anthony Connelly, prin. Fax 341-1817
Marian HS 700/9-12
7400 Military Ave 68134 402-571-2618
Elizabeth Kish, hdmstr. Fax 571-1952
Mercy HS 300/9-12
1501 S 48th St 68106 402-553-9424
Carolyn Jaworski, prin. Fax 553-0394
Metropolitan Community College Post-Sec.
30th & Fort Sts 68111 402-449-8300
Metropolitan Community College Post-Sec.
204th & Dodge St 68103 402-457-2000
Metropolitan Community College Post-Sec.
PO Box 3777 68103 402-449-8400
Nebraska Methodist College Post-Sec.
720 N 87th St 68114 402-354-7200
Omaha Christian Academy 300/PK-12
5612 L St 68117 402-399-9565
Timothy Koehn, supt. Fax 399-0248
Omaha School of Massage Therapy Post-Sec.
9748 Park Dr 68127 402-331-3694

Roncalli HS 300/9-12
6401 Sorensen Pkwy 68152 402-571-7670
Curt Feilmeier, prin. Fax 571-3216
St. Peter Claver Cristo Rey HS 9-12
5301 S 36th St 68107 402-734-1802
Lori Soto, prin. Fax 734-1835
Skutt Catholic HS 700/9-12
3131 S 156th St 68130 402-333-0818
Patrick J. Slattery, prin. Fax 333-1790
The Creative Center Post-Sec.
10850 Emmet St 68164 402-898-1000
University of Nebraska at Omaha Post-Sec.
60th And Dodge St 68182 402-554-2800
University of Nebraska Medical Center Post-Sec.
987020 Nebraska Medical Ctr 68198 402-559-4200
Vatterott College Post-Sec.
11818 I St 68137 402-891-9411
Xenon Intl School of Hair Design Post-Sec.
8516 Park Dr 68127 402-393-2933

O Neill, Holt, Pop. 3,721
O'Neill SD 900/K-12
PO Box 230, 402-336-3775
Amy Shane, supt. Fax 336-4890
oneill.esu8.org/
O'Neill JSHS 400/7-12
PO Box 230, 402-336-1544
Steven Brosz, prin. Fax 336-1105

St. Mary S PK-12
326 E Benton St, 402-336-4455
Norman Hale, prin. Fax 336-1281

Orchard, Antelope, Pop. 359
Nebraska USD 1
Supt. — See Royal
Orchard JSHS 100/7-12
PO Box 269 68764 402-893-3215
Dale Martin, prin. Fax 893-2065

Ord, Valley, Pop. 2,129
Ord SD 600/K-12
320 N 19th St 68862 308-728-5013
Max Kroger, supt. Fax 728-5108
www.ord.esu10.k12.ne.us/
Ord JSHS 300/7-12
1800 K St 68862 308-728-3241
Mark Hagge, prin. Fax 728-5108

Osceola, Polk, Pop. 902
Osceola SD 300/K-12
PO Box 198 68651 402-747-3121
Kenneth Heinz, supt. Fax 747-3041
www.esu7.org/~oweb/osceola.html
Osceola HS 100/9-12
PO Box 198 68651 402-747-3121
Russ Gade, prin. Fax 747-3041
Osceola MS 50/7-8
PO Box 198 68651 402-747-3121
Russ Gade, prin. Fax 747-3041

Oshkosh, Garden, Pop. 766
Garden County SD 300/K-12
PO Box 230 69154 308-772-3242
Paula Sissel, supt. Fax 772-3039
www.gardencountyschools.org/
Garden County HS 100/9-12
PO Box 230 69154 308-772-3242
Greg Stanfield, prin. Fax 772-3039
Other Schools – See Lewellen

Osmond, Pierce, Pop. 746
Osmond SD 300/K-12
PO Box 458 68765 402-748-3777
Ted Hillman, supt. Fax 748-3210
osmond.esu8.org/
Osmond JSHS 200/7-12
PO Box 458 68765 402-748-3777
Randy Jochum, prin. Fax 748-3210

Overton, Dawson, Pop. 655
Overton SD 300/PK-12
PO Box 310 68863 308-987-2424
Mark Aten, supt. Fax 987-2349
www.ovr.esu10.k12.ne.us/
Overton JSHS 100/7-12
PO Box 310 68863 308-987-2424
Mitch Kubicek, prin. Fax 987-2349

Oxford, Furnas, Pop. 806
Southern Valley SD 500/K-12
43739 Highway 89 68967 308-868-2222
Chuck Lambert, supt. Fax 868-2223
teachers.esu11.org/sovalley/
Southern Valley JSHS 300/7-12
43739 Highway 89 68967 308-868-2222
Brent Hollinger, prin. Fax 868-2223

Palmer, Merrick, Pop. 458
Palmer SD 200/K-12
PO Box 248 68864 308-894-3065
Shawn A. Scott, supt. Fax 894-8245
www.palmer.esu7.org/school/school.html
Palmer JSHS 100/7-12
PO Box 248 68864 308-894-3065
Shawn A. Scott, prin. Fax 894-8245

Palmyra, Otoe, Pop. 543
Palmyra SD 500/K-12
PO Box 130 68418 402-780-5327
Clyde Childers, supt. Fax 780-5328
www.district or1.org/
Palmyra JSHS 200/7-12
PO Box 130 68418 402-780-5327
David Bottrell, prin. Fax 780-5328

Papillion, Sarpy, Pop. 20,431
Papillion-La Vista SD 8,500/PK-12
420 S Washington St 68046 402-537-9998
Harlan Metschke, supt. Fax 537-6216
www.paplv.esu3.org

Papillion JHS 600/7-8
423 S Washington St 68046 402-898-0424
John McGill, prin. Fax 898-0430
Papillion-Lavista HS 1,500/9-12
402 E Centennial Rd 68046 402-898-0400
James Glover, prin. Fax 898-0415
Papillion-La Vista South HS 1,300/9-12
10799 Highway 370 68046 402-829-4600
Dr. Enid Schonewise, prin. Fax 827-1330
Other Schools – See La Vista

Nebraska Christian College Post-Sec.
12550 S 114th St 68046 402-935-9400

Pawnee City, Pawnee, Pop. 946
Pawnee City SD 300/K-12
PO Box 393 68420 402-852-2988
Wayne Kohler, supt. Fax 852-2993
www.pawnee.esu6.org/
Pawnee City JSHS 100/7-12
PO Box 393 68420 402-852-2988
Robert West, prin. Fax 852-2993

Paxton, Keith, Pop. 548
Paxton Consolidated SD 200/K-12
PO Box 368 69155 308-239-4283
Delbert F. Dack, supt. Fax 239-4359
www.paxton.k12.ne.us/
Paxton JSHS 100/7-12
PO Box 368 69155 308-239-4283
Sheri M. Chittenden, prin. Fax 239-4359

Pender, Thurston, Pop. 1,165
Pender SD 400/K-12
PO Box 629 68047 402-385-3244
Joe Sherwood, supt. Fax 385-3342
www.penderschools.org/
Pender JSHS 200/7-12
PO Box 629 68047 402-385-3244
Jason Dolliver, prin. Fax 385-3342

Peru, Nemaha, Pop. 778

Peru State College Post-Sec.
PO Box 10 68421 402-872-3815

Petersburg, Boone, Pop. 340
Boone Central SD
Supt. — See Albion
Boone Central MS 100/7-8
PO Box 240 68652 402-386-5302
Mary Thieman, prin. Fax 386-5464

Pierce, Pierce, Pop. 1,730
Pierce SD 700/K-12
201 N Sunset St 68767 402-329-4677
Daniel Navrkal, supt. Fax 329-4678
www.piercepublic.org/
Pierce JSHS 400/7-12
201 N Sunset St 68767 402-329-6217
Mark Brahmer, prin. Fax 329-4678

Pilger, Stanton, Pop. 372
Wisner-Pilger SD
Supt. — See Wisner
Wisner-Pilger MS 7-8
PO Box 325 68768 402-396-3566
David Ludwig, prin. Fax 529-3477

Plainview, Pierce, Pop. 1,279
Plainview SD 400/K-12
PO Box 638 68769 402-582-4993
David Hamm, supt. Fax 582-4665
www.plainviewschools.org/
Plainview JSHS 200/7-12
PO Box 638 68769 402-582-4991
Randall Klooz, prin. Fax 582-4665

Plattsmouth, Cass, Pop. 7,023
Plattsmouth SD 1,800/PK-12
1912 E Highway 34 68048 402-296-3361
Renee Jacobson, supt. Fax 296-2667
www.plattsmouthschools.org/
Plattsmouth HS 500/9-12
1916 E Highway 34 68048 402-296-3322
Jeffery Wiles, prin. Fax 296-3342
Plattsmouth MS 500/5-8
1724 8th Ave 68048 402-296-3174
Mark Smith, prin. Fax 296-2910

Pleasanton, Buffalo, Pop. 344
Pleasanton SD 200/K-12
PO Box 190 68866 308-388-2041
Ronald Wymore, supt. Fax 388-5502
www.pleasanton.k12.ne.us/
Pleasanton JSHS 100/7-12
PO Box 190 68866 308-388-2041
Ronald Wymore, prin. Fax 388-5502

Polk, Polk, Pop. 301
High Plains Community SD 300/K-12
PO Box 29 68654 402-765-2271
Dennis Gray, supt. Fax 765-3332
www.hpc.esu7.org/
High Plains HS 100/9-12
PO Box 29 68654 402-765-3331
Cletus Arasmith, prin. Fax 765-3332
Other Schools – See Clarks

Ponca, Dixon, Pop. 1,042
Ponca SD 500/K-12
PO Box 568 68770 402-755-2241
William Thompson, supt. Fax 755-2992
www.poncaschool.org/
Ponca JSHS 200/7-12
PO Box 568 68770 402-755-2241
Michelle Rinas, prin. Fax 755-2992

Potter, Cheyenne, Pop. 411
Potter-Dix SD 200/K-12
PO Box 189 69156 308-879-4434
Kevin Thomas, supt. Fax 879-4566
www.pdcoyotes.com

Potter-Dix HS 100/7-12
PO Box 189 69156 308-879-4434
Bryce Jorgenson, prin. Fax 879-4566

Prague, Saunders, Pop. 331
Prague SD 100/K-12
PO Box 98 68050 402-663-4388
Gene L. Burton, supt. Fax 663-4312
www.praguepublicschools.org/
Prague JSHS 100/7-12
PO Box 98 68050 402-663-4388
Raymond Collins, prin. Fax 663-4312

Ralston, Douglas, Pop. 6,193
Ralston SD 3,000/PK-12
8545 Park Dr 68127 402-331-4700
Dr. Virginia Moon, supt. Fax 331-4843
www.ralstonschools.org/
Ralston HS 1,000/9-12
8969 Park Dr 68127 402-331-7373
Greg Shepard, prin. Fax 898-3511
Ralston MS 500/7-8
8202 Lakeview St 68127 402-331-4701
Kathleen Krzycki, prin. Fax 331-5376

Randolph, Cedar, Pop. 888
Randolph SD 45 400/K-12
PO Box 755 68771 402-337-0252
Ted Hillman, supt. Fax 337-0235
www.randolphpublic.org/
Randolph JSHS 200/7-12
PO Box 755 68771 402-337-0252
Steven Rinehart, prin. Fax 337-0235

Ravenna, Buffalo, Pop. 1,281
Ravenna SD 400/K-12
PO Box 8400 68869 308-452-3249
Dwaine Uttecht, supt. Fax 452-3172
Ravenna JSHS 200/7-12
PO Box 8400 68869 308-452-3249
Devon Huebert, prin. Fax 452-3172

Raymond, Lancaster, Pop. 195
Raymond Central SD 700/K-12
1800 W Agnew Rd 68428 402-785-2615
Gary Oxley, supt. Fax 785-2097
www.rcentral.org
Raymond JSHS 400/7-12
1800 W Agnew Rd 68428 402-785-2685
Ivan Dixon, prin. Fax 785-2097

Red Cloud, Webster, Pop. 1,029
Red Cloud Community SD 200/K-12
334 N Cherry St 68970 402-746-3413
Joan Reznicek, supt. Fax 746-3690
www.esu9.org/%7Eredcloud/
Washington JSHS 100/7-12
121 W 7th Ave 68970 402-746-2818
Marlyn Washburn, prin. Fax 746-2817

Rising City, Butler, Pop. 381
Rising City SD 200/PK-12
PO Box 160 68658 402-542-2216
Daniel Alberts, supt. Fax 542-2265
www.risingcityschools.org/
Rising City JSHS 100/7-12
PO Box 160 68658 402-542-2216
Michael Derr, prin. Fax 542-2265

Roseland, Adams, Pop. 254
Silver Lake SD 300/K-12
PO Box 8 68973 402-756-6611
Gale McDonald, supt. Fax 756-6613
Silver Lake JSHS 200/7-12
PO Box 8 68973 402-756-6611
Kenneth Mahoney, prin. Fax 756-6613

Royal, Antelope, Pop. 70
Nebraska USD 1 600/K-12
PO Box 98 68773 402-893-2068
William Kuester, supt. Fax 893-9949
neunified1.esu8.org/
Other Schools – See Clearwater, Orchard, Verdigre

Rushville, Sheridan, Pop. 902
Gordon-Rushville SD
Supt. — See Gordon
Gordon-Rushville MS 100/6-8
PO Box 590 69360 308-327-2491
William Paul, prin. Fax 327-2504

Saint Edward, Boone, Pop. 757
Saint Edward SD 200/K-12
PO Box C 68660 402-678-2282
Kevin Lyons, supt. Fax 678-2284
teachers.esu7.org/stedweb/
Saint Edward JSHS 100/7-12
PO Box C 68660 402-678-2282
Kevin Lyons, prin. Fax 678-2284

Saint Paul, Howard, Pop. 2,257
Saint Paul SD 700/K-12
PO Box 325 68873 308-754-4433
Douglas Ackles, supt. Fax 754-5374
www.stpaul.k12.ne.us/
Saint Paul JSHS 300/7-12
PO Box 325 68873 308-754-4433
John Weitzel, prin. Fax 754-5374

Sargent, Custer, Pop. 612
Sargent SD 200/K-12
PO Box 366 68874 308-527-4119
Robert Brown, supt. Fax 527-3332
sites.sargent.k12.ne.us/sargent/
Sargent JSHS 100/7-12
PO Box 366 68874 308-527-4119
Cory Grant, prin. Fax 527-3332

Schuyler, Colfax, Pop. 5,327
Schuyler SD 1,500/PK-12
401 Adam St 68661 402-352-3527
Robin Stevens, supt. Fax 352-5552
Schuyler Central HS 400/9-12
401 Adam St 68661 402-352-3527
Joyce Baumert, prin. Fax 352-5552

Scotia, Greeley, Pop. 287
North Loup Scotia SD 200/K-12
PO Box 307 68875 308-245-3201
Gene Haddix, supt. Fax 245-9133
userweb.esu10.org/~scotia@esu10.org/
Scotia JSHS 100/7-12
PO Box 307 68875 308-245-3201
Richard Johnson, prin. Fax 245-9133

Scottsbluff, Scotts Bluff, Pop. 14,814
Scottsbluff SD 2,800/PK-12
2601 Broadway 69361 308-635-6200
Dr. Gary Reynolds, supt. Fax 635-6217
www.sbps.net/
Bluffs MS 600/6-8
23rd & Broadway 69361 308-635-6270
Dr. James Schmucker, prin. Fax 635-6271
Scottsbluff HS 900/9-12
313 E 27th St 69361 308-635-6230
Charles Nighswonger, prin. Fax 635-6240

Regional West Medical Center Post-Sec.
4021 Avenue B 69361 308-635-3711
Western Nebraska Community College Post-Sec.
1601 E 27th St 69361 308-635-3606

Scribner, Dodge, Pop. 968
Scribner-Snyder SD 300/PK-12
PO Box L 68057 402-664-2567
Richard A. Alt, supt. Fax 664-2708
www.sstrojans.esu2.org/
Scribner-Snyder JSHS 200/7-12
PO Box L 68057 402-664-2567
Alfred Ivey, prin. Fax 664-2708

Seward, Seward, Pop. 6,776
Seward SD 1,400/PK-12
410 South St 68434 402-643-2941
Marlene Uhing, supt. Fax 643-4986
www.sewardpublicschools.org
Seward HS 500/9-12
532 Northern Heights Dr 68434 402-643-2988
Ronald Lamberty, prin. Fax 643-2599
Seward MS 400/5-8
237 S 3rd St 68434 402-643-2986
Steven Schrad, prin. Fax 643-6686

Concordia University Post-Sec.
800 N Columbia Ave 68434 402-643-3651

Shelby, Polk, Pop. 648
Shelby SD 300/K-12
PO Box 218 68662 402-527-5946
Larry Stick, supt. Fax 527-5133
www.shelby.esu7.org
Shelby JSHS 100/7-12
PO Box 218 68662 402-527-5946
William Curry, prin. Fax 527-5133

Shelton, Buffalo, Pop. 1,125
Shelton SD 400/K-12
PO Box 610 68876 308-647-6742
Kendall Steffensen, supt. Fax 647-5233
sites.shelton.k12.ne.us/sheltonpublic/
Shelton JSHS 200/7-12
PO Box 610 68876 308-647-5459
Gale Dunkhas, prin. Fax 647-5233

Platte Valley Academy 50/1-12
19338 W Campus Dr 68876 308-647-5151
Jim Goodchild, prin. Fax 647-5368

Shickley, Fillmore, Pop. 358
Shickley SD 100/K-12
PO Box 407 68436 402-627-3375
Paul Sheffield, supt. Fax 627-2003
www.shickley.esu6.k12.ne.us/
Shickley JSHS 100/7-12
PO Box 407 68436 402-627-3375
Randall Kort, prin. Fax 627-2003

Sidney, Cheyenne, Pop. 6,442
Sidney SD 1,200/K-12
2103 King St 69162 308-254-5855
John Hakonson, supt. Fax 254-5756
www.sidneyraiders.com/
Sidney HS 400/9-12
1122 19th Ave 69162 308-254-5893
Jay Ehler, prin. Fax 254-5992
Sidney MS 200/7-8
1122 19th Ave 69162 308-254-5853
Jill Finkey, prin. Fax 254-5854

Western Nebraska Community College Post-Sec.
69162 800-221-9682

South Sioux City, Dakota, Pop. 11,979
South Sioux City SD 3,500/PK-12
PO Box 158 68776 402-494-2425
Steve Rector, supt. Fax 494-3916
www.sioux.esu1.org
South Sioux City HS 1,000/9-12
3301 G St 68776 402-494-2433
Patrick Nauroth, prin. Fax 494-2464
South Sioux City MS 800/6-8
3625 G St 68776 402-494-3061
John Laughhunn, prin. Fax 494-8427

Spalding, Greeley, Pop. 502
Spalding SD 100/K-12
PO Box 220 68665 308-497-2431
Joan Carraher, supt. Fax 497-2141
sites.spalding.k12.ne.us/
Spalding JSHS 100/7-12
PO Box 220 68665 308-497-2431
Joan Carraher, prin. Fax 497-2141

Spalding Academy 100/K-12
PO Box 310 68665 308-497-2103
Kevin Kirwan, prin. Fax 497-2105

Spencer, Boyd, Pop. 504
West Boyd SD 100/K-12
PO Box 109 68777 402-589-2040
Duane Lechtenberg, supt. Fax 589-2041
West Boyd-Spencer-Naper HS 100/5-12
PO Box 109 68777 402-589-1333
Duane Lechtenberg, prin. Fax 589-1142

Springfield, Sarpy, Pop. 1,497
South Sarpy SD 46 1,000/K-12
14801 S 108th St 68059 402-592-1300
Charles Chevalier, supt. Fax 597-8551
www.sarpy46.org/
Platteview Central JHS 200/7-8
14801 S 108th St 68059 402-339-5052
Ralph Glock, prin. Fax 339-3166
Platteview HS 300/9-12
14801 S 108th St 68059 402-339-3606
Scott Shepard, prin. Fax 339-3751

Springview, Keya Paha, Pop. 217
Keya Paha County SD 100/K-12
PO Box 219 68778 402-497-3501
Katherine Meink, supt. Fax 497-4321
www.esu17.org/%7Ekphshome/index.html
Keya Paha County HS 50/9-12
PO Box 219 68778 402-497-3501
Katherine Meink, prin. Fax 497-4321

Stanton, Stanton, Pop. 1,629
Stanton Community SD 500/K-12
PO Box 749 68779 402-439-2233
Michael Sieh, supt. Fax 439-2270
www.scs-ne.org/
Stanton MSHS 200/7-12
PO Box 749 68779 402-439-2250
Chris Stogdill, prin. Fax 439-2270

Stapleton, Logan, Pop. 288
Stapleton SD 200/PK-12
PO Box 128 69163 308-636-2252
Daniel Hutchison, supt. Fax 636-2618
Stapleton JSHS 100/7-12
PO Box 128 69163 308-636-2252
Adam Boettcher, prin. Fax 636-2618

Stella, Richardson, Pop. 207
SE Nebraska Consolidated SD 100/K-12
71829 642 Blvd 68442 402-883-2600
Michael Montgomery, supt. Fax 883-2020
www.southeast.esu6.org/
SE Nebraska Cons HS 100/7-12
71829 642 Blvd 68442 402-883-2400
Michael Montgomery, prin. Fax 883-2020

Sterling, Johnson, Pop. 495
Sterling SD 200/K-12
PO Box 39 68443 402-866-4761
James Duval, supt. Fax 866-4771
www.sterlingjets.org/
Sterling JSHS 100/7-12
PO Box 39 68443 402-866-4761
Gregory Peterson, prin. Fax 866-4771

Stromsburg, Polk, Pop. 1,165
Cross County Community SD 400/K-12
PO Box 525 68666 402-764-2156
Rady Page, supt. Fax 764-2156
Cross County HS - Stromsburg 100/9-12
PO Box 525 68666 402-764-5521
Evan Wieseman, prin. Fax 764-8294
Other Schools – See Benedict

Stuart, Holt, Pop. 577
Stuart SD 200/K-12
PO Box 99 68780 402-924-3302
Robert J. Hanzlik, supt. Fax 924-3676
stuart.esu8.org/
Stuart JSHS 100/7-12
PO Box 99 68780 402-924-3302
Robert J. Hanzlik, prin. Fax 924-3676

Sumner, Dawson, Pop. 241
Sumner-Eddyville-Miller SD 200/K-12
PO Box 126 68878 308-752-2925
Dennis Chipman, supt. Fax 752-2600
sites.sem.k12.ne.us/
SEM JSHS 100/7-12
PO Box 126 68878 308-752-2925
James Langin, prin. Fax 752-2600

Superior, Nuckolls, Pop. 1,903
South Central Nebraska Unified SD
Supt. — See Fairfield
Superior JSHS 200/7-12
PO Box 288 68978 402-879-3257
Robert Cook, prin. Fax 879-3022

Sutherland, Lincoln, Pop. 1,223
Sutherland SD 400/PK-12
PO Box 217 69165 308-386-4656
Michael Cunning, supt. Fax 386-2426
userweb.esu16.org/~shs/
Sutherland JSHS 200/7-12
PO Box 217 69165 308-386-4656
Brian Maschmann, prin. Fax 386-2426

Sutton, Clay, Pop. 1,394
Sutton SD 400/PK-12
PO Box 590 68979 402-773-5569
Larry Weaver, supt. Fax 773-5578
sites.esu9.org/sutton/
Sutton JSHS 200/7-12
PO Box 590 68979 402-773-4303
Dana Wiseman, prin. Fax 773-5578

Syracuse, Otoe, Pop. 1,835
Syracuse-Dunbar-Avoca SD 800/PK-12
PO Box P 68446 402-269-2383
Bradley Buller, supt. Fax 269-2224
www.sdarockets.org/
Syracuse JSHS 400/7-12
PO Box P 68446 402-269-2381
Joy Stilmock, prin. Fax 269-3028

Table Rock, Pawnee, Pop. 249
Humboldt & Table Rock Steinauer USD 2007
Supt. — See Humboldt
Humboldt & Table Rock Steinauer MS 100/5-8
PO Box F 68447 402-839-2085
Don Day, prin. Fax 839-2088

Taylor, Loup, Pop. 195
Loup County SD 100/K-12
PO Box 170 68879 308-942-6115
Wayne Ruppert, supt. Fax 942-6248
Loup County JSHS 100/7-12
PO Box 170 68879 308-942-6115
Ken Sheets, prin. Fax 942-6248

Tecumseh, Johnson, Pop. 1,951
Tecumseh SD 400/K-12
PO Box 338 68450 402-335-3320
Randall Marymee, supt. Fax 335-3346
www.tecumseh.esu6.k12.ne.us/
Tecumseh JSHS 200/7-12
PO Box 338 68450 402-335-3328
Richard Lester, prin. Fax 335-3346

Tekamah, Burt, Pop. 1,814
Tekamah-Herman SD 600/PK-12
112 N 13th St 68061 402-374-2157
Kevin Nolan, supt. Fax 374-2155
www.tekamah.esu2.org/
Tekamah JSHS 300/7-12
112 N 13th St 68061 402-374-2156
Daniel Gross, prin. Fax 374-2155

Thedford, Thomas, Pop. 180
Thedford SD 100/PK-12
PO Box 248 69166 308-645-2230
Henry Eggert, supt. Fax 645-2618
webquests.esu16.org:8080/ttrojans/
Thedford Rural JSHS 100/7-12
PO Box 248 69166 308-645-2230
Henry Eggert, prin. Fax 645-2618

Tilden, Madison, Pop. 1,053
Elkhorn Valley SD 300/K-12
PO Box 430 68781 402-368-5301
Ken Navratil, supt. Fax 368-5338
falcon.esu8.org/
Elkhorn Valley JSHS 200/7-12
PO Box 430 68781 402-368-5301
Beth Johnsen, prin. Fax 368-5338

Trenton, Hitchcock, Pop. 477
Hitchcock County USD 200/K-12
PO Box 368 69044 308-334-5575
Cynthia Huff, supt. Fax 334-5381
www.hcfalcons.org/
Hitchcock County HS 100/9-12
PO Box 368 69044 308-334-5575
John Varilek, prin. Fax 334-5381

Tryon, McPherson
McPherson County SD 100/K-12
PO Box 38 69167 308-587-2262
R. Todd Porter, supt. Fax 587-2571
athena.esu16.org/~mchs/
McPherson County HS 50/9-12
PO Box 38 69167 308-587-2262
R. Todd Porter, prin. Fax 587-2571

Utica, Seward, Pop. 825
Centennial SD 600/PK-12
PO Box 187 68456 402-534-2291
Brian Maher, supt. Fax 534-2291
www.centennialpublic.org/
Centennial JSHS 300/7-12
PO Box 187 68456 402-534-2321
Ryan Ruhl, prin. Fax 534-2291

Valentine, Cherry, Pop. 2,786
Valentine SD 800/K-12
431 N Green St 69201 402-376-2730
Jamie Isom, supt. Fax 376-2736
www.vhs.esu17.org
Valentine MS 200/6-8
239 N Wood St 69201 402-376-3367
Ron Billings, prin. Fax 376-3386
Valentine Rural HS 300/9-12
431 N Green St 69201 402-376-2730
Dave Renning, prin. Fax 376-2736

Valley, Douglas, Pop. 1,829
Douglas County West Community SD 500/K-12
PO Box 378 68064 402-359-2583
George Conrad, supt. Fax 359-4371
www.dcwest.org/
Douglas County West HS 200/9-12
PO Box 378 68064 402-359-2121
JoAnn Stevens, prin. Fax 359-4371
Other Schools – See Waterloo

Verdigre, Knox, Pop. 486
Nebraska USD 1
Supt. — See Royal
Verdigre JSHS 100/7-12
204 2nd St 68783 402-668-2275
Michael Zulkoski, prin. Fax 668-2276

Waco, York, Pop. 261

Nebraska Lutheran HS 100/9-12
203 Kendall St 68460 402-728-5236
Craig Charron, prin. Fax 728-5433

Wahoo, Saunders, Pop. 4,063
Wahoo SD 900/PK-12
2201 N Locust St 68066 402-443-3051
Edward Rastovski, supt. Fax 443-4731
www.wahooschools.org/
Wahoo HS 300/9-12
2201 N Locust St 68066 402-443-4332
Chris Arent, prin. Fax 443-4731
Wahoo MS 200/6-8
2201 N Locust St 68066 402-443-3101
Timothy Farley, prin. Fax 443-4731

Bishop Neumann Central HS 300/7-12
202 S Linden St 68066 402-443-4151
Brian Kane, prin. Fax 443-5551

Wakefield, Dixon, Pop. 1,340
Wakefield SD 500/K-12
PO Box 330 68784 402-287-2012
Michael Moody, supt. Fax 287-2014
www.wakefieldschools.org/
Wakefield JSHS 200/7-12
PO Box 330 68784 402-287-2012
Bill Heimann, prin. Fax 287-2014

Wallace, Lincoln, Pop. 321
Wallace SD 65 R 200/K-12
PO Box 127 69169 308-387-4323
Wendel L. Cass, supt. Fax 387-4322
Wallace JSHS 100/7-12
PO Box 127 69169 308-387-4323
Larry Seger, prin. Fax 387-4322

Walthill, Thurston, Pop. 917
Walthill SD 300/K-12
PO Box 3C 68067 402-846-5432
Dan Schiefelbein, supt. Fax 846-5029
walthweb.esu1.org/
Walthill JSHS 100/7-12
PO Box 3C 68067 402-846-5432
Carol Hilker, prin. Fax 846-5029

Waterloo, Douglas, Pop. 506
Douglas County West Community SD
Supt. — See Valley
Douglas County West MS 50/5-8
PO Box 328 68069 402-779-2646
Mitch Mollring, prin. Fax 779-2534

Wauneta, Chase, Pop. 577
Wauneta-Palisade SD 300/K-12
PO Box 368 69045 308-394-5700
Charles Isom, supt. Fax 394-5962
www.geocities.com/wauneta.geo
Wauneta-Palisade HS 100/9-12
PO Box 368 69045 308-394-5650
Randy Geier, prin. Fax 394-5962
Wauneta Palisade JHS 100/7-8
PO Box 368 69045 308-394-5650
Randy Geier, prin. Fax 394-5962

Wausa, Knox, Pop. 587
Wausa SD 200/K-12
PO Box 159 68786 402-586-2255
Robert Marks Ed.D., supt. Fax 586-2406
wausaweb.esu1.org/
Wausa JSHS 100/7-12
PO Box 159 68786 402-586-2255
Robert Marks, prin. Fax 586-2406

Waverly, Lancaster, Pop. 2,693
Waverly SD 1,300/K-12
PO Box 426 68462 402-786-2321
Dan Ernst, supt. Fax 786-2799
www.dist145.esu6.org/
Waverly HS 600/9-12
PO Box 426 68462 402-786-2765
Philip Warrick, prin. Fax 786-2760
Waverly MS 400/6-8
PO Box 426 68462 402-786-2348
Phillip Picquet, prin. Fax 786-2760

Wayne, Wayne, Pop. 5,163
Wayne SD 900/K-12
611 W 7th St 68787 402-375-3150
Joseph Reinert, supt. Fax 375-5251
schools.waynene.org/
Wayne HS 300/9-12
611 W 7th St 68787 402-375-3150
Mark Hanson, prin. Fax 375-5251
Wayne MS 300/5-8
611 W 7th St 68787 402-375-2230
Timothy Krupicka, prin. Fax 375-2342

Wayne State College Post-Sec.
1111 Main St 68787 402-375-7000

Weeping Water, Cass, Pop. 1,118
Weeping Water SD 400/K-12
PO Box 206 68463 402-267-2445
Brian Gegg, supt. Fax 267-5217
www.weepingwaterps.org/
Weeping Water JSHS 200/7-12
PO Box 206 68463 402-267-4265
Keith Leckron, prin. Fax 267-5217

West Point, Cuming, Pop. 3,476
West Point SD 800/PK-12
PO Box 188 68788 402-372-5860
Theodore De Turk, supt. Fax 372-5458
www.wpcadets.org/
West Point-Beemer JSHS 400/7-12
PO Box 188 68788 402-372-5546
Stephen Grizzle, prin. Fax 372-5458

Central Catholic HS 200/9-12
419 E Decatur St 68788 402-372-5326
Ken Hajek, prin. Fax 372-5327

Wilber, Saline, Pop. 1,799
Wilber-Clatonia SD 500/K-12
PO Box 487 68465 402-821-2266
David Rokusek, supt. Fax 821-3013
Wilber-Clatonia JSHS 300/7-12
PO Box 487 68465 402-821-2508
Ronald Oltman, prin. Fax 821-3013

Wilcox, Kearney, Pop. 351
Wilcox-Hildreth SD 300/K-12
PO Box 190 68982 308-478-5265
Roger Boyer, supt. Fax 478-5260
www.esu11.org/wilcohildr/home.htm
Wilcox-Hildreth HS 100/9-12
PO Box 190 68982 308-478-5265
Victor Young, prin. Fax 478-5260
Other Schools – See Hildreth

Winnebago, Thurston, Pop. 798
Winnebago SD 400/K-12
PO Box KK 68071 402-878-2224
Fred Williams, supt. Fax 878-2472
winnebago.esu1.org/
Winnebago JSHS 100/7-12
PO Box KK 68071 402-878-2224
Dan Fehringer, prin. Fax 878-2472

Little Priest Tribal College Post-Sec.
PO Box 720 68071 402-878-2380

Winside, Wayne, Pop. 433
Winside SD 300/K-12
PO Box 158 68790 402-286-4466
Donavon Leighton, supt. Fax 286-4466
winside.esu1.org/
Winside JSHS 100/7-12
PO Box 158 68790 402-286-4465
Jeffrey Messersmith, prin. Fax 286-4466

Wisner, Cuming, Pop. 1,200
Wisner-Pilger SD 300/K-12
PO Box 580 68791 402-529-3249
Alan Harms, supt. Fax 529-3477
www.wisnerpilger.org/
Wisner HS 200/9-12
PO Box 580 68791 402-529-3249
Christopher Uttecht, prin. Fax 529-3477
Other Schools – See Pilger

Wolbach, Greeley, Pop. 267
Greeley-Wolbach SD
Supt. — See Greeley
Greeley-Wolbach JHS 50/7-8
PO Box 67 68882 308-246-5232
Todd Beck, prin. Fax 246-5234

Wood River, Hall, Pop. 1,200
Wood River Rural SD 600/K-12
PO Box 518 68883 308-583-2249
Larry Harnish, supt. Fax 583-2395
Wood River MS 200/6-8
PO Box 518 68883 308-583-2249
Tom Moore, prin. Fax 583-2395
Wood River Rural HS 200/9-12
PO Box 518 68883 308-583-2249
Tom Moore, prin. Fax 583-2395

Wymore, Gage, Pop. 1,615
Southern SD 1 500/K-12
PO Box 237 68466 402-645-3326
William Shimeall, supt. Fax 645-8049
www.southernschools.org/
Southern JSHS 200/7-12
PO Box 237 68466 402-645-3326
Steven Whitwer, prin. Fax 645-8049

Wynot, Cedar, Pop. 175
Wynot SD 200/K-12
PO Box 157 68792 402-357-2121
Marvin Johnson, supt. Fax 357-2524
Wynot HS 100/9-12
PO Box 157 68792 402-357-2121
Richard Higgins, prin. Fax 357-2524
Wynot MS 50/5-8
PO Box 157 68792 402-357-2121
Richard Higgins, prin. Fax 357-2524

York, York, Pop. 7,888
York SD 1,200/K-12
2918 N Delaware Ave 68467 402-362-6655
Terrence Keneal̲y, supt. Fax 362-6943
york.ne.schoolwebpages.com
York HS 500/9-12
1005 Duke Dr 68467 402-362-6655
Dan Endorf, prin. Fax 362-2994
York MS 300/6-8
1200 N East Ave 68467 402-362-6655
Brian Tonniges, prin. Fax 362-6831

York College Post-Sec.
912 Kiplinger Ave 68467 402-363-5600

Yutan, Saunders, Pop. 1,217
Yutan SD 500/K-12
1200 2nd St 68073 402-625-2243
Kevin Johnson, supt. Fax 625-2812
www.yutan.esu2.org/
Yutan JSHS 200/7-12
1200 2nd St 68073 402-625-2241
Dan Schnoes, prin. Fax 625-2812

NEVADA

NEVADA DEPARTMENT OF EDUCATION
700 E Fifth St, Carson City 89701-5096
Telephone 775-687-9200
Fax 775-687-9101
Website http://www.doe.nv.gov/

Superintendent of Instruction Keith Rheault

NEVADA BOARD OF EDUCATION
700 E Fifth St, Carson City 89701-5096

President Cliff Ferry

PUBLIC, PRIVATE AND CATHOLIC SECONDARY SCHOOLS

Alamo, Lincoln
Lincoln County SD
Supt. — See Panaca
Pahranagat Valley HS 100/9-12
PO Box 298 89001 775-725-3321
Steven Hansen, prin. Fax 725-3334
Pahranagat Valley MS 100/6-8
PO Box 539 89001 775-725-3601
Ken Higbee, prin. Fax 725-3358

Austin, Lander
Lander County SD
Supt. — See Battle Mountain
Austin JSHS 50/6-12
PO Box 160 89310 775-964-2467
Toby Melver, prin. Fax 964-1206

Battle Mountain, Lander, Pop. 3,542
Lander County SD 1,200/K-12
PO Box 1300 89820 775-635-2886
Curtis Jordan, supt. Fax 635-5347
www.lander.k12.nv.us
Battle Mountain HS 400/9-12
PO Box 1330 89820 775-635-5436
Amy Kester, prin. Fax 635-5459
Battle Mountain JHS 200/7-8
PO Box 1360 89820 775-635-2415
Lorraine Sparks, prin. Fax 635-6118
Other Schools – See Austin

Beatty, Nye, Pop. 1,623
Nye County SD
Supt. — See Tonopah
Beatty HS 100/9-12
PO Box 806 89003 775-553-2595
Nancy Hein, prin. Fax 553-2887

Boulder City, Clark, Pop. 15,177
Clark County SD
Supt. — See Las Vegas
Boulder City HS 800/9-12
1101 5th St 89005 702-799-8200
Jeanne M. Donadio, prin. Fax 799-8230
Garrett MS 600/6-8
1200 Avenue G 89005 702-799-8290
Jamey Lynn Hood, prin. Fax 799-8252

Carlin, Elko, Pop. 2,083
Elko County SD
Supt. — See Elko
Carlin S 200/K-12
PO Box 730 89822 775-754-6317
Norm Mahlberg, prin. Fax 754-2175

Carson City, Carson City, Pop. 54,311
Carson City SD 8,700/K-12
PO Box 603 89702 775-283-2000
Dr. Mary Pierczynski, supt. Fax 283-2090
www.carsoncityschools.com
Carson HS 2,600/9-12
1111 N Saliman Rd 89701 775-283-1600
Fred Perdomo, prin. Fax 283-1790
Carson MS 1,100/6-8
1140 W King St 89703 775-283-2800
Sam Santillo, prin. Fax 283-2890
Eagle Valley MS 900/6-8
4151 E Fifth St 89701 775-283-2600
F. Mariani, prin. Fax 283-2690

Carson City Beauty Academy Post-Sec.
2531 N Carson St 89706 775-885-9853
Western Nevada Community College Post-Sec.
2201 W College Pkwy 89703 775-445-3000

Dayton, Lyon, Pop. 2,217
Lyon County SD
Supt. — See Yerington
Dayton HS 700/9-12
335 Dayton Valley Rd 89403 775-246-6240
Jose Delfin, prin. Fax 246-6245
Dayton IS 600/6-8
315 Dayton Valley Rd 89403 775-246-6250
Neal Freitas, prin. Fax 246-6253

Dyer, Esmeralda

Deep Springs College Post-Sec.
HC 72 Box 45001 89010 760-872-2000

Elko, Elko, Pop. 16,685
Elko County SD 8,800/K-12
PO Box 1012 89803 775-738-5196
Antoinette Cavanaugh, supt. Fax 738-5857
www.elko.k12.nv.us
Elko HS 1,300/9-12
987 College Ave 89801 775-738-7281
Mike Altenburg, prin. Fax 738-9616
Elko JHS 700/7-8
777 Country Club Dr 89801 775-738-7236
Mollie Keller, prin. Fax 753-3876
Adult HS Adult
PO Box 1012 89803 775-753-2233
Susan Jones, lead tchr. Fax 753-2257
Other Schools – See Carlin, Jackpot, Owyhee, Spring Creek, Wells, West Wendover

---

Great Basin College Post-Sec.
1500 College Pkwy 89801 800-343-2724

Ely, White Pine, Pop. 3,918
White Pine County SD 1,300/K-12
1135 Avenue C 89301 775-289-4851
Bob Dolezal, supt. Fax 289-3999
www.whitepine.k12.nv.us
White Pine County HS 400/9-12
1800 Bobcat Dr 89301 775-289-4811
Adam Young, prin. Fax 289-1542
White Pine County MS 300/6-8
844 Aultman St 89301 775-289-4841
Aaron Hansen, prin. Fax 289-1565
Other Schools – See Lund

Eureka, Eureka
Eureka County SD 200/K-12
PO Box 249 89316 775-237-5373
Ben Zunino, supt. Fax 237-5014
www.eureka.k12.nv.us
Eureka County JSHS 100/7-12
PO Box 237 89316 775-237-5361
Ken Fujii, prin. Fax 237-5113

Fallon, Churchill, Pop. 8,103
Churchill County SD 4,500/K-12
545 E Richards St 89406 775-423-5184
Dr. Carolyn Ross, supt. Fax 423-2959
www.churchill.k12.nv.us
Churchill County HS 1,400/9-12
1222 S Taylor St 89406 775-423-2181
John Riley, prin. Fax 423-8968
Churchill County JHS 700/7-8
650 S Maine St 89406 775-423-7701
Judy Pratt, prin. Fax 423-8010
Lahontan Valley HS 9-12
690 S Maine St 89406 775-423-6322
Keith Boone, prin. Fax 423-6364

Fernley, Lyon, Pop. 11,342
Lyon County SD
Supt. — See Yerington
Fernley HS 700/9-12
1300 US Highway 95A S 89408 775-575-3400
Sue Segura, prin. Fax 575-3406
Fernley IS 700/5-8
320 US Highway 95A S 89408 775-575-3390
Ryan Cross, prin. Fax 575-3394
Fernley Adult Education Center Adult
1300 US Highway 95A S 89408 775-575-3409
Kathleen Jameson, prin. Fax 575-3399

Gabbs, Nye, Pop. 947
Nye County SD
Supt. — See Tonopah
Gabbs S 50/K-12
PO Box 147 89409 775-285-2692
Selway Mulkey, prin. Fax 285-2381

Gardnerville, Douglas, Pop. 2,177
Douglas County SD
Supt. — See Minden
Carson Valley MS 900/7-9
PO Box 157 89410 775-782-2265
Kerry Pope, prin. Fax 782-7341
Pau-Wa-Lu MS 900/7-9
PO Box 157 89410 775-265-6100
Keith Lewis, prin. Fax 265-1653

Gerlach, Washoe
Washoe County SD
Supt. — See Reno
Gerlach MSHS 50/6-12
555 East Sunset Blvd 89412 775-557-2326
Carol Kaufmann, prin. Fax 557-2587

Hawthorne, Mineral, Pop. 4,162
Mineral County SD 500/K-12
PO Box 1540 89415 775-945-2403
Steven Cook, supt. Fax 945-3709
www.gohawthorne.com
Mineral County HS 200/7-12
PO Box 938 89415 775-945-3332
Margaret Ruybalid, prin. Fax 945-3371

Henderson, Clark, Pop. 232,146
Clark County SD
Supt. — See Las Vegas
Basic HS 2,200/9-12
400 Palo Verde Dr 89015 702-799-8000
Susan Segal, prin. Fax 799-8966
Brown JHS 1,200/6-8
307 Cannes St 89015 702-799-8900
Kimberly Bass Davis, prin. Fax 799-3511
Burkholder MS 6-8
355 W Van Wagenen St 89015 702-799-8080
Jessie Phee, prin. Fax 799-8088
Community College HS South 100/11-12
700 College Dr, 702-651-3080
Dennis Birr, prin. Fax 651-3075
Coronado HS 2,500/9-12
1001 Coronado Center Dr 89052 702-799-6800
Lee Koelliker, prin. Fax 799-6839
Foothill HS 2,100/9-12
800 College Dr, 702-799-3500
Gretchen K. Crehan, prin. Fax 799-3524
Greenspun JHS 1,600/6-8
140 N Valle Verde Dr 89074 702-799-0920
Elizabeth Howe, prin. Fax 799-0925
Green Valley HS 2,800/9-12
460 N Arroyo Grande Blvd 89014 702-799-0950
Jeffrey Horn, prin. Fax 799-0717
Liberty HS 1,100/9-12
3700 Liberty Heights Ave 89052 702-799-2270
Rosalind Gibson, prin. Fax 799-6858
Mannion MS 1,800/6-8
155 E Paradise Hills Dr, 702-799-3020
David W. Erbach, prin. Fax 799-3501
Miller MS 1,800/6-8
2400 Cozy Hill Cir 89052 702-799-2260
Tamathy Larnerd, prin. Fax 799-1309
Webb MS 6-8
2200 Reunion Ave 89052 702-799-1305
Paula Naegle, prin. Fax 799-1310
White MS 1,700/6-8
1661 Galleria Dr 89014 702-799-0777
Danielle Miller, prin. Fax 799-7690

Art Institute of Las Vegas Post-Sec.
2350 Corporate Cir 89074 702-369-9944
DeVry University Post-Sec.
2490 Paseo Verde Pkwy #150 89074 702-933-9700
Henderson International S 200/5-12
1165 Sandy Ridge Ave 89052 702-818-2100
Rod Kehl, hdmstr.
ITT Technical Institute Post-Sec.
168 N Gibson Rd 89014 702-558-5404
Lake Mead Christian Academy 500/K-12
PO Box 90099 89009 702-565-5831
Gayle Sue Blakeley, admin. Fax 566-6206
Las Vegas College Post-Sec.
170 N Stephanie St Ste 145 89074 702-368-6200
Touro Univ. Coll. / Osteopathic Medicine Post-Sec.
874 American Pacific Dr 89014 702-856-3262

Incline Village, Washoe, Pop. 7,119
Washoe County SD
Supt. — See Reno
Incline HS 400/9-12
499 Village Blvd 89451 775-832-4260
John Clark, prin. Fax 832-4208
Incline MS 300/6-8
931 Southwood Blvd 89451 775-832-4220
Kathleen Watty, prin. Fax 832-4210

Sierra Nevada College-Lake Tahoe Post-Sec.
999 Tahoe Blvd 89451 800-332-8666

Indian Springs, Clark, Pop. 1,164
Clark County SD
Supt. — See Las Vegas
Indian Springs HS 9-12
PO Box 1088 89018 702-799-0932
Katherine Christensen, prin. Fax 879-3142
Indian Springs MS 6-8
400 Sky Rd 89018 702-799-0932
Katherine Christensen, prin. Fax 879-3142
Indian Springs Conservation Adult HS Adult
PO Box 208 89070 702-486-3888
Reid Kimoto, prin. Fax 486-3398

Jackpot, Elko
Elko County SD
Supt. — See Elko
Jackpot S 200/K-12
PO Box 463 89825 775-755-2374
Brian Messmer, prin. Fax 755-2291

Las Vegas, Clark, Pop. 545,147
Clark County SD 274,700/PK-12
5100 W Sahara Ave 89146 702-799-5000
Walt Rulffes, supt. Fax 799-5505
www.ccsd.net/
Advance Technologies Academy 1,000/9-12
2501 Vegas Dr 89106 702-799-7870
Karen Diamond, prin. Fax 799-0656
Arbor View HS 9-12
7500 Whispering Sands Dr 89131 702-799-6660
Patrick Hayden, prin. Fax 799-6669
Bailey MS 6-8
2500 N Hollywood Blvd 89156 702-799-4811
Karen Stansfield-Paquett, prin. Fax 799-4807
Becker MS 1,500/6-8
9151 Pinewood Hills Dr 89134 702-799-4460
Karen L. West, prin. Fax 799-4470
Bonanza HS 2,400/9-12
6665 Del Rey Ave 89146 702-799-4000
Dawn L. Shupe, prin. Fax 799-4078
Brinley MS 1,200/6-8
2480 Maverick St 89108 702-799-4550
Sharon Beatty, prin. Fax 799-4549
Cadwallader MS 1,400/6-8
7775 Elkhorn Rd 89131 702-799-6692
Kathryn Singer, prin. Fax 799-4536
Canarelli MS 1,600/6-8
7808 S Torrey Pines Dr 89139 702-799-1340
Kristy Keller, prin. Fax 799-5715
Cannon JHS 1,100/6-8
5850 Euclid St 89120 702-799-5600
Elmer Manzanares, prin. Fax 799-5644
Cashman MS 1,100/6-8
4622 W Desert Inn Rd 89102 702-799-5880
Misti Taton, prin. Fax 799-5947
Centennial HS 2,600/9-12
10200 Centennial Pkwy 89149 702-799-3440
Trent Day, prin. Fax 799-3443
Chaparral HS 2,200/9-12
3850 Annie Oakley Dr 89121 702-799-7580
Kevin McPartlin, prin. Fax 799-0776
Cimarron-Memorial HS 2,900/9-12
2301 N Tenaya Way 89128 702-799-4400
Karen Stanley, prin. Fax 799-4425
Clark HS 2,600/9-12
4291 Pennwood Ave 89102 702-799-5800
Ronnie Smith, prin. Fax 799-5813
Community College HS West 200/11-12
6375 W Charleston Blvd 89146 702-651-5030
Dennis Birr, prin. Fax 651-5035
Cortney JHS 1,700/6-8
5301 E Hacienda Ave 89122 702-799-2400
Teresa Holden, prin. Fax 799-2407
Del Sol HS 1,600/9-12
3100 E Patrick Ln 89120 702-799-6830
John A. Barlow, prin. Fax 799-2235
Desert Pines HS 3,200/9-12
3800 Harris Ave 89110 702-799-2196
Timothy Stephens, prin. Fax 799-2198
Durango HS 2,300/9-12
7100 W Dewey Dr 89113 702-799-5850
Mark Gums, prin. Fax 799-5855
Eldorado HS 2,900/9-12
1139 Linn Ln 89110 702-799-7200
Richard Carranza, prin. Fax 799-7255
Escobedo MS 6-8
9501 Echelon Point Dr 89149 702-799-4560
Taylor Powers, prin. Fax 799-4568
Faiss MS 6-8
9525 W Maule Ave 89148 702-799-6850
Joy Lea, prin. Fax 799-6852
Fertitta MS 1,500/6-8
9905 W Mesa Vista Ave 89148 702-799-1900
Patricia LaMonica, prin. Fax 799-5688
Fremont MS 1,400/6-8
1100 E Saint Louis Ave 89104 702-799-5558
Shawn Boyle, prin. Fax 799-5566
Garside JHS 1,500/6-8
300 S Torrey Pines Dr 89107 702-799-4245
Stephanie Wong, prin. Fax 799-4296
Gibson MS 1,200/6-8
3900 W Washington Ave 89107 702-799-4700
Linda Archambault, prin. Fax 799-4705
Guinn MS 1,100/6-8
4150 S Torrey Pines Dr 89103 702-799-5900
Georgia Taton, prin. Fax 799-5905
Harney MS 1,800/6-8
1580 S Hollywood Blvd 89142 702-799-3240
John Scott, prin. Fax 799-3286
Hyde Park MS 1,700/6-8
900 Hinson St 89107 702-799-4260
James Kuzma, prin. Fax 799-0348
Johnson JHS 1,500/6-8
7701 Ducharme Ave 89145 702-799-4480
Terry Ann Sobrero, prin. Fax 799-4497
Keller MS 1,900/6-8
301 Fogg St 89110 702-799-3220
April Key, prin. Fax 799-3226
Knudson MS 1,400/6-8
2400 Atlantic St 89104 702-799-7470
Northey Henderson, prin. Fax 799-0157
Las Vegas Academy HS 1,500/9-12
315 S 7th St 89101 702-799-7800
Stephen T. Clark, prin. Fax 799-7948
Las Vegas HS 3,200/9-12
6500 E Sahara Ave 89142 702-799-0180
Patrice Johnson, prin. Fax 799-0192
Lawrence JHS 1,600/6-8
4410 S Juliano Rd 89147 702-799-2540
Kathryn Mead, prin. Fax 799-2563
Leavitt MS 1,700/6-8
4701 Quadrel St 89129 702-799-4699
Shanna Mack, prin. Fax 799-4528
Lied MS 1,300/6-8
5350 W Tropical Pkwy 89130 702-799-4620
Kimberly Bauman, prin. Fax 799-4626
Mack MS 6-8
4250 Karen Ave 89121 702-799-2005
Joseph Murphy, prin. Fax 799-2412
Martin MS 1,600/6-8
2800 Stewart Ave 89101 702-799-7922
Regina J. Adams, prin. Fax 799-7959
Molasky JHS 1,600/6-8
7801 W Gilmore Ave 89129 702-799-3400
Bart Mangino, prin. Fax 799-3407
Monaco MS 1,700/6-8
1870 N Lamont St 89115 702-799-3670
Russ Ramirez, prin. Fax 799-3202
Northwest Career & Technical Academy 9-12
8200 W Tropical Pkwy 89149 702-799-4640
Frank Pesce, prin. Fax 799-4644
O'Callaghan MS 1,900/6-8
1450 Radwick Dr 89110 702-799-7340
Susan Echols, prin. Fax 799-8870
Orr MS 1,200/6-8
1562 E Katie Ave 89119 702-799-5573
George Leavens, prin. Fax 799-0297
Palo Verde HS 3,000/9-12
333 S Pavilion Center Dr 89144 702-799-1450
Daniel Phillips, prin. Fax 799-1455
Rancho HS 3,100/9-12
1900 Searles Ave 89101 702-799-7000
Robert Chesto, prin. Fax 799-8316
Robison MS 1,600/6-8
825 Marion Dr 89110 702-799-7300
Elena Baker, prin. Fax 799-7302
Rogich MS 1,400/6-8
235 N Pavilion Center Dr 89144 702-799-6040
Susan Harrison, prin. Fax 799-6094
Saville MS 1,000/6-8
8101 N Torrey Pines Dr 89131 702-799-3460
Kathy A. Kulas, prin. Fax 799-4511
Sawyer MS 1,600/6-8
5450 Redwood St 89118 702-799-5980
Kim Friel, prin. Fax 799-5969
Schofield MS 1,600/6-8
8625 Spencer St 89123 702-799-2290
Elizabeth C. Angelcor, prin. Fax 799-5717
Shadow Ridge HS 2,600/9-12
5050 Brent Ln 89131 702-799-6699
Thomas Barberini, prin. Fax 799-4698
Sierra Vista HS 2,600/9-12
8100 W Robindale Rd 89113 702-799-6820
Emil T. Wozniak, prin. Fax 799-6847
Silverado HS 2,700/9-12
1650 Silver Hawk Ave 89123 702-799-5790
Kim Grytdahl, prin. Fax 799-5744
Silvestri JHS 1,800/6-8
1055 E Silverado Ranch Blvd, 702-799-2240
Debbie Brockett, prin. Fax 799-2247
Southern Nevada Vocational Technical Ctr Vo/Tech
5710 Mountain Vista St 89120 702-799-7500
Richard Arguello, prin. Fax 799-2007
Spring Valley HS 1,900/9-12
3750 S Buffalo Dr 89147 702-799-2580
Robert A. Gerye, prin. Fax 799-1288
Tarkanian MS 6-8
5800 W Pyle Ave 89141 702-799-6801
Brenda Larsen-Mitchell, prin. Fax 799-6805
Valley HS 2,800/9-12
2839 Burnham Ave, 702-799-5450
Ron Montoya, prin. Fax 799-1074
Von Tobel MS 1,400/6-8
2436 N Pecos Rd 89115 702-799-7280
Rogelio Gonzalez, prin. Fax 799-7286
Western HS 2,300/9-12
4601 W Bonanza Rd 89107 702-799-4080
Lillie Pearl Morgan, prin. Fax 799-4104
West Prep S 1,000/K-10
2050 Saphire Stone Ave 89106 702-799-3120
Mike Barton, prin. Fax 799-3126
Woodbury MS 1,100/6-8
3875 E Harmon Ave 89121 702-799-7660
Greg Snelling, prin. Fax 799-0805
Desert Rose Adult HS Adult
1251 Robin St 89106 702-799-6240
Sandra Ransel, prin. Fax 799-6260
Other Schools – See Boulder City, Henderson, Indian Springs, Laughlin, Logandale, Mesquite, North Las Vegas, Overton, Sandy Valley

---

Academy of Hair Design Post-Sec.
5191 W Charleston Blvd #150 89146 702-878-1185
Aces-Full Academy for Casino Dealers Post-Sec.
557 E Sahara Ave Ste 220 89104 702-369-1194
American Career Institute Post-Sec.
2340 Paseo Del Prado #D-208 89102 702-222-3522
Associated Pathologist Laboratories Post-Sec.
4230 Burnham Ave 89119 702-733-7866
Bishop Gorman HS 900/9-12
1801 S Maryland Pkwy 89104 702-732-1945
Dr. Paul Sullivan, prin. Fax 732-2856
Calvary Chapel Christian S 600/K-12
7175 W Oquendo Rd 89113 702-248-8879
John Weaver, admin. Fax 220-8694
Faith Lutheran JSHS 1,200/6-12
2015 S Hualapai Way 89117 702-804-4400
Kevin Dunning, dir. Fax 804-4488
Heritage College Post-Sec.
3315 Spring Mountain Rd 89102 702-368-2338
High-Tech Institute Post-Sec.
2320 S Rancho Dr 89102 702-385-6700
House of Knowledge S 50/K-12
PO Box 270097 89127 702-326-5931
Cynthia Watson, admin.
Las Vegas Junior Academy 100/K-10
6059 W Oakey Blvd 89146 702-871-7208
Janet Block, prin. Fax 364-5456
Le Cordon Bleu College of Culinary Arts Post-Sec.
1451 Center Crossing Rd 89144 702-365-7690
Marinello School of Beauty Post-Sec.
5001 E Bonanza Rd Ste 110 89110 702-796-6200
Meadows S 800/K-12
8601 Scholar Ln 89128 702-254-1610
Carolyn Goodman, hdmstr. Fax 254-2452
Mountain View Christian S 700/PK-12
3900 E Bonanza Rd 89110 702-452-1300
Crystal McClanahan, prin. Fax 452-0499
Paradise Christian Academy 200/PK-12
2525 Emerson Ave 89121 702-732-8256
Teena Oglesby, admin. Fax 732-8515
PCI Dealers School Post-Sec.
920 S Valley View Blvd 89107 702-877-4724
Pima Medical Institute Post-Sec.
3333 E Flamingo Rd 89121 702-458-7650
Southern Nevada Univ of Cosmetology Post-Sec.
3430 E Tropicana Ave 89121 702-458-6333
Trinity Christian S 300/PK-12
950 E Sahara Ave 89104 702-735-5778
Thurban Warrick, prin. Fax 731-0961
University of Nevada Las Vegas Post-Sec.
4505 S Maryland Pkwy 89154 800-334-8658
Word of Life Christian Academy 100/PK-10
3520 N Buffalo Dr 89129 702-645-1180
Kelly Marchello, prin. Fax 396-0293

Laughlin, Clark, Pop. 4,791
Clark County SD
Supt. — See Las Vegas
Laughlin MSHS 400/6-12
1900 Cougar Dr 89029 702-298-1996
Richard Edwards, prin. Fax 298-5493

Logandale, Clark
Clark County SD
Supt. — See Las Vegas
Moapa Valley HS 600/9-12
2400 St Joseph St 89021 702-397-2611
Grant Hanevold, prin. Fax 397-2892

Lovelock, Pershing, Pop. 1,878
Pershing County SD 800/K-12
PO Box 389 89419 775-273-7819
Daniel Fox, supt. Fax 273-2668
www.pershing.k12.nv.us
Pershing County HS 200/9-12
PO Box 990 89419 775-273-2625
Russell Fecht, prin. Fax 273-2163
Pershing County MS 100/7-8
PO Box 1020 89419 775-273-1200
Charles Safford, prin. Fax 273-3191

Lund, White Pine
White Pine County SD
Supt. — See Ely
Lund JSHS 7-12
PO Box 129 89317 775-238-5200
Alan Hedges, prin. Fax 238-0208

Mc Dermitt, Humboldt, Pop. 373
Humboldt County SD
Supt. — See Winnemucca
Mc Dermitt JSHS 100/7-12
PO Box 98 89421 775-532-8761
John Moddrell, prin. Fax 532-8017

Mesquite, Clark, Pop. 13,523
Clark County SD
Supt. — See Las Vegas
Hughes MS 500/6-8
550 Hafen Ln 89027 702-346-3250
Clifford Hughes, prin. Fax 346-3095
Virgin Valley HS 600/9-12
820 Valley View Dr 89027 702-346-2780
M. DeLos Perkins, prin. Fax 346-7265

Minden, Douglas, Pop. 1,441
Douglas County SD 7,100/K-12
PO Box 1888 89423 775-782-5134
Carol Lark, supt. Fax 782-3162
www.dcsd.k12.nv.us
Douglas HS 1,600/10-12
PO Box 1888 89423 775-782-5136
Marty Swisher, prin. Fax 782-7039
Other Schools – See Gardnerville, Zephyr Cove

Sierra Lutheran HS 50/9-12
1617 Water St Ste S 89423 775-782-0060
Debbie Conner, admin. Fax 782-0454

North Las Vegas, Clark, Pop. 176,635
Clark County SD
Supt. — See Las Vegas
Area Technical Trade Center — Vo/Tech
444 W Brooks Ave 89030 — 702-799-8300
Cynthia Morris, prin. — Fax 799-8371
Bridger MS — 1,300/6-8
2505 N Bruce St 89030 — 702-799-7185
Milana Winter, prin. — Fax 799-7074
Canyon Springs HS — 1,800/9-12
350 E Alexander Rd 89032 — 702-799-1870
Ronan Matthew, prin. — Fax 799-1876
Cheyenne HS — 2,800/9-12
3200 W Alexander Rd 89032 — 702-799-4830
Jeffrey Geihs, prin. — Fax 799-4856
Community College HS East — 100/11-12
3200 E Cheyenne Ave 89030 — 702-651-4071
Dennis Birr, prin. — Fax 651-4627
Cram MS — 1,400/6-8
1900 W Deer Springs Way 89084 — 702-799-7020
Jeri Plunkett, prin. — Fax 799-8346
Findlay MS — 1,700/6-8
333 W Tropical Pkwy 89031 — 702-799-3160
David Bechtel, prin. — Fax 799-3169
Johnston MS — 6-8
5855 Lawrence St, — 702-799-7001
Kenneth Fowler, prin. — Fax 799-7010
Legacy HS — 9-12
150 W Deer Springs Way 89084 — 702-799-1777
Tammy Malich, prin. — Fax 799-1701
Mojave HS — 2,800/9-12
5302 Goldfield St 89031 — 702-799-0432
Charity Varnado, prin. — Fax 799-0437
Sedway MS — 1,500/6-8
3465 Engelstad St 89032 — 702-799-3880
Stanley Allen, prin. — Fax 799-1785
Smith MS — 1,100/6-8
1301 E Tonopah Ave 89030 — 702-799-7080
Neddy Alvarez, prin. — Fax 799-7195
Swainston MS — 1,500/6-8
3500 W Gilmore Ave 89032 — 702-799-4860
Bevelyn Smothers, prin. — Fax 799-4806

American Institute of Technology — Post-Sec.
4020 E Lone Mountain Rd, — 702-644-1234
Community College of Southern Nevada — Post-Sec.
3200 E Cheyenne Ave 89030 — 702-651-4000
University Baptist Academy — 100/K-12
3770 W Washburn Rd 89031 — 702-732-3385
Elizabeth Scafani, prin. — Fax 734-0747

Overton, Clark
Clark County SD
Supt. — See Las Vegas
Lyon MS — 500/6-8
179 S Anderson 89040 — 702-397-8610
David Wilson, prin. — Fax 397-2754

Owyhee, Elko, Pop. 908
Elko County SD
Supt. — See Elko
Owyhee S — K-12
PO Box 100 89832 — 775-757-3400
Teola Blossom, prin. — Fax 757-3663

Pahrump, Nye, Pop. 7,424
Nye County SD
Supt. — See Tonopah
Clarke MS — 1,100/6-8
4201 N Blagg Rd 89060 — 775-727-5546
Joe Peters, prin. — Fax 727-7104
Pahrump Valley HS — 1,100/9-12
501 E Calvada Blvd 89048 — 775-727-7737
Kent Roberts, prin. — Fax 727-7722

New Hope Christian Academy — 100/PK-12
781 West St 89048 — 775-751-1867
Julie Schmidt, admin. — Fax 751-3387

Panaca, Lincoln
Lincoln County SD — 800/K-12
PO Box 118 89042 — 775-728-4471
Clark M. Hardy, supt. — Fax 728-4435
www.lincoln.k12.nv.us
Lincoln County HS — 200/9-12
PO Box 268 89042 — 775-728-4481
Craig Babcock, prin. — Fax 728-4484
Meadow Valley MS — 100/7-8
PO Box 567 89042 — 775-728-4655
Marty Soderborg, prin. — Fax 728-4302
Other Schools – See Alamo

Reno, Washoe, Pop. 203,550
Washoe County SD — 60,800/K-12
PO Box 30425 89520 — 775-348-0200
Paul Dugan, supt. — Fax 348-0304
www.washoe.k12.nv.us
Billinghurst MS — 900/7-8
6685 Chesterfield Ln 89523 — 775-746-5870
Ken Cervantes, prin. — Fax 746-5875
Clayton MS — 700/7-8
1295 Wyoming Ave 89503 — 775-746-5860
Daniel Garfinkle, prin. — Fax 746-5864
Cold Springs MS — 6-8
18235 Cody Ct, — 775-677-5433
Roberta Duval, prin. — Fax 677-5439
Damonte Ranch MSHS — 900/7-12
10500 Rio Wrangler Pkwy, — 775-851-5656
Denise Hausauer, prin. — Fax 851-5663
Galena HS — 1,500/9-12
3600 Butch Cassidy Dr 89511 — 775-851-5630
Tom Brown, prin. — Fax 851-5607
Hare Occupational Center — Vo/Tech
350 Hunter Lake Dr 89509 — 775-857-4947
Heather Murray, admin.
Hug HS — 1,300/9-12
2880 Sutro St 89512 — 775-333-5300
Andrew Kelley, prin. — Fax 333-5312
McQueen HS — 2,000/9-12
6055 Lancer St 89523 — 775-746-5880
John Carlson, prin. — Fax 747-6883
North Valleys HS — 2,000/9-12
1470 E Golden Valley Rd, — 775-677-5499
Cinda Gifford, prin. — Fax 677-5497
O'Brien MS — 1,300/7-8
10500 Stead Blvd 89506 — 775-677-5420
Scott Grange, prin. — Fax 677-5423
Pine MS — 900/7-8
4800 Neil Rd 89502 — 775-689-2550
Brad Boudreau, prin. — Fax 689-2539
Regional Technical Institute — Vo/Tech
380 Edison Way 89502 — 775-861-4418
Heather Murray, prin. — Fax 861-4415
Reno HS — 1,800/9-12
395 Booth St 89509 — 775-333-5050
Bob Sullivan, prin. — Fax 333-5058
Swope MS — 900/7-8
901 Keele Dr 89509 — 775-333-5330
Dr. Michele Collins, prin. — Fax 333-5083
TMCC Magnet SHS — 200/11-12
7000 Dandini Blvd 89512 — 775-674-7660
Heather Murray, prin. — Fax 674-7931
Traner MS — 600/7-8
1700 Carville Dr 89512 — 775-333-5130
Lauren Ford, prin. — Fax 333-5135
Vaughn MS — 800/7-8
1200 Bresson Ave 89502 — 775-333-5160
Dr. Ginny Knowles, prin. — Fax 333-5118
Washoe MSHS — 600/7-12
777 W 2nd St 89503 — 775-333-5150
Michael Doering, prin. — Fax 333-5122
Wooster HS — 1,500/9-12
1331 E Plumb Ln 89502 — 775-333-5100
Jess Castillo, prin. — Fax 333-5108
Other Schools – See Gerlach, Incline Village, Sparks

Bishop Manogue HS — 9-12
110 Bishop Manogue Dr 89511 — 775-336-6000
Tim Petersen, prin. — Fax 336-6015
Career College of Northern Nevada — Post-Sec.
1195 Corporate Blvd Ste A 89502 — 775-856-2266
Church Academy — 100/K-12
1205 N McCarran Blvd 89512 — 775-329-5848
Ron Poe, prin. — Fax 329-3360
Morrison University — Post-Sec.
10315 Professional Cir #201, — 775-850-0700
Reno Tahoe Job Training Academy — Post-Sec.
3702 S Virginia St Ste H2 89502 — 775-329-5665
Sierra Nevada HS — 500/9-12
5005 Echo Ave 89506 — 775-789-0951
Dr. Joseph Reading, prin.
Silver State Adventist S — 100/K-10
PO Box 11950 89510 — 775-322-0714
Fax 322-8064
Truckee Meadows Community College — Post-Sec.
7000 Dandini Blvd 89512 — 775-673-7000
University of Nevada 89557 — Post-Sec.
775-784-1110

Round Mountain, Nye
Nye County SD
Supt. — See Tonopah
Round Mountain JSHS — 100/6-12
PO Box 1427 89045 — 775-377-2690
Barbara Floto, prin. — Fax 377-1239

Sandy Valley, Clark
Clark County SD
Supt. — See Las Vegas
Sandy Valley MS — 100/6-8
HC 31 Box 111 89019 — 702-723-5344
Marilyn Miks, prin. — Fax 723-5251

Silver Springs, Lyon, Pop. 2,253
Lyon County SD
Supt. — See Yerington
Silver Stage HS — 400/9-12
3755 W Spruce Ave 89429 — 775-577-5071
Patrick Peters, prin. — Fax 577-5079
Silver Stage MS — 400/5-8
3800 W Spruce Ave 89429 — 775-577-5050
Rob Jacobson, prin. — Fax 577-5053

Smith, Lyon, Pop. 1,033
Lyon County SD
Supt. — See Yerington
Smith Valley JSHS — 100/7-12
20 Day Ln 89430 — 775-465-2332
Keri Pommerening, prin. — Fax 465-2681

Sparks, Washoe, Pop. 82,051
Washoe County SD
Supt. — See Reno
Dilworth MS — 600/7-8
255 Prater Way 89431 — 775-353-5740
Laurie Gray, prin. — Fax 353-5584
Mendive MS — 1,100/7-8
1900 Whitewood Dr 89434 — 775-353-5990
Juliana Annand, prin. — Fax 353-5994
Reed HS — 2,500/9-12
1350 Baring Blvd 89434 — 775-353-5700
Mary Vesco, prin. — Fax 353-5708
Shaw MS — 900/7-8
600 Eagle Canyon Dr, — 775-425-7777
Dave Fullenwider, prin.
Spanish Springs HS — 1,900/9-12
1065 Eagle Canyon Dr, — 775-425-7733
Ross Gregory, prin. — Fax 425-7735
Sparks HS — 1,100/9-12
820 15th St 89431 — 775-353-5550
Nancy Sanger, prin. — Fax 353-5514
Sparks MS — 600/7-8
2275 18th St 89431 — 775-353-5770
Andrew Yoxsimer, prin. — Fax 353-5585

Excel Christian S — 100/K-12
740 Baring Blvd 89434 — 775-356-9995
Bonnie Krupa, admin. — Fax 356-9527
Legacy Christian HS — 100/7-12
816 Holman Way 89431 — 775-358-1112
Gregory Root, admin. — Fax 358-5030
Milan Institute — Post-Sec.
950 Industrial Way 89431 — 775-348-7200

Spring Creek, Elko, Pop. 5,866
Elko County SD
Supt. — See Elko
Spring Creek HS — 900/9-12
14550 Lamoille Hwy 89815 — 775-753-5575
Betty Fobes, prin. — Fax 753-5956
Spring Creek MS — 700/6-8
14650 Lamoille Hwy 89815 — 775-777-1688
Karen Branzell, prin. — Fax 777-1738

Tonopah, Nye, Pop. 3,616
Nye County SD — 5,600/K-12
PO Box 113 89049 — 775-482-6258
Dr. William Roberts, supt. — Fax 482-8573
www.nye.k12.nv.us
Tonopah HS — 200/9-12
PO Box 1349 89049 — 775-482-3698
Alvin Eiseman, prin. — Fax 482-3935
Other Schools – See Beatty, Gabbs, Pahrump, Round Mountain

Virginia City, Storey
Storey County SD — 500/K-12
PO Box C 89440 — 775-847-0983
Dr. Robert Slaby, supt. — Fax 847-0989
www.storey.k12.nv.us
Virginia City HS — 200/9-12
PO Box C 89440 — 775-847-0992
Patrick Beckwith, prin. — Fax 847-0994
Virginia City MS — 100/6-8
PO Box C 89440 — 775-847-0980
Todd Hess, prin. — Fax 847-0913

Wells, Elko, Pop. 1,295
Elko County SD
Supt. — See Elko
Wells S — 200/K-12
PO Box 338 89835 — 775-752-3837
Leslie Lotspeich, prin. — Fax 752-2470

West Wendover, Elko, Pop. 4,966
Elko County SD
Supt. — See Elko
West Wendover JSHS — 500/7-12
PO Box 3830 89883 — 775-664-3940
Keith Walz, prin. — Fax 664-3944

Winnemucca, Humboldt, Pop. 7,726
Humboldt County SD — 3,400/K-12
310 E 4th St 89445 — 775-623-8100
Dr. Del Jarman, supt. — Fax 623-8102
www.humboldt.k12.nv.us
Lowry HS — 1,000/9-12
5375 Kluncy Canyon Rd 89445 — 775-623-8130
Deborah Watts, prin. — Fax 623-8185
Winnemucca JHS — 500/7-8
451 Reinhart St 89445 — 775-623-8120
Ray Garrison, prin. — Fax 623-8208
Other Schools – See Mc Dermitt

Yerington, Lyon, Pop. 3,486
Lyon County SD — 8,000/K-12
25 E Goldfield Ave 89447 — 775-463-6800
Nat Lommori, supt. — Fax 463-6808
lyon.k12.nv.us
Yerington HS — 500/9-12
114 Pearl St 89447 — 775-463-6822
Jerry Ogolin, prin. — Fax 463-6828
Yerington IS — 500/5-8
215 Pearl St 89447 — 775-463-6833
Harriet Hasbrouck, prin. — Fax 463-6840
Other Schools – See Dayton, Fernley, Silver Springs, Smith

Zephyr Cove, Douglas, Pop. 1,434
Douglas County SD
Supt. — See Minden
Kingsbury MS — 200/6-8
PO Box 648 89448 — 775-588-6281
Dan Wold, prin. — Fax 588-8893
Whittell HS — 200/9-12
PO Box 677 89448 — 775-588-2446
Sue Shannon, prin. — Fax 588-2443

NEW HAMPSHIRE

NEW HAMPSHIRE DEPT. OF EDUCATION
101 Pleasant St, Concord 03301-3852
Telephone 603-271-3494
Fax 603-271-1953
Website http://www.ed.state.nh.us

Commissioner of Education Lyonel Tracy

NEW HAMPSHIRE BOARD OF EDUCATION
101 Pleasant St, Concord 03301-3852

Chairperson John Lyons

SCHOOL ADMINISTRATIVE UNITS (SAU)

SAU 1
Keith Burke, supt., 106 Hancock Rd 603-924-3336
Peterborough 03458 Fax 924-6707
www.conval.edu/

SAU 2
Dr. Phillip McCormack, supt. 603-279-7947
103 Main St Ste 2, Meredith 03253 Fax 279-3044
www.sau2.k12.nh.us/

SAU 3
John Moulis, supt. 603-752-6500
183 Hillside Ave, Berlin 03570 Fax 752-2528
www.sau3.org/

SAU 4
Marie Ross, supt. 603-744-5555
20 N Main St, Bristol 03222 Fax 744-6659
www.newfound.k12.nh.us

SAU 5
Howard Colter, supt. 603-868-5100
36 Coe Dr, Durham 03824 Fax 868-6668
www.orcsd.org

SAU 6
Jacqueline Guillette, supt. 603-543-4200
165 Broad St, Claremont 03743 Fax 543-4244
www.sau6.k12.nh.us/

SAU 7
Robert Mills, supt. 603-237-5571
21 Academy St, Colebrook 03576 Fax 237-5126

SAU 8
Dr. Christine Rath, supt. 603-225-0811
16 Rumford St, Concord 03301 Fax 226-2187
www.concord.k12.nh.us

SAU 9
Dr. Carl Nelson, supt. 603-356-5533
19 Pine St, North Conway 03860 Fax 356-5144

SAU 10
Mary Ellen Hannon, supt. 603-432-1210
18 S Main St, Derry 03038 Fax 432-1264
www.derry.k12.nh.us

SAU 11
Dr. John O'Connor, supt. 603-516-6800
288 Central Ave, Dover 03820 Fax 516-6809
www.dover.k12.nh.us/

SAU 12
Dr. Nathan Greenberg, supt. 603-432-6920
268 Mammoth Rd Fax 425-1049
Londonderry 03053

SAU 13
Dr. Gwen Poirer, supt. 603-539-2610
626 Plains Rd, Silver Lake 03875 Fax 539-9064

SAU 14
Barbara Munsey, supt. 603-679-5402
213 Main St, Epping 03042 Fax 679-1237

SAU 15
Dr. Charles Littlefield, supt. 603-622-3731
90 Farmer Rd, Hooksett 03106 Fax 669-4352

SAU 16
Dr. Arthur Hanson, supt. 603-775-8653
24 Front St Ste 1, Exeter 03833 Fax 775-8673
www.sau16.org/

SAU 17
Dr. Keith Pfeifer, supt. 603-642-3688
178 Main St, Kingston 03848 Fax 642-7885

SAU 18
Jo Ellen Divoll, supt. 603-934-3108
119 Central St, Franklin 03235 Fax 934-3462

SAU 19
Dr. Darrell Lockwood, supt. 603-497-4818
11 School St, Goffstown 03045 Fax 497-8425
www.goffstown.k12.nh.us

SAU 20
Paul Bousquet, supt. 603-466-3632
123 Main St, Gorham 03581 Fax 466-3870
www.sau20.org/

SAU 21
James F. Gaylord, supt. 603-926-8992
2 Alumni Dr, Hampton 03842 Fax 926-5157
www.sau21.k12.nh.us

SAU 23
Bruce Labs, supt. 603-787-2113
2975 Dartmouth College Hwy Fax 787-2118
North Haverhill 03774
www.sau23.k12.nh.us

SAU 24
Dr. Christine Tyrie, supt. 603-428-3269
PO Box 2417, Henniker 03242 Fax 428-3850

SAU 25
Timothy Mayes, supt. 603-472-3755
103 County Rd, Bedford 03110 Fax 472-2567
www.sau25.net/

SAU 26
Marjorie Chiafery, supt. 603-424-6200
36 McElwain St, Merrimack 03054 Fax 424-6229
www.merrimack.k12.nh.us

SAU 27
Catherine M. Hamblett, supt. 603-578-3570
1 Highlander Ct, Litchfield 03052 Fax 578-1267

SAU 28
Dr. Frank Bass, supt. 603-425-1976
PO Box 510, Windham 03087 Fax 425-1719

SAU 29 603-357-9002
, 34 West St, Keene 03431 Fax 357-9012
www.sau29.k12.nh.us/

SAU 30
Robert Champlin, supt. 603-524-5710
PO Box 309, Laconia 03247 Fax 528-8442

SAU 31
Kathleen Murphy, supt. 603-659-5020
186A Main St, Newmarket 03857 Fax 659-5022

SAU 32
Russell W. Collins, supt. 603-469-3442
92 Bonner Rd, Meriden 03770 Fax 469-3985

SAU 33
Michael Shore, supt. 603-895-4299
43 Harriman Hill Rd Fax 895-0147
Raymond 03077
www.raymond.k12.nh.us

SAU 34
Dr. Barbara Baker, supt. 603-464-4466
PO Box 2190, Deering 03244 Fax 464-4053
www.hdsd.org

SAU 35
Patrick Low, supt. 603-444-3925
262 Cottage St Ste 230 Fax 444-6299
Littleton 03561
www.sau35.k12.nh.us

SAU 36
Dr. Dean Cascadden, supt. 603-837-9363
14 King Sq, Whitefield 03598 Fax 837-2326
www.sau36.org

SAU 37
Dr. Michael Ludwell, supt. 603-624-6300
286 Commercial St Fax 644-0357
Manchester 03101
www.mansd.org

SAU 38
Dr. Kenneth Dassau, supt. 603-352-6955
600 Old Homestead Hwy Fax 358-6708
East Swanzey 03446
www.mrsd.org/

SAU 39
Dr. Mary Jennings, supt. 603-673-2690
PO Box 849, Amherst 03031 Fax 672-1786
www.sprise.com/

SAU 40
Robert Suprenant, supt. 603-673-2202
100 West St, Milford 03055 Fax 673-2237

SAU 41
Richard Pike, supt. 603-465-7118
PO Box 1588, Hollis 03049 Fax 465-3933
www.sau41.k12.nh.us

SAU 42
Julia Earl, supt. 603-594-4300
PO Box 687, Nashua 03061 Fax 594-4350
www.nashua.edu

SAU 43
William J. Mealey, supt. 603-863-3540
9 Depot St Ste 2, Newport 03773 Fax 863-5368

SAU 44
Judy McGann, supt. 603-942-1290
569 1st NH Tpke Fax 942-1295
Northwood 03261

SAU 45
Michael Lancor, supt., PO Box 419 603-476-5247
Moultonborough 03254 Fax 476-8009
www.moultonborough.k12.nh.us

SAU 46
Dr. Michael Martin, supt. 603-753-6561
105 Community Dr Fax 753-6023
Penacook 03303

SAU 47
James O'Neill, supt. 603-532-8100
81 Fitzgerald Dr Unit 2 Fax 532-8149
Jaffrey 03452
www.sau47.k12.nh.us

SAU 48
Mark Halloran, supt. 603-536-1254
47 Old Ward Bridge Rd Fax 536-3545
Plymouth 03264
www.sau48.k12.nh.us/

SAU 49
John Robertson, supt. 603-569-1658
PO Box 190, Wolfeboro Falls 03896 Fax 569-6983
www.govwentworth.k12.nh.us

SAU 50
Dr. George Cushing, supt. 603-422-9572
48 Post Rd, Greenland 03840 Fax 422-9575
www.sau50.k12.nh.us/

SAU 51
Dr. William Compton, supt. 603-435-5526
175 Barnstead Rd Unit 3 Fax 435-5331
Pittsfield 03263
www.barnstead.k12.nh.us

SAU 52
Dr. Robert Lister, supt. 603-431-5080
50 Clough Dr, Portsmouth 03801 Fax 431-6753
www.cityofportsmouth.com/school/

SAU 53
Thomas Haley, supt. 603-485-5188
267 Pembroke St, Pembroke 03275 Fax 485-9529
www.sau53.org

SAU 54
Michael Hopkins, supt. 603-332-3678
150 Wakefield St Ste 8 Fax 335-7367
Rochester 03867
www.rochesterschools.com

SAU 55
Dr. Douglas McDonald, supt. 603-382-6119
30 Greenough Rd, Plaistow 03865 Fax 382-3334

SAU 56
Karen Soule, supt. 603-692-4450
51 W High St, Somersworth 03878 Fax 692-9100

SAU 57
Michael Dalahanty, supt. 603-893-7040
38 Geremonty Dr, Salem 03079 Fax 893-7080

SAU 58
Sherwood Fluery, supt. 603-636-1437
8 Preble St, Groveton 03582 Fax 636-6102

SAU 59
Tammy Davis, supt. 603-286-4116
433 W Main St, Northfield 03276 Fax 286-7402
www.winnisquam.k12.nh.us/Sau/index.htm

SAU 60
Joseph Della Badia, supt. 603-826-7756
PO Box 600, Charlestown 03603 Fax 826-4430

SAU 61
Michelle Langa, supt. 603-755-2627
356 Main St, Farmington 03835 Fax 755-2060

SAU 62
Barbara Tremblay, supt. 603-632-5563
PO Box 789, Enfield 03748 Fax 632-4181
mascoma.k12.nh.us

SAU 63
Francine Fullam, supt. 603-878-1026
659 Turnpike Rd Ste 120 Fax 878-3871
New Ipswich 03071

SAU 64
William Lander, supt. 603-473-2326
39 Main St, Union 03887 Fax 473-2218
www.sau64.k12.nh.us

SAU 65
Dr. Thomas Brennan, supt. 603-526-2051
169 Main St, New London 03257 Fax 526-2145

SAU 66
Brian Blake, supt. 603-746-5186
204 Maple St, Contoocook 03229 Fax 746-5714

SAU 67
Kathleen Holt, supt. 603-224-4728
32 White Rock Hill Rd, Bow 03304 Fax 224-4111

SAU 68
Michael Cosgriff, supt. 603-745-2051
PO Box 846, Lincoln 03251 Fax 745-2351
www.lin-wood.k12.nh.us

SAU 70
Wayne Gersen, supt. 603-643-6050
45 Lyme Rd Ste 207 Fax 643-3073
Hanover 03755

SAU 71
Dr. John Handfield, supt. 603-863-2420
29 School Rd, Lempster 03605 Fax 863-2451

SAU 72
Normand Tanguay, supt. 603-875-7890
252 Suncook Valley Rd Fax 875-0391
Alton 03809
www.alton.k12.nh.us

SAU 73
Dr. Paul P. DeMinico, supt. 603-527-9215
47 Cherry Valley Rd, Gilford 03249 Fax 527-9216

SAU 74
Michael Morgan, supt. 603-664-2715
41 Province Ln, Barrington 03825 Fax 664-2609
www.barrington.k12.nh.us

SAU 75
John Moses, supt. 603-863-9689
PO Box 287, Grantham 03753 Fax 863-9684

SAU 76
Dr. Gordon Schnare, supt. 603-795-4431
PO Box 117, Lyme 03768 Fax 795-9407

SAU 77
Karen Stewart, admin. 603-638-2800
PO Box 130, Monroe 03771 Fax 638-2031

SAU 78
Noelle Vitt, supt. 603-353-2170
PO Box 153, Orford 03777 Fax 353-2189
SAU 79
Dr. Harry Fensom, supt. 603-267-9097
PO Box 309, Gilmanton 03237 Fax 267-9498
SAU 80
W. Michael Cozort, supt. 603-267-9223
58 School St, Belmont 03220 Fax 267-9225
www.shaker.k12.nh.us
SAU 81
Philip Bell, supt. 603-886-1235
20 Library St, Hudson 03051 Fax 886-1236

SAU 82
Dr. Victor Petzy, supt. 603-887-3621
22 Murphy Dr, Chester 03036 Fax 887-4961
www.chesteracademy.org/
SAU 83
Normand Tanguay, supt. 603-895-2511
432 Main St, Fremont 03044 Fax 895-1106
SAU 88
Dr. Michael Harris, supt. 603-448-1634
PO Box 488, Lebanon 03766 Fax 448-0602
www.lebanon.k12.nh.us

SAU 201
David Smith, hdmstr. 603-942-5531
907 1st NH Tpke Fax 942-7537
Northwood 03261
www.coebrownacademy.com
SAU 202
Mary Anderson, hdmstr. 603-437-5200
5 Pinkerton St, Derry 03038 Fax 432-5328
www.pinkertonacademy.net
SAU 301
Normand Tanguay, supt. 603-875-3800
242 Suncook Valley Rd Fax 875-8200
Alton 03809
www.pmhschool.com

PUBLIC, PRIVATE AND CATHOLIC SECONDARY SCHOOLS

Allenstown, Merrimack
Allenstown SD
Supt. — See Pembroke
Dupont MS 300/5-8
10 School St 03275 603-485-4474
Betsey Cox-Buteau, prin. Fax 485-1806

Alstead, Cheshire
Fall Mountain Regional SD
Supt. — See Charlestown
Vilas MS 100/5-8
PO Box 670 03602 603-835-6351
Carol Bennett, prin. Fax 835-2052

Alton, Belknap
Prospect Mountain SD 100/9-12
242 Suncook Valley Rd 03809 603-875-3800
Normand Tanguay, supt. Fax 875-8200
www.pmhschool.com
Prospect Mountain HS 9-12
242 Suncook Valley Rd 03809 603-875-3800
Russell Holden, prin. Fax 875-8200

Amherst, Hillsborough
Amherst SD 1,700/K-8
PO Box 849 03031 603-673-2690
Dr. Mary Jennings, supt. Fax 672-1786
www.sprise.com
Amherst MS 900/5-8
PO Box 966 03031 603-673-8944
Porter Dodge, prin. Fax 673-6774

Souhegan Cooperative SD 1,000/9-12
PO Box 849 03031 603-673-2690
Dr. Mary Jennings, supt. Fax 672-1786
Souhegan Coop. HS 1,000/9-12
PO Box 1152 03031 603-673-9940
Scott Prescott, prin. Fax 673-0318

Andover, Merrimack

Proctor Academy 300/9-12
PO Box 500 03216 603-735-6000
Mike Henryques, hdmstr. Fax 735-5129

Antrim, Hillsborough, Pop. 1,325
Contoocook Valley SD
Supt. — See Peterborough
Great Brook MS 400/5-8
16 School St 03440 603-588-6630
G. Bruce West, prin. Fax 588-3207

Barrington, Strafford
Barrington SD 800/PK-8
41 Province Ln 03825 603-664-2715
Michael Morgan, supt. Fax 664-2609
www.barrington.k12.nh.us
Barrington MS 300/5-8
20 Haley Dr 03825 603-664-2127
Michael Tursi, prin. Fax 664-5739

Good Shepherd S 200/K-12
37 Province Ln 03825 603-664-2742
Elizabeth Shortle, prin. Fax 664-7196

Bedford, Hillsborough
Bedford SD 2,900/PK-8
103 County Rd 03110 603-472-3755
Timothy Mayes, supt. Fax 472-2567
www.sau25.net/
McKelvie MS 900/6-8
108 Liberty Hill Rd 03110 603-472-3951
Jan Raudonis, prin. Fax 472-4503

Michael's School of Hair Design Post-Sec.
73 S River Rd Ste 26 03110 603-668-4300
Mount Zion Christian S 200/K-12
469 S River Rd 03110 603-606-7930
Robert Carter, hdmstr. Fax 606-7935

Belmont, Belknap
Shaker Regional SD 1,500/PK-12
58 School St 03220 603-267-9223
W. Michael Cozort, supt. Fax 267-9225
www.shaker.k12.nh.us
Belmont HS 500/9-12
255 Seavey Rd 03220 603-267-6525
Marcia Hayward, prin. Fax 267-5962
Belmont MS 500/5-8
38 School St 03220 603-267-9220
Robert Gadomski, prin. Fax 267-9221

Berlin, Coos, Pop. 10,097
Berlin SD 1,600/K-12
183 Hillside Ave 03570 603-752-6500
John Moulis, supt. Fax 752-2528
www.sau3.org/
Berlin HS 600/9-12
550 Willard St 03570 603-752-4122
Gary Bisson, prin. Fax 752-8566
Berlin JHS 300/7-8
200 State St 03570 603-752-5311
Beverly Dupont, prin. Fax 752-8580
Berlin Regional Vocational Center Vo/Tech
550 Willard St 03570 603-752-4122
Roland Pinette, prin. Fax 752-8566

New Hampshire Community Tech College Post-Sec.
2020 Riverside Dr 03570 603-752-1113

Bethlehem, Grafton
Profile SD 300/7-12
691 Profile Rd 03574 603-444-3925
Patrick Low, supt. Fax 444-6299
www.profile.k12.nh.us/
Profile HS 200/9-12
691 Profile Rd 03574 603-823-7411
Richard Larcom, prin. Fax 823-7490
Profile JHS 100/7-8
691 Profile Rd 03574 603-823-7411
Richard Larcom, prin. Fax 823-7490

White Mountain S 100/9-12
371 W Farm Rd 03574 603-444-2928
Alan T. Popp, hdmstr. Fax 444-1258

Bow, Merrimack
Bow SD 1,800/PK-12
32 White Rock Hill Rd 03304 603-224-4728
Kathleen Holt, supt. Fax 224-4111
www.bownet.org
Bow HS 600/9-12
32 White Rock Hill Rd 03304 603-228-2210
John House-Myers, prin. Fax 228-2212
Bow Memorial MS 600/5-8
20 Bow Center Rd 03304 603-225-3212
Kirk Spofford, prin. Fax 228-2228

Brentwood, Rockingham

Lighthouse Christian Academy 100/K-12
263 Route 125 03833 603-642-3756
Linda Brown, admin. Fax 642-7845

Bristol, Grafton, Pop. 1,483
Newfound Area SD 1,500/PK-12
20 N Main St 03222 603-744-5555
Marie Ross, supt. Fax 744-6659
www.newfound.k12.nh.us
Newfound Memorial MS 400/6-8
155 N Main St 03222 603-744-8162
Eric Chase, prin. Fax 744-8037
Newfound Regional HS 500/9-12
150 Newfound Rd 03222 603-744-6006
Michael O'Malley, prin. Fax 744-2526

Canaan, Grafton
Mascoma Valley Regional SD
Supt. — See Enfield
Indian River MS 500/5-8
45 Royal Rd 03741 603-632-4357
Dorothy Campbell, prin. Fax 632-4262
Mascoma Valley Regional HS 500/9-12
27 Royal Rd 03741 603-632-4308
Patrick Andrew, prin. Fax 632-5419

Cardigan Mountain S 200/6-9
62 Alumni Dr 03741 603-523-4321
Fax 523-7227

Candia, Rockingham

Remington HS 50/9-12
PO Box 62 03034 603-483-5664
Jeffrey Philbrick, hdmstr. Fax 483-4811

Charlestown, Sullivan, Pop. 1,173
Fall Mountain Regional SD 1,900/PK-12
PO Box 600 03603 603-826-7756
Joseph Della Badia, supt. Fax 826-4430
www.fall-mountain.k12.nh.us
Charlestown MS 200/6-8
PO Box 325 03603 603-826-7711
Paula Stevens, prin. Fax 826-3102
Other Schools – See Alstead, Langdon, Walpole

Chester, Rockingham

Chester College of New England Post-Sec.
40 Chester St 03036 603-887-4401

Claremont, Sullivan, Pop. 13,388
Claremont SD 2,000/PK-12
165 Broad St 03743 603-543-4200
Jacqueline Guillette, supt. Fax 543-4244
www.sau6.k12.nh.us
Claremont MS 500/6-8
107 South St 03743 603-543-4250
Donald Hart, prin. Fax 543-4289
Stevens HS 700/9-12
175 Broad St 03743 603-543-4220
Leo Couture, prin. Fax 543-4220
Sugar River Valley Regional Ctr West Vo/Tech
111 South St 03743 603-543-4291
John Doherty, dir. Fax 543-4296

Claremont Christian Academy 50/K-12
97 Maple Ave 03743 603-542-8759
Rev. Stephen Cook, dir. Fax 542-8759
New Hampshire Community Tech College Post-Sec.
1 College Dr 03743 603-542-7744

Colebrook, Coos
Colebrook SD 500/K-12
21 Academy St 03576 603-237-5571
Robert Mills, supt. Fax 237-5126
www.colebrook.k12.nh.us/
Colebrook Academy 200/9-12
13 Academy St 03576 603-237-4280
Priscilla McGuire, prin. Fax 237-5717

Pittsburg SD 200/K-12
21 Academy St 03576 603-237-5571
Robert Mills, supt. Fax 237-5126
Other Schools – See Pittsburg

Concord, Merrimack, Pop. 42,336
Concord SD 5,300/PK-12
16 Rumford St 03301 603-225-0811
Dr. Christine Rath, supt. Fax 226-2187
www.concord.k12.nh.us
Concord HS 1,800/9-12
170 Warren St 03301 603-225-0800
Gene Connolly, prin. Fax 223-2054
Concord Regional Technical Center Vo/Tech
170 Warren St 03301 603-225-0800
Donna Nelson, prin. Fax 223-2050
Rundlett MS 1,300/6-8
144 South St 03301 603-225-0865
George Rogers, prin. Fax 226-3288

Merrimack Valley SD 2,800/PK-12
105 Community Dr 03303 603-753-6561
Michael Martin, supt. Fax 753-6023
www.mv.k12.nh.us
Other Schools – See Penacook

Bishop Brady HS 400/9-12
25 Columbus Ave 03301 603-224-7418
Jean Barker, prin. Fax 228-6664
Concord Academy of Hair Design Post-Sec.
20 S Main St 03301 603-224-2211
Franklin Pierce College Post-Sec.
5 Chenell Dr 03301 603-228-1155
Franklin Pierce Law Center Post-Sec.
2 White St 03301 603-228-9217
Granite State College Post-Sec.
8 Old Suncook Rd 03301 603-228-3000
Hesser College Post-Sec.
25 Hall St 03301 603-225-9200
New Hampshire Technical Institute Post-Sec.
11 Institute Dr 03301 603-271-6484
St. Paul's S 500/9-12
325 Pleasant St 03301 603-229-4600
William Matthews, prin. Fax 229-4892
Trinity Christian S 300/K-12
80 Clinton St 03301 603-225-5410
Peter Flint, prin. Fax 225-3235

Contoocook, Merrimack, Pop. 1,334
Hopkinton SD 1,000/PK-12
204 Maple St 03229 603-746-5186
Brian Blake, supt. Fax 746-5714
www.hopkintonschools.org/
Hopkinton HS 400/9-12
297 Park Ave 03229 603-746-4167
Steven Chamberlin, prin. Fax 746-5109
Hopkinton MS 200/7-8
297 Park Ave 03229 603-746-4167
Steven Chamberlin, prin. Fax 746-5109

Conway, Carroll, Pop. 1,604
Conway SD
Supt. — See North Conway
Kennett HS 1,000/9-12
176 Main St 03818 603-447-6364
John Loynd, prin. Fax 447-6842
Kennett MS 400/7-8
176 Main St 03818 603-447-5408
Kevin M. Richard, prin. Fax 447-6842
Mt. Washington Career & Technical Center Vo/Tech
176 Main St 03818 603-447-5209
Neal Moylan, prin. Fax 447-1735

Deering, Hillsborough
Hillsboro-Deering Cooperative SD 1,400/PK-12
2300 2nd NH Tpke 03244 603-464-4466
Dr. Barbara Baker, supt. Fax 464-4053
www.hdsd.org
Other Schools – See Hillsborough

Derry, Rockingham, Pop. 20,446
Derry Cooperative SD 4,100/PK-8
18 S Main St 03038 603-432-1210
Mary Ellen Hannon, supt. Fax 432-1264
www.derry.k12.nh.us
Hood Memorial MS 900/6-8
5 Hood Rd 03038 603-432-1224
Austin Garofalo, prin. Fax 432-1227
West Running Brook MS 800/6-8
1 W Running Brook Ln 03038 603-432-1250
Leslie Saucier, prin. Fax 432-1243

Pinkerton Academy 3,300/9-12
5 Pinkerton St 03038 603-437-5200
Mary Anderson, hdmstr. Fax 432-5328
www.pinkertonacademy.net
Pinkerton Academy 3,300/9-12
5 Pinkerton St 03038 603-437-5200
Mary Anderson, hdmstr. Fax 432-5328

Calvary Christian S 300/K-12
145 Hampstead Rd 03038 603-434-1501
Donald Batchelder, prin. Fax 437-8096

Dover, Strafford, Pop. 28,486
Dover SD 4,100/PK-12
288 Central Ave 03820 603-516-6800
Dr. John O'Connor, supt. Fax 516-6809
www.dover.k12.nh.us

Dover HS 1,600/9-12
25 Alumni Dr 03820 603-516-6900
Christopher George, prin. Fax 516-6926
Dover MS 1,100/5-8
16 Daley Dr 03820 603-516-7200
Lawrence DeYoung, prin. Fax 516-5747
Dover Vocational Center Vo/Tech
25 Alumni Dr 03820 603-516-6976
Jim Stopa, dir. Fax 516-6975

McIntosh College Post-Sec.
23 Cataract Ave 03820 603-742-1234
Portsmouth Christian Academy 800/PK-12
20 Seaborne Dr 03820 603-742-3617
Dr. Connie Lawrence, hdmstr. Fax 750-0490
St. Thomas Aquinas HS 700/9-12
197 Dover Point Rd 03820 603-742-3206
Jeffrey Quinn, prin. Fax 749-7822

Dublin, Cheshire

Dublin Christian Academy 100/K-12
PO Box 521 03444 603-563-8505
Kevin Moody, prin. Fax 563-8008
Dublin S 100/9-12
PO Box 522 03444 603-563-8584
Christopher Horgan, prin. Fax 563-7121

Durham, Strafford, Pop. 9,236
Oyster River Cooperative SD 2,200/K-12
36 Coe Dr 03824 603-868-5100
Howard Colter, supt. Fax 868-6668
www.orcsd.org
Oyster River HS 700/9-12
55 Coe Dr 03824 603-868-2375
Laura Rogers, prin. Fax 868-2049
Oyster River MS 700/5-8
1 Coe Dr 03824 603-868-2155
Marcia Ross, prin. Fax 868-3469

University of New Hampshire 03824 Post-Sec.
603-862-1234

East Swanzey, Cheshire
Hinsdale SD 700/PK-12
600 Old Homestead Hwy 03446 603-352-6955
Dr. Kenneth Dassau, supt. Fax 358-6708
www.mrsd.org
Other Schools – See Hinsdale

Monadnock Regional SD 2,400/PK-12
600 Old Homestead Hwy 03446 603-352-6955
Dr. Kenneth Dassau, supt. Fax 358-6708
www.mrsd.org
Monadnock Regional HS 900/9-12
580 Old Homestead Hwy 03446 603-352-6575
Joseph Smith, prin. Fax 355-1209
Monadnock Regional MS 400/7-8
580 Old Homestead Hwy 03446 603-352-6575
Matthew Young, prin. Fax 357-6520

Winchester SD 500/PK-8
600 Old Homestead Hwy 03446 603-352-6955
Dr. Kenneth Dassau, supt. Fax 358-6708
www.mrsd.org
Other Schools – See Winchester

Enfield, Grafton, Pop. 1,560
Mascoma Valley Regional SD 1,500/PK-12
PO Box 789 03748 603-632-5563
Barbara Tremblay, supt. Fax 632-4181
www.mascoma.k12.nh.us/
Other Schools – See Canaan

Epping, Rockingham, Pop. 1,384
Epping SD 1,100/PK-12
213 Main St 03042 603-679-5402
Barbara Munsey, supt. Fax 679-1237
www.sau14.k12.nh.us/
Epping HS 400/9-12
21 Prospect St 03042 603-679-5472
Dixie Tremblay, prin. Fax 679-2966
Epping MS 300/6-8
21 Prospect St 03042 603-679-5472
Lyn Healy, prin. Fax 679-2966

Exeter, Rockingham, Pop. 9,556
Exeter Region Cooperative SD 2,900/6-12
24 Front St Ste 1 03833 603-775-8653
Dr. Arthur Hanson, supt. Fax 775-8673
www.sau16.org/
Exeter HS 1,600/9-12
315 Epping Rd 03833 603-395-2555
Victor Sokul, prin. Fax 395-2499
Other Schools – See Stratham

Exeter SD 1,000/PK-5
24 Front St Ste 1 03833 603-775-8653
Dr. Arthur Hanson, supt. Fax 775-8673
www.sau16.org/
Seacoast School of Tech Vo/Tech
40 Linden St 03833 603-775-8461
Nancy Pierce, prin. Fax 775-8983

Phillips Exeter Academy 1,000/9-12
20 Main St 03833 603-772-4311
Tyler Tingley, prin. Fax 777-4393

Farmington, Strafford, Pop. 3,567
Farmington SD 1,500/PK-12
356 Main St 03835 603-755-2627
Michelle Langa, supt. Fax 755-2060
www.sau61.com/
Farmington HS 500/9-12
1 Thayer Dr 03835 603-755-2811
G. Michael Lee, prin. Fax 755-3252
Wilson Memorial MS 600/4-8
51 School St 03835 603-755-2181
Clayton Lewis, prin. Fax 755-9473

Franklin, Merrimack, Pop. 8,763
Franklin SD 1,400/PK-12
119 Central St 03235 603-934-3108
Jo Ellen Divoll, supt. Fax 934-3462
www.franklin.k12.nh.us/
Franklin HS 500/9-12
115 Central St 03235 603-934-5441
Robert Braman, prin. Fax 934-7445
Franklin MS 400/5-8
200 Sanborn St 03235 603-934-5828
James Friel, prin. Fax 934-2432

Gilford, Belknap
Gilford SD 1,300/K-12
47 Cherry Valley Rd 03249 603-527-9215
Dr. Paul DeMinico, supt. Fax 527-9216
www.sau.gilford.k12.nh.us
Gilford HS 500/9-12
88 Alvah Wilson Rd 03249 603-524-7135
Kenneth Wiswell, prin. Fax 524-3867
Gilford MS 300/5-8
72 Alvah Wilson Rd 03249 603-527-2460
James Kemmerer, prin. Fax 527-2461

Goffstown, Hillsborough, Pop. 14,621
Goffstown SD 3,100/PK-12
11 School St 03045 603-497-4818
Dr. Darrell Lockwood, supt. Fax 497-8425
www.goffstown.k12.nh.us
Goffstown Area HS 1,300/9-12
27 Wallace Rd 03045 603-497-4841
Frank McBride, prin. Fax 497-5257
Mountain View MS 1,100/5-8
41 Lauren Ln 03045 603-497-8288
James Hunt, prin. Fax 497-4987

Gorham, Coos, Pop. 1,910
Gorham Randolph Shelburne Cooperative SD 600/K-12
123 Main St 03581 603-466-3632
Paul Bousquet, supt. Fax 466-3870
www.sau20.org/
Gorham HS 200/9-12
120 Main St 03581 603-466-2776
Keith Parent, prin. Fax 466-3111
Gorham MS 100/6-8
120 Main St 03581 603-466-2776
Keith Parent, prin. Fax 466-3111

Greenland, Rockingham
Rye SD 600/PK-8
48 Post Rd 03840 603-422-9572
Dr. George Cushing, supt. Fax 422-9575
Other Schools – See Rye

Groveton, Coos, Pop. 1,255
Northumberland SD 500/K-12
8 Preble St 03582 603-636-1437
Sherwood Fluery, supt. Fax 636-6102
Groveton HS 200/9-12
65 State St 03582 603-636-1619
Pierce Couture, prin. Fax 636-9752
Groveton MS 100/7-8
65 State St 03582 603-636-1619
Pierre Couture, prin. Fax 636-9752

Stratford SD 200/K-12
8 Preble St 03582 603-636-1437
Sherwood Fluery, supt. Fax 636-6102
Other Schools – See North Stratford

Hampstead, Rockingham
Hampstead SD
Supt. — See Plaistow
Hampstead MS 600/5-8
26 School St 03841 603-329-6743
Patricia Grassbaugh, prin. Fax 329-4120

Hampton, Rockingham, Pop. 7,989
Hampton SD 1,500/PK-8
2 Alumni Dr 03842 603-926-8992
James Gaylord, supt. Fax 926-5157
www.sau21.k12.nh.us
Hampton Academy 500/6-8
29 Academy Ave 03842 603-926-2000
Manfred Muscara, prin. Fax 926-1855

Seabrook SD 900/PK-8
2 Alumni Dr 03842 603-926-8992
James Gaylord, supt. Fax 926-5157
www.sau21.k12.nh.us
Other Schools – See Seabrook

Winnacunnet Cooperative SD 1,200/9-12
2 Alumni Dr 03842 603-926-8992
James Gaylord, supt. Fax 926-5157
www.sau21.k12.nh.us
Winnacunnet HS 1,200/9-12
1 Alumni Dr 03842 603-926-3395
Randall Zito, prin. Fax 926-7824

Hanover, Grafton, Pop. 6,538
Dresden SD 1,200/6-12
45 Lyme Rd Ste 207 03755 603-643-6050
Wayne Gersen, supt. Fax 643-3073
Hanover HS 700/9-12
41 Lebanon St 03755 603-643-3431
Deborah Gillespie, prin. Fax 643-0661
Richmond MS 400/6-8
63 Lyme Rd 03755 603-643-6040
Susan Finer, prin. Fax 643-0662

Dartmouth College 03755 Post-Sec.
603-646-1110

Henniker, Merrimack, Pop. 1,693
John Stark Regional SD 900/9-12
PO Box 2417 03242 603-428-3269
Dr. Christine Tyrie, supt. Fax 428-3850
Other Schools – See Weare

Weare SD 1,300/PK-8
PO Box 2417 03242 603-428-3269
Dr. Christine Tyrie, supt. Fax 428-3850
sau24.k12.nh.us
Other Schools – See Weare

New England College Post-Sec.
98 Bridge St 03242 603-428-2211

Hillsborough, Hillsborough, Pop. 1,826
Hillsboro-Deering Cooperative SD
Supt. — See Deering
Hillsboro-Deering HS 500/9-12
12 Hillcat Dr 03244 603-464-1130
Jon Ingrahm, prin. Fax 464-4028
Hillsboro-Deering MS 400/6-8
6 Hillcat Dr 03244 603-464-1120
Richard Nannicelli, prin. Fax 464-5759

Hinsdale, Cheshire, Pop. 1,718
Hinsdale SD
Supt. — See East Swanzey
Hinsdale HS 200/9-12
PO Box 46 03451 603-336-5984
John Hartnett, prin. Fax 336-7497
Hinsdale JHS 100/7-8
PO Box 46 03451 603-336-5984
John Harnett, prin. Fax 336-7497

Holderness, Grafton

Holderness S 300/9-12
Chapel Ln 03245 603-536-1257
Phillip Peck, hdmstr. Fax 536-1267

Hollis, Hillsborough
Hollis/Brookline Cooperative SD 1,200/7-12
PO Box 1588 03049 603-465-7118
Richard Pike, supt. Fax 465-3933
www.sau41.k12.nh.us
Hollis/Brookline HS 800/9-12
24 Cavalier Ct 03049 603-465-2269
Timothy Kelley, prin. Fax 465-2485
Hollis/Brookline MS 400/7-8
25 Main St 03049 603-465-2223
Patricia Goyette, prin. Fax 465-7523

Hooksett, Merrimack, Pop. 2,573
Hooksett SD 1,200/PK-8
90 Farmer Rd 03106 603-622-3731
Dr. Charles Littlefield, supt. Fax 669-4352
Cawley MS 500/6-8
89 Whitehall Rd 03106 603-485-9959
Ronald Pedro, prin. Fax 485-5291

Southern New Hampshire University Post-Sec.
2500 N River Rd 03106 603-668-2211

Hudson, Hillsborough, Pop. 7,626
Hudson SD 4,100/PK-12
20 Library St 03051 603-886-1235
Philip Bell, supt. Fax 886-1236
www.sau81.org/
Alvirne HS 1,400/9-12
200 Derry Rd 03051 603-886-1260
Bryan Lane, prin. Fax 595-1525
Hudson Memorial MS 1,100/6-8
1 Memorial Dr 03051 603-886-1240
Susan Nadeau, prin. Fax 883-1252
Palmer Vocational Tech Center Vo/Tech
200 Derry Rd 03051 603-886-1260
Jane Parkin, dir. Fax 595-1513

Continental Academie of Hair Design Post-Sec.
PO Box 370 03051 603-889-1614

Jaffrey, Cheshire, Pop. 2,558
Jaffrey-Rindge Cooperative SD 1,700/PK-12
81 Fitzgerald Dr Unit 2 03452 603-532-8100
James O'Neill, supt. Fax 532-8149
www.sau47.k12.nh.us
Conant HS 500/9-12
3 Conant Way 03452 603-532-8131
John Barth, prin. Fax 532-8102
Jaffrey-Rindge MS 400/6-8
1 Conant Way 03452 603-532-8122
Richard Haywood, prin. Fax 532-8124

Keene, Cheshire, Pop. 22,778
Keene SD 3,800/PK-12
34 West St 03431 603-357-9002
Fax 357-9012
www.sau29.k12.nh.us/
Cheshire Career Center Vo/Tech
43 Arch St 03431 603-352-0640
Wayne Cotton, prin. Fax 357-9061
Keene HS 1,800/9-12
43 Arch St 03431 603-352-0640
Alan Chmiel, prin. Fax 357-1512
Keene MS 800/6-8
17 Washington St 03431 603-357-9023
Dorothy Frazier, prin. Fax 357-9045

Antioch University New England Post-Sec.
40 Avon St 03431 603-357-3122
Franklin Pierce College Post-Sec.
17 Bradco St 03431 603-357-0079
Keene Beauty Academy Post-Sec.
800 Park Ave 03431 603-357-3736
Keene State College Post-Sec.
229 Main St 03435 603-352-1909

Kingston, Rockingham
Sanborn Regional SD 1,800/PK-12
178 Main St 03848 603-642-3688
Dr. Keith Pfeifer, supt. Fax 642-7885
sanborn.k12.nh.us
Sanborn Regional HS 600/9-12
17 Danville Rd 03848 603-642-3341
Gail Sudduth, prin. Fax 642-6947
Other Schools – See Newton

Laconia, Belknap, Pop. 17,060
Laconia SD 2,500/PK-12
PO Box 309 03247 603-524-5710
Robert Champlin, supt. Fax 528-8442
www.laconia.k12.nh.us
Huot Technical Center Vo/Tech
345 Union Ave 03246 603-528-8693
Scott Davis, prin. Fax 524-5711
Laconia HS 800/9-12
345 Union Ave 03246 603-524-3350
Jonathan Freeman, prin. Fax 528-8683
Memorial MS 600/6-8
150 Mcgrath St 03246 603-524-4632
James McCollum, prin. Fax 528-8675

Empire Beauty School Post-Sec.
556 Main St 03246 603-524-8777
Laconia Christian S 100/PK-12
1386 Meredith Center Rd 03246 603-524-3250
Rick Duba, prin. Fax 524-3285
New Hampshire Technical College Post-Sec.
379 Belmont Rd 03246 603-524-3207

Langdon, Sullivan
Fall Mountain Regional SD
Supt. — See Charlestown
Fall Mountain Regional HS 700/9-12
134 Fmrhs Rd 03602 603-835-6318
Thomas Ferenc, prin. Fax 835-6254

Fall Mountain Regional Vocational Center Vo/Tech
134 Fmrhs Rd 03602 603-835-6319
Heidi Gove, prin. Fax 835-6254

Lebanon, Grafton, Pop. 12,606
Lebanon SD 2,000/PK-12
PO Box 488 03766 603-448-1634
Dr. Michael Harris, supt. Fax 448-0602
www.lebanon.k12.nh.us
Lebanon HS 700/9-12
195 Hanover St 03766 603-448-2055
James Nourse, prin. Fax 448-0605
Lebanon JHS 300/7-8
75 Bank St 03766 603-448-3056
Anne Evensen, prin. Fax 448-0616

Upper Valley Teacher Institute Post-Sec.
1 Court St Ste 210 03766 603-448-6507

Lincoln, Grafton
Lincoln-Woodstock Cooperative SD 200/K-12
PO Box 846 03251 603-745-2051
Michael Cosgriff, supt. Fax 745-2351
www.lin-wood.k12.nh.us
Lin-Wood S 200/K-12
PO Box 97 03251 603-745-2214
Robert Nelson, prin. Fax 745-6797

Lisbon, Grafton, Pop. 1,246
Lisbon Regional SD 200/K-12
25 Highland Ave 03585 603-444-3925
Patrick Low, supt. Fax 444-6299
www.lisbon.k12.nh.us/
Lisbon Regional S 200/K-12
24 Highland Ave 03585 603-838-5506
Robert Butson, prin. Fax 838-5012

Litchfield, Hillsborough
Litchfield SD 1,700/PK-12
1 Highlander Ct 03052 603-578-3570
Catherine Hamblett, supt. Fax 578-1267
Campbell HS 500/9-12
1 Highlander Ct 03052 603-546-0300
Michael Parent, prin. Fax 546-0310
Litchfield MS 600/5-8
19 McElwain Dr 03052 603-424-0566
Thomas Lecklider, prin. Fax 424-1296

Tabernacle Christian S 200/K-12
242 Derry Rd 03052 603-883-6310
Harold McGrath, prin. Fax 883-2413

Littleton, Grafton, Pop. 4,633
Littleton SD 900/K-12
262 Cottage St Ste 230 03561 603-444-3925
Patrick Low, supt. Fax 444-6299
www.high.littleton.k12.nh.us/metadot/
Bronson JHS 200/7-8
96 School St 03561 603-444-3361
George Brodeur, prin. Fax 444-3009
Gallen Regional Vocational Center Vo/Tech
159 Oak Hill Ave 03561 603-444-5186
Forrest Goodwin, prin. Fax 444-0167
Littleton HS 300/9-12
159 Oak Hill Ave 03561 603-444-5601
Alan Smith, prin. Fax 444-3009

Londonderry, Rockingham, Pop. 10,114
Londonderry SD 5,600/PK-12
268 Mammoth Rd 03053 603-432-6920
Dr. Nathan Greenberg, supt. Fax 425-1049
www.londonderry.org
Londonderry HS 1,700/9-12
295 Mammoth Rd 03053 603-432-6941
James Elefante, prin. Fax 425-1022
Londonderry MS 1,400/6-8
313 Mammoth Rd 03053 603-432-6925
Andrew Corey, prin. Fax 432-0714

Manchester, Hillsborough, Pop. 109,691
Manchester SD 17,400/PK-12
286 Commercial St 03101 603-624-6300
Michael Ludwell Ph.D., supt. Fax 624-6337
www.mansd.org
Hillside MS 1,000/6-8
112 Reservoir Ave 03104 603-624-6352
Steven Donohue, prin. Fax 628-6049
Manchester Central HS 2,400/9-12
207 Lowell St 03104 603-624-6363
John Rist, prin. Fax 624-6376
Manchester Memorial HS 2,100/9-12
1 Crusader Way 03103 603-624-6378
Arthur Adamakos, prin. Fax 628-6009
Manchester School of Tech Vo/Tech
530 S Porter St 03103 603-624-6490
Karen White, dir. Fax 628-6146
Manchester West HS 2,100/9-12
9 Notre Dame Ave 03102 603-624-6384
Janice Thompson, prin. Fax 628-6153
McLaughlin MS 800/6-8
290 S Mammoth Rd 03109 603-628-6247
Barry Albert, prin. Fax 628-6274
Parkside MS 800/6-8
75 Parkside Ave 03102 603-624-6356
Dawn Smith-Michaud, prin. Fax 624-6355
Southside MS 1,000/6-8
140 S Jewett St 03103 603-624-6359
Mark Willis, prin. Fax 624-6361

Continental Academie of Hair Design Post-Sec.
228 Maple St 03103 603-622-5851
Derryfield S 400/6-12
2108 River Rd 03104 603-669-4524
Randle Richardson, prin. Fax 625-9715
Franklin Pierce College Post-Sec.
670 N Commercial St Ste 206 03101 - -
Hesser College Post-Sec.
3 Sundial Ave 03103 603-668-6660
Jolicoeur S 100/1-12
1 Mammoth Rd 03109 603-621-3599
Noel J. Sullivan, prin. Fax 623-6940
New England EMS Institute Post-Sec.
1 Elliot Way 03103 603-628-2220
New Hampshire Community Tech College Post-Sec.
1066 Front St 03102 603-668-6706
St. Anselm College Post-Sec.
100 Saint Anselms Dr 03102 603-641-7000
St. Joseph Regional JHS 300/7-8
460 Pine St 03104 603-624-4811
Fax 624-6670

Trinity HS 500/9-12
581 Bridge St 03104 603-668-2910
Denis Mailloux, prin. Fax 668-2913
University of New Hampshire Post-Sec.
400 Commercial St 03101 603-668-0700

Meredith, Belknap, Pop. 1,654
Inter-Lakes Cooperative SD 1,300/PK-12
103 Main St Ste 2 03253 603-279-7947
Dr. Phillip McCormack, supt. Fax 279-3044
inter-lakes.k12.nh.us
Inter-Lakes HS 400/9-12
1 Laker Ln 03253 603-279-6162
Patricia Kennelly, prin. Fax 279-5302
Inter-Lakes MS 400/5-8
1 Laker Ln 03253 603-279-6162
Everett Bennett, prin. Fax 279-6344

Meriden, Sullivan

Kimball Union Academy 300/9-12
PO Box 188 03770 603-469-2000
Michael J. Schafer, hdmstr. Fax 469-2040

Merrimack, Hillsborough, Pop. 22,156
Merrimack SD 3,500/PK-12
36 McElwain St 03054 603-424-6200
Marjorie Chiafery, supt. Fax 424-6229
www.merrimack.k12.nh.us
Merrimack HS 1,600/9-12
38 Mcelwain St 03054 603-424-6204
Kenneth Johnson, prin. Fax 424-6230
Merrimack MS 7-8
31 Madeline Bennett Ln 03054 603-424-6289
Thomas Levesque, prin. Fax 423-1109

South Merrimack Christian Academy 300/K-12
517 Boston Post Rd 03054 603-880-6832
Brian Burbach, prin. Fax 598-7085
Thomas More College of Liberal Arts Post-Sec.
6 Manchester St 03054 603-880-8308

Milford, Hillsborough, Pop. 8,015
Milford SD 2,300/PK-12
100 West St 03055 603-673-2202
Robert Suprenant, supt. Fax 673-2237
www.milfordschools.net
Milford Applied Technology Center Vo/Tech
100 West St 03055 603-673-4201
Rosie Deloge, prin. Fax 673-4201
Milford HS 900/9-12
100 West St 03055 603-673-4201
Bradford Craven, prin. Fax 673-4201
Milford MS 600/6-8
33 Osgood Rd 03055 603-673-5221
Anthony DeMarco, prin. Fax 673-5221

Milford Christian Academy 100/1-12
273 Elm St 03055 603-673-9324
Fax 673-4539

Milton, Strafford
Milton SD
Supt. — See Union
Nute HS 200/9-12
PO Box 337 03851 603-652-4591
John T. Parkhurst, prin. Fax 652-9926
Nute JHS 100/6-8
PO Box 337 03851 603-652-4591
John T. Parkhurst, prin. Fax 652-9926

Moultonborough, Carroll
Moultonborough SD 700/PK-12
PO Box 419 03254 603-476-5247
Michael Lancor, supt. Fax 476-8009
www.moultonborough.k12.nh.us
Moultonborough Academy 100/7-8
PO Box 228 03254 603-476-5517
Andrew Coppinger, prin. Fax 476-5153
Moultonborough Academy 200/9-12
PO Box 228 03254 603-476-5517
Andrew Coppinger, prin. Fax 476-5153

Nashua, Hillsborough, Pop. 87,321
Nashua SD 11,100/PK-12
PO Box 687 03061 603-594-4300
Julia Earl, supt. Fax 594-4350
www.nashua.edu
Academy of Learning & Technology 100/6-10
47 Grand Ave 03060 603-594-4326
Patricia Place, prin.
Elm Street MS 900/6-8
117 Elm St 03060 603-594-4322
Pauline Caron, prin. Fax 594-4370
Fairgrounds MS 600/6-8
27 Cleveland St 03060 603-594-4393
John Nelson, prin. Fax 594-4355
Nashua HS North 2,000/9-12
10 Chuck Druding Dr 03063 603-589-6400
David Ryan, prin. Fax 589-6449
Nashua HS South 1,100/9-12
36 Riverside Dr 03062 603-594-4311
Jennifer Seusing, prin. Fax 589-8722
Pennichuck MS 500/6-8
207 Manchester St 03064 603-594-4308
Paul F. Asbell, prin. Fax 594-4413

Bishop Guertin HS 900/9-12
194 Lund Rd 03060 603-889-4107
Linda Brodeur, prin. Fax 889-0701
Daniel Webster College Post-Sec.
20 University Dr 03063 603-577-6000
Hesser College Post-Sec.
410 Amherst St 03063 603-883-0404
Nashua Catholic Regional JHS 300/7-8
6 Bartlett Ave 03064 603-883-6707
Thomas Kelleher, prin. Fax 594-8955
Nashua Christian Academy 300/K-12
34 Franklin St 03064 603-889-8892
Christine Urban, admin. Fax 821-7451
New Hampshire Community Tech College Post-Sec.
505 Amherst St 03063 603-882-6923
Rivier College Post-Sec.
420 S Main St 03060 603-888-1311

New Hampton, Belknap

New Hampton S 300/9-12
PO Box 579 03256 603-677-3400
Andrew Menke, hdmstr. Fax 677-3482

New Ipswich, Hillsborough
Mascenic Regional SD 1,400/PK-12
659 Turnpike Rd Ste 120 03071 603-878-1026
Francine Fullam, supt. Fax 878-2657
www.mascenic.com/
Boynton MS 500/5-8
500 Turnpike Rd 03071 603-878-4800
Thomas Starratt, prin. Fax 878-0525
Mascenic Regional HS 400/9-12
175 Turnpike Rd 03071 603-878-1113
Craig Mueller, prin. Fax 878-3344

Wilton-Lyndeborough SD 400/7-12
659 Turnpike Rd Ste 120 03071 603-878-1026
Francine Fullam, supt. Fax 878-2657
Other Schools – See Wilton

New London, Merrimack
Kearsarge Regional SD 2,100/K-12
169 Main St 03257 603-526-2051
Dr. Thomas Brennan, supt. Fax 526-2145
www.kearsarge.k12.nh.us/
Kearsarge Regional MS 500/6-8
114 Cougar Ct 03257 603-526-6415
Donald West, prin. Fax 526-2934
Other Schools – See North Sutton

Colby-Sawyer College Post-Sec.
100 Main St 03257 603-526-3000

Newmarket, Rockingham, Pop. 4,917
Newmarket SD 800/PK-12
186 Main St 03857 603-659-5020
Kathleen Murphy, supt. Fax 659-5022
Newmarket Central JSHS 300/6-12
213 S Main St 03857 603-659-3271
Deborah Brooks, prin. Fax 659-5304

Newport, Sullivan, Pop. 3,772
Newport SD 1,200/K-12
9 Depot St Ste 2 03773 603-863-3540
William J. Mealey, supt. Fax 863-5368
Newport HS 400/9-12
245 N Main St 03773 603-863-2414
Barry Connell, prin. Fax 863-0887
Newport MS 300/6-8
245 N Main St 03773 603-863-2414
Barry Connell, prin. Fax 863-0887
Sugar River Valley Reg Voc Ctr Vo/Tech
243 N Main St 03773 603-863-3759
Cathryn Baird, prin. Fax 863-7104

Sunapee SD 500/K-12
9 Depot St Ste 2 03773 603-863-3540
William Mealey, supt. Fax 863-5368
Other Schools – See Sunapee

Newton, Rockingham
Sanborn Regional SD
Supt. — See Kingston
Sanborn Regional MS 500/6-8
31 W Main St Ste A 03858 603-382-6226
Kathleen Laureti, prin. Fax 382-9771

North Conway, Carroll, Pop. 2,032
Conway SD 2,200/K-12
19 Pine St 03860 603-356-5533
Dr. Carl Nelson, supt. Fax 356-5144
www.kennett.k12.nh.us
Other Schools – See Conway

Northfield, Merrimack
Winnisquam Regional SD 1,800/PK-12
433 W Main St 03276 603-286-4116
Tammy Davis, supt. Fax 286-7402
www.winnisquam.k12.nh.us
Other Schools – See Tilton

North Haverhill, Grafton
Haverhill Cooperative SD 800/PK-12
2975 Dartmouth College Hwy 03774 603-787-2113
Bruce Labs, supt. Fax 787-2118
www.sau23.k12.nh.us
Haverhill Cooperative MS 300/4-8
175 Morrill Dr 03774 603-787-2100
Brent Walker, prin. Fax 787-6117
Other Schools – See Woodsville

North Stratford, Coos
Stratford SD
Supt. — See Groveton
Stratford HS 100/9-12
19 School St 03590 603-922-3387
Georgia Caron, prin. Fax 922-3303

North Sutton, Merrimack
Kearsarge Regional SD
Supt. — See New London
Kearsage Regional HS 700/9-12
PO Box 182 03260 603-927-4261
Carlton J. Fitzgerald, prin. Fax 927-4453

Northwood, Rockingham
Coe-Brown Northwood Academy 700/9-12
907 1st NH Tpke 03261 603-942-5531
David Smith, hdmstr. Fax 942-7537
www.coebrownacademy.com
Coe-Brown Northwood Academy 700/9-12
907 1st NH Tpke 03261 603-942-5531
David Smith, hdmstr. Fax 942-7537

Orford, Grafton
Rivendell Interstate SD 300/K-12
PO Box 153 03777 603-353-2170
Noelle Vitt, supt. Fax 353-2189
www.rivendellschool.org
Rivendell Academy 300/6-12
2972 Route 25A 03777 603-353-4321
Robert Sampson, prin. Fax 353-4414

Pelham, Hillsborough
Pelham SD
Supt. — See Windham
Pelham HS 600/9-12
85 Marsh Rd 03076 603-635-2115
Dr. Dorothy Mohr, prin. Fax 635-3994
Pelham Memorial MS 600/6-8
59 Marsh Rd 03076 603-635-2321
Catherine Pinsonneaut, prin. Fax 635-2369

Pembroke, Merrimack, Pop. 6,561
Allenstown SD 500/K-8
267 Pembroke St 03275 603-485-5188
Thomas Haley, supt. Fax 485-9529
www.sau53.org
Other Schools – See Allenstown

Pembroke SD 1,900/K-12
267 Pembroke St 03275 603-485-5188
Thomas Haley, supt. Fax 485-9529
www.sau53.org
Pembroke Academy 1,000/9-12
209 Academy Rd 03275 603-485-7881
Michael A. Reardon, prin. Fax 485-1824
Three Rivers MS 400/5-8
243 Academy Rd 03275 603-485-9539
Deborah Bulkley, prin. Fax 485-1829

Penacook, See Concord
Merrimack Valley SD
Supt. — See Concord
Merrimack Valley HS 900/9-12
106 Village St 03303 603-753-4311
Michael Jette, prin. Fax 753-6423
Merrimack Valley MS 600/6-8
14 Allen St 03303 603-753-6336
Mary R. Estee, prin. Fax 753-8107

Peterborough, Hillsborough, Pop. 2,685
Contoocook Valley SD 3,100/PK-12
106 Hancock Rd 03458 603-924-3336
Keith R. Burke, supt. Fax 924-6707
www.conval.edu
Applied Technology Center Region 14 Vo/Tech
182 Hancock Rd 03458 603-371-0310
Chester Bowles, prin. Fax 924-9176
ConVal Regional HS 1,200/9-12
184 Hancock Rd 03458 603-924-3869
Susan Dell, prin. Fax 924-9176
South Meadow MS 500/5-8
108 Hancock Rd 03458 603-924-7105
Richard Dunning, prin. Fax 924-2064
Other Schools – See Antrim

Pittsburg, Coos
Pittsburg SD
Supt. — See Colebrook
Pittsburg HS 100/9-12
12 School St 03592 603-538-6536
Mark Ekberg, prin. Fax 538-6996

Pittsfield, Merrimack, Pop. 1,717
Pittsfield SD 800/PK-12
175 Barnstead Rd Unit 3 03263 603-435-5526
Dr. William Compton, supt. Fax 435-5331
Pittsfield HS 300/9-12
23 Oneida St 03263 603-435-6701
Karen Erlandson, prin. Fax 435-7087
Pittsfield MS 100/7-8
23 Oneida St 03263 603-435-6701
Karen Erlandson, prin. Fax 435-7087

Plaistow, Rockingham
Hampstead SD 1,100/PK-8
30 Greenough Rd 03865 603-382-6119
Dr. Douglas McDonald, supt. Fax 382-3334
www.hampstead.k12.nh.us
Other Schools – See Hampstead

Timberlane Regional SD 4,500/PK-12
30 Greenough Rd 03865 603-382-6119
Dr. Douglas McDonald, supt. Fax 382-3334
www.timberlane.net/
Timberlane Regional HS 1,400/9-12
36 Greenough Rd 03865 603-382-6541
Donald Woodworth, prin. Fax 382-8086
Timberlane Regional MS 1,200/6-8
44 Greenough Rd 03865 603-382-7131
Michael Hogan, prin. Fax 382-2781

Plymouth, Grafton, Pop. 3,967
Pemi-Baker Regional HSD 900/9-12
47 Old Ward Bridge Rd 03264 603-536-1254
John True, supt. Fax 536-3545
Plymouth Applied Technology Center Vo/Tech
86 Old Ward Bridge Rd 03264 603-536-1444
Dr. Gwen Blair, prin. Fax 536-9086
Plymouth Regional HS 900/9-12
86 Old Ward Bridge Rd 03264 603-536-1444
Bruce Parsons, prin. Fax 536-9086

Calvary Christian S 100/K-12
115 Yeaton Rd 03264 603-536-4022
Richard Anderson, prin. Fax 536-9896
Plymouth State University Post-Sec.
17 High St 03264 603-535-5000

Portsmouth, Rockingham, Pop. 20,674
Portsmouth SD 2,700/PK-12
50 Clough Dr 03801 603-431-5080
Dr. Robert Lister, supt. Fax 431-6753
www.portsmouth.k12.nh.us
Portsmouth Career-Tech Center 19 Vo/Tech
50 Andrew Jarvis Dr 03801 603-436-7100
Pamela MacArtney, prin. Fax 436-6793
Portsmouth HS 1,100/9-12
50 Andrew Jarvis Dr 03801 603-436-7100
Jeffrey Collins, prin. Fax 427-2320
Portsmouth MS 500/6-8
155 Parrott Ave 03801 603-436-5781
John Stokel, prin. Fax 427-2326

Franklin Pierce College Post-Sec.
73 Corporate Dr 03801 603-433-2000
Hesser College Post-Sec.
170 Commerce Way 03801 603-436-5300
Portsmouth Beauty School of Hair Design Post-Sec.
140 Congress St 03801 603-436-7775

Raymond, Rockingham, Pop. 2,516
Raymond SD 1,600/PK-12
43 Harriman Hill Rd 03077 603-895-4299
Michael Shore, supt. Fax 895-0147
www.raymond.k12.nh.us
Gove MS 500/5-8
1 Stephen K Batchelder Pkwy 03077 603-895-3394
Caesar Meledandri, prin. Fax 895-9856
Raymond HS 600/9-12
45 Harriman Hill Rd 03077 603-895-6616
James Beitler, prin. Fax 895-1582

Rindge, Cheshire

Franklin Pierce College Post-Sec.
20 College Rd 03461 800-437-0048
Hampshire Country S 50/4-12
122 Hampshire Rd 03461 603-899-3325
William Dickerman, hdmstr. Fax 899-6521
Meeting S 50/9-12
120 Thomas Rd 03461 603-899-3366
Jacqueline Stillwell, prin. Fax 899-6216

Rochester, Strafford, Pop. 30,004
Rochester SD 4,800/PK-12
150 Wakefield St Ste 8 03867 603-332-3678
Michael Hopkins, supt. Fax 335-7367
www.rochesterschools.com
Creteau Regional Technology Center Vo/Tech
140 Wakefield St 03867 603-335-7351
Richard Towne, prin. Fax 335-7365
Rochester MS 1,100/6-8
47 Brock St 03867 603-332-4090
Steven Beals, prin. Fax 332-9384
Spaulding HS 1,600/9-12
130 Wakefield St 03867 603-332-0757
Robert Pedersen, prin. Fax 330-0251

Rye, Rockingham
Rye SD
Supt. — See Greenland
Rye JHS 200/6-8
501 Washington Rd 03870 603-964-5591
Janice Yost, prin. Fax 964-3881

Salem, Rockingham, Pop. 27,400
Salem SD 5,300/PK-12
38 Geremonty Dr 03079 603-893-7040
Michael Delahanty, supt. Fax 893-7080
www.salemschooldistrictnh.com
Salem HS 2,200/9-12
44 Geremonty Dr 03079 603-893-7069
William Hagen, prin. Fax 893-7087
Salem Regional Vocational Center Vo/Tech
44 Geremonty Dr 03079 603-893-7069
Robert Pariseau, prin. Fax 898-0208
Woodbury MS, 206 Main St 03079 1,200/6-8
Maura Palmer, prin. 603-893-7055

Hesser College Post-Sec.
11 Manor Pkwy 03079 603-898-3480

Sanbornton, Belknap

Sant Bani S 200/K-12
19 Ashram Rd 03269 603-934-4240
Kent Bicknell, prin. Fax 934-2970

Seabrook, Rockingham
Seabrook SD
Supt. — See Hampton
Seabrook MS 400/5-8
236 Walton Rd 03874 603-474-9221
Stanley Shupe, prin. Fax 474-8020

Somersworth, Strafford, Pop. 11,720
Somersworth SD 1,800/PK-12
51 W High St 03878 603-692-4450
Dr. Charles Ott, supt. Fax 692-9100
Somersworth HS 600/9-12
11 Memorial Dr 03878 603-692-2431
Brian Flanagan, prin. Fax 692-7326
Somersworth MS 600/5-8
7 Memorial Dr 03878 603-692-2126
Paul Maskwa, prin. Fax 692-9101
Somersworth Regional Vocational Center Vo/Tech
18 Cemetery Rd 03878 603-692-2242
Barney Share, dir. Fax 692-9116

Empire Beauty School Post-Sec.
362 Route 108 03878 603-692-1515
Tri-City Christian Academy 300/K-12
150 W High St 03878 603-692-2093
Paul Edgar, prin. Fax 692-6305

South Tamworth, Carroll

Community S 50/7-12
1164 Bunker Hill Rd 03883 603-323-7000
Jennifer Rowe, dir. Fax 323-8240

Stratham, Rockingham
Exeter Region Cooperative SD
Supt. — See Exeter
Cooperative MS 1,400/6-8
100 Academic Way 03885 603-775-8700
Thomas O'Malley, prin. Fax 775-0151

New Hampshire Community Tech College Post-Sec.
277 Portsmouth Ave 03885 603-772-1194

Sunapee, Sullivan
Sunapee SD
Supt. — See Newport
Sunapee HS 200/9-12
10 North Rd 03782 603-763-5615
Sean Moynihan, prin. Fax 763-3055
Sunapee MS 100/6-8
10 North Rd 03782 603-763-5615
Sean Moynihan, prin. Fax 763-3055

Mount Royal Academy 100/K-12
26 Seven Hearths Ln 03782 603-763-9010
John Donohue, hdmstr. Fax 763-5390

Tilton, Belknap, Pop. 3,081
Winnisquam Regional SD
Supt. — See Northfield
Winnisquam Regional HS 500/9-12
435 W Main St 03276 603-286-4531
Judith Farr, prin. Fax 286-2006
Winnisquam Regional HS Vo/Tech
435 W Main St 03276 603-286-4531
Janet Rosequist, dir. Fax 286-2006
Winnisquam Regional MS 500/6-8
76 Winter St 03276 603-286-7143
Thomas Croteau, prin. Fax 286-7410

Tilton S 200/9-12
30 School St 03276 603-286-4342
James Clements, hdmstr. Fax 286-3137

Union, Carroll
Milton SD 600/K-12
39 Main St 03887 603-473-2326
William Lander, supt. Fax 473-2218
Other Schools – See Milton

Walpole, Cheshire, Pop. 3,304
Fall Mountain Regional SD
Supt. — See Charlestown
Walpole MS 200/5-8
PO Box 549 03608 603-756-4728
Samuel Jacobs, prin. Fax 756-3343

Warner, Merrimack

Magdalen College Post-Sec.
511 Kearsarge Mountain Rd 03278 603-456-2656

Weare, Hillsborough
John Stark Regional SD
Supt. — See Henniker
Stark Regional HS 900/9-12
618 N Stark Hwy 03281 603-529-7675
Arthur Aaronson, prin. Fax 529-4646

Weare SD
Supt. — See Henniker
Weare MS 600/5-8
16 East Rd 03281 603-529-7555
David Pabst, prin. Fax 529-0464

West Lebanon, See Lebanon

New England School of Hair Design Post-Sec.
12 Interchange Dr 03784 603-298-5199

Westmoreland, Cheshire

Pioneer Junior Academy 50/1-12
13 Mount Gilboa Rd 03467 603-399-4803
Brianna Perry, prin. Fax 399-4803

Whitefield, Coos, Pop. 1,041
White Mountains Regional SD 1,500/PK-12
14 King Sq 03598 603-837-9363
Dr. Dean Cascadden, supt. Fax 837-2326
www.sau36.org
White Mountain Reg HS Vo/Tech
PO Box 338 03598 603-837-2528
Lori Lane, prin. Fax 837-3811
White Mountains Regional HS 400/9-12
PO Box 338 03598 603-837-2528
Ryan Earley, prin. Fax 837-3811

Wilton, Hillsborough, Pop. 1,165
Wilton-Lyndeborough SD
Supt. — See New Ipswich
Wilton-Lyndeborough HS 200/9-12
PO Box 255 03086 603-654-6123
Trevor Ebel, prin. Fax 654-2104
Wilton-Lyndeborough MS 100/7-8
PO Box 255 03086 603-654-6123
Trevor Ebel, prin. Fax 654-2104

High Mowing S 100/9-12
222 Isaac Frye Hwy 03086 603-654-2391
Cary Hughes, dean Fax 654-6588

Winchester, Cheshire, Pop. 1,735
Winchester SD
Supt. — See East Swanzey
Winchester MS 200/6-8
PO Box 7 03470 603-239-4381
David Funkhouser, prin. Fax 239-4457

Windham, Rockingham
Pelham SD 2,000/1-12
PO Box 510 03087 603-425-1976
Dr. Frank Bass, supt. Fax 425-1719
www.pelhamsd.org
Other Schools – See Pelham

Windham SD 1,600/PK-PK, 1-
PO Box 510 03087 603-425-1976
Dr. Frank Bass, supt. Fax 425-1719
www.windhamsd.org
Windham MS 600/6-8
112 Lowell Rd 03087 603-893-2636
Stephen Plocharczyk, prin. Fax 870-9007

Wolfeboro, Carroll, Pop. 2,783
Governor Wentworth Regional SD 2,900/PK-12
26 Bay St 03894 603-569-1658
John Robertson, supt. Fax 569-6983
www.govwentworth.k12.nh.us
Kingswood Regional HS 1,000/9-12
396 S Main St 03894 603-569-2055
Paul MacMillan, prin. Fax 569-8104
Kingswood Regional MS 500/7-8
404 S Main St 03894 603-569-3689
Kirkland Ross, prin. Fax 569-8113
Region 9 Vocational Technical Center Vo/Tech
384 S Main St 03894 603-569-4361
Stephen Guyer, prin. Fax 569-9243

Brewster Academy 400/9-12
80 Academy Dr 03894 603-569-1600
Dr. Michael Cooper, hdmstr. Fax 569-7199

Woodsville, Grafton, Pop. 1,122
Haverhill Cooperative SD
Supt. — See North Haverhill
Woodsville HS 300/9-12
9 High St 03785 603-747-2781
Jack Upton, prin. Fax 747-2766

NEW JERSEY

NEW JERSEY DEPARTMENT OF EDUCATION

100 River View Plz #CN500, Trenton 08611
Telephone 609-292-4469
Fax 609-777-4099
Website http://www.state.nj.us/education

Commissioner of Education Lucille Davy

NEW JERSEY BOARD OF EDUCATION

100 River View Plz #CN500, Trenton 08611

President Arnold Hyndman

COUNTY SUPERINTENDENTS OF SCHOOLS

Atlantic County Office of Education
Dr. Daniel Loggi, supt. 609-625-0004
6260 Old Harding Hwy Ste 1 Fax 625-6539
Mays Landing 08330
www.aclink.org/education/homepage.asp
Bergen County Office of Education
Dr. Aaron Graham, supt. 201-336-6875
1 Bergen County Plz Ste 350 Fax 336-6880
Hackensack 07601
Burlington County Office of Education
Walter Keiss, supt. 609-265-5060
2 Academy Dr, Westampton 08060 Fax 265-5922
Camden County Office of Education
Dr. Albert Monillas, supt. 856-401-2400
509 Lakeland Rd Fax 401-2410
Blackwood 08012
Cape May County Office of Education
Dr. Albert Monillas, supt. 609-465-1283
4 Moore Rd Fax 465-2094
Cape May Court House
Cumberland County Office of Education
Dr. Daniel Mastrobuono, supt. 856-451-0211
19 Landis Ave, Bridgeton 08302 Fax 455-9523

Essex County Office of Education
Anthony Marino, supt. 973-395-4677
7 Glenwood Ave Ste 404 Fax 395-4696
East Orange 07017
Gloucester County Office of Education
Dr. H. Mark Stanwood, supt. 856-468-6500
1492 Tanyard Rd, Sewell 08080 Fax 468-9115
www.co.gloucester.nj.us
Hudson County Office of Education
Robert Osak, supt. 201-319-3850
595 Newark Ave, Jersey City 07306 Fax 319-3650
Hunterdon County Office of Education
Frank Dragotta, supt. 908-788-1414
PO Box 2900, Flemington 08822 Fax 788-1457
www.co.hunterdon.nj.us/schools.htm
Mercer County Office of Education
Michael Klavon, supt. 609-588-5884
1075 Old Trenton Rd Fax 588-5849
Trenton 08690
Middlesex County Office of Education
Dr. Patrick Piegari, supt. 732-249-2900
1460 Livingston Ave Fax 296-0683
North Brunswick 08902
Monmouth County Office of Education
Eugenia Lawson, supt. 732-431-7816
PO Box 1264, Freehold 07728 Fax 577-0679

Morris County Office of Education
Dr. Kathleen Serafino, supt. 973-285-8332
PO Box 900, Morristown 07963 Fax 285-8341
Ocean County Office of Education
Dr. Bruce Greenfield, supt. 732-929-2078
212 Washington St Fax 506-5336
Toms River 08753
Passaic County Office of Education
Dr. Robert Gilmartin, supt. 973-569-2110
501 River St, Paterson 07524 Fax 754-0241
Salem County Office of Education
Michael Elwell, supt. 856-339-8611
94 Market St, Salem 08079 Fax 935-6290
Somerset County Office of Education
David Livingston, supt. 908-541-5700
PO Box 3000, Somerville 08876 Fax 722-6902
Sussex County Office of Education
Barry Worman, supt. 973-579-6996
262 White Lake Rd, Sparta 07871 Fax 579-6476
www.sussex.nj.us/
Union County Office of Education
Dr. Carmen Centuolo, supt. 908-654-9860
300 North Ave E, Westfield 07090 Fax 654-9869
Warren County Office of Education
William King, supt. 908-475-6327
537 Oxford St, Belvidere 07823 Fax 475-6394
www.warrennet.org/wcdoe/

PUBLIC, PRIVATE AND CATHOLIC SECONDARY SCHOOLS

Aberdeen, Monmouth, Pop. 17,038
Matawan-Aberdeen Regional SD 3,600/K-12
1 Crest Way 07747 732-290-2705
Bruce Quinn, supt. Fax 290-0751
www.marsd.k12.nj.us
Matawan Regional HS 1,100/9-12
450 Atlantic Ave 07747 732-290-2800
Michael D'Anna, prin. Fax 566-2404
Other Schools – See Cliffwood

Monmouth County Vocational SD
Supt. — See Freehold
Aberdeen Vocational S Vo/Tech
450 Atlantic Ave 07747 732-566-5599
James Johnson, prin. Fax 566-2392

Absecon, Atlantic, Pop. 7,989
Absecon CSD 900/K-8
800 Irelan Ave 08201 609-641-5375
James Giaquinto, supt. Fax 641-8692
www.abseconschools.org
Attales MS 400/5-8
800 Irelan Ave 08201 609-641-5375
Karen Woods, prin. Fax 641-8692

Holy Spirit HS 9-12
500 S New Rd 08201 609-646-3000
Fr. Joseph Perreault, prin. Fax 646-1770

Adelphia, Monmouth

Talmudical Academy of New Jersey Post-Sec.
Route 524 07710 732-431-1600
Talmudical Academy of NJ 50/9-12
PO Box 7 07710 732-431-1600
Mendy Nestlebaum, prin. Fax 431-3951

Allendale, Bergen, Pop. 6,754
Allendale SD 1,100/K-8
100 Brookside Ave 07401 201-327-2020
Jerilyn Caprio Ed.D., supt. Fax 785-9735
www.allendaleschoolsnj.com
Brookside MS 700/4-8
100 Brookside Ave 07401 201-327-2021
Bruce Winkelstein, prin. Fax 825-6553

Northern Highlands Regional HSD 1,300/9-12
298 Hillside Ave 07401 201-327-8700
Dr. Robert McGuire, supt. Fax 327-5274
www.northernhighlands.org
Northern Highlands Regional HS 1,300/9-12
298 Hillside Ave 07401 201-327-8700
John Keenan, prin. Fax 327-3370

Allentown, Monmouth, Pop. 1,858
Upper Freehold Regional SD 2,100/PK-12
27 High St 08501 609-259-7292
Dr. Robert Smith, supt. Fax 259-0881
www.ufrsd.net
Allentown HS 1,000/9-12
27 High St 08501 609-259-2160
Christopher Nagy, prin. Fax 259-0390

Annandale, Hunterdon, Pop. 1,074
North Hunterdon/Vorhees Regional HSD 2,900/9-12
1445 State Route 31 S 08801 908-735-2846
Dr. Charles Shaddow, supt. Fax 735-6914
www.nhvweb.net
North Hunterdon HS 1,700/9-12
1445 State Route 31 S 08801 908-735-5191
Michael Hughes, prin. Fax 735-5191
Other Schools – See Glen Gardner

Asbury, Hunterdon
Bethlehem Township SD 700/K-8
940 Iron Bridge Rd 08802 908-537-4044
Dr. Mario Barbiere, supt. Fax 537-7224
www.btschools.org
Hoppock MS 300/5-8
280 Asbury West Portal Rd 08802 908-479-6336
Edward Keegan, prin. Fax 479-1021

Asbury Park, Monmouth, Pop. 16,624
Asbury Park SD 2,700/PK-12
407 Lake Ave 07712 732-776-2606
Dr. Antonio N. Lewis, supt. Fax 774-8067
asburypark.usschoolnet.com/
Asbury Park HS 600/9-12
1003 Sunset Ave 07712 732-776-2638
Dr. Linda Palumbo, prin. Fax 776-3119
Asbury Park MS 600/6-8
1200 Bangs Ave 07712 732-776-2559
Fax 776-7503
Asbury Evening HS Adult
1003 Sunset Ave 07712 732-776-2666
Fax 776-2667

Monmouth County Vocational SD
Supt. — See Freehold
Culinary Education Center Vo/Tech
101 Drury Ln 07712 732-988-3299
Michael Sirianni, prin. Fax 776-8096

Atco, Camden
Winslow Township SD 5,900/PK-12
30 Cooper Folly Rd 08004 856-767-2850
Dr. Daniel Swirsky, supt. Fax 768-2765
www.winslow-schools.com
Winslow Township HS 1,600/9-12
200 Coopers Folly Rd 08004 856-767-1850
Glen Jackson, prin.
Winslow Township MS 1,300/6-8
30 Cooper Folly Rd 08004 856-767-7222
Dr. Mary Alimenti, prin.

Atlantic City, Atlantic, Pop. 40,368
Atlantic City SD 6,600/PK-12
1300 Atlantic Ave 08401 609-343-7200
Fredrick Nickles, supt. Fax 345-3268
www.acboe.org/
Atlantic City HS 2,600/9-12
1400 N Albany Ave 08401 609-343-7300
Oscar Torres, prin. Fax 343-7345
Atlantic City Evening HS Adult
1400 N Albany Ave 08401 609-343-7300
LaKecia Hyman, admin. Fax 343-7345

Audubon, Camden, Pop. 9,047
Audubon SD 1,600/K-12
350 Edgewood Ave 08106 856-547-1325
Mary Ann Rende, supt. Fax 546-8550
www.audubon.k12.nj.us/
Audubon JSHS 900/7-12
350 Edgewood Ave 08106 856-547-7695
John Ross, prin. Fax 547-4073

Augusta, Sussex

Veritas Christian Academy 50/9-10
PO Box 182 07822 973-579-6333
Dr. Eric Mindrebo, admin. Fax 579-6293

Avenel, Middlesex, Pop. 15,504
Woodbridge Township SD
Supt. — See Woodbridge
Avenel MS 700/6-8
85 Woodbine Ave 07001 732-396-7020
Gary Kuzniak, prin. Fax 574-0573

Barnegat, Ocean, Pop. 1,160
Barnegat Township SD 2,400/K-12
550 Barnegat Blvd N 08005 609-698-5800
Dr. Thomas C. McMahon, supt. Fax 698-6638
www.barnegatschools.com
Barnegat HS 300/9-12
180 Bengal Blvd 08005 609-660-7510
Joseph Saxton, prin. Fax 660-7598
Brackman MS 800/6-8
600 Barnegat Blvd N 08005 609-698-5880
Stephen Nichol, prin. Fax 698-7965

Barrington, Camden, Pop. 7,050
Barrington Borough SD 400/K-8
311 Reading Ave 08007 856-547-8467
Dr. Loyola Garcia, supt. Fax 547-5533
www.barringtonschools.net/
Woodland MS 200/6-8
1 School Ln 08007 856-547-8402
Patricia Moore, prin. Fax 522-1248

Basking Ridge, Somerset, Pop. 4,000
Bernards Township SD 5,100/K-12
101 Peachtree Rd 07920 908-204-2600
Dr. Valerie A. Goger, supt. Fax 766-7641
www.bernardsboe.com/
Annin MS 1,200/6-8
70 Quincy Rd 07920 908-204-2610
Nick Markarian, prin. Fax 204-0244
Ridge HS 1,400/9-12
268 S Finley Ave 07920 908-204-2585
Frank Howlett, prin. Fax 204-2582

Bayonne, Hudson, Pop. 59,987
Bayonne SD 8,400/PK-12
669 Avenue A 07002 201-858-5800
Dr. Patricia McGeehan, supt. Fax 858-6289
www.bhs.bboed.org/
Bayonne HS 2,300/9-12
667 Avenue A 07002 201-858-5900
Richard Baccarella, prin. Fax 858-6263
Public S 14 200/4-8
101 W 23rd St 07002 201-858-6281
Janice Lo Re, prin. Fax 436-5079
ACC Evening HS Adult
Avenue A & 28th St 07002 201-858-5851
Monica Flynn, dir.

Hudson County Vocational SD
Supt. — See North Bergen
Hudson County AVTS - Bayonne Vo/Tech
Ave A & 28th St 07002 201-854-2107
Joseph Sirangelo, prin.

Bayonne Hospital School of Nursing Post-Sec.
29 E 29th St 07002 201-339-9656
Holy Family Academy 300/9-12
239 Avenue A 07002 201-339-7341
Sr. Mary Ford, prin. Fax 339-9295
Marist HS 500/9-12
1241 Kennedy Blvd 07002 201-437-4544
Br. Stephen Schlitte, prin. Fax 437-6013
Yeshiva Gedola of Bayonne 100/9-12
735 Avenue C 07002 201-339-7187
Shmuel Horowitz, prin. Fax 339-8339

Bayville, Ocean
Central Regional SD 2,200/7-12
509 Forest Hills Pkwy 08721 732-269-1100
David Trethaway, supt. Fax 269-7723
www.centralreg.k12.nj.us
Central Regional HS 1,400/9-12
509 Forest Hills Pkwy 08721 732-269-1100
Bruce Orsino, prin. Fax 269-7723
Central Regional MS 800/7-8
509 Forest Hills Pkwy 08721 732-269-1100
Tommy Parlapanides, prin. Fax 269-7723

Beachwood, Ocean, Pop. 10,738
Toms River Regional SD
Supt. — See Toms River
Toms River IS South 6-8
1675 Pinewald Rd 08722 732-818-8570
Paul Gluck, prin.

Belleville, Essex, Pop. 36,300
Belleville SD 4,400/K-12
102 Passaic Ave 07109 973-450-3500
Dr. Edward Kliszus, supt. Fax 450-3504
www.belleville.k12.nj.us/
Belleville HS 1,600/9-12
100 Passaic Ave 07109 973-450-3500
Victor DePauw, prin. Fax 450-3196
Belleville MS 700/7-8
279 Washington Ave 07109 973-450-3532
Carmine Guinta, prin. Fax 450-5001

Bellmawr, Camden, Pop. 11,159
Bellmawr Borough SD 900/K-8
256 Anderson Ave 08031 856-931-3620
Fax 931-9326
bellmawrschools.org
Bell Oaks MS 400/5-8
256 Anderson Ave 08031 856-931-6273
Anthony Farinelli, prin. Fax 931-9326

Belmar, Monmouth, Pop. 5,962

St. Rose HS 600/9-12
607 7th Ave 07719 732-681-2858
Dr. Michele Campbell, prin. Fax 280-2745

Belvidere, Warren, Pop. 2,732
Belvidere SD 1,000/K-12
809 Oxford St 07823 908-475-6600
Dirk Swaneveld, supt. Fax 475-6619
www.belvideresd.org
Belvidere HS 600/9-12
809 Oxford St 07823 908-475-4025
Joseph Flynn, prin. Fax 475-1685
Oxford Street MS 200/4-8
807 Oxford St 07823 908-475-4001
Karl Rice, prin. Fax 475-6619

Bergenfield, Bergen, Pop. 26,056
Bergenfield SD 3,600/K-12
100 S Prospect Ave 07621 201-385-8202
Dr. Michael Kuchar, supt. Fax 385-3718
www.bergenfield.org/
Bergenfield HS 1,200/9-12
80 S Prospect Ave 07621 201-385-8600
Hank Sinatra, prin. Fax 439-0978
Brown MS 900/6-8
130 S Washington Ave 07621 201-385-8847
Ronald Kopec, prin. Fax 385-0219

Berkeley Heights, Union, Pop. 11,980
Berkeley Heights SD 2,800/PK-12
345 Plainfield Ave 07922 908-464-1718
Judith Rattner, supt. Fax 464-7673
www.bhs.k12.nj.us
Columbia MS 600/6-8
345 Plainfield Ave 07922 908-464-1600
Dr. John Dennis, prin. Fax 464-0017
Livingston HS 900/9-12
175 Watchung Blvd 07922 908-464-3100
Gregory Meissner, prin. Fax 464-7508

Bernardsville, Somerset, Pop. 7,612
Somerset Hills Regional SD 1,900/K-12
25 Olcott Ave 07924 908-204-1930
Peter Miller, supt. Fax 953-0567
www.shsd.org/
Bernards HS 700/9-12
25 Olcott Ave 07924 908-630-3001
Dr. Lynn Caravello, prin. Fax 766-8223
Bernardsville MS 600/5-8
141 Seney Dr 07924 908-204-1916
Dr. Lynn Kratz, prin. Fax 953-2184

Blackwood, Camden, Pop. 5,120
Black Horse Pike Regional SD 4,000/9-12
580 Erial Rd 08012 856-227-4106
Ralph Ross, supt. Fax 227-6835
www.bhprsd.org

Highland HS 1,100/9-12
450 Erial Rd 08012 856-227-4100
Frank Palatucci, prin. Fax 227-3619
Other Schools – See Erial, Runnemede

Gloucester Township SD 7,700/K-8
17 Erial Rd 08012 856-227-1400
Thomas Seddon, supt. Fax 228-1422
www.gloucestertownshipschools.org/
Glen Landing MS 900/6-8
85 Little Gloucester Rd 08012 856-227-3534
Andrea Stubbs, prin. Fax 228-5260
Lewis MS 700/6-8
875 Erial Rd 08012 856-227-8400
Alan Gansert, prin. Fax 228-5130
Other Schools – See Sicklerville

Camden County College Post-Sec.
PO Box 200 08012 856-227-7200
Helene Fuld School of Nursing Post-Sec.
PO Box 1669 08012 856-374-0100
Pennco Tech Post-Sec.
99 Erial Rd 08012 856-232-0310

Blairstown, Warren
North Warren Regional SD 1,100/7-12
PO Box 410 07825 908-362-9342
Dr. John Toleno, supt. Fax 362-8744
www.northwarren.org
North Warren Regional JSHS 1,100/7-12
PO Box 410 07825 908-362-8211
Dr. Ken Greene, prin. Fax 362-7353

Blair Academy 400/9-12
PO Box 600 07825 908-362-6121
T. Chandler Hardwick, hdmstr. Fax 362-5157

Bloomfield, Essex, Pop. 48,200
Bloomfield Township SD 5,800/PK-12
155 Broad St 07003 973-680-8555
Frank Digesere, supt. Fax 680-0263
www.bloomfield.k12.nj.us
Bloomfield HS 1,800/9-12
160 Broad St 07003 973-680-8600
Christopher Jennings, prin. Fax 680-8684
Bloomfield MS 1,000/7-8
60 Huck Rd 07003 973-680-8620
Patricia Pelikan, prin. Fax 338-6523

Essex County Vocational SD
Supt. — See Verona
Essex County Vocational HS-Bloomfield Vo/Tech
209 Franklin St 07003 973-429-8893
Eric Love, prin. Fax 429-7330

Bloomfield College Post-Sec.
467 Franklin St 07003 973-748-9000
Concorde School of Hair Design Post-Sec.
9 Ward St 07003 973-680-0099

Bloomingdale, Passaic, Pop. 7,654
Bloomingdale SD 700/K-8
31 Captolene Ave 07403 973-838-3282
Thomas Comiciotto, supt. Fax 838-6397
www.bloomingdaleschools.org
Bergen MS 300/5-8
225 Glenwild Ave 07403 973-838-4835
Dr. Fredda Rosenberg, prin. Fax 283-1893

Bogota, Bergen, Pop. 8,150
Bogota SD 1,100/K-12
1 Henry C Luthin Pl 07603 201-441-4800
Jose Negron, supt. Fax 489-5759
www.bogotaonline.org/
Bogota JSHS 500/7-12
1 Henry C Luthin Pl 07603 201-441-4808
Arnold Oftedal, prin. Fax 441-4849

Boonton, Morris, Pop. 8,555
Boonton SD 1,300/K-12
434 Lathrop Ave 07005 973-335-3994
Mario Cardinale, supt. Fax 335-8281
www.boonton.org/schools/schools/index.htm
Boonton HS 600/9-12
306 Lathrop Ave 07005 973-335-9700
Augustus Modla, prin. Fax 402-5135
Boonton MS 100/7-8
306 Lathrop Ave 07005 973-335-9700
Jennifer Spitzer, prin. Fax 402-5135

Bordentown, Burlington, Pop. 3,989
Bordentown Regional SD 1,200/K-12
318 Ward Ave 08505 609-298-0025
John Polomano, supt. Fax 298-2515
www.bordentown.k12.nj.us
Bordentown Regional HS 600/9-12
318 Ward Ave 08505 609-298-0025
Frederick D'Antoni, prin. Fax 291-0347
Bordentown Regional MS 6-8
50 Dunns Mill Rd 08505 609-298-0674
Dr. Norine Gerepka, prin. Fax 291-1929

Bound Brook, Somerset, Pop. 10,168
Bound Brook Borough SD 600/PK-12
W 2nd St LaMonte Building 08805 732-652-2500
Dr. Edward Hoffman, supt. Fax 271-9097
www.bbrook.k12.nj.us
Bound Brook HS 500/9-12
111 W Union Ave 08805 732-652-7950
Dr. Daniel Gallagher, prin. Fax 356-6445
Smalley MS 100/6-8
Cherry Ave 08805 732-652-7940
Edward Gordon, prin. Fax 271-4879

Branchburg, Somerset
Branchburg Township SD 2,000/K-8
240 Baird Rd 08876 908-722-3335
Kenneth Knops, supt. Fax 526-6144
www.branchburg.k12.nj.us
Branchburg Central MS 700/6-8
220 Baird Rd 08876 908-526-1415
William Feldman, prin. Fax 526-7486

Brick, Ocean, Pop. 78,300
Brick Township SD 10,800/PK-12
101 Hendrickson Ave 08724 732-785-3000
Melindo Persi, supt. Fax 840-9089
www.brickschools.org/
Brick Township HS 1,700/9-12
346 Chambersbridge Rd 08723 732-262-2500
Dennis Filippone, prin. Fax 920-5907

Brick Township Memorial HS 1,900/9-12
2001 Lanes Mill Rd 08724 732-785-3090
Richard Caldes, prin. Fax 458-2748
Lake Riviera MS 1,200/6-8
171 Beaverson Blvd 08723 732-262-2600
Susan McNamara, prin. Fax 477-0392
Veteran's Memorial MS 1,400/6-8
105 Hendrickson Ave 08724 732-785-3030
John VanDerslice, prin. Fax 458-9777

Ocean County Vocational SD
Supt. — See Toms River
Ocean County Voc-Tech S - Brick Vo/Tech
350 Chambersbridge Rd 08723 732-920-0050
Vern Beadle, prin. Fax 920-0108

Capri Institute of Hair Design Post-Sec.
268 Brick Blvd 08723 732-920-3600

Bridgeton, Cumberland, Pop. 23,959
Bridgeton SD 4,100/PK-12
PO Box 657 08302 856-455-8030
Dr. H. Victor Gilson, supt. Fax 451-0815
www.bridgeton.k12.nj.us/
Bridgeton HS 1,000/9-12
111 N West Ave 08302 856-455-8030
Lynn Williams, prin. Fax 455-0486
ExCEL S 6-8
7 Washington St 08302 856-455-8030
Sam Hull, prin. Fax 459-0280
Adult Learning Center Adult
111 N West Ave 08302 856-455-8030
Sam Hull, prin. Fax 455-4217

Cumberland County Vocational SD
601 Bridgeton Ave 08302 856-451-9000
Darlene Barber, supt. Fax 453-1118
www.cumberland.tec.nj.us
Cumberland Co. Technical Education Ctr Vo/Tech
601 Bridgeton Ave 08302 856-451-9000
Dave Hitchner, prin. Fax 453-1118

Cumberland Co. Tech. Education Center Post-Sec.
601 Bridgeton Ave 08302 856-451-9000

Bridgewater, Somerset, Pop. 36,400
Bridgewater-Raritan Regional SD 7,900/PK-12
PO Box 6030 08807 908-685-2777
J. Michael Schilder Ed.D., supt. Fax 231-8496
www.brrsd.k12.nj.us
Bridgewater-Raritan HS 2,400/9-12
PO Box 6569 08807 908-231-8660
Dr. James Riccobono, prin. Fax 231-0467
Bridgewater-Raritan MS 2,100/6-8
PO Box 6933 08807 908-231-8661
Nancy Mahoney, prin. Fax 575-0847

Somerset County Vocational SD
PO Box 6350 08807 908-526-8900
Michael Maddaluna, supt. Fax 704-0784
www.scti.org
Somerset County Vo-Tech HS Vo/Tech
PO Box 6350 08807 908-526-8900
Edmund Jones, prin. Fax 704-0784
Somerset County Adult Tech Inst Adult
PO Box 6350 08807 908-526-8900
Joseph Malone, dir. Fax 526-9494

Brigantine, Atlantic, Pop. 12,861
Brigantine CSD 1,000/K-8
PO Box 947 08203 609-266-7671
Dr. Robert Previti, supt. Fax 266-4748
www.brigantine.atlnet.org
Brigantine North MS 500/5-8
PO Box 947 08203 609-266-3603
William Gussie, prin. Fax 266-7062

Brookside, Morris
Mendham Township SD 900/K-8
W Main St 07926 973-543-7107
Christine Johnson, supt. Fax 543-5537
www.mendhamtwp.org
Mendham Twp. MS 400/5-8
16 Washington Valley Rd 07926 973-543-2505
Patrick Ciccone, prin. Fax 543-0701

Budd Lake, Morris, Pop. 7,272
Mt. Olive Township SD 4,600/K-12
89 US Highway 46 07828 973-691-4008
Rosalie S. Lamonte Ph.D., supt. Fax 691-4022
www.mtoliveboe.org
Mt. Olive MS 1,100/6-8
160 Wolfe Rd 07828 973-691-4006
Dr. Tracey Severns, prin. Fax 691-4029
Other Schools – See Flanders

Buena, Atlantic, Pop. 3,848
Buena Regional SD 2,400/K-12
PO Box 309 08310 856-697-0800
Diane DeGiacomo, supt. Fax 697-4963
www.buena.k12.nj.us/
Buena Regional HS 1,000/9-12
125 Weymouth Rd 08310 856-697-2400
Ken Soboloski, prin. Fax 697-4701
Other Schools – See Minotola

Burlington, Burlington, Pop. 9,791
Burlington CSD 1,800/PK-12
518 Locust Ave 08016 609-387-5874
Dr. Edward Gola, supt. Fax 386-6971
www.burlington-nj.net
Burlington City JSHS 800/7-12
100 Blue Devil Way 08016 609-387-5800
Julian Jenkins, prin. Fax 387-4287

Burlington Township SD 3,800/PK-12
PO Box 428 08016 609-387-3955
Dr. Christopher Manno, supt. Fax 239-2192
www.burltwpsch.org/
Burlington Township HS 1,100/9-12
610 Fountain Ave 08016 609-387-1713
Fax 387-0439
Hopkins MS 600/7-8
700 Jacksonville Rd Ste 1 08016 609-387-3774
Lawrence Penny, prin. Fax 387-1314

Institute of Logistical Management Post-Sec.
PO Box 427 08016 609-747-1515
Life Center Academy 400/PK-12
2045 Columbus Rd 08016 609-499-2100
Robert Newman, dean Fax 499-4905

St. Mary's Hall/Doane Academy 200/PK-12
350 Riverbank 08016 609-386-3500
John McGee, hdmstr. Fax 386-5878

Butler, Morris, Pop. 8,091
Butler SD 1,100/K-12
38 Bartholdi Ave 07405 973-492-2000
Dr. Rene Rovtar, supt. Fax 492-1016
pegasus.butlerboe.org/
Butler HS 500/9-12
38 Bartholdi Ave 07405 973-492-2000
William Hanisch, prin. Fax 492-8672
Butler MS 300/5-8
34 Pearl Pl 07405 973-492-2079
Andrea Vladichak, prin. Fax 492-9774

Morris County Vocational SD
Supt. — See Denville
Academy for Law & Public Safety Vo/Tech
Bartholdi Ave 07405 973-492-2000
William Hanisch, prin.

Caldwell, Essex, Pop. 7,489
Caldwell-West Caldwell SD
Supt. — See West Caldwell
Cleveland MS, 36 Academy Rd 07006 600/6-8
Casey Shorter, prin. 973-228-9115

Caldwell College Post-Sec.
9 Ryerson Ave 07006 973-618-3000
Mt. St. Dominic Academy 300/9-12
3 Ryerson Ave 07006 973-226-0660
Sr. Frances Sullivan, hdmstr. Fax 226-2693

Califon, Hunterdon, Pop. 1,055
Lebanon Township SD 800/K-8
70 Bunnvale Rd 07830 908-638-4521
Judith Burd, supt. Fax 638-5511
www.lebtwpk8.org
Woodglen MS 400/5-8
70 Bunnvale Rd 07830 908-638-4111
Michael Rubright, prin. Fax 638-8418

Tewksbury Township SD 300/PK-8
173 County Road 517 07830 908-439-2010
Dr. Gayle M. Carrick, supt. Fax 439-2655
www.tewksburyschools.org
Old Turnpike MS 300/5-8
171 County Road 517 07830 908-439-2010
William Petrick, prin. Fax 439-3160

Camden, Camden, Pop. 80,010
Camden CSD 13,900/PK-12
201 N Front St 08102 856-966-2040
Dr. Leonard Fitts, supt. Fax 966-2138
www.camden.k12.nj.us
Brimm Medical Arts HS 300/9-12
1626 Copewood St 08103 856-966-2500
Thurselle Treece, prin. Fax 966-2489
Camden HS 1,000/9-12
1700 Park Blvd 08103 856-966-5100
Al Davis, prin. Fax 966-4756
Creative & Performing Arts HS 200/9-12
1701 S 6th St 08104 856-966-8955
Dr. Davida Coe-Brockington, prin. Fax 964-9759
East Camden MS 500/5-8
3064 Stevens St 08105 856-966-5111
Patricia Kenny, prin. Fax 964-9791
Hatch MS 400/6-8
1875 Park Blvd 08103 856-966-5122
Kathleen Avant, prin. Fax 964-0778
Met East HS 9-12
1151 Kaighns Ave 08103 856-966-8950
Fax 966-2388
Morgan Village MS 500/5-8
1000 Morgan Blvd 08104 856-966-5330
Louis Mason, prin. Fax 964-8443
Pyne Poynt MS 400/4-8
800 Erie St 08102 856-966-5360
Tyrone Richards, prin. Fax 964-8462
Veterans Memorial MS 500/5-8
800 N 26th St 08105 856-966-5090
Ellen Anderson, prin. Fax 541-5141
Wilson HS 1,200/9-12
3100 Federal St 08105 856-966-5300
Calvin Gunning, prin. Fax 966-4755
Riggs Adult Education S Adult
1656 Kaighns Ave 08103 856-966-5223
John Randall, prin. Fax 541-8671

Cooper Hospital/Univ Medical Center Post-Sec.
1 Cooper Plz # 217 08103 856-342-2416
Our Lady of Lourdes School of Nursing Post-Sec.
1600 Haddon Ave 08103 856-757-3729
Rowan University Post-Sec.
200 N Broadway 08102 856-757-2857
Rutgers-The State University of N.J. Post-Sec.
311 N 5th St 08102 856-225-6026
San Miguel S 50/6-8
836 S 4th St 08103 856-342-6707
Dr. Mary Burke, prin. Fax 968-0483
West Jersey Health System Post-Sec.
1000 Atlantic Ave 08104 856-342-4600

Cape May, Cape May, Pop. 3,760
Lower Cap May Regional SD 1,700/7-12
687 Route 9 08204 609-884-3475
Jack Pfizenmayer, supt. Fax 884-7067
lcmrschool.org/lcmr/index.htm
Lower Cape May Regional HS 1,200/9-12
687 Route 9 08204 609-884-3475
Joe Castellucci, prin. Fax 884-0546
Teitelman MS 500/7-8
687 Route 9 08204 609-884-3475
Eugene Sole, prin. Fax 884-4311

Cape May Court House, Cape May, Pop. 4,426
Cape May County Technical SD
188 Crest Haven Rd, 609-465-2161
William Desmond, supt. Fax 465-3069
www.capemaytech.com
Cape May County Tech HS Vo/Tech
188 Crest Haven Rd, 609-465-2161
Robert Matthies, prin.
Cape May County Tech Evening HS Adult
188 Crest Haven Rd, 609-465-2161
George Miller, prin.

Dennis Township SD 700/K-8
601 Hagen Rd, 609-861-0549
George Papp, supt. Fax 861-1833
dennis.capemayschools.com/
Other Schools – See Dennisville

Middle Township SD 2,900/PK-12
216 S Main St, 609-465-1800
Michael Kopakowski, supt. Fax 465-7058
middle.capemayschools.com/
Middle Township HS 1,100/9-12
300 E Atlantic Ave, 609-465-1852
David Salvo, prin. Fax 465-3415
Middle Township MS 4 600/6-8
300 E Pacific Ave, 609-465-1834
Amos Kraybill, prin. Fax 465-5524

Burdette Tomlin Memorial Hospital Post-Sec.
2 Stone Harbor Blvd, 609-463-2180
Cape Christian Academy 100/PK-12
10 Oyster Rd, 609-465-4132
James Patterson, admin. Fax 465-0170
Cape May County Technical Institute Post-Sec.
188 Crest Haven Rd, 609-465-2161

Carlstadt, Bergen, Pop. 6,018
Carlstadt SD 400/PK-8
550 Washington St 07072 201-939-6502
Frank Legato, supt. Fax 939-5710
www.carlstadt.org
Washington MS 300/3-8
550 Washington St 07072 201-939-6506
Steve Kollinok, prin. Fax 939-8371

Carneys Point, Salem, Pop. 7,686
Penns Grove-Carneys Point Regional SD
Supt. — See Penns Grove
Penns Grove HS 500/9-12
334 Harding Hwy 08069 856-299-6300
Dr. Paul Rufino, prin. Fax 299-5192

Salem Community College Post-Sec.
460 Hollywood Ave 08069 856-299-2100

Carteret, Middlesex, Pop. 21,460
Carteret Borough SD 3,800/PK-12
599 Roosevelt Ave 07008 732-541-8960
Kevin Ahearn, supt. Fax 541-0433
www.carteretschools.org
Carteret HS 1,000/9-12
199 Washington Ave 07008 732-541-8960
Lamont Repollet, prin. Fax 969-4004
Carteret MS 1,000/6-8
300 Carteret Ave 07008 732-541-8960
Mary Spiga, prin. Fax 541-0483

Cedar Grove, Essex, Pop. 12,053
Cedar Grove Township SD 1,500/K-12
520 Pompton Ave 07009 973-239-1550
Dr. Eugene Polles, supt. Fax 239-2994
www.cedargrove.k12.nj.us
Cedar Grove HS 400/9-12
90 Rugby Rd 07009 973-239-6400
Judith Nappi, prin. Fax 857-9833
Cedar Grove Memorial MS 500/5-8
500 Ridge Rd 07009 973-239-2646
Lawrence Neugebauer, prin. Fax 239-2003

Chatham, Morris, Pop. 8,439
School District of the Chathams 3,200/K-12
58 Meyersville Rd 07928 973-635-5656
James O'Neill, supt. Fax 701-0146
www.chatham-nj.org/coin
Chatham HS 900/9-12
255 Lafayette Ave 07928 973-635-9075
Michael LaSusa, prin. Fax 635-8670
Chatham MS 700/6-8
480 Main St 07928 973-635-7200
Kenneth Wark, prin. Fax 635-7190

Cherry Hill, Camden, Pop. 70,100
Cherry Hill Township SD 11,300/K-12
PO Box 5015 08034 856-429-5600
Dr. David Campbell, supt. Fax 354-1864
www.cherryhill.k12.nj.us/
Beck MS 1,000/6-8
936 Cropwell Rd 08003 856-424-4505
Dr. Dennis Perry, prin. Fax 424-8602
Carusi MS 900/6-8
315 Roosevelt Dr 08002 856-667-1220
Kirk Rickansrud, prin. Fax 779-0613
Cherry Hill HS - East 2,100/9-12
1750 Kresson Rd 08003 856-424-2222
John O'Breza, prin. Fax 424-0637
Cherry Hill HS - West 1,600/9-12
2101 Chapel Ave W 08002 856-663-8006
Joseph Meloche, prin. Fax 663-5746
Rosa International MS 800/6-8
485 Browning Ln 08003 856-616-8787
Ed Canzanese, prin.

Camden Catholic HS 1,000/9-12
300 Cuthbert Rd 08002 856-663-2247
Thomas Kiely, prin. Fax 661-0632
Chubb Institute Post-Sec.
2100 Route 38 08002 856-988-9880
Empire Beauty School Post-Sec.
2100 State Highway #38 08002 856-667-8887
Harris School of Business Post-Sec.
1 Mall Dr Ste 700 08002 856-662-5300
Kings Christian S 400/PK-12
5 Carnegie Plz 08003 856-489-6724
Dr. Rebecca Stiegel, hdmstr. Fax 489-6727
Living Faith Christian Academy 200/K-12
202 Park Blvd 08002 856-665-5507
Gail Foster, prin. Fax 665-5601

Chester, Morris, Pop. 1,653
Chester Township SD 1,300/K-8
415 State Route 24 Ste 11 07930 908-879-7373
Michael Roth, supt. Fax 879-5887
www.chester-nj.org
Black River MS 400/6-8
North Rd 07930 908-879-6363
Robert Mullen, prin. Fax 879-9085

West Morris Regional HSD 2,500/9-12
10 S Four Bridges Rd 07930 908-879-6404
Anthony di Battista, supt. Fax 879-8861
www.wmrhsd.org
West Morris Central HS 1,300/9-12
259 Bartley Rd 07930 908-879-5212
Michael Reilly, prin. Fax 879-2741
Other Schools – See Mendham

Chesterfield, Burlington

Meadow View Junior Academy 100/K-12
241 Bordentown Chstrfeld Rd, 609-298-1122
Sadrail Saint-Ulysse, prin. Fax 298-7550

Cinnaminson, Burlington, Pop. 14,583
Cinnaminson Township SD 2,500/K-12
PO Box 224 08077 856-829-7600
Salvatore Illuzzi, supt. Fax 786-9618
www.cinnaminson.com
Cinnaminson HS 900/9-12
1197 Riverton Rd 08077 856-829-7770
Michael Zank, prin. Fax 829-7777
Cinnaminson MS 600/6-8
312 N Fork Landing Rd 08077 856-786-8012
Gay Moceri, prin. Fax 786-1860

Clark, Union, Pop. 14,629
Clark Township SD 2,300/K-12
365 Westfield Ave 07066 732-574-9600
Dr. Brian Zychowski, supt. Fax 382-5957
www.clarkschools.org
Johnson HS 900/9-12
365 Westfield Ave 07066 732-382-0910
Robert Taylor, prin. Fax 382-5957
Kumpf MS 500/6-8
59 Mildred Ter 07066 732-381-0400
Richard Delmonaco, prin. Fax 381-0262

Mother Seton Regional HS 400/9-12
Valley Rd 07066 732-382-1952
Sr. Regina Martin, prin. Fax 382-4725

Clarksburg, Monmouth
Millstone Township SD 1,700/K-8
18 Schoolhouse Rd 08510 732-446-0890
Dr. Mary Anne Donahue, supt. Fax 792-2948
www.millstone.k12.nj.us
Millstone Township MS 800/5-8
308 Millstone Rd 08510 732-446-6802
Michelle Vella, prin. Fax 792-9754

Clayton, Gloucester, Pop. 7,447
Clayton SD 1,000/PK-12
300 W Chestnut St 08312 856-881-8700
Cleve Bryan, supt. Fax 863-8196
www.clayton.k12.nj.us
Clayton MSHS 300/7-12
350 E Clinton St 08312 856-881-8701
Marc Meillier, prin. Fax 863-0808

Cliffside Park, Bergen, Pop. 23,035
Cliffside Park SD 2,400/K-12
525 Palisade Ave 07010 201-313-2310
Robert J. Paladino, supt. Fax 943-7050
www.cliffsidepark.edu
Cliffside Park HS 1,000/9-12
64 Riverview Ave 07010 201-313-2370
Michael Romagnino, prin. Fax 313-7961

Cliffwood, Monmouth, Pop. 1,500
Matawan-Aberdeen Regional SD
Supt. — See Aberdeen
Matawan Aberdeen MS 1,000/6-8
469 Matawan Ave 07721 732-290-2850
Joanne Avella, prin. Fax 765-0894

Clifton, Passaic, Pop. 79,922
Clifton SD, PO Box 2209 07015 9,600/K-12
Michael Rice Ph.D., supt. 973-470-2260
www.clifton.k12.nj.us
Clifton HS 3,200/9-12
333 Colfax Ave 07013 973-470-2312
Richard Tardalo, prin. Fax 458-9290
Columbus MS 1,200/6-8
350 Piaget Ave 07011 973-470-2360
Jimmie Warren, prin. Fax 470-2365
Wilson MS 1,100/6-8
1400 Van Houten Ave 07013 973-470-2350
William Hahn, prin. Fax 470-2607

Capri Institute of Hair Design Post-Sec.
1595 Main Ave 07011 973-772-4610
KeySkills Learning Post-Sec.
50 Mount Prospect Ave 07013 973-778-8136

Closter, Bergen, Pop. 8,669
Closter SD 1,300/K-8
340 Homans Ave 07624 201-768-3001
Joanne Newberry, supt. Fax 768-1903
www.nvnet.org/k8/closter
Tenakill MS 700/5-8
275 High St 07624 201-768-1332
Alfred Baffa, prin. Fax 784-0726

Collingswood, Camden, Pop. 14,083
Collingswood Borough SD 1,900/K-12
200 Lees Ave 08108 856-962-5732
James Bathurst, supt. Fax 962-5723
collingswood.k12.nj.us
Collingswood HS 800/9-12
424 W Collings Ave 08108 856-962-5701
Charles Earling, prin. Fax 962-5565
Collingswood MS 300/7-8
414 W Collings Ave 08108 856-962-5702
John McMullin, prin. Fax 962-5751

Colonia, Middlesex, Pop. 18,238
Woodbridge Township SD
Supt. — See Woodbridge
Colonia HS 1,400/9-12
180 East St 07067 732-499-6500
Robert McLaughlin, prin. Fax 574-2575
Colonia MS 600/6-8
100 Delaware Ave 07067 732-396-7000
Gregg Miller, prin. Fax 574-0772

Colts Neck, Monmouth
Colts Neck Township SD 1,500/K-8
70 Conover Rd 07722 732-946-0055
Dr. Richard Fitzpatrick, supt. Fax 946-4792
www.coltsneckschools.org

Cedar Drive MS 600/6-8
73 Cedar Dr 07722 732-946-0055
Maggie Maziarz, prin. Fax 462-4108

Freehold Regional HSD
Supt. — See Englishtown
Colts Neck HS 1,600/9-12
59 Five Points Rd 07722 732-761-0190
R. McChesney, prin. Fax 761-0193

Columbus, Burlington
Northern Burlington County Regional SD 1,900/7-12
160 Mansfield Rd E 08022 609-298-3900
Dr. James Sarruda, supt. Fax 298-3154
www.nburlington.com
Northern Burlington County Regional HS 1,200/9-12
160 Mansfield Rd E 08022 609-298-3900
Dr. Scott Oswald, prin. Fax 298-8563
Northern Burlington County Regional JHS 700/7-8
160 Mansfield Rd E 08022 609-298-3900
Eric Barnett, prin. Fax 291-1563

Convent Station, Morris

Academy of St. Elizabeth 200/9-12
PO Box 297 07961 973-605-3200
Sr. Patricia Costello, prin.

Cranford, Union, Pop. 22,624
Cranford Township SD 3,500/K-12
132 Thomas St 07016 908-709-6202
Dr. Lawrence S. Feinsod, supt. Fax 272-7735
www.cranfordschools.org
Cranford HS 1,100/9-12
201 W End Pl 07016 908-709-6272
Carol Grossi, prin. Fax 276-6552
Orange Avenue S 700/3-8
901 Orange Ave 07016 908-709-6257
Kathleen Gorski, prin. Fax 272-3025

Union County College Post-Sec.
1033 Springfield Ave 07016 908-709-7000

Creamridge, Monmouth

New Jersey United Christian Academy 50/8-12
73 Holmes Mill Rd 08514 609-738-2121
Donna Torres, prin. Fax 738-2151

Cresskill, Bergen, Pop. 8,449
Cresskill SD 1,600/K-12
1 Lincoln Dr 07626 201-567-5919
Dr. Charles Khoury, supt. Fax 567-7976
www.cresskillboe.k12.nj.us
Cresskill JSHS 700/7-12
1 Lincoln Dr 07626 201-567-5479
Peter Eftychiou, prin. Fax 567-0028

Delanco, Burlington, Pop. 3,316
Delanco Township SD 400/K-8
411 Walnut St 08075 856-461-0859
Michael Livengood, supt. Fax 461-6903
www.delanco.com
Walnut Street MS 100/6-8
411 Walnut St 08075 856-461-0874
Maureen Kelly, prin. Fax 461-6903

Delran, Burlington, Pop. 13,178
Delran Township SD 2,600/K-12
52 Hartford Rd 08075 856-461-6800
Dr. George Sharp, supt. Fax 461-6125
www.delran.k12.nj.us
Delran HS 800/9-12
50 Hartford Rd 08075 856-461-6100
John Fricke, prin. Fax 764-6177
Delran MS 700/6-8
905 S Chester Ave 08075 856-461-8822
James Duda, prin. Fax 461-0311

Holy Cross HS 800/9-12
5035 Route 130 08075 856-461-5400
Dennis Guida, prin. Fax 461-0323

Demarest, Bergen, Pop. 5,005
Demarest SD 700/K-8
568 Piermont Rd 07627 201-768-6060
Lawrence V. Hughes, supt. Fax 767-9122
www.nvnet.org
Demarest MS 400/5-8
568 Piermont Rd 07627 201-768-6061
Michael Fox, prin. Fax 768-9122

Northern Valley Regional SD 2,400/9-12
162 Knickerbocker Rd 07627 201-768-2200
Dr. Jan Furman, supt. Fax 768-7356
www.nvnet.org/nvhs/
Northern Valley Regional HS 1,100/9-12
150 Knickerbocker Rd 07627 201-768-3200
Dr. Bruce Sabatini, prin. Fax 768-5438
Other Schools – See Old Tappan

Academy of the Holy Angels 500/9-12
315 Hillside Ave 07627 201-768-7822
Jennifer Moran, prin. Fax 768-6933

Dennisville, Cape May
Dennis Township SD
Supt. — See Cape May Court House
Dennis Township MS 300/6-8
165 Academy Rd 08214 609-861-2821
James DiCarlo, prin. Fax 861-5229

Denville, Morris, Pop. 13,812
Denville Township SD 1,900/K-8
501 Openaki Rd 07834 973-983-6530
John Sakala, supt. Fax 366-2481
www.denville.org
Valleyview MS 600/6-8
320 Diamond Spring Rd 07834 973-983-6535
George Deamer, prin. Fax 627-0632

Morris County Vocational SD
400 E Main St 07834 973-627-4600
James Rogers, supt. Fax 627-4958
www.mcvts.org
Academy for Visual & Performing Arts Vo/Tech
400 E Main St 07834 973-627-4600
Miriam Faber, prin.
Morris County School of Technology Vo/Tech
400 E Main St 07834 973-627-4600
Thomas Barnard, prin. Fax 627-4958

Other Schools – See Butler, Rockaway

Morris Catholic HS 400/9-12
200 Morris Ave 07834 973-627-6660
Dr. Jeanne Gradone, prin. Fax 627-4351

Deptford, Gloucester
Deptford Township SD 4,000/PK-12
2022 Good Intent Rd 08096 856-232-2700
Dr. Joseph Canataro, supt. Fax 227-7473
www.deptford.k12.nj.us/
Deptford Township HS 1,100/9-12
575 Fox Run Rd 08096 856-232-2713
Gary Swenson, prin. Fax 374-9145
Other Schools – See Sewell

Lincoln Technical Institute Post-Sec.
1450 Clements Bridge Rd 08096 856-384-2888

Dover, Morris, Pop. 18,441
Dover Town SD 2,900/PK-12
100 Grace St 07801 973-989-2000
Robert Becker, supt. Fax 989-1662
www.dover-nj.org
Dover HS 900/9-12
100 Grace St 07801 973-989-2010
Elaine Simpson, prin. Fax 989-1662
East Dover MS 500/7-8
302 E McFarlan St 07801 973-989-2040
Robert Franks, prin. Fax 361-2117

Dover Business College Post-Sec.
15 E Blackwell St 07801 973-285-8400
Joe Kubert Sch of Cartoon & Graphic Arts Post-Sec.
37 Myrtle Ave 07801 973-361-1327

Dumont, Bergen, Pop. 17,474
Dumont SD 2,600/K-12
25 Depew St 07628 201-387-3082
Dr. James Montesano, supt. Fax 387-0259
www.dumontnj.org
Dumont HS 800/9-12
101 New Milford Ave 07628 201-387-3000
Maria Poidomani, prin. Fax 387-8461

Dunellen, Middlesex, Pop. 6,994
Dunellen SD 1,000/K-12
High & Lehigh Sts 08812 732-968-3226
Pio Pennisi, supt. Fax 968-3513
www.dunellenschools.org/
Dunellen HS 300/9-12
411 First St 08812 732-968-0885
Gene Mosley, prin. Fax 968-3138
Lincoln MS 200/6-8
411 First St 08812 732-968-0885
Joseph Moran, prin. Fax 968-3138

Eastampton, Burlington
Eastampton Township SD 800/K-8
1 Student Dr 08060 609-267-9172
Robert Krastek, supt. Fax 267-7895
www.eastampton.k12.nj.us
Eastampton Township MS 500/4-8
1 Student Dr 08060 609-267-9172
Robert Krastek, prin. Fax 261-3338

East Brunswick, Middlesex, Pop. 47,400
East Brunswick Township SD 8,800/PK-12
760 State Route 18 08816 732-613-6705
Dr. JoAnn Magistro, supt. Fax 698-9871
www.ebnet.org
Churchill JHS 1,500/8-9
18 Norton Rd 08816 732-613-6800
Mark Sutor, prin. Fax 257-0087
East Brunswick SHS 2,200/10-12
380 Cranbury Rd 08816 732-613-6904
Robert Murphy, prin. Fax 254-1938

Middlesex County Vocational SD
PO Box 1070 08816 732-257-3300
Dr. Karen McCloud-Hjazeh, supt. Fax 651-0618
www.mcvts.net
East Brunswick Vocational HS Vo/Tech
PO Box 1070 08816 732-254-8700
Paul LaPilusa, prin. Fax 613-9608
Adult HS - East Brunswick Adult
112 Rues Ln 08816 732-257-3300
Judy Alexander, contact Fax 613-9608
Other Schools – See Edison, Perth Amboy, Piscataway, Woodbridge

East Hanover, Morris, Pop. 9,926
East Hanover Township SD 1,100/K-8
20 School Ave 07936 973-887-2112
Larry Santos, supt. Fax 887-2773
www.easthanoverschools.org/
East Hanover MS 400/6-8
477 Ridgedale Ave 07936 973-887-8810
Robert Allen, prin. Fax 887-5079

Hanover Park Regional HSD 1,500/9-12
75 Mount Pleasant Ave 07936 973-887-0320
Dr. John Adamus, supt. Fax 887-9247
Hanover Park HS 800/9-12
63 Mount Pleasant Ave 07936 973-887-0300
Edward Franko, prin. Fax 515-7680
Other Schools – See Whippany

East Orange, Essex, Pop. 68,190
East Orange SD 10,400/PK-12
715 Park Ave 07017 973-266-5760
Laval S. Wilson, supt. Fax 678-4865
www.eastorange.k12.nj.us
Costley MS 500/6-8
116 Hamilton St 07017 973-266-5660
Amaila Trono, prin. Fax 266-2956
East Orange Campus 9 HS 800/9-9
34 N Walnut St 07017 973-266-5800
Dr. Nicholas Del Tufo, prin. Fax 266-2954
East Orange Campus HS 1,800/10-12
340 Prospect St 07017 973-266-7360
Dr. Kelvin Harris, prin. Fax 266-7368
Healy MS 600/6-8
116 Hamilton St 07017 973-266-5670
Janis Burchell, prin. Fax 675-5094
Sojourner Truth MS 600/6-8
116 Hamilton St 07017 973-266-5665
Vincent Stallings, prin. Fax 395-3586
Tyson JSHS 700/6-12
161 Elmwood Ave 07018 973-266-5970
Laura Trimmings, prin. Fax 414-0154

Edmonson Comm. Education Ctr. Adult
74 Halsted St 07018 973-266-5640
Arlene King, dir. Fax 266-2890

Ahlus Sunnah S 300/PK-12
215 N Oraton Pkwy 07017 973-672-4124
Umar Abdallah, prin. Fax 672-3919
Best Care Training Institute Post-Sec.
68 S Harrison St 07017 973-673-3900
Joy's School of Hair Design Post-Sec.
PO Box 2269 07019 973-673-4141

East Rutherford, Bergen, Pop. 8,960
Carlstadt-East Rutherford Regional HSD 500/9-12
120 Paterson Ave 07073 201-935-4155
Dr. Sam Feldman, supt. Fax 935-5639
Becton Regional HS 500/9-12
120 Paterson Ave 07073 201-935-3007
James Jencarelli, prin. Fax 935-5639

East Rutherford SD 400/PK-8
Grove & Uhland Sts 07073 201-804-3100
Dr. Gayle Strauss, supt. Fax 804-3131
www.erboe.net/
Faust MS 200/5-8
Grove St & Uhland St 07073 201-804-3110
Henry Srednicki Ph.D., prin. Fax 804-3131

East Windsor, Mercer, Pop. 22,353
East Windsor Regional SD
Supt. — See Hightstown
Kreps MS 1,100/6-8
5 Kent Ln 08520 609-443-7767
Virginia Kearns, prin. Fax 443-8972

Eatontown, Monmouth, Pop. 14,088
Eatontown SD 1,200/K-8
215 Broad St 07724 732-542-1310
Barbara Struble, supt. Fax 542-1700
www.eatontown.org
Memorial MS 300/7-8
7 Grant Ave 07724 732-542-5013
Ron Danielson, prin. Fax 389-1364

Edgewater Park, Burlington, Pop. 8,388
Edgewater Park Township SD 800/K-8
25 Washington Ave 08010 609-877-2122
Scott Streckbein, supt. Fax 877-3941
www.edgewaterpark.k12.nj.us
Ridgeway MS 400/5-8
300 Delanco Rd 08010 609-871-3434
Dennis Corbett, prin. Fax 871-2434

Edison, Middlesex, Pop. 99,500
Edison Township SD 13,300/K-12
312 Pierson Ave 08837 732-452-4900
Dr. Vincent Capraro, supt. Fax 452-4993
www.edison.k12.nj.us
Adams MS 800/6-8
1081 New Dover Rd 08820 732-452-2920
Daniel Donnelly, prin. Fax 452-2922
Edison HS 2,000/9-12
50 Boulevard Of Eagles 08817 732-650-5200
Joseph Kovacs, prin. Fax 650-5259
Hoover MS 800/6-8
174 Jackson Ave 08837 732-452-2940
Lou Figueroa, prin. Fax 452-2949
Jefferson MS 700/6-8
450 Division St 08817 732-650-5290
Joseph Drew, prin. Fax 652-5295
Stevens HS 2,200/9-12
855 Grove Ave 08820 732-452-2800
Gail Pawlikowski, prin. Fax 452-2863
Wilson MS 800/6-8
50 Woodrow Wilson Dr 08820 732-452-2870
Daniel Donnelly, prin. Fax 452-2876

Middlesex County Vocational SD
Supt. — See East Brunswick
Academy of Science and Technology Vo/Tech
100 Technology Dr 08837 732-452-2600
Glenn Methner, prin. Fax 906-8421

Bishop George Ahr HS 900/9-12
1 Tingley Ln 08820 732-549-1108
Sr. Donna Trukowski, prin. Fax 494-2229
Cittone Institute Post-Sec.
1697 Oak Tree Rd 08820 732-548-8798
Middlesex County College Post-Sec.
2600 Woodbridge Ave 08837 732-548-6000
Rabbi Jacob Joseph School Post-Sec.
1 Plainfield Ave 08817 732-985-6533
Rabbi Jacob Joseph S 100/9-12
1 Plainfield Ave 08817 732-985-6533
Yitzchok Weintraub, dir. Fax 985-6553
Wardlaw-Hartridge S 400/PK-12
1295 Inman Ave 08820 908-754-1882
Andrew Webster, hdmstr. Fax 754-9678

Egg Harbor City, Atlantic, Pop. 4,497
Egg Harbor City SD 500/PK-8
527 Philadelphia Ave 08215 609-965-1034
John Gilly, supt. Fax 965-6719
www.ehcs.k12.nj.us
Rittenberg MS 200/5-8
528 Philadelphia Ave 08215 609-965-1034
Jack Griffith, prin. Fax 965-4742

Pilgrim Academy 500/K-12
PO Box 322 08215 609-965-2866
Dr. Hubert Hartzler, hdmstr. Fax 965-3379

Egg Harbor Township, Atlantic
Egg Harbor Township SD
Supt. — See Pleasantville
Egg Harbor Township HS 1,900/9-12
24 High School Dr 08234 609-653-0100
Kim Gruccio, prin. Fax 927-8844
Egg Harbor Township MS 1,100/7-8
4034 Fernwood Ave 08234 609-383-3355
Mildred Peretti, prin. Fax 383-0628

Atlantic Christian S 500/PK-12
391 Zion Rd 08234 609-653-1199
Joseph Sanelli, admin. Fax 653-1435
Star Technical Institute Post-Sec.
3003 Englsh Crk Ave #212 08234 609-407-2999
Trocki Hebrew Academy 300/PK-12
6814 Black Horse Pike 08234 609-383-8484
Dr. Cyla Trocki-Videll, admin. Fax 383-1114

Elberon, See Long Branch

Ilan HS 50/9-12
82 Norwood Ave 07740 732-870-2800
Raizi Chechik, hdmstr. Fax 870-0885

Elizabeth, Union, Pop. 125,809
Elizabeth SD 19,100/PK-12
500 N Broad St 07208 908-436-5000
Pablo Munoz, supt. Fax 436-5037
www.elizabeth.k12.nj.us
Battin MS 500/6-8
300 S Broad St 07202 908-436-6300
Debra DeMattia, prin. Fax 436-6293
Cleveland MS 500/6-8
436 1st Ave 07206 908-436-6030
James Carter, prin. Fax 436-6012
Elizabeth HS 5,100/9-12
600 Pearl St 07202 908-436-6868
Ann Marie Remus, prin. Fax 436-6850
Hamilton MS 800/6-8
310 Cherry St 07208 908-436-6100
Marianela Martin, prin. Fax 436-6082
Holmes MS 500/6-8
436 1st Ave 07206 908-436-6070
Manuel Gonzalez, prin. Fax 436-6052
McAuliffe MS 500/6-8
300 S Broad St 07202 908-436-6340
Berthenia Harmon, prin. Fax 436-6328

Benedictine Academy 200/9-12
840 N Broad St 07208 908-352-0670
Sr. Germaine Fritz, pres. Fax 352-0698
Bruriah HS for Girls 400/7-12
35 North Ave 07208 908-355-4850
Chaya Newman, prin. Fax 351-5420
Drake College of Business Post-Sec.
125 Broad St 07201 908-352-5509
Elizabeth General Medical Center School Post-Sec.
925 E Jersey St 07201 908-965-7390
Jewish Educational Center 1,000/PK-12
330 Elmora Ave 07208 908-355-4850
Rav Elazar Teitz, dean Fax 355-9554
St. Mary of the Assumption HS 300/9-12
237 S Broad St 07202 908-352-4350
Janet Malko, prin. Fax 352-2359
St. Patrick Academy 100/5-8
227 Court St 07206 908-351-2188
Joseph Picaro, prin. Fax 351-6086
St. Patrick HS 200/9-12
221 Court St 07206 908-353-5220
Joseph Picaro, prin. Fax 629-1123
Trinity Christian Academy 200/PK-12
417 Pennington St 07202 908-352-9725
Union County College Post-Sec.
12 W Jersey St 07201 908-965-6000

Elmwood Park, Bergen, Pop. 18,905
Elmwood Park SD 2,100/K-12
465 Boulevard Ste 1 07407 201-796-8700
Joseph Casapulla, supt. Fax 703-9337
www.epps.org/
Memorial HS 600/9-12
375 River Dr 07407 201-796-8700
Richard Tomko, prin. Fax 797-1405
Memorial MS 500/6-8
375 River Dr 07407 201-794-2823
Lawrence DeSantis, prin. Fax 791-3438

Elwood, Atlantic, Pop. 1,487
Mullica Township SD 800/K-8
PO Box 318 08217 609-561-3868
Richard Goldberg, supt. Fax 561-7133
www.mullica.k12.nj.us
Mullica Township MS 400/5-8
PO Box 318 08217 609-561-3868
Brenda Harring-Marro, prin. Fax 561-7133

Emerson, Bergen, Pop. 7,334
Emerson SD 1,100/PK-12
131 Main St 07630 201-599-4178
Dr. Vincent Taffaro, supt. Fax 599-4160
www.emerson.k12.nj.us
Emerson JSHS 500/7-12
131 Main St 07630 201-262-4447
Dr. Paula Valenti, prin. Fax 262-1041

Englewood, Bergen, Pop. 26,207
Englewood CSD 2,400/PK-12
12 Tenafly Rd 07631 201-862-6000
Carol Lisa, supt. Fax 569-6099
www.epsd.org
Dismus MS 500/6-8
325 Tryon Ave 07631 201-862-6025
Peter Elbert, prin. Fax 833-9103
Liberty S 9-12
12 Tenafly Rd 07631 201-862-6249
Joseph Bell, prin. Fax 871-5931
Morrow HS 900/9-12
274 Knickerbocker Rd 07631 201-862-6049
James Smith, prin. Fax 833-9620

Dwight-Englewood S 1,000/PK-12
315 E Palisade Ave 07631 201-569-9500
Dr. Rodney DeJarnett, hdmstr. Fax 568-9451
Englewood Hospital & Medical Center Post-Sec.
350 Engle St 07631 201-894-3002
Yeshiva Ohr Simcha of Englewood 100/9-12
101 W Forest Ave 07631 201-816-1800
Rabbi Yosef Strassfeld, prin. Fax 567-6013

Englewood Cliffs, Bergen, Pop. 5,738
Englewood Cliffs SD 400/K-8
143 Charlotte Pl 07632 201-567-7292
Philomena Pezzano Ed.D., supt. Fax 567-2738
www.englewoodcliffs.org
Upper S 300/3-8
143 Charlotte Pl 07632 201-567-6151
Joseph Spano, prin. Fax 541-8672

St. Peter's College 07632 Post-Sec.
201-568-7730

Englishtown, Monmouth, Pop. 1,790
Freehold Regional HSD 11,000/9-12
11 Pine St 07726 732-792-7300
Dr. James Wasser, supt. Fax 446-9126
www.frhsd.com
Other Schools – See Colts Neck, Farmingdale, Freehold, Manalapan, Marlboro

Manalapan-Englishtown Regional SD 4,800/K-8
54 Main St 07726 732-786-2500
Maureen Lally Ed.D., supt. Fax 786-2542
www.mers.k12.nj.us
Other Schools – See Manalapan

Erial, Camden, Pop. 2,500
Black Horse Pike Regional SD
Supt. — See Blackwood
Timber Creek Regional HS 1,400/9-12
501 Jarvis Rd 08081 856-232-9703
Mae Robinson, prin. Fax 232-5267

Divers Academy International Post-Sec.
1500 Liberty Pl 08081 800-238-3483

Ewing, Mercer, Pop. 36,000
Ewing Township SD 3,900/K-12
1331 Lower Ferry Rd 08618 609-538-9800
Raymond Broach Ed.D., supt. Fax 538-0041
www.ewing.k12.nj.us
Ewing HS 1,200/9-12
900 Parkway Ave 08618 609-538-9800
Dr. Rodney Logan, prin. Fax 882-8172
Fisher MS 900/6-8
1325 Lower Ferry Rd 08618 609-538-9800
Barbara Brower, prin. Fax 637-9753

College of New Jersey Post-Sec.
PO Box 7718 08628 609-771-1855
Mercer Christian Academy 200/PK-12
11 Buttonwood Dr 08638 609-882-7300
Gregg Garman, hdmstr. Fax 883-2816
Villa Victoria Academy - Upper 100/7-12
376 W Upper Ferry Rd 08628 609-882-1700
Sr. Mary Ann Gecina, prin. Fax 882-8421

Fairfield, Essex, Pop. 7,615

StenoTech Career Institute Post-Sec.
20 Just Rd 07004 973-882-4875
The Institute for Health Education Post-Sec.
7 Spielman Rd 07004 973-808-1666

Fair Haven, Monmouth, Pop. 5,899
Fair Haven Borough SD 900/PK-8
224 Hance Rd 07704 732-747-2294
William Presutti, supt. Fax 747-7441
www.fairhaven.edu
Knollwood MS 600/4-8
224 Hance Rd 07704 732-747-0320
Thomas Famulary, prin. Fax 747-7441

Fair Lawn, Bergen, Pop. 31,408
Fair Lawn SD 4,500/K-12
37-01 Fair Lawn Ave 07410 201-794-5500
Bruce Watson, supt. Fax 797-9296
www.fairlawnschools.org/
Fair Lawn HS 1,500/9-12
14-00 Berdan Ave 07410 201-794-5455
James Marcella, prin. Fax 794-8107
Jefferson MS 700/6-8
35-01 Morlot Ave 07410 201-703-2240
Dr. John Dunay, prin. Fax 475-9185
Memorial MS 400/6-8
12-00 1st St 07410 201-794-5470
John Immerman, prin. Fax 703-2237

Artistic Academy of Hair Design Post-Sec.
21 Broadway 07410 201-794-3502

Farmingdale, Monmouth, Pop. 1,572
Freehold Regional HSD
Supt. — See Englishtown
Howell HS 1,800/9-12
405 Squankum Yellowbrook Rd 07727 732-919-2131
Zina Duerbig, prin. Fax 919-1964

Howell Township SD 6,900/K-8
200 Squankum Yellowbrook Rd 07727 732-751-2480
Dr. Enid Golden, supt. Fax 919-1060
www.howell.k12.nj.us
Howell Township MS North 900/6-8
501 Squankum Yellowbrook Rd 07727 732-919-0095
Joe Isola, prin. Fax 919-1008
Other Schools – See Freehold, Howell

Flanders, Morris, Pop. 1,200
Mt. Olive Township SD
Supt. — See Budd Lake
Mt. Olive HS 1,300/9-12
18 Corey Rd 07836 973-927-2208
Kevin Stansberry, prin. Fax 927-2204

Flemington, Hunterdon, Pop. 4,171
Flemington-Raritan Regional SD 2,200/K-8
50 Court St 08822 908-284-7561
Jack Farr, supt. Fax 284-7514
www.frsd.k12.nj.us/
Case MS, 301 Case Blvd 08822 7-8
Nancy Gartenberg, prin. 908-284-5101

Hunterdon Central Regional HSD 2,700/9-12
84 State Route 31 08822 908-284-7135
Dr. LeRoy Seitz, supt. Fax 284-7138
www.hcrhs.k12.nj.us
Hunterdon Central Regional HS 2,700/9-12
84 State Route 31 08822 908-284-7155
Peter Karycki, prin. Fax 284-7313

Hunterdon County Vocational SD
8 Bartles Corner Rd Ste 2 08822 908-788-1119
Richard Van Gulik, supt. Fax 788-1457
www.hcpolytech.org/
Hunterdon County Polytech S Vo/Tech
8 Bartles Corner Rd Ste 2 08822 908-788-1119
Richard Van Gulik, prin.
Hunterdon County Vocational S Vo/Tech
84 State Route 31 08822 908-284-1444
Dan Kerr, prin. Fax 284-9824
Hunterdon County Vocational S - Bartles Vo/Tech
8 Bartles Corner Rd 08822 908-806-3855
Dan Kerr, prin.

Hunterdon Christian Academy 100/K-12
116 Main St 08822 908-782-9700
Shannon Nusser, supt. Fax 782-4857

Florence, Burlington, Pop. 8,564
Florence Township SD 1,500/K-12
201 Cedar St 08518 609-499-4600
Dr. Louis G. Talarico, supt. Fax 499-9679
www.florence.k12.nj.us
Florence Township Memorial HS 400/9-12
1050 Cedar Ln 08518 609-499-4600
Stephen Falcone, prin. Fax 499-3424
Florence Township MS 400/6-8
250 Pine St 08518 609-499-4647
Stephen Falcone, prin. Fax 499-8356

Florham Park, Morris, Pop. 12,626
Florham Park SD 1,000/K-8
PO Box 39 07932 973-822-3880
Dr. William Ronzitti, supt. Fax 822-0716
www.fpks.org
Ridgedale MS 300/6-8
71 Ridgedale Ave 07932 973-822-3855
Mark Majeski, prin. Fax 822-7963

Fords, Middlesex, Pop. 14,392
Woodbridge Township SD
Supt. — See Woodbridge
Fords MS, 100 Fanning St 08863 600/6-8
Cynthia Lagunovich, prin. 732-417-5400

Forked River, Ocean, Pop. 4,243
Lacey Township SD
Supt. — See Lanoka Harbor
Lacey Township MS 600/6-8
660 Denton Ave 08731 609-242-2100
V. Clark, prin. Fax 242-2114

Fort Lee, Bergen, Pop. 37,175
Fort Lee SD 3,400/K-12
255 Whiteman St 07024 201-585-4610
Joanne Calabro, supt. Fax 585-0691
www.fortlee-boe.net
Cole MS 600/7-8
467 Stillwell Ave 07024 201-585-4660
Rosemarie Giacomelli, prin. Fax 585-1688
Fort Lee HS 1,100/9-12
3000 Lemoine Ave 07024 201-585-4675
Jay Berman, prin. Fax 585-2296

Franklin Lakes, Bergen, Pop. 11,302
Franklin Lakes SD 1,400/K-8
490 Pulis Ave 07417 201-891-1856
Roger Bayersdorfer, supt. Fax 891-9333
www.franklinlakes.k12.nj.us/
Franklin Avenue MS 500/6-8
755 Franklin Ave 07417 201-891-0202
Georgiann Gongora, prin. Fax 848-5190

Ramapo Indian Hills Regional HSD
Supt. — See Oakland
Ramapo HS 1,200/9-12
331 George St 07417 201-891-1500
Michael Jordan, prin. Fax 891-6844

Franklinville, Gloucester
Delsea Regional SD 1,800/7-12
PO Box 405 08322 856-694-0100
Frank Borelli, supt. Fax 694-4417
www.delsea.k12.nj.us
Delsea Regional HS 1,200/9-12
PO Box 405 08322 856-694-0100
Joseph Sottosanti, prin. Fax 694-2046
Delsea Regional MS 600/7-8
PO Box 405 08322 856-694-0100
Piera Gravenor, prin. Fax 694-4417

Freehold, Monmouth, Pop. 11,439
Freehold Borough SD 1,300/PK-8
280 Park Ave 07728 732-761-2100
Philip Meara, supt. Fax 462-8954
www.freeholdboro.k12.nj.us
Freehold IS 400/6-8
280 Park Ave 07728 732-761-2156
Nelson Ribon, prin. Fax 761-2181

Freehold Regional HSD
Supt. — See Englishtown
Freehold Borough HS 1,200/9-12
2 Robertsville Rd 07728 732-431-8360
Linda Jewell, prin. Fax 577-8228
Freehold Township HS 2,000/9-12
281 Elton Adelphia Rd 07728 732-431-8460
Elizabeth Higley, prin. Fax 780-5314
Freehold Evening HS Adult
2 Robertsville Rd 07728 732-431-8589
Sam Grove, prin.

Freehold Township SD 4,300/PK-8
384 W Main St 07728 732-866-8400
William Setaro Ed.D., supt. Fax 761-1809
www.freeholdtwp.k12.nj.us/
Barkalow MS 800/6-8
498 Stillwells Corner Rd 07728 732-431-4403
John Soviero, prin. Fax 294-5560
Eisenhower MS 800/6-8
279 Burlington Rd 07728 732-431-3910
Dianne Brethauer, prin. Fax 294-7180

Howell Township SD
Supt. — See Farmingdale
Memorial MS 500/6-8
458 Adelphia Rd 07728 732-919-1085
Chuck Welsh, prin. Fax 751-0325

Monmouth County Vocational SD
PO Box 5033 07728 732-431-7942
Brian McAndrew Ed.D., supt. Fax 409-6736
www.mcvsd.org
Biotechnology HS Vo/Tech
5000 Kozloski Rd 07728 732-431-6443
Linda Eno, prin. Fax 409-6736
Freehold Vocational S Vo/Tech
21 Robertsville Rd 07728 732-462-7570
James Johnson, prin. Fax 294-0569
Monmouth County Career Center Vo/Tech
1000 Kozloski Rd 07728 732-431-3773
Anthony Schaible, prin. Fax 409-7292
Other Schools – See Aberdeen, Asbury Park, Hazlet, Highlands, Keyport, Lincroft, Long Branch, Middletown, Neptune, Wall

Frenchtown, Hunterdon, Pop. 1,503
Delaware Valley Regional HSD 900/9-12
19 Senator Stout Rd 08825 908-996-2131
Robert Walsh, supt. Fax 996-4527
www.dvrhs.org

Delaware Valley Regional HS 900/9-12
19 Senator Stout Rd 08825 908-996-2131
Brian Fogelson, prin. Fax 996-6653

Galloway, Atlantic
Galloway Township SD 3,500/K-8
101 S Reeds Rd 08205 609-748-1250
Douglas Groff, supt. Fax 748-1796
www.gtps.k12.nj.us
Galloway Township MS 900/7-8
100 S Reeds Rd 08205 609-748-1250
Dr. Donald Gross, prin.

Greater Egg Harbor Regional HSD
Supt. — See Mays Landing
Absegami HS 2,200/9-12
201 S Wrangleboro Rd 08205 609-652-1372
Raymond Dolton, prin. Fax 652-0139

Garfield, Bergen, Pop. 29,772
Garfield SD 4,200/PK-12
125 Outwater Ln 07026 973-340-5000
Nicholas Perrapato, supt. Fax 340-4620
www.garfield.k12.nj.us/
Garfield HS 1,300/9-12
500 Palisade Ave 07026 973-340-5010
Doug Petrie, prin. Fax 546-8430
Jefferson MS 600/7-8
62 Alpine St 07026 973-340-5039
Marilyn Martorano, prin. Fax 340-1963

Gibbstown, Gloucester, Pop. 3,902
Greenwich Township SD 500/PK-8
415 Swedesboro Rd 08027 856-224-4920
Francine Marteski Ed.D., supt. Fax 224-5761
www.greenwich.k12.nj.us
Nehaunsey MS 200/5-8
415 Swedesboro Rd 08027 856-224-4920
Suzanne Gibson, prin. Fax 224-5765

Gillette, Morris
Long Hill Township SD 1,100/K-8
759 Valley Rd 07933 908-647-1200
Arthur DiBenedetto, supt. Fax 647-7818
www.longhill.org
Other Schools – See Stirling

Gladstone, Somerset, Pop. 2,086

Gill St. Bernard's S 600/PK-12
PO Box 604 07934 908-234-1611
Sidney Rowell, hdmstr. Fax 234-1715
Montgomery Academy 100/1-12
PO Box 710 07934 908-234-2840
Marcie Fiorentino, prin. Fax 234-2817

Glassboro, Gloucester, Pop. 19,290
Glassboro SD 2,300/PK-12
560 Joseph Bowe Memorial Bl 08028 856-881-0123
Fax 881-0884
www.glassboro.k12.nj.us
Glassboro HS 700/9-12
550 Bowe Blvd 08028 856-881-2200
Santina Haldeman, prin. Fax 307-1189
Glassboro IS 400/7-8
202 Delsea Dr N 08028 856-881-2313
Marianne Carver, prin. Fax 881-3751

Rowan University Post-Sec.
201 Mullica Hill Rd 08028 856-256-4000

Glen Gardner, Hunterdon, Pop. 1,999
North Hunterdon/Vorhees Regional HSD
Supt. — See Annandale
Voorhees HS 1,200/9-12
256 County Road 513 08826 908-638-6116
David Steffan, prin. Fax 638-8689

Glen Ridge, Essex, Pop. 7,020
Glen Ridge SD 1,800/PK-12
12 High St 07028 973-429-8302
Daniel Fishbein Ed.D., supt. Fax 429-5750
www.glenridge.org
Glen Ridge HS 700/7-12
200 Ridgewood Ave 07028 973-429-8303
Kenneth Rota, prin. Fax 429-3531

Glen Rock, Bergen, Pop. 11,457
Glen Rock SD 2,400/K-12
620 Harristown Rd 07452 201-445-7700
George Connelly, supt. Fax 389-5019
www.glenrocknj.org/
Glen Rock HS 700/9-12
600 Harristown Rd 07452 201-445-7700
James McCarthy, prin. Fax 389-5015
Glen Rock MS 600/6-8
400 Hamilton Ave 07452 201-445-7700
Edward Thompson, prin. Fax 389-5042

Gloucester City, Camden, Pop. 11,582
Gloucester City SD 2,000/PK-12
520 Cumberland St 08030 856-456-9394
Dr. Mary Stansky, supt. Fax 742-8815
www.gcsd.k12.nj.us
Gloucester City JSHS 800/7-12
1300 Market St 08030 856-456-7000
Jack Don, prin. Fax 456-2348
Gloucester City Adult HS Adult
520 Cumberland St 08030 856-456-3374
George Henry, prin. Fax 742-8570

Gloucester Catholic HS 800/9-12
333 Ridgeway St 08030 856-456-4400
John Colman, prin. Fax 456-0506
P.B. Cosmetology Education Centre Post-Sec.
110 Monmouth St 08030 856-456-4927

Great Meadows, Warren, Pop. 1,108
Great Meadows Regional SD 1,000/K-8
PO Box 74 07838 908-637-6576
Jason Bing, supt. Fax 637-6356
www.gmrsd.com
Great Meadows Regional MS 400/6-8
273 US Highway 46 07838 908-637-4584
Mark Ippolito, prin. Fax 637-4492

Green Brook, Somerset
Green Brook Township SD 900/K-8
132 Jefferson Ave 08812 732-968-1171
Stephanie Bilenker, supt. Fax 968-1869
www.gbtps.org
Green Brook MS 500/4-8
132 Jefferson Ave 08812 732-968-1051
Linda Pollard, prin. Fax 752-1086

Hackensack, Bergen, Pop. 43,735
Bergen County Vocational SD
Supt. — See Paramus
Bergen County Academies Vo/Tech
200 Hackensack Ave 07601 201-343-6000
Patricia Cosgrove, prin. Fax 996-6955

Hackensack SD 5,700/PK-12
355 State St 07601 201-646-7830
Dr. Joseph Montesano, supt. Fax 646-7827
www.hackensackelementary.org
Hackensack HS 2,100/9-12
135 1st St 07601 201-646-7900
Mark Porto, prin. Fax 646-7922
Hackensack MS 800/7-8
360 Union St 07601 201-646-7842
Andrea Parchment, prin. Fax 646-7840

Academy of Massage Therapy Post-Sec.
321 Main St 07601 201-568-3220
American Business Academy Post-Sec.
66 Moore St 07601 201-488-9400
Fairleigh Dickinson University Post-Sec.
150 Kotte Pl 07601 201-692-2675
Hackensack Univ Medical Center Post-Sec.
30 Prospect Ave 07601 201-996-2000
Parisian Academy Post-Sec.
362 State St 07601 201-487-2203

Hackettstown, Warren, Pop. 9,375
Hackettstown SD 1,900/K-12
PO Box 465 07840 908-850-6500
Robert Gratz, supt. Fax 850-4985
www.hackettstown.org
Hackettstown HS 1,000/9-12
701 Warren St 07840 908-852-8150
Brian Purzak, prin. Fax 852-6214
Hackettstown MS 400/5-8
500 Washington St 07840 908-852-8554
Marie Griffin, prin. Fax 850-6544

Centenary College Post-Sec.
400 Jefferson St 07840 908-852-1400

Haddonfield, Camden, Pop. 11,591
Haddonfield Borough SD 2,500/K-12
1 Lincoln Ave 08033 856-429-4130
Joseph O'Brien Ed.D., supt. Fax 354-2179
www.haddonfield.k12.nj.us
Haddonfield Memorial HS 900/9-12
401 Kings Hwy E 08033 856-429-3960
Priscilla Vimislik, prin. Fax 795-8910
Haddonfield MS 600/6-8
5 Lincoln Ave 08033 856-429-5851
Noah Tennant, prin. Fax 429-2006

Pope Paul VI HS 1,000/9-12
901 Hopkins Rd Ste B 08033 856-858-4900
Sr. Marianne McCann, prin. Fax 858-6832

Haddon Heights, Camden, Pop. 7,427
Haddon Heights SD 1,300/K-12
300 2nd Ave 08035 856-547-1412
Dr. Nancy Hacker, supt. Fax 547-3868
hhsd.k12.nj.us
Haddon Heights JSHS 800/7-12
301 2nd Ave 08035 856-547-1920
David Sandowich, prin. Fax 547-6808

Baptist S 400/K-12
Third & Station Ave 08035 856-547-2996
Lynn Conahan, admin. Fax 547-6584

Haledon, Passaic, Pop. 8,398
Passaic County Manchester Regional HSD 800/9-12
70 Church St 07508 973-389-2820
Dr. Raymond Kwak, supt. Fax 956-8805
www.mrhs.net
Manchester Regional HS 800/9-12
70 Church St 07508 973-389-2820
Richard Ney, prin. Fax 956-8805

Hamburg, Sussex, Pop. 3,567
Hardyston Township SD 800/PK-8
183 Wheatsworth Rd 07419 973-823-7000
Dennis Tobin, supt. Fax 823-7011
www.htps.org
Hardyston MS 300/6-8
183 Wheatsworth Rd 07419 973-823-7000
Dennis Tobin, prin. Fax 823-7011

Wallkill Valley Regional SD 800/9-12
10 Grumm Rd 07419 973-827-4100
Joseph DiPasquale, supt. Fax 827-8318
www.wallkill.k12.nj.us
Wallkill Valley Regional HS 800/9-12
10 Grumm Rd 07419 973-827-4100
Joseph DiPasquale, prin. Fax 827-8318

Hamilton, Mercer
Hamilton Township SD 12,700/K-12
90 Park Ave 08690 609-631-4100
Neil Bencivengo, supt. Fax 631-4103
www.hamilton.k12.nj.us
Crockett MS 900/6-8
2631 Kuser Rd 08691 609-631-4149
Barbara Panfili, prin. Fax 631-4116
Grice MS 1,000/6-8
901 Whitehorse Hamilton Sq 08610 609-631-4152
David Innocenzi, prin. Fax 631-4119
Hamilton East-Steinert HS 1,500/9-12
2900 Klockner Rd 08690 609-631-4150
Michael Gilbert, prin. Fax 631-4117
Hamilton North-Nottingham HS 1,300/9-12
1055 Klockner Rd 08619 609-631-4161
Neal Campeas, prin. Fax 631-4129
Hamilton West-Watson HS 1,300/9-12
2720 S Clinton Ave 08610 609-631-4168
David McWilliam, prin. Fax 631-4137
Reynolds MS 1,200/6-8
2145 Yrdvll Hamilton Squ Rd 08690 609-631-4162
Joseph Slavin, prin. Fax 631-4130
Accredited Evening HS Adult
90 Park Ave 08690 609-890-3600
Dr. Lois Braender, prin. Fax 631-4106

Trenton Catholic Academy 300/9-12
175 Leonard Ave 08610 609-586-3705
James Foley, prin. Fax 586-6584

Hammonton, Atlantic, Pop. 13,585
Hammonton SD 3,200/PK-12
PO Box 631 08037 609-567-7000
Mary Lou DeFrancisco, supt. Fax 561-3567
www.hammontonps.org/
Hammonton HS 1,300/9-12
566 Old Forks Rd 08037 609-567-7000
James Donoghue, prin. Fax 567-5985
Hammonton MS 600/7-8
75 N Liberty St 08037 609-567-7007
Gene Miller, prin. Fax 561-3974

St. Joseph HS 9-12
328 Vine St 08037 609-561-8700
Jeffrey Taylor, prin. Fax 561-8701

Hampton, Hunterdon, Pop. 1,608
Union Township SD 600/PK-8
165 Perryville Rd 08827 908-735-5511
Dr. Jeffrey Bender, supt. Fax 735-6657
www.uniontwpschool.org
Union Township MS 300/5-8
165 Perryville Rd 08827 908-735-5511
Frances Suchovic, prin. Fax 735-6657

Harrison, Hudson, Pop. 14,060
Harrison SD, 430 William St 07029 1,900/K-12
Anthony Comprelli, supt. 973-483-4627
www.harrison.k12.nj.us
Harrison HS 700/9-12
1 N 5th St 07029 973-482-5050
Ronald Shields, prin. Fax 482-3625
Washington MS 400/6-8
223 Hamilton St 07029 973-483-2285
Alan Doffont, prin.

Hasbrouck Heights, Bergen, Pop. 11,643
Hasbrouck Heights SD 1,500/K-12
379 Boulevard 07604 201-288-6150
Joseph Luongo, supt. Fax 288-0289
www.hhschools.org
Hasbrouck Heights HS 500/9-12
365 Boulevard 07604 201-288-3971
Peter O'Hare, prin. Fax 288-2083
Hasbrouck Heights MS 400/6-8
365 Boulevard 07604 201-393-8190
Edward Bolcar, prin. Fax 288-2083

Hawthorne, Passaic, Pop. 18,268
Hawthorne SD 2,200/PK-12
PO Box 2 07507 973-427-1300
Dr. Richard Spirito, supt. Fax 427-1757
www.hawthorne.k12.nj.us
Hawthorne HS 700/9-12
160 Parmelee Ave 07506 973-423-6415
Dr. David Browne, prin. Fax 423-6422
Lincoln MS 500/6-8
230 Hawthorne Ave 07506 973-423-6460
Douglas Alexander, prin. Fax 427-5393

Hawthorne Christian Academy 500/K-12
2000 State Rt 208 07506 973-423-3331
Donald J.Klingen, hdmstr. Fax 238-1718
Roman Academy of Beauty Culture Post-Sec.
431 Lafayette Ave 07506 973-423-2223

Hazlet, Monmouth, Pop. 21,976
Hazlet Township SD 3,300/K-12
421 Middle Rd 07730 732-264-8402
Renae LaPrete, supt. Fax 264-1599
www.hazlet.org
Hazlet MS 600/7-8
1639 Union Ave 07730 732-264-0940
John DeGenito, prin. Fax 264-0571
Raritan HS 1,000/9-12
419 Middle Rd 07730 732-264-8411
Colleen Rafter, prin. Fax 264-3214

Monmouth County Vocational SD
Supt. — See Freehold
Hazlet Vocational S Vo/Tech
417 Middle Rd 07730 732-264-4995
James Johnson, prin. Fax 264-3846

Hibernia, Morris, Pop. 200
Rockaway Township SD 2,700/K-8
PO Box 500 07842 973-627-8200
Dr. Gary Vita, supt. Fax 627-7968
www.morris.k12.nj.us/rocktwp
Other Schools – See Rockaway

High Bridge, Hunterdon, Pop. 3,770
High Bridge SD 400/K-8
50 Thomas St 08829 908-638-4103
Dr. Patricia Ash, supt. Fax 638-4211
www.hbschools.org
High Bridge MS 100/6-8
50 Thomas St 08829 908-638-4101
Patricia Ash, prin. Fax 638-4211

Highland Park, Middlesex, Pop. 14,268
Highland Park SD 1,500/PK-12
435 Mansfield St 08904 732-572-6990
David Ottaviano, supt. Fax 393-1174
www.highlandpark.k12.nj.us
Highland Park HS 500/9-12
102 N 5th Ave 08904 732-572-2400
Frederick Williams, prin. Fax 819-7041
Highland Park MS 200/7-8
102 N 5th Ave 08904 732-572-2400
Richard Horowitz, prin. Fax 819-7041

Highlands, Monmouth, Pop. 4,998
Henry Hudson Regional SD 400/7-12
1 Grand Tour 07732 732-872-0900
Dr. Kathryn Fedina, supt. Fax 708-1409
www.henryhudsonreg.k12.nj.us/
Hudson Regional JSHS 400/7-12
1 Grand Tour 07732 732-872-0900
Dr. Kathryn Fedina, prin. Fax 708-1409

Monmouth County Vocational SD
Supt. — See Freehold
Marine Academy of Science & Technology Vo/Tech
Building 305 07732 732-291-0995
Paul Christopher, prin. Fax 291-9367

Hightstown, Mercer, Pop. 5,293
East Windsor Regional SD 4,600/PK-12
25A Leshin Ln 08520 609-443-7717
Ronald Bolandi, supt. Fax 443-8040
www.eastwindsorregionalschools.com/
Hightstown HS 1,300/9-12
25 Leshin Ln 08520 609-443-7738
Alix Arvizu, prin. Fax 443-7880
Other Schools – See East Windsor

Peddie S 500/9-12
PO Box A 08520 609-490-7500
John Green, hdmstr. Fax 944-7912

Hillsborough, Somerset
Hillsborough Township SD 7,400/PK-12
379 S Branch Rd 08844 908-369-0030
Karen Lake Ed.D., supt. Fax 369-8286
www.hillsborough.k12.nj.us
Hillsborough HS 2,300/9-12
466 Raider Blvd 08844 908-874-4200
Karen Bingert, prin. Fax 874-3762
Hillsborough MS 1,200/6-8
260 Triangle Rd 08844 908-874-3420
Joseph Trybulski, prin. Fax 874-3492

Hillsdale, Bergen, Pop. 10,089
Hillsdale SD 1,300/K-8
32 Ruckman Rd 07642 201-664-0282
Anthony DeNorchia, supt. Fax 664-9049
www.hillsdaleschools.com
White MS 600/5-8
120 Magnolia Ave 07642 201-664-0286
Noreen Hajinlian, prin. Fax 664-2715

Pascack Valley Regional HSD
Supt. — See Montvale
Pascack Valley HS 1,000/9-12
200 Piermont Ave 07642 201-358-7060
Barbara Sapienza, prin. Fax 358-7060

Hillside, Union, Pop. 21,044
Hillside Township SD 3,100/K-12
195 Virginia St 07205 908-352-7664
Raymond Bandlow Ph.D., supt. Fax 282-5831
www.hillsidek12.org
Hillside HS 1,000/9-12
1085 Liberty Ave 07205 908-352-7664
Eva Marie Raleigh, prin. Fax 352-4246
Krumbiegel MS 500/7-8
145 Hillside Ave 07205 908-352-7664
Martin Dickerson, prin. Fax 282-5840

Hoboken, Hudson, Pop. 39,900
Hoboken SD, 1115 Clinton St 07030 1,800/PK-12
Patrick Gagliardi, supt. 201-356-3600
www.hoboken.k12.nj.us
Brandt MS 200/7-8
215 9th St 07030 201-356-3690
Elizabeth Falco, prin. Fax 356-3697
Hoboken HS 600/9-12
900 Clinton St 07030 201-356-3700
Patrick Gagliardi, prin. Fax 356-3704

Hudson S 200/5-12
601 Park Ave 07030 201-659-8335
Suellen Newman, dir. Fax 222-3669
Stevens Institute of Technology Post-Sec.
Castle Point on Hudson 07030 201-216-5100

Holmdel, Monmouth
Holmdel Township SD 3,500/K-12
PO Box 407 07733 732-946-1800
Barbara Duncan, supt. Fax 946-1875
www.holmdelschools.org
Holmdel HS 1,200/9-12
36 Crawfords Corner Rd 07733 732-946-1832
Fax 946-0093
Satz IS 600/7-8
24 Crawfords Corner Rd 07733 732-946-1808
Arthur Howard, prin. Fax 834-0089

St. John Vianney HS 1,000/9-12
540 Line Rd 07733 732-739-0800
Joseph Deroba, prin. Fax 739-0824

Hopatcong, Sussex, Pop. 16,001
Hopatcong Borough SD 2,400/K-12
PO Box 1029 07843 973-398-8801
Dr. Wayne Threlkeld, supt. Fax 398-1961
www.hopatcongschools.org/
Hopatcong HS 800/9-12
PO Box 1029 07843 973-398-8803
Emil Binotto, prin. Fax 398-9048
Hopatcong MS 600/6-8
PO Box 1029 07843 973-398-8804
Theresa Williams, prin. Fax 398-4184

Howell, Monmouth
Howell Township SD
Supt. — See Farmingdale
Howell Township MS South 1,100/6-8
1 Kuzminski Way 07731 732-836-1327
Thomas Feaster, prin. Fax 836-0698

Monmouth Academy 200/K-12
152 Lanes Mill Rd 07731 732-364-2812
Barbara Anastos, dir. Fax 364-4004

Irvington, Essex, Pop. 60,600
Irvington Township SD 7,400/PK-12
1 University Pl 07111 973-399-6800
Ethel Davion, supt. Fax 372-3724
www.irvington.k12.nj.us
Irvington HS 1,900/9-12
1253 Clinton Ave 07111 973-399-6899
Dr. Neely Hackett, prin. Fax 371-7045
Union Avenue MS 700/6-8
427 Union Ave 07111 973-399-6885
Ron Bligh, prin. Fax 371-0957
University MS 700/6-8
255 Myrtle Ave 07111 973-399-6879
Theodore Boler, prin. Fax 351-1025
Irvington Adult HS Adult
1 University Pl 07111 973-399-1083

Iselin, Middlesex, Pop. 16,141
Woodbridge Township SD
Supt. — See Woodbridge
Iselin MS, 900 Woodruff St 08830 700/6-8
Jacqueline Miller, prin. 732-602-8450

Kennedy Memorial HS 1,000/9-12
200 Washington Ave 08830 732-602-8650
Michael Cilento, prin. Fax 634-1112

Ultrasound Diagnostic School Post-Sec.
675 US Route 1 2nd Flr 08830 732-634-1131

Jackson, Ocean, Pop. 800
Jackson Township SD 9,200/K-12
151 Don Connor Blvd 08527 732-833-4600
Thomas Gialanella, supt. Fax 833-4609
www.jacksonsd.org
Goetz MS 1,200/6-8
835 Patterson Rd 08527 732-833-4610
Faith Lessig, prin. Fax 833-4749
Jackson Liberty HS 9-12
125 N Hope Chapel Rd 08527 732-833-4700
Maureen Butler, prin. Fax 833-7099
Jackson Memorial HS 2,800/9-12
101 Don Connor Blvd 08527 732-833-4621
Anthony Gaita, prin. Fax 833-4629
McAuliffe MS 1,000/6-8
35 S Hope Chapel Rd 08527 732-833-4701
Kevin Dieugenio, prin. Fax 833-4729
Jackson Adult HS Adult
101 Don Connor Blvd 08527 732-833-4638
Laura Wheaton, dir. Fax 833-4629

Ocean County Vocational SD
Supt. — See Toms River
Ocean County Voc-Tech S - Jackson Vo/Tech
850 Toms River Rd 08527 732-928-3830
Thomas McInerney, prin. Fax 928-0490

Jamesburg, Middlesex, Pop. 6,521
Jamesburg SD 600/PK-8
13 Augusta St 08831 732-521-0303
Fax 521-1267
www.jamesburg.org
Breckwedel MS 200/6-8
13 Augusta St 08831 732-521-0640
Fax 521-1267

Yeshiva Tiferes Naftoli of Central NJ 100/9-12
3059 Englishtown Rd 08831 732-446-5841
Rabbi Asa Minkowich, prin.

Jersey City, Hudson, Pop. 239,614
Hudson County Vocational SD
Supt. — See North Bergen
County Prep HS Vo/Tech
525 Montgomery St 07302 201-631-6302
Barbara Mendolla, prin.
Explore 2000 Vo/Tech
525 Montgomery St 07302 201-631-6395
Charles Matthews, prin. Fax 369-5562

Jersey City SD 25,500/PK-12
346 Claremont Ave 07305 201-915-6202
Dr. Charles T. Epps, supt.
www.jcboe.org/
Conwell MS, 107 Bright St 07302 100/6-8
W. DeFelippo, prin. 201-946-5740
Dickinson HS 2,800/9-12
2 Palisade Ave 07306 201-714-4400
James Burke, prin. Fax 792-2292
Ferris HS 1,300/9-12
35 Colgate St 07302 201-915-6660
Nicole Hazel, prin. Fax 333-2060
Lincoln HS 800/9-12
60 Crescent Ave 07304 201-915-6700
Dr. Michael Winds, prin. Fax 435-4493
Martin S 200/7-8
59 Wilkinson Ave 07305 201-915-6590
Donald Howard, prin. Fax 915-6596
McNair Academic HS 600/9-12
123 Coles St 07302 201-418-7618
Edward Slattery, prin. Fax 792-1498
Nolan MS 600/6-8
88 Gates Ave 07305 201-915-6570
Anna Ortiz-Rivas, prin. Fax 369-3749
Snyder HS 900/9-12
239 Bergen Ave 07305 201-915-6600
Ellen Ruane, prin. Fax 946-1562
Adult Education Center Adult
299 Sip Ave 07306 201-217-7883
Margaret DiNardo, coord. Fax 395-9215
Adult Evening HS Adult
2 Palisade Ave 07306 201-714-4440
Margaret DiNardo, coord.

Christ Hospital School of Nursing Post-Sec.
176 Palisade Ave 07306 201-795-8360
Chubb Institute Post-Sec.
40 Journal Sq 07306 201-876-3800
Hudson Area School of Radiologic Tech. Post-Sec.
176 Palisade Ave 07306 201-795-8246
Hudson Catholic HS 600/9-12
790 Bergen Ave 07306 201-332-5970
Dr. Paul Ward, prin. Fax 332-6373
Hudson County Community College Post-Sec.
25 Journal Sq 07306 201-656-2020
Micro Tech Training Center Post-Sec.
3000 John F Kennedy Blvd 07306 201-216-9901
Natural Motion Institute of Hair Design Post-Sec.
2800 John F Kennedy Blvd 07306 201-659-0303
New Jersey City University Post-Sec.
2039 John F Kennedy Blvd 07305 201-200-6000
New Jersey School of Locksmithing Post-Sec.
392 Summit Ave 07306 201-963-9688
St. Aloysius HS 300/9-12
721 W Side Ave 07306 201-435-9240
Donna Marciano, prin. Fax 435-2115
St. Anthony HS 200/9-12
175 8th St 07302 201-653-5739
Edward Santana, prin. Fax 653-8120
St. Dominic Academy 500/9-12
2572 John F Kennedy Blvd 07304 201-434-5938
Deborah Egan, prin. Fax 434-2603
St. Francis Hospital Post-Sec.
1 McWilliams Pl 07302 201-795-7001
St. Mary HS 200/9-12
209 3rd St 07302 201-656-8008
Beatriz Esteban-Messina, prin. Fax 653-4518
St. Peter Prep S 9-12
144 Grand St 07302 201-434-4400
Kevin Cuddihy, prin. Fax 547-2341
St. Peter's College Post-Sec.
2627 John F Kennedy Blvd 07306 201-915-9000

Keansburg, Monmouth, Pop. 10,619
Keansburg Borough SD 1,900/PK-12
100 Palmer Pl 07734 732-787-2007
Barbara Trzeszkowski, supt. Fax 495-6714
www.keansburg.k12.nj.us
Bolger MS 500/5-8
100 Palmer Pl 07734 732-787-2007
Nicholas Eremita, prin. Fax 495-7906
Keansburg HS 500/9-12
140 Port Monmouth Rd 07734 732-787-2007
Thomas Normile, prin. Fax 495-5401

Kearny, Hudson, Pop. 38,771
Kearny SD 5,200/PK-12
100 Davis Ave 07032 201-955-5021
Robert Mooney, supt. Fax 955-0544
www.kearnyschools.com/
Kearny HS 1,700/9-12
336 Devon St 07032 201-955-5048
Alfred Somma, prin. Fax 998-9653

Kearny Christian Academy 100/PK-12
172 Midland Ave 07032 201-998-0788
Jane Botelho, admin. Fax 998-1102

Kenilworth, Union, Pop. 7,743
Kenilworth SD 1,300/PK-12
426 Boulevard 07033 908-276-1644
Dr. Lloyd Leschuk, supt. Fax 276-7598
www.kenilworthschools.com
Brearley JSHS 700/7-12
401 Monroe Ave 07033 908-931-9696
Charles Capello, prin. Fax 931-1618

Capri Institute of Hair Design Post-Sec.
660 N Michigan Ave 07033 908-964-1330

Keyport, Monmouth, Pop. 7,505
Keyport SD 1,100/PK-12
335 Broad St 07735 732-264-0561
Dr. C. Dan Blachford, supt. Fax 888-3343
www.keyportschools.org/
Keyport JSHS 500/8-12
351 Broad St 07735 732-264-0902
Miguel Hernandez, prin. Fax 888-3342

Monmouth County Vocational SD
Supt. — See Freehold
Keyport Vocational S Vo/Tech
280 Atlantic St 07735 732-739-0592
James Johnson, prin. Fax 739-1470

Kinnelon, Morris, Pop. 9,631
Kinnelon Borough SD 2,100/K-12
109 Kiel Ave 07405 973-838-1418
James Opiekun, supt. Fax 838-5527
www.kinnelonpublicschools.org/
Kinnelon HS 600/9-12
121 Kinnelon Rd 07405 973-838-5500
Wayne Merckling, prin. Fax 838-0261
Miller MS 500/6-8
117 Kiel Ave 07405 973-838-5250
Adam Silverstein, prin. Fax 838-3998

Lake Hopatcong, Morris, Pop. 3,000
Jefferson Township SD 3,500/K-12
28 Bowling Green Pkwy 07849 973-663-5780
Joseph Kraemer, supt. Fax 663-2790
www.jefftwp.org/
Other Schools – See Oak Ridge

Lakehurst, Ocean, Pop. 2,683
Ocean County Vocational SD
Supt. — See Toms River
Ocean County Voc-Tech S - Navy Lakehurst Vo/Tech
PO Box 1125 08733 732-657-4000
Karen Homiek, prin. Fax 657-4500

Lakewood, Ocean, Pop. 38,800
Lakewood Township SD 5,000/PK-12
655 Princeton Ave 08701 732-905-3633
Edward Luick, supt. Fax 364-1657
www.lakewood.k12.nj.us/
Lakewood HS 1,300/9-12
855 Somerset Ave 08701 732-905-3502
Dr. David Clauser, prin. Fax 905-0895
Lakewood MS 700/7-8
755 Somerset Ave 08701 732-905-3600
Josue Falaise, prin. Fax 905-3695
Evening HS Adult
655 Princeton Ave 08701 732-905-3600
Dr. David Weintraub, prin. Fax 905-6985

Bais Kaila Torah Prep HS 200/9-12
PO Box 952 08701 732-370-4300
Naomi Weitzner, prin. Fax 367-0389
Bais Shaindel HS 50/9-12
685 River Ave 08701 732-363-7074
Devorah Eckstein, prin. Fax 363-3399
Bais Yaakov HS 50/9-12
277 James St 08701 732-370-8200
Ettil Yagod, prin. Fax 370-2076
Beth Medrash Govoha Post-Sec.
617 6th St 08701 732-367-1060
Calvary Academy 300/PK-12
1133 E County Line Rd 08701 732-363-3633
Melissa Payne, hdmstr. Fax 363-7337
Georgian Court University Post-Sec.
900 Lakewood Ave 08701 732-364-2200
Lakewood Cheder S Bais Faga 1,200/3-8
350 Courtney Rd 08701 732-363-5070
Suri Jacobovitch, prin. Fax 370-1195
Mesivta Keren HaTorah 100/9-12
299 Monmouth Ave 08701 732-942-7300
Rabbi Moshe Rabinowitz, prin. Fax 363-4222
Mesivta Keser Torah 100/9-12
455 14th St 08701 732-681-5656
Rev. David Heinemann, prin. Fax 681-7171
Mesivta of Lakewood 50/8-12
415 6th St 08701 732-905-8370
Rabbi Zvi Yosef Bursztyn, prin. Fax 363-9052
Star Technical Institute Post-Sec.
1255 Highway 70 Ste 12N 08701 732-901-9710
Yeshiva Bais Aharon 100/9-12
1430 14th St 08701 732-367-7604
Binyomin Schulgasser, admin. Fax 367-1777
Yeshiva Gedola Ohr HaTalmud 50/9-12
PO Box 826 08701 732-364-7062
Rabbi Chesky Schonfeld, dir. Fax 364-1754
Yeshivas Bais Pinchos 50/9-12
1951 New Central Ave 08701 732-367-2880
Rabbi Yaakov Licht, prin. Fax 364-5258

Lambertville, Hunterdon, Pop. 3,840
South Hunterdon Regional HSD 400/7-12
301 Mt Airy Harbourton Rd 08530 609-397-1888
Lisa Brady, supt. Fax 397-2366
www.shrhs.org
South Hunterdon Regional HS 400/7-12
301 Mt Airy Harbourton Rd 08530 609-397-2060
Donald Woodring, prin. Fax 397-2366

Lanoka Harbor, Ocean
Lacey Township SD 4,300/K-12
PO Box 216 08734 609-971-2000
Richard Starodub, supt. Fax 242-9406
www.laceyschools.org/home.aspx
Lacey Township HS 1,500/9-12
PO Box 206 08734 609-971-2020
William Zylinski, prin. Fax 242-0873
Other Schools – See Forked River

Laurel Springs, Camden, Pop. 1,939

Empire Beauty School Post-Sec.
1305 Blackwood Clementon Rd 08021
856-435-8100

Lawrenceville, Mercer, Pop. 6,446
Lawrence Township SD 4,200/PK-12
2565 Princeton Pike 08648 609-671-5500
Philip Meara, supt. Fax 883-4225
www.ltps.org
Lawrence HS 1,500/9-12
2525 Princeton Pike 08648 609-671-5510
David Roman, prin. Fax 771-4095
Lawrence MS 600/7-8
2455 Princeton Ave 08648 609-671-5520
Andrew Zuckerman, prin. Fax 637-0768

Empire Beauty School Post-Sec.
1719 Brunswick Ave 08648 609-392-4545
Lawrenceville S 800/9-12
PO Box 6008 08648 609-896-0400
Elizabeth Duffy, hdmstr. Fax 895-2161
Notre Dame HS 1,300/9-12
601 Lawrenceville Rd 08648 609-882-7900
Mary Liz Ivins, prin. Fax 882-5723
Rider University Post-Sec.
2083 Lawrenceville Rd 08648 609-896-5000

Lebanon, Hunterdon, Pop. 1,749
Clinton Township SD 1,700/PK-8
PO Box 362 08833 908-236-7235
Dr. Elizabeth Nastus, supt. Fax 236-6358
www.ctsd.k12.nj.us
Round Valley MS 700/6-8
128 Cokesbury Rd 08833 908-236-6341
Gerard Dalton, prin. Fax 236-2847

Leonardo, Monmouth, Pop. 3,788
Middletown Township SD
Supt. — See Middletown
Bayshore MS 700/6-8
834 Leonardville Rd 07737 732-291-1380
Carol Force, prin.

Leonia, Bergen, Pop. 8,853
Leonia SD 1,700/K-12
570 Grand Ave 07605 201-947-0230
Dr. Bernard Josefsberg, supt. Fax 947-4782
www.leoniaschools.org
Leonia HS 600/9-12
100 Christie Heights St 07605 201-461-7441
Edward Bertolini, prin. Fax 461-8957
Leonia MS 400/6-8
500 Broad Ave 07605 201-461-9100
Maureen Willis, prin. Fax 461-1510

Lincoln Park, Morris, Pop. 10,899
Lincoln Park Borough SD 900/K-8
92 Ryerson Rd 07035 973-696-5500
Dr. Joyce J. Valenza, supt. Fax 696-9273
www.lincolnparkboe.org
Lincoln Park MS 400/5-8
90 Ryerson Rd 07035 973-696-5520
Michael Meyer, prin. Fax 872-8930

Craig Upper S 100/9-12
200 Comly Rd 07035 973-305-8085
David Blanchard, hdmstr. Fax 305-8086

Lincroft, Monmouth, Pop. 6,193
Monmouth County Vocational SD
Supt. — See Freehold
High Technology HS Vo/Tech
PO Box 119 07738 732-842-8444
Daniel Simon, prin. Fax 219-9418

Brookdale Community College Post-Sec.
765 Newman Springs Rd 07738 732-842-1900
Christian Brothers Academy 900/9-12
850 Newman Springs Rd 07738 732-747-1959
Br. Stephen Olert, prin. Fax 747-1643

Linden, Union, Pop. 40,014
Linden SD 5,900/PK-12
2 E Gibbons St 07036 908-486-2800
Joseph Martino, supt. Fax 486-6331
www.linden.k12.nj.us
Linden HS 1,800/9-12
121 W Saint Georges Ave 07036 908-486-5432
Barry Black, prin. Fax 486-3242
McManus MS 700/6-8
300 Edgewood Rd 07036 908-486-7751
Denise Cleary, prin. Fax 587-0607
Soehl MS 600/6-8
300 E Henry St 07036 908-486-0550
Diana Braisted, prin. Fax 486-3478
Linden Adult Evening S Adult
121 W Saint Georges Ave 07036 908-486-2212
Jean Forstenhausler, contact Fax 925-4427

Micropower Computer Institute Post-Sec.
1203 W Saint Georges Ave 07036 908-587-9070
Victory Christian Academy 100/PK-12
2301 Grier Ave 07036 908-925-7920

Lindenwold, Camden, Pop. 17,265
Lindenwold SD 2,300/PK-12
1017 E Linden Ave 08021 856-784-4071
Geraldine Carroll, supt. Fax 435-5887
www.lindenwold.k12.nj.us/
Lindenwold HS 700/9-12
801 Egg Harbor Rd 08021 856-741-0320
Dr. Scott Oswald, prin. Fax 741-0350
Lindenwold MS 700/5-8
40 White Horse Ave 08021 856-346-3330
J. Scott Strong, prin. Fax 346-0554

Linwood, Atlantic, Pop. 7,398
Linwood CSD 1,000/PK-8
51 Belhaven Ave 08221 609-926-6703
Thomas Baruffi Ed.D., supt. Fax 926-6705
www.linwoodschools.org/
Belhaven MS 500/5-8
51 Belhaven Ave 08221 609-926-6700
Frank Rudnesky Ed.D., prin. Fax 926-6705

Mainland Regional HSD 1,600/9-12
1301 Oak Ave 08221 609-927-2461
Dr. Russell Dever, supt. Fax 927-1942
www.mainlandregional.net
Mainland Regional HS 1,600/9-12
1301 Oak Ave 08221 609-927-4151
Dr. Robert Blake, prin. Fax 927-1942

Little Falls, Passaic, Pop. 11,294
Little Falls Township SD 800/K-8
560 Main St 07424 973-256-1034
Bruce deLyon, supt. Fax 256-6542
www.lfnjschools.org/
Little Falls MS 1 400/5-8
32 Stevens Ave 07424 973-256-1033
Jennifer Montesano, prin. Fax 785-4857

Passaic Valley Regional HSD 1 1,300/9-12
100 E Main St 07424 973-890-2560
Dr. Viktor Joganow, supt. Fax 890-0512
www.pvhs.k12.nj.us
Passaic Valley Regional HS 1,300/9-12
100 E Main St 07424 973-890-2500
John Wallace, prin. Fax 890-0512

Little Silver, Monmouth, Pop. 6,137
Little Silver Borough SD 800/K-8
124 Willow Dr 07739 732-741-2188
Marjorie Heller, supt. Fax 741-3644
www.littlesilverschools.org/lss
Markham Place MS 400/5-8
95 Markham Pl 07739 732-741-7112
Don Merce, prin. Fax 741-3562

Red Bank Regional HSD 1,100/9-12
101 Ridge Rd 07739 732-842-8000
Dr. Edward Westervelt, supt. Fax 842-8504
www.redbankregional.k12.nj.us
Red Bank Regional HS 1,100/9-12
101 Ridge Rd 07739 732-842-8000
Jim Stefankiewicz, prin. Fax 842-8504

Livingston, Essex, Pop. 27,500
Livingston Township SD 5,100/K-12
11 Foxcroft Dr 07039 973-535-8000
Brad Draeger, supt. Fax 535-1254
www.livingston.org
Heritage MS 800/7-8
20 Foxcroft Dr 07039 973-535-8000
Pat Boland, prin. Fax 597-9492
Livingston HS 1,600/9-12
30 Robert H Harp Dr 07039 973-535-8000
Pam Clause-McGroarty, prin. Fax 994-4297

Gibbs College Post-Sec.
630 W Mount Pleasant Ave 07039 973-744-2010
Kushner Hebrew Academy 800/PK-12
110 S Orange Ave 07039 973-597-1115
Susan Dworken, hdmstr. Fax 597-3363
Newark Academy 500/6-12
91 S Orange Ave 07039 973-992-7000
Elizabeth Riegelman, hdmstr. Fax 992-8962
St. Barnabas Medical Center Post-Sec.
94 Old Short Hills Rd 07039 973-533-5628

Lodi, Bergen, Pop. 24,310
Lodi SD 3,000/PK-12
8 Hunter St 07644 973-778-4620
Frank Quatrone, supt. Fax 778-6393
www.lodi.k12.nj.us
Jefferson MS 700/6-8
75 1st St 07644 973-478-8662
Robert Sciolaro, prin. Fax 478-0358
Lodi HS 800/9-12
99 Putnam St 07644 973-478-6100
Joan Fragala, prin. Fax 478-4012

Felician College Post-Sec.
262 S Main St 07644 210-559-6000
Immaculate Conception HS 200/9-12
258 S Main St 07644 973-773-2400
Sr. Mary Alicia Adametz, prin. Fax 614-0893

Logan, Gloucester
Logan Township SD 900/PK-8
110 School Ln 08085 856-467-5133
John Herbst, supt. Fax 467-9012
www.logan.k12.nj.us
Logan MS 400/5-8
110 School Ln 08085 856-467-5133
Terry Jacobs, prin. Fax 467-9012

Long Branch, Monmouth, Pop. 32,091
Long Branch SD 2,400/PK-12
540 Broadway 07740 732-571-2868
Joseph Ferraina, supt. Fax 229-0797
www.longbranch.k12.nj.us
Leadership Academy 6-8
350 Indiana Ave 07740 732-229-5533
Donald Colvin, prin. Fax 229-4898
S of Digital Sciences & Complex Math 9-12
391 Westwood Ave 07740 732-229-7300
Ron Polakowski, prin. Fax 229-2825
9th Grade Academy 9-9
391 Westwood Ave 07740 732-229-7300
Elford Rawls, prin. Fax 229-2825
School of Leadership 9-12
391 Westwood Ave 07740 732-229-7300
Alvin Freeman, prin. Fax 229-2825
School of Visual & Performing Arts 9-12
391 Westwood Ave 07740 732-229-7300
Matthew Johnson, prin. Fax 229-2825
Science and Computer Technology Academy 6-8
364 Indiana Ave 07740 732-229-5533
Francisco Rodriguez, prin. Fax 229-4898
Visual and Performing Arts Academy 6-8
364 Indiana Ave 07740 732-229-5533
John Perri, prin. Fax 229-4898

Monmouth County Vocational SD
Supt. — See Freehold
Adult Technical Center Vo/Tech
255 W End Ave 07740 732-229-3019
Assunta Paulisko, prin. Fax 229-5727

Monmouth Medical Center Post-Sec.
300 2nd Ave 07740 732-222-5200

Long Valley, Morris, Pop. 1,744
Washington Township SD 2,100/PK-8
53 W Mill Rd 07853 908-876-4172
Gerald Vernotica Ed.D., supt. Fax 876-9392
www.wtschools.org
Long Valley MS 700/6-8
51 W Mill Rd 07853 908-876-3434
Dr. Kevin Walsh, prin. Fax 876-3436

Lumberton, Burlington
Lumberton Township SD 1,700/K-8
33 Municipal Dr 08048 609-267-1406
Frank Logandro, supt. Fax 267-0002
www.lumberton.k12.nj.us/
Lumberton MS 600/6-8
30 Dimsdale Dr 08048 609-265-0123
Patricia Hutchinson, prin. Fax 265-0476

Lyndhurst, Bergen, Pop. 18,262
Lyndhurst Township SD 2,200/PK-12
1050 Wall St W Ste 645 07071 201-438-5683
Joseph Abate, supt. Fax 896-2118
Lyndhurst HS 600/9-12
400 Weart Ave 07071 201-896-2100
Anita Pescevich, prin. Fax 896-2088

Madison, Morris, Pop. 15,918
Madison SD 2,200/PK-12
359 Woodland Rd 07940 973-593-3100
Richard Noonan, supt. Fax 301-2170
www.madisonpublicschools.org
Madison HS 700/9-12
170 Ridgedale Ave 07940 973-593-3117
Greg Robertson, prin. Fax 593-3141
Madison JHS 300/7-8
285 Main St 07940 973-593-3149
Ann Marie Hodges, prin. Fax 966-1908

Drew University Post-Sec.
36 Madison Ave 07940 973-408-3000
Fairleigh Dickinson University Post-Sec.
285 Madison Ave 07940 800-338-8803

Mahwah, Bergen, Pop. 17,905
Mahwah Township SD 3,300/PK-12
60 Ridge Rd 07430 201-882-2400
Charles Montesano, supt. Fax 529-1287
www.mahwah.k12.nj.us
Mahwah HS 800/9-12
50 Ridge Rd 07430 201-882-2300
John Pascale, prin. Fax 512-0949
Ramapo Ridge MS 800/6-8
150 Ridge Rd 07430 201-882-2380
Brian Miller, prin. Fax 529-6790

Lincoln Technical Institute Post-Sec.
70 McKee Dr 07430 201-529-1414
National Tax Training School Post-Sec.
PO Box 767 07430 201-684-0828
Ramapo College of New Jersey Post-Sec.
505 Ramapo Valley Rd 07430 201-684-7500

Manahawkin, Ocean, Pop. 1,594
Ocean County Vocational SD
Supt. — See Toms River
Ocean County Voc-Tech S - MATES Academy Vo/Tech
195 Cedar Bridge Rd 08050 609-978-8439
Peg Roma, prin. Fax 978-8540

Southern Regional SD 3,600/7-12
105 Cedar Bridge Rd 08050 609-597-9481
James Kerfoot, supt. Fax 978-0298
www.srsd.net
Southern Regional HS 1,300/9-10
600 N Main St 08050 609-597-9481
Eric Wilhelm, prin. Fax 978-5375
Southern Regional HS 1,300/11-12
90 Cedar Bridge Rd 08050 609-597-9481
Eric Wilhelm, prin. Fax 978-5357
Southern Regional MS 1,000/7-8
75 Cedar Bridge Rd 08050 609-597-9481
Lorraine Airey, prin. Fax 978-8209
Adult Evening HS Adult
105 Cedar Bridge Rd 08050 609-597-9481
Jan Kristbergs, prin. Fax 978-5352

Manalapan, Monmouth
Freehold Regional HSD
Supt. — See Englishtown
Manalapan HS 2,100/9-12
30 Church Ln 07726 732-792-7200
Dr. Anthony Procopio, prin. Fax 446-4981

Manalapan-Englishtown Regional SD
Supt. — See Englishtown
Manalapan-Englishtown MS 1,400/7-8
155 Millhurst Rd 07726 732-786-2650
Robert Williams, prin. Fax 786-2660

Manasquan, Monmouth, Pop. 6,201
Manasquan SD 1,700/K-12
169 Broad St 08736 732-528-8800
Carole Morris, supt. Fax 223-6286
www.manasquanboe.org/
Manasquan HS 1,000/9-12
167 Broad St 08736 732-528-8820
Cary McCormack, prin. Fax 528-0316

Manchester, Ocean
Manchester Township SD
Supt. — See Whiting
Manchester Township HS 1,100/9-12
101 S Colonial Dr 08759 732-657-2121
David Walling, prin. Fax 657-2781
Manchester Township MS 700/6-8
2759 Ridgeway Rd 08759 732-657-1717
Thomas Baxter, prin. Fax 657-0326

Manville, Somerset, Pop. 10,404
Manville Borough SD 1,300/PK-12
410 Brooks Blvd 08835 908-231-8500
Dr. Donald Burkhardt, supt. Fax 707-3963
www.manvilleschools.org
Batcho IS, 100 N 13th Ave 08835 300/6-8
Dr. James Brunn, prin. 908-231-8521
Manville HS 400/9-12
1100 Brooks Blvd 08835 908-231-6806
Mary McLoughlin, prin. Fax 231-8532

Maple Shade, Burlington, Pop. 19,211
Maple Shade Township SD 1,900/K-12
170 Frederick Ave 08052 856-779-1750
Cheryl Smith, supt. Fax 779-1054
www.mapleshade.org/
Maple Shade JSHS 900/7-12
180 Frederick Ave 08052 856-779-2880
Randy Hepler, prin. Fax 779-8849

Maplewood, Essex, Pop. 21,756
South Orange-Maplewood SD 6,200/K-12
525 Academy St 07040 973-762-5600
Peter Horoschak, supt. Fax 378-9464
www.somsd.k12.nj.us
Columbia HS 2,000/9-12
17 Parker Ave 07040 973-378-5266
Lovie Lilly, prin. Fax 378-5234
Maplewood MS 700/6-8
7 Burnett St 07040 973-378-7660
Kristopher Harrison, prin. Fax 378-5247
Other Schools – See South Orange

Margate City, Atlantic, Pop. 8,666
Margate City SD 600/K-8
8103 Winchester Ave 08402 609-822-1686
Dominick Potena, supt. Fax 822-3399
www.margateschools.org
Tighe MS 200/6-8
7804 Amherst Ave 08402 609-822-2353
James Rhoads, prin. Fax 822-8456

Marlboro, Monmouth
Freehold Regional HSD
Supt. — See Englishtown
Marlboro HS 2,200/9-12
95 N Main St 07746 732-671-8393
James Mullevey, prin. Fax 972-6615

Marlboro Township SD 5,900/PK-8
1980 Township Dr 07746 732-972-2000
Dr. David Abbott, supt. Fax 972-2003
www.marlboro.k12.nj.us
Marlboro MS 1,200/6-8
355 County Road 520 07746 732-972-2100
Patricia Nieliwocki, prin. Fax 972-6765
Other Schools – See Morganville

Marlton, Burlington, Pop. 10,228
Evesham Township SD 5,000/K-8
25 S Maple Ave 08053 856-983-1800
Patricia Lucas, supt. Fax 983-2939
www.evesham.k12.nj.us
DeMasi MS 800/6-8
199 Evesboro Medford Rd 08053 856-988-0777
Virginia Grossman, prin.
Marlton MS 1,100/6-8
150 Tomlinson Mill Rd 08053 856-988-0684
Gary Hoffman, prin.

Lenape Regional HSD
Supt. — See Shamong Township
Cherokee HS 2,400/9-12
120 Tomlinson Mill Rd 08053 856-983-5140
Linda Roher, prin. Fax 596-6495

Rizzieri Aveda School Post-Sec.
6001 Lincoln Dr W 08053 856-988-8600

Martinsville, Somerset

Pingry S 700/7-12
PO Box 366 08836 908-647-5555
Nathaniel Conard, prin. Fax 647-3703

Matawan, Monmouth, Pop. 8,819
Old Bridge Township SD 9,800/K-12
4207 Highway 516 07747 732-290-3976
Dr. Simon Bosco, supt. Fax 441-3816
www.oldbridgeadmin.org
Old Bridge HS 3,100/9-12
4209 Highway 516 07747 732-290-3900
Dr. James Hickey, prin. Fax 566-1263
Other Schools – See Old Bridge

Mays Landing, Atlantic, Pop. 2,090
Atlantic County Vocational SD
5080 Atlantic Ave 08330 609-625-2249
Dr. Philip Guenther, supt. Fax 625-2876
www.acitech.org
Atlantic County Institute of Technology Vo/Tech
5080 Atlantic Ave 08330 609-625-2249
Ronald DeFelice, prin. Fax 625-0707
Atlantic County Adult Education Adult
5080 Atlantic Ave 08330 609-625-2249
Maryann Sakamoto, prin. Fax 625-8622

Greater Egg Harbor Regional HSD 3,700/9-12
1824 Dr Dennis Foreman Dr 08330 609-625-1456
Adam Pfeffer Ed.D., supt. Fax 625-0045
www.gehrhsd.net/
Oakcrest HS 1,600/9-12
1824 Dr Dennis Foreman Dr 08330 609-909-2600
Anthony Mongelluzzo, prin. Fax 625-0872
Other Schools – See Galloway

Hamilton Township SD 2,400/PK-8
1876 Dr Dennis Foreman Dr 08330 609-476-6300
Frederick Donatucci, supt. Fax 625-4847
www.hamiltonschools.org
Davies MS 700/6-8
1876 Dr Dennis Foreman Dr 08330 609-625-6600
Michael Muldoon, prin. Fax 625-2267

Atlantic Cape Community College Post-Sec.
5100 Black Horse Pike 08330 609-343-4900
Atlantic Co. Vocational Technical School Post-Sec.
5080 Atlantic Ave 08330 609-625-2249

Maywood, Bergen, Pop. 9,442
Maywood SD 700/PK-8
452 Maywood Ave 07607 201-845-9110
Dr. Robert Otinsky, supt. Fax 845-7146
www.maywoodschools.org
Maywood Avenue MS 400/4-8
452 Maywood Ave 07607 201-845-9110
Gerald Bossard, prin. Fax 291-1917

Medford, Burlington
Burlington Co. Institute of Technology
Supt. — See Mount Holly
Burlington Co. Institute of Technology Vo/Tech
10 Hawkin Rd 08055 609-654-0200
Joseph Porter, prin. Fax 654-1081

Lenape Regional HSD
Supt. — See Shamong Township
Lenape HS 1,900/9-12
235 Hartford Rd 08055 609-654-5111
Barry Croll, prin. Fax 953-6779
Shawnee HS 1,500/9-12
600 Tabernacle Rd 08055 609-654-7544
Matthew Campbell, prin. Fax 654-5611

Medford Township SD 2,900/K-8
128 Route 70 Ste 1 08055 609-654-6416
Joseph J. Del Rossi Ed.D., supt. Fax 654-7436
www.medford.k12.nj.us/
Medford Township Memorial MS 700/7-8
55 Mill St 08055 – Phillip Petru, prin. 609-654-7707

Medford Lakes, Burlington, Pop. 4,185
Medford Lakes Borough SD 500/PK-8
135 Mudjekeewis Trl 08055 609-654-0991
Diane Bacher, supt. Fax 654-7629
www.medford-lakes.k12.nj.us
Neeta S 400/3-8
44 Neeta Trl 08055 609-654-5155
Karen Rockhill, prin. Fax 953-8258

Mendham, Morris, Pop. 5,172
Mendham Borough SD 700/K-8
12 Hilltop Rd 07945 973-543-2295
Dr. Janie Edmonds, supt. Fax 543-2805
www.mendhamboro.org
Mountain View MS 300/5-8
100 Dean Rd 07945 973-543-7075
Patricia Lambert, prin. Fax 543-7993

West Morris Regional HSD
Supt. — See Chester
West Morris Mendham HS 1,200/9-12
65 E Main St 07945 973-543-2501
Michael Matyas, prin. Fax 543-6739

Assumption College for Sisters Post-Sec.
350 Bernardsville Rd 07945 973-543-6528

Metuchen, Middlesex, Pop. 13,383
Metuchen SD 1,900/PK-12
16 Simpson Pl 08840 732-321-8700
T. Pollifrone-Sinatra, supt. Fax 321-6567
www.metuchenschools.org/metuchen
Edgar MS 600/5-8
49 Brunswick Ave 08840 732-321-8770
Katherine Glutz, prin. Fax 452-0571
Metuchen HS 600/9-12
400 Grove Ave 08840 732-321-8743
John Novak, prin. Fax 549-6415

St. Joseph HS 800/9-12
145 Plainfield Rd 08840 732-549-7600
John Anderson, prin. Fax 549-0664

Middlesex, Middlesex, Pop. 13,938
Middlesex Borough SD 2,000/K-12
300 John F Kennedy Dr 08846 732-317-6000
Dr. James C. Baker, supt. Fax 317-6006
www.middlesex.k12.nj.us
Mauger MS 800/4-8
Fisher Ave 08846 732-317-6000
Robert Heidt, prin. Fax 317-6002
Middlesex HS 700/9-12
300 John F Kennedy Dr 08846 732-317-6000
Gregory Freeman, prin. Fax 317-6008

Middletown, Monmouth, Pop. 24,000
Middletown Township SD 9,900/K-12
59 Tindall Rd 07748 732-671-3850
Karen Bilbao, supt. Fax 615-9351
www.middletownk12.org/
Middletown-North HS 1,600/9-12
63 Tindall Rd 07748 732-706-6061
Patricia Cartier, prin. Fax 706-6067
Middletown-South HS 1,400/9-12
900 Nutswamp Rd 07748 732-706-6111
Mark Kelly, prin. Fax 706-8058
Thompson MS 900/6-8
1001 Middletown Lincroft Rd 07748 732-671-2212
Patrick Houston, prin.
Other Schools – See Leonardo, Port Monmouth

Monmouth County Vocational SD
Supt. — See Freehold
Middletown Vocational S Vo/Tech
2 Swartzel Dr 07748 732-671-0650
James Johnson, prin. Fax 671-7455

Midland Park, Bergen, Pop. 6,952
Midland Park Borough SD 800/K-12
31 Highland Ave 07432 201-444-1400
August DePreker, supt. Fax 444-3051
www.midlandparkschools.k12.nj.us
Midland Park JSHS 500/7-12
250 Prospect St 07432 201-444-7400
Patricia Terraciano, prin. Fax 444-0352

Milford, Hunterdon, Pop. 1,215
Holland Township SD 600/K-8
710 Milford Warren Glen Rd 08848 908-995-2401
Dr. Eugene Costa, supt. Fax 995-2011
hts.k12.nj.us
Holland Township MS 300/5-8
710 Milford Warren Glen Rd 08848 908-995-2401
Nancy Yard, prin.

Millburn, Essex, Pop. 18,630
Millburn Township SD 4,300/K-12
434 Millburn Ave 07041 973-376-3600
Dr. Richard L. Brodow, supt. Fax 912-9396
www.millburn.org
Millburn HS 1,200/9-12
462 Millburn Ave 07041 973-376-3600
Dr. Keith Neigel, prin. Fax 912-8633
Millburn MS 1,100/6-8
25 Old Short Hills Rd 07041 973-379-2600
Michael Cahill, prin. Fax 912-0939

Milburn School for Hearing Handicapped Post-Sec.
Spring & Willow Sts 07041 973-376-9439

Milltown, Middlesex, Pop. 7,130
Milltown SD 600/K-8
80 Violet Ter 08850 732-214-2360
Dr. Linda Madison, supt. Fax 214-2376
www.milltownps.org
Kilmer S 400/4-8
21 W Church St 08850 732-214-2370
Janet Ferlazzo, prin. Fax 214-2378

Millville, Cumberland, Pop. 27,886
Millville SD 5,900/PK-12
PO Box 5010 08332 856-327-7575
Dr. Shelly Schneider, supt. Fax 825-1545
www.millville.org
Memorial Freshman HS 1,000/8-9
504 E Broad St 08332 856-327-6072
Al Johnson, prin. Fax 825-4480
Millville SHS 1,500/10-12
200 N Wade Blvd 08332 856-327-6040
Dr. Christy Thompson, prin. Fax 293-1342

Minotola, See Buena
Buena Regional SD
Supt. — See Buena
Cleary MS 500/6-8
1501 Central Ave 08341 856-697-0100
Kenneth Nelson, prin. Fax 697-9580

Monmouth Junction, Middlesex, Pop. 1,570
South Brunswick Township SD
Supt. — See North Brunswick
Crossroads North MS 800/6-8
635 Georges Rd 08852 732-329-4191
Judith Black, prin. Fax 329-1907
Crossroads South MS 1,200/6-8
195 Major Rd 08852 732-329-4633
Dr. James Warfel, prin. Fax 329-1906
South Brunswick HS 2,400/9-12
750 Ridge Rd 08852 732-329-4044
Timothy Matheney, prin. Fax 274-1237

Noor Ul-Iman S 300/PK-12
PO Box 271 08852 732-329-1306
Janet Nazif, prin. Fax 329-8703

Monroe Township, Middlesex
Monroe Township SD 4,200/K-12
423 Buckelew Ave 08831 732-521-2111
Ralph P. Ferrie, supt. Fax 521-2719
monroe.k12.nj.us
Applegarth MS 600/7-8
227 Applegarth Rd 08831 609-655-0604
Jeff Gorman, prin. Fax 655-4314
Monroe Township HS 1,300/9-12
1629 Perrineville Rd 08831 732-521-2882
Robert Goodall, prin. Fax 521-2976

Montclair, Essex, Pop. 39,200
Montclair SD 6,300/K-12
22 Valley Rd 07042 973-509-4000
Dr. Frank Alvarez, supt. Fax 509-0586
www.montclair.k12.nj.us/
Glenfield MS 700/6-8
25 Maple Ave 07042 973-509-4171
Alex Anemone, prin. Fax 509-4179
Montclair HS 1,900/9-12
100 Chestnut St 07042 973-509-4069
Mel Katz, prin. Fax 509-4098
Mt. Hebron MS 500/6-8
173 Bellevue Ave 07043 973-509-4220
Dr. Mark Jennings, prin. Fax 509-4218
Renaissance MS 200/6-8
17 Munn St 07042 973-509-5741
Charles Cobb, prin. Fax 509-5752

Eastern School of Acupuncture Post-Sec.
427 Bloomfield Ave Ste 301 07042 973-746-8717
Immaculate Conception HS 9-12
33 Cottage Pl 07042 973-744-7445
Joann Degnan, prin. Fax 744-3926
Lacordaire Academy 100/9-12
155 Lorraine Ave 07043 973-744-1156
Sr. Suzanne McCaffrey, prin. Fax 783-9521
Montclair Kimberley Academy 400/4-8
201 Valley Rd 07042 973-746-9800
Thomas Nammack, hdmstr. Fax 783-5777
Montclair Kimberley Academy - Upper S 400/9-12
6 Lloyd Rd 07042 973-783-8300
Thomas Nammack, hdmstr. Fax 744-4051
Montclair State University Post-Sec.
Montclair State University 07043 973-655-4000
Mountainside Hospital Post-Sec.
1 Bay Ave 07042 973-429-6850

Montvale, Bergen, Pop. 7,306
Montvale SD 1,000/PK-8
47 Spring Valley Rd 07645 201-391-1662
Dr. Susan King, supt. Fax 391-8935
www.montvale.k12.nj.us
Fieldstone MS 500/5-8
47 Spring Valley Rd 07645 201-391-9000
Dr. Paul Semendinger, prin. Fax 391-8935

Pascack Valley Regional HSD 1,700/9-12
46 Akers Ave 07645 201-358-7006
Dr. Benedict Tantillo, supt. Fax 505-4858
www.pascack.k12.nj.us
Pascack Hills HS 600/9-12
225 W Grand Ave 07645 201-358-7020
Sarah Van Gunten, prin. Fax 358-7020
Other Schools – See Hillsdale

St. Joseph Regional HS 9-12
40 Chestnut Ridge Rd 07645 201-391-3300
John Job, prin. Fax 391-8073

Montville, Morris, Pop. 15,600
Montville Township SD
Supt. — See Pine Brook
Lazar MS 900/6-8
123 Changebridge Rd 07045 973-331-7140
John Gallucci, prin. Fax 331-9279

Montville Township HS 1,100/9-12
100 Horseneck Rd 07045 973-331-7100
Marianne Laux, prin. Fax 334-0753

Trinity Christian S 200/PK-12
160 Changebridge Rd 07045 973-334-1785
Douglas Prol, prin. Fax 334-9282

Moorestown, Burlington, Pop. 13,242
Moorestown Township SD 4,100/K-12
803 N Stanwick Rd 08057 856-778-6600
Fax 235-0961
www.mtps.com
Allen III MS 700/7-8
801 N Stanwick Rd 08057 856-778-6620
Sharon Vitella, prin. Fax 727-9309
Moorestown HS 1,300/9-12
350 Bridgeboro Rd 08057 856-778-6610
David Yates, prin. Fax 722-8983

Moorestown Friends S 700/PK-12
110 E Main St 08057 856-235-2900
Laurence R. Van Meter, hdmstr. Fax 235-6684

Morganville, Monmouth
Marlboro Township SD
Supt. — See Marlboro
Marlboro Memorial MS 900/6-8
71 Nolan Rd 07751 732-617-5602
Joanmarie Penney, prin. Fax 972-7118

Morris Plains, Morris, Pop. 5,629
Morris Plains SD 600/PK-8
500 Speedwell Ave 07950 973-538-1650
Vicki Pede, supt. Fax 540-1983
www.morrisplainsschools.com/
Borough MS 400/3-8
500 Speedwell Ave 07950 973-538-1650
Rosalie Haller, prin. Fax 538-8367

Parsippany-Troy Hills Township SD
Supt. — See Parsippany
Parsippany Hills HS 1,200/9-12
20 Rita Dr 07950 973-682-2815
Dr. Richard Konet, prin. Fax 682-2855

Morristown, Morris, Pop. 18,851
Morris SD 4,400/K-12
31 Hazel St 07960 973-292-2300
Thomas Ficarra, supt. Fax 292-2057
www.morrisschooldistrict.org
Frelinghuysen MS 900/6-8
200 W Hanover Ave 07960 973-292-2200
Ethel Minchello, prin. Fax 292-2458
Morristown HS 1,500/9-12
50 Early St 07960 973-292-2100
Linda Murphy, prin. Fax 539-5573

College of Saint Elizabeth Post-Sec.
2 Convent Rd 07960 973-290-4000
Delbarton S 500/7-12
230 Mendham Rd 07960 973-538-3231
Rev. Luke Travers, hdmstr. Fax 538-8836
Morristown-Beard S 500/6-12
70 Whippany Rd 07960 973-539-3032
Dr. Alex Curtis, hdmstr. Fax 539-1590
Morristown Memorial Hospital Post-Sec.
100 Madison Ave 07960 973-971-5177
Rabbinical College of America Post-Sec.
226 Sussex Ave 07960 973-267-9404
Shepard HS 100/9-12
10 Columbia St 07960 973-984-1600
Jay Gavitt, prin. Fax 984-9722
Villa Walsh Academy 7-12
455 Western Ave 07960 973-538-3680
Sr. Patricia Pompa, prin. Fax 538-6733

Mountain Lakes, Morris, Pop. 4,336
Mountain Lakes SD 1,500/K-12
400 Boulevard Ste 3 07046 973-334-8280
Dr. John Kazmark, supt. Fax 334-2316
www.mtlakes.org
Briarcliff MS 300/6-8
93 Briarcliff Rd 07046 973-334-0342
Constance Sakala, prin. Fax 334-6857
Mountain Lakes HS 700/9-12
96 Powerville Rd 07046 973-334-8400
Lew Ludwig, prin. Fax 334-3550

Craig S 200/3-12
10 Tower Hill Rd 07046 973-334-1295
David Blanchard, hdmstr. Fax 334-1299

Mountainside, Union, Pop. 6,635
Mountainside SD 400/PK-8
1497 Woodacres Dr 07092 908-232-3232
Dr. Richard O'Malley, admin. Fax 232-1743
mountainsideschools.net/
Deerfield S 400/3-8
302 Central Ave 07092 908-232-8828
Robert Burkhardt, prin. Fax 232-7338

Mount Arlington, Morris, Pop. 5,332
Mount Arlington SD 400/K-8
446 Howard Blvd 07856 973-398-6400
Jane Mullins Jameson, supt. Fax 398-3614
www.gti.net/mtas/
Mount Arlington MS 300/3-8
235 Howard Blvd 07856 973-398-4400
Martha Weber, prin. Fax 398-5726

Mount Ephraim, Camden, Pop. 4,467
Mount Ephraim Borough SD 400/K-8
125 S Black Horse Pike 08059 856-931-1634
Joseph Rafferty, supt. Fax 931-0202
mtephraimschools.org/
Kershaw MS 200/5-8
125 S Black Horse Pike 08059 856-931-1634

Mount Holly, Burlington, Pop. 10,639
Burlington Co. Institute of Technology
695 Woodlane Rd 08060 609-267-4226
Dolores Szymanski, supt. Fax 267-9788
www.bcit.cc/
Burlington Co. Institute of Tech Evening Vo/Tech
695 Woodlane Rd 08060 609-654-2000
John Karaska, prin. Fax 654-2698
Burlington Co. Institute of Technology Vo/Tech
695 Woodlane Rd 08060 609-267-4226
Daniel Money, prin. Fax 267-3752
Other Schools – See Medford

Mount Holly Township SD 1,000/PK-8
330 Levis Dr 08060 609-267-7108
Paul Spaventa, supt. Fax 702-9082
www.mtholly.k12.nj.us
Holbein MS 400/5-8
333 Levis Dr 08060 609-267-7200
John Dileo, prin. Fax 702-9775

Rancocas Valley Regional HSD 2,300/9-12
520 Jacksonville Rd 08060 609-267-0830
Dr. Michael Moskalski, supt. Fax 265-9204
www.rancocasvalley.k12.nj.us
Rancocas Valley Regional HS 2,200/9-12
520 Jacksonville Rd 08060 609-267-0830
Dr. Michael Moskalski, prin. Fax 265-9204
Rancocas Valley Regional Adult S Adult
520 Jacksonville Rd 08060 609-267-0830
Camille Rosenberg, dir.

Burlington County Inst. of Technology Post-Sec.
695 Woodlane Rd 08060 609-267-4226

Mount Laurel, Burlington
Mount Laurel Township SD 4,400/K-8
330 Mount Laurel Rd 08054 856-235-3387
Dr. Antoinette Rath, supt. Fax 235-1837
mtlaurelschools.org
Harrington MS 1,000/7-8
514 Mount Laurel Rd 08054 856-234-1610
Robert Mitchell, prin. Fax 222-9754

Cittone Institute Post-Sec.
1000 Howard Blvd # 2 08054 856-722-9333
Heritage Christian Academy 100/PK-12
530 Union Mill Rd 08054 856-234-1145
Ron Hamilton, prin.

Mullica Hill, Gloucester, Pop. 1,117
Clearview Regional HSD 2,200/7-12
420 Cedar Rd 08062 856-223-2765
Patricia Carroll, supt. Fax 478-0409
www.clearviewregional.edu
Clearview Regional HS 1,400/9-12
625 Breakneck Rd 08062 856-223-2790
Kevin Kitchenman, prin. Fax 478-6705
Clearview Regional MS 800/7-8
595 Jefferson Rd 08062 856-223-2740
David Kelk, prin. Fax 223-9068

Neptune, Monmouth, Pop. 5,062
Monmouth County Vocational SD
Supt. — See Freehold
Monmouth Co. Acad of Allied Health & Sci Vo/Tech
2325 Heck Ave 07753 732-775-0058
Robert Cancro, prin. Fax 775-6646

Neptune Township SD 4,000/PK-12
60 Neptune Blvd 07753 732-776-2000
David Mooij, supt. Fax 776-2003
www.neptune.k12.nj.us/education/district/district.php
Neptune HS 1,200/9-12
55 Neptune Blvd 07753 732-776-2200
Richard Allen, prin. Fax 776-2253
Neptune MS 900/6-8
2300 Heck Ave 07753 732-776-2200
Mark Alfone, prin. Fax 776-2254

Jersey Shore Medical Center Post-Sec.
1945 State Route 33 07753 732-776-4603

Newark, Essex, Pop. 280,666
Essex County Vocational SD
Supt. — See Verona
Essex County Vocational HS-13th Street Vo/Tech
300 N 13th St 07107 973-483-5466
John Dolan, prin. Fax 483-6606
Newark Tech HS Vo/Tech
91 W Market St 07103 973-622-1100
Baruti Kafele, prin. Fax 623-2010

Newark SD 37,200/PK-12
2 Cedar St Ste 1 07102 973-733-7333
Marion Bolden, supt. Fax 733-6834
www.nps.k12.nj.us/
Academy of Vocational Careers Vo/Tech
74 Montgomery St 07103 973-733-6911
Dr. Caesar Previdi, prin. Fax 733-6917
Arts HS 600/9-12
550 Martin Luther King Jr B 07102 973-733-7391
Dr. Norma Fair-Brown, prin. Fax 733-7395
Barringer 9th Grade Academy 500/9-9
24 Crane St 07104 973-268-5101
Donna Marable-Ship, prin. Fax 268-5324
Barringer HS 1,200/10-12
90 Parker St 07104 973-268-5125
Carmen Ruiz, prin. Fax 268-5128
Brown Academy MS 400/6-8
695 Bergen St 07108 973-733-6844
Kevin Guyton, prin. Fax 733-6887
Camden MS, 321 Bergen St 07103 500/5-8
Josephine McDowell, prin. 973-733-8351
Central HS 700/9-12
100 Summit St 07103 973-733-6897
Gregory Stewart, prin. Fax 733-8212
Chancellor Avenue MS 300/3-8
321 Chancellor Ave 07112 973-705-3870
Eugene Brown, prin. Fax 705-3003
East Side HS 1,400/9-12
238 Van Buren St 07105 973-465-4900
Mario Santos, prin. Fax 465-4936
Maple Avenue S 300/4-8
33 Maple Ave 07112 973-705-3850
Daneen Washington, prin. Fax 705-3013
Marin MS 800/5-8
663 Broadway 07104 973-268-5330
Sylvia Esteves, prin. Fax 268-5972
Morton Street MS 300/6-8
75 Morton St 07103 973-733-6938
Gerald Samuels, prin. Fax 733-7287
Newark Vocational S Vo/Tech
301 W Kinney St 07103 973-733-7256
Deborah DeBerry, prin. Fax 242-5431
Science HS 600/9-12
40 Rector St 07102 973-733-8689
Christine Taylor, prin. Fax 733-8236
Shabazz HS 1,200/9-12
80 Johnson Ave 07108 973-733-6760
Leila Dinkins, prin. Fax 430-9163
Technology HS Vo/Tech
223 Broadway 07104 973-481-5962
Mona Dana, prin. Fax 497-5786

University JSHS 500/7-12
55 Clinton Pl 07108 973-351-2010
Roger Leon, prin. Fax 351-2003
Vailsburg MS 400/6-8
107 Ivy St 07106 973-351-2121
Talibah Sun, prin. Fax 374-2102
Weequahic HS 700/9-12
279 Chancellor Ave 07112 973-705-3900
Ronald Stone, prin. Fax 923-4095
West Side 9th Grade Academy 400/9-9
301 W Kinney St 07103 973-733-7018
Dr. Kenneth Watts, prin.
West Side HS 900/10-12
403 S Orange Ave 07103 973-733-6977
Otis Brown, prin. Fax 733-8941
Adult Learning Center Adult
32 Warren Pl 07102 973-733-7028
Newark Evening HS Adult
403 S Orange Ave 07103 973-374-2090
Edna Bailey, prin.

Alpha & Omega Christian S 100/PK-12
4 Fleming Ave 07105 973-465-5333
Rev. José Torres, dir. Fax 465-5335
Bethel Christian Academy 200/K-12
580 Mount Prospect Ave 07104 973-484-6646
Dr. Jim Bentley, prin. Fax 484-5328
Essex County College Post-Sec.
303 University Ave 07102 973-877-3000
Link Community S 100/7-8
120 Livingston St 07103 973-642-0529
Marnie McKoy, prin. Fax 642-1978
McEllis Training Institute Post-Sec.
800 Broad St 07102 973-643-6917
Newark Boys Chorus S 100/4-8
1016 Broad St 07102 973-621-8900
Lawrence Emery, hdmstr. Fax 621-1343
New Community Workforce Development Ctr. Post-Sec.
201 Bergen St 07103 973-824-6484
New Jersey Institute of Technology Post-Sec.
University Heights 07102 973-596-3000
New Testament Church S 50/K-12
511 Orange St 07107 973-268-1310
Mollie Haynes, prin. Fax 485-4738
Rutgers-The State University of N.J. Post-Sec.
07102 973-353-5568
St. Benedict Prep S 600/7-12
520 Mrtn Lther King Jr Blvd 07102 973-643-4800
Rev. Edwin Leahy, prin. Fax 792-5721
St. Vincent Academy 300/9-12
228 W Market St 07103 973-622-1613
Sr. June Favata, dir. Fax 622-1128
Seton Hall University School of Law Post-Sec.
1 Newark Ctr 07102 973-642-8747
UMDNJ Grad. Sch. of Biomedical Sciences Post-Sec.
185 S Orange Ave 07103 973-972-4511
UMDNJ-New Jersey Dental School Post-Sec.
110 Bergen St 07103 973-972-4633
UMDNJ-New Jersey Medical School Post-Sec.
185 S Orange Ave 07103 973-972-4539
UMDNJ-Sch. of Health Related Professions Post-Sec.
65 Bergen St 07107 973-972-5453
UMDNJ-School of Nursing Post-Sec.
30 Bergen St 07107 973-972-4322
UMDNJ-University of Medicine & Dentistry Post-Sec.
65 Bergen St 07107 973-982-4300

New Brunswick, Middlesex, Pop. 50,156
New Brunswick SD 5,700/PK-12
PO Box 2683 08903 732-745-5300
Richard Kaplan, supt. Fax 745-5459
www.nbps.k12.nj.us
New Brunswick HS 1,300/9-12
1125 Livingston Ave 08901 732-745-5300
David Aderhold, prin. Fax 937-7580
New Brunswick MS 50/6-8
30 Van Dyke Ave 08901 732-745-5300
Faye Warren, prin. Fax 565-7621
Adult HS Adult
268 Baldwin St 08901 732-846-5300
Marlene Lederman, prin. Fax 745-5325

New Brunswick Theological Seminary Post-Sec.
17 Seminary Pl 08901 732-247-5241
Rutgers-The State University of N.J. Post-Sec.
35 College Ave 08901 732-932-4636

New Egypt, Ocean, Pop. 2,327
Plumsted Township SD 1,600/PK-12
117 Evergreen Rd 08533 609-758-6800
Jerry North, supt. Fax 758-6808
www.newegypt.us
New Egypt HS 500/9-12
117 Evergreen Rd 08533 609-758-6800
Richard Caldes, prin. Fax 758-5683
New Egypt MS 400/6-8
115 Evergreen Rd 08533 609-758-6800
Jerry Jellig, prin. Fax 758-5538

Newfield, Gloucester, Pop. 1,661

Our Lady of Mercy Academy 200/9-12
1001 Main Rd 08344 856-697-2008
Sr. Grace Marie, prin. Fax 697-2887

New Milford, Bergen, Pop. 16,318
New Milford SD 1,900/K-12
145 Madison Ave 07646 201-261-2952
Bert Ammerman, supt. Fax 261-8018
www.newmilfordschools.org
New Milford HS 600/9-12
1 Snyder Cir 07646 201-262-0172
Bert Ammerman, prin. Fax 262-4445
Owens MS 500/6-8
470 Marion Ave 07646 201-265-8661
Tony Grasso, prin. Fax 265-5680

Transfiguration Academy - Upper 100/5-8
1092 Carnation Dr 07646 201-836-7074
Salvatore Tralongo, prin. Fax 836-4475

New Monmouth, Monmouth

Mater Dei HS 400/9-12
538 Church St 07748 732-671-9100
Roger Harding, prin. Fax 671-9214

New Providence, Union, Pop. 11,905
New Providence SD 2,200/K-12
356 Elkwood Ave 07974 908-464-9050
David Miceli Ed.D., supt. Fax 464-9041
www.npsd.k12.nj.us
New Providence HS 700/9-12
35 Pioneer Dr 07974 908-464-4700
Dr. Deborah Feinberg, prin. Fax 464-8556
New Providence MS 300/7-8
35 Pioneer Dr 07974 908-464-9161
Gina Hansen, prin. Fax 464-5927

Newton, Sussex, Pop. 8,416
Andover Regional SD 700/PK-8
707 Limecrest Rd 07860 973-383-3746
Jerry A. Clymer, supt. Fax 579-3972
www.andoverregional.org
Long Pond S 300/5-8
707 Limecrest Rd 07860 973-940-1234
T. Jon Sinclair, prin. Fax 579-2690

Kittatinny Regional SD 1,300/7-12
77 Halsey Rd 07860 973-383-1800
Robert Walker, supt. Fax 383-6218
www.krhs.net
Kittatinny Regional JSHS 1,300/7-12
77 Halsey Rd 07860 973-383-1800
Susan Kappler, prin. Fax 383-4392

Newton SD 1,700/PK-12
57 Trinity St 07860 973-383-1900
Mark Miller, supt. Fax 383-5378
www.newtonnj.org
Halsted Street MS 300/6-8
59 Halsted St 07860 973-383-7440
Martin Fleming, prin. Fax 383-7432
Newton HS 900/9-12
44 Ryerson Ave 07860 973-383-7573
Paul DiRupo, prin. Fax 383-1153

Sussex County Community College Post-Sec.
1 College Hill Rd 07860 973-300-2100

North Arlington, Bergen, Pop. 15,179
North Arlington SD 1,500/PK-12
222 Ridge Rd 07031 201-991-6800
Dr. Oliver Stringham, supt. Fax 991-1656
www.narlington.k12.nj.us
North Arlington HS 500/9-12
222 Ridge Rd 07031 201-991-6800
Robert Kinloch, prin. Fax 991-0188
North Arlington MS 400/6-8
45 Beech St 07031 201-991-6800
Daniel DiGuglielmo, prin. Fax 246-0703

Queen of Peace HS 700/9-12
191 Rutherford Pl 07031 201-998-8227
Cathy Condon, prin. Fax 998-3040

North Bergen, Hudson, Pop. 59,000
Hudson County Vocational SD
8511 Tonnelle Ave 07047 201-662-6700
Frank Gargiulo, supt.
www.hcstonline.org
High Tech HS Vo/Tech
2000 85th St 07047 201-662-6801
Karol Brancato, prin. Fax 854-4129
Hudson County AVTS Adult Evening HS Vo/Tech
2000 85th St 07047 201-662-6761
James Doran, prin.
Other Schools – See Bayonne, Jersey City

North Bergen SD 7,100/K-12
7317 Kennedy Blvd 07047 201-295-2706
Peter Fischbach, supt.
www.northbergen.k12.nj.us/
North Bergen HS 2,300/9-12
7417 Kennedy Blvd 07047 201-295-2783
Paschal Tennaro, prin. Fax 295-9521

Mesivta Ohr Naftoli 100/9-12
8410 4th Ave 07047 845-357-5609
Rabbi Aron Milstein, prin. Fax 357-5601
North Hudson Academy 50/1-12
PO Box 390 07047 201-865-9577

North Brunswick, Middlesex, Pop. 37,400
North Brunswick Township SD 5,200/K-12
PO Box 6016 08902 732-289-3030
Geraldine Margin, supt. Fax 297-8567
www.nbtschools.org
Linwood MS 1,300/6-8
25 Linwood Pl 08902 732-289-3600
J. Peter Clark, prin. Fax 247-7033
North Brunswick Township HS 1,600/9-12
98 Raider Rd 08902 732-289-3700
Salvatore Mistretta, prin. Fax 821-8342

South Brunswick Township SD 8,400/K-12
231 Black Horse Ln 08902 732-297-7800
Gary P. McCartney Ed.D., supt. Fax 297-8456
www.sbschools.org
Other Schools – See Monmouth Junction

Chubb Institute Post-Sec.
651 US Highway 1 08902 732-448-2600
DeVry College of Technology Post-Sec.
630 US Highway 1 08902 732-435-4880

North Caldwell, Essex, Pop. 7,284
West Essex Regional SD 1,500/7-12
65 W Greenbrook Rd 07006 973-582-1600
Dr. Donald Merachnik, supt. Fax 228-0559
www.westex.org
West Essex JHS 800/7-9
65 W Greenbrook Rd 07006 973-228-1200
David Montgomery, prin. Fax 228-5852
West Essex SHS 700/10-12
65 W Greenbrook Rd 07006 973-228-1200
Barbara Longo, prin. Fax 364-1872

Northfield, Atlantic, Pop. 8,025
Northfield CSD 1,200/K-8
2000 New Rd 08225 609-407-4000
Richard Stepura Ed.D., supt. Fax 646-0608
www.ncs-nj.org/index.php?module=ContentExpress&func=d
Northfield Community MS 600/5-8
2000 New Rd 08225 609-407-4008
Maria Caiafa, prin. Fax 641-2646

North Haledon, Passaic, Pop. 9,073
North Haledon SD 600/K-8
515 High Mountain Rd 07508 973-427-8993
Dr. Charles Ferraro, supt. Fax 427-4357
www.northhaledonschools.com
High Mountain MS 300/5-8
515 High Mountain Rd 07508 973-427-1220
Donna Cardiello, prin. Fax 427-7685

Eastern Christian HS 400/9-12
50 Oakwood Ave 07508 973-427-0900
Jan Lucas, prin. Fax 427-3716
Mary Help of Christians Academy 200/9-12
659 Belmont Ave 07508 973-790-6200
Sr. Theresa Kelly, prin. Fax 790-6125

North Plainfield, Somerset, Pop. 21,608
North Plainfield Borough SD 3,200/K-12
33 Mountain Ave 07060 908-769-6060
Dr. Marilyn Birnbaum, supt. Fax 755-5490
www.nplainfield.org
North Plainfield HS 1,500/7-12
34 Wilson Ave 07060 908-769-6000
Jerard Stephenson, prin. Fax 769-6032
Adult HS Adult
12 Harrison Ave 07060 908-769-6090
Rosemary McGuinness, prin. Fax 769-6116

Reignbow Hair Fashion Institute Post-Sec.
121 Watchung Ave 07060 908-754-4247

Northvale, Bergen, Pop. 4,564
Northvale SD 400/K-8
441 Tappan Rd 07647 201-768-8484
Sylvan Hershey, supt. Fax 768-4948
www.nvnet.org
Hale MS 200/4-8
441 Tappan Rd 07647 201-768-8484
Michael Pinajian, dean Fax 768-4948

Nutley, Essex, Pop. 27,400
Nutley SD 4,100/K-12
375 Bloomfield Ave 07110 973-661-8798
Joseph Zarra, supt. Fax 661-3447
www.nutleyschools.org
Franklin MS 700/7-8
325 Franklin Ave 07110 973-661-8871
John Calicchio, prin. Fax 661-3775
Nutley HS 1,300/9-12
300 Franklin Ave 07110 973-661-8832
Gregory Catrambone, prin. Fax 661-3664

Abundant Life Academy 400/PK-12
390 Washington Ave 07110 973-667-9700
Suzanne Bruno, prin. Fax 667-1278
Hohokus School - RETS Nutley Post-Sec.
103 Park Ave 07110 973-661-0600

Oakhurst, Monmouth, Pop. 4,130
Ocean Township SD 4,300/K-12
163 Monmouth Rd 07755 732-531-5600
Thomas Pagano, supt. Fax 531-3874
www.ocean.k12.nj.us
Ocean Township HS 1,400/9-12
550 W Park Ave 07755 732-531-5650
Julia Davidow, prin. Fax 571-4009
Other Schools – See Ocean

Oakland, Bergen, Pop. 13,645
Oakland SD 1,700/K-8
315 Ramapo Valley Rd 07436 201-337-6156
Dr. Richard Heflich, supt. Fax 405-1237
www.oaklandschoolsnj.org/
Valley MS 600/6-8
71 Oak St 07436 201-337-8185
Dr. Christopher Lane, prin. Fax 337-7089

Ramapo Indian Hills Regional HSD 2,200/9-12
131 Yawpo Ave 07436 201-416-8100
Paul Saxton, supt. Fax 891-9672
www.rih.org
Indian Hills HS 1,000/9-12
97 Yawpo Ave 07436 201-337-0100
Albert Evangelista, prin. Fax 337-1031
Other Schools – See Franklin Lakes

Barnstable Academy 100/5-12
8 Wright Way 07436 201-651-0200
Lizanne Coyne, hdmstr. Fax 337-9797

Oaklyn, Camden, Pop. 4,116
Oaklyn Borough SD 500/K-9
156 Kendall Blvd 08107 856-858-0335
Tommie Stringer, supt. Fax 869-3474
www.oaklyn.k12.nj.us
Oaklyn JHS 200/7-9
156 Kendall Blvd 08107 856-858-0335
James Sanders, prin. Fax 858-1623

Oak Ridge, Passaic
Jefferson Township SD
Supt. — See Lake Hopatcong
Jefferson Township HS 1,000/9-12
1010 Weldon Rd 07438 973-697-3535
Virginia Jones, prin. Fax 208-8409
Jefferson Township MS 900/6-8
1000 Weldon Rd 07438 973-697-1980
Jeanne Howe, prin. Fax 697-1348

Ocean, Monmouth, Pop. 26,700
Ocean Township SD
Supt. — See Oakhurst
Ocean Township IS 1,400/5-8
1200 W Park Ave 07712 732-531-5630
Larry Kostula, prin. Fax 493-1891

Concorde School of Hair Design Post-Sec.
Route 35 & Sunset Ave 07712 732-918-0505
Deal Yeshiva 100/K-12
1515 Logan Rd 07712 732-663-1717
Rabbi Isaac Dwek, dean Fax 663-1700
Hillel Yeshiva HS 300/9-12
1027 Deal Rd 07712 732-493-0420
Rabbi Howard Bald, hdmstr. Fax 493-2718

Ocean City, Cape May, Pop. 15,330
Ocean City SD 2,100/K-12
501 Atlantic Ave Ste 1 08226 609-399-5150
Dr. Kathleen Taylor, supt. Fax 399-4656
www.ocean.city.k12.nj.us
Ocean City HS 1,400/9-12
501 Atlantic Ave 08226 609-399-1290
Matthew Jamison, prin. Fax 399-1966
Ocean City IS 400/4-8
1801 Bay Ave 08226 609-399-5611
Dr. Pamela Vaughan, prin. Fax 398-7089

Oceanport, Monmouth, Pop. 5,780
Oceanport Borough SD 800/K-8
Wolf Hill Ave 07757 732-544-8588
James DiGiovanna, supt. Fax 544-0386
www.oceanport.k12.nj.us
Maple Place MS 300/5-8
2 Maple Pl 07757 732-229-0267
Dr. John Amato, prin. Fax 229-0961

Old Bridge, Middlesex, Pop. 22,151
Old Bridge Township SD
Supt. — See Matawan
Salk MS 1,200/6-8
155 W Greystone Rd 08857 732-360-4519
David Cittadino, prin. Fax 251-1690
Sandburg MS 1,200/6-8
3439 Highway 516 08857 732-360-0505
Dr. Joseph Gannon, prin. Fax 360-9676
Old Bridge Adult HS Adult
3098 Highway 516 08857 732-679-0900
Evan Jenkins, prin. Fax 360-1349

Old Tappan, Bergen, Pop. 5,903
Northern Valley Regional SD
Supt. — See Demarest
Northern Valley Regional HS 1,200/9-12
100 Central Ave 07675 201-784-1600
Fred Hessler, prin. Fax 768-7724

Old Tappan SD 800/K-8
277 Old Tappan Rd 07675 201-664-1421
William Ward, supt. Fax 664-4418
www.oldtappan.nvnet.org
DeWolf MS 400/5-8
275 Old Tappan Rd 07675 201-664-1475
Dennis Rossi, prin. Fax 664-8101

Oradell, Bergen, Pop. 8,005
River Dell Regional HSD
Supt. — See River Edge
River Dell Regional HS 900/9-12
55 Pyle St 07649 201-599-7240
Lorraine Brooks, prin. Fax 261-3809

Bergen Catholic HS 800/9-12
1040 Oradell Ave 07649 201-261-1844
Timothy McElhinney, prin. Fax 599-9507

Orange, Essex, Pop. 33,300
Orange Township SD 4,000/K-12
451 Lincoln Ave 07050 973-677-4040
Dr. Nathan Parker, supt. Fax 677-2518
www.orange.k12.nj.us
Orange HS 1,100/9-12
400 Lincoln Ave 07050 973-677-4050
Dr. Lee McCaskill, prin. Fax 677-3069
Orange MS 600/7-8
400 Central Ave 07050 973-677-4135
Dr. Judith Kronin, prin. Fax 677-2439

Palisades Park, Bergen, Pop. 18,857
Palisades Park SD 1,300/K-12
270 1st St 07650 201-947-3560
Dr. Mark Hayes, supt. Fax 947-4079
www.palpk.k12.nj.us
Palisades Park JSHS 500/8-12
1 Veterans Plz 07650 201-941-1100
Nicholas Cipriano, prin. Fax 947-1280

Palmyra, Burlington, Pop. 7,641
Palmyra Borough SD 1,100/K-12
301 Delaware Ave 08065 856-786-2963
Dr. Walter Rudder, supt. Fax 829-9638
www.palmyra.k12.nj.us
Palmyra HS 600/7-12
311 W 5th St 08065 856-786-9400
Dr. Richard Perry, prin. Fax 786-3014
Evening HS Adult
311 W 5th St 08065 856-786-8050
Clifton Matthew, prin. Fax 303-1664

Paramus, Bergen, Pop. 26,545
Bergen County Vocational SD
327 E Ridgewood Ave 07652 201-343-6000
Robert Aloia, supt. Fax 225-9182
www.bergen.org
Bergen County Technical HS - Paramus Vo/Tech
285 Pascack Rd 07652 201-986-0009
Gregory Walters Ed.D., prin. Fax 996-6935
Other Schools – See Hackensack, Teterboro

Paramus SD 4,100/K-12
145 Spring Valley Rd 07652 201-261-7800
Janice Dime Ph.D., supt. Fax 261-5861
www.paramus.k12.nj.us
East Brook MS 700/5-8
190 Spring Valley Rd 07652 201-261-7800
Willis Bott Ed.D., prin. Fax 262-1541
Paramus HS 1,300/9-12
99 E Century Rd 07652 201-261-7800
Lina Gudelis, prin. Fax 261-3833
West Brook MS 700/5-8
550 Roosevelt Blvd 07652 201-261-7800
Joan Broe, prin. Fax 652-0376

Bergen Community College Post-Sec.
400 Paramus Rd 07652 201-447-7100
Berkeley College Post-Sec.
64 E Midland Ave 07652 800-446-5400
Capri Institute of Hair Design Post-Sec.
615 Winters Ave 07652 201-599-0880
Cittone Institute Post-Sec.
160 E State Rt 4 07652 201-828-5911
Dover Business College Post-Sec.
East 81 Route 4 W 07652 201-843-8500
Frisch S 500/9-12
243 Frisch Ct 07652 201-845-0555
Dr. Kalman Stein, prin. Fax 845-4941
Paramus Catholic HS 1,400/9-12
425 Paramus Rd 07652 201-445-6465
Joseph Agostino, prin. Fax 445-3952

Park Ridge, Bergen, Pop. 8,959
Park Ridge SD 1,300/K-12
2 Park Ave 07656 201-573-6000
Dr. Patricia Johnson, supt. Fax 391-6511
www.parkridge.k12.nj.us
Park Ridge HS 600/7-12
2 Park Ave 07656 201-573-6000
Richard Martinez, prin. Fax 930-4874

Parlin, Middlesex
Sayreville SD
Supt. — See South Amboy
Sayreville MS 1,300/6-8
800 Washington Rd 08859 732-525-5290
Donna Jakubik, prin. Fax 727-5621
Sayreville War Memorial HS 1,700/9-12
820 Washington Rd 08859 732-525-5252
James Brown, prin. Fax 316-0720

Parsippany, Morris, Pop. 51,000
Parsippany-Troy Hills Township SD 6,800/PK-12
PO Box 52 07054 973-263-7250
LeRoy Seitz Ed.D., supt. Fax 263-7230
www.pthsd.k12.nj.us
Brooklawn MS 900/6-8
250 Beachwood Rd 07054 973-428-7551
Eileen Hoehne, prin. Fax 781-0309
Central MS 700/6-8
1602 US Highway 46 07054 973-263-7125
Jeffrey Rutzky, prin. Fax 402-1579
Parsippany HS 1,000/9-12
309 Baldwin Rd 07054 973-263-7001
Anthony Sciaino, prin. Fax 263-7347
PACE S, 577 Vail Rd 07054 Adult
Joanne Caponegro, dir. 973-263-7180
Other Schools – See Morris Plains

Chubb Institute Post-Sec.
8 Sylvan Way 07054 973-630-4900
Parsippany Christian S 200/PK-12
PO Box 5365 07054 973-539-7012
Rev. Philip Thibault, prin. Fax 539-2527

Passaic, Passaic, Pop. 68,338
Passaic CSD 11,400/PK-12
PO Box 388 07055 973-470-5500
Dr. Robert Holster, supt. Fax 470-8984
passaic-city.k12.nj.us
Lincoln MS 1,500/7-8
291 Lafayette Ave 07055 973-470-5504
John Scozzaro, prin. Fax 470-5128
Passaic HS 2,600/9-12
170 Paulison Ave 07055 973-470-5600
Carlist Creech, prin. Fax 470-5135

Bais Yaakov of Passaic HS 100/9-12
181 Pennington Ave 07055 973-365-0100
Baila Stern, prin. Fax 365-0570
Collegiate S 200/PK-12
22 Kent Ct 07055 973-777-1714
Paula Grassie, hdmstr. Fax 777-3255
Mesivta Tiferes Rav Zvi Aryeh Zemel 100/9-12
15 Temple Pl 07055 973-594-9001
Rabbi Yisroel Cohn, prin. Fax 594-0101

Paterson, Passaic, Pop. 149,843
Paterson SD, 33 Church St 07505 24,700/PK-12
Dr. Michael Glascoe, supt. 973-321-1000
www.paterson.k12.nj.us
Academy of Performing Arts 5-8
45 Smith St 07505 973-321-0570
Cora Quince, admin. Fax 321-0577
B.U.I.L.D. Academy 6-8
202 Union Ave 07502 973-321-1000
Florencio Moran, prin. Fax 321-0587
Eastside HS 3,200/9-12
150 Park Ave 07501 973-321-0510
Karen Johnson, prin. Fax 321-0516
Great Falls Academy 9-12
259 Alabama Ave 07513 973-321-2380
Zatiti Moody, admin. Fax 321-2387
HARP Academy 9-12
175 Main St 07505 973-321-0561
Fax 321-0565
International HS 9-12
202 Union Ave 07502 973-321-2281
Yolanda Burgos, prin. Fax 321-0398
Kennedy HS 2,700/9-12
61 Preakness Ave 07522 973-321-0500
Richard Roberto, prin. Fax 321-0507
Morgan Academy 9-12
32 Spruce St 07501 973-321-2540
Michael Gowdy, coord. Fax 321-2547
MPACT Academy 9-12
175 Main St 07505 973-321-0563
Fax 321-0376
PANTHER Academy 9-12
201 Memorial Dr 07505 973-321-2290
Fax 321-2297
Parks HS of Fine & Performing Arts 300/9-12
413 12th Ave 07514 973-321-0520
Sharon Smith, prin. Fax 321-0527
Paterson City S 4 500/5-8
55 Clinton St 07522 973-321-0040
David Cozart, prin. Fax 321-0047
Paterson City S 7 200/5-8
106 Ramsey St 07501 973-321-0070
Courtney Glover, prin. Fax 321-0077
Paterson Pre-Collegiate Teaching Academy 9-12
137 Ellison St 07505 973-321-0550
Fax 321-0556
Public Safety Academy 9-12
47 State St 07501 973-321-2392
John Tyson, prin. Fax 321-2396
Sports Business Academy 9-12
47 State St 07501 973-321-2390
John Tyson, prin. Fax 321-2396
Silk City 2000 Academy/Adult S Adult
151 Ellison St 07505 973-321-0760
Kathleen Kellett, prin. Fax 321-0767

Al-Huda S 200/K-12
154 Ellison St 07505 973-742-7474
Mohammad Abutayeb, prin. Fax 742-3434
HoHoKus Sch of Trade/Technical Sciences Post-Sec.
634 Market St 07513 800-646-9353
Madison Avenue Baptist Academy 200/K-12
900 Madison Ave 07501 973-279-5800
Brandon Black, prin. Fax 684-6289
Passaic Co. Community College Post-Sec.
1 College Blvd 07505 973-684-6800

Paterson Catholic HS 400/9-12
764 11th Ave 07514 973-278-1024
Richard Garibell, prin. Fax 684-7244

Paulsboro, Gloucester, Pop. 6,096
Paulsboro SD 1,300/PK-12
662 N Delaware St 08066 856-423-5515
Dr. Frank Scambia, supt. Fax 423-4602
www.paulsboro.k12.nj.us/
Paulsboro JSHS 600/7-12
670 N Delaware St 08066 856-423-2222
Lucia Pollino, prin. Fax 423-8915

Pemberton, Burlington, Pop. 1,323
Pemberton Township SD 4,900/PK-12
PO Box 228 08068 609-893-8141
Dr. Michael Gorman, supt. Fax 894-0933
www.pemberton.k12.nj.us
Fort MS 800/7-8
301 Fort Dix Rd 08068 609-893-8141
Mary Hutchinson, prin. Fax 894-9287
Pemberton Township HS 1,400/9-12
148 Arneys Mount Road 08068 609-893-8141
Richard Nolan, prin. Fax 894-0126
Evening HS Adult
148 Arneys Mount Rd 08068 609-893-8141

Burlington County College Post-Sec.
County Route 530 08068 609-894-9311

Pennington, Mercer, Pop. 2,696
Hopewell Valley Regional SD 3,900/K-12
425 S Main St 08534 609-737-4000
Dr. Judith Ferguson, supt. Fax 737-1418
www.hvrsd.k12.nj.us
Central HS 1,100/9-12
259 Pennington Titusville 08534 609-737-4000
Michael Daher, prin. Fax 737-1581
Timberlane MS 1,000/6-8
51 Timberlane Dr 08534 609-737-4000
Patricia Coats, prin. Fax 737-2718

Mercer County Vocational SD
Supt. — See Trenton
MCVS Sypek Center Vo S Vo/Tech
129 Bull Run Rd 08534 609-737-9785
Sharon Nesmith, prin. Fax 737-3951

Pennington S 500/6-12
112 W Delaware Ave 08534 609-737-1838
Penny Townsend, hdmstr. Fax 730-1405

Pennsauken, Camden, Pop. 35,900
Camden County Technical Schools
Supt. — See Sicklerville
Pennsauken Technical HS Vo/Tech
6008 Browning Rd 08109 856-663-1040
Patricia Fitzgerald, prin. Fax 655-8011

Pennsauken Township SD 5,000/PK-12
1695 Hylton Rd 08110 856-662-8505
James Chapman Ed.D., supt. Fax 663-5865
www.pennsauken.net/
Pennsauken HS 1,700/9-12
800 Hylton Rd 08110 856-662-8500
William Clarke, prin. Fax 910-2612
Phifer MS 900/7-8
8201 Park Ave 08109 856-662-8500
Curt Wrzeszczinski, prin. Fax 486-1422

Bishop Eustace Prep S 800/9-12
5552 Marlton Pike 08109 856-662-2160
Cyril Bleistine, prin. Fax 662-0802
JDT Christian Academy 50/K-12
3600 Earle St 08110 856-910-2815
Tangela Lane, admin.
Omega Institute Post-Sec.
7050 Kaighns Ave 08109 856-663-4299
Urban Promise Academy 50/9-12
3700 Rudderow St 08110 856-486-0367
Lynne Rogers, admin. Fax 661-1954

Penns Grove, Salem, Pop. 4,824
Penns Grove-Carneys Point Regional SD 2,100/PK-12
100 Iona Ave 08069 856-299-4250
Joseph A. Massare Ed.D., supt. Fax 299-5226
www.pennsgrove.k12.nj.us
Penns Grove MS 400/6-8
351 E Maple Ave 08069 856-299-0576
Jean Spinelli, prin. Fax 299-4378
Other Schools – See Carneys Point

Pennsville, Salem, Pop. 12,218
Pennsville Township SD 2,000/K-12
30 Church St 08070 856-540-6200
Dr. Mark Jones, supt. Fax 678-7565
www.psdnet.org/SchoolDistrict/framesindex.html
Pennsville Memorial HS 600/9-12
110 S Broadway 08070 856-540-6220
Steven Hindman, prin. Fax 678-2715
Pennsville MS 500/6-8
4 William Penn Ave 08070 856-540-6240
Sheila Burris, prin. Fax 678-2908

Park Bible Academy 200/PK-12
104 Sparks Ave 08070 856-678-9464
Edward W. Riley, prin. Fax 678-3696

Perth Amboy, Middlesex, Pop. 48,797
Middlesex County Vocational SD
Supt. — See East Brunswick
Perth Amboy Vocational HS Vo/Tech
457 High St 08861 732-376-6300
Gerald Bohrer, prin. Fax 376-6391
Adult HS - Perth Amboy Adult
457 High St 08861 732-257-3300
Dawn Lystad, contact Fax 376-6391

Perth Amboy SD 9,200/PK-12
178 Barracks St 08861 732-376-6200
John Rodecker, supt. Fax 826-1644
www.perthamboy.k12.nj.us/
McGinnis MS 1,500/7-8
271 State St 08861 732-376-6040
Roland H. Jenkins, prin. Fax 376-6047
Perth Amboy HS 2,000/9-12
300 Eagle Ave 08861 732-376-6030
Rozalia Czaban, prin. Fax 376-6275
Perth Amboy Accredited Adult HS Adult
178 Barracks St 08861 732-376-6240
Senovia Robles, prin. Fax 376-6245

Raritan Bay Medical Center Post-Sec.
530 New Brunswick Ave 08861 732-324-5232
Reignbow Beauty Academy Post-Sec.
312 State St 08861 732-442-6007
Yeshiva Gedolah of Perth Amboy 100/9-12
PO Box 2506 08862 732-826-5507
Rabbi E. Gruskin, prin. Fax 826-0130

Petersburg, See Woodbine
Upper Township SD 1,500/K-8
525 Perry Rd 08270 609-628-3513
Dr. Larry Hobdell, supt. Fax 628-2002
upperschools.org/
Upper Township MS 600/6-8
525 Perry Rd 08270 609-628-3500
Fax 628-3506

Phillipsburg, Warren, Pop. 14,920
Lopatcong Township SD 800/PK-8
263 State Route 57 08865 908-859-0800
Dr. Michael Rossi, supt. Fax 213-1339
www.warrennet.org/lopatcongschool
Lopatcong MS 400/5-8
321 Stonehenge Dr 08865 908-213-2955
Ms. Rosemary Kowalchuk, prin. Fax 213-1339

Phillipsburg SD 3,000/PK-12
445 Marshall St 08865 908-454-3400
Dr. H. Gordon Pethick, supt. Fax 454-1746
www.pburg.k12.nj.us
Phillipsburg HS 1,600/9-12
200 Hillcrest Blvd 08865 908-454-6551
Mary Jane Deutsch, prin. Fax 213-2427
Phillipsburg MS 600/6-8
525 Warren St 08865 908-454-5577
Dr. John Milone, prin. Fax 213-2546

Pilesgrove, Salem
Salem County Vocational Technical SD
880 Route 45 08098 856-769-0101
William Adams Ed.D., supt. Fax 769-3602
www.scvts.org/
Salem Co. Arts Science & Technology HS Vo/Tech
880 Route 45 08098 856-769-0101
Fax 769-3602
Salem County Career & Technical HS Vo/Tech
880 Route 45 08098 856-769-0101
Todd Bonsall, prin. Fax 769-4214

Pine Brook, Morris
Montville Township SD 3,900/K-12
328 Changebridge Rd 07058 973-331-7117
Dr. Gary Bowen, supt. Fax 331-1307
www.montville.net
Other Schools – See Montville

Pine Hill, Camden, Pop. 11,305
Pine Hill Borough SD 2,000/PK-12
1003 Turnerville Rd 08021 856-783-6900
Kenneth Koczur, supt. Fax 783-2955
www.pinehill.k12.nj.us
Overbrook Regional HS 900/9-12
1200 Turnerville Rd 08021 856-767-8000
Paul Harmelin, prin. Fax 767-3082
Pine Hill MS 400/6-8
1100 Turnerville Rd 08021 856-210-0200
Kate Klemick, prin. Fax 210-0195

Piscataway, Middlesex, Pop. 48,900
Middlesex County Vocational SD
Supt. — See East Brunswick
Piscataway Vocational HS Vo/Tech
21 Suttons Ln 08854 732-985-0717
Dr. Linda Russo, prin. Fax 985-7717

Piscataway Township SD 6,600/K-12
PO Box 1332 08855 732-572-2289
Robert L. Copeland, supt. Fax 777-1361
www.piscatawayschools.org/
Conackamack MS 600/6-8
5205 Witherspoon St 08854 732-699-1577
Dr. Suzanne Westberg, prin. Fax 699-0118
Piscataway Twp. HS 2,200/9-12
100 Behmer Rd 08854 732-981-0700
Dr. Michael Wanko, prin. Fax 981-1985
Quibbletown MS 500/6-8
99 Academy St 08854 732-752-0444
Deidre Ortiz, prin. Fax 752-5798
Schor MS 500/6-8
243 N Randolphville Rd 08854 732-752-4457
Richard Hueston, prin. Fax 424-9445

An-Noor Academy 300/PK-12
120 Ethel Rd W Ste A 08854 732-287-1530
Dr. Ahmed Salem, prin. Fax 287-1564
Katharine Gibbs School Post-Sec.
180 Centennial Ave 08854 732-885-1580
Timothy Christian S 600/K-12
2008 Ethel Rd 08854 732-985-0300
Michael Keller, supt. Fax 985-8008
UMDNJ-Robert Wood Johnson Medical School Post-Sec.
671 Hoes Ln W 08854 732-235-5600
UMDNJ School of Public Health Post-Sec.
170 Frelinghuysen Rd Rm 236 08854 732-445-0199

Pitman, Gloucester, Pop. 9,251
Pitman SD 1,500/K-12
420 Hudson Ave 08071 856-589-2145
Thomas Shulte, supt. Fax 582-5465
www.pitman.k12.nj.us
Pitman HS 500/9-12
225 Linden Ave 08071 856-589-2121
Cherie Lombardo, prin. Fax 589-8855
Pitman MS, 138 E Holly Ave 08071 300/6-8
Eileen Salmon, prin. 856-589-0636

Pittsgrove, Salem
Pittsgrove Township SD 1,900/PK-12
1076 Almond Rd 08318 856-358-3094
Dr. David Moyer, supt. Fax 358-6020
www.pittsgrove.org
Pittsgrove Township MS 600/5-8
1082 Almond Rd 08318 856-358-8529
Michael Clarke, prin. Fax 358-2686
Schalick HS 600/9-12
718 Centerton Rd 08318 856-358-2054
Matthew Jamison, prin. Fax 358-7063

Pittstown, Hunterdon
Alexandria Township SD 700/K-8
557 County Road 513 08867 908-996-6811
Dr. Wendy Schadt, supt. Fax 996-3375
www.alexandria.k12.nj.us
Alexandria MS 400/4-8
557 County Road 513 08867 908-996-6811
David Pawlowski, prin. Fax 996-7963

Plainfield, Union, Pop. 47,642
Plainfield SD 7,100/PK-12
504 Madison Ave 07060 908-731-4335
Dr. Paula Howard, supt. Fax 731-4336
www.plainfieldnjk12.org
Hubbard MS 700/6-8
661 W 8th St 07060 908-731-4320
Doris Williams, prin. Fax 731-4315
Maxson MS 1,000/6-8
920 E 7th St 07062 908-731-4310
Phillip Williamson, prin. Fax 731-4306
Plainfield HS 1,800/9-12
950 Park Ave 07060 908-731-4390
Frank Ingargiola, prin. Fax 731-4394

Du Cret School of the Arts Post-Sec.
1030 Central Ave 07060 908-757-7171
Koinonia Academy 200/K-12
1040 Plainfield Ave 07060 908-668-9002
Muhlenberg Regional Medical Center Post-Sec.
Park Avenue And Randolph Rd 07060 908-668-2400
Union County College Post-Sec.
232 E 2nd St 07060 908-412-3559

Plainsboro, Middlesex
West Windsor-Plainsboro Regional SD
Supt. — See Princeton Junction
Community MS 1,100/6-8
55 Grovers Mill Rd 08536 609-716-5300
Dr. Arthur Downs, prin. Fax 716-5333
West Windsor-Plainsboro HS North 1,300/9-12
90 Grovers Mill Rd 08536 609-716-5100
Michael Zapicchi, prin. Fax 716-5142

Pleasantville, Atlantic, Pop. 19,032
Egg Harbor Township SD 6,700/PK-12
202 Naples Ave 08232 609-646-7911
Dr. Phillip Heery, supt. Fax 383-8749
www.eht.k12.nj.us
Other Schools – See Egg Harbor Township

Pleasantville SD 3,200/PK-12
PO Box 960 08232 609-383-6800
Dr. Clarence Alston, supt. Fax 677-8122
www.pleasantville.k12.nj.us
Pleasantville HS 900/9-12
701 Mill Rd 08232 609-383-6900
Stephen Townsend, prin. Fax 383-9934
Pleasantville MS 700/6-8
801 Mill Rd 08232 609-383-6800
Briggitte White, prin. Fax 677-0852

Shore Beauty School Post-Sec.
103 W Washington Ave 08232 609-645-3635

Point Pleasant, Ocean, Pop. 19,861
Point Pleasant Borough SD 3,100/PK-12
2100 Panther Path 08742 732-701-1900
Robert Ciliento, supt. Fax 892-8403
www.pointpleasant.k12.nj.us/
Memorial MS 800/6-8
Laura Herbert Dr 08742 732-701-1900
Robert Alfonse, prin. Fax 892-0984
Point Pleasant Borough HS 1,000/9-12
Laura Herbert Dr 08742 732-701-1900
John Staryak, dir. Fax 892-1252

Pt Pleas Bch, Ocean, Pop. 5,302
Point Pleasant Beach SD 900/K-12
299 Cooks Ln 08742 732-899-8840
Dr. John Ravally, supt. Fax 899-1730
www.ptpleasantbch.k12.nj.us/
Point Pleasant Beach HS 400/9-12
700 Trenton Ave 08742 732-899-1817
Dr. Raymond Ellis, prin. Fax 899-1145

Pomona, Atlantic, Pop. 2,624

Richard Stockton College of New Jersey Post-Sec.
PO Box 195 08240 609-652-1776

Pompton Lakes, Passaic, Pop. 11,313
Pompton Lakes SD 1,800/K-12
237 Van Ave 07442 973-835-4334
Dr. Terrance R. Brennan, supt. Fax 835-1748
www.plps.org
Lakeside MS 400/6-8
316 Lakeside Ave 07442 973-835-2221
Dr. Paul Amoroso, prin. Fax 835-8088
Pompton Lakes HS 700/9-12
44 Lakeside Ave 07442 973-835-7100
Vincent Przybylinski, prin. Fax 835-1054

Institute for Therapeutic Massage Post-Sec.
125 Wanaque Ave 07442 973-839-6131

Pompton Plains, Morris
Pequannock Township SD 2,500/K-12
538 Newark Pompton Tpke 07444 973-616-6040
Larrie Reynolds, supt. Fax 616-6043
www.pequannock.org
Pequannock Twp. HS 800/9-12
85 Sunset Rd 07444 973-616-6000
John Lavagnino, prin. Fax 616-6029
Pequannock Valley MS 600/6-8
493 Newark Pompton Tpke 07444 973-616-6050
Dr. William Trusheim, prin. Fax 616-8370

Chancellor Academy 100/9-12
PO Box 338 07444 973-835-4989
Dr. Richard Sheridan, dir. Fax 835-0768
Netherlands Reformed Christian S 200/PK-12
164 Jacksonville Rd 07444 973-628-7400
John Vanderbrink, prin. Fax 628-0461

Port Monmouth, Monmouth, Pop. 3,558
Middletown Township SD
Supt. — See Middletown
Thorne MS, 70 Murphy Rd 07758 900/6-8
V. McKenzie, prin. 732-787-1220

Port Norris, Cumberland, Pop. 1,701
Commercial Township SD 700/PK-8
PO Box 650 08349 856-785-0840
Barry Ballard, supt. Fax 785-2354
www.commercial.k12.nj.us
Port Norris MS 200/6-8
PO Box 670 08349 856-785-1611
Peter Koza, prin. Fax 785-2556

Pottersville, Hunterdon

Purnell S 100/9-12
PO Box 500 07979 908-439-2154
Ayanna Hill-Gill, hdmstr. Fax 439-2090

Princeton, Mercer, Pop. 13,495
Princeton Regional SD 3,200/K-12
25 Valley Rd 08540 609-806-4220
Judith A. Wilson, supt. Fax 806-4221
www.prs.k12.nj.us
Princeton HS 1,200/9-12
151 Moore St 08540 609-806-4280
Gary Snyder, prin. Fax 806-4281
Witherspoon MS 700/6-8
217 Walnut Ln 08540 609-806-4270
William Johnson, prin. Fax 806-4271

American Boychoir S 100/5-8
19 Lambert Dr 08540 609-924-5858
Fax 924-5812
Hun S of Princeton 600/6-12
176 Edgerstoune Rd 08540 609-921-7600
Dr. James Byer, hdmstr. Fax 683-4410
Princeton Day S 900/PK-12
PO Box 75 08542 609-924-6700
Dr. Judith R. Fox, hdmstr. Fax 924-8944
Princeton Theological Seminary Post-Sec.
PO Box 821 08542 609-921-8300
Princeton University 08544 Post-Sec.
609-258-3000
Raritan Valley Flying School Post-Sec.
Route 206 08540 609-921-3100
Stuart Country Day S 500/PK-12
1200 Stuart Rd 08540 609-921-2330
Ann Soos, prin. Fax 497-0784
Westminster Choir College of Rider Univ. Post-Sec.
101 Walnut Ln 08540 609-921-7100

Princeton Junction, Mercer, Pop. 2,362
West Windsor-Plainsboro Regional SD 8,900/K-12
PO Box 505 08550 609-716-5000
Robert Loretan Ph.D., supt. Fax 716-5012
www.ww-p.org
Grover MS 1,200/6-8
10 Southfield Rd 08550 609-716-5250
Steven Mayer, prin. Fax 716-5270
West Windsor-Plainsboro HS South 1,500/9-12
346 Clarksville Rd 08550 609-716-5050
Charles Rudnick, prin. Fax 716-5092
Other Schools – See Plainsboro

Rahway, Union, Pop. 27,563
Rahway SD 3,900/PK-12
1200 Kline Pl 07065 732-396-1020
Frank Buglione, supt. Fax 396-1391
www.rahway.net
Rahway HS 1,200/9-12
1012 Madison Ave 07065 732-396-1101
Amod Field, prin. Fax 396-2630
Rahway MS 900/6-8
1200 Kline Pl 07065 732-396-1025
Elaine Ross, prin. Fax 396-2633

Ramsey, Bergen, Pop. 14,558
Ramsey SD 2,000/K-12
266 E Main St 07446 201-785-2300
Dr. Roy Montesano, supt. Fax 934-6623
www.ramsey.k12.nj.us
Ramsey HS 800/9-12
266 E Main St 07446 201-785-2300
Dr. Thomas Melville, prin. Fax 818-2656
Smith MS 700/6-8
2 Monroe St 07446 201-785-2313
Dr. Richard Weiner, prin. Fax 785-2320

Don Bosco Prep HS 9-12
492 N Franklin Tpke 07446 201-327-8003
John Stanczak, prin. Fax 327-3397
HoHoKus School Post-Sec.
10 S Franklin Tpke 07446 201-327-8877

Randolph, Morris, Pop. 19,974
Randolph Township SD 5,300/K-12
25 Schoolhouse Rd 07869 973-361-0808
Dr. Max Riley, supt. Fax 361-2405
www.rtnj.org
Randolph HS 1,500/9-12
511 Millbrook Ave 07869 973-361-2400
Carol Strowbridge, prin. Fax 361-1661
Randolph MS 1,300/6-8
507 Millbrook Ave 07869 973-366-8700
Georgiana Walsh, prin.

County College of Morris Post-Sec.
214 Center Grove Rd 07869 973-328-5000

Red Bank, Monmouth, Pop. 11,876
Red Bank Borough SD 800/PK-8
76 Branch Ave 07701 732-758-1507
Laura Morana, supt. Fax 212-1356
www.rbb.k12.nj.us
Red Bank MS 300/4-8
101 Harding Rd 07701 732-758-1515
Terence Wilkins, prin. Fax 758-1518

Red Bank Catholic HS 9-12
112 Broad St 07701 732-747-1774
Robert Abatemarco, prin. Fax 747-1936

Richland, Atlantic

St. Augustine Prep S 500/9-12
PO Box 279 08350 856-697-2600
Rev. Francis Horn, prin. Fax 697-8389

Ridgefield, Bergen, Pop. 11,014
Ridgefield SD 1,400/K-12
555 Chestnut St 07657 201-945-9236
Dr. Richard Brockel, supt. Fax 945-7830
Ridgefield Memorial JSHS 600/8-12
555 Walnut St 07657 201-945-4455
Marcella Gleie, prin. Fax 945-3505

Ridgefield Park, Bergen, Pop. 12,746
Ridgefield Park SD 1,900/K-12
712 Lincoln Ave 07660 201-641-0800
Dr. John Richardson, supt. Fax 641-2203
www.rpps.net
Ridgefield Park JSHS 1,000/7-12
1 Ozzie Nelson Dr 07660 201-440-1440
Eric Koenig, prin. Fax 641-6861

Ridgewood, Bergen, Pop. 24,790
Ridgewood Village SD 5,400/PK-12
49 Cottage Pl 07450 201-670-2700
Dr. Paul Arilotta, supt. Fax 670-2668
www.ridgewood.k12.nj.us
Franklin MS 600/6-8
335 N Van Dien Ave 07450 201-670-2780
Anthony Orsini, prin.
Ridgewood HS 1,600/9-12
627 E Ridgewood Ave 07450 201-670-2800
John Lorenz, prin. Fax 444-7008
Washington MS 700/6-8
155 Washington Pl 07450 201-670-2790
Katie Kashmanian, prin.

Valley Hospital Post-Sec.
223 N Van Dien Ave 07450 201-447-8002

Ringwood, Passaic, Pop. 12,809
Ringwood SD 1,400/K-8
121 Carletondale Rd 07456 973-962-7028
Dr. Patrick Martin, supt. Fax 962-9211
www.ringwoodschools.org/
Ryerson MS 500/6-8
130 Valley Rd 07456 973-962-7063
Paul Scutti, prin. Fax 962-6905

River Edge, Bergen, Pop. 10,911
River Dell Regional HSD 1,400/7-12
230 Woodland Ave 07661 201-599-7206
Patrick Fletcher, supt. Fax 261-3809
www.riverdell.k12.nj.us
River Dell MS 500/7-8
230 Woodland Ave 07661 201-599-7250
Richard Freedman, prin. Fax 599-7257
Other Schools – See Oradell

Riverside, Burlington, Pop. 7,974
Riverside Township SD 1,400/PK-12
112 E Washington St 08075 856-461-1255
Robert Goldschmidt, supt. Fax 461-5168
www.riverside.k12.nj.us
Riverside HS 500/9-12
112 E Washington St 08075 856-461-1255
Lawrence Talbot, prin. Fax 461-7277
Riverside MS 300/6-8
112 E Washington St 08075 856-461-1255
Robin Ehrich, prin. Fax 461-7277

River Vale, Bergen, Pop. 9,410
River Vale SD 1,400/K-8
609 Westwood Ave 07675 201-358-4000
David Verducci Ph.D., supt. Fax 358-8319
www.rivervaleschools.com/
Holdrum MS 400/6-8
393 Rivervale Rd 07675 201-358-4016
Jayellen Jenkins, prin. Fax 358-8427

Robbinsville, Mercer
Washington Township SD 1,900/K-12
155 Robbinsville Edinburg 08691 609-632-0910
Dr. John Szabo, supt. Fax 371-7964
www.wtpsmercer.k12.nj.us
Pond Road MS 900/4-8
150 Pond Rd 08691 609-632-0940
Paul Gizzo, prin. Fax 918-9011
Robbinsville HS 200/9-12
155 Robbinsville Edinburg 08691 609-632-0950
Deborah Fadde, prin. Fax 371-7961

Rockaway, Morris, Pop. 6,419
Morris County Vocational SD
Supt. — See Denville
Academy for Math-Science & Engineering Vo/Tech
520 W Main St 07866 973-664-2301
Joseph Cacciaguida, prin.

Morris Hills Regional SD 2,700/9-12
48 Knoll Dr 07866 973-664-2291
Dr. Ernest Palestis, supt. Fax 627-6588
www.mhrd.k12.nj.us
Morris Hills HS, 520 W Main St 07866 1,100/9-12
Joseph Cacciaguida, prin. 973-664-2301
Morris Knolls HS 1,600/9-12
50 Knoll Dr 07866 973-664-2201
William Cleffi, prin. Fax 586-3550
Morris Hills Adult HS Adult
48 Knoll Dr 07866 973-664-2250

Rockaway Borough SD 500/K-8
103 E Main St 07866 973-625-8601
Emil Suarez, supt. Fax 625-7355
Jefferson MS, 95 E Main St 07866 300/5-8
Rodney Seifert, prin. 973-625-8603

Rockaway Township SD
Supt. — See Hibernia
Copeland MS 900/6-8
100 Lake Shore Dr 07866 973-627-2465
Scott Allshouse, prin.

Roselle, Union, Pop. 21,265
Roselle Borough SD 2,300/K-12
710 Locust St 07203 908-298-2040
Katie LaMar, supt. Fax 298-3353
www.roselleschools.org
Clark HS 1,100/8-12
122 E 6th Ave 07203 908-298-2004
Nathan Fisher, prin. Fax 259-0782

Roselle Catholic HS 800/9-12
1 Raritan Rd 07203 908-245-2350
Br. Owen Ormsby, prin. Fax 241-3869

Roselle Park, Union, Pop. 13,189
Roselle Park SD 2,000/K-12
510 Chestnut St 07204 908-245-1197
Patrick Spagnoletti, supt. Fax 245-1226
www.roselleparkschools.org

Roselle Park HS 800/8-12
185 W Webster Ave 07204 908-241-4550
Sarah Costa, prin. Fax 245-6609

Rumson, Monmouth, Pop. 7,233
Rumson Borough SD 1,000/K-8
60 Forrest Ave 07760 732-842-4747
Richard Noonan, supt. Fax 842-4877
www.rumson.k12.nj.us
Forrestdale MS, 60 Forrest Ave 07760 600/4-8
Kathi Cronin, prin. 732-842-0383

Rumson-Fair Haven Regional HSD 900/9-12
74 Ridge Rd 07760 732-842-5456
Dr. Peter Righi, supt. Fax 842-3139
www.rfhrhs.org
Rumson-Fair Haven HS 900/9-12
74 Ridge Rd 07760 732-842-1597
Elizabeth Panella, prin. Fax 741-1712

Runnemede, Camden, Pop. 8,520
Black Horse Pike Regional SD
Supt. — See Blackwood
Triton HS 1,500/9-12
250 Schubert Ave 08078 856-939-4500
Edward Stahl, prin. Fax 939-4724

Runnemede Borough SD 700/K-8
505 W 3rd Ave 08078 856-931-5365
Joseph Sweeney, supt. Fax 931-4446
Volz MS, 505 W 3rd Ave 08078 400/4-8
David Gentile, prin. 856-931-5353

Rutherford, Bergen, Pop. 17,967
Rutherford SD 1,700/K-12
176 Park Ave 07070 201-939-1717
Leslie O'Keefe, supt. Fax 939-6350
www.rutherford.k12.nj.us
Pierrepont S 400/4-8
70 E Pierrepont Ave 07070 201-438-7675
Margaret Vaccarino, prin. Fax 842-0452
Rutherford HS 800/9-12
54 Elliott Pl 07070 201-438-7675
John Hurley, prin. Fax 438-7293
Union S 400/4-8
359 Union Ave 07070 201-438-7675
Richard Curci, prin. Fax 804-8248

St. Mary HS 9-12
64 Chestnut St 07070 201-933-8410
Monica D'Alessio, prin. Fax 933-0834
Yeshivas Mesillah 6-8
185 Montross Ave 07070 201-372-0020
Miriam Wolfson, prin. Fax 372-0702

Saddle Brook, Bergen, Pop. 13,296
Saddle Brook Township SD 1,700/K-12
355 Mayhill St 07663 201-843-2133
Dr. Harry Groveman, supt. Fax 843-8265
www.saddlebrookschools.org/
Saddle Brook MSHS 800/7-12
355 Mayhill St 07663 201-843-2880
Jim Sarto, prin. Fax 843-4305

Helma Institute Massage Therapy Post-Sec.
190 Midland Ave 07663 201-226-0056

Saddle River, Bergen, Pop. 3,766

Saddle River Day S 300/K-12
147 Chestnut Ridge Rd 07458 201-327-4050
John O'Brien, hdmstr. Fax 327-6161

Salem, Salem, Pop. 5,812
Salem CSD 1,500/PK-12
205 Walnut St 08079 856-935-3800
Margaret Nicolosi, supt. Fax 935-6977
www.salemnj.org
Salem HS 600/9-12
219 Walnut St 08079 856-935-3900
Gregory Dunham, prin. Fax 935-3288
Salem MS 500/3-8
51 New Market St 08079 856-935-2700
John Mulhorn, prin. Fax 935-2284

Scotch Plains, Union, Pop. 21,160
Scotch Plains-Fanwood SD 4,900/PK-12
Evergreen Ave & Cedar St 07076 908-232-6161
Dr. Margaret Hayes, supt. Fax 889-1769
www.spfk12.org
Park MS 800/5-8
580 Park Ave 07076 908-322-4445
Lisa Rebimbas, prin. Fax 561-5929
Scotch Plains-Fanwood HS 1,400/9-12
641 Westfield Rd 07076 908-889-8600
David Heisey, prin. Fax 889-8254
Terrill MS 800/5-8
1301 Terrill Rd 07076 908-322-5215
Kevin Holloway, prin. Fax 322-6813

Union County Vocational Technical SD
1776 Raritan Rd 07076 908-889-2900
Dr. Thomas Bistocchi, supt. Fax 889-4336
www.ucvts.tec.nj.us
Academy for Allied Health Sciences Vo/Tech
1776 Raritan Rd 07076 908-889-2403
Gloria Griffith, prin.
Academy for Information Technology Vo/Tech
1776 Raritan Rd 07076 908-889-8288
Paul Munz, prin. Fax 889-6831
Union County Magnet HS Vo/Tech
1776 Raritan Rd 07076 908-889-8288
Gwendolyn Seneschal, prin. Fax 889-3196
Union County Vo-Tech HS Vo/Tech
1776 Raritan Rd 07076 908-889-8288
Patrick Mauro, prin. Fax 889-4399
Union County Adult HS Adult
1776 Raritan Rd 07076 908-889-8288
Robert Glowacky, prin. Fax 889-4940

Union Catholic Regional HS 9-12
1600 Martine Ave 07076 908-889-1600
Sr. Percylee Hart, prin. Fax 889-7867

Seabrook, Cumberland, Pop. 1,457
Cumberland Regional SD 1,400/9-12
PO Box 5115 08302 856-451-9400
Katherine A. Kelk, supt. Fax 455-8514
www.crhsd.org/

Cumberland Regional HS 1,400/9-12
PO Box 5115 08302 856-451-9400
John J. Mitchell, prin. Fax 455-8514

Upper Deerfield Township SD 900/K-8
1369 Highway 77 08302 856-455-2267
Dr. Philip Exley, supt. Fax 455-0419
Woodruff MS 300/6-8
1373 Highway 77 08302 856-455-2267
Dr. James Turner, prin. Fax 453-7077

Secaucus, Hudson, Pop. 15,623
Secaucus SD 1,900/PK-12
PO Box 1496 07096 201-974-2004
Constantino Scerbo, supt. Fax 974-1911
www.sboe.org
Secaucus HS 500/9-12
11 Millridge Rd 07094 201-974-2033
Patrick Impreveduto, prin. Fax 974-0026
Secaucus MS 300/7-8
Millridge Rd 07094 201-974-2025
Pasquale Cocucci, prin. Fax 974-0026

Sewell, Gloucester
Deptford Township SD
Supt. — See Deptford
Monongahela MS 700/7-8
890 Bankbridge Rd 08080 856-415-9540
Michael Adams, prin. Fax 464-9284

Gloucester County Vocational SD
1360 Tanyard Rd 08080 856-468-1445
Frederick Keating, supt. Fax 468-3397
www.gcit.org
Gloucester Co. Institute of Technology Vo/Tech
1360 Tanyard Rd 08080 856-468-1445
Ted Frett, prin. Fax 468-1035

Washington Township SD 9,200/K-12
206 E Holly Ave 08080 856-589-6644
Dr. Cheryl Simone, supt. Fax 582-1918
www.wtps.org
Bunker Hill MS 800/6-8
372 Pitman Downer Rd 08080 856-881-7007
Mark Ebner, prin.
Chestnut Ridge MS 700/6-8
641 Hurffville Crosskeys Rd 08080 856-582-3535
James Barnes, prin. Fax 589-0683
Orchard Valley MS 700/6-8
238 Pitman Downer Rd 08080 856-582-5353
Stephan Buono, prin. Fax 589-0197
Washington Township HS 3,000/9-12
519 Hurffville Crosskeys Rd 08080 856-589-8500
Rosemarie Farrow, prin. Fax 589-4057

Gloucester County Christian S 400/PK-12
151 Golf Club Rd 08080 856-589-1665
Donald Netz, prin. Fax 582-4989
Gloucester County College Post-Sec.
1400 Tanyard Rd 08080 856-468-5000

Shamong Township, Burlington, Pop. 5,765
Lenape Regional HSD 7,100/9-12
93 Willow Grove Rd 08088 609-268-2000
Dr. Daniel Hicks, supt. Fax 268-6642
www.lrhsd.org/
Other Schools – See Marlton, Medford, Tabernacle

Shamong Township SD 900/K-8
295 Indian Mills Rd 08088 609-268-0120
Thomas P. Christensen, supt. Fax 268-1229
www.ims.k12.nj.us
Indian Mills Memorial MS 400/5-8
295 Indian Mills Rd 08088 609-268-0440
Timothy Carroll, prin. Fax 268-1229

Sicklerville, Camden
Camden County Technical Schools
343 Berlin Cross Keys Rd 08081 856-767-7000
Gary Bennett Ed.D., supt. Fax 767-3589
www.ccts.tec.nj.us
Gloucester Township Technical HS Vo/Tech
343 Berlin Cross Keys Rd 08081 856-767-7000
Charles Buchheim, prin. Fax 767-3638
Camden County Technical Adult S Adult
343 Berlin Cross Keys Rd 08081 856-767-7000
Teri Stallone, prin. Fax 753-4879
Other Schools – See Pennsauken

Gloucester Township SD
Supt. — See Blackwood
Mullen MS 1,200/6-8
1400 Sicklerville Rd 08081 856-875-8777
Joanne Acerba, prin. Fax 875-0902

Gloucester Township Technical School Post-Sec.
343 Berlin Cross Keys Rd 08081 856-767-7000

Skillman, Somerset
Montgomery Township SD 4,000/K-12
1014 Route 601 08558 609-466-7601
Dr. Samuel Stewart, supt. Fax 466-0944
www.mtsd.k12.nj.us
Montgomery HS 1,400/9-12
1016 Route 601 08558 609-466-7602
James Misek, prin. Fax 466-0243
Montgomery Upper MS 800/7-8
375 Burnt Hill Rd 08558 609-466-7603
William Robbins, prin. Fax 874-7045

Somerdale, Camden, Pop. 5,155
Sterling HSD 900/9-12
501 S Warwick Rd 08083 856-784-1287
Jack McCulley, supt. Fax 435-1530
www.sterling.k12.nj.us
Sterling HS 900/9-12
501 S Warwick Rd 08083 856-784-1333
Dr. Dennis Vespe, prin. Fax 784-7661

Somerset, Somerset, Pop. 22,070
Franklin Township SD 5,400/PK-12
1755 Amwell Rd 08873 732-873-2400
William Westfield, supt. Fax 873-2132
www.franklinboe.org
Franklin HS, 500 Elizabeth Ave 08873 1,700/9-12
Orvyl Wilson, prin. 732-302-4200
Franklin MS 1,100/7-8
415 Francis St 08873 732-249-6410
Dr. Dianne Lotz, prin. Fax 246-0770
Adult HS Adult
415 Francis St 08873 732-249-6410
Fax 873-8393

Rutgers Prep S 700/PK-12
1345 Easton Ave 08873 732-545-5600
Dr. Steven Loy, hdmstr. Fax 214-1819

Somers Point, Atlantic, Pop. 11,701

Shore Memorial Hospital Post-Sec.
Shore Rd 08244 609-653-3545

Somerville, Somerset, Pop. 12,478
Somerville Borough SD 2,100/K-12
51 W Cliff St 08876 908-218-4101
Dr. Carolyn Leary, supt. Fax 526-9668
Somerville HS 1,000/9-12
222 Davenport St 08876 908-218-4108
Timothy O'Halloran, prin. Fax 707-0971
Somerville MS, 51 W Cliff St 08876 300/6-8
Michael Ryan, prin. 908-218-4107

Immaculata HS 900/9-12
240 Mountain Ave 08876 908-722-0200
Sr. Regina Havens, prin. Fax 218-7765
Raritan Valley Community College Post-Sec.
PO Box 3300 08876 908-526-1200

South Amboy, Middlesex, Pop. 7,975
Sayreville SD 5,500/PK-12
150 Lincoln St 08879 732-525-5224
Dr. Frank Alfano, supt. Fax 727-5769
www.sayrevillek12.net/
Other Schools – See Parlin

South Amboy SD 1,100/PK-12
240 John St 08879 732-525-2102
Robert Sheedy, supt. Fax 727-0730
www.saboe.k12.nj.us/
South Amboy MSHS 500/7-12
200 Gvrnr Hrold G Hffmn Plz 08879 732-316-7669
Dr. Patrick McCabe, prin.

Cardinal McCarrick HS 500/9-12
310 Augusta St 08879 732-721-0748
Jean Kline, prin. Fax 727-7018

Southampton Township MS 3 300/6-8
100 Warrior Way 08088 609-859-2256
Jennifer Horner, prin. Fax 801-0754

South Orange, Essex, Pop. 16,390
South Orange-Maplewood SD
Supt. — See Maplewood
South Orange MS 700/6-8
70 N Ridgewood Rd 07079 973-378-2772
Kirk Smith, prin. Fax 378-2775

Immaculate Conception Seminary Post-Sec.
400 S Orange Ave 07079 973-761-9575
Marylawn of the Oranges Academy 200/9-12
445 Scotland Rd 07079 973-762-9222
Mary O'Connor, prin. Fax 378-7975
Seton Hall University Post-Sec.
400 S Orange Ave 07079 973-761-9000

South Plainfield, Middlesex, Pop. 23,064
South Plainfield SD 3,800/K-12
125 Jackson Ave 07080 908-754-4620
Robert J. Rosado Ed.D., supt. Fax 754-3960
www.spnet.k12.nj.us
South Plainfield HS 1,200/9-12
200 Lake St 07080 908-754-4620
Dr. Kenneth May, prin. Fax 756-7659
South Plainfield MS 600/7-8
2201 Plainfield Ave 07080 908-754-4620
Steven Novak, prin. Fax 791-1152
Adult HS Adult
125 Jackson Ave 07080 908-754-4620
Sophia Domogala, prin. Fax 561-2859

Central Career School Post-Sec.
126 Corporate Blvd 07080 908-412-8600
Engine City Technical Institute Post-Sec.
901 Hadley Rd 07080 800-305-3487

South River, Middlesex, Pop. 16,060
South River SD 1,900/K-12
15 Montgomery St 08882 732-613-4000
Ronald Grygo, supt. Fax 613-4756
www.srivernj.org
South River HS 600/9-12
11 Montgomery St 08882 732-613-4014
Kevin Kidney, prin. Fax 613-4044
South River MS 500/6-8
3 Montgomery St 08882 732-613-4073
Dr. Richard Sternberg, prin. Fax 698-9305

Moshe Aaron Yeshiva HS 200/9-12
34 Charles St 08882 732-613-7460
Dovid Wadler, prin. Fax 613-7464

Sparta, Sussex, Pop. 15,157
Sparta Township SD 4,000/K-12
18 Mohawk Ave 07871 973-729-7886
Dr. J. Thomas Morton, supt. Fax 729-0576
www.sparta.org
Sparta HS 1,100/9-12
70 W Mountain Rd 07871 973-729-6191
Richard Lio, prin. Fax 729-3258
Sparta MS 1,100/6-8
350 Main St 07871 973-729-3151
Linda Nick, prin. Fax 729-0573

Sussex County Technical SD
105 N Church Rd 07871 973-383-6700
Dr. Mark Toback, supt. Fax 383-4272
www.sussex.tec.nj.us
Sussex County Technical S Vo/Tech
105 N Church Rd 07871 973-383-6700
Dr. Mark Toback, prin. Fax 383-4272

Pope John XXIII HS 9-12
28 Andover Rd 07871 973-729-6125
Fr. Kieran McHugh, prin. Fax 729-3487

Spotswood, Middlesex, Pop. 8,237
Spotswood SD 1,600/PK-12
105 Summerhill Rd 08884 732-723-2200
John Krewer Ed.D., supt. Fax 251-7666
www.spotswood.k12.nj.us

Spotswood HS 800/9-12
105 Summerhill Rd 08884 732-723-2201
Thomas Calder, prin. Fax 251-7666
Spotswood Memorial MS 300/6-8
115 Summerhill Rd 08884 732-723-2227
Thomas Weaver, prin. Fax 251-7666

Springfield, Union, Pop. 13,420
Springfield SD 1,600/PK-12
PO Box 210 07081 973-376-1025
Michael Davino, supt. Fax 912-9229
www.springfieldschools.com
Dayton HS 600/9-12
101 Mountain Ave 07081 973-376-1025
Elizabeth Cresci, prin. Fax 376-4570
Gaudineer MS 400/6-8
75 S Springfield Ave 07081 973-376-1025
Timothy Kielty, prin. Fax 376-3259

Stanhope, Sussex, Pop. 3,701
Byram Township SD 1,200/K-8
12 Mansfield Dr 07874 973-347-6663
Joseph Pezak, supt. Fax 347-9001
www.byramschools.org
Byram IS 500/5-8
12 Mansfield Dr 07874 973-347-1019
Jack Leonard, prin. Fax 347-9001

Lenape Valley Regional HSD 900/9-12
PO Box 578 07874 973-347-7600
Paul Palik, admin. Fax 347-2536
www.lvhs.org
Lenape Valley Regional HS 900/9-12
PO Box 578 07874 973-347-7600
Douglas deMarrais, prin. Fax 347-2536

Stewartsville, Warren
Greenwich Township SD 900/K-8
101 Wydham Farm Blvd 08886 908-859-2022
Kevin Brennan, supt. Fax 859-4522
www.greenwichschool.org
Stewartsville MS 300/6-8
642 S Main St 08886 908-859-2023
Patty Lantz, prin. Fax 859-1809

Stirling, Morris
Long Hill Township SD
Supt. — See Gillette
Central MS 400/6-8
90 Central Ave 07980 908-647-2311
Richard Cimino, prin. Fax 647-0610

Stratford, Camden, Pop. 7,184
Stratford Borough SD 800/K-8
111 Warwick Rd 08084 856-783-2555
Albert Brown, supt. Fax 309-0304
www.stratford.k12.nj.us
Yellin MS 500/4-8
111 Warwick Rd 08084 856-783-1094
Carol Vita, prin. Fax 309-0304

Star Technical Institute Post-Sec.
43 S White Horse Pike 08084 856-435-7827
UMDNJ-School of Osteopathic Medicine Post-Sec.
1 Medical Center Dr # 210 08084 856-566-7050

Succasunna, Morris, Pop. 11,781
Roxbury Township SD 4,400/K-12
42 N Hillside Ave 07876 973-584-6867
Dennis Mack, supt. Fax 252-1434
www.roxbury.org
Eisenhower MS 700/7-8
47 Eyland Ave 07876 973-584-2973
Daniel Johnson, prin. Fax 584-4529
Roxbury HS 1,500/9-12
1 Bryant Dr 07876 973-584-1200
Jeffrey Swanson, prin. Fax 252-1494

Capri Institute of Hair Design Post-Sec.
Roxbury Mall Route 10 E 07876 973-584-9030

Summit, Union, Pop. 21,200
Summit CSD 3,600/K-12
90 Maple St 07901 908-918-2100
Dr. Carolyn Deacon, supt. Fax 273-3656
www.summit.k12.nj.us
Summit HS 1,000/9-12
125 Kent Place Blvd 07901 908-273-1494
Paul Sears, prin. Fax 273-2832
Summit MS 800/6-8
272 Morris Ave 07901 908-273-1190
Dr. Theodore Stanik, prin. Fax 273-8320

Kent Place S 600/PK-12
42 Norwood Ave 07901 908-273-0900
Susan Bosland, hdmstr. Fax 273-9390
Oak Knoll S of the Holy Child K-12
44 Blackburn Rd 07901 908-522-8100
Timothy Saburn, hdmstr. Fax 273-4616
Oratory Prep S 300/7-12
1 Beverly Rd 07901 908-273-1084
Timothy Lynch, hdmstr. Fax 273-5505

Sussex, Sussex, Pop. 2,189
High Point Regional SD 1,300/9-12
299 Pidgeon Hill Rd 07461 973-875-7204
Dr. John Hannum, supt. Fax 875-0904
www.hpregional.org
High Point Regional HS 1,300/9-12
299 Pidgeon Hill Rd 07461 973-875-3101
Gregory Youngman, prin. Fax 875-2756

Sussex-Wantage Regional SD 1,600/K-8
31 Ryan Rd 07461 973-875-3175
Raymond Nazzaro, supt. Fax 875-7175
swregional.org
Sussex MS 600/6-8
10 Loomis Ave 07461 973-875-4138
Joseph Mulford, prin. Fax 875-6790

Tabernacle, Burlington
Lenape Regional HSD
Supt. — See Shamong Township
Seneca HS 1,200/9-12
110 Carranza Rd 08088 609-268-4600
John Furgione, prin. Fax 268-4635

Tabernacle Township SD 1,000/K-8
132 New Rd 08088 609-268-0153
Bernice Blum-Bart, supt. Fax 268-1006
www.tabernacle.k12.nj.us
Olson MS 500/5-8
132 New Rd 08088 609-268-0153
Susan Grosser, prin. Fax 268-1006

Teaneck, Bergen, Pop. 39,500
Teaneck SD 4,100/PK-12
1 Merrison St 07666 201-833-5510
John Czeterko, supt. Fax 837-9468
www.teaneckschools.org/
Franklin MS, 1315 Taft Rd 07666 600/5-8
Barbara Pinsak, prin. 201-833-5451
Jefferson MS, 655 Teaneck Rd 07666 700/5-8
Antoine Green, prin. 201-833-5471
Teaneck HS 1,400/9-12
100 Elizabeth Ave 07666 201-833-5400
Angela Davis, prin. Fax 833-5403

Fairleigh Dickinson University Post-Sec.
1000 River Rd 07666 201-692-2000
Holy Name Hospital School of Nursing Post-Sec.
690 Teaneck Rd 07666 201-833-3005
Ma'ayanot Yeshiva HS for Girls 200/9-12
1650 Palisade Ave 07666 201-833-4307
Rookie Billet, prin. Fax 833-0816
Metropolitan Schechter HS 100/9-12
800 Broad St 07666 201-837-8357
Fax 837-6773
Torah Academy of Bergen County 200/9-12
1600 Queen Anne Rd 07666 201-837-7696
Arthur Poleyeff, prin. Fax 837-9027

Tenafly, Bergen, Pop. 14,362
Tenafly SD 3,100/K-12
500 Tenafly Rd 07670 201-816-4508
Dr. Morton Sherman, supt. Fax 569-3678
www.tenafly.k12.nj.us
Tenafly HS 1,000/9-12
19 Columbus Dr 07670 201-816-6614
Dr. Dora Kontogiannis, prin. Fax 871-9184
Tenafly MS 700/6-8
10 Sunset Ln 07670 201-816-4900
William Belluzzi, prin. Fax 569-0327

Teterboro, Bergen, Pop. 18
Bergen County Vocational SD
Supt. — See Paramus
Bergen County Technical HS - Teterboro Vo/Tech
504 State Rt 46 07608 201-440-0011
Andrea Sheridan, prin. Fax 996-6925

Teterboro School of Aeronautics Post-Sec.
80 Moonachie Ave 07608 201-288-6300

Tinton Falls, Monmouth, Pop. 17,274
Monmouth Regional HSD 1,100/9-12
1 Norman J Field Way 07724 732-542-1170
James Cleary, supt. Fax 542-5815
www.monmouthregional.net/
Monmouth Regional HS 1,100/9-12
1 Norman J Field Way 07724 732-542-1170
Andrew Teeple, prin. Fax 542-5815

Monmouth-Ocean Ed. Serv. Comm. SD 50/9-12
100 Tornillo Way Ste 1, 732-389-5555
Timothy Nogueira, supt.
www.moesc.org/
Monmouth Adult Education Commission Adult
100 Tornillo Way Ste 1, 732-389-5555
Maria Penzimer, prin. Fax 542-0302

Tinton Falls SD 1,700/K-8
658 Tinton Ave 07724 732-460-2400
Dr. Leonard R. Kelpsh, supt. Fax 542-1158
www.tfs.k12.nj.us
Tinton Falls MS 600/6-8
674 Tinton Ave 07724 732-542-0775
Dr. Marion Lamberti, prin. Fax 542-8723

Ranney S 800/PK-12
235 Hope Rd 07724 732-542-4777
Lawrence Sykoff, hdmstr. Fax 544-1629

Toms River, Ocean, Pop. 7,524
Ocean County Vocational SD
137 Bey Lea Rd 08753 732-240-6414
William Hoey, supt. Fax 505-8929
www.ocvts.org
Ocean County Voc-Tech S - Toms River Vo/Tech
1299 Old Freehold Rd 08753 732-473-3100
Craig Coleman, prin. Fax 349-9788
Other Schools – See Brick, Jackson, Lakehurst, Manahawkin, Waretown

Toms River Regional SD 15,800/K-12
1144 Hooper Ave 08753 732-505-5510
Michael Ritacco, supt. Fax 505-9330
www.trschools.com
Toms River HS - East 1,800/9-12
1225 Raider Way 08753 732-505-5666
Maureen Madden, prin. Fax 270-0909
Toms River HS - North 2,300/9-12
1245 Old Freehold Rd 08753 732-505-5702
James Hauenstein, prin. Fax 341-6249
Toms River HS - South 1,500/9-12
55 Hyers St 08753 732-505-5738
Leonard Stanziano, prin. Fax 341-1321
Toms River IS East 1,500/6-8
1519 Hooper Ave 08753 732-505-5777
Jack Sohl, prin. Fax 286-1290
Toms River IS North 1,300/6-8
150 Intermediate North Way 08753 732-505-5800
Irene Benn, prin. Fax 286-1291
Other Schools – See Beachwood

Monsignor Donovan HS 9-12
711 Hooper Ave 08753 732-349-8801
Dr. Edward Gere, prin. Fax 349-8956
Ocean County College Post-Sec.
College Dr 08754 732-255-0400
Performance Training Post-Sec.
1012 Cox Cro Rd 08755 732-505-9119

Totowa, Passaic, Pop. 10,592
Totowa SD 700/K-8
10 Crews St 07512 973-956-0010
Vincent Varcadipane, supt. Fax 956-9859
www.totowa.k12.nj.us
Memorial MS 400/3-8
294 Totowa Rd 07512 973-942-0010
John Vanderberg, prin. Fax 904-1082

Trenton, Mercer, Pop. 84,639
Mercer County Vocational SD
1085 Old Trenton Rd 08690 609-586-2129
Dr. Kimberly Schneider, supt. Fax 586-8966
www.mctec.net
MCVS Assunpink Center Vo/Tech
1085 Old Trenton Rd 08690 609-586-5144
Lucille Jones, prin. Fax 586-1709
MCVS Health Careers Center Vo/Tech
1070 Klockner Rd 08619 609-587-7640
Virginia Clevenger, prin. Fax 587-3304
MCVS School of Performing Arts Vo/Tech
1200 Old Trenton Rd 08690 609-586-3550
Ryan Killeen, prin. Fax 586-4985
MCVS Adult Evening S Adult
1085 Old Trenton Rd 08690 609-586-5146
Peter Frascella, dir. Fax 586-1709
Other Schools – See Pennington

Trenton SD 10,800/PK-12
108 N Clinton Ave 08609 609-656-4900
Rodney Lofton, supt. Fax 989-2682
www.trenton.k12.nj.us
Career Education Center Vo/Tech
37 Sherman Ave 08638 609-278-2585
William Simpson, prin. Fax 278-2586
Dunn MS 700/6-8
401 Dayton St 08610 609-656-4707
Maryann Klaus, prin. Fax 989-9693
Hedgepeth-Williams MS 600/6-8
301 Gladstone Ave 08629 609-656-4760
Edna Margolin, prin. Fax 989-2927
TCHS - Medical Arts Academy Vo/Tech
50 N Clinton Ave 08609 609-278-5102
James Earle, prin.
Trenton Central HS 3,000/9-12
400 Chambers St 08609 609-278-7260
James Earle, prin. Fax 989-2940
Trenton Central HS - West 9-12
1001 W State St 08618 609-656-4770
Hope Witter, prin.
Daylight/Twilight HS Adult
720 Bellevue Ave 08618 609-989-2494
William Tracy, prin. Fax 656-6062

Helene Fuld Medical Center Post-Sec.
750 Brunswick Ave 08638 609-394-3174
Marie Katzenbach School for the Deaf Post-Sec.
PO Box 535 08625 609-530-3100
Mercer County Community College Post-Sec.
N Broad & Academy Sts 08608 609-586-0505
Mercer County Community College Post-Sec.
PO Box B 08690 609-586-4800
Mercer County Vocational-Tech. School Post-Sec.
1085 Old Trenton Rd 08690 609-586-2129
Mercer Medical Center Post-Sec.
PO Box 1658 08607 609-394-4050
St. Francis Medical Center Post-Sec.
601 Hamilton Ave 08629 609-599-5000
Thomas Edison State College Post-Sec.
101 W State St 08608 609-984-1100

Tuckerton, Ocean, Pop. 3,780
Pinelands Regional SD 1,800/7-12
PO Box 248 08087 609-296-3106
Dr. Detlef Kern, supt. Fax 294-9519
www.pinelandsregional.org/
Pinelands Regional HS 800/10-12
PO Box 248 08087 609-296-3106
Thomas Procopio, prin. Fax 296-6905
Pinelands Regional JHS 1,000/7-9
PO Box 248 08087 609-296-3106
Michael Melega, prin. Fax 296-2626

Union, Union, Pop. 55,000
Township of Union SD 7,700/PK-12
2369 Morris Ave 07083 908-851-6420
Dr. Theodore Jakubowski, supt. Fax 851-6421
www.twpunionschools.org
Burnet MS 1,100/6-8
1000 Caldwell Ave 07083 908-851-6490
Raymond Salvatore, prin. Fax 687-2645
Kawameeh MS 800/6-8
490 David Ter 07083 908-851-6570
Harold Bell, prin. Fax 687-5941
Union HS 2,500/9-12
2350 N 3rd St 07083 908-851-6500
Samuel Fortunato, prin. Fax 687-5204

European Academy of Cosmetology Post-Sec.
1126 Morris Ave 07083 908-686-4422
Healthcare Training Institute Post-Sec.
1969 Morris Ave 07083 908-851-7711
Kean University Post-Sec.
1000 Morris Ave 07083 908-527-2000
Lincoln Technical Institute Post-Sec.
2299 Vauxhall Rd 07083 908-964-7800

Union Beach, Monmouth, Pop. 6,659
Union Beach Borough SD 900/PK-8
1207 Florence Ave 07735 732-264-5405
Arthur J. Waltz Ed.D., supt. Fax 264-6109
www.ub.k12.nj.us
Adult HS Adult
1205 Florence Ave 07735 732-264-5313
Virginia Grezner, prin. Fax 264-8297

Union City, Hudson, Pop. 65,128
Union City SD, 3912 32nd St 07087 9,500/PK-12
Stanley Sanger, supt. 201-348-5852
www.union-city-nj.org/modules/AMS/
Emerson HS 1,400/9-12
318 18th St 07087 201-348-5900
Robert Fazio, prin. Fax 864-2262
Marti MS 500/6-8
1800 Summit Ave 07087 201-348-5400
Geraldine Perez, prin. Fax 348-5405
Union City Career Academy Vo/Tech
1901 West St 07087 201-271-6264
Richard Quagliarello, dir. Fax 864-7705
Union Hill HS 1,500/9-12
3808 Hudson Ave 07087 201-348-5936
David Wilcomes, prin. Fax 348-5866

Evening HS, 318 18th St 07087 — Adult
Dosinda Perez, prin. — 201-392-3618

Mesivta Sanz Hudson County S — 300/K-12
3400 New York Ave 07087 — 201-867-8690
Cheskel Rosenberg, admin. — Fax 867-2848
Miftaahul Uloom S — 200/PK-12
4607 Cottage Pl 07087 — 201-223-9920

Upper Saddle River, Bergen, Pop. 8,509
Upper Saddle River SD — 1,400/K-8
395 W Saddle River Rd 07458 — 201-961-6502
Dr. Joyce Snider, supt. — Fax 934-4923
www.usronline.org
Cavallini MS — 500/6-8
392 W Saddle River Rd 07458 — 201-961-6400
Gene Solomon Ed.D., prin. — Fax 236-9662

Ventnor City, Atlantic, Pop. 12,737
Ventnor City SD — 900/K-8
400 N Lafayette Ave 08406 — 609-487-7918
Carmine Bonanni, supt. — Fax 823-4036
www.vecc.atlnet.org
Ventnor MS — 300/6-8
400 N Lafayette Ave 08406 — 609-487-7900
Robert Baker, prin. — Fax 823-4036

Vernon, Sussex
Vernon Township SD — 5,200/K-12
PO Box 99 07462 — 973-764-2900
Anthony J. Macerino, supt. — Fax 764-0033
www.vtsd.com
Glen Meadow MS — 900/7-8
PO Box 516 07462 — 973-764-8981
Carol Nelson Ed.D., prin. — Fax 764-3295
Vernon Twp. HS — 1,700/9-12
PO Box 800 07462 — 973-764-2960
Timothy Dunnigan, prin. — Fax 764-2961

Verona, Essex, Pop. 13,597
Essex County Vocational SD
900 Bloomfield Ave 07044 — 973-228-0377
Ivan Holmes, supt. — Fax 228-5910
www.essextech.org
Other Schools – See Bloomfield, Newark, West Caldwell

Verona SD — 2,000/K-12
121 Fairview Ave 07044 — 973-239-2100
Earl Kim, supt. — Fax 239-2496
www.veronaschools.org
Verona HS — 600/9-12
151 Fairview Ave 07044 — 973-239-3300
Glenn Cesa, prin. — Fax 857-7543
Whitehorne MS — 600/5-8
600 Bloomfield Ave 07044 — 973-239-1300
Yvette McNeal, prin. — Fax 857-1611

Vineland, Cumberland, Pop. 58,164
Vineland CSD — 7,900/PK-12
625 E Plum St 08360 — 856-794-6700
Charles Ottinger, supt. — Fax 794-9464
www.vineland.org
Landis IS — 600/6-8
61 W Landis Ave 08360 — 856-794-6925
Donald Kohaut, prin. — Fax 507-8763
Rossi IS — 500/6-8
2572 Palermo Ave 08361 — 856-794-6961
Lawrence Ricci, prin. — Fax 507-8786
Veterans Memorial MS — 600/6-8
424 S Main Rd 08360 — 856-794-6918
Rusty Phillips, prin. — Fax 507-8759
Vineland HS North — 1,500/9-10
3010 E Chestnut Ave 08361 — 856-794-6800
Fax 507-8781
Vineland HS South — 1,200/11-12
2880 E Chestnut Ave 08361 — 856-794-6800
Dr. Thomas McCann, prin. — Fax 507-8751
Wallace MS — 6-8
688 N Mill Rd 08360 — 856-362-8887
Belinda Hall, prin. — Fax 362-8980
Vineland Adult Learning Center — Adult
48 W Landis Ave 08360 — 856-794-6943
Joseph Camardo, prin. — Fax 794-1120

Cumberland Christian S — 500/K-12
1100 W Sherman Ave 08360 — 856-696-1600
Wayne Baker, hdmstr. — Fax 696-0631
Cumberland County College — Post-Sec.
PO Box 1500 08362 — 856-691-8600
Sacred Heart HS — 300/9-12
15 N East Ave 08360 — 856-691-4491
Fr. Edward Namiotka, prin. — Fax 563-1644

Voorhees, Camden, Pop. 24,559
Eastern Camden County Regional HSD — 2,200/9-12
PO Box 2500 08043 — 856-346-6740
Dr. Harold Melleby, supt. — Fax 627-7894
www.eastern.k12.nj.us
Eastern Intermediate HS — 1,100/9-10
PO Box 2500 08043 — 856-784-4441
Dr. James Talarico, prin. — Fax 784-3527
Eastern SHS — 1,100/11-12
PO Box 2500 08043 — 856-346-6720
Robert Tull, prin. — Fax 784-1322

Voorhees Township SD — 3,400/PK-8
329 Route 73 08043 — 856-751-8446
Raymond Brosel, supt. — Fax 751-3666
www.voorhees.k12.nj.us/
Voorhees MS — 1,200/6-8
1000 Holly Oak Dr 08043 — 856-795-2025
Charles Ronkin, prin.

Waldwick, Bergen, Pop. 9,650
Waldwick SD — 1,500/PK-12
155 Summit Ave 07463 — 201-445-3131
Dr. Robert Penna, supt. — Fax 445-0584
www.waldwick.k12.nj.us/
Waldwick HS — 400/9-12
155 Wyckoff Ave 07463 — 201-652-9000
Paul Fried, prin. — Fax 652-5053
Waldwick MS — 400/6-8
155 Wyckoff Ave 07463 — 201-652-9000
Michael Meyers, prin. — Fax 652-5053

Waldwick SDA S — 100/PK-12
70 Wyckoff Ave 07463 — 201-652-6078
Alipia Gonzalez, prin. — Fax 652-4652

Wall, Monmouth, Pop. 5,201
Monmouth County Vocational SD
Supt. — See Freehold
Communications HS of Monmouth Co. — Vo/Tech
1740 New Bedford Rd 07719 — 732-681-1010
James Gleason, prin. — Fax 681-6780

Wall Township SD — 4,300/PK-12
PO Box 1199 07719 — 732-556-2000
Dr. James F. Habel, supt. — Fax 556-2101
www.wall.k12.nj.us
Wall HS — 1,300/9-12
PO Box 1199 07719 — 732-556-2000
Steve Genco, prin. — Fax 556-2104
Wall IS — 1,100/6-8
PO Box 1199 07719 — 732-556-2500
Rosaleen Sirchio, prin. — Fax 556-2535

Stuart School of Business Administration — Post-Sec.
2400 Belmar Blvd 07719 — 732-681-7200

Wallington, Bergen, Pop. 11,491
Wallington SD — 1,100/K-12
30 Pine St 07057 — 973-777-4421
Dr. Frank Cocchiola, supt. — Fax 614-9391
www.wboe.org
Wallington JSHS — 500/7-12
234 Main Ave 07057 — 973-777-0808
Dr. Joseph Pompeo, prin. — Fax 777-1434

Wanaque, Passaic, Pop. 10,616
Lakeland Regional HSD — 1,100/9-12
205 Conklintown Rd 07465 — 973-835-1900
Albert Guazzo, supt. — Fax 835-2834
www.lakeland.k12.nj.us
Lakeland Regional HS — 1,100/9-12
205 Conklintown Rd 07465 — 973-835-1900
Joseph LoCascio, prin. — Fax 835-6369

Waretown, Ocean, Pop. 1,283
Ocean County Vocational SD
Supt. — See Toms River
Ocean County Voc-Tech S - Waretown — Vo/Tech
423 Wells Mill Rd 08758 — 609-693-3434
James Rizzolo, prin. — Fax 693-1514

Warren, Somerset
Warren Township SD — 2,200/K-8
213 Mount Horeb Rd 07059 — 732-560-8700
Dr. James Crisfield, supt. — Fax 560-8801
www.warrentboe.org
Warren MS — 800/6-8
100 Old Stirling Rd 07059 — 908-753-5300
Robert Comba, prin. — Fax 753-4789

Watchung Hills Regional SD — 1,800/9-12
108 Stirling Rd 07059 — 908-647-4890
Frances Strumsland, supt. — Fax 647-4852
www.whrhs.org
Watchung Hills Regional HS — 1,800/9-12
108 Stirling Rd 07059 — 908-647-4800
Dr. Thomas DiGanci, prin. — Fax 647-4852

Washington, Warren, Pop. 6,876
Warren County Vocational SD
1500 State Route 57 W 07882 — 908-835-2813
Dr. Alan Naimoli, supt. — Fax 689-9283
www.warrennet.org/warrentech
Warren County Vo-Tech Institute — Vo/Tech
1500 State Route 57 W 07882 — 908-835-2839
Dr. Alan Naimoli, prin. — Fax 689-7699
Warren County Technical Adult HS — Adult
1500 State Route 57 W 07882 — 908-689-0122
Geta Vogel, prin. — Fax 689-7699

Warren Hills Regional HSD — 2,100/7-12
89 Bowerstown Rd 07882 — 908-689-3143
Peter Merluzzi, supt. — Fax 689-4814
www.warrenhills.org
Warren Hills Regional HS — 1,300/9-12
41 Jackson Valley Rd 07882 — 908-689-3050
Tim O'Brien, prin. — Fax 689-9640
Warren Hills Regional MS — 700/7-8
64 Carlton Ave 07882 — 908-689-0750
Jack Paulus, prin. — Fax 689-3663

Warren County Community College — Post-Sec.
475 State Route 57 W 07882 — 908-835-9222

Washington Township, Bergen, Pop. 9,245
Westwood Regional SD — 2,600/K-12
701 Ridgewood Rd 07676 — 201-664-0880
Geoffrey Zoeller, supt. — Fax 664-7642
www.westwood.k12.nj.us
Westwood Regional JSHS — 1,100/7-12
701 Ridgewood Rd 07676 — 201-664-0880
Patrick Bower, prin. — Fax 722-1542

Immaculate Heart Academy — 800/9-12
500 Van Emburgh Ave 07676 — 201-445-6800
Sr. Ellen Cronan, prin. — Fax 445-7416

Watchung, Somerset, Pop. 6,170
Watchung Borough SD — 700/K-8
1 Dr Parenty Way 07069 — 908-755-8121
Dr. Mary Louise Malyska, supt. — Fax 755-6946
www.watchungschools.com
Valley View MS — 300/5-8
50 Valley View Rd 07069 — 908-755-4422
Pat Dye, prin. — Fax 755-4035

Mt. St. Mary Academy — 400/9-12
1645 US Highway 22 07069 — 908-757-0108
Sr. Lisa Gambacorto, dir. — Fax 756-5751

Wayne, Passaic, Pop. 55,000
Passaic County Vocational SD
45 Reinhardt Rd 07470 — 973-790-6000
Diana Lobosco, supt.
www.pcti.tec.nj.us
Passaic County Technical Institute — Vo/Tech
45 Reinhardt Rd 07470 — 973-790-6000
Diana Lobosco, prin.
Passaic County Adult HS — Adult
45 Reinhardt Rd 07470 — 973-790-6000
Diana Lobosco, prin.

Wayne Township SD — 8,400/K-12
50 Nellis Dr 07470 — 973-633-3000
Dr. Maria Nuccetelli, supt. — Fax 628-8058
www.wayneschools.com
Schuyler-Colfax MS — 1,000/6-8
1500 Hamburg Tpke 07470 — 973-633-3130
Dorothy Sherwood, prin. — Fax 633-3195
Washington MS — 1,000/6-8
68 Lenox Rd 07470 — 973-633-3140
MaryJane Tierney, prin. — Fax 633-7590
Wayne Hills HS — 1,300/9-12
272 Berdan Ave 07470 — 973-633-3090
Frank Markowick, prin. — Fax 633-2589
Wayne MS — 6-8
201 Garside Ave 07470 — 973-389-2120
Diane Pandolfi, prin. — Fax 389-2130
Wayne Valley HS — 1,400/9-12
551 Valley Rd 07470 — 973-633-3067
Robert Reis, prin. — Fax 633-3082

Berdan Institute — Post-Sec.
201 Willowbrook Blvd 07470 — 973-837-1818
De Paul Catholic HS — 600/9-12
1512 Alps Rd 07470 — 973-694-3702
Thomas Smithling, prin. — Fax 633-5381
William Paterson University — Post-Sec.
300 Pompton Rd 07470 — 973-720-2000

Weehawken, Hudson, Pop. 12,385
Weehawken Township SD — 1,200/PK-12
53 Liberty Pl 07086 — 201-422-6130
Kevin McLellan, supt.
www.weehawken.k12.nj.us
Weehawken JSHS — 500/7-12
53 Liberty Pl 07086 — 201-422-6130
Dr. Peter Olivieri, prin. — Fax 867-9370

Westampton, Burlington, Pop. 60,004
Westampton Township SD — 900/K-8
710 Rancocas Rd 08060 — 609-267-2053
Dr. Kenneth Hamilton, supt. — Fax 267-2760
www.westampton.k12.nj.us
Westampton MS — 500/5-8
700 Rancocas Rd 08060 — 609-267-2722
Anne Lipsett, prin. — Fax 702-9017

West Berlin, Camden, Pop. 3,000
Berlin Township SD — 600/PK-8
225 Grove Ave 08091 — 856-767-9480
Brian Betze, supt. — Fax 767-8235
berlintwp.k12.nj.us
Eisenhower MS — 300/5-8
235 Grove Ave 08091 — 856-767-0203
Leslie Koller, prin. — Fax 767-7992

West Caldwell, Essex, Pop. 10,422
Caldwell-West Caldwell SD — 2,600/K-12
104 Gray St 07006 — 973-228-6979
Daniel Gerardi, supt. — Fax 228-8716
www.cwcboe.org/
Caldwell HS — 800/9-12
265 Westville Ave 07006 — 973-228-6981
Kevin Barnes, prin. — Fax 228-1116
Other Schools – See Caldwell

Essex County Vocational SD
Supt. — See Verona
Essex County Vocational S-West Caldwell — Vo/Tech
620 Passaic Ave 07006 — 973-575-7740
Dr. Anthony Ingenito, prin. — Fax 575-6958

Essex County College — Post-Sec.
730 Bloomfield Ave 07006 — 973-403-2560

West Deptford, Gloucester, Pop. 19,380
West Deptford Township SD — 3,100/K-12
675 Grove Rd 08066 — 856-848-4300
Edward J. Wasilewski, supt. — Fax 845-5743
www.wdeptford.k12.nj.us/
West Deptford MS — 1,000/5-8
675 Grove Rd 08066 — 856-848-1200
Donna Martello, prin. — Fax 848-2325
Other Schools – See Westville

Westfield, Union, Pop. 29,918
Westfield SD — 5,800/K-12
302 Elm St 07090 — 908-789-4420
William Foley, supt. — Fax 789-4192
www.westfieldnjk12.org
Edison IS — 700/6-8
800 Rahway Ave 07090 — 908-789-4470
Cheryl O'Brien, prin. — Fax 789-1506
Roosevelt IS — 700/6-8
301 Clark St 07090 — 908-789-4560
Stewart Carey, prin. — Fax 789-4193
Westfield HS — 1,700/9-12
550 Dorian Rd 07090 — 908-789-4500
Dennis Fyffe, prin. — Fax 789-4230

West Long Branch, Monmouth, Pop. 8,286
Shore Regional HSD — 700/9-12
132 State Route 36 07764 — 732-222-9300
Leonard Schnappauf, supt. — Fax 222-8849
www.shoreregional.org
Shore Regional HS — 700/9-12
132 State Route 36 07764 — 732-222-9300
Leonard Schnappauf, prin. — Fax 222-8849

West Long Branch Borough SD — 700/K-8
135 Locust Ave 07764 — 732-222-5900
Elizabeth Keshish Ed.D., supt. — Fax 222-9325
www.wlbschools.com
Antonides MS — 500/4-8
135 Locust Ave 07764 — 732-222-5080
Lawrence Farley, prin. — Fax 222-8154

Deal Yeshiva — 300/K-12
PO Box 98 07764 — 732-229-1717
Dr. Judith Shoner, prin. — Fax 728-1400
Monmouth University — Post-Sec.
400 Cedar Ave 07764 — 732-571-3400

West Milford, Passaic, Pop. 26,600
West Milford Township SD — 4,500/PK-12
46 Highlander Dr 07480 — 973-697-1700
Glenn Kamp, supt. — Fax 697-8351
www.wmtps.org
Macopin MS — 800/7-8
70 Highlander Dr 07480 — 973-697-5691
Raymond Johnson, prin. — Fax 697-0301
West Milford HS — 1,500/9-12
67 Highlander Dr 07480 — 973-697-1701
Maureen Bernstock, prin. — Fax 208-0912

Westmont, Camden, Pop. 5,500
Haddon Township SD — 2,200/PK-12
500 Rhoads Ave 08108 — 856-869-7700
Mark Raivetz, supt. — Fax 854-7792
www.haddon.k12.nj.us

Haddon Township HS 700/9-12
406 Memorial Ave 08108 856-869-7750
Gary O'Brien, prin.
Rohrer MS, 101 MacArthur Blvd 08108 500/6-8
Joseph Rafferty, prin. 856-869-7770

West New York, Hudson, Pop. 46,667
West New York SD 6,100/PK-12
6028 Broadway 07093 201-553-4000
Anthony Yankovich, supt. Fax 865-2725
www.wnyschools.net
Memorial HS 1,600/9-12
5501 Park Ave 07093 201-553-4110
Robert Sanchez, prin. Fax 864-2151
West New York MS 800/7-8
201 57th St 07093 201-563-4160
Tony Ferrainolo, prin. Fax 863-6698

New Horizons Beauty School Post-Sec.
5518 Bergenline Ave 07093 201-866-4000
St. Joseph of the Palisades HS 300/9-12
5400 Broadway 07093 201-864-9700
Bruce Segall, prin. Fax 864-0229

West Orange, Essex, Pop. 45,500
West Orange SD 6,100/K-12
179 Eagle Rock Ave 07052 973-669-5400
Jerry Tarnoff, supt. Fax 669-1432
www.westorange.k12.nj.us
Edison MS 700/6-8
75 William St 07052 973-669-5360
Xavier Fitzgerald, prin. Fax 243-9802
Liberty MS 6-8
1 Kelly Dr 07052 973-243-2007
John Vogler, prin. Fax 243-2743
Roosevelt MS 700/6-8
36 Gilbert Pl 07052 973-669-5373
Frank Corrado, prin. Fax 243-9807
West Orange HS 1,900/9-12
51 Conforti Ave 07052 973-669-5301
Arthur Alloggiamento, prin. Fax 669-1260

Seton Hall Preparatory HS 1,000/9-12
120 Northfield Ave 07052 973-325-6624
Rev. Michael Kelly, prin. Fax 325-6652
Solomon Schecter Day S - Upper S 400/6-12
1418 Pleasant Valley Way 07052 973-669-8000
Joyce Raynor Ph.D., hdmstr. Fax 669-0034

West Paterson, Passaic, Pop. 11,245
West Paterson SD 900/K-8
853 McBride Ave 07424 973-278-5535
Scott Rixford, supt. Fax 278-2568
wpschools.org
Memorial MS 400/5-8
15 Memorial Dr 07424 973-256-5800
Charles Silverstein, prin. Fax 256-5644

Berkeley College Post-Sec.
44 Rifle Camp Rd 07424 973-278-5400

Westville, Gloucester, Pop. 4,466
West Deptford Township SD
Supt. — See West Deptford
West Deptford HS 1,100/9-12
1600 Crown Point Rd 08093 856-848-6110
Howard Cohen, prin. Fax 845-5774

St. John of God Community Services Post-Sec.
1145 Delsea Dr 08093 856-848-4700

Westwood, Bergen, Pop. 10,994

Pascack Valley Hospital Post-Sec.
250 Old Hook Rd 07675 201-358-3010

Wharton, Morris, Pop. 6,222
Wharton Borough SD 700/K-8
137 E Central Ave 07885 973-361-2592
Richard Bitondo, supt. Fax 895-2187
www.wpbs.org
MacKinnon MS 200/6-8
137 E Central Ave 07885 973-361-1253
Christopher Herdman, prin. Fax 361-4805

Whippany, Morris
Hanover Park Regional HSD
Supt. — See East Hanover
Whippany Park HS 600/9-12
165 Whippany Rd 07981 973-887-3004
John Manning, prin. Fax 887-0451

Hanover Township SD 1,500/K-8
61 Highland Ave 07981 973-515-2404
Scott R. Pepper, supt. Fax 540-1023
www.hanovertwpschools.com/
Memorial JHS 500/6-8
61 Highland Ave 07981 973-515-5510
Michael J. Wasko, prin. Fax 515-2481

White House Station, Hunterdon, Pop. 1,287
Readington Township SD 2,000/K-8
PO Box 807 08889 908-534-2195
Jordan Schiff Ed.D., supt. Fax 534-9551
www.readington.k12.nj.us
Readington MS 800/6-8
PO Box 700 08889 908-534-2113
Johanna Ruberto Ed.D., prin. Fax 534-6802

Whiting, Ocean
Manchester Township SD 3,100/K-12
121 Route 539 08759 732-350-5900
William DeFeo, supt. Fax 350-0436
www.manchestertwp.org
Other Schools – See Manchester

Wildwood, Cape May, Pop. 5,291
Wildwood CSD 900/PK-12
4300 Pacific Ave 08260 609-522-4157
Dennis Anderson, supt. Fax 523-8161
Wildwood HS 300/9-12
4300 Pacific Ave 08260 609-522-7922
Dr. Gladys Lauriello, prin. Fax 522-7914
Wildwood MS 200/5-8
4300 Pacific Ave 08260 609-522-7922
Dr. Gladys Lauriello, prin. Fax 522-7914

Wildwood Catholic HS 400/9-12
1500 Central Ave 08260 609-522-7257
Richard Turco, prin. Fax 522-2453

Williamstown, Gloucester, Pop. 10,891
Monroe Township SD 4,800/K-12
75 E Academy St 08094 856-629-6400
Robert Terrill Ed.D., supt. Fax 262-2499
www.monroetwp.k12.nj.us
Williamstown HS 1,600/9-12
700 N Tuckahoe Rd 08094 856-262-8200
Stephen F. Stumpo, prin. Fax 262-0869
Williamstown MS 1,400/5-8
561 Clayton Rd 08094 856-629-7444
Charles D. Folker, prin. Fax 875-6757

Victory Christian S 200/PK-12
PO Box 806 08094 856-629-4300
Chris Peria, prin. Fax 875-7703

Willingboro, Burlington, Pop. 32,400
Willingboro Township SD 3,300/PK-12
440 Beverly Rancocas Rd 08046 609-835-8600
Ed Kern, supt. Fax 835-3880
www.willingboroschools.org/
Levitt MS 400/7-8
50 Salem Rd 08046 609-835-8900
Michael White, prin. Fax 835-3974
Willingboro HS 1,300/9-12
20 S John F Kennedy Way 08046 609-835-8800
Teresa-Anne Lucas, prin. Fax 835-8877
Adult HS, 50 Salem Rd 08046 Adult
Jack McGee, prin. 609-835-3810

Woodbridge, Middlesex, Pop. 17,434
Middlesex County Vocational SD
Supt. — See East Brunswick
Woodbridge Vocational HS Vo/Tech
1 Convery Blvd 07095 732-634-5858
Hector Montes, prin. Fax 632-7073

Woodbridge Township SD 12,800/K-12
PO Box 428 07095 732-602-8550
Vincent Smith, supt. Fax 750-3493
www.woodbridge.k12.nj.us
Woodbridge HS 1,600/9-12
25 Samuel Lupo Pl 07095 732-602-8600
Arthur Lee Warren, prin. Fax 602-8612
Woodbridge MS 500/6-8
525 Barron Ave 07095 732-602-8690
James Sullivan, prin. Fax 855-0326
Other Schools – See Avenel, Colonia, Fords, Iselin

Berkeley College Post-Sec.
430 Rahway Ave 07095 800-446-5400

Woodbury, Gloucester, Pop. 10,435
Woodbury SD 1,400/PK-12
25 N Broad St 08096 856-853-0123
Joseph Jones, supt. Fax 853-0704
www.woodburysch.com
Woodbury JSHS 700/6-12
25 N Broad St 08096 856-853-0123
Denise Dunham, prin. Fax 853-2684

Woodbury Heights, Gloucester, Pop. 3,022
Gateway Regional SD 1,000/7-12
775 Tanyard Rd, 856-848-8172
Joyce Stumpo, supt. Fax 848-2049
www.gatewayhs.com
Gateway Regional MSHS 1,000/7-12
775 Tanyard Rd, 856-848-8200
Dr. Ronald Davis, prin. Fax 251-9813

Woodcliff Lake, Bergen, Pop. 5,887
Woodcliff Lake SD 900/PK-8
100 Dorchester Rd 07677 201-930-5600
Peter Lisi, supt. Fax 930-0488
www.woodcliff-lake.com
Woodcliff MS 300/6-8
134 Woodcliff Ave 07677 201-930-5600
Lauren Barbelet, prin. Fax 391-7932

Wood Ridge, Bergen, Pop. 7,607
Wood-Ridge SD 1,100/K-12
89 Hackensack St 07075 201-933-6777
Elaine Giugliano, supt. Fax 804-9204
www.wood-ridgeschools.org
Ostrovsky MS 200/6-8
540 Windsor Rd 07075 201-939-2103
Robert Recchione, prin. Fax 939-0259
Wood-Ridge HS 400/9-12
258 Hackensack St 07075 201-939-0810
Dr. Ronald Frederick, prin. Fax 939-1195

Woodstown, Salem, Pop. 3,312
Woodstown-Pilesgrove Regional SD 1,600/PK-12
135 East Ave 08098 856-769-0144
Robert Bumpus, supt. Fax 769-4549
www.woodstown.org
Woodstown HS 600/9-12
140 East Ave 08098 856-769-0144
Dr. Scott Hoopes, prin. Fax 769-4102
Woodstown MS 500/5-8
15 Lincoln Ave 08098 856-769-0144
John Fargnoli, prin. Fax 769-9425

Woolwich, Gloucester
Kingsway Regional SD 1,800/7-12
213 Kings Hwy 08085 856-467-4600
Ave Altersitz, supt. Fax 467-5382
www.kingsway.k12.nj.us
Kingsway Regional HS 1,300/9-12
201 Kings Hwy 08085 856-467-3300
Thomas Coleman, prin. Fax 241-1932
Kingsway Regional MS 500/7-8
203 Kings Hwy 08085 856-467-3300
Troy Walton, prin.

Wyckoff, Bergen, Pop. 15,372
Wyckoff Township SD 2,500/K-8
241 Morse Ave 07481 201-848-5701
Dr. Janet Razze, supt. Fax 848-5695
www.wyckoffschools.org
Eisenhower MS 900/6-8
344 Calvin Ct 07481 201-848-5750
Richard Kuder, prin. Fax 848-5682

Eastern Christian MS 300/5-8
518 Sicomac Ave 07481 201-891-3663
Richard VanYperen, prin. Fax 847-0902

Zarephath, Somerset

Somerset Christian Academy 200/K-12
595 Weston Canal Rd 08890 732-356-3488
Lia Diorio, prin. Fax 868-0386
Somerset Christian College Post-Sec.
PO Box 9035 08890 800-234-9305

NEW MEXICO

NEW MEXICO PUBLIC EDUCATION DEPARTMENT

300 Don Gaspar Ave, Santa Fe 87501-2786
Telephone 505-827-5800
Fax 505-827-6696
Website http://www.sde.state.nm.us

Secretary of Education — Veronica Garcia

NEW MEXICO BOARD OF EDUCATION

300 Don Gaspar Ave, Santa Fe 87501-2786

REGIONAL EDUCATION COOPS (REC) & REGIONAL CENTER COOPS (RCC)

Central REC 5
Nina Tafoya, dir. — 505-889-3412
PO Box 37440, Albuquerque 87176 — Fax 889-3422
www.crecnm.org/

High Plains REC 3
Stephen Aguirre, dir. — 505-445-7090
101 N 2nd St, Raton 87740 — Fax 445-7663
hprec.com

Northeast REC 4
Lorenzo Marquez, dir. — 505-426-2085
PO Box 927, Las Vegas 87701 — Fax 454-1473
www.rec4.com

Pecos Valley REC 8
Janet Sistrunk, dir. — 505-748-6100
PO Box 155, Artesia 88211 — Fax 748-6160
www.pvrec8.com/

REC 2
Kris Baca, dir. — 505-638-5491
PO Box 230, Gallina 87017 — Fax 638-0131

REC 6
Patti Harrelson, dir. — 505-562-4455
1500 S Avenue K Ste 9 — Fax 562-4460
Portales 88130
www.rec6.net

REC 7
Belinda Morris, dir. — 505-393-0755
315 E Clinton St, Hobbs 88240 — Fax 393-0249

REC 9
Sandy Gladden, dir. — 505-257-2368
1400 Sudderth Dr, Ruidoso 88345 — Fax 257-2141
www.recixnm.org/

Southwest REC 10
Cathe North, dir., PO Box 4075 — 505-894-7589
Truth or Consequences 87901 — Fax 894-7584
www.swrecnm.org

PUBLIC, PRIVATE AND CATHOLIC SECONDARY SCHOOLS

Alamogordo, Otero, Pop. 36,245

Alamogordo SD — 6,600/PK-12
PO Box 650 88311 — 505-439-3270
Michael Harris, supt. — Fax 439-3373
aps4kids.org

Alamogordo HS — 1,900/9-12
PO Box 650 88311 — 505-443-2000
Joe Jaramillo, prin. — Fax 443-2018

Chaparral MS — 700/6-8
PO Box 650 88311 — 505-439-3350
Cheryl Kullman, prin. — Fax 439-3354

Mountain View MS — 500/6-8
PO Box 650 88311 — 505-439-3330
Mike Farley, prin. — Fax 439-3355

Other Schools – See Holloman AFB

Community Christian S — 200/PK-12
2907 Thunder Rd 88310 — 505-434-0352
Connie Higgs, admin. — Fax 437-1320

New Mexico School Visually Handicapped — Post-Sec.
1900 N White Sands Blvd 88310 — 505-437-3505

New Mexico State University — Post-Sec.
2400 Scenic Dr 88310 — 505-439-3600

Olympian University of Cosmetology — Post-Sec.
1810 10th St 88310 — 505-437-2221

Albuquerque, Bernalillo, Pop. 494,236

Albuquerque SD — 85,900/PK-12
PO Box 25704 87125 — 505-880-3700
Dr. Elizabeth Everitt, supt. — Fax 872-8855
ww2.aps.edu

Adams MS — 900/6-8
5401 Glenrio Rd NW 87105 — 505-831-0400
Stanley Agustin, prin. — Fax 836-7760

Albuquerque HS — 1,800/9-12
800 Odelia Rd NE 87102 — 505-843-6400
Linda Sink, prin. — Fax 848-9432

Career Enrichment Ctr — Vo/Tech
807 Mountain Rd NE 87102 — 505-247-3658
Katherine Sandoval, prin. — Fax 243-2447

Carter MS — 1,100/6-8
8901 Bluewater Rd NW 87121 — 505-833-7540
Rita Martinez, prin. — Fax 833-7559

Cibola HS — 2,900/9-12
1510 Ellison Dr NW 87114 — 505-897-0110
Grace Brown, prin. — Fax 897-4251

Cleveland MS — 800/6-8
6910 Natalie Ave NE 87110 — 505-881-9227
Susan Labarge, prin. — Fax 881-9441

Del Norte HS — 1,700/9-12
5323 Montgomery Blvd NE 87109 — 505-883-7222
Rebecca Almeter, prin. — Fax 880-3965

Desert Ridge MS — 1,100/6-8
8400 Barstow St NE 87122 — 505-857-9282
Sean Joyce, prin. — Fax 857-0201

Eisenhower MS — 1,000/6-8
11001 Camero Ave NE 87111 — 505-292-2530
Debra Hamilton, prin. — Fax 291-6884

Eldorado HS — 2,200/9-12
11300 Montgomery Blvd NE 87111 — 505-296-4871
Yvonne Garcia, prin. — Fax 291-6809

Garfield MS — 400/6-8
3501 6th St NW 87107 — 505-344-1647
Rhonda Sandoval, prin. — Fax 344-6562

Grant MS — 800/6-8
1111 Easterday Dr NE 87112 — 505-299-2113
Ed Briggs, prin. — Fax 291-6881

Harrison MS — 600/6-8
3912 Isleta Blvd SW 87105 — 505-877-1279
Sam Obenshain, prin. — Fax 877-6797

Hayes MS — 500/6-8
1100 Texas St NE 87110 — 505-265-7741
Jimmie Lueder, prin. — Fax 260-6108

Highland HS — 2,000/9-12
4700 Coal Ave SE 87108 — 505-265-3711
Nicki Dennis, prin. — Fax 348-8503

Hoover MS — 800/6-8
12015 Tivoli Ave NE Ste A 87111 — 505-298-6896
Wayne Knight, prin. — Fax 291-6880

Jackson MS — 700/6-8
10600 Indian School Rd NE 87112 — 505-299-7377
Ann Piper, prin. — Fax 291-6877

Jefferson MS — 900/6-8
712 Girard Blvd NE 87106 — 505-255-8691
Ivy Langan, prin. — Fax 268-2334

Johnson MS — 1,000/6-8
6811 Taylor Ranch Rd NW 87120 — 505-898-1492
Marcie Johnson, prin. — Fax 898-7150

Kennedy MS — 500/6-8
721 Tomasita St NE 87123 — 505-298-6701
Ruby Ethridge, prin. — Fax 291-6879

La Cueva HS — 2,200/9-12
7801 Wilshire Ave NE 87122 — 505-823-2327
Jo Ann Coffee, prin. — Fax 857-0177

Madison MS — 800/6-8
3501 Moon St NE 87111 — 505-299-4735
Jim Steinhubel, prin. — Fax 323-9512

Manzano HS — 2,000/9-12
12200 Lomas Blvd NE 87112 — 505-559-2200
Tim Whalen, prin. — Fax 291-6854

McKinley MS — 800/6-8
4500 Comanche Rd NE 87110 — 505-881-9390
Scott Elder, prin. — Fax 880-3968

Monroe MS — 1,200/6-8
6100 Paradise Blvd NW 87114 — 505-897-0101
Vernon Martinez, prin. — Fax 897-2371

Polk MS — 400/6-8
2220 Raymac Rd SW 87105 — 505-877-6444
Theresa Baca, prin. — Fax 877-1618

Pyle MS — 700/6-8
1820 Valdora Rd SW 87105 — 505-877-3770
B. Cordoba Martinez, prin. — Fax 873-8540

Rio Grande HS — 1,800/9-12
2300 Arenal Rd SW 87105 — 505-873-0220
Al Sanchez, prin. — Fax 873-8523

Sandia HS — 2,200/9-12
7801 Candelaria Rd NE 87110 — 505-294-1511
Michael Bachicha, prin. — Fax 291-6878

Taft MS — 700/6-8
620 Schulte Rd NW 87107 — 505-344-4389
Stephanie Williams, prin. — Fax 761-8440

Taylor MS — 600/6-8
8200 Guadalupe Trl NW 87114 — 505-898-3666
Nancy Romero, prin. — Fax 897-5165

Truman MS — 900/6-8
9400 Benavides Rd SW 87121 — 505-836-3030
Judith Martin-Tafoya, prin. — Fax 836-7745

Valley HS — 2,000/9-12
1505 Candelaria Rd NW 87107 — 505-345-9021
Anthony Griego, prin. — Fax 761-8429

Van Buren MS — 600/6-8
700 Louisiana Blvd SE 87108 — 505-268-3833
Maria Carmen Graham, prin. — Fax 260-6104

Washington MS — 500/6-8
1101 Park Ave SW 87102 — 505-764-2000
Cynthia Challberg-Hale, prin. — Fax 764-2022

West Mesa HS — 2,600/9-12
6701 Fortuna Rd NW 87121 — 505-831-6993
Blanca Lopez, prin. — Fax 836-7756

Wilson MS — 600/6-8
1138 Cardenas Dr SE 87108 — 505-268-3961
Connie Hansen, prin. — Fax 260-2000

Albuquerque Evening HS — Adult
800 Odelia Rd NE 87102 — 505-848-9424
Dave Wells, prin. — Fax 848-9454

Other Schools – See Tijeras

Albuquerque Academy — 1,100/6-12
6400 Wyoming Blvd NE 87109 — 505-828-3200
Andrew T. Watson, hdmstr. — Fax 828-3322

Albuquerque Barber College — Post-Sec.
601 San Pedro Dr NE Ste 100 87108 — 505-266-4900

Albuquerque TVI Community College — Post-Sec.
525 Buena Vista Dr SE 87106 — 505-224-3000

Apollo College — Post-Sec.
1001 Menaul Blvd NE Ste C 87107 — 800-368-7246

Bosque S — 500/6-12
4000 Learning Rd NW 87120 — 505-898-6388
Andrew Wooden, hdmstr. — Fax 922-0392

Calvary Christian Academy — 200/PK-12
1404 Lead Ave SE 87106 — 505-842-8681

DeWolff Coll of Hairstyling\Cosmetology — Post-Sec.
1500 Eubank Blvd NE 87112 — 505-296-4100

Evangel Christian Academy — 200/PK-12
4501 Montgomery Blvd NE 87109 — 505-883-4674
Nick Olona, prin. — Fax 883-1229

Hope Christian S — 1,400/K-12
8005 Louisiana Blvd NE 87109 — 505-822-8868
Kelly McEachran, hdmstr. — Fax 822-8260

International Institute of the Americas — Post-Sec.
4201 Central Ave NW Ste J 87105 — 505-880-2877

ITT Technical Institute — Post-Sec.
5100 Masthead St NE 87109 — 505-828-1114

Menaul S — 200/6-12
301 Menaul Blvd NE 87107 — 505-345-7727
Lindsey Gilbert, hdmstr. — Fax 344-2517

National American University — Post-Sec.
4775 Indian Sch Rd NE #200 87110 — 505-265-7517

New Life Baptist Academy — 200/PK-12
6900 Los Volcanes Rd NW 87121 — 505-352-2628
Lille Allen, prin. — Fax 352-2684

New Mexico Aveda Inst de Bellas Artes — Post-Sec.
2614 Pennsylvania St NE 87110 — 505-294-5333

Olympian University of Cosmetology — Post-Sec.
6300 San Mateo Blvd NE # J 87109 — 505-765-1044

Pima Medical Institute — Post-Sec.
2201 San Pedro Dr NE 87110 — 505-881-1234

St. Pius X HS — 1,000/9-12
5301 Saint Josephs Dr NW 87120 — 505-831-8400
Barbara Rothweiler, prin. — Fax 831-8413

Sandia Prep S — 600/6-12
532 Osuna Rd NE 87113 — 505-338-3000
Dick Heath, hdmstr. — Fax 338-3099

Southwestern Indian Polytechnic Inst. — Post-Sec.
PO Box 10146 87184 — 505-346-2347

Temple Baptist Academy — 200/PK-12
1621 Arizona St NE 87110 — 505-262-0969
David Baker, admin. — Fax 262-0996

The Art Center Design College — Post-Sec.
5000 Marble Ave NE 87110 — 505-254-7575

Universal Therapeutic Massage Institute — Post-Sec.
3410 Aztec Rd NE 87107 — 505-888-0020

University of New Mexico — Post-Sec.
1 University Campus 87131 — 505-277-0111

University of Phoenix-NM Division | Post-Sec.
7471 Pan Amrcan West Fwy NE 87109 | 505-821-4800

Victory Christian S | 200/K-12
220 El Pueblo Rd NW 87114 | 505-898-3060
Glenn Frey, admin. | Fax 898-6690

Animas, Hidalgo
Animas SD | 300/PK-12
PO Box 85 88020 | 505-548-2299
Jerry Birdwell, supt. | Fax 548-2388
www.animask12.net
Animas HS | 100/9-12
PO Box 90 88020 | 505-548-2296
Ruben Aguallo, prin. | Fax 548-2649
Animas MS | 100/5-8
PO Box 68 88020 | 505-548-2296
Karla Stinehart, prin. | Fax 548-2388

Anthony, Dona Ana, Pop. 5,160
Gadsden ISD
Supt. — See Santa Teresa
Gadsden HS | 2,400/9-12
6301 Highway 28 88021 | 505-882-6300
George Foster, prin. | Fax 882-2370
Gadsden MS | 1,000/7-8
1301 Washington St 88021 | 505-882-2372
Dr. David Garcia, prin. | Fax 882-5227

Anton Chico, Guadalupe
Santa Rosa Consolidated SD
Supt. — See Santa Rosa
Anton Chico MS | 50/6-8
PO Box 169 87711 | 505-427-6038
Ted Hearn, prin. | Fax 427-4246

Artesia, Eddy, Pop. 10,481
Artesia SD | 3,500/PK-12
1106 W Quay Ave 88210 | 505-746-3585
Mike Phipps, supt. | Fax 746-6232
www.bulldogs.org
Artesia HS | 700/10-12
1006 W Richardson Ave 88210 | 505-746-9816
Crit Caton, prin. | Fax 746-4365
Park JHS | 600/8-9
15th & Cannon 88210 | 505-746-9892
Mike Nuanes, prin. | Fax 746-4462

Aztec, San Juan, Pop. 7,084
Aztec Municipal SD | 3,200/PK-12
1118 W Aztec Blvd 87410 | 505-334-9474
Dr. Linda Paul, supt. | Fax 334-9861
www.aztecschools.com
Aztec HS | 1,000/9-12
500 E Chaco St 87410 | 505-334-9414
Kirk Carpenter, prin. | Fax 599-4387
Koogler MS | 700/6-8
455 N Light Plant Rd 87410 | 505-334-6102
Richard Vogel, prin. | Fax 599-4385

Bayard, Grant, Pop. 2,397
Cobre Consolidated SD | 1,400/PK-12
PO Box 1000 88023 | 505-537-4010
Harrell Holder, supt. | Fax 537-5455
www.cobre.k12.nm.us
Cobre HS | 500/9-12
PO Box 749 88023 | 505-537-4020
Eric Martinez, prin. | Fax 537-5503
Snell MS | 200/7-8
PO Box 729 88023 | 505-537-4030
Jeff Gorum, prin. | Fax 537-3358

Belen, Valencia, Pop. 7,121
Belen Consolidated SD | 4,700/PK-12
520 N Main St 87002 | 505-966-1000
Kenneth Griego, supt. | Fax 966-1005
www.belen.k12.nm.us
Belen HS | 1,400/9-12
520 N Main St 87002 | 505-966-1300
Tamie Pargas, prin. | Fax 966-1350
Belen MS | 800/7-8
520 N Main St 87002 | 505-966-1600
Aubrey Tucker, prin. | Fax 966-1650

Bernalillo, Sandoval, Pop. 6,938
Bernalillo SD | 3,200/PK-12
224 N Camino Del Pueblo 87004 | 505-867-2317
Barbara Vigil-Lowder Ed.D., supt. | Fax 867-7850
www.bernalillo-schools.org
Bernalillo HS | 900/9-12
250 Isidora Sanchez 87004 | 505-867-2388
Orlando Rodriguez, prin. | Fax 867-7826
Bernalillo MS | 600/6-8
485 Camino don Tomas 87004 | 505-867-3309
Allan Tapia, prin. | Fax 867-7819
Other Schools – See Santo Domingo Pueblo

Bloomfield, San Juan, Pop. 7,442
Bloomfield SD | 2,900/PK-12
325 N Bergin Ln 87413 | 505-632-3316
Randy Allison, supt. | Fax 632-4371
www.bsin.k12.nm.us
Bloomfield HS | 900/9-12
520 N 1st St 87413 | 505-634-3400
Nancy Radford, prin. | Fax 634-3413
Mesa Alta JHS | 500/7-8
329 N Bergin Ln 87413 | 505-632-4350
Ricardo Sanchez, prin. | Fax 634-3835

Capitan, Lincoln, Pop. 1,500
Capitan Municipal SD | 600/PK-12
PO Box 278 88316 | 505-354-2239
Dr. Larry Miller, supt. | Fax 354-2240
www.capitan.k12.nm.us
Capitan HS | 200/9-12
PO Box 278 88316 | 505-354-2567
Gary Salazar, prin. | Fax 354-2240
Capitan MS | 200/6-8
PO Box 278 88316 | 505-354-2096
Bill Miller, prin. | Fax 354-2240

Carlsbad, Eddy, Pop. 25,300
Carlsbad Municipal SD | 5,800/K-12
408 N Canyon St 88220 | 505-234-3300
Charlotte Neill, supt. | Fax 234-3367
www.carlsbad.k12.nm.us
Alta Vista MS | 600/6-8
408 N Canyon St 88220 | 505-234-3316
Theodor Cordova, prin. | Fax 234-3478
Carlsbad HS | 1,700/9-12
408 N Canyon St 88220 | 505-234-3319
Tom Quintela, prin. | Fax 234-3393
Leyva MS | 800/6-8
408 N Canyon St 88220 | 505-234-3318
Janet Hunt, prin. | Fax 234-3452

Eddy County Beauty College | Post-Sec.
1115 W Mermod St 88220 | 505-885-4545
New Mexico State University | Post-Sec.
1500 University Dr 88220 | 505-234-9200

Carrizozo, Lincoln, Pop. 1,063
Carrizozo Municipal SD | 200/PK-12
PO Box 99 88301 | 505-648-2348
Sergio Castanon, supt. | Fax 648-2216
www.cmsgrizzlies.org/
Carrizozo HS | 100/9-12
PO Box 99 88301 | 505-648-2346
Mel Holland, prin. | Fax 648-3255
Carrizozo MS | 100/5-8
PO Box 99 88301 | 505-648-2346
Mel Holland, prin. | Fax 648-3255

Casa Blanca, Cibola
Grants-Cibola County SD
Supt. — See Grants
Laguna Acoma JSHS | 300/7-12
PO Box 689 87007 | 505-285-2673
Jim Reed, prin. | Fax 552-7184

Chama, Rio Arriba, Pop. 1,173
Chama Valley ISD
Supt. — See Tierra Amarilla
Chama MS | 100/6-8
PO Box 337 87520 | 505-756-2161
Larkin Vigil, prin. | Fax 756-2538

Chaparral, Dona Ana, Pop. 2,962
Gadsden ISD
Supt. — See Santa Teresa
Chaparral HS | 9-12
800 County Line Dr, | 505-824-6700
James Diggs, prin.
Chaparral MS | 500/7-8
290 E Lisa Dr, | 505-824-4847
Marti Muela, prin. | Fax 824-4045

Cimarron, Colfax, Pop. 877
Cimarron Municipal SD | 500/K-12
125 N Collison Ave 87714 | 505-376-2445
Dr. Annette Johnson, supt. | Fax 376-2442
cimarronschools.org/
Cimarron HS | 100/9-12
125 N Collison Ave 87714 | 505-376-2241
Penny Coppedge, prin. | Fax 376-2428
Cimarron MS | 100/5-8
125 N Collison Ave 87714 | 505-376-2512
James Gallegos, prin. | Fax 376-2217
Other Schools – See Eagle Nest

Clayton, Union, Pop. 2,186
Clayton Municipal SD | 500/PK-12
323 S 5th St 88415 | 505-374-9611
Jack Wiley, supt. | Fax 374-9881
www.claytonschools.us/
Clayton HS | 200/9-12
323 S 5th St 88415 | 505-374-2596
John Burgess, prin. | Fax 374-6012
Clayton JHS | 100/7-8
323 S 5th St 88415 | 505-374-9543
Terrell Jones, prin. | Fax 374-9469

Cliff, Grant
Silver Consolidated SD
Supt. — See Silver City
Cliff JSHS | 200/7-12
PO Box 9 88028 | 505-535-2051
Clayton Ellwanger, prin. | Fax 535-2054

Cloudcroft, Otero, Pop. 764
Cloudcroft Municipal SD | 500/PK-12
PO Box 198 88317 | 505-682-2361
Tommy Hancock, supt. | Fax 682-2921
www.cmsbears.org
Cloudcroft HS | 200/9-12
PO Box 198 88317 | 505-682-2524
Roman Renteria, prin. | Fax 682-1343
Cloudcroft MS | 100/6-8
PO Box 198 88317 | 505-682-3336
Fred Wright, prin. | Fax 682-2776

Clovis, Curry, Pop. 33,357
Clovis SD | 8,100/K-12
PO Box 19000 88102 | 505-769-4300
Dr. Rhonda Seidenwurm, supt. | Fax 769-4333
www.cms.k12.nm.us
Clovis SHS | 1,600/10-12
PO Box 19000 88102 | 505-769-4350
Jody Balch, prin. | Fax 769-4366
Gattis JHS | 500/7-9
PO Box 19000 88102 | 505-769-4400
Craig Terry, prin. | Fax 769-4403
Marshall JHS | 600/7-9
PO Box 19000 88102 | 505-769-4410
Diana Russell, prin. | Fax 769-4413
Yucca JHS | 800/7-9
PO Box 19000 88102 | 505-769-4420
Alan Dropps, prin. | Fax 769-4421

Clovis Christian S | 300/K-12
PO Box 608 88102 | 505-763-5311
Steve Medeiros, admin. | Fax 763-4469
Clovis Community College | Post-Sec.
417 Schepps Blvd 88101 | 505-769-2811

Corona, Lincoln, Pop. 170
Corona SD | 100/PK-12
PO Box 258 88318 | 505-849-1911
Travis Lightfoot, supt. | Fax 849-2026
www.coronacardinals.com
Corona JSHS | 50/7-12
PO Box 258 88318 | 505-849-1911
Rick Cogdill, prin. | Fax 849-2026

Corrales, Sandoval, Pop. 7,638

Sandia View S | 100/9-12
65 Sandia View Ln 87048 | 505-898-0717
Leon M. Hill, prin. | Fax 897-7053

Crownpoint, McKinley, Pop. 2,108
Gallup-McKinley County SD
Supt. — See Gallup
Crownpoint HS | 400/9-12
PO Box 700 87313 | 505-786-5664
Bruce Helms, prin. | Fax 786-5316
Crownpoint MS | 300/6-8
PO Box 700 87313 | 505-786-5663
Rozelyn Carroll, prin. | Fax 786-5685

Cuba, Sandoval, Pop. 616
Cuba ISD | 700/PK-12
PO Box 70 87013 | 505-289-3211
Pancho Guardiola, supt. | Fax 289-3314
cuba.k12.nm.us/
Cuba HS | 400/9-12
PO Box 70 87013 | 505-289-3211
Victor Velarde, prin. | Fax 289-3314
Cuba MS | 100/6-8
PO Box 70 87013 | 505-289-3211
Edward Atencio, prin. | Fax 289-3314

Deming, Luna, Pop. 14,876
Deming SD | 5,300/PK-12
1001 S Diamond Ave 88030 | 505-546-8841
Harvielee Moore, supt. | Fax 546-8517
www.demingps.org
Deming HS | 1,200/9-12
1100 S Nickel St 88030 | 505-546-2678
Janean Garney, prin. | Fax 544-0918
Hofacket MS | 900/8-9
1400 S Iron St 88030 | 505-546-4863
Robin Parnell, prin. | Fax 544-7217

Des Moines, Union, Pop. 154
Des Moines Municipal SD | 100/K-12
PO Box 38 88418 | 505-278-2611
Jaynee Burchard, supt. | Fax 278-2617
Des Moines JSHS | 100/7-12
PO Box 38 88418 | 505-278-2611
Jaynee Burchard, prin. | Fax 278-2617

Dexter, Chaves, Pop. 1,230
Dexter Consolidated SD | 1,200/PK-12
PO Box 159 88230 | 505-734-5420
Patricia Parsons, supt. | Fax 734-6813
www.dexterdemons.org
Dexter HS | 400/9-12
PO Box 159 88230 | 505-734-5420
Eddie Ward, prin. | Fax 734-6709
Dexter MS | 300/6-8
PO Box 159 88230 | 505-734-5420
Lesa Dodd, prin. | Fax 734-6811

Dora, Roosevelt, Pop. 127
Dora Consolidated SD | 200/PK-12
PO Box 327 88115 | 505-477-2216
Steve Barron, supt. | Fax 477-2464
www.doraschools.com
Dora JSHS | 100/7-12
PO Box 327 88115 | 505-477-2211
David Bass, prin. | Fax 477-2464

Dulce, Rio Arriba, Pop. 2,438
Dulce ISD | 700/K-12
PO Box 547 87528 | 505-759-3353
Dr. Ralph Friedly, supt. | Fax 759-3533
www.dulceschools.com/
Dulce HS | 200/9-12
PO Box 547 87528 | 505-759-3282
Rose Kartchner, prin. | Fax 759-3535
Dulce MS | 200/6-8
PO Box 547 87528 | 505-759-3646
Pam Siders, prin. | Fax 759-1349

Eagle Nest, Colfax, Pop. 292
Cimarron Municipal SD
Supt. — See Cimarron
Eagle Nest MS | 100/5-8
PO Box 287 87718 | 505-377-6991
Lee Mills, prin. | Fax 377-3646

Elida, Roosevelt, Pop. 178
Elida Municipal SD | 100/K-12
PO Box 8 88116 | 505-274-6211
Jack Burch, supt. | Fax 274-6213
www.elida.k12.nm.us/
Elida JSHS | 100/7-12
PO Box 8 88116 | 505-274-6211
Jim Daugherty, prin. | Fax 274-6213

El Rito, Rio Arriba
Mesa Vista Consolidated SD | 500/PK-12
PO Box 6 87530 | 505-581-4504
Robert Archuleta, supt. | Fax 581-4613
Other Schools – See Ojo Caliente

Northern New Mexico Community College | Post-Sec.
87530 | 505-581-4501

Espanola, Rio Arriba, Pop. 9,655
Espanola SD | 4,500/PK-12
714 Calle Don Diego 87532 | 505-753-2254
Dr. David Cockerham, supt. | Fax 753-2321
www.k12espanola.org

Espanola MS East 300/7-8
714 Calle Don Diego 87532 505-753-2293
Lewis Johnson, prin. Fax 747-3211
Espanola Valley HS 800/10-12
714 Calle Don Diego 87532 505-753-7357
Bruce Hopmeier, prin. Fax 753-6177
Vigil MS 600/8-9
714 Calle Don Diego 87532 505-753-1348
Alfred Garcia, prin. Fax 747-3083

McCurdy S 400/PK-12
261 S Mccurdy Rd 87532 505-753-7221
Fred Pomeroy, supt. Fax 753-7830
Northern New Mexico College Post-Sec.
921 N Paseo De Onate 87532 505-747-2100
Victory Christian Academy 100/K-12
PO Box 540 87532 505-753-0039

Estancia, Torrance, Pop. 1,552
Estancia Municipal SD 900/PK-12
PO Box 68 87016 505-384-2001
Dr. Bruce Peterson, supt. Fax 384-2015
www.estancia.k12.nm.us
Estancia HS 300/9-12
PO Box 68 87016 505-384-2002
Doreen Winn, prin. Fax 384-2015
Estancia MS 100/7-8
PO Box 68 87016 505-384-2003
Doreen Winn, prin. Fax 384-2015

Liberty Ranch Christian S 50/PK-12
Blue Grass Rd 87016 505-384-2530
Edward Bragg, prin. Fax 384-2530

Eunice, Lea, Pop. 2,602
Eunice SD 600/PK-12
PO Box 129 88231 505-394-2524
Larry Harvey, supt. Fax 394-3006
www.eunice.org/
Caton MS 100/6-8
PO Box 129 88231 505-394-3338
Dwain Haynes, prin. Fax 394-3661
Eunice HS 200/9-12
PO Box 129 88231 505-394-2332
Richard Hayes, prin. Fax 394-3140

Farmington, San Juan, Pop. 43,161
Farmington Municipal SD 10,000/PK-12
PO Box 5850 87499 505-324-9840
Janel Ryan, supt. Fax 599-8806
www.fms.k12.nm.us/home_body.html
Farmington HS 1,600/9-12
2200 N Sunset Ave 87401 505-324-0352
Mark Driskell, prin. Fax 599-8832
Heights MS 700/6-8
3700 College Blvd 87402 505-599-8611
Dave Willden, prin. Fax 599-8673
Hermosa MS 600/6-8
1500 E 25th St 87401 505-599-8612
Bob Rank, prin. Fax 599-8681
Mesa View MS 600/6-8
4451 Wildflower Dr 87401 505-599-8622
Kim Salazar, prin. Fax 599-8646
Piedra Vista HS 1,100/9-12
5700 College Blvd 87402 505-599-8880
Ann Gattis, prin. Fax 599-8891
Tibbetts MS 600/6-8
312 E Apache St 87401 505-599-8613
Dr. Anthony Smagacz, prin. Fax 599-8675

San Juan College Post-Sec.
4601 College Blvd 87402 505-326-3311

Floyd, Roosevelt, Pop. 76
Floyd Municipal SD 300/PK-12
PO Box 65 88118 505-478-2211
Paul Benoit, supt. Fax 478-2811
www.floydbroncos.com/
Floyd HS 100/9-12
PO Box 65 88118 505-478-2211
Chris Duncan, prin. Fax 478-2811
Floyd MS 100/5-8
PO Box 65 88118 505-478-2211
Chris Duncan, prin. Fax 478-2811

Fort Sumner, DeBaca, Pop. 1,060
Fort Sumner Municipal SD 300/PK-12
PO Box 387 88119 505-355-7734
Patricia Miller, supt. Fax 355-7716
www.ftsumnerk12.com/
Fort Sumner HS 100/9-12
PO Box 387 88119 505-355-2231
Patti Scott, prin. Fax 355-7663
Fort Sumner MS 100/6-8
PO Box 387 88119 505-355-2231
Patti Scott, prin. Fax 355-7663

Gallina, Rio Arriba
Jemez Mountain SD 300/K-12
PO Box 230 87017 505-638-5419
Adan Delgado, supt. Fax 638-5571
www.jmsk12.com/
Coronado MSHS 100/6-12
PO Box 230 87017 505-638-5549
Richard Perea, prin. Fax 638-5571

Gallup, McKinley, Pop. 19,378
Gallup-McKinley County SD 13,000/PK-12
PO Box 1318 87305 505-722-7711
Karen White, supt. Fax 721-1199
www.gmcs.k12.nm.us/
Gallup HS 1,600/10-12
1055 Rico St 87301 505-721-2525
Mike Butkovich, prin. Fax 721-2556
Gallup JHS 1,500/8-9
680 S Boardman Ave 87301 505-721-1900
Frank Chiapetti, prin. Fax 721-1910
Other Schools – See Crownpoint, Navajo, Ramah, Thoreau, Tohatchi

---

Gallup Catholic HS 100/9-12
514 Park Ave 87301 505-722-6089
Angelo DiPalo, prin. Fax 863-5139
University of New Mexico Post-Sec.
200 College Rd 87301 505-863-7500

Grady, Curry, Pop. 97
Grady Municipal SD 100/PK-12
PO Box 71 88120 505-357-2192
Joel Shirley, supt. Fax 357-2000
Grady HS 50/9-12
PO Box 71 88120 505-357-2192
Darrel Bollinger, prin. Fax 357-2000
Grady MS 50/6-8
PO Box 71 88120 505-357-2192
Darrel Bollinger, prin. Fax 357-2000

Grants, Cibola, Pop. 9,043
Grants-Cibola County SD 3,600/PK-12
PO Box 8 87020 505-285-2600
Kilino Marquez, supt. Fax 285-2628
www.gccs.cc/
Grants HS 1,000/9-12
500 Mountain Rd 87020 505-285-2651
Rick Horacek, prin. Fax 287-3126
Los Alamitos MS 500/7-8
1100 Mount Taylor Ave 87020 505-285-2683
Joan Gilmore, prin. Fax 285-2692
Other Schools – See Casa Blanca

New Mexico State University Post-Sec.
1500 N 3rd St 87020 505-287-7981

Hagerman, Chaves, Pop. 1,162
Hagerman Municipal SD 400/PK-12
PO Box B 88232 505-752-3254
Louis Mestas, supt. Fax 752-3255
bobcat.net
Hagerman HS 100/9-12
PO Box B 88232 505-752-3283
Guyla Maples, prin. Fax 752-3306
Hagerman MS 100/6-8
PO Box B 88232 505-752-3283
Mark Lovas, prin. Fax 752-0241

Hatch, Dona Ana, Pop. 1,654
Hatch Valley SD 1,500/K-12
PO Box 790 87937 505-267-8200
Dane Kennon, supt. Fax 267-8210
www.hatch.k12.nm.us/
Hatch Valley HS 400/9-12
PO Box 790 87937 505-267-8232
Michael Gaume, prin. Fax 267-8235
Hatch Valley MS 400/6-8
PO Box 790 87937 505-267-8252
Claud Gobble, prin. Fax 267-8255
ACE HS Adult
PO Box 790 87937 505-267-8225
Fax 267-8226

Hobbs, Lea, Pop. 29,006
Hobbs Municipal SD 7,400/PK-12
PO Box 1030 88241 505-433-0100
Cliff Burch, supt. Fax 433-0140
www.hobbsschools.net
Highland JHS 700/7-8
2500 N Jefferson St 88240 505-433-1200
John Notaro, prin. Fax 433-1203
Hobbs Freshman HS Heizer Campus 600/9-9
100 E Stanolind Rd 88240 505-433-1100
Pat McMurray, prin. Fax 433-1109
Hobbs HS 1,500/10-12
800 N Jefferson St 88240 505-433-0200
Eppie Calderon, prin. Fax 433-0203
Houston JHS 500/7-8
300 N Houston St 88240 505-433-1300
Jeff Cearley, prin. Fax 433-1304

College of the Southwest Post-Sec.
6610 N Lovington Hwy 88240 505-392-6561
New Mexico Junior College Post-Sec.
5317 N Lovington Hwy 88240 505-392-4510

Holloman AFB, Otero, Pop. 5,891
Alamogordo SD
Supt. — See Alamogordo
Holloman MS 200/6-8
381 1st St Bldg 768 88330 505-479-2282
Maria Showalter, prin. Fax 479-4041

Hondo, Lincoln
Hondo Valley SD 100/PK-12
PO Box 55 88336 505-653-4411
John MacCallum, supt. Fax 653-4414
Hondo HS 100/7-12
PO Box 55 88336 505-653-4411
John MacCallum, prin. Fax 653-4414

House, Quay, Pop. 64
House Municipal SD 100/K-12
PO Box 673 88121 505-279-7353
Dr. Art Brokenbek, supt. Fax 279-6201
www.houseschools.net
House JSHS 100/7-12
PO Box 673 88121 505-279-7353
Dr. Art Brokenbek, prin. Fax 279-6201

Jal, Lea, Pop. 2,021
Jal SD 400/PK-12
PO Box 1386 88252 505-395-2101
Rick Ferguson, supt. Fax 395-2146
Jal JSHS 200/7-12
PO Box 1386 88252 505-395-2277
Elaine O'Neal, prin. Fax 395-3177

Jemez Pueblo, Sandoval, Pop. 1,301
Jemez Valley SD 400/PK-12
8501 Highway 4 87024 505-834-7391
Sandra Henson, supt. Fax 834-7394
www.jvps.org
Jemez Valley HS 100/9-12
8501 Highway 4 87024 505-834-7392
Claudie Thompson, prin. Fax 834-7676
Jemez Valley MS 100/6-8
8501 Highway 4 87024 505-834-7393
Claudie Thompson, prin. Fax 834-7130

Kirtland, San Juan, Pop. 3,552
Central Consolidated SD 22
Supt. — See Shiprock
Kirtland Central HS 1,000/9-12
550 Rd 6100 87417 505-598-5881
Fax 598-9712
Kirtland MS 600/7-8
538 Rd 6100 87417 505-598-6114
Charles Trujillo, prin. Fax 598-9497

Lake Arthur, Chaves, Pop. 432
Lake Arthur Municipal SD 200/PK-12
PO Box 98 88253 505-365-2001
Michael Grossman, supt. Fax 365-2002
Lake Arthur HS 50/9-12
PO Box 98 88253 505-365-2001
Dale Ballard, prin. Fax 365-2002
Lake Arthur MS 50/6-8
PO Box 98 88253 505-365-2001
Dale Ballard, prin. Fax 365-2002

Las Cruces, Dona Ana, Pop. 82,671
Las Cruces SD 22,900/PK-12
505 S Main St Ste 249 88001 505-527-5807
Stan Rounds, supt. Fax 527-5972
www.lcps.k12.nm.us
Camino Real MS 1,000/6-8
505 S Main St Ste 249 88001 505-527-6030
Angie Holguin-Dotson, prin. Fax 527-6031
Las Cruces HS 2,300/9-12
505 S Main St Ste 249 88001 505-527-9400
Nyeta Haines, prin. Fax 527-9767
Lynn MS 800/6-8
505 S Main St Ste 249 88001 505-527-9445
Gina Rivera, prin. Fax 527-9454
Mayfield HS 2,400/9-12
505 S Main St Ste 249 88001 505-527-9415
Chris Cook, prin. Fax 527-9420
Onate HS 1,900/9-12
505 S Main St Ste 249 88001 505-527-9430
David del Toro, prin. Fax 527-9444
Picacho MS 700/6-8
505 S Main St Ste 249 88001 505-527-9455
Michael Montoya, prin. Fax 527-9459
Sierra MS 1,000/6-8
505 S Main St Ste 249 88001 505-527-9640
Brenda Lewis, prin. Fax 527-9768
Vista MS 900/6-8
505 S Main St Ste 249 88001 505-527-9465
Dan Davis, prin. Fax 527-9470
Zia MS 900/6-8
505 S Main St Ste 249 88001 505-527-9475
John Hendee, prin. Fax 527-9479
Other Schools – See White Sands

Business Skills Institute Post-Sec.
1400 El Paseo Rd 88001 505-526-5579
Mesilla Valley Christian S 500/PK-12
3850 Stern Dr 88001 505-525-8515
John Foreman, admin. Fax 526-2713
New Mexico State Univ. Dona Ana Branch Post-Sec.
PO Box 30001 88003 505-527-7500
New Mexico State University Post-Sec.
PO Box 30001 88003 505-646-0111
Olympian University of Cosmetology Post-Sec.
1460 Missouri Ave # 5 88001 505-523-7181

Las Vegas, San Miguel, Pop. 14,020
Las Vegas City SD 2,100/PK-12
901 Douglas Ave 87701 505-454-5700
Dr. Pete Campos, supt. Fax 454-6965
cybercardinal.com/
Memorial MS 500/6-8
901 Douglas Ave 87701 505-454-5710
Sandra Madrid, prin. Fax 426-0303
Robertson HS 700/9-12
901 Douglas Ave 87701 505-454-5770
Richard Lopez, prin. Fax 425-6852

West Las Vegas SD 1,900/K-12
179 Bridge St 87701 505-426-2300
Joe Baca, supt. Fax 426-2332
West Las Vegas HS 500/9-12
179 Bridge St 87701 505-426-2500
Gene Parson, prin. Fax 426-2501
West Las Vegas MS 400/6-8
179 Bridge St 87701 505-426-2541
Victor Sanchez, prin. Fax 426-2542
Other Schools – See Ribera

Luna Community College Post-Sec.
366 Luna Dr 87701 505-454-2500
New Mexico Highlands University Post-Sec.
PO Box 9000 87701 505-454-3434

La Union, Dona Ana

Covenant Christian Academy 50/7-12
7048 McNutt Rd 88021 505-589-3538
Jeffrey Miller, hdmstr.

Logan, Quay, Pop. 986
Logan Municipal SD 200/PK-12
PO Box 67 88426 505-487-2252
Carolyn Franklin, supt. Fax 487-9479
Logan HS 100/9-12
PO Box 67 88426 505-487-2252
Gary Miller, prin. Fax 487-9479
Logan MS 6-8
PO Box 67 88426 505-487-2252
Gary Miller, prin. Fax 487-9479

Lordsburg, Hidalgo, Pop. 2,815
Lordsburg Municipal SD 700/PK-12
PO Box 430 88045 505-542-9361
Jim Barentine, supt. Fax 542-9364
www.lmsed.org
Dugan-Tarango MS 100/7-8
1352 Hardin St 88045 505-542-9806
David Lackey, prin. Fax 542-9811
Lordsburg HS 200/9-12
501 W 4th St 88045 505-542-3782
J. Vance Lee, prin. Fax 542-3712

Los Alamos, Los Alamos, Pop. 11,455
Los Alamos SD 3,600/PK-12
PO Box 90 87544 505-663-2222
Dr. James Anderson, supt. Fax 661-6300
www.laschools.net
Los Alamos HS 1,200/9-12
1300 Diamond Dr 87544 505-663-2510
Lynne Saccaro, prin. Fax 662-6846
Los Alamos MS 600/7-8
1 Hawk Dr 87544 505-663-2375
Garrett Bosarge, prin. Fax 662-4270

University of New Mexico Post-Sec.
4000 University Dr 87544 505-662-5919

Los Lunas, Valencia, Pop. 11,338
Los Lunas SD 8,500/PK-12
PO Box 1300 87031 505-866-8231
Walter Gibson, supt. Fax 865-7766
www.llschools.net/
Career Academy Vo/Tech
PO Box 1300 87031 505-565-8755
Fax 565-8762
Los Lunas HS 2,400/9-12
PO Box 1300 87031 505-865-4646
Dr. Dan Webb, prin. Fax 565-2847
Los Lunas MS 800/7-8
PO Box 1300 87031 505-865-7273
Russell Hague, prin. Fax 865-9742
Manzano Vista MS 700/7-8
PO Box 1300 87031 505-865-1750
David Yates, prin. Fax 866-8921
Valencia HS 9-12
PO Box 1300 87031 505-565-8755
Mario Zuniga, prin. Fax 565-8762

Christ the King S 50/K-12
700 Camelot Blvd SW 87031 505-865-9226
Rev. Alan R. Coleman, prin. Fax 865-9226
University of New Mexico Post-Sec.
280 La Entrada Rd 87031 505-925-8500

Loving, Eddy, Pop. 1,313
Loving Municipal SD 600/PK-12
PO Box 98 88256 505-745-2000
David Chavez, supt. Fax 745-2002
www.lovingschools.org
Loving HS 200/9-12
PO Box 98 88256 505-745-2020
Ricky Williams, prin. Fax 745-2002
Loving MS 100/6-8
PO Box 98 88256 505-745-2050
Jesse Fuentes, prin. Fax 745-2052

Lovington, Lea, Pop. 9,603
Lovington Municipal SD 2,900/PK-12
PO Box 1537 88260 505-739-2200
Jimmy Derrick, supt. Fax 739-2205
lovington.nm.schoolwebpages.com
Lovington JHS 400/8-9
500 W Jefferson Ave 88260 505-739-2330
Darin Manes, prin. Fax 739-2330
Lovington SHS 500/10-12
701 W Avenue K 88260 505-739-2230
Robert Brown, prin. Fax 739-2242

Magdalena, Socorro, Pop. 877
Magdalena Municipal SD 500/PK-12
PO Box 24 87825 505-854-2241
Mike Chambers, supt. Fax 854-2294
www.magdalena.k12.nm.us
Magdalena HS 100/9-12
PO Box 629 87825 505-854-2241
Regina Lane, prin. Fax 854-2531
Magdalena MS 100/6-8
PO Box 629 87825 505-854-2241
Regina Lane, prin. Fax 854-2531

Maxwell, Colfax, Pop. 262
Maxwell Municipal SD 100/PK-12
PO Box 275 87728 505-375-2371
Jim Bowie, supt. Fax 375-2375
www.maxwellp12.com/
Maxwell HS 50/9-12
PO Box 275 87728 505-375-2371
Christiana Hidalgo, prin. Fax 375-2375
Maxwell MS 50/7-8
PO Box 275 87728 505-375-2371
Christiana Hidalgo, prin. Fax 375-2375

Melrose, Curry, Pop. 728
Melrose SD 200/PK-12
PO Box 275 88124 505-253-4269
Dr. Ronald Windom, supt. Fax 253-4291
www.melroseschools.org
Melrose JSHS 100/7-12
PO Box 275 88124 505-253-4267
Jamie Widner, prin. Fax 253-4291

Montezuma, San Miguel

Hammer United World College 200/11-12
PO Box 248 87731 505-454-4200
Lisa Darling, pres. Fax 454-4274

Mora, Mora
Mora ISD 600/K-12
PO Box 179 87732 505-387-3101
Anita Roybal, supt. Fax 387-3111
www.mora.k12.nm.us/
Mora HS 200/9-12
PO Box 180 87732 505-387-3122
Danny Chavez, prin. Fax 387-3121
Mora MS 200/6-8
PO Box 687 87732 505-387-3125
Loretta Chavez, prin. Fax 387-3126

Moriarty, Torrance, Pop. 1,808
Moriarty Municipal SD 4,100/PK-12
PO Box 2000 87035 505-832-4471
Karen Couch, supt. Fax 832-4472
www.moriarty.k12.nm.us
Edgewood MS 400/7-8
PO Box 2000 87035 505-281-7181
Barbara Gradner, prin. Fax 832-7210
Moriarty HS 1,300/9-12
PO Box 2000 87035 505-832-4254
Wayne Marshall, prin. Fax 832-4939
Moriarty MS 300/7-8
PO Box 2000 87035 505-832-6200
Dawn Tinsley, prin. Fax 832-5919

Mosquero, Harding, Pop. 95
Mosquero Municipal SD 100/PK-12
PO Box 258 87733 505-673-2271
Nelda Isaacs, supt. Fax 673-2305
www.mms.k12.nm.us
Mosquero JSHS 50/7-12
PO Box 258 87733 505-673-2271
Nelda Isaacs, prin. Fax 673-2305

Mountainair, Torrance, Pop. 1,078
Mountainair SD 300/PK-12
PO Box 456 87036 505-847-2333
Jay Mortensen, supt. Fax 847-2843
Mountainair HS 100/6-12
PO Box 456 87036 505-847-2211
Travis Dempsey, prin. Fax 847-2843

Navajo, McKinley, Pop. 1,985
Gallup-McKinley County SD
Supt. — See Gallup
Navajo MS 200/6-8
PO Box 1286 87328 505-777-2390
Pauletta White, prin. Fax 777-2375
Navajo Pine HS 200/9-12
PO Box 1286 87328 505-777-2288
Fax 777-2375

Newcomb, San Juan, Pop. 388
Central Consolidated SD 22
Supt. — See Shiprock
Newcomb HS 300/9-12
PO Box 7973 87455 505-696-3417
Glen Haven, prin. Fax 696-3487
Newcomb MS 200/6-8
PO Box 7973 87455 505-696-3417
Leland Roundy, prin. Fax 696-3487

Ojo Caliente, Taos
Mesa Vista Consolidated SD
Supt. — See El Rito
Mesa Vista HS 200/9-12
PO Box 50 87549 505-583-2275
Felix Garcia, prin. Fax 583-9133
Mesa Vista MS 100/7-8
PO Box 50 87549 505-583-2275
Felix Garcia, prin. Fax 583-9133

Pecos, San Miguel, Pop. 1,407
Pecos ISD 800/PK-12
PO Box 368 87552 505-757-4700
Roy Herrera, supt. Fax 757-8721
www.pecos.k12.nm.us/
Pecos HS 200/9-12
PO Box 368 87552 505-757-4720
Cynthia Luna, prin. Fax 757-2772
Pecos MS 200/6-8
PO Box 368 87552 505-757-4620
Michael Chavez, prin. Fax 757-2561

Penasco, Taos, Pop. 648
Penasco ISD 500/PK-12
PO Box 520 87553 505-587-2230
Dorothy Sanchez, supt. Fax 587-2513
www.penasco.k12.nm.us
Penasco HS 200/9-12
PO Box 520 87553 505-587-2503
Frank Fast Wolf, prin. Fax 587-9908
Penasco MS 100/5-8
PO Box 520 87553 505-587-2503
Frank Fast Wolf, prin. Fax 587-9910

Portales, Roosevelt, Pop. 11,295
Portales Municipal SD 2,900/PK-12
501 S Abilene Ave 88130 505-356-7000
Randy Fowler, supt. Fax 356-4377
www.portalesschools.com
Portales HS 700/9-12
201 S Knoxville St 88130 505-356-5831
Melvin Nusser, prin. Fax 356-8082
Portales JHS 400/7-8
700 E 3rd St 88130 505-356-7045
Steve Harris, prin. Fax 359-0826

Eastern New Mexico University 88130 Post-Sec.
505-562-1011

Quemado, Catron
Quemado ISD 200/PK-12
PO Box 128 87829 505-773-4700
Bill Green, supt. Fax 773-4717
www.quemadoschools.org
Quemado JSHS 100/7-12
PO Box 128 87829 505-773-4645
Valerie Brea, prin. Fax 773-4717

Questa, Taos, Pop. 1,913
Questa ISD 500/K-12
PO Box 440 87556 505-586-0421
Richard Romero, supt. Fax 586-0531
www.questa.k12.nm.us
Questa HS 200/9-12
PO Box 529 87556 505-586-1604
Kevin Hubka, prin. Fax 586-2282
Questa JHS 100/7-8
PO Box 529 87556 505-586-1604
Kevin Hubka, prin. Fax 586-2282

Ramah, McKinley
Gallup-McKinley County SD
Supt. — See Gallup
Ramah JSHS 200/7-12
PO Box 849 87321 505-783-4211
Tim Bond, prin. Fax 783-4261

Raton, Colfax, Pop. 6,944
Raton SD 1,500/PK-12
PO Box 940 87740 505-445-9111
Bill Walz, supt. Fax 445-5641
Raton HS 400/9-12
1535 Tiger Cir 87740 505-445-3541
Mike Sparaco, prin. Fax 445-2237
Raton MS 400/6-8
500 S 3rd St 87740 505-445-9881
David Castillo, prin. Fax 445-3682

Rehoboth, McKinley

Rehoboth Christian S 400/K-12
PO Box 41 87322 505-863-4412
Ron Polinder, supt. Fax 863-2185

Reserve, Catron, Pop. 338
Reserve ISD 200/PK-12
PO Box 350 87830 505-533-6241
Loren Cushman, supt. Fax 533-6647
www.reserve.k12.nm.us/
Reserve JSHS 100/7-12
PO Box 350 87830 505-533-6242
Cindy Shellhorn, prin. Fax 533-6900

Ribera, San Miguel
West Las Vegas SD
Supt. — See Las Vegas
Valley MS 100/6-8
HC 72 Box 205 87560 505-426-2581
Becky Gallegos, prin. Fax 426-2582

Rio Rancho, Sandoval, Pop. 66,599
Rio Rancho SD 12,200/PK-12
500 Laser Dr NE 87124 505-896-0667
Dr. V. Sue Cleveland, supt. Fax 896-0662
www.rrps.net
Rio Rancho HS 2,600/10-12
301 Loma Colorado St NE 87124 505-896-5600
Richard Von Ancken, prin. Fax 896-5901
Rio Rancho Mid HS 2,100/8-9
1600 40th St NE, 505-891-5335
Lisa Dobson, prin. Fax 891-1180

National American University Post-Sec.
1601 Rio Rancho Dr SE # 200 87124 505-891-1111

Roswell, Chaves, Pop. 45,199
Roswell ISD 8,900/PK-12
PO Box 1437 88202 505-627-2500
Michael Gottlieb, supt. Fax 627-2512
www.risd.k12.nm.us
Berrendo MS 600/6-8
800 Marion Richards Rd 88201 505-627-2775
Laura Herrera, prin. Fax 625-8248
Goddard HS 1,300/9-12
701 E Country Club Rd 88201 505-627-4800
Fax 627-4853
Mesa MS 400/6-8
1601 E Bland St 88203 505-627-2800
Ruben Bolanos, prin. Fax 625-8263
Mountain View MS 500/6-8
312 E Mountain View Rd 88203 505-627-2825
Glenda Grant, prin. Fax 625-8260
Roswell HS 1,400/9-12
500 W Hobbs St 88203 505-637-3200
Brian Shea, prin. Fax 637-3268
Sierra MS 600/6-8
615 S Sycamore Ave 88203 505-627-2850
Josie Turner, prin. Fax 625-8283

Aladdin Beauty College Post-Sec.
108 S Union Ave 88203 505-623-6331
Eastern New Mexico University Post-Sec.
PO Box 6000 88202 505-624-7000
Gateway Christian S 200/PK-12
PO Box 1642 88202 505-622-9710
Rick Rapp, admin. Fax 622-9739
New Mexico Military Institute Post-Sec.
101 W College Blvd 88201 800-421-5376
New Mexico Military Institute 400/9-12
101 W College Blvd 88201 505-624-8020
Don Beard, prin. Fax 624-8027

Roy, Harding, Pop. 239
Roy Municipal SD 100/PK-12
PO Box 430 87743 505-485-2242
Richard Hazen, supt. Fax 485-2497
www.roy-nm-schools.net/
Roy JSHS 100/7-12
PO Box 430 87743 505-485-2242
Richard Hazen, prin. Fax 485-2497

Ruidoso, Lincoln, Pop. 8,812
Ruidoso Municipal SD 2,400/PK-12
200 Horton Cir 88345 505-257-4051
Paul Wirth Ed.D., supt. Fax 257-4150
www.ruidoso.k12.nm.us
Ruidoso HS 700/9-12
200 Horton Cir 88345 505-258-4910
Shirley Crawford, prin. Fax 258-3516

Ruidoso MS 400/7-8
200 Horton Cir 88345 505-257-7324
George Heaton, prin. Fax 257-3946

San Jon, Quay, Pop. 274
San Jon Municipal SD 200/PK-12
PO Box 5 88434 505-576-2466
Gary Salazar, supt. Fax 576-2772
www.sanjonschools.com/
San Jon HS 100/9-12
PO Box 5 88434 505-576-2466
DeLoyce Smith, prin. Fax 576-2772
San Jon MS 100/6-8
PO Box 5 88434 505-576-2466
DeLoyce Smith, prin. Fax 576-2772

Santa Fe, Santa Fe, Pop. 70,631
Pojoaque Valley SD 1,900/PK-12
PO Box 3468 87501 505-455-2282
Toni Nolan-Trujillo, supt. Fax 455-7152
pvs.k12.nm.us/
Pojoaque Valley HS 700/9-12
PO Box 3468 87501 505-455-2234
Gloria Salazar Shuttles, prin. Fax 455-3471
Pojoaque Valley MS 400/7-8
PO Box 3468 87501 505-455-2238
Eileen Chavez, prin. Fax 455-3392

Santa Fe SD 12,400/PK-12
610 Alta Vista St 87505 505-467-2000
Dr. Leslie Carpenter, supt. Fax 995-3300
www.sfps.info
Alameda MS 300/7-8
450 La Madera St 87501 505-467-4500
Norma Cavazos, prin. Fax 995-3305
Capital HS 1,300/9-12
4851 Paseo Del Sol 87507 505-467-1000
Melanie Romero, prin. Fax 995-3311
Capshaw MS 400/7-8
351 W Zia Rd 87505 505-467-4300
Sue Lujan, prin. Fax 989-5439
De Vargas MS 600/7-8
1720 Llano St 87505 505-467-3300
Winifred Krause, prin. Fax 995-3307
Ortiz MS 700/6-8
4164 S Meadows Rd 87507 505-467-2300
Denine Mares, prin. Fax 989-5597
Santa Fe HS 1,700/9-12
2100 Yucca St 87505 505-467-2400
Dr. Daniel Webb, prin. Fax 995-3309

Christian Life Academy 100/K-12
121 Siringo Rd 87505 505-984-1001
Solomon Sedillo, prin. Fax 988-4781
College of Santa Fe Post-Sec.
1600 Saint Michaels Dr 87505 505-473-6011
Desert Academy 200/7-12
313 Camino Alire 87501 505-992-8284
Terry Passalacqua, hdmstr. Fax 992-8270
Institute of American Indian Arts Post-Sec.
83 A Van Nu Po 87508 505-424-2330
New Mexico Academy for Science & Math 100/6-12
7300 Old Santa Fe Trl 87505 505-954-4000
Milton Griggs, hdmstr. Fax 986-9095
New Mexico School for the Deaf Post-Sec.
1060 Cerrillos Rd 87505 505-827-6739
St. John's College Post-Sec.
1160 Camino De Cruz Blanca 87505 505-984-6000
St. Michael HS 800/7-12
100 Siringo Rd 87505 505-983-7353
Bill Armijo Ed.D., prin. Fax 982-8722
Santa Fe Community College Post-Sec.
6401 S Richards Ave 87508 505-428-1000
Santa Fe Prep S 300/7-12
1101 Camino De Cruz Blanca 87505 505-982-1829
James Leonard, hdmstr. Fax 982-2897
Sante Fe Waldorf S 200/PK-12
26 Puesta Del Sol 87508 505-983-9727
Fax 983-7416
Southwest Acupuncture College Post-Sec.
1622 Galisteo St 87505 505-438-8884
Southwestern College Post-Sec.
PO Box 4788 87502 505-471-5756

Santa Rosa, Guadalupe, Pop. 2,509
Santa Rosa Consolidated SD 700/PK-12
344 S 4th St 88435 505-472-3171
Dan Flores, supt. Fax 472-5609
www.santarosa.k12.nm.us
Santa Rosa HS 200/9-12
717 S 3rd St 88435 505-472-3422
Michael Tillman, prin. Fax 472-3169
Santa Rosa MS 100/6-8
244 S 4th St 88435 505-472-3633
Joseph M. Salas, prin. Fax 472-3132
Other Schools – See Anton Chico

Santa Teresa, Dona Ana, Pop. 900
Gadsden ISD 13,500/PK-12
4950 McNutt Rd 88008 505-882-6200
Cynthia Nava, supt. Fax 882-6229
www.gisd.k12.nm.us
Santa Teresa HS 1,200/9-12
100 Airport Rd 88008 505-589-5300
Ralph Gallegos, prin. Fax 589-5311
Santa Teresa MS 700/7-8
PO Box 778 88008 505-874-7200
Rosa Lovelace, prin. Fax 589-2780
Other Schools – See Anthony, Chaparral

Santo Domingo Pueblo, Sandoval, Pop. 2,866
Bernalillo SD
Supt. — See Bernalillo
Santo Domingo MS 100/6-8
PO Box 459 87052 505-867-4441
Richard Torralba, prin. Fax 867-7862

Shiprock, San Juan, Pop. 7,687
Central Consolidated SD 22 7,000/PK-12
PO Box 1199 87420 505-368-4984
Fax 368-5232
www.centralschools.org/
Shiprock HS 900/9-12
PO Box 3578 87420 505-368-5161
Floyd Ashley, prin. Fax 368-5796
Tse' Bit'ai MS 500/7-8
PO Box 1703 87420 505-368-4741
Fax 368-5105
Other Schools – See Kirtland, Newcomb

Silver City, Grant, Pop. 9,999
Silver Consolidated SD 3,200/PK-12
2810 N Swan St 88061 505-956-2000
Dick Pool, supt. Fax 956-2039
La Plata MS 700/6-8
3500 N Silver St 88061 505-956-2060
John Carter, prin. Fax 956-2098
Silver HS 900/9-12
3200 N Silver St 88061 505-388-1563
James Graham, prin. Fax 388-2927
Other Schools – See Cliff

Agape Community Christian S 50/K-12
1301 N Santa Rita St 88061 505-538-3467
Douglas Bryant, prin. Fax 538-2906
Western New Mexico University Post-Sec.
PO Box 680 88062 505-538-6011

Socorro, Socorro, Pop. 8,621
Socorro Consolidated SD 1,900/PK-12
PO Box 1157 87801 505-835-0300
Dr. Cheryl Wilson, supt. Fax 835-1682
www.socorro.k12.nm.us/
Sarracino MS 400/6-8
1425 El Camino Real St 87801 505-835-0283
Charles Zimmerly, prin. Fax 835-0360
Socorro HS 600/9-12
PO Box 1367 87801 505-835-0700
Daniel Padilla, prin. Fax 835-0704

New Mexico Institute Mining & Technology Post-Sec.
801 Leroy Pl 87801 505-835-5011

Springer, Colfax, Pop. 1,224
Springer Municipal SD 200/K-12
PO Box 308 87747 505-483-3432
Zita Rae Lopez, supt. Fax 483-2387
www.springerschools.org
Miranda JHS 50/6-8
PO Box 308 87747 505-483-3485
Glenda Moore, prin. Fax 483-5012
Springer HS 100/9-12
PO Box 308 87747 505-483-3464
Secundino Esquibel, prin. Fax 483-3970

Sunland Park, Dona Ana, Pop. 14,089

International School Post-Sec.
141 Quinella Dr 88063 505-589-1414

Taos, Taos, Pop. 5,126
Taos Municipal SD 2,400/PK-12
213 Paseo Del Canon E 87571 505-758-5202
Dr. Marc Space, supt. Fax 758-5298
www.taosschools.org/
Taos HS 1,000/9-12
134 Cervantes St 87571 505-751-8000
Tom Trujillo, prin. Fax 751-8001
Taos MS 700/6-8
235 Paseo Del Canon E 87571 505-737-6000
Reynaldo Quintana, prin. Fax 737-6001

National College of Midwifery Post-Sec.
209 State Road 240 87571 505-758-8914
University of New Mexico Post-Sec.
115 Civic Plaza Dr 87571 505-737-6200

Tatum, Lea, Pop. 693
Tatum Municipal SD 200/PK-12
PO Box 685 88267 505-398-4455
T.J. Parks, supt. Fax 398-8220
www.tatumschools.org/
Tatum JSHS 100/7-12
PO Box 685 88267 505-398-4555
Lisa Medlin, prin. Fax 398-8220

Texico, Curry, Pop. 1,060
Texico Municipal SD 500/PK-12
PO Box 237 88135 505-482-3801
Dr. R. L. Richards, supt. Fax 482-3650
www.texicoschools.com
Texico HS 200/9-12
PO Box 237 88135 505-482-3305
Buddy Little, prin. Fax 482-3650
Texico MS 100/6-8
PO Box 237 88135 505-482-9520
Rick Stanley, prin. Fax 482-3650

Thoreau, McKinley
Gallup-McKinley County SD
Supt. — See Gallup
Thoreau HS 600/9-12
PO Box 96 87323 505-862-7488
Monique Siedschiag, prin. Fax 862-7742
Thoreau MS 400/6-8
PO Box 787 87323 505-862-7463
Alberta Noize, prin. Fax 862-7464

Tierra Amarilla, Rio Arriba
Chama Valley ISD 500/PK-12
PO Box 10 87575 505-588-7285
Manuel Valdez, supt. Fax 588-7860
www.eschs.k12.nm.us
Escalante HS 200/9-12
PO Box 157 87575 505-588-7201
Fred Trujillo, prin. Fax 588-7911
Tierra Amarilla MS 100/6-8
PO Box 159 87575 505-588-7297
Rebecca Truelove, prin. Fax 588-7021
Other Schools – See Chama

Tijeras, Bernalillo, Pop. 499
Albuquerque SD
Supt. — See Albuquerque
Roosevelt MS 500/6-8
11799 State Highway 337 87059 505-281-3316
Lee Roy Martinez, prin. Fax 281-5120

Eastern Hills Christian Academy 100/PK-12
PO Box 1779 87059 505-286-1482
Dede Ferguson, prin. Fax 286-7609

Tohatchi, McKinley, Pop. 661
Gallup-McKinley County SD
Supt. — See Gallup
Tohatchi HS 500/9-12
PO Box 248 87325 505-733-2216
Fax 733-2216
Tohatchi MS 300/6-8
PO Box 322 87325 505-733-2555
Bart Stanley, prin. Fax 733-2556

Truth or Consequences, Sierra, Pop. 7,071
Truth or Consequences Municipal SD 1,500/PK-12
180 N Date St 87901 505-894-8150
Jim Nesbitt, supt. Fax 894-7532
www.torc.k12.nm.us
Hot Springs HS 400/9-12
180 N Date St 87901 505-894-8350
Ron Williams, prin. Fax 894-0471
Truth or Consequences MS 400/6-8
180 N Date St 87901 505-894-8380
Randy Piper, prin. Fax 894-0606

Tucumcari, Quay, Pop. 5,335
Tucumcari SD 1,100/PK-12
PO Box 1046 88401 505-461-3910
Aaron McKinney, supt. Fax 461-3554
www.gorattlers.org
Tucumcari HS, 1100 S 7th St 88401 300/9-12
Susan Montoya, prin. 505-461-3830
Tucumcari MS, 914 S 5th St 88401 300/6-8
Roberta Segura, prin. 505-461-2310

Mesalands Community College Post-Sec.
911 S 10th St 88401 505-461-4413

Tularosa, Otero, Pop. 2,858
Tularosa Municipal SD 900/K-12
504 1st St 88352 505-585-8800
Brenda Vigil, supt. Fax 585-4439
www.tularosa.k12.nm.us
Tularosa HS 300/9-12
504 1st St 88352 505-585-8866
Pam Miller, prin. Fax 585-8112
Tularosa MS 200/7-8
504 1st St 88352 505-585-8803
Diane Baker, prin. Fax 585-4739

Vaughn, Guadalupe, Pop. 469
Vaughn Municipal SD 100/PK-12
PO Box 489 88353 505-584-2283
Lorena Garcia, supt. Fax 584-2355
www.vaughn.k12.nm.us/
Vaughn JSHS 50/7-12
PO Box 489 88353 505-584-2313
Diana White, prin. Fax 584-2355

Wagon Mound, Mora, Pop. 352
Wagon Mound SD 200/K-12
PO Box 158 87752 505-666-3000
Albert Martinez, supt. Fax 666-9001
www.nnmt.net/~wmps/
Wagon Mound JSHS 100/7-12
PO Box 158 87752 505-666-3001
Albert Martinez, prin. Fax 666-9001

White Sands, Dona Ana, Pop. 2,616
Las Cruces SD
Supt. — See Las Cruces
White Sands MS 100/6-8
1 Viking St 88002 505-678-1064
Larry Davis, prin. Fax 678-8515

Zuni, McKinley, Pop. 5,857
Zuni SD 1,700/K-12
PO Box A 87327 505-782-5511
Dr. Kaye Peery, supt. Fax 782-5870
www.zuni.k12.nm.us
Twin Buttes HS 100/7-12
PO Box 680 87327 505-782-4446
Fax 782-4944
Zuni HS 400/9-12
PO Box 550 87327 505-782-4451
Joe Westmoreland, prin. Fax 782-5551
Zuni MS 300/7-8
PO Box 447 87327 505-782-5885
Terri Sebastian, prin. Fax 782-4370

NEW YORK

NEW YORK EDUCATION DEPARTMENT
111 Education, Albany 12234-0001
Telephone 518-474-5844
Fax 518-473-4909
Website http://www.nysed.gov

Commissioner of Education — Richard Mills

NEW YORK BOARD OF REGENTS
Washington Ave, Albany 12234-0001

Chancellor — Robert Bennett

BOARDS OF COOPERATIVE EDUCATIONAL SERVICES (BOCES)

Broome-Delaware-Tioga BOCES
Dr. Joseph R. Busch, supt. — 607-763-3309
435 Glenwood Rd — Fax 763-3215
Binghamton 13905
www.btboces.stier.org/

Capital Region BOCES
Dr. Barbara Nagler, supt. — 518-862-4900
1031 Watervliet Shaker Rd — Fax 862-4903
Albany 12205
www.capregboces.org

Cattaraugus/Allegany/Erie/Wy BOCES
Dr. Robert Olczak, supt. — 585-376-8246
1825 Windfall Rd, Olean 14760 — Fax 376-8452
caew-boces.wnyric.org/

Cayuga/Onondaga BOCES
Gary Gilchrist, supt. — 315-253-0361
5980 S Street Rd, Auburn 13021 — Fax 252-6493
cayboces.org

Champlain Valley Educational Services
Craig King, supt. — 518-561-0100
PO Box 455, Plattsburgh 12901 — Fax 562-1471
www.cves.org/

Delaware/Chenango/Mdsn/Otsg BOCES
Alan Pole, supt. — 607-335-1233
6678 County Road 32 — Fax 334-9848
Norwich 13815
www.dcmoboces.com

Dutchess BOCES
Dr. John Pennoyer, supt. — 845-486-4800
5 Boces Rd, Poughkeepsie 12601 — Fax 486-4981
www.dcboces.org

Eastern Suffolk BOCES
Edward Zero, supt. — 631-289-2200
201 Sunrise Hwy, Patchogue 11772 — Fax 289-2381
www.esboces.org/

Erie 1 BOCES
Donald Ogilvie, supt. — 716-821-7000
355 Harlem Rd — Fax 821-7242
West Seneca 14224
www.erie1boces.org

Erie 2-Chautauqua-Cattaraugus BOCES
Robert Guiffreda, supt. — 716-549-4454
8685 Erie Rd, Angola 14006 — Fax 549-1758
e2ccboces.wnyric.org/

Franklin-Essex-Hamilton BOCES
David DeSantis, supt. — 518-483-6420
PO Box 28, Malone 12953 — Fax 483-2178
www.fehb.org/

Genesee Valley BOCES
Dr. Michael Glover, supt. — 585-344-7905
80 Munson St, Le Roy 14482 — Fax 658-7910
www.gvboces.org

Greater Southern Tier BOCES
Anthony Micha, supt. — 607-962-3175
9579 Vocational Dr — Fax 962-1579
Painted Post 14870
www.gstboces.org/index.cfm

Hamilton-Fulton-Montgomery BOCES
Dr. Geoffrey Davis, supt. — 518-762-4634
PO Box 665, Johnstown 12095 — Fax 762-4724
www.hfmboces.org/indexmap.html

Herkimer-Fulton-Hamilton-Otsego BOCES
Sandra Simpson, supt. — 315-867-2023
352 Gros Blvd, Herkimer 13350 — Fax 867-2002
www.herkimer-boces.org

Jeffrsn-Lws-Hmltn-Hrkmr-Oneida BOCES
Jack Boak, supt. — 315-779-7010
20104 State Route 3 — Fax 785-8300
Watertown 13601
www.boces.com/

Madison-Oneida BOCES
Jacklin Starks, supt. — 315-361-5500
PO Box 168, Verona 13478 — Fax 361-5595
www.moboces.org

Monroe 1 BOCES
Dr. Frederick Wille, supt. — 585-383-2200
41 OConnor Rd, Fairport 14450 — Fax 383-6404
www.monroe.edu/

Monroe 2 - Orleans BOCES
Dr. Joseph Marinelli, supt. — 585-352-2400
3599 Big Ridge Rd — Fax 352-2442
Spencerport 14559
www.monroe2boces.org

Nassau BOCES
Dr. James D. Mapes, supt. — 516-396-2200
PO Box 9195, Garden City 11530 — Fax 997-8742
www.nassauboces.org

Oneida-Herkimer-Madison BOCES
Howard Mettelman, supt. — 315-793-8560
PO Box 70, New Hartford 13413 — Fax 793-8541
www.oneida-boces.org/

Onondaga-Cortland-Madison BOCES
Dr. Jessica Cohen, supt. — 315-433-2600
PO Box 4754, Syracuse 13221 — Fax 434-9347
www.ocmboces.org/

Orange-Ulster BOCES
Dr. Robert Hanna, supt. — 845-291-0110
53 Gibson Rd, Goshen 10924 — Fax 291-0118
www.ouboces.org/

Orleans-Niagara BOCES
Dr. Clark Godshall, admin. — 800-836-7510
4232 Shelby Basin Rd — Fax 798-1317
Medina 14103
www.onboces.org

Oswego BOCES
Dr. Joseph Camerino, supt. — 315-963-4222
179 County Route 64 — Fax 963-7131
Mexico 13114
www.oswegoboces.org/

Otsego-Delaware-Schoharie-Greene BOCES
Dr. Marie Wiles, supt. — 607-652-1209
159 W Main St, Stamford 12167 — Fax 652-1215
www.oncboces.org

Putnam Northern Westchester BOCES
Dr. James T. Langlois, supt. — 914-248-2300
200 BOCES Dr — Fax 248-2308
Yorktown Heights 10598
www.pnwboces.org

Questar III BOCES
James Baldwin, supt. — 518-477-8771
10 Empire State Blvd — Fax 477-9833
Castleton on Hudson 12033
www.questar.org/

Rockland BOCES
Dr. James Ryan, supt. — 845-627-4701
65 Parrott Rd, West Nyack 10994 — Fax 624-1764
www.rocklandboces.org/

St. Lawrence-Lewis BOCES
Linda Gush Ph.D., supt. — 315-386-4504
PO Box 231, Canton 13617 — Fax 386-2099
www.sllboces.org/

Sullivan County BOCES
Dr. Martin Handler, supt. — 845-292-0082
6 Wierk Ave, Liberty 12754 — Fax 292-8694
www.scboces.com

Tompkins-Seneca-Tioga BOCES
Dr. Ellen A. O'Donnell, supt. — 607-257-1551
555 Warren Rd, Ithaca 14850 — Fax 257-2825
www.tstboces.org/

Ulster BOCES
Martin Ruglis, supt. — 845-255-3040
175 State Route 32 N — Fax 255-7942
New Paltz 12561
www.ulsterboces.org/

Washington-Srtg-Warren-Hmltn-Essex BOCES
Dr. John Stoothoff, supt. — 518-746-3310
1153 Burgoyne Ave Ste 2 — Fax 746-3309
Fort Edward 12828
wswheboces.org/

Wayne-Finger Lakes BOCES
Dr. Joseph Marinelli, supt. — 315-332-7284
131 Drumlin Ct, Newark 14513 — Fax 332-7425
www.wflboces.org/wflboces/index.cfm

Westchester BOCES
Ronald Smalls, supt. — 914-937-3820
17 Berkley Dr, Rye Brook 10573 — Fax 937-7850
www.swboces.org/

Western Suffolk BOCES
Dr. James Mapes, supt. — 631-549-4900
507 Deer Park Rd, Dix Hills 11746 — Fax 423-1821
www.wsboces.org/

PUBLIC, PRIVATE AND CATHOLIC SECONDARY SCHOOLS

Accord, Ulster

Rondout Valley Central SD — 2,800/K-12
PO Box 9 12404 — 845-687-2400
Eileen Camasso, supt. — Fax 687-9577
www.rondout.k12.ny.us

Rondout Valley HS — 1,000/9-12
PO Box 9 12404 — 845-687-2400
William Cafiero, prin. — Fax 687-7665

Rondout Valley MS — 1,000/5-8
PO Box 9 12404 — 845-687-2400
Raymond Palmer, prin. — Fax 687-8980

Adams, Jefferson, Pop. 1,663

South Jefferson Central SD
Supt. — See Adams Center

Clarke MS — 500/6-8
11060 US Route 11 13605 — 315-232-4531
Tom O'Brien, prin. — Fax 232-4620

South Jefferson HS — 600/9-12
11060 US Route 11 13605 — 315-232-4531
Karen Denny, prin. — Fax 232-3728

Adams Center, Jefferson, Pop. 1,675

South Jefferson Central SD — 2,000/K-12
13180 US Route 11 13606 — 315-583-6104
Jamie Moesel, supt. — Fax 583-6381
www.spartanpride.org
Other Schools – See Adams

Addison, Steuben, Pop. 1,765

Addison Central SD — 1,200/PK-12
1 Colwell St 14801 — 607-359-2244
Betsy Stiker, supt. — Fax 359-2246
www.addison.wnyric.org/

Addison JSHS — 600/7-12
1 Colwell St 14801 — 607-359-2241
Joseph Dioguardi, prin. — Fax 359-3443

Afton, Chenango, Pop. 831

Afton Central SD — 700/K-12
PO Box 5 13730 — 607-639-8229
Elizabeth Briggs, supt. — Fax 639-1801
www.afton.stier.org

Afton JSHS — 400/6-12
PO Box 5 13730 — 607-639-8202
David Glover, prin. — Fax 639-8257

Airmont, Rockland, Pop. 8,600

Mesifta Beth Shraga S — 100/9-12
28 Saddle River Rd, — 845-356-1980
S. Feivel Mendlowitz, admin. — Fax 425-2604

Rabbinical College Beth Shraga — Post-Sec.
28 Saddle River Rd, — 845-356-1980

Akron, Erie, Pop. 3,067

Akron Central SD — 1,700/PK-12
47 Bloomingdale Ave 14001 — 585-542-5010
Ronald DeCarli, supt. — Fax 542-3863
www.akronschools.org

Akron HS — 500/9-12
47 Bloomingdale Ave 14001 — 585-542-5030
Joseph Lucenti, prin. — Fax 542-3863

Akron MS — 400/6-8
47 Bloomingdale Ave 14001 — 585-542-5040
Virginia Williams, prin. — Fax 542-3863

Albany, Albany, Pop. 93,523

Albany CSD — 8,600/PK-12
1 Academy Park 12207 — 518-475-6000
Dr. Eva C. Joseph, supt. — Fax 475-6009
www.albanyschools.org

Abrookin Voc-Tech Center — Vo/Tech
99 Kent St 12206 — 518-462-7278
Fax 462-7174

Albany HS — 2,400/9-12
700 Washington Ave 12203 — 518-454-3987
Maxine Fantroy-Ford, prin. — Fax 437-0476

Hackett MS — 800/6-8
45 Delaware Ave 12202 — 518-462-7186
Kenneth Newman, prin. — Fax 462-7161

Livingston Magnet Academy 700/6-8
315 Northern Blvd 12210 518-462-7154
Tracy Ford, prin. Fax 465-6530
Myers MS 6-8
100 Elbel Ct 12209 518-475-6425
Kimberly Wilkins, prin. Fax 475-6427
Adult Learning Center Adult
27 Western Ave 12203 518-462-7254
Michael Cioffi, prin. Fax 462-7253

South Colonie Central SD 5,700/K-12
102 Loralee Dr 12205 518-869-3576
Michael Marcelle, supt. Fax 869-6517
www.southcolonieschools.org
Colonie Central HS 1,800/9-12
1 Raider Blvd 12205 518-459-1220
David Wetzel, prin. Fax 459-8524
Lisha Kill MS 900/5-8
68 Waterman Ave 12205 518-456-2306
Francis Cocozza, prin. Fax 452-8165
Sand Creek MS 1,100/5-8
329 Sand Creek Rd 12205 518-459-1333
David Perry, prin. Fax 459-1404

Academy of the Holy Names 300/9-12
1075 New Scotland Rd 12208 518-489-2559
Mary Ann Vigliante, prin. Fax 438-7368
Albany Academy 400/PK-12
135 Academy Rd 12208 518-465-1461
Caroline Mason, hdmstr. Fax 427-7016
Albany Academy for Girls 400/PK-12
140 Academy Rd 12208 518-463-2201
Caroline Mason, hdmstr. Fax 463-5096
Albany College of Pharmacy Post-Sec.
106 New Scotland Ave 12208 518-445-7390
Albany Law School of Union University Post-Sec.
80 New Scotland Ave 12208 518-445-2326
Austin Beauty School Post-Sec.
527 Central Ave 12206 518-438-7879
Bishop Maginn HS 400/9-12
99 Slingerland St 12202 518-463-2247
Joseph Grasso, prin. Fax 463-9880
Bryant & Stratton College Post-Sec.
1259 Central Ave 12205 518-437-1802
Center for Natural Wellness School Post-Sec.
3 Cerone Commercial Dr 12205 518-449-2737
Christian Brothers Academy 500/6-12
12 Airline Dr 12205 518-452-9809
David McGuire, prin. Fax 452-9804
College of Saint Rose Post-Sec.
432 Western Ave 12203 518-454-5150
Doane Stuart S 300/PK-12
799 S Pearl St 12202 518-465-5222
Dr. Richard Enemark, hdmstr. Fax 465-5230
Excelsior College Post-Sec.
7 Columbia Cir 12203 518-464-8500
La Salle S 200/6-12
391 Western Ave 12203 518-242-4731
James Meyer, dir. Fax 242-4747
Maimonides Hebrew Day S 100/PK-12
PO Box 8806 12208 518-453-9363
Marcia Rosenfield, admin. Fax 453-9362
Maria College of Albany Post-Sec.
700 New Scotland Ave 12208 518-438-3111
Memorial Hospital School of Nursing Post-Sec.
600 Northern Blvd 12204 518-471-3260
Orlo School of Hair Design & Cosmetology Post-Sec.
232 N Allen St 12206 518-459-7832
Sage College of Albany Post-Sec.
140 New Scotland Ave 12208 518-292-1717
St. Anne Institute 100/7-12
160 N Main Ave 12206 518-437-6661
John Schumann, prin. Fax 437-6532
SUNY at Albany Post-Sec.
1400 Washington Ave 12222 518-442-3300

Albertson, Nassau, Pop. 5,166
Herricks UFD
Supt. — See New Hyde Park
Herricks MS 1,000/6-8
7 Hilldale Dr 11507 516-625-6463
Joseph Leccese, prin. Fax 248-3281

Albion, Orleans, Pop. 5,766
Albion Central SD 2,400/PK-12
324 East Ave 14411 585-589-2050
Dr. Ada Grabowski, supt. Fax 589-2059
www.albionk12.org/
Bergerson MS, 254 East Ave 14411 600/5-8
Kim Houserman, prin. 585-589-2020
D'Amico HS, 302 East Ave 14411 800/9-12
Daniel Monacelli, prin. 585-589-2040

Alden, Erie, Pop. 2,613
Alden Central SD 1,900/K-12
13190 Park St 14004 716-937-9116
Lynn Fusco Ph.D., supt. Fax 937-1864
www.aldenschools.org
Alden HS 700/9-12
13190 Park St 14004 716-937-9116
Kevin Ryan, prin. Fax 937-1740
Alden MS 500/6-8
13250 Park St 14004 716-937-9116
Adam Stoltman, prin. Fax 937-3563

Alexander, Genesee, Pop. 497
Alexander Central SD 1,000/K-12
3314 Buffalo St 14005 585-591-1551
Dick Young, supt. Fax 591-2257
www.alexander.k12.ny.us
Alexander JSHS 600/7-12
3314 Buffalo St 14005 585-591-1551
Kathleen Maerten, prin. Fax 591-2257

Alexandria Bay, Jefferson, Pop. 1,100
Alexandria Central SD 600/K-12
34 Bolton Ave 13607 315-482-9971
Peter Morgante, supt. Fax 482-9973
Alexandria Central JSHS 300/5-12
34 Bolton Ave 13607 315-482-5113
Ronald Hockmuth, prin. Fax 482-9973

Alfred, Allegany, Pop. 5,009

Alfred University Post-Sec.
1 Saxon Dr 14802 607-871-2111
Alfred Univ.-NY State Coll. of Ceramics Post-Sec.
2 Pine St 14802 607-871-2411
SUNY College of Technology 14802 Post-Sec.
607-587-4215

Allegany, Cattaraugus, Pop. 1,831
Allegany-Limestone Central SD 1,400/PK-12
3131 Five Mile Rd 14706 585-375-6600
Diane Munro, supt.
www.alli.wnyric.org/
Allegany-Limestone HS 500/9-12
3131 Five Mile Rd 14706 585-375-6600
Cynthia Havers, prin. Fax 375-6630
Allegany-Limestone MS 400/6-8
3131 Five Mile Rd 14706 585-375-6600
Timothy McMullen, prin. Fax 375-6630

Almond, Allegany, Pop. 446
Alfred-Almond Central SD 700/K-12
6795 State Route 21 14804 607-276-2981
Richard Nicol, supt. Fax 276-6304
www.aacs.wnyric.org
Alfred-Almond JSHS 400/7-12
6795 State Route 21 14804 607-276-2961
Richard Calkins, prin. Fax 276-6304

Amenia, Dutchess, Pop. 1,057
Northeast Central SD 800/K-12
PO Box N 12501 845-373-4100
Dr. Richard Johns, supt. Fax 373-4102
Webutuck MSHS 500/6-12
194 Haight Rd 12501 845-373-4114
Ken Sauer, prin. Fax 373-8529

Kildonan S 100/2-12
425 Morse Hill Rd 12501 845-373-8111
Ronald Wilson, hdmstr. Fax 373-9793

Amherst, Erie, Pop. 45,800
Amherst Central SD 3,100/K-12
55 Kings Hwy 14226 716-362-3000
Dennis Ford, supt. Fax 836-2537
amherstschools.org
Amherst Central HS 1,000/9-12
4301 Main St 14226 716-362-8100
Jo Ann Balazs, prin. Fax 836-4972
Amherst MS 700/6-8
55 Kings Hwy 14226 716-362-7100
Diane Klein, prin. Fax 836-0193

Sweet Home Central SD 3,800/PK-12
1901 Sweet Home Rd 14228 716-250-1402
Geoffrey M. Hicks, supt. Fax 250-1374
www.sweethomeschools.com
Sweet Home HS 1,300/9-12
1901 Sweet Home Rd 14228 716-250-1200
Fax 250-1362
Sweet Home MS 900/6-8
4150 Maple Rd 14226 716-250-1450
Gregory Smorol, prin. Fax 250-1490

Bryant & Stratton College Post-Sec.
40 Hazelwood Dr 14228 716-691-0012
Daemen College Post-Sec.
4380 Main St 14226 716-839-3600
University at Buffalo SUNY Post-Sec.
408 Capen Hall 14260 716-645-2000

Amityville, Suffolk, Pop. 9,477
Amityville UFD 2,800/PK-12
150 Park Ave 11701 631-598-6507
Dr. Brian Desorbe, supt. Fax 691-4108
www.amityville.com/School/
Amityville Memorial HS 800/9-12
250 Merrick Rd 11701 631-598-6550
Dr. Scott Andrews, prin. Fax 264-4489
Miles MS 700/6-8
501 Broadway 11701 631-789-6200
Jack Lenson, prin. Fax 789-1655

Island Drafting & Technical Institute Post-Sec.
128 Broadway 11701 631-691-8733

Amsterdam, Montgomery, Pop. 17,749
Broadalbin-Perth Central SD
Supt. — See Broadalbin
Broadalbin-Perth MS 400/7-8
1870 County Highway 107 12010 518-954-2700
Susan Casper, prin. Fax 954-2709

Greater Amsterdam SD 3,500/K-12
11 Liberty St 12010 518-843-5217
Ronald E. Limoncelli, supt. Fax 842-0012
www.gasd.org
Amsterdam HS 1,200/9-12
140 Saratoga Ave 12010 518-843-4932
Gavin Murdoch, prin. Fax 843-5432
Lynch MS 900/6-8
55 Brandt Pl 12010 518-843-3716
Thomas Perillo, prin. Fax 843-6287

Perth Bible Christian Academy 100/PK-12
1863 County Highway 107 12010 518-843-0734
Bonnie Howard, prin. Fax 843-3304

Andes, Delaware, Pop. 278
Andes Central SD 100/K-12
PO Box 248 13731 845-676-3167
John Bernhardt, supt. Fax 676-3181
www.andescentralschool.org
Andes Central S 100/K-12
PO Box 248 13731 845-676-3166
John Bernhardt, prin. Fax 676-3181

Andover, Allegany, Pop. 1,037
Andover Central SD 400/PK-12
31-35 Elm St 14806 607-478-8491
William Berg, supt. Fax 478-8833
www.andovercsd.org/
Andover S 400/PK-12
31-35 Elm St 14806 607-478-8491
Richard McInroy, prin. Fax 478-8833

Angola, Erie, Pop. 2,194
Evans-Brant Central SD (Lake Shore) 3,100/K-12
959 Beach Rd 14006 716-926-2201
Jeffrey Rabey, supt. Fax 549-6407
www.lakeshore.wnyric.org
Lake Shore Central MS 800/6-8
8855 Erie Rd 14006 716-549-2302
Scott Smith, prin. Fax 549-4374
Lake Shore HS 1,100/9-12
959 Beach Rd 14006 716-549-2301
R. Terrence Redman, prin. Fax 549-4033

Annandale on Hudson, Dutchess

Bard College 12504 Post-Sec.
845-758-6822

Ardsley, Westchester, Pop. 4,815
Ardsley UFD 2,200/K-12
500 Farm Rd 10502 914-693-6300
Dr. Richard Maurer, supt. Fax 693-8340
www.ardsleyschools.org
Ardsley HS 700/9-12
300 Farm Rd 10502 914-693-6300
Dr. James Haubner, prin. Fax 693-6822
Ardsley MS 700/5-8
700 Ashford Ave 10502 914-693-7564
Jeffrey O'Donnell, prin. Fax 693-7896

Argyle, Washington, Pop. 287
Argyle Central SD 600/K-12
5023 State Route 40 12809 518-638-8243
Ryan Sherman, supt. Fax 638-6373
Argyle Central HS 300/9-12
5023 State Route 40 12809 518-638-8243
Ryan Sherman, prin. Fax 638-6373

Arkport, Steuben, Pop. 828
Arkport Central SD 600/K-12
35 East Ave 14807 607-295-7471
William Locke, supt. Fax 295-7473
www.stev.net
Arkport Central S 600/K-12
35 East Ave 14807 607-295-9823
Jack Wraight, prin. Fax 295-7473

Armonk, Westchester, Pop. 2,745
Byram Hills Central SD 2,800/K-12
10 Tripp Ln Ste 1 10504 914-273-4082
John Chambers, supt. Fax 273-2516
www.byramhills.org
Byram Hills HS 800/9-12
12 Tripp Ln Ste 1 10504 914-273-9200
Dr. William Donohue, prin. Fax 273-8099
Crittenden MS 700/6-8
10 MacDonald Ave 10504 914-273-4250
Dr. H. Evan Powderly, prin. Fax 273-4618

Astoria, See New York
NYC Department of Education
Supt. — See New York
IS 10 1,000/6-8
4511 31st Ave 11103 718-278-7054
Clemente Lopes, prin. Fax 274-1578
IS 235 200/6-8
3014 30th St 11102 718-932-5876
Carmen Rivera, prin. Fax 932-5990
Baccalaureate S for Global Education 7-12
3412 36th Ave 11106 718-361-5275
William Stroud, prin. Fax 361-5395
Long Island City HS 3,700/9-12
1430 Broadway 11106 718-545-7095
William Bassell, prin. Fax 545-2980

Learning Institute for Beauty Sciences Post-Sec.
3815 Broadway 11103 718-726-8383
St. Demetrios S 700/PK-12
3003 30th Dr 11102 718-728-1754
Anastasios Koularmanis, prin. Fax 726-3482
St. John's Prep HS 1,300/9-12
2121 Crescent St 11105 718-721-7200
William Higgins, prin. Fax 545-9385

Athol Springs, Erie

St. Francis HS 600/9-12
4129 Lake Shore Rd 14010 716-627-1200
Rev. Michael Sajda, pres. Fax 627-4610

Attica, Wyoming, Pop. 2,496
Attica Central SD 1,700/K-12
3338 E Main Street Rd 14011 585-591-0400
Bryce Thompson, supt. Fax 591-2681
www.atticacsd.org
Attica HS 600/9-12
3338 E Main Street Rd 14011 585-591-0400
Kathleen Ballard, prin. Fax 591-2681
Attica JHS 600/5-8
3338 E Main Street Rd 14011 585-591-0400
Kenneth Hammel, prin. Fax 591-2681

Auburn, Cayuga, Pop. 27,941
Auburn CSD 4,800/K-12
78 Thornton Ave 13021 315-255-8800
John Plume, supt. Fax 253-6068
www.auburn.cnyric.org/
Auburn HS 1,500/9-12
250 Lake Ave 13021 315-255-8300
David Roth, prin. Fax 255-5876
East MS 600/6-8
191 Franklin St 13021 315-255-8480
Diane Dolcemascolo, prin. Fax 255-5910
West MS 600/6-8
217 Genesee St 13021 315-255-8540
Deborah Carey, prin. Fax 255-8559

SUNY Cayuga County Community College Post-Sec.
197 Franklin St 13021 315-255-1743

Aurora, Cayuga, Pop. 659
Southern Cayuga Central SD 1,000/K-12
2384 State Route 34B 13026 315-364-7211
Larry Hayes, supt. Fax 364-7863
www.southerncayuga.org

Southern Cayuga MS 300/5-8
2384 State Route 34B 13026 315-364-7098
Patricia Reilley, prin. Fax 364-7863
Southern Cayuga Secondary S 400/9-12
2384 State Route 34B 13026 315-364-7111
Karen Simon, prin. Fax 364-7863

Wells College Post-Sec.
PO Box 500 13026 315-364-3266

Averill Park, Rensselaer, Pop. 1,656
Averill Park Central SD 3,500/K-12
8439 Miller Hill Rd 12018 518-674-7050
Josephine Moccia Ed.D., supt. Fax 674-3802
www.averillpark.k12.ny.us/
Algonquin MS 900/6-8
333 NY Highway 351 12018 518-674-7100
Steve Beebie, prin. Fax 674-0671
Averill Park HS 1,200/9-12
146 Gettle Rd 12018 518-674-7000
Colleen Gomes, prin. Fax 674-7046

Avoca, Steuben, Pop. 986
Avoca Central SD 700/K-12
PO Box G 14809 607-566-2221
R. Christopher Roser, supt. Fax 566-2398
www.avoca.wnyric.org
Avoca Central S 700/K-12
PO Box G 14809 607-566-2221
M. Sullivan, prin. Fax 566-8384

Avon, Livingston, Pop. 2,972
Avon Central SD 1,100/K-12
191 Clinton St 14414 585-226-2455
Bruce Amey, supt. Fax 226-8202
www.avoncsd.org
Avon HS 400/9-12
245 Clinton Street Ext 14414 585-226-2455
Christopher Salinas, prin. Fax 226-8202
Avon MS 300/5-8
191 Clinton St 14414 585-226-2455
Jennifer Miller, prin. Fax 226-8202

Babylon, Suffolk, Pop. 12,659
Babylon UFD 2,000/K-12
50 Railroad Ave 11702 631-893-7925
Ellen Best-Laimit, supt. Fax 893-7935
www.babylonsd.org
Babylon JSHS 900/7-12
50 Railroad Ave 11702 631-893-7910
Robert Visbal, prin. Fax 893-7936

Bainbridge, Chenango, Pop. 1,354
Bainbridge-Guilford Central SD 900/K-12
18 Juliand St 13733 607-967-6321
Karl Brown, supt. Fax 967-4231
www.bgcsd.org
Bainbridge-Guilford HS 300/9-12
18 Juliand St 13733 607-967-6323
William Zakrajsek, prin. Fax 967-4231
Bainbridge-Guilford MS 200/6-8
18 Juliand St 13733 607-967-6300
Victoria Gullo, prin. Fax 967-4231

Baldwin, Nassau, Pop. 22,719
Baldwin UFD 5,300/K-12
960 Hastings St 11510 516-377-9271
Dr. Robert Britto, supt. Fax 377-9421
www.baldwin.k12.ny.us/
Baldwin HS 1,700/9-12
841 Ethel T Kloberg Dr 11510 516-377-9204
Susan Knors, prin. Fax 377-9208
Baldwin MS 1,200/6-8
3211 Schreiber Pl 11510 516-377-9321
James Brown, prin. Fax 377-9432

Baldwinsville, Onondaga, Pop. 7,149
Baldwinsville Central SD 6,000/K-12
29 E Oneida St 13027 315-638-6043
Jeanne Dangle, supt. Fax 638-6041
www.bville.org
Baker SHS 1,300/10-12
29 E Oneida St 13027 315-638-6000
Olivia Cambs, prin. Fax 638-6150
Durgee JHS 1,000/8-9
29 E Oneida St 13027 315-638-6086
Bonnie VanBenschoten, prin. Fax 635-3970

Ballston Spa, Saratoga, Pop. 5,574
Ballston Spa Central SD 4,400/K-12
70 Malta Ave 12020 518-884-7195
Dr. Raymond Colucciello, supt. Fax 884-7101
www.bscsd.org
Ballston Spa HS 1,400/9-12
220 Ballston Ave 12020 518-884-7150
Kristi Jensen, prin. Fax 884-7199
Ballston Spa MS 1,100/6-8
210 Ballston Ave 12020 518-884-7200
Dr. Helen Stuetzel, prin. Fax 884-7234

Bardonia, Rockland, Pop. 4,487

Albertus Magnus HS 500/9-12
798 Route 304 10954 845-623-8842
Joseph Troy, prin. Fax 623-0009

Barker, Niagara, Pop. 557
Barker Central SD 1,100/PK-12
1628 Quaker Rd 14012 716-795-3832
Steven LaRock, supt. Fax 795-3283
barkercsd.net
Barker HS 300/9-12
1628 Quaker Rd 14012 716-795-3201
John Hoar, prin. Fax 795-3911
Barker MS 300/5-8
1628 Quaker Rd 14012 716-795-3203
Cheryl Cardone, prin. Fax 795-9437

Barrytown, Dutchess

Unification Theological Seminary Post-Sec.
30 Seminary Dr 12507 845-752-3100

Batavia, Genesee, Pop. 15,661
Batavia CSD 2,500/K-12
PO Box 677 14021 585-343-2480
Richard G. Stutzman, supt. Fax 344-8204
www.bataviacsd.org
Batavia HS 800/9-12
260 State St 14020 585-343-2480
Pamela Buresch, prin. Fax 344-8609
Batavia MS 600/6-8
96 Ross St 14020 585-343-2480
Sandra Griffin, prin. Fax 344-8626

Continental School of Beauty Culture Post-Sec.
215 Main St 14020 585-344-0886
Genesee Community College Post-Sec.
1 College Rd 14020 585-343-0055
New York State School for the Blind Post-Sec.
2A Richmond Ave 14020
Notre Dame HS 200/9-12
73 Union St 14020 585-343-2783
Dr. Joseph Scanlon, prin. Fax 343-7323

Bath, Steuben, Pop. 5,589
Bath Central SD 2,000/PK-12
25 Ellis Ave 14810 607-776-3301
Marion Tunney, supt. Fax 776-5021
www.bathcsd.org
Haverling HS 600/9-12
25 Ellis Ave 14810 607-776-4107
Randy Brzezinski, prin. Fax 776-5021
Haverling MS 500/6-8
25 Ellis Ave 14810 607-776-4110
Michael Siebert, prin. Fax 776-5625

Bayport, Suffolk, Pop. 7,702
Bayport-Blue Point UFD 2,500/K-12
189 Academy St 11705 631-472-7860
Anthony J. Annunziato, supt. Fax 472-7817
www.b-bp.k12.ny.us
Bayport-Blue Point HS 700/9-12
200 Snedecor Ave 11705 631-472-7800
Peter Sellitto Ed.D., prin. Fax 472-7814
Young MS 600/6-8
602 Sylvan Ave 11705 631-472-7820
Susan Haske, prin. Fax 472-7849

Bay Shore, Suffolk, Pop. 21,279
Bay Shore UFD 5,600/K-12
75 Perkal St 11706 631-968-1115
Evelyn Holman Ph.D., supt. Fax 968-1129
www.bayshore.k12.ny.us
Bay Shore HS 1,700/9-12
155 3rd Ave 11706 631-968-1156
Edmund Frazier, prin. Fax 968-2332
Bay Shore MS 1,300/6-8
393 Brook Ave 11706 631-968-1208
LaQuita Outlaw, prin. Fax 968-2342

Brentwood UFD
Supt. — See Brentwood
West MS 800/6-8
2030 Udall Rd 11706 631-434-2371
Adrienne Ratuszny, prin. Fax 242-3992

Bayside, See New York
NYC Department of Education
Supt. — See New York
Bayside HS 3,400/9-12
3224 Corporal Kennedy St 11361 718-229-7600
Judith Tarlo, prin. Fax 423-9566
MS 158 1,100/6-8
4635 Oceania St 11361 718-423-8100
Marie Nappi, prin. Fax 423-8135

Beacon, Dutchess, Pop. 14,836
Beacon CSD 3,700/PK-12
10 Education Dr 12508 845-838-6900
Dr. Jean Parr, supt. Fax 838-6905
www.beaconcityk12.org/
Beacon HS 1,100/9-12
101 Matteawan Rd 12508 845-838-6900
Edward Mancari, prin. Fax 838-0796
Rombout MS 900/6-8
84 Matteawan Rd 12508 845-838-6900
Brian Archer, prin. Fax 231-0474

Beaver Falls, Lewis
Beaver River Central SD 1,000/K-12
PO Box 179 13305 315-346-1211
Francine Shea, supt. Fax 346-6775
www.brcsd.org/
Beaver River MSHS 600/6-12
PO Box 179 13305 315-346-1211
Debra Smith, prin. Fax 346-6775

Bedford, Westchester, Pop. 1,828
Bedford Central SD 4,200/K-12
632 S Bedford Rd 10506 914-241-6000
Dr. Debra Jackson, supt. Fax 241-6004
www.bedford.k12.ny.us
Fox Lane HS 1,300/9-12
PO Box 390 10506 914-241-6085
Deborah Talbot, prin. Fax 241-6064
Fox Lane MS 900/6-8
S Bedford Rd 10506 914-241-6143
Anne Marie Berardi, prin. Fax 241-6129

Rippowam Cisqua S 200/5-9
439 Cantitoe St 10506 914-244-1250
Eileen F. Lambert, hdmstr. Fax 244-1245

Bedford Hills, Westchester, Pop. 3,200

Yeshiva & Mesivta Ohel Shmuel 50/11-12
165 Haines Rd Stop 1 10507 914-241-2700
Rabbi M. Waldman, prin. Fax 666-0280

Belfast, Allegany
Belfast Central SD 400/PK-12
1 King St 14711 585-365-9940
Judy May, supt. Fax 365-2648
www.belfast.wnyric.org
Belfast Central S 400/PK-12
1 King St 14711 585-365-8285
Jennifer Amos, prin. Fax 365-2648

Belle Harbor, Queens

Yeshiva Merkaz Hatorah of Belle Harbor 50/9-12
505 Beach 129th St, 718-474-3064
Rabbi Levi Dicker, admin. Fax 634-4510

Bellerose, Queens, Pop. 1,153
NYC Department of Education
Supt. — See New York
HS of Teaching Liberal Arts & Science 600/9-12
7420 Commonwealth Blvd 11426 718-736-7100
Nigel Pugh, dir. Fax 736-7125

Belleville, Jefferson
Belleville Henderson Central SD 600/PK-12
PO Box 158 13611 315-846-5411
Robert Ike Ed.D., supt. Fax 846-5826
Belleville Henderson Central S 600/PK-12
PO Box 158 13611 315-846-5121
Shawn Baker, prin. Fax 846-5826

Bellmore, Nassau, Pop. 16,438
Bellmore-Merrick Central HSD
Supt. — See North Merrick
Grand Avenue MS 1,100/7-8
2301 Grand Ave 11710 516-992-1100
Lewis Serra, prin. Fax 679-5068
Kennedy HS 1,300/9-12
3000 Bellmore Ave 11710 516-992-1400
Lorraine Poppe, prin. Fax 826-0526
Mepham HS 1,300/9-12
2401 Camp Ave 11710 516-992-1500
John Didden, prin. Fax 785-7590

Bellport, Suffolk, Pop. 2,359
South Country Central SD
Supt. — See East Patchogue
Bellport MS 1,100/6-8
35 Kreamer St 11713 631-730-1657
Gerard Cairns, prin. Fax 286-4460

Belmont, Allegany, Pop. 912
Genesee Valley Central SD 800/PK-12
1 Jaguar Dr 14813 585-268-7900
Michael Taylor, supt. Fax 268-7990
www.gvcs.wnyric.org/
Genesee Valley HS 200/9-12
1 Jaguar Dr 14813 585-268-7900
Mary Kay Worth, prin. Fax 268-5012
Genesee Valley MS 200/5-8
1 Jaguar Dr 14813 585-268-7900
Mary Kay Worth, prin. Fax 268-5012

Bemus Point, Chautauqua, Pop. 338
Bemus Point Central SD 900/K-12
PO Box 468 14712 716-386-2375
Albert D'Attilio, supt. Fax 386-2376
www.bemusptcsd.org
Maple Grove JSHS 500/7-12
PO Box 468 14712 716-386-2855
Edward Turkasz, prin. Fax 386-2376

Bergen, Genesee, Pop. 1,195
Byron-Bergen Central SD 1,200/K-12
6917 W Bergen Rd 14416 585-494-1220
Dr. Gregory Geer, supt. Fax 494-2613
www.bbcs.k12.ny.us
Byron-Bergen HS 400/9-12
6917 W Bergen Rd 14416 585-494-1220
David Pescrillo, prin. Fax 494-2613
Byron-Bergen MS 400/5-8
6917 W Bergen Rd 14416 585-494-1220
Daniel Bedette, prin. Fax 494-2613

Berlin, Rensselaer
Berlin Central SD 1,000/K-12
PO Box 259 12022 518-658-2690
Maria A. Diamond, supt. Fax 658-3822
www.berlincentral.org/
Berlin Central JSHS 600/6-12
PO Box 259 12022 518-658-2515
Frances DelSignore, prin. Fax 658-2535

Berne, Albany
Berne-Knox-Westerlo Central SD 1,100/K-12
1738 Helderberg Trl 12023 518-872-1293
Steven Schrade, supt. Fax 872-0341
www.bkwcsd.k12.ny.us/
Berne-Knox-Westerlo JSHS 700/6-12
1738 Helderberg Trl 12023 518-872-1482
Mary Petrilli, prin. Fax 872-0341

Bethpage, Nassau, Pop. 15,761
Bethpage UFD 3,000/K-12
10 Cherry Ave 11714 516-644-4000
Dr. Richard S. Marsh, supt. Fax 931-8783
www.bethpagecommunity.com
Bethpage HS 900/9-12
10 Cherry Ave 11714 516-644-4100
John DeTommaso, prin. Fax 937-6076
Kennedy MS 700/6-8
500 Broadway 11714 516-644-4200
Kerri McCarthy, prin. Fax 937-0540

Plainedge UFD
Supt. — See North Massapequa
Plainedge MS 800/6-8
200 Stewart Ave 11714 516-992-7650
Stephanie Clagnaz, prin. Fax 992-7645

Briarcliffe College Post-Sec.
1055 Stewart Ave 11714 516-918-3600

Binghamton, Broome, Pop. 45,492
Binghamton CSD 6,100/PK-12
PO Box 2126 13902 607-762-8100
Peggy J. Wozniak, supt. Fax 762-8112
www.binghamtonschools.org
Binghamton HS 1,700/9-12
31 Main St 13905 607-762-8200
Albert Penna, prin. Fax 762-6072
East MS 700/6-8
167 E Frederick St 13904 607-762-8300
Michael O'Branski, prin. Fax 762-8398
West MS 700/6-8
W Middle Ave 13905 607-763-8400
Michael Holly, prin. Fax 763-8429

Chenango Forks Central SD 1,800/PK-12
1 Gordon Dr 13901 607-648-7543
Robert Bundy Ed.D., supt. Fax 648-7560
www.cforks.org
Chenango Forks HS 600/9-12
1 Gordon Dr 13901 607-648-7544
Diane Wheeler-Busch, prin. Fax 648-7560
Chenango Forks MS 500/6-8
1 Gordon Dr 13901 607-648-7576
William Burke, prin. Fax 648-7560

Chenango Valley Central SD 2,000/PK-12
1160 Chenango St 13901 607-779-4710
Carmen Ciullo, supt. Fax 779-8610
www.cvcsd.stier.org/
Chenango Valley HS 600/9-12
1160 Chenango St 13901 607-779-4743
R. Glenn Reich, prin. Fax 779-4777
Chenango Valley MS 300/7-8
1160 Chenango St 13901 607-779-4755
David Gill, prin. Fax 779-4784

Broome Community College Post-Sec.
907 Upper Front St 13905 607-778-5000
Ridley-Lowell Business & Technical Inst. Post-Sec.
116 Front St 13905 607-724-2941
Seton Catholic Central HS 400/9-12
70 Seminary Ave 13905 607-723-5307
Kathleen Dwyer, prin. Fax 723-4811
SUNY at Binghamton Post-Sec.
PO Box 6001 13902 607-777-2000

Blauvelt, Rockland, Pop. 4,838
South Orangetown Central SD 3,400/K-12
160 Van Wyck Rd 10913 845-680-1050
Dr. Joseph Zambito, supt. Fax 680-1900
www.socsd.org
South Orangetown MS 800/6-8
160 Van Wyck Rd 10913 845-680-1100
Dr. William Lee, prin. Fax 680-1905
Other Schools – See Orangeburg

Bloomfield, Ontario, Pop. 1,325
Bloomfield Central SD 1,100/K-12
Oakmount Ave 14469 585-657-6121
Thomas Strining, supt. Fax 657-6060
www.bloomfieldcsd.org
Bloomfield HS 400/9-12
Oakmount Ave 14469 585-657-6121
Michael Reho, prin. Fax 657-4771
Bloomfield MS 300/6-8
Oakmount Ave 14469 585-657-6121
Janet Starwald, prin. Fax 657-4771

Bohemia, Suffolk, Pop. 9,556
Connetquot Central SD 7,100/K-12
780 Ocean Ave 11716 631-244-2215
Alan Groveman, supt. Fax 589-0683
www.connetquot.k12.ny.us/
Connetquot HS 2,200/9-12
190 7th St 11716 631-244-2226
Gregory Murtha, prin. Fax 244-2287
Other Schools – See Oakdale, Ronkonkoma

Boiceville, Ulster
Onteora Central SD 2,100/K-12
PO Box 300 12412 845-657-8851
Jack Jordan, supt. Fax 657-8742
onteora.schoolwires.com/
Onteora HS 800/9-12
4166 State Route 28 12412 845-657-2373
Barbara Ruben, prin. Fax 657-8430
Onteora MS 400/7-8
4166 State Route 28 12412 845-657-1100
Gayle Kavanagh, prin. Fax 657-7763

Bolivar, Allegany, Pop. 1,139
Bolivar-Richburg Central SD 1,000/PK-12
100 School St 14715 585-928-2561
Joseph Decerbo, supt. Fax 928-2411
www.brcs.wnyric.org
Bolivar-Richburg JSHS 500/6-12
100 School St 14715 585-928-2561
John Marshall, prin. Fax 928-1368

Bolton Landing, Warren
Bolton Central SD 300/K-12
PO Box 120 12814 518-644-2400
Raymond Ciccarelli, supt. Fax 644-2124
Bolton Central S 300/K-12
PO Box 120 12814 518-644-2400
James Donahue, prin. Fax 644-2124

Boonville, Oneida, Pop. 2,095
Adirondack Central SD 1,400/K-12
110 Ford St 13309 315-942-9200
Frederick Morgan, supt. Fax 942-5522
www.adirondackcsd.org
Adirondack HS 500/9-12
8181 State Route 294 13309 315-942-9250
Eric Vernold, prin. Fax 942-9254
Adirondack MS 400/6-8
8181 State Route 294 13309 315-942-9202
Patricia Thomas, prin. Fax 942-9211

Bradford, Schuyler
Bradford Central SD 300/K-12
2820 State Route 226 14815 607-583-4616
Charles Clemens, supt. Fax 583-4013
www.bradfordcsd.org/bcs/site/default.asp
Bradford Central S 300/K-12
2820 State Route 226 14815 607-583-4616
Geri Furterer, prin. Fax 583-4013

Brasher Falls, Saint Lawrence, Pop. 1,271
Brasher Falls Central SD 1,000/PK-12
PO Box 307 13613 315-389-5131
Stephen Putman, supt. Fax 389-5245
bfcsd.org
St. Lawrence Central HS 300/9-12
PO Box 307 13613 315-389-5131
Tracy Davison, prin. Fax 389-5245
St. Lawrence Central MS 300/5-8
PO Box 307 13613 315-389-5131
Christoper Rose, prin. Fax 389-5245

Brentwood, Suffolk, Pop. 55,000
Brentwood UFD 15,700/PK-12
52 3rd Ave 11717 631-434-2323
Donna Jones, supt. Fax 273-6575
www.bufsd.org/
Brentwood Freshman Center 1,200/9-9
33 Leahy Ave 11717 631-434-2541
Jose Suarez, prin. Fax 434-2549
Brentwood SHS 3,000/10-12
2 6th Ave 11717 631-434-2204
Thomas O'Brien, prin. Fax 434-2206
East MS 1,000/6-8
70 Hilltop Dr 11717 631-434-2473
Kyrie Siegel, prin. Fax 434-2171
North MS 1,100/6-8
350 Wicks Rd 11717 631-434-2356
Mae Lane, prin. Fax 952-9249
South MS 900/6-8
785 Candlewood Rd 11717 631-434-2341
Dana Gutierrez, prin. Fax 434-2560
Other Schools – See Bay Shore

Academy of St. Joseph 300/PK-12
1725 Brentwood Rd 11717 631-273-2406
Katharine Ventura, prin. Fax 231-4155
Long Island University Post-Sec.
100 2nd Ave 11717 631-273-5112
SUNY Suffolk County Community College Post-Sec.
1001 Crooked Hill Rd 11717 631-851-6700

Brewster, Putnam, Pop. 2,158
Brewster Central SD 3,700/K-12
30 Farm To Market Rd 10509 845-279-8000
Dr. Jane Sandbank, supt. Fax 279-3510
www.brewsterschools.org
Brewster HS 1,200/9-12
50 Foggintown Rd 10509 845-279-5051
Matthew Byrnes, prin. Fax 279-6730
Wells MS 900/6-8
570 Route 312 10509 845-279-3702
JoAnne Januzzi, prin. Fax 279-7634

Briarcliff Manor, Westchester, Pop. 7,938
Briarcliff Manor UFD 1,800/K-12
45 Ingham Rd 10510 914-941-8880
Dr. Frances Wills, supt. Fax 941-2177
www.briarcliffschools.org
Briarcliff Manor HS 600/9-12
444 Pleasantville Rd 10510 914-769-6299
James Kaishian, prin. Fax 769-2509
Briarcliff MS 400/6-8
444 Pleasantville Rd 10510 914-769-6343
Susan Howard, prin. Fax 769-6375

Bridgehampton, Suffolk, Pop. 1,997
Bridgehampton UFD 200/PK-12
PO Box 3021 11932 631-537-0271
Dr. Dianne Youngblood, supt. Fax 537-9038
www.bridgehampton.k12.ny.us/
Bridgehampton S 200/PK-12
PO Box 3021 11932 631-537-0271
John Pryor, prin. Fax 537-0443

Broadalbin, Fulton, Pop. 1,407
Broadalbin-Perth Central SD 1,900/K-12
14 School St 12025 518-954-2500
Robert Munn, supt. Fax 954-2509
www.bpcsd.org
Broadalbin-Perth HS 600/9-12
100 Bridge St 12025 518-954-2600
Robin Blowers, prin. Fax 954-2609
Other Schools – See Amsterdam

Brockport, Monroe, Pop. 8,134
Brockport Central SD 4,400/K-12
40 Allen St 14420 585-637-1810
James Fallon, supt. Fax 637-0165
brockport.k12.ny.us
Brockport HS 1,500/9-12
40 Allen St 14420 585-637-1877
Gary Levandowski, prin. Fax 637-1867
Oliver MS 1,100/6-8
40 Allen St 14420 585-637-1860
Rob Banzer, prin. Fax 637-1869

Cornerstone Christian Academy 100/K-12
60 Holley St 14420 585-637-4540
Christopher Johnson, admin. Fax 637-4518
SUNY College at Brockport Post-Sec.
350 New Campus Dr 14420 585-395-2211

Brocton, Chautauqua, Pop. 1,487
Brocton Central SD 700/K-12
138 W Main St 14716 716-792-2173
John Skahill, supt. Fax 792-9965
www.brocton.wnyric.org/
Brocton MSHS 400/6-12
138 W Main St 14716 716-792-2190
Stephen Keefe, prin. Fax 792-2246

Bronx, See New York
NYC Department of Education
Supt. — See New York
Academy of Applied Math & Technology 6-8
345 Brook Ave 10454 718-292-3883
Rose-Marie Mills, prin.
Acad for Scholarship & Entrepreneurship 6-12
1619 Boston Rd 10460 718-935-3168
Zenobia White Farrell, prin.
Accion Academy 6-8
1825 Prospect Ave 10457 718-378-6744
Sharon Spann, prin. Fax 837-8674
Addams Academic Careers HS Vo/Tech
900 Tinton Ave 10456 718-292-4513
Ellen O'Grady, prin. Fax 292-1947
Aspire Preparatory S 6-8
2441 Wallace Ave 10467 718-935-3497
Steven Cobb, prin.
Astor Collegiate Academy 200/9-12
925 Astor Ave 10469 718-944-3419
Richard Cintron, prin. Fax 519-1565
Belmont Preparatory HS 300/9-12
500 E Fordham Rd 10458 718-733-8100
Garner Bass, prin. Fax 295-3655
Bronx Academy of Health Careers 200/9-12
800 E Gun Hill Rd 10467 718-881-6147
Marvia Lindsay, prin. Fax 547-1321
Bronx Academy of Letters 200/9-12
339 Morris Ave 10451 718-292-1052
Joan Sullivan, prin. Fax 401-6626
Bronx Aerospace Academy 200/9-12
800 E Gun Hill Rd 10467 718-994-7823
Barbara Kirkweg, prin. Fax 994-4974
Bronx Center for Science & Mathematics 9-12
1363 Fulton Ave 10456 718-992-7089
Edward Tom, prin. Fax 590-1052
Bronx Coalition Community HS 400/9-12
1300 Boynton Ave 10472 718-860-8200
Gloria McDuffie, prin. Fax 842-5151
Bronx Dance Academy 300/6-8
3617 Bainbridge Ave 10467 718-515-0410
Amy Jones, prin. Fax 515-0345
Bronx Early College Academy 6-12
3333 Henry Hudson Pkwy 10463 718-432-0537
Constantino Trillana, prin.
Bronx Engineering & Technology Academy 100/9-12
99 Terrace View Ave Rm 544 10463 718-563-6678
Carine Davis, prin. Fax 563-6975
Bronx Expeditionary Learning HS 100/9-11
240 E 172nd St 10457 718-293-9569
Talana Bradley, prin. Fax 293-9567
Bronx Green MS 6-8
2441 Wallace Ave 10467 718-935-3198
Emily Becker, prin.
Bronx Guild HS 200/9-12
1980 Lafayette Ave 10473 718-597-1587
Sam Decker, prin. Fax 597-1371
Bronx Health Sciences HS 100/9-12
750 Baychester Ave 10475 718-548-1349
Miriam Rivas, prin.
HS for Contemporary Arts 200/9-12
800 E Gun Hill Rd 10467 718-944-5610
Francisco Sanchez, prin. Fax 944-5650
HS for Excellence 300/9-12
1100 Boston Rd 10456 718-860-1385
Wade Fuller, prin. Fax 860-4882
Bronx HS for Law & Community Service 300/9-12
500 E Fordham Rd 10458 718-733-8100
Gail Joyner-White, prin. Fax 584-6695
Bronx HS for Performance & Stagecraft 9-12
1619 Boston Rd 10460 718-991-0860
Mark Sweeting, prin.
HS for Teaching & Professions 400/9-12
2780 Reservoir Ave 10468 718-364-7400
Maxine Johnson-Harris, prin. Fax 295-3535
HS for Violin & Dance 9-12
1100 Boston Rd 10456 718-542-3700
Tanya Lippold, prin. Fax 589-9849
Bronx HS for Visual Arts 300/9-12
50 Mercy College Pl 10462 718-319-5160
Dr. George York, prin. Fax 319-5165
Bronx HS for Writing & Communication 100/9-12
800 E Gun Hill Rd 10467 718-944-5660
Steven Chernigoff, prin. Fax 944-5690
HS of American Studies 200/9-12
2925 Goulden Ave 10468 718-329-2144
Alessandro Weiss, prin. Fax 329-0792
Bronx HS of Business 300/9-12
240 E 172nd St 10457 718-410-4060
Enrique Lizardi, prin. Fax 992-5760
HS of Computers & Technology 100/9-12
800 E Gun Hill Rd 10467 718-696-3930
Bruce Abramowitz, prin. Fax 798-2875
Bronx HS of Science 2,500/9-12
75 Bronx Science Blvd 10468 718-817-7700
Valerie Reidy, prin. Fax 733-7951
HS of World Cultures 400/9-12
1300 Boynton Ave 10472 718-860-8121
Dr. Ramon Namnum, prin. Fax 893-7152
IS 117 1,000/6-8
1865 Morris Ave 10453 718-583-7750
Delise Jones, prin. Fax 583-7658
IS 129 200/6-8
2055 Mapes Ave 10460 718-933-5976
Yvette Beasley, prin. Fax 933-8132
IS 158 200/8-9
800 Home St 10456 718-542-1155
Marsha Elliott, prin. Fax 589-8067
IS 174 1,300/5-8
456 White Plains Rd 10473 718-617-5293
Sharon Delaney, prin. Fax 328-3124
IS 180 1,000/5-8
700 Baychester Ave 10475 718-904-5650
Frank Uzzo, prin. Fax 904-5655
IS 181 700/5-8
800 Baychester Ave 10475 718-904-5600
Stephen Bennett, prin. Fax 904-5620
IS 184 300/8-8
778 Forest Ave 10456 718-292-1684
Alejandro M. Soto, prin. Fax 292-5861
IS 190 300/6-8
1550 Crotona Park E 10460 718-620-9423
Diana J. Santiago, prin. Fax 620-9927
IS 192 1,000/6-8
650 Hollywood Ave 10465 718-822-5317
Jeanette Vargas, prin. Fax 239-3124
IS 206 500/5-8
2280 Aqueduct Ave 10468 718-584-1570
David Neering, prin. Fax 584-7928
IS 219 1,000/6-8
3630 3rd Ave 10456 718-681-7093
Dominic Cipollone, prin. Fax 681-7324
IS 224 200/6-8
345 Brook Ave 10454 718-665-9804
Jennifer Apodaca, prin. Fax 665-0078
IS 228 - Jonas Bronck Academy 6-8
4525 Manhattan College Pkwy 10471 718-884-6773
Maria Esponda, prin. Fax 884-6775
IS 229 500/5-8
275 Harlem River Park Brg 10453 718-583-6266
Dr. Ezra Matthias, prin. Fax 583-6325
IS 232 800/6-8
1700 Macombs Rd 10453 718-583-7007
Marcella Lilley, prin. Fax 583-4864
IS 254 500/6-8
2452 Washington Ave 10458 718-220-8700
Wilfred Heymans, prin. Fax 220-4881
IS 303 300/6-8
1700 Macombs Rd 10453 718-583-5466
Patricia Bentley, prin. Fax 583-2463
IS 313 500/6-8
1600 Webster Ave 10457 718-583-1736
Lauren Wilkens, prin. Fax 583-0281

IS 318 400/6-8
1919 Prospect Ave 10457 718-294-8504
Maria Lopez, prin. Fax 901-0778

IS 339 800/6-8
1600 Webster Ave 10457 718-583-6767
Jason Levy, prin. Fax 583-0281

Bronx International HS 300/9-12
1100 Boston Rd 10456 718-620-1053
Joaquin Vega, prin. Fax 620-1056

JHS 22 700/5-8
270 E 167th St 10456 718-681-6850
Shimon Waronker, prin. Fax 681-6895

JHS 45 1,300/6-8
2502 Lorillard Pl 10458 718-584-1660
Anna Maria Giordano, prin. Fax 584-7968

JHS 80 1,000/6-8
149 E Mosholu Pkwy N 10467 718-405-6300
Lovey Mazique-Rivera, prin. Fax 405-6324

JHS 98 500/5-8
1619 Boston Rd 10460 718-589-8200
Claralee Irobunda, prin. Fax 589-8179

JHS 113 600/8-8
3710 Barnes Ave 10467 718-653-2130
Angela Green, prin. Fax 547-5377

JHS 118 1,200/6-8
577 E 179th St 10457 718-584-2330
Giulia Cox, prin. Fax 584-7763

JHS 123 500/6-8
1025 Morrison Ave 10472 718-328-2105
Virginia Connelly, prin. Fax 328-8561

JHS 125 900/5-8
1111 Pugsley Ave 10472 718-822-5186
Hilda Bairan, prin. Fax 239-3121

JHS 127 900/5-8
1560 Purdy St 10462 718-892-8600
Harry Sherman, prin. Fax 892-8300

JHS 131 1,200/5-8
885 Bolton Ave 10473 718-991-7490
Rudolph Rupnarain, prin. Fax 328-6705

JHS 142 1,000/6-8
3750 Baychester Ave 10466 718-231-0100
Alan Borer, prin. Fax 231-3046

JHS 144 1,200/6-8
2545 Gunther Ave 10469 718-379-7400
Katina Lotakis, prin. Fax 320-0595

JHS 145 500/5-8
1000 Teller Ave 10456 718-681-7219
Robert Hannibal, prin. Fax 681-6913

JHS 151 400/6-8
250 E 156th St 10451 718-292-0260
John Piazza, prin. Fax 292-5704

JHS 162 1,200/6-8
600 Saint Anns Ave 10455 718-292-0880
Maryann Manzolillo, prin. Fax 292-5735

JHS 166 1,100/5-8
250 E 164th St 10456 718-681-6334
Lauren Reiss-Meredith, prin. Fax 681-6377

Bronx Lab S 100/9-12
800 E Gun Hill Rd 10467 718-696-3700
Marc Sternberg, prin. Fax 696-3730

Bronx Latin S 100/6-12
800 Home St 10456 718-991-6349
Leticia Pineiro, prin. Fax 991-6627

Bronx Leadership Academy II 300/9-12
1100 Boston Rd 10456 718-842-0173
Paulette Franklin, prin. Fax 893-7368

Bronx Leadership HS 600/9-12
1710 Webster Ave 10457 718-299-4274
Kenneth Gaskins, prin. Fax 299-4707

MS 101 600/5-8
2750 Lafayette Ave 10465 718-829-6372
Kim Hampton-Hewitt, prin. Fax 829-6594

MS 201 400/6-8
730 Bryant Ave 10474 718-328-1972
Talbert Thomas, prin. Fax 328-7330

MS 203 500/6-8
339 Morris Ave 10451 718-292-1052
William Hewlett, prin. Fax 292-5765

MS 223 300/6-8
360 E 145th St 10454 718-292-8627
Ramon Gonzalez, prin. Fax 292-7435

MS 273 100/6-8
2111 Crotona Ave 10457 718-561-1617
Deborah Cimini, prin. Fax 561-2184

MS 301 500/6-8
890 Cauldwell Ave 10456 718-585-2950
Benjamin Basile, prin. Fax 401-2567

MS 302 1,100/5-8
681 Kelly St 10455 718-292-6070
Angel Rodriguez, prin. Fax 401-2958

MS 327 200/6-8
580 Crotona Park S 10456 718-402-8327
Manuel Ramirez, prin. Fax 993-2990

MS 331 6-8
40 W Tremont Ave 10453 718-583-4146
John Barnes, prin. Fax 583-4292

MS 390 600/5-8
1930 Andrews Ave 10453 718-583-5502
Robert Mercedes, prin. Fax 583-5556

MS 391 1,100/6-8
2225 Webster Ave 10457 718-584-0980
Pedro Santana, prin. Fax 294-7208

MS 399 700/6-8
120 E 184th St 10468 718-584-0350
Yolanda Torres, prin. Fax 584-0730

Bronx MSHS for Medical Science 300/6-12
240 E 172nd St 10457 718-293-7200
William Quintana, prin. Fax 992-4129

Bronx School Law Government & Justice 500/7-12
244 E 163rd St 10451 718-410-3430
Meisha Ross-Porter, prin. Fax 410-3950

Bronx S of Law & Finance 200/9-12
99 Terrace View Ave Rm 804 10463 718-561-0113
Evan Schwartz, prin. Fax 561-0595

Bronx Studio S 6-12
1180 Tinton Ave 10456 718-861-8704
David Vazquez, prin. Fax 861-8703

Bronx Theatre HS 200/9-12
99 Terrace View Ave Rm 716 10463 718-329-2902
Deborah Effinger, prin. Fax 329-0433

Bronx Writing Academy 700/6-8
270 E 167th St 10456 718-293-9048
Nick Marinacci, prin. Fax 293-9748

Business S for Entrepreneurial Studies 600/5-8
977 Fox St 10459 718-991-8489
Domingo Martinez, prin. Fax 378-3352

Childs HS 2,000/9-12
800 E Gun Hill Rd 10467 718-519-7700
Monica Ortiz-Urena, prin. Fax 547-1321

Clinton HS 4,300/9-12
100 W Mosholu Pkwy S 10468 718-543-1000
Geraldine Ambrosio, prin. Fax 548-0036

Collegiate Institute of Math & Science 200/9-12
925 Astor Ave 10469 718-944-3431
Estelle Hans, prin. Fax 652-3525

Columbus HS 2,600/9-12
925 Astor Ave 10469 718-944-3400
Lisa Maffei, prin. Fax 519-1565

Community S for Social Justice 200/9-12
350 Gerard Ave 10451 718-402-8650
Sue Ann Rosch, prin. Fax 402-8650

Cruz Bronx HS of Music 9-12
2780 Reservoir Ave 10468 718-733-3781
Dr. William Rodriguez, prin. Fax 733-3865

Curie MSHS 100/7-12
120 W 231st St 10463 718-432-6491
Rodney Fisher, prin. Fax 432-6553

Discovery HS 200/9-12
2780 Reservoir Ave 10468 718-733-3872
Scott Goldner, prin. Fax 733-3621

Dodge Career & Technology HS Vo/Tech
2474 Crotona Ave 10458 718-584-2700
Craig Shapiro, prin. Fax 584-7490

Douglass Academy III 200/6-12
3630 3rd Ave 10456 718-538-9726
Rahesha Amon, prin. Fax 538-9796

Dreamyard Preparatory S 9-12
240 E 172nd St 10457 718-410-4242
Rod Bowen, prin. Fax 410-4312

Eagle Academy for Young Men 9-12
244 E 163rd St 10451 718-402-8481
David Banks, prin. Fax 402-8650

East Bronx Academy for the Future 6-12
1716 Southern Blvd 10460 718-861-8641
Sarah Scrogin, prin. Fax 861-8634

Eximius College Preparatory Academy 6-12
1363 Fulton Ave 10456 718-992-7154
Tammy Smith, prin. Fax 590-1081

Explorations Academy 9-12
1595 Bathgate Ave 10457 718-466-5790
John Nassivera, prin. Fax 466-5791

Fordham HS for the Arts 300/9-12
500 E Fordham Rd 10458 718-733-8100
Iris Blige, prin. Fax 295-3605

Fordham Leadership Academy 400/9-12
500 E Fordham Rd 10458 718-733-8100
Richard Bost, prin. Fax 584-6695

Foreign Langugage Academy\Global Study 400/9-12
470 Jackson Ave 10455 718-585-4024
Leba Augone, prin. Fax 585-4239

Gateway S of Environmental Research 9-12
1980 Lafayette Ave 10473 718-824-9327
Cliff Siegel, prin. Fax 824-4368

Global Enterprise HS 200/9-12
925 Astor Ave 10469 718-944-3548
Rick Levine, prin.

Globe S for Environmental Research 6-12
3710 Barnes Ave 10467 718-994-1395
Barbara Hartnett, prin. Fax 994-1316

Gompers Career & Technical HS Vo/Tech
455 Southern Blvd 10455 718-665-0950
Joyce Kittrell, prin. Fax 292-3164

Hamer Freedom HS 400/9-12
1021 Jennings St 10460 718-861-0521
Nancy Mann, prin. Fax 861-0619

Hamer MS 100/6-8
1001 Jennings St 10460 718-860-2707
Lorraine Chanon, prin. Fax 860-3212

Health Opportunities HS 600/9-12
350 Gerard Ave 10451 718-401-1826
Carron Staple, prin. Fax 401-1632

Hostos-Lincoln Academy 500/6-12
475 Grand Concourse 10451 718-518-4333
Nick Paarlberg, prin. Fax 518-4321

Institute for Law and Public Policy 9-12
1440 Story Ave 10473 718-935-3165
Grismaldy Laboy, prin. Fax 860-5081

International Community HS 9-12
968 Cauldwell Ave 10456 718-893-0249
Berena Cabarcas, prin. Fax 893-0891

International S of Liberal Arts 7-12
2780 Reservoir Ave 10468 718-562-9083
Karen Maldonado, prin. Fax 562-9369

KAPPA 5-8
3630 3rd Ave 10456 718-590-5455
Sheri Warren, prin. Fax 681-4266

Kappa III S, 2055 Mapes Ave 10460 6-8
Elisa Alvarez, prin.

Kelly HS 200/9-12
965 Longwood Ave 10459 718-860-1242
Joshua Laub, prin. Fax 860-1934

Kennedy HS 3,700/9-12
99 Terrace View Ave Rm 422 10463 718-817-7400
Anthony Rotunno, prin. Fax 562-5132

Kingsbridge International HS 9-12
2780 Reservoir Ave 10468 718-562-9157
Ronald Newlon, prin. Fax 562-9413

Leadership Institute 9-12
1701 Fulton Ave 10457 718-299-7490
Ronald Gonzalez, prin.

Lehman HS 3,800/9-12
3000 E Tremont Ave 10461 718-904-4200
Robert Leder, prin. Fax 904-4285

Levin HS for Media & Communications 300/9-12
240 E 172nd St 10457 718-992-3709
Nasib Hoxha, prin. Fax 992-4170

Marble Hill HS for International Studies 300/9-12
99 Terrace View Ave Rm 822 10463 718-561-0973
Iris Zucker, prin. Fax 561-5612

Metropolitan HS 9-10
1121 Intervale Ave 10459 718-991-4634
Carla Theodorou, prin. Fax 542-7294

Millenium Art Academy 200/9-12
1980 Lafayette Ave 10473 718-824-0978
Maxine Nodel, prin. Fax 824-0963

Monroe Academy for Business & Law 500/9-12
1300 Boynton Ave 10472 718-860-8140
Benito Herrero, prin. Fax 893-3262

Monroe Academy for Visual Arts & Design 500/9-12
1300 Boynton Ave 10472 718-860-8160
Richard Massel, prin. Fax 860-8110

Morris Academy for Collaborative Studies 200/9-12
1100 Boston Rd 10456 718-542-3700
Charles Osewalt, prin. Fax 542-3958

Mott Hall Bronx HS 9-12
1595 Bathgate Ave 10457 718-588-0918
David Tinagero, prin. Fax 588-0328

Mott Hall III 6-8
450 Saint Pauls Pl 10456 718-992-9506
Jorisis Stupart, prin. Fax 681-6905

Mott Haven Village Prep HS 200/9-12
701 Saint Anns Ave 10455 718-402-0571
Ana Maldonado, prin. Fax 402-0917

MSHS 141 1,200/6-12
660 W 237th St 10463 718-796-8516
Daniella Phillips, prin. Fax 796-8657

MSHS 368 900/6-12
2975 Tibbett Ave 10463 718-432-4300
Rose Clunie, prin. Fax 432-4310

Neruda Academy 9-12
1980 Lafayette Ave 10473 718-918-2700
Dina Heisler, prin. Fax 823-7858

New Day Academy 6-12
800 Home St 10456 718-542-1155
Paul Schwarz, prin.

New Explorers HS 200/9-12
701 Saint Anns Ave 10455 718-993-3634
Cindy Franza, prin. Fax 993-3614

New Millenium Business Academy 6-8
1000 Teller Ave 10456 718-588-8308
Melody Morgan, prin. Fax 681-6913

New School for Arts & Sciences 400/9-12
965 Longwood Ave 10459 718-617-1252
Donald Amaker, prin. Fax 617-0894

New S for Leadership and Journalism 6-8
120 W 231st St 10463 718-601-2869
Dolores Peterson, prin. Fax 601-2867

New World HS 9-12
50 Mercy College Pl 10462 718-319-5175
Fausto Salazar, prin. Fax 319-5179

Peace & Diversity Academy 100/9-12
3000 E Tremont Ave 10461 718-430-6395
Andrew Turay, prin. Fax 430-6335

Pelham Preparatory Academy 300/9-12
925 Astor Ave 10469 718-944-3401
Jane Aronoff, prin. Fax 944-3479

Renaissance HS of Musical Theater 200/9-12
3000 E Tremont Ave 10461 718-430-6390
Bernardo Ascona, prin. Fax 430-6308

Rucker S of Community Research 9-12
916 Eagle Ave 10456 718-935-3399
Sharif Rucker, prin.

School for Community Research & Learning 200/9-12
1980 Lafayette Ave 10473 347-892-2054
William Mulqueen, prin. Fax 892-3580

School for Inquiry & Social Justice 100/6-8
1025 Morrison Ave 10472 718-860-4181
Andrea Cyprys, prin. Fax 860-4163

School of Performing Arts 500/5-8
977 Fox St 10459 718-589-4844
Louis Corominas, prin. Fax 589-7998

Smith HS Vo/Tech
333 E 151st St 10451 718-993-5000
Rene Cassanova, prin. Fax 292-1944

South Bronx Academy for Applied Media 6-8
778 Forest Ave 10456
Roshone Ault, prin.

South Bronx Preparatory HS 6-12
360 E 145th St 10454 718-292-2211
Brian Rosenbloom, prin. Fax 292-2172

Sports Professions HS 9-12
2545 Gunther Ave 10469 718-319-2740
Janet Gallardo, prin. Fax 319-2744

Stevenson HS 2,700/9-12
1980 Lafayette Ave 10473 718-918-2700
Gerard Martori, prin. Fax 792-7983

Theatre Arts Production Company S 6-12
2225 Webster Ave 10457 718-584-0832
Lynn Passarella, prin. Fax 584-5102

Truman HS 2,800/9-12
750 Baychester Ave 10475 718-904-5400
Sana Nasser, prin. Fax 904-5502

University Heights HS 400/9-12
W 181st St & University Ave 10453 718-289-5300
Dr. Brenda Bravo, prin. Fax 295-7572

Urban Assembly Academy 9-12
240 E 172nd St 10457 718-293-6768
Jonathan Foy, prin.

Urban Assembly Math & Science MSHS 100/6-12
1595 Bathgate Ave Ste 250 10457 718-432-0537
Kenneth Baum, prin. Fax 432-0467

Urban Assembly S for Careers in Sports 300/9-12
701 Saint Anns Ave 10455 718-993-0255
Felice Lepore, prin. Fax 993-1567

Urban Assembly S for Performing Arts 9-12
339 Morris Ave 10451 718-401-4891
Fia Davis, prin. Fax 585-3726

Urban Science Academy 500/5-8
1000 Teller Ave 10456 718-588-8221
Patrick Kelly, prin. Fax 588-8268

Validus Preparatory Academy 9-12
1595 Bathgate Ave 10457 718-466-4000
Brady Smith, prin. Fax 466-4001

Walton HS 2,600/9-12
2780 Reservoir Ave 10468 718-364-7400
John Tornifolio, prin. Fax 295-3535

West Bronx Academy for the Future 6-12
500 E Fordham Rd 10458 718-733-8100
Wilper Morales, prin.

Wings Academy 500/9-12
1122 E 180th St 10460 718-597-1751
Wayne Cox, prin. Fax 931-8366

Young Women's Leadership Academy 7-12
2060 Lafayette Ave 10473 718-828-4555
Arnette Crocker, prin.

Academy of Mt. St. Ursula 9-12
330 Bedford Park Blvd 10458 718-364-5353
Sr. Mary Read, prin. Fax 364-2354

All Hallows S 500/9-12
111 E 164th St 10452 718-293-4545
Sean Sullivan, prin. Fax 410-8298

Aquinas HS 800/9-12
685 E 182nd St 10457 718-367-2113
Sr. Catherine Rose Quigley, prin. Fax 295-5864

Bronx Lebanon Hospital Center — Post-Sec.
1650 Grand Concourse 10457 — 718-518-1800
Cardinal Hayes HS — 1,100/9-12
650 Grand Concourse 10451 — 718-292-6100
Christopher Keogan, prin. — Fax 292-9178
Cardinal Spellman HS — 1,400/9-12
1 Cardinal Spellman Pl 10466 — 718-881-8000
Dr. Neil McCarthy, prin. — Fax 515-6615
College of Mount Saint Vincent — Post-Sec.
6301 Riverdale Ave 10471 — 718-405-3200
College of New Rochelle — Post-Sec.
332 E 149th St 10451 — 718-665-1310
College of New Rochelle — Post-Sec.
755 Co Op City Blvd 10475 — 718-320-0300
CUNY Bronx Community College — Post-Sec.
W 181st And University Ave 10453 — 718-289-5100
CUNY Lehman College — Post-Sec.
250 Bedford Park Blvd W 10468 — 718-960-8000
Fieldston S — 800/7-12
3901 Fieldston Rd 10471 — 718-329-7300
Dr. John Love, prin. — Fax 329-7305
Fordham Preparatory HS — 900/9-12
441 E Fordham Rd 10458 — 718-367-7500
Robert Gomprecht, prin. — Fax 367-7598
Fordham University — Post-Sec.
441 E Fordham Rd 10458 — 718-817-1000
Hostos Community College - CUNY — Post-Sec.
500 Grand Concourse 10451 — 718-518-6633
Lavelle School/Blind-Visually Impaired — Post-Sec.
E 221 St & Paulding Ave 10469
Manhattan College — Post-Sec.
4513 Manhattan College Pkwy 10471 — 718-862-8000
Mercy College — Post-Sec.
1200 Waters Pl 10461 — 718-798-8952
Monroe College — Post-Sec.
2501 Jerome Ave 10468 — 718-933-6700
Monsignor Scanlan HS — 600/9-12
915 Hutchinson River Pkwy 10465 — 718-430-0100
Sr. Marie O'Donnell, prin. — Fax 892-8845
Montefiore Medical Center — Post-Sec.
111 E 210th St 10467 — 718-920-4001
Mt. St. Michael Academy — 200/6-8
4300 Murdock Ave 10466 — 718-515-6400
Lillian Dippolito, prin. — Fax 515-4486
Mt. St. Michael Academy — 1,000/9-12
4300 Murdock Ave 10466 — 718-515-6400
Br. Lawrence Lavallee, prin. — Fax 994-7729
New York Institute for Special Education — Post-Sec.
999 Pelham Pkwy N 10469 — 718-519-7000
Our Saviour Lutheran S — 400/PK-12
1734 Williamsbridge Rd 10461 — 718-792-5665
Lewis Williams, prin. — Fax 409-3877
Preston HS — 600/9-12
2780 Schurz Ave 10465 — 718-863-9134
Sr. Lucille Coldrick, prin. — Fax 863-6125
St. Barnabas HS — 300/9-12
425 E 240th St 10470 — 718-325-8800
Michael Musante, prin. — Fax 325-8820
St. Catharine Academy — 700/9-12
2250 Williamsbridge Rd 10469 — 718-882-2882
Sr. Anne Welch, prin. — Fax 231-9099
St. Ignatius Academy — 50/5-8
740 Manida St 10474 — 718-861-9084
Lourdes Torres, prin. — Fax 861-9096
St. Pius V HS — 200/9-12
500 Courtlandt Ave 10451 — 718-292-3636
Sr. Mary Jo Lynch, prin. — Fax 402-1704
St. Raymond Academy — 9-12
2380 E Tremont Ave 10462 — 718-824-4220
Sr. Mary Ann D'Antonio, prin. — Fax 829-3571
St. Raymond Boys HS — 800/9-12
2151 Saint Raymonds Ave 10462 — 718-824-5050
Br. Daniel Gardner, prin. — Fax 863-8808
Salanter Akiba Riverdale HS — 100/9-12
5900 Netherland Ave 10471 — 718-548-2727
Rabbi Tully Harcsztark, prin. — Fax 548-4400
SUNY Maritime College — Post-Sec.
6 Pennyfield Ave 10465 — 718-409-7200
Veterans Affairs Medical Center — Post-Sec.
130 W Kingsbridge Rd 10468 — 718-579-1640
Yeshiva of the Telshe Alumni — Post-Sec.
4904 Independence Ave 10471 — 718-601-3523

Bronxville, Westchester, Pop. 6,455
Bronxville UFD — 1,500/K-12
177 Pondfield Rd 10708 — 914-395-0500
David Quattrone, supt. — Fax 337-7109
www.bronxville.k12.ny.us
Bronxville HS — 400/9-12
177 Pondfield Rd 10708 — 914-395-0500
Terence Barton, prin. — Fax 337-1904
Bronxville MS — 400/6-8
177 Pondfield Rd 10708 — 914-395-0500
Dr. Barry Richelsoph, prin. — Fax 337-1904

Concordia College — Post-Sec.
171 White Plains Rd 10708 — 914-337-9300
Sarah Lawrence College — Post-Sec.
1 Meadway 10708 — 914-337-0700

Brookfield, Madison
Brookfield Central SD — 200/K-12
PO Box 60 13314 — 315-899-3323
Sherri Morris-Schiebel, supt. — Fax 899-8902
Brookfield Central S — 200/K-12
PO Box 60 13314 — 315-899-3323
Sherri Morris-Schiebel, prin. — Fax 899-8902

Brookhaven, Suffolk, Pop. 3,118
South Country Central SD
Supt. — See East Patchogue
Bellport HS — 1,400/9-12
205 Beaver Dam Rd 11719 — 631-730-1575
Lois Etzel, prin. — Fax 286-5336

Brooklyn, See New York
NYC Department of Education
Supt. — See New York
Academy for College Preparation — 9-12
911 Flatbush Ave 11226 — 718-935-3183
Ditta Korbeogo, prin.
Academy for Environmental Leadership — 9-12
400 Irving Ave 11237 — 718-381-7100
Nilda Gomez-Katz, prin.

Academy for Urban Planning — 300/9-12
400 Irving Ave 11237 — 718-381-7100
Monique A. Darrisaw, prin. — Fax 418-0314
Academy for Young Writers — 9-12
183 S 3rd St 11211 — 718-935-3185
Carolyn Yaffe, prin.
Academy of Business & Tech - Erasmus — 600/9-12
911 Flatbush Ave 11226 — 718-282-7804
Myrna Walters, prin. — Fax 462-1890
Academy of Hospitality & Tourism — 9-12
911 Flatbush Ave 11226 — 718-564-2580
Adam Brier, prin. — Fax 564-2581
Academy of Humanities - Erasmus — 600/9-12
911 Flatbush Ave 11226 — 718-282-8428
Dr. Richard A. Forman, prin. — Fax 462-1974
Acorn Community HS — 600/9-12
561 Grand Ave 11238 — 718-789-2258
Dr. Andrea D. Lewis, dir. — Fax 789-2260
Acorn HS for Social Justice — 600/9-12
1396 Broadway 11221 — 718-919-1256
Joseph Parker, prin. — Fax 852-4593
All City Leadership Academy — 200/6-12
1474 Gates Ave 11237 — 718-381-9653
E. Estevez, prin. — Fax 381-9680
Automotive HS — Vo/Tech
50 Bedford Ave 11222 — 718-218-9301
Melissa Silberman, prin. — Fax 599-4351
Banneker Academy — 800/9-12
77 Clinton Ave 11205 — 718-797-3702
Daryl Rock, prin. — Fax 797-3862
Barton Vocational HS — Vo/Tech
901 Classon Ave 11225 — 718-636-4900
Jacqueline Foster, prin. — Fax 857-3688
B.A.S.E. — 200/9-12
883 Classon Ave 11225 — 718-636-5800
Veronica Peterson, prin. — Fax 789-7279
Bedford Academy HS — 9-12
1119 Bedford Ave 11216 — 718-398-3061
George Leonard, prin. — Fax 636-3819
Boys & Girls HS — 3,900/9-12
1700 Fulton St 11213 — 718-467-1700
Spencer Holder, prin. — Fax 221-0645
Brooklyn College Academy — 600/7-12
2900 Bedford Ave 11210 — 718-951-5941
Nick Mazzarella, prin. — Fax 951-4441
Brooklyn Collegiate HS — 100/6-12
2021 Bergen St 11233 — 718-922-1145
Amote Sias, prin. — Fax 922-2347
Brooklyn Community HS of Arts & Media — 9-12
70 Tompkins Ave 11206 — 718-302-5092
James O'Brien, prin. — Fax 302-5098
Brooklyn Comprehensive Night HS — 12-12
6565 Flatlands Ave 11236 — 718-968-4200
Catherine Paparelli, prin. — Fax 629-2718
HS for Civil Rights — 100/9-12
400 Pennsylvania Ave 11207 — 718-922-6289
Michael Steele, prin. — Fax 922-7253
HS for Global Citizenship — 9-12
883 Classon Ave 11225 — 718-230-6300
Brad Haggerty, prin. — Fax 230-6301
HS for Public Service — 200/9-12
600 Kingston Ave 11203 — 718-467-7400
Marisa Boan, prin. — Fax 604-3029
HS for Service & Learning — 9-12
911 Flatbush Ave 11226 — 718-564-2551
Leonard Kassan, prin. — Fax 564-2552
Brooklyn HS for the Arts — 700/9-12
345 Dean St 11217 — 718-855-2412
Robert Finley, prin. — Fax 852-8734
HS for Youth & Community Development — 100/9-12
911 Flatbush Ave 11226 — 718-564-2470
Mary Prendergast, prin. — Fax 564-2471
HS of Enterprise - Business & Tech — 800/9-12
850 Grand St 11211 — 718-387-2701
Juan Mendez, prin. — Fax 387-2748
HS of Legal Studies — 800/9-12
850 Grand St 11211 — 718-387-2800
Denise Morgan, prin. — Fax 387-3281
HS of Sports Management — 9-12
2865 W 19th St 11224 — 718-946-6812
Robin Pitts, prin. — Fax 946-6825
HS of Telecommunications Arts & Tech — 1,100/9-12
350 67th St 11220 — 718-759-3400
Philip Weinberg, prin. — Fax 759-3490
IS 30 — 300/6-8
415 Ovington Ave 11209 — 718-491-5684
Linda Guarneri, prin. — Fax 491-0071
IS 35 — 300/6-8
272 Macdonough St 11233 — 718-574-2345
Jacklyn Charles, prin. — Fax 452-1273
IS 55 — 300/7-8
2021 Bergen St 11233 — 718-495-7736
Alma Summors, prin. — Fax 270-8725
IS 68 — 1,100/6-8
956 E 82nd St 11236 — 718-241-4800
Alex Fralin, prin. — Fax 241-5582
IS 96 — 1,300/6-8
99 Avenue P 11204 — 718-236-1344
Barry Fein, prin. — Fax 236-2397
IS 98 — 1,100/6-8
1401 Emmons Ave 11235 — 718-891-9005
Marian Nagler, prin. — Fax 891-3865
IS 136 — 6-8
4004 4th Ave 11232 — 718-965-3333
Ronnie Block - Lyons, prin. — Fax 965-9567
IS 171 — 1,000/5-8
528 Ridgewood Ave 11208 — 718-647-0111
Joan Beckman, prin. — Fax 827-5834
IS 187 — 1,000/6-8
1171 65th St 11219 — 718-236-3394
Justin Berman, prin. — Fax 236-3638
IS 211 — 800/6-8
1001 E 100th St 11236 — 718-251-4411
Buffie Simmons-Peart, prin. — Fax 241-2503
IS 228 — 1,200/6-8
228 Avenue S 11223 — 718-375-7635
Rose Caniglia, prin. — Fax 998-4013
IS 232 — 800/6-8
905 Winthrop St 11203 — 718-773-2662
Ingrid Thomas-Clark, prin. — Fax 953-4592
IS 239 — 1,200/6-8
2401 Neptune Ave 11224 — 718-266-0814
Carol Moore, prin. — Fax 266-1693
IS 240 — 1,800/6-8
2500 Nostrand Ave 11210 — 718-253-3700
Elena O'Sullivan, prin. — Fax 253-0356

IS 246 — 1,200/6-8
72 Veronica Pl 11226 — 718-282-5230
Bently Warrington, prin. — Fax 284-6429
IS 252 — 500/6-8
1084 Lenox Rd 11212 — 718-342-1144
Mendis Brown, prin. — Fax 485-8117
IS 271 — 500/7-8
1137 Herkimer St 11233 — 718-495-7787
Rosemarie Sinclair, prin. — Fax 495-7831
IS 281 — 1,200/6-8
8787 24th Ave 11214 — 718-996-6706
Stephen Rosenblum, prin. — Fax 996-4186
IS 285 — 1,100/6-8
5909 Beverley Rd 11203 — 718-451-2200
Edward Gentile, prin. — Fax 451-0229
IS 303 — 1,100/6-8
501 West Ave 11224 — 718-996-0100
Gary Ingrassia, prin. — Fax 996-3785
IS 311 — 300/6-8
590 Sheffield Ave 11207 — 718-272-8371
Gail Gaines, prin. — Fax 272-8372
IS 340 — 400/6-8
227 Sterling Pl 11238 — 718-857-5516
Gloria Dupree, prin. — Fax 230-5479
IS 347 — 500/6-8
35 Starr St 11221 — 718-821-4248
John Barbella, prin. — Fax 821-1332
IS 349 — 500/6-8
35 Starr St 11221 — 718-418-6389
Roy Parris, prin. — Fax 418-6146
IS 364 — 400/6-8
1426 Freeport Loop 11239 — 718-642-3007
Dale Kelly, prin. — Fax 642-8516
IS 381 — 500/6-8
1599 E 22nd St 11210 — 718-252-0058
Mary Harrington, prin. — Fax 252-0035
IS 392 — 300/5-8
104 Sutter Ave 11212 — 718-498-2491
Shirley Wheeler, prin. — Fax 346-2804
Brooklyn International HS — 300/9-12
49 Flatbush Ave 11217 — 718-643-9315
Pamela Taranto, prin. — Fax 643-9516
JHS 14 — 900/6-8
2424 Batchelder St 11235 — 718-743-0220
Anne Tully, prin. — Fax 769-8632
JHS 49 — 500/6-8
223 Graham Ave 11206 — 718-387-7697
Claytisha Walden, prin. — Fax 302-2318
JHS 50 — 700/6-8
183 S 3rd St 11211 — 718-387-4184
Denise Jamison, prin. — Fax 302-2320
JHS 57 — 400/6-8
125 Stuyvesant Ave 11221 — 718-574-2357
Celeste Douglas, prin. — Fax 453-0577
JHS 62 — 1,300/6-8
700 Cortelyou Rd 11218 — 718-941-5450
Barry Kevorkian, prin. — Fax 693-7433
JHS 78 — 1,500/6-8
1420 E 68th St 11234 — 718-763-4701
William Woods, prin. — Fax 251-3439
JHS 88 — 800/6-8
544 7th Ave 11215 — 718-788-4482
Ailene Altman-Mitchell, prin. — Fax 768-0213
JHS 113 — 900/6-8
300 Adelphi St 11205 — 718-834-6734
Khalek Kirkland, prin. — Fax 596-2802
JHS 117 — 500/6-8
300 Willoughby Ave 11205 — 718-230-5400
Alander Hasty, prin. — Fax 622-3570
JHS 126 — 600/6-8
424 Leonard St 11222 — 718-782-2527
Dr. Sheldon Toback, prin. — Fax 302-2319
JHS 162 — 700/6-8
1390 Willoughby Ave 11237 — 718-821-4860
Barbara DeMartino, prin. — Fax 821-1728
JHS 166 — 900/6-8
800 Van Siclen Ave 11207 — 718-649-0765
Maria Ortega, prin. — Fax 927-2172
JHS 201 — 1,500/6-8
8010 12th Ave 11228 — 718-833-9363
Madeleine Brennan, prin. — Fax 836-1786
JHS 218 — 1,100/6-8
370 Fountain Ave 11208 — 718-647-9050
Joseph Costa, prin. — Fax 827-5839
JHS 220 — 1,300/6-8
4812 9th Ave 11220 — 718-633-8200
L. M. Witek, prin. — Fax 871-7466
JHS 223 — 700/6-8
4200 16th Ave 11204 — 718-438-0155
Gertrude Adduci, prin. — Fax 871-7477
JHS 227 — 1,400/6-8
6500 16th Ave 11204 — 718-256-8218
Brenda Champion, prin. — Fax 331-7378
JHS 234 — 1,700/6-8
1875 E 17th St 11229 — 718-645-1334
Susan Schaeffer, prin. — Fax 645-7759
JHS 258 — 600/6-8
141 Macon St 11216 — 718-398-3764
Stanley Walker, prin. — Fax 857-3422
JHS 259 — 1,300/6-8
7301 Fort Hamilton Pkwy 11228 — 718-833-1000
Janice Geary, prin. — Fax 833-3419
JHS 278 — 1,100/6-8
1925 Stuart St 11229 — 718-375-3523
Debra Garofalo, prin. — Fax 998-7324
JHS 291 — 1,000/6-8
231 Palmetto St 11221 — 718-574-0361
Sean Walsh, prin. — Fax 574-1364
JHS 292 — 900/6-8
301 Vermont St 11207 — 718-498-6560
Everett Hughes, prin. — Fax 345-3327
JHS 296 — 1,000/6-8
125 Covert St 11207 — 718-574-0288
Maria De Los Barreto, prin. — Fax 574-1368
JHS 302 — 1,200/6-8
350 Linwood St 11208 — 718-647-9500
Martin Weinstein, prin. — Fax 827-3294
JHS 318 — 1,200/6-8
101 Walton St 11206 — 718-782-0589
Fortunato Rubino, prin. — Fax 384-7867
JHS 383 — 1,300/5-8
1300 Greene Ave 11237 — 718-574-0390
Barbara Sanders, prin. — Fax 574-1366
Brooklyn Latin S — 9-12
325 Bushwick Ave 11206 — 718-366-0154
Jason Griffiths, prin. — Fax 381-3012

MS 2 900/6-8
655 Parkside Ave 11226 718-462-6992
Adrienne Spencer, prin. Fax 284-7717

MS 51 900/6-8
350 5th Ave 11215 718-369-7603
Lenore Berner, prin. Fax 499-4948

MS 61 1,200/6-8
400 Empire Blvd 11225 718-774-1002
Rhonda Taylor, prin. Fax 467-4335

MS 143 300/7-8
800 Gates Ave 11221 718-574-2424
Adofo Muhammad, prin. Fax 453-0383

MS 266 200/6-8
62 Park Pl 11217 718-857-2291
Michele Robinson, prin. Fax 857-2347

MS 267 500/6-8
800 Gates Ave 11221 718-574-2319
Patricia King, prin. Fax 574-2320

MS 385 300/6-8
125 Stuyvesant Ave 11221 718-602-3271
Glyn Marryshow, prin. Fax 602-3274

MS 447 6-8
345 Dean St 11217 718-330-9328
Lisa Gioe-Cordi, prin. Fax 330-0944

MS 571 200/6-8
80 Underhill Ave 11238 718-834-6790
Linda Patterson-Weston, prin. Fax 638-0295

MS 582 200/6-8
207 Bushwick Ave 11206 718-456-8218
Brian Walsh, prin. Fax 456-8220

MS 584 200/6-8
130 Rochester Ave 11213 718-604-1380
Verone Kennedy, prin. Fax 604-3678

MS for Academic and Social Excellence 6-8
1224 Park Pl 11213
Kathleen Clarke-Glover, prin.

MS of the Arts 200/6-8
790 E New York Ave 11203 718-493-8920
Susan Hobson-Ransom, prin.

MS School of Integrated Learning 6-8
1224 Park Pl 11213 718-774-0362
Monique Campbell, prin. Fax 774-0521

Brooklyn Preparatory HS 100/9-12
300 Willoughby Ave 11205 718-789-6126
Janet Price, prin. Fax 789-6148

Brooklyn S for Collaborative Studies 400/6-12
610 Henry St 11231 718-923-4750
Alyce Barr, prin. Fax 923-4730

Brooklyn S for Global Studies 600/6-12
284 Baltic St 11201 718-694-9741
Lisa Gibbs, prin. Fax 694-9745

Brooklyn S for Music & Theater 200/9-12
883 Classon Ave 11225 718-230-6250
Kieran McGuire, prin. Fax 230-6262

Brooklyn Studio Secondary S 700/6-12
8310 21st Ave 11214 718-266-5032
Martin Fiasconaro, prin. Fax 266-5093

Brooklyn Tech HS 4,100/9-12
29 Fort Greene Pl 11217 718-804-6400
Randy Asher, prin. Fax 260-9254

Bushwick HS for Social Justice 200/9-12
400 Irving Ave 11237 718-381-7100
Terry C. Byam, prin. Fax 418-0192

Bushwick Leaders HS 200/9-12
797 Bushwick Ave 11221 718-919-4212
Catherine Reilly, prin. Fax 919-4217

Campos Secondary S 600/6-11
215 Heyward St 11206 718-302-7900
Howard Finemen, prin. Fax 302-7979

Canarsie HS 2,500/9-12
1600 Rockaway Pkwy 11236 718-290-8600
David Harris, prin. Fax 290-8681

Carson HS for Coastal Studies 9-10
521 West Ave 11224 718-265-0329
Joanne Pierre, prin. Fax 372-2514

Cobble Hill S of American Studies 900/9-12
347 Baltic St 11201 718-403-9544
Kenneth Cuthbert, prin. Fax 403-9553

Dewey HS 3,200/9-12
50 Avenue X 11223 718-373-6400
Barry Fried, prin. Fax 266-4385

Douglas Academy 200/6-10
1014 Lafayette Ave 11221 718-574-2820
Marian Bowden, prin. Fax 574-2821

Douglas Academy VII HS 100/9-12
226 Bristol St 11212 718-485-3789
Tamika Matheson, prin. Fax 922-1160

Douglass Academy VIII MS 6-8
1400 Pennsylvania Ave 11239 718-642-4305
Tamara Thomas, prin. Fax 642-4537

East NY Family Academy 400/6-12
2057 Linden Blvd 11207 718-927-0012
Sheila Richards, prin. Fax 927-0411

Ebbets Field MS 6-8
46 McKeever Pl 11225 718-941-5097
Margaret Baker, prin.

EBC/ENY HS for Public Safety & Law 500/9-12
1495 Herkimer St 11233 718-498-7163
Beverly Faison, prin. Fax 498-7170

EBC-HS for Public Service 600/9-12
1155 Dekalb Ave 11221 718-452-3440
Victor Capellan, prin. Fax 452-3544

Edmonds Learning Center II 6-8
430 Howard Ave 11233 718-467-0306
Herbert Daughtry, prin. Fax 953-0682

Evers Preparatory S 900/6-12
1186 Carroll St 11225 718-703-5400
Dr. Michael Wiltshire, prin. Fax 703-5600

FDNY S for Fire & Life Safety 100/9-12
400 Pennsylvania Ave 11207 718-922-0389
Ray Palmer, prin. Fax 922-0593

Ft. Hamilton HS 4,500/9-12
8301 Shore Rd 11209 718-748-1537
Joann Chester, prin. Fax 836-3955

Foundations Academy 9-10
265 Ralph Ave 11233 718-452-6315
Gary Biedleman, prin. Fax 602-3985

Freedom Academy 200/9-12
116 Nassau St 11201 718-694-8357
Coran James, prin. Fax 694-8360

Goldstein - Sciences HS 900/9-12
1830 Shore Blvd 11235 718-368-8500
Joseph Zaza, prin. Fax 368-8555

Grady HS Vo/Tech
25 Brighton 4th Rd 11235 718-332-5000
Stephen Jackson, prin. Fax 332-2544

Green S Academy for Environmental Career 9-12
223 Graham Ave 11206 718-599-1207
Karali Pitzele, prin. Fax 387-7945

International Arts & Business HS 200/9-12
600 Kingston Ave 11203 718-467-7400
Leonard Trerotola, prin. Fax 604-3029

International HS 9-12
755 E 100th St 11236 718-345-0854
Michael Soet, prin. Fax 342-2352

International HS at Prospect Heights 100/9-12
883 Classon Ave 11225 718-230-6333
Alexandra Anormaliza, prin. Fax 230-6322

Kappa V S, 985 Rockaway Ave 11212 100/6-8
Anthony Shepherd, prin. 718-922-4690

Kingsborough Early College S 6-12
2001 Oriental Blvd 11235 718-332-0084
Connie Hamilton, prin. Fax 332-2677

Lafayette HS 2,000/9-12
2630 Benson Ave 11214 718-372-3480
Jolanta Rohloff, prin. Fax 996-6684

Lane HS 3,200/9-12
999 Jamaica Ave 11208 718-647-2100
Evan Ahern, prin. Fax 235-4877

Lincoln HS 2,600/9-12
2800 Ocean Pkwy 11235 718-333-7400
Ari Hoogenboom, prin. Fax 946-5035

Madison HS 4,200/9-12
3787 Bedford Ave 11229 718-758-7200
Joseph A. Gogliormella, prin. Fax 758-7341

Maxwell Career and Technical HS Vo/Tech
145 Pennsylvania Ave 11207 718-345-9100
Zipora Steiner, prin. Fax 345-5470

McKinney S of the Arts 700/6-12
101 Park Ave 11205 718-834-6760
Paula Holmes, prin. Fax 834-6776

Metropolitan Corporate Academy 400/9-12
362 Schermerhorn St 11217 718-222-6200
Michael Fienga, prin. Fax 222-6296

Midwood HS 3,800/9-12
2839 Bedford Ave 11210 718-724-8500
David Cohen, prin. Fax 724-8515

Mott Hall IV MS 100/6-8
1137 Herkimer St 11233 718-485-5240
Lajuan White, prin.

Murrow HS 3,700/9-12
1600 Avenue L 11230 718-258-9283
Anthony Lodico, prin. Fax 252-2611

New Horizons S 200/6-8
317 Hoyt St 11231 718-330-9227
Mary Lou Aranyos, dir. Fax 330-9251

New Utrecht HS 2,700/9-12
1601 80th St 11214 718-232-2500
Dr. Howard Lucks, prin. Fax 259-5526

New Voices S of Academic & Creative Arts 400/6-8
330 18th St 11215 718-965-0390
Frank Giordano, prin. Fax 965-0603

New York Harbor HS 200/9-12
400 Irving Ave 11237 718-381-7100
Nathan Dudley, prin. Fax 418-0128

Performing Arts & Technology HS 100/9-12
400 Pennsylvania Ave 11207 718-922-0762
Lottie Almonte, prin. Fax 922-0953

Progress HS 1,000/9-12
850 Grand St 11211 718-387-0228
William Jusino, prin. Fax 782-0911

Public MS 577 300/6-8
320 Manhattan Ave 11211 718-302-1609
Maria Masullo, prin. Fax 302-1662

Robeson HS 1,400/9-12
150 Albany Ave 11213 718-774-0300
Ira Weston, prin. Fax 467-3692

Roosevelt HS 3,400/9-12
5800 20th Ave 11204 718-256-1346
Geri Maione, prin. Fax 232-9513

Satellite East 300/6-8
344 Monroe St 11216 718-789-4251
Kim Mcpherson, prin. Fax 789-4823

Satellite III S 300/6-8
170 Gates Ave 11238 718-789-5835
Kenyatte Reid, prin. Fax 789-5814

Satellite West MS 300/6-8
209 York St 11201 718-834-6774
Charles Adams, prin. Fax 834-2979

School for Democracy & Leadership 6-12
600 Kingston Ave 11203 718-771-4865
Nancy Gannon, prin. Fax 771-5847

School for Human Rights 6-12
600 Kingston Ave 11203 718-771-4793
Kevin Dotson, prin. Fax 771-4815

School for International Studies 500/6-12
284 Baltic St 11201 718-330-9390
Fred Walsh, prin. Fax 875-7522

Science Skills Center HS 900/9-12
49 Flatbush Ave 11217 718-243-9413
Denise Jennings, prin. Fax 243-9399

Science Technology & Research HS 200/9-12
911 Flatbush Ave 11226 718-564-2540
Henrietta Coursey, prin. Fax 564-2541

Secondary S for Journalism 500/6-12
237 7th Ave 11215 718-832-4201
Abbie Reif, prin. Fax 832-0273

Secondary S for Law 600/6-12
237 7th Ave 11215 718-832-4250
Larry Woodbridge, prin. Fax 499-3947

Secondary S for Research 400/6-12
237 7th Ave 11215 718-832-4300
Jill Bloomberg, prin. Fax 788-8127

Sheepshead Bay HS 3,200/9-12
3000 Avenue X 11235 718-332-2003
Reesa Levy, prin. Fax 648-9349

South Brooklyn Community HS 200/9-12
173 Conover St 11231 718-422-1915
Vanda Belusic, dir. Fax 422-1927

South Shore HS 2,000/9-12
6565 Flatlands Ave 11236 718-968-4100
Judy Henry, prin. Fax 251-0248

Stroud MS 100/6-8
750 Classon Ave 11238 718-638-3067
Claudette Essor, prin. Fax 638-3515

Sunset Park Prep MS 300/6-8
4004 4th Ave 11232 718-965-3331
Lola Padin, prin. Fax 965-3330

Teachers Preparatory HS 500/6-12
226 Bristol St 11212 718-498-2605
Dr. Michael Alcoff, prin. Fax 345-8069

Tilden HS 2,200/9-12
5800 Tilden Ave 11203 718-629-4523
Diane Varano, prin. Fax 629-0165

Transit Tech HS Vo/Tech
1 Wells St 11208 718-647-5204
Larry Kalvar, prin. Fax 647-4458

Urban Assembly Academy of Business 6-12
141 Macon St 11216 718-783-4842
Clyde Cole, prin. Fax 783-4869

Urban Assembly Institute Math & Science 6-12
960 Prospect Pl 11213 718-778-5890
Kelly Demonaco, prin. Fax 778-5895

Urban Assembly S for Law & Justice 100/9-12
50 Navy St 11201 718-858-1160
Elana Karopkin, prin. Fax 858-4733

Urban Assembly S for Music & Art 9-10
49 Flatbush Avenue Ext 11201 718-858-0249
Paul Thompson, prin. Fax 858-0492

Urban Assembly S for Urban Environment 6-12
70 Tompkins Ave 11206 718-599-0371
Kourtney Boyd, prin. Fax 388-0872

WATCH HS 100/9-12
400 Pennsylvania Ave 11207 718-922-0650
Kim Lawrence, prin. Fax 922-0709

W.E.B. DuBois Academic HS 300/9-12
402 Eastern Pkwy 11225 718-773-7765
Catherine Hartnett, prin. Fax 773-7849

West Brooklyn Community HS 10-12
1053 41st St 11219 718-686-1444
Liliana Polo, prin. Fax 686-1189

Westinghouse Vo & Tech HS Vo/Tech
105 Johnson St 11201 718-625-6130
John Widlund, prin. Fax 596-9434

Williamsburg HS Architecture & Design 9-12
257 N 6th St 11211 718-388-1260
Steve Farini, prin. Fax 486-2580

Williamsburg Prep S 100/9-12
257 N 6th St 11211 718-302-2306
Kathleen Elvin, prin. Fax 302-3726

Adelphi Academy 300/PK-12
8515 Ridge Blvd 11209 718-238-3308
Todd Marsh, dean Fax 238-2894

Advanced Software Analysis Post-Sec.
151 Lawrence St Ste 2 11201 718-522-9073

Al-Noor S 700/PK-12
675 4th Ave 11232 718-768-7181
Nidal Abuasi, prin. Fax 768-7088

Bais Brocha Stolin Karlin 400/PK-12
4314 10th Ave 11219 718-853-1222
Rabbi Ephraim Scherman, admin. Fax 851-0112

Bais Rochel HS 900/9-12
62 Harrison Ave 11211 718-963-9287
Leah Schorr, prin. Fax 963-9571

Bais Rochel S of Boro Park 1,500/K-12
5301 14th Ave 11219 718-438-7822
Mindy Margulies, prin. Fax 438-3153

Bais Sarah Girls S 600/PK-12
1363 50th St 11219 718-871-7571
B. Schwartz, prin. Fax 871-3615

Bais Tziporah S 400/PK-12
1449 39th St 11218 718-436-8336
Moshe Melamed, dir. Fax 436-1201

Bais Yaakov Academy 700/PK-12
1213 Elm Ave 11230 718-339-4747
Lisa Wadler, prin. Fax 998-5766

Bais Yaakov Adas Yereim 300/PK-12
563 Bedford Ave 11211 718-782-2486
D. Ausch, prin. Fax 384-5885

Bais Yaakov Adas Yereim 300/PK-12
1169 43rd St 11219 718-435-5111
Chaya Brikman, prin. Fax 435-5446

Bais Yaakov D'Gur HS 100/9-12
1975 51st St 11204 718-338-5600
Leah Lederman, prin. Fax 338-5974

Be'er Hagolah Institute 700/K-12
671 Louisiana Ave 11239 718-642-6800
Pearl Kaufman, dir. Fax 642-4740

Beikvei Hatzoin S 200/PK-12
31 Division Ave 11211 718-486-6363
Shaindy Gross, prin. Fax 486-6639

Beis Chaya Mushka 100/PK-12
1505 Carroll St 11213 718-756-0770
Rabbi Levi Plotkin, prin. Fax 493-9336

Belz Girls S 800/PK-12
600 McDonald Ave 11218 718-871-0500
R. Grussgott, prin. Fax 435-4456

Berkeley Carroll S 500/5-12
181 Lincoln Pl 11217 718-789-6060
Robert Vitalo, hdmstr. Fax 398-3640

Berk Trade School Post-Sec.
383 Pearl St 11201 718-625-6037

Beth Chana S 300/1-12
712 Bedford Ave 11206 718-935-1845
Rabbi Mordechai Scheiner, prin. Fax 935-1863

Beth HaMedrash Shaarei Yosher Post-Sec.
4102 16th Ave # 10 11204 718-854-2290

Beth Hamedrash Shaarei Yosher 100/9-12
4102 16th Ave 11204 718-854-2290
Rabbi Aaron Steinburg, admin. Fax 436-9045

Beth HaTalmud Rabbinical College Post-Sec.
2127 82nd St 11214 718-259-2525

Beth Jacob HS 800/9-12
4420 15th Ave 11219 718-851-2255
D. Wolf, prin. Fax 435-3736

Beth Jacob S 800/PK-12
85 Parkville Ave 11230 718-633-6555
Rabbi Michoel Levi, prin. Fax 633-2930

Beth Rivkah HS 1,800/9-12
310 Crown St 11225 718-735-0400
Chaya Lane, prin. Fax 735-0422

Bet Yaakov Ateret Torah HS 100/9-12
2166 Coney Island Ave 11223 718-382-7002
Rebecca Weiss, prin. Fax 732-7767

Bishop Ford Central Catholic HS 1,000/9-12
500 19th St 11215 718-360-2500
Frank Brancato, prin. Fax 360-2595

Bishop Kearney HS 1,100/9-12
2202 60th St 11204 718-236-6363
Sr. M. Thomasine Stagnitta, prin. Fax 236-7784

Bishop Loughlin Memorial HS 900/9-12
357 Clermont Ave 11238 718-857-2700
Br. Dennis Cronin, prin. Fax 398-4227

Bnos Menachem S for Girls 300/PK-10
739 E New York Ave 11203 718-493-1100
R. Katz, prin. Fax 493-4836
Bnos Yaakov Educational Center 50/1-12
62 Harrison Ave 11211 718-387-7905
Gitty Lichtman, prin. Fax 387-7124
Bnos Yaakov of Boro Park 900/PK-12
1402 40th St 11218 718-851-0316
Yehudis Weiser, dean Fax 436-7280
Bnos Yaakov S for Girls 600/1-12
62 Harrison Ave 11211 718-963-3940
Rabbi M. H. Samet, prin.
Bnos Yisroel Viznitz S 700/PK-12
12 Franklin Ave 11211 718-330-0222
Eva Rozman, prin. Fax 858-7387
Bnos Zion of Bobov 1,400/PK-12
5000 14th Ave 11219 718-438-3080
Rabbi Moshe Zenwirth, admin. Fax 438-3144
Bobover Yeshiva Bnei Zion S 50/6-8
1533 48th St 11219 718-435-8033
Rabbi Shlomo Kessler, prin. Fax 972-5305
Boricua College Post-Sec.
186 N 6th St 11211 718-782-2200
Brooklyn Amity S 200/K-10
1501 Hendrickson St 11234 718-891-6100
Metin Cetiner, prin. Fax 891-6841
Brooklyn Friends S 600/PK-12
375 Pearl St 11201 718-852-1029
Michael Nill, hdmstr. Fax 643-4868
Brooklyn Hospital Post-Sec.
121 Dekalb Ave 11201 718-250-8005
Brooklyn Law School Post-Sec.
250 Joralemon St 11201 718-780-7906
Career & Educational Consultants Post-Sec.
270 Flatbush Avenue Ext 11201 718-858-8500
Career Institute of Health & Technology Post-Sec.
340 Flatbush Avenue Ext 11201 718-422-1212
Central Yeshiva Tomchei Tmimim Lubavitz Post-Sec.
841 Ocean Pkwy 11230 718-434-0784
Centurion Professional Training Post-Sec.
2619 E 16th St 11235 718-646-4507
Charles Stuart School of Locksmithing Post-Sec.
1420 Kings Hwy 11229 718-339-2640
Christian Heritage Academy 300/PK-12
1100 E 42nd St 11210 718-377-9406
Rev. Albert Delmadge, hdmstr. Fax 338-9870
College of New Rochelle Post-Sec.
1368 Fulton St 11216 718-638-2500
CUNY Brooklyn College Post-Sec.
2900 Bedford Ave 11210 718-951-5000
CUNY Kingsborough Community College Post-Sec.
2001 Oriental Blvd 11235 718-368-5000
CUNY Medgar Evers College Post-Sec.
1650 Bedford Ave 11225 718-270-4900
Darkei Noam Rabbinical College Post-Sec.
2822 Avenue J 11210 718-338-6464
Educational Institute Oholei Torah 100/9-12
667 Eastern Pkwy 11213 718-363-0019
Rabbi Zushe Wilhelm, prin. Fax 778-0784
Elite HS 9-12
2115 Benson Ave 11214 718-373-0960
Rabbi Yehuda Braun, dean Fax 373-0962
Followers of Jesus S 100/1-12
3065 Atlantic Ave 11208 718-235-5493
James Gochnauer, prin. Fax 484-1477
Fontbonne Hall Academy 500/9-12
9901 Shore Rd 11209 718-748-2244
Sr. Anne Clancy, prin. Fax 745-3841
Franklin Career Institute Post-Sec.
5323 5th Ave 11220 718-535-3333
Gamla College Post-Sec.
1213 Elm Ave 11230 718-339-4747
Gerer Mesivta Bais Yisroel 50/9-12
5407 16th Ave 11204 718-854-8777
Rabbi Dovid Olewski, prin. Fax 851-1265
Hair Design Institute at Fifth Avenue Post-Sec.
6711 5th Ave 11220 718-745-1000
Harma Religious Institute Yeshiva HS 200/12-12
30 Lancaster Ave 11223 718-743-3141
Rabbi Hanania Elbaz, dean Fax 743-7990
Institute of Design and Construction Post-Sec.
141 Willoughby St 11201 718-855-3661
Kehilath Yakov Rabbinical Seminary Post-Sec.
206 Wilson St 11211 718-963-1212
Learning Institute for Beauty Sciences Post-Sec.
2384 86th St 11214 718-373-2400
Long Island College Hospital Post-Sec.
339 Hicks St 11201 718-780-1000
Long Island University-Brooklyn Campus Post-Sec.
1 University Plz 11201 718-488-1000
Lubavitcher S Chabad 300/PK-12
841 Ocean Pkwy 11230 718-859-7600
Rabbi S. Dechter, prin. Fax 434-0845
Machon Bais Yaakov S 400/9-12
1683 42nd St 11204 718-972-7900
Rabbi Moshe Yanofsky, prin. Fax 633-4636
Machzikei Hadath Rabbinical College Post-Sec.
5407 16th Ave 11204 718-854-8777
Magen David Yeshiva HS 500/9-12
7801 Bay Pkwy 11214 718-331-4002
Norman Fisher, prin. Fax 331-2174
Masores Bais Yaakov S 500/PK-12
1395 Ocean Ave 11230 718-692-2424
Joseph Gelman, prin. Fax 692-3162
McAuley HS 200/9-12
710 E 37th St 11203 718-462-7282
Margaret Lake, prin. Fax 462-7284
Merkaz Bnos - Business School Post-Sec.
2115 Benson Ave 11214 718-234-4000
Merkaz Bnos HS 100/9-12
1400 W 6th St 11204 718-259-5600
Rabbi Chaim Waldman, dir. Fax 259-8024
Mesifta V'Yoel Moshei S 600/9-12
5301 14th Ave 11219 718-438-7109
Rabbi Roseburg, prin.
Mesivta Eastern Parkway Rabbinical Sem. Post-Sec.
510 Dahill Rd 11218 718-438-1002
Mesivta Eitz Chaim S 300/9-12
1577 48th St 11219 718-438-2018
Rabbi Israel Licht, prin. Fax 871-9031
Mesivta Imrei Yosef Spinka 400/9-12
1460 56th St 11219 718-851-1600
Rabbi Aaron Weiss, prin. Fax 851-2915
Mesivta Lev Bonim 100/9-12
8700 Avenue K 11236 718-444-5996
Rabbi Yisroel Pearl, prin. Fax 209-0608
Mesivta Nachlas Yakov of Adas Yereim 100/9-12
185 Wilson St 11211 718-388-1751
Laslo Goldberger, prin. Fax 388-3531
Mesivta of Manhattan Beach 100/9-12
59 W End Ave 11235 718-368-1333
Rabbi Chaim Zelikovitz, prin. Fax 368-1969
Mesivta Rabbi Chaim Berlin 200/9-12
1585 Coney Island Ave 11230 718-377-8400
Rabbi Yaakov Shulman, prin. Fax 377-5883
Mesivta Sholom Shachne 9-12
129 Elmwood Ave 11230 718-252-6333
Rabbi Meir Gutfreund, prin. Fax 252-4574
Mesivta Tiferes Elimelech S 50/9-12
4407 12th Ave 11219 718-854-3062
Rabbi Yosef Leizerson, prin. Fax 854-3062
Mesivta Torah Vodaath Seminary Post-Sec.
425 E 9th St 11218 718-941-8000
Mesivta Veretzky 100/9-12
1102 Avenue L 11230 718-252-7777
Rabbi Efraim Nussbaum, prin. Fax 252-0808
Mesivta Zichron Eliezer S 100/9-12
1543 E 9th St 11230 718-336-9629
Rabbi Zelig Friedman, prin. Fax 615-4780
Mikdash Shelomo HS 50/9-12
1532 E 10th St 11230 718-382-1152
Rabbi Moshe Benzecry, prin. Fax 382-1142
Mirrer Yeshiva Central Institute Post-Sec.
1795 Ocean Pkwy 11223 718-645-0536
Mirrer Yeshiva Mesivta HS 200/9-12
1795 Ocean Pkwy 11223 718-375-0771
Rabbi Dovid Rockove, prin. Fax 375-6342
Mosdos Chasidei Square 400/K-12
1373 43rd St 11219 718-436-2550
Moshe Melamid, admin. Fax 436-2658
Nazareth Regional HS 600/9-12
475 E 57th St 11203 718-763-1100
Dr. Robert Muccigrosso, prin. Fax 629-5382
Nefesh Academy 300/PK-12
1750 E 18th St 11229 718-627-4463
Sandra Newhouse, prin. Fax 645-8755
New Vistas Academy 300/PK-12
3321 Glenwood Rd 11210 718-421-1786
Harry Moore, dir. Fax 282-9089
New York City College of Technology CUNY Post-Sec.
300 Jay St 11201 718-260-5000
New York Methodist Hospital Post-Sec.
506 6th St 11215 718-780-3706
Northside Catholic Academy - Mt. Carmel 6-8
10 Withers St 11211 718-782-1110
Beverly D'Angelo, prin. Fax 782-1110
Packer Collegiate Institute 900/PK-12
170 Joralemon St 11201 718-250-0281
Bruce Dennis, hdmstr. Fax 875-1363
Poly Prep Country Day S 800/5-12
9216 7th Ave 11228 718-836-9800
David B. Harman, prin. Fax 921-5112
Polytechnic University Post-Sec.
6 Metrotech Ctr 11201 718-260-3600
Pratt Institute Post-Sec.
200 Willoughby Ave 11205 718-636-3600
Prospect Park Bnos Leah HS 400/9-12
1601 Avenue R 11229 718-376-3337
Zlata Press, prin. Fax 376-4497
Rabbinical Academy Mesivta Rabbi Chaim Post-Sec.
1605 Coney Island Ave 11230 718-377-0777
Rabbinical Coll. Bobovr Yeshiva Bnei Zn. Post-Sec.
1577 48th St 11219 718-438-2018
Rabbinical Coll. Ch' San Sofer of NY Post-Sec.
1876 50th St 11204 718-236-1171
Rabbinical College of Ohr Shimon Yisroel Post-Sec.
215 Hewes St 11211 718-855-4092
Rabbinical Seminary Adas Yereim Post-Sec.
185 Wilson St 11211 718-388-1751
Rabbinical Seminary M'Kor Chaim Post-Sec.
1571 55th St 11219 718-851-0183
St. Ann's S 1,000/PK-12
129 Pierrepont St 11201 718-522-1660
Dr. Larry Weiss, prin. Fax 522-2599
St. Edmund Prep HS 400/9-12
2474 Ocean Ave 11229 718-743-6100
John Lorenzetti, prin. Fax 743-5243
St. Francis College Post-Sec.
180 Remsen St 11201 718-522-2300
St. Joseph HS 300/9-12
80 Willoughby St 11201 718-624-3618
Sr. Eugenia Calabrese, prin. Fax 624-2792
St. Joseph's College Post-Sec.
245 Clinton Ave 11205 718-636-6800
St. Saviour HS 400/9-12
588 6th St 11215 718-768-4406
Sr. Valeria Belanger, prin. Fax 369-2688
Shalsheles Bais Yaakov S 100/K-10
1681 42nd St 11204 718-436-1122
Esther Goodstein, prin. Fax 436-9073
Shulamith S for Girls 200/9-12
1277 E 14th St 11230 718-338-7154
Dr. Susan Katz, prin. Fax 258-9626
Sinai Academy 100/9-12
2025 79th St 11214 718-256-7400
Rabbi Moshe Silber, prin. Fax 256-7786
Soille Bais Yaakov HS 100/9-12
2600 Ocean Ave 11229 718-769-8160
Sora Bulka, prin. Fax 769-8640
SUNY Health Science Center Post-Sec.
450 Clarkson Ave 11203 718-270-1000
Talmudical Seminary Oholei Torah Post-Sec.
667 Eastern Pkwy 11213 718-774-5050
Talmud Torah Imrei Chaim 700/PK-12
1824 53rd St 11204 718-234-2000
Mayer Taub, admin. Fax 236-0970
Tomer Dvora HS 300/9-12
5801 16th Ave 11204 718-633-4125
Rivkah Taub, prin. Fax 633-3529
Torah Academy HS of Brooklyn 100/9-12
2066 E 9th St 11223 718-339-8844
Rabbi Avi Davidowitz, prin. Fax 339-9701
Torah Temimah Talmudical Seminary Post-Sec.
507 Ocean Pkwy 11218 718-853-8500
United Lubavitcher Yeshiva 100/9-12
PO Box 130347 11213 718-735-6607
Rabbi Menachem Minsky, prin. Fax 778-7161
United Talmudical Academy 50/K-12
82 Lee Ave 11211 718-963-9260
Rabbi Skaist, prin. Fax 963-9498
United Talmudical Academy 400/7-9
1346 53rd St 11219 718-438-7038
Rabbi Zurech Spira, prin. Fax 438-5552
United Talmudical Seminary Post-Sec.
82 Lee Ave 11211 718-963-9770
Xaverian HS 9-12
7100 Shore Rd 11209 718-836-7100
Dr. Joseph Marino, prin. Fax 836-7114
Yeshiva Ahavas Yisroel 50/K-12
2 Lee Ave 11211 718-388-0848
Shlomo Levine, dir. Fax 628-2545
Yeshiva and Kollel Harbotzas Torah Post-Sec.
1049 E 15th St 11230 718-692-0208
Yeshiva & Mesivta Torah Temimah 1,000/K-12
555 Ocean Pkwy 11218 718-853-8500
Rabbi Yisroel Hisiger, prin. Fax 438-5779
Yeshiva Bais Yitzchok D'Spinka 500/PK-12
575 Bedford Ave 11211 718-387-4597
Rabbi Zalman Horowitz, dean Fax 486-6645
Yeshiva Beis Meir 200/9-12
1327 38th St 11218 718-437-5844
Rabbi Mayer Altman, dir. Fax 437-4883
Yeshiva Chanoch Lenaar 100/8-12
876 Eastern Pkwy 11213 718-774-8456
Rabbi Raphael Jaworowski, prin. Fax 493-2424
Yeshiva Chemdas Yisroel Kerem 50/10-12
1149 38th St 11218 718-686-5500
Rabbi Yosef Meisels, prin. Fax 437-4946
Yeshiva Congregation Toras Yufa S 100/10-10
1056 54th St 11219 718-436-5683
Yeshiva Darchai Menachem 4-9
823 Eastern Pkwy 11213 718-953-2919
Rabbi Chaim Perl, admin.
Yeshiva Derech Chaim Post-Sec.
1573 39th St 11218 718-438-5476
Yeshiva Gedolah Bais Yisroel Post-Sec.
2002 Avenue J 11210 718-258-7400
Yeshiva Gedolah Bais Yisroel 50/9-12
2002 Avenue J 11210 718-258-7400
Rabbi Yehuda Mintz, prin. Fax 258-2394
Yeshiva Gedolah Imrei Yosef D'Spinka Post-Sec.
1460 56th St 11219 718-972-1989
Yeshiva Gedolah of Midwood 100/11-12
201 Avenue F 11218 718-853-2400
Rabbi Avrohom Pinter, prin. Fax 853-7826
Yeshivah of Flatbush Braverman HS 800/9-12
1609 Avenue J 11230 718-377-1100
Rabbi Ronald Levy, prin. Fax 258-0933
Yeshiva Karlin Stolin Post-Sec.
1818 54th St 11204 718-232-7800
Yeshiva Ketana Toldos Yaakov 300/9-12
87 Heyward St 11206 718-852-0502
Rabbi Shimon Biston, prin. Fax 852-0512
Yeshiva Machzikei Hadas Belz 500/PK-12
1601 42nd St 11204 718-436-4445
Rabbi Aharon Friedman, dir. Fax 435-9046
Yeshiva Mesivta Arugath Habosem 400/K-12
40 Lynch St 11206 718-237-4500
George Cohen, prin. Fax 237-6064
Yeshiva Mesivta Karlin Stolin 400/PK-12
1818 54th St 11204 718-232-7800
Rabbi Dovid Stein, admin. Fax 331-4833
Yeshiva Mesivta Rabbi Shlomo Kluger 500/K-12
1876 50th St 11204 718-236-1171
Rabbi Mayer Weinberger, dir. Fax 236-1119
Yeshiva Mesivta Tiferes Yisroel S 400/K-12
1271 E 35th St 11210 718-258-9006
David Schonbrun, prin. Fax 258-9055
Yeshiva Mesivta Torah Vodaath 700/K-12
425 E 9th St 11218 718-941-8000
Chaim Schilit, prin. Fax 941-8032
Yeshiva Minchas Eluzar S 50/9-12
4706 14th Ave 11219 718-438-7633
Rabbi Joshua Horowitz, prin. Fax 438-0868
Yeshiva M'Kor Chaim 50/9-12
1571 55th St 11219 718-851-0183
Rabbi Simcha Paler, prin. Fax 853-2967
Yeshiva Nesivos Chaim 100/9-12
221 Avenue F 11218 718-633-4760
Rabbi Yisroel Brown, admin. Fax 633-2468
Yeshiva Novominsk Post-Sec.
1569 47th St 11219 718-438-2727
Yeshiva of Brooklyn-Girls 1,000/PK-12
1470 Ocean Pkwy 11230 718-376-3775
G. Bresler, prin. Fax 376-4280
Yeshiva of Nitra Rabbinical College Post-Sec.
194 Division Ave 11211 718-387-0422
Yeshiva Ohr Eliezer 100/6-12
511 Avenue R 11223 718-336-2898
Sharon Hagler, prin. Fax 336-3583
Yeshiva Ohr Hatorah 50/9-12
5822 11th Ave 11219 718-851-7956
Rabbi David Eichenstein, dir.
Yeshiva R'tzahd S 400/5-8
8700 Avenue K 11236 718-444-5996
Rabbi David Lapp, prin. Fax 209-0608
Yeshivas Boyan Tiferes Mordechai Shlomo 400/PK-12
1205 44th St 11219 718-435-6060
Rabbi David Endzweig, admin. Fax 435-4060
Yeshiva Shir Chodosh 50/9-10
5014 16th Ave Ste 195 11204 718-744-4510
Rabbi Yehuda Langsam, prin. Fax 854-9436
Yeshivas Novominsk-Kol Yehuda 200/9-12
1569 47th St 11219 718-438-2727
Rabbi Shlomo Spira, prin. Fax 438-2472
Yeshivas Tiferes Academy 50/9-12
1960 Schenectady Ave 11234 718-252-0801
Rabbi Moshe Aronov, dean Fax 252-6787
Yeshivas Vyelipol HS 100/9-12
860 E 27th St 11210 718-951-1800
Zalman Friedman, prin. Fax 951-3414
Yeshivat Ateret Torah 1,000/PK-12
901 Quentin Rd 11223 718-375-7100
Rabbi Chaim Weinberg, prin. Fax 645-5097
Yeshiva Tiferes Shmiel D'Aleksander 100/9-12
PO Box 190738 11219 718-438-1818
Rabbi Boruch Singer, prin. Fax 438-7826
Yeshivat Mikdash Melech Post-Sec.
1326 Ocean Pkwy 11230 718-339-1090
Yeshiva Toldos Yitzchok Bnei Mordechai 100/PK-10
1413 45th St 11219 718-633-4802
Philip Gross, prin. Fax 972-2595
Yeshiva Toras Chesed S 200/9-12
5506 16th Ave 11204 718-972-3077
Fax 972-3078

Yeshiva Toras Emes Kamenitz 500/PK-12
1904 Avenue N 11230 718-375-0900
Irving Frank, prin. Fax 375-0272
Yeshivat Or Hatorah S 50/9-12
2119 Homecrest Ave 11229 718-645-4645
Rabbi Elya Travis, prin. Fax 645-4693
Yeshivat Shaare Torah Boys S 600/PK-12
1202 Avenue P 11229 718-645-1216
Rabbi Nachman Cohen, coord. Fax 645-9529
Yeshivat Shaare Torah Girls HS 100/9-12
321 Avenue N 11230 718-382-4000
Leah Diskind, prin. Fax 382-7999
Yeshiva Yesode Hatorah 50/9-12
620 Bedford Ave 11211 718-802-1613
S.L. Felderbaum, prin. Fax 852-4364
Zvi Dov Roth Academy 200/7-12
3300 Kings Hwy 11234 718-338-6921
Chana Kartaginer, prin. Fax 677-7703

Brookville, Nassau, Pop. 3,439

Long Island Lutheran HS 600/6-12
131 Brookville Rd 11545 516-626-1700
Dr. David M. Hahn, hdmstr. Fax 626-7459

Brushton, Franklin, Pop. 471
Brushton-Moira Central SD 800/K-12
758 County Route 7 12916 518-529-8948
Robin Jones, supt. Fax 529-6062
www.bmcsd.org
Brushton-Moira Central JSHS 400/7-12
758 County Route 7 12916 518-529-7342
Steve Grenville, prin. Fax 529-6062

Buffalo, Erie, Pop. 279,745
Buffalo CSD 34,600/PK-12
713 City Hall 14202 716-816-3600
James Williams Ed.D., supt. Fax 851-3535
www.buffaloschools.org/
Drew Science Magnet S 7-8
1 N Meadow Dr 14214 716-816-4440
Delcene West, prin.
Public HS 187 900/5-12
333 Clinton St 14204 716-851-3868
Kevin Kazmierczak, prin. Fax 851-3863
Public HS 195 900/5-12
186 E North St 14204 716-816-4230
Dr. William Kresse, prin. Fax 888-7145
Public HS 200 1,100/9-12
2885 Main St 14214 716-816-4250
Ramona Reynolds, prin. Fax 838-7490
Public HS 202 1,100/9-12
110 14th St 14213 716-816-4300
Kevin Eberle, prin. Fax 888-7158
Public HS 204 1,000/9-12
370 Lafayette Ave 14213 716-816-4340
Jacquelyn Baldwin, prin. Fax 888-7096
Public HS 205 1,400/9-12
51 Ontario St 14207 716-816-4360
Michael Mogavero, prin. Fax 871-6046
Public HS 206 1,000/9-12
150 Southside Pkwy 14220 716-816-4828
Patricia Thomas, prin. Fax 828-4905
Public HS 301 Vo/Tech
400 Kensington Ave 14214 716-816-4450
James Pautler, prin. Fax 838-7546
Public HS 302A 300/9-12
70 W Chippewa St 14202 716-816-3018
James Weimer, admin. Fax 851-3017
Public HS 304, 319 Suffolk St 14215 Vo/Tech
David Greco, prin. 716-816-4330
Public HS 305 Vo/Tech
1500 Elmwood Ave 14207 716-816-4480
Crystal Barton, prin. Fax 871-6073
Public HS 306 Vo/Tech
666 E Delavan Ave 14215 716-816-4500
Fax 897-8058
Public HS 307 9-12
820 Northampton St 14211 716-816-4520
Geraldine Horton, prin.
Public HS 415 9-10
106 Appenheimer Ave 14214 716-851-3763
Susan Doyle, prin. Fax 851-3766
Public MS 56 200/5-8
716 W Delavan Ave 14222 716-888-7100
Michael Gruber, prin. Fax 888-7104
Public MS 66 400/5-8
780 Parkside Ave 14216 716-816-3440
Angela Elmore, prin. Fax 838-7448
Public MS 79, 225 Lawn Ave 14207 800/5-8
Michael O'Brien, prin. 716-816-4040
Public MS 94 600/5-8
489 Hertel Ave 14207 716-816-4150
Sharon Ruffin, prin. Fax 871-6071
Public MS 97 5-8
1405 Sycamore St 14211 716-816-4460
Brigette Gillespie, prin.
Public MS 131 200/5-8
1369 Broadway St 14212 716-816-3270
Gregory Mott, prin. Fax 871-6071
Public S 69 300/3-8
1515 S Park Ave 14220 716-816-4777
Elaine Vandi, prin. Fax 828-4797
Public S 76 500/3-8
300 S Elmwood Ave 14201 716-816-3848
Donna Jackson, prin. Fax 851-3853
Public S 402 Vo/Tech
2495 Main St 14214 716-816-3250
Thomas Vitale, prin. Fax 838-2226

Cheektowago-Sloan UFD 1,600/PK-12
166 Halstead Ave 14212 716-891-6402
James Mazgajewski, supt. Fax 891-6435
www.sloan.wnyric.org
Other Schools – See Cheektowaga

Kenmore-Tonawanda UFSD 8,300/K-12
1500 Colvin Blvd 14223 716-874-8400
Mark Mondanaro, supt. Fax 874-8624
www.kenton.k12.ny.us/
Franklin MS 500/6-8
540 Parkhurst Blvd 14223 716-874-8404
Dennis Priore, prin. Fax 874-8480
Hoover MS 700/6-8
249 Thorncliff Rd 14223 716-874-8405
Margaret Hollstein, prin. Fax 874-8470
Kenmore West HS 1,600/9-12
33 Highland Pkwy 14223 716-874-8401
Douglas Smith, prin. Fax 874-8527
Other Schools – See Kenmore, Tonawanda

Bishop Timon-St. Jude HS 300/9-12
601 McKinley Pkwy 14220 716-826-3610
Thomas Sullivan, prin. Fax 824-5833
Bryant & Stratton College Post-Sec.
465 Main St Ste 400 14203 716-884-9120
Buffalo Seminary 200/9-12
205 Bidwell Pkwy 14222 716-885-6780
Sandra Gilmor, hdmstr. Fax 885-6785
Canisius College Post-Sec.
2001 Main St 14208 716-883-7000
Canisius HS 800/9-12
1180 Delaware Ave 14209 716-882-0466
William Kopas, prin. Fax 883-1870
Central Catholic S 6-8
1955 Genesee St 14211 716-852-6854
Rev. James Joyce, prin. Fax 852-8410
Continental School of Beauty Culture Post-Sec.
326 Kenmore Ave 14223 716-833-5016
Darul-Uloom Al Madania 200/PK-10
182 Sobieski St 14212 716-892-2606
M. Ibrihim Memon, prin. Fax 892-6621
D'Youville College Post-Sec.
320 Porter Ave 14201 716-881-3200
Erie Community College Post-Sec.
121 Ellicott St 14203 716-842-2770
Finney HS 100/9-12
260 Eggert Rd 14215 716-362-0770
Susan Thorington, prin. Fax 895-2383
Holy Angels Academy 300/9-12
24 Shoshone St 14214 716-834-7120
Jo Anne Grippi, prin. Fax 834-7128
Medaille College Post-Sec.
18 Agassiz Cir 14214 716-884-3281
Mt. Mercy Academy 500/9-12
88 Red Jacket Pkwy 14220 716-825-8796
Paulette Gaske, prin. Fax 825-0976
Nardin Academy 500/9-12
135 Cleveland Ave 14222 716-881-6262
Rebecca Reeder, prin. Fax 881-0086
National Tractor Trailer School Post-Sec.
175 Katherine St 14210 716-849-6887
New York Institute of Massage Post-Sec.
PO Box 645 14231 716-633-0355
Nichols S 600/5-12
1250 Amherst St 14216 716-876-3500
Richard C. Bryan, hdmstr. Fax 877-1090
Park S of Buffalo 200/PK-12
4625 Harlem Rd 14226 716-839-1242
Donald Grace, prin. Fax 839-2014
St. Mary's School for the Deaf Post-Sec.
2253 Main St 14214
SUNY College at Buffalo Post-Sec.
1300 Elmwood Ave 14222 716-878-4000
SUNY Educational Opportunity Center Post-Sec.
465 Washington St 14203 716-849-6725
Trocaire College Post-Sec.
360 Choate Ave 14220 716-826-1200
University at Buffalo SUNY Post-Sec.
Ellicott Complex Mfac # 220 14261 716-645-6900
Villa Maria College of Buffalo Post-Sec.
240 Pine Ridge Rd 14225 716-896-0700

Burnt Hills, Saratoga
Burnt Hills-Ballston Lake Central SD
Supt. — See Scotia
Burnt Hills-Ballston Lake HS 1,100/9-12
88 Lake Hill Rd 12027 518-399-9141
Maryellen Symer, prin. Fax 399-4341
O'Rourke MS 800/6-8
173 Lake Hill Rd 12027 518-399-9141
Donald Germain, prin. Fax 384-2588

Cairo, Greene, Pop. 1,273
Cairo-Durham Central SD 1,800/K-12
PO Box 780 12413 518-622-8534
Sally Sharkey, supt. Fax 622-9566
www.cairodurham.org
Cairo-Durham HS 600/9-12
PO Box 598 12413 518-622-8543
William Toussaint, prin. Fax 622-8857
Cairo-Durham MS 500/6-8
PO Box 1139 12413 518-622-0490
Simon Williams, prin. Fax 622-0493

Caledonia, Livingston, Pop. 2,223
Caledonia-Mumford Central SD 1,100/K-12
99 North St 14423 585-538-3400
David Dinolfo, supt. Fax 538-3450
www.cal-mum.org
Caledonia-Mumford HS 400/9-12
99 North St 14423 585-538-3483
Thomas Woodruff, prin. Fax 538-3470
Caledonia-Mumford MS 300/6-8
99 North St 14423 585-538-3482
Robert Molisani, prin. Fax 538-3430

Cambridge, Washington, Pop. 1,875
Cambridge Central SD 1,100/K-12
23 W Main St 12816 518-677-2653
Melody Troy, supt. Fax 677-3889
www.cambridgecsd.org
Cambridge HS 600/7-12
24 S Park St 12816 518-677-8527
Daniel Severson, prin. Fax 677-3246

Camden, Oneida, Pop. 2,288
Camden Central SD 2,700/K-12
51 3rd St 13316 315-245-4075
Richard Keville, supt. Fax 245-1622
www.camdenschools.org/
Camden HS 900/9-12
55 Oswego St 13316 315-245-3168
Jeffrey Bryant, prin. Fax 245-4173
Camden MS 400/7-8
32 Union St 13316 315-245-0080
Mary Barker, prin. Fax 245-0083

Camillus, Onondaga, Pop. 1,211
West Genesee Central SD 5,000/K-12
300 Sanderson Dr 13031 315-487-4562
Dr. Rudolph Rubeis, supt. Fax 487-2999
www.westgenesee.org
Camillus MS 600/6-8
5525 Ike Dixon Rd 13031 315-672-3159
Robert Honcharski, prin. Fax 672-3309
West Genesee HS 1,600/9-12
5201 W Genesee St 13031 315-487-4601
Barry Copeland, prin. Fax 487-4582
West Genesee MS 700/6-8
500 Sanderson Dr 13031 315-487-4615
Earl Sanderson, prin. Fax 487-4618

Campbell, Steuben
Campbell-Savona Central SD 900/K-12
8455 County Route 125 14821 607-527-4550
Lynn Lyndes, supt. Fax 527-8363
www.campbellsavona.wnyric.org
Campbell-Savona JSHS 400/7-12
8455 County Route 125 14821 607-527-4550
Lisa Hawken, prin. Fax 527-8363

Canaan, Columbia
Berkshire UFD 200/7-12
13640 State Route 22 12029 518-781-3500
James Gaudette, supt. Fax 781-4890
Berkshire JSHS 7-12
13640 State Route 22 12029 518-781-3500
Bruce Potter, prin. Fax 781-4890

Canajoharie, Montgomery, Pop. 2,191
Canajoharie Central SD 1,100/PK-12
136 Scholastic Way 13317 518-673-6302
Richard Rose, supt. Fax 673-3177
www.canajoharieschools.org
Canajoharie HS 400/9-12
136 Scholastic Way 13317 518-673-6330
Dr. Donald Bowden, prin. Fax 673-3177
Canajoharie MS 200/6-8
25 School District Rd 13317 518-673-6320
Thomas Sincavage, prin. Fax 673-5557

Canandaigua, Ontario, Pop. 11,391
Canandaigua CSD 4,100/K-12
143 N Pearl St 14424 585-396-3700
Donald Raw, supt. Fax 396-7306
www.canandaiguaschools.org/
Canandaigua Academy 1,300/9-12
435 East St 14424 585-396-3800
Lynne Erdle, prin. Fax 396-3806
Canandaigua MS 1,000/6-8
215 Granger St 14424 585-396-3850
Ralph Undercoffler, prin. Fax 396-3863

Finger Lakes Community College Post-Sec.
4355 Lakeshore Dr 14424 585-394-3500

Canaseraga, Allegany, Pop. 574
Canaseraga Central SD 300/K-12
PO Box 230 14822 607-545-6421
Marie Blum, supt. Fax 545-6265
www.canaseraga.wnyric.org
Canaseraga S 300/K-12
PO Box 230 14822 607-545-6421
James Anderson, prin. Fax 545-6265

Canastota, Madison, Pop. 4,429
Canastota Central SD 1,500/K-12
120 Roberts St 13032 315-697-2025
Frederick Bragan, supt. Fax 697-6368
www.canastotacsd.org
Canastota JSHS 700/7-12
102 Roberts St 13032 315-697-2003
Donna Marie Norton, prin. Fax 697-6368

Utica School of Commerce Post-Sec.
PO Box 462 13032 315-697-8200

Candor, Tioga, Pop. 830
Candor Central SD 900/K-12
PO Box 145 13743 607-659-5010
Jeffrey Kisloski, supt. Fax 659-7112
candor.org
Candor JSHS 400/7-12
PO Box 145 13743 607-659-5020
Ryan Dougherty, prin. Fax 659-4692

Canisteo, Steuben, Pop. 2,281
Canisteo-Greenwood Central SD 1,000/PK-12
84 Greenwood St 14823 607-698-4225
Lorraine Patti, supt. Fax 698-2833
www.cg.wnyric.org
Canisteo-Greenwood JSHS 7-12
84 Greenwood St 14823 607-698-4225
Michael Wright, prin. Fax 698-2833

Canton, Saint Lawrence, Pop. 6,060
Canton Central SD 1,400/PK-12
99 State St 13617 315-386-8561
Dr. Katrina Jacobson, supt. Fax 386-1323
www.ccsdk12.org/
McKenney MS 500/4-8
99 State St 13617 315-386-8561
Arthur Quackenbush, prin. Fax 386-1323
Williams HS 500/9-12
99 State St 13617 315-386-8561
William Gregory, prin. Fax 386-1323

St. Lawrence University Post-Sec.
2501 Saint Lawrence Univ 13617 315-229-5011
SUNY Canton - College of Technology Post-Sec.
34 Cornell Dr 13617 315-386-7011

Carle Place, Nassau, Pop. 5,107
Carle Place UFD 1,500/K-12
168 Cherry Ln 11514 516-622-6442
W. Michael Mahoney, supt. Fax 622-6447
www.cps.k12.ny.us
Carle Place MSHS 700/7-12
168 Cherry Ln 11514 516-622-6400
Neil Connolly, prin. Fax 622-6489

Carmel, Putnam, Pop. 4,800
Carmel Central SD
Supt. — See Patterson
Carmel HS 1,600/9-12
30 Fair St 10512 845-225-8441
Kevin Carroll, prin. Fax 228-2308

Fischer MS — 1,600/5-8
281 Fair St 10512 — 845-228-2300
Les Weintraub, prin. — Fax 228-2304

Carthage, Jefferson, Pop. 3,790
Carthage Central SD — 2,900/K-12
25059 County Route 197 13619 — 315-493-5000
Carl Militello, supt. — Fax 493-5069
www.carthagecsd.org
Carthage HS — 900/9-12
36500 State Route 26 13619 — 315-493-5030
Peter Turner, prin. — Fax 493-5039
Carthage MS — 700/5-8
21986 Cole Rd 13619 — 315-493-5020
Andrea Miller, prin. — Fax 493-5029

Castleton on Hudson, Rensselaer, Pop. 1,525
Schodack Central SD — 1,200/K-12
1216 Maple Hill Rd 12033 — 518-732-2297
Douglas Hamlin, supt. — Fax 732-7710
www.schodack.k12.ny.us/
Maple Hill HS — 400/9-12
1216 Maple Hill Rd 12033 — 518-732-7701
Robert Horan, prin. — Fax 732-0494
Maple Hill MS — 500/4-8
1477 S Schodack Rd 12033 — 518-732-7736
Heather Lansing, prin. — Fax 732-0493

Cato, Cayuga, Pop. 592
Cato-Meridian Central SD — 1,200/PK-12
2851 State Route 370 13033 — 315-626-3439
Deborah D. Bobo, supt. — Fax 626-2888
www.catomeridian.org/
Cato-Meridian HS — 400/9-12
2851 State Route 370 13033 — 315-626-3317
Joseph Coleman, prin. — Fax 626-2551
Cato-Meridian MS — 400/5-8
2851 State Route 370 13033 — 315-626-3319
Sean Gleason, prin. — Fax 626-2888

Catskill, Greene, Pop. 4,367
Catskill Central SD — 1,700/K-12
343 W Main St 12414 — 518-943-4696
Kathleen Farrell Ph.D., supt. — Fax 943-7116
www.catskillcsd.org
Catskill HS — 600/9-12
341 W Main St 12414 — 518-943-2300
William Ball, prin. — Fax 943-1451
Catskill MS — 300/7-8
345 W Main St 12414 — 518-943-5665
Marielena Davis, prin. — Fax 943-3001

Columbia-Greene Beauty School — Post-Sec.
342 Main St 12414 — 518-943-2224

Cattaraugus, Cattaraugus, Pop. 1,029
Cattaraugus-Little Valley Central SD
Supt. — See Little Valley
Cattaraugus-Little Valley HS — 400/9-12
25 N Franklin St 14719 — 716-257-3483
Paul Stetz, prin. — Fax 257-5108
Cattaraugus-Little Valley MS — 200/6-8
25 N Franklin St 14719 — 716-257-3483
Lawrence Studd, prin. — Fax 257-5108

Cazenovia, Madison, Pop. 2,698
Cazenovia Central SD — 1,800/K-12
31 Emory Ave 13035 — 315-655-1317
Robert Dubik, supt. — Fax 655-1375
www.caz.cnyric.org
Cazenovia JSHS — 800/8-12
31 Emory Ave 13035 — 315-655-1314
Eric Schnabl, prin. — Fax 655-1371

Cazenovia College 13035 — Post-Sec.
800-654-3210

Cedarhurst, Nassau, Pop. 6,082
Lawrence UFD
Supt. — See Lawrence
Lawrence HS — 1,200/9-12
2 Reilly Rd 11516 — 516-295-8000
Geoffrey Touretz, prin. — Fax 295-2754

Hebrew Academy of Five Towns HS — 500/9-12
635 Central Ave 11516 — 516-569-3807
Stanley Blumenstein, prin. — Fax 374-5761
Yeshiva Zichron Aryeh — Post-Sec.
100 Cedarhurst Ave 11516 — 516-295-5700

Centereach, Suffolk, Pop. 27,400
Middle Country Central SD — 11,400/PK-12
8 43rd St 11720 — 631-285-8005
Dr. Roberta Gerold, supt. — Fax 738-2719
www.middlecountry.k12.ny.us/
Centereach HS — 1,700/9-12
14 43rd St 11720 — 631-285-8100
Thomas Bell, prin. — Fax 285-8101
Dawnwood MS, 10 43rd St 11720 — 1,300/6-8
Linda Peyser, prin. — 631-285-8200
Selden MS, 22 Jefferson Ave 11720 — 1,300/6-8
Barbara Phillipson, prin. — 631-285-8400
Other Schools – See Selden

Our Savior New American S — 300/PK-12
140 Mark Tree Rd 11720 — 631-588-2757
Dolores Reade, prin. — Fax 588-2617

Center Moriches, Suffolk, Pop. 5,987
Center Moriches UFD — 1,400/K-12
529 Main St 11934 — 631-878-0052
Donald James, supt. — Fax 878-4326
www.cmschools.org
Center Moriches HS — 500/9-12
311 Frowein Rd 11934 — 631-878-0092
Lino Bracco, prin. — Fax 878-1796
Center Moriches MS — 300/6-8
311 Frowein Rd 11934 — 631-878-2519
Patricia Cunningham, prin. — Fax 878-0362

Burket Christian S — 200/PK-12
34 Oak St 11934 — 631-878-1727
Dominick Scibetta, admin. — Fax 878-8968

Central Islip, Suffolk, Pop. 33,400
Central Islip UFD — 6,500/PK-12
50 Wheeler Rd 11722 — 631-348-5001
Fadhilika Atiba-Weza, supt. — Fax 348-0366
www.cischools.us
Central Islip HS — 1,900/9-12
85 Wheeler Rd 11722 — 631-348-5078
Anthony Servedio, prin. — Fax 342-0161
Reed MS — 1,000/7-8
200 Half Mile Rd 11722 — 631-348-5065
Carmen Garcia-Collins, prin. — Fax 348-5159

New York Institute of Technology — Post-Sec.
211 Carleton Ave 11722 — 631-348-3000
Touro College — Post-Sec.
225 Eastview Dr 11722 — 631-421-2244

Central Square, Oswego, Pop. 1,658
Central Square Central SD — 4,900/K-12
642 S Main St 13036 — 315-668-4220
Dr. Carolyn Costello, supt. — Fax 676-4437
www.centralsquareschools.org/
Central Square MS — 1,300/6-8
248 US Route 11 13036 — 315-668-4216
Paul Schoeneck, prin. — Fax 668-8410
Moore HS — 1,500/9-12
44 School Dr 13036 — 315-668-4231
Thomas Douglas, prin. — Fax 668-4346

Central Valley, Orange, Pop. 1,929
Monroe-Woodbury Central SD — 7,300/K-12
278 Route 32 10917 — 845-460-6200
Joseph DiLorenzo, supt. — Fax 460-6080
www.mw.k12.ny.us
Monroe-Woodbury HS — 2,400/9-12
155 Dunderberg Rd 10917 — 845-460-7000
Aldo Filippone, prin. — Fax 460-7090
Monroe-Woodbury MS — 1,700/6-8
199 Dunderberg Rd 10917 — 845-460-6400
Elsie Rodriguez, prin. — Fax 460-6044

Champlain, Clinton, Pop. 1,159
Northeastern Clinton Central SD — 1,600/K-12
103 State Route 276 12919 — 518-298-8242
Robert J. Hebert, supt. — Fax 298-4293
www.nccscougars.org/
Northeastern Clinton HS — 600/9-12
103 State Route 276 12919 — 518-298-8638
Christine Crowley, prin. — Fax 298-4293
Northeastern Clinton MS — 400/6-8
103 State Route 276 12919 — 518-298-8681
Thomas Brandell, prin. — Fax 298-4293

Chappaqua, Westchester, Pop. 6,400
Chappaqua Central SD — 4,200/K-12
PO Box 21 10514 — 914-238-7200
David A. Fleishman, supt. — Fax 238-7218
www.ccsd.ws
Bell MS — 700/5-8
50 Senter St 10514 — 914-238-6170
Martin Fitzgerald, prin. — Fax 238-2085
Greeley HS — 1,200/9-12
70 Roaring Brook Rd 10514 — 914-861-9400
Andrew Salesnick, prin. — Fax 238-4291
Seven Bridges MS — 700/5-8
PO Box 22 10514 — 914-666-7330
Donna Raskin, prin. — Fax 666-7306

Chateaugay, Franklin, Pop. 786
Chateaugay Central SD — 600/K-12
PO Box 904 12920 — 518-497-6420
Paul Harrica, supt. — Fax 497-3170
www.chateaugay.org/
Chateaugay JSHS — 300/7-12
PO Box 904 12920 — 518-497-6611
Dale Breault, prin. — Fax 497-3170

Chatham, Columbia, Pop. 1,761
Chatham Central SD — 1,400/K-12
50 Woodbridge Ave 12037 — 518-392-1501
Scott Hunter, supt. — Fax 392-2413
www.chathamcentralschools.com/
Chatham HS — 500/9-12
50 Woodbridge Ave 12037 — 518-392-4142
Ronald Davis, prin. — Fax 392-0908
Chatham MS — 500/5-8
50 Woodbridge Ave 12037 — 518-392-1560
Gordon Fitting, prin. — Fax 392-1559

Chaumont, Jefferson, Pop. 606
Lyme Central SD — 400/K-12
PO Box 219 13622 — 315-649-2417
Donnalee Dodson, supt. — Fax 649-2812
www.lymecsd.org
Lyme Central S — 400/K-12
PO Box 219 13622 — 315-649-2417
Joseph O'Donnell, prin. — Fax 649-2812

Chazy, Clinton
Chazy Central UFD — 600/K-12
609 Miner Farm Rd 12921 — 518-846-7135
Kevin Mulligan, supt. — Fax 846-8322
www.chazy.org
Chazy Central Rural JSHS — 300/7-12
609 Miner Farm Rd 12921 — 518-846-7135
Kevin Mulligan, prin. — Fax 846-8322

Cheektowaga, Erie, Pop. 79,200
Cheektowaga Central SD — 2,400/PK-12
3600 Union Rd 14225 — 716-686-3606
Delia Bonenberger, supt. — Fax 681-5232
www.cheektowagacentral.org
Cheektowaga Central HS — 800/9-12
3600 Union Rd 14225 — 716-686-3602
Steven Wright, prin. — Fax 686-3619
Cheektowaga Central MS — 600/6-8
3600 Union Rd 14225 — 716-686-3660
Cheryl Buggs, prin. — Fax 686-3669

Cheektowaga-Maryvale UFD — 2,500/K-12
1050 Maryvale Dr 14225 — 716-631-7407
Gary Brader, supt. — Fax 635-4699
www.maryvale.wnyric.org
Maryvale HS — 800/9-12
1050 Maryvale Dr 14225 — 716-631-7481
Renee Salvadore, prin. — Fax 631-7404
Maryvale MS — 600/6-8
1050 Maryvale Dr 14225 — 716-631-7425
Jeffrey Barthelme, prin. — Fax 631-7499

Cheektowago-Sloan UFD
Supt. — See Buffalo
Kennedy HS — 500/9-12
305 Cayuga Creek Rd 14227 — 716-891-6407
Stephen Bovino, prin. — Fax 891-6430
Kennedy MS — 400/6-8
305 Cayuga Creek Rd 14227 — 716-897-7300
David Peters, prin. — Fax 891-6430

Cleveland Hill UFD — 1,200/K-12
105 Mapleview Rd 14225 — 716-836-7200
Bruce Inglis, supt. — Fax 836-0675
www.clevehill.wnyric.org/
Cleveland Hill MSHS — 500/6-12
105 Mapleview Rd 14225 — 716-836-7200
Jill Sherman, prin. — Fax 836-0675

SUNY Empire State College — Post-Sec.
2875 Union Rd Ste 34 14227 — 716-853-7700

Cherry Valley, Otsego, Pop. 561
Cherry Valley-Springfield Central SD — 700/PK-12
PO Box 485 13320 — 607-264-9332
Nicholas J. Savin, supt. — Fax 264-9023
www.cvscs.org
Cherry Valley-Springfield JSHS — 300/7-12
PO Box 485 13320 — 607-264-9012
Charles Strange, prin. — Fax 264-3458

Chester, Orange, Pop. 3,604
Chester UFD — 1,000/K-12
64 Hambletonian Ave 10918 — 845-469-5052
Helen Anne Livingston, supt. — Fax 469-2377
chesterufsd.org
Chester Academy — 600/6-12
64 Hambletonian Ave 10918 — 845-469-2231
Fax 469-3547

Chestertown, Warren
North Warren Central SD — 600/PK-12
6110 State Route 8 12817 — 518-494-3015
Joseph Murphy, supt. — Fax 494-2929
www.northwarren.k12.ny.us
North Warren Central S — 600/PK-12
6110 State Route 8 12817 — 518-494-3015
Theresa Andrew, prin. — Fax 494-2929

Chestnut Ridge, Rockland, Pop. 7,843
East Ramapo Central SD
Supt. — See Spring Valley
Chestnut Ridge MS — 500/7-8
892 Chestnut Ridge Rd 10977 — 845-577-6300
Maria Vergez, prin. — Fax 426-1063

Green Meadow Waldorf S — 400/PK-12
307 Hungry Hollow Rd 10977 — 845-356-2514
Kay Hoffman, prin. — Fax 356-2921

Chittenango, Madison, Pop. 4,901
Chittenango Central SD — 2,500/K-12
1732 Fyler Rd 13037 — 315-687-2669
Thomas E. Marzeski, supt. — Fax 687-9830
www.chittenangoschools.org
Chittenango HS — 900/9-12
150 Genesee St 13037 — 315-687-2621
Derek Sajnog, prin. — Fax 687-5182
Chittenango MS — 600/6-8
1732 Fyler Rd 13037 — 315-687-2648
Linda LLewellyn, prin. — Fax 687-5482

Churchville, Monroe, Pop. 1,901
Churchville-Chili Central SD — 4,400/K-12
139 Fairbanks Rd 14428 — 585-293-1800
Anne Spadafora, supt. — Fax 293-1013
www.cccsd.org
Churchville-Chili JHS — 1,200/7-9
137 Fairbanks Rd 14428 — 585-293-4541
David Hamilton, prin. — Fax 293-4501
Churchville-Chili SHS — 1,100/10-12
5786 Buffalo Rd 14428 — 585-293-4540
Bill Geraci, prin. — Fax 293-4508

Cicero, Onondaga
North Syracuse Central SD
Supt. — See North Syracuse
Cicero-North Syracuse SHS — 2,200/10-12
6002 State Route 31 13039 — 315-218-4100
James Froio, prin. — Fax 218-4185

Cincinnatus, Cortland
Cincinnatus Central SD — 700/K-12
2809 Cincinnatus Rd 13040 — 607-863-4069
Steven Hubbard, supt. — Fax 863-4109
www.cincynet.cnyric.org
Cincinnatus HS — 200/9-12
2809 Cincinnatus Rd 13040 — 607-863-3200
Karen Heffernan, prin. — Fax 863-4559
Cincinnatus MS — 200/5-8
2809 Cincinnatus Rd 13040 — 607-863-3200
Joseph Mack, prin. — Fax 863-4559

Circleville, Orange, Pop. 1,350
Pine Bush Central SD
Supt. — See Pine Bush
Circleville MS — 600/6-8
PO Box 143 10919 — 845-744-2031
Ralph LaRocca, prin. — Fax 361-3811

Clarence, Erie
Clarence Central SD — 5,000/K-12
9625 Main St 14031 — 716-407-9100
Thomas Coseo Ed.D., supt. — Fax 407-9126
www.clarenceschools.org
Clarence HS, 9625 Main St 14031 — 1,600/9-12
Joseph Gentile, prin. — 716-407-9020
Clarence MS — 1,200/6-8
10150 Greiner Rd 14031 — 716-407-9200
Jeff White, prin.

Clayton, Jefferson, Pop. 1,866
Thousand Islands Central SD — 1,100/K-12
PO Box 1000 13624 — 315-686-5594
Dr. John Slattery, supt. — Fax 686-5511
www.1000islandsschools.org

Thousand Islands HS 400/9-12
8481 Country Route 9 13624 315-686-5594
Joseph Gilfus, prin. Fax 654-5039
Thousand Islands MS 300/6-8
8487 County Route 9 13624 315-686-5594
Debra Percy, prin. Fax 654-5038

Clifton Park, Saratoga
Shenendehowa Central SD 9,500/K-12
5 Chelsea Pl 12065 518-881-0600
R. Oliver Robinson, supt. Fax 371-9393
www.shenet.org/
Acadia MS 800/6-8
970 Route 146 Ste 54 12065 518-881-0450
Jonathan Burns, prin. Fax 371-3981
Gowana MS 700/6-8
970 Route 146 Ste 55 12065 518-881-0460
Jill Bush, prin. Fax 383-1490
Koda MS 700/6-8
970 Route 146 Ste 59 12065 518-881-0470
Bruce Ballan, prin. Fax 383-1532
Shenendehowa HS West 800/9-9
970 Route 146 Ste 56 12065 518-881-0330
Frank Tedesco, prin. Fax 383-5768
Shenendehowa SHS East 2,100/10-12
970 Route 146 12065 518-881-0310
Frank Tedesco, prin. Fax 383-1670

Clifton Springs, Ontario, Pop. 2,195
Phelps-Clifton Springs Central SD 2,000/K-12
1490 State Route 488 14432 315-548-6420
Michael Ford, supt. Fax 548-6429
www.midlakes.org
Midlakes HS 700/9-12
1554 State Route 488 14432 315-548-6300
L. Rick Bley, prin. Fax 548-6319
Midlakes MS 500/6-8
1550 State Route 488 14432 315-548-6600
Kathy DeMay, prin. Fax 548-6619

Climax, Greene

Grapeville Christian S 100/K-12
2416 County Route 26 12042 518-966-5037
Nicole Orsino, prin. Fax 966-4265

Clinton, Oneida, Pop. 1,918
Clinton Central SD 1,600/K-12
75 Chenango Ave 13323 315-557-2253
Jeffrey Roudebush, supt. Fax 853-8727
www.ccs.edu
Clinton HS 600/9-12
75 Chenango Ave 13323 315-557-2232
Richard Hunt, prin. Fax 853-8727
Clinton MS 400/6-8
75 Chenango Ave 13323 315-557-2260
Martin Cross, prin. Fax 853-8727

Hamilton College Post-Sec.
198 College Hill Rd 13323 315-859-4011

Clinton Corners, Dutchess

Upton Lake Christian S 100/K-12
PO Box 63 12514 845-266-3497
Dietlind Hoiem, admin. Fax 266-3828

Clintonville, Clinton
Au Sable Valley Central SD 1,300/K-12
1273 Route 9N 12924 518-834-2845
Paul Savage, supt. Fax 834-2843
www.avcs.org
Au Sable Valley HS 400/9-12
1490 Route 9N 12924 518-834-2800
Laura Marlow, prin. Fax 834-2847
Au Sable Valley MS 300/7-8
1490 Route 9N 12924 518-834-2800
Philip Mero, prin. Fax 834-2847

Clyde, Wayne, Pop. 2,181
Clyde-Savannah Central SD 1,000/K-12
215 Glasgow St 14433 315-902-3000
Marilyn Barr, supt. Fax 923-2560
www.clydesavannah.org/
Clyde JSHS 500/7-12
215 Glasgow St 14433 315-902-3050
Dr. Craig Pawlak, prin. Fax 923-7906

Clymer, Chautauqua
Clymer Central SD 500/K-12
8672 E Main St 14724 716-355-4444
Ralph Wilson, supt. Fax 355-4467
www.clymer.wnyric.org/
Clymer Central S 500/K-12
8672 E Main St 14724 716-355-4444
Edward Bailey, prin. Fax 355-4467

Cobleskill, Schoharie, Pop. 4,706
Cobleskill-Richmondville Central SD 2,100/K-12
155 Washington Ave 12043 518-234-4032
Samuel Shevat, supt. Fax 234-7721
www.crcs.k12.ny.us/
Golding MS 600/6-8
193 Golding Dr 12043 518-234-8368
Scott McDonald, prin. Fax 234-1018
Other Schools – See Richmondville

SUNY College of Agriculture & Technology Post-Sec.
107 Schenectady Ave 12043 518-255-5011

Cohoes, Albany, Pop. 15,085
Cohoes CSD 2,200/K-12
7 Bevan St 12047 518-237-0100
Charles Dedrick, supt. Fax 237-2912
www.cohoes.org/
Cohoes HS 700/9-12
1 Tiger Cir 12047 518-237-9100
Joseph Rajczak, prin. Fax 238-0169
Cohoes MS 500/6-8
7 Bevan St 12047 518-237-4131
Mark Perry, prin. Fax 237-2253

Cold Spring, Putnam, Pop. 2,009
Haldane Central SD 800/K-12
15 Craigside Dr 10516 845-265-9254
Dr. John DiNatale, supt. Fax 265-9213
www2.lhric.org/haldane
Haldane JSHS 400/7-12
15 Craigside Dr 10516 845-265-9254
J. Andy Irvin, prin. Fax 265-9213

Cold Spring Harbor, Suffolk, Pop. 4,789
Cold Spring Harbor Central SD 2,100/K-12
75 Goose Hill Rd 11724 631-692-8036
Whitney Vantine Ed.D., supt. Fax 367-3108
www.csh.k12.ny.us
Cold Spring Harbor JSHS 1,000/7-12
82 Turkey Ln 11724 631-692-8600
Jay Matuk, prin. Fax 692-8016

College Point, See New York

St. Agnes Academic HS 400/9-12
1320 124th St 11356 718-353-6068
Sr. Joan Martin, prin.

Colton, Saint Lawrence
Colton-Pierrepont Central SD 400/PK-12
4921 State Highway 56 13625 315-262-2100
Martin Bregg, supt. Fax 262-2644
www.cpcs.k12.ny.us
Colton-Pierrepont JSHS 200/7-12
4921 State Highway 56 13625 315-262-2100
Randy Johnson, prin. Fax 262-2644

Commack, Suffolk, Pop. 36,400
Commack UFD
Supt. — See East Northport
Commack HS, 1 Scholar Ln 11725 2,100/9-12
Ronald Vale, prin. 631-912-2100
Commack MS 1,800/6-8
700 Vanderbilt Pkwy 11725 631-858-3500
Pamela Travis-Moore, prin.

Long Island Business Institute Post-Sec.
6500 Jericho Tpke 11725 631-499-7100

Congers, Rockland, Pop. 8,003

Rockland Country Day S 200/PK-12
34 Kings Hwy 10920 845-268-6802
James Handlin Ed.D., hdmstr. Fax 268-4644

Conklin, Broome
Susquehanna Valley Central SD 1,800/K-12
PO Box 200 13748 607-775-9100
Carol Boyce, supt. Fax 775-4575
www.svsabers.org/
Stank MS 500/6-8
1040 Conklin Rd 13748 607-775-0303
Gerardo Tagliaferri, prin. Fax 775-9142
Susquehanna Valley HS 700/9-12
1040 Conklin Rd 13748 607-775-0304
David Daniels, prin. Fax 775-4575

Cooperstown, Otsego, Pop. 1,938
Cooperstown Central SD 1,100/K-12
39 Linden Ave 13326 607-547-5364
Mary Jo McPhail, supt. Fax 547-5100
Cooperstown Central HS 400/9-12
39 Linden Ave 13326 607-547-8181
Gary Kuch, prin. Fax 547-5100
Cooperstown MS 300/6-8
39 Linden Ave 13326 607-547-5512
Michael Cring, prin. Fax 547-5100

Copenhagen, Lewis, Pop. 812
Copenhagen Central SD 600/K-12
PO Box 30 13626 315-688-4411
Lisa Parsons, supt. Fax 688-2001
www.ccsknights.org/
Copenhagen Central S 600/K-12
PO Box 30 13626 315-688-4411
Patricia Gibbons, prin. Fax 688-2001

Copiague, Suffolk, Pop. 20,769
Copiague UFD 4,600/K-12
2650 Great Neck Rd 11726 631-842-4015
Dr. William Bolton, supt. Fax 841-4614
www.copiague.k12.ny.us/
Copiague MS 1,100/6-8
2650 Great Neck Rd 11726 631-842-4011
Albert Voorneveld, prin. Fax 841-4630
O'Connell - Copiague HS 1,400/9-12
1100 Dixon Ave 11726 631-842-4010
Michael Hodgkiss, prin. Fax 841-4642

Corfu, Genesee, Pop. 763
Pembroke Central SD 1,400/PK-12
PO Box 308 14036 585-599-4525
Gary Mix, supt. Fax 762-9993
www.pembroke.k12.ny.us
Pembroke JSHS 700/7-12
PO Box 308 14036 585-599-4525
Keith Palmer, prin. Fax 762-9993

Corinth, Saratoga, Pop. 2,472
Corinth Central SD 1,300/K-12
105 Oak St 12822 518-654-2601
Dr. Daniel Starr, supt. Fax 654-6266
www.corinthcsd.com/
Corinth HS 400/9-12
105 Oak St 12822 518-654-9005
Brian Testani, prin. Fax 654-6266
Corinth MS 400/5-8
105 Oak St 12822 518-654-9005
Gregory Kreis, prin. Fax 654-6266

Corning, Steuben, Pop. 10,551
Corning CSD
Supt. — See Painted Post
Corning Free Academy MS 700/6-8
11 W 3rd St 14830 607-936-3788
Richard Kimble, prin. Fax 654-2809
Corning-Painted Post East HS 800/9-12
201 Cantigney St 14830 607-936-3746
Joseph Tobia, prin. Fax 654-2787
Northside Blodgett MS 600/6-8
143 Princeton Ave 14830 607-936-3791
Robert Rossi, prin. Fax 654-2798

Corning Christian Academy 200/PK-12
11 Aisne St 14830 607-962-4220
Dean Everhart, admin. Fax 962-4410
Corning Community College Post-Sec.
1 Academic Dr 14830 607-962-9011

Cornwall, Orange, Pop. 11,270
Cornwall Central SD
Supt. — See Cornwall on Hudson
Cornwall Central MS 1,100/5-8
122 Main St 12518 845-534-8009
Diana Musich, prin. Fax 534-7809

Cornwall on Hudson, Orange, Pop. 3,110
Cornwall Central SD 3,200/K-12
24 Idlewild Ave 12520 845-534-8009
Timothy Rehm, supt. Fax 534-4231
www.cornwallschools.com/
Other Schools – See Cornwall, New Windsor

New York Military Academy 200/7-12
78 Academy Ave 12520 845-534-3710
Dr. Christopher Hennen, hdmstr. Fax 534-7121
Storm King S 100/7-12
314 Mountain Rd 12520 845-534-7892
Helen Chinitz, prin. Fax 534-2709

Corona, See New York
NYC Department of Education
Supt. — See New York
Arts & Business HS 800/9-12
10525 Horace Harding Expy 11368 718-271-8383
Vivian Selenikas, prin. Fax 271-7196
IS 61 1,900/6-8
9850 50th Ave 11368 718-760-3233
John O'Mahoney, prin. Fax 760-5220

Cortland, Cortland, Pop. 18,522
Cortland CSD 2,800/K-12
1 Valley View Dr 13045 607-758-4100
Laurence Spring, supt. Fax 758-4128
www.cortlandschools.org
Cortland JSHS 1,300/7-12
8 Valley View Dr 13045 607-758-4100
Steve Woodard, prin.

Cortland Christian Academy 100/K-12
15 West Rd 13045 607-756-5838
Craig Miller, admin. Fax 756-7716
SUNY College at Cortland Post-Sec.
PO Box 2000 13045 607-753-2011

Cortlandt Manor, See Peekskill
Hendrick Hudson Central SD
Supt. — See Montrose
Blue Mountain MS 700/6-8
7 Furnace Woods Rd 10567 914-736-5300
Dr. John Sieverding, prin. Fax 736-3513

Lakeland Central SD
Supt. — See Shrub Oak
Panas HS 800/9-12
300 Croton Ave 10567 914-739-2823
Susan Strauss, prin. Fax 739-3545

Ohr Hameir Seminary Tifereth Israel HS 100/9-12
141 Furnace Woods Rd 10567 914-736-1500
Joseph Willner, prin. Fax 736-1055

Coxsackie, Greene, Pop. 2,853
Coxsackie-Athens Central SD 1,600/K-12
24 Sunset Blvd 12051 518-731-1710
Dr. Earle Gregory, supt. Fax 731-1729
www.coxsackie-athens.org
Coxsackie-Athens HS 500/9-12
24 Sunset Blvd 12051 518-731-1800
Dr. James Maxwell, prin. Fax 731-1809
Coxsackie-Athens MS 500/5-8
24 Sunset Blvd 12051 518-731-1850
Joseph Posillico, prin. Fax 731-1859

Craryville, Columbia
Taconic Hills Central SD 1,800/K-12
PO Box 482 12521 518-325-0310
David Paciencia, supt. Fax 325-3557
www.taconichills.k12.ny.us/
Taconic Hills HS 700/9-12
PO Box 536 12521 518-325-0390
John Gulisane, prin. Fax 325-9051
Taconic Hills MS 600/5-8
PO Box 535 12521 518-325-0420
Steve Drescher, prin. Fax 325-9051

Cross River, Westchester
Katonah-Lewisboro UFD
Supt. — See South Salem
Jay HS 1,300/9-12
60 N Salem Rd 10518 914-763-7200
Richard Leprine, prin. Fax 763-7494
Jay MS 1,000/6-8
40 N Salem Rd 10518 914-763-7500
Alice Cronin, prin. Fax 763-7665

Croton on Hudson, Westchester, Pop. 7,134
Croton-Harmon UFD 1,600/K-12
10 Gerstein St 10520 914-271-4793
Dr. Marjorie Castro, supt. Fax 271-8685
www.croton-harmonschools.org
Croton-Harmon HS 400/9-12
36 Old Post Rd S 10520 914-271-2147
Joel Adelberg, prin. Fax 271-6643
Van Cortlandt MS 400/6-8
3 Glen Pl 10520 914-271-2191
Don Slater, prin. Fax 271-6618

Crown Point, Essex
Crown Point Central SD 300/K-12
PO Box 35 12928 518-597-4200
Shari Brannock, supt. Fax 597-4121
Crown Point Central S 300/K-12
PO Box 35 12928 518-597-3285
Agatha Mace, prin. Fax 597-4121

Cuba, Allegany, Pop. 1,586
Cuba-Rushford Central SD 1,000/K-12
5476 Route 305 14727 585-968-2650
Anne Brungard, supt. Fax 968-2651
www.crcs.wnyric.org/

Cuba-Rushford HS 300/9-12
5476 Route 305 14727 585-968-2650
Carlos Gildemeister, prin. Fax 968-2651
Cuba-Rushford MS 300/6-8
5476 Route 305 14727 585-968-2650
Barbara Funk, prin. Fax 968-2651

Cutchogue, Suffolk, Pop. 2,627
Mattituck-Cutchogue UFD 1,500/1-12
385 Depot Ln 11935 631-298-4242
James McKenna, supt. Fax 298-8573
Other Schools – See Mattituck

Dannemora, Clinton, Pop. 4,108
Saranac Central SD 1,500/K-12
32 Emmons St 12929 518-565-5600
Kenneth Cringle, supt. Fax 565-5617
www.saranac.org
Other Schools – See Saranac

Dansville, Livingston, Pop. 4,640
Dansville Central SD 1,700/K-12
284 Main St 14437 585-335-4000
Matthew McGarrity, supt. Fax 335-4002
www.dansvillecsd.org
Dansville HS 600/9-12
282 Main St 14437 585-335-4010
Shannon Whitcombe, prin. Fax 335-4080
Dansville MS 400/6-8
31 Clara Barton St 14437 585-335-4020
Amy Schiavi, prin. Fax 335-4021

Davenport, Delaware
Charlotte Valley Central SD 500/K-12
15611 State Highway 23 13750 607-278-5511
Mark Dupra, supt. Fax 278-5900
www.charlottevalleycs.org
Charlotte Valley S 500/K-12
15611 State Highway 23 13750 607-278-5511
Edgar Whaley, prin. Fax 278-5900

Deer Park, Suffolk, Pop. 28,300
Deer Park UFD 4,400/PK-12
1881 Deer Park Ave 11729 631-274-4000
Elizabeth Marino, supt. Fax 242-6762
www.deerparkschools.org/
Deer Park HS 1,200/9-12
30 Rockaway Ave 11729 631-274-4100
Nanine Cuttitta, prin. Fax 243-4225
Frost MS 1,100/6-8
450 Half Hollow Rd 11729 631-274-4200
James Cummings, prin. Fax 242-0035

De Kalb Junction, Saint Lawrence
Hermon-DeKalb Central SD 400/PK-12
709 E DeKalb Rd 13630 315-347-3442
Ann Adams, supt. Fax 347-3817
Hermon-DeKalb Central S 400/PK-12
709 E DeKalb Rd 13630 315-347-3442
Mark White, prin. Fax 347-3817

Delanson, Schenectady, Pop. 404
Duanesburg Central SD 900/K-12
133 School Rd 12053 518-895-2279
Dr. Mark Villanti, supt. Fax 895-2626
dcs.neric.org
Duanesburg JSHS 500/6-12
163 School Rd 12053 518-895-2355
Wilford LeForestier, prin. Fax 895-9971

Delhi, Delaware, Pop. 2,720
Delhi Central SD 900/K-12
2 Sheldon Dr 13753 607-746-1300
Jack Mulholland, supt. Fax 746-6028
www.delhischools.org
Delaware Academy HS 400/9-12
2 Sheldon Dr 13753 607-746-1281
Judith Byam, prin. Fax 746-1324
Delhi MS 200/6-8
2 Sheldon Dr 13753 607-746-1282
Richard Hughes, prin. Fax 746-1210

SUNY College of Technology Post-Sec.
2 Main St 13753 607-746-4000

Delmar, Albany, Pop. 8,360
Bethlehem Central SD 5,100/K-12
90 Adams Pl 12054 518-439-7098
Leslie Loomis, supt. Fax 475-0352
bcsd.k12.ny.us
Bethlehem Central HS 1,700/9-12
700 Delaware Ave 12054 518-439-4921
Charles Abba, prin. Fax 439-2837
Bethlehem Central MS 1,200/6-8
332 Kenwood Ave 12054 518-439-7460
Jodi Monroe, prin. Fax 475-0092

Depew, Erie, Pop. 15,798
Depew UFD 2,300/K-12
591 Terrace Blvd 14043 716-686-2253
Robert F. DeFilippo, supt. Fax 686-2269
www.depewschools.org/
Depew HS 800/9-12
5201 Transit Rd 14043 716-686-2421
Carol Townsend, prin. Fax 686-2478
Depew MS 800/5-8
5201 Transit Rd 14043 716-686-2440
Joseph D'Amato, prin. Fax 686-2410

Deposit, Delaware, Pop. 1,636
Deposit Central SD 600/K-12
171 2nd St 13754 607-467-5380
Bonnie Hauber, supt. Fax 467-5535
Deposit JSHS 300/7-12
171 2nd St 13754 607-467-2197
John Murphy, prin. Fax 467-5504

DeRuyter, Madison, Pop. 518
De Ruyter Central SD 500/PK-12
711 Railroad St 13052 315-852-3410
Bruce Sharpe, supt. Fax 852-9600
De Ruyter JSHS 300/6-12
711 Railroad St 13052 315-852-3400
David Hubman, prin. Fax 852-9600

De Witt, Onondaga, Pop. 8,244
Jamesville-DeWitt Central SD 2,800/K-12
PO Box 606 13214 315-445-8304
Alice Kendrick, supt. Fax 445-8477
www.jamesvilledewitt.org
Jamesville-DeWitt HS 900/9-12
6845 Edinger Dr 13214 315-445-8340
Paul Gasparini, prin. Fax 445-8307
Other Schools – See Jamesville

Manlius Pebble Hill S 600/PK-12
5300 Jamesville Rd 13214 315-446-2452
Baxter Ball, prin. Fax 446-2620

Dexter, Jefferson, Pop. 1,138
General Brown Central SD 1,500/K-12
PO Box 500 13634 315-639-4711
Stephan Vigliotti, supt. Fax 639-6916
www.gblions.org
Brown JSHS 800/7-12
17643 Cemetery Rd 13634 315-639-6234
Mary Margaret Zehr, prin. Fax 639-3444

Dix Hills, Suffolk, Pop. 26,100
Half Hollow Hills Central SD 9,600/K-12
525 Half Hollow Rd 11746 631-592-3000
Dr. Sheldon Karnilow, supt. Fax 592-3900
www.hhh.k12.ny.us
Candlewood MS 1,000/6-8
1200 Carlls Straight Path 11746 631-592-3300
Andrew Greene, prin. Fax 592-3921
Half Hollow Hills HS East 1,500/9-12
50 Vanderbilt Pkwy 11746 631-592-3100
Al Kindelmann, prin. Fax 592-3907
Half Hollow Hills HS West 1,200/9-12
375 Wolf Hill Rd 11746 631-592-3200
Dr. James Lofrese, prin. Fax 592-3923
Other Schools – See Melville

Five Towns College Post-Sec.
305 N Service Rd 11746 631-424-7000
Upper Room Christian S 300/PK-12
722 Deer Park Rd 11746 631-242-5359
Gregory Eck, prin. Fax 242-5418

Dobbs Ferry, Westchester, Pop. 11,070
Dobbs Ferry UFD 1,300/K-12
505 Broadway 10522 914-693-1506
Debra Kaplan, supt. Fax 693-1787
www.dfsd.org
Dobbs Ferry HS 400/9-12
505 Broadway 10522 914-693-7645
Keith Yi, prin. Fax 693-1115
Dobbs Ferry MS 300/6-8
505 Broadway 10522 914-693-7640
Marjorie Holderman, prin. Fax 693-1115

Greenburgh 11 UFD 300/K-12
PO Box 501 10522 914-693-8500
Sandra Mallah, supt. Fax 693-4029
Greenburgh Eleven HS 9-12
PO Box 501 10522 914-693-8500
Sandra Strang, prin. Fax 693-4029

Long Island University Post-Sec.
555 Broadway 10522 914-693-4500
Masters S 500/5-12
49 Clinton Ave 10522 914-479-6400
Dr. Maureen Fonseca, hdmstr. Fax 693-1230
Mercy College Post-Sec.
555 Broadway 10522 914-674-7600
Our Lady of Victory Academy 400/9-12
565 Broadway 10522 914-693-1633
Sr. Joan Agro, prin. Fax 693-5250

Dolgeville, Herkimer, Pop. 2,095
Dolgeville Central SD 1,000/PK-12
38 Slawson St 13329 315-429-3155
Theodore Kawryga, supt. Fax 429-8473
www.dolgeville.org
Green MSHS 500/7-12
38 Slawson St 13329 315-429-3155
James D. Donnelly, prin. Fax 429-8473

Dover Plains, Dutchess, Pop. 1,847
Dover UFD 1,700/K-12
2368 Route 22 12522 845-832-4500
Dr. Craig Onofry, supt. Fax 832-4511
www.doverschools.org
Dover HS 600/9-12
2368 Route 22 12522 845-832-4520
Michael Tierney, prin. Fax 832-3924
Dover MS 500/6-8
2368 Route 22 12522 845-832-4521
Michael Tierney, prin. Fax 832-3924

Downsville, Delaware
Downsville Central SD 400/K-12
PO Box J 13755 607-363-2100
Robert Mackey, supt.
www.dcseagles.org
Downsville Central S 400/K-12
PO Box J 13755 607-363-2111
Ron Whipple, prin. Fax 363-2105

Dryden, Tompkins, Pop. 1,833
Dryden Central SD 1,700/K-12
PO Box 88 13053 607-844-8694
Mark J. Crawford, supt. Fax 844-4733
www.dryden.k12.ny.us
Dryden HS 600/9-12
PO Box 88 13053 607-844-8694
Richard During, prin. Fax 844-9004
Dryden MS 500/6-8
PO Box 88 13053 607-844-8694
Edmund Walsh, prin. Fax 844-5174

Tompkins Cortland Community College Post-Sec.
PO Box 139 13053 607-844-8211

Dundee, Yates, Pop. 1,645
Dundee Central SD 900/K-12
55 Water St 14837 607-243-5533
Nancy Zimar, supt. Fax 243-7912
www.dundeecs.org
Dundee JSHS 400/7-12
55 Water St 14837 607-243-5534
Eric Sturtz, prin. Fax 243-7912

Dunkirk, Chautauqua, Pop. 12,493
Dunkirk CSD 2,000/K-12
620 Marauder Dr 14048 716-366-9300
J. Richard Rodriguez, supt. Fax 366-9399
www.dunkirk.wnyric.org
Dunkirk HS 700/9-12
75 W 6th St 14048 716-366-9390
David Pulley, prin. Fax 366-0321
Dunkirk MS 500/6-8
525 Eagle St 14048 716-366-9380
David Boyda, prin. Fax 366-9357

East Amherst, Erie
Williamsville Central SD 10,700/K-12
PO Box 5000 14051 716-626-8000
Dr. Howard Smith, supt. Fax 626-8089
www.williamsvillek12.org
Casey MS 900/5-8
105 Casey Rd 14051 716-626-8585
Francis McGreevy, prin. Fax 626-8562
Transit MS 1,000/5-8
8730 Transit Rd 14051 716-626-8701
Jill Pellis, prin. Fax 626-8796
Williamsville East HS 1,000/9-12
151 Paradise Rd 14051 716-626-8404
Neal Miller, prin. Fax 626-8408
Other Schools – See Williamsville

East Aurora, Erie, Pop. 6,418
East Aurora UFD 2,100/K-12
430 Main St 14052 716-687-2302
James Bodziak, supt. Fax 652-8581
www.eaur.wnyric.org/
East Aurora HS 700/9-12
1003 Center St 14052 716-687-2505
Dr. James Hoagland, prin. Fax 687-2552
East Aurora MS 500/6-8
430 Main St 14052 716-687-2453
Jeffrey Banks, prin. Fax 652-8581

Christ the King Seminary Post-Sec.
PO Box 607 14052 585-652-8900

Eastchester, Westchester, Pop. 18,537
Eastchester UFD 2,700/K-12
580 White Plains Rd 10709 914-793-6130
Dr. Robert Siebert, supt. Fax 793-9006
www2.lhric.org/eastchester/
Eastchester HS 700/9-12
2 Stewart Pl 10709 914-793-6130
Dr. Jeffrey Capuano, prin. Fax 793-9000
Eastchester MS 600/6-8
550 White Plains Rd 10709 914-793-6130
Dr. Walter Moran, prin. Fax 793-1699

Tuckahoe UFD
Supt. — See Tuckahoe
Tuckahoe HS 300/9-12
65 Siwanoy Blvd 10709 914-337-5376
Bart Linehan, prin. Fax 337-5168
Tuckahoe MS 200/6-8
65 Siwanoy Blvd 10709 914-337-5376
Carl Albano, prin. Fax 337-5236

East Elmhurst, See New York
NYC Department of Education
Supt. — See New York
IS 227 1,400/5-8
3202 Junction Blvd 11369 718-335-7500
Renee David, prin. Fax 779-7186

Monsignor McClancy Memorial HS 9-12
7106 31st Ave 11370 718-898-3800
James Carey, prin. Fax 898-3929

East Greenbush, Rensselaer, Pop. 3,784
East Greenbush Central SD 4,500/K-12
29 Englewood Ave 12061 518-477-2755
Terrance Brewer, supt. Fax 477-4833
www.egcsd.org
Columbia HS 1,500/9-12
962 Luther Rd 12061 518-207-2000
Michael Kuzdzal, prin. Fax 207-2009
Goff MS 1,100/6-8
35 Gilligan Rd 12061 518-477-2731
Deborah Marcil, prin. Fax 477-2667

East Hampton, Suffolk, Pop. 1,357
East Hampton UFD 2,000/PK-12
4 Long Ln 11937 631-329-4104
Dr. Raymond Gualtieri, supt. Fax 324-0109
www.ehufsd.org
East Hampton HS 1,000/9-12
2 Long Ln 11937 631-329-4130
Dr. Scott Farina, prin. Fax 329-4210
East Hampton MS 500/5-8
76 Newtown Ln 11937 631-329-4116
Dr. Thomas Lamorgese, prin. Fax 329-4187

East Meadow, Nassau, Pop. 37,600
East Meadow UFD
Supt. — See Westbury
East Meadow HS 1,700/9-12
101 Carman Ave 11554 516-228-5331
Mark Scher, prin. Fax 228-5339
Woodland MS 1,300/6-8
690 Wenwood Dr 11554 516-564-6523
James Lethbridge, prin. Fax 564-6519

East Moriches, Suffolk, Pop. 4,021
East Moriches UFD 800/K-8
9 Adelaide Ave 11940 631-878-0162
Dr. Charles Russo, supt. Fax 878-0186
www.eastmoriches.k12.ny.us
East Moriches MS 400/5-8
9 Adelaide Ave 11940 631-878-0162
Robert McIntyre, prin. Fax 874-0096

East Northport, Suffolk, Pop. 20,411
Commack UFD 7,400/K-12
480 Clay Pitts Rd 11731 631-912-2000
Dr. James Feltman, supt. Fax 266-2406
www.commack.k12.ny.us

Other Schools – See Commack

Northport-East Northport UFD
Supt. — See Northport
East Northport MS 700/6-8
1075 5th Ave 11731 631-262-6770
Joanne Kroon, prin. Fax 262-6773

East Norwich, Nassau, Pop. 2,698
Oyster Bay-East Norwich Central SD
Supt. — See Oyster Bay
Vernon S 500/3-8
880 Oyster Bay Rd 11732 516-624-6562
Martin Malone, prin. Fax 624-6522

East Patchogue, Suffolk, Pop. 20,195
South Country Central SD 4,800/PK-12
189 N Dunton Ave 11772 631-730-1510
Dr. Susan Agruso, supt. Fax 286-6394
www.southcountry.org/
Other Schools – See Bellport, Brookhaven

Victory Christian Academy 100/PK-12
1343 Montauk Hwy 11772 631-654-9284
Barbara Seaton, prin. Fax 654-9297

East Rochester, Monroe, Pop. 6,366
East Rochester UFD 1,100/PK-12
222 Woodbine Ave 14445 585-248-6302
Howard Maffucci, supt.
www.erschools.org
East Rochester JSHS 600/5-12
200 Woodbine Ave 14445 585-248-6350
Christopher Barker, prin. Fax 248-6383

East Rockaway, Nassau, Pop. 10,263
East Rockaway UFD 1,200/K-12
443 Ocean Ave 11518 516-887-8300
Arnold Dodge Ph.D., supt. Fax 887-8308
www.eastrockawayschools.org
East Rockaway JSHS 600/7-12
443 Ocean Ave 11518 516-887-8300
William Fortgang, prin. Fax 887-8308

East Setauket, See Setauket
Three Village Central SD 8,000/K-12
PO Box 9050 11733 631-730-4000
Frank Carasiti, supt.
www.3villagecsd.k12.ny.us
Melville HS 1,800/10-12
380 Old Town Rd 11733 631-730-4900
Thomas Colletti, prin. Fax 730-4901
Other Schools – See Setauket, Stony Brook

East Syracuse, Onondaga, Pop. 3,076
East Syracuse-Minoa Central SD 3,700/PK-12
407 Fremont Rd 13057 315-656-7205
Dr. Donna DeSiato, supt. Fax 656-3241
www.esmschools.org
East Syracuse-Minoa Central HS 1,200/9-12
6400 Fremont Rd 13057 315-656-7242
Francis Murphy, prin. Fax 656-4307
Pine Grove MS 900/6-8
6318 Fremont Rd 13057 315-656-7265
Lee Carulli, prin. Fax 656-2530

Bishop Grimes JSHS 600/7-12
6653 Kirkville Rd 13057 315-437-0356
Sr. James Therese Downey, prin. Fax 437-0358

Eden, Erie, Pop. 3,088
Eden Central SD 1,800/K-12
PO Box 267 14057 716-992-3629
Robert Zimmerman, supt. Fax 992-3682
www.edencentral.org/
Eden JSHS 900/7-12
PO Box 267 14057 716-992-3641
Ron Buggs, prin. Fax 992-3652

Edmeston, Otsego
Edmeston Central SD 600/K-12
11 North St 13335 607-965-8931
David Rowley, supt. Fax 965-8942
edmestoncentralschool.net
Edmeston Central S 600/K-12
11 North St 13335 607-965-8931
Martha Winsor, prin. Fax 965-8942

Eggertsville, Erie

Buffalo Academy of the Sacred Heart 400/9-12
3860 Main St 14226 716-834-2101
Barbara Ochterski Ph.D., hdmstr. Fax 834-2944

Elba, Genesee, Pop. 667
Elba Central SD 600/K-12
PO Box 370 14058 585-757-9967
Joan Cole, supt. Fax 757-2713
www.elbacsd.org
Elba JSHS 300/7-12
PO Box 370 14058 585-757-9967
Jason Smith, prin. Fax 757-6683

Eldred, Sullivan
Eldred Central SD 700/K-12
PO Box 249 12732 845-557-6141
Charlotte Gregory, supt. Fax 557-3672
www.eldredschools.org
Eldred Central JSHS 400/7-12
PO Box 249 12732 845-557-6014
Scott Krebs, prin. Fax 557-3672

Elizabethtown, Essex
Elizabethtown-Lewis Central SD 400/K-12
PO Box 158 12932 518-873-6371
Gail S. Else, supt. Fax 873-9552
Elizabethtown-Lewis Central S 400/K-12
PO Box 158 12932 518-873-6371
Amy L. Tyo, prin. Fax 873-9552

Ellenburg Depot, Clinton
Northern Adirondack Central SD 1,100/K-12
PO Box 164 12935 518-594-7060
William Scott, supt. Fax 594-7255
Northern Adirondack JSHS 700/6-12
PO Box 164 12935 518-594-3962
John Coughenour, prin. Fax 594-7255

Ellenville, Ulster, Pop. 3,954
Ellenville Central SD 1,800/K-12
28 Maple Ave 12428 845-647-0100
Lisa Wiles, supt. Fax 647-0105
www.ecs.k12.ny.us
Ellenville HS 600/9-12
28 Maple Ave 12428 845-647-0123
Ronald Chaisson, prin. Fax 647-5972
Ellenville MS 500/5-8
28 Maple Ave 12428 845-647-0126
Glenn Bollin, prin. Fax 647-0230

Ellicottville, Cattaraugus, Pop. 538
Ellicottville Central SD 700/PK-12
5873 Route 219 S 14731 716-699-2368
Patricia Haynes, supt. Fax 699-6017
Ellicottville MSHS 400/6-12
5873 Route 219 S 14731 716-699-2316
Robert Miller, prin.

Elma, Erie
Iroquois Central SD 2,900/K-12
PO Box 32 14059 716-652-3000
Neil Rochelle, supt. Fax 652-9305
www.iroquois.wnyric.org
Iroquois HS 1,000/9-12
PO Box 32 14059 716-652-3000
Dennis Kenney, prin. Fax 995-2440
Iroquois MS 700/6-8
PO Box 32 14059 716-652-3000
Brian Wiesinger, prin. Fax 995-2335

Elmhurst, See New York
NYC Department of Education
Supt. — See New York
IS 5 1,500/6-8
5040 Jacobus St 11373 718-205-6788
Debra Van Nostrandt, prin. Fax 429-6518
Newtown HS 4,100/9-12
4801 90th St 11373 718-595-8400
John Ficalora, prin. Fax 699-8584

Cathedral Prep Seminary 200/9-12
5625 92nd St 11373 718-592-6800
Rev. Joseph Calise, prin. Fax 592-5574

Elmira, Chemung, Pop. 29,928
Elmira CSD 6,900/PK-12
951 Hoffman St 14905 607-735-3000
Dr. Raymond Bryant, supt. Fax 735-3002
www.elmiracityschools.com
Broadway MS 900/6-8
1000 Broadway St 14904 607-735-3300
Brian LeBaron, prin. Fax 735-3309
Davis MS 700/6-8
610 Lake St 14901 607-735-3400
Derek Almy, prin. Fax 735-3409
Elmira Free Academy 1,000/9-12
933 Hoffman St 14905 607-735-3100
Scott Williams, prin. Fax 735-3109
Southside HS 1,200/9-12
777 S Main St 14904 607-735-3200
Christopher Krantz, prin. Fax 735-3209

Arnot-Ogden Medical Center Post-Sec.
600 Roe Ave 14905 607-737-4289
Arnot-Ogden Medical Center Post-Sec.
600 Roe Ave 14905 607-737-4153
Elmira Business Institute Post-Sec.
303 N Main St 14901 800-843-1812
Elmira Christian Academy 100/K-12
235 E Miller St 14904 607-734-7195
David Cook, prin. Fax 734-7195
Elmira College Post-Sec.
1 Park Pl 14901 607-735-1800
Holy Family JHS 200/7-8
1010 Davis St 14901 607-734-0336
Elizabeth Berliner, prin. Fax 734-4977
Notre Dame HS 400/9-12
1400 Maple Ave 14904 607-734-2267
Sr. Mary Walter Hickey, prin. Fax 737-8903

Elmira Heights, Chemung, Pop. 4,011
Elmira Heights Central SD 1,100/K-12
100 Robinwood Ave 14903 607-734-7114
Mary Beth Fiore, supt. Fax 734-7134
www.heightsschools.com
Cohen MS 300/6-8
100 Robinwood Ave 14903 607-734-5078
Terry DeVine, prin. Fax 734-9382
Edison HS 400/9-12
2083 College Ave 14903 607-733-5604
Al Turshman, prin. Fax 737-7976

Elmont, Nassau, Pop. 33,600
Sewanhaka Central HSD
Supt. — See Floral Park
Elmont Memorial HS 2,000/7-12
555 Ridge Rd 11003 516-488-9200
John Capozzi, prin. Fax 488-9213

Elmsford, Westchester, Pop. 4,727
Elmsford UFD 1,000/PK-12
98 S Goodwin Ave 10523 914-592-8440
Dr. Carol Franks-Randall, supt. Fax 592-2181
www.elmsd.org
Hamilton JSHS 500/7-12
98 S Goodwin Ave 10523 914-592-7311
Leonard Mecca, prin. Fax 592-2181

Elwood, Suffolk, Pop. 10,916
Elwood UFD
Supt. — See Greenlawn
Elwood/Glenn HS 700/9-12
478 Elwood Rd 11731 631-266-5410
Vincent Mulieri, prin. Fax 368-5038
Elwood MS 600/6-8
478 Elwood Rd 11731 631-266-5420
Patrick Scarola, prin. Fax 266-3987

Endicott, Broome, Pop. 12,639
Union-Endicott Central SD 4,500/K-12
1100 E Main St 13760 607-757-2811
Dr. James P. Coon, supt. Fax 757-2809
www.uetigers.stier.org
Snapp MS 1,000/6-8
101 S Loder Ave 13760 607-757-2156
Ann Marie Foley, prin. Fax 658-7117
Union-Endicott HS 1,400/9-12
1200 E Main St 13760 607-757-2181
Pamela Sellitto, prin. Fax 757-2535

Endwell, Broome, Pop. 12,602
Maine-Endwell Central SD 2,600/K-12
712 Farm To Market Rd 13760 607-754-1400
Joseph Stoner, supt. Fax 754-1650
www.me.stier.org//main.html
Maine-Endwell HS 800/9-12
750 Farm To Market Rd 13760 607-754-1400
Jason Van Fossen, prin. Fax 786-8209
Maine-Endwell MS 700/6-8
1119 Farm To Market Rd 13760 607-786-8271
Richard Otis, prin. Fax 786-5137

Fabius, Onondaga, Pop. 344
Fabius-Pompey Central SD 900/K-12
1211 Mill St 13063 315-683-5301
Martin Swenson, supt. Fax 683-5827
www.fabiuspompey.org
Fabius-Pompey JSHS 500/6-12
1211 Mill St 13063 315-683-5811
Robert Hughes, prin. Fax 683-5569

Fairport, Monroe, Pop. 5,576
Fairport Central SD 7,100/K-12
38 W Church St 14450 585-421-2004
Barbara Gregory, supt. Fax 421-3421
www.fairport.org
Brown MS 1,000/6-8
665 Ayrault Rd 14450 585-421-2065
David Dunn, prin. Fax 421-2136
Fairport HS 1,600/10-12
1358 Ayrault Rd 14450 585-421-2100
David Paddock, prin. Fax 421-4645
Minerva-Deland JHS 600/9-9
140 Hulburt Rd 14450 585-421-2030
Pat Moriarty, prin. Fax 421-1985
Perrin MS 800/6-8
85 Potter Pl 14450 585-421-2080
Brett Provenzano, prin. Fax 421-2097

Falconer, Chautauqua, Pop. 2,419
Falconer Central SD 1,400/PK-12
2 East Ave N 14733 716-665-6624
Jane R. Fosberg, supt. Fax 665-9265
www.falconer.wnyric.org/
Falconer HS 500/9-12
2 East Ave N 14733 716-665-6624
Charles Nebral, prin. Fax 665-9265
Falconer MS 300/6-8
2 East Ave N 14733 716-665-6624
Judy Roach, prin. Fax 665-9265

Fallsburg, Sullivan
Fallsburg Central SD 1,400/PK-12
PO Box 124 12733 845-434-5884
Ivan Katz, supt. Fax 434-8346
www.fallsburgcsd.net/
Fallsburg HS 700/7-12
PO Box 124 12733 845-434-6800
Mark Plescia, prin. Fax 434-0418

Farmingdale, Nassau, Pop. 8,668
Farmingdale UFD 6,300/K-12
50 Van Cott Ave 11735 631-752-6510
Dr. Roberta A. Gerold, supt.
www.farmingdaleschools.org
Farmingdale HS 1,900/9-12
150 Lincoln St 11735 631-752-6600
Allan Bauer, prin. Fax 454-6196
Howitt MS 1,600/6-8
70 Van Cott Ave 11735 631-752-6525
Luis Pena, prin. Fax 752-7013

Farmingdale SUNY Post-Sec.
2350 Broadhollow Rd 11735 631-420-2000
New Jerusalem Christian Academy 50/1-12
816 Main St 11735 516-249-0955
Alan Brandenburg, prin. Fax 249-0955

Farmingville, Suffolk, Pop. 14,842
Sachem Central SD
Supt. — See Holbrook
Sachem HS East 9-12
177 Granny Rd 11738 631-716-8200
John Aleksak, prin. Fax 716-8207

Faith Academy 200/PK-12
1070 Portion Rd 11738 631-732-7088
Karen Warren, admin. Fax 696-2799

Far Rockaway, See New York
NYC Department of Education
Supt. — See New York
Douglass Academy VI HS 9-12
821 Bay 25th St 11691 718-471-2890
Linda Alfred, prin.
Far Rockaway HS 1,100/9-12
821 Bay 25th St 11691 718-327-6000
Denise Hallet, prin. Fax 327-8836
IS 53 900/6-8
1045 Nameoke St 11691 718-471-6900
Claude Monereau, prin. Fax 471-6955
Knowledge & Power Preparatory Academy VI 6-8
821 Bay 25th St 11691 718-471-6934
Peter Dalton, prin. Fax 471-6938

Beis Medrash Heichal Dovid Post-Sec.
275 Beach 17th St 11691 718-868-2300
Clarke JHS, Beach 112th St 11694 7-8
Ann Cordes, prin. 718-449-9413
Global Business Institute Post-Sec.
1931 Mott Ave 11691 718-327-2220
Mesivta Chaim Shlomo S 200/9-12
257 Beach 17th St 11691 718-868-2300
Rabbi Menachem Gold, prin. Fax 868-0517
Stella Maris HS 500/7-12
140 Beach 112th St 11694 718-634-4994
Geri Martinez, prin. Fax 634-5267

Tichon Meir Moshe S 50/9-12
613 Beach 9th St 11691 718-327-6645
Adina Mandel, prin. Fax 327-1391
Torah Academy HS for Girls 300/9-12
636 Lanett Ave 11691 718-327-1300
Rabbi Michoel Shepard, prin. Fax 327-2315
Yeshiva of Far Rockaway S 200/9-12
802 Hicksville Rd 11691 718-327-7600
Rabbi Aaron Brafman, prin. Fax 327-1430

Fayetteville, Onondaga, Pop. 4,171
Fayetteville-Manlius Central SD
Supt. — See Manlius
Wellwood MS 700/5-8
700 S Manlius St 13066 315-692-1300
John Almonte, prin. Fax 692-1049

Fillmore, Allegany, Pop. 450
Fillmore Central SD 700/K-12
PO Box 177 14735 585-567-2251
David Hanks, supt. Fax 567-2541
www.fillmore.wnyric.org/
Fillmore Central S 700/K-12
PO Box 177 14735 585-567-2289
Kyle Faulkner, prin. Fax 567-2541

Fishers Island, Suffolk
Fishers Island UFD 50/PK-12
PO Box A 06390 631-788-7444
Jeanne Schultz, supt. Fax 788-5562
www.fischool.com
Fishers Island Central S 50/PK-12
PO Box A 06390 631-788-7444
Jeanne Schultz, prin. Fax 788-5562

Floral Park, Nassau, Pop. 15,737
NYC Department of Education
Supt. — See New York
MS 172 1,100/6-8
8114 257th St 11004 718-831-4000
Jeffrey Slivko, prin. Fax 831-4008

Sewanhaka Central HSD 8,600/7-12
77 Landau Ave 11001 516-488-9800
Warren Meierdiercks, supt. Fax 488-7738
www.sewanhaka.k12.ny.us/
Floral Park Memorial HS 1,500/7-12
210 Locust St 11001 516-488-9300
Kathleen Sottile, prin. Fax 488-9214
Sewanhaka HS 1,600/7-12
500 Tulip Ave 11001 516-488-9600
Debra Lidowsky, prin. Fax 488-9215
Other Schools – See Elmont, Franklin Square, New Hyde Park

Florida, Orange, Pop. 2,781
Florida UFD 900/K-12
PO Box 757 10921 845-651-3095
Douglas Burnside, supt. Fax 651-6801
www.floridaufsd.org
Seward Institute 500/6-12
PO Box 757 10921 845-651-4038
Michael Rheaume, prin. Fax 651-7166

Flushing, See New York
NYC Department of Education
Supt. — See New York
Bowne HS 3,600/9-12
6325 Main St 11367 718-263-1919
Howie Kwait, prin. Fax 575-4069
East-West S of International Studies 6-12
4621 Colden St 11355 718-353-0009
Ben Sherman, prin. Fax 353-3772
Flushing HS 2,600/9-12
3501 Union St 11354 718-888-7500
Cornelia Gutwein, prin. Fax 886-4255
IS 25 900/7-8
3465 192nd St 11358 718-961-3480
Joseph Catone, prin. Fax 358-1563
IS 237 1,000/7-9
4621 Colden St 11355 718-353-6464
Joseph Cantara, prin. Fax 460-6427
IS 250 200/5-8
7540 Parsons Blvd 11366 718-591-3015
Marc Rosenberg, prin. Fax 591-3237
Flushing International HS 100/9-12
14480 Barclay Ave 11355 718-463-2348
Joseph Luft, prin. Fax 463-3514
JHS 168 600/7-9
15840 76th Rd 11366 718-591-9000
Judy Gewuerz, prin. Fax 591-2340
JHS 185 800/7-9
14726 25th Dr 11354 718-445-3232
Valerie Sawinski, prin. Fax 359-5352
JHS 189 700/7-8
14480 Barclay Ave 11355 718-359-6676
Cindy Diaz-Burgos, prin. Fax 358-0155
JHS 216 1,400/6-8
6420 175th St 11365 718-358-2005
Reginald Landeau, prin. Fax 358-2070
Harris HS 1,100/9-12
14911 Melbourne Ave 11367 718-575-5580
Tom Cunningham, prin. Fax 575-1366
Kennedy Community HS 400/9-12
7540 Parsons Blvd 11366 718-969-5510
Ira Pernick, prin. Fax 969-5524
Lewis HS 4,100/9-12
5820 Utopia Pkwy 11365 718-357-7740
Jeffrey Scherr, prin. Fax 357-5903
World Journalism Preparatory S 9-12
3465 192nd St 11358 718-935-3330
Cynthia Schneider, prin.

CUNY Queens College Post-Sec.
6530 Kissena Blvd 11367 718-997-5000
Holy Cross HS 1,000/9-12
2620 Francis Lewis Blvd 11358 718-886-7250
Joseph Giannuzzi, prin. Fax 886-7257
Long Island Business Institute Post-Sec.
136-18 39th Ave 11354 718-939-5100
Mesivta Yesodei Yeshurun 100/9-12
14161 71st Ave 11367 718-261-4738
Dr. Yaakov Nierman, prin. Fax 793-1546
Rabbinical Seminary Chofetz Chaim HS 100/9-12
7601 147th St 11367 718-263-1445
Matt Linger, prin. Fax 263-4918

St. Vincent Catholic Medical Center Post-Sec.
17505 Horace Harding Expy 11365 718-357-0500
Vaughn College of Aeronautics and Tech Post-Sec.
8601 23rd Ave 11369 718-429-6600
Windsor S 200/6-12
4160 Kissena Blvd 11355 718-359-8300
James Seery, hdmstr. Fax 359-1876

Fonda, Montgomery, Pop. 779
Fonda-Fultonville Central SD 1,600/K-12
PO Box 1501 12068 518-853-4415
James Hoffman, supt. Fax 853-4461
www.fondafultonvilleschools.org
Fonda-Fultonville HS 600/9-12
PO Box 1501 12068 518-853-3182
David Ziskin, prin. Fax 853-1239
Fonda-Fultonville MS 500/5-8
PO Box 1501 12068 518-853-4747
Elizabeth Donovan, prin. Fax 853-4461

Forest Hills, See New York
NYC Department of Education
Supt. — See New York
Forest Hills HS 3,500/9-12
6701 110th St 11375 718-268-3137
Stephen Frey, prin. Fax 793-7850
JHS 190 1,100/7-9
6817 Austin St 11375 718-830-4970
Marilyn Grant, prin. Fax 830-4960

Bramson O R T College Post-Sec.
6930 Austin St 11375 718-261-5800
Ezra Academy 300/7-12
11945 Union Tpke 11375 718-263-5500
Francine Hirschman, prin. Fax 520-9424
Kew-Forest S 400/K-12
11917 Union Tpke 11375 718-268-4667
Peter Lewis, hdmstr. Fax 268-9121
Rabbinical Seminary of America Post-Sec.
9215 69th Ave 11375 718-268-4700

Forestville, Chautauqua, Pop. 733
Forestville Central SD 600/K-12
12 Water St 14062 716-965-2742
John O'Connor, supt. Fax 965-2117
www.forestville.com
Forestville Central JSHS 400/6-12
4 Academy St 14062 716-965-2711
Charles Leichner, prin. Fax 965-2102

Fort Ann, Washington, Pop. 469
Fort Ann Central SD 600/K-12
1 Catherine St 12827 518-639-5594
Maureen VanBuren, supt. Fax 639-8911
www.fortannschool.org/
Fort Ann S 600/K-12
1 Catherine St 12827 518-639-5594
Dan Ward, prin. Fax 639-8911

Fort Covington, Franklin
Salmon River Central SD 1,600/PK-12
637 County Route 1 12937 518-358-6610
Glenn Bellinger, supt. Fax 358-3492
Salmon River JSHS 700/7-12
637 County Route 1 12937 518-358-6620
John Simons, prin. Fax 358-9787

Fort Edward, Washington, Pop. 3,120
Fort Edward UFD 600/PK-12
220 Broadway 12828 518-747-4594
Stanley Maziejka, supt. Fax 747-4289
www.fortedward.org
Fort Edward S 600/PK-12
220 Broadway 12828 518-747-4529
John Godfrey, prin. Fax 747-4289

Fort Montgomery, Orange, Pop. 1,450
Highland Falls Ft. Montgomery Central SD 1,100/PK-12
21 Morgan Farm Rd 10922 845-446-9575
Dr. Philip Arbolino, supt. Fax 446-3321
www.hffmcsd.org/
O'Neill HS 600/9-12
21 Morgan Rd 10922 845-446-4914
Louis Trombetta, prin. Fax 446-2123
Other Schools – See Highland Falls

Fort Plain, Montgomery, Pop. 2,211
Fort Plain Central SD 900/PK-12
25 High St 13339 518-993-4000
Douglas Burton, supt. Fax 993-3393
www.fortplain.org
Fort Plain JSHS 400/7-12
1 West St 13339 518-993-4000
Deborah Larrabee, prin. Fax 993-2897

Frankfort, Herkimer, Pop. 2,452
Frankfort-Schuyler Central SD 1,200/K-12
605 Palmer St 13340 315-894-5083
Robert Reina, supt. Fax 895-7011
www.frankfort-schuyler.org
Frankfort-Schuyler Central JSHS 600/6-12
605 Palmer St 13340 315-895-7461
Donald Stankavage, prin. Fax 895-4032

Franklin, Delaware, Pop. 384
Franklin Central SD 300/PK-12
PO Box 888 13775 607-829-3551
Gordon Daniels, supt. Fax 829-2101
www.franklincsd.org
Franklin Central S 300/PK-12
PO Box 888 13775 607-829-3551
Jason Thomson, prin. Fax 829-2101

Franklin Square, Nassau, Pop. 29,500
Sewanhaka Central HSD
Supt. — See Floral Park
Carey HS 1,800/7-12
230 Poppy Ave 11010 516-539-9400
Douglas Monaghan, prin. Fax 565-4351

Valley Stream Central HSD
Supt. — See Valley Stream
Valley Stream North JSHS 1,200/7-12
750 Herman Ave 11010 516-564-5510
Dr. Thomas Troisi, prin. Fax 564-5539

Franklinville, Cattaraugus, Pop. 1,778
Franklinville Central SD 900/K-12
31 N Main St 14737 716-676-8029
Dennis Johnson, supt. Fax 676-3779
www.franklinville.wnyric.org
Franklinville JSHS 500/7-12
31 N Main St 14737 716-676-8060
Angelo Melaro, prin. Fax 676-2798

New Life Christian S 50/K-12
6323 Route 16 14737 585-676-2412
Dwight Coords, admin. Fax 676-3995

Fredonia, Chautauqua, Pop. 10,735
Fredonia Central SD 1,800/PK-12
425 E Main St 14063 716-679-1581
Paul J. DiFonzo, supt. Fax 679-1555
www.fredonia.wnyric.org
Fredonia HS 600/9-12
425 E Main St 14063 716-679-1581
Todd Crandall, prin. Fax 672-8687
Fredonia MS 500/6-8
425 E Main St 14063 716-679-1581
Andrew Ludwig, prin. Fax 672-2686

SUNY College at Fredonia 14063 Post-Sec.
716-673-3111

Freeport, Nassau, Pop. 43,519
Freeport UFD 6,900/PK-12
235 N Ocean Ave 11520 516-867-5200
Dr. Eric L. Eversley, supt. Fax 623-4759
www.freeportschools.org
Dodd MS 1,100/7-8
25 Pine St 11520 516-867-5280
John O'Mard, prin. Fax 379-6794
Freeport HS 2,200/9-12
50 S Brookside Ave 11520 516-867-5300
Kimberlee Pierre, prin. Fax 379-7592

De LaSalle S 5-8
87 Pine St 11520 516-379-8660
Roseann Petruccio, prin. Fax 379-8806
Freeport Christian Academy 100/PK-10
50 N Main St 11520 516-546-2020
Tito Mattei, hdmstr. Fax 546-8394

Fresh Meadows, See New York
NYC Department of Education
Supt. — See New York
Queens S of Inquiry 6-12
15840 76th Rd 11366 718-380-6929
Elizabeth Ophals, prin. Fax 380-6809

St. Francis Prep S 2,700/9-12
6100 Francis Lewis Blvd 11365 718-423-8810
Br. Leonard Conway, prin. Fax 224-2108

Frewsburg, Chautauqua, Pop. 1,817
Frewsburg Central SD 1,000/K-12
26 Institute St 14738 716-569-9241
Stephen Vanstrom, supt. Fax 569-4681
frewsburg.wnyric.org
Frewsburg JSHS 500/7-12
26 Institute St 14738 716-569-3255
Kathleen Anderson, prin. Fax 569-4681

Friendship, Allegany, Pop. 1,423
Friendship Central SD 400/PK-12
46 W Main St 14739 585-973-3534
Maureen Donahue, supt. Fax 973-2023
Friendship Central S 400/PK-12
46 W Main St 14739 585-973-3311
John Marshall, prin. Fax 973-2023

Fulton, Oswego, Pop. 11,525
Fulton CSD 3,800/K-12
167 S 4th St 13069 315-593-5510
William Lynch, supt. Fax 598-6351
www.fulton.cnyric.org/
Bodley HS 1,100/9-12
6 Gillard Dr 13069 315-593-5400
Dennis Dumas, prin. Fax 593-5427
Fulton JHS 600/7-8
129 Curtis St 13069 315-593-5440
Mark Slosek, prin. Fax 593-5459

Gainesville, Wyoming, Pop. 292
Letchworth Central SD 1,200/K-12
5550 School Rd 14066 585-493-5450
Joseph Backer, supt. Fax 493-2762
www.letchworth.k12.ny.us/
Letchworth HS 400/9-12
5550 School Rd 14066 585-493-2571
Matthew Wilkins, prin. Fax 493-2762
Letchworth MS 400/5-8
5550 School Rd 14066 585-493-2592
Jonathan Retz, prin. Fax 493-2762

Galway, Saratoga, Pop. 213
Galway Central SD 1,100/K-12
5317 Sacandaga Rd 12074 518-882-1033
Clifford Moses, supt.
www.galwaycsd.org/
Galway HS 400/9-12
5317 Sacandaga Rd 12074 518-882-1221
Paul Jenkins, prin. Fax 882-5250
Galway MS 200/7-8
5317 Sacandaga Rd 12074 518-882-5047
Paul Berry, prin. Fax 882-5850

Garden City, Nassau, Pop. 21,697
Garden City UFD 4,200/K-12
56 Cathedral Ave 11530 516-478-1000
Robert Feirsen, supt. Fax 294-1045
www.gardencity.k12.ny.us
Garden City HS 1,200/9-12
170 Rockaway Ave 11530 516-478-2000
Francis Banta, prin. Fax 294-2639
Garden City MS 1,000/6-8
98 Cherry Valley Ave 11530 516-478-3000
Peter Osroff, prin. Fax 294-0732

Adelphi University Post-Sec.
1 South Ave 11530 516-877-3000

Career Institute of Health & Technology — Post-Sec.
200 Garden City Plz Ste 100 11530 — 516-877-1225
Nassau Community College — Post-Sec.
1 Education Dr 11530 — 516-572-7501
Ultrasound Diagnostic School — Post-Sec.
711 Stewart Ave Ste 200 11530 — 516-248-6060
Waldorf S of Garden City — 400/PK-12
225 Cambridge Ave 11530 — 516-742-3434
Susan Braun, admin. — Fax 742-3457

Garden City Park, Nassau, Pop. 7,437
Mineola UFD
Supt. — See Mineola
Mineola HS — 800/9-12
10 Armstrong Rd 11040 — 516-237-2600
Edward Escobar, prin. — Fax 739-4765

Garnerville, See West Haverstraw
North Rockland Central SD — 8,000/PK-12
65 Chapel St 10923 — 845-942-3000
Brian Monahan, supt. — Fax 942-3047
www.nrcsd.org
Other Schools – See Thiells

Geneseo, Livingston, Pop. 7,809
Geneseo Central SD — 900/K-12
4050 Avon Rd 14454 — 585-243-3450
Dr. Jon Hunter, supt. — Fax 243-9481
Geneseo JSHS — 500/6-12
4050 Avon Rd 14454 — 585-243-3450
Tim Hayes, prin. — Fax 243-9481

SUNY College at Geneseo — Post-Sec.
1 College Cir 14454 — 585-245-5211

Geneva, Ontario, Pop. 13,509
Geneva CSD — 2,500/K-12
649 Exchange St 14456 — 315-781-0400
Dr. Robert Young, supt. — Fax 781-4128
www.genevacsd.org
Geneva HS — 800/9-12
101 Carter Rd 14456 — 315-781-0402
David Pullen, prin. — Fax 781-0695
Geneva MS — 600/6-8
101 Carter Rd 14456 — 315-781-0404
Ann Goldfarb, prin. — Fax 781-0694

De Sales HS — 100/9-12
90 Pulteney St 14456 — 315-789-5111
Rev. Joseph Grasso, prin. — Fax 789-8230
Hobart & William Smith Colleges — Post-Sec.
Pulteney St 14456 — 315-781-3000

Germantown, Columbia
Germantown Central SD — 700/K-12
123 Main St 12526 — 518-537-6280
Patrick Gabriel, supt. — Fax 537-6283
www.germantowncsd.org
Germantown Central HS — 400/7-12
123 Main St 12526 — 518-537-6281
Karol Harlow, prin. — Fax 537-6893

Getzville, Erie, Pop. 2,300

ITT Technical Institute — Post-Sec.
PO Box 327 14068 — 716-689-2200

Ghent, Columbia

Hawthorne Valley S — 300/PK-12
330 Route 21C 12075 — 518-672-7092
Roderick Sipe, admin. — Fax 672-0181

Gilbertsville, Otsego, Pop. 351
Gilbertsville-Mount Upton Central SD — 500/K-12
693 State Highway 51 13776 — 607-783-2207
Douglas Exley, supt. — Fax 783-2254
Gilbertsville-Mount Upton JSHS — 300/7-12
693 State Highway 51 13776 — 607-783-2207
Tonda Dunbar, prin. — Fax 783-2254

Gilboa, Schoharie
Gilboa-Conesville Central SD — 400/K-12
132 Wyckoff Rd 12076 — 607-588-7541
M. Matthew Murray, supt. — Fax 588-6820
Gilboa-Conesville Central S — 400/K-12
132 Wyckoff Rd 12076 — 607-588-7555
Virginia Keegan, prin. — Fax 588-6820

Glen Cove, Nassau, Pop. 26,633
Glen Cove CSD — 2,800/PK-12
150 Dosoris Ln 11542 — 516-759-7217
Dr. Laurence Aronstein, supt. — Fax 759-1679
www.glencove.k12.ny.us
Finley MS — 700/6-8
Forest Ave 11542 — 516-759-7241
Anael Alston, prin. — Fax 759-8774
Glen Cove HS — 1,000/9-12
150 Dosoris Ln 11542 — 516-759-7261
Joseph Hinton, prin. — Fax 759-8778

Solomon Schechter HS of Long Island — 400/6-12
27 Cedar Swamp Rd 11542 — 516-656-5500
Allan Dalfen, prin. — Fax 656-9822
Webb Institute — Post-Sec.
298 Crescent Beach Rd 11542 — 516-671-2213

Glendale, See New York
NYC Department of Education
Supt. — See New York
IS 119 — 1,100/6-8
7401 78th Ave 11385 — 718-326-8261
Mary Aloisio, prin. — Fax 456-9523

Glen Head, Nassau, Pop. 4,488
North Shore Central SD
Supt. — See Sea Cliff
North Shore HS — 800/9-12
450 Glen Cove Ave 11545 — 516-705-0200
Richard Rozakis, prin. — Fax 705-0259
North Shore MS — 600/6-8
505 Glen Cove Ave 11545 — 516-705-0300
Marc Ferris, prin. — Fax 705-0324

Glens Falls, Warren, Pop. 14,108
Glens Falls CSD — 2,500/K-12
15 Quade St 12801 — 518-792-1212
Thomas McGowan, supt. — Fax 792-1538
www.gfsd.org
Glens Falls HS — 900/9-12
10 Quade St 12801 — 518-792-6564
Jeffrey Ziegler, prin. — Fax 743-1164
Glens Falls MS — 600/6-8
20 Quade St 12801 — 518-793-3418
Christopher Reed, prin. — Fax 793-4888

Adirondack Beauty School — Post-Sec.
108 Dix Ave 12801 — 518-745-1646
Glens Falls Hospital — Post-Sec.
100 Park St 12801 — 518-792-3151

Gloversville, Fulton, Pop. 15,283
Gloversville CSD — 3,100/PK-12
PO Box 593 12078 — 518-775-5700
Daniel Connor, supt. — Fax 725-8793
www.gloversvilleschools.org
Gloversville HS — 900/9-12
199 Lincoln St 12078 — 518-725-0671
Robert Orsino, prin. — Fax 773-3674
Gloversville MS — 700/6-8
234 Lincoln St 12078 — 518-773-7351
Peter Glaser, prin. — Fax 773-9865

Goshen, Orange, Pop. 5,437
Goshen Central SD — 2,900/K-12
227 Main St 10924 — 845-294-2410
Roy Reese, supt. — Fax 294-8486
www.goshenschoolsny.org
Goshen Central HS — 900/9-12
222 Scotchtown Rd 10924 — 845-294-2434
Robert Litz, prin. — Fax 294-7696
Hooker MS — 700/6-8
41 Lincoln Ave 10924 — 845-294-2470
Kent Maslin, prin. — Fax 294-2473

Burke Catholic HS — 9-12
80 Fletcher St 10924 — 845-294-5481
Fr. James Byrnes, prin. — Fax 294-7957

Gouverneur, Saint Lawrence, Pop. 4,127
Gouverneur Central SD — 1,700/K-12
133 E Barney St 13642 — 315-287-4870
Christine LaRose, supt. — Fax 287-4736
gcs.neric.org/newweb/
Gouveneur MS — 300/6-8
113 E Barney St 13642 — 315-287-1903
Lauren French, prin.
Gouverneur HS — 500/9-12
113 E Barney St 13642 — 315-287-1900
John Dixon, prin.

Gowanda, Cattaraugus, Pop. 2,716
Gowanda Central SD — 1,500/PK-12
10674 Prospect St 14070 — 716-532-3325
Charles Rinaldi, supt. — Fax 995-2156
www.gowcsd.com
Gowanda HS — 500/9-12
10674 Prospect St 14070 — 716-532-3325
Kimberly Moritz, prin. — Fax 995-2107
Gowanda MS — 500/5-8
10674 Prospect St 14070 — 716-532-3325
David Smith, prin. — Fax 995-2127

Grahamsville, Sullivan
Tri-Valley Central SD — 1,200/PK-12
34 Moore Hill Rd 12740 — 845-985-2296
Nancy George, supt. — Fax 985-0310
tvcs.k12.ny.us
Tri-Valley MS — 200/5-8
34 Moore Hill Rd 12740 — 845-985-2296
Thomas Palmer, prin. — Fax 985-7261
Tri-Valley Secondary S — 600/7-12
34 Moore Hill Rd 12740 — 845-985-2296
Robert Worden, prin. — Fax 985-7261

Grand Island, Erie
Grand Island Central SD — 3,200/K-12
1100 Ransom Rd 14072 — 716-773-8800
Dr. Thomas Ramming, supt. — Fax 773-8843
www.grandisland-cs.k12.ny.us
Connor MS — 800/6-8
1100 Ransom Rd 14072 — 716-773-8830
Bruce Benson, prin. — Fax 773-8983
Grand Island HS — 1,000/9-12
1100 Ransom Rd 14072 — 716-773-8820
Sandra Anzalone, prin. — Fax 773-8951

Granville, Washington, Pop. 2,623
Granville Central SD — 1,500/K-12
58 Quaker St 12832 — 518-642-1051
Daniel Teplesky, supt. — Fax 642-2491
www.granvillecsd.org
Granville JSHS — 800/7-12
58 Quaker St 12832 — 518-642-1051
Daryl Hammond, prin. — Fax 642-4544

Great Neck, Nassau, Pop. 9,605
Great Neck UFD — 6,100/PK-12
345 Lakeville Rd 11020 — 516-773-1405
Dr. Ronald L. Friedman, supt. — Fax 773-6685
www.greatneck.k12.ny.us
Great Neck South HS — 1,200/9-12
341 Lakeville Rd 11020 — 516-773-1600
Randolph Ross, prin. — Fax 773-8269
Great Neck South MS — 800/6-8
349 Lakeville Rd 11020 — 516-773-1660
Dr. James R. Welsch, prin. — Fax 773-1770
Miller Great Neck North HS — 900/9-12
35 Polo Rd 11023 — 516-773-1513
Bernard Kaplan, prin. — Fax 773-8271
Sherman Great Neck North MS — 600/6-8
77 Polo Rd 11023 — 516-773-1570
Barbara Andrews, prin. — Fax 773-1760

North Shore Hebrew Academy — 50/6-8
26 Old Mill Rd 11023 — 516-487-9163
Francine Ballan, prin. — Fax 829-3933

Greene, Chenango, Pop. 1,690
Greene Central SD — 1,400/K-12
40 S Canal St 13778 — 607-656-4161
Gary Smith, supt. — Fax 656-7933
www.greenecsd.org
Greene HS — 500/9-12
40 S Canal St 13778 — 607-656-4161
Terry Heller, prin. — Fax 656-8872
Greene MS — 400/6-8
40 S Canal St 13778 — 607-656-4161
Judy Gorton, prin. — Fax 656-4520

Green Island, Albany, Pop. 2,572
Green Island UFD — 300/K-12
171 Hudson Ave 12183 — 518-273-1422
John McKinney, supt. — Fax 270-0818
www.greenisland.org
Heatly S — 300/K-12
171 Hudson Ave 12183 — 518-273-1422
Erin Peteani, prin. — Fax 270-0818

Greenlawn, Suffolk, Pop. 13,208
Elwood UFD — 2,600/K-12
100 Kenneth Ave 11740 — 631-266-5402
Dr. William Swart, supt. — Fax 266-3834
www.elwood.k12.ny.us
Other Schools – See Elwood

Harborfields Central SD — 3,600/K-12
2 Oldfield Rd 11740 — 631-754-5320
Dr. Janet Ceparano Wilson, supt. — Fax 261-0068
www.harborfieldscsd.net
Harborfields HS — 1,000/9-12
98 Taylor Ave 11740 — 631-754-5360
David Bennardo, prin. — Fax 754-6237
Oldfield MS — 900/6-8
2 Oldfield Rd 11740 — 631-754-5310
Joanne Giordano, prin. — Fax 754-2677

Greenport, Suffolk, Pop. 2,079
Greenport UFD — 700/K-12
720 Front St 11944 — 631-477-1950
Dr. Charles Kozora, supt. — Fax 477-2164
www.greenport.k12.ny.us/
Greenport JSHS — 400/7-12
720 Front St 11944 — 631-477-1950
Michael Comanda, prin. — Fax 477-2164

Greenvale, Nassau

Long Island University-C. W. Post Campus — Post-Sec.
720 Northern Blvd 11548 — 516-299-2000

Greenville, Greene, Pop. 9,528
Greenville Central SD — 1,300/K-12
4976 Route 81 12083 — 518-966-5070
Cheryl Dudley, supt. — Fax 966-8346
www.greenville.k12.ny.us
Greenville HS — 500/9-12
4976 Route 81 12083 — 518-966-5070
Michael Laster, prin. — Fax 966-4054
Greenville MS — 300/6-8
4976 Route 81 12083 — 518-966-5070
Colleen Hall, prin. — Fax 966-5408

Greenwich, Washington, Pop. 1,886
Greenwich Central SD — 1,200/K-12
10 Gray Ave 12834 — 518-692-9542
John McGuire, supt. — Fax 692-9547
www.greenwichcsd.org/
Greenwich JSHS — 600/7-12
10 Gray Ave 12834 — 518-692-9542
Matthias Donnelly, prin. — Fax 692-8503

Greenwood Lake, Orange, Pop. 3,461
Greenwood Lake UFD — 600/K-8
PO Box 8 10925 — 845-477-7395
John Guarracino, supt. — Fax 477-7398
Other Schools – See Monroe

Groton, Tompkins, Pop. 2,432
Groton Central SD — 1,100/K-12
PO Box 99 13073 — 607-898-5301
Dr. Brenda Myers, supt. — Fax 898-4647
www.grotoncs.org
Groton HS — 300/9-12
400 Peru Rd 13073 — 607-898-5802
Eric Hartz, prin. — Fax 898-5824
Groton MS — 300/6-8
400 Peru Rd 13073 — 607-898-5803
Connie Filzen, prin. — Fax 898-5824

Guilderland, Albany
Guilderland Central SD — 5,600/K-12
6076 State Farm Rd 12084 — 518-456-6200
Gregory Aidala Ed.D., supt. — Fax 456-1152
www.guilderlandschools.org/
Farnsworth MS — 1,400/6-8
6072 State Farm Rd 12084 — 518-456-6010
Mary Summermatter, prin. — Fax 456-3747
Other Schools – See Guilderland Center

Guilderland Center, Albany
Guilderland Central SD
Supt. — See Guilderland
Guilderland Center HS — 1,900/9-12
8 School Rd 12085 — 518-861-8591
Michael Piccirillo, prin. — Fax 861-5874

Hadley, Saratoga

King's S — 100/PK-12
6087 State Route 9N 12835 — 518-654-6230
Deborah Hersey, prin. — Fax 654-7310

Hamburg, Erie, Pop. 9,637
Frontier Central SD — 5,500/K-12
5120 Orchard Ave 14075 — 716-926-1711
David Kurzawa, supt. — Fax 926-1776
www.frontier.wnyric.org
Frontier HS — 1,700/9-12
4432 Bay View Rd 14075 — 716-926-1720
Michael Baumann, prin. — Fax 646-2195
Frontier MS — 1,400/6-8
2751 Amsdell Rd 14075 — 716-926-1730
M. Kerry Courtney, prin. — Fax 646-2207

Hamburg Central SD 3,800/PK-12
5305 Abbott Rd 14075 716-646-3220
Dr. Peter Roswell, supt. Fax 646-3209
www.hamburg.wnyric.org/
Hamburg HS 1,100/9-12
4111 Legion Dr 14075 716-646-3302
Michael Gallagher, prin. Fax 646-3028
Hamburg MS 900/6-8
360 Division St 14075 716-646-3250
Geoffrey Grace, prin. Fax 646-6380

Hopevale UFD 100/7-12
3780 Howard Rd 14075 716-648-1930
David Frahm, supt. Fax 648-2361
www.hopevale.com
Hopevale JSHS 100/7-12
3780 Howard Rd 14075 716-648-1930
Cynthia Stachowski, prin. Fax 648-2361

Hilbert College Post-Sec.
5200 S Park Ave 14075 716-649-7900
Immaculata Academy 200/9-12
5138 S Park Ave 14075 716-649-6161
David Christian, prin. Fax 646-1782

Hamilton, Madison, Pop. 3,550
Hamilton Central SD 700/K-12
47 W Kendrick Ave 13346 315-824-3721
Diana Bowers, supt. Fax 824-3745
Hamilton JSHS 400/6-12
47 W Kendrick Ave 13346 315-824-2009
Dana Chapman, prin. Fax 824-3745

Colgate University Post-Sec.
13 Oak Dr 13346 315-228-1000

Hammond, Saint Lawrence, Pop. 294
Hammond Central SD 300/K-12
PO Box 185 13646 315-324-5931
Douglas McQueer, supt. Fax 324-6057
Hammond Central S 300/K-12
PO Box 185 13646 315-324-5931
Douglas McQueer, prin. Fax 324-6057

Hammondsport, Steuben, Pop. 707
Hammondsport Central SD 600/K-12
PO Box 368 14840 607-569-5200
Christopher Brown, supt. Fax 569-5212
www.hammondsportcsd.org
Hammondsport JSHS 300/7-12
8272 Main Street Ext 14840 607-569-5287
Tad Rounds, prin. Fax 569-5279

Hampton Bays, Suffolk, Pop. 7,893
Hampton Bays UFD 1,800/K-12
86 Argonne Rd E 11946 631-723-2100
Joanne Loewenthal, supt. Fax 723-2109
www.hbschools.us
Hampton Bays Secondary S 800/7-12
88 Argonne Rd E 11946 631-723-2110
Dan Nolan, prin. Fax 723-2120

Hancock, Delaware, Pop. 1,139
Hancock Central SD 500/PK-12
67 Education Ln 13783 607-637-1301
Terrance Dougherty, supt. Fax 637-2512
Hancock JSHS 300/5-12
67 Education Ln 13783 607-637-1306
Michael Williams, prin. Fax 637-2512

Hannibal, Oswego, Pop. 527
Hannibal Central SD 1,700/K-12
PO Box 66 13074 315-564-7900
Michael DiFabio, supt. Fax 564-7263
www.hannibalcsd.org/
Hannibal HS 500/9-12
928 Cayuga St 13074 315-564-7910
Danielle Mahoney, prin. Fax 564-7973
Kenney MS 600/5-8
846 Cayuga St 13074 315-564-7955
Robert Wren, prin. Fax 564-7509

Harpursville, Broome
Harpursville Central SD 1,000/PK-12
PO Box 147 13787 607-693-8101
Kathleen M. Wood, supt. Fax 693-1480
www.hcs.stier.org/
Harpursville HS 400/9-12
PO Box 147 13787 607-693-8105
Glenn Hamilton, prin. Fax 693-1480
Harpursville MS 200/6-8
PO Box 147 13787 607-693-8110
Joshua Quick, prin. Fax 693-1480

Harrison, Westchester, Pop. 25,827
Harrison Central SD 3,400/K-12
50 Union Ave 10528 914-835-3300
Louis Wool, supt. Fax 835-2950
www.harrisoncsd.org
Harrison HS 900/9-12
255 Union Ave 10528 914-630-3095
Dr. James Ruck, prin. Fax 835-5471
Klein MS 800/6-8
50 Union Ave 10528 914-630-3033
Scott Fried, prin. Fax 777-1346

Harrisville, Lewis, Pop. 612
Harrisville Central SD 400/K-12
PO Box 200 13648 315-543-2707
Rolf Waters, supt. Fax 543-2360
Harrisville JSHS 200/7-12
PO Box 200 13648 315-543-2920
Mary Curcio, prin. Fax 543-2360

Hartford, Washington
Hartford Central SD 600/PK-12
4704 State Route 149 12838 518-632-5931
Thomas Abraham, supt. Fax 632-5231
www.hartfordcsd.org
Hartford Central HS 400/6-12
4704 State Route 149 12838 518-632-5923
Patrick Sweeney, prin. Fax 632-5231

Hartsdale, Westchester, Pop. 9,587
Greenburgh Central SD 7 1,800/PK-12
475 W Hartsdale Ave 10530 914-761-6000
Dr. Josephine Moffett, supt. Fax 761-2354
www.greenburgh.k12.ny.us
Woodland MS 300/7-8
475 W Hartsdale Ave 10530 914-761-6052
Michael Chambless, prin. Fax 761-7670
Woodlands HS 500/9-12
475 W Hartsdale Ave 10530 914-761-6052
Robert Chakar, prin. Fax 761-7387

Cristo Rey HS 9-12
112 E 106th St, 212-996-7000
William Ford, prin. Fax 427-7444
Maria Regina HS 500/9-12
500 W Hartsdale Ave 10530 914-761-3300
Sr. Danielle Baran, prin. Fax 761-0860
Solomon Schechter S of Westchester 500/6-12
555 W Hartsdale Ave 10530 914-948-8333
Dr. Elliot Spiegel, hdmstr. Fax 948-7979
SUNY Empire State College Post-Sec.
200 N Central Ave 10530 914-948-6206

Hastings on Hudson, Westchester, Pop. 8,021
Greenburgh-Graham UFD 400/1-12
1 S Broadway 10706 914-478-1106
James G. Donlevy, supt. Fax 478-0904
King HS 200/9-12
1 S Broadway 10706 914-478-1161
Dr. Vijay Giles, prin. Fax 478-2321

Hastings-on-Hudson UFD 1,700/K-12
27 Farragut Ave 10706 914-478-6200
Robert Shaps, supt. Fax 478-6209
www.hastings.k12.ny.us
Farragut MS 500/5-8
27 Farragut Ave 10706 914-478-6230
Gail Kipper, prin. Fax 478-6314
Hastings HS 600/9-12
1 Mount Hope Blvd 10706 914-478-6250
Dr. Thomas Fazio, prin. Fax 478-7842

Hauppauge, Suffolk, Pop. 19,750
Hauppauge UFD 4,100/K-12
PO Box 6006 11788 631-265-3630
Patricia Sullivan-Kriss, supt. Fax 265-3649
www.hauppauge.k12.ny.us
Hauppauge HS 1,200/9-12
PO Box 6006 11788 631-265-3630
Dean Schlanger, prin. Fax 979-0926
Hauppauge MS 900/6-8
PO Box 6006 11788 631-265-3630
Maryann Fletcher, prin. Fax 265-9546

Learning Institute for Beauty Sciences Post-Sec.
544 Route 111 11788 631-724-0440

Hawthorne, Westchester, Pop. 4,764

Polytechnic University Post-Sec.
40 Saw Mill River Rd 10532 914-323-2000

Hempstead, Nassau, Pop. 52,829
Hempstead UFD 6,500/PK-12
185 Peninsula Blvd 11550 516-292-7111
Dr. Nathaniel Clay, supt. Fax 292-9471
www.hempsteadschools.org/
Hempstead HS 1,800/9-12
201 President St 11550 516-292-7111
Reginald Stroughn, prin. Fax 292-7770
Schultz MS 1,500/6-8
70 Greenwich St 11550 516-292-7111
Julius Brown, prin. Fax 483-2549

Uniondale UFD
Supt. — See Uniondale
Lawrence Road MS 900/6-8
50 Lawrence Rd 11550 516-918-1500
Dexter Hodge, prin. Fax 565-5023

Franklin Career Institute Post-Sec.
91 N Franklin St 11550 516-481-4444
Hofstra University Post-Sec.
100 Hofstra University 11549 516-463-6600
Learning Institute for Beauty Sciences Post-Sec.
173A Fulton Ave 11550 516-483-6259
Sacred Heart Academy 800/9-12
47 Cathedral Ave 11550 516-483-7383
Sr. Jeanne Ross, prin. Fax 483-1016
Suburban Technical School Post-Sec.
175 Fulton Ave 11550 516-481-6660

Henrietta, Monroe
Rush-Henrietta Central SD 5,700/K-12
2034 Lehigh Station Rd 14467 585-359-5012
Dr. J. Kenneth Graham, supt. Fax 359-5045
www.rhnet.org
Ninth Grade Academy 500/9-9
2000 Lehigh Station Rd 14467 585-359-5550
Greg Lane, prin. Fax 359-5559
Roth MS 800/6-8
4000 E Henrietta Rd 14467 585-359-5108
Denise Zeh, prin. Fax 359-5164
Rush-Henrietta HS 1,400/10-12
1799 Lehigh Station Rd 14467 585-359-5208
Beth Patton, prin. Fax 359-5290
Other Schools – See West Henrietta

Herkimer, Herkimer, Pop. 7,264
Herkimer Central SD 1,300/K-12
801 W German St 13350 315-866-2230
Carol Zygo, supt.
www.herkimercsd.org/
Herkimer JSHS 700/7-12
801 W German St 13350 315-866-2230
Terry Dangle, prin. Fax 866-2234

Herkimer County Community College Post-Sec.
100 Reservoir Rd 13350 315-866-0300

Heuvelton, Saint Lawrence, Pop. 777
Heuvelton Central SD 600/K-12
PO Box 375 13654 315-344-2414
Susan Todd, supt. Fax 344-2349
www.heuvelton.k12.ny.us/
Heuvelton Central S 600/K-12
PO Box 375 13654 315-344-2414
Michael Warden, prin. Fax 344-2349

Hewlett, Nassau, Pop. 6,620
Hewlett-Woodmere UFD
Supt. — See Woodmere
Hewlett HS 1,100/9-12
60 Everit Ave 11557 516-374-8005
David Gutmann, prin. Fax 374-8173
Woodmere MS 800/6-8
1170 Peninsula Blvd 11557 516-374-8068
Claudette Tableman, prin. Fax 374-4571

Abraham HS for Girls 300/9-12
291 Meadowview Ave 11557 516-374-7195
Helen Spirn, prin. Fax 374-2532
Mesivta Ateres Yaakov HS 200/9-12
1170 William St Ste A 11557 516-374-6465
Rabbi Sam Rudansky, prin. Fax 374-1834

Hicksville, Nassau, Pop. 41,400
Hicksville UFD 5,200/PK-12
200 Division Ave 11801 516-733-6600
Maureen K. Bright, supt. Fax 733-6584
www.hicksvillepublicschools.com
Hicksville HS 1,600/9-12
180 Division Ave 11801 516-733-6621
Brijinder Singh, prin. Fax 733-6626
Hicksville MS 1,200/6-8
215 Jerusalem Ave 11801 516-733-6521
Stephen Aronowitz, prin. Fax 733-6528

Holy Trinity Diocesan HS 1,700/9-12
98 Cherry Ln 11801 516-433-2900
Gene Fennell, prin. Fax 433-2827

Highland, Ulster, Pop. 4,492
Highland Central SD 1,900/K-12
320 Pancake Hollow Rd 12528 845-691-1012
John McCarthy, supt. Fax 691-1039
www.highland-k12.org/
Highland HS 600/9-12
320 Pancake Hollow Rd 12528 845-691-1020
David Evans, prin. Fax 691-2096
Highland MS 500/6-8
71 Main St 12528 845-691-1081
Jo Burruby, prin. Fax 691-2074

Highland Residential Center 200/7-12
629 N Chodikee Lake Rd 12528 845-691-6006
Ronald VanKleeck, admin. Fax 691-8726

Highland Falls, Orange, Pop. 3,761
Highland Falls Ft. Montgomery Central SD
Supt. — See Fort Montgomery
Highland Falls MS 300/5-8
PO Box 287 10928 845-446-4761
Ellen Connors, prin. Fax 446-0858

Hillburn, Rockland, Pop. 890
Ramapo Central SD 4,700/K-12
45 Mountain Ave 10931 845-357-7783
Robert MacNaughton Ph.D., supt. Fax 357-5707
www.ramapocentral.org
Other Schools – See Suffern

Hilton, Monroe, Pop. 5,957
Hilton Central SD 4,400/K-12
225 West Ave 14468 585-392-1000
David Dimbleby, supt. Fax 392-1038
www.hilton.k12.ny.us
Hilton HS 1,500/9-12
400 East Ave 14468 585-392-1000
Brian Bartalo, prin. Fax 392-1052
Williams MS 800/7-8
200 School Ln 14468 585-392-1000
Carol Stehm, prin. Fax 392-1054

Hinsdale, Cattaraugus
Hinsdale Central SD 500/K-12
3701 Main St 14743 716-557-2227
Judi McCarthy, supt. Fax 557-2259
www.hinsdale.wnyric.org/working.htm
Hinsdale Central S 500/K-12
3701 Main St 14743 716-557-2227
Laurie Edmonston, prin. Fax 557-2259

Holbrook, Suffolk, Pop. 27,900
Sachem Central SD 12,200/K-12
245 Union Ave 11741 631-471-1336
Dr. Charles Murphy, supt. Fax 471-1341
www.sachem.edu
Seneca MS 800/6-8
850 Main St 11741 631-471-1850
Gemma Salvia, prin. Fax 471-1849
Other Schools – See Farmingville, Holtsville, Lake Ronkonkoma

Holland, Erie, Pop. 1,288
Holland Central SD 1,200/K-12
103 Canada St 14080 716-537-8222
Garry Stone, supt. Fax 537-2453
Holland HS 400/9-12
103 Canada St 14080 716-537-8220
James Biryla, prin. Fax 537-2453
Holland MS 400/5-8
11720 Partridge Rd 14080 716-537-8277
Eric Lawton, prin. Fax 537-2453

Holland Patent, Oneida, Pop. 459
Holland Patent Central SD 1,800/K-12
9601 Main St 13354 315-865-7221
Kathleen Davis, supt. Fax 865-4057
Holland Patent Central HS 600/9-12
9601 Main St 13354 315-865-8154
Gordon Garrett, prin. Fax 865-4069
Holland Patent MS 400/6-8
9601 Main St 13354 315-865-8152
Nancy Nowicki, prin. Fax 865-7243

Holley, Orleans, Pop. 1,750
Holley Central SD 1,300/K-12
3800 N Main Street Rd 14470 585-638-6316
Robert D'Angelo, supt. Fax 638-7409
Holley JSHS 700/7-12
Lynch Rd 14470 585-638-6335
Terrance McCarthy, prin. Fax 638-7925

Hollis, See New York
NYC Department of Education
Supt. — See New York
IS 238 1,700/6-8
8815 182nd St 11423 718-297-9821
Joseph Gates, prin. Fax 658-5288

Midrash L'man Achai 100/7-12
18815 McLaughlin Ave 11423 718-464-2080
Chaim Slomnicki, prin. Fax 464-2070
Yeshiva University HS - Girls 300/9-12
8686 Palo Alto St 11423 718-479-8550
Rochelle Brand, prin. Fax 479-8686

Holtsville, Suffolk, Pop. 14,972
Sachem Central SD
Supt. — See Holbrook
Sagamore MS 900/6-8
57 Division St 11742 631-696-8600
Steve Siciliano, prin. Fax 696-8620
Sequoya MS 900/6-8
750 Waverly Ave 11742 631-207-7100
Frank Panasci, prin. Fax 207-7115

Homer, Cortland, Pop. 3,303
Homer Central SD 2,300/K-12
PO Box 500 13077 607-749-7241
Douglas Larison, supt. Fax 749-2312
www.homercentral.org
Homer HS 700/9-12
80 S West St 13077 607-749-7246
Fred Farah, prin. Fax 749-2312
Homer JHS 400/7-8
58 Clinton St 13077 607-749-1230
Tom Turck, prin. Fax 749-1238

Honeoye, Ontario
Honeoye Central SD 1,000/K-12
PO Box 170 14471 585-229-4125
William Schofield, supt. Fax 229-5633
www.honeoye.org
Honeoye JSHS, PO Box 170 14471 700/6-12
Mike Mead, prin. 585-229-5171

Honeoye Falls, Monroe, Pop. 2,571
Honeoye Falls-Lima Central SD 2,600/K-12
20 Church St 14472 585-624-7000
Dr. Michelle Kavanaugh, supt. Fax 624-7003
www.hflcsd.org/
Honeoye Falls-Lima HS 800/9-12
83 East St 14472 585-624-7051
Kathy Walling, prin. Fax 624-7118
Honeoye Falls-Lima MS 700/6-8
619 Quaker Meeting House Rd 14472 585-624-7100
Shawn Williams, prin. Fax 624-7121

Hoosick, Rensselaer

Hoosac S 100/8-12
PO Box 9 12089 518-686-7331
Richard Lomuscio, hdmstr. Fax 686-3370

Hoosick Falls, Rensselaer, Pop. 3,350
Hoosick Falls Central SD 1,200/K-12
PO Box 192 12090 518-686-7012
Roger Thompson, supt. Fax 686-9060
www.hoosick-falls.k12.ny.us
Hoosick Falls HS 600/7-12
PO Box 192 12090 518-686-7321
Richard Potter, prin. Fax 686-9060

Hopewell Junction, Dutchess, Pop. 1,786
Wappingers Central SD
Supt. — See Wappingers Falls
Jay HS 2,000/9-12
2012 Route 52 12533 845-897-6700
Paul Tobin, prin. Fax 897-6719

Hornell, Steuben, Pop. 8,762
Hornell CSD 1,900/K-12
25 Pearl St 14843 607-324-1302
George Kiley, supt. Fax 324-4060
www.hornell.wnyric.org
Hornell HS 900/7-12
134 Seneca St 14843 607-324-1303
David Glover, prin. Fax 324-3702

St. James Mercy Hospital Post-Sec.
411 Canisteo St 14843 607-324-3900

Horseheads, Chemung, Pop. 6,366
Horseheads Central SD 4,300/K-12
1 Raider Ln 14845 607-739-5601
Ralph Marino, supt. Fax 739-5832
www.horseheadsdistrict.org
Horseheads HS 1,500/9-12
401 Fletcher St 14845 607-739-5601
James Abrams, prin. Fax 795-2505
Horseheads MS 700/7-8
950 Sing Sing Rd 14845 607-739-6356
Jay Hillman, prin. Fax 795-2525

Houghton, Allegany, Pop. 1,740

Houghton Academy 200/7-12
9790 Thayer St 14744 585-567-8115
Philip Stockin, hdmstr. Fax 567-8048
Houghton College Post-Sec.
PO Box 128 14744 585-567-9200

Hudson, Columbia, Pop. 7,145
Hudson CSD 2,100/K-12
215 Harry Howard Ave 12534 518-828-4360
Marilyn Barry, supt. Fax 697-8777
www.hudsoncityschooldistrict.com/
Hudson HS 700/9-12
215 Harry Howard Ave 12534 518-828-4132
Steven Spicer, prin. Fax 697-8418
Hudson MS 700/5-8
102 Harry Howard Ave 12534 518-828-4650
Ryan Groat, prin. Fax 697-8434

Columbia-Greene Community College Post-Sec.
4400 State Route 23 12534 518-828-4181

Hudson Falls, Washington, Pop. 6,864
Hudson Falls Central SD 2,300/K-12
PO Box 710 12839 518-747-2121
Mark Doody, supt. Fax 747-0951
www.hfcsd.org
Hudson Falls HS 700/9-12
80 E La Barge St 12839 518-747-2121
C.J. Hebert, prin. Fax 746-9033
Hudson Falls MS 500/6-8
131 Notre Dame St 12839 518-747-2121
Todd Gonyeau, prin. Fax 746-2790

Huntington, Suffolk, Pop. 18,243
Huntington UFD
Supt. — See Huntington Station
Finley JHS 700/7-8
20 Greenlawn Rd 11743 631-673-2020
John Amato, prin. Fax 425-4746
Huntington HS 1,100/9-12
188 Oakwood Rd 11743 631-673-2003
Dr. Carmela Leonardi, prin. Fax 425-4730

Hebrew Academy S of Academic Excellence 100/PK-12
755 Park Ave 11743 631-425-2426
Rabbi Moshe Labrie, dean Fax 367-0177
Seminary of the Immaculate Conception Post-Sec.
440 W Neck Rd 11743 631-423-0483

Huntington Station, Suffolk, Pop. 30,200
Huntington UFD 4,200/K-12
50 Tower St 11746 631-673-2038
John Finello, supt. Fax 423-3447
www.hufsd.edu/
Other Schools – See Huntington

South Huntington UFD 5,700/K-12
60 Weston St 11746 631-425-5300
Thomas C. Shea Ed.D., supt. Fax 425-5362
www.shufsd.org
Stimson MS 900/7-8
401 Oakwood Rd 11746 631-425-5432
Faye Robins, prin. Fax 425-5449
Whitman HS 1,900/9-12
301 W Hills Rd 11746 631-425-5387
James Polansky, prin. Fax 425-5378

St. Anthony HS 2,300/9-12
275 Wolf Hill Rd 11747 631-271-2020
Br. Gary Cregan, prin. Fax 547-6820

Hurley, Ulster, Pop. 4,644

Coleman HS 200/9-12
430 Hurley Ave 12443 845-338-2750
John P. Traverse, prin. Fax 338-0250

Hyde Park, Dutchess, Pop. 21,230
Hyde Park Central SD 4,500/K-12
PO Box 2033 12538 845-229-4000
Carole Pickering, supt. Fax 229-4056
www.hydeparkschools.org
Haviland MS 1,100/6-8
PO Box 721 12538 845-229-4030
Matt Latvis, prin. Fax 229-2475
Other Schools – See Staatsburg on Hudson

Beauty School of Middletown Post-Sec.
RR 9 12538 845-229-6541
Culinary Institute of America Post-Sec.
1946 Campus Dr 12538 845-451-1368

Ilion, Herkimer, Pop. 8,330
Ilion Central SD 1,700/PK-12
PO Box 480 13357 315-894-9934
Robert Service, supt. Fax 894-2716
www.ilioncsd.org/
Ilion JSHS 800/7-12
1 Golden Bomber Dr 13357 315-895-7471
Renee Rudd, prin. Fax 894-2716

Indian Lake, Hamilton
Indian Lake Central SD 200/K-12
28 W Main St 12842 518-648-5024
Mark Brand, supt. Fax 648-6346
ilcsd.org
Indian Lake Central S 200/K-12
28 W Main St 12842 518-648-5024
David Snide, prin. Fax 648-6346

Irvington, Westchester, Pop. 6,615
Irvington UFD 2,000/K-12
40 N Broadway 10533 914-591-8501
Dr. Kathleen Matusiak, supt. Fax 591-9781
www.irvingtonschools.org
Irvington HS 600/9-12
40 N Broadway 10533 914-591-8648
Dr. Scott Mosenthal, prin. Fax 591-6714
Irvington MS 500/6-8
40 N Broadway 10533 914-591-9494
Joe Witazek, prin. Fax 591-8535

Island Park, Nassau, Pop. 4,741
Island Park UFD 800/K-8
150 Trafalgar Blvd 11558 516-431-8100
Dr. Edward J. Price, supt. Fax 431-7550
www.ips.k12.ny.us
Island Park/Lincoln Orens MS 400/5-8
150 Trafalgar Blvd 11558 516-431-7194
Dr. Thalia Vendetti, prin. Fax 431-7550

Islip, Suffolk, Pop. 18,924
Islip UFD 3,600/K-12
215 Main St 11751 631-859-2200
Alan Van Cott, supt. Fax 859-2224
www.islipufsd.org/
Islip HS 1,100/9-12
2508 Union Blvd 11751 631-859-2234
Ellen Rossman, prin. Fax 859-2227
Islip MS 900/6-8
211 Main St 11751 631-859-2274
Timothy Martin, prin. Fax 859-2277

Islip Terrace, Suffolk, Pop. 5,530
East Islip UFD 5,100/PK-12
1 Craig B Gariepy Ave 11752 631-224-2000
Dennis P. Maloney, supt. Fax 581-1617
www.eischools.org
East Islip HS 1,600/9-12
1 Redmen St 11752 631-224-2100
Miriam Flynn, prin. Fax 581-4410
East Islip MS 900/6-8
100 Redmen St 11752 631-224-2170
Mark Bernard, prin. Fax 859-3745

Ithaca, Tompkins, Pop. 29,766
Ithaca CSD 5,500/PK-12
400 Lake St 14850 607-274-2101
Dr. Judith Pastel, supt. Fax 274-2271
www.icsd.k12.ny.us
Boynton MS 600/6-8
1601 N Cayuga St 14850 607-274-2241
Jason Trumble, prin. Fax 274-2357
De Witt MS 600/6-8
560 Warren Rd 14850 607-257-3222
Ronald Acerra, prin. Fax 266-3502
Ithaca HS 1,600/9-12
1401 N Cayuga St 14850 607-274-2145
Joe Wilson, prin. Fax 277-3061

Cornell University Post-Sec.
410 Thurston Ave 14850 607-255-2000
Ithaca College Post-Sec.
953 Danby Rd 14850 607-274-3011

Jackson Heights, See New York
NYC Department of Education
Supt. — See New York
IS 145 1,900/6-8
3334 80th St 11372 718-457-1242
Delores Beckham, prin. Fax 335-0601
IS 230 1,100/6-8
7310 34th Ave 11372 718-335-7648
Sharon Terry, prin. Fax 335-7513

Garden S 400/PK-12
3316 79th St 11372 718-335-6363
Dr. Richard Marotta, hdmstr. Fax 565-1169
Plaza College Post-Sec.
7409 37th Ave 11372 718-779-1430

Jamaica, See New York
NYC Department of Education
Supt. — See New York
Business/Computer Applications S 500/9-12
20701 116th Ave 11411 718-978-2807
Raymond H. Warmsley, prin. Fax 978-3402
Edison Career & Tech HS Vo/Tech
16565 84th Ave 11432 718-297-6580
Ilona S. Posner, prin. Fax 658-0365
Hillcrest HS 3,200/9-12
16005 Highland Ave 11432 718-658-5407
Steven Duch, prin. Fax 739-5137
Humanities & the Arts Magnet HS 500/9-12
20701 116th Ave 11411 718-978-2135
Mercedes Qualls, prin. Fax 978-2309
Jamaica HS 2,400/9-12
16701 Gothic Dr 11432 718-739-5942
Jay Dickler, prin. Fax 739-4826
HS for Law Enforcement & Public Safety 400/9-12
11625 Guy R Brewer Blvd 11434 718-977-4800
Diahann E. Malcolm, dir. Fax 977-4802
JHS 8 1,000/6-8
10835 167th St 11433 718-739-6883
John Murphy, prin. Fax 526-2727
JHS 72 800/6-8
13325 Guy R Brewer Blvd 11434 718-723-6200
Chandra Williams, prin. Fax 527-1675
JHS 217 1,300/6-8
8505 144th St 11435 718-657-1120
Jeannette Reed, prin. Fax 291-3668
Law 500/9-12
20701 116th Ave 11411 718-978-6432
Carole Kelly, prin. Fax 978-6749
Martin HS 1,600/9-12
15610 Baisley Blvd 11434 718-528-2920
Anthony Cromer, prin. Fax 276-1846
Math Science Research & Tech Magnet HS 500/9-12
20701 116th Ave 11411 718-978-1837
Andrea Holt, prin. Fax 978-2063
Queens Gateway to the Health Sciences 600/7-12
15091 87th Rd 11432 718-739-8080
Cynthia Edwards, prin. Fax 739-8778
Queens HS for Science 300/9-12
9450 159th St 11451 718-657-3181
Jie Zhang, prin. Fax 657-2579
York Early College Academy 6-12
13325 Guy R Brewer Blvd 11434 718-978-1127
Deborah Burnett, prin. Fax 978-1994
Young Womens Leadership S 7-12
10920 Union Hall St 11433 718-725-0402
Avionne Gumbs, prin. Fax 725-0390

Al-Iman S 300/PK-12
8989 Van Wyck Expy 11435 718-297-6520
Sr. Iman Dakmak-Rakka, prin. Fax 658-5530
Allen School Post-Sec.
16318 Jamaica Ave 11432 718-291-2200
Archbishop Molloy HS 1,500/9-12
8353 Manton St 11435 718-441-2100
Br. Roy George, prin. Fax 849-8251
CUNY York College Post-Sec.
9420 Guy R Brewer Blvd 11451 718-262-2000
Jon Louis School of Beauty Post-Sec.
9114 Merrick Blvd 11432 718-658-6240
Louis Academy 1,000/9-12
17621 Wexford Ter 11432 718-297-2120
Sr. Kathleen McKinney, prin. Fax 739-0037
Machon Academy 200/9-12
13906 86th Ave 11435 718-658-1862
Rabbi Yitzchok Young, prin. Fax 658-1804
Nail Academy Post-Sec.
16204 Jamaica Ave 11432 718-297-6330

New York Automotive & Diesel Institute — Post-Sec.
17818 Liberty Ave 11433 — 718-361-1300
St. John's University — Post-Sec.
8000 Utopia Pkwy 11439 — 718-990-6161

Jamestown, Chautauqua, Pop. 30,381
Jamestown CSD — 5,000/PK-12
201 E 4th St 14701 — 716-483-4420
Raymond Fashano, supt. — Fax 483-4421
www.jamestown.wnyric.org
Jamestown HS — 1,400/9-12
350 E 2nd St 14701 — 716-483-3470
Joseph Yelich, prin. — Fax 483-4399
Jefferson MS — 500/5-8
195 Martin Rd 14701 — 716-483-4411
Carm Proctor, prin. — Fax 483-4273
Persell MS — 500/5-8
375 Baker St 14701 — 716-483-4406
Philip Cammarata, prin. — Fax 483-4417
Washington MS — 600/5-8
159 Buffalo St 14701 — 716-483-4413
Daniel Bracey, prin. — Fax 483-4268

Southwestern Central SD — 1,700/K-12
600 Hunt Rd 14701 — 716-484-1136
Daniel George, supt. — Fax 488-2442
swcs.wnyric.org/
Southwestern HS — 600/9-12
600 Hunt Rd 14701 — 716-664-6273
Jon Peterson, prin. — Fax 484-1167
Southwestern MS — 400/6-8
600 Hunt Rd 14701 — 716-664-6270
Gregory Paterniti, prin. — Fax 487-0855

Bethel Baptist Christian Academy — 100/K-12
200 Hunt Rd 14701 — 716-484-7420
Clarence Lee, admin. — Fax 484-0087
Jamestown Business College — Post-Sec.
PO Box 429 14702 — 716-664-5100
Jamestown Community College — Post-Sec.
PO Box 20 14702 — 716-665-5220
Woman's Christian Assoc. Hospital — Post-Sec.
207 Foote Ave 14701 — 716-664-8110

Jamesville, Onondaga
Jamesville-DeWitt Central SD
Supt. — See De Witt
Jamesville-DeWitt MS — 900/5-8
6280 Randall Rd 13078 — 315-445-8360
Jeffrey Craig, prin. — Fax 445-8421

Jasper, Steuben
Jasper-Troupsburg Central SD — 600/PK-12
PO Box 81 14855 — 607-792-3675
Chad Groff, supt. — Fax 792-3749
Jasper-Troupsburg JSHS — 300/7-12
PO Box 81 14855 — 607-792-3675
Mary Vanetten, prin. — Fax 792-3749

Jefferson, Schoharie
Jefferson Central SD — 300/K-12
1332 State Route 10 12093 — 607-652-7821
Carl Mummenthey, supt. — Fax 652-7806
www.jeffersoncs.org
Jefferson Central S — 300/K-12
1332 State Route 10 12093 — 607-652-7821
Carl Mummenthey, prin. — Fax 652-7806

Jeffersonville, Sullivan, Pop. 412
Sullivan West Central SD — 900/K-12
PO Box 308 12748 — 845-482-4610
Alan Derry, supt.
www.swcsd.org/
Other Schools – See Lake Huntington

Jericho, Nassau, Pop. 13,141
Jericho UFD — 3,200/K-12
99 Old Cedar Swamp Rd 11753 — 516-203-3600
Henry Grishman, supt. — Fax 933-2047
www.jerichoschools.org
Jericho HS — 1,100/9-12
99 Old Cedar Swamp Rd 11753 — 516-203-3610
Joe Prisinzano, prin. — Fax 681-2895
Jericho MS — 800/6-8
99 Old Cedar Swamp Rd 11753 — 516-203-3620
Donald Gately, prin. — Fax 681-8984

Johnson City, Broome, Pop. 14,955
Johnson City Central SD — 2,600/K-12
666 Reynolds Rd 13790 — 607-763-1230
Mary Kay Frys, supt. — Fax 729-2767
www.jcschools.com
Johnson City HS — 800/9-12
666 Reynolds Rd 13790 — 607-763-1256
Jackie O'Donnell, prin. — Fax 763-1211
Johnson City MS — 600/6-8
601 Columbia Dr 13790 — 607-763-1240
Margaret Kucko, prin. — Fax 763-1297

Davis College — Post-Sec.
400 Riverside Dr 13790 — 607-729-1581
St. James MS — 200/4-8
143 Main St 13790 — 607-797-5444
George Clancy, prin. — Fax 797-6794
United Health Services Hospital — Post-Sec.
33-57 Harrison St 13790 — 607-763-6000

Johnstown, Fulton, Pop. 8,572
Johnstown CSD — 1,900/PK-12
2 Wright Dr Ste 101 12095 — 518-762-4611
John Whelan, supt. — Fax 762-6379
www.johnstownschools.org/
Johnstown HS — 600/9-12
2 Wright Dr 12095 — 518-762-4661
Michael Beatty, prin. — Fax 736-1489
Knox JHS — 300/7-8
400 S Perry St 12095 — 518-762-3711
David Carr, prin. — Fax 762-2775

Fulton-Montgomery Community College — Post-Sec.
2805 State Highway 67 12095 — 518-762-4651

Jordan, Onondaga, Pop. 1,346
Jordan-Elbridge Central SD — 1,700/K-12
PO Box 902 13080 — 315-689-8500
Marilyn Dominick, supt. — Fax 689-0084
www.jecsd.org
Jordan-Elbridge HS — 600/9-12
PO Box 901 13080 — 315-689-8510
David Zehner, prin. — Fax 689-1985
Jordan-Elbridge MS — 400/6-8
PO Box 1150 13080 — 315-689-8520
David Shafer, prin. — Fax 689-6524

Jordanville, Herkimer

Holy Trinity Orthodox Seminary — Post-Sec.
PO Box 36 13361 — 315-858-0945

Katonah, Westchester

Harvey S — 300/6-12
260 Jay St 10536 — 914-232-3161
Barry Fenstermacher, prin. — Fax 232-2986
Montfort Academy — 9-12
99 Valley Rd 10536 — 914-767-0325
Dave Petrillo, prin.

Keene Valley, Essex
Keene Central SD — 200/K-12
PO Box 67 12943 — 518-576-4555
Cynthia Ford-Johnston, supt. — Fax 576-4599
Keene Central S — 200/K-12
PO Box 67 12943 — 518-576-4555
Cynthia Ford-Johnston, prin. — Fax 576-4599

Kendall, Orleans
Kendall Central SD — 1,000/K-12
1932 Kendall Rd 14476 — 585-659-2741
Dr. Michael O'Laughlin, supt. — Fax 659-8903
www.monroe2boces.org/kendal
Kendall JSHS — 500/7-12
16887 Roosevelt Hwy 14476 — 585-659-2706
Carol D'Agostino, prin. — Fax 659-8988

Kenmore, Erie, Pop. 15,555
Kenmore-Tonawanda UFSD
Supt. — See Buffalo
Kenmore MS — 700/6-8
155 Delaware Rd 14217 — 716-874-8403
Elaine Thomas, prin. — Fax 874-8650

Mt. St. Mary Academy — 300/9-12
3756 Delaware Ave 14217 — 716-877-1358
Dawn Riggie, prin. — Fax 877-0548
St. Joseph Collegiate Institute — 900/9-12
845 Kenmore Ave 14223 — 716-874-4024
Robert Scott, prin. — Fax 874-4956

Keuka Park, Yates

Keuka College — Post-Sec.
PO Box 98 14478 — 315-536-4411

Kew Garden Hills, See New York

Shaarey B'nos Chayil - Shevach HS — 200/9-12
7509 Main St, — 718-263-0525
Kalman Scheinwald, dir. — Fax 263-3759

Kew Gardens, See New York

Yeshiva Shaar Hatorah-Grodno — 100/9-12
11706 84th Ave 11418 — 718-846-1940
Rabbi Azriel Hoschander, prin. — Fax 850-7916
Yeshiva Tifereth Moshe Dov Revel Center — 500/4-8
8306 Abingdon Rd 11415 — 718-846-7300
Rabbi Yaakov May, prin. — Fax 441-3962

Kings Park, Suffolk, Pop. 17,773
Kings Park Central SD — 4,000/K-12
101 Church St 11754 — 631-269-3210
Dr. Mary DeRose, supt. — Fax 269-0750
www.kpcsd.k12.ny.us
Kings Park HS — 1,200/9-12
200 Route 25a 11754 — 631-269-3245
Thomas Fasano, prin. — Fax 269-7472
Rogers MS — 1,000/6-8
97 Old Dock Rd 11754 — 631-269-3269
Ralph Cartisano, prin. — Fax 269-3282

Kings Point, Nassau, Pop. 5,257

United States Merchant Marine Academy — Post-Sec.
300 Steamboat Rd 11024 — 516-773-5000

Kingston, Ulster, Pop. 23,067
Kingston CSD — 8,000/PK-12
61 Crown St 12401 — 845-339-3000
Gerard Gretzinger, supt. — Fax 339-2249
www.kingstoncityschools.org/
Bailey MS — 1,000/6-8
Merilina Ave Ext 12401 — 845-338-6390
Alvin Goren, prin. — Fax 338-6312
Kingston HS — 2,400/9-12
403 Broadway 12401 — 845-331-1970
Marie Anderson, prin. — Fax 331-1628
Other Schools – See Lake Katrine

Gloden Hall Health Care Center — Post-Sec.
Golden Hill Dr 12401 — 845-339-4540

Lackawanna, Erie, Pop. 18,175
Lackawanna CSD — 1,900/PK-12
245 S Shore Blvd 14218 — 716-827-6767
Paul G. Hashem, supt. — Fax 827-6710
www.lackawannaschools.org
Lackawanna HS — 600/9-12
550 Martin Rd 14218 — 716-827-6727
Peter Hazzan, prin. — Fax 827-6724
Lackawanna MS — 300/7-8
550 Martin Rd 14218 — 716-827-6704
Michael Jakubowski, prin. — Fax 827-6784

Baker Hall S — 100/7-12
777 Ridge Rd 14218 — 716-828-9737
Nancy Pankow, dir. — Fax 828-9798

La Fargeville, Jefferson
La Fargeville Central SD — 600/K-12
PO Box 138 13656 — 315-658-2241
Susan Whitney, supt. — Fax 658-4223
www.lafargevillecsd.org
La Fargeville Central HS — 300/7-12
PO Box 138 13656 — 315-658-2241
Kisun Peters, prin. — Fax 658-4223

La Fayette, Onondaga
La Fayette Central SD — 1,000/K-12
5955 US Route 20 13084 — 315-677-9728
Mark Mondanaro, supt. — Fax 677-3372
www.lafayetteschools.com
La Fayette JSHS — 500/7-12
3122 US Route 11 13084 — 315-677-5506
Paula Cowling, prin. — Fax 677-5507

Lagrangeville, Dutchess
Arlington Central SD
Supt. — See Poughkeepsie
Arlington HS — 3,100/9-12
1157 Route 55 12540 — 845-486-4860
Thomas Brooks, prin. — Fax 486-4879
Lagrange MS — 900/6-8
110 Stringham Rd 12540 — 845-486-4880
Eric Schetter, prin. — Fax 486-8863
Union Vale MS — 1,000/6-8
1657 E Noxon Rd 12540 — 845-223-8600
Steven Kerins, prin.

Lake George, Warren, Pop. 991
Lake George Central SD — 1,100/K-12
381 Canada St 12845 — 518-668-5456
Bruce Levin, supt. — Fax 668-2285
www.lkgeorge.org
Lake George JSHS — 600/7-12
381 Canada St 12845 — 518-668-5452
David Eagle, prin. — Fax 668-2285

Lake Grove, Suffolk, Pop. 10,670

Lake Grove School — Post-Sec.
PO Box 712 11755 — 888-585-9007

Lake Huntington, Sullivan
Sullivan West Central SD
Supt. — See Jeffersonville
Sullivan West JSHS — 500/7-12
PO Box 309 12752 — 845-932-8401
Rod McLaughlin, prin.

Lake Katrine, Ulster, Pop. 1,998
Kingston CSD
Supt. — See Kingston
Miller MS — 1,000/6-8
65 Fording Place Rd 12449 — 845-382-2960
Robert Pritchard, prin. — Fax 382-6069

Lake Luzerne, Warren, Pop. 2,042
Hadley-Luzerne Central SD — 1,000/K-12
27 Ben Rosa Park 12846 — 518-696-2112
Irwin Sussman, supt. — Fax 696-5402
www.hlcs.org
Hadley-Luzerne HS — 300/9-12
273 Lake Ave 12846 — 518-696-2112
Beecher Baker, prin. — Fax 696-2356
Townsend MS — 500/3-8
27 Hyland Dr 12846 — 518-696-2378
Patrick Cronin, prin. — Fax 696-2485

Lake Placid, Essex, Pop. 2,757
Lake Placid Central SD — 800/K-12
50 Cummins Rd 12946 — 518-523-2475
Dr. Ernest Stretton, supt. — Fax 523-4971
lakeplacidcsd.net
Lake Placid JSHS — 500/6-12
34 School St 12946 — 518-523-2474
Dr. David Messner, prin. — Fax 523-2896

Mountain Lake Children's Residence — Post-Sec.
50 Riverside Dr 12946 — 888-585-9007
National Sports Academy — 100/8-12
821 Mirror Lake Dr 12946 — 518-523-3460
Dave Wenn, hdmstr. — Fax 523-3488
North Country S — 100/4-9
PO Box 187 12946 — 518-523-9329
Libby Doan, dean — Fax 523-4858
Northwood S — 200/8-12
PO Box 1070 12946 — 518-523-3357
Edward Good, hdmstr. — Fax 523-3405

Lake Ronkonkoma, Suffolk, Pop. 18,997
Sachem Central SD
Supt. — See Holbrook
Sachem HS North — 2,300/9-12
212 Smith Rd 11779 — 631-471-1400
James Nolan, prin. — Fax 471-1408
Samoset MS — 800/6-8
51 School St 11779 — 631-471-1700
Mary Cavanaugh, prin. — Fax 471-1706

Lancaster, Erie, Pop. 11,490
Lancaster Central SD — 5,800/K-12
177 Central Ave 14086 — 716-686-3201
Thomas Markle, supt. — Fax 686-3350
lancasterschools.org
Lancaster HS — 2,000/9-12
1 Forton Dr 14086 — 716-686-3250
Dan Paveljack, prin. — Fax 686-3347
Lancaster MS — 1,000/7-8
148 Aurora St 14086 — 716-686-3220
Peter Kruszynski, prin. — Fax 686-3223

St. Mary HS — 9-12
142 Laverack Ave 14086 — 716-683-4824
Dr. Joseph Casimino, prin. — Fax 683-4996

Lansing, Tompkins, Pop. 3,417
Lansing Central SD — 1,300/K-12
264 Ridge Rd 14882 — 607-533-4294
Dr. Mark Lewis, supt. — Fax 533-3602
www.lansingschools.org
Lansing HS — 500/9-12
300 Ridge Rd 14882 — 607-533-4652
Michelle Stone, prin. — Fax 533-4612

Lansing MS 400/5-8
6 Ludlowville Rd 14882 607-533-4271
James Thomas, prin. Fax 533-3543

Larchmont, Westchester, Pop. 6,487
Mamaroneck UFD
Supt. — See Mamaroneck
Hommocks MS 1,100/6-8
10 Hommocks Rd 10538 914-220-3300
Dr. Seth Weitzman, prin. Fax 220-3315

French-American S of NY 700/PK-10
111 Larchmont Ave 10538 914-834-3002
Robert M. Leonhardt, hdmstr. Fax 834-1284

Latham, Albany, Pop. 10,131
North Colonie Central SD 5,600/K-12
91 Fiddlers Ln Ste 1 12110 518-785-8591
Randy A. Ehrenberg, supt. Fax 785-8502
www.northcolonie.org
Shaker HS 2,000/9-12
445 Watervliet Shaker Rd 12110 518-785-5511
Richard Murphy, prin. Fax 783-5905
Shaker JHS 900/7-8
475 Watervliet Shaker Rd 12110 518-785-1341
Russell Moore, prin. Fax 783-8877

Mildred Elley the College for Careers Post-Sec.
800 New Loudon Rd Ste 5120 12110 518-786-0855
SUNY Empire State College Post-Sec.
21 British American Blvd 12110 518-783-6203

Laurelton, See New York
NYC Department of Education
Supt. — See New York
IS 231 1,500/7-8
14500 Springfield Blvd 11413 718-276-5140
Robert Brisbane, prin. Fax 276-2259

Laurens, Otsego, Pop. 263
Laurens Central SD 400/K-12
PO Box 301 13796 607-432-2050
Romona Wenck, supt. Fax 432-4388
laurenscs.org
Laurens Central S 400/K-12
PO Box 301 13796 607-432-2050
Bill Dorritie, prin. Fax 432-4388

Lawrence, Nassau, Pop. 6,501
Lawrence UFD 3,500/PK-12
PO Box 477 11559 516-295-7030
Dr. John Fitzsimons, supt. Fax 239-7164
www.lawrence.org/
Lawrence MS 800/6-8
195 Broadway 11559 516-295-7000
George Akst, prin. Fax 295-7196
Other Schools – See Cedarhurst

Hebrew Academy of Five Towns MS 300/6-8
44 Frost Ln 11559 516-569-6352
Naomi Lippman, prin. Fax 569-6457
Rambam Mesivta 200/9-12
15 Frost Ln 11559 516-371-5824
Rabbi Yotav Eliach, prin. Fax 371-4706
Shor Yoshuv Institute Post-Sec.
1 Cedarlawn Ave 11559 516-239-9002

Le Roy, Genesee, Pop. 4,290
Le Roy Central SD 1,400/K-12
2 Trigon Park 14482 585-768-8133
Mary Jane Brooke, supt. Fax 768-8929
www.leroy.k12.ny.us
Le Roy JSHS 700/7-12
9300 S Street Rd 14482 585-768-8131
Charles Herring, prin. Fax 768-8929

Levittown, Nassau, Pop. 53,000
Island Trees UFD 2,800/K-12
74 Farmedge Rd 11756 516-520-2100
James Parla, supt. Fax 520-2113
www.islandtrees.org
Island Trees HS 900/9-12
59 Straight Ln 11756 516-520-2135
William Kealy, prin. Fax 520-9199
Island Trees MS 900/5-8
45 Wantagh Ave 11756 516-520-2157
Jon Segerdahl, prin. Fax 520-2168

Levittown UFD 7,800/K-12
150 Abbey Ln 11756 516-520-8300
Herman Sirois, supt. Fax 520-8314
www.levittownschools.com
Division Avenue HS 1,100/9-12
120 Division Ave 11756 516-520-8350
Kathleen Valentino, prin. Fax 520-8364
MacArthur HS 1,300/9-12
3369 N Jerusalem Rd 11756 516-520-8450
John Bifolco, prin. Fax 520-8466
Salk MS 1,000/6-8
3359 N Jerusalem Rd 11756 516-520-8470
Debbie Rifkin, prin. Fax 520-8479
Wisdom Lane MS 900/6-8
120 Center Ln 11756 516-520-8370
Dr. Robert Tymann, prin. Fax 520-8380

Hunter Business School Post-Sec.
3601 Hempstead Tpke 11756 516-796-1000
Learning Institute for Beauty Sciences Post-Sec.
2981 Hempstead Tpke 11756 516-731-8300

Liberty, Sullivan, Pop. 3,923
Liberty Central SD 1,800/PK-12
115 Buckley St 12754 845-292-6990
Edward Rhine, supt. Fax 292-1164
www.libertyk12.org
Liberty JSHS 800/8-12
125 Buckley St 12754 845-292-5400
Jack Strassman, prin. Fax 292-7262

Lido Beach, Nassau, Pop. 2,786
Long Beach CSD 4,400/PK-12
235 Lido Blvd 11561 516-897-2104
Dr. Robert Greenberg, supt. Fax 897-2107
www.lbeach.org
Long Beach HS 1,400/9-12
322 Lagoon Dr W 11561 516-897-2012
Nicholas Restivo, prin. Fax 897-2052
Long Beach MS 1,000/6-8
239 Lido Blvd 11561 516-897-2166
Joane Tom, prin. Fax 897-2145

Lima, Livingston, Pop. 2,425

Lima Christian S 200/K-12
1574 Rochester St 14485 585-624-3841
Ralph Dewey, prin. Fax 624-8293

Lincolndale, Westchester
Somers Central SD
Supt. — See Somers
Somers HS 900/9-12
PO Box 640 10540 914-248-8585
Irene Perrella, prin. Fax 248-8186

Ives S 200/7-11
PO Box 600 10540 914-248-7474
Dr. Frank McGowan, prin. Fax 248-5673

Lindenhurst, Suffolk, Pop. 28,248
Lindenhurst UFD 7,300/K-12
350 Daniel St 11757 631-226-6441
Neil Lederer, supt. Fax 226-6865
www.lindenhurstschools.org
Lindenhurst HS 2,300/9-12
300 Charles St 11757 631-226-6445
Daniel Giordano, prin. Fax 226-6577
Lindenhurst MS 1,800/6-8
350 S Wellwood Ave 11757 631-226-6521
Frank Naccarato, prin. Fax 226-6554

Lisbon, Saint Lawrence
Lisbon Central SD 500/K-12
6866 County Route 10 13658 315-393-4951
Ernest Witkowski, supt. Fax 393-7666
lisboncs.schoolwires.com
Lisbon Central S 500/K-12
6866 County Route 10 13658 315-393-4951
Christopher Todd, prin. Fax 393-7666

Little Falls, Herkimer, Pop. 5,026
Little Falls CSD 1,200/K-12
15 Petrie St 13365 315-823-1470
William Gokey, supt. Fax 823-0321
www.lfcsd.org
Little Falls HS 400/9-12
1 High School Rd 13365 315-823-1167
Louis Patrei, prin. Fax 823-1209
Little Falls MS 300/6-8
1 High School Rd 13365 315-823-4300
Kathryn Faber, prin. Fax 823-3920

Little Neck, See New York
NYC Department of Education
Supt. — See New York
JHS 67 1,000/6-8
5160 Marathon Pkwy 11362 718-423-8138
Zoi McGrath, prin. Fax 423-8281

Little Valley, Cattaraugus, Pop. 1,090
Cattaraugus-Little Valley Central SD 1,000/K-12
207 Rock City St 14755 716-938-9155
Louis McIntosh, supt. Fax 938-6576
www.cattlv.wnyric.org/
Other Schools – See Cattaraugus

Liverpool, Onondaga, Pop. 2,415
Liverpool Central SD 7,700/PK-12
195 Blackberry Rd 13090 315-622-7125
Janice H. Matousek, supt. Fax 622-7124
www.liverpool.k12.ny.us
Chestnut Hill MS 300/7-8
204 Saslon Park Dr 13088 315-453-0245
Scott Krell, prin. Fax 453-0278
Liverpool HS 2,100/10-12
4338 Wetzel Rd 13090 315-453-1112
Fax 453-1246
Liverpool MS 500/7-8
700 7th St 13088 315-453-0258
Robert Gaetano, prin. Fax 453-0281
Ninth Grade Annex 9-9
4340 Wetzel Rd 13090 315-453-1275
Ted Phillips, prin.
Soule Road MS 500/7-8
8340 Soule Rd 13090 315-453-1283
Robert Sheitz, prin. Fax 453-1286

Bryant & Stratton College Post-Sec.
8687 Carling Rd 13090 315-472-6603
National Tractor Trailer School Post-Sec.
4650 Buckley Rd 13088 315-451-2430

Livingston Manor, Sullivan, Pop. 1,482
Livingston Manor Central SD 600/PK-12
PO Box 947 12758 845-439-4400
Debra Lynker, supt. Fax 439-4717
lmcs.k12.ny.us
Livingston Manor JSHS 300/7-12
PO Box 947 12758 845-439-4400
David Richards, prin. Fax 439-4717

Livonia, Livingston, Pop. 1,527
Livonia Central SD 2,100/K-12
PO Box E 14487 585-346-4000
Scott Bischoping, supt. Fax 346-6145
www.livoniacsd.org
Livonia HS 700/9-12
PO Box E 14487 585-346-4040
Karen Bennett, prin. Fax 346-9605
Livonia JHS 400/7-8
PO Box E 14487 585-346-4050
Charles D'Imperio, prin. Fax 346-6835

Loch Sheldrake, Sullivan

SUNY Sullivan County Community College Post-Sec.
112 College Rd 12759 845-434-5750

Lockport, Niagara, Pop. 21,271
Lockport CSD 5,400/PK-12
130 Beattie Ave 14094 716-478-4800
Terry Carbone, supt. Fax 478-4863
www.lockport.k12.ny.us
Belknap MS, 491 High St 14094 700/6-8
Gary Wilson, prin. 716-478-4550
Lockport HS, 250 Lincoln Ave 14094 1,700/9-12
Frank Movalli, prin. 716-478-4450
North Park MS 600/6-8
160 Passaic Ave 14094 716-478-4700
James Snyder, prin.

Starpoint Central SD 2,800/K-12
4363 Mapleton Rd 14094 716-210-2352
Dr. C. Douglas Whelan, supt.
www.starpointcsd.org/
Starpoint HS 900/9-12
4363 Mapleton Rd 14094 716-210-2300
Gil Licata, prin.
Starpoint MS 700/6-8
4363 Mapleton Rd 14094 716-210-2200
James Bryer, prin.

Christian Academy of Western New York 100/PK-12
120 Main St 14094 716-433-1652
Patricia Poeller, admin. Fax 438-0751

Locust Valley, Nassau, Pop. 3,963
Locust Valley Central SD 2,300/K-12
22 Horse Hollow Rd 11560 516-674-6390
Richard Hirt, supt. Fax 674-0138
www.lvcsd.k12.ny.us/
Locust Valley HS 700/9-12
99 Horse Hollow Rd 11560 516-674-6305
Sean Feeney, prin. Fax 671-1096
Locust Valley MS 500/6-8
99 Horse Hollow Rd 11560 516-674-6370
Matt Sanzone, prin. Fax 674-3795

Friends Academy 700/PK-12
Duck Pond Rd 11560 516-676-0393
William Morris, hdmstr. Fax 393-4276
Portledge S 400/PK-12
355 Duck Pond Rd 11560 516-750-3100
Stephen Hahn, hdmstr. Fax 671-2039

Long Beach, Nassau, Pop. 35,336

Mesivta of Long Beach 100/9-12
205 W Beech St 11561 516-255-4700
Rabbi Harvey Krasnow, prin. Fax 255-4701
Rabbinical College of Long Island Post-Sec.
205 W Beech St 11561 516-255-4700

Long Island City, See New York
NYC Department of Education
Supt. — See New York
Academy of Finance & Enterprise 9-10
3020 Thomson Ave 11101 718-389-3623
Gilberto Vega, prin. Fax 389-3724
Applied Communication HS 9-10
3020 Thomson Ave 11101 718-389-3163
Mary Ellen Kociszewski, prin. Fax 389-3427
Aviation Career & Technical HS Vo/Tech
4530 36th St 11101 718-361-2032
Eileen Taylor, prin. Fax 784-8654
Bryant HS 3,600/9-12
4810 31st Ave 11103 718-721-5404
C. Pellettieri, prin. Fax 728-3478
Information Technology HS 500/9-12
2116 44th Rd 11101 718-937-4270
Noralee Montemarano, dir. Fax 937-5236
International HS at Laguardia College 500/9-12
3110 Thomson Ave 11101 718-482-5455
Lee Pan, prin. Fax 392-6904
IS 126 800/6-8
3151 21st St 11106 718-274-8316
Dr. Candice Scott, prin. Fax 278-6512
IS 141 1,000/6-8
3711 21st Ave 11105 718-278-6403
Anthony Aldorasi, prin. Fax 278-2884
IS 204 900/6-8
3641 28th St 11106 718-937-1463
Thomas Semanski, prin. Fax 937-7964
Middle College HS 500/9-12
3110 Thomson Ave Ste L101 11101 718-349-4000
Aaron Listhaus, prin. Fax 349-4003
Newcomers HS 900/9-12
2801 41st Ave 11101 718-937-6005
Mary Burke, prin. Fax 937-6316
Queens Vocational HS Vo/Tech
3702 47th Ave 11101 718-937-3010
Denise Vittor, prin. Fax 392-8397
Sinatra HS 500/9-12
3020 Thomson Ave 11101 718-361-9920
Donna Finn, prin. Fax 361-9995
Wagner HS 400/9-12
4707 30th Pl 11101 718-472-5671
Bruce Noble, prin. Fax 472-9117
Young Womens Leadership S 6-12
2370 31st St 11105 845-671-0458
Laura Mitchell, prin.

DeVry Institute of Technology Post-Sec.
3020 Thomson Ave 11101 718-472-2728
Evangel Christian S 500/PK-12
3921 Crescent St 11101 718-937-9600
Rev. Robert Johansson, hdmstr. Fax 937-1613
LaGuardia Community College / CUNY Post-Sec.
31-10 Thompson Ave 11101 718-482-7200
New York School for Medical Dental Asst. Post-Sec.
3310 Queens Blvd 11101 718-793-2330

Long Lake, Hamilton
Long Lake Central SD 100/PK-12
PO Box 217 12847 518-624-2147
Kevin Crampton, supt. Fax 624-3896
Long Lake Central S 100/PK-12
PO Box 217 12847 518-624-2147
Kevin Crampton, prin. Fax 624-3896

Loudonville, Albany, Pop. 10,822

Loudonville Christian S 300/PK-12
374 Loudon Rd 12211 518-434-6051
Valyn Anderson, hdmstr. Fax 935-2258
Siena College Post-Sec.
515 Loudon Rd 12211 518-783-2300

Lowville, Lewis, Pop. 3,250
Lowville Central SD 1,400/K-12
7668 N State St 13367 315-376-9000
Kenneth McAuliffe, supt. Fax 376-1933
www.lacs-ny.org
Lowville HS 400/9-12
7668 N State St 13367 315-376-9015
Daniel Cushing, prin. Fax 376-1933
Lowville MS 300/6-8
7668 N State St 13367 315-376-9010
Leueen Smithling, prin. Fax 376-9011

Lynbrook, Nassau, Pop. 19,640
Lynbrook UFD 3,100/K-12
111 Atlantic Ave 11563 516-887-0253
Dr. Philip Cicero, supt. Fax 887-3263
www.lynbrook.k12.ny.us
Lynbrook HS 1,000/9-12
9 Union Ave 11563 516-887-0200
Joseph Rainis, prin. Fax 887-8079
Lynbrook North MS 300/6-8
529 Merrick Rd 11563 516-887-0282
Dr. Shawn Robertson, prin. Fax 887-0286
Lynbrook South MS 500/6-8
333 Union Ave 11563 516-887-0266
Margaret Ronai Ed.D., prin. Fax 887-0268

Lyndonville, Orleans, Pop. 847
Lyndonville Central SD 800/K-12
PO Box 540 14098 585-765-3101
Barbara Deane-Williams, supt. Fax 765-2106
Lyndonville JHS 300/5-8
PO Box 540 14098 585-765-3142
Mathew Penrod, prin. Fax 765-2106
Webber HS 300/9-12
PO Box 540 14098 585-765-3164
Kenneth Smith, prin. Fax 765-2106

Lyons, Wayne, Pop. 3,553
Lyons Central SD 1,100/K-12
10 Clyde Rd 14489 315-946-2200
Richard Amundson, supt. Fax 946-2205
www.lyonscsd.org
Lyons HS 300/9-12
10 Clyde Rd 14489 315-946-2220
Harold Decook, prin. Fax 946-2221
Lyons MS 200/7-8
10 Clyde Rd 14489 315-946-2200
Celine Olgin, prin. Fax 946-2221

Mc Graw, Cortland, Pop. 1,032
Mc Graw Central SD 600/K-12
PO Box 556 13101 607-836-3636
Maria S. Fragnoli-Ryan, supt. Fax 836-3635
www.mcgrawschools.org
Mc Graw JSHS 300/7-12
PO Box 556 13101 607-836-3600
Curt Czarniak, prin. Fax 836-3635

Madison, Madison, Pop. 312
Madison Central SD 500/K-12
7303 State Route 20 13402 315-893-1878
Cynthia DeDominick, supt. Fax 893-7111
www.madisoncentralny.org
Madison Central S 500/K-12
7303 State Route 20 13402 315-893-1878
Charles Chafee, prin. Fax 893-7111

Madrid, Saint Lawrence
Madrid-Waddington Central SD 800/K-12
PO Box 67 13660 315-322-5746
Lynn Roy, supt. Fax 322-4462
www.mwcsk12.org
Madrid-Waddington JSHS 500/6-12
PO Box 67 13660 315-322-5746
Joseph Ruddy, prin. Fax 322-4462

Mahopac, Putnam, Pop. 7,755
Mahopac Central SD 5,400/K-12
179 E Lake Blvd 10541 845-628-3415
Robert J. Reidy Ph.D., supt. Fax 628-5502
www.mahopac.k12.ny.us
Mahopac HS 1,700/9-12
421 Baldwin Place Rd 10541 845-628-3256
Aaron Trummer, prin. Fax 628-4380
Mahopac MS 1,300/6-8
425 Baldwin Place Rd 10541 845-621-1330
Ira Gurkin, prin. Fax 628-5847

Malone, Franklin, Pop. 5,929
Malone Central SD 2,400/PK-12
PO Box 847 12953 518-483-7800
Stephen Shafer, supt. Fax 483-3071
malone.k12.ny.us/
Franklin Academy HS 800/9-12
42 Huskie Ln 12953 518-483-7807
Jerry Griffin, prin. Fax 483-7813
Malone MS 500/6-8
15 Francis St 12953 518-483-7801
Lynn Latreille, prin. Fax 483-9497

Malverne, Nassau, Pop. 8,832
Malverne UFD 1,600/K-12
301 Wicks Ln 11565 516-887-6405
Dr. Mary Ellen Freeley, supt. Fax 596-2910
www.malverne.k12.ny.us
Herber MS 500/5-8
75 Ocean Ave 11565 516-887-6444
David Zimbler, prin. Fax 596-0525
Malverne HS 600/9-12
80 Ocean Ave 11565 516-887-6420
Glenda Good, prin. Fax 887-6479

Mamaroneck, Westchester, Pop. 18,350
Mamaroneck UFD 4,800/PK-12
1000 W Boston Post Rd 10543 914-220-3000
Dr. Paul R. Fried, supt. Fax 220-3010
www.mamkschools.org
Mamaroneck HS 1,400/9-12
1000 W Boston Post Rd 10543 914-220-3100
Dr. Mark Orfinger, prin. Fax 220-3115
Other Schools – See Larchmont

Rye Neck UFD 1,400/K-12
310 Hornidge Rd 10543 914-777-5200
Dr. Peter Mustich, supt. Fax 777-5201
www.ryeneck.k12.ny.us/
Rye Neck HS 400/9-12
300 Hornidge Rd 10543 914-777-5200
Dr. Barbara Ferraro, prin. Fax 777-4801
Rye Neck MS 500/5-8
300 Hornidge Rd 10543 914-777-5200
Eric Lutinski, prin. Fax 777-4701

Westchester Hebrew HS 100/9-12
856 Orienta Ave 10543 914-698-0806
Rabbi Jeffery Beer, hdmstr. Fax 698-1330

Manhasset, Nassau, Pop. 7,718
Manhasset UFD 2,800/K-12
200 Memorial Pl 11030 516-267-7700
Charles Cardillo, supt. Fax 627-1618
www.manhasset.k12.ny.us
Manhasset HS 800/9-12
200 Memorial Pl 11030 516-267-7600
Richard McMahon, prin. Fax 627-4604
Manhasset MS 400/7-8
200 Memorial Pl 11030 516-267-7500
Richard McMahon, prin. Fax 627-8157

St. Mary HS 900/9-12
51 Clapham Ave 11030 516-627-2711
Dr. Kevin McBride, prin. Fax 627-3209

Manlius, Onondaga, Pop. 4,695
Fayetteville-Manlius Central SD 4,700/K-12
8199 E Seneca Tpke 13104 315-692-1200
Corliss Kaiser, supt. Fax 692-1227
www.fmschools.org
Eagle Hill MS 900/5-8
4645 Enders Rd 13104 315-692-1400
Mary Coughlin, prin. Fax 692-1046
Fayetteville-Manlius HS 1,600/9-12
8201 E Seneca Tpke 13104 315-692-1900
James Chupaila, prin. Fax 692-1028
Other Schools – See Fayetteville

Manorville, Suffolk, Pop. 6,198
Eastport-South Manor Central SD 3,400/K-12
149 Dayton Ave 11949 631-874-6720
B. Allen Mannella, supt. Fax 878-6308
www.esmonline.org
Eastport/South Manor JSHS 7-12
543 Moriches Middle Isle Rd 11949 631-874-6500
Joseph Steimel, prin. Fax 874-6787

Marathon, Cortland, Pop. 1,034
Marathon Central SD 1,000/K-12
PO Box 339 13803 607-849-3251
Timothy Turecek, supt. Fax 849-3305
Marathon JSHS 500/7-12
PO Box 339 13803 607-849-3251
David Rosetti, prin. Fax 849-3305

Marcellus, Onondaga, Pop. 1,793
Marcellus Central SD 2,200/K-12
2 Reed Pkwy 13108 315-673-0201
Dr. Craig Tice, supt. Fax 673-1727
marcellusschools.org
Driver MS 900/4-8
2 Reed Pkwy 13108 315-673-0219
Patrick Collier, prin. Fax 673-1727
Marcellus HS 700/9-12
1 Mustang Hl 13108 315-673-0296
John Durkee, prin. Fax 673-0312

Marcy, Oneida, Pop. 8,685
Whitesboro Central SD
Supt. — See Yorkville
Whitesboro HS 1,200/9-12
6000 State Route 291 13403 315-266-3200
Curt Woodcock, prin. Fax 266-3223

Margaretville, Delaware, Pop. 653
Margaretville Central SD 500/K-12
PO Box 319 12455 845-586-2647
John P. Riedl, supt. Fax 586-2949
www.margaretvillecs.org
Margaretville Central S 500/K-12
PO Box 319 12455 845-586-2647
Linda Taylor, prin. Fax 586-2949

Marion, Wayne
Marion Central SD 1,100/K-12
4034 Warner Rd 14505 315-926-2300
Dr. J. Richard Boyes, supt. Fax 926-5797
www.marioncs.org/
Marion JSHS 600/7-12
4034 Warner Rd 14505 315-926-4228
Duane Perry, prin. Fax 926-3114

Marlboro, Ulster, Pop. 2,200
Marlboro Central SD 1,700/K-12
50 Cross Rd 12542 845-236-5802
Dr. Lou Ciota, supt. Fax 236-5817
www.marlboroschools.org
Marlboro Central HS 700/9-12
50 Cross Rd 12542 845-236-5810
Paul Hughes, prin. Fax 236-2638
Marlboro MS 500/6-8
1375 Route 9W 12542 845-236-5842
Jose Sanchez, prin. Fax 236-3634

Maspeth, See New York
NYC Department of Education
Supt. — See New York
IS 73 1,800/6-8
7002 54th Ave 11378 718-639-3817
Patricia Reynolds, prin. Fax 429-5162

Martin Luther HS 400/9-12
6002 Maspeth Ave 11378 718-894-4000
Elizabeth Crowe, prin. Fax 894-1469

Massapequa, Nassau, Pop. 22,018
Massapequa UFD 8,200/K-12
4925 Merrick Rd 11758 516-797-6600
Dr. Maureen Flaherty, supt. Fax 797-6072
www.msd.k12.ny.us
Berner MS 1,300/7-8
50 Carman Mill Rd 11758 516-797-6080
Stephen Scarallo, prin. Fax 797-6638
Massapequa HS 1,700/10-12
4925 Merrick Rd 11758 516-797-6110
Dr. James Grossane, prin. Fax 797-6663
Massapequa HS Ames Campus 600/9-9
198 Baltimore Ave 11758 516-797-6530
Barbara Williams, prin. Fax 797-6534

Plainedge UFD
Supt. — See North Massapequa
Plainedge HS 1,100/9-12
241 Wyngate Dr 11758 516-992-7550
Robert Amster, prin. Fax 992-7545

Massena, Saint Lawrence, Pop. 10,859
Massena Central SD 2,800/K-12
84 Nightengale Ave 13662 315-764-3700
Douglas Huntley, supt. Fax 764-3701
www.mcs.k12.ny.us
Leary JHS 500/7-8
84 Nightengale Ave 13662 315-764-3720
Roger Clough, prin. Fax 764-3723
Massena HS 1,000/9-12
84 Nightengale Ave 13662 315-764-3710
Cathryn McDevitt, prin. Fax 764-3719

Mastic Beach, Suffolk, Pop. 10,293
William Floyd UFD 10,000/K-12
240 Mastic Beach Rd 11951 631-874-1100
Dr. Richard Hawkins, supt. Fax 281-3047
www.wfsd.k12.ny.us
Floyd HS 3,200/9-12
240 Mastic Beach Rd 11951 631-874-1120
Robert Feeney, prin. Fax 281-3047
Paca MS 1,300/6-8
338 Blanco Dr 11951 631-874-1414
Barbara Butler, prin. Fax 281-3047
Other Schools – See Moriches

Mattituck, Suffolk, Pop. 3,902
Mattituck-Cutchogue UFD
Supt. — See Cutchogue
Mattituck-Cutchogue JSHS 800/7-12
15125 Main Rd 11952 631-298-8460
Shawn Petretti, prin. Fax 298-8544

Mayfield, Fulton, Pop. 800
Mayfield Central SD 1,200/PK-12
27 School St 12117 518-661-8207
Ralph Acquaro, supt. Fax 661-7666
www.mayfieldk12.com/
Mayfield JSHS 600/7-12
27 School St 12117 518-661-8200
Robert Husain, prin. Fax 661-7666

Mayville, Chautauqua, Pop. 1,721
Chautauqua Lake SD 1,000/PK-12
100 N Erie St 14757 716-753-5808
Benjamin Spitzer, supt. Fax 753-5813
www.clake.org
Chautauqua Lake Central HS 300/9-12
100 N Erie St 14757 716-753-5882
Rosemary Andrews, prin. Fax 753-5886
Chautauqua Lake MS 200/6-8
100 N Erie St 14757 716-753-5872
John Panebianco, prin. Fax 753-5876

Mechanicville, Saratoga, Pop. 4,997
Mechanicville CSD 1,300/K-12
25 Kniskern Ave 12118 518-664-5727
Michael McCarthy, supt. Fax 514-2101
www.mechanicville.org/
Mechanicville HS 400/9-12
25 Kniskern Ave 12118 518-664-9888
G. Michael Apostol, prin. Fax 514-2107
Mechanicville MS 300/6-8
25 Kniskern Ave 12118 518-664-6303
Kevin Duffy, prin. Fax 514-2104

Medford, Suffolk, Pop. 21,274
Patchogue-Medford UFD
Supt. — See Patchogue
Oregon MS 800/6-9
109 Oregon Ave 11763 631-687-6800
Timothy Mundell, prin. Fax 758-1126
Patchogue-Medford HS 2,200/10-12
181 Buffalo Ave 11763 631-687-6500
Manuel Sanzone, prin. Fax 758-1126

Medina, Orleans, Pop. 6,235
Medina Central SD 1,900/K-12
1 Mustang Dr 14103 585-798-2700
Richard Galante, supt. Fax 798-5676
www.medinacsd.org
Medina HS 600/9-12
2 Mustang Dr 14103 585-798-2710
Wes Pickreign, prin. Fax 798-2787
Wise MS 500/6-8
1016 Gwinn St 14103 585-798-2100
Marc Graff, prin. Fax 798-1062

Orleans County Christian S 50/K-12
PO Box 349 14103 585-798-2992
Linda Strickland, admin. Fax 798-3766

Melville, Suffolk, Pop. 12,586
Half Hollow Hills Central SD
Supt. — See Dix Hills
West Hollow MS 1,300/6-8
250 Old East Neck Rd 11747 631-592-3400
Mary Rettaliata, prin. Fax 592-3922

Katharine Gibbs School Post-Sec.
320 S Service Rd 11747 516-370-3510
Polytechnic University Post-Sec.
105 Maxess Rd Ste 201N 11747 631-755-4300

Merrick, Nassau, Pop. 23,042
Bellmore-Merrick Central HSD
Supt. — See North Merrick

Calhoun HS 1,300/9-12
1786 State St 11566 516-992-1300
David Seinfeld, prin. Fax 867-7390
Merrick Avenue MS 1,000/7-8
1870 Merrick Ave 11566 516-992-1200
Caryn Frange, prin. Fax 867-6391

Mexico, Oswego, Pop. 1,560
Mexico Central SD 2,600/K-12
40 Academy St 13114 315-963-8400
Nelson Bauersfeld, supt. Fax 963-3325
www.mexico.cnyric.org
Mexico HS 900/9-12
3338 Main St 13114 315-963-8400
Judy Belfield, prin. Fax 963-8887
Mexico MS 800/5-8
16 Fravor Rd 13114 315-963-8400
Kim Willix, prin. Fax 963-3848

Middleburgh, Schoharie, Pop. 1,554
Middleburgh Central SD 1,000/PK-12
PO Box 606 12122 518-827-3600
Douglas Kelley, supt. Fax 827-6632
teacherweb.com/NY/MiddleburghCentralSchool/District/
Middleburgh HS 300/9-12
PO Box 400 12122 518-827-3600
Lori Petrosino, prin. Fax 827-5192
Middleburgh MS 200/6-8
PO Box 400 12122 518-827-3600
Maura Green, prin. Fax 827-9533

Middle Island, Suffolk, Pop. 7,848
Longwood Central SD 9,600/K-12
35 Yaphank Middle Island Rd 11953 631-345-2172
Dr. Allan Gerstenlauer, supt. Fax 345-2166
www.longwood.k12.ny.us
Longwood HS 3,200/9-12
100 Longwood Rd 11953 631-345-9200
Donald Murphy, prin. Fax 345-9279
Longwood JHS 1,600/7-8
198 Longwood Rd 11953 631-345-2701
Levi McIntyre, prin. Fax 345-9281

Middleport, Niagara, Pop. 1,826
Royalton-Hartland Central SD 900/K-12
54 State St 14105 716-735-3031
Paul Bona, supt. Fax 735-3660
royhart.org/
Royalton-Hartland HS 500/9-12
56 State St 14105 716-735-3800
Kevin Shanley, prin. Fax 735-6128
Royalton-Hartland MS 100/5-8
78 State St 14105 716-735-3722
Sean Kinsley, prin. Fax 735-0047

Middletown, Orange, Pop. 26,067
Middletown CSD 6,400/K-12
223 Wisner Ave 10940 845-326-1130
Dr. Kenneth Eastwood, supt. Fax 326-9938
www.middletowncityschools.org/
Middletown HS 2,100/9-12
20 Gardner Ave Ext 10940 845-341-5900
Alan Gonzalez, prin. Fax 326-1605
Monhagen MS 800/6-8
555 County Highway 78 10940 845-346-4800
Tracey Sorrentino, prin. Fax 346-4868
Twin Towers MS 800/6-8
112 Grand Ave 10940 845-341-5400
Gordon Dean, prin. Fax 343-4515

Beauty School of Middletown Post-Sec.
225 Dolson Ave Ste 100 10940 845-343-2171
Harmony Christian S 300/PK-12
1790 Route 211 E 10941 845-692-5353
Kevin Barry, admin. Fax 692-7140
SUNY Orange County Community College Post-Sec.
115 South St 10940 845-344-6222

Middle Village, See New York

Christ the King Regional HS 1,600/9-12
6802 Metropolitan Ave 11379 718-366-7400
Peter Mannarino, prin. Fax 366-1165

Milford, Otsego, Pop. 485
Milford Central SD 500/K-12
PO Box 237 13807 607-286-3341
Peter Livshin, supt. Fax 286-7879
Milford Central S 500/K-12
PO Box 237 13807 607-286-3349
Ben Badurina, prin. Fax 286-7879

Millbrook, Dutchess, Pop. 1,559
Millbrook Central SD 1,100/K-12
PO Box AA 12545 845-677-4200
Dr. R. Lloyd Jaeger, supt. Fax 677-4206
www.millbrookcsd.org/
Millbrook HS, PO Box AA 12545 300/9-12
Jeffrey Matteson, prin. 845-677-2510
Millbrook MS 200/6-8
PO Box AA 12545 845-677-4210
Brian Fried, prin. Fax 677-6913

Millbrook S 200/9-12
131 Millbrook School Rd 12545 845-677-8261
Drew Casertano, hdmstr. Fax 677-8598

Miller Place, Suffolk, Pop. 9,315
Miller Place UFD 3,100/K-12
275 Route 25A Unit 43 11764 631-474-2700
Dr. Grace Brindley, supt. Fax 474-0686
www.millerplace.k12.ny.us
Miller Place HS 900/9-12
15 Memorial Dr 11764 631-474-2723
Seth Lipshie, prin. Fax 474-1734
North Country Road MS 700/6-8
191 N Country Rd 11764 631-474-2710
Matthew Clark, prin. Fax 474-5178

Mill Neck, Nassau, Pop. 852

Mill Neck Lutheran School Post-Sec.
Frost Mill Rd B12 11765

Millwood, Westchester, Pop. 1,000

Yeshiva Kehilath Yaakov 50/11-12
PO Box 501 10546 914-762-3010
Rabbi Shimshon Katz, admin. Fax 762-3010

Mineola, Nassau, Pop. 18,978
Mineola UFD 2,800/PK-12
121 Jackson Ave 11501 516-237-2001
Dr. Lorenzo Licopoli, supt. Fax 739-4783
www.mineola.k12.ny.us
Mineola MS 700/6-8
200 Emory Rd 11501 516-237-2500
Mark Barth, prin. Fax 739-4129
Other Schools – See Garden City Park

Chaminade HS 9-12
340 Jackson Ave 11501 516-742-5555
Br. Joseph Bellizzi, prin. Fax 742-1989
NY College Traditional Chinese Medicine Post-Sec.
155 1st St 11501 516-739-1545
Winthrop University Hospital Post-Sec.
259 1st St 11501 516-663-2201

Mohawk, Herkimer, Pop. 2,569
Mohawk Central SD 1,000/K-12
28 Grove St 13407 315-867-2904
Joyce Caputo, supt. Fax 867-2918
www.mohawk.k12.ny.us
Mohawk JSHS 500/7-12
28 Grove St 13407 315-866-2620
Edward Rinaldo, prin. Fax 867-2909

Monroe, Orange, Pop. 8,127
Greenwood Lake UFD
Supt. — See Greenwood Lake
Greenwood Lake MS 300/5-8
1247 Lakes Rd 10950 845-986-8624
Allan Lipsky, prin. Fax 782-2004

Kiryas Joel Village UFSD 200/PK-12
PO Box 398, 845-782-2300
Dr. Steven Benardo, supt. Fax 782-4176
Kiryas Joel Village S 200/PK-12
PO Box 398, 845-782-7510
Susan Gartenberg, prin. Fax 782-4176

Bnei Yoel S 300/PK-12
PO Box 255, 845-783-8036
Fax 782-7039
UTA Mesivta of Kiryas Joel Post-Sec.
PO Box 2009, 845-783-9901
UTA of Kiryas Joel 5,800/K-12
PO Box 477, 845-783-5800
Rabbi Baruch Weinberger, prin. Fax 782-1922

Monsey, Rockland, Pop. 13,986

Ateres Bais Yaakov 200/PK-12
236 Cherry Ln 10952 845-368-2200
Rabbi Aaron Fink, dean Fax 357-2343
Bais Malka Girls S of Belz 300/PK-12
PO Box 977 10952 845-371-0500
C. Levine, prin. Fax 425-2629
Bais Shifra Miriam S 300/K-12
PO Box 682 10952 845-356-0061
Gabriel Kramarsky, admin. Fax 356-0223
Bais Yaakov D'Rav Hirsch 100/9-12
PO Box 671 10952 845-371-6750
Rabbi Z. Gelley, dean Fax 371-6618
Bais Yaakov HS of Spring Valley 400/9-12
11 Smolley Dr 10952 845-356-3113
M. Paretzky, prin. Fax 356-3132
Bais Yaakov of Ramapo HS 100/9-12
16 Hershel Ter 10952 845-356-0580
Gitty Kramer, admin. Fax 356-0584
Beth Rochel School for Girls 800/K-12
145 Saddle River Rd 10952 845-352-5000
Rabbi Jacob Przewozman, admin. Fax 352-6571
Bnos Yisroel Girls S of Viznitz 1,000/1-12
1 School Ter 10952 845-731-3700
Rabbi Hershy Moskowitz, admin. Fax 731-3751
Kol Yaakov Torah Center Post-Sec.
29 W Maple Ave 10952 845-425-3863
Mesivta Shaarei Arazim 100/9-12
PO Box 523 10952 845-426-6401
Rabbi Zev Freundlich, admin. Fax 426-6389
Mesivta Yesodei Yisroel 100/9-12
51 Carlton Rd 10952 845-425-2520
Dr. Yaakov Zvi Nierman, prin. Fax 425-0317
Mesivta Ziev Hatorah 100/9-12
PO Box 814 10952 845-426-6868
Yizchok Weinberger, dir. Fax 356-5651
Monsey Academy for Girls 100/9-12
58 Parker Blvd 10952 845-356-3929
Rivka Shear, prin. Fax 364-0328
Ohr Somayach Tanenbaum Educational Ctr. Post-Sec.
PO Box 334 10952 845-425-1370
Yeshiva and Kolel Bais Medrash Elyon Post-Sec.
73 Main St 10952 845-356-7064
Yeshiva Beth David S 500/K-12
PO Box 136 10952 845-352-3100
Rabbi Yehuda Lichter, prin. Fax 352-0153
Yeshiva D'Monsey Rabbinical College Post-Sec.
2 Roman Blvd 10952 845-426-3276
Yeshiva Gedola of South Monsey 100/9-12
10 Algonquin Cir 10952 845-356-4030
Rabbi Eliezer Abish, prin. Fax 352-7436
Yeshiva Shaar Ephraim S 100/9-12
PO Box 253 10952 845-426-3110
Y. Oshry, prin. Fax 425-4721
Yeshivath Viznitz Post-Sec.
PO Box 446 10952 845-356-1010
Yeshiva Toras Chaim 50/9-11
PO Box 1112 10952 845-352-9126
Mayer Schlesinger, dir.
Yeshiva Viznitz 1,600/PK-12
PO Box 446 10952 845-356-1010
Rabbi Berl Rosenfeld, admin. Fax 356-7359

Montgomery, Orange, Pop. 4,238
Valley Central SD 5,200/K-12
944 State Route 17K 12549 845-457-2400
Richard M. Hooley Ed.D., supt. Fax 457-4319
www.vcsd.k12.ny.us
Valley Central HS 1,800/9-12
1175 State Route 17K 12549 845-457-2400
Darryl Imperati, prin. Fax 457-4056
Valley Central MS 1,200/6-8
1189 State Route 17K 12549 845-457-2400
Ned Hayes, prin. Fax 457-4311

Monticello, Sullivan, Pop. 6,649
Monticello Central SD 3,500/K-12
237 Forestburgh Rd 12701 845-794-7700
Dr. Patrick Michel, supt. Fax 794-7710
www.monticelloschools.net
Kaiser MS 900/6-8
45 Breakey Ave 12701 845-796-3058
Deborah Wood, prin. Fax 796-3099
Monticello HS 1,100/9-12
39 Breakey Ave 12701 845-794-8840
Arlene Siegel-Lerner, prin. Fax 794-8133

Montrose, Westchester
Hendrick Hudson Central SD 2,900/K-12
61 Trolley Rd 10548 914-736-5200
Dr. Daniel McCann, supt. Fax 736-5242
www.henhudschools.org/
Hendrick Hudson HS 900/9-12
2166 Albany Post Rd 10548 914-736-5250
James Mackin, prin. Fax 737-6746
Other Schools – See Cortlandt Manor

Moravia, Cayuga, Pop. 1,326
Moravia Central SD 1,100/K-12
PO Box 1189 13118 315-497-2670
William Tammaro, supt. Fax 497-2260
www.moraviaschool.org/
Moravia JSHS 500/7-12
PO Box 1189 13118 315-497-2670
Brian Morgan, prin. Fax 497-3852

Moriches, Suffolk
William Floyd UFD
Supt. — See Mastic Beach
Floyd MS 1,200/6-8
630 Moriches Middle Island 11955 631-874-5500
Carolyn Schick, prin.

Morris, Otsego, Pop. 561
Morris Central SD 400/K-12
PO Box 40 13808 607-263-6100
Michael Virgil, supt. Fax 263-2483
morriscs.org
Morris Central S 400/K-12
PO Box 40 13808 607-263-6100
Leone Schermerhorn, prin. Fax 263-2483

Morristown, Saint Lawrence, Pop. 441
Morristown Central SD 400/K-12
PO Box 217 13664 315-375-8814
Beverly Ouderkirk, supt. Fax 375-8604
Morristown Central S 400/K-12
PO Box 217 13664 315-375-8814
Michael Willis, prin. Fax 375-8604

Morrisville, Madison, Pop. 2,304
Morrisville-Eaton Central SD 800/K-12
PO Box 990 13408 315-684-9300
Michael Drahos, supt. Fax 684-9399
www.m-ecs.org
Morrisville-Eaton MSHS 400/7-12
PO Box 990 13408 315-684-9121
Jonathan Bryant, prin. Fax 684-9192

SUNY College of Agriculture & Technology Post-Sec.
13408 315-684-6000

Mount Kisco, Westchester, Pop. 10,331

Yeshiva Farm Settlement S 400/9-12
PO Box 1050 10549 914-666-9702
Yitzchak Schwartz, admin.

Mount Morris, Livingston, Pop. 2,978
Mount Morris Central SD 600/K-12
30 Bonadonna Ave 14510 585-658-2568
Renee Garrett, supt. Fax 658-4814
www.mt-morris.k12.ny.us
Mount Morris JSHS 300/7-12
30 Bonadonna Ave 14510 585-658-3331
Mark Valentino, prin. Fax 658-4814

Mount Sinai, Suffolk, Pop. 8,023
Mount Sinai UFD 2,400/K-12
150 N Country Rd 11766 631-870-2550
Jonathan Van Eyk, supt. Fax 473-0905
www.mtsinai.k12.ny.us
Mount Sinai HS 800/9-12
Gertrude Goodman Dr 11766 631-870-2800
Peter Ferenz, prin. Fax 928-3668
Mount Sinai MS 800/5-8
150 N Country Rd 11766 631-870-2700
Robert Grable, prin. Fax 928-3129

Mount Vernon, Westchester, Pop. 67,924
Mount Vernon CSD 8,900/PK-12
165 N Columbus Ave 10553 914-665-5000
Dr. Welton Sawyer, supt. Fax 665-6077
www.lhric.org/mtvernon
Davis MS 900/7-8
350 Gramatan Ave 10552 914-665-5120
Murdisia Orr, prin. Fax 665-5128
Longfellow MS 7-8
624 S 3rd Ave 10550 914-665-5151
Cleveland Person, prin. Fax 665-5152
Mount Vernon HS 2,700/9-12
100 California Rd 10552 914-665-5300
Stephen Jackson, prin. Fax 665-5281

Fortress Christian Academy 50/K-12
51 N 10th Ave 10550 914-699-9039
Rev. Dennis Karaman, admin. Fax 699-6819
Hopfer School of Nursing Post-Sec.
53 Valentine St 10550 914-664-8000
Westchester School of Beauty Culture Post-Sec.
6 Gramatan Ave 10550 914-699-2344

Munnsville, Madison, Pop. 426
Stockbridge Valley Central SD 500/K-12
PO Box 732 13409 315-495-4400
Dr. Randy Richards, supt. Fax 495-4492
www.stockbridgevalley.org
Stockbridge Valley Central S 500/K-12
PO Box 732 13409 315-495-4445
Mary Anne Iritz, prin. Fax 495-4492

Nanuet, Rockland, Pop. 14,065
Nanuet UFD 1,900/K-12
101 Church St 10954 845-627-9880
Dr. Mark McNeill, supt. Fax 624-5338
nanunet.lhric.org/
Barr MS 600/5-8
143 Church St 10954 845-627-4040
Roger Guccione, prin. Fax 624-3138
Nanuet HS 600/9-12
103 Church St 10954 845-627-9800
Dr. Vin Carella, prin. Fax 624-5520

Capri Cosmetology Learning Center Post-Sec.
251 W Route 59 10954 845-623-6339

Naples, Ontario, Pop. 1,050
Naples Central SD 900/K-12
136 N Main St 14512 585-374-7900
Brenda Keith, supt. Fax 374-5859
www.naples.k12.ny.us
Naples HS 400/7-12
136 N Main St 14512 585-374-7905
Kenneth Foster, prin. Fax 374-5859

Nedrow, Onondaga, Pop. 2,700
Onondaga Central SD 1,100/PK-12
4466 S Onondaga Rd 13120 315-492-1701
Joseph Rotella, supt. Fax 492-4650
www.ocs.cnyric.org
Onondaga JSHS 500/7-12
4479 S Onondaga Rd 13120 315-492-1705
William Rasbeck, prin. Fax 492-8567

Nesconset, Suffolk, Pop. 10,712
Smithtown Central SD
Supt. — See Smithtown
Great Hollow MS 900/6-8
150 Southern Blvd 11767 631-382-2800
Daniel Goitia, prin. Fax 382-2807

Newark, Wayne, Pop. 9,411
Newark Central SD 2,500/PK-12
100 E Miller St Ste 5 14513 315-332-3217
Robert Christmann, supt. Fax 332-3523
newarkcsd.schoolwires.com
Newark HS 800/9-12
625 Peirson Ave 14513 315-332-3242
Kevin Whitaker, prin. Fax 332-3567
Newark MS 600/6-8
701 Peirson Ave 14513 315-332-3295
Mark Miller, prin. Fax 332-3584

Newark Valley, Tioga, Pop. 1,038
Newark Valley Central SD 1,400/K-12
PO Box 547 13811 607-642-3221
Mary Ellen Grant, supt. Fax 642-8821
www.nvcs.stier.org/
Newark Valley JSHS 600/8-12
68 Wilson Creek Rd 13811 607-642-8351
Christopher Tennant, prin. Fax 642-5292

New Berlin, Chenango, Pop. 1,123
Unadilla Valley Central SD 1,000/PK-12
PO Box F 13411 607-847-7500
Rexford Hurlburt, supt. Fax 847-6924
Unadilla Valley HS 400/9-12
PO Box F 13411 607-847-7500
Franklin Johnson, prin. Fax 847-8045
Unadilla Valley MS 200/6-8
PO Box F 13411 607-847-7500
Stephen Griffin, prin. Fax 847-8045

Newburgh, Orange, Pop. 28,548
Newburgh Enlarged CSD 12,000/PK-12
124 Grand St 12550 845-563-3500
Dr. Annette Saturnelli, supt. Fax 563-3501
www.newburghschools.org/newburgh/newburgh.cfm
Newburgh Free Academy 2,400/10-12
201 Fullerton Ave 12550 845-563-5400
Peter Copeletti, prin. Fax 563-5405
North JHS 1,000/7-9
301 Robinson Ave 12550 845-563-8400
Ronald Jackson, prin. Fax 563-8409
South JHS 1,000/7-9
33 Monument St 12550 845-563-7000
Edward Mucci, prin. Fax 563-7019
Other Schools – See New Windsor

Mt. St. Mary College Post-Sec.
330 Powell Ave 12550 845-561-0800

New City, Rockland, Pop. 34,100
Clarkstown Central SD 9,400/K-12
62 Old Middletown Rd 10956 845-639-6419
Dr. William Heebink, supt. Fax 639-6488
www.ccsd.edu
Clarkstown North HS 1,500/9-12
151 Congers Rd 10956 845-639-6504
Harry Leonardatos, prin. Fax 638-6916
Other Schools – See West Nyack

Newcomb, Essex
Newcomb Central SD 100/PK-12
PO Box 418 12852 518-582-3341
Clark Hults, supt. Fax 582-2163
www.newcombcsd.org
Newcomb Central S 100/PK-12
PO Box 418 12852 518-582-3341
Clark Hults, prin. Fax 582-2163

Newfane, Niagara, Pop. 3,001
Newfane Central SD 2,100/PK-12
6273 Charlotteville Rd 14108 716-778-6850
Dr. James Mills, supt. Fax 778-6852
www.newfane.wnyric.org
Newfane HS, 1 Panther Dr 14108 600/9-12
Steve Burley, prin. 716-778-6551
Newfane MS, 2700 Transit Rd 14108 500/6-8
Gary Pogorzelski, prin. 716-778-6452

Newfield, Tompkins
Newfield Central SD 1,000/PK-12
247 Main St 14867 607-564-9955
William Hurley, supt. Fax 564-0055
www.newfieldschools.org
Newfield HS 300/9-12
247 Main St 14867 607-564-9955
Suzanne France, prin. Fax 564-3624
Newfield MS 300/6-8
247 Main St 14867 607-564-9955
Catherine Griggs, prin. Fax 564-3403

New Hartford, Oneida, Pop. 1,843
New Hartford Central SD 2,700/K-12
33 Oxford Rd 13413 315-624-1218
Daniel Gilligan, supt. Fax 724-8940
www.newhartfordschools.org
New Hartford SHS 700/10-12
33 Oxford Rd 13413 315-624-1214
Jennifer Spring, prin. Fax 738-9209
Perry JHS 600/7-9
9499 Weston Rd 13413 315-738-9300
Keith Levatino, prin. Fax 738-9349

New Hyde Park, Nassau, Pop. 9,472
Herricks UFD 4,100/K-12
999 Herricks Rd 11040 516-248-3105
Dr. John Bierwirth, supt. Fax 248-3108
www.herricks.org/
Herricks HS 1,400/9-12
100 Shelter Rock Rd 11040 516-248-3142
Dr. Jane Modoono, prin. Fax 248-3282
Other Schools – See Albertson

Sewanhaka Central HSD
Supt. — See Floral Park
New Hyde Park Memorial HS 1,600/7-12
500 Leonard Blvd 11040 516-488-9500
Loretta Nugent, prin. Fax 488-9506

New Lebanon, Columbia
New Lebanon Central SD 600/K-12
14665 State Route 22 12125 518-794-9016
Patrick Gabriel, supt. Fax 766-5574
www.newlebanoncsd.org
New Lebanon JSHS 300/7-12
14665 State Route 22 12125 518-794-7600
Patricia Ackley, prin. Fax 766-6265

Darrow S 100/9-12
110 Darrow Rd 12125 518-794-6000
Nancy Wolf, hdmstr. Fax 794-7065

New Paltz, Ulster, Pop. 6,765
New Paltz Central SD 2,300/K-12
196 Main St 12561 845-256-4020
Maria Rice, supt. Fax 256-4025
www.newpaltz.k12.ny.us
New Paltz HS 800/9-12
196 Main St 12561 845-256-4100
Barbara Clinton, prin. Fax 256-4109
New Paltz MS 600/6-8
196 Main St 12561 845-256-4200
Richard Wiesenthal, prin. Fax 256-4209

SUNY College at New Paltz Post-Sec.
1 Hawk Dr 12561 845-257-2121

Newport, Herkimer, Pop. 619
West Canada Valley Central SD 900/K-12
5447 State Route 28 13416 315-845-6800
Kenneth Slentz, supt.
www.westcanada.org/
West Canada Valley JSHS 500/7-12
5447 State Route 28 13416 315-845-6802
Frank Sutliff, prin. Fax 845-8652

New Rochelle, Westchester, Pop. 72,967
New Rochelle CSD 10,600/PK-12
515 North Ave 10801 914-576-4300
Richard Organisciak, supt. Fax 632-4144
www.nred.org
Leonard MS 1,300/6-8
25 Gerada Ln 10804 914-576-4339
William Evans, prin. Fax 576-4784
New Rochelle HS 3,200/9-12
265 Clove Rd 10801 914-576-4502
Don Conetta, prin. Fax 576-4284
Young MS 1,200/6-8
270 Centre Ave 10805 914-576-4360
Anthony Bongo, prin. Fax 632-2738

Blessed Sacrament-St. Gabriel HS 300/9-12
24 Shea Pl 10801 914-632-2595
Edward Sullivan, prin. Fax 632-3321
College of New Rochelle Post-Sec.
29 Castle Pl 10805 914-654-5000
Hallen S 300/K-12
97 Centre Ave 10801 914-636-6600
Carol Locascio, dir. Fax 636-2844
Iona College Post-Sec.
715 North Ave 10801 914-633-2000
Iona Preparatory S 700/9-12
255 Wilmot Rd 10804 914-632-0714
Maureen Kiers, hdmstr. Fax 632-9760
Monroe College Post-Sec.
434 Main St 10801 914-632-5400
Salesian HS 9-12
148 E Main St 10801 914-632-0248
John Flaherty, prin. Fax 632-1362
Thornton-Donovan S 200/K-12
100 Overlook Cir 10804 914-632-8836
Douglas Fleming, hdmstr. Fax 576-7936
Ursuline HS 600/9-12
1354 North Ave 10804 914-636-3950
Sr. Jean Nicholson, prin. Fax 636-3949

New Square, Rockland, Pop. 6,332

Avir Yaakov Girl's S 800/K-12
15 N Roosevelt Ave 10977 845-354-0874
Zlaty Hoffman, prin. Fax 354-5920

New Windsor, Orange, Pop. 8,898
Cornwall Central SD
Supt. — See Cornwall on Hudson
Cornwall Central HS 1,000/9-12
10 Dragon Dr 12553 845-534-8009
Michael Brooksl, prin. Fax 565-2754

Newburgh Enlarged CSD
Supt. — See Newburgh
Heritage JHS 800/7-9
405 Union Ave 12553 845-563-3750
Joseph Raiti, prin. Fax 563-3759

Woodland Montessori S 50/PK-10
1145 Little Britain Rd #200 12553 845-567-6383
Parinaz Mokhtari, prin. Fax 567-0097

New York, New York, Pop. 8,143,197
NYC Department of Education 910,800/PK-12
52 Chambers St 10007 718-935-2000
Joel Klein, chncllr.
www.nycenet.edu
Academy for Environmental Science 300/9-12
410 E 100th St 10029 212-860-5854
David Grodsky, prin. Fax 860-6008
Academy of Collaborative Education 6-8
222 W 134th St 10030 212-935-3188
Yvonne El-Amin, prin.
Art & Design HS 1,300/9-12
1075 2nd Ave 10022 212-752-4340
Scott Feltzin, prin. Fax 752-4945
Arts & Technology HS 500/9-12
122 Amsterdam Ave 10023 212-501-1198
Anne Geiger, prin. Fax 441-3693
Ballet Tech / School for Dance 200/4-12
890 Broadway Fl 3 10003 212-254-1803
John Treadwell, prin. Fax 477-5048
Bard HS Early College 9-12
525 E Houston St 10002 212-995-8479
Raymond Peterson, prin. Fax 777-4702
Baruch College Campus HS 9-12
17 Lexington Ave 10010 212-660-6400
Alicia Katz, prin. Fax 660-6401
Bayard Rustin HS for the Humanities 2,000/9-12
351 W 18th St 10011 212-675-5350
John Angelet, prin. Fax 255-5701
Beacon HS 1,000/9-12
227 W 61st St 10023 212-245-2807
Ruth Lacey, prin. Fax 245-2179
Bergtraum HS 2,800/9-12
411 Pearl St 10038 212-964-9610
Barbara Esmilla, prin. Fax 732-6622
Brandeis HS 2,500/9-12
145 W 84th St 10024 212-441-5600
Dr. Eloise Messineo, prin. Fax 877-1959
Bread & Roses Integrated Arts HS 400/9-12
6 Edgecombe Ave 10030 212-926-4152
Larry Wilson, prin. Fax 926-4317
Central Park East HS 300/9-12
1573 Madison Ave 10029 212-860-5929
Bennett Lieberman, prin. Fax 860-2938
Chelsea Career & Technical Education HS Vo/Tech
131 Avenue Of The Americas 10013 212-925-1080
Timothy Timberlake, prin. Fax 941-7934
Choir Academy of Harlem 500/4-12
2005 Madison Ave 10035 212-289-6227
Ashanti Chimurenga, prin. Fax 289-4195
City College Academy of the Arts 6-12
4600 Broadway 10040 212-567-3164
Bernadette Drysdale, prin. Fax 567-3958
Community Health Academy of the Heights 6-12
511 W 182nd St 10033 212-568-3401
Sandra Maldonado, prin. Fax 928-1716
Douglas Academy 1,300/6-12
2581 Adam Clayton Powell Jr 10039 212-491-4107
Dr. Gregory Hodge, prin. Fax 491-4414
Douglass Academy II 300/6-12
215 W 114th St 10026 212-865-9260
Latasha Greer, prin. Fax 865-9281
East Side Community HS 500/6-12
420 E 12th St 10009 212-460-8467
Mark Federman, prin. Fax 260-9657
Essex Street Academy 9-12
350 Grand St 10002 347-475-4773
Alex Shub, prin. Fax 674-2058
Facing History S 9-12
525 W 50th St 10019 718-757-2680
Gillian Smith, prin. Fax 757-2156
Fashion Industries HS 1,600/9-12
225 W 24th St 10011 212-255-1235
Hilda Nieto, prin. Fax 255-4756
Food & Finance HS 100/9-12
525 W 50th St 10019 212-586-2943
Roger E. Turgeon, prin. Fax 586-4205
Green HS of Teaching 700/9-12
421 E 88th St 10128 212-722-5240
Isabel Dimola, prin. Fax 427-8069
Greenwich Village MS 6-8
490 Hudson St 10014 212-691-7384
Kelly McGuire, prin. Fax 691-9489
Harbor Heights MS 6-8
549 Audubon Ave 10040 212-927-1841
Monica Klehr, prin.
Health Professions & Human Services HS 1,600/9-12
345 E 15th St 10003 212-780-9175
Marta Jimenez, prin. Fax 979-7261
Henry Street S for International Studies 200/6-12
220 Henry St 10002 212-406-9411
Hoa Tu, prin. Fax 406-9417
Heritage S 300/9-12
1680 Lexington Ave 10029 212-828-2858
Vivian Orlen, prin. Fax 828-2861
Humanities Preparatory S 200/9-12
351 W 18th St 10011 212-929-4433
Barnaby Spring, prin. Fax 929-4445
Institute for Collaborative Education 400/6-12
345 E 15th St 10003 212-475-7972
John Pettinato, prin. Fax 475-0459
Irving HS 2,900/9-12
40 Irving Pl 10003 212-674-5000
Dr. Denise DiCarlo, prin. Fax 674-9569
Kappa II S 100/6-8
144 E 128th St 10035 212-828-6892
Kendra Washington Bass, prin. Fax 828-6896

Kappa IV S 100/6-8
6 Edgecombe Ave 10030 212-690-4963
Panorea Panagiosoulis, prin. Fax 690-5020
Kennedy-Onassis HS 600/9-12
120 W 46th St 10036 212-391-0041
Edward Demeo, prin. Fax 391-1293
La Guardia HS 2,500/9-12
100 Amsterdam Ave 10023 212-496-0700
Kim Bruno, prin. Fax 724-5748
Landmark HS 400/9-12
220 W 58th St 10019 212-247-3414
Trevor Naidoo, prin. Fax 247-0602
Law Advocacy & Community Justice HS 500/9-12
122 Amsterdam Ave 10023 212-501-1201
Miriam Nightengale, prin. Fax 441-3697
Leadership & Public Service HS 600/9-12
90 Trinity Pl 10006 212-346-0007
Frank Brancato, prin. Fax 346-0612
Legacy S for Integrated Studies 400/9-12
34 W 14th St 10011 212-645-1980
Gregory Rodrigues, prin. Fax 645-2596
Life Science Secondary S 600/6-12
320 E 96th St 10128 212-348-1694
Genevieve Stanislaus, prin. Fax 348-4293
Lower Manhattan Arts Academy 9-12
350 Grand St 10002 212-505-0143
John Wenk, prin. Fax 475-2486
Luperon HS of Science & Math 400/9-12
516 W 181st St 10033 212-927-2561
Juan Villar, prin. Fax 927-2763
Manhattan Bridges HS 200/9-12
525 W 50th St 10019 212-757-5274
Mirza Sanchez-Medina, prin. Fax 757-5411
Manhattan HS for Science/Math 1,500/9-12
260 Pleasant Ave 10029 212-876-4639
Corinne Vinal, prin. Fax 996-5946
Manhattan/Hunter Science HS 300/9-12
122 Amsterdam Ave 10023 212-501-1235
Susan Kreisman, prin. Fax 501-1171
Manhattan International H1S 300/9-12
317 E 67th St, 212-517-6728
Alan Krull, prin. Fax 517-7147
Manhattan Theatre Lab HS 9-12
122 Amsterdam Ave 10023 212-690-7367
Evelyn Collins, prin. Fax 690-8053
Manhattan Village Academy 300/9-12
43 W 22nd St 10010 212-242-8752
Hector Geager, prin. Fax 242-7630
Marshall Academy 500/7-12
200 W 135th St 10030 212-283-8055
Dr. Sandye Johnson, prin. Fax 283-8109
Marte Valle Model HS 500/6-12
145 Stanton St 10002 212-473-8152
Jayne Godlewski, prin. Fax 475-7588
Milk HS 100/9-12
2 Astor Pl 10003 212-477-1555
Daniel Rossi, prin. Fax 674-8650
Millenium HS 300/9-12
75 Broad St 10004 212-825-9008
Robert Rhodes, prin. Fax 825-9095
Mott Hall HS 100/9-12
6 Edgecombe Ave 10030 212-690-5501
John Sullivan, prin. Fax 690-5047
Mott Hall II 300/6-8
234 W 109th St 10025 212-678-2960
Mary Moss, prin. Fax 222-0560
New Design HS 200/9-12
350 Grand St 10002 212-475-4148
Scott Conti, prin. Fax 674-2128
New Explorations Sci Tech/Math S 600/K-12
111 Columbia St 10002 212-677-5190
Olga Livanis, prin. Fax 260-8124
Newton JHS for Science Math Tech 400/6-8
260 Pleasant Ave 10029 212-860-6006
Lisa Nelson, prin. Fax 987-4197
HS Arts 200/9-12
122 Amsterdam Ave 10023 212-799-4064
Stephen Noonan, prin. Fax 799-4171
HS for Dual Language & Asian Studies 100/9-12
350 Grand St 10002 212-475-4097
Li Yan, prin. Fax 674-1392
New York HS for Economic & Finance 700/9-12
100 Trinity Pl 10006 212-346-0708
Dr. Craig Peck, prin. Fax 346-0712
New York HS for Environmental Studies 1,400/9-12
444 W 56th St 10019 212-262-8113
Shirley Matthews, prin. Fax 262-0702
HS for Math Science Engineering 300/9-12
138 Convent Ave 10031 212-281-6490
William Dugan, prin. Fax 281-6918
HS Health Careers & Science 600/9-12
549 Audubon Ave 10040 212-927-1841
Harris Marmor, prin. Fax 927-2179
HS International Business & Finance 600/9-12
549 Audubon Ave 10040 212-927-1841
Juan Alvarez, prin. Fax 923-4974
HS Law & Public Service 600/9-12
549 Audubon Ave 10040 212-927-2380
Nicholas Politis, prin. Fax 781-9516
HS Media & Communications 600/9-12
549 Audubon Ave 10040 212-927-1841
Janet Saraceno, prin. Fax 923-4974
HS of Graphic Communication Arts 2,000/9-12
439 W 49th St 10019 212-245-5925
Jerod Resnick, prin. Fax 265-1552
HS of Hospitality Management 100/9-12
525 W 50th St 10019 212-586-1819
Matthew Angrisani, prin. Fax 586-2713
IS 131 800/6-8
100 Hester St 10002 212-219-1204
Jane Lehrach, prin. Fax 925-6386
IS 195 900/6-8
625 W 133rd St 10027 212-690-5848
Aura Rivera, prin. Fax 690-5999
IS 218 1,600/6-8
4600 Broadway 10040 212-567-2322
June Barnett, prin. Fax 569-7221
IS 223 400/4-8
71 Convent Ave 10027 212-927-9466
Cynthia Arndt, prin. Fax 491-3451
IS 286 300/6-8
509 W 129th St 10027 212-690-5972
Sandra Small, prin. Fax 694-4124
IS 289 300/6-8
201 Warren St 10282 212-571-5659
Ellen Foote, prin. Fax 571-0739

IS 528 300/6-8
180 Wadsworth Ave 10033 212-740-4900
Norma Perez, prin. Fax 781-7302
JHS 13 400/6-8
1573 Madison Ave 10029 212-860-8935
Jacob Michelman, prin. Fax 860-5933
JHS 44 500/6-8
100 W 77th St 10024 212-441-1163
Liza Ortiz, prin. Fax 501-0912
JHS 45 600/6-8
2351 1st Ave 10035 212-860-5838
Maria Aviles, prin. Fax 860-5837
JHS 52 1,400/5-8
650 Academy St 10034 212-567-9162
Salvador Fernandez, prin. Fax 942-4952
JHS 54 900/6-8
103 W 107th St 10025 212-678-2861
Dr. Elana Elster, prin. Fax 316-0883
JHS 104 1,100/6-8
330 E 21st St 10010 212-674-4545
Rosemarie Gaetani, prin. Fax 477-2205
JHS 117 500/6-8
240 E 109th St 10029 212-860-5872
Major Fareed, prin. Fax 876-3782
JHS 143 1,600/6-8
511 W 182nd St 10033 212-927-7739
Ourania Pappas, prin. Fax 781-5539
JHS 167 1,200/6-8
220 E 76th St 10021 212-535-8610
Jennifer Rehn, prin. Fax 472-9385
MS 114 300/6-8
1458 York Ave, 212-439-6278
David Getz, prin. Fax 717-5606
MS 224 200/6-8
410 E 100th St 10029 212-860-6047
Lillian Sarro, prin. Fax 410-0678
MS 243 200/5-8
270 W 70th St 10023 212-678-2791
Elaine Schwartz, prin. Fax 579-9728
MS 244 200/6-8
100 W 77th St 10024 212-441-1191
Rodney Murphy, prin. Fax 501-7235
MS 245 300/6-8
100 W 77th St 10024 212-441-0873
Henry Zymeck, prin. Fax 678-5908
MS 246 200/6-8
234 W 109th St 10025 212-678-5850
Rodney Murphy, prin. Fax 678-4275
MS 247 200/6-8
32 W 92nd St 10025 212-799-2653
Claudia Aguirre, prin. Fax 579-2407
MS 250 200/6-8
735 W End Ave 10025 212-866-6313
Jeanne Rotunda, dir. Fax 678-5295
MS 255 300/6-8
319 E 19th St 10003 212-614-8785
Rhonda Perry, prin. Fax 614-0095
MS 256 200/6-8
154 W 93rd St 10025 212-222-2857
Cheryl Rosen, prin. Fax 531-0586
MS 258 200/6-8
154 W 93rd St 10025 212-678-5888
John Curry, prin. Fax 961-1613
MS 260 200/6-8
320 W 21st St 10011 212-255-8860
Joseph Cassidy, prin. Fax 807-0421
MS 319 100/6-8
21 Jumel Pl 10032 212-923-3827
Ysidro Abreu, prin. Fax 923-3676
MS 321 100/6-8
21 Jumel Pl 10032 212-923-5129
Pamela Glover, prin. Fax 923-5180
MS 322 6-8
4600 Broadway 10040 212-304-0853
Erica Zigelman, prin. Fax 567-3016
MS 324 100/6-8
21 Jumel Pl 10032 212-923-4057
Janet Heller, prin. Fax 923-4626
MS 326 200/6-8
401 W 164th St 10032 917-521-8175
Sharon Weissbrot, prin. Fax 521-1705
MS 328 200/6-8
401 W 164th St 10032 917-521-2508
Jorge A. Estrella, prin. Fax 521-7797
MS 332 100/6-8
220 Henry St 10002 212-267-5701
Cyndi Kerr, prin. Fax 267-5703
NYC Lab School for Collaborative Studies 400/6-8
333 W 17th St 10011 212-691-6119
Gary Eisinger, prin. Fax 691-6219
NYC Museum S 300/9-12
333 W 17th St 10011 212-675-6204
Darlene Miller, dir. Fax 675-6524
Pace HS 100/9-12
100 Hester St 10002 212-334-4663
Yvette Sy, prin. Fax 334-4919
Park East HS 300/9-12
230 E 105th St 10029 212-831-1517
Kevin McCarthy, prin. Fax 348-6097
Powell MS for Law & Social Justice 600/6-8
509 W 129th St 10027 212-690-5977
Winston Riley, prin. Fax 690-5980
Professional Performing Arts HS 400/6-12
328 W 48th St 10036 212-247-8652
Keith Ryan, prin. Fax 247-7514
Public MS 345 - CASTLE 400/6-8
220 Henry St 10002 212-227-0762
Mauriciere Degovia, prin. Fax 577-9785
Randolph HS 1,800/9-12
443 W 135th St 10031 212-926-0113
Maurice Collins, prin. Fax 281-2726
Repertory Company HS for Theatre Arts 200/9-12
123 W 43rd St 10036 212-382-1875
Michael Mehmet, prin. Fax 382-2306
Roosevelt HS 300/9-12
411 E 76th St 10021 212-772-1220
Susan Elliott, prin. Fax 772-1440
School for the Physical City 300/9-12
55 E 25th St 10010 212-683-7440
Junior Miller, prin. Fax 683-7338
School of the Future 600/6-12
127 E 22nd St 10010 212-475-8086
C. Delaura, dir. Fax 475-9273
Stuyvesant HS 2,900/9-12
345 Chambers St 10282 212-312-4800
Stanley Teitel, prin. Fax 587-3874

Talent Unlimited HS 400/9-12
317 E 67th St, 212-737-1530
Deena Forman, prin. Fax 737-2863
Technology Arts & Sciences Studio 6-8
185 1st Ave 10003 212-982-1836
George Morgan, prin. Fax 982-0528
Thomas HS 2,800/9-12
111 E 33rd St 10016 212-576-0500
Steven Satin, prin. Fax 545-9648
Tompkins Square MS 200/6-8
600 E 6th St 10009 212-995-1430
Mark Pingitore, prin. Fax 995-9671
Unity Center for Urban Technologies 200/9-12
121 Avenue Of The Americas 10013 212-343-8038
Maritza Tamayo, prin. Fax 343-8044
University Neighborhood HS 400/9-12
200 Monroe St 10002 212-962-4341
Robert Miller, prin. Fax 267-5611
Urban Academy Laboratory S 100/9-12
317 E 67th St, 212-570-5284
Herb Mack, prin. Fax 570-5366
Urban Assembly Media HS 100/9-12
122 Amsterdam Ave 10023 212-501-1110
Lynette Delgado, prin. Fax 501-1111
Urban Assembly of Government & Law 9-12
350 Grand St 10002 718-935-3356
Joaquin Tamayo, prin.
Urban Assembly S Design & Construction 100/9-12
525 W 50th St 10019 212-586-0981
Lawrence Pendergast, prin. Fax 586-1731
Urban Assembly S of Business 9-12
420 E 12th St 10009 917-475-1071
Patricia Minaya, prin. Fax 475-1739
Urban Peace Academy 300/9-12
2351 1st Ave 10035 212-987-1906
Flora Greenaway, prin. Fax 987-1915
Vanguard HS 400/9-12
317 E 67th St, 212-517-5175
Louis Delgado, prin. Fax 517-5334
Wadleigh Arts HS 800/6-12
215 W 114th St 10026 212-749-5800
Karen Watts, prin. Fax 749-6463
Washington Hts. Expeditionary Learning S 6-12
511 W 182nd St 10033 212-781-0524
Brett Kimmel, prin. Fax 781-0742
Young Womens Leadership HS 9-12
105 E 106th St 10029 212-289-7593
Kathleen Ponze, prin. Fax 289-7728
Manhattan Comprehensive Night & Day HS Adult
240 2nd Ave 10003 212-353-2010
Howard Friedman, prin. Fax 353-1673
Other Schools – See Astoria, Bayside, Bellerose, Bronx, Brooklyn, Corona, East Elmhurst, Elmhurst, Far Rockaway, Floral Park, Flushing, Forest Hills, Fresh Meadows, Glendale, Hollis, Jackson Heights, Jamaica, Laurelton, Little Neck, Long Island City, Maspeth, Oakland Gardens, Ozone Park, Queens Village, Rego Park, Richmond Hill, Ridgewood, Rockaway Park, Saint Albans, South Ozone Park, Springfield Gardens, Staten Island, Whitestone, Woodside

---

American Academy McAllister Institute Post-Sec.
619 W 54th St Fl 6 10019 212-757-1190
American Academy of Dramatic Arts Post-Sec.
120 Madison Ave 10016 212-686-9244
American Barber Institute Post-Sec.
252 W 29th St 10001 212-290-2289
American University in Cairo Post-Sec.
420 5th Ave Fl 3 10018 212-730-8800
Apex Technical School Post-Sec.
635 Avenue Of The Americas 10011 212-645-3300
Art Institute of New York City Post-Sec.
75 Varick St Fl 16 10013 212-226-5500
Bank Street College of Education Post-Sec.
610 W 112th St 10025 212-875-4404
Barnard College Post-Sec.
3009 Broadway 10027 212-854-5262
Bellevue Hospital Center Post-Sec.
462 1st Ave 10016 212-561-4132
Birch Wathen Lenox S 400/K-12
210 E 77th St, 212-861-0404
Frank Carnabuci, prin. Fax 879-5309
Boricua College Post-Sec.
3755 Broadway 10032 212-694-1000
Brearley S 700/K-12
610 E 83rd St 10028 212-744-8582
Dr. Stephanie Hull, prin. Fax 472-8020
Browning S 400/K-12
52 E 62nd St, 212-838-6280
Stephen Clement, prin. Fax 355-5602
Calhoun S 700/2-12
433 W End Ave 10024 212-497-6500
Steven Nelson, hdmstr. Fax 497-6530
Caliber Training Institute Post-Sec.
500 Fashion Ave Frnt 2 10018 212-564-0500
Cathedral HS 900/9-12
350 E 56th St 10022 212-688-1545
Sr. Elizabeth Graham, prin. Fax 754-2024
Chapin S 600/K-12
100 E End Ave 10028 212-744-2335
Patricia Hayot, hdmstr. Fax 535-8138
Chubb Institute Post-Sec.
498 Fashion Ave Fl 17 10018 212-659-2116
Churchill S and Center 400/K-12
301 E 29th St 10016 212-722-0610
Wendy Federico, dir. Fax 722-1387
College of New Rochelle Post-Sec.
125 Barclay St 10007 212-815-1710
College of New Rochelle Post-Sec.
144 W 125th St 10027 212-662-7500
Collegiate S 600/K-12
260 W 78th St 10024 212-812-8500
Lee Levison, hdmstr. Fax 812-8522
Columbia Grammar & Prep S 1,000/PK-12
5 W 93rd St 10025 212-749-6200
Richard Soghoian, prin. Fax 865-4278
Columbia University Post-Sec.
168th & Broadway 10032 212-305-5756
Columbia University Post-Sec.
2960 Broadway 10027 212-854-1754
Connelly Center for Education 100/5-8
220 E 4th St 10009 212-982-2287
Kimberly Morcate, prin. Fax 984-0547

Convent of the Sacred Heart S PK-12
1 E 91st St 10128 212-722-4745
Patricia Hult, hdmstr. Fax 996-1784
Cooper Union Post-Sec.
30 Cooper Sq 10003 212-353-4100
Cope Institute Post-Sec.
225 Broadway Fl 2 10007 212-809-5935
County Univ. Sch. of Dental & Oral Surg. Post-Sec.
630 W 168th St 10032
Culinary Academy of New York Post-Sec.
154 W 14th St 10011 212-675-6655
CUNY Bernard M. Baruch College Post-Sec.
17 Lexington Ave 10010 212-802-2000
CUNY Borough/Manhattan Comm. College Post-Sec.
199 Chambers St 10007 212-346-8800
CUNY City College Post-Sec.
160 Convent Ave 10031 212-650-7000
CUNY Graduate Center Post-Sec.
365 5th Ave 10016 212-817-7000
CUNY Hunter College Post-Sec.
695 Park Ave 10021 212-772-4000
CUNY John Jay College Criminal Justice Post-Sec.
899 10th Ave 10019 212-237-8000
Dalton S 1,300/K-12
108 E 89th St 10128 212-423-5200
Ellen Stein, hdmstr. Fax 423-5259
De La Salle Academy 100/6-8
202 W 97th St 10025 212-316-5840
Br. Brian Carty, prin. Fax 316-5998
Dominican Academy 200/9-12
44 E 68th St, 212-744-0195
Sr. Joan Franks, prin. Fax 744-0375
Dwight S 500/PK-12
291 Central Park W 10024 212-724-6360
Stephen Spahn, prin. Fax 874-7232
Fashion Institute of Technology Post-Sec.
227 W 27th St 10001 212-217-7999
FEGS Trades & Business School Post-Sec.
80 Vandam St 10013 212-366-8466
Folk Art Institute Post-Sec.
45 E 53rd St 10022 212-977-7170
Fordham University Post-Sec.
113 W 60th St 10023 212-636-6000
French Culinary Institute Post-Sec.
462 Broadway 10013 212-219-8890
Friends Seminary S 700/K-12
222 E 16th St 10003 212-979-5030
Robert Lauder, prin. Fax 979-5034
Gemological Institute of America Post-Sec.
580 5th Ave 10036 212-944-5900
General Theological Seminary Post-Sec.
175 9th Ave 10011 212-243-5150
Global Business Institute Post-Sec.
209 W 125th St 10027 212-663-1500
Globe Institute of Technology Post-Sec.
291 Broadway Fl 2 10007 212-349-4330
Harlem International Community S 50/PK-12
2116 Adam Clayton Powell Jr 10027 212-222-7798
Ms. Wallie Simpson, prin. Fax 222-7798
Harlem School of Technology Post-Sec.
215 W 125th St 10027 212-932-2849
Hebrew Union College Post-Sec.
1 W 4th St 10012 212-674-5300
Helene Fuld College of Nursing Post-Sec.
1879 Madison Ave 10035 212-423-2700
Heschel MS 100/6-8
314 W 91st St 10024 212-595-7817
Lori Skopp, prin. Fax 595-6281
Heschel S 700/PK-12
270 W 89th St 10024 212-595-7087
Roanna Shorofsky, dir. Fax 595-7252
Hewitt S 500/K-12
45 E 75th St 10021 212-288-1919
Linda MacMurray Gibbs, hdmstr. Fax 472-7531
Hunter College Campus S 1,600/K-12
71 E 94th St 10128 212-860-1267
Dr. John Mucciolo, dir. Fax 289-2209
Institute of Allied Medical Professions Post-Sec.
405 Park Ave 10022 212-758-1410
Institute of Audio Research Post-Sec.
64 University Pl 10003 212-677-7590
Interboro Institute Post-Sec.
450 W 56th St 10019 212-399-0091
Jewish Theological Seminary of America Post-Sec.
3080 Broadway 10027 212-678-8000
Juilliard School Post-Sec.
60 Lincoln Center Plz 10023 212-799-5000
Katharine Gibbs School Post-Sec.
50 W 40th St 10018 212-867-9300
Keller Graduate School Post-Sec.
120 W 45th St Ste 200 10036 212-556-0002
Kings Academy 200/PK-12
2345 3rd Ave 10035 212-348-7380
Thomas Streitferdt, prin. Fax 348-0515
Laboratory Institute of Merchandising Post-Sec.
12 E 53rd St 10022 212-752-1530
LaSalle Academy 600/9-12
44 E 2nd St 10003 212-475-8940
John Quinn, prin. Fax 529-3598
La Scuola New York G. Marconi S 200/PK-12
12 E 96th St 10128 212-369-3290
B. Padolecchia Goodrich, prin. Fax 369-1164
Learning Institute for Beauty Sciences Post-Sec.
22 W 34th St 10001 212-695-4555
Lia Schorr Inst of Cosmetic Skin Care Post-Sec.
686 Lexington Ave 10022 212-486-9541
Lookstein Upper S 500/9-12
60 E 78th St, 212-774-8000
Kenneth Rochlin, dir. Fax 774-8099
Loyola S 200/9-12
980 Park Ave 10028 212-288-3522
James Lyness, hdmstr. Fax 861-1021
LREI Little Red School House 600/PK-12
272 Avenue of the Americas 10014 212-477-5316
Philip Kassen, dir. Fax 677-9159
Lycee Francais De New York 1,300/PK-12
505 E 75th St 10021 212-369-1400
Yves Theze, prin. Fax 439-4210
Lyceum Kennedy S 200/PK-12
225 E 43rd St 10017 212-681-1877
Yves Rivaud, hdmstr. Fax 681-1922
Mandl School College of Allied Health Post-Sec.
254 W 54th St 10019 212-247-3434
Manhattan HS for Girls 200/9-12
154 E 70th St 10021 212-737-6800
Ruth Assaf, prin. Fax 737-0766

Manhattan School of Computer Technology Post-Sec.
42 Broadway Fl 22 10004 212-349-9768
Manhattan School of Music Post-Sec.
120 Claremont Ave 10027 212-749-2802
Mannes College of Music Post-Sec.
150 W 85th St 10024 212-580-0210
Marymount Manhattan College Post-Sec.
221 E 71st St 10021 212-517-0400
Marymount S 500/PK-12
1026 5th Ave 10028 212-744-4486
Concepcion Alvar, hdmstr. Fax 744-0163
Memorial Sloan Kettering Cancer Center Post-Sec.
1275 York Ave, 212-639-6561
Mercy College - Manhattan Campus Post-Sec.
66 W 35th St 10001 212-615-3351
Mesivta Tifereth Jerusalem of America Post-Sec.
145 E Broadway 10002 212-964-2830
Mesivta Tifereth Jerusalem S 200/PK-12
145 E Broadway 10002 212-964-2830
Rabbi Stanley Bronfeld, prin. Fax 349-5213
Metropolitan College of New York Post-Sec.
75 Varick St 10013 212-343-1234
Mother Cabrini HS 500/9-12
701 Fort Washington Ave 10040 212-923-3540
Brian Donahue, prin. Fax 781-2051
Mt. Sinai School of Medicine Post-Sec.
1 Gustave L Levy Pl 10029 212-241-6546
Nativity Mission MS 100/6-8
204 Forsyth St 10002 212-477-2472
Nick Romero, prin. Fax 473-0538
New School University Post-Sec.
66 W 12th St 10011 212-229-5600
New York Academy of Art Post-Sec.
111 Franklin St 10013 212-966-0300
New York Career Institute Post-Sec.
11 Park Pl Fl 4 10007 212-962-0002
New York College of Podiatric Medicine Post-Sec.
1800 Park Ave 10035 212-410-8000
New York Eye & Ear Infirmary Post-Sec.
310 E 14th St 10003 212-979-4375
New York Institute of Technology Post-Sec.
1855 Broadway 10023 212-261-1508
New York Inst. of Business Technology Post-Sec.
248 W 35th St 10001 212-725-9400
New York International Beauty School Post-Sec.
500 8th Ave Rm 803 10018 212-868-7171
New York Law School Post-Sec.
57 Worth St 10013 212-431-2888
New York Paralegal School Post-Sec.
299 Broadway Ste 200 10007 212-349-8800
New York Presbyterian Hospital Post-Sec.
525 E 68th St, 212-746-4000
New York School of Interior Design Post-Sec.
170 E 70th St 10021 212-472-1500
New York Theological Seminary Post-Sec.
475 Riverside Dr Ste 500 10115 212-870-1211
New York University Post-Sec.
70 Washington Sq S 10012 212-998-1212
New York University Medical Center Post-Sec.
550 1st Ave 10016 212-263-5111
Nightingale-Bamford S 600/K-12
20 E 92nd St 10128 212-289-5020
Dorothy Hutcheson, hdmstr. Fax 876-1045
Northeastern Academy 200/9-12
532 W 215th St 10034 212-569-4800
Marlene Alvarez, prin. Fax 569-6145
Notre Dame HS 200/9-12
327 W 13th St 10014 212-620-5575
Maureen Ryan, prin. Fax 620-0432
Pace University Post-Sec.
1 Pace Plz 10038 212-346-1200
Pacific College of Oriental Medicine Post-Sec.
915 Broadway Fl 3 10010 212-982-3456
Parsons School of Design Post-Sec.
66 5th Ave 10011 212-229-8953
Phillips Beth Israel School of Nursing Post-Sec.
776 Avenue of the Americas 10001 212-614-6110
Professional Business College Post-Sec.
125 Canal St 10002 212-226-7300
Professional Children's S 200/6-12
132 W 60th St 10023 212-582-3116
Dr. James Dawson, hdmstr. Fax 956-3295
Rabbi Isaac Elchanan Theological Sem. Post-Sec.
2495 Amsterdam Ave 10033 212-960-5344
Ramaz MS 200/5-8
114 E 85th St 10028 212-774-8040
Rabbi Jeffrey Kobrin, hdmstr. Fax 774-8061
Regis HS 500/9-12
55 E 84th St 10028 212-288-1100
Dr. Gary Tocchet, prin. Fax 794-1221
Rice HS 400/9-12
74 W 124th St Frnt 1 10027 212-369-4100
Br. John Walderman, hdmstr. Fax 348-4631
Rockefeller University Post-Sec.
1230 York Ave, 212-327-8000
St. Agnes Boys HS 300/9-12
555 W End Ave 10024 212-873-9100
Br. Richard Van Houten, prin. Fax 873-9292
St. George Academy HS 100/9-12
215 E 6th St 10003 212-473-3323
Peter Shyshka, prin. Fax 534-0819
St. Jean Baptiste HS 400/9-12
173 E 75th St 10021 212-288-1645
Sr. Ona Bessette, prin. Fax 288-6540
St. John's University Post-Sec.
101 Murray St 10007 212-962-4111
St. Michael Academy 400/9-12
425 W 33rd St 10001 212-563-2547
Sr. Kathleen Cusack, prin. Fax 563-9892
St. Thomas Choir S 50/3-8
202 W 58th St 10019 212-247-3311
Charles Wallace, hdmstr. Fax 247-3393
St. Vincent Ferrer HS 500/9-12
151 E 65th St, 212-535-4680
Sr. Gail Morgan, prin. Fax 988-3455
St. Vincent's Hospital & Medical Center Post-Sec.
153 W 11th St 10011 212-604-7500
School for the Deaf Post-Sec.
225 E 23rd St 10010
School of Visual Arts Post-Sec.
209 E 23rd St 10010 212-592-2000
Sessions.edu Online School of Design Post-Sec.
350 7th Ave Rm 1203 10001 212-239-3080
Sotheby's Institute of Art Post-Sec.
1334 York Ave 10021 212-894-1111

Spanish-American Institute Post-Sec.
215 W 43rd St 10036 212-840-7111
Spence S 600/K-12
22 E 91st St 10128 212-289-5940
Ellanor Brize, hdmstr. Fax 860-2652
Steiner Upper S 100/7-12
15 E 78th St, 212-879-1101
Josh Eisen, prin. Fax 794-1554
Studio Jewelers Post-Sec.
32 E 31st St 10016 212-686-1944
SUNY College of Optometry Post-Sec.
33 W 42nd St 10036 212-780-4900
SUNY Empire State College Post-Sec.
325 Hudson St Flr 5 10013 212-647-7800
Swedish Institute Post-Sec.
226 W 26th St Fl 5 10001 212-924-5900
TCI Institute The College of Technology Post-Sec.
320 W 31st St 10001 212-594-4000
Teachers College of Columbia University Post-Sec.
525 W 120th St 10027 212-678-3000
The Institute of Culinary Education Post-Sec.
50 W 23rd St 10010 212-847-0711
Touro College Post-Sec.
27 W 23rd St # 33 10010 212-463-0400
Touro College Post-Sec.
240 E 123rd St 10035 212-722-1575
Trevor Day S 200/6-12
1 W 88th St 10024 212-426-3360
Pam Clarke, dir. Fax 873-8520
Trinity S 1,000/K-12
139 W 91st St 10024 212-873-1650
Henry Moses, hdmstr. Fax 799-3417
Tri-State College of Acupuncture Post-Sec.
265 W 14th St Ste 400 10011 212-242-2255
Ultrasound Diagnostic School Post-Sec.
120 E 16th St Fl 2 10003 212-645-9116
U.N. International S 1,500/K-12
2450 FDR Dr Frnt 2 10010 212-684-7400
Dr. Kenneth Wrye, dir. Fax 684-1382
Union Theological Seminary Post-Sec.
3041 Broadway 10027 212-662-7100
Weill Medical College of Cornell Univ Post-Sec.
1300 York Ave, 212-746-5454
Winston Preparatory S 200/6-12
126 W 17th St 10011 646-638-2705
Scott Bezsylko, hdmstr. Fax 638-2706
Wood Tobe-Coburn School Post-Sec.
8 E 40th St 10016 212-686-9040
Xavier HS 900/9-12
30 W 16th St 10011 212-924-7900
Michael Livigni, hdmstr. Fax 924-0303
Yeshiva Rabbi S.R. Hirsch 500/PK-12
91 Bennett Ave 10033 212-568-6200
Jonathan Simon, admin. Fax 928-4422
Yeshiva University Post-Sec.
55 5th Ave 10003 212-790-0274
Yeshiva University Post-Sec.
500 W 185th St 10033 212-960-5400
Yeshiva University HS 300/9-12
2540 Amsterdam Ave 10033 212-960-5345
Yaacov Sklar, prin. Fax 960-0027
York Prep S 300/6-12
40 W 68th St 10023 212-362-0400
Ronald Stewart, hdmstr. Fax 362-7106

New York Mills, Oneida, Pop. 3,146
New York Mills UFD 600/K-12
1 Marauder Blvd 13417 315-768-8127
Dave Langone, supt. Fax 768-3521
www.newyorkmills.org
New York Mills JSHS 300/7-12
1 Marauder Blvd 13417 315-768-8124
Gary Hadfield, prin. Fax 768-3521

Niagara Falls, Niagara, Pop. 52,866
Niagara Falls CSD 8,200/PK-12
607 Walnut Ave 14301 716-286-4205
Carmen Granto, supt. Fax 286-4283
www.nfschools.net/
Gaskill MS 800/6-8
910 Hyde Park Blvd 14301 716-278-5820
Joseph Colburn, prin. Fax 278-5829
La Salle MS 700/6-8
7436 Buffalo Ave 14304 716-278-5880
Richard Carella, prin. Fax 283-2494
Niagara Falls HS 2,400/9-12
4455 Porter Rd 14305 716-278-5800
Mark Laurrie, prin. Fax 286-7964
Niagara MS 600/6-8
6431 Girard Ave 14304 716-278-9120
Maria Chille-Zafuto, prin. Fax 278-9122

Niagara-Wheatfield Central SD 4,000/PK-12
6700 Schultz St 14304 716-215-3003
Dr. Judith Howard, supt. Fax 215-3039
www.nwcsd.k12.ny.us
Other Schools – See Sanborn

Cheryl Fell's School of Business Post-Sec.
2541 Military Rd 14304 716-297-2750
Niagara Catholic JSHS 200/7-12
520 66th St 14304 716-283-8771
Robert DiFrancesco, prin. Fax 283-8774
St. Dominic Savio MS 200/6-8
504 66th St 14304 716-215-1461
Rose Mary Buscaglia, prin. Fax 215-1465

Niagara University, Niagara

Niagara University Post-Sec.
PO Box 9999 14109 716-285-1212

North Babylon, Suffolk, Pop. 18,081
North Babylon UFD 5,200/K-12
5 Jardine Pl 11703 631-321-3226
Dr. Joseph Laria, supt. Fax 321-3295
www.nbsd.org
Moses MS 1,300/6-8
250 Phelps Ln 11703 631-321-3251
Kathleen Hartnett, prin. Fax 587-2619
North Babylon HS 1,500/9-12
1 Phelps Ln 11703 631-321-3233
Donald Shevlin, prin. Fax 321-3327

North Collins, Erie, Pop. 1,033
North Collins Central SD 700/K-12
2045 School St 14111 716-337-0101
Benjamin Halsey, supt. Fax 337-3457
www.northcollins.com
North Collins JSHS 400/7-12
2045 School St 14111 716-337-0101
Annie Metcalf, prin. Fax 337-3457

North Creek, Warren
Johnsburg Central SD 400/K-12
PO Box 380 12853 518-251-2814
Michael Markwica, supt. Fax 251-2562
www.johnsburg.k12.ny.us
Johnsburg Central S 400/K-12
PO Box 380 12853 518-251-3504
Nadine Allard, prin. Fax 251-2562

North Massapequa, Nassau, Pop. 19,365
Plainedge UFD 3,600/K-12
241 Wyngate Dr 11758 516-992-7455
Dr. John Richman, supt. Fax 992-7446
www.plainedgeschools.org
Other Schools – See Bethpage, Massapequa

North Merrick, Nassau, Pop. 12,113
Bellmore-Merrick Central HSD 5,900/7-12
1260 Meadowbrook Rd 11566 516-992-1000
Dr. Henry Kiernan, supt. Fax 623-0151
www.bellmore-merrick.k12.ny.us
Other Schools – See Bellmore, Merrick

Northport, Suffolk, Pop. 7,587
Northport-East Northport UFD 6,500/PK-12
PO Box 210 11768 631-262-6604
Marylou McDermott, supt. Fax 262-6607
northport.k12.ny.us
Northport HS 1,900/9-12
154 Laurel Hill Rd 11768 631-262-6652
Irene McLaughlin, prin. Fax 262-6736
Northport MS 800/6-8
11 Middleville Rd 11768 631-262-6750
Thomas Heinegg, prin. Fax 262-6793
Other Schools – See East Northport

Northport VA Medical Center Post-Sec.
79 Middleville Rd 11768 631-261-4400

North Salem, Westchester
North Salem Central SD 1,400/K-12
230 June Rd 10560 914-669-5414
Dr. Ken Freeston, supt. Fax 669-8753
northsalem.k12.ny.us
North Salem MSHS 700/6-12
230 June Rd 10560 914-669-5414
Dr. Patricia Cyganovich, prin. Fax 669-5663

North Syracuse, Onondaga, Pop. 6,726
North Syracuse Central SD 9,800/PK-12
5355 W Taft Rd 13212 315-218-2151
Jerome Melvin, supt. Fax 218-2185
www.nscsd.org
North Syracuse JHS 1,700/8-9
5353 W Taft Rd 13212 315-218-3600
Constance Turose, prin. Fax 218-3685
Other Schools – See Cicero

North Tonawanda, Niagara, Pop. 32,072
North Tonawanda CSD 4,400/PK-12
175 Humphrey St 14120 716-807-3599
Vincent Vecchiarella, supt. Fax 807-3525
www.ntcityschools.wnyric.org
North Tonawanda HS 1,600/9-12
405 Meadow Dr 14120 716-807-3600
James Fisher, prin. Fax 807-3639
North Tonawanda MS 800/7-8
1500 Vanderbilt Ave 14120 716-807-3700
Richard Barone, prin. Fax 807-3701

North Tonawanda Catholic S 100/4-8
75 Keil St 14120 716-693-2828
Sr. Rosemarie Kutsko, prin. Fax 693-0169

Northville, Fulton, Pop. 1,159
Northville Central SD 500/PK-12
PO Box 608 12134 518-863-7000
Dr. Harry Brooks, supt. Fax 863-7011
northvillecsd.k12.ny.us
Northville MSHS 300/6-12
PO Box 608 12134 518-863-7000
Michael Healey, prin. Fax 863-7011

Norwich, Chenango, Pop. 7,233
Norwich CSD 2,300/PK-12
19 Eaton Ave Ste 500 13815 607-334-1600
Gerard O'Sullivan, supt. Fax 336-8652
www.norwichcityschooldistrict.com/
Norwich HS 700/9-12
19 Eaton Ave Ste 500 13815 607-334-1600
Fax 334-6680
Norwich MS 400/7-8
19 Eaton Ave Ste 500 13815 607-334-1600
Lisa Schuchman, prin. Fax 334-6210

Valley Heights Christian Academy 100/PK-12
75 Calvary Dr 13815 607-336-8422
Eric Schimke, prin.

Norwood, Saint Lawrence, Pop. 1,627
Norwood-Norfolk Central SD 1,100/K-12
PO Box 194 13668 315-353-9951
Elizabeth Kirnie, supt. Fax 353-2467
www.nncsk12.org/
Norwood HS 400/9-12
PO Box 194 13668 315-353-6631
Robin Fetter, prin. Fax 353-2480
Norwood-Norfolk MS 400/5-8
PO Box 194 13668 315-353-6674
Robert Stewart, prin.

Nunda, Livingston, Pop. 1,280
Keshequa Central SD 900/K-12
PO Box 517 14517 585-468-2541
Edward Stores, supt. Fax 468-3814
www.keshequa.org
Keshequa HS 300/9-12
PO Box 517 14517 585-468-2513
Doris Marsh, prin. Fax 468-5493
Keshequa MS 200/6-8
PO Box 517 14517 585-468-2513
Doris Marsh, prin. Fax 468-3814

Nyack, Rockland, Pop. 6,676
Nyack UFD 2,900/K-12
13A Dickinson Ave 10960 845-353-7015
Dr. Valencia Douglas, supt. Fax 353-0508
www.nyackschools.com
Nyack MS 600/6-8
98 S Highland Ave 10960 845-353-7200
Jacqueline Gonzalez, prin. Fax 353-0506
Other Schools – See Upper Nyack

Alliance Theological Seminary Post-Sec.
350 N Highland Ave 10960 845-353-2020
Nyack College Post-Sec.
1 South Blvd 10960 845-358-1710

Oakdale, Suffolk, Pop. 7,875
Connetquot Central SD
Supt. — See Bohemia
Oakdale-Bohemia Road MS 800/6-8
60 Oakdale Bohemia Rd 11769 631-244-2268
Dr. Terry Earley, prin. Fax 563-6167

Dowling College Post-Sec.
150 Idle Hour Blvd 11769 631-244-3000

Oakfield, Genesee, Pop. 1,721
Oakfield-Alabama Central SD 1,100/K-12
7001 Lewiston Rd 14125 585-948-5211
Robert McIntosh, supt. Fax 948-9362
www.oahornets.org
Oakfield-Alabama JSHS 600/6-12
7001 Lewiston Rd 14125 585-948-5211
Lynn Muscarella, prin. Fax 948-9362

Oakland Gardens, See New York
NYC Department of Education
Supt. — See New York
Cardozo HS 4,100/9-12
5700 223rd St 11364 718-279-6500
Richard Hallman, prin. Fax 631-7880
JHS 74 1,000/6-8
6115 Oceania St 11364 718-631-6800
Andrea Dapolito, prin. Fax 631-6899

CUNY Queensborough Community College Post-Sec.
22205 56th Ave 11364 718-631-6262

Oceanside, Nassau, Pop. 32,800
Oceanside UFD 6,300/PK-12
145 Merle Ave 11572 516-678-1215
Dr. Herb Brown, supt. Fax 678-7503
www.oceanside.k12.ny.us/
Oceanside HS 2,000/9-12
3160 Skillman Ave 11572 516-678-7526
Dorie Ciulla, prin. Fax 678-6790
Oceanside MS 1,000/7-8
186 Alice Ave 11572 516-678-8518
Robert Fenter, prin. Fax 594-2365

Hochstim School of Radiography Post-Sec.
PO Box 9007 11572 516-763-2030

Odessa, Schuyler, Pop. 608
Odessa-Montour Central SD 600/K-12
PO Box 430 14869 607-594-3341
James Frame, supt. Fax 594-3976
www.omschools.org
Odessa-Montour MSHS 300/6-12
PO Box 430 14869 607-594-3341
Andy Morrow, prin. Fax 594-3438

Ogdensburg, Saint Lawrence, Pop. 11,422
Ogdensburg CSD 1,700/K-12
1100 State St 13669 315-393-0900
Maurice Barry, supt. Fax 393-2767
www.ogdensburgk12.org/
Ogdensburg Free Academy HS 900/7-12
1100 State St 13669 315-393-0900
Cynthia Centofanti, prin. Fax 393-7412

Old Forge, Herkimer
Town of Webb UFD 400/K-12
PO Box 38 13420 315-369-3222
Donald Gooley, supt. Fax 369-6216
www.towschool.org
Town of Webb S 400/K-12
PO Box 38 13420 315-369-3222
Marie Schoonover, prin. Fax 369-6216

Old Westbury, Nassau, Pop. 5,035
East Williston UFD 1,800/K-12
11 Bacon Rd 11568 516-333-3758
Dr. Carolyn Harris, supt.
www.ewsdonline.org/
Wheatley HS, 11 Bacon Rd 11568 700/8-12
Richard Simon, prin. 516-333-7804

Westbury UFD 4,000/PK-12
2 Hitchcock Ln 11568 516-874-1829
Dr. Constance Clark, supt. Fax 876-5187
www.westburyschools.org
Westbury HS 1,100/9-12
1 Post Rd 11568 516-876-5047
Manuel Arias, prin. Fax 876-5079
Other Schools – See Westbury

New York Institute of Technology Post-Sec.
PO Box 8000 11568 516-686-7520
New York Institute of Technology Post-Sec.
PO Box 8000 11568 516-686-7516
SUNY College at Old Westbury Post-Sec.
PO Box 210 11568 516-876-3000
SUNY Empire State College Post-Sec.
PO Box 130 11568 516-997-4700

Olean, Cattaraugus, Pop. 14,799
Olean CSD 2,300/PK-12
410 W Sullivan St 14760 716-375-8018
Mark Ward, supt. Fax 375-8047
www.oleanschools.org
Olean HS 800/9-12
410 W Sullivan St 14760 716-375-8010
Barbara Lias, prin. Fax 375-8048
Olean MS 500/6-8
401 Wayne St 14760 716-375-8061
Gerald Trietley, prin. Fax 375-8070

Archbishop Walsh HS 100/9-12
208 N 24th St 14760 585-372-8122
Rev. Barry Allaire, prin. Fax 372-6707
Continental School of Beauty Culture Post-Sec.
515 N Union St 14760 716-372-5095
Jamestown Community College 14760 Post-Sec.
585-372-1661
Olean Business Institute Post-Sec.
301 N Union St 14760 716-372-7978

Olmstedville, Essex
Minerva Central SD 100/PK-12
PO Box 39 12857 518-251-2000
Timothy Farrell, supt. Fax 251-2395
Minerva Central S 100/PK-12
PO Box 39 12857 518-251-2000
Heidi Kelly, prin. Fax 251-2395

Oneida, Madison, Pop. 10,923
Oneida CSD 2,400/K-12
PO Box 327 13421 315-363-2550
Ronald R. Spadafora, supt. Fax 363-6728
www.oneidany.org
Oneida HS 800/9-12
560 Seneca St 13421 315-363-6901
Brian Gallagher, prin. Fax 366-0619
Other Schools – See Wampsville

Oneonta, Otsego, Pop. 13,206
Oneonta CSD 2,200/PK-12
189 Main St 13820 607-433-8200
Michael Shea, supt. Fax 433-8290
oneontacsd.org
Oneonta HS 700/9-12
130 East St 13820 607-433-8243
Nancy Osborn, prin. Fax 433-8204
Oneonta MS 400/7-8
130 East St 13820 607-433-8262
Kevin Johnson, prin. Fax 433-8203

Hartwick College Post-Sec.
West St 13820 607-431-4000
Lighthouse Christian Academy 50/K-12
12 Grove St 13820 607-432-2031
Jacqueline Yarborough, admin. Fax 432-3403
SUNY College at Oneonta 13820 Post-Sec.
607-436-3500
Utica School of Commerce Post-Sec.
17 Elm St 13820 607-432-7003

Ontario Center, Wayne
Wayne Central SD 2,700/K-12
6076 Ontario Center Rd 14520 315-524-1001
Michael Havens, supt. Fax 524-4233
www.wayne.k12.ny.us
Armstrong MS 700/6-8
6076 Ontario Center Rd 14520 315-524-1080
Robert Armocida, prin. Fax 524-1119
Beneway HS 900/9-12
6200 Ontario Center Rd 14520 315-524-1050
Joseph Siracuse, prin. Fax 524-1079

Orangeburg, Rockland, Pop. 3,583
South Orangetown Central SD
Supt. — See Blauvelt
Tappan Zee HS 1,000/9-12
15 Dutch Hill Rd 10962 845-680-1600
Edward Bolan, prin. Fax 680-1950

Dominican College of Blauvelt Post-Sec.
470 Western Hwy 10962 845-359-7800
Long Island University-Rockland Campus Post-Sec.
70 Route 340 10962 845-359-7200

Orchard Park, Erie, Pop. 3,147
Orchard Park Central SD 5,200/K-12
3330 Baker Rd 14127 716-209-6222
Joan Thomas, supt. Fax 209-6353
www.opschools.org
Orchard Park HS 1,600/9-12
4040 Baker Rd 14127 716-209-6242
Robert Farwell, prin.
Orchard Park MS 1,300/6-8
60 S Lincoln Ave 14127 716-209-6227
James Higgins, prin.

Bryant & Stratton College Post-Sec.
200 Red Tail 14127 716-677-9500
Erie Community College South Post-Sec.
4041 Southwestern Blvd 14127 716-648-5400

Oriskany, Oneida, Pop. 1,423
Oriskany Central SD 800/K-12
PO Box 539 13424 315-768-2058
Michael Deuel, supt. Fax 768-1733
Oriskany JSHS 400/7-12
PO Box 539 13424 315-768-2063
Andy Brown, prin. Fax 768-4496

Ossining, Westchester, Pop. 23,547
Ossining UFD 4,200/PK-12
190 Croton Ave 10562 914-941-7700
Dr. Robert Roelle, supt. Fax 941-2794
ossiningufsd.org
Dorner MS 900/6-8
90 Van Cortlandt Ave 10562 914-762-5740
Regina Cellio, prin. Fax 762-5246
Ossining HS 1,300/9-12
29 S Highland Ave 10562 914-762-5760
Joshua Mandel, prin. Fax 762-4011

Oswego, Oswego, Pop. 17,705
Oswego CSD 4,700/K-12
120 E 1st St Ste 1 13126 315-341-2001
David Fischer, supt. Fax 341-2910
www.oswego.org
Oswego HS 1,700/9-12
2 Buccaneer Blvd 13126 315-341-2200
Pete Myles, prin. Fax 341-2920
Oswego MS 800/7-8
100 Mark Fitzgibbons Dr 13126 315-341-2300
Constance Evelyn, prin. Fax 341-2390

SUNY College at Oswego 13126 Post-Sec.
315-312-2500

Otego, Otsego, Pop. 1,007
Otego-Unadilla Central SD 1,200/K-12
2641 State Highway 7 13825 607-988-5038
Dr. Rebecca Furlong, supt. Fax 988-1039
unatego.org
Unatego JSHS 700/6-12
2641 State Highway 7 13825 607-988-5000
Julie Lambiaso, prin. Fax 988-1039

Ovid, Seneca, Pop. 609
South Seneca Central SD 900/PK-12
7263 Main St 14521 607-869-9636
Janie Nusser, supt. Fax 532-8540
www.southseneca.com/
South Seneca HS 300/9-12
7263 Main St 14521 607-869-9636
Robert Waller, prin. Fax 869-9553
South Seneca MS 200/7-8
7263 Main St 14521 607-869-9636
Robert Fitzsimmons, prin. Fax 532-8540

Owego, Tioga, Pop. 3,794
Owego-Apalachin Central SD 2,300/K-12
36 Talcott St 13827 607-687-6224
Dr. William Russell, supt. Fax 687-6313
www.oacsd.org
Owego-Apalachin MS 600/6-8
100 Elm St 13827 607-687-6248
Robert Devan, prin. Fax 687-6259
Owego Free Academy 800/9-12
1 Sheldon Guile Blvd 13827 607-687-6230
Ronald Pierce, prin. Fax 687-6247

Oxford, Chenango, Pop. 1,571
Oxford Academy & Central SD 900/K-12
PO Box 192 13830 607-843-7185
Randall Squier, supt. Fax 843-3241
www.oxac.org
Oxford Academy HS 300/9-12
PO Box 192 13830 607-843-2025
Christine Pierce, prin. Fax 843-3231
Oxford Academy MS 300/5-8
PO Box 192 13830 607-843-7185
Kathleen Hansen, prin. Fax 843-3241

Oyster Bay, Nassau, Pop. 6,687
Oyster Bay-East Norwich Central SD 1,600/PK-12
1 McCouns Ln 11771 516-624-6505
Dr. Phyllis Harrington, supt. Fax 624-6520
oben.powertolearn.com/
Oyster Bay JSHS 700/7-12
150 E Main St 11771 516-624-6524
Dennis O'Hara, prin. Fax 624-6684
Other Schools – See East Norwich

St. Dominic HS 500/9-12
110 Anstice St 11771 516-922-4888
Robert Lowenberg, prin. Fax 922-4898

Ozone Park, See New York
NYC Department of Education
Supt. — See New York
Adams HS 3,200/9-12
10101 Rockaway Blvd 11417 718-322-0500
Grace Zwillenberg, prin. Fax 738-9077
Cypress Hills Collegiate Preparatory S 9-12
9406 104th St 11416 718-935-3214
Alex Maysonet, prin.
HS for Construction Engineering & Arch 9-12
9406 104th St 11416 718-846-6280
Quintin Cedeno, prin. Fax 846-6283
JHS 202 1,100/6-8
13830 Lafayette St 11417 718-848-0001
William Moore, prin. Fax 848-8082
JHS 210 2,200/6-8
9311 101st Ave 11416 718-845-5942
Rosalyn Allman-Manning, prin. Fax 845-4037
MS 137 1,900/6-8
10915 98th St 11417 718-659-0471
Laura Mastrogiovanni, prin. Fax 659-4594

Painted Post, Steuben, Pop. 1,805
Corning CSD 5,700/PK-12
165 Charles St 14870 607-936-3704
Judith Staples Ed.D., supt. Fax 654-2735
www.corningareaschools.com
Corning-Painted Post West HS 1,000/9-12
201 Victory Hwy 14870 607-936-3794
John Wood, prin. Fax 654-2771
Other Schools – See Corning

Palisades, Rockland

Lamont-Doherty Earth Observatory Post-Sec.
10964 845-365-8550

Palmyra, Wayne, Pop. 3,429
Palmyra-Macedon Central SD 2,200/K-12
151 Hyde Pkwy 14522 315-597-3401
Harold Ferguson, supt. Fax 597-3898
www.palmaccsd.org
Palmyra-Macedon HS 700/9-12
151 Hyde Pkwy 14522 315-597-3420
Barb Persia, prin. Fax 597-3898
Palmyra-Macedon MS 500/6-8
163 Hyde Pkwy 14522 315-597-3450
Darcy Smith, prin. Fax 597-3460

Panama, Chautauqua, Pop. 471
Panama Central SD 600/K-12
41 North St 14767 716-782-2455
Carol Hay, supt. Fax 782-4281
www.pancent.org
Panama HS 300/7-12
41 North St 14767 716-782-2455
Bert Lictus, prin. Fax 782-4281

Parish, Oswego, Pop. 496
Altmar-Parish-Williamstown Central SD 1,600/K-12
PO Box 97 13131 315-625-5251
Deborah Haab, supt. Fax 625-7952
www.apw.cnyric.org
Altmar-Parish-Williamstown HS 500/9-12
639 County Route 22 13131 315-625-5222
Mark Potter, prin. Fax 625-4638
Altmar-Parish-Williamstown MS 400/6-8
640 County Route 22 13131 315-625-5200
Jamie Coppola, prin. Fax 625-4937

Parishville, Saint Lawrence
Parishville-Hopkinton Central SD 500/K-12
PO Box 187 13672 315-265-4642
Thomas Burns, supt. Fax 268-1309
phcs.neric.org
Parishville-Hopkinton JSHS 200/7-12
PO Box 187 13672 315-265-4642
Darin P. Saiff, prin. Fax 268-1309

Patchogue, Suffolk, Pop. 11,901
Patchogue-Medford UFD 8,300/PK-12
241 S Ocean Ave 11772 631-687-6380
Michael Mostow, supt. Fax 758-1126
pat-med.k12.ny.us
Saxton MS 800/6-9
121 Saxton St 11772 631-687-6700
Linda Pickford, prin. Fax 758-1126
South Ocean MS 600/6-9
225 S Ocean Ave 11772 631-687-6600
Randy Rusielewicz, prin. Fax 758-1126
Other Schools – See Medford

Briarcliffe College Post-Sec.
225 W Main St 11772 631-654-5300
St. Joseph's College Post-Sec.
155 W Roe Blvd 11772 631-447-3200

Patterson, Putnam
Carmel Central SD 4,800/K-12
PO Box 296 12563 845-878-2094
Dr. Marilyn Terranova, supt. Fax 878-4337
www.ccsd.k12.ny.us
Other Schools – See Carmel

Pattersonville, Schenectady

Spencer Business & Technical Institute Post-Sec.
795 Pattersonville Rd 12137 518-374-7619

Paul Smiths, Franklin

Paul Smith's College 12970 Post-Sec.
800-421-2605

Pavilion, Genesee
Pavilion Central SD 900/K-12
7014 Big Tree Rd 14525 585-584-3115
Edward Orman, supt. Fax 584-3421
Pavilion JSHS 500/6-12
7014 Big Tree Rd 14525 585-584-3070
Dr. Sheila Stellrecht, prin. Fax 584-3421

Pawling, Dutchess, Pop. 2,313
Pawling Central SD 1,400/K-12
7 Haight St 12564 845-855-4600
Joseph Sciortino, supt. Fax 855-4659
www.pawlingschools.org
Pawling HS 400/9-12
7 Haight St 12564 845-855-4620
Frank Tolan, prin. Fax 855-4617
Pawling MS 500/5-8
7 Haight St 12564 845-855-4653
Cheryl Thomas, prin. Fax 855-4134

Trinity-Pawling S 300/7-12
700 Route 22 12564 845-855-3100
Archibald Smith, hdmstr. Fax 855-3816

Pearl River, Rockland, Pop. 15,314
Pearl River UFD 2,500/K-12
275 E Central Ave 10965 845-620-3900
Dr. Frank V. Auriemma, supt. Fax 620-3927
www.pearlriver.org
Pearl River HS 1,000/8-12
275 E Central Ave 10965 845-620-3800
William Furdon, prin. Fax 620-3904

Iona College at Blue Hill Post-Sec.
PO Box 1522 10965 845-620-1350

Peekskill, Westchester, Pop. 24,044
Peekskill CSD 3,000/PK-12
1031 Elm St 10566 914-737-3300
Judith Johnson, supt. Fax 737-3912
www.peekskillcsd.org
Peekskill HS 900/9-12
1072 Elm St 10566 914-737-0201
Vincent Burruano, prin. Fax 737-2550
Peekskill MS 400/7-8
212 Ringgold St 10566 914-737-4542
Walter Chadwick, prin. Fax 737-3253

Northern Westchester Sch of Hairdressing Post-Sec.
19 Bank St 10566 914-739-8400
Ohr HaMeir Theological Seminary Post-Sec.
PO Box 2130 10566 914-736-1500

Pelham, Westchester, Pop. 6,364
Pelham UFD 2,600/K-12
18 Franklin Pl 10803 914-738-3434
Dr. Charles Wilson, supt. Fax 738-7223
www.pelhamschools.org
Pelham Memorial HS 700/9-12
575 Colonial Ave 10803 914-738-8110
Jeannine Clark, prin. Fax 738-8122
Pelham MS 600/6-8
28 Franklin Pl 10803 914-738-8190
Joseph Longobardi, prin. Fax 738-8132

Penfield, Monroe, Pop. 30,219
Penfield Central SD 4,900/K-12
PO Box 900 14526 585-249-5700
G. Susan Gray, supt. Fax 248-8412
www.penfield.edu
Bay Trail MS 1,200/6-8
1760 Scribner Rd 14526 585-249-6450
Ronald Marro, prin. Fax 248-0735
Penfield HS 1,600/9-12
25 High School Dr 14526 585-249-6700
Mark Van Vliet, prin. Fax 248-2810

Penn Yan, Yates, Pop. 5,170
Penn Yan Central SD 2,000/PK-12
1 School Dr 14527 315-536-3371
Ann Orman, supt. Fax 536-0068
www.pycsd.org
Penn Yan Academy HS 600/9-12
305 Court St 14527 315-536-4408
Keith Mathews, prin. Fax 536-0341
Penn Yan MS 500/6-8
515 Liberty St 14527 315-536-3366
Linda Raide, prin. Fax 536-7769

Perry, Wyoming, Pop. 3,792
Perry Central SD 1,100/PK-12
33 Watkins Ave 14530 585-237-0270
Daniel White, supt. Fax 237-6172
Perry HS 400/9-12
33 Watkins Ave 14530 585-237-0270
Josua Audsley, prin. Fax 237-6350
Perry MS 300/5-8
50 Olin Ave 14530 585-237-0270
Katherine Waite, prin. Fax 237-3483

Peru, Clinton, Pop. 1,565
Peru Central SD 2,100/K-12
PO Box 68 12972 518-643-6000
A. Paul Scott, supt. Fax 643-2043
www.peru.com
Peru HS 700/9-12
PO Box 68 12972 518-643-6400
Jeannie Henry, prin. Fax 643-2043
Peru MS 500/6-8
PO Box 68 12972 518-643-6300
Christopher Mazzella, prin. Fax 643-6313

Philadelphia, Jefferson, Pop. 1,560
Indian River Central SD 3,500/K-12
32735 County Route 29 Ste B 13673 315-642-3441
Roger W. Adams, supt. Fax 642-3738
www.ircsd.org/
Indian River HS 900/9-12
32925 US Route 11 13673 315-642-3427
Troy Decker, prin. Fax 642-5658
Indian River MS 800/6-8
32735 County Route 29 13673 315-642-0125
Nancy Taylor-Schmitt, prin. Fax 642-0802

Phoenix, Oswego, Pop. 2,198
Phoenix Central SD 2,400/K-12
116 Volney St 13135 315-695-1519
Rita Racette, supt. Fax 695-1201
www.phoenix.k12.ny.us
Birdlebough HS 800/9-12
552 Main St 13135 315-695-1631
James McLaughlin, prin. Fax 695-1618
Dillon MS 600/6-8
116 Volney St 13135 315-695-1521
Susan Anderson, prin. Fax 695-1523

Pine Bush, Orange, Pop. 1,445
Pine Bush Central SD 6,000/K-12
PO Box 700 12566 845-744-2031
Rosemarie Stark, supt. Fax 744-6189
www.pinebushschools.org
Crispell MS 800/6-8
PO Box 780 12566 845-744-2031
John Boyle, prin. Fax 744-2261
Pine Bush HS 2,000/9-12
PO Box 670 12566 845-744-2031
Jeannette Greene, prin. Fax 744-3488
Other Schools – See Circleville

AEF Chapel Field S 200/6-12
211 Fleury Rd 12566 845-778-1881
William Spanjer, prin. Fax 778-5841

Pine Plains, Dutchess, Pop. 1,312
Pine Plains Central SD 1,400/K-12
2829 Church St 12567 518-398-7181
Linda L. Kaumeyer, supt. Fax 398-6592
www.pineplainsschools.org
Stissing Mountain HS 500/9-12
2829 Church St 12567 518-398-7181
John Howe, prin. Fax 398-6592
Stissing Mountain MS 400/6-8
2829 Church St 12567 518-398-7181
Robert Hess, prin. Fax 398-6592

Pittsford, Monroe, Pop. 1,352
Pittsford Central SD 5,900/K-12
42 W Jefferson Rd 14534 585-267-1000
Mary Alice Price, supt. Fax 267-1088
www.pittsfordschools.org
Barker Road MS 1,400/6-8
75 Barker Rd 14534 585-267-1800
Michael Pero, prin. Fax 385-5960
Calkins Road MS 6-8
1899 Calkins Rd 14534 585-267-1900
Scott Reinhart, prin. Fax 264-0053
Pittsford-Mendon HS 1,000/9-12
472 Mendon Rd 14534 585-267-1600
Karl Thielking, prin. Fax 267-1679
Pittsford-Sutherland HS 900/9-12
55 Sutherland St 14534 585-267-1100
Elizabeth Konar, prin. Fax 381-7687

Plainview, Nassau, Pop. 25,600
Plainview-Old Bethpage Central SD 5,000/K-12
106 Washington Ave 11803 516-937-6301
Dr. Martin Brooks, supt. Fax 937-6303
www.pob.k12.ny.us/
Mattlin MS 800/5-8
100 Washington Ave 11803 516-937-6393
Dean Mittleman, prin. Fax 937-6431
Plainview-Old Bethpage/JFK HS 1,600/9-12
50 Kennedy Dr 11803 516-937-6370
James Murray, prin. Fax 937-6433
Plainview-Old Bethpage MS 800/5-8
121 Central Park Rd 11803 516-349-4750
Dr. Edward Metzendorf, prin. Fax 349-4777

Plattsburgh, Clinton, Pop. 19,181
Beekmantown Central SD
Supt. — See West Chazy
Beekmantown HS 700/9-12
6944 Route 22 12901 518-563-8787
Garth Frechette, prin. Fax 563-8132
Beekmantown MS 500/6-8
6944 Route 22 12901 518-563-8690
Sue Coonrod, prin. Fax 563-8132

Plattsburgh CSD 2,000/PK-12
49 Broad St 12901 518-957-6002
James Short, supt. Fax 561-6605
www.plattscsd.org/
Plattsburgh HS 700/9-12
1 Clifford Dr 12901 518-561-7500
John Fairchild, prin. Fax 561-1895
Stafford MS 500/6-8
15 Broad St 12901 518-563-6800
Patricia Amo, prin. Fax 563-8520

Champlain Valley Physicians Hospital Post-Sec.
75 Beekman St 12901 518-561-2000
Clinton Community College Post-Sec.
136 Clinton Point Dr 12901 518-562-4200
New Life Christian Academy 50/PK-12
164 Prospect Ave 12901 518-563-2842
Rev. James Miller, admin. Fax 563-8331
Seton Catholic Central JSHS 300/7-12
206 New York Rd 12903 518-561-4031
Rev. Robert Aucoin, prin. Fax 563-1193
SUNY College at Plattsburgh 12901 Post-Sec.
518-564-2000

Pleasantville, Westchester, Pop. 7,130
Pleasantville UFD 1,800/K-12
60 Romer Ave 10570 914-741-1400
Dr. Donald Antonecchia, supt. Fax 741-1499
www.pleasantvilleschools.com
Pleasantville HS 500/9-12
60 Romer Ave 10570 914-741-1420
Dr. George Cancro, prin. Fax 741-2546
Pleasantville MS 600/5-8
40 Romer Ave 10570 914-741-1450
Vivian Ossowski, prin. Fax 741-1476

Pace University Post-Sec.
861 Bedford Rd 10570 914-773-3200

Poland, Herkimer, Pop. 449
Poland Central SD 800/PK-12
74 Cold Brook St 13431 315-826-0203
John Stewart, supt. Fax 826-7516
www.polandcs.org
Poland JSHS 300/7-12
74 Cold Brook St 13431 315-826-7900
Jon Speich, prin. Fax 826-7516

Port Byron, Cayuga, Pop. 1,268
Port Byron Central SD 1,200/K-12
30 Maple Ave 13140 315-776-5728
Neil O'Brien, supt. Fax 776-4050
portbyron.cnyric.org/
Lehn MS 400/5-8
30 Maple Ave 13140 315-776-8939
Sarah Feinberg, prin. Fax 776-4050
West HS 400/9-12
30 Maple Ave 13140 315-776-4598
Shawn Bissetta, prin. Fax 776-4050

Port Chester, Westchester, Pop. 27,886
Port Chester-Rye UFD
Supt. — See Rye Brook
Port Chester HS 900/9-12
1 Tamarack Rd 10573 914-934-7950
Dr. Mitchell Combs, prin. Fax 934-2998
Port Chester MS 800/6-8
113 Bowman Ave 10573 914-934-7930
Carmen Macchia, prin. Fax 934-7886

Port Henry, Essex, Pop. 1,089
Moriah Central SD 800/K-12
39 Viking Ln 12974 518-546-3301
William Larrow, supt. Fax 546-7895
Moriah JSHS 400/7-12
39 Viking Ln 12974 518-546-3301
Kathy Carr, prin. Fax 546-7895

Port Jefferson, Suffolk, Pop. 7,935
Port Jefferson UFD 1,300/PK-12
550 Scraggy Hill Rd 11777 631-476-4404
Dr. Robert Aloise, supt. Fax 476-4409
www.portjeff.k12.ny.us
Port Jefferson MS 300/6-8
350 Old Post Rd 11777 631-474-4440
Roseann Cirnigliaro, prin. Fax 476-4430
Vandermuelen HS 400/9-12
350 Old Post Rd 11777 631-476-4400
Mark Sidman, prin. Fax 476-4408

Port Jefferson Station, See Port Jefferson
Comsewogue SD 3,900/K-12
290 Norwood Ave 11776 631-474-8105
Dr. Shelley Saffer, supt. Fax 474-3568
www.comsewogue.k12.ny.us
Comsewogue HS 1,100/9-12
565 Bicycle Path 11776 631-474-8182
Jennifer Reph, prin. Fax 474-8175
Kennedy MS, 200 Jayne Blvd 11776 900/6-8
Michael Fama, prin. 631-474-8160

Port Jervis, Orange, Pop. 9,202
Port Jervis CSD 3,300/K-12
9 Thompson St 12771 845-858-3175
Joseph Dilorenzo, supt. Fax 856-1885
www.portjerviscsd.k12.ny.us/
Port Jervis HS 1,100/9-12
Route 209 12771 845-858-3100
Anthony Di Marco, prin. Fax 858-2895
Port Jervis MS 500/7-8
118 E Main St 12771 845-858-3148
Thomas Bongiovi, prin. Fax 858-2893

Portville, Cattaraugus, Pop. 994
Portville Central SD 1,000/K-12
500 Elm St 14770 585-933-7141
Peter Tigh Ph.D., supt. Fax 933-7161
www.portville.wnyric.org/
Portville JSHS 500/7-12
500 Elm St 14770 585-933-6704
Kevin Curran, prin. Fax 933-7161

Port Washington, Nassau, Pop. 15,387
Port Washington UFD 4,800/K-12
100 Campus Dr 11050 516-767-5000
Dr. Geoffrey Gordon, supt. Fax 767-5007
www.portnet.k12.ny.us
Schreiber HS 1,400/9-12
101 Campus Dr 11050 516-767-5800
John Lewis, prin. Fax 767-5807
Weber JHS 1,100/6-8
Port Washington Blvd 11050 516-767-5500
Marilyn Rodahan, prin. Fax 767-5507

Smith S 100/5-12
322 Port Washington Blvd 11050 516-365-4900
Veronica McCue, prin. Fax 627-5648

Potsdam, Saint Lawrence, Pop. 9,705
Potsdam Central SD 1,400/PK-12
29 Leroy St 13676 315-265-2000
Patrick Brady;, supt. Fax 265-2048
www.potsdam.k12.ny.us
Kingston MS 400/5-8
29 Leroy St 13676 315-265-2000
Richard Evans, prin. Fax 265-8103
Potsdam HS 500/9-12
29 Leroy St 13676 315-265-2000
J. Gregory Jadlos, prin. Fax 265-8134

Clarkson University Post-Sec.
PO Box 5500 13699 315-268-6400
SUNY College at Potsdam 13676 Post-Sec.
315-267-2000

Pottersville, Warren

Word of Life Bible Institute Post-Sec.
PO Box 129 12860 518-494-4723

Poughkeepsie, Dutchess, Pop. 30,355
Arlington Central SD 10,200/K-12
696 Dutchess Tpke Ste J 12603 845-486-4460
Frank V. Pepe, supt. Fax 486-4457
www.arlingtonschools.org
Arlington MS 600/6-8
601 Dutchess Tpke 12603 845-486-4480
Brendan Lyons, prin. Fax 486-4446
Other Schools – See Lagrangeville

Poughkeepsie CSD 4,600/K-12
11 College Ave 12603 845-451-4900
Dr. Laval Wilson, supt. Fax 451-4955
www.poughkeepsieschools.org/
Poughkeepsie HS 1,200/9-12
70 Forbus St 12603 845-451-4850
Linda Melton Mann, prin. Fax 451-4853
Poughkeepsie MS 1,100/6-8
55 College Ave 12603 845-451-4800
Edgar Glascott, prin. Fax 451-4836

Spackenkill UFD 1,800/K-12
15 Croft Rd 12603 845-463-7800
Dr. Lois Colletta, supt. Fax 463-7804
www.dcboces.org/sufsd/
Spackenkill HS 600/9-12
112 Spackenkill Rd 12603 845-463-7810
Paul Fanuele, prin. Fax 463-7826
Todd MS 400/6-8
11 Croft Rd 12603 845-463-7830
Steven Malkischer, prin. Fax 462-1109

Dutchess Community College Post-Sec.
53 Pendell Rd 12601 845-431-8000
Marist College Post-Sec.
3399 North Rd 12601 845-575-3000
Oakwood Friends S 200/6-12
22 Spackenkill Rd 12603 845-462-4200
Peter Baily, hdmstr. Fax 462-4251
Our Lady of Lourdes HS 900/9-12
131 Boardman Rd 12603 845-463-0400
Rev. John Lagiovane, prin. Fax 463-0174
Poughkeepsie Day S 300/PK-12
260 Boardman Rd 12603 845-462-7600
Josie Holford, hdmstr. Fax 462-7603
Ridley-Lowell Business & Technical Inst. Post-Sec.
26 S Hamilton St 12601 845-471-0330
Tabernacle Christian Academy 100/K-12
155 Academy St 12601 845-454-2792
Timothy Hostetter, prin. Fax 483-0926
Vassar College Post-Sec.
124 Raymond Ave 12604 845-437-7000

Prattsburgh, Steuben
Prattsburg Central SD 500/PK-12
1 Academy St 14873 607-522-3795
Jeffrey Black, supt. Fax 522-6221
Prattsburg Central S 500/PK-12
1 Academy St 14873 607-522-3795
Fax 522-6221

Pulaski, Oswego, Pop. 2,345
Pulaski Central SD 1,100/K-12
2 Hinman Rd 13142 315-298-5188
Dr. Marshall Marshall, supt. Fax 298-4390
www.pacs.cnyric.org
Pulaski JSHS 600/7-12
4624 Salina St 13142 315-298-5103
Joseph McGrath, prin. Fax 298-2371

Purchase, See Harrison

Keio Academy of New York 400/9-12
3 College Rd 10577 914-694-4825
Sumio Sakomura, hdmstr. Fax 694-4830
Long Island University-Westchester Post-Sec.
735 Anderson Hill Rd 10577 800-472-3548
Manhattanville College Post-Sec.
2900 Purchase St 10577 914-694-2200
Purchase College SUNY Post-Sec.
735 Anderson Hill Rd 10577 914-251-6000

Putnam Valley, Putnam
Putnam Valley Central SD 1,900/K-12
146 Peekskill Hollow Rd 10579 845-528-8143
Gary Tutty, supt. Fax 528-0274
www.putnamvalleyschools.org
Putnam Valley HS 600/9-12
146 Peekskill Hollow Rd 10579 845-526-7847
Raymond Cooper, prin. Fax 528-4456
Putnam Valley MS 600/5-8
142 Peekskill Hollow Rd 10579 845-528-8101
Edward Hallisey, prin. Fax 528-8145

Queensbury, Warren
Queensbury UFD 3,900/K-12
429 Aviation Rd 12804 518-824-5600
Dr. Brian Howard, supt. Fax 793-4476
www.queensburyschool.org/
Queensbury HS 1,300/9-12
409 Aviation Rd 12804 518-742-6026
Michael Patton, prin. Fax 742-6043
Queensbury MS 1,000/6-8
455 Aviation Rd 12804 518-742-6035
Douglas Silvernell, prin. Fax 742-6053

SUNY Adirondack Community College Post-Sec.
640 Bay Rd 12804 518-743-2200

Queens Village, See New York
NYC Department of Education
Supt. — See New York
IS 109 1,500/6-8
21310 92nd Ave 11428 718-465-0651
Shango Blake, prin. Fax 264-1246
Van Buren HS 3,300/9-12
23017 Hillside Ave 11427 718-776-4728
Marilyn Shevell, prin. Fax 776-6807

Bethel Christian Academy 400/PK-12
21532 Jamaica Ave 11428 718-978-4357
Dr. Gail Johnson, prin.

Randolph, Cattaraugus, Pop. 1,266
Randolph Central SD 1,000/PK-12
18 Main St 14772 716-358-7005
Sandra Craft, supt. Fax 358-7072
www.randolphcsd.org/
Randolph HS 300/9-12
18 Main St 14772 716-358-7007
Dave Davison, prin. Fax 358-7072
Randolph MS 300/5-8
22 Main St 14772 716-358-7028
William Caldwell, prin. Fax 358-7060

Ravena, Albany, Pop. 3,323
Ravena-Coeymans-Selkirk Central SD
Supt. — See Selkirk
Ravena-Coeymans-Selkirk HS 800/9-12
2025 US Route 9W 12143 518-756-5200
Hakim Jones, prin. Fax 756-3534
Ravena-Coeymans-Selkirk MS 500/5-8
2025 Route 9W 12143 518-756-5200
Pam Black, prin. Fax 756-1988

Red Creek, Wayne, Pop. 503
Red Creek Central SD 1,100/K-12
PO Box 190 13143 315-754-2010
David Sholes, supt. Fax 754-8169
www.rccsd.org
Red Creek HS 400/9-12
PO Box 190 13143 315-754-2040
Noel Patterson, prin. Fax 754-2068
Red Creek MS 300/6-8
PO Box 190 13143 315-754-2070
Randall Lawrence, prin. Fax 754-2077

Red Hook, Dutchess, Pop. 1,825
Red Hook Central SD 2,300/K-12
7401 S Broadway 12571 845-758-2241
Paul Finch Ed.D., supt. Fax 758-3366
www.redhookcentralschools.org/
Linden Avenue MS 600/6-8
65 W Market St 12571 845-758-2241
Steven Chaikin, prin. Fax 758-0688
Red Hook HS 700/9-12
103 W Market St 12571 845-758-2241
Roy Paisley, prin. Fax 758-0482

Devereux Center in New York Post-Sec.
40 Devereux Way 12571 845-758-1899
Northern Dutchess Christian S 100/K-12
59 Fisk St 12571 845-876-7300
Nancy Aierstok, prin. Fax 758-4476

Rego Park, See New York
NYC Department of Education
Supt. — See New York
JHS 157 1,100/6-9
6355 102nd St 11374 718-830-4910
Vincent Suraci, prin. Fax 830-4993

Career Institute of Health & Technology Post-Sec.
9525 Queens Blvd Ste 600 11374 718-897-4868
Metropolitan Learning Institute Post-Sec.
9745 Queens Blvd Ste 401 11374 718-897-0482

Remsen, Oneida, Pop. 522
Remsen Central SD 600/K-12
PO Box 406 13438 315-831-3797
Ann Turner, supt. Fax 831-2172
www.remsencsd.org/

Remsen JSHS 300/7-12
PO Box 406 13438 315-831-3851
Aaron Carey, prin. Fax 831-2172

Rensselaer, Rensselaer, Pop. 7,859
Rensselaer CSD 1,100/PK-12
555 Broadway 12144 518-465-7509
Gordon Reynolds, supt. Fax 436-0479
www.rcsd.k12.ny.us
Rensselaer HS 300/9-12
555 Broadway 12144 518-436-8561
Dr. Michael Dawkins, prin. Fax 436-0479
Rensselaer MS 300/6-8
555 Broadway 12144 518-436-8561
Karen Urbanski, prin. Fax 436-0479

Retsof, Livingston
York Central SD 700/K-12
PO Box 102 14539 585-243-1730
Thomas Manko, supt. Fax 243-5269
www.yorkcsd.org/
York JSHS 300/6-12
PO Box 102 14539 585-243-1730
David Sylvester, prin. Fax 243-5269

Rhinebeck, Dutchess, Pop. 3,126
Rhinebeck Central SD 1,200/K-12
PO Box 351 12572 845-871-5520
Joseph Phelan, supt. Fax 876-4276
www.rhinebeckcsd.org/
Bulkeley MS 300/6-8
PO Box 351 12572 845-871-5500
John Kemnitzer, prin. Fax 871-5553
Rhinebeck HS 400/9-12
PO Box 351 12572 845-871-5500
Edwin Davenport, prin. Fax 876-8755

Richfield Springs, Otsego, Pop. 1,194
Richfield Springs Central SD 600/K-12
PO Box 631 13439 315-858-0610
Robert Barraco, supt. Fax 858-2440
www.richfieldcsd.org
Richfield Springs Central S 600/K-12
PO Box 631 13439 315-858-0610
Penny Harrington, prin. Fax 858-2440

Richmond Hill, See New York
NYC Department of Education
Supt. — See New York
Richmond Hill HS 3,200/9-12
8930 114th St 11418 718-846-3335
Frances Desanctis, prin. Fax 847-0980

Yeshiva Shaar HaTorah - Grodno Post-Sec.
8396 117th St 11418 718-846-1940

Richmondville, Schoharie, Pop. 798
Cobleskill-Richmondville Central SD
Supt. — See Cobleskill
Cobleskill-Richmondville HS 700/9-12
1353 State Route 7 12149 518-234-3565
David Zacher, prin. Fax 234-1018

Ridgewood, See New York
NYC Department of Education
Supt. — See New York
Cleveland HS 2,800/9-12
2127 Himrod St 11385 718-381-9600
Dominick Scarola, prin. Fax 417-8457
IS 77 1,200/6-8
976 Seneca Ave 11385 718-366-7120
Joseph Miller, prin. Fax 456-9512
IS 93 1,400/6-8
6656 Forest Ave 11385 718-821-4882
George Foley, prin. Fax 456-9521

Midway Paris Beauty School Post-Sec.
5440 Myrtle Ave 11385 718-418-2790

Ripley, Chautauqua, Pop. 1,189
Ripley Central SD 400/PK-12
PO Box 688 14775 716-736-6201
Dr. John Hamels, supt. Fax 736-6226
www.ripleycsd.wnyric.org
Ripley Central S 400/PK-12
PO Box 688 14775 716-736-2631
Susan Hammond, prin. Fax 736-6226

Riverdale, See New York

Mann HS 900/6-12
231 W 246th St 10471 718-432-4000
Dr. Thomas Kelly, hdmstr. Fax 548-2089
Riverdale Country S 1,100/PK-12
5250 Fieldston Rd 10471 718-549-8810
John Johnson, hdmstr. Fax 519-2795
Yeshiva of Telshe Alumni 100/9-12
4904 Independence Ave 10471 718-601-3523
Rabbi Noson Joseph, admin. Fax 601-2141
Yeshiva Ohavei Torah 100/9-12
450 W 250th St 10471 718-432-2600
Rabbi Avrumi Portowicz, prin. Fax 548-4106

Riverhead, Suffolk, Pop. 8,814
Riverhead Central SD 4,800/K-12
700 Osborn Ave 11901 631-369-6716
Paul R. Doyle, supt. Fax 369-6816
www.riverhead.net
Riverhead HS 1,400/9-12
700 Harrison Ave 11901 631-369-6723
James McCaffrey, prin. Fax 369-5164
Riverhead MS 800/7-8
600 Harrison Ave 11901 631-369-6759
Andrea Pekar, prin. Fax 369-6829

Central Suffolk Hospital Post-Sec.
1300 Roanoke Ave 11901 631-548-6000
Long Island University Post-Sec.
121 Speonk Riverhead Rd 11901 631-287-8010
McGann-Mercy HS 400/7-12
1225 Ostrander Ave 11901 631-727-5900
Dr. Steven Cheeseman, prin. Fax 727-8483
SUNY Suffolk County Community College Post-Sec.
2 Speonk Riverhead Rd 11901 631-548-2500

Rochester, Monroe, Pop. 211,091
Brighton Central SD 3,600/K-12
2035 Monroe Ave 14618 585-242-5080
Dr. Christopher Manaseri, supt. Fax 242-5164
www.bcsd.org
Brighton HS 1,300/9-12
1150 Winton Rd S 14618 585-242-5000
Nancy Hackett, prin. Fax 242-7364
Twelve Corners MS 900/6-8
2643 Elmwood Ave 14618 585-242-5100
Terence Quinn, prin. Fax 242-2540

East Irondequoit Central SD 3,500/K-12
600 Pardee Rd 14609 585-339-1210
Susan Allen, supt. Fax 288-0713
www.eicsd.k12.ny.us/
East Irondequoit MS 900/6-8
155 Densmore Rd 14609 585-339-1400
Deborah Decker, prin. Fax 339-1409
Eastridge HS 1,100/9-12
2350 Ridge Rd E 14622 585-339-1450
Matthew Laniak, prin. Fax 339-1459

Gates-Chili Central SD 4,900/K-12
3 Spartan Way 14624 585-247-5050
Richard Stein, supt. Fax 340-5569
www.gateschili.org
Gates-Chili HS 1,600/9-12
1 Spartan Way 14624 585-247-5050
Tim Clasgens, prin. Fax 340-5518
Gates-Chili MS 1,300/6-8
2 Spartan Way 14624 585-247-5050
Gerard Iuppa, prin. Fax 340-5532

Greece Central SD 13,200/PK-12
750 Maiden Ln 14615 585-621-1000
Steven Achramovitch, supt. Fax 621-6967
www.greece.k12.ny.us
Apollo MS 1,000/6-8
750 Maiden Ln 14615 585-966-5200
Cindy Neth, prin. Fax 966-5239
Arcadia MS 900/6-8
130 Island Cottage Rd 14612 585-966-3300
Karen D'Angelo, prin. Fax 966-3339
Greece Arcadia HS 1,400/9-12
120 Island Cottage Rd 14612 585-966-3000
Leslie Flick, prin. Fax 966-3039
Greece Athena HS 1,400/9-12
800 Long Pond Rd 14612 585-966-4000
Richard Snyder, prin. Fax 966-4039
Greece Athena MS 1,000/6-8
800 Long Pond Rd 14612 585-966-4200
John Rivers, prin. Fax 966-4239
Greece Olympia HS 1,400/9-12
1139 Maiden Ln 14615 585-966-5000
Christina Sloane, prin. Fax 966-5039

Rochester CSD 31,700/PK-12
131 W Broad St 14614 585-262-8100
Dr. Manuel Rivera, supt. Fax 262-5151
www.rcsdk12.org/
BioScience & Health Careers HS Vo/Tech
950 Norton St 14621 585-324-3730
Bernadette Regan, prin. Fax 336-8018
Business Finance & Entrepreneurship S Vo/Tech
655 Colfax St 14606 585-324-9781
Joseph Baldino, prin.
Charlotte HS 1,000/7-12
4115 Lake Ave 14612 585-663-7070
Deborah Rider, prin. Fax 621-0275
Douglass Preparatory S 1,000/7-9
940 Fernwood Park 14609 585-482-2000
Vicky Ramos, prin. Fax 654-1039
East HS 2,000/7-12
1801 E Main St 14609 585-288-3130
Kathleen Lamb, prin. Fax 654-1066
Global Media Arts HS @ Franklin Vo/Tech
950 Norton St 14621 585-324-3720
Dennis Francione, prin. Fax 336-5549
Intl Finance & Economic Dev Career HS Vo/Tech
950 Norton St 14621 585-324-3725
Ali Abdulmateen, prin. Fax 336-5562
Jefferson HS 1,100/7-12
1 Edgerton Park 14608 585-458-2280
Mary Andrecolich-Diaz, prin. Fax 277-0038
Marshall HS 1,300/7-12
180 Ridgeway Ave 14615 585-458-2110
Joseph Munno, prin. Fax 277-0077
Monroe JSHS 1,200/7-12
164 Alexander St 14607 585-232-1530
Linda Dianetti, prin. Fax 262-8965
Northeast College Preparatory HS 7-12
625 Scio St 14605 585-262-8850
Robert Goldsberry, prin.
Northwest College Preparatory HS 7-12
180 Ridgeway Ave 14615 585-458-2110
Toyia Wilson, prin.
School of Applied Technology at Edison Vo/Tech
655 Colfax St 14606 585-324-9783
Kathryn Hargis, prin.
School of Engineering & Manufacturing Vo/Tech
655 Colfax St 14606 585-324-9782
Eldridge Moore, prin.
School of Imaging & Information Tech Vo/Tech
655 Colfax St 14606 585-324-9794
Bonnie Atkins, prin.
School of the Arts 1,100/7-12
45 Prince St 14607 585-242-7682
Brenda Pacheco-Rivera, prin. Fax 256-6580
School Without Walls Foundation Academy 7-8
111 Clinton Ave N 14604 585-324-3111
Daniel Drmacich, prin.
Thomas HS 500/7-12
625 Scio St 14605 585-262-8850
Sandra Jordan, prin. Fax 262-8872
Wilson Commencement Acad @ Wilson 800/10-12
501 Genesee St 14611 585-328-3440
Barbara Hasler, prin. Fax 464-6153
Wilson Foundation Acad @ James Madison 1,000/7-9
200 Genesee St 14611 585-463-4100
Barbara Hasler, prin. Fax 463-4103

West Irondequoit Central SD 3,900/K-12
321 List Ave 14617 585-342-5500
Jeffrey B. Crane, supt. Fax 266-1556
www.westirondequoit.org
Dake MS 700/7-8
350 Cooper Rd 14617 585-342-2140
Timothy Terranova, prin. Fax 336-3034
Irondequoit HS 1,400/9-12
260 Cooper Rd 14617 585-336-2914
Patrick McCue, prin. Fax 336-2929

Allendale Columbia S 500/PK-12
519 Allens Creek Rd 14618 585-381-4560
Charles Hertrick, hdmstr. Fax 383-1191
All Saints Catholic Academy 200/7-8
170 Spencerport Rd 14606 585-429-6010
Monette Mahoney, prin. Fax 429-6761
Aquinas Institute 900/9-12
1127 Dewey Ave 14613 585-254-2020
Dennis Sadler, prin. Fax 254-7401
Bexley Hall Seminary Post-Sec.
26 Broadway 14607 585-546-2160
Bishop Kearney HS 500/9-12
125 Kings Hwy S 14617 585-342-4000
Louis Angelo, prin. Fax 342-4694
Bryant & Stratton College Post-Sec.
150 Bellwood Dr 14606 585-720-0660
Bryant & Stratton College Post-Sec.
1225 Jeffson Rd 14623 585-292-5627
Colgate Rochester Crozer Divinity School Post-Sec.
1100 Goodman St S 14620 585-271-1320
Continental School Post-Sec.
633 Jefferson Rd 14623 585-272-8060
David Hochstein Memorial Music School Post-Sec.
50 Plymouth Ave N 14614 585-454-4596
Eastman School of Music Post-Sec.
26 Gibbs St 14604 585-274-1060
Harley S 500/PK-12
1981 Clover St 14618 585-442-1770
Dr. Timothy Cottrell, hdmstr. Fax 442-5758
Howard S 200/5-12
275 Pinnacle Rd 14623 585-334-8010
Linda Lawrence, prin. Fax 334-8073
McQuaid Jesuit HS 900/7-12
1800 Clinton Ave S 14618 585-473-1130
William Hobbs, prin. Fax 256-6171
Monroe Community College Post-Sec.
1000 E Henrietta Rd 14623 585-292-2000
Nazareth Academy 300/9-12
1001 Lake Ave 14613 585-458-8583
Louis Zona, prin. Fax 647-8717
Nazareth College of Rochester Post-Sec.
4245 East Ave 14618 585-389-2525
Nazareth Hall MS 200/6-8
1001 Lake Ave 14613 585-647-8716
Sr. Elizabeth Snyder, dir. Fax 254-5468
Northstar Christian Academy 400/PK-12
332 Spencerport Rd 14606 585-429-5530
David Stein, prin. Fax 429-7913
Ora Academy 50/9-12
600 East Ave 14607 585-271-8711
Rabbi Reuven Feinberg, hdmstr. Fax 271-8158
Our Lady of Mercy HS 600/7-12
1437 Blossom Rd 14610 585-288-7120
Vilma Goetting, prin. Fax 288-7966
Roberts Wesleyan College Post-Sec.
2301 Westside Dr 14624 585-594-6000
Rochester Business Institute Post-Sec.
1630 Portland Ave 14621 585-266-0430
Rochester General Hospital Post-Sec.
1425 Portland Ave 14621 585-338-4430
Rochester Institute of Technology (NTID) Post-Sec.
52 Lomb Memorial Dr 14623 585-475-6585
Rochester Institute of Technology Post-Sec.
1 Lomb Memorial Dr 14623 585-475-2411
Rochester School for the Deaf Post-Sec.
1545 Saint Paul St 14621 585-544-1240
Rochester SDA Junior Academy 100/PK-12
309 Jefferson Ave 14611 585-436-5915
James Duberry, prin. Fax 436-5921
St. Bernard's Sch of Theology & Ministry Post-Sec.
120 French Rd 14618 585-271-3657
St. John Fisher College Post-Sec.
3690 East Ave 14618 585-385-8000
Shear Ego Intl School of Hair Design Post-Sec.
525 Titus Ave 14617 585-342-0070
Siena Catholic Academy 300/7-8
2617 East Ave 14610 585-381-1220
Timothy Leahy, prin. Fax 381-1223
SUNY Empire State College Post-Sec.
1475 Winton Rd N 14609 585-244-3884
Talmudical Institute of Upstate New York Post-Sec.
769 Park Ave 14607 585-473-2810
Talmudical Institute of Upstate New York 100/9-12
769 Park Ave 14607 585-473-2810
Rabbi M. Davidowitz, dean Fax 442-0417
University of Rochester Post-Sec.
Wallis Hall 14627 585-275-2121
University of Rochester Medical Center Post-Sec.
14642 585-275-8831

Rockaway Park, See New York
NYC Department of Education
Supt. — See New York
Beach Channel HS 2,300/9-12
10000 Beach Channel Dr 11694 718-945-6900
Dr. David Morris, prin. Fax 474-7682
Channel View S for Research 400/6-12
10000 Beach Channel Dr 11694 718-634-1970
Patricia Tubridy, prin. Fax 634-2896
Scholars Academy 6-8
320 Beach 104th St 11694 718-474-6918
Brian O'Connell, prin. Fax 474-6957

Rockville Centre, Nassau, Pop. 24,237
Rockville Centre UFD 3,600/K-12
128 Shepherd St 11570 516-255-8957
Dr. William Johnson, supt. Fax 255-8810
www.rvcschools.org
South Side HS 1,200/9-12
140 Shepherd St 11570 516-255-8944
Dr. Carol Burris, prin. Fax 766-7934
South Side MS 800/6-8
67 Hillside Ave 11570 516-255-8976
Shelagh McGinn, prin. Fax 763-0914

Mercy Medical Center Post-Sec.
PO Box 9024 11571 516-705-2525
Molloy College Post-Sec.
PO Box 5002 11571 516-678-5000

Rocky Point, Suffolk, Pop. 8,596
Rocky Point UFD 3,500/K-12
170 Route 25A 11778 631-744-1600
Dr. Carla D'ambrosio, supt. Fax 744-0817
www.rockypointschools.org
Rocky Point HS 1,000/9-12
82 Rocky Point Yaphank Rd 11778 631-744-1600
William Caulfield, prin. Fax 209-0204
Rocky Point MS 800/6-8
76 Rocky Point Yaphank Rd 11778 631-744-1600
Joseph Tanen Centamore, prin. Fax 886-0000

Rome, Oneida, Pop. 34,344
Rome CSD 5,800/PK-12
112 E Thomas St 13440 315-338-6500
Thomas Gallagher, supt. Fax 334-7409
www.romecsd.org/
Rome Free Academy 1,800/9-12
95 Dart Cir 13441 315-334-7200
Mark Benson, prin. Fax 334-7236
Staley Upper ES 700/6-8
620 E Bloomfield St 13440 315-338-5300
Michael Stalteri, prin. Fax 338-5306
Strough MS 700/6-8
801 Laurel St 13440 315-338-5200
Riccardo Ripa, prin. Fax 334-7465

New York State School for the Deaf Post-Sec.
401 Turin St 13440
Rome Catholic S 100/PK-12
800 Cypress St 13440 315-336-6190
Chris Mominey, prin. Fax 336-6194

Romulus, Seneca
Romulus Central SD 600/PK-12
5705 State Route 96 14541 866-810-0345
Michael Midey, supt. Fax 869-5961
www.rcs.k12.ny.us
Romulus Central HS 300/7-12
5705 State Route 96 14541 866-810-0345
Lynn Rhone, prin. Fax 869-5961

Ronkonkoma, Suffolk, Pop. 20,391
Connetquot Central SD
Supt. — See Bohemia
Ronkonkoma MS 900/6-8
501 Peconic St 11779 631-467-6000
Charles Morea, prin. Fax 467-6003

Roosevelt, Nassau, Pop. 15,030
Roosevelt UFD 2,700/PK-12
240 Denton Pl 11575 516-867-8616
Ronald Ross, supt. Fax 379-0178
www.rooseveltufsd.com/
Roosevelt HS 700/9-12
240 Denton Pl 11575 516-345-7200
Donald Humphrey, prin. Fax 867-2471
Roosevelt MS 500/7-8
1 Wagner Ave 11575 516-345-7300
Brodrick Spencer, prin. Fax 771-0376

Roscoe, Sullivan
Roscoe Central SD 300/PK-12
6 Academy St 12776 607-498-4126
Carmine Giangreco, supt. Fax 498-5609
www.roscoe.k12.ny.us
Roscoe Central S 300/PK-12
6 Academy St 12776 607-498-4126
Scott Haberli, prin. Fax 498-5609

Roslyn, Nassau, Pop. 2,879
Roslyn UFD 3,400/PK-12
PO Box 367 11576 516-625-6303
Gerard Dempsey, supt. Fax 625-8201
www.roslynschools.org
Other Schools – See Roslyn Heights

Mesivta of Roslyn 50/9-12
2 Shelter Rock Rd 11576 516-877-2131
Dr. William Muller, prin. Fax 877-2174

Roslyn Heights, Nassau, Pop. 6,405
Roslyn UFD
Supt. — See Roslyn
Roslyn HS 1,000/9-12
475 Round Hill Rd 11577 516-625-6337
Kevin Scanlon, prin. Fax 625-8191
Roslyn MS 800/6-8
375 Locust Ln 11577 516-625-6410
Jack Palmadesso, prin. Fax 625-6597

Roxbury, Delaware
Roxbury Central SD 300/K-12
53729 State Highway 30 12474 607-326-4151
Dr. Craig G. Carr, supt. Fax 326-4154
www.roxburycs.org
Roxbury Central S 300/K-12
53729 State Highway 30 12474 607-326-4151
Thomas O'Brien, prin. Fax 326-4154

Rushville, Ontario, Pop. 634
Marcus Whitman Central SD 1,500/K-12
4100 Baldwin Rd 14544 585-554-4848
Oren Cook, supt. Fax 554-4882
www.mwcsd.org/
Whitman HS 500/9-12
4100 Baldwin Rd 14544 585-554-6441
Susan Wissick, prin. Fax 554-5201
Whitman MS 400/6-8
4100 Baldwin Rd 14544 585-554-6442
Alan DeGroote, prin. Fax 554-3414

Russell, Saint Lawrence
Edwards-Knox Central SD 600/K-12
PO Box 630 13684 315-562-8326
Dr. William Cartwright, supt. Fax 562-2477
www.ekcsk12.org
Edwards-Knox JSHS 300/7-12
PO Box 630 13684 315-562-3227
Jeff Davis, prin. Fax 562-8433

Rye, Westchester, Pop. 14,992
Rye CSD 2,800/K-12
324 Midland Ave 10580 914-967-6100
Dr. Edward Shine, supt. Fax 967-6957
www.ryecityschools.lhric.org
Rye HS 700/9-12
1 Parsons St 10580 914-967-6100
Dr. Jim Rooney, prin. Fax 967-4380
Rye MS 600/6-8
3 Parsons St 10580 914-967-6100
Dr. Ann Edwards, prin. Fax 921-6189

Rye Country Day S 800/PK-12
Cedar St 10580 914-967-1417
Scott Nelson, hdmstr. Fax 967-1418
School of the Holy Child 200/9-12
2225 Westchester Ave 10580 914-967-5622
Ann Sullivan, prin. Fax 967-6476

Rye Brook, Westchester, Pop. 9,471
Blind Brook-Rye UFD 1,400/K-12
390 N Ridge St 10573 914-937-3600
Dr. Ronald Valenti, supt. Fax 937-5871
blindbrook.org
Blind Brook HS 400/9-12
840 King St 10573 914-937-3600
Anthony Baxter, prin. Fax 937-4509
Blind Brook MS, 840 King St 10573 300/6-8
Dr. Thomas Wolf, prin. 914-937-3600

Port Chester-Rye UFD 3,400/K-12
113 Bowman Ave 10573 914-934-7901
Dr. Donald Carlisle, supt. Fax 934-0727
www.portchesterschools.org/
Other Schools – See Port Chester

Sackets Harbor, Jefferson, Pop. 1,418
Sackets Harbor Central SD 500/K-12
PO Box 290 13685 315-646-3575
Suzanne Tingley, supt. Fax 646-1038
Sackets Harbor Central S 500/K-12
PO Box 290 13685 315-646-3575
Robert Wagoner, prin. Fax 646-1038

Sag Harbor, Suffolk, Pop. 2,368
Sag Harbor UFD 900/K-12
200 Jermain Ave 11963 631-725-5300
Kathryn Holden, supt. Fax 725-5307
www.sagharborschools.org
Pierson JSHS 500/6-12
200 Jermain Ave 11963 631-725-5302
Jeff Nichols, prin. Fax 725-5314

Saint Albans, See New York
NYC Department of Education
Supt. — See New York
Pathways College Preparatory S 6-12
10989 204th St 11412 718-454-4957
Michelle Shannon, prin. Fax 454-4892
IS 192 900/6-8
10989 204th St 11412 718-479-5540
Harriett Diaz, prin. Fax 217-4645

Saint Bonaventure, Cattaraugus, Pop. 2,397

St. Bonaventure University 14778 Post-Sec.
585-375-2000

Saint James, Suffolk, Pop. 12,703
Smithtown Central SD
Supt. — See Smithtown
Nesaquake MS 900/6-8
478 Edgewood Ave 11780 631-382-5100
Steven Podd, prin. Fax 382-5107
Smithtown HS East 9-12
10 School St 11780 631-382-2700
Edwin Thompson, prin. Fax 382-2707

Knox S 100/6-12
541 Long Beach Rd 11780 631-686-1600
David Stephens, hdmstr. Fax 686-1650

Saint Johnsville, Montgomery, Pop. 1,650
Oppenheim-Ephratah Central SD 400/PK-12
6486 State Highway 29 13452 518-568-2014
Dan Russom, supt. Fax 568-2941
oecs.k12.ny.us
Oppenheim-Ephratah Central S 400/PK-12
6486 State Highway 29 13452 518-568-2014
Michele Weaver, prin. Fax 568-2941

Saint Johnsville Central SD 500/PK-12
61 Monroe St 13452 518-568-7023
Christine Battisti, supt. Fax 568-5407
www.sjcsd.org/
Saint Johnsville MSHS 300/6-12
44 Center St 13452 518-568-2011
Greg Sova, prin. Fax 568-2797

Saint Regis Falls, Franklin
Saint Regis Falls Central SD 300/PK-12
PO Box 309 12980 518-856-9421
Patricia Dovi, supt. Fax 856-0142
Saint Regis Falls S 300/PK-12
PO Box 309 12980 518-856-9421
Richard Hansen, prin. Fax 856-0142

Salamanca, Cattaraugus, Pop. 5,851
Salamanca CSD 1,400/K-12
50 Iroquois Dr 14779 716-945-2403
Rick Moore, supt. Fax 945-3964
www.salamancany.org/
Salamanca HS 400/9-12
50 Iroquois Dr 14779 716-945-2404
Donnald Hensel, prin. Fax 945-5983
Salamanca MS 300/6-8
50 Iroquois Dr 14779 716-945-2405
Laurence Whitcomb, prin. Fax 945-5738

Salem, Washington, Pop. 911
Salem Central SD 800/K-12
PO Box 517 12865 518-854-7855
Richard Wheeler, supt. Fax 854-3957
Salem JSHS 400/7-12
PO Box 517 12865 518-854-7600
Daniel Jordan, prin. Fax 854-3957

Sanborn, Niagara
Niagara-Wheatfield Central SD
Supt. — See Niagara Falls
Niagara-Wheatfield HS 1,300/9-12
2292 Saunders Settlement Rd 14132 716-215-3100
Michelle Spasiano, prin. Fax 215-3125
Town MS 1,000/6-8
2292 Saunders Settlement Rd 14132 716-215-3150
Dr. Laura Palka, prin. Fax 215-3160

SUNY Niagara County Community College Post-Sec.
3111 Saunders Settlement Rd 14132 716-614-6222

Sandy Creek, Oswego, Pop. 771
Sandy Creek Central SD 1,000/K-12
PO Box 248 13145 315-387-3445
Stewart Amell, supt. Fax 387-2196
www.sccs.cnyric.org/
Sandy Creek HS 400/9-12
PO Box 248 13145 315-387-3465
Maureen Shiel, prin. Fax 387-2196
Sandy Creek MS 300/6-8
PO Box 248 13145 315-387-3465
Joanne Shelmidine, prin. Fax 387-2196

Saranac, Clinton
Saranac Central SD
Supt. — See Dannemora
Saranac HS 600/9-12
60 Picketts Corners Rd 12981 518-565-5800
Jonathan Parks, prin. Fax 565-5809
Saranac JHS 300/7-8
70 Picketts Corners Rd 12981 518-565-5700
James Gratto, prin. Fax 565-5706

Saranac Lake, Franklin, Pop. 4,923
Saranac Lake Central SD 1,600/PK-12
79 Canaras Ave 12983 518-891-5460
Scott A. Amo, supt. Fax 891-5140
www.slcs.org
Petrova MS 400/6-8
79 Canaras Ave 12983 518-891-4221
Patricia Kenyon, prin. Fax 891-6615
Saranac Lake HS 600/9-12
79 Canaras Ave 12983 518-891-4450
Bruce VanWeelden, prin. Fax 891-6813

North Country Community College Post-Sec.
PO Box 89 12983 518-891-2915

Saratoga Springs, Saratoga, Pop. 28,036
Saratoga Springs CSD 6,900/K-12
3 Blue Streak Blvd 12866 518-583-4709
John MacFadden, supt. Fax 584-6624
www.saratogaschools.org
Maple Ave MS 1,700/6-8
515 Maple Ave 12866 518-587-4551
Stuart Byrne, prin. Fax 587-5759
Saratoga Springs HS 2,100/9-12
1 Blue Streak Blvd 12866 518-587-6690
Frank Crowley, prin. Fax 583-1671

Saratoga Central Catholic HS 7-12
247 S Broadway 12866 518-587-7070
Chris Signor, prin. Fax 587-0678
Skidmore College Post-Sec.
815 N Broadway 12866 518-580-5000
SUNY Empire State College Post-Sec.
1 Union Ave 12866 800-847-3000
Waldorf S of Saratoga Springs 200/PK-12
122 Regent St 12866 518-587-0549
Sydney Morrell, admin. Fax 581-1682

Saugerties, Ulster, Pop. 3,930
Saugerties Central SD 3,300/K-12
PO Box A 12477 845-247-6550
Richard Rhau, supt. Fax 246-8364
www.saugerties.k12.ny.us
Saugerties HS 1,200/9-12
PO Box A 12477 845-247-6650
Timothy Price, prin. Fax 246-4312
Saugerties JHS 600/7-8
PO Box A 12477 845-247-6560
Donald Farris, prin. Fax 246-4322

Sauquoit, Oneida
Sauquoit Valley Central SD 1,200/K-12
2601 Oneida St 13456 315-839-6311
Deborah Flack, supt. Fax 839-5352
www.svcsd.org
Sauquoit Valley HS 400/9-12
2601 Oneida St 13456 315-839-6316
John Kolczynski, prin. Fax 839-6397
Sauquoit Valley MS 300/6-8
2601 Oneida St 13456 315-839-6371
Ron Wheelock, prin. Fax 839-6390

Sayville, Suffolk, Pop. 16,550
Sayville UFD 3,500/K-12
99 Greeley Ave 11782 631-244-6510
Dr. Rosemary Jones, supt. Fax 244-6504
www.sayville.k12.ny.us
Sayville MS 900/6-8
291 Johnson Ave 11782 631-244-6650
Dr. Walter Schartner, prin. Fax 244-6655
Other Schools – See West Sayville

Scarsdale, Westchester, Pop. 17,763
Edgemont UFD 1,900/K-12
300 White Oak Ln 10583 914-472-7768
Nancy Taddiken, supt. Fax 472-6846
www.edgemont.org/
Edgemont JSHS 900/7-12
200 White Oak Ln 10583 914-725-1500
William Manfredonia, prin. Fax 725-1057

Scarsdale UFD 4,600/K-12
2 Brewster Rd Ste 2 10583 914-721-2412
Michael McGill, supt. Fax 722-2822
www.scarsdaleschools.k12.ny.us
Scarsdale HS 1,300/9-12
1057 Post Rd 10583 914-721-2450
John Klemme, prin. Fax 721-2549
Scarsdale MS 1,100/6-8
134 Mamaroneck Rd 10583 914-721-2600
Michael McDermott, prin. Fax 721-2655

Schaghticoke, Rensselaer, Pop. 675
Hoosic Valley Central SD 1,300/K-12
2 Pleasant Ave 12154 518-753-4450
Dr. James Seeley, supt. Fax 753-7665
www.hoosicvalley.k12.ny.us/
Hoosic Valley HS 400/9-12
1548 State Route 67 12154 518-753-4432
Patti Sawyer, prin. Fax 753-7491
Hoosic Valley MS 400/5-8
Route 67 12154 518-753-4432
Amy Goodell, prin. Fax 753-7491

Schenectady, Schenectady, Pop. 61,280
Mohonasen Central SD 3,300/K-12
2072 Curry Rd 12303 518-356-8200
Kathleen Spring, supt. Fax 356-8247
www.mohonasen.org
Draper MS 900/6-8
2070 Curry Rd 12303 518-356-8350
Debra Male, prin. Fax 356-8359
Mohonasen HS 1,100/9-12
2072 Curry Rd 12303 518-356-8300
Patrick McGrath, prin. Fax 356-8309

Niskayuna Central SD 4,300/K-12
1239 Van Antwerp Rd 12309 518-377-4666
Dr. Kevin Baughman, supt. Fax 377-4074
www.nisk.k12.ny.us
Iroquois MS 600/6-8
2495 Rosendale Rd 12309 518-377-2233
David Crandall, prin. Fax 377-2219
Niskayuna HS 1,500/9-12
1626 Balltown Rd 12309 518-382-2521
John Rickert, prin. Fax 382-2539
Van Antwerp MS 500/6-8
2253 Story Ave 12309 518-370-1243
Luke Rakoczy, prin. Fax 370-4610

Schalmont Central SD 2,200/K-12
401 Duanesburg Rd 12306 518-355-9200
Dr. Valerie Kelsey, supt. Fax 355-9203
www.schalmont.org
Schalmont HS 800/9-12
1 Sabre Dr 12306 518-355-6110
Terence Nash, prin. Fax 355-8720
Schalmont MS 600/6-8
2 Sabre Dr 12306 518-355-6110
Michael Kondratowicz, prin. Fax 355-5329

Schenectady CSD 9,000/PK-12
108 Education Dr 12303 518-370-8100
Eric Ely, supt. Fax 370-8173
www.schenectady.k12.ny.us
Central Park MS 800/6-8
421 Elm St 12304 518-881-3660
Tonya Federico, prin. Fax 881-3662
Mont Pleasant MS 700/6-8
1121 Forest Rd 12303 518-370-8160
Nicola DiLeva, prin. Fax 370-8339
Oneida MS 700/6-8
1629 Oneida St 12308 518-370-8260
Karmen McEvoy, prin. Fax 370-8267
Schenectady HS 2,600/9-12
1445 The Plz 12308 518-370-8167
Gary Comley, prin. Fax 370-8169

Ellis Hospital School of Nursing Post-Sec.
1101 Nott St 12308 518-243-4471
Mid-America Baptist Theological Seminary Post-Sec.
2810 Curry Rd 12303 518-355-4000
Modern Welding School Post-Sec.
1842 State St 12304 518-374-1216
Notre Dame-Bishop Gibbons HS 400/6-12
2600 Albany St 12304 518-393-3131
Michael Piatek, prin. Fax 370-3817
SUNY Schenectady County Community Coll. Post-Sec.
78 Washington Ave 12305 518-381-1200
Union College 12308 Post-Sec.
518-388-6000

Schenevus, Otsego, Pop. 529
Schenevus Central SD 400/K-12
159 Main St 12155 607-638-5530
Lynda Bookhard, supt. Fax 638-5600
Schenevus Central S 400/K-12
159 Main St 12155 607-638-5881
Marie McCrea, prin. Fax 638-5600

Schoharie, Schoharie, Pop. 988
Schoharie Central SD 1,100/K-12
PO Box 430 12157 518-295-8132
Brian Sherman, supt. Fax 295-8178
www.schoharie.k12.ny.us
Schoharie JSHS 600/7-12
PO Box 430 12157 518-295-8188
Stacey Birdsall, prin. Fax 295-8161

Schroon Lake, Essex
Schroon Lake Central SD 300/K-12
PO Box 338 12870 518-532-7164
Michael Bonnewell, supt. Fax 532-0284
www.schroonschool.org
Schroon Lake Central S 300/K-12
PO Box 338 12870 518-532-7164
Michael Bonnewell, prin. Fax 532-0284

Schuylerville, Saratoga, Pop. 1,389
Schuylerville Central SD 1,700/K-12
14 Spring St 12871 518-695-3255
Dr. Leon Reed, supt. Fax 695-6491
www.schuylervilleschools.org
Schuylerville JSHS 800/7-12
14 Spring St 12871 518-695-3255
Matthew Sickles, prin. Fax 695-3103

Scio, Allegany
Scio Central SD 500/PK-12
3968 Washington St 14880 585-593-5076
Michael J. McArdle, supt. Fax 593-3468
www.scio.wnyric.org
Scio Central S 500/PK-12
3968 Washington St 14880 585-593-5510
Thomas Simon, prin. Fax 593-0653

Scotia, Schenectady, Pop. 7,958
Burnt Hills-Ballston Lake Central SD 3,400/K-12
50 Cypress Dr Ste 4 12302 518-399-9141
Jim Schultz, supt. Fax 399-1882
www.bhbl.org
Other Schools – See Burnt Hills

Scotia-Glenville Central SD 2,900/K-12
900 Preddice Pkwy 12302 518-382-1215
Susan Swartz, supt. Fax 382-1222
www.sgcsd.neric.org
Scotia-Glenville HS 1,000/9-12
1 Tartan Way 12302 518-382-1231
Lynda Castronovo, prin. Fax 382-1251
Scotia-Glenville MS 700/6-8
10 Prestige Pkwy 12302 518-382-1263
Sharyll Keller, prin. Fax 382-1263

Schenectady Christian S 300/K-12
36-38 Sacandaga Rd 12302 518-370-4272
John Bishop, hdmstr. Fax 370-4778

Scottsville, Monroe, Pop. 2,071
Wheatland-Chili Central SD 800/K-12
13 Beckwith Ave 14546 585-889-6246
Thomas Gallagher, supt. Fax 889-6284
www.wheatland.k12.ny.us
Wheatland-Chili MSHS 400/6-12
940 North Rd 14546 585-889-6245
Patrick Brimstein, prin. Fax 889-6217

Sea Cliff, Nassau, Pop. 4,996
North Shore Central SD 2,800/K-12
112 Franklin Ave 11579 516-705-0350
Edward Melnick, supt. Fax 705-0353
www.northshore.k12.ny.us/
Other Schools – See Glen Head

Seaford, Nassau, Pop. 15,597
Seaford UFD 2,700/K-12
1600 Washington Ave 11783 516-592-4000
Michael Maina, supt.
www.seaford.k12.ny.us/
Seaford HS 800/9-12
1575 Seamans Neck Rd 11783 516-592-4300
Michael Ragon, prin.
Seaford MS, 3940 Sunset Ave 11783 700/6-8
Roseanne Careri, prin. 516-592-4200

Selden, Suffolk, Pop. 20,608
Middle Country Central SD
Supt. — See Centereach
Newfield HS 1,700/9-12
145 Marshall Dr 11784 631-285-8300

SUNY Suffolk County Community College Post-Sec.
533 College Rd 11784 631-451-4110

Selkirk, Albany
Ravena-Coeymans-Selkirk Central SD 2,300/PK-12
26 Thatcher St 12158 518-756-5200
Vicki Wright, supt. Fax 767-2644
www.rcscsd.org
Other Schools – See Ravena

Seneca Falls, Seneca, Pop. 6,837
Seneca Falls Central SD 1,400/K-12
PO Box 268 13148 315-568-5500
Gerald Macaluso, supt. Fax 712-0535
www.sfcs.k12.ny.us/
Mynderse Academy 500/9-12
105 Troy St 13148 315-568-5500
Anthony Ferrara, prin. Fax 712-0523
Seneca Falls MS 300/6-8
95 Troy St 13148 315-568-5500
Robert McKeveny, prin. Fax 712-0524

Finger Lakes Christian S 100/PK-12
2291 State Route 89 13148 315-568-2216
Scott VanKirk, admin. Fax 568-6638
New York Chiropractic College Post-Sec.
PO Box 800 13148 315-568-3000

Setauket, Suffolk, Pop. 13,634
Three Village Central SD
Supt. — See East Setauket
Gelinas JHS, 25 Mud Rd 11733 1,000/7-9
Gustave Hueber, prin. 631-730-4700

Sharon Springs, Schoharie, Pop. 540
Sharon Springs Central SD 400/K-12
PO Box 218 13459 518-284-2266
Patterson Green, supt. Fax 284-9033
www.sharonsprings.org/
Sharon Springs Central S 400/K-12
PO Box 218 13459 518-284-2267
Patterson Green, prin. Fax 284-9075

Shelter Island, Suffolk, Pop. 1,193
Shelter Island UFD 200/K-12
PO Box 2015 11964 631-749-0302
Sharon Clifford, supt. Fax 749-1262
Shelter Island Central S 200/K-12
PO Box 2015 11964 631-749-0302
Sharon Clifford, prin. Fax 749-1262

Sherburne, Chenango, Pop. 1,446
Sherburne-Earlville Central SD 1,700/K-12
15 School St 13460 607-674-7300
Gayle Hellert, supt. Fax 674-9742
secsd.org
Sherburne-Earlville HS 500/9-12
13 School St 13460 607-674-7380
Keith Reed, prin. Fax 674-7368
Sherburne-Earlville MS 400/6-8
13 School St 13460 607-674-7350
Jill Lee, prin. Fax 674-7392

Sherman, Chautauqua, Pop. 679
Sherman Central SD 500/K-12
PO Box 950 14781 716-761-6121
Thomas Schmidt, supt. Fax 761-6119
www.sherman.wnyric.org
Sherman HS 200/7-12
PO Box 950 14781 716-761-6121
David Hickey, dean Fax 761-6119

Shoreham, Suffolk, Pop. 423
Shoreham-Wading River Central SD 2,700/K-12
250b Route 25a 11786 631-821-8100
Harriet Copel Ed.D., supt. Fax 929-3001
www.swrcsd.org
Prodell MS 700/6-8
100 Randall Rd 11786 631-821-8212
Linda Anthony, prin. Fax 821-8275
Shoreham-Wading River HS 800/9-12
250a Route 25a 11786 631-821-8264
Ismael Colon, prin. Fax 821-8162

Shortsville, Ontario, Pop. 1,298
Manchester-Shortsville Central SD 900/K-12
1506 State Route 21 14548 585-289-3964
Robert Leiby, supt. Fax 289-6660
www.redjacket.org
Red Jacket HS 300/9-12
1506 State Route 21 14548 585-289-3966
Timothy Benjamin, prin. Fax 289-4755
Red Jacket MS 200/6-8
1506 State Route 21 14548 585-289-3967
Charlene Harvey, prin. Fax 289-8715

Shrub Oak, Westchester
Lakeland Central SD 6,100/K-12
1086 E Main St 10588 914-245-1700
Kenneth Connolly, supt. Fax 245-7817
www.lakelandschools.org
Lakeland HS 1,100/9-12
1349 E Main St 10588 914-528-0600
Cheryl Champ, prin. Fax 528-0521
Other Schools – See Cortlandt Manor, Yorktown Heights

Sidney, Delaware, Pop. 3,905
Sidney Central SD 1,100/K-12
95 W Main St 13838 607-563-2135
Sandra Cooper, supt. Fax 563-2386
Sidney HS, 95 W Main St 13838 400/9-12
Annette Hammond, prin. 607-563-2135
Sidney MS, 13 Pearl St E 13838 400/6-8
Allen Bilofsky, prin. 607-563-2135

Silver Creek, Chautauqua, Pop. 2,863
Silver Creek Central SD 1,200/K-12
1 Dickinson St 14136 716-934-2603
Gordon Salisbury, supt. Fax 934-2103
www.silvercreek.wnyric.org/
Silver Creek HS 400/9-12
1 Dickinson St 14136 716-934-2603
John Hertlein, prin. Fax 934-2103
Silver Creek MS 300/6-8
1 Dickinson St 14136 716-934-2603
Patricia Krenzer, prin. Fax 934-2103

Sinclairville, Chautauqua, Pop. 635
Cassadaga Valley Central SD 1,300/PK-12
PO Box 540 14782 716-962-5155
John C. Brown, supt. Fax 962-5976
cvweb.wnyric.org/
Cassadaga Valley MSHS 700/6-12
PO Box 540 14782 716-962-8581
Jud Foy, prin. Fax 962-5788

Skaneateles, Onondaga, Pop. 2,589
Skaneateles Central SD 1,800/K-12
49 E Elizabeth St 13152 315-291-2221
Philip D'Angelo, supt. Fax 685-0347
www.scs.cnyric.org/
Skaneateles HS 600/9-12
49 E Elizabeth St 13152 315-291-2231
Georgette Hoskins, prin. Fax 685-0347
Skaneateles MS 400/6-8
35 East St 13152 315-291-2241
Timothy Chiavara, prin. Fax 685-0347

Slate Hill, Orange
Minisink Valley Central SD 4,600/K-12
PO Box 217 10973 845-355-5110
Dr. Martha Murray, supt. Fax 355-5119
www.minisink.com
Minisink Valley HS 1,500/9-12
PO Box 217 10973 845-355-5150
John Latini, prin. Fax 355-5198
Minisink Valley MS 1,100/6-8
PO Box 217 10973 845-355-5200
Robert Peters, prin. Fax 355-5205

Sleepy Hollow, Westchester, Pop. 9,977
Tarrytown UFD 2,500/PK-12
200 N Broadway 10591 914-631-9404
Dr. Howard Smith, supt. Fax 332-6283
www.tufsd.org
Sleepy Hollow MSHS 1,100/7-12
210 N Broadway 10591 914-631-8838
Carol Conklin, prin. Fax 332-6219

Smithtown, Suffolk, Pop. 27,100
Smithtown Central SD 8,900/K-12
26 New York Ave 11787 631-382-2006
Edward Ehmann, supt. Fax 382-2010
www.smithtown.k12.ny.us
Accompsett MS 6-8
660 Meadow Rd 11787 631-382-2300
John Nocero, prin. Fax 382-2307
Smithtown HS West 2,100/9-12
100 Central Rd 11787 631-382-2905
John Dolan, prin. Fax 382-2910
Other Schools – See Nesconset, Saint James

Smithtown Christian S 600/PK-12
1 Higbie Dr 11787 631-265-3334
Rev. Salvatore Greco Ed.D., supt. Fax 265-1079

Sodus, Wayne, Pop. 1,673
Sodus Central SD 1,100/PK-12
PO Box 220 14551 315-483-5201
Susan Kay Salvaggio, supt. Fax 483-4755
www.soduscsd.org
Sodus HS 500/9-12
PO Box 220 14551 315-483-5203
Eugene Hoskins, prin. Fax 483-6168
Sodus MS 200/7-8
PO Box 220 14551 315-483-5214
Nelson Kise, prin. Fax 483-6168

Solvay, Onondaga, Pop. 6,606
Solvay UFD 1,200/K-12
103 3rd St 13209 315-468-1111
J. Francis Manning, supt. Fax 468-2755
www.solvayschools.org
Solvay HS 700/9-12
600 Gertrude Ave 13209 315-468-2551
Joseph Rotella, prin. Fax 484-1404
Other Schools – See Syracuse

Somers, Westchester
Somers Central SD 3,300/K-12
334 Route 202 10589 914-277-2400
Dr. Joanne Marien, supt. Fax 248-7886
www.somers.k12.ny.us/
Somers MS 800/6-8
250 Route 202 10589 914-277-3399
Geraldine Paige, prin. Fax 277-2236
Other Schools – See Lincolndale

Kennedy HS 600/9-12
54 Route 138 10589 914-232-5061
Stephen Schmidt, prin. Fax 232-3416

Southampton, Suffolk, Pop. 4,109
Southampton UFD 1,700/PK-12
70 Leland Ln 11968 631-591-4510
Dr. Linda J. Bruno, supt. Fax 591-4528
www.southampton.k12.ny.us
Southampton HS 600/9-12
141 Narrow Ln 11968 631-591-4600
Nicholas Dyno, prin. Fax 283-6313
Southampton IS 400/5-8
70 Leland Ln 11968 631-591-4700
Timothy Frazier, prin. Fax 283-6899

South Dayton, Chautauqua, Pop. 637
Pine Valley Central SD 700/K-12
7755 Route 83 14138 716-988-3293
Jerry Williams, supt. Fax 988-3139
www.pval.org/
Pine Valley Central JSHS 400/7-12
7827 Route 83 14138 716-988-3276
Carol Smith, prin. Fax 988-3139

South Fallsburg, Sullivan, Pop. 2,115

Yeshiva Gedola Zichron Moshe 300/9-12
PO Box 580 12779 845-434-5240
Rabbi Meshulim Gorelick, prin. Fax 434-1009
Yeshivath Zichron Moshe Post-Sec.
Laurel Park Rd 12779 845-434-5240

South Glens Falls, Saratoga, Pop. 3,445
South Glens Falls Central SD 3,400/PK-12
6 Bluebird Rd 12803 518-793-9617
Dr. James McCarthy, supt. Fax 761-0723
www.sgfallssd.org/
South Glens Falls HS 1,000/9-12
42 Merritt Rd 12803 518-792-9987
Fax 792-5412
Winch MS 800/6-8
99 Hudson St 12803 518-792-5891
Mark Fish, prin. Fax 793-9505

South Kortright, Delaware
South Kortright Central SD 400/K-12
PO Box 113 13842 607-538-9111
Benjamin Berliner, supt. Fax 538-9205
www.skcs.org
South Kortright Central S 400/K-12
PO Box 113 13842 607-538-9111
John J. Bonhotal, prin. Fax 538-9205

Southold, Suffolk, Pop. 5,192
Southold UFD 1,000/K-12
PO Box 40 11971 631-765-5400
Dr. Christopher Gallagher, supt. Fax 765-5086
www.northfork.net/shs
Southold JSHS 500/7-12
PO Box 40 11971 631-765-5081
Mary Fitzpatrick, prin. Fax 765-5086

South Otselic, Chenango
Georgetown-South Otselic Central SD 400/K-12
PO Box 161 13155 315-653-7591
Larry Thomas, supt. Fax 653-7500
Otselic Valley JSHS 200/7-12
PO Box 161 13155 315-653-7218
Scott Poreda, prin. Fax 653-7500

South Ozone Park, See New York
NYC Department of Education
Supt. — See New York
JHS 226 2,000/6-8
12110 Rockaway Blvd 11420 718-843-2260
Sonia Nieves, prin. Fax 835-6317

Al-Ihsan Academy 400/1-12
13008 Rockaway Blvd 11420 718-322-3154
Refeek Mohamed, prin. Fax 322-7069

South Salem, Westchester
Katonah-Lewisboro UFD 4,100/K-12
1 Shady Ln 10590 914-763-7000
Dr. Robert V. Lichtenfeld, supt. Fax 763-7033
www.k-lschools.org
Other Schools – See Cross River

South Wales, Erie

Gow S 100/7-12
PO Box 85 14139 585-652-3450
M. Rogers, hdmstr. Fax 652-3457

Sparkill, Rockland

St. Thomas Aquinas College Post-Sec.
125 Route 340 10976 845-398-4000

Spencer, Tioga, Pop. 709
Spencer-Van Etten Central SD
Supt. — See Van Etten
Spencer-Van Etten HS 400/9-12
PO Box 307 14883 607-589-7140
Ann Sincock, prin. Fax 589-3010
Spencer-Van Etten MS 400/5-8
1 Center St 14883 607-589-7120
Marcia Bishop, prin. Fax 589-3020

Spencerport, Monroe, Pop. 3,519
Spencerport Central SD 4,200/K-12
71 Lyell Ave 14559 585-349-5000
Mary Anne Kermis, supt. Fax 349-5011
www.spencerportschools.org
Cosgrove MS 1,100/6-8
2749 Spencerport Rd 14559 585-349-5300
Michael Canny, prin. Fax 349-5346
Spencerport HS 1,400/9-12
2707 Spencerport Rd 14559 585-349-5200
Ty Zinkiewich, prin. Fax 349-5266

Springfield Gardens, See New York
NYC Department of Education
Supt. — See New York
Carver HS for the Sciences 300/9-12
14310 Springfield Blvd 11413 718-525-6439
Dr. Janice Sutton, prin. Fax 525-6482
Excelsior Preparatory HS 100/9-12
14310 Springfield Blvd 11413 718-525-6507
Derek Jones, prin. Fax 525-6276
Preparatory Academy for Writers 9-12
14310 Springfield Blvd 11413 718-935-3513
Michael Renna, prin.
Queens Preparatory Academy 9-10
14310 Springfield Blvd 11413 718-712-2304
Tashon Haywood, prin. Fax 712-3273
Springfield Gardens HS 800/9-12
14310 Springfield Blvd 11413 718-341-3033
Elizabeth McCullough, prin. Fax 525-8495
IS 59 1,200/6-8
13255 Ridgedale St 11413 718-527-3501
Carleton Gordon, prin. Fax 276-1364

Spring Valley, Rockland, Pop. 25,355
East Ramapo Central SD 8,200/PK-12
105 S Madison Ave 10977 845-577-6000
Dr. Mitchell Schwartz, supt. Fax 577-6168
www.ercsd.k12.ny.us/
Ramapo Freshman Center 600/9-9
465 Viola Rd 10977 845-577-6100
Jean Fields, prin. Fax 426-1059
Ramapo HS 1,100/10-12
400 Viola Rd 10977 845-577-6400
Jean Fields, prin. Fax 426-1124
Spring Valley HS 1,200/9-12
361 Route 59 10977 845-577-6500
Beverly Davis, prin. Fax 426-1127
Other Schools – See Chestnut Ridge, Suffern

Sunbridge College Post-Sec.
285 Hungry Hollow Rd 10977 845-425-0055
SUNY Rockland Community College Post-Sec.
766 N Main St 10977 845-352-5535
SUNY Rockland Community College Post-Sec.
185 N Main St 10977 845-352-5535
United Talmudical Academy 1,300/K-12
89 S Main St 10977 845-425-0392
Yidel Spitzer, admin. Fax 352-7253
Yeshiva Avir Yaakov 2,200/PK-12
PO Box 840 10977 845-362-6600
Fax 354-6809
Yeshiva Degel Hatorah 200/K-12
111 Maple Ave 10977 845-356-4610
Rabbi Moshe Schwab, prin. Fax 356-4507
Yeshiva Tzoin Yosef-Pupa 400/PK-12
4 Widman Ct 10977 845-371-1220
J. Kohn, prin. Fax 371-1237
Yeshiva Zichron Yaakov 9-12
720 Union Rd 10977 845-362-4990
Rabbi Dov Shapiro, prin. Fax 362-4979

Springville, Erie, Pop. 4,311
Springville-Griffith Inst. Central SD 2,300/K-12
307 Newman St 14141 716-592-3230
Dr. Brenda Peters, supt. Fax 592-3209
www.springvillegi.wnyric.org
Griffith Institute HS 800/9-12
290 N Buffalo St 14141 716-592-3237
Philip Benson, prin. Fax 592-0674
Griffith Institute MS 500/6-8
267 Newman St 14141 716-592-3270
Gary Cerne, prin. Fax 592-0746

Staatsburg on Hudson, Dutchess
Hyde Park Central SD
Supt. — See Hyde Park
Roosevelt HS 1,500/9-12
154 S Cross Rd 12580 845-229-4020
Barbara Marrine, prin. Fax 229-4029

Stamford, Delaware, Pop. 1,269
Stamford Central SD, 1 River St 12167 500/K-12
Gregory Sanik, supt. 607-652-7301
Stamford Central S 500/K-12
1 River St 12167 607-652-7301
Julie Mable, prin. Fax 652-3446

Star Lake, Saint Lawrence, Pop. 1,092
Clifton-Fine Central SD 400/PK-12
11 Hall Ave 13690 315-848-3333
Dr. Paul Alioto, supt. Fax 848-3350
Clifton-Fine JSHS 200/7-12
11 Hall Ave 13690 315-848-3333
Susan Shene, prin. Fax 848-3350

Staten Island, See New York
NYC Department of Education
Supt. — See New York
CSI HS for International Studies 9-10
2800 Victory Blvd 10314 718-982-3460
Aimee Horowitz, prin. Fax 982-3482
Curtis HS 2,400/9-12
105 Hamilton Ave 10301 718-390-1800
Aurelia Curtis, prin. Fax 556-4800
McKee Career and Technical HS Vo/Tech
290 Saint Marks Pl 10301 718-420-2600
Linda Waite, prin. Fax 981-8776
New Dorp HS 2,200/9-12
465 New Dorp Ln 10306 718-667-8686
Deirdre DeAngelis, prin. Fax 987-4889
Port Richmond HS 2,500/9-12
85 Saint Josephs Ave 10302 718-273-3600
Tim Gannon, prin. Fax 981-6203
Public S 80 1,200/K-12
715 Ocean Ter 10301 718-815-0186
Joanne Buckheit, prin. Fax 815-9638
IS 2 900/6-8
333 Midland Ave 10306 718-987-5336
Michelena Dibuono, prin. Fax 987-6937
IS 7 1,300/6-8
1270 Huguenot Ave 10312 718-356-2314
Dr. Nora Derosa-Karby, prin. Fax 967-0809
IS 24 1,500/6-8
225 Cleveland Ave 10308 718-356-4200
Rosemarie O'Neill, prin. Fax 356-5834
IS 27 800/6-8
11 Clove Lake Pl 10310 718-981-8800
Tracey Kornish, prin. Fax 815-4677
IS 34 1,100/6-8
528 Academy Ave 10307 718-984-0772
Jeffrey Preston, prin. Fax 227-4074
IS 49 1,100/6-8
101 Warren St 10304 718-727-6040
Linda Hill, prin. Fax 876-8207
IS 51 1,400/6-8
20 Houston St 10302 718-981-0502
Emma Della Rocca, prin. Fax 815-3957
IS 61 1,200/6-8
445 Castleton Ave 10301 718-727-8481
Richard Gallo, prin. Fax 447-2112
IS 72 1,800/6-8
33 Ferndale Ave 10314 718-698-5757
Peter Macellari, prin. Fax 761-5928
IS 75 1,500/6-8
455 Huguenot Ave 10312 718-356-0130
Mark Cannizzaro, prin. Fax 984-5302
Staten Island Tech HS Vo/Tech
485 Clawson St 10306 718-667-5725
Vincent Maniscalco, prin. Fax 987-5872
Tottenville HS 3,800/9-12
100 Luten Ave 10312 718-356-2220
John Tuminaro, prin. Fax 317-0962
Wagner HS 2,700/9-12
1200 Manor Rd 10314 718-698-4200
Gary M. Giordano, prin. Fax 698-5213

CUNY College of Staten Island Post-Sec.
2800 Victory Blvd 10314 718-982-2000
Francis HS 200/9-12
4240 Amboy Rd 10308 718-967-0400
Constance Costa, prin. Fax 227-7766
Monsignor Farrell HS 1,200/9-12
2900 Amboy Rd 10306 718-987-2900
Fr. John Paddock, prin. Fax 987-4241
Moore Catholic HS 900/9-12
100 Merrill Ave 10314 718-761-9200
Douglas McManus, prin. Fax 982-7779
Notre Dame Academy 400/9-12
134 Howard Ave 10301 718-447-8878
Dr. Gregory Rossicone, prin. Fax 447-2926
St. John's University Post-Sec.
300 Howard Ave 10301 718-447-4343
St. John Villa Academy 600/9-12
26 Landis Ave 10305 718-442-6240
Sr. Antonia Zuffante, prin. Fax 447-6729
St. Joseph by the Sea HS 9-12
5150 Hylan Blvd 10312 718-984-6500
Rev. Joseph Ansaldi, prin. Fax 984-6503
St. Joseph Hill Academy 9-12
850 Hylan Blvd 10305 718-447-1374
Angela Ferrando, prin. Fax 447-3041
St. Peter's Boys HS 800/9-12
200 Clinton Ave 10301 718-447-1676
John Fodera, prin. Fax 447-4027
St. Peter's Girls HS 9-12
300 Richmond Ter 10301 718-447-0304
Evelyn Lacagnino, prin. Fax 447-0832
St. Vincent's Medical Center Post-Sec.
355 Bard Ave 10310 718-876-2413
Sisters of Charity Medical Center Post-Sec.
75 Vanderbilt Ave 10304 718-818-6470
Staten Island Academy 400/PK-12
715 Todt Hill Rd 10304 718-987-8100
Diane J. Hulse, hdmstr. Fax 979-7641
Wagner College Post-Sec.
1 Campus Rd 10301 718-390-3100
Yeshiva & Mesivta of Staten Island 50/9-12
1870 Drumgoole Rd E 10309 718-356-4323
Shloma Eidelman, dir. Fax 356-5200

Stillwater, Saratoga, Pop. 1,706
Stillwater Central SD 1,200/K-12
334 Hudson Ave 12170 518-373-6100
Donald Flynt, supt. Fax 664-9134
Stillwater MSHS 700/6-12
334 Hudson Ave 12170 518-373-6100
Mario Fernandez, prin. Fax 664-1832

Stone Ridge, Ulster

Ulster County Community College Post-Sec.
12484 845-687-5000

Stony Brook, Suffolk, Pop. 13,726
Three Village Central SD
Supt. — See East Setauket
Murphy JHS, 351 Oxhead Rd 11790 900/7-9
Vincent Vizzo, prin. 631-730-4800

Stony Brook S 300/7-12
1 Chapman Pkwy 11790 631-751-1800
Robert Gustafson, hdmstr. Fax 751-4211
SUNY at Stony Brook 11794 Post-Sec.
631-689-6000

Suffern, Rockland, Pop. 10,897
East Ramapo Central SD
Supt. — See Spring Valley
Pomona MS 400/8-9
101 Pomona Rd 10901 845-577-6200
Brenda Shannon, prin. Fax 577-6245

Ramapo Central SD
Supt. — See Hillburn
Suffern HS 1,500/9-12
49 Viola Rd 10901 845-357-3800
Patrick Faherty, prin. Fax 357-5035
Suffern JHS 1,100/6-8
80 Hemion Rd 10901 845-357-7400
Diana Jabis, prin. Fax 357-4563

Bat Torah - Alisa M. Flatow Yeshiva HS 100/9-12
4 Campbell Ave 10901 845-357-0774
Miriam Bak, prin. Fax 357-9482
Shaarei Torah of Rockland 100/9-12
91 Carlton Rd W 10901 845-352-3431
Rabbi Mordechai Wolmark, admin. Fax 352-3433
SUNY Rockland Community College Post-Sec.
145 College Rd 10901 845-574-4000
Yeshiva Ohr Reuven 100/9-12
259 Grandview Ave 10901 845-362-8362
Rabbi Bezalel Rudinsky, prin. Fax 354-4830
Yeshiva Shaarei Torah of Rockland Post-Sec.
91 Carlton Rd W 10901 845-352-3431

Syosset, Nassau, Pop. 18,967
Syosset Central SD 6,600/K-12
99 Pell Ln 11791 516-364-5600
Dr. Carole Hankin, supt. Fax 921-5616
www.syosset.k12.ny.us
South Woods MS 700/6-8
99 Pell Ln 11791 516-364-5621
Michelle Burget, prin. Fax 921-5616
Syosset HS 2,100/9-12
70 Southwoods Rd 11791 516-364-5675
Dr. Jorge Schneider, prin. Fax 921-5616
Thompson MS 900/6-8
98 Ann Dr 11791 516-364-5760
James Kassebaum, prin. Fax 921-5616

Culinary Academy of Long Island Post-Sec.
125 Michael Dr 11791 516-364-4344
New York College of Health Professions Post-Sec.
6801 Jericho Tpke 11791 516-364-0808
Our Lady of Mercy Academy 500/9-12
815 Convent Rd 11791 516-921-1047
Joan Gordon, prin. Fax 921-3634

Syracuse, Onondaga, Pop. 141,683
Solvay UFD
Supt. — See Solvay
Solvay MS 4-8
299 Bury Dr 13209 315-487-7061
James Werbeck, prin. Fax 484-1444

Syracuse CSD 20,300/K-12
725 Harrison St 13210 315-435-4161
Daniel Lowengard, supt. Fax 435-4015
www.syracusecityschools.com/
Bellevue MS Academy 7-8
1607 S Geddes St 13207 315-435-4480
Anthony Williams, prin. Fax 435-6232
Central Technical-Vocational Center Vo/Tech
258 E Adams St 13202 315-435-4300
John Dittmann, prin. Fax 435-5816
Clary Magnet MS 500/6-8
100 Amidon Dr 13205 315-435-4411
Pamela Odom-Cain, prin. Fax 435-5832
Corcoran HS 1,500/9-12
919 Glenwood Ave 13207 315-435-4321
Brian Nolan, prin. Fax 435-4024
Danforth Magnet MS 400/6-8
309 W Brighton Ave 13205 315-435-4535
Florence Williams, prin. Fax 435-6208
Fowler HS 1,300/9-12
227 Magnolia St 13204 315-435-4376
Laura Vieira-Suarez, prin. Fax 435-6313
Grant MS 800/6-8
2400 Grant Blvd 13208 315-435-4433
Steven Wolf, prin. Fax 435-4856
Henninger HS 1,700/9-12
600 Robinson St 13206 315-435-4343
David Cecile, prin. Fax 435-6277
Levy MS 500/7-8
111 Fellows Ave 13210 315-435-4444
Deborah Meyer, prin. Fax 435-4443
Lincoln MS 600/6-8
1613 James St 13203 315-435-4450
Dean DeSantis, prin. Fax 435-4455
Nottingham HS 1,300/9-12
3100 E Genesee St 13224 315-435-4380
Debra Mastropaolo, prin. Fax 435-4177

Westhill Central SD 2,000/K-12
400 Walberta Rd 13219 315-426-3218
Stephen Bocciolatt, supt. Fax 488-6411
www.westhillschools.org/
Onondaga Hill MS 600/5-8
4860 Onondaga Rd 13215 315-426-3400
Douglas Hutson, prin. Fax 492-0156
Westhill HS 700/9-12
4501 Onondaga Blvd 13219 315-426-3100
Grenardo Avellino, prin. Fax 475-0319

Bishop Ludden JSHS 800/7-12
815 Fay Rd 13219 315-468-2591
Dennis Meehan, prin. Fax 468-0097
Bryant & Stratton College Post-Sec.
953 James St 13203 315-472-6603
Christian Brothers Academy 700/7-12
6245 Randall Rd 13214 315-446-5960
Br. Thomas Zoppo, prin. Fax 446-3393
Crouse Hospital School of Nursing Post-Sec.
736 Irving Ave 13210 315-470-7481
Faith Heritage S 400/PK-12
3740 Midland Ave 13205 315-469-7777
Jeff Shaver, dir. Fax 492-7440
Le Moyne College Post-Sec.
1419 Salt Springs Rd 13214 315-445-4100
Living Word Academy 200/PK-12
6101 Court Street Rd 13206 315-437-6744
Philip Mastroleo, prin. Fax 437-6766
Onondaga Community College Post-Sec.
4941 Onondaga Rd 13215 315-498-2622
Phillips Hairstyling Institute Post-Sec.
709 E Genesee St 13210 315-422-9656

St. Joseph's Hospital College of Nursing Post-Sec.
206 Prospect Ave 13203 315-448-5040
Simmons Institute of Funeral Service Post-Sec.
1828 South Ave 13207 315-475-5142
SUNY College Environ. Science - Forestry Post-Sec.
1 Forestry Dr 13210 315-470-6500
SUNY Empire State College Post-Sec.
219 Walton St Fl 1 13202 315-472-5799
SUNY Upstate Medical University Post-Sec.
750 E Adams St 13210 315-464-5540
Syracuse University 13244 Post-Sec.
315-443-1870

Tannersville, Greene, Pop. 446
Hunter-Tannersville Central SD 500/PK-12
PO Box 1018 12485 518-589-5400
Ralph Marino, supt. Fax 589-5403
www.htcsd.org/
Tannersville MSHS 300/7-12
6094 Main St 12485 518-589-5880
Thomas Averill, prin. Fax 589-7071

Tarrytown, Westchester, Pop. 11,346

Hackley S 800/K-12
293 Benedict Ave 10591 914-631-0128
Walter Johnson, hdmstr. Fax 366-2636
Marymount College Post-Sec.
100 Marymount Ave 10591 914-631-3200

Thiells, Rockland, Pop. 5,204
North Rockland Central SD
Supt. — See Garnerville
Fieldstone Secondary S 1,300/8-9
100 Fieldstone Dr 10984 845-942-7900
Frank Parrino, prin. Fax 942-7910
North Rockland HS 1,900/10-12
106 Hammond Rd 10984 845-942-3300
Dennis Hand, prin. Fax 942-3365

Thornwood, Westchester, Pop. 7,025
Mount Pleasant Central SD 1,900/K-12
825 Westlake Dr 10594 914-769-5500
Dr. Alfred Lodovico, supt. Fax 769-3733
www.mtplcsd.org
Westlake HS 500/9-12
825 Westlake Dr 10594 914-769-8540
Frank Viteritti, prin. Fax 769-0596
Westlake MS 600/5-8
825 Westlake Dr 10594 914-769-8540
Jerry Schulman, prin. Fax 769-8550

Ticonderoga, Essex, Pop. 2,726
Ticonderoga Central SD 1,000/K-12
9 Amherst Ave 12883 518-585-6674
John McDonald, supt. Fax 585-2682
www.ticonderogak12.org
Ticonderoga HS 400/9-12
5 Calkins Pl 12883 518-585-6661
Michael Graney, prin. Fax 585-5282
Ticonderoga MS 200/6-8
116 Alexandria Ave 12883 518-585-7442
Bruce Tubbs, prin. Fax 585-2716

SUNY North Country Community College Post-Sec.
PO Box 311 12883 518-585-4454

Tioga Center, Tioga
Tioga Central SD 1,200/K-12
PO Box 241 13845 607-687-8000
Patrick Dougherty, supt. Fax 687-8007
www.tiogacentral.org/
Tioga HS 400/9-12
PO Box 241 13845 607-687-8001
Scot Taylor, prin. Fax 687-8010
Tioga MS 400/5-8
PO Box 241 13845 607-687-8004
Cynthia Bennett, prin. Fax 687-6910

Tonawanda, Erie, Pop. 15,335
Kenmore-Tonawanda UFSD
Supt. — See Buffalo
Kenmore East HS 1,200/9-12
350 Fries Rd 14150 716-874-8402
LuAnn Ostanski, prin. Fax 874-8443

Tonawanda CSD 2,200/K-12
202 Broad St 14150 716-694-7784
Barbara Peters Ed.D., supt. Fax 695-8738
www.tona.wnyric.org
Tonawanda HS 700/9-12
150 Hinds St 14150 716-694-7670
Susan Frey, prin. Fax 694-7692
Tonawanda MS 500/6-8
600 Fletcher St 14150 716-694-7660
James Newton, prin. Fax 694-4597

Cardinal O'Hara HS 200/9-12
39 Ohara Rd 14150 716-695-2600
Michael Powers, prin. Fax 692-8697
MarJon School of Beauty Culture Post-Sec.
1154 Niagara Falls Blvd 14150 716-836-6240

Troy, Rensselaer, Pop. 48,310
Brunswick Central SD 1,400/K-12
3992 State Highway 2 12180 518-279-4600
David Burnham, supt. Fax 279-1918
www.brittonkill.k12.ny.us
Tamarac MSHS 900/6-12
3992 State Highway 2 12180 518-279-4600
Richard Pogue, prin. Fax 279-3888

Lansingburgh Central SD 2,300/K-12
576 5th Ave 12182 518-233-6850
Lee Bordick, supt.
www.lansingburgh.org
Knickerbacker MS 500/6-8
320 7th Ave 12182 518-233-6811
Shaun Paolino, prin. Fax 238-2518
Lansingburgh HS 700/9-12
320 7th Ave 12182 518-233-6806
Angelina Bergin, prin. Fax 233-6826

Troy CSD 4,000/PK-12
2920 5th Ave 12180 518-271-5200
Lonnie Palmer, supt. Fax 271-5229
www.troy.k12.ny.us/
Doyle MS 700/6-8
1976 Burdett Ave 12180 518-271-5350
Diana Germain, prin. Fax 271-8160
Troy HS 1,400/9-12
1950 Burdett Ave 12180 518-271-5300
John Carmello, prin. Fax 274-2341

Catholic Central HS 500/7-12
625 7th Ave 12182 518-235-7100
Christopher Bott, prin. Fax 237-1796
La Salle Institute 600/6-12
174 Williams Rd 12180 518-283-2500
Robert Herzog, prin. Fax 283-6265
Oakwood Christian S 200/PK-12
260 Oakwood Ave 12182 518-271-0526
Rev. James DuJack, hdmstr. Fax 270-1659
Rensselaer Polytechnic Institute Post-Sec.
110 8th St 12180 518-276-6000
Russell Sage College Post-Sec.
45 Ferry St 12180 518-244-2000
Russell Sage Graduate School Post-Sec.
45 Ferry St 12180 518-244-2264
Samaritan Hospital School of Nursing Post-Sec.
2215 Burdett Ave 12180 518-271-3285
SUNY Hudson Valley Community College Post-Sec.
80 Vandenburgh Ave 12180 518-629-4822
Troy School of Beauty Culture Post-Sec.
15 Highland Ct 12180 518-273-7741
Willard S 300/9-12
285 Pawling Ave 12180 518-833-1300
Trudy Hall, prin. Fax 833-1800

Trumansburg, Tompkins, Pop. 1,588
Trumansburg Central SD 1,400/K-12
100 Whig St 14886 607-387-7551
Cosimo Tangorra, supt. Fax 387-2807
www.tburg.k12.ny.us
Dickerson HS 500/9-12
100 Whig St 14886 607-387-7551
Paula Hurley, prin. Fax 387-2807
Doig MS 500/5-8
100 Whig St 14886 607-387-7551
Gary Astles, prin. Fax 387-2807

Tuckahoe, Westchester, Pop. 6,256
Tuckahoe UFD 1,000/K-12
29 Elm St 10707 914-337-6600
Michael Yazurlo Ed.D., supt. Fax 337-3072
www.tuckahoeschools.org/
Other Schools – See Eastchester

St. Vladimir's Orthodox Theological Sem. Post-Sec.
575 Scarsdale Rd 10707 914-961-8313

Tully, Onondaga, Pop. 891
Tully Central SD 1,200/K-12
PO Box 628 13159 315-696-6204
Kraig Pritts, supt. Fax 883-1343
www.tullyschools.org/
Tully JSHS 600/7-12
PO Box 628 13159 315-696-6235
Peter Cardamone, prin. Fax 696-6237

Tupper Lake, Franklin, Pop. 3,856
Tupper Lake Central SD 1,000/K-12
294 Hosley Ave 12986 518-359-3371
Daniel Bower, supt. Fax 359-7862
www.tupperlakecsd.net/
Tupper Lake MSHS 500/7-12
25 Chaney Ave 12986 518-359-3322
Pamela Martin, prin. Fax 359-7862

Turin, Lewis, Pop. 246
South Lewis Central SD 1,200/K-12
PO Box 10 13473 315-348-2500
Frank House, supt. Fax 348-2510
www.southlewis.org
South Lewis HS 400/9-12
PO Box 40 13473 315-348-2520
Dr. Dan McPhail, prin. Fax 348-2510
South Lewis MS 300/6-8
PO Box 70 13473 315-348-2570
Philomena Goss, prin. Fax 348-2510

Tuxedo Park, Orange, Pop. 732
Tuxedo UFD 600/K-12
PO Box 2002 10987 845-351-4799
Joseph Zanetti, supt. Fax 351-5296
tuxedoschooldistrict.com
Baker HS 400/9-12
PO Box 2002 10987 845-351-4786
Denis Petrilak, prin. Fax 351-4823

Uniondale, Nassau, Pop. 20,328
Uniondale UFD 6,200/K-12
933 Goodrich St 11553 516-560-8824
William Lloyd Ph.D., supt. Fax 292-2659
www.uniondale.k12.ny.us
Turtle Hook MS 700/6-8
975 Jerusalem Ave 11553 516-918-1300
Annette O'Ferrall, prin. Fax 505-2533
Uniondale HS 1,800/9-12
933 Goodrich St 11553 516-560-8831
Florence Simmons, prin. Fax 564-8464
Other Schools – See Hempstead

Hebrew Academy of Nassau County 400/7-12
215 Oak St 11553 516-538-8161
Rabbi Elliot Hecht, prin. Fax 489-1142
Kellenberg Memorial HS 2,500/6-12
1400 Glenn Curtiss Blvd 11553 516-292-0200
Br. Ken Hoagland, prin. Fax 292-0877

Union Springs, Cayuga, Pop. 1,069
Union Springs Central SD 1,000/K-12
239 Cayuga St 13160 315-889-4101
Linda Rice, supt. Fax 889-4108
www.uscsd.info/
Union Springs HS 400/9-12
239 Cayuga St 13160 315-889-4110
Kimberle Ward, prin. Fax 889-4118

Union Springs MS 200/7-8
239 Cayuga St 13160 315-889-4112
Thomas Eldridge, prin. Fax 889-4108

Union Springs Academy 50/9-12
PO Box 524 13160 315-889-7314
John Baker, prin. Fax 889-7188

Upper Nyack, Rockland, Pop. 1,873
Nyack UFD
Supt. — See Nyack
Nyack HS 1,000/9-12
360 Christian Herald Rd 10960 845-353-7100
Phyllis Aliberto, prin. Fax 353-7119

Utica, Oneida, Pop. 59,336
Utica CSD 8,500/K-12
1115 Mohawk St 13501 315-792-2222
Marilyn Skermont, supt. Fax 792-2200
www.uticaschools.org
Donovan MS 1,000/6-8
1701 Noyes St 13502 315-792-2007
John Licari, prin. Fax 792-2077
Kennedy MS 1,000/6-8
500 Deerfield Dr E 13502 315-792-2086
Elizabeth Paul, prin. Fax 792-2084
Proctor HS, 1203 Hilton Ave 13501 2,300/9-12
Dolores Chainey, prin. 315-368-6100

Faxton-St. Luke's Healthcare Post-Sec.
PO Box 479 13503 315-624-6136
Mohawk Valley Community College Post-Sec.
1101 Sherman Dr 13501 315-792-5400
Munson-Williams-Proctor Institute Post-Sec.
310 Genesee St 13502 315-797-8260
Notre Dame JSHS 600/7-12
2 Notre Dame Ln 13502 315-724-5118
Sr. Anna Collins, prin. Fax 724-9460
St. Elizabeth College of Nursing Post-Sec.
2215 Genesee St 13501 315-798-8125
SUNY Institute of Technology Utica/Rome Post-Sec.
PO Box 3050 13504 315-792-7100
Tilton S at the House of Good Shepherd 100/1-11
1550 Champlin Ave 13502 315-235-7671
David Williams, dir. Fax 235-7609
Utica College Post-Sec.
1600 Burrstone Rd 13502 315-792-3111
Utica School of Commerce Post-Sec.
201 Bleecker St 13501 315-733-2307

Valatie, Columbia, Pop. 1,910
Kinderhook Central SD 2,200/K-12
2910 Route 9 12184 518-758-7575
James Dexter, supt. Fax 758-7579
www.berk.com/~ichabod/
Crane HS 700/9-12
2910 US Highway 9 12184 518-758-7577
William Schneider, prin. Fax 758-2181
Crane MS 600/5-8
2910 US Highway 9 12184 518-758-7676
Maureen Van Duesen, prin. Fax 758-7579

Academy of Christian Leadership 50/7-12
3429 Route 9 12184 518-784-2222
Jim Ogden, admin. Fax 784-2224

Valhalla, Westchester, Pop. 6,200
Valhalla UFD 1,500/K-12
316 Columbus Ave 10595 914-683-5040
Dr. Diane Ramos-Kelly, supt. Fax 683-5075
Valhalla HS 400/9-12
300 Columbus Ave 10595 914-683-5014
Jonathan Thomas, prin. Fax 683-5003
Valhalla MS 300/6-8
300 Columbus Ave 10595 914-683-5011
Steven Garcia, prin. Fax 683-5003

New York Medical College 10595 Post-Sec.
914-594-4000
Westchester Community College Post-Sec.
75 Grasslands Rd 10595 914-785-6600
Westchester County Medical Center Post-Sec.
Grasslands Rd 10595 914-285-7276

Valley Stream, Nassau, Pop. 35,799
Valley Stream Central HSD 4,600/7-12
1 Kent Rd 11580 516-872-5601
Dr. R. Marc Bernstein, supt. Fax 872-5658
vschsd.org
Valley Stream Central SHS 1,000/10-12
135 Fletcher Ave 11580 516-561-4410
Joseph Pompilio, prin. Fax 561-4490
Valley Stream Memorial JHS 1,000/7-9
320 Fletcher Ave 11580 516-872-7710
Dr. Kathleen Walsh, prin. Fax 872-7711
Valley Stream South JSHS 1,400/7-12
150 Jedwood Pl 11581 516-791-0310
Dr. Stephen Lando, prin. Fax 791-0305
Other Schools – See Franklin Square

Business Informatics Center Post-Sec.
134 S Central Ave 11580 516-561-0050
Mesivta Or Chadash 100/9-12
322 N Corona Ave 11580 516-561-5090
Rabbi Boruch Gottesman, prin. Fax 561-5091
Valley Stream Christian Academy 100/K-12
12 E Fairview Ave 11580 516-823-0022
Leslie Fowley, admin. Fax 823-0228

Van Etten, Chemung, Pop. 564
Spencer-Van Etten Central SD 1,100/PK-12
PO Box 307 14889 607-589-7100
Steven Schoonmaker, supt. Fax 589-3010
www.s-ve.org
Other Schools – See Spencer

Van Hornesville, Herkimer
Van Hornesville-Owen D. Young Central SD 200/K-12
PO Box 125 13475 315-858-0729
James Christmann, supt. Fax 858-2019
Young Central S 200/K-12
PO Box 125 13475 315-858-0729
James Christmann, prin. Fax 858-2019

Verona, Oneida
Vernon-Verona-Sherrill Central SD 2,400/PK-12
PO Box 128 13478 315-829-2520
Norman Reed, supt. Fax 829-4949
www.vvscentralschools.org/
Vernon-Verona-Sherrill HS 800/9-12
PO Box 128 13478 315-829-2520
Mark Wixson, prin. Fax 829-4465
Vernon-Verona-Sherrill MS 400/7-8
PO Box 128 13478 315-829-2520
James Kramer, prin. Fax 829-5966

Vestal, Broome, Pop. 5,000
Vestal Central SD 4,200/K-12
201 Main St Ste 6 13850 607-757-2241
Mark Capobianco, supt. Fax 757-2227
www.vestal.k12.ny.us/
Vestal HS 1,400/9-12
205 Woodlawn Dr 13850 607-757-2281
Catherine Hepler, prin. Fax 757-2301
Vestal MS 1,000/6-8
600 S Benita Blvd 13850 607-757-2331
Ann Marie Loose, prin. Fax 757-2229

Ross Corners Christian Academy 200/PK-12
2101 Owego Rd 13850 607-748-3301
Toby Wyse, admin. Fax 748-3301

Victor, Ontario, Pop. 2,547
Victor Central SD 3,700/PK-12
953 High St 14564 585-924-3252
Timothy McElheran, supt. Fax 742-7090
www.victorschools.org
Victor HS 1,100/9-12
953 High St 14564 585-924-3252
Yvonne O'Shea, prin. Fax 924-9536
Victor JHS 500/7-8
953 High St 14564 585-924-3252
Carl Christensen, prin. Fax 924-9535

Voorheesville, Albany, Pop. 2,782
Voorheesville Central SD 1,200/K-12
432 New Salem Rd 12186 518-765-3313
Linda Langevin, supt. Fax 765-2751
vcsd.neric.org/
Bouton MSHS 700/7-12
432 New Salem Rd 12186 518-765-3314
Mark Diefendorf, prin. Fax 765-5547

Wallkill, Ulster, Pop. 2,125
Wallkill Central SD 3,500/K-12
PO Box 310 12589 845-895-7100
Anthony Argulewicz, supt. Fax 895-3630
www.wallkillcsd.k12.ny.us
Wallkill HS 1,200/9-12
PO Box 310 12589 845-895-7150
David Bernsley, prin. Fax 895-8003
Wallkill MS 600/7-8
PO Box 310 12589 845-895-7175
Yvonne Herrington, prin. Fax 895-8036

Walton, Delaware, Pop. 2,951
Walton Central SD 1,100/K-12
47-49 Stockton Ave 13856 607-865-4116
Jonathan Buhner, supt. Fax 865-8568
www.waltoncsd.stier.org/
Walton HS 400/9-12
47-49 Stockton Ave 13856 607-865-4116
Michael Snider, prin. Fax 865-6130
Walton MS 300/6-8
47-49 Stockton Ave 13856 607-865-4116
Michael A. MacDonald, prin. Fax 865-8568

Walworth, Wayne
Gananda Central SD 1,200/K-12
1500 Dayspring Rdg 14568 315-986-3521
Patricia Roach, supt. Fax 986-2003
www.Gananda.org
Gananda / Cirillo HS 300/9-12
3195 Wiedrick Rd 14568 315-986-3521
Ken Dehn, prin. Fax 986-2003
Gananda MS 300/6-8
1500 Dayspring Rdg 14568 315-986-3521
Matthew Mahoney, prin. Fax 986-2003

Wampsville, Madison, Pop. 569
Oneida CSD
Supt. — See Oneida
Shortell MS 400/7-8
PO Box 716 13163 315-363-1050
Robin Price, prin. Fax 366-0622

Wantagh, Nassau, Pop. 18,567
Wantagh UFD 3,700/K-12
3301 Beltagh Ave 11793 516-781-8000
Carl Bonuso, supt. Fax 781-6076
www.wantaghschools.org
Wantagh HS 1,000/9-12
3297 Beltagh Ave 11793 516-679-6402
Terrance O'Connor, prin. Fax 679-6432
Wantagh MS 800/6-8
3299 Beltagh Ave 11793 516-679-6350
Dr. Jeannette Stern, prin. Fax 679-6311

Wappingers Falls, Dutchess, Pop. 5,085
Wappingers Central SD 12,300/K-12
167 Myers Corners Rd 12590 845-298-5000
Richard Powell, supt. Fax 298-5041
www.wappingersschools.org
Ketcham HS 1,900/9-12
99 Myers Corners Rd 12590 845-298-5100
Sherrill Lazarus, prin. Fax 298-5099
Van Wyck JHS 1,500/6-8
10 Hillside Lake Rd 12590 845-227-1700
Steve Shuchat, prin. Fax 227-1748
Wappingers Falls JHS 1,000/7-8
30 Major MacDonald Way 12590 845-298-5200
Cheryl Musante, prin. Fax 298-5156
Other Schools – See Hopewell Junction

Warrensburg, Warren, Pop. 3,204
Warrensburg Central SD 900/K-12
103 Schroon River Rd 12885 518-623-2861
Timothy Lawson, supt. Fax 623-2436
www.wcsd.org/
Warrensburg JSHS 400/7-12
103 Schroon River Rd 12885 518-623-2862
Daniel Roberts, prin. Fax 623-5089

Warsaw, Wyoming, Pop. 3,701
Warsaw Central SD 1,200/K-12
153 W Buffalo St 14569 585-786-8000
Philip D'Angelo, supt. Fax 786-8008
www.warsaw.k12.ny.us/
Warsaw HS 400/9-12
81 W Court St 14569 585-786-8000
Marc Czadzeck, prin. Fax 786-3193
Warsaw MS 300/6-8
81 W Court St 14569 585-786-8000
Gregory Feller, prin. Fax 786-3193

Warwick, Orange, Pop. 6,571
Warwick Valley Central SD 4,500/K-12
PO Box 595 10990 845-987-3000
Dr. Frank Greenhall, supt. Fax 987-1147
www.warwickvalleyschools.com
Warwick Valley HS 1,500/9-12
PO Box 595 10990 845-987-3050
Randy Barbarash, prin. Fax 987-8982
Warwick Valley MS 1,200/6-8
PO Box 595 10990 845-987-3100
John Kolesar, prin. Fax 986-6942

Washingtonville, Orange, Pop. 6,236
Washingtonville Central SD 4,900/K-12
52 W Main St 10992 845-497-2200
Roberta Greene, supt. Fax 496-2330
www.ws.k12.ny.us
Washingtonville HS 1,700/9-12
54 W Main St 10992 845-497-2200
Michael Rossi, prin. Fax 496-2212
Washingtonville MS 1,200/6-8
38 W Main St 10992 845-497-2200
Maureen Peterson, prin. Fax 496-2099

Waterford, Saratoga, Pop. 2,182
Waterford-Halfmoon UFD 900/K-12
125 Middletown Rd 12188 518-237-0800
Carl Klossner, supt. Fax 237-7335
www.whufsd.org
Waterford-Halfmoon HS 300/9-12
125 Middletown Rd 12188 518-237-0800
Fax 237-7335
Waterford-Halfmoon MS 300/5-8
125 Middletown Rd 12188 518-237-0800
Christine Barry, prin. Fax 237-7335

Waterloo, Seneca, Pop. 5,134
Waterloo Central SD 2,000/K-12
109 Washington St 13165 315-539-1500
Terry MacNabb, supt. Fax 539-1504
www.waterloocsd.org/
Waterloo HS 600/9-12
96 Stark St 13165 315-539-1550
John Butler, prin. Fax 539-1536
Waterloo MS 500/6-8
65 Center St 13165 315-539-1540
Michael Ferrara, prin. Fax 539-1504

Watertown, Jefferson, Pop. 27,220
Watertown CSD 4,000/K-12
1351 Washington St 13601 315-785-3700
Terry Fralick, supt. Fax 785-6855
www.watertowncsd.org
Case MS 700/7-8
1237 Washington St 13601 315-785-3870
Donald Whitney, prin. Fax 785-3731
Watertown HS 1,200/9-12
1335 Washington St 13601 315-785-3800
Stephen Williamson, prin. Fax 785-3733

Faith Fellowship Christian S 100/PK-12
131 Moore Ave 13601 315-782-9342
Donald Cronk, prin. Fax 786-0309
Immaculate Heart Central JSHS 7-12
1316 Ives St 13601 315-788-4670
Pat Fontana, prin. Fax 788-4672
Jefferson Community College Post-Sec.
1220 Coffeen St 13601 315-786-2200
Samaritan Medical Center Post-Sec.
830 Washington St 13601 315-785-4000

Waterville, Oneida, Pop. 1,682
Waterville Central SD 1,000/K-12
381 Madison St 13480 315-841-3900
James Van Wormer, supt. Fax 841-3939
www.watervilleschools.org/
Waterville JSHS 600/6-12
381 Madison St 13480 315-841-3800
Sherri Walczak, prin. Fax 841-3838

Watervliet, Albany, Pop. 9,889
Watervliet CSD 1,400/K-12
1245 Hillside Dr 12189 518-629-3200
Paul Padalino, supt. Fax 629-3265
vliet.neric.org/
Watervliet JSHS 600/7-12
1245 Hillside Dr 12189 518-629-3200
Lori Caplan, prin. Fax 273-1707

Watkins Glen, Schuyler, Pop. 2,099
Watkins Glen Central SD 1,300/K-12
303 12th St 14891 607-535-3219
Thomas Phillips, supt. Fax 535-4629
www.watkinsglenschools.org/
Watkins Glen Central HS 500/9-12
301 12th St 14891 607-535-3210
David Warren, prin. Fax 535-4629
Watkins Glen MS 400/5-8
200 10th St 14891 607-535-3230
Kristine Somerville, prin. Fax 535-4532

Waverly, Tioga, Pop. 4,493
Waverly Central SD 1,800/K-12
15 Frederick St 14892 607-565-2841
Michael McMahon, supt. Fax 565-4997
www.waverlyschools.com/
Waverly HS 600/9-12
1 Frederick St 14892 607-565-8101
Dave Mastrantuono, prin. Fax 565-4997
Waverly MS 300/7-8
1 Frederick St 14892 607-565-3410
Diane Tymoski, prin. Fax 565-4997

Wawarsing, Ulster, Pop. 12,348

Wawarsing Christian Academy 100/PK-12
PO Box 338 12489 845-647-3810
Ronald Mahany, admin. Fax 647-1041

Wayland, Steuben, Pop. 1,842
Wayland-Cohocton Central SD 1,900/PK-12
2350 State Route 63 14572 585-728-2211
Michael Wetherbee, supt. Fax 728-3566
www.wccsk12.org
Wayland-Cohocton HS 600/9-12
2350 State Route 63 14572 585-728-2366
William Whyte, prin. Fax 728-2425
Wayland-Cohocton MS 600/5-8
2350 State Route 63 14572 585-728-2551
Eileen Feinman, prin. Fax 728-3556

Webster, Monroe, Pop. 5,089
Webster Central SD 8,600/K-12
119 South Ave 14580 585-265-3600
Adele Bovard, supt. Fax 265-6561
www.websterschools.org
Spry MS 1,100/6-8
119 South Ave 14580 585-265-6500
David Swinson, prin. Fax 265-6512
Thomas HS 1,400/9-12
800 Five Mile Line Rd 14580 585-670-8000
John Walker, prin. Fax 671-1884
Webster Schroeder HS 1,500/9-12
875 Ridge Rd 14580 585-671-1880
Joseph Pustulka, prin. Fax 671-8681
Willink MS 1,100/6-8
900 Publishers Pkwy 14580 585-670-1030
Joseph Morgan, prin. Fax 671-1978

Webster Christian S 300/PK-12
675 Holt Rd 14580 585-872-5150
Keith Bell, admin. Fax 872-5932

Weedsport, Cayuga, Pop. 1,970
Weedsport Central SD 1,000/K-12
2821 E Brutus Street Rd 13166 315-834-6637
Shaun O'Connor, supt.
Weedsport JSHS 600/6-12
2821 E Brutus Street Rd 13166 315-834-6652
Phillip Grome, prin. Fax 834-8693

Wells, Hamilton
Wells Central SD 200/PK-12
PO Box 300 12190 518-924-6000
Paul Williamson, supt. Fax 924-9246
wells.neric.org
Wells S 200/PK-12
PO Box 300 12190 518-924-6000
Paul Williamson, prin. Fax 924-9246

Wellsville, Allegany, Pop. 4,773
Wellsville Central SD 1,400/K-12
126 W State St 14895 585-596-2170
Byron Chandler Ed.D., supt. Fax 596-2177
www.wellsville.wnyric.org
Wellsville HS 500/9-12
126 W State St 14895 585-596-2188
Connie Synakowski, prin. Fax 596-2180
Wellsville MS 300/6-8
126 W State St 14895 585-596-2144
Mary Ellen O'Connell, prin. Fax 596-2142

West Babylon, Suffolk, Pop. 43,700
West Babylon UFD 4,800/K-12
10 Farmingdale Rd 11704 631-321-3142
Melvin Noble, supt. Fax 661-5166
www.westbabylon.k12.ny.us
West Babylon HS 1,500/9-12
500 Great East Neck Rd 11704 631-321-3003
Dr. Ellice Vassallo, prin. Fax 321-3168
West Babylon JHS 1,100/6-8
200 Old Farmingdale Rd 11704 631-321-3084
Michael Rizzo, prin. Fax 321-3079

Commercial Driver Training School Post-Sec.
600 Patton Ave 11704 631-249-1330

Westbury, Nassau, Pop. 14,691
East Meadow UFD 7,800/K-12
718 The Plain Rd 11590 516-478-5776
Robert Dillon Ed.D., supt.
www.eastmeadow.k12.ny.us
Clarke HS 900/9-12
740 Edgewood Dr 11590 516-876-7450
Timothy Voels, prin. Fax 876-7416
Clarke MS 700/6-8
740 Edgewood Dr 11590 516-876-7401
Stacey Breslin, prin. Fax 876-7407
Other Schools – See East Meadow

Westbury UFD
Supt. — See Old Westbury
Westbury MS 900/6-8
455 Rockland St 11590 516-876-5082
Darnel Powell, prin. Fax 876-5141

West Chazy, Clinton
Beekmantown Central SD 2,100/K-12
37 Eagle Way 12992 518-563-8250
Mark Sposato Ed.D., supt. Fax 563-8132
www.bcsdk12.org
Other Schools – See Plattsburgh

Westfield, Chautauqua, Pop. 3,464
Westfield Central SD 900/K-12
203 E Main St 14787 716-326-2151
Laura Chabe, supt. Fax 326-2195
www.wacs.wnyric.org/
Westfield HS 300/9-12
203 E Main St 14787 716-326-2151
Kevin Davenport, prin. Fax 326-2157
Westfield MS 200/6-8
203 E Main St 14787 716-326-2151
Kevin Davenport, prin. Fax 326-2157

Westhampton Beach, Suffolk, Pop. 1,957
Westhampton Beach UFD 1,700/K-12
340 Mill Rd 11978 631-288-3800
Lynn Schwartz, supt. Fax 288-8351
www.westhamptonbeach.k12.ny.us
Westhampton Beach HS 900/9-12
49 Lilac Rd 11978 631-288-3800
Edward W. Casswell, prin. Fax 288-3915
Westhampton Beach MS 400/6-8
340 Mill Rd 11978 631-288-3800
Charisse Miller, prin. Fax 288-5496

West Hempstead, Nassau, Pop. 17,689
West Hempstead UFD 2,400/K-12
252 Chestnut St 11552 516-390-3107
Dr. Carol Eisenburg, supt. Fax 489-1776
www.westhempstead.k12.ny.us
West Hempstead HS 900/9-12
400 Nassau Blvd 11552 516-390-3214
Thomas Lee, prin. Fax 489-1769
West Hempstead MS 500/6-8
450 Nassau Blvd 11552 516-390-3160
Joseph Cirnigliaro, prin. Fax 489-8946

West Henrietta, Monroe
Rush-Henrietta Central SD
Supt. — See Henrietta
Burger MS 600/6-8
639 Erie Station Rd 14586 585-359-5308
Shawn Nelms, prin. Fax 359-5333

West Islip, Suffolk, Pop. 29,000
West Islip UFD 5,800/K-12
100 Sherman Ave 11795 631-893-3200
Beth Virginia Blau Ed.D., supt. Fax 893-3212
www.westislipufsd.k12.ny.us/
Beach Street MS 600/6-8
1765 Beach St 11795 631-893-3310
Anne Shierant, prin. Fax 893-3318
Udall Road MS 800/6-8
900 Udall Rd 11795 631-893-3290
Bernadette Burns, prin. Fax 893-3301
West Islip HS 1,700/9-12
3 Higbie Ln 11795 631-893-3250
Kenneth Hartill, prin. Fax 893-3318

St. John the Baptist Diocesan HS 9-12
1170 Montauk Hwy 11795 631-587-8000
Walter Lace, prin. Fax 587-8996

Westmoreland, Oneida
Westmoreland Central SD 1,100/K-12
5176 State Route 233 13490 315-557-2601
Antoinette Kulak, supt. Fax 853-4602
Westmoreland HS 400/9-12
5176 State Route 233 13490 315-557-2616
Rocco Migliori, prin. Fax 853-4602
Westmoreland MS 400/5-8
5176 State Route 233 13490 315-557-2618
Brian Kavanagh, prin. Fax 853-4602

West Nyack, Rockland, Pop. 3,437
Clarkstown Central SD
Supt. — See New City
Clarkstown South HS 1,400/9-12
31 Demarest Mill Rd 10994 845-624-3400
James Vitale, prin. Fax 623-5470
Festa MS 2,200/6-8
30 Parrott Rd 10994 845-639-6339
Dianne Basso, prin. Fax 634-5874

West Point, Orange, Pop. 8,024

United States Military Academy Post-Sec.
646 Swift Rd 10996 845-938-4041

Westport, Essex, Pop. 524
Westport Central SD 200/K-12
PO Box 408 12993 518-962-8244
Karen Tromblee, supt. Fax 962-4571
www.westportcs.org
Westport Central S 200/K-12
PO Box 408 12993 518-962-8244
Karen Tromblee, prin. Fax 962-4571

West Sayville, Suffolk, Pop. 4,680
Sayville UFD
Supt. — See Sayville
Sayville HS 1,100/9-12
20 Brook St 11796 631-244-6600
Joseph Buderman, prin. Fax 244-6779

West Seneca, Erie, Pop. 45,600
West Seneca Central SD 7,600/K-12
1397 Orchard Park Rd 14224 716-677-3101
James Brotz, supt. Fax 677-3104
www.wscschools.org/
East MS 600/7-8
1445 Center Rd 14224 716-677-3530
Monica Witman, prin. Fax 674-1046
West MS 700/7-8
395 Center Rd 14224 716-677-3500
Brian Graham, prin. Fax 675-6134
West Seneca East HS 1,100/9-12
4760 Seneca St 14224 716-677-3300
Angela LaPaglia, prin. Fax 677-2933
West Seneca West HS 1,400/9-12
3330 Seneca St 14224 716-677-3350
Jon MacSwan, prin. Fax 674-3551

Continental School of Beauty Culture Post-Sec.
1050 Union Rd 14224 716-675-8205
Houghton College Post-Sec.
910 Union Rd 14224 716-674-6363
West Seneca Christian S 300/K-12
511 Union Rd 14224 716-674-1820
Russell Baun, admin. Fax 674-4894

West Valley, Cattaraugus
West Valley Central SD 400/PK-12
PO Box 290 14171 716-942-3293
Edward Ahrens, supt. Fax 942-3440
www.wvalley.wnyric.org
West Valley Central S 400/PK-12
PO Box 290 14171 716-942-3293
Edward Ahrens, prin. Fax 942-3480

West Winfield, Herkimer, Pop. 843
Bridgewater-West Winfield Central SD 1,400/K-12
500 Fairground Rd 13491 315-822-6161
Casey Barduhn, supt. Fax 822-6162
www.mmcsd.org
Mount Markham HS 500/9-12
500 Fairground Rd 13491 315-822-6343
Russell Kissinger, prin. Fax 822-3486
Mount Markham MS 500/5-8
500 Fairground Rd 13491 315-822-6361
Dawn Yerkie, prin. Fax 822-6125

Whitehall, Washington, Pop. 2,648
Whitehall Central SD 900/K-12
87 Buckley Rd 12887 518-499-1772
James Watson, supt. Fax 499-1759
Whitehall JSHS 400/7-12
87 Buckley Rd 12887 518-499-1770
Kelly McHugh, prin. Fax 499-1759

White Plains, Westchester, Pop. 56,733
White Plains CSD 6,300/K-12
5 Homeside Ln 10605 914-422-2019
Timothy P. Connors, supt. Fax 422-2024
www.wpcsd.k12.ny.us
White Plains HS 1,900/9-12
550 North St 10605 914-422-2182
Ivan Toper, prin. Fax 422-2196
White Plains MS (Eastview Campus) 6-8
350 Main St 10601 914-422-2223
Joseph Cloherty, prin. Fax 422-2222
White Plains MS (Highlands Campus) 1,500/6-8
128 Grandview Ave 10605 914-422-2092
Diana Knight, prin. Fax 422-2273

Academy of Our Lady of Good Counsel HS 300/9-12
52 N Broadway 10603 914-949-0178
Sr. Carol Peterson, prin. Fax 682-3531
Archbishop Stepinac HS 700/9-12
950 Mamaroneck Ave 10605 914-946-4800
Paul Carty, prin. Fax 684-2591
Berkeley College - Westchester Campus Post-Sec.
99 Church St 10601 914-694-1122
German S 400/K-12
50 Partridge Rd 10605 914-948-6514
Udo Bochinger, hdmstr. Fax 948-6529
Mercy College Post-Sec.
277 Martine Ave 10601 914-948-3666
Music Conservatory of Westchester Post-Sec.
216 Central Ave 10606 914-761-3715
New York School for the Deaf Post-Sec.
555 Knollwood Rd 10603
Pace University Post-Sec.
78 N Broadway 10603 914-422-4000
Pace University Post-Sec.
1 Martine Ave 10606 914-442-2000
Sanford-Brown Institute Post-Sec.
333 Westchester Ave 10604 914-347-6817
The College of Westchester Post-Sec.
PO Box 710 10602 914-948-4442
Windward S 300/5-12
40 W Red Oak Ln 10604 914-949-6968
Dr. John Russell, hdmstr. Fax 949-8220

Whitesboro, Oneida, Pop. 3,854
Whitesboro Central SD
Supt. — See Yorkville
Whitesboro MS 600/7-8
75 Oriskany Blvd 13492 315-266-3100
Sheryl Griffith, prin. Fax 768-9770

Whitestone, See New York
NYC Department of Education
Supt. — See New York
JHS 194 900/7-9
15460 17th Ave 11357 718-746-0818
Anne Marie Iannizzi, prin. Fax 746-7618

Whitesville, Allegany
Whitesville Central SD 300/K-12
692 Main St 14897 607-356-3301
Douglas Wyant, supt. Fax 356-3598
www.whitesville.wnyric.org
Whitesville Central S 300/K-12
692 Main St 14897 607-356-3301
Jennifer Fisk, prin. Fax 356-3598

Whitney Point, Broome, Pop. 939
Whitney Point Central SD 1,700/PK-12
PO Box 249 13862 607-692-8202
Dr. Carol Eaton, supt. Fax 692-4434
www.wpcsd.org
Whitney Point HS 600/9-12
PO Box 249 13862 607-692-8201
Fred Rothman, prin. Fax 692-4434
Whitney Point MS 400/6-8
PO Box 249 13862 607-692-8232
Dan Sweeney, prin. Fax 692-4434

Williamson, Wayne
Williamson Central SD 1,300/K-12
PO Box 900 14589 315-589-9661
Maria Ehresman, supt. Fax 589-7611
www.williamsoncentral.org
Williamson HS 400/9-12
PO Box 900 14589 315-589-9621
Douglas Lauf, prin. Fax 589-8310
Williamson MS 400/5-8
PO Box 900 14589 315-589-9665
John Fulmer, prin. Fax 589-8314

Williamsville, Erie, Pop. 5,315
Williamsville Central SD
Supt. — See East Amherst
Heim MS 700/5-8
175 Heim Rd 14221 716-626-8600
Charles Kramer, prin. Fax 626-8626
Mill MS 800/5-8
505 Mill St 14221 716-626-8300
Michael Calandra, prin. Fax 626-8326
Williamsville North HS 1,500/9-12
1595 Hopkins Rd 14221 716-626-8505
Fax 626-8597
Williamsville South HS 900/9-12
5950 Main St 14221 716-626-8200
Elvin Simmons, prin. Fax 626-8207

Christian Central Academy 400/K-12
39 Academy St 14221 716-634-4821
Nurline Lawrence, hdmstr. Fax 634-5851
Erie Community College North Post-Sec.
6205 Main St 14221 716-634-0800

Leon Studio One School of Hair Design — Post-Sec.
5221 Main St 14221 — 716-631-3878

Willsboro, Essex
Willsboro Central SD — 400/PK-12
PO Box 180 12996 — 518-963-4456
Stephen Broadwell, supt. — Fax 963-7577
www.willsborocsd.org/
Willsboro Central S — 400/PK-12
PO Box 180 12996 — 518-963-4456
Stephen Broadwell, prin. — Fax 963-7577

Wilson, Niagara, Pop. 1,167
Wilson Central SD — 1,500/K-12
PO Box 648 14172 — 716-751-9341
Dr. Michael Wendt, supt. — Fax 751-6556
www.wilson.wnyric.org/
Wilson HS — 500/9-12
PO Box 648 14172 — 716-751-9341
Daniel Johnson, prin. — Fax 751-9597
Wilson MS — 400/6-8
PO Box 648 14172 — 716-751-9341
Peter Rademacher, prin. — Fax 751-9597

Windham, Greene
Windham-Ashland-Jewett Central SD — 500/K-12
PO Box 429 12496 — 518-734-3400
John Wiktorko, supt. — Fax 734-6050
Windham-Ashland Central S — 500/K-12
PO Box 429 12496 — 518-734-3400
Dr. John Gratto, prin. — Fax 734-6050

Windsor, Broome, Pop. 872
Windsor Central SD — 1,900/K-12
215 Main St 13865 — 607-655-8216
Jason Andrews, supt. — Fax 655-3553
www.windsor-csd.org
Windsor Central HS — 600/9-12
1191 State Route 79 13865 — 607-655-8250
Christopher Haynes, prin. — Fax 655-3622

Wolcott, Wayne, Pop. 1,664
North Rose-Wolcott Central SD — 1,600/K-12
11669 Salter Colvin Rd 14590 — 315-594-3141
Daniel Starr, supt. — Fax 594-2352
www.nrwcs.org/
North Rose-Wolcott HS — 500/9-12
11631 Salter Colvin Rd 14590 — 315-594-3100
William Rotenberg, prin. — Fax 594-6235
North Rose-Wolcott MS — 400/6-8
5957 New Hartford St 14590 — 315-594-3130
John Boogaard, prin. — Fax 594-3120

Woodmere, Nassau, Pop. 15,578
Hewlett-Woodmere UFD — 3,300/PK-12
1 Johnson Pl 11598 — 516-374-8100
Les M. Omotani, supt. — Fax 374-8101
www.hewlett-woodmere.net
Other Schools – See Hewlett

Davis Renov Stahler Yeshiva HS for Boys — 300/9-12
700 Ibsen St 11598 — 516-295-7700
Harvey Feldman, prin. — Fax 295-2929
Woodmere Academy — 400/PK-12
336 Woodmere Blvd 11598 — 516-374-9000
Alan Bernstein, hdmstr. — Fax 374-4707

Woodside, See New York
NYC Department of Education
Supt. — See New York

IS 125 — 1,700/5-8
4602 47th Ave 11377 — 718-937-0320
Judy Mittler, prin. — Fax 361-2451

Greater New York Academy — 200/9-12
4132 58th St 11377 — 718-639-1752
Lillian Mitchell, prin. — Fax 639-8992
Razi S — 500/PK-12
5511 Queens Blvd 11377 — 718-779-0711
Dr. Ghassan Elcheikhali, prin. — Fax 779-0103

Woodstock, Ulster, Pop. 1,870

Woodstock Day S — 200/PK-12
PO Box 1 12498 — 845-246-3744
Steve Coleman, hdmstr. — Fax 246-0053

Worcester, Otsego
Worcester Central SD — 400/K-12
198 Main St 12197 — 607-397-8785
John Selover, supt. — Fax 397-9454
www.worcestercs.org
Worcester Central S — 400/K-12
198 Main St 12197 — 607-397-8785
Dr. Ann Cole, prin. — Fax 397-9454

Wyandanch, Suffolk, Pop. 8,950
Wyandanch UFD — 1,600/PK-12
1445 Straight Path 11798 — 631-491-1012
Dr. Sherman Roberts, supt. — Fax 253-0522
www.wyandanch.k12.ny.us/
Olive MS — 500/6-8
140 Garden City Ave 11798 — 631-491-1047
Gina Talbert, prin. — Fax 491-1917
Wyandanch Memorial HS — 600/9-12
54 S 32nd St 11798 — 631-491-1022
Kester Hodge, prin. — Fax 491-1728

Wynantskill, Rensselaer, Pop. 3,329

Vanderheyden Hall — 100/7-12
PO Box 219 12198 — 518-283-6500
Dawn Graham, dir. — Fax 286-2132

Yonkers, Westchester, Pop. 196,425
Yonkers CSD — 23,600/PK-12
1 Larkin Ctr 10701 — 914-376-8000
Bernard Pierorazio, supt. — Fax 376-8062
www.yonkerspublicschools.org
Emerson MS — 1,000/6-8
160 Bolmer Ave 10703 — 914-376-8300
Robert Riccuiti, prin. — Fax 376-8499
Gorton HS — 1,300/9-12
100 Shonnard Pl 10703 — 914-376-8350
Rocco Grassi, prin. — Fax 376-8377
Lincoln HS — 1,400/9-12
375 Kneeland Ave 10704 — 914-376-8400
Edwin Quezada, prin. — Fax 376-8414
Museum MS — 1,000/6-8
565 Warburton Ave 10701 — 914-376-8425
Dr. Catherine Mayus, prin. — Fax 376-8475
Roosevelt HS — 1,600/9-12
631 Tuckahoe Rd 10710 — 914-376-8500
Jade Sharp, prin. — Fax 779-7632
Saunders Trades & Tech HS — Vo/Tech
183 Palmer Rd 10701 — 914-376-8150
Steve Mazzola, prin. — Fax 376-8154
Twain MS — 900/6-8
160 Woodlawn Ave 10704 — 914-376-8540
Eileen Rivera-Shapiro, prin. — Fax 376-8552
Yonkers HS — 500/6-11
150 Rockland Ave 10705 — 914-376-8191
Ralph Vigliotti, prin. — Fax 376-4856
Yonkers MS — 1,100/6-8
150 Rockland Ave 10705 — 914-376-8200
Anthony Cioffi, prin. — Fax 376-8245

Cochran School of Nursing — Post-Sec.
967 N Broadway 10701 — 914-964-4283
Sacred Heart HS — 400/9-12
34 Convent Ave 10703 — 914-965-3114
Agnes McNamara, prin. — Fax 965-4510
St. Joseph's Seminary — Post-Sec.
201 Seminary Ave 10704 — 914-968-6200

Yorkshire, Cattaraugus, Pop. 1,340
Yorkshire-Pioneer Central SD — 2,800/K-12
PO Box 579 14173 — 585-492-9300
Jeffrey Bowen Ed.D., supt. — Fax 492-9360
www.pioneerschools.org/
Pioneer HS — 900/9-12
PO Box 639 14173 — 585-492-9328
Sharon Huff Ed.D., prin. — Fax 492-1825
Pioneer MS — 900/5-8
PO Box 619 14173 — 585-492-9375
Ravo Root, prin. — Fax 492-9372

Yorktown Heights, Westchester, Pop. 7,690
Lakeland Central SD
Supt. — See Shrub Oak
Lakeland-Copper Beech MS — 1,500/6-8
3401 Old Yorktown Rd 10598 — 914-245-1885
Jean Miccio, prin. — Fax 245-1259

Yorktown Central SD — 4,200/K-12
2725 Crompond Rd 10598 — 914-243-8000
Dr. Vincent Ziccolella, supt. — Fax 243-8003
www.yorktown.org
Strang MS — 1,000/6-8
2701 Crompond Rd 10598 — 914-243-8100
Linda Grimm, prin. — Fax 243-0016
Yorktown HS — 1,400/9-12
2727 Crompond Rd 10598 — 914-243-8050
John Sullivan, prin. — Fax 245-9256

Mercy College — Post-Sec.
2651 Strang Blvd 10598 — 914-245-6100

Yorkville, Oneida, Pop. 2,613
Whitesboro Central SD — 3,700/K-12
PO Box 304 13495 — 315-266-3300
Arnold Kaye, supt. — Fax 768-9730
www.wboro.org
Other Schools – See Marcy, Whitesboro

Youngstown, Niagara, Pop. 1,901
Lewiston-Porter Central SD — 2,300/K-12
4061 Creek Rd 14174 — 716-286-7241
Don Rappold, supt. — Fax 754-2755
lew-port.com
Lewiston-Porter HS — 900/9-12
4061 Creek Rd 14174 — 716-286-7263
Paul Casseri, prin. — Fax 286-7852
Lewiston-Porter MS — 600/6-8
4061 Creek Rd 14174 — 716-286-7201
Vincent Dell'Oso, prin. — Fax 286-7204

NORTH CAROLINA

NORTH CAROLINA DEPT. PUBLIC INSTRUCTION
301 N Wilmington St, Raleigh 27601-1058
Telephone 919-807-3300
Fax 919-807-3445
Website http://www.dpi.state.nc.us

Superintendent of Public Instruction June Atkinson

NORTH CAROLINA BOARD OF EDUCATION
301 N Wilmington St, Raleigh 27601-1058

Chairperson Howard Lee

PUBLIC, PRIVATE AND CATHOLIC SECONDARY SCHOOLS

Aberdeen, Moore, Pop. 4,794
Moore County SD
Supt. — See Carthage
Southern MS 700/6-8
717 Johnson St 28315 910-693-1550
Debbie Warren, prin. Fax 693-1544

Ahoskie, Hertford, Pop. 4,324
Hertford County SD
Supt. — See Winton
Hertford County HS 1,100/9-12
1500 1st St W 27910 252-332-4096
Larry Cooper, prin. Fax 332-6176

Ahoskie Christian S 200/K-12
500 Kiwanis St 27910 252-332-2764
Elaine Pool, prin.
Ridgecroft S 300/PK-12
PO Box 1008 27910 252-332-2964
Elton Winslow, prin. Fax 332-7586
Roanoke-Chowan Community College Post-Sec.
109 Community College Rd 27910 252-862-1200

Albemarle, Stanly, Pop. 15,325
Stanly County SD 9,800/PK-12
1000 N 1st St Ste 4 28001 704-983-5151
Dr. Samuel DePaul, supt. Fax 982-3618
www.scs.k12.nc.us
Albemarle HS 700/9-12
311 Park Ridge Rd 28001 704-982-3711
David Bright, prin. Fax 982-9645
Albemarle MS 500/6-8
1811 Badin Rd 28001 704-982-5480
Todd Thorpe, prin. Fax 983-2600
Stanley Early College HS 9-12
141 College Dr 28001 704-991-0128
Curtis Parker, dean Fax 991-0255
Other Schools – See New London, Norwood, Oakboro

Stanly Community College Post-Sec.
141 College Dr 28001 704-982-0121

Andrews, Cherokee, Pop. 1,703
Cherokee County SD
Supt. — See Murphy
Andrews HS 300/9-12
50 High School Dr 28901 828-321-5415
S. Tim Coffey, prin. Fax 321-3986
Andrews MS 200/6-8
2750 Business 19 28901 828-321-5762
DavAnn Hubbard, prin. Fax 321-2009

Angier, Harnett, Pop. 4,107
Harnett County SD
Supt. — See Lillington
Harnett Central HS 1,400/9-12
2911 Harnett Central Rd 27501 919-639-6161
Ken Jernigan, prin. Fax 639-3642
Harnett Central MS 1,200/6-8
2529 Harnett Central Rd 27501 919-639-6000
Chris Mace, prin. Fax 639-9617

Apex, Wake, Pop. 28,551
Wake County SD
Supt. — See Raleigh
Apex HS 2,200/9-12
1501 Laura Duncan Rd 27502 919-387-2208
Matthew Wight, prin. Fax 387-3023
Apex MS 1,000/6-8
400 E Moore St 27502 919-387-2181
Timothy Locklair, prin. Fax 387-2203
Lufkin Road MS 1,000/6-8
1002 Lufkin Rd, 919-387-4465
Dr. Jessie Dingle, prin. Fax 363-1095
Middle Creek HS 1,800/9-12
123 Middle Creek Park Ave, 919-773-3838
John Williams, prin. Fax 773-3880
Salem MS 700/6-8
6150 Old Jenks Rd, 919-363-1870
Herbert Ellzey, prin. Fax 363-1876
West Lake MS 1,400/6-8
4600 W Lake Rd, 919-662-2900
Dr. Gregory Decker, prin. Fax 662-2906

Archdale, Randolph, Pop. 9,428

Mount Calvary Christian S 100/K-12
6551 Weant Rd 27263 336-434-6800
Dr. Bruce Phillips, prin. Fax 434-5267

Arden, Buncombe
Buncombe County SD
Supt. — See Asheville
Valley Springs MS 800/6-8
224 Long Shoals Rd 28704 828-654-1785
Thomas Keever, prin. Fax 654-1789

Christ S 200/8-12
500 Christ School Rd 28704 828-684-6232
Paul Krieger, hdmstr. Fax 684-2745

Asheboro, Randolph, Pop. 23,639
Asheboro CSD 4,500/PK-12
PO Box 1103 27204 336-625-5104
Dr. Diane Frost, supt. Fax 625-9238
www.asheboro.k12.nc.us
Asheboro HS 1,300/9-12
1221 S Park St 27203 336-625-6185
Dr. Larry Riggan, prin. Fax 625-9320
North Asheboro MS 500/6-8
1861 N Asheboro School Rd 27203 336-672-1900
Ronald Coley, prin. Fax 672-6267
South Asheboro MS 600/6-8
523 W Walker Ave 27203 336-629-4141
Gwendolyn Williams, prin. Fax 629-3761

Randolph County SD 18,300/K-12
2222 S Fayetteville St 27205 336-318-6100
Donald Andrews, supt. Fax 318-6155
www.randolph.k12.nc.us
Randolph Early College HS 9-12
629 Industrial Park Ave 27205 336-625-1137
Cathy Waddell, prin. Fax 625-3186
Southwestern Randolph HS 1,300/9-12
1641 Hopewell Friends Rd 27205 336-381-7747
Chris Vecchione, prin. Fax 381-7743
Southwestern Randolph MS 600/6-8
1509 Hopewell Friends Rd 27205 336-381-3900
Michael Nicholson, prin. Fax 381-3905
Other Schools – See Liberty, Ramseur, Randleman, Trinity

Fayetteville Street Christian S 200/K-12
151 W Pritchard St 27203 336-629-1383
Mike Brown, prin. Fax 629-0067
Randolph Community College Post-Sec.
PO Box 1009 27204 336-633-0200

Asheville, Buncombe, Pop. 72,231
Asheville CSD 3,800/PK-12
85 Mountain St 28801 828-350-7000
Robert L. Logan, supt. Fax 255-5131
www.asheville.k12.nc.us
Asheville HS 1,200/9-12
419 Mcdowell St 28803 828-255-5352
Judd Porter, prin. Fax 255-5316
Asheville MS 700/6-8
197 S French Broad Ave 28801 828-350-6200
Pam Cocke, prin. Fax 255-5311

Buncombe County SD 25,200/K-12
175 Bingham Rd 28806 828-255-5921
Cliff Dodson, supt. Fax 255-5923
www.buncombe.k12.nc.us/
Career Education Center Vo/Tech
175 Bingham Rd 28806 828-251-0499
Magnolia Thomas, prin. Fax 255-5275
Erwin HS 1,200/9-12
60 Lees Creek Rd 28806 828-232-4251
Eddie Burchfiel, prin. Fax 251-2893
Erwin MS 1,000/6-8
20 Erwin Hills Rd 28806 828-232-4264
Andy Peoples, prin. Fax 232-4267
Reynolds HS 1,500/9-12
1 Rocket Dr 28803 828-298-2500
Regina Lambert, prin. Fax 298-2002
Reynolds MS 700/6-8
2 Rocket Dr 28803 828-298-7484
Robbie Adell, prin. Fax 298-7503
Roberson HS 1,500/9-12
250 Overlook Rd 28803 828-654-1765
Rob Weinkle, prin. Fax 654-1768
Other Schools – See Arden, Black Mountain, Candler, Fletcher, Swannanoa, Weaverville

---

Asheville Buncombe Technical Comm. Coll. Post-Sec.
340 Victoria Rd 28801 828-254-1921
Asheville S 200/9-12
360 Asheville School Rd 28806 828-254-6345
Archibald Montgomery, hdmstr. Fax 210-6109
Atlantic University of Chinese Medicine Post-Sec.
64 Westgate Pkwy 28806 828-225-8550
Carolina Christian S 200/PK-12
48 Woodland Hills Rd 28804 828-658-8964
Dema Barishnikov, admin. Fax 658-8965
Carolina Day S 700/PK-12
1345 Hendersonville Rd 28803 828-274-0757
Dr. Beverly Sgro, hdmstr. Fax 274-0756
North Asheville Christian S 200/PK-10
20 Reynolds Mountain Blvd 28804 828-645-8053
Susie Hepler, admin. Fax 645-2973
South College Post-Sec.
29 Turtle Creek Dr 28803 828-277-5521
Temple Baptist S 200/K-12
985 1/2 Patton Ave 28806 828-252-3712
William Spence, prin. Fax 254-5119
University of North Carolina Post-Sec.
1 University Hts 28804 828-251-6600
Warren Wilson College Post-Sec.
PO Box 9000 28815 828-298-3325

Aurora, Beaufort, Pop. 581
Beaufort County SD
Supt. — See Washington
Aurora MS 100/6-8
693 N 7th St 27806 252-322-4524
Ted Overton, prin. Fax 322-4474

Ayden, Pitt, Pop. 4,798
Pitt County SD
Supt. — See Greenville
Ayden-Grifton HS 700/9-12
7653 NC 11 S 28513 252-746-4183
Bill Frazier, prin. Fax 746-2120
Ayden MS 400/5-8
192 3rd St 28513 252-746-3672
Seth Brown, prin. Fax 746-9923

Bailey, Nash, Pop. 675
Nash-Rocky Mount SD
Supt. — See Nashville
Southern Nash HS 1,300/9-12
6446 Southern Nash High Rd 27807 252-478-5450
Rosalie Bardin, prin. Fax 478-5953

Bakersville, Mitchell, Pop. 353
Mitchell County SD 2,300/K-12
72 Ledger School Rd 28705 828-688-4432
Dr. William Sears, supt. Fax 688-4095
central.mitchell.k12.nc.us
Bowman MS 200/5-8
PO Box 46 28705 828-688-2752
Angela Burleson, prin. Fax 688-6002
Mitchell HS 700/9-12
416 Ledger School Rd 28705 828-688-2101
Jack Brooks, prin. Fax 688-4847
Other Schools – See Spruce Pine

Banner Elk, Avery, Pop. 958

Lees-McRae College Post-Sec.
PO Box 128 28604 828-898-5241

Barco, Currituck
Currituck County SD
Supt. — See Currituck
Currituck County HS 1,100/9-12
4203 Caratoke Hwy 27917 252-453-0014
Dr. Harper Donahoe, prin. Fax 453-0017
Currituck County MS 400/6-8
4263 Caratoke Hwy 27917 252-453-2171
Bill Wicks, prin. Fax 453-0019

Battleboro, Edgecombe, Pop. 559
Edgecombe County SD
Supt. — See Tarboro
Phillips MS 500/4-8
1407 Legett-Battleboro Rd 27809 252-446-2031
William Etheridge, prin. Fax 446-1629

Nash-Rocky Mount SD
Supt. — See Nashville
Red Oak MS 1,000/6-8
3170 Red Oak Battleboro Rd 27809 252-451-5500
Connie Bobbitt, prin. Fax 451-5510

Bayboro, Pamlico, Pop. 716
Pamlico County SD 1,700/PK-12
507 Anderson Dr 28515 252-745-4171
Rick Sherrill, supt. Fax 745-4172
www.pamlico.k12.nc.us
Pamlico County HS 700/9-12
PO Box 699 28515 252-745-3151
Tom Frazier, prin. Fax 745-3153
Pamlico County MS 400/6-8
15526 NC Highway 55 28515 252-745-4061
Henry Rice, prin. Fax 745-5583

Bear Creek, Chatham
Chatham County SD
Supt. — See Pittsboro

Chatham Central HS 500/9-12
14950 NC Highway 902 27207 919-837-2251
Mitch Stensland, prin. Fax 837-2975

Beaufort, Carteret, Pop. 4,119
Carteret County SD 8,300/PK-12
107 Safrit Dr 28516 252-728-4583
Brad Sneeden, supt. Fax 728-3028
www.carteretcountyschools.org
Beaufort MS 300/6-8
100 Carraway Dr 28516 252-728-4520
Greg Guthrie, prin. Fax 728-3392
East Carteret HS 600/9-12
3263 US Highway 70 E 28516 252-728-3514
Ralph Holloway, prin. Fax 728-3487
Other Schools – See Morehead City, Newport

Belhaven, Beaufort, Pop. 1,965

Pungo Christian Academy 100/PK-12
983 W Main St 27810 252-943-2678
Marcy S. Morgan, prin. Fax 943-3292

Belmont, Gaston, Pop. 8,779
Gaston County SD
Supt. — See Gastonia
Belmont MS 700/6-8
110 N Central Ave 28012 704-825-9619
Audrey Devine, prin. Fax 825-6951
South Point HS 1,200/9-12
906 Southpoint Rd 28012 704-825-3351
Sheri Little, prin. Fax 825-2820

Belmont Abbey College Post-Sec.
100 Belmont Mount Holly Rd 28012 704-825-6700
Gaston Christian S 700/PK-12
200 Mercy Dr 28012 704-825-9000
Daniel Patton, hdmstr. Fax 825-9101

Benson, Johnston, Pop. 3,282
Johnston County SD
Supt. — See Smithfield
Benson MS 500/5-8
1600 N Wall St 27504 919-894-3889
Sheila Singleton, prin. Fax 894-1551
McGee's Crossroads MS 600/6-8
13353 NC Highway 210 27504 919-894-6003
Barretta Haynes, prin. Fax 894-6007
West Johnston HS 1,600/9-12
5935 Raleigh Rd 27504 919-934-7333
Brookie Honeycutt, prin. Fax 934-6906

Bessemer City, Gaston, Pop. 5,319
Gaston County SD
Supt. — See Gastonia
Bessemer City HS 800/9-12
119 Yellow Jacket Rd 28016 704-629-2258
Ted Saunders, prin. Fax 629-2775
Bessemer City MS 600/6-8
525 Ed Wilson Rd 28016 704-629-3281
Lance Frady, prin. Fax 629-4501

Bethel, Pitt, Pop. 1,689
Pitt County SD
Supt. — See Greenville
North Pitt HS 900/9-12
5659 NC Highway 11 N 27812 252-825-0054
Marty Baker, prin. Fax 825-1310

Beulaville, Duplin, Pop. 1,098
Duplin County SD
Supt. — See Kenansville
East Duplin HS 800/9-12
PO Box 188 28518 910-298-4535
Ben Thigpen, prin. Fax 298-2021

Biscoe, Montgomery, Pop. 1,715
Montgomery County SD
Supt. — See Troy
East MS 500/6-8
1834 US Highway 220 Alt S 27209 910-428-3278
Sandra Lampros, prin. Fax 428-1279
East Montgomery HS 600/9-12
157 Eagle Ln 27209 910-428-9641
Travis Reeves, prin. Fax 428-1197

Black Mountain, Buncombe, Pop. 7,650
Buncombe County SD
Supt. — See Asheville
Owen HS 900/9-12
99 Lake Eden Rd 28711 828-686-3852
Don Johnson, prin. Fax 686-8442

Bladenboro, Bladen, Pop. 1,713
Bladen County SD
Supt. — See Elizabethtown
Bladenboro MS 400/5-8
910 S Main St 28320 910-863-3232
Wilbert Stokes, prin. Fax 863-4683
West Bladen HS 900/9-12
1600 NC 410 Hwy 28320 910-862-2130
Rick Helms, prin. Fax 862-3328

Boiling Springs, Cleveland, Pop. 3,883

Gardner-Webb University Post-Sec.
PO Box 817 28017 704-406-2361

Bolivia, Brunswick, Pop. 168
Brunswick County SD 11,100/PK-12
35 Referendum Dr NE 28422 910-253-2900
Dr. Katie McGee, supt. Fax 253-2983
www.bcswan.net
Brunswick County Early College HS 9-12
1109 Old Ocean Hwy 28422 910-754-8565
Vicky Snyder, prin. Fax 754-8567
Other Schools – See Leland, Shallotte, Southport

Boone, Watauga, Pop. 13,192
Watauga County SD 4,600/PK-12
PO Box 1790 28607 828-264-7190
Dr. Bobbie Short, supt. Fax 264-7196
www.watauga.k12.nc.us
Watauga HS 1,500/9-12
400 High School Dr 28607 828-264-2407
Angela Quick, prin. Fax 264-9030

Appalachian State University Post-Sec.
Asu Sta 28608 828-262-2000

Boonville, Yadkin, Pop. 1,113
Yadkin County SD
Supt. — See Yadkinville

Starmount HS 800/9-12
2516 Longtown Rd 27011 336-468-2891
Tony George, prin. Fax 468-6434

Bostic, Rutherford, Pop. 327
Rutherford County SD
Supt. — See Forest City
East Rutherford MS 800/6-8
PO Box 189 28018 828-245-4836
Brad Teague, prin. Fax 245-1491

Brevard, Transylvania, Pop. 6,643
Transylvania County SD 3,800/K-12
400 Rosenwald Ln 28712 828-884-6173
Dr. Sonna Lyda, supt. Fax 884-9524
www.transylvania.k12.nc.us
Brevard HS 800/9-12
747 Country Club Rd 28712 828-884-4103
Douglas Odom, prin. Fax 885-7355
Brevard MS 600/6-8
400 Fisher Rd 28712 828-884-2091
David Williams, prin. Fax 883-3150
Other Schools – See Rosman

Brevard College Post-Sec.
1 Brevard College Dr 28712 828-883-8292

Browns Summit, Guilford
Guilford County SD
Supt. — See Greensboro
Brown Summit MS 200/6-8
4720 E NC Highway 150 27214 336-656-0432
Terri Spears, prin. Fax 656-0439

Bryson City, Swain, Pop. 1,361
Swain County SD 1,700/K-12
PO Box 2340 28713 828-488-3129
Robert White, supt. Fax 488-8510
www.swaincountyschools.com
Swain County HS 500/9-12
1415 Fontana Rd 28713 828-488-2152
Regina Mathis, prin. Fax 488-0523
Swain County MS 400/6-8
135 Arlington Ave 28713 828-488-3480
Os Waters, prin. Fax 488-0949
Swain Co. S for Applied Sci Math & Tech 9-12
1415 Fontana Rd 28713 828-488-0190
Jeff Payne, prin. Fax 488-0680

Buies Creek, Harnett, Pop. 2,085

Campbell University Post-Sec.
PO Box 546 27506 910-893-1200

Bunn, Franklin, Pop. 391
Franklin County SD
Supt. — See Louisburg
Bunn HS 900/9-12
PO Box 146 27508 919-496-3975
George Kelley, prin. Fax 496-1639
Bunn MS 700/6-8
4742 NC 39 Hwy S 27508 919-496-7700
David Hawks, prin. Fax 496-1404

Burgaw, Pender, Pop. 3,756
Pender County SD 7,200/PK-12
925 Penderlea Hwy 28425 910-259-2187
Dr. Ted Kaniuka, supt. Fax 259-0133
www.edline.net/pages/pender_county_schools
Burgaw MS 300/6-8
500 S Wright St 28425 910-259-0149
Harold Vann Blakes, prin. Fax 259-0150
Pender Early College HS 9-12
100 Industrial Dr 28425 910-259-7178
Angela Jeffrey, prin.
Pender HS 700/9-12
5380 NC Highway 53 W 28425 910-259-0162
Robbie Cauley, prin. Fax 259-0166
West Pender MS 300/6-8
10750 NC Highway 53 W 28425 910-283-5626
June Robbins, prin. Fax 283-9537
Other Schools – See Hampstead, Rocky Point

Burlington, Alamance, Pop. 47,592
Alamance-Burlington SD 21,800/PK-12
1712 Vaughn Rd 27217 336-570-6060
Randy Bridges Ed.D., supt. Fax 570-6218
www.abss.k12.nc.us
Broadview MS 700/6-8
2229 Broadview Dr 27217 336-570-6195
Nakia Hardy, prin. Fax 570-6202
Cummings HS 900/9-12
2200 N Mebane St 27217 336-570-6100
Lynn Briggs, prin. Fax 570-6107
Sellars-Gunn Educational Center Vo/Tech
612 Apple St 27217 336-570-6130
James Pegues, prin. Fax 570-6208
Turrentine MS 1,000/6-8
1710 Edgewood Ave 27215 336-570-6150
Dr. John Swajkoski, prin. Fax 570-6210
Williams HS 1,300/9-12
1307 S Church St 27215 336-570-6161
Nola Taylor, prin. Fax 570-6214
Other Schools – See Elon, Graham, Mebane

Burnsville, Yancey, Pop. 1,628
Yancy County SD 2,500/K-12
PO Box 190 28714 828-682-6101
Dr. Barbara Tipton, supt. Fax 682-7110
www.yanceync.net
Cane River MS 300/6-8
1128 Cane River School Rd 28714 828-682-2202
Beverly Brown, prin. Fax 682-3754
East Yancey MS 300/6-8
285 Georges Fork Rd 28714 828-682-2281
Rick Tipton, prin. Fax 682-3513
Mountain Heritage HS 800/9-12
PO Box 70 28714 828-682-6103
Alton Robinson, prin. Fax 682-4287

Butner, Granville, Pop. 4,679
Granville County SD
Supt. — See Oxford
Butner-Stem MS 500/6-8
501 E D St 27509 919-575-9429
Donna McLamb, prin. Fax 575-5894

Buxton, Dare
Dare County SD
Supt. — See Nags Head
Cape Hatteras JSHS 400/6-12
PO Box 948 27920 252-995-5730
Lou Tonelson, prin. Fax 995-6161

Calypso, Duplin, Pop. 474
Duplin County SD
Supt. — See Kenansville
North Duplin JSHS 500/7-12
1388 W NC Highway 403 28325 919-658-3051
Debra Hunter, prin. Fax 658-9971

Camden, Camden
Camden County SD 1,700/PK-12
174 NC Highway 343 N 27921 252-335-0831
John Dunn, supt. Fax 331-2300
www.camden.k12.nc.us
Camden County HS 500/9-12
103 US Highway 158 W 27921 252-338-0114
Kathy Goins, prin. Fax 331-6792
Camden MS 400/6-8
248 Scotland Rd 27921 252-338-3349
Jean Gray, prin. Fax 331-2253
Cam Tech HS 9-12
103 US Highway 158 W Ste A 27921 252-335-7219
Ina Lane, prin. Fax 335-4219

Cameron, Moore, Pop. 157
Moore County SD
Supt. — See Carthage
New Century MS 900/6-8
1577 Union Church Rd 28326 910-947-1301
Cindy Holland, prin. Fax 947-1227
Union Pines HS 1,200/9-12
1981 Union Church Rd 28326 910-947-5511
Robin Lea, prin. Fax 947-5117

Candler, Buncombe
Buncombe County SD
Supt. — See Asheville
Enka HS 1,300/9-12
475 Enka Lake Rd 28715 828-670-5000
Don Icenhower, prin. Fax 670-5007
Enka MS 1,000/6-8
390 Asbury Rd 28715 828-670-5010
Pam Fourtenbary, prin. Fax 670-5015

Mt. Pisgah Academy 200/9-12
75 Academy Dr 28715 828-667-2535
Rick Anderson, prin. Fax 667-0657

Canton, Haywood, Pop. 4,002
Haywood County SD
Supt. — See Waynesville
Canton MS 500/6-8
60 Penland St 28716 828-646-3467
Greg Bailey, prin. Fax 648-9558
Pisgah HS 1,000/9-12
1 Black Bear Dr 28716 828-646-3440
Danny Miller, prin. Fax 648-8618

Bethel Christian Academy 200/K-12
100 Park St 28716 828-648-4492
Paula Rhodarmer, prin. Fax 648-4498

Carrboro, Orange, Pop. 16,425
Chapel Hill-Carrboro CSD
Supt. — See Chapel Hill
Carrboro HS 9-12
201 Rock Haven Rd 27510 919-918-2200
Jeff Thomas, prin. Fax 918-2507

Carthage, Moore, Pop. 1,935
Moore County SD 12,000/K-12
PO Box 1180 28327 910-947-2976
Susan Purser Ed.D., supt. Fax 947-3011
www.mcs.k12.nc.us/
Pinckney Academy Vo/Tech
PO Box 1180 28327 910-947-2603
Mike Metcalf, prin. Fax 947-2404
Other Schools – See Aberdeen, Cameron, Robbins, Southern Pines, West End

Cary, Wake, Pop. 106,439
Wake County SD
Supt. — See Raleigh
Cary HS 2,400/9-12
638 Walnut St 27511 919-460-3549
Dr. David Dennis, prin. Fax 460-3573
Davis Drive MS 1,100/6-8
2101 Davis Dr 27519 919-387-3033
Linda Bird, prin. Fax 387-3039
Green Hope HS 2,100/9-12
2500 Carpenter Upchurch Rd 27519 919-380-3700
James Hedrick, prin. Fax 380-3712
Panther Creek HS 9-10
6770 McCrimmon Pkwy 27519 919-463-8656
Rodney Nelson, prin. Fax 463-8695
Reedy Creek MS 700/6-8
930 Reedy Creek Rd 27513 919-460-3504
Carla Jernigan, prin. Fax 460-3391
West Cary MS 900/6-8
1000 Evans Rd 27513 919-460-3528
Douglas Thilman, prin. Fax 460-3540

Cary Academy 700/6-12
1500 N Harrison Ave 27513 919-677-3873
Donald S. Berger, hdmstr. Fax 677-4002
Cary Christian S 800/K-12
1330 Old Apex Rd 27513 919-303-2560
Larry Stephenson, admin. Fax 367-7558
Miller-Motte Technical College Post-Sec.
2205 Walnut St 27518 919-532-7171

Cashiers, Jackson
Jackson County SD
Supt. — See Sylva
Blue Ridge S 300/PK-12
95 Bobcat Dr 28717 828-743-2646
Carol Rector, prin. Fax 743-5320

Castle Hayne, New Hanover, Pop. 1,182
New Hanover County SD
Supt. — See Wilmington
Wilmington Early College HS 9-12
4500 Blue Clay Rd 28429 910-362-7786
Ivy Murrain, prin. Fax 362-7424

Catawba, Catawba, Pop. 739
Catawba County SD
Supt. — See Newton
Bandys HS 1,100/9-12
5040 E Bandys Xrd 28609 828-241-3171
Todd Black, prin. Fax 241-9402

Cerro Gordo, Columbus, Pop. 240
Columbus County SD
Supt. — See Whiteville

West Columbus HS 600/9-12
PO Box 130 28430 910-654-6111
Mark Brown, prin. Fax 654-4082

Chadbourn, Columbus, Pop. 2,105
Columbus County SD
Supt. — See Whiteville
Chadbourn MS 300/5-8
801 W Smith St 28431 910-654-4300
Georgia Spaulding, prin. Fax 654-6809

Chapel Hill, Orange, Pop. 49,543
Chapel Hill-Carrboro CSD 10,700/PK-12
750 S Merritt Mill Rd 27516 919-967-8211
Dr. Neil Pedersen, supt. Fax 933-4560
www.chccs.k12.nc.us
Chapel Hill HS 1,800/9-12
1709 High School Rd 27516 919-929-2106
Jacqueline Ellis, prin. Fax 929-2455
East Chapel Hill HS 1,600/9-12
500 Weaver Dairy Rd 27514 919-969-2482
David Thaden, prin. Fax 969-2492
Grey Culbreth MS 600/6-8
225 Culbreth Rd 27516 919-929-7161
Susan Wells, prin. Fax 969-2412
McDougle MS 600/6-8
900 Old Fayetteville Rd 27516 919-933-1556
Debra Scott, prin. Fax 969-2433
Phillips MS 700/6-8
606 N Estes Dr 27514 919-929-2188
Eileen Tulley, prin. Fax 969-2477
Smith MS 600/6-8
9201 Seawell School Rd 27516 919-918-2145
Valerie Reinhardt, prin. Fax 918-2079
Other Schools – See Carrboro

Emerson Waldorf S 300/PK-12
6211 New Jericho Rd 27516 919-967-1858
Edward Schuldt, prin. Fax 967-2732
University of North Carolina 27599 Post-Sec.
919-962-2211
University of North Carolina Hospitals Post-Sec.
101 Manning Dr 27514 919-966-5111

Charlotte, Mecklenburg, Pop. 610,949
Charlotte/Mecklenburg County SD 118,100/PK-12
PO Box 30035 28230 980-343-3000
Dr. Peter Gorman, supt. Fax 343-3647
www.cms.k12.nc.us/
Albemarle Road MS 900/6-8
6900 Democracy Dr 28212 980-343-6420
Betty Bauknight, prin. Fax 343-6501
Berry Academy of Technology Vo/Tech
1430 Alleghany St 28208 980-343-5992
Dr. David Baldaia, prin. Fax 343-5994
Biotechnolgy Health & Public Admin @ OHS 9-12
4301 Sandy Porter Rd Ste E 28273 980-343-1110
Jerry Brown, prin. Fax 343-1114
Bishop Spaugh Academy 600/6-8
1901 Herbert Spaugh Ln 28208 980-343-6025
Tyrone McDonal, prin. Fax 343-6124
Carmel MS 1,200/6-8
5001 Camilla Dr 28226 980-343-6705
Nancy Hicks, prin. Fax 343-6749
Cochrane MS 500/6-8
6200 Starhaven Dr 28215 980-343-6460
Terry M. Brown, prin. Fax 343-6521
Community House MS 6-8
9500 Community House Rd 28277 980-343-0689
Gifford Lockley, prin. Fax 343-0691
Coulwood MS 1,200/6-8
500 Kentberry Dr 28214 980-343-6090
Robert Folk, prin. Fax 343-6142
Davis MS 400/6-8
3343 Griffith St 28203 980-343-5832
Patricia Collins, prin. Fax 343-5860
East Mecklenburg HS 2,200/9-12
6800 Monroe Rd 28212 980-343-6430
Mark Nixon, prin. Fax 343-5227
Eastway MS 6-8
1501 Norland Rd 28205 980-343-6410
Nancy Barkemeyer, prin. Fax 343-6406
Garinger HS 1,700/9-12
1100 Eastway Dr 28205 980-343-6450
Jo Ella Ferrell, prin. Fax 343-6454
Graham MS 1,000/6-8
1800 Runnymede Ln 28211 980-343-5810
William Leach, prin. Fax 343-5868
Harding University HS 1,500/9-12
2001 Alleghany St 28208 980-343-6007
Curtis Carroll, prin. Fax 343-6015
Independence HS 2,500/9-12
1967 Patriot Dr 28227 980-343-6900
Nancy Bartles, prin. Fax 343-6907
International Studies @ GHS HS 9-9
1100 Eastway Dr Ste B 28205 980-343-1092
Natasha Thompson, prin. Fax 343-1096
Interntnl Business & Communication @ OHS 9-12
4301 Sandy Porter Rd Ste C 28273 980-343-1104
Todd Pipkin, prin. Fax 343-1108
Intl Studies & Global Economics @ OHS HS 9-12
4301 Sandy Porter Rd Ste A 28273 980-343-1113
Matthew Hayes, prin. Fax 343-3808
Kell HS 9-12
10220 Ardrey Kell Rd 28277 980-343-0860
Mike Mathews, prin. Fax 343-0862
Kennedy MS 800/6-8
4000 Gallant Ln 28273 980-343-5540
Dr. Johnnie Gordon, prin. Fax 343-5412
King MS 1,000/6-8
500 Bilmark Ave 28213 980-343-0698
Dr. Mark Robinson, prin. Fax 343-0700
Mallard Creek HS 9-12
3825 Johnston Oehler Rd 28269 980-343-1341
Katherine Rea, prin. Fax 343-1342
Martin MS 1,600/6-8
7800 IBM Dr 28262 980-343-5382
Raynard Lee, prin. Fax 343-5135
Math Sci Pre-Engineering Tech S @ OHS 9-12
4301 Sandy Porter Rd Ste B 28273 980-343-1101
Ayinde Rudolph, prin. Fax 343-3803
McClintock MS 1,000/6-8
2101 Rama Rd 28212 980-343-6425
Andrew Thiel, prin. Fax 343-6509
Myers Park HS 2,700/9-12
2400 Colony Rd 28209 980-343-5800
Tom Spivey, prin. Fax 343-5803
New Technology HS @ Garinger 9-12
1100 Eastway Dr Ste C 28205 980-343-1093
Barry Blair, prin. Fax 343-0000
Northeast MS 1,100/6-8
5960 Brickstone Dr 28227 980-343-6920
David Switzer, prin. Fax 343-6153
Northridge MS 1,200/6-8
7601 The Plz 28215 980-343-5015
Jamal Crawford, prin. Fax 343-5174
Northwest S of the Arts 1,100/6-12
1415 Beatties Ford Rd 28216 980-343-5500
Dr. Charles LaBorde, prin. Fax 343-5593
Northwest S of the Arts at Spirit Square 6-12
1415 Beatties Ford Rd 28216 980-343-3235
Charles LaBorde, prin. Fax 343-5593
Olympic HS 1,600/9-12
4301 Sandy Porter Rd 28273 980-343-3800
Pam Espinosa, prin. Fax 343-3803
Piedmont Open MS 900/6-8
1241 E 10th St 28204 980-343-5435
Deirdta Gardner, prin. Fax 343-5557
Providence HS 2,500/9-12
1800 Pineville Matthews Rd 28270 980-343-5390
Dr. Terri Cockerham, prin. Fax 343-3956
Quail Hollow MS 1,200/6-8
2901 Smithfield Church Rd 28210 980-343-3620
Mark Bosco, prin. Fax 343-3622
Randolph MS 800/6-8
4400 Water Oak Rd 28211 980-343-6700
Jackie Menser, prin. Fax 343-6741
Ranson MS 900/6-8
5850 Statesville Rd 28269 980-343-6800
Kevin Carr, prin. Fax 343-6796
Renaissance S @ Olympic 9-12
4301 Sandy Porter Rd Ste D 28273 980-343-3800
Melody Sears, prin. Fax 343-3803
Robinson MS 1,200/6-8
5925 Ballantyne Commons Pky 28277 980-343-6944
Dr. Maureen Furr, prin. Fax 343-6947
Sedgefield MS 600/6-8
2700 Dorchester Pl 28209 980-343-5840
Darius Adamson, prin. Fax 343-5862
South Charlotte MS 1,100/6-8
8040 Strawberry Ln 28277 980-343-3670
V. Christine Waggoner, prin. Fax 343-3725
South Mecklenburg HS 2,300/9-12
8900 Park Rd 28210 980-343-3600
Marian Yates, prin. Fax 343-3607
Southwest MS 1,000/6-8
13624 Steele Creek Rd 28273 980-343-5006
Valerie Williams, prin. Fax 343-3239
Vance HS 2,200/9-12
7600 IBM Dr 28262 980-343-5284
Philip Cauthen, prin. Fax 343-5286
Waddell HS 1,100/9-12
7030 Nations Ford Rd 28217 980-343-6769
Dr. Edward Ellis, prin. Fax 949-6771
West Charlotte HS 1,700/9-12
2219 Senior Dr 28216 980-343-6060
John Modest, prin. Fax 343-6049
West Mecklenburg HS 1,600/9-12
7400 Tuckaseegee Rd 28214 980-343-6080
Charity Bell, prin. Fax 343-6079
Williams MS 700/6-8
2400 Carmine St 28206 980-343-5544
Angela Bozeman, prin. Fax 343-5601
Wilson MS 500/6-8
7020 Tuckaseegee Rd 28214 980-343-6070
Shelley Hinton, prin. Fax 343-6129
Other Schools – See Cornelius, Davidson, Huntersville, Matthews

---

Adventist Christian Academy 100/PK-12
4601 Emory Ln 28211 704-366-4351
Fax 367-1872
Art Institute of Charlotte Post-Sec.
2110 Water Ridge Pkwy 28217 704-357-8020
Brookstone College of Business Post-Sec.
10125 Berkeley Place Dr 28262 704-547-8600
Carolina Beauty College Post-Sec.
5430 N Tryon St Ste O 28213 704-597-5503
Carolinas College of Health Sciences Post-Sec.
PO Box 32861 28232 704-355-5043
Central Piedmont Community College Post-Sec.
PO Box 35009 28235 704-330-2722
Charlotte Catholic HS 1,000/9-12
7702 Pineville Matthews Rd 28226 704-543-1127
Jerry Healy, prin. Fax 543-1217
Charlotte Christian S 1,000/PK-12
7301 Sardis Rd 28270 704-366-5657
Dr. Leo Orsino, hdmstr. Fax 366-5678
Charlotte Country Day S 1,600/PK-12
1440 Carmel Rd 28226 704-943-4500
Margaret Gragg, hdmstr. Fax 943-4577
Charlotte Latin S 1,400/PK-12
9502 Providence Rd 28277 704-846-1100
Arch N. McIntosh, hdmstr. Fax 846-1712
DeVry University Post-Sec.
4521 Sharon Rd Ste 145 28211 704-362-2345
Dore Academy 100/K-12
1727 Providence Rd 28207 704-365-5490
Roberta Smith, hdmstr. Fax 365-5087
Dudley Beauty College Post-Sec.
1950 John McDonald Ave 28216 704-392-2564
ECPI College of Technology Post-Sec.
4800 Airport Center Pkwy 28208 704-399-1010
Fletcher S 200/K-12
8500 Sardis Rd 28270 704-365-4658
Margaret Sigmon, hdmstr. Fax 364-2978
Hairstyling Institute of Charlotte Post-Sec.
209B S Kings Dr 28204 704-334-5511
Hickory Grove Baptist Christian S 1,100/K-12
6050 Hickory Grove Rd 28215 704-531-4008
Rev. Henry Ward, admin. Fax 531-4082
Holy Trinity Catholic MS 1,000/6-8
3100 Park Rd 28209 704-527-7822
Carole Breerwood, prin. Fax 525-7288
Johnson & Wales University Post-Sec.
801 W Trade St 28202 980-598-1000
Johnson C. Smith University Post-Sec.
100 Beatties Ford Rd 28216 704-378-1000
King's College Post-Sec.
322 Lamar Ave 28204 704-372-0266
Lee University Charlotte Center Post-Sec.
1209 Little Rock Rd 28214 704-394-2307
Mercy School of Nursing Post-Sec.
701 Forest Point Cir Ste B 28273 704-512-2010
New Life Theological Seminary Post-Sec.
PO Box 790106 28206 704-334-6882
Northside Christian Academy 800/PK-12
333 Jeremiah Blvd 28262 704-596-4074
David Kilgore, hdmstr. Fax 921-1384
Presbyterian Hospital Post-Sec.
PO Box 33549 28233 704-384-4141
Providence Day S 1,500/PK-12
5800 Sardis Rd 28270 704-887-7041
Eugene Bratek, prin. Fax 887-7042
Queens University of Charlotte Post-Sec.
1900 Selwyn Ave 28274 704-337-2212
Reformed Theological Seminary Post-Sec.
2101 Carmel Rd 28226 704-366-5066
Resurrection Christian S 100/PK-12
2940 Commonwealth Ave 28205 704-334-9898
Janet Atwell, prin. Fax 347-0811
Southeastern School of Neuromuscular Post-Sec.
4 Woodlawn Green #200 28217 704-527-4979
United Faith Christian Academy 300/PK-12
8617 Providence Rd 28277 704-541-1742
Mark Starnes, hdmstr. Fax 540-7926
Universal College of Beauty Post-Sec.
1701 W Trade St 28216 704-333-6969
University of North Carolina Post-Sec.
9201 University City Blvd 28223 704-547-2000
Victory Christian S 400/K-12
1501 Carrier Dr 28216 704-391-7339
Michael Pratt, prin. Fax 391-0494

Cherokee, Swain

Oconaluftee Job Corps Center Post-Sec.
502 Ocnaluftee Job Corps Rd 28719 828-497-5411

Cherryville, Gaston, Pop. 5,455
Gaston County SD
Supt. — See Gastonia
Chavis MS 600/6-8
103 S Chavis Dr 28021 704-435-6045
James Montgomery, prin. Fax 435-6168
Cherryville HS 600/9-12
PO Box 779 28021 704-435-4506
Steve Huffstetler, prin. Fax 435-4989

China Grove, Rowan, Pop. 3,714
Rowan-Salisbury County SD
Supt. — See Salisbury
China Grove MS 600/6-8
1013 N Main St 28023 704-857-7038
Donald Bost, prin. Fax 857-6650
South Rowan HS 1,800/9-12
1655 Patterson St 28023 704-857-1161
Juddson Starling, prin. Fax 855-1420

Chocowinity, Beaufort, Pop. 731
Beaufort County SD
Supt. — See Washington
Chocowinity MS 400/5-8
3831 US Highway 17 S 27817 252-946-6191
Rick Anderson, prin. Fax 975-3812
Southside HS 500/9-12
5700 NC Highway 33 E 27817 252-940-1881
Todd Blumenreich, prin. Fax 940-1888

Claremont, Catawba, Pop. 1,104
Catawba County SD
Supt. — See Newton
Bunker Hill HS 900/9-12
4675 Oxford School Rd 28610 828-241-3355
Jeff Taylor, prin. Fax 241-9401
Mill Creek MS 600/7-8
1041 Shiloh Rd 28610 828-241-2711
Rob Rucker, prin. Fax 241-2743
River Bend MS 500/7-8
4670 Oxford School Rd 28610 828-241-2754
Donna Heavner, prin. Fax 241-2820

Clarkton, Bladen, Pop. 702
Bladen County SD
Supt. — See Elizabethtown
Clarkton MS of Discovery 400/6-8
PO Box 127 28433 910-647-6531
Michelle Mena, prin. Fax 647-6671

Clayton, Johnston, Pop. 12,943
Johnston County SD
Supt. — See Smithfield
Clayton HS 1,500/9-12
600 S Fayetteville St 27520 919-553-4064
Jerry Smith, prin. Fax 553-2563
Clayton MS 700/6-8
490 Guy Rd 27520 919-553-5811
Deborah Woodruff, prin. Fax 553-6978
Riverwood MS 800/6-8
204 Athletic Club Blvd, 919-359-2769
Phillip Lee, prin. Fax 359-1519

Clemmons, Forsyth, Pop. 16,430
Winston-Salem/Forsyth SD
Supt. — See Winston Salem
West Forsyth HS 2,300/9-12
1735 Lewisville Clemmons Rd 27012 336-712-4400
Kurt Telford, prin. Fax 712-4416

Cleveland, Rowan, Pop. 823

Clearview Christian Academy 100/PK-12
200 Clearview Dr 27013 704-278-0420
Lori Jarvis, dir. Fax 278-0480

Clinton, Sampson, Pop. 8,768
Clinton CSD 2,800/PK-12
606 College St 28328 910-592-3132
Gene Hales Ed.D., supt. Fax 592-2011
www.clinton.k12.nc.us
Clinton HS 800/9-12
1201 W Elizabeth St 28328 910-592-2067
Jeff Bell, prin. Fax 592-6185
Sampson Early College HS 9-12
PO Box 318 28329 910-592-8081
Linda Jewell-Carr Ed.D., prin. Fax 592-8048
Sampson MS 700/6-8
505 Sunset Ave 28328 910-592-3327
Terrace Miller, prin. Fax 592-2292

Sampson County SD 8,300/PK-12
PO Box 439 28329 910-592-1401
Dr. Leslie Stewart Hobbs, supt. Fax 590-2445
www.sampson.k12.nc.us/
Union HS 500/9-12
455 River Rd 28328 910-592-4026
Stuart Daugherty, prin. Fax 592-8226
Union MS 500/6-8
1190 Edmond Matthis Rd 28328 910-592-4547
Peggy Carter, prin. Fax 592-4211
Other Schools – See Dunn, Newton Grove, Roseboro, Salemburg

Sampson Community College Post-Sec.
PO Box 318 28329 910-592-8081

Clyde, Haywood, Pop. 1,357
Haywood County SD
Supt. — See Waynesville
Central Haywood HS 100/9-12
PO Box 249 28721 828-627-9944
Phil Pressley, prin. Fax 627-8935
Haywood Early College HS 9-12
185 Freedlander Dr 28721 828-565-4000
Doris Hipps, prin. Fax 565-4074

Haywood Community College — Post-Sec.
185 Freedlander Dr 28721 — 828-627-2821

Columbia, Tyrrell, Pop. 784
Tyrrell County SD — 700/PK-12
PO Box 328 27925 — 252-796-1121
Nelson Smith, supt. — Fax 796-1492
www.tyrrell.k12.nc.us
Columbia HS — 200/9-12
PO Box 419 27925 — 252-796-0191
Jana Rawls, prin. — Fax 796-0143
Columbia MS — 200/6-8
PO Box 839 27925 — 252-796-0369
Marcia Manning, prin. — Fax 796-3639

Columbus, Polk, Pop. 994
Polk County SD — 2,200/PK-12
PO Box 638 28722 — 828-894-3051
William Miller, supt. — Fax 894-8153
www.polk.k12.nc.us
Polk County HS — 700/9-12
1681 NC 108 Hwy E 28722 — 828-894-2525
Aaron Greene, prin. — Fax 894-2093
Other Schools – See Mill Spring

Concord, Cabarrus, Pop. 61,092
Cabarrus County SD — 22,500/PK-12
PO Box 388 28026 — 704-262-6191
Dr. Harold Winkler, supt. — Fax 786-6141
www.cabarrus.k12.nc.us
Central Cabarrus HS — 1,600/9-12
505 Highway 49 S 28025 — 704-786-0125
Brad Hinson, prin. — Fax 782-1239
Concord HS — 1,200/9-12
481 Burrage Rd NE 28025 — 704-786-4161
Carla Black, prin. — Fax 782-7539
Concord MS — 1,000/6-8
1500 Gold Rush Dr 28025 — 704-786-4121
James Carroll, prin. — Fax 782-8632
Fries MS — 800/6-8
133 Stonecrest Cir 28027 — 704-788-4140
Kecia Coln, prin. — Fax 784-2086
Griffin MS — 1,100/6-8
7650 Griffins Gate Dr SW 28025 — 704-455-4700
Dr. Jim Williams, prin. — Fax 455-4780
Harris Road MS — 900/6-8
1251 Patriot Plantation Blv 28027 — 704-782-2002
Susan Cline, prin. — Fax 262-4298
Northwest Cabarrus HS — 1,200/9-12
5130 NW Cabarrus Dr 28027 — 704-788-4111
Sharon Abercrombie, prin. — Fax 723-4114
Northwest Cabarrus MS — 800/6-8
5140 NW Cabarrus Dr 28027 — 704-788-4135
Tim Farrar, prin. — Fax 784-2649
Robinson HS — 1,600/9-12
300 Pitts School Rd SW 28027 — 704-788-4500
Todd Smith, prin. — Fax 262-3630
Other Schools – See Mount Pleasant

Cabarrus College of Health Sciences — Post-Sec.
401 Medical Park Dr 28025 — 704-783-1556
Cannon S — 900/PK-12
5801 Poplar Tent Rd 28027 — 704-786-8171
Matthew Gossage, hdmstr. — Fax 788-7779
Covenant Classical S — 200/PK-12
3200 Patrick Henry Dr S 28027 — 704-792-1854
Corie Crouch, hdmstr. — Fax 792-2102
Empire Beauty School — Post-Sec.
10075 Weddington Road Ext 28027 — 800-575-5983
First Assembly Christian S — 800/PK-12
154 Warren C Coleman Blvd N 28027 — 704-793-4750
Blenda Snodderly, hdmstr. — Fax 793-4784

Connellys Springs, Burke, Pop. 1,494
Burke County SD
Supt. — See Morganton
East Burke HS — 2,000/9-12
3695 E Burke Blvd 28612 — 828-397-5541
Rexana Lowman, prin. — Fax 397-7652

Conover, Catawba, Pop. 7,093

Tri-City Christian S — 300/PK-12
PO Box 1690 28613 — 828-465-0475
Bob Templeton, admin. — Fax 466-3749

Conway, Northampton, Pop. 704
Northampton County SD
Supt. — See Jackson
Conway MS — 500/6-8
400 E Main St 27820 — 252-585-0312
Jerry Simmons, prin. — Fax 585-0335
Northampton County HS East — 600/9-12
750 Northamptn County HS Rd 27820 — 252-585-0627
Michael McIntosh, prin. — Fax 585-9019

Cornelius, Mecklenburg, Pop. 18,870
Charlotte/Mecklenburg County SD
Supt. — See Charlotte
Bailey MS — 6-8
12334 Bailey Rd 28031 — 980-343-1068
Angela Baucom, prin. — Fax 343-1069

Cramerton, Gaston, Pop. 3,005
Gaston County SD
Supt. — See Gastonia
Cramerton MS — 800/6-8
601 Cramer Mountain Rd 28032 — 704-824-2907
Cristi Bostic, prin. — Fax 824-0228

Cramerton Christian Academy — 400/K-12
426 Woodlawn Ave 28032 — 704-824-2840
Kyle Brown, prin. — Fax 824-9642

Creedmoor, Granville, Pop. 3,155
Granville County SD
Supt. — See Oxford
Hawley MS — 600/6-8
2173 Brassfield Rd 27522 — 919-528-0091
Beth Cook, prin. — Fax 528-0051
South Granville HS — 1,200/9-12
701 Crescent Dr 27522 — 919-528-1507
Harold Carver, prin. — Fax 528-3389
South Granville S of Health & Life Sci — 9-12
701 Crescent Dr 27522 — 919-693-5510
Catherine Brooks, prin.

Christian Faith Center Academy — 100/K-12
PO Box 510 27522 — 919-528-1581
Gloria McKain, prin. — Fax 528-4380

Creswell, Washington, Pop. 267
Washington County SD
Supt. — See Plymouth
Creswell JSHS — 100/7-12
PO Box 188 27928 — 252-797-4766
Wayne Talley, prin. — Fax 797-4651

Cullowhee, Jackson, Pop. 4,029

Western Carolina University — Post-Sec.
University Dr 28723 — 828-227-7211

Currituck, Currituck
Currituck County SD — 3,900/PK-12
2958 Caratoke Hwy 27929 — 252-232-2223
C. Michael Warren, supt. — Fax 232-3655
www.currituck.k12.nc.us
Other Schools – See Barco, Moyock

Dallas, Gaston, Pop. 3,411
Gaston County SD
Supt. — See Gastonia
Friday MS — 700/6-8
1221 Ratchford Dr 28034 — 704-922-5297
Jessica McGee, prin. — Fax 922-9841
North Gaston HS — 1,100/9-12
1133 Ratchford Dr 28034 — 704-922-5285
Brent Boone, prin. — Fax 922-7486

Gaston College — Post-Sec.
201 Highway 321 S 28034 — 704-922-6200
Tabernacle Christian Academy — 200/K-12
2128 Dallas Cherryville Hwy 28034 — 704-922-9143
Patricia Hedrick, prin. — Fax 922-9988

Danbury, Stokes, Pop. 108
Stokes County SD — 7,400/PK-12
PO Box 50 27016 — 336-593-8146
Nelson Jessup, supt. — Fax 593-2041
www.stokes.k12.nc.us
North Stokes HS — 400/9-12
1350 N Stokes School Rd 27016 — 336-593-8134
Ronnie Mendenhall, prin. — Fax 593-8882
Other Schools – See King, Lawsonville, Walnut Cove

Davidson, Mecklenburg, Pop. 8,581
Charlotte/Mecklenburg County SD
Supt. — See Charlotte
Davidson International Baccalaureate MS — 200/6-8
PO Box 369 28036 — 980-343-5185
Dr. Mary Louise Jones, prin. — Fax 343-5187

Davidson College — Post-Sec.
PO Box 7156 28035 — 704-892-2000
Davidson Day S, 412 Armour St 28036 — 200/K-10
Bonnie Coffer, prin. — 704-896-3585

Deep Run, Lenoir
Lenoir County SD
Supt. — See Kinston
South Lenoir HS — 800/9-12
3355 Old Hwy 11 28525 — 252-568-6161
Jay Thomas, prin. — Fax 568-6015

Delco, Columbus
Columbus County SD
Supt. — See Whiteville
Acme-Delco MS — 200/6-8
PO Box 40 28436 — 910-655-3200
Miriam Davis, prin. — Fax 655-6865

Denton, Davidson, Pop. 1,472
Davidson County SD
Supt. — See Lexington
South Davidson HS — 500/9-12
14956 S NC Highway 109 27239 — 336-859-3533
Keith Overcash, prin. — Fax 859-2789
South Davidson MS — 400/6-8
14954 S NC Highway 109 27239 — 336-850-0575
Kimberly Loflin, prin. — Fax 859-0267

Denver, Lincoln
Lincoln County SD
Supt. — See Lincolnton
East Lincoln HS — 800/9-12
6471 Highway 73 28037 — 704-483-5681
Todd Black, prin. — Fax 483-6751

Dobson, Surry, Pop. 1,508
Surry County SD — 8,800/PK-12
PO Box 364 27017 — 336-386-8211
Dr. Ashley Hinson, supt. — Fax 386-4279
www.surry.k12.nc.us/
Central MS — 600/6-8
PO Box 768 27017 — 336-386-4018
Vickie Cameron, prin. — Fax 386-4371
Surry Central HS — 900/9-12
PO Box 8 27017 — 336-386-8842
Kerin Via, prin. — Fax 386-4424
Other Schools – See Mount Airy, Pilot Mountain

Surry Community College — Post-Sec.
630 S Main St 27017 — 336-386-8121

Dublin, Bladen, Pop. 250

Bladen Community College — Post-Sec.
PO Box 266 28332 — 910-862-2164

Dudley, Wayne
Wayne County SD
Supt. — See Goldsboro
Brogden MS — 500/5-8
3761 US Hwy 117 South Alt 28333 — 919-705-6010
Earl Moore, prin. — Fax 705-6000
Southern Wayne HS — 1,100/9-12
124 Walter Fulcher Rd 28333 — 919-705-6060
Tim Harrell, prin. — Fax 731-5982

Dunn, Harnett, Pop. 9,889
Harnett County SD
Supt. — See Lillington
Coats-Erwin MS — 700/6-8
2833 NC Highway 55 E 28334 — 910-230-0300
Whit Bradham, prin. — Fax 230-0306
Dunn MS — 500/6-8
1301 Meadow Lark Rd 28334 — 910-892-1017
Stan Williams, prin. — Fax 892-7923

Sampson County SD
Supt. — See Clinton
Midway HS — 600/9-12
15375 Spiveys Corner Hwy 28334 — 910-567-6664
O.C. Holland, prin. — Fax 567-5989
Midway MS — 600/6-8
1115 Roberts Grove Rd 28334 — 910-567-5879
Joan Jones, prin. — Fax 567-5131

Heritage Bible College — Post-Sec.
PO Box 1628 28335 — 910-892-3178

Durham, Durham, Pop. 204,845
Durham County SD — 30,300/PK-12
PO Box 30002 27702 — 919-560-2000
Dr. Carl Harris, supt. — Fax 560-2422
www.dpsnc.net
Brogden MS — 800/6-8
1001 Leon St 27704 — 919-560-3906
Alexis Spann, prin. — Fax 560-3957
Carrington MS — 1,300/6-8
227 Milton Rd 27712 — 919-560-3916
Julie Spencer, prin. — Fax 560-3522
Chewning MS — 700/6-8
5001 Red Mill Rd 27704 — 919-560-3914
Everette Johnson, prin. — Fax 477-9189
Clement Early College HS — 9-12
1801 Fayetteville St 27707 — 919-560-2696
Dr. Nicholas King, prin. — Fax 560-5328
Durham School of the Arts — 1,400/6-12
400 N Duke St 27701 — 919-560-3926
Ron Roukema, prin. — Fax 560-2217
Githens MS — 1,000/6-8
4800 Old Chapel Hill Rd 27707 — 919-560-3966
Emmett Tilley, prin. — Fax 560-3454
Hillside HS — 1,600/9-12
3727 Fayetteville St 27707 — 919-560-3925
Earl Pappy, prin. — Fax 560-2312
Jordan HS — 1,800/9-12
6806 Garrett Rd 27707 — 919-560-3912
Richard Webber, prin. — Fax 493-2620
Lowes Grove MS — 700/6-8
4418 S Alston Ave 27713 — 919-560-3946
Eric Johnson, prin. — Fax 560-2102
Middle College HS at DTCC — 11-12
1637 E Lawson St 27703 — 919-686-3815
Dr. Charles Nolan, prin. — Fax 686-3624
Neal MS — 800/6-8
201 Baptist Rd 27704 — 919-560-3955
Myron Wilson, prin. — Fax 560-3451
Northern HS — 1,600/9-12
117 Tom Wilkinson Rd 27712 — 919-560-3956
John Colclough, prin. — Fax 479-3001
Riverside HS — 1,800/9-12
3218 Rose Of Sharon Rd 27712 — 919-560-3965
James Key, prin. — Fax 560-3798
Rogers-Herr MS — 600/6-8
911 W Cornwallis Rd 27707 — 919-560-3970
Drew Sawyer, prin. — Fax 560-2439
Shepard MS — 400/6-8
2401 Dakota St 27707 — 919-560-3938
Kenneth Barnes, prin. — Fax 560-3945
Southern HS — 1,500/9-12
800 Clayton Rd 27703 — 919-560-3968
Rodriguez Teal, prin. — Fax 596-1951

Apex School of Theology — Post-Sec.
2945 S Miami Blvd Ste 114 27703 — 919-572-1625
Carolina Beauty College — Post-Sec.
5106 N Roxboro St 27704 — 919-477-1444
Carolina Friends S — 500/K-12
4809 Friends School Rd 27705 — 919-383-6602
Mike Hanas, prin. — Fax 383-6009
Cresset Christian Academy — 300/PK-12
3707 Garrett Rd 27707 — 919-489-2655
Gail Murphy, admin. — Fax 493-8102
Duke University 27706 — Post-Sec.
919-684-8111
Durham Academy — 1,100/PK-12
3501 Ridge Rd 27705 — 919-493-9595
Edward Costello, hdmstr.
Durham Technical Community College — Post-Sec.
1637 E Lawson St 27703 — 919-686-3300
Hill Center — 200/K-12
3200 Pickett Rd 27705 — 919-489-7464
Sharon Maskel Ed.D., prin. — Fax 489-7466
Liberty Christian S — 200/K-12
3864 Guess Rd 27705 — 919-471-5522
Loren Kurtz, prin.
Mt. Zion Christian Academy — 200/K-12
3519 Fayetteville St 27707 — 919-688-4245
Peggy McIlwain, prin. — Fax 688-2201
North Carolina Central University — Post-Sec.
PO Box 19617 27707 — 919-560-6100

East Bend, Yadkin, Pop. 666
Yadkin County SD
Supt. — See Yadkinville
Forbush HS — 1,000/9-12
1525 Falcon Rd 27018 — 336-961-4644
Jeff Wallace, prin. — Fax 961-2575

East Flat Rock, Henderson, Pop. 3,218
Henderson County SD
Supt. — See Hendersonville
East Henderson HS — 1,100/9-12
110 Old Upward Rd 28726 — 828-697-4768
Matthew Gruebmeyer, prin. — Fax 698-6123
Flat Rock MS — 800/6-8
191 Preston Ln 28726 — 828-697-4775
Bill Reedy, prin. — Fax 698-6124

Eden, Rockingham, Pop. 15,679
Rockingham County SD — 14,700/PK-12
511 Harrington Hwy 27288 — 336-627-2600
Dr. Rodney Shotwell, supt. — Fax 627-2660
www.rock.k12.nc.us
Holmes MS — 900/6-8
211 N Pierce St 27288 — 336-623-9791
George Murphy, prin. — Fax 627-0075
Morehead HS — 1,200/9-12
134 N Pierce St 27288 — 336-627-7731
Betty Harrington, prin. — Fax 623-5462
Other Schools – See Madison, Mayodan, Reidsville

Edenton, Chowan, Pop. 5,001
Edenton/Chowan County SD — 2,500/PK-12
PO Box 206 27932 — 252-482-4436
Allan Smith, supt. — Fax 482-7309
www.ecps.k12.nc.us
Holmes HS — 700/9-12
PO Box 409 27932 — 252-482-8426
William Moore, prin. — Fax 482-2010
Other Schools – See Tyner

Efland, Orange
Orange County SD
Supt. — See Hillsborough
Gravelly Hill MS 6-8
4819 W Ten Rd 27243 919-732-8126
Jason Johnson, prin.

Elizabeth City, Pasquotank, Pop. 18,456
Elizabeth City/Pasquotank County SD 6,100/PK-12
PO Box 2247 27906 252-335-2981
Dr. Tony Stewart, supt. Fax 335-0974
www.ecpps.k12.nc.us
Elizabeth City MS 700/6-8
306 N Road St 27909 252-335-2974
Gerri Hill, prin. Fax 335-1751
Northeastern HS 900/9-12
963 Oak Stump Rd 27909 252-335-2932
Don Sisson, prin. Fax 335-1005
Pasquotank County HS 1,000/9-12
1064 Northside Rd 27909 252-337-6880
Patti Hamler, prin. Fax 337-6890
River Road MS 700/6-8
1701 River Rd 27909 252-333-1454
Carolyn Jennings, prin. Fax 331-1339

Albemarle Academy 200/K-12
1210 US Highway 17 S 27909 252-338-0883
Melvin Hooker, prin. Fax 338-1222
College of the Albemarle Post-Sec.
PO Box 2327 27906 252-335-0821
Elizabeth City State University Post-Sec.
1704 Weeksville Rd 27909 252-335-3400
Roanoke Bible College Post-Sec.
715 N Poindexter St 27909 252-334-2070
Victory Christian S 200/PK-12
684 Old Hertford Hwy 27909 252-264-2011
R.L. Parker, admin. Fax 264-4155

Elizabethtown, Bladen, Pop. 3,844
Bladen County SD 5,900/PK-12
PO Box 37 28337 910-862-4136
Dr. Kenneth Dinkins, supt. Fax 862-4277
bladencounty.nc.schoolwebpages.com
East Bladen HS 700/9-12
5600 NC Highway 87 E 28337 910-645-2500
Rob Spainhour, prin. Fax 645-2509
Elizabethtown MS 500/5-8
PO Box 639 28337 910-862-4071
Linda Baldwin, prin. Fax 862-7426
Other Schools – See Bladenboro, Clarkton, Tar Heel

Elkin, Surry, Pop. 4,315
Elkin CSD 1,200/PK-12
202 W Spring St 28621 336-835-3135
Dr. Barry C. Shepherd, supt. Fax 835-3376
www.elkincityschools.com
Elkin HS 400/9-12
334 Elk Spur St 28621 336-835-3858
Misty Walker, prin. Fax 835-3253
Elkin MS 200/7-8
300 Elk Spur St 28621 336-835-3858
Pam Helms, prin. Fax 835-3253

Elk Park, Avery, Pop. 448
Avery County SD
Supt. — See Newland
Cranberry MS 200/6-8
PO Box 38 28622 828-733-2932
Kim Davis, prin. Fax 733-6863

Ellerbe, Richmond, Pop. 993
Richmond County SD
Supt. — See Hamlet
Ellerbe JHS 300/6-9
128 W Ballard St 28338 910-652-3231
William Kelley, prin. Fax 652-3106

Elm City, Wilson, Pop. 1,381
Wilson County SD
Supt. — See Wilson
Elm City MS 500/6-8
215 Church St E 27822 252-236-4148
David Lyndon, prin. Fax 236-3754

Elon, Alamance, Pop. 7,100
Alamance-Burlington SD
Supt. — See Burlington
Western Alamance HS 1,100/9-12
1731 N NC Highway 87 27244 336-538-6020
Terri Spears, prin. Fax 538-6014
Western MS 800/6-8
2100 Eldon Dr 27244 336-538-6010
Dr. Lizzie Alston, prin. Fax 538-6012

Elon University Post-Sec.
2700 Campus Box 27244 336-278-2000

Enfield, Halifax, Pop. 2,302
Halifax County SD
Supt. — See Halifax
Eastman MS 300/6-8
20212 NC Highway 48 27823 252-445-3720
Linda Bulluck, prin. Fax 445-2410
Enfield MS 300/6-8
PO Box 128 27823 252-445-5502
Ruzalia Vines, prin. Fax 445-3600

Erwin, Harnett, Pop. 4,792
Harnett County SD
Supt. — See Lillington
Triton HS 1,400/9-12
215 Maynard Lake Rd 28339 910-897-8121
Brooks Matthews, prin. Fax 897-3148

Cape Fear Christian Academy 300/PK-12
138 Erwin Chapel Rd 28339 910-897-5423
Pat Sandel, hdmstr. Fax 897-2150

Fairmont, Robeson, Pop. 2,618
Robeson County SD
Supt. — See Lumberton
Fairgrove MS 400/4-8
1953 Fairgrove Rd 28340 910-628-8290
Craig Lowry, prin. Fax 628-6181
Fairmont HS 800/9-12
5419 Old Stage Rd 28340 910-628-6727
Lannie Edwards, prin. Fax 628-0652
Fairmont MS 500/5-8
402 Iona St 28340 910-628-4363
Joyce Canady, prin. Fax 628-0335
Lumberton JHS 600/7-8
1953 Fairgrove Rd 28340 910-735-2108
Gary Patrick, prin. Fax 671-4350

Farmville, Pitt, Pop. 4,546
Pitt County SD
Supt. — See Greenville
Farmville Central HS 800/9-12
3308 E Wilson St 27828 252-753-5138
Valerie Galbreth, prin. Fax 753-7873
Farmville MS 700/6-8
3914 Grimmersburg St 27828 252-753-2116
Mary Carter, prin. Fax 753-7995

Fayetteville, Cumberland, Pop. 129,928
Cumberland County SD 53,200/PK-12
PO Box 2357 28302 910-678-2300
William C. Harrison Ed.D., supt. Fax 678-2339
www.ccs.k12.nc.us
Abbott MS 1,000/6-8
590 Winding Creek Rd 28305 910-323-2201
Myra Holloway, prin. Fax 485-0841
Britt HS 1,700/9-12
7403 Rockfish Rd 28306 910-429-2800
Conrad Lopes, prin. Fax 429-2810
Byrd HS 1,300/9-12
1624 Ireland Dr 28304 910-484-8121
Jackie Warner, prin. Fax 323-4127
Byrd MS 800/7-8
1616 Ireland Dr 28304 910-483-3101
Lodies Gloston, prin. Fax 483-3741
Cape Fear HS 1,500/9-12
4762 Clinton Rd, 910-483-0191
Jeffery Jernigan, prin. Fax 483-1679
Chesnutt MS 700/6-8
2121 Skibo Rd 28314 910-867-9147
Tom Hatch, prin. Fax 868-3695
Cross Creek Early College HS 9-12
1200 Murchison Rd 28301 910-672-1499
Melinda Vickers, prin. Fax 672-1590
Cumberland Health & Life Sciences HS 9-12
1624 Ireland Dr 28304 910-485-1634
Katrenna Rich, prin. Fax 483-5754
Griffin MS 1,200/6-8
5551 Fisher Rd 28304 910-424-7678
Mike Magnum, prin. Fax 424-7602
Jeralds MS 600/6-8
2517 Ramsey St 28301 910-822-2570
Shirley Gamble, prin. Fax 822-1534
Lewis Chapel MS 800/6-8
2150 Skibo Rd 28314 910-864-1407
Kathia Ennett, prin. Fax 864-8298
Massey Hill Classical HS 300/9-12
1062 Southern Ave 28306 910-485-8761
Mark Culbreath, prin. Fax 485-7950
Pine Forest HS 1,700/9-12
525 Andrews Rd 28311 910-488-2384
Cindy McCormic, prin. Fax 488-0790
Pine Forest MS 800/6-8
6901 Ramsey St 28311 910-488-2711
Dan Krumanocker, prin. Fax 630-2357
Ross Classical JSHS 900/6-12
3200 Ramsey St 28301 910-488-8415
Debbie Poulk, prin. Fax 488-6209
Sanford HS 1,500/9-12
2301 Fort Bragg Rd 28303 910-484-1151
Diane Antolak, prin. Fax 484-7203
Seventy-First Classical MS 500/6-8
6830 Raeford Rd 28304 910-864-0092
Scott Pope, prin. Fax 487-8547
Seventy-First HS 1,800/9-12
6764 Raeford Rd 28304 910-867-3116
Tina Poltrock, prin. Fax 867-1445
Smith HS 1,500/9-12
1800 Seabrook Rd 28301 910-483-0153
Rene Corders, prin. Fax 483-7696
Westover HS 1,300/9-12
277 Bonanza Dr 28303 910-864-0190
Mark Smith, prin. Fax 864-5924
Westover MS 800/6-8
275 Bonanza Dr 28303 910-864-0813
Myron Williams, prin. Fax 864-7906
Williams MS 1,200/6-8
4464 Clinton Rd, 910-483-8222
Donna Hancock, prin. Fax 483-4831
Other Schools – See Hope Mills, Spring Lake

Berean Baptist Academy 300/PK-12
518 Glensford Dr 28314 910-868-2511
Donald Adams, prin. Fax 868-1550
Cornerstone Christian Academy 100/PK-12
3000 Scotty Hill Rd 28303 910-867-1166
Greg DeBruler, prin. Fax 867-2166
Fayetteville Academy 400/PK-12
3200 Cliffdale Rd 28303 910-868-5131
Richard Cameron, hdmstr. Fax 868-7351
Fayetteville Adventist Christian S 50/K-12
PO Box 64397 28306 910-484-6091
Phyllis Knight, prin.
Fayetteville Beauty College Post-Sec.
3442 Bragg Blvd 28303 910-487-0227
Fayetteville Christian S 600/PK-12
1422 Ireland Dr 28304 910-483-3905
Tammi Peters, prin. Fax 483-6966
Fayetteville State University Post-Sec.
1200 Murchison Rd 28301 910-486-1111
Fayetteville Technical Community College Post-Sec.
PO Box 35236 28303 910-678-8400
Liberty Christian Academy 300/PK-12
6548 Rockfish Rd 28306 910-424-1205
Duncan Edge, prin. Fax 424-8049
Methodist College Post-Sec.
5400 Ramsey St 28311 910-630-7000
Mitchell's Hairstyling Academy Post-Sec.
222 Tallywood Shopping Ctr 28303 910-485-6310
New Life Christian Academy 50/PK-12
1420 Hoke Loop Rd 28314 910-868-9640
Connie McLauchlin, prin. Fax 868-3300
Northwood Temple Academy 400/PK-12
4200 Ramsey St 28311 910-822-7711
Renee McLamb, hdmstr. Fax 488-7299
Trinity Christian S 200/K-12
3727 Rosehill Rd 28311 910-488-6779
Dennis Vandevender, prin.
Village Christian Academy 800/K-12
908 S McPherson Church Rd 28303 910-483-5500
Joan Dayton, admin. Fax 483-5335

Flat Rock, Henderson, Pop. 2,750

Blue Ridge Community College Post-Sec.
College Ave 28731 828-694-1700

Fletcher, Henderson, Pop. 4,522
Buncombe County SD
Supt. — See Asheville
Cane Creek MS 800/6-8
570 Lower Brush Creek Rd 28732 828-628-0824
Kathy Noyes, prin. Fax 628-9833

Fletcher Academy 100/9-12
PO Box 5440 28732 828-687-5100
Rob Gettys, prin. Fax 687-5102
Veritas Christian Academy 300/K-12
17 Cane Creek Rd 28732 828-681-0546
Kay Belknap, hdmstr. Fax 681-0547

Forest City, Rutherford, Pop. 7,273
Rutherford County SD 9,700/K-12
382 W Main St 28043 828-245-0252
Dr. John Kinlaw, supt. Fax 245-4151
www.rutherford.k12.nc.us
Chase HS 900/9-12
1603 Chase High Rd 28043 828-245-7668
Robert Smith, prin. Fax 248-3584
Chase MS 700/6-8
840 Chase High Rd 28043 828-247-1044
Greg Lovelace, prin. Fax 247-0551
East Rutherford HS 900/9-12
PO Box 668 28043 828-245-6424
Janet Mason, prin. Fax 247-0039
Other Schools – See Bostic, Rutherfordton, Spindale

Master's Academy 100/PK-12
120 School Dr 28043 828-245-7203
Tami Schultz, admin.

Four Oaks, Johnston, Pop. 1,765
Johnston County SD
Supt. — See Smithfield
Four Oaks MS 500/6-8
1475 Boyette Rd 27524 919-963-4022
Lisa Edwards, prin. Fax 963-4123
South Johnston HS 1,000/9-12
10381 US Highway 301 S 27524 919-894-3146
Barry Honeycutt, prin. Fax 894-3229

Franklin, Macon, Pop. 3,611
Macon County SD 4,200/K-12
PO Box 1029 28744 828-524-3314
Dan Brigman, supt. Fax 524-5938
www.mcsk-12.org
Early College HS 9-12
4178 Murphy Rd 28734 828-524-3314
Gary Brown, prin.
Franklin HS 1,100/9-12
100 Panther Dr 28734 828-524-6467
Gary Sheilds, prin. Fax 524-0684
Macon MS 900/6-8
1345 Wells Grove Rd 28734 828-524-3766
Todd Gibbs, prin. Fax 349-3900
Other Schools – See Highlands, Topton

Trimont Christian Academy 100/PK-12
98 Promise Ln 28734 828-369-6756
Robert Ricotta, admin. Fax 524-0622

Franklinton, Franklin, Pop. 1,899
Franklin County SD
Supt. — See Louisburg
Franklinton HS 700/9-12
PO Box 520 27525 919-494-2332
Charles Fuller, prin. Fax 494-5140

Fremont, Wayne, Pop. 1,441
Wayne County SD
Supt. — See Goldsboro
Norwayne MS 1,000/6-8
1394 Norwayne School Rd 27830 919-242-3414
Mario Re, prin. Fax 242-3418

Fuquay Varina, Wake, Pop. 6,525
Wake County SD
Supt. — See Raleigh
Fuquay-Varina HS 1,600/9-12
201 Bengal Dr 27526 919-557-2511
William Blanchard, prin. Fax 557-2512
Fuquay-Varina MS 900/6-8
109 N Ennis St 27526 919-557-2727
William Holley, prin. Fax 557-2732

Hilltop Christian S 200/K-12
5309 Umstead Rd 27526 919-552-5612
Travis Moots, prin.

Garner, Wake, Pop. 22,364
Johnston County SD
Supt. — See Smithfield
Cleveland MS 700/6-8
2323 Cornwallis Rd 27529 919-553-7500
Kathleen McLamb, prin. Fax 553-7798

Wake County SD
Supt. — See Raleigh
East Garner MS 900/6-8
6301 Jones Sausage Rd 27529 919-662-2339
Cathy Williams, prin. Fax 662-2357
Garner Magnet HS 1,900/9-12
2101 Spring Dr 27529 919-662-2379
Isaac Holton, prin. Fax 662-2397
North Garner MS 900/6-8
720 Powell Dr 27529 919-662-2434
John Wall, prin. Fax 662-5637

EnVisionary I-Care Post-Sec.
133 Highway 70 W 27529 919-661-7773

Gaston, Northampton, Pop. 936
Northampton County SD
Supt. — See Jackson
Gaston MS 300/6-8
PO Box J 27832 252-537-2520
Martha Paige, prin. Fax 535-5692
Northampton County HS West 500/9-12
152 Hurricane Ln 27832 252-537-1910
Willie Bell, prin. Fax 537-9028

Gastonia, Gaston, Pop. 68,964
Gaston County SD 31,700/PK-12
PO Box 1397 28053 704-866-6100
L. Reeves McGlohon, supt. Fax 866-6321
www.gaston.k12.nc.us/
Ashbrook HS 1,500/9-12
2222 S New Hope Rd 28054 704-866-6600
Page Carver, prin. Fax 866-6203
Forestview HS 1,300/9-12
5545 Union Rd 28056 704-861-2625
Robert Carpenter, prin. Fax 853-3323
Grier MS 700/6-8
1622 E Garrison Blvd 28054 704-866-6086
Laura Dixon, prin. Fax 866-6116

Highland School of Technology Vo/Tech
1600 N Morris St 28052 704-810-8818
Lee Dedmon, prin. Fax 866-6105
Huss HS 1,100/9-12
1518 Edgefield Ave 28052 704-866-6610
Kelly Gwaltney, prin. Fax 866-6103
Southwest MS 1,000/6-8
1 Roadrunner Dr 28052 704-866-6290
Jacob Barr, prin. Fax 866-6293
York-Chester MS 500/6-8
601 S Clay St 28052 704-866-6297
Cindy White, prin. Fax 866-6319
Other Schools – See Belmont, Bessemer City, Cherryville, Cramerton, Dallas, Lowell, Mount Holly, Stanley

---

Gaston Day S 400/PK-12
2001 Gaston Day School Rd 28056 704-864-7744
Dr. Richard E. Rankin, prin. Fax 865-3813
Victory Christian Academy 100/K-12
310 Carolina Ave 28052 704-865-7132
Willa McGhee, prin. Fax 867-1731

Gatesville, Gates, Pop. 297
Gates County SD 1,900/PK-12
PO Box 125 27938 252-357-1113
Fax 357-0207
coserver.gates.k12.nc.us/
Central MS 500/6-8
362 US Highway 158 W 27938 252-357-0470
Shirley Vinson, prin. Fax 357-1319
Gates County HS 700/9-12
88 US Highway 158 W 27938 252-357-0720
Fax 357-2058

Gibsonville, Guilford, Pop. 4,569
Guilford County SD
Supt. — See Greensboro
Eastern Guilford HS 1,000/9-12
415 Peeden Dr 27249 336-274-8461
Dr. Lisa Cooke, prin. Fax 449-7392
Eastern MS 900/6-8
435 Peeden Dr 27249 336-697-3199
Michael Ferrell, prin. Fax 449-0728

Goldsboro, Wayne, Pop. 38,670
Wayne County SD 18,700/K-12
PO Box 1797 27533 919-731-5900
Dr. Steven Taylor, supt. Fax 705-6199
www.waynecountyschools.org
Dillard MS 200/7-8
1101 Devereaux St 27530 919-580-9360
Sylvester Townsend, prin. Fax 736-1121
Eastern Wayne HS 1,300/9-12
1135 E New Hope Rd 27534 919-751-7120
Eugene Byrd, prin. Fax 751-7107
Eastern Wayne MS 700/6-8
3518 Central Heights Rd 27534 919-751-7110
Catherine Eubanks, prin. Fax 751-7114
Goldsboro HS 800/9-12
PO Box 1757 27533 919-731-5930
Patricia Burden, prin. Fax 731-5914
Greenwood MS 600/5-8
3209 E Ash St 27534 919-751-7100
Larry Dean, prin. Fax 751-7201
Rosewood HS 600/9-12
900 Rosewood Rd 27530 919-705-6050
David Lewis, prin. Fax 705-6055
Rosewood MS 400/6-8
541 NC Highway 581 S 27530 919-736-5050
Francis Southerland, prin. Fax 736-5055
Wayne Early Middle College HS 11-12
PO Box 1797 27533 919-735-5151
Lee Johnson, prin. Fax 581-1011
Other Schools – See Dudley, Fremont, Mount Olive, Pikeville, Seven Springs

---

Faith Christian Academy 300/K-12
1200 W Grantham St 27530 919-734-8701
Walter Sloan, prin. Fax 734-9658
Mitchell's Hairstyling Academy Post-Sec.
1021 N Spence Ave 27534 919-778-8200
Wayne Christian S 500/PK-12
1201 Patetown Rd 27530 919-735-5605
Lynn Mooring, prin. Fax 735-5229
Wayne Community College Post-Sec.
PO Box 8002 27533 919-735-5151
Wayne Country Day S 300/PK-12
480 Country Day Rd 27530 919-736-1045
Todd Anderson, prin. Fax 583-9493

Graham, Alamance, Pop. 13,952
Alamance-Burlington SD
Supt. — See Burlington
Graham HS 900/9-12
903 Trollinger Rd 27253 336-570-6440
Todd Wirt, prin. Fax 570-6446
Graham MS 700/6-8
311 E Pine St 27253 336-570-6460
Teresa Faucette, prin. Fax 570-6464
Southern Alamance HS 1,400/9-12
631 Southern High School Rd 27253 336-570-6400
Dawn Madren, prin. Fax 570-6404
Southern MS 800/6-8
771 Southern High School Rd 27253 336-570-6500
Heather Ward, prin. Fax 570-6504

Alamance Christian S 300/K-12
PO Box 838 27253 336-578-0318
Daniel Freeman, admin. Fax 578-7200
Alamance Community College Post-Sec.
PO Box 8000 27253 336-578-2002

Granite Falls, Caldwell, Pop. 4,573
Caldwell County SD
Supt. — See Lenoir
Granite Falls MS 700/6-8
90 N Main St 28630 828-396-2341
Brian Suddreth, prin. Fax 396-7072

Grantsboro, Pamlico, Pop. 734

Pamlico Community College Post-Sec.
PO Box 185 28529 252-249-1851

Greensboro, Guilford, Pop. 231,962
Guilford County SD 67,700/PK-12
PO Box 880 27402 336-370-8100
Dr. Terry Grier, supt. Fax 370-8299
www.gcsnc.com/
Academy at Smith 10-12
2407 S Holden Rd - Bldg B 27407 336-316-5866
Sharonda Murrell, prin. Fax 294-7313
Allen MS 800/6-8
1108 Glendale Dr 27406 336-294-7325
Jesse Pratt, prin. Fax 294-7315
Arts Academy at Weaver Ed Ctr 200/9-12
300 S Spring St 27401 336-370-8282
Anna Brady, prin. Fax 370-8287
Aycock MS 700/6-8
811 Cypress St 27405 336-370-8110
Marilyn Foley, prin. Fax 370-8044
Dudley HS 1,400/9-12
1200 Lincoln St 27401 336-370-8130
Phyllis Martin, prin. Fax 370-8979
Greenboro Middle College HS 100/11-12
108 Odell Pl Ste 1 27403 336-370-8300
Denise Francisco, prin. Fax 370-8918
Grimsley HS 1,800/9-12
801 Westover Ter 27408 336-370-8180
Robert M. Gasparello, prin. Fax 370-8194
GTCC East Middle College HS 9-12
501 W Washington St 27401 336-370-8984
Pete Kashubara, prin. Fax 230-1516
Guilford Early College HS 200/9-12
5608 W Friendly Ave 27410 336-316-2860
Tony Burks, prin. Fax 316-2858
Guilford MS 900/4-8
401 College Rd 27410 336-316-5833
Cynthia Kremer, prin. Fax 316-5837
Hairston MS 800/6-8
3911 Naco Rd 27401 336-370-8250
Lewis Ferebee, prin. Fax 370-8153
Jackson MS 600/6-8
2200 Ontario St 27403 336-294-7350
Rodney Wilds, prin. Fax 294-7316
Kernodle MS 1,000/6-8
3600 Drawbridge Pkwy 27410 336-545-3717
Charles L. Burns, prin. Fax 545-3714
Kiser MS 800/6-8
716 Benjamin Pkwy 27408 336-370-8240
Sharon McCants, prin. Fax 370-8248
Lincoln Academy 4-8
1016 Lincoln St 27401 336-370-3471
Rodney Boone, prin. Fax 370-3480
Mendenhall MS 900/6-8
205 Willoughby Blvd 27408 336-545-2000
Nola Taylor, prin. Fax 545-2004
Middle College HS at Bennett 100/9-12
600 Gorrell St 27406 336-370-8636
Esther Coble, prin. Fax 370-8637
Middle College HS at NC A&T 100/9-12
1601 E Market St 27411 336-691-0941
Russell Harper, prin. Fax 691-0952
Northern HS 9-12
7101 Spencer Dixon Rd 27455 336-370-8100
Joe Yeager, prin.
Northern MS 6-8
616 Simpson Calhoun Rd 27455 336-605-3342
Sam Misher, prin. Fax 605-3343
Northwest Guilford HS 2,100/9-12
5240 NW School Rd 27409 336-605-3300
Angelo Kidd, prin. Fax 605-3314
Northwest Guilford MS 1,200/6-8
5300 NW School Rd 27409 336-605-3333
Dr. William Stewart, prin. Fax 605-3325
Page HS 1,700/9-12
201 Alma Pinnix Dr 27405 336-370-8200
Dr. Terry Worrell, prin. Fax 370-8219
Smith HS 1,700/9-12
2407 S Holden Rd 27407 336-294-7300
Noah Rogers, prin. Fax 294-7313
Southeast Guilford HS 1,300/9-12
4530 SE School Rd 27406 336-674-4300
Keith D. Kremer, prin. Fax 674-4290
Southeast Guilford MS 1,000/6-8
4825 Woody Mill Rd 27406 336-674-4280
Sam Foust, prin. Fax 674-4276
Southern Guilford HS 900/9-12
5700 Drake Rd 27406 336-674-4250
James Gibson, prin. Fax 674-4254
Western Guilford HS 1,500/9-12
409 Friendway Rd 27410 336-316-5800
Richard Armstrong, prin. Fax 316-5813
Other Schools – See Browns Summit, Gibsonville, High Point, Jamestown, Mc Leansville

---

American Hebrew Academy 200/9-12
4334 Hobbs Rd 27410 336-217-7015
Dr. Gary Grandon, prin. Fax 217-7011
Bennett College Post-Sec.
900 E Washington St 27401 336-273-4431
Brookstone College of Business Post-Sec.
7815 National Service Rd 27409 336-668-2627
Caldwell Academy 600/K-12
2900 Horse Pen Creek Rd 27410 336-665-1161
Mark Guthrie, hdmstr. Fax 665-1178
Carolina Beauty College Post-Sec.
1917 E Wendover Ave 27405 336-886-4712
Carolina Beauty College Post-Sec.
2001 E Wendover Ave 27405 336-272-2966
ECPI College of Technology Post-Sec.
7802 Airport Center Dr 27409 336-665-1400
Greensboro College Post-Sec.
815 W Market St 27401 336-272-7102
Greensboro Day S 900/PK-12
5401 Lawndale Dr 27455 336-288-8590
Mark Hale, prin. Fax 282-2905
Guilford College Post-Sec.
5800 W Friendly Ave 27410 336-316-2000
Guilford Day S 100/1-12
3310 Horse Pen Creek Rd 27410 336-282-7044
Laura B. Mlatac, hdmstr. Fax 282-2048
Leon's Beauty School Post-Sec.
1410 W Lee St 27403 336-274-4601
Moses H. Cone Memorial Hospital Post-Sec.
1200 N Elm St 27401 336-574-7881
New Garden Friends S 300/PK-12
1128 New Garden Rd 27410 336-299-0964
Marty Goldstein, prin. Fax 292-0347
North Carolina A&T State University Post-Sec.
1601 E Market St 27411 336-334-7500
Shining Light Academy 200/K-12
4530 W Wendover Ave 27409 336-299-9688
Rev. Steve Kilby, prin.
University of North Carolina Post-Sec.
1000 Spring Garden St 27412 336-334-5000
Vandalia Christian S 700/PK-12
3919 Pleasant Garden Rd 27406 336-379-8380
Mark Weatherford, admin. Fax 379-8671

Greenville, Pitt, Pop. 69,517
Pitt County SD 21,400/PK-12
1717 W 5th St 27834 252-830-4200
Dr. Beverly Reep, supt. Fax 830-4239
www.pitt.k12.nc.us/
Aycock MS 900/6-8
1325 Red Banks Rd 27858 252-756-4181
Julie Cary, prin. Fax 756-2408
Conley HS 1,200/9-12
2006 Worthington Rd 27858 252-756-3440
Michael Lutz, prin. Fax 756-3028
Eppes MS 500/6-8
1100 S Elm St 27858 252-757-2160
Charlie Langley, prin. Fax 757-2163
Hope MS 6-8
2995 Mills Rd 27858 252-355-7071
Pat Clark, prin. Fax 355-6055
Rose HS 1,700/9-12
600 W Arlington Blvd 27834 252-321-3640
Dr. George Frazier, prin. Fax 321-3653
Wellcome MS 500/6-8
3101 N Memorial Dr 27834 252-752-5938
Jeff Theus, prin. Fax 752-1685
Other Schools – See Ayden, Bethel, Farmville, Winterville

East Carolina University Post-Sec.
Admissions 27858 252-328-6131
Greenville Christian Academy 400/K-12
1621 Greenville Blvd SW 27834 252-756-0939
Paul Aynes, prin.
Mitchell's Hairstyling Academy Post-Sec.
426 E Arlington Blvd 27858 252-756-3050
Oakwood S 300/K-10
4000 MacGregor Downs Rd 27834 252-931-0760
Dr. Raymond Bailey, prin.
Pitt Community College Post-Sec.
PO Box 7007 27835 252-321-4200
Trinity Christian S 400/PK-12
3111 Golden Rd 27858 252-758-0037
Denise Mills, prin. Fax 758-0767

Grifton, Lenoir, Pop. 2,066
Lenoir County SD
Supt. — See Kinston
Savannah MS 300/6-8
2583 Cameron Langston Rd 28530 252-527-8897
Anita Sykes, prin. Fax 527-9175

Halifax, Halifax, Pop. 325
Halifax County SD 5,400/PK-12
PO Box 468 27839 252-583-5111
Geraldine Middleton, supt. Fax 583-1474
www.halifax.k12.nc.us/
Halifax County S of Ecology 9-12
16685 NC Highway 125 27839 252-445-2333
Flora Pitchford, prin. Fax 445-2260
Southeast Halifax HS 700/9-12
16683 NC Highway 125 27839 252-445-2027
Fax 445-3463
Other Schools – See Enfield, Littleton, Roanoke Rapids, Scotland Neck

Weldon CSD
Supt. — See Weldon
Weldon MS 300/6-8
4489 US Highway 301 27839 252-536-2571
James Harfield, prin. Fax 536-3485

Hallsboro, Columbus
Columbus County SD
Supt. — See Whiteville
Hallsboro MS 400/5-8
PO Box 248 28442 910-646-4192
Michael Mobley, prin. Fax 646-5072

Hamlet, Richmond, Pop. 5,824
Richmond County SD 8,200/PK-12
PO Box 1259 28345 910-582-5860
Dr. Larry Weatherly, supt. Fax 582-7921
www.richmond.k12.nc.us
Hamlet JHS 700/7-9
1406 Mcdonald Ave 28345 910-582-7903
Carl Ransom, prin. Fax 582-5730
Other Schools – See Ellerbe, Rockingham

Richmond Community College Post-Sec.
PO Box 1189 28345 910-582-7000

Hampstead, Pender
Pender County SD
Supt. — See Burgaw
Topsail HS 700/9-12
17445 US Highway 17 N 28443 910-270-2755
Fax 270-9290
Topsail MS 600/6-8
17385 US Highway 17 N 28443 910-270-2612
Markus Skipper, prin. Fax 270-3190

Harrells, Sampson, Pop. 209

Harrells Christian Academy 400/K-12
PO Box 88 28444 910-532-4575
Dr. Ronald Montgomery, prin. Fax 532-2958

Havelock, Craven, Pop. 21,827
Craven County SD
Supt. — See New Bern
Havelock HS 1,200/9-12
101 Webb Blvd 28532 252-444-5112
Jeffrey Murphy, prin. Fax 444-5119
Havelock MS 500/6-8
102 High School Dr 28532 252-444-5125
Thomas McCarthy, prin. Fax 444-5129
Tucker Creek MS 500/6-8
200 Sermons Rd 28532 252-444-7200
Danny Tripp, prin. Fax 444-7206

Liberty Christian S 100/K-12
81 Shepard St 28532 252-447-4185
Bryan Roberts, prin. Fax 447-6736

Hayesville, Clay, Pop. 469
Clay County SD 1,300/PK-12
PO Box 178 28904 828-389-8513
Douglas Penland, supt. Fax 389-3437
www.clayschools.org/
Hayesville HS 400/9-12
205 Yellow Jacket Dr 28904 828-389-6532
Dr. Gail Criss, prin. Fax 389-6251
Hayesville MS 400/5-8
135 School Dr 28904 828-389-9924
Mickey Noe, prin. Fax 389-1706

Hays, Wilkes, Pop. 1,522
Wilkes County SD
Supt. — See North Wilkesboro
North Wilkes HS 700/9-12
PO Box 430 28635 336-957-8601
Annette Greene, prin. Fax 957-4787

Henderson, Vance, Pop. 16,213
Vance County SD 8,500/PK-12
PO Box 7001 27536 252-492-2127
Dr. Norman Shearin, supt. Fax 438-6119
www.vcs.k12.nc.us
Eaton-Johnson MS 1,100/6-8
500 N Beckford Dr 27536 252-438-5017
Michael Talley, prin. Fax 738-0250
Henderson MS 900/6-8
219 Charles St 27536 252-492-0054
Victor Fenner, prin. Fax 430-8588
Northern Vance HS 1,100/9-12
293 Warrenton Rd 27537 252-492-6041
Hugh Brady, prin. Fax 492-7878
Southern Vance HS 1,100/9-12
925 Garrett Rd 27537 252-430-6000
James Pickens, prin. Fax 430-0308

Crossroads Christian S 400/PK-12
583 Old County Home Rd 27537 252-431-1333
Jon Hughes, hdmstr. Fax 431-0333
Kerr-Vance Academy 400/PK-12
700 Vance Academy Rd 27537 252-492-0018
Paul Villatico, hdmstr. Fax 438-4652
Maria Parham Hospital Post-Sec.
566 Ruin Creek Rd 27536 252-436-1130
Vance-Granville Community College Post-Sec.
PO Box 917 27536 252-492-2061
Victory Baptist S 100/K-12
PO Box 592 27536 252-492-6079
Rev. Ricky Easter, prin. Fax 492-4683

Hendersonville, Henderson, Pop. 11,396
Henderson County SD 12,500/PK-12
414 4th Ave W 28739 828-697-4733
Stephen Page Ed.D., supt. Fax 697-5541
www.henderson.k12.nc.us
Apple Valley MS 800/6-8
43 Fruitland Rd 28792 828-697-4545
Caroline Patterson, prin. Fax 698-6119
Hendersonville HS 700/9-12
311 8th Ave W 28791 828-697-4802
W. Robert Wilkins, prin. Fax 698-6126
Hendersonville MS 500/6-8
825 N Whitted St 28791 828-697-4800
Jenny Moreno, prin. Fax 698-6127
North Henderson HS 900/9-12
35 Fruitland Rd 28792 828-697-4500
Frank Edney, prin. Fax 698-6129
Rugby MS 800/6-8
3345 Haywood Rd 28791 828-891-6566
Beverly Davis, prin. Fax 891-6589
West Henderson HS 1,100/9-12
3600 Haywood Rd 28791 828-891-6571
Dean Jones, prin. Fax 891-6590
Other Schools – See East Flat Rock

Hendersonville Christian S 100/K-12
708 Old Spartanburg Rd 28792 828-692-0556
Kenny Young, prin. Fax 692-0557

Hertford, Perquimans, Pop. 2,104
Perquimans County SD 1,800/PK-12
PO Box 337 27944 252-426-5741
Dr. Kenneth W. Wells, supt. Fax 426-4913
www.pcs.k12.nc.us/
Perquimans County HS 600/9-12
PO Box 398 27944 252-426-5778
James Bunch, prin. Fax 426-1663
Other Schools – See Winfall

Hickory, Catawba, Pop. 40,232
Catawba County SD
Supt. — See Newton
Arndt MS 700/7-8
3350 34th Street Dr NE 28601 828-256-9545
Cynthia McKee, prin. Fax 256-6748
Catawba Valley Early College HS 9-12
2550 US Highway 70 SE 28602 828-485-2980
Dr. Eddy Daniel, prin. Fax 485-2981
St. Stephens HS 1,200/9-12
3205 34th Street Dr NE 28601 828-256-9841
DeAnna Taylor, prin. Fax 256-7159

Hickory CSD 4,500/PK-12
432 4th Ave SW 28602 828-322-2855
Dr. Ric Vandett, supt. Fax 322-1834
www.hickory.k12.nc.us
Grandview MS 400/6-8
451 Catawba Valley Blvd 28602 828-328-2289
Dr. Vanessa Howerton, prin. Fax 328-2992
Hickory HS 1,300/9-12
1234 3rd St NE 28601 828-322-5860
Dr. Kim Mattox, prin. Fax 326-7101
Northview MS 500/6-8
302 28th Ave NE 28601 828-327-6300
Dr. Martha Hill, prin. Fax 327-6367

Catawba Valley Community College Post-Sec.
2550 US Highway 70 SE 28602 828-327-7000
Christian Family Academy 200/K-12
PO Box 5353 28603 828-324-4204
David Gruver, prin.
Hickory Christian Academy 200/K-12
PO Box 5203 28603 828-324-5405
Tracy Robinson, prin.
Lenoir-Rhyne College Post-Sec.
7th Ave and 8th St 28603 828-328-1741
Tabernacle Christian S 200/K-12
1225 29th Avenue Dr NE 28601 828-324-9936
Dr. Gordon Fenlason, prin. Fax 324-8921

Hiddenite, Alexander
Alexander County SD
Supt. — See Taylorsville
East Alexander MS 700/6-8
1285 White Plains Rd 28636 828-632-7565
Sheila Jenkins, prin. Fax 632-4508

Highlands, Macon, Pop. 941
Macon County SD
Supt. — See Franklin
Highlands S 400/K-12
PO Box 940 28741 828-526-2147
Brian Jetter, prin. Fax 526-0615

High Point, Guilford, Pop. 95,086
Guilford County SD
Supt. — See Greensboro
Academy at High Point Central 10-12
801 Ferndale Blvd 27262 336-885-7905
Bonnie Kosiczky, prin.
Andrews HS 1,200/9-12
1920 McGuinn Dr 27265 336-819-2800
Monique Brooks, prin. Fax 887-5585
Ferndale MS 600/6-8
701 Ferndale Blvd 27262 336-819-2855
Lori Braxton, prin. Fax 885-2854
High Point Central HS 1,400/9-12
801 Ferndale Blvd 27262 336-819-2825
Revonda Johnson, prin. Fax 819-2991
Jay MS 700/6-8
1201 E Fairfield Rd 27263 336-434-8470
Kevin Wheat, prin. Fax 431-5530
Middle College of Entrtnmnt/Tech @ GTCC 9-12
901 S Main St 27260 336-819-4111
Ralph Kitley, prin. Fax 819-4116
Penn-Griffin MS 700/6-8
825 E Washington Dr 27260 336-819-2870
Bobby Ann Hayes, prin. Fax 889-4841
Southwest Guilford HS 1,200/9-12
4364 Barrow Rd 27265 336-819-2970
George Allen Parker, prin. Fax 454-5175
Southwest Guilford MS 1,000/6-8
4368 Barrow Rd 27265 336-819-2985
William Farkas, prin. Fax 454-4015
Welborn MS 800/6-8
1710 McGuinn Dr 27265 336-819-2880
Lori Bolds, prin. Fax 819-2878

Hayworth Christian S 200/PK-12
1696 Westchester Dr 27262 336-882-3126
Mickey Briles, admin. Fax 882-9157
High Point Christian Academy 800/PK-12
307 N Rotary Dr 27262 336-841-8702
Richard Hardee, admin. Fax 841-8701
High Point University Post-Sec.
933 Montlieu Ave 27262 336-841-9000
John Wesley College Post-Sec.
2314 N Centennial St 27265 336-889-2262
Tri-City Junior Academy 100/K-10
8000 Clinard Farms Rd 27265 336-665-9822
Clint Sutton, prin. Fax 665-9834
Wesleyan Christian Academy 1,300/PK-12
1917 N Centennial St 27262 336-884-3333
Joel Farlow, admin. Fax 884-8232
Westchester Country Day S 400/K-12
2045 N Old Greensboro Rd 27265 336-869-2128
Charles Hamblet, hdmstr. Fax 869-6685

Hillsborough, Orange, Pop. 5,382
Orange County SD 6,700/K-12
200 E King St 27278 919-732-8126
Dr. Shirley Carraway, supt. Fax 732-8120
www.orange.k12.nc.us
Cedar Ridge HS 1,100/9-12
1125 New Grady Brown Sch Rd 27278
919-245-4000
Gary Thornburg, prin. Fax 245-4010
Orange HS 1,000/9-12
500 Orange High School Rd 27278 919-732-6133
Jeffrey Dishmon, prin. Fax 644-7699
Stanback MS 700/6-8
3700 NC Highway 86 S 27278 919-644-3200
Clara Daniels, prin. Fax 644-3226
Stanford MS 900/6-8
308 Orange High School Rd 27278 919-732-6121
Richard Kozak, prin. Fax 732-6910
Other Schools – See Efland

Hobgood, Halifax, Pop. 389

Hobgood Academy 200/K-12
201 S Beech St 27843 252-826-4116
William Whitehurst, prin. Fax 826-2265

Holly Ridge, Onslow, Pop. 761
Onslow County SD
Supt. — See Jacksonville
Dixon HS 600/9-12
160 Dixon School Rd 28445 910-347-2958
John Shannon, prin. Fax 347-3932
Dixon MS 500/6-8
200 Dixon School Rd 28445 910-347-2738
Dr. Laurie Spring, prin. Fax 347-4399

Holly Springs, Wake, Pop. 15,228
Wake County SD
Supt. — See Raleigh
Holly Ridge MS 1,000/6-8
950 Holly Springs Rd 27540 919-577-1335
Kenneth Proulx, prin. Fax 577-1379
Holly Springs HS 9-10
5329 Cass Holt Rd 27540 919-577-1444
Luther Johnson, prin. Fax 577-1773

Hookerton, Greene, Pop. 489

Mount Calvary Christian Academy 200/K-12
PO Box 250 28538 252-747-8111
Michael Fulcher, prin. Fax 747-8112

Hope Mills, Cumberland, Pop. 12,782
Cumberland County SD
Supt. — See Fayetteville
Grays Creek HS 1,000/9-12
5301 Celebration Dr 28348 910-424-8589
Joyce Adams, prin. Fax 424-7411
Grays Creek MS 500/6-8
2964 School Rd 28348 910-483-4124
Sara Whitaker, prin. Fax 483-5296
Hope Mills MS 700/6-8
4975 Cameron Rd 28348 910-425-5106
Patsy Ray, prin. Fax 423-5887
South View HS 1,800/9-12
4184 Elk Rd 28348 910-425-8181
Robert Barnes, prin. Fax 425-2962
South View MS 1,000/6-8
4100 Elk Rd 28348 910-424-3131
Garda Tatum, prin. Fax 424-2402

Hudson, Caldwell, Pop. 3,061
Caldwell County SD
Supt. — See Lenoir
Caldwell County Career Center HS Vo/Tech
2857 Hickory Blvd 28638 828-726-2606
Debbie Kincaid, prin. Fax 726-2463
Caldwell Early College HS 9-12
2855 Hickory Blvd 28638 828-759-4636
Teresa Branch, prin.
Hudson MS 800/6-8
291 Pine Mountain Rd 28638 828-728-4281
Jeff Church, prin. Fax 726-8157
South Caldwell HS 1,600/9-12
7035 Spartan Dr 28638 828-396-2188
Michael Peake, prin. Fax 396-3329

Caldwell Community Coll. & Tech. Inst. Post-Sec.
2855 Hickory Blvd 28638 828-726-2200
Harris Chapel Christian Academy 100/K-12
1444 Cajah Mountain Rd 28638 828-728-3721
Allen Norrod, prin. Fax 728-2375
Heritage Christian S 200/K-12
239 Mount Herman Rd 28638 828-726-0055
Robert Setzer, prin.

Huntersville, Mecklenburg, Pop. 36,377
Charlotte/Mecklenburg County SD
Supt. — See Charlotte
Alexander MS 1,700/6-8
12201 Hambright Rd 28078 980-343-3830
Joanna Smith, prin. Fax 343-3851
Bradley MS 1,700/6-8
13345 Beatties Ford Rd 28078 980-343-5750
Alicisa Johnson, prin. Fax 343-5743
Hopewell HS 2,200/9-12
11530 Beatties Ford Rd 28078 980-343-5988
Kendra March, prin. Fax 343-5990
North Mecklenburg HS 2,700/9-12
11201 Old Statesville Rd 28078 980-343-3840
Joey Burch, prin. Fax 343-3845

SouthLake Christian Academy 800/K-12
13901 Hagers Ferry Rd 28078 704-949-2200
C. Wayne Parker, hdmstr. Fax 949-2203

Icard, Burke, Pop. 2,553
Burke County SD
Supt. — See Morganton
East Burke MS 800/6-8
PO Box 1150 28666 828-397-7446
Jim Childers, prin. Fax 397-1086

Indian Trail, Union, Pop. 16,473
Union County SD
Supt. — See Monroe
Porter Ridge HS 9-12
2839 Ridge Rd 28079 704-292-7662
Sam Basden, prin. Fax 296-9733
Porter Ridge MS 6-8
2827 Ridge Rd 28079 704-225-7555
Timothy Conner, prin. Fax 226-9844
Sun Valley MS 1,400/6-8
1409 Wesley Chapel Rd 28079 704-296-3009
Blaire Brigham-Traywick, prin. Fax 296-3045

Lake Park Christian Academy 100/K-12
3624 Lake Park Rd 28079 704-882-6267
William Kamm, admin. Fax 882-4651
Metrolina Christian Academy 700/PK-12
PO Box 1460 28079 704-882-3375
Rick Calloway, admin. Fax 882-0631

Iron Station, Lincoln
Lincoln County SD
Supt. — See Lincolnton
East Lincoln MS 600/6-8
4137 Highway 73 28080 704-732-0761
Dr. Vista Rainey, prin. Fax 732-4456

Jackson, Northampton, Pop. 672
Northampton County SD 3,100/PK-12
PO Box 158 27845 252-534-1371
Dr. Kathi Gibson, supt. Fax 534-1268
www.northampton.k12.nc.us/
Other Schools – See Conway, Gaston

Jacksonville, Onslow, Pop. 62,628
Onslow County SD 22,200/PK-12
PO Box 99 28541 910-455-2211
Dr. Kathy Spencer, supt. Fax 455-1965
www.onslow.k12.nc.us
Hunters Creek MS 800/6-8
85 Hunters Trl 28546 910-353-2147
Tim Foster, prin. Fax 353-7939
Jacksonville Commons MS 700/6-8
315 Commons Dr S 28546 910-346-6888
Lynn Jackson, prin. Fax 938-1682
Jacksonville HS 1,300/9-12
1021 Henderson Dr 28540 910-989-2048
Susie Barrett, prin. Fax 989-2046
New Bridge MS 500/6-8
401 New Bridge St 28540 910-346-5144
Brent Anderson, prin. Fax 346-5402
Northside HS 800/9-12
365 Commons Dr S 28546 910-455-4868
Albert James, prin. Fax 455-4987
Northwoods Park MS 700/6-8
904 Sioux Dr 28540 910-347-1202
Christina Baldwin, prin. Fax 347-0713
Southwest HS 800/9-12
1420 Burgaw Hwy 28540 910-455-4888
Debra Bryan, prin. Fax 455-3949
Southwest MS 500/6-8
3000 Furia Dr 28540 910-455-1105
Pam Baldwin, prin. Fax 455-4082
White Oak HS 1,200/9-12
1001 Piney Green Rd 28546 910-455-1541
Meghan Doyle, prin. Fax 938-2302
Other Schools – See Holly Ridge, Richlands, Swansboro

Cheveux School Hair Design and Hairport Post-Sec.
4781 Gum Branch Rd # 1 28540 910-455-5767
Coastal Carolina Community College Post-Sec.
444 Western Blvd 28546 910-455-1221
Jacksonville Christian Academy 200/K-12
919 Gum Branch Rd 28540 910-347-2358
Rev. Earl Hanna, prin.
Living Water Christian S 200/K-12
3980 Gum Branch Rd 28540 910-938-7017
Barbara Koebbe, prin. Fax 938-7025

Jamestown, Guilford, Pop. 2,997
Guilford County SD
Supt. — See Greensboro
GTCC Middle College HS 100/9-12
601 High Point Rd 27282 336-819-2957
Tony Watlington, prin. Fax 819-2961
Jamestown MS 1,200/6-8
4401 Vickery Chapel Rd N 27282 336-819-2100
Denise Richmond, prin. Fax 454-6734
Ragsdale HS 1,400/9-12
602 High Point Rd 27282 336-819-2960
Kathy Rogers, prin. Fax 454-6767

Guilford Technical Community College Post-Sec.
PO Box 309 27282 336-334-4822

Jamesville, Martin, Pop. 478
Martin County SD
Supt. — See Williamston
Jamesville JSHS 300/7-12
PO Box 189 27846 252-792-4428
Clarence Pointe, prin. Fax 809-4812

Jefferson, Ashe, Pop. 1,366
Ashe County SD 3,300/PK-12
PO Box 604 28640 336-246-7175
Donnie Johnson, supt. Fax 246-7609
www.ashe.k12.nc.us/
Other Schools – See Warrensville, West Jefferson

Kannapolis, Cabarrus, Pop. 39,041
Kannapolis CSD 3,600/K-12
100 Denver St 28083 704-938-1131
Jo Anne A. Byerly, supt. Fax 933-6370
www.kannapolis.k12.nc.us
Brown HS 1,300/9-12
415 E 1st St 28083 704-932-6125
Debra Morris, prin. Fax 933-1862
Kannapolis MS 7-8
1445 Oakwood Ave 28081 704-932-4102
Daron Buckwell, prin. Fax 932-4104

Kenansville, Duplin, Pop. 881
Duplin County SD 9,000/PK-12
PO Box 128 28349 910-296-1521
Dr. Wiley Doby, supt. Fax 296-1396
www.duplinschools.net
Smith MS 400/6-8
PO Box 369 28349 910-296-0309
Angela Britt, prin. Fax 296-0086
Other Schools – See Beulaville, Calypso, Rose Hill, Teachey, Warsaw

---

James Sprunt Community College Post-Sec.
PO Box 398 28349 910-296-2500

Kenly, Johnston, Pop. 1,830
Johnston County SD
Supt. — See Smithfield
North Johnston HS 700/9-12
PO Box 339 27542 919-284-2031
Ross Renfrow, prin. Fax 284-6224

Kernersville, Forsyth, Pop. 21,361
Winston-Salem/Forsyth SD
Supt. — See Winston Salem
East Forsyth HS 1,900/9-12
2500 W Mountain St 27284 336-703-6735
Patricia Gainey, prin. Fax 727-8546
East Forsyth MS 6-8
810 Bagley Rd 27284 336-703-6765
Dossie Poteat, prin. Fax 607-8531
Glenn HS 1,700/9-12
1600 Union Cross Rd 27284 336-771-4500
Adolphus Coplin, prin. Fax 771-4507
Kernersville MS 1,200/6-8
110 Brown Rd 27284 336-996-5566
Deborah Brooks, prin. Fax 996-1966
Southeast MS 1,100/6-8
1200 Old Salem Rd 27284 336-996-5848
Debbie Blanton-Warren, prin. Fax 996-0148

Bishop McGuiness HS 500/9-12
1725 NC Highway 66 S 27284 336-564-1010
George Repass, prin. Fax 564-1060
Dudley Cosmetology University Post-Sec.
900 E Mountain St 27284 336-996-2030
Kerwin Baptist Christian S 100/PK-12
4520 Old Hollow Rd 27284 336-993-3791
Dr. Ron Carrell, prin. Fax 996-1850

Kill Devil Hills, Dare, Pop. 6,550
Dare County SD
Supt. — See Nags Head
First Flight HS 800/9-12
PO Box 1758 27948 252-449-7000
Arty Tillett, prin. Fax 449-7004
First Flight MS 700/6-8
109 Run Hill Rd 27948 252-441-8888
Adrienne Palma, prin. Fax 441-7694

King, Stokes, Pop. 6,353
Stokes County SD
Supt. — See Danbury
Chestnut Grove MS 800/6-8
2185 Chestnut Grove Rd 27021 336-983-2106
Todd Martin, prin. Fax 983-2725
West Stokes HS 1,000/9-12
1400 Priddy Rd 27021 336-983-2099
Charles McAninch, prin. Fax 983-6076

Calvary Christian S 200/K-12
748 Spainhour Rd 27021 336-983-3743
Sid Main, prin. Fax 983-8426

Kings Mountain, Cleveland, Pop. 10,862
Cleveland County SD
Supt. — See Shelby
Kings Mountain HS 9-12
500 Phifer Rd 28086 704-734-5647
Ronny Funderburke, prin. Fax 734-1723
Kings Mountain MS 7-8
1000 Phifer Rd 28086 704-734-5667
Stephen Fisher, prin. Fax 734-5615

Hope Christian Academy 200/K-12
PO Box 6 28086 – Tim Barrett, prin. 704-734-0051

Kinston, Lenoir, Pop. 22,851
Lenoir County SD 10,000/PK-12
PO Box 729 28502 252-527-1109
Dr. John Frossard, supt. Fax 527-6884
www.lenoir.k12.nc.us
Kinston HS 1,100/9-12
2601 N Queen St 28501 252-527-8067
Craig Hill, prin. Fax 527-4090
Rochelle MS 700/6-8
301 N Rochelle Blvd 28501 252-527-4290
Edwin Jones, prin. Fax 527-6498
Woodington MS 800/6-8
4939 US Highway 258 S 28504 252-527-9570
Diane Heath, prin. Fax 527-3883
Other Schools – See Deep Run, Grifton, La Grange

Arendell Parrott Academy 700/PK-12
PO Box 1297 28503 252-522-4222
Dr. Ike Southerland, hdmstr. Fax 522-0672
Bethel Christian Academy 400/K-12
1936 Banks School Rd 28504 252-522-4636
Michael Fulcher, prin. Fax 523-7290
Lenoir Community College Post-Sec.
PO Box 188 28502 252-527-6223
Lenoir Memorial Hospital Post-Sec.
100 Airport Rd 28501 252-522-7797

Knightdale, Wake, Pop. 6,319
Wake County SD
Supt. — See Raleigh
Knightdale HS 700/9-12
100 Bryan Chalk Ln 27545 919-217-5350
Marvin Connelly, prin. Fax 217-5357

La Grange, Lenoir, Pop. 2,804
Lenoir County SD
Supt. — See Kinston
Frink MS 700/6-8
102 Martin Luther King Jr 28551 252-566-3326
Brent Williams, prin. Fax 566-4027
North Lenoir HS 1,000/9-12
2400 Institute Rd 28551 252-527-9184
Dexter Simms, prin. Fax 527-8672

Lake Waccamaw, Columbus, Pop. 1,460
Columbus County SD
Supt. — See Whiteville
East Columbus HS 600/9-12
PO Box 401 28450 910-646-4094
Mark Bridgers, prin. Fax 646-3779

Landis, Rowan, Pop. 3,064
Rowan-Salisbury County SD
Supt. — See Salisbury
Corriher-Lipe MS 700/6-8
214 W Rice St 28088 704-857-7946
Dr. Beverly S. Pugh, prin. Fax 855-2670

Lasker, Northampton, Pop. 99

Northeast Academy 300/PK-12
210 Church St 27845 252-539-2461
Russell Leake, hdmstr. Fax 539-3919

Laurel Hill, Scotland
Scotland County SD
Supt. — See Laurinburg
Carver MS 500/6-8
18601 Fieldcrest Rd 28351 910-462-4669
Gary Dwyer, prin. Fax 462-4674

Laurinburg, Scotland, Pop. 15,810
Scotland County SD 7,000/PK-12
322 S Main St 28352 910-276-1138
Dr. Shirley Prince, supt. Fax 277-4310
www.scsnc.org
Scotland HS 1,800/9-12
1000 W Church St 28352 910-276-7370
Roger Edwards, prin. Fax 277-4444
Scotland HS of Business & Finance 9-12
1000 W Church St 28352 910-276-7370
Fred Thomas, prin. Fax 277-4444
Scotland HS of Engineering/Skill Trades 9-12
1000 W Church St 28352 910-276-7370
David Kincaid, prin. Fax 277-4444
Scotland HS of Health & Sciences 9-12
1000 W Church St 28352 910-276-7370
Billy Simpson, prin. Fax 277-4444
Scotland HS of Leadership & Public Srvc 9-12
1000 W Church St 28352 910-276-7370
Kay Fuller, prin. Fax 277-4444
Scotland HS of Math Science & Technology 9-12
1000 W Church St 28352 910-276-7370
Dr. Jean Honeycutt, prin. Fax 277-4444
Scotland HS of Visual & Performing Arts 9-12
1000 W Church St 28352 910-273-7370
Rodney Hassler, prin. Fax 277-4444
Spring Hill MS 500/6-8
22801 Airbase Rd 28352 910-369-0590
Harriet Jackson, prin. Fax 369-0595
Sycamore Lane MS 600/6-8
2100 Sycamore Ln 28352 910-277-4350
Rick Singletary, prin. Fax 277-4321
Other Schools – See Laurel Hill

St. Andrews Presbyterian College Post-Sec.
1700 Dogwood Mile St 28352 910-277-5000
Scotland Christian Academy 200/K-12
10300 McColl Rd 28352 910-276-7722
Phillip Cline, prin.

Lawndale, Cleveland, Pop. 636
Cleveland County SD
Supt. — See Shelby
Burns HS 1,300/9-12
307 E Stagecoach Trl 28090 704-538-7403
Dr. Collette Deviney, prin. Fax 538-3895
Burns MS 1,000/6-8
215 Shady Grove Rd 28090 704-538-3126
Gary Blake, prin. Fax 538-3944

Lawsonville, Stokes
Stokes County SD
Supt. — See Danbury
Piney Grove MS 400/6-8
3415 Piney Grove Church Rd 27022 336-593-4000
Roger Tucker, prin. Fax 593-4003

Leland, Brunswick, Pop. 4,440
Brunswick County SD
Supt. — See Bolivia
Leland MS 600/6-8
927 Old Fayetteville Rd NE 28451 910-371-3030
Rob Knuschke, prin. Fax 371-0647
North Brunswick HS 800/9-12
114 Scorpion Dr 28451 910-371-2261
Deanne Meadows, prin. Fax 371-0879

Lenoir, Caldwell, Pop. 17,912
Caldwell County SD 13,000/PK-12
1914 Hickory Blvd SW 28645 828-728-8407
Dr. Steve Stone, supt. Fax 728-0012
www.caa.k12.nc.us
Gamewell MS 600/6-8
3210 Gamewell School Rd 28645 828-754-6204
Keith Hindman, prin. Fax 754-6278
Hibriten HS 1,000/9-12
550 East Blvd 28645 828-758-7376
Fax 758-9708
Lenoir MS 600/6-8
332 Greenhaven Dr NW 28645 828-758-2500
Dr. Pete Yount, prin. Fax 758-1570
West Caldwell HS 1,100/9-12
300 W Caldwell Dr 28645 828-758-5583
David Colwell, prin. Fax 754-2783
Other Schools – See Granite Falls, Hudson

Lewisville, Forsyth, Pop. 9,547

Forsyth Country Day S 1,000/PK-12
PO Box 549 27023 336-945-3151
Henry Battle, prin. Fax 945-2907

Lexington, Davidson, Pop. 20,398
Davidson County SD 19,600/PK-12
PO Box 2057 27293 336-249-8181
Fred Mock, supt. Fax 249-1062
www.davidson.k12.nc.us
Central Davidson HS 900/9-12
2747 NC Highway 47 27292 336-357-2920
Emily Lipe, prin. Fax 357-5175
Central Davidson MS 900/6-8
2591 NC Highway 47 27292 336-357-2310
Crystal Clodfelter, prin. Fax 357-5965
Davidson Early College HS 9-12
PO Box 1287 27293 336-242-5686
Dr. Larry Allred, prin. Fax 242-5688
North Davidson HS 1,500/9-12
7227 Old US Highway 52 27295 336-731-8431
Gary Fishel, prin. Fax 731-2642
North Davidson MS 1,300/6-8
333 Critcher Dr 27295 336-731-2331
Dr. Denise Hedrick, prin. Fax 731-2328
Tyro MS 700/6-8
2749 Michael Rd 27295 336-853-7795
Harry Mock, prin. Fax 853-7357
West Davidson HS 800/9-12
200 Dragon Dr 27295 336-853-8082
Catherine Gentry, prin. Fax 857-7315
Other Schools – See Denton, Thomasville

Lexington CSD 3,100/PK-12
1010 Fair St 27292 336-242-1527
Rebecca Bloxam, supt. Fax 249-3206
lexcs.org
Lexington HS 800/9-12
26 Penry St 27292 336-242-1574
Greg Newlin, prin. Fax 242-1285
Lexington MS 700/6-8
100 E Hemstead St 27292 336-242-1557
Patti Kroh, prin. Fax 242-1372

Davidson County Community College Post-Sec.
PO Box 1287 27293 336-249-8186
Sheets Memorial Christian S 300/PK-12
307 Holt St 27292 336-249-4224
Dan Hightower, admin. Fax 249-6985
Union Grove Christian S 300/K-12
2295 Union Grove Rd 27295 336-764-3105
Pete Steinhaus, prin. Fax 764-8657

Liberty, Randolph, Pop. 2,712
Randolph County SD
Supt. — See Asheboro
Northeastern Randolph MS 500/6-8
3493 Ramseur Julian Rd 27298 336-622-5808
Kristen Miller, prin. Fax 622-5868

Lillington, Harnett, Pop. 3,162
Harnett County SD 17,000/K-12
PO Box 1029 27546 910-893-8151
Dan Honeycutt, supt. Fax 893-5816
www.harnett.k12.nc.us/
Western Harnett HS 1,100/9-12
10637 NC 27 W 27546 919-499-5113
Terry Hinson, prin. Fax 499-1537
Western Harnett MS 1,000/6-8
11135 NC 27 W 27546 919-499-4497
Janice Harrington, prin. Fax 499-1788
Other Schools – See Angier, Dunn, Erwin, Spring Lake

Lincolnton, Lincoln, Pop. 10,393
Lincoln County SD 11,100/PK-12
PO Box 400 28093 704-732-2261
Dr. Jim Watson, supt. Fax 736-4321
www.lincoln.k12.nc.us
Lincoln County School of Technology Vo/Tech
1 Timpken Dr 28092 704-732-4084
David Bynum, prin. Fax 735-8292
Lincolnton HS 900/9-12
803 N Aspen St 28092 704-735-3089
Tony Worley, prin. Fax 736-4234
Lincolnton MS 700/6-8
2361 Startown Rd 28092 704-735-1120
Scott Carpenter, prin. Fax 732-6811
North Lincoln HS 900/9-12
2737 Lee Lawing Rd 28092 704-736-1969
Richard Freeman, prin. Fax 736-1966
Pumpkin Center MS 600/6-8
3980 King Wilkinson Rd 28092 704-736-0262
Rhonda Hager, prin. Fax 736-9812
West Lincoln HS 1,000/9-12
172 Shoal Rd 28092 704-276-1402
Mitchell Sherrill, prin. Fax 276-2004
West Lincoln MS 800/6-8
260 Shoal Rd 28092 704-276-1760
Glenda Walker, prin. Fax 276-2293
Other Schools – See Denver, Iron Station

Lincoln Christian Academy 100/K-12
280 Car Farm Rd 28092 704-735-5997
Dr. Clyde Smith, admin. Fax 732-3514

Littleton, Halifax, Pop. 662
Halifax County SD
Supt. — See Halifax
Northwest HS 900/9-12
8492 NC Highway 48 27850 252-586-4125
Sharon Arrington, prin. Fax 586-6240

Louisburg, Franklin, Pop. 3,356
Franklin County SD 7,800/K-12
PO Box 449 27549 919-496-4159
Dr. Bert L'Homme, supt. Fax 496-3341
www.fcschools.net
Louisburg HS 600/9-12
201 Allen Ln 27549 919-496-3725
Chris Blice, prin. Fax 496-2505
Terrell Lane MS 500/6-8
101 Terrell Ln 27549 919-496-1855
Novella Brown, prin. Fax 496-1370
Other Schools – See Bunn, Franklinton, Youngsville

Louisburg College Post-Sec.
501 N Main St 27549 919-496-2521

Lowell, Gaston, Pop. 2,671
Gaston County SD
Supt. — See Gastonia
Holbrook MS 800/6-8
418 S Church St 28098 704-824-2381
Gary Ford, prin. Fax 824-4529

Lucama, Wilson, Pop. 865
Wilson County SD
Supt. — See Wilson
Springfield MS 500/6-8
5551 Wiggins Mill Rd 27851 252-239-1347
Donna Simms, prin. Fax 239-1686

Lumberton, Robeson, Pop. 21,591
Robeson County SD 24,600/PK-12
PO Box 2909 28359 910-671-6000
Johnny Hunt, supt. Fax 671-6024
www.robeson.k12.nc.us
Early College HS 9-12
5160 N Fayetteville Rd 28360 910-737-5232
Wesley Revels, prin. Fax 737-5231
Littlefield MS 700/4-8
9674 NC Highway 41 N 28358 910-671-6065
David Evans, prin. Fax 671-6068
Lumberton HS 2,100/9-12
3901 Fayetteville Rd 28358 910-671-6050
Gregory Killingsworth, prin. Fax 671-6067
Robeson County Career Center Vo/Tech
PO Box 2909 28359 910-671-6095
Daniel Ryberg, prin. Fax 671-6097
Other Schools – See Fairmont, Maxton, Orrum, Pembroke, Red Springs, Rowland, Saint Pauls

---

Robeson Community College Post-Sec.
PO Box 1420 28359 910-738-7101

Mc Leansville, Guilford, Pop. 1,154
Guilford County SD
Supt. — See Greensboro
Northeast Guilford HS 1,100/9-12
6700 Mcleansville Rd 27301 336-375-2500
Anitra Walker, prin. Fax 375-2520
Northeast Guilford MS 900/6-8
6720 Mcleansville Rd 27301 336-375-2525
Melissa Harrelson, prin. Fax 375-2534

Madison, Rockingham, Pop. 2,239
Rockingham County SD
Supt. — See Eden
Western Rockingham MS 800/6-8
915 Ayersville Rd 27025 336-548-2168
Jonathan Craig, prin. Fax 548-1799

Maiden, Catawba, Pop. 3,264
Catawba County SD
Supt. — See Newton
Maiden HS 600/9-12
600 W Main St 28650 828-428-8197
Dwayne Finger, prin. Fax 428-8341
Maiden MS 7-8
518 N C Ave 28650 828-428-2326
Nan VanHoy, prin. Fax 428-5389

Manteo, Dare, Pop. 1,301
Dare County SD
Supt. — See Nags Head
Manteo HS 500/9-12
PO Box 280 27954 252-473-5841
John Luciano, prin. Fax 473-2263
Manteo MS 300/6-8
264 N Highway 64 27954 252-473-5549
Terry McGinnis, prin. Fax 473-2612

Marion, McDowell, Pop. 5,013
McDowell County SD 6,500/K-12
334 S Main St 28752 828-652-4535
Dr. Ira Trollinger, supt. Fax 659-2238
www.mcdowell.k12.nc.us/
East McDowell JHS 700/7-9
676 State St 28752 828-652-7711
Becky Pearson, prin. Fax 652-1469
McDowell Early College 9-12
54 College Dr 28752 828-652-6021
Lisa Robinson, prin. Fax 652-1014
McDowell HS 1,400/9-12
600 McDowell High Dr 28752 828-652-7920
Ben Talbert, prin. Fax 652-1101
West McDowell JHS 800/7-9
346 W McDowell Jr High Sch 28752 828-652-3390
Coy Gibson, prin. Fax 659-1964

Marion Christian Academy 200/K-12
PO Box 1045 28752 828-652-2033
Lincoln Walters, admin. Fax 652-1853
McDowell Technical Community College Post-Sec.
54 College Dr 28752 828-652-6021

Marshall, Madison, Pop. 837
Madison County SD 2,600/K-12
5738 US Hwy 25-70 28753 828-649-9276
Ronald Wilcox Ed.D., supt. Fax 649-9334
www.madison.k12.nc.us
Madison HS 800/9-12
5740 US Highway 25-70 28753 828-649-2876
Daniel Metcalf, prin. Fax 649-0104
Madison MS 600/6-8
95 Upper Brush Creek Rd 28753 828-649-2269
Carolyn Franklin, prin. Fax 649-9015

Mars Hill, Madison, Pop. 1,834

Mars Hill College 28754 Post-Sec.
800-543-1514

Marshville, Union, Pop. 2,820
Union County SD
Supt. — See Monroe
East Union MS 800/6-8
6010 W Marshville Blvd 28103 704-624-2114
Kevin Plue, prin. Fax 624-9302
Forest Hills HS 1,000/9-12
100 Forest Hills School Rd 28103 704-233-4001
Dr. Mike Zezech, prin. Fax 233-4003

Matthews, Mecklenburg, Pop. 25,306
Charlotte/Mecklenburg County SD
Supt. — See Charlotte
Butler HS 2,200/9-12
1810 Matthews Mint Hill Rd 28105 980-343-6300
Joel Ritchie, prin. Fax 343-6315
Crestdale MS 1,200/6-8
940 Sam Newell Rd 28105 980-343-5755
Avery Mitchell, prin. Fax 343-5761
Mint Hill MS 1,000/6-8
11501 Idlewild Rd 28105 980-343-5439
Denise Watts, prin. Fax 343-5442

Union County SD
Supt. — See Monroe
Weddington HS 1,600/9-12
4901 Monroe Weddington Rd 28104 704-708-5530
Brad Breedlove, prin. Fax 708-6218
Weddington MS 1,400/6-8
5903 Deal Rd 28104 704-814-9772
Jan Hollis, prin. Fax 814-9775

Bible Baptist Christian S 100/PK-12
2724 Margaret Wallace Rd 28105 704-535-1694
David King, prin. Fax 536-1289
Covenant Day S 800/K-12
800 Fullwood Rd 28105 704-847-2385
Dr. Marni Halvorson, hdmstr. Fax 708-6137
Empire Beauty School Post-Sec.
11032 E Independence Blvd 28105 800-575-5983
Southern Evangelical Seminary Post-Sec.
3000 Tilley Morris Rd 28105 704-847-5600

Maxton, Robeson, Pop. 2,629
Robeson County SD
Supt. — See Lumberton
Townsend MS 300/5-8
105 W Carolina St 28364 910-844-5086
Walter Jackson, prin. Fax 844-4292

Mayodan, Rockingham, Pop. 2,497
Rockingham County SD
Supt. — See Eden
McMichael HS 1,100/9-12
6845 NC Highway 135 27027 336-427-5165
Mavis Dillon, prin. Fax 427-5776

Mebane, Alamance, Pop. 8,945
Alamance-Burlington SD
Supt. — See Burlington
Eastern Alamance HS 1,100/9-12
4040 Mebane Rogers Rd 27302 919-563-5991
Dave Ebert, prin. Fax 563-6114
Hawfields MS 600/6-8
1948 S NC Highway 119 27302 919-563-5303
Amy Walker, prin. Fax 563-1351
Woodlawn MS 600/6-8
3970 Mebane Rogers Rd 27302 919-563-3222
Fax 563-6807

Merry Hill, Bertie

Lawrence Academy 400/PK-12
PO Box 70 27957 252-482-4748
Eric Meadows, hdmstr. Fax 482-2215

Micro, Johnston, Pop. 502
Johnston County SD
Supt. — See Smithfield
North Johnston MS 600/6-8
PO Box 69 27555 919-284-3374
Ray Stott, prin. Fax 284-3399

Millers Creek, Wilkes, Pop. 1,787
Wilkes County SD
Supt. — See North Wilkesboro
West Wilkes HS 700/9-12
6598 Boone Trl 28651 336-973-4503
Hal Gatewood, prin. Fax 973-7323

Mill Spring, Polk
Polk County SD
Supt. — See Columbus
Polk County MS 300/6-8
321 Wolverine Trl 28756 828-894-2215
Hank Utz, prin. Fax 894-0191

Misenheimer, Stanly, Pop. 617

Pfeiffer University Post-Sec.
PO Box 960 28109 704-463-1360

Mocksville, Davie, Pop. 4,464
Davie County SD 6,200/PK-12
220 Cherry St 27028 336-751-5921
Dr. Steve Lane, supt. Fax 751-9013
www.davie.k12.nc.us
Davie County HS 1,700/9-12
1200 Salisbury Rd 27028 336-751-5905
Penny Hedrick, prin. Fax 751-4597
North Davie MS 800/6-8
497 Farmington Rd 27028 336-998-5555
Wanda Shaffner, prin. Fax 998-7233
South Davie MS 800/6-8
700 Hardison St 27028 336-751-5941
Dr. Danny Cartner, prin. Fax 751-5656

Trinity Baptist Academy 100/K-12
2722 US Highway 601 S 27028 336-284-2832
Dr. Darrell Cox, prin.

Monroe, Union, Pop. 29,987
Union County SD 28,600/PK-12
500 N Main St Ste 700 28112 704-283-3733
Dr. Ed Davis, supt. Fax 289-1536
www.ucps.k12.nc.us
Central Academy of Technology and Arts Vo/Tech
600 Brewer Dr 28112 704-296-3088
Dr. Linda Presley, prin. Fax 296-3090
Monroe HS 1,000/9-12
1 High School Dr 28112 704-296-3130
Dr. Mike Webb, prin. Fax 296-3138
Monroe MS 800/6-8
601 E Sunset Dr 28112 704-296-3120
Montrio Belton, prin. Fax 296-3122
Parkwood HS 1,300/9-12
3220 Parkwood School Rd 28112 704-764-2900
Rob Jackson, prin. Fax 764-2907
Parkwood MS 900/6-8
3219 Parkwood School Rd 28112 704-764-2910
Neil Hawkins, prin. Fax 764-2914
Piedmont HS 1,400/9-12
3006 Sikes Mill Rd 28110 704-753-2810
Wanda Little, prin. Fax 753-2815
Piedmont MS 1,200/6-8
2816 Sikes Mill Rd 28110 704-753-2840
Anne Radke, prin. Fax 753-2846
Sun Valley HS 1,600/9-12
5211 Old Charlotte Hwy 28110 704-296-3020
Ken Roess, prin. Fax 296-3029
Union County Early College HS 9-12
4209A Old Charlotte Hwy 28110 704-290-1565
Victoria McGovern, prin. Fax 282-0956
Other Schools – See Indian Trail, Marshville, Matthews, Waxhaw

---

Sunset Park Christian S 50/K-12
1320 S Hayne St 28112 704-283-2414
Davena Carnes, prin. Fax 226-9595
Tabernacle Christian S 200/K-12
2900 Walkup Ave 28110 704-283-4395
Stephen Leonard, prin.

Montreat, Buncombe, Pop. 661

Montreat College Post-Sec.
PO Box 1267 28757 828-669-8011

Mooresville, Iredell, Pop. 20,488
Iredell-Statesville SD
Supt. — See Statesville
Brawley MS 800/6-8
664 Brawley School Rd 28117 704-664-4430
Roberta Ellis, prin. Fax 664-9846
Lake Norman HS 1,400/9-12
186 Doolie Rd 28117 704-799-8555
David Blattner, prin. Fax 799-1512
Lakeshore MS 600/6-8
244 Lakeshore School Dr 28117 704-799-0187
Jim Gaghan, prin. Fax 663-6431

Mooresville CSD 4,200/PK-12
305 N Main St 28115 704-664-5553
Dr. Bruce Boyles, supt. Fax 663-3005
www.mgsd.k12.nc.us
Mooresville HS 1,300/9-12
659 E Center Ave 28115 704-664-5545
Dr. Mark Rendell, prin. Fax 664-4381
Mooresville MS 800/7-8
160 S Magnolia St 28115 704-663-3841
Stephen Mauney, prin. Fax 664-5101
Woods Adv Tech / Arts Center Vo/Tech
574 W McLelland Ave 28115 704-663-3274
Devry Gibbs, prin. Fax 664-5102

Mooresville Christian Academy 100/K-12
PO Box 114 28115 704-663-4690
Betsy Harris, hdmstr. Fax 663-2908
NASCAR Technical Institute Post-Sec.
220 Byers Creek Rd 28117 704-658-1950

Moravian Falls, Wilkes, Pop. 1,736
Wilkes County SD
Supt. — See North Wilkesboro
Central Wilkes MS 800/6-8
3541 S NC Highway 16 28654 336-667-7453
Teresa Foster, prin. Fax 667-5825

Morehead City, Carteret, Pop. 8,847
Carteret County SD
Supt. — See Beaufort
Morehead City MS 500/6-8
400 Barbour Rd 28557 252-726-1126
Suzanne Kreuser, prin. Fax 726-4980
West Carteret HS 1,200/9-12
4700 Country Club Rd 28557 252-726-1176
Carolyn Heller, prin. Fax 726-6290

Carteret Community College Post-Sec.
3505 Arendell St 28557 252-222-6000

Morganton, Burke, Pop. 17,041
Burke County SD 14,900/PK-12
PO Box 989 28680 828-439-4312
David Burleson, supt. Fax 439-4314
www.burke.k12.nc.us
Freedom HS 2,300/9-12
511 Independence Blvd 28655 828-433-1310
Brian Oliver, prin. Fax 439-8420
Johnson MS 600/6-8
701 Lenoir Rd 28655 828-430-7340
Jack Leonard, prin. Fax 430-4801
Liberty MS 600/6-8
529 Enola Rd 28655 828-437-1330
Angela Williams, prin. Fax 432-2124
Patton HS 9-12
701 Enola Rd 28655 828-433-3000
Shanda McFarlin, prin. Fax 433-3001
Table Rock MS 700/6-8
1581 NC 126 28655 828-437-5212
Sharon Colaw, prin. Fax 439-5702
Other Schools – See Connellys Springs, Icard, Valdese

Morganton Christian Academy 100/PK-12
201 Believers Way 28655 828-437-1897
Greg Zolninger, prin. Fax 439-8948
North Carolina School for the Deaf Post-Sec.
517 W Fleming Dr 28655 828-433-2971
Western Piedmont Community College Post-Sec.
1001 Burkemont Ave 28655 828-438-6000

Mount Airy, Surry, Pop. 8,454
Mt. Airy CSD 1,900/PK-12
130 Rawley Ave 27030 336-786-8355
Tim Farley, supt. Fax 786-7553
www.mtairy.k12.nc.us
Mount Airy HS 600/9-12
1011 N South St 27030 336-789-5147
Sandy George, prin. Fax 719-2341
Mount Airy MS 500/6-8
249 Hamburg St 27030 336-789-9021
Ross Scott, prin. Fax 789-6074

Surry County SD
Supt. — See Dobson
Gentry MS 500/6-8
1915 W Pine St 27030 336-786-4155
Tom Hemmings, prin. Fax 786-6863
Meadowview MS 400/6-8
1282 Mckinney Rd 27030 336-789-0276
Angela Carson, prin. Fax 789-0449
North Surry HS 1,100/9-12
2440 W Pine St 27030 336-789-5055
Bill Goins, prin. Fax 786-8630

Northern Hospital of Surry County Post-Sec.
PO Box 1101 27030 336-719-7124
White Plains Christian S 100/K-12
609 Old Highway 601 27030 336-786-9585
David Tucker, prin.

Mount Gilead, Montgomery, Pop. 1,387
Montgomery County SD
Supt. — See Troy

West MS 600/6-8
129 NC Highway 109 S 27306 910-572-9378
Jerry Michael Penninger, prin. Fax 572-2114
West Montgomery HS 700/9-12
147 Warrior Rd 27306 910-439-6191
David Cassady, prin. Fax 439-4600

Mount Holly, Gaston, Pop. 9,676
Gaston County SD
Supt. — See Gastonia
East Gaston HS 1,500/9-12
1744 Lane Rd 28120 704-827-7251
Marty Starnes, prin. Fax 827-5974
Mount Holly MS 700/6-8
124 S Hawthorne St 28120 704-827-4811
Judy Moore, prin. Fax 822-1049

Mount Olive, Wayne, Pop. 4,442
Wayne County SD
Supt. — See Goldsboro
Mount Olive MS 300/6-8
309 Wooten St 28365 919-658-7320
Craig Uzzell, prin. Fax 658-7325

Mt. Olive College Post-Sec.
634 Henderson St 28365 919-658-2502

Mount Pleasant, Cabarrus, Pop. 1,429
Cabarrus County SD
Supt. — See Concord
Mount Pleasant HS 900/9-12
700 Walker Rd 28124 704-436-9321
Edith Sayewich, prin. Fax 436-2909
Mount Pleasant MS 700/6-8
8325 Highway 49 N 28124 704-436-9302
Sam Treadaway, prin. Fax 436-6112

Mount Ulla, Rowan
Rowan-Salisbury County SD
Supt. — See Salisbury
West Rowan HS 1,400/9-12
8050 NC Highway 801 28125 704-278-9233
Jamie Durant, prin. Fax 278-9733

Moyock, Currituck
Currituck County SD
Supt. — See Currituck
Moyock MS 600/5-8
216 Survey Rd 27958 252-435-2566
Virginia Arrington, prin. Fax 435-2576

Murfreesboro, Hertford, Pop. 2,221
Hertford County SD
Supt. — See Winton
Hertford County MS 600/7-8
1850 NC Highway 11 27855 252-398-4091
Carson Watford, prin. Fax 398-5570

Chowan University Post-Sec.
1 University Dr 27855 800-488-4101

Murphy, Cherokee, Pop. 1,565
Cherokee County SD 3,800/PK-12
911 Andrews Rd 28906 828-837-2722
Dr. Jeanette Hedrick, supt. Fax 837-5799
www.cherokee.k12.nc.us
Hiwassee Dam HS 200/9-12
267 Blue Eagle Cir 28906 828-644-5916
Kenny Garland, prin. Fax 644-9463
Murphy HS 600/9-12
234 High School Cir 28906 828-837-2426
Jerry Brackett, prin. Fax 837-2555
Murphy MS 400/6-8
65 Middle School Dr 28906 828-837-0160
Michael Rogers, prin. Fax 837-5814
Tri-County Early College HS 9-12
4610 E US Highway 64 28906 828-835-4298
Sue Ledford, prin. Fax 835-4319
Other Schools – See Andrews

Murphy Adventist S 50/PK-12
PO Box 620 28906 828-837-5857
Joan Bilbo, prin. Fax 835-9300
Tri-County Community College Post-Sec.
2300 E US Highway 64 28906 828-837-6810

Nags Head, Dare, Pop. 3,076
Dare County SD 4,900/PK-12
PO Box 1508 27959 252-480-8888
Dr. Sue Burgess, supt. Fax 480-8889
www.dare.k12.nc.us
Other Schools – See Buxton, Kill Devil Hills, Manteo

Nashville, Nash, Pop. 4,477
Nash-Rocky Mount SD 17,600/PK-12
930 Eastern Ave 27856 252-459-5220
Rick McMahon, supt. Fax 459-6404
www.nrms.k12.nc.us
Nash Central MS 800/6-8
1638 S 1st St 27856 252-459-5292
Lorenza Morgan, prin. Fax 459-5297
Other Schools – See Bailey, Battleboro, Rocky Mount, Spring Hope

New Bern, Craven, Pop. 24,106
Craven County SD 14,700/PK-12
3600 Trent Rd 28562 252-514-6300
William Rivenbark, supt. Fax 514-6351
www.craven.k12.nc.us
Craven Early College HS 9-12
800 College Ct 28562 252-637-5706
Dr. Annette Brown, prin. Fax 637-4459
Fields MS 600/6-8
2000 Dr M L King Jr Blvd 28560 252-514-6438
Thomasine Hassell, prin. Fax 514-6443
MacDonald MS 900/6-8
3127 Elizabeth Ave 28562 252-514-6450
Karen Barrow, prin. Fax 514-6456
New Bern HS 1,900/9-12
4200 Academic Dr 28562 252-514-6400
Stuart Blount, prin. Fax 514-6412
West Craven MS 900/6-8
515 NW Crvn Mddle School Rd 28562 252-514-6488
Renee Franklin, prin. Fax 514-6491
Other Schools – See Havelock, Vanceboro

Craven Community College Post-Sec.
PO Box 885 28563 252-638-4131
Ruths Chapel Christian S 200/K-12
2709 Oaks Rd 28560 252-638-1297
David Thompson, prin. Fax 638-5770

Newland, Avery, Pop. 686
Avery County SD 2,400/PK-12
PO Box 1360 28657 828-733-6006
Grace Calhoun, supt. Fax 733-8943
www.averyschools.net
Avery County HS 700/9-12
PO Box 1300 28657 828-733-0151
Mark Garrett, prin. Fax 733-1742
Avery County MS 400/6-8
PO Box 729 28657 828-733-0145
David Wright, prin. Fax 733-3506
Other Schools – See Elk Park

New London, Stanly, Pop. 320
Stanly County SD
Supt. — See Albemarle
New London Choice MS 300/6-8
PO Box 68 28127 704-463-7962
Jessie Morton, prin. Fax 463-5340
North Stanly HS 800/9-12
40206 US Highway 52 N 28127 704-463-7358
Joyce Steele, prin. Fax 463-1962

Christ the King Christian Academy 100/K-12
PO Box 279 28127 704-463-7285
John Kahl, prin. Fax 463-7285

Newport, Carteret, Pop. 3,840
Carteret County SD
Supt. — See Beaufort
Broad Creek MS 600/6-8
2382 Highway 24 28570 252-247-3135
Cathy Tomon, prin. Fax 247-5114
Croatan HS 800/9-12
1 Cougar Ln 28570 252-393-7022
Matthew Bottoms, prin. Fax 393-1223
Newport MS 500/6-8
500 E Chatham St 28570 252-223-3482
Bud Lanning, prin. Fax 223-4914

Gramercy Christian S 200/K-12
8170 Highway 70 28570 252-223-5199
Vicki Bishop, hdmstr. Fax 223-2359

Newton, Catawba, Pop. 13,016
Catawba County SD 16,700/PK-12
PO Box 1010 28658 828-464-8333
Tim Markley, supt. Fax 464-0925
www.catawba.k12.nc.us
Foard HS 1,200/9-12
3407 Plateau Rd 28658 704-462-1496
Sally Bradshaw, prin. Fax 462-1988
Jacobs Fork MS 700/7-8
3431 Plateau Rd 28658 704-462-1827
Lisa Thompson, prin. Fax 462-1600
Other Schools – See Catawba, Claremont, Hickory, Maiden

Newton-Conover CSD 2,900/PK-12
605 N Ashe Ave 28658 828-464-3191
Dr. Barry Redmond, supt. Fax 466-0063
www.nccs.k12.nc.us
Newton-Conover HS 900/9-12
338 W 15th St 28658 828-465-0920
Richard Armstrong, prin. Fax 464-1412
Newton-Conover MS 700/6-8
221 W 26th St 28658 828-464-4221
Sylvia White, prin. Fax 464-5238

Newton Grove, Sampson, Pop. 623
Sampson County SD
Supt. — See Clinton
Hobbton HS 500/9-12
12201 Hobbton Hwy 28366 910-594-0242
Wesley Johnson, prin. Fax 594-1115
Hobbton MS 400/6-8
12081 Hobbton Hwy 28366 910-594-1420
Kevin Hunter, prin. Fax 594-0049

Norlina, Warren, Pop. 1,060

Norlina Christian S 100/PK-12
PO Box 757 27563 252-456-3385
Abidan Shah, admin. Fax 456-3354

North Wilkesboro, Wilkes, Pop. 4,204
Wilkes County SD 10,300/PK-12
613 Cherry St 28659 336-667-1121
Dr. Stephen Laws, supt. Fax 667-0871
www.wilkes.k12.nc.us
North Wilkes MS 600/6-8
2776 Yellow Banks Rd 28659 336-696-2724
Wayne Shepherd, prin. Fax 696-4183
Other Schools – See Hays, Millers Creek, Moravian Falls, Ronda, Wilkesboro

---

Wilkes Regional Medical Center Post-Sec.
PO Box 609 28659 336-651-8100

Norwood, Stanly, Pop. 2,160
Stanly County SD
Supt. — See Albemarle
South Stanly HS 500/9-12
40488 S Stanly School Rd 28128 704-474-3155
Mike Campbell, prin. Fax 474-7436
South Stanly MS 400/6-8
12492 Cottonville Rd 28128 704-474-5355
Sam Basden, prin. Fax 474-5579

Oakboro, Stanly, Pop. 1,180
Stanly County SD
Supt. — See Albemarle
West Stanly HS 1,000/9-12
306 E Red Cross Rd 28129 704-485-3012
Larry Smith, prin. Fax 485-4509

Oak Ridge, Guilford, Pop. 4,196

Oak Ridge Military Academy 200/6-12
PO Box 498 27310 336-643-4131
Dr. Roy Berwick, pres. Fax 643-1797

Ocracoke, Hyde
Hyde County SD
Supt. — See Swanquarter
Ocracoke S 100/K-12
PO Box 189 27960 252-928-3251
George Ortman, prin. Fax 928-5380

Olin, Iredell
Iredell-Statesville SD
Supt. — See Statesville

North Iredell HS 1,100/9-12
156 Raider Rd 28660 704-876-4191
Mark Byrd, prin. Fax 876-1053
North Iredell MS 600/6-8
2467 Jennings Rd 28660 704-876-4802
Kelly Cooper, prin. Fax 876-6190

Orrum, Robeson, Pop. 81
Robeson County SD
Supt. — See Lumberton
Orrum MS 400/5-8
PO Box 129 28369 910-628-6285
Kent Lovett, prin. Fax 628-8408

Oxford, Granville, Pop. 8,530
Granville County SD 8,700/PK-12
101 Delacroix St 27565 919-693-4613
Thomas Williams, supt. Fax 693-7391
eclipse.gcs.k12.nc.us/
Northern Granville MS 800/7-8
3144 Webb School Rd 27565 919-693-1483
Daniel Callaghan, prin. Fax 693-1716
Webb HS 1,300/9-12
3200 Webb School Rd 27565 919-693-2521
Roy Winslow, prin. Fax 693-2589
Webb S of Health & Life Sciences 10-12
3200 Webb School Rd 27565 919-693-6411
Dr. Elizabeth Lee, prin.
Other Schools – See Butner, Creedmoor

Pantego, Beaufort, Pop. 170

Terra Ceia Christian S 200/K-12
4428 Christian School Rd 27860 252-943-2485
Ken Leys, prin. Fax 943-2139

Pembroke, Robeson, Pop. 2,693
Robeson County SD
Supt. — See Lumberton
Information Technology HS 9-12
11344 Deep Branch Rd 28372 910-521-4764
Sheila Gasque, prin. Fax 522-1791
Pembroke MS 700/6-8
PO Box 1148 28372 910-522-5013
Tommy Lowry, prin. Fax 522-5010
Swett HS 1,600/9-12
PO Box 1210 28372 910-521-3253
Antonio Wilkins, prin. Fax 521-2956

University of North Carolina at Pembroke Post-Sec.
PO Box 1510 28372 910-521-6000

Pfafftown, Forsyth
Winston-Salem/Forsyth SD
Supt. — See Winston Salem
Reagan HS 9-12
3750 Transou Rd 27040 336-703-6776
Stan Elrod, prin. Fax 922-1752

Pikeville, Wayne, Pop. 709
Wayne County SD
Supt. — See Goldsboro
Aycock HS 1,200/9-12
PO Box 159 27863 919-242-3400
Eddie Radford, prin. Fax 242-6994

Pilot Mountain, Surry, Pop. 1,277
Surry County SD
Supt. — See Dobson
East Surry HS 700/9-12
801 W Main St 27041 336-368-2251
Tony Hall, prin. Fax 368-3035
Pilot Mountain MS 500/6-8
202 Friends St 27041 336-368-2641
Dennis Lawson, prin. Fax 368-3935

Pinehurst, Moore, Pop. 11,437

Sandhills Community College Post-Sec.
3395 Airport Rd 28374 910-692-6185

Pinetops, Edgecombe, Pop. 1,320
Edgecombe County SD
Supt. — See Tarboro
South Edgecombe MS 600/5-8
230 Pinetops Crisp Rd 27864 252-827-5083
William Wright, prin. Fax 827-2811
Southwest Edgecombe HS 1,000/9-12
5912 NC Highway 43 27864 252-827-5016
Tim Pittman, prin. Fax 827-2815

Pinetown, Beaufort
Beaufort County SD
Supt. — See Washington
Northside HS 500/9-12
7868 Free Union Church Rd 27865 252-943-6341
John Smith, prin. Fax 943-6344

Pisgah Forest, Transylvania

Schenck Civilian Conservation Center Post-Sec.
98 Schenck Dr 28768 828-862-6100

Pittsboro, Chatham, Pop. 2,452
Chatham County SD 7,400/K-12
PO Box 128 27312 919-542-3626
Dr. Ann Hart, supt. Fax 542-1380
www.chatham.k12.nc.us
Horton MS 400/5-8
PO Box 639 27312 919-542-2303
Mervin Jenkins, prin. Fax 542-7099
Northwood HS 1,000/9-12
310 Northwood School Rd 27312 919-542-4181
Carrie Little, prin. Fax 542-4934
Other Schools – See Bear Creek, Siler City

Plymouth, Washington, Pop. 3,964
Washington County SD 2,300/PK-12
802 Washington St 27962 252-793-5171
Julius Walker, supt. Fax 793-5062
www.washingtonco.k12.nc.us/
Plymouth HS 500/9-12
PO Box 827 27962 252-793-3031
Gloria McCray, prin. Fax 793-3986
Other Schools – See Creswell, Roper

Polkton, Anson, Pop. 2,514
Anson County SD
Supt. — See Wadesboro
Anson Early College S 9-10
680 US Highway 74 W 28135 704-272-5395
Deborah Davis, prin.

South Piedmont Community College Post-Sec.
PO Box 126 28135 704-272-7635

Powellsville, Bertie, Pop. 250
Bertie County SD
Supt. — See Windsor
White MS 200/6-8
503 E Main St 27967 252-332-2491
Wayne Mayo, prin. Fax 209-0994

Princeton, Johnston, Pop. 1,200
Johnston County SD
Supt. — See Smithfield
Princeton S 1,300/PK-12
PO Box 38 27569 919-936-5011
W. Kirk Denning, prin. Fax 936-2962

Raeford, Hoke, Pop. 3,594
Hoke County SD 7,000/PK-12
PO Box 370 28376 910-875-4106
Dr. Freddie Williamson, supt. Fax 875-3362
www.hcs.k12.nc.us
East Hoke MS 900/6-8
4702 Fayetteville Rd 28376 910-875-5048
Dr. Althea Taylor, prin. Fax 875-9307
Hoke County HS 1,600/9-12
505 S Bethel Rd 28376 910-875-2156
Steve Hagen, prin. Fax 904-1644
Sandhoke Early College HS 9-12
505 S Bethel Rd 28376 910-875-1380
Lakisha Rice, prin. Fax 875-2302
West Hoke MS 700/6-8
200 NC Highway 211 28376 910-875-3411
Sam Queen, prin. Fax 875-0332

Raleigh, Wake, Pop. 341,530
Wake County SD 113,200/PK-12
PO Box 28041 27611 919-850-1600
Dr. Del Burns, supt. Fax 850-1819
www.wcpss.net
Athens Drive HS 1,800/9-12
1420 Athens Dr 27606 919-233-4050
WIlliam Crockett, prin. Fax 233-4082
Broughton HS 2,100/9-12
723 Saint Marys St 27605 919-856-7810
Roy Teel, prin. Fax 856-7822
Carnage MS 1,000/6-8
1425 Carnage Dr 27610 919-856-7600
Delores Fogg, prin. Fax 856-7619
Carroll MS 600/6-8
4520 Six Forks Rd 27609 919-881-1370
Mary Rich, prin. Fax 881-5016
Centennial MS 500/6-8
1900 Main Campus Dr 27606 919-233-4217
Edye Bryant, prin. Fax 233-4268
Daniels MS 1,000/6-8
2816 Oberlin Rd 27608 919-881-4860
Stephen Mares, prin. Fax 881-1418
Dillard Drive MS 1,000/6-8
5200 Dillard Dr 27606 919-233-4228
Teresa Abron, prin. Fax 854-1615
Durant Road MS 1,400/6-8
10401 Durant Rd 27614 919-870-4098
Robert E. Smith, prin. Fax 518-0021
East Millbrook MS 1,000/6-8
3801 Spring Forest Rd 27616 919-850-8755
David Ansbacher, prin. Fax 850-8770
East Wake MS 900/6-8
2700 Old Milburnie Rd 27604 919-266-8500
Bradford Shackelford, prin. Fax 266-8506
Enloe HS 2,300/9-12
128 Clarendon Cres 27610 919-856-7918
A. Beth Cochran, prin. Fax 856-7917
Leesville Road HS 2,200/9-12
8409 Leesville Rd 27613 919-870-4250
Stephen Gainey, prin. Fax 870-4287
Leesville Road MS 1,200/6-8
8405 Leesville Rd 27613 919-870-4141
Floyd Lowman, prin. Fax 870-4166
Ligon MS 1,100/6-8
706 E Lenoir St 27601 919-856-7929
Scott Lyons, prin. Fax 856-3745
Martin MS 1,000/6-8
1701 Ridge Rd 27607 919-881-4970
Wade Martin, prin. Fax 881-1416
Millbrook HS 2,000/9-12
2201 Spring Forest Rd 27615 919-850-8787
Dana King, prin. Fax 850-8803
Moore Square MS 600/6-8
301 S Person St 27601 919-664-5737
Elizabeth Colbert, prin. Fax 856-8194
River Oaks MS 6-8
4700 New Bern Ave 27610 919-231-5600
Susanne Warren, prin. Fax 231-5607
Sanderson HS 1,800/9-12
5500 Dixon Dr 27609 919-881-4800
Cathy Moore, prin. Fax 881-5006
Southeast Raleigh HS 2,200/9-12
2600 Rock Quarry Rd 27610 919-856-2800
Beulah Wright, prin. Fax 856-2827
Wake Early College of Health & Sciences 9-12
2901 Holston Ln 27610 919-212-5800
Dr. Jim Palermo, prin. Fax 212-5810
Wakefield HS 1,900/9-12
2200 Wakefield Pines Dr 27614 919-562-3600
Steve Takacs, prin. Fax 562-3623
Wakefield MS 1,100/6-8
2300 Wakefield Pines Dr 27614 919-562-3500
Mark Savage, prin. Fax 562-3527
West Millbrook MS 1,100/6-8
8115 Strickland Rd 27615 919-870-4050
Melda Smith, prin. Fax 870-4064
Other Schools – See Apex, Cary, Fuquay Varina, Garner, Holly Springs, Knightdale, Wake Forest, Wendell, Zebulon

---

Cardinal Gibbons HS 1,000/9-12
1401 Edwards Mill Rd 27607 919-834-1625
Jason Curtis, prin. Fax 834-9771
ECPI College of Technology Post-Sec.
4101 Doie Cope Rd 27613 919-571-0057
Fletcher Academy 100/1-12
400 Cedarview Ct 27609 919-782-5082
Junell Blaylock, prin. Fax 782-5980
Friendship Christian S 300/PK-12
5510 Falls of Neuse Rd 27609 919-872-2133
Dan Perryman, admin. Fax 872-7451
GRACE Christian S 400/PK-12
801 Buck Jones Rd 27606 919-783-6618
Kathie Thompson, prin. Fax 783-0856
Meredith College Post-Sec.
3800 Hillsborough St 27607 919-760-8600
Neuse Baptist Christian S 200/K-12
8700 Capital Blvd 27616 919-876-0990
Kenneth Bartholomew, admin. Fax 876-3168
North Carolina State University Post-Sec.
PO Box 7001 27695 919-515-2011
North Raleigh Christian Academy 1,200/K-12
7300 Perry Creek Rd 27616 919-573-7900
Dr. S.L. Sherrill, supt. Fax 573-7901
Peace College Post-Sec.
15 E Peace St 27604 919-508-2000
Raleigh Christian Academy 400/PK-12
2110 Trawick Rd 27604 919-872-2215
Dwight Ausley, admin. Fax 861-1000
Ravenscroft S 1,100/PK-12
7409 Falls Of Neuse Rd 27615 919-847-0900
Doreen Kelly, hdmstr. Fax 846-2371
St. Augustine's College Post-Sec.
1315 Oakwood Ave 27610 919-516-4000
St. David's S 500/K-12
3400 White Oak Rd 27609 919-782-3331
Kevin Lockerbie, hdmstr. Fax 571-3330
St. Mary's College Prep S 300/9-12
900 Hillsborough St 27603 919-424-4000
Theo Coonrod, hdmstr. Fax 424-4122
School of Communication Arts Post-Sec.
3000 Wakefield Crossing Dr 27614 800-288-7442
Shaw University Post-Sec.
118 E South St 27601 919-546-8200
Strayer University Post-Sec.
3200 Spring Forest Rd 27616 919-878-9900
Trinity Academy of Raleigh 200/K-12
10224 Baileywick Rd 27613 919-786-0114
Dr. Robert Littlejohn, prin.
Wake Christian Academy 900/K-12
5500 Wake Academy Dr 27603 919-772-6264
Mike Woods, admin. Fax 779-0948
Wake Technical Community College Post-Sec.
9101 Fayetteville Rd 27603 919-662-3400
Word of God Christian Academy 200/PK-12
3000 Rock Quarry Rd 27610 919-834-8200
Anesha Pittman, prin. Fax 899-3640

Ramseur, Randolph, Pop. 1,704
Randolph County SD
Supt. — See Asheboro
Eastern Randolph HS 1,400/9-12
390 Eastern Randolph Rd 27316 336-824-2351
Parks Allen, prin. Fax 824-6164
Southeastern Randolph MS 700/6-8
5302 Foushee Rd 27316 336-824-6700
Stephanie Bridges, prin. Fax 824-6705

Faith Christian S 300/PK-12
5449 Brookhaven Rd 27316 336-824-4156
William Hohneisen, prin. Fax 824-1012

Randleman, Randolph, Pop. 3,653
Randolph County SD
Supt. — See Asheboro
Randleman HS 1,100/9-12
4396 Tigers Den Rd 27317 336-498-2682
Tim Setzer, prin. Fax 498-2609
Randleman MS 900/6-8
800 High Point St 27317 336-498-2606
Dennis Hamilton, prin. Fax 498-8015

Red Springs, Robeson, Pop. 3,484
Robeson County SD
Supt. — See Lumberton
Red Springs HS 700/9-12
509 N Vance St 28377 910-843-4211
Melissa Flowers, prin. Fax 843-2825
Red Springs MS 600/5-8
302 W 2nd Ave 28377 910-843-3883
Richard Dixon, prin. Fax 843-3765

Macdonald Academy 200/PK-12
200 N College St 28377 910-843-4995
Jonathon Good, hdmstr. Fax 843-8102

Reidsville, Rockingham, Pop. 14,778
Rockingham County SD
Supt. — See Eden
Reidsville HS 1,000/9-12
1901 S Park Dr 27320 336-349-6361
Janet King, prin. Fax 349-3205
Reidsville MS 800/6-8
1903 S Park Dr 27320 336-342-4726
Louise Uziel, prin. Fax 342-9434
Rockingham County HS 1,200/9-12
180 High School Rd 27320 336-634-3220
Wayne Barnett, prin. Fax 342-7794
Rockingham County MS 900/6-8
182 High School Rd 27320 336-616-0073
Steve Hall, prin. Fax 616-0870

Community Baptist S 200/K-12
509 Triangle Rd 27320 336-342-5991
Celeste Bailey, prin. Fax 342-7180

Richlands, Onslow, Pop. 827
Onslow County SD
Supt. — See Jacksonville
Richlands HS 800/9-12
PO Box 218 28574 910-324-4191
Maria Johnson, prin. Fax 324-6688
Trexler MS 600/6-8
PO Box 188 28574 910-324-4414
Susanne Long, prin. Fax 324-3963

Roanoke Rapids, Halifax, Pop. 16,458
Halifax County SD
Supt. — See Halifax
Davie MS 500/6-8
4391 US Highway 158 27870 252-519-0300
Claude Cooper, prin. Fax 519-0222

Roanoke Rapids CSD 3,000/PK-12
536 Hamilton St 27870 252-519-7100
Dennis Sawyer, supt. Fax 535-5919
www.rrgsd.org
Chaloner MS 700/6-8
2100 Virginia Ave 27870 252-519-7600
Jimmy Kearney, prin. Fax 537-9947
Roanoke Rapids HS 900/9-12
800 Hamilton St 27870 252-519-7200
Monica Smith-Woofter, prin. Fax 537-3606

Halifax Academy 500/PK-12
1400 Three Bridges Rd 27870 252-537-8527
Glenn Wiggs, hdmstr. Fax 308-0555

Robbins, Moore, Pop. 1,217
Moore County SD
Supt. — See Carthage
Elise MS 200/6-8
PO Box 850 27325 910-948-2421
Brenda Cassady, prin. Fax 948-4112
North Moore HS 600/9-12
PO Box 9 27325 910-464-3105
Michael Tylavsky, prin. Fax 464-6016

Robbinsville, Graham, Pop. 736
Graham County SD 1,300/PK-12
52 Moose Branch Rd 28771 828-479-3413
Rick Davis, supt. Fax 479-7950
www.gcsk12.com
Robbinsville HS 400/9-12
PO Box 625 28771 828-479-3330
Scott Perkins, prin. Fax 479-1052
Robbinsville MS 200/7-8
PO Box 940 28771 828-479-8488
Bruce Snyder, prin. Fax 479-6847

Robersonville, Martin, Pop. 1,637
Martin County SD
Supt. — See Williamston
Roanoke HS 400/9-12
21077 NC Highway 903 27871 252-795-4081
Vicki Dixon, prin. Fax 795-4187
Roanoke MS 300/6-8
21230 NC Highway 903 27871 252-795-3910
David Jenkins, prin. Fax 795-3890

Rockingham, Richmond, Pop. 9,220
Richmond County SD
Supt. — See Hamlet
Richmond SHS 1,500/10-12
PO Box 1748 28380 910-997-9812
Cory Satterfield, prin. Fax 997-9816
Rockingham JHS 800/7-9
415 Wall St 28379 910-997-9827
Linwood Huffman, prin. Fax 997-9859
Rohanen JHS 300/7-9
252 School St 28379 910-997-9839
T. K. Thrower, prin. Fax 997-8172

Temple Christian S 200/K-12
165 Airport Rd 28379 910-997-3179
Rev. Joey Byrd, prin.

Rockwell, Rowan, Pop. 1,982

Rockwell Christian S 200/K-12
PO Box 609 28138 704-279-8854
Ken Prater, prin. Fax 279-1442

Rocky Mount, Edgecombe, Pop. 56,626
Edgecombe County SD
Supt. — See Tarboro
West Edgecombe MS 700/4-8
6301 Nobles Mill Pond Rd 27801 252-446-2030
Laverne Daniels, prin. Fax 446-1592

Nash-Rocky Mount SD
Supt. — See Nashville
Edwards MS 1,000/6-8
720 Edwards St 27803 252-977-3328
Beezie Whitaker, prin. Fax 446-5527
Nash Central HS 1,200/9-12
4279 Nash Central High Rd 27804 252-451-2860
LeRoy Hartsfield, prin. Fax 451-1279
Northern Nash HS 1,300/9-12
4230 Green Hills Rd 27804 252-937-5600
Chip Hodges, prin. Fax 443-5448
Parker MS 600/6-8
1500 E Virginia St 27801 252-977-3486
Charles Davis, prin. Fax 446-5756
Rocky Mount HS 1,300/9-12
308 S Tillery St 27804 252-977-3085
Judy Bradshaw, prin. Fax 985-4321

Faith Christian S 300/K-12
PO Box 8165 27804 252-443-1700
Keith Griffin, hdmstr. Fax 443-2456
Falls Road Baptist Church S 200/K-12
113 Trevathan St 27804 252-977-2401
Jonathan Wright, prin. Fax 977-3493
Nash Community College Post-Sec.
PO Box 7488 27804 252-443-4011
North Carolina Wesleyan College Post-Sec.
3400 N Wesleyan Blvd 27804 252-985-5100
Rocky Mount Academy 400/PK-12
1313 Avondale Ave 27803 252-443-4126
Thomas Stevens, hdmstr. Fax 937-7922

Rocky Point, Pender
Pender County SD
Supt. — See Burgaw
Cape Fear MS 500/6-8
1886 NC Highway 133 28457 910-602-3334
Leah Dove, prin. Fax 602-3036
Trask HS 600/9-12
14328 NC Highway 210 28457 910-602-6810
Randy Richardson, prin. Fax 602-6662

Ronda, Wilkes, Pop. 467
Wilkes County SD
Supt. — See North Wilkesboro
East Wilkes HS 500/9-12
PO Box 368 28670 336-835-4772
Eric Barker, prin. Fax 835-9298
East Wilkes MS 500/6-8
2202 Macedonia Church Rd 28670 336-928-9800
Jodi Weatherman, prin. Fax 957-8734

Roper, Washington, Pop. 588
Washington County SD
Supt. — See Plymouth
Washington County Union MS 600/5-8
PO Box 309 27970 252-793-2835
Earnell Purington, prin. Fax 793-4411

Roseboro, Sampson, Pop. 1,297
Sampson County SD
Supt. — See Clinton
Roseboro-Salemburg MS 500/6-8
PO Box 976 28382 910-525-4764
Lisa Reynolds, prin. Fax 525-3471

Rose Hill, Duplin, Pop. 1,377
Duplin County SD
Supt. — See Kenansville
Charity MS 600/6-8
PO Box 70 28458 910-289-3323
Janice Wynn, prin. Fax 289-2064

Rosman, Transylvania, Pop. 483
Transylvania County SD
Supt. — See Brevard

Rosman HS 400/9-12
749 Pickens Hwy 28772 828-862-4284
Larry Clayton, prin. Fax 862-4765
Rosman MS 300/6-8
749 Pickens Hwy 28772 828-862-4286
Jenny Moreno, prin. Fax 885-8222

Rowland, Robeson, Pop. 1,148
Robeson County SD
Supt. — See Lumberton
Rowland MS 200/6-8
408 W Chapel St 28383 910-422-3983
Dr. Penny Britt, prin. Fax 422-8369
South Robeson HS 500/9-12
3268 S Robeson Rd 28383 910-422-3987
DeRay Cole, prin. Fax 422-3221

Roxboro, Person, Pop. 8,755
Person County SD 5,800/PK-12
304 S Morgan St Ste 25 27573 336-599-2191
Ronnie Bugnar, supt. Fax 599-2194
www.person.k12.nc.us
Northern MS 800/6-8
1935 Carver Dr, 336-599-6344
Jerry Caricofe, prin. Fax 598-9207
Person HS 1,800/9-12
1010 Ridge Rd 27573 336-599-8321
Margaret Bradsher, prin. Fax 599-6583
Southern MS 700/6-8
209 Southern Middle School 27573 336-599-6995
Bill Boston, prin. Fax 503-0587

Piedmont Community College Post-Sec.
PO Box 1197 27573 336-599-1181
Roxboro Christian Academy 200/K-12
PO Box 1357 27573 336-599-0208
Nena Morton, prin.

Ruffin, Rockingham

Rhema Christian Academy 50/K-12
6901 NC Highway 700 27326 336-939-7070
Debra Carter, pres.

Rutherfordton, Rutherford, Pop. 4,099
Rutherford County SD
Supt. — See Forest City
R-S Central HS 1,100/9-12
PO Box 1119 28139 828-287-3304
Tim Davis, prin. Fax 286-2024
R-S MS 800/6-8
545 Charlotte Rd 28139 828-286-4461
Greg Carter, prin. Fax 286-4882

Saint Pauls, Robeson, Pop. 2,235
Robeson County SD
Supt. — See Lumberton
Saint Pauls HS 1,000/9-12
648 N Stage Rd 28384 910-865-4177
Stephen Gaskins, prin. Fax 737-9750
Saint Pauls MS 500/6-8
526 W Shaw St 28384 910-865-4070
Barbara Thompson, prin. Fax 737-9360

Salemburg, Sampson, Pop. 480
Sampson County SD
Supt. — See Clinton
Lakewood HS 500/9-12
245 Lakewood School Rd 28385 910-525-5171
Gerald Johnson, prin. Fax 525-3344

Salisbury, Rowan, Pop. 27,563
Rowan-Salisbury County SD 20,900/PK-12
PO Box 2349 28145 704-636-7500
Dr. Judy Grissom, supt. Fax 630-6129
www.rss.k12.nc.us
East Rowan HS 1,400/9-12
175 Saint Luke Church Rd 28146 704-279-5232
G. Kelly Sparger, prin. Fax 279-4549
Erwin MS 900/6-8
170 Saint Luke Church Rd 28146 704-279-7265
Ray Whitaker, prin. Fax 279-7954
Henderson Independent HS 200/8-12
1215 N Main St 28144 704-639-3103
Robert Pulliam, prin. Fax 639-3118
Knox MS 600/6-8
1625 W Park Rd 28144 704-633-2922
Susan Heaggans, prin. Fax 638-3538
Salisbury HS 900/9-12
500 Lincolnton Rd 28144 704-636-1221
Dr. N. Windsor Eagle, prin. Fax 639-3029
Southeast MS 700/6-8
1570 Peeler Rd 28146 704-638-5561
Fax 638-5719
West Rowan MS 800/6-8
5925 Statesville Blvd 28147 704-633-4775
Cynthia Misenheimer, prin. Fax 633-3157
Other Schools – See China Grove, Landis, Mount Ulla, Spencer

Catawba College Post-Sec.
2300 W Innes St 28144 704-637-4111
Hood Theological Seminary Post-Sec.
1810 Lutheran Synod Dr 28144 704-636-6823
Livingstone College Post-Sec.
701 W Monroe St 28144 704-797-1000
North Hills Christian S 200/PK-12
2970 W Innes St 28144 704-636-3005
Carolyn Barker, hdmstr. Fax 636-3597
Rowan-Cabarrus Community College Post-Sec.
PO Box 1595 28145 704-637-0760

Sanford, Lee, Pop. 26,710
Lee County SD 9,200/K-12
PO Box 1010 27331 919-774-6226
Dr. James McCormick, supt. Fax 776-0443
www.lee.k12.nc.us
East Lee MS 1,100/6-8
1337 Broadway Rd 27332 919-776-8441
Dr. Tom Harvley-Felder, prin. Fax 774-7451
Lee County HS 2,600/9-12
1708 Nash St 27330 919-776-7541
Greg Batten, prin. Fax 718-7170
Lee Early College S 9-12
1105 Kelly Dr 27330 919-718-7259
Robert Dietrich, prin. Fax 718-7519
Southern Lee HS 9-12
2301 Tramway Rd 27332 919-718-2400
Hans Lassiter, prin. Fax 718-2410
West Lee MS 1,100/6-8
3301 Wicker St 27330 919-775-7351
Stella Farrow, prin. Fax 776-3694

Central Carolina Community College Post-Sec.
1105 Kelly Dr 27330 919-775-5401
Grace Christian S 300/K-12
2601 Jefferson Davis Hwy 27332 919-774-4415
William Carver, admin. Fax 718-6777
Lee Christian S 400/PK-12
3220 Keller Andrews Rd 27330 919-708-5115
Stephen Coble, prin. Fax 708-6933

Scotland Neck, Halifax, Pop. 2,240
Halifax County SD
Supt. — See Halifax
Brawley MS 300/6-8
PO Box 449 27874 252-826-4513
Allen Sledge, prin. Fax 826-5098

Selma, Johnston, Pop. 6,646
Johnston County SD
Supt. — See Smithfield
Selma MS 600/5-8
1533 US Highway 301 N 27576 919-965-2555
Jennifer Moore, prin. Fax 202-0116

Seven Springs, Wayne, Pop. 85
Wayne County SD
Supt. — See Goldsboro
Spring Creek JSHS 1,000/6-12
4340 Indian Springs Rd 28578 919-751-7160
Steve Clingan, prin. Fax 751-7202

Shallotte, Brunswick, Pop. 1,588
Brunswick County SD
Supt. — See Bolivia
Shallotte MS 900/6-8
225 Village Rd 28470 910-754-6882
Jerry Small, prin. Fax 754-3108
West Brunswick HS 1,300/9-12
550 Whiteville Rd NW 28470 910-754-4338
Jim Jordan, prin. Fax 754-3110

Shelby, Cleveland, Pop. 21,263
Cleveland County SD 9,800/PK-12
130 S Post Rd Ste 2 28152 704-476-8000
Dr. Bruce Boyles, supt. Fax 476-8300
www.clevelandcountyschools.org
Crest HS 1,600/9-12
800 Old Boiling Springs Rd 28152 704-482-5354
Roger Harris, prin. Fax 482-1187
Crest MS of Technology 1,300/6-8
315 Beaver Dam Church Rd 28152 704-482-0343
Jeff Benfield, prin. Fax 487-0378
Shelby HS 9-12
230 E Dixon Blvd 28152 704-482-3409
Dianna Bridges, prin. Fax 487-2869
Shelby MS 6-8
400 W Marion St 28150 704-482-6331
Tim Quattlebaum, prin. Fax 487-2889
Other Schools – See Kings Mountain, Lawndale

Cleveland Community College Post-Sec.
137 S Post Rd 28152 704-484-4000

Siler City, Chatham, Pop. 8,079
Chatham County SD
Supt. — See Pittsboro
Chatham MS 500/5-8
2025 S 2nd Avenue Ext 27344 919-663-2414
Brenda Griffin, prin. Fax 663-2871
Jordan-Matthews HS 700/9-12
910 E Cardinal St 27344 919-742-2916
Norma Boone, prin. Fax 742-2201

Smithfield, Johnston, Pop. 11,970
Johnston County SD 26,100/PK-12
PO Box 1336 27577 919-934-6031
Anthony L. Parker Ed.D., supt. Fax 934-6035
www.johnston.k12.nc.us
Smithfield MS 800/6-8
1455 Buffalo Rd 27577 919-934-4696
Anne Meredith, prin. Fax 934-7552
Smithfield-Selma HS 1,500/9-12
700 E Booker Dairy Rd 27577 919-934-5191
Patrick Jacobs, prin. Fax 934-3001
Other Schools – See Benson, Clayton, Four Oaks, Garner, Kenly, Micro, Princeton, Selma

---

Johnston Christian Academy 200/PK-12
PO Box 1599 27577 919-934-1248
John Floyd, prin. Fax 934-1289
Johnston Community College Post-Sec.
PO Box 2350 27577 919-934-3051

Snow Hill, Greene, Pop. 1,442
Greene County SD 3,300/PK-12
301 Kingold Blvd 28580 252-747-3425
Dr. Steve Mazingo, supt. Fax 747-5942
www.gcsedu.org/
Greene Central HS 900/9-12
140 School Dr 28580 252-747-3814
Dr. Randy Bledsoe, prin. Fax 747-5972
Greene County MS 800/6-8
485 Middle School Rd 28580 252-747-8191
Gregory Monroe, prin. Fax 747-8696
Greene Early College HS 9-12
818 Hwy 91 28580 252-747-9044
Steve Bryant, prin. Fax 747-9046

Southern Pines, Moore, Pop. 11,881
Moore County SD
Supt. — See Carthage
Pinecrest HS 2,000/9-12
250 Voit Gilmore Rd 28387 910-692-6554
Joel County, prin. Fax 692-0606

Calvary Christian S 200/K-12
400 S Bennett St 28387 910-692-8311
Dwight Creech, prin. Fax 692-1992
O'Neal S 400/PK-12
PO Box 290 28388 910-692-6920
John Neiswender, hdmstr. Fax 692-6930

Southport, Brunswick, Pop. 2,725
Brunswick County SD
Supt. — See Bolivia
South Brunswick HS 1,000/9-12
280 Cougar Rd 28461 910-845-2204
Van Pennell, prin. Fax 845-8974
South Brunswick MS 900/6-8
100 Cougar Rd 28461 910-845-2771
Patricia Underwood, prin. Fax 845-8972

Brunswick Christian Academy 50/6-8
4928 Southport Supply Rd SE 28461
Debra Hill, dir. 910-457-7000

Sparta, Alleghany, Pop. 1,797
Alleghany County SD 1,600/PK-12
85 Peachtree St 28675 336-372-4345
Dr. Jeff Cox, supt. Fax 372-4204
www.alleghany.k12.nc.us
Alleghany HS 400/9-12
404 Trojan Ave 28675 336-372-4554
Paul Crouse, prin. Fax 372-2680

Spencer, Rowan, Pop. 3,345
Rowan-Salisbury County SD
Supt. — See Salisbury
North Rowan HS 800/9-12
300 N Whitehead Ave 28159 704-636-4420
Rodney Bass, prin. Fax 639-3033
North Rowan MS 700/6-8
512 Charles St 28159 704-639-3018
Darrell McDowell, prin. Fax 639-3099

Spindale, Rutherford, Pop. 3,921
Rutherford County SD
Supt. — See Forest City
REaCH S 9-12
PO Box 804 28160 828-286-3636
Dr. Laura Thomas, prin. Fax 286-8109

Isothermal Community College Post-Sec.
PO Box 804 28160 828-286-3636

Spring Hope, Nash, Pop. 1,272
Nash-Rocky Mount SD
Supt. — See Nashville
Southern Nash MS 1,100/6-8
5301 S NC Highway 581 27882 252-478-4807
Carina Bissette, prin. Fax 478-4861

Spring Lake, Cumberland, Pop. 8,197
Cumberland County SD
Supt. — See Fayetteville
Spring Lake MS 600/6-8
612 Spring Ave 28390 910-497-1175
James Ellerbe, prin. Fax 497-1598

Harnett County SD
Supt. — See Lillington
Overhills HS 900/9-12
2495 Ray Rd 28390 910-436-1436
John Castranio, prin. Fax 436-0413
Overhills MS 900/6-8
2711 Ray Rd 28390 910-436-0009
Rose Cooper, prin. Fax 436-0948

Spruce Pine, Mitchell, Pop. 1,998
Mitchell County SD
Supt. — See Bakersville
Harris MS 300/6-8
121 Harris St 28777 828-765-2321
Chad Calhoun, prin. Fax 765-1595

Altapass Christian S 50/K-12
50 Altapass Trl 28777 828-765-0660
Debbie McKinney, prin. Fax 765-0660
Mayland Community College Post-Sec.
PO Box 547 28777 828-765-7351

Stanley, Gaston, Pop. 3,094
Gaston County SD
Supt. — See Gastonia
Stanley MS 600/6-8
317 Hovis Rd 28164 704-263-2941
Staci Bradley, prin. Fax 263-0993

Statesville, Iredell, Pop. 24,875
Iredell-Statesville SD 19,500/PK-12
PO Box 911 28687 704-872-8931
Dr. Terry Holliday, supt. Fax 871-2834
www.iss.k12.nc.us
Collaborative College for Technology 9-12
500 W Broad St 28677 704-978-5450
Lisa Miller, prin. Fax 978-5452
East Iredell MS 700/6-8
590 Chestnut Grove Rd 28625 704-872-4666
Dr. Katherine Stillerman, prin. Fax 873-6602
South Iredell HS 900/9-12
299 Old Mountain Rd 28677 704-528-4536
David Dixon, prin. Fax 528-0882
Statesville HS 1,200/9-12
474 N Center St 28677 704-873-3491
Larry Rogers, prin. Fax 878-6195
Statesville MS 500/6-8
321 Clegg St 28677 704-872-2135
Terry Jonas, prin. Fax 871-9279
West Iredell HS 1,100/9-12
213 Warrior Dr 28625 704-873-2181
Todd Holden, prin. Fax 873-0356
West Iredell MS 800/6-8
303 Watermelon Rd 28625 704-873-2887
Pat Svanson, prin. Fax 881-0582
Other Schools – See Mooresville, Olin, Troutman

Crossroads Christian S 100/PK-12
PO Box 706 28687 704-873-5484
June Gaither, admin. Fax 871-1596
Gardner-Webb University Post-Sec.
PO Box 908 28687 704-872-3664
Mitchell Community College Post-Sec.
500 W Broad St 28677 704-878-3200
Southview Christian S 100/K-12
625 Wallace Springs Rd 28677 704-872-9554
Walter Wagner, prin. Fax 872-4359
Statesville Christian S 500/PK-12
1210 Museum Rd 28625 704-873-9511
C. David Balik, hdmstr. Fax 873-0841

Stokesdale, Guilford, Pop. 3,524

Oak Level Baptist Academy 100/K-12
1569 Oak Level Church Rd 27357 336-643-9288
Clay Walker, prin.

Sugar Grove, Watauga

Jung Tao School of Chinese Medicine Post-Sec.
207 Dale Adams Rd 28679 828-297-4181

Supply, Brunswick

Brunswick Community College — Post-Sec.
PO Box 30 28462 — 910-755-7300

Swannanoa, Buncombe, Pop. 3,538
Buncombe County SD
Supt. — See Asheville
Owen MS — 700/6-8
730 Old US 70 Hwy 28778 — 828-686-7739
Vicky Matthews, prin. — Fax 686-7938

Asheville Christian Academy — 500/PK-12
PO Box 1089 28778 — 828-581-2200
William George, hdmstr. — Fax 581-2218

Swanquarter, Hyde
Hyde County SD — 700/PK-12
PO Box 217 27885 — 252-926-3281
Gregory Todd, supt. — Fax 926-3083
www.hyde.k12.nc.us/
Mattamuskeet HS — 200/9-12
20392 US Highway 264 27885 — 252-926-0221
Linwood Smith, prin. — Fax 926-0224
Mattamuskeet MS — 100/6-8
20400 US Highway 264 27885 — 252-926-0015
Rosemary Mann, prin. — Fax 926-0016
Other Schools – See Ocracoke

Swansboro, Onslow, Pop. 1,338
Onslow County SD
Supt. — See Jacksonville
Swansboro HS — 1,000/9-12
161 Queens Creek Rd 28584 — 910-326-4300
Christine Andre, prin. — Fax 326-1674
Swansboro MS — 800/6-8
1240 W Corbett Ave 28584 — 910-326-3601
Darin Cloninger, prin. — Fax 326-5848

Sylva, Jackson, Pop. 2,398
Jackson County SD — 3,600/PK-12
398 Hospital Rd 28779 — 828-586-2311
Sue Nations, supt. — Fax 586-5450
www.jcps.k12.nc.us
Smoky Mountain HS — 1,000/9-12
100 Smoky Mountain Dr 28779 — 828-586-2177
Alex Bell, prin. — Fax 586-2374
Other Schools – See Cashiers

Southwestern Community College — Post-Sec.
447 College Dr 28779 — 828-586-4091

Tabor City, Columbus, Pop. 2,629
Columbus County SD
Supt. — See Whiteville
South Columbus HS — 800/9-12
40 Stallion Dr 28463 — 910-653-4073
Dr. Maudie Davis, prin. — Fax 653-9461
Tabor City MS — 300/6-8
701 W 6th St 28463 — 910-653-3637
Dale Norris, prin. — Fax 653-2093

Tarboro, Edgecombe, Pop. 10,600
Edgecombe County SD — 7,800/PK-12
PO Box 7128 27886 — 252-641-2600
Roland Whitted, supt. — Fax 641-5714
www.ecps.us/community/
Martin MS — 500/7-8
400 E Johnston St 27886 — 252-641-5710
Douglas Edwards, prin. — Fax 641-5713
North Edgecombe HS — 400/9-12
7589 NC Highway 33 NW 27886 — 252-823-3562
Derrick Jordan, prin. — Fax 823-7847
Tarboro HS — 800/9-12
1400 W Howard Ave 27886 — 252-823-4284
Michael Lutz, prin. — Fax 823-0862
Other Schools – See Battleboro, Pinetops, Rocky Mount

Edgecombe Community College — Post-Sec.
2009 W Wilson St 27886 — 252-823-5166

Tar Heel, Bladen, Pop. 69
Bladen County SD
Supt. — See Elizabethtown
Tar Heel MS — 400/5-8
PO Box 128 28392 — 910-862-2475
Susan Inman, prin. — Fax 872-5599

Taylorsville, Alexander, Pop. 1,855
Alexander County SD — 5,700/PK-12
700 Liledoun Rd 28681 — 828-632-7001
Jack Hoke, supt. — Fax 632-8862
www.alexander.k12.nc.us
Alexander Central HS — 1,600/9-12
223 School Dr 28681 — 828-632-7063
Steve Bumgarner, prin. — Fax 632-5387
West Alexander MS — 700/6-8
85 Bulldog Ln 28681 — 828-495-4611
Susan Gantt, prin. — Fax 495-3527
Other Schools – See Hiddenite

Teachey, Duplin, Pop. 254
Duplin County SD
Supt. — See Kenansville
Wallace-Rose Hill HS — 700/9-12
602 High School Rd 28464 — 910-285-7501
M.D. Guthrie, prin. — Fax 285-1116

Thomasville, Davidson, Pop. 25,872
Davidson County SD
Supt. — See Lexington
Brown MS — 800/6-8
1140 Kendall Mill Rd 27360 — 336-475-8845
Randy Holmes, prin. — Fax 475-3842
East Davidson HS — 900/9-12
1408 Lake Rd 27360 — 336-476-4814
Cathi Smith, prin. — Fax 476-2982
Ledford HS — 900/9-12
140 Jesse Green Rd 27360 — 336-769-9671
Bill Butts, prin. — Fax 769-0650
Ledford MS — 900/6-8
3954 N NC Highway 109 27360 — 336-476-4816
J. Evan Myers, prin. — Fax 476-1479

Thomasville CSD — 2,500/K-12
400 Turner St 27360 — 336-474-4200
Daniel Cockman, supt. — Fax 475-0356
www.tcs.k12.nc.us
Thomasville HS — 700/9-12
410 Unity St 27360 — 336-474-4250
Dirk Gurley, prin. — Fax 476-7430
Thomasville MS — 600/6-8
400 Unity St 27360 — 336-474-4120
Georgia Marshall, prin. — Fax 472-5081

Carolina Christian Academy — 100/K-12
367 Academy Dr 27360 — 336-472-8950
Daniel Lee, prin. — Fax 472-8920

Topton, Macon
Macon County SD
Supt. — See Franklin
Nantahala S — 100/K-12
213 Winding Stairs Rd 28781 — 828-321-4388
Chris Baldwin, prin. — Fax 321-4834

Trenton, Jones, Pop. 253
Jones County SD — 1,400/PK-12
320 W Jones St 28585 — 252-448-2531
Dr. Ethan Lenker, supt. — Fax 448-1394
www.jonesnc.net
Jones HS — 400/9-12
1490 NC Highway 58 S 28585 — 252-448-2451
Joletha White, prin. — Fax 448-1034
Jones MS — 400/6-8
190 Old New Bern Rd 28585 — 252-448-3956
Steve Hill, prin. — Fax 448-1044

Trinity, Randolph, Pop. 6,915
Randolph County SD
Supt. — See Asheboro
Archdale-Trinity MS — 800/7-8
PO Box 232 27370 — 336-431-2589
Andrea Haynes, prin. — Fax 431-1809
Trinity HS — 1,400/9-12
5746 Trinity High School Dr 27370 — 336-861-6870
Daryl Barnes, prin. — Fax 861-8613
Uwharrie MS — 400/6-8
1463 Pleasant Union Rd 27370 — 336-241-3900
Linda Johnson, prin. — Fax 241-3904

Troutman, Iredell, Pop. 1,706
Iredell-Statesville SD
Supt. — See Statesville
Troutman MS — 500/6-8
PO Box 807 28166 — 704-528-5137
Judy Gaghan, prin. — Fax 528-4006

Troy, Montgomery, Pop. 3,269
Montgomery County SD — 4,700/PK-12
PO Box 427 27371 — 910-576-6511
Dr. Donna Cox Peters, supt. — Fax 576-2044
www.montgomery.k12.nc.us
Other Schools – See Biscoe, Mount Gilead

Montgomery Community College — Post-Sec.
1011 Page St 27371 — 910-576-6222

Tyner, Chowan
Edenton/Chowan County SD
Supt. — See Edenton
Chowan MS — 600/6-8
2845 Virginia Rd 27980 — 252-221-4131
Tanya Turner, prin. — Fax 221-8033

Valdese, Burke, Pop. 4,530
Burke County SD
Supt. — See Morganton
Heritage MS — 700/6-8
1951 Enon Rd 28690 — 828-874-0731
Doug Rhoney, prin. — Fax 879-6330

Vanceboro, Craven, Pop. 846
Craven County SD
Supt. — See New Bern
West Craven HS — 1,100/9-12
2600 Streets Ferry Rd 28586 — 252-244-3200
Leon Farrow, prin. — Fax 244-3207

Wadesboro, Anson, Pop. 5,263
Anson County SD — 4,400/PK-12
PO Box 719 28170 — 704-694-4417
Dr. George Truman, supt. — Fax 694-7470
www.anson.k12.nc.us
Anson HS — 1,200/9-12
96 Anson High School Rd 28170 — 704-694-9301
Michael McLeod, prin. — Fax 694-4570
Anson MS — 700/7-8
832 US Highway 52 N 28170 — 704-694-3945
Howard McLean, prin. — Fax 694-5209
Other Schools – See Polkton

Anson College of Cosmetology — Post-Sec.
1217 E Caswell St 28170 — 704-694-6677

Wake Forest, Wake, Pop. 20,126
Wake County SD
Supt. — See Raleigh
Heritage MS — 700/6-8
3500 Rogers Rd 27587 — 919-562-6204
LaVaughan Buchanan, prin. — Fax 562-6227
Wake Forest-Rolesville HS — 1,800/9-12
420 Stadium Dr 27587 — 919-554-8611
Andre Smith, prin. — Fax 554-8617
Wake Forest-Rolesville MS — 1,000/6-8
1800 S Main St 27587 — 919-554-8440
Elaine Hanzer, prin. — Fax 554-8435

Southeastern Baptist Theological Sem. — Post-Sec.
PO Box 1889 27588 — 919-761-2280

Walkertown, Forsyth, Pop. 4,294
Winston-Salem/Forsyth SD
Supt. — See Winston Salem
Walkertown MS — 700/6-8
PO Box 1149 27051 — 336-595-2161
Piper Hendrix, prin. — Fax 595-3423

Walnut Cove, Stokes, Pop. 1,571
Stokes County SD
Supt. — See Danbury
Southeastern Stokes MS — 500/6-8
1044 N Main St 27052 — 336-591-4371
Jo Beth Clark, prin. — Fax 591-8164
South Stokes HS — 700/9-12
1100 S Stokes High Dr 27052 — 336-994-2995
Debbie Whitaker, prin. — Fax 994-2608

Wanchese, Dare, Pop. 1,380

Wanchese Christian Academy — 100/PK-12
PO Box 201 27981 — 252-473-5797
Cherie Peters, prin. — Fax 473-1640

Warrensville, Ashe
Ashe County SD
Supt. — See Jefferson
Ashe County MS — 500/7-8
PO Box 259 28693 — 336-384-3591
W. Bobby Ashley, prin. — Fax 384-2112

Warrenton, Warren, Pop. 770
Warren County SD — 3,100/K-12
PO Box 110 27589 — 252-257-3184
Dr. Ray Spain, supt. — Fax 257-5357
www.wcsk12.org
Warren County HS — 1,000/9-12
149 Campus Dr 27589 — 252-257-4413
Dr. Tony Cozart, prin. — Fax 257-1019
Warren County MS — 800/6-8
118 Campus Dr 27589 — 252-257-3751
Danylu Hundley, prin. — Fax 257-4532

Warsaw, Duplin, Pop. 3,092
Duplin County SD
Supt. — See Kenansville
Kenan HS — 600/9-12
1241 NC Highway 24 50 28398 — 910-293-4218
Fax 293-6744
Warsaw MS — 200/6-8
738 W College St 28398 — 910-293-7997
Kenneth Houston, prin. — Fax 293-7397

Washington, Beaufort, Pop. 9,841
Beaufort County SD — 7,400/PK-12
321 Smaw Rd 27889 — 252-946-6593
Dr. Jeffrey C. Moss, supt. — Fax 946-3255
www.beaufort.k12.nc.us
B.C. Education Technical Center — Vo/Tech
511 N Harvey St 27889 — 252-946-5382
Victoria Mallison, prin. — Fax 946-7964
Jones MS — 900/6-8
4105 Market Street Ext 27889 — 252-946-0874
Donna Moore, prin. — Fax 946-7604
Washington HS — 1,100/9-12
400 Slatestone Rd 27889 — 252-946-0858
Charles Blanchard, prin. — Fax 946-9633
Other Schools – See Aurora, Chocowinity, Pinetown

Beaufort County Community College — Post-Sec.
PO Box 1069 27889 — 252-946-6194

Waxhaw, Union, Pop. 3,207
Union County SD
Supt. — See Monroe
Marvin Ridge HS — 9-12
2825 Crane Rd 28173 — 704-290-1520
Bill Cook, prin. — Fax 843-6911
Marvin Ridge MS — 6-8
2831 Crane Rd 28173 — 704-290-1510
Dr. Tom Bulla, prin. — Fax 243-2586

Waynesville, Haywood, Pop. 9,386
Haywood County SD — 7,900/K-12
1230 N Main St 28786 — 828-456-2400
Bill Upton, supt. — Fax 456-2438
www.haywood.k12.nc.us
Bethel MS — 300/6-8
730 Sonoma Rd 28786 — 828-646-3442
Jan Nesbitt, prin. — Fax 648-6259
Tuscola HS — 1,300/9-12
564 Tuscola School Rd 28786 — 828-456-2708
Dale McDonald, prin. — Fax 456-2434
Waynesville MS — 1,100/6-8
495 Brown Ave 28786 — 828-456-2403
Keith Roden, prin. — Fax 452-7905
Other Schools – See Canton, Clyde

Weaverville, Buncombe, Pop. 2,508
Buncombe County SD
Supt. — See Asheville
North Buncombe HS — 1,200/9-12
890 Clarks Chapel Rd 28787 — 828-645-4221
Jack Evans, prin. — Fax 645-4367
North Buncombe MS — 600/7-8
51 N Buncombe School Rd 28787 — 828-645-7944
Vicki Biggers, prin. — Fax 645-2509

Weldon, Halifax, Pop. 1,315
Weldon CSD — 1,000/PK-12
301 Mulberry St 27890 — 252-536-4821
Dr. Elie Bracy, supt. — Fax 536-3062
www.weldoncityschools.k12.nc.us
Weldon HS — 300/9-12
415 County Rd 27890 — 252-536-4829
Cory Moore, prin. — Fax 536-0168
Other Schools – See Halifax

Halifax Community College — Post-Sec.
PO Box 809 27890 — 252-536-2551

Wendell, Wake, Pop. 4,516
Wake County SD
Supt. — See Raleigh
East Wake HS — 1,600/9-12
5101 Rolesville Rd 27591 — 919-365-2625
Dr. Herman G. Norman, prin. — Fax 365-2628
East Wake S of Integrated Technology — Vo/Tech
5101 Rolesville Rd 27591 — 919-365-2657
Kristin Cuilla, prin. — Fax 365-2693

Wentworth, Rockingham, Pop. 2,777

Rockingham Community College — Post-Sec.
PO Box 38 27375 — 336-342-4261

West End, Moore
Moore County SD
Supt. — See Carthage
West Pine MS — 700/6-8
144 Archie Rd 27376 — 910-673-1464
Jeff Maples, prin. — Fax 673-1272

West Jefferson, Ashe, Pop. 1,082
Ashe County SD
Supt. — See Jefferson
Ashe County HS — 1,000/9-12
PO Box 450 28694 — 336-246-2400
Phil Howell, prin. — Fax 246-2411

Whiteville, Columbus, Pop. 5,212
Columbus County SD — 7,000/PK-12
PO Box 729 28472 — 910-642-5168
Dr. Dan Strickland, supt. — Fax 640-1010
www.columbus.k12.nc.us/
Other Schools – See Cerro Gordo, Chadbourn, Delco, Hallsboro, Lake Waccamaw, Tabor City

Whiteville CSD 2,800/PK-12
PO Box 609 28472 910-642-4116
Dr. Danny D. McPherson, supt. Fax 642-0564
www.whiteville.k12.nc.us
Central MS 600/6-8
310 S Mrtn Lthr King Jr Ave 28472 910-642-3546
Dr. Beverly Boone, prin. Fax 642-7484
Whiteville HS 800/9-12
413 N Lee St 28472 910-914-4189
Kyle Ramey, prin. Fax 914-4186

Carolina Adventist Academy 50/K-10
3710 James B White Hwy S 28472 910-640-0855
Evelyn Tucker, prin.
Columbus Christian Academy 200/K-12
115 W Calhoun St 28472 910-642-6196
Debra Edwards, prin. Fax 642-3066
Southeastern Community College Post-Sec.
PO Box 151 28472 910-642-7141
Waccamaw Academy 200/K-12
PO Box 507 28472 910-642-7530
Denning Buchter, hdmstr. Fax 642-6938

Wilkesboro, Wilkes, Pop. 3,204
Wilkes County SD
Supt. — See North Wilkesboro
Career and Technical Magnet HS of Wilkes Vo/Tech
374 Lincoln Heights Rd 28697 336-667-3653
Joey Ortiz, prin. Fax 838-8947
West Wilkes MS 500/6-8
1677 N NC Highway 16 28697 336-973-1700
Cynthia Altemueller, prin. Fax 973-7423
Wilkes Central HS 1,000/9-12
1179 Moravian Falls Rd 28697 336-667-5277
Stephen Moree, prin. Fax 667-2091

Wilkes Community College Post-Sec.
PO Box 120 28697 336-838-6100

Williamston, Martin, Pop. 5,650
Martin County SD 4,500/PK-12
300 N Watts St 27892 252-792-1575
Dr. Thomas Daly, supt. Fax 792-1965
www.martin.k12.nc.us/
Bear Grass JSHS 300/7-12
6344 E Bear Grass Rd 27892 252-792-3721
Hal Davis, prin. Fax 809-4814
Williamston HS 600/9-12
1260 Godwin Dr 27892 252-792-7881
Linda Cherry, prin. Fax 809-4807
Williamston MS 500/6-8
600 N Smithwick St 27892 252-792-1111
Clay Wagner, prin. Fax 792-6644
Other Schools – See Jamesville, Robersonville

Martin Community College Post-Sec.
1161 Kehukee Park Rd 27892 252-792-1521

Wilmington, New Hanover, Pop. 95,476
New Hanover County SD 23,200/PK-12
6410 Carolina Beach Rd 28412 910-763-5431
Dr. Alfred Lerch, supt. Fax 254-4479
www.nhcs.net
Ashley HS 1,600/9-12
555 Halyburton Memorial Pky 28412 910-790-2360
James McAdams, prin. Fax 790-2356
Bear Early College HS 9-12
630 MacMillian Ave 28403 910-350-1387
Tilley Gurley, prin. Fax 350-1392
Hoggard HS 1,800/9-12
4305 Shipyard Blvd 28403 910-350-2072
Dave Spencer, prin. Fax 350-2066
Lakeside JSHS 300/6-12
1805 S 13th St 28401 910-251-6161
Jerry Oates, prin. Fax 251-6022
Laney HS 1,800/9-12
2700 N College Rd 28405 910-350-2089
Al O'Briant, prin. Fax 350-2083
Murray MS 900/6-8
655 Halyburton Memorial Pky 28412 910-790-2363
LaChawn Smith, prin. Fax 790-2351
Myrtle Grove MS 800/6-8
901 Piner Rd 28409 910-350-2100
Robin Meiers, prin. Fax 350-2104
New Hanover HS 1,700/9-12
1307 Market St 28401 910-251-6100
Chris Furr, prin. Fax 251-6114
Noble MS 800/6-8
6520 Market St 28405 910-350-2112
Wade Smith, prin. Fax 350-2109
Roland-Grise MS 800/6-8
4412 Lake Ave 28403 910-350-2136
Will Hatch, prin. Fax 350-2133
Trask MS 800/6-8
2900 N College Rd 28405 910-350-2142
Sharon Dousharm, prin. Fax 350-2144
Virgo MS 400/6-8
813 Nixon St 28401 910-251-6150
Megan Silvey, prin. Fax 251-6055
Williston MS 900/6-8
401 S 10th St 28401 910-815-6906
Mary Beall, prin. Fax 815-6904
Other Schools – See Castle Hayne

Cape Fear Academy 700/PK-12
3900 S College Rd 28412 910-791-0287
John Meehl, hdmstr. Fax 791-0290
Cape Fear Community College Post-Sec.
411 N Front St 28401 910-251-5100
Coastal Christian HS 50/9-12
709 George Anderson Dr 28412 910-395-9995
D. Kirk Nielsen, admin. Fax 395-9995
Life Christian Academy 50/1-12
606 S College Rd 28403 910-798-5778
Dr. Christina Gray, hdmstr. Fax 790-5316
Miller-Motte Technical College Post-Sec.
5000 Market St 28405 800-784-2110
Mr. David's School of Hair Design Post-Sec.
4348 Market St # N-17 28403 910-763-4418
New Hanover Regional Medical Center Post-Sec.
2131 S 17th St 28401 910-343-7074

University of North Carolina Post-Sec.
601 S College Rd 28403 910-962-3000
Wilmington Christian Academy 600/K-12
1401 N College Rd 28405 910-791-4248
Barren Nobles, admin. Fax 791-4276

Wilson, Wilson, Pop. 46,967
Wilson County SD 12,800/PK-12
PO Box 2048 27894 252-399-7700
Dr. Larry Price, supt. Fax 399-2776
www.wilson.k12.nc.us/
Beddingfield HS 1,100/9-12
4510 Old Stantonsburg Rd 27893 252-399-7880
Glenn Reaves, prin. Fax 399-7850
Darden MS 400/6-8
1665 Lipscomb Rd E 27893 252-206-4973
Charles Chestnut, prin. Fax 206-1508
Fike HS 1,200/9-12
500 Harrison Dr N 27893 252-399-7905
Steve Ellis, prin. Fax 399-7893
Forest Hills MS 600/6-8
1210 Forest Hills Rd NW 27896 252-399-7913
Scott Sage, prin. Fax 399-7894
Hunt HS 1,200/9-12
4559 Lamm Rd SW 27893 252-399-7930
Joe Davis, prin. Fax 399-7897
Speight MS 500/6-8
5514 Old Stantonsburg Rd, 252-238-3983
Sarah Ellington, prin. Fax 238-2104
Toisnot MS 600/6-8
1301 Corbett Ave N 27893 252-399-7973
Craig Harris, prin. Fax 399-7749
Other Schools – See Elm City, Lucama

Barton College Post-Sec.
PO Box 5000 27893 252-399-6300
Community Christian S 300/PK-12
5160 Packhouse Rd 27896 252-399-1376
Renita Petway, hdmstr. Fax 243-6973
Eastern North Carolina Sch. for the Deaf Post-Sec.
PO Box 2768 27894
Greenfield S 200/PK-12
PO Box 3525 27895 252-237-8046
Janet Beaman, hdmstr. Fax 237-1825
Mitchell's Hairstyling Academy Post-Sec.
2620 Forest Hills Rd #A 27893 252-243-3158
Wilson Christian Academy 400/K-12
PO Box 3818 27895 252-237-8064
Shirley Pierce, prin. Fax 234-9164
Wilson Technical Community College Post-Sec.
PO Box 4305 27893 252-291-1195

Windsor, Bertie, Pop. 2,231
Bertie County SD 3,200/PK-12
PO Box 10 27983 252-794-3173
Dr. Nettie Collins-Hart, supt. Fax 794-9727
www.bertieschools.com
Bertie HS 1,100/9-12
715 US Highway 13 N 27983 252-794-3034
Sharon Bond, prin. Fax 794-1932
Southwestern MS 500/6-8
819 Governors Rd 27983 252-794-2358
Sandra Hardy, prin. Fax 794-3407
Other Schools – See Powellsville

Bethel Assembly Christian Academy 200/K-12
105 Askewville Bryant St 27983 252-794-4034
Chris Howerton, prin.

Winfall, Perquimans, Pop. 567
Perquimans County SD
Supt. — See Hertford
Perquimans County MS 400/6-8
PO Box 39 27985 252-426-7355
Jamie Liverman, prin. Fax 426-1424

Wingate, Union, Pop. 2,866

Wingate University Post-Sec.
201 E Wilson St 28174 704-233-8000

Winston Salem, Forsyth, Pop. 188,934
Winston-Salem/Forsyth SD 48,200/PK-12
PO Box 2513 27102 336-727-2816
Dr. Donald Martin, supt. Fax 727-2008
wsfcs.k12.nc.us
Career Center Vo/Tech
1615 Miller St 27103 336-727-8181
Dr. Dennis Moser, prin. Fax 727-2115
Carter Vocational S Vo/Tech
2700 S Main St 27127 336-771-4590
Dr. Jan Floyd, prin. Fax 771-4554
Carver HS 1,100/9-12
3545 Carver School Rd 27105 336-727-2987
Carol Montague, prin. Fax 727-8211
Clemmons MS 1,100/6-8
3785 Fraternity Church Rd 27127 336-774-4677
Sandra Hunter, prin. Fax 774-4678
Hanes MS 600/6-8
2900 Indiana Ave 27105 336-727-2252
Joe Childers, prin. Fax 748-4138
Hill MS 400/6-8
2200 Tryon St 27107 336-771-4515
Becky Hodges, prin. Fax 771-4519
Jefferson MS 1,100/6-8
3500 Sally Kirk Rd 27106 336-774-4630
Frank Martin, prin. Fax 774-4635
Meadowlark MS 1,100/6-8
301 Meadowlark Dr 27106 336-922-1730
Loretta Rowland-Kitley, prin. Fax 922-1745
Mineral Springs MS 500/6-8
4559 Ogburn Ave 27105 336-661-4870
Randy Fulton, prin. Fax 661-4857
Mt. Tabor HS 1,800/9-12
342 Petree Rd 27106 336-703-6700
Martha Land, prin. Fax 774-4606
North Forsyth HS 1,800/9-12
5705 Shattalon Dr 27105 336-661-4880
Ron Jessup, prin. Fax 661-4869
Northwest MS 1,000/6-8
5501 Murray Rd 27106 336-924-5126
Sharon Richardson, prin. Fax 924-5128

Paisley MS 600/6-10
1400 Grant Ave 27105 336-727-2775
Marion Couch, prin. Fax 727-8315
Parkland HS 1,300/9-12
1600 Brewer Rd 27127 336-771-4700
Dr. Tim Lee, prin. Fax 771-4703
Philo MS 500/6-8
410 Haverhill St 27127 336-771-4570
Valarie Williams, prin. Fax 771-4578
Reynolds HS 1,900/9-12
301 N Hawthorne Rd 27104 336-727-2061
Dr. Art Paschal, prin. Fax 727-2053
School of Biotechnology 9-12
3605 Old Greensboro Rd 27101 336-703-6754
Carolyn Preyar, prin. Fax 748-3565
School of Computer Technology 9-12
3605 Old Greensboro Rd 27101 336-703-6754
Brad Craddock, prin. Fax 748-3565
School of Pre-Engineering 9-12
3605 Old Greensboro Rd 27101 336-703-6754
Doug Geringer, prin. Fax 748-3565
Wiley MS 800/6-8
1400 W Northwest Blvd 27104 336-727-2378
Ed Weiss, prin. Fax 727-2303
Other Schools – See Clemmons, Kernersville, Pfafftown, Walkertown

---

Calvary Baptist Day S 700/PK-12
5000 Country Club Rd 27104 336-765-5546
Martha Lennon, admin. Fax 714-5577
Carolina Beauty College Post-Sec.
7736 N Point Blvd Ste C 27106 336-759-7969
Cosmetology Inst of Beauty Arts & Sci. Post-Sec.
807 Silas Creek Pkwy 27127 336-773-1472
Forsyth Technical Community College Post-Sec.
2100 Silas Creek Pkwy 27103 336-723-0371
Gospel Light Christian S 400/K-12
4940 Gospel Light Church Rd 27101 336-722-6100
Bobby Roberson, prin. Fax 722-9640
North Carolina School of the Arts Post-Sec.
PO Box 12189 27117 336-770-3291
Piedmont Baptist College Post-Sec.
716 Franklin St 27101 336-725-8344
Salem Academy 200/9-12
500 E Salem Ave 27101 336-721-2646
Gordon Bondurant, hdmstr. Fax 917-5340
Salem Baptist Christian S 300/PK-12
429 S Broad St 27101 336-725-6113
Martha Drake, hdmstr. Fax 725-8455
Salem College Post-Sec.
PO Box 10548 27108 800-327-2536
Wake Forest University Post-Sec.
Medical Center Blvd 27157 336-748-4424
Wake Forest University Post-Sec.
PO Box 7305 27109 336-759-5000
Winston-Salem Barber School Post-Sec.
1531 Silas Creek Pkwy 27127 336-724-1459
Winston-Salem Bible College Post-Sec.
PO Box 777 27102 336-774-0900
Winston-Salem State University Post-Sec.
601 S Mrtn Lther King Jr Dr 27110 336-750-2000
Woodland Baptist Christian S 200/PK-12
3665 N Patterson Ave 27105 336-767-6176
Steve Holley, admin. Fax 767-9116

Winterville, Pitt, Pop. 4,688
Pitt County SD
Supt. — See Greenville
Cox MS 1,000/6-8
2657 Church St 28590 252-756-3105
Tracy Cole-Williams, prin. Fax 756-1081
South Central HS 1,100/9-12
570 Forlines Rd 28590 252-321-3232
John Coleman, prin. Fax 321-7909

Winton, Hertford, Pop. 920
Hertford County SD 3,700/PK-12
PO Box 158 27986 252-358-1761
Dr. Mary Jo Allen, supt. Fax 358-4745
www.hertford.k12.nc.us
Other Schools – See Ahoskie, Murfreesboro

Yadkinville, Yadkin, Pop. 2,867
Yadkin County SD 6,100/PK-12
121 Washington St 27055 336-679-2051
Barbara Todd, supt. Fax 679-4013
www.yadkin.k12.nc.us
Other Schools – See Boonville, East Bend

Yanceyville, Caswell, Pop. 2,147
Caswell County SD 3,400/PK-12
PO Box 160 27379 336-694-4116
Douglas N. Barker, supt. Fax 694-5154
www.caswell.k12.nc.us/
Bartlett Yancey HS 1,000/9-12
PO Box 190 27379 336-694-4212
Dr. Gary Cone, prin. Fax 694-5285
Dillard MS 800/6-8
PO Box 310 27379 336-694-4941
Frank Scott, prin. Fax 694-6353

Youngsville, Franklin, Pop. 712
Franklin County SD
Supt. — See Louisburg
Cedar Creek MS 700/6-8
2228 Cedar Creek Rd 27596 919-554-4848
Brooke Wheeler, prin. Fax 570-5143

American Institute of Applied Science Post-Sec.
100 Hunter Pl 27596 919-554-2500

Zebulon, Wake, Pop. 4,218
Wake County SD
Supt. — See Raleigh
Zebulon MS 1,000/6-8
1000 Shepard School Rd 27597 919-404-3630
Dalphine Perry, prin. Fax 404-3651

Heritage Christian Academy 100/K-12
615 Mack Todd Rd 27597 919-269-6915
Rev. David Dupree, prin.

NORTH DAKOTA

NORTH DAKOTA DEPT. OF PUBLIC INSTRUCTION
600 E Boulevard Ave, Bismarck 58505-0660
Telephone 701-328-2260
Fax 701-328-2461
Website http://www.dpi.state.nd.us

Superintendent of Public Instruction Wayne Sanstead

NORTH DAKOTA BOARD OF EDUCATION
600 E Boulevard Ave, Bismarck 58505-0660

COUNTY SUPERINTENDENTS OF SCHOOLS

Adams County Office of Education
Patricia Carroll, supt. 701-567-4363
PO Box 589, Hettinger 58639 Fax 567-2910
Barnes County Office of Education
Edward McGough, supt. 701-845-8500
230 4th St NW, Valley City 58072 Fax 845-8548
Benson County Office of Education
Jean Olson, supt. 701-473-5370
PO Box 347, Minnewaukan 58351 Fax 473-5571
www.tradecorridor.com/minnewaukan/
Billings County Office of Education
Virginia Bares, supt. 701-623-4366
PO Box 334, Medora 58645 Fax 623-4896
Bottineau County Office of Education
Dwane Getzlaff, supt. 701-228-2815
314 5th St W Ste 8A Fax 228-3658
Bottineau 58318
www.tradecorridor.com/bottineaucounty/index.html
Bowman County Office of Education
Lois Anderson, supt. 701-523-3478
PO Box 380, Bowman 58623 Fax 523-3428
Burke County Office of Education
Teri Baumann, supt. 701-377-2861
PO Box 310, Bowbells 58721 Fax 377-2020
Burleigh County Office of Education
Karen Kautzmann, supt. 701-667-3315
210 2nd Ave NW, Mandan 58554 Fax 667-3348
www.co.burleigh.nd.us
Cass County Office of Education
Mike Montplaisir, supt. 701-241-5601
PO Box 2806, Fargo 58108 Fax 241-5728
www.co.cass.nd.us
Cavalier County Office of Education
Dawn Roppel, supt. 701-256-2229
901 3rd St, Langdon 58249 Fax 256-2546
Dickey County Office of Education
Tom Strand, supt. 701-349-3249
PO Box 148, Ellendale 58436 Fax 349-4639
Divide County Office of Education
Donald Nielsen, supt. 701-965-6313
PO Box G, Crosby 58730 Fax 965-6004
Dunn County Office of Education
Reinhard Hauck, supt. 701-573-4448
PO Box 105, Manning 58642 Fax 573-4444
Eddy County Office of Education
Joan Schaefer, supt. 701-947-5615
524 Central Ave Fax 947-2279
New Rockford 58356
Emmons County Office of Education
Del Svalen, supt. 701-254-4486
PO Box 338, Linton 58552 Fax 254-4322
Foster County Office of Education
Roger Schlotman, supt. 701-652-2441
PO Box 80, Carrington 58421 Fax 652-2173
Golden Valley County Office of Education
Virginia Bares, supt. 701-872-4543
PO Box 35, Beach 58621 Fax 872-4383
www.beachnd.com

Grand Forks County Office of Education
David Godfread, supt. 701-795-2777
500 Stanford Rd Fax 795-2770
Grand Forks 58203
Grant County Office of Education
Judy Zins, supt. 701-622-3238
PO Box 279, Carson 58529 Fax 622-3717
Griggs County Office of Education
Ardis Oettle, supt. 701-797-2411
PO Box 340, Cooperstown 58425 Fax 797-3587
www.cooperstownnd.com
Hettinger County Office of Education
Sheila Steiner, supt. 701-824-2500
PO Box 668, Mott 58646 Fax 824-2717
ndaco.org
Kidder County Office of Education
Ruth Graf, supt. 701-475-2632
PO Box 66, Steele 58482 Fax 475-2202
www.ndaco.org
La Moure County Office of Education
Margaret Witt, supt. 701-883-5301
PO Box 128, La Moure 58458 Fax 883-5304
Logan County Office of Education
Gary Schumacher, supt. 701-754-2756
301 Broadway, Napoleon 58561 Fax 754-2270
McHenry County Office of Education
Maxine Rognlien, supt. 701-537-5642
PO Box 147, Towner 58788 Fax 537-5969
McIntosh County Office of Education
Coreen Schumacher, supt. 701-684-7631
PO Box 290, Ashley 58413 Fax 288-3671
McKenzie County Office of Education
Carol Kieson, supt. 701-444-3456
PO Box 503, Watford City 58854 Fax 444-4113
www.4eyes.net
McLean County Office of Education
Lori Foss, supt. 701-462-8541
PO Box 1108, Washburn 58577 Fax 462-3542
www.tradecorridor.com/mcleancounty/
Mercer County Office of Education
Phil Eastgate, supt. 701-873-2298
1021 Arthur St, Stanton 58571
Morton County Office of Education
Karen Kautzmann, supt. 701-667-3315
210 2nd Ave NW, Mandan 58554 Fax 667-3348
www.co.morton.nd.us/
Mountrail County Office of Education
Karen Eliason, supt. 701-628-2145
PO Box 69, Stanley 58784 Fax 628-3975
Nelson County Office of Education
Sharon Young, supt. 701-247-2472
210 B Ave W, Lakota 58344 Fax 247-2943
Oliver County Office of Education
Barbara Fleming, supt. 701-794-8721
PO Box 188, Center 58530 Fax 794-3476
Pembina County Office of Education
Dorothy L. Robinson, supt. 701-265-4336
301 Dakota St W, Cavalier 58220 Fax 265-4876

Pierce County Office of Education
Karin Fursather, supt. 701-776-5225
240 2nd St SE, Rugby 58368 Fax 776-5707
Ramsey County Office of Education
Lisa Diseth, supt. 701-662-7062
524 4th Ave, Devils Lake 58301 Fax 662-7049
Ransom County Office of Education
Suzanne Anderson, supt. 701-683-5823
PO Box 112, Lisbon 58054 Fax 683-5827
Renville County Office of Education
LeAnn Fisher, supt. 701-756-6301
PO Box 68, Mohall 58761 Fax 756-7158
www.renvillecounty.org
Richland County Office of Education
Bailey Harris, supt. 701-642-7700
418 2nd Ave N, Wahpeton 58075 Fax 642-7701
Rolette County Office of Education
Dwane Getzlaff, supt. 701-477-5265
PO Box 939, Rolla 58367 Fax 477-6339
www.tradecorridor.com/rolettecounty
Sargent County Office of Education
Sherry Hosford, supt. 701-724-6241
PO Box 177, Forman 58032 Fax 724-6244
Sheridan County Office of Education
Tracy Laib, supt. 701-363-2205
PO Box 636, Mc Clusky 58463 Fax 363-2953
www.ndaco.org
Sioux County Office of Education
Barb Hettich, supt. 701-854-3481
PO Box L, Fort Yates 58538 Fax 854-3854
Slope County Office of Education
Kathy Walser, supt. 701-879-6277
PO Box MM, Amidon 58620 Fax 879-6278
Stark County Office of Education
Alice Schultz, supt. 701-456-7630
PO Box 130, Dickinson 58602 Fax 456-7634
Steele County Office of Education
Linda Leadbetter, supt. 701-524-2110
PO Box 275, Finley 58230 Fax 524-1715
Stutsman County Office of Education
Noel Johnson, supt. 701-252-9035
511 2nd Ave SE, Jamestown 58401 Fax 251-1603
Towner County Office of Education
D. Allen Halley, supt. 701-968-4346
PO Box 603, Cando 58324 Fax 968-4342
Traill County Office of Education
Rebecca Braaten, supt. 701-636-4458
PO Box 429, Hillsboro 58045 Fax 636-0429
Walsh County Office of Education
Janelle Beneda, supt. 701-352-1060
600 Cooper Ave, Grafton 58237 Fax 352-1104
Ward County Office of Education
Jodi Johnson, supt. 701-857-6495
PO Box 5005, Minot 58702 Fax 857-6424
Wells County Office of Education
Evelyn Faul, supt. 701-547-3221
PO Box 408, Fessenden 58438 Fax 547-3719
Williams County Office of Education
Grant Archer, supt. 701-577-4580
PO Box 2047, Williston 58802 Fax 577-4579

PUBLIC, PRIVATE AND CATHOLIC SECONDARY SCHOOLS

Alexander, McKenzie, Pop. 213
Alexander SD 2 50/K-12
PO Box 66 58831 701-828-3335
Murray Kline, supt. Fax 828-3134
www.alexander.k12.nd.us/
Alexander HS 50/7-12
PO Box 66 58831 701-828-3335
Michelle Simonson, prin. Fax 828-3134

Anamoose, McHenry, Pop. 264
Anamoose SD 14 100/K-12
706 3rd St W 58710 701-465-3258
Steven Heim, supt. Fax 465-3259
www.anamoose.k12.nd.us
Anamoose JSHS 100/7-12
706 3rd St W 58710 701-465-3258
Steve Heim, prin. Fax 465-3259

Ashley, McIntosh, Pop. 783
Ashley SD 9 200/K-12
703 W Main St 58413 701-288-3456
Leslie Dale, supt. Fax 288-3457
www.ashley.k12.nd.us/
Ashley HS 100/7-12
703 W Main St 58413 701-288-3456
Kendra Becker, prin. Fax 288-3457

Beach, Golden Valley, Pop. 1,000
Beach SD 3 300/K-12
PO Box 368 58621 701-872-4161
Larry Helvik, supt. Fax 872-3801
www.beach.k12.nd.us
Beach JSHS 200/7-12
PO Box 368 58621 701-872-4161
Brandt Gaugler, prin. Fax 872-3801

Belcourt, Rolette, Pop. 2,458
Belcourt SD 7 1,700/K-12
PO Box 440 58316 701-477-6471
Dr. Viola LaFontaine, supt. Fax 477-6470
www.belcourt.k12.nd.us
Turtle Mountain Community HS 600/9-12
PO Box 440 58316 701-477-6471
Rosemary Jaros, prin. Fax 477-8821
Turtle Mountain Community MS 400/6-8
PO Box 440 58316 701-477-6471
Louis Dauphinais, prin. Fax 477-3973

Turtle Mountain Community College Post-Sec.
PO Box 340 58316 701-477-7862

Belfield, Stark, Pop. 820
Belfield SD 13 200/K-12
PO Box 97 58622 701-575-4275
Darrel Remington, supt. Fax 575-8533
www.belfield.k12.nd.us/

Belfield JSHS 100/7-12
PO Box 97 58622 701-575-4275
Jeffrey Lamprecht, prin. Fax 575-8533

Berthold, Ward, Pop. 442
Lewis and Clark SD 161 400/K-12
PO Box 185 58718 701-453-3484
Brian Nelson, supt. Fax 453-3488
www.lewisandclark.k12.nd.us/
Berthold HS, PO Box 185 58718 100/9-12
Margaret Person, prin. 701-453-3484
Other Schools – See Makoti

Beulah, Mercer, Pop. 3,036
Beulah SD 27 800/K-12
204 5th St NW 58523 701-873-2261
Al Liebersbach, supt. Fax 873-5273
www.beulah.k12.nd.us
Beulah HS 300/9-12
204 5th St NW 58523 701-873-2261
Todd Kaylor, prin. Fax 873-5273
Beulah MS 300/5-8
1700 Central Ave N 58523 701-873-4325
Gail Wold, prin. Fax 873-2844

Binford, Griggs, Pop. 178
Midkota SD 7 100/K-12
PO Box 38 58416 701-676-2511
Kerwin Borgen, supt. Fax 676-2510
www.midkota.k12.nd.us
Other Schools – See Glenfield

Bisbee, Towner, Pop. 150
Bisbee-Egeland SD 2 100/K-12
PO Box 217 58317 701-656-3536
Brent Bautz, supt. Fax 656-3205
bisbeehs.utma.com
Bisbee-Egeland JSHS 50/7-12
PO Box 217 58317 701-656-3536
Eric Koogen, prin. Fax 656-3205

Bismarck, Burleigh, Pop. 57,377
Bismarck SD 1 10,600/PK-12
806 N Washington St 58501 701-355-3000
Dr. Paul Johnson, supt. Fax 355-3001
www.bismarck.k12.nd.us
Bismarck Career & Technical Center Vo/Tech
1500 Edwards Ave 58501 701-224-5402
Dale Hoerauf, prin. Fax 224-5552
Bismarck SHS 1,400/10-12
800 N 8th St 58501 701-221-3500
Ken Erickson, prin. Fax 221-3742
Century SHS 1,100/10-12
1000 E Century Ave 58503 701-250-4000
Mike Heilman, prin. Fax 250-4099
Horizon MS 800/7-9
500 Ash Coulee Dr 58503 701-221-3555
Rudolph Steidl, prin. Fax 221-3569
Simle MS 800/7-9
1215 N 19th St 58501 701-221-3570
Russ Riehl, prin. Fax 221-3584
Wachter MS 800/7-9
1107 S 7th St 58504 701-221-3585
Brian Beehler, prin. Fax 221-3592
Adult Learning Center Adult
806 N Washington St 58501 701-221-3791
Scott Halvorson, prin. Fax 221-3793

Bismarck State College Post-Sec.
PO Box 5587 58506 701-224-5400
Dakota Adventist Academy 100/9-12
15905 Sheyenne Cir 58503 701-258-9000
Leonard Quaile, admin. Fax 258-0110
Medcenter One College of Nursing Post-Sec.
512 N 7th St 58501 701-323-6271
Medcenter One Health System Post-Sec.
222 N 7th St 58501 701-222-5413
R.D. Hairstyling College Post-Sec.
124 N 4th St 58501 701-223-8804
St. Alexius Medical Center Post-Sec.
PO Box 5510 58506 701-224-7600
St. Marys Central HS 400/9-12
1025 N 2nd St 58501 701-223-4113
Tom Eberle, prin. Fax 223-8629
Shiloh Christian S 300/PK-12
1915 Shiloh Dr 58503 701-221-2104
Ross Reinhiller, admin. Fax 224-8221
United Tribes Technical College Post-Sec.
3315 University Dr 58504 701-255-3285
University of Mary Post-Sec.
7500 University Dr 58504 701-255-7500

Bottineau, Bottineau, Pop. 2,157
Bottineau SD 1 800/K-12
301 Brander St 58318 701-228-2266
Jason Kersten, supt. Fax 228-2021
www.bottineau.k12.nd.us/
Bottineau JSHS 400/7-12
301 Brander St 58318 701-228-2266
Ross Roemmich, prin. Fax 228-2021

Minot State University-Bottineau Campus Post-Sec.
105 Simrall Blvd 58318 701-228-2277

Bowbells, Burke, Pop. 361
Bowbells SD 14 100/K-12
PO Box 279 58721 701-377-2396
Brent Johnston, supt. Fax 377-2399
www.bowbells.k12.nd.us
Bowbells HS 50/7-12
PO Box 279 58721 701-377-2396
Celeste Thingvold, prin. Fax 377-2399

Bowman, Bowman, Pop. 1,513
Bowman County SD 1 400/K-12
PO Box H 58623 701-523-3283
Tony Duletski, supt. Fax 523-3849
www.bowman.k12.nd.us
Bowman HS 200/9-12
PO Box H 58623 701-523-3283
Wayne Olson, prin. Fax 523-3849

Buxton, Traill, Pop. 348
Central Valley SD 3 300/K-12
1556 Highway 81 NE 58218 701-847-2220
Marcia Hall, supt. Fax 847-2407
www.centralvalley.k12.nd.us/
Central Valley HS 100/7-12
1556 Highway 81 NE 58218 701-847-2220
Robert Schneck, prin. Fax 847-2407

Cando, Towner, Pop. 1,172
Southern SD 8 200/K-12
PO Box 489 58324 701-968-4416
Mark Lindahl, supt. Fax 968-4418
www.cando.k12.nd.us/
Cando HS 100/7-12
PO Box 489 58324 701-968-4416
Jeff Hagler, prin. Fax 968-4418

Carrington, Foster, Pop. 2,148
Carrington SD 49 600/PK-12
PO Box 48 58421 701-652-3136
Brian Duchscherer, supt. Fax 652-1243
www.carrington.k12.nd.us/
Carrington JSHS 300/8-12
PO Box 48 58421 701-652-3136
Chuck Kessler, prin. Fax 652-1243

Casselton, Cass, Pop. 1,920
Central Cass SD 17 800/K-12
802 5th St N 58012 701-347-5352
Michael Severson, supt. Fax 347-5354
www.central-cass.k12.nd.us/
Central Cass HS 200/9-12
802 5th St N 58012 701-347-5352
Steve Lorentzen, prin. Fax 347-5354
Central Cass MS 100/6-8
802 5th St N 58012 701-347-5352
Pete Pogatshnik, prin. Fax 347-5354

Cavalier, Pembina, Pop. 1,443
Cavalier SD 6 500/K-12
PO Box 410 58220 701-265-8417
Francis Schill, supt. Fax 265-8106
cavalier.nd.schoolwebpages.com/
Cavalier HS 200/9-12
PO Box 410 58220 701-265-8417
Daniel Stutlien, prin. Fax 265-8106

Center, Oliver, Pop. 593
Center-Stanton SD 1 200/PK-12
PO Box 248 58530 701-794-8778
Royal D. Lyson, supt. Fax 794-3659
www.center.k12.nd.us/
Center S 100/K-12
PO Box 248 58530 701-794-8778
Lyle Krueger, prin. Fax 794-3659

Colfax, Richland, Pop. 91
Richland SD 44 300/K-12
PO Box 49 58018 701-372-3713
Wayne Ulven, supt. Fax 372-3718
www.richland.k12.nd.us
Richland JSHS 200/7-12
PO Box 49 58018 701-372-3713
Neil Race, prin. Fax 372-3718

Cooperstown, Griggs, Pop. 945
Griggs County Central SD 18 200/K-12
1207 Foster Ave NE 58425 701-797-3114
Wade Faul, supt. Fax 797-3130
www.griggs-co.k12.nd.us/
Griggs County Central JSHS 200/7-12
1207 Foster Ave NE 58425 701-797-3114
Jeremy Larson, prin. Fax 797-3130

Crosby, Divide, Pop. 1,017
Divide County SD 1 300/K-12
PO Box G 58730 701-965-6313
Donald Nielsen, supt. Fax 965-6004
www.divide-co.k12.nd.us/
Divide County JSHS 200/7-12
PO Box G 58730 701-965-6392
Lee Lampert, prin. Fax 965-6942

Des Lacs, Ward, Pop. 193
United SD 7 600/PK-12
PO Box 117 58733 701-725-4334
Clarke Ranum, supt. Fax 725-4375
www.united.k12.nd.us/
Des Lacs Burlington HS 200/9-12
PO Box 117 58733 701-725-4334
Andrew Schafer, prin. Fax 725-4375

Devils Lake, Ramsey, Pop. 6,816
Devils Lake SD 1 1,900/PK-12
1601 College Dr N 58301 701-662-7640
Steven W. Swiontek, supt. Fax 662-7646
www.dlschools.org/
Central MS 600/5-8
325 7th St NE 58301 701-662-7664
Robert Gibson, prin. Fax 662-7649
Devils Lake HS 600/9-12
1601 College Dr N 58301 701-662-1200
Ryan Hanson, prin. Fax 662-1208
Lake Area Career & Technology Center Vo/Tech
205 16th St NW 58301 701-662-7650
Denise Wolf, prin. Fax 662-7658

Lake Region State College Post-Sec.
1801 College Dr N 58301 701-662-1600

Dickinson, Stark, Pop. 15,666
Dickinson SD 1 2,600/K-12
PO Box 1057 58602 701-456-0002
Dr. Paul Stremick, supt. Fax 456-0035
www.dickinson.k12.nd.us
Dickinson HS 900/9-12
PO Box 1057 58602 701-456-0030
Ron Dockter, prin. Fax 456-0019
Hagen JHS 500/7-8
PO Box 1057 58602 701-456-0020
Perry Braunagel, prin. Fax 456-0023
Southwest Community HS Adult
PO Box 1057 58602 701-456-0042
Eileen Rowe, prin. Fax 456-0042

Dickinson State University 58601 Post-Sec.
701-483-2507
Trinity HS 300/7-12
PO Box 1177 58602 701-483-6081
Kelly Koppinger, admin. Fax 483-1450

Drake, McHenry, Pop. 287
Drake SD 57 100/K-12
PO Box 256 58736 701-465-3732
Brent Engebretson, supt. Fax 465-3634
Drake HS, PO Box 256 58736 100/7-12
Jason Wolsky, prin. 701-465-3732

Drayton, Pembina, Pop. 852
Drayton SD 19 200/K-12
108 S 5th St 58225 701-454-3324
Robert Klein, supt. Fax 454-3485
Drayton JSHS 100/7-12
108 S 5th St 58225 701-454-3324
Kerri Stegman, prin. Fax 454-3485

Dunseith, Rolette, Pop. 748
Dunseith SD 1 400/K-12
PO Box 789 58329 701-244-0480
Lanelia DeCoteau, supt. Fax 244-5129
www.dunseith.k12.nd.us/
Dunseith JSHS 200/7-12
PO Box 789 58329 701-244-5249
Jorgen Knutson, prin. Fax 244-5129

Edgeley, LaMoure, Pop. 578
Edgeley SD 3 200/K-12
PO Box 37 58433 701-493-2292
Richard Diegel, supt. Fax 493-2411
www.edgeley.k12.nd.us/
Edgeley HS 100/7-12
PO Box 37 58433 701-493-2292
Todd Kosel, prin. Fax 493-2411

Edinburg, Walsh, Pop. 233
Edinburg SD 106 100/K-12
PO Box 6 58227 701-993-8312
David Monson, supt. Fax 993-8313
www.edinburg.k12.nd.us/
Edinburg HS 100/7-12
PO Box 6 58227 701-993-8312
Gene LaFromboise, prin. Fax 993-8313

Edmore, Ramsey, Pop. 239
Edmore SD 2 100/7-12
PO Box 188 58330 701-644-2282
Keith Arneson, supt. Fax 644-2222
www.adams-edmore.k12.nd.us
Adams-Edmore JSHS 100/7-12
PO Box 188 58330 701-644-2282
Wade Schock, prin. Fax 644-2222

Elgin, Grant, Pop. 600
Elgin - New Leipzig SD 49 200/K-12
PO Box 70 58533 701-584-2374
Martin Schock, supt. Fax 584-3018
www.elgin.k12.nd.us
Grant County HS 100/9-12
PO Box 70 58533 701-584-2374
Terry Bentz, prin. Fax 584-3018

Ellendale, Dickey, Pop. 1,500
Ellendale SD 40 400/K-12
PO Box 400 58436 701-349-3232
Jeff Fastnacht, supt. Fax 349-3447
www.ellendale.k12.nd.us
Ellendale JSHS 200/7-12
PO Box 400 58436 701-349-4148
Matthew Herman, prin. Fax 349-3447

Trinity Bible College Post-Sec.
50 6th Ave S 58436 701-349-3621

Enderlin, Ransom, Pop. 1,055
Enderlin SD 22 300/K-12
410 Bluff St 58027 701-437-2240
Patrick Feist, supt. Fax 437-2242
www.enderlin.k12.nd.us/
Enderlin HS 200/7-12
410 Bluff St 58027 701-437-2240
Timothy Michaelson, prin. Fax 437-2242

Fairmount, Richland, Pop. 386
Fairmount SD 18 100/K-12
PO Box 228 58030 701-474-5469
Clarke Johnson, supt. Fax 474-5862
www.fairmount.k12.nd.us/
Fairmount HS 100/7-12
PO Box 228 58030 701-474-5469
Clarke Johnson, prin. Fax 474-5862

Fargo, Cass, Pop. 90,672
Fargo SD 1 8,000/PK-12
415 4th St N 58102 701-446-1000
Rick Buresh, supt. Fax 446-1200
www.fargo.k12.nd.us/
Discovery MS 500/6-8
1717 40th Ave S 58104 701-446-3300
Linda Davis, prin. Fax 446-3599
Eielson MS 6-8
1601 13th Ave S 58103 701-446-1700
Brad Larson, prin. Fax 446-1799
Fargo North HS 900/9-12
801 17th Ave N 58102 701-446-2400
Andrew Dahlen, prin. Fax 446-2799

Fargo South SHS 1,600/10-12
1840 15th Ave S 58103 701-446-2000
Todd Bertsch, prin. Fax 446-2399
Franklin MS 600/6-8
1420 8th St N 58102 701-446-3600
John Nelson, prin. Fax 446-3899
South Campus II 9-9
1305 9th Ave S 58103 701-446-3200
Marcy Blikre, prin. Fax 446-3299
Evaluation & Training Center Adult
424 9th Ave S 58103 701-241-4858
Terry Paulson, prin. Fax 241-4896

Aakers College Post-Sec.
4012 19th Ave S 58103 701-277-3889
Josef's School of Hair Design Post-Sec.
627 NP Ave N 58102 701-235-0011
Moler Barber College of HairStyling Post-Sec.
16 8th St S 58103 701-232-6773
North Dakota State University 58105 Post-Sec.
701-237-7211
Oak Grove Lutheran HS 300/6-12
124 N Terrace N 58102 701-237-0210
Morgan Forness, prin. Fax 237-4217
Shanley HS 300/9-12
5600 25th St S 58104 701-893-3200
Don Bunce, prin. Fax 893-3277
Sr. Rosalind Gefre School of Massage Post-Sec.
3101 39th St S Ste E 58104 701-297-5993
Sullivan MS 300/6-8
5600 25th St S 58104 701-893-3200
Sean Safranski, prin. Fax 893-3277
Tri-College University 58105 Post-Sec.
701-231-8170

Fessenden, Wells, Pop. 547
Fessenden-Bowdon SD 25 200/K-12
PO Box 67 58438 701-547-3296
Terry Olschlager, supt. Fax 547-3125
www.fessenden-bowdon.k12.nd.us/
Fessenden-Bowdon HS 100/9-12
PO Box 67 58438 701-547-3296
Terry Olschlager, prin. Fax 547-3125

Finley, Steele, Pop. 447
Finley-Sharon SD 19 200/K-12
PO Box 448 58230 701-524-2420
Merlin H. Dahl, supt. Fax 524-2588
www.finley.k12.nd.us/
Finley-Sharon HS 100/7-12
PO Box 448 58230 701-524-2420
Merlin H. Dahl, prin. Fax 524-2588

Flasher, Morton, Pop. 272
Flasher SD 39 200/K-12
PO Box 267 58535 701-597-3355
John Barry, supt. Fax 597-3781
www.flasher.k12.nd.us/
Flasher HS 100/7-12
PO Box 267 58535 701-597-3355
John Barry, prin. Fax 597-3781

Fordville, Walsh, Pop. 246
Fordville-Lankin SD 5 100/K-12
PO Box 127 58231 701-229-3297
Gaillord Peltier, supt. Fax 229-3231
www.fordville-lankin.k12.nd.us/
Fordville Lankin HS 100/7-12
PO Box 127 58231 701-229-3297
Gaillord Peltier, prin. Fax 229-3231

Forman, Sargent, Pop. 476
Sargent Central SD 6 300/K-12
575 5th St SW 58032 701-724-3205
Michael D. Campbell, supt. Fax 724-3559
www.sargent.k12.nd.us
Sargent Central HS 200/7-12
575 5th St SW 58032 701-724-3205
Brenda Grothe, prin. Fax 724-3559

Fort Totten, Benson, Pop. 867
Fort Totten SD 30 200/9-12
PO Box 239 58335 701-766-1435
Wayne Trottier, supt. Fax 766-1475
Four Winds Community HS 200/9-12
PO Box 239 58335 701-766-1412
John Laducer, prin. Fax 766-1435

Cankdeska Cikana Community College Post-Sec.
PO Box 269 58335 701-766-4415

Fort Yates, Sioux, Pop. 236
Fort Yates SD 4 200/6-8
9189 Highway 24 58538 701-854-2142
Dr. Harold Larson, supt. Fax 854-2145
Fort Yates MS 200/6-8
9189 Highway 24 58538 701-854-3819
Lunda Vail, prin. Fax 854-7467

Sitting Bull College Post-Sec.
1341 92nd St 58538 701-854-3861

Gackle, Logan, Pop. 298
Gackle-Streeter SD 56 100/K-12
PO Box 375 58442 701-485-3692
Norman Fries, supt. Fax 485-3620
www.gacklestreeter.k12.nd.us/
Gackle-Streeter HS 100/7-12
PO Box 375 58442 701-485-3692
Ron Groth, prin. Fax 485-3620

Garrison, McLean, Pop. 1,216
Garrison SD 51 400/PK-12
PO Box 249 58540 701-463-2818
Steve M. Brannan, supt. Fax 463-2067
www.garrison.k12.nd.us/
Garrison JSHS 200/7-12
PO Box 249 58540 701-463-2818
Mark Larson, prin. Fax 463-2067

Glenburn, Renville, Pop. 338
Glenburn SD 26 300/K-12
PO Box 138 58740 701-362-7426
David Wisthoff, supt. Fax 362-7349
www.glenburn.k12.nd.us/
Glenburn HS 200/7-12
PO Box 138 58740 701-362-7426
David Wisthoff, prin. Fax 362-7349

Glenfield, Foster, Pop. 132
Midkota SD 7
Supt. — See Binford
Midkota HS 100/7-12
PO Box 98 58443 701-785-2126
Gilbert Black, prin. Fax 785-2226

Glen Ullin, Morton, Pop. 829
Glen Ullin SD 48 200/K-12
PO Box 548 58631 701-348-3590
Richard Ott, supt. Fax 348-3084
www.glen-ullin.k12.nd.us
Glen Ullin JSHS 100/7-12
PO Box 548 58631 701-348-3365
Larry Sebastian, prin. Fax 348-3084

Golden Valley, Mercer, Pop. 174
Golden Valley SD 20 50/7-12
PO Box 158 58541 701-983-4256
David Bicknese, supt. Fax 983-4257
www.goldenvalley.k12.nd.us/
Golden Valley JSHS 50/7-12
PO Box 158 58541 701-983-4256
David Bicknese, prin. Fax 983-4257

Goodrich, Sheridan, Pop. 133
Goodrich SD 16 50/K-12
PO Box 159 58444 701-884-2469
Rodney Scherbenske, supt. Fax 884-2496
Goodrich HS 50/7-12
PO Box 159 58444 701-884-2469
Daniel Klemisch, prin. Fax 884-2496

Grafton, Walsh, Pop. 4,248
Grafton SD 3 900/K-12
1548 School Rd 58237 701-352-1930
Jack Maus, supt. Fax 352-1943
www.grafton.k12.nd.us/
Grafton Central MS 200/5-8
725 Griggs Ave 58237 701-352-1469
Dennis G. Hammer, prin. Fax 352-1120
Grafton HS 300/9-12
1548 School Rd 58237 701-352-1930
Darren Albrecht, prin. Fax 352-1943
North Valley Area Career & Tech Vo/Tech
1540 School Rd 58237 701-352-3705
Elizabeth Daby, prin. Fax 352-3170

Grand Forks, Grand Forks, Pop. 49,792
Grand Forks SD 1 7,500/PK-12
PO Box 6000 58206 701-746-2200
Mark Sanford, supt. Fax 772-7739
www.gfschools.org
Central HS 1,100/9-12
115 N 4th St 58203 701-746-2375
Jeffrey Schatz, prin. Fax 746-2387
Red River HS 1,300/9-12
2211 17th Ave S 58201 701-746-2400
James Stenehjem, prin. Fax 746-2406
Schroeder MS 500/6-8
800 32nd Ave S 58201 701-746-2330
Ken Schill, prin. Fax 746-2332
South MS 500/6-8
1999 47th Ave S 58201 701-746-2345
Nancy Dutot, prin. Fax 746-2355
Valley MS 500/6-8
2100 5th Ave N 58203 701-746-2360
Kevin Ohnstad, prin. Fax 746-2363
Other Schools – See Grand Forks AFB

Josef's School of Hair Design Post-Sec.
2011 S Washington St 58201 701-772-2728
North Dakota School for the Blind Post-Sec.
500 Stanford Rd 58203
University of North Dakota Post-Sec.
Box 8193 University Station 58203 701-777-2011

Grand Forks AFB, Grand Forks, Pop. 9,343
Grand Forks SD 1
Supt. — See Grand Forks
Twining S 100/4-8
1422 Louisiana St 58204 701-787-5100
Barry Lentz, prin. Fax 787-5143

Granville, McHenry, Pop. 255
TGU SD 60
Supt. — See Towner
TGU Granville HS 100/7-12
210 6th St SW 58741 701-728-6641
Tonya Hunskor, prin. Fax 728-6386

Grenora, Williams, Pop. 194
Grenora SD 99 100/K-12
PO Box 38 58845 701-694-2711
Nancy Wisness, supt. Fax 694-2717
www.grenora.k12.nd.us/
Grenora HS 50/7-12
PO Box 38 58845 701-694-2711
Nancy Wisness, prin. Fax 694-2717

Gwinner, Sargent, Pop. 709
North Sargent SD 3 200/K-12
PO Box 289 58040 701-678-2492
Harlan Heinrich, supt. Fax 678-2311
www.northsargent.k12.nd.us
North Sargent HS 100/7-12
PO Box 289 58040 701-678-2492
Randal Brockman, prin. Fax 678-2311

Halliday, Dunn, Pop. 215
Halliday SD 19 50/K-12
PO Box 188 58636 701-938-4391
David Lee, supt. Fax 938-4373
www.halliday.k12.nd.us/
Halliday HS 50/7-12
PO Box 188 58636 701-938-4391
Maureen Olson, prin. Fax 938-4373

Hankinson, Richland, Pop. 1,011
Hankinson SD 8 300/K-12
PO Box 220 58041 701-242-7516
Jess Smith, supt. Fax 242-7434
www.hankinson.k12.nd.us/
Hankinson HS 200/7-12
PO Box 220 58041 701-242-7138
Chad Benson, prin. Fax 242-7434

Harvey, Wells, Pop. 1,759
Harvey SD 38 400/K-12
811 Burke Ave 58341 701-324-4692
Robert Marthaller, supt. Fax 324-4414
www.harvey.k12.nd.us/
Harvey HS 200/9-12
200 North St E 58341 701-324-2267
Shane Sagert, prin. Fax 324-2424

Hatton, Traill, Pop. 684
Hatton SD 7 200/K-12
PO Box 200 58240 701-543-3455
Kevin Rogers, supt. Fax 543-3459
www.hatton.k12.nd.us/
Hatton HS 100/7-12
PO Box 200 58240 701-543-3455
Kevin Rogers, prin. Fax 543-3459

Hazelton, Emmons, Pop. 210
Hazelton-Moffit-Braddock SD 6 100/K-12
PO Box 209 58544 701-782-6231
Brad Rinas, supt. Fax 782-6245
Hazelton-Moffit-Braddock HS 100/7-12
PO Box 209 58544 701-782-6231
Brad Rinas, prin. Fax 782-6245

Hazen, Mercer, Pop. 2,356
Hazen SD 3 700/PK-12
PO Box 487 58545 701-748-2345
Michael Ness, supt. Fax 748-2342
www.hazen.k12.nd.us
Hazen HS 300/9-12
PO Box 487 58545 701-748-2345
Ed Boger, prin. Fax 748-2342
Hazen MS 200/6-8
PO Box 487 58545 701-748-6649
Jerry Obenauer, prin. Fax 748-6650

Hebron, Morton, Pop. 754
Hebron SD 13 100/K-12
PO Box Q 58638 701-878-4442
Jeffrey Watts, supt. Fax 878-4345
www.hebron.k12.nd.us/
Hebron HS 100/7-12
PO Box Q 58638 701-878-4442
Steven Maerschbecker, prin. Fax 878-4345

Hettinger, Adams, Pop. 1,231
Hettinger SD 13 300/K-12
PO Box 1188 58639 701-567-5315
John Campbell, supt. Fax 567-5094
www.hettinger.k12.nd.us
Hettinger HS 200/7-12
PO Box 1188 58639 701-567-4502
Brian Christopherson, prin. Fax 567-2796

Hillsboro, Traill, Pop. 1,529
Hillsboro SD 9 400/K-12
PO Box 579 58045 701-636-4360
Mike Bitz, supt. Fax 636-4362
www.hillsboro.k12.nd.us/
Hillsboro JSHS 200/7-12
PO Box 579 58045 701-636-4360
Kevin Coles, prin. Fax 636-4362

Hoople, Walsh, Pop. 270
Valley SD 12 200/PK-12
PO Box 150 58243 701-894-6226
John Oistad, supt. Fax 894-6146
www.valley.k12.nd.us/
Valley HS 100/9-12
PO Box 150 58243 701-894-6226
Douglas Bertsch, prin. Fax 894-6146

Hope, Steele, Pop. 268
Hope SD 10 100/7-12
PO Box 100 58046 701-945-2511
Arthur Mitzel, supt. Fax 945-2511
www.hope-page.k12.nd.us/
Hope-Page HS 100/7-12
PO Box 100 58046 701-945-2473
Dale Krueger, prin. Fax 945-2511

Hunter, Cass, Pop. 307
Northern Cass SD 97 400/K-12
16021 18th St SE 58048 701-874-2322
Allen Burgad, supt. Fax 874-2422
www.northerncass.k12.nd.us
Northern Cass HS 200/7-12
16021 18th St SE 58048 701-874-2322
Terry Baesler, prin. Fax 874-2422

Inkster, Grand Forks, Pop. 97
Midway SD 128 300/K-12
3202 33rd Ave NE 58244 701-869-2432
Roger Abbe, supt. Fax 869-2688
midway.nd.schoolwebpages.com
Midway HS 100/9-12
3202 33rd Ave NE 58244 701-869-2432
George Lee, prin. Fax 869-2688
Midway MS 100/6-8
3202 33rd Ave NE 58244 701-869-2432
Nancy Brueckner, prin. Fax 869-2688

Jamestown, Stutsman, Pop. 14,826
Jamestown SD 1 — 2,200/PK-12
PO Box 269 58402 — 701-252-1950
David Smette, supt. — Fax 251-2011
www.jamestown.k12.nd.us
Jamestown HS — 900/9-12
PO Box 269 58402 — 701-252-0559
William Nold, prin. — Fax 252-8580
Jamestown MS — 400/6-8
PO Box 269 58402 — 701-252-0317
Joseph Hegland, prin. — Fax 252-3310
James Valley Area Vo-Tech Center — Vo/Tech
PO Box 269 58402 — 701-252-8841
Dan Schneibel, prin. — Fax 252-3646

Carlsen Center for Children — 50/K-12
701 3rd St NW 58401 — 800-568-5175
Marcia Gums, prin. — Fax 952-5154
Jamestown College — Post-Sec.
6000 College Ln 58405 — 701-252-3467

Kenmare, Ward, Pop. 1,098
Kenmare SD 28 — 300/K-12
PO Box 667 58746 — 701-385-4996
Greg Haugland, supt. — Fax 385-4390
www.kenmare.k12.nd.us/
Kenmare JSHS — 200/7-12
PO Box 667 58746 — 701-385-4996
Arnold Jordan, prin. — Fax 385-4390

Kensal, Stutsman, Pop. 153
Kensal SD 19 — 100/K-12
803 1st Ave 58455 — 701-435-2484
Tom Tracy, supt. — Fax 435-2486
www.kensal.k12.nd.us/
Kensal HS — 50/7-12
803 1st Ave 58455 — 701-435-2484
Allan Zerr, prin. — Fax 435-2486

Killdeer, Dunn, Pop. 683
Killdeer SD 16 — 400/K-12
PO Box 579 58640 — 701-764-5877
Gary Wilz, supt. — Fax 764-5648
www.killdeer.k12.nd.us
Killdeer HS — 200/7-12
PO Box 579 58640 — 701-764-5877
Steve Quintus, prin. — Fax 764-5648

Kindred, Cass, Pop. 574
Kindred SD 2 — 700/K-12
55 1st Ave S 58051 — 701-428-3177
Steve Hall, supt. — Fax 428-3149
www.kindred.k12.nd.us/
Kindred HS — 300/7-12
55 1st Ave S 58051 — 701-428-3177
Kent Packer, prin. — Fax 428-3149

Kulm, LaMoure, Pop. 391
Kulm SD 7 — 100/K-12
PO Box G 58456 — 701-647-2303
Daniel Bauer, supt. — Fax 647-2304
www.kulm.k12.nd.us/
Kulm JSHS — 100/7-12
PO Box G 58456 — 701-647-2341
Thomas Nitschke, prin. — Fax 647-2457

Lakota, Nelson, Pop. 754
Lakota SD 66 — 200/K-12
PO Box 388 58344 — 701-247-2992
Joe Harder, supt. — Fax 247-2910
www.lakota.k12.nd.us
Lakota JSHS — 100/7-12
PO Box 388 58344 — 701-247-2992
Joe Harder, prin. — Fax 247-2910

La Moure, LaMoure, Pop. 892
La Moure SD 8 — 300/K-12
PO Box 656 58458 — 701-883-5396
Brett Gibbs, supt. — Fax 883-5144
www.lamoure.k12.nd.us/
La Moure JSHS — 200/7-12
PO Box 656 58458 — 701-883-5397
Mitchell Carlson, prin. — Fax 883-5144

Langdon, Cavalier, Pop. 1,863
Langdon Area SD 23 — 400/PK-12
715 14th Ave 58249 — 701-256-5291
Rich Rogers, supt. — Fax 256-2606
lhs.utma.com/
Langdon Area JSHS — 200/7-12
715 14th Ave 58249 — 701-256-5291
Jason Schwabe, prin. — Fax 256-2606

Larimore, Grand Forks, Pop. 1,325
Larimore SD 44 — 500/PK-12
PO Box 769 58251 — 701-343-2366
Roger Abbe, supt. — Fax 343-2908
larimore.nd.schoolwebpages.com/
Larimore JSHS — 300/7-12
PO Box 769 58251 — 701-343-2366
Pamela Cronin, prin. — Fax 343-2908

Leeds, Benson, Pop. 452
Leeds SD 6 — 200/K-12
PO Box 189 58346 — 701-466-2461
Joel Braaten, supt. — Fax 466-2422
Leeds JSHS — 100/7-12
PO Box 189 58346 — 701-466-2461
Jason Gullickson, prin. — Fax 466-2422

Lidgerwood, Richland, Pop. 746
Lidgerwood SD 28 — 200/K-12
PO Box 468 58053 — 701-538-7341
Tony Grubb, supt. — Fax 538-4483
www.lidgerwood.k12.nd.us/
Lidgerwood HS — 100/7-12
PO Box 468 58053 — 701-538-7341
Tony Grubb, prin. — Fax 538-4483

Lignite, Burke, Pop. 158
Burke Central SD 36 — 100/K-12
PO Box 91 58752 — 701-933-2821
Mike Klabo, supt. — Fax 933-2823
Burke Central HS — 50/7-12
PO Box 91 58752 — 701-933-2821
Mike Klabo, prin. — Fax 933-2823

Linton, Emmons, Pop. 1,158
Linton SD 36 — 300/K-12
PO Box 970 58552 — 701-254-4138
Steven Nelson, supt. — Fax 254-4313
www.linton.k12.nd.us
Linton HS — 100/9-12
PO Box 970 58552 — 701-254-4717
Steven Nelson, prin. — Fax 254-4313
Linton MS — 100/6-8
PO Box 970 58552 — 701-254-4173
Brian Flyberg, prin. — Fax 254-0159

Lisbon, Ransom, Pop. 2,237
Lisbon SD 19 — 600/K-12
PO Box 593 58054 — 701-683-4106
Steven Johnson, supt. — Fax 683-4414
www.lisbon.k12.nd.us/
Lisbon HS — 200/9-12
PO Box 593 58054 — 701-683-4106
Philip Martin, prin. — Fax 683-4414
Lisbon MS — 200/5-8
PO Box 593 58054 — 701-683-4108
Elinor Meckle, prin. — Fax 683-4111

Mc Clusky, Sheridan, Pop. 428
Mc Clusky SD 19 — 100/K-12
PO Box 499 58463 — 701-363-2470
Rodney Scherbenske, supt. — Fax 363-2239
mcclusky.nd.schoolwebpages.com/
Mc Clusky JSHS — 100/7-12
PO Box 499 58463 — 701-363-2470
Daniel Klemisch, prin. — Fax 363-2239

Maddock, Benson, Pop. 483
Maddock SD 9 — 200/K-12
PO Box 398 58348 — 701-438-2531
Brian Bubach, supt. — Fax 438-2620
www.maddock.k12.nd.us/
Maddock HS — 100/9-12
PO Box 398 58348 — 701-438-2531
Kimberly Anderson, prin. — Fax 438-2620

Makoti, Ward, Pop. 139
Lewis and Clark SD 161
Supt. — See Berthold
North Shore HS — 100/7-12
PO Box 127 58756 — 701-726-5591
Janene M. Lee, prin. — Fax 726-5701

Mandan, Morton, Pop. 17,225
Mandan SD 1 — 3,300/PK-12
309 Collins Ave 58554 — 701-663-9531
Wilfred Volesky, supt. — Fax 663-0328
www.mandan.k12.nd.us
Mandan HS — 1,100/9-12
905 8th Ave NW 58554 — 701-663-9532
Mark Andresen, prin. — Fax 663-5398
Mandan JHS — 500/7-8
406 4th St NW 58554 — 701-663-7491
Harlan Haak, prin. — Fax 667-0984

Mandaree, McKenzie, Pop. 367
Mandaree SD 36 — 200/K-12
PO Box 488 58757 — 701-759-3311
Carolyn Bluestone, supt. — Fax 759-3493
www.mandaree.k12.nd.us/
Mandaree HS — 100/9-12
PO Box 488 58757 — 701-759-3311
Carolyn Bluestone, prin. — Fax 759-3493
Mandaree MS — 50/7-8
PO Box 488 58757 — 701-759-3188
Carolyn Bluestone, prin. — Fax 759-3493

Marion, LaMoure, Pop. 131
Litchville-Marion SD 46 — 200/K-12
PO Box 159 58466 — 701-669-2262
Steven Larson, supt. — Fax 669-2316
www.litchville-marion.k12.nd.us/
Litchville-Marion JSHS — 100/7-12
PO Box 159 58466 — 701-669-2262
Steven Larson, prin. — Fax 669-2316

Max, McLean, Pop. 262
Max SD 50 — 200/K-12
PO Box 297 58759 — 701-679-2685
Elroy Burkle, supt. — Fax 679-2245
www.max.k12.nd.us/
Max HS — 100/7-12
PO Box 297 58759 — 701-679-2685
Elroy Burkle, prin. — Fax 679-2245

Mayville, Traill, Pop. 1,931
May-Port CG SD 14 — 600/K-12
900 Main St W 58257 — 701-788-2281
Michael Bradner, supt. — Fax 788-2959
www.mayportcg.com/
Mayville-Portland CG HS — 200/9-12
900 Main St W 58257 — 701-788-2281
Scott Ulland, prin. — Fax 788-2959
Mayville-Portland CG MS — 100/6-8
900 Main St W 58257 — 701-788-2281
Jeffrey Houdek, prin. — Fax 788-2959

Mayville State University — Post-Sec.
330 3rd St NE 58257 — 701-786-2301

Medina, Stutsman, Pop. 310
Medina SD 3 — 100/PK-12
PO Box 547 58467 — 701-486-3121
James Dunnigan, supt. — Fax 486-3138
www.medina.k12.nd.us/
Medina HS — 50/9-12
PO Box 547 58467 — 701-486-3121
James Dunnigan, prin. — Fax 486-3138

Milnor, Sargent, Pop. 676
Milnor SD 2 — 300/K-12
PO Box 369 58060 — 701-427-5237
Diann Aberle, supt. — Fax 427-5304
www.milnor.k12.nd.us/
Milnor HS — 100/7-12
PO Box 369 58060 — 701-427-5237
Patrick Adair, prin. — Fax 427-5304

Minnewaukan, Benson, Pop. 307
Minnewaukan SD 5 — 200/K-12
PO Box 348 58351 — 701-473-5306
Myron Jury, supt. — Fax 473-5420
www.minnewaukan.k12.nd.us/
Minnewaukan HS — 100/7-12
PO Box 348 58351 — 701-473-5306
Ronald Carlson, prin. — Fax 473-5420

Minot, Ward, Pop. 34,984
Minot SD 1 — 6,700/PK-12
215 2nd St SE 58701 — 701-857-4422
Dr. David Looysen, supt. — Fax 857-4432
www.minot.k12.nd.us/
Central Campus HS — 1,000/9-10
215 1st St SE 58701 — 701-857-4660
Keith Altendorf, prin. — Fax 857-4636
Hill MS — 600/6-8
1000 6th St SW 58701 — 701-857-4477
Leslie Anderson, prin. — Fax 857-4479
Magic City Campus HS — 1,000/11-12
1100 11th Ave SW 58701 — 701-857-4500
Mark Vollmer, prin. — Fax 857-4521
Memorial MS — 200/7-8
1 Rocket Rd 58704 — 701-727-3300
Tom Holtz, prin. — Fax 727-3303
Ramstad MS — 500/6-8
501 Lincoln Ave 58703 — 701-857-4465
Jim Tschetter, prin. — Fax 857-4464

Bishop Ryan S — 300/K-12
316 11th Ave NW 58703 — 701-838-3355
Terry Voiles, prin. — Fax 837-8914
Headquarters Academy of Hair Design — Post-Sec.
108 Main St S 58701 — 701-852-8329
Minot State University — Post-Sec.
500 University Ave W 58707 — 701-858-3350
Our Redeemer's Christian S — 300/PK-12
700 16th Ave SE 58701 — 701-839-0772
Julie Smesrud, admin. — Fax 858-0994
Trinity Medical Center — Post-Sec.
3 Burdick Expy 58701 — 701-857-5000

Minto, Walsh, Pop. 626
Minto SD 20 — 200/K-12
PO Box 377 58261 — 701-248-3479
Harold Mach, supt. — Fax 248-3001
www.minto.k12.nd.us/
Minto HS — 100/7-12
PO Box 377 58261 — 701-248-3400
Frank Mitzel, prin. — Fax 248-3001

Mohall, Renville, Pop. 754
Mohall-Lansford-Sherwood SD 1 — 300/PK-12
PO Box 187 58761 — 701-756-6896
Kelly Taylor, supt. — Fax 756-6549
www.mohall.k12.nd.us/
Mohall HS — 100/7-12
PO Box 187 58761 — 701-756-6660
Lenora Stevenson, prin. — Fax 756-6549
Other Schools – See Sherwood

Montpelier, Stutsman, Pop. 95
Montpelier SD 14 — 100/K-12
PO Box 10 58472 — 701-489-3348
Lynn Krueger, supt. — Fax 489-3349
www.montpelier.k12.nd.us
Montpelier HS — 100/7-12
PO Box 10 58472 — 701-489-3348
Lynn Krueger, prin. — Fax 489-3349

Mott, Hettinger, Pop. 718
Mott-Regent SD 1 — 300/K-12
205 Dakota Ave 58646 — 701-824-2249
Myron Schweitzer, supt. — Fax 824-2249
mott.nd.schoolwebpages.com/
Mott / Regent HS — 100/9-12
205 Dakota Ave 58646 — 701-824-2795
Myron Schweitzer, prin. — Fax 824-2249
Other Schools – See Regent

Munich, Cavalier, Pop. 235
Munich SD 19 — 100/K-12
PO Box 39 58352 — 701-682-5321
Kevin Baumgarn, supt. — Fax 682-5323
www.munich.k12.nd.us/
Munich HS — 100/7-12
PO Box 39 58352 — 701-682-5321
Kurt Hayes, prin. — Fax 682-5323

Napoleon, Logan, Pop. 750
Napoleon SD 2 — 200/K-12
PO Box 69 58561 — 701-754-2244
Jon C. Starkey, supt. — Fax 754-2233
www.napoleon.k12.nd.us/
Napoleon HS — 100/7-12
PO Box 69 58561 — 701-754-2244
Kip R. Schmidt, prin. — Fax 754-2233

Newburg, Bottineau, Pop. 84
Newburg - United SD 54 — 100/K-12
PO Box 427 58762 — 701-272-6151
Jason Kertsen, supt. — Fax 272-6117
www.newburg.k12.nd.us/
Newburg United HS — 50/7-12
PO Box 427 58762 — 701-272-6151
Carl Selvig, prin. — Fax 272-6117

New England, Hettinger, Pop. 543
New England SD 9 200/K-12
PO Box 307 58647 701-579-4160
Kelly Rasch, supt. Fax 579-4462
www.new-england.k12.nd.us
New England HS 100/7-12
PO Box 307 58647 701-579-4160
Lawrence Lechler, prin. Fax 579-4462

New Rockford, Eddy, Pop. 1,372
New Rockford-Sheyenne SD 2 400/K-12
437 1st Ave N 58356 701-947-5036
Kurt Eddy, supt. Fax 947-2195
www.newrockford.k12.nd.us/
New Rockford HS 200/7-12
437 1st Ave N 58356 701-947-5036
Craig Peterson, prin. Fax 947-2195

New Salem, Morton, Pop. 890
New Salem SD 7 400/PK-12
PO Box 378 58563 701-843-7846
Gordon Davis, supt. Fax 843-7011
www.newsalem.k12.nd.us/
New Salem JSHS 200/7-12
PO Box 378 58563 701-843-7610
Keith Jacobson, prin. Fax 843-7011

New Town, Mountrail, Pop. 1,415
New Town SD 1 700/PK-12
PO Box 700 58763 701-627-3650
Marc Bluestone, supt. Fax 627-3689
www.new-town.k12.nd.us/
New Town HS 200/9-12
PO Box 700 58763 701-627-3658
Spencer Wilkinson, prin. Fax 627-3689
New Town MS 200/6-8
PO Box 700 58763 701-627-3660
Fax 627-3689

Fort Berthold Community College Post-Sec.
PO Box 490 58763 701-627-4738

Northwood, Grand Forks, Pop. 884
Northwood SD 129 300/K-12
PO Box 250 58267 701-587-5221
Paula Pederson, supt. Fax 587-5423
www.northwood.k12.nd.us
Northwood HS 200/7-12
PO Box 250 58267 701-587-5221
Matthew Strinden, prin. Fax 587-5423

Oakes, Dickey, Pop. 1,848
Oakes SD 41 500/PK-12
804 Main Ave 58474 701-742-3234
Arthur Conklin, supt. Fax 742-2812
www.oakes.k12.nd.us
Oakes JSHS 300/7-12
804 Main Ave 58474 701-742-3234
Donald Warren, prin. Fax 742-2812
Southeast Regional Career & Tech Center Vo/Tech
PO Box 372 58474 701-742-3248
Kraig Steinhoff, prin. Fax 742-3152

Park River, Walsh, Pop. 1,438
Park River SD 78 400/K-12
PO Box 240 58270 701-284-7164
Kirk Ham, supt. Fax 284-7936
www.parkriver.k12.nd.us/
Park River HS 200/7-12
PO Box 240 58270 701-284-7164
David Beckman, prin. Fax 284-7936

Parshall, Mountrail, Pop. 1,027
Parshall SD 3 300/PK-12
PO Box 158 58770 701-862-3129
Stephen R. Cascaden, supt. Fax 862-3801
Parshall JSHS 100/7-12
PO Box 158 58770 701-862-3129
Mark Grueneich, prin. Fax 862-3801

Pembina, Pembina, Pop. 599
North Border SD 100 300/K-12
155 S 3rd St 58271 701-825-6261
Wade Defoe, supt. Fax 825-6645
Pembina HS 100/9-12
PO Box 409 58271 701-825-6261
Jeff Carpenter, prin. Fax 825-6645
Pembina MS 7-8
PO Box 409 58271 701-825-6261
Jeff Carpenter, prin. Fax 825-6645
Other Schools – See Walhalla

Petersburg, Nelson, Pop. 179
Dakota Prairie SD 1 300/K-12
PO Box 37 58272 701-345-8233
Janet Edlund, supt. Fax 345-8251
www.dakotaprairie.k12.nd.us/
Dakota Prairie HS 200/7-12
PO Box 37 58272 701-345-8233
Curt Herman, prin. Fax 345-8251

Pingree, Stutsman, Pop. 61
Pingree-Buchanan SD 10 100/K-12
111 Lincoln Ave 58476 701-252-5563
Dennis Adair, supt. Fax 252-2245
www.pingree.k12.nd.us/
Pingree Buchanan JSHS 100/8-12
111 Lincoln Ave 58476 701-252-5563
Shannon Faller, prin. Fax 252-2245

Powers Lake, Burke, Pop. 273
Powers Lake SD 27 100/K-12
PO Box 346 58773 701-464-5432
Ruth Ann Larshus, supt. Fax 464-5435
Powers Lake JSHS 100/7-12
PO Box 346 58773 701-464-5432
Ruth Ann Larshus, prin. Fax 464-5435

Ray, Williams, Pop. 525
Nesson SD 2 200/K-12
PO Box 564 58849 701-568-3301
Daniel Anderson, supt. Fax 568-3302
www.ray.k12.nd.us
Ray HS 100/7-12
PO Box 564 58849 701-568-3301
Arley Larson, prin. Fax 568-3302

Regent, Hettinger, Pop. 182
Mott-Regent SD 1
Supt. — See Mott
Mott/Regent MS at Regent 100/5-8
PO Box 219 58650 701-563-4315
Deb Vining, prin. Fax 563-4315

Rhame, Bowman, Pop. 176
Rhame SD 17 100/K-12
PO Box 250 58651 701-279-5523
Anthony T. Duletski, supt. Fax 279-5750
www.rhame.k12.nd.us/
Rhame HS 50/9-12
PO Box 250 58651 701-279-5523
Niel R. Hinek, prin. Fax 279-5750

Richardton, Stark, Pop. 581
Richardton-Taylor SD 34 300/K-12
PO Box 289 58652 701-974-2111
Gerald Quintus, supt. Fax 974-2161
Richardton-Taylor HS 100/7-12
PO Box 289 58652 701-974-2111
Ron Dazell, prin. Fax 974-2161

Rocklake, Towner, Pop. 167
North Central SD 28 100/K-12
PO Box 188 58365 701-266-5539
Dean Ralston, supt. Fax 266-5533
www.rocklake.k12.nd.us/
North Central HS 50/7-12
PO Box 188 58365 701-266-5539
Dean Ralston, prin. Fax 266-5533

Rogers, Barnes, Pop. 58
North Central SD 65 100/K-12
10860 20 1/2 St SE 58479 701-646-6202
Doug Jacobson, supt. Fax 646-6566
www.rogers.k12.nd.us/
North Central HS 100/7-12
10860 20 1/2 St SE 58479 701-646-6202
Daren Christianson, prin. Fax 646-6566

Rolette, Rolette, Pop. 540
Rolette SD 29 200/K-12
PO Box 97 58366 701-246-3595
Bradley N. Webster, supt. Fax 246-3452
www.rolettepublicschools.com
Rolette JSHS 100/7-12
PO Box 97 58366 701-246-3595
Bradley Webster, prin. Fax 246-3452

Rolla, Rolette, Pop. 1,442
Mt. Pleasant SD 4 300/PK-12
201 5th St NE 58367 701-477-3151
Robert Lech, supt. Fax 477-5001
www.rolla.k12.nd.us
Mt. Pleasant HS 200/7-12
201 5th St NE 58367 701-477-3151
Randy Loing, prin. Fax 477-5001

Roseglen, McLean
White Shield SD 85 100/K-12
2 2nd Ave W 58775 701-743-4350
Ioane Schmidt, supt. Fax 743-4501
www.white-shield.k12.nd.us/
White Shield HS 50/9-12
2 2nd Ave W 58775 701-743-4350
Karen Groninger, prin. Fax 743-4501

Rugby, Pierce, Pop. 2,688
Rugby SD 5 600/PK-12
1123 S Main Ave 58368 701-776-5201
Jeffery Lind, supt. Fax 776-5091
www.rugby.k12.nd.us/
Rugby JSHS 300/7-12
1123 S Main Ave 58368 701-776-5201
David Zwingel, prin. Fax 776-5091

Saint John, Rolette, Pop. 357
St. John SD 3 200/K-12
PO Box 200 58369 701-477-5651
Donald Davis, supt. Fax 477-8195
www.stjohn.k12.nd.us
Saint John HS 100/9-12
PO Box 200 58369 701-477-5651
Randall Cale, prin. Fax 477-8195

Saint Thomas, Pembina, Pop. 424
Saint Thomas SD 43 100/K-12
PO Box 150 58276 701-257-6424
Larry Durand, supt. Fax 257-6461
Saint Thomas HS 100/7-12
PO Box 150 58276 701-257-6424
David Hanson, prin. Fax 257-6461

Sawyer, Ward, Pop. 348
Sawyer SD 16 100/K-12
PO Box 167 58781 701-624-5167
Daniel Larson, supt. Fax 624-5482
Sawyer HS 100/7-12
PO Box 167 58781 701-624-5167
Daniel D. Larson, prin. Fax 624-5482

Scranton, Bowman, Pop. 286
Scranton SD 33 200/K-12
PO Box 126 58653 701-275-8897
John Pretzer, supt. Fax 275-6221
www.scrantonpublicschool.homestead.com/
Scranton HS 100/7-12
PO Box 126 58653 701-275-8266
Dennis Schaff, prin. Fax 275-6221

Selfridge, Sioux, Pop. 220
Selfridge SD 8 100/K-12
PO Box 45 58568 701-422-3353
James Gross, supt. Fax 422-3348
Selfridge HS 100/7-12
PO Box 45 58568 701-422-3353
James Gross, prin. Fax 422-3348

Sherwood, Renville, Pop. 230
Mohall-Lansford-Sherwood SD 1
Supt. — See Mohall
Sherwood HS 50/7-12
PO Box 9 58782 701-459-2214
Lenora Stevenson, prin. Fax 459-2749

Solen, Sioux, Pop. 89
Solen SD 3 200/PK-12
PO Box 128 58570 701-445-3331
Alan Bjornson, supt. Fax 445-3323
Solen HS 100/7-12
PO Box 128 58570 701-445-3331
Alan Bjornson, prin. Fax 445-3323

South Heart, Stark, Pop. 296
South Heart SD 9 200/K-12
PO Box 159 58655 701-677-5671
Loren Mathson, supt. Fax 677-5616
www.southheart.k12.nd.us/
South Heart HS 100/7-12
PO Box 159 58655 701-677-5671
Curt M. Pierce, prin. Fax 677-5616

Stanley, Mountrail, Pop. 1,222
Stanley SD 2 300/K-12
PO Box 10 58784 701-628-3811
Wayne Stanley, supt. Fax 628-3358
Stanley JSHS 200/7-12
PO Box 10 58784 701-628-2342
Kevin Hoherz, prin. Fax 628-3358

Starkweather, Ramsey, Pop. 147
Starkweather SD 44 100/K-12
PO Box 45 58377 701-292-4381
Kevin Baumgarn, supt. Fax 292-5714
www.starkweather.k12.nd.us/
Starkweather HS 100/7-12
PO Box 45 58377 701-292-4381
Dennis Dockter, prin. Fax 292-5714

Steele, Kidder, Pop. 694
Steele-Dawson SD 26 300/K-12
PO Box 380 58482 701-475-2243
Ken Miller, supt. Fax 475-2737
Steele-Dawson HS 100/7-12
PO Box 380 58482 701-475-2243
Darnell Schmidt, prin. Fax 475-2737

Strasburg, Emmons, Pop. 491
Strasburg SD 15 200/K-12
PO Box 308 58573 701-336-2667
James Eiseman, supt. Fax 336-7490
www.strasburg.k12.nd.us/
Strasburg JSHS 100/7-12
PO Box 308 58573 701-336-2667
Joel Hedtke, prin. Fax 336-7490

Surrey, Ward, Pop. 870
Surrey SD 41 400/PK-12
PO Box 40 58785 701-839-8867
Robert Briggs, supt. Fax 838-8822
www.surrey.k12.nd.us
Surrey HS 200/7-12
PO Box 40 58785 701-838-3282
David Gerding, prin. Fax 838-1262

Tappen, Kidder, Pop. 188
Tappen SD 28 100/K-12
PO Box 127 58487 701-327-4256
Gerald Christianson, admin. Fax 327-4255
www.tappen.k12.nd.us
Tappen HS 50/9-12
PO Box 127 58487 701-327-4256
Tom Six, prin. Fax 327-4255

Thompson, Grand Forks, Pop. 962
Thompson SD 61 400/K-12
PO Box 269 58278 701-599-2765
Jerry Bartholomay, supt. Fax 599-2819
www.thompson.k12.nd.us
Thompson HS 200/7-12
PO Box 269 58278 701-599-2765
Jim Larson, prin. Fax 599-2819

Tioga, Williams, Pop. 1,090
Tioga SD 15 200/K-12
PO Box 69 58852 701-664-2333
David Rust, supt. Fax 664-4441
www.tioga.k12.nd.us
Tioga HS 100/7-12
PO Box 279 58852 701-664-3606
Todd Lee, prin. Fax 664-3356

Tower City, Cass, Pop. 240
Maple Valley SD 4 300/K-12
PO Box 168 58071 701-749-2570
Roger Mulvaney, supt. Fax 749-2313
www.maple-valley.k12.nd.us/
Maple Valley HS 100/7-12
PO Box 168 58071 701-749-2570
Gary Milbrandt, prin. Fax 749-2313

Towner, McHenry, Pop. 516
TGU SD 60 400/K-12
PO Box 270 58788 701-537-5414
Debby Marshall, supt. Fax 537-5413
TGU Towner HS 100/9-12
PO Box 270 58788 701-537-5414
Greg Foster, prin. Fax 537-5413
Other Schools – See Granville

Turtle Lake, McLean, Pop. 527
Turtle Lake - Mercer SD 72 200/K-12
PO Box 160 58575 701-448-2365
Timothy Ketterling, supt. Fax 448-2368
www.tlm.k12.nd.us/
Turtle Lake Mercer HS 100/7-12
PO Box 160 58575 701-448-2365
Robert Martin, prin. Fax 448-2368

Tuttle, Kidder, Pop. 95
Tuttle-Pettibone SD 20 50/7-12
PO Box 8 58488 701-867-2564
Robert Stringer, supt. Fax 867-2565
www.tuttle-pettibone.k12.nd.us/
Tuttle-Pettibone JSHS 50/7-12
PO Box 8 58488 701-867-2564
Lee Kelm, prin. Fax 867-2565

Underwood, McLean, Pop. 739
Underwood SD 8 200/K-12
PO Box 100 58576 701-442-3201
Dale Ekstrom, supt. Fax 442-3704
www.underwood.k12.nd.us/
Underwood HS 100/7-12
PO Box 100 58576 701-442-3201
Gene Utecht, prin. Fax 442-3704

Valley City, Barnes, Pop. 6,439
Valley City SD 2 1,000/PK-12
460 Central Ave N 58072 701-845-0483
Dean Koppelman, supt. Fax 845-4109
www.valley-city.k12.nd.us
Sheyenne Valley Area Career & Tech Ctr. Vo/Tech
PO Box 30 58072 701-845-0256
Jeffrey Bopp, prin. Fax 845-0003
Valley City HS 400/9-12
493 Central Ave N 58072 701-845-0483
Kim Knodle, prin. Fax 845-2762
Valley City JHS 200/7-8
493 Central Ave N 58072 701-845-0483
Al Cruchet, prin. Fax 845-2762

Valley City State University Post-Sec.
101 College St SW 58072 701-845-7990

Velva, McHenry, Pop. 966
Velva SD 1 400/K-12
PO Box 179 58790 701-338-2022
Steven Dick, supt. Fax 338-2023
velva.nd.schoolwebpages.com/
Velva HS 200/7-12
PO Box 179 58790 701-338-2022
Kelly D. Peters, prin. Fax 338-2023

Wahpeton, Richland, Pop. 8,220
Wahpeton SD 37 1,400/PK-12
1505 11th St N 58075 701-642-6741
Michael Connell, supt. Fax 642-4908
www.wahpeton.k12.nd.us
Southeast Region Career & Technology Ctr Vo/Tech
2101 9th St N 58075 701-642-8701
Dan Rood, dir. Fax 642-3811
Wahpeton HS 500/9-12
1021 11th St N 58075 701-642-2604
Clark Gripentrog, prin. Fax 642-1330
Wahpeton MS 300/6-8
1209 Loy Ave 58075 701-642-6687
Beverly Jacobson, prin. Fax 642-5622

North Dakota State College of Science Post-Sec.
800 6th St N 58076 701-671-1130

Walhalla, Pembina, Pop. 982
North Border SD 100
Supt. — See Pembina
Walhalla HS 100/9-12
PO Box 558 58282 701-549-3751
Cynthia Gendreau, prin. Fax 549-3753

Warwick, Benson, Pop. 76
Warwick SD 29 200/K-12
PO Box 7 58381 701-294-2561
Charles Guthrie, supt. Fax 294-2626
Warwick HS 100/7-12
PO Box 7 58381 701-294-2561
Gene Riedinger, prin. Fax 294-2626

Washburn, McLean, Pop. 1,264
Washburn SD 4 300/K-12
PO Box 280 58577 701-462-3228
Robert Tollefson, supt. Fax 462-3561
www.washburn.k12.nd.us
Washburn HS 200/7-12
PO Box 280 58577 701-462-3221
Glen Weinmann, prin. Fax 462-3561

Watford City, McKenzie, Pop. 1,357
McKenzie County SD 1 600/K-12
PO Box 589 58854 701-444-3626
Steven Holen, supt. Fax 444-6345
Watford City JSHS 300/7-12
PO Box 589 58854 701-444-3624
Jay Diede, prin. Fax 444-3612

West Fargo, Cass, Pop. 19,487
West Fargo SD 6 5,400/PK-12
207 Main Ave W 58078 701-356-2000
Dana Wallace, supt. Fax 356-2009
www.west-fargo.k12.nd.us
Cheney MS 1,300/6-8
825 17th Ave E 58078 701-356-2090
Rob Kaspari, prin. Fax 356-2099
West Fargo HS 1,500/9-12
801 9th St E 58078 701-356-2050
Gary Clark, prin. Fax 356-2060

Westhope, Bottineau, Pop. 492
Westhope SD 17, 395 Main St 58793 100/K-12
Robert Thom, supt. 701-245-6444
www.westhope.k12.nd.us/
Westhope HS, 395 Main St 58793 100/7-12
Robert Thom, prin. 701-245-6444

Williston, Williams, Pop. 12,193
Williston SD 1 2,200/K-12
PO Box 1407 58802 701-572-1580
Warren Larson, supt. Fax 572-3547
www.williston.k12.nd.us
Williston HS 800/9-12
PO Box 1407 58802 701-572-0967
Chris Kittleson, prin. Fax 572-5449
Williston JHS 400/7-8
PO Box 1407 58802 701-572-5618
Marcia Armogost, prin. Fax 774-3109

Trinity Christian S 200/PK-12
2419 9th Ave W 58801 701-774-9056
Doug Black, admin. Fax 774-3158
Williston State College Post-Sec.
PO Box 1326 58802 701-774-4200

Wilton, McLean, Pop. 745
Montefiore SD 1 200/K-12
PO Box 249 58579 701-734-6559
Robert Tollefson, supt. Fax 734-6944
www.wilton.k12.nd.us
Wilton HS 100/7-12
PO Box 249 58579 701-734-6331
Roger Norris, prin. Fax 734-6944

Wimbledon, Barnes, Pop. 216
Wimbledon-Courtenay SD 82 200/K-12
PO Box 255 58492 701-435-2494
Douglas Jacobson, supt. Fax 435-2365
www.wimbledoncourtenay.k12.nd.us/
Wimbledon Courtenay HS 100/7-12
PO Box 255 58492 701-435-2494
Darrin Roach, prin. Fax 435-2365

Wing, Burleigh, Pop. 117
Wing SD 28 100/K-12
PO Box 130 58494 701-943-2310
Gene Kotaska, supt. Fax 943-2318
www.wing.k12.nd.us/
Wing HS 50/7-12
PO Box 130 58494 701-943-2319
Gary Simmons, prin. Fax 943-2318

Wishek, McIntosh, Pop. 1,000
Wishek SD 19 200/K-12
PO Box 247 58495 701-452-2892
Terrence Erholtz, supt. Fax 452-4273
www.wishek.k12.nd.us
Wishek JSHS 100/7-12
PO Box 247 58495 701-452-2995
Perry Turner, prin. Fax 452-4273

Wolford, Pierce, Pop. 47
Wolford SD 1 50/K-12
PO Box 478 58385 701-583-2387
Larry Zavada, supt. Fax 583-2519
www.wolford.k12.nd.us/
Wolford HS 50/7-12
PO Box 478 58385 701-583-2387
Diane Fritel, prin. Fax 583-2519

Wyndmere, Richland, Pop. 503
Wyndmere SD 42 300/K-12
PO Box 190 58081 701-439-2287
Rick Jacobson, supt. Fax 439-2804
www.wyndmere.k12.nd.us/
Wyndmere HS 200/7-12
PO Box 190 58081 701-439-2287
Chris Swenson, prin. Fax 439-2804

Zeeland, McIntosh, Pop. 127
Zeeland SD 4 100/K-12
PO Box 2 58581 701-423-5429
Corbley Ogren, supt. Fax 423-5465
www.zeeland.k12.nd.us/
Zeeland HS 50/7-12
PO Box 2 58581 701-423-5429
Corbley Ogren, prin. Fax 423-5465

OHIO

OHIO DEPARTMENT OF EDUCATION
25 S Front St, Columbus 43215-4183
Telephone 877-644-6338
Website http://www.ode.state.oh.us

Superintendent of Public Instruction Susan Tave Zelman

OHIO BOARD OF EDUCATION
25 S Front St, Columbus 43215-4104

President Jennifer Sheets

EDUCATIONAL SERVICE CENTERS (ESC)

Allen County ESC
Brian Rockhold, supt. 419-222-1836
1920 Slabtown Rd, Lima 45801 Fax 224-0718
www.noacsc.org/allen/ac/

Ashtabula County ESC
Richard Crepage, supt. 440-576-9023
PO Box 186, Jefferson 44047 Fax 576-3065
www.ashtabulaesc.org/

Athens-Meigs Counties ESC
John Costanzo, supt. 740-593-8001
507 Richland Ave Ste 108 Fax 593-5968
Athens 45701

Auglaize County ESC
Patrick Niekamp, supt. 419-738-3422
1045 Dearbaugh Ave Ste 2 Fax 738-1267
Wapakoneta 45895
www.auglaizeesc.k12.oh.us/

Belmont County ESC
Michael Crawford, supt. 740-695-9773
101 N Market St Fax 695-2177
Saint Clairsville 43950
www.belmontcountyesc.k12.oh.us/

Brown County ESC
James Frazier, supt. 937-378-6118
325 W State St, Georgetown 45121 Fax 378-4286
www.browncountyesc.org/

Butler County ESC
Daniel Hare, supt. 513-887-3710
1910 Fairgrove Ave Ste B Fax 887-3709
Hamilton 45011
www.bcesc.org

Clark County ESC
Stacia Smith, supt. 937-325-7671
30 Warder St Ste 120 Fax 325-9915
Springfield 45504
www.clarkesc.k12.oh.us/

Clermont County ESC
Glenn Alexander, supt. 513-735-8300
2400 Clermont Center Dr Fax 735-8371
Batavia 45103
www.clermontcountyschools.org

Columbiana County ESC
Anna Vaughn, supt. 330-424-9591
38720 Saltwell Rd, Lisbon 44432 Fax 424-9481
www.ccesc.k12.oh.us/

Cuyahoga County ESC
Harry Eastridge, supt. 216-524-3000
5811 W Canal Rd Fax 524-3683
Valley View 44125
www.cuyahoga.k12.oh.us/

Darke County ESC
Michael Gray, supt. 937-548-4915
5279 Education Dr Fax 548-8920
Greenville 45331
www.darke.k12.oh.us

Delaware-Union Counties ESC
Dr. James Crawford, supt. 740-548-7880
4565 Columbus Pike Fax 548-4465
Delaware 43015
www.duesc.org/

Erie-Huron-Ottawa Counties ESC
William B. Lally, supt. 419-625-6274
2900 Columbus Ave Fax 627-1104
Sandusky 44870
www.ehoesc.org/

Fairfield County ESC
J. Larry Miller, supt. 740-653-3193
995 Liberty Dr, Lancaster 43130 Fax 653-4053

Franklin County ESC
Bart Anderson, supt. 614-445-3750
2080 Citygate Dr, Columbus 43219 Fax 445-3767
www.fcesc.org/

Gallia-Vinton Counties ESC
Denise Shockley, supt. 740-245-0593
PO Box 178, Rio Grande 45674 Fax 245-0596

Geauga County ESC
Matthew Galemmo, supt. 440-279-1700
470 Center St Bldg 2 Fax 286-7106
Chardon 44024
www.gcesc.k12.oh.us/

Greene County ESC
Terry Thomas, supt., 360 E Enon Rd 937-767-1303
Yellow Springs 45387 Fax 767-1025
www.greene.k12.oh.us/

Hamilton County ESC
David Distel, supt. 513-674-4200
11083 Hamilton Ave Fax 742-8339
Cincinnati 45231
www.hcesc.org/

Hancock County ESC
Larry Busdeker, supt. 419-422-7525
7746 County Road 140 Fax 422-8766
Findlay 45840
www.hancockcountyesc.org/

Hardin County ESC
Ron Morrison, supt. 419-674-2288
1211 W Lima St Ste A Fax 675-3309
Kenton 43326

Jefferson County ESC
Frederick Burns, supt. 740-283-3347
2023 Sunset Blvd Fax 283-2709
Steubenville 43952
www.jcesc.k12.oh.us/

Knox County ESC
David Southward, supt. 740-393-6767
308 Martinsburg Rd Fax 393-6812
Mount Vernon 43050
www.treca.org/schools/knoxesc/ppp.html

Lake County ESC
Linda Williams, supt. 440-350-2563
30 S Park Pl Ste 320 Fax 350-2566
Painesville 44077
www.lcesc.k12.oh.us/

Lawrence County ESC
Harold Shafer, supt. 740-532-4223
111 S 4th St, Ironton 45638 Fax 532-7226

Licking County ESC
Nelson McCray, supt. 740-349-6084
675 Price Rd NE, Newark 43055 Fax 349-6107
www.lcesc.org/

Logan County ESC
Joyce Roberts, supt. 937-599-5195
121 S Opera St Fax 599-1959
Bellefontaine 43311
www.loganesc.k12.oh.us/

Lorain County ESC
Thomas Rockwell, supt. 440-324-5777
1885 Lake Ave, Elyria 44035 Fax 324-7355

Lucas County ESC
Sandra Frisch, supt. 419-245-4150
2275 Collingwood Blvd Fax 245-4186
Toledo 43620
www.lucas.k12.oh.us/

Madison-Champaign Counties ESC
Judy Saylor, supt. 937-484-1557
1512 S US Highway 68 Fax 484-1571
Urbana 43078
www.mccesc.k12.oh.us/

Mahoning County ESC
Richard Denaman, supt. 330-965-7828
100 DeBartolo Pl Ste 105 Fax 965-7902
Youngstown 44512
www.mcesc.k12.oh.us

Medina County ESC
William J. Koran, supt. 330-723-6393
124 W Washington St Fax 723-0573
Medina 44256
www.medina-esc.k12.oh.us

Mercer County ESC
Andrew Smith, supt. 419-586-6628
441 E Market St, Celina 45822 Fax 586-3377
www.noacsc.org/mercer/mc/

Miami County ESC
John Decker, supt. 937-339-5100
2000 W Stanfield Rd, Troy 45373 Fax 339-3256
www.miami.k12.oh.us/

Mid-Ohio ESC
Robert Alexander, supt. 419-774-5520
890 W 4th St, Mansfield 44906 Fax 774-5523
www.moesc.k12.oh.us/

Montgomery County ESC
Donald R. Thompson, supt. 937-225-4598
200 S Keowee St, Dayton 45402 Fax 496-7426
www.montgomery.k12.oh.us

Muskingum Valley ESC
Richard Murry, supt. 740-452-4518
205 N 7th St, Zanesville 43701 Fax 455-6702
www.mvesc.k12.oh.us/

North Central Ohio ESC
James Lahoski, supt. 419-447-2927
65 Saint Francis Ave, Tiffin 44883 Fax 447-2825
www.ncoesc.esu.k12.oh.us/

Northwest Ohio ESC
John Wilhelm, supt. 419-335-1070
PO Box 552, Wauseon 43567 Fax 335-5464
www.nwoesc.k12.oh.us/

Ohio Valley ESC
Carol Austin, supt. 740-439-3558
128 E 8th St, Cambridge 43725 Fax 439-0012

Perry-Hocking Counties ESC
Dale Dickson, supt., 1605 Airport Rd 740-342-3502
New Lexington 43764 Fax 342-1961
www.gmntrico4u.org/counties/perry/phesc.html

Pickaway County ESC
Tyrus Ankrom, supt. 740-474-7529
2050 Stoneridge Dr Fax 474-7251
Circleville 43113
pickawayesc.org/

Portage County ESC
Dewey Chapman, supt. 330-297-1436
326 E Main St, Ravenna 44266 Fax 297-1113
www.portagenet.sparcc.org/

Preble County ESC
Paul L. Erslan, supt. 937-456-1187
597 Hillcrest Dr, Eaton 45320 Fax 456-3253
www.preble.k12.oh.us/

Putnam County ESC
Jan Osborn, supt. 419-523-5951
124 Putnam Pkwy, Ottawa 45875 Fax 523-6126
putnam.noacsc.org/

Ross-Pike Counties ESC
Philip Satterfield, supt. 740-702-3120
475 Western Ave Ste E Fax 702-3123
Chillicothe 45601
gsn.k12.oh.us/RossCO/

Sandusky County ESC
Douglas Picciuto, supt. 419-332-8214
500 W State St, Fremont 43420 Fax 332-6707
www.sandusky.k12.oh.us/

Shelby County ESC
Mary Lou Holly, supt. 937-498-1354
129 E Court St, Sidney 45365 Fax 498-4850
www.scesc.k12.oh.us

South Central Ohio ESC
Darren C. Jenkins, supt. 740-354-7761
411 Court St Rm 105 Fax 353-1882
Portsmouth 45662
www.scoesc.k12.oh.us/

Southern Ohio ESC
Robert Dalton, supt. 937-382-6921
3321 Airborne Rd Fax 383-3171
Wilmington 45177
www.cfhesd.k12.oh.us/

Stark County ESC
Larry Morgan, supt. 330-492-8136
2100 38th St NW, Canton 44709 Fax 492-6381
www.stark.k12.oh.us/

Summit County ESC
Linda Fuline, supt. 330-945-5600
420 Washington Ave Ste 200 Fax 945-6222
Cuyahoga Falls 44221
www.cybersummit.org/

Tri-County ESC
Eugene Linton, supt. 330-345-6771
741 Winkler Dr, Wooster 44691 Fax 345-7622
www.youresc.k12.oh.us/

Trumbull County ESC
Anthony D'Ambrosio Ed.D., supt. 330-505-2800
6000 Youngstown Warren Rd Fax 505-2814
Niles 44446
www.trumbull.k12.oh.us/

Tuscarawas-Carroll-Harrison Counties ESC
Robert Fogler, supt., 834 E High Ave 330-308-9939
New Philadelphia 44663 Fax 308-0964
www.tchesc.k12.oh.us/

Warren County ESC
John Lazares, supt. 513-695-2900
320 E Silver St, Lebanon 45036 Fax 695-2961
www.warren.k12.oh.us/

Washington County ESC
Roger L. Bartunek, supt. 740-373-6669
PO Box 1A, Marietta 45750 Fax 376-5809
www.gmntrico4u.org/counties/washington/wcesc.html

Western Buckeye ESC
Kevin Dangler, supt. 419-399-4711
PO Box 176, Paulding 45879 Fax 399-3346
www.noacsc.org/vanwert/wb/

Wood County ESC
Douglas Garman, supt. 419-354-9010
1867 N Research Dr Fax 354-1146
Bowling Green 43402
www.wood.k12.oh.us/

PUBLIC, PRIVATE AND CATHOLIC SECONDARY SCHOOLS

Aberdeen, Brown, Pop. 1,670
Ripley-Union-Lewis-Huntington Local SD
Supt. — See Ripley
Ripley-Union-Lewis-Huntington MS 5-8
2300 Rains Eitel Rd 45101 937-795-8001
Machael Kennedy, prin. Fax 795-8035

Ada, Hardin, Pop. 5,847
Ada EVD 900/K-12
435 Grand Ave 45810 419-634-6421
Raymond Getz, supt. Fax 634-0311
www.ada.k12.oh.us
Ada JSHS 400/7-12
435 Grand Ave 45810 419-634-2746
Gary Ludwig, prin. Fax 634-4153

Ohio Northern University Post-Sec.
525 S Main St 45810 419-772-2000

Akron, Summit, Pop. 210,795
Akron CSD 27,500/K-12
70 N Broadway St 44308 330-761-1661
Dr. Sylvester Small, supt. Fax 761-3225
www.akronschools.com
Adult Vocational Services Vo/Tech
147 Park St 44308 330-761-1385
Minni Carter-Page, dir. Fax 761-1388
Buchtel HS 700/9-12
1040 Copley Rd 44320 330-873-3300
Deborah Houchins, prin. Fax 873-3307
Central-Hower HS 900/9-12
123 S Forge St 44308 330-761-1605
Norris Kelly, prin. Fax 761-1614
East HS 700/9-12
80 Brittain Rd 44305 330-794-4100
Anthony Lane, prin. Fax 794-4107
Ellet HS 1,200/9-12
309 Woolf Ave 44312 330-794-4120
M. Constance Hardy, prin. Fax 794-4130
Firestone HS 1,200/9-12
333 Rampart Ave 44313 330-873-3315
LaVonne Humphrey, prin. Fax 873-3318
Garfield HS 1,300/9-12
435 N Firestone Blvd 44301 330-773-6831
Ronald Stuecher, prin. Fax 773-3403
Goodrich MS 700/6-8
700 Lafollette St 44306 330-773-6689
Jo Anne Orlando, prin. Fax 773-7807
Goodyear MS 700/6-8
49 N Martha Ave 44305 330-794-4135
Michelle Marquess-Kearns, prin. Fax 794-4142
Hyre MS 900/6-8
2443 Wedgewood Dr 44312 330-794-4144
Cynthia Wilhite, prin. Fax 794-4143
Innes MS 900/6-8
1999 East Ave 44314 330-848-5210
James McCoy, prin. Fax 848-5217
Jennings MS 600/6-8
225 E Tallmadge Ave 44310 330-761-1715
Nicki Embly, prin. Fax 761-1713
Kenmore HS 800/9-12
2140 13th St SW 44314 330-848-4141
Elizabeth Neidert, prin. Fax 848-5270
Kent MS 800/6-8
1445 Hammel St 44306 330-773-7631
Larry Petry, prin. Fax 773-6442
Litchfield MS 600/6-8
1540 Fairfax Rd 44313 330-873-3330
H. James Dieringer, prin. Fax 873-3337
Miller-South Education Center MS 400/4-8
1055 East Ave 44307 330-761-1765
Kathleen Ashcroft, prin. Fax 761-1764
North HS 700/9-12
985 Gorge Blvd 44310 330-761-2665
Addie Veasley, prin. Fax 761-2661
Perkins MS 600/6-8
630 Mull Ave 44313 330-873-3340
Felisha Cheatem, prin. Fax 873-3347
Riedinger MS 500/6-8
77 W Thornton St 44311 330-761-1345
Traci Buckner, prin. Fax 761-1349
Evening HS Adult
985 Gorge Blvd 44310 330-761-2680
Frank Kalain, coord. Fax 761-2661
School of Practical Nursing Adult
619 Sumner St 44311 330-761-3255
Marilyn Barkley, prin. Fax 761-3254

Coventry Local SD 2,200/K-12
3257 Cormany Rd 44319 330-644-8489
Gary Zoldesy, supt. Fax 644-0159
www.coventrylocalschools.com
Coventry JHS 400/8-9
3257 Cormany Rd 44319 330-644-2232
Cynthia McDonald, prin. Fax 644-0331
Coventry SHS 600/10-12
3089 Manchester Rd 44319 330-644-3004
Jon Hibian, prin. Fax 644-4222

Manchester Local SD 1,500/K-12
6075 Manchester Rd 44319 330-882-6926
Sam Reynolds, supt. Fax 882-0013
www.panthercountry.org/
Manchester HS 500/9-12
437 W Nimisila Rd 44319 330-882-3291
James France, prin. Fax 882-5696
Manchester MS 500/5-8
760 W Nimisila Rd 44319 330-882-3812
James Miller, prin. Fax 882-2013

Springfield Local SD 3,000/K-12
2960 Sanitarium Rd 44312 330-798-1111
Jerome Pecko, supt. Fax 798-1161
www.springfield-lucas.k12.oh.us/
Springfield HS 900/9-12
2966 Sanitarium Rd 44312 330-798-1002
Cynthia Frola, prin. Fax 798-1162
Spring Hill JHS 600/7-8
660 Lessig Ave 44312 330-798-1003
Robert Bauer, prin. Fax 798-1163

Akron General Medical Center Post-Sec.
400 Wabash Ave 44307 330-846-6548
Akron Institute Post-Sec.
1600 S Arlington St Ste 100 44306 330-724-1600
Archbishop Hoban HS 800/9-12
1 Holy Cross Blvd 44306 330-773-6658
Mary Anne Beiting, prin. Fax 773-9100
Brown Mackie College Post-Sec.
755 White Pond Dr Ste 101 44320 330-733-8766
Children's Hospital & Medical Center Post-Sec.
1 Perkins Sq 44308 330-379-8293
Cooperative Medical Technology Program Post-Sec.
1 Perkins Sq 44308 330-543-8720
Mogadore Christian Academy 100/K-12
3603 Carper Ave 44312 330-628-8482
Dennis Calaway, prin. Fax 628-2677
Our Lady of the Elms HS 200/9-12
1375 W Exchange St 44313 330-867-0880
Lisa K. Massello, prin. Fax 864-6488
Our Lady of the Elms JHS 100/7-8
1375 W Exchange St 44313 330-867-0880
Lisa K. Massello, prin. Fax 864-6488
St. Vincent-St. Mary HS 600/9-12
15 N Maple St 44303 330-253-9113
David Rathz, prin. Fax 996-0020
University of Akron Post-Sec.
381 Buchtel Mall 44304 330-972-7111

Albany, Athens, Pop. 815
Alexander Local SD 1,700/PK-12
6091 Ayers Rd 45710 740-698-8831
Robert Bray, supt. Fax 698-2038
www.alexanderschools.org/
Alexander HS 500/9-12
6125 School Rd 45710 740-698-8831
Frank Doudna, prin. Fax 698-3614
Alexander MS 400/6-8
6115 School Rd 45710 740-698-8831
Frank Doudna, prin. Fax 698-8833

Alliance, Stark, Pop. 22,801
Alliance CSD 3,100/K-12
200 Glamorgan St 44601 330-821-2100
Stephen Stohla, supt. Fax 821-0202
www.aviators.stark.k12.oh.us/
Alliance HS 900/9-12
400 Glamorgan St 44601 330-829-2245
Robert Gress, prin. Fax 823-4920
Alliance MS 800/6-8
3205 S Union Ave 44601 330-829-2254
Rae Ellen Dale, prin. Fax 823-0872

Marlington Local SD 2,700/K-12
10320 Moulin Ave NE 44601 330-823-7458
Tony D. Scott, supt. Fax 823-7759
www.dukes.stark.k12.oh.us/
Marlington HS 900/9-12
10450 Moulin Ave NE 44601 330-823-1300
Jim Nicodemo, prin. Fax 829-1986
Marlington MS 600/6-8
10325 Moulin Ave NE 44601 330-823-7566
Steve Viscounte, prin.

Good Shepherd S 50/K-12
7775 Pontius St NE 44601 330-935-0623
Rev. Gary Spencer, admin. Fax 935-0433
Mt. Union College Post-Sec.
1972 Clark Ave 44601 330-821-5320

Amanda, Fairfield, Pop. 722
Amanda-Clearcreek Local SD 1,400/K-12
328 E Main St 43102 740-969-7250
James Dick, supt. Fax 969-7620
www.amanda.k12.oh.us
Amanda-Clearcreek HS 500/9-12
328 E Main St 43102 740-969-7251
Jon Saxton, prin. Fax 969-7669
Other Schools – See Stoutsville

Amherst, Lorain, Pop. 11,872
Amherst EVD 4,200/K-12
185 Forest St 44001 440-988-4406
Robert Boynton, supt. Fax 988-4413
www.amherst.k12.oh.us
Amherst JHS 700/7-8
548 Milan Ave 44001 440-988-0324
Michael Diamond, prin. Fax 988-0328
Steele HS 1,400/9-12
450 Washington St 44001 440-988-4433
Michael Gillam, prin. Fax 988-5087

Andover, Ashtabula, Pop. 1,247
Pymatuning Valley Local SD 1,400/K-12
PO Box 1180 44003 440-293-6488
Dr. John Rose, supt. Fax 293-7654
www.pvschools.k12.oh.us/
Pymatuning Valley HS 500/9-12
PO Box 1180 44003 440-293-6263
Jeffrey Meddock, prin. Fax 293-7214
Pymatuning Valley MS 600/4-8
PO Box 1180 44003 440-293-6981
Andrew Kuthy, prin. Fax 293-7237

Anna, Shelby, Pop. 1,442
Anna Local SD 1,200/K-12
PO Box 169 45302 937-394-2011
Andrew Bixler, supt. Fax 394-7658
www.anna.k12.oh.us
Anna MSHS 700/6-12
PO Box 169 45302 937-394-2011
Glenn Honeycutt, prin. Fax 394-7658

Ansonia, Darke, Pop. 1,115
Ansonia Local SD 600/K-12
PO Box 279 45303 937-337-4000
James Atchley, supt. Fax 337-9520
www.ansonia.k12.oh.us/
Ansonia HS 200/9-12
PO Box 279 45303 937-337-5591
Steve Garman, prin. Fax 337-9520
Ansonia MS 100/7-8
PO Box 279 45303 937-337-5591
Stephen Garman, prin. Fax 337-9520

Antwerp, Paulding, Pop. 1,649
Antwerp Local SD 600/K-12
303 S Harrmann Rd 45813 419-258-5421
Mark Hartman, supt. Fax 258-4041
www.noacsc.org/paulding/aw/
Antwerp Local HS 300/9-12
303 S Harrmann Rd 45813 419-258-5421
Stephen Arnold, prin. Fax 258-4041
Antwerp Local MS 6-8
303 S Harrmann Rd 45813 419-258-5420
Stephen Arnold, prin. Fax 258-4041

Apple Creek, Wayne, Pop. 983
Southeast Local SD 1,700/K-12
9048 Dover Rd 44606 330-698-3001
Steven A. Sayers, supt. Fax 698-5000
www.southeast.k12.oh.us
Lea MS 200/7-8
9130 Dover Rd 44606 330-698-3151
Matt Payment, prin. Fax 698-1922
Waynedale HS 400/9-12
9050 Dover Rd 44606 330-698-3071
William Seder, prin. Fax 698-1432

Arcadia, Hancock, Pop. 596
Arcadia Local SD 500/K-12
19033 State Route 12 44804 419-894-6431
Laurie Walles, supt. Fax 894-6970
www.noacsc.org/hancock/ad/
Arcadia JSHS 200/7-12
19033 State Route 12 44804 419-894-6431
Cathy Romick, prin. Fax 894-6970

Arcanum, Darke, Pop. 2,032
Arcanum Butler Local SD 1,100/PK-12
2 Weisenbarger Ct 45304 937-692-5174
Wayne Combs, supt. Fax 692-5959
www.arcanum-butler.k12.oh.us
Arcanum HS 400/9-12
310 N Main St 45304 937-692-5175
Phil Reuch, prin. Fax 692-5959
Butler MS 300/6-8
1481 State Route 127 45304 937-678-6571
Kirby Tippla, prin. Fax 678-6581

Archbold, Fulton, Pop. 4,505
Archbold Area Local SD 1,400/K-12
600 Lafayette St 43502 419-445-5579
David Deskins, supt. Fax 445-8536
www.archbold.k12.oh.us
Archbold HS 500/9-12
600 Lafayette St 43502 419-445-5579
Tim Meister, prin. Fax 445-8536
Archbold MS 400/5-8
306 Stryker St 43502 419-446-2726
Mike Pressler, prin. Fax 445-8402

Four County JVSD
22900 State Route 34 43502 419-267-3331
Dr. David A. Nicholls, supt. Fax 267-5234
www.fourcounty.net
Four County Career Center Vo/Tech
22900 State Route 34 43502 419-267-3331
William Spiess, prin. Fax 267-5234

Northwest State Community College Post-Sec.
22600 State Route 34 43502 419-267-5511

Arlington, Hancock, Pop. 1,293
Arlington Local SD 600/K-12
PO Box 260 45814 419-365-5121
David A. Rossman, supt. Fax 365-1282
www.noacsc.org/hancock/ag
Arlington JSHS 300/7-12
PO Box 260 45814 419-365-5121
Teri Kubbs, prin. Fax 365-1282

Ashland, Ashland, Pop. 21,550
Ashland CSD 3,600/K-12
PO Box 160 44805 419-289-1117
James Jones, supt. Fax 289-9534
www.ashland-city.k12.oh.us
Ashland HS 1,200/9-12
1440 King Rd 44805 419-289-7968
Robert Lake, prin. Fax 281-8796
Ashland MS 600/7-8
345 Cottage St 44805 419-289-7966
Mike Heimann, prin. Fax 289-2303

Ashland County-West Holmes JVSD
1783 State Route 60 44805 419-289-3313
Michael McDaniel, supt. Fax 289-3729
www.acwhcc-jvs.k12.oh.us
Ashland Co. - West Holmes JVS Career Ctr Vo/Tech
1783 State Route 60 44805 419-289-3313
David Feola, prin. Fax 289-3729

Crestview Local SD 1,200/PK-12
1575 State Route 96 44805 419-895-1700
Steven Willeke, supt. Fax 895-1733
www.crestview-richland.k12.oh.us
Crestview HS 400/9-12
1575 State Route 96 44805 419-895-1700
Debbie Reidy, prin. Fax 895-3103
Crestview MS 400/4-8
1575 State Route 96 44805 419-895-1700
John McNeely, prin. Fax 895-1733

Mapleton Local SD 800/K-12
1 Mountie Dr 44805 419-945-2188
Lori Lytle, supt. Fax 945-8114
www.mapleton.k12.oh.us/
Mapleton HS 300/7-12
1 Mountie Dr 44805 419-945-2188
Scott Young, prin. Fax 945-2123

Ashland County-West Holmes Career Center Post-Sec.
1783 State Route 60 44805 419-289-3313
Ashland Theological Seminary Post-Sec.
910 Center St 44805 419-289-5161

Ashland University Post-Sec.
401 College Ave 44805 419-289-4142

Ashtabula, Ashtabula, Pop. 20,321
Ashtabula Area CSD 4,100/K-12
PO Box 290 44005 440-993-2500
Joseph Donatone, supt. Fax 993-2626
www.aacs.net
Lakeside HS 1,000/9-12
6600 Sanborn Rd 44004 440-993-2522
James Candela, prin. Fax 993-2647
Lakeside JHS 300/7-8
401 W 44th St 44004 440-993-2618
Sylvia Atkinson, prin. Fax 992-0331
West JHS 400/7-8
1231 W 47th St 44004 440-993-2577
Patricia Craft, prin. Fax 993-2585

Buckeye Local SD 2,300/K-12
3436 Edgewood Dr 44004 440-998-4411
Nancy L. Williams, supt. Fax 992-8369
www.buckeyeschools.net/
Braden JHS 400/7-8
3436 Edgewood Dr 44004 440-998-0550
Steven Kofol, prin.
Edgewood HS 800/9-12
2428 Blake Rd 44004 440-997-5301
Timothy Essig, prin. Fax 998-6143

Kent State University-Ashtabula Campus Post-Sec.
3325 W 13th St 44004 440-964-3322
SS. John & Paul HS 200/7-12
541 W 34th St 44004 440-997-5531
Albina Larson, prin. Fax 998-1661

Ashville, Pickaway, Pop. 3,252
Teays Valley Local SD 3,300/K-12
385 Circleville Ave 43103 740-983-4111
Jeff Sheets, supt. Fax 983-4158
www.teays-valley.k12.oh.us
Teays Valley HS 1,000/9-12
3887 State Route 752 43103 740-983-3131
John Keel, prin. Fax 983-4158
Teays Valley MS 900/6-8
383 Circleville Ave 43103 740-983-4074
Kyle Wolfe, prin. Fax 983-4158

Athens, Athens, Pop. 20,918
Athens CSD
Supt. — See The Plains
Athens MS 500/7-8
51 W State St 45701 740-593-7107
Paul Grippa, prin. Fax 594-6506

Ohio University Post-Sec.
120 Chubb Hall 45701 740-593-1000

Attica, Seneca, Pop. 925
Seneca East Local SD 900/K-12
PO Box 462 44807 419-426-7041
Michael Wank, supt. Fax 426-5514
www.seneca-east.k12.oh.us/
Seneca East HS 300/9-12
PO Box 462 44807 419-426-3312
Judy Watson, prin. Fax 426-5400
Other Schools – See Republic

Atwater, Portage
Waterloo Local SD 1,400/K-12
1464 Industry Rd 44201 330-947-2664
Robert Wolf, supt. Fax 947-2847
www.viking.portage.k12.oh.us
Waterloo HS 500/9-12
1464 Industry Rd 44201 330-947-2124
Nick Hulea, prin. Fax 947-1911
Waterloo MS 400/6-8
1464 Industry Rd 44201 330-947-0033
Paul Woodard, prin. Fax 947-4073

Aurora, Portage, Pop. 14,353
Aurora CSD 2,700/PK-12
102 E Garfield Rd 44202 330-995-7702
Russell Bennett, supt. Fax 562-4892
www.aurora-schools.org
Aurora HS 800/9-12
109 W Pioneer Trl 44202 330-562-3501
Pat Ciccantelli, prin. Fax 562-3588
Harmon MS 700/6-8
130 Aurora Hudson Rd 44202 330-562-3375
Will Laine, prin. Fax 562-4796

Austinburg, Ashtabula

Grand River Academy 100/9-12
PO Box 222 44010 440-275-2811
Randy Blum, hdmstr. Fax 275-1825

Austintown, Mahoning, Pop. 31,500

Hair Academy Post-Sec.
6000 Mahoning Ave 44515 330-792-6504

Avon, Lorain, Pop. 15,741
Avon Local SD 2,200/K-12
35573 Detroit Rd 44011 440-937-4680
Jim Reitenbach, supt. Fax 937-4688
www.avon.k12.oh.us
Avon HS, 37545 Detroit Rd 44011 700/9-12
Chad Coffman, prin. 440-934-6171
Avon MS 400/7-8
3075 Stoney Ridge Rd 44011 440-934-3800
Craig Koehler, prin.

Avon Lake, Lorain, Pop. 20,608
Avon Lake CSD 3,400/K-12
175 Avon Belden Rd 44012 440-933-6210
Robert D. Scott, supt. Fax 933-6711
www.avonlakecityschools.org
Avon Lake HS 1,100/9-12
175 Avon Belden Rd 44012 440-933-6290
Joanie Hines Ed.D., prin. Fax 930-2798
Learwood MS 500/7-8
340 Lear Rd 44012 440-933-8142
Jane Ramsay, prin. Fax 933-8406

Bainbridge, Ross, Pop. 1,048
Paint Valley Local SD 1,100/K-12
7454 US Highway 50 W 45612 740-634-2826
Gary E. Uhrig, supt. Fax 634-2890
gsn.k12.oh.us/PaintValley/index.htm
Paint Valley HS 400/9-12
7454 US Highway 50 W 45612 740-634-3582
H. Dwight Goins, prin. Fax 634-3518
Paint Valley MS 300/6-8
7454 US Highway 50 W 45612 740-634-3454
Brent Taylor, prin. Fax 634-3459

Baltimore, Fairfield, Pop. 2,919
Liberty Union-Thurston Local SD 1,400/K-12
621 W Washington St 43105 740-862-4171
Paul E. Mathews, supt. Fax 862-2015
www.libertyunion.org
Liberty Union HS 400/9-12
500 W Washington St 43105 740-862-4107
Mark Fullen, prin. Fax 862-4100
Liberty Union MS 400/5-8
600 W Washington St 43105 740-862-4126
Henry Gavarkavich, prin. Fax 862-2015

Barberton, Summit, Pop. 27,192
Barberton CSD 3,900/K-12
479 Norton Ave 44203 330-753-1025
Dr. Elizabeth J. Lolli, supt. Fax 848-0884
www.barbertonschools.org
Barberton HS 1,200/9-12
555 Barber Rd 44203 330-753-1084
Kirk Koennecke, prin. Fax 848-5517
Highland MS 400/6-8
1152 Belleview Ave 44203 330-848-4243
Fax 848-4221
Light MS 500/6-8
292 Robinson Ave 44203 330-848-4236
Jason Ondrus, prin. Fax 848-1272

Barnesville, Belmont, Pop. 4,149
Barnesville EVD 1,200/K-12
210 W Church St 43713 740-425-3615
Randy Lucas, supt. Fax 425-5000
www.barnesville.k12.oh.us/
Barnesville HS 400/9-12
910 Shamrock Dr 43713 740-425-3617
Jeff Crosier, prin. Fax 425-9254
Barnesville MS 400/5-8
970 Shamrock Dr 43713 740-425-3116
Erin Olexo, prin. Fax 425-9204

Olney Friends S 100/9-12
61830 Sandy Ridge Rd 43713 740-425-3655
Richard Sidwell, hdmstr. Fax 425-3202

Bascom, Seneca
Hopewell-Loudon Local SD 900/K-12
PO Box 400 44809 419-937-2216
Geoffrey Palmer, supt. Fax 937-2516
www.hlschool.org/
Hopewell-Loudon Local JSHS 400/7-12
PO Box 400 44809 419-937-2216
Bill Dobbins, prin. Fax 937-2516

Batavia, Clermont, Pop. 1,669
Batavia Local SD 1,900/K-12
800 Bauer Ave 45103 513-732-2343
Barbara Bradley Ed.D., supt. Fax 732-3221
www.bataviaschools.org
Batavia HS 600/9-12
1 Bull Dog Pl 45103 513-732-2341
Jamie Corrill, prin. Fax 732-3221
Batavia MS, 800 Bauer Ave 45103 600/5-8
Karyn Strong, prin. 513-732-9534

Clermont Northeastern Local SD 1,900/PK-12
2792 US Highway 50 45103 513-625-5478
Ralph Shell, supt. Fax 625-6080
www.cneschools.org
Clermont Northeastern HS 700/9-12
5327 Hutchinson Rd 45103 513-625-1211
Frank Chapin, prin. Fax 625-3328
Clermont Northeastern MS 600/5-8
5347 Hutchinson Rd 45103 513-625-7075
Kathy Sabo, prin. Fax 625-3325

West Clermont Local SD
Supt. — See Cincinnati
Amelia HS 1,300/9-12
1351 Clough Pike 45103 513-947-7400
Keith Hickman, prin. Fax 753-2419
Amelia MS 1,100/6-8
1341 Clough Pike 45103 513-947-7500
David Mack, prin. Fax 753-7851

University of Cincinnati Post-Sec.
4200 Clermont College Dr 45103 513-732-5200

Bath, Summit
Revere Local SD
Supt. — See Richfield
Revere MS 700/6-8
PO Box 339 44210 330-666-4155
Frank Surace, prin. Fax 659-3795

Bay Village, Cuyahoga, Pop. 15,236
Bay Village CSD 2,500/K-12
377 Dover Center Rd 44140 440-617-7300
Clinton Keener, supt. Fax 617-7301
www.bayvillageschools.com
Bay HS 800/9-12
29230 Wolf Rd 44140 440-617-7400
James Cahoon, prin. Fax 617-7401
Bay MS 700/5-8
27725 Wolf Rd 44140 440-617-7600
Sean McAndrews, prin. Fax 617-7601

Beachwood, Cuyahoga, Pop. 11,535
Beachwood CSD 1,500/PK-12
24601 Fairmount Blvd 44122 216-464-2600
Dr. Richard A. Markwardt, supt. Fax 292-2340
www.beachwood.k12.oh.us
Beachwood HS 600/9-12
25100 Fairmount Blvd 44122 216-831-2080
Robert Hardis, prin. Fax 292-4169
Beachwood MS 200/7-8
2860 Richmond Rd 44122 216-831-0355
Linda LoGalbo, prin. Fax 831-1891

Stone Yavne HS 200/7-12
2475 S Green Rd 44122 216-691-5838
Lois Mager, prin.

Beallsville, Monroe, Pop. 422
Switzerland of Ohio Local SD
Supt. — See Woodsfield
Beallsville JSHS 200/7-12
PO Box 262 43716 740-926-1302
Todd Christman, prin. Fax 926-1394

Beaver, Pike, Pop. 466
Eastern Local SD 800/K-12
1170 Tile Mill Rd 45613 740-226-4851
Dr. Charles Shreve, supt. Fax 226-1331
www.ep.k12.oh.us
Eastern HS 300/9-12
1170 Tile Mill Rd 45613 740-226-1544
Steve Kempf, prin. Fax 226-6322
Eastern MS 200/6-8
1170 Tile Mill Rd 45613 740-226-1544
Steve Kempf, prin. Fax 226-6322

Beavercreek, Greene, Pop. 39,655
Beavercreek CSD 7,400/PK-12
3040 Kemp Rd 45431 937-426-1522
Dennis A. Morrison, supt. Fax 429-7517
www.beavercreek.k12.oh.us/
Ankeney MS 800/6-8
4085 Shakertown Rd 45430 937-429-7567
Pam Taiclet, prin. Fax 429-7685
Beavercreek HS 2,500/9-12
2660 Dayton Xenia Rd 45434 937-429-7547
Marian West, prin. Fax 429-7546
Ferguson MS 900/6-8
2680 Dayton Xenia Rd 45434 937-429-7577
Gary Creviston, prin. Fax 429-7686

Bedford, Cuyahoga, Pop. 13,571
Bedford CSD 3,700/K-12
475 Northfield Rd 44146 440-439-1500
Martha A. Motsco, supt. Fax 439-4850
www.bedford.k12.oh.us
Bedford HS 1,200/9-12
481 Northfield Rd 44146 440-786-3521
Kevin Gibaldi, prin. Fax 439-4627
Other Schools – See Bedford Heights

St. Peter Chanel HS 400/9-12
480 Northfield Rd 44146 440-232-5900
Roger Abood, pres. Fax 232-9283

Bedford Heights, Cuyahoga, Pop. 10,855
Bedford CSD
Supt. — See Bedford
Heskett MS 700/7-8
5771 Perkins Rd 44146 440-439-4450
Virginia Golden, prin. Fax 786-3572

Bellaire, Belmont, Pop. 4,738
Bellaire Local SD 1,500/K-12
340 34th St 43906 740-676-1826
John Stinoski, supt. Fax 671-6002
www.bellaire.k12.oh.us
Bellaire HS 500/9-12
349 35th St 43906 740-676-3652
Michael Sherwood, prin. Fax 671-6004
Bellaire MS 500/5-8
54555 Bellaire-Neffs Rd 43906 740-676-1635
Fax 676-3014

St. John Central HS 300/9-12
3625 Guernsey St 43906 740-676-4932
Marc Kajfez, prin. Fax 676-4934

Bellbrook, Greene, Pop. 6,960
Sugarcreek Local SD 2,500/PK-12
60 E South St 45305 937-848-6251
Keith St. Pierre, supt. Fax 848-5018
www.sugarcreek.k12.oh.us
Bellbrook HS 900/9-12
3737 Upper Bellbrook Rd 45305 937-848-3737
Christopher Baker, prin. Fax 848-5016
Bellbrook MS 700/6-8
3600 Feedwire Rd 45305 937-848-2141
Jenness Sigman, prin. Fax 848-2152

Bellefontaine, Logan, Pop. 13,009
Bellefontaine CSD 2,800/K-12
820 Ludlow Rd 43311 937-593-9060
Larry Anderson, supt. Fax 599-1346
www.bellefontaine.k12.oh.us/
Bellefontaine HS 900/9-12
555 E Lake Ave 43311 937-593-0545
Maureen Yoder, prin. Fax 593-0575
Bellefontaine MS 600/6-8
509 N Park St 43311 937-593-9010
Michael Hassel, prin. Fax 593-9030

Benjamin Logan Local SD 1,900/K-12
4740 County Road 26 43311 937-593-9211
Stanley P. Mounts, supt. Fax 599-4059
www.benlogan.k12.oh.us
Logan HS 600/9-12
6609 State Route 47 E 43311 937-592-1666
Scott Albert, prin. Fax 599-4061
Logan MS 600/5-8
4626 County Road 26 43311 937-599-2386
James Cox, prin. Fax 599-4062

Ohio Hi-Point Career Center
2280 State Route 540 43311 937-599-3010
Kimberly Wilson, supt. Fax 599-2318
www.ohp.k12.oh.us
Ohio Hi-Point Career Center Vo/Tech
2280 State Route 540 43311 937-599-3010
Vicci Elder, dir. Fax 599-2318

Bellevue, Huron, Pop. 8,029
Bellevue CSD 2,300/K-12
125 North St 44811 419-484-5000
Stephen Schumm, supt. Fax 483-0723
www.bellevueschools.org
Bellevue HS 800/9-12
200 Oakland Ave 44811 419-484-5070
Francis Scruci, prin. Fax 483-7157
Bellevue JHS, 215 North St 44811 400/7-8
John Redd, prin. 419-484-5060

Bellville, Richland, Pop. 1,754
Clear Fork Valley Local SD 1,900/K-12
92 Hines Ave 44813 419-886-3855
Daniel Freund, supt. Fax 886-2237
www.clearfork.k12.oh.us
Clear Fork HS 600/9-12
987 State Route 97 E 44813 419-886-2601
Debra Ruhl, prin. Fax 886-4749
Clear Fork MS 500/6-8
987 State Route 97 E 44813 419-886-3111
Brian Brown, prin. Fax 886-4749

Belmont, Belmont, Pop. 518
Union Local SD
Supt. — See Morristown
Union Local HS 500/9-12
66779 Belmont Morristown Rd 43718 740-782-1181
Joel Davia, prin. Fax 782-1346
Union Local MS 400/6-8
66859 Belmont Morristown Rd 43718 740-782-1388
Dan Wesson, prin. Fax 782-1474

Faith Community Christian HS 50/9-12
321 3rd St 43718 740-484-1437
April Woods, admin. Fax 484-1435

Beloit, Mahoning, Pop. 1,016
West Branch Local SD 2,200/K-12
14277 S Main St 44609 330-938-9324
Dr. Scott Weingart, supt. Fax 938-6815
www.westbranch.k12.oh.us/
West Branch HS 800/9-12
14277 S Main St 44609 330-938-2183
Joseph Knoll, prin. Fax 938-6815
West Branch MS 600/6-8
14409 Beloit Snodes Rd 44609 330-938-4300
Matthew Manley, prin. Fax 938-6815

Belpre, Washington, Pop. 6,560
Belpre CSD 1,300/K-12
2014 Washington Blvd 45714 740-423-9511
Harry Fleming, supt. Fax 423-3050
www.belpre.k12.oh.us
Belpre HS 400/9-12
612 3rd St 45714 740-423-3000
Bob Hattman, prin. Fax 423-3003
Belpre MS 500/4-8
2000 Rockland Ave 45714 740-423-3010
Bernie Boice, prin. Fax 423-3012

Berea, Cuyahoga, Pop. 18,242
Berea CSD 7,400/K-12
390 Fair St 44017 440-243-6000
Derran Wimer, supt. Fax 234-2309
www.berea.k12.oh.us
Berea HS 1,200/9-12
165 E Bagley Rd 44017 440-234-5418
Vincenzo Ruggiero, prin. Fax 891-0317
Roehm MS 700/6-8
7220 Pleasant Ave 44017 440-234-1326
Harold Booker, prin. Fax 891-3764
Other Schools – See Brook Park, Middleburg Heights

Baldwin-Wallace College Post-Sec.
275 Eastland Rd 44017 440-826-2900

Bergholz, Jefferson, Pop. 753
Edison Local SD
Supt. — See Hammondsville
Springfield MS 400/5-8
4569 County Road 75 43908 740-768-2420
Richard Wilinski, prin. Fax 768-2403

Berlin, Holmes
East Holmes Local SD 1,700/PK-12
PO Box 182 44610 330-893-2610
Joe Wengerd, supt. Fax 893-2838
www.eastholmes.k12.oh.us
Hiland JSHS 400/7-12
PO Box 275 44610 330-893-2626
Matthew Johnson, prin. Fax 893-3570
Other Schools – See Charm

Berlin Center, Mahoning
Western Reserve Local SD 800/K-12
13850 W Akron Canfield Rd 44401 330-547-4100
Charles Swindler, supt. Fax 547-9302
www.westernreserve.k12.oh.us
Western Reserve HS 300/9-12
13850 W Akron Canfield Rd 44401 330-547-3911
Jeffrey Zatchok, prin. Fax 547-9302
Western Reserve MS 300/5-8
15904 W Akron Canfield Rd 44401 330-547-3941
Deborah Farelli, prin. Fax 547-9302

Berlin Heights, Erie, Pop. 658
Berlin-Milan Local SD
Supt. — See Milan
Berlin-Milan MS 400/6-8
20 Center St 44814 419-588-2078
Douglas Crooks, prin. Fax 588-3212

Bethel, Clermont, Pop. 2,590
Bethel-Tate Local SD 2,000/K-12
112 N Union St 45106 513-734-2271
James Smith, supt. Fax 734-4792
www.betheltate.org
Bethel-Tate HS 600/9-12
3420 State Route 125 45106 513-734-2271
Kimberley Mcguire, prin. Fax 734-1355
Bethel-Tate MS 500/6-8
649 W Plane St 45106 513-734-2271
Steve Gill, prin. Fax 734-0888

U.S. Grant JVSD
718 W Plane St 45106 513-734-6222
Ken Morrison, supt. Fax 734-4758
www.grantcareer.com
Grant Career Center Vo/Tech
718 W Plane St 45106 513-734-6222
Kenneth Kappel, prin. Fax 734-4758

Bettsville, Seneca, Pop. 761
Bettsville Local SD 200/K-12
PO Box 6 44815 419-986-5166
Randy Pawlowski, supt. Fax 986-6039
www.bettsville.k12.oh.us/
Bettsville HS 100/9-12
PO Box 6 44815 419-986-5166
David Madaras, prin. Fax 986-6039
Bettsville MS 100/5-8
PO Box 6 44815 419-986-5166
David Madaras, prin. Fax 986-6039

Beverly, Washington, Pop. 1,272
Fort Frye Local SD 1,200/K-12
PO Box 1149 45715 740-984-2497
Robert Heinlein, supt. Fax 984-8784
www.fortfrye.k12.oh.us/
Ft. Frye JSHS 600/7-12
PO Box 1089 45715 740-984-2376
Susan Rauch, prin. Fax 984-4361

Bexley, Franklin, Pop. 12,322
Bexley CSD 2,200/K-12
348 S Cassingham Rd 43209 614-231-7611
Michael Johnson, supt. Fax 231-8448
www.bexley.k12.oh.us/
Bexley HS 800/9-12
326 S Cassingham Rd 43209 614-231-4591
John Kellogg, prin. Fax 338-2087
Bexley MS 400/7-8
300 S Cassingham Rd 43209 614-237-4277
Harley Williams, prin. Fax 338-2090

Blanchester, Clinton, Pop. 4,348
Blanchester Local SD 1,800/K-12
951 Cherry St 45107 937-783-3523
Brian Ruckel, supt. Fax 783-2990
www.blanchester.k12.oh.us/
Blanchester HS 600/9-12
953 Cherry St 45107 937-783-2461
George Rise, prin. Fax 783-5666
Blanchester MS 400/6-8
955 Cherry St 45107 937-783-3642
Martin Paeltz, prin. Fax 783-3477

Bloomdale, Wood, Pop. 709
Elmwood Local SD 1,200/K-12
7650 Jerry City Rd 44817 419-655-2583
Steven Pritts, supt. Fax 655-3995
www.elmwood.k12.oh.us
Elmwood HS 400/9-12
7650 Jerry City Rd 44817 419-655-2583
Tom Bentley, prin.
Elmwood MS 400/5-8
7650 Jerry City Rd 44817 419-655-2583
Jesse Steiner, prin.

Bloomingburg, Fayette, Pop. 850
Miami Trace Local SD
Supt. — See Washington Court House
Miami Trace JHS 500/7-8
103 Main St 43106 740-437-7344
Eric Wayne, prin. Fax 437-6061

Bloomingdale, Jefferson, Pop. 214
Jefferson County JVSD
1509 County Road 22A 43910 740-264-5545
Dale Edwards, supt. Fax 264-3144
www.jcjvs.k12.oh.us
Jefferson County Joint Vocational HS Vo/Tech
1509 County Road 22A 43910 740-264-5545
Todd Phillipson, prin. Fax 264-3144

Bluffton, Allen, Pop. 4,013
Bluffton EVD 1,200/K-12
102 S Jackson St 45817 419-358-5901
Rodney Russell, supt. Fax 358-4871
www.bluffton.noacsc.org/
Bluffton HS 400/9-12
106 W College Ave 45817 419-358-7941
Gregory Denecker, prin. Fax 358-6586
Bluffton MS 300/6-8
116 S Jackson St 45817 419-358-7961
Dean Giesige, prin. Fax 358-4871

Bluffton University Post-Sec.
1 University Dr 45817 419-358-3000

Boardman, Mahoning, Pop. 37,100

Hondros College Post-Sec.
7410 South Ave 44512 330-896-9666

Botkins, Shelby, Pop. 1,181
Botkins Local SD 600/K-12
PO Box 550 45306 937-693-4241
Connie Schneider, supt. Fax 693-2557
www.botkins.k12.oh.us
Botkins JSHS 300/7-12
PO Box 550 45306 937-693-4241
Cheryl Fark, prin. Fax 693-2557

Bowerston, Harrison, Pop. 424
Conotton Valley Union Local SD
Supt. — See Sherrodsville
Connotton Valley JSHS 300/7-12
7205 Cumberland Rd SW 44695 740-269-2711
Al Kennedy, prin. Fax 269-4405

Bowling Green, Wood, Pop. 29,793
Bowling Green CSD 3,000/K-12
140 S Grove St 43402 419-352-3576
Hugh Caumartin, supt. Fax 352-1701
www.bgcs.k12.oh.us
Bowling Green HS 1,100/9-12
530 W Poe Rd 43402 419-354-0100
Jeff Dever, prin. Fax 354-1839
Bowling Green JHS 500/7-8
215 W Wooster St 43402 419-354-0200
Lee Vincent, prin. Fax 353-1958

Bowling Green State University Post-Sec.
110 McFall Ctr 43403 419-372-2478

Bradford, Miami, Pop. 1,891
Bradford EVD 600/K-12
760 Railroad Ave 45308 937-448-2770
Barbara Townsend, supt. Fax 448-2493
www.bradford.k12.oh.us/
Bradford JSHS 300/6-12
750 Railroad Ave 45308 937-448-2719
Brad Greer, prin. Fax 448-2742

Brecksville, Cuyahoga, Pop. 13,250
Brecksville-Broadview Heights CSD 4,700/K-12
6638 Mill Rd 44141 440-740-4010
Thomas Diringer Ed.D., supt. Fax 740-4014
www.bbhcsd.org
Other Schools – See Broadview Heights

Cuyahoga Valley Career Center
8001 Brecksville Rd 44141 440-526-5200
Roscoe Schlachter, supt. Fax 746-8298
www.cvcc.k12.oh.us
Cuyahoga Valley Career Center Vo/Tech
8001 Brecksville Rd 44141 440-526-5200
Richard Rybak, prin. Fax 838-8929

Bridgeport, Belmont, Pop. 2,107
Bridgeport EVD 800/K-12
501 Bennett St 43912 740-635-1713
Mark Matz, supt. Fax 635-6003
www.bevs.k12.oh.us/
Bridgeport HS 300/9-12
501 Bennett St 43912 740-635-0853
Rob Zitzelsberger, prin. Fax 635-6008
Kirkwood MS 200/6-8
501 Bennett St 43912 740-635-0853
Rob Zitzelsberger, prin. Fax 635-6003

Brilliant, Jefferson, Pop. 1,604
Buckeye Local SD
Supt. — See Dillonvale
Buckeye North MS 200/6-8
1004 3rd St 43913 740-598-4540
Sharon Wallace, prin. Fax 598-4145

Bristolville, Trumbull
Bristol Local SD 800/K-12
PO Box 260 44402 330-889-3882
Dr. Marty Santillo, supt. Fax 889-2529
www.bristol.k12.oh.us
Bristol HS 400/7-12
PO Box 260 44402 330-889-2621
Gene Jones, prin. Fax 889-2529

Broadview Heights, Cuyahoga, Pop. 17,505
Brecksville-Broadview Heights CSD
Supt. — See Brecksville
Brecksville-Broadview Heights HS 1,600/9-12
6380 Mill Rd 44147 440-740-4700
Brian Wilch, prin. Fax 740-4704
Brecksville-Broadview Heights MS 1,200/6-8
6376 Mill Rd 44147 440-740-4400
Wendy Baker, prin. Fax 740-4404

Lawrence S 200/1-12
1551 E Wallings Rd 44147 440-526-0003
Mary Mayer, prin. Fax 526-0595
Vatterott College Post-Sec.
5025 E Royalton Rd 44147 440-526-1660

Brookfield, Trumbull
Brookfield Local SD 1,400/K-12
PO Box 209 44403 330-448-4930
Michael Notar, supt. Fax 448-5026
www.brookfield.k12.oh.us/
Brookfield HS, PO Box 209 44403 500/9-12
John Yensick, prin. 330-448-3001
Brookfield MS 400/5-8
PO Box 209 44403 330-448-3003
Tim Filipovich, prin. Fax 448-5028

Brooklyn, Cuyahoga, Pop. 10,901
Brooklyn CSD 1,400/K-12
9200 Biddulph Rd 44144 216-485-8110
Jefferey Lampert, supt. Fax 485-8118
www.brooklyn.k12.oh.us/
Brooklyn HS 400/9-12
9200 Biddulph Rd 44144 216-485-8163
Marsha Miller, prin. Fax 485-8124
Brooklyn MS 300/6-8
9200 Biddulph Rd 44144 216-485-8126
Tom Russo, prin. Fax 485-8118

Brook Park, Cuyahoga, Pop. 20,059
Berea CSD
Supt. — See Berea
Ford MS 1,100/6-8
17001 Holland Rd 44142 216-433-1133
Michael Pelegrino, prin. Fax 676-2072

Brookville, Montgomery, Pop. 5,317
Brookville Local SD 1,400/K-12
325 Simmons Ave 45309 937-833-2181
Timothy Hopkins, supt. Fax 833-2787
www.brookville.k12.oh.us/
Brookville HS 500/9-12
1 Blue Pride Dr 45309 937-833-6761
Chris Bronner, prin. Fax 833-6302
Brookville IS 500/4-8
2 Blue Pride Dr 45309 937-833-6731
Rebecca Hagan, prin. Fax 833-6756

Brunswick, Medina, Pop. 35,159
Brunswick CSD 7,300/K-12
3643 Center Rd 44212 330-225-7731
James Hayas, supt. Fax 273-0507
www.bcsoh.org
Brunswick HS 2,400/9-12
3581 Center Rd 44212 330-225-7731
Michael Mayell, prin. Fax 225-5393

Edwards MS 500/6-8
1497 Pearl Rd 44212 330-225-7731
Kent Morgan, prin. Fax 273-0519
Visintainer MS 600/6-8
1459 Pearl Rd 44212 330-225-7731
Carol Yost, prin. Fax 273-0400
Willetts MS 700/6-8
1045 Hadcock Rd 44212 330-225-7731
Mike Hodson, prin. Fax 273-0222

Bryan, Williams, Pop. 8,360
Bryan CSD 2,300/PK-12
1350 Fountain Grove Dr 43506 419-636-6973
James Gunner, supt. Fax 633-6280
www.bryan.k12.oh.us
Bryan HS 700/9-12
150 S Portland St 43506 419-636-4536
Norm Glismann, prin. Fax 633-6281
Bryan MS 800/4-8
1301 Center St 43506 419-636-6766
Beth Hollabaugh, prin. Fax 633-6282

Bucyrus, Crawford, Pop. 12,885
Bucyrus CSD 1,500/PK-12
117 E Mansfield St 44820 419-562-4045
John Roller, supt. Fax 562-3990
www.bucyrus.k12.oh.us
Bucyrus HS 600/9-12
900 W Perry St 44820 419-562-7721
James C. Oyster, prin. Fax 562-7819
Bucyrus MS 400/5-8
245 Woodlawn Ave 44820 419-562-0003
Wm. Todd Roll, prin. Fax 562-1773

Wynford Local SD 1,200/K-12
3288 Holmes Center Rd 44820 419-562-7828
Steve Mohr, supt. Fax 562-7825
www.wynford.k12.oh.us
Wynford JSHS 500/7-12
3288 Holmes Center Rd 44820 419-562-7828
Scott Langenderfer, prin. Fax 562-7825

Burton, Geauga, Pop. 1,446
Berkshire Local SD 1,200/K-12
PO Box 364 44021 440-834-4123
James Knapp, supt. Fax 834-2058
www.berkshire.k12.oh.us
Berkshire JSHS 700/7-12
PO Box 365 44021 440-834-4110
Steve Reedy, prin. Fax 834-0440

Kent State University-Geauga Campus Post-Sec.
14111 Claridon Troy Rd 44021 440-834-4187

Byesville, Guernsey, Pop. 2,597
Rolling Hills Local SD
Supt. — See Cambridge
Meadowbrook HS 700/9-12
58615 Marietta Rd 43723 740-685-2566
Charles Chippi, prin. Fax 685-2797
Meadowbrook MS 500/6-8
58607 Marietta Rd 43723 740-685-2561
Larry Touvell, prin. Fax 685-2628

Cadiz, Harrison, Pop. 3,396
Belmont-Harrison Area JVSD
Supt. — See Saint Clairsville
Harrison Career Center Vo/Tech
82500 Cadiz Jewett Rd 43907 740-942-2148
Kenneth Woodford, prin. Fax 695-4866

Harrison Hills CSD
Supt. — See Hopedale
Harrison Central HS 600/9-12
440 E Market St 43907 740-912-7700
James Rocchi, prin. Fax 942-7705

Caldwell, Noble, Pop. 1,911
Caldwell EVD 1,000/K-12
516 Fairground St 43724 740-732-5637
William Brelsford, supt. Fax 732-7303
www.caldwell.k12.oh.us/
Caldwell HS, 516 Fairground St 43724 300/9-12
H. Dalton Summers, prin. 740-732-5634

Caledonia, Marion, Pop. 556
River Valley Local SD 1,800/K-12
197 Brocklesby Rd 43314 740-725-5400
Thomas G. Shade, supt. Fax 725-5499
www.rivervalley.k12.oh.us
River Valley HS 500/9-12
4280 Marion Mount Gilead Rd 43314 740-725-5800
David Gorenflo, prin. Fax 725-5899
River Valley MS 400/6-8
4334 Marion Mount Gilead Rd 43314 740-725-5700
Glenn Crawford, prin. Fax 725-5799

Cambridge, Guernsey, Pop. 11,562
Cambridge CSD 2,700/K-12
6111 Fairdale Dr 43725 740-439-5021
Regis Woods, supt. Fax 439-3796
www.cambridge.k12.oh.us/
Cambridge HS 800/9-12
65328 Creek Rd 43725 740-435-1100
Frank Blake, prin. Fax 435-1101
Cambridge MS 600/6-8
65370 Creek Rd 43725 740-435-1140
William Lee, prin. Fax 435-1141

Rolling Hills Local SD 2,200/K-12
60851 Southgate Rd 43725 740-432-5370
Gary Norris, supt. Fax 435-8312
www.omeresa.net/Schools/Meadowbrook/
Other Schools – See Byesville

Camden, Preble, Pop. 2,264
Preble Shawnee Local SD 1,200/K-12
124 Bloomfield St 45311 937-452-3323
Dale Robertson, supt. Fax 452-3926
www.preble-shawnee.k12.oh.us
Preble Shawnee HS 500/9-12
5495 Somers Gratis Rd 45311 937-787-3541
Richard McKee, prin. Fax 787-3664
Preble Shawnee JHS 200/7-8
5495 Somers Gratis Rd 45311 937-787-3519
Dianna Whitis, prin. Fax 787-3664

Campbell, Mahoning, Pop. 8,888
Campbell CSD 1,600/K-12
280 6th St 44405 330-799-8777
Thomas Robey, supt. Fax 799-0875
www.campbell.k12.oh.us
Campbell MS 500/5-8
2002 Community Cir 44405 330-799-0054
Marcia Norris, prin. Fax 799-8259
Memorial HS 500/9-12
280 6th St 44405 330-799-1515
Richard Gozur, prin. Fax 799-6390

Canal Fulton, Stark, Pop. 5,054
Northwest Local SD 2,000/K-12
8614 Erie Ave N 44614 330-854-2291
Dennis Lambes, supt.
www.northwest.sparcc.org/
Northwest HS 800/9-12
8580 Erie Ave N 44614 330-854-2205
Stephen Jones, prin. Fax 854-2030
Northwest MS 400/7-8
8614 Erie Ave N 44614 330-854-3303
Robert Venables, prin. Fax 854-5883

Canal Winchester, Franklin, Pop. 5,652
Canal Winchester Local SD 2,800/K-12
290 Washington St 43110 614-837-4533
Jeff Childers, supt. Fax 833-2165
www.canalwin.k12.oh.us
Canal Winchester HS 800/9-12
300 Washington St 43110 614-833-2157
Lynn Landis, prin. Fax 833-2163
Canal Winchester MS 400/7-8
100 Washington St 43110 614-833-2151
Cassandra Miller, prin. Fax 833-2173

Harvest Preparatory S 600/PK-12
4595 Gender Rd 43110 614-837-1990
Jack Johnson, hdmstr. Fax 837-9591

Canfield, Mahoning, Pop. 7,153
Canfield Local SD 3,100/K-12
100 Wadsworth St 44406 330-533-3303
Dante J. Zambrini, supt. Fax 533-6827
canfield.access-k12.org
Canfield HS 1,100/9-12
100 Cardinal Dr 44406 330-533-5507
Abby Barone, prin. Fax 533-1919
Canfield Village MS 1,000/5-8
42 Wadsworth St 44406 330-533-5544
Ronald Infante, prin. Fax 702-7064

Mahoning County Career & Technical Ctr 330-729-4000
7300 N Palmyra Rd 44406 Fax 729-4050
Roan Craig, supt.
Mahoning County Career & Technical Ctr Vo/Tech
7300 N Palmyra Rd 44406 330-729-4000
Jane Hogan, dir. Fax 729-4015

Canton, Stark, Pop. 79,478
Canton CSD 11,200/PK-12
617 Mckinley Ave SW 44707 330-438-2500
Marva Jones, supt. Fax 455-0682
www.ccsdistrict.org
Crenshaw MS 800/6-8
2525 19th St NE 44705 330-454-7717
Edward Rehfus, prin. Fax 588-2120
Early College HS 9-12
231 McKinley Ave NW 44702 330-458-3950
Tom Forbes, prin. Fax 458-3980
Freshman Academy 9-9
1510 Clarendon Ave NW 44708 330-451-3334
Marilyn Van Almen, prin. Fax 438-2782
Hartford MS 400/6-8
1824 3rd St SE 44707 330-453-6012
Stephanie Patrick, prin. Fax 453-5096
Lehman MS 700/6-8
1400 Broad Ave NW 44708 330-456-1963
Valerie Pack, prin. Fax 456-8121
McKinley HS 1,900/9-12
2323 17th St NW 44708 330-438-2712
Jeffrey Talbert, prin. Fax 580-2712
Souers MS 600/6-8
2800 13th St SW 44710 330-456-8779
Barbara Maceyak, prin. Fax 438-2788
Timken HS 900/9-12
521 Tuscarawas St W 44702 330-438-2602
Kim Redmond, prin. Fax 580-3508
Community Educational Services Adult
617 Mckinley Ave SW 44707 330-438-2559
Kim Redmond, prin. Fax 454-6767

Canton Local SD 1,800/K-12
4526 Ridge Ave SE 44707 330-484-8010
Teresa Purses, supt. Fax 484-8032
www.cantonlocal.org
Canton South HS 800/9-12
600 Faircrest St SE 44707 330-484-8000
G. Ira Wentworth, prin. Fax 484-8013
Faircrest Memorial MS 600/6-8
616 Faircrest St SW 44706 330-484-8015
Timothy Welker, prin. Fax 484-8033

Plain Local SD 1,500/K-12
901 44th St NW 44709 330-492-3500
Christopher Smith, supt. Fax 493-5542
www.plainlocal.org/
Glenoak HS 9-12
1801 Schneider St NE 44721 330-491-3800
Mark Hartman, prin. Fax 491-3801
Glenwood MS 6-8
1015 44th St NW 44709 330-491-3780
Cindy Donnelly, prin. Fax 491-3781
Oakwood MS 6-8
2300 Schneider St NE 44721 330-491-3790
Mark Filicky, prin. Fax 491-3791

Aultman Hospital Post-Sec.
2600 6th St SW 44710 330-438-6241
Central Catholic HS 600/9-12
4824 Tuscarawas St W 44708 330-478-2131
Fr. Robert Kaylor, prin. Fax 478-6086
Heritage Christian S 300/PK-12
2107 6th St SW 44706 330-452-8271
Howard Pizor, prin. Fax 452-0672

Malone College Post-Sec.
515 25th St NW 44709 330-471-8100
National Beauty College Post-Sec.
4642 Cleveland Ave NW 44709 330-499-9444
Timken Mercy Medical Center Post-Sec.
1320 Mercy Dr NW 44708 330-489-1001

Cardington, Morrow, Pop. 1,992
Cardington-Lincoln Local SD 1,100/K-12
121 Nichols St 43315 419-864-3691
Mark Wilcheck, supt. Fax 864-0946
www.cardington.k12.oh.us/
Cardington-Lincoln HS 400/9-12
349 Chesterville Ave 43315 419-864-2691
Taylor Gerhardt, prin. Fax 864-9515
Cardington-Lincoln JHS 200/7-8
349 Chesterville Ave 43315 419-864-0609
Rick Smith, prin. Fax 864-3168

Carey, Wyandot, Pop. 3,868
Carey EVD 900/K-12
357 E South St 43316 419-396-7922
Raymond Funk, supt. Fax 396-3158
carey.k12.oh.us/
Carey JSHS 500/7-12
357 E South St 43316 419-396-7638
Karl Vehre, prin. Fax 396-3158

Carlisle, Warren, Pop. 5,688
Carlisle Local SD 1,800/K-12
724 Fairview Dr 45005 937-746-0710
Timothy J. McLinden, supt. Fax 746-0438
www.carlisle-local.k12.oh.us
Carlisle HS 500/9-12
250 Jamaica Rd 45005 937-746-4481
Matt Bishop, prin. Fax 937-6578
Chamberlain MS 400/6-8
720 Fairview Dr 45005 937-746-3227
Mike Milner, prin. Fax 746-0519

Carroll, Fairfield, Pop. 474
Bloom-Carroll Local SD 1,500/K-12
PO Box 338 43112 614-837-6560
Lynn Dildine, supt. Fax 756-7466
www.bloom-carroll.k12.oh.us
Bloom-Carroll HS 500/9-12
5240 Plum Rd 43112 740-756-4318
Roger Mace, prin. Fax 756-9525
Bloom-Carroll MS 300/6-8
PO Box 338 43112 740-756-9231
Mark Fenik, prin. Fax 756-7466

Eastland-Fairfield Career & Technical SD
Supt. — See Groveport
Fairfield Career Center Vo/Tech
4000 Columbus Lncster Rd NW 43112
614-837-9443
Bonnie Hopkins, prin. Fax 837-9447

Carrollton, Carroll, Pop. 3,297
Carrollton EVD 2,500/PK-12
252 3rd St NE 44615 330-627-2181
Kevin J. Spears, supt. Fax 627-2182
www.carrollton.k12.oh.us
Bell-Herron MS, 252 3rd St NE 44615 500/6-8
Robert Mehno, prin. 330-627-7188
Carrollton HS, 252 3rd St NE 44615 900/9-12
David Davis, prin. 330-627-2134

Casstown, Miami, Pop. 326
Miami East Local SD 1,400/K-12
3825 N State Route 589 45312 937-335-7505
Todd Rappold, supt. Fax 335-6309
www.miamieast.k12.oh.us
Miami East HS 500/9-12
3825 N State Route 589 45312 937-335-7070
Tim Williams, prin. Fax 335-7505
Miami East JHS 300/6-8
4025 N State Route 589 45312 937-335-5439
Allen Mack, prin. Fax 332-7927

Castalia, Erie, Pop. 906
Margaretta Local SD 1,500/K-12
305 S Washington St 44824 419-684-5322
Edward Kurt, supt. Fax 684-9003
www.margaretta.k12.oh.us/
Margaretta JSHS, 209 Lowell St 44824 700/7-12
Keith Bonnigson, prin. 419-684-5351

Cedarville, Greene, Pop. 4,037
Cedar Cliff Local SD 700/K-12
PO Box 45 45314 937-766-6000
David Baits, supt. Fax 766-4717
www.cedarcliffschools.org
Cedarville MSHS 400/6-12
PO Box 45 45314 937-766-1871
Virginia Potter, prin. Fax 766-5211

Cedarville University Post-Sec.
251 N Main St 45314 937-766-2211

Celina, Mercer, Pop. 10,348
Celina CSD 2,900/K-12
585 E Livingston St 45822 419-586-8300
Matt Miller, supt. Fax 586-7046
www.celinaschools.org
Celina HS 1,000/9-12
715 E Wayne St 45822 419-586-8300
Curt Shellabarger, prin. Fax 584-0307
Celina MS 500/7-8
615 Holly St 45822 419-586-8300
Ann Esselstein, prin. Fax 586-9166

Harbor Christian S 50/9-12
PO Box 357 45822 419-586-9029
Nancy Head, prin. Fax 586-8961
Wright State University Post-Sec.
7600 State Route 703 45822 419-586-0300

Centerburg, Knox, Pop. 1,483
Centerburg Local SD 1,200/K-12
175 Union St 43011 740-625-6346
Dorothy B. Holden, supt. Fax 625-9939
Centerburg HS 400/9-12
3782 Columbus Rd 43011 740-625-6055
John Morgan, prin. Fax 625-5799

Centerburg MS 300/6-8
3782 Columbus Rd 43011 740-625-6055
Mike Hebenthal, prin. Fax 625-5799

Centerville, Montgomery, Pop. 23,162
Centerville CSD 8,100/K-12
111 Virginia Ave 45458 937-433-8841
Gary P. Smiga, supt. Fax 438-6057
www.centerville.k12.oh.us
Centerville HS 2,700/9-12
500 E Franklin St 45459 937-439-3500
Eileen Booher, prin. Fax 439-3574
Magsig MS 600/6-8
192 W Franklin St 45459 937-433-0965
S. Westendorf-Wozniak, prin. Fax 433-5256
Tower Heights MS 600/6-8
195 N Johanna Dr 45459 937-434-0383
Clint Freese, prin. Fax 434-3033
Other Schools – See Dayton

RETS Technical Center Post-Sec.
555 E Alex Bell Rd 45459 937-433-3410
Spring Valley Academy 400/K-12
1461 E Spring Valley Pike 45458 937-433-0790
Bradley Durby, prin. Fax 433-0914

Chagrin Falls, Cuyahoga, Pop. 3,808
Chagrin Falls EVD 2,000/PK-12
400 E Washington St 44022 440-247-4363
Dr. David Axner, supt. Fax 247-5883
www.chagrin-falls.k12.oh.us
Chagrin Falls HS 700/9-12
400 E Washington St 44022 440-247-2072
Robert Hunt, prin. Fax 247-2071
Chagrin Falls MS 300/7-8
342 E Washington St 44022 440-247-4746
Lisa Bontempo, prin. Fax 247-4855

Kenston Local SD 2,200/K-12
17419 Snyder Rd 44023 440-543-9677
Robert Lee, supt. Fax 543-8634
www.kenstonlocal.com
Kenston HS 1,000/9-12
9500 Bainbridge Rd 44023 440-543-9821
Christopher Lewis, prin. Fax 543-9021
Kenston MS 700/6-8
17425 Snyder Rd 44023 440-543-8241
Patricia Brockway, prin. Fax 543-4851

English Nanny and Governess School Post-Sec.
37 S Franklin St 44022 440-247-0600

Chardon, Geauga, Pop. 5,280
Chardon Local SD 3,300/K-12
428 North St 44024 440-285-4052
Joseph Bergant, supt. Fax 285-7229
www.chardon.k12.oh.us
Chardon HS 1,100/9-12
151 Chardon Ave 44024 440-285-4057
Doug Delong, prin. Fax 285-9463
Chardon MS 800/6-8
424 North St 44024 440-285-4062
Tom Solet, prin. Fax 286-0461

Notre Dame-Cathedral Latin HS 800/9-12
13000 Auburn Rd 44024 440-286-6226
Joseph Waler, prin. Fax 286-7199

Charm, Holmes
East Holmes Local SD
Supt. — See Berlin
Wise MS, PO Box 159 44617 50/5-8
Jon Wilson, prin. 330-893-2505

Chesapeake, Lawrence, Pop. 879
Chesapeake Union EVD 1,300/K-12
10183 County Road 1 45619 740-867-3135
Samuel Hall, supt. Fax 867-3136
www.peake.k12.oh.us
Chesapeake HS 400/9-12
10181 County Road 1 45619 740-867-5958
Joseph Rase, prin. Fax 867-1130
Chesapeake MS 400/5-8
10335 County Road 1 45619 740-867-3972
Kim Wells, prin. Fax 867-1120

Lawrence County JVSD
11627 State Route 243 45619 740-867-6641
Stephen Dodgion, supt. Fax 867-2009
www.collins-cc.k12.oh.us
Lawrence County Joint Vocational SHS Vo/Tech
11627 State Route 243 45619 740-867-6641
Fax 867-2009

Collins Career Center Post-Sec.
11627 State Route 243 45619 740-867-6641

Cheshire, Gallia, Pop. 84
Gallia County Local SD
Supt. — See Gallipolis
Kyger Creek MS 200/5-8
350 Watson Grove Rd 45620 740-367-7721
Silos Johnson, prin. Fax 367-5005
River Valley HS 600/9-12
1428 Little Kyger Rd 45620 740-367-7377
J. Michael Jacobs, prin. Fax 367-7249

Chesterland, Geauga, Pop. 2,078
West Geauga Local SD 2,500/K-12
8615 Cedar Rd 44026 440-729-5900
Anthony Podojil, supt. Fax 729-5939
www.westgeauga.k12.oh.us
West Geauga HS 900/9-12
13401 Chillicothe Rd 44026 440-729-5950
Joseph Mueller, prin. Fax 729-5959
West Geauga MS 700/6-8
8611 Cedar Rd 44026 440-729-5940
James Kish, prin. Fax 729-5909

Chillicothe, Ross, Pop. 22,081
Chillicothe CSD 3,200/K-12
235 Cherry St 45601 740-775-4250
Roger Crago, supt. Fax 775-4270
www.chillicothe.k12.oh.us
Chillicothe HS 1,000/9-12
381 Yoctangee Pkwy 45601 740-702-2287
John Payne, prin. Fax 773-1097
Smith MS 600/6-8
345 Arch St 45601 740-773-2241
Robert Crabtree, prin. Fax 774-9482

Huntington Local SD 1,400/K-12
188 Huntsman Rd 45601 740-663-5892
John Barr, supt. Fax 663-6078
www.hunt.k12.oh.us/
Huntington HS 500/9-12
188 Huntsman Rd 45601 740-663-2230
Tim Butler, prin. Fax 663-5042
Huntington MS 300/6-8
188 Huntsman Rd 45601 740-663-6079
Alice Kellough, prin. Fax 663-6080

Pickaway-Ross County JVSD
895 Crouse Chapel Rd 45601 740-642-1200
Brett Smith, supt. Fax 642-1399
www.pickawayross.com
Pickaway-Ross Career & Technology Center Vo/Tech
895 Crouse Chapel Rd 45601 740-642-1200
Judy Wells, prin. Fax 642-1399

Southeastern Local SD 300/K-12
2003 Lancaster Rd 45601 740-774-2003
Brian Justice, supt. Fax 774-1687
www.sepanthers.k12.oh.us/
Southeastern HS 300/9-12
2003 Lancaster Rd 45601 740-774-2003
Leonard Steyer, prin. Fax 774-1684
Southeastern MS 50/5-8
2003 Lancaster Rd 45601 740-774-2003
David Shea, prin. Fax 774-1684

Union-Scioto Local SD 2,000/K-12
1565 Egypt Pike 45601 740-773-4102
Dwight Garrett, supt. Fax 775-2852
gsn.k12.oh.us/unioto/index.htm
Unioto HS 600/9-12
14193 Pleasant Valley Rd 45601 740-773-4105
James Osborne, prin. Fax 774-9158
Unioto JHS 300/7-8
160 Moundsville Rd 45601 740-773-5211
Ron Lovely, prin. Fax 772-2974

Zane Trace Local SD 1,600/K-12
946 State Route 180 45601 740-775-1355
Carolyn Everidge, supt. Fax 773-0249
gsn.k12.oh.us/zanetrace/index.html
Zane Trace HS 500/9-12
946 State Route 180 45601 740-775-1809
Todd Holdren, prin. Fax 775-1301
Zane Trace MS 500/5-8
946 State Route 180 45601 740-773-9854
Bret Mavis, prin.

Ohio University Post-Sec.
PO Box 629 45601 740-774-7200
Recording Workshop Post-Sec.
455 Massieville Rd 45601 740-663-1000
Southeastern Business College Post-Sec.
1410 Industrial Dr 45601 740-774-6300

Cincinnati, Hamilton, Pop. 308,728
Cincinnati CSD, PO Box 5381 45201 34,100/PK-12
Rosa Blackwell, supt. 513-363-0000
www.cps-k12.org
Aiken College & Career HS 600/9-12
5641 Belmont Ave 45224 513-363-6760
Eric Thomas, prin. Fax 363-6767
Aiken Traditional HS 300/9-12
5641 Belmont Ave 45224 513-363-6600
Susan Raudabaugh, prin. Fax 363-6620
Clark Montessori S 700/7-12
3030 Erie Ave 45208 513-363-7100
Rupashree Townsend, prin. Fax 363-7120
Dater HS 700/7-12
2146 Ferguson Rd 45238 513-363-7200
Martha Dupree-Gibson, prin. Fax 363-7220
Hughes Center HS 1,500/9-12
2515 Clifton Ave 45219 513-363-7500
Mary Hahn, prin. Fax 363-7520
Riverview East S 100/PK-10
3555 Kellogg Ave 45226 513-363-3400
Eugene Smith, prin. Fax 363-3420
School for Creative & Performing Arts 1,000/4-12
1310 Sycamore St 45202 513-363-8000
John Carlisle, prin. Fax 363-8020
Shroder Paideia Academy 600/7-12
3500 Lumford Pl 45213 513-363-6900
Yenetta Harper, prin. Fax 363-6920
Taft HS 700/9-12
420 Ezzard Charles Dr 45214 513-363-8200
Anthony Smith, prin. Fax 363-8220
Walnut Hills JSHS 1,900/7-12
3250 Victory Pkwy 45207 513-363-8400
Marvin Koenig, prin. Fax 363-8420
Western Hills University HS 500/9-12
2144 Ferguson Rd 45238 513-363-8900
Stephanie Morton, prin. Fax 363-8920
Woodward Career Technical S Vo/Tech
7005 Reading Rd 45237 513-363-9300
J. Larry Ballew, prin. Fax 363-9320
Woodward SHS 200/11-12
7001 Reading Rd 45237 513-363-9500
Sammy Yates, prin. Fax 363-9520

Deer Park Community CSD 1,400/K-12
8688 Donna Ln 45236 513-891-0222
Kimberlee Gray, supt. Fax 891-2930
www.deerparkcityschools.org
Deer Park JSHS 700/7-12
8351 Plainfield Rd 45236 513-891-0010
Mark Lutz, prin. Fax 891-3845

Finneytown Local SD 1,800/K-12
8916 Fontainebleau Ter 45231 513-728-3700
Randall Parsons, supt. Fax 931-0986
www.finneytown.org
Finneytown HS 900/7-12
8916 Fontainebleau Ter 45231 513-931-0712
Jack Fisher, prin. Fax 728-7230

Forest Hills Local SD 7,500/K-12
7550 Forest Rd 45255 513-231-3600
John B. Patzwald Ph.D., supt. Fax 231-3830
www.foresthills.edu
Anderson HS 1,500/9-12
7560 Forest Rd 45255 513-232-2772
Diana Carter, prin. Fax 232-3146
Nagel MS 1,200/7-8
1500 Nagel Rd 45255 513-474-5407
Natasha Adams, prin. Fax 474-5584
Turpin HS 1,100/9-12
2650 Bartels Rd 45244 513-232-7770
Peggy Johnson, prin. Fax 232-9047

Great Oaks Institute of Technology
3254 E Kemper Rd Unit 3 45241 513-771-8840
Roberta White, supt. Fax 771-6575
Diamond Oaks CDC Vo/Tech
6375 Harrison Ave 45247 513-574-1300
Rober Schnur, prin. Fax 574-3953
Scarlet Oaks CDC Vo/Tech
3254 E Kemper Rd Unit 2 45241 513-771-8810
Craig Williams, prin. Fax 771-4928
Other Schools – See Milford, Wilmington

Indian Hill EVD 2,200/K-12
6855 Drake Rd 45243 513-272-4500
Jane Knudson Ed.D., supt. Fax 272-4512
www.ih.k12.oh.us
Indian Hill HS 700/9-12
6865 Drake Rd 45243 513-272-4550
Nancy Striebich, prin. Fax 272-4557
Indian Hill MS 500/6-8
6845 Drake Rd 45243 513-272-4642
Brian Frank, prin. Fax 272-4690

Lockland Local SD 700/K-12
210 N Cooper Ave 45215 513-563-5000
Donna Hubbard, supt. Fax 563-9611
www.locklandschools.org
Other Schools – See Lockland

Madeira CSD 1,300/PK-12
7465 Loannes Dr 45243 513-985-6070
Stephen M. Kramer, supt. Fax 985-6072
www.madeiracityschools.org
Madeira HS 500/9-12
7465 Loannes Dr 45243 513-891-8222
Chris Mate, prin. Fax 985-6089
Madeira MS 200/5-8
6612 Miami Ave 45243 513-561-5555
Robert Kramer, prin. Fax 272-4145

Mariemont CSD 1,700/K-12
6743 Chestnut St 45227 513-272-7500
Gerald Harris, supt. Fax 527-3436
www.mariemontschools.org
Mariemont HS 500/9-12
3812 Pocahontas Ave 45227 513-272-7600
Jim Renner, prin. Fax 527-5991
Mariemont JHS 300/7-8
6743 Chestnut St 45227 513-272-7300
Keith Koehne, prin. Fax 527-3432

Mt. Healthy CSD 3,400/PK-12
7615 Harrison Ave 45231 513-729-0077
David Horine, supt. Fax 728-4692
www.mthcs.org/
Mt. Healthy HS 1,100/9-12
2046 Adams Rd 45231 513-728-7644
D. Wayne Sawyers, prin. Fax 728-4695
North MS 300/7-8
2170 Struble Rd 45231 513-742-6016
David Kennedy, prin. Fax 728-4691
South MS 300/7-8
1917 Miles Rd 45231 513-742-0666
Stephanie Patton, prin. Fax 742-2797

North College Hill CSD 1,500/PK-12
1498 W Galbraith Rd 45231 513-728-4770
Gary Gellert, supt. Fax 728-4774
www.nchcityschools.org
North College Hill JSHS 800/7-12
1620 W Galbraith Rd 45239 513-728-4783
Kelly Hughes, prin. Fax 728-4791

Northwest Local SD 10,800/PK-12
3240 Banning Rd 45239 513-923-1000
Richard Glatfelter, supt. Fax 923-3644
www.nwlsd.org
Colerain HS 2,300/9-12
8801 Cheviot Rd 45251 513-385-6424
Maureen Heintz, prin. Fax 741-5032
Colerain MS 700/6-8
4700 Poole Rd 45251 513-385-8490
Chris Shisler, prin. Fax 385-6685
Northwest HS 1,200/9-12
10761 Pippin Rd 45231 513-851-7300
Todd Bowling, prin. Fax 742-6376
Pleasant Run MS 1,000/6-8
11770 Pippin Rd 45231 513-851-2400
David Maine, prin. Fax 851-7071
White Oak MS 800/6-8
3130 Jessup Rd 45239 513-741-4300
Traci Rea, prin. Fax 741-0717

Oak Hills Local SD 8,200/K-12
6325 Rapid Run Rd 45233 513-574-3200
Patricia Brenneman, supt. Fax 598-2947
www.oakhills.k12.oh.us
Bridgetown MS 600/6-8
3900 Race Rd 45211 513-574-3511
Tim Cybulski, prin. Fax 574-6689
Delhi MS 600/6-8
5280 Foley Rd 45238 513-922-8400
Marni Durham, prin. Fax 922-8472
Oak Hills HS 3,100/9-12
3200 Ebenezer Rd 45248 513-922-2300
Jeff Brandt, prin. Fax 451-3795
Rapid Run MS 600/6-8
6345 Rapid Run Rd 45233 513-574-3200
Robert Sehlhorst, prin.

Princeton CSD 5,800/PK-12
25 W Sharon Rd 45246 513-771-8560
Aaron Mackey, supt. Fax 771-3454
www.princeton.k12.oh.us
Princeton Community MS 1,300/6-8
11157 Chester Rd 45246 513-552-8500
Mario Basora, prin. Fax 552-8511
Princeton HS 1,900/9-12
11080 Chester Rd 45246 513-552-8200
Raymond Spicher, prin. Fax 552-8224

Sycamore Community CSD 5,600/K-12
4881 Cooper Rd 45242 513-686-1700
Dr. Adrienne James, supt. Fax 791-4873
www.sycamoreschools.org
Sycamore HS 1,900/9-12
7400 Cornell Rd 45242 513-686-1770
Kenji Matsudo, prin. Fax 489-7425
Sycamore JHS 1,000/7-8
5757 Cooper Rd 45242 513-686-1760
Karen Naber, prin. Fax 891-3162

West Clermont Local SD 9,100/K-12
4350 Aicholtz Rd 45245 513-943-5000
Gary Brooks, supt. Fax 752-6158
www.westcler.k12.oh.us
Glen Este HS 1,500/9-12
4342 Glen Este Wthmsvlle Rd 45245 513-947-7600
Dennis Ashworth, prin. Fax 943-7090
Glen Este MS 1,000/6-8
4342 Glen Este Wthmsvlle Rd 45245 513-947-7700
Kevin Thacker, prin. Fax 753-3462
Other Schools – See Batavia

Winton Woods CSD 4,100/K-12
1215 W Kemper Rd 45240 513-619-2300
Camille Nasbe, supt. Fax 619-2309
www.wintonwoods.org
Winton Woods HS 1,300/9-12
1231 W Kemper Rd 45240 513-619-2420
Anita Williams, prin.
Winton Woods MS 700/7-8
147 Farragut Rd 45218 513-619-2240
Erroll Campbell, prin.

Aldersgate Christian Academy 100/K-12
1810 Young St 45202 513-721-7944
David Crosley, prin. Fax 721-1357
Antonelli College Post-Sec.
124 E 7th St 45202 800-505-4338
Art Academy of Cincinnati Post-Sec.
1212 Jackson St 45202 513-562-6262
Art Institute of Cincinnati Post-Sec.
1171 E Kemper Rd 45246 513-751-1206
Art Institute of Ohio - Cincinnati Post-Sec.
1011 Glendale Milford Rd 45215 513-771-2829
Athenaeum of Ohio Post-Sec.
6616 Beechmont Ave 45230 513-231-2223
Bacon HS 800/9-12
4320 Vine St 45217 513-641-1300
Thomas Devolve, prin. Fax 641-0498
Brown Mackie College Post-Sec.
1011 Glendale Milford Rd 45215 513-771-2424
Central Baptist Academy 200/K-12
7645 Winton Rd 45224 513-521-5481
Richard Voiles, admin. Fax 521-5481
Christ Hospital Post-Sec.
2139 Auburn Ave 45219 513-369-2201
Christian Center Academy 200/PK-12
717 Barg Salt Run Rd 45244 513-575-4673
Pamela Walling, prin.
Cincinnati Christian University Post-Sec.
PO Box 4320 45204 513-244-8100
Cincinnati College of Mortuary Science Post-Sec.
645 W North Bend Rd 45224 513-761-2020
Cincinnati Country Day S 900/K-12
6905 Given Rd 45243 513-979-0274
Dr. Robert Macrae, hdmstr. Fax 527-7645
Cincinnati Hills Christian Academy 400/5-8
11525 Snider Rd 45249 513-247-0900
Rob Hall, prin. Fax 247-9362
Cincinnati Hills Christian Academy 400/9-12
11525 Snider Rd 45249 513-247-0900
Burr Storrs, prin. Fax 247-0982
Cincinnati Junior Academy 100/K-10
3798 Clifton Ave 45220 513-751-1255
Sherry Herdman, prin. Fax 751-1224
Cincinnati State Technical & Comm Coll Post-Sec.
3520 Central Pkwy 45223 513-569-1500
College of Mount Saint Joseph Post-Sec.
5701 Delhi Rd 45233 513-244-4200
Elder HS 1,000/9-12
3900 Vincent Ave 45205 513-921-3744
Thomas Otten, prin. Fax 921-8123
Galen College of Nursing Post-Sec.
100 E-Business Way Ste 200 45241 513-475-3600
God's Bible School and College Post-Sec.
1810 Young St 45202 513-721-7944
Good Samaritan Hospital Post-Sec.
375 Dixmyth Ave 45220 513-872-1983
Hebrew Union College Post-Sec.
3101 Clifton Ave 45220 513-221-1875
Hillside Christian Academy 50/K-12
5554 Muddy Creek Rd 45238 513-451-3777
Terrance Bledsoe, admin.
Hondros College Post-Sec.
4675 Cornell Rd Ste 175 45241 513-247-9711
Institute of Medical & Dental Technology Post-Sec.
375 Glensprings Dr Ste 201 45246 513-851-8500
International Academy of Hair Design Post-Sec.
8419 Colerain Ave 45239 513-741-4777
ITT Technical Institute Post-Sec.
4750 Wesley Ave 45212 513-531-8300
La Salle HS 800/9-12
3091 N Bend Rd 45239 513-741-3000
Thomas Luebbe, prin. Fax 741-2666
Marinello-Eastern Hills Academy Post-Sec.
7681 Beechmont Ave 45255 513-231-8621
McAuley HS 800/9-12
6000 Oakwood Ave 45224 513-681-1800
Cheryl Sucher, prin. Fax 681-1802
McNicholas HS 900/9-12
6536 Beechmont Ave 45230 513-231-3500
Thomas Bill, prin. Fax 231-1351

Miami Valley Christian Academy 400/K-12
6830 School St 45244 513-272-6822
Matthew Long, hdmstr. Fax 272-3711
Moeller HS 1,000/9-12
9001 Montgomery Rd 45242 513-791-1680
Blane M. Collison, prin. Fax 792-3343
Moler-Hollywood Beauty College Post-Sec.
130 E 6th St Fl 2 45202 513-621-5262
Mother of Mercy HS 600/9-12
3036 Werk Rd 45211 513-661-2740
Sr. Nancy Merkle, prin. Fax 661-1842
Ohio Center for Broadcasting Post-Sec.
6703 Madison Rd 45227 513-271-6060
Purcell-Marian HS 9-12
2935 Hackberry St 45206 513-751-1230
Albert Early, prin. Fax 751-1395
Reg Inst for Torah & Secular Studies 50/9-12
2209 Losantiville Ave 45237 513-631-0083
Rabbi E. Dzialoszynsky, prin. Fax 631-0947
St. Rita School for the Deaf Post-Sec.
1720 Glendale Milford Rd 45215 513-771-7600
St. Ursula Academy 700/9-12
1339 E Mcmillan St 45206 513-961-3410
Frances Romweber, prin. Fax 961-3856
St. Xavier HS 1,500/9-12
600 W North Bend Rd 45224 513-761-7600
David Mueller, prin. Fax 842-1610
Seton HS 600/9-12
3901 Glenway Ave 45205 513-471-2600
Susan Gibbons, prin. Fax 471-0529
Seven Hills S 1,100/PK-12
5400 Red Bank Rd 45227 513-271-9027
Sandra Theunick, hdmstr. Fax 271-2471
Sevenstar Academy 100/6-12
7155 E Kemper Rd 45249 707-276-3472
Fax 618-3334
Southwestern College of Business Post-Sec.
630 Vine St Ste 200 45202 513-421-3212
Southwestern College of Business Post-Sec.
149 Northland Blvd 45246 513-874-0432
Summit Country Day S 1,100/PK-12
2161 Grandin Rd 45208 513-871-4700
Dr. Patricia White, prin. Fax 871-6558
Temple Baptist College Post-Sec.
11965 Kenn Rd 45240 513-851-3800
Tri County Beauty College Post-Sec.
111 W Kemper Rd 45246 513-671-8340
Union Institute & University Post-Sec.
440 E McMillan St 45206 513-861-6400
University of Cincinnati Post-Sec.
2700 Clifton Ave 45220 513-556-6000
University of Cincinnati Post-Sec.
9555 Plainfield Rd 45236 513-745-5600
University of Cincinnati/OMI College Post-Sec.
2220 Victory Pkwy 45206 513-556-6567
Univ. of Cincinnati Coll. Allied Health Post-Sec.
PO Box 670394 45267 513-558-7495
Ursuline Academy 700/9-12
5535 Pfeiffer Rd 45242 513-791-5791
Adele Iwanusa, prin. Fax 791-5802
Western Hills Sch of Beauty & Hair Dsgn. Post-Sec.
6490 Glenway Ave 45211 513-574-3818
Xavier University Post-Sec.
3800 Victory Pkwy 45207 513-745-3000

Circleville, Pickaway, Pop. 13,559
Circleville CSD 1,600/K-12
388 Clark Dr 43113 740-474-4340
Tyrus Ankrom, supt. Fax 474-6600
www.circlevillecityschools.org/
Circleville HS 700/9-12
380 Clark Dr 43113 740-474-4846
Paul Vitartas, prin. Fax 474-3987
Everts MS 600/6-8
520 S Court St 43113 740-474-2345
Kirk McMahon, prin. Fax 477-6384

Logan Elm Local SD 2,300/K-12
9579 Tarlton Rd 43113 740-474-7501
C. Asa Bradbury, supt. Fax 477-6525
www.loganelmschools.com/
Logan Elm HS 700/9-12
9575 Tarlton Rd 43113 740-474-7503
Sally Kleon, prin. Fax 477-6525
McDowell-Exchange JHS 400/7-8
9579 Tarlton Rd 43113 740-474-7538
Rodney Brobst, prin. Fax 477-6525

Circleville Bible College Post-Sec.
PO Box 458 43113 740-474-8896

Clarksville, Clinton, Pop. 498
Clinton-Massie Local SD 1,800/K-12
2556 Lebanon Rd 45113 937-289-2471
Ronald Rudduck, supt. Fax 289-3313
www.clinton-massie.k12.oh.us
Clinton-Massie HS 600/9-12
2556 Lebanon Rd 45113 937-289-2109
Randy Dunlap, prin. Fax 289-7019
Clinton-Massie MS 400/6-8
2556 Lebanon Rd 45113 937-289-2932
Mark McCormick, prin. Fax 289-8100

Clayton, Montgomery, Pop. 13,194
Miami Valley Career Technology Center
6800 Hoke Rd 45315 937-837-7781
John Boggess, supt. Fax 837-5318
www.mvctc.com
Miami Valley Career Tech Center Vo/Tech
6800 Hoke Rd 45315 937-837-7781
Kristy Taylor, prin. Fax 837-5318

Northmont CSD
Supt. — See Englewood
Northmont HS 2,000/9-12
4916 National Rd 45315 937-832-6000
P. Eugene Klaus, prin. Fax 832-6001
Northmont MS 1,000/7-8
4810 National Rd 45315 937-832-6500
David Weekley, prin. Fax 832-6501

Cleveland, Cuyahoga, Pop. 452,208
Cleveland Municipal SD 56,000/PK-12
1380 E 6th St 44114 216-574-8000
Dr. Eugene Sanders, supt. Fax 574-8193
www.cmsdnet.net

Academy of Business Law & Technology 9-12
1349 E 79th St 44103 216-431-5361
Michelle Madison, prin. Fax 432-4543
Academy of Creative Expression 9-12
1349 E 79th St 44103 216-431-5361
Denetris Anderson, prin. Fax 432-4543
Adams HS 9-12
3817 Martin Luther King Jr 44105 216-491-5700
Carol Lockhart, prin. Fax 491-5701
Addams Business Career Center 600/9-12
2373 E 30th St 44115 216-621-2131
Gerard Leslie, prin. Fax 696-8843
Business Entrepreneurship & Tech Academy 9-12
17100 Harvard Ave 44128 216-921-1450
Perry Myles, prin. Fax 295-2455
Center for Urban & Environmental Studies 9-12
5515 Ira Ave 44144 216-351-8862
Karl Williamson, prin. Fax 778-6571
Cleveland Schl of Architecture & Design 9-12
2075 Stokes Blvd 44106 216-229-0232
Stacy Griffin-Cooper, prin.
Cleveland School of Arts HS 600/6-12
2064 Stearns Rd 44106 216-791-2496
Barbara Walton, prin. Fax 421-7689
Cleveland School of Science & Medicine 9-12
2075 Stokes Blvd 44106 216-229-0232
Edward Weber, prin.
Cleveland Skills & Career Center Vo/Tech
3122 Euclid Ave 44115 216-664-4673
Valerie Biggs-Hill, coord. Fax 361-1664
Collinwood HS 1,500/6-12
15210 Saint Clair Ave 44110 216-451-8782
Deborah Moore, prin. Fax 268-6057
East HS 1,100/9-12
1349 E 79th St 44103 216-431-5361
Brenda Washington, admin. Fax 432-4543
East Tech Annex Vo/Tech
1935 Euclid Ave 44115 216-621-5202
Gene Zuckerman, prin. Fax 795-8880
East Tech HS Vo/Tech
2439 E 55th St 44104 216-431-2626
Dale Laux, admin. Fax 431-4631
Glenville HS 1,700/9-12
650 E 113th St 44108 216-268-6000
Jacqueline Bell, admin. Fax 541-7666
Hayes HS Vo/Tech
4600 Detroit Ave 44102 216-631-1528
David Volosin, prin. Fax 634-2175
Hay HS, 2075 Stokes Blvd 44106 9-12
Kathleen Freilino, admin. 216-229-0232
High Tech Academy 10-12
2900 Community College Ave 44115 216-987-3549
Stacy Hutchinson, prin. Fax 987-4397
Kennedy HS 1,900/9-12
17100 Harvard Ave 44128 216-921-1450
Charita Crockrom, admin. Fax 295-2455
King S for Law 900/6-12
1651 E 71st St 44103 216-431-6858
Donald Jolly, prin. Fax 431-5180
Leadership & Human Services Institute Vo/Tech
2439 E 55th St 44104 216-431-2626
David Reiman, prin. Fax 431-4631
Leadership Urban Academy 9-12
17100 Harvard Ave 44128 216-921-1450
Erin Frew, prin. Fax 295-2455
Lighthouse Academy Vo/Tech
2439 E 55th St 44104 216-431-2626
Cheryl Taylor, prin. Fax 431-4631
Lincoln-West HS 1,600/9-12
3202 W 30th St 44109 216-631-1505
Valentina Mickey, prin. Fax 634-2403
Marshall HS 2,000/9-12
3952 W 140th St 44111 216-251-5740
Rhonda Saegert, prin. Fax 476-6862
Morgan S of Science 400/6-9
4016 Woodbine Ave 44113 216-281-6188
Laverne Hooks, prin. Fax 634-2113
Renaissance S of Fine Arts 9-12
650 E 113th St 44108 216-268-6000
Teresa Conley, prin. Fax 541-7666
Rhodes HS 1,700/9-12
5100 Biddulph Ave 44144 216-351-6285
Wayne Marok, admin. Fax 749-8130
Rhodes HS at Harper 9-12
5515 Ira Ave 44144 216-351-8862
Jennifer Rhone, prin. Fax 778-6571
School of Applied Design & Technology 9-12
1349 E 79th St 44103 216-431-5361
Patrick McNichols, prin. Fax 432-4543
School of Business & Internatnl Affairs 9-12
650 E 113th St 44108 216-268-6000
Anthony Riccio, prin. Fax 541-7666
School of Dreams Academy 9-12
17100 Harvard Ave 44128 216-921-1450
Christy Nickerson, prin. Fax 295-2455
School of Health Leadership & Wellness 9-12
650 E 113th St 44108 216-268-6000
Sophronia Hairston, prin. Fax 541-7666
School of Inquiry/Innovation & Tech 9-12
5100 Biddulph Ave 44144 216-351-6285
Donald Strinka, prin. Fax 749-8130
School of Leadership 9-12
5100 Biddulph Ave 44144 216-351-6285
Craig Strom, prin. Fax 749-8130
School of Medicine Pub Health & Justice 9-12
5515 Ira Ave 44144 216-351-8862
Jennifer Rhone, prin. Fax 778-6571
School of Science & Technology 9-12
650 E 113th St 44108 216-268-6000
Marion Wallace, prin. Fax 541-7666
Shuler MS 700/6-10
13501 Terminal Ave 44135 216-671-0272
Marilyn Cargile, prin. Fax 476-4212
South HS 1,500/9-12
7415 Broadway Ave 44105 216-641-0410
Timothy Bigenho, prin. Fax 441-8242
Technology Institute Vo/Tech
2439 E 55th St 44104 216-431-2626
Brian Register, prin. Fax 431-4631
Young S 400/6-11
17900 Harvard Ave 44128 216-283-5220
Alisa McKinnie, prin. Fax 295-3547
Cleveland Extension HS Adult
4600 Detroit Ave 44102 216-651-3840
Steven Mietus, prin. Fax 634-7143

Orange CSD 2,300/PK-12
32000 Chagrin Blvd 44124 216-831-8600
Daniel Lukich, supt. Fax 831-8029
www.orangeschools.org
Brady MS 500/6-8
32000 Chagrin Blvd 44124 216-831-8600
Stephen Hegner, prin. Fax 839-1335
Orange HS 800/9-12
32000 Chagrin Blvd 44124 216-831-8581
Daniel Hanstein, prin. Fax 831-4846

Academy of Court Reporting Post-Sec.
2044 Euclid Ave 44115 216-861-3222
ATS Institute of Technology Post-Sec.
301 Alpha Park 44143 440-449-1700
Beatrice Academy of Beauty Post-Sec.
10500 Cedar Ave 44106 216-421-2313
Benedictine HS 400/9-12
2900 Martin Luther King Jr 44104 216-421-2080
Sal Miroglotta, prin. Fax 421-1100
Bryant & Stratton College Post-Sec.
12955 Snow Rd 44130 216-265-3151
Bryant & Stratton College Post-Sec.
1700 E 13th St 44114 216-771-1700
Case Western Reserve University Post-Sec.
10900 Euclid Ave 44106 216-368-2000
Cleveland Central Catholic HS 400/9-12
6550 Baxter Ave 44105 216-441-4700
Karl Ertle, prin. Fax 441-8353
Cleveland Clinic Foundation Post-Sec.
9500 Euclid Ave 44195 216-445-5719
Cleveland Institute Dental Medical Asst. Post-Sec.
2450 Prospect Ave E 44115 216-241-2930
Cleveland Institute of Art Post-Sec.
11141 East Blvd 44106 216-421-7000
Cleveland Institute of Electronics Post-Sec.
1776 E 17th St 44114 216-781-9400
Cleveland Institute of Music Post-Sec.
11021 East Blvd 44106 216-795-3107
Cleveland State University Post-Sec.
2121 Euclid Ave 44115 216-687-2000
Cleveland Veterans Affairs Medical Ctr Post-Sec.
10701 East Blvd 44106 216-421-3028
Community of Faith Christian S 50/PK-12
356 Eddy Rd 44108 216-451-9240
Edwin Sanders, prin. Fax 451-3865
Cuyahoga Community College Post-Sec.
2900 Community College Ave 44115 216-987-4000
Fairview General Hospital Post-Sec.
18101 Lorain Ave 44111 216-476-7000
John Carroll University Post-Sec.
20700 N Park Blvd 44118 216-397-1886
Keller Graduate School Post-Sec.
200 Public Sq Ste 150 44114 216-781-8000
Laura/Alvin Siegal Coll Judaic Studies Post-Sec.
26500 Shaker Blvd 44122 216-464-4050
Meridia Health System Post-Sec.
17325 Euclid Ave 44112 440-446-8260
MetroHealth Medical Center Post-Sec.
2500 Metrohealth Dr 44109 216-459-5700
Myers University Post-Sec.
3921 Chester Ave 44114 216-361-2769
Notre Dame College Post-Sec.
4545 College Rd 44121 216-381-1680
Ohio College of Podiatric Medicine Post-Sec.
10515 Carnegie Ave 44106 216-231-3300
Ohio Technical College Post-Sec.
1374 E 51st St 44103 216-881-1700
Remington College Post-Sec.
14445 Broadway Ave 44125 216-475-7520
St. Ignatius HS 1,400/9-12
1911 W 30th St 44113 216-651-0222
Peter H. Corrigan, prin. Fax 651-6313
St. Joseph Academy 600/9-12
3430 Rocky River Dr 44111 216-251-6788
Audrey Menard, prin. Fax 251-5809
St. Luke's Medical Center Post-Sec.
2351 E 22nd St 44115 216-368-7000
St. Martin de Porres HS 9-12
6111 Lausche Ave 44103 216-881-1689
Mary Ann Vogel, prin. Fax 881-8303
Sanford-Brown College Post-Sec.
17535 Rosbough Blvd Ste 100 44130 440-239-9640
Southwest General Hospital Post-Sec.
18697 Bagley Rd 44130 440-816-6801
Total Technical Institute Post-Sec.
8720 Brookpark Rd 44129 216-485-0900
University Hospital of Cleveland Post-Sec.
11100 Euclid Ave 44106 216-844-7565
Ursuline College Post-Sec.
2550 Lander Rd 44124 440-449-4200
Villa Angela-St. Joseph HS 500/9-12
18491 Lake Shore Blvd 44119 216-481-8414
Janice Roccosalva, prin. Fax 486-1035

Cleveland Heights, Cuyahoga, Pop. 48,029
Cleveland Hts - University Hts CSD
Supt. — See University Heights
Cleveland Heights HS 2,000/9-12
13263 Cedar Rd 44118 216-371-7101
Darcel Williams, prin. Fax 371-6506
Monticello MS 500/6-8
3665 Monticello Blvd 44121 216-371-6520
Renee Cavor, prin. Fax 397-5967
Roxboro MS 600/6-8
2400 Roxboro Rd 44106 216-371-7440
Brian Sharosky, prin. Fax 397-3857

Beaumont HS 500/9-12
3301 N Park Blvd 44118 216-321-2954
Margaret Connell, prin. Fax 321-3947
Hebrew Academy of Cleveland 700/PK-12
1860 S Taylor Rd 44118 216-321-5838
Rabbi Simcha Dessler, dir. Fax 932-4597
Lutheran East HS 100/9-12
3565 Mayfield Rd 44118 216-382-6100
Clarence Griffin, prin. Fax 382-6119
Mosdos Ohr HaTorah S - Girls 300/PK-12
1700 S Taylor Rd 44118 216-321-1547
Brina Fried, prin. Fax 321-7505
Saperstein HS for Boys 100/7-12
1975 Lyndway Rd 44121 216-382-6495
Rabbi N.W. Dessler, dean Fax 291-5127

Cleves, Hamilton, Pop. 2,574
Three Rivers Local SD 1,300/PK-12
92 Cleves Ave 45002 513-941-6400
Rhonda Bohannon, supt. Fax 467-3207
www.threeriversschools.org
Three Rivers MS 500/5-8
8575 Bridgetown Rd 45002 513-467-3500
Thomas Huber, prin. Fax 467-3504
Other Schools – See North Bend

Clyde, Sandusky, Pop. 6,143
Clyde-Green Springs EVD 2,300/K-12
106 S Main St 43410 419-547-0588
Todd Helms, supt. Fax 547-8644
www.clyde.k12.oh.us
Clyde HS 800/9-12
1015 Race St 43410 419-547-9511
Joe Webb, prin. Fax 547-7593
McPherson MS 400/7-8
201 Spring St 43410 419-547-9150
Jon Detwiler, prin. Fax 547-9173

Coal Grove, Lawrence, Pop. 2,081
Dawson-Bryant Local SD 1,300/K-12
222 Lane St 45638 740-532-6451
James Payne, supt. Fax 533-6006
Dawson-Bryant HS 400/9-12
1 Hornet Ln 45638 740-532-6345
Steven Easterling, prin. Fax 533-6013
Dawson-Bryant MS 300/6-8
1 Hornet Ln 45638 740-532-1664
Gary Dutey, prin. Fax 533-6003

Coldwater, Mercer, Pop. 4,438
Coldwater EVD 1,500/K-12
310 N 2nd St 45828 419-678-2611
Richard Seas, supt. Fax 678-3100
cw.noacsc.org
Coldwater HS 500/9-12
310 N 2nd St 45828 419-678-4821
Steve Keller, prin. Fax 678-3100
Coldwater MS 500/5-8
310 N 2nd St 45828 419-678-3331
Jerry Kanney, prin. Fax 678-3100

Collins, Huron
Western Reserve Local SD 1,300/K-12
3765 State Route 20 44826 419-660-8508
Donald Barnes, supt. Fax 660-8429
www.western-reserve.org
Western Reserve HS 400/9-12
3841 State Route 20 44826 419-668-8470
Thomas Lehman, prin. Fax 663-5916
Western Reserve MS 200/7-8
3841 State Route 20 44826 419-668-1924
Thomas Lehman, prin.

Columbiana, Columbiana, Pop. 5,807
Columbiana EVD 1,000/K-12
700 Columbiana Waterford Rd 44408 330-482-5352
Ronald Iarussi, supt. Fax 482-5361
www.columbiana.k12.oh.us
Columbiana HS 300/9-12
700 Columbiana Waterford Rd 44408 330-482-3818
Timothy Saxton, prin. Fax 482-5360
South Side MS 300/5-8
720 Columbiana Waterford Rd 44408 330-482-5354
David Cappuzzello, prin. Fax 482-6332

Crestview Local SD 1,100/K-12
44100 Crestview Rd Ste A 44408 330-482-5526
John Dilling, supt. Fax 482-5367
www.crestviewlocal.k12.oh.us/
Crestview HS 400/9-12
44100 Crestview Rd Ste B 44408 330-482-4744
John Gecina, prin. Fax 482-5369
Crestview MS 400/5-8
44100 Crestview Rd Ste C 44408 330-482-4648
David Mackay, prin. Fax 482-5374

Heartland Christian S 300/PK-12
28 Pittsburgh St 44408 330-482-2331
Dallas Lehman, admin. Fax 482-2413

Columbia Station, Lorain
Columbia Local SD 1,100/K-12
25796 Royalton Rd 44028 440-236-5008
John Kuhn, supt. Fax 236-8817
www.columbia.k12.oh.us/
Columbia HS 400/9-12
14168 W River Rd 44028 440-236-5001
Graig Bansek, prin. Fax 236-3081
Columbia MS 400/5-8
13646 W River Rd 44028 440-236-5741
James Cottom, prin. Fax 236-9274

Columbus, Franklin, Pop. 730,657
Columbus CSD 55,500/K-12
270 E State St 43215 614-365-5000
Gene T. Harris, supt. Fax 365-5689
www.columbus.k12.oh.us/
Beechcroft HS 800/9-12
6100 Beechcroft Rd 43229 614-365-5364
Anthony Alston, prin. Fax 365-6963
Beery MS 500/6-8
2740 Lockbourne Rd 43207 614-365-5414
Edmund Baker, prin. Fax 365-5412
Briggs HS 900/9-12
2555 Briggs Rd 43223 614-365-5915
Kurt Yancey, prin. Fax 365-6964
Brookhaven HS 1,100/9-12
4077 Karl Rd 43224 614-365-5985
Talisha Dixon, prin. Fax 365-6965
Buckeye MS 700/6-8
2950 Parsons Ave 43207 614-365-5417
Marianne Minshall, prin. Fax 365-5895
Centennial HS 800/9-12
1441 Bethel Rd 43220 614-365-5491
Frances L. Hershey, prin. Fax 365-6967
Champion MS 400/6-8
1270 Hawthorne Ave 43203 614-365-6082
Joseph Santa-Emma, prin. Fax 365-6080
Clinton MS 700/6-8
3940 Karl Rd 43224 614-365-5996
Patricia Dubose, prin. Fax 365-5999
Dominion MS 500/6-8
330 E Dominion Blvd 43214 614-365-6020
Dorothy Flanagan, prin. Fax 365-6018
East HS 900/9-12
100 E Arcadia Ave 43202 614-365-5233
Edward P. Johnson, prin. Fax 365-5809
Eastmoor Academy HS 700/9-12
417 S Weyant Ave 43213 614-365-6158
Darryl Sanders, prin. Fax 365-6960
Eastmoor MS 700/6-8
3450 Medway Ave 43213 614-365-6166
Debra Odom, prin. Fax 365-6164
Fort Hayes Career Center Vo/Tech
546 Jack Gibbs Blvd 43215 614-365-6681
Milton Ruffin, dir. Fax 365-6988
Hilltonia MS 700/6-8
2345 W Mound St 43204 614-365-5937
Jerrilyn Eddington, prin. Fax 365-8015
Independence HS 1,000/9-12
5175 Refugee Rd 43232 614-365-5372
Michael Dodds, prin. Fax 365-8286
Indianola MS 400/6-8
420 E 19th Ave 43201 614-365-5575
Donna LeBeau, prin. Fax 365-5577
Johnson Park MS 600/6-8
1130 S Waverly St 43227 614-365-6501
Charmaine W. Tinker, prin. Fax 365-8698
Linden-McKinley HS 700/9-12
1320 Duxberry Ave 43211 614-365-5583
Fax 365-6968
Linmoor MS 300/6-8
2001 Hamilton Ave 43211 614-365-5595
Michelle Myles, prin. Fax 365-5594
Marion-Franklin HS 1,000/9-12
1265 Koebel Rd 43207 614-365-5432
Brian J. Terrell, prin. Fax 365-6625
Medina MS 700/6-8
1425 Huy Rd 43224 614-365-6050
Sherri C. Edwards, prin. Fax 365-8136
Mifflin HS 800/9-12
3245 Oak Spring St 43219 614-365-5466
Laura Commodore-Young, prin. Fax 365-6628
Northeast Career Ctr Vo/Tech
3871 Stelzer Rd 43219 614-365-5478
Joy Waldron, dir. Fax 365-5484
Northland HS 1,300/9-12
1919 Northcliff Dr 43229 614-365-5342
Duane R. Bland, prin. Fax 365-6479
Ridgeview MS 500/6-8
4241 Rudy Rd 43214 614-365-5506
Keith M. Harris, prin. Fax 365-5505
Sherwood MS 500/6-8
1400 Shady Lane Rd 43227 614-365-5393
Anthony J. Wade, prin. Fax 365-8351
Southeast Career Center Vo/Tech
3500 Alum Creek Dr 43207 614-365-5442
James Price, dir. Fax 365-6985
Southmoor MS 400/6-8
1201 Moler Rd 43207 614-365-5550
Cary Cordell, prin. Fax 365-6637
South Urban Academy HS 800/9-12
1160 Ann St 43206 614-365-5541
Johnetta D. Wiley, prin. Fax 365-5538
Starling MS 600/6-8
120 S Central Ave 43222 614-365-5945
Mark Hayward, prin. Fax 365-5942
Walnut Ridge HS 1,100/9-12
4841 E Livingston Ave 43227 614-365-5400
Timothy Carpenter, prin. Fax 365-5662
Wedgewood MS 600/6-8
3771 Eakin Rd 43228 614-365-5947
Stephen Hoffman, prin. Fax 365-5950
West HS 1,100/9-12
179 S Powell Ave 43204 614-365-5956
Arnold Holmes, prin. Fax 365-6970
Westmoor MS 700/6-8
3001 Valleyview Dr 43204 614-365-5974
Kathleen E. Squires, prin. Fax 365-6705
Whetstone HS 1,000/9-12
4405 Scenic Dr 43214 614-365-6060
Chris Shaffer, prin. Fax 365-6971
Woodward Park MS 1,000/6-8
5151 Karl Rd 43229 614-365-5354
Jill Spanheimer, prin. Fax 365-5357
Yorktown MS 700/6-8
5600 E Livingston Ave 43232 614-365-5408
Pamela Smith, prin. Fax 365-5411
Other Schools – See Dublin

Hamilton Local SD 2,900/K-12
775 Rathmell Rd 43207 614-491-8044
Christopher Lester, supt. Fax 491-8323
www.hamilton-local.k12.oh.us
Hamilton MS 500/7-8
775 Rathmell Rd 43207 614-491-3468
Terry McCray, prin. Fax 491-0260
Hamilton Township HS 800/9-12
4999 Lockbourne Rd 43207 614-491-3330
Jeffrey Endres, prin. Fax 492-1495

South-Western CSD
Supt. — See Grove City
Finland MS 800/7-8
1825 Finland Ave 43223 614-801-3600
Paul Smathers, prin. Fax 278-6334
Franklin Heights HS 1,200/9-12
1001 Demorest Rd 43204 614-801-3200
Brian Lidle, prin. Fax 278-6303
Norton MS 600/7-8
215 Norton Rd 43228 614-801-3700
Scott Cunningham, prin. Fax 870-5528

Worthington CSD
Supt. — See Worthington
McCord MS 400/7-8
1500 Hard Rd 43235 614-883-3550
Michael Kuri, prin. Fax 883-3560
Worthington Kilbourne HS 1,600/9-12
1499 Hard Rd 43235 614-883-2550
Ed Dunaway, prin. Fax 883-2560

Academy of Court Reporting Post-Sec.
630 E Broad St 43215 614-221-7770
American Inst. of Alternative Medicine Post-Sec.
6685 Doubletree Ave 43229 614-825-6278

American School of Technology Post-Sec.
2100 Morse Rd # 4599 43229 614-436-4820
Arthur James Cancer Hospital Post-Sec.
300 W 10th Ave 43210 614-293-5485
Bexley Hall Seminary Post-Sec.
583 Sheridan Ave 43209 614-231-3095
Bishop Hartley HS 600/9-12
1285 Zettler Rd 43227 614-237-5421
Mike Winters, prin. Fax 237-2809
Bishop Ready HS 400/9-12
707 Salisbury Rd 43204 614-276-5263
Celene Seamen, prin. Fax 276-5116
Bishop Waterson HS 1,100/9-12
99 E Cooke Rd 43214 614-268-8671
Marian Hutson, prin. Fax 268-0551
Bradford School Post-Sec.
2469 Stelzer Rd 43219 614-416-6200
Capital University Post-Sec.
2199 E Main St 43209 614-236-6011
Capital University Law School Post-Sec.
303 E Broad St 43215 614-236-6500
Columbus College of Art & Design Post-Sec.
107 N 9th St 43215 614-224-9101
Columbus School for Girls 700/PK-12
56 S Columbia Ave 43209 614-252-0781
Diane B. Cooper, hdmstr. Fax 252-0571
Columbus State Community College Post-Sec.
550 E Spring St 43215 614-287-2400
Columbus Torah Academy 300/K-12
181 Noe Bixby Rd 43213 614-864-0299
Marcia Hershfield, prin. Fax 864-2218
DeVry University Post-Sec.
1350 Alum Creek Dr 43209 614-253-7291
Franklin University Post-Sec.
201 S Grant Ave 43215 614-341-6300
HARDI Home Study Institute Post-Sec.
1389 Dublin Rd 43215 614-488-1835
Keller Graduate School Post-Sec.
8800 Lyra Dr Ste 120 43240 614-252-8850
Liberty Christian Academy 500/PK-12
4938 Beatrice Dr 43227 614-864-5332
LaVonne McIlrath, admin. Fax 864-5381
Marburn Academy 100/K-12
1860 Walden Dr 43229 614-433-0822
Earl Oremus, prin.
Mt. Carmel College of Nursing Post-Sec.
127 S Davis Ave 43222 614-234-5800
Nationwide Beauty Academy Post-Sec.
5300 WestPointe Plaza Dr 43228 614-921-9109
Ohio Dominican University Post-Sec.
1216 Sunbury Rd 43219 614-253-2741
Ohio Institute of Health Careers Post-Sec.
1880 E Dublin Granville Rd 43229 614-891-5030
Ohio School for the Deaf Post-Sec.
500 Morse Rd 43214
Ohio State College of Barber Styling Post-Sec.
4614 E Broad St 43213 614-868-1015
Ohio State Sch of Cosmetology Northland Post-Sec.
4390 Karl Rd 43224 614-263-1861
Ohio State School for the Blind Post-Sec.
5220 N High St 43214
Ohio State School of Cosmetology Post-Sec.
3717 S High St 43207 614-491-0492
Ohio State University Post-Sec.
154 W 12th Ave 43210 614-292-6446
Ohio State University Hospitals Post-Sec.
450 W 10th Ave 43210 614-293-5555
Pontifical College Josephinum Post-Sec.
7625 N High St 43235 614-885-5585
St. Charles Prep S 600/9-12
2010 E Broad St 43209 614-252-6714
Dominic Cavello, prin. Fax 265-3375
St. Francis De Sales HS 900/9-12
4212 Karl Rd 43224 614-267-7808
Dan Garrick, prin. Fax 265-3375
Spa School Post-Sec.
5050 N High St 43214 614-888-1092
Technology Education College Post-Sec.
2745 Winchester Pike 43232 614-759-7700
Tree of Life Christian HS 300/6-12
935 Northridge Rd 43224 614-263-2688
Todd Marrah, prin. Fax 263-6450
Trinity Lutheran Seminary Post-Sec.
2199 E Main St 43209 614-235-4136
Wellington S 600/K-12
3650 Reed Rd 43220 614-457-7883
Richard O'Hara, hdmstr. Fax 442-3286

Columbus Grove, Putnam, Pop. 2,178
Columbus Grove Local SD 900/K-12
201 W Cross St 45830 419-659-2639
Robert Jennell, supt. Fax 659-5134
Columbus Grove HS 300/9-12
201 W Cross St 45830 419-659-2156
Chris Pfahler, prin. Fax 659-5134
Columbus Grove MS 200/5-8
201 W Cross St 45830 419-659-2631
James Kincaid, prin. Fax 659-5134

Concord, Lake
Auburn JVSD
8140 Auburn Rd 44077 440-357-7542
G. Thomas Schultz, supt. Fax 357-0310
www.auburncc.org
Auburn Career Center Vo/Tech
8140 Auburn Rd 44077 440-357-7542
Suzanne Gucciardo, dir. Fax 357-0227

Conneaut, Ashtabula, Pop. 12,648
Conneaut Area CSD 2,400/K-12
400 Mill St Ste B 44030 440-593-7200
Mary Zappitelli, supt. Fax 593-6253
www.conneautschools.org
Conneaut HS 700/9-12
381 Mill St 44030 440-593-7210
Kent Houston, prin. Fax 593-6899
Conneaut MS 700/6-8
230 Gateway Ave 44030 440-593-7240
Linda Bernay, prin. Fax 593-6253

Continental, Putnam, Pop. 1,188
Continental Local SD 700/K-12
5211 State Route 634 45831 419-596-3671
Gary Jones, supt. Fax 596-3861
cn2.noacsc.org
Continental HS 200/9-12
5211 State Route 634 45831 419-596-3871
Larry Claypool, prin. Fax 596-2651
Continental MS 200/6-8
5211 State Route 634 45831 419-596-4571
Larry Claypool, prin. Fax 596-2651

Convoy, Van Wert, Pop. 1,065
Crestview Local SD 1,000/K-12
531 E Tully St 45832 419-749-9100
John Basinger, supt. Fax 749-4235
www.crestviewknights.com/
Crestview JSHS 500/7-12
531 E Tully St 45832 419-749-9100
Mike Biro, prin. Fax 749-2484

Copley, Summit, Pop. 11,130
Copley-Fairlawn CSD 3,300/K-12
3797 Ridgewood Rd 44321 330-664-4800
Edward Myracle, supt. Fax 664-4811
www.copley-fairlawn.org
Copley-Fairlawn MS 1,100/5-8
1531 S Clvland Massillon Rd 44321 330-664-4875
JoAnn Berkowitz, prin. Fax 664-4912
Copley HS 1,000/9-12
3807 Ridgewood Rd 44321 330-664-4822
William Steffen, prin. Fax 664-4951

Ohio College of Massotherapy Post-Sec.
225 Heritage Woods Dr 44321 330-665-1084

Corning, Perry, Pop. 616
Southern Local SD 1,000/K-12
10397 State Route 155 SE 43730 740-394-2402
Cindy Hartman, supt. Fax 394-2083
www.spsd.k12.oh.us/
Miller HS 300/9-12
10397 State Route 155 SE 43730 740-394-2426
Ralph Holbert, prin. Fax 394-2083
Miller MS 300/5-8
10397 State Route 155 SE 43730 740-394-1173
Larry Hoover, prin. Fax 394-2083

Cortland, Trumbull, Pop. 6,640
Lakeview Local SD 2,200/K-12
300 Hillman Dr 44410 330-637-8741
Robert Wilson, supt. Fax 638-1060
www.lakeviewlocal.org
Lakeview HS 800/9-12
300 Hillman Dr 44410 330-637-4921
Fred Kunar, prin. Fax 638-1060
Lakeview MS 500/6-8
640 Wakefield Dr 44410 330-637-4360
Nancy Krygowski, prin. Fax 638-1060

Maplewood Local SD 1,100/K-12
2414 Greenville Rd 44410 330-637-7506
Perry Nicholas, supt. Fax 637-6616
www.maplewood.k12.oh.us/
Maplewood HS 300/9-12
2414 Greenville Rd 44410 330-637-8466
Ruth Zitnik, prin. Fax 637-0496
Maplewood MS 300/5-8
4174 Greenville Rd 44410 330-924-2431
Kevin Spicher, prin. Fax 924-5151

Coshocton, Coshocton, Pop. 11,632
Coshocton CSD 1,900/K-12
1207 Cambridge Rd 43812 740-622-1901
Wade Lucas, supt. Fax 623-5803
www.coshoctonredskins.com/
Coshocton JSHS 900/7-12
1205 Cambridge Rd 43812 740-622-9433
Bill Hartmeyer, prin. Fax 623-0774

Coshocton County JVSD
23640 Airport Rd 43812 740-622-0211
Donna Johnson, supt. Fax 623-4651
www.coshocton-jvs.k12.oh.us
Coshocton County Career Center Vo/Tech
23640 Airport Rd 43812 740-622-0211
Eddie Dovenbarger, prin. Fax 623-4651

Coshocton Christian S 100/PK-12
23891 Airport Rd 43812 740-622-5052
Wesley Courser, prin. Fax 622-9244

Covington, Miami, Pop. 2,575
Covington EVD 900/K-12
25 N Grant St 45318 937-473-2249
Randy G. Earl, supt. Fax 473-3730
www.covington.k12.oh.us
Covington HS 300/9-12
807 Chestnut St 45318 937-473-3746
Chad Mason, prin. Fax 473-3889
Covington MS 200/6-8
25 N Grant St 45318 937-473-2833
Paula Jurgens, prin. Fax 473-8189

Crestline, Crawford, Pop. 4,964
Crestline EVD 800/K-12
PO Box 350 44827 419-683-3647
Mark Stock, supt. Fax 683-2330
www.crestline.k12.oh.us
Crestline HS 300/8-12
7854 Oldfield Rd 44827 419-683-3647
Douglas Potts, prin. Fax 683-9063

Creston, Wayne, Pop. 2,140
North Central Local SD 1,400/K-12
350 S Main St 44217 330-435-6382
Larry Acker, supt. Fax 435-4633
www.northcentral.k12.oh.us/
Creston MS 400/5-8
PO Box 4443 44217 330-435-4255
Karen O'Hare, prin. Fax 435-4633
Norwayne HS 500/9-12
350 S Main St 44217 330-435-4276
Douglas Zimmerly, prin. Fax 435-4633

Crooksville, Perry, Pop. 2,485
Crooksville EVD 1,100/K-12
4065 School Dr 43731 740-982-7040
Steven Pompey, supt. Fax 982-3551
www.crooksville.k12.oh.us/
Crooksville HS 300/9-12
4075 Ceramic Way 43731 740-982-7015
Jacqueline Bolyard, prin. Fax 982-3086
Crooksville MS 300/6-8
12400 Tunnel Hill Rd 43731 740-982-7010
Gary Stall, prin. Fax 982-5087

Crown City, Gallia, Pop. 434
Gallia County Local SD
Supt. — See Gallipolis
South Gallia HS 200/9-12
266 Mercerville Rd 45623 740-256-6379
Scot West, prin. Fax 256-6007

Cutler, Washington
Warren Local SD
Supt. — See Vincent
Bartlett S 100/4-8
2035 State Route 550 45724 740-551-2461
Michelle Hiser, prin. Fax 551-2237

Cuyahoga Falls, Summit, Pop. 50,494
Cuyahoga Falls CSD 4,600/K-12
PO Box 396 44222 330-926-3800
Dr. Edwin S. Holland, supt. Fax 920-1074
www.cfalls.summit.k12.oh.us
Bolich MS 600/6-8
2630 13th St 44223 330-926-3801
Chris McBurney, prin. Fax 920-3737
Cuyahoga Falls HS 1,700/9-12
2300 4th St 44221 330-926-3808
Nicholas Valentine, prin. Fax 916-6013
Roberts MS 300/6-8
3333 Charles St 44221 330-926-3809
Thomas Ratcliff, prin. Fax 920-3748

Cuyahoga Valley Christian Academy 900/7-12
4687 Wyoga Lake Rd 44224 330-929-0575
Jon Holley, hdmstr. Fax 929-0156

Cuyahoga Heights, Cuyahoga, Pop. 559
Cuyahoga Heights Local SD 900/PK-12
4820 E 71st St 44125 216-429-5700
Peter Guerrera, supt. Fax 341-3737
www.cuyhts.k12.oh.us
Cuyahoga Heights HS 300/9-12
4820 E 71st St 44125 216-429-5707
Lora Garrett, prin. Fax 429-5706
Cuyahoga Heights MS 200/6-8
4840 E 71st St 44125 216-429-5757
Tom Burton, prin. Fax 429-5735

Dalton, Wayne, Pop. 1,582
Dalton Local SD 1,000/K-12
PO Box 514 44618 330-828-2267
Scott Beatty, supt. Fax 828-2800
www.dalton.k12.oh.us
Dalton IS 200/6-8
PO Box 514 44618 330-828-2405
Broc Bidlack, prin. Fax 828-2801
Dalton Local HS 300/9-12
PO Box 514 44618 330-828-2261
Larry Case, prin. Fax 828-2904

Danville, Knox, Pop. 1,096
Danville Local SD 700/K-12
PO Box 30 43014 740-599-6116
Damien Bawn, supt. Fax 599-5417
www.danville.k12.oh.us/
Danville HS 200/9-12
PO Box 30 43014 740-599-6116
Linda Rex, prin. Fax 599-5418
Danville MS, PO Box 30 43014 100/7-8
Linda Rex, prin. 740-599-6116

Dayton, Montgomery, Pop. 158,873
Centerville CSD
Supt. — See Centerville
Watts MS 600/6-8
7056 McEwen Rd 45459 937-434-0370
Brian Miller, prin. Fax 434-2907

Dayton CSD 15,200/PK-12
115 S Ludlow St 45402 937-542-3000
Percy Mack Ph.D., supt. Fax 542-3188
www.dps.k12.oh.us
Belmont HS 1,100/9-12
2323 Mapleview Ave 45420 937-542-6460
Joye Stier, prin. Fax 542-6461
Dunbar HS 900/9-12
2222 Richley Dr 45408 937-542-6760
Phyllis Combs, prin. Fax 542-6761
Fairview MS 700/7-8
2408 Philadelphia Dr 45406 937-542-6050
Vondia Jackson, prin. Fax 542-6051
Meadowdale HS 1,000/9-12
4417 Williamson Dr 45416 937-542-7030
Dora A. Carson, prin. Fax 542-7031
Patterson Career Center Vo/Tech
441 River Corridor Dr 45402 937-542-7180
Sheryl Lenehan, prin. Fax 542-7181
Stivers School for the Arts 900/7-12
325 Homewood Ave 45405 937-542-7380
Erin Dooley, prin. Fax 542-7381
White HS 1,100/9-12
501 Niagara Ave 45405 937-542-6610
Duane Davis Ed.D., prin. Fax 542-6611
Wright MS 600/7-8
1361 Huffman Ave 45403 937-542-6380
Shawna Welch, prin. Fax 542-6381

Jefferson Township Local SD 700/K-12
2625 S Union Rd 45418 937-835-5682
Dr. Norris Brown, supt. Fax 835-5955
www.jeffersontwp.k12.oh.us/
Jefferson HS 400/7-12
2701 S Union Rd 45418 937-295-5691
Don Kuntz, prin. Fax 835-5693

Mad River Local SD 2,400/K-12
801 Old Harshman Rd 45431 937-259-6606
Michael Eaglowski, supt. Fax 259-6607
www.madriver.k12.oh.us
Mad River MS 50/7-8
1801 Harshman Rd 45424 937-237-4265
Mark Henderson, prin. Fax 237-4273

Stebbins HS 1,100/9-12
1900 Harshman Rd 45424 937-237-4250
Dr. Todd Nichols, prin. Fax 237-4262

Northridge Local SD 1,700/K-12
2011 Timber Ln 45414 937-278-5885
Tod Perez, supt. Fax 276-8351
www.northridge-montgomery.k12.oh.us
Dennis MS 400/6-8
5120 N Dixie Dr 45414 937-274-2135
Timothy Whitestone, prin. Fax 276-8354
Northridge HS 500/9-12
2251 Timber Ln 45414 937-275-7469
David Jackson, prin. Fax 275-8434

Oakwood CSD 2,100/K-12
20 Rubicon Rd 45409 937-297-5332
Mary Jo Scalzo Ph.D., supt. Fax 297-5345
www.oakwoodschools.org
Oakwood HS 600/9-12
1200 Far Hills Ave 45419 937-297-5325
Joseph Boyle, prin. Fax 297-5348
Oakwood JHS 300/7-8
1200 Far Hills Ave 45419 937-297-5328
John Kronour, prin. Fax 297-7807

Trotwood-Madison CSD
Supt. — See Trotwood
Trotwood-Madison MS 500/7-8
3594 N Snyder Rd 45426 937-854-0017
Gerry Griffith, prin. Fax 854-8433

Vandalia-Butler CSD
Supt. — See Vandalia
Smith MS 500/5-8
3625 Little York Rd 45414 937-415-7000
Shannon White, prin. Fax 415-7051

Carousel Beauty College Post-Sec.
125 E 2nd St 45402 937-223-3572
Carroll HS 1,000/9-12
4524 Linden Ave 45432 937-253-8188
Joseph Sens, prin. Fax 258-7001
Chaminade-Julienne HS 1,000/9-12
505 S Ludlow St 45402 937-461-3740
John Marshall, prin. Fax 461-6256
Dayton Barber College Post-Sec.
28 W 5th St 45402 937-222-9101
Dominion Academy of Dayton 100/4-12
925 N Main St 45405 937-224-8555
Fax 224-4485
International College of Broadcasting Post-Sec.
6 S Smithville Rd 45431 937-258-8251
ITT Technical Institute Post-Sec.
3325 Stop 8 Rd 45414 937-454-2267
Miami-Jacobs College Post-Sec.
110 N Patterson Blvd 45402 937-222-7337
Miami Valley Hospital Post-Sec.
1 Wyoming St 45409 937-223-6192
Miami Valley S 500/PK-12
5151 Denise Dr 45429 937-434-4444
Peter Benedict, hdmstr. Fax 434-1033
Ohio Institute of Photography & Tech Post-Sec.
2029 Edgefield Rd 45439 937-294-6155
Sinclair Community College Post-Sec.
444 W 3rd St 45402 937-512-2500
Southwestern College of Business Post-Sec.
111 W 1st St Ste 1140 45402 937-224-0061
University of Dayton Post-Sec.
300 College Park Ave 45469 937-229-1000
Wright State University Post-Sec.
3640 Colonel Glenn Hwy 45435 937-775-3333

Defiance, Defiance, Pop. 16,150
Ayersville Local SD 900/K-12
28046 Watson Rd 43512 419-395-1111
Tod A. Hug, supt. Fax 395-9990
www.ayersville.k12.oh.us
Ayersville HS 300/9-12
28046 Watson Rd 43512 419-395-1111
Cameron VanArsdalen, prin. Fax 395-2566
Ayersville MS 300/5-8
28046 Watson Rd 43512 419-395-1111
Bruce Brown, prin. Fax 395-9990

Defiance CSD 2,500/K-12
629 Arabella St 43512 419-782-0070
Michael Struble, supt. Fax 782-4395
www.defiancecityschools.org
Defiance HS 900/9-12
1755 Palmer Dr 43512 419-784-2777
Fred Boring, prin. Fax 784-0102
Defiance JHS 400/7-8
629 Arabella St 43512 419-782-0050
Kelly Davis, prin. Fax 782-0060

Northeastern Local SD 1,200/K-12
5921 Domersville Rd 43512 419-497-3461
James Roach, supt. Fax 497-3401
www.tinora.k12.oh.us
Tinora HS 400/9-12
5921 Domersville Rd 43512 419-497-2621
Philip Nofziger, prin. Fax 497-3401
Tinora JHS 200/7-8
5921 Domersville Rd 43512 419-497-2361
G. Kent Adams, prin. Fax 497-3401

Defiance College Post-Sec.
701 N Clinton St 43512 419-784-4010

De Graff, Logan, Pop. 1,174
Riverside Local SD 700/K-12
2096 County Road 24 S 43318 937-585-5981
Bernie Pachmayer, supt. Fax 585-4599
www.riverside.k12.oh.us
Riverside HS 200/9-12
2096 County Road 24 S 43318 937-585-5981
Mike Edwards, prin. Fax 585-4599
Riverside MS 100/5-8
2096 County Road 24 S 43318 937-585-5981
Tim Walls, prin. Fax 585-4599

Delaware, Delaware, Pop. 31,322
Buckeye Valley Local SD 2,200/K-12
679 Coover Rd 43015 740-369-8735
John Schiller, supt. Fax 363-7654
www.buckeyevalley.k12.oh.us
Buckeye Valley HS 700/9-12
901 Coover Rd 43015 740-363-1349
Dave Heflinger, prin. Fax 363-9380
Buckeye Valley MS 500/6-8
683 Coover Rd 43015 740-363-6626
Andrew Miller, prin. Fax 363-4483

Delaware Area Career Center
4565 Columbus Pike 43015 740-548-0708
Patricia Foor, supt. Fax 549-1397
www.delawareareacc.org
Delaware Area Career Center North Campus Vo/Tech
1610 State Route 521 43015 740-363-1993
Mary Paulins, prin. Fax 362-6461
Delaware Area Career Center South Campus Vo/Tech
4565 Columbus Pike 43015 740-548-0708
Dale Hayes, prin. Fax 548-0710
Delaware Area Career Ctr Adult Education Adult
4565 Columbus Pike 43015 740-548-0708
Sue Rowland, prin. Fax 549-1397

Delaware CSD 4,500/K-12
248 N Washington St 43015 740-833-1100
Dr. Mary Anne Ashworth, supt. Fax 833-1149
www.dcs.k12.oh.us
Dempsey MS 700/7-8
599 Pennsylvania Ave 43015 740-833-1800
Paul King, prin. Fax 833-1899
Hayes HS 1,300/9-12
289 Euclid Ave 43015 740-833-1010
James Peterson, prin. Fax 833-1099

Bethany Academy 100/K-10
500 N Liberty St 43015 740-362-5540
Jerry Smith, admin.
Delaware Christian S 300/K-12
45 Belle Ave 43015 740-363-8425
Gordon McDonald, admin. Fax 369-8378
Methodist Theological School in Ohio Post-Sec.
3081 Columbus Pike 43015 740-363-1146
Ohio Wesleyan University Post-Sec.
61 S Sandusky St 43015 740-368-2000

Delphos, Allen, Pop. 6,820
Delphos CSD 1,100/K-12
234 N Jefferson St 45833 419-692-2509
Bruce Sommers, supt. Fax 692-2653
www.noacsc.org/allen/dl/
Jefferson HS 400/9-12
901 Wildcat Ln 45833 419-695-1786
Robert Kiracofe, prin. Fax 692-2287
Jefferson MS 200/6-8
227 N Jefferson St 45833 419-695-2523
Terry Moreo, prin. Fax 692-2302

St. John HS 400/9-12
515 E 2nd St 45833 419-692-5371
Donald Huysman, prin. Fax 879-6874

Delta, Fulton, Pop. 2,927
Pike-Delta-York Local SD 1,500/K-12
504 Fernwood St 43515 419-822-3391
Robin Rayfield, supt. Fax 822-4478
www.pdy.k12.oh.us
Pike-Delta-York HS 500/9-12
605 Taylor St 43515 419-822-8247
Randall Lintermoot, prin. Fax 822-5921
Pike-Delta-York MS 400/6-8
1101 Panther Pride Dr 43515 419-822-9118
Dennis Ford, prin. Fax 822-8490

Dennison, Tuscarawas, Pop. 2,927
Claymont CSD 2,200/K-12
201 N 3rd St 44621 740-922-5478
Gary Hunter, supt. Fax 922-7325
www.claymont.k12.oh.us
Other Schools – See Uhrichsville

Diamond, Mahoning
Southeast Local SD
Supt. — See Ravenna
Southeast MS 500/6-8
8540 Tallmadge Rd 44412 330-654-5842
James Ries, prin. Fax 654-9110

TDDS Technical Institute Post-Sec.
1688 N Pricetown Rd 44412 330-538-2216

Dillonvale, Jefferson, Pop. 750
Buckeye Local SD 2,400/K-12
6899 State Route 150 43917 740-769-7395
Joseph Pielech, supt. Fax 769-2361
www.omeresa.net/schools/buckeye/
Other Schools – See Brilliant, Rayland, Tiltonsville

Dola, Hardin
Hardin Northern Local SD 500/K-12
11589 State Route 81 45835 419-759-2331
Jeff Price, supt. Fax 759-2581
Hardin Northern JSHS 200/7-12
11589 State Route 81 45835 419-759-3515
Bradd Molk, prin. Fax 759-2581

Dover, Tuscarawas, Pop. 12,516
Dover CSD 2,600/K-12
219 W 6th St 44622 330-364-1906
Robert Hamm, supt. Fax 343-7070
www.dover.k12.oh.us/
Dover HS 900/9-12
520 N Walnut St 44622 330-364-7148
Karie McCrate, prin. Fax 364-7142
Dover MS 600/6-8
2131 N Wooster Ave 44622 330-364-7121
Thomas Jones, prin. Fax 364-7127

Doylestown, Wayne, Pop. 2,851
Chippewa Local SD 1,400/K-12
56 N Portage St 44230 330-658-6368
Steve Caples, supt. Fax 658-5842
www.chippewa.k12.oh.us
Chippewa HS 500/9-12
100 Valley View Rd 44230 330-658-2011
Shawn Bramen, prin. Fax 658-3339
Chippewa MS 400/5-8
257 High St 44230 330-658-2214
Sandy Stebly, prin. Fax 658-5842

Dresden, Muskingum, Pop. 1,427
Tri-Valley Local SD 3,100/K-12
36 E Muskingum Ave 43821 740-754-1572
C. Douglas Spade, supt. Fax 754-6400
www.tri-valley.k12.oh.us
Tri-Valley HS 1,000/9-12
46 E Muskingum Ave 43821 740-754-2921
James Pottmeyer, prin. Fax 754-6409
Tri-Valley MS 500/7-8
1358 Main St 43821 740-754-3531
Margaret Wilcox, prin. Fax 754-1879

Dublin, Franklin, Pop. 34,964
Columbus CSD
Supt. — See Columbus
Northwest Career Ctr Vo/Tech
2960 Cranston Dr 43017 614-365-6622
Steve Kalliantas, dir. Fax 365-5621

Dublin CSD 12,600/K-12
7030 Coffman Rd 43017 614-764-5913
Dr. David Axner, supt. Fax 761-5899
www.dublinschools.net
Davis MS 700/6-8
2400 Sutter Pkwy 43016 614-761-5820
David Nosker, prin. Fax 761-5893
Dublin Coffman HS 1,500/9-12
6780 Coffman Rd 43017 614-764-5900
Tracey Miller, prin. Fax 764-5925
Dublin Jerome HS 900/9-12
8300 Hyland Croy Rd 43016 614-764-5913
Cathy Sankey, prin. Fax 873-1937
Dublin Scioto HS 1,400/9-12
4000 Hard Rd 43016 614-717-2464
Marina Davis, prin. Fax 717-2484
Grizzell MS 900/6-8
8705 Avery Rd 43017 614-798-3569
Timothy Barton, prin. Fax 761-6514
Karrer MS 800/6-8
7245 Tullymore Dr 43016 614-873-0459
Rick Weininger, prin. Fax 718-8505
Sells MS 600/6-8
150 W Bridge St 43017 614-764-5919
Rich Baird, prin. Fax 764-5923

Duncan Falls, Muskingum
Franklin Local SD 2,400/K-12
PO Box 428 43734 740-674-5203
David N. Branch, supt. Fax 674-5214
www.franklin-local.k12.oh.us
Other Schools – See Philo, Roseville

East Canton, Stark, Pop. 1,619
Osnaburg Local SD 900/K-12
310 Browning Ct N 44730 330-488-1609
Tom Davis, supt. Fax 488-4001
ecweb.sparcc.org
East Canton HS 300/9-12
310 Browning Ct N 44730 330-488-0316
Chris Corbi, prin. Fax 488-4001
East Canton MS 400/4-8
310 Browning Ct N 44730 330-488-0229
Erica Knowles, prin. Fax 488-4001

East Cleveland, Cuyahoga, Pop. 25,708
East Cleveland CSD 4,700/K-12
15305 Terrace Rd 44112 216-268-6570
Myrna Loy Corley, supt. Fax 268-6676
www.east-cleveland.k12.oh.us
Heritage MS, 14410 Terrace Rd 44112 400/8-8
Beverly Bright-Lloyd, prin. 216-268-6610
Shaw HS 1,300/9-12
15320 Euclid Ave 44112 216-268-6500
Sandra Brown, prin. Fax 268-6676

Huron School of Nursing Post-Sec.
13951 Terrace Rd 44112 216-761-7996

Eastlake, Lake, Pop. 19,795
Willoughby-Eastlake CSD
Supt. — See Willoughby
Eastlake MS 600/6-8
35972 Lake Shore Blvd 44095 440-942-5696
Ralph Young, prin. Fax 918-8973
North HS 1,600/9-12
34041 Stevens Blvd 44095 440-975-3666
Mark Beaumier, prin. Fax 975-3671

East Liverpool, Columbiana, Pop. 12,396
East Liverpool CSD 2,600/K-12
500 Maryland St 43920 330-385-7132
Ken Halbert, supt. Fax 386-8763
eastliverpool.k12.oh.us
East Liverpool HS 1,000/9-12
100 Maine Blvd 43920 330-386-8750
Linda Henderson, prin. Fax 386-8753
East Liverpool MS 700/6-8
810 W 8th St 43920 330-386-8765
Patrick Poling, prin. Fax 382-7670

East Liverpool Christian S 200/PK-12
46682 Florence St 43920 330-385-5588
Janice Moegerle, prin. Fax 385-1267
Kent State University-East Liverpool Post-Sec.
400 E 4th St 43920 330-385-3805
Ohio Valley College of Technology Post-Sec.
PO Box 7000 43920 330-385-1070

East Palestine, Columbiana, Pop. 4,805
East Palestine CSD 1,400/K-12
200 W North Ave 44413 330-426-4191
Jeffrey Richardson, supt. Fax 426-9592
www.epschools.k12.oh.us/
East Palestine HS 500/9-12
360 W Grant St 44413 330-426-9401
Gary Contini, prin. Fax 426-5105
East Palestine MS 300/6-8
320 W Grant St 44413 330-426-9451
Lynn Campbell, prin.

Eaton, Preble, Pop. 8,242
Eaton Community SD 2,300/K-12
307 N Cherry St 45320 937-456-1107
Dr. Joe DeLuca, supt. Fax 472-1057
www.eaton.k12.oh.us/index.htm
Eaton HS 700/9-12
600 Hillcrest Dr 45320 937-456-1141
Brad Neavin, prin. Fax 456-1143
Eaton MS 500/6-8
311 N Cherry St 45320 937-456-2286
Kern Carpenter, prin. Fax 456-2022

Edgerton, Williams, Pop. 2,015
Edgerton Local SD 500/K-12
111 E River St 43517 419-298-2112
J. Richard Gieringer, supt. Fax 298-2281
www.edgerton.k12.oh.us/
Edgerton HS 300/7-12
111 E River St 43517 419-298-2331
Jeffrey Snyder, prin. Fax 298-1322

Edon, Williams, Pop. 863
Edon-Northwest Local SD 700/K-12
802 W Indiana St 43518 419-272-3213
Thomas Lammers, supt. Fax 272-2240
www.edon.k12.oh.us/
Edon HS 300/9-12
802 W Indiana St 43518 419-272-3113
Robert Morton, prin. Fax 272-2240
Edon MS 200/5-8
802 W Indiana St 43518 419-272-3213
Robert Morton, prin. Fax 272-2240

Elida, Allen, Pop. 1,894
Elida Local SD 1,800/K-12
4380 Sunnydale St 45807 419-331-4155
Don Diglia, supt. Fax 331-1656
home.elida.k12.oh.us/
Elida HS 800/9-12
101 E North St 45807 419-331-4115
Sarah Burden, prin. Fax 339-3523
Elida MS 600/6-8
4500 Sunnydale St 45807 419-331-2505
Herbert Purton, prin. Fax 331-6822

Elmore, Ottawa, Pop. 1,408
Woodmore Local SD
Supt. — See Woodville
Woodmore JSHS 600/7-12
633 Fremont St 43416 419-862-2721
Anthony Anastasio, prin. Fax 862-3835

Elyria, Lorain, Pop. 56,061
Elyria CSD 7,700/K-12
42101 Griswold Rd 44035 440-284-8000
Paul Rigda, supt. Fax 284-0678
www.elyriaschools.org
Eastern Heights JHS 400/7-8
528 Garford Ave 44035 440-284-8015
Kimberly Benetto, prin. Fax 323-0827
Elyria HS 2,100/9-12
311 6th St 44035 440-284-8300
Dianne Quinn, prin. Fax 323-2543
Northwood JHS 400/7-8
700 Gulf Rd 44035 440-284-8016
Thomas Jama, prin. Fax 284-1546
Westwood JHS 400/7-8
42350 Adelbert St 44035 440-284-8017
Darren Conley, prin. Fax 284-1055

Elyria Catholic HS 500/9-12
725 Gulf Rd 44035 440-365-1821
Andrew Krakowiak, prin. Fax 365-7536
First Baptist Christian S 200/PK-12
11400 Lagrange Rd 44035 440-458-5185
Brenda Milam, prin. Fax 458-8717
Lorain County Community College Post-Sec.
1005 Abbe Rd N 44035 440-365-5222
Ohio Institute of Health Careers Post-Sec.
631 Griswold Rd 44035 866-636-4734
Open Door Christian S 600/K-12
8287 W Ridge Rd 44035 440-322-6386
Walter Sheffield, pres. Fax 284-6033

Englewood, Montgomery, Pop. 12,727
Northmont CSD 5,900/K-12
4001 Old Salem Rd 45322 937-832-5000
Dr. Gale Mabry, supt. Fax 832-5001
www.northmontschools.com/
Other Schools – See Clayton

Enon, Clark, Pop. 2,581
Greenon Local SD 2,000/K-12
500 Enon-Xenia Rd 45323 937-864-1202
Denny Howell, supt. Fax 864-2470
www.greenon.k12.oh.us
Indian Valley MS 700/5-8
510 Enon-Xenia Rd 45323 937-864-7348
Cathie Scott, prin. Fax 864-6009
Other Schools – See Springfield

Euclid, Cuyahoga, Pop. 49,619
Euclid CSD 6,400/K-12
651 E 222nd St 44123 216-261-2900
Dr. Joffrey Jones, supt. Fax 261-3120
www.euclid.k12.oh.us
AIID 9-12
711 E 222nd St 44123 216-797-7825
Stephen Hardaway, prin. Fax 797-7900
Business & Communications S 9-12
711 E 222nd St 44123 216-797-7821
Ed Klein, prin. Fax 797-7900
Euclid Academy of the Arts 9-12
711 E 222nd St 44123 216-797-7813
Tina Elliott, prin. Fax 797-7900
Euclid Central MS 800/6-8
20701 Euclid Ave 44117 216-797-5300
Mike Mennel, prin. Fax 797-5333
Forest Park MS 800/6-8
27000 Elinore Ave 44132 216-797-4700
Charlie Smialek, prin. Fax 797-4710
International Academy 9-12
711 E 222nd St 44123 216-797-7831
Claudia Spencer, prin. Fax 797-7900
Professional Path S 9-12
711 E 222nd St 44123 216-797-7809
Elie Thomas, prin. Fax 797-7900
Science Technology Engineering & Math S 2,000/9-12
711 E 222nd St 44123 216-797-7801
Ron Seymour, prin. Fax 797-7900

Fairborn, Greene, Pop. 31,650
Fairborn CSD 4,500/PK-12
306 E Whittier Ave 45324 937-878-3961
Dave Scarberry, supt. Fax 879-8180
www.fairborn.k12.oh.us
Baker MS 800/6-8
200 Lincoln Dr 45324 937-878-4681
William Howard, prin. Fax 879-8193
Fairborn HS 1,500/9-12
900 E Dayton Yellow Springs 45324 937-879-3611
Robert Cotter, prin. Fax 879-8190

Creative Images-Matrix Design Academy Post-Sec.
1076 Kauffman Ave 45324 937-878-9555
Hondros College Post-Sec.
1810 Successful Dr 45324 937-431-1808

Fairfield, Butler, Pop. 42,294
Butler Technology/Career Development SD
3603 Hamilton Middletown Rd 45011 513-868-1911
Robert Sommers, supt. Fax 868-9348
www.butlertech.org
Lee Career-Technology Center Vo/Tech
3603 Hamilton Middletown Rd 45011 513-868-6300
Bob Thompson, prin. Fax 868-1701
Options Arts Academy Vo/Tech
101 S Monument Ave 45011 513-863-8873
Jackie Quay, prin.
Other Schools – See Hamilton, Monroe

Fairfield CSD 9,500/K-12
211 Donald Dr 45014 513-829-6300
Robert Farrell, supt. Fax 829-0148
www.fairfieldcityschools.com
Fairfield Freshman HS 800/9-9
5050 Dixie Hwy 45014 513-829-8300
Dan Beckenhaupt, prin. Fax 829-4733
Fairfield MS 1,600/7-8
1111 Nilles Rd 45014 513-829-4433
Megan Graham, prin. Fax 829-6480
Fairfield SHS 2,200/10-12
8800 Holden Blvd 45014 513-942-2999
Paul Waller, prin. Fax 942-3288

Moler-Pickens Beauty College Post-Sec.
5951 Boymel Dr Ste S 45014 513-874-5116

Fairlawn, Summit, Pop. 7,202

Academy of Court Reporting Post-Sec.
2930 W Market St 44333 330-867-4030
Gerber Akron Beauty School Post-Sec.
33 Shiawassee Ave 44333 330-867-6200

Fairport Harbor, Lake, Pop. 3,223
Fairport Harbor EVD 600/K-12
329 Vine St 44077 440-354-5400
Domenic Paolo, supt. Fax 354-1724
www.fairport.k12.oh.us/home.htm
Fairport Harding JSHS 300/7-12
329 Vine St 44077 440-354-3592
Miki Steigerwald, prin. Fax 354-5426

Fairview Park, Cuyahoga, Pop. 16,528
Fairview Park CSD 1,800/K-12
20770 Lorain Rd 44126 440-331-5500
Brion Deitsch, supt. Fax 356-3545
www.leeca.org/fairview
Fairview HS 700/9-12
4507 W 213th St 44126 440-356-3500
Cary Willgren, prin. Fax 356-3529
Mayer MS 300/7-8
21200 Campus Dr 44126 440-356-3510
Thomas Kairis, prin. Fax 895-2191

Fairview Academy Post-Sec.
22610 Lorain Rd 44126 440-734-5555

Fayette, Fulton, Pop. 1,326
Gorham Fayette Local SD 500/K-12
PO Box 309 43521 419-237-2573
David Hankins, supt. Fax 237-3125
www.gorham-fayette.k12.oh.us
Gorham Fayette JSHS 200/7-12
PO Box 309 43521 419-237-2114
James Marquette, prin. Fax 237-3125

Fayetteville, Brown, Pop. 390
Fayetteville-Perry Local SD 1,000/K-12
501 S Apple St 45118 513-875-2423
Roy Hill, supt. Fax 875-2703
www.fp.k12.oh.us
Fayetteville-Perry HS 300/9-12
501 S Apple St 45118 513-875-3520
Raegan White, prin. Fax 875-4512
Fayetteville-Perry MS 300/5-8
601 S Apple St 45118 513-875-2829
David Tatman, prin. Fax 875-4523

Chatfield College Post-Sec.
20918 State Route 251 45118 513-875-3344

Felicity, Clermont, Pop. 915
Felicity-Franklin Local SD 1,200/PK-12
PO Box 839 45120 513-876-2113
William Shepherd, supt. Fax 876-2519
www.felicityfranklinschools.org/
Felicity-Franklin Local HS 400/9-12
PO Box 839 45120 513-876-2113
Guy Hopkins, prin. Fax 876-2560
Felicity-Franklin Local MS 400/5-8
PO Box 839 45120 513-876-2113
James Danner, prin. Fax 876-2519

Findlay, Hancock, Pop. 39,118
Findlay CSD 6,200/K-12
227 S West St 45840 419-425-8212
Dr. Dean Wittwer, supt. Fax 425-8203
www.findlaycityschools.org
Central MS 500/6-8
200 W Main Cross St 45840 419-425-8257
Christopher Renn, prin. Fax 427-5453
Donnell MS 500/6-8
301 Baldwin Ave 45840 419-425-8370
Donald Williams, prin. Fax 427-5454
Findlay HS 1,900/9-12
1200 Broad Ave 45840 419-425-8289
Craig Kupferberg, prin. Fax 427-5448
Glenwood MS 400/6-8
1715 N Main St 45840 419-425-8373
David Alvarado, prin. Fax 427-5455
Millstream East Vocational S Vo/Tech
620 Lynn St 45840 419-425-8214
Edith Wannemacher, prin. Fax 427-5461
Millstream South Vocational S Vo/Tech
1100 Broad Ave 45840 419-425-8277
Kathy Siebenaler-Wilson, prin. Fax 427-5469

Liberty-Benton Local SD 1,300/K-12
9190 County Road 9 45840 419-422-8526
Dennis Recker, supt. Fax 422-5108
www.noacsc.org/hancock/lb/
Liberty-Benton HS 400/9-12
9190 County Road 9 45840 419-424-5351
Brenda Frankart, prin. Fax 422-5108
Liberty Benton MS 300/6-8
9050 W State Route 12 45840 419-422-9166
Bruce Otley, prin. Fax 422-5108

Brown Mackie College Post-Sec.
1700 Fostoria Ave Ste 100 45840 888-296-5059
Owens Community College Post-Sec.
3200 Bright Rd 45840 567-429-3500
University of Findlay Post-Sec.
1000 N Main St 45840 419-422-8313
Winebrenner Theological Seminary Post-Sec.
950 N Main St 45840 419-434-4200

Fort Jennings, Putnam, Pop. 431
Jennings Local SD 500/K-12
PO Box 98 45844 419-286-2238
Frank Sukup, supt. Fax 286-2240
Fort Jennings JSHS 200/7-12
PO Box 98 45844 419-286-2238
Nicholas Langhals, prin. Fax 286-2240

Fort Loramie, Shelby, Pop. 1,459
Fort Loramie Local SD 800/K-12
PO Box 26 45845 937-295-3931
Larry Ludlow, supt. Fax 295-2758
www.loramie.k12.oh.us/
Fort Loramie JSHS 400/7-12
PO Box 290 45845 937-295-3342
Michael Roche, prin. Fax 295-2758

Fort Recovery, Mercer, Pop. 1,323
Fort Recovery Local SD 1,100/PK-12
PO Box 604 45846 419-375-4139
David R. Riel, supt. Fax 375-1058
www.noacsc.org/mercer/fr/
Fort Recovery HS 300/9-12
PO Box 604 45846 419-375-4111
David Warvel, prin. Fax 375-2039
Fort Recovery MS 200/6-8
865 Sharpsburg Rd 45846 419-375-2815
Ted Shuttleworth, prin. Fax 375-1126

Fostoria, Seneca, Pop. 13,395
Fostoria CSD 2,200/PK-12
500 Parkway Dr 44830 419-435-8163
Dr. Cynthia A. Lemmerman, supt. Fax 436-4109
www.fostoria.k12.oh.us/
Fostoria HS 700/9-12
1001 Park Ave 44830 419-436-4110
Jude Meyers, prin. Fax 436-4118
Fostoria MS 500/6-8
1202 H L Ford Dr 44830 419-436-4120
Kathleen Leitzy, prin. Fax 436-4169

Lakota Local SD
Supt. — See Risingsun
Lakota JHS 200/7-8
8351 W County Road 28 44830 419-435-2497
James Balsizer, prin. Fax 435-9401

St. Wendelin HS 200/9-12
533 N Countyline St 44830 419-435-8144
Angela Joseph, prin. Fax 436-4042

Fowler, Trumbull
Mathews Local SD
Supt. — See Vienna
Neal MS, PO Box 179 44418 200/6-8
Michael King, prin. 330-637-3066

Frankfort, Ross, Pop. 1,040
Adena Local SD 1,200/K-12
3367 County Road 550 45628 740-998-4633
Michael Kinnamon, supt. Fax 998-4632
adena.k12.oh.us/
Adena HS 400/9-12
3367 County Road 550 45628 740-998-2313
Michael Francis, prin. Fax 998-2314
Adena MS 300/6-8
3367 County Road 550 45628 740-998-2313
Richard Clark, prin. Fax 998-2314

Franklin, Warren, Pop. 12,410
Franklin CSD 3,000/K-12
150 E 6th St 45005 937-746-1699
Steven Buerschen, supt. Fax 743-4135
www.franklin-city.k12.oh.us
Franklin HS 900/9-12
750 E 4th St 45005 937-743-8610
Dave Gregory, prin. Fax 743-8623
Franklin MS 800/6-8
136 E 6th St 45005 937-743-8630
James Martin, prin. Fax 743-8637

Fenwick HS 400/9-12
4855 State Route 122 45005 513-423-0723
Catherine Mulligan, prin. Fax 420-8690
Middletown Christian S 600/PK-12
3011 Union Rd 45005 513-423-4542
Mark Spradling, supt. Fax 261-6841

Southwestern College Post-Sec.
201 E 2nd St 45005 937-746-6633

Franklin Furnace, Scioto, Pop. 1,212
Green Local SD 700/K-12
4070 Gallia Pike 45629 740-354-9221
Ronald Lindsay, supt. Fax 355-8975
www.green.k12.oh.us
Green JSHS 300/7-12
4057 Gallia Pike 45629 740-354-9150
David Hopper, prin. Fax 355-4094

Fredericktown, Knox, Pop. 2,526
Fredericktown Local SD 1,200/K-12
134 W 2nd St 43019 740-694-2956
Dan Humphrey, supt. Fax 694-0956
www.fredericktown.net/schools.htm
Fredericktown HS 400/9-12
117 Columbus Rd 43019 740-694-2726
Gary Chapman, prin. Fax 694-5618
Fredericktown IS 500/4-8
31 Taylor St 43019 740-694-2966
Emily Funston, prin. Fax 694-4160

Fremont, Sandusky, Pop. 17,049
Fremont CSD 4,400/K-12
1220 Cedar St Ste A 43420 419-332-6454
Traci McCaudy, supt. Fax 334-5454
www.fremont.k12.oh.us
Fremont MS 1,000/7-9
501 Croghan St 43420 419-332-5569
Anthony Walker, prin. Fax 334-5494
Fremont Ross SHS 1,000/10-12
1100 North St 43420 419-332-8221
Sandra Werling, prin. Fax 334-5450

Vanguard-Sentinel JVSD
1306 Cedar St 43420 419-332-2626
David Danhoff, supt. Fax 334-4308
www.vscc.k12.oh.us/
Technology Center Vo/Tech
1220 Cedar St Ste C 43420 419-334-5698
Thomas Gerschutz, prin. Fax 334-2609
Vanguard Career Center Vo/Tech
1306 Cedar St 43420 419-332-2626
Terri Clark, dir. Fax 334-5692
Other Schools – See Tiffin

St. Joseph Central HS 300/9-12
702 Croghan St 43420 419-332-9947
Mike Gabel, prin. Fax 332-4945
Terra State Community College Post-Sec.
2830 Napoleon Rd 43420 419-334-8400

Gahanna, Franklin, Pop. 33,077
Gahanna-Jefferson CSD 6,900/K-12
160 S Hamilton Rd 43230 614-471-7065
Gregg Morris, supt. Fax 478-5568
www.gahannaschools.org
Gahanna MS East 600/6-8
730 Clotts Rd 43230 614-478-5550
Dwight Carter, prin. Fax 478-5544
Gahanna MS South 500/6-8
349 Shady Spring Dr 43230 614-337-3730
Angie Adrean, prin. Fax 337-3734
Gahanna MS West 600/6-8
350 N Stygler Rd 43230 614-478-5570
John Rathburn, prin. Fax 337-3771
Lincoln HS 2,300/9-12
140 S Hamilton Rd 43230 614-478-5500
Mark White, prin. Fax 337-3769

Columbus Academy 1,000/PK-12
PO Box 30745 43230 614-475-2311
John MacKenzie, prin. Fax 475-0396
Gahanna Christian Academy 500/PK-12
817 N Hamilton Rd 43230 614-471-9270
Rev. Lawrence Bates, supt. Fax 471-9201

Galena, Delaware, Pop. 505
Big Walnut Local SD 2,600/K-12
PO Box 218 43021 740-965-2706
April Domine, supt.
www.bigwalnut.k12.oh.us/
Other Schools – See Sunbury

Galion, Crawford, Pop. 11,449
Galion CSD 1,500/PK-12
200 W Church St 44833 419-468-3432
Dennis Rose, supt. Fax 468-4333
www.ncocc-k12.org/galion
Galion HS 700/9-12
200 N Union St 44833 419-468-6500
Joe Gotchall, prin. Fax 468-4333
Galion MS 400/6-8
200 W Walnut St 44833 419-468-3134
Andrew Johnson, prin. Fax 468-4333

Northmor Local SD 1,300/K-12
5247 County Road 29 44833 419-946-8861
Brent Winand, supt. Fax 947-6255
www.ncocc-k12.org/northmor
Northmor HS 600/7-12
5353 County Road 29 44833 419-946-3946
Dennis Ervin, prin. Fax 947-7545

Gallipolis, Gallia, Pop. 4,212
Gallia County Local SD 2,500/K-12
230 Shawnee Ln 45631 740-446-7917
Charla C. Evans, supt. Fax 446-3187
gallialocal.org
Other Schools – See Cheshire, Crown City

Gallipolis CSD 2,300/K-12
61 State St 45631 740-446-3211
Jack Payton, supt. Fax 446-6433
gallipoliscityschools.k12.oh.us
Gallia Academy JSHS 1,000/7-12
340 4th Ave 45631 740-446-3212
Bruce Wilson, prin. Fax 446-3436

Gallipolis Career College Post-Sec.
1176 Jackson Pike # 312 45631 740-446-4367
Gallipolis State Institute 45631 Post-Sec.

Ohio Valley Christian S 100/K-12
455 3rd Ave 45631 740-446-0374
Dr. Frederick Williams, admin. Fax 446-8593

Galloway, Franklin
South-Western CSD
Supt. — See Grove City
Westland HS 1,600/9-12
146 Galloway Rd 43119 614-851-7000
James Grube, prin. Fax 870-5531

Gambier, Knox, Pop. 2,050

Kenyon College Post-Sec.
1 Kenyon College 43022 740-427-5000

Garfield Heights, Cuyahoga, Pop. 29,042
Garfield Heights CSD 4,000/K-12
5640 Briarcliff Dr 44125 216-475-8100
Jeanne Sternad, supt. Fax 475-1824
www.garfieldheightscityschools.com/
Garfield Heights HS 1,300/9-12
4900 Turney Rd 44125 216-662-2800
Terrance Olszewski, prin. Fax 271-6183
Garfield Heights MS 1,000/6-8
12000 Mapleleaf Dr 44125 216-475-8105
Marlene Remesch, prin. Fax 475-8146

Archbishop Lyke-St Timothy S 200/5-8
4351 E 131st St 44105 216-581-3517
Margarete Smith, prin. Fax 581-6204
Trinity HS 600/9-12
12425 Granger Rd 44125 216-581-1644
Carla Fritsch, prin. Fax 581-9348

Garrettsville, Portage, Pop. 2,222
James A. Garfield Local SD 1,600/K-12
10235 State Route 88 44231 330-527-4336
Charles Klamer, supt. Fax 527-5941
garfield.sparcc.org/
Garfield HS 500/9-12
10233 State Route 88 44231 330-527-4341
Neil Wallace, prin. Fax 527-5636
Garfield MS 300/7-8
10231 State Route 88 44231 330-527-2151
Rosalice Manlove, prin. Fax 527-2601

Gates Mills, Cuyahoga, Pop. 2,370

Gilmour Academy 9-12
34001 Cedar Rd 44040 440-473-8090
Br. Robert Lavelle, prin. Fax 473-8093
Gilmour Academy MS 7-8
34001 Cedar Rd 44040 440-473-8111
Yvonne Saunders, prin. Fax 473-8112
Hawken S 400/9-12
PO Box 8002 44040 440-423-4446
Scott Looney, hdmstr. Fax 423-2975

Geneva, Ashtabula, Pop. 6,478
Geneva CSD 2,800/K-12
135 S Eagle St 44041 440-466-4831
Ronald Donatone, supt. Fax 466-0908
www.genevaschools.org/
Geneva HS 1,000/9-12
1031 S Ridge Rd E 44041 440-466-4831
Joanna Daniels, prin. Fax 466-8547
Geneva JHS 500/7-8
839 Sherman St 44041 440-466-4831
Richard Belconis, prin. Fax 466-5692

Genoa, Ottawa, Pop. 2,351
Genoa Area Local SD 1,700/K-12
2810 N Genoa Clay Center Rd 43430 419-855-7741
Dennis Mock, supt. Fax 855-4030
www.genoaschools.com
Genoa Area HS 500/9-12
2980 N Genoa Clay Center Rd 43430 419-855-7735
James Henline, prin. Fax 855-7739
Genoa Area MS 400/6-8
2950 N Genoa Clay Center Rd 43430 419-855-7781
Kevin Katafias, prin. Fax 855-7784

Georgetown, Brown, Pop. 3,720
Georgetown EVD 1,100/K-12
1043 Mount Orab Pike 45121 937-378-3730
Richrd Spindler, supt. Fax 378-2219
www.gtownschools.org/
Georgetown JSHS 500/7-12
987 Mount Orab Pike 45121 937-378-6730
Perianne Germann, prin. Fax 378-2442

Southern Hills JVSD
9193 Hamer Rd 45121 937-378-6131
Charles Guarino, supt. Fax 378-4577
www.shcc.k12.oh.us
Southern Hills Career Center Vo/Tech
9193 Hamer Rd 45121 937-378-6131
Tim Chadwell, prin. Fax 378-4577

Germantown, Montgomery, Pop. 5,157
Valley View Local SD 2,000/K-12
64 Comstock St 45327 937-855-6581
Sherry Parr, supt. Fax 855-7156
www.valleyview.k12.oh.us
Valley View HS 600/9-12
6027 Frmrsvll Germantn Pike 45327 937-855-4116
Steve Anderson, prin. Fax 855-4739
Valley View MS 500/6-8
64 Comstock St 45327 937-855-4203
Harold Bowman, prin. Fax 855-7156

Germantown Christian S 100/PK-12
9440 Eby Rd 45327 937-855-7334
Patricia Proctor, prin. Fax 855-7746

Gibsonburg, Sandusky, Pop. 2,460
Gibsonburg EVD 1,300/PK-12
301 S Sunset Ave 43431 419-637-2479
Richard Freeborn, supt. Fax 637-3029
www.gibsonburg.k12.oh.us/
Gibsonburg HS 400/9-12
740 S Main St 43431 419-637-2873
Thom Loomis, prin. Fax 637-2046
Gibsonburg MS 300/6-8
740 S Main St 43431 419-637-7954
Danny Kissell, prin. Fax 637-2046

Girard, Trumbull, Pop. 10,490
Girard CSD 1,800/K-12
704 E Prospect St 44420 330-545-2596
Joseph Jeswald, supt. Fax 545-2597
Girard HS 600/9-12
31 N Ward Ave 44420 330-545-5431
Ronald Ragozine, prin. Fax 545-5440
Girard JHS 300/7-8
31 N Ward Ave 44420 330-545-5431
William Ryser, prin. Fax 545-5440

Glouster, Athens, Pop. 2,029
Trimble Local SD 1,000/K-12
1 Tomcat Dr 45732 740-767-4444
Cindy Johnston, supt. Fax 767-4901
trimble.k12.oh.us/
Trimble HS 300/9-12
1 Tomcat Dr 45732 740-767-3434
Joseph Hemsley, prin. Fax 767-4901
Trimble MS 300/5-8
18500 Jacksonville Rd 45732 740-767-2810
Darrell Dugan, prin. Fax 767-9523

Gnadenhutten, Tuscarawas, Pop. 1,294
Indian Valley Local SD 1,100/K-12
PO Box 171 44629 740-254-4334
Randall Cadle, supt. Fax 254-9271
www.ivschools.org/
Indian Valley HS 600/7-12
PO Box 130 44629 740-254-4262
Martha Roudebush, prin. Fax 254-4911

Goshen, Clermont
Goshen Local SD 2,600/K-12
6694 Goshen Rd 45122 513-722-2222
Charlene Thomas, supt. Fax 722-3767
www.goshenlocalschools.org
Goshen HS 800/9-12
6707 Goshen Rd 45122 513-722-2227
John Strathern, prin. Fax 722-2247
Goshen MS 600/6-8
6692 Goshen Rd 45122 513-722-2226
Troy Smith, prin. Fax 722-2246

Cozaddale Baptist Academy 100/K-12
10632 Eltzroth Rd 45122 513-722-2064
C. Lee Carr, admin. Fax 722-0096

Grafton, Lorain, Pop. 5,855
Midview Local SD 3,500/K-12
1010 Vivian Dr 44044 440-926-3737
Howard Dulmage, supt. Fax 926-2675
www.midviewk12.org
Midview HS 1,100/9-12
38199 Capel Rd 44044 440-748-2124
Susan Bobola, prin. Fax 748-5277
Midview MS 600/7-8
37999 Capel Rd 44044 440-748-2122
Scott Goggin, prin. Fax 748-0131

Grand Rapids, Wood, Pop. 998
Otsego Local SD
Supt. — See Tontogany
Otsego MS 300/7-8
23939 2nd St 43522 419-832-2261
Ray Graves, prin. Fax 832-0487

Grandview Heights, Franklin, Pop. 6,273
Grandview Heights CSD 1,200/K-12
1587 W 3rd Ave 43212 614-481-3600
Dr. David Mancini, supt. Fax 481-3648
www.grandviewschools.org/
Grandview Heights HS 400/9-12
1587 W 3rd Ave 43212 614-481-3620
Steven Andersson, prin. Fax 481-3648
Grandview Heights MS 200/7-8
1240 Oakland Ave 43212 614-481-3632
Robert Baeslack, prin. Fax 481-3648

Granville, Licking, Pop. 5,281
Granville EVD 2,200/K-12
PO Box 417 43023 740-587-8101
Scot Prebles, supt. Fax 587-8191
www.granville.k12.oh.us/
Granville HS 700/9-12
248 New Burg St 43023 740-587-8105
Charles Dilbone, prin. Fax 587-8195
Granville MS 400/7-8
210 New Burg St 43023 740-587-8104
Lisa Sealover-Ormond, prin. Fax 587-8194

Denison University Post-Sec.
PO Box B 43023 740-587-0810
Granville Christian Academy 300/K-12
1820 Newark Granville Rd 43023 740-587-4423
Nancy Warner, prin. Fax 587-1266

Green, Summit, Pop. 23,463
Green Local SD 3,200/PK-12
PO Box 218 44232 330-896-7500
David Macali, supt. Fax 896-7580
www.green.summit.k12.oh.us
Other Schools – See Uniontown

Portage Lakes JVSD
PO Box 248 44232 330-896-8200
Mark Lukens, supt. Fax 896-8297
Portage Lakes Career Center Vo/Tech
PO Box 248 44232 330-896-8200
Paulette Prince, prin. Fax 896-8297

Green Camp, Marion, Pop. 323
Elgin Local SD
Supt. — See Marion
Elgin JHS 300/7-8
PO Box 214 43322 740-528-2320
Brian Napper, prin. Fax 528-2618

Greenfield, Highland, Pop. 5,146
Greenfield EVD 2,200/PK-12
200 N 5th St 45123 937-981-2152
Terrence Fouch, supt. Fax 981-4395
greenfield.k12.oh.us

Greenfield MS 600/5-8
200 N 5th St 45123 937-981-2197
Howard Zody, prin. Fax 981-0417
McClain HS 700/9-12
200 N 5th St 45123 937-981-7731
Dan Strain, prin. Fax 981-4395

Greenville, Darke, Pop. 13,166
Greenville CSD 3,300/K-12
215 W 4th St 45331 937-548-3185
Greg Taylor, supt. Fax 548-6943
www.greenville.k12.oh.us
Greenville HS 1,100/9-12
100 Greenwave Way 45331 937-548-4188
Chris Mortensen, prin. Fax 548-3082
Greenville JHS 500/7-8
131 Central Ave 45331 937-548-3202
Jack Schulte, prin. Fax 548-3315

Greenwich, Huron, Pop. 1,549
South Central Local SD 900/K-12
3305 Greenwich Angling Rd 44837 419-752-3815
Ben Chaffee, supt. Fax 752-0182
buford.willard-oh.com/southcentral/
South Central HS 300/9-12
3305 Greenwich Angling Rd 44837 419-752-3354
Denise Dilsaver, prin. Fax 752-6927

Grove City, Franklin, Pop. 30,892
South-Western CSD 21,100/PK-12
3805 Marlane Dr 43123 614-801-3000
Dr. R. Kirk Hamilton, supt. Fax 871-2781
www.swcs.us
Brookpark MS 500/7-8
2803 Southwest Blvd 43123 614-801-3500
Bob Rains, prin. Fax 871-6512
Central Crossing HS 1,500/9-12
4500 Big Run South Rd 43123 614-801-6500
Ed Palmer, prin. Fax 801-6690
Grove City HS 1,600/9-12
4665 Hoover Rd 43123 614-801-3300
Kathryn Buckerfield, prin. Fax 871-6563
Jackson MS 600/7-8
2271 Holton Rd 43123 614-801-3800
Elizabeth Watkins, prin. Fax 801-3818
Pleasant View MS 800/7-8
7255 Kropp Rd 43123 614-801-3900
Thom Gamertsfelder, prin. Fax 870-5530
South-Western Career Academy Vo/Tech
4750 Big Run South Rd 43123 614-801-3400
Shirley Moore, prin. Fax 801-6138
Other Schools – See Columbus, Galloway

Grove City Christian S 700/K-12
PO Box 728 43123 614-875-3000
Joyce Schneider, admin. Fax 875-8933

Groveport, Franklin, Pop. 4,753
Eastland-Fairfield Career & Technical SD
4300 Amalgamated Pl 43125 614-836-4530
Dr. Mark Weedy, supt. Fax 836-0203
www.eastland-fairfield.com
Eastland Career Center Vo/Tech
4465 S Hamilton Rd 43125 614-836-5725
Deb Stephenson, prin. Fax 836-4525
Adult Workforce Development Adult
4300 Amalgamated Pl Ste 100 43125 614-836-4541
Jane Hines, dir. Fax 836-0203
Other Schools – See Carroll

Groveport Madison Local SD 5,200/K-12
5940 Clyde Moore Dr 43125 614-492-2520
Scott McKenzie, supt. Fax 492-2533
www.gocruisers.org
Groveport Madison HS 1,800/9-12
4475 S Hamilton Rd 43125 614-836-4964
Donis Toler, prin. Fax 836-4690
Groveport Madison JHS 500/8-8
751 Main St 43125 614-836-4957
Zoraba Ross, prin. Fax 836-4999

Fairfield Career Center Post-Sec.
4465 S Hamilton Rd 43125 614-836-5725
Madison Christian S 500/PK-12
3565 Bixby Rd 43125 614-497-3456
Gary Ramin, prin. Fax 497-3057

Hamilton, Butler, Pop. 61,943
Butler Technology/Career Development SD
Supt. — See Fairfield
Options Business Academy Vo/Tech
105 N 2nd St 45011 513-887-0001
Harold Niehaus, prin.

Edgewood CSD
Supt. — See Trenton
Edgewood MS 900/6-8
3440 Busenbark Rd 45011 513-867-7430
Judith Scherrer, prin. Fax 867-7571

Hamilton CSD 9,000/K-12
PO Box 627 45012 513-887-5000
Janet Baker, supt. Fax 887-5014
hamiltoncityschools.com/
Garfield MS 800/7-8
250 N Fair Ave 45011 513-887-5035
Patricia Blake, prin. Fax 887-4700
Hamilton Freshman HS 700/9-9
2260 NW Washington Blvd 45013 513-896-3400
Gregory Rulon, prin. Fax 896-3402
Hamilton SHS 1,800/10-12
1165 Eaton Ave 45013 513-868-7700
Dennis Malone, prin. Fax 887-4810
Wilson MS 600/7-8
714 Eaton Ave 45013 513-887-5170
Sheryl Burk, prin. Fax 887-5186

New Miami Local SD 900/K-12
600 Seven Mile Ave 45011 513-863-0833
Robert Bierly, supt. Fax 863-0497
New Miami JSHS 400/7-12
600 Seven Mile Ave 45011 513-863-4917
Tom Alf, prin. Fax 896-3956

Ross Local SD 2,700/PK-12
3371 Hamilton Cleves Rd 45013 513-863-1253
M. Todd Yohey, supt. Fax 863-6250
www.rosd.k12.oh.us
Ross HS 900/9-12
3601 Hamilton Cleves Rd 45013 513-863-1252
Keith Klinefelter, prin. Fax 863-8340
Ross MS 800/5-8
3425 Hamilton Cleves Rd 45013 513-863-1251
Christopher Saylor, prin. Fax 863-0066

Badin HS 700/9-12
571 Hamilton New London Rd 45013 513-863-3993
Frank M. Margello, prin. Fax 785-2844
Cincinnati Christian HS 400/6-12
7474 Morris Rd 45011 513-892-8500
Dan Bragg, supt. Fax 892-0516
Miami University-Hamilton Campus Post-Sec.
1601 University Blvd 45011 513-785-3000

Hamler, Henry, Pop. 678
Patrick Henry Local SD 1,000/K-12
6900 State Route 18 43524 419-274-5451
Susan Miko, supt. Fax 274-1641
www.patrickhenry.k12.oh.us/
Henry HS 400/9-12
6900 State Route 18 43524 419-274-3015
Gregg Pettit, prin. Fax 274-8365
Henry MS 200/5-8
E050 County Road 7 43524 419-274-3431
Jennifer Ripke, prin. Fax 274-1890

Hammondsville, Jefferson
Edison Local SD 2,700/PK-12
14890 State Route 213 43930 330-532-3199
Lisa Carmichael, supt. Fax 532-2860
www.edisonlocal.k12.oh.us/
Stanton MS 400/5-8
14890 State Route 213 43930 330-532-1594
Troy Radinsky, prin. Fax 532-1594
Other Schools – See Bergholz, Richmond

Hannibal, Monroe
Switzerland of Ohio Local SD
Supt. — See Woodsfield
River HS 300/9-12
PO Box 37 43931 740-483-1358
Vincent Monseau, prin. Fax 483-2321

Hanoverton, Columbiana, Pop. 385
United Local SD 1,400/K-12
8143 State Route 9 44423 330-223-1521
Thomas Davis, supt. Fax 223-2363
www.united.k12.oh.us/
United JSHS 700/7-12
8143 State Route 9 44423 330-223-7102
William Young, prin. Fax 223-2363

Harrison, Hamilton, Pop. 7,821
Southwest Local SD 3,900/K-12
230 S Elm St 45030 513-367-4139
Daniel Lawler, supt. Fax 367-2287
www.southwestschools.org
Harrison HS 1,400/9-12
9860 West Rd 45030 513-367-4169
Susan Thomas, prin. Fax 367-7251
Harrison MS 700/7-8
9830 West Rd 45030 513-367-4831
Don Jostworth, prin. Fax 367-0370

Christ Centered S 100/PK-12
220 Sunset Ave 45030 513-367-4564
Jerry Goodbar, admin. Fax 367-7981

Harrod, Allen, Pop. 482
Allen East Local SD 1,100/K-12
9520 Harrod Rd 45850 419-648-3333
Michael Richards, supt. Fax 648-5282
www.noacsc.org/allen/ae
Allen East MS 400/4-8
9520 Harrod Rd 45850 419-648-3571
Larry Altenburger, prin. Fax 648-5282
Other Schools – See Lafayette

Hartville, Stark, Pop. 2,389
Lake Local SD
Supt. — See Uniontown
Lake MS 800/6-8
12001 Market Ave N 44632 330-877-4290
Jeffrey Durbin, prin. Fax 877-1384

Lake Center Christian S 600/K-12
12893 Kaufman Ave NW 44632 330-877-2049
Matthew McMullen, supt. Fax 877-2040

Haviland, Paulding, Pop. 171
Wayne Trace Local SD 1,100/PK-12
4915 US Route 127 45851 419-263-2415
Brian Gerber, supt. Fax 263-2377
www.noacsc.org/paulding/wt/
Wayne Trace JSHS 600/7-12
4915 US Route 127 45851 419-399-4100
Kevin Wilson, prin. Fax 622-3037

Heath, Licking, Pop. 8,888
Heath CSD 1,700/K-12
107 Lancaster Dr 43056 740-522-2816
Tom Forman, supt. Fax 522-4697
www.heath.k12.oh.us/
Heath HS 500/9-12
300 Licking View Dr 43056 740-788-3300
Terry Kopchak, prin. Fax 788-3322
Heath MS 400/6-8
310 Licking View Dr 43056 740-788-3200
Tim Winland, prin. Fax 788-3209

Hebron, Licking, Pop. 2,149
Lakewood Local SD 2,300/K-12
PO Box 70 43025 740-928-5878
Jay Gault, supt. Fax 928-3152
www.lakewoodlocal.k12.oh.us/
Lakewood HS 700/9-12
PO Box 70 43025 740-928-4526
Larry Bevard, prin. Fax 928-3731

Lakewood MS 500/6-8
PO Box 70 43025 740-928-8330
Jim Riley, prin. Fax 928-5627

Hicksville, Defiance, Pop. 3,533
Hicksville EVD 1,000/K-12
105 E Smith St 43526 419-542-7665
Kevin Miller, supt. Fax 542-8534
www.hicksvilleschools.org/
Hicksville JSHS 500/7-12
105 E Smith St 43526 419-542-7636
Sue Dangler, prin. Fax 542-8534

Highland Heights, Cuyahoga, Pop. 8,621
Mayfield CSD
Supt. — See Mayfield Heights
CEVEC Vo/Tech
211 Alpha Park 44143 440-995-7451
Robert Ross, prin. Fax 995-7455

Highland Hills, Cuyahoga, Pop. 1,421

Cuyahoga Community College Post-Sec.
25444 Harvard Rd 44122 216-987-2019

Hilliard, Franklin, Pop. 26,656
Hilliard CSD 14,300/PK-12
5323 Cemetery Rd 43026 614-771-4273
Dale McVey, supt. Fax 777-2424
www.hilliard.k12.oh.us
Hilliard Darby HS 2,300/9-12
4200 Leppert Rd 43026 614-527-4200
David Stewart, prin. Fax 527-4206
Hilliard Davidson HS 1,900/9-12
5100 Davidson Rd 43026 614-771-2299
John Bandow, prin. Fax 529-7406
Hilliard Heritage MS 800/7-8
5670 Scioto Darby Rd 43026 614-771-2800
Suzanne McCoy, prin. Fax 771-2808
Hilliard Memorial MS 700/7-8
5600 Scioto Darby Rd 43026 614-334-3057
Douglas Lowery, prin. Fax 334-3058
Weaver MS 700/7-8
4600 Avery Rd 43026 614-529-7424
Steve Estepp, prin. Fax 529-7425

Hillsboro, Highland, Pop. 6,677
Hillsboro CSD 2,500/K-12
338 W Main St 45133 937-393-3475
Art Reiber, supt. Fax 393-5841
www.hillsboro.k12.oh.us
Hillsboro HS 900/9-12
358 W Main St 45133 937-393-3485
Larry Stall, prin. Fax 393-5842
Hillsboro MS 400/6-8
358 W Main St 45133 937-393-9877
Rick Earley, prin. Fax 393-5843

Southern State Community College Post-Sec.
100 Hobart Dr 45133 937-393-3431

Hiram, Portage, Pop. 1,192

Hiram College Post-Sec.
PO Box 96 44234 330-569-3211

Holgate, Henry, Pop. 1,165
Holgate Local SD 500/K-12
801 Joe E Brown Ave 43527 419-264-5141
James Reiter, supt. Fax 264-1965
www.holgate.k12.oh.us/
Holgate JSHS 300/6-12
103 Frazier Ave 43527 419-264-2521
Bruce Kidder, prin. Fax 264-1965

Holland, Lucas, Pop. 1,326
Springfield Local SD 3,800/K-12
6900 Hall St 43528 419-867-5600
Dr. Cynthia Beekley, supt. Fax 867-5700
www.springfield-lucas.k12.oh.us
Springfield HS 1,200/9-12
1470 S Mccord Rd 43528 419-867-5633
Michael O'Shea, prin. Fax 867-5618
Springfield MS 900/6-8
7001 Madison Ave 43528 419-867-5644
Matt Geha, prin. Fax 867-5732

Hondros College Post-Sec.
6135 Trust Dr Ste 110 43528 419-865-0070

Hopedale, Harrison, Pop. 994
Harrison Hills CSD 2,000/PK-12
PO Box 356 43976 740-942-7800
Jim Drexler, supt. Fax 942-7808
www.harrisonhills.k12.oh.us/
Other Schools – See Cadiz, Scio

Houston, Shelby
Hardin-Houston Local SD 900/K-12
5300 Houston Rd 45333 937-295-3010
John Schey, supt. Fax 295-3737
www.houston.k12.oh.us
Houston JSHS 400/7-12
5300 Houston Rd 45333 937-295-3010
Rick Russell, prin. Fax 295-3737

Howard, Knox
East Knox Local SD 1,200/K-12
PO Box 68 43028 740-599-7493
John Marschhausen, supt. Fax 599-5863
www.ekschools.com
East Knox HS 600/7-12
PO Box 128 43028 740-599-7007
Gary Comstock, prin. Fax 599-2922

Hoytville, Wood, Pop. 296
Mc Comb Local SD
Supt. — See Mc Comb
Mc Comb Local MS 200/6-8
PO Box 157 43529 419-278-8194
Jerry Wolford, prin. Fax 278-7166

Hubbard, Trumbull, Pop. 8,006
Hubbard EVD 2,300/K-12
150 Hall Ave 44425 330-534-1921
Richard J. Buchenic, supt. Fax 534-0522
www.hubbard.k12.oh.us/
Hubbard HS 800/9-12
350 Hall Ave 44425 330-534-1113
Ronald Garrett, prin. Fax 534-2865
Reed MS 700/5-8
150 Hall Ave 44425 330-534-1129
Jon Young, prin. Fax 534-0522

Huber Heights, Montgomery, Pop. 38,089
Huber Heights CSD 6,700/K-12
5954 Longford Rd 45424 937-237-6300
William Kirby, supt. Fax 237-6307
www.huberheights.k12.oh.us/
Studebaker MS 800/6-8
5950 Longford Rd 45424 937-237-6345
Tom Heid, prin.
Wayne HS 2,300/9-12
5400 Chambersburg Rd 45424 937-233-6431
John Allen, prin. Fax 237-6321
Weisenborn MS 800/6-8
6061 Troy Pike 45424 937-237-6350
Kathy Leary, prin.

Carousel of Miami Valley Beauty College Post-Sec.
7809 Waynetowne Blvd 45424 937-233-8818

Hudson, Summit, Pop. 23,084
Hudson CSD 5,500/PK-12
2400 Hudson Aurora Rd 44236 330-653-1200
Louis Thomas, supt. Fax 653-1474
www.hudson.edu
Hudson HS 1,800/9-12
2500 Hudson Aurora Rd 44236 330-653-1416
Jay Tyree, prin. Fax 653-1481
Hudson MS 1,400/6-8
77 N Oviatt St 44236 330-653-1316
Charles DiLauro, prin. Fax 653-1368

Brighton College Post-Sec.
85 S Main St Ste B 44236 800-231-3803
Western Reserve Academy 400/9-12
115 College St 44236 330-650-4400
Henry Flanagan, hdmstr. Fax 650-9754

Hunting Valley, Cuyahoga, Pop. 711

University S 400/9-12
2785 Som Center Rd 44022 216-831-2200
Stephen Murray, hdmstr. Fax 831-0402

Huron, Erie, Pop. 7,581
Huron CSD 1,600/PK-12
712 Cleveland Rd E 44839 419-433-3911
Fred Fox, supt. Fax 433-7095
www.huron-city.k12.oh.us/
Huron HS 500/9-12
710 Cleveland Rd W 44839 419-433-3171
John Ruf, prin. Fax 433-2339
McCormick MS 500/5-8
325 Ohio St 44839 419-433-5658
Mark Doughty, prin. Fax 433-8427

Bowling Green State University Post-Sec.
1 University Dr 44839 419-433-5560

Independence, Cuyahoga, Pop. 6,869
Independence Local SD 1,200/PK-12
7733 Stone Rd 44131 216-642-5850
David Laurenzi, supt. Fax 642-3482
www.independence.k12.oh.us
Independence HS 400/9-12
6001 Archwood Rd 44131 216-642-5860
Roger Howard, prin. Fax 642-5886
Independence MS 400/5-8
6111 Archwood Rd 44131 216-642-5865
Edward Vittardi, prin. Fax 520-7002

Ironton, Lawrence, Pop. 11,417
Ironton CSD 1,600/K-12
105 S 5th St 45638 740-532-4133
Dean Nance, supt. Fax 532-2314
www.tigertown.com
Ironton HS 500/9-12
1701 S 7th St 45638 740-532-3911
Joseph Rowe, prin. Fax 533-6027
Ironton JHS 200/7-8
1701 S 7th St 45638 740-532-9458
Toben Schreck, prin. Fax 533-6039

Rock Hill Local SD 1,900/K-12
2325 County Road 26 Unit A 45638 740-532-7030
Lloyd Evans, supt. Fax 532-2092
rockhill.org/
Rock Hill HS 600/9-12
2415 County Road 26 45638 740-533-7012
Steve Lambert, prin.
Rock Hill MS 500/6-8
2171 County Road 26 45638 740-532-7026
Wes Hairston, prin.

Ohio University Southern Campus Post-Sec.
1804 Liberty Ave 45638 740-533-4600
St. Joseph Central HS 100/7-12
912 S 6th St 45638 740-532-0485
James Mains, prin. Fax 532-3699

Irwin, Union

Rosedale Bible College Post-Sec.
2270 Rosedale Rd 43029 740-857-1311

Jackson, Jackson, Pop. 6,240
Jackson CSD 2,600/K-12
450 Vaughn St 45640 740-286-6442
Stephen P. Anderson, supt. Fax 286-6445
www.jcs.k12.oh.us
Jackson HS 900/9-12
500 Vaughn St 45640 740-286-7575
Kevin Rice, prin. Fax 286-8197
Jackson MS 700/6-8
21 Tropic St 45640 740-286-7586
Mark Broermann, prin. Fax 286-8637

Southeastern Business College Post-Sec.
504 McCarty Ln 45640 740-286-1554

Jackson Center, Shelby, Pop. 1,459
Jackson Center Local SD 500/K-12
PO Box 849 45334 937-596-6053
Jerry Harmon, supt. Fax 596-6490
Jackson Center JSHS 300/7-12
PO Box 849 45334 937-596-6149
William Reichert, prin. Fax 596-6490

Jacksontown, Licking

Excel Academy, PO Box 109 43030 100/K-12
Marlene Jacob, prin. 740-323-1102

Jamestown, Greene, Pop. 1,854
Greeneview Local SD 1,400/K-12
4 S Charleston Rd 45335 937-675-2728
Valerie Browning Ph.D., supt. Fax 675-6807
www.greeneview.k12.oh.us
Greeneview IS 400/4-8
53 N Limestone St 45335 937-675-9391
Harold Farley, prin. Fax 675-6866
Greenview HS 500/9-12
4710 Cottonville Rd 45335 937-675-9711
Wallace Campbell, prin. Fax 675-6805

Jefferson, Ashtabula, Pop. 3,514
Ashtabula County JVSD
1565 State Route 167 44047 440-576-6015
Jerome Brockway, supt. Fax 576-6502
www.acjvs.org
Ashtabula County Joint Vocational S Vo/Tech
1565 State Route 167 44047 440-576-6015
Jon Whipple, prin. Fax 576-6502

Jefferson Area Local SD 2,200/K-12
45 E Satin St 44047 440-576-9180
Douglas Hladek, supt. Fax 576-9876
www.jefferson.k12.oh.us/
Jefferson Area JSHS 1,100/7-12
125 S Poplar St 44047 440-576-4731
Thomas Harrison, prin. Fax 576-9876

Jeromesville, Ashland, Pop. 485
Hillsdale Local SD 1,200/K-12
485 Township Rd 1902 44840 419-368-8231
Joel Roscoe, supt. Fax 368-7504
www.hillsdale.k12.oh.us/
Hillsdale HS 400/9-12
485 Township Rd 1902 44840 419-368-6841
Kevin Reidy, prin. Fax 368-7504
Hillsdale MS 400/5-8
PO Box 57 44840 419-368-4911
Tom Gaus, prin. Fax 368-3613

Johnstown, Licking, Pop. 3,883
Johnstown-Monroe Local SD 1,500/K-12
441 S Main St 43031 740-967-6846
Tom Suriano, supt. Fax 967-1106
johnstown.k12oh.us
Adams MS 400/6-8
80 W Maple St 43031 740-967-8766
Angela Pollock, prin. Fax 967-0051
Johnstown-Monroe HS 400/9-12
401 S Oregon St 43031 740-967-2721
Kim Jakeway, prin. Fax 967-1140

Northridge Local SD 1,500/K-12
6097 Johnstown Utica Rd 43031 740-967-6631
Jacqueline Henderson, supt. Fax 967-5022
northridge.k12.oh.us
Northridge HS 500/9-12
6066 Johnstown Utica Rd 43031 740-967-6651
Chris Vail, prin. Fax 967-6958
Northridge MS 300/6-8
6066 Johnstown Utica Rd 43031 740-967-6671
Amy Anderson, prin. Fax 967-7083

Kalida, Putnam, Pop. 1,124
Kalida Local SD 700/K-12
PO Box 269 45853 419-532-3534
Mark Neal, supt. Fax 532-2277
www.kalida.k12.oh.us
Kalida JSHS 300/7-12
PO Box 269 45853 419-532-3529
Donald Horstman, prin. Fax 532-2277

Kansas, Sandusky
Lakota Local SD
Supt. — See Risingsun
Lakota HS 400/9-12
5186 County Road 13 44841 419-986-5161
Timothy Bodnarik, prin. Fax 986-5436

Kelleys Island, Erie, Pop. 384
Kelleys Island Local SD 50/K-12
PO Box 349 43438 419-746-2730
Phil Thiede, supt. Fax 746-2271
www.kelleys.k12.oh.us/
Kelleys Island S 50/K-12
PO Box 349 43438 419-746-2730
Phil Thiede, prin. Fax 746-2271

Kent, Portage, Pop. 28,135
Kent CSD 3,600/PK-12
321 N Depeyster St 44240 330-673-6515
Marc Crail, supt. Fax 677-6166
kent.k12.oh.us
Central HS 9-12
200 N Mantua St 44240 330-676-4181
Tom Larkin, prin. Fax 676-4303
Roosevelt HS 1,200/9-12
1400 N Mantua St 44240 330-673-9595
Roger Sidoti, prin. Fax 673-9217
Stanton MS 800/6-8
1175 Hudson Rd 44240 330-673-6693
Dr. Timothy Dortch, prin. Fax 673-1561

Kent State University Post-Sec.
PO Box 5190 44242 330-672-2444

Kenton, Hardin, Pop. 8,169
Kenton CSD 2,100/PK-12
222 W Carrol St 43326 419-673-0775
Doug Roberts, supt. Fax 673-3180
www.kentoncityschools.org/
Kenton HS 700/9-12
200 Harding Ave 43326 419-673-1286
Archibald Rodgers, prin. Fax 675-5200
Kenton MS 500/6-8
300 Oriental St 43326 419-673-1237
Steven Ickes, prin. Fax 673-1626

Kettering, Montgomery, Pop. 55,481
Kettering CSD 7,400/K-12
3750 Far Hills Ave 45429 937-499-1400
Robert Mengerink, supt. Fax 499-1519
www.kettering.k12.oh.us
Kettering-Fairmont HS 2,400/9-12
3301 Shroyer Rd 45429 937-499-1600
James Schoenlein, prin. Fax 499-1661
Kettering MS 1,100/6-8
3000 Glengarry Dr 45420 937-499-1550
James Justice, prin. Fax 499-1598
Van Buren JHS 700/6-8
3775 Shroyer Rd 45429 937-499-1800
Matthew Rugh, prin. Fax 499-1820

Archbishop Alter HS 700/9-12
940 E David Rd 45429 937-434-4434
Sr. Katie Hoelscher, prin. Fax 434-0507
Carousel Beauty College Post-Sec.
3120 Woodman Dr 45420 937-298-5752
Kettering College of Medical Arts Post-Sec.
3737 Southern Blvd 45429 800-433-5262
School of Advertising Art Post-Sec.
1725 E David Rd 45440 937-294-0592

Kidron, Wayne

Central Christian S, PO Box 9 44636 300/5-12
Joyce Taylor, prin. 330-857-7311

Kings Mills, Warren
Kings Local SD 3,800/K-12
PO Box 910 45034 513-398-8050
Charles Mason, supt. Fax 229-7590
www.kingslocal.k12.oh.us
Kings HS 1,100/9-12
5500 Columbia Rd 45034 513-398-8050
Doug Mader, prin. Fax 459-2941
Kings JHS 600/7-8
5620 Columbia Rd 45034 513-398-8050
James Acton, prin. Fax 459-2951

Kinsman, Trumbull
Joseph Badger Local SD 600/K-12
7119 State Route 7 44428 330-876-2800
David D. Bair, supt. Fax 876-2810
www.joseph-badger.k12.oh.us/
Badger HS 300/9-12
7119 State Route 7 44428 330-876-2820
Edwin Baldwin, prin. Fax 876-2821
Badger MS 300/5-8
7119 State Route 7 44428 330-876-2840
Robert Moon, prin. Fax 876-2841

Kirtland, Lake, Pop. 7,251
Kirtland Local SD 1,100/K-12
9252 Chillicothe Rd 44094 440-256-3311
Stan Lipinski, supt. Fax 256-3831
www.kirtland.k12.oh.us
Kirtland HS 300/9-12
9150 Chillicothe Rd 44094 440-256-3366
Jack Thompson, prin. Fax 256-1042
Kirtland MS 200/6-8
9152 Chillicothe Rd 44094 440-256-3358
Harry Siskind, prin. Fax 256-3928

Lakeland Community College Post-Sec.
7700 Clocktower Dr 44094 440-953-7000

Lafayette, Allen, Pop. 298
Allen East Local SD
Supt. — See Harrod
Allen East HS 300/9-12
PO Box 7186 45854 419-649-6311
Gary DeLuca, prin. Fax 649-8900

La Grange, Lorain, Pop. 1,551
Keystone Local SD 1,200/K-12
PO Box 65, 440-355-5131
Dr. Gary Friedt, supt. Fax 355-6052
www.keystonelocalschools.org/
Keystone HS 600/9-12
PO Box 65, 440-355-5132
Thomas Clary, prin. Fax 355-6052
Keystone MS 600/5-8
PO Box 65, 440-355-5133
Timothy Jenkins, prin. Fax 355-6052

Lakeside, Ottawa
Danbury Local SD 600/K-12
9451 E Harbor Rd 43440 419-798-5185
Martin Fanning, supt. Fax 798-2260
www.danbury.k12.oh.us
Danbury JSHS 300/7-12
9451 E Harbor Rd 43440 419-798-4037
Karen Abbott, prin. Fax 798-2262

Lakewood, Cuyahoga, Pop. 53,244
Lakewood CSD 4,800/K-12
1470 Warren Rd 44107 216-529-4092
David Estrop, supt. Fax 228-8327
www.lakewoodcityschools.org/
Garfield MS 6-8
13114 Detroit Ave 44107 216-529-4241
Mark Walter, prin. Fax 529-4301
Harding MS 500/6-8
16600 Hilliard Rd 44107 216-529-4261
Meredith Wojtkun, prin. Fax 529-4708
Lakewood HS 2,200/9-12
14100 Franklin Blvd 44107 216-529-4021
Dr. William Wagner, prin. Fax 529-4459

St. Edward HS 900/9-12
13500 Detroit Ave 44107 216-221-3776
Eugene Boyer, prin. Fax 221-4609
Virginia Marti College of Art & Design Post-Sec.
11724 Detroit Ave 44107 216-221-8584

Lancaster, Fairfield, Pop. 36,063
Fairfield Union Local SD
Supt. — See Rushville
Fairfield Union HS 600/9-12
6401 Cincinnati Zanesville 43130 740-536-7306
Dale Ferbrache, prin. Fax 536-7911
Fairfield Union JHS 300/7-8
6401 Cincinnati Zanesville 43130 740-536-7846
Matthew McPhail, prin. Fax 536-7911

Lancaster CSD 5,200/K-12
345 E Mulberry St 43130 740-687-7300
Denise Callihan, supt. Fax 687-7303
www.lancaster.k12.oh.us
Ewing JHS 500/6-8
825 E Fair Ave 43130 740-687-7347
John Zishka, prin. Fax 687-3446
Lancaster HS 1,800/9-12
1312 Granville Pike 43130 740-681-7500
Steve Wigton, prin. Fax 681-7505
Sherman JHS 500/6-8
701 Union St 43130 740-687-7344
Greg Stickel, prin. Fax 687-3443

Fairfield Christian Academy 700/PK-12
1965 N Columbus St 43130 740-654-2889
Megan Peters, supt. Fax 654-7689
Fisher Catholic HS 300/9-12
1803 Granville Pike 43130 740-654-1231
James Condron, prin. Fax 654-1233
Ohio University Post-Sec.
1570 Granville Pike 43130 740-654-6711
Southeastern Business College Post-Sec.
1522 Sheridan Dr 43130 740-687-6126

Latham, Pike
Western Local SD 900/K-12
PO Box 130 45646 740-493-3113
Joseph Morrison, supt. Fax 493-2065
Western JSHS 400/7-12
PO Box 130 45646 740-493-2514
Phillip Howard, prin. Fax 493-8513

Leavittsburg, Trumbull
LaBrae Local SD 1,100/K-12
1001 N Leavitt Rd 44430 330-898-0800
Ronald Joseph, supt. Fax 898-6112
LaBrae HS 400/9-12
1001 N Leavitt Rd 44430 330-898-0800
Douglas Hitchcock, prin. Fax 898-6112
LaBrae MS, 1001 N Leavitt Rd 44430 300/6-8
Alex Geordan, prin. 330-898-0800

Lebanon, Warren, Pop. 19,978
Lebanon CSD 4,200/K-12
700 Holbrook Ave 45036 513-934-5770
Mark North, supt. Fax 932-5906
www.lebanon.k12.oh.us
Lebanon HS 1,500/9-12
1916 Drake Rd 45036 513-934-5100
Dr. Samuel Ison, prin. Fax 933-2150
Lebanon JHS 800/7-8
160 Miller Rd 45036 513-934-5300
Tom Olson, prin. Fax 932-9436

Warren County JVSD
3525 N State Route 48 45036 513-932-5677
Margaret Hess, supt. Fax 932-3810
www.wccareercenter.com
Warren County Career Center Vo/Tech
3525 N State Route 48 45036 513-932-5677
Gary Patton, dir. Fax 932-3810

Leesburg, Highland, Pop. 1,341
Fairfield Local SD 900/K-12
11611 State Route 771 45135 937-780-2221
Scott Wilson, supt. Fax 780-6900
www.fairfield-highland.k12.oh.us
Fairfield HS 300/9-12
11611 State Route 771 45135 937-780-2966
Daniel Staggs, prin. Fax 780-2841
Fairfield MS 300/5-8
11611 State Route 771 45135 937-780-2977
Michael Daye, prin. Fax 780-2841

Lees Creek, Clinton
East Clinton Local SD 1,500/K-12
97 College St 45138 937-584-2461
Gary West, supt. Fax 584-2817
www.east-clinton.k12.oh.us
East Clinton HS 500/9-12
PO Box 19 45138 937-584-2474
Dean Lynch, prin. Fax 584-4842
East Clinton MS 400/6-8
PO Box 19 45138 937-584-9267
Terry Enochs, prin. Fax 584-9558

Leetonia, Columbiana, Pop. 2,043
Leetonia EVD 800/K-12
450 Walnut St 44431 330-427-6594
Robert Rostan, supt. Fax 427-1136
www.leetonia.k12.oh.us
Leetonia HS 300/9-12
450 Walnut St 44431 330-427-2115
Michael Ferguson, prin. Fax 427-6904
Leetonia MS 300/5-8
450 Walnut St 44431 330-427-2444
Elizabeth Goerig, prin. Fax 427-2549

Leipsic, Putnam, Pop. 2,232
Leipsic Local SD 700/K-12
232 Oak St 45856 419-943-2165
Alice L. Dewar, supt. Fax 943-4331
www.noacsc.org/putnam/1p/
Leipsic JSHS 400/7-12
232 Oak St 45856 419-943-2164
Nancey Schortgen, prin. Fax 943-2185

Lewisburg, Preble, Pop. 1,784
Tri-County North Local SD 1,200/K-12
PO Box 40 45338 937-962-2671
Stephen Grant, supt. Fax 962-4731
Tri-County North HS 400/9-12
PO Box 610 45338 937-962-2675
Jeff Parker, prin. Fax 833-4860
Tri-County North MS 400/5-8
PO Box 699 45338 937-962-2631
Joseph Finkbine, prin. Fax 833-4860

Lewis Center, Delaware, Pop. 300
Olentangy Local SD 9,300/K-12
814 Shanahan Rd Ste 100 43035 740-657-4050
Scott Davis, supt. Fax 657-4099
www.olentangy.k12.oh.us
Olentangy HS 1,100/9-12
675 Lewis Center Rd 43035 740-657-4100
Melinda Farry, prin. Fax 657-4199
Olentangy Orange MS 600/6-8
2680 E Orange Rd 43035 740-657-5300
James Wightman, prin. Fax 657-5399
Olentangy Shanahan MS 600/6-8
814 Shanahan Rd 43035 740-657-4300
Dennis Harden, prin. Fax 657-4398
Other Schools – See Powell

Lewistown, Logan
Indian Lake Local SD 2,000/K-12
6210 State Route 235 N 43333 937-686-8601
Dr. William McGlothlin, supt. Fax 686-8421
www.indianlake.k12.oh.us
Indian Lake HS 600/9-12
6210 State Route 235 N 43333 937-686-8851
Denny Shaner, prin. Fax 686-0024
Indian Lake MS 700/5-8
8920 County Road 91 43333 937-686-8833
Diane Gillespie, prin. Fax 686-8993

Lexington, Richland, Pop. 4,224
Lexington Local SD 2,700/K-12
103 Clever Ln 44904 419-884-2132
James Ziegelhofer, supt. Fax 884-3129
www.lexington.k12.oh.us
Lexington HS 1,000/9-12
103 Clever Ln 44904 419-884-1111
James Goode, prin. Fax 884-3129
Lexington JHS 400/7-8
90 Frederick St 44904 419-884-2112
William Ferguson, prin. Fax 884-3129

Liberty, Butler
Lakota Local SD 14,400/PK-12
5572 Princeton Rd, 513-874-5505
Michael Taylor, supt. Fax 644-1167
www.lakotaonline.com
Lakota Plains JHS 600/7-8
5500 Princeton Rd, 513-644-1130
Michael Holbrook, prin. Fax 644-1135
Other Schools – See Middletown, West Chester

Liberty Center, Henry, Pop. 1,117
Liberty Center Local SD 1,200/K-12
PO Box 434 43532 419-533-5011
Jack Loudin, supt. Fax 533-5036
www.libertycenter.k12.oh.us/
Liberty Center HS 400/9-12
PO Box 434 43532 419-533-6641
Beverly Jump, prin. Fax 533-5036
Liberty Center MS 400/5-8
PO Box 434 43532 419-533-0020
Beverly Jump, prin. Fax 533-5036

Lima, Allen, Pop. 38,608
Apollo JVSD
3325 Shawnee Rd 45806 419-998-2908
J. Chris Pfister, supt. Fax 998-2929
www.apollocareercenter.com
Apollo Career Ctr Joint Vocational JSHS Vo/Tech
3325 Shawnee Rd 45806 419-998-2908
Doug Bodey, dir. Fax 998-2929

Bath Local SD 2,000/K-12
2650 Bible Rd 45801 419-221-0807
William Lodermeier, supt. Fax 221-0983
www.noacsc.org/allen/ba
Bath HS 600/9-12
2850 Bible Rd 45801 419-221-0366
Richard Gross, prin. Fax 221-0766
Bath MS 600/5-8
2700 Bible Rd 45801 419-221-1839
Bradley Clark, prin. Fax 221-2431

Lima CSD 4,900/K-12
515 Calumet Ave 45804 419-996-3400
Karel Oxley, supt. Fax 996-3401
www.limacityschools.org
HS for Multiple Intelligences 9-12
1 Spartan Way 45801 419-996-3000
Jeffrey McClellan, prin. Fax 996-3001
Lima Performance Based HS 1,400/9-12
1 Spartan Way 45801 419-996-3000
Douglas Kent, prin. Fax 996-3001
North MS 500/5-8
1135 N West St 45801 419-996-3100
Mark Vaughn, prin. Fax 996-3101
Progressive Academy HS 9-12
1 Spartan Way 45801 419-996-3000
Judy Shisler, prin. Fax 996-3001
South MS 600/5-8
755 Saint Johns Ave 45804 419-996-3190
Mitchell Black, prin. Fax 996-3191
West MS 500/5-8
503 N Cable Rd 45805 419-996-3150
Rise Light, prin. Fax 996-3151

Perry Local SD 800/K-12
2770 E Breese Rd 45806 419-221-2770
Michael Lamb, supt. Fax 221-2773
www.noacsc.org/allen/pe/index.htm
Perry HS 400/7-12
2770 E Breese Rd 45806 419-221-2775
Michael Minnig, prin. Fax 221-2773

Shawnee Local SD 2,600/K-12
3255 Zurmehly Rd 45806 419-998-8031
Paul Nardini, supt. Fax 998-8050
shawnee.noacsc.org/
Shawnee HS 900/9-12
3333 Zurmehly Rd 45806 419-998-8000
Don Wade, prin. Fax 998-8026
Shawnee MS 800/5-8
3235 Zurmehly Rd 45806 419-998-8057
Tony Cox, prin. Fax 998-8050

James A. Rhodes State Coll Post-Sec.
4240 Campus Dr 45804 419-995-8000
Liberty Christian S 50/PK-12
801 Bellefontaine Ave 45801 419-229-6266
Nadine Wagner, admin. Fax 229-6266
Lima Central Catholic HS 400/9-12
720 S Cable Rd 45805 419-222-4276
Richard Mitterholzer, pres. Fax 222-6933
Ohio State Beauty Academy Post-Sec.
57 Town Sq 45801 419-229-7896
Ohio State University-Lima Campus Post-Sec.
4240 Campus Dr 45804 419-221-1641
Temple Christian S 200/PK-12
982 Brower Rd 45801 419-227-1644
Bruce Bowman, supt. Fax 227-6635
University of Northwestern Ohio Post-Sec.
1441 N Cable Rd 45805 419-227-3141

Lisbon, Columbiana, Pop. 3,082
Beaver Local SD 2,400/K-12
13093 State Route 7 44432 330-385-6831
Willard Adkins, supt. Fax 386-8711
www.beaver.k12.oh.us/
Beaver Local HS 800/9-12
13187 State Route 7 44432 330-386-8700
Janet Christen, prin. Fax 386-8720
Beaver Local MS 800/5-8
13052 State Route 7 44432 330-386-8707
Thomas Sapp, prin. Fax 382-0317

Columbiana County JVSD
9364 State Route 45 44432 330-424-9561
Edna Anderson, supt. Fax 424-9719
Columbiana County Joint Vocational SHS Vo/Tech
9364 State Route 45 44432 330-424-9561
Rick Istnick, prin. Fax 424-9719

Lisbon EVD 1,000/K-12
317 N Market St 44432 330-424-7714
Donald Thompson, supt. Fax 424-0135
www.lisbon.k12.oh.us/
Anderson JSHS 600/6-12
260 W Pine St 44432 330-424-3215
Donald Mook, prin. Fax 424-1004

Lockland, Hamilton, Pop. 3,393
Lockland Local SD
Supt. — See Cincinnati
Lockland JSHS 300/7-12
249 W Forrer St 45215 513-563-5000
Ben Hubbard, prin. Fax 733-0800

Lodi, Medina, Pop. 3,287
Cloverleaf Local SD 3,400/K-12
8525 Friendsville Rd 44254 330-948-2500
Dr. Bruce Hulme, supt. Fax 948-1034
www.cls.k12.oh.us
Cloverleaf HS 1,200/9-12
8525 Friendsville Rd 44254 330-948-2500
Robert Hevener, prin. Fax 948-4068
Other Schools – See Seville

Logan, Hocking, Pop. 7,090
Logan-Hocking Local SD 3,600/PK-12
121 S Spring St 43138 740-385-8517
Stephen Stirn, supt. Fax 385-3683
www.loganhocking.k12.oh.us
Logan-Hocking HS 1,300/9-12
50 North St 43138 740-385-2069
Jeff Daubenmire, prin. Fax 385-9564
Logan-Hocking MS 1,000/6-8
1 Middleschool Dr 43138 740-385-8764
Myles Kiphen, prin. Fax 385-9547

London, Madison, Pop. 9,396
London CSD 2,100/PK-12
60 S Walnut St 43140 740-852-5700
Thomas Coyne, supt. Fax 852-7360
www.london.k12.oh.us/
London HS 600/9-12
336 Elm St 43140 740-852-5705
Jeff Thompson, prin. Fax 852-3078
London JHS 300/7-8
60 S Walnut St 43140 740-852-5700
Mark Elliott, prin. Fax 845-2869

Madison-Plains Local SD 1,500/K-12
55 Linson Rd 43140 740-852-3712
Janice Streit, supt. Fax 852-5895
www.madison-plains.k12.oh.us
Madison-Plains HS 500/9-12
800 Linson Rd 43140 740-852-0364
Chris Clark, prin. Fax 852-3046
Madison-Plains MS 400/6-8
9940 State Route 38 SW 43140 740-852-1707
John Woodason, prin. Fax 852-6351

Madison Clark Christian Academy 100/K-12
2600 US Highway 40 NE 43140 740-845-1175
Karen Keigley, prin.

Lorain, Lorain, Pop. 67,820
Clearview Local SD 1,500/K-12
4700 Broadway 44052 440-233-5412
Rick Buckosh, supt. Fax 233-6034
www.clearview.k12.oh.us/
Clearview HS 500/9-12
4700 Broadway 44052 440-233-6313
Daniel Parent, prin. Fax 233-6311
Durling MS 500/5-8
100 N Ridge Rd W 44053 440-233-6869
Jerome Davis, prin. Fax 233-6204

Lorain CSD 4,600/PK-12
2350 Pole Ave 44052 440-233-2271
Dr. Dee Morgan, supt. Fax 282-9151
www.lorainschools.org
King HS - ExCEL 9-12
2600 Ashland Ave 44052 440-282-2288
David Hall, prin. Fax 282-3056
King HS - Global Enterprise & Tech 9-12
2600 Ashland Ave 44052 440-282-8599
Steven Sturgill, prin. Fax 282-3046
King HS - Renaissance 9-12
2600 Ashland Ave 44052 440-282-7117
Tom Tucker, prin. Fax 282-3036
Longfellow MS - Lake Erie 7-8
305 Louisiana Ave 44052 440-288-1025
Alexis Hayden, prin. Fax 288-1116
Longfellow MS - Lorain Lighthouse 7-8
305 Louisiana Ave 44052 440-288-1002
Michelle Spotts, prin. Fax 288-1149
Southview HS - Leadership Academy 9-12
2270 E 42nd St 44055 440-277-7506
Sam Newsome, prin. Fax 277-1537
Southview HS - PRIDE S 9-12
2270 E 42nd St 44055 440-277-7912
Marilyn Stano, prin. Fax 277-9854
Southview HS - School of the Arts 9-12
2270 E 42nd St 44055 440-277-0107
Iris Morales, prin. Fax 277-9947
Whittier MS - Ambassadors 6-8
3201 Seneca Ave 44055 440-277-7261
Roberta Davila, prin. Fax 277-5565
Whittier MS - Tornadoes 6-8
3201 Seneca Ave 44055 440-277-7261
Aliceson Humphries, prin. Fax 277-5566
Wilson MS - Monarch 6-8
602 Washington Ave 44052 440-246-1020
Chris Pankey, prin. Fax 246-0180
Wilson MS - North Shore 6-8
602 Washington Ave 44052 440-246-1021
Romy Adams, prin. Fax 246-1016

Sheffield-Sheffield Lake CSD
Supt. — See Sheffield Lake
Brookside HS 700/9-12
1812 Harris Rd 44054 440-949-4220
Burton Daugherty, prin. Fax 949-4204
Sheffield MS 500/6-8
1919 Harris Rd 44054 440-949-4228
David Riley, prin. Fax 949-4204

Northern Institute of Cosmetology Post-Sec.
667 Broadway 44052 440-244-4282
Ohio Business College Post-Sec.
1907 N Ridge Rd E 44055 440-277-0021

Lore City, Guernsey, Pop. 305
East Guernsey Local SD
Supt. — See Old Washington
Buckeye Trail HS 400/9-12
65555 Wintergreen Rd 43755 740-489-5005
Timothy VanCamp, prin. Fax 489-9839
Buckeye Trail MS 300/6-8
65553 Wintergreen Rd 43755 740-489-5100
Lonnie Caudill, prin. Fax 489-9049

Loudonville, Ashland, Pop. 2,982
Loudonville-Perrysville EVD 1,300/K-12
210 E Main St 44842 419-994-3912
John Miller, supt. Fax 994-3912
www.lpschools.k12.oh.us
Loudonville HS 500/9-12
421 Campus Ave 44842 419-994-4101
Ben Blubaugh, prin. Fax 994-3485
Other Schools – See Perrysville

Louisville, Stark, Pop. 9,367
Louisville CSD 3,300/K-12
418 E Main St 44641 330-875-1666
Clyde Lepley, supt. Fax 875-7603
www.leopard.sparcc.org
Louisville HS 1,000/9-12
1201 S Nickelplate St 44641 330-875-1438
Polly Doyle, prin. Fax 875-7606
Louisville MS 800/6-8
1300 S Chapel St 44641 330-875-5597
Jason Rimmele, prin. Fax 875-7620

St. Thomas Aquinas HS 9-12
2121 Reno Dr 44641 330-875-1631
Joseph Vagedes, prin. Fax 875-8469

Loveland, Hamilton, Pop. 11,219
Loveland CSD 4,400/PK-12
757 S Lebanon Rd 45140 513-683-5600
Kevin S. Boys Ed.D., supt. Fax 683-5697
www.lovelandschools.org/
Loveland HS 1,300/9-12
1 Tiger Trl 45140 513-683-1920
Molly Moorhead, prin. Fax 677-7952
Loveland MS 700/7-8
801 S Lebanon Rd 45140 513-683-3100
Erica Kramer, prin. Fax 677-7986

Lowellville, Mahoning, Pop. 1,200
Lowellville Local SD 600/K-12
52 Rocket Pl 44436 330-536-6318
Rocco Nero, supt. Fax 536-8221
www.lowellville.k12.oh.us/
Lowellville JSHS 300/7-12
52 Rocket Pl 44436 330-536-8426
Rocco Nero, prin. Fax 536-8468

Lucas, Richland, Pop. 608
Lucas Local SD 600/PK-12
84 Lucas North Rd 44843 419-892-2338
William Huber, supt. Fax 892-1138
www.lucascubs.org
Lucas HS 200/8-12
5 1st Ave 44843 419-892-2338
Steve Dickerson, prin. Fax 892-1138

Lucasville, Scioto, Pop. 1,575
Scioto County JVSD
951 Vern Riffe Dr 45648 740-259-5522
Stan Jennings, supt. Fax 259-2632
www.scjvs.com

Scioto County Joint Vocational HS Vo/Tech
951 Vern Riffe Dr 45648 740-259-5522
Don Gibson, dir. Fax 259-2632

Valley Local SD 1,200/K-12
1821 State Route 728 45648 740-259-3115
Paul Miller, supt. Fax 259-2314
www.valley.k12.oh.us/
Valley HS 300/9-12
1821 State Route 728 45648 740-259-5551
Michael Yeagle, prin. Fax 259-2314
Valley MS, 393 Indian Dr 45648 400/5-8
Lisa Harley, prin. 740-259-2651

Lynchburg, Highland, Pop. 1,432
Lynchburg-Clay Local SD 1,300/K-12
PO Box 515 45142 937-364-2338
Gregory Hawk, supt. Fax 364-2339
www.lynchclay.k12.oh.us
Lynchburg-Clay HS 400/9-12
6762 State Route 134 45142 937-364-2250
Michelle Williamson, prin. Fax 364-6133
Lynchburg-Clay MS 300/6-8
8250 State Route 134 45142 937-364-2811
Eric Magee, prin. Fax 364-2159

Lyndhurst, Cuyahoga, Pop. 14,450
South Euclid-Lyndhurst CSD 4,500/K-12
5044 Mayfield Rd 44124 216-691-2000
William Zelei, supt. Fax 691-2033
www.sel.k12.oh.us
Brush HS 1,600/9-12
4875 Glenlyn Rd 44124 216-691-2065
Elaine Vrabel, prin. Fax 691-2064
Memorial JHS 700/7-8
1250 Professor Rd 44124 216-691-2140
Tim Jarvie, prin. Fax 691-2159

Cleveland Institute Dental Medical Asst. Post-Sec.
5564 Mayfield Rd 44124 440-473-6273
Inner State Beauty School Post-Sec.
5150 Mayfield Rd 44124 440-442-4500

Mc Arthur, Vinton, Pop. 1,645
Vinton County Local SD 2,700/PK-12
307 W High St 45651 740-596-5218
John Simmons, supt. Fax 596-3142
vinton.k12.oh.us/
Vinton County HS 800/9-12
63910 US Highway 50 45651 740-596-5258
Kevin Waddell, prin. Fax 596-3003
Vinton County JHS 400/7-8
57710 US Highway 50 45651 740-596-5243
Dee Caudill, prin. Fax 596-3815

Mc Comb, Hancock, Pop. 1,632
Mc Comb Local SD 800/K-12
PO Box 877 45858 419-293-3979
Timothy Scherer, supt. Fax 293-2412
www.noacsc.org/hancock/mb
Mc Comb Local HS 300/9-12
PO Box 877 45858 419-293-3853
Bill McFarland, prin. Fax 293-3107
Other Schools – See Hoytville

Mc Connelsville, Morgan, Pop. 1,829
Morgan Local SD 2,200/K-12
PO Box 509 43756 740-962-2782
Lori Snyder-Lowe, supt. Fax 962-4931
www.mlsd.k12.oh.us/
Morgan HS 700/9-12
800 Raider Dr 43756 740-962-2944
Anita Eldridge, prin. Fax 962-6005
Morgan JHS 400/7-8
820 Junior Raider Dr 43756 740-962-2833
Timothy Hopkins, prin. Fax 962-3389

Mc Dermott, Scioto
Northwest Local SD 1,700/K-12
800 Mohawk Dr 45652 740-259-5558
Ruth Teeters, supt. Fax 259-3476
www.northwest.k12.oh.us
Northwest HS 600/9-12
914 Mohawk Dr 45652 740-259-2366
Rick Scarberry, prin. Fax 259-5655
Northwest MS 400/6-8
692 Mohawk Dr 45652 740-259-2528
Gregory Tipton, prin. Fax 259-5731

Mc Donald, Trumbull, Pop. 3,501
McDonald Local SD 900/K-12
600 Iowa Ave 44437 330-530-8051
Michael Wasser, supt. Fax 530-7041
www.mcdonald.k12.oh.us
McDonald JSHS 400/7-12
600 Iowa Ave 44437 330-530-8051
John Larocca, prin. Fax 530-7041

Macedonia, Summit, Pop. 10,314
Nordonia Hills CSD
Supt. — See Northfield
Nordonia HS 1,300/9-12
8006 S Bedford Rd 44056 330-468-4601
Charles Vrabel, prin. Fax 468-0045

Mc Guffey, Hardin, Pop. 572
Upper Scioto Valley Local SD 800/K-12
PO Box 305 45859 419-757-4451
Nancy Wood Allison, supt. Fax 757-0590
www.usv.k12.oh.us/
Upper Scioto Valley HS 200/9-12
PO Box 305 45859 419-757-3231
Craig Hurley, prin. Fax 757-0135
Upper Scioto Valley MS 200/6-8
PO Box 305 45859 419-757-3231
Craig Hurley, prin. Fax 757-0135

Madison, Lake, Pop. 3,070
Madison Local SD 3,500/K-12
6741 N Ridge Rd 44057 440-428-2166
James Herrholtz, supt. Fax 946-6472
www.madisonschools.net/
Madison HS 1,100/9-12
3100 Burns Rd 44057 440-428-2161
William Fisher, prin. Fax 428-2165
Madison MS 900/6-8
1941 Red Bird Rd 44057 440-428-1196
Heidi Stark, prin. Fax 428-9389

Magnolia, Stark, Pop. 935
Sandy Valley Local SD 1,500/K-12
5362 State Route 183 NE 44643 330-866-3339
David Janofa, supt. Fax 866-5238
cardweb.stark.k12.oh.us/
Sandy Valley JSHS 700/7-12
5362 State Route 183 NE 44643 330-866-9371
David Fischer, prin. Fax 866-2490

Malvern, Carroll, Pop. 1,229
Brown Local SD 900/K-12
401 W Main St 44644 330-863-1170
Connie Griffin, supt. Fax 863-1172
www.hornet.sparcc.org
Malvern HS 300/9-12
401 W Main St 44644 330-863-1355
Douglas Schmidt, prin. Fax 863-1915
Malvern MS 200/6-8
401 W Main St 44644 330-863-1355
Jane Swinderman, prin. Fax 863-1915

Manchester, Adams, Pop. 2,082
Manchester Local SD 900/K-12
130 Wayne Frye Dr 45144 937-549-4777
Robert Ralstin, supt. Fax 549-4744
www.manchester.k12.oh.us/
Manchester HS 400/7-12
130 Wayne Frye Dr 45144 937-549-3971
Donald Stricklett, prin. Fax 549-2872

Mansfield, Richland, Pop. 50,615
Madison Local SD 3,300/K-12
1379 Grace St 44905 419-589-2600
Dr. David Williamson, supt. Fax 589-3653
www.madison-richland.k12.oh.us
Madison Comprehensive HS 800/10-12
600 Esley Ln 44905 419-589-2112
Allen Pease, prin. Fax 589-2533
Madison JHS 800/7-9
690 Ashland Rd 44905 419-522-0471
Scott Kullman, prin. Fax 522-1463

Mansfield CSD 5,600/K-12
PO Box 1448 44901 419-525-6400
Dr. P. Joseph Madak, supt. Fax 525-6415
www.tygerpride.com
Malabar MS 800/6-8
205 W Cook Rd 44907 419-525-6374
Joann Hipsher, prin. Fax 525-6376
Mansfield HS 1,600/9-12
124 N Linden Rd 44906 419-525-6369
Virginia Dias, prin. Fax 524-2210
Simpson MS 500/6-8
218 W 4th St 44903 419-525-6348
Shawn Perry, prin. Fax 525-6350

Ontario Local SD 1,800/PK-12
457 Shelby Ontario Rd 44906 419-747-4311
Daryl Hall, supt. Fax 747-6859
www.ncocc-k12.org/ontario
Ontario HS 600/9-12
467 Shelby Ontario Rd 44906 419-529-3969
Jim Klenk, prin. Fax 529-5649
Ontario MS 400/6-8
447 Shelby Ontario Rd 44906 419-529-5507
Monty Perry, prin. Fax 529-7058

Mansfield Christian S 700/PK-12
500 Logan Rd 44907 419-756-5651
Kris Schottleutner, supt. Fax 756-7470
MedCentral College of Nursing Post-Sec.
335 Glessner Ave 44903 419-520-2600
North Central State College Post-Sec.
PO Box 698 44901 419-755-4800
Ohio State University-Mansfield Campus Post-Sec.
1680 University Dr 44906 419-755-4011
St. Peter HS 200/9-12
104 W 1st St 44902 419-524-0979
Tressa Reith, prin. Fax 524-3336
Temple Christian S 300/K-12
752 Stewart Rd N 44905 419-589-9707
Dave Cook, prin. Fax 589-7213

Mantua, Portage, Pop. 1,026
Crestwood Local SD 2,600/K-12
4565 W Prospect St 44255 330-274-8511
Joseph Iacano, supt. Fax 274-3710
www.crestwood.sparcc.org/
Crestwood HS 900/9-12
10919 Main St 44255 330-274-2214
Aaron Sable, prin. Fax 274-3150
Crestwood MS 700/6-8
10880 John Edward Dr 44255 330-274-2249
Carl Smilan, prin. Fax 274-3705

Maple Heights, Cuyahoga, Pop. 24,739
Maple Heights CSD 2,400/PK-12
14605 Granger Rd 44137 216-587-6100
Dr. Charles Keenan, supt. Fax 518-2674
www.mapleheightsk12.com
Maple Heights HS 1,100/9-12
5500 Clement Ave 44137 216-587-3200
Nancy Santilli, prin. Fax 587-3259
Milkovich MS 700/7-8
5460 West Blvd 44137 216-587-3200
Tracy Williams, prin. Fax 587-6166

Marengo, Morrow, Pop. 314
Highland Local SD 1,800/K-12
6506 State Route 229 43334 419-768-2206
Timothy Hilborn, supt. Fax 768-3115
www.highland.k12.oh.us/
Other Schools – See Sparta

Maria Stein, Mercer
Marion Local SD 1,000/K-12
7956 State Route 119 45860 419-925-4294
Carl Metzger, supt. Fax 925-0212
marionlocal.k12.oh.us/
Marion HS 300/9-12
1901 State Route 716 45860 419-925-4597
Michael Pohlman, prin. Fax 925-5111

Marietta, Washington, Pop. 14,270
Marietta CSD 3,100/K-12
111 Academy Dr 45750 740-374-6500
Dr. Doug Baker, supt. Fax 374-6506
mariettacityschools.k12.oh.us
Marietta HS 1,100/9-12
208 Davis Ave 45750 740-374-6540
Michael Elliott, prin. Fax 376-2462
Marietta MS 700/6-8
242 N 7th St 45750 740-374-6530
Mark Doebrich, prin. Fax 374-6531

Washington County JVSD
21740 State Route 676 45750 740-373-2766
Roger Bartunek, supt. Fax 373-9026
www.thecareercenter.net
Washington County Career Center Vo/Tech
21740 State Route 676 45750 740-373-2766
Dennis Blatt, prin. Fax 373-9026

Marietta College Post-Sec.
215 5th St 45750 740-376-4600
Memorial Hospital Post-Sec.
401 Matthew St 45750 740-374-1412
Valley Beauty School Post-Sec.
1315 Cisler Dr 45750 740-373-3617
Washington State Community College Post-Sec.
710 Colegate Dr 45750 740-374-8716

Marion, Marion, Pop. 36,494
Elgin Local SD 1,600/K-12
4616 Larue Prospect Rd W 43302 740-382-1101
Doug Ute, supt. Fax 382-1672
www.treca.org/schools/elgin/
Elgin HS 500/9-12
1239 Keener Rd S 43302 740-383-5118
Robert Britton, prin. Fax 383-4225
Other Schools – See Green Camp

Marion CSD 4,300/K-12
910 E Church St 43302 740-387-3300
Dr. William Zwick, supt. Fax 223-4400
www.marioncityschools.org/
Grant MS, 420 Presidential Dr 43302 1,300/6-8
Mike Terry, prin. 740-223-4900
Harding HS 1,600/9-12
1500 Harding Hwy E 43302 740-223-4700
Mike McCreary, prin.

Pleasant Local SD 1,300/K-12
1107 Owens Rd W 43302 740-389-4476
John Bruno, supt. Fax 389-6985
www.pleasant.treca.org/index.html
Pleasant HS 500/9-12
1101 Owens Rd W 43302 740-389-2389
Brian Sparling, prin. Fax 389-3904
Pleasant MS 300/6-8
3507 Smeltzer Rd 43302 740-389-5167
Joe Kume, prin. Fax 389-5111

Tri-Rivers Career Center
2222 Marion Mount Gilead Rd 43302 740-389-4681
Charles Barr, supt. Fax 389-2963
www.tririvers.com
Tri-Rivers Career Center Vo/Tech
2222 Marion Mount Gilead Rd 43302 740-389-4681
Larry Hickman, dir. Fax 389-2963

Marion Catholic Preparatory JSHS 100/7-12
1001 Mount Vernon Ave 43302 740-389-2381
Fran Voll, prin. Fax 389-5243
Marion General Hospital Post-Sec.
1000 McKinley Park Dr 43302 740-383-8700
Marion Technical College Post-Sec.
1467 Mount Vernon Ave 43302 740-389-4636
Ohio State University-Marion Post-Sec.
1465 Mount Vernon Ave 43302 740-389-6786

Martins Ferry, Belmont, Pop. 6,860
Martins Ferry CSD 1,600/K-12
633 Hanover St 43935 740-633-1732
Nick Stankovich, supt. Fax 633-5666
www.mfcsd.k12.oh.us/
Martins Ferry HS 700/8-12
810 Hanover St 43935 740-633-0684
Jeff Oberdick, prin. Fax 635-6103

Marysville, Union, Pop. 17,483
Marysville EVD 4,900/K-12
1000 Edgewood Dr 43040 937-644-8105
Larry Zimmerman, supt. Fax 644-1849
www.marysville.k12.oh.us
Marysville HS 1,400/9-12
800 Amrine Mill Rd 43040 937-642-0010
Gregory Hanson, prin. Fax 642-2033
Marysville MS 800/7-8
833 N Maple St 43040 937-642-1721
Kathy McKinniss, prin. Fax 642-2170

Christian Academy 50/PK-12
PO Box 435 43040 937-644-0911
Donna Moceri, prin. Fax 644-0911

Mason, Warren, Pop. 28,847
Mason CSD 8,400/PK-12
211 N East St 45040 513-398-0474
Kevin Bright, supt. Fax 398-4554
www.masonohioschools.com
Mason HS 2,400/9-12
6100 S Mason Montgomery Rd 45040 513-398-5025
Dr. Dave Allen, prin. Fax 459-7348
Mason MS 1,400/7-8
6370 S Mason Montgomery Rd 45040 513-398-9035
Tonya McCall, prin. Fax 459-0904

Mars Hill Academy 200/K-12
4230 Aero Dr 45040 513-770-3223
Tim McCoy, hdmstr. Fax 770-3443

Massillon, Stark, Pop. 32,150
Jackson Local SD 5,600/K-12
7984 Fulton Dr NW 44646 330-830-8000
Cheryl Haschak, supt. Fax 830-8008
jackson.stark.k12.oh.us
Jackson HS 1,800/9-12
7600 Fulton Dr NW 44646 330-837-3501
Rick Campbell, prin. Fax 830-8069
Jackson Memorial MS 1,300/6-8
7355 Mudbrook Rd NW 44646 330-830-8034
Christopher Diloreto, prin. Fax 830-8068

Massillon CSD 3,500/K-12
207 Oak Ave SE 44646 330-830-1810
Fred Blosser, supt. Fax 830-0953
www.massillon.sparcc.org
Massillon MS 600/5-8
250 29th St NW 44647 330-830-3902
Diane Lukac, prin. Fax 830-3952
Washington HS 1,400/9-12
1 Paul E Brown Dr SE 44646 330-830-1800
Mark Fortner, prin. Fax 832-1954

Perry Local SD 4,700/PK-12
4201 13th St SW 44646 330-477-8121
John Richard, supt. Fax 478-6184
perrynet.stark.k12.oh.us
Edison JHS 800/8-9
4201 13th St SW 44646 330-478-6167
Jamie Morckel, prin. Fax 477-4612
Perry SHS 1,100/10-12
3737 13th St SW 44646 330-477-3486
Mark Dean, prin. Fax 478-6180

Stark County Area JVSD
6805 Richville Dr SW 44646 330-832-1591
Larry Morgan, supt. Fax 832-9850
www.drage.stark.k12.oh.us
Drage Career-Technical Center Vo/Tech
6805 Richville Dr SW 44646 330-832-9856
Richard Faiello, prin. Fax 832-9850

Tuslaw Local SD 800/K-12
1835 Manchester Ave NW 44647 330-837-7813
Alan Osler, supt. Fax 837-7804
Tuslaw HS 500/9-12
1847 Manchester Ave NW 44647 330-837-7800
Robert Sattler, prin. Fax 837-6016
Tuslaw MS 200/3-8
1723 Manchester Ave NW 44647 330-837-7807
David Ryder, prin. Fax 837-6015

Massillon Christian S 100/K-12
965 Overlook Ave SW 44647 330-833-1039
Carol Crowley, prin. Fax 830-5981

Maumee, Lucas, Pop. 14,285
Maumee CSD 2,800/K-12
2345 Detroit Ave 43537 419-893-3200
Gregory Smith, supt. Fax 891-5387
www.maumee.k12.oh.us
Gateway MS 700/6-8
900 Gibbs St 43537 419-893-3386
Christopher Conroy, prin. Fax 893-2263
Maumee HS 1,000/9-12
1147 Saco St 43537 419-893-8778
Larry Caffro, prin. Fax 893-5621

Stautzenberger College Post-Sec.
1796 Indian Wood Cir 43537 419-866-0261

Mayfield, Cuyahoga, Pop. 3,242
Mayfield CSD
Supt. — See Mayfield Heights
Mayfield HS 1,600/8-12
6116 Wilson Mills Rd 44143 440-995-6900
Tony Loewer, prin. Fax 995-6805

Mayfield Heights, Cuyahoga, Pop. 18,380
Mayfield CSD 3,700/K-12
1101 SOM Center RD 44124 440-995-6800
Phillip Price Ph.D., supt. Fax 995-7205
www.mayfield.k12.oh.us
Other Schools – See Highland Heights, Mayfield

Mechanicsburg, Champaign, Pop. 1,716
Mechanicsburg EVD 800/K-12
60 High St 43044 937-834-2453
Michael Nutter, supt. Fax 834-3954
www.mechanicsburg.k12.oh.us
Mechanicsburg HS 400/7-12
60 High St 43044 937-834-2453
Lou Kramer, prin. Fax 834-7103

Medina, Medina, Pop. 26,461
Buckeye Local SD 2,100/PK-12
3044 Columbia Rd 44256 330-722-8257
Craig Bailey, supt. Fax 722-5793
www.buckeye.k12.oh.us
Buckeye HS 800/9-12
3084 Columbia Rd 44256 330-722-3604
Dennis Honkala, prin. Fax 722-8257
Buckeye JHS 400/7-8
3024 Columbia Rd 44256 330-725-0118
Roger Cramer, prin. Fax 722-8257

Highland Local SD 2,900/PK-12
3880 Ridge Rd 44256 330-239-1901
Bruce Armstrong, supt. Fax 239-2456
www.highlandschools.org
Highland HS 900/9-12
4150 Ridge Rd 44256 330-239-1901
Daryl Kubilus, prin. Fax 239-2807
Highland MS 700/6-8
3880 Ridge Rd 44256 330-239-1901
John Deuber, prin. Fax 239-2487

Medina CSD 7,500/PK-12
140 W Washington St 44256 330-725-8831
Randy Steep, supt. Fax 764-3501
www.mcsoh.org
Claggett MS 800/6-8
420 E Union St 44256 330-636-3600
Jo Maurer, prin. Fax 725-9349
Medina HS 2,300/9-12
777 E Union St 44256 330-636-3200
Susan Huth, prin. Fax 725-3521
Root MS 900/6-8
333 W Sturbridge Dr 44256 330-636-3500
Chad Wise, prin. Fax 764-1471

Medina County JVSD
1101 W Liberty St 44256 330-725-8461
Thomas Horwedel, supt. Fax 725-5870
www.mcjvs.org
Medina County Career Center Vo/Tech
1101 W Liberty St 44256 330-725-8461
Fax 725-5870

Hamrick Truck Driving School Post-Sec.
1156 Medina Rd 44256 330-239-2229
Medina County Career Center Post-Sec.
1101 W Liberty St 44256 330-725-8461

Mentor, Lake, Pop. 51,485
Mentor EVD 9,000/K-12
6451 Center St 44060 440-255-4444
Dr. Jacqueline Hoynes, supt. Fax 255-4622
www.mentorschools.org
Memorial JHS 800/7-9
8979 Mentor Ave 44060 440-974-2250
Patrick McKenrick, prin. Fax 974-2259
Mentor SHS 2,400/10-12
6477 Center St 44060 440-974-5300
Joseph Spiccia, prin. Fax 974-5216
Ridge JHS 700/7-9
7860 Johnnycake Ridge Rd 44060 440-974-5400
Megan Kinsey, prin. Fax 974-5285
Shore JHS 900/7-9
5670 Hopkins Rd 44060 440-257-8750
Douglas Baker, prin. Fax 257-8761

Brown Aveda Institute Post-Sec.
8816 Mentor Ave 44060 440-255-9494
Cleveland Institute Dental Medical Asst. Post-Sec.
5733 Hopkins Rd 44060 440-946-9530
Hondros College Post-Sec.
7350 Industrial Park Blvd 44060 440-918-0080
Lake Catholic HS 800/9-12
6733 Reynolds Rd 44060 440-951-0077
Christine Paul, prin. Fax 974-9087

Metamora, Fulton, Pop. 607
Evergreen Local SD 800/K-12
14544 County Road 6 43540 419-644-3521
Kenneth L. Jones, supt. Fax 644-6070
www.evergreen.k12.oh.us
Evergreen HS 500/9-12
14544 County Road 6 43540 419-644-2951
Mark Basilius, prin. Fax 644-6070
Evergreen MS 300/6-8
14544 County Road 6 43540 419-644-2331
Thomas Shafer, prin. Fax 644-9203

Miamisburg, Montgomery, Pop. 19,796
Miamisburg CSD 5,500/K-12
540 Park Ave 45342 937-866-3381
Dr. Gary Schomburg, supt. Fax 865-5250
www.miamisburgcityschools.org
Miamisburg HS 1,600/9-12
1860 Belvo Rd 45342 937-866-0771
Jim Ingham, prin. Fax 865-5267
Wantz MS 900/7-8
117 S 7th St 45342 937-866-3431
Susan Jandes, prin. Fax 866-6891

Dayton Christian HS 500/9-12
9391 Washington Church Rd 45342 937-291-7201
David Rough, prin. Fax 291-7202
Dayton Christian MS 300/5-8
9391 Washington Church Rd 45342 937-291-7201
Rich Garrett, prin. Fax 291-7202
Miamisburg Christian Academy 50/K-12
8500 S Union Rd 45342 937-866-6226
Charles Maqsud, prin. Fax 866-0112

Middleburg Heights, Cuyahoga, Pop. 15,437
Berea CSD
Supt. — See Berea
Midpark HS 1,300/9-12
7000 Paula Dr 44130 216-676-8400
Bela Molnar, prin. Fax 676-2070

Polaris JVSD
7285 Old Oak Blvd 44130 440-891-7600
Linda Schwarzbach, supt. Fax 826-4330
www.polaris.edu
Polaris Career Center Vo/Tech
7285 Old Oak Blvd 44130 440-891-7600
John Walker, prin. Fax 243-3952

Middlefield, Geauga, Pop. 2,411
Cardinal Local SD 1,200/K-12
PO Box 188 44062 440-632-0261
James Campbell, supt. Fax 632-5886
www.cardinal.k12.oh.us
Cardinal HS 400/9-12
PO Box 7 44062 440-632-0264
Richard Zigarovich, prin. Fax 632-1734
Cardinal MS 300/6-8
PO Box 879 44062 440-632-0263
James Millet, prin. Fax 632-0294

Middletown, Butler, Pop. 51,472
Lakota Local SD
Supt. — See Liberty
Lakota East SHS 1,700/10-12
6840 Lakota Ln 45044 513-755-7211
Keith Kline, prin. Fax 759-8633
Liberty JHS 800/7-8
7055 Dutchland Blvd 45044 513-777-4420
Gabriel Lofton, prin. Fax 777-7950

Madison Local SD 1,600/K-12
1324 Middletown Eaton Rd 45042 513-420-4750
Dr. Chris Cline, supt. Fax 420-4781
www.madison-local.k12.oh.us/
Madison JSHS 800/7-12
5797 W Alexandria Rd 45042 513-420-4760
Curtis Philpot, prin. Fax 420-4914

Middletown CSD 5,900/PK-12
1515 Girard Ave 45044 513-423-0781
Dr. Steve Price, supt. Fax 420-4579
www.middletowncityschools.com
Middletown HS 1,800/9-12
601 N Breiel Blvd 45042 513-420-4500
Dennis Newell, prin. Fax 420-4648
Vail MS 700/6-8
1415 Girard Ave 45044 513-420-4528
Michael Valenti, prin. Fax 420-4527
Verity MS 500/6-8
1900 Johns Rd 45044 513-420-4635
Greg Williams, prin. Fax 420-4615

Carousel Beauty College Post-Sec.
633 S Breiel Blvd 45044 513-422-2962
Miami University-Middletown Campus Post-Sec.
4200 N University Blvd 45042 513-727-3200
Middletown Regional Hospital Post-Sec.
105 McKnight Dr 45044 513-420-5100

Milan, Erie, Pop. 1,381
Berlin-Milan Local SD 1,800/PK-12
140 S Main St 44846 419-499-4272
David Snook, supt. Fax 499-4859
www.berlin-milan.org
Edison HS 600/9-12
2603 State Route 113 E 44846 419-499-4652
Jeffrey Goodwin, prin. Fax 499-2035
Other Schools – See Berlin Heights

EHOVE JVSD
316 Mason Rd W 44846 419-499-4663
Sharon Mastroianni, supt. Fax 499-4076
www.ehove.net
EHOVE Career Center Vo/Tech
316 Mason Rd W 44846 419-499-4663
Greg Edinger, dir. Fax 499-5390

Milford, Clermont, Pop. 6,325
Great Oaks Institute of Technology
Supt. — See Cincinnati
Live Oaks CDC Vo/Tech
5956 Buckwheat Rd 45150 513-575-1900
Joseph Moon, prin. Fax 575-0805

Milford EVD 6,300/K-12
777 Garfield Ave 45150 513-831-1314
John Frye, supt. Fax 831-3208
www.milfordschools.org
Milford HS 2,000/9-12
1 Eagles Way 45150 513-831-2990
Dr. Ray Bauer, prin. Fax 831-9714
Milford JHS 900/7-8
5735 Pleasant Hill Rd 45150 513-831-1900
Chris Davis, prin. Fax 248-3451

St. Andrew/St. Elizabeth Ann Seton S 200/5-8
555 Main St 45150 513-831-5277
Donna Beebe, prin. Fax 831-8436

Milford Center, Union, Pop. 684
Fairbanks Local SD 900/K-12
11158 State Route 38 43045 937-349-3731
Jim Craycraft, supt. Fax 349-8885
www.fairbanks.k12.oh.us/
Fairbanks HS 400/9-12
11158 State Route 38 43045 937-349-3721
Tom Montgomery, prin. Fax 349-2011
Fairbanks MS 300/5-8
11158 State Route 38 43045 937-349-6841
Patricia Lucas, prin. Fax 349-2013

Millbury, Wood, Pop. 1,156
Lake Local SD 1,800/K-12
PO Box 151 43447 419-836-2552
Jim Witt, supt. Fax 836-1755
www.lakelocal.k12.oh.us
Lake HS 600/9-12
28080 Lemoyne Rd 43447 419-661-6640
Marty Schloegl, prin. Fax 661-6650
Lake JHS 400/6-8
28100 Lemoyne Rd 43447 419-661-6660
Lee Herman, prin. Fax 661-6664

Miller City, Putnam, Pop. 130
Miller City-New Cleveland Local SD 500/K-12
PO Box 38 45864 419-876-3172
William Kreinbrink, supt. Fax 876-3849
web.ml.noacsc.org/
Miller City-New Cleveland HS 100/9-12
PO Box 38 45864 419-876-3173
Kevin McGlaughlin, prin. Fax 876-2020
Miller City-New Cleveland MS 100/6-8
PO Box 38 45864 419-876-3174
Kevin McGlaughlin, prin. Fax 876-2020

Millersburg, Holmes, Pop. 3,582
West Holmes Local SD 2,800/K-12
28 W Jackson St 44654 330-674-3546
Joseph Parish, supt. Fax 674-1177
www.westholmes.k12.oh.us
West Holmes HS 900/9-12
10909 State Route 39 44654 330-674-6085
Jay Arbaugh, prin. Fax 674-0818
West Holmes MS 600/6-8
10901 State Route 39 44654 330-674-4761
Maureen Businger, prin. Fax 674-2311

Millersport, Fairfield, Pop. 967
Walnut Township Local SD 800/K-12
PO Box 278 43046 740-467-2802
S. Edward Abram, supt. Fax 467-3494
Millersport JSHS 400/7-12
PO Box 278 43046 740-467-2929
Roger Montgomery, prin. Fax 467-3494

Mineral Ridge, Trumbull, Pop. 3,928
Weathersfield Local SD 1,000/K-12
3750 Main St 44440 330-652-0287
Michael Hanshaw, supt. Fax 544-7476
www.weathersfield.k12.oh.us/
Mineral Ridge HS 300/9-12
1334 Seaborn St 44440 330-652-1451
Lew Lowery, prin. Fax 505-9374
Mineral Ridge MS 300/5-8
3750 Main St 44440 330-652-2120
Bill Koppel, prin. Fax 544-7476

Minerva, Stark, Pop. 3,976
Minerva Local SD 2,200/K-12
303 Latzer Ave 44657 330-868-4332
Douglas Marrah Ed.D., supt. Fax 868-4731
lion.stark.k12.oh.us/
Minerva HS 600/9-12
501 Almeda Ave 44657 330-868-4134
Carl Michael, prin. Fax 868-6555
Minerva MS 600/6-8
600 E Line St 44657 330-868-4497
Richard Mikes, prin. Fax 868-6122

Minford, Scioto
Minford Local SD 1,700/K-12
PO Box 204 45653 740-820-3896
Dennis Meade, supt. Fax 820-3334
www.minford.k12.oh.us/
Minford HS 500/9-12
PO Box 204 45653 740-820-3445
Robert Shaffer, prin. Fax 820-4484
Minford MS 600/4-8
PO Box 204 45653 740-820-2181
Kevin Lloyd, prin. Fax 820-2191

Mingo Junction, Jefferson, Pop. 3,426
Indian Creek Local SD
Supt. — See Wintersville
Indian Creek JHS 300/7-8
110 Steuben St 43938 740-266-2916
Mark Furda, prin. Fax 535-9100

Jefferson County Christian S 200/PK-12
2501 Commercial Ave 43938 740-535-1337
Diane Hutchison, prin.

Minster, Auglaize, Pop. 2,820
Minster Local SD 300/K-12
100 E 7th St 45865 419-628-3397
Gayl Ray, supt. Fax 628-2495
www.minster.k12.oh.us
Minster MSHS 200/7-12
50 E 7thSt 45865 419-628-4174
Michael Lee, prin. Fax 628-2482

Mogadore, Summit, Pop. 3,966
Field Local SD 2,200/K-12
1473 Saxe Rd 44260 330-673-2659
David Redd, supt. Fax 677-2513
www.field.sparcc.org/
Field HS 700/9-12
2900 State Route 43 44260 330-673-9591
Michael Harris, prin. Fax 677-2510
Field MS 400/6-8
1379 Saxe Rd 44260 330-673-4176
Beth Coleman, prin. Fax 673-0942

Mogadore Local SD 700/K-12
1 S Cleveland Ave 44260 330-628-9946
Terry Byers, supt. Fax 628-6661
www.mogadore.summit.k12.oh.us
Mogadore JSHS 300/7-12
130 S Cleveland Ave 44260 330-628-9943
Terry Byers, prin. Fax 628-6657

Monclova, Lucas

Monclova Christian Academy 200/K-12
PO Box 15 43542 419-866-7630
Russell Merin, supt. Fax 868-1062

Monroe, Butler, Pop. 10,410
Butler Technology/Career Development SD
Supt. — See Fairfield
Greentree Health Science Academy Vo/Tech
225 Macready Ave 45050 513-539-0818
Tod Baldwin, prin. Fax 539-1129

Monroe Local SD 1,700/K-12
231 Macready Ave 45050 513-539-2536
Arnol Elam, supt. Fax 539-2648
www.monroelocalschools.com/
Monroe HS, 220 Yankee Rd 45050 500/9-12
Robert Leahy, prin. 513-539-8471
Monroe JHS, 210 Yankee Rd 45050 300/7-8
Steven Jackson, prin. 513-539-8471

Monroeville, Huron, Pop. 1,396
Monroeville Local SD 700/K-12
101 West St 44847 419-465-2610
Carol Girton, supt. Fax 465-4263
www.monroeville.k12.oh.us
Monroeville JSHS 400/7-12
101 West St 44847 419-465-2531
David Stubblebine, prin. Fax 465-4580

Montpelier, Williams, Pop. 4,135
Montpelier EVD 1,100/K-12
PO Box 193 43543 419-485-6700
Pam Campbell, supt. Fax 485-6700
www.montpelier.k12.oh.us/
Montpelier HS 300/9-12
PO Box 193 43543 419-485-6700
Ed Ewers, prin. Fax 485-6700
Montpelier MS 400/4-8
PO Box 193 43543 419-485-6700
Randy Stuckey, prin. Fax 485-6700

Morral, Marion, Pop. 385
Ridgedale Local SD 900/PK-12
3103 Hillman Ford Rd 43337 740-382-6065
Eric Hoffman, supt. Fax 383-6538
www.treca.org/schools/ridge/
Ridgedale JSHS 500/6-12
3165 Hillman Ford Rd 43337 740-382-6065
Clayton Born, prin. Fax 387-8525

Morristown, Belmont, Pop. 302
Union Local SD 1,500/K-12
PO Box 300 43759 740-782-1978
H. Kirk Glasgow, supt. Fax 695-5066
www.union-local.k12.oh.us
Other Schools – See Belmont

Morrow, Warren, Pop. 1,500
Little Miami Local SD 3,400/K-12
5819 Morrow Rossburg Rd 45152 513-899-2264
Daniel Bennett, supt. Fax 899-3244
www.littlemiamischools.com
Little Miami HS 900/9-12
3001 E US Highway 22 And 3 45152 513-899-3781
John Spieser, prin. Fax 899-4912
Little Miami JHS 600/7-8
605 Welch Rd 45152 513-899-3408
Brian Bailey, prin. Fax 899-3196

Mount Blanchard, Hancock, Pop. 461
Riverdale Local SD 800/K-12
20613 State Route 37 45867 419-694-4994
Dr. Joyce Plummer, supt. Fax 694-6465
www.riverdale.k12.oh.us
Riverdale HS 300/9-12
20613 State Route 37 45867 419-694-2211
Deb Frey, prin. Fax 694-5008
Riverdale MS 300/6-8
20613 State Route 37 45867 419-694-2211
Deb Frey, prin. Fax 694-5008

Mount Gilead, Morrow, Pop. 3,547
Mt. Gilead EVD 1,400/K-12
145 1/2 N Cherry St 43338 419-946-1646
Robert P. Alexander, supt. Fax 946-3651
www.treca.org/schools/mtg/
Mount Gilead HS 500/9-12
338 W Park Ave 43338 419-947-6065
Debra Clauss, prin. Fax 946-3263
Mount Gilead MS 300/6-8
145 N Cherry St 43338 419-947-9517
Sean Smith, prin. Fax 947-9518

Gilead Christian S South Campus 100/7-12
3613 Township Road 115 43338 419-946-5990
Jim McMillan, admin. Fax 946-1103

Mount Orab, Brown, Pop. 2,909
Western Brown Local SD 3,400/K-12
524 W Main St 45154 937-444-2044
Jeffrey Royalty, supt. Fax 444-4303
www.wb.k12.oh.us/
Mount Orab MS 800/5-8
472 W Main St 45154 937-444-2529
Kevin Kratzer, prin. Fax 444-4268
Western Brown HS 1,000/9-12
476 W Main St 45154 937-444-2544
Ray Wisby, prin. Fax 444-4355

Mount Vernon, Knox, Pop. 16,000
Knox County JVSD
306 Martinsburg Rd 43050 740-397-5820
Ray Richardson, supt. Fax 397-7040
Knox County Career Center Vo/Tech
306 Martinsburg Rd 43050 740-397-5820
Rick Hornick, dir. Fax 397-7040

Mt. Vernon CSD 4,000/K-12
300 Newark Rd 43050 740-397-7422
R. Jeff Maley, supt. Fax 393-5949
www.mt-vernon.k12.oh.us
Mount Vernon HS 1,400/9-12
300 Martinsburg Rd 43050 740-393-5900
Kathy Kasler, prin. Fax 397-6018
Mount Vernon MS 1,000/6-8
298 Martinsburg Rd 43050 740-392-6867
Deborah McDaniel, prin. Fax 392-3369

Christian Star Academy 50/PK-12
7 E Sugar St 43050 740-393-0251
Suzanne Feasel, admin. Fax 393-0067
Knox County Career Center Post-Sec.
306 Martinsburg Rd 43050 740-397-5820
Mount Vernon Academy 200/9-12
PO Box 311 43050 740-397-5411
David Daniels, prin. Fax 397-3901
Mt. Vernon Nazarene University Post-Sec.
800 Martinsburg Rd 43050 740-397-9000

Mount Victory, Hardin, Pop. 605
Ridgemont Local SD 600/PK-12
330 Taylor St W 43340 937-354-2441
Bruce Gast, supt. Fax 354-2194
www.ridgemont.k12.oh.us
Other Schools – See Ridgeway

Mowrystown, Highland, Pop. 392
Bright Local SD 700/PK-12
PO Box 9 45155 937-442-3114
Dee Wright, supt. Fax 442-6655
www.bright.k12.oh.us/
Whiteoak JSHS 300/7-12
PO Box 297 45155 937-442-2241
J. R. Roush, prin. Fax 442-6655

Munroe Falls, Summit, Pop. 5,300
Stow-Munroe Falls CSD
Supt. — See Stow
Kimpton MS 1,000/7-8
380 N River Rd 44262 330-689-5288
Fax 686-4718

Napoleon, Henry, Pop. 9,169
Napoleon Area CSD 2,300/K-12
701 Briarheath Ave Ste 108 43545 419-599-7015
David Watson, supt. Fax 599-7035
www.napoleon.k12.oh.us/default.htm
Napoleon HS 900/9-12
701 Briarheath Ave Ste 123 43545 419-599-1050
Jeffrey Schlade, prin. Fax 599-8537
Napoleon MS 500/6-8
303 W Main St 43545 419-592-6991
Tony Borton, prin. Fax 599-7638

Navarre, Stark, Pop. 1,431
Fairless Local SD 1,900/K-12
11885 Navarre Rd SW 44662 330-767-3577
Mona Fair, supt. Fax 767-3298
falcon.stark.k12.oh.us
Fairless HS 600/9-12
11885 Navarre Rd SW 44662 330-767-3444
Larry Chambliss, prin. Fax 767-3298

Fairless JHS 300/7-8
11885 Navarre Rd SW 44662 330-767-3444

Nelsonville, Athens, Pop. 5,444
Nelsonville-York CSD 1,400/PK-12
2 Buckeye Dr 45764 740-753-4441
Ted Bayat, supt. Fax 753-1968
www.nelsonvilleyork.k12.oh.us/
Nelsonville-York HS 400/9-12
1 Buckeye Dr 45764 740-753-4441
Charles McClelland, prin. Fax 753-1420
Nelsonville-York JHS 200/7-8
14455 Kimberley Rd 45764 740-753-4441
Joseph Malesick, prin. Fax 753-1087

Tri-County Career Center
15676 State Route 691 45764 740-753-3511
William Wittman, supt. Fax 753-5376
www.tricountyhightech.com
Tri-County Career Center Vo/Tech
15676 State Route 691 45764 740-753-3511
Linda Fife, prin. Fax 753-5376

Hocking College Post-Sec.
3301 Hocking Pkwy 45764 800-282-4163

New Albany, Franklin, Pop. 5,827
New Albany - Plain Local SD 3,200/K-12
55 N High St 43054 614-855-2040
Dr. Steve Castle, supt. Fax 855-2043
www.new-albany.k12.oh.us
New Albany HS 700/9-12
7600 Fodor Rd 43054 614-413-8300
Scott Stewart, prin. Fax 413-8301
New Albany MS 800/6-8
6600 E Dublin Granville Rd 43054 614-413-8500
Andrew Culp, prin. Fax 413-8501

Newark, Licking, Pop. 47,301
Career & Technology Educational Centers
150 Price Rd 43055 740-366-3351
Ronald Cassidy, supt. Fax 366-6215
Career & Technology Educational Center Vo/Tech
150 Price Rd 43055 740-366-3351
Mary Andrews, dir. Fax 366-6215

Licking Valley Local SD 2,200/K-12
1379 Licking Valley Rd 43055 740-763-3525
Susan Hatcher, supt. Fax 763-0471
www.lickingvalley.k12.oh.us/
Licking Valley HS 700/9-12
100 Hainsview Dr 43055 740-763-3721
David Hile, prin. Fax 763-0847
Licking Valley MS 500/6-8
1379 Licking Valley Rd 43055 740-763-3396
Rick Nabors, prin. Fax 763-2612

Newark CSD 4,600/K-12
85 E Main St 43055 740-345-9891
Keith Richards, supt. Fax 345-7495
www.newarkcityschools.org
Heritage MS 200/6-8
471 E Main St 43055 740-345-4440
Les Richards, prin. Fax 328-2042
Liberty MS 6-8
1055 Evans Blvd 43055 740-670-7325
Diane Henry, prin. Fax 670-7329
Newark HS 1,800/9-12
314 Granville St 43055 740-345-9831
Jesse Truett, prin. Fax 328-2232
Wilson MS 400/6-8
621 Mount Vernon Rd 43055 740-349-2315
John Davis, prin. Fax 328-2045

Central Ohio Technical College Post-Sec.
1179 University Dr 43055 740-366-1351
Newark Catholic HS 300/9-12
1 Green Wave Dr 43055 740-344-3594
Beth Hill, prin. Fax 344-0421
Ohio State University-Newark Post-Sec.
1179 University Dr 43055 740-366-3321

New Boston, Scioto, Pop. 2,189
New Boston Local SD 400/K-12
522 Glenwood Ave 45662 740-456-4626
Jerry Skiver, supt. Fax 456-5252
Glenwood HS 200/7-12
522 Glenwood Ave 45662 740-456-4559
Melinda Burnside, prin. Fax 456-5252

Southeastern Business College Post-Sec.
3879 Rhodes Ave Ste A 45662 740-456-4124

New Bremen, Auglaize, Pop. 2,993
New Bremen Local SD 1,000/K-12
901 E Monroe St 45869 419-629-8606
Ann Harvey, supt. Fax 629-0115
www.bremen.k12.oh.us
New Bremen HS 300/9-12
901 E Monroe St 45869 419-629-8606
Frank Borchers, prin. Fax 629-2973

Newbury, Geauga
Newbury Local SD 800/K-12
14775 Auburn Rd 44065 440-564-5501
Richard Wagner, supt. Fax 564-9460
newbury.k12.oh.us
Newbury JSHS 400/7-12
14775 Auburn Rd 44065 440-564-2281
Judith Miller, prin. Fax 564-9788

New Carlisle, Clark, Pop. 5,639
Tecumseh Local SD 2,400/PK-12
9760 W National Rd 45344 937-845-3576
Jim Gay, supt. Fax 845-4453
www.tecumseh.k12.oh.us
Tecumseh HS 1,100/9-12
9830 W National Rd 45344 937-845-4500
Michael Ostendorf, prin. Fax 845-4547
Tecumseh MS 6-8
10000 W National Rd 45344 937-845-4465
Brad Martin, prin. Fax 845-4484

Newcomerstown, Tuscarawas, Pop. 3,952
Newcomerstown EVD 1,200/K-12
702 S River St 43832 740-498-8373
Jeffrey Staggs, supt. Fax 498-8375
www.nct.k12.oh.us
Newcomerstown HS 400/9-12
659 Beaver St 43832 740-498-5111
Randy Addy, prin. Fax 498-4994
Newcomerstown MS 300/6-8
325 W State St 43832 740-498-8151
Timothy Sherman, prin. Fax 498-4991

New Concord, Muskingum, Pop. 2,660
East Muskingum Local SD 2,100/K-12
13505 John Glenn School Rd 43762 740-826-7655
Jim Heagen, supt. Fax 826-7194
www.east-muskingum.k12.oh.us
East Muskingum MS 500/6-8
13120 John Glenn School Rd 43762 740-826-7631
David Scholl, prin. Fax 826-4392
Glenn HS 700/9-12
13115 John Glenn School Rd 43762 740-826-7641
Frank Gregory, prin. Fax 826-3039

Muskingum College Post-Sec.
147 Center St 43762 740-826-8211

New Knoxville, Auglaize, Pop. 915
New Knoxville Local SD 400/K-12
PO Box 476 45871 419-753-2431
Charles Rowen, supt. Fax 753-2333
www.nk.k12.oh.us
New Knoxville HS 200/7-12
PO Box 476 45871 419-753-2431
Linda Tebbe, prin. Fax 753-2333

New Lebanon, Montgomery, Pop. 4,208
New Lebanon Local SD 1,300/K-12
320 S Fuls Rd 45345 937-687-1301
Dr. Barbara Curry, supt. Fax 687-7321
www.newlebanon.k12.oh.us/
Dixie HS 400/9-12
300 S Fuls Rd 45345 937-687-1366
Douglas Dunham, prin. Fax 687-7074
Dixie MS 400/5-8
200 S Fuls Rd 45345 937-687-3508
Thomas Sarver, prin. Fax 687-7705

New Lexington, Perry, Pop. 4,632
New Lexington CSD 1,900/K-12
101 3rd Ave 43764 740-342-4133
Larry Rentschler, supt. Fax 342-6051
www.nlcs.k12.oh.us/
New Lexington HS 600/9-12
2547 Panther Dr NE 43764 740-342-3528
Tonya Sherburne, prin. Fax 342-4765
New Lexington MS 500/6-8
2549 Panther Dr NE 43764 740-342-4128
Tonya Cline, prin. Fax 342-6071

New London, Huron, Pop. 2,668
New London Local SD 1,200/PK-12
2 Wildcat Dr 44851 419-929-8433
Gary Graham, supt. Fax 929-4108
www.newlondon.k12.oh.us/
New London HS 400/9-12
1 Wildcat Dr 44851 419-929-1586
Mary Lou Harris, prin. Fax 929-9513
New London MS 300/6-8
1 Wildcat Dr 44851 419-929-5409
Mary Lou Harris, prin. Fax 929-9513

New Madison, Darke, Pop. 780
Tri-Village Local SD 800/K-12
PO Box 31 45346 937-996-6261
Anthony Thomas, supt. Fax 996-5537
www.tri-village.k12.oh.us
Tri-Village JSHS 400/7-12
PO Box 31 45346 937-996-1511
William Moore, prin. Fax 996-0307

New Matamoras, Washington, Pop. 1,019
Frontier Local SD 900/K-12
44870 State Route 7 45767 740-865-3473
Troy Thacker, supt. Fax 865-2010
www.flsd.k12.oh.us/
Frontier HS 300/9-12
44870 State Route 7 45767 740-865-3441
Troy Thacker, prin. Fax 865-2011

New Middletown, Mahoning, Pop. 1,620
Springfield Local SD 1,200/K-12
PO Box 549 44442 330-542-2929
Debra Mettee, supt. Fax 542-9453
www.springfield.k12.oh.us
Springfield HS 400/9-12
11335 Yngstwn Pittsburgh Rd 44442 330-542-3626
Anthony De Felice, prin. Fax 542-9453
Springfield IS 400/5-8
11333 Yngstwn Pittsburgh Rd 44442 330-542-3624
Jerome Hiznay, prin. Fax 542-2159

New Paris, Preble, Pop. 1,546
National Trail Local SD 1,100/K-12
6940 Oxford Gettysburg Rd 45347 937-437-3333
Clinton Moore, supt. Fax 437-7865
National Trail HS 400/9-12
6940 Oxford Gettysburg Rd 45347 937-437-3333
Mark Wiseman, prin. Fax 437-8270
National Trail MS 300/5-8
6940 Oxford Gettysburg Rd 45347 937-437-3333
Mark Wiseman, prin. Fax 437-7306

New Philadelphia, Tuscarawas, Pop. 17,430
Buckeye JVSD
545 University Dr NE 44663 330-339-2288
Paul Hickman, supt. Fax 339-5159
www.bjvs.k12.oh.us/
Buckeye Career Center Vo/Tech
545 University Dr NE 44663 330-339-2288
Fax 339-5159

New Philadelphia CSD 3,000/K-12
248 Front Ave SW 44663 330-364-0600
Richard J. Varrati, supt. Fax 364-9310
www.npschools.org
New Philadelphia HS 1,000/9-12
343 Ray Ave NW 44663 330-364-0644
Bob Alsept, prin. Fax 364-0633
Welty MS 700/6-8
315 4th St NW 44663 330-364-0645
Sallie Stroup, prin. Fax 364-0633

Central Catholic HS 200/9-12
777 3rd St NE 44663 330-343-3302
David DiDonato, prin. Fax 343-6388
Kent State University Post-Sec.
330 University Dr NE 44663 330-339-3391

New Richmond, Clermont, Pop. 2,463
New Richmond EVD 2,500/K-12
212 Market St 45157 513-553-2616
Thomas Durbin, supt. Fax 553-6431
www.nrschools.org
New Richmond HS 800/9-12
1131 Bethel New Richmond Rd 45157 513-553-3191
Diana Spinnati, prin. Fax 553-2531
New Richmond MS 400/7-8
1135 Bethel New Richmond Rd 45157 513-553-3161
Adam Bird, prin. Fax 553-6412

New Riegel, Seneca, Pop. 218
New Riegel Local SD 400/K-12
44 N Perry St 44853 419-595-2265
Ronald Jump, supt. Fax 595-2901
www.new-riegel.k12.oh.us
New Riegel JSHS 200/7-12
44 N Perry St 44853 419-595-2256
David Rombach, prin. Fax 595-2901

Newton Falls, Trumbull, Pop. 4,833
Newton Falls EVD 1,300/K-12
909 1/2 Milton Blvd 44444 330-872-5445
David Wilson, supt. Fax 872-3351
www.newton-falls.k12.oh.us/
Newton Falls JSHS 500/7-12
907 Milton Blvd 44444 330-872-5121
John Crowder, prin. Fax 872-3351

New Washington, Crawford, Pop. 960
Buckeye Central Local SD 700/K-12
306 S Kibler St 44854 419-492-2864
Ronald Cirata, supt. Fax 492-2039
www.buckeye-central.k12.oh.us
Buckeye Central JSHS 400/7-12
306 S Kibler St 44854 419-492-2266
Jay Zeiter, prin. Fax 492-2039

Niles, Trumbull, Pop. 20,016
Niles CSD 2,900/K-12
100 West St 44446 330-652-2509
Rocco Adduci, supt. Fax 652-3522
www.niles.k12.oh.us/
McKinley HS 900/9-12
616 Dragon Dr 44446 330-652-9968
Mark Pallante, prin. Fax 505-0755
Niles MS 700/6-8
411 Brown St 44446 330-652-5656
Robert Marino, prin. Fax 652-9158

ETI Technical College Post-Sec.
2076 Youngstown Warren Rd 44446 330-652-9919
Raphael's School of Beauty Culture Post-Sec.
1324 Youngstown Warren Rd 44446 330-652-1559
Victory Christian S 100/K-12
2053 Pleasant Valley Rd 44446 330-539-9827
Rhonda Buie, prin. Fax 539-9828

North Baltimore, Wood, Pop. 3,343
North Baltimore Local SD 800/K-12
201 S Main St 45872 419-257-3531
Kyle Clark, supt. Fax 257-2008
www.northbaltimoreschools.org/
North Baltimore HS 300/9-12
124 S 2nd St 45872 419-257-3464
Jason Kozina, prin. Fax 257-3601
North Baltimore MS 100/7-8
124 S 2nd St 45872 419-257-3464
Jason Kozina, prin. Fax 257-3044

North Bend, Hamilton, Pop. 612
Three Rivers Local SD
Supt. — See Cleves
Taylor HS 600/9-12
36 E Harrison Ave 45052 513-467-3200
Randal Mechlenborg, prin. Fax 467-3204

North Bloomfield, Trumbull
Bloomfield-Mespo Local SD 400/K-12
2077 Park West Rd 44450 440-685-4710
Frank DiPiero, supt. Fax 685-4751
www.bloomfield.k12.oh.us
Bloomfield MSHS 200/6-12
2077 Park West Rd 44450 440-685-4711
Steve Kobus, prin. Fax 685-4751

North Canton, Stark, Pop. 16,780
North Canton CSD 4,900/PK-12
525 7th St NE 44720 330-497-5600
Michael Gallina, supt. Fax 497-5618
www.northcanton.sparcc.org/~nccs/
Hoover HS 1,700/9-12
525 7th St NE 44720 330-497-5620
Anthony Pallija, prin. Fax 497-5606
North Canton MS 1,200/6-8
605 Fair Oaks Ave SW 44720 330-497-5635
John Stanley, prin. Fax 497-5659

Brown Mackie College Post-Sec.
1320 W Maple St 44720 330-494-1214
Kent State University-Stark Campus Post-Sec.
6000 Frank Ave NW 44720 330-499-9600
Stark State College of Technology Post-Sec.
6200 Frank Ave NW 44720 330-494-6170
Walsh University Post-Sec.
2020 E Maple St 44720 800-362-9846

North Eaton, Lorain

Christian Community S 200/K-12
35716 Royalton Rd 44044 440-748-6224
Richard Willis, hdmstr. Fax 748-1007

Northfield, Summit, Pop. 3,722
Nordonia Hills CSD 3,800/K-12
9370 Olde 8 Rd 44067 330-467-0580
J. Wayne Blankenship, supt. Fax 468-0152
www.nordonia.summit.k12.oh.us
Nordonia MS 600/7-8
73 Leonard Ave 44067 330-467-0584
Dave Wilson, prin. Fax 468-6719
Other Schools – See Macedonia

North Jackson, Mahoning
Jackson-Milton Local SD 900/K-12
14110 Mahoning Ave 44451 330-538-3232
Warne Palmer, supt. Fax 538-2259
www.jacksonmilton.k12.oh.us/
Jackson-Milton HS 300/9-12
10748 Mahoning Ave 44451 330-538-3308
Joseph Malmisur, prin. Fax 538-0821
Jackson-Milton MS 200/6-8
10748 Mahoning Ave 44451 330-538-4054
Fax 538-0821

North Lewisburg, Union, Pop. 1,590
Triad Local SD 1,100/K-12
7920 Brush Lake Rd 43060 937-826-4961
Dan Kaffenbarger, supt. Fax 826-3281
www.triad.k12.oh.us
Triad HS 300/9-12
8099 Brush Lake Rd 43060 937-826-3771
Kyle Huffman, prin. Fax 826-2002
Triad MS 400/5-8
7941 Brush Lake Rd 43060 937-826-3071
Scott Blackburn, prin. Fax 826-1000

North Lima, Mahoning
South Range Local SD 1,300/K-12
11836 South Ave 44452 330-549-5226
Dennis Dunham, supt. Fax 549-4740
www.southrange.k12.oh.us/
South Range HS 400/9-12
11836 South Ave 44452 330-549-2163
Phillip Latessa Ed.D., prin. Fax 549-0214
Other Schools – See Salem

Tri-State College of Massotherapy Post-Sec.
9159 Market St # 26 44452 330-629-9998

North Olmsted, Cuyahoga, Pop. 32,653
North Olmsted CSD 4,600/PK-12
27425 Butternut Ridge Rd 44070 440-779-3549
Dr. Kurt Stanic, supt. Fax 779-3505
www.northolmstedschools.org/
North Olmsted HS 1,600/9-12
5755 Burns Rd 44070 440-779-8825
Paul Sink, prin. Fax 777-2216
North Olmsted MS 800/7-8
27351 Butternut Ridge Rd 44070 440-779-8501
Steve Barrett, prin. Fax 779-8510

Hearts for Jesus Christ Christian S 200/K-12
26654 Brookpark Road Ext 44070 440-552-6952
Deborah Brown, admin.
Remington College Post-Sec.
26350 Brookpark Rd 44070 440-777-2560

North Ridgeville, Lorain, Pop. 26,108
North Ridgeville CSD 3,100/K-12
5490 Mills Creek Ln 44039 440-327-4444
Larry Bowersox, supt. Fax 327-9774
www.nrcs.k12.oh.us
North Ridgeville HS 1,100/9-12
34600 Bainbridge Rd 44039 440-327-1992
Patricia Bahr, prin. Fax 327-4056
North Ridgeville MS 800/6-8
35895 Center Ridge Rd 44039 440-353-1180
John Komperda, prin. Fax 353-1144

Lake Ridge Academy 400/K-12
37501 Center Ridge Rd 44039 440-327-1175
Stanley Way, hdmstr. Fax 353-0324

North Robinson, Crawford, Pop. 203
Colonel Crawford Local SD 1,000/PK-12
PO Box 7 44856 419-562-4666
Ted Bruner, supt. Fax 562-3304
www.colonel-crawford.k12.oh.us/
Crawford HS 400/9-12
PO Box 7 44856 419-562-4666
James Trainer, prin. Fax 562-3304
Crawford IS 200/6-8
PO Box 20 44856 419-562-5753
Kevin Ruth, prin. Fax 562-3304

North Royalton, Cuyahoga, Pop. 29,538
North Royalton CSD 4,500/PK-12
6579 Royalton Rd 44133 440-237-8800
Randy S. Boroff, supt. Fax 582-7336
www.northroyaltonsd.org
North Royalton HS 1,500/9-12
14713 Ridge Rd 44133 440-582-7801
Carol Moehring, prin. Fax 582-7337
North Royalton MS 1,400/5-8
14709 Ridge Rd 44133 440-582-9120
Donald DiLillo, prin. Fax 582-7229

Northwood, Wood, Pop. 5,499
Northwood Local SD 1,000/K-12
600 Lemoyne Rd 43619 419-691-3888
Gregory Clark, supt. Fax 697-2470
www.northwood.k12.oh.us
Northwood HS 300/9-12
700 Lemoyne Rd 43619 419-691-4651
Joe Gagel, prin. Fax 691-2846
Northwood MS 200/6-8
500 Lemoyne Rd 43619 419-691-4621
Amy Klinger, prin. Fax 697-2479

Toledo Academy of Beauty Culture - East Post-Sec.
2592 Woodville Rd 43619 419-693-7257

Norton, Summit, Pop. 11,563
Norton CSD 2,400/PK-12
4128 Cleveland Massillon Rd 44203 330-825-0863
Karen Wilson, supt. Fax 825-0929
www.nortonschools.org
Norton HS 800/9-12
4108 Cleveland Massillon Rd 44203 330-825-7300
Rolland Gerstenmaier, prin. Fax 825-4275
Norton MS 800/5-8
3390 Cleveland Massillon Rd 44203 330-825-5607
Joyce Gerber, prin. Fax 825-1461

Akron Machining Institute Post-Sec.
2959 Barber Rd 44203 330-745-1111

Norwalk, Huron, Pop. 16,505
Norwalk CSD 2,900/K-12
134 Benedict Ave 44857 419-668-2779
Dr. Wayne Babcanec, supt. Fax 663-3302
www.norwalk-city.k12.oh.us
Norwalk HS 800/9-12
350 Shady Lane Dr 44857 419-668-2079
Robert Duncan, prin.
Norwalk MS, 64 Christie Ave 44857 400/7-8
James Hagemeyer, prin. 419-668-8370

St. Paul JSHS 7-12
93 E Main St 44857 419-668-3005
James Tokarsky, prin. Fax 668-6417

Norwood, Hamilton, Pop. 19,997
Norwood CSD 2,400/K-12
2132 Williams Ave Ste 1 45212 513-924-2500
Steve L. Collier, supt. Fax 396-6420
www.norwoodschools.org
Norwood HS 800/9-12
2020 Sherman Ave 45212 513-924-2800
Terri Holden, prin. Fax 396-5559
Norwood MS 400/7-8
2060 Sherman Ave 45212 513-924-2700
Matt Freeman, prin. Fax 396-5537

Oak Harbor, Ottawa, Pop. 2,816
Benton Carroll Salem Local SD 2,000/K-12
11685 W State Route 163 43449 419-898-6210
Diane Kershaw, supt. Fax 898-4303
www.bcs.k12.oh.us/
Oak Harbor HS 700/9-12
11661 W State Route 163 43449 419-898-6216
Keith Thorbahn, prin. Fax 898-0116
Oak Harbor MS 500/6-8
315 N Church St 43449 419-898-6217
Marie Wittman, prin. Fax 898-1613

Oak Hill, Jackson, Pop. 1,656
Oak Hill Union Local SD 1,300/K-12
205 Western Ave 45656 740-682-7595
William Ramsey, supt. Fax 682-6998
www.oakhill.k12.oh.us
Oak Hill MSHS 700/6-12
5063 State Road 93 45656 740-682-7055
Regina Boggs, prin. Fax 682-6075

Oberlin, Lorain, Pop. 8,280
Firelands Local SD 2,100/K-12
11970 Vermilion Rd 44074 440-965-5821
Max Shoff, supt. Fax 965-5990
www.firelandsschools.org/
Firelands HS 700/9-12
10643 Vermilion Rd 44074 440-965-5351
Richard Reighley, prin. Fax 965-5296
Other Schools – See South Amherst

Lorain County JVSD
15181 State Route 58 44074 440-774-1051
William Randall, supt. Fax 774-2144
www.lcjvs.com/
Burton Vocational Center HS Vo/Tech
15181 State Route 58 44074 440-774-1051
Jo Ann Kuebbeler, prin. Fax 774-2144

Oberlin CSD 1,100/K-12
153 N Main St 44074 440-774-1458
Geoffrey Andrews, supt. Fax 774-4492
www.oberlin.k12.oh.us
Langston MS 300/6-8
150 N Pleasant St 44074 440-775-7961
Jomill Wiley, prin. Fax 776-4520
Oberlin HS 300/9-12
281 N Pleasant St 44074 440-774-1295
William Baylis, prin. Fax 774-5099

Oberlin College Post-Sec.
101 N Professor St 44074 440-775-8121

Old Fort, Seneca
Old Fort Local SD 600/K-12
PO Box 64 44861 419-992-4291
Laura Keller, supt. Fax 992-4293
www.old-fort.k12.oh.us/
Old Fort JSHS 300/7-12
PO Box 64 44861 419-992-4291
Thomas Weaver, prin. Fax 992-4293

Old Washington, Guernsey, Pop. 267
East Guernsey Local SD 1,000/K-12
PO Box 128 43768 740-489-5190
Robert Greenwood, supt. Fax 489-9813
www.eguernsey.k12.oh.us
Other Schools – See Lore City

Olmsted Falls, Cuyahoga, Pop. 8,437
Olmsted Falls CSD 3,300/K-12
PO Box 38010 44138 440-427-6000
Dr. Todd Hoadley, supt. Fax 427-6010
www.ofcs.k12.oh.us/
Olmsted Falls HS 1,100/9-12
26939 Bagley Rd 44138 440-427-6100
Robert Trapp, prin. Fax 427-6110
Olmsted Falls MS 800/6-8
27045 Bagley Rd 44138 440-427-6200
Mark Kurz, prin. Fax 427-6210

Oregon, Lucas, Pop. 19,175
Oregon CSD 3,800/K-12
5721 Seaman St 43616 419-693-0661
John Hall, supt. Fax 698-6016
www.oregon.k12.oh.us
Clay HS 1,200/9-12
5665 Seaman St 43616 419-693-0665
Michael Zalar, prin. Fax 698-6047
Eisenhower MS 400/6-8
331 N North Curtice Rd 43618 419-836-8498
Mark Verroco, prin. Fax 836-2005
Fassett MS 500/6-8
3025 Starr Ave 43616 419-693-0455
Dean Ensey, prin. Fax 698-6048

Cardinal Stritch HS 400/9-12
3225 Pickle Rd 43616 419-693-0465
Tim Mahoney, prin. Fax 693-0465
St. Charles Hospital Post-Sec.
2600 Navarre Ave 43616 419-698-7341

Orrville, Wayne, Pop. 8,485
Orrville CSD 1,800/K-12
815 N Ella St 44667 330-682-4651
James Ritchie, supt. Fax 682-0073
www.orrville.k12.oh.us
Orrville HS 600/9-12
841 N Ella St 44667 330-682-4661
Richard Gardner, prin. Fax 682-4662
Orrville JHS 300/7-8
217 E Church St 44667 330-682-1791
David Sovacool, prin. Fax 682-2743

Kingsway Christian S 200/K-12
11138 Old Lincoln Way E 44667 330-683-0012
James Williams, admin. Fax 683-0017
University of Akron-Wayne College Post-Sec.
1901 Smucker Rd 44667 330-683-2010

Orwell, Ashtabula, Pop. 1,515
Grand Valley Local SD 900/K-12
111 Grand Valley Ave Ste A 44076 440-437-6260
John Sheets, supt. Fax 437-1025
www.grand-valley.k12.oh.us
Grand Valley HS 400/9-12
111 Grand Valley Ave Ste C 44076 440-437-6260
Stephen Sisko, prin. Fax 437-6254
Grand Valley MS 400/5-8
111 Grand Valley Ave Ste D 44076 440-437-6260
Lowell Moodt, prin. Fax 437-6156

Ottawa, Putnam, Pop. 4,479
Ottawa-Glandorf Local SD 1,600/K-12
630 Glendale Ave 45875 419-523-5261
Kevin Brinkman, supt. Fax 523-5978
og.noacsc.org/
Ottawa-Glandorf HS 600/9-12
630 Glendale Ave 45875 419-523-5702
William Hanna, prin. Fax 523-6346

Ottoville, Putnam, Pop. 864
Ottoville Local SD 600/K-12
PO Box 248 45876 419-453-3356
Kenneth Amstutz, supt. Fax 453-3367
www.noacsc.org/putnam/ov/
Ottoville JSHS 300/7-12
PO Box 248 45876 419-453-3358
Wilbur Altenburger, prin. Fax 453-3367

Oxford, Butler, Pop. 22,123
Talawanda CSD 3,100/PK-12
131 W Chestnut St 45056 513-273-3333
Dr. Philip Cagwin, supt. Fax 273-3113
www.talawanda.org
Talawanda HS 1,100/9-12
101 W Chestnut St 45056 513-273-3200
Vicki Brunn, prin. Fax 273-3203
Talawanda MS 800/6-8
4030 Oxford Reily Rd 45056 513-273-3300
Sharon Lytle, prin. Fax 273-3303

Miami University Post-Sec.
E High St 45056 513-529-1809

Painesville, Lake, Pop. 17,789
Painesville City Local SD 2,800/K-12
58 Jefferson St 44077 440-392-5060
Michael Hanlon Ph.D., supt. Fax 392-5089
www.painesville-city.k12.oh.us
Harvey HS 600/9-12
167 W Washington St 44077 440-392-5110
Kimberly Martin, prin. Fax 392-5119
Hobart MS 600/6-8
200 W Walnut Ave 44077 440-392-5250
Denise Ward, prin. Fax 392-5259

Painesville Township Local SD 4,600/K-12
585 Riverside Dr 44077 440-352-0668
Dr. Michael Shoaf, supt. Fax 639-1959
www.townshipschools.com
Riverside JSHS 1,900/8-12
585 Riverside Dr 44077 440-352-3341
David Toth, prin. Fax 352-0695

Lake Erie College Post-Sec.
391 W Washington St 44077 440-352-3361

Pandora, Putnam, Pop. 1,214
Pandora-Gilboa Local SD 600/K-12
PO Box 389 45877 419-384-3227
Dale Lewellen, supt. Fax 384-3230
www.pg.noacsc.org
Pandora-Gilboa HS 200/9-12
PO Box 389 45877 419-384-3225
Mel Heitmeyer, prin. Fax 384-3230
Pandora-Gilboa MS 200/5-8
PO Box 389 45877 419-384-3225
John Stoner, prin. Fax 384-3230

Parma, Cuyahoga, Pop. 81,469
Parma CSD 13,100/K-12
5311 Longwood Ave 44134 440-842-5300
Dr. Sarah Zatik, supt. Fax 885-2452
www.parmacityschools.org/

Greenbriar MS 800/7-8
11810 Huffman Rd 44130 440-885-2368
Frank Spisak, prin. Fax 885-8353
Normandy HS 1,300/9-12
2500 W Pleasant Valley Rd 44134 440-885-2400
Chris Jayjack, prin. Fax 885-2402
Parma HS 1,700/9-12
6285 W 54th St 44129 440-885-2300
Cassandra Johnson, prin. Fax 885-8684
Shiloh MS 800/7-8
2303 Grantwood Dr 44134 440-885-8485
Phyllis Spears, prin. Fax 885-8486
Other Schools – See Parma Heights, Seven Hills

Padua Franciscan HS 1,100/9-12
6740 State Rd 44134 440-845-2444
David Stec, prin. Fax 845-5710
Parma Community General Hospital Post-Sec.
7007 Powers Blvd 44129 440-743-3000

Parma Heights, Cuyahoga, Pop. 20,657
Parma CSD
Supt. — See Parma
Valley Forge HS 1,800/9-12
9999 Independence Blvd 44130 440-885-2330
Janine Andrzejewski, prin. Fax 885-8412

Cuyahoga Community College Post-Sec.
11000 W Pleasant Valley Rd 44130 440-842-7773
Holy Name HS 800/9-12
6000 Queens Hwy 44130 440-886-0300
Benjamin Farmer, prin. Fax 886-1267

Pataskala, Licking, Pop. 12,624
Licking Heights Local SD
Supt. — See Summit Station
Licking Heights Central MS 300/6-8
6565 Summit Rd SW 43062 740-927-3365
Charles Leedle, prin. Fax 927-5845
Licking Heights HS 500/9-12
4000 Mink St SW 43062 740-927-9046
Stephen Hackett, prin. Fax 927-3197

Southwest Licking Local SD 3,400/K-12
927A South St 43062 740-927-3941
Forest Yocum, supt. Fax 927-4648
www.swl.k12.oh.us
Watkins Memorial HS 1,000/9-12
8868 Watkins Rd SW 43062 740-927-3846
Steve Donahue, prin. Fax 964-0088
Watkins MS 800/6-8
8808 Watkins Rd SW 43062 740-927-5767
G. Chris Kyre, prin. Fax 927-2337

Paulding, Paulding, Pop. 3,430
Paulding EVD 1,800/PK-12
405 N Water St 45879 419-399-4656
William Shugars, supt. Fax 399-2404
pv.noacsc.org
Paulding HS 500/9-12
405 N Water St 45879 419-399-4656
Todd Harmon, prin. Fax 399-2404
Paulding MS 400/6-8
405 N Water St 45879 419-399-4656
David Stallkamp, prin. Fax 399-2404

Peebles, Adams, Pop. 1,845
Adams County/Ohio Valley Local SD
Supt. — See West Union
Peebles HS 500/7-12
25719 State Route 41 45660 937-587-2681
Eric Meredith, prin. Fax 587-5236

Pemberville, Wood, Pop. 1,351
Eastwood Local SD 1,900/K-12
4800 Sugar Ridge Rd 43450 419-833-6411
Brent Welker, supt. Fax 833-4915
www.eastwood.k12.oh.us/
Eastwood HS 600/9-12
4900 Sugar Ridge Rd 43450 419-833-3611
Jeff Hill, prin. Fax 833-6014
Eastwood MS 400/6-8
4800 Sugar Ridge Rd 43450 419-833-6011
John Obrock, prin. Fax 833-7454

Peninsula, Summit, Pop. 664
Woodridge Local SD 1,700/K-12
4411 Quick Rd 44264 330-928-9074
Dr. Jeffrey Graham, supt. Fax 928-1542
www.woodridge.k12.oh.us/
Woodridge HS 500/9-12
4440 Quick Rd 44264 330-929-3191
Mic Becerra, prin. Fax 928-5036
Woodridge MS 500/6-8
4451 Quick Rd 44264 330-928-7420
Linda Ocepek, prin. Fax 928-5645

Perry, Lake, Pop. 1,267
Perry Local SD 1,900/K-12
4325 Manchester Rd 44081 440-259-3881
Michael Sawyers, supt. Fax 259-3607
www.perry-lake.k12.oh.us
Perry HS 600/9-12
1 Success Blvd 44081 440-259-3511
Doug Jenkins, prin. Fax 259-9290
Perry MS 600/5-8
2 Learning Ln 44081 440-259-3026
Ann Spurrier, prin. Fax 259-5149

Perrysburg, Wood, Pop. 16,980
Penta Career Center
30095 Oregon Rd 43551 419-666-1120
Frederick Susor, supt. Fax 666-6049
www.pentacareercenter.org
Penta Career Center Vo/Tech
30095 Oregon Rd 43551 419-666-1120
Jeffrey Kurtz, prin. Fax 666-6049

Perrysburg EVD 4,400/K-12
140 E Indiana Ave 43551 419-874-9131
Michael L. Cline, supt. Fax 872-8820
www.perrysburg.k12.oh.us
Perrysburg HS 1,400/9-12
13385 Roachton Rd 43551 419-874-3181
Michael Short, prin. Fax 872-8813
Perrysburg JHS 1,100/6-8
550 E South Boundary St 43551 419-874-9193
Patrick Calvin, prin. Fax 872-8812

Perrysville, Ashland, Pop. 822
Loudonville-Perrysville EVD
Supt. — See Loudonville
Perrysville JHS 200/7-8
PO Box 426 44864 419-938-7193
John Lance, prin. Fax 938-3304

Pettisville, Fulton
Pettisville Local SD 600/K-12
PO Box 53001 43553 419-446-2705
Stephen Switzer, supt. Fax 445-2992
blackbirds.pettisville.k12.oh.us/
Pettisville JSHS 300/7-12
PO Box 53001 43553 419-446-2705
Michael Lane, prin. Fax 445-2992

Philo, Muskingum, Pop. 769
Franklin Local SD
Supt. — See Duncan Falls
Philo HS 700/9-12
200 Broad St 43771 740-674-4355
Michael Dorman, prin. Fax 674-5202
Philo JHS 400/6-8
225 Market St 43771 740-674-5210
Tony Sines, prin. Fax 674-5217

Pickerington, Fairfield, Pop. 15,878
Pickerington Local SD 9,000/K-12
777 Long Rd 43147 614-833-2110
Dr. Robert H. Thiede, supt. Fax 833-2143
www.pickerington.k12.oh.us
Pickerington HS Central 1,100/9-12
300 Opportunity Way 43147 614-833-3025
Charles Kemper, prin. Fax 833-3062
Pickerington HS North 1,700/9-12
7800 Refugee Rd 43147 614-830-2700
Mike Smith, prin. Fax 833-3660
Pickerington Lakeview JHS 800/7-8
12445 Ault Rd 43147 614-830-2200
Jim Sotlar, prin. Fax 834-3267
Pickerington Ridgeview JHS 600/7-8
130 Hill Rd S 43147 614-833-2100
Charles Byers, prin. Fax 833-2127

Piketon, Pike, Pop. 1,973
Pike County Area JVSD
PO Box 577 45661 740-289-2721
Stephen E. Martin, supt. Fax 289-8891
www.pikectc.org
Riffe Career Technology Center Vo/Tech
PO Box 577 45661 740-289-2721
Elizabeth Prince Ph.D., dir. Fax 289-2527

Scioto Valley Local SD 1,700/K-12
PO Box 600 45661 740-289-4456
Dennis Thompson, supt. Fax 289-3065
www.piketon.k12.oh.us/
Piketon JSHS 800/7-12
PO Box 488 45661 740-289-2254
Steve McCann, prin. Fax 289-1514

Miracle City Academy 100/PK-12
204 Commercial Blvd 45661 740-289-2787
Malcolm Cisco, prin. Fax 289-2013

Pioneer, Williams, Pop. 1,428
North Central Local SD 700/K-12
400 E Baubice St 43554 419-737-2392
Kenneth Boyer, supt. Fax 737-3361
www.ncschool.k12.oh.us/
North Central JSHS 300/7-12
400 E Baubice St 43554 419-737-2366
Paul Allison, prin. Fax 737-3361

Piqua, Miami, Pop. 20,883
Piqua CSD 3,900/K-12
719 E Ash St 45356 937-773-4321
Dr. Karen Mantia, supt. Fax 778-4518
portal2.piqua.org/
Piqua HS 1,300/9-12
1 Indian Trl 45356 937-773-6314
Katherine Davisson, prin. Fax 778-4514
Piqua JHS 600/7-8
1 Tomahawk Trl 45356 937-778-2997
Edward McCord, prin. Fax 773-3574

Upper Valley JVSD
8811 Career Dr 45356 937-778-1980
Karl Wilson, supt. Fax 778-0103
www.uvjvs.org
Upper Valley Joint Vocational S Vo/Tech
8811 Career Dr 45356 937-778-1980
Michael Shellabarger, dir. Fax 778-4677

Edison State Community College Post-Sec.
1973 Edison Dr 45356 937-778-8600
Piqua Catholic S - North 200/4-8
503 W North St 45356 937-773-1564
Anthony Frierott, prin. Fax 773-0380

Pitsburg, Darke, Pop. 393
Franklin Monroe Local SD 800/K-12
PO Box 78 45358 937-692-8637
David Gray, supt. Fax 692-6547
www.franklin-monroe.k12.oh.us/
Franklin Monroe JSHS 400/7-12
PO Box 78 45358 937-692-8761
Kent Shafer, prin. Fax 692-8740

Plain City, Madison, Pop. 3,462
Jonathan Alder Local SD 1,700/PK-12
9200 US Highway 42 S 43064 614-873-5621
Douglas Carpenter Ph.D., supt. Fax 873-8462
www.alder.k12.oh.us
Alder HS 600/9-12
9200 US Highway 42 S 43064 614-873-4642
Phil Harris, prin. Fax 873-4252
Alder JHS 300/7-8
6440 Kilbury Huber Rd 43064 614-873-4635
Jud Ross, prin. Fax 873-0845

Tolles Career & Technical Center
7877 US Highway 42 S 43064 614-873-4666
Carl J. Berg, supt. Fax 873-8761
www.tollestech.com
Tolles Career & Technical Center Vo/Tech
7877 US Highway 42 S 43064 614-873-4666
Steve Hull, prin. Fax 873-6909

Pleasant Hill, Miami, Pop. 1,140
Newton Local SD 600/K-12
PO Box 803 45359 937-676-3271
Pat McBride, supt. Fax 676-2054
Newton JSHS 300/7-12
PO Box 803 45359 937-676-3081
Andrew White, prin. Fax 676-3258

Pleasant Plain, Warren, Pop. 164

Village Christian S 200/PK-12
PO Box 48 45162 513-877-2143
Dwight Hesson, supt. Fax 877-2102

Plymouth, Huron, Pop. 1,860
Plymouth-Shiloh Local SD 1,000/K-12
365 Sandusky St 44865 419-687-4733
James Metcalf, supt. Fax 687-1541
www.plymouth.k12.oh.us/
Plymouth HS 300/9-12
400 Trux St 44865 419-687-8200
John Hart, prin. Fax 687-8175
Shiloh MS 300/6-8
400 Trux St 44865 419-687-4061
Bradley Turson, prin. Fax 887-8175

Poland, Mahoning, Pop. 2,750
Poland Local SD 2,500/K-12
30 Riverside Dr 44514 330-757-7000
Robert Zorn, supt. Fax 757-2390
www.polandbulldogs.com/
Poland MS 400/7-8
47 College St 44514 330-757-7003
Susan Sause, prin. Fax 757-2390
Poland Seminary HS 900/9-12
3199 Dobbins Rd 44514 330-757-7018
Robert Rostan, prin. Fax 757-2390

Pomeroy, Meigs, Pop. 1,999
Meigs Local SD 1,600/K-12
PO Box 272 45769 740-992-2153
William Buckley, supt. Fax 992-7814
www.ml.k12.oh.us/
Meigs HS 700/9-12
42091 Pomeroy Pike 45769 740-992-2158
Dennis Eichinger, prin. Fax 992-5839
Meigs MS 500/6-8
42353 Charles Chancey Dr 45769 740-992-3058
Mary Hawk, prin. Fax 992-6952

Port Clinton, Ottawa, Pop. 6,336
Port Clinton CSD 1,900/K-12
431 Portage Dr 43452 419-732-2102
Patrick Adkins, supt. Fax 734-4527
www.port-clinton.k12.oh.us
Port Clinton HS 700/9-12
821 Jefferson St 43452 419-734-2147
Gaylord Moore, prin. Fax 734-4276
Port Clinton MS 300/7-8
110 E 4th St 43452 419-734-4448
Robert Nobles, prin. Fax 734-4440

Portsmouth, Scioto, Pop. 20,101
Clay Local SD 600/K-12
44 Clay High St 45662 740-354-6645
Anthony Mantell, supt. Fax 354-5746
clay.k12.oh.us/
Clay HS 300/7-12
44 Clay High St 45662 740-354-6644
Todd Warnock, prin. Fax 354-5746

Portsmouth CSD 800/K-12
923 Findlay St 45662 740-354-5663
Wyvonna Broughton, supt. Fax 354-8872
www.portsmouth.k12.oh.us
Portsmouth JSHS 500/7-12
1225 Gallia St 45662 740-353-2398
Ann Charles, prin. Fax 354-3494

Washington-Nile Local SD
Supt. — See West Portsmouth
Portsmouth West HS 500/9-12
15332 US Highway 52 45663 740-858-1103
Anthony Bazler, prin. Fax 858-1110

Notre Dame JSHS 200/7-12
2220 Sunrise Ave 45662 740-353-0719
Kathy Milligan, prin. Fax 353-2526
Paramount Beauty Academy Post-Sec.
1745 11th St 45662 740-353-2436
Shawnee State University Post-Sec.
940 2nd St 45662 740-354-3205

Powell, Delaware, Pop. 10,504
Olentangy Local SD
Supt. — See Lewis Center
Olentangy Liberty HS 1,100/9-12
3584 Home Rd 43065 740-657-4200
Mark Raiff, prin. Fax 657-4299
Olentangy Liberty MS 1,000/6-8
7940 Liberty Rd N 43065 740-657-4400
Gena Williams, prin. Fax 657-4499

Learning Unlimited-Village Academy 400/K-12
284 S Liberty St 43065 614-841-0050
Susan Lasley, prin. Fax 841-0501

Proctorville, Lawrence, Pop. 629
Fairland Local SD 1,900/K-12
228 Private Drive 10010 45669 740-886-3100
Jerry McConnell, supt. Fax 886-7253
fairland.k12.oh.us/
Fairland HS 600/9-12
21360 State Route 243 45669 740-886-3250
Roni Hayes, prin. Fax 886-6738
Fairland MS 400/6-8
7875 State Route 7 45669 740-886-3200
Michael Whitley, prin. Fax 886-5125

Put in Bay, Ottawa, Pop. 135
Put-in-Bay Local SD — 100/K-12
PO Box 659 43456 — 419-285-3614
Steven Poe, supt. — Fax 285-2137
www.put-in-bay.k12.oh.us
Put-in-Bay JSHS — 50/7-12
PO Box 659 43456 — 419-285-3614
Steven Poe, prin. — Fax 285-2137

Racine, Meigs, Pop. 757
Southern Local SD — 700/K-12
920 Elm St 45771 — 740-949-2669
Mark Miller, supt. — Fax 949-3309
www.seovec.org/southern/
Southern HS — 300/9-12
920 Elm St 45771 — 740-949-2611
Tony Deem, prin. — Fax 949-3309

Ravenna, Portage, Pop. 11,510
Maplewood Career Center
7075 State Route 88 44266 — 330-296-2892
Craig Morgan, dir. — Fax 296-5680
www.maplenet.sparcc.org
Maplewood Career Center — Vo/Tech
7075 State Route 88 44266 — 330-296-2892
Fax 296-5680

Ravenna CSD — 3,200/PK-12
507 E Main St 44266 — 330-296-9679
Dr. Tim Calfee, supt. — Fax 297-4158
www.ravenna.portage.k12.oh.us
Brown MS — 500/7-8
228 S Scranton St 44266 — 330-296-3849
Judy Paydock, prin. — Fax 297-4146
Ravenna HS — 900/9-12
345 E Main St 44266 — 330-296-3844
Michael Bradley, prin. — Fax 296-1855

Southeast Local SD — 2,100/K-12
8245 Tallmadge Rd 44266 — 330-654-5841
Dewey Chapman, supt. — Fax 654-9110
se-web.portage.k12.oh.us/
Southeast HS — 700/9-12
8423 Tallmadge Rd 44266 — 330-654-5841
Gregory Newell, prin. — Fax 654-9110
Other Schools – See Diamond

Bohecker's Business College — Post-Sec.
653 Enterprise Pkwy 44266 — 800-794-2856

Rawson, Hancock, Pop. 462
Cory-Rawson Local SD — 500/K-12
3930 County Road 26 45881 — 419-963-3415
Richard Steiner, supt. — Fax 963-4400
cory-rawson.k12.oh.us
Cory-Rawson HS — 300/7-12
3930 County Road 26 45881 — 419-963-2611
Mark Willeke, prin. — Fax 963-4400

Rayland, Jefferson, Pop. 412
Buckeye Local SD
Supt. — See Dillonvale
Buckeye HS — 800/9-12
10692 State Route 150 43943 — 740-859-2196
Scott Celestin, prin. — Fax 859-2857

Reading, Hamilton, Pop. 10,320
Reading Community CSD — 1,400/K-12
1301 Bonnell St 45215 — 513-554-1800
L. Scott Inskeep, supt. — Fax 483-6754
www.readingschools.org
Reading Community JSHS — 700/7-12
810 E Columbia Ave 45215 — 513-733-4422
Charles LaFata, prin. — Fax 483-6766

Mt. Notre Dame HS — 800/9-12
711 E Columbia Ave 45215 — 513-821-3044
Maureen Baldock, prin. — Fax 821-6068

Reedsville, Meigs
Eastern Local SD — 800/K-12
50008 State Route 681 45772 — 740-667-6079
Ricky D. Edwards, supt. — Fax 667-3978
Eastern HS — 300/9-12
38900 State Route 7 45772 — 740-985-3329
Scot Gheen, prin. — Fax 667-3978

Republic, Seneca, Pop. 595
Seneca East Local SD
Supt. — See Attica
Seneca East JHS — 200/7-8
PO Box 39 44867 — 419-585-4291
Fax 585-5010

Reynoldsburg, Franklin, Pop. 33,059
Reynoldsburg CSD — 6,700/K-12
7244 E Main St 43068 — 614-501-1020
Dr. Richard Ross, supt. — Fax 501-1050
reynoldsburg.schoolnet.com
Reynoldsburg HS — 2,100/9-12
6699 E Livingston Ave 43068 — 614-501-4000
Diane Mankins, prin. — Fax 575-3098
Reynoldsburg JHS — 1,100/7-8
2300 Baldwin Pl 43068 — 614-367-1600
Tyrone Olverson, prin. — Fax 367-1625

Ohio State School of Cosmetology East — Post-Sec.
6320 E Livingston Ave 43068 — 614-868-1601

Richfield, Summit, Pop. 3,553
Revere Local SD — 2,800/K-12
3496 Everett Rd 44286 — 330-666-4155
Elisabeth McNicholas, supt. — Fax 659-3127
www.revere.k12.oh.us
Revere HS — 900/9-12
3420 Everett Rd 44286 — 330-659-6111
Bill Adams, prin. — Fax 659-6407
Other Schools – See Bath

Richmond, Jefferson, Pop. 466
Edison Local SD
Supt. — See Hammondsville
Edison HS — 800/9-12
9890 State Route 152 43944 — 740-765-4313
Doug Thoburn, prin. — Fax 765-4961

Richmond Heights, Cuyahoga, Pop. 10,521
Richmond Heights Local SD — 1,100/K-12
447 Richmond Rd 44143 — 216-692-8485
Walter Calinger, supt. — Fax 692-2820
www.richmond-heights.k12.oh.us
Richmond Heights HS — 300/9-12
447 Richmond Rd 44143 — 216-692-0094
Terry Wallace, prin. — Fax 692-8495
Richmond Heights MS — 300/6-8
447 Richmond Rd 44143 — 216-692-7395
Betty Mateen, prin. — Fax 692-2820

Richwood, Union, Pop. 2,132
North Union Local SD — 800/K-12
12920 State Route 739 43344 — 740-943-2509
Rick Smith, supt. — Fax 943-2534
www.n-union.k12.oh.us
North Union HS — 400/9-12
401 N Franklin St 43344 — 740-943-3012
Eric Holman, prin. — Fax 943-2534
North Union MS — 400/6-8
16 Norris St 43344 — 740-943-2369
Diana Martin, prin. — Fax 943-9279

Ridgeway, Hardin, Pop. 351
Ridgemont Local SD
Supt. — See Mount Victory
Ridgemont JSHS — 300/7-12
162 E Hale St 43345 — 937-363-2701
Chad Cunningham, prin. — Fax 363-2066

Rio Grande, Gallia, Pop. 875
Gallia-Jackson-Vinton JVSD
PO Box 157 45674 — 740-245-5334
Daniel Lewis, supt. — Fax 245-9465
Buckeye Hills Career Center — Vo/Tech
PO Box 157 45674 — 740-245-5334
Truman Noe, dir. — Fax 245-9465

University of Rio Grande — Post-Sec.
General Delivery 45674 — 740-245-5353

Ripley, Brown, Pop. 1,813
Ripley-Union-Lewis-Huntington Local SD — 900/K-12
120 Main St 45167 — 937-392-4396
Dr. C. Stephen Oborn, supt. — Fax 392-7003
www.ripley.k12.oh.us
Ripley-Union-Lewis-Huntington HS — 500/9-12
1317 S 2nd St 45167 — 937-392-4384
Gary Scarth, prin. — Fax 392-7017
Other Schools – See Aberdeen

Risingsun, Wood, Pop. 607
Lakota Local SD — 1,100/PK-12
PO Box 5 43457 — 419-457-2911
Rebecca Heimlich, supt. — Fax 457-0535
www.lakota-sandusky.k12.oh.us
Other Schools – See Fostoria, Kansas

Rittman, Wayne, Pop. 6,311
Rittman EVD — 900/K-12
75 N Main St 44270 — 330-927-7400
Orville Ullman, supt. — Fax 927-7405
www.rittman.k12.oh.us/
Rittman HS — 300/8-12
100 Saurer St 44270 — 330-927-7140
Joseph Magnacca, prin. — Fax 927-7145

Eastern Road Christian Academy — 50/K-12
2600 Eastern Rd 44270 — 330-925-5437
Faron Cole, prin. — Fax 927-0448

Rockford, Mercer, Pop. 1,118
Parkway Local SD — 900/K-12
400 Buckeye St 45882 — 419-363-3045
Douglas Karst, supt. — Fax 363-2595
www.parkwayschools.org/
Parkway HS — 300/9-12
400 Buckeye St 45882 — 419-363-3045
Gregory Puthoff, prin. — Fax 363-2596
Parkway MS — 300/6-8
400 Buckeye St 45882 — 419-363-3045
Steve Baumgartner, prin. — Fax 363-2597

Rocky River, Cuyahoga, Pop. 19,681
Rocky River CSD — 2,600/K-12
21600 Center Ridge Rd 44116 — 440-333-6000
Dennis Allen, supt. — Fax 356-6014
www.lnoca.org/~rrcs/
Rocky River HS — 800/9-12
20951 Detroit Rd 44116 — 440-356-6800
Debra Bernard, prin. — Fax 331-2189
Rocky River MS — 600/6-8
1631 Lakeview Ave 44116 — 440-356-6870
David Root, prin. — Fax 356-6881

Lutheran West HS — 400/9-12
3850 Linden Rd 44116 — 440-333-1660
John Buetow, prin. — Fax 333-1729
Magnificat HS — 800/9-12
20770 Hilliard Blvd 44116 — 440-331-1572
Sr. Mary Pat Cook, prin. — Fax 331-7257

Rootstown, Portage
Rootstown Local SD — 1,300/K-12
4140 State Route 44 44272 — 330-325-9911
William M. Stauffer, supt. — Fax 325-4105
rootstown.sparcc.org
Rootstown HS — 400/9-12
4140 State Route 44 44272 — 330-325-7911
Andrew Hawkins, prin. — Fax 325-8506
Rootstown MS — 300/6-8
4140 State Route 44 44272 — 330-325-9956
Neal Beans, prin. — Fax 325-8505

Northeastern Ohio Univ Coll of Medicine — Post-Sec.
PO Box 95 44272 — 330-325-2511

Roseville, Perry, Pop. 1,922
Franklin Local SD
Supt. — See Duncan Falls
Roseville MS — 200/5-8
76 W Athens Rd 43777 — 740-697-7317
Bruce King, prin. — Fax 697-7186

Rossford, Wood, Pop. 6,387
Rossford EVD — 2,000/PK-12
601 Superior St 43460 — 419-666-2010
Luci Gernot, supt. — Fax 661-2856
www.rossford.k12.oh.us
Rossford HS — 600/9-12
701 Superior St 43460 — 419-666-5262
Ronald Grimm, prin. — Fax 661-2831
Rossford JHS — 300/7-8
651 Superior St 43460 — 419-666-5254
Lester Pierson, prin. — Fax 661-2890

Rushville, Fairfield, Pop. 273
Fairfield Union Local SD — 2,000/K-12
7698 Main St 43150 — 740-536-7384
James Herd, supt. — Fax 536-9132
www.fairfield-union.k12.oh.us/
Other Schools – See Lancaster

Russia, Shelby, Pop. 611
Russia Local SD — 500/K-12
PO Box 8 45363 — 937-295-3454
Michael Moore, supt. — Fax 526-9519
Russia JSHS — 200/7-12
PO Box 8 45363 — 937-295-3454
Vernon Rosenbeck, prin. — Fax 526-9519

Saint Bernard, Hamilton, Pop. 4,640
St. Bernard-Elmwood Place CSD — 1,100/PK-12
105 Washington Ave 45217 — 513-482-7121
Dr. Mimi Webb, supt. — Fax 641-0066
stbernard.hccanet.org/
Saint Bernard-Elmwood Place JSHS — 500/7-12
4615 Tower Ave 45217 — 513-482-7100
Janie Acra, prin. — Fax 641-4878

Saint Clairsville, Belmont, Pop. 5,025
Belmont-Harrison Area JVSD
110 Fox Shannon Pl 43950 — 740-695-9130
Charles Bizzari, supt. — Fax 695-5340
Belmont Career Center — Vo/Tech
110 Fox Shannon Pl 43950 — 740-695-9130
Charles Strahl, prin. — Fax 695-5340
Other Schools – See Cadiz

St. Clairsville-Richland CSD — 1,600/K-12
108 Woodrow Ave 43950 — 740-695-1624
F. William Zanders, supt. — Fax 695-1627
www.stcs.k12.oh.us/
St. Clairsville HS — 600/9-12
102 Woodrow Ave 43950 — 740-695-1584
Walt Skaggs, prin. — Fax 695-2513
St. Clairsville MS — 400/6-8
104 Woodrow Ave 43950 — 740-695-1591
Diane Thompson, prin. — Fax 695-2317

Belmont Technical College — Post-Sec.
120 Fox Shannon Pl 43950 — 740-695-9500
Ohio University — Post-Sec.
45425 National Rd W 43950 — 740-695-1720

Saint Henry, Mercer, Pop. 2,301
St. Henry Consolidated Local SD — 1,100/K-12
391 E Columbus St 45883 — 419-678-4834
Rodney Moorman, supt. — Fax 678-1724
noacsc.org/mercer/sh
Saint Henry HS — 400/9-12
391 E Columbus St 45883 — 419-678-4834
Frank Griesdorn, prin. — Fax 678-1724
Saint Henry MS — 400/5-8
381 E Columbus St 45883 — 419-678-4834
Julie Laipply, prin. — Fax 678-1724

Saint Marys, Auglaize, Pop. 8,276
St. Mary's CSD — 2,300/K-12
101 W South St 45885 — 419-394-4312
Kenneth Baker, supt. — Fax 394-5638
www.ridertown.com/news/pages/mainsch.html
McBroom MS — 400/7-8
210 S Front St 45885 — 419-394-2112
Newton Triplett, prin. — Fax 394-3022
Memorial HS — 800/9-12
101 W South St 45885 — 419-394-4011
Michael Makley, prin. — Fax 394-1932

Grand Lake Christian S — 50/PK-12
1001 Holly St Ste A 45885 — 419-300-9001
Teresa Howell, prin.

Saint Paris, Champaign, Pop. 1,984
Graham Local SD — 2,200/K-12
370 E Main St 43072 — 937-663-4123
James Zerkle, supt. — Fax 663-4670
www.graham.k12.oh.us
Graham HS — 700/9-12
7800 US Highway 36 43072 — 937-663-4127
Larry Moore, prin. — Fax 663-0396
Graham MS — 500/6-8
9644 US Highway 36 43072 — 937-663-5339
Jacob Conley, prin. — Fax 663-4674

Operation Rebirth Christian Academy — 50/7-12
1638 Apple Rd 43072 — 937-663-5765
James Brian, dir. — Fax 663-4949

Salem, Columbiana, Pop. 12,005
Salem CSD — 1,800/K-12
1226 E State St 44460 — 330-332-0316
Stephen Larcomb, supt. — Fax 332-8936
www.salem.k12.oh.us
Salem HS — 800/9-12
1200 E 6th St 44460 — 330-332-8905
Joseph Shivers, prin. — Fax 332-8943
Salem JHS — 400/7-8
1200 E 6th St 44460 — 330-332-8914
Sean Kirkland, prin. — Fax 332-8923

South Range Local SD
Supt. — See North Lima
South Range MS — 500/4-8
7600 W South Range Rd 44460 — 330-533-3335
Albert Toth, prin. — Fax 533-7593

Allegheny Wesleyan College — Post-Sec.
2161 Woodsdale Rd 44460 — 800-292-3153

Kent State University-Salem Campus Post-Sec.
2491 State Route 45 S 44460 330-332-0361
Salem Wesleyan Academy 100/K-12
1095 Newgarden Ave 44460 330-332-4819
Dan Forrider, prin. Fax 332-4819

Salineville, Columbiana, Pop. 1,363
Southern Local SD 400/K-12
38095 State Route 39 43945 330-679-2343
James Herring, supt. Fax 679-0193
www.southern.k12.oh.us
Southern Local JSHS 400/7-12
38095 State Route 39 43945 330-679-2305
Dennis Spisak, prin. Fax 679-3005

Sandusky, Erie, Pop. 26,666
Perkins Local SD 2,200/K-12
1210 E Bogart Rd 44870 419-625-0484
Sharon Buccieri, supt. Fax 621-2052
www.perkins.k12.oh.us
Perkins HS 800/9-12
3714 Campbell St 44870 419-625-1252
Chris Gastier, prin. Fax 621-2057
Perkins MS 500/6-8
3700 South Ave 44870 419-625-0132
Dean Janitzki, prin. Fax 625-0523

Sandusky CSD 3,800/K-12
407 Decatur St 44870 419-626-6940
William F. Pahl, supt. Fax 621-2784
www.scs-k12.net
Jackson JHS 300/8-8
314 W Madison St 44870 419-621-2818
Scott Matheny, prin. Fax 621-2824
Sandusky Career Center Vo/Tech
2130 Hayes Ave 44870 419-625-9294
Viki Kaszonyi, dir. Fax 621-2893
Sandusky HS 1,200/9-12
2130 Hayes Ave 44870 419-621-2743
Dan Poggiali, prin. Fax 621-2751

Firelands Regional Medical Center Post-Sec.
1912 Hayes Ave 44870 419-557-7111
Ohio Business College Post-Sec.
5202 Timber Commons Dr 44870 419-627-8345
St. Mary Central Catholic HS 9-12
410 W Jefferson St 44870 419-626-1892
Doug Solet, prin. Fax 621-2252
Sandusky Central Catholic S-St. Mary S 300/4-8
530 Decatur St 44870 419-626-1648
Douglas Solet, prin. Fax 621-0404

Sarahsville, Noble, Pop. 195
Noble Local SD 1,200/K-12
20977 Zep Rd E 43779 740-732-2084
Daniel Doyle, supt. Fax 732-7669
www.gozeps.org/
Shenandoah HS 400/9-12
49346 Seneca Lake Rd 43779 740-732-2361
Sharon Miller, prin. Fax 732-6479

Sardinia, Brown, Pop. 901
Eastern Local SD 1,600/K-12
PO Box 500 45171 937-378-3981
Alan Simmons, supt. Fax 695-9046
www.eb.k12.oh.us
Eastern HS 500/9-12
PO Box 49 45171 937-378-6016
Ted Downing, prin. Fax 695-0303
Eastern JHS 300/7-8
PO Box 25 45171 937-378-6720
Rob Beucler, prin. Fax 695-1299

Southern State Community College Post-Sec.
12681 US Route 62 45171 937-695-0307

Scio, Harrison, Pop. 781
Harrison Hills CSD
Supt. — See Hopedale
Harrison JHS 300/7-8
322 W Main St 43988 740-942-7600
Fax 942-7605

Seaman, Adams, Pop. 1,084
Adams County/Ohio Valley Local SD
Supt. — See West Union
North Adams HS 500/7-12
96 Green Devil Dr 45679 937-386-2528
Rodney Wallace, prin. Fax 386-2888

Sebring, Mahoning, Pop. 4,706
Sebring Local SD 700/K-12
510 N 14th St 44672 330-938-6165
Howard Friend, supt. Fax 938-4701
McKinley JSHS 300/7-12
225 E Indiana Ave 44672 330-938-2963
Vito Weeda, prin. Fax 938-4702

Senecaville, Guernsey, Pop. 454
Mid-East Career & Technology Centers
Supt. — See Zanesville
Mid-East Career & Tech Ctr - Buffalo Vo/Tech
57090 Vocational Rd 43780 740-685-2516
Joseph Smith, dir. Fax 685-2518

Seven Hills, Cuyahoga, Pop. 12,041
Parma CSD
Supt. — See Parma
Hillside MS 600/7-8
1 Educational Park Dr 44131 440-885-2373
Jeff Cook, prin. Fax 885-8448

DeVry University Post-Sec.
6000 Lombardo Ctr 44131 216-328-8754
Hondros College Post-Sec.
4100 Rockside Rd 44131 216-524-1143

Seville, Medina, Pop. 2,462
Cloverleaf Local SD
Supt. — See Lodi
Cloverleaf MS 600/7-8
7500 Buffham Rd 44273 330-948-2500
Ronald Tisher, prin. Fax 721-3619

Shadyside, Belmont, Pop. 3,562
Shadyside Local SD 800/K-12
3890 Lincoln Ave 43947 740-676-3121
Terry Brinker, supt. Fax 676-6616
www.shadyside.k12.oh.us
Shadyside JSHS 400/7-12
3890 Lincoln Ave 43947 740-676-3235
Lawrence Falbo, prin. Fax 676-6616

Shaker Heights, Cuyahoga, Pop. 27,723
Shaker Heights CSD 5,700/K-12
15600 Parkland Dr 44120 216-295-4000
Mark Freeman, supt. Fax 295-4340
www.shaker.org
Shaker Heights HS 1,800/9-12
15911 Aldersyde Dr 44120 216-295-4200
Michael Griffith, prin. Fax 295-4277
Shaker Heights MS 1,000/7-8
20600 Shaker Blvd 44122 216-295-4100
Randall Yates, prin. Fax 295-4129

Hathaway Brown S 800/PK-12
19600 N Park Blvd 44122 216-932-4214
William Christ, hdmstr. Fax 371-1501
Laurel S 700/K-12
1 Lyman Cir 44122 216-464-1441
Ann Klotz, prin. Fax 464-8483

Sheffield Lake, Lorain, Pop. 9,157
Sheffield-Sheffield Lake CSD 2,000/K-12
1824 Harris Rd 44054 440-949-6181
Will Folger, supt. Fax 949-4204
www.sheffield.k12.oh.us
Other Schools – See Lorain

Shelby, Richland, Pop. 9,471
Pioneer Career & Technology Center
27 Ryan Rd 44875 419-347-7926
Glenna Cannon, supt. Fax 347-4709
www.pctc.k12.oh.us/
Pioneer Career & Technology Center Vo/Tech
27 Ryan Rd 44875 419-347-7744
Fax 347-4977

Shelby CSD 1,600/K-12
25 High School Ave 44875 419-342-3520
Charles A. Speelman, supt. Fax 347-3586
www.shelbyk12.org
Shelby HS 800/9-12
109 W Smiley Ave 44875 419-342-5065
John Gies, prin. Fax 342-5095
Shelby MS 400/7-8
16 Park Ave 44875 419-347-5451
Tim Tarvin, prin. Fax 347-2095

Sherrodsville, Carroll, Pop. 317
Conotton Valley Union Local SD 600/K-12
PO Box 187 44675 740-269-2000
Jeff Bleininger, supt. Fax 269-7901
www.conottonvalley.k12.oh.us
Other Schools – See Bowerston

Sherwood, Defiance, Pop. 807
Central Local SD 1,200/K-12
6289 US Highway 127 43556 419-658-2808
David E. Bagley, supt. Fax 658-4010
www.centrallocal.k12.oh.us/default.htm
Fairview HS 400/9-12
6289 US Highway 127 43556 419-658-2378
Troy Merillat, prin. Fax 658-4011
Fairview MS 300/6-8
6289 US Highway 127 43556 419-658-2331
Robert Lloyd, prin. Fax 658-4010

Sidney, Shelby, Pop. 20,188
Fairlawn Local SD 500/K-12
18800 Johnston Rd 45365 937-492-1974
Steve Mascho, supt. Fax 492-8613
www.fairlawn.k12.oh.us
Fairlawn MSHS 300/6-12
18800 Johnston Rd 45365 937-492-5930
Jo DeMotte, prin. Fax 492-8613

Sidney CSD 3,800/K-12
750 S 4th Ave 45365 937-497-2200
Dr. Michael Trego, supt. Fax 497-2211
www.sidney.k12.oh.us
Sidney HS 1,100/9-12
1215 Campbell Rd 45365 937-497-2238
Jeff Hobbs, prin. Fax 497-2216
Sidney MS 900/6-8
980 Fair Rd 45365 937-497-2225
Gene Gooding, prin. Fax 497-2204

Christian Academy S 200/K-12
2151 W Russell Rd 45365 937-492-7556
Mary Smith, supt. Fax 492-5399
Lehman HS 300/9-12
2400 Saint Marys Rd 45365 937-498-1161
David M. Barhorst, prin. Fax 492-9877

Smithville, Wayne, Pop. 1,312
Green Local SD 1,400/K-12
PO Box 438 44677 330-669-3921
Larry Brown, supt. Fax 669-2121
www.green-local.k12.oh.us/
Greene MS 400/5-8
PO Box 367 44677 330-669-2751
Edward Kosek, prin. Fax 669-2121
Smithville HS 400/9-12
PO Box 156 44677 330-669-3165
Rich Bellanco, prin. Fax 669-2999

Wayne County JVSD
518 W Prospect St 44677 330-669-7000
Kip Crain, supt. Fax 669-7001
www.wcscc.org
Wayne County Schools Career Center Vo/Tech
518 W Prospect St 44677 330-669-7000
Michael Hall, prin. Fax 669-7001

Solon, Cuyahoga, Pop. 22,335
Solon CSD 5,300/PK-12
33800 Inwood Dr 44139 440-248-1600
Joseph Regano, supt. Fax 248-7665
www.solonschools.org
Solon HS 1,800/9-12
33600 Inwood Dr 44139 440-349-6230
George Steyer, prin. Fax 349-8041
Solon MS 800/7-8
6835 Som Center Rd 44139 440-349-3848
Eugenia Robinson-Green, prin. Fax 349-8034

South Amherst, Lorain, Pop. 1,800
Firelands Local SD
Supt. — See Oberlin
South Amherst MS 700/5-8
152 W Main St 44001 440-986-7021
Tony Reaser, prin. Fax 986-7022

South Charleston, Clark, Pop. 1,821
Southeastern Local SD 800/K-12
PO Box Z 45368 937-462-8388
Glenn Kiefer, supt. Fax 462-7915
www.sels.us
Miami View MS 200/5-8
230 Clifton Rd 45368 937-462-8364
Sara Suver, prin. Fax 462-7914
Southeastern HS 300/9-12
PO Box Z 45368 937-462-8308
Susan Cline, prin. Fax 462-8394

South Euclid, Cuyahoga, Pop. 22,210

Regina HS 300/9-12
1857 S Green Rd 44121 216-382-2110
Sr. Maureen Burke, prin. Fax 382-3555

Southington, Trumbull
Southington Local SD 700/K-12
4432 State Route 305 44470 330-898-7480
Frank Danso, supt. Fax 898-4828
www.southington.k12.oh.us/
Chalker HS 200/9-12
4432 State Route 305 44470 330-898-1781
Nicholas Roberts, prin. Fax 898-4828
Southington MS 200/5-8
4432 State Route 305 44470 330-898-1781
Fax 898-4828

South Point, Lawrence, Pop. 3,922
South Point Local SD 1,900/K-12
203 Park Ave 45680 740-377-4315
Ken Cook, supt. Fax 377-9735
www.southpoint.k12.oh.us
South Point HS 600/9-12
302 High St 45680 740-377-4323
Eddie Scott, prin. Fax 377-4325
South Point MS, 201 Park Ave 45680 400/6-8
George York, prin. 740-377-4343

South Vienna, Clark, Pop. 504
Northeastern Local SD
Supt. — See Springfield
South Vienna MS 400/6-8
140 W Main St 45369 937-568-4765
Ted Williams, prin. Fax 568-4988

South Webster, Scioto, Pop. 751
Bloom-Vernon Local SD 1,000/K-12
PO Box 237 45682 740-778-2281
Rick Carrington, supt. Fax 778-2526
www.bv.k12.oh.us/
South Webster JSHS 500/7-12
PO Box 100 45682 740-778-2320
Robert Johnson, prin. Fax 778-3227

Sparta, Morrow, Pop. 202
Highland Local SD
Supt. — See Marengo
Highland HS 600/9-12
PO Box 98 43350 419-768-3101
Tony Deluliis, prin. Fax 768-3560
Highland MS 400/6-8
PO Box 68 43350 419-768-2781
Rob Terrill, prin. Fax 768-2742

Spencerville, Allen, Pop. 2,209
Spencerville Local SD 900/K-12
600 School St 45887 419-647-4111
Joel Hatfield, supt. Fax 647-6498
www.spencervillebearcats.com
Spencerville HS 300/9-12
2500 Wisher Dr 45887 419-647-4111
Shawn Brown, prin. Fax 647-6498
Spencerville MS 200/5-8
2500 Wisher Dr 45887 419-647-4112
Dennis Fuge, prin. Fax 647-6498

Springboro, Warren, Pop. 16,403
Springboro Community CSD 2,700/K-12
1685 S Main St 45066 937-748-3960
David Baker Ph.D., supt. Fax 748-3956
www.springboro.org
Springboro HS 1,300/9-12
1675 S Main St 45066 937-748-3950
Dr. Ron Malone, prin. Fax 748-3983
Springboro JHS 700/7-8
1605 S Main St 45066 937-748-3953
Andrea Cook, prin. Fax 748-3964

Ridgeville Christian S 300/PK-12
946 E Lower Springboro Rd 45066 513-932-6407
Marvin Retzer, admin. Fax 932-8453

Springfield, Clark, Pop. 63,302
Clark-Shawnee Local SD 2,500/K-12
3680 Selma Rd 45502 937-328-5378
Debbie Finkes, supt. Fax 328-5379
www.clark-shawnee.k12.oh.us/
Shawnee HS 900/9-12
1675 E Possum Rd 45502 937-325-9296
Nathan Dockter, prin. Fax 328-5389

Greenon Local SD
Supt. — See Enon
Greenon HS 600/9-12
3950 S Tecumseh Rd 45502 937-325-7343
Robert McClure, prin. Fax 328-7527

Northeastern Local SD 3,700/K-12
1414 Bowman Rd 45502 937-325-7615
Richard Broderick, supt. Fax 328-6592
www.northeastern.k12.oh.us
Kenton Ridge HS 700/9-12
4444 Middle Urbana Rd 45503 937-390-1274
Charles Foss, prin. Fax 390-0013
Northeastern HS 500/9-12
1480 Bowman Rd 45502 937-328-6575
Mark Klopfenstein, prin. Fax 328-6581
Northridge MS 500/6-8
4445 Ridgewood Rd E 45503 937-399-2852
Sharon Beck, prin. Fax 342-4631
Other Schools – See South Vienna

Northwestern Local SD 1,900/K-12
5610 Troy Rd 45502 937-964-1318
Kevin Lacey, supt. Fax 964-6019
www.northwestern.k12.oh.us
Northwestern HS 700/9-12
5650 Troy Rd 45502 937-964-1324
Lori Swafford, prin. Fax 964-6006
Northwestern MS 600/5-8
5610 Troy Rd 45502 937-964-1391
Rick Yontz, prin. Fax 964-6000

Springfield CSD 8,400/K-12
700 S Limestone St 45505 937-505-2800
Dr. Edna Jean Harper, supt. Fax 328-6855
www.spr.k12.oh.us/
Clark MS 400/6-8
1500 W Jefferson St 45506 937-505-4170
Michael Renkiewicz, prin. Fax 325-9358
Hayward MS 400/6-8
1700 Clifton Ave 45505 937-505-4190
Susie Samuels, prin. Fax 323-9812
Roosevelt MS 600/6-8
721 E Home Rd 45503 937-505-4370
Monte Brigham, prin. Fax 342-0280
Schaefer MS 500/6-8
147 S Fostoria Ave 45505 937-505-4390
Kathy Klosterman, prin. Fax 325-8974
Springfield North HS 1,400/9-12
701 E Home Rd 45503 937-342-4100
JoEtta Cooper, prin. Fax 342-4121
Springfield South HS 1,000/9-12
700 S Limestone St 45505 937-328-2027
Pauline Swan, prin. Fax 328-6866

Springfield-Clark County JVSD
1901 Selma Rd 45505 937-325-7368
Randall Richardson, supt. Fax 325-7452
www.sccjvs.org/
Springfield-Clark Co. Joint Vocational S Vo/Tech
1901 Selma Rd 45505 937-325-7368
Susan Backus, dir. Fax 325-7452

Carousel Beauty College Post-Sec.
1475 Upper Valley Pike #956 45504 937-323-0277
Catholic Central JSHS 200/7-12
1200 E High St 45505 937-325-9204
Jeanne Kunay, prin. Fax 328-7426
Clark State Community College Post-Sec.
570 E Leffel Ln 45505 937-325-0691
Community Hospital School of Nursing Post-Sec.
2615 E High St 45505 937-328-8905
Emmanuel Christian Academy 400/K-12
2177 Emmanuel Way 45502 937-390-3777
George Simon Ph.D., admin. Fax 390-0966
Nightingale Montessori S 100/K-12
1106 E High St 45505 937-324-0336
Nancy Schwab, prin. Fax 398-0086
Wittenberg University Post-Sec.
PO Box 720 45501 937-327-6231

Steubenville, Jefferson, Pop. 19,314
Steubenville CSD 2,200/PK-12
PO Box 189 43952 740-283-3767
Richard Ranallo, supt. Fax 283-8930
www.steubenville.k12.oh.us/
Harding MS 500/6-8
2002 Sunset Blvd 43952 740-282-3481
Rob Rembold, prin. Fax 283-8949
Steubenville HS 700/9-12
420 N 4th St 43952 740-282-9741
Shawn Crosier, prin. Fax 283-8943

Catholic Central HS 400/9-12
320 West View Ave 43952 740-264-5538
Denise McKeown, prin. Fax 264-5443
Century School of Cosmetology Post-Sec.
434 Market St 43952 740-282-3312
Franciscan University of Steubenville Post-Sec.
100 Franciscan Way 43952 800-783-6220
Jefferson Community College Post-Sec.
4000 Sunset Blvd 43952 740-264-5591
Ohio Valley Hospital Post-Sec.
1 Ross Park Blvd 43952 740-283-7273
Trinity Medical Center East Post-Sec.
380 Summit Ave 43952 740-283-7213

Stewart, Athens
Federal Hocking Local SD 1,400/PK-12
PO Box 117 45778 740-662-6691
James R. Patsey, supt. Fax 662-5065
www.federalhocking.k12.oh.us
Federal Hocking HS 500/9-12
8461 State Route 144 45778 740-662-6691
John Wryst, prin. Fax 662-3805
Federal Hocking MS 300/6-8
8461 State Route 144 45778 740-662-6691
Sonya White, prin. Fax 662-5065

Stoutsville, Fairfield, Pop. 593
Amanda-Clearcreek Local SD
Supt. — See Amanda
Amanda-Clearcreek MS 300/6-8
9096 Walnut St 43154 740-969-7252
Kenneth Dille, prin. Fax 969-7638

Stow, Summit, Pop. 34,404
Stow-Munroe Falls CSD 6,000/PK-12
4350 Allen Rd 44224 330-689-5445
Dr. Russell Jones, supt. Fax 688-1629
www.smfcsd.org
Stow-Munroe Falls HS 2,000/9-12
3227 Graham Rd 44224 330-689-5300
Rick Bailey, prin. Fax 678-3899
Other Schools – See Munroe Falls

Walsh Jesuit HS 900/9-12
4550 Wyoga Lake Rd 44224 330-929-4205
Fr. James Prehn, prin. Fax 929-9749

Strasburg, Tuscarawas, Pop. 2,607
Strasburg-Franklin Local SD 700/K-12
140 N Bodmer Ave 44680 330-878-5571
Palmer Fogler, supt. Fax 878-7900
Strasburg-Franklin HS 300/7-12
140 N Bodmer Ave 44680 330-878-5571
Jeff Gyurko, prin. Fax 878-7900

Streetsboro, Portage, Pop. 14,210
Streetsboro CSD 2,100/K-12
9000 Kirby Ln 44241 330-626-4900
Thomas M. Giovangnoli, supt. Fax 626-8102
www.rockets.sparcc.org
Streetsboro HS 600/9-12
1900 Annalane Dr 44241 330-626-4902
James Montaquila, prin. Fax 626-8103
Streetsboro MS 400/7-8
1951 Annalane Dr 44241 330-626-4905
George Hammond, prin. Fax 626-8104

Strongsville, Cuyahoga, Pop. 43,949
Strongsville CSD 7,300/PK-12
13200 Pearl Rd 44136 440-572-7010
James Gray, supt. Fax 572-7041
strongnet.org
Albion MS 600/7-8
11109 Webster Rd 44136 440-572-7070
Jeff Stanton, prin. Fax 572-7079
Center MS 600/7-8
13200 Pearl Rd 44136 440-572-7090
Jeff Martin, prin. Fax 572-7094
Strongsville HS 2,500/9-12
20025 Lunn Rd 44149 440-572-7100
Karen Hollo, prin. Fax 572-7107

ITT Technical Institute Post-Sec.
14955 W Sprague Rd 44136 440-234-9091

Struthers, Mahoning, Pop. 11,240
Struthers CSD 2,000/K-12
99 Euclid Ave 44471 330-750-1061
Dr. Sandra DiBacco-Tusinac, supt. Fax 750-5516
www.struthers.k12.oh.us/
Struthers HS 600/9-12
111 Euclid Ave 44471 330-750-1062
Mary Ann Meadows, prin. Fax 755-4525
Struthers MS 600/5-8
800 5th St 44471 330-750-1064
Jacqueline Kuffel, prin. Fax 755-4749

Youngstown College of Massotherapy Post-Sec.
14 Highland Ave 44471 330-755-1406

Stryker, Williams, Pop. 1,391
Stryker Local SD 500/K-12
400 S Defiance St 43557 419-682-6961
Russ Griggs, supt. Fax 682-2646
www.nwoca.org/~stryker_www/
Stryker JSHS 300/7-12
400 S Defiance St 43557 419-682-4591
Denise Meyer, prin. Fax 682-3508

Living Word Christian S 100/K-12
22754 County Road B50 43557 419-682-1750
James Garrett, admin. Fax 682-2231

Sugarcreek, Tuscarawas, Pop. 2,159
Garaway Local SD 1,200/K-12
146 Dover Rd NW 44681 330-852-2421
Ted Gerber, supt. Fax 852-2991
www.garaway.k12.oh.us/
Garaway JSHS 600/7-12
146 Dover Rd NW 44681 330-852-4292
Teresa Alberts, prin. Fax 852-4382

Sugar Grove, Fairfield, Pop. 443
Berne Union Local SD 1,000/K-12
PO Box 187 43155 740-746-8341
Thomas Wolfe, supt. Fax 746-9824
www.berne-union.k12.oh.us
Berne Union HS 300/9-12
PO Box 187 43155 740-746-9956
Robert Starr, prin. Fax 746-9824
Berne Union MS 300/5-8
PO Box 187 43155 740-746-9738
Sara Hayes, prin. Fax 746-9824

Sullivan, Ashland
Black River Local SD 1,700/PK-12
257A County Road 40 44880 419-736-3300
Janice Wyckoff, supt. Fax 736-3308
www.blackriver.k12.oh.us/
Black River HS 500/9-12
233 County Road 40 44880 419-736-3303
Bruce Lorincz, prin. Fax 736-3302
Black River MS 400/6-8
257 County Road 40 44880 419-736-3304
Cathy Aviles, prin. Fax 736-3309

Summit Station, Licking, Pop. 1,380
Licking Heights Local SD 1,200/K-12
6539 Summit Rd SW 43073 740-927-6926
Ernest Husarik, supt. Fax 927-9043
www.licking-heights.k12.oh.us/
Other Schools – See Pataskala

Sunbury, Delaware, Pop. 3,225
Big Walnut Local SD
Supt. — See Galena
Big Walnut HS, PO Box 5001 43074 900/9-12
Charles Workman, prin. 740-965-3766
Big Walnut MS, PO Box 5002 43074 600/6-8
Steve House, prin. 740-965-3006

Swanton, Fulton, Pop. 3,557
Swanton Local SD 1,500/K-12
108 N Main St 43558 419-826-7085
Neil Weber, supt. Fax 825-1197
www.swanton.k12.oh.us
Swanton HS 500/9-12
601 N Main St 43558 419-826-3045
Paulette Baz, prin. Fax 826-1611
Swanton MS 300/6-8
206 Cherry St 43558 419-826-4016
Steve Smith, prin. Fax 826-5176

Sycamore, Wyandot, Pop. 894
Mohawk Local SD 900/K-12
295 State Highway 231 44882 419-927-2414
Sam Martin, supt. Fax 927-2393
www.mohawk.k12.oh.us/
Mohawk HS 400/7-12
295 State Highway 231 44882 419-927-6292
Carol Koehler, prin.

Sylvania, Lucas, Pop. 19,069
Sylvania CSD 7,700/K-12
PO Box 608 43560 419-824-8500
Bradley Rieger, supt. Fax 824-8503
www.sylvania.k12.oh.us
Arbor Hills JHS 700/6-8
5334 Whiteford Rd 43560 419-824-8640
Scott Nelson, prin. Fax 824-8659
McCord JHS 700/6-8
4304 N Mccord Rd 43560 419-824-8650
Jeff Robbins, prin. Fax 824-8619
Northview HS 1,300/9-12
5403 Silica Dr 43560 419-824-8570
Stewart Jesse, prin. Fax 824-8698
Southview HS 1,300/9-12
7225 Sylvania Ave 43560 419-824-8580
Dave McMurray, prin. Fax 824-8678
Timberstone JHS 600/6-8
9000 Sylvania Ave 43560 419-824-8680
Jack Smith, prin. Fax 824-8690

Lourdes College Post-Sec.
6832 Convent Blvd 43560 419-885-3211

Tallmadge, Summit, Pop. 17,408
Tallmadge CSD 2,700/K-12
486 East Ave 44278 330-633-3291
Jeffrey Ferguson, supt. Fax 633-5331
www.tallmadge.k12.oh.us/index.htm
Tallmadge HS 900/9-12
484 East Ave 44278 330-633-5505
Rebecca Decapua, prin. Fax 630-5986
Tallmadge MS 700/6-8
76 North Ave 44278 330-633-4994
Gregory Misch, prin. Fax 630-5984

The Plains, Athens, Pop. 2,644
Athens CSD 2,900/K-12
25 S Plains Rd 45780 740-797-4544
Carl Martin, supt. Fax 797-2486
athenscity.k12.oh.us/
Athens HS 900/9-12
1 High School Rd 45780 740-797-4521
Mike Meek, prin. Fax 797-1421
Other Schools – See Athens

Thompson, Geauga
Ledgemont Local SD 700/K-12
16200 Burrows Rd 44086 440-298-3341
John Marshall, supt. Fax 298-3342
www.ledgemont.k12.oh.us
Ledgemont HS 200/9-12
16700 Thompson Rd 44086 440-298-3343
Beto Gage, prin. Fax 298-1481

Thornville, Perry, Pop. 1,034
Northern Local SD 2,300/K-12
8700 Sheridan Dr 43076 740-743-1303
Jack Porter, supt. Fax 743-3301
www.nlsd.k12.oh.us
Sheridan HS 800/9-12
8660 Sheridan Dr 43076 740-743-1335
Rick Caldwell, prin. Fax 743-3311
Sheridan MS 600/6-8
8700 Sheridan Dr 43076 740-743-1315
Thomas Dorman, prin. Fax 743-3319

Tiffin, Seneca, Pop. 17,438
Tiffin CSD 2,900/K-12
244 S Monroe St 44883 419-447-2515
Donald Coletta, supt. Fax 448-5202
www.tiffin.k12.oh.us
Columbian HS 1,000/9-12
300 S Monroe St 44883 419-447-6331
Larry Kisabeth, prin. Fax 448-5252
Tiffin MS 700/6-8
103 Shepherd Dr 44883 419-447-3358
J. Kevin Campbell, prin. Fax 448-5250

Vanguard-Sentinel JVSD
Supt. — See Fremont
Sentinel Career Center Vo/Tech
793 E Township Road 201 44883 419-448-1212
Henry Elchert, prin. Fax 447-2544

Calvert HS 200/9-12
152 Madison St 44883 419-447-3844
Anthony Mass, prin. Fax 447-2922
Heidelberg College Post-Sec.
310 E Market St 44883 419-448-2000
Tiffin Academy of Hair Design Post-Sec.
104 E Market St 44883 419-447-3117
Tiffin University Post-Sec.
155 Miami St 44883 800-968-6446

Tiltonsville, Jefferson, Pop. 1,244
Buckeye Local SD
Supt. — See Dillonvale
Buckeye Southwest MS 400/6-8
100 Walden Ave 43963 740-859-2357
George Bell, prin. Fax 859-2660

Tipp City, Miami, Pop. 9,357
Bethel Local SD 900/K-12
7490 State Route 201 45371 937-845-9414
Kevin Turner, supt. Fax 845-5007
www.bethel.k12.oh.us
Bethel HS 300/9-12
7490 State Route 201 45371 937-845-9487
David Vail, prin. Fax 845-5007
Bethel JHS 200/7-8
7490 State Route 201 45371 937-845-9430
Mike Johnston, prin. Fax 845-5007

Tipp City EVD 2,600/K-12
90 S Tippecanoe Dr 45371 937-667-8444
John Zigler, supt. Fax 667-6886
www.tippcityschools.com/
Tippecanoe HS 800/9-12
615 E Kessler Cowlesville 45371 937-667-8448
Charles Wray, prin. Fax 667-0912
Tippecanoe MS 700/6-8
555 N Hyatt St 45371 937-667-8454
Greg Southers, prin. Fax 667-0874

Toledo, Lucas, Pop. 301,285
Ottawa Hills Local SD 1,000/K-12
3600 Indian Rd 43606 419-536-6371
Cathleen Heidelberg, supt. Fax 534-5380
www.ohschools.k12.oh.us
Ottawa Hills JSHS 500/7-12
2532 Evergreen Rd 43606 419-534-5376
Katherine Hurst, prin. Fax 534-5384

Toledo CSD 29,300/PK-12
420 E Manhattan Blvd 43608 419-729-8200
John Foley, supt. Fax 729-8425
www.tps.org
Allied Health Academy 9-12
2400 Collingwood Blvd 43620 419-671-4112
Jose Hernandez, prin. Fax 249-8248
Arts & Media Academy 9-12
2400 Collingwood Blvd 43620 419-671-4110
Harriett Grier, prin. Fax 249-8248
Bowsher HS 1,400/9-12
3548 S Detroit Ave 43614 419-385-5776
Larry Black, prin. Fax 389-5055
Business Technology Industry Academy 9-12
2400 Collingwood Blvd 43620 419-671-4111
Phyllis Jones, prin. Fax 249-8248
Byrnedale JHS 800/7-8
3645 Glendale Ave 43614 419-382-3427
Karen Schultz-Gray, prin. Fax 385-3911
Cowboy Academy of Business 9-12
1250 Western Ave 43609 419-671-5113
Gayle Schaber, prin. Fax 385-8246
DeVeaux JHS 1,000/7-8
2626 W Sylvania Ave 43613 419-472-6320
James Gault, prin. Fax 473-2123
Early College HS 9-12
2225 Nebraska Ave 43607 419-530-3003
Jacqueline Quinn, prin. Fax 530-3040
East Broadway MS 6-8
1755 E Broadway St 43605 419-671-7200
R.C. Morrison, prin. Fax 671-7260
Gateway Academy 9-12
1250 Western Ave 43609 419-671-5110
Howard Brown, prin. Fax 385-8246
Humanities Academy 9-12
1250 Western Ave 43609 419-671-5112
Patricia Lewinski, prin. Fax 385-8246
Human Services Academy 9-12
2400 Collingwood Blvd 43620 419-671-4113
Keith Miller, prin. Fax 249-8248
Jones JHS 500/7-8
1250 Western Ave 43609 419-671-5200
Pamela King, prin. Fax 385-2737
Leverette JHS 600/7-8
1111 E Manhattan Blvd 43608 419-726-3449
Steve Riddle, prin. Fax 729-8826
Libbey HS 1,000/9-12
1250 Western Ave 43609 419-671-5110
Fax 385-8246
McTigue JHS 600/7-8
5700 Hill Ave 43615 419-531-4264
Cheryl King, prin. Fax 534-5829
Robinson JHS 600/7-8
1075 Horace St 43606 419-244-3753
Deborah Rivers, prin. Fax 255-6002
Rogers HS 1,200/9-12
222 McTigue Dr 43615 419-671-1000
Tony Brashear, prin. Fax 671-1060
Scott HS 1,300/9-12
2400 Collingwood Blvd 43620 419-244-8303
Jose Hernandez, prin. Fax 249-8248
Smart Academy 9-12
2010 Tremainsville Rd 43613 419-671-5111
Daphne Derden, prin. Fax 385-8246
Start HS 1,800/9-12
2100 Tremainsville Rd 43613 419-473-1446
Raymond Russell, prin. Fax 479-3151
Toledo Technology Academy Vo/Tech
3301 Upton Ave 43613 419-479-3161
Gary Thompson, dir. Fax 479-3192
Waite HS 1,400/9-12
301 Morrison Dr 43605 419-691-4687
David Yenrick, prin. Fax 697-2511
Woodward HS 1,200/9-12
600 E Streicher St 43608 419-729-7131
Ron Spitulski, prin. Fax 729-7055
Adult Education Center Adult
1530 N Superior St 43604 419-671-8700
Joan Reasonover, dir. Fax 671-8704

Washington Local SD 6,800/K-12
3505 W Lincolnshire Blvd 43606 419-473-8220
Michael Carmean, supt. Fax 473-8247
www.washloc.k12.oh.us
Washington JHS 600/8-10
5700 Whitmer Dr 43613 419-473-8449
Lynita Bigelow, prin. Fax 473-8340
Whitmer HS 2,200/9-12
5601 Clegg Dr 43613 419-473-8490
Brad Faust, prin. Fax 473-8461

Central Catholic HS 9-12
2550 Cherry St 43608 419-255-2280
Michael Kaucher, prin. Fax 259-2848
Davis College Post-Sec.
4747 Monroe St 43623 419-473-2700
Emmanuel Christian S 400/PK-12
4607 W Laskey Rd 43623 419-885-3558
Robert Flamm, prin. Fax 885-0139
Maumee Valley Country Day S 500/PK-12
1715 S Reynolds Rd 43614 419-381-1313
Gary Boehm, hdmstr. Fax 381-9941
Mercy College of Northwest Ohio Post-Sec.
2221 Madison Ave 43604 419-251-1279
Notre Dame Academy 600/9-12
3535 W Sylvania Ave 43623 419-475-9359
Kim Grilliot, prin. Fax 724-2640
Owens Community College Post-Sec.
PO Box 10000 43699 567-661-7000
Professional Skills Institute Post-Sec.
20 Arco Dr 43607 419-531-9610
Riverside Hospital Post-Sec.
3404 W Sylvania Ave 43623 419-729-6059
St. Francis De Sales HS 700/9-12
2323 W Bancroft St 43607 419-531-1618
Andy Hill, prin. Fax 531-9740
St. John's Jesuit Academy 7-8
5901 Airport Hwy 43615 419-865-5743
Christopher Knight, prin. Fax 861-5002
St. John's Jesuit HS 800/9-12
5901 Airport Hwy 43615 419-865-5743
Tim Malone, prin. Fax 861-5002
St. Ursula Academy 600/9-12
4025 Indian Rd 43606 419-531-1693
Jane McGee, prin. Fax 534-5777
Toledo Academy of Beauty Culture - North Post-Sec.
5020 Lewis Ave 43612 419-478-5325
Toledo Academy of Beauty Culture - South Post-Sec.
1554 S Byrne Rd 43614 419-381-7218
Toledo Christian S 800/PK-12
2303 Brookford Dr 43614 419-389-8700
James Ellinger, supt. Fax 724-2117
Toledo Islamic Academy 200/K-12
4404 Secor Rd 43623 419-292-1491
Carolyn al-Qadi, prin. Fax 292-0444
University of Toledo Post-Sec.
3000 Arlington Ave 43614 419-383-4000
University of Toledo Post-Sec.
2801 W Bancroft St 43606 419-530-4636

Tontogany, Wood, Pop. 371
Otsego Local SD 1,700/K-12
PO Box 290 43565 419-823-4381
Joseph Long, supt. Fax 823-3035
www.otsegoknights.org
Otsego HS 500/9-12
PO Box 290 43565 419-823-4911
David Drewyor, prin. Fax 823-6421
Other Schools – See Grand Rapids

Toronto, Jefferson, Pop. 5,402
Toronto CSD 900/PK-12
300 Myers St 43964 740-537-2456
Frank Vostatek, supt. Fax 537-1102
www.torontocityschools.k12.oh.us
Karaffa MS, 1307 Dennis Way 43964 200/5-8
Jerome Vinci, prin. 740-537-2471
Toronto HS, 300 Myers St 43964 300/9-12
Robert Reeves, prin. 740-537-2442

Trenton, Butler, Pop. 10,488
Edgewood CSD 3,700/PK-12
3500 Busenbark Rd 45067 513-863-4692
Tom York, supt. Fax 867-7421
www.edgewoodschools.com/index.cfm
Edgewood HS 1,100/9-12
5005 Trenton Oxford Rd 45067 513-867-7425
Bob Buchheim, prin. Fax 867-7428
Other Schools – See Hamilton

Trotwood, Montgomery, Pop. 26,608
Trotwood-Madison CSD 2,900/K-12
444 S Broadway St 45426 937-854-3050
Lowell Draffen, supt. Fax 854-3057
www.trotwood.k12.oh.us/
Trotwood-Madison HS 1,100/9-12
4440 N Union Rd 45426 937-854-0878
Gerald Cox, prin. Fax 854-0594
Other Schools – See Dayton

United Theological Seminary Post-Sec.
4501 Denlinger Rd 45426 800-322-5817

Troy, Miami, Pop. 22,343
Troy CSD 3,900/K-12
500 N Market St 45373 937-332-6700
Tom Dunn, supt. Fax 332-6771
www.troy.k12.oh.us
Troy HS 1,500/9-12
151 Staunton Rd 45373 937-332-6710
Eric Herman, prin. Fax 332-6738
Troy JHS 700/7-8
556 Adams St 45373 937-332-6720
Stephanie Johnson, prin. Fax 332-3812

Hobart Institute of Welding Technology Post-Sec.
400 Trade Sq E 45373 800-332-9448
Troy Christian HS 400/7-12
700 S Dorset Rd 45373 937-339-5692
Steve Peterson, prin. Fax 335-6258

Twinsburg, Summit, Pop. 17,380
Twinsburg CSD 4,000/PK-12
11136 Ravenna Rd 44087 330-486-2000
Steve Marlow, supt. Fax 425-7216
twinsburg.k12.oh.us
Chamberlin MS 700/7-8
10270 Ravenna Rd 44087 330-486-2281
Belinda Scott, prin. Fax 963-8313
Twinsburg HS 1,200/9-12
10084 Ravenna Rd 44087 330-486-2400
Michael Swank, prin. Fax 405-7406

Uhrichsville, Tuscarawas, Pop. 5,647
Claymont CSD
Supt. — See Dennison
Claymont HS 700/9-12
4205 Indian Hill Rd SE 44683 740-922-3471
Larry Amicone, prin. Fax 922-1031
Claymont JHS 400/7-8
215 E 6th St 44683 740-922-5241
Michael Wright, prin. Fax 922-7330

Union City, Darke, Pop. 1,701
Mississinawa Valley Local SD 700/K-12
1469 State Road 47 E 45390 937-968-5656
W. Joe Scholler, supt. Fax 968-6731
www.mississinawa.k12.oh.us
Mississinawa Valley JSHS 300/7-12
10480 Staudt Rd 45390 937-968-4464
Clarence Perry, prin. Fax 968-3434

Uniontown, Stark, Pop. 3,074
Green Local SD
Supt. — See Green
Green HS 1,400/9-12
1474 Boettler Rd 44685 330-896-7575
Gary Geis, prin. Fax 896-7549
Green MS 700/7-8
1711 Steese Rd 44685 330-896-7710
Brian Reed, prin. Fax 896-7760

Lake Local SD 3,400/K-12
11936 King Church Ave NW 44685 330-877-9383
William Stetler, supt. Fax 877-4754
lake.stark.k12.oh.us/
Lake HS 1,100/9-12
1025 Lake Center St NW 44685 330-877-4282
Jeffrey Wendorf, prin. Fax 877-0853
Other Schools – See Hartville

Hondros College Post-Sec.
1505 Crprt Woods Pky #100 44685 330-896-9666

University Heights, Cuyahoga, Pop. 13,242
Cleveland Hts - University Hts CSD 6,500/K-12
2155 Miramar Blvd 44118 216-371-7171
Deborah Delisle, supt. Fax 397-3880
www.chuh.org
Wiley MS 500/6-8
2181 Miramar Blvd 44118 216-371-7270
Denine Goolsby, prin. Fax 397-5968
Other Schools – See Cleveland Heights

Fuchs Mizrachi S 400/PK-12
2301 Fenwick Rd 44118 216-932-0220
Rabbi Pinchos Hecht, hdmstr. Fax 932-0345

Upper Arlington, Franklin, Pop. 31,550
Upper Arlington CSD 5,200/K-12
1950 N Mallway Dr 43221 614-487-5000
Jeffrey Weaver Ph.D., supt. Fax 487-5012
www.uaschools.org
Hastings MS 700/6-8
1850 Hastings Ln 43220 614-487-5100
Beverly Von Zielonka, prin. Fax 487-5116
Jones MS 600/6-8
2100 Arlington Ave 43221 614-487-5080
Karen Pettus, prin. Fax 487-5307
Upper Arlington HS 1,900/9-12
1650 Ridgeview Rd 43221 614-487-5200
Kip Greenhill, prin. Fax 487-5238

Upper Sandusky, Wyandot, Pop. 6,455
Upper Sandusky EVD 1,700/K-12
800 N Sandusky Ave Ste A 43351 419-294-2307
Kenneth Doseck, supt. Fax 294-6891
www.uppersandusky.k12.oh.us
Union MS 600/4-8
390 W Walker St 43351 419-294-5721
James Wheeler, prin. Fax 294-2586
Upper Sandusky HS 600/9-12
800 N Sandusky Ave 43351 419-294-2308
James Clifford, prin. Fax 294-6889

Urbana, Champaign, Pop. 11,561
Urbana CSD 2,300/K-12
711 Wood St 43078 937-653-1402
Dr. Susan McCarty, supt. Fax 652-3845
www.urbana.k12.oh.us
Urbana HS 600/9-12
500 Washington Ave 43078 937-653-1412
Charles Thiel, prin. Fax 653-1487
Urbana JHS 400/7-8
500 Washington Ave 43078 937-653-1439
Kristin Mays, prin.

Urbana University Post-Sec.
579 College Way 43078 937-484-1301

Utica, Licking, Pop. 2,109
North Fork Local SD 1,900/K-12
PO Box 497 43080 740-892-3666
Thomas Slater, supt. Fax 892-2937
www.northfork.k12.oh.us
Utica HS 600/9-12
PO Box 677 43080 740-892-2855
C. Mark McDaniel, prin. Fax 892-2090
Utica JHS 300/7-8
PO Box 647 43080 740-892-2691
Paul Galloway, prin. Fax 892-2203

Valley View, Cuyahoga, Pop. 2,099

Ohio Center for Broadcasting Post-Sec.
9000 Sweet Valley Dr 44125 216-447-9117

Van Buren, Hancock, Pop. 304
Van Buren Local SD 900/K-12
217 S Main St 45889 419-299-3578
Timothy Myers, supt. Fax 299-3668
www.noacsc.org/hancock/vb/
Van Buren HS 300/9-12
217 S Main St 45889 419-299-3384
Michael Brand, prin. Fax 299-3340
Van Buren MS 200/6-8
217 S Main St 45889 419-299-3385
Jason Clark, prin. Fax 299-3340

Vandalia, Montgomery, Pop. 14,298
Vandalia-Butler CSD 3,400/K-12
306 S Dixie Dr 45377 937-415-6400
Dr. Christy Donnelly, supt. Fax 415-6429
www.vandaliabutlerschools.org
Butler HS 1,200/9-12
600 S Dixie Dr 45377 937-415-6300
Chad Hill, prin. Fax 415-6457
Morton MS 500/5-8
231 W National Rd 45377 937-415-6600
Gary Miller, prin. Fax 415-6648
Other Schools – See Dayton

Vanlue, Hancock, Pop. 360
Vanlue Local SD 300/K-12
PO Box 250 45890 419-387-7724
Timothy Kruse, supt. Fax 387-7722
www.noacsc.org/hancock/vl/
Vanlue JSHS 200/7-12
PO Box 250 45890 419-387-7724
Scott Hall, prin. Fax 387-7722

Van Wert, Van Wert, Pop. 10,435
Lincolnview Local SD 800/K-12
15945 Middle Point Rd 45891 419-238-6493
Doug Fries, supt. Fax 968-2227
www.noacsc.org/vanwert/lv/main.html
Lincolnview JSHS 400/7-12
15945 Middle Point Rd 45891 419-238-1289
Kelly Dye, prin. Fax 968-2227

Van Wert CSD 1,800/K-12
205 W Crawford St 45891 419-238-0648
Cathy Hoffman, supt. Fax 238-3974
www.vanwertcougars.net
Van Wert HS 700/9-12
205 W Crawford St 45891 419-238-3350
William Clifton, prin. Fax 238-0526
Van Wert MS 400/6-8
305 W Crawford St 45891 419-238-0727
Mary Riepenhoff, prin. Fax 238-7166

Vantage JVSD
818 N Franklin St 45891 419-238-5411
Dr. Stephen Mercer, supt. Fax 238-4058
www.vantagecareercenter.com
Vantage Career Center Vo/Tech
818 N Franklin St 45891 419-238-5411
Bob Vennekotter, dir. Fax 238-4058

Vermilion, Erie, Pop. 11,000
Vermilion Local SD 2,400/K-12
1230 Beechview Dr 44089 440-967-5210
Bruce Keller, supt. Fax 967-0740
vermilionschools.org
Sailorway MS 600/6-8
5355 Sailorway Dr 44089 440-967-6196
Heidi Riddle, prin. Fax 967-5720
Vermilion HS 800/9-12
1250 Sanford St 44089 440-967-3183
Michael Colatruglio, prin. Fax 967-8317

Versailles, Darke, Pop. 2,539
Versailles EVD 1,400/K-12
PO Box 313 45380 937-526-4773
Tom Doseck, supt. Fax 526-5745
www.versailles.k12.oh.us
Versailles JSHS 700/7-12
PO Box 313 45380 937-526-4427
Roger McEldowney, prin. Fax 526-4356

Vienna, Trumbull, Pop. 1,067
Mathews Local SD 900/K-12
4434 Warren Sharon Rd Ste B 44473 330-394-1800
Lee Seiple, supt. Fax 394-1930
www.mathews.k12.oh.us
Mathews HS 300/9-12
4429 Warren Sharon Rd 44473 330-394-1138
Louis Demarco, prin.
Other Schools – See Fowler

Vincent, Washington
Warren Local SD 2,700/K-12
220 Sweetapple Rd 45784 740-678-2366
Thomas Gibbs, supt. Fax 678-8275
www.warrenlocal.k12.oh.us/
Warren HS 800/9-12
130 Warrior Dr 45784 740-678-2393
Dan Leffingwell, prin. Fax 678-2783
Other Schools – See Cutler

Wadsworth, Medina, Pop. 19,951
Wadsworth CSD 4,700/PK-12
360 College St 44281 330-336-3571
Dale Fortner, supt. Fax 334-5242
www.wadsworth.k12.oh.us/
Wadsworth HS 1,500/9-12
625 Broad St 44281 330-335-1400
Brian Williams, prin. Fax 335-1376
Wadsworth MS 700/7-8
150 Silvercreek Rd 44281 330-335-1410
Roger Wright, prin. Fax 336-3820

Reimer Road Baptist Christian S 200/PK-12
1055 Reimer Rd 44281 330-334-1480
Rev. James Newton, hdmstr. Fax 336-3064

Wapakoneta, Auglaize, Pop. 9,602
Auglaize County ESC
1045 Dearbaugh Ave Ste 2 45895 419-738-3422
Patrick Niekamp, supt. Fax 738-1267
www.auglaizeesc.k12.oh.us/
Auglaize County HS 7-12
1045 Dearbaugh Ave 45895 419-739-7489

Wapakoneta CSD 3,100/K-12
1102 Gardenia Dr 45895 419-739-2900
Keith Horner, supt. Fax 739-2918
www.noacsc.org/auglaize/wk/
Wapakoneta HS, 1 Redskin Trl 45895 1,300/8-12
Aaron Rex, prin. 419-739-5200

Warren, Trumbull, Pop. 45,796
Champion Local SD 1,700/K-12
5759 Mahoning Ave NW 44483 330-847-2330
Pamela Hood, supt. Fax 847-2336
www.champion.k12.oh.us
Champion HS 600/9-12
5976 Mahoning Ave NW 44483 330-847-2305
Michele Bonno, prin. Fax 847-2353
Champion MS 500/5-8
5435 Kuszmaul Ave NW 44483 330-847-2340
Mary Rose Walker, prin. Fax 847-3624

Howland Local SD 3,300/K-12
8200 South St SE 44484 330-856-8200
John Rubesich, supt. Fax 856-8214
www.howlandschools.com
Howland HS 1,100/9-12
200 Shaffer Dr NE 44484 330-856-8220
Frank Thomas, prin. Fax 856-7827
Howland MS 800/6-8
8100 South St SE 44484 330-856-8250
Barbara Sullivan, prin. Fax 856-2157

Lordstown Local SD 600/K-12
1824 Salt Springs Rd W 44481 330-824-2534
William Pfahler, supt. Fax 824-2847
www.lordstown.k12.oh.us/
Lordstown JSHS 200/7-12
1824 Salt Springs Rd W 44481 330-824-2581
Anthony J. Calderone, prin. Fax 824-2586

Trumbull Career & Technical Center
528 Educational Hwy NW 44483 330-847-0503
Wayne McClain, supt. Fax 847-6817
www.tctc.k12.oh.us
Trumbull Career & Technical Center Vo/Tech
528 Educational Hwy NW 44483 330-847-0503
Gary Hoffman, dir. Fax 847-0339

Warren CSD 6,300/K-12
261 Monroe St NW 44483 330-841-2321
Dr. Kathryn Hellweg, supt. Fax 395-4728
www.warrenschools.k12.oh.us
East MS 600/5-8
1470 South St SE 44483 330-841-2255
James Mitolo, prin. Fax 841-2257
Harding HS 1,800/9-12
860 Elm Rd NE 44483 330-841-2316
Fax 841-2289
Turner MS 500/5-8
1443 Mahoning Ave NW 44483 330-841-2379
Fax 841-2378
Warren Western Reserve MS 900/5-8
200 Loveless Ave SW 44485 330-841-2345
Linda Reigelman, prin. Fax 373-6065

Kennedy HS 400/7-12
2550 Central Parkway Ave SE 44484 330-369-1804
June Drennen, prin. Fax 369-1125
Kent State University-Trumbull Campus Post-Sec.
4314 Mahoning Ave NW 44483 330-678-4281
Trumbull Business College Post-Sec.
3200 Ridge Ave SE 44484 330-369-3200
Warren Christian S 200/K-12
2640 Parkman Rd NW 44485 330-898-3840
Dwight Long, admin. Fax 898-1757

Warrensville Heights, Cuyahoga, Pop. 14,223
Warrensville Heights CSD 2,800/K-12
4500 Warrensville Center Rd 44128 216-295-7710
Elaine Davis, supt. Fax 921-5902
www.warrensville.k12.oh.us
Warrensville Heights HS 900/9-12
4270 Northfield Rd 44128 216-752-8585
Henry Pettiegrew, prin. Fax 752-8116
Warrensville Heights MS 400/7-8
4285 Warrensville Center Rd 44128 216-752-4050
Phyllis Wren, prin. Fax 752-5813

ITT Technical Institute Post-Sec.
4700 Richmond Rd 44128 216-896-6500

Warsaw, Coshocton, Pop. 787
River View Local SD 2,500/K-12
26496 State Route 60 43844 740-824-3521
Kyle Kanuckel, supt. Fax 824-3760
www.river-view.k12.oh.us
River View HS 900/9-12
26496 State Route 60 43844 740-824-3522
David Hire, prin. Fax 824-4746
River View JHS 400/7-8
26546 State Route 60 43844 740-824-3523
Alan English, prin. Fax 824-5241

Washington Court House, Fayette, Pop. 13,471
Miami Trace Local SD 2,700/K-12
1400 US Highway 22 NW 43160 740-335-3010
Daniel W. Roberts, supt. Fax 335-5675
www.miamitrace.k12.oh.us/
Miami Trace HS 900/9-12
3722 State Route 41 NW 43160 740-335-5891
Jeff Spears, prin. Fax 636-2010
Other Schools – See Bloomingburg

Washington Court House CSD 2,300/K-12
306 Highland Ave 43160 740-335-6620
Keith Brown, supt. Fax 335-1245
www.washingtonch.k12.oh.us
Washington HS 600/9-12
1200 Willard St 43160 740-335-0820
Jeff Hodson, prin. Fax 335-0842
Washington MS 500/6-8
318 N North St 43160 740-335-0291
Steve Ross, prin. Fax 333-3606

Waterford, Washington
Wolf Creek Local SD 700/K-12
PO Box 67 45786 740-984-2373
Robert Caldwell, supt. Fax 984-4420
www.wolfcreek.k12.oh.us
Waterford HS 200/9-12
PO Box 67 45786 740-984-2373
Randy Shrider, prin. Fax 984-4420

Wauseon, Fulton, Pop. 7,311
Wauseon EVD 2,100/K-12
126 S Fulton St 43567 419-335-6616
Marc Robinson, supt. Fax 335-3978
www.wauseon.k12.oh.us
Burr Road MS 500/6-8
717 Burr Rd 43567 419-335-2701
William Friess, prin. Fax 335-0089
Wauseon HS 700/9-12
840 Parkview St 43567 419-335-5756
Joseph Sevenich, prin. Fax 335-4228

Waverly, Pike, Pop. 5,086
Waverly CSD 2,100/K-12
1 Tiger Dr 45690 740-947-4770
Cheryl Francis, supt. Fax 947-4483
www.waverly.k12.oh.us
Waverly HS 700/9-12
1 Tiger Dr 45690 740-947-7701
David Surrey, prin. Fax 947-8877
Waverly JHS 500/6-8
3 Tiger Dr 45690 740-947-4527
Bill Hoover, prin. Fax 947-8047

Waynesfield, Auglaize, Pop. 819
Waynesfield-Goshen Local SD 700/K-12
500 N Westminster St 45896 419-568-2391
Earnie Jones, supt. Fax 568-8024
www.waynesfield.k12.oh.us/
Waynesfield-Goshen Local HS 300/6-12
500 N Westminster St 45896 419-568-5261
Thomas Winkler, prin. Fax 568-6282

Waynesville, Warren, Pop. 2,980
Wayne Local SD 1,400/K-12
659 Dayton Rd 45068 513-897-6971
Thomas Isaacs, supt. Fax 897-9605
www.wayne-local.k12.oh.us
Waynesville HS 500/9-12
735 Dayton Rd 45068 513-897-2776
Randy Gebhardt, prin. Fax 897-2713
Waynesville MS 300/6-8
723 Dayton Rd 45068 513-897-4706
Shawn Lenney, prin. Fax 897-9605

Wellington, Lorain, Pop. 4,648
Wellington EVD 1,600/K-12
201 S Main St 44090 440-647-4286
Victor Cardenzana, supt. Fax 647-4806
www.wellington.k12.oh.us
McCormick MS 600/4-8
201 S Main St 44090 440-647-2342
Tom Durham, prin. Fax 647-7310
Wellington HS 500/9-12
629 N Main St 44090 440-647-3734
Robert Klinar, prin. Fax 647-7318

Wellston, Jackson, Pop. 6,025
Wellston CSD 1,800/PK-12
1 E Broadway St 45692 740-384-2152
Lee Kaple, supt. Fax 384-3948
www.wcs.k12.oh.us
Wellston HS 500/9-12
200 Golden Rocket Dr 45692 740-384-2162
Tony Meinerding, prin. Fax 384-9581
Wellston MS 400/6-8
227 Golden Rocket Dr 45692 740-384-2251
Barbara White, prin. Fax 384-9801

Wellsville, Columbiana, Pop. 4,034
Wellsville Local SD 700/K-12
929 Center St 43968 330-532-2643
Richard Bereschik, supt. Fax 532-6204
www.wellsville.k12.oh.us
Daw MS, 929 Center St 43968 300/4-8
David Buzzard, prin. 330-532-1372
Wellsville HS 300/9-12
1 Bengal Blvd 43968 330-532-1188
Greg Davis, prin. Fax 532-9004

West Alexandria, Preble, Pop. 1,343
Twin Valley Community Local SD 1,100/K-12
100 Education Dr 45381 937-839-4688
Richard Brownlee, supt. Fax 839-4898
www.tvs.k12.oh.us
Twin Valley South HS 400/9-12
100 Education Dr 45381 937-839-4693
Scott Cottingim, prin. Fax 839-4898
Twin Valley South MS 200/6-8
100 Education Dr 45381 937-839-4165
Eva Howard, prin. Fax 839-4898

West Carrollton, Montgomery, Pop. 14,072
West Carrollton CSD 3,900/PK-12
430 E Pease Ave 45449 937-859-5121
Rusty Clifford, supt. Fax 859-5250
www.westcarrolltonschools.com
West Carrollton HS 1,100/9-12
5833 Student St 45449 937-859-5121
Fred Gehron, prin. Fax 435-2315
West Carrollton MS 900/6-8
424 E Main St 45449 937-859-5121
John Runzo, prin. Fax 859-2780

West Chester, Butler
Lakota Local SD
Supt. — See Liberty
Hopewell JHS 500/7-8
8200 Cox Rd 45069 513-777-2258
David Pike, prin. Fax 777-1908
Lakota Freshman HS 1,300/9-9
5050 Tylersville Rd 45069 513-874-8390
Keith Kline, prin. Fax 874-8236
Lakota Ridge JHS 700/7-8
6199 Beckett Ridge Blvd 45069 513-777-0552
Andre Gendreau, prin. Fax 777-0919
Lakota West SHS 1,900/10-12
8940 Union Centre Blvd 45069 513-874-5699
Richard Hamilton, prin. Fax 682-4134

Westerville, Franklin, Pop. 34,722
Westerville CSD 13,900/K-12
336 S Otterbein Ave 43081 614-797-5700
Fax 797-5701
www.westerville.k12.oh.us
Blendon MS 600/6-8
223 S Otterbein Ave 43081 614-797-6400
David Baker, prin. Fax 797-6401
Genoa MS 900/6-8
5948 S Old 3C Hwy 43082 614-797-6500
Suzanne Kile, prin. Fax 797-6501

Heritage MS — 900/6-8
390 N Spring Rd 43082 — 614-797-6600
Felicia Harper, prin. — Fax 797-6601
Walnut Springs MS — 900/6-8
888 E Walnut St 43081 — 614-797-6700
Matt Lutz, prin. — Fax 797-6701
Westerville Central HS — 1,100/9-12
7118 Mount Royal Ave 43082 — 614-797-6800
Todd Spinner, prin. — Fax 797-6801
Westerville-North HS — 1,700/9-12
950 County Line Rd 43081 — 614-797-6200
Kurt Yancey, prin. — Fax 797-6201
Westerville-South HS — 1,500/9-12
303 S Otterbein Ave 43081 — 614-797-6000
Keith Bell, prin. — Fax 797-6001

Hondros College — Post-Sec.
4140 Executive Pkwy 43081 — 614-508-7277
Ohio State Cosmetology School — Post-Sec.
5970 Westerville Rd 43081 — 614-890-3535
Otterbein College — Post-Sec.
78 W Home St 43081 — 614-890-3000
Worthington Christian MS — 200/6-8
8225 Worthington Galena Rd 43081 — 614-431-8230
Richard Dray, prin. — Fax 431-8216

West Jefferson, Madison, Pop. 4,287
Jefferson Local SD — 1,000/PK-12
906 W Main St 43162 — 614-879-7654
William Mullett, supt. — Fax 879-5376
www.west-jefferson.k12.oh.us
Memorial MS — 300/6-8
177 S Frey Ave 43162 — 614-879-8345
Debbie Omen, prin. — Fax 879-5399
West Jefferson HS — 400/9-12
1 Roughrider Dr 43162 — 614-879-7681
Dave Metz, prin. — Fax 879-5381

West Lafayette, Coshocton, Pop. 2,535
Ridgewood Local SD — 1,400/PK-12
301 S Oak St 43845 — 740-545-6354
William Caudill, supt. — Fax 545-6336
www.ridgewood.k12.oh.us
Ridgewood HS — 500/9-12
602 Johnson St 43845 — 740-545-6345
Rick Raach, prin. — Fax 545-5311
Ridgewood MS — 400/6-8
517 S Oak St 43845 — 740-545-6335
Mike Masloski, prin. — Fax 545-5300

Westlake, Cuyahoga, Pop. 31,331
Westlake CSD — 3,900/K-12
27200 Hilliard Blvd 44145 — 440-871-7300
James Costanza, supt. — Fax 871-6034
www.westlake.k12.oh.us
Burneson MS — 700/7-8
2240 Dover Center Rd 44145 — 440-835-6340
G. Newman, prin. — Fax 835-5987
Westlake HS — 1,300/9-12
27830 Hilliard Blvd 44145 — 440-250-1002
Tim Freeman, prin. — Fax 835-5572

West Liberty, Champaign, Pop. 1,760
West Liberty-Salem Local SD — 1,200/K-12
7208 US Highway 68 N 43357 — 937-465-1075
Steve Thompson, supt. — Fax 465-1095
www.wls.k12.oh.us
West Liberty-Salem MSHS — 700/6-12
7208 US Highway 68 N 43357 — 937-465-1060
Greg Johnson, prin. — Fax 465-1095

West Milton, Miami, Pop. 4,684
Milton-Union EVD — 1,700/K-12
112 S Spring St 45383 — 937-884-7910
Dr. James Barney, supt. — Fax 884-7911
www.milton-union.k12.oh.us
Milton-Union HS — 600/9-12
221 Jefferson St 45383 — 937-884-7940
Brian Powderly, prin. — Fax 884-7941
Milton-Union MS — 400/6-8
146 S Spring St 45383 — 937-884-7930
Dr. Ginny Rammel, prin. — Fax 884-7931

West Portsmouth, Scioto, Pop. 3,551
Washington-Nile Local SD — 1,700/K-12
15332 US Highway 52 45663 — 740-858-1111
Patricia Ciraso, supt. — Fax 858-1110
www.west.k12.oh.us
Portsmouth West MS — 400/6-8
1420 13th St 45663 — 740-858-6668
Christopher Jordan, prin. — Fax 858-4101
Other Schools – See Portsmouth

West Salem, Wayne, Pop. 1,488
Northwestern Local SD — 1,500/K-12
7571 N Elyria Rd 44287 — 419-846-3151
Jeffrey Layton, supt. — Fax 846-3361
www.northwestern-wayne.k12.oh.us
Northwestern HS — 500/9-12
7473 N Elyria Rd 44287 — 419-846-3833
Michael Burkholder, prin. — Fax 846-3163
Northwestern MS — 400/6-8
7569 N Elyria Rd 44287 — 419-846-3974
Robert Dorety, prin. — Fax 846-3750

West Union, Adams, Pop. 3,108
Adams County/Ohio Valley Local SD — 4,100/K-12
141 Lloyd Rd 45693 — 937-544-5586
Charles Kimble, supt. — Fax 544-3720
www.ohiovalley.k12.oh.us
Ohio Valley Career & Technical Center — Vo/Tech
175 Lloyd Rd 45693 — 937-544-2336
Tad Mitchell, prin. — Fax 544-5176
West Union HS — 600/7-12
97 Dragon Lair Dr 45693 — 937-544-5553
Dennis Sizemore, prin. — Fax 544-5361
Other Schools – See Peebles, Seaman

Adams County Christian S — 100/K-12
187 Willow Dr 45693 — 937-544-5502
Shirley Lewis, admin. — Fax 544-5503

West Unity, Williams, Pop. 1,803
Millcreek-West Unity Local SD — 700/K-12
113 S Defiance St 43570 — 419-924-2365
Deb Piotrowski, supt. — Fax 924-2367
www.hilltop.k12.oh.us
Hilltop HS — 300/7-12
113 S Defiance St 43570 — 419-924-2365
Mick Belcher, prin. — Fax 924-2367

Wheelersburg, Scioto, Pop. 5,113
Wheelersburg Local SD — 1,500/K-12
PO Box 340 45694 — 740-574-8484
Mark Knapp, supt. — Fax 574-6134
www.burg.k12.oh.us
Wheelersburg HS — 400/9-12
701 Pirate Dr 45694 — 740-574-2527
Matthew McCorkle, prin. — Fax 574-6178
Wheelersburg MS — 400/5-8
1731 Dogwood Ridge Rd 45694 — 740-574-2515
Amber Fannin, prin. — Fax 574-9201

Whitehall, Franklin, Pop. 18,052
Whitehall CSD — 2,900/K-12
625 S Yearling Rd 43213 — 614-417-5000
Judyth Dobbert-Meloy, supt. — Fax 417-5023
www.whitehall.k12.oh.us
Rosemore MS — 700/6-8
4735 Kae Ave 43213 — 614-417-5200
Mark Trace, prin. — Fax 417-5212
Whitehall-Yearling HS — 800/9-12
675 S Yearling Rd 43213 — 614-417-5100
Dondra Maney, prin. — Fax 417-5133

Whitehouse, Lucas, Pop. 3,303
Anthony Wayne Local SD — 4,000/K-12
PO Box 2487 43571 — 419-877-5377
John Granger, supt. — Fax 877-9352
www.anthonywayneschools.org
Wayne HS — 1,300/9-12
5967 Finzel Rd 43571 — 419-877-0466
James Conner, prin. — Fax 877-5028
Wayne JHS — 600/7-8
6035 Finzel Rd 43571 — 419-877-5342
Jeffrey Schwerer, prin. — Fax 877-4908

Wickliffe, Lake, Pop. 13,205
Wickliffe CSD — 1,600/K-12
2221 Rockefeller Rd 44092 — 440-943-6900
Robert Smith, supt. — Fax 943-7738
www.wickliffe-city.k12.oh.us
Wickliffe HS — 500/9-12
2255 Rockefeller Rd 44092 — 440-944-0800
Vicki Wheatley, prin. — Fax 943-7738
Wickliffe MS — 500/5-8
29240 Euclid Ave 44092 — 440-943-3220
A. William Kermavner, prin. — Fax 943-7755

Bryant & Stratton College — Post-Sec.
27557 Chardon Rd 44092 — 440-944-6800
Rabbinical College of Telshe — Post-Sec.
28400 Euclid Ave 44092 — 440-943-5300
St. Mary Seminary/Graduate Sch. Theology — Post-Sec.
28700 Euclid Ave 44092 — 440-943-7600
Telshe HS — 100/9-12
28400 Euclid Ave 44092 — 440-943-5300
Rabbi Zev Poss, prin. — Fax 943-5303

Wilberforce, Greene, Pop. 2,639

Central State University — Post-Sec.
PO Box 1004 45384 — 937-376-6011
Payne Theological Seminary — Post-Sec.
PO Box 474 45384 — 937-376-2946
Wilberforce University — Post-Sec.
PO Box 1001 45384 — 937-376-2911

Willard, Huron, Pop. 6,818
Willard CSD — 2,300/PK-12
PO Box 150 44890 — 419-935-1541
Dennis Doughty, supt. — Fax 935-8491
www.willard.k12.oh.us
Willard HS — 700/9-12
PO Box 410 44890 — 419-935-0181
Jeff Ritz, prin. — Fax 933-6701
Willard MS, 949 S Main St 44890 — 600/5-8
Dan Major, prin. — 419-933-8312

Williamsburg, Clermont, Pop. 2,332
Williamsburg Local SD — 1,000/K-12
549 W Main St Ste A 45176 — 513-724-3077
Jeffery Weir, supt. — Fax 724-1504
www.burgschools.org
Williamsburg MSHS — 600/6-12
500 S 5th St 45176 — 513-724-2211
Matthew Earley, prin. — Fax 724-6577

Williamsport, Pickaway, Pop. 1,020
Westfall Local SD — 1,600/K-12
19463 Pherson Pike 43164 — 740-986-3671
Randall Cotner, supt. — Fax 986-8375
gsn.k12.oh.us/westfall/default.htm
Westfall HS — 500/9-12
19463 Pherson Pike 43164 — 740-986-2911
Dennis Karshner, prin. — Fax 986-6311
Westfall MS — 400/6-8
19545 Pherson Pike 43164 — 740-986-2941
Kent Wolfe, prin. — Fax 986-6751

Willoughby, Lake, Pop. 22,336
Willoughby-Eastlake CSD — 8,700/K-12
37047 Ridge Rd 44094 — 440-946-5000
Dr. Keith Miller, supt. — Fax 946-4671
www.willoughby-eastlake.k12.oh.us
South HS — 1,300/9-12
5000 Shankland Rd 44094 — 440-975-3647
Paul Lombardo, prin. — Fax 975-3645
Willoughby-Eastlake Tech Ctr — Vo/Tech
25 Public Sq 44094 — 440-946-7085
Richard Hart, prin. — Fax 975-3741
Willoughby MS — 900/4-8
36901 Ridge Rd 44094 — 440-975-3600
William Porter, prin. — Fax 975-3618
Other Schools – See Eastlake, Willowick

Andrews S — 200/6-12
38588 Mentor Ave 44094 — 440-942-3600
David Rath, hdmstr. — Fax 942-3660
Cornerstone Christian Academy — 300/K-12
2846 SOM Center Rd 44094 — 440-943-9260
Daniel Buell Ph.D., admin. — Fax 943-9262

Willowick, Lake, Pop. 14,004
Willoughby-Eastlake CSD
Supt. — See Willoughby
Willowick MS — 700/6-8
31500 Royalview Dr 44095 — 440-943-2950
Loretta Rodman, prin. — Fax 943-9964

Willow Wood, Lawrence
Symmes Valley Local SD — 900/K-12
14778 State Route 141 45696 — 740-643-2451
Thomas Ben, supt. — Fax 643-1219
www.symmesvalley.k12.oh.us
Symmes Valley HS — 300/9-12
14778 State Route 141 45696 — 740-643-2371
Jeff Saunders, prin. — Fax 643-1606

Wilmington, Clinton, Pop. 12,474
Great Oaks Institute of Technology
Supt. — See Cincinnati
Laurel Oaks CDC — Vo/Tech
300 Oak Dr 45177 — 937-382-1411
Dr. Robert Bowermeister, prin. — Fax 383-2095

Wilmington CSD — 3,200/K-12
341 S Nelson Ave 45177 — 937-382-1641
Philip Warner, supt. — Fax 382-1645
www.wilmingtoncityschool.com
O'Borror MS — 700/6-8
275 Thorne Ave 45177 — 937-382-7556
Nicole Quallen, prin. — Fax 382-3295
Wilmington HS — 1,000/9-12
300 Richardson Pl 45177 — 937-382-7716
Ronald Sexton, prin. — Fax 382-1139

Southern State Community College — Post-Sec.
1850 Davids Dr 45177 — 937-382-6645
Wilmington College — Post-Sec.
1870 Quaker Way 45177 — 937-382-6661

Windham, Portage, Pop. 2,749
Windham EVD — 1,000/PK-12
9530 Bauer Ave 44288 — 330-326-2711
Ronald Niemiec, supt. — Fax 326-2134
Windham HS — 300/9-12
9530 Bauer Ave 44288 — 330-326-3916
Carol Kropinak, prin. — Fax 326-2052
Windham JHS — 200/6-8
9530 Bauer Ave 44288 — 330-326-3490
Carol Kropinak, prin. — Fax 326-3713

Wintersville, Jefferson, Pop. 3,889
Indian Creek Local SD — 2,200/PK-12
587 Bantam Ridge Rd 43953 — 740-264-3502
Jene Watkins, supt. — Fax 266-2915
www.indian-creek.k12.oh.us
Indian Creek HS — 700/9-12
200 Park Dr 43953 — 740-264-1163
John Craig, prin. — Fax 266-2929
Other Schools – See Mingo Junction

Woodsfield, Monroe, Pop. 2,501
Switzerland of Ohio Local SD — 2,700/K-12
304 Mill St 43793 — 740-472-5801
Mike Staggs, supt. — Fax 472-5806
www.swissohio.k12.oh.us/switzerland_of_ohio.htm
Monroe Central HS — 300/9-12
46605 State Route 78 43793 — 740-458-1246
Marc Ring, prin. — Fax 458-9079
Swiss Hills Career Center — Vo/Tech
46601 State Route 78 43793 — 740-472-0722
Marc Ring, prin. — Fax 472-0367
Other Schools – See Beallsville, Hannibal

Woodville, Sandusky, Pop. 2,003
Woodmore Local SD — 1,200/K-12
708 W Main St 43469 — 419-849-2381
Jane Garling, supt. — Fax 849-2132
www.woodmore.k12.oh.us/
Other Schools – See Elmore

Wooster, Wayne, Pop. 25,668
Triway Local SD — 2,100/K-12
3205 Shreve Rd 44691 — 330-264-9491
David Rice, supt. — Fax 262-3955
www.tccsa.net/dp/trwy
Triway HS — 700/9-12
3205 Shreve Rd 44691 — 330-264-8685
Scott Wharton, prin. — Fax 262-3955
Triway JHS — 300/7-8
3145 Shreve Rd 44691 — 330-264-2114
Mitchell Caraway, prin. — Fax 264-6025

Wooster CSD — 4,000/K-12
144 N Market St 44691 — 330-264-0869
Dr. Dan Good, supt. — Fax 262-3407
www.wooster.k12.oh.us
Edgewood MS — 700/7-8
2695 Graustark Path 44691 — 330-345-6475
Anita Jorney-Gifford, prin. — Fax 345-8237
Wooster HS — 1,300/9-12
515 Oldman Rd 44691 — 330-345-4000
Jerry Parsons, prin. — Fax 345-3501

College of Wooster — Post-Sec.
1189 Beall Ave 44691 — 330-263-2000
Ohio State University-A & T Institute — Post-Sec.
1328 Dover Rd 44691 — 330-264-3911

Worthington, Franklin, Pop. 13,202
Worthington CSD — 9,200/K-12
200 E Wilson Bridge Rd 43085 — 614-883-3000
Melissa Conrath, supt. — Fax 883-3010
www.worthington.k12.oh.us
Kilbourne MS — 400/7-8
50 E Dublin Granville Rd 43085 — 614-883-3500
Pamela VanHorn, prin. — Fax 883-3510
Perry MS — 400/7-8
2341 Snouffer Rd 43085 — 614-883-3600
Jeff Maddox, prin. — Fax 883-3610

Worthington HS 1,700/9-12
300 W Dublin Granville Rd 43085 614-883-2250
Richard Littell, prin. Fax 883-2260
Worthingway MS 400/7-8
6625 Guyer St 43085 614-883-3650
Santha Stall, prin. Fax 883-3660
Other Schools – See Columbus

Worthington Christian HS 400/9-12
6670 Worthington Galena Rd 43085 614-431-8210
Thomas Anglea, prin. Fax 431-8213

Wyoming, Hamilton, Pop. 7,719
Wyoming CSD 2,000/K-12
420 Springfield Pike 45215 513-772-2343
Dr. Gail Kist-Kline, supt. Fax 672-3355
www.wyomingcityschools.org
Wyoming HS 700/9-12
106 Pendery Ave 45215 513-761-7722
Annie Wade, prin. Fax 679-3611
Wyoming MS 700/5-8
17 Wyoming Ave 45215 513-761-7248
Kathy Ryan, prin. Fax 761-7319

Xenia, Greene, Pop. 23,600
Greene County JVSD
2960 W Enon Rd 45385 937-372-6941
Marsha Leonard, supt. Fax 372-8283
www.greeneccc.com
Greene County Career Center Vo/Tech
2960 W Enon Rd 45385 937-372-6941
Manfred Stamguts, prin. Fax 372-8283

Xenia Community CSD 5,100/K-12
578 E Market St 45385 937-376-2961
Jeffrey K. Lewis Ed.D., supt. Fax 372-4701
www.xenia.k12.oh.us
Central MS 600/6-8
425 Edison Blvd 45385 937-372-7635
Mike Earley, prin. Fax 374-4410
Warner MS 600/6-8
600 Buckskin Trl 45385 937-376-9488
Dr. Peg McAtee, prin. Fax 374-4228
Xenia HS 1,500/9-12
303 Kinsey Rd 45385 937-372-6983
Reinhold Finkes, prin. Fax 374-4390

Dayton Christian S - Xenia Christian HS 300/7-12
1101 Wesley Ave 45385 937-372-9754
Alan Stock, prin. Fax 372-0098
Freedom Christian Academy 50/K-12
1067 US Route 68 S 45385 937-372-9399
Charles Savage, prin.
Xenia Nazarene Christian S 200/K-12
1204 W 2nd St 45385 937-372-4362
Charlene Crisp, prin. Fax 372-1074

Yellow Springs, Greene, Pop. 3,665
Yellow Springs EVD 700/K-12
201 S Walnut St 45387 937-767-7381
Anthony Armocida Ph.D., supt. Fax 767-6604
www.yellow-springs.k12.oh.us/
Yellow Springs HS / McKinney MS 400/7-12
420 E Enon Rd 45387 937-767-7224
John Gudgel, prin. Fax 767-6154

Antioch University McGregor Post-Sec.
800 Livermore St 45387 937-767-6321

Youngstown, Mahoning, Pop. 82,837
Austintown Local SD 5,000/K-12
225 Idaho Rd 44515 330-797-3900
Douglas Heuer, supt. Fax 797-3943
www.austintown.k12.oh.us
Austintown MS 900/5-8
5800 Mahoning Ave 44515 330-797-3900
Daniel Bokesch, prin. Fax 797-3965
Fitch HS 1,600/9-12
4560 Falcon Dr 44515 330-797-3900
Douglas McGlynn, prin. Fax 797-3944
Ohl MS 700/5-8
255 Idaho Rd 44515 330-797-3900
Dennis Rice, prin. Fax 797-3964

Boardman Local SD 4,900/K-12
7410 Market St 44512 330-726-3404
Frank Lazzeri, supt. Fax 726-3432
www.boardman.k12.oh.us
Boardman HS 1,700/9-12
7777 Glenwood Ave 44512 330-758-7511
Tim Saxton, prin. Fax 758-7515
Center MS, 7410 Market St 44512 900/5-8
Randall Ebie, prin. 330-726-3400
Glenwood MS 700/5-8
7635 Glenwood Ave 44512 330-726-3414
Anthony Alvino, prin. Fax 758-8067

Liberty Local SD 1,800/K-12
4115 Shady Rd 44505 330-759-0807
Lawrence Prince, supt. Fax 759-1209
www.liberty.k12.oh.us
Guy MS 600/5-8
4115 Shady Rd 44505 330-759-1733
Mark Lucas, prin. Fax 759-4507
Liberty HS 700/9-12
1 Leopard Way 44505 330-759-2301
John Young, prin. Fax 759-4506

Youngstown CSD 7,100/K-12
PO Box 550 44501 330-744-6915
Wendy Webb Ed.D., supt. Fax 743-1557
www.youngstown.k12.oh.us/
Alpha: S of Excellence for Boys 7-9
2546 Hillman St 44507 330-744-7535
Jerome Harrell, prin.
Athena: S of Excellence for Girls 100/7-9
164 W Myrtle Ave 44507 330-480-1995
Michele Dotson, prin.
Berry MS, 940 Bryn Mawr Ave 44505 5-8
Robert Kearns, prin. 330-744-8646
Chaney HS 900/9-12
731 S Hazelwood Ave 44509 330-744-8822
Robert Spencer, dean Fax 480-1909
East MS 600/5-8
1544 E High Ave 44505 330-744-8845
Sandra Mislevy, prin. Fax 480-1910
Hayes MS 500/5-8
1616 Ford Ave 44504 330-744-7602
Carol Staten, prin. Fax 480-1905
Rayen HS 900/9-12
250 Benita Ave 44504 330-744-8550
Henrietta Williams, dean Fax 480-1912
Volney Rogers JHS 500/7-8
2400 S Schenley Ave 44511 330-744-7996
Marilyn Mastronardi, prin. Fax 480-1908
Wilson HS 800/9-12
2725 Gibson St 44502 330-744-8525
Kenya Harrington, dean Fax 480-1911
Youngstown Early College HS 100/9-12
Fedor Hall Elm St 44555 330-480-5878
Larry Johnson, prin. Fax 480-5875
Choffin Career & Technical Center Adult
200 E Wood St 44503 330-744-8706
Joseph Meranto, prin. Fax 744-8705

Cardinal Mooney HS 600/9-12
2545 Erie St 44507 330-788-5007
Sr. Jane Kudlacz, prin. Fax 788-4511
ITT Technical Institute Post-Sec.
1030 N Meridian Rd 44509 330-270-1600
St. Elizabeth Hospital Post-Sec.
PO Box 1790 44501 330-746-7211
Ursuline HS 500/9-12
750 Wick Ave 44505 330-744-4563
Patricia Fleming, prin. Fax 744-3358
Watkins Christian Academy 200/K-12
2122 E High Ave 44505 330-746-5626
Raymond McElroy, prin.
Western Reserve Care System Post-Sec.
345 Oak Hill Ave 44502 330-747-0777
Youngstown Christian S 400/PK-12
4425 Southern Blvd 44512 330-788-8088
Anthony Agresta, prin. Fax 788-2875
Youngstown State University Post-Sec.
1 University Plz 44555 330-742-3000

Zanesville, Muskingum, Pop. 25,253
Maysville Local SD 2,200/K-12
PO Box 1818 43702 740-453-0754
Monte Bainter, supt. Fax 455-4081
maysvillelsd.schoolwires.com/
Maysville HS, 3725 Panther Dr 43701 600/9-12
Mark Ulbrich, prin. 740-454-7999
Maysville MS, 3725 Panther Dr 43701 500/6-8
Mark Ulbrich, prin. 740-454-7982

Mid-East Career & Technology Centers
400 Richards Rd 43701 740-454-0105
William Bussey, supt. Fax 454-0731
www.mid-east.k12.oh.us/
Mid-East Career & Tech Ctr - Zanesville Vo/Tech
400 Richards Rd 43701 740-454-0101
Alice Hite, dir. Fax 454-0723
Other Schools – See Senecaville

West Muskingum Local SD 1,800/K-12
4880 West Pike 43701 740-455-4052
Sharon Smith, supt. Fax 455-4063
www.westm.k12.oh.us
West Muskingum HS 600/9-12
150 Kimes Rd 43701 740-455-4050
Ed Miller, prin. Fax 452-7648
West Muskingum MS 400/6-8
100 Kimes Rd 43701 740-455-4055
Jim Spisak, prin. Fax 455-9717

Zanesville CSD 3,100/PK-12
160 N 4th St 43701 740-454-9751
Fax 455-4325
www.zanesville.k12.oh.us
Cleveland MS, 968 Pine St 43701 300/6-8
Flora Martin, prin. 740-453-0636
Roosevelt MS, 1429 Blue Ave 43701 300/6-8
Charlene Lewis, prin. 740-453-0711
Zanesville HS 1,100/9-12
1701 Blue Ave 43701 740-453-0335
Richard Sykes, prin. Fax 455-4329

Bishop Fenwick S 100/6-8
1030 E Main St 43701 740-453-2637
Mary Walsh, prin. Fax 454-0653
Bishop Rosecrans HS 200/9-12
1040 E Main St 43701 740-452-7504
Richard Smith Ed.D., prin. Fax 455-5080
Muskingum Christian Academy 100/K-12
1018 Marietta St 43701 740-454-7116
Ralph Weaver, prin. Fax 454-7174
Ohio University Post-Sec.
1425 Newark Rd 43701 740-453-0762
Valley Beauty School Post-Sec.
627 Main St 43701 740-452-6821
Zane State College Post-Sec.
1555 Newark Rd 43701 740-454-2501

Zoarville, Tuscarawas
Tuscarawas Valley Local SD 1,700/PK-12
2637 Tusky Valley Rd NE 44656 330-859-2213
Mark A. Murphy, supt. Fax 859-2706
www.tuskyvalley.k12.oh.us
Tuscarawas Valley HS 500/9-12
2637 Tusky Valley Rd NE 44656 330-859-2421
Jeff Raynor, prin. Fax 859-8805
Tuscarawas Valley MS 500/5-8
2633 Tusky Valley Rd NE 44656 330-859-2427
Timothy McCrate, prin. Fax 859-8845

OKLAHOMA

OKLAHOMA DEPARTMENT OF EDUCATION

2500 N Lincoln Blvd Rm 112, Oklahoma City 73105-4596
Telephone 405-521-3301
Fax 405-521-6205
Website http://www.sde.state.ok.us

Superintendent of Public Instruction Sandy Garrett

OKLAHOMA BOARD OF EDUCATION

2500 N Lincoln Blvd Rm 112, Oklahoma City 73105-4596

Chairperson Sandy Garrett

INTERLOCAL COOPERATIVES (IC)

Atoka-Coal Counties IC
Kris Hall, dir. 580-889-2664
PO Box 1231, Atoka 74525 Fax 889-6302
Cherokee County IC
Sheryl Lynn Rountree, dir. 918-456-1064
15481 N Jarvis Rd Fax 456-1041
Tahlequah 74464
Choctaw Nation IC
Terry Ragan, dir. 580-931-0691
PO Box 602, Durant 74702 Fax 931-0683
Five Star IC
Nancy Anderson, dir. 918-225-5600
1405 E Moses St, Cushing 74023 Fax 225-3026
www.fsilc.k12.ok.us

Garfield County IC
Gerald Hoeltzel, dir. 580-233-3071
PO Box 10036, Enid 73706 Fax 233-3072
McCurtain County IC
Cindy Duncan, dir. 580-286-3344
103 NE A Ave, Idabel 74745 Fax 286-5598
www.mccareok.com/
NewNet 66 IC
Mike Pennell, dir. 918-633-6896
310 N Weenonah Ave
Claremore 74017

Osage County IC
Gerald Harris, dir. 918-885-2667
207 E Main St, Hominy 74035 Fax 885-6742
www.ocic.k12.ok.us/
Pooled Investment IC
Jack Harrell, pres. 405-375-3696
2901 N Lincoln Blvd Fax 375-3696
Oklahoma City 73105
Seminole County IC
Dr. Audie Woodard, dir. 405-382-6121
630 Golf Rd, Seminole 74868 Fax 382-5254
Tri-County IC
Ty Harman, dir. 580-673-2310
PO Box 217, Fox 73435 Fax 673-2309

PUBLIC, PRIVATE AND CATHOLIC SECONDARY SCHOOLS

Achille, Bryan, Pop. 520
Achille ISD 400/PK-12
PO Box 280 74720 580-283-3775
Dr. Charles Caughern, supt. Fax 283-3787
Achille HS, PO Box 280 74720 100/9-12
Steve Evans, prin. 580-283-3775

Ada, Pontotoc, Pop. 15,999
Ada ISD 2,500/PK-12
PO Box 1359 74821 580-310-7200
Pat Harrison, supt. Fax 310-7206
www.adapss.com/
Ada JHS, 223 W 18th St 74820 600/7-9
David Smith, prin. 580-310-7260
Ada SHS, 1400 Stadium Dr 74820 500/10-12
Charlie Golightly, prin. 580-310-7220

Byng ISD 1,600/PK-12
500 S New Bethel Blvd 74820 580-436-3020
Steven Crawford, supt. Fax 436-3052
www.byngschools.com
Byng JHS 300/7-9
500 S New Bethel Blvd 74820 580-310-6743
Jim Wright, prin. Fax 310-6741
Byng SHS 300/10-12
500 S New Bethel Blvd 74820 580-310-6732
Alex Souza, prin. Fax 310-6730

Latta ISD 700/PK-12
13925 County Road 1560 74820 580-332-2092
Cliff Johnson, supt. Fax 332-3116
www.latta.k12.ok.us/
Latta JHS 200/7-9
13925 County Road 1560 74820 580-332-8180
Stan Cochran, prin.
Latta SHS 100/10-12
13925 County Road 1560 74820 580-332-3300
Stan Cochran, prin.

OK Dept. of Voc. & Tech. Education
Supt. — None
Pontotoc Technology Center Vo/Tech
601 W 33rd St 74820 580-310-2200
Greg Pierce, supt. Fax 436-0236

Vanoss ISD 500/PK-12
4665 County Road 1555 74820 580-759-2251
Cheryl Melton, supt. Fax 759-3080
www.vanoss.k12.ok.us
Vanoss HS 200/9-12
4665 County Road 1555 74820 580-759-2503
Gary Self, prin. Fax 759-3080

East Central University Post-Sec.
1100 E 14th St 74820 580-332-8000
Valley View Regional Hospital Post-Sec.
430 N Monte Vista St 74820 580-332-2323

Adair, Mayes, Pop. 708
Adair ISD 900/PK-12
PO Box 197 74330 918-785-2424
Tom Linihan, supt. Fax 785-2491
adairschools.org
Adair HS 300/9-12
PO Box 197 74330 918-785-2424
Clifton Collins, prin. Fax 785-2491
Adair MS 200/6-8
PO Box 197 74330 918-785-2425
Brad Rogers, prin. Fax 785-2491

Afton, Ottawa, Pop. 1,106
Afton ISD 400/K-12
PO Box 100 74331 918-257-8303
Randy Gardner, supt. Fax 257-4846
www.aftonschools.net/
Afton HS 200/9-12
PO Box 100 74331 918-257-8305
Alan Lauchner, prin. Fax 257-4846

OK Dept. of Voc. & Tech. Education
Supt. — None
Northeast Oklahoma Tech Center N Campus Vo/Tech
PO Box 219 74331 918-257-8324
Carol Farris, prin. Fax 257-4342

Agra, Lincoln, Pop. 358
Agra ISD 400/PK-12
PO Box 279 74824 918-375-2262
Wesley McFarland, supt. Fax 375-2263
www.agra.k12.ok.us/
Agra HS 100/9-12
PO Box 279 74824 918-375-2261
John Lazenby, prin. Fax 375-2260

Alex, Grady, Pop. 657
Alex ISD 300/K-12
PO Box 188 73002 405-785-2605
Norvel Heston, supt. Fax 785-2914
www.alex.k12.ok.us/
Alex JSHS 100/7-12
PO Box 188 73002 405-785-2264
Tim Persinger, prin. Fax 785-9976

Aline, Alfalfa, Pop. 197
Aline-Cleo ISD 200/PK-12
PO Box 49 73716 580-463-2255
Dwayne Noble, supt. Fax 463-2256
www.alinecleo.k12.ok.us
Aline-Cleo Springs HS 100/9-12
PO Box 49 73716 580-463-2256
Jim Patton, prin. Fax 463-2256

Allen, Pontotoc, Pop. 957
Allen ISD 400/PK-12
PO Box 430 74825 580-857-2417
David Lassiter, supt. Fax 857-2636
www.allen.k12.ok.us/
Allen HS 100/9-12
PO Box 430 74825 580-857-2416
Rip Garcia, prin. Fax 857-2636

Altus, Jackson, Pop. 19,899
Altus ISD 4,200/PK-12
PO Box 558 73522 580-481-2100
Bob Drury, supt. Fax 481-2129
www.altusschools.k12.ok.us
Altus JHS 700/8-9
PO Box 558 73522 580-481-2173
Roe Worbes, prin. Fax 481-2547
Altus SHS 800/10-12
PO Box 558 73522 580-481-2167
Mark Haught, prin. Fax 481-2545

CareerTech Skills Centers
Supt. — None
Dom Garrison, supt.
Altus Skills Center Vo/Tech
PO Box 668 73522 580-477-1617

Navajo ISD 400/K-12
15695 S County Road 210 73521 580-482-7742
Gary Montgomery, supt. Fax 482-7749
www.navajo.k12.ok.us
Navajo JSHS 100/7-12
15695 S County Road 210 73521 580-482-7742
Floyd Roach, prin. Fax 482-7749

OK Dept. of Voc. & Tech. Education
Supt. — None
Southwest Technology Center Vo/Tech
711 W Tamarack Rd 73521 580-477-2250
Dr. June Knight, supt. Fax 477-0138

Western Oklahoma State College Post-Sec.
2801 N Main St 73521 580-477-2000

Alva, Woods, Pop. 4,900
Alva ISD 1,000/PK-12
418 Flynn St 73717 580-327-4823
Don Rader, supt. Fax 327-2965
www.alvaschools.com
Alva HS 300/9-12
501 14th St 73717 580-327-3682
Steve Parkhurst, prin. Fax 327-4240
Alva MS 200/6-8
800 Flynn St 73717 580-327-0608
Terry Conder, prin. Fax 327-4255

CareerTech Skills Centers
Supt. — None
Dom Garrison, supt.
Alva Skills Center Vo/Tech
1856 E Flynn St 73717 580-327-0783

OK Dept. of Voc. & Tech. Education
Supt. — None
Northwest Technology Center Vo/Tech
1801 11th St 73717 580-327-0344
Freelin Roberts, supt. Fax 327-5467

Northwestern Oklahoma State University Post-Sec.
709 Oklahoma Blvd 73717 580-327-1700

Amber, Grady, Pop. 522
Amber-Pocasset ISD 300/PK-12
PO Box 38 73004 405-224-5768
Jack Jerman, supt. Fax 224-5115
Amber-Pocasset HS 100/10-12
PO Box 38 73004 405-224-4017
Chad Hance, prin. Fax 224-5115
Amber-Pocasset JHS 7-9
PO Box 38 73004 405-224-4017
Chad Hance, prin. Fax 224-5115

Anadarko, Caddo, Pop. 6,584
Anadarko ISD 2,000/PK-12
1400 S Mission St 73005 405-247-6605
Tom Cantrell, supt. Fax 247-6819
Anadarko HS 600/9-12
1400 Warrior Dr 73005 405-247-2486
Lynn Bellamy, prin. Fax 247-7066
Anadarko MS 400/6-8
900 W College St 73005 405-247-6671
Doug Hall, prin. Fax 247-3666

Antlers, Pushmataha, Pop. 2,508
Antlers ISD 1,000/K-12
PO Box 627 74523 580-298-5504
Mark Virden, supt. Fax 298-4006
www.antlers.k12.ok.us
Antlers HS 300/9-12
PO Box 627 74523 580-298-2141
Bryan McNutt, prin. Fax 298-4019
Obuch MS 200/6-8
PO Box 627 74523 580-298-3308
Jerry Brown, prin. Fax 298-4012

Apache, Caddo, Pop. 1,597
Boone-Apache ISD 600/PK-12
PO Box 354 73006 580-588-3369
James Hooper, supt. Fax 588-3400
www.apache.k12.ok.us/
Apache HS 200/9-12
PO Box 354 73006 580-588-3358
Karen Rodenberg, prin. Fax 588-2079
Apache MS, PO Box 354 73006 100/7-8
Jayne Ivy, prin. 580-588-2122

Arapaho, Custer, Pop. 709
Arapaho ISD 300/PK-12
PO Box 160 73620 580-323-3261
Fax 323-5886
www.arapaho.k12.ok.us/
Arapaho HS 100/9-12
PO Box 160 73620 580-323-3261
Ken Downs, prin. Fax 323-3469

Ardmore, Carter, Pop. 24,280
Ardmore ISD 3,100/PK-12
PO Box 1709 73402 580-226-7650
Dr. Ruth Ann Carr, supt. Fax 226-7652
www.ardmore.k12.ok.us
Ardmore HS 800/9-12
PO Box 1709 73402 580-226-7680
Bobby Upshaw, prin. Fax 221-3012
Ardmore MS 700/6-8
PO Box 1709 73402 580-223-2475
Ron Beach, prin. Fax 221-3060

CareerTech Skills Centers
Supt. — None
Dom Garrison, supt.
Ardmore Skills Center Vo/Tech
204 Scenic State Highway 77 73401 580-223-4049

Dickson ISD 1,200/PK-12
4762 State Highway 199 73401 580-223-9557
Sherry Howe, supt. Fax 223-7947
www.dickson.k12.ok.us/
Dickson HS 400/9-12
4762 State Highway 199 73401 580-226-0633
Mike Martin, prin. Fax 223-7011
Dickson JHS 200/7-8
4762 State Highway 199 73401 580-223-2700
Brad Jones, prin. Fax 223-7947

OK Dept. of Voc. & Tech. Education
Supt. — None
Southern Oklahoma Technology Center Vo/Tech
2610 Sam Noble Pkwy 73401 580-223-2070
David Powell, supt. Fax 223-2120

Plainview ISD 1,300/PK-12
1140 S Plainview Rd 73401 580-223-6319
Steve Merlyn, supt. Fax 490-3190
www.plainview.k12.ok.us/
Plainview HS 400/9-12
1140 S Plainview Rd 73401 580-223-5877
Tim Parham, prin. Fax 490-3191
Plainview MS 300/6-8
1140 S Plainview Rd 73401 580-223-6502
Lisa Hartman, prin.

Ardmore Adventist Academy 50/1-12
154 Beaver Academy Rd 73401 580-223-4948
Oklahoma State Horseshoeing School Post-Sec.
4802 Dogwood Rd 73401 580-223-0064

Arkoma, LeFlore, Pop. 2,191
Arkoma ISD 400/PK-12
PO Box 349 74901 918-875-3351
Katie Blagg, supt. Fax 875-3780
www.arkoma.k12.ok.us/
Arkoma HS 100/9-12
PO Box 349 74901 918-875-3353
Katie Blagg, prin. Fax 875-3780

Arnett, Ellis, Pop. 497
Arnett ISD 200/PK-12
PO Box 317 73832 580-885-7811
Rusty Puffinbarger, supt. Fax 885-7922
www.arnett.k12.ok.us/
Arnett HS 100/9-12
PO Box 317 73832 580-885-7285
Bob Dobrinski, prin. Fax 885-7922

Asher, Pottawatomie, Pop. 434
Asher ISD, PO Box 168 74826 200/PK-12
Terry Grissom, supt. 405-784-2332
www.asher.k12.ok.us
Asher HS, PO Box 168 74826 100/9-12
Jamie Chambers, prin. 405-784-2331

Atoka, Atoka, Pop. 3,044
Atoka ISD 900/PK-12
PO Box 720 74525 580-889-6611
Mark McPherson, supt. Fax 889-2513
atoka.org
Atoka HS 400/9-12
PO Box 720 74525 580-889-3361
Brian Armstrong, prin. Fax 889-6453
McCall MS 200/6-8
PO Box 720 74525 580-889-5640
Chad Graham, prin. Fax 889-4064

OK Dept. of Voc. & Tech. Education
Supt. — None
Kiamichi Technology Center Vo/Tech
PO Box 240 74525 580-889-7321
Elaine Gee, dir. Fax 889-5642

Tushka ISD 400/PK-12
204 S Pecan St 74525 580-889-7355
Bill Pingleton, supt. Fax 889-6144
Tushka HS 200/9-12
204 S Pecan St 74525 580-889-7355
Matt Simpson, prin. Fax 889-6144

Balko, Beaver
Balko ISD 100/PK-12
RR 1 Box 37 73931 580-646-3385
Brent Phelps, supt. Fax 646-3499
Balko HS 50/9-12
RR 1 Box 37 73931 580-646-3385
Brent Phelps, prin. Fax 646-3499

Barnsdall, Osage, Pop. 1,280
Barnsdall ISD 400/K-12
PO Box 629 74002 918-847-2271
Rick Loggins, supt. Fax 847-3029
www.barnsdall.k12.ok.us/
Barnsdall HS, PO Box 629 74002 100/10-12
Sam Wofford, prin. 918-847-2721
Barnsdall JHS, PO Box 629 74002 100/7-9
Sam Wofford, prin. 918-847-2721

Bartlesville, Washington, Pop. 34,734
Bartlesville ISD 5,900/PK-12
PO Box 1357 74005 918-336-8600
Dr. Gary Quinn, supt. Fax 337-3643
www.bps-ok.org
Bartlesville Mid HS 1,000/9-10
PO Box 1357 74005 918-333-4444
Jason Langham, prin. Fax 335-6311
Bartlesville SHS 900/11-12
PO Box 1357 74005 918-336-3311
Chuck McCauley, prin. Fax 337-6226
Central MS 700/6-8
PO Box 1357 74005 918-336-9302
LaDonna Chancellor, prin. Fax 337-6270
Madison MS 700/6-8
PO Box 1357 74005 918-333-3176
Lexie Radebaugh, prin. Fax 335-6377

OK Dept. of Voc. & Tech. Education
Supt. — None
Tri-County Technology Center Vo/Tech
6101 Nowata Rd 74006 918-333-2422
Anita Risner, supt. Fax 331-3274

American Christian S of Bartlesville 100/PK-12
396980 W 2400 Rd 74006 918-331-0500
Danny Reich, hdmstr. Fax 331-0501
Oklahoma Wesleyan University Post-Sec.
2201 Silver Lake Rd 74006 918-333-6151
Wesleyan Christian S 200/PK-12
1780 Silver Lake Rd 74006 918-333-8631
Curtis Cloud, prin. Fax 333-8632

Battiest, McCurtain
Battiest ISD 300/PK-12
PO Box 199 74722 580-241-7810
Lendall Martin, supt. Fax 241-7847
www.battiest.k12.ok.us/
Battiest HS 100/9-12
PO Box 199 74722 580-241-5550
Lendall Martin, prin. Fax 241-7847

Beaver, Beaver, Pop. 1,414
Beaver ISD 400/PK-12
PO Box 580 73932 580-625-3444
Scott Kinsey, supt. Fax 625-3690
Beaver HS 100/9-12
PO Box 580 73932 580-625-3444
Michael McVay, prin. Fax 625-3690

Beggs, Okmulgee, Pop. 1,375
Beggs ISD 1,000/PK-12
1201 W 9th St 74421 918-267-3628
Marsha Norman, supt. Fax 267-3635
www.beggs.k12.ok.us
Beggs HS 300/9-12
1201 W 9th St 74421 918-267-3625
Merrill Masters, prin. Fax 267-3624
Beggs MS 200/5-8
1201 W 9th St 74421 918-267-4916
Cindy Swearingen, prin. Fax 267-4779

Bennington, Bryan, Pop. 296
Bennington ISD 300/K-12
729 N Perry St 74723 580-847-2737
James Parrish, supt. Fax 847-2787
www.benningtonisd.org/
Bennington HS 100/9-12
729 N Perry St 74723 580-847-2310
David Dewalt, prin. Fax 847-2787

Bethany, Oklahoma, Pop. 19,786
Bethany ISD 1,400/PK-12
6721 NW 42nd St 73008 405-789-3801
Dr. Kent Shellenberger, supt. Fax 499-4606
www.bps.k12.ok.us
Bethany HS 400/9-12
6721 NW 42nd St 73008 405-789-6370
Rocky George, prin. Fax 499-4634
Bethany MS, 6721 NW 42nd St 73008 300/6-8
Sherry Adkison, prin. 405-787-3240

Putnam City ISD
Supt. — See Oklahoma City
Western Oaks MS 600/6-8
7210 NW 23rd St 73008 405-789-4434
Lynette Thompson, prin. Fax 491-7616

Southern Nazarene University Post-Sec.
6729 NW 39th Expy 73008 405-789-6400
Southwestern Christian University Post-Sec.
PO Box 340 73008 405-789-7661

Billings, Noble, Pop. 562
Billings ISD 100/PK-12
PO Box 39 74630 580-725-3271
Les Justus, supt. Fax 725-3278
www.billings.k12.ok.us
Billings HS 50/9-12
PO Box 39 74630 580-725-3271
Les Justus, prin. Fax 725-3278

Binger, Caddo, Pop. 708
Binger-Oney ISD 300/K-12
PO Box 280 73009 405-656-2304
Sharon Kniffin, supt. Fax 656-2267
www.binger-oney.k12.ok.us/
Binger-Oney HS 100/9-12
PO Box 280 73009 405-656-2304
Kevin Sims, prin. Fax 656-2267

Bixby, Tulsa, Pop. 18,600
Bixby ISD 4,000/PK-12
109 N Armstrong St 74008 918-366-2200
Dr. Mary Jane Bias, supt. Fax 366-4241
www.bixbyps.org
Bixby HS 1,200/9-12
109 N Armstrong St 74008 918-366-2234
Lou Gregorio, prin. Fax 366-2350
Bixby MS 600/7-8
109 N Armstrong St 74008 918-366-2201
Sean Spellecy, prin. Fax 366-2337

Blackwell, Kay, Pop. 7,297
Blackwell ISD 1,400/PK-12
201 E Blackwell Ave 74631 580-363-2570
Lesa Ward, supt. Fax 363-5513
www.blackwell.k12.ok.us/
Blackwell HS 500/9-12
303 E Coolidge Ave 74631 580-363-3553
Dan Bringham, prin. Fax 363-2133
Blackwell MS 300/6-8
1041 S 1st St 74631 580-363-2100
Eric Webb, prin. Fax 363-7010

Blair, Jackson, Pop. 823
Blair ISD 300/PK-12
PO Box 428 73526 580-563-2632
Gary McLaughlin, supt. Fax 563-9166
www.blairschool.org
Blair HS 100/9-12
PO Box 428 73526 580-563-2486
Mike Rutherford, prin. Fax 563-9166

Blanchard, McClain, Pop. 3,678
Blanchard ISD 1,300/K-12
211 N Tyler Ave 73010 405-485-3391
Sandra Park, supt. Fax 485-2985
www.blanchard.k12.ok.us/
Blanchard HS 400/9-12
400 N Harrison Ave 73010 405-485-3392
Glen Castle, prin. Fax 485-9549
Blanchard MS 300/6-8
400 N Harrison Ave 73010 405-485-3393
Joseph Billington, prin. Fax 485-9103

Bridge Creek ISD 1,100/K-12
2209 E Sooner Rd 73010 405-387-4880
Randy Davenport, supt. Fax 387-4882
www.bridgecreek.k12.ok.us/
Bridge Creek HS 300/9-12
2209 E Sooner Rd 73010 405-387-3981
K.B. Wedel, prin.
Bridge Creek MS 300/6-8
2209 E Sooner Rd 73010 405-387-9681
David Morrow, prin.

Bluejacket, Craig, Pop. 285
Bluejacket ISD 200/PK-12
PO Box 29 74333 918-784-2365
Almeda Carroll, supt. Fax 784-2130
www.bluejacket.k12.ok.us
Bluejacket HS 100/9-12
PO Box 29 74333 918-784-2365
Shellie Baker, prin. Fax 784-2130
Bluejacket MS, PO Box 29 74333 50/6-8
Shellie Baker, prin. 918-784-2365

Boise City, Cimarron, Pop. 1,322
Boise City ISD 300/K-12
PO Box 1116 73933 580-544-3110
Dan Faulkner, supt. Fax 544-2972
www.boisecity.k12.ok.us/
Boise City HS, PO Box 1115 73933 100/9-12
Kim Jenkins, prin. 580-544-3111

Bokchito, Bryan, Pop. 570
Rock Creek SD 500/PK-12
200 E Steakley St 74726 580-295-3137
Preston Burns, supt. Fax 295-3762
www.rockcreekisd.net
Rock Creek HS 100/9-12
200 E Steakley St 74726 580-295-3761
John Cartwright, prin. Fax 295-3854

Bokoshe, LeFlore, Pop. 462
Bokoshe ISD 200/PK-12
PO Box 158 74930 918-969-2491
Dennis Shoup, supt. Fax 969-2493
www.bokoshe.k12.ok.us
Bokoshe HS, PO Box 158 74930 100/10-12
Jeremy Dyer, prin. 918-969-2341
Bokoshe MS, PO Box 158 74930 100/7-9
Jeremy Dyer, prin. 918-969-2341

Boley, Okfuskee, Pop. 1,102
Boley ISD 100/PK-12
PO Box 248 74829 918-667-3324
Gretana Gonzales, supt. Fax 667-3476
Boley HS 50/9-12
PO Box 248 74829 918-667-3324
Gretana Gonzales, prin. Fax 667-3476

CareerTech Skills Centers
Supt. — None
Dom Garrison, supt.
Boley Skills Center Vo/Tech
PO Box 185 74829 918-667-3768

Boswell, Choctaw, Pop. 701
Boswell ISD 400/PK-12
PO Box 839 74727 580-566-2558
Gerald Stegall, supt. Fax 566-2265
www.boswell.k12.ok.us/
Boswell HS 100/9-12
PO Box 839 74727 580-566-2735
Cindy Duncan, prin. Fax 566-2265
Boswell MS 100/7-8
PO Box 839 74727 580-566-2785
Keith Edge, prin. Fax 566-2265

Bowlegs, Seminole, Pop. 371
Bowlegs ISD, PO Box 88 74830 — 300/PK-12
Bobbette Hamilton, supt. — 405-398-4172
www.bowlegs.k12.ok.us
Bowlegs HS — 100/9-12
PO Box 88 74830 — 405-398-4321
David Morris, prin. — Fax 398-4327

Boynton, Muskogee, Pop. 278
Boynton-Moton ISD — 200/PK-12
PO Box 97 74422 — 918-472-7330
Fax 472-7410
Boynton-Moton HS — 100/9-12
PO Box 97 74422 — 918-472-7310
Gary Calip, prin. — Fax 472-7410

Braggs, Muskogee, Pop. 307
Braggs ISD — 200/PK-12
PO Box 59 74423 — 918-487-5265
Harry Atkins, supt. — Fax 487-7171
www.braggs.k12.ok.us
Braggs HS — 100/9-12
PO Box 59 74423 — 918-487-5265
Kenneth Pattison, prin. — Fax 487-7171

Braman, Kay, Pop. 239
Braman ISD — 100/K-12
PO Box 130 74632 — 580-385-2191
Mat Luse, supt. — Fax 385-2193
Braman HS — 50/9-12
PO Box 130 74632 — 580-385-2191
Mat Luse, prin. — Fax 385-2193

Bristow, Creek, Pop. 4,397
Bristow ISD — 1,600/PK-12
420 N Main St 74010 — 918-367-5555
Dr. Jeanene Barnett, supt. — Fax 367-5848
www.bristow.k12.ok.us
Bristow HS — 500/9-12
420 N Main St 74010 — 918-367-2241
Rick Gaines, prin. — Fax 367-5849
Bristow MS — 400/6-8
420 N Main St 74010 — 918-367-3551
Brian Lomenick, prin. — Fax 367-1362

Broken Arrow, Tulsa, Pop. 86,228
Broken Arrow ISD — 14,700/PK-12
601 S Main St 74012 — 918-259-4300
Dr. Jim Sisney, supt. — Fax 258-0399
www.baschools.org/
Broken Arrow North Intermediate HS — 1,100/9-10
808 E College St 74012 — 918-259-4320
Steven Nida, prin. — Fax 258-0796
Broken Arrow SHS — 2,100/11-12
1901 E Albany St 74012 — 918-259-4310
Rob Armstrong, prin. — Fax 355-3676
Broken Arrow South Intermediate HS — 1,200/9-10
301 W New Orleans St 74011 — 918-259-4330
Richard Dale, prin. — Fax 451-1964
Centennial MS — 700/6-8
225 E Omaha St 74012 — 918-259-4340
Amy Fichtner, prin. — Fax 251-8347
Childers MS — 600/6-8
301 E Tucson St 74011 — 918-259-4350
Elizabeth Burns, prin. — Fax 451-5465
Haskell MS — 900/6-8
412 S 9th St 74012 — 918-259-4360
Phil Tucker, prin. — Fax 251-8685
Oliver MS — 800/6-8
3100 W New Orleans St 74011 — 918-259-4590
Tom Sorrells, prin. — Fax 250-8185
Sequoyah MS — 600/6-8
2701 S Elm Pl 74012 — 918-259-4370
Heidi McAnulty, prin. — Fax 451-2167

OK Dept. of Voc. & Tech. Education
Supt. — None
Tulsa Tech Center Broken Arrow Campus — Vo/Tech
4600 S Olive Ave 74011 — 918-828-3000
Brad Wayman, dir. — Fax 828-3009

Union ISD
Supt. — See Tulsa
Union Eighth Grade Center — 1,100/8-8
6501 S Garnett Rd 74012 — 918-250-9541
Marla Robinson, prin. — Fax 461-3899
Union Intermediate HS — 2,200/9-10
7616 S Garnett Rd 74012 — 918-254-8644
John Chargois, prin. — Fax 252-4779

Broken Arrow Beauty College — Post-Sec.
400 S Elm Pl 74012 — 918-251-9660
Grace Christian S — 400/PK-12
9610 S Garnett Rd 74012 — 918-249-9100
Dr. Ken Stewart, supt. — Fax 317-5156
Summit Christian Academy — 400/K-12
200 E Broadway St 74012 — 918-251-1997

Broken Bow, McCurtain, Pop. 4,170
Broken Bow ISD — 1,800/PK-12
108 W 5th St 74728 — 580-584-3306
Carolyn Davis, supt. — Fax 584-9482
www.bbisd.org
Broken Bow HS — 700/9-12
108 W 5th St 74728 — 580-584-3365
Daryl Williams, prin. — Fax 584-2064
Rector Johnson MS — 300/6-8
108 W 5th St 74728 — 580-584-9603
David Williams, prin. — Fax 584-2549

Buffalo, Harper, Pop. 1,102
Buffalo ISD — 100/K-12
PO Box 130 73834 — 580-735-2419
Terry Chapman, supt. — Fax 735-2619
www.buffalo.k12.ok.us
Buffalo S — 100/K-12
PO Box 130 73834 — 580-735-2448
Sarah Yauk, prin. — Fax 735-2619

Bunch, Adair
Cave Springs SD — 300/PK-12
PO Box 200 74931 — 918-775-2364
Steve Adair, supt. — Fax 776-2052
www.cavesprings.k12.ok.us
Cave Springs HS, PO Box 200 74931 — 100/9-12
Darlene Adair, prin. — 918-696-8604

Burlington, Alfalfa, Pop. 146
Burlington ISD — 200/PK-12
PO Box 17 73722 — 580-431-2501
Glen Elliott, supt. — Fax 431-2237
www.burlingtonschool.com/
Burlington HS, PO Box 17 73722 — 100/9-12
Joe Feely, prin. — 580-431-2222

Burneyville, Love
Turner ISD — 300/PK-12
PO Box 159 73430 — 580-276-1307
James Gilmartin, supt. — Fax 276-2006
www.turnerisd.org
Turner HS, PO Box 159 73430 — 100/9-12
Michael Palmer, prin. — 580-276-3873

Burns Flat, Washita, Pop. 1,731
Burns Flat-Dill City ISD — 600/PK-12
PO Box 129 73624 — 580-562-4844
Rick E. Garrison, supt. — Fax 562-4847
Burns Flat-Dill City JSHS — 100/9-12
PO Box 129 73624 — 580-562-4846
Ron Hughes, prin.

OK Dept. of Voc. & Tech. Education
Supt. — None
Western Technology Center — Vo/Tech
PO Box 1469 73624 — 580-562-3181
Gene Orsack, supt. — Fax 562-4476

Butler, Custer, Pop. 334
Butler ISD — 100/PK-12
PO Box 127 73625 — 580-664-3295
Rod McDonald, supt. — Fax 664-5286
www.butler.k12.ok.us/
Butler HS — 50/9-12
PO Box 127 73625 — 580-664-3295
Leon Beall, prin. — Fax 664-5286

Cache, Comanche, Pop. 2,406
Cache ISD — 1,400/PK-12
201 W H Ave 73527 — 580-429-3266
Randy Batt, supt. — Fax 429-3271
www.cache.k12.ok.us
Cache HS, 201 W H Ave 73527 — 400/9-12
Gary Michael, prin. — 580-429-3214
Cache MS, 201 W H Ave 73527 — 300/6-8
Debbie Hoffman, prin. — 580-429-8489

Caddo, Bryan, Pop. 965
Caddo ISD — 500/PK-12
PO Box 128 74729 — 580-367-2208
Richard Thomas, supt. — Fax 367-2837
www.caddoisd.org
Caddo HS — 100/9-12
PO Box 128 74729 — 580-367-2208
Patrick Mitchell, prin. — Fax 367-2837

Calera, Bryan, Pop. 1,784
Calera ISD — 600/PK-12
PO Box 386 74730 — 580-434-5700
Aaron Newcomb, supt. — Fax 434-5800
www.caleraisd.k12.ok.us
Calera HS, PO Box 386 74730 — 200/9-12
Karen Hughes, prin. — 580-434-5158

Calumet, Canadian, Pop. 534
Calumet ISD — 200/K-12
PO Box 10 73014 — 405-893-2222
Keith Weldon, supt. — Fax 893-8019
Calumet HS — 100/9-12
PO Box 10 73014 — 405-893-2222
Jimmie Smith, prin. — Fax 893-8019
Calumet JHS — 50/7-8
PO Box 10 73014 — 405-893-2222
Jimmie Smith, prin. — Fax 893-8019

Calvin, Hughes, Pop. 269
Calvin ISD — 200/PK-12
PO Box 127 74531 — 405-645-2411
Jon Tuck, supt. — Fax 645-2384
www.calvin.k12.ok.us
Calvin HS — 100/9-12
PO Box 127 74531 — 405-645-2411
Curtis Fitzgerald, prin. — Fax 645-2384

Cameron, LeFlore, Pop. 320
Cameron ISD — 500/PK-12
PO Box 190 74932 — 918-654-3225
John Long, supt. — Fax 654-7387
www.cameron.k12.ok.us/
Cameron HS — 200/9-12
PO Box 190 74932 — 918-654-3412
Edward Martin, prin. — Fax 654-3826

Canadian, Pittsburg, Pop. 243
Canadian ISD — 400/PK-12
PO Box 168 74425 — 918-339-7251
Rodney Karch, supt. — Fax 339-2393
Canadian HS, PO Box 168 74425 — 100/9-12
Bud Rattan, prin. — 918-339-2705

Caney, Atoka, Pop. 208
Caney ISD — 200/PK-12
PO Box 60 74533 — 580-889-1996
Tommy Johnson, supt. — Fax 889-5033
www.caneyisd.org/
Caney HS — 100/9-12
PO Box 60 74533 — 580-889-6607
Phil Daniel, prin. — Fax 889-7922

Canton, Blaine, Pop. 602
Canton ISD — 400/PK-12
PO Box 639 73724 — 580-886-3516
Gayle Hajny, supt. — Fax 886-3501
www.canton.k12.ok.us
Canton HS, PO Box 639 73724 — 100/9-12
Darrell Gunsaulis, prin. — 580-886-2256

Canute, Washita, Pop. 528
Canute ISD — 200/PK-12
PO Box 490 73626 — 580-472-3295
Mike Maddox, supt. — Fax 472-3187
Canute HS — 100/9-12
PO Box 490 73626 — 580-472-3782
Kevin Merz, prin. — Fax 472-3187

Carnegie, Caddo, Pop. 1,603
Carnegie ISD — 600/K-12
315 S Carnegie St 73015 — 580-654-1470
Donny Darrow, supt. — Fax 654-1644
www.carnegieschools.com
Carnegie JHS — 200/7-9
315 S Carnegie St 73015 — 580-654-1766
Donny Darrow, dean — Fax 654-2281
Carnegie SHS — 100/10-12
315 S Carnegie St 73015 — 580-654-1266
Lonnie Bliss, prin. — Fax 654-2772

Carney, Lincoln, Pop. 644
Carney ISD — 200/PK-12
PO Box 240 74832 — 405-865-2344
Dewayne Osborn, supt. — Fax 865-2345
Carney HS, PO Box 240 74832 — 100/9-12
Mike Parsons, prin. — 405-865-2344

Cashion, Kingfisher, Pop. 716
Cashion ISD — 400/K-12
PO Box 100 73016 — 405-433-2741
Todd Garrison, supt. — Fax 433-2646
Cashion HS — 100/9-12
PO Box 100 73016 — 405-433-2575
Marva Oard, prin. — Fax 433-2646

Catoosa, Rogers, Pop. 6,440
Catoosa SD — 2,300/PK-12
2000 S Cherokee St 74015 — 918-266-8603
Larry Cale, supt. — Fax 266-1525
www.catoosa.k12.ok.us
Catoosa HS — 700/9-12
2000 S Cherokee St 74015 — 918-266-8619
Connie Cypert, prin. — Fax 266-1486
Wells MS — 600/6-8
2000 S Cherokee St 74015 — 918-266-8623
George Linihan, prin. — Fax 266-1282

Cement, Caddo, Pop. 530
Cement ISD — 200/PK-12
PO Box 60 73017 — 405-489-3216
Connie Claborn, supt. — Fax 489-3219
Cement HS — 100/9-12
PO Box 60 73017 — 405-489-3218
Marion Claborn, prin. — Fax 489-3219

Chandler, Lincoln, Pop. 2,859
Chandler ISD — 1,100/PK-12
901 S CHS 74834 — 405-258-1450
Don Gray, supt. — Fax 258-2657
www.chandler.k12.ok.us/
Chandler HS — 300/9-12
901 S CHS 74834 — 405-258-1269
Rod Pitts, prin. — Fax 240-5715
Chandler JHS — 200/7-8
901 S CHS 74834 — 405-258-0183
Mark Howard, prin. — Fax 258-1850

Chattanooga, Comanche, Pop. 431
Chattanooga ISD — 300/PK-12
PO Box 129 73528 — 580-597-3347
Chuck Hood, supt. — Fax 597-3344
www.chatty.k12.ok.us/
Chattanooga HS, PO Box 129 73528 — 100/9-12
Jerry Brown, prin. — 580-597-3347

Checotah, McIntosh, Pop. 3,533
Checotah ISD — 1,300/PK-12
PO Box 289 74426 — 918-473-5610
Robert Bible, supt. — Fax 473-1020
Checotah HS — 400/9-12
PO Box 289 74426 — 918-473-2239
Pam Keeter, prin. — Fax 473-2532
Checotah MS — 300/6-8
PO Box 289 74426 — 918-473-5912
Brian Terry, prin. — Fax 473-1020

Chelsea, Rogers, Pop. 2,262
Chelsea ISD — 1,100/PK-12
206 E 4th St 74016 — 918-789-2528
Mike Martin, supt. — Fax 789-3271
www.chelseadragons.net
Chelsea HS, 206 E 4th St 74016 — 400/9-12
Paul Gruenberg, prin. — 918-789-2533
Chelsea JHS, 206 E 4th St 74016 — 200/7-8
Meg Moss, prin. — 918-789-2521

Cherokee, Alfalfa, Pop. 1,485
Cherokee ISD — 300/PK-12
PO Box 325 73728 — 580-596-3391
Lance Miller, supt. — Fax 596-2217
Cherokee HS, PO Box 325 73728 — 100/9-12
Darral Barnett, prin. — 580-596-3391

Cheyenne, Roger Mills, Pop. 733
Cheyenne ISD — 300/PK-12
PO Box 650 73628 — 580-497-2666
Alton Rawlins, supt. — Fax 497-3373
www.cheyenne.k12.ok.us
Cheyenne HS, PO Box 650 73628 — 100/9-12
Phillip Butler, prin. — 580-497-3371

Chickasha, Grady, Pop. 16,849
Chickasha ISD — 2,800/PK-12
900 W Choctaw Ave 73018 — 405-222-6500
Jim Glaze, supt. — Fax 222-6590
chickasha.ok.schoolwebpages.com
Chickasha HS — 900/9-12
900 W Choctaw Ave 73018 — 405-222-6550
Beth Reigh-Edwards, prin. — Fax 222-6558
Chickasha MS — 600/6-8
900 W Choctaw Ave 73018 — 405-222-6530
Debra Reynolds, prin. — Fax 222-6594

OK Dept. of Voc. & Tech. Education
Supt. — None
Canadian Valley Technology Center — Vo/Tech
1401 W Michigan Ave 73018 — 405-224-7220
Earl Cowan, supt. — Fax 222-3839

Academy of Cosmetology — Post-Sec.
607 W Grand Ave 73018 — 405-222-2323
University of Sciences & Arts of OK — Post-Sec.
PO Box 82345 73018 — 405-224-3140

Choctaw, Oklahoma, Pop. 10,529
Choctaw/Nicoma Park ISD 4,600/PK-12
12880 NE 10th St 73020 405-769-4859
Dr. Jim McCharen, supt. Fax 769-9821
www.cnpschools.org
Choctaw HS 1,100/10-12
14300 NE 10th St 73020 405-390-8899
Donny Black, prin. Fax 390-2275
Choctaw JHS 600/7-9
14667 NE 3rd St 73020 405-390-2207
JeanAnn Gaona, prin. Fax 390-4439
Nicoma Park JHS 500/7-9
1321 Hickman Ave 73020 405-769-3106
David Reid, prin. Fax 769-9355

OK Dept. of Voc. & Tech. Education
Supt. — None
Eastern Oklahoma County Technology Ctr Vo/Tech
4601 N Choctaw Rd 73020 405-390-9591
Dr. Terry Underwood, supt. Fax 390-9598

Chouteau, Mayes, Pop. 1,992
Chouteau-Mazie ISD 1,000/PK-12
PO Box 969 74337 918-476-8336
Tom Turner, supt. Fax 476-8538
Chouteau-Mazie HS 300/9-12
PO Box 969 74337 918-476-8336
Donny Trammell, prin. Fax 476-8372
Chouteau-Mazie MS 200/6-8
PO Box 969 74337 918-476-8336
Charles Arnall, prin. Fax 476-8306

Claremore, Rogers, Pop. 17,161
Claremore ISD 4,000/PK-12
310 N Weenonah Ave 74017 918-699-7300
J. Michael McClaren, supt. Fax 341-8447
www.claremore.k12.ok.us
Claremore HS 1,200/9-12
1910 N Florence Ave 74017 918-341-0724
Fax 343-6331
Rogers JHS 600/7-8
1915 N Florence Ave 74017 918-341-7411
Terry Adams, prin. Fax 343-6332

Justus-Tiawah SD 500/PK-8
14902 E School Rd, 918-341-3626
David Garroutte, supt. Fax 341-4920
www.justus.k12.ok.us
Justus-Tiawah MS North Campus 100/7-8
15011 E 523 Rd, 918-341-1252
David Garroutte, prin. Fax 341-4920

Sequoyah ISD 1,400/PK-12
16441 S 4180 Rd 74017 918-341-5472
Terry Saul, supt. Fax 341-5764
www.sequoyaheagles.net
Sequoyah MS 300/7-9
16405 S 4180 Rd 74017 918-341-5537
Troy Steidley, prin. Fax 343-8102
Sequoyah SHS 300/10-12
16401 S 4180 Rd 74017 918-341-0642
Steve Johnson, prin. Fax 343-8105

Verdigris ISD 1,100/PK-12
8104 E 540 Rd, 918-266-7227
Michael Payne, supt. Fax 266-3910
vps.k12.ok.us
Verdigris HS 300/9-12
8104 E 540 Rd, 918-266-2336
Randall Risenhoover, prin. Fax 266-3910
Verdigris MS 300/5-8
8104 E 540 Rd, 918-266-6343
Denton Holland, prin. Fax 266-1554

Claremore Beauty College Post-Sec.
200 N Cherokee Ave 74017 918-341-4370
Claremore Christian S 100/PK-12
1055 W Blue Starr Dr 74017 918-341-1805
Ryan Mullins, prin. Fax 341-1011
Rogers State University Post-Sec.
1701 W Will Rogers Blvd 74017 918-343-7777

Clarita, Coal
Olney ISD 100/PK-12
PO Box 129 74535 580-428-3293
Jerry Romines, supt. Fax 428-3310
www.olney.k12.ok.us/
Olney HS 50/9-12
PO Box 129 74535 580-428-3293
Jerry Romines, prin. Fax 428-3310

Clayton, Pushmataha, Pop. 724
Clayton ISD 300/PK-12
PO Box 190 74536 918-569-4492
Jim Dominick, supt. Fax 569-7757
www.clayton.k12.ok.us
Clayton HS 100/9-12
PO Box 190 74536 918-569-4156
Lyndon Howze, prin. Fax 569-4680

Cleveland, Pawnee, Pop. 3,247
Cleveland ISD 1,700/PK-12
600 N Gilbert Ave 74020 918-358-2210
Dennis Smith, supt. Fax 358-3071
www.clevelandtigers.com/
Cleveland HS 500/9-12
323 N Gilbert Ave 74020 918-358-2210
Alan Baker, prin. Fax 358-2141
Cleveland MS 400/6-8
322 N Gilbert Ave 74020 918-358-2210
Noel Nation, prin. Fax 358-2534

Clinton, Custer, Pop. 8,363
Clinton ISD 1,800/PK-12
PO Box 729 73601 580-323-1800
Perry Adams, supt. Fax 323-1804
www.clinton.k12.ok.us/
Clinton HS 500/9-12
PO Box 729 73601 580-323-1230
Steve Hill, prin. Fax 323-1236
Clinton MS 300/7-8
PO Box 729 73601 580-323-4228
Peggy Constien, prin. Fax 323-3896

Coalgate, Coal, Pop. 1,889
Coalgate ISD 700/PK-12
PO Box 368 74538 580-927-2351
Joe A. McCulley, supt. Fax 927-2694
www.coalgateschools.org
Byrd MS 100/7-8
PO Box 368 74538 580-927-3560
Adam Beauchamp, prin. Fax 927-4031
Coalgate HS 200/9-12
PO Box 368 74538 580-927-2592
Jim Girten, prin. Fax 927-4020

Colbert, Bryan, Pop. 1,094
Colbert ISD 900/PK-12
PO Box 310 74733 580-296-2624
Jarvis Dobbs, supt. Fax 296-2088
www.colbert.k12.ok.us/
Colbert HS, PO Box 310 74733 200/9-12
William Goodson, prin. 580-296-2590
Colbert MS, PO Box 310 74733 100/7-8
Andy Goodson, prin. 580-296-2590

Colcord, Delaware, Pop. 851
Colcord ISD 800/PK-12
PO Box 188 74338 918-326-4116
Kelly Hampton, supt. Fax 326-4471
Colcord HS 300/9-12
PO Box 188 74338 918-326-4107
Jerry Swank, prin. Fax 326-4493
Colcord MS 200/6-8
PO Box 188 74338 918-326-4852
Robert Hampton, prin. Fax 326-4468

Coleman, Johnston
Coleman ISD 200/PK-12
PO Box 188 73432 580-937-4418
Rick Webb, supt. Fax 937-4866
Coleman HS 100/9-12
PO Box 188 73432 580-937-4418
Rick Webb, prin. Fax 937-4866

Collinsville, Tulsa, Pop. 4,325
Collinsville ISD 2,100/PK-12
1119 W Broadway St 74021 918-371-2386
Pat Herald, supt. Fax 371-4285
www.collinsville.k12.ok.us/
Collinsville HS 600/9-12
2400 W Broadway St 74021 918-371-3382
Cory Slagle, prin. Fax 371-6904
Collinsville MS 500/6-8
1415 W Center St 74021 918-371-2541
Kelly Hamlin, prin. Fax 371-1302

Comanche, Stephens, Pop. 1,516
Comanche ISD 1,000/K-12
1030 Ash Ave 73529 580-439-2900
Terry Davidson, supt. Fax 439-2907
Comanche HS 300/9-12
1030 Ash Ave 73529 580-439-2933
Steven Dunham, prin. Fax 439-2950
Comanche MS 200/6-8
1030 Ash Ave 73529 580-439-2922
Brent Crow, prin. Fax 439-2979

Commerce, Ottawa, Pop. 2,573
Commerce ISD 800/PK-12
420 D St 74339 918-675-4316
Jim Haynes, supt. Fax 675-4464
www.commercetigers.net
Commerce HS 200/9-12
420 D St 74339 918-675-4343
Jim Buttram, prin. Fax 675-4682
Commerce MS 200/6-8
500 Commerce St 74339 918-675-4101
Herb Logan, prin. Fax 675-5353

Copan, Washington, Pop. 809
Copan ISD 400/PK-12
PO Box 429 74022 918-532-4490
Steve Stanley, supt. Fax 532-4568
www.copan.k12.ok.us/
Copan HS, PO Box 429 74022 100/9-12
Jay Vernon, prin. 918-532-4344

Cordell, Washita, Pop. 2,809
Cordell ISD 700/PK-12
PO Box 290 73632 580-832-3420
Tim Puett, supt. Fax 832-4108
www.cordell.k12.ok.us
Cordell JHS, PO Box 290 73632 100/7-9
Larry Johnson, prin. 580-832-2233
Cordell SHS, PO Box 290 73632 100/10-12
Larry Johnson, prin. 580-832-3432

Corn, Washita, Pop. 578
Washita Heights ISD 200/PK-12
PO Box 8 73024 580-343-2228
Tim Merchant, supt. Fax 343-2259
www.whchiefs.k12.ok.us/
Washita Heights HS 100/9-12
PO Box 8 73024 580-343-2298
Jim Shelton, prin. Fax 343-2259

Corn Bible Academy 100/7-12
PO Box 38 73024 580-343-2262
Mark Thiessen, prin. Fax 343-2261

Council Hill, Muskogee, Pop. 131
Midway ISD 200/PK-12
PO Box 127 74428 918-474-3434
Don Ford, supt. Fax 474-3636
Midway HS 100/9-12
PO Box 127 74428 918-474-3434
Curt Been, prin. Fax 474-3636

Covington, Garfield, Pop. 542
Covington-Douglas ISD 300/PK-12
PO Box 9 73730 580-864-7481
Darren Sharp, supt. Fax 864-7644
www.c-d.k12.ok.us
Covington-Douglas HS 100/9-12
PO Box 9 73730 580-864-7482
Dena Stewart, prin. Fax 864-7644

Coweta, Wagoner, Pop. 8,352
Coweta ISD 2,900/PK-12
PO Box 550 74429 918-486-6506
Sean McDaniel, supt. Fax 486-4167
www.cowetaps.com/
Coweta JHS 700/7-9
PO Box 550 74429 918-486-2127
Mike Lingo, prin. Fax 486-7307
Coweta SHS 600/10-12
PO Box 550 74429 918-486-4474
Randy Craven, prin. Fax 486-1062

Coyle, Logan, Pop. 360
Coyle ISD 400/PK-12
PO Box 287 73027 405-466-2242
Rick Kibbe, supt. Fax 466-2448
www.coyle.k12.ok.us
Coyle HS 100/9-12
PO Box 287 73027 405-466-2242
Josh Sumrall, prin. Fax 466-2448

Crescent, Logan, Pop. 1,336
Crescent ISD 600/PK-12
PO Box 719 73028 405-969-3738
Steve Shiever, supt. Fax 969-2003
www.crescentok.com/
Crescent HS 200/9-12
PO Box 719 73028 405-969-2545
Rick McCombs, prin. Fax 969-2003
Crescent JHS 100/6-8
PO Box 719 73028 405-969-2190
Wayne Owens, prin. Fax 969-2003

Cromwell, Seminole, Pop. 264
Butner ISD 300/PK-12
PO Box 157 74837 405-944-5530
Dr. Ron Ledford, supt. Fax 944-5746
Butner HS 100/9-12
PO Box 157 74837 405-944-5526
Ken Victory, prin. Fax 944-5746

Crowder, Pittsburg, Pop. 440
Crowder ISD 400/PK-12
PO Box B 74430 918-334-3203
David Jones, supt. Fax 334-3295
Crowder HS, PO Box B 74430 100/9-12
Jennifer Smith, prin. 918-334-3204

Cushing, Payne, Pop. 8,267
Cushing ISD 1,800/PK-12
PO Box 1609 74023 918-225-3425
Eddie L. Williams, supt. Fax 225-5256
Cushing HS, 1700 E Walnut St 74023 600/9-12
James Lauerman, prin. 918-225-6622
Cushing MS, 316 N Steele Ave 74023 400/6-8
Terry Morgan, prin. 918-225-1311

Cyril, Caddo, Pop. 1,169
Cyril ISD 400/PK-12
PO Box 449 73029 580-464-2419
Jim Conger, supt. Fax 464-2445
Cyril HS 100/9-12
PO Box 449 73029 580-464-2272
Jason James, prin. Fax 464-2445

Dale, Pottawatomie, Pop. 100
Dale ISD 700/PK-12
300 Smith Ave 74851 405-964-5558
Charles Dickinson, supt. Fax 964-5559
www.dale.k12.ok.us
Dale HS 200/10-12
300 Smith Ave 74851 405-964-5555
Harold Jones, prin. Fax 964-5539
Dale JHS, 300 Smith Ave 74851 200/7-9
Harold Jones, prin. 405-964-5555

Davenport, Lincoln, Pop. 886
Davenport ISD 400/PK-12
PO Box 849 74026 918-377-2277
John Greenfield, supt. Fax 377-2553
www.davenport.k12.ok.us/
Davenport HS 100/9-12
PO Box 849 74026 918-377-2278
Daniel Accord, prin. Fax 377-2553

Davidson, Tillman, Pop. 345
Davidson ISD 100/PK-12
PO Box 338 73530 580-568-2423
Phillip Ratcliff, supt. Fax 568-2423
Davidson HS 50/9-12
PO Box 338 73530 580-568-2261
Phillip Ratcliff, prin. Fax 568-2423

Davis, Murray, Pop. 2,648
Davis ISD 800/PK-12
400 E Atlanta Ave 73030 580-369-2386
Monte Thompson, supt. Fax 369-3507
www.davis.k12.ok.us/
Davis HS 300/9-12
400 E Atlanta Ave 73030 580-369-5541
Jack Kapella, prin. Fax 369-3071
Davis MS 200/5-8
400 E Atlanta Ave 73030 580-369-5565
Sheri Knight, prin. Fax 369-3289

Del City, Oklahoma, Pop. 21,945
Midwest City-Del City ISD
Supt. — See Midwest City
Del City SHS 1,100/10-12
1900 S Sunnylane Rd 73115 405-677-5777
Annette Nantois, prin. Fax 671-8675
Del Crest JHS 600/7-9
4731 Judy Dr 73115 405-671-8615
Jason Brown, prin. Fax 671-8618
Kerr JHS 700/7-9
2300 Linda Ln 73115 405-671-8625
Brian Eccellente, prin. Fax 671-8626

Christian Heritage Academy 600/PK-12
4400 SE 27th St 73115 405-672-1787
Josh Bullard, hdmstr. Fax 672-1839
Mid-Del Christian S 400/PK-12
3801 SE 29th St 73115 405-677-6000
Jim Howard, admin. Fax 677-6066

Depew, Creek, Pop. 569
Depew ISD — 300/PK-12
PO Box 257 74028 — 918-324-5466
Bruce Terronez, supt. — Fax 324-5336
Depew HS — 100/9-12
PO Box 257 74028 — 918-324-5543
Bruce McKinzie, prin. — Fax 324-5336

Dewar, Okmulgee, Pop. 908
Dewar ISD — 500/PK-12
PO Box 790 74431 — 918-652-9625
Billy Green, supt. — Fax 652-3096
www.dewar.k12.ok.us/
Dewar HS — 100/9-12
PO Box 790 74431 — 918-652-9625
Todd Been, prin. — Fax 652-3096
Dewar MS — 100/6-8
PO Box 790 74431 — 918-652-9625
Kate McDonald, prin. — Fax 652-3096

Dewey, Washington, Pop. 3,288
Dewey ISD — 1,100/K-12
1 Bulldogger Rd 74029 — 918-534-2241
Paul Smith, supt. — Fax 534-0149
www.dewey.k12.ok.us
Dewey HS, 1 Bulldogger Rd 74029 — 400/9-12
Jack Golden, prin. — 918-534-0933
Dewey MS, 1 Bulldogger Rd 74029 — 300/6-8
Leta Moreland, prin. — 918-534-0111

Dibble, McClain, Pop. 295
Dibble ISD — 700/PK-12
PO Box 9 73031 — 405-344-6375
Bill Bentley, supt. — Fax 344-6977
www.dibble.k12.ok.us
Dibble HS, PO Box 9 73031 — 200/9-12
Chad Clanton, prin. — 405-344-6380
Dibble MS — 200/6-8
PO Box 9 73031 — 405-344-6380
Mark Howe, prin. — Fax 344-7275

Dover, Kingfisher, Pop. 367
Dover ISD — 200/PK-12
PO Box 195 73734 — 405-828-4206
Floyd Kirk, supt. — Fax 828-7150
www.dover.k12.ok.us
Dover S — 200/PK-12
PO Box 195 73734 — 405-828-4205
Wade Detrick, prin. — Fax 828-8019

Drummond, Garfield, Pop. 386
Drummond ISD — 300/PK-12
PO Box 240 73735 — 580-493-2216
Vic Woods, supt. — Fax 493-2273
www.drummond.k12.ok.us/
Drummond HS, PO Box 240 73735 — 100/9-12
Greg Kokojan, prin. — 580-493-2271

Drumright, Creek, Pop. 2,877
Drumright SD — 600/PK-12
301 S Pennsylvania Ave 74030 — 918-352-2492
H.T. Gee, supt. — Fax 352-4430
www.drumright.k12.ok.us/
Drumright HS — 200/9-12
301 S Pennsylvania Ave 74030 — 918-352-2152
Jim Frazier, prin. — Fax 352-9845
Edison MS — 100/6-8
300 E Pine St 74030 — 918-352-2318
Kevin Bilyeu, prin. — Fax 352-4033

OK Dept. of Voc. & Tech. Education
Supt. — None
Central Tech — Vo/Tech
3 Central Tech Cir 74030 — 918-352-2551
Phil Waul, supt. — Fax 352-2441

Olive ISD — 400/PK-12
9352 S 436th West Ave 74030 — 918-352-9567
Charles Lewis, supt. — Fax 352-4379
www.olive.k12.ok.us/
Olive HS — 100/9-12
9352 S 436th West Ave 74030 — 918-352-9568
Sam Ahtone, prin.

Duke, Jackson, Pop. 392
Duke ISD — 200/PK-12
PO Box 160 73532 — 580-679-3014
Steven Peretto, supt. — Fax 679-3017
www.dukeschools.com/
Duke HS, PO Box 160 73532 — 100/9-12
Kevin Cansler, prin. — 580-679-3311

Duncan, Stephens, Pop. 22,306
Duncan ISD — 3,500/PK-12
PO Box 1548 73534 — 580-255-0686
Dr. Sherry Labyer, supt. — Fax 252-2453
www.duncanpublicschools.org
Duncan HS — 1,100/9-12
PO Box 1548 73534 — 580-255-0700
Gary Reed, prin. — Fax 252-2445
Duncan MS — 800/6-8
PO Box 1548 73534 — 580-470-8106
Mike Toone, prin. — Fax 470-8743

Empire ISD — 500/PK-12
9450 W Cherokee Rd 73533 — 580-252-5392
Jim Motes, supt. — Fax 252-4231
www.empireschools.org
Empire HS — 200/9-12
9450 W Cherokee Rd 73533 — 580-255-7515
Robert Grider, prin.

OK Dept. of Voc. & Tech. Education
Supt. — None
Red River Technology Center — Vo/Tech
PO Box 1807 73534 — 580-255-2903
Jerry Morris, supt. — Fax 255-0491

Durant, Bryan, Pop. 14,795
Durant ISD — 2,900/PK-12
PO Box 1160 74702 — 580-924-1276
Terry James Ph.D., supt. — Fax 924-6019
www.durantisd.org
Durant HS — 900/9-12
802 W Walnut St 74701 — 580-924-4424
Steve Wlodarczyk, prin. — Fax 924-3642
Durant MS — 400/7-8
410 N 6th Ave 74701 — 580-924-1321
Jim Corley, prin. — Fax 924-8278

OK Dept. of Voc. & Tech. Education
Supt. — None
Kiamichi Technology Center — Vo/Tech
810 Waldron Dr 74701 — 580-924-7081
Michael Goodwin, dir. — Fax 924-2790

Silo ISD — 500/PK-12
122 W Bourne St 74701 — 580-924-7003
Tim Smith, supt. — Fax 920-7988
www.siloisd.org
Silo HS — 100/9-12
122 W Bourne St 74701 — 580-924-7000
Kim Marlow, prin. — Fax 924-7045
Silo JHS — 100/6-8
122 W Bourne St 74701 — 580-924-7000
Billy Bowen, prin. — Fax 920-7983

Southeastern Oklahoma State University — Post-Sec.
Station A 74701 — 580-924-0121
Southern School of Beauty — Post-Sec.
140 W Main St 74701 — 580-924-1049
Victory Life Academy — 300/K-12
3412 W University Blvd 74701 — 580-920-0850
Sue Sheriff, prin. — Fax 920-1794

Dustin, Hughes, Pop. 445
Dustin ISD — 100/PK-12
PO Box 390660 74839 — 918-656-3230
Barry Nault, supt. — Fax 656-3242
www.dustin.k12.ok.us/
Dustin HS, PO Box 390660 74839 — 50/9-12
Barry Nault, prin. — 918-656-3230

Eagletown, McCurtain
Eagletown ISD — 200/PK-12
PO Box 38 74734 — 580-835-2242
Kent Hendon, supt. — Fax 835-7420
Eagletown HS — 100/8-12
PO Box 38 74734 — 580-835-2242
Mike Bryan, prin. — Fax 835-7420

Earlsboro, Pottawatomie, Pop. 657
Earlsboro ISD — 200/K-12
PO Box 10 74840 — 405-997-5616
Terry Brown, supt. — Fax 997-3181
Earlsboro HS — 100/9-12
PO Box 10 74840 — 405-997-5252
Mark Maloy, prin. — Fax 997-3181

Edmond, Oklahoma, Pop. 74,881
Deer Creek ISD — 2,300/PK-12
20701 N MacArthur Blvd, — 405-348-6100
Rebecca Wilkinson, supt. — Fax 348-3049
www.deercreekschools.org/
Deer Creek HS — 600/9-12
6101 NW 206th St, — 405-348-5720
Sheli McAdoo, prin. — Fax 359-3155
Deer Creek MS — 500/6-8
21175 N Macarthur Blvd, — 405-348-4830
Toni Jones, prin. — Fax 359-3163

Edmond ISD — 18,500/PK-12
1001 W Danforth Rd 73003 — 405-340-2800
Dr. David Goin, supt. — Fax 340-2835
www.edmondschools.net/
Central MS — 900/6-8
500 E 9th St 73034 — 405-340-2890
Tara Fair, prin. — Fax 340-3961
Cheyenne MS — 800/6-8
1271 W Covell Rd 73003 — 405-330-7380
Dr. Debbie Bendick, prin. — Fax 330-7397
Cimarron MS — 700/6-8
3701 S Bryant Ave 73013 — 405-340-2935
Susie Schinnerer, prin. — Fax 330-3398
Edmond Memorial HS — 2,000/9-12
1000 E 15th St 73013 — 405-340-2850
Kyle Heath, prin. — Fax 340-2856
Edmond North HS — 2,100/9-12
215 W Danforth Rd 73003 — 405-340-2875
Jan Keirns, prin. — Fax 330-7349
Edmond Santa Fe HS — 1,800/9-12
1901 W 15th St 73013 — 405-340-2230
Jason Brown, prin. — Fax 340-2240
Sequoyah MS — 900/6-8
1125 E Danforth Rd 73034 — 405-340-2900
Jeff Edwards, prin. — Fax 340-2909
Summit MS — 700/6-8
1703 NW 150th St 73013 — 405-340-2920
Desarae Witmer, prin. — Fax 340-2933

Oklahoma Christian S — 800/PK-12
PO Box 509 73083 — 405-341-2265
Dallas Caldwell, hdmstr. — Fax 330-7615
University of Central Oklahoma — Post-Sec.
100 N University Dr 73034 — 405-974-2000

Eldorado, Jackson, Pop. 498
Eldorado ISD — 100/PK-12
PO Box J 73537 — 580-633-2219
Mark Baumann, supt. — Fax 633-2316
Eldorado HS — 50/9-12
PO Box J 73537 — 580-633-2219
Pam Charlson, prin. — Fax 633-2316

Elgin, Comanche, Pop. 1,278
Elgin ISD — 1,300/PK-12
PO Box 369 73538 — 580-492-3663
Tom Crimmins, supt. — Fax 492-4084
www.elgin.k12.ok.us/
Elgin HS — 400/9-12
PO Box 369 73538 — 580-492-3670
Shari Pillow, prin. — Fax 492-3697
Elgin MS — 300/5-8
PO Box 369 73538 — 580-492-3655
Sammy Jackson, prin. — Fax 492-3658

Elk City, Beckham, Pop. 10,743
CareerTech Skills Centers
Supt. — None
Dom Garrison, supt.
Elk City Skills Center — Vo/Tech
PO Box 1071 73648 — 580-243-5517

Elk City ISD — 1,900/PK-PK, 1-
222 W Broadway Ave 73644 — 580-225-0175
Galeard Roper, supt. — Fax 225-8644
www.elkcityschools.com/
Elk City HS — 500/10-12
222 W Broadway Ave 73644 — 580-225-0105
Rick McNeil, prin. — Fax 225-1359
Elk City JHS — 300/8-9
222 W Broadway Ave 73644 — 580-225-0476
Jamey Cook, prin. — Fax 225-0208

Merritt ISD — 500/PK-12
RR 4 Box 7195 73644 — 580-225-5460
Gary Higgins, supt. — Fax 225-5469
Merritt HS — 100/9-12
RR 4 Box 7195 73644 — 580-225-5460
Jeff Daugherty, prin. — Fax 225-5469

Elmore City, Garvin, Pop. 763
Elmore City-Pernell ISD — 500/PK-12
100 N Muse Ave 73433 — 580-788-2566
Jim Smith, supt. — Fax 788-4665
www.ecphs.k12.ok.us
Elmore City-Pernell HS — 100/9-12
100 N Muse Ave 73433 — 580-788-2565
Burl Solie, prin. — Fax 788-4665

El Reno, Canadian, Pop. 16,097
El Reno ISD — 2,500/PK-12
PO Box 580 73036 — 405-262-1703
Dr. Jeff Mills, supt. — Fax 262-8620
www.elreno.k12.ok.us
Dale JHS — 400/8-9
PO Box 580 73036 — 405-262-3253
Matt Goucher, prin. — Fax 262-8650
El Reno HS — 600/10-12
PO Box 580 73036 — 405-262-3254
Matt Goucher, prin. — Fax 262-8629

OK Dept. of Voc. & Tech. Education
Supt. — None
Canadian Valley Technology Center — Vo/Tech
6505 E US Highway 66 73036 — 405-422-2200
Dr. Earl Cowan, supt. — Fax 422-2354

Canadian Valley Area Voc-Tech School — Post-Sec.
6505 E US Highway 66 73036 — 405-262-2629
Redlands Community College — Post-Sec.
1300 S Country Club Rd 73036 — 405-262-2552

Enid, Garfield, Pop. 46,416
Chisholm ISD — 900/PK-12
300 Colorado Ave 73701 — 580-237-5512
Roydon Tilley, supt. — Fax 234-5334
www.chisholm.k12.ok.us
Chisholm HS — 300/9-12
4018 W Carrier Rd 73703 — 580-233-2852
Jaymie Morley, prin. — Fax 233-9325
Chisholm MS — 200/6-8
4202 W Carrier Rd 73703 — 580-234-0234
Shane Dent, prin. — Fax 234-0343

Enid ISD — 6,300/PK-12
500 S Independence St 73701 — 580-234-5270
Dr. Garland Keithly, supt. — Fax 249-3565
www.enidpublicschools.org/
Emerson JHS — 500/7-9
700 W Elm Ave 73701 — 580-237-3017
Kimberly Jones, prin. — Fax 249-3587
Enid HS — 1,300/10-12
611 W Wabash Ave 73701 — 580-234-2404
Jim Beierschmitt, prin. — Fax 249-3576
Longfellow JHS — 400/7-9
900 E Broadway Ave Bldg 2 73701 — 580-234-7022
Ron Few, prin. — Fax 249-3586
Waller JHS — 600/7-9
2604 W Randolph Ave 73703 — 580-234-5931
John Garvie, prin. — Fax 249-3585

OK Dept. of Voc. & Tech. Education
Supt. — None
Autry Technology Center — Vo/Tech
1201 W Willow Rd 73703 — 580-242-2750
Dr. Jim Strate, supt. — Fax 233-8262

Enid Beauty College — Post-Sec.
1601 E Broadway Ave 73701 — 580-237-6677
Oklahoma Bible Academy — 300/7-12
5913 W Chestnut Ave 73703 — 580-242-4104
Tim Kuhns, hdmstr. — Fax 242-4106
O T Autry Area Vocational Tech Center — Post-Sec.
1201 W Willow Rd 73703 — 580-242-2750
St. Mary's Hospital — Post-Sec.
305 S 5th St 73701 — 580-233-6100

Erick, Beckham, Pop. 1,045
Erick ISD — 200/K-12
PO Box 9 73645 — 580-526-3476
Phil Compton, supt. — Fax 526-3308
Erick HS, PO Box 9 73645 — 100/9-12
Darrel Humphries, prin. — 580-526-3351

Eucha, Delaware

New Life S — 50/7-12
PO Box 670 74342 — 918-435-8206
Carrie Collins, prin. — Fax 435-8209

Eufaula, McIntosh, Pop. 2,789
Eufaula ISD — 1,100/K-12
PO Box 609 74432 — 918-689-2152
Bill Wilson, supt. — Fax 689-1080
www.eufaula.k12.ok.us/
Eufaula HS — 400/9-12
PO Box 609 74432 — 918-689-2556
Steve Butcher, prin. — Fax 689-1099
Eufaula MS — 300/6-8
PO Box 609 74432 — 918-689-2711
Chris Whelan, prin. — Fax 689-2874

Fairfax, Osage, Pop. 1,505
Woodland SD — 500/PK-12
PO Box 487 74637 — 918-642-3295
David Payne, supt. — Fax 642-5754

Woodland HS 100/9-12
PO Box 487 74637 918-642-3295
Joe Sindelar, prin. Fax 642-5754
Other Schools – See Ralston

Fairland, Ottawa, Pop. 1,012
Fairland ISD 500/PK-12
PO Box 689 74343 918-676-3811
Charles Thomas, supt. Fax 676-3594
www.fairlandowls.com
Fairland HS, PO Box 689 74343 100/9-12
Mark Malcom, prin. 918-676-3246

Fairview, Major, Pop. 2,629
Fairview ISD 700/PK-12
408 E Broadway 73737 580-227-2531
Rocky Burchfield, supt. Fax 227-2642
www.fairviewhigh.com
Chamberlain MS 200/6-8
1000 E Elm St 73737 580-227-2555
Billy Sacket, prin. Fax 227-2642
Fairview HS 200/9-12
316 N 8th Ave 73737 580-227-4446
Mark Van Meter, prin. Fax 227-1004

OK Dept. of Voc. & Tech. Education
Supt. — None
Northwest Technology Center Vo/Tech
PO Box 250 73737 580-227-3708
Jane Bowen, dir. Fax 227-2651

Fargo, Ellis, Pop. 318
Fargo ISD 200/PK-12
PO Box 200 73840 580-698-2298
Mike Woods, supt. Fax 698-8019
www.fargo.k12.ok.us
Fargo HS 50/9-12
PO Box 200 73840 580-698-2298
Sherri Long, prin. Fax 698-8019

Felt, Cimarron
Felt ISD 100/PK-12
PO Box 47 73937 580-426-2220
Barbalee Blair, supt. Fax 426-2799
www.felt.k12.ok.us
Felt HS 50/9-12
PO Box 47 73937 580-426-2220
Lewetta Hefley, prin. Fax 426-2799

Fittstown, Pontotoc
Stonewall ISD
Supt. — See Stonewall
McLish MS PK-PK, 5-
PO Box 29 74842 580-777-2221
Jack Wofford, prin. Fax 777-2222

Fletcher, Comanche, Pop. 1,038
Fletcher ISD 400/PK-12
PO Box 489 73541 580-549-6015
Kathryn Turner, supt. Fax 549-6016
www.fletcherschools.org/
Fletcher JHS 100/7-9
PO Box 489 73541 580-549-6015
Julia Poteete, prin. Fax 549-6016
Fletcher SHS, PO Box 489 73541 100/10-12
Julia Poteete, prin. 580-549-6015

Forgan, Beaver, Pop. 493
Forgan ISD 200/PK-12
PO Box 406 73938 580-487-3366
Travis Smalts, supt. Fax 487-3368
www.forgan.k12.ok.us
Forgan HS 50/9-12
PO Box 406 73938 580-487-3366
Todd Kerr, prin. Fax 487-3368

Fort Cobb, Caddo, Pop. 651
Fort Cobb-Broxton ISD 400/PK-12
PO Box 130 73038 405-643-2336
Dennis Klugh, supt. Fax 643-2547
Fort Cobb-Broxton HS 100/9-12
PO Box 130 73038 405-643-2820
Kyle Lierle, prin. Fax 643-3115
Fort Cobb-Broxton MS 100/6-8
PO Box 130 73038 405-643-2820
James Biddy, prin.

OK Dept. of Voc. & Tech. Education
Supt. — None
Caddo-Kiowa Technology Center Vo/Tech
PO Box 190 73038 405-643-5511
Jerry Martin, supt. Fax 643-2144

Fort Gibson, Muskogee, Pop. 4,252
Fort Gibson ISD 1,800/PK-12
500 Ross Ave 74434 918-478-2474
Derald Glover, supt. Fax 478-8533
www.ftgibson.k12.ok.us
Fort Gibson HS 600/9-12
500 Ross Ave 74434 918-478-2452
Gary Sparks, prin. Fax 478-6244
Fort Gibson MS 400/6-8
500 Ross Ave 74434 918-478-2471
Gregory Phares, prin. Fax 478-6412

Fort Supply, Woodward, Pop. 328
CareerTech Skills Centers
Supt. — None
Dom Garrison, supt.
Fort Supply Skills Center Vo/Tech
PO Box 130 73841 580-766-2089

Fort Supply ISD 100/PK-12
PO Box 160 73841 580-766-2611
Pat Howell, supt. Fax 766-8019
Fort Supply HS, PO Box 160 73841 50/9-12
Pat Howell, prin. 580-766-2611

Fort Towson, Choctaw, Pop. 611
Fort Towson ISD 400/PK-12
PO Box 39 74735 580-873-2712
Jo Miller, supt. Fax 873-1053
www.forttowson.k12.ok.us/
Fort Towson HS 100/9-12
PO Box 39 74735 580-873-2325
Phillip Ware, prin. Fax 873-2712

Fox, Carter
Fox ISD 300/PK-12
PO Box 248 73435 580-673-2081
James Miller, supt. Fax 673-2389
www.foxps.k12.ok.us
Fox HS 100/9-12
PO Box 248 73435 580-673-2082
David Cole, prin. Fax 673-2389

Foyil, Rogers, Pop. 266
Foyil ISD 500/PK-12
PO Box 49 74031 918-341-1113
Michael Mcgregor, supt. Fax 341-1223
www.foyil.k12.ok.us
Foyil JSHS 100/7-12
PO Box 49 74031 918-342-1782
Rick Antle, prin. Fax 341-1223

Frederick, Tillman, Pop. 4,195
Frederick ISD 1,000/PK-12
PO Box 370 73542 580-335-5516
Tony O'Brien, supt. Fax 335-2324
www.frederickbombers.net
Frederick HS, PO Box 610 73542 300/9-12
Ruth Ann Hoover, prin. 580-335-5521
Frederick MS, PO Box 490 73542 200/6-8
Randy Biggs, prin. 580-335-2014

OK Dept. of Voc. & Tech. Education
Supt. — None
Great Plains Technology Center Vo/Tech
2001 E Gladstone Ave 73542 580-335-5525
Gary Tyler, dir. Fax 335-2209

Freedom, Woods, Pop. 262
Freedom ISD 100/PK-12
PO Box 5 73842 580-621-3271
Gary Parris, supt. Fax 621-3699
www.freedom.k12.ok.us
Freedom HS 50/9-12
PO Box 5 73842 580-621-3272
James Todd, prin. Fax 621-3699

Gage, Ellis, Pop. 408
Gage ISD 100/K-12
PO Box 60 73843 580-923-7666
Doug Taylor, supt. Fax 923-7907
www.gage.k12.ok.us/
Gage JSHS 50/7-12
PO Box 60 73843 580-923-7909
Doug Taylor, prin. Fax 923-7907

Gans, Sequoyah, Pop. 214
Gans ISD 400/PK-12
PO Box 70 74936 918-775-2236
Brenda Taylor, supt. Fax 775-5145
www.gans.k12.ok.us
Gans HS 100/9-12
PO Box 70 74936 918-775-2236
Larry Calloway, prin. Fax 775-5145

Garber, Garfield, Pop. 802
Garber ISD 300/PK-12
PO Box 539 73738 580-863-2220
Jim Lamer, supt. Fax 863-2259
www.garber.k12.ok.us/
Garber HS, PO Box 539 73738 100/9-12
Marc Hatton, prin. 580-863-2231

Geary, Blaine, Pop. 1,290
Geary ISD 500/PK-12
PO Box 188 73040 405-884-2989
Bill Caruthers, supt. Fax 884-2099
www.geary.k12.ok.us
Geary JHS, PO Box 188 73040 100/7-9
Tom Deighan, prin. 405-884-2362
Geary SHS, PO Box 188 73040 100/10-12
Tom Deighan, prin. 405-884-2362

Geronimo, Comanche, Pop. 950
Geronimo ISD 300/PK-12
PO Box 99 73543 580-355-3160
Danny McCuiston, supt. Fax 357-8307
www.geronimo.k12.ok.us
Geronimo HS 100/9-12
PO Box 99 73543 580-355-3160
Amy Wilcox, prin. Fax 355-9670

Glencoe, Payne, Pop. 562
Glencoe ISD 400/PK-12
201 E Lone Chimney Rd 74032 580-669-2261
Pat Gougler, supt. Fax 669-2961
www.glencoe.k12.ok.us
Glencoe HS 100/9-12
201 E Lone Chimney Rd 74032 580-669-2261
Pat Gougler, prin. Fax 669-2961

Glenpool, Tulsa, Pop. 8,960
Glenpool ISD 2,200/PK-12
PO Box 1149 74033 918-322-9500
Kathy Coley, supt. Fax 322-1529
www.glenpool.k12.ok.us
Glenpool HS 600/9-12
PO Box 1149 74033 918-322-9500
Bruce Snider, prin. Fax 322-1012
Glenpool MS 500/6-8
PO Box 1149 74033 918-322-9500
Danna Garland, prin. Fax 322-9333

Goodwell, Texas, Pop. 1,129
Goodwell ISD 200/PK-12
PO Box 580 73939 580-349-2271
Robert Miller, supt. Fax 349-2531
www.gpseagles.org
Goodwell HS 50/9-12
PO Box 580 73939 580-349-2271
Micah Davis, prin. Fax 349-2531

Yarbrough ISD 100/PK-12
RR 1 Box 31 73939 580-545-3327
Jim Wiggin, supt. Fax 545-3392
Yarbrough HS 50/9-12
RR 1 Box 31 73939 580-545-3328
Terry Mulbery, prin. Fax 545-3392

Oklahoma Panhandle State University Post-Sec.
PO Box 430 73939 580-349-2611

Gore, Sequoyah, Pop. 907
Gore ISD 600/K-12
PO Box 580 74435 918-489-5587
Patricia Cox, supt. Fax 489-5664
www.gore.k12.ok.us/
Gore HS 200/9-12
PO Box 580 74435 918-489-5587
Steven Barrick, prin. Fax 489-5664
Gore MS 200/6-8
PO Box 580 74435 918-487-5191
Richard Moseley, prin. Fax 489-5664

Gracemont, Caddo, Pop. 336
Gracemont ISD 200/PK-12
PO Box 5 73042 405-966-2236
Larry Mills, supt. Fax 966-2395
Gracemont HS 100/9-12
PO Box 5 73042 405-966-2234
Wayne Taggart, prin. Fax 966-2395

Grandfield, Tillman, Pop. 1,007
Grandfield ISD 300/PK-12
PO Box 639 73546 580-479-5237
Ed Turlington, supt. Fax 479-3381
www.grandfield.k12.ok.us/
Grandfield HS 100/9-12
PO Box 639 73546 580-479-3140
Judd Matthes, prin. Fax 479-5563

Granite, Greer, Pop. 1,797
CareerTech Skills Centers
Supt. — None
Dom Garrison, supt.
Granite Skills Center Vo/Tech
PO Box 86 73547 580-480-3700

Granite ISD 300/PK-12
PO Box 98 73547 580-535-2104
Loren Tackett, supt. Fax 535-2106
Granite HS 100/9-12
PO Box 98 73547 580-535-2104
Janice Crume, prin. Fax 535-2106

Grove, Delaware, Pop. 5,752
Grove ISD 2,300/PK-12
PO Box 450789 74345 918-786-3003
Tom Steen, supt. Fax 786-9365
www.ridgerunners.net
Grove HS, PO Box 450789 74345 700/9-12
Mike Teel, prin. 918-786-2208
Grove MS, PO Box 450789 74345 500/6-8
Don Barr, prin. 918-786-2209

Guthrie, Logan, Pop. 10,800
Guthrie ISD 3,000/PK-12
802 E Vilas Ave 73044 405-282-8900
Terry Simpson, supt. Fax 282-5904
www.guthrie.k12.ok.us
Guthrie HS 900/9-12
200 N Crooks Dr 73044 405-282-5906
Carl Clark, prin. Fax 282-8823
Guthrie JHS 500/7-8
705 E Oklahoma Ave 73044 405-282-5936
Tim Rawls, prin. Fax 282-5985

Guymon, Texas, Pop. 10,643
Guymon ISD 2,300/PK-12
PO Box 1307 73942 580-338-4340
Doug Melton, supt. Fax 338-3812
156.110.79.11/
Central JHS, PO Box 1307 73942 300/7-8
Kenny Mason, prin. 580-338-4360
Guymon HS 600/9-12
PO Box 1307 73942 580-338-4350
Lowell Doss, prin. Fax 338-0994

Haileyville, Pittsburg, Pop. 899
Haileyville ISD 400/PK-12
PO Box 29 74546 918-297-2626
David Cravens, supt. Fax 297-7136
haileyville.ok.schoolwebpages.com
Haileyville HS, PO Box 29 74546 100/9-12
Roger Hemphill, prin. 918-297-2627

Hammon, Roger Mills, Pop. 454
Hammon ISD 200/PK-12
PO Box 279 73650 580-473-2221
Randy Ann Stickney, supt. Fax 473-2464
www.hammon.k12.ok.us/
Hammon HS 100/9-12
PO Box 279 73650 580-473-2737
Richard Megli, prin. Fax 473-2464

Hanna, McIntosh, Pop. 135
Hanna ISD 100/PK-12
PO Box 10 74845 918-657-2523
Patricia Berry, supt. Fax 657-2424
Hanna HS, PO Box 10 74845 50/9-12
Scott Vincent, prin. 918-657-2527

Hardesty, Texas, Pop. 277
Hardesty ISD 100/PK-12
PO Box 129 73944 580-888-4258
Wade Stafford, supt. Fax 888-4560
www.hardesty.k12.ok.us
Hardesty HS 50/9-12
PO Box 129 73944 580-888-4258
Wade Stafford, prin. Fax 888-4560

Harrah, Oklahoma, Pop. 4,939
Harrah ISD 2,200/PK-12
20670 Walker St 73045 405-454-6244
Dr. Dean Hughes, supt. Fax 454-0022
www.harrahschools.com
Harrah HS 500/10-12
20370 Elm St 73045 405-454-2416
Dale Munyon, prin. Fax 454-6842
Harrah JHS 400/8-9
1480 N Dobbs Rd 73045 405-454-6331
John Hunt, prin. Fax 454-6361

Hartshorne, Pittsburg, Pop. 2,073
Hartshorne ISD 800/PK-12
520 S 5th St 74547 918-297-2534
James Barnes, supt. Fax 297-2698
www.hartshorne.k12.ok.us
Hartshorne JHS 200/7-9
520 S 5th St 74547 918-297-2433
John Bernardi, prin. Fax 297-2698

Hartshorne SHS 200/10-12
520 S 5th St 74547 918-297-2536
Mark Ichord, prin. Fax 297-2025

Haskell, Muskogee, Pop. 1,776
Haskell ISD 900/PK-12
PO Box 278 74436 918-482-5221
Dr. Landon Berry, supt. Fax 482-3346
www.haskell.k12.ok.us
Beavers MS 200/6-8
PO Box 278 74436 918-482-5221
Michael Broyles, prin. Fax 482-3346
Haskell HS 300/9-12
PO Box 278 74436 918-482-5223
John Munger, prin. Fax 482-3346

Haworth, McCurtain, Pop. 351
Haworth ISD 600/PK-12
HC 73 Box 1 74740 580-245-1406
Donald Ray, supt. Fax 245-2265
www.haworth.k12.ok.us
Haworth JHS 100/7-9
HC 73 Box 1 74740 580-245-1461
John Crabtree, prin. Fax 245-4911
Haworth SHS 100/10-12
HC 73 Box 1 74740 580-245-1440
Craig Wall, prin. Fax 245-4913

Healdton, Carter, Pop. 2,777
Healdton ISD 500/PK-12
PO Box 490 73438 580-229-0566
Don Lewis, supt. Fax 229-1522
Healdton HS, PO Box 490 73438 200/9-12
Greg Raper, prin. 580-229-0540
Healdton MS 100/6-8
PO Box 490 73438 580-229-0303
Greg Raper, prin. Fax 229-1475

Heavener, LeFlore, Pop. 3,246
Heavener ISD 900/PK-12
PO Box 698 74937 918-653-7223
Edward Wilson, supt. Fax 653-7843
www.heavener.k12.ok.us
Heavener HS, PO Box 698 74937 300/9-12
Jerry Williams, prin. 918-653-4436

Helena, Alfalfa, Pop. 1,392
CareerTech Skills Centers
Supt. — None
Dom Garrison, supt.
Helena Skills Center Vo/Tech
PO Box 286 73741 580-852-3221

Timberlake ISD 300/PK-12
PO Box 287 73741 580-852-3307
Roy Rousey, supt. Fax 852-3280
www.tlake.k12.ok.us
Timberlake HS 100/9-12
PO Box 287 73741 580-852-3281
Cliff Benson, prin. Fax 852-3280

Hennessey, Kingfisher, Pop. 2,050
Hennessey ISD 800/PK-12
604 E Oklahoma St 73742 405-853-4321
Lyle Young, supt. Fax 853-4439
www.hps.k12.ok.us
Hennessey HS 200/9-12
707 E Oklahoma St 73742 405-853-4394
Brady Barnes, prin. Fax 853-4644
Hennessey MS 200/5-8
120 N Mitchell Rd 73742 405-853-4303
David Garner, prin. Fax 853-4848

Henryetta, Okmulgee, Pop. 6,110
Henryetta ISD 1,200/PK-12
1801 W Troy Aikman Dr 74437 918-652-6523
Dan Edwards, supt. Fax 652-6510
www.henryetta.k12.ok.us
Henryetta HS 300/9-12
1800 W Troy Aikman Dr 74437 918-652-6571
Brad Wion, prin. Fax 652-6572
Henryetta MS 300/6-8
1700 W Troy Aikman Dr 74437 918-652-6578
Keith Flanary, prin. Fax 652-6506

Wilson ISD 300/PK-12
8867 Chestnut Rd 74437 918-652-3374
Rick Hatfield, supt. Fax 652-8140
www.wpstigers.k12.ok.us
Wilson HS 100/9-12
8867 Chestnut Rd 74437 918-652-3384
Andrea James, prin. Fax 650-9725

Hinton, Caddo, Pop. 2,183
Hinton ISD 500/PK-12
PO Box 1036 73047 405-542-3257
Harvey Mead, supt. Fax 542-3286
www.hinton.k12.ok.us
Hinton HS 100/9-12
PO Box 1036 73047 405-542-3235
Jeff Thompson, prin. Fax 542-3286
Hinton MS 100/6-8
PO Box 1036 73047 405-542-3235
Jason Reece, prin. Fax 542-3286

Hobart, Kiowa, Pop. 3,805
Hobart ISD 900/PK-12
PO Box 899 73651 580-726-5691
Roger Hill, supt. Fax 726-2855
www.hobart.k12.ok.us
Hobart HS, PO Box 899 73651 300/9-12
Rod Maynard, prin. 580-726-5611
Hobart MS, PO Box 899 73651 200/6-8
Benny Barnett, prin. 580-726-5615

Hodgen, LeFlore
CareerTech Skills Centers
Supt. — None
Dom Garrison, supt.
Hamilton Skills Center Vo/Tech
PO Box 250 74939 918-653-7831

Holdenville, Hughes, Pop. 5,538
Holdenville ISD 1,100/PK-12
210 Grimes Ave 74848 405-379-5483
Shellie Gammill, supt. Fax 379-5874
www.holdenville.k12.ok.us
Holdenville HS 300/9-12
210 Grimes Ave 74848 405-379-6893
Daniel Pittman, prin. Fax 379-2012
Holdenville JHS 200/7-8
210 Grimes Ave 74848 405-379-3387
Les White, prin. Fax 379-2012

Moss ISD 300/PK-12
8087 E 134 Rd 74848 405-379-7251
Louis Maggia, supt. Fax 379-2333
www.mossps.k12.ok.us/
Moss HS 100/9-12
8087 E 134 Rd 74848 405-379-7251
Bob Sifers, prin. Fax 379-2333

Hollis, Harmon, Pop. 2,087
Hollis ISD 600/PK-12
PO Box 193 73550 580-688-3450
Wilmer Cooper, supt. Fax 688-2532
www.hollis.k12.ok.us
Hollis HS, PO Box 193 73550 200/9-12
Ron Smith, prin. 580-688-2707
Hollis MS, PO Box 193 73550 100/6-8
Ron Smith, prin. 580-688-2707

Hominy, Osage, Pop. 3,733
Hominy ISD 700/PK-12
200 S Pettit Ave 74035 918-885-6511
Russell Hall, supt. Fax 885-2538
www.hominy.k12.ok.us/
Hominy HS, 200 S Pettit Ave 74035 200/9-12
Doyle Edwards, prin. 918-885-2141
Hominy MS, 200 S Pettit Ave 74035 100/7-8
Pat Drummond, prin. 918-885-6253

Hooker, Texas, Pop. 1,721
Hooker ISD 500/PK-12
PO Box 247 73945 580-652-2162
Freida Burgess, supt. Fax 652-3118
Hooker HS, PO Box 247 73945 200/9-12
Joe Oliver, prin. 580-652-2516

Howe, LeFlore, Pop. 715
Howe ISD 400/PK-12
PO Box 259 74940 918-658-3666
Scott Parks, supt. Fax 658-2233
www.howeschools.org
Howe HS 100/9-12
PO Box 259 74940 918-658-3368
Brooks Cawhorn, prin. Fax 658-2233

Hugo, Choctaw, Pop. 5,521
Hugo ISD 1,200/K-12
208 N 2nd St 74743 580-326-6483
Tony Daugherty, supt. Fax 326-2480
Hugo HS 300/9-12
201 E Brown St 74743 580-326-9648
Tommie Cummings, prin. Fax 326-4811
Hugo MS 200/7-8
208 N 2nd St 74743 580-326-3365
Darnell Shanklin, prin. Fax 326-7352

OK Dept. of Voc. & Tech. Education
Supt. — None
Kiamichi Technology Center Vo/Tech
PO Box 699 74743 580-326-6491
Dr. Charles Wibben, dir. Fax 326-5696

School of Hair Design Post-Sec.
116 W Jackson St 74743 580-326-7338

Hulbert, Cherokee, Pop. 533
Hulbert ISD 500/PK-12
PO Box 188 74441 918-772-2501
Wayne Ryals, supt. Fax 772-2766
www.hulbertriders.com
Hulbert JSHS 200/7-12
PO Box 188 74441 918-772-2565
Erik Puckett, prin. Fax 772-1275

Hydro, Caddo, Pop. 1,045
Hydro-Eakly SD 500/PK-12
529 E 6th St 73048 405-663-2774
Delbo Leach, supt. Fax 663-2139
www.hydroeakly.k12.ok.us/
Hydro-Eakly HS 100/9-12
529 E 6th St 73048 405-663-2246
Kim Hale, prin. Fax 663-2139
Hydro-Eakly MS 100/6-8
529 E 6th St 73048 405-663-2246
Kim Hale, prin. Fax 663-2139

Idabel, McCurtain, Pop. 6,916
Idabel ISD 1,500/PK-12
200 NE Ave C 74745 580-286-7639
Jane Wooten, supt. Fax 286-5585
www.idabelps.org
Idabel HS 500/9-12
901 E Lincoln Rd 74745 580-286-7693
Ted Brewer, prin. Fax 286-6755
Idabel MS 300/6-8
100 NE Ave D 74745 580-286-6558
Curtis Fuller, prin. Fax 286-8272

OK Dept. of Voc. & Tech. Education
Supt. — None
Kiamichi Technology Center Vo/Tech
3205 NE Lincoln Rd 74745 580-286-7555
Johnnie Meredith, dir. Fax 286-3753

School of Hair Design Post-Sec.
1437 SE Washington St 74745 580-286-7840

Indiahoma, Comanche, Pop. 360
Indiahoma ISD 200/PK-12
PO Box 8 73552 580-246-3448
Deanna Voegeli, supt. Fax 246-3372
www.indiahoma.k12.ok.us
Indiahoma HS 100/9-12
PO Box 8 73552 580-246-3202
Ken Latham, prin. Fax 246-3372

Indianola, Pittsburg, Pop. 193
Indianola ISD 300/PK-12
PO Box 119 74442 918-823-4231
Dr. Jeff Maddox, supt. Fax 823-4234
Indianola HS, PO Box 119 74442 100/9-12
Gina Barlow, prin. 918-823-4231

Inola, Rogers, Pop. 1,725
Inola ISD 1,300/PK-12
PO Box 1149 74036 918-543-2255
Jake Crutchfield, supt. Fax 543-8754
www.inola.k12.ok.us
Inola HS 400/9-12
PO Box 789 74036 918-543-2404
Robert Kinnick, prin. Fax 543-2345
Inola MS 400/5-8
PO Box 819 74036 918-543-2434
Vickie Johnson, prin. Fax 543-6268

Jay, Delaware, Pop. 2,840
Jay ISD 1,700/K-12
PO Box 630 74346 918-253-4293
David Schachle, supt. Fax 253-8970
www.jay.k12.ok.us
Jay HS 500/9-12
PO Box 630 74346 918-253-4466
Dennis Snell, prin. Fax 253-6249
Jay MS 400/6-8
PO Box 630 74346 918-253-8510
Judy Larmon, prin. Fax 253-3342

Jenks, Tulsa, Pop. 13,095
Jenks ISD 9,200/PK-12
205 E B St 74037 918-299-4411
Dr. Kirby Lehman, supt. Fax 299-9197
jenksps.org
Jenks Freshman Academy 800/9-9
205 E B St 74037 918-299-4411
Stephen Mathews, prin. Fax 298-0807
Jenks HS 2,100/10-12
205 E B St 74037 918-299-4411
Mike Means, prin. Fax 298-0336
Other Schools – See Tulsa

Jenks Beauty College Post-Sec.
535 W Main St 74037 918-299-0901

Jones, Oklahoma, Pop. 2,611
Jones ISD 1,000/PK-12
412 SW 3rd St 73049 405-399-9215
Mike Steele, supt. Fax 399-9212
www.joneshs.k12.ok.us
Jones HS 300/9-12
304 Hawaii St 73049 405-399-9122
Carl Johnson, prin. Fax 399-9212
Jones MS 200/7-8
16011 E Wilshire Blvd 73049 405-399-9114
Pam Lucas, prin. Fax 399-6101

Kansas, Delaware, Pop. 709
Kansas ISD 900/K-12
PO Box 196 74347 918-868-2562
Jim Burgess, supt. Fax 868-3103
www.kansasokschools.com/
Kansas HS 300/9-12
PO Box 196 74347 918-868-3308
Ned Phillips, prin. Fax 868-3103
Kansas JHS 200/6-8
PO Box 196 74347 918-868-5308
Bryon Arnold, prin. Fax 868-5582

OK Dept. of Voc. & Tech. Education
Supt. — None
Northeast Oklahoma Tech Center E Campus Vo/Tech
PO Box 30 74347 918-868-3535
Rick Craig, prin. Fax 868-3530

Kellyville, Creek, Pop. 918
Kellyville ISD 1,300/PK-12
PO Box 99 74039 918-247-6133
Ronald Jackson, supt. Fax 247-6120
www.kellyvilleschools.org/
Kellyville HS, PO Box 99 74039 400/9-12
Charles Nance, prin. 918-247-6333
Kellyville MS, PO Box 99 74039 200/7-8
John Castillo, prin. 918-247-6333

Keota, Haskell, Pop. 530
Keota ISD 400/PK-12
PO Box 640 74941 918-966-3950
Charles Brown, supt. Fax 966-3247
www.keota.k12.ok.us
Keota HS 100/9-12
PO Box 640 74941 918-966-3950
Terry Shaw, prin. Fax 966-3247

Ketchum, Mayes, Pop. 293
Ketchum ISD 700/PK-12
PO Box 720 74349 918-782-3241
Mark Alexander, supt. Fax 782-9018
www.ketchumwarriors.com
Ketchum HS 200/9-12
PO Box 720 74349 918-782-4481
Jim Owen, prin. Fax 782-4848
Ketchum MS, PO Box 720 74349 200/6-8
Rick Pool, prin. 918-782-3242

Keyes, Cimarron, Pop. 367
Keyes ISD 100/PK-12
PO Box 47 73947 580-546-7231
Ricky McCullough, supt. Fax 546-7338
www.keyes.k12.ok.us
Keyes HS 50/9-12
PO Box 47 73947 580-546-7231
Ricky McCullough, prin. Fax 546-7338

Kiefer, Creek, Pop. 1,313
Kiefer ISD 400/PK-12
PO Box 850 74041 918-321-3421
Charles Montalbano, supt. Fax 321-5216
www.kiefer.k12.ok.us/
Kiefer HS, PO Box 850 74041 100/9-12
Gayla Johnson, prin. 918-321-3533
Rongey MS, PO Box 850 74041 100/7-8
Gayla Johnson, prin. 918-321-3421

Kingfisher, Kingfisher, Pop. 4,501
Kingfisher ISD 1,200/PK-12
PO Box 29 73750 405-375-4194
Max Thomas, supt. Fax 375-5565
www.kingfisher.k12.ok.us
Kingfisher HS 400/9-12
PO Box 29 73750 405-375-4191
Charles Willis, prin. Fax 375-4456

Kingfisher MS — 300/5-8
PO Box 29 73750 — 405-375-6607
Andy Evans, prin. — Fax 375-6410

Kingston, Marshall, Pop. 1,526
Kingston ISD — 1,100/PK-12
PO Box 370 73439 — 580-564-9033
Jay McAdams, supt. — Fax 564-9516
www.kingston.k12.ok.us
Kingston HS — 300/9-12
PO Box 370 73439 — 580-564-2384
Donna Anderson, prin. — Fax 564-0901
Kingston MS — 300/6-8
PO Box 370 73439 — 580-564-2996
Ron Slawson, prin. — Fax 564-0902

Kinta, Haskell, Pop. 250
Kinta ISD — 200/PK-12
PO Box 219 74552 — 918-768-3338
Patricia Deville, supt. — Fax 768-3221
Kinta HS, PO Box 219 74552 — 100/9-12
Gerald Fishinghawk, prin. — 918-768-3339

Kiowa, Pittsburg, Pop. 701
Kiowa ISD — 300/PK-12
PO Box 6 74553 — 918-432-5631
Michael W. Kellogg, supt. — Fax 432-5683
www.kiowa.k12.ok.us
Kiowa HS, PO Box 6 74553 — 100/9-12
Garry Walden, prin. — 918-432-5641

Konawa, Seminole, Pop. 1,434
Konawa ISD — 500/PK-12
701 W South St 74849 — 580-925-3244
Dr. Jim Beckham, supt. — Fax 925-2146
www.konawa.k12.ok.us
Konawa JHS — 6-9
701 W South St 74849 — 580-925-3222
Larry Marlow, prin. — Fax 925-2146
Konawa SHS — 100/10-12
701 W South St 74849 — 580-925-3221
Gary Stidham, prin. — Fax 925-2146

Kremlin, Garfield, Pop. 230
Kremlin-Hillsdale ISD — 300/PK-12
PO Box 198 73753 — 580-874-2284
Steve Hoffsommer, supt. — Fax 874-4488
Kremlin-Hillsdale HS — 100/9-12
PO Box 198 73753 – Kurt Neal, prin. — 580-874-2281

Lahoma, Garfield, Pop. 562
Cimarron ISD — 300/PK-12
PO Box 8 73754 — 580-796-2204
Steve Walker, supt. — Fax 796-2350
www.cimarron.k12.ok.us
Cimarron HS — 100/9-12
PO Box 8 73754 — 580-796-2204
Gene Novosad, prin. — Fax 796-2350

Lamont, Grant, Pop. 436
Deer Creek-Lamont ISD — 200/PK-12
PO Box 10 74643 — 580-388-4335
Mark Taylor, supt. — Fax 388-4341
www.dcla.k12.ok.us/
Deer Creek-Lamont HS — 100/9-12
PO Box 10 74643 — 580-388-4333
David Zachary, prin.

Lane, Atoka
CareerTech Skills Centers
Supt. — None
Dom Garrison, supt.
McLeod Skills Center — Vo/Tech
PO Box 156 74555 — 580-889-7275

Langston, Logan, Pop. 1,688

Langston University — Post-Sec.
PO Box 907 73050 — 405-466-2231

Laverne, Harper, Pop. 1,016
Laverne ISD — 300/PK-12
PO Box 40 73848 — 580-921-3362
Ed Thomas, supt. — Fax 921-3636
www.laverne.k12.ok.us
Laverne HS — 100/9-12
PO Box 40 73848 — 580-921-3361
Todd Overstreet, prin. — Fax 921-3936

Lawton, Comanche, Pop. 90,234
CareerTech Skills Centers
Supt. — None
Dom Garrison, supt.
Lawton Skills Center — Vo/Tech
605 SW Coombs Rd 73501 — 580-355-4921

Lawton ISD — 14,800/PK-12
PO Box 1009 73502 — 580-357-6900
Barry Beauchamp, supt. — Fax 585-6319
www.lawtonps.org
Central MS — 600/6-8
1201 NW Fort Sill Blvd 73507 — 580-355-8544
Gene Shelkett, prin. — Fax 585-6452
Eisenhower JHS — 1,200/7-9
5702 W Gore Blvd 73505 — 580-353-1040
Rick Owens, prin. — Fax 585-6436
Eisenhower SHS — 1,300/10-12
5202 W Gore Blvd 73505 — 580-355-9144
Maria Anderson, prin. — Fax 585-6329
Lawton HS — 1,200/9-12
601 NW Fort Sill Blvd 73507 — 580-355-5170
Rick Kitzrow, prin. — Fax 585-6433
MacArthur HS — 1,100/9-12
4402 E Gore Blvd 73501 — 580-355-5230
Robert Roshell, prin. — Fax 585-6434
MacArthur MS — 600/6-8
510 NE 45th St 73507 — 580-353-5111
Mark Mattingly, prin. — Fax 585-6435
Tomlinson MS — 600/6-8
702 NW Homestead Dr 73505 — 580-585-6416
Dick Adams, prin. — Fax 585-6451

OK Dept. of Voc. & Tech. Education
Supt. — None
Great Plains Technology Center — Vo/Tech
4500 SW Lee Blvd 73505 — 580-355-6371
James Nesbitt, supt. — Fax 250-5677

Cameron University — Post-Sec.
2800 W Gore Blvd 73505 — 580-581-2200
Comanche Co. Memorial Hospital — Post-Sec.
PO Box 129 73502 — 580-355-8620
Eve's College of Hairstyling — Post-Sec.
912 SW C Ave 73501 — 580-355-6620
Great Plains Area Voc. Tech. School — Post-Sec.
4500 SW Lee Blvd 73505 — 580-355-6371
Lawton Christian HS — 200/7-12
1 NW Crusader Dr 73505 — 580-536-6885
Lani Malcolm, admin. — Fax 536-5242
Platt College — Post-Sec.
112 SW 11th St 73501 — 580-355-4416

Leedey, Dewey, Pop. 333
Leedey ISD — 200/PK-12
PO Box 67 73654 — 580-488-3424
Marc Montrose, supt. — Fax 488-3428
Leedey HS, PO Box 67 73654 — 100/9-12
Ronnie Dupree, prin. — 580-488-3377

Le Flore, LeFlore, Pop. 172
LeFlore SD — 200/PK-12
PO Box 147, — 918-753-2345
James Caughern, supt. — Fax 753-2604
www.lefloreps.k12.ok.us/
LeFlore HS — 100/9-12
PO Box 147, — 918-753-2253
L.D. Boatright, prin. — Fax 753-2604

Lexington, Cleveland, Pop. 2,079
CareerTech Skills Centers
Supt. — None
Dom Garrison, supt.
Harp Skills Center — Vo/Tech
PO Box 550 73051 — 405-527-4848
Lexington Skills Center — Vo/Tech
PO Box 550 73051 — 405-527-2191

Lexington ISD — 1,100/PK-12
420 NE 4th St 73051 — 405-527-7236
Denny Prince, supt. — Fax 527-9517
www.lexington.k12.ok.us/
Lexington HS — 300/9-12
420 NE 4th St 73051 — 405-527-7236
Randall Fuller, prin. — Fax 527-9517
Lexington MS — 200/7-8
420 NE 4th St 73051 — 405-527-7236
Gary Jones, prin. — Fax 527-9517

Lindsay, Garvin, Pop. 2,890
Lindsay ISD — 1,100/PK-12
800 W Creek St 73052 — 405-756-3131
Doyle Greteman, supt. — Fax 756-8819
www.lindsay.k12.ok.us
Lindsay HS, 800 W Creek St 73052 — 300/9-12
Tom Inman, prin. — 405-756-3132
Lindsay MS, 800 W Creek St 73052 — 200/6-8
Bob Ashley, prin. — 405-756-3133

Locust Grove, Mayes, Pop. 1,576
Locust Grove ISD — 1,500/PK-12
PO Box 399 74352 — 918-479-5243
David Cash, supt. — Fax 479-6468
www.lg.k12.ok.us
Locust Grove HS — 500/9-12
PO Box 399 74352 — 918-479-5247
Howard Hill, prin. — Fax 479-2743
Locust Grove MS — 300/6-8
PO Box 399 74352 — 918-479-5244
Charles Coleman, prin. — Fax 479-2930

Lone Grove, Carter, Pop. 5,075
Lone Grove ISD — 1,100/PK-12
PO Box 1330 73443 — 580-657-3131
Gary Scott, supt. — Fax 657-4355
www.lonegrove.k12.ok.us/
Lone Grove HS — 300/9-12
PO Box 1330 73443 — 580-657-3133
Russell Noland, prin. — Fax 657-6624
Lone Grove MS, PO Box 1330 73443 — 200/6-8
Ted Clardy, prin. — 580-657-3132

Lone Wolf, Kiowa, Pop. 474
Lone Wolf ISD — 100/PK-12
PO Box 158 73655 — 580-846-9091
James Sutherland, supt. — Fax 846-5266
Lone Wolf HS — 50/9-12
PO Box 158 73655 — 580-846-9091
James Sutherland, prin. — Fax 846-5266

Lookeba, Caddo, Pop. 132
Lookeba-Sickles ISD — 200/PK-12
RR 1 Box 34 73053 — 405-457-6623
Dennis Byrd, supt. — Fax 457-6619
Lookeba-Sickles HS — 100/9-12
RR 1 Box 34 73053 — 405-457-6621
Kirk Wilson, prin.

Luther, Oklahoma, Pop. 1,083
Luther ISD — 800/K-12
PO Box 430 73054 — 405-277-3233
W.B. Wilson, supt. — Fax 277-3498
lutherlions.org
Luther HS — 200/9-12
PO Box 430 73054 — 405-277-3263
Jan Scheffler, prin. — Fax 277-3630
Luther MS — 200/6-8
PO Box 430 73054 — 405-277-3264
Barry Gunn, prin. — Fax 277-3877

Mc Alester, Pittsburg, Pop. 17,566
CareerTech Skills Centers
Supt. — None
Dom Garrison, supt.
Brannon Skills Center — Vo/Tech
PO Box 1999, — 918-423-9212

McAlester ISD — 2,000/PK-12
PO Box 1027, — 918-423-4771
Jim Northcutt, supt. — Fax 423-8166
www.mcalester.k12.ok.us/
McAlester HS — 700/9-12
PO Box 1027, — 918-423-4776
Allen Wadsworth, prin. — Fax 423-8689
Puterbaugh MS — 400/7-8
PO Box 1027, — 918-423-5445
Randy Hughes, prin. — Fax 423-7021

OK Dept. of Voc. & Tech. Education
Supt. — None
Kiamichi Technology Center — Vo/Tech
301 Kiamichi Dr, — 918-426-0940
Fred Probis, dir. — Fax 426-1626

Mc Curtain, Haskell, Pop. 474
McCurtain SD — 300/PK-12
PO Box 189, — 918-945-7237
Darrell Adcock, supt. — Fax 945-7064
www.mccurtain.k12.ok.us/
McCurtain HS, PO Box 189, — 100/9-12
Perry Arnwine, prin. — 918-945-7236

Mc Loud, Pottawatomie, Pop. 2,821
CareerTech Skills Centers
Supt. — None
Dom Garrison, supt.
Bassett Skills Center — Vo/Tech
29501 Kickapoo Rd, — 405-964-5540

Mc Loud ISD — 1,300/K-12
PO Box 240, — 405-964-3314
Ronnie Renfrow, supt. — Fax 964-2801
www.mcloud.k12.ok.us
Mc Loud HS — 500/9-12
PO Box 60, — 405-964-3311
Leigh Todd, prin. — Fax 964-3498
Mc Loud JHS — 300/7-8
PO Box 730, — 405-964-3312
Doug Van Scoyoc, prin. — Fax 964-7530

Macomb, Pottawatomie, Pop. 63
Macomb ISD — 400/PK-12
36591 State Highway 59B 74852 — 405-598-3892
Randy Cottrell, supt. — Fax 598-8041
Macomb HS — 100/9-12
36591 State Highway 59B 74852 — 405-598-5420
Doran Smith, prin. — Fax 598-3295

Madill, Marshall, Pop. 3,688
Madill ISD — 1,500/K-12
601 W McArthur St 73446 — 580-795-3303
Jon Dotson, supt. — Fax 795-3210
www.madillok.com
Madill HS — 400/9-12
700 S 5th Ave 73446 — 580-795-3339
Monte Womack, prin. — Fax 795-2657
Madill MS — 300/6-8
601 W McArthur St 73446 — 580-795-7373
Steve Wilburn, prin. — Fax 795-6930

Mangum, Greer, Pop. 2,745
Mangum ISD — 700/PK-12
400 N Pennsylvania Ave 73554 — 580-782-3371
Mike Southall, supt. — Fax 782-2313
www.mangum.k12.ok.us/
Mangum HS — 200/10-12
301 N Oklahoma Ave 73554 — 580-782-3343
Micky Lively, prin. — Fax 782-3265
Mangum JHS — 100/7-9
400 N Oklahoma Ave 73554 — 580-782-2702
Mary Jane Scott, prin. — Fax 782-5911

Mannford, Creek, Pop. 2,758
Mannford ISD — 1,600/K-12
PO Box 100 74044 — 918-865-4062
Dr. Emet Callaway, supt. — Fax 865-3405
www.mannford.k12.ok.us
Mannford HS — 600/9-12
PO Box 100 74044 — 918-865-3841
Roger Moore, prin. — Fax 865-2813
Mannford MS — 400/6-8
PO Box 100 74044 — 918-865-4680
Molly Gregory, prin. — Fax 865-2862

Marietta, Love, Pop. 2,526
Marietta ISD — 900/PK-12
PO Box 289 73448 — 580-276-9444
James Howard, supt. — Fax 276-4037
www.marietta.k12.ok.us
Marietta HS — 300/9-12
PO Box 289 73448 — 580-276-3204
Larry Case, prin. — Fax 276-1208
Marietta MS — 200/6-8
PO Box 289 73448 — 580-276-3886
Jeff Dooley, prin. — Fax 276-1203

Marlow, Stephens, Pop. 4,531
Bray-Doyle ISD — 500/PK-12
1205 S Brooks Rd 73055 — 580-658-5076
R. Kevin McKinley, supt. — Fax 658-5888
Bray-Doyle HS — 100/9-12
1205 S Brooks Rd 73055 — 580-658-5071
Jack Williams, prin.

Central High ISD — 400/PK-12
RR 3 Box 249 73055 — 580-658-6858
Bennie Newton, supt. — Fax 658-8010
www.centralhighpublicschools.com/
Central HS — 100/9-12
RR 3 Box 249 73055 — 580-658-2929
Mark Perry, prin. — Fax 658-8010

Marlow ISD — 1,400/PK-12
PO Box 73 73055 — 580-658-2719
George E. Coffman, supt. — Fax 658-6455
www.marlow.k12.ok.us
Marlow HS — 400/9-12
PO Box 73 73055 — 580-658-1516
Tom Cosgrove, prin. — Fax 658-1520
Marlow MS — 300/6-8
PO Box 73 73055 — 580-658-2619
Tommy Williams, prin. — Fax 658-1169

Mason, Okfuskee
Mason ISD — 300/PK-12
RR 1 Box 143B 74859 — 918-623-0231
John Cope, supt. — Fax 623-0884
www.mason.k12.ok.us/
Mason HS — 100/9-12
RR 1 Box 143B 74859 — 918-623-0107
Eddie Weaver, prin. — Fax 623-0147

Maud, Pottawatomie, Pop. 1,159
Maud ISD 300/PK-12
PO Box 130 74854 405-374-2416
J.E. Pryor, supt. Fax 374-2628
www.maud.k12.ok.us/
Maud HS 100/9-12
PO Box 130 74854 405-374-2425
David Shelton, prin. Fax 374-2895

Maysville, Garvin, Pop. 1,296
Maysville ISD 500/PK-12
600 1st St 73057 888-806-5220
William Martin, supt. Fax 867-4864
Maysville HS 100/9-12
600 1st St 73057 888-806-5330
Shelly Hildebrand, prin. Fax 867-4864

Medford, Grant, Pop. 1,072
Medford ISD 200/PK-12
301 N Main St 73759 580-395-2392
Jason Sternberger, supt. Fax 395-2391
www.medford.k12.ok.us/
Medford JSHS 100/7-12
301 N Main St 73759 580-395-2392
Mickey Geurkink, prin. Fax 395-2391

Meeker, Lincoln, Pop. 989
Meeker SD 900/PK-12
214 E Carl Hubbell Blvd 74855 405-279-3511
Robert Hightower, supt. Fax 279-2765
www.meeker.k12.ok.us/
Meeker HS 300/9-12
214 E Carl Hubbell Blvd 74855 405-279-2113
Rita Palmer, prin.
Meeker MS 200/6-8
214 E Carl Hubbell Blvd 74855 405-279-2414
Mike Hill, prin.

Miami, Ottawa, Pop. 13,565
Miami ISD 2,300/K-12
26 N Main St 74354 918-542-8455
William Stephens, supt. Fax 542-1236
www.miami.k12.ok.us
Miami HS 700/9-12
2000 E Central Ave 74354 918-542-4421
Mike Reece, prin. Fax 542-7421
Rogers MS 600/6-8
504 Goodrich Blvd 74354 918-542-5588
Mark Stanton, prin. Fax 542-4400

Northeastern Oklahoma A&M College Post-Sec.
200 I St NE 74354 918-542-8441

Midwest City, Oklahoma, Pop. 54,890
Midwest City-Del City ISD 14,400/PK-12
7217 SE 15th St 73110 405-737-4461
William Scoggan M.Ed., supt. Fax 739-1615
www.mid-del.net
Albert JHS 900/7-9
2515 S Post Rd 73130 405-739-1761
Joyce Honey, prin. Fax 739-1780
Albert SHS 800/10-12
2009 S Post Rd 73130 405-739-1726
Silvya Kirk Ph.D., prin. Fax 739-1685
Eubanks Mid-Del Technology Center Vo/Tech
1621 Maple Dr 73110 405-739-1707
Debbie Neugent, prin. Fax 739-1716
Jarman JHS 500/7-9
5 W McArthur Dr 73110 405-739-1771
Rick Croslin, prin. Fax 739-1773
Midwest City SHS 1,200/10-12
213 Elm St 73110 405-739-1741
Ron Stearns, prin. Fax 739-1675
Monroney JHS 700/7-9
7400 E Reno Ave 73110 405-739-1786
Chris Reynolds, prin. Fax 739-1789
Other Schools – See Del City

OK Dept. of Voc. & Tech. Education
Supt. — None
Mid-Del Technology Center Vo/Tech
1621 Maple Dr 73110 405-739-1707
Fax 739-1716

Rose State College Post-Sec.
6420 SE 15th St 73110 405-733-7300

Milburn, Johnston, Pop. 301
Milburn ISD 200/PK-12
PO Box 429 73450 580-443-5522
Jon Holmes, supt. Fax 443-5303
www.milburn.k12.ok.us
Milburn HS 100/9-12
PO Box 429 73450 580-443-5522
Jon Holmes, prin. Fax 443-5303

Mill Creek, Johnston, Pop. 329
Mill Creek ISD 200/PK-12
PO Box 118 74856 580-384-5514
Richard Bowen, supt. Fax 384-3920
www.millcreek.k12.ok.us
Mill Creek HS 50/9-12
PO Box 118 74856 580-384-5447
Barbara McDonald, prin. Fax 384-3920

Minco, Grady, Pop. 1,767
Minco ISD 500/PK-12
PO Box 428 73059 405-352-4867
Richard Brownen, supt. Fax 352-4006
www.minco.k12.ok.us
Minco HS 200/9-12
PO Box 428 73059 405-352-4377
Robert Odam, prin. Fax 352-4006
Minco MS 100/6-8
PO Box 428 73059 405-352-4377
Troy Wittrock, prin. Fax 352-4006

Moore, Cleveland, Pop. 47,697
Moore ISD 19,300/PK-12
1500 SE 4th St 73160 405-735-4200
Deborah Arato, supt. Fax 735-4392
www.mooreschools.com/
Central JHS 900/7-9
400 N Broadway St 73160 405-793-3265
David Peak, prin. Fax 895-7398
Highland East JHS 900/7-9
1200 SE 4th St 73160 405-735-4580
John Marren, prin. Fax 793-3198
Highland West JHS 700/7-9
901 N Santa Fe Ave 73160 405-735-4600
Peggy Pate, prin. Fax 793-3218
Moore SHS 1,900/10-12
300 N Eastern Ave 73160 405-793-3100
Mike Coyle, prin. Fax 793-3140
Other Schools – See Oklahoma City

Hillsdale Free Will Baptist College Post-Sec.
PO Box 7208 73153 405-912-9000
Oklahoma Health Academy Post-Sec.
1939 N Moore Ave 73160 405-912-2777
Southwest Christian Academy 100/PK-12
1005 SW 4th St Ste A 73160 405-794-9000
Janet Moran, prin. Fax 794-7558

Mooreland, Woodward, Pop. 1,221
Mooreland ISD 500/PK-12
PO Box 75 73852 580-994-5388
Terry Kellner, supt. Fax 994-5900
www.mooreland.k12.ok.us
Mooreland HS 100/9-12
PO Box 75 73852 580-994-5426
Ron Wilson, prin. Fax 994-2344

Morris, Okmulgee, Pop. 1,326
Morris ISD 1,000/PK-12
PO Box 80 74445 918-733-9072
James Lyons, supt. Fax 733-4205
Morris HS 400/9-12
PO Box 80 74445 918-733-4198
Andrew Ewton, prin. Fax 733-2857
Morris MS 200/6-8
PO Box 80 74445 918-733-4551
Greg Large, prin. Fax 733-4618

Morrison, Noble, Pop. 625
Morrison ISD 500/PK-12
PO Box 176 73061 580-724-3341
Dennis Casey, supt. Fax 724-3004
www.morrison.k12.ok.us
Morrison HS, PO Box 176 73061 100/9-12
David Cartmell, prin. 580-724-3307

Mounds, Creek, Pop. 1,278
Liberty ISD 500/PK-12
2727 E 201st St S 74047 918-366-8496
Dr. Kent Holbrook, supt. Fax 366-8497
www.liberty.k12.ok.us
Liberty HS, 2727 E 201st St S 74047 200/9-12
Randy Hess, prin. 918-366-8784

Mounds ISD 800/PK-12
PO Box 189 74047 918-827-6100
Dr. Jim Gray, supt. Fax 827-3704
www.mounds.k12.ok.us/
Mounds HS, PO Box 189 74047 200/9-12
Beverly Carile, prin. 918-827-6200
Mounds MS, PO Box 189 74047 300/5-8
Tod Williams, prin. 918-827-6300

Mountain View, Kiowa, Pop. 830
Mountain View-Gotebo ISD 300/PK-12
RR 2 Box 88 73062 580-347-2211
Paula Squires, supt. Fax 347-2869
Mountain View-Gotebo HS 100/9-12
RR 2 Box 88 73062 580-347-2211
Brad Logan, prin.

Moyers, Pushmataha
Moyers SD 100/K-12
PO Box 88 74557 580-298-5549
Donna Dudley, supt. Fax 298-2022
www.moyers.k12.ok.us/
Moyers HS 100/9-12
PO Box 88 74557 580-298-6951
LaWanda Vaughn, prin. Fax 298-2022

Muldrow, Sequoyah, Pop. 3,168
Muldrow ISD 1,700/PK-12
PO Box 660 74948 918-427-7406
Roger Sharp, supt. Fax 427-6088
www.muldrow.k12.ok.us
Muldrow HS 500/9-12
PO Box 660 74948 918-427-3274
David Rhodes, prin. Fax 427-1035
Muldrow MS 500/5-8
PO Box 660 74948 918-427-5421
Montea Wight, prin. Fax 427-1034

Muskogee, Muskogee, Pop. 39,766
Hilldale ISD 1,800/PK-12
500 E Smith Ferry Rd 74403 918-683-0273
D. B. Merrill, supt. Fax 683-8725
www.hilldale.k12.ok.us
Hilldale HS 500/9-12
300 E Smith Ferry Rd 74403 918-683-3253
Dwayne Pemberton, prin. Fax 683-0622
Hilldale MS 400/6-8
400 E Smith Ferry Rd 74403 918-683-0763
John Engelbrecht, prin. Fax 683-0766

Muskogee ISD 6,200/PK-12
202 W Broadway St 74401 918-684-3700
Michael Garde, supt. Fax 684-3827
www.mpsi20.org
Muskogee 7th & 8th Grade Center 900/7-8
Callahan & North S St 74403 918-684-3775
Dr. Kathryn Turlington, prin. Fax 684-3776
Muskogee HS 1,700/9-12
3200 E Shawnee Rd 74403 918-684-3750
Gary Bivin, prin. Fax 684-3751

OK Dept. of Voc. & Tech. Education
Supt. — None
Indian Capital Technology Center Vo/Tech
2403 N 41st St E 74403 918-686-7565
Tom Stiles, supt. Fax 686-7564
Indian Capital Technology Center Vo/Tech
2403 N 41st St E 74403 918-687-6383
Jerry Belton, dir. Fax 687-6624

Bacone College Post-Sec.
2299 Old Bacone Rd 74403 918-781-7340
Muskogee General Hospital Post-Sec.
300 Rockefeller Dr 74401 918-682-5501
Parkview School OK School for the Blind Post-Sec.
3300 Gibson St 74403 918-682-6641
Virgil's Beauty College Post-Sec.
111 S 9th St 74401 918-682-9429

Mustang, Canadian, Pop. 15,887
Mustang ISD 7,400/PK-12
906 S Heights Dr 73064 405-376-2461
Karl Springer, supt. Fax 376-7333
www.mustangps.org
Mustang HS 1,600/10-12
906 S Heights Dr 73064 405-376-2404
Terry Tipton, prin. Fax 376-7347
Mustang MS 900/6-8
906 S Heights Dr 73064 405-376-2448
Linda Wilkes, prin. Fax 376-7373
Mustang Mid HS 600/9-9
906 S Heights Dr 73064 405-376-7855
Kenny Nelson, prin. Fax 376-7852
Mustang North MS 800/6-8
906 S Heights Dr 73064 405-324-2236
Ralph Smith, prin. Fax 324-2258

Mutual, Woodward, Pop. 78
Sharon-Mutual ISD 300/PK-12
RR 1 Box 290 73853 580-989-3210
Doug Evans, supt. Fax 989-3241
www.smps.k12.ok.us
Sharon-Mutual HS 100/9-12
RR 1 Box 290 73853 580-989-3231
Clint Ford, prin.

Newcastle, McClain, Pop. 6,303
Newcastle ISD 1,200/K-12
101 N Main St 73065 405-387-2890
Robert Everett, supt. Fax 387-3482
www.newcastle.k12.ok.us
Newcastle HS 400/9-12
101 N Main St 73065 405-387-4304
Joe Cox, prin. Fax 387-3461
Newcastle MS 300/6-8
418 NW 10th St 73065 405-387-3139
Randy Scott, prin. Fax 387-5563

Newkirk, Kay, Pop. 2,162
Newkirk ISD 700/PK-12
PO Box 91 74647 580-362-2388
Carl Barnes, supt. Fax 362-3413
www.newkirk.k12.ok.us
Newkirk HS 200/9-12
PO Box 91 74647 580-362-6241
Dwight Winburn, prin. Fax 362-6242
Newkirk MS 200/6-8
PO Box 485 74647 580-362-2516
Jim Wiersig, prin. Fax 362-1150

Ninnekah, Grady, Pop. 1,046
Ninnekah ISD 500/PK-12
PO Box 275 73067 405-224-4092
Todd Bunch, supt. Fax 224-4096
Ninnekah HS 100/9-12
PO Box 275 73067 405-224-4299
David Pitts, prin. Fax 224-4665
Ninnekah JHS 100/7-8
PO Box 275 73067 405-224-4299
David Pitts, prin. Fax 224-4665

Noble, Cleveland, Pop. 5,518
Noble ISD 2,800/PK-12
PO Box 499 73068 405-872-3452
Curtis Inge, supt. Fax 872-3271
www.nobleps.com
Noble HS 800/9-12
4601 E Etowah Rd 73068 405-872-3441
Frank Soloman, prin. Fax 872-9824
Noble MS 700/6-8
1201 N 8th St 73068 405-872-3495
Gary Lundy, prin. Fax 872-8670

Norman, Cleveland, Pop. 101,719
Little Axe ISD 1,200/PK-12
2000 168th Ave NE 73026 405-329-7691
Barry Damrill, supt. Fax 579-2929
littleaxe.k12.ok.us
Little Axe HS 400/9-12
2000 168th Ave NE 73026 405-329-1612
Jim Klepper, prin. Fax 329-2914
Little Axe MS 300/6-8
2000 168th Ave NE 73026 405-329-2156
Dalton Griffin, prin. Fax 579-2937

Norman ISD 12,700/PK-12
131 S Flood Ave 73069 405-364-1339
Dr. Joseph Siano, supt. Fax 366-5851
www.norman.k12.ok.us
Alcott MS 600/6-8
1919 W Boyd St 73069 405-366-5845
Dana Morris, prin. Fax 447-6572
Irving MS 600/6-8
125 Vicksburg Ave 73071 405-366-5941
Jerry Privett, prin. Fax 366-5944
Longfellow MS 600/6-8
215 N Ponca Ave 73071 405-366-5948
Darien Moore, prin. Fax 366-5952
Norman HS 1,800/9-12
911 W Main St 73069 405-366-5812
Dr. Lynne Chesley, prin. Fax 366-5945
Norman North HS 2,100/9-12
1809 Stubbeman Ave 73069 405-366-5954
Jerry Winkle, prin. Fax 573-3590
Whittier MS 900/6-8
2000 W Brooks St 73069 405-366-5956
Sharon Dean, prin. Fax 447-6562

OK Dept. of Voc. & Tech. Education
Supt. — None
Moore Norman Technology Center Vo/Tech
4701 12th Ave NW 73069 405-364-5763
Dr. John Hunter, supt. Fax 217-8277

Blue Eagle Christian Academy 50/PK-12
2404 Classen Blvd 73071 405-364-7200
Bertha Symes, admin.

Community Christian S 700/PK-12
3002 Broce Dr 73072 405-329-2500
Barbara Ohsfeldt, admin. Fax 329-3510
University of Oklahoma at Norman Post-Sec.
660 Parrington Oval 73019 405-325-0311

Nowata, Nowata, Pop. 4,034
Nowata ISD 1,100/PK-12
707 W Osage Ave 74048 918-273-3425
Fred Bailey, supt. Fax 273-2105
www.nowataps.k12.ok.us/
Nowata HS, 707 W Osage Ave 74048 300/9-12
Michelle Miller, prin. 918-273-2221
Nowata MS, 707 W Osage Ave 74048 300/6-8
Kathy Berry, prin. 918-273-1346

Oaks, Delaware, Pop. 422
Oaks-Mission ISD 300/PK-12
PO Box 160 74359 918-868-2183
Wyman Thompson, supt. Fax 868-2707
Oaks-Mission HS, PO Box 160 74359 100/9-12
David Hampton, prin. 918-868-2499

Oilton, Creek, Pop. 1,143
Oilton ISD 400/PK-12
PO Box 130 74052 918-862-3954
Matt Posey, supt. Fax 862-3955
Oilton HS 100/9-12
PO Box 130 74052 918-862-3272
Tony McCool, prin. Fax 862-3763

Okarche, Kingfisher, Pop. 1,158
Okarche ISD 300/PK-12
PO Box 276 73762 405-263-7300
Robert Barnett, supt. Fax 263-7515
www.okarche.k12.ok.us/
Okarche HS 100/10-12
PO Box 276 73762 405-263-7212
Wynona Knopp, prin. Fax 263-7515
Okarche JHS, PO Box 276 73762 100/7-9
Wynona Knopp, prin. 405-263-7212

Okay, Wagoner, Pop. 593
Okay ISD 500/PK-12
PO Box 830 74446 918-682-2548
Mickey Igert, supt. Fax 683-8331
www.okayschool.k12.ok.us/
Okay HS 200/9-12
PO Box 830 74446 918-682-0371
Donald Branscum, prin. Fax 682-7653

Okeene, Blaine, Pop. 1,210
Okeene ISD 300/K-12
PO Box 409 73763 580-822-3268
Ron Pittman, supt. Fax 822-4123
Okeene JSHS 100/7-12
PO Box 409 73763 580-822-3219
Jeremy Osmus, prin. Fax 822-4123

Okemah, Okfuskee, Pop. 2,970
Okemah ISD 900/PK-12
107 W Date St 74859 918-623-1874
Tom Condict, supt. Fax 623-1203
www.okemah.k12.ok.us
Okemah HS 300/9-12
704 E Date St 74859 918-623-1274
Tom Howell, prin. Fax 623-1884
Okemah MS 200/4-8
107 W Date St 74859 918-623-0212
Tony Dean, prin. Fax 623-9151

Oklahoma City, Oklahoma, Pop. 531,324
CareerTech Skills Centers
Supt. — None
Dom Garrison, supt.
Hillside Skills Center Vo/Tech
3300 N Martin Luther King 73111 405-425-2942

Crooked Oak ISD 1,100/PK-12
1901 SE 15th St 73129 405-677-5252
Shannon Goodsell, supt. Fax 670-8070
www.crookedoak.org/
Crooked Oak HS 300/9-12
1901 SE 15th St 73129 405-677-4063
Verna Shelton, prin. Fax 677-8072
Crooked Oak MS 300/6-8
1901 SE 15th St 73129 405-672-0231
Ken Attebery, prin. Fax 670-2256

Millwood ISD 1,200/PK-12
6724 N Martin Luther King 73111 405-478-1336
Dr. Gloria Griffin, supt. Fax 478-4698
www.millwood.k12.ok.us
Millwood Arts Academy 4-8
6700 N Martin Luther King 73111 405-478-0630
Christine Harrison, prin.
Millwood HS 300/9-12
6718 N Martin Luther King 73111 405-478-0504
Nanette Thomas, prin.

Moore ISD
Supt. — See Moore
Brink JHS 1,100/7-9
11420 S Western Ave 73170 405-692-5620
Janet Southard, prin. Fax 692-5634
West JHS 1,000/7-9
9400 S Pennsylvania Ave 73159 405-735-4620
Dr. Michaele Benn, prin. Fax 692-5660
Westmoore SHS 2,100/10-12
12613 S Western Ave 73170 405-735-4800
Mark Hunt, prin. Fax 692-5711

OK Dept. of Voc. & Tech. Education
Supt. — None
Metro Tech Vo/Tech
1900 Springlake Dr 73111 405-424-8324
Dr. James Branscum, supt. Fax 424-5419
Metro Tech-Aviation Career Center Vo/Tech
5600 S MacArthur Blvd 73179 405-685-0008
Peter Lee, dir. Fax 681-5644
Metro Tech South Bryant Campus Vo/Tech
4901 S Bryant Ave 73129 405-424-8324
Jeanne Webb, dir. Fax 670-6895
Metro Tech-Springlake Campus Vo/Tech
1900 Springlake Dr 73111 405-424-8324
Fax 528-1512

Tuttle-Portland Campus Vo/Tech
12777 N Rockwell Ave 73142 405-717-7799
Dr. Kay Martin, supt. Fax 755-0028
Tuttle-Rockwell Campus Vo/Tech
12777 N Rockwell Ave 73142 405-717-7799
Dr. Kay Martin, supt. Fax 717-4112

Oklahoma City ISD 33,900/PK-12
900 N Klein Ave 73106 405-587-0000
Fax 587-0443
www.okcps.org/
Belle Isle MS 400/6-8
5904 N Villa Ave 73112 405-843-0888
Lynn Kellert, prin. Fax 841-3127
Capitol Hill HS 1,100/9-12
500 SW Grand Blvd 73109 405-616-1210
Donna Lay, prin. Fax 636-5007
Classen S of Advanced Studies 400/6-12
1901 N Ellison Ave 73106 405-556-5070
Dr. Ronald Maxfield, prin. Fax 556-5080
Douglass HS 500/7-12
900 N Martin Luther King Av 73117 405-587-4200
Vallene Cooks, prin. Fax 425-4656
Grant HS 1,500/9-12
5016 S Pennsylvania Ave 73119 405-685-6621
Phillip Wallace, prin. Fax 686-4006
Jackson MS 600/6-8
2601 S Villa Ave 73108 405-634-6357
Steve Johnson, prin. Fax 636-5078
Jefferson MS 1,000/6-8
6800 S Blackwelder Ave 73159 405-632-2341
Gloria Torres, prin. Fax 636-5084
Marshall HS 600/10-12
9017 N University Ave 73114 405-848-6871
Cleo McGlory, prin. Fax 841-3109
New John Marshall HS 7-12
12201 N Portland Ave 73120 405-587-0402
Trina Liles, prin.
Northeast Academy for Health Sci./Eng. 500/6-12
3100 N Kelley Ave 73111 405-424-1491
Dr. Brian Staples, prin. Fax 425-4609
Northwest Classen HS 1,200/9-12
2801 NW 27th St 73107 405-942-5551
Tami Sanders, prin. Fax 942-3900
Oklahoma Centennial HS 7-12
9017 N University Ave 73114 405-751-1210
Carole Thompson, prin.
Roosevelt MS 900/6-8
3233 SW 44th St 73119 405-685-7795
Marilyn Vrooman, prin. Fax 686-4059
Southeast HS 800/9-12
5401 S Shields Blvd 73129 405-636-5008
Dr. Michael Maples, prin. Fax 636-5024
Taft MS 1,000/6-8
2901 NW 23rd St 73107 405-946-1431
Lisa Johnson, prin. Fax 945-1126
Webster MS 800/6-8
6708 S Santa Fe Ave 73139 405-632-6653
Richard Brown, prin. Fax 636-5094
Other Schools – See Spencer

Oklahoma School of Science & Math 200/11-12
1141 N Lincoln Blvd 73104 405-521-6436
Dr. Edna Manning, pres. Fax 521-6442
www.ossm.edu/
Oklahoma School of Science & Math 11-12
1141 N Lincoln Blvd 73104 405-521-6436
Dr. Edna Manning, pres. Fax 521-6442

Putnam City ISD 19,000/PK-12
5401 NW 40th St 73122 405-495-5200
Dr. Jim Capps, supt. Fax 495-8648
www.putnamcityschools.org
Capps MS 900/6-8
4020 N Grove Ave 73122 405-787-3660
Christie Baker, prin. Fax 491-7536
Cooper MS 900/6-8
8001 River Bend Blvd 73132 405-720-9887
Jennifer DeSouza, prin. Fax 728-5632
Hefner MS 1,200/6-8
8400 N Macarthur Blvd 73132 405-721-2411
Lise Finley, prin. Fax 728-5645
Mayfield MS 700/6-8
1600 N Purdue Ave 73127 405-947-8693
Dr. Dick Balenseifen, prin. Fax 948-9000
Putnam City HS 2,000/9-12
5300 NW 50th St 73122 405-789-4350
Dr. Don Wentroth, prin. Fax 789-1662
Putnam City North HS 2,200/9-12
11800 N Rockwell Ave 73162 405-722-4220
Dr. Brian Chastain, prin. Fax 721-4946
Putnam City West HS 1,700/9-12
8500 NW 23rd St 73127 405-787-1140
Buster Meeks, prin. Fax 491-7602
Other Schools – See Bethany

Western Heights ISD 3,100/PK-12
8401 SW 44th St 73179 405-350-3410
Joe Kitchens, supt. Fax 745-6322
www.westernheights.k12.ok.us
Western Heights HS 800/9-12
8201 SW 44th St 73179 405-350-3435
Jean Adams, prin. Fax 745-6315
Western Heights MS 700/6-8
8435 SW 44th St 73179 405-350-3455
Dewayne White, prin. Fax 745-6341

ATI Career Training Center Post-Sec.
2401 NW 23rd St Ste 14 73107 405-445-5740
Bishop McGuinness HS 700/9-12
801 NW 50th St 73118 405-842-6638
David Morton, prin. Fax 858-9550
Casady S 900/PK-12
PO Box 20390 73156 405-749-3100
Charles Britton, hdmstr. Fax 749-3214
CC's Cosmetology College Post-Sec.
4439 NW 50th St 73112 405-943-2300
Central State Beauty Academy Post-Sec.
8494 NW Expressway St 73162 405-722-4499
Heritage College Post-Sec.
7100 S I 35 Srvce Rd #7118 73149 405-631-3399
Heritage Hall S 800/PK-12
1800 NW 122nd St 73120 405-749-3001
Guy Bramble, hdmstr. Fax 751-7372
Hollywood Cosmetology Center Post-Sec.
PO Box 890488 73189 405-364-3375

ITT Technical Institute Post-Sec.
1900 NW Expressway St #305R 73118
405-810-4100
Metro Area Vocational Technical School Post-Sec.
1900 Springlake Dr 73111 405-424-8324
Mid-America Christian University Post-Sec.
3500 SW 119th St 73170 405-691-3800
Mt. St. Mary's HS 200/9-12
2801 S Shartel Ave 73109 405-631-8865
Talita DeNegri, prin. Fax 631-9209
Oklahoma Christian University Post-Sec.
PO Box 11000 73136 405-425-5000
Oklahoma City Community College Post-Sec.
7777 S May Ave 73159 405-682-1611
Oklahoma City University Post-Sec.
2501 N Blackwelder Ave 73106 405-521-5000
Oklahoma State University-Oklahoma City Post-Sec.
900 N Portland Ave 73107 405-947-4421
Parkview Adventist Academy 50/K-10
4201 N Martin Luther King 73111 405-427-6525
Fax 427-1154
Platt College Post-Sec.
309 S Ann Arbor Ave 73128 405-946-7799
Platt College Post-Sec.
2727 W Memorial Rd 73134 405-749-2433
State Barber and Hair Design College Post-Sec.
2514 S Agnew Ave 73108 405-631-8621
Tuttle Vocational Technical Center Post-Sec.
12777 N Rockwell Ave 73142 405-722-7799
University Hospital of Oklahoma City Post-Sec.
PO Box 26307 73126 405-271-4000
University of Oklahoma Health Sciences Post-Sec.
1000 Stanton L Young Blvd 73190 405-271-4000
Vatterott College Post-Sec.
4621 NW 23rd St 73127 405-945-0088
Wright Business School Post-Sec.
2219 SW 74th St Ste 122 73159 405-681-2300

Okmulgee, Okmulgee, Pop. 12,854
OK Dept. of Voc. & Tech. Education
Supt. — None
Green Country Technology Center Vo/Tech
PO Box 1217 74447 918-758-0840
Danne Spurlock, supt. Fax 758-0422

Okmulgee ISD 1,900/PK-12
PO Box 1346 74447 918-758-2000
Paul McGee, supt. Fax 758-2088
www.okmulgee.k12.ok.us
Okmulgee HS 600/9-12
415 W 3rd St 74447 918-758-2075
David Parker, prin. Fax 758-2096
Okmulgee MS 400/6-8
1421 Martin Luther King Dr 74447 918-758-2050
John Whitfield, prin. Fax 758-2095

Oklahoma State University-Okmulgee Post-Sec.
1801 E 4th St 74447 800-722-4471

Oktaha, Muskogee, Pop. 334
Oktaha ISD 600/PK-12
PO Box 9 74450 918-687-7556
Jerry Needham, supt. Fax 687-0074
Oktaha HS, PO Box 9 74450 200/9-12
Neoma Buckley, prin. 918-687-3672

Olustee, Jackson, Pop. 645
Olustee ISD 200/PK-12
PO Box 70 73560 580-648-2243
Roger Allen, supt. Fax 648-2501
Olustee HS 100/9-12
PO Box 70 73560 580-648-2243
Darinda Welch, prin. Fax 648-2501

Omega, Kingfisher
Lomega ISD 200/PK-12
RR 1 Box 46 73764 405-729-4215
Steve Mendell, supt. Fax 729-4666
www.lomega.k12.ok.us
Lomega HS 50/9-12
RR 1 Box 46 73764 405-729-4281
Karen Castonguay, prin. Fax 729-4666

OK Dept. of Voc. & Tech. Education
Supt. — None
Chisholm Trail Technology Center Vo/Tech
RR 1 Box 60 73764 405-729-8324
Tim Geis, supt. Fax 729-8335

Oologah, Rogers, Pop. 1,121
Oologah-Talala ISD 1,700/K-12
PO Box 189 74053 918-443-6000
Rick Thomas, supt. Fax 443-9088
www.oologah.k12.ok.us
Oologah HS 600/9-12
PO Box 189 74053 918-443-6211
Jack Chambers, prin. Fax 443-2418
Oologah MS 400/6-8
PO Box 189 74053 918-443-6151
Melissa Overcash, prin. Fax 443-2875

Orlando, Logan, Pop. 215
Mulhall-Orlando ISD 300/PK-12
PO Box 8 73073 580-455-2211
Dr. Don Sjoberg, supt. Fax 455-8019
www.mulhall-orlando.k12.ok.us
Mulhall-Orlando HS 100/9-12
PO Box 8 73073 580-455-2212
Pat Smith, prin. Fax 455-8019

Owasso, Tulsa, Pop. 23,771
Owasso ISD 7,600/K-12
1501 N Ash St 74055 918-272-5367
Dr. Clark Ogilvie, supt. Fax 272-8111
www.owasso.k12.ok.us
Owasso Eighth Grade Center 600/8-8
1501 N Ash St 74055 918-272-6274
Deirdre Hodge, prin. Fax 272-5562
Owasso HS 1,000/11-12
1501 N Ash St 74055 918-272-5334
Sam Herriman, prin. Fax 272-8108
Owasso Mid HS 1,200/9-10
1501 N Ash St 74055 918-274-3000
Don Huggins, prin. Fax 274-3006

Rejoice Christian S 600/PK-10
13413 E 106th St N 74055 918-272-7235
Charles Horstman, admin. Fax 516-0062

Paden, Okfuskee, Pop. 430
Paden ISD 300/PK-12
PO Box 370 74860 405-932-5053
Keith Kincade, supt. Fax 932-4132
www.paden.k12.ok.us/
Paden HS, PO Box 370 74860 100/9-12
Jeremy Ramsey, prin. 405-932-4465

Panama, LeFlore, Pop. 1,396
Panama ISD 800/PK-12
PO Box 1680 74951 918-963-2217
Darthur Drummonds, supt. Fax 963-4860
Panama HS 200/9-12
PO Box 1680 74951 918-963-2215
Larry Brooks, prin. Fax 963-2638
Panama MS 200/6-8
PO Box 1680 74951 918-963-2213
Grant Ralls, prin. Fax 963-2463

Panola, Latimer
Panola ISD 300/PK-12
PO Box 6 74559 918-465-3298
Alan Lumpkins, supt. Fax 465-3656
www.panola.k12.ok.us/
Panola HS 100/9-12
PO Box 6 74559 918-465-3813
Linda Albright, prin. Fax 465-2996

Paoli, Garvin, Pop. 654
Paoli ISD 300/PK-12
PO Box 278 73074 405-484-7336
Rick Worden, supt. Fax 484-7268
www.paoli.k12.ok.us/
Paoli HS, PO Box 278 73074 100/9-12
Greg Benson, prin. 405-484-7336

Park Hill, Cherokee
Keys SD 800/PK-12
26622 S 520 Rd 74451 918-458-1835
Jerry Hood, supt. Fax 456-7502
www.keys.k12.ok.us
Keys HS 300/9-12
26622 S 520 Rd 74451 918-458-1835
Calvin Klugh, prin. Fax 456-7502

Pauls Valley, Garvin, Pop. 6,178
Pauls Valley ISD 1,300/PK-12
PO Box 780 73075 405-238-6453
Bobby D. Russell, supt. Fax 238-9178
www.paulsvalley.k12.ok.us
Pauls Valley JHS 300/7-9
PO Box 780 73075 405-238-1239
Martha Graham, prin. Fax 238-1410
Pauls Valley SHS 300/10-12
PO Box 780 73075 405-238-6497
Pete Campbell, prin. Fax 238-1236

Pawhuska, Osage, Pop. 3,533
Pawhuska ISD 1,000/PK-12
1801 McKenzie St 74056 918-287-1281
Ben West, supt. Fax 287-4461
pawhuska.k12.ok.us
Pawhuska HS 300/9-12
621 E 15th St 74056 918-287-1262
Robert Schornick, prin. Fax 287-1236
Pawhuska JHS 100/7-8
615 E 15th St 74056 918-287-1264
Jon Culver, prin. Fax 287-2062

Pawnee, Pawnee, Pop. 2,204
Pawnee ISD 800/PK-12
615 Denver St 74058 918-762-3676
Ned Williams, supt. Fax 762-2704
Pawnee HS, 615 Denver St 74058 200/9-12
David Tanner, prin. 918-762-3055
Pawnee MS, 605 Denver St 74058 200/6-8
David Tanner, prin. 918-762-3055

Perkins, Payne, Pop. 2,186
Perkins-Tryon ISD 1,300/PK-12
PO Box 549 74059 405-547-5703
James Ramsey, supt. Fax 547-2020
www.p-t.k12.ok.us
Perkins-Tryon HS 300/10-12
PO Box 549 74059 405-547-5724
Margaret Hrencher, prin. Fax 547-5760
Perkins-Tryon JHS 300/7-9
PO Box 549 74059 405-547-5715
Mark Shelton, prin. Fax 547-5761

Perry, Noble, Pop. 5,105
Perry ISD 1,000/PK-12
900 Fir St 73077 580-336-4511
Brent Koontz, supt. Fax 336-5185
www.perry.k12.ok.us/
Perry Middle HS, 901 Elm St 73077 100/8-9
Scott Chenoweth, prin. 580-336-2265
Perry SHS 300/10-12
900 Fir St 73077 580-336-4415
Dr. Linda Powers, prin. Fax 336-5185

Picher, Ottawa, Pop. 1,625
Picher-Cardin ISD 300/PK-12
PO Box 280 74360 918-673-1714
Robert Walker, supt. Fax 673-1718
Picher-Cardin HS, PO Box 280 74360 100/9-12
Robert Walker, prin. 918-673-1713

Piedmont, Canadian, Pop. 4,685
Piedmont ISD 1,700/PK-12
713 Piedmont Rd N 73078 405-373-2311
Mike Hyatt, supt. Fax 373-0912
piedmont.k12.ok.us
Piedmont HS 500/9-12
1055 Edmond Rd NW 73078 405-373-5011
Todd Glasgow, prin. Fax 373-3055
Piedmont MS 400/6-8
823 2nd St NW 73078 405-373-1315
Jacky Parish, prin. Fax 373-5006

Pittsburg, Pittsburg, Pop. 283
Pittsburg ISD 200/PK-12
PO Box 200 74560 918-432-5062
Tony Potts, supt. Fax 432-5312
Pittsburg HS, PO Box 200 74560 100/9-12
Jimmy Harwood, prin. 918-432-5513

Pocola, LeFlore, Pop. 4,373
Pocola ISD 900/PK-12
PO Box 640 74902 918-436-2424
James Warden, supt. Fax 436-2437
www.pocola.k12.ok.us
Pocola HS 200/9-12
PO Box 640 74902 918-436-2042
Randy Ragland, prin. Fax 436-2920
Pocola MS, PO Box 640 74902 200/6-8
Mark McKenzie, prin. 918-436-2091

Ponca City, Kay, Pop. 25,070
OK Dept. of Voc. & Tech. Education
Supt. — None
Pioneer Technology Center Vo/Tech
2101 N Ash St 74601 580-762-8336
Dr. Doug Major, supt. Fax 762-1175

Ponca City ISD 5,100/PK-12
111 W Grand Ave 74601 580-767-8000
David Pennington, supt. Fax 767-8007
www.poncacity.k12.ok.us
East MS 500/8-8
612 E Grand Ave 74601 580-767-8010
Barbara Davis, prin. Fax 762-5301
Ponca City HS 1,600/9-12
927 N 5th St 74601 580-767-9500
John Woody, prin. Fax 767-9515

Ponca City Beauty College Post-Sec.
122 N 1st St 74601 888-557-6709

Pond Creek, Grant, Pop. 824
Pond Creek-Hunter ISD 300/PK-12
PO Box 56 73766 580-532-4242
Joel Quinn, supt. Fax 532-4965
www.pondcreek-hunter.k12.ok.us
Pond Creek-Hunter HS 100/7-12
PO Box 56 73766 580-532-4241
Joe Kelsey, prin. Fax 532-4965

Porter, Wagoner, Pop. 581
Porter Consolidated SD 500/PK-12
PO Box 120 74454 918-483-2401
Mark Fenton, supt. Fax 483-2310
Porter Consolidated HS 100/9-12
PO Box 120 74454 918-483-7011
Larry Shackelford, prin. Fax 483-2310

Porum, Muskogee, Pop. 733
Porum ISD 500/PK-12
PO Box 189 74455 918-484-5121
Mark Calavan, supt. Fax 484-2310
www.porum.k12.ok.us/
Porum HS 200/9-12
PO Box 189 74455 918-484-5122
Don Cox, prin. Fax 484-5121

Poteau, LeFlore, Pop. 8,152
OK Dept. of Voc. & Tech. Education
Supt. — None
Kiamichi Technology Center Vo/Tech
PO Box 825 74953 918-647-4525
Doug Hall, dir. Fax 647-4527

Poteau ISD 2,100/PK-12
100 Mockingbird Ln 74953 918-647-7700
Dr. Alice Smith, supt. Fax 647-9357
www.poteau.k12.ok.us
Kidd MS 400/6-8
100 Mockingbird Ln 74953 918-647-7741
Lorraine Caldwell, prin. Fax 647-4286
Poteau HS 600/9-12
100 Mockingbird Ln 74953 918-647-7716
John Spencer, prin. Fax 647-4383

Carl Albert State College Post-Sec.
1507 S McKenna St 74953 918-647-1200
Poteau Beauty College Post-Sec.
301 Turman St 74953 918-647-4119

Prague, Lincoln, Pop. 2,124
Prague ISD 1,000/PK-12
3504 NBU 74864 405-567-4455
Rick Martin, supt. Fax 567-3095
Prague HS 300/9-12
3504 NBU 74864 405-567-2281
David Smith, prin. Fax 567-4982
Prague MS 200/6-8
3504 NBU 74864 405-567-2281
Andrea Sealock, prin. Fax 567-3095

Preston, Okmulgee
Preston ISD 500/PK-12
PO Box 40 74456 918-756-3388
Mark Hudson, supt. Fax 756-2122
www.preston.k12.ok.us/
Preston HS 200/9-12
PO Box 40 74456 918-756-8636
Pam Snowden, prin. Fax 756-2122

Prue, Osage, Pop. 438
Prue ISD 400/PK-12
PO Box 130 74060 918-242-3351
Joe Hulsey, supt. Fax 242-3392
www.prue.k12.ok.us/
Prue HS 100/9-12
PO Box 130 74060 918-242-3384
Deborah Tennison, prin. Fax 242-3888

Pryor, Mayes, Pop. 8,921
OK Dept. of Voc. & Tech. Education
Supt. — None
Northeast Oklahoma Tech Center S Campus Vo/Tech
PO Box 825 74362 918-825-5555
Greg Mitchell, dir. Fax 825-6281
Northeast Oklahoma Technology Center Vo/Tech
PO Box 487 74362 918-825-7040
Dell Heavener, supt. Fax 825-3176

Pryor ISD 2,400/PK-12
PO Box 548 74362 918-825-1255
Dr. Larry Burdick, supt. Fax 825-3938
www.pryor.k12.ok.us
Pryor JHS 500/7-9
PO Box 548 74362 918-825-2371
Terry Gwartney, prin. Fax 825-3950
Pryor SHS 500/10-12
PO Box 548 74362 918-825-2340
Bill Gage, prin. Fax 825-3914

Bradford Christian S 100/K-12
2320 NE 1st St 74361 918-825-7038
Patrick Mayer, prin. Fax 825-7037
Pryor Beauty College Post-Sec.
330 W Graham Ave 74361 918-825-2795

Purcell, McClain, Pop. 5,858
Purcell ISD 1,400/PK-12
919 N 9th Ave Ste 1 73080 405-527-2146
Dr. Tony Christian, supt. Fax 527-6366
www.purcellps.k12.ok.us/
Purcell JHS 300/7-9
711 N 9th Ave 73080 405-527-2146
Bret Petty, prin. Fax 527-4454
Purcell SHS 300/10-12
201 Lester Ln 73080 405-527-6591
Don Schneberger, prin. Fax 527-6593

Quapaw, Ottawa, Pop. 975
Quapaw ISD 700/PK-12
305 W 1st St 74363 918-674-2501
Dennis Earp, supt. Fax 674-2721
Quapaw HS 200/9-12
305 W 1st St 74363 918-674-2474
Terry Tyree, prin. Fax 674-2721
Quapaw MS 200/6-8
305 W 1st St 74363 918-674-2496
Larry Radford, prin. Fax 674-2721

Quinton, Pittsburg, Pop. 1,081
Quinton ISD 500/PK-12
PO Box 670 74561 918-469-3100
Sherri A. Prentice, supt. Fax 469-3308
www.quinton.k12.ok.us/
Quinton HS 200/9-12
PO Box 670 74561 918-469-3309
J. David Smith, prin. Fax 469-2310

Ralston, Pawnee, Pop. 360
Woodland SD
Supt. — See Fairfax
Woodland MS 200/5-8
6th & McKinley 74650 918-738-4286
Bobby Rose, prin. Fax 738-4287

Ramona, Washington, Pop. 574
Caney Valley ISD 800/K-12
PO Box 410 74061 918-536-2500
James Knox, supt. Fax 536-2600
www.cvalley.k12.ok.us/
Caney Valley HS 300/9-12
PO Box 410 74061 918-536-3425
Debra Keil, prin. Fax 536-7105
Caney Valley MS, PO Box 410 74061 200/6-8
James Farrell, prin. 918-536-2705

Randlett, Cotton, Pop. 518
Big Pasture ISD 300/PK-12
PO Box 167 73562 580-281-3831
Ernest Copus, supt. Fax 281-3299
Big Pasture HS 100/9-12
PO Box 167 73562 580-281-3276
Jimmy Smith, prin. Fax 281-3299

Rattan, Pushmataha, Pop. 242
Rattan ISD 500/PK-12
PO Box 44 74562 580-587-2546
Bruce Lawless, supt. Fax 587-4000
www.rattan.k12.ok.us
Rattan JHS 100/7-8
PO Box 44 74562 580-587-2715
Neil Birchfield, prin. Fax 587-2476
Rattan SHS 100/9-12
PO Box 44 74562 580-587-2715
Neil Birchfield, prin. Fax 587-2476

Red Oak, Latimer, Pop. 572
Red Oak ISD 200/PK-12
PO Box 310 74563 918-754-2426
Bryan Deatherage, supt. Fax 754-2898
Red Oak HS 100/9-12
PO Box 310 74563 918-754-2283
Lane Jackson, prin. Fax 754-2898

Red Rock, Noble, Pop. 291
Frontier SD 400/PK-12
PO Box 130 74651 580-723-4361
Terri Taflinger, supt. Fax 723-4516
www.frontierok.com
Frontier HS 100/9-12
PO Box 130 74651 580-723-4360
Randy Robinson, prin. Fax 723-4516

Reydon, Roger Mills, Pop. 171
Reydon ISD 100/PK-12
PO Box 10 73660 580-655-4375
Phil Drouhard, supt. Fax 655-4622
Reydon HS, PO Box 10 73660 50/9-12
Jeff Kelly, prin. 580-655-4375

Ringling, Jefferson, Pop. 1,082
Ringling ISD 500/PK-12
PO Box 1010 73456 580-662-2385
Richard Gleave, supt. Fax 662-2683
www.ringling.k12.ok.us/
Ringling HS, PO Box 1010 73456 100/10-12
Jim Cooper, prin. 580-662-2386
Ringling JHS, PO Box 1010 73456 100/7-9
Jim Cooper, prin. 580-662-2386

Ringwood, Major, Pop. 419
Ringwood ISD 400/PK-12
PO Box 239 73768 580-883-2202
Ray Johnson, supt. Fax 883-2220
www.ringwood.k12.ok.us/

Ringwood HS 100/9-12
PO Box 239 73768 580-883-2201
C.W. White, prin. Fax 883-2220

Ripley, Payne, Pop. 426
Ripley ISD 400/PK-12
PO Box 97 74062 918-372-4567
Dr. Kenny Beams, supt. Fax 372-4608
www.ripley.k12.ok.us/
Ripley HS 100/9-12
PO Box 97 74062 918-372-4245
Les Tilley, prin. Fax 372-4608

Roff, Pontotoc, Pop. 724
Roff ISD 300/PK-12
PO Box 157 74865 580-456-7663
Ron Brown, supt. Fax 456-7245
www.geocities.com/roffschool
Roff HS 100/9-12
PO Box 157 74865 580-456-7252
George Tidwell, prin. Fax 456-7499

Roland, Sequoyah, Pop. 3,110
Roland ISD 1,300/PK-12
301 Ranger Blvd 74954 918-427-4601
Paul R. Wood, supt. Fax 427-1785
www.rolandschools.org
Roland JHS 300/7-9
301 Ranger Blvd 74954 918-427-4631
Charles Morton, prin. Fax 427-0093
Roland SHS 300/10-12
301 Ranger Blvd 74954 918-427-7419
Gary Lattimore, prin. Fax 427-6993

Rush Springs, Grady, Pop. 1,324
Rush Springs ISD 600/PK-12
PO Box 308 73082 580-476-3929
David Divine, supt. Fax 476-2018
www.rushsprings.k12.ok.us
Rush Springs HS 200/9-12
PO Box 308 73082 580-476-3596
Mike Zurline, prin. Fax 476-2018
Rush Springs MS 100/6-8
PO Box 308 73082 580-476-3447
Shawn Haskins, prin. Fax 476-2148

Ryan, Jefferson, Pop. 854
Ryan ISD 300/PK-12
PO Box 369 73565 580-757-2308
Larry Ninman, supt. Fax 757-2609
Ryan HS, PO Box 369 73565 100/9-12
Pete Maples, prin. 580-757-2296

Salina, Mayes, Pop. 1,454
Salina ISD 800/PK-12
PO Box 98 74365 918-434-5091
Vol Woods, supt. Fax 434-5346
www.salina.k12.ok.us
Salina HS 200/9-12
PO Box 98 74365 918-434-5347
Tony Thomas, prin. Fax 434-5537
Salina MS 200/6-8
PO Box 98 74365 918-434-5311
Sally Cox, prin. Fax 434-5173

Sallisaw, Sequoyah, Pop. 8,621
Central ISD 500/PK-12
RR 1 Box 36 74955 918-775-5525
Max Tanner, supt. Fax 775-8557
centralps.k12.ok.us
Central HS 200/9-12
RR 1 Box 36 74955 918-775-5525
Ron Winans, prin. Fax 775-8557

OK Dept. of Voc. & Tech. Education
Supt. — None
Indian Capital Technology Center Vo/Tech
HC 61 Box 12 74955 918-775-9119
Curtis Shumaker, dir. Fax 775-7305

Sallisaw ISD 2,100/PK-12
701 J T Stites Blvd 74955 918-775-5544
Ronald Wyrick, supt. Fax 775-1257
Sallisaw HS 600/9-12
2301 W Ruth Ave 74955 918-775-7761
Ernie Martens, prin. Fax 775-1275
Spear MS, 211 S Main St 74955 500/6-8
Greg Cast, prin. 918-775-3015

Sand Springs, Tulsa, Pop. 17,667
Sand Springs ISD 4,600/PK-12
PO Box 970 74063 918-246-1400
Lloyd Snow, supt. Fax 246-1401
www.sandites.org/
Boyd JHS 1,200/6-8
PO Box 970 74063 918-246-1535
Dr. Richard Rosenberger, prin. Fax 246-1544
Central 9th Grade Center 400/9-9
PO Box 970 74063 918-246-1440
Randy Dean, prin. Fax 246-1446
Page HS 1,100/9-12
PO Box 970 74063 918-246-1470
Janice Bayouth, prin. Fax 246-1480

Moriah Christian Academy 100/PK-12
680 E 41st St 74063 918-241-8410
Kim Ervin, admin.
Sand Springs Beauty College Post-Sec.
28 E 2nd St 74063 918-245-6627

Sapulpa, Creek, Pop. 20,619
OK Dept. of Voc. & Tech. Education
Supt. — None
Central Tech Vo/Tech
1720 S Main St 74066 918-224-9300
David Main, dir. Fax 224-3190

Sapulpa ISD 4,300/PK-12
1 S Mission St 74066 918-224-3400
Dr. Joe W. Crowder, supt. Fax 227-3287
www.sapulpa.k12.ok.us
Sapulpa JHS 700/8-9
7 S Mission St 74066 918-224-6710
Derald Buckley, prin. Fax 227-0473
Sapulpa SHS 1,100/10-12
3 S Mission St 74066 918-224-6560
Jenyfer Glisson, prin. Fax 224-0174

Sasakwa, Seminole, Pop. 149
Sasakwa ISD 200/PK-12
PO Box 323 74867 405-941-3213
Jim Mathews, supt. Fax 941-3163
Sasakwa HS 100/9-12
PO Box 323 74867 405-941-3250
Buddy Canning, prin. Fax 941-3561

Savanna, Pittsburg, Pop. 744
Savanna ISD 500/PK-12
PO Box 266 74565 918-548-3777
Mitch Tidwell, supt. Fax 548-3836
www.savanna.k12.ok.us/
Savanna HS 300/9-12
PO Box 266 74565 918-548-3887
Gary Reeder, prin. Fax 548-3836

Sayre, Beckham, Pop. 2,836
OK Dept. of Voc. & Tech. Education
Supt. — None
Western Technology Center Vo/Tech
RR 4 Box 132 73662 580-928-2097
Andy Humble, dir. Fax 928-9827

Sayre ISD 700/PK-12
716 NE Highway 66 73662 580-928-5531
Todd Winn, supt. Fax 928-5538
www.sayre.k12.ok.us
Sayre HS 200/9-12
716 NE Highway 66 73662 580-928-5576
Danny Crabb, prin. Fax 928-3045
Sayre MS 200/6-8
716 NE Highway 66 73662 580-928-5578
Monica Brower, prin. Fax 928-3045

Southwestern Oklahoma State University Post-Sec.
409 E Mississippi Ave 73662 580-928-5533

Schulter, Okmulgee, Pop. 607
Schulter ISD 200/PK-12
PO Box 203 74460 918-652-8219
Alfred Gaches, supt. Fax 652-8474
Schulter HS 100/9-12
PO Box 203 74460 918-652-8200
Allen Callahan, prin. Fax 652-8474

Seiling, Dewey, Pop. 821
Seiling ISD 300/PK-12
PO Box 780 73663 580-922-7383
Bob Bush, supt. Fax 922-8019
www.seiling.k12.ok.us
Seiling JSHS 100/7-12
PO Box 780 73663 580-922-7382
C. Oakes, prin. Fax 922-8019

Seminole, Seminole, Pop. 6,913
Seminole ISD 1,100/PK-12
PO Box 1031 74818 405-382-5085
Jeff Pritchard, supt. Fax 382-8281
www.sps.k12.ok.us
Seminole HS 400/9-12
PO Box 1031 74818 405-382-1415
John Walker, prin. Fax 382-1062
Seminole MS 200/7-8
PO Box 1031 74818 405-382-5065
Michelle Sneed, prin. Fax 382-8653

Strother ISD 300/PK-12
36085 EW 1140 74868 405-382-4014
Lowell Wallace, supt. Fax 382-3339
Strother HS 100/9-12
36085 EW 1140 74868 405-382-0982
John Turner, prin. Fax 382-9430

Varnum ISD 300/PK-12
11929 NS 3550 74868 405-382-1448
Gary Larman, supt. Fax 382-8618
Varnum HS 100/9-12
11929 NS 3550 74868 405-382-1408
Mark Wynn, prin. Fax 382-8618

Seminole State College Post-Sec.
PO Box 351 74818 405-382-9950

Sentinel, Washita, Pop. 860
Sentinel ISD 300/K-12
PO Box 640 73664 580-393-2101
Hal Holt, supt. Fax 393-2101
www.sentinel.k12.ok.us/
Thomas HS 100/9-12
PO Box 640 73664 580-393-2112
Paula Combs, prin. Fax 393-4334

Shattuck, Ellis, Pop. 1,235
Shattuck ISD 200/PK-12
PO Box 159 73858 580-938-2586
Mack Morse, supt. Fax 938-8019
www.shattuck.k12.ok.us/
Shattuck HS 100/9-12
PO Box 159 73858 580-938-2586
Randy Holley, prin. Fax 938-8019

Shawnee, Pottawatomie, Pop. 29,824
Bethel ISD 1,200/K-12
36000 Clearpond Rd 74801 405-273-0385
David Glover, supt. Fax 273-5056
www.bethel.k12.ok.us
Bethel HS 400/9-12
36000 Clearpond Rd 74801 405-273-3633
Steve Carpenter, prin. Fax 273-5056
Bethel MS 300/6-8
36000 Clearpond Rd 74801 405-273-5944
Gary Cartwright, prin. Fax 273-5056

OK Dept. of Voc. & Tech. Education
Supt. — None
Cooper Technology Center Vo/Tech
1 John C Bruton Blvd 74804 405-273-7493
Marty Lewis, supt. Fax 273-4704

Shawnee ISD 3,800/PK-12
326 N Union Ave 74801 405-273-0653
Marilyn Bradford, supt. Fax 273-6818
www.shawnee.k12.ok.us
Shawnee HS 1,200/9-12
1001 N Kennedy Ave 74801 405-275-3084
Lee Hamilton, prin.
Shawnee MS 900/6-8
4300 N Union Ave 74804 405-273-0403
Dr. Marsha Gore, prin.

Family of Faith Christian S 100/K-12
PO Box 1442 74802 405-273-5331
Christopher Belyeu, admin. Fax 273-5331
Family of Faith College Post-Sec.
PO Box 1805 74802 405-273-5331
Liberty Academy 300/PK-12
PO Box 1176 74802 405-273-3022
Lenore Matthews, admin. Fax 273-3029
Oklahoma Baptist University Post-Sec.
500 W University St 74804 405-275-2850
St. Gregory's University Post-Sec.
1900 W Macarthur St 74804 405-878-5100
Shawnee Beauty College Post-Sec.
410 E Main St 74801 405-275-3182

Shidler, Osage, Pop. 520
Shidler ISD 200/K-12
PO Box 85 74652 918-793-2021
Donna Campo, supt. Fax 793-2061
www.shidler.k12.ok.us
Shidler HS 100/7-12
PO Box 85 74652 918-793-2461
Bob Campo, prin. Fax 793-2062

Skiatook, Tulsa, Pop. 6,290
Skiatook ISD 2,300/PK-12
355 S Osage St 74070 918-396-1792
Gary Johnson, supt. Fax 396-1799
www.skiatookschools.org
Newman MS 500/6-8
355 S Osage St 74070 918-396-2307
Steve Cantrell, prin. Fax 396-1799
Skiatook HS 700/9-12
355 S Osage St 74070 918-396-1790
Donna Brogan, prin. Fax 396-1799

Smithville, McCurtain, Pop. 111
Smithville ISD 300/PK-12
PO Box 8 74957 580-244-3333
Delbert McBroom, supt. Fax 244-7214
www.smithville.k12.ok.us
Smithville HS 100/9-12
PO Box 8 74957 580-244-3281
Curtis McDaniel, prin. Fax 244-7277
Smithville MS, PO Box 8 74957 100/6-8
Stacy Nichols, prin. 580-244-7212

Snyder, Kiowa, Pop. 1,452
Snyder ISD 500/PK-12
PO Box 368 73566 580-569-2773
Dr. DeDe Graham, supt. Fax 569-4205
www.snyder.k12.ok.us
Snyder HS, PO Box 368 73566 200/9-12
Robert Trammell, prin. 580-569-2730
Snyder MS, PO Box 368 73566 200/4-8
Carol McPhail, prin. 580-569-2691

Soper, Choctaw, Pop. 300
Soper ISD 300/PK-12
PO Box 149 74759 580-345-2757
Olen Jestis, supt. Fax 345-2896
www.soperisd.org
Soper HS 100/9-12
PO Box 149 74759 580-345-2212
Monte Sill, prin. Fax 345-2896

South Coffeyville, Nowata, Pop. 801
Oklahoma Union SD 600/PK-12
RR 1 Box 377-7 74072 918-255-6550
Dr. Robert Jobe, supt. Fax 255-6817
www.okunion.k12.ok.us/
Oklahoma Union HS 200/9-12
RR 1 Box 377-7 74072 918-255-6550
Steve Barth, prin. Fax 255-6817
Oklahoma Union MS 200/6-8
RR 1 Box 377-7 74072 918-255-6550
Teresa Kelley, prin. Fax 255-6817

South Coffeyville ISD 300/PK-12
PO Box 190 74072 918-255-6202
Colt Shaw, supt. Fax 255-6230
South Coffeyville HS 100/9-12
PO Box 190 74072 918-255-6087
Clem Haddox, prin. Fax 255-6230

Spencer, Oklahoma, Pop. 3,840
Oklahoma City ISD
Supt. — See Oklahoma City
Rogers MS 300/6-8
4000 Spencer Rd 73084 405-771-3205
Michael Brown, prin. Fax 771-2114
Star Spencer HS 600/9-12
3001 Spencer Rd 73084 405-587-8800
Dr. Sally Cole, prin. Fax 771-2105

Sperry, Tulsa, Pop. 1,017
Sperry ISD 1,300/PK-12
PO Box 610 74073 918-288-6258
Jerry Burd, supt. Fax 288-7067
www.sperry.k12.ok.us
Sperry HS 300/9-12
PO Box 610 74073 918-288-7213
James White, prin. Fax 288-7230
Sperry MS 300/6-8
PO Box 610 74073 918-288-7213
Dennis Holland, prin. Fax 288-7231

Oklahoma Farriers College Post-Sec.
PO Box 788 74073 918-288-7221

Spiro, LeFlore, Pop. 2,287
OK Dept. of Voc. & Tech. Education
Supt. — None
Kiamichi Technology Center Vo/Tech
610 SW 3rd St 74959 918-962-3722
Doug Hall, dir. Fax 962-4627

Spiro ISD 1,200/K-12
600 W Broadway St 74959 918-962-2463
J. L. Williams, supt. Fax 962-2757
www.spiro.k12.ok.us/
Spiro HS, 600 W Broadway St 74959 300/9-12
Tracy Saling, prin. 918-962-2493

Spiro MS, 600 W Broadway St 74959 — 300/6-8
Russell Thornton, prin. — 918-962-2488

Springer, Carter, Pop. 592
Springer ISD — 200/PK-12
PO Box 249 73458 — 580-653-2656
Rick Peters, supt. — Fax 653-2666
www.springer.k12.ok.us/
Springer HS, PO Box 249 73458 — 100/9-12
Brenda Foster, prin. — 580-653-2471

Sterling, Comanche, Pop. 748
Sterling ISD — 400/PK-12
PO Box 158 73567 — 580-365-4307
Jay Zehr, supt. — Fax 365-4705
www.sterling.k12.ok.us/
Sterling HS, PO Box 158 73567 — 100/9-12
Richard McCauley, prin. — 580-365-4303

Stigler, Haskell, Pop. 2,821
OK Dept. of Voc. & Tech. Education
Supt. — None
Kiamichi Technology Center — Vo/Tech
1410 Old Military Rd 74462 — 918-967-2801
Joe Carrick, dir. — Fax 967-2803

Stigler ISD — 1,200/PK-12
309 NW E St 74462 — 918-967-2805
Bill Self, supt. — Fax 967-4550
www.stigler.k12.ok.us
Stigler HS — 400/9-12
309 NW E St 74462 — 918-967-8834
David Morgan, prin. — Fax 967-8974
Stigler MS — 300/5-8
309 NW E St 74462 — 918-967-2521
Rick Prentice, prin. — Fax 967-5125

Stillwater, Payne, Pop. 40,906
OK Dept. of Voc. & Tech. Education
Supt. — None
Meridian Technology Center — Vo/Tech
1312 S Sangre Rd 74074 — 405-377-3333
Dr. Andrea Kelly, supt. — Fax 372-3466
Other Schools – See Ada OK, Afton OK, Altus OK, Alva OK, Ardmore OK, Atoka OK, Bartlesville OK, Broken Arrow OK, Burns Flat OK, Chickasha OK, Choctaw OK, Drumright OK, Duncan OK, Durant OK, El Reno OK, Enid OK, Fairview OK, Fort Cobb OK, Frederick OK, Hugo OK, Idabel OK, Kansas OK, Lawton OK, Mc Alester OK, Midwest City OK, Muskogee OK, Norman OK, Oklahoma City OK, Okmulgee OK, Omega OK, Ponca City OK, Poteau OK, Pryor OK, Sallisaw OK, Sapulpa OK, Sayre OK, Shawnee OK, Spiro OK, Stigler OK, Stilwell OK, Tahlequah OK, Talihina OK, Tinker AFB OK, Tulsa OK, Wayne OK, Wetumka OK, Wilburton OK, Woodward OK

Stillwater ISD — 5,300/PK-12
PO Box 879 74076 — 405-533-6300
Dr. Walter Swanson, supt. — Fax 743-6311
www.stillwater.k12.ok.us
Stillwater JHS — 700/7-9
PO Box 879 74076 — 405-533-6420
Trent Swanson, prin. — Fax 743-6444
Stillwater SHS — 1,100/10-12
PO Box 879 74076 — 405-533-6450
Uwe Gordon, prin. — Fax 743-6488

Indian Meridian Vocational Tech School — Post-Sec.
1312 S Sangre Rd 74074 — 405-377-3333
Oklahoma State University 74078 — Post-Sec.
405-744-5000
Stillwater Beauty Academy — Post-Sec.
1684 Cimarron Plz 74075 — 405-377-4100
Sunnybrook Christian S — 100/PK-12
421 E Richmond Rd 74075 — 405-377-3748
Genevieve Hurst, admin. — Fax 372-2505

Stilwell, Adair, Pop. 3,472
OK Dept. of Voc. & Tech. Education
Supt. — None
Indian Capital Technology Center — Vo/Tech
RR 4 Box 3320 74960 — 918-696-3111
Tony Pivec, dir. — Fax 696-3111

Stilwell ISD — 1,500/PK-12
1801 W Locust St 74960 — 918-696-7001
Marion Bayles, supt. — Fax 696-2193
www.stilwell.k12.ok.us
Stilwell HS — 600/9-12
1801 W Locust St 74960 — 918-696-7276
Alicia Ketcher, prin. — Fax 696-4695
Stilwell MS — 300/5-8
12 N 7th St 74960 — 918-696-2685
Chris McMullen, prin. — Fax 696-7761

Stonewall, Pontotoc, Pop. 471
Stonewall ISD — 200/PK-12
600 Highschool 74871 — 580-265-4241
Kevin Flowers, supt. — Fax 265-4536
Stonewall HS — 100/9-12
600 Highschool 74871 — 580-265-4242
Tamara Newberry, prin. — Fax 265-4231
Other Schools – See Fittstown

Stratford, Garvin, Pop. 1,484
Stratford ISD — 400/PK-12
PO Box 589 74872 — 580-759-3615
Brent Walden, supt. — Fax 759-2669
www.stratfordisd.org
Stratford JSHS — 100/7-12
PO Box 589 74872 — 580-759-2381
Chad Hall, prin. — Fax 759-2669

Stringtown, Atoka, Pop. 412
CareerTech Skills Centers
Supt. — None
Dom Garrison, supt.
Stringtown Skills Center — Vo/Tech
PO Box 159 74569 — 580-346-7411

Stringtown ISD — 200/PK-12
PO Box 130 74569 — 580-346-7423
Richard Quaid, supt. — Fax 346-7726
www.stringtown.k12.ok.us
Stringtown HS — 100/9-12
PO Box 130 74569 — 580-346-7423
Richard Quaid, dean — Fax 346-7949

Stroud, Lincoln, Pop. 2,755
Stroud ISD — 800/PK-12
212 W 7th St 74079 — 918-968-2541
Rick McDaniel, supt. — Fax 968-2582
www.stroud.k12.ok.us
Stroud HS — 200/9-12
212 W 7th St 74079 — 918-968-2542
Joe VanTuyl, prin. — Fax 968-3656
Stroud MS — 200/6-8
212 W 7th St 74079 — 918-968-2200
Marsha Thompson, prin. — Fax 968-2391

Stuart, Hughes, Pop. 213
Stuart ISD — 300/PK-12
8837 4th St 74570 — 918-546-2476
Bill San Millan, supt. — Fax 546-2329
www.stuart.k12.ok.us/
Stuart HS — 100/9-12
8837 4th St 74570 — 918-546-2474
Tracy Blasengame, prin. — Fax 546-2329

Sulphur, Murray, Pop. 4,877
Sulphur ISD — 1,400/PK-12
1021 W 9th St 73086 — 580-622-2061
Keith Foreman, supt. — Fax 622-6789
www.sulphur.k12.ok.us
Sulphur HS — 400/9-12
1021 W 9th St 73086 — 580-622-3174
Greg Hinkle, prin. — Fax 622-5735
Sulphur JHS — 200/7-8
1021 W 9th St 73086 — 580-622-4010
Kristie Jessop, prin. — Fax 622-3900

Oklahoma School for the Deaf — Post-Sec.
1100 E Oklahoma Ave 73086 — 580-622-4900

Sweetwater, Roger Mills, Pop. 70
Sweetwater ISD — 100/PK-12
RR 1 Box 6 73666 — 580-534-2272
Don Riley, supt. — Fax 534-2273
Sweetwater HS — 50/9-12
RR 1 Box 6 73666 — 580-534-2272
Don Riley, prin. — Fax 534-2273

Taft, Muskogee, Pop. 476
CareerTech Skills Centers
Supt. — None
Dom Garrison, supt.
Taft Skills Center Dunn Campus — Vo/Tech
PO Box 245 74463 — 918-683-8669
Taft Skills Center Warrior Campus — Vo/Tech
PO Box 245 74463 — 918-683-8365

Tahlequah, Cherokee, Pop. 16,075
OK Dept. of Voc. & Tech. Education
Supt. — None
Indian Capital Technology Center — Vo/Tech
PO Box 497 74465 — 918-456-2594
Wilson Fargo, dir. — Fax 456-0140

Tahlequah ISD — 2,700/PK-12
PO Box 517 74465 — 918-458-4100
Paul Hurst, supt. — Fax 458-4103
www.tahlequah.k12.ok.us
Tahlequah HS — 900/9-12
591 Pendleton St 74464 — 918-458-4150
Dr. Nick Migliorino, prin. — Fax 458-4135
Tahlequah MS — 500/5-8
871 Pendleton St 74464 — 918-458-4140
Fax 458-4108

Beauty Technical College — Post-Sec.
PO Box 1506 74465 — 918-456-6360
Northeastern State University — Post-Sec.
600 N Grand Ave 74464 — 918-456-5511

Talihina, Latimer, Pop. 1,234
Buffalo Valley ISD — 200/K-12
4384 SE Highway 63 74571 — 918-522-4426
Ira Harris, supt. — Fax 522-4287
www.buffalovalley.k12.ok.us
Buffalo Valley HS — 100/9-12
4384 SE Highway 63 74571 — 918-522-4803
Betty Smallwood, prin. — Fax 522-4287

OK Dept. of Voc. & Tech. Education
Supt. — None
Kiamichi Technology Center — Vo/Tech
13224 SE 202nd Rd 74571 — 918-567-2264
Shelley Free, dir. — Fax 567-3359

Talihina ISD — 600/PK-12
PO Box 38 74571 — 918-567-2259
Robert Perryman, supt. — Fax 567-3507
www.talihina.k12.ok.us/
Talihina JHS, PO Box 38 74571 — 100/7-9
Jason Lockhart, prin. — 918-567-2138
Talihina SHS, PO Box 38 74571 — 200/10-12
Jason Lockhart, prin. — 918-567-2266

Taloga, Dewey, Pop. 361
Taloga ISD — 100/PK-12
PO Box 158 73667 — 580-328-5577
Rick Ruckman, supt. — Fax 328-5237
www.taloga.k12.ok.us
Taloga HS — 50/9-12
PO Box 158 73667 — 580-328-5586
Rick Ruckman, prin. — Fax 328-5237

Tecumseh, Pottawatomie, Pop. 6,516
Tecumseh ISD — 2,000/K-12
1301 E Highland St 74873 — 405-598-3739
Tom Wilsie, supt. — Fax 598-2861
www.tecumseh.k12.ok.us
Tecumseh HS — 700/9-12
901 N 13th St 74873 — 405-598-2113
James Blue, prin. — Fax 598-2432
Tecumseh MS — 500/6-8
315 W Park St 74873 — 405-598-3744
Karen Kinsey, prin. — Fax 598-1948

Temple, Cotton, Pop. 1,149
Temple ISD — 300/PK-12
PO Box 400 73568 — 580-342-6230
David Brewer, supt. — Fax 342-6463
www.temple.k12.ok.us/
Temple HS — 100/9-12
PO Box 400 73568 — 580-342-6221
Darrell Lamar, prin. — Fax 342-6463

Texhoma, Texas, Pop. 928
Texhoma ISD — 200/PK-12
PO Box 648 73949 — 580-423-7433
Eric Smith, supt. — Fax 423-7096
www.texhoma61.net/
Texhoma HS — 100/9-12
PO Box 648 73949 — 580-423-7371
Steve Neptune, prin. — Fax 423-7096

Thackerville, Love, Pop. 417
Thackerville ISD — 300/PK-12
PO Box 377 73459 — 580-276-2630
David Herron, supt. — Fax 276-2638
www.thackervilleschools.org
Thackerville HS — 100/9-12
PO Box 377 73459 — 580-276-3610
Jamie Mitchell, prin. — Fax 276-2638

Thomas, Custer, Pop. 1,150
Thomas-Fay-Custer USD — 400/PK-12
PO Box 190 73669 — 580-661-3527
Rob Royalty, supt. — Fax 661-3589
Thomas JSHS — 100/7-12
PO Box 190 73669 — 580-661-3522
Craig McVay, prin. — Fax 661-3589

Tinker AFB, See Oklahoma City
OK Dept. of Voc. & Tech. Education
Supt. — None
Mid-Del-Tinker Career Tech — Vo/Tech
Building 1 D Ave 73145 — 405-734-7266
Dave Williams, dir. — Fax 737-2330

Tipton, Tillman, Pop. 841
Tipton ISD — 300/K-12
PO Box 340 73570 — 580-667-5268
Brad Overton, supt. — Fax 667-5267
www.tiptonps.k12.ok.us
Tipton HS — 100/9-12
PO Box 340 73570 — 580-667-5268
Cliff McCown, prin. — Fax 667-5478
Tipton MS — 100/7-8
PO Box 340 73570 — 580-667-5268
Cliff McCown, prin. — Fax 667-5325

Tishomingo, Johnston, Pop. 3,136
Tishomingo ISD — 900/PK-12
1300 E Main St 73460 — 580-371-9190
Ronald Hutchings, supt. — Fax 371-3765
www.tishomingo.k12.ok.us/
Tishomingo HS, 1300 E Main St 73460 — 300/9-12
Leo McCallay, prin. — 580-371-2322
Tishomingo MS, 1300 E Main St 73460 — 200/6-8
Larry Davis, prin. — 580-371-3602

Murray State College — Post-Sec.
1 Murray Campus St 73460 — 580-371-2371

Tonkawa, Kay, Pop. 3,132
Tonkawa ISD — 600/PK-12
500 E North Ave 74653 — 580-628-3597
Rod Reese, supt. — Fax 628-5132
www.tonkawa.k12.ok.us/
Tonkawa JSHS — 200/6-12
500 E North Ave 74653 — 580-628-2566
Kyle Simpson, prin. — Fax 628-3646

Northern Oklahoma College — Post-Sec.
PO Box 310 74653 — 580-628-6200

Tulsa, Tulsa, Pop. 382,457
Berryhill ISD — 1,100/PK-12
3128 S 63rd West Ave 74107 — 918-446-1966
Mike Campbell, supt. — Fax 446-6370
www.berryhill.k12.ok.us
Berryhill JHS — 300/7-9
3128 S 63rd West Ave 74107 — 918-446-8765
Kevin Collins, prin. — Fax 445-6018
Berryhill SHS — 300/10-12
3128 S 63rd West Ave 74107 — 918-446-1636
JoEtta Terrell, prin. — Fax 445-6015

Jenks ISD
Supt. — See Jenks
Jenks MS, 3019 E 101st St 74137 — 1,400/7-8
Rob Miller, prin. — 918-299-4411

OK Dept. of Voc. & Tech. Education
Supt. — None
Tulsa County Technology Center — Vo/Tech
PO Box 477200 74147 — 918-828-5000
Dr. Gene Callahan, supt. — Fax 828-5009
Tulsa Tech Center Peoria — Vo/Tech
PO Box 477200 74147 — 918-828-2000
Sharon Schaub, dir. — Fax 828-2009
Tulsa Tech Center Riverside Campus — Vo/Tech
PO Box 477200 74147 — 918-828-4000
Michael Highland, dir. — Fax 828-4009
Tulsa Technology Center-Lemley — Vo/Tech
PO Box 477200 74147 — 918-828-1000
Sandee Tackett, dir. — Fax 828-1009

Tulsa ISD — 39,300/PK-12
PO Box 470208 74147 — 918-746-6800
Michael Zolkoski Ed.D., supt. — Fax 746-6850
www.tulsaschools.org
Byrd MS — 800/6-8
7502 E 57th St 74145 — 918-833-9520
Garry Nichols, prin. — Fax 833-9551
Carver MS — 600/6-8
624 E Oklahoma Pl 74106 — 918-925-1420
Cleta Driver, prin. — Fax 925-1450

Central HS 1,000/9-12
3101 W Edison St 74127 918-833-8400
Jean Keeton, prin. Fax 833-8417
Cleveland MS 600/6-8
724 N Birmingham Ave 74110 918-746-9400
John Maxwell, prin. Fax 746-9426
Clinton MS, 2224 W 41st St 74107 500/6-8
Lisa Lawrence, prin. 918-746-8640
East Central HS 1,100/9-12
12150 E 11th St 74128 918-746-9700
Tom O'Malley, prin. Fax 746-9760
Edison Preparatory HS 1,100/9-12
2906 E 41st St 74105 918-746-8500
Steve Mayfield, prin.
Edison Preparatory MS 900/6-8
2906 E 41st St 74105 918-746-8500
Steve Mayfield, prin.
Foster MS, 12121 E 21st St 74129 700/6-8
Darin Schmidt, prin. 918-746-9500
Hale HS 900/9-12
6960 E 21st St 74129 918-925-1200
Chris Johnson, prin. Fax 925-1262
Hamilton MS 500/6-8
2316 N Norwood Pl 74115 918-746-9440
Debra Wiggins, prin. Fax 746-9447
Lewis & Clark MS 600/6-8
737 S Garnett Rd 74128 918-746-9540
Ginger Bunnell, prin.
Madison MS 400/6-8
4132 W Cameron St 74127 918-833-8860
Ava Hicks, prin.
McLain School for Science & Technology Vo/Tech
4929 N Peoria Ave 74126 918-833-8500
Jerome Williams, prin. Fax 833-8559
Memorial HS 1,500/9-12
5840 S Hudson Ave 74135 918-833-9600
Elizabeth Martin, prin.
Monroe MS, 2010 E 48th St N 74130 400/7-8
Jolly Meadows, prin. 918-833-8900
Nimitz MS 400/6-8
3111 E 56th St 74105 918-746-8800
Earlene Gathright, prin. Fax 746-8826
Rogers HS, 3909 E 5th Pl 74112 1,200/9-12
Kevin Burr, prin. 918-833-9000
Thoreau Demonstration Academy 500/6-8
7370 E 71st St 74133 918-833-9700
Thomas Padalino, prin.
Washington HS 1,300/9-12
1514 E Zion St 74106 918-925-1000
Debi Boyles, prin. Fax 928-1001
Webster HS 600/9-12
1919 W 40th St 74107 918-746-8000
Phillip Garland, prin. Fax 746-8056
Whitney MS 800/6-8
2177 S 67th East Ave 74129 918-746-9260
Derrick Schmidt, prin.
Wilson MS 600/6-8
1127 S Columbia Ave 74104 918-833-9340
Oliver Wallace, prin.

Union ISD, 8506 E 61st St 74133 13,900/PK-12
Cathy Burden, supt. 918-357-4321
www.unionps.org
Union HS 1,900/11-12
6636 S Mingo Rd 74133 918-459-2638
Dave Stauffer, prin. Fax 459-5510
Other Schools – See Broken Arrow

Bishop Kelley HS 900/9-12
3905 S Hudson Ave 74135 918-627-3390
Alan Weyland, pres. Fax 664-2134
Career Point Institute Post-Sec.
3138 S Garnett Rd 74146 918-622-4100
Cascia Hall Prep S 6-12
2520 S Yorktown Ave 74114 918-746-2600
Rev. Bernard Scianna, hdmstr. Fax 746-2636
CC's Cosmetology College Post-Sec.
11630 E 21st St 74129 918-234-9444
Evangelistic Temple S 200/PK-12
1339 E 55th St 74105 918-743-5597
Randy Fulmer, prin. Fax 747-3457
Holland Hall 1,000/PK-12
5666 E 81st St 74137 918-481-1111
Mark Desjardins Ph.D., hdmstr. Fax 481-1145
Lincoln Christian S 600/K-12
1003 N 129th East Ave 74116 918-234-8863
Br. Jim Wideman, admin. Fax 234-8864
Metro Christian Academy 1,000/K-12
6363 S Trenton Ave 74136 918-745-9868
Tim Cameron, hdmstr. Fax 747-8724
Mingo Valley Christian S 300/PK-12
8720 E 61st St 74133 918-294-0404
Dennis Queen, prin. Fax 294-0555
Oklahoma Health Academy Post-Sec.
2865 E Skelly Dr Ste 224 74105 918-748-9900
Oral Roberts University Post-Sec.
7777 S Lewis Ave 74171 918-495-6161
OSU College of Osteopathic Medicine Post-Sec.
1111 W 17th St 74107 918-582-1972
Phillips Theological Seminary Post-Sec.
901 N Mingo Rd 74116 918-610-8303
Platt College Post-Sec.
3801 S Sheridan Rd 74145 918-663-9000
St. Francis Hospital Post-Sec.
6161 S Yale Ave 74136 918-494-1370
Spartan Coll of Aeronautics & Technology Post-Sec.
8820 E Pine St 74115 800-331-1204
Technical Institute of Cosmetology Arts Post-Sec.
822 E 6th St 74120 918-660-8828
Tulsa Adventist Jr Academy 50/K-10
900 S New Haven Ave 74112 918-834-1107
Fax 834-2151
Tulsa Community College Post-Sec.
3727 E Apache St 74115 918-595-7000
Tulsa Community College Metro Campus Post-Sec.
909 S Boston Ave 74119 918-595-7000
Tulsa Community College Southeast Campus Post-Sec.
10300 E 81st St 74133 918-595-7000
Tulsa Community College West Campus Post-Sec.
7505 W 41st St 74107 918-595-7000
Tulsa County Area Voc Tech District 18 Post-Sec.
3420 S Memorial Dr 74145 918-627-7200
Tulsa Welding School Post-Sec.
2545 E 11th St 74104 918-587-6789
University of Tulsa Post-Sec.
600 S College Ave 74104 918-631-2000

Vatterott College Post-Sec.
4343 S 118th East Ave 74146 918-835-8288
Victory Christian S 1,300/K-12
7700 S Lewis Ave 74136 918-491-7720
Dr. Dennis Demuth, supt. Fax 491-7727
Wright Christian Academy 300/PK-12
11391 E Admiral Pl 74116 918-438-0922
Jeff Brown, admin. Fax 438-0700

Tupelo, Coal, Pop. 360
Tupelo ISD 200/PK-12
PO Box 239 74572 580-845-2460
Tony Stevens, supt. Fax 845-2565
www.tupelo.k12.ok.us
Tupelo HS 100/9-12
PO Box 239 74572 580-845-2381
Kevin Mann, prin. Fax 845-2565

Turpin, Beaver
Turpin SD 400/PK-12
PO Box 187 73950 580-778-3333
Glyndel Holland, supt. Fax 778-3179
www.turpin.k12.ok.us
Turpin HS 100/9-12
PO Box 187 73950 580-778-3333
Bret Rider, prin. Fax 778-3733

Tuttle, Grady, Pop. 5,365
Tuttle ISD 1,400/K-12
PO Box 780 73089 405-381-2605
Lee Coker, supt. Fax 381-4008
www.tuttleschools.info/
Tuttle HS 400/9-12
PO Box 780 73089 405-381-2396
Pat Ragsdale, prin. Fax 381-4637
Tuttle MS 300/6-8
PO Box 780 73089 405-381-2062
Jim Stewart, prin. Fax 381-4630

Tyrone, Texas, Pop. 857
Tyrone ISD 200/PK-12
PO Box 168 73951 580-854-6298
Dave Easterday, supt. Fax 854-6474
Tyrone HS 100/9-12
PO Box 168 73951 580-854-6298
Melea Welch, prin. Fax 854-6474

Union City, Canadian, Pop. 1,387
Union City ISD 300/PK-12
PO Box 279 73090 405-483-3531
Todd Carel, supt. Fax 483-5599
Union City HS 100/9-12
PO Box 279 73090 405-483-5326
Todd Carel, prin. Fax 483-5199

Valliant, McCurtain, Pop. 759
Valliant ISD 1,100/PK-12
604 E Lucas St 74764 580-933-7232
Debbie Golden, supt. Fax 933-7289
www.vpsd.org
Valliant HS 300/9-12
604 E Lucas St 74764 580-933-7292
Don Mullenix, prin. Fax 933-7278
Valliant MS 300/6-8
604 E Lucas St 74764 580-933-4253
Tim Weaver, prin. Fax 933-4254

Velma, Stephens, Pop. 693
Velma-Alma ISD 300/K-12
PO Box 8 73491 580-444-3355
Jerry Garrett, supt. Fax 444-2554
Velma-Alma HS 200/9-12
PO Box 8 73491 580-444-3356
Mike Thompson, prin. Fax 444-2554

Verden, Grady, Pop. 682
Verden ISD 300/PK-12
PO Box 99 73092 405-453-7247
David Davidson, supt. Fax 453-7246
www.verden.k12.ok.us/
Verden HS 100/9-12
PO Box 99 73092 405-453-7836
Clint Shirley, prin. Fax 453-7246

Vian, Sequoyah, Pop. 1,460
Vian ISD 1,000/PK-12
PO Box 434 74962 918-773-5798
Lawrence Barnes, supt. Fax 773-3051
www.vian.k12.ok.us/
Vian HS 300/9-12
PO Box 434 74962 918-773-5475
Bob Thomas, prin. Fax 773-3051
Vian MS 200/6-8
PO Box 434 74962 918-773-8631
Dr. Carla Wortman, prin. Fax 773-3051

Vici, Dewey, Pop. 647
Vici ISD 300/PK-12
PO Box 60 73859 580-995-4744
Kim Stephens, supt. Fax 995-3101
www.vicischools.k12.ok.us
Vici HS 100/9-12
PO Box 60 73859 580-995-4251
Greg Gregory, prin. Fax 995-3101

Vinita, Craig, Pop. 6,017
Vinita ISD 1,700/PK-12
PO Box 408 74301 918-256-6778
Michael Garde, supt. Fax 256-5617
www.vinitahornets.com
Vinita HS, PO Box 408 74301 500/9-12
Rusty Rankin, prin. 918-256-6777
Vinita MS, PO Box 408 74301 400/6-8
Jeff Williams, prin. 918-256-2402

White Oak ISD 200/PK-12
27355 S 4340 Rd 74301 918-256-4484
J.D. Parkerson, supt. Fax 256-4486
White Oak HS 100/9-12
27355 S 4340 Rd 74301 918-256-4484
J.D. Parkerson, prin.

Ketchum Adventist Junior Academy 50/1-10
35369 S Highway 82 74301 918-782-2986
Fax 782-1567

Wagoner, Wagoner, Pop. 7,877
Wagoner ISD 2,400/PK-12
PO Box 508 74477 918-485-4046
Janice Aldridge, supt. Fax 485-8710
www.wagonerps.org
Wagoner HS 600/9-12
300 Bulldog Cir 74467 918-485-5553
Jerry Adams, prin. Fax 485-8886
Wagoner MS 600/6-8
500 Bulldog Cir 74467 918-485-9541
Darrell Morgan, prin. Fax 485-4149

Wakita, Grant, Pop. 396
Wakita ISD 100/PK-12
PO Box 45 73771 580-594-2261
Gerald Miller, supt. Fax 594-2263
www.wakita.k12.ok.us
Wakita HS 50/9-12
PO Box 45 73771 580-594-2262
Kelly Childress, prin. Fax 594-2263

Walters, Cotton, Pop. 2,610
Walters ISD 700/PK-12
418 S Broadway St 73572 580-875-2568
Jimmie Dedmon, supt. Fax 875-2831
blued.org
Walters HS 200/9-12
418 S Broadway St 73572 580-875-3257
Chuck Karpe, prin. Fax 875-6097
Walters MS, 418 S Broadway St 73572 200/6-8
Laurie Graham, prin. 580-875-3214

Wanette, Pottawatomie, Pop. 418
Wanette ISD 200/PK-12
PO Box 161 74878 405-383-2656
Rick Riggs, supt. Fax 383-2449
www.wanette.k12.ok.us/
Wanette HS, PO Box 161 74878 100/9-12
Rick Riggs, prin. 405-383-2254

Wapanucka, Johnston, Pop. 432
Wapanucka ISD 200/PK-12
PO Box 188 73461 580-937-4466
Stanley Williams, supt. Fax 937-4804
Wapanucka HS, PO Box 188 73461 100/9-12
Max Rowland, prin. 580-937-4288

Warner, Muskogee, Pop. 1,443
Warner ISD 700/PK-12
1008 N 5th St 74469 918-463-5171
Monte Madewell, supt. Fax 463-2542
www.warner.k12.ok.us/
Warner HS 200/9-12
1008 N 5th St 74469 918-463-5172
Steve McGinnis, prin. Fax 463-2378
Warner MS, 1008 N 5th St 74469 200/6-8
Brenda Bales, prin. 918-463-2197

Connors State College Post-Sec.
RR 1 Box 1000 74469 918-463-2931

Washington, McClain, Pop. 530
Washington ISD 900/PK-12
PO Box 98 73093 405-288-6190
A.J. Brewer, supt. Fax 288-6214
www.washington.k12.ok.us/
Washington HS 200/9-12
PO Box 98 73093 405-288-2354
David Crabbe, prin. Fax 288-6214
Washington MS 200/6-8
PO Box 98 73093 405-288-2428
Stuart McPherson, prin. Fax 288-6214

Watonga, Blaine, Pop. 5,588
Watonga ISD 800/PK-12
PO Box 310 73772 580-623-7364
Dr. Craig Cummins, supt. Fax 623-7370
www.watonga.k12.ok.us
Watonga HS 300/9-12
PO Box 310 73772 580-623-7362
Curtis Janko, prin. Fax 623-8019
Watonga MS 200/6-8
PO Box 310 73772 580-623-7361
Robin Roof, prin. Fax 623-7371

Watts, Adair, Pop. 328
Watts ISD 400/PK-12
RR 2 Box 1 74964 918-422-5311
Rita Bunch, supt. Fax 422-5556
www.wattsschool.com
Watts HS 100/9-12
RR 2 Box 1 74964 918-422-5132
Martin Bradford, prin. Fax 422-5556

Waukomis, Garfield, Pop. 1,201
Pioneer-Pleasant Vale ISD 500/PK-12
6520 E Wood Rd 73773 580-758-3282
Bill Noak, supt. Fax 758-1541
www.ppv.k12.ok.us/
Pioneer-Pleasant Vale HS 100/9-12
6520 E Wood Rd 73773 580-758-3282
Randy Schneider, prin.
Pioneer-Pleasant Vale JHS 100/7-8
6520 E Wood Rd 73773 580-758-3282
Randy Schneider, prin.

Waukomis ISD 300/PK-12
PO Box 729 73773 580-758-3247
Dwain Jindra, supt. Fax 758-3834
www.waukomis.k12.ok.us
Waukomis HS 100/6-12
PO Box 729 73773 580-758-3245
Janet Blocker, prin. Fax 758-3256

Waurika, Jefferson, Pop. 1,857
Waurika ISD 300/PK-12
PO Box 330 73573 580-228-3373
Roxie Terry, supt. Fax 228-3428
Waurika MSHS 100/6-12
PO Box 330 73573 580-228-3373
Dale Spradlin, prin. Fax 228-3428

Wayne, McClain, Pop. 727
OK Dept. of Voc. & Tech. Education
Supt. — None
Mid-America Technology Center Vo/Tech
PO Box H 73095 405-449-3391
Dusty Ricks, supt. Fax 449-7321

Wayne ISD 500/PK-12
PO Box 40 73095 405-449-3646
David Powell, supt. Fax 449-7095
www.wayne.k12.ok.us
Wayne HS 100/9-12
PO Box 40 73095 405-449-3317
James Lewis, prin. Fax 449-7095
Wayne MS 100/6-8
PO Box 40 73095 405-449-7047
Billy Lucas, prin. Fax 449-7095

Waynoka, Woods, Pop. 930
Waynoka ISD 200/PK-12
2134 Lincoln St 73860 580-824-6561
Dale Ross, supt. Fax 824-0656
www.waynoka.k12.ok.us/
Waynoka HS, 2134 Lincoln St 73860 100/9-12
Michael Meriwether, prin. 580-824-4341

Weatherford, Custer, Pop. 9,738
Weatherford ISD 1,700/PK-12
516 N Broadway St 73096 580-772-3327
Bill Seitter, supt. Fax 774-0821
www.wpsok.org
Weatherford HS 500/9-12
1500 N Washington St 73096 580-772-3385
James Ritz, prin. Fax 774-1939
Weatherford MS 400/6-8
509 N Custer St 73096 580-772-2270
Mark Shadid, prin. Fax 774-1981

Southwestern Oklahoma State University Post-Sec.
100 Campus Dr 73096 580-772-6611

Webbers Falls, Muskogee, Pop. 724
Webbers Falls ISD 300/PK-12
PO Box 300 74470 918-464-2580
Dudley Hume, supt. Fax 464-2313
www.webbersfalls.k12.ok.us/
Webbers Falls HS 100/9-12
PO Box 300 74470 918-464-2383
Judy Morton, prin. Fax 464-2313

Welch, Craig, Pop. 600
Welch ISD 300/PK-12
PO Box 189 74369 918-788-3319
Dr. Clark McKeon, supt. Fax 788-3734
welchwildcats.net
Welch JSHS 100/7-12
PO Box 189 74369 918-788-3222
Bruce Chrz, prin. Fax 788-3734

Weleetka, Okfuskee, Pop. 954
Graham ISD 100/PK-12
RR 1 Box 91 74880 918-652-8935
Dusty Chancey, supt. Fax 652-2422
www.graham.k12.ok.us
Graham HS 50/9-12
RR 1 Box 91 74880 918-652-8935
Dusty Chancey, prin. Fax 652-2422

Weleetka ISD 500/PK-12
PO Box 278 74880 405-786-2442
Dan Parrish, supt. Fax 786-2625
www.weleetka.k12.ok.us
Weleetka HS 100/10-12
PO Box 278 74880 405-786-2203
Ron Hunter, prin. Fax 786-2625
Weleetka JHS, PO Box 278 74880 100/7-9
Ron Hunter, prin. 405-786-2204

Wellston, Lincoln, Pop. 826
Wellston ISD 700/PK-12
PO Box 60 74881 405-356-2534
Dwayne Danker, supt. Fax 356-2838
www.wellston.k12.ok.us/
Wellston HS 200/9-12
PO Box 60 74881 405-356-2533
Ethel Grubbs, prin. Fax 356-2838
Wellston MS 100/6-8
PO Box 60 74881 405-356-2533
Mark Grubbs, prin. Fax 356-2838

Westville, Adair, Pop. 1,652
Westville ISD 1,100/PK-12
PO Box 410 74965 918-723-3181
Dan Collins, supt. Fax 723-3042
www.westville.k12.ok.us
Westville JHS 300/7-9
PO Box 410 74965 918-723-3432
Shawn Gillespie, prin. Fax 723-3042
Westville SHS 200/10-12
PO Box 410 74965 918-723-5644
Brent McKee, prin. Fax 723-5644

Wetumka, Hughes, Pop. 1,420
OK Dept. of Voc. & Tech. Education
Supt. — None
West Watkins Technology Center Vo/Tech
7892 Highway 9 74883 405-452-5500
Jim Moore, supt. Fax 452-5706

Wetumka ISD 400/PK-12
410 E Benson St 74883 405-452-5150
Michael Jaggars, supt. Fax 452-3052
www.wetumka.k12.ok.us/
Wetumka HS 100/9-12
410 E Benson St 74883 405-452-3291
David Dean, prin. Fax 452-5836

Wewoka, Seminole, Pop. 3,437
New Lima ISD 300/PK-12
116 Gross St 74884 405-257-5771
Carroll Brooksher, supt. Fax 257-2587
www.newlima.k12.ok.us
New Lima HS 100/7-12
116 Gross St 74884 405-257-5771
Gil Turpin, prin. Fax 257-2587

Wewoka ISD 700/PK-12
PO Box 870 74884 405-257-5475
Sam McElvany, supt. Fax 257-2303
www.wps.k12.ok.us/
Wewoka HS 200/9-12
PO Box 870 74884 405-257-5473
Kenneth Pattison, prin. Fax 257-2303
Wewoka MS 200/6-8
PO Box 870 74884 405-257-2340
Darrell Brown, prin. Fax 257-2303

Whitesboro, LeFlore
Whitesboro ISD 200/PK-12
PO Box 150 74577 918-567-2556
Dr. John Turner, supt. Fax 567-2842
Whitesboro HS, PO Box 150 74577 100/9-12
Rocky Farris, prin. 918-567-2624

Wilburton, Latimer, Pop. 2,934
OK Dept. of Voc. & Tech. Education
Supt. — None
Kiamichi Technology Center Vo/Tech
PO Box 548 74578 918-465-2324
Dr. Greg Winters, supt. Fax 465-3666

Wilburton ISD 1,000/PK-12
1201 W Blair Ave 74578 918-465-2100
Charles Enis, supt. Fax 465-3086
Wilburton JHS 200/7-9
1201 W Blair Ave 74578 918-465-2281
Tressa Taylor Moore, prin.
Wilburton SHS 200/10-12
1201 W Blair Ave 74578 918-465-3125
Nancy Taylor, prin.

Eastern Oklahoma State College Post-Sec.
1301 W Main St 74578 918-465-2361

Wilson, Carter, Pop. 1,623
Wilson ISD 400/PK-12
1860 Hewitt Rd 73463 580-668-2306
Lynn Henderson, supt. Fax 668-2170
www.wilson.k12.ok.us/
Wilson HS 100/9-12
1860 Hewitt Rd 73463 580-668-2317
Gary Labeth, prin. Fax 668-2170

Wister, LeFlore, Pop. 1,025
Wister ISD 600/PK-12
201 Logan St 74966 918-655-3132
Jerry Carpenter, supt. Fax 655-7402
www.wisterschools.org/
Wister HS 100/9-12
201 Logan St 74966 918-655-7276
Robert Craig, prin. Fax 655-7402

Woodward, Woodward, Pop. 11,931
OK Dept. of Voc. & Tech. Education
Supt. — None
High Plains Technology Center Vo/Tech
3921 34th St 73801 580-256-6618
Dr. Don Dale, supt. Fax 571-6190

Woodward ISD 2,500/PK-12
PO Box 668 73802 580-256-6063
Bill Denton, supt. Fax 256-4391
www.woodwardps.net
Woodward HS 700/9-12
PO Box 668 73802 580-256-5329
Kirk Warnick, prin. Fax 256-8716
Woodward MS South 300/7-8
PO Box 668 73802 580-256-7901
Frank Harrington, prin. Fax 256-8014

Woodward Beauty College Post-Sec.
502 Texas St 73801 580-256-7520

Wright City, McCurtain, Pop. 814
Wright City ISD 500/PK-12
PO Box 329 74766 580-981-2824
David Hawkins, supt. Fax 981-2115
Wright City HS 100/9-12
PO Box 329 74766 580-981-2558
Bob Finley, prin. Fax 981-2329
Wright City JHS 100/7-8
PO Box 329 74766 580-981-2558
Bob Finley, prin. Fax 981-2329

Wyandotte, Ottawa, Pop. 359
Wyandotte ISD 600/PK-12
PO Box 360 74370 918-678-2255
Duane Thomas, supt. Fax 678-2304
www.wyandotteschools.net
Wyandotte HS 300/9-12
PO Box 360 74370 918-678-2222
Marcia Kruse, prin. Fax 678-3906
Wyandotte MS 6-8
PO Box 360 74370 918-678-2222
Chris Gwartney, prin. Fax 678-3906

Wynnewood, Garvin, Pop. 2,314
Wynnewood ISD 700/PK-12
702 E Kerr Blvd 73098 405-665-2004
Bill Weldon, supt. Fax 665-5425
www.wynnewood.k12.ok.us/
Wynnewood HS 200/9-12
702 E Kerr Blvd 73098 405-665-2045
Steve Musgrove, prin.
Wynnewood MS 200/5-8
702 E Kerr Blvd 73098 405-665-4105
Mitzi Winters, prin.

Wynona, Osage, Pop. 535
Wynona ISD 200/PK-12
PO Box 700 74084 918-846-2467
Dixie Hurd, supt. Fax 846-2883
Wynona HS, PO Box 700 74084 50/9-12
Mark Allgood, prin. 918-846-2467

Yale, Payne, Pop. 1,254
Yale ISD 600/PK-12
315 E Chicago Ave 74085 918-387-2434
Mike Wilson, supt. Fax 387-2503
www.yale.k12.ok.us/
Yale HS 200/9-12
315 E Chicago Ave 74085 918-387-2282
Dodds Terrell, prin. Fax 387-2503
Yale JHS 100/7-8
315 E Chicago Ave 74085 918-387-2118
Dodds Terrell, prin. Fax 387-2503

Yukon, Canadian, Pop. 22,032
Yukon ISD 4,900/K-12
600 Maple St 73099 405-354-2587
Dr. Larry Birden, supt. Fax 354-4208
www.yukonps.com
Independence MS 700/6-8
500 E Vandament Ave 73099 405-354-5274
Tresa Smith, prin. Fax 354-0921
Lakeview MS 800/6-8
2700 N Mustang Rd 73099 405-350-2630
Angie Walton, prin. Fax 350-2632
Yukon HS 9-10
1029 Garth Brooks Blvd 73099 405-354-6692
Shirley Tucker, prin. Fax 354-6640
Yukon HS 800/11-12
1000 Yukon Ave 73099 405-354-6661
Dyton Coleman, prin. Fax 354-8411

Southwest Covenant S 200/K-12
2250 N Mustang Rd 73099 405-354-0772
G. Max DeWeese, hdmstr. Fax 350-2670
Yukon Beauty College Post-Sec.
1231 Garth Brooks Blvd 73099 405-354-3172

OREGON

OREGON DEPARTMENT OF EDUCATION
255 Capitol St NE, Salem 97310-0406
Telephone 503-947-5600
Fax 503-378-5156
Website http://www.ode.state.or.us

Superintendent of Public Instruction Susan Castillo

OREGON BOARD OF EDUCATION
255 Capitol St NE, Salem 97310-0406

Jerry Berger Chairperson

EDUCATION SERVICE DISTRICTS (ESD)

Clackamas ESD
Milt Dennison, supt. 503-675-4000
4011 SE Lake Rd, Milwaukie 97222 Fax 675-4200
www.clackesd.k12.or.us
Douglas ESD
Jonathan Hill, supt. 541-440-4777
1871 NE Stephens St Fax 440-4771
Roseburg 97470
www.douglasesd.k12.or.us
Grant ESD
Anthony Lanni, supt. 541-575-1349
835 S Canyon Blvd Fax 575-3601
John Day 97845
www.grantesd.k12.or.us
Harney ESD
Dennis Mills, supt. 541-573-2426
450 N Buena Vista Ave Fax 573-1822
Burns 97720
www.harneyesd.k12.or.us
High Desert ESD
Dennis Dempsey, supt. 541-693-5600
145 SE Salmon Ave Ste A Fax 693-5601
Redmond 97756
www.hdesd.k12.or.us
Jefferson ESD
Guy Fisher, supt. 541-475-2804
295 SE Buff St, Madras 97741 Fax 475-2827

Lake ESD
Judith May, supt. 541-947-3371
357 N L St, Lakeview 97630 Fax 947-3373
www.lakeesd.k12.or.us/
Lane ESD
Debbie Egan, supt. 541-461-8200
1200 Highway 99 N, Eugene 97402 Fax 461-8298
www.lane.k12.or.us
Linn-Benton-Lincoln ESD
Susan Waddell, supt. 541-812-2600
905 4th Ave SE, Albany 97321 Fax 926-6047
www.lblesd.k12.or.us
Malheur ESD
Tim Labrousse, supt. 541-473-3138
363 A St W, Vale 97918 Fax 473-3915
www.malesd.k12.or.us
Multnomah ESD
Edward Schmitt, supt. 503-255-1841
PO Box 301039, Portland 97294 Fax 257-1525
www.mesd.k12.or.us
North Central ESD
Anthony Lanni, supt. 541-384-2732
PO Box 637, Condon 97823 Fax 384-2752
www.ncesd.k12.or.us
Northwest Regional ESD
Jim Mabbott, supt. 503-614-1428
5825 NE Ray Cir, Hillsboro 97124 Fax 614-1440
www.nwresd.k12.or.us

Region 9 ESD
James Carnes Ed.D., supt. 541-298-5155
400 E Scenic Dr Ste 207 Fax 296-2965
The Dalles 97058
www.r9esd.k12.or.us
Region 18 ESD
Edward Jensen, supt. 541-426-4997
107 SW 1st St Ste 105 Fax 426-3732
Enterprise 97828
www.wallowaesd.k12.or.us/
South Coast ESD
Rick Howell, supt. 541-269-1611
1350 Teakwood Ave Fax 266-4040
Coos Bay 97420
www.scesd.k12.or.us
Southern Oregon ESD
Steve Boyarsky, supt. 541-776-8590
101 N Grape St, Medford 97501 Fax 779-2018
www.soesd.k12.or.us
Umatilla-Morrow ESD
George Murdock, supt. 541-276-6616
2001 SW Nye Ave Fax 276-4252
Pendleton 97801
www.umesd.k12.or.us
Union-Baker ESD
Mary Apple, supt. 541-963-4106
10100 N McAlister Rd Fax 963-7256
La Grande 97850
www.ubesd.k12.or.us
Willamette ESD
Maureen Casey, supt. 503-588-5330
2611 Pringle Rd SE, Salem 97302 Fax 363-5787
www.wesd.org

PUBLIC, PRIVATE AND CATHOLIC SECONDARY SCHOOLS

Adel, Lake
Adel SD 21
Supt. — See Lakeview
Adel S 50/4-8
PO Box 117 97620 541-947-3818
John Griffin, prin. Fax 947-5419

Adrian, Malheur, Pop. 143
Adrian SD 61 300/K-12
PO Box 108 97901 541-372-3744
Gene Mills, supt. Fax 372-5380
www.adriansd.com
Adrian HS 100/9-12
PO Box 108 97901 541-372-2335
Gene Mills, prin. Fax 372-5380

Albany, Linn, Pop. 44,797
Greater Albany SD 8J 8,500/K-12
718 7th Ave SW 97321 541-967-4501
Pat Bedore, supt. Fax 967-4587
albany.k12.or.us
Calapooia MS 800/6-8
830 24th Ave SE, 541-967-4555
Pat Wiedmann, prin. Fax 924-3702
Memorial MS 600/6-8
1050 Queen Ave SW 97321 541-967-4537
Kathleen Jackson, prin. Fax 924-3703
North Albany MS 600/6-8
1205 NW North Albany Rd 97321 541-967-4541
Randy Lary, prin. Fax 924-3704
South Albany HS 1,200/9-12
3705 Columbus St SE, 541-967-4522
Chris Equinoa, prin. Fax 924-3700
West Albany HS 1,300/9-12
1130 Queen Ave SW 97321 541-967-4545
Susie Orsborn, prin. Fax 924-3701

Fairview Christian S 100/K-12
35100 Goltra Rd SE, 541-928-4219
Ray Allen, prin. Fax 928-2140
Linn-Benton Community College Post-Sec.
6500 Pacific Blvd SW 97321 541-917-4999

Aloha, Washington, Pop. 43,600

Life Christian S 300/PK-12
5585 SW 209th Ave 97007 503-259-1329
Adam Kronberger, admin. Fax 649-5484

Magee Brothers Beaverton Sch of Beauty Post-Sec.
18295A SW Tualatin Valley 97007 503-649-1388

Alsea, Benton
Alsea SD 7J 100/K-12
PO Box B 97324 541-487-4305
Jason Larson, supt. Fax 487-4089
www.alsea.k12.or.us/
Alsea HS, PO Box B 97324 100/9-12
Jason Larson, prin. 541-487-4305

Amity, Yamhill, Pop. 1,463
Amity SD 4J 800/K-12
PO Box 138 97101 503-835-2171
Reg McShane, supt. Fax 835-5050
www.amity.k12.or.us
Amity HS 300/9-12
PO Box 138 97101 503-835-2181
Mike Solem, prin. Fax 835-6113
Amity MS 200/6-8
PO Box 138 97101 503-835-0518
Dave Lund, prin. Fax 835-0418

Perrydale SD 21 300/K-12
7445 Perrydale Rd 97101 503-835-3184
Robin Stoutt, supt. Fax 835-0631
www.perrydale.k12.or.us
Perrydale JSHS 200/6-12
7445 Perrydale Rd 97101 503-835-3184
Justin Huntley, prin. Fax 835-0631

Arlington, Gilliam, Pop. 490
Arlington SD 3 100/K-12
PO Box 10 97812 541-454-2632
Raymon Smith, supt. Fax 454-2137
www.honkernet.net
Arlington HS 50/9-12
PO Box 10 97812 541-454-2632
Raymon Smith, prin. Fax 454-2137

Ashland, Jackson, Pop. 20,829
Ashland SD 5 2,700/K-12
885 Siskiyou Blvd 97520 541-482-2811
Juli DiChiro, supt. Fax 482-2185
www.ashland.k12.or.us/splash/
Ashland HS 1,200/9-12
201 S Mountain Ave 97520 541-482-8771
Jeff Schlecht, prin. Fax 482-2172

Ashland MS 700/6-8
100 Walker Ave 97520 541-482-1611
Dale Rooklyn, prin. Fax 482-8112

Southern Oregon University Post-Sec.
1250 Siskiyou Blvd 97520 541-552-7672

Astoria, Clatsop, Pop. 9,784
Astoria SD 1 2,100/K-12
785 Alameda Ave 97103 503-325-6441
Michael Sowder, supt. Fax 325-6524
www.astoria.k12.or.us/
Astoria HS 800/9-12
1001 W Marine Dr 97103 503-325-3911
Larry Lockett, prin. Fax 325-2891
Astoria MS 300/7-8
1100 Klaskanine Ave 97103 503-325-4331
Ron Alley, prin. Fax 325-3040

Knappa SD 4 600/K-12
41535 Old Highway 30 97103 503-458-6166
Rick Pass, supt. Fax 458-5466
www.knappasd.k12.or.us
Knappa HS 200/9-12
41535 Old Highway 30 97103 503-458-6166
Nanette Hagen, prin. Fax 458-5466

Astoria Beauty College Post-Sec.
1180 Commercial St 97103 503-325-3163
Clatsop Community College Post-Sec.
1653 Jerome Ave 97103 503-325-0910

Athena, Umatilla, Pop. 1,218
Athena-Weston SD 29RJ 600/K-12
375 S 5th St 97813 541-566-3551
Richard Hensel, supt. Fax 566-9454
www.athwest.k12.or.us/
Weston-McEwen HS 200/9-12
540 E Main St 97813 541-566-3555
Brian Schimel, prin. Fax 566-2751
Other Schools – See Weston

Aurora, Marion, Pop. 879
North Marion SD 15 1,400/PK-12
20256 Grim Rd NE 97002 503-678-5835
Linda Reeves, supt. Fax 678-1473
www.nmarion.k12.or.us

North Marion HS 600/9-12
20167 Grim Rd NE 97002 503-678-7123
Glenn Elliott, prin. Fax 678-7186
North Marion MS 50/6-8
20246 Grim Rd NE 97002 503-678-7118
Sharon Baum, prin. Fax 678-7185

Baker City, Baker, Pop. 9,703
Baker SD 5J 2,000/PK-12
2090 4th St 97814 541-524-2260
Don Ulrey, supt. Fax 524-2564
www.baker.k12.or.us
Baker HS 700/9-12
2500 E St 97814 541-524-2600
Jerry Peacock, prin. Fax 524-2699
Baker MS 300/7-8
2320 Washington Ave 97814 541-524-2500
Minda Vaughan, prin. Fax 524-2563

Bandon, Coos, Pop. 2,908
Bandon SD 54 800/K-12
455 9th St SW 97411 541-347-4411
Diane Buche, supt. Fax 347-3974
www.bandon.k12.or.us/
Bandon HS 300/9-12
550 9th St SW 97411 541-347-4413
Gaye Knapp, prin. Fax 347-3714
Harbor Lights MS 300/5-8
390 9th St SW 97411 541-347-4415
Gerald Prickett, prin. Fax 347-1280

Banks, Washington, Pop. 1,562
Banks SD 13 1,200/K-12
450 S Main St 97106 503-324-8591
Marvin Ott, supt. Fax 324-6969
www.banks.k12.or.us
Banks HS 400/9-12
450 S Main St 97106 503-324-2281
Jim Foster, prin. Fax 324-8221
Banks JHS 200/7-8
450 S Main St 97106 503-324-3111
Mark Everett, prin. Fax 324-7441

Beaver, Tillamook
Nestucca Valley SD 101
Supt. — See Cloverdale
Nestucca Valley MS 100/6-8
PO Box 77 97108 503-398-5545
Jim Gadberry, prin. Fax 398-5831

Beaverton, Washington, Pop. 85,775
Beaverton SD 48J 35,600/K-12
16550 SW Merlo Rd 97006 503-591-8000
Jerome Colonna, supt. Fax 591-4415
www.beavton.k12.or.us
Aloha HS 1,900/9-12
18550 SW Kinnaman Rd 97007 503-259-4700
Vicki Lukich, prin. Fax 259-4713
Beaverton HS 2,000/9-12
13000 SW 2nd St 97005 503-259-5000
Janice Adams, prin. Fax 259-4990
Conestoga MS 1,000/6-8
12250 SW Conestoga Dr 97008 503-524-1345
Dan Zenor, prin. Fax 524-1349
Five Oaks MS 1,100/6-8
1600 NW 173rd Ave 97006 503-533-1890
Mike Chamberlain, prin. Fax 533-1898
Highland Park MS 1,000/6-8
7000 SW Wilson Ave 97008 503-672-3640
Allan Deckard, prin. Fax 672-3644
International S of Beaverton 6-12
17770 SW Blanton St 97007 503-259-3600
Sheila Baumgardner, prin. Fax 259-3603
Meadow Park MS 900/6-8
14100 SW Downing St 97006 503-672-3660
Jill O'Neill, prin. Fax 672-3664
Mountain View MS 1,100/6-8
17500 SW Farmington Rd 97007 503-259-3890
Joann Hulquist, prin. Fax 259-3894
School of Science & Technology Vo/Tech
1841 SW Merlo Dr 97006 503-259-5575
Gregory Parcher, prin. Fax 259-5588
Southridge HS 2,000/9-12
9625 SW 125th Ave 97008 503-259-5400
Amy Gordon, prin. Fax 259-5425
Whitford MS 900/6-8
7935 SW Scholls Ferry Rd 97008 503-672-3680
Matthew Casteel, prin. Fax 672-3684
Other Schools – See Portland

Cor Deo Christian Academy 100/1-10
9100 SW 135th Ave 97008 503-524-1866
Bill Sweitzer, prin. Fax 579-9129
Oregon Graduate Institute/Science & Tech Post-Sec.
20000 NW Walker Rd 97006 503-748-1121
St. Stephens Academy 100/K-12
7275 SW Hall Blvd 97008 503-929-9711
Raelene Meeker, prin. Fax 626-1522
Valley Catholic HS 500/7-12
4275 SW 148th Ave 97007 503-644-3745
Ross Thomas, prin. Fax 646-4054

Bend, Deschutes, Pop. 67,152
Bend-LaPine Administrative SD 1 14,000/K-12
520 NW Wall St 97701 541-383-6000
Douglas Nelson, supt. Fax 383-6003
www.bend.k12.or.us
Bend HS 1,300/9-12
230 NE 6th St 97701 541-383-6290
Mark Neffendorf, prin. Fax 383-6465
Cascade MS 700/6-8
19619 SW Mountaineer Way 97702 541-383-6230
Michael Hecker, prin. Fax 383-6255
High Desert MS 700/6-8
61111 27th St 97702 541-383-6480
Gary DeFrang, prin. Fax 383-6499
Mountain View HS 1,500/9-12
2755 NE 27th St 97701 541-383-6360
Kathryn Legace, prin. Fax 383-6469
Pilot Butte MS 600/6-8
1501 NE Neff Rd 97701 541-383-6260
Stephanie Bennett, prin. Fax 383-6286

Sky View MS 600/6-8
63555 18th St 97701 541-383-6479
D. Scott Edmondson, prin. Fax 322-5217
Summit HS 1,300/9-12
2855 NW Clearwater Dr 97701 541-322-3300
Alfred Hulbert, prin. Fax 322-3310
Other Schools – See La Pine

Central Oregon Community College Post-Sec.
2600 NW College Way 97701 541-383-7500
Morning Star Christian S 200/PK-12
19741 Baker Rd 97702 541-382-5091
Rev. Ken Marks, admin. Fax 382-0268
Phagans' Central Oregon Beauty College Post-Sec.
355 NE 2nd St 97701 541-382-6171
Three Sisters SDA S 50/K-10
21155 Tumalo Rd 97701 541-389-2091
Randy Thornton, prin. Fax 389-2091

Blachly, Lane
Blachly SD 90 100/K-12
20264 Blachly Grange Rd 97412 541-925-3262
Bob De La Vergne, supt. Fax 925-3062
www.blachly.k12.or.us/
Triangle Lake S 100/K-12
20264 Blachly Grange Rd 97412 541-925-3262
Bob De La Vergne, prin. Fax 925-3062

Boardman, Morrow, Pop. 3,051
Morrow SD 1
Supt. — See Lexington
Riverside JSHS 500/7-12
210 NE Boardman Ave 97818 541-481-2525
Dirk Dirksen, prin. Fax 481-2047

Bonanza, Klamath, Pop. 416
Klamath County SD
Supt. — See Klamath Falls
Bonanza S K-12
PO Box 128 97623 541-545-6581
Charlene Soule, prin. Fax 545-1719

Klamath-Lake Co. Youth Ranch 50/9-12
5800 Happy Hollow Ln 97623 541-545-6742
James Yoder, prin. Fax 545-3025

Boring, Clackamas
Oregon Trail SD 46
Supt. — See Sandy
Boring MS 400/6-8
27801 SE Dee St 97009 503-668-9393
Scott Maltman, prin. Fax 668-5291

Brookings, Curry, Pop. 6,297
Brookings-Harbor SD 17-C 1,800/K-12
629 Easy St 97415 541-469-7443
Chris Nichols, supt. Fax 469-6599
www.brookings.k12.or.us
Azalea MS 500/6-8
629 Easy St 97415 541-469-7427
Michael Dillenburg, prin. Fax 469-7080
Brookings-Harbor HS 600/9-12
629 Easy St 97415 541-469-2108
Emmalie Lee, prin. Fax 469-6570

Brookings Harbor Christian S 100/PK-12
PO Box 5809 97415 541-469-6478
Christine Hudson, admin. Fax 412-7242

Brooks, Marion

Willamette Valley Christian S 200/K-12
PO Box 9088 97305 503-393-5236
Gary Glassco, admin. Fax 485-8203

Brownsville, Linn, Pop. 1,517
Central Linn SD 552 600/K-12
331 E Blakely Ave 97327 541-466-3105
Max Harrell, supt. Fax 466-3180
www.centrallinn.k12.or.us
Other Schools – See Halsey

Burns, Harney, Pop. 2,755
Harney County SD 3 1,000/K-12
550 N Court Ave 97720 541-573-6811
David L. Courtney, supt. Fax 573-7557
www.burnsschools.k12.or.us
Burns HS 300/9-12
1100 Oregon Ave 97720 541-573-2044
Ron Wassom, prin. Fax 573-5456
Other Schools – See Hines

Butte Falls, Jackson, Pop. 433
Butte Falls SD 91 200/K-12
PO Box 228 97522 541-865-3563
Steve Pine, supt. Fax 865-3217
www.buttefallsschools.org/
Butte Falls MSHS 100/7-12
PO Box 167 97522 541-865-3563
Steve Pine, prin. Fax 865-7810

Canby, Clackamas, Pop. 14,989
Canby SD 86 5,300/K-12
1130 S Ivy St 97013 503-266-7861
Deborah Sommer, supt. Fax 266-0022
www.canby.k12.or.us
Ackerman MS 1,000/6-8
350 SE 13th Ave 97013 503-263-7140
Joel Sebastian, prin. Fax 266-7489
Baker Prairie MS 6-8
1859 S Township Rd 97013 503-263-7170
Lou Bailey, prin. Fax 263-7189
Canby HS 1,700/9-12
721 SW 4th Ave 97013 503-263-7200
Pat Johnson, prin. Fax 263-7211

Canyon City, Grant, Pop. 595
Grant SD 3 800/K-12
401 N Canyon City Blvd 97820 541-575-1280
Newell Cleaver, supt. Fax 575-0928
www.grantesd.k12.or.us
Other Schools – See John Day, Mount Vernon

Canyonville, Douglas, Pop. 1,397

Canyonville Christian Academy 200/7-12
PO Box 1100 97417 541-839-4401
Cathy Lovato, supt. Fax 839-6228

Cascade Locks, Hood River, Pop. 1,109
Hood River County SD
Supt. — See Hood River
Cascade Locks S 200/K-12
PO Box 279 97014 541-374-8467
Ed Drew, prin. Fax 374-8446

Cave Junction, Josephine, Pop. 1,380
Three Rivers County SD
Supt. — See Grants Pass
Byrne MS 300/6-8
101 S Junction Ave 97523 541-592-2163
Tom Hewkin, prin. Fax 592-4851
Illinois Valley HS 500/9-12
625 E River St 97523 541-592-2116
JoAnn Bethany, prin. Fax 592-4853

Central Point, Jackson, Pop. 15,672
Central Point SD 6 4,600/K-12
300 Ash St 97502 541-494-6200
Randal Gravon, supt. Fax 664-1637
www.district6.org
Crater HS 1,500/9-12
655 N 3rd St 97502 541-494-6300
Kirk Gibson, prin. Fax 664-7589
Scenic MS 800/6-8
1955 Scenic Ave 97502 541-494-6400
Sheila Henson, prin. Fax 664-8534
Other Schools – See Gold Hill

Chiloquin, Klamath, Pop. 723
Klamath County SD
Supt. — See Klamath Falls
Chiloquin JSHS 300/7-12
PO Box 397 97624 541-783-2321
Doug Wilson, prin. Fax 783-2792

Christmas Valley, Lake

Solid Rock Christian S 50/K-12
PO Box 745 97641 541-576-2895
Dell Renee Wilson, prin.

Clackamas, Clackamas, Pop. 2,578
North Clackamas SD 12
Supt. — See Milwaukie
Clackamas HS 2,000/9-12
14486 SE 122nd Ave 97015 503-353-5812
Jan Miner, prin. Fax 353-5815
Sunrise MS 1,100/7-8
14331 SE 132nd Ave 97015 503-353-5755
Terrence Smyth, prin. Fax 353-5765

Pioneer Pacific College Post-Sec.
8800 SE Sunnyside Rd 97015 503-654-8000

Clatskanie, Columbia, Pop. 1,631
Clatskanie SD 6J 900/K-12
PO Box 678 97016 503-728-0587
Ed Serra, supt. Fax 728-0608
www.clat6j.k12.or.us/
Clatskanie MSHS 500/7-12
PO Box 68 97016 503-728-2146
Gary Mounce, prin. Fax 728-4632

Cloverdale, Tillamook
Nestucca Valley SD 101 600/K-12
36925 Highway 101 S 97112 503-392-4892
Bob Simonson, supt. Fax 392-9061
www.nestucca.k12.or.us
Nestucca HS 200/9-12
PO Box 38 97112 503-392-3194
Randy Wharton, prin. Fax 392-3724
Other Schools – See Beaver

Colton, Clackamas
Colton SD 53 800/K-12
30429 S Grays Hill Rd 97017 503-824-3535
Linda Johnson, supt. Fax 824-3530
www.colton.k12.or.us
Colton HS 300/9-12
30205 S Wall St 97017 503-824-2311
David Gilbertson, prin. Fax 824-2312
Colton MS 200/6-8
21580 S Schieffer Rd 97017 503-824-2319
Beth Lund, prin. Fax 824-2309

Condon, Gilliam, Pop. 708
Condon SD 25J 100/K-12
PO Box 615 97823 541-384-2581
Gene Carlson, supt. Fax 384-2585
www.condon.k12.or.us
Condon HS 100/8-12
PO Box 575 97823 541-384-2441
Gene Carlson, prin. Fax 384-2504

Coos Bay, Coos, Pop. 15,823
Coos Bay SD 9 3,700/K-12
PO Box 509 97420 541-267-3104
Karen Gray, supt. Fax 269-5366
www.coos-bay.k12.or.us
Marshfield HS 1,200/9-12
PO Box 509 97420 541-267-1405
Travis Howard, prin. Fax 269-0161
Sunset MS 600/7-8
PO Box 509 97420 541-888-1242
Jon Mishra, prin. Fax 888-9814

Southwestern Oregon Community College Post-Sec.
1988 Newmark Ave 97420 541-888-2525

Coquille, Coos, Pop. 4,254
Coquille SD 8 900/K-12
790 W 17th St 97423 541-396-2181
John Kinnee, supt. Fax 396-5015
www.coquille.k12.or.us/

Coquille HS 400/9-12
499 W Central St 97423 541-396-2163
Patrick Royal, prin. Fax 396-4635
Coquille Valley S 200/4-8
1115 N Baxter St 97423 541-396-2914
Mark Nortness, prin. Fax 396-4543

Corbett, Multnomah
Corbett SD 39 600/K-12
35800 Historic Columbia Riv 97019 503-695-3612
Robert Dunton, supt. Fax 695-3641
www.corbett.k12.or.us
Corbett HS 200/10-12
35800 Historic Columbia Riv 97019 503-695-3600
Randy Trani, prin. Fax 695-3641
Corbett MS 200/7-9
35800 Historic Columbia Riv 97019 503-695-3636
Randy Trani, prin. Fax 695-3641

Corvallis, Benton, Pop. 49,553
Corvallis SD 509J 6,700/K-12
PO Box 3509J 97339 541-757-5811
Dawn Tarzian, supt. Fax 757-5703
www.csd509j.net/
Cheldelin MS 600/6-8
987 NE Conifer Blvd 97330 541-757-5971
Dawn Granger, prin. Fax 757-4596
Corvallis HS 1,400/9-12
1400 NW Buchanan Ave 97330 541-757-5871
Suzanne Dalton, prin. Fax 757-5875
Crescent Valley HS 1,100/9-12
4444 NW Highland Dr 97330 541-757-5801
Cherie Stroud, prin. Fax 757-4522
Pauling MS 700/6-8
1111 NW Cleveland Ave 97330 541-757-5961
James Wickman, prin. Fax 757-4598

Oregon State University 97333 Post-Sec.
541-737-0123
Phagans' Beauty College Post-Sec.
142 SW 2nd St 97333 541-753-6466
Santiam Christian S 900/PK-12
7220 NE Arnold Ave 97330 541-745-5524
Stanton Baker, supt. Fax 745-6338

Cottage Grove, Lane, Pop. 8,724
South Lane SD 45J3 2,700/K-12
PO Box 218 97424 541-942-3381
Krista Parent, supt. Fax 942-8098
www.slane.k12.or.us/dsc
Cottage Grove HS 900/9-12
PO Box 160 97424 541-942-3391
Donn Pollard, prin. Fax 942-7492
Lincoln MS 600/6-8
1565 S 4th St 97424 541-942-3316
Brian McCasline, prin. Fax 942-9801

Cove, Union, Pop. 606
Cove SD 15 200/K-12
PO Box 68 97824 541-568-4424
Jeff Clark, supt. Fax 568-4251
Cove S 200/K-12
PO Box 68 97824 541-568-4424
Toby Koehn, prin. Fax 568-4251

Crane, Harney
Harney County UNHSD 1J 100/9-12
PO Box 828 97732 541-493-2641
Jeff Walker, supt. Fax 493-2051
Crane Union HS 100/9-12
PO Box 828 97732 541-493-2641
Jeff Walker, prin. Fax 493-2051

Creswell, Lane, Pop. 4,632
Creswell SD 40 1,000/K-12
998 A St 97426 541-895-6000
Rick Stuber, supt. Fax 895-6019
www.creswell.k12.or.us
Creswell HS 300/9-12
33390 Nieblock Ln 97426 541-895-6020
Jan Ophus, prin. Fax 895-6089
Creswell MS 300/6-8
655 W Oregon Ave 97426 541-895-6090
Shirley Burrus, prin. Fax 895-6139

Culver, Jefferson, Pop. 898
Culver SD 4 600/K-12
PO Box 228 97734 541-546-2541
Linda Florence, supt. Fax 546-7517
www.culver.k12.or.us/
Culver HS 200/9-12
PO Box 228 97734 541-546-2251
Bill Perkins, prin. Fax 546-2201
Culver MS 200/6-8
PO Box 228 97734 541-546-3090
Alice Smith, prin. Fax 546-2137

Dallas, Polk, Pop. 14,001
Dallas SD 2 3,000/K-12
111 SW Ash St 97338 503-623-5594
Christy Perry, supt. Fax 623-5597
www.dallas.k12.or.us
Dallas HS 1,000/9-12
1250 SE Holman Ave 97338 503-623-8336
Keith Ussery, prin. Fax 623-4669
LaCreole MS 700/6-8
701 SE Lacreole Dr 97338 503-623-6662
Steve Spencer, prin. Fax 623-8477

Damascus, Clackamas, Pop. 9,454
Gresham-Barlow SD 10J
Supt. — See Gresham
Damascus MS 400/5-8
14151 SE 242nd Ave, 503-658-3171
Lori Walter, prin. Fax 658-6275

Damascus Christian S 300/K-12
14251 SE Rust Way, 503-658-4100
Timothy Oakley, admin. Fax 658-5827

Days Creek, Douglas

Milo Adventist Academy 100/9-12
PO Box 278 97429 541-825-3200
Randy Bovee, prin. Fax 825-3723

Dayton, Yamhill, Pop. 2,206
Dayton SD 8 1,000/K-12
526 Ferry St 97114 503-864-2215
Janelle Beers, supt. Fax 864-3927
www.dayton.k12.or.us
Dayton HS 300/9-12
801 Ferry St 97114 503-864-2273
Roger Lorenzen, prin. Fax 864-2932
Dayton JHS 300/6-8
801 Ferry St 97114 503-864-2246
Jami Fluke, prin. Fax 864-3697

Dayville, Grant, Pop. 122
Dayville SD 16J 100/K-12
PO Box C 97825 541-987-2412
Maurice Thorne, supt. Fax 987-2155
Dayville S 100/K-12
PO Box C 97825 541-987-2412
Maurice Thorne, prin. Fax 987-2155

Drain, Douglas, Pop. 1,039
North Douglas SD 22 400/K-12
PO Box 428 97435 541-836-2223
Dan Forbess, supt. Fax 836-7558
www.northdouglas.k12.or.us
North Douglas HS 100/9-12
PO Box 488 97435 541-836-2222
Lesa Haley, prin. Fax 836-2387

Dufur, Wasco, Pop. 582
Dufur SD 29 300/K-12
802 NE 5th St 97021 541-467-2509
Jack Henderson, supt. Fax 467-2589
www.dufur.k12.or.us
Dufur S 300/K-12
802 NE 5th St 97021 541-467-2509
Bert Wyatt, prin. Fax 467-2589

Eagle Point, Jackson, Pop. 7,496
Jackson County SD 9 4,200/K-12
PO Box 548 97524 541-830-1200
Cynda Rickert, supt. Fax 830-6550
www.eaglepnt.k12.or.us
Eagle Point HS 1,200/9-12
PO Box 198 97524 541-830-1300
Mari Brabbin, prin. Fax 830-6682
Eagle Point MS 500/6-8
PO Box 218 97524 541-830-1250
Dan Johnson, prin. Fax 830-6086
Other Schools – See Shady Cove, White City

Echo, Umatilla, Pop. 691
Echo SD 5 200/K-12
600 E Gerone St 97826 541-376-8436
Rob Waite, supt. Fax 376-8473
www.echo.k12.or.us/
Echo S 200/K-12
600 E Gerone St 97826 541-376-8436
Norm Stewart, prin. Fax 376-8473

Elgin, Union, Pop. 1,642
Elgin SD 23 400/K-12
PO Box 68 97827 541-437-1211
Kerma Berry, supt. Fax 437-1231
www.elgin.k12.or.us
Elgin HS 100/9-12
PO Box 68 97827 541-437-2021
Kerma Berry, prin. Fax 437-1705

Elkton, Douglas, Pop. 150
Elkton SD 34 200/PK-12
PO Box 390 97436 541-584-2228
Robert Allen, supt. Fax 584-2227
www.elkton.k12.or.us/
Elkton HS 100/9-12
PO Box 390 97436 541-584-2228
Robert Allen, prin. Fax 584-2227

Elmira, Lane
Fern Ridge SD 28J 1,500/K-12
88834 Territorial Rd 97437 541-935-2253
Ivan Hernandez, supt. Fax 935-8222
www.fernridge.k12.or.us
Elmira HS 500/9-12
24936 Fir Grove Ln 97437 541-935-8200
Karen McKenzie, prin. Fax 935-8205
Fern Ridge MS 400/6-8
88831 Territorial Rd 97437 541-935-8230
Doug Kartub, prin. Fax 935-8234

Enterprise, Wallowa, Pop. 1,800
Enterprise SD 21 400/K-12
201 SE 4th St 97828 541-426-3193
Brad Royse, supt. Fax 426-3504
www.enterprise.k12.or.us/
Enterprise HS 200/7-12
201 SE 4th St 97828 541-426-3193
Blake Carlsen, prin. Fax 426-3504

Enterprise SDA S 50/K-10
PO Box N 97828 541-426-8339
Fax 426-8339

Estacada, Clackamas, Pop. 2,435
Estacada SD 108 2,200/K-12
255 NE 6th Ave 97023 503-630-6871
Michael Call, supt. Fax 630-8513
www.estacada.k12.or.us
Estacada HS 700/9-12
355 NE 6th Ave 97023 503-630-8515
Rick Slater, prin. Fax 630-8699
Estacada JHS 400/7-8
500 NE Main St 97023 503-630-8516
Kevin Olds, prin. Fax 630-8693

Eugene, Lane, Pop. 144,515
Bethel SD 52 5,700/K-12
4640 Barger Dr 97402 541-689-3280
Steve Hull, supt. Fax 689-0719
www.bethel.k12.or.us
Cascade MS 500/6-8
1525 Echo Hollow Rd 97402 541-689-0641
Glen Martz, prin. Fax 689-9622
Kalapuya HS 100/9-12
1200 N Terry St 97402 541-607-9853
Fred Crisman, prin. Fax 607-9857
Shasta MS 500/6-8
4656 Barger Dr 97402 541-688-9611
Bert Eliason, prin. Fax 689-9382
Willamette HS 1,500/9-12
1801 Echo Hollow Rd 97402 541-689-0731
Jim Jamieson, prin. Fax 689-7119

Crow-Applegate-Lorane SD 66 300/K-12
85955 Territorial Hwy 97402 541-935-2100
Eileen Palmer, supt. Fax 935-6107
www.cal.k12.or.us
Crow MSHS 100/7-12
25863 Crow Rd 97402 541-935-2227
Ron Osibov, prin. Fax 935-6829

Eugene SD 4J 17,800/K-12
200 N Monroe St 97402 541-687-3123
George Russell, supt. Fax 687-3691
www.4j.lane.edu
Churchill HS 1,400/9-12
1850 Bailey Hill Rd 97405 541-687-3421
Dennis Biggerstaff, prin. Fax 687-3682
Jefferson MS 400/6-8
1650 W 22nd Ave 97405 541-687-3221
Jeff Johnson, prin. Fax 687-3675
Kelly MS 500/6-8
850 Howard Ave 97404 541-687-3224
Tim Rochholz, prin. Fax 687-3676
Kennedy MS 500/6-8
2200 Bailey Hill Rd 97405 541-687-3241
Charlie Smith, prin. Fax 687-3677
Madison MS 400/6-8
875 Wilkes Dr 97404 541-687-4300
Nancy Pollard, prin. Fax 687-4320
Monroe MS 600/6-8
2800 Bailey Ln 97401 541-687-3254
Rick Gaultney, prin. Fax 687-3679
North Eugene HS 1,300/9-12
200 Silver Ln 97404 541-687-3261
Laurie Henry, prin. Fax 687-3683
Roosevelt MS 700/6-8
680 E 24th Ave 97405 541-687-3227
Morley Hegstrom, prin. Fax 687-3680
Sheldon HS 1,600/9-12
2455 Willakenzie Rd 97401 541-687-3381
Bob Bolden, prin. Fax 687-3684
South Eugene HS 1,700/9-12
400 E 19th Ave 97401 541-687-3201
Randy Bernstein, prin. Fax 687-3685
Spencer Butte MS 400/6-8
500 E 43rd Ave 97405 541-687-3237
Cydney Vandercar, prin. Fax 687-3681
Young MS 600/6-8
2555 Gilham Rd 97408 541-687-5400
Sara Cramer, prin. Fax 687-5456

Eugene Bible College Post-Sec.
2155 Bailey Hill Rd 97405 541-485-1780
Gutenberg College Post-Sec.
1883 University St 97403 541-683-5141
Lane Community College Post-Sec.
4000 E 30th Ave 97405 541-747-4501
Lifegate Christian S 100/K-12
1052 Fairfield Ave 97402 541-689-5847
Tom Gregersen, admin. Fax 689-6028
Marist HS 500/9-12
1900 Kingsley Rd 97401 541-686-2234
Perry Martin, prin. Fax 342-6451
Northwest Christian College Post-Sec.
828 E 11th Ave 97401 541-343-1641
Oak Hill S 100/K-12
86397 Eastway Dr 97405 541-744-0954
Elliott Grey, hdmstr. Fax 741-6968
University of Oregon Post-Sec.
1217 University Of Oregon 97403 541-346-1000
Wellsprings Friends S 100/9-12
3590 W 18th Ave 97402 541-686-1223
Dennis Hoerner, hdmstr. Fax 687-1493

Fairview, Multnomah, Pop. 9,327
Reynolds SD 7 10,100/K-12
1204 NE 201st Ave 97024 503-661-7200
Terry Kneisler, supt. Fax 667-6932
www.reynolds.k12.or.us
Reynolds MS 1,000/6-8
1200 NE 201st Ave 97024 503-665-8166
Yuki Monteith, prin. Fax 667-6751
Other Schools – See Portland, Troutdale

Falls City, Polk, Pop. 1,014
Falls City SD 57 200/K-12
111 N Main St 97344 503-787-3521
Peter Tarzian, supt. Fax 787-1507
www.fallscity.k12.or.us
Falls City HS 100/9-12
111 N Main St 97344 503-787-3521
Peter Tarzian, prin. Fax 787-1507

Finn Rock, Lane
McKenzie SD 68 200/K-12
51187 Blue River Dr, Vida OR 97488 541-822-3338
Susan Taylor Greene, supt. Fax 822-8014
www.mckenzie.k12.or.us
McKenzie JSHS 100/6-12
51187 Blue River Dr, Vida OR 97488 541-822-3313
Jim Seversen, prin. Fax 822-8014

Florence, Lane, Pop. 7,841
Siuslaw SD 97J 1,500/K-12
2111 Oak St 97439 541-997-2651
Gerald Hamilton, supt. Fax 997-6748
www.siuslaw.k12.or.us

Siuslaw HS 600/9-12
2975 Oak St 97439 541-997-3448
Larry Martindale, prin. Fax 997-4160
Siuslaw MS 400/6-8
2525 Oak St 97439 541-997-8241
Nancy Larson, prin. Fax 997-4161

Forest Grove, Washington, Pop. 19,689
Forest Grove SD 15 5,800/K-12
1728 Main St 97116 503-357-6171
Jack Musser, supt. Fax 359-2520
www.fgsd.k12.or.us
Armstrong MS 900/7-8
1777 Mountain View Ln 97116 503-359-2465
Sherry Adams, prin. Fax 359-2560
Forest Grove HS 1,700/9-12
1401 Nichols Ln 97116 503-359-2432
John O'Neill, prin. Fax 359-2521

Pacific University Post-Sec.
2043 College Way 97116 800-635-0561

Fossil, Wheeler, Pop. 435
Fossil SD 21J 100/K-12
PO Box 206 97830 541-763-4384
Mike Hughes, supt. Fax 763-2099
Wheeler HS 50/9-12
PO Box 266 97830 541-763-4146
Mike Hughes, prin. Fax 763-4010

Gaston, Washington, Pop. 765
Gaston SD 511J 500/K-12
PO Box 68 97119 503-985-0210
Terry Mahler, supt. Fax 985-3366
www.gaston.k12.or.us
Gaston JSHS 300/7-12
PO Box 68 97119 503-985-7516
Mike Durbin, prin. Fax 985-3279

Gervais, Marion, Pop. 2,292
Gervais SD 1 1,100/K-12
PO Box 100 97026 503-792-3801
Larry Glaze, supt. Fax 792-3809
www.gervais.k12.or.us
Gervais HS 300/9-12
PO Box 195 97026 503-792-3656
Chuck Borberg, prin. Fax 792-3770
Gervais MS 300/5-8
PO Box 176 97026 503-792-3624
Ken Stott, prin. Fax 792-3626

Gilchrist, Klamath
Klamath County SD
Supt. — See Klamath Falls
Gilchrist S K-12
PO Box 668 97737 541-433-2295
Christie Gestvang, prin. Fax 433-2688

Gladstone, Clackamas, Pop. 12,117
Gladstone SD 115 2,200/K-12
17789 Webster Rd 97027 503-655-2777
Bob Stewart, supt. Fax 655-5201
www.gladstone.k12.or.us
Gladstone HS 800/9-12
18800 Portland Ave 97027 503-655-2544
Stu Evans, prin. Fax 655-0320
Kraxberger MS 700/5-8
17777 Webster Rd 97027 503-655-3636
Joni Cesario, prin. Fax 650-2596

Grace Christian S 200/PK-12
6460 Glen Echo Ave 97027 503-655-1702
Mardel Watterud, prin. Fax 655-1702

Glendale, Douglas, Pop. 897
Glendale SD 77 500/K-12
PO Box E 97442 541-832-2133
Lloyd Hartley, supt. Fax 832-3183
www.glendale.k12.or.us
Glendale JSHS 300/7-12
PO Box E 97442 541-832-2171
Tom McCormick, prin. Fax 832-2486

Glide, Douglas
Glide SD 12 800/PK-12
301 Glide Loop Dr 97443 541-496-3521
Don Schrader, supt. Fax 496-4300
www.glide.k12.or.us
Glide HS 300/9-12
18990 N Umpqua Hwy 97443 541-496-3554
Pam Maurice, prin. Fax 496-4304
Glide MS 100/7-8
301 Glide Loop Dr 97443 541-496-3516
Ira Weir, prin. Fax 496-4302

Gold Beach, Curry, Pop. 1,930
Central Curry SD 1 700/K-12
29516 Ellensburg Ave 97444 541-247-6648
Jeff Davis, supt. Fax 247-9717
www.ccsd.k12.or.us
Gold Beach HS 200/9-12
29516 Ellensburg Ave 97444 541-247-6647
Jennifer Dukek, prin. Fax 247-4557

Gold Hill, Jackson, Pop. 1,062
Central Point SD 6
Supt. — See Central Point
Hanby MS 300/6-8
806 6th Ave 97525 541-494-6800
Dennis Allen, prin. Fax 855-1120

Grand Ronde, Polk
Willamina SD 30J
Supt. — See Willamina
Willamina MS at Grand Ronde 200/6-8
PO Box 7 97347 503-879-5210
Kathy Long, prin. Fax 879-5249

Grants Pass, Josephine, Pop. 28,882
Grants Pass SD 7 5,800/K-12
725 NE Dean Dr 97526 541-474-5700
Steve Iverson, supt. Fax 474-5705
www.grantspass.k12.or.us
Grants Pass HS 1,900/9-12
830 NE 9th St 97526 541-474-5710
Aaron Anderson, prin. Fax 474-5717
North MS 700/6-8
1725 NW Highland Ave 97526 541-474-5740
Dan Smith, prin. Fax 474-5739
South MS 700/6-8
350 W Harbeck Rd 97527 541-474-5750
Renee Cardiff, prin. Fax 474-9742

Three Rivers County SD 5,900/K-12
8550 New Hope Rd 97527 541-862-3111
Jerry C. Fritts, supt. Fax 862-3119
www.threerivers.k12.or.us
Fleming MS 500/6-8
6001 Monument Dr 97526 541-476-8284
John George, prin. Fax 471-2458
Hidden Valley HS 900/9-12
651 Murphy Creek Rd 97527 541-862-2124
Dennis Misner, prin. Fax 862-2872
Lincoln Savage MS 500/6-8
8551 New Hope Rd 97527 541-862-2171
Tom Wiik, prin. Fax 862-2713
North Valley HS 800/9-12
6741 Monument Dr 97526 541-479-3388
Linda Hugle, prin. Fax 471-2462
Other Schools – See Cave Junction

Grants Pass SDA Junior Academy 100/K-10
2250 NW Heidi Ln 97526 541-479-2293
Roger Knauff, prin. Fax 479-8412
New Hope Christian S 300/PK-12
5961 New Hope Rd 97527 541-476-4588
Terell Bowdoin, admin. Fax 474-7626
Phagans' Grants Pass College of Beauty Post-Sec.
304 NE Agness Ave Ste F 97526 541-479-6678
Rogue Community College Post-Sec.
3345 Redwood Hwy 97527 541-956-7500
Vineyard Christian S 100/PK-12
275 Potts Way 97526 541-479-9649
Doug Thomas, prin. Fax 479-3506

Gresham, Multnomah, Pop. 96,072
Centennial SD 28J
Supt. — See Portland
Centennial HS 1,800/9-12
3505 SE 182nd Ave 97030 503-661-7612
Mark Baier, prin. Fax 661-5296

Gresham-Barlow SD 10J 11,900/K-12
1331 NW Eastman Pkwy 97030 503-618-2450
Ken Noah, supt. Fax 661-1589
www.gresham.k12.or.us
Barlow HS 1,800/9-12
5105 SE 302nd Ave 97080 503-674-5600
James Hiu, prin. Fax 674-5645
Clear Creek MS 700/6-8
219 NE 219th Ave 97030 503-492-6700
John Koch, prin. Fax 492-6707
Gresham HS 1,800/9-12
1200 N Main Ave 97030 503-674-5500
Carol Daiberl, prin. Fax 674-5549
McCarty MS 600/6-8
1400 SE 5th St 97080 503-665-0148
Tim Tutty, prin. Fax 669-1892
Russell MS 800/6-8
3625 SE Powell Valley Rd 97080 503-667-6900
Randy Bryant, prin. Fax 492-6708
Springwater Trail HS 200/9-12
1440 SE Fleming Ave 97080 503-667-4669
Larry Bentz, prin. Fax 667-3697
West Orient MS 400/6-8
29805 SE Orient Dr 97080 503-663-3323
Teresa Ketelson, prin. Fax 663-2504
Other Schools – See Damascus

Mt. Hood Community College Post-Sec.
26000 SE Stark St 97030 503-491-6422

Halfway, Baker, Pop. 319
Pine Eagle SD 61 200/K-12
375B N Main St 97834 541-742-2811
Mike Corley, supt. Fax 742-2810
www.pineeagle.k12.or.us/
Pine Eagle HS 100/9-12
400 Cornucopia Hwy 97834 541-742-2421
Mike Corley, prin. Fax 742-2422

Halsey, Linn, Pop. 745
Central Linn SD 552
Supt. — See Brownsville
Central Linn HS 300/7-12
32433 Highway 228 97348 541-369-2811
Julie Knoedler, prin. Fax 369-3455

Happy Valley, Clackamas, Pop. 8,282

Northwest College of Hair Design Post-Sec.
8307 SE Monterey Ave, 503-659-2834

Harper, Malheur
Harper SD 66 100/K-12
PO Box 800 97906 541-358-2473
Dennis Savage, supt. Fax 358-2488
www.harper.k12.or.us
Harper S 100/K-12
PO Box 800 97906 541-358-2473
Dennis Savage, prin. Fax 358-2488

Harrisburg, Linn, Pop. 3,265
Harrisburg SD 7J 800/K-12
PO Box 208 97446 541-995-6626
Ron Worrell, supt. Fax 995-3453
www.harrisburg.k12.or.us
Harrisburg HS 300/9-12
PO Box 209 97446 541-995-6626
Larry Cote, prin. Fax 995-6697
Harrisburg MS 200/6-8
PO Box 317 97446 541-995-6551
Jon St. Germaine, prin. Fax 995-5120

Helix, Umatilla, Pop. 183
Helix SD 1 200/K-12
PO Box 398 97835 541-457-2175
Barbara Ceniga, supt. Fax 457-2481
www.helix.k12.or.us/
Helix S 200/K-12
PO Box 398 97835 541-457-2175
Barbara Ceniga, prin. Fax 457-2481

Heppner, Morrow, Pop. 1,438
Morrow SD 1
Supt. — See Lexington
Heppner JSHS 200/7-12
PO Box 67 97836 541-676-9138
Daye Stone, prin. Fax 676-5836

Hermiston, Umatilla, Pop. 14,657
Hermiston SD 8 4,600/K-12
341 NE 3rd St 97838 541-667-6000
Darce Driskel, supt. Fax 667-6050
www.hermiston.k12.or.us
Hermiston HS 1,300/9-12
600 S 1st St 97838 541-667-6100
Sean Gallagher, prin. Fax 667-6150
Larive MS 500/6-8
199 E Ridgeway Ave 97838 541-667-6200
Phil Starkey, prin. Fax 667-6250
Sandstone MS 600/6-8
400 NE 10th St 97838 541-667-6300
Pat Consoliver, prin. Fax 667-6350

Hillsboro, Washington, Pop. 84,533
Hillsboro SD 1J 19,000/K-12
3083 NE 49th Pl 97124 503-844-1500
Jeremy Lyon, supt. Fax 844-1540
www.hsd.k12.or.us
Brown MS 900/7-8
1505 SW Cornelius Pass Rd 97123 503-844-1070
Don Brown, prin. Fax 693-1171
Century HS 1,400/9-12
2000 SE Century Blvd 97123 503-848-6500
Ted Zehr, prin. Fax 848-1825
Evergreen MS 800/7-8
29850 NW Evergreen Rd 97124 503-844-1400
Ruben Degollado, prin. Fax 693-1706
Glencoe HS 1,400/9-12
2700 NW Glencoe Rd 97124 503-844-1900
Carol Loughner, prin. Fax 640-5604
Hillsboro HS 1,400/9-12
3285 SE Rood Bridge Rd 97123 503-844-1980
Sloan Presidio, prin. Fax 693-0645
Liberty HS 1,200/9-12
21945 NW Wagon Way 97124 503-844-1250
Gregg O'Mara, prin. Fax 848-5851
Poynter MS 800/7-8
1535 NE Grant St 97124 503-844-1580
Greg Timmons, prin. Fax 640-8965
Thomas MS 500/7-8
645 NE Lincoln St 97124 503-844-1050
Dave Parker, prin. Fax 640-6347

Airman Proficiency Center Post-Sec.
3565 NE Cornell Rd 97124 503-648-2831
Faith Bible Christian HS 100/9-12
2299 SE 45th Ave 97123 503-681-8254
Jim Cochran, prin. Fax 681-9274
Heritage Christian S 200/K-12
1679 SE Enterprise Cir 97123 503-640-1027
Todd Pfaff, hdmstr. Fax 846-0609
Northwest College of Hair Design Post-Sec.
210 SE 4th Ave 97123 503-844-7320
Tualatin Valley Junior Academy 300/K-10
21975 SW Baseline Rd 97123 503-649-5518
Jesse Cone, prin. Fax 642-7654

Hines, Harney, Pop. 1,493
Harney County SD 3
Supt. — See Burns
Hines MS 200/6-8
PO Box 38 97738 541-573-6436
Katie Baltzor, prin. Fax 573-7255

Hood River, Hood River, Pop. 6,480
Hood River County SD 3,900/K-12
1011 Eugene St 97031 541-386-2511
Dr. Pat Evenson-Brady, supt. Fax 387-5099
www.hoodriver.k12.or.us/
Hood River MS 400/6-8
1602 May St 97031 541-386-2114
Robert Dias, prin. Fax 386-5070
Hood River Valley HS 1,200/9-12
1220 Indian Creek Rd 97031 541-386-4500
Steve Fisk, prin. Fax 386-2400
Wy'East MS 400/6-8
3000 Wyeast Rd 97031 541-354-1548
Catherine Dalbey, prin. Fax 354-5120
Other Schools – See Cascade Locks

Horizon Christian S 200/K-12
700 Pacific Ave 97031 541-387-3200
Christopher Herring, admin. Fax 387-3651
Mid-Columbia Adventist Academy 50/K-10
1100 22nd St 97031 541-386-3187
Fax 386-5702

Huntington, Baker, Pop. 481
Huntington SD 16J 100/K-12
520 3rd St E 97907 541-869-2204
Brian Wolf, supt. Fax 869-2444
www.huntington.k12.or.us/
Huntington S 100/K-12
520 3rd St E 97907 541-869-2204
Brian Wolf, prin. Fax 869-2444

Imbler, Union, Pop. 282
Imbler SD 11 300/K-12
PO Box 164 97841 541-534-5331
Doug Hislop, supt. Fax 534-9560
www.imbler.k12.or.us
Imbler JSHS 200/7-12
PO Box 164 97841 541-534-5331
Mike Mills, prin. Fax 534-9560

Independence, Polk, Pop. 8,193
Central SD 13J 2,600/K-12
1610 Monmouth St 97351 503-838-0030
Joseph Hunter, supt. Fax 838-0033
www.central.k12.or.us
Central HS 800/9-12
1530 Monmouth St 97351 503-838-0480
Sylvia Warren, prin. Fax 838-0483
Talmadge MS 400/7-8
510 S 16th St 97351 503-838-1424
Beau Horn, prin. Fax 606-2436

Irrigon, Morrow, Pop. 1,777
Morrow SD 1
Supt. — See Lexington
Irrigon JSHS 200/7-12
315 E Wyoming Ave 97844 541-922-5551
Tom Crane, prin. Fax 922-5558

Jacksonville, Jackson, Pop. 2,230

Cascade Christian HS 300/9-12
525 E St 97530 541-899-2060
Melvin Ray Johnson, admin. Fax 899-2230

Jefferson, Marion, Pop. 2,607
Jefferson SD 14J 900/K-12
1328 N 2nd St 97352 541-327-3337
Bob Wadlow, supt. Fax 327-2960
www.jefferson.k12.or.us
Jefferson HS 300/9-12
2200 Talbot Rd SE 97352 541-327-3337
Cathy Emmert, prin. Fax 327-1867
Jefferson MS 200/6-8
1334 N 2nd St 97352 541-327-3337
Monica Lawson, prin. Fax 327-2960

John Day, Grant, Pop. 1,605
Grant SD 3
Supt. — See Canyon City
Grant Union HS 300/9-12
911 S Canyon Blvd 97845 541-575-1799
Mark Witty, prin. Fax 575-2754

Jordan Valley, Malheur, Pop. 233
Jordan Valley SD 3 100/K-12
PO Box 99 97910 541-586-2213
Michael Sessions, supt. Fax 586-2568
Jordan Valley HS 100/7-12
PO Box 99 97910 541-586-2213
Michael Sessions, prin. Fax 586-2569

Joseph, Wallowa, Pop. 1,005
Joseph SD 6 300/K-12
PO Box W 97846 541-432-7311
Rhonda Shirley, supt. Fax 432-1100
www.joseph.k12.or.us/
Joseph HS 100/9-12
PO Box W 97846 541-432-7311
Sherri Kilgore, prin. Fax 432-1100
Joseph MS 100/5-8
PO Box W 97846 541-432-7311
Sherri Kilgore, prin. Fax 432-1100

Junction City, Lane, Pop. 5,369
Junction City SD 69 1,800/K-12
325 Maple St 97448 541-998-6311
Kathleen Rodden-Nord, supt. Fax 998-3926
www.junctioncity.k12.or.us
Junction City HS 600/9-12
1135 W 6th Ave 97448 541-998-2343
Kathryn Hedrick, prin. Fax 998-6303
Oaklea MS 500/5-8
1515 Rose St 97448 541-998-3381
Tom Endersby, prin. Fax 998-3383

Keizer, Marion, Pop. 34,644
Salem-Keizer SD 24J
Supt. — See Salem
Claggett Creek MS 1,000/6-8
1810 Alder Dr NE 97303 503-399-3701
Melissa Cole, prin. Fax 399-3708
McNary HS 2,000/9-12
595 Chemawa Rd N 97303 503-399-3233
Ken Parshall, prin. Fax 391-4025
Whiteaker MS 800/6-8
1605 Lockhaven Dr NE 97303 503-399-3224
Larry Goss, prin. Fax 375-7872

Klamath Falls, Klamath, Pop. 19,882
Klamath County SD 5,600/K-12
10501 Washburn Way 97603 541-883-5000
Greg Thede, supt. Fax 883-6677
www.kcsd.k12.or.us
Brixner JHS 500/7-8
4727 Homedale Rd 97603 541-883-5025
Larry Headden, prin. Fax 883-5019
Henley HS 700/9-12
8245 Highway 39 97603 541-883-5040
Mark Greif, prin. Fax 883-6663
Henley MS 500/7-8
7925 Highway 39 97603 541-883-5050
Polly Beam, prin. Fax 883-5012
Other Schools – See Bonanza, Chiloquin, Gilchrist, Merrill

Klamath Falls CSD 4,000/K-12
1336 Avalon St 97603 541-883-4700
Cecilia Amuchastegui, supt. Fax 850-2766
www.kfalls.k12.or.us
Klamath Union HS 1,000/9-12
1300 Monclaire St 97601 541-883-4710
Jeff Bullock, prin. Fax 885-4276
Mazama HS 1,000/9-12
3009 Summers Ln 97603 541-883-4730
Terry Bennett, prin. Fax 885-6760
Ponderosa JHS 500/7-8
2554 Main St 97601 541-883-4740
Bob Vian, prin. Fax 885-4286
Klamath Adult Learning Ctr. Adult
2856 Eberlein Ave 97603 541-883-4719
Fax 885-4281

College of Cosmetology Post-Sec.
357 E Main St 97601 541-882-6644
Hosanna Christian S 300/PK-12
5000 Hosanna Way 97603 541-882-7732
Dan Dickey, admin. Fax 882-6940
Klamath Community College Post-Sec.
7390 S 6th St 97603 541-882-3521
Oregon Institute of Technology Post-Sec.
3201 Campus Dr 97601 541-885-1000
Triad S 200/PK-12
4849 S 6th St 97603 541-885-7940
David Wehr, hdmstr. Fax 884-8725

La Grande, Union, Pop. 12,440
La Grande SD 1 1,900/K-12
708 K Ave Ste 100 97850 541-663-3202
Jay Rowell, supt. Fax 663-3211
www.lagrande.k12.or.us
La Grande HS 700/9-12
708 K Ave 97850 541-663-3301
Doug Potter, prin. Fax 663-3313
La Grande MS 400/6-8
1108 4th St 97850 541-663-3421
Jim Boen, prin. Fax 663-3422

Eastern Oregon University Post-Sec.
1 University Blvd 97850 541-962-3393

Lake Oswego, Clackamas, Pop. 36,502
Lake Oswego SD 7J 6,900/K-12
PO Box 70 97034 503-534-2000
William Korach, supt. Fax 534-2030
www.loswego.k12.or.us
Lake Oswego HS 1,300/9-12
PO Box 310 97034 503-534-2313
Bruce Plato, prin. Fax 534-2327
Lake Oswego JHS 600/7-8
2500 Country Club Rd 97034 503-534-2335
Ann Gerson, prin. Fax 534-2341
Lakeridge HS 1,100/9-12
PO Box 739 97034 503-534-2319
Mike Lehman, prin. Fax 534-2392
Waluga JHS 600/7-8
4700 Jean Rd 97035 503-534-2343
Steve Sherrell, prin. Fax 534-2276

Westside Christian HS 300/9-12
4565 Carman Dr 97035 503-697-4711

Lakeview, Lake, Pop. 2,378
Adel SD 21 50/4-8
357 N L St 97630 541-947-5418
Fax 947-3373
Other Schools – See Adel

Lakeview SD 7 800/K-12
1341 S 1st St 97630 541-947-3347
Judy Graham, supt. Fax 947-3386
www.lkv.k12.or.us/
Daly MS 100/7-8
220 S H St 97630 541-947-2257
Lane Stratton, prin. Fax 947-3506
Lakeview HS 300/9-12
906 S 3rd St 97630 541-947-2287
Robert Nash, prin. Fax 947-3601

La Pine, Deschutes
Bend-LaPine Administrative SD 1
Supt. — See Bend
La Pine HS 500/9-12
PO Box 306 97739 541-322-5360
Jay Mathisen, prin. Fax 322-5352
La Pine MS 500/5-8
PO Box 305 97739 541-536-5967
Patricia Yaeger, prin. Fax 536-5787

Lebanon, Linn, Pop. 13,834
Lebanon Community SD 9 4,200/K-12
485 S 5th St 97355 541-451-8511
James Robinson, supt. Fax 451-8519
www.lebanon.k12.or.us
Lebanon HS 1,300/9-12
1700 S 5th St 97355 541-451-8555
Ken Ray, prin. Fax 451-8550
Seven Oak MS 600/6-8
550 Cascade Dr 97355 541-451-8416
Ed Sansom, prin. Fax 451-8431

East Linn Christian Academy 100/7-12
31498 SW 5th St 97355 541-259-2324
Jim Hill, prin. Fax 451-3800

Lexington, Morrow, Pop. 273
Morrow SD 1 2,100/K-12
PO Box 368 97839 541-989-8202
Mark Burrows, supt. Fax 989-8470
www.morrow.k12.or.us
Other Schools – See Boardman, Heppner, Irrigon

Lincoln City, Lincoln, Pop. 7,849
Lincoln County SD
Supt. — See Newport
Taft HS 600/7-12
3780 SE Spy Glass Ridge Dr 97367 541-996-2115
Steve Kilduff, prin. Fax 996-4335

Lincoln City SDA Junior Academy 100/1-12
2126 NE Surf Ave 97367 541-994-5181
Fax 994-9034

Long Creek, Grant, Pop. 202
Long Creek SD 17 100/PK-12
PO Box 429 97856 541-421-3896
Tim Sprenger, supt. Fax 421-3012
Long Creek S 100/PK-12
PO Box 429 97856 541-421-3896
Tim Sprenger, prin. Fax 421-3012

Lowell, Lane, Pop. 923
Lowell SD 71 200/K-12
65 S Pioneer 97452 541-937-8405
Aaron Brown, supt. Fax 937-2112
www.lowell.k12.or.us
Lowell JSHS 100/8-12
65 S Pioneer 97452 541-937-2124
Aaron Brown, prin. Fax 937-2112

Mc Minnville, Yamhill, Pop. 23,136
McMinnville SD 40 5,800/K-12
1500 NE Baker St, 503-565-4000
Maryalice Russell, supt. Fax 565-4030
www.msd.k12.or.us
Duniway MS 600/6-8
575 NW Michelbook Ln, 503-565-4400
Cathy Carnahan, prin. Fax 565-4414
McMinnville HS 1,800/9-12
615 NE 15th St, 503-565-4200
Kris Olsen, prin. Fax 565-4244
Patton MS 700/6-8
1175 NE 19th St, 503-565-4500
Jim Torgerson, prin. Fax 565-4515

Linfield College Post-Sec.
900 SE Baker St, 503-434-2200
Mc Minnville Christian HS 50/9-12
PO Box 622, 503-472-0086
Leon Mayer, contact

Madras, Jefferson, Pop. 5,300
Jefferson County SD 509J 3,000/K-12
445 SE Buff St 97741 541-475-6192
Guy Fisher, supt. Fax 475-6856
www.whitebuffalos.net/
Jefferson County MS 700/6-8
1180 SE City View St 97741 541-475-7253
Ken Clark, prin. Fax 475-4825
Madras HS 900/9-12
390 SE 10th St 97741 541-475-7265
Gary Carlton, prin. Fax 475-7744

Mapleton, Lane
Mapleton SD 32 200/K-12
10868 E Mapleton Rd 97453 541-268-4312
Kyle Tucker, supt. Fax 268-4632
www.mapleton.k12.or.us
Mapleton MSHS 100/7-12
10868 E Mapleton Rd 97453 541-268-4322
Kyle Tucker, prin. Fax 268-4632

Marcola, Lane
Marcola SD 79J 300/K-12
38300 Wendling Rd 97454 541-933-2817
W. Rolla Weber, supt. Fax 933-2338
www.marcola.k12.or.us
Mohawk HS 100/9-12
38300 Wendling Rd 97454 541-933-2512
W. Rolla Weber, prin. Fax 933-2338

Marylhurst, Clackamas

Marylhurst University Post-Sec.
PO Box 261 97036 800-634-9982

Maupin, Wasco, Pop. 406
South Wasco County SD 1 200/K-12
PO Box 346 97037 541-395-2645
Dennis Hickey, supt. Fax 395-2679
www.swasco.net
South Wasco County HS 100/7-12
PO Box 347 97037 541-395-2225
Dennis Hickey, prin. Fax 395-2223

Medford, Jackson, Pop. 70,147
Medford SD 549C 12,400/K-12
500 Monroe St 97501 541-842-3636
Dr. Philip Long, supt. Fax 842-1087
www.medford.k12.or.us
Hedrick MS 1,000/7-8
1501 E Jackson St 97504 541-842-3700
Paul Cataldo, prin. Fax 842-1548
McLoughlin MS 1,000/7-8
320 W 2nd St 97501 541-842-3720
Amy Tiger, prin. Fax 842-1652
North Medford HS 2,000/9-12
1900 N Keene Way Dr 97504 541-842-3670
Patrick Royal, prin. Fax 842-5206
South Medford HS 1,900/9-12
815 S Oakdale Ave 97501 541-842-3680
Kevin Campbell, prin. Fax 842-1513

Abdill Career College Post-Sec.
843 E Main St Ste 203 97504 541-779-8384
Harvest Baptist Christian S 100/PK-10
2001 S Columbus Ave 97501 541-773-6974
Bill Whittington, admin. Fax 773-4331
Phagans' Medford Beauty School Post-Sec.
2320 Poplar Dr 97504 541-772-6155
Rogue Valley Adventist Academy 200/K-12
3675 S Stage Rd 97501 541-773-2988
Fax 779-7575
St. Mary's HS 6-12
816 Black Oak Dr 97504 541-773-7877
Frank Phillips, prin. Fax 772-8973

Merrill, Klamath, Pop. 897
Klamath County SD
Supt. — See Klamath Falls
Lost River JSHS 300/7-12
23330 Highway 50 97633 541-798-5666
William Starkweather, prin. Fax 798-5072

Mill City, Linn, Pop. 1,593
Santiam Canyon SD 129J 700/K-12
PO Box 197 97360 503-897-2321
Brad Yates, supt. Fax 897-4004
www.santiam.k12.or.us
Mill City MS 200/5-8
PO Box 198 97360 503-897-2368
James Beck, prin. Fax 897-4034

Santiam HS 200/9-12
PO Box 199 97360 503-897-2311
David Plotts, prin. Fax 897-3154

Milton Freewater, Umatilla, Pop. 5,886
Milton-Freewater USD 7 1,900/K-12
138 S Main St 97862 541-938-3551
Marilyn McBride, supt. Fax 938-6704
www.miltfree.k12.or.us
Central MS 400/6-8
306 SW 2nd Ave 97862 541-938-5504
Steve Carnes, prin. Fax 938-6615
McLoughlin HS 500/9-12
120 S Main St 97862 541-938-5591
Ralph Brown, prin. Fax 938-5593

Milwaukie, Clackamas, Pop. 20,810
North Clackamas SD 12 15,900/K-12
4444 SE Lake Rd 97222 503-353-6000
Ron Naso, supt. Fax 353-6007
www.nclack.k12.or.us
Alder Creek MS 800/7-8
13801 SE Webster Rd 97267 503-353-5700
Christine Garcia, prin. Fax 353-5715
Milwaukie HS 1,400/9-12
11300 SE 23rd Ave 97222 503-353-5830
Kelly Carlisle, prin. Fax 353-5845
Putnam HS 1,400/9-12
4950 SE Roethe Rd 97267 503-353-5872
Cindy Quintanilla, prin. Fax 353-5875
Rowe MS 800/7-8
3606 SE Lake Rd 97222 503-353-5725
Larry Becker, prin. Fax 353-5740
Other Schools – See Clackamas, Portland

LaSalle HS 9-12
11999 SE Fuller Rd 97222 503-659-4155
Tom Dudley, prin. Fax 659-2535
Phagans' School of Hair Design Post-Sec.
16550 SE McLoughlin Blvd 97267 503-652-2668
Portland Waldorf S 100/PK-12
2300 SE Harrison St 97222 503-654-2200
Fax 652-5162

Mitchell, Wheeler, Pop. 158
Mitchell SD 55 100/K-12
PO Box 247 97750 541-462-3311
Susan Horton, supt. Fax 462-3849
www.mitchell.k12.or.us
Mitchell S 100/K-12
PO Box 247 97750 541-462-3311
Michael Carroll, prin. Fax 462-3849

Molalla, Clackamas, Pop. 6,737
Molalla River SD 35 2,900/K-12
PO Box 188 97038 503-829-2359
Wayne Kostur, supt. Fax 829-5540
www.molallariv.k12.or.us
Molalla HS 900/9-12
PO Box 309 97038 503-829-2355
Kevin Ricker, prin. Fax 829-6382
Molalla River MS 700/6-8
PO Box 225 97038 503-829-6133
Robert Espenel, prin. Fax 829-5680

Monmouth, Polk, Pop. 8,987

Mid Valley Christian Academy 100/PK-12
1483 N 16th St 97361 503-838-2818
Candice Thomas, admin.
Western Oregon University Post-Sec.
345 Monmouth Ave N 97361 877-877-1593

Monroe, Benton, Pop. 581
Monroe SD 1J 400/K-12
365 N 5th St 97456 541-847-6292
Randall Crowson, supt. Fax 847-6290
www.monroe.k12.or.us/sd1j.htm
Monroe HS 100/9-12
365 N 5th St 97456 541-847-5161
Bill Crowson, prin. Fax 847-6161

Monument, Grant, Pop. 134
Monument SD 8 50/K-12
PO Box 127 97864 541-934-2646
Scott Langkamp, supt. Fax 934-2005
Monument S 50/K-12
PO Box 127 97864 541-934-2646
Scott Langkamp, prin. Fax 934-2005

Moro, Wasco, Pop. 301
Sherman County SD
Supt. — See Wasco
Sherman JSHS 200/7-12
65912 High School Loop 97039 541-565-3500
Wes Owens, prin. Fax 565-3319

Mount Angel, Marion, Pop. 3,355
Mt. Angel SD 91 800/K-12
PO Box 1129 97362 503-845-2345
Robert Young, supt. Fax 845-2789
masd.mtangel.k12.or.us
Kennedy HS 200/9-12
890 E Marquam St 97362 503-845-6128
Bryan Starr, prin. Fax 845-2789
Mount Angel MS 200/6-8
460 E Marquam St 97362 503-845-6137
Dave Carlson, prin. Fax 845-2856

Mount Vernon, Grant, Pop. 531
Grant SD 3
Supt. — See Canyon City
Mount Vernon MS 200/6-8
PO Box 648 97865 541-932-4733
Monty Nash, prin. Fax 932-4980

Myrtle Creek, Douglas, Pop. 3,528
South Umpqua SD 19 1,800/K-12
558 Chadwick Ln 97457 541-863-3115
Beverly Parsons, supt. Fax 863-5212
www.susd.k12.or.us
Coffenberry MS 400/6-8
591 Rice St 97457 541-863-3104
Doug Park, prin. Fax 863-5187

South Umpqua HS 600/9-12
501 Chadwick Ln 97457 541-863-3118
Brody Guthrie, prin. Fax 863-5486

Myrtle Point, Coos, Pop. 2,509
Myrtle Point SD 41 700/K-12
212 Spruce St 97458 541-572-2811
Robert Smith, supt. Fax 572-5401
www.mpsd.k12.or.us/
Myrtle Point JSHS 400/7-12
717 4th St 97458 541-572-2811
Greg Tippett, prin. Fax 572-5221

Newberg, Yamhill, Pop. 20,681
Newberg SD 29J 4,900/K-12
714 E 6th St 97132 503-554-5000
Dr. Paula Radich, supt. Fax 537-9474
www.newberg.k12.or.us
Chehalem Valley MS 700/6-8
403 W Foothills Dr 97132 503-554-4600
Kevin Engelen, prin. Fax 537-3239
Mountain View MS 500/6-8
2015 N Emery Dr 97132 503-554-4500
Wayne Strong, prin. Fax 537-3337
Newberg HS 1,600/9-12
2400 Douglas Ave 97132 503-554-4400
Bill Smethurst, prin. Fax 538-6560

George Fox University Post-Sec.
414 N Meridian St 97132 503-538-8383
Lewis Academy 200/PK-12
PO Box 3250 97132 503-538-0114
Wade Witherspoon, supt. Fax 538-4113
Open Bible Christian S 100/K-12
1605 N College St 97132 503-538-9833
Frank Canepa, prin. Fax 538-4649

Newport, Lincoln, Pop. 9,833
Lincoln County SD 4,300/K-12
PO Box 1110 97365 541-265-9211
Tom Rinearson, supt. Fax 265-3231
www.lincoln.k12.or.us
Newport HS 700/9-12
322 NE Eads St 97365 541-265-9281
Suzanne Dalton, prin. Fax 574-2228
Newport MS 400/6-8
825 NE 7th St 97365 541-265-6601
Marsha Eckelman, prin. Fax 265-6493
Newton Magnet S 100/6-8
825 NE 7th St 97365 541-574-2238
Marsha Eckelman, prin.
Other Schools – See Lincoln City, Toledo, Waldport

Phagans' Newport Academy of Cosmetology Post-Sec.
158 E Olive St 97365 541-265-3083

North Bend, Coos, Pop. 9,843
North Bend SD 13 1,900/K-12
1913 Meade St 97459 541-756-2521
B.J. Hollensteiner, supt. Fax 756-1313
www.nbend.k12.or.us
North Bend HS 700/9-12
2323 Pacific St 97459 541-756-8328
Bill Lucero, prin. Fax 756-6945
North Bend MS 500/5-8
1500 16th St 97459 541-756-8341
Scott Edmondson, prin. Fax 756-6460

Kingsview Christian S 100/PK-12
1850 Clark St 97459 541-756-1411
Rick Wetherell, supt. Fax 756-0105

North Powder, Union, Pop. 485
North Powder SD 8J 200/K-12
PO Box 10 97867 541-898-2244
Lance Dixon, supt. Fax 898-2046
www.npowder.k12.or.us
Powder Valley S 200/K-12
PO Box 10 97867 541-898-2244
Lance Dixon, prin. Fax 898-2046

Nyssa, Malheur, Pop. 3,068
Nyssa SD 26 1,100/K-12
804 Adrian Blvd 97913 541-372-2275
Donald Grotting, supt. Fax 372-2204
www.nyssa.k12.or.us
Nyssa HS 300/9-12
824 Adrian Blvd 97913 541-372-2287
Ken Ball, prin. Fax 372-5634
Nyssa MS 300/6-8
101 S 11th St 97913 541-372-3891
Jana Iverson, prin. Fax 372-3260

Oakland, Douglas, Pop. 973
Oakland SD 1 600/K-12
PO Box 390 97462 541-459-4341
Dan Forbess, supt. Fax 459-4120
www.oakland.k12.or.us
Lincoln MS 200/5-8
PO Box 420 97462 541-459-3407
Larry Watts, prin. Fax 459-9167
Oakland HS 200/9-12
PO Box 479 97462 541-459-2597
Greg Knee, prin. Fax 459-4765

Oakridge, Lane, Pop. 3,147
Oakridge SD 76 600/K-12
76499 Rose St 97463 541-782-2813
Donald Kordosky, supt. Fax 782-2982
www.oakridge.k12.or.us/
Oakridge HS 200/9-12
47997 W 1st St 97463 541-782-2231
Donald Kordosky, prin. Fax 782-4692
Other Schools – See Westfir

Ontario, Malheur, Pop. 11,125
Ontario SD 8C 2,700/K-12
195 SW 3rd Ave 97914 541-889-5374
Dr. Dennis Carter, supt. Fax 889-8553
www.ontario.k12.or.us
Ontario HS 800/9-12
1115 W Idaho Ave 97914 541-889-5309
Bret Uptmor, prin. Fax 889-8117

Ontario MS 700/6-8
573 SW 2nd Ave 97914 541-889-5377
LaVelle Cornwell, prin. Fax 881-0060

Treasure Valley Community College Post-Sec.
650 College Blvd 97914 541-881-8822

Oregon City, Clackamas, Pop. 30,221
Oregon City SD 62 8,000/K-12
PO Box 2110 97045 503-785-8000
Roger Rada, supt. Fax 657-2492
www.orecity.k12.or.us
Gardiner MS 600/7-8
180 Ethel St 97045 503-785-8200
Chris Mills, prin. Fax 650-5482
Ogden MS 700/7-8
14133 Donovan Rd 97045 503-785-8300
John Olson, prin. Fax 657-2508
Oregon City HS 2,300/9-12
19761 Beavercreek Rd 97045 503-785-8900
Nancy Bush-Lange, prin. Fax 785-8578

Clackamas Community College Post-Sec.
19600 Molalla Ave 97045 503-657-6958
North Clackamas Christian S 300/PK-12
19575 Sebastian Way 97045 503-655-5961
Joseph Morgan, admin. Fax 655-4875

Paisley, Lake, Pop. 242
Paisley SD 11 100/K-12
PO Box 97 97636 541-943-3111
Mark Jeffrey, supt. Fax 943-3129
Paisley S 100/K-12
PO Box 97 97636 541-943-3111
Mark Jeffery, prin. Fax 943-3129

Pendleton, Umatilla, Pop. 16,636
Pendleton SD 16 3,300/K-12
1207 SW Frazer Ave 97801 541-276-6711
Jim Keene, supt. Fax 278-3208
www.pendleton.k12.or.us
Pendleton HS 1,000/9-12
1800 NW Carden Ave 97801 541-276-3621
Tom Lovell, prin. Fax 966-9268
Sunridge MS 800/6-8
700 SW Runnion Ave 97801 541-276-4560
Susan DeMarsh, prin. Fax 276-4724

Blue Mountain Community College Post-Sec.
PO Box 100 97801 541-276-1260
Harris Junior Academy 50/K-10
3121 SW Hailey Ave 97801 541-276-0615
Fax 276-3465

Philomath, Benton, Pop. 4,213
Philomath SD 17J 1,700/K-12
1620 Applegate St 97370 541-929-3169
Pete Tuana, supt. Fax 929-3991
www.philomath.k12.or.us
Philomath HS 600/9-12
2054 Applegate St 97370 541-929-3211
Kent Sherwood, prin. Fax 929-3244
Philomath MS 500/6-8
2021 Chapel Dr 97370 541-929-3167
Larry Sleeman, prin. Fax 929-3180

Phoenix, Jackson, Pop. 4,375
Phoenix-Talent SD 4 2,800/K-12
PO Box 698 97535 541-535-1517
Ben Bergreen, supt. Fax 535-3928
www.phoenix.k12.or.us
Phoenix HS 800/9-12
PO Box 697 97535 541-535-1526
Jani Hale, prin. Fax 535-7511
Other Schools – See Talent

Pilot Rock, Umatilla, Pop. 1,525
Pilot Rock SD 2 400/K-12
PO Box BB 97868 541-443-8291
Gordon Munck, supt. Fax 443-8000
www.pilotrock.k12.or.us
Pilot Rock JSHS 200/7-12
PO Box BB 97868 541-443-2671
Ed Sherman, prin. Fax 443-2120

Pleasant Hill, Lane
Pleasant Hill SD 1 800/K-12
36386 Highway 58 97455 541-746-9646
Steve Waddell, supt. Fax 746-2537
www.pleasanthill.k12.or.us/
Pleasant Hill HS 400/9-12
36386 Highway 58 97455 541-747-4541
Tony Scurto, prin. Fax 744-3351
Pleasant Hill MS 200/5-8
36386 Highway 58 97455 541-736-0400
Mary Ritter, prin. Fax 736-0446

Emerald Christian Academy 100/K-10
35582 Zephyr Way 97455 541-746-1708
Fax 746-8353

Portland, Multnomah, Pop. 533,427
Beaverton SD 48J
Supt. — See Beaverton
Cedar Park MS 1,000/6-8
11100 SW Park Way 97225 503-672-3620
Linda Hall, prin. Fax 672-3626
Stoller MS 1,100/6-8
14141 NW Laidlaw Rd 97229 503-533-1910
Florence Richey, prin. Fax 533-1914
Sunset HS 2,000/9-12
13840 NW Cornell Rd 97229 503-259-5050
Todd McKee, prin. Fax 259-5066
Westview HS 2,400/9-12
4200 NW 185th Ave 97229 503-259-5218
Matt Coleman, prin. Fax 259-5230

Centennial SD 28J 6,400/K-12
18135 SE Brooklyn St 97236 503-760-7990
Robert McKean, supt. Fax 762-3689
www.centennial.k12.or.us
Centennial MS 1,000/7-8
17650 SE Brooklyn St 97236 503-762-3206
Doug Cook, prin. Fax 762-3236
Other Schools – See Gresham

David Douglas SD 40 8,500/K-12
1500 SE 130th Ave 97233 503-252-2900
Barbara Rommel, supt. Fax 261-8208
www.ddouglas.k12.or.us
Douglas HS 2,600/9-12
1001 SE 135th Ave 97233 503-261-8300
Randy Hutchinson, prin. Fax 261-8399
Light MS 800/6-8
10800 SE Washington St 97216 503-256-6511
Mark Gaulke, prin. Fax 261-8423
Ott MS 700/6-8
12500 SE Ramona St 97236 503-256-6510
Natalie Osburn, prin. Fax 261-8403
Russell MS 6-8
3955 SE 112th Ave 97266 503-256-6519
Charlene Bassine, prin. Fax 761-7246

North Clackamas SD 12
Supt. — See Milwaukie
Sabin-Schellenberg Professional-Tech Ctr Vo/Tech
14450 SE Johnson Rd 97267 503-353-5900
Cinda Morrison, prin. Fax 353-5915

Parkrose SD 3 3,500/K-12
10636 NE Prescott St 97220 503-408-2100
Dr. Karen Fischer Giray, supt. Fax 408-2140
www.parkrose.k12.or.us
Parkrose HS 1,100/9-12
12003 NE Shaver St 97220 503-408-2600
Roy Reynolds, prin. Fax 408-2739
Parkrose MS 900/6-8
11800 NE Shaver St 97220 503-408-2700
Ana Gonzalez, prin. Fax 408-2998

Portland SD 1J 41,200/PK-12
PO Box 3107 97208 503-916-3200
Vicki Phillips, supt. Fax 916-3110
www.pps.k12.or.us/
Beaumont MS 500/6-8
4043 NE Fremont St 97212 503-916-5610
Sherie Knutsen, prin. Fax 916-2609
Benson Polytechnic HS Vo/Tech
546 NE 12th Ave 97232 503-916-5100
Christie Plinski, prin. Fax 916-2690
Binnsmead MS 700/6-8
2225 SE 87th Ave 97216 503-916-5700
John Hinds, prin. Fax 916-2610
Cleveland HS 1,300/9-12
3400 SE 26th Ave 97202 503-916-5120
Paul Cook, prin. Fax 916-2692
East Sylvan MS 6-8
1849 SW 58th Ave 97221 503-916-5560
Allison Couch, prin. Fax 916-5565
Fernwood MS 600/6-8
1915 NE 33rd Ave 97212 503-916-6480
Linda Kapranos, prin. Fax 916-2626
Franklin HS 1,500/9-12
5405 SE Woodward St 97206 503-916-5140
Charles Hopson, prin. Fax 916-2694
George MS 500/6-8
10000 N Burr Ave 97203 503-916-6262
Beth Madison, prin. Fax 916-2627
Grant HS 1,800/9-12
2245 NE 36th Ave 97212 503-916-5160
Toni Hunter, prin. Fax 916-2695
Gray MS 500/6-8
5505 SW 23rd Ave, 503-916-5676
Larry Dashiell, prin. Fax 916-2629
Gregory Heights MS 600/6-8
7334 NE Siskiyou St 97213 503-916-5600
Bonnie Hobson, prin. Fax 916-2631
Hosford International MS 400/6-8
2303 SE 28th Pl 97214 503-916-5640
Melissa Sandven, prin. Fax 916-2637
Jackson MS 800/6-8
10625 SW 35th Ave 97219 503-916-5680
John Danielson, prin. Fax 916-2640
Jefferson-Academy of Arts & Technology 9-12
5210 N Kerby Ave 97217 503-916-5180
Juanita Valder, admin. Fax 916-2698
Jefferson - Academy of Science & Tech 9-12
5210 N Kerby Ave 97217 503-916-5180
Leon Dudley, prin. Fax 916-2698
Kellogg MS 400/7-8
3330 SE 69th Ave 97206 503-916-5707
Margaret Lewis, prin. Fax 916-2643
Lane MS 600/6-8
7200 SE 60th Ave 97206 503-916-6355
Karl Logan, prin. Fax 916-2648
Lincoln HS 1,400/9-12
1600 SW Salmon St 97205 503-916-5200
Peyton Chapman, prin. Fax 916-2700
Madison HS 1,100/9-12
2735 NE 82nd Ave 97220 503-916-5220
Patricia Thompson, prin. Fax 916-2702
Marshall - Biz-Tech HS 200/9-12
3905 SE 91st Ave 97266 503-916-5241
Travis Fantz, admin. Fax 916-2703
Marshall - Pauling Academy 200/9-12
3905 SE 91st Ave 97266 503-916-5243
Stevie Newcomer, admin. Fax 916-2703
Marshall - Renaissance Arts Academy 200/9-12
3905 SE 91st Ave 97266 503-916-5244
Fred Locke, admin. Fax 916-2703
Mt. Tabor MS 700/6-8
5800 SE Ash St 97215 503-916-5646
Van Troung, prin. Fax 916-2659
Portsmouth MS 300/7-8
5103 N Willis Blvd 97203 503-916-5666
Paul Steger, prin. Fax 916-2663
Roosevelt - ACT 9-12
6941 N Central St 97203 503-916-5260
Tim Taylor, prin. Fax 916-2704
Roosevelt - POWER 9-12
6941 N Central St 97203 503-916-5260
Brandy Byers, admin. Fax 916-2704
Roosevelt - SEIS HS 9-12
6941 N Central St 97203 503-916-5260
Lorna Fast Buffalo Horse, admin. Fax 916-2704
Sellwood MS 600/6-8
8300 SE 15th Ave 97202 503-916-5656
Helen Nolen, prin. Fax 916-2672
Tubman MS 200/7-8
2231 N Flint Ave 97227 503-916-5630
Aurora Lora, prin. Fax 916-2677
West Sylvan MS 900/6-8
8111 SW West Slope Dr 97225 503-916-5690
Allison Couch, prin. Fax 916-2681
Wilson HS 1,500/9-12
1151 SW Vermont St 97219 503-916-5280
Susan Brent, prin. Fax 916-2705
Portland Evening HS Adult
546 NE 12th Ave 97232 503-916-5720
Macaree Traynham, admin. Fax 916-2691
Portland Night S Adult
2245 NE 36th Ave 97212 503-916-6486
Charlene Turenne, prin. Fax 916-2696

Reynolds SD 7
Supt. — See Fairview
Lee MS 800/6-8
1121 NE 172nd Ave 97230 503-255-5686
Carla Sosanya, prin. Fax 252-0522

Riverdale SD 51J 500/K-12
11733 SW Breyman Ave 97219 503-636-8611
Dr. Thomas Hagerman, supt. Fax 635-6342
www.riverdale.k12.or.us
Riverdale HS 200/9-12
9727 SW Terwilliger Blvd 97219 503-892-0722
Sue Higgens, prin. Fax 892-0723

Apollo College Post-Sec.
2004 Lloyd Ctr Fl 3 97232 503-761-6100
Art Institute of Portland Post-Sec.
1122 NW Davis St 97209 503-228-6528
Australasian College of Health Sciences Post-Sec.
5940 SW Hood Ave, 503-244-0726
Beau Monde College Acad of Cosmetology Post-Sec.
11131 NE Halsey St 97220 503-252-7444
Beau Monde College of Hair Design Post-Sec.
1221 SW 12th Ave 97205 503-226-7355
Birthingway College of Midwifery Post-Sec.
12113 SE Foster Rd 97266 503-760-3131
Cascade College Post-Sec.
9101 E Burnside St 97216 800-550-7678
Catlin Gabel S 700/PK-12
8825 SW Barnes Rd 97225 503-297-1894
Dr. Lark Palma, prin. Fax 297-0139
Central Catholic HS 800/9-12
2401 SE Stark St 97214 503-235-3138
Ronald Edwards, prin. Fax 233-0073
City Christian S 300/PK-12
9200 NE Fremont St 97220 503-252-5207
Ed Mason, prin. Fax 257-2221
College of Legal Arts Post-Sec.
8909 SW Barbur Blvd 97219 503-223-5100
Columbia Christian S 300/PK-12
413 NE 91st Ave 97220 503-252-8577
Morgan Outlaw, prin. Fax 252-2108
Concorde Career Institute Post-Sec.
1827 NE 44th Ave 97213 503-281-4181
Concordia University Post-Sec.
2811 NE Holman St 97211 503-288-9371
De La Salle North HS 200/9-12
7654 N Delaware Ave 97217 503-285-9385
John Huelskamp, prin. Fax 285-9546
DeVry University Post-Sec.
9755 SW Barnes Rd Ste 150 97225 503-296-7468
Edison HS 100/9-12
9020 SW Bvrtn Hillsdale Hwy 97225 503-297-2336
Patrick Maguire, dir. Fax 297-2527
George Fox University Post-Sec.
12753 SW 68th Ave 97223 503-639-0559
Heald College Post-Sec.
625 SW Broadway Ste 400 97205 503-229-0492
ITT Technical Institute Post-Sec.
6035 NE 78th Ct 97218 503-255-6500
Jesuit HS 1,100/9-12
9000 SW Beaverton Hillsdale 97225 503-292-2663
Sandy Satterberg, prin. Fax 291-5464
Lewis & Clark College Post-Sec.
0615 SW Palatine Hill Rd 97219 503-768-7000
Linfield College Post-Sec.
2215 NW Northrup St 97210 503-229-7161
Multnomah Bible Coll. & Biblical Sem. Post-Sec.
8435 NE Glisan St 97220 503-255-0332
National Coll. of Naturopathic Medicine Post-Sec.
049 SW Porter St 97201 503-499-4343
Open Meadow Alternative S 100/9-12
7654 N Crawford St 97203 503-285-0508
Rosemary Donnelly, prin. Fax 285-0798
Oregon College of Art & Craft Post-Sec.
8245 SW Barnes Rd 97225 503-297-5544
Oregon College of Oriental Medicine Post-Sec.
10525 SE Cherry Blossom Dr 97216 503-253-3443
Oregon Episcopal S 800/PK-12
6300 SW Nicol Rd 97223 503-246-7771
Matthew Hanly, hdmstr. Fax 293-1105
Oregon Health & Science University Post-Sec.
3181 SW Sam Jackson Park Rd, 503-494-7800
Pacific Northwest College of Art Post-Sec.
1241 NW Johnson St 97209 503-821-8972
Phagans' School of Hair Design Post-Sec.
1542 NE Weidler St 97232 503-239-0838
Portland Adventist Academy 300/9-12
1500 SE 96th Ave 97216 503-255-8372
Gale Crosby, prin. Fax 255-5132
Portland Christian JSHS 400/7-12
12425 NE San Rafael St 97230 503-256-3960
Kevin Barrows, prin. Fax 256-2773
Portland Community College Post-Sec.
PO Box 19000 97280 503-244-6111
Portland Lutheran S 300/PK-12
740 SE 182nd Ave 97233 503-667-3199
Donn Maier, prin. Fax 667-4520
Portland State University Post-Sec.
PO Box 751 97207 503-725-3000
Reed College Post-Sec.
3202 SE Woodstock Blvd 97202 503-771-1112
St. Andrew Nativity S 100/6-8
806 NE Alberta St 97211 503-335-9600
Fr. Jeff McDougall, prin. Fax 335-9494
St. Mary Academy 600/9-12
1615 SW 5th Ave 97201 503-228-8306
Pat Barr, prin. Fax 223-0995
St. Vincent Hospital & Medical Center Post-Sec.
9205 SW Barnes Rd 97225 503-216-3031
Serendipity Center 100/K-12
PO Box 33350 97292 503-761-7139
Patrick Sliger, prin. Fax 761-7917
University of Portland Post-Sec.
5000 N Willamette Blvd 97203 503-943-7911
Veterans Administration Medical Center Post-Sec.
PO Box 1034 97207 503-220-8262
Walla Walla University School of Nursing Post-Sec.
10345 SE Market St 97216 503-251-6115
Warner Pacific College Post-Sec.
2219 SE 68th Ave 97215 503-517-1000
Western Business College Post-Sec.
425 SW Washington St 97204 503-222-3225
Western Culinary Institute Post-Sec.
921 SW Morrison St Ste 400 97205 503-223-2245
Western Seminary Post-Sec.
5511 SE Hawthorne Blvd 97215 503-517-1800
Western States Chiropractic College Post-Sec.
2900 NE 132nd Ave 97230 503-256-3180

Port Orford, Curry, Pop. 1,180
Port Orford-Langlois SD 2CJ 400/K-12
PO Box 8 97465 541-348-2337
Ruby Price, supt. Fax 348-2228
www.2cj.com
Pacific HS 100/9-12
PO Box 8 97465 541-348-2293
Ruby Price, prin. Fax 348-2389

Powers, Coos, Pop. 754
Powers SD 31 100/K-12
PO Box 479 97466 541-439-2291
Matt Shorb, supt. Fax 439-2875
www.powers.k12.or.us
Powers HS 100/7-12
PO Box 479 97466 541-439-2291
Jody Cyr, prin. Fax 439-2875

Prairie City, Grant, Pop. 965
Prairie City SD 4 200/K-12
PO Box 345 97869 541-820-3314
Kevin Purnell, supt. Fax 820-4352
www.grantesd.k12.or.us
Prairie City S 200/K-12
PO Box 345 97869 541-820-3314
Kevin Purnell, prin. Fax 820-4352

Prineville, Crook, Pop. 8,908
Crook County SD 3,200/K-12
471 NE Ochoco Plaza Dr 97754 541-447-5664
Steve Swisher, supt. Fax 447-3645
www.crookcounty.k12.or.us
Crook County HS 1,000/9-12
1100 SE Lynn Blvd 97754 541-416-6900
Jim Golden, prin. Fax 416-6907
Crook County MS 700/6-8
100 NE Knowledge St 97754 541-447-6283
Rocky Miner, prin. Fax 447-3293

Crook County Christian S 200/PK-12
839 S Main St 97754 541-416-0114
Sue Uptain, prin. Fax 416-0330

Prospect, Jackson
Prospect SD 59 200/K-12
PO Box 40 97536 541-560-3653
Don Alexander, supt. Fax 560-3644
Prospect S 200/K-12
PO Box 40 97536 541-560-3653
Wayne Gallagher, prin. Fax 560-3644

Rainier, Columbia, Pop. 1,816
Rainier SD 13 1,100/K-12
28168 Old Rainier Rd 97048 503-556-3777
R. Michael Carter, supt. Fax 556-3778
www.rainier.k12.or.us
Rainier JSHS 600/7-12
28170 Old Rainier Rd 97048 503-556-4215
Jeff Gilbert, prin. Fax 556-1120

Redmond, Deschutes, Pop. 19,771
Redmond SD 2J 5,800/K-12
145 SE Salmon Ave 97756 541-923-5437
Vickie Fleming, supt. Fax 923-5142
www.redmond.k12.or.us
Gregory MS 6-8
1220 NW Upas Ave 97756 541-526-6440
Mike McIntosh, prin. Fax 526-6441
Obsidian MS 700/6-8
1335 SW Obsidian Ave 97756 541-923-4900
Joe Beck, prin. Fax 923-6509
Redmond HS 1,800/9-12
675 SW Rimrock Way 97756 541-923-4800
Jon Bullock, prin. Fax 548-0809

Central Christian S 200/PK-12
PO Box 639 97756 541-548-7803
Bill Mahnke, prin. Fax 548-2801

Reedsport, Douglas, Pop. 4,361
Reedsport SD 105 800/K-12
100 Ranch Rd 97467 541-271-3656
Forrest Bell, supt. Fax 271-3658
Reedsport JSHS 400/7-12
2260 Longwood Dr 97467 541-271-2141
Patrick Gross, prin. Fax 271-2143

Riddle, Douglas, Pop. 1,023
Riddle SD 70 500/K-12
PO Box 45 97469 541-874-3131
Dave Gianotti, supt. Fax 874-2345
Riddle JSHS, PO Box 45 97469 200/7-12
Terry Prestianni, prin. 541-874-2251

Rockaway, Tillamook, Pop. 1,074
Neah-Kah-Nie SD 56 700/K-12
PO Box 28 97136 503-355-2222
Jay Kosik, supt. Fax 355-3434
www.neahkahnie.k12.or.us
Neah-Kah-Nie HS 300/9-12
24705 Highway 101 N 97136 503-355-2272
Kristi Woika, prin. Fax 355-8200
Neah-Kah-Nie MS 100/6-8
25111 Highway 101 N 97136 503-355-2990
Allen Boyle, prin. Fax 355-8514

Rogue River, Jackson, Pop. 1,941
Rogue River SD 35 1,100/K-12
PO Box 1045 97537 541-582-3235
Dave Orr, supt. Fax 582-1600
www.rogueriver.k12.or.us
Rogue River HS 400/9-12
PO Box 1045 97537 541-582-3297
Dave Orr, prin. Fax 582-6005
Rogue River MS 300/6-8
PO Box 1045 97537 541-582-3233
Kathi Sue Summers, prin. Fax 582-6004

Roseburg, Douglas, Pop. 20,727
Douglas County SD 4 6,600/K-12
1419 NW Valley View Dr 97470 541-440-4015
Lee Paterson, supt. Fax 440-4003
www.roseburg.k12.or.us
Fremont MS 800/6-8
850 W Keady Ct 97470 541-440-4055
Keith Kronser, prin. Fax 440-4060
Lane MS 800/6-8
2153 NE Vine St 97470 541-440-4104
Doug Freeman, prin. Fax 440-4100
Roseburg HS 2,100/9-12
400 W Harvard Ave 97470 541-440-4142
Karen Goirigolzarri, prin. Fax 440-8296

Roseburg Beauty College Post-Sec.
700 SE Stephens St 97470 541-673-5533
Roseburg Junior Academy 100/K-10
1653 NW Troost St 97470 541-673-5278
Thom Harder, prin. Fax 672-9785
Umpqua Community College Post-Sec.
PO Box 967 97470 541-440-4600
Umpqua Valley Christian S 300/PK-12
359 Roberts Creek Rd 97470 541-679-4964
Doug Tharp, admin. Fax 679-1881

Saint Benedict, Marion, Pop. 55

Mt. Angel Seminary Post-Sec.
1 Abbey Dr 97373 503-845-3951

Saint Helens, Columbia, Pop. 11,209
Saint Helens SD 502 3,400/K-12
474 N 16th St 97051 503-397-3085
Patricia Adams, supt. Fax 397-1907
www.sthelens.k12.or.us
Saint Helens HS 1,100/9-12
2375 Gable Rd 97051 503-397-1900
Brian Heinze, prin. Fax 397-1828
Saint Helens MS 600/7-8
354 N 15th St 97051 503-366-7300
Paul Berg, prin. Fax 366-7306

Saint Paul, Marion, Pop. 395
St. Paul SD 45 200/PK-12
20449 Main St NE 97137 503-633-2541
Bruce Shull, supt. Fax 633-2540
www.stpaul.k12.or.us
Saint Paul HS 100/7-12
20449 Main St NE 97137 503-633-2541
Debbie Eder, prin. Fax 633-2540

Salem, Marion, Pop. 148,751
Salem-Keizer SD 24J 37,200/K-12
PO Box 12024 97309 503-399-3000
Sandy Husk, supt. Fax 399-5579
www.salkeiz.k12.or.us
Crossler MS 800/6-8
1155 Davis Rd S 97306 503-399-3444
Jim Adams, prin. Fax 391-4005
Early College HS 9-12
4071 Winema Pl NE 97305 503-365-4800
Terri Gregory, coord.
Houck MS 1,100/6-8
1155 Connecticut Ave SE, 503-399-3446
Elizabeth Ryan, prin. Fax 391-4167
Judson MS 900/6-8
4512 Jones Rd SE 97302 503-399-3201
Debra Faber, prin. Fax 391-4041
Leslie MS 800/6-8
3850 Pringle Rd SE 97302 503-399-3206
Steve Nelson, prin. Fax 399-3479
McKay HS 1,900/9-12
2440 Lancaster Dr NE 97305 503-399-3080
Cynthia Richardson, prin. Fax 375-7807
North Salem HS 1,900/9-12
765 14th St NE 97301 503-399-3241
John Honey, prin. Fax 375-7808
Parrish MS 700/6-8
802 Capitol St NE 97301 503-399-3210
Harold Kaiser, prin. Fax 391-4004
South Salem HS 1,800/9-12
1910 Church St SE 97302 503-399-3252
Willese Everson, prin. Fax 375-7805
Sprague HS 1,800/9-12
2373 Kuebler Rd S 97302 503-399-3261
Cheryl Bower, prin. Fax 391-4046
Stephens MS 1,000/6-8
4962 Hayesville Dr NE 97305 503-399-3442
Neil Anderson, prin. Fax 391-4079
Waldo MS 700/6-8
2805 Lansing Ave NE 97301 503-399-3215
Joe LaFountaine, prin. Fax 391-4070
Walker MS 1,000/6-8
1075 8th St NW 97304 503-399-3220
Tricia Nelson, prin. Fax 399-5540
West Salem HS 1,400/9-12
1776 Titan Dr NW 97304 503-399-5533
Ed John, prin. Fax 584-5004
Other Schools – See Keizer

Academy of Hair Design Post-Sec.
305 Court St NE 97301 503-585-8122
Blanchet S 300/7-12
4373 Market St NE 97301 503-391-2639
Robert Weber, prin. Fax 399-1259
Chemeketa Community College Post-Sec.
PO Box 14007 97309 503-399-5000
College of Hair Design Careers Post-Sec.
1684 Clay St NE 97301 503-588-5888
Corban College Post-Sec.
5000 Deer Park Dr SE, 503-581-8600
Livingstone Adventist Academy 300/K-12
5771 Fruitland Rd NE, 503-363-9408
Barbara Livesay, prin. Fax 363-5721
Oregon State School for the Blind Post-Sec.
700 Church St SE 97301
Oregon State School for the Deaf Post-Sec.
999 Locust St NE 97301
Phagans' School of Beauty Post-Sec.
622 Lancaster Dr NE 97301 503-363-6800
Salem Academy 400/PK-12
942 Lancaster Dr NE 97301 503-378-1219
Dr. Benjamin Potloff, supt. Fax 375-3522
Western Mennonite S 200/6-12
9045 Wallace Rd NW 97304 503-363-2000
Darrel Camp, prin. Fax 370-9455
Willamette University Post-Sec.
900 State St 97301 503-370-6300

Sandy, Clackamas, Pop. 7,871
Oregon Trail SD 46 4,200/K-12
PO Box 547 97055 503-668-5541
Clementina Salinas, supt. Fax 668-7906
www.ortrail.k12.or.us
Cedar Ridge MS 400/6-8
17225 Smith Ave 97055 503-668-8067
Molly Knudsen, prin. Fax 668-3977
Sandy HS 1,400/9-12
17100 SE Bluff Rd 97055 503-668-8011
Jim Saxton, prin. Fax 668-7646
Other Schools – See Boring, Welches

Scappoose, Columbia, Pop. 5,913
Scappoose SD 1J 2,200/K-12
33589 High School Way 97056 503-543-6374
Paul Peterson, supt. Fax 543-7011
www.scappoose.k12.or.us
Scappoose HS 700/9-12
33700 High School Way 97056 503-543-6376
Sue Hays, prin. Fax 543-3796
Scappoose MS 400/7-8
52265 Columbia River Hwy 97056 503-543-7163
Neal Lordos, prin. Fax 543-7917

Scio, Linn, Pop. 704
Scio SD 95 600/K-12
38875 NW 1st Ave 97374 503-394-3261
Gary Tempel, supt. Fax 394-3920
www.scio.k12.or.us/
Scio HS 200/9-12
38875 NW 1st Ave 97374 503-394-3276
Scott Linenberger, prin. Fax 394-3236
Scio MS 100/6-8
38875 NW 1st Ave 97374 503-394-3271
Kerry Lau, prin. Fax 394-4042

Seaside, Clatsop, Pop. 6,116
Jewell SD 8 200/K-12
83874 Highway 103 97138 503-755-2451
John Seeley, supt. Fax 755-0616
www.jewell.k12.or.us/
Jewell S 200/K-12
83874 Highway 103 97138 503-755-2451
John Seeley, prin. Fax 755-0616

Seaside SD 10 1,700/K-12
1801 S Franklin St 97138 503-738-5591
Doug Dougherty, supt. Fax 738-3471
www.seaside.k12.or.us/
Broadway MS 400/6-8
1120 Broadway St 97138 503-738-6892
Sheila Roley, prin. Fax 738-3900
Seaside HS 600/9-12
1901 N Holladay Dr 97138 503-738-5586
Don Wickersham, prin. Fax 738-5589

Shady Cove, Jackson, Pop. 2,301
Jackson County SD 9
Supt. — See Eagle Point
Shady Cove S 300/3-8
PO Box 138 97539 541-878-1400
Tiffany O'Donnell, prin. Fax 830-6226

Sheridan, Yamhill, Pop. 5,570
Sheridan SD 48J 900/K-12
435 S Bridge St 97378 503-843-2433
Roy Williams, supt. Fax 843-3505
www.sheridan.k12.or.us
Sheridan HS 300/9-12
433 S Bridge St 97378 503-843-2162
A.J. Grauer, prin. Fax 843-3466

Delphian S 200/PK-12
20950 SW Rock Creek Rd 97378 800-626-6610
Fax 843-4158
West Valley Academy 100/K-12
PO Box 127 97378 503-843-4123
Janice Davidson, prin. Fax 843-2080

Sherwood, Washington, Pop. 15,398
Sherwood SD 88J 3,600/K-12
23295 SW Main St 97140 503-625-8100
Dan Jamison, supt. Fax 625-8101
www.sherwood.k12.or.us
Sherwood HS 900/9-12
16956 SW Meinecke Rd 97140 503-625-8200
Michelle DeBoard, prin. Fax 625-8201
Sherwood MS 800/6-8
21970 SW Sherwood Blvd 97140 503-925-2600
Anna Pittioni, prin. Fax 925-2601

Silver Lake, Lake
North Lake SD 14 200/K-12
56566 Fort Rock Rd 97638 541-576-2121
Ryan Mattingly, supt. Fax 576-2705
North Lake S 200/K-12
56566 Fort Rock Rd 97638 541-576-2121
Ryan Mattingly, prin. Fax 576-2705

Silverton, Marion, Pop. 8,233
Silver Falls SD 4J 3,400/K-12
1456 Pine St 97381 503-873-5303
Craig Roessler, supt. Fax 873-2936
ww3.silverfalls.k12.or.us/
Silverton HS Pine Street Campus 300/9-9
1456 Pine St 97381 503-873-1970
Jodi Drescher, prin. Fax 873-1441
Silverton HS Schlador Street Campus 800/10-12
802 Schlador St 97381 503-873-6331
Jodi Drescher, prin. Fax 873-8606
Twain MS 300/7-8
425 N Church St 97381 503-873-5317
Andy Bellando, prin. Fax 873-7108

Sisters, Deschutes, Pop. 1,212
Sisters SD 6 1,200/K-12
525 E Cascade Ave 97759 541-549-8521
Ted Thonstad, supt. Fax 549-8951
www.outlawnet.com/outlaw/ssd
Sisters HS 500/9-12
1700 W McKinney Butte Rd 97759 541-549-4045
Bob Macauley, prin. Fax 549-4051
Sisters MS 300/5-8
15200 McKenzie Rd 97759 541-549-2099
Kathy Miner, prin. Fax 549-2098

Spray, Wheeler, Pop. 130
Spray SD 1 100/K-12
PO Box 230 97874 541-468-2226
Paul Young, supt. Fax 468-2630
www.spray.k12.or.us
Spray S 100/K-12
PO Box 230 97874 541-468-2226
Paul Young, prin. Fax 468-2630

Springfield, Lane, Pop. 55,641
Springfield SD 19 11,100/K-12
525 Mill St 97477 541-747-3331
Nancy Golden, supt. Fax 726-3312
www.sps.lane.edu
Briggs MS 500/6-8
2355 Yolanda Ave 97477 541-744-6350
Brooke Wagner, prin. Fax 744-6354
Hamlin MS 500/6-8
326 Centennial Blvd 97477 541-744-6356
Mike Riplinger, prin. Fax 744-6360
Springfield HS 1,600/9-12
875 7th St 97477 541-744-4700
Chris Reiersgaard, prin. Fax 744-4144
Springfield MS 300/6-8
1084 G St 97477 541-744-6362
Jeff Mather, prin. Fax 744-6366
Stewart MS 700/6-8
900 S 32nd St 97478 541-988-2520
Dawn Strong, prin. Fax 988-2530
Thurston HS 1,500/9-12
333 58th St 97478 541-744-5000
Ed Mendelssohn, prin. Fax 744-5029
Thurston MS 500/6-8
6300 Thurston Rd 97478 541-744-6368
Carl Swan, prin. Fax 744-6372

Pioneer Pacific College Post-Sec.
3800 Sports Way 97477 541-684-4644
Springfield College of Beauty Post-Sec.
307 Q St 97477 541-746-4473

Stanfield, Umatilla, Pop. 1,979
Stanfield SD 61 600/K-12
1120 N Main St 97875 541-449-8766
Dale Nees, supt. Fax 449-8768
www.stanfield.k12.or.us
Stanfield Secondary S 200/7-12
1120 N Main St 97875 541-449-3851
Steve Staniak, prin. Fax 449-8751

Stayton, Marion, Pop. 7,184
North Santiam SD 29J 2,300/K-12
1155 N 3rd Ave 97383 503-769-6924
Dr. Jack Adams, supt. Fax 769-3578
www.nsantiam.k12.or.us
Stayton HS 800/9-12
757 W Locust St 97383 503-769-2171
Charlotte Klampe, prin. Fax 769-6050
Stayton MS 500/4-8
1021 Shaff Rd 97383 503-769-2198
Randy LaFollett, prin. Fax 769-9524

Regis HS 200/9-12
550 W Regis St 97383 503-769-2159
Doug Ierardi, prin. Fax 769-1706

Sutherlin, Douglas, Pop. 7,281
Sutherlin SD 130 1,500/K-12
531 E Central Ave 97479 541-459-2228
John Lahley, supt. Fax 459-2484
www.sutherlin.k12.or.us
Sutherlin HS 500/9-12
500 E Fourth Ave 97479 541-459-9551
Marty Gary, prin. Fax 459-4887

Sutherlin MS 200/7-8
649 E Fourth Ave 97479 541-459-2668
Steve Perkins, prin. Fax 459-2047

Sweet Home, Linn, Pop. 8,389
Sweet Home SD 55 2,300/K-12
1920 Long St 97386 541-367-7126
Larry Horton, supt. Fax 367-7105
www.sweethome.k12.or.us
Sweet Home HS 800/9-12
1641 Long St 97386 541-367-7145
Patricia Stineff, prin. Fax 367-7196
Sweet Home JHS 400/7-8
880 22nd Ave 97386 541-367-7187
Hal Huschka, prin. Fax 367-7107

Talent, Jackson, Pop. 6,018
Phoenix-Talent SD 4
Supt. — See Phoenix
Talent MS 700/6-8
PO Box 359 97540 541-535-1552
Patti Kinney, prin. Fax 535-7532

Tangent, Linn, Pop. 968

Central Valley Junior Academy 50/1-10
31630 Highway 34 97389 541-928-7820
Fax 967-4410

The Dalles, Wasco, Pop. 11,317
North Wasco County SD 21 2,300/K-12
3632 W 10th St 97058 541-296-6149
Candy Armstrong, supt. Fax 298-6018
www.nwasco.k12.or.us
The Dalles MS 6-8
1100 E 12th St 97058 541-296-4616
Jan Anderson, prin. Fax 298-6196
The Dalles - Wahtonka HS 10-12
220 E 10th St 97058 541-296-4601
Stephen Jupe, prin. Fax 298-4964
Wahtonka 9th Grade S 9-9
3601 W 10th St 97058 541-296-4633
Tim McGlothlin, prin. Fax 296-2358

Tigard, Washington, Pop. 47,968
Tigard-Tualatin SD 23J 12,000/K-12
6960 SW Sandburg St 97223 503-431-4000
Rob Saxton, supt. Fax 431-4047
www.ttsd.k12.or.us
Fowler MS 900/6-8
10865 SW Walnut St 97223 503-431-5000
Shelley Corry, prin. Fax 431-5010
Tigard HS 2,000/9-12
9000 SW Durham Rd 97224 503-431-5400
Pam Henslee, prin. Fax 431-5410
Twality MS 900/6-8
14650 SW 97th Ave 97224 503-431-5200
Pat Sharp, prin. Fax 431-5210
Other Schools – See Tualatin

Phagans' Tigard Beauty School Post-Sec.
8820 SW Center St 97223 503-639-6107

Tillamook, Tillamook, Pop. 4,471
Tillamook SD 9 2,000/K-12
6825 Officer Row 97141 503-842-4414
Randy Schild, supt. Fax 842-6854
www.tillamook.k12.or.us
Tillamook HS 700/9-12
2605 12th St 97141 503-842-2566
Bruce Rhodes, prin. Fax 842-1340
Tillamook JHS 300/7-8
3906 Alder Ln 97141 503-842-7531
Elroy Thompson, prin. Fax 842-1349

Tillamook Adventist S 100/K-12
4300 12th St 97141 503-842-6533
Steven McKeone, prin. Fax 842-6236

Toledo, Lincoln, Pop. 3,434
Lincoln County SD
Supt. — See Newport
Toledo HS 400/7-12
1800 NE Sturdevant Rd 97391 541-336-5104
Paula Priest, prin. Fax 336-2970

Mid Coast Christian S 50/K-12
PO Box 1408 97391 541-336-2234
Martha Eisele, prin. Fax 336-2702

Troutdale, Multnomah, Pop. 14,898
Reynolds SD 7
Supt. — See Fairview
Morey MS 700/6-8
2801 SW Lucas Ave 97060 503-491-1935
Tony Mann, prin. Fax 491-0245
Reynolds HS 2,500/9-12
1698 SW Cherry Park Rd 97060 503-667-3186
Kevin Kannier, prin. Fax 669-0776

Tualatin, Washington, Pop. 25,881
Tigard-Tualatin SD 23J
Supt. — See Tigard
Hazelbrook MS 1,000/6-8
11300 SW Hazelbrook Rd 97062 503-431-5100
Elizabeth Ryan, prin. Fax 431-5110
Tualatin HS 1,800/9-12
22300 SW Boones Ferry Rd 97062 503-431-5600
Jeff Smith, prin. Fax 431-5610

West Linn-Wilsonville SD 3J 7,900/K-12
22210 SW Stafford Rd 97062 503-673-7000
Roger Woehl, supt. Fax 673-7001
www.wlwv.k12.or.us
Other Schools – See West Linn, Wilsonville

Horizon Christian S 500/PK-12
PO Box 4190 97062 503-612-6521
Dr. Robert Tinnin, supt. Fax 691-9677

Turner, Marion, Pop. 1,571
Cascade SD 5 2,300/PK-12
10226 Marion Rd SE 97392 503-749-8488
F. James McBride, supt. Fax 749-8321
www.cascade.k12.or.us
Cascade HS 800/9-12
10226 Marion Rd SE 97392 503-749-8490
Darin Drill, prin. Fax 749-8324
Cascade JHS 600/6-8
10226 Marion Rd SE 97392 503-749-8489
Leanne Deffenbaugh, prin. Fax 749-8323

Ukiah, Umatilla, Pop. 255
Ukiah SD 80R 100/K-12
PO Box 218 97880 541-427-3731
Dan Korber, supt. Fax 427-3730
www.ukiah.k12.or.us
Ukiah S 100/K-12
PO Box 218 97880 541-427-3731
Dan Korber, prin. Fax 427-3730

Umatilla, Umatilla, Pop. 6,306
Umatilla SD 6R 1,300/K-12
1001 6th St 97882 541-922-6500
Brian Say, supt. Fax 922-6507
www.umatilla.k12.or.us/
Brownell MS 300/6-8
1460 7th St 97882 541-922-6625
Bill Varady, prin. Fax 922-6507
Umatilla HS 300/9-12
1460 7th St 97882 541-922-6525
John Thomas, prin. Fax 922-6599

Union, Union, Pop. 1,945
Union SD 5 500/K-12
PO Box K 97883 541-562-6115
Mike Wood, supt. Fax 562-8116
www.union.k12.or.us
Union JSHS 200/7-12
PO Box 908 97883 541-562-5166
James Taylor, prin. Fax 562-8116

Unity, Baker, Pop. 124
Burnt River SD 30J 50/K-12
PO Box 8 97884 541-446-3466
Robert Otheim, supt. Fax 446-3581
Burnt River S 50/K-12
PO Box 8 97884 541-446-3336
Robert Otheim, prin. Fax 446-3581

Vale, Malheur, Pop. 1,926
Vale SD 84 900/K-12
403 E St W 97918 541-473-0201
Matthew Hawley, supt. Fax 473-3294
www.vale.k12.or.us
Vale HS 300/9-12
505 Viking Dr 97918 541-473-3181
Les Keele, prin. Fax 473-2364
Vale MS 100/7-8
403 E St W 97918 541-473-0241
Mary Jo Sharp, prin. Fax 473-3293

Vernonia, Columbia, Pop. 2,287
Vernonia SD 47J 700/K-12
475 Bridge St 97064 503-429-5891
Kenneth Cox, supt. Fax 429-7742
www.vernonia.k12.or.us/
Vernonia HS 200/9-12
299 Bridge St 97064 503-429-3521
Nate Underwood, prin. Fax 429-7049
Vernonia MS 200/6-8
249 Bridge St 97064 503-429-0487
Fax 429-4731

Vida, Lane

McKenzie River Christian S 100/K-12
PO Box I 97488 541-896-0554
Russ Conklin, prin. Fax 896-0554

Waldport, Lincoln, Pop. 2,094
Lincoln County SD
Supt. — See Newport
Waldport HS 300/9-12
PO Box 370 97394 541-563-3243
Von Taylor, prin. Fax 563-4145

Wallowa, Wallowa, Pop. 824
Wallowa SD 12 300/K-12
PO Box 425 97885 541-886-2061
Marc Thielman, supt. Fax 886-7355
www.wallowa.k12.or.us/
Wallowa JSHS 100/7-12
PO Box 425 97885 541-886-2951
John Nesemann, prin. Fax 886-7355

Warrenton, Clatsop, Pop. 4,310
Warrenton-Hammond SD 30 800/K-12
820 SW Cedar Ave 97146 503-861-2281
Craig Brewington, supt. Fax 861-2911
www.whsd.k12.or.us/
Warrenton HS 300/9-12
1700 S Main Ave 97146 503-861-3317
Rod Heyen, prin. Fax 861-2997

Wasco, Sherman, Pop. 341
Sherman County SD 300/K-12
PO Box 66 97065 541-442-5777
Dale Coles, supt. Fax 442-5778
www.sherman.k12.or.us/District/
Other Schools – See Moro

Welches, Clackamas
Oregon Trail SD 46
Supt. — See Sandy
Welches MS 200/6-8
24903 E Salmon River Rd 97067 503-622-3166
Mike Sutton, prin. Fax 622-3398

Westfir, Lane, Pop. 277
Oakridge SD 76
Supt. — See Oakridge
Oakridge JHS 100/7-8
46433 Westfir Rd 97492 541-782-2731
Donald Kordosky, prin. Fax 782-4647

West Linn, Clackamas, Pop. 25,094
West Linn-Wilsonville SD 3J
Supt. — See Tualatin
Athey Creek MS 600/6-8
2900 SW Borland Rd 97068 503-673-7400
Carolyn Miller, prin. Fax 638-8302
Rosemont Ridge MS 700/6-8
20001 S Salamo Rd 97068 503-673-7550
Debi Briggs Crispin, prin. Fax 657-8720
West Linn HS 1,600/9-12
5464 W A St 97068 503-673-7800
Kim Noah, prin. Fax 657-8710

Weston, Umatilla, Pop. 714
Athena-Weston SD 29RJ
Supt. — See Athena
Athena-Weston MS 200/6-8
PO Box 158 97886 541-566-3548
Mary Pilgreen, prin. Fax 566-2326

White City, Jackson, Pop. 5,891
Jackson County SD 9
Supt. — See Eagle Point
White Mountain MS 400/6-8
550 Wilson Way 97503 541-830-6315
Lynn Eccleston, prin. Fax 830-6751

Willamina, Yamhill, Pop. 1,874
Willamina SD 30J 1,000/K-12
324 SE Adams St 97396 503-876-4525
Gus Forster, supt. Fax 876-3610
www.willamina.k12.or.us
Willamina HS 400/9-12
1100 NE Oaken Hills Dr 97396 503-876-2545
Tim France, prin. Fax 876-2511
Other Schools – See Grand Ronde

Wilsonville, Clackamas, Pop. 16,075
West Linn-Wilsonville SD 3J
Supt. — See Tualatin
Wilsonville HS 1,000/9-12
PO Box 3770 97070 503-673-7600
Andy Sommer, prin. Fax 682-0917
Wood MS 600/6-8
PO Box 705 97070 503-673-7500
Barbara Soisson, prin. Fax 682-9109

Pioneer Pacific College Post-Sec.
27501 SW Parkway Ave 97070 503-682-3903
Pioneer Pacific College Post-Sec.
27375 SW Parkway Ave 97070 503-682-1862

Winston, Douglas, Pop. 4,764
Winston-Dillard SD 116 1,500/K-12
620 Elwood St 97496 541-679-3000
Duane Yecha, supt. Fax 679-4819
www.wdsd.org
Douglas HS 500/9-12
1381 NW Douglas Blvd 97496 541-679-3001
Kevin McDaniel, prin. Fax 679-7284
Winston MS 200/7-8
330 Thompson Ave 97496 541-679-3002
Charan Cline, prin. Fax 679-3026

Woodburn, Marion, Pop. 21,736
Woodburn SD 103 3,400/K-12
965 N Boones Ferry Rd 97071 503-981-9555
Walt Blomberg, supt. Fax 981-8018
www.woodburn.k12.or.us
Academy of International Studies 9-12
1785 N Front St 97071 503-981-2600
Chuck Ransom, prin. Fax 981-2675
French Prairie MS 500/6-8
1025 N Boones Ferry Rd 97071 503-981-2650
Eric Swenson, prin. Fax 981-2724
Valor MS 500/6-8
450 Parr Rd 97071 503-981-2750
Bill Rhoades, prin. Fax 981-2790
Wellness Business and Sports S 9-12
1785 N Front St 97071 503-981-2600
Leo Colegio, prin. Fax 981-2675
Woodburn Academy of Art/Science & Tech 9-12
1785 N Front St 97071 503-981-2600
Geri Federico, prin. Fax 981-2675
Woodburn Arts and Communication Academy 9-12
1785 N Front St 97071 503-981-2600
Jennifer Dixon, prin. Fax 981-2675

Yamhill, Yamhill, Pop. 823
Yamhill-Carlton SD 1 1,200/K-12
PO Box 68 97148 503-662-4911
Steve Chiovaro, supt. Fax 662-4931
www.ycsd.k12.or.us
Yamhill-Carlton HS 400/9-12
275 N Maple St 97148 503-852-7600
James Orth, prin. Fax 662-3220

Yoncalla, Douglas, Pop. 1,059
Yoncalla SD 32 400/K-12
PO Box 568 97499 541-849-2782
Art Johns, supt. Fax 849-2190
www.yoncalla.k12.or.us
Yoncalla HS 100/9-12
PO Box 568 97499 541-849-2175
Brian Berry, prin. Fax 849-2669

PENNSYLVANIA

PENNSYLVANIA DEPARTMENT OF EDUCATION
333 Market St Fl 9, Harrisburg 17101-2215
Telephone 717-783-6788
Fax 717-787-7222
Website http://www.pde.psu.edu

Secretary of Education Gerald Zahorchak

PENNSYLVANIA BOARD OF EDUCATION
333 Market St Fl 10, Harrisburg 17101-2215

Chairperson Karl Girton

INTERMEDIATE UNITS (IU)

Allegheny IU 3
Dr. Donna Durno, dir. 412-394-5700
475 Waterfront Dr E Fax 394-5706
Homestead 15120
www.aiu3.net/

Appalachia IU 8
Dr. Michael Dillon, dir. 814-940-0223
4500 6th Ave, Altoona 16602 Fax 472-5033
www.iu08.org/

ARIN IU 28
Dr. Robert Coad, dir. 724-463-5300
2895 W Pike Rd, Indiana 15701 Fax 463-5315
www.arin.k12.pa.us

Beaver Valley IU 27
Thomas Zelesnik, dir. 724-774-7800
225 Center Grange Rd Fax 774-4751
Aliquippa 15001
www.bviu.org/bviu/site/default.asp

Berks County IU 14
Dr. Nancy G. Almon, dir. 610-987-2248
PO Box 16050, Reading 19612 Fax 987-8400
www.berksiu.org

Blast IU 17
Thomas Shivetts, dir. 570-323-8561
PO Box 3609, Williamsport 17701
www.iu17.org

Bucks County IU 22
Richard Coe Ed.D., dir. 215-348-2940
705 N Shady Retreat Rd Fax 489-7874
Doylestown 18901
www.bciu.k12.pa.us

Capital Area IU 15
Dr. Glenn Zehner, dir. 717-732-8400
PO Box 489, Summerdale 17093 Fax 732-8421
www.caiu.org/caiu/site/default.asp

Carbon-Lehigh IU 21
Robert Keegan, dir. 610-769-4111
4750 Orchard Rd Fax 769-1290
Schnecksville 18078
www.cliu.org

Central IU 10
Dr. Nancy Robbins, dir. 814-342-0884
345 Link Rd, West Decatur 16878 Fax 342-5137
www.ciu10.com

Central Susquehanna IU 16
Dr. Robert Witten, dir. 570-523-1155
PO Box 213, Lewisburg 17837 Fax 524-7104
www.csiu.org/

Chester County IU 24
Dr. John Baillie, dir. 484-237-5000
455 Boot Rd, Downingtown 19335 Fax 237-5154
www.cciu.org/

IU 1
Dr. Lawrence J. O'Shea, dir. 724-938-3241
1 Intermediate Unit Dr Fax 938-8722
Coal Center 15423
www.iu1.k12.pa.us/

Colonial IU 20
Dr. Charlene Brennan, dir. 610-252-5550
6 Danforth Rd, Easton 18045 Fax 252-5740
www.ciu20.org

Delaware County IU 25
Christopher McGinley, dir. 610-938-9000
200 Yale Ave, Morton 19070 Fax 565-1315
www.dciu.org/

Lancaster-Lebanon IU 13
Dr. James Scott, dir. 717-606-1600
1020 New Holland Ave
Lancaster 17601
www.iu13.k12.pa.us

Lincoln IU 12
Dr. Michael Thew, dir. 717-624-4616
PO Box 70, New Oxford 17350 Fax 624-6519
www.iu12.org

Luzerne IU 18
Michael Ostrowski, dir. 570-762-8884
PO Box 1649, Kingston 18704
www.liu18.org/

Midwestern IU 4
Angelo Pezzuolo, dir. 724-458-6700
453 Maple St, Grove City 16127 Fax 458-5083
www.miu4.k12.pa.us/

Montgomery County IU 23
Dr. Jerry Shiveley, dir. 610-539-8550
1605 W Main St Ste B Fax 539-5973
Norristown 19403
www.mciu.k12.pa.us

Northeastern Educational IU 19
Dr. Fred Rosetti, dir. 570-876-9200
1200 Line St, Archbald 18403 Fax 876-8660
www.neiu.org

Northwest Tri-County IU 5
Dr. Marjorie Wallace, dir. 814-734-5610
252 Waterford St, Edinboro 16412 Fax 734-5806
www.iu5.org/

Philadelphia IU 26
Paul G. Vallas, dir. 215-400-4000
440 N Broad St, Philadelphia 19130

Pittsburgh/Mt. Oliver IU 2
Mark Roosevelt, dir. 412-363-0851
515 N Highland Ave Fax 488-7271
Pittsburgh 15206

Riverview IU 6
Dr. William Kaufman, dir. 814-226-7103
270 Mayfield Rd, Clarion 16214 Fax 226-4850
www.riu6.org/

Schuylkill IU 29
Dr. Gerald Achenbach, dir. 570-544-9131
PO Box 130, Mar Lin 17951 Fax 544-6412
www.iu29.org/

Seneca Highlands IU 9
M. Wetzel, dir. 814-887-5512
PO Box 1566, Smethport 16749 Fax 887-2157
www.iu9.org

Tuscarora IU 11
Richard Daubert, dir. 717-899-7143
2527 US Highway 522 S
Mc Veytown 17051
www.tiu.k12.pa.us/

Westmoreland IU 7
Bruce Paul, dir. 724-836-2460
102 Equity Dr, Greensburg 15601 Fax 836-1747
wiu.k12.pa.us/

PUBLIC, PRIVATE AND CATHOLIC SECONDARY SCHOOLS

Abington, Montgomery, Pop. 56,600
Abington SD 7,200/K-12
970 Highland Ave 19001 215-884-4700
Amy Sichel Ph.D., supt. Fax 881-2545
www.abington.k12.pa.us
Abington JHS 1,900/7-9
2056 Susquehanna Rd 19001 215-884-4700
Cornelius McCarthy, prin. Fax 517-2894
Abington SHS 1,900/10-12
900 Highland Ave 19001 215-884-4700
Robert Burt, prin. Fax 886-1871

Abington Memorial Hospital Post-Sec.
1200 Old York Rd 19001 215-576-2000
Pennsylvania State University Post-Sec.
1600 Woodland Rd 19001 215-881-7300

Albion, Erie, Pop. 1,558
Northwestern SD 1,800/K-12
100 Harthan Way 16401 814-756-9400
Patrick Kelley, supt. Fax 756-9414
www.nwsd.org
Northwestern HS 600/9-12
200 Harthan Way 16401 814-756-9400
Daniel Shreve, prin. Fax 756-9411
Northwestern MS 400/6-8
150 Harthan Way 16401 814-756-9400
Sandi Shaner, prin. Fax 756-9415

Alexandria, Huntingdon, Pop. 382
Juniata Valley SD 800/K-12
PO Box 318 16611 814-669-9150
James Foster, supt. Fax 669-4492
www.tiu11.org/~jvweb/
Juniata Valley JSHS 400/7-12
PO Box 318 16611 814-669-4401
Mark Loucks, prin. Fax 669-4421

Aliquippa, Beaver, Pop. 11,105
Aliquippa SD 1,400/K-12
100 Harding Ave 15001 724-857-7500
John Thomas, supt. Fax 857-3404
www.aliquippa.k12.pa.us
Aliquippa HS 500/9-12
100 Harding Ave 15001 724-857-7500
Gary Monahan, prin. Fax 375-0593
Aliquippa MS 400/5-8
100 Harding Ave 15001 724-857-7500
Peter Carbone, prin. Fax 857-3404

Hopewell Area SD 2,800/K-12
2354 Brodhead Rd 15001 724-375-6691
Dr. Charles Reina, supt. Fax 375-0942
www.hopewell.k12.pa.us
Hopewell HS 1,000/9-12
1215 Longvue Ave 15001 724-378-8565
Michael Allison, prin. Fax 378-4952
Hopewell JHS 900/5-8
2354 Brodhead Rd 15001 724-375-7765
Edward Katkich, prin. Fax 378-2594

Allentown, Lehigh, Pop. 106,992
Allentown CSD 17,000/PK-12
PO Box 328 18105 484-765-4000
Karen Angello Ph.D., supt. Fax 765-4225
www.allentownsd.org/
Allen HS 3,500/9-12
126 N 17th St 18104 484-765-5000
Keith Falko, prin. Fax 765-5010
Dieruff HS 1,900/9-12
815 N Irving St 18109 484-765-5500
James Moniz, prin. Fax 765-5512
Harrison-Morton MS 800/6-8
137 N 2nd St 18101 484-765-5700
Burdette Chapel, prin. Fax 765-5715
Raub MS 1,000/6-8
102 S Saint Cloud St 18104 484-765-5300
Regina Finlayson, prin. Fax 765-5310

South Mountain MS 1,300/6-8
709 W Emaus Ave 18103 484-765-4300
Ralph Lovelidge, prin. Fax 765-4310
Trexler MS 1,000/6-8
851 N 15th St 18102 484-765-4600
Karl Foerster, prin. Fax 765-4610

Parkland SD 8,800/K-12
1210 Springhouse Rd 18104 610-351-5503
Dr. Louise Donohue, supt. Fax 351-5509
www.parklandsd.org
Parkland HS 3,000/9-12
2700 N Cedar Crest Blvd 18104 610-351-5600
Richard Sniscak, prin. Fax 351-5656
Springhouse MS 900/6-8
1200 Springhouse Rd 18104 610-351-5700
Michelle Minotti, prin. Fax 351-5748
Other Schools – See Orefield

Salisbury Township SD 1,800/K-12
1140 Salisbury Rd 18103 610-797-2062
Mary Anne Wright, supt. Fax 791-9983
www.salisbury.k12.pa.us/
Salisbury HS 500/10-12
500 E Montgomery St 18103 610-797-4107
J. William Hume, prin. Fax 797-1972
Salisbury MS 600/6-9
3301 Devonshire Rd 18103 610-791-0830
Robert Cassidy, prin. Fax 797-9648

Allentown Central Catholic HS 900/9-12
301 N 4th St 18102 610-437-4601
Kathy Hanlon, prin. Fax 437-6760
Allentown School of Cosmetology Post-Sec.
1921 Union Blvd 18109 610-437-4626
Cedar Crest College Post-Sec.
100 College Dr 18104 610-437-4471
Lehigh Valley Christian HS 200/9-12
1414 E Cedar St 18109 610-821-9443
Charles Bloomfield, prin. Fax 821-5527

Lehigh Valley Hospital & Health Network — Post-Sec.
PO Box 7017 18105 — 610-402-2556
Lincoln Technical Institute — Post-Sec.
5151 W Tilghman St 18104 — 610-398-5300
Muhlenberg College — Post-Sec.
2400 W Chew St 18104 — 610-821-3100
Pennsylvania School of Business — Post-Sec.
406 W Hamilton St 18101 — 610-264-8029
Sacred Heart Hospital — Post-Sec.
421 W Chew St 18102 — 610-776-4745
Welder Training & Testing Institute — Post-Sec.
729 E Highland St 18109 — 610-437-9720

Allison Park, Allegheny, Pop. 6,000
Area Vocational Technical School
Supt. — None
Beattie Career Center — Vo/Tech
9600 Babcock Blvd 15101 — 412-366-2800
Kathryn Bamberger, prin. — Fax 366-9600

Hampton Township SD — 3,200/K-12
4591 School Dr 15101 — 412-492-6302
John Hoover, supt. — Fax 487-6898
www.htsd.k12.pa.us
Hampton HS — 1,100/9-12
2929 McCully Rd 15101 — 412-492-6376
Jeffrey Finch, prin. — Fax 486-7050
Hampton MS, 4589 School Dr 15101 — 700/6-8
Kenneth DiDonato, prin. — 412-492-6356

Altoona, Blair, Pop. 47,176
Altoona Area SD — 8,400/PK-12
1415 6th Ave 16602 — 814-946-8211
Dr. Dennis Murray, supt. — Fax 946-8375
www.aasdcat.com/aasd/
Altoona Area SHS — 1,900/10-12
1415 6th Ave 16602 — 814-946-8273
Sharon Fasenmyer, prin.
Keith JHS — 1,000/7-9
1318 19th Ave 16601 — 814-946-8355
John Wilson, prin. — Fax 946-8557
Roosevelt JHS — 1,000/7-9
1501 7th Ave 16602 — 814-946-8340
Lori Mangan, prin. — Fax 946-8429

Area Vocational Technical School
Supt. — None
Greater Altoona CTC — Vo/Tech
1500 4th Ave 16602 — 814-946-8450
Dr. Lanny Ross, prin. — Fax 946-8351

Altoona Beauty School — Post-Sec.
1528 Valley View Blvd 16602 — 814-942-3141
Altoona Hospital — Post-Sec.
620 Howard Ave 16601 — 814-946-2223
Bishop Guilfoyle HS — 400/9-12
2400 Pleasant Valley Blvd 16602 — 814-944-4014
Robert Gervinski, prin. — Fax 944-8695
Computer Learning Network — Post-Sec.
2900 Fairway Dr 16602 — 814-944-5643
Great Commission S — 100/K-12
1100 6th Ave 16602 — 814-942-9710
Van Wiedemann, admin. — Fax 942-7147
Pennsylvania State University — Post-Sec.
3000 Ivyside Park 16601 — 814-949-5000
Pruonto's Hair Design Institute — Post-Sec.
705 12th St 16602 — 814-944-4494
South Hills School of Business & Tech. — Post-Sec.
508 58th St 16602 — 814-944-6134

Alverton, Westmoreland
Southmoreland SD
Supt. — See Scottdale
Southmoreland HS — 700/9-12
PO Box A 15612 — 724-887-2019
Carolyn Adams, prin. — Fax 887-2980
Southmoreland JHS — 400/7-8
PO Box B 15612 — 724-887-2034
Timothy Scott, prin. — Fax 887-2032

Ambler, Montgomery, Pop. 6,349
Wissahickon SD — 4,600/K-12
601 Knight Rd 19002 — 215-619-8000
Dr. Stanley Durtan, supt. — Fax 619-8002
wsdweb.org
Wissahickon HS — 1,400/9-12
521 Houston Rd 19002 — 215-619-8112
William Hayes, prin. — Fax 619-8113
Wissahickon MS — 1,100/6-8
500 Houston Rd 19002 — 215-619-8110
Lynda Fields, prin. — Fax 619-8111

Ambler Beauty Academy — Post-Sec.
50 E Butler Ave 19002 — 215-643-5994
Temple University 19002 — Post-Sec.
215-283-1252

Ambridge, Beaver, Pop. 7,329
Ambridge Area SD — 3,100/K-12
740 Park Rd 15003 — 724-266-2833
Dr. Kenneth Voss, supt. — Fax 266-3981
www.ambridge.k12.pa.us
Ambridge Area HS — 1,000/9-12
909 Duss Ave 15003 — 724-266-2833
Alan Fritz, prin. — Fax 266-5056
Other Schools – See Freedom

Trinity Episcopal School for Ministry — Post-Sec.
311 11th St 15003 — 724-266-3838

Annville, Lebanon, Pop. 4,294
Annville-Cleona SD — 1,700/K-12
520 S White Oak St 17003 — 717-867-7600
Marsha Zehner, supt. — Fax 867-7610
www.acschools.org
Annville-Cleona JSHS — 800/7-12
500 S White Oak St 17003 — 717-867-7700
Bernard Kepler, prin. — Fax 867-7720

Lebanon Valley College — Post-Sec.
101 N College Ave 17003 — 717-867-6100

Apollo, Armstrong, Pop. 1,672
Apollo-Ridge SD — 1,600/K-12
Star Route 15613 — 724-478-6000
Fax 478-1149
www.apolloridge.com/
Other Schools – See Spring Church

Orchard Hills Christian Academy — 50/1-12
385 Kings Rd 15613 — 724-478-3455
Sandra Cornell, prin. — Fax 478-1174

Archbald, Lackawanna, Pop. 6,290
Valley View SD — 2,600/K-12
1 Columbus Dr 18403 — 570-876-5080
Joseph Daley, supt. — Fax 876-6365
www.valleyviewsd.org/
Valley View HS — 800/9-12
1 Columbus Dr 18403 — 570-876-4110
Donald Kanavy, prin. — Fax 803-0217
Valley View MS — 600/6-8
1 Columbus Dr 18403 — 570-876-6461
Gary Violanti, prin. — Fax 803-0276

Ardmore, Montgomery, Pop. 12,646
Lower Merion SD — 6,800/K-12
301 E Montgomery Ave 19003 — 610-645-1800
Dr. Jamie Savedoff, supt. — Fax 645-9772
www.lmsd.org
Lower Merion HS — 1,600/9-12
245 E Montgomery Ave 19003 — 610-645-1810
David Piperato, prin.
Other Schools – See Bala Cynwyd, Narberth, Rosemont

Armagh, Indiana, Pop. 125
United SD — 1,300/K-12
10780 Route 56 Hwy E 15920 — 814-446-5618
Dr. Kathy Myers Wunder, supt. — Fax 446-6615
www.unitedsd.net/
United JSHS — 600/7-12
10780 Route 56 Hwy E 15920 — 814-446-5615
Lewis Kindja, prin. — Fax 446-6615

Arnold, Westmoreland, Pop. 5,401
New Kensington-Arnold SD
Supt. — See New Kensington
Valley MS — 600/6-8
1701 Alcoa Dr 15068 — 724-335-2511
Kim Crummie, prin. — Fax 339-5532

Ashland, Schuylkill, Pop. 3,159
North Schuylkill SD — 2,000/K-12
15 Academy Ln 17921 — 570-874-0466
Robert Franklin, supt. — Fax 874-3334
www.northschuylkill.net
North Schuylkill JSHS — 1,000/7-12
15 Academy Ln 17921 — 570-874-0495
Sharon J. Snyder, prin. — Fax 874-1531

Cardinal Brennan JHSH — 300/7-12
130 Academy Ln 17921 — 570-874-3921
Dr. Jaclyn M. Fowler, prin. — Fax 874-2239

Aston, Delaware
Area Vocational Technical School
Supt. — None
Delaware County Technical HS Aston — Vo/Tech
700 Crozerville Rd 19014 — 610-459-3050
James Rogers, prin.

Chichester SD — 3,700/K-12
401 Cherry Tree Rd 19014 — 610-485-6881
Michael T. Golde, supt. — Fax 485-3086
www.chichesterschools.net
Other Schools – See Boothwyn

Penn-Delco SD — 3,400/K-12
2821 Concord Rd 19014 — 610-497-6300
Dr. Leslye Abrutyn, supt. — Fax 497-1798
www.pdsd.org
Northley MS — 800/6-8
2801 Concord Rd 19014 — 610-497-6300
Pete Donaghy, prin. — Fax 497-5737
Sun Valley HS — 1,200/9-12
2881 Pancoast Ave 19014 — 610-497-6300
Tom Jakubczwk, prin. — Fax 497-2863

American Christian S — 300/K-12
4150 Market St 19014 — 610-497-0700
Vicki Conteh, admin. — Fax 497-0785
Neumann College — Post-Sec.
1 Neumann Dr 19014 — 610-459-0905

Atglen, Chester, Pop. 1,350
Octorara Area SD — 2,700/K-12
228 Highland Rd Ste 1 19310 — 610-593-8238
Dr. Thomas Newcome, supt. — Fax 593-6425
www.octorara.k12.pa.us
Octorara Area HS — 800/9-12
226 Highland Rd 19310 — 610-593-8253
Scott Rohrer, prin. — Fax 593-8256
Octorara Area MS — 700/6-8
228 Highland Rd 19310 — 610-593-8223
Douglas Groover, prin. — Fax 593-5185

Athens, Bradford, Pop. 3,301
Athens Area SD — 2,400/K-12
204 Willow St 18810 — 570-888-7766
Douglas A. Ulkins, supt. — Fax 888-3186
www.athensasd.k12.pa.us
Athens Area HS — 500/10-12
401 W Frederick St 18810 — 570-888-7766
Beth Schulze, prin. — Fax 888-4038
Rowe JHS — 400/8-9
116 W Pine St Ste 1 18810 — 570-888-7766
Scott Webster, prin. — Fax 888-9536

Austin, Potter, Pop. 597
Austin Area SD — 200/PK-12
138 Costello Ave 16720 — 814-647-8603
Matthew Hutcheson, supt. — Fax 647-8869
www.austinsd.com
Austin Area JSHS — 100/7-12
138 Costello Ave 16720 — 814-647-8603
Matthew Hutcheson, prin. — Fax 647-8869

Avella, Washington
Avella Area SD — 700/K-12
1000 Avella Rd 15312 — 724-356-2218
Wayde Killmeyer, supt. — Fax 356-2207
www.avella.hky.com/
Avella Area JSHS — 400/7-12
1000 Avella Rd 15312 — 724-356-2216
Timothy Beck, prin. — Fax 356-7905

Avis, Clinton, Pop. 1,472

Walnut Street Christian S — 200/PK-12
PO Box 616 17721 — 570-398-1080
Kathy Gottschall, prin. — Fax 753-5728

Baden, Beaver, Pop. 4,172

Quigley HS — 200/9-12
200 Quigley Dr 15005 — 724-869-2188
Dr. Madonna Helbling, prin. — Fax 869-3091

Bala Cynwyd, Montgomery, Pop. 8,000
Lower Merion SD
Supt. — See Ardmore
Bala-Cynwyd MS — 900/6-8
510 Bryn Mawr Ave 19004 — 610-645-1480
Dr. Patricia Haupt, prin.

Bangor, Northampton, Pop. 5,305
Bangor Area SD — 3,600/K-12
123 Five Points Richmond Rd 18013 — 610-588-2163
John Reinhart, supt. — Fax 599-7040
www.bangor.k12.pa.us
Bangor Area HS — 1,200/9-12
187 Five Points Richmond Rd 18013 — 610-599-7011
Frank DeFelice, prin. — Fax 599-7043
Bangor Area MS — 600/7-8
401 Five Points Richmond Rd 18013 — 610-599-7012
Joseph Gunnels, prin. — Fax 599-7045

Bartonsville, Monroe
Area Vocational Technical School
Supt. — None
Monroe Career & Tech Institute — Vo/Tech
PO Box 66 18321 — 570-629-2001
Patricia Moyer, dir. — Fax 629-9698

Beaver, Beaver, Pop. 4,550
Beaver Area SD — 2,100/K-12
855 2nd St Ste 6 15009 — 724-774-4010
Dr. John Hansen, supt. — Fax 774-8770
www.basd.k12.pa.us/index2.php
Beaver Area HS — 700/9-12
Gypsy Glen Rd 15009 — 724-774-0251
Dan Taormina, prin. — Fax 774-3926
Beaver Area MS — 300/7-8
Gypsy Glen Rd 15009 — 724-774-0253
Dan Taormina, prin. — Fax 774-3926

Medical Center of Beaver County — Post-Sec.
1000 Dutch Ridge Rd 15009 — 724-728-7000

Beaver Falls, Beaver, Pop. 9,402
Big Beaver Falls Area SD — 1,900/K-12
1503 8th Ave 15010 — 724-843-3470
Donna Nugent, supt. — Fax 843-2360
www.tigerweb.org
Beaver Falls Area HS — 700/9-12
1701 8th Ave 15010 — 724-843-7470
Thomas Karczewski, prin. — Fax 843-0892
Beaver Falls MS — 500/6-8
1601 8th Ave 15010 — 724-846-5470
Thomas House, prin. — Fax 846-2579

Blackhawk SD — 2,800/K-12
500 Blackhawk Rd 15010 — 724-846-6600
Dr. Alan Guandolo, supt. — Fax 846-2021
www.bsd.k12.pa.us
Blackhawk JSHS — 1,200/8-12
500 Blackhawk Rd 15010 — 724-846-9600
Scott Nelson, prin. — Fax 891-7113

Beaver County Christian HS — 100/9-12
510 37th St 15010 — 724-843-3002
Doug Carson, prin. — Fax 843-5224
Beaver Falls Beauty Academy — Post-Sec.
720 13th St 15010 — 724-843-7700
Geneva College — Post-Sec.
3200 College Ave 15010 — 724-846-5100

Beaver Springs, Snyder
Midd-West SD
Supt. — See Middleburg
West Snyder MS — 300/5-8
645 Snyder Ave 17812 — 570-658-8144
David Harrison, prin. — Fax 658-7287

Bedford, Bedford, Pop. 3,051
Bedford Area SD — 2,300/K-12
330 E John St 15522 — 814-623-4295
Dr. Glenn Thompson, supt. — Fax 623-4299
www.bedford.k12.pa.us
Bedford HS — 600/9-12
330 E John St 15522 — 814-623-4250
Dan Webb, prin. — Fax 623-4265
Bedford MS — 500/6-8
440 E Watson St 15522 — 814-623-4200
Max Shoemaker, prin. — Fax 623-4214
Other Schools – See Hyndman

Bellefonte, Centre, Pop. 6,161
Bellefonte Area SD — 3,000/K-12
318 N Allegheny St 16823 — 814-355-4814
James T. Masullo, supt. — Fax 353-5342
www.basd.net
Bellefonte Area HS — 1,000/9-12
830 E Bishop St 16823 — 814-355-4833
Anne Hutcheson, prin. — Fax 353-5320
Bellefonte Area MS — 800/6-8
100 N School St 16823 — 814-355-5466
Karen Krisch, prin. — Fax 353-5350

Belle Vernon, Fayette, Pop. 1,163
Belle Vernon Area SD — 2,900/K-12
270 Crest Ave 15012 — 724-929-5262
Robert Nagy, supt. — Fax 930-9460
www.bvasd.net/
Belle Vernon Area HS — 1,000/9-12
425 Crest Ave 15012 — 724-929-9800
Gregory Zborovancik, prin.
Bellmar MS, 500 Perry Ave 15012 — 400/6-8
Stephen Russell, prin. — 724-929-9030
Rostraver MS, 250 Crest Ave 15012 — 400/6-8
Dr. John Fohmar, prin. — 724-929-2993

Belleville, Mifflin, Pop. 1,589

Belleville Mennonite S 200/PK-12
PO Box 847 17004 717-935-2184
R. Ann Kanagy, supt. Fax 935-5641

Bellwood, Blair, Pop. 1,916
Bellwood-Antis SD 1,300/K-12
400 Martin St 16617 814-742-2271
G. Brian Toth, supt. Fax 742-9049
www.blwd.k12.pa.us
Bellwood-Antis HS 400/9-12
400 Martin St 16617 814-742-2274
Diane Williams, prin. Fax 742-9817
Bellwood-Antis MS 400/5-8
400 Martin St 16617 814-742-2273
Robert Fisher, prin. Fax 742-9817

Bensalem, Bucks, Pop. 59,700
Bensalem Township SD 5,800/K-12
3000 Donallen Dr 19020 215-750-2800
Dr. James Lombardo, supt. Fax 359-0181
www.bensalemsd.org/
Bensalem HS 2,000/9-12
4319 Hulmeville Rd 19020 215-750-2800
Francis Perry, prin. Fax 245-4875
Shafer MS 400/7-8
3333 Hulmeville Rd 19020 215-750-2800
William Incollingo, prin. Fax 244-2964
Snyder MS 300/7-8
3330 Hulmeville Rd 19020 215-750-2800
Patrick Lyons, prin. Fax 244-2851

Bensalem Baptist S 100/K-12
3351 Richlieu Rd 19020 215-639-5433
Tammy Rivera, dir. Fax 639-5469
De La Salle Vocational HS Vo/Tech
PO Box 344 19020 215-464-0344
Ann Walker, prin. Fax 638-3767
Holy Family University Post-Sec.
1311 Bristol Pike 19020 215-637-7700
Holy Ghost Prep S 500/9-12
2429 Bristol Pike 19020 215-639-2102
Paul Pomeroy, prin. Fax 639-4225
ITT Technical Institute Post-Sec.
3330 Tillman Dr 19020 215-244-8871

Bentleyville, Washington, Pop. 2,448
Bentworth SD 1,200/K-12
150 Bearcat Dr 15314 724-239-2861
Charles Baker, supt. Fax 239-2865
bentworth.org
Bentworth HS 400/9-12
75 Bearcat Dr 15314 724-239-5911
Kevin Fortuna, prin. Fax 239-4010
Other Schools – See Ellsworth

Benton, Columbia, Pop. 923
Benton Area SD 800/K-12
600 Green Acres Rd 17814 570-925-6651
Gary Powlus, supt. Fax 925-6973
www.bentonsd.k12.pa.us/
Benton Area MSHS 400/7-12
600 Green Acres Rd 17814 570-925-2651
Joseph Goode, prin. Fax 925-0956

Berlin, Somerset, Pop. 2,130
Berlin-Brothersvalley SD 900/K-12
1025 Main St 15530 814-267-4621
Margie Zorn, supt. Fax 267-6060
www.bbsd.com/
Berlin-Brothersvalley HS 300/9-12
1025 Main St 15530 814-267-4622
Thomas Vent, prin. Fax 267-6060
Berlin Brothersvalley MS 300/5-8
1025 Main St 15530 814-267-6931
Martin Mudry, prin. Fax 267-6060

Bernville, Berks, Pop. 881
Tulpehocken Area SD 1,700/K-12
428 New Schaefferstown Rd 19506 610-488-9555
Elizabeth Massar, supt. Fax 488-7914
www.tulpehocken.org
Tulpehocken Area JSHS 900/7-12
430 New Schaefferstown Rd 19506 610-488-6286
Greg Protzman, prin. Fax 488-7976

Berwick, Columbia, Pop. 10,352
Berwick Area SD 3,200/K-12
500 Line St 18603 570-759-6400
James Kraky, supt. Fax 759-6439
www.berwicksd.org
Berwick Area HS 900/9-12
1100 Fowler Ave 18603 570-759-6400
Richard Walton, prin. Fax 759-6466
Berwick Area MS 900/6-8
1100 Evergreen Dr 18603 570-759-6400
Ralph Norce, prin. Fax 759-7978

Berwyn, See Devon
Tredyffrin-Easttown SD 5,800/K-12
738 1st Ave 19312 610-240-1900
Dr. Daniel Waters, supt. Fax 240-1965
www.tesd.net/
Conestoga HS 1,800/9-12
200 Irish Rd 19312 610-240-1000
Timothy Donovan, prin. Fax 240-1055
Tredyffrin-Easttown MS 900/5-8
801 Conestoga Rd 19312 610-240-1200
Mark Cataldi, prin. Fax 240-1225
Other Schools – See Wayne

Bessemer, Lawrence, Pop. 1,126
Mohawk Area SD 2,000/K-12
PO Box 25 16112 724-667-7723
Dr. Timothy McNamee, supt. Fax 667-0602
www.mohawk.k12.pa.us
Mohawk JSHS 1,000/7-12
PO Box 25 16112 724-667-7782
Charles Shoop, prin. Fax 667-0602

Bethel Park, Allegheny, Pop. 32,313
Bethel Park SD 5,200/K-12
301 Church Rd 15102 412-854-8402
Dr. Thomas Knight, supt. Fax 854-8430
www.bpsd.org
Bethel Park HS 1,900/9-12
309 Church Rd 15102 412-854-8581
David Helsinki, prin. Fax 854-8559
Independence MS 800/7-8
2807 Bethel Church Rd 15102 412-854-8677
David Muench, prin. Fax 854-8732

Bethlehem, Northampton, Pop. 72,895
Area Vocational Technical School
Supt. — None
Bethlehem AVTS Vo/Tech
3300 Chester Ave 18020 610-866-8013
Brian Williams, prin. Fax 866-6124

Bethlehem Area SD 15,000/K-12
1516 Sycamore St 18017 610-861-0500
Dr. Joseph Lewis, supt. Fax 807-5599
www.beth.k12.pa.us/
Broughal MS 600/6-8
125 W Packer Ave 18015 610-866-5041
Joseph Santoro, prin. Fax 807-5909
East Hills MS 1,300/6-8
2005 Chester Rd 18017 610-867-0541
Edward J. Crawford, prin. Fax 807-5941
Freedom HS 2,000/9-12
3149 Chester Ave 18020 610-867-5843
Michael LaPorta, prin. Fax 867-7360
Liberty HS Freshman Campus 800/9-9
1110 Fernwood St 18018 610-807-5995
JoAnne Durante, prin. Fax 849-0200
Liberty SHS 2,000/10-12
1115 Linden St 18018 610-691-7200
JoAnne Durante, prin. Fax 691-0741
Nitschmann MS 900/6-8
909 W Union Blvd 18018 610-866-5781
Jacqueline Santarasto, prin. Fax 866-1435
Northeast MS 800/6-8
1170 Fernwood St 18018 610-868-8581
Joseph Rahs, prin. Fax 807-5997

Bethlehem Catholic HS 700/9-12
2133 Madison Ave 18017 610-866-0791
Richard Culver, prin. Fax 866-9892
Lehigh University Post-Sec.
27 Memorial Dr W 18015 610-758-3000
Moravian Academy MS 200/6-8
11 W Market St 18018 610-866-6677
George King, hdmstr. Fax 866-6337
Moravian Academy - Upper S Campus 300/9-12
4313 Green Pond Rd 18020 610-691-1600
George King, hdmstr. Fax 691-3354
Moravian College Post-Sec.
1200 Main St 18018 610-861-1300
Moravian Theological Seminary Post-Sec.
1200 Main St 18018 610-861-1516
Northampton Co. Area Community College Post-Sec.
3835 Green Pond Rd 18020 610-861-5300
St. Luke's Hospital Post-Sec.
801 Ostrum St 18015 610-954-3400

Biglerville, Adams, Pop. 1,152
Upper Adams SD 1,400/K-12
PO Box 847 17307 717-677-7191
Eric Eshbach, supt. Fax 677-9807
www.uasd.k12.pa.us
Biglerville HS 600/9-12
161 N Main St 17307 717-677-7191
Richard Sterner, prin. Fax 677-0142
Upper Adams MS 300/7-8
161 N Main St 17307 717-677-7191
David Zinn, prin. Fax 677-0219

Birdsboro, Berks, Pop. 5,191
Daniel Boone Area SD 3,600/K-12
PO Box 490 19508 610-582-6140
David Robbins, supt. Fax 582-0059
www.dboone.k12.pa.us/
Boone Area HS 1,100/9-12
PO Box 450 19508 610-582-6100
William McIlmoyle, prin. Fax 582-5400
Other Schools – See Douglassville

Berks Christian S 100/K-12
926 Philadelphia Ter 19508 610-582-1000
Robert Becker, admin. Fax 404-0126

Blairsville, Indiana, Pop. 3,460
Blairsville-Saltsburg SD 2,200/K-12
102 School Ln 15717 724-459-5500
H. Robert Mencer Ed.D., supt. Fax 459-9209
www.b-ssd.org
Blairsville HS 400/9-12
100 School Ln 15717 724-459-8882
Timothy Haselhoff, prin. Fax 459-3392
Blairsville MS 300/6-8
104 School Ln 15717 724-459-8880
Joyce Henderson, prin. Fax 459-0213
Other Schools – See Saltsburg

WyoTech Blairsville Post-Sec.
500 Innovation Dr 15717 724-459-9500

Bloomsburg, Columbia, Pop. 12,915
Area Vocational Technical School
Supt. — None
Columbia-Montour AVTS Vo/Tech
5050 Sweppenheiser Dr 17815 570-784-8040
Cosmas Curry, prin. Fax 784-3565

Bloomsburg Area SD 1,800/K-12
728 E 5th St 17815 570-784-5000
Joseph Kelly, supt. Fax 387-8832
bloomsburgasd.schoolwires.com
Bloomsburg Area HS 500/9-12
1200 Railroad St 17815 570-784-6100
Daniel Bonomo, prin. Fax 387-3492
Bloomsburg Area MS 500/6-8
1100 Railroad St 17815 570-784-9100
Lee Gump, prin. Fax 387-3491

Central Columbia SD 2,200/K-12
4777 Old Berwick Rd 17815 570-784-2850
Harry Mathias, supt. Fax 387-0192
www.centralcolumbia.k12.pa.us/
Central Columbia HS 700/9-12
4777 Old Berwick Rd 17815 570-784-2833
Jeffrey Groshek, prin. Fax 784-0863
Central Columbia MS 700/5-8
4777 Old Berwick Rd 17815 570-784-2850
John Kurelia, prin. Fax 784-4935

Bloomsburg University of Pennsylvania Post-Sec.
400 E 2nd St 17815 570-389-4000
Columbia County Christian S 200/PK-12
123 Schoolhouse Rd 17815 570-784-2977
Scott Shaw, admin. Fax 784-1755
Keystone National High School Post-Sec.
420 W 5th St 17815 570-784-5220

Blossburg, Tioga, Pop. 1,477
Southern Tioga SD 2,300/K-12
241 Main St 16912 570-638-2183
Joseph M. Kalata, supt. Fax 638-3512
www.southerntioga.org
North Penn JSHS 300/7-12
300 Morris St 16912 570-638-2158
Albert Lindner, prin. Fax 638-2150
Other Schools – See Liberty, Mansfield

Blue Bell, Montgomery, Pop. 6,091

Montgomery County Community College Post-Sec.
340 Dekalb Pike 19422 215-641-6300
Reformed Episcopal Seminary Post-Sec.
826 2nd Ave 19422 610-292-9852

Boiling Springs, Cumberland, Pop. 1,978
South Middleton SD 2,200/K-12
4 Forge Rd 17007 717-240-2618
Patricia B. Sanker Ed.D., supt. Fax 258-1214
www.bubblers.k12.pa.us
Boiling Springs HS 700/9-12
4 Forge Rd 17007 717-258-6484
Joseph Mancuso, prin. Fax 258-5014
Yellow Breeches MS 500/6-8
4 Forge Rd 17007 717-258-6484
Frederick Withum, prin. Fax 258-0301

Boothwyn, Delaware, Pop. 5,069
Chichester SD
Supt. — See Aston
Chichester HS 1,200/9-12
PO Box 2100 19061 610-485-6881
James Donnelly, prin. Fax 485-6510
Chichester MS 1,200/5-8
PO Box 2100 19061 610-485-6881
Salvatore Salamone, prin. Fax 494-3064

Boswell, Somerset, Pop. 1,290
North Star SD 1,100/K-12
1200 Morris Ave 15531 814-629-5631
Dennis P. Leyman, supt. Fax 629-6181
www.northstar.k12.pa.us
North Star HS 400/9-12
400 Ohio St 15531 814-629-6651
Joseph Bradley, prin. Fax 629-9346

Boyertown, Berks, Pop. 3,946
Boyertown Area SD 7,000/K-12
911 Montgomery Ave 19512 610-367-6031
Dr. Harry Morgan, supt. Fax 369-7620
basd.netjunction.com
Boyertown Area JHS West 900/7-9
380 S Madison St 19512 610-369-7471
Gregory Galtere, prin.
Boyertown Area SHS 1,600/10-12
120 N Monroe St 19512 610-369-7435
Daniel Goffredo, prin. Fax 369-7533
Other Schools – See Gilbertsville

Bradford, McKean, Pop. 8,651
Bradford Area SD 2,900/PK-12
PO Box 375 16701 814-362-3841
Sandra Romanowski, supt. Fax 362-2552
www.bradfordareaschools.org
Bradford Area HS 1,000/9-12
81 Interstate Pkwy 16701 814-362-3845
Kenneth Coffman, prin. Fax 362-1765
Fretz MS 800/6-8
140 Lorana Ave 16701 814-362-3500
Tina Slaven, prin. Fax 362-1812

Bradford Regional Medical Center Post-Sec.
116 Interstate Pkwy 16701 814-362-8292
University of Pittsburgh at Bradford Post-Sec.
300 Campus Dr 16701 814-362-7500

Bridgeville, Allegheny, Pop. 5,022
Chartiers Valley SD
Supt. — See Pittsburgh
Chartiers Valley HS 1,100/9-12
50 Thoms Run Rd 15017 412-429-2273
Dr. Terri Flynn, prin. Fax 276-5808
Chartiers Valley MS 800/6-8
50 Thoms Run Rd 15017 412-429-2220
Betsy Sapienza, prin. Fax 429-2226

Bristol, Bucks, Pop. 9,810
Bristol Borough SD 1,300/PK-12
420 Buckley St 19007 215-781-1010
Dr. Broadus Davis, supt. Fax 781-1012
www.bbsd.org/
Bristol HS, 1801 Wilson Ave 19007 400/9-12
Thomas Shaffer, prin. 215-781-1030
Bristol MS, 1801 Wilson Ave 19007 200/7-8
Thomas Shaffer, prin. 215-781-1034

Bristol Township SD
Supt. — See Levittown
Roosevelt MS 500/7-9
1001 New Rodgers Rd 19007 215-788-0436
Ruth Geisel, prin. Fax 788-2629

Pennco Tech Post-Sec.
3815 Otter St 19007 215-824-3200

Brockway, Jefferson, Pop. 2,101
Brockway Area SD 1,200/K-12
40 North St 15824 814-265-8411
Stephen Zarlinski, supt. Fax 265-8498
www.brockway.k12.pa.us/
Brockway Area JSHS 500/7-12
100 Alexander St 15824 814-265-8414
Denise Carlini, prin. Fax 265-8413

Brodheadsville, Monroe, Pop. 1,389
Pleasant Valley SD 5,200/K-12
1 School Ln 18322 570-402-1000
Dr. Frank Pullo, supt. Fax 992-7275
www.pvbears.org/
Pleasant Valley MS 600/8-9
Route 115 18322 570-402-1000
Howard Drake, prin. Fax 992-6968
Pleasant Valley SHS 1,700/10-12
Route 209 18322 570-402-1000
John Gress, prin. Fax 992-7733

Brookhaven, Delaware, Pop. 7,849

Christian Academy 500/K-12
4301 Chandler Dr 19015 610-872-7600
Anita Gray, prin. Fax 876-2173

Brookville, Jefferson, Pop. 4,077
Brookville Area SD 1,900/K-12
PO Box 479 15825 814-849-8372
John Johnson, supt. Fax 849-6842
www.brookville.k12.pa.us
Brookville Area JSHS 900/7-12
PO Box 479 15825 814-849-1106
Keith Wolfe, prin. Fax 849-1117

Broomall, Delaware, Pop. 10,930
Marple Newtown SD
Supt. — See Newtown Square
Paxon Hollow MS 800/6-8
815 Paxon Hollow Rd 19008 610-359-4320
Stephen Subers Ed.D., prin.

CHI Institute/RETS Campus Post-Sec.
1991 Sproul Rd Ste 42 19008 610-353-7630

Brownstown, Lancaster, Pop. 834
Area Vocational Technical School
Supt. — None
Lancaster County CTC-Brownstown Vo/Tech
PO Box 519 17508 717-859-5100
Douglas Lyons, prin. Fax 859-4529

Brownsville, Fayette, Pop. 2,690
Brownsville Area SD 1,900/K-12
1025 Lewis St 15417 724-785-2021
Lawrence Golembiewski, supt. Fax 785-6988
www.basd.org
Brownsville Area HS 600/9-12
1 Falcon Dr 15417 724-785-8200
Richard Gates, prin. Fax 785-8930
Brownsville MS 300/7-8
2 Falcon Dr 15417 724-785-2155
Vincent Nosser, prin. Fax 785-2502

Bryn Athyn, Montgomery, Pop. 1,354

Academy of the New Church-Boys 100/9-12
PO Box 707 19009 267-502-2538
Scott Daum, prin. Fax 502-2617
Academy of the New Church-Girls 100/9-12
PO Box 707 19009 267-502-2556
Margaret Gladish, prin. Fax 502-2617
Bryn Athyn College of the New Church Post-Sec.
PO Box 717 19009 215-938-2543

Bryn Mawr, Montgomery, Pop. 3,271

American College Post-Sec.
270 S Bryn Mawr Ave 19010 610-526-1000
Baldwin S 600/PK-12
701 Montgomery Ave 19010 610-525-2700
Sally Powell, hdmstr. Fax 525-7534
Bryn Mawr College Post-Sec.
101 N Merion Ave 19010 610-526-5000
Country Day S of the Sacred Heart 400/PK-12
480 S Bryn Mawr Ave 19010 610-527-3915
Sr. Matthew MacDonald, hdmstr. Fax 527-0942
Harcum Junior College Post-Sec.
750 Montgomery Ave 19010 610-525-4100
Rosemont College Post-Sec.
1400 Montgomery Ave 19010 610-527-0200
Shipley S 900/PK-12
814 Yarrow St 19010 610-525-4300
Steven Piltch, prin. Fax 525-5082

Burgettstown, Washington, Pop. 1,521
Burgettstown Area SD 1,600/K-12
100 Bavington Rd 15021 724-947-8136
Deborah Jackson, supt. Fax 947-8143
www.burgettstown.k12.pa.us
Burgettstown MSHS 800/7-12
104 Bavington Rd 15021 724-947-8100
Tracy Schooley, prin. Fax 947-3325

Tri State Christian Academy 100/K-12
750 Steubenville Pike 15021 724-947-8722
J.R. Wright, admin. Fax 947-0821

Butler, Butler, Pop. 14,521
Area Vocational Technical School
Supt. — None
Butler County AVTS Vo/Tech
210 Campus Ln 16001 724-282-0735
Dr. Joseph Cunningham, prin. Fax 282-7448

Butler Area SD 8,200/K-12
110 Campus Ln 16001 724-287-8721
Dr. Edward Fink, supt.
www.butler.k12.pa.us
Butler Area Intermediate HS 1,400/9-10
551 Fairground Hill Rd 16001 724-287-8721
John Wyllie, prin.
Butler Area JHS 1,200/7-8
225 E North St 16001 724-287-8721
James Allen, prin. Fax 287-4996
Butler Area SHS 1,300/11-12
120 Campus Ln 16001 724-287-8721
Fax 287-1596

Butler Beauty School Post-Sec.
233 S Main St 16001 724-287-0708
Butler County Community College Post-Sec.
PO Box 1203 16003 724-287-8711

First Baptist Christian S 100/PK-12
221 New Castle St 16001 724-287-1188
Kenneth Kisler, prin. Fax 287-6934

Cairnbrook, Somerset
Shade-Central CSD 600/K-12
203 McGreagor Ave 15924 814-754-4648
Hubert Donahue Ph.D., supt. Fax 754-5848
www.shade.k12.pa.us
Shade JSHS 300/7-12
203 McGreagor Ave 15924 814-754-4648
Joseph Kimmel, prin.

California, Washington, Pop. 5,072
California Area SD 1,000/K-12
750 Orchard St 15419 724-938-2511
Dr. Robert T. Marks, supt. Fax 938-2587
www.calsd.k12.pa.us/
Other Schools – See Coal Center

California University of Pennsylvania Post-Sec.
250 University Ave 15419 724-938-4000

Cambridge Springs, Crawford, Pop. 2,282
Penncrest SD
Supt. — See Saegertown
Cambridge Springs JSHS 600/7-12
698 Venango Ave 16403 814-398-4631
David Nuhfer, prin. Fax 398-8343

Camp Hill, Cumberland, Pop. 7,424
Camp Hill SD 1,100/K-12
2627 Chestnut St 17011 717-901-2400
Connie R. Kindler, supt. Fax 901-2416
www.camphillsd.k12.pa.us
Camp Hill HS 400/9-12
100 S 24th St 17011 717-901-2500
James Robertson, prin. Fax 901-2614
Camp Hill MS 300/6-8
2401 Chestnut St 17011 717-901-2450
Mark Dolan, prin. Fax 901-2573

West Shore SD
Supt. — See Lewisberry
Allen MS, 4225 Gettysburg Rd 17011 500/6-8
Tammi Jones, prin. 717-901-9552
Cedar Cliff HS 1,400/9-12
1301 Carlisle Rd 17011 717-737-8654
Robert Savidge, prin. Fax 737-0874

Holy Spirit Hospital Post-Sec.
505 N 21st St 17011 717-763-2106
Trinity HS 600/9-12
3601 Simpson Ferry Rd 17011 717-761-1116
Dr. Nancy Burke, admin. Fax 761-7309

Canonsburg, Washington, Pop. 8,810
Area Vocational Technical School
Supt. — None
Western Area CTC Vo/Tech
688 Western Ave 15317 724-746-2890
Dr. Joseph Iannetti, prin. Fax 746-0817

Canon-McMillan SD 4,500/K-12
1 N Jefferson Ave 15317 724-746-2940
Nick Bayat Ed.D., supt. Fax 746-9184
www.cmsd.k12.pa.us
Canon-McMillan HS 1,400/9-12
314 Elm Street Ext 15317 724-745-1400
Dave Helinski, prin. Fax 745-2258
Canonsburg MS 700/7-8
25 E College St 15317 724-745-9030
Greg Taranto, prin. Fax 873-5230

Canton, Bradford, Pop. 1,745
Canton Area SD 1,200/K-12
139 E Main St 17724 570-673-3191
W. Jeffrey Johnston, supt. Fax 673-3680
www.canton.k12.pa.us
Canton JSHS 600/7-12
139 E Main St 17724 570-673-5134
Chris Bigger, prin. Fax 673-3680

Carbondale, Lackawanna, Pop. 9,348
Carbondale Area SD 1,500/K-12
101 Brooklyn St 18407 570-282-4660
Dominick Famularo, supt. Fax 282-6988
gateway.ca.k12.pa.us
Carbondale Area JSHS 800/7-12
101 Brooklyn St 18407 570-282-4500
Joseph Farrell, prin. Fax 282-7341

Carlisle, Cumberland, Pop. 18,108
Carlisle Area SD 4,800/K-12
623 W Penn St 17013 717-240-6800
Mary Kay Durham, supt. Fax 240-6898
www.carlisleschools.org
Carlisle HS 1,700/9-12
623 W Penn St 17013 717-240-6800
Gary Worley, prin. Fax 240-7145
Lamberton MS 500/6-8
623 W Penn St 17013 717-240-6800
Keith Colestock, prin. Fax 240-2066
Wilson MS 600/6-8
623 W Penn St 17013 717-240-6800
Wilfred Brousse, prin. Fax 240-2050

Carlisle Christian Academy 100/PK-12
1412 Holly Pike, 717-249-3692
Matthew Tuckey, admin. Fax 240-0644
Dickinson College Post-Sec.
PO Box 1773 17013 717-243-5121
Penn State Dickinson School of Law Post-Sec.
150 S College St 17013 717-240-5000

Carmichaels, Greene, Pop. 525
Carmichaels Area SD 1,100/K-12
225 N Vine St 15320 724-966-5045
Craig Baily, supt. Fax 966-8793
www.carmarea.org/Carm_Web/MainIndex.htm
Carmichaels Area JSHS 500/7-12
300 W Greene St 15320 724-966-5045
Lyn Shlosky, prin. Fax 966-5556

Carnegie, Allegheny, Pop. 8,149
Carlynton SD 1,600/K-12
435 Kings Hwy 15106 412-429-8400
Michael Panza, supt. Fax 429-2502
www.carlynton.k12.pa.us

Carlynton JSHS 800/7-12
435 Kings Hwy 15106 412-429-2500
Robert Susini, prin. Fax 429-2508

Catasauqua, Lehigh, Pop. 6,553
Catasauqua Area SD 1,700/K-12
201 N 14th St 18032 610-264-5571
Robert Spengler, supt. Fax 264-5618
www.cattysd.org
Catasauqua MS 600/5-8
850 Pine St 18032 610-264-4341
Melissa Inselmann, prin. Fax 264-5458
Other Schools – See Northampton

Catawissa, Columbia, Pop. 1,557
Southern Columbia Area SD 1,400/K-12
800 Southern Dr 17820 570-356-2331
Richard Beierschmitt, supt. Fax 356-2892
www.scasd.us/
Southern Columbia HS 500/9-12
812 Southern Dr 17820 570-356-3450
Paul Caputo, prin. Fax 356-2835
Southern Columbia MS 400/5-8
810 Southern Dr 17820 570-356-3400
Roger Nunkester, prin. Fax 356-2835

Center Valley, Lehigh
Southern Lehigh SD 3,000/K-12
5775 Main St 18034 610-282-3121
Joseph Liberati, supt. Fax 282-0193
www.slsd.org
Southern Lehigh HS 1,000/9-12
5800 Main St Unit 1 18034 610-282-1421
Christine Siegfried, prin. Fax 282-2965
Southern Lehigh MS 700/6-8
3715 Preston Ln 18034 610-282-3700
R. Ann Pope, prin. Fax 282-2963

DeSales University Post-Sec.
2755 Station Ave 18034 610-282-1100
Lehigh Valley College Post-Sec.
2809 Saucon Valley Rd 18034 800-227-9109

Chalfont, Bucks, Pop. 4,198
Central Bucks SD
Supt. — See Doylestown
Unami MS 900/7-9
160 Moyer Rd 18914 267-893-3400
David Bolton, prin. Fax 893-5820

Chambersburg, Franklin, Pop. 17,961
Area Vocational Technical School
Supt. — None
Franklin County CTC Vo/Tech
2463 Loop Rd, 717-263-9033
Jim Duffy, prin. Fax 263-6568

Chambersburg Area SD 8,200/PK-12
435 Stanley Ave 17201 717-263-9281
Dr. Joseph Padasak, supt.
www.chambersburg.k12.pa.us
Chambersburg Area SHS 1,800/10-12
511 S 6th St 17201 717-261-3328
Dr. Barry Purvis, prin. Fax 261-3490
Faust JHS 1,400/8-9
1957 Scotland Ave 17201 717-261-3369
David Shank, prin. Fax 261-3379

Cumberland Valley Christian S 400/PK-12
600 Miller St 17201 717-264-3266
Rev. Carl McKee, prin. Fax 264-0416
Shalom Christian Academy 500/PK-12
126 Social Island Rd, 717-375-2223
Conrad Swartzentruber, admin. Fax 375-2224
Wilson College Post-Sec.
1015 Philadelphia Ave 17201 717-264-4141
Wrightco Technologies Tech Training Inst Post-Sec.
225 Sollenberger Rd, 717-263-8142

Champion, Fayette

Champion Christian S 100/PK-12
2166 Indian Head Rd 15622 724-455-2122
Merle Skinner, pres. Fax 455-6651

Charleroi, Washington, Pop. 4,696
Area Vocational Technical School
Supt. — None
Mon Valley CTC Vo/Tech
1 Guttman Blvd 15022 724-489-9581
Bradley Deicas, prin.

Charleroi SD 1,700/K-12
125 Fecsen Dr 15022 724-483-3509
Dr. Brad Ferko, supt. Fax 483-3776
www.charleroisd.org
Charleroi Area HS 500/9-12
100 Fecsen Dr 15022 724-483-3575
Vince Vitori, prin. Fax 483-2294
Charleroi Area MS 400/6-8
100 Fecsen Dr 15022 724-483-3600
Mary Tickner, prin. Fax 489-9128

Chester, Delaware, Pop. 37,058
Chester-Upland SD 3,700/K-12
1720 Melrose Ave 19013 610-447-3600
Dr. Gloria Grantham, supt. Fax 447-3616
www.chesteruplandsd.org/
Chester HS 1,600/9-12
200 W 9th St 19013 610-447-3772
John Vann, prin. Fax 447-3682
Smedley MS 400/6-8
1701 Upland St 19013 610-447-3660
Howard Johnson, prin. Fax 447-3661

Widener University Post-Sec.
1 University Pl 19013 610-499-4000

Chesterbrook, Chester, Pop. 4,561

DeVry University Post-Sec.
701 Lee Rd Ste 103 19087 610-889-9980

Cheswick, Allegheny, Pop. 1,790
Allegheny Valley SD 1,200/K-12
300 Pearl Ave 15024 724-274-5300
Gabriel Ziccarelli Ph.D., supt. Fax 274-8040
www.avsd.k12.pa.us
Other Schools – See Springdale

Cheswick Christian Academy 200/K-12
1407 Pittsburgh St 15024 724-274-4846

Cheyney, Delaware

Cheyney University of Pennsylvania Post-Sec.
PO Box 200 19319 610-399-2000

Clairton, Allegheny, Pop. 8,081
Area Vocational Technical School
Supt. — None
Steel Center AVTS Vo/Tech
565 N Lewis Run Rd 15025 412-469-3200
John Sandrene, prin.

Clairton CSD 900/K-12
502 Mitchell Ave 15025 412-233-7090
Dr. Robert David, supt. Fax 233-4755
www.clairton.k12.pa.us/
Clairton HS 300/9-12
501 Waddell Ave 15025 412-233-9200
Donald MacFann, prin. Fax 233-3243
Clairton MS 200/5-8
501 Waddell Ave 15025 412-233-9200
Daniel Stephens, prin. Fax 233-3243

Claridge, Westmoreland
Penn-Trafford SD
Supt. — See Harrison City
Penn MS 700/6-8
PO Box 399 15623 724-744-4431
Ronald Darragh, prin. Fax 744-1215

Clarion, Clarion, Pop. 5,507
Clarion Area SD 900/K-12
221 Liberty St 16214 814-226-6110
George White, supt. Fax 226-9292
www.clarion-schools.com
Clarion Area JSHS 500/7-12
219 Liberty St 16214 814-226-8112
Todd MacBeth, prin. Fax 226-9004

Clarion University of Pennsylvania Post-Sec.
840 Wood St 16214 814-393-2000

Clarks Summit, Lackawanna, Pop. 5,010
Abington Heights SD 3,600/K-12
200 E Grove St 18411 570-586-2511
Michael Mahon, supt. Fax 586-1756
www.ahsd.org
Abington Heights HS 1,200/9-12
222 Noble Rd 18411 570-585-5300
Susan Sallavanti, prin. Fax 586-9093
Abington Heights MS 1,200/5-8
1555 Newton Ransom Blvd 18411 570-586-1281
Edward Kairis, prin. Fax 586-6361

Baptist Bible College and Seminary Post-Sec.
538 Venard Rd 18411 570-586-2400
Summit Christian Academy 100/PK-12
660 Griffin Pond Rd 18411 570-587-1545
Tim Connor, admin. Fax 586-5849

Claysburg, Blair, Pop. 1,399
Claysburg-Kimmel SD 900/K-12
RR 1 Box 522 16625 814-239-5141
James O'Harrow, supt. Fax 239-5896
www.cksd.k12.pa.us
Claysburg-Kimmel JSHS 400/7-12
RR 1 Box 522 16625 814-239-5141
Dr. Gunter Moritz, prin. Fax 239-8949

Claysville, Washington, Pop. 695
McGuffey SD 2,300/K-12
PO Box 431 15323 724-663-7745
Joseph Stefka, supt. Fax 663-5465
mcguffey.k12.pa.us
McGuffey HS 800/9-12
86 McGuffey Dr 15323 724-948-3328
Keith Kucherawy, prin. Fax 948-3344
McGuffey MS 600/6-8
86 McGuffey Dr 15323 724-948-3323
Beverly Arbore, prin. Fax 948-2413

Clearfield, Clearfield, Pop. 6,339
Area Vocational Technical School
Supt. — None
Clearfield County CTC Vo/Tech
1620 River Rd 16830 814-765-5308
Lois Richards, prin. Fax 765-5474

Clearfield Area SD 2,700/K-12
PO Box 710 16830 814-765-5511
Dr. Denise Keltz, supt. Fax 765-5515
www.clearfield.org
Clearfield Area HS 1,000/9-12
PO Box 910 16830 814-765-2401
John Law, prin. Fax 765-2405
Clearfield Area MS 700/5-8
PO Box 710 16830 814-765-5302
Timothy Meckey, prin. Fax 765-4604

Clearfield Alliance Christian S 100/K-12
56 Alliance Rd 16830 814-765-0216
Clearfield Beauty Academy Post-Sec.
22 N 3rd St 16830 814-765-2022
Clearfield Hospital Post-Sec.
PO Box 992 16830 814-768-2496
Lock Haven University-Clearfield Campus Post-Sec.
PO Box 1410 16830 814-765-0559

Clymer, Indiana, Pop. 1,467
Penns Manor Area SD 1,000/K-12
6003 Route 553 Hwy 15728 724-254-2666
Dr. Thomas Sgriccia, supt. Fax 254-3418
www.pennsmanor.org/
Penns Manor Area JSHS 500/7-12
6003 Route 553 Hwy 15728 724-254-2666
Daren Johnston, prin. Fax 254-3418

Coal Center, Washington, Pop. 130
California Area SD
Supt. — See California
California Area HS 400/9-12
293 Malden Rd 15423 724-785-5800
Brian Jackson, prin. Fax 785-8860
California Area MS 300/6-8
293 Malden Rd 15423 724-785-5800
Raymond Huffman, prin. Fax 785-5458

Coal Township, Northumberland, Pop. 9,922
Area Vocational Technical School
Supt. — None
Northumberland County AVTS Vo/Tech
1700 W Montgomery St 17866 570-644-0304
Robert Beierschmitt, prin.

Shamokin Area SD 2,500/PK-12
2000 W State St 17866 570-648-5752
James Zack, supt. Fax 648-2592
www.indians.k12.pa.us/
Shamokin Area JSHS 1,300/7-12
2000 W State St 17866 570-648-5731
Chris Venna, prin.

Our Lady of Lourdes Regional S 200/K-12
2001 Clinton Ave 17866 570-644-0375
John McKay, admin. Fax 644-7655

Coatesville, Chester, Pop. 11,495
Area Vocational Technical School
Supt. — None
Center for Arts & Tech - Brandywine Vo/Tech
1635 E Lincoln Hwy 19320 610-384-1585
Richard Saylor, prin.

Coatesville Area SD 7,200/K-12
545 E Lincoln Hwy 19320 610-466-2400
Richard Como, supt. Fax 383-1426
www.coatesville.k12.pa.us/
Coatesville Area 9-10 Center 1,300/9-10
1425 E Lincoln Hwy 19320 610-383-3735
Robert Fisher, prin. Fax 383-3723
Coatesville Area SHS 1,100/11-12
1445 E Lincoln Hwy 19320 610-383-3730
Robert Fisher, prin. Fax 383-3725
North Brandywine MS 600/6-8
256 Reeceville Rd 19320 610-383-3745
Chamise Taylor, prin. Fax 383-3749
Scott MS 600/6-8
800 Olive St 19320 610-383-6946
Teresa Powell, prin. Fax 383-7110
South Brandywine MS 600/6-8
600 Doe Run Rd 19320 610-383-3750
John Reid, prin. Fax 383-3754

Brandywine Hospital Post-Sec.
201 Reeceville Rd 19320 610-383-9000
Lan-Chester Christian S 100/PK-12
200 Airport Rd 19320 610-383-5784
Fax 383-5894

Cochranton, Crawford, Pop. 1,092
Crawford Central SD
Supt. — See Meadville
Cochranton JSHS 400/7-12
PO Box 127 16314 814-425-7421
Donald K. Wigton, prin. Fax 425-2071

Collegeville, Montgomery, Pop. 5,055
Perkiomen Valley SD 5,100/K-12
3 Iron Bridge Dr 19426 610-489-8506
Dr. Priscilla Feir, supt. Fax 489-2974
www.pvsd.org
Perkiomen Valley East MS 600/6-8
100 Kagey Rd 19426 610-409-8580
Jeferey Madden, prin. Fax 409-0625
Perkiomen Valley HS 1,300/9-12
509 Gravel Pike 19426 610-489-1230
John Romanoski, prin. Fax 489-1921
Other Schools – See Zieglerville

Spring-Ford Area SD 6,800/K-12
199 Bechtel Rd 19426 610-705-6000
Marsha Hurda Ed.D., supt. Fax 705-6245
www.spring-ford.net
Other Schools – See Royersford

Ursinus College Post-Sec.
PO Box 1000 19426 610-409-3000
Valley Forge Baptist Academy 200/K-12
616 S Trappe Rd 19426 610-792-1884
Lois Rall, prin. Fax 948-6423

Columbia, Lancaster, Pop. 10,092
Columbia Borough SD 1,500/K-12
200 N 5th St 17512 717-684-2283
Barry Clippinger, supt. Fax 681-2617
www.columbia.k12.pa.us
Columbia JSHS 700/7-12
901 Ironville Pike 17512 717-684-7500
Virginia Babic, prin. Fax 681-2219

NAWCC School of Horology Post-Sec.
514 Poplar St 17512 717-684-8261

Commodore, Indiana
Purchase Line SD, PO Box 374 15729 1,200/K-12
Dr. Richard Makin, supt. 724-254-4312
www.plsd.k12.pa.us/
Purchase Line JSHS 600/7-12
PO Box 374 15729 724-254-4312
James Price, prin.

Confluence, Somerset, Pop. 793
Turkeyfoot Valley Area SD 400/K-12
172 Turkeyfoot Rd 15424 814-395-3621
Ric Toner, supt. Fax 395-3366
www.turkeyfoot.k12.pa.us
Turkeyfoot Valley Area JSHS 200/7-12
172 Turkeyfoot Rd 15424 814-395-3622
Darlene Sherrard, prin. Fax 395-3366

Conneaut Lake, Crawford, Pop. 676
Conneaut SD
Supt. — See Linesville
Conneaut Lake JSHS 600/7-12
10331 US Highway 6 16316 814-382-5315
Richard Rossi, prin. Fax 382-0165

Conneautville, Crawford, Pop. 807
Conneaut SD
Supt. — See Linesville
Conneaut Valley JSHS 400/7-12
22154 Highway 18 16406 814-587-2091
Kevin Burns, prin. Fax 587-2094

Connellsville, Fayette, Pop. 8,644
Area Vocational Technical School
Supt. — None
Connellsville Area CTC Vo/Tech
720 Locust St 15425 724-626-0236
Albert Kanaan, prin.

Connellsville Area SD 5,600/K-12
732 Rockridge Rd 15425 724-628-3300
James Duncan, supt. Fax 628-9002
www.casdfalcons.org
Connellsville Area SHS 1,400/10-12
201 Falcon Dr 15425 724-628-1350
Tammy Duncan, prin. Fax 628-0280
Connellsville JHS East 800/7-9
710 Locust St 15425 724-628-8910
Charles Geyer, prin.
Connellsville JHS West 600/7-9
215 Falls Ave 15425 724-628-4497
John Schroyer, prin.

Geibel Catholic HS 300/9-12
611 E Crawford Ave 15425 724-628-5600
Vincent Mascia, prin. Fax 626-5700

Coraopolis, Allegheny, Pop. 5,754
Cornell SD 500/K-12
1099 Maple Street Ext 15108 412-264-5010
Dr. Erv Weischedel, supt. Fax 264-1445
www.cornell.k12.pa.us
Cornell JSHS 100/7-12
1099 Maple Street Ext 15108 412-264-5010
Donna Belas, prin. Fax 264-1445

Montour SD
Supt. — See Mc Kees Rocks
Williams MS 1,000/5-8
0 Porters Hollow Rd 15108 412-771-8802
Melissa Heasley, prin. Fax 771-3772

Moon Area SD 3,800/K-12
8353 University Blvd 15108 412-264-9440
Dr. Alexander Meta, supt. Fax 264-3268
www.masd.k12.pa.us
Other Schools – See Moon Township

Our Lady of Sacred Heart HS 300/9-12
1504 Woodcrest Ave 15108 412-264-5140
Sr. Francine Horos, prin. Fax 264-4143
Robert Morris University Post-Sec.
6001 University Blvd 15108 412-262-8200

Corry, Erie, Pop. 6,548
Corry Area SD 2,500/K-12
800 E South St 16407 814-664-4677
Dr. Brian M. Dougherty, supt. Fax 664-9645
www.corrysd.net
Corry Area HS 800/9-12
534 E Pleasant St 16407 814-665-8297
Kelly Cragg, prin. Fax 664-3650
Corry MS 400/7-8
534 E Pleasant St 16407 814-665-8297
Gail Swank, prin. Fax 664-3650

Coudersport, Potter, Pop. 2,551
Coudersport Area SD 1,000/K-12
698 Dwight St 16915 814-274-9480
George Nuffer, supt. Fax 274-7551
www.coudersportschools.com
Coudersport Area JSHS 500/7-12
698 Dwight St 16915 814-274-8500
Alanna Huck, prin. Fax 274-8053

Cranberry Township, Butler

Pittsburgh Technical Institute Post-Sec.
850 Cranberry Woods Dr 16066 866-233-5556

Cresson, Cambria, Pop. 1,538
Penn Cambria SD 1,800/K-12
201 6th St 16630 814-886-8121
Mary Beth Whited, supt. Fax 886-4809
www.pcam.org
Penn Cambria HS 700/9-12
401 Linden Ave 16630 814-886-8188
Guy Monica, prin. Fax 884-3977
Other Schools – See Gallitzin

Mount Aloysius College Post-Sec.
7373 Admiral Peary Hwy 16630 814-886-4131

Curwensville, Clearfield, Pop. 2,540
Curwensville Area SD 1,200/K-12
650 Beech St 16833 814-236-1101
Norman Hatten, supt. Fax 236-1103
www.curwensville.org/
Curwensville Area JSHS 600/7-12
650 Beech St 16833 814-236-1100
Alan Nichol, prin. Fax 236-2392

Dallas, Luzerne, Pop. 2,508
Dallas SD 2,600/K-12
PO Box 2000 18612 570-674-7221
Frank P. Galicki, supt. Fax 674-7295
www.dallassd.com/
Dallas HS 800/9-12
PO Box 2000 18612 570-674-7230
Deborah Morgantini, prin. Fax 674-6843
Dallas MS 700/6-8
PO Box 2000 18612 570-674-7245
Anthony Martinelli, prin. Fax 674-7219

College Misericordia Post-Sec.
301 Lake St 18612 570-674-6400

Dallastown, York, Pop. 4,080
Dallastown Area SD — 5,500/K-12
700 New School Ln 17313 — 717-244-4021
Dr. Stewart Weinberg, supt. — Fax 246-0597
www.dallastown.net/
Dallastown Area HS — 1,700/9-12
700 New School Ln 17313 — 717-244-4021
Dr. Alan Fauth, prin. — Fax 244-8813
Dallastown Area MS — 1,400/6-8
700 New School Ln 17313 — 717-244-4021
Dr. Robert Krantz, prin. — Fax 244-0350

Danville, Montour, Pop. 4,640
Danville Area SD — 2,600/K-12
600 Walnut St 17821 — 570-271-3268
Steven P. Keifer, supt. — Fax 275-7712
www.danville.k12.pa.us
Danville Area HS — 800/9-12
600 Walnut St 17821 — 570-271-3268
Craig Burger, prin. — Fax 275-5463
Danville Area MS — 700/6-8
120 Northumberland St 17821 — 570-271-3268
Kevin Duckworth, prin. — Fax 275-1281

Geisinger Medical Center — Post-Sec.
100 N Academy Ave 17822 — 570-271-5200

Darby, Delaware, Pop. 10,046
William Penn SD
Supt. — See Lansdowne
Penn Wood West MS — 500/7-8
121 Summit St 19023 — 610-586-1804
Brian Wilson, prin. — Fax 586-7372

Davidsville, Somerset, Pop. 1,167
Conemaugh Township Area SD — 1,100/K-12
PO Box 407 15928 — 814-479-7575
Dr. Joseph DiBartola, supt. — Fax 479-2620
www.ctasd.org
Conemaugh Township Area JSHS — 600/7-12
PO Box 407 15928 — 814-479-4014
David Koba, prin. — Fax 479-2038

Denver, Lancaster, Pop. 3,646
Cocalico SD — 3,600/K-12
PO Box 800 17517 — 717-336-1413
Bruce Sensenig, supt. — Fax 336-1415
www.cocalico.k12.pa.us/
Cocalico HS — 1,200/9-12
PO Box 800 17517 — 717-336-1421
Andrew Terry, prin. — Fax 336-1486
Cocalico MS — 900/6-8
PO Box 800 17517 — 717-336-1471
Donald Jones, prin. — Fax 336-1482

Gehmans Mennonite S — 200/K-12
650 Gehman School Rd 17517 — 717-484-4222
Melvin Weaver, prin. — Fax 484-4222

Derry, Westmoreland, Pop. 2,869
Derry Area SD — 2,700/K-12
982 N Chestnut Street Ext 15627 — 724-694-1401
Joseph Bellissimo, supt. — Fax 694-1429
wiu.k12.pa.us/derry
Derry Area HS — 900/9-12
988 N Chestnut Street Ext 15627 — 724-694-2780
Kathy Perry, prin. — Fax 694-1489
Derry Area MS — 700/6-8
994 N Chestnut Street Ext 15627 — 724-694-8231
David Sroka, prin. — Fax 694-1459

Devon, Chester, Pop. 5,019

Devon Preparatory S — 300/6-12
363 N Valley Forge Rd 19333 — 610-688-7337
Rev. James Shea, hdmstr. — Fax 688-2409

Dillsburg, York, Pop. 2,321
Northern York County SD — 3,200/K-12
149 S Baltimore St 17019 — 717-432-8691
Brian Small, supt. — Fax 432-1421
www.northernpolarbears.com
Northern HS — 1,100/9-12
653 S Baltimore St 17019 — 717-432-8691
Steve Bowman, prin. — Fax 432-0375
Northern MS — 800/6-8
655 S Baltimore St 17019 — 717-432-8691
Sylvia Murray, prin. — Fax 432-5889

Dimock, Susquehanna
Area Vocational Technical School
Supt. — None
Susquehanna County Career & Tech. Center — Vo/Tech
PO Box 100 18816 — 570-278-9229
Alice Davis, dir. — Fax 278-3913

Elk Lake SD — 1,500/K-12
PO Box 100 18816 — 570-278-1106
William Bush, supt. — Fax 278-4838
www.elklakeschool.org
Elk Lake JSHS — 800/7-12
PO Box 100 18816 — 570-278-1106
Kenneth Cuomo, prin. — Fax 278-4838

Dingmans Ferry, Pike
Delaware Valley SD
Supt. — See Milford
Dingman-Delaware MS — 700/6-8
1365 Route 739 18328 — 570-296-3140
Joseph Caramanica, prin. — Fax 296-3170

East Stroudsburg Area SD
Supt. — See East Stroudsburg
East Stroudsburg HS North — 1,200/9-12
HC 12 Box 690 18328 — 570-588-4420
Patricia Mulroy, prin. — Fax 588-4421
Lehman IS — 900/6-8
HC 12 Box 695 18328 — 570-588-4410
Stephen Zall, prin. — Fax 588-4411

Douglassville, Berks
Daniel Boone Area SD
Supt. — See Birdsboro
Boone Area MS — 900/6-8
1845 Weavertown Rd 19518 — 610-689-6300
Thomas Hankel, prin. — Fax 689-6306

Dover, York, Pop. 1,922
Dover Area SD — 3,400/K-12
2 School Ln 17315 — 717-292-3671
Dr. Richard D. Nilsen, supt. — Fax 292-9659
www.dover.k12.pa.us
Dover Area HS — 1,000/9-12
46 W Canal St 17315 — 717-292-3671
Joel Riedel, prin. — Fax 292-7303
Dover Area IS — 600/7-8
4500 Intermediate Ave 17315 — 717-292-3671
Kenneth Walter, prin. — Fax 292-9849

Downingtown, Chester, Pop. 7,858
Downingtown Area SD — 11,000/K-12
126 Wallace Ave 19335 — 610-269-8460
Dr. Sandra Griffin, supt. — Fax 873-1404
www.dasd.org
Downingtown HS - West Campus — 1,800/9-12
445 Manor Ave 19335 — 610-269-4400
Dr. Tony Watson, prin. — Fax 269-1801
Downingtown MS — 1,300/6-8
115 Rock Raymond Rd 19335 — 610-518-0685
Thomas Mulvey, prin. — Fax 518-0685
Other Schools – See Exton

Bishop Shanahan HS — 1,300/9-12
220 Woodbine Rd 19335 — 610-518-1300
Sr. Maureen McDermott, prin. — Fax 343-6220

Doylestown, Bucks, Pop. 8,225
Central Bucks SD — 19,400/K-12
16 Weldon Dr 18901 — 267-893-2000
Dr. N. Robert Laws, supt. — Fax 893-5800
www.cbsd.org
Central Bucks SHS - East — 2,200/10-12
2804 Holicong Rd, — 267-893-2300
Abram Lucabaugh, prin. — Fax 794-5446
Central Bucks SHS - West — 2,200/10-12
375 W Court St 18901 — 267-893-2500
J. Kevin Munnelly, prin. — Fax 348-9832
Holicong MS — 1,100/7-9
2900 Holicong Rd, — 267-893-2700
Jason Bucher, prin. — Fax 893-5816
Lenape MS — 800/7-9
313 W State St 18901 — 267-893-2800
H. Nicholas Chubb Ed.D., prin. — Fax 345-4699
Tohickon MS — 1,100/7-9
5051 Old Easton Rd 18901 — 267-893-3300
John L. Skari, prin. — Fax 893-5819
Other Schools – See Chalfont, Warrington

Delaware Valley College — Post-Sec.
700 E Butler Ave 18901 — 215-345-1500

Dresher, Montgomery
Upper Dublin SD
Supt. — See Maple Glen
Sandy Run MS — 1,100/6-8
520 Twining Rd 19025 — 215-576-3251
Neil Evans, prin. — Fax 572-3886

Bethel Seminary of the East — Post-Sec.
1605 Limekiln Pike 19025 — 215-641-4801

Drexel Hill, Delaware, Pop. 29,300
Upper Darby SD — 12,000/K-12
4611 Bond Ave 19026 — 610-789-7200
Joseph Galli, supt. — Fax 789-8671
www.udsd.k12.pa.us
Drexel Hill MS, 3001 State Rd 19026 — 1,500/6-8
Jonathan Ross, prin. — 610-853-4580
Upper Darby HS — 4,000/9-12
601 N Lansdowne Ave 19026 — 610-622-7000
Geoffrey Kramer, prin. — Fax 622-7844
Other Schools – See Upper Darby

Archbishop Prendergast HS — 900/9-12
401 N Lansdowne Ave 19026 — 610-259-0265
Sr. Catherine Robinson, prin. — Fax 259-3676
Monsignor Bonner HS — 1,000/9-12
403 N Lansdowne Ave 19026 — 610-259-0280
William Brannick, prin. — Fax 259-1630

Du Bois, Clearfield, Pop. 8,117
Du Bois Area SD — 4,400/K-12
500 Liberty Blvd 15801 — 814-371-2700
Sharon Kirk, supt. — Fax 371-2544
www.dasd.k12.pa.us
Du Bois Area HS — 1,400/9-12
425 Orient Ave 15801 — 814-371-8111
Timothy Glunt, prin. — Fax 371-3928
Du Bois Area MS — 1,100/6-8
404 Liberty Blvd 15801 — 814-375-8770
Daniel Hawkins, prin. — Fax 375-8780

DuBois Business College — Post-Sec.
1 Beaver Dr 15801 — 814-371-6920
Du Bois Central Catholic HS — 200/9-12
PO Box 567 15801 — 814-371-3060
Kathleen Kunkle, admin. — Fax 371-3215
Du Bois Central Catholic MS — 100/6-8
PO Box 567 15801 — 814-371-3060
Deborah Heigel, admin. — Fax 371-3215
DuBois Christian S — 100/PK-12
199 Eastern Ave 15801 — 814-371-7395
Greg Reese, prin. — Fax 371-7399
PA Academy of Cosmetic Arts & Sciences — Post-Sec.
19 N Brady St 15801 — 814-371-4151
Pennsylvania State University — Post-Sec.
College Place 15801 — 814-375-4700
Triangle Tech — Post-Sec.
PO Box 551 15801 — 814-371-2090

Duke Center, McKean
Otto-Eldred SD — 800/K-12
143 Sweitzer Dr 16729 — 814-966-3214
Robert Falk, supt. — Fax 966-3911
www.ottoeldred.org
Otto-Eldred JSHS — 400/7-12
143 Sweitzer Dr 16729 — 814-966-3212
Matthew Splain, prin. — Fax 966-3911

Duncannon, Perry, Pop. 1,496
Susquenita SD — 2,200/K-12
1725 Schoolhouse Rd 17020 — 717-957-6000
Dr. Daniel Sheats, supt. — Fax 834-5523
www.susq.k12.pa.us/
Susquenita HS — 700/9-12
1725 Schoolhouse Rd 17020 — 717-957-6000
Nancy Valdez, prin. — Fax 834-6653
Susquenita MS — 800/5-8
1725 Schoolhouse Rd 17020 — 717-957-6000
Steve Blasco, prin. — Fax 957-9334

Duncansville, Blair, Pop. 1,194

Blair County Christian S — 100/PK-12
PO Box 840 16635 — 814-696-3702
Stephen Ashmore, prin. — Fax 696-2783

Dunmore, Lackawanna, Pop. 13,968
Dunmore SD — 1,700/K-12
300 W Warren St 18512 — 570-343-2110
Richard McDonald, supt. — Fax 343-1458
www.dunmoreschooldistrict.net/
Dunmore HS — 600/9-12
300 W Warren St 18512 — 570-346-2043
James Forgione, prin. — Fax 343-1458
Dunmore MS — 300/7-8
300 W Warren St 18512 — 570-346-2043
John Barrett, prin. — Fax 343-1458

Holy Cross HS - Bishop O'Hara Campus — 300/9-12
501 E Drinker St 18512 — 570-346-7541
Anita Sirak, prin. — Fax 348-1070
Pennsylvania State University — Post-Sec.
120 Ridgeview Dr 18512 — 570-963-4757

Duquesne, Allegheny, Pop. 6,875
Duquesne CSD — 900/PK-12
300 Kennedy Ave 15110 — 412-466-5300
Jacquelyn D. Webb Ph.D., supt. — Fax 466-7599
Duquesne MSHS — 400/6-12
300 Kennedy Ave 15110 — 412-466-0714
Daniel Stephens, prin. — Fax 466-2197

Dushore, Sullivan, Pop. 613
Sullivan County SD — 800/K-12
PO Box 346 18614 — 570-928-8194
Dr. Kathryn Gruber, supt. — Fax 928-8196
www.sulcosd.k12.pa.us
Other Schools – See Laporte

East Greenville, Montgomery, Pop. 3,085
Upper Perkiomen SD — 3,300/K-12
201 W 5th St 18041 — 215-679-7961
Dr. Timothy Kirby, supt. — Fax 679-0885
www.upsd.org/
Upper Perkiomen MS — 1,000/5-8
510 Jefferson St 18041 — 215-679-6288
Duane Wickard, prin. — Fax 679-3091
Other Schools – See Pennsburg

Easton, Northampton, Pop. 26,267
Area Vocational Technical School
Supt. — None
Career Inst of Technology — Vo/Tech
5335 Kesslersville Rd 18040 — 610-258-2857
Ronald Roth, prin.

Easton Area SD — 8,600/K-12
1801 Bushkill Dr 18040 — 610-250-2400
Dennis Riker, supt. — Fax 923-8954
www.eastonsd.org
Easton Area HS — 2,800/9-12
2601 William Penn Hwy 18045 — 610-250-2481
William Rider, prin. — Fax 250-2483
Shawnee MS — 1,400/7-8
1010 Echo Trl 18040 — 610-250-2460
Stephen Furst, prin. — Fax 250-2613

Wilson Area SD — 2,200/K-12
2040 Washington Blvd 18042 — 484-373-6000
Douglas Wagner, supt. — Fax 258-6421
www.wilsonareasd.org
Lauer MS — 600/6-8
2400 Firmstone St 18042 — 484-373-6110
Dennis Harper, prin. — Fax 258-4014
Wilson Area HS — 700/9-12
424 Warrior Ln 18042 — 484-373-6030
John Martuscelli, prin. — Fax 258-8831

Lafayette College — Post-Sec.
High St 18042 — 610-330-5000
Notre Dame HS — 600/9-12
3417 Church Rd 18045 — 610-868-1431
Joseph Kramer, prin. — Fax 868-6710
Rock Christian Academy — 50/PK-12
PO Box 636 18044 — 610-253-8161
Arlene Santos, admin. — Fax 250-8794

East Stroudsburg, Monroe, Pop. 10,621
East Stroudsburg Area SD — 7,900/K-12
PO Box 298 18301 — 570-424-8500
Dr. Rachael Heath, supt. — Fax 424-5646
www.esasd.net
East Stroudsburg HS South — 1,400/9-12
279 N Courtland St 18301 — 570-424-8471
Lois Palio, prin. — Fax 420-8353
Lambert IS — 1,100/6-8
2000 Milford Rd 18301 — 570-424-8430
Michael Catrillo, prin. — Fax 476-0464
Other Schools – See Dingmans Ferry

East Stroudsburg University of PA — Post-Sec.
200 Prospect St 18301 — 570-424-3211
Notre Dame JSHS — 400/5-12
60 Spangenburg Ave 18301 — 570-421-0466
Jeffrey Lyons, prin. — Fax 476-0629

Ebensburg, Cambria, Pop. 2,938
Area Vocational Technical School
Supt. — None
Admiral Peary AVTS — Vo/Tech
948 Ben Franklin Hwy 15931 — 814-472-6490
Mark Kudlawiec, prin. — Fax 472-6494

Central Cambria SD — 1,900/K-12
208 Schoolhouse Rd 15931 — 814-472-8870
Dr. Susan Makosy, supt. — Fax 472-9695
www.cchs.k12.pa.us/
Central Cambria HS — 700/9-12
204 Schoolhouse Rd 15931 — 814-472-8860
Kenneth Bussard, prin. — Fax 472-8886

Central Cambria MS 400/6-8
205 W Highland Ave 15931 814-472-6505
Kimberly McDermott, prin. Fax 472-4187

Bishop Carroll HS 300/9-12
728 Ben Franklin Hwy 15931 814-472-7500
Kristie Wolfe, prin. Fax 472-8020
Pennsylvania Institute of Taxidermy Post-Sec.
118 Industrial Park Rd 15931 814-472-4510
Wrightco Technologies Tech Training Inst Post-Sec.
728 Ben Franklin Hwy 15931 814-472-5211

Edinboro, Erie, Pop. 6,737
General McLane SD 2,400/K-12
11771 Edinboro Rd 16412 814-734-1033
Alan J. Karns, supt. Fax 734-4635
www.generalmclane.org
McLane HS 900/9-12
11761 Edinboro Rd 16412 814-734-1602
Richard Scaletta, prin. Fax 734-5250
Parker MS 700/5-8
11781 Edinboro Rd 16412 814-734-1151
Annette Rilling, prin. Fax 734-7485

Edinboro University of Pennsylvania Post-Sec.
16444 814-732-2000

Elderton, Armstrong, Pop. 343
Armstrong SD
Supt. — See Ford City
Elderton JSHS 400/7-12
Lytle St 15736 724-354-2153
David Kristofic, prin. Fax 354-4303

Elizabeth, Allegheny, Pop. 1,505
Elizabeth Forward SD 2,900/K-12
401 Rock Run Rd 15037 412-896-2300
Michael Latusek, supt. Fax 751-9483
www.efsd.net
Elizabeth Forward HS 1,000/9-12
1000 Weigles Hill Rd 15037 412-896-2349
Dr. David Bowlin, prin. Fax 384-2030
Elizabeth Forward MS 800/6-8
401 Rock Run Rd 15037 412-896-2335
Jennifer Meliton, prin. Fax 751-6669

Elizabethtown, Lancaster, Pop. 11,892
Elizabethtown Area SD 4,000/K-12
600 E High St 17022 717-367-1521
Dr. Allan Thrush, supt. Fax 367-1920
www.etown.k12.pa.us
Elizabethtown Area HS 1,300/9-12
600 E High St 17022 717-367-1533
Richard Schwarzman, prin. Fax 367-4149
Elizabethtown Area MS 1,000/6-8
600 E High St 17022 717-361-7525
Richard Schwarzman, prin. Fax 361-2597

Elizabethtown College Post-Sec.
1 Alpha Dr 17022 717-361-1000
Mt. Calvary Christian S 400/PK-12
629 Holly St 17022 717-367-1649
Kenneth Howard, admin. Fax 367-5672

Elizabethville, Dauphin, Pop. 1,295
Upper Dauphin Area SD
Supt. — See Lykens
Upper Dauphin Area HS 400/9-12
220 N Church St 17023 717-362-8181
Timothy Foley, prin. Fax 362-8088

Elkins Park, Montgomery, Pop. 4,700
Cheltenham Township SD 4,700/K-12
1000 Ashbourne Rd 19027 215-886-9500
Dr. William Kiefer, supt. Fax 884-3029
www.cheltenham.org
Other Schools – See Wyncote

Medical College Hospitals Post-Sec.
60 Township Line Rd 19027 215-663-6150
Pennsylvania College of Optometry Post-Sec.
8360 Old York Rd 19027 215-780-1400
Temple University Tyler School of Art Post-Sec.
7725 Penrose Ave 19027 215-782-2875

Elkland, Tioga, Pop. 1,722
Northern Tioga SD 2,500/K-12
117 Coates Ave 16920 814-258-5642
Timothy Bowers, supt. Fax 258-7083
www.ntiogasd.org
Elkland Area JSHS 300/7-12
110 Ellison Rd 16920 814-258-5115
Thomas Butler, prin. Fax 258-7700
Other Schools – See Tioga, Westfield

Elliottsburg, Perry
West Perry SD 2,800/K-12
2606 Shermans Valley Rd 17024 717-789-3934
Dr. David R. Hoover, supt. Fax 789-4997
www.westperry.k12.pa.us/
West Perry HS 900/9-12
2608 Shermans Valley Rd 17024 717-789-3931
Fax 789-2110
West Perry MS 700/6-8
2620 Shermans Valley Rd 17024 717-789-3012
Bernard Danko, prin. Fax 789-3393

Ellsworth, Washington, Pop. 1,039
Bentworth SD
Supt. — See Bentleyville
Bentworth MS 200/7-8
89 Pine St 15331 724-239-4431
David Schreiber, prin. Fax 239-5889

Ellwood City, Lawrence, Pop. 8,262
Ellwood City Area SD 2,100/K-12
501 Crescent Ave 16117 724-752-1591
Frank Aloi, supt. Fax 752-0743
www.ellwood.k12.pa.us
Lincoln JSHS 1,000/7-12
501 Crescent Ave 16117 724-752-1591
Joseph Mancini, prin. Fax 752-0743

Riverside Beaver County SD 1,600/K-12
318 Country Club Dr 16117 724-758-7512
Dr. David J. Parry, supt. Fax 758-2070
www.riverside.k12.pa.us
Riverside HS 700/9-12
300 Country Club Dr 16117 724-758-7512
Michael Leitera, prin. Fax 758-7519
Riverside MS 300/7-8
302 Country Club Dr 16117 724-758-7512
Raymond Santillo, prin. Fax 758-0919

Elverson, Chester, Pop. 1,164
Twin Valley SD 3,200/K-12
4851 N Twin Valley Rd 19520 610-286-8600
Dr. Judith Funk, supt. Fax 286-8608
www.tvsd.org
Twin Valley HS 1,000/9-12
4897 N Twin Valley Rd 19520 610-286-8614
Kate Long, prin. Fax 286-8604
Twin Valley MS 800/6-8
770 Clymer Hill Rd 19520 610-286-8660
Kim Donahue, prin. Fax 286-8662

Emmaus, Lehigh, Pop. 11,351
East Penn SD 6,800/K-12
800 Pine St 18049 610-966-8300
Dr. George Ziolkowski, supt. Fax 966-8339
www.eastpenn.k12.pa.us/
Emmaus HS 2,500/9-12
500 N Macungie St 18049 610-966-1651
Elizabeth Drake, prin.
Other Schools – See Macungie

Emporium, Cameron, Pop. 2,362
Cameron County SD 900/K-12
601 Woodland Ave 15834 814-486-4000
Clyde Moate, supt. Fax 486-1721
www.cameroncountyschools.org/
Cameron County JSHS 500/7-12
601 Woodland Ave 15834 814-486-4000
Myron Crumrine, prin. Fax 486-3643

Enola, Cumberland, Pop. 5,961
East Pennsboro Area SD 2,800/K-12
890 Valley St 17025 717-732-3601
Dr. Linda Bigos, supt. Fax 732-8927
www.epasd.k12.pa.us
East Pennsboro Area HS 900/9-12
425 W Shady Ln 17025 717-732-0723
Craig Robbins, prin. Fax 732-8932
East Pennsboro Area MS 900/5-8
529 N Enola Dr 17025 717-732-0771
Stephen Andrejack, prin.

Ephrata, Lancaster, Pop. 13,092
Ephrata Area SD 4,000/K-12
803 Oak Blvd 17522 717-721-1400
Dr. Gerald B. Rosati, supt. Fax 733-1841
easdpa.org
Ephrata HS 1,400/9-12
803 Oak Blvd 17522 717-721-1478
Joane Eby, prin. Fax 721-1129
Ephrata MS 900/6-8
957 Hammon Ave 17522 717-721-1468
Kevin Fillgrove, prin. Fax 738-1930
Washington Educational Center Adult
26 Marshall St 17522 717-721-1150
Paul Murr, dir. Fax 721-1152

Ephrata Mennonite S 200/K-10
598 Stevens Rd 17522 717-738-4266
David Sauder, prin. Fax 738-4266
Grandview Heights Christian Academy 100/K-12
110 Durlach Rd 17522 717-738-0895
Jeanne Weber, prin. Fax 738-1002
Pleasant Valley Mennonite S 200/1-12
144 Pleasant Valley Rd 17522 717-738-1833
Larry Weaver, prin. Fax 738-3941

Erdenheim, Montgomery
Springfield Township SD
Supt. — See Oreland
Springfield Township HS 900/8-12
1801 Paper Mill Rd 19038 215-233-6000
Joseph Roy, prin. Fax 233-0691

Antonelli Institute - Art & Photography Post-Sec.
300 Montgomery Ave 19038 215-836-2222
Philadelphia-Montgomery Christian Acad. 400/PK-12
35 Hillcrest Rd 19038 215-233-0782
Tom Sorkness, hdmstr. Fax 233-0829

Erie, Erie, Pop. 102,612
Area Vocational Technical School
Supt. — None
City of Erie Regional Career & Tech S Vo/Tech
3325 Cherry St 16508 814-874-6225
David Kranking, dir.
Erie County Technical S Vo/Tech
8500 Oliver Rd 16509 814-864-0641
Aldo Jackson Ph.D., dir. Fax 864-9400

Erie CSD 12,600/K-12
148 W 21st St 16502 814-874-6000
Dr. James Barker, supt. Fax 874-6010
esd.iu5.org/
Central HS 1,200/9-12
3325 Cherry St 16508 814-874-6200
Gerald Mifsud, prin. Fax 874-6207
East HS 1,100/9-12
1001 Atkins St 16503 814-874-6400
Thomas James, prin. Fax 874-6407
Northwest Pennsylvania Collegiate Acad 700/9-12
2825 State St 16508 814-874-6300
Lori Gornall, dean Fax 874-6305
Roosevelt MS 700/6-8
2300 Cranberry St 16502 814-874-6800
Ina Fisher, prin. Fax 874-6807
Vincent HS 800/9-12
1330 W 8th St 16502 814-874-6500
Kenneth Brasington, prin. Fax 874-6507
Wilson MS 800/6-8
718 E 28th St 16504 814-874-6600
Pat Dean, prin. Fax 874-6607
Adult Learning Center Adult
444 W 18th St 16502 814-874-6175
David Kranking, prin. Fax 874-6117

Iroquois SD 1,200/K-12
4231 Morse St 16511 814-899-7643
Joseph Buzanowski Ed.D., supt. Fax 898-2099
Iroquois JSHS 600/7-12
4301 Main St 16511 814-899-7643
Brian Uplinger, prin. Fax 898-4105

Millcreek Township SD 7,000/K-12
3740 W 26th St 16506 814-835-5300
Dr. Dean Maynard, supt. Fax 835-5371
www.mtsd.org
McDowell Intermediate HS 1,200/9-10
3320 Caughey Rd 16506 814-835-5487
Thomas Maciulewicz, prin. Fax 835-5417
McDowell SHS 1,100/11-12
3580 W 38th St 16506 814-835-5403
Timothy Rankin, prin. Fax 835-5521
Westlake MS 500/6-8
4330 W Lake Rd 16505 814-835-5756
Marty Kaverman, prin. Fax 835-5770
Wilson MS 500/6-8
900 W 54th St 16509 814-835-5569
David Koma, prin. Fax 835-5582
Other Schools – See Fairview

Wattsburg Area SD 1,600/K-12
10782 Wattsburg Rd 16509 814-824-3400
Frank Bova, supt. Fax 824-5200
www.wattsburg.org/
Seneca HS 500/9-12
10770 Wattsburg Rd 16509 814-824-3400
Tom Rinke, prin. Fax 825-2262
Wattsburg Area MS 500/5-8
10774 Wattsburg Rd 16509 814-824-3400
Kenneth Berlin, prin. Fax 825-6337

Bethel Christian S of Erie 100/K-12
1781 W 38th St 16508 814-868-2365
Dennis Gillenwater, prin. Fax 864-7674
Cathedral Prep HS 600/9-12
225 W 9th St 16501 814-453-7737
Rev. Scott Jabo, hdmstr. Fax 455-5462
Erie Business Center Post-Sec.
246 W 9th St 16501 814-456-7504
Erie First Christian Academy 300/PK-12
8150 Oliver Rd 16509 814-866-6979
John Richardson, admin. Fax 866-5829
Erie Institute of Technology Post-Sec.
940 Millcreek Mall 16565 814-868-9900
Gannon University Post-Sec.
109 University Sq 16541 814-871-7000
GECAC Training Institute Post-Sec.
1006 W 10th St 16502 814-451-5610
Great Lakes Institute of Technology Post-Sec.
5100 Peach St 16509 814-864-6666
Lake Erie College\Osteopathic Medicine Post-Sec.
1858 W Grandview Blvd 16509 814-866-6641
Mercyhurst College Post-Sec.
501 E 38th St 16546 814-824-2000
Mercyhurst Prep S 800/9-12
538 E Grandview Blvd 16504 814-824-2210
Margaret Aste, prin. Fax 824-3638
Pennsylvania State University Post-Sec.
5091 Station Rd 16563 814-898-6000
Toni & Guy Hairdressing Academy Post-Sec.
930 Peach St 16501 800-775-4187
Triangle Tech Post-Sec.
2000 Liberty St 16502 814-453-6016
Tri-State Business Institute Post-Sec.
5757 W Ridge Rd 16506 814-838-7673
Villa Maria Academy 500/9-12
2403 W 8th St 16505 814-838-2061
Sr. Mary Drexler, prin. Fax 836-0881

Everett, Bedford, Pop. 1,888
Area Vocational Technical School
Supt. — None
Bedford Co. Technical Center Vo/Tech
195 Pennknoll Rd 15537 814-623-2760
Allen Sell, prin. Fax 623-7234

Everett Area SD 1,500/K-12
427 E South St 15537 814-652-9114
Rodney L. Green, supt. Fax 652-6191
everett.k12.pa.us
Everett Area JSHS 800/7-12
1 Renaissance Cir 15537 814-652-9114
Jonathan Donelson, prin. Fax 652-0107

Exeter, Luzerne, Pop. 6,007
Wyoming Area SD 2,700/K-12
20 Memorial St 18643 570-655-3733
Raymond Bernardi, supt. Fax 883-1280
www.wyomingarea.org
Wyoming Area JSHS 1,300/7-12
20 Memorial St 18643 570-655-2836
Vito Quaglia, prin. Fax 883-1280

Exton, Chester, Pop. 2,550
Downingtown Area SD
Supt. — See Downingtown
Downingtown HS - East Campus 1,700/9-12
50 Devon Dr 19341 610-363-6400
Linwood Smith, prin. Fax 903-1047
Lionville MS 1,400/6-8
550 W Uwchlan Ave 19341 610-524-6300
Judy Groh, prin. Fax 524-0152

Automotive Training Center Post-Sec.
114 Pickering Way 19341 610-363-6716
CFS the School at Church Farm 200/7-12
1001 E Lincoln Hwy 19341 610-363-7500
Charles Shreiner, hdmstr. Fax 363-5367
Universal Technical Institute Post-Sec.
750 Pennsylvania Dr 19341 877-884-3986

Factoryville, Wyoming, Pop. 1,197
Lackawanna Trail SD 1,400/K-12
PO Box 85 18419 570-945-5184
Robert Jurbala, supt. Fax 945-3154
Lackawanna Trail JSHS 700/7-12
PO Box 85 18419 570-945-5181
Matthew Rakauskas, prin. Fax 945-3832

New Hope Academy 50/9-12
PO Box 295 18419 570-945-0161
Rev. Nick Gatoura, prin. Fax 945-0163

Fairfield, Adams, Pop. 511
Fairfield Area SD 1,300/K-12
4840 Fairfield Rd 17320 717-642-8228
Dr. Gary Miller, supt. Fax 642-2036
www.fairfieldpaschools.org/
Fairfield Area HS 400/9-12
4840 Fairfield Rd 17320 717-642-8228
Wayne Sherrard, prin. Fax 642-2004
Fairfield Area MS 400/5-8
4840 Fairfield Rd 17320 717-642-8228
Beth Bender, prin. Fax 642-2005

Fairless Hills, Bucks, Pop. 9,026
Area Vocational Technical School
Supt. — None
Bucks County Technical HS Vo/Tech
610 Wistar Rd 19030 215-949-1700
Scott Parks, prin.

Bristol Township SD
Supt. — See Levittown
Armstrong MS 400/7-9
475 Wistar Rd 19030 215-945-4940
Larry Funk, prin. Fax 945-1664

Pennsbury SD
Supt. — See Fallsington
Pennsbury HS East 1,600/11-12
705 Hood Blvd 19030 215-949-6700
David Bowman, prin. Fax 949-3896
Pennsbury HS West 1,800/9-10
608 S Olds Blvd 19030 215-949-6780
Lisa Becker, prin. Fax 949-6857

Conwell-Egan HS 1,000/9-12
611 Wistar Rd 19030 215-945-6200
Maryjane McHugh, prin. Fax 945-6206

Fairview, Erie, Pop. 212
Fairview SD 1,600/K-12
7460 McCray Rd 16415 814-474-2600
Larry D. Kessler, supt. Fax 474-5497
www.fairviewschools.org/
Fairview HS 500/9-12
7460 McCray Rd 16415 814-474-2600
Sam Signorio, prin. Fax 474-1367
Fairview MS 600/5-8
4967 Avonia Rd 16415 814-474-2600
Steve Ferringer, prin. Fax 474-1640

Millcreek Township SD
Supt. — See Erie
Walnut Creek MS 700/6-8
5901 Sterrettania Rd 16415 814-835-5700
Timothy Stoops, prin. Fax 835-5710

Fallsington, Bucks
Pennsbury SD 11,200/K-12
134 Yardley Ave 19054 215-428-4100
Paul Long, admin. Fax 295-8912
www.pennsbury.k12.pa.us
Other Schools – See Fairless Hills, Yardley

Farmington, Fayette

New Meadow Run Parochial S 100/PK-10
PO Box 240 15437 724-329-8573
F. Dwight Wareham, prin. Fax 329-8674

Farrell, Mercer, Pop. 5,999
Farrell Area SD 1,100/PK-12
1600 Roemer Blvd 16121 724-346-6585
Richard R. Rubano, supt. Fax 346-0223
www.farrellareaschools.com
Farrell Area MSHS 500/7-12
1700 Roemer Blvd 16121 724-346-6585
Lee Vincent McFerren, prin. Fax 346-2381

Fawn Grove, York, Pop. 465
South Eastern SD 3,300/K-12
377 Main St 17321 717-382-4843
Dr. Tracy Shank, supt. Fax 382-4769
www.sesdweb.net/
Kennard-Dale HS 1,000/9-12
393 Main St 17321 717-382-4871
Fax 382-4869
South Eastern MS - East 600/7-8
375 Main St 17321 717-382-4851
Shelton Mooney, prin. Fax 382-9033

Feasterville, Bucks, Pop. 6,696
Neshaminy SD
Supt. — See Langhorne
Poquessing MS 700/6-9
300 Heights Ln 19053 215-322-0350
Ron Sayre, prin.

Bucks County School of Beauty Culture Post-Sec.
1761 Bustleton Pike 19053 215-322-0666

Finleyville, Washington, Pop. 452
Ringgold SD
Supt. — See New Eagle
Finley MS 600/6-8
6023 State Route 88 15332 724-348-7154
Wendy Burke, prin. Fax 348-8839

Fishertown, Bedford
Chestnut Ridge SD 1,800/K-12
3281 Valley Rd 15539 814-839-4195
Dr. Thomas Otis, supt. Fax 839-2088
www.crsd.k12.pa.us/
Chestnut Ridge MS 500/5-8
3281 Valley Rd 15539 814-839-4195
David Goodin, prin. Fax 839-2088
Other Schools – See New Paris

Fleetwood, Berks, Pop. 4,006
Fleetwood Area SD 2,600/K-12
801 N Richmond St 19522 610-944-9598
Dr. Paul B. Eaken, supt. Fax 944-9408
www.fleetwoodasd.k12.pa.us
Fleetwood Area HS 900/9-12
803 N Richmond St 19522 610-944-7656
Robert Dziedzic, prin. Fax 944-6952
Fleetwood Area MS 800/5-8
407 N Richmond St 19522 610-944-7634
Christopher Redding, prin. Fax 944-5307

Flinton, Cambria
Glendale SD 900/K-12
1466 Beaver Valley Rd 16640 814-687-3402
Dr. Dennis Bruno, supt. Fax 687-3341
www.gsd1.org
Glendale JSHS 400/7-12
1466 Beaver Valley Rd 16640 814-687-4261
Gary Walstrom, prin. Fax 687-4718

Flourtown, Montgomery, Pop. 4,754

Mt. St. Joseph Academy 600/9-12
120 W Wissahickon Ave 19031 215-233-3177
Sr. Karen Dietrich, prin. Fax 233-4734

Fogelsville, Lehigh

Pennsylvania State University Post-Sec.
8380 Mohr Ln 18051 610-285-5000

Folcroft, Delaware, Pop. 6,906
Area Vocational Technical School
Supt. — None
Delaware County Technical HS - Folcroft Vo/Tech
701 Henderson Blvd 19032 610-583-7620
Dr. Darla Glantz, prin. Fax 583-6537

Southeast Delco SD 3,800/K-12
1560 Delmar Dr 19032 610-522-4300
Dr. Trudie Bennett, supt. Fax 461-4874
www.sedelco.k12.pa.us
Other Schools – See Sharon Hill

Folsom, Delaware, Pop. 8,173
Ridley SD 5,700/K-12
901 Morton Ave 19033 610-534-1900
Dr. Nicholas Ignatuk, supt. Fax 534-2335
www.ridleysd.k12.pa.us
Ridley HS 2,000/9-12
901 Morton Ave 19033 610-237-8034
William Mills, prin. Fax 237-9641
Other Schools – See Ridley Park

Ford City, Armstrong, Pop. 3,258
Area Vocational Technical School
Supt. — None
Lenape AVTS Vo/Tech
2215 Chaplin Ave 16226 724-763-7116
Dawn Kocher-Taylor, prin.

Armstrong SD 5,900/K-12
410 Main St 16226 724-763-7151
Dr. William Kerr, supt. Fax 763-7295
www.asd.k12.pa.us
Ford City JSHS 800/7-12
1100 4th Ave 16226 724-763-5289
Timothy Sedgwick, prin. Fax 763-7813
Other Schools – See Elderton, Kittanning, Rural Valley

Forest City, Susquehanna, Pop. 1,795
Forest City Regional SD 900/PK-12
100 Susquehanna St 18421 570-785-2400
Dr. Robert Vadella, supt. Fax 785-9557
www.forestcityschool.org/
Forest City Regional JSHS 500/7-12
100 Susquehanna St 18421 570-785-2402
Anthony Rusnak, prin. Fax 785-3785

Fort Washington, Montgomery, Pop. 3,699
Upper Dublin SD
Supt. — See Maple Glen
Upper Dublin HS 1,600/9-12
800 Loch Alsh Ave 19034 215-643-8900
Charles Rittenhouse, prin. Fax 643-0229

DeVry University Post-Sec.
1140 Virginia Dr 19034 215-591-5700
Germantown Academy 1,100/PK-12
PO Box 287 19034 215-646-3300
James Connor, prin. Fax 646-1216

Forty Fort, Luzerne, Pop. 4,331

Allied Medical & Technical Institute Post-Sec.
166 Slocum St 18704 570-288-8400

Foxburg, Clarion, Pop. 269
Allegheny-Clarion Valley SD 1,000/K-12
PO Box 100 16036 724-659-5820
Dr. Patrick Lukasavich, supt. Fax 659-2963
www.acvsd.org/
Allegheny-Clarion Valley JSHS 500/7-12
PO Box 345 16036 724-659-4661
Robert Collett, prin. Fax 659-4774

Frackville, Schuylkill, Pop. 4,199
Area Vocational Technical School
Supt. — None
Schuylkill Technology Center - North Vo/Tech
101 Technology Dr 17931 570-874-1034
Brent Borzak, prin. Fax 874-4028

Franklin, Venango, Pop. 6,879
Franklin Area SD 2,300/K-12
417 13th St 16323 814-432-8917
Ronald Paranick, supt. Fax 437-5754
www.fasd.k12.pa.us/
Franklin Area HS 800/9-12
246 Pone Ln 16323 814-432-2121
William Vonada, prin. Fax 432-5031
Franklin Area MS 400/7-8
246 Pone Ln 16323 814-432-2224
Dale Ishman, prin. Fax 437-1491

Valley Grove SD 1,000/K-12
429 Wiley Ave 16323 814-432-4919
Jeffrey A. Clark, supt. Fax 437-1243
Rocky Grove JSHS 500/7-12
403 Rocky Grove Ave 16323 814-437-3759
James Smith, prin. Fax 437-1062

Fredericksburg, Lebanon, Pop. 3,607
Northern Lebanon SD 2,500/K-12
PO Box 100 17026 717-865-2117
Dr. Don Bell, supt. Fax 865-0606
www.norleb.k12.pa.us
Northern Lebanon HS 800/9-12
PO Box 100 17026 717-865-2117
David Woods, prin. Fax 865-7818
Northern Lebanon MS 400/7-8
PO Box 100 17026 717-865-2117
David Yavoich, prin. Fax 865-5835

Fredericktown, Washington, Pop. 1,237
Bethlehem-Center SD 1,400/K-12
194 Crawford Rd 15333 724-267-4910
Karen Downie Ed.D., supt. Fax 267-4904
www.bc.k12.pa.us
Bethlehem-Center HS 400/9-12
179 Crawford Rd 15333 724-267-4944
Dr. Richard Martin, prin. Fax 267-4907
Bethlehem-Center MS 300/6-8
136 Crawford Rd 15333 724-267-4935
Rick Showalter, prin. Fax 267-4937

Freedom, Beaver, Pop. 1,665
Ambridge Area SD
Supt. — See Ambridge
Ambridge Area JHS 500/7-8
401 1st St 15042 724-266-2833
Megan Mealie, prin. Fax 869-5321

Freedom Area SD 1,700/K-12
1701 8th Ave 15042 724-775-7644
Dr. Ronald Sofo, supt. Fax 775-7434
www.freedom.k12.pa.us
Freedom Area HS 600/9-12
1190 Bulldog Dr 15042 724-775-7400
Dr. Robert Staub, prin. Fax 775-7753
Freedom Area MS 600/5-8
1701 8th Ave 15042 724-775-7641
Robert Gallagher, prin. Fax 775-7748

Freeland, Luzerne, Pop. 3,455

MMI Prep S 200/6-12
154 Centre St 18224 570-636-1108
William Shergalis Ph.D., pres. Fax 636-0742

Freeport, Armstrong, Pop. 1,854
Freeport Area SD
Supt. — See Sarver
Freeport Area JHS 300/7-8
325 4th St 16229 724-295-9020
Robert Isenberg, prin. Fax 295-4630

Galeton, Potter, Pop. 1,301
Galeton Area SD 400/PK-12
25 Bridge St 16922 814-435-6571
Michael Schwarz, supt. Fax 435-1187
www.gasd.net
Galeton Area S 400/PK-12
25 Bridge St 16922 814-435-6571
Kay Stuart, prin. Fax 435-6981

Gallitzin, Cambria, Pop. 1,666
Penn Cambria SD
Supt. — See Cresson
Penn Cambria MS 400/6-8
401 Division St 16641 814-886-4181
Jeff Baird, prin. Fax 886-9308

Gap, Lancaster, Pop. 1,226

Fairhaven Christian S 100/1-12
1031 Simmontown Rd 17527 717-442-9840
Curtis Stoltzfus, prin.

Geigertown, Berks

High Point Baptist Academy 300/PK-12
200 Chapel Rd 19523 610-286-5942
Ken Lang, prin. Fax 286-7525

Gettysburg, Adams, Pop. 8,014
Gettysburg Area SD 3,300/K-12
900 Biglerville Rd 17325 717-334-6254
Dr. David Mowery, supt. Fax 334-5220
www.gettysburg.k12.pa.us
Gettysburg Area HS 1,200/9-12
1130 Old Harrisburg Rd 17325 717-334-6254
Richard Gulas, prin. Fax 334-9190
Gettysburg Area MS 800/6-8
37 Lefever St 17325 717-334-6254
Steven Litten, prin. Fax 334-6999

Adams County Christian Academy 100/PK-12
1865 Biglerville Rd 17325 717-334-9177
Kimberly Mentzer, admin. Fax 334-7691
Freedom Christian S 100/K-12
3185 York Rd 17325 717-624-3884
Karen Trout, admin. Fax 624-1562
Gettysburg College Post-Sec.
300 N Washington St 17325 717-337-6000
Lutheran Theological Seminary Post-Sec.
61 Seminary Rdg 17325 717-334-6286

Gibsonia, Allegheny, Pop. 3,500
Pine-Richland SD 4,000/K-12
702 Warrendale Rd 15044 724-625-7773
Dr. James Manley, supt. Fax 625-1490
www.pinerichland.org
Pine-Richland HS 1,200/9-12
700 Warrendale Rd 15044 724-625-4444
Dr. Laura Davis, prin. Fax 625-4640
Pine-Richland MS 1,000/6-8
100 Logan Rd 15044 724-625-3111
Dr. Kathleen Harrington, prin. Fax 625-3144

Aquinas Academy 200/K-12
2308 W Hardies Rd 15044 724-444-0722
Leslie Mitros, hdmstr. Fax 444-0750

Gilbertsville, Montgomery, Pop. 3,994
Boyertown Area SD
Supt. — See Boyertown
Boyertown Area JHS East 800/7-9
2020 Big Rd 19525 610-754-9550
Andrew Ruppert, prin.

Girard, Erie, Pop. 3,017
Girard SD 2,000/K-12
1203 Lake St 16417 814-774-5666
Dr. James Tracy, supt. Fax 774-4220
www.gsd.k12.pa.us
Girard HS 600/9-12
1135 Lake St 16417 814-774-5607
Gregg McClelland, prin. Fax 774-2239
Rice Avenue MS 700/5-8
1100 Rice Ave 16417 814-774-5604
Don Stark, prin. Fax 774-5259

Girard Alliance Christian Academy 100/K-12
229 Rice Ave 16417 814-774-9537
Karen Brumagin, admin. Fax 774-2552

Glen Mills, Delaware
Garnet Valley SD, 80 Station Rd 19342 4,200/K-12
Dr. Anthony Costello, supt. 610-579-7300
www.garnetvalleyschools.com/
Garnet Valley HS 1,200/9-12
552 Smithbridge Rd 19342 610-579-7745
Dr. Joseph Hook, prin.
Garnet Valley MS 1,000/6-8
601 Smithbridge Rd 19342 610-579-5100
Christopher Marchese, prin.

Glenmoore, Chester

Upattinas Open Community S 100/K-12
429 Greenridge Rd 19343 610-458-5138
Richard Bull, prin. Fax 458-8688

Glen Rock, York, Pop. 1,853
Southern York County SD 3,300/K-12
PO Box 128 17327 717-235-4811
Thomas Hensley, supt. Fax 235-0863
www.syc.k12.pa.us
Southern MS 600/7-8
PO Box 128 17327 717-235-4811
Kevin L. Helmeczi, prin. Fax 227-9681
Susquehannock HS 1,100/9-12
PO Box 128 17327 717-235-4811
Brian Cashman, prin. Fax 227-1951

Glenshaw, Allegheny
Shaler Area SD 5,600/K-12
1800 Mount Royal Blvd 15116 412-492-1200
Donald Lee, supt. Fax 492-1293
www.sasd.k12.pa.us
Shaler Area IS 1,000/8-9
1810 Mount Royal Blvd 15116 412-492-1200
David McQuade, prin. Fax 492-1237
Other Schools – See Pittsburgh

Glenside, Montgomery, Pop. 8,704

Arcadia University Post-Sec.
450 S Easton Rd 19038 215-572-2900
LaSalle College HS 1,100/9-12
8605 Cheltenham Ave 19038 215-233-2911
Joseph Marchese, prin. Fax 233-1418
Princeton Information Technology Center Post-Sec.
137 S Easton Rd 19038 215-576-7377
Won Institute of Graduate Studies Post-Sec.
137 S Easton Rd 19038 215-884-8942

Grantham, Cumberland

Messiah College Post-Sec.
1 S College Ave 17027 717-766-2511

Greencastle, Franklin, Pop. 3,838
Greencastle-Antrim SD 2,800/K-12
500 Leitersburg St 17225 717-597-2187
Dr. Preston D. Rearick, supt. Fax 597-2180
www.greencastle.k12.pa.us
Greencastle-Antrim HS 900/9-12
300 S Ridge Ave 17225 717-597-2186
Edward Rife, prin. Fax 597-2912
Greencastle-Antrim MS 700/6-8
370 S Ridge Ave 17225 717-597-2185
Robert Crider, prin. Fax 597-6468

Green Lane, Montgomery, Pop. 585

Intl Academy of Advanced Reflexology Post-Sec.
1701 Snyder Rd 18054 215-234-0307

Greensboro, Greene, Pop. 279
Southeastern Greene SD 700/K-12
1000 Mapletown Rd 15338 724-943-3630
Dr. Philip Savini, supt. Fax 943-3052
Mapletown JSHS 300/7-12
1000 Mapletown Rd 15338 724-943-3401
Richard Hauger, prin. Fax 943-4769

Greensburg, Westmoreland, Pop. 15,569
Greensburg Salem SD 3,400/K-12
1 Academy Hill Pl 15601 724-832-2901
Thomas Yarabinetz, supt. Fax 832-2968
www.greensburgsalem.org
Greensburg Salem HS 1,200/9-12
65 Mennel Dr 15601 724-832-2960
Dr. Lisa Mason, prin. Fax 832-2971
Greensburg Salem MS 900/6-8
301 N Main St 15601 724-832-2930
Tammy Wolicki, prin. Fax 832-2939

Hempfield Area SD 6,400/K-12
4347 State Route 136 15601 724-834-2590
Terry Foriska, supt. Fax 837-8681
www.hempfieldarea.k12.pa.us
Harrold MS 500/6-8
1368 Middletown Rd 15601 724-850-2301
Rebecca Gardner, prin. Fax 850-2302
Hempfield Area HS 2,100/9-12
4345 State Route 136 15601 724-834-9000
Kathy Charlton, prin. Fax 850-2090
Wendover MS 500/6-8
425 Arthur Pl 15601 724-838-4070
Deanna Mikesic, prin. Fax 838-4071
Other Schools – See Irwin

Dominion Christian Academy 50/9-12
PO Box 1611 15601 724-837-1000
Roy Smith, admin. Fax 837-0220

Greensburg Central Catholic HS 500/9-12
911 Armory Dr 15601 724-834-0310
Rev. Daniel Blout, prin. Fax 834-2472
Seton Hill University Post-Sec.
Seton Hill Dr 15601 724-834-2200
Triangle Tech Post-Sec.
222 E Pittsburgh St # A 15601 724-832-1050
University of Pittsburgh Post-Sec.
150 Finoli Dr 15601 724-837-7040
Westmoreland Christian Academy 100/PK-12
122 Elgin Dr 15601 724-853-8308
Dr. David Erdman, admin. Fax 853-8308

Greenville, Mercer, Pop. 6,355
Greenville Area SD 1,600/K-12
9 Donation Rd 16125 724-588-2502
Dr. Patricia Homer, supt. Fax 588-5024
www.greenville.k12.pa.us
Greenville JSHS 800/7-12
9 Donation Rd 16125 724-588-2500
Stephen Ross, prin. Fax 588-4397

Reynolds SD 1,500/K-12
531 Reynolds Rd 16125 724-646-5501
Maddox Stokes Ph.D., supt. Fax 646-5505
www.reynolds.k12.pa.us
Reynolds JSHS 700/7-12
531 Reynolds Rd 16125 724-646-5701
Joseph Torck, prin. Fax 646-5705

Thiel College Post-Sec.
75 College Ave 16125 724-589-2000

Grove City, Mercer, Pop. 7,764
Grove City Area SD 2,600/K-12
511 Highland Ave 16127 724-458-6733
Dr. Robert Post, supt. Fax 458-5868
www.grovecity.k12.pa.us
Grove City Area HS 800/9-12
511 Highland Ave 16127 724-458-5456
Joseph Skibinski, prin. Fax 450-0678
Grove City Area MS 400/7-8
130 E Main St 16127 724-458-8040
James Anderson, prin. Fax 450-0780
Republic JSHS 300/5-12
200 George Junior Rd 16127 724-458-9330
Tammi Martin, prin. Fax 458-7455

Grove City Christian Academy 100/PK-10
107 Breckenridge St 16127 724-458-5253
Bobbie VanTil, prin.
Grove City College Post-Sec.
100 Campus Dr 16127 724-458-2000

Guys Mills, Crawford
Penncrest SD
Supt. — See Saegertown
Maplewood JSHS 700/7-12
30383 Guys Mills Rd 16327 814-789-3666
Michael Henegan, prin. Fax 789-2409

Faith Builders Christian S 100/K-12
PO Box 127 16327 814-789-2303
Gerald Miller, prin. Fax 789-3396

Gwynedd Valley, Montgomery

Gwynedd-Mercy Academy 400/9-12
PO Box 902 19437 215-646-8815
Sr. Kathleen Boyce, prin. Fax 646-4361
Gwynedd-Mercy College Post-Sec.
PO Box 901 19437 215-646-7300

Hadley, Mercer
Commodore Perry SD 700/K-12
3002 Perry Hwy 16130 724-253-3255
Michael Stahlman, supt. Fax 253-3467
www.cpanthers.org/
Perry JSHS 400/7-12
3002 Perry Hwy 16130 724-253-2232
Doug Mays, prin. Fax 253-3467

Halifax, Dauphin, Pop. 844
Halifax Area SD 1,200/K-12
3940 Peters Mountain Rd 17032 717-896-3416
James Dull, supt. Fax 896-3976
www.hasd.us
Halifax Area HS 400/9-12
3940 Peters Mountain Rd 17032 717-896-3416
David Hatfield, prin. Fax 896-3976
Halifax Area MS 300/6-8
3940 Peters Mountain Rd 17032 717-896-3416
Robert Hassinger, prin. Fax 896-3976

Hamburg, Berks, Pop. 4,183
Hamburg Area SD 2,300/K-12
Windsor St 19526 610-562-2241
Dr. William N. Kiefer, supt. Fax 562-2634
www.hasdhawks.org
Hamburg Area HS, Windsor St 19526 900/9-12
Christopher Spohn, prin. 610-562-3861
Hamburg Area MS, Windsor St 19526 700/6-8
Stephen Seier, prin. 610-562-3990

Blue Mountain Academy 200/9-12
2363 Mountain Rd 19526 610-562-2291
Spencer Hannah, prin. Fax 562-8050

Hanover, York, Pop. 14,990
Hanover Public SD 1,700/K-12
403 Moul Ave 17331 717-637-9000
Dr. Jill Dillon, supt. Fax 630-4617
www.hpsd.k12.pa.us
Hanover HS 500/9-12
401 Moul Ave 17331 717-637-9000
Karen Schoonover, prin. Fax 630-4634
Hanover MS 500/5-8
300 Keagy Ave 17331 717-637-9000
Pamela Smith, prin. Fax 630-4632

South Western SD 3,700/K-12
225 Bowman Rd Ste 2 17331 717-632-2500
Barbara Rupp, supt. Fax 632-7993
www.swsd.k12.pa.us/
Markle IS 1,100/6-8
225 Bowman Rd Ste 1 17331 717-632-2500
Alan Moyer, prin. Fax 633-7073

South Western HS 1,300/9-12
200 Bowman Rd 17331 717-632-2500
Walt Graves, prin. Fax 633-4819

Empire Beauty School Post-Sec.
1000 Carlisle St 17331 717-633-6201
St. Joseph MS 100/6-8
5125 Grandview Rd 17331 717-632-0118
Susan Mummert, prin. Fax 632-0030

Hanover Area JSHS 1,000/7-12
1600 Sans Souci Pkwy 18706 570-831-2300
David Fisher, prin. Fax 831-2316

Harborcreek, Erie
Harbor Creek SD 2,100/K-12
6375 Buffalo Rd 16421 814-897-2100
Dr. David Smith, supt. Fax 897-2142
www.hcsd.iu5.org
Harbor Creek HS 700/9-12
6375 Buffalo Rd 16421 814-897-2100
Ed Zenewicz, prin. Fax 898-4245
Harbor Creek JHS 400/7-8
6375 Buffalo Rd 16421 814-897-2100
Linda Allen, prin. Fax 897-2121

Harmony, Butler, Pop. 902
Seneca Valley SD 7,700/K-12
124 Seneca School Rd 16037 724-452-6040
Dr. Donald Tylinski, supt. Fax 452-6105
www.svsd.net/
Seneca Valley Intermediate HS 1,200/9-10
126 Seneca School Rd 16037 724-452-6040
Alan Cumo, prin. Fax 452-3718
Seneca Valley MS 1,200/7-8
122 Seneca School Rd 16037 724-452-6040
Tracy Vitale, prin. Fax 452-0331
Seneca Valley SHS 1,100/11-12
128 Seneca School Rd 16037 724-452-6040
Mark Korcinsky, prin. Fax 452-8357

Harrisburg, Dauphin, Pop. 47,472
Area Vocational Technical School
Supt. — None
Dauphin County AVTS Vo/Tech
6001 Locust Ln 17109 717-652-3170
Dr. Robert Clark, prin. Fax 652-9326

Central Dauphin SD 11,100/K-12
600 Rutherford Rd 17109 717-545-4703
John Scola, supt. Fax 545-5624
www.cdschools.org
Central Dauphin East HS 1,500/9-12
626 Rutherford Rd 17109 717-541-1662
Todd Neuhard, prin. Fax 545-7139
Central Dauphin East MS 900/6-8
628 Rutherford Rd 17109 717-545-4703
Robert Holbrook, prin. Fax 657-4987
Central Dauphin HS 2,000/9-12
437 Piketown Rd 17112 717-703-5360
Richard Mazzatesta, prin. Fax 703-5730
Central Dauphin MS 800/6-8
4600 Locust Ln 17109 717-540-4606
Dr. Pamela Boyd, prin. Fax 545-6931
Linglestown MS 700/6-8
1200 N Mountain Rd 17112 717-657-3060
Carol Johnson, prin. Fax 657-0537
Other Schools – See Steelton

Harrisburg SD 7,700/PK-12
2101 N Front St Bldg 2 17110 717-703-4000
Dr. Gerald W. Kohn, supt. Fax 703-4115
www.hbgsd.k12.pa.us
Harrisburg Career & Technology Academy Vo/Tech
2915 N 3rd St 17110 717-703-4350
Stuart Kermes, prin. Fax 703-4355
Harrisburg HS 2,100/9-12
2451 Market St 17103 717-703-4300
Evangeline Kimber, prin. Fax 703-4333
Harrisburg University Science & Tech HS 9-12
215 Market St 17101 717-703-1900
Michael Reed, dir.

Susquehanna Township SD 3,100/K-12
3550 Elmerton Ave 17109 717-657-5100
David W. Volkman, supt. Fax 657-2919
www.hannasd.org
Susquehanna Twp. HS 1,000/9-12
3500 Elmerton Ave 17109 717-657-5117
Judy Baumgardner, prin. Fax 657-2919
Susquehanna Twp. MS 800/6-8
801 Wood St 17109 717-657-5125
Michael Jones, prin. Fax 657-2919

Bishop McDevitt HS 800/9-12
2200 Market St 17103 717-236-7973
Sr. Mary Anne Bednar, prin. Fax 234-1270
Covenant Christian Academy 200/K-12
6098 Locust Ln 17109 717-540-9885
Dr. Christopher Perrin, prin. Fax 540-7176
Empire Beauty School Post-Sec.
3941 Jonestown Rd 17109 717-652-8500
Harrisburg Area Community College Post-Sec.
1 Hacc Dr 17110 717-780-2300
Harrisburg Christian S 300/K-12
PO Box 6464 17112 717-545-3728
Tom Wieland, hdmstr. Fax 545-9370
Kaplan Career Institute Post-Sec.
5650 Derry St 17111 717-564-4112
Keystone Technical Institute Post-Sec.
2301 Academy Dr 17112 717-545-4747
Widener University School of Law Post-Sec.
PO Box 69380 17106 717-541-3900

Harrison City, Westmoreland
Penn-Trafford SD 4,700/K-12
PO Box 530 15636 724-744-4496
Dr. Deborah Kolonay, supt. Fax 744-4016
www.penntrafford.org
Penn-Trafford HS 1,600/9-12
PO Box 530 15636 724-744-4471
Scott Inglese, prin. Fax 744-1214
Other Schools – See Claridge, Trafford

Hatboro, Montgomery, Pop. 7,288
Upper Moreland Township SD
Supt. — See Willow Grove

Upper Moreland MS 800/6-8
4000 Orangemans Rd 19040 215-674-4185
Charles Hafele, prin. Fax 956-1906

Hatfield, Montgomery, Pop. 2,872
North Penn SD
Supt. — See Lansdale
Pennfield MS 900/7-9
726 Forty Foot Rd 19440 215-368-9600
Dr. Barbara Galloway, prin. Fax 368-9791

Biblical Theological Seminary Post-Sec.
200 N Main St 19440 800-235-4021

Haverford, Montgomery, Pop. 6,000

Haverford College Post-Sec.
370 Lancaster Ave 19041 610-896-1000
Haverford S 1,000/PK-12
450 Lancaster Ave 19041 610-642-3020
Joseph Cox, prin. Fax 649-4898

Havertown, Delaware, Pop. 30,000
Haverford Township SD 5,200/K-12
1801 Darby Rd 19083 610-853-5900
William Keilbaugh Ed.D., supt. Fax 789-5379
www.haverford.k12.pa.us
Haverford HS 1,900/9-12
200 Mill Rd 19083 610-853-5900
Jeffrey Nesbitt, prin. Fax 853-5952
Haverford MS 1,300/6-8
1701 Darby Rd 19083 610-853-5900
Carol Restifo, prin. Fax 853-5937

Talent Academy Post-Sec.
1345 W Chester Pike 19083 610-352-1401

Hawley, Pike, Pop. 1,292
Wallenpaupack Area SD 4,000/K-12
HC 6 Box 6075 18428 570-226-4557
Michael Silsby, supt. Fax 226-0638
www.paupack.ptd.net
Wallenpaupack Area HS 1,300/9-12
HC 6 Box 6075 18428 570-226-4557
Jay Starnes, prin. Fax 251-3153
Wallenpaupack Area MS 1,000/6-8
HC 6 Box 6071 18428 570-226-4557
Diane Szader, prin. Fax 251-3165

Hazleton, Luzerne, Pop. 22,125
Area Vocational Technical School
Supt. — None
Hazleton Area Career Center Vo/Tech
1451 W 23rd St 18202 570-459-3172

Hazleton Area SD 9,500/K-12
1515 W 23rd St 18202 570-459-3111
Frank Victor, supt. Fax 459-3118
www.hasd.k12.pa.us
Hazleton Area Career Center Vo/Tech
1451 W 23rd St 18202 570-459-3172
Clarence John, prin. Fax 459-3181
Hazleton Area HS 3,200/9-12
1601 W 23rd St 18202 570-459-3221
Robert Stefanovich, prin. Fax 459-3242

Academy of Hair Design Post-Sec.
1057 N Church St # A 18202 570-784-1020
Immanuel Christian S 100/K-12
725 N Locust St 18201 570-459-1111
Kelly Knowlden, prin. Fax 459-6920
Pennsylvania State University Post-Sec.
Hazelton Campus 18201 570-450-3000

Hegins, Schuylkill
Tri-Valley SD
Supt. — See Valley View
Tri-Valley JSHS 500/7-12
155 E Main St 17938 570-682-3125
Mark Snyder, prin. Fax 682-9873

Hellertown, Northampton, Pop. 5,615
Saucon Valley SD 2,400/K-12
2097 Polk Valley Rd 18055 610-838-7026
Sandra Fellin, supt. Fax 838-6419
www.svpanthers.org
Saucon Valley HS 800/9-12
2100 Polk Valley Rd 18055 610-838-7001
Todd Gombos, prin. Fax 838-2365
Saucon Valley MS 600/6-8
2095 Polk Valley Rd 18055 610-838-7071
Pamela Bernardo, prin. Fax 838-7473

Herminie, Westmoreland
Yough SD 2,400/K-12
915 Lowber Rd 15637 724-446-7272
Lawrence Nemec, supt. Fax 446-5017
www.yough.net
Yough HS 800/9-12
919 Lowber Rd 15637 724-446-5520
Earl Thompson, prin. Fax 446-6008
Other Schools – See Ruffs Dale

Hermitage, Mercer, Pop. 16,571
Hermitage SD 2,200/K-12
411 N Hermitage Rd 16148 724-981-8750
Karen Ionta, supt. Fax 981-5080
www.hermitage.k12.pa.us
Hermitage MS 300/7-8
123 N Hermitage Rd 16148 724-981-8750
William Roth, prin. Fax 347-4514
Hickory HS 800/9-12
640 N Hermitage Rd 16148 724-981-8750
Eric Trosch, prin. Fax 347-4558

Kennedy Catholic HS 9-12
2120 Shenango Valley Fwy 16148 724-346-5531
Dr. Peter P. Iacino, prin. Fax 346-3011
Penn State Cosmetology Academy Post-Sec.
2200 E State St 16148 724-347-4503

Herndon, Northumberland, Pop. 362
Line Mountain SD
Supt. — See Trevorton
Line Mountain JSHS 600/7-12
RR 1 Box 1660 17830 570-758-2011
Karen Wiest, prin. Fax 758-1514

Hershey, Dauphin, Pop. 11,860
Derry Township SD 3,500/K-12
PO Box 898 17033 717-534-2501
Dr. Linda Brewer, supt. Fax 533-4357
www.hershey.k12.pa.us
Hershey HS 1,100/9-12
PO Box 898 17033 717-531-2244
Mike Murphy, prin. Fax 534-2684
Hershey MS 900/6-8
PO Box 898 17033 717-531-2222
Sue King, prin. Fax 531-2245

Hershey S 1,500/PK-12
PO Box 830 17033 717-520-2000
John O'Brien, pres. Fax 520-2002
Milton S. Hershey Medical Center Hosp. Post-Sec.
PO Box 850 17033 717-531-8803
Penn State Hershey College of Medicine Post-Sec.
500 University Dr 17033 717-534-8521

Hilltown, Bucks

St. Agnes-Sacred Heart S 200/5-8
Route 152 & Broad St 18927 215-822-9174
Margaret Graham, prin. Fax 822-7942

Holland, Bucks, Pop. 5,300
Council Rock SD
Supt. — See Newtown
Council Rock HS South 2,100/9-12
2002 Rock Way 18966 215-944-1100
Al Funk, prin. Fax 944-1145
Holland MS 700/7-8
400 E Holland Rd 18966 215-968-0854
Michael Lecker, prin. Fax 968-1475

Villa Joseph Marie HS 300/9-12
1180 Holland Rd 18966 215-357-8810
Mary Elaine, prin. Fax 357-2477

Hollidaysburg, Blair, Pop. 5,519
Hollidaysburg Area SD 3,800/K-12
201 Jackson St 16648 814-695-8702
Dr. Paul Gallagher, supt. Fax 695-2315
www.tigerwires.com
Hollidaysburg Area JHS 900/7-9
1000 Hewit St 16648 814-695-4426
Edward Barton, prin. Fax 696-2959
Hollidaysburg Area SHS 1,100/10-12
1500 N Montgomery St 16648 814-695-4416
Linda McCall, prin. Fax 696-2958

Hollsopple, Somerset

Johnstown Christian S 300/PK-12
125 Christian School Rd 15935 814-288-2588
Linda Gundlach, admin. Fax 288-1447

Homer City, Indiana, Pop. 1,755
Homer-Center SD 1,000/K-12
65 Wildcat Ln 15748 724-479-8080
Dr. Joseph Marcoline, supt. Fax 479-3967
homercenter.org/
Homer-Center JSHS 500/7-12
70 Wildcat Ln 15748 724-479-8026
Rick Foust, prin. Fax 479-4236

Honesdale, Wayne, Pop. 4,849
Wayne Highlands SD 3,300/K-12
474 Grove St 18431 570-253-4661
Thomas Jenkins, supt. Fax 253-9409
www.waynehighlands.org
Honesdale HS 1,100/9-12
459 Terrace St 18431 570-253-2046
James Rodda, prin. Fax 253-1502
Wayne Highlands MS 600/6-8
482 Grove St 18431 570-253-5900
Kurt Eisele, prin. Fax 253-5259

Hookstown, Beaver, Pop. 144
South Side Area SD 1,400/K-12
4949 Route 151 15050 724-573-9581
Dr. Robert Del Greco, supt. Fax 573-0414
www.sssd.k12.pa.us/
South Side HS 500/9-12
4949 State Route 151 15050 724-573-9581
Vincent Trombetta, prin. Fax 573-0449
South Side MS 300/6-8
4949 State Route 151 15050 724-573-9581
Timothy Strader, prin. Fax 573-0449

Horsham, Montgomery, Pop. 15,051
Hatboro-Horsham SD 5,500/K-12
229 Meetinghouse Rd 19044 215-672-5660
Dr. William A. Lessa, supt. Fax 675-2201
www.hatboro-horsham.org
Hatboro-Horsham HS 1,900/9-12
899 Horsham Rd 19044 215-441-7900
Dennis Williams, prin. Fax 441-7940
Keith Valley MS 1,300/6-8
227 Meetinghouse Rd 19044 215-956-2910
Jonathan Kircher, prin. Fax 674-0762

Houston, Washington, Pop. 1,276
Chartiers-Houston SD 1,200/K-12
2020 W Pike St 15342 724-746-1400
Charles Mahoney, supt. Fax 746-3971
www.chbucs.k12.pa.us/
Chartiers-Houston JSHS 600/7-12
2050 W Pike St 15342 724-745-3350
Philip Mary, prin. Fax 745-3495

Houtzdale, Clearfield, Pop. 902
Moshannon Valley SD 1,100/K-12
4934 Green Acre Rd 16651 814-378-7609
Michael Slavinski Ed.D., supt. Fax 378-7100
www.movalley.org
Moshannon Valley JSHS 600/7-12
4934 Green Acre Rd 16651 814-378-7616
Dr. Jack Cunning, prin. Fax 378-5205

Hughesville, Lycoming, Pop. 2,114
Area Vocational Technical School
Supt. — None
Lycoming CTC Vo/Tech
293 Cemetery St 17737 570-584-2300
John Pulver, prin.

East Lycoming SD 1,800/K-12
349 Cemetery St 17737 570-584-2131
David L. Price, supt. Fax 584-5701
www.eastlycoming.net
Hughesville JSHS 900/7-12
349 Cemetery St 17737 570-584-5111
Ron Lorson, prin. Fax 584-5378

Hummelstown, Dauphin, Pop. 4,402
Lower Dauphin SD 3,900/K-12
291 E Main St 17036 717-566-5300
Sherri Smith, supt. Fax 566-3670
www.ldsd.org
Lower Dauphin HS 1,200/9-12
201 S Hanover St 17036 717-566-5330
Jeffrey Hughes, prin. Fax 566-3970
Lower Dauphin MS 1,000/6-8
251 Quarry Rd 17036 717-566-5310
Robert K. Schultz, prin. Fax 566-5383

Hershey Christian S 300/K-12
330 Hilltop Rd 17036 717-533-4900
Timothy D. Rockafellow, admin. Fax 533-0908

Huntingdon, Huntingdon, Pop. 6,876
Huntingdon Area SD 2,300/K-12
2400 Cassady Ave Ste 2 16652 814-643-4140
Jill Adams, supt. Fax 643-6244
www.hasd.tiu.k12.pa.us/
Huntingdon Area HS 800/9-12
2400 Cassady Ave 16652 814-643-1080
Arthur Waleski, prin. Fax 643-3800
Huntingdon Area MS 600/6-8
2500 Cassady Ave 16652 814-643-2900
Patricia Wargo, prin. Fax 643-6513

Calvary Christian Academy 100/K-12
300 Standing Stone Ave 16652 814-643-4075
Donald Kidd, prin. Fax 643-4094
DuBois Business College Post-Sec.
1001 Moore St 16652 814-641-0440
Juniata College Post-Sec.
1700 Moore St 16652 814-641-3000

Huntingdon Valley, Montgomery, Pop. 10,000
Lower Moreland Township SD 1,900/K-12
2551 Murray Ave 19006 215-938-0270
Dr. Mary Feeley, supt. Fax 947-6933
www.lmtsd.org
Lower Moreland HS 600/9-12
555 Red Lion Rd 19006 215-938-0220
Gregory Doviak, prin. Fax 947-0333
Murray Avenue MS 700/4-8
2551 Murray Ave 19006 215-938-0230
Frank McKee, prin. Fax 947-3697

Huntingdon Valley Christian Academy 100/PK-10
1845 Byberry Rd 19006 215-947-6595
Gary Davis, prin. Fax 947-4277

Hyndman, Bedford, Pop. 978
Bedford Area SD
Supt. — See Bedford
Hyndman MSHS 200/7-12
PO Box 695 15545 814-842-3918
Paul Ruhlman, prin. Fax 842-6246

Immaculata, Chester

Immaculata University 19345 Post-Sec.
610-647-4400

Imperial, Allegheny, Pop. 3,449
West Allegheny SD
Supt. — See Oakdale
West Allegheny HS 1,000/9-12
205 W Allegheny Rd 15126 724-695-5245
Daniel Smith, prin. Fax 695-8690
West Allegheny MS 800/6-8
207 W Allegheny Rd 15126 724-695-8979
Rick Smith, prin. Fax 695-8211

Indiana, Indiana, Pop. 15,016
Area Vocational Technical School
Supt. — None
Indiana County Technology Center Vo/Tech
441 Hamill Rd 15701 724-349-6700
Carol Fry, prin.

Indiana Area SD 3,100/K-12
501 E Pike Rd 15701 724-463-8713
Dr. Deborah Clawson, supt. Fax 463-0868
www.iasd.cc
Indiana Area JHS 900/7-9
245 N 5th St 15701 724-463-8568
Jill Piper, prin. Fax 463-2133
Indiana Area SHS 800/10-12
450 N 5th St 15701 724-463-8562
Paula Daskivich, prin. Fax 463-9709

Cambria-Rowe Business College Post-Sec.
422 S 13th St 15701 724-463-0222
Indiana University of Pennsylvania Post-Sec.
15705 724-357-2100

Industry, Beaver, Pop. 1,845
Western Beaver County SD
Supt. — See Midland
Western Beaver County JSHS 500/7-12
216 Engle Rd 15052 724-643-8500
Rob Postupac, prin. Fax 643-8504

Irwin, Westmoreland, Pop. 4,187
Hempfield Area SD
Supt. — See Greensburg
West Hempfield MS 500/6-8
156 Northumberland Dr 15642 724-850-2140
David Waryanka, prin. Fax 850-2141

Norwin SD
Supt. — See North Huntingdon
Norwin MS 900/7-8
10870 Mockingbird Dr 15642 724-863-5707
Robert Randolph, prin. Fax 863-5408

Jamestown, Mercer, Pop. 604
Jamestown Area SD 700/K-12
PO Box 217 16134 724-932-5557
Dr. Douglas Allen, supt. Fax 932-5632
Jamestown Area JSHS 400/7-12
PO Box 217 16134 724-932-3186
Brian Keyser, prin.

Jamison, Bucks
Area Vocational Technical School
Supt. — None
Middle Bucks Institute of Tech Vo/Tech
2740 York Rd 18929 215-343-2480
Dr. Michael Erwin, dir.

Jeannette, Westmoreland, Pop. 10,196
Jeannette CSD 1,400/K-12
Park St 15644 724-523-5497
Vincent Aiello, supt. Fax 523-3289
wiu.k12.pa.us/jeannette/
Jeannette HS 400/9-12
200 Florida Ave 15644 724-523-5591
Sharon Marks, prin. Fax 523-5534
Jeannette McKee MS 300/6-8
1000 Lowry Ave 15644 724-527-1591
Matthew Jones, prin. Fax 523-6792

Christian Fellowship Academy 200/PK-12
2005 Ridge Rd 15644 724-523-2358
Sharon Herbster, prin. Fax 523-5439
Monsour Medical Center Post-Sec.
70 Lincoln Hwy E 15644 724-527-0600

Jefferson, Allegheny, Pop. 979
Jefferson-Morgan SD 900/K-12
1351 Jefferson Rd 15344 724-883-2310
Donna Furnier Ph.D., supt. Fax 883-4942
www.jmsd.org/
Jefferson-Morgan HS 300/9-12
1351 Jefferson Rd 15344 724-883-2310
Thomas Katruska, prin. Fax 883-3786
Jefferson-Morgan MS 100/7-8
1351 Jefferson Rd 15344 724-883-2310
Carol Korber, prin. Fax 883-3786

Jefferson Hills, Allegheny, Pop. 9,642
West Jefferson Hills SD 2,900/K-12
835 Old Clairton Rd 15025 412-655-8450
Dr. John P. Lozosky, supt. Fax 655-9544
www.wjhsd.net
Jefferson HS 1,100/9-12
310 Old Clairton Rd 15025 412-655-8610
Dr. Bart Rocco, prin. Fax 655-8618
Other Schools – See Pittsburgh

Jenkintown, Montgomery, Pop. 4,404
Jenkintown SD 500/K-12
325 Highland Ave 19046 215-885-3722
Dr. Raymond J. Boccuti, supt. Fax 885-2090
www.jenkintown.org/
Jenkintown JSHS 200/7-12
325 Highland Ave 19046 215-884-1801
Dr. Lorraine Trollinger, prin. Fax 885-2090

Abington Friends S 700/PK-12
575 Washington Ln 19046 215-886-4350
Richard Nourie, hdmstr. Fax 886-9143
Manor College Post-Sec.
700 Fox Chase Rd 19046 215-885-2360
St. Basil Academy 400/9-12
711 Fox Chase Rd 19046 215-885-3771
Sr. Carla Hernandez, prin. Fax 885-4025

Jermyn, Lackawanna, Pop. 2,244
Lakeland SD 1,700/K-12
1593 Lakeland Dr 18433 570-254-9485
Dr. Margaret Billings-Jones, supt. Fax 254-9224
www.lakelandsd.org
Lakeland JSHS 900/7-12
1593 Lakeland Dr 18433 570-254-9485
Joseph Hanni, prin. Fax 254-6730

Jersey Shore, Lycoming, Pop. 4,426
Jersey Shore Area SD 2,900/K-12
175 A and P Dr 17740 570-398-1561
Richard Emery, supt. Fax 398-5089
www.jsasd.k12.pa.us
Jersey Shore Area HS 1,000/9-12
701 Cemetery St 17740 570-398-7170
Mary Thomas, prin. Fax 398-5612
Jersey Shore Area MS 700/6-8
601 Thompson St 17740 570-398-7400
Reed Mellinger, prin. Fax 398-5618

Jim Thorpe, Carbon, Pop. 4,892
Area Vocational Technical School
Supt. — None
Carbon Career & Technical Institute Vo/Tech
150 W 13th St 18229 570-325-3682
Dr. Robert Mauro, prin.

Jim Thorpe Area SD 1,900/K-12
410 Center Ave 18229 570-325-3691
Keith Boyer, supt. Fax 325-3699
www.jtasd.org/
Jim Thorpe Area HS 800/7-12
1 Olympian Way 18229 570-325-3663
Thomas Lesisko, prin. Fax 325-8973

Adventure Learning Center 100/7-12
1398 State Route 903 Ste 3 18229 570-325-5681
Richard Kerzner, dir.

Johnsonburg, Elk, Pop. 2,817
Johnsonburg Area SD 800/K-12
315 High School Rd 15845 814-965-2536
Walter Fitch, supt. Fax 965-5809
Johnsonburg Area JSHS 400/7-12
315 High School Rd 15845 814-965-2556
Donald Wismar, prin. Fax 965-5809

Johnstown, Cambria, Pop. 22,539
Area Vocational Technical School
Supt. — None
Greater Johnstown AVTS Vo/Tech
445 Schoolhouse Rd 15904 814-269-4545
Joseph Rizzo, prin.

Conemaugh Valley SD 900/K-12
1451 Frankstown Rd 15902 814-535-3957
William Rushin, supt. Fax 536-8902
Conemaugh Valley JSHS 400/7-12
1342 William Penn Ave 15906 814-535-5523
James Cekada, prin. Fax 536-4025

Ferndale Area SD 800/K-12
100 Dartmouth Ave 15905 814-535-1507
Dr. Christine Oldham, supt. Fax 535-8527
www.fasdk12.org/index800600.html
Ferndale Area JSHS 400/7-12
600 Harlan Ave 15905 814-288-5757
Kathy Nagle, prin. Fax 288-5224

Greater Johnstown SD 3,300/PK-12
1091 Broad St 15906 814-533-5651
Barbara Parkins, supt. Fax 533-5655
www.gjsd.net
Greater Johnstown HS 1,000/9-12
222 Central Ave 15902 814-533-5603
Dan Resenic, prin. Fax 533-5698
Greater Johnstown MS 700/6-8
280 Decker Ave 15906 814-533-5570
Darren Buchko, prin. Fax 533-5564

Richland SD 1,600/K-12
220 Highfield St Ste 102 15904 814-266-6063
Gerald Davitch, supt. Fax 266-7349
www.richlandsd.com/
Richland HS 700/8-12
220 Highfield St 15904 814-266-6081
Thomas Fleming, prin. Fax 269-9506

Westmont Hilltop SD 1,700/K-12
827 Diamond Blvd 15905 814-255-6751
Dr. Susan Anderson, supt. Fax 255-7735
Westmont Hilltop HS 600/9-12
200 Fair Oaks Dr 15905 814-255-8726
William Marshall, prin. Fax 255-2704
Westmont Hilltop MS 500/5-8
827 Diamond Blvd 15905 814-255-8704
Carole Kakabar, prin. Fax 255-8783

Bishop McCort HS 500/9-12
25 Osborne St 15905 814-536-8991
Kenneth Salem, prin. Fax 535-4118
Cambria County Christian S 100/K-12
561 Pike Rd 15909 814-749-7406
Charlie Fenchak, admin. Fax 749-7028
Cambria-Rowe Business College Post-Sec.
221 Central Ave 15902 814-536-5168
Commonwealth Technical Institute Post-Sec.
727 Goucher St 15905 814-255-8200
Conemaugh Valley Memorial Hospital Post-Sec.
1086 Franklin St 15905 814-534-9118
Davidsville Christian S 50/PK-12
197 Pender Rd 15905 814-479-2525
Melissa Allison, admin. Fax 479-7908
Greater Johnstown Area Voc Tech School Post-Sec.
445 Schoolhouse Rd 15904 814-266-6073
PA Academy of Cosmetic Arts & Sciences Post-Sec.
2445 Bedford St 15904 814-269-3444
Pennsylvania Highlands Community College Post-Sec.
PO Box 68 15907 814-532-5300
University of Pittsburgh at Johnstown Post-Sec.
450 Schoolhouse Rd 15904 814-269-7000

Jonestown, Lebanon, Pop. 1,008

Blue Mountain Christian S 100/K-12
14 Silvertown Rd 17038 717-865-9650
Janet Catani, admin. Fax 865-4732

Kane, McKean, Pop. 3,893
Kane Area SD 1,400/K-12
400 W Hemlock Ave 16735 814-837-9570
Sandra Chlopecki, supt. Fax 837-7450
www.kasd.net
Kane Area HS 400/9-12
300 Hemlock Ave 16735 814-837-6821
Jeff Kepler, prin. Fax 837-6158
Kane Area MS 400/6-8
400 W Hemlock Ave 16735 814-837-6030
James Fryzlewicz, prin. Fax 837-9133

Karns City, Butler, Pop. 234
Karns City Area SD 1,800/K-12
1446 Kittanning Pike 16041 724-756-2030
Larry Henry, supt. Fax 756-2121
www.karnscity.k12.pa.us
Karns City JSHS 900/7-12
1446 Kittanning Pike 16041 724-756-2030
Dave Beck, prin. Fax 756-2121

Kennett Square, Chester, Pop. 5,292
Kennett Consolidated SD 4,000/K-12
300 E South St 19348 610-444-6600
Dr. Rudolph Karkosak, supt. Fax 444-6614
kcsd.org
Kennett HS 1,100/9-12
100 E South St 19348 610-444-6623
Wesley McDowell, prin. Fax 444-6237
Other Schools – See Landenberg

Unionville-Chadds Ford SD 3,900/K-12
740 Unionville Rd 19348 610-347-0970
Sharon Parker, supt. Fax 347-0976
www.ucfsd.org
Patton MS 1,000/6-8
760 Unionville Rd 19348 610-347-2000
Bruce Vosburgh, prin. Fax 347-0421
Unionville HS 1,300/9-12
750 Unionville Rd 19348 610-347-1600
Jim Fulginti, prin. Fax 347-1890

Kimberton, Chester

Kimberton Waldorf S 300/PK-12
PO Box 350 19442 610-933-3635
Paula Moraine, chrpsn. Fax 935-6985

King of Prussia, Montgomery, Pop. 18,406
Upper Merion Area SD 3,500/K-12
435 Crossfield Rd 19406 610-205-6401
Dr. Melinda Jamula, supt. Fax 205-6433
www.umasd.org
Upper Merion HS 1,100/9-12
440 Crossfield Rd 19406 610-205-3801
Jonathan Bauer, prin. Fax 205-3993
Upper Merion MS 1,100/5-8
450 Crossfield Rd 19406 610-205-8801
John Adiletto, prin. Fax 205-8999

ITT Technical Institute Post-Sec.
760 Moore Rd 19406 610-491-8004

Kingsley, Susquehanna
Mountain View SD 1,400/K-12
RR 1 Box 339A 18826 570-434-2180
Dr. Andrew Chichura, supt. Fax 434-2404
www.mvsd.net
Mountain View JSHS 800/7-12
RR 1 Box 339 18826 570-434-2501
Fax 434-9582

Kingston, Luzerne, Pop. 13,176
Area Vocational Technical School
Supt. — None
West Side AVTS, 75 Evans St 18704 Vo/Tech
Peter Halesey, prin. 570-288-8493

Wyoming Valley West SD 5,000/K-12
450 N Maple Ave 18704 570-288-6551
Dr. Michael Garzella, supt. Fax 288-1564
www.wvwspartans.org
Wyoming Valley West MS 1,400/6-8
201 Chester St 18704 570-287-2131
David Tosh, prin. Fax 287-6343
Other Schools – See Plymouth

Wyoming Seminary 400/9-12
201 N Sprague Ave 18704 570-270-2100
Jeremy Packard, hdmstr. Fax 270-2199

Kintnersville, Bucks
Palisades SD 2,100/K-12
39 Thomas Free Dr 18930 610-847-5131
Francis V. Barnes Ph.D., supt. Fax 847-8116
www.palisadessd.org
Palisades HS 700/9-12
35 Church Hill Rd 18930 610-847-5131
Richard Heffernan, prin. Fax 847-2562
Palisades MS 500/6-8
4710 Durham Rd 18930 610-847-5131
Edward Baumgartner, prin. Fax 847-2691

Kinzers, Lancaster
Pequea Valley SD 1,900/K-12
PO Box 130 17535 717-768-5530
Patrick Hallock, supt. Fax 768-7176
www.pvsd.k12.pa.us
Pequea Valley HS 600/9-12
PO Box 287 17535 717-768-5500
Brian Bliss, prin. Fax 768-5523
Pequea Valley IS 500/6-8
PO Box 257 17535 717-768-5535
Erik Orndorff, prin. Fax 768-5656

Kittanning, Armstrong, Pop. 4,454
Armstrong SD
Supt. — See Ford City
Kittanning Area MS 600/6-8
210 N Mckean St 16201 724-543-1295
Michael S. Cominos, prin. Fax 543-1155
Kittanning HS 700/9-12
1200 Orr Ave 16201 724-543-1591
James Rummel, prin. Fax 543-1712

Armstrong County Memorial Hospital Post-Sec.
1 Nolte Dr 16201 724-543-8404
Kittanning Beauty School Post-Sec.
120 Market St 16201 800-833-4247

Knox, Clarion, Pop. 1,122
Keystone SD 1,200/K-12
451 Huston Ave 16232 814-797-5921
Dr. Jean Gool, supt. Fax 797-2382
www.keyknox.com
Keystone JSHS 600/7-12
700 Beatty Ave 16232 814-797-1261
Vicky Walters, prin. Fax 797-2868

Kutztown, Berks, Pop. 4,926
Kutztown Area SD 1,800/K-12
50 Trexler Ave 19530 610-683-7361
Dr. Brenda Winkler, supt. Fax 683-7230
www.kasd.org
Kutztown Area HS 600/9-12
50 Trexler Ave 19530 610-683-7346
Eric Erb, prin. Fax 894-4801
Kutztown Area MS 500/6-8
10 Deisher Ln 19530 610-683-3575
Matthew Smith, prin. Fax 683-5460

Kutztown University of Pennsylvania Post-Sec.
19530 610-683-4000

Lake Ariel, Wayne
Western Wayne SD
Supt. — See South Canaan
Western Wayne HS 800/9-12
1970A Easton Tpke 18436 570-937-4113
R. Jay Starnes, prin. Fax 937-4707
Western Wayne MS 600/6-8
1970B Easton Tpke 18436 570-937-3010
Peter Chapla, prin. Fax 937-3440

Canaan Christian Academy 200/PK-12
30 Hemlock Rd 18436 570-937-4848
David Marquette, prin. Fax 937-4800

Lampeter, Lancaster
Lampeter-Strasburg SD 3,200/K-12
PO Box 428 17537 717-464-3311
Dr. Robert A. Frick, supt. Fax 464-4699
www.l-spioneers.org
Lampeter-Strasburg HS 1,000/9-12
PO Box 428 17537 717-464-3311
Carroll Staub, prin. Fax 464-2367
Meylin MS 800/6-8
PO Box 428 17537 717-464-3311
Michael Burcin, prin. Fax 509-0289

Lancaster, Lancaster, Pop. 54,757
Conestoga Valley SD 3,900/K-12
2110 Horseshoe Rd 17601 717-397-2421
Dr. Gerald Huesken, supt. Fax 397-0442
www.cvsd.k12.pa.us
Conestoga Valley HS 1,200/9-12
2110 Horseshoe Rd 17601 717-397-5231
Brian Ginter, prin. Fax 397-8841
Conestoga Valley MS 700/7-8
500 Mount Sidney Rd 17602 717-397-1294
Robert Houghton, prin. Fax 397-4404

Hempfield SD
Supt. — See Landisville
Centerville MS 700/7-8
865 Centerville Rd 17601 717-898-5580
William Cackovic, prin. Fax 898-5513

Lancaster SD 11,100/K-12
1020 Lehigh Ave 17602 717-291-6121
Fax 396-6844
www.lancaster.k12.pa.us
Hand MS 600/6-8
431 S Ann St 17602 717-291-6161
Larry Mays, prin. Fax 399-6407
Lincoln MS 700/6-8
1001 Lehigh Ave 17602 717-291-6187
Josh Keene, prin. Fax 399-6408
McCaskey East HS 9-12
1051 Lehigh Ave 17602 717-291-6172
Damaso Albino, prin. Fax 391-8601
McCaskey HS 3,000/9-12
445 N Reservoir St 17602 717-291-6211
Dwight Nolt, prin. Fax 390-2567
Reynolds MS 600/6-8
605 W Walnut St 17603 717-291-6257
Arnold Raffone, prin. Fax 399-6409
Wheatland MS 700/6-8
919 Hamilton Park Dr 17603 717-291-6285
Marty Slaugh, prin. Fax 399-6411

Manheim Township SD
Supt. — See Lititz
Manheim Twp. HS 1,700/9-12
PO Box 5134 17606 717-560-3097
David Hanna, prin. Fax 569-2806
Manheim Twp. MS 900/6-8
PO Box 5134 17606 717-560-3111
Christopher Adams, prin. Fax 569-1670

Penn Manor SD 5,400/K-12
2950 Charlestown Rd 17603 717-872-9500
Donald F. Stewart, supt. Fax 872-9505
www.pennmanor.net
Manor MS 500/7-8
2950 Charlestown Rd 17603 717-872-9510
Dana Edwards, prin. Fax 872-9505
Other Schools – See Millersville, Pequea

Consolidated School of Business Post-Sec.
2124 Ambassador Cir 17603 717-394-6211
Dayspring Christian Academy 300/PK-12
1008 New Holland Ave 17601 717-295-6400
Michael Myers, hdmstr. Fax 295-6410
Empire Beauty School Post-Sec.
1801 Columbia Ave 17603 717-394-8561
Franklin & Marshall College Post-Sec.
PO Box 3003 17604 717-291-3911
Lancaster Bible College Post-Sec.
901 Eden Rd 17601 717-569-7071
Lancaster Christian S 300/K-12
651 Lampeter Rd 17602 717-392-8092
Dr. Sandy Outlar, hdmstr. Fax 509-3094
Lancaster Country Day S 500/PK-12
725 Hamilton Rd 17603 717-392-2916
Michael Mersky, prin. Fax 392-0425
Lancaster General College of Nursing Post-Sec.
410 N Lime St 17602 717-544-6912
Lancaster HS 700/9-12
650 Juliette Ave 17601 717-509-0315
Dermot Garrett, prin. Fax 509-0312
Lancaster Mennonite S 1,300/K-12
2176 Lincoln Hwy E 17602 717-299-0436
J. Richard Thomas, supt. Fax 299-0823
Lancaster School of Cosmetology Post-Sec.
50 Ranck Ave 17602 717-299-0200
Lancaster Theological Seminary Post-Sec.
555 W James St 17603 717-393-0654
Living Word Academy 300/PK-12
2384 New Holland Pike 17601 717-556-0711
Mark Cote, hdmstr. Fax 656-4868
Pennsylvania College of Art and Design Post-Sec.
PO Box 59 17608 717-396-7833
Resurrection MS 200/4-8
521 E Orange St 17603 717-392-3083
Brenda Weaver, prin. Fax 735-7793
Thaddeus Stevens College of Technology Post-Sec.
750 E King St 17602 717-299-7730
York Technical Institute Post-Sec.
3050 Hempland Rd 17601 800-227-9675

Landenberg, Chester
Kennett Consolidated SD
Supt. — See Kennett Square
Kennett MS, 195 Sunny Dell Rd 19350 1,000/6-8
John Carr, prin. 610-268-5800

Landisville, Lancaster, Pop. 4,239
Hempfield SD 7,300/K-12
200 Church St 17538 717-898-5500
Dr. David Poore, supt. Fax 898-5628
www.hempfieldsd.org
Hempfield HS 2,400/9-12
200 Stanley Ave 17538 717-898-5510
John Sparmblack, prin. Fax 898-5518
Landisville MS 600/7-8
340 Mumma Dr 17538 717-898-5607
Dr. Nancy Herr, prin. Fax 898-1603
Other Schools – See Lancaster

Langhorne, Bucks, Pop. 1,974
Neshaminy SD 9,300/K-12
2001 Old Lincoln Hwy 19047 215-752-6300
Paul Kadri, supt. Fax 752-6374
www.neshaminy.k12.pa.us
Maple Point MS 1,100/6-9
2250 Langhorne Yardley Rd 19047 215-752-6900
Mark Collins, prin.
Neshaminy MS 700/6-9
1200 Langhorne Newtown Rd 19047 215-752-3600
Karen Wychock, prin. Fax 702-0363
Neshaminy SHS 2,300/10-12
2001 Old Lincoln Hwy 19047 215-752-6451
Alex Menio, prin. Fax 752-6320
Other Schools – See Feasterville, Levittown

Philadelphia Biblical University Post-Sec.
200 Manor Ave 19047 215-752-5800
Woods Services Post-Sec.
PO Box 36 19047 800-782-3646

Lansdale, Montgomery, Pop. 15,913
Area Vocational Technical School
Supt. — None
North Montco Tech Career Center Vo/Tech
1265 Sumneytown Pike 19446 215-368-1177
Michael Lucas, prin.

North Penn SD 13,300/K-12
401 E Hancock St 19446 215-368-0400
Dr. Robert Hassler, supt. Fax 368-3161
www.npenn.org
North Penn SHS 3,300/10-12
1340 S Valley Forge Rd 19446 215-368-9800
Burton Hynes, prin. Fax 855-0632
Penndale MS 1,500/7-9
400 Penn St 19446 215-368-2700
Dr. Sean O'Sullivan, prin. Fax 368-6817
Other Schools – See Hatfield, North Wales

Calvary Baptist Christian S 300/PK-12
1380 S Valley Forge Rd 19446 215-368-1100
Randy Thaxton, prin. Fax 368-1003
Calvary Baptist Theological Seminary Post-Sec.
1380 S Valley Forge Rd 19446 215-368-7538
Dock Mennonite HS 400/9-12
1000 Forty Foot Rd 19446 215-362-2675
Elaine Moyer, prin. Fax 362-2943
Lansdale Catholic HS 800/9-12
700 Lansdale Ave 19446 215-362-6160
Linda Robinson, prin. Fax 362-5746
Lansdale School of Cosmetology Post-Sec.
215 W Main St 19446 215-362-2322

Lansdowne, Delaware, Pop. 10,789
William Penn SD 4,900/K-12
100 Green Ave 19050 610-284-8000
Dana Bedden, supt. Fax 284-8054
www.wpsd.k12.pa.us
Penn Wood SHS 1,200/10-12
100 Green Ave 19050 610-284-8080
John Leary, prin. Fax 284-2141
Other Schools – See Darby, Yeadon

Lansford, Carbon, Pop. 4,210
Panther Valley SD 1,500/K-12
PO Box 40 18232 570-645-4248
J. Christopher West, supt. Fax 645-6232
www.panthervalley.org/
Panther Valley HS 500/9-12
PO Box 40 18232 570-645-2171
George Gillespie, prin. Fax 645-2507
Panther Valley MS 400/6-8
PO Box 40 18232 570-645-2175
Amanda Zaremba, prin. Fax 645-9723

La Plume, Lackawanna

Keystone College Post-Sec.
PO Box 50 18440 570-945-5141

Laporte, Sullivan, Pop. 276
Sullivan County SD
Supt. — See Dushore
Sullivan County JSHS 400/7-12
PO Box 98 18626 570-946-7001
Linda Rogers, prin. Fax 946-5070

Latrobe, Westmoreland, Pop. 8,654
Area Vocational Technical School
Supt. — None
Eastern Westmoreland CTC Vo/Tech
4904 State Route 982 15650 724-539-9788
Marie Bowers, prin. Fax 539-1907

Greater Latrobe SD 4,300/K-12
410 Main St 15650 724-539-4200
Dr. William Stavisky, supt. Fax 539-4202
grlatrobe.k12.pa.us/
Greater Latrobe JHS 1,100/7-9
130 High School Rd 15650 724-539-4265
Carla Baldwin, prin. Fax 539-4223
Greater Latrobe SHS 1,100/10-12
131 High School Rd 15650 724-539-4225
Dr. Georgia Teppert, prin. Fax 539-4295

Latrobe Area Hospital Post-Sec.
101 W 2nd Ave 15650 724-537-1001
St. Vincent College Post-Sec.
300 Fraser Purchase Rd 15650 724-539-9761
St. Vincent Seminary Post-Sec.
300 Fraser Purchase Rd 15650 724-537-4592

Laureldale, Berks, Pop. 3,752
Muhlenberg SD 3,100/K-12
801 E Bellevue Ave 19605 610-921-8000
Dr. Theresa Haught, supt. Fax 921-8076
www.muhlsd.berksiu.k12.pa.us/
Muhlenberg HS 1,000/9-12
Sharp Ave & Frances St 19605 610-921-8078
Scott Schwenk, prin. Fax 921-7925
Muhlenberg MS 800/6-8
801 E Bellevue Ave 19605 610-921-8034
Donna Albright, prin. Fax 921-8038

Lebanon, Lebanon, Pop. 23,986
Area Vocational Technical School
Supt. — None
Lebanon County CTC Vo/Tech
833 Metro Dr 17042 717-273-8551
George Custer, dir. Fax 273-0534

Cornwall-Lebanon SD 4,800/K-12
105 E Evergreen Rd 17042 717-272-2031
Thomas Sherk, supt. Fax 274-2786
www.clsd.k12.pa.us
Cedar Crest HS 1,600/9-12
115 E Evergreen Rd 17042 717-272-2033
David Helsel, prin. Fax 273-3250
Cedar Crest MS 1,100/6-8
101 E Evergreen Rd 17042 717-272-2032
Philip Domencic, prin. Fax 228-1437

Lebanon SD 4,300/PK-12
1000 S 8th St 17042 717-273-9391
Dr. Marianne T. Bartley, supt. Fax 270-6778
www.lebanon.k12.pa.us
Lebanon HS 1,100/9-12
1000 S 8th St 17042 717-273-9391
Thomas Jordan, prin. Fax 270-6778
Lebanon MS 1,000/6-8
350 N 8th St 17046 717-273-9391
Mary Garrett, prin. Fax 270-6859

Empire Beauty School Post-Sec.
1776 Quentin Rd 17042 717-272-3323
Lebanon Catholic S 500/K-12
1400 Chestnut St 17042 717-273-3731
Michele Ambrosia, admin. Fax 274-5167
Lebanon Christian Academy 100/K-12
875 Academy Dr 17046 717-273-8114
Jeff Griffith, prin. Fax 272-1886
Lebanon County Career School Post-Sec.
18 E Weidman St 17046 800-694-8804
New Covenant Christian S 200/PK-12
452 Ebenezer Rd 17046 717-274-2423
Dr. Timothy Deibler, admin. Fax 274-9830

Leechburg, Armstrong, Pop. 2,269
Kiski Area SD 4,500/K-12
250 Hyde Park Rd 15656 724-845-2022
Dr. John Meighan, supt. Fax 842-0444
www.kiskiarea.com
Kiski Area HS 1,500/9-12
250 Hyde Park Rd 15656 724-845-8181
William McClarnon, prin. Fax 842-0403
Kiski Area IS 800/7-8
260 Hyde Park Rd 15656 724-845-2219
Patrick Hefflin, prin. Fax 845-3208

Leechburg Area SD 800/K-12
210 Penn Ave 15656 724-842-9681
James Budzilek, supt. Fax 845-2241
www.leechburg.k12.pa.us
Leechburg Area HS 200/9-12
215 1st St 15656 724-842-0571
Karen Hulse, prin. Fax 845-4761
Leechburg Area MS 200/6-8
215 1st St 15656 724-842-0571
Karen Hulse, prin. Fax 845-4761

Leesport, Berks, Pop. 1,916
Area Vocational Technical School
Supt. — None
Berks CTC - West Vo/Tech
1057 County Road 19533 610-374-4073
James Casper, prin. Fax 987-6106

Schuylkill Valley SD 2,000/K-12
929 Lakeshore Dr 19533 610-916-0957
Dr. Solomon Lausch, supt. Fax 926-3960
www.schuylkillvalley.org/
Schuylkill Valley HS 700/9-12
929 Lakeshore Dr 19533 610-926-1706
David Haughney, prin. Fax 926-8341
Schuylkill Valley MS 500/6-8
114 Ontelaunee Dr 19533 610-926-7111
Judith Sargent, prin. Fax 926-3321

Leetsdale, Allegheny, Pop. 1,152
Quaker Valley SD
Supt. — See Sewickley
Quaker Valley SHS 500/10-12
625 Beaver St 15056 412-749-6000
Fax 749-6011

Lehighton, Carbon, Pop. 5,523
Lehighton Area SD 2,400/K-12
1000 Union St 18235 610-377-4490
Lamar Snyder, supt. Fax 377-2423
www.lehighton.org/
Lehighton Area HS, 1 Indian Ln 18235 800/9-12
Dr. Gary Von Norman, prin. 610-377-6180
Lehighton Area MS 800/5-8
301 Beaver Run Rd 18235 610-377-6535
Timothy Kach, prin.

Lehman, Luzerne
Lake-Lehman SD 2,200/K-12
PO Box 38 18627 570-675-2165
James McGovern, supt. Fax 675-7657
www.lake-lehman.k12.pa.us/
Lake-Lehman JSHS 1,100/7-12
PO Box 38 18627 570-675-7458
Tracey Wagner, prin. Fax 675-2951

Pennsylvania State University Post-Sec.
PO Box PSU 18627 570-675-2171

Lemoyne, Cumberland, Pop. 3,952
West Shore SD
Supt. — See Lewisberry
Lemoyne MS, 701 Market St 17043 400/6-8
Thomas Haupt, prin. 717-761-6345

Leola, Lancaster, Pop. 5,685

Veritas Academy 100/K-12
26 Hillcrest Ave 17540 717-556-0690
G. Tyler Fischer, hdmstr. Fax 556-0736

Lester, Delaware

All-State Career School Post-Sec.
501 Seminole St 19029 610-521-1818

Levittown, Bucks, Pop. 53,700
Bristol Township SD 5,500/K-12
6401 Mill Creek Rd 19057 215-943-3200
Ellen Budman, supt. Fax 949-2210
www.bucksiu.org/btsd/
Franklin MS 300/7-9
6403 Mill Creek Rd 19057 215-949-8903
Stanley Vitale, prin. Fax 547-8415
Truman HS 1,500/10-12
3001 Green Ln 19057 215-547-3000
William Haws, prin. Fax 547-4802
Other Schools – See Bristol, Fairless Hills

Neshaminy SD
Supt. — See Langhorne
Sandburg MS, 30 Harmony Rd 19056 700/6-9
Dawn Kelly, prin. 215-943-0360

Levittown Beauty Academy Post-Sec.
8919 New Falls Rd 19054 215-943-0298

Lewisberry, York, Pop. 389
West Shore SD 8,200/K-12
507 Fishing Creek Rd 17339 717-938-9577
Dr. Richard Domencic, supt. Fax 938-2779
www.wssd.k12.pa.us
Crossroads MS 800/6-8
535 Fishing Creek Rd 17339 717-932-1295
David Zuilkoski, prin.
Red Land HS 1,200/9-12
560 Fishing Creek Rd 17339 717-938-6561
Edward Novosel, prin. Fax 938-0886
Other Schools – See Camp Hill, Lemoyne, New Cumberland

Lewisburg, Union, Pop. 5,562
Lewisburg Area SD 1,800/K-12
PO Box 351 17837 570-523-3220
Dr. Mark DiRocco, supt. Fax 522-3278
www.dragon.k12.pa.us
Eichhorn MS 400/6-8
2057 Washington Ave 17837 570-523-3220
Tracy Krum, prin. Fax 522-3331
Lewisburg Area HS 600/9-12
815 Market St 17837 570-523-3220
David Himes, prin. Fax 524-9484

Bucknell University 17837 Post-Sec.
570-577-2000

Lewistown, Mifflin, Pop. 8,649
Area Vocational Technical School
Supt. — None
Mifflin-Juniata CTC, 700 Pitt St 17044 Vo/Tech
Kevin O'Donnell, prin. 717-248-3933

Mifflin County SD 5,900/K-12
201 8th St 17044 717-248-0148
David Runk, supt. Fax 248-5345
www.mcsdk12.org
Indian Valley HS 1,000/9-12
700 Cedar St 17044 717-248-5441
Ronald Varner, prin. Fax 242-5806
Lewistown Area HS 900/9-12
2 Manor Dr 17044 717-242-1401
Vance Varner, prin. Fax 242-5810
Lewistown MS 400/6-8
212 Green Ave 17044 717-242-5801
D. Robert Reeder, prin. Fax 242-5804
Other Schools – See Mc Veytown, Reedsville

Mifflin-Juniata Career & Technology Ctr Post-Sec.
700 Pitt St 17044 717-248-3933
South Hills School of Business & Tech. Post-Sec.
124 E Market St 17044 717-248-8140

Liberty, Tioga, Pop. 2,810
Southern Tioga SD
Supt. — See Blossburg
Liberty JSHS 300/7-12
PO Box 135 16930 570-324-2071
Francis Jaquish, prin. Fax 324-2313

Ligonier, Westmoreland, Pop. 1,622
Ligonier Valley SD 2,100/K-12
339 W Main St 15658 724-238-5696
Stephen Whisdosh Ed.D., supt. Fax 238-7877
wiu.k12.pa.us/ligonier/
Ligonier Valley HS 500/9-12
40 Springer Rd 15658 724-238-9531
Ronald Baldonieri, prin. Fax 238-2675
Ligonier Valley MS 400/5-8
536 Bell St 15658 724-238-6412
David Steimer, prin. Fax 238-2358
Other Schools – See New Florence

Limerick, Montgomery
Area Vocational Technical School
Supt. — None
Western Center for Technical Study Vo/Tech
77 Gratersford Rd 19468 610-489-7272
Maryann Jukubczyk, prin.

Chapel Christian Academy 200/K-12
378 W Ridge Pike 19468 610-489-6215
Robert Spare, prin.

Lincoln University, Chester

Lincoln University Post-Sec.
PO Box 179 19352 610-932-8300

Linesville, Crawford, Pop. 1,122
Conneaut SD 2,800/K-12
219 W School Dr 16424 814-683-5900
Dick Astor, supt. Fax 683-4127
connwww.iu5.org
Linesville HS 500/7-12
302 W School Dr 16424 814-683-5551
Sharon Sielski, prin. Fax 683-5221
Other Schools – See Conneaut Lake, Conneautville

Lititz, Lancaster, Pop. 9,008
Manheim Township SD 5,400/K-12
2933 Lititz Pike 17543 717-569-8231
Dr. Kevin Singer, supt. Fax 569-3729
www.mtwp.k12.pa.us
Other Schools – See Lancaster

Warwick SD 4,600/K-12
301 W Orange St 17543 717-626-3734
Dr. John George, supt. Fax 626-3850
www.warwick.k12.pa.us/
Warwick HS 1,500/9-12
301 W Orange St 17543 717-626-3700
Penny Mason, prin. Fax 626-6199
Warwick MS 800/7-8
401 Maple St 17543 717-626-3701
Michael O'Hara, prin. Fax 627-6089

Linden Hall S for Girls 100/6-12
212 E Main St 17543 717-626-8512
Dr. Vincent Stumpo, hdmstr. Fax 627-1384
Lititz Christian S 300/1-12
501 W Lincoln Ave 17543 717-626-9518
Rick Bernhardt, admin. Fax 626-5683

Littlestown, Adams, Pop. 4,131
Littlestown Area SD 2,500/K-12
162 Newark St 17340 717-359-4146
Dr. Robert McConaghy, supt. Fax 359-9617
www.lasd.k12.pa.us
Littlestown HS 700/9-12
200 E Myrtle St 17340 717-359-4146
Bryant Meckley, prin. Fax 359-9461
Maple Avenue MS 700/6-8
75 Maple Ave 17340 717-359-4146
Eric Naylor, prin. Fax 359-9617

Lock Haven, Clinton, Pop. 8,784
Keystone Central SD 4,400/K-12
95 W 4th St Ofc 1 17745 570-893-4900
Dr. Donald Wills, supt. Fax 893-4923
www.kcsd.k12.pa.us
Other Schools – See Mill Hall, Renovo

Lock Haven University Post-Sec.
401 N Fairview St 17745 570-893-2011

Loretto, Cambria, Pop. 1,166

St. Francis University Post-Sec.
PO Box 600 15940 814-472-3000

Lower Burrell, Westmoreland, Pop. 12,444
Burrell SD 2,200/K-12
1021 Puckety Church Rd 15068 724-334-1406
Anna Mary Palermo Ph.D., supt. Fax 334-1429
www.burrell.k12.pa.us
Burrell HS 700/9-12
1021 Puckety Church Rd 15068 724-334-1403
John Boylan, prin. Fax 334-1420
Huston MS 500/6-8
1020 Puckety Church Rd 15068 724-334-1443
Shannon Wagner, prin. Fax 334-1434

Newport Business Institute Post-Sec.
945 Greensburg Rd 15068 724-339-7542
Oakbridge Academy of Arts Post-Sec.
1250 Greensburg Rd 15068 724-335-5336

Loysburg, Bedford
Northern Bedford County SD 1,200/PK-12
152 NBC Dr 16659 814-766-2221
William Wade, supt. Fax 766-3772
Northern Bedford County MSHS 600/6-12
152 NBC Dr 16659 814-766-2221
Wayne Sherlock, prin. Fax 766-3772

Lykens, Dauphin, Pop. 1,862
Upper Dauphin Area SD 1,300/K-12
5668 State Route 209 17048 717-362-8134
Elaine Eib Ed.D., supt. Fax 362-3050
www.udasd.org/
Upper Dauphin Area MS 400/5-8
5668 State Route 209 17048 717-362-8177
Daniel Bulinski, prin. Fax 362-6567
Other Schools – See Elizabethville

Mc Alisterville, Juniata
Juniata County SD
Supt. — See Mifflintown
East Juniata JSHS 600/7-12
RR 2 Box 2411 17049 717-463-2111
Benjamin Fausey, prin. Fax 463-3268

Juniata Mennonite S 200/K-12
PO Box 278 17049 717-463-2898
Andrew Meiser, prin. Fax 463-0134

Mc Clellandtown, Fayette
Albert Gallatin Area SD
Supt. — See Uniontown
Gallatin North MS 500/6-8
113 College Ave 15458 724-737-5423
James Patitucci, prin. Fax 737-5312

Mc Clure, Snyder, Pop. 1,056

Mifflin County Christian Academy 100/PK-12
5113 Back Maitland Rd 17841 717-543-2200
Craig Todd, admin. Fax 543-2207

Mc Connellsburg, Fulton, Pop. 1,079
Area Vocational Technical School
Supt. — None
Fulton County AVTS Vo/Tech
145 E Cherry St 17233 717-485-5813
Elizabeth Cheatle, prin.

Central Fulton SD 1,000/PK-12
151 E Cherry St 17233 717-485-3183
Dr. Julia Cigola, supt. Fax 485-5984
www.cfsd.info
Mc Connellsburg HS 300/9-12
151 E Cherry St 17233 717-485-3195
Todd Beatty, prin. Fax 485-0175
Mc Connellsburg MS 200/6-8
151 E Cherry St 17233 717-485-4209
Todd Beatty, prin. Fax 485-0175

Mc Donald, Washington, Pop. 2,246
Fort Cherry SD 1,300/K-12
110 Fort Cherry Rd 15057 724-796-1551
Robert Dinnen Ph.D., supt. Fax 796-0065
www.fortcherry.org
Fort Cherry JSHS 700/7-12
110 Fort Cherry Rd 15057 724-796-1551
Timothy Royall, prin. Fax 356-2769

South Fayette Township SD 1,900/K-12
3660 Old Oakdale Rd 15057 412-221-4542
Dr. Linda Hippert, supt. Fax 693-0490
www.southfayette.org
South Fayette Township HS 500/9-12
3640 Old Oakdale Rd 15057 412-221-4542
Ann Bisignani, prin. Fax 693-9843
South Fayette Township MS 600/5-8
3700 Old Oakdale Rd 15057 412-221-4542
Karen Labutta, prin. Fax 693-0860

Mc Keesport, Allegheny, Pop. 23,343
Area Vocational Technical School
Supt. — None
McKeesport Area Tech Center Vo/Tech
1960 Eden Park Blvd 15132 412-664-3693
Dr. Julia Stewart, prin.

McKeesport Area SD 4,600/K-12
3590 Oneil Blvd 15132 412-664-3610
Patrick A. Risha, supt. Fax 664-3638
www.mckasd.com
Founders Hall MS 800/7-8
3600 Oneil Blvd 15132 412-664-3690
Dr. Timothy Gabauer, prin.
McKeesport Area HS 1,500/9-12
1960 Eden Park Blvd 15132 412-664-3650
Harry Bauman, prin.

South Allegheny SD 1,700/K-12
2743 Washington Blvd 15133 412-675-3070
Elaine M. Brown, supt. Fax 672-2836
www.southallegheny.org
South Allegheny HS 600/9-12
2743 Washington Blvd 15133 412-675-3070
Keith Gephart, prin. Fax 673-4903
South Allegheny MS 300/7-8
2743 Washington Blvd 15133 412-675-3070
Jeff Solomon, prin. Fax 673-4905

Pennsylvania State University Post-Sec.
0 University Dr 15132 412-675-9000
Serra Catholic HS 300/9-12
200 Hershey Dr 15132 412-751-2020
Michael Luft, prin. Fax 751-3488

Mc Kees Rocks, Allegheny, Pop. 7,235
Montour SD 3,200/K-12
223 Clever Rd 15136 412-490-6500
Dr. Carl DeJulio, supt. Fax 490-0828
www.montourschools.com
Montour HS 1,100/9-12
223 Clever Rd 15136 412-490-6500
Patrick Dworakowski, prin. Fax 494-9747
Other Schools – See Coraopolis

Sto-Rox SD 1,500/K-12
600 Russellwood Ave 15136 412-778-8871
Fran Serenka, supt. Fax 771-5205
www.srsd.k12.pa.us
Sto-Rox HS 500/9-12
1105 Valley St 15136 412-771-3213
Dr. Melanie Kerber, prin. Fax 771-8395
Sto-Rox MS 300/6-8
298 Ewing Rd 15136 412-771-3213
Janell Logue-Belden, prin. Fax 771-3848

Ohio Valley General Hospital Post-Sec.
25 Heckel Rd 15136 412-777-6207
Robinson Township Christian S 100/PK-12
77 Phillips Ln 15136 412-787-5919
Bob Alouise, prin. Fax 787-1558

Mc Murray, Washington, Pop. 4,082
Peters Township SD 4,000/K-12
631 E McMurray Rd 15317 724-941-6251
Dr. Timm Mackley, supt. Fax 941-6565
www.ptsd.k12.pa.us
Peters Township HS 1,300/9-12
264 E McMurray Rd 15317 724-941-6250
Dr. Thomas Hajzus, prin. Fax 942-0915
Peters Township MS 700/7-8
625 E McMurray Rd 15317 724-941-2688
Dr. Anthony Merante, prin. Fax 941-1426

Mc Sherrystown, Adams, Pop. 3,702

Delone Catholic HS 9-12
140 S Oxford Ave 17344 717-637-5969
Dr. Maureen Thiec, prin. Fax 637-0442

Macungie, Lehigh, Pop. 3,111
East Penn SD
Supt. — See Emmaus
Eyer MS, 5616 Buckeye Rd 18062 700/6-8
Dr. Douglas Wells, prin. 610-965-1600
Lower Macungie MS 1,100/6-8
6299 Lower Macungie Rd 18062 610-395-8593
Robert Misko, prin.

Salem Christian S 200/K-12
8031 Salem Bible Church Rd 18062 610-966-5823
Warren Skuret, admin. Fax 965-8368

Mc Veytown, Mifflin, Pop. 389
Mifflin County SD
Supt. — See Lewistown
Strodes Mills MS 200/6-8
205 Chestnut Ridge Rd 17051 717-248-5488
E. Terry Styers, prin. Fax 242-5839

Mahanoy City, Schuylkill, Pop. 4,462
Mahanoy Area SD 1,100/K-12
1 Golden Bear Dr 17948 570-773-3443
Anthony Crimaldi, supt. Fax 773-2913
Mahanoy Area HS 400/9-12
1 Golden Bear Dr 17948 570-773-3443
Charlotte Golden, prin.

Mahanoy Area MS 400/5-8
1 Golden Bear Dr 17948 570-773-3443
Joie Green, prin.

McCann School of Business & Technology Post-Sec.
47 S Main St 17948 570-773-1820

Malvern, Chester, Pop. 3,100
Great Valley SD 4,000/K-12
47 Church Rd 19355 610-889-2100
Rita Jones Ed.D., supt. Fax 889-2120
www.gvsd.org
Great Valley HS 1,200/9-12
225 Phoenixville Pike 19355 610-889-1900
John Fidler, prin. Fax 695-8901
Great Valley MS 1,000/6-8
255 Phoenixville Pike 19355 610-644-6440
Stephen Swymer Ed.D., prin. Fax 889-1166

Devereux Beneto Center Post-Sec.
655 Sugartown Rd # 297 19355 800-935-6789
Malvern Prep S 600/6-12
418 S Warren Ave 19355 484-595-1100
James Stewart, hdmstr. Fax 595-1124
Penn State Great Valley School Post-Sec.
30 E Swedesford Rd 19355 610-648-3200
Phelps S 200/7-12
583 Sugartown Rd 19355 610-644-1754
Christopher Chirielson, hdmstr. Fax 644-6679
Villa Maria Academy 400/9-12
370 Old Lincoln Hwy 19355 610-644-2551
Sr. Marita Carmel, prin. Fax 644-2866

Manchester, York, Pop. 2,436
Northeastern York SD 3,200/PK-12
41 Harding St 17345 717-266-3667
Dr. Dennis Baughman, supt. Fax 266-5792
www.nesd.k12.pa.us
Northeastern HS 900/9-12
300 High St 17345 717-266-3644
Dennis Ashton, prin. Fax 266-0616
Northeastern MS 600/7-8
198 N Hartman St 17345 717-266-3676
Michael Alessandroni, prin. Fax 266-9735

Manheim, Lancaster, Pop. 4,659
Manheim Central SD 3,100/K-12
71 N Hazel St 17545 717-665-3422
Carol Saylor, supt. Fax 665-7631
www.manheimcentral.org
Manheim Central HS 1,100/9-12
400 Adele Ave 17545 717-665-2451
Arlen Mummau, prin. Fax 665-9174
Manheim Central MS 500/7-8
123 E Gramby St 17545 717-665-2246
Dr. Scott Deisley, prin. Fax 665-9108

Mansfield, Tioga, Pop. 3,354
Southern Tioga SD
Supt. — See Blossburg
Mansfield JSHS 600/7-12
73 W Wellsboro St 16933 570-662-2674
Denise Drabick, prin. Fax 662-2808

Mansfield University of Pennsylvania Post-Sec.
Academy St 16933 570-662-4000
New Covenant Academy 100/PK-12
310 Extension St 16933 570-662-2996
Terry Mickey, hdmstr. Fax 662-0272

Maple Glen, Montgomery, Pop. 5,881
Upper Dublin SD 4,400/K-12
1580 Fort Washington Ave 19002 215-643-8800
Michael Pladus Ed.D., supt. Fax 643-8803
www.udsd.org
Other Schools – See Dresher, Fort Washington

Marienville, Forest
Forest Area SD
Supt. — See Tionesta
East Forest JSHS 100/7-12
120 W Birch St 16239 814-927-6688
Michael Hardy, prin. Fax 927-8452

Marietta, Lancaster, Pop. 2,603
Donegal SD
Supt. — See Mount Joy
Donegal MS 700/6-8
1175 River Rd 17547 717-426-4915
Judy Sammet, prin. Fax 426-2417

Marion Center, Indiana, Pop. 428
Marion Center Area SD 1,400/PK-12
PO Box 156 15759 724-397-5551
Francis Fregly, supt. Fax 397-9144
www.mcasd.net/
Marion Center Area HS 500/7-12
PO Box 209 15759 724-397-5551
Thomas Trunzo, prin.

Markleysburg, Fayette, Pop. 273
Uniontown Area SD
Supt. — See Uniontown
McMullen MS 200/6-8
4773 National Pike 15459 724-329-8811
Edward Fearer, prin.

Mar Lin, Schuylkill
Area Vocational Technical School
Supt. — None
Schuylkill Technology Center - South Vo/Tech
PO Box 110 17951 570-544-4748
Kurt Lynch, prin. Fax 544-3895

Mars, Butler, Pop. 1,707
Mars Area SD 2,900/K-12
545 Route 228 16046 724-625-1518
Dr. William Pettigrew, supt. Fax 625-1060
www.marsk12.org
Mars Area HS 900/9-12
520 Route 228 16046 724-625-1581
Anna Saker, prin. Fax 625-4477
Mars Area MS 700/6-8
1775 Three Degree Rd 16046 724-625-3145
Richard Cornell, prin. Fax 625-4470

Martinsburg, Blair, Pop. 2,157
Spring Cove SD
Supt. — See Roaring Spring

Central HS, RR 1 Box 420 16662 600/9-12
David Crumrine, prin. 814-793-2111

Meadville, Crawford, Pop. 13,368
Area Vocational Technical School
Supt. — None
Crawford County AVTS Vo/Tech
860 Thurston Rd 16335 814-724-6024
Neil Donovan, prin. Fax 337-0602

Crawford Central SD 4,100/K-12
11280 Mercer Pike 16335 814-724-3960
Michael E. Dolecki, supt. Fax 333-8731
www.craw.org
Meadville Area HS 1,000/9-12
930 North St 16335 814-336-1121
James T. Morgan, prin. Fax 337-1486
Meadville Area MS 500/7-8
974 North St 16335 814-333-1188
Rebecca James, prin. Fax 333-2799
Other Schools – See Cochranton

Allegheny College Post-Sec.
520 N Main St 16335 814-332-3100
Business Institute of Pennsylvania Post-Sec.
632 Arch St 16335 814-724-0700
Calvary Baptist Christian Academy 200/PK-12
543 Randolph St 16335 814-724-6606
Durwood Abbey, prin. Fax 724-6606

Mechanicsburg, Cumberland, Pop. 8,818
Area Vocational Technical School
Supt. — None
Cumberland-Perry AVTS Vo/Tech
110 Old Willow Mill Rd 17050 717-697-0354
Mary Rodman, prin. Fax 697-0592

Cumberland Valley SD 7,700/K-12
6746 Carlisle Pike 17050 717-697-8261
B. Jean Walker, supt. Fax 795-7084
www.cvschools.org
Cumberland Valley HS 2,500/9-12
6746 Carlisle Pike 17050 717-766-0217
Steven Kirkpatrick, prin. Fax 795-8940
Eagle View MS 1,100/6-8
6746 Carlisle Pike 17050 717-766-0217
Kaye Wishard, prin. Fax 697-3738
Good Hope MS 800/6-8
451 Skyport Rd 17050 717-761-1865
Matthew LaBuda, prin. Fax 761-5910

Mechanicsburg Area SD 3,200/K-12
100 E Elmwood Ave 17055 717-691-4500
Joseph Hood, supt. Fax 691-3438
www.mbgsd.org
Mechanicsburg Area HS 1,200/9-12
500 S Broad St 17055 717-691-4530
David Harris, prin. Fax 691-7632
Mechanicsburg Area MS 900/6-8
1750 S Market St 17055 717-691-4560
Leonard Ference, prin. Fax 791-7977

Computer Learning Network Post-Sec.
401 E Winding Hill Rd # 101 17055 717-761-1481
Emmanuel Baptist Christian Academy 100/PK-12
4681 E Trindle Rd 17050 717-761-7000
F. Ross Ritchey, prin. Fax 761-3207
Faith Tabernacle S 100/1-12
1410 Good Hope Rd 17050 717-975-0641
Lon Feaser, prin. Fax 975-9920
ITT Technical Institute Post-Sec.
5020 Louise Dr 17055 717-691-9263

Media, Delaware, Pop. 5,451
Rose Tree Media SD 4,000/K-12
308 N Olive St 19063 610-627-6000
Dr. Denise Kerr, supt. Fax 565-5317
www.rtmsd.org
Penncrest HS 1,300/9-12
134 Barren Rd 19063 610-627-6200
Kenneth Batchelor, prin. Fax 891-0898
Springton Lake MS 1,000/6-8
1900 N Providence Rd 19063 610-627-6500
Joyce Jeuell, prin. Fax 566-8665

Delaware County Community College Post-Sec.
901 Media Line Rd 19063 610-359-5000
Pennsylvania Institute of Technology Post-Sec.
800 Manchester Ave 19063 610-892-1500
Pennsylvania State University Post-Sec.
25 Yearsley Mill Rd 19063 610-892-1350
Williamson Free School of Mech. Trades Post-Sec.
106 S New Middletown Rd 19063 610-566-1776

Melrose Park, Montgomery, Pop. 6,500

Gratz College Post-Sec.
7605 Old York Rd 19027 215-635-7300
Saligman MS 100/6-8
7613 Old York Rd 19027 215-635-3303
Susan Friedman, prin. Fax 635-3325

Mercer, Mercer, Pop. 2,297
Area Vocational Technical School
Supt. — None
Mercer County Career Center Vo/Tech
PO Box 152 16137 724-662-3000
Rachel Martin, prin. Fax 662-1025

Mercer Area SD 1,500/K-12
545 W Butler St 16137 724-662-5100
Dr. William Gathers, supt. Fax 662-5109
www.mercer.k12.pa.us
Mercer Area HS 500/9-12
545 W Butler St 16137 724-662-5104
Dr. Hendley Hoge, prin. Fax 662-2993
Mercer Area MS 200/7-8
545 W Butler St 16137 724-662-5105
Timothy Dadich, prin. Fax 662-2993

Mercersburg, Franklin, Pop. 1,549
Tuscarora SD 2,700/K-12
118 E Seminary St 17236 717-328-3127
Dr. Thomas A. Stapleford, supt. Fax 328-9316
www.tus.k12.pa.us/

Buchanan HS 800/9-12
4773 Fort Loudon Rd 17236 717-328-2146
Rodney Benedick, prin. Fax 328-5428
Buchanan MS 600/6-8
5191 Fort Loudon Rd 17236 717-328-5221
Charles Rahauser, prin. Fax 328-9081

Mercersburg Academy 400/9-12
300 E Seminary St 17236 717-328-6113
Douglas Hale, hdmstr. Fax 328-9072

Merion Station, Montgomery, Pop. 700

Akiba Hebrew Academy 300/6-12
223 N Highland Ave 19066 610-667-4070
Rabbi Philip Field, prin. Fax 667-1046
Episcopal Academy 1,100/PK-12
376 N Latches Ln 19066 610-667-9612
Hamilton Clark, hdmstr. Fax 667-8629
Merion Mercy Academy 500/9-12
511 Montgomery Ave 19066 610-664-6655
Sr. Regina Ward, prin. Fax 664-6322

Mertztown, Berks
Brandywine Heights Area SD
Supt. — See Topton
Brandywine Heights Area HS 700/9-12
103 Old Topton Rd 19539 610-682-5102
Demetrios Thermenos, prin. Fax 682-5139

Gateway Christian S 100/K-12
245 Fredericksville Rd 19539 610-682-2748
Arthur Dexter, prin. Fax 682-9670

Meyersdale, Somerset, Pop. 2,340
Meyersdale Area SD 1,000/K-12
309 Industrial Park Rd 15552 814-634-5123
Curtis Kerns, supt. Fax 634-0832
www.masd.net
Meyersdale Area HS 400/9-12
1349 Shaw Mines Rd 15552 814-634-8311
John Wiltrout, prin. Fax 634-5100
Meyersdale Area MS 200/6-8
1353 Shaw Mines Rd 15552 814-634-1437

Middleburg, Snyder, Pop. 1,356
Midd-West SD 2,400/K-12
568 E Main St 17842 570-837-0046
William L. Houser, supt. Fax 837-3018
www.mwsd.cc
Middleburg MS 400/6-8
10 Dock Hill Rd 17842 570-837-0551
Donna Samuelson, prin. Fax 837-5061
Midd-West HS 800/9-12
540 E Main St 17842 570-837-0046
Ronald Renshaw, prin. Fax 837-5267
Other Schools – See Beaver Springs

Middletown, Dauphin, Pop. 8,944
Middletown Area SD 2,500/K-12
55 W Water St Ste 2 17057 717-948-3300
Richard Weinstein Ed.D., supt. Fax 948-3329
www.raiderweb.org
Middletown Area HS 700/9-12
1155 N Union St 17057 717-948-3333
Patrick Hruz, prin. Fax 948-3359
Middletown Area MS 700/6-8
215 Oberlin Rd 17057 717-948-3390
Russ Eppinger, prin. Fax 948-3392

Pennsylvania State University Post-Sec.
777 W Harrisburg Pike 17057 717-948-6000

Midland, Beaver, Pop. 2,969
Western Beaver County SD 900/K-12
343 Ridgemont Dr 15059 724-643-9310
Enrico Antonini, supt. Fax 643-8048
www.westernbeaver.org/
Other Schools – See Industry

Mifflinburg, Union, Pop. 3,578
Mifflinburg Area SD 2,300/K-12
PO Box 285 17844 570-966-8200
Barry Tomasetti, supt. Fax 966-8210
www.mifflinburg.org
Mifflinburg Area HS 800/9-12
75 Market St 17844 570-966-8230
Glenn Fogel, prin. Fax 966-8260
Mifflinburg Area MS 600/6-8
100 Mabel St 17844 570-966-8290
Marion Lynn, prin. Fax 966-8304

Mifflintown, Juniata, Pop. 846
Juniata County SD 3,100/K-12
HC 63 Box 7D 17059 717-436-2111
Dr. Kenneth Albaugh, supt. Fax 436-2777
www.jcsd.k12.pa.us
Juniata HS 600/9-12
RR 4 Box 259 17059 717-436-2193
Edward Apple, prin. Fax 436-2858
Tuscarora MS 500/6-8
RR 4 Box 118 17059 717-436-2165
Ralph Baker, prin. Fax 436-5999
Other Schools – See Mc Alisterville

Milford, Pike, Pop. 1,214
Delaware Valley SD 5,300/K-12
236 Route 6 And 209 18337 570-296-1800
Dr. Candis Finan, supt. Fax 296-3172
www.dvsd.org
Delaware Valley HS 9-10 900/9-10
256 Route 6 and 209 18337 570-409-2001
Michael Lacika, prin. Fax 409-2002
Delaware Valley HS 11-12 800/11-12
252 Route 6 And 209 18337 570-296-1850
Joseph Casmus, prin. Fax 296-3160
Delaware Valley MS 500/7-8
258 Route 6 And 209 18337 570-296-1830
Peter Ioppolo, prin. Fax 296-3162
Other Schools – See Dingmans Ferry

Mill Creek, Huntingdon, Pop. 335
Area Vocational Technical School
Supt. — None
Huntingdon County CTC Vo/Tech
PO Box E 17060 814-643-0951
Kenneth Parker, prin.

Millersburg, Dauphin, Pop. 2,491
Millersburg Area SD 900/K-12
799 Center St 17061 717-692-2108
John Fronk, supt. Fax 692-2895
www.mlbgsd.k12.pa.us/
Millersburg Area HS 300/9-12
799 Center St 17061 717-692-2108
S. Kirk Miller, prin.
Millersburg Area MS 200/6-8
799 Center St 17061 717-692-2108
Jeffrey Prouse, prin.

Millerstown, Perry, Pop. 682
Greenwood SD 900/K-12
405 E Sunbury St 17062 717-589-3117
Ed Burns, supt. Fax 589-3013
www.greenwoodsd.org
Greenwood HS 300/9-12
405 E Sunbury St 17062 717-589-3116
Nicholas Guarente, prin. Fax 589-7096
Greenwood MS 100/7-8
405 E Sunbury St 17062 717-589-3116
Nicholas Guarente, prin. Fax 589-7096

Millersville, Lancaster, Pop. 7,583
Penn Manor SD
Supt. — See Lancaster
Penn Manor HS 1,900/9-12
PO Box 1001 17551 717-872-9520
Janice Mindish, prin. Fax 872-0934

Millersville University of Pennsylvania Post-Sec.
PO Box 1002 17551 717-872-3024

Mill Hall, Clinton, Pop. 1,490
Area Vocational Technical School
Supt. — None
Keystone Central CTC Vo/Tech
64 Keystone Central Dr 17751 570-748-6584
Samuel Marolo, prin. Fax 748-5467

Keystone Central SD
Supt. — See Lock Haven
Central Mountain HS 1,400/9-12
64 Keystone Central Dr 17751 570-893-4646
Karen Probst, prin. Fax 893-4946
Central Mountain MS 1,000/6-8
200 Ben Ave 17751 570-726-3141
Norman Palovecsik, prin. Fax 726-7227

Millville, Columbia, Pop. 957
Millville Area SD 800/K-12
PO Box 260 17846 570-458-5538
Kathleen Stark Ed.D., supt. Fax 458-5584
www.millville.k12.pa.us
Millville Area JSHS 400/7-12
PO Box 260 17846 570-458-5538
Brian Seely, prin. Fax 458-5583

Milton, Northumberland, Pop. 6,484
Milton Area SD 2,400/K-12
700 Mahoning St 17847 570-742-7614
Dr. William Clark, supt. Fax 742-4523
www.milton.k12.pa.us
Milton Area HS 800/9-12
700 Mahoning St 17847 570-742-7611
Bryan Noaker, prin. Fax 742-4928
Milton Area MS 600/6-8
700 Mahoning St 17847 570-742-7685
V. David Brown, prin. Fax 742-4857

Meadowbrook Christian S 300/PK-12
363 Stamm Rd 17847 570-742-2638
W. Randall Reddinger, admin. Fax 742-4710

Minersville, Schuylkill, Pop. 4,337
Minersville Area SD 1,000/PK-12
PO Box 787 17954 570-544-4764
M. Joseph Brady, supt. Fax 544-6162
www.battlinminers.com
Minersville Area JSHS 500/7-12
PO Box 787 17954 570-544-4761
Carl McBreen, prin. Fax 544-5866

Mohrsville, Berks

King's Academy 200/K-12
1562 Main St 19541 610-926-9639
Barbara Ann Wilcox, admin. Fax 926-8089

Monaca, Beaver, Pop. 5,973
Area Vocational Technical School
Supt. — None
Beaver County AVTS Vo/Tech
145 Poplar Dr 15061 724-728-5800
Robert George, prin. Fax 775-2299

Center Area SD 2,000/K-12
160 Baker Rd Ext 15061 724-775-5600
Dr. Daniel Matsook, supt. Fax 775-4302
www.casd.k12.pa.us
Center Area HS 700/9-12
160 Baker Rd Ext 15061 724-775-4300
Anthony Mendicino, prin. Fax 775-4302
Center Area MS 500/6-8
160 Baker Rd Ext 15061 724-775-8200
Michael McCullough, prin. Fax 775-4302

Monaca SD 800/K-12
1500 Allen Ave 15061 724-775-3252
Dr. Michael Thomas, supt. Fax 775-3633
Monaca JSHS 400/7-12
1500 Allen Ave 15061 724-775-4320
Shawn McCreary, prin. Fax 770-9074

Community College of Beaver County Post-Sec.
1 Campus Dr 15061 724-775-8561
Pennsylvania State University Post-Sec.
Broadhead Rd 15061 724-773-3500

Monessen, Westmoreland, Pop. 8,307
Monessen CSD 1,100/K-12
1275 Rostraver St 15062 724-684-3600
Dr. Cynthia Chelen, supt. Fax 684-6782
www.monessen.k12.pa.us/index.html
Monessen HS 400/9-12
1245 State Rd 15062 724-684-7100
Randall Marino, prin. Fax 684-7925
Monessen MS 300/6-8
1245 State Rd 15062 724-684-6282
Randall Marino, prin. Fax 684-7925

Douglas Education Center Post-Sec.
130 7th St 15062 724-684-3684

Monongahela, Washington, Pop. 4,562
Ringgold SD
Supt. — See New Eagle
Carroll MS 300/6-8
120 Alexander Ave 15063 724-258-8454
Deborah DiMaglio, prin. Fax 258-4109
Ringgold HS 1,200/9-12
1 Ram Dr 15063 724-258-2200
Dwane Homa, prin. Fax 258-7360

Monroeville, Allegheny, Pop. 28,591
Area Vocational Technical School
Supt. — None
Forbes Road CTC Vo/Tech
607 Beatty Rd 15146 412-373-8100
Quentin Martin, prin. Fax 373-8106

Gateway SD 4,300/K-12
9000 Gateway Campus Blvd 15146 412-372-5300
Dr. Cleveland Steward, supt. Fax 373-5731
www.gatewayk12.org
Gateway HS 1,600/9-12
3000 Gateway Campus Blvd 15146 412-373-5744
William Short, prin. Fax 373-5872
Gateway MS 700/7-8
4450 Old William Penn Hwy 15146 412-373-5780
Andrew Leopold, prin. Fax 373-5794

Career Training Academy Post-Sec.
4314 Old William Penn # 103 15146 412-373-3900
Community College of Allegheny County Post-Sec.
595 Beatty Rd 15146 724-325-1327
Empire Beauty School Post-Sec.
320 Mall Blvd 15146 412-373-7727
Greater Works Christian S 200/PK-12
301 College Park Dr 15146 724-327-6500
J. R. Gardner, hdmstr. Fax 325-4602
ITT Technical Institute Post-Sec.
105 Mall Blvd # 200 15146 412-856-5920
Western School of Health & Bus. Careers Post-Sec.
1 Monroeville Ctr 15146 412-373-6400

Mont Alto, Franklin, Pop. 1,760

Pennsylvania State University Post-Sec.
Mont Alto Campus 17237 717-749-6000

Montgomery, Lycoming, Pop. 1,619
Montgomery Area SD 1,000/K-12
120 Penn St 17752 570-547-1608
Daphne Ross, supt. Fax 547-6271
www.montasd.org
Montgomery HS 300/9-12
120 Penn St 17752 570-547-1608
Linda Gutkowski, prin. Fax 547-6755
Montgomery MS 200/6-8
120 Penn St 17752 570-547-1608
Linda Gutkowski, prin. Fax 547-6755

Montoursville, Lycoming, Pop. 4,628
Loyalsock Township SD 1,400/K-12
1720 Sycamore Rd 17754 570-326-6508
Richard Mextorf Ed.D., supt. Fax 326-0770
www.ltsd.k12.pa.us
Other Schools – See Williamsport

Montoursville Area SD 2,100/K-12
50 N Arch St 17754 570-368-2491
Dr. Albert Cunningham, supt. Fax 368-3501
www.montoursville.k12.pa.us/
McCall MS 700/5-8
600 Willow St 17754 570-368-2441
Jeffrey Moore, prin. Fax 368-3521
Montoursville Area HS 700/9-12
100 N Arch St 17754 570-368-2611
C. Raymond Huff, prin. Fax 368-2768

Montrose, Susquehanna, Pop. 1,596
Montrose Area SD 1,900/K-12
80 High School Rd 18801 570-278-3731
Michael Ognosky, supt. Fax 278-4798
www.masd.info/
Montrose JSHS 900/7-12
50 High School Rd 18801 570-278-3731
James Tallarico, prin. Fax 278-9143

Moon Township, Allegheny, Pop. 10,187
Moon Area SD
Supt. — See Coraopolis
Moon Area MS 900/6-8
8353 University Blvd 15108 412-262-4140
Julie Moore, prin. Fax 264-3013
Moon HS 1,200/9-12
904 Beaver Grade Rd 15108 412-262-9040
Michael Hauser, prin. Fax 264-1271

Moosic, Lackawanna, Pop. 5,738

Empire Beauty School Post-Sec.
3370 Birney Ave 18507 570-823-5987

Morgantown, Lancaster

Conestoga Christian S 300/K-12
2760 Main St 19543 610-286-0353
Susan Yoder, admin. Fax 286-0350

Morrisdale, Clearfield
West Branch Area SD 1,300/K-12
356 Allport Cutoff 16858 814-345-6832
Arleen Multhauf, supt. Fax 345-5220
www.westbranch.org
West Branch Area JSHS 600/7-12
356 Allport Cutoff 16858 814-345-5615
Sean Wechtenhiser, prin. Fax 345-6116

Morrisville, Bucks, Pop. 9,810
Morrisville Borough SD 900/K-12
550 W Palmer St 19067 215-736-2681
Elizabeth Hammond Yonson Ed.D., supt. Fax 736-2413
mv.org
Morrisville Borough JSHS 500/6-12
550 W Palmer St 19067 215-736-5260
Melanie Gehrens, prin. Fax 736-3958

Morton, Delaware, Pop. 2,665
Area Vocational Technical School
Supt. — None
Delaware County AVTS Vo/Tech
200 Yale Ave 19070 610-938-9000
Dr. Philip Lachimia, prin.

Moscow, Lackawanna, Pop. 1,916
North Pocono SD 3,200/K-12
701 Church St 18444 570-842-7659
Dr. Louis DeFazio, supt. Fax 842-0886
www.npsd.net
North Pocono HS 1,100/9-12
701 Church St 18444 570-842-7606
Colin Fureaux, prin. Fax 842-2163
North Pocono MS 800/6-8
701 Church St 18444 570-842-4588
Edward Bugno, prin. Fax 842-1783

St. Gregory's Academy 100/9-12
RR 8 Box 8214 18444 570-842-8112
E. Howard Clark, hdmstr. Fax 842-4513

Mountain Top, Luzerne
Crestwood SD 3,100/K-12
281 S Mountain Blvd 18707 570-474-6888
Richard Duffy, supt. Fax 474-2254
www.edline.net/pages/crestwood_sd
Crestwood HS 1,100/9-12
281 S Mountain Blvd 18707 570-474-6782
Christopher Gegaris, prin. Fax 474-1175
Crestwood MS 500/7-8
281 S Mountain Blvd 18707 570-474-6782
Brian Waite, prin. Fax 474-2254

Mount Braddock, Fayette

West Virginia Career Institute Post-Sec.
PO Box 278 15465 724-437-4600

Mount Carmel, Northumberland, Pop. 6,053
Mt. Carmel Area SD 1,700/PK-12
600 W 5th St 17851 570-339-1500
Cheryl Latorre, supt. Fax 339-0487
www.mca.k12.pa.us
Mt. Carmel Area JSHS 900/7-12
600 W 5th St 17851 570-339-1500
Mary John, prin. Fax 339-0487

Mount Joy, Lancaster, Pop. 6,944
Area Vocational Technical School
Supt. — None
Lancaster County CTC-Mt. Joy Vo/Tech
PO Box 537 17552 717-653-3000
Bridget Mazzocchi, prin. Fax 653-0901

Donegal SD 2,700/K-12
1051 Koser Rd 17552 717-653-1447
Linda Abele, supt. Fax 492-1350
www.donegal.k12.pa.us
Donegal HS 900/9-12
915 Anderson Ferry Rd 17552 717-653-1871
John Felix, prin. Fax 492-1241
Other Schools – See Marietta

Janus S 100/1-12
205 Lefever Rd 17552 717-653-0025
Christopher Harris, dir. Fax 653-0696

Mount Pleasant, Westmoreland, Pop. 4,531
Mt. Pleasant Area SD 2,100/K-12
271 State St 15666 724-547-4100
Frank Watson, supt. Fax 547-0629
www.mpasd.net
Mount Pleasant Area JSHS 800/7-12
265 State St 15666 724-547-4100
Terry Struble, prin. Fax 547-0526

Mount Carmel Christian S 100/K-12
1231 Mount Pleasant Rd 15666 724-887-7169
Sherwood Edward, prin.

Mount Union, Huntingdon, Pop. 2,392
Mt. Union Area SD 1,500/K-12
28 W Market St 17066 814-542-8631
Dr. Jerry Dunkle, supt. Fax 542-8633
www.muasd.org/
Mt. Union Area JSHS 700/7-12
706 N Shaver St 17066 814-542-2518
Curt Whitsel, prin. Fax 542-5451

Muncy, Lycoming, Pop. 2,533
Muncy SD 1,100/K-12
46 S Main St Ste 1 17756 570-546-3125
Lawrence Potash, supt. Fax 546-6676
www.muncysd.org
Muncy JSHS 500/7-12
200 W Penn St 17756 570-546-3127
Calvin Barto, prin. Fax 546-7688

Munhall, Allegheny, Pop. 11,513
Steel Valley SD 2,100/K-12
220 E Oliver Rd 15120 412-464-3600
Dr. William Kinavey, supt. Fax 464-3626
www.svsd.k12.pa.us
Steel Valley HS 700/9-12
3113 Main St 15120 412-464-3600
Leo Schlanger, prin. Fax 464-3609
Steel Valley MS 500/6-8
3114 Main St 15120 412-464-3600
Kevin Walsh, prin. Fax 464-3642

Murrysville, Westmoreland, Pop. 19,098
Franklin Regional SD 3,800/K-12
3210 School Rd 15668 724-327-5456
Dr. Peter D'Arcangelo, supt. Fax 327-6149
www.franklinregional.k12.pa.us

Franklin Regional HS 1,300/9-12
3200 School Rd 15668 724-327-5456
Tina Burns, prin. Fax 327-9256
Franklin Regional MS 900/6-8
4660 Old William Penn Hwy 15668 724-327-5456
Shelley Shaneyfelt, prin. Fax 733-0949

Myerstown, Lebanon, Pop. 3,106
Eastern Lebanon County SD 2,400/K-12
180 Elco Dr 17067 717-866-7117
Dr. Ronald Hetrick, supt. Fax 866-7084
www.elco.k12.pa.us
Eastern Lebanon County HS 800/9-12
180 Elco Dr 17067 717-866-7447
Randall Grove, prin. Fax 866-7287
Eastern Lebanon County MS 600/6-8
60 Evergreen Dr 17067 717-866-6591
Keith DuBois, prin. Fax 866-5837

Evangelical School of Theology Post-Sec.
121 S College St 17067 717-866-5775
Lebanon Valley Christian S 100/1-12
7821 Lancaster Ave 17067 717-933-5171
Daniel Moyer, prin. Fax 933-1616
Myerstown Mennonite S 100/1-12
739 E Lincoln Ave 17067 717-866-5667
Anthony Hurst, prin. Fax 866-8652

Nanticoke, Luzerne, Pop. 10,382
Greater Nanticoke Area SD 2,100/K-12
427 Kosciuszko St 18634 570-735-1270
Anthony Perrone, supt. Fax 735-1350
www.gnasd.com
Greater Nanticoke Area HS 900/8-12
425 Kosciuszko St 18634 570-735-7781
Mary Ann Jarolen, prin. Fax 733-1002

Luzerne County Community College Post-Sec.
1333 S Prospect St 18634 570-740-0200

Nanty Glo, Cambria, Pop. 3,024
Blacklick Valley SD 700/K-12
555 Birch St 15943 814-749-9211
Donald Thomas, supt. Fax 749-8627
bvsd.k12.pa.us
Blacklick Valley JSHS 400/7-12
555 Birch St 15943 814-749-9213
Michael McDermott, prin.

Narberth, Montgomery, Pop. 4,154
Lower Merion SD
Supt. — See Ardmore
Welsh Valley MS, 325 Tower Ln 19072 800/6-8
Dr. Deitra Spence, prin. 610-658-3920

Natrona Heights, Allegheny, Pop. 11,400
Highlands SD 2,900/PK-12
PO Box 288 15065 724-226-2400
Dr. Karol Galcik, supt. Fax 226-8437
www.goldenrams.com
Highlands HS 900/9-12
1500 Pacific Ave 15065 724-226-1000
Thomas Shirey, prin. Fax 226-9611
Highlands MS 700/6-8
1350 Broadview Blvd 15065 724-226-0600
Shauna Zukowski, prin. Fax 226-3287

Allegheny Valley Hospital Post-Sec.
1301 Carlisle St 15065 724-226-7000
St. Joseph HS 100/9-12
800 Montana Ave 15065 724-224-5552
Beverly Kaniecki, prin. Fax 224-3205

Nazareth, Northampton, Pop. 6,023
Nazareth Area SD 4,500/K-12
1 Education Plz 18064 610-759-1170
Dr. Victor Lesky, supt. Fax 759-9637
www.nazarethasd.k12.pa.us
Nazareth Area HS 1,600/9-12
501 E Center St 18064 610-759-1730
Alan Davis, prin. Fax 746-2599
Nazareth Area MS 1,100/6-8
355 Tatamy Rd 18064 610-759-3350
Robert Kern, prin. Fax 759-3725

Needmore, Fulton

Fulton County Community Christian S 100/PK-12
PO Box 235 17238 717-573-4400
Russell Cheek, prin. Fax 573-2731

New Berlin, Union, Pop. 830
Area Vocational Technical School
Supt. — None
SUN Area Career & Technology Center Vo/Tech
PO Box 527 17855 570-966-1034
John Bohn, dir. Fax 966-9492

New Bethlehem, Clarion, Pop. 1,007
Redbank Valley SD 1,400/K-12
920 Broad St 16242 814-275-2426
John M. Cornish Ed.D., supt. Fax 275-2428
www.redbankvalley.net/
Redbank Valley JSHS 700/7-12
910 Broad St 16242 814-275-2424
Stephen Dobransky, prin. Fax 275-2428

New Bloomfield, Perry, Pop. 1,084

Carson Long Military Institute 200/6-12
PO Box 98 17068 717-582-2121
Col. Matthew Brown, pres. Fax 582-8763

New Brighton, Beaver, Pop. 6,275
New Brighton Area SD 1,900/K-12
3225 43rd St 15066 724-843-1795
John Osheka Ed.D., supt. Fax 843-6144
www.nbsd.k12.pa.us
New Brighton Area HS 600/9-12
3200 43rd St Ste 2 15066 724-846-1050
Edward Kasparek, prin.
New Brighton Area MS 500/6-8
901 Penn Ave 15066 724-846-8100
Dr. David Pietro, prin.

New Castle, Lawrence, Pop. 25,030
Area Vocational Technical School
Supt. — None
Lawrence County CTC Vo/Tech
750 Phelps Way 16101 724-658-3583
Andrew Tommelleo, prin. Fax 658-8530

Laurel SD 1,400/K-12
2497 Harlansburg Rd 16101 724-658-8940
Dr. Sandra L. Hennon, supt. Fax 658-2992
www.laurel.k12.pa.us
Laurel JSHS 700/7-12
2497 Harlansburg Rd 16101 724-658-9056
Harold Dunn, prin. Fax 658-2992

Neshannock Township SD 1,300/K-12
3834 Mitchell Rd 16105 724-658-4793
Dr. Mary Todora, supt. Fax 658-1828
www.neshannock.k12.pa.us
Neshannock JSHS 600/7-12
3834 Mitchell Rd 16105 724-658-5513
Scott Seltzer, prin. Fax 657-8169

New Castle Area SD 3,600/PK-12
420 Fern St 16101 724-656-4756
George J. Gabriel, supt. Fax 656-4767
www.ncasd.com
New Castle HS 900/9-12
300 E Lincoln Ave 16101 724-656-4700
John Sarandrea, prin. Fax 658-3916
New Castle JHS 700/7-8
310 E Lincoln Ave 16101 724-656-4700
Jacqueline Respress, prin. Fax 658-6276

Shenango Area SD 1,400/K-12
2501 Old Pittsburgh Rd 16101 724-658-7287
Lawrence Connelly, supt. Fax 658-5370
Shenango HS 700/7-12
2550 Ellwood Rd 16101 724-658-5537
Michael Schreck, prin. Fax 658-7584

Union Area SD 600/K-12
500 S Scotland Ln 16101 724-658-4775
Dr. Dean A. Casello, supt. Fax 658-5151
www.union.k12.pa.us
Union Area MSHS 200/5-12
2106 Camden Ave 16101 724-658-4501
David Nerti, prin. Fax 658-8617

Erie Business Center South Post-Sec.
170 Cascade Galleria 16101 724-658-9066
Jameson Memorial Hosp School of Nursing Post-Sec.
1211 Wilmington Ave 16105 724-656-4240
New Castle School of Beauty Culture Post-Sec.
314 E Washington St 16101 724-654-6611

New Cumberland, Cumberland, Pop. 7,127
West Shore SD
Supt. — See Lewisberry
New Cumberland MS 400/6-8
331 8th St 17070 717-774-0162
Karen Hertzler, prin.

New Eagle, Washington, Pop. 2,276
Ringgold SD 3,600/K-12
400 Main St 15067 724-258-9329
Edward Repka, supt. Fax 258-5363
www.ringgold.org
Other Schools – See Finleyville, Monongahela

New Florence, Westmoreland, Pop. 749
Ligonier Valley SD
Supt. — See Ligonier
Laurel Valley MSHS 400/7-12
114 Education Ln 15944 724-238-4034
Matthew McNickle, prin. Fax 235-9415

New Holland, Lancaster, Pop. 5,140
Eastern Lancaster County SD 3,500/K-12
PO Box 609 17557 717-354-1500
Dr. Saundra Hoover, supt. Fax 354-1512
www.elanco.k12.pa.us
Garden Spot HS 1,200/9-12
PO Box 609 17557 717-354-1555
Donald Reed, prin. Fax 354-1534
Garden Spot MS, PO Box 609 17557 600/7-8
Joyce Wilkinson, prin. 717-354-1561

New Hope, Bucks, Pop. 2,276
New Hope-Solebury SD 1,100/K-12
180 W Bridge St 18938 215-862-2552
Barbara Burke-Stevenson, supt. Fax 744-6012
www.nhsd.org/
New Hope-Solebury HS 400/9-12
180 W Bridge St 18938 215-862-2028
Stephen Young, prin. Fax 862-3198
New Hope-Solebury MS 300/6-8
180 W Bridge St 18938 215-862-0608
Joyce Mundy, prin. Fax 862-2862

Solebury S 200/7-12
6832 Phillips Mill Rd 18938 215-862-5261
John Brown, hdmstr. Fax 862-3366

New Kensington, Westmoreland, Pop. 14,085
Area Vocational Technical School
Supt. — None
Northern Westmoreland County AVTS Vo/Tech
705 Stevenson Blvd 15068 724-335-9389
Marsha Welsh, prin. Fax 337-9010

New Kensington-Arnold SD 2,500/PK-12
701 Stevenson Blvd 15068 724-335-8581
Thomas Wilczek, supt. Fax 337-6519
nkasd.com
Valley HS 800/9-12
703 Stevenson Blvd 15068 724-337-4536
Kellie Abbott, prin. Fax 337-6519
Other Schools – See Arnold

Career Training Academy Post-Sec.
950 5th Ave 15068 724-337-1000
Citizens General Hospital Post-Sec.
651 4th Ave 15068 724-337-5090
Pennsylvania State University Post-Sec.
3550 7th Street Rd 15068 724-334-5466

Newmanstown, Lebanon, Pop. 1,410

Millbach Mennonite S 100/1-10
601 State Route 419 17073 717-949-2111
Bruce Good, prin.

New Milford, Susquehanna, Pop. 845
Blue Ridge SD 1,200/K-12
RR 3 Box 220 18834 570-465-3141
Robert McNamara, supt. Fax 465-3148
brsd.org
Blue Ridge HS 400/9-12
RR 3 Box 220 18834 570-465-3144
John Manchester, prin. Fax 465-3148
Blue Ridge MS 300/6-8
RR 3 Box 220 18834 570-465-3177
Matthew Nebzydoski, prin. Fax 465-3148

New Oxford, Adams, Pop. 1,773
Conewago Valley SD 2,900/K-12
130 Berlin Rd 17350 717-624-2157
Dr. Daniel Trimmer, supt. Fax 624-5020
www.conewago.k12.pa.us
New Oxford HS 1,200/9-12
130 Berlin Rd 17350 717-624-2157
Michael O'Brien, prin. Fax 624-5021
New Oxford MS 600/7-8
130 Berlin Rd 17350 717-624-2157
Gretchen Gates, prin. Fax 624-6560

New Paris, Bedford, Pop. 205
Chestnut Ridge SD
Supt. — See Fishertown
Chestnut Ridge HS 600/9-12
2588 Quaker Valley Rd 15554 814-839-4195
George Knisely, prin. Fax 839-0018

Newport, Perry, Pop. 1,467
Newport SD 1,300/K-12
PO Box 9 17074 717-567-3806
Dr. Kerry Helm, supt. Fax 567-6468
www.newportsd.org
Newport JSHS 600/7-12
PO Box 9 17074 717-567-3806
Lori Gallagher, prin. Fax 567-7402

Greater Perry Comm Christian Academy 50/K-10
55 W Shortcut Rd 17074 717-567-9990
Denise Long, prin. Fax 567-9950

New Stanton, Westmoreland, Pop. 2,055
Area Vocational Technical School
Supt. — None
Central Westmoreland CTC Vo/Tech
240 Arona Rd 15672 724-925-3532
Clentin Martin, prin. Fax 925-1423

Newtown, Bucks, Pop. 2,256
Council Rock SD 12,500/K-12
30 N Chancellor St 18940 215-944-1000
Mark Klein, supt. Fax 944-1031
www.crsd.org
Council Rock HS North 2,200/9-12
62 Swamp Rd 18940 215-944-1300
Susan McCarthy, prin. Fax 944-1387
Newtown MS 800/7-8
116 Richboro Newtown Rd 18940 215-968-7200
Richard Hollahan, prin. Fax 968-1476
Other Schools – See Holland, Richboro

Bucks County Community College Post-Sec.
Swamp Rd 18940 215-968-8000
George S 500/9-12
PO Box 4000 18940 215-579-6500
Nancy Starmer, hdmstr. Fax 579-6507
Holy Family University 18940 Post-Sec.
215-504-2000
La Salle University Post-Sec.
33 University Dr 18940 215-579-7335

Newtown Square, Delaware, Pop. 11,300
Marple Newtown SD 3,500/K-12
40 Media Line Rd Ste 206 19073 610-359-4200
Merle Horowitz, supt. Fax 723-3340
www.mnsd.net
Marple Newtown HS 1,200/9-12
120 Media Line Rd 19073 610-359-4218
John Sanville, prin. Fax 356-2194
Other Schools – See Broomall

Delaware County Christian S 900/PK-12
462 Malin Rd 19073 610-353-6522
Dr. Stephen Dill, hdmstr. Fax 356-9684

New Tripoli, Lehigh
Northwestern Lehigh SD 2,300/K-12
6493 Route 309 18066 610-298-8661
John M. Gould Ph.D., supt. Fax 298-8002
www.nwlehighsd.org
Northwestern Lehigh HS 800/9-12
6493 Route 309 18066 610-298-8661
Dennis Nemes, prin. Fax 298-4645
Northwestern Lehigh MS 700/5-8
6636 Northwest Rd 18066 610-298-8661
Kathleen Kelley, prin. Fax 298-8178

Newville, Cumberland, Pop. 1,323
Big Spring SD 3,100/K-12
45 Mount Rock Rd 17241 717-776-2000
Richard Fry, supt. Fax 776-4428
www.bigspring.k12.pa.us
Big Spring HS 1,000/9-12
100 Mount Rock Rd 17241 717-776-2000
John Scudder, prin. Fax 776-2433
Big Spring MS 800/6-8
47 Mount Rock Rd 17241 717-776-2000
Linda Wilson, prin. Fax 776-2468

New Wilmington, Lawrence, Pop. 2,480
Wilmington Area SD 1,600/K-12
300 Wood St 16142 724-656-8866
C. Joyce Nicksick, supt. Fax 946-8982
www.wilmington.k12.pa.us/
Wilmington Area HS 600/9-12
350 Wood St 16142 724-656-8866
William Lyon, prin.

Wilmington Area MS 500/5-8
400 Wood St 16142 724-656-8866
Benjamin Fennick, prin.

Westminster College 16172 Post-Sec.
724-946-7100

Norristown, Montgomery, Pop. 30,689
Methacton SD 5,300/K-12
1001 Kriebel Mill Rd 19403 610-489-5000
Dr. Jeffrey A. Miller, supt. Fax 489-5019
www.methacton.org
Arcola IS 1,300/6-8
4000 Eagleville Rd 19403 610-489-5000
Mary Anne DelCollo, prin. Fax 831-5317
Methacton HS 1,700/9-12
1001 Kriebel Mill Rd 19403 610-489-5000
Frederick Cummins, prin. Fax 489-8165

Norristown Area SD 6,000/K-12
401 N Whitehall Rd 19403 610-630-5000
Dr. Lisa J. Andrejko, supt. Fax 630-5013
www.nasd.k12.pa.us
East Norriton MS 400/5-8
330 Roland Dr 19401 610-275-6520
Gary Engler, prin. Fax 272-0531
Eisenhower MS 500/5-8
1601 Markley St 19401 610-277-8720
Nicole Poncheri, prin. Fax 270-2901
Norristown Area HS 1,900/9-12
1900 Eagle Dr 19403 610-630-5090
Joseph Howell, prin. Fax 630-5115
Stewart MS 700/5-8
1315 W Marshall St 19401 610-275-6870
Rachel Holler, prin. Fax 272-0560

Kennedy-Kenrick HS 600/9-12
250 E Johnson Hwy 19401 610-275-2846
Rosemary Naab, prin. Fax 277-6699
Pathway School Post-Sec.
162 Egypt Rd 19403 610-277-0660

Northampton, Northampton, Pop. 9,699
Catasauqua Area SD
Supt. — See Catasauqua
Catasauqua HS 600/9-12
2500 W Bullshead Rd 18067 610-697-0111
David Ascani, prin. Fax 697-0116

Northampton Area SD 5,700/K-12
2014 Laubach Ave 18067 610-262-7811
Dr. Linda J. Firestone, supt. Fax 262-1150
www.northampton.k12.pa.us
Northampton Area HS 1,900/9-12
1619 Laubach Ave 18067 610-262-7812
Dr. Kathleen Ott, prin. Fax 262-3024
Northampton Area MS 1,000/7-8
1617 Laubach Ave 18067 610-262-7817
Joseph Kovalchik, prin. Fax 262-6583

North East, Erie, Pop. 4,331
North East SD 1,900/K-12
50 E Division St 16428 814-725-8671
Dr. Judith A. Miller, supt. Fax 725-9380
www.nesd1.k12.pa.us/
North East HS 700/9-12
1901 Freeport Rd 16428 814-725-8672
Regan Tanner, prin. Fax 725-3357
North East MS 500/6-8
1903 Freeport Rd 16428 814-725-8672
Gregory Beardsley, prin. Fax 725-1086

Northern Cambria, Cambria, Pop. 4,022
Northern Cambria SD 1,200/K-12
601 Joseph St 15714 814-948-5481
Dr. Thomas Estep, supt. Fax 948-6058
www.ncsd.k12.pa.us/
Northern Cambria HS 400/9-12
813 35th St 15714 814-948-6800
Dennis Colbert, prin. Fax 948-9810
Northern Cambria MS 300/6-8
601 Joseph St 15714 814-948-5880
Thomas Rocco, prin.

North Huntingdon, Westmoreland, Pop. 28,158
Norwin SD 5,200/K-12
281 McMahon Dr 15642 724-861-3000
Dr. John C. Boylan, supt. Fax 863-9467
www.norwinsd.org
Norwin HS 1,700/9-12
251 Mcmahon Dr 15642 724-861-3005
Dr. Edward Federinko, prin. Fax 861-0581
Other Schools – See Irwin

Northumberland, Northumberland, Pop. 3,586

Northumberland Christian S 200/K-12
351 5th St 17857 570-473-9786
John Rees, prin. Fax 473-8405
Sunbury Christian Academy 200/PK-12
135 Spruce Hollow Rd 17857 570-473-7592
Nancy Gross, admin. Fax 473-7531

North Versailles, Allegheny, Pop. 12,302
East Allegheny SD 1,900/K-12
1150 Jacks Run Rd 15137 412-824-8012
Roger D'Emidio, supt. Fax 824-1062
www.eawildcats.net
East Allegheny JSHS 900/7-12
1150 Jacks Run Rd 15137 412-824-9700
Gary Peiffer, prin. Fax 825-4570

All-State Career School Post-Sec.
97 2nd St 15137 412-823-1818

North Wales, Montgomery, Pop. 3,299
North Penn SD
Supt. — See Lansdale
Pennbrook MS 1,000/7-9
1201 E Walnut St 19454 215-699-9287
Allyn Roche, prin. Fax 699-0151

Lansdale School of Business Post-Sec.
201 Church Rd 19454 215-699-5700

North Warren, Warren
Warren County SD 4,700/K-12
185 Hospital Dr Ste F 16365 814-723-6900
Fax 723-4244
www.wcsdpa.org
Other Schools – See Russell, Sheffield, Warren, Youngsville

Oakdale, Allegheny, Pop. 1,466
Area Vocational Technical School
Supt. — None
Parkway West CTC Vo/Tech
7101 Steubenville Pike 15071 412-923-1772
Jack Highfield, prin. Fax 787-7257

West Allegheny SD 3,300/K-12
600 Donaldson Rd 15071 724-695-3422
John S. DiSanti Ph.D., supt. Fax 695-3788
www.westallegheny.k12.pa.us/
Other Schools – See Imperial

Pittsburgh Technical Institute Post-Sec.
1111 McKee Rd 15071 800-784-9675

Oakmont, Allegheny, Pop. 6,587
Riverview SD 1,200/K-12
701 10th St 15139 412-828-1800
C. Erdeljac, supt. Fax 828-9346
www.rsd.k12.pa.us
Riverview HS 700/7-12
100 Hulton Rd 15139 412-828-1800
Thomas Graham, prin. Fax 828-6296

Oil City, Venango, Pop. 10,942
Area Vocational Technical School
Supt. — None
Venango Technology Center Vo/Tech
1 Vo Tech Dr 16301 814-677-3097
Rod Tarr, dir. Fax 676-0075

Oil City Area SD 2,400/K-12
PO Box 929 16301 814-676-1867
Joseph Carrico, supt. Fax 676-2211
www.ocasd.org
Oil City Area MS 600/6-8
8 Lynch Blvd 16301 814-676-5702
Scott Stahl, prin. Fax 676-2306
Oil City HS 800/9-12
10 Lynch Blvd 16301 814-676-2771
Richard Breene, prin. Fax 677-7256

Clarion University - Venango Campus Post-Sec.
1801 W 1st St 16301 814-676-6591
DuBois Business College Post-Sec.
701 E 3rd St 16301 814-677-1322
Venango Catholic HS 100/9-12
1505 W 1st St 16301 814-677-3098
Rev. John Malthaner, prin. Fax 676-4453

Old Forge, Lackawanna, Pop. 8,558
Old Forge SD 900/K-12
300 Marion St 18518 570-457-6721
Dr. Gene Camoni, supt. Fax 457-8389
www.ofsd.cc/
Old Forge JSHS 400/7-12
300 Marion St 18518 570-457-6721
Jeffery Hatala, prin. Fax 414-0997

Triboro Christian Academy 100/PK-12
100 S Main St 18518 570-457-5392
Erika Weber, prin. Fax 451-0807

Oley, Berks
Area Vocational Technical School
Supt. — None
Berks CTC - East Vo/Tech
3307 Friedensburg Rd 19547 610-987-6201
Lisa Greenawalt, prin. Fax 987-6106

Oley Valley SD 2,100/K-12
17 Jefferson St 19547 610-987-4100
Jeffrey Zackon Ed.D., supt. Fax 987-4138
www.oleyvalleysd.org
Oley Valley HS 700/9-12
17 Jefferson St 19547 610-987-4100
Darrell Markley, prin. Fax 987-4138
Oley Valley MS 500/6-8
3247 Friedensburg Rd 19547 610-987-4100
Eileen Lightcap, prin. Fax 987-4240

Orefield, Lehigh
Parkland SD
Supt. — See Allentown
Orefield MS 1,300/6-8
2675 PA Route 309 18069 610-351-5750
Rodney Troutman, prin. Fax 351-5799

Oreland, Montgomery, Pop. 5,695
Springfield Township SD 2,100/K-12
1901 Paper Mill Rd 19075 215-233-6000
Roseann B. Nyiri Ed.D., supt. Fax 233-5815
www.sdst.org
Other Schools – See Erdenheim

Orwigsburg, Schuylkill, Pop. 2,995
Blue Mountain SD 2,900/K-12
PO Box 188 17961 570-366-0515
Dr. William H. Hall, supt. Fax 366-0838
www.bmsd.org
Blue Mountain MS 700/6-8
PO Box 279 17961 570-366-0546
James McGonigle, prin. Fax 366-2513
Other Schools – See Schuylkill Haven

Oxford, Chester, Pop. 4,682
Oxford Area SD 3,300/K-12
125 Bell Tower Ln 19363 610-932-6600
Dr. Mary Jane Gales, supt. Fax 932-6648
www.oxford.k12.pa.us
Oxford Area HS 1,100/9-12
705 Waterway Rd 19363 610-932-6640
David Madden, prin. Fax 932-6649
Penn's Grove S 600/7-8
602 Garfield St 19363 610-932-6615
David Hamburg, prin. Fax 932-6619

Palmerton, Carbon, Pop. 5,279
Palmerton Area SD 2,000/K-12
PO Box 350 18071 610-826-2364
Michael W. Michaels, supt. Fax 826-4958
www.palmerton.org/
Palmerton Area HS 600/9-12
3525 Fireline Rd 18071 610-826-3155
Kathleen Egan, prin. Fax 826-4929
Palmerton Area JHS 300/7-8
3529 Fireline Rd 18071 610-826-2492
Thaddeus Kosciolek, prin. Fax 826-2366

Palmyra, Lebanon, Pop. 6,957
Palmyra Area SD 3,000/K-12
1125 Park Dr 17078 717-838-3144
Dr. Larry Schmidt, supt. Fax 838-5105
www.palmyra.k12.pa.us/
Palmyra Area HS 1,000/9-12
1125 Park Dr 17078 717-838-1331
Kelly Harbaugh, prin. Fax 838-7915
Palmyra Area MS 700/6-8
50 W Cherry St 17078 717-838-2119
Chris Demers, prin. Fax 838-4402

Paoli, Chester, Pop. 5,603

Delaware Valley Friends S 200/7-12
19 E Central Ave 19301 610-640-4150
Katherine Schantz, hdmstr. Fax 296-9970
Royer-Greaves School for Blind Post-Sec.
118 S Valley Rd 19301

Patton, Cambria, Pop. 1,923
Cambria Heights SD 1,500/K-12
PO Box 6 16668 814-674-6076
Dr. Lawrence Wess, supt. Fax 674-6076
chsd.k12.pa.us
Cambria Heights HS 500/9-12
PO Box 6 16668 814-674-3601
Timothy Laurito, prin. Fax 674-5605
Cambria Heights MS 400/6-8
PO Box 216 16668 814-674-6290
David Caldwell, prin. Fax 674-5054

Pen Argyl, Northampton, Pop. 3,670
Pen Argyl Area SD 2,000/K-12
1620 Teels Rd 18072 610-863-3191
William Haberl Ed.D., supt. Fax 863-7040
www.penargyl.k12.pa.us
Pen Argyl Area HS 700/9-12
501 W Laurel Ave 18072 610-863-1293
John Smith, prin. Fax 863-7660
Wind Gap MS 800/4-8
1620 Teels Rd 18072 610-863-9093
Terry Barry, prin. Fax 863-3817

Pennsburg, Montgomery, Pop. 3,371
Upper Perkiomen SD
Supt. — See East Greenville
Upper Perkiomen HS 1,100/9-12
2 Walt Rd 18073 215-679-5935
John Semet, prin. Fax 679-0911

Perkiomen S 300/5-12
PO Box 130 18073 215-679-9511
George Allison, hdmstr. Fax 679-9101

Penns Creek, Snyder

Penn View Christian Academy 100/PK-12
125 Penn View Dr 17862 570-837-1855
Nathaniel Tucker, prin. Fax 837-1865

Pequea, Lancaster
Penn Manor SD
Supt. — See Lancaster
Marticville MS 400/7-8
356 Frogtown Rd 17565 717-291-9854
Anne Carroll, prin. Fax 284-5954

Perkasie, Bucks, Pop. 8,736
Area Vocational Technical School
Supt. — None
Upper Bucks County AVTS Vo/Tech
3115 Ridge Rd 18944 215-795-2911
David Warren, prin. Fax 795-0530

Pennridge SD 7,200/K-12
1506 N 5th St 18944 215-257-5011
Dr. Robert Kish, supt. Fax 453-8699
www.bucksiu.org/pennridge/psd/psd.htm
Pennridge Central MS 700/7-8
144 N Walnut St 18944 215-258-0939
Dr. Thomas Rutter, prin. Fax 258-0938
Pennridge HS 2,400/9-12
1228 N 5th St 18944 215-453-2744
Thomas Creeden, prin. Fax 257-4986
Pennridge South MS 500/7-8
610 S 5th St 18944 215-257-0467
Dr. Margaret Kantes, prin. Fax 257-3094

Perryopolis, Fayette, Pop. 1,748
Frazier SD 1,200/K-12
142 Constitution St 15473 724-736-4432
Dennis Spinella Ph.D., supt. Fax 736-0688
www.frazierschooldistrict.org
Frazier HS 400/9-12
142 Constitution St 15473 724-736-4426
Donald Martin, prin. Fax 736-0688
Frazier MS 300/6-8
142 Constitution St 15473 724-736-4428
Kathleen Janci, prin. Fax 736-0688

Philadelphia, Philadelphia, Pop. 1,463,281
Area Vocational Technical School
Supt. — None
Bok Technical HS Vo/Tech
1901 S 9th St 19148 215-952-6200
Larry Melton, prin. Fax 952-6410
Communications Technology HS Vo/Tech
81st & Lyons Ave 19153 215-492-6958
Barbara McCreery, prin.
Dobbins AVTS Vo/Tech
2150 W Lehigh Ave 19132 215-227-4421
Charles Whiting, prin. Fax 227-5087
Edison/Fareira Skills HS Vo/Tech
151 W Luzerne St 19140 215-324-9440
Dr. Jose Lebron, prin.

Kensington Culinary Arts S Vo/Tech
2449 Emerald St 19125 215-291-4700
Dr. Reuben Yarmus, prin.
Mastbaum AVTS Vo/Tech
3116 Frankford Ave 19134 215-291-4707
M. Sandra Dean, prin.
Philadelphia AVTS Vo/Tech
440 N Broad St 19130 215-400-5984
Dr. Larry Aniloff, prin.
Randolph AVTS Vo/Tech
3101 Henry Ave 19129 215-227-4407
Peggy Johnson, prin. Fax 227-5087
Saul Agriculture S Vo/Tech
7100 Henry Ave 19128 215-487-4467
Thomas Scott, prin.
School for Exceptional Adults AVTS Vo/Tech
1400 W Olney Ave 19141 215-299-3699
Swenson Arts & Technology HS Vo/Tech
2750 Red Lion Rd 19114 215-961-2009
David Kipphut, prin. Fax 961-2081

Philadelphia CSD 171,600/PK-12
440 N Broad St 19130 215-400-4000
Paul Vallas, supt.
www.phila.k12.pa.us
Academy at Palumbo 9-9
1122 Catharine St 19147 215-351-7618
Adrienne Chew, prin.
Baldi MS 1,200/6-8
8801 Verree Rd 19115 215-961-2003
Eugene McLaughlin, prin. Fax 961-2116
Barratt MS 500/5-8
1599 Wharton St 19146 215-952-6217
Roy McKinney, prin. Fax 952-8583
Bartram HS 1,900/9-12
2401 S 67th St 19142 215-492-6450
Constance McAlister, prin. Fax 492-6117
Beeber MS 800/6-8
5925 Malvern Ave 19131 215-581-5513
Deborah Jumpp, prin. Fax 581-5694
Bodine HS for International Affairs 500/9-12
1101 N 4th St 19123 215-351-7332
Dr. Ann Gardner, prin. Fax 351-7370
Carver HS for Engineering & Science 700/9-12
1600 W Norris St 19121 215-684-5079
Linda Ahmed, prin. Fax 684-5151
Central East MS 1,100/5-8
238 E Wyoming Ave 19120 215-456-3012
Ralph Burnley, prin. Fax 456-0122
Central HS 2,300/9-12
1700 W Olney Ave 19141 215-276-5262
Dr. Sheldon Pavel, prin. Fax 276-4721
Clemente MS 1,300/5-8
122 W Erie Ave 19140 215-291-5400
Carmen Garcia-Collins, prin. Fax 291-5036
Conwell MS 900/5-8
1849 E Clearfield St 19134 215-291-4722
Ed Hoffman, prin. Fax 291-5019
Cooke MS 800/5-8
1300 W Louden St 19141 215-456-3002
Gerald Branch, prin. Fax 456-3185
Creative & Performing Arts HS 700/9-12
901 S Broad St 19147 215-952-2462
Johnny Whaley, prin. Fax 952-6472
Elverson MS 100/8-8
2118 N 13th St 19122 215-684-5091
Bruce Ryan, prin. Fax 684-5507
Fels HS 1,400/9-12
901 Devereaux Ave 19111 215-537-2516
Greg Hailey, prin. Fax 537-2556
Fitzsimons HS 500/7-12
2601 W Cumberland St 19132 215-227-4431
Richard Jenkins, prin. Fax 227-8662
Frankford HS 2,200/9-12
5000 Oxford Ave 19124 215-537-2519
Richard Mantell, prin. Fax 537-2598
Franklin HS 1,200/9-12
550 N Broad St 19130 215-299-4662
Chris Johnson, prin. Fax 299-7285
Furness HS 1,100/9-12
1900 S 3rd St 19148 215-952-6226
Hiromi Stone, prin. Fax 952-8635
Germantown HS 1,300/9-12
40 E High St 19144 215-951-4004
Dr. Rose Ford, prin. Fax 843-8946
Gillespie MS 600/6-8
1801 W Pike St 19140 215-227-4409
Nancy Hatchett, prin. Fax 227-4676
Girard Academic Music Program 500/5-12
2136 W Ritner St 19145 215-952-8589
Angelo Milicia, prin. Fax 952-6544
Gratz HS 1,600/9-12
1798 W Hunting Park Ave 19140 215-227-4408
Dr. Delores Williams, prin. Fax 227-7194
Harding MS 1,300/6-8
2000 Wakeling St 19124 215-537-2528
Terri Hargett, prin. Fax 537-2850
Jones MS 1,000/5-8
2950 Memphis St 19134 215-291-4709
Ernest Lowe, prin. Fax 291-4754
Kensington Business Finance HS 1,300/9-12
2051 E Cumberland St 19125 215-291-4700
Eileen Maicon-Weissman, prin. Fax 291-5833
Kensington CAPA 9-12
2051 E Cumberland St 19125 215-291-4700
Adele Pride, prin. Fax 291-5833
Kensington Culinary Arts HS 9-12
2463 Emerald St 19125 215-291-5185
Dr. Reuben Yarmus, prin. Fax 291-6320
King HS 1,700/9-12
6100 Stenton Ave 19138 215-276-5253
Jane Adams, prin. Fax 276-5844
LaBrum MS 400/6-8
10800 Hawley Rd 19154 215-281-2607
Lois Forrester Frye, prin. Fax 281-5800
Lamberton HS 500/9-12
7501 Woodbine Ave 19151 215-581-5647
Darlene Tolbert, prin. Fax 581-5648
Lankenau HS 100/9-12
201 Spring Ln 19128 215-487-4465
Jacqueline Bentley, prin. Fax 487-4879
Leeds MS 500/6-8
1100 E Mount Pleasant Ave 19150 215-248-6602
Stephanie Mitchell, prin. Fax 248-6623
Lewis MS 700/6-8
6199 Ardleigh St 19138 215-276-5830
Woolworth Davis, prin. Fax 549-5213

Lincoln HS 2,200/9-12
3201 Ryan Ave 19136 215-335-5653
Dr. Donald Donley, prin. Fax 335-5997
Masterman MSHS 1,200/5-12
1699 Spring Garden St 19130 215-299-4661
Marjorie Neff, prin. Fax 299-3425
Meehan MS 1,000/6-8
3001 Ryan Ave 19152 215-335-5654
Mary Jackson, prin. Fax 335-5992
Northeast HS 3,500/9-12
1601 Cottman Ave 19111 215-728-5018
Linda Carroll, prin. Fax 728-5004
Olney HS East 2,200/9-12
100 E Duncannon Ave 19120 215-456-3014
Newton Brown, prin. Fax 456-3064
Olney HS West 9-12
100 E Duncannon Ave 19120 215-456-0109
Rita Hardy, prin. Fax 456-0442
Overbrook HS 1,900/9-12
5898 Lancaster Ave 19131 215-581-5507
Ethelyn Young, prin. Fax 581-3406
Partnership HS for Law Democracy 9-12
18 S 7th St 19106
Tom Davidson, prin.
Peirce MS 300/6-8
2400 Christian St 19146 215-875-5743
Joseph Ritvalski, prin. Fax 875-5757
Penn HS 1,300/9-12
1333 N Broad St 19122 215-684-5900
Patricia Randzo, prin. Fax 684-8976
Penn Treaty MS 700/5-8
600 E Thompson St 19125 215-291-4715
Dr. Donald Anticoli, prin. Fax 291-5172
Pepper MS 1,200/5-8
2901 S 84th St 19153 215-492-6457
Yolanda Armstrong, prin. Fax 492-1844
Philadelphia Center City HS 400/9-12
9 S 12th St 19107 215-299-8801
Catherine Blount, prin. Fax 299-8816
Philadelphia HS for Business/Technology 9-12
540 N 13th St 19123 215-351-7375
Sam Gottlieb, prin.
Philadelphia HS for Girls 1,200/9-12
1400 W Olney Ave 19141 215-276-5258
Dr. Geraldine Myles, prin. Fax 276-5738
HS of the Future 9-9
4021 Parkside Ave 19104 215-823-5500
Dr. Shirley Grover, prin. Fax 823-5504
Philadelphia Military Academy 9-10
2118 N 13th St 19122 215-684-5091
Robert Manning, prin.
Philadelphia Military Academy 200/9-10
1100 E Mount Pleasant Ave 19150 215-248-6602
Ozzie Wright, prin.
Philadelphia Regional HS 300/9-12
1118 Market St 19107 215-299-3510
Ernestine Caldwell, prin. Fax 299-3513
Pickett MS 600/5-8
5700 Wayne Ave 19144 215-951-4002
Judy Seibert Burns, prin. Fax 951-4177
Rhodes Academy 900/6-12
2900 W Clearfield St 19132 215-227-4402
Linda Wayman, prin. Fax 227-4926
Robeson HS for Human Services 9-12
4125 Ludlow St 19104 215-823-8207
Jon Council, prin. Fax 823-8252
Roosevelt MS 700/6-8
430 E Washington Ln 19144 215-951-4170
Stefanie Ressler, prin. Fax 951-7762
Roxborough HS 1,300/9-12
6498 Ridge Ave 19128 215-487-4464
Dr. Rebecca Mitchell, prin. Fax 487-4843
Rush MS 1,000/6-8
3801 Woodhaven Rd 19154 215-281-2603
Gene McLaughlin, prin. Fax 281-3334
Saul HS for Agricultural Sciences 9-12
7100 Henry Ave 19128 215-487-4467
Thomas Scott, prin. Fax 487-4844
Sayre HS 300/9-12
5800 Walnut St 19139 215-471-2904
Joseph Starinieri, prin. Fax 471-3486
Shaw MS 800/5-8
5400 Warrington Ave 19143 215-727-2161
Sharif El-Mekki, prin. Fax 727-2248
Shoemaker MS 300/7-8
5301 Media St 19131 215-581-5501
Margaret Holloman, prin. Fax 581-5929
South Philadelphia HS 1,400/9-12
2101 S Broad St 19148 215-952-6220
Dr. Kevin King, prin. Fax 551-2275
Stetson MS 900/5-8
3200 B St 19134 215-291-4720
Kathleen Fitzpatrick, prin. Fax 291-4168
Stoddart-Fleisher MS 200/7-8
540 N 13th St 19123 215-351-7375
Thomas Davidson, prin. Fax 351-7377
Strawberry Mansion HS 900/9-12
3133 Ridge Ave Ste 2 19121 215-684-5089
Lois Powell-Mondesire, prin. Fax 684-5380
Sulzberger MS 700/6-8
4725 Fairmount Ave 19139 215-581-5510
Adrienne Wooden, prin. Fax 878-8006
Thomas MS 300/5-8
927 Johnston St 19148 215-952-6225
Roslynn Sample Green, prin. Fax 952-8514
Tilden MS 1,100/5-8
6601 Elmwood Ave 19142 215-492-6454
Michelle Burns, prin. Fax 492-6128
Turner MS 600/6-8
5900 Baltimore Ave 19143 215-471-2906
Veronica Alston, prin. Fax 471-8745
University City HS 2,000/9-12
3601 Filbert St 19104 215-387-5100
Anthony Irvin, prin. Fax 387-6362
Vare MS 600/5-8
2100 S 24th St 19145 215-952-8611
Dr. Patricia Cox, prin. Fax 952-8520
Vaux MSHS 400/8-12
2300 W Master St 19121 215-684-5068
Sandra Pearson, prin. Fax 684-5430
Wagner MS 800/6-8
1701 W Chelten Ave 19126 215-276-5252
Penny Nixon, prin. Fax 276-5849
Wanamaker MS 100/8-8
1111 Cecil B Moore Ave 19122 215-684-5210
Dr. Bea Mickey, prin.

Washington HS 2,500/9-12
10175 Bustleton Ave 19116 215-961-2001
Alan E. Liebowitz, prin. Fax 961-2545
Washington Jr. MS 1,200/5-8
201 E Olney Ave 19120 215-456-0422
Michael Rosenberg, prin. Fax 456-2181
West Philadelphia HS 1,400/9-12
4700 Walnut St 19139 215-471-2902
Clifton James, prin. Fax 471-6402
Wilson MS 1,200/6-8
1800 Cottman Ave 19111 215-728-5015
James McWilliams, prin. Fax 728-5051

Al-Aqsa Islamic S 300/PK-12
1501 Germantown Ave 19122 215-765-6660
Claude Crumpton, prin. Fax 765-6640
Albert Einstein Medical Center Post-Sec.
5501 Old York Rd 19141 215-456-7010
American Beauty Academy Post-Sec.
6912 Frankford Ave 19135 215-331-1515
ARAMARK Healthcare Support Services Post-Sec.
1101 Market St Fl 12 19107 610-687-8600
Archbishop Ryan HS 2,600/9-12
11201 Academy Rd 19154 215-637-1800
Helen Chaykowsky, prin. Fax 637-8833
Art Institute of Philadelphia Post-Sec.
1622 Chestnut St 19103 215-567-7080
Aviation Institute of Maintenance Post-Sec.
3001 Grant Ave 19114 215-676-7700
Berean Institute Post-Sec.
1901 W Girard Ave 19130 215-763-4833
Bethel Baptist Academy 100/K-12
2210 E Susquehanna Ave 19125 215-426-1909
Joseph White, prin. Fax 426-6758
Better Way Christian Academy 50/K-12
8253 Bustleton Ave 19152 215-844-5000
Patrice Johnson, dean
Blair Christian Academy 200/PK-12
220 W Upsal St 19119 215-438-6557
Dr. Karen Jenkins, admin. Fax 438-0661
Calvary Christian Academy 1,000/PK-12
13500 Philmont Ave 19116 215-969-1579
Dr. Samuel Pennington, hdmstr. Fax 969-9732
Cardinal Dougherty HS 1,200/9-12
6301 N 2nd St 19120 215-276-2300
Dr. Thomas Rooney, prin. Fax 276-2306
Center for Innovative Training & Educ. Post-Sec.
714 Market St Ste 433 19106 215-922-6555
Chalutzim Academy 100/PK-12
7501 Haverford Ave 19151 215-477-4443
Linda Brown, admin. Fax 477-8710
Chestnut Hill Academy 500/PK-12
500 W Willow Grove Ave 19118 215-247-4700
Francis Steel, hdmstr. Fax 247-8516
Chestnut Hill College Post-Sec.
9601 Germantown Ave 19118 215-248-7000
Christ's Christian Academy 50/1-12
520 W Roosevelt Blvd 19120 215-457-4974
Darla James, admin. Fax 457-4741
City Center Academy 100/9-12
315 S 17th St 19103 215-731-1930
Raymond Withers, prin. Fax 735-3960
Community College of Philadelphia Post-Sec.
1700 Spring Garden St 19130 215-751-8000
Crefeld S 100/7-12
8836 Crefeld St 19118 215-242-5545
Mark Piechota, dir. Fax 242-8869
Crooked Places Made Straight Chr Academy 100/K-12
711 S 50th St 19143 215-726-4151
Dr. Winona Stewart, prin. Fax 726-5241
Curtis Institute of Music Post-Sec.
1726 Locust St 19103 215-893-5252
Delaware Valley Academy-Medical & Dental Post-Sec.
3330 Grant Ave 19114 215-676-1200
DeVry University Post-Sec.
1800 JFK Blvd Ste 104 19103 866-863-3879
Drexel University Post-Sec.
3141 Chestnut St 19104 215-895-2000
Empire Beauty School Post-Sec.
2632 S Broad St 19145 215-465-8803
Empire Beauty School Post-Sec.
4026 Woodhaven Rd 19154 215-637-3700
Empire Beauty School Post-Sec.
1522 Chestnut St 19102 215-568-3980
Faith Tabernacle S 200/1-12
3611 N Randolph St Ste 15 19140 215-221-0909
Fax 229-3204
Father Judge HS 9-12
3301 Solly Ave 19136 215-338-9494
Dr. Joseph DeAngelis, prin. Fax 338-0250
First Century Gospel S 100/1-10
6807 Rising Sun Ave 19111 215-742-6615
Dick Wakefield, prin. Fax 742-7009
Frankford Hospital Post-Sec.
4918 Penn St 19124 215-831-2362
Friends Select S 500/PK-12
17th St & Benjamin Franklin 19103 215-561-5900
Rose Hagan, hdmstr. Fax 864-2979
Germantown Friends S 900/K-12
31 W Coulter St 19144 215-951-2300
Richard Wade, hdmstr. Fax 951-2312
Girard College S 700/1-12
2101 S College Ave 19121 215-787-2600
Dominic M. Cermele, pres. Fax 787-4435
Graves Christian Academy 100/K-12
5447 Chester Ave 19143 215-727-7795
Sharon Flythe, prin. Fax 727-7804
Hallahan HS 700/9-12
311 N 19th St 19103 215-563-8930
Margaret Gallagher, prin. Fax 563-3809
Holy Family University Post-Sec.
9801 Frankford Ave 19114 215-637-7700
Hope Church S 200/PK-12
6707 Old York Rd 19126 215-927-7770
Dr. Suzette Ajedho, prin. Fax 927-8070
Hussian School of Art Post-Sec.
1118 Market St 19107 215-981-0900
International Christian HS 200/9-12
413 E Tabor Rd 19120 215-455-9334
Robert DiStefano, prin. Fax 455-7198
Ivy Leaf S 200/4-8
6929 N Broad St 19126 215-549-2670
Denise Baker, prin. Fax 549-3646
Jean Madeline Educ. Ctr. for Cosmetology Post-Sec.
315A Bainbridge St 19147 215-238-9998
JNA Institute of Culinary Arts Post-Sec.
1212 S Broad St 19146 215-468-8800

La Salle University — Post-Sec.
1900 W Olney Ave 19141 — 215-951-1000
Lincoln Technical Institute — Post-Sec.
9191 Torresdale Ave 19136 — 215-335-0800
Lincoln Technical Institute — Post-Sec.
3600 Market St 19104 — 215-382-1553
Little Flower HS — 800/9-12
1000 W Lycoming St 19140 — 215-455-6900
Sr. Kathleen Klarich, prin. — Fax 329-0478
L.T. International Beauty School — Post-Sec.
830 N Broad St 19130 — 215-922-4478
Lutheran Theological Seminary — Post-Sec.
7301 Germantown Ave 19119 — 215-248-4616
Mercy Vocational HS — Vo/Tech
2900 W Hunting Park Ave 19129 — 215-226-1225
Sr. Rosemary Herron, prin. — Fax 228-6337
Messiah College — Post-Sec.
2026 N Broad St 19121 — 215-769-2526
Methodist Hospital — Post-Sec.
2301 S Broad St 19148 — 215-952-9402
Metropolitan Career Center — Post-Sec.
162 W Chelten Ave 19144 — 215-843-6615
Metropolitan Career Center — Post-Sec.
100 S Broad St Ste 830 19110 — 215-568-9215
Moore College of Art and Design — Post-Sec.
20th & Race St 19103 — 215-568-4000
Nazareth Academy — 400/9-12
4001 Grant Ave 19114 — 215-637-7676
Sr. Mary Joan Jacobs, prin. — Fax 637-8523
Nazareth Hospital — Post-Sec.
2601 Holme Ave 19152 — 215-335-6000
Northeast Catholic HS — 800/9-12
1842 Torresdale Ave 19124 — 215-831-1234
Rev. Nicholas Waseline, prin. — Fax 743-0926
Northeastern Hospital School of Nursing — Post-Sec.
2301 E Allegheny Ave 19134 — 215-291-3145
Northeast Prep S — 100/7-12
1309 Cottman Ave 19111 — 215-342-5500
Howard Schwartz, dir. — Fax 342-8866
Orleans Technical Institute — Post-Sec.
1330 Rhawn St 19111 — 215-728-4700
Orleans Technical Institute Center City — Post-Sec.
1845 Walnut St Ste 700 19103 — 215-854-1853
Overbrook School for the Blind — Post-Sec.
6333 Malvern Ave 19151 — 215-877-0313
Peirce College — Post-Sec.
1420 Pine St 19102 — 215-545-6400
Pennsylvania Academy of the Fine Arts — Post-Sec.
118 N Broad St 19102 — 215-972-7600
Pennsylvania Hospital — Post-Sec.
800 Spruce St 19107 — 215-829-3312
Pennsylvania School for the Deaf — Post-Sec.
100 W School House Ln 19144
Philadelphia Coll. Osteopathic Medicine — Post-Sec.
4170 City Ave 19131 — 215-871-6700
Philadelphia Mennonite HS — 100/9-12
860 N 24th St 19130 — 215-769-5363
Dr. Barbara Moses, prin. — Fax 769-4063
Philadelphia University — Post-Sec.
4201 Henry Ave 19144 — 215-951-2700
Restaurant School at Walnut Hill College — Post-Sec.
4207 Walnut St 19104 — 215-222-4200
Roman Catholic HS — 900/9-12
301 N Broad St 19107 — 215-627-1270
Robert O'Neill, prin. — Fax 627-4979
Roxborough Memorial Hospital — Post-Sec.
5800 Ridge Ave 19128 — 215-487-4459
St. Hubert HS — 9-12
7320 Torresdale Ave 19136 — 215-624-6840
Sr. Marie Hart, prin. — Fax 624-5940
St. John Neumann/St. Maria Goretti HS — 700/9-12
1736 S 10th St 19148 — 215-465-8437
Patricia Sticco, prin. — Fax 462-2410
St. Joseph's Prep S — 1,000/9-12
1733 W Girard Ave 19130 — 215-978-1950
Dr. Michael J. Coury, pres. — Fax 765-1710
St. Joseph's University — Post-Sec.
5600 City Ave 19131 — 610-660-1000
St. Monica MS — 300/5-8
16th & Porter Sts 19145 — 215-467-5338
Sr. Rita Murphy, prin. — Fax 467-4599
Settlement Music School — Post-Sec.
416 Queen St 19147 — 215-336-0400
Springside S — 700/PK-12
8000 Cherokee St 19118 — 215-247-7200
Priscilla G. Sands, hdmstr. — Fax 248-6377
Star Technical Institute — Post-Sec.
9121 Roosevelt Blvd 19114 — 215-969-5877
Talmudical Yeshiva of Philadelphia — Post-Sec.
6063 Drexel Rd 19131 — 215-477-1000
Talmudical Yeshiva of Philadelphia — 100/9-12
6063 Drexel Rd 19131 — 215-477-1000
Rabbi Uri Mandelbaum, prin. — Fax 477-5065
Temple University — Post-Sec.
Broad St & Montgomery Ave 19122 — 215-204-7000
Temple University — Post-Sec.
3307 N Broad St 19140 — 215-787-7000
Temple University Center City — Post-Sec.
1515 Market St 19102 — 215-204-8822
Temple Univ School of Podiatric Medicine — Post-Sec.
8th & Race St 19107 — 215-629-0300
Thomas Jefferson University — Post-Sec.
111 S 11th St 19107 — 215-955-6000
Thompson Institute — Post-Sec.
3010 Market St 19104 — 215-387-1530
University of Pennsylvania — Post-Sec.
3400 Spruce St 19104 — 215-898-5000
University of the Arts — Post-Sec.
320 S Broad St 19102 — 215-717-6000
University of the Sciences Philadelphia — Post-Sec.
600 S 43rd St 19104 — 215-596-8800
Westminster Theological Seminary — Post-Sec.
PO Box 27009 19118 — 215-887-5511
West Philadelphia Catholic HS — 700/9-12
4501 Chestnut St 19139 — 215-386-2244
Sr. Mary Bur, prin. — Fax 222-1651

Philipsburg, Centre, Pop. 2,942
Philipsburg-Osceola Area SD — 2,000/K-12
200 Short St 16866 — 814-342-1050
W. Charles Young, supt. — Fax 342-7208
www.pomounties.org/
Philipsburg-Osceola Area HS — 700/9-12
502 Philips St 16866 — 814-342-1521
Samuel Witt, prin. — Fax 342-7521
Philipsburg-Osceola JHS — 400/7-8
100 N 6th St 16866 — 814-342-4860
Robert Rocco, prin. — Fax 342-7529

South Hills School of Business & Tech. — Post-Sec.
200 Shadylane Dr 16866 — 814-342-7427

Phoenixville, Chester, Pop. 15,420
Area Vocational Technical School
Supt. — None
Center for Arts & Tech - Pickering — Vo/Tech
1580 Charlestown Rd 19460 — 610-933-8877
Dr. Ronald Husband, prin.

Phoenixville Area SD — 3,200/K-12
PO Box 809 19460 — 484-927-5000
David R. Noyes Ed.D., supt. — Fax 983-9537
www.pasd.com
Phoenixville Area HS — 900/9-12
1200 Gay St 19460 — 484-927-5100
Richard Kaskey, prin. — Fax 933-6009
Phoenixville Area MS — 800/6-8
1330 Main St 19460 — 484-927-5200
Dr. Troy Czukoski, prin. — Fax 933-6121

Valley Forge Christian College — Post-Sec.
1401 Charlestown Rd 19460 — 610-935-0450

Pine Forge, Berks

Pine Forge Academy — 200/9-12
PO Box 338 19548 — 610-326-5800
Cynthia Pool-Gibson, prin. — Fax 326-4260

Pine Grove, Schuylkill, Pop. 2,079
Pine Grove Area SD — 1,700/K-12
103 School St 17963 — 570-345-2731
Dr. Terence Maher, supt. — Fax 345-6473
www.pgasd.com
Pine Grove Area HS — 600/9-12
101 School St 17963 — 570-345-2731
David Jones, prin. — Fax 345-8326
Pine Grove Area MS — 600/5-8
105 School St 17963 — 570-345-2731
Steve Brill, prin. — Fax 345-6075

Pittsburgh, Allegheny, Pop. 316,718
Area Vocational Technical School
Supt. — None
Pittsburgh AVTS — Vo/Tech
850 Boggs Ave 15211 — 412-488-2500
Darla DelDuca, prin.

Avonworth SD — 1,400/K-12
258 Josephs Ln 15237 — 412-369-8738
Dr. Valerie McDonald, supt. — Fax 369-8746
www.avonworth.k12.pa.us
Avonworth HS — 400/9-12
304 Josephs Ln 15237 — 412-366-6360
Kenneth Lockette, prin. — Fax 366-7603
Avonworth MS — 300/6-8
256 Josephs Ln 15237 — 412-366-9650
Thomas Ralston, prin. — Fax 358-9621

Baldwin-Whitehall SD — 4,400/K-12
4900 Curry Rd 15236 — 412-885-7810
Dr. Donna Milanovich, supt. — Fax 885-7802
www.bwschools.net/
Baldwin HS — 1,700/9-12
4653 Clairton Blvd 15236 — 412-885-7500
Dr. Todd Keruskin, prin. — Fax 885-6652
Harrison MS — 1,000/6-8
129 Windvale Dr 15236 — 412-885-7530
Andrea Dorfzaun, prin. — Fax 885-6766

Brentwood Borough SD — 1,300/K-12
3601 Brownsville Rd 15227 — 412-881-2227
Dr. Ronald DuFalla, supt. — Fax 881-1640
www.brentwoodpgh.k12.pa.us
Brentwood HS — 500/9-12
3601 Brownsville Rd 15227 — 412-881-4940
Jason Olexa, prin. — Fax 881-4170
Brentwood MS — 300/6-8
3601 Brownsville Rd 15227 — 412-881-4940
Lawrence Kushner Ph.D., prin. — Fax 881-4170

Chartiers Valley SD — 3,500/K-12
2030 Swallow Hill Rd 15220 — 412-429-2201
Anthony Skender, supt. — Fax 429-2237
www.cvsd.net
Other Schools – See Bridgeville

Fox Chapel Area SD — 4,600/K-12
611 Field Club Rd 15238 — 412-963-9600
Dr. Anne Stephens, supt. — Fax 967-0697
www.fcasd.edu
Dorseyville MS — 1,100/6-8
3732 Saxonburg Blvd 15238 — 412-967-2520
Rox Serrao, prin. — Fax 967-2531
Fox Chapel Area HS — 1,600/9-12
611 Field Club Rd 15238 — 412-967-2433
Kenneth Williams, prin. — Fax 967-0697

Keystone Oaks SD — 2,400/K-12
1000 Kelton Ave 15216 — 412-571-6000
Dr. William Urbanek, supt. — Fax 571-6006
www.kosd.org
Keystone Oaks HS — 900/9-12
1000 Kelton Ave 15216 — 412-571-6040
Scott Hagy, prin. — Fax 571-6043
Keystone Oaks MS — 600/6-8
1002 Kelton Ave 15216 — 412-571-6146
Annette Todd, prin. — Fax 571-6092

Mt. Lebanon SD — 5,500/K-12
7 Horsman Dr 15228 — 412-344-2077
Dr. George Wilson, supt. — Fax 344-2047
www.mtlsd.org
Jefferson MS — 600/6-8
21 Moffett St 15243 — 412-344-2123
Joan Zacharias, prin. — Fax 344-1252
Mellon MS — 700/6-8
11 Castle Shannon Blvd 15228 — 412-344-2122
Vincent Barone, prin. — Fax 344-0590
Mt. Lebanon HS — 1,900/9-12
155 Cochran Rd 15228 — 412-344-2003
Dr. Zeb Jansante, prin. — Fax 344-2021

North Allegheny SD — 8,200/K-12
200 Hillvue Ln 15237 — 412-366-2100
Dr. Patricia Green, supt. — Fax 369-5513
www.northallegheny.org
Carson MS — 700/6-8
200 Hillvue Ln 15237 — 412-369-5520
Brian Miller, prin. — Fax 630-5819
Ingomar MS — 500/6-8
1521 Ingomar Heights Rd 15237 — 412-348-1470
Kevin Deitrick, prin. — Fax 366-4487
North Allegheny Intermediate HS — 1,400/9-10
350 Cumberland Rd 15237 — 412-369-5530
Brendan Hyland, prin. — Fax 369-4825
Other Schools – See Wexford

North Hills SD — 4,800/K-12
135 6th Ave 15229 — 412-318-6000
Dr. Joseph Clapper, supt. — Fax 318-1084
www.nhsd.k12.pa.us
North Hills JHS — 1,300/7-9
55 Rochester Rd 15229 — 412-318-1450
John Kreider, prin. — Fax 318-1453
North Hills SHS — 1,300/10-12
53 Rochester Rd 15229 — 412-318-1400
Patrick Mannarino, prin. — Fax 318-1403

Northgate SD — 1,500/K-12
591 Union Ave 15202 — 412-734-8001
Dr. Reggie Bonfield, supt. — Fax 734-8008
www.northgate.k12.pa.us
Northgate MSHS — 800/7-12
589 Union Ave 15202 — 412-734-8002
Bryan Kyle, prin. — Fax 734-8086

Penn Hills SD — 5,600/K-12
309 Collins Dr 15235 — 412-793-7000
Dr. Patricia Gennari, supt. — Fax 793-6402
www.phsd.k12.pa.us
Linton MS — 1,900/6-9
250 Aster St 15235 — 412-795-3000
Fax 795-6087
Penn Hills SHS — 1,400/10-12
12200 Garland Dr 15235 — 412-793-7000
Nancy Hines, prin. — Fax 793-9401

Pittsburgh SD — 26,100/PK-12
341 S Bellefield Ave 15213 — 412-622-3600
Mark Roosevelt, supt. — Fax 622-3604
www.pghboe.net
Allderdice HS — 1,500/9-12
2409 Shady Ave 15217 — 412-422-4800
Kevin McGuire, prin. — Fax 422-4803
Allegheny Traditional Academy — 300/6-8
810 Arch St 15212 — 412-323-4115
Toni Kendrick, prin. — Fax 323-4114
Arlington IS — 200/3-8
2500 Jonquil St 15210 — 412-488-3641
Dr. Cindi Muehlbauer, prin. — Fax 488-3760
Arsenal MS — 400/6-8
220 40th St 15201 — 412-622-5740
Debra Rucki, prin. — Fax 622-5743
Brashear HS — 1,400/9-12
590 Crane Ave 15216 — 412-571-7300
Dr. Ruthanne Reginella, prin. — Fax 571-7305
Carrick HS — 1,300/9-12
125 Parkfield St 15210 — 412-885-7700
Anita Burley, prin. — Fax 885-7708
Faison Arts IS — 50/5-8
8080 Bennett St 15221 — 412-247-7840
Dr. Marvine Garrett, prin. — Fax 247-7850
Frick International Studies Academy — 700/6-8
107 Thackeray St 15213 — 412-622-5980
Wayne Walters, prin. — Fax 622-5983
Langley HS — 800/9-12
2940 Sheraden Blvd 15204 — 412-778-2100
Linda Baehr, prin. — Fax 778-2106
Lincoln IS — 100/5-8
7109 Hermitage St 15208 — 412-247-7880
Dr. Regina Holley, prin. — Fax 247-7888
Oliver HS — 1,000/9-12
2323 Brighton Rd 15212 — 412-323-3250
Tawayne Weems, prin. — Fax 323-3294
Peabody HS — 700/9-12
515 N Highland Ave 15206 — 412-665-2050
John Vater, prin. — Fax 665-2077
Perry Traditional Academy — 1,100/9-12
3875 Perrysville Ave 15214 — 412-323-3400
Jacqueline Blakey-Tate, prin. — Fax 323-3404
Pittsburgh Classical Academy — 300/6-8
1463 Chartiers Ave 15220 — 412-928-3110
Valerie Merlo, prin. — Fax 928-3106
Pittsburgh HS / Creative & Perform. Arts — 500/9-12
111 9th St 15222 — 412-338-6100
Dr. Rhonda Taliaferro, prin. — Fax 338-6143
Rogers Creative & Performing Arts S — 300/6-8
5525 Columbo St 15206 — 412-665-2000
Dr. Lynda Lewis, prin. — Fax 665-2006
Rooney MS — 300/6-8
3530 Fleming Ave 15212 — 412-732-6700
Merridith Murray, prin. — Fax 732-6706
Schaeffer IS — 100/4-8
3128 Allendale St 15204 — 412-778-2170
LaVerne Anthony, prin. — Fax 778-2174
Schenley HS — 1,400/9-12
4101 Bigelow Blvd 15213 — 412-622-8200
Sophia Facaros, prin. — Fax 622-8226
Schiller Classical Academy — 300/6-8
1018 Peralta St 15212 — 412-323-4190
Scott Grosh, prin. — Fax 323-4192
South Brook MS — 400/6-8
779 Dunster St 15226 — 412-572-8170
Gina Reichert, prin. — Fax 572-8177
South Hills MS — 400/6-8
595 Crane Ave 15216 — 412-572-8130
Dr. Deborah Ann Cox, prin. — Fax 572-8148
Sterrett Classical Academy — 400/6-8
7100 Reynolds St 15208 — 412-247-7870
Sarah Sumpter, prin. — Fax 247-7877
Westinghouse HS — 600/9-12
1101 N Murtland St 15208 — 412-665-3940
Dr. Shemeca Crenshaw, prin. — Fax 665-4977

Plum Borough SD 4,400/K-12
200 School Rd 15239 412-795-0100
George Cooke Ed.D., supt. Fax 795-9115
www.pbsd.k12.pa.us
O'Block JHS 700/7-8
440 Presque Isle Dr 15239 724-733-2400
Joseph Fishell, prin. Fax 327-6880
Plum HS 1,500/9-12
900 Elicker Rd 15239 412-795-4880
Pamela Kinzler, prin. Fax 795-6823

Shaler Area SD
Supt. — See Glenshaw
Shaler Area HS 1,600/10-12
381 Wible Run Rd 15209 412-492-1200
William Suit, prin. Fax 684-1076

Upper St. Clair SD
Supt. — See Upper Saint Clair
Ft. Couch MS 700/7-8
515 Fort Couch Rd 15241 412-833-1600
Joseph DeMar, prin. Fax 854-3095
Upper Saint Clair HS 1,400/9-12
1825 Mclaughlin Run Rd 15241 412-833-1600
Dr. Michael Ghilani, prin. Fax 833-4889

West Jefferson Hills SD
Supt. — See Jefferson Hills
Pleasant Hills MS 700/6-8
404 National Dr 15236 412-655-8680
Suzan Petersen, prin. Fax 655-5691

Woodland Hills SD 5,600/K-12
2430 Greensburg Pike 15221 412-731-1300
Roslynne H. Wilson Ed.D., supt. Fax 731-1562
www.whsd.k12.pa.us
Woodland Hills HS 1,900/9-12
2550 Greensburg Pike 15221 412-244-1100
Robert Scherrer, prin. Fax 242-2344
Woodland Hills JHS - West 600/7-8
7600 Evans St 15218 412-351-0698
Linda Marcolini, prin. Fax 351-5841
Other Schools – See Turtle Creek

Art Institute of Pittsburgh Post-Sec.
420 Blvd Of The Allies 15219 412-263-6600
Bidwell Training Center Post-Sec.
1815 Metropolitan St 15233 412-323-4000
Bishop Canevin Catholic HS 400/9-12
2700 Morange Rd 15205 412-922-7400
Kenneth Sinagra, prin. Fax 922-7403
Bradford School Post-Sec.
125 W Station Square Dr 15219 412-391-6710
Career Training Academy Post-Sec.
1500 Northway Mall 15237 412-367-4000
Carlow University Post-Sec.
3333 5th Ave 15213 412-578-6000
Carnegie Mellon University Post-Sec.
5000 Forbes Ave 15213 412-268-2000
Center for Emergency Medicine/Western PA Post-Sec.
230 McKee Pl # 500 15213 412-647-4665
Central Catholic HS 900/9-12
4720 5th Ave 15213 412-621-8189
Br. Richard Grzeskiewicz, prin. Fax 208-0555
Chatham College Post-Sec.
Woodland Rd 15232 412-365-1100
Community College of Allegheny County Post-Sec.
808 Ridge Ave 15212 412-237-2525
Community College of Allegheny County Post-Sec.
8701 Perry Hwy 15237 412-366-7000
Craig Academy 100/1-12
751 N Negley Ave 15206 412-361-2801
Denise Sedlacek, dir. Fax 361-6775
Dean Institute of Technology Post-Sec.
1501 W Liberty Ave 15226 412-531-4433
DeVry University Post-Sec.
210 6th Ave Ste 200 15222 412-642-9072
Duffs Business Institute Post-Sec.
100 Forbes Ave # 1200 15222 412-261-4520
Duquesne University Post-Sec.
600 Forbes Ave 15282 412-396-6000
Ellis S 500/PK-12
6425 5th Ave 15206 412-661-5992
Mary H. Grant, hdmstr. Fax 661-3979
Empire Beauty School Post-Sec.
1000 McKnight Park Dr #1006 15237 800-575-5983
Grace Academy 50/7-12
8610 Bricelyn St 15221 412-244-8233
Ronald Malamisuro, admin. Fax 243-1465
Hillel Academy of Pittsburgh 300/K-12
5685 Beacon St 15217 412-521-8131
Rabbi Moshe Isaacs, hdmstr. Fax 521-5150
Home for Crippled Children Post-Sec.
1426 Denniston St 15217
ICM School of Business & Medical Careers Post-Sec.
10 Wood St 15222 412-261-2647
Imani Christian Academy 200/K-12
235 Eastgate Dr 15235 412-731-7982
Edward Matthews, admin. Fax 731-7343
International Academy of Design & Tech Post-Sec.
555 Grant St 15219 412-391-4197
ITT Technical Institute Post-Sec.
10 Parkway Ctr 15220 412-937-9150
La Roche College Post-Sec.
9000 Babcock Blvd 15237 412-536-1272
Mercy Hospital School of Nursing Post-Sec.
1401 Blvd Of The Allies 15219 412-232-7940
Mt. Alvernia HS 100/9-12
146 Hawthorne Rd 15209 412-821-3858
Fax 821-2910
North Catholic HS 400/9-12
1400 Troy Hill Rd 15212 412-321-4823
Fax 321-0599
North Hills Beauty Academy Post-Sec.
813 W View Park Dr 15229 412-931-8563
Oakland Catholic HS 500/9-12
144 N Craig St 15213 412-682-6633
Dr. Maureen Marsteller, prin. Fax 682-2496
Pennsylvania Culinary Institute Post-Sec.
717 Liberty Ave 15222 412-566-2433
Pennsylvania Gunsmith School Post-Sec.
812 Ohio River Blvd 15202 412-766-1812
PIA School of Specialized Technology Post-Sec.
PO Box 10897 15236 412-462-9011
Pittsburgh Institute of Mortuary Science Post-Sec.
5808 Baum Blvd 15206 412-362-8500
Pittsburgh Theological Seminary Post-Sec.
616 N Highland Ave 15206 412-362-5610

Point Park University Post-Sec.
201 Wood St 15222 412-391-4100
Point Park Univ.-St. Francis Med. Ctr. Post-Sec.
201 Wood St 15222 412-392-3879
Pressley Ridge School Post-Sec.
530 Marshall Ave 15214 412-442-4468
Reformed Presbyterian Theological Sem. Post-Sec.
7418 Penn Ave 15208 412-731-8690
Robert Morris College Post-Sec.
600 5th Ave 15219 412-227-6800
Rosedale Technical Institute Post-Sec.
215 Beecham Dr Ste 2 15205 412-521-6200
St. Margaret School of Nursing Post-Sec.
221 7th St Ste 100 15238 412-784-4980
Seton-LaSalle HS 500/9-12
1000 McNeilly Rd 15226 412-561-3583
Sr. Patricia Laffey, prin. Fax 561-9097
Shady Side Academy 400/9-12
423 Fox Chapel Rd 15238 412-968-3000
Thomas Southard, pres. Fax 968-3006
Shady Side Academy MS 100/6-8
500 Squaw Run Rd E 15238 412-968-3100
Amy Mindlin, hdmstr. Fax 968-3008
Shadyside Hospital Post-Sec.
5230 Centre Ave 15232 412-622-2010
South Hills Beauty Academy Post-Sec.
3269 W Liberty Ave 15216 412-561-3381
Triangle Tech Post-Sec.
1940 Perrysville Ave 15214 412-359-1000
Trinity Christian S 400/K-12
299 Ridge Ave 15221 412-242-8886
Dale McLane, supt. Fax 242-8859
University Health Center Post-Sec.
300 Halket St 15213 412-641-4664
University of Pittsburgh Post-Sec.
4200 5th Ave 15260 412-624-4141
UPMC School of Medical Imaging Post-Sec.
3434 Forbes Ave 15213 412-647-3528
Vet Tech Institute Post-Sec.
125 7th St 15222 412-391-7021
Vincentian Academy 300/9-12
8200 McKnight Rd 15237 412-364-1616
Sr. Camille Panich, prin. Fax 367-5722
Western Pennsylvania Hospital Post-Sec.
4900 Friendship Ave 15224 412-578-5538
Western Pennsylvania School for Blind Post-Sec.
Bayard at Bellefield 15213
Western Pennsylvania School for the Deaf Post-Sec.
300 E Swissvale Ave 15218 412-371-7000
Western School of Health & Bus. Careers Post-Sec.
421 7th Ave 15219 412-281-2600
Winchester Thurston S 600/PK-12
555 Morewood Ave 15213 412-578-7500
Gary J. Niels, hdmstr. Fax 578-7504
Yeshiva S 400/PK-12
PO Box 81868 15217 412-422-7300
Rabbi Yisroel Rosenfeld, dean Fax 422-5930

Pittston, Luzerne, Pop. 7,689
Pittston Area SD 3,200/K-12
5 Stout St 18640 570-654-2271
Dr. Ross Scarantino, supt. Fax 654-5548
www.pittstonarea.com
Pittston Area HS 1,100/9-12
5 Stout St 18640 570-654-3541
Dr. John Lussi, prin. Fax 602-0823
Pittston Area MS 800/6-8
120 New St 18640 570-655-2927
George Cosgrove, prin. Fax 654-0862

Seton Catholic HS 200/9-12
37 William St 18640 570-654-4831
James Redington, prin. Fax 654-2599

Plains, Luzerne, Pop. 4,694
Wilkes-Barre Area SD
Supt. — See Wilkes Barre
Solomon/Plains JHS 600/7-8
43 Abbott St 18705 570-826-7224
Gina Bartoletti, prin. Fax 820-3715

Pleasant Gap, Centre, Pop. 1,699
Area Vocational Technical School
Supt. — None
Central PA Institute of Science & Tech. Vo/Tech
540 N Harrison Rd 16823 814-359-2793
Dr. Gregory Michelone, dir. Fax 359-2599

Plumsteadville, Bucks

Plumstead Christian HS 300/6-12
PO Box 216 18949 215-766-8073
Dean Whiteway, hdmstr. Fax 766-2033

Plymouth, Luzerne, Pop. 6,161
Wyoming Valley West SD
Supt. — See Kingston
Wyoming Valley West HS 1,500/9-12
150 Wadham St 18651 570-779-5361
Irvin DeRemer, prin. Fax 779-9510

Plymouth Meeting, Montgomery, Pop. 6,241
Area Vocational Technical School
Supt. — None
Center for Tech Studies-Montgomery Co. Vo/Tech
821 Plymouth Rd 19462 610-277-2301
Walter Slauch, prin.

Colonial SD 4,700/K-12
230 Flourtown Rd 19462 610-834-1670
Vincent F. Cotter, supt. Fax 834-7535
www.colonialsd.org
Colonial MS 1,100/6-8
716 Belvoir Rd 19462 610-275-5100
Robert Fahler, prin. Fax 278-2447
Plymouth-Whitemarsh HS 1,600/9-12
201 E Germantown Pike 19462 610-825-1500
Monica Sullivan, prin. Fax 832-0766

Pocono Summit, Monroe
Pocono Mountain SD
Supt. — See Swiftwater
Pocono Mountain West HS 1,600/10-12
HC 89 Box 2002 18346 570-839-7121
Jawn Herman, prin. Fax 839-5968
Pocono Mountain West JHS 600/8-9
HC 89 Box 2002 18346 570-839-7121
Dr. Eric Vogt, prin.

Point Marion, Fayette, Pop. 1,276
Albert Gallatin Area SD
Supt. — See Uniontown
Gallatin South MS 400/6-8
224 New Geneva Rd 15474 724-725-5241
Ralph Garcia, prin. Fax 725-5424

Portage, Cambria, Pop. 2,686
Portage Area SD 1,000/PK-12
84 Mountain Ave 15946 814-736-9636
Richard Bernazzoli, supt. Fax 736-9634
portage.schoolwires.com
Portage Area JSHS 400/8-12
85 Mountain Ave 15946 814-736-9636
Thomas Kakabar, prin. Fax 736-9597

Port Allegany, McKean, Pop. 2,260
Area Vocational Technical School
Supt. — None
Seneca Highlands AVTS Vo/Tech
219 Edison Bates Dr 16743 814-642-2573
Donald Raydo, prin.

Port Allegany SD 1,100/K-12
20 Oak St 16743 814-642-2596
Martin Flint, supt. Fax 642-9574
www.pahs.net
Port Allegany JSHS 600/7-12
20 Oak St 16743 814-642-2544
Marc Budd, prin. Fax 642-9574

Portersville, Butler, Pop. 261

Portersville Christian S 300/K-12
343 E Portersville Rd 16051 724-368-8787
Patricia Watters, admin. Fax 368-3100

Pottstown, Montgomery, Pop. 21,551
Owen J. Roberts SD 4,300/K-12
901 Ridge Rd 19465 610-469-5100
Dr. Myra Forrest, supt. Fax 469-0748
www.ojrsd.com
Roberts HS 1,300/9-12
981 Ridge Rd 19465 610-469-5101
George Carlino, prin. Fax 469-5898
Roberts MS 1,000/6-8
881 Ridge Rd 19465 610-469-5102
Dr. David Blozowich, prin. Fax 469-5832

Pottsgrove SD 3,300/K-12
1301 Kauffman Rd 19464 610-327-2277
Dr. Sharon Richardson, supt. Fax 327-2530
www.pgsd.org
Pottsgrove HS 1,000/9-12
1345 Kauffman Rd 19464 610-326-5105
Joyce Wishart, prin. Fax 970-6191
Pottsgrove MS 800/6-8
1351 N Hanover St 19464 610-326-8243
Dr. Regina Hove, prin. Fax 718-0581

Pottstown SD 3,200/PK-12
PO Box 779 19464 610-323-8200
David Krem, supt. Fax 326-6540
pottstownschools.com
Pottstown HS 900/9-12
750 N Washington St 19464 610-970-6700
Stephen Rodriguez, prin. Fax 970-1363
Pottstown MS 700/6-8
600 N Franklin St 19464 610-970-6665
Gail Cooper, prin. Fax 970-8738

Antonelli Medical & Professional Inst Post-Sec.
1700 Industrial Hwy 19464 610-323-7270
Coventry Christian S 400/PK-12
962 E Schuylkill Rd 19465 610-326-3366
Mark E. Niehls, supt. Fax 326-9370
Empire Beauty School Post-Sec.
141 E High St 19464 610-327-1313
Hill S 500/9-12
717 E High St 19464 610-326-1000
David Dougherty, hdmstr. Fax 705-1753
St. Pius X HS 600/9-12
844 N Keim St 19464 610-326-8990
Rev. Joseph Bongard, prin. Fax 323-8594
West-Mont Christian Academy 300/PK-12
873 S Hanover St 19465 610-326-7690
Dr. James Smock, admin. Fax 326-7126

Pottsville, Schuylkill, Pop. 14,764
Area Vocational Technical School
Supt. — None
Schuylkill Technology Center - Airport Vo/Tech
240 Airport Rd 17901 570-544-4904
Albert Gurka, prin.

Pottsville Area SD 3,100/K-12
1501 Laurel Blvd 17901 570-621-2900
Dr. James Gallagher, supt. Fax 621-2025
www.pottsville.k12.pa.us/
Lengel MS 900/5-8
1541 Laurel Blvd 17901 570-621-2923
Edward Hauck, prin. Fax 621-2999
Pottsville Area HS 1,200/9-12
16th and Elk Ave 17901 570-621-2960
Joseph Opalenick, prin. Fax 621-2037

Empire Beauty School Post-Sec.
324 N Centre St 17901 570-622-6060
McCann School of Business & Technology Post-Sec.
2650 Woodglen Rd 17901 570-622-7622
Nativity BVM HS 300/9-12
1 Lawtons Hl 17901 570-622-8110
Rev. Ronald Jankaitis, prin. Fax 622-0454
Pottsville Hospital School of Nursing Post-Sec.
420 S Jackson St 17901 570-621-5027
Schuylkill Institute of Business & Tech. Post-Sec.
118 S Centre St Ste 2 17901 570-622-4835

Prospect Park, Delaware, Pop. 6,449
Interboro SD 3,900/K-12
900 Washington Ave 19076 610-461-6700
Dr. Lois Snyder, supt. Fax 583-1678
www.interboro.k12.pa.us
Interboro HS 1,400/9-12
500 16th Ave 19076 610-237-6410
Paul S. Gibson Ed.D., prin. Fax 237-8103

Pulaski, Lawrence

New Castle School of Trades — Post-Sec.
New Castle Youngstown Rd 16143 — 724-964-8811

Punxsutawney, Jefferson, Pop. 6,036
Punxsutawney Area SD — 2,500/K-12
475 Beyer Ave 15767 — 814-938-5151
Dr. J. Frantz, supt. — Fax 938-6677
www.punxsy.k12.pa.us/
Punxsutawney Area HS — 900/9-12
450 N Findley St 15767 — 814-938-5151
David E. London, prin. — Fax 938-5101
Punxsutawney Area MS — 500/7-8
465 Beyer Ave 15767 — 814-938-5151
Richard Galluzzi, prin.

Punxsutawney Christian S — 200/PK-12
105 W Mahoning St 15767 — 814-939-7010
Pat Woods, admin. — Fax 939-7011
Punxy Beauty School of Cosmetology Arts — Post-Sec.
222 N Findley St 15767 — 814-938-8811

Quakertown, Bucks, Pop. 8,823
Quakertown Community SD — 4,900/K-12
600 Park Ave 18951 — 215-529-2000
James Scanlon Ed.D., supt. — Fax 529-2042
www.qcsd.org/
Freshman Center — 9-9
349 S 9th St 18951 — 267-371-1200
Suzanne Vincent, prin. — Fax 371-1201
Milford MS — 500/6-8
2255 Allentown Rd 18951 — 215-529-2210
Derek Peiffer, prin. — Fax 529-2211
Quakertown Community HS — 1,300/10-12
600 Park Ave 18951 — 215-529-2060
Mario Galante, prin. — Fax 529-2061
Strayer MS — 800/6-8
1200 Ronald Reagan Dr 18951 — 215-529-2290
Richard Zinck Ed.D., prin. — Fax 529-2291

Quarryville, Lancaster, Pop. 2,101
Solanco SD — 3,900/K-12
121 S Hess St 17566 — 717-786-8401
Jon Rednak Ed.D., supt. — Fax 786-8245
www.solanco.k12.pa.us
Smith MS — 500/6-8
645 Kirkwood Pike 17566 — 717-786-2244
James Close, prin. — Fax 786-8796
Solanco HS — 1,400/9-12
585 Solanco Rd 17566 — 717-786-2151
Gerard Rosolie, prin. — Fax 786-1808
Swift MS — 500/6-8
1866 Robert Fulton Hwy 17566 — 717-548-2187
Suzanne Herr, prin. — Fax 548-3350

Radnor, Delaware, Pop. 31,300
Radnor Township SD
Supt. — See Wayne
Radnor HS — 1,100/9-12
130 King Of Prussia Rd 19087 — 610-293-0855
Joane Eby, prin. — Fax 989-9146

Archbishop Carroll HS — 1,100/9-12
211 Matsonford Rd 19087 — 610-688-7610
Carol Ann Blair, prin. — Fax 688-8326
Cabrini College — Post-Sec.
610 King Of Prussia Rd 19087 — 610-902-8100

Reading, Berks, Pop. 80,855
Antietam SD — 1,100/K-12
100 Antietam Rd 19606 — 610-779-0554
Dr. Lawrence Mayes, supt. — Fax 779-4424
www.antietamsd.org
Antietam MSHS — 500/7-12
100 Antietam Rd 19606 — 610-779-3545
Melissa Brewer, prin. — Fax 779-0378

Area Vocational Technical School
Supt. — None
Reading-Muhlenberg AVTS — Vo/Tech
PO Box 13068 19612 — 610-921-7306
Gerard Cunningham, admin. — Fax 921-7367

Exeter Township SD — 3,900/K-12
3650 Perkiomen Ave 19606 — 610-779-0700
Nicholas Corbo, supt. — Fax 779-7104
www.exeter.k12.pa.us/
Exeter Township HS — 1,000/9-12
201 E 37th St 19606 — 610-779-3060
James Smith, prin. — Fax 370-0518
Exeter Township JHS — 700/7-8
151 E 39th St 19606 — 610-779-3320
Eric Flamm, prin. — Fax 370-0678

Reading SD — 17,000/PK-12
800 Washington St 19601 — 610-371-5611
Dr. Thomas Chapman, supt. — Fax 371-5971
www.readingsd.org
Northeast MS — 1,300/6-8
1216 N 13th St 19604 — 610-371-5774
Alexander Brown, prin. — Fax 371-5784
Northwest MS — 1,100/6-8
1000 N Front St 19601 — 610-371-5882
Dennis Campbell, prin. — Fax 371-5881
Reading HS — 4,300/9-12
801 N 13th St 19604 — 610-371-5710
Wynton Butler, prin. — Fax 371-8723
Southern MS — 900/6-8
931 Chestnut St 19602 — 610-371-5802
Joel Brigel, prin. — Fax 371-5814
Southwest MS — 800/6-8
300 Chestnut St 19602 — 610-371-5934
Yolanda Williams, prin. — Fax 371-5950

Albright College — Post-Sec.
PO Box 15234 19612 — 800-225-1856
Alvernia College — Post-Sec.
400 Saint Bernardine St 19607 — 610-796-8200
Central Catholic HS — 400/9-12
1400 Hill Rd 19602 — 610-373-4178
Thomas Mirabella, prin. — Fax 375-4898
Empire Beauty School — Post-Sec.
2302 N 5th Street Hwy 19605 — 610-372-2777
Fairview Christian S — 100/K-12
410 S 14th St 19602 — 610-372-8826
Jay Fox, prin. — Fax 478-0896
Holy Name HS — 500/9-12
955 E Wyomissing Blvd 19611 — 610-374-8361
Keith Laser, prin. — Fax 374-4309
Pace Institute — Post-Sec.
606 Court St 19601 — 610-375-7223
Pennsylvania State University — Post-Sec.
PO Box 7009 19610 — 610-320-4800
Reading Adventist Junior Academy — 100/1-10
309 N Kenhorst Blvd 19607 — 610-777-8424
Lee Stahl, prin. — Fax 603-0129
Reading Area Community College — Post-Sec.
PO Box 1706 19603 — 610-372-4721
Reading Hospital & Medical Center — Post-Sec.
PO Box 16052 19612 — 610-378-6664
St. Joseph's Hospital — Post-Sec.
PO Box 316 19603 — 610-378-2000

Red Lion, York, Pop. 6,084
Red Lion Area SD — 5,600/K-12
696 Delta Rd 17356 — 717-244-4518
Larry Macaluso, supt. — Fax 244-2196
www.rlasd.k12.pa.us
Red Lion Area JHS — 1,000/7-8
200 Country Club Rd 17356 — 717-244-1448
Kurt Fassnacht, prin. — Fax 244-6160
Red Lion Area SHS — 1,700/9-12
200 Horace Mann Ave 17356 — 717-246-1611
Charles Humberd, prin. — Fax 246-9181

Red Lion Christian S — 300/K-12
105 Springvale Rd 17356 — 717-244-3905
Steve Schmuck, prin. — Fax 246-3738

Reedsville, Mifflin, Pop. 1,030
Mifflin County SD
Supt. — See Lewistown
Indian Valley MS — 800/6-8
125 Kish Rd 17084 — 717-667-2123
Mark Crosson, prin. — Fax 667-6608

Renovo, Clinton, Pop. 1,243
Keystone Central SD
Supt. — See Lock Haven
Bucktail Area JSHS — 200/7-12
1300 Bucktail Ave 17764 — 570-923-1166
Kurt Smith, prin. — Fax 923-2233

Reynoldsville, Jefferson, Pop. 2,609
Area Vocational Technical School
Supt. — None
Jefferson County-Dubois AVTS — Vo/Tech
576 Vo Tech Rd 15851 — 814-653-8265
W. Barnett Knorr, prin. — Fax 653-8425

Richboro, Bucks, Pop. 5,332
Council Rock SD
Supt. — See Newtown
Richboro MS — 500/7-8
98 Upper Holland Rd 18954 — 215-355-0500
William Bell, prin. — Fax 355-3230

Ridgway, Elk, Pop. 4,302
Ridgway Area SD — 1,000/K-12
PO Box 447 15853 — 814-773-3146
Brent Rhoads, supt. — Fax 776-4299
www.ridgwayareaschooldistrict.com/
Ridgway Area HS — 400/9-12
PO Box 447 15853 — 814-773-3164
Heather Vargas, prin. — Fax 776-4247
Ridgway Area MS — 200/6-8
PO Box 447 15853 — 814-773-3156
William Connelly, prin. — Fax 776-4239

North Central Industrial Tech. Ed. Ctr. — Post-Sec.
651 Montmorenci Rd 15853 — 814-772-1012

Ridley Park, Delaware, Pop. 7,062
Ridley SD
Supt. — See Folsom
Ridley MS — 1,400/6-8
400 Free St 19078 — 610-237-8034
Gail Heinemeyer, prin. — Fax 237-8032

Rimersburg, Clarion, Pop. 1,018
Union SD — 800/K-12
354 Baker St Ste 2 16248 — 814-473-6311
Lawrence Bornak, supt. — Fax 473-8201
www.unionsd.net/
Union JSHS, 354 Baker St Ste 1 16248 — 400/7-12
Stephen Shutters, prin. — 814-473-3121

Roaring Spring, Blair, Pop. 2,309
Spring Cove SD — 1,900/K-12
1100 E Main St 16673 — 814-224-5124
Fax 224-5516
springcove.schoolnet.com
Spring Cove MS — 500/6-8
1150 E Main St 16673 — 814-224-2106
Frank Pannebaker, prin.
Other Schools – See Martinsburg

Robesonia, Berks, Pop. 2,059
Conrad Weiser Area SD — 2,900/K-12
44 Big Spring Rd 19551 — 610-693-8545
Dr. Robert Urzillo, supt. — Fax 693-8586
www.conradweiser.org
Weiser HS — 1,000/9-12
44 Big Spring Rd 19551 — 610-693-8521
Dr. Betsy Adams, prin. — Fax 693-8511
Weiser MS — 1,000/5-8
347 E Penn Ave 19551 — 610-693-8514
Joseph Torchia, prin. — Fax 693-8543

Rochester, Beaver, Pop. 3,804
Rochester Area SD — 1,100/K-12
540 Reno St 15074 — 724-775-7500
Dr. C. Dean Galitsis, supt. — Fax 775-6942
www.rasd.net/
Rochester Area HS — 400/9-12
540 Reno St 15074 — 724-775-7500
Walter Gaida, prin. — Fax 775-9268
Rochester Area MS — 300/6-8
540 Reno St 15074 — 724-775-7500
Marianne LeDonne, prin. — Fax 775-9267

Rockwood, Somerset, Pop. 933
Rockwood Area SD — 900/K-12
439 Somerset Ave 15557 — 814-926-4913
Vincent Capricci, supt. — Fax 926-2880
www.rockwoodschools.org
Rockwood Area JSHS — 400/7-12
437 Somerset Ave 15557 — 814-926-4631
Mark Bower, prin. — Fax 926-2631

Rome, Bradford, Pop. 373
Northeast Bradford SD — 900/K-12
RR 1 Box 211B 18837 — 570-744-2521
G. Mathew Gordon, supt. — Fax 744-2933
www.neb.k12.pa.us
Northeast Bradford JSHS — 500/7-12
RR 1 Box 211B 18837 — 570-744-2521
Heather McPherson, prin. — Fax 744-2933

Rosemont, Montgomery
Lower Merion SD
Supt. — See Ardmore
Harriton HS, 600 N Ithan Ave 19010 — 900/9-12
Steven Kline, prin. — 610-658-3950

Hill Top Preparatory S — 100/6-12
737 S Ithan Ave 19010 — 610-527-3230
Tom Needham, hdmstr. — Fax 527-7683
Irwin S — 600/K-12
S Ithan Ave & Conestoga Rd 19010 — 610-525-8400
Martha Cutts, dir. — Fax 525-8908

Roseto, Northampton, Pop. 1,662

Faith Christian S — 200/K-12
122 Dante St 18013 — 610-588-3414
Robert Tomlinson, admin. — Fax 588-8103
Pius X HS — 200/7-12
580 3rd Ave 18013 — 610-588-3291
Thomas Klepeisz, prin. — Fax 599-3048

Royersford, Montgomery, Pop. 4,330
Spring-Ford Area SD
Supt. — See Collegeville
Spring-Ford HS — 1,800/9-12
350 S Lewis Rd 19468 — 610-705-6001
Patrick Nugent, prin. — Fax 705-6258
Spring-Ford MS 8th Grade Center — 500/8-8
700 Washington St 19468 — 610-705-6002
Michael Siggins, prin. — Fax 705-6255

Ruffs Dale, Westmoreland
Yough SD
Supt. — See Herminie
Yough MS — 700/5-8
171 State Route 31 15679 — 724-872-5164
Thomas Paterline, prin. — Fax 872-5319

Rural Valley, Armstrong, Pop. 874
Armstrong SD
Supt. — See Ford City
West Shamokin JSHS — 700/7-12
178 Wolf Dr 16249 — 724-783-7040
Rick Burns, prin. — Fax 783-6747

Russell, Warren
Warren County SD
Supt. — See North Warren
Eisenhower MSHS — 600/7-12
3700 Route 957 16345 — 814-757-8878
Kelly Martin, prin. — Fax 757-8516

Calvary Chapel Christian S — 100/PK-12
PO Box 579 16345 — 814-757-8744
James Hunt, prin. — Fax 757-8745

Russellton, Allegheny, Pop. 1,691
Deer Lakes SD — 2,100/K-12
PO Box 10 15076 — 724-265-5300
Mark King, supt. — Fax 265-5025
www.deerlakes.net
Deer Lakes HS — 700/9-12
PO Box 40 15076 — 724-265-5320
Michael Pendred, prin. — Fax 265-3970
Deer Lakes MS — 500/6-8
PO Box 20 15076 — 724-265-5310
Dr. Thomas Lesniewski, prin. — Fax 265-3711

Saegertown, Crawford, Pop. 1,057
Penncrest SD — 3,900/K-12
PO Box 808 16433 — 814-763-2323
Richard Borchilo, supt. — Fax 763-5129
www.penncrest.iu5.org
Saegertown JSHS — 600/7-12
18079 Mook Rd 16433 — 814-763-2615
Randall Deemer, prin. — Fax 763-6702
Other Schools – See Cambridge Springs, Guys Mills

French Creek Valley Christian S — 100/PK-12
420 North St 16433 — 814-763-3282
Wendy Horning, prin. — Fax 763-3283

Saint Davids, Delaware

Eastern University — Post-Sec.
1300 Eagle Rd 19087 — 610-341-5800

Saint Marys, Elk, Pop. 14,182
Saint Marys Area SD — 2,500/K-12
977 S Saint Marys St 15857 — 814-834-7831
Murray Neeper, supt. — Fax 781-2190
smasd.org
Saint Marys Area HS — 900/9-12
977 S Saint Marys St 15857 — 814-834-7831
Joshua Williams, prin. — Fax 781-2190
Saint Marys Area MS — 600/6-8
979 S Saint Marys St 15857 — 814-834-7831
James Wortman, prin. — Fax 781-2191

Elk County Catholic HS — 400/9-12
600 Maurus St 15857 — 814-834-7800
John Kowach, hdmstr. — Fax 781-3441
St. Marys Catholic MS — 300/6-8
325 Church St 15857 — 814-834-2665
Mary Agnes Marshall, prin. — Fax 834-5339

Salisbury, Somerset, Pop. 829
Salisbury-Elk Lick SD — 400/PK-12
PO Box 68 15558 — 814-662-2733
Dr. David Welling, supt. — Fax 662-2544
www.selsd.com
Salisbury-Elk Lick JSHS — 200/7-12
PO Box 68 15558 — 814-662-2741
Eugene Wengerd, prin. — Fax 662-2091

Saltsburg, Indiana, Pop. 907
Blairsville-Saltsburg SD
Supt. — See Blairsville
Saltsburg MSHS 500/7-12
84 Trojan Ln 15681 724-639-3547
Eric Kostic, prin. Fax 639-0071

Kiski S 200/9-12
1888 Brett Ln 15681 724-639-3586
Christopher Brueningsen, hdmstr. Fax 639-8467

Sarver, Butler
Freeport Area SD 2,000/K-12
621 S Pike Rd 16055 724-295-5141
Stan Chapp Ed.D., supt. Fax 295-3001
www.freeport.k12.pa.us
Freeport Area HS 600/9-12
625 S Pike Rd 16055 724-295-5143
Robert Schleiden, prin. Fax 295-2390
Other Schools – See Freeport

Evangel Heights Christian Academy 300/PK-12
120 Beale Rd 16055 724-295-9199
Gary Bracewell, dir. Fax 295-9009

Saxonburg, Butler, Pop. 1,636
South Butler County SD 2,900/K-12
328 Knoch Rd 16056 724-352-1700
Dr. Patrick T. O'Toole, supt. Fax 352-3622
www.southbutler.k12.pa.us
Knoch HS 1,000/9-12
345 Knoch Rd 16056 724-352-1700
Frank Moxie, prin. Fax 352-0160
Knoch MS 700/6-8
754 Dinnerbell Rd 16056 724-352-1700
James George, prin. Fax 352-0170

Saxton, Bedford, Pop. 772
Tussey Mountain SD 1,200/K-12
199 Front St 16678 814-635-3670
Dr. Ronald D. McCahan, supt. Fax 635-3928
www.tmsd.net/
Tussey Mountain JSHS 600/7-12
199 Front St 16678 814-635-2975
Mike Panek, prin.

Sayre, Bradford, Pop. 5,606
Sayre Area SD 1,200/PK-12
333 W Lockhart St 18840 570-888-7615
Dean Hosterman, supt. Fax 888-8248
www.sayresd.org
Sayre Area JSHS 600/7-12
331 W Lockhart St 18840 570-888-6622
Samuel Cessna, prin. Fax 882-9385

Robert Packer Hospital Post-Sec.
1 Guthrie Sq 18840 570-888-6666

Schnecksville, Lehigh, Pop. 1,780
Area Vocational Technical School
Supt. — None
Lehigh Career & Technical Institute Vo/Tech
4500 Education Park Dr 18078 610-799-1323
Dr. Clyde Hornberger, prin.

Lehigh Carbon Community College Post-Sec.
4525 Education Park Dr 18078 610-799-2121

Schuylkill Haven, Schuylkill, Pop. 5,283
Blue Mountain SD
Supt. — See Orwigsburg
Blue Mountain HS 1,000/9-12
1076 W Market St 17972 570-366-0511
Dr. Cynthia Knauer, prin. Fax 366-1965

Schuylkill Haven Area SD 1,300/K-12
120 Haven St 17972 570-385-6705
Richard Rada, supt. Fax 385-6736
www.haven.k12.pa.us/
Schuylkill Haven Area HS 500/8-12
120 Haven St 17972 570-385-6717
Charles Grabusky, prin. Fax 385-6745

Pennsylvania State University Post-Sec.
200 University Dr 17972 570-385-6000

Scottdale, Westmoreland, Pop. 4,567
Southmoreland SD 2,300/K-12
609 Parker Ave 15683 724-887-2000
Dr. John Halfhill, supt. Fax 887-2055
www.southmoreland.net
Other Schools – See Alverton

Scranton, Lackawanna, Pop. 73,120
Area Vocational Technical School
Supt. — None
CTC of Lackawanna County Vo/Tech
3201 Rockwell Ave 18508 570-346-8471
Vincent Nallo, prin. Fax 342-4251

Scranton SD 9,000/PK-12
425 N Washington Ave 18503 570-348-3400
Michael Sheridan, supt. Fax 348-3563
www.scrsd.org/
Northeast IS, 721 Adams Ave 18510 900/6-8
Barbara Dixon, prin. 570-348-3651
Scranton HS 1,900/9-12
63 Munchak Way 18508 570-348-3481
Robert McTiernan, prin. Fax 348-3561
South Scranton IS 500/6-8
355 Maple St 18505 570-348-3631
Charles Gahwiler, prin.
West Scranton HS 1,000/9-12
1201 Luzerne St 18504 570-348-3616
Kevin Rogan, prin. Fax 348-3594
West Scranton IS 800/6-8
Fellows St & Parrott Ave 18504 570-348-3475
Dr. Charlotte Slocum, prin.

Allied Medical & Technical Careers Post-Sec.
517 Ash St 18509 570-558-1818
Bais Yaakov of Scranton 100/9-12
1025 Vine St 18510 570-347-5003
Esther Elefant, prin. Fax 353-5003
Center for Innovative Training & Educ. Post-Sec.
135 Franklin Ave 18503 570-922-6555

Education Direct Post-Sec.
925 Oak St 18515 570-342-7701
Eisner Yeshiva HS 100/9-12
930 Hickory St 18505 570-346-1747
Charles Gahwiler, prin. Fax 346-2251
Holy Cross HS - Bishop Hannan Campus 300/9-12
330 Wyoming Ave 18503 570-346-4643
James Marcks, prin. Fax 346-0048
Johnson College Post-Sec.
3427 N Main Ave 18508 570-342-6404
Lackawanna College Post-Sec.
501 Vine St 18509 570-961-7810
Marywood University Post-Sec.
2300 Adams Ave 18509 570-348-6211
St. Paul S 200/4-8
1527 Penn Ave 18509 570-343-7880
Elizabeth Murray, prin. Fax 343-0069
Scranton Prep S 800/9-12
1000 Wyoming Ave 18509 570-941-7737
Patrick Marx, prin. Fax 941-6118
Scranton State School for the Deaf Post-Sec.
1800 N Washington Ave 18509
University of Scranton Post-Sec.
800 Linden St 18510 570-941-7400
Yeshiva Beth Moshe Post-Sec.
930 Hickory St 18505 570-346-1747
Yeshiva Beth Moshe 100/9-12
PO Box 1141 18501 570-346-1747
Rabbi Chaim Bressler, prin. Fax 346-2251

Selinsgrove, Snyder, Pop. 5,417
Selinsgrove Area SD 2,600/K-12
401 18th St 17870 570-374-1144
Dr. Frederick C. Johnson, supt. Fax 372-2222
www.seal-pa.org/
Selinsgrove Area HS 1,000/9-12
500 N Broad St 17870 570-372-2230
Reed Messmore, prin. Fax 372-2240
Selinsgrove Area MS 700/6-8
401 18th St 17870 570-372-2250
George Pyle, prin. Fax 372-2251

Gospel Christian Academy 50/PK-12
50 Gospel Way 17870 570-743-7754
Kii Fisher, admin. Fax 743-7746
Susquehanna University Post-Sec.
514 University Ave 17870 570-374-0101

Sellersville, Bucks, Pop. 4,496

Faith Christian Academy 300/K-12
700 N Main St 18960 215-257-5031
Robert Clymer, prin. Fax 257-3327
Upper Bucks Christian S 300/K-12
754 E Rockhill Rd 18960 215-536-9200
Russ Baun, prin. Fax 536-2229

Seneca, Venango, Pop. 1,029
Cranberry Area SD 1,200/K-12
3 Education Dr 16346 814-676-5628
Dr. Nicholas A. Bodnar, supt. Fax 677-5728
www.cranberrysd.org/
Cranberry Area JSHS 700/7-12
1 Education Dr 16346 814-676-8504
John Irvine, prin. Fax 676-5156

Christian Life Academy 100/K-12
PO Box 207 16346 814-676-9360
Michael Lloyd, admin. Fax 676-2908
Northwest Medical Center Post-Sec.
100 Fairfield Dr 16346 814-677-1711

Sewickley, Allegheny, Pop. 3,674
Quaker Valley SD 1,600/K-12
203 Graham St 15143 412-749-3600
Dr. R. Longo, supt. Fax 749-3601
www.qvsd.org/qvsd/site/default.asp
Quaker Valley MS 300/7-9
201 Graham St 15143 412-749-5079
Dr. Kenneth Powell, prin.
Other Schools – See Leetsdale

Eden Christian Academy 100/7-12
318 Nicholson Rd 15143 412-741-2825
Thomas Aiken, hdmstr. Fax 324-1101
Sewickley Academy 800/PK-12
315 Academy Ave 15143 412-741-2230
Kolia J. O'Connor, hdmstr. Fax 741-1411
Sewickley Valley Hospital Post-Sec.
700 Blackburn Rd 15143 412-741-6600
The Education Center at Watson Inst. Post-Sec.
301 Campmeeting Rd 15143 412-741-1800

Shamokin Dam, Snyder, Pop. 1,466

Empire Beauty School Post-Sec.
PO Box 397 17876 570-743-1410

Shanksville, Somerset, Pop. 230
Shanksville-Stonycreek SD 400/PK-12
PO Box 128 15560 814-267-4649
Mr. Thomas McInroy, supt. Fax 267-4372
www.sssd.com
Shanksville-Stonycreek MSHS 200/6-12
PO Box 128 15560 814-267-4649
Timothy Kretchman, prin. Fax 267-4372

Sharon, Mercer, Pop. 15,504
Sharon CSD 2,300/K-12
215 Forker Blvd 16146 724-981-6390
Michael Calla, supt. Fax 981-0844
sharoncitysd.schoolwires.com
Sharon MSHS 1,100/7-12
1129 E State St 16146 724-983-4030
Leonard Rich, prin. Fax 981-0840

Business Institute of Pennsylvania Post-Sec.
335 Boyd Dr 16146 724-983-0700
Pennsylvania State University Post-Sec.
147 Shenango Ave 16146 724-983-5800
Sharon Regional Health System Post-Sec.
740 E State St 16146 724-983-3865

Sharon Hill, Delaware, Pop. 5,357
Southeast Delco SD
Supt. — See Folcroft

Academy Park HS 1,300/9-12
300 Calcon Hook Rd 19079 610-522-4330
Eric Turman, prin. Fax 522-4335

Venus Beauty Academy Post-Sec.
1033 Chester Pike 19079 610-586-2500

Sharpsville, Mercer, Pop. 4,281
Sharpsville Area SD 1,400/K-12
701 S 7th St 16150 724-962-7874
Mark Ferrara, supt. Fax 962-7873
www.sharpsville.k12.pa.us/
Sharpsville Area HS 500/9-12
301 Blue Devil Way 16150 724-962-7861
Kirk Scurpa, prin. Fax 962-7730
Sharpsville Area MS 300/6-8
303 Blue Devil Way 16150 724-962-7863
John Vannoy, prin. Fax 962-7891

Sheffield, Warren, Pop. 1,294
Warren County SD
Supt. — See North Warren
Sheffield Area MSHS 400/6-12
6760 Route 6 16347 814-968-3720
James Evers, prin. Fax 968-4233

Shelocta, Armstrong, Pop. 122

Wrightco Technologies Tech Training Inst Post-Sec.
Route 422 W 15774 724-354-5162

Shenandoah, Schuylkill, Pop. 5,296
Shenandoah Valley SD 1,000/PK-12
805 W Centre St 17976 570-462-1936
Dr. Stanley Rakowsky, supt. Fax 462-4611
www.shenandoah.k12.pa.us
Shenandoah Valley JSHS 500/7-12
805 W Centre St 17976 570-462-1957
Phillip Andras, prin. Fax 462-2982

Shickshinny, Luzerne, Pop. 907
Northwest Area SD 1,400/K-12
243 Thorne Hill Rd 18655 570-542-4126
Nancy Tkatch, supt. Fax 542-0187
www.northwest.k12.pa.us/
Northwest Area JSHS 700/7-12
243 Thorne Hill Rd 18655 570-542-4126
Joseph Gorham, prin. Fax 542-4825

Shillington, Berks, Pop. 5,031
Governor Mifflin SD 4,200/K-12
10 S Waverly St 19607 610-775-1461
Dr. Mary T. Weiss, supt. Fax 775-6586
www.governormifflinsd.org
Mifflin HS 1,400/9-12
101 S Waverly St 19607 610-775-5089
John Sengia, prin. Fax 796-7471
Mifflin MS 700/7-8
130 E Lancaster Ave 19607 610-775-1465
Kevin Hohl, prin. Fax 685-3760

Shinglehouse, Potter, Pop. 1,190
Oswayo Valley SD 400/PK-12
PO Box 610 16748 814-697-7175
Charles Wicker, supt. Fax 697-7439
www.oswayo.com/
Oswayo Valley MSHS 200/6-12
PO Box 610 16748 814-697-6132
Gary Elder, prin. Fax 697-6375

Shippensburg, Cumberland, Pop. 5,605
Shippensburg Area SD 3,100/K-12
317 N Morris St 17257 717-530-2700
Dr. Jacqueline Lesney, supt. Fax 530-2724
www.ship.k12.pa.us
Shippensburg Area HS 1,000/9-12
201 Eberly Dr 17257 717-530-2730
Dr. H. Frederick Shilling, prin. Fax 530-2835
Shippensburg Area MS 800/6-8
101 Park Pl W 17257 717-530-2750
Teri Mowery, prin. Fax 530-2757

Shippensburg University Post-Sec.
1871 Old Main Dr 17257 717-477-7447

Shippenville, Clarion, Pop. 483
Area Vocational Technical School
Supt. — None
Clarion County Career Center Vo/Tech
447 Career Ln 16254 814-226-4391
William Powell, dir. Fax 226-7350

Shiremanstown, Cumberland, Pop. 1,480

Bible Baptist S 500/PK-12
201 W Main St 17011 717-737-3550
George Wiedman, admin. Fax 761-3977

Sidman, Cambria, Pop. 1,189
Forest Hills SD 2,300/K-12
PO Box 158 15955 814-487-7613
Donald Bailey, supt. Fax 487-7775
www.fhsd.k12.pa.us/
Forest Hills HS 600/10-12
PO Box 325 15955 814-487-7613
Edwin Bowser, prin. Fax 487-2371
Forest Hills MS 600/7-9
1427 Frankstown Rd 15955 814-495-4611
Raymond Wotkowski, prin. Fax 495-7367

Sinking Spring, Berks, Pop. 3,443
Wilson SD
Supt. — See West Lawn
Wilson Southern JHS 700/7-9
3100 Iroquois Ave 19608 610-670-0180
Luke Hadfield, prin. Fax 670-4815

Slatington, Lehigh, Pop. 4,413
Northern Lehigh SD 2,100/K-12
1201 Shadow Oaks Ln 18080 610-767-9800
Dr. Nicholas P. Sham, supt. Fax 767-9809
www.nlsd.org
Northern Lehigh HS 700/9-12
1 Bulldog Ln 18080 610-767-9833
Aileen Yadush, prin. Fax 767-9853
Northern Lehigh MS 400/7-8
600 Diamond St 18080 610-767-9812
David Papay, prin. Fax 767-9850

Slippery Rock, Butler, Pop. 3,210
Slippery Rock Area SD 2,500/K-12
201 Kiester Rd 16057 724-794-2960
Dr. Marianne Lee Beaton, supt. Fax 794-2001
www.slipperyrock.k12.pa.us
Slippery Rock Area HS 800/9-12
201 Kiester Rd 16057 724-794-2960
Harry Beil, prin. Fax 794-1952
Slippery Rock Area MS 600/6-8
201 Kiester Rd 16057 724-794-2960
Joseph Raykle, prin. Fax 794-6265

Slippery Rock University Post-Sec.
14 Maltby Ave 16057 724-738-9000

Smethport, McKean, Pop. 1,617
Smethport Area SD 1,000/K-12
414 S Mechanic St 16749 814-887-5543
George J. Romanowski, supt. Fax 887-5544
www.smethporthubbers.net
Smethport Area JSHS 500/7-12
412 S Mechanic St 16749 814-887-5545
Robert Miller, prin. Fax 887-5546

Somerset, Somerset, Pop. 6,500
Area Vocational Technical School
Supt. — None
Somerset County Technology Center Vo/Tech
281 Technology Dr 15501 814-443-3651
Georgia Yeager, prin. Fax 445-6716

Somerset Area SD 2,700/K-12
645 S Columbia Ave Ste 110 15501 814-443-2831
Dr. David Pastrick, supt. Fax 443-1964
sasdpa.net
Somerset Area JHS 700/7-9
645 S Columbia Ave Ste 120 15501 814-443-2831
Jeff Boyer, prin. Fax 444-3301
Somerset Area SHS 700/10-12
645 S Columbia Ave Ste 130 15501 814-443-2831
Mark Gross, prin. Fax 444-3202

Somerset Community Hospital Post-Sec.
225 S Center Ave 15501 814-443-5221

Souderton, Montgomery, Pop. 6,691
Souderton Area SD 6,700/K-12
760 Lower Rd 18964 215-723-6061
Charles D. Amuso Ed.D., supt. Fax 723-8897
www.soudertonsd.org
Indian Crest JHS 1,100/8-9
139 Harleysville Pike 18964 215-723-9193
Jeff Pammer, prin. Fax 723-8897
Souderton Area HS 1,500/10-12
41 N School Ln 18964 215-723-2808
Sam Varano, prin. Fax 723-6352

Southampton, Bucks, Pop. 11,500
Centennial SD
Supt. — See Warminster
Klinger MS 700/6-8
1415 2nd Street Pike 18966 215-364-5950
Khalid Mumin, prin.

CHI Institute Post-Sec.
520 Street Rd 18966 215-357-5100

South Canaan, Wayne
Western Wayne SD 2,500/PK-12
PO Box 220 18459 570-937-4270
Andrew Falonk, supt. Fax 937-4105
www.westernwayne.org
Other Schools – See Lake Ariel

St. Tikhon's Orthodox Theological Sem. Post-Sec.
PO Box 130 18459 570-937-4411

South Park, Allegheny
South Park SD 2,200/K-12
2005 Eagle Ridge Dr 15129 412-655-3111
Richard Bucchianeri, supt. Fax 655-2952
www.sparksd.org
South Park HS 800/9-12
2005 Eagle Ridge Dr 15129 412-655-4900
Dr. Patricia Smith, prin. Fax 655-1463
South Park MS 700/5-8
2500 Stewart Rd 15129 412-831-7200
Douglas Broglie, prin. Fax 831-7204

South Williamsport, Lycoming, Pop. 6,189
South Williamsport Area SD 1,400/K-12
515 W Central Ave 17702 570-327-1581
Thomas C. Farr, supt. Fax 326-0641
www.mounties.k12.pa.us
South Williamsport Area JSHS 700/7-12
700 Percy St 17702 570-326-2684
Paul Anderson, prin. Fax 326-2687

Spring Church, Armstrong
Apollo-Ridge SD
Supt. — See Apollo
Apollo-Ridge HS 500/9-12
1825 State Route 56 15686 724-478-6000
Christopher Clark, prin. Fax 478-9775
Apollo-Ridge MS 400/6-8
1829 State Route 56 15686 724-478-6000
Donna Sybert, prin. Fax 478-3730

Springdale, Allegheny, Pop. 3,597
Allegheny Valley SD
Supt. — See Cheswick
Springdale JSHS 600/7-12
501 Butler Rd 15144 724-274-8100
Janice Nuzzo Ph.D., prin. Fax 274-2106

Springfield, Delaware, Pop. 24,160
Springfield SD 3,400/K-12
111 W Leamy Ave 19064 610-938-6000
Dr. James Capolupo, supt. Fax 938-6005
www.springfieldsd-delco.org
Richardson MS 1,000/5-8
20 W Woodland Ave 19064 610-938-6300
Frank McKnight, prin. Fax 938-6305
Springfield HS 1,200/9-12
49 W Leamy Ave 19064 610-938-6100
Dr. Bridget Kelly, prin. Fax 938-6105

Cardinal O'Hara HS 2,000/9-12
1701 S Sproul Rd 19064 610-544-3800
William Miles Ed.D., prin. Fax 544-1189
Chubb Institute-Keystone School Post-Sec.
400 S State Rd 19064 610-543-1747

Spring Grove, York, Pop. 2,212
Spring Grove Area SD 3,900/K-12
100 E College Ave 17362 717-225-4731
Dr. David Stricker, supt. Fax 225-6028
www.sgasd.org
Spring Grove Area MS 700/7-8
1472 Roth Church Rd 17362 717-225-4731
Rosemary Aldinger, prin. Fax 225-0146
Spring Grove HS 1,300/9-12
Hanover & Jackson Sts 17362 717-225-4731
Steven Brown, prin. Fax 225-0736

Spring Mills, Centre
Penns Valley Area SD 1,400/K-12
4528 Penns Valley Rd 16875 814-422-8814
Dr. John DiNunzio, supt. Fax 422-8020
www.pennsvalley.org
Penns Valley Area JSHS 800/7-12
4545 Penns Valley Rd 16875 814-422-8854
Albert D'Ambrosia, prin. Fax 422-8280

State College, Centre, Pop. 38,720
State College Area SD 7,300/K-12
131 W Nittany Ave 16801 814-231-1011
Dr. Patricia Best, supt. Fax 231-4130
www.scasd.org
Mount Nittany MS 900/6-8
656 Brandywine Dr 16801 814-466-5133
Jason Perrin, prin. Fax 466-5140
Park Forest MS 900/6-8
2180 School Dr 16803 814-237-5301
David Dolbin, prin. Fax 272-0196
State College Area HS 2,700/9-12
653 Westerly Pkwy 16801 814-231-1111
Craig Butler, prin. Fax 231-5024

Empire Beauty School Post-Sec.
206 W Hamilton Ave 16801 814-238-1961
Grace Prep S 50/9-12
1117 William St 16801 814-867-1177
Robert Gresh, admin. Fax 867-3555
South Hills School of Business & Tech. Post-Sec.
480 Waupelani Dr 16801 888-282-7427

Steelton, Dauphin, Pop. 5,667
Central Dauphin SD
Supt. — See Harrisburg
Swatara MS 600/6-8
1101 Highland St 17113 717-939-9363
Michael Jordan, prin. Fax 939-2156

Steelton-Highspire SD 1,300/K-12
PO Box 7645 17113 717-939-9823
Dr. Norma Mateer, supt. Fax 939-8241
www.shsd.k12.pa.us
Steelton-Highspire JSHS 600/7-12
250 Reynders St 17113 717-939-9895
Paul Cronin, prin. Fax 939-8241

Stoneboro, Mercer, Pop. 1,061
Lakeview SD 1,300/K-12
2482 Mercer St 16153 724-376-7911
Dr. Paulette Savolskis, supt. Fax 376-7910
Lakeview HS 400/9-12
2482 Mercer St 16153 724-376-7911
David Sapala, prin. Fax 376-7910
Lakeview MS 400/5-8
2482 Mercer St 16153 724-376-7911
Fred McConnell, prin. Fax 376-7910

Stoneboro Wesleyan Methodist S 100/K-12
947 Fredonia Rd 16153 724-376-3319
Roger Patterson, prin. Fax 376-3319

Strafford, Chester, Pop. 4,500

Woodlynde S 300/1-12
445 Upper Gulph Rd 19087 610-687-9660
John Murray, hdmstr. Fax 687-4752

Strattanville, Clarion, Pop. 515
Clarion-Limestone Area SD 1,100/K-12
4091 C L School Rd 16258 814-764-5111
Theodore Pappas, supt. Fax 764-5729
www.clarion-limestoneschool.com
Clarion-Limestone JSHS 500/7-12
4091 C L School Rd 16258 814-764-5111
Michael Drzewiecki, prin. Fax 764-5274

Stroudsburg, Monroe, Pop. 6,264
Stroudsburg Area SD 4,800/K-12
123 Linden St 18360 570-421-1990
Frederick Hackett, supt. Fax 424-5986
www.sburg.org
Stroudsburg HS 1,300/10-12
1100 W Main St 18360 570-421-1991
Jeff Sodi, prin. Fax 424-1383
Stroudsburg JHS 1,000/8-9
1198 Chipperfield Dr 18360 570-424-4848
Dr. Maryellen Mross, prin. Fax 424-4839

Stroudsburg School of Cosmetology Post-Sec.
100 N 8th St 18360 570-421-3387

Summerdale, Cumberland

Central Pennsylvania College Post-Sec.
College Hill & Valley Rds 17093 717-732-0702

Sunbury, Northumberland, Pop. 10,086
Shikellamy SD 3,200/K-12
200 Island Blvd 17801 570-286-3720
Dr. Alan Lonoconus, supt. Fax 286-3776
www.shikbraves.org
Rice MS 400/6-8
4th & Hanover Sts, 570-473-3547
Frank Boyer, prin. Fax 473-4483
Shikellamy HS 1,100/9-12
600 Walnut St 17801 570-286-3713
Terry Roden, prin. Fax 286-3775
Sunbury MS 400/6-8
115 Fairmount Ave 17801 570-286-3736
Michael Hubicki, prin. Fax 286-3780

McCann School of Business & Technology Post-Sec.
1147 N 4th St 17801 570-286-3058
Triangle Tech Post-Sec.
RR 1 Box 51 17801 570-988-0700

Susquehanna, Susquehanna, Pop. 1,702
Susquehanna Community SD 900/K-12
RR 3 Box 5A 18847 570-853-4921
Bronson Stone, supt. Fax 853-3768
www.scschools.org/
Susquehanna Community JSHS 500/7-12
RR 3 Box 5A 18847 570-853-4921
Michael Lisowski, prin. Fax 853-3918

Swarthmore, Delaware, Pop. 6,146

Swarthmore College Post-Sec.
500 College Ave 19081 610-328-8000

Swiftwater, Monroe
Pocono Mountain SD 10,800/K-12
PO Box 200 18370 570-839-7121
Dr. Dwight Pfennig, supt. Fax 895-4768
www.pmsd.org
Pocono Mountain East HS 2,000/9-12
PO Box 200 18370 570-839-7121
Todd Burns, prin. Fax 839-5934
Swiftwater IS 900/7-8
PO Box 200 18370 570-839-7121
Tom Barbush, prin. Fax 839-5935
Other Schools – See Pocono Summit

Tamaqua, Schuylkill, Pop. 6,754
Tamaqua Area SD 2,100/K-12
PO Box 112 18252 570-668-2570
Carol Makuta, supt. Fax 668-6850
www.tamaqua.k12.pa.us/
Tamaqua Area HS 700/9-12
PO Box 90 18252 570-668-1901
Raymond Kinder, prin. Fax 668-2970
Tamaqua Area MS 500/6-8
PO Box 90 18252 570-668-1210
Ruth Ann Gardiner, prin. Fax 668-5027

Marian HS 300/9-12
166 Marian Ave 18252 570-467-3335
Sr. Bernard Agnes Smith, prin. Fax 467-0186

Taylor, Lackawanna, Pop. 6,227
Riverside SD 1,500/K-12
300 Davis St 18517 570-562-2121
Salvatore F. Luzio, supt. Fax 562-3205
ns.neiu.k12.pa.us/WWW/RS/index.html
Riverside JSHS 800/7-12
310 Davis St 18517 570-562-2121
Joseph Moceyunas, prin. Fax 562-7551

Three Springs, Huntingdon, Pop. 428
Southern Huntingdon County SD 1,400/K-12
RR 2 Box 1124 17264 814-447-5529
Grant Stiffler, supt. Fax 447-3967
www.shcsd.k12.pa.us
Southern Huntingdon County MSHS 700/6-12
RR 2 Box 1124 17264 814-447-5529
Fred Foster, prin. Fax 447-3750

Throop, Lackawanna, Pop. 3,949
Mid Valley SD 1,600/K-12
52 Underwood Rd 18512 570-307-1119
Dr. Joseph Crotti, supt. Fax 307-1107
www.mvsd.us
Mid Valley JSHS 800/7-12
52 Underwood Rd 18512 570-307-2180
Randy Parry, prin.

Tioga, Tioga, Pop. 605
Northern Tioga SD
Supt. — See Elkland
Williamson JSHS 600/7-12
33 Jct Cross Rd 16946 570-827-2191
Diana Barnes, prin. Fax 827-3557

Tionesta, Forest, Pop. 592
Forest Area SD 700/K-12
HC 2 Box 16 16353 814-755-4491
Duane Vicini, supt. Fax 755-2426
www.forestareaschools.org/
West Forest JSHS 300/7-12
HC 2 Box 15 16353 814-755-3611
Kevin Sprong, prin. Fax 755-2427
Other Schools – See Marienville

North Clarion County SD 700/K-12
10439 Route 36 16353 814-744-8536
David Stake, supt. Fax 744-9378
www.northclarion.org/
North Clarion County JSHS 400/7-12
10439 Route 36 16353 814-744-8544
Steven Young, prin. Fax 744-8762

Titusville, Crawford, Pop. 5,862
Titusville Area SD 2,300/PK-12
221 N Washington St 16354 814-827-2715
Karen Jez, supt. Fax 827-7761
www.gorockets.org/
Titusville HS 800/9-12
302 E Walnut St 16354 814-827-2715
Stephanie Keebler, prin. Fax 827-7761
Titusville MS, 415 Water St 16354 600/6-8
Michael McGaughey, prin. 814-827-2715

University of Pittsburgh at Titusville Post-Sec.
504 E Main St # 287 16354 814-827-4400

Topton, Berks, Pop. 1,975
Brandywine Heights Area SD 2,000/K-12
200 W Weis St 19562 610-682-5100
Dr. John Curtin, supt. Fax 682-5136
www.bhasd.org/
Brandywine Heights Area MS 700/5-8
200 W Weis St 19562 610-682-5131
Kathy Johnson, prin. Fax 682-5105
Other Schools – See Mertztown

Towanda, Bradford, Pop. 2,915
Area Vocational Technical School
Supt. — None
Northern Tier Career Center — Vo/Tech
RR 1 Box 157A 18848 — 570-265-8111
Walter Becker, prin.

Towanda Area SD — 1,200/K-12
PO Box 231 18848 — 570-265-9894
Diane Cantellops, supt. — Fax 265-4881
www.tsd.k12.pa.us/
Towanda Area JSHS — 900/7-12
1 High School Dr 18848 — 570-265-3690
Steven Gobble, prin. — Fax 268-2069

Tower City, Schuylkill, Pop. 1,343
Williams Valley SD — 1,100/K-12
10330 Route 209 Rd 17980 — 717-647-2167
Diane M. Niederriter, supt. — Fax 647-2055
www.wvsd.k12.pa.us
Williams Valley JSHS — 600/7-12
10330 Route 209 Rd 17980 — 717-647-2167
Diane Niederriter, dean — Fax 647-2055

Trafford, Westmoreland, Pop. 3,106
Penn-Trafford SD
Supt. — See Harrison City
Trafford MS — 400/6-8
100 Brinton Ave 15085 — 412-372-6600
James Simpson, prin. — Fax 372-1554

Transfer, Mercer

Winner Institute of Arts & Sciences — Post-Sec.
1 Winner Rd 16154 — 724-646-2433

Trevorton, Northumberland, Pop. 2,058
Line Mountain SD — 1,300/K-12
500 W Shamokin St 17881 — 570-797-4672
Ned Sodrick, supt. — Fax 797-4688
www.linemountain.com
Other Schools – See Herndon

Trevose, Bucks

Strayer University — Post-Sec.
3600 Horizon Blvd Ste 100 19053 — 215-953-5999
Ultrasound Diagnostic School — Post-Sec.
3600 Horizon Blvd 19053 — 215-244-4906

Troy, Bradford, Pop. 1,485
Troy Area SD — 1,800/K-12
310 Elmira St 16947 — 570-297-2750
Robert W. Grantier, supt. — Fax 297-1600
www.troyareasd.org/
Troy Area HS — 600/9-12
250 High St 16947 — 570-297-2176
R. Mark Strzelecki, prin. — Fax 297-2868
Troy Area MS, 350 High St 16947 — 600/5-8
Rebecca Stanfield, prin. — 570-297-4565

Martha Lloyd School — Post-Sec.
190 W Main St 16947

Tunkhannock, Wyoming, Pop. 1,825
Tunkhannock Area SD — 3,100/K-12
41 Philadelphia Ave 18657 — 570-836-3111
Michael Healey, supt. — Fax 836-2942
www.tasd.net/
Tunkhannock HS — 1,000/9-12
120 W Tioga St 18657 — 570-836-8223
Michael Thornton, prin. — Fax 836-4719
Tunkhannock MS — 1,000/5-8
200 Franklin Ave 18657 — 570-836-8235
Joseph Papi, prin. — Fax 836-5796

Turbotville, Northumberland, Pop. 662
Warrior Run SD — 1,800/K-12
4800 Susquehanna Trl 17772 — 570-649-5138
Daniel B. Scheaffer, supt. — Fax 649-5475
www.wrsd.org
Warrior Run HS — 600/9-12
4800 Susquehanna Trl 17772 — 570-649-5166
Patricia Cross, prin. — Fax 649-5591
Warrior Run MS — 600/5-8
4800 Susquehanna Trl 17772 — 570-649-5135
Larry Boyer, prin.

Turtle Creek, Allegheny, Pop. 5,704
Woodland Hills SD
Supt. — See Pittsburgh
Woodland Hills JHS - East — 300/7-8
126 Monroeville Ave 15145 — 412-824-2450
Janet Wilson Carter, prin. — Fax 824-6738

Tyrone, Blair, Pop. 5,324
Tyrone Area SD — 1,700/PK-12
701 Clay Ave 16686 — 814-684-0710
Dr. William Miller, supt. — Fax 684-2678
www.tyrone.k12.pa.us/
Tyrone Area HS — 700/9-12
1001 Clay Ave 16686 — 814-684-4240
Dr. Rebecca Erb, prin. — Fax 684-4245
Tyrone Area MS — 500/5-8
1001 Clay Ave 16686 — 814-684-4240
Dr. John Vendetti, prin. — Fax 682-1013

Grier S — 200/7-12
PO Box 308 16686 — 814-684-3000
Andrea Hollnagel, hdmstr. — Fax 684-2177

Ulster, Bradford

North Rome Christian S — 100/K-12
RR 1 Box 190A 18850 — 570-247-2800
Lee Ann Carmichael, admin. — Fax 247-7288

Ulysses, Potter, Pop. 669
Northern Potter SD — 700/K-12
745 Northern Potter Rd 16948 — 814-848-7506
Robert C. Smith, supt. — Fax 848-7431
www.npschools.com
Northern Potter JSHS — 300/7-12
763 Northern Potter Rd 16948 — 814-848-7534
Susan Valentine, prin. — Fax 848-9671

Union City, Erie, Pop. 3,364
Union City Area SD — 1,300/K-12
107 Concord St 16438 — 814-438-3804
Sandra Myers, supt. — Fax 438-2030
www.ucasd.org/
Union City HS — 400/9-12
105 Concord St 16438 — 814-438-7673
Joseph Neuch, prin. — Fax 438-8079
Union City MS — 300/6-8
105 Concord St 16438 — 814-438-7673
Joseph Neuch, prin. — Fax 438-8079

Uniontown, Fayette, Pop. 11,935
Albert Gallatin Area SD — 3,800/K-12
2625 Morgantown Rd 15401 — 724-564-7190
Walter Vicinelly, supt. — Fax 564-7195
www.albertgallatin.k12.pa.us/
Gallatin Area HS — 1,200/9-12
1119 Township Dr 15401 — 724-564-2024
Joetta Britvich, prin. — Fax 564-4525
Other Schools – See Mc Clellandtown, Point Marion

Area Vocational Technical School
Supt. — None
Fayette County AVTS — Vo/Tech
175 Georges Fairchance Rd 15401 — 724-437-2721
Dr. Edward Jeffreys, prin.

Laurel Highlands SD — 3,400/K-12
304 Bailey Ave 15401 — 724-437-2821
Dr. Ronald Sheba, supt. — Fax 437-8929
www.hhs.net/lhsdl
Laurel Highlands HS — 1,200/9-12
300 Bailey Ave 15401 — 724-437-4741
John K. Diamond, prin. — Fax 437-5653
Laurel Highlands MS — 600/7-8
18 Hookton Ave 15401 — 724-437-2865
Mary Macar, prin. — Fax 437-8518

Uniontown Area SD — 3,500/K-12
23 E Church St 15401 — 724-438-4501
Charles D. Machesky, supt. — Fax 437-7007
www.uniontown.k12.pa.us
Uniontown Area HS — 1,100/9-12
146 E Fayette St 15401 — 724-439-5000
Thomas Colebank, prin. — Fax 439-5004
Other Schools – See Markleysburg

Chestnut Ridge Christian Academy — 100/PK-12
115 Downer Ave 15401 — 724-439-1090
Patricia D. Cowsert, prin. — Fax 439-4540
Laurel Business Institute — Post-Sec.
11 E Penn St 15401 — 724-439-4900
Penn State Fayette Eberly Campus — Post-Sec.
PO Box 519 15401 — 724-430-4100
Wrightco Technologies Tech Training Inst — Post-Sec.
2 W Main St Ste 200 15401 — 724-439-2080

University Park, See State College

Pennsylvania State University — Post-Sec.
PO Box 3000 16802 — 814-865-4700

Upper Darby, See Darby
Upper Darby SD
Supt. — See Drexel Hill
Beverly Hills MS — 1,500/6-8
1400 Garrett Rd 19082 — 610-626-9317
Edgar Speer, prin.

PJA School — Post-Sec.
7900 W Chester Pike 19082 — 610-789-6700
Star Technical Institute — Post-Sec.
1570 Garrett Rd 19082 — 610-626-2700

Upper Saint Clair, Allegheny, Pop. 19,692
Upper St. Clair SD — 4,100/K-12
1820 McLaughlin Run Rd 15241 — 412-833-1600
Dr. James D. Lombardo, supt. — Fax 833-5535
www.uscsd.k12.pa.us
Other Schools – See Pittsburgh

Valley View, Schuylkill, Pop. 4,660
Tri-Valley SD — 900/K-12
110 W Main St 17983 — 570-682-9013
Jack L. Herb, supt. — Fax 682-9544
www.tri-valley.k12.pa.us
Other Schools – See Hegins

Villanova, Delaware

Academy of Notre Dame De Namur — 500/6-12
560 Sproul Rd 19085 — 610-687-0650
Maria Marino, prin. — Fax 687-1912
Devereux Foundation in Pennsylvania — Post-Sec.
444 Devereux Dr 19085 — 610-542-3030
Villanova University — Post-Sec.
800 E Lancaster Ave 19085 — 610-519-4500

Wallingford, Delaware
Wallingford-Swarthmore SD — 3,600/K-12
200 S Providence Rd 19086 — 610-892-3470
Dr. George Slick, supt. — Fax 892-3493
www.wssd.org
Strath Haven HS — 1,300/9-12
205 S Providence Rd 19086 — 610-892-3470
Mary Jo Yannacone, prin. — Fax 892-3494
Strath Haven MS — 800/6-8
200 S Providence Rd 19086 — 610-892-3470
A. Ferguson Abbott, prin. — Fax 892-3492

Warfordsburg, Fulton
Southern Fulton SD — 900/K-12
3072 Great Cove Rd Ste 100 17267 — 717-294-2203
Ralph Scott, supt. — Fax 294-2207
sfsd.k12.pa.us
Southern Fulton JSHS — 400/7-12
13083 Buck Valley Rd 17267 — 717-294-3251
Brett Gilliland, prin. — Fax 294-6248

Warminster, Bucks, Pop. 32,400
Centennial SD — 6,300/K-12
433 Centennial Rd 18974 — 215-441-6000
David P. Blatt, supt. — Fax 441-8055
www.centennialsd.org/
Log College MS — 800/6-8
730 Norristown Rd 18974 — 215-441-6075
Dr. Harry Clark, prin.
Tennent HS, 333 Centennial Rd 18974 — 2,100/9-12
Eileen Poroszok, prin. — 215-441-6181
Other Schools – See Southampton

Archbishop Wood HS — 1,200/9-12
655 York Rd 18974 — 215-672-5050
Mary Harkins, prin. — Fax 672-9572
Automotive Training Center — Post-Sec.
900 Johnsville Blvd 18974 — 877-411-8041
Empire Beauty School — Post-Sec.
435 York Rd 18974 — 215-443-8446

Warren, Warren, Pop. 9,648
Area Vocational Technical School
Supt. — None
Warren County AVTS — Vo/Tech
347 E 5th Ave 16365 — 814-726-1260
Delores Berry, prin. — Fax 726-9673

Warren County SD
Supt. — See North Warren
Beaty-Warren MS — 700/6-8
2 E 3rd Ave 16365 — 814-723-5200
Gary Weber, prin. — Fax 723-9503
Warren Area HS — 900/9-12
345 E 5th Ave 16365 — 814-723-3370
James Miller, prin. — Fax 726-3126

Warrington, Bucks, Pop. 7,000
Central Bucks SD
Supt. — See Doylestown
Central Bucks SHS - South — 10-12
1100 Folly Rd 18976 — 267-893-3000
W. Rodney Stone, prin. — Fax 893-5824
Tamanend MS — 800/7-9
1492 Stuckert Rd 18976 — 267-893-2900
Alan R. Hershman, prin. — Fax 893-5818

SS. Joseph & Robert S — 200/5-8
850 Euclid Ave 18976 — 215-343-5100
Donna Maria Meyers, prin. — Fax 343-7434

Washington, Washington, Pop. 15,136
Trinity Area SD — 3,800/K-12
231 Park Ave 15301 — 724-225-9880
Dr. Thomas Turnbaugh, supt. — Fax 228-2640
www.trinitypride.k12.pa.us
Trinity HS, 231 Park Ave 15301 — 1,300/9-12
Donald Snoke, prin. — 724-225-5380
Trinity MS, 50 Scenic Dr 15301 — 900/6-8
Peter Keruskin, prin. — 724-228-2112

Washington SD — 2,000/K-12
201 Allison Ave 15301 — 724-223-5010
Roberta DiLorenzo Ed.D., supt. — Fax 223-5024
www.washington.k12.pa.us
Washington HS — 600/9-12
201 Allison Ave 15301 — 724-223-5080
Ronald Junko, prin. — Fax 223-5046
Washington Park MS — 500/6-8
801 E Wheeling St 15301 — 724-223-5060
Jason Minnitti, prin. — Fax 223-5123

Faith Christian S — 100/PK-12
524 E Beau St 15301 — 724-222-5440
Lucy Hall, prin. — Fax 222-5442
First Love Christian Academy — 50/9-12
PO Box 109 15301 — 724-225-3522
Kathleen Klein, pres. — Fax 229-2797
Penn Commercial Business/Technical Sch. — Post-Sec.
242 Oak Spring Rd 15301 — 724-222-5330
Washington & Jefferson College — Post-Sec.
60 S Lincoln St 15301 — 724-222-4400
Washington Hospital — Post-Sec.
155 Wilson Ave 15301 — 724-223-3167

Waterfall, Fulton
Forbes Road SD — 500/K-12
159 Red Bird Dr 16689 — 814-685-3866
Dr. Merrill Arnold, supt. — Fax 685-3159
Forbes Road JSHS — 200/7-12
159 Red Bird Dr 16689 — 814-685-3866
James Heroux, prin. — Fax 685-3159

Waterford, Erie, Pop. 1,420
Ft. LeBoeuf SD — 2,200/K-12
PO Box 810 16441 — 814-796-2638
Dr. Michele Campbell, supt. — Fax 796-6459
flb.fortleboeuf.net
Ft. LeBoeuf HS — 800/9-12
931 N High St 16441 — 814-796-2616
Rick Fessler, prin. — Fax 796-2141
Ft. LeBoeuf MS — 600/6-8
PO Box 516 16441 — 814-796-2681
Matthew Bennett, prin. — Fax 796-4712

Watsontown, Northumberland, Pop. 2,148

Watsontown Christian Academy — 100/K-12
1225 8th Street Dr 17777 — 570-538-9276
H. William Wilhelm, prin. — Fax 538-9148

Wayne, Delaware
Radnor Township SD — 3,400/K-12
135 S Wayne Ave Ste 1 19087 — 610-688-8100
Dr. Gary Cooper, supt. — Fax 971-0742
www.rtsd.org/
Radnor MS — 900/6-8
131 S Wayne Ave 19087 — 610-386-6300
William Laffey, prin. — Fax 688-2491
Other Schools – See Radnor

Tredyffrin-Easttown SD
Supt. — See Berwyn
Valley Forge MS — 1,000/5-8
105 W Walker Rd 19087 — 610-240-1300
Matthew Gibson, prin. — Fax 240-1325

Valley Forge Military Academy — 600/7-12
1001 Eagle Rd 19087 — 610-989-1200
Anthony McGeorge, pres. — Fax 989-1595
Valley Forge Military College — Post-Sec.
1001 Eagle Rd 19087 — 800-234-8362

Waynesboro, Franklin, Pop. 9,700
Waynesboro Area SD 4,100/K-12
210 Clayton Ave 17268 717-762-1191
Barry Dallara, supt. Fax 762-0028
www.wasd.k12.pa.us
Waynesboro Area HS 1,300/9-12
550 E 2nd St 17268 717-762-1191
Jon Bilbo, prin. Fax 762-3787
Waynesboro Area MS 700/7-8
702 E 2nd St 17268 717-762-1191
Larry Bricker, prin. Fax 762-6566

Waynesburg, Greene, Pop. 4,142
Area Vocational Technical School
Supt. — None
Greene County CTC Vo/Tech
60 Zimmerman Dr 15370 724-627-3106
Janice Quailey, prin.

Central Greene SD 2,300/K-12
PO Box 472 15370 724-627-8151
Dr. Jerome Bartley, supt. Fax 627-9591
www.cgsd.org
Miller MS 600/6-8
126 E Lincoln St 15370 724-852-2722
Matt Blair, prin. Fax 627-0637
Waynesburg Central HS 700/9-12
30 Zimmerman Dr 15370 724-852-1050
Albert Veverka, prin. Fax 852-2109

West Greene SD 600/K-12
1367 Hargus Creek Rd 15370 724-499-5183
Thelma Szarell, supt. Fax 499-5623
www.wgsd.org/
West Greene MSHS 200/6-12
1352 Hargus Creek Rd 15370 724-499-5051
A.J. McGivern, prin. Fax 499-5492

Open Door Christian S 100/K-12
793 Lippencott Rd 15370 724-852-1871
Kevin Roberts, admin.
Waynesburg College Post-Sec.
51 W College St 15370 724-627-8191

Weatherly, Carbon, Pop. 2,621
Weatherly Area SD 800/K-12
602 6th St 18255 570-427-8681
Gene Freeman Ed.D., supt. Fax 427-8918
www.weatherlysd.org
Weatherly Area HS 300/9-12
601 6th St 18255 570-427-8521
Brian Baddick, prin. Fax 427-4642
Weatherly Area MS 200/6-8
602 6th St 18255 570-427-8689
Deborah Popson, prin. Fax 427-8918

Wellsboro, Tioga, Pop. 3,342
Wellsboro Area SD 1,700/K-12
2 Charles St 16901 570-724-4424
Philip Waber, supt. Fax 724-5103
www.wellsborosd.k12.pa.us
Butler MS 500/5-8
9 Nichols St 16901 570-724-2306
David Krick, prin. Fax 724-4143
Wellsboro Area HS 600/9-12
225 Nichols St 16901 570-724-3547
Patrick Hewitt, prin. Fax 724-3027

Pennsylvania College of Technology Post-Sec.
Mansfield Rd 16901 570-724-7703

West Chester, Chester, Pop. 18,047
West Chester Area SD 11,700/K-12
829 Paoli Pike 19380 484-266-1000
Dr. Alan G. Elko, supt. Fax 266-1178
www.wcasd.k12.pa.us
Fugett MS 900/6-8
500 Ellis Ln 19380 484-266-2900
Joseph Morris, prin. Fax 266-2999
Pierce MS 1,000/6-8
1314 Burke Rd 19380 484-266-2500
Dr. Anthony Barber, prin. Fax 266-2599
Stetson MS 900/6-8
1060 Wilmington Pike 19382 484-266-2700
Leroy Whitehead, prin. Fax 266-2799
West Chester East HS 1,800/9-12
450 Ellis Ln 19380 484-266-3800
Dr. Richard F. Dunlap, prin. Fax 266-3899
West Chester Henderson HS 2,000/9-12
400 Montgomery Ave 19380 484-266-3300
Marc Bertrando, prin. Fax 266-3399
West Chester Rustin HS 9-12
1100 Shiloh Rd 19382 484-266-4300
Dr. Phyllis Simmons, prin.

Devereux Kanner Center Post-Sec.
390 E Boot Rd 19380 866-532-2212
Empire Beauty School Post-Sec.
313 W Market St 19382 610-344-7665
West Chester Christian S 200/K-12
1237 Paoli Pike 19380 610-692-3700
David Douglass, admin. Fax 692-9480
West Chester University of Pennsylvania Post-Sec.
S High St 19383 610-436-1000

Westfield, Tioga, Pop. 1,158
Northern Tioga SD
Supt. — See Elkland
Cowanesque Valley JSHS 400/7-12
51 N Fork Rd 16950 814-367-2233
Matthew Sottolano, prin. Fax 367-5874

West Grove, Chester, Pop. 2,640
Avon-Grove SD 5,000/K-12
375 S Jennersville Rd 19390 610-869-2441
Dr. Augustus Massaro, supt. Fax 869-4335
www.avongrove.org/
Avon-Grove HS 1,600/9-12
257 State Rd 19390 610-869-2446
Thomas Alexander, prin. Fax 869-4511
Engle MS 800/7-8
107 Schoolhouse Rd 19390 610-869-3022
Robert Fraser, prin. Fax 869-0827

West Lawn, Berks, Pop. 1,578
Wilson SD 5,300/K-12
2601 Grandview Blvd 19609 610-670-0180
Dr. Lawrence Mussoline, supt. Fax 670-9101
www.wilson.k12.pa.us
Wilson Central JHS 700/7-9
2601 Grandview Blvd 19609 610-670-0180
Steven Leever, prin. Fax 670-4783
Wilson SHS 1,300/10-12
2601 Grandview Blvd 19609 610-670-0185
E. Wayne Foley, prin. Fax 670-9101
Other Schools – See Sinking Spring

West Middlesex, Mercer, Pop. 884
West Middlesex Area SD 1,200/K-12
3591 Sharon Rd 16159 724-634-3030
Alan Baldarelli, supt. Fax 528-0380
www.wmasd.k12.pa.us
West Middlesex JSHS 600/7-12
3591 Sharon Rd 16159 724-634-3030
Larry Ellison, prin. Fax 528-0380

West Mifflin, Allegheny, Pop. 21,236
West Mifflin Area SD 3,300/K-12
515 Camp Hollow Rd 15122 412-466-9131
Dr. Frank Prazenica, supt. Fax 466-9260
www.wmasd.org
West Mifflin Area HS 1,100/9-12
91 Commonwealth Ave 15122 412-466-7220
Dr. Mark Hoover, prin. Fax 466-4595
West Mifflin Area MS 800/6-8
371 Camp Hollow Rd 15122 412-466-3200
Cliford Bowers, prin. Fax 466-0836

Community College of Allegheny County Post-Sec.
1750 Clairton Rd 15122 412-469-1100
Empire Beauty School Post-Sec.
2393 Mountain View Dr 15122 800-575-5983
Wilson Christian Academy 400/PK-12
1900 Clairton Rd 15122 412-466-1919
Mark Minkus, supt. Fax 466-0303

Westover, Clearfield, Pop. 437
Harmony Area SD 400/PK-12
5239 Ridge Rd 16692 814-845-7918
Scott King, supt. Fax 845-2305
www.harmonyowls.com/
Harmony Area MS 100/7-9
5239 Ridge Rd 16692 814-845-7655
Ted Focht, prin. Fax 845-7811
Harmony Area SHS 100/10-12
5239 Ridge Rd 16692 814-845-7918
Scott King, prin. Fax 845-2305

West Sunbury, Butler, Pop. 100
Moniteau SD 1,700/K-12
1810 W Sunbury Rd 16061 724-637-2117
Dr. Trudy Peterman, supt. Fax 637-3862
www.moniteau.k12.pa.us
Moniteau JSHS 900/7-12
1810 W Sunbury Rd 16061 724-637-2091
Stephen Puskar, prin. Fax 637-3862

Westtown, Chester

Westtown S 700/PK-12
PO Box 1799 19395 610-399-0123
John Baird, hdmstr. Fax 399-3760

Wexford, Allegheny
North Allegheny SD
Supt. — See Pittsburgh
Marshall MS 700/6-8
5145 Wexford Run Rd 15090 724-934-6060
Cynthia Kainaroi, prin. Fax 935-2474
North Allegheny SHS 1,400/11-12
10375 Perry Hwy 15090 724-934-7200
Dr. Lawrence Butterini, prin. Fax 935-5846

Whitehall, Lehigh, Pop. 13,744
Whitehall-Coplay SD 4,100/K-12
2940 Macarthur Rd 18052 610-439-1431
John Corby, supt. Fax 435-0124
www.whitehallcoplay.org
Whitehall-Coplay MS 1,300/5-8
2930 Macarthur Rd 18052 610-439-1439
Peter Bugbee, prin. Fax 740-9308
Whitehall HS 1,400/9-12
3800 Mechanicsville Rd 18052 610-437-5081
James Davis, prin. Fax 820-7520

Empire Beauty School Post-Sec.
1634 MacArthur Rd 18052 610-776-8908
Intl Academy of Advanced Reflexology Post-Sec.
1177 6th St 18052 215-234-0307

Wilkes Barre, Luzerne, Pop. 42,021
Area Vocational Technical School
Supt. — None
Wilkes-Barre AVTS Vo/Tech
PO Box 1699 18705 570-822-4131
Dr. Thomas O'Donnell, prin.

Wilkes-Barre Area SD 6,800/K-12
730 S Main St 18702 570-826-7182
Jeffrey Namey Ed.D., supt. Fax 829-5031
www.wbasd.k12.pa.us
Coughlin HS 1,100/9-12
80 N Washington St 18701 570-826-7201
Andrew Kuhl, prin. Fax 826-7252
G.A.R. Memorial JSHS 900/7-12
250 S Grant St 18702 570-826-7165
Dino Galella, prin. Fax 826-7164
Meyers JSHS 900/7-12
341 Carey Ave 18702 570-826-7145
Anthony Schwab, prin. Fax 820-3770
Other Schools – See Plains

Academy of Creative Hair Design Post-Sec.
125 N Wilkes Barre Blvd 18702 570-288-4574
Holy Redeemer HS 700/9-12
159 S Pennsylvania Ave 18701 570-829-2424
Rev. Walter E. Jenkins, prin. Fax 829-4412
King's College Post-Sec.
133 N River St 18711 570-208-5900
Wilkes Barre General Hospital Post-Sec.
575 N River St 18764 570-829-8111

Wilkes University Post-Sec.
170 S Franklin St 18766 570-408-5000

Wilkinsburg, Allegheny, Pop. 18,008
Wilkinsburg Borough SD 1,600/PK-12
718 Wallace Ave 15221 412-371-9667
Archie Perrin, supt. Fax 371-4058
www.wilkinsburg.k12.pa.us
Wilkinsburg HS 400/9-12
747 Wallace Ave 15221 412-371-9500
Ella Rawlings, prin. Fax 371-3981
Wilkinsburg MS 300/7-8
747 Wallace Ave 15221 412-244-9303
Ella Rawlings, prin. Fax 871-2277

Williamsburg, Blair, Pop. 1,276
Williamsburg Community SD 600/K-12
515 W 3rd St 16693 814-832-2125
Dr. Lee Swinsburg, supt. Fax 832-3657
www.williamsburg.k12.pa.us/
Williamsburg Community JSHS 300/7-12
515 W 3rd St 16693 814-832-2125
Maureen Letcher, prin. Fax 832-0115

Williamsport, Lycoming, Pop. 30,112
Loyalsock Township SD
Supt. — See Montoursville
Loyalsock Twp. HS 500/9-12
1801 Loyalsock Dr 17701 570-326-3581
Allen DiMarco, prin. Fax 322-3952
Loyalsock Twp. MS 400/6-8
2101 Loyalsock Dr 17701 570-323-9439
Timothy Fausnaught, dean Fax 323-5303

Williamsport Area SD 5,900/K-12
201 W 3rd St 17701 570-327-5500
Dr. Patricia Lowery, supt. Fax 327-8122
www.wasd.org
Curtin MS 500/6-8
85 Eldred St 17701 570-323-4785
Kevin Harris, prin. Fax 323-4974
Lycoming Valley MS 500/6-8
1825 Hayes Ave 17701 570-494-1700
James Dougherty, prin. Fax 494-1706
Roosevelt MS 500/6-8
2800 W 4th St 17701 570-323-6177
Reginald Fatherly, prin. Fax 326-6851
Williamsport Area HS 1,900/9-12
2990 W 4th St 17701 570-323-8411
Bruce Elliott, prin. Fax 322-4150

Divine Providence Hospital Post-Sec.
1100 Grampian Blvd 17701 570-326-8101
Empire Beauty School Post-Sec.
1808 E 3rd St 17701 570-322-8243
Keystone Christian S 100/PK-12
PO Box 756 17703 570-323-7071
Wayne Stebbins, admin. Fax 323-7071
Lycoming College Post-Sec.
700 College Pl 17701 570-321-4000
Newport Business Institute Post-Sec.
941 W 3rd St 17701 570-326-2869
Pennsylvania College of Technology Post-Sec.
1 College Ave 17701 570-326-3761
St. John Neumann Regional Academy 200/7-12
901 Penn St 17701 570-323-9953
Paul Ward, prin. Fax 321-7146
Williamsport Hospital Post-Sec.
777 Rural Ave 17701 570-326-8101

Willow Grove, Montgomery, Pop. 16,325
Area Vocational Technical School
Supt. — None
Eastern Center for Arts & Tech Vo/Tech
3075 Terwood Rd 19090 215-784-4800
Dr. Joseph Colaneri, prin. Fax 784-4801

Upper Moreland Township SD 3,100/K-12
2900 Terwood Rd 19090 215-659-6800
Robert Milrod Ph.D., supt. Fax 659-3421
www.umtsd.org/
Upper Moreland HS 1,000/9-12
3000 Terwood Rd 19090 215-830-1500
David DeVido, prin. Fax 830-1581
Other Schools – See Hatboro

Willow Hill, Franklin
Fannett-Metal SD 500/K-12
PO Box 91 17271 717-349-7172
Dr. Dana Baker, supt. Fax 349-2748
www.edline.net/pages/fannett-metal
Fannett-Metal JSHS 200/6-12
PO Box 91 17271 717-349-2363
Bradley Ocker, prin. Fax 349-2173

Willow Street, Lancaster, Pop. 5,817
Area Vocational Technical School
Supt. — None
Lancaster County CTC-Willow Street Vo/Tech
PO Box 527 17584 717-464-7050
Dr. Timothy Bianchi, prin. Fax 464-9518

Windber, Somerset, Pop. 4,119
Windber Area SD 1,400/PK-12
2301 Graham Ave 15963 814-467-5551
Rick Huffman, supt. Fax 467-4208
Windber Area HS 400/9-12
2301 Graham Ave 15963 814-467-4567
Virgil Palumbo, prin. Fax 467-0677
Windber Area MS 400/6-8
2301 Graham Ave 15963 814-467-4620
Gary Buchsen, prin.

Wingate, Centre
Bald Eagle Area SD 2,000/K-12
751 S Eagle Valley Rd 16823 814-355-4860
Daniel Fisher, supt. Fax 355-1028
www.beasd.org/
Bald Eagle Area JSHS 1,000/7-12
751 S Eagle Valley Rd 16823 814-355-4868
David Reichelderfer, prin. Fax 355-2146

Woodlyn, Delaware, Pop. 10,151

Woodlyn Christian S 100/PK-12
1121 MacDade Blvd 19094 610-833-2253
Nancy Dyson, dir. Fax 833-2253

Wormleysburg, Cumberland, Pop. 2,651

Harrisburg Academy 500/PK-12
10 Erford Rd 17043 717-763-7811
Dr. James Newman, hdmstr. Fax 975-0894

Wrightsville, York, Pop. 2,255
Eastern York SD 2,700/K-12
PO Box 150 17368 717-252-1555
Dr. Darla Pianowski, supt. Fax 478-6000
www.easternyork.com/
Eastern York HS 700/9-12
PO Box 2002 17368 717-252-1551
Mark Shue, prin. Fax 252-4808
Eastern York MS 700/6-8
PO Box 2003 17368 717-252-3400
Fax 252-4891

Wyalusing, Bradford, Pop. 549
Wyalusing Area SD 1,500/K-12
PO Box 157 18853 570-746-1605
Ray Fleming, supt. Fax 746-9156
www.wyalusingrams.com/
Wyalusing Valley JSHS 700/7-12
RR 2 Box 7 18853 570-746-1218
Martin Weisgold, prin.

Wyncote, Montgomery, Pop. 2,960
Cheltenham Township SD
Supt. — See Elkins Park
Cedarbrook MS 800/7-8
300 Longfellow Rd 19095 215-881-6423
Iris Parker, prin.
Cheltenham HS 1,700/9-12
500 Rices Mill Rd 19095 215-881-6400
Dr. Elliott Lewis, prin. Fax 881-6406

Bishop McDevitt HS 800/9-12
125 Royal Ave 19095 215-887-5575
Harry Neenhold, prin. Fax 887-1371
Reconstructionist Rabbinical College Post-Sec.
1299 Church Rd 19095 215-576-0800

Wynnewood, Montgomery, Pop. 7,800

Friends' Central S 1,000/PK-12
1101 City Ave 19096 610-649-7440
David Felsen, hdmstr. Fax 649-5669
Lankenau Hospital Post-Sec.
100 E Lancaster Ave 19096 610-526-3019
Palmer Theological Seminary Post-Sec.
6 E Lancaster Ave 19096 610-896-5000
St. Charles Borromeo Seminary Post-Sec.
100 E Wynnewood Rd 19096 610-667-3394
Torah Academy of Greater Philadelphia 400/K-12
742 Argyle Rd 19096 610-642-7870
Rabbi Joshua Levy, prin. Fax 642-2265

Wyomissing, Berks, Pop. 10,434
Wyomissing Area SD 1,900/K-12
630 Evans Ave 19610 610-374-0739
Dr. Helen Larson, supt. Fax 374-0948
www.wyoarea.org/
Wyomissing Area JSHS 900/7-12
630 Evans Ave 19610 610-374-0739
William Hartman, prin. Fax 374-6012

Berks Technical Institute Post-Sec.
2205 Ridgewood Rd 19610 610-372-1722

Yardley, Bucks, Pop. 2,542
Pennsbury SD
Supt. — See Fallsington
Boehm MS 800/6-8
866 Big Oak Rd 19067 215-428-4220
Theresa Ricci, prin. Fax 428-9605
Penn MS 1,000/6-8
1524 Derbyshire Rd 19067 215-428-4280
Larry Ricci, prin. Fax 428-1549
Pennwood MS 1,000/6-8
1523 Makefield Rd 19067 215-428-4237
Dr. Kevin McHugh, prin. Fax 428-4265

Yeadon, Delaware, Pop. 11,506
William Penn SD
Supt. — See Lansdowne
Ninth Grade Academy 300/9-9
600 Cypress St 19050 610-626-3223
Dr. John Coyle, prin. Fax 284-8061

York, York, Pop. 40,418
Area Vocational Technical School
Supt. — None
York County School of Technology Vo/Tech
2179 S Queen St 17402 717-741-0820
Dr. James Kraft, prin. Fax 741-0694

Central York SD 4,500/K-12
775 Marion Rd 17406 717-846-6789
Dr. Linda Estep, supt. Fax 840-0451
www.cysd.k12.pa.us
Central York HS 1,500/9-12
601 Mundis Mill Rd 17406 717-846-6789
Jay Butterfield, prin. Fax 848-4684
Central York MS 1,200/6-8
1950 N Hills Rd 17406 717-846-6789
Edmund McManama, prin.

West York Area SD 3,100/K-12
2605 W Market St 17404 717-792-2796
Dr. Emilie Lonardi, supt. Fax 792-5114
www.wyasd.k12.pa.us
West York Area HS 900/9-12
1800 Bannister St 17404 717-845-6634
Janet May, prin. Fax 845-6634
West York Area MS 800/6-8
1700 Bannister St 17404 717-845-1671
Leslie Trimmer, prin. Fax 845-1671

York CSD 6,600/K-12
PO Box 1927 17405 717-845-3571
Dr. Tresa Diggs, supt. Fax 849-1394
www.ycs.k12.pa.us
Penn HS, 101 W College Ave 17401 1,800/9-12
Jesse Rawls, prin. 717-845-3571
Penn MS 1,100/6-8
415 E Boundary Ave 17403 717-845-3571
Rona Kaufmann, prin. Fax 849-1362
Smith MS 900/6-8
701 Texas Ave 17404 717-845-3571
Eric Holmes, prin. Fax 849-1418

York Suburban SD 2,700/K-12
1800 Hollywood Dr 17403 717-848-2814
Dr. William Hartman, supt. Fax 843-6899
www.yshs.k12.pa.us
York Suburban HS 800/9-12
1800 Hollywood Dr 17403 717-843-3881
Daniel Roesch, prin. Fax 848-3845
York Suburban MS 700/6-8
455 Sundale Dr 17402 717-755-2841
Victoria Gross, prin. Fax 751-0496

Baltimore School of Massage-York Campus Post-Sec.
170 Red Rock Rd 17406 717-268-1881
Bradley Academy for the Visual Arts Post-Sec.
1409 Williams Rd 17402 717-755-2300
Christian S of York 400/PK-12
907 Greenbriar Rd 17404 717-767-6842
Dr. Michael R. Leaming, supt. Fax 767-4904
Consolidated School of Business Post-Sec.
1605 Clugston Rd 17404 717-764-9550
Empire Beauty School Post-Sec.
2592 Eastern Blvd 17402 717-600-8111
Pennsylvania State University Post-Sec.
1031 Edgecomb Ave 17403 717-771-4000
York Catholic HS 700/7-12
601 E Springettsbury Ave 17403 717-846-8871
George Andrews, prin. Fax 843-4588
York College of Pennsylvania Post-Sec.
PO Box 15199 17405 717-846-7788
York Country Day S 300/PK-12
1071 Regents Glen Blvd 17403 717-843-9805
Nat Coffman, hdmstr. Fax 815-6769
York Hospital Post-Sec.
1001 S George St 17403 717-851-2942
York Technical Institute Post-Sec.
1405 Williams Rd 17402 717-757-1100
Yorktowne Business Institute Post-Sec.
W 7th Ave 17404 717-846-5000

York Springs, Adams, Pop. 653
Bermudian Springs SD 2,100/K-12
PO Box 501 17372 717-528-4113
Dr. William K. Shoemaker, supt. Fax 528-7981
www.bermudian.org
Bermudian Springs HS 700/9-12
PO Box 501 17372 717-528-4113
Russell Greenholt, prin. Fax 528-4124
Bermudian Springs MS 700/5-8
PO Box 501 17372 717-528-4113
Clifton Vanartsdalen, prin. Fax 528-0034

Youngsville, Warren, Pop. 1,723
Warren County SD
Supt. — See North Warren
Youngsville HS 500/8-12
227 College St 16371 814-563-7573
Darrell Jaskolka, prin. Fax 563-4459

Warren County Christian S 100/K-12
RR 1 Box 270B 16371 814-563-4457
Richard Kolcharno, prin. Fax 563-7647

Youngwood, Westmoreland, Pop. 3,171

Westmoreland County Community College Post-Sec.
145 Pavilion Ln 15697 724-925-4000

Zieglerville, Montgomery
Perkiomen Valley SD
Supt. — See Collegeville
Perkiomen Valley West MS 500/6-8
220 Big Rd 19492 484-977-7210
Ryan Stanson-Marsh, prin. Fax 977-7212

RHODE ISLAND

RHODE ISLAND DEPARTMENT OF EDUCATION
255 Westminster St, Providence 02903-3400
Telephone 401-222-4600
Fax 401-277-6178
Website http://www.ridoe.net

Commissioner of Education Peter McWalters

RHODE ISLAND BOARD OF REGENTS
255 Westminster St, Providence 02903-3414

Chairperson James Di Prete

PUBLIC, PRIVATE AND CATHOLIC SECONDARY SCHOOLS

Barrington, Bristol, Pop. 15,849
Barrington SD 3,400/PK-12
PO Box 95 02806 401-245-5000
Ralph Malafronte, supt. Fax 245-5003
barringtonschools.org
Barrington HS 1,100/9-12
220 Lincoln Ave 02806 401-247-3150
John Gray, prin. Fax 245-6170
Barrington MS 900/6-8
261 Middle Hwy 02806 401-247-3160
Richard Wheeler, prin. Fax 247-3164

St. Andrew's S 200/6-12
63 Federal Rd 02806 401-246-1230
John Martin, hdmstr. Fax 246-0510
Zion Bible College Post-Sec.
27 Middle Hwy 02806 401-246-0900

Block Island, Washington
New Shoreham SD 100/K-12
PO Box 1890 02807 401-466-7732
Leslie Ryan, supt. Fax 466-3249
www.bi.k12.ri.us
Block Island S 100/K-12
PO Box 1890 02807 401-466-5600
Marlee Lacoste, admin. Fax 466-5610

Bristol, Bristol, Pop. 21,625
Bristol Warren Regional SD 3,300/PK-12
151 State St 02809 401-253-4000
Edward Mara Ed.D., supt. Fax 253-1740
www2.bw.k12.ri.us/
Mt. Hope HS 1,200/9-12
199 Chestnut St 02809 401-254-5980
Margaret Ferreira, prin. Fax 254-5925
Other Schools – See Warren

Roger Williams University Post-Sec.
1 Old Ferry Rd 02809 401-253-1040

Central Falls, Providence, Pop. 19,159
Central Falls SD 3,400/PK-12
21 Hedley Ave 02863 401-727-7700
Dr. William Holland, supt. Fax 727-7722
www.cfschools.net/
Calcutt MS 800/6-8
112 Washington St 02863 401-727-7726
Elizabeth Legault, prin. Fax 724-0870
Central Falls HS 1,000/9-12
24 Summer St 02863 401-727-7710
John Kennedy, prin. Fax 727-6157

Chepachet, Providence
Foster-Glocester SD 1,700/6-12
PO Box D 02814 401-568-4175
Mario Cirillo Ed.D., supt. Fax 568-4178
www.fg.k12.ri.us/
Other Schools – See North Scituate

Coventry, Kent, Pop. 31,083
Coventry SD 5,500/PK-12
9 Foster Dr 02816 401-822-9400
Kenneth DiPietro, supt. Fax 822-9406
www.coventryschools.net
Career & Technical Center Vo/Tech
40 Reservoir Rd 02816 401-822-9499
John Canole, prin. Fax 822-9492
Coventry HS 1,900/9-12
40 Reservoir Rd 02816 401-822-9499
Michael Hobin, prin. Fax 822-9492
Flat River MS 500/6-8
1675 Flat River Rd 02816 401-822-9466
Alan Yanku, prin. Fax 822-9456
Knotty Oak MS 600/7-8
15 Foster Dr 02816 401-822-9426
Michael Convery, prin. Fax 822-9469

Cranston, Providence, Pop. 81,614
Cranston SD 10,800/PK-12
845 Park Ave 02910 401-270-8000
Catherine Ciarlo, supt. Fax 270-8703
www.cpsed.net
Bain MS 700/6-8
135 Gansett Ave 02910 401-270-8010
Thomas Barbieri, prin. Fax 270-8567
Cranston Area Career & Technical Center Vo/Tech
100 Metropolitan Ave 02920 401-270-8070
Lynda Wagner, prin. Fax 270-8611
Cranston HS East 1,700/9-12
899 Park Ave 02910 401-270-8126
Sean Kelly, prin. Fax 270-8509
Cranston HS West 1,800/9-12
80 Metropolitan Ave 02920 401-270-8049
Steven Knowlton, prin. Fax 270-8526
Park View MS 900/6-8
25 Park View Blvd 02910 401-270-8090
Melinda Thies, prin. Fax 270-8527
Western Hills MS 1,100/6-8
400 Phenix Ave 02920 401-270-8030
Norma Cole, prin. Fax 270-8635

Katharine Gibbs School Post-Sec.
85 Garfield Ave 02920 401-861-1420

Cumberland, Providence
Cumberland SD 5,100/PK-12
2602 Mendon Rd 02864 401-658-1600
Donna Morelle Ed.D., supt. Fax 658-4620
www.cumberlandschools.org/
Cumberland HS 1,500/9-12
2600 Mendon Rd 02864 401-658-2600
Stephen R. Driscoll, prin. Fax 658-3124
McCourt MS 600/6-8
45 Highland Ave 02864 401-725-2092
Armand Pires, prin. Fax 723-1188
North Cumberland MS 700/6-8
400 Nate Whipple Hwy 02864 401-333-6306
Thomas Kenworthy, prin. Fax 333-1926

East Greenwich, Kent, Pop. 11,865
East Greenwich SD 2,400/K-12
111 Peirce St 02818 401-398-1205
Charles Meyers, supt. Fax 886-3203
www.egsd.net/
Cole MS 500/7-8
100 Cedar Ave 02818 401-398-1203
Joseph Militello, prin. Fax 886-3283
East Greenwich HS 700/9-12
300 Avenger Dr 02818 401-886-3292
Michael Levine, prin. Fax 885-1336

Rocky Hill S 300/PK-12
530 Ives Rd 02818 401-884-9070
James Young, hdmstr. Fax 885-4985

East Providence, Providence, Pop. 49,515
East Providence SD 6,000/PK-12
80 Burnside Ave 02915 401-433-6222
Jacqueline Forbes Ph.D., supt. Fax 433-6256
epschoolsri.com
East Providence Career & Technical Ctr Vo/Tech
1998 Pawtucket Ave 02914 401-435-7815
Charles Rocha, dir. Fax 435-7854
East Providence HS 2,000/9-12
2000 Pawtucket Ave 02914 401-435-7806
Edward Daft, prin. Fax 435-7864
Martin MS 1,000/6-8
111 Brown St 02914 401-435-7819
Frank DeVall, prin. Fax 435-7851
Other Schools – See Riverside

MTTI - MotoRing Technical Training Inst. Post-Sec.
54 Water St 02914 401-434-4840
Providence Country Day S 300/5-12
660 Waterman Ave 02914 401-438-5170
Susan Haberlandt, hdmstr. Fax 435-4514
St. Mary Academy-Bay View 900/6-12
3070 Pawtucket Ave 02915 401-434-0113
Colleen Gribbin, prin. Fax 438-5936

Esmond, Providence, Pop. 4,400
Smithfield SD 2,600/PK-12
49 Farnum Pike 02917 401-231-6606
Robert O'Brien, supt. Fax 232-0870
www.ri.net/schools/Smithfield/District/
Other Schools – See Smithfield

Harrisville, Providence, Pop. 1,654
Burrillville SD 2,500/PK-12
2300 Broncos Hwy 02830 401-568-1301
Steven Welford, supt. Fax 568-4111
www.bsd-ri.net/
Burrillville HS 800/9-12
425 East Ave 02830 401-568-1310
Donald Rebello, prin. Fax 568-1363
Burrillville MS 600/6-8
2220 Broncos Hwy 02830 401-568-1320
Lois Short, prin. Fax 568-1317

Jamestown, Newport, Pop. 4,999
Jamestown SD 500/PK-8
76 Melrose Ave 02835 401-423-7020
Dr. Robert Power, supt. Fax 423-7022
www.jamestownri.com/school
Jamestown MS 300/5-8
55 Lawn Ave 02835 401-423-7010
Kathleen Almanzor, prin. Fax 423-7012

Johnston, Providence, Pop. 26,542
Johnston SD 3,300/PK-12
10 Memorial Ave 02919 401-233-1900
Margaret A. Iacovelli, supt. Fax 233-1907
www.ri.net/schools/johnston
Ferri MS 900/6-8
10 Memorial Ave 02919 401-233-1930
Joan Fargnoli, prin. Fax 233-1943
Johnston SHS 900/9-12
345 Cherry Hill Rd 02919 401-233-1920
Dr. Elizabeth Mantelli, prin. Fax 233-0031

Kingston, Washington, Pop. 6,504

University of Rhode Island 02881 Post-Sec.
401-874-1000

Lincoln, Providence, Pop. 18,045
Lincoln SD 4,100/PK-12
1624 Lonsdale Ave 02865 401-721-3300
Joseph Nasif, supt. Fax 726-1813
www.lincolnps.org/
Davies Career-Technical HS Vo/Tech
50 Jenckes Hill Rd 02865 401-728-1500
Victoria Garrick, prin. Fax 728-8910
Lincoln HS 1,100/9-12
135 Old River Rd 02865 401-333-1850
Robert Martin, prin. Fax 334-8753
Lincoln MS 600/6-8
152 Jenckes Hill Rd 02865 401-721-3400
Bruce Macksoud, prin. Fax 333-9977

Community College of Rhode Island Post-Sec.
1762 Louisquisset Pike 02865 401-333-7000
Computer-Ed Business Institute Post-Sec.
622 George Washington Hwy 02865 401-334-2430

Middletown, Newport, Pop. 3,400
Middletown SD 2,500/PK-12
26 Oliphant Ln 02842 401-849-2122
Rosemarie Kraeger, supt. Fax 849-0202
www.ri.net/middletown/
Gaudet MS 800/5-8
1113 Aquidneck Ave 02842 401-846-6395
Vincent Giuliano, prin. Fax 847-7580
Middletown HS 700/9-12
130 Valley Rd 02842 401-846-7250
Steven Ruscito, prin. Fax 849-7170

St. George's S 300/9-12
372 Purgatory Rd 02842 401-847-7565
Eric Peterson, hdmstr. Fax 842-6677

Narragansett, Washington, Pop. 3,721
Narragansett SD 1,600/PK-12
25 5th Ave 02882 401-792-9450
Katherine Sipala, supt. Fax 792-9439
www.narragansett.k12.ri.us/
Narragansett HS 500/9-12
245 S Pier Rd 02882 401-792-9400
Daniel Warner, prin. Fax 792-9410
Narragansett Pier MS 500/5-8
235 S Pier Rd 02882 401-792-9430
Marie Ahern, prin. Fax 792-9436

Newport, Newport, Pop. 25,340
Newport SD 2,300/PK-12
437 Broadway 02840 401-847-2100
John Ambrogi Ed.D., supt. Fax 849-0170
www.newportrischools.org/
Newport Area Career & Technical Center Vo/Tech
15 Wickham Rd 02840 401-849-3608
Mary Beth Pike, dir. Fax 849-4670
Rogers HS 800/9-12
15 Wickham Rd 02840 401-847-6235
Patricia DiCenso, prin. Fax 849-3295
Thompson MS 600/6-8
55 Broadway 02840 401-847-1493
Eric Thomas Ed.D., prin. Fax 849-3426

International Yacht Restoration School Post-Sec.
449 Thames St 02840 401-848-5777
Salve Regina University Post-Sec.
100 Ochre Point Ave 02840 401-847-6650

North Kingstown, Washington, Pop. 2,800
North Kingstown SD 3,700/K-12
100 Fairway Dr 02852 401-268-6200
James Halley, supt. Fax 268-6405
www.nksd.net
Davisville MS 600/6-8
200 School St 02852 401-541-6300
Ruthanne Logan, prin. Fax 541-6310
North Kingstown HS 1,500/9-12
150 Fairway Dr 02852 401-268-6236
Gerald Foley, prin. Fax 268-6210
Wickford MS 500/6-8
250 Tower Hill Rd 02852 401-268-6470
Kathleen Mort, prin. Fax 268-6480

North Providence, Providence, Pop. 32,500
North Providence SD 3,500/PK-12
2240 Mineral Spring Ave 02911 401-233-1100
Donna Ottaviano Ed.D., supt. Fax 233-1106
Birchwood MS 400/6-8
10 Birchwood Dr 02904 401-233-1120
Kenneth Ferrara, prin. Fax 353-6903
North Providence HS 1,200/9-12
1828 Mineral Spring Ave 02904 401-233-1150
Joseph Goho, prin. Fax 233-1166
Ricci MS 500/6-8
51 Intervale Ave 02911 401-233-1170
Patricia Hines, prin. Fax 232-5421

St. Joseph's Hospital Post-Sec.
200 High Service Ave 02904 401-456-3050

North Scituate, Providence
Foster-Glocester SD
Supt. — See Chepachet
Ponaganset HS 1,000/9-12
137 Anan Wade Rd 02857 401-647-3377
Edmond Lemoi, prin. Fax 647-5743
Ponaganset MS 700/6-8
91 Anan Wade Rd 02857 401-647-3361
Patricia Marcotte, prin. Fax 647-9080

Scituate SD 1,800/PK-12
PO Box 188 02857 401-647-4100
Paul Lescault, supt. Fax 647-4102
www.scituateri.net
Scituate HS 600/9-12
94 Trimtown Rd 02857 401-647-4120
David Light, prin. Fax 647-4126
Scituate MS 500/6-8
94 Trimtown Rd 02857 401-647-4123
Lawrence Filippelli, prin. Fax 647-4104

North Smithfield, Providence, Pop. 10,497
North Smithfield SD
Supt. — See Slatersville
North Smithfield JSHS 800/7-12
412 Greenville Rd 02896 401-766-2500
David Silva, prin. Fax 765-8629

Pawtucket, Providence, Pop. 73,742
Pawtucket SD 9,300/PK-12
PO Box 388 02862 401-729-6315
Dr. Hans Dellith, supt. Fax 727-1641
www.psdri.net
Goff JHS 500/7-8
974 Newport Ave 02861 401-729-6500
Lisa Benedetti Ramzi, prin. Fax 721-2105
Jenks JHS 700/6-8
350 Division St 02860 401-729-6520
Susan Pfeil, prin. Fax 729-6524
Shea HS 1,200/9-12
485 East Ave 02860 401-729-6445
Dr. Christopher Lord, prin. Fax 729-6454
Slater JHS 700/6-8
281 Mineral Spring Ave 02860 401-729-6480
Meredith Caswell, prin. Fax 729-6490
Tolman HS 1,300/9-12
150 Exchange St 02860 401-729-6400
Fred Silva, prin. Fax 729-6403

Bishop Keough Regional HS 100/9-12
145 Power Rd 02860 401-726-0335
Jeanne Leclerc, prin. Fax 726-0336

New England Tractor Trailer Training Post-Sec.
600 Mshssuck Valley Ind Hwy 02860 401-725-1220
Newport School of Hairdressing Post-Sec.
226 Main St 02860 401-725-6882
St. Raphael Academy 500/9-12
122 Walcott St 02860 401-723-8100
Richard A. Rouleau, prin. Fax 723-8740
Sawyer School Post-Sec.
101 Main St 02860 401-272-8400

Peace Dale, See Wakefield
South Kingstown SD
Supt. — See Wakefield
Curtis Corner MS 500/6-8
301 Curtis Corner Rd 02879 401-360-1333
Michele Humbyrd, prin. Fax 360-1334

Portsmouth, Newport, Pop. 3,600
Portsmouth SD 3,000/PK-12
29 Middle Rd 02871 401-683-1039
Susan Lusi Ph.D., supt. Fax 683-5204
portsmouthrischools.tripod.com
Portsmouth HS 1,000/9-12
126 Education Ln 02871 401-683-2124
Robert Littlefield, prin. Fax 683-6404
Portsmouth MS 900/5-8
125 Jepson Ln 02871 401-849-3700
Natalie Dunning, prin. Fax 841-8420

Aquidneck Island Christian Academy 100/K-12
321 E Main Rd 02871 401-849-5550
Stephen Bailey, admin. Fax 849-6811
Portsmouth Abbey S 300/9-12
285 Corys Ln 02871 401-683-2000
Dr. James De Vecchi, hdmstr. Fax 683-5888

Providence, Providence, Pop. 176,862
Providence SD 24,400/PK-12
797 Westminster St 02903 401-456-9100
Donnie Evans Ed.D., supt. Fax 456-9252
www.providenceschools.org
Adelaide Avenue HS 200/9-9
155 Harrison St 02907 401-456-0676
Dr. Mator Kpangbai, dir. Fax 456-0679
Birch Vocational Center Vo/Tech
434 Mount Pleasant Ave 02908 401-456-9198
Larry Roberti, admin. Fax 453-8655
Bridgham MS 600/6-8
1655 Westminster St 02909 401-456-9360
Dr. Dinah Larbi, prin. Fax 453-8632
Central HS 1,600/9-12
70 Fricker St 02903 401-456-9111
Elaine Almagno, prin. Fax 456-9113
Classical HS 1,100/9-12
770 Westminster St 02903 401-456-9145
Cheryl Gomes, prin. Fax 456-9155
Del Sesto HS 9-12
152 Springfield St 02909 401-278-0527
Albert Paranzino, prin. Fax 278-0564
E-Cubed Academy 300/9-12
812 Branch Ave 02904 401-456-0694
Wobberson Torchon, prin. Fax 456-0696
Feinstein HS 300/9-12
544 Elmwood Ave 02907 401-456-1706
Kenneth Perry, dir. Fax 453-8698
Greene MS 800/6-8
721 Chalkstone Ave 02908 401-456-9347
Dr. Nicole Mathis-Thomas, prin. Fax 453-8630
Hanley Career And Technology Vo/Tech
91 Fricker St 02903 401-456-9136
Ramon Torres, prin. Fax 456-9172
Hope Arts HS 400/9-12
324 Hope St 02906 401-456-9405
Scott Sutherland, prin. Fax 456-9329
Hope Leadership HS 400/9-12
324 Hope St 02906 401-453-8686
Wayne Montague, prin. Fax 456-9163
Hope Technology HS 500/9-12
324 Hope St 02906 401-456-9164
Dr. Arthur Petrosinelli, prin. Fax 456-9162
Hopkins MS 600/6-8
480 Charles St 02904 401-456-9203
Thomas Montaquila, prin. Fax 456-9226
MET Equality S 600/9-12
325 Public St 02905 401-752-2600
Chris Hempel, prin. Fax 752-2612
MET Justice Campus 9-12
325 Public St 02905 401-752-2600
Phil Price, prin. Fax 752-2612
MET Liberty S 9-12
325 Public St 02905 401-752-2600
Jodi Woodruff, prin. Fax 752-2612
MET Peace Street Campus 9-12
362 Dexter St 02907 401-742-3400
Charlie Plant, prin. Fax 752-3425
MET Shepard Building S 9-12
80 Washington St 02903 401-277-5046
Charles Adler, prin. Fax 277-5049
MET Unity S 9-12
325 Public St 02905 401-752-2600
Nancy Diaz, prin. Fax 752-2612
Mt. Pleasant HS 1,500/9-12
434 Mount Pleasant Ave 02908 401-456-9181
Maureen Crisafulli, prin. Fax 453-8655
Perry MS 700/6-8
370 Hartford Ave 02909 401-456-9352
Frances Rotella, prin. Fax 453-8634
Springfield MS 400/6-8
152 Springfield St 02909 401-278-0557
Albert Paranzino, prin. Fax 278-0564
Stuart MS 800/6-8
188 Princeton Ave 02907 401-456-9341
Marc Catone, prin. Fax 453-8659
Williams MS 900/6-8
278 Thurbers Ave 02905 401-456-9355
Rudolph Mosely, prin. Fax 453-8631

Angelo School of Cosmetology Hair Design Post-Sec.
151 Broadway 02903 401-272-4300
Brown S 800/PK-12
250 Lloyd Ave 02906 401-831-7350
Joanne Hoffman, hdmstr. Fax 455-0084
Brown University Post-Sec.
1 Prospect St 02912 401-863-1000
Community College of Rhode Island Post-Sec.
1 Hilton St 02905 401-455-6000
Community Preparatory S 200/3-8
126 Somerset St 02907 401-521-9696
Judith Ryan, hdmstr. Fax 521-9715
Johnson & Wales University Post-Sec.
8 Abbott Park Pl 02903 401-598-1000
LaSalle Academy 1,300/7-12
612 Academy Ave 02908 401-351-7750
Donald Kavanagh, prin. Fax 444-1782
Lincoln S 400/PK-12
301 Butler Ave 02906 401-331-9696
Julia Eells, hdmstr. Fax 751-6670
Providence College Post-Sec.
549 River Ave 02918 401-865-1000
Providence Hebrew S 100/PK-12
450 Elmgrove Ave 02906 401-331-5327
Rabbi Peretz Scheinerman, dean Fax 331-0030
Rhode Island College Post-Sec.
600 Mount Pleasant Ave 02908 401-456-8000
Rhode Island Hospital Post-Sec.
593 Eddy St 02903 401-444-5123
Rhode Island School of Design Post-Sec.
2 College St 02903 401-454-6100
Roger Williams University Post-Sec.
150 Washington St 02903 401-274-2200
Sawyer School Post-Sec.
550 Hartford Ave 02909 401-272-3280
School One 100/9-12
220 University Ave 02906 401-331-2497
Beverly Vileno, hdmstr. Fax 421-8869
Wheeler S 800/PK-12
216 Hope St 02906 401-421-8100
Dan Miller, hdmstr. Fax 751-7674
Women & Infants Hospital Post-Sec.
101 Dudley St 02905 401-274-1100

Riverside, See East Providence
East Providence SD
Supt. — See East Providence
Riverside MS 500/6-8
179 Forbes St 02915 401-433-6230
Michael Almeida, prin. Fax 433-6261

Slatersville, Providence
North Smithfield SD 1,800/PK-12
PO Box 72 02876 401-769-5492
Stephen Lindberg, supt. Fax 769-5493
www.northsmithfieldschools.com/
Other Schools – See North Smithfield

Smithfield, Providence, Pop. 19,163
Smithfield SD
Supt. — See Esmond
Gallagher MS 700/6-8
10 Indian Run Trl 02917 401-949-2056
Karl Smith Ed.D., prin. Fax 949-5697
Smithfield HS 800/9-12
90 Pleasant View Ave 02917 401-949-2050
Daniel Kelley, prin. Fax 949-2052

Bryant University Post-Sec.
1150 Douglas Pike 02917 401-232-6000
Masters Regional Academy 100/7-12
915 Douglas Pike 02917 401-232-7061
Michael Dube, prin. Fax 233-9267

Tiverton, Newport, Pop. 7,259
Tiverton SD 2,200/K-12
100 N Brayton Rd 02878 401-624-8475
William J. Rearick, supt. Fax 624-4086
www.tivschools.com
Tiverton HS 800/9-12
100 N Brayton Rd 02878 401-624-8494
Steven Fezette, prin. Fax 624-8495
Tiverton MS 700/5-8
10 Quintal Dr 02878 401-624-6668
Patricia Aull, prin. Fax 624-6669

Wakefield, Washington, Pop. 7,134
South Kingstown SD 3,800/PK-12
307 Curtis Corner Rd 02879 401-360-1307
Robert A. Hicks Ed.D., supt. Fax 360-1330
www.skschools.net/
Broad Rock MS 500/6-8
351 Broad Rock Rd 02879 401-782-6223
Sheila Sullivan, prin. Fax 782-6282
South Kingston HS 1,300/9-12
215 Columbia St 02879 401-360-1000
Robert McCarthy, prin. Fax 789-5180
Other Schools – See Peace Dale

Prout S 500/7-12
4640 Tower Hill Rd 02879 401-789-9262
Gary Delneo, prin. Fax 782-2262

Warren, Bristol, Pop. 11,385
Bristol Warren Regional SD
Supt. — See Bristol
Kickemuit MS 800/6-8
525 Child St 02885 401-245-2010
Michael Carbone, prin. Fax 254-5960

Our Lady of Fatima HS 200/7-12
360 Market St 02885 401-245-4449
Sr. Mary Margaret Souza, prin. Fax 245-1380

Warwick, Kent, Pop. 87,233
Warwick SD 11,700/PK-12
34 Warwick Lake Ave 02889 401-734-3100
Robert Shapiro, supt. Fax 734-3105
www.warwickschools.org
Aldrich JHS 700/7-8
789 Post Rd 02888 401-734-3500
William Sangster, prin. Fax 734-3508
Gorton JHS 600/7-8
69 Draper Ave 02889 401-734-3350
Kenneth Sheehan, prin. Fax 734-3359
Pilgrim HS 1,400/9-12
111 Pilgrim Pkwy 02888 401-734-3250
Dennis Mullen, prin. Fax 734-3264
Toll Gate HS 1,200/9-12
575 Centerville Rd Ste 1 02886 401-734-3300
Stephen Chrabaszcz, prin. Fax 734-3314
Warwick Area Career & Technical Center Vo/Tech
575 Centerville Rd 02886 401-734-3150
Joseph Crowley, dir. Fax 734-3160
Warwick Veterans Memorial HS 1,300/9-12
2401 W Shore Rd 02889 401-734-3200
Gerry Habershaw, prin. Fax 734-3214
Winman JHS 700/7-8
575 Centerville Rd Ste 2 02886 401-734-3375
Joanne McInerney, prin. Fax 734-3385

Bishop Hendricken HS 1,000/9-12
2615 Warwick Ave 02889 401-739-3450
Vincent Mancuso, prin. Fax 732-8261
Community College of Rhode Island Post-Sec.
400 East Ave 02886 401-825-1000
New England Institute of Technology Post-Sec.
2500 Post Rd 02886 401-739-5000
Overbrook Academy 200/6-9
836 Warwick Neck Ave 02889 401-737-2850
Kristina Pinero, prin. Fax 737-2884
Warwick Academy of Beauty Culture Post-Sec.
1276 Bald Hill Rd Unit 100 02886 401-737-4946

Westerly, Washington, Pop. 16,477
Westerly SD 3,600/PK-12
15 Highland Ave 02891 401-348-2700
Thomas DiPaola Ph.D., supt. Fax 348-2707
www.westerly.k12.ri.us
Westerly HS 1,200/9-12
23 Ward Ave 02891 401-596-2109
Paula Fusco, prin. Fax 596-5098
Westerly MS 800/6-8
10 Sandy Hill Rd 02891 401-348-2750
Dennis Curran, prin. Fax 348-2752

West Greenwich, Kent, Pop. 3,492
Exeter-West Greenwich SD 2,100/PK-12
940 Nooseneck Hill Rd 02817 401-397-5125
James DiPrete, supt. Fax 397-2407
www.ewg.k12.ri.us
Exeter-West Greenwich Regional HS 700/9-12
930 Nooseneck Hill Rd 02817 401-397-6893
Denise Boule', prin. Fax 392-0134
Exeter-West Greenwich Regional JHS 300/7-8
930 Nooseneck Hill Rd 02817 401-397-6897
Mark Thompson, prin. Fax 392-0109

West Warwick, Kent, Pop. 29,600
West Warwick SD 3,700/PK-12
10 Harris Ave 02893 401-821-1180
David Raiche, supt. Fax 822-8463
www.westwarwickpublicschools.com/
Deering MS 900/6-8
2 Webster Knight Dr 02893 401-822-8445
Karen Wilson, prin. Fax 822-8474
West Warwick HS 1,100/9-12
4 Webster Knight Dr 02893 401-821-6596
Wayne Talbot, prin. Fax 822-8473

Wood River Junction, Washington
Chariho SD 3,700/PK-12
455A Switch Rd 02894 401-364-7575
Barry Ricci, supt. Fax 364-1176
www.chariho.k12.ri.us/
Chariho Area Career & Technical Center Vo/Tech
459 Switch Rd 02894 401-364-6869
Susan Chandler, dir. Fax 364-1191
Chariho Regional HS 1,200/9-12
453 Switch Rd 02894 401-364-7778
Robert Mitchell, prin. Fax 364-1190
Chariho Regional MS 1,100/5-8
455b Switch Rd 02894 401-364-0651
Carol Blanchette, prin. Fax 364-1189

Woonsocket, Providence, Pop. 44,328
Woonsocket SD 6,500/K-12
108 High St 02895 401-767-4600
Maureen Macera Ph.D., supt. Fax 767-4607
www.woonsocketschools.com/
Woonsocket Area Career & Tech. Center Vo/Tech
400 Aylsworth Ave 02895 401-767-4662
Andrew Riley, prin. Fax 767-4665
Woonsocket HS 2,000/9-12
777 Cass Ave 02895 401-767-4700
George Nasuti, prin. Fax 767-4748
Woonsocket MS 1,600/6-8
357 Park Pl 02895 401-767-4600
Patrick McGee, prin. Fax 767-4771

Good Shepherd Regional MS 300/4-8
1210 Mendon Rd 02895 401-767-5906
Lawrence Poitras, prin. Fax 767-5905
Mt. St. Charles Academy 1,000/7-12
800 Logee St 02895 401-769-0310
Herve Richer, prin. Fax 762-2327

SOUTH CAROLINA

SOUTH CAROLINA DEPARTMENT OF EDUCATION

1429 Senate St Ste 100, Columbia 29201-3799
Telephone 803-734-8500
Fax 803-734-3389
Website ed.sc.gov/

Superintendent of Education Jim Rex

SOUTH CAROLINA BOARD OF EDUCATION

1429 Senate St Ste 100, Columbia 29201-3730

Chairperson John Tindal

PUBLIC, PRIVATE AND CATHOLIC SECONDARY SCHOOLS

Abbeville, Abbeville, Pop. 5,732
Abbeville County SD 3,700/K-12
400 Greenville St 29620 864-366-5427
Ivan Randolph, supt. Fax 366-8531
www.acsd.k12.sc.us/
Abbeville County Career Center Vo/Tech
100 Old Calhoun Falls Rd 29620 864-366-9069
Nick Hyduke, prin. Fax 366-4774
Abbeville HS 500/9-12
701 Washington St 29620 864-366-5916
Steve Glenn, prin. Fax 366-4939
Wright MS 500/6-8
111 Highway 71 29620 864-366-5998
Barry Jacks, prin. Fax 366-4282
Other Schools – See Calhoun Falls, Due West

Aiken, Aiken, Pop. 27,490
Aiken County SD 24,300/K-12
1000 Brookhaven Dr 29803 803-641-2428
Fax 642-8903
www.aiken.k12.sc.us
Aiken HS 1,500/9-12
449 Rutland Dr NE 29801 803-641-2500
Garen Cofer, prin. Fax 641-2501
Aiken MS 800/6-8
101 Gator Ln 29801 803-641-2570
Brooks Smith, prin. Fax 641-2578
Kennedy MS 1,000/6-8
274 E Pine Log Rd 29803 803-641-2470
Ben Osborne, prin. Fax 641-2405
Schofield MS 800/6-8
224 Kershaw St NE 29801 803-641-2770
Carl White, prin. Fax 641-2529
Silver Bluff HS 900/9-12
64 Desoto Dr 29803 803-652-8100
Todd Bornshever, prin. Fax 652-8104
South Aiken HS 1,400/9-12
232 E Pine Log Rd 29803 803-641-2600
Dr. Janice Nashatker, prin. Fax 641-2607
Other Schools – See Graniteville, Jackson, Monetta, New Ellenton, North Augusta, Wagener, Warrenville

---

Aiken Christian S 100/6-12
142 Talatha Church Rd 29803 803-642-0286
Clark Ballard, prin. Fax 642-0485
Aiken Preparatory S 200/PK-12
619 Barnwell Ave NW 29801 803-648-3223
Deborah Boehner, hdmstr. Fax 648-6482
Aiken Technical College Post-Sec.
PO Box 696 29802 803-593-9231
Lacy Cosmetology School Post-Sec.
3084 Whiskey Rd 29803 803-648-6181
South Aiken Baptist Christian S 400/K-10
980 Dougherty Rd 29803 803-648-7871
Randy Martin, prin. Fax 643-9533
University of South Carolina Post-Sec.
471 University Pkwy 29801 803-648-6851

Allendale, Allendale, Pop. 3,897
Allendale County SD 1,700/PK-12
PO Box 458 29810 803-584-4603
Dr. W. Duck Hucks, supt. Fax 584-5303
www.acs.k12.sc.us
Allendale County Adult Learning Center Adult
PO Box 498 29810 803-584-3107
Janice Robertson, dir.
Other Schools – See Fairfax

University of South Carolina Post-Sec.
PO Box 617 29810 803-584-6314

Anderson, Anderson, Pop. 25,899
Anderson SD 5 11,800/PK-12
PO Box 439 29622 864-260-5000
Betty Bagley, supt. Fax 260-5896
www.anderson5.net
Hanna HS 1,600/9-12
2600 N Highway 81 29621 864-260-5110
Michael Sams, prin. Fax 260-5213
Hanna-Westside Extension Campus Vo/Tech
1225 S McDuffie St 29624 864-260-5160
Rick Mascaro, prin. Fax 260-5685
Lakeside MS 1,000/6-8
315 Pearman Dairy Rd 29625 864-260-5135
Martha Hanwell, prin. Fax 260-5885
McCants MS 1,300/6-8
2123 Marchbanks Ave 29621 864-260-5145
Jacky Stamps, prin. Fax 260-5846
Southwood MS 600/6-8
1110 Southwood St 29624 864-260-5205
Evelyn Murphy, prin. Fax 964-2607
Westside HS 1,700/9-12
806 Pearman Dairy Rd 29625 864-260-5230
Henry Adair, prin. Fax 260-5007

Anderson College Post-Sec.
316 Boulevard 29621 864-231-2000
Anderson Memorial Hospital Post-Sec.
800 N Fant St 29621 864-261-1109
Forrest Junior College Post-Sec.
601 E River St 29624 864-225-7653

Andrews, Georgetown, Pop. 3,110
Georgetown County SD
Supt. — See Georgetown
Andrews HS 700/9-12
12890 County Line Rd 29510 843-264-3414
Michelle Staggers, prin. Fax 264-3326
Rosemary MS 700/6-8
12804 County Line Rd 29510 843-264-9780
Michael Caviris, prin. Fax 264-9787

Aynor, Horry, Pop. 587
Horry County SD
Supt. — See Conway
Aynor HS 400/10-12
201 Jordanville Rd 29511 843-358-6261
Marion Shaw, prin. Fax 358-7401

Bamberg, Bamberg, Pop. 3,552
Bamberg SD 1 1,600/K-12
PO Box 526 29003 803-245-3053
Phyllis Schwarting, supt. Fax 245-3056
www.bamberg1.com
Bamberg-Ehrhardt HS 500/9-12
PO Box 89 29003 803-245-3030
Randall L. Maxwell, prin. Fax 245-6502
Bamberg-Ehrhardt MS 400/6-8
PO Box 548 29003 803-245-3058
Robert Kearse, prin. Fax 245-6501

Bamberg Job Corps Center Post-Sec.
PO Box 967 29003 803-245-5101

Barnwell, Barnwell, Pop. 4,874
Barnwell SD 45 2,700/K-12
660 Hagood Ave 29812 803-541-1300
Carolyne Williams, supt. Fax 541-1348
www.barnwell45.k12.sc.us
Barnwell HS 800/9-12
474 Jackson St 29812 803-541-1390
Linda Zionkowski, prin. Fax 541-0726
Guinyard-Butler MS 500/7-8
779 Allen St 29812 803-541-1370
Dr. John Bass, prin. Fax 541-1306

Batesburg, Lexington, Pop. 6,189
Lexington County SD 3 2,200/K-12
338 W Columbia Ave 29006 803-532-4423
Dr. William Gummerson, supt. Fax 532-8000
www.lex3.k12.sc.us
Batesburg-Leesville HS 600/9-12
600 Summerland Ave 29006 803-532-9251
Raymond Padgett, prin. Fax 532-3232
Batesburg-Leesville MS 600/6-8
425 Shealy Rd 29006 803-532-3831
Herbert Smith, prin. Fax 532-8021

King Academy 300/K-12
1046 Sardis Rd 29006 803-532-6682
Dennis Gibson, prin. Fax 604-0409

Beaufort, Beaufort, Pop. 12,058
Beaufort County SD 18,400/PK-12
PO Box 309 29901 843-322-2300
Dr. Valerie Page Truesdale, supt. Fax 322-2371
www.beaufort.k12.sc.us/
Battery Creek HS 1,400/9-12
1 Blue Dolphin Dr 29906 843-322-5500
Edmond Burnes, prin. Fax 322-5608
Beaufort HS 1,600/9-12
84 Sea Island Pkwy, 843-322-2000
Dan Durbin, prin. Fax 322-2158
Beaufort MS 600/6-8
2501 Mossy Oaks Rd 29902 843-322-5700
Carole Ingram, prin. Fax 322-5723
Smalls MS 700/6-8
43 W K Alston Dr 29906 843-322-2500
Denise Smith, prin. Fax 322-2564
Other Schools – See Bluffton, Hilton Head Island, Ladys Island, Seabrook

---

Beaufort Academy 400/PK-12
240 Sams Point Rd, 843-524-3393
Timothy Johnston, prin. Fax 524-1171
Beaufort Christian S 100/K-12
378 Parris Island Gtwy 29906 843-525-0635
Douglas Wadsworth, prin. Fax 525-0635
Technical College of the Lowcountry Post-Sec.
PO Box 1288 29901 843-525-8324
University of South Carolina Post-Sec.
801 Carteret St 29902 843-521-4100

Belton, Anderson, Pop. 4,568
Anderson SD 2
Supt. — See Honea Path
Belton MS 600/6-8
102 Cherokee Rd 29627 864-338-6595
Margaret Spivey, prin. Fax 338-3301

Bennettsville, Marlboro, Pop. 9,351
Marlboro County SD 5,000/PK-12
PO Box 947 29512 843-479-4016
Dr. David A. Sherbine, supt. Fax 479-5944
www.marlboro.k12.sc.us
Bennettsville MS 500/6-8
701 Cheraw St 29512 843-479-5941
Fannie Mason, prin. Fax 479-5943
Marlboro County HS 1,300/9-12
951 Fayetteville Avenue Ext 29512 843-479-5900
Rocky Peterkin, prin. Fax 479-5916

Bishopville, Lee, Pop. 3,831
Lee County SD 2,500/K-12
521 Park St 29010 803-484-5327
Dr. Lloyd Hunter, supt. Fax 484-9107
www.leeschoolsk12.org/home.asp
Dennis MS 100/6-8
321 Roland St 29010 803-484-5386
Kwamine Simpson, prin. Fax 484-5825
Lee Central HS 700/9-12
1800 Wisacky Hwy 29010 803-428-4010
Leevette Malloy, prin. Fax 428-4062
Lee County Career & Technical Center Vo/Tech
310 Roland St 29010 803-484-5337
Bryan Durant, prin. Fax 484-4171
Other Schools – See Elliott

Lee Academy 800/K-12
630 Cousar St 29010 803-484-5532
Phil Rizzo, prin. Fax 484-9491

Blacksburg, Cherokee, Pop. 1,898
Cherokee SD
Supt. — See Gaffney
Blacksburg HS 500/9-12
201 W Ramseur Dr 29702 864-839-6371
Jim Touchberry, prin. Fax 839-2960
Blacksburg MS 500/6-8
101 London St 29702 864-839-6476
Virgil Hampton, prin. Fax 839-2390

Blackville, Barnwell, Pop. 2,919
Area Vocational Schools
Supt. — None
Barnwell County Career Center Vo/Tech
5214 Reynolds Rd 29817 803-259-5512
H. Samuel McKay, dir. Fax 541-4701

Barnwell SD 19 1,000/PK-12
PO Box 185 29817 803-284-5605
Teresa Pope Ph.D., supt. Fax 284-4417
www.barnwell19.k12.sc.us/
Blackville-Hilda HS 300/9-12
PO Box 245 29817 803-284-5700
Elliott Willingham, prin. Fax 284-3766
Blackville-Hilda JHS 100/7-8
PO Box 186 29817 803-284-5900
Mary Ella Brown, prin. Fax 284-0961

Barnwell Christian S 50/1-12
5675 SC Highway 70 29817 803-259-2100
Andrew Korver, prin.
Davis Academy 300/K-12
5061 Hilda Rd 29817 803-284-2017
Robert Len Frederick, hdmstr. Fax 284-5544

Bluffton, Beaufort, Pop. 2,341
Beaufort County SD
Supt. — See Beaufort
Bluffton HS 1,100/9-12
12 HE McCracken Cir 29910 843-706-8800
Fax 706-8819
McCracken MS 1,000/6-8
250 HE McCracken Cir 29910 843-706-8700
Phillip Shaw, prin. Fax 706-8778

Blythewood, Richland, Pop. 655
Richland SD 2
Supt. — See Columbia
Blythewood HS 9-12
10901 Wilson Blvd 29016 803-691-4090
Keith Price, prin. Fax 691-4097
Blythewood MS 800/6-8
2351 Longtown Rd E 29016 803-691-6850
Nancy Gregory, prin. Fax 691-6860
Kelly Mill MS 800/6-8
1141 Kelly Mill Rd 29016 803-691-7210
Dr. Michaele Lemrow, prin. Fax 691-7211

South Carolina Criminal Justice Academy Post-Sec.
PO Box 1993 29016 803-896-7779

Boiling Springs, Spartanburg, Pop. 3,522
Spartanburg SD 2 8,400/K-12
4606 Parris Bridge Rd 29316 864-578-0128
Scott Mercer, supt. Fax 578-8924
www.spartanburg2.k12.sc.us
Boiling Springs HS 9th Grade Campus 600/9-9
3655 Boiling Springs Rd 29316 864-578-2610
Eddie Cole, prin. Fax 578-2620
Boiling Springs HS 1,300/10-12
2251 Old Furnace Rd 29316 864-578-8465
Chuck Gordon, prin. Fax 578-6825
Other Schools – See Chesnee, Inman

Bowman, Orangeburg, Pop. 1,179

Bowman Academy 100/1-12
PO Box 98 29018 803-829-2770
Ada Smith, prin. Fax 829-2770

Branchville, Orangeburg, Pop. 1,052
Orangeburg Consolidated SD 4
Supt. — See Cope
Branchville HS 300/7-12
PO Box 188 29432 803-274-8875
George Benton, prin. Fax 274-8645

Calhoun Falls, Abbeville, Pop. 2,264
Abbeville County SD
Supt. — See Abbeville
Calhoun Falls JSHS 300/6-12
205 Edgefield St 29628 864-447-8014
Tammy Hollingsworth, prin. Fax 447-9379

Camden, Kershaw, Pop. 7,000
Kershaw County SD 10,300/PK-12
PO Box 7008 29020 803-432-8416
Dr. Herbert Berg, supt. Fax 425-8918
www.kershaw.k12.sc.us
Applied Technical Education Campus Vo/Tech
874 Vocational Ln 29020 803-425-8982
Allen Teal, dir. Fax 425-8983
Camden HS 1,000/9-12
1022 Ehrenclou Dr 29020 803-425-8930
Edward Dean, prin. Fax 424-2861
Camden MS 900/6-8
416 Laurens St 29020 803-425-8975
Jeff Jordan, prin. Fax 425-8954
Kershaw County Adult Education Adult
874 Vocational Ln 29020 803-425-8980
Dr. Carolyn Ham, dir. Fax 425-8988
Other Schools – See Elgin, Kershaw, Lugoff

Camden Military Academy 300/7-12
520 Highway 1 N 29020 803-432-6001
Eric Boland, hdmstr. Fax 425-1020

Campobello, Spartanburg, Pop. 464
Spartanburg SD 1 4,500/K-12
PO Box 218 29322 864-468-4542
James Littlefield, supt. Fax 472-4118
www.spartanburg1.k12.sc.us/
Landrum HS 400/9-12
18818 Asheville Hwy 29322 864-457-2606
Susan Vasquez, prin. Fax 457-3148
Other Schools – See Inman, Landrum

Cayce, Lexington, Pop. 12,432
Lexington County SD 2
Supt. — See West Columbia
Brookland-Cayce HS 1,200/9-12
1300 State St 29033 803-791-5000
Scott Newman, prin. Fax 739-4970
Busbee Creative Arts Academy 400/6-8
501 Bulldog Blvd 29033 803-739-4070
Angela Burns, prin. Fax 739-4133

Columbia Beauty School Post-Sec.
1824 Airport Blvd 29033 803-796-5252

Central, Pickens, Pop. 4,039
Pickens County SD
Supt. — See Easley
Daniel HS 1,000/9-12
1819 Six Mile Hwy 29630 864-624-4430
Sharon Huff, prin. Fax 624-4428
Edwards MS 800/6-8
1157 Madden Bridge Rd 29630 864-624-4423
Mike Sanders, prin. Fax 624-4426

Southern Wesleyan University Post-Sec.
PO Box 1020 29630 864-644-5000

Chapin, Lexington, Pop. 676
Lexington/Richland Counties SD 5
Supt. — See Irmo
Chapin HS 1,100/9-12
300 Columbia Ave 29036 803-345-2246
Mike Satterfield, prin. Fax 345-7111
Chapin MS 800/6-8
1130 Old Lexington Hwy 29036 803-345-1466
Jane Crawford, prin. Fax 345-7117

Charleston, Charleston, Pop. 106,712
Charleston County SD 39,000/PK-12
75 Calhoun St Fl 2 29401 843-937-6300
Dr. Maria Goodloe-Johnson, supt. Fax 937-6307
www.ccsdschools.com/
Academic Magnet HS 500/9-12
1525 Avenue B S 29405 843-746-1300
Michael Tolley, prin. Fax 746-1310
Birney MS 800/6-8
7750 Pinehurst St 29420 843-764-2212
Robert Cook, prin. Fax 569-5466
Burke HS 700/9-12
244 President St 29403 843-579-4815
Charles Benton, prin. Fax 579-4855
Burke MS 6-8
244 President St 29403 843-579-4352
Blondell Gadsden, prin. Fax 579-4347
Ft. Johnson MS 500/6-8
1825 Camp Rd 29412 843-762-2740
David Parler, prin. Fax 762-6212
James Island MS 600/6-8
1484 Camp Rd 29412 843-762-2784
Phillip Davie, prin. Fax 762-6209
St. Andrews MS 400/6-8
721 Wappoo Rd 29407 843-763-1533
Benjamin Bragg, prin. Fax 763-1599
Toole Military Magnet S 500/6-11
2950 Carner Ave 29405 843-745-7102
Anderson Townsend, prin. Fax 566-7791
West Ashley HS 2,100/9-12
4060 Wildcat Blvd 29414 843-573-1201
Bob Olson, prin. Fax 573-1223
West Ashley MS 800/7-8
1776 Kennerty Dr 29407 843-763-1546
Jennifer Coker, prin. Fax 852-6557
Williams MS 700/5-8
640 Butte St 29414 843-763-1529
Judith Peterson, prin. Fax 763-5955
Other Schools – See Hollywood, Johns Island, Mc Clellanville, Mount Pleasant, North Charleston

---

Academy of Cosmetology Post-Sec.
5117 Dorchester Rd 29418 843-552-3241
Ashley Hall 700/PK-12
172 Rutledge Ave 29403 843-722-4088
Jill Muti, hdmstr. Fax 720-2868
Bishop England HS 900/9-12
363 Seven Farms Dr 29492 843-849-9599
David Held, prin. Fax 849-9221
Cathedral Academy 300/PK-12
PO Box 41129 29423 843-760-1192
Donna Lewis, admin. Fax 760-1197
Charleston Cosmetology Institute Post-Sec.
8484 Dorchester Rd 29420 843-552-3670
Charleston Southern University Post-Sec.
PO Box 118087 29423 800-947-7474
College of Charleston Post-Sec.
66 George St 29424 843-953-5500
First Baptist Church S 500/K-12
48 Meeting St 29401 843-722-6646
Thomas E. Mullins, hdmstr. Fax 720-2521
James Island Christian S 300/PK-12
15 Crosscreek Dr 29412 843-795-1762
William Smith, hdmstr. Fax 762-1619
Medical University of South Carolina Post-Sec.
PO Box 250402 29425 843-792-2300
Northside Christian S 500/PK-12
7800 Northside Dr 29420 843-797-2690
Dr. Cecil Beach, admin. Fax 797-7402
Porter-Gaud S 900/K-12
300 Albemarle Rd 29407 843-556-3620
Liza Lee, hdmstr. Fax 769-9926
The Citadel Post-Sec.
171 Moultrie St 29409 843-953-5000
Trident Technical College Post-Sec.
PO Box 118067 29423 843-574-6111

Cheraw, Chesterfield, Pop. 5,474
Chesterfield County SD
Supt. — See Chesterfield
Cheraw HS 900/9-12
649 Chesterfield Hwy 29520 843-921-1000
Dr. Henry Cobb, prin. Fax 921-1006
Long MS 700/6-8
1010 W Greene St 29520 843-921-1010
Dannie Blair, prin. Fax 921-1017

Jesus is Lord Christian S 200/PK-12
PO Box 639 29520 843-537-2033
Glenda Kimrey, admin. Fax 537-5055

Northeastern Technical College Post-Sec.
PO Box 1007 29520 843-921-6900

Chesnee, Spartanburg, Pop. 1,022
Spartanburg SD 2
Supt. — See Boiling Springs
Chesnee HS 600/9-12
795 S Alabama Ave 29323 864-461-7318
Thomas Ezell, prin. Fax 461-4137
Chesnee MS 500/6-8
805 S Alabama Ave 29323 864-461-3900
Dale Campbell, prin. Fax 461-3950

Chester, Chester, Pop. 6,199
Chester County SD 5,900/K-12
109 Hinton St 29706 803-385-6122
Larry Heath, supt. Fax 581-0863
www.chester.k12.sc.us/
Chester County Career Center Vo/Tech
1324 J A Cochran Byp 29706 803-377-1991
Lee Green, prin. Fax 581-0912
Chester HS 900/9-12
1330 J A Cochran Byp 29706 803-377-3161
Curtis Dunbar, prin. Fax 581-2363
Chester MS 900/6-8
1014 McCandless Rd 29706 803-377-8192
Steven Cummings, prin. Fax 581-1875
Other Schools – See Great Falls, Richburg

Chesterfield, Chesterfield, Pop. 1,338
Chesterfield County SD 7,800/K-12
401 West Blvd 29709 843-623-2175
Dr. John Williams, supt. Fax 623-3434
www.chesterfield.k12.sc.us
Chesterfield HS 500/9-12
401 N Page St 29709 843-623-2161
Scott Radkin, prin. Fax 623-2050
Chesterfield-Ruby MS 400/6-8
14445 Highway 9 29709 843-623-9401
Dr. Andrea Hampton, prin. Fax 623-9429
Other Schools – See Cheraw, Jefferson, Mc Bee, Pageland

Clemson, Pickens, Pop. 12,364

Clemson University Post-Sec.
105 Sikes Hall 29634 864-656-3311

Clinton, Laurens, Pop. 9,071
Laurens SD 56 3,300/K-12
600 E Florida St 29325 864-833-0800
John Taylor, supt. Fax 833-0804
www.laurens56.k12.sc.us
Bell Street MS 600/7-8
600 Peachtree St 29325 864-833-0807
Maureen Tiller, prin. Fax 833-0810
Clinton HS 1,000/9-12
800 N Adair St 29325 864-833-0817
Dr. A. Keith Bridges, prin. Fax 833-0825

Presbyterian College Post-Sec.
503 S Broad St 29325 864-833-8230

Clover, York, Pop. 4,251
Clover SD 2 5,400/PK-12
604 Bethel St 29710 803-222-7191
Vicki Phelps, supt. Fax 222-8010
www.clover2.k12.sc.us
Clover HS 1,500/9-12
1625 Highway 55 E 29710 803-222-4591
Ron Wright, prin. Fax 222-8021
Clover JHS 900/7-8
1555 Highway 55 E 29710 803-222-4521
Ron Thompson, prin. Fax 222-8034

Columbia, Richland, Pop. 117,088
Lexington/Richland Counties SD 5
Supt. — See Irmo
Irmo HS 1,900/9-12
6671 Saint Andrews Rd 29212 803-732-8100
Eddie Walker, prin. Fax 732-8110
Irmo MS 1,100/7-8
6051 Wescott Rd 29212 803-732-8200
Marie Waldrop, prin. Fax 732-8208

Richland SD 1 25,900/PK-12
1616 Richland St 29201 803-231-7000
Dr. Allen Coles, supt. Fax 231-7505
www.richlandone.org/
Alcorn MS 500/6-8
5125 Fairfield Rd 29203 803-735-3439
Anthony Graham, prin. Fax 735-3487
Columbia HS 800/9-12
1701 Westchester Dr 29210 803-731-8950
Dr. Sean Alford, prin. Fax 731-8953
Crayton MS 1,100/6-8
5000 Clemson Ave 29206 803-738-7224
Susan Childs, prin. Fax 738-7901
Dreher HS 1,200/9-12
701 Adger Rd 29205 803-253-7000
Jeanne Stiglbauer, prin. Fax 253-7007
Eau Claire HS 1,000/9-12
4800 Monticello Rd 29203 803-735-7600
Rodney Zimmerman, prin. Fax 735-7629
Flora HS 1,800/9-12
100 Falcon Dr 29204 803-738-7300
Richard McClure, prin. Fax 738-7307
Gibbes MS 400/6-8
3602 Thurmond St 29204 803-343-2942
Rick Coleman, prin. Fax 733-3040
Hand MS 1,000/6-8
2600 Wheat St 29205 803-343-2947
Marisa Vickers, prin. Fax 733-6173
Heyward Career & Technology Center Vo/Tech
3560 Lynhaven Dr 29204 803-735-3343
Sherry Rivers, prin. Fax 691-4253
Johnson Preparatory Academy 600/9-12
2219 Barhamville Rd 29204 803-253-7092
Dr. Kathie Greer, prin. Fax 253-5713

Keenan HS 900/9-12
3455 Pine Belt Rd 29204 803-738-7232
Dr. Steve Wilson, prin. Fax 738-7589
Perry MS 400/6-8
2600 Barhamville Rd 29204 803-256-6347
Demetria Clemons, prin. Fax 255-2262
St. Andrews MS 900/6-8
1231 Blue Field Dr 29210 803-731-8910
Ken Richardson, prin. Fax 731-8913
Sanders MS 600/6-8
136 Alida St 29203 803-735-3445
Andrenna Smith, prin. Fax 735-3679
Adult & Community Education Adult
2612 Covenant Rd 29204 803-343-2935
Ericka Hursey, dir. Fax 212-1453
Other Schools – See Hopkins

Richland SD 2 20,500/PK-12
6831 Brookfield Rd 29206 803-787-1910
Stephen W. Hefner Ed.D., supt. Fax 738-7393
www.richland2.org
Dent MS 1,200/6-8
2721 Decker Blvd 29206 803-699-2750
Randall Gary, prin. Fax 699-2754
Richland Northeast HS 1,600/9-12
7500 Brookfield Rd 29223 803-699-2800
Ralph Schmidt, prin. Fax 699-3679
Ridge View HS 2,300/9-12
4801 Hard Scrabble Rd 29229 803-699-2999
Dr. Marty Martin, prin. Fax 699-2888
Spring Valley HS 2,000/9-12
120 Sparkleberry Ln 29229 803-699-3500
Dr. Greg Owings, prin. Fax 699-3541
Summit Parkway MS 1,000/6-8
200 Summit Pkwy 29229 803-699-3580
Sig Tanner, prin. Fax 699-3682
Wright MS 1,300/6-8
2740 Alpine Rd 29223 803-736-8740
Lori Marrero, prin. Fax 736-8798
Rogers Adult Continuing Center Adult
750 Old Clemson Rd 29229 803-736-8787
Curtis Watson, prin. Fax 736-8785
Other Schools – See Blythewood

Allen University Post-Sec.
1530 Harden St 29204 803-376-5701
Baptist Medical Center Post-Sec.
1519 Marion St 29201 803-771-5042
Benedict College Post-Sec.
1600 Harden St 29204 803-256-4220
Beta Tech Post-Sec.
7500 Two Notch Rd 29223 803-754-7544
Cardinal Newman HS 400/7-12
4701 Forest Dr 29206 803-782-2814
Jacquie Kasprowski, prin. Fax 782-9314
Columbia Biblical Seminary Post-Sec.
PO Box 3122 29230 800-845-2721
Columbia College Post-Sec.
1301 Columbia College Dr 29203 803-786-3871
Columbia International University Post-Sec.
PO Box 3122 29230 803-754-4100
Covenant Christian S 200/PK-12
2801 Stepp Dr 29204 803-787-0225
T. Chris Crain, hdmstr. Fax 782-7309
ECPI College of Technology Post-Sec.
250 Berryhill Rd Ste 300 29210 803-772-3333
Hammond S 1,000/PK-12
854 Galway Ln 29209 803-776-0295
Adam de Pencier, prin. Fax 776-0122
Heathwood Hall Episcopal S 900/PK-12
3000 S Beltline Blvd 29201 803-765-2309
Stephen Hickman, hdmstr. Fax 748-4755
Kenneth Shuler's School of Cosmetology Post-Sec.
449 Saint Andrews Rd 29210 803-772-6042
Lippen Middle and HS 500/6-12
PO Box 3999 29230 803-786-7200
Les Lehman, prin. Fax 744-1387
Lutheran Theological Southern Seminary Post-Sec.
4201 Main St 29203 803-786-5150
Midlands Technical College Post-Sec.
PO Box 2408 29202 803-738-8324
Sloans S 200/K-12
171 Starlight Dr 29210 803-772-1677
Southeastern School of Neuromuscular Post-Sec.
1420 Colonial Life Blvd #80 29210 803-798-8800
South University Post-Sec.
9 Science Ct 29203 800-688-0932
Strayer University Post-Sec.
200 Center Point Cir # 300 29210 803-750-2500
University of South Carolina 29208 Post-Sec.
803-777-7700
W.L. Bonner Bible College Post-Sec.
4430 Argent Ct 29203 803-754-3950

Conway, Horry, Pop. 13,442
Horry County SD 31,800/PK-12
PO Box 260005 29528 843-488-6700
Dr. Bobby Nalley, supt. Fax 488-6722
www.hcs.k12.sc.us
Academy for Technology and Academics Vo/Tech
5639 Highway 701 N 29526 843-488-6600
David Stoudenmire, prin. Fax 488-6601
Black Water MS 6-8
900 E Cox Ferry Rd 29526 843-903-8440
Connie Huddle, prin. Fax 903-8441
Conway HS 1,500/9-12
2301 Church St 29526 843-488-0662
Porter Kennington, prin. Fax 488-0686
Conway MS 600/6-8
1104 Elm St 29526 843-488-6040
Mary Clark, prin. Fax 488-0611
Early College HS 9-12
2050 E Highway 501 29526 843-349-7102
Joan Grimmett, dir. Fax 349-7895
Scholars Academy 9-12
215 University Hall 29526 843-349-4117
Anita Huggins, prin. Fax 349-6144
Whittemore Park MS 700/6-8
1808 Rhue St 29527 843-488-0669
Robbie Watkins, prin. Fax 488-0669
Other Schools – See Aynor, Galivants Ferry, Green Sea, Little River, Loris, Murrells Inlet, Myrtle Beach

---

Coastal Carolina University Post-Sec.
PO Box 261954 29528 843-347-3161
Conway Christian S 300/K-12
PO Box 1245 29528 843-365-2005
Connie Smith, prin. Fax 365-2021
Horry-Georgetown Technical College Post-Sec.
PO Box 261966 29528 843-349-5277

Cope, Orangeburg, Pop. 103
Orangeburg Consolidated SD 4 4,200/PK-12
PO Box 68 29038 803-534-8081
Darrell Johnson, supt. Fax 531-5614
www.orangeburg4.com
Cope Area Career Center Vo/Tech
PO Box 128 29038 803-534-7661
Sandra Jameson, prin. Fax 535-4301
Other Schools – See Branchville, Cordova, Neeses

Cordova, Orangeburg, Pop. 147
Orangeburg Consolidated SD 4
Supt. — See Cope
Carver-Edisto MS 700/6-8
PO Box 65 29039 803-536-0231
Chris Nettles, prin. Fax 535-0934
Edisto HS 900/9-12
PO Box 101 29039 803-534-0098
Baron Davis, prin. Fax 531-5615

Cowpens, Spartanburg, Pop. 2,330
Spartanburg SD 3
Supt. — See Glendale
Cowpens MS 500/6-8
150 Foster St 29330 864-463-3310
Rodney Goode, prin. Fax 463-3306

Cross, Berkeley
Berkeley County SD
Supt. — See Moncks Corner
Cross JSHS 500/7-12
1293 Old Highway 6 29436 843-899-8900
Robb Streeter, prin. Fax 899-8910

Dalzell, Sumter
Sumter SD 2
Supt. — See Sumter
Hillcrest MS 500/6-8
PO Box 151 29040 803-499-3341
Robert Barth, prin. Fax 499-3353

Sumter Academy 600/PK-12
PO Box 869 29040 803-499-3378
Dr. Robert Mayfield, hdmstr. Fax 499-3391

Darlington, Darlington, Pop. 6,525
Darlington County SD 10,200/K-12
PO Box 1117 29540 843-398-5100
Dr. Rainey Knight, supt. Fax 398-5207
www.darlington.k12.sc.us
Darlington Co. Institute of Technology Vo/Tech
160 Pinedale Dr 29532 843-398-4796
Bert Guerry, dir. Fax 398-3500
Darlington HS 1,100/9-12
525 Spring St 29532 843-398-5140
Pearl Jeffords, prin. Fax 398-2739
Darlington MS 900/6-8
150 Pinedale Dr 29532 843-398-5088
Carlita Davis, prin. Fax 398-3390
Mayo HS for Math Science & Technology 300/9-12
405 Chestnut St 29532 843-398-5050
Arlene Johnson, prin. Fax 398-2647
Other Schools – See Hartsville, Lamar

Trinity Collegiate S 100/7-12
5001 Hoffmeyer Rd 29532 843-395-9124
Dr. Robert Vito, hdmstr. Fax 395-6495

Denmark, Bamberg, Pop. 3,130
Bamberg SD 2 1,000/PK-12
62 Holly Ave 29042 803-793-3346
Sacaida Howell Ph.D., supt. Fax 793-2006
www.bamberg2.org/
Denmark-Olar HS 300/9-12
PO Box 98 29042 803-793-3307
Hughie Peterson, prin. Fax 793-2004
Denmark-Olar MS 200/6-8
PO Box 383 29042 803-793-3383
Gwendolyn Harris, prin. Fax 793-2038

Denmark Technical College Post-Sec.
PO Box 327 29042 803-793-5149
Voorhees College Post-Sec.
Voorhees Rd 29042 803-793-3351

Dillon, Dillon, Pop. 6,366
Area Vocational Schools
Supt. — None
Dillon County Applied Tech. Center Vo/Tech
PO Box 1130 29536 843-774-5143
Jerry Strickland, prin. Fax 774-7711

Dillon SD 2 3,700/PK-12
405 W Washington St 29536 843-774-1200
D. Ray Rogers, supt. Fax 774-1203
www.dillon2.k12.sc.us
Dillon HS 900/9-12
1730 Highway 301 N 29536 843-774-1230
Dr. Julia Von Frank, prin. Fax 774-1234
Martin JHS 600/7-8
301 Martin Luther King Jr 29536 843-774-1212
Danny Price, prin. Fax 841-3616

Dillon Christian S 400/K-12
PO Box 151 29536 843-841-1000
Dr. David Bult, hdmstr. Fax 841-0810

Dorchester, Dorchester
Area Vocational Schools
Supt. — None
Dorchester County Career S Vo/Tech
507 Schoolhouse Rd 29437 800-454-8101
James Villeponteaux, prin. Fax 563-9038
Other Schools – See Blackville SC, Dillon SC, Manning SC, Marion SC, Ridgeland SC, Sumter SC, Williamston SC

Dorchester SD 4
Supt. — See Saint George
Woodland HS 700/9-12
4128 Highway 78 29437 843-563-5956
James Peterson, prin. Fax 563-5997

Due West, Abbeville, Pop. 1,287
Abbeville County SD
Supt. — See Abbeville
Dixie HS 400/8-12
PO Box 158 29639 864-379-2186
Tracy Carter, prin. Fax 379-8187

Erskine College & Seminary Post-Sec.
PO Box 176 29639 864-379-8838

Duncan, Spartanburg, Pop. 2,977
Spartanburg SD 5 6,400/K-12
PO Box 307 29334 864-949-2350
Scott Turner, supt. Fax 439-0051
www.spart5.k12.sc.us
Byrnes HS 1,800/9-12
PO Box 187 29334 864-949-2355
Jeff Rogers, prin. Fax 949-2362
Florence Chapel MS 600/7-8
290 Shoals Rd 29334 864-949-2310
Steve Gambrell, prin. Fax 949-2315
Hill MS 600/7-8
PO Box 277 29334 864-949-2370
Terry Glasgow, prin. Fax 949-2369

Easley, Pickens, Pop. 18,852
Pickens County SD 16,100/K-12
1348 Griffin Mill Rd 29640 864-855-8150
Dr. Lee D'Andrea, supt. Fax 855-8159
www.pickens.k12.sc.us
Dacusville MS 400/6-8
899 Thomas Mill Rd 29640 864-859-6049
Ellen Smith, prin. Fax 850-2094
Easley HS 1,500/9-12
PO Box 129 29641 864-855-8180
Betty Garrison, prin. Fax 855-8194
Gettys MS 1,400/6-8
105 Stewart Dr 29640 864-855-8170
Michael Corey, prin. Fax 855-6413
Skelton Career Center Vo/Tech
1400 Griffin Mill Rd 29640 864-855-8195
Leonard Williams, dir. Fax 855-8192
Pickens Lifelong Learning Adult Educ Adult
200 W D Ave 29640 864-855-8198
Mary Gaston, dir. Fax 850-8116
Other Schools – See Central, Liberty, Pickens

Landmark Christian Academy 100/K-12
116 Landmark Ct 29640 864-859-0793
Jeremy Hodge, prin.
Siloam Christian S 400/PK-12
229 Siloam Rd 29642 864-295-6949
Tim Cockrell, admin. Fax 295-4179

Elgin, Kershaw, Pop. 954
Kershaw County SD
Supt. — See Camden
Stover MS 600/6-8
PO Box 1200 29045 803-438-7414
Dennis Reeder, prin. Fax 438-7014

Elliott, Lee
Lee County SD
Supt. — See Bishopville
Mt. Pleasant MS 400/6-8
PO Box 177 29046 803-428-3610
Linda Norton, prin. Fax 428-3656

Estill, Hampton, Pop. 2,394
Hampton SD 2 1,400/K-12
PO Box 1028 29918 803-625-5000
Dennis Thompson, supt. Fax 625-2573
www.hampton2.k12.sc.us
Estill HS 400/9-12
PO Box 757 29918 803-625-5100
George Yeldell, prin. Fax 625-4695
Estill MS 400/6-8
PO Box 817 29918 803-625-5200
Dr. Fayette Nick, prin. Fax 625-3588

Henry Academy 300/PK-12
8766 Savannah Hwy 29918 803-625-2440
Dr. Terry D. King, hdmstr. Fax 625-3110

Fairfax, Allendale, Pop. 3,178
Allendale County SD
Supt. — See Allendale
Allendale-Fairfax HS 400/9-12
3581 Allendale Fairfax Hwy 29827 803-584-2311
James Jones, prin. Fax 584-1787
Allendale-Fairfax MS 400/6-8
3581 Allendale Fairfax Hwy 29827 803-584-3489
Clarence Jackson, prin. Fax 584-5331

Florence, Florence, Pop. 31,269
Florence SD 1 14,700/K-12
319 S Dargan St 29506 843-669-4141
Larry Jackson, supt. Fax 673-1108
www.fsd1.org

Florence Career Ctr — Vo/Tech
126 E Howe Springs Rd 29505 — 843-664-8465
Alphonso Bradley, prin. — Fax 413-4688
Sneed MS — 900/7-8
1102 S Ebenezer Rd 29501 — 843-673-1199
Tony Lunsford, prin. — Fax 679-6890
South Florence HS — 1,500/9-12
3200 S Irby St 29505 — 843-664-8190
Neal Vincent, prin. — Fax 664-8184
Southside MS — 1,000/7-8
200 E Howe Springs Rd 29505 — 843-664-8467
Erik Lowry, prin. — Fax 673-5766
West Florence HS — 1,600/9-12
221 N Beltline Dr 29501 — 843-664-8472
Pamela Quick, prin. — Fax 664-8475
Williams MS — 800/7-8
1119 N Irby St 29501 — 843-664-8162
Leon McCray, prin. — Fax 664-8178
Wilson HS — 1,300/9-12
1411 E Old Marion Hwy 29506 — 843-664-8440
Gerard Edwards, prin. — Fax 664-8176

Byrnes Schools — 300/PK-12
1201 E Ashby Rd 29506 — 843-662-0131
William Bugg, hdmstr. — Fax 669-2466
Christian Assembly S — 200/K-12
401 Pamplico Hwy 29505 — 843-667-1975
Audrey Streit, prin. — Fax 664-0389
Florence Christian S — 700/PK-12
PO Box 12809 29504 — 843-662-0454
Jim Berry, prin. — Fax 661-4301
Florence-Darlington Technical College — Post-Sec.
PO Box 100548 29501 — 843-661-8324
Francis Marion University — Post-Sec.
PO Box 100547 29501 — 843-661-1362
King's Academy — 300/K-12
1015 S Ebenezer Rd 29501 — 843-661-7464
Karen Rainwater, prin. — Fax 661-7647
Maranatha Christian S — 300/PK-12
2624 W Palmetto St 29501 — 843-665-6395
Chad Reel, prin. — Fax 629-0510
McLeod Regional Medical Center — Post-Sec.
555 E Cheves St 29506 — 843-667-2297

Fort Mill, York, Pop. 8,257
Lancaster County SD
Supt. — See Lancaster
Indian Land HS — 400/9-12
8361 Charlotte Hwy, — 803-547-7571
Kathy Faris, prin. — Fax 547-7366

York SD 4 — 6,900/K-12
120 E Elliott St 29715 — 803-548-2527
Dr. V. Keith Callicutt, supt. — Fax 547-4696
www.fort-mill.k12.sc.us
Fort Mill HS — 2,100/9-12
225 Munn Rd E 29715 — 803-548-1900
Dee Christopher, prin. — Fax 548-1911
Fort Mill MS — 700/6-8
200 Springfield Pkwy 29715 — 803-547-5553
Tommy Schmolze, prin. — Fax 548-2911
Gold Hill MS — 900/6-8
1025 Dave Gibson Blvd 29708 — 803-548-8300
Tommy Johnston, prin. — Fax 548-8322
Springfield MS — 6-8
1711 Springfield Pkwy 29715 — 803-548-8199
Keith Griffin, prin. — Fax 547-1013

Fountain Inn, Greenville, Pop. 6,729

Pleasant Grove Christian Academy — 100/PK-12
1269 S Frontage Rd 29644 — 864-862-7793
Dr. George Hopson, admin. — Fax 862-0198

Gaffney, Cherokee, Pop. 12,934
Cherokee SD — 9,100/PK-12
PO Box 460 29342 — 864-902-3500
Dr. William B. James, supt. — Fax 902-3541
www.cherokee1.k12.sc.us
Cherokee Technology Center — Vo/Tech
3206 Cherokee Ave 29340 — 864-489-3191
Ray Bedford, prin. — Fax 487-1287
Ewing MS — 600/6-8
171 E Junior High Rd 29340 — 864-489-3176
Amanda Burnette, prin. — Fax 489-8534
Gaffney HS — 2,100/9-12
149 Twin Lake Rd 29341 — 864-902-3600
Quincie Moore, prin. — Fax 902-3628
Gaffney MS — 700/6-8
805 E Frederick St 29340 — 864-902-3630
Herman Thompson, prin. — Fax 902-3637
Granard MS — 500/6-8
815 W Rutledge Ave 29341 — 864-489-6833
Charles Wright, prin. — Fax 488-1553
Limestone Learning Center - Adult — Adult
130 Leadmine St 29340 — 864-487-7152
Lisa Hanron, prin. — Fax 487-1260
Other Schools – See Blacksburg

Limestone College — Post-Sec.
1115 College Dr 29340 — 864-489-7151

Galivants Ferry, Horry
Horry County SD
Supt. — See Conway
Aynor MS — 500/6-9
400 Frye Rd 29544 — 843-358-6000
Milton Frink, prin. — Fax 358-5065

Gaston, Lexington, Pop. 1,389
Lexington County SD 4
Supt. — See Swansea
Sandhills MS — 600/7-8
582 Meadowfield Rd 29053 — 803-926-1890
Angie Rye, prin. — Fax 926-1910

Georgetown, Georgetown, Pop. 8,941
Georgetown County SD — 10,500/PK-12
2018 Church St 29440 — 843-436-7000
Dr. Randy Dozier, supt. — Fax 436-7171
www.gcsd.k12.sc.us
Georgetown HS — 1,100/9-12
2500 Anthuan Maybank St 29440 — 843-546-8516
Dr. Mike Cafaro, prin. — Fax 546-8521
Georgetown MS — 900/6-8
2400 Anthuan Maybank St 29440 — 843-527-4495
Rosemary Gray, prin. — Fax 527-2290
Other Schools – See Andrews, Hemingway, Pawleys Island

Gilbert, Lexington, Pop. 552
Lexington County SD 1
Supt. — See Lexington
Gilbert HS — 800/9-12
840 Main St 29054 — 803-892-1100
Paul Shealy, prin. — Fax 892-1133
Gilbert MS — 700/6-8
120 Rikard Cir 29054 — 803-892-1050
Benji Ricard, prin. — Fax 892-1067

Glendale, Spartanburg
Spartanburg SD 3 — 3,100/K-12
PO Box 267 29346 — 864-579-8000
Dr. Jim Ray, supt. — Fax 579-8005
www.spa3.k12.sc.us
Other Schools – See Cowpens, Pacolet, Spartanburg

Goose Creek, Berkeley, Pop. 32,516
Berkeley County SD
Supt. — See Moncks Corner
Goose Creek HS — 1,700/9-12
1137 Red Bank Rd 29445 — 843-553-5300
John Fulmer, prin. — Fax 820-4064
Marrington MS — 200/5-8
109 Gearing St 29445 — 843-572-0313
Arnold Coull, prin. — Fax 820-4063
Sedgefield MS — 1,000/6-8
131 Charles B Gibson Blvd 29445 — 843-797-2620
Don Brown, prin. — Fax 820-5401
Stratford HS — 2,800/9-12
951 Crowfield Blvd 29445 — 843-820-4000
Jim Spencer, prin. — Fax 820-4042
Westview MS — 1,200/6-8
101 Westview Dr 29445 — 843-572-1700
Rex Whitcomb, prin. — Fax 820-3728

Graniteville, Aiken
Aiken County SD
Supt. — See Aiken
Leavelle-McCampbell MS — 500/6-8
82 Canal St 29829 — 803-663-4300
Al Lamback, prin. — Fax 663-4302
Midland Valley HS — 1,200/9-12
227 Mustang Dr 29829 — 803-593-7100
Dr. Doris Hickson, prin. — Fax 593-7106

Gray Court, Laurens, Pop. 1,005
Laurens SD 55
Supt. — See Laurens
Gray Court-Owings S — 500/3-8
PO Box 187 29645 — 864-876-2171
Marilyn Ramsey, prin. — Fax 876-2965
Hickory Tavern MS — 400/6-8
163 Neely Ferry Rd 29645 — 864-575-4301
Russell Scott, prin. — Fax 575-4305

Great Falls, Chester, Pop. 2,095
Chester County SD
Supt. — See Chester
Great Falls HS — 300/9-12
411 Sunset Ave 29055 — 803-482-2210
Howard Rheiner, prin. — Fax 482-4896
Great Falls MS — 300/5-8
409 Sunset Ave 29055 — 803-482-2220
Wendell Sumter, prin. — Fax 482-6025

Greeleyville, Williamsburg, Pop. 419
Williamsburg County SD
Supt. — See Kingstree
Murray JSHS — 600/7-12
PO Box 188 29056 — 843-426-2121
Sam Giles, prin. — Fax 426-2151

Green Sea, Horry
Horry County SD
Supt. — See Conway
Green Sea-Floyds JSHS — 600/7-12
5625 Highway 9 29545 — 843-392-3131
Chip Hennecy, prin. — Fax 392-9805

Greenville, Greenville, Pop. 56,676
Anderson SD 1
Supt. — See Williamston
Powdersville MS — 500/6-8
135 Hood Rd 29611 — 864-269-1821
Monty Oxendine, prin. — Fax 269-0795

Greenville County SD — 62,600/PK-12
PO Box 2848 29602 — 864-355-3100
Dr. Phinnize Fisher, supt. — Fax 241-4195
www.greenville.k12.sc.us/
Beck Academy — 600/6-8
901 Woodruff Rd 29607 — 864-241-3268
Dr. J. Brodie Bricker, prin. — Fax 241-3282
Berea HS — 1,100/9-12
201 Burdine Dr 29617 — 864-355-1600
Bill Roach, prin. — Fax 355-1625
Berea MS — 900/6-8
151 Berea Middle School Rd 29617 — 864-355-1700
Dr. Judy Davis, prin. — Fax 355-1777
Carolina Academy — 700/9-12
2725 Anderson Rd 29611 — 864-355-2300
Lillie Lewis, prin. — Fax 355-7375
Donaldson Career Center — Vo/Tech
100 Vocational Dr 29605 — 864-355-4650
Cheryl McClure, prin. — Fax 355-4683
Enoree Career Center — Vo/Tech
108 Scalybark Rd 29617 — 864-355-7400
Fax 355-7407
Fine Arts Center — 11-12
102 Pine Knoll Dr 29609 — 864-241-3327
Dr. Roy Fluhrer, prin. — Fax 241-3502
Golden Strip Career Ctr — Vo/Tech
1120 E Butler Rd 29607 — 864-355-1050
Leroy Elrod, prin. — Fax 355-1058
Greenville Academy — 800/6-8
100 Blassingame Rd 29605 — 864-241-3360
Dr. Robert Palmer, prin. — Fax 241-3366
Greenville Academy — 1,300/9-12
1 Vardry St 29601 — 864-241-3220
Dalton Lucas, prin. — Fax 241-3227
Hampton HS — 1,200/9-12
100 Pine Knoll Dr 29609 — 864-355-0100
Lance Radford, prin. — Fax 355-0194
Hughes Academy — 1,000/6-8
122 Deoyley Ave 29605 — 864-355-6200
Dr. Lorraine Watson, prin. — Fax 355-6275
League Academy — 800/6-8
125 Twin Lake Rd 29609 — 864-292-7688
Merry Cox, prin. — Fax 292-8681
Mann Academy — 1,300/9-12
61 Isbell Ln 29607 — 864-281-1150
Susan Hughes, prin. — Fax 281-1173
Sevier MS — 600/6-8
1004 Piedmont Park Rd 29609 — 864-355-8200
Karen Kapp, prin. — Fax 355-8255
Southside HS — 800/9-12
6630 Frontage Rd 29605 — 864-299-8393
Paulette Payne, prin. — Fax 299-8395
Tanglewood MS — 600/6-8
44 Merriwoods Dr 29611 — 864-355-4500
Dennis Dotterer, prin. — Fax 355-4512
Adult Education/Lifelong Learning — Adult
206 Wilkins St 29605 — 864-241-3388
Dr. Chuck Welch, prin. — Fax 241-3548
Other Schools – See Greer, Mauldin, Piedmont, Simpsonville, Taylors, Travelers Rest

---

Academy of Hair Technology — Post-Sec.
3715 E North St Ste F 29615 — 864-322-0300
Bob Jones University — Post-Sec.
1700 Wade Hampton Blvd 29614 — 864-242-5100
Christ Church Episcopal S — 1,000/K-12
245 Cavalier Dr 29607 — 864-299-1522
Dr. Leland H. Cox, dir. — Fax 299-8094
ECPI College of Technology — Post-Sec.
1001 Keys Dr # 100 29615 — 864-288-2828
Furman University — Post-Sec.
3300 Poinsett Hwy 29613 — 864-294-2000
Greenville Technical College — Post-Sec.
PO Box 5616 29606 — 864-250-8000
Hampton Park Christian S — 800/K-12
875 State Park Rd 29609 — 864-233-0556
Bruce Mizell, admin. — Fax 235-5621
ITT Technical Institute — Post-Sec.
6 Independence Pt 29615 — 864-288-0777
Jones Academy — 500/9-12
1700 Wade Hampton Blvd 29614 — 864-242-5100
Dr. Sid Cates, prin. — Fax 271-7278
Jones JHS — 300/7-8
1700 Wade Hampton Blvd 29614 — 864-770-1393
Fax 271-7278
St. Joseph's HS — 300/9-12
100 Saint Josephs Dr 29607 — 864-234-9009
Keith Kiser, hdmstr. — Fax 234-5516
Shannon Forest Christian S — 600/PK-12
829 Garlington Rd 29615 — 864-678-5107
Brenda Hillman, hdmstr. — Fax 281-9372

Greenwood, Greenwood, Pop. 22,378
Greenwood SD 50 — 9,100/K-12
PO Box 248 29648 — 864-941-5400
Darrell Johnson, supt. — Fax 941-5427
www.gwd50.k12.sc.us
Brewer MS, 1000 Emerald Rd 29646 — 600/6-8
Anthony Holland, prin. — 864-941-5500
Emerald HS, 150 Bypass 225 29646 — 900/9-12
Les Gamble, prin. — 864-941-5730
Greenwood HS — 1,700/9-12
1816 Cokesbury Rd 29649 — 864-941-5600
Beth Taylor, prin. — Fax 941-5498
Northside MS — 900/6-8
431 Deadfall Rd 29649 — 864-941-5780
Beth Pinson, prin. — Fax 941-3434
Russell Career Center — Vo/Tech
601 Northside Dr E 29649 — 864-941-5750
Charles Graves, prin.
Westview MS — 800/6-8
1410 W Alexander Ave 29646 — 864-941-5400
Cynthia Storer, prin.

Calvary Christian S — 100/K-12
2775 Montague Ext 29649 — 864-229-6553
Cindy Stanley, prin.
Cambridge Academy — 200/PK-12
103 Eastman St 29649 — 864-229-2875
Dr. R.J. Steeley, hdmstr. — Fax 229-6712
Greenwood Christian S — 400/PK-12
2026 Woodlawn Rd 29649 — 864-229-2427
Michael Edds, hdmstr. — Fax 943-0876
Lander University — Post-Sec.
320 Stanley Ave 29649 — 864-388-8000
Piedmont Technical College — Post-Sec.
PO Box 1467 29648 — 864-941-8324

Greer, Greenville, Pop. 21,421
Greenville County SD
Supt. — See Greenville
Blue Ridge HS — 1,100/8-12
2151 Fews Chapel Rd 29651 — 864-355-1800
Reena Watson, prin. — Fax 355-1821

Blue Ridge MS 900/6-8
2423 E Tyger Bridge Rd 29651 864-355-1900
Tony Poole, prin. Fax 355-1966
Bonds Career Center Vo/Tech
505 N Main St 29650 864-355-8080
Wayne Rhodes, prin. Fax 355-8264
Greer HS 1,200/9-12
3000 E Gap Creek Rd 29651 864-355-5700
Marion Waters, prin. Fax 355-5725
Greer MS 1,000/6-8
3032 E Gap Creek Rd 29651 864-355-5800
Rita Mantooth, prin. Fax 355-5880
Riverside HS 1,400/9-12
794 Hammett Bridge Rd 29650 864-355-7800
Andy Crowley, prin. Fax 355-7898
Riverside MS 1,000/6-8
615 Hammett Bridge Rd 29650 864-355-7900
Ron Harrison, prin. Fax 355-7918

Hanahan, Berkeley, Pop. 13,818
Berkeley County SD
Supt. — See Moncks Corner
Hanahan HS 800/9-12
6015 Murray Dr 29410 843-820-3710
Rodney Thompson, prin. Fax 820-3716
Hanahan MS 600/5-8
5815 Murray Dr 29410 843-820-3800
Robin Rogers, prin. Fax 820-3804

Hartsville, Darlington, Pop. 7,414
Darlington County SD
Supt. — See Darlington
Hartsville HS 1,400/9-12
701 Lewellyn Ave 29550 843-383-3130
Dr. Charlie Burry, prin. Fax 857-3715
Hartsville MS 900/6-8
1427 14th St 29550 843-383-3121
Chris Rogers, prin. Fax 857-4510

State Supported Schools
Supt. — None
Governers School Science/Math 11-12
401 Railroad Ave 29550 843-383-3900

Coker College Post-Sec.
300 E College Ave 29550 843-383-8000
Emmanuel Christian S 500/PK-12
1001 N Marquis Hwy 29550 843-332-0164
Randy Down, admin. Fax 878-0501

Hemingway, Williamsburg, Pop. 524
Georgetown County SD
Supt. — See Georgetown
Carvers Bay HS 500/9-12
13002 Choppee Rd 29554 843-545-5837
Daryl Brown, prin. Fax 558-6927
Carvers Bay MS 400/6-8
13000 Choppee Rd 29554 843-545-0918
Darryl Stanley, prin. Fax 558-6937

Williamsburg County SD
Supt. — See Kingstree
Hemingway AVC Vo/Tech
1593 Hemingway Hwy 29554 843-558-5813
John Gardner, prin. Fax 558-5991
Hemingway HS 400/9-12
PO Box 1509 29554 843-558-9413
Grady Richardson, prin. Fax 558-9335

Hilton Head Island, Beaufort, Pop. 34,497
Beaufort County SD
Supt. — See Beaufort
Hilton Head Island HS 1,200/9-12
70 Wilborn Rd 29926 843-689-4800
Amanda O'Nan, prin. Fax 689-4947
Hilton Head MS 1,000/6-8
55 Wilborn Rd 29926 843-689-4500
Sherry DeSimone, prin. Fax 689-4600

Hilton Head Christian Academy 500/K-12
55 Gardner Dr 29926 843-681-2878
Mike Lindsay, hdmstr. Fax 681-9758
Hilton Head Prep S 500/K-12
8 Foxgrape Rd 29928 843-671-2286
Susan Groesbeck, hdmstr. Fax 671-7624

Holly Hill, Orangeburg, Pop. 1,364
Orangeburg Consolidated SD 3 2,300/K-12
PO Box 98 29059 803-496-3288
David Longshore, supt. Fax 496-5850
www.obg3.k12.sc.us
Holly Hill-Roberts MS 700/6-8
PO Box 879 29059 803-496-3818
JoAnne Lawton, prin. Fax 496-7584
Other Schools – See Santee

Holly Hill Academy 400/K-12
PO Box 757 29059 803-496-3243
John Gasque, hdmstr. Fax 496-9778

Hollywood, Charleston, Pop. 4,307
Charleston County SD
Supt. — See Charleston
Baptist Hill HS 400/9-12
5117 Baptist Hill Rd 29449 843-889-2276
James Winbush, prin. Fax 889-2101
Schroder MS 400/6-8
7224 Highway 162 29449 843-889-2391
Raymond Davis, prin. Fax 889-6539

St. Paul's Academy 100/K-12
5139 Gibson Rd 29449 843-889-2702
Cliff Bell, prin. Fax 889-6290

Honea Path, Anderson, Pop. 3,597
Anderson SD 2 3,800/K-12
10990 Belton Honea Path Hwy 29654 864-369-7364
Thomas Chapman, supt. Fax 369-4006
www.anderson2.k12.sc.us
Belton-Honea Path HS 1,000/9-12
11000 Belton Honea Path Hwy 29654 864-369-7382
Jimmy Ouzts, prin. Fax 369-4011
Honea Path MS 400/5-8
107 Brock Ave 29654 864-369-7641
John Snead, prin. Fax 369-4034
Other Schools – See Belton

Hopkins, Richland
Richland SD 1
Supt. — See Columbia
Hopkins MS 600/6-8
1601 Clarkson Rd 29061 803-695-3331
Goler Collins, prin. Fax 695-3320
Lower Richland HS 1,600/9-12
2615 Lower Richland Blvd 29061 803-695-3000
Marvin Byers, prin. Fax 695-3062
Southeast MS 800/6-8
731 Horrell Hill Rd 29061 803-695-5700
Jeannetta Scott, prin. Fax 695-5703

Inman, Spartanburg, Pop. 1,918
Spartanburg SD 1
Supt. — See Campobello
Chapman HS 900/9-12
1420 Compton Bridge Rd 29349 864-472-2836
Dr. Ron Garner, prin. Fax 472-0914
Mabry JHS 400/7-8
10 W Miller St 29349 864-472-8402
Michael Blackwell, prin. Fax 472-7438
Swofford Career Center Vo/Tech
5620 Highway 11 29349 864-592-2790
Tommy Campbell, dir. Fax 592-1469

Spartanburg SD 2
Supt. — See Boiling Springs
Boiling Springs JHS 1,100/7-8
4801 Highway 9 29349 864-578-5954
Donald Barnette, prin. Fax 599-5489

Irmo, Richland, Pop. 11,223
Lexington/Richland Counties SD 5 16,500/PK-12
1020 Dutch Fork Rd 29063 803-732-8000
Dr. Scott Andersen, supt. Fax 732-8017
www.lex5.k12.sc.us
Dutch Fork HS 2,000/9-12
1400 Old Tamah Rd 29063 803-732-8050
Gregory Morton, prin. Fax 732-8064
Dutch Fork MS 1,100/7-8
1528 Old Tamah Rd 29063 803-732-8167
Roderic Taylor, prin. Fax 732-8171
Other Schools – See Chapin, Columbia

Islandton, Colleton

New Hope Christian S of Islandton 100/K-12
PO Box 55 29929 843-866-2608
Mark Givens, prin.

Iva, Anderson, Pop. 1,180
Anderson SD 3 2,700/K-12
PO Box 118 29655 864-348-6196
L. Hugh Smith, supt. Fax 348-6198
www.anderson3.k12.sc.us
Crescent HS 700/9-12
9104 Highway 81 S 29655 864-352-6175
Devon Smith, prin. Fax 348-2308
Other Schools – See Starr

Jackson, Aiken, Pop. 1,644
Aiken County SD
Supt. — See Aiken
Jackson MS 500/6-8
8217 Atomic Rd 29831 803-279-3525
Marc Funderburk, prin. Fax 471-2202

Jefferson, Chesterfield, Pop. 703
Chesterfield County SD
Supt. — See Chesterfield
New Heights MS 600/6-8
5738 Highway 151 29718 843-658-6830
Matthew Brantley, prin. Fax 658-6812

Johns Island, Charleston
Charleston County SD
Supt. — See Charleston
Haut Gap MS 300/6-8
1861 Bohicket Rd 29455 843-559-6418
Deborah Fickling, prin. Fax 559-6439
St. Johns HS 400/9-12
1518 Main Rd 29455 843-559-6400
Kenneth Wilson, prin. Fax 559-6409

Charleston Collegiate S 300/PK-12
2024 Academy Rd 29455 843-559-5506
Robert Shirley, prin. Fax 559-6172

Johnsonville, Florence, Pop. 1,460
Florence SD 5 1,500/PK-12
PO Box 98 29555 843-386-2358
A. Dale Strickland, supt. Fax 386-3139
Johnsonville HS 400/9-12
237 S Georgetown Hwy 29555 843-386-2707
James Berry, prin. Fax 386-9058
Johnsonville MS 500/5-8
PO Box 67 29555 843-386-2066
Stevie Phillips, prin. Fax 386-3786

Johnston, Edgefield, Pop. 2,352
Edgefield County SD 3,800/K-12
3 Par Dr 29832 803-275-4601
Sharon Keesley, supt. Fax 275-4426
www.edgefield.k12.sc.us
JET MS 600/6-8
1095 Columbia Rd 29832 803-275-1997
Louis Scott, prin. Fax 275-1783
Thurmond Career Center Vo/Tech
17 Par Dr 29832 803-275-1767
Carroll Wates, prin. Fax 275-1766
Thurmond HS 1,000/9-12
1131 Columbia Rd 29832 803-275-1768
Greg Thompson, prin. Fax 275-1764
Other Schools – See North Augusta

Wardlaw Academy 200/PK-12
1296 Columbia Rd 29832 803-275-4794
Ben Couch, prin. Fax 275-4873

Jonesville, Union, Pop. 927
Union County SD
Supt. — See Union
Jonesville JSHS 400/7-12
131 N Main St 29353 864-674-5272
Cindy Langley, prin. Fax 674-5280

Kershaw, Lancaster, Pop. 1,631
Kershaw County SD
Supt. — See Camden
North Central HS 500/9-12
3000 Lockhart Rd 29067 803-432-9858
Keith McAlister, prin. Fax 425-8992
North Central MS 500/6-8
805 Keys Ln 29067 803-424-2740
Burchell Richardson Ed.D., prin. Fax 424-2742

Lancaster County SD
Supt. — See Lancaster
Jackson HS 500/9-12
6925 Kershaw Camden Hwy 29067 803-475-2381
Alisa Goodman, prin. Fax 475-7317
Jackson MS 500/6-8
6865 Kershaw Camden Hwy 29067 803-475-6021
Mary Barry, prin. Fax 475-8256

Kingstree, Williamsburg, Pop. 3,363
Williamsburg County SD 5,500/K-12
PO Box 1067 29556 843-355-5571
Ralph Fennell, supt. Fax 355-3213
www.wcsd.k12.sc.us/
Kingstree HS 900/9-12
615 Martin Luther King Ave 29556 843-355-6525
Roberta Cumbee, prin. Fax 355-7730
Kingstree JHS 500/7-8
710 3rd Ave 29556 843-355-6823
Margie Myers, prin. Fax 355-9207
Adult Education Adult
400 Lexington Ave 29556 843-355-6887
Glen Kennedy, dir.
Other Schools – See Greeleyville, Hemingway

Williamsburg Academy 400/K-12
PO Box 770 29556 843-355-9400
Joan Thompson, prin. Fax 355-7734
Williamsburg Technical College Post-Sec.
601 Martin Luther King Ave 29556 843-354-2021

Ladys Island, Beaufort
Beaufort County SD
Supt. — See Beaufort
Ladys Island MS 700/6-8
30 Cougar Dr, 843-322-3100
Terry Bennett, prin. Fax 322-3179

Ladson, Berkeley, Pop. 13,540
Berkeley County SD
Supt. — See Moncks Corner
College Park MS 800/6-8
713 College Park Rd 29456 843-553-8300
Ingrid Dukes, prin. Fax 820-4026
Sangaree MS 700/6-8
1050 Discovery Dr 29456 843-821-4028
Jude Gehlmann, prin. Fax 871-8974

Dorchester SD 2
Supt. — See Summerville
Oakbrook MS 1,000/6-8
286 Old Fort Dr 29456 843-873-9750
Garland Crump, prin. Fax 821-3931

Grace Christian Academy 100/PK-12
PO Box 749 29456 843-553-1373
Rev. Randy Wade, prin. Fax 553-1378

Lake City, Florence, Pop. 6,690
Florence County SD 3 3,800/K-12
PO Box 1389 29560 843-374-8652
Beth Wright, supt. Fax 374-2946
www.florence3.k12.sc.us/
Lake City HS 1,100/9-12
PO Box 1569 29560 843-374-3321
Stan Yarborough, prin. Fax 374-3138
McNair MS 500/6-8
PO Box 1209 29560 843-374-8651
David Scurry, prin. Fax 374-8504
Truluck MS 400/6-8
PO Box 1239 29560 843-374-8685
Laura Hickson, prin. Fax 374-7341

Carolina Academy 300/K-12
351 N Country Club Rd 29560 843-374-5485
Anna Floyd, prin. Fax 374-0164

Lake View, Dillon, Pop. 792
Dillon SD 1 900/K-12
PO Box 644 29563 843-759-3001
Stephen Laird, supt. Fax 759-3000
www.lakeviewschools.com
Lake View JSHS 300/8-12
PO Box 624 29563 843-759-3009
Edison Arnette, prin. Fax 759-3016

Lamar, Darlington, Pop. 1,003
Darlington County SD
Supt. — See Darlington
Lamar HS 400/9-12
216 N Darlington St 29069 843-326-5543
Kathy Gainey, prin. Fax 326-7507

Spaulding MS 200/6-8
400 Cartersville Hwy 29069 843-326-5335
Fran Knotts, prin. Fax 326-7656

Lancaster, Lancaster, Pop. 8,371
Lancaster County SD 11,300/PK-12
PO Box 130 29721 803-286-6972
R. Gene Moore, supt. Fax 286-4865
www.lancasterscschools.org/
Buford HS 500/9-12
4290 Tabernacle Rd 29720 803-286-7068
Richard Porter, prin. Fax 286-8147
Buford MS 500/6-8
1890 N Rocky River Rd 29720 803-285-8473
Sheri Wells, prin. Fax 283-2023
Lancaster County Vocational S Vo/Tech
625 Normandy Rd 29720 803-285-7404
Fax 285-2720
Lancaster HS 1,800/9-12
617 Normandy Rd 29720 803-283-2001
Joseph Keenan, prin. Fax 286-6962
Rucker MS 600/6-8
422 Old Dixie Rd 29720 803-416-8555
Jonathan Phipps, prin. Fax 285-1534
South MS 800/6-8
1551 Billings Dr 29720 803-283-8416
Joyce Crimminger, prin. Fax 283-8417
Adult Education Adult
610 E Meeting St 29720 803-285-7660
James Howey, dir. Fax 285-9281
Other Schools – See Fort Mill, Kershaw

University of South Carolina Post-Sec.
PO Box 889 29721 803-285-7471

Landrum, Spartanburg, Pop. 2,518
Spartanburg SD 1
Supt. — See Campobello
Landrum MS 200/6-8
104 Redland Rd 29356 864-457-2629
Crystral McSwain, prin. Fax 457-5372

Latta, Dillon, Pop. 1,462
Dillon SD 3 1,500/K-12
205 King St 29565 843-752-7101
Dr. John Kirby, supt. Fax 752-2081
www.dillon3.k12.sc.us
Latta HS 400/9-12
618 N Richardson St 29565 843-752-5751
George Liebenrood, prin. Fax 752-2707
Latta MS 400/6-8
612 N Richardson St 29565 843-752-7117
Martha Heyward, prin. Fax 752-2722

Laurens, Laurens, Pop. 9,824
Laurens SD 55 5,800/K-12
1029 W Main St 29360 864-984-3568
Edgar C. Taylor, supt. Fax 984-8100
www.laurens55.k12.sc.us/
Laurens District 55 HS 1,600/9-12
5058 Highway 76 W 29360 864-682-3151
John Hendricks, prin. Fax 682-7426
Laurens MS 400/6-8
1035 W Main St 29360 864-984-2400
Rhett Harris, prin. Fax 984-6013
Sanders MS 300/6-8
609 Green St 29360 864-984-0354
George Ward, prin. Fax 984-2452
Other Schools – See Gray Court

Lexington, Lexington, Pop. 13,586
Lexington County SD 1 19,000/K-12
PO Box 1869 29071 803-359-4178
Karen Woodward, supt. Fax 359-8807
www.lexington1.net
Lexington HS 2,200/9-12
2463 Augusta Hwy 29072 803-359-5565
B. Creig Tyler, prin. Fax 359-8726
Lexington MS 1,700/6-8
702 N Lake Dr 29072 803-359-6169
Laura McMahan, prin. Fax 359-7233
Lexington Technology Center Vo/Tech
2421 Augusta Hwy 29072 803-359-4151
Kenneth Lake, prin. Fax 359-4073
Pleasant Hill MS 6-8
660 Rawl Rd 29072 803-996-4200
Dr. William Coon, prin. Fax 996-4250
White Knoll HS 1,700/9-12
5643 Platt Springs Rd 29073 803-996-4500
Jo Mayer, prin. Fax 996-4581
Other Schools – See Gilbert, Pelion, West Columbia

Columbia Adventist Academy 100/K-10
241 Riverchase Way 29072 803-796-0277
Nancy Chang, prin. Fax 936-9161

Liberty, Pickens, Pop. 3,004
Pickens County SD
Supt. — See Easley
Liberty HS 600/9-12
319 Summit Dr 29657 864-843-5800
Randy Gilstrap, prin. Fax 843-5828
Liberty MS 700/5-8
310 W Main St 29657 864-843-5855
Donivan Edwards, prin. Fax 843-5857

Little River, Horry, Pop. 3,470
Horry County SD
Supt. — See Conway
North Myrtle Beach HS 1,200/9-12
3750 Sea Mountain Hwy 29566 843-399-6171
Daryl Brown, prin. Fax 399-6509
North Myrtle Beach MS 1,000/6-8
11240 Highway 90 29566 843-399-6136
Virginia Horton, prin. Fax 399-2233

Lobeco, Beaufort

Agape Christian Academy 100/K-12
PO Box 719 29931 843-846-4835
Charles Lightsey, prin.

Lockhart, Union, Pop. 507
Union County SD
Supt. — See Union
Lockhart JSHS 200/7-12
PO Box 220 29364 864-545-6501
Kevin Morrow, prin. Fax 545-2175

Loris, Horry, Pop. 2,305
Horry County SD
Supt. — See Conway
Loris HS 800/9-12
301 Loris Lions Rd 29569 843-756-4040
Trevor Strawderman, prin. Fax 756-5331
Loris MS 700/6-8
5209 Highway 66 29569 843-756-2181
Judy Beard, prin. Fax 756-0522

Lugoff, Kershaw, Pop. 3,211
Kershaw County SD
Supt. — See Camden
Lugoff-Elgin HS 1,300/9-12
1284 Highway 1 S 29078 803-438-3481
Thomas Gladden, prin. Fax 438-8005
Lugoff-Elgin MS 600/6-8
1244 Highway 1 S 29078 803-438-3591
Dave Matthews, prin. Fax 438-8027

Mc Bee, Chesterfield, Pop. 674
Chesterfield County SD
Supt. — See Chesterfield
Mc Bee JSHS 400/7-12
PO Box 218 29101 843-335-8251
Skip Gering, prin. Fax 335-6515

Mc Clellanville, Charleston, Pop. 334
Charleston County SD
Supt. — See Charleston
Lincoln HS 100/9-12
714 Lincoln Rd 29458 843-577-0970
Michell Glover, prin. Fax 887-3116
Mc Clellanville MS 200/6-8
711 Pinckney St 29458 843-577-0325
William Price, prin. Fax 887-3002

Rutledge Academy 100/K-12
1011 Old Cemetery Rd 29458 843-887-3323
Inda Johnson, hdmstr. Fax 887-3525

Mc Cormick, McCormick, Pop. 1,736
McCormick SD 800/K-12
821 N Mine St 29835 864-852-2435
Sandra Calliham Ed.D., supt. Fax 852-2883
www.mccormick.k12.sc.us/
Mc Cormick HS 300/9-12
516 Mims Dr 29835 864-852-2302
Bobby Cunningham, prin. Fax 852-6256
Mc Cormick MS 200/6-8
6979 SC Highway 28 S 29835 864-443-2243
Cecily Morris, prin. Fax 443-3298

Manning, Clarendon, Pop. 4,025
Area Vocational Schools
Supt. — None
Dubose Career Center Vo/Tech
PO Box 1249 29102 803-473-2531
Dr. Tim Hardee, prin. Fax 473-4320

Clarendon SD 2 3,400/PK-12
PO Box 1252 29102 803-435-4435
John Tindal, supt. Fax 435-8172
www.clarendon2.k12.sc.us
Manning HS 1,000/9-12
2155 Paxville Hwy 29102 803-435-4417
Mike Shorter, prin. Fax 435-4404
Manning JHS 600/7-8
1101 W L Hamilton Rd 29102 803-435-8195
Preston Threatt, prin. Fax 435-6848

Marion, Marion, Pop. 6,997
Area Vocational Schools
Supt. — None
Marion Co. Technical Education Center Vo/Tech
PO Box 890 29571 843-423-1941
Paul Crandall, dir. Fax 423-1943

Marion SD 1 3,100/K-12
719 N Main St 29571 843-423-1811
Michael Lupo, supt. Fax 423-8328
www.marion1.k12.sc.us
Johnakin MS 700/6-8
601 Gurley St 29571 843-423-8360
Patrice Holmes, prin. Fax 423-8383
Marion HS 900/9-12
1205 S Main St 29571 843-423-2571
Alfred McFadden, prin. Fax 423-8330

Marion SD 7
Supt. — See Mullins
Creek Bridge HS 500/7-12
6641 S Highway 41 29571 843-362-3500
Burnie Bell, prin. Fax 362-3506

Mauldin, Greenville, Pop. 19,343
Greenville County SD
Supt. — See Greenville
Mauldin HS 2,200/9-12
701 E Butler Rd 29662 864-355-6500
Ann Miller, prin. Fax 355-6657

Moncks Corner, Berkeley, Pop. 6,525
Berkeley County SD 27,500/PK-12
PO Box 608 29461 843-899-8600
Dr. Chester Floyd, supt. Fax 899-8791
www.berkeley.k12.sc.us
Berkeley HS 1,600/9-12
406 W Main St 29461 843-899-8800
Ben Hodges Ph.D., prin. Fax 899-8810
Berkeley MS 1,300/6-8
320 N Live Oak Dr 29461 843-899-8840
Dr. Susan Gehlmann, prin. Fax 899-8846
Macedonia MS 600/5-8
200 Macedonia Foxes Cir 29461 843-899-8940
Janie Langley, prin. Fax 899-8929
Other Schools – See Cross, Goose Creek, Hanahan, Ladson, Saint Stephen

St. John Christian Academy 400/PK-12
204 W Main St 29461 843-761-8539
Eric Denton, prin. Fax 899-5514
Trident Technical College Post-Sec.
1001 S Live Oak Dr 29461 843-899-8033

Monetta, Aiken, Pop. 219
Aiken County SD
Supt. — See Aiken
Ridge Spring-Monetta HS 300/9-12
10 J P Kneece Dr 29105 803-685-2100
William Ward, prin. Fax 685-2108

Moore, Spartanburg
Spartanburg SD 6
Supt. — See Roebuck
Anderson Applied Technology Center Vo/Tech
PO Box 248 29369 864-576-5020
Sherri Yarborough, prin. Fax 576-8642
Dawkins MS 900/6-8
1300 E Blackstock Rd 29369 864-576-8088
Kenneth Kiser, prin. Fax 595-2418

Mount Pleasant, Charleston, Pop. 57,932
Charleston County SD
Supt. — See Charleston
Cario MS 1,000/6-8
3500 Thomas Cario Blvd 29466 843-856-4595
Carol Bartlett, prin. Fax 856-4599
Laing MS 500/6-8
2213 N Highway 17 29466 843-849-2809
Deborah Price, prin. Fax 849-2895
Moultrie MS 800/6-8
1560 Mathis Ferry Rd 29464 843-849-2819
Jean Siewicki, prin. Fax 849-2891
Wando HS 2,700/9-12
1000 Warrior Way 29466 843-849-2830
Lucy Beckham, prin. Fax 849-2890

First Baptist Church S of Mt. Pleasant 400/K-12
681 McCants Dr 29464 843-884-3663
Chad Moore, prin. Fax 884-9608
Palmetto Christian Academy 500/K-10
361 Egypt Rd 29464 843-881-9967
Rev. L. Joe Shorter Ph.D., admin. Fax 881-4662
Trident Academy 100/K-12
1455 Wakendaw Rd 29464 843-884-7046
Joe Ferber, hdmstr. Fax 881-8320

Mullins, Marion, Pop. 4,855
Marion SD 2 1,700/PK-PK, 1-
PO Box 689 29574 843-464-3700
Dr. Nathaniel Miller, supt. Fax 464-3705
www.marion2.k12.sc.us
Mullins HS 600/9-12
747 Millers Rd 29574 843-464-3710
Theodore Greene, prin. Fax 464-3717
Palmetto MS 500/6-8
305 ONeal St 29574 843-464-3730
Tim Felder, prin. Fax 464-3736

Marion SD 7 900/K-12
3559 S Highway 501 29574 843-423-2891
Everette M. Dean Ed.D., supt. Fax 423-7987
www.marion7.k12.sc.us
Other Schools – See Marion

Pee Dee Academy 400/K-12
PO Box 449 29574 843-423-1771
Hal Townsend, prin. Fax 423-0301

Murrells Inlet, Georgetown, Pop. 3,334
Horry County SD
Supt. — See Conway
St. James HS 1,100/9-12
10800 Highway 707 29576 843-650-5600
Joe Dowling, prin. Fax 650-1004

Myrtle Beach, Horry, Pop. 26,593
Horry County SD
Supt. — See Conway
Academy for Arts Science & Technology Vo/Tech
895 International Dr 29579 843-839-1412
Ronnie Burgess, prin. Fax 839-1419
Carolina Forest HS 1,500/9-12
700 Gardner Lacy Rd 29579 843-236-7997
Velna Allen, prin. Fax 236-7504
Forestbrook MS 1,000/6-8
4430 Gator Ln 29588 843-236-7300
Margaret Sordian, prin. Fax 236-8065
Myrtle Beach HS 1,200/9-12
3302 Robert M Grissom Pkwy 29577 843-448-7149
Nona Kerr, prin. Fax 445-2036
Myrtle Beach MS 900/6-8
950 Seahawk Way 29577 843-448-3932
Roger Gray, prin. Fax 448-1182
Ocean Bay MS 6-8
905 International Dr 29579 843-903-8420
Dr. Cindy Thibodeau, prin. Fax 903-8421
St. James MS 900/6-8
9775 Saint James Rd 29588 843-650-5543
Dr. Dwight Boykin, prin. Fax 650-5610
Socastee HS 1,300/9-12
4900 Socastee Blvd 29588 843-293-2513
Dr. Paul Browning, prin. Fax 293-3393

Calvary Christian S 300/PK-12
4511 Dick Pond Rd 29588 843-650-2829
Danny Martin, prin. Fax 215-4125
Christian Academy 200/K-12
3013 Theatre Dr 29579 843-236-6222
Todd Underwood, prin. Fax 236-7044
Golf Academy of the Carolinas Post-Sec.
3268 Waccamaw Blvd 29579 800-342-7342
Horry-Georgetown Technical College Post-Sec.
743 Hemlock Ave 29577 843-477-0808
Strand College of Hair Design Post-Sec.
423 79th Ave N 29572 843-449-1017

Neeses, Orangeburg, Pop. 402
Orangeburg Consolidated SD 4
Supt. — See Cope
Hunter-Kinard-Tyler HS 300/7-12
7066 Norway Rd 29107 803-263-4832
Fred Moore, prin. Fax 263-4467

Newberry, Newberry, Pop. 10,659
Newberry County SD 5,500/K-12
PO Box 718 29108 803-321-2600
Bennie Bennett, supt. Fax 321-2604
www.newberry.k12.sc.us/
Newberry Career Ctr Vo/Tech
3413 Main St 29108 803-321-2674
Donald Lawrimore, prin. Fax 321-2676
Newberry HS 900/9-12
3113 Main St 29108 803-321-2621
Barry Rosenberg, prin. Fax 321-2633
Newberry MS 700/6-8
125 ONeal St 29108 803-321-2640
Katrina Singletary, prin. Fax 321-2647
Newberry Adult Learning Center Adult
591 McSwain St 29108 803-321-2112
David Green, dir. Fax 321-2186
Other Schools – See Prosperity, Whitmire

Newberry Academy 300/K-12
2055 Smith Rd 29108 803-276-2760
Bob Dawkins, hdmstr. Fax 276-2401
Newberry College Post-Sec.
2100 College St 29108 800-845-4955

New Ellenton, Aiken, Pop. 2,259
Aiken County SD
Supt. — See Aiken
New Ellenton MS 200/6-8
814 Main St S 29809 803-652-8200
Elisa Sanders-Pee, prin. Fax 652-8203

Ninety Six, Greenwood, Pop. 1,922
Greenwood SD 52 1,700/PK-12
605 Johnston Rd 29666 864-543-3100
Dan Powell Ph.D., supt. Fax 543-3704
www.greenwood52.org
Edgewood MS 400/6-8
200 Edgewood Cir 29666 864-543-3511
Wallace Hall, prin. Fax 543-4994
Ninety Six HS 500/9-12
601 Johnston Rd 29666 864-543-2911
Jo Anne Campbell, prin. Fax 543-3132

North, Orangeburg, Pop. 788
Orangeburg Consolidated SD 5
Supt. — See Orangeburg
North MSHS 300/7-12
692 Cromer Ave 29112 803-247-2541
Sterling Harris, prin. Fax 247-5090

North Augusta, Aiken, Pop. 19,467
Aiken County SD
Supt. — See Aiken
Knox MS 700/6-8
1804 Wells Rd 29841 803-442-6300
Brenda Smith, prin. Fax 442-6302
North Augusta HS 1,500/9-12
2000 Knobcone Ave 29841 803-442-6100
Kyle Smith, prin. Fax 442-6127
North Augusta MS 600/6-8
725 Old Edgefield Rd 29841 803-442-6200
Barry Head, prin. Fax 442-6202

Edgefield County SD
Supt. — See Johnston
Merriwether MS 400/6-8
PO Box 7010 29861 803-279-2511
Gaye Holmes, prin. Fax 279-1710

Kenneth Shuler's School of Cosmetology Post-Sec.
736 Martintown Rd 29841 803-278-1200
Victory Christian S 200/K-12
620 W Martintown Rd 29841 803-278-2138
Dr. Ed Martin, prin. Fax 442-9355

North Charleston, Charleston, Pop. 86,313
Charleston County SD
Supt. — See Charleston
Brentwood MS 700/6-8
2685 Leeds Ave 29405 843-745-7094
LaWanda Glears, prin. Fax 566-1838
Charleston County S of the Arts 600/6-9
1600 Saranac St 29405 843-529-4990
Rose Myers, prin. Fax 529-4991
Charlestowne Academy 400/K-12
5841 Rivers Ave 29406 843-746-1349
Edward Tichi, prin. Fax 746-1354
Garrett Academy of Technology Vo/Tech
2731 Gordon St 29405 843-745-7126
David Parson, prin. Fax 529-3914
Morningside MS 900/6-8
1999 Singley St 29405 843-745-2000
Kala Goodwine, prin. Fax 745-7191
North Charleston HS 1,300/9-12
1087 E Montague Ave 29405 843-745-7140
David Colwell, prin. Fax 566-1954

Stall HS 1,000/9-12
7749 Pinehurst St 29420 843-764-2200
Dan Conner, prin. Fax 764-2240

Dorchester SD 2
Supt. — See Summerville
Fort Dorchester HS 2,200/9-12
8500 Patriot Blvd 29420 843-760-4450
Jim Atkinson, prin. Fax 760-4852
River Oaks MS 6-8
8642 River Oaks Dr 29420 843-695-2470
Kathy Sobolewski, prin.

Beta Tech Post-Sec.
8088 Rivers Ave 29406 843-569-0889
ECPI College of Technology Post-Sec.
7410 Northside Dr Ste G101 29420 843-414-0350
Ferndale Baptist S 200/K-12
4870 Piedmont Ave 29406 843-744-3307
Milton Ashley, prin. Fax 744-3308
Miller-Motte Technical College Post-Sec.
8085 Rivers Ave 29406 843-574-0101
Northwood Academy 300/6-12
2263 Otranto Rd 29406 843-764-2284
Dr. Darlene Anderson, prin. Fax 764-3713
Southeastern School of Neuromuscular Post-Sec.
4600 Goer Dr Ste 105 29406 843-747-1279

Orangeburg, Orangeburg, Pop. 14,460
Orangeburg Consolidated SD 5 6,400/K-12
578 Ellis Ave 29115 803-534-5454
Melvin Smoak, supt. Fax 533-7953
www.orangeburg5.k12.sc.us/
Clark MS 800/5-8
919 Bennett St 29115 803-531-2200
Lana Williams, prin. Fax 533-6503
Howard MS 600/5-8
1255 Belleville Rd 29115 803-534-5470
Dr. Jacqueline Vogt, prin. Fax 535-1606
Orangeburg 5 Tech Center Vo/Tech
3720 Magnolia St 29118 803-536-4473
Abbiegail Hugine, prin. Fax 533-6365
Orangeburg-Wilkinson HS 1,700/9-12
601 Bruin Pkwy 29118 803-534-6180
Rodney Zimmerman, prin. Fax 533-6310
Other Schools – See North, Rowesville

Claflin University Post-Sec.
700 College Ave 29115 803-535-5000
Orangeburg-Calhoun Technical College Post-Sec.
3250 Saint Matthews Rd 29118 803-536-0311
Orangeburg Prep S 800/K-12
2651 North Rd 29118 803-534-7970
Kelley Mims, prin. Fax 535-2190
South Carolina State University Post-Sec.
PO Box 7127 29117 803-536-7000
Southern Methodist College Post-Sec.
PO Box 1027 29116 803-534-7826

Pacolet, Spartanburg, Pop. 2,727
Spartanburg SD 3
Supt. — See Glendale
Pacolet MS 200/6-8
850 Sunny Acres Rd 29372 864-474-4080
Cynthia James, prin. Fax 474-4085

Pageland, Chesterfield, Pop. 2,544
Chesterfield County SD
Supt. — See Chesterfield
Central HS 600/9-12
200 Zion Church Rd 29728 843-672-6115
J.R. Green, prin. Fax 672-2694

New Covenent Christian S 200/PK-12
PO Box 188 29728 843-672-2760
Gayle Mills, prin. Fax 672-3913

Pamplico, Florence, Pop. 1,158
Florence SD 2 1,200/K-12
2121 S Pamplico Hwy 29583 843-493-2502
Steve Quick, supt. Fax 493-1912
www.flo2.k12.sc.us/
Hannah-Pamplico HS 300/9-12
2055 S Pamplico Hwy 29583 843-493-5781
Henry Dixon, prin. Fax 493-5424

New Prospect Christian S 200/K-12
4221 Sheminally Rd 29583 843-493-2189
Gwen Ard, prin. Fax 493-0899

Pawleys Island, Georgetown, Pop. 144
Georgetown County SD
Supt. — See Georgetown
Waccamaw HS 600/9-12
2412 Kings River Rd 29585 843-237-9899
Robert Brown, prin. Fax 237-9883
Waccamaw MS 500/6-8
247 Wildcat Way 29585 843-237-0106
Leonard Nelson, prin. Fax 237-0237

Pelion, Lexington, Pop. 587
Lexington County SD 1
Supt. — See Lexington
Pelion HS 700/9-12
600 Lydia Dr 29123 803-894-2100
Jean Haggard, prin. Fax 894-2101
Pelion MS 900/5-8
758 Magnolia St 29123 803-894-2050
Dr. Sandra Jowers, prin. Fax 894-2051

Pendleton, Anderson, Pop. 3,050
Anderson SD 4 2,700/K-12
PO Box 545 29670 864-646-8000
Dr. Gary Burgess, supt. Fax 646-8555
www.anderson4.k12.sc.us
Pendleton HS 800/9-12
PO Box 869 29670 864-646-8040
Rodney Graves, prin. Fax 646-8066

Riverside MS 700/6-8
458 Riverside St 29670 864-646-8020
Kevin Black, prin. Fax 646-8025

Tri-County Tech College Post-Sec.
PO Box 587 29670 864-646-8361

Pickens, Pickens, Pop. 2,974
Pickens County SD
Supt. — See Easley
Pickens HS 1,400/9-12
111 Blue Flame Dr 29671 864-878-8730
Marion Lawson, prin. Fax 898-5611
Pickens MS 1,000/6-8
467 Sparks Ln 29671 864-878-8735
Tim Mullis, prin. Fax 878-8734

Piedmont, Greenville, Pop. 4,143
Anderson SD 1
Supt. — See Williamston
Wren HS 1,500/9-12
905 Wren School Rd 29673 864-850-5900
Robbie Binnicker, prin. Fax 850-5929
Wren MS 800/6-8
1010 Wren School Rd 29673 864-850-5930
Robin Fulbright, prin. Fax 850-5941

Greenville County SD
Supt. — See Greenville
Woodmont HS 1,000/9-12
2831 W Georgia Rd 29673 864-355-8600
Leroy Hamilton, prin. Fax 355-8694
Woodmont MS 900/6-8
150 Woodmont School Rd 29673 864-299-8373
Kira Geter, prin. Fax 299-8408

Prosperity, Newberry, Pop. 1,098
Newberry County SD
Supt. — See Newberry
Mid-Carolina HS 600/9-12
6794 US Highway 76 29127 803-364-2134
Lynn Cary, prin. Fax 364-4395
Mid-Carolina MS 600/6-8
6834 US Highway 76 29127 803-364-3634
Buddy Livingston, prin. Fax 364-4877

Richburg, Chester, Pop. 321
Chester County SD
Supt. — See Chester
Lewisville HS 400/9-12
3971 Lewisville High School 29729 803-789-5131
James Knox, prin. Fax 789-3188
Lewisville MS 400/6-8
PO Box 280 29729 803-789-5858
H.L. Erwin, prin. Fax 789-6159

Ridgeland, Jasper, Pop. 2,618
Area Vocational Schools
Supt. — None
Academy for Career Excellence Vo/Tech
80 Lowcountry Dr 29936 843-987-8107
Catherine M. Smith, dir. Fax 987-4136

Jasper County SD 3,000/K-12
PO Box 848 29936 843-717-1100
Dr. William Singleton, supt. Fax 717-1199
www.jcsd.net
Jasper County HS 800/9-12
913 Grays Hwy 29936 843-717-1500
Marc Grant, prin. Fax 717-1599
Ridgeland MS 700/5-8
PO Box 250 29936 843-717-1400
Benjamin Gadsden, prin. Fax 717-1499

Heyward Academy 500/PK-12
PO Box 2233 29936 843-726-3673
John Rogers, prin. Fax 726-5773

Ridgeville, Dorchester, Pop. 1,960
Dorchester SD 2
Supt. — See Summerville
Givhans Community S Adult
273 Highway 61 29472 843-832-5559
Joyce Dearing, prin. Fax 821-3944

Dorchester SD 4
Supt. — See Saint George
Clay Hill MS 6-8
387 S Railroad Ave 29472 843-851-7386
Kenneth Pinkney, prin. Fax 873-0571

Rock Hill, York, Pop. 59,554
Rock Hill SD 3 16,300/PK-12
PO Box 10072 29731 803-981-1000
Fax 981-1094
www.rock-hill.k12.sc.us/
Castle Heights MS 1,000/6-8
2382 Firetower Rd 29730 803-981-1400
Kelly Kane, prin. Fax 981-1430
Northwestern HS 2,500/9-12
2503 W Main St 29732 803-981-1200
James Blake, prin. Fax 981-1250
Rawlinson Road MS 1,100/6-8
2631 W Main St 29732 803-981-1500
Jean Dickson, prin. Fax 981-1532
Rock Hill Applied Technology Center Vo/Tech
2399 W Main St 29732 803-981-1100
Don Gillman, dir. Fax 981-1125
Rock Hill HS 2,400/9-12
320 W Springdale Rd 29730 803-981-1300
Judy Mobley, prin. Fax 981-1343
Saluda Trail MS 900/6-8
2300 Saluda Rd 29730 803-981-1800
Brenda Campbell, prin. Fax 981-1819
South Pointe HS 9-12
801 Neely Rd 29730 803-980-2100
Al Leonard, prin. Fax 980-2105
Sullivan MS 1,100/6-8
1825 Eden Ter 29730 803-981-1450
Dr. Bob Heath, prin. Fax 981-1456

Adult Education | Adult
217 Orange St 29730 | 803-981-1375
Sandy Andrews, prin. | Fax 981-1397

Clinton Junior College | Post-Sec.
1029 Crawford Rd 29730 | 803-327-7402
Plaza School of Beauty Culture | Post-Sec.
946 Oakland Ave 29730 | 803-328-5166
Trinity Christian S | 200/PK-12
505 University Dr 29730 | 803-366-3121
Thomas Krauter, admin. | Fax 366-8339
Westminster Catawba Christian S | 600/PK-12
2650 India Hook Rd 29732 | 803-366-4119
Dr. John Blumenstein, hdmstr. | Fax 328-5465
Winthrop University | Post-Sec.
701 W Oakland Ave 29733 | 803-323-2211
York Technical College | Post-Sec.
452 Anderson Rd S 29730 | 803-327-8000

Roebuck, Spartanburg, Pop. 1,966
Spartanburg SD 6 | 9,600/K-12
1390 Cavalier Way 29376 | 864-576-4212
Dr. Darryl Owings, supt. | Fax 574-6265
www.spartanburg6.k12.sc.us
Dorman HS | 2,000/10-12
1050 Cavalier Way 29376 | 864-582-4347
Jerry Wyatt, prin. | Fax 587-8738
Dorman HS - Freshman Campus | 900/9-9
1225 Cavalier Way 29376 | 864-582-3479
Fax 342-8997
Gable MS | 700/6-8
198 Otts Shoals Rd 29376 | 864-576-3500
Karen Bush, prin. | Fax 595-2428
Other Schools – See Moore, Spartanburg

Rowesville, Orangeburg, Pop. 366
Orangeburg Consolidated SD 5
Supt. — See Orangeburg
Bethune-Bowman MSHS | 400/6-12
4857 Charleston Hwy 29133 | 803-516-6011
Parrie Hook, prin. | Fax 516-6013

Ruffin, Colleton
Colleton County SD
Supt. — See Walterboro
Ruffin MS | 400/6-8
155 Patriot Ln 29475 | 843-562-2291
Harry Jenkins, prin. | Fax 562-8028

Saint George, Dorchester, Pop. 2,097
Dorchester SD 4 | 2,500/PK-12
500 Ridge St 29477 | 843-563-4535
Jerry Montjoy, supt. | Fax 563-9269
www.dorchester4.k12.sc.us
Saint George MS | 600/6-8
600 Minus St 29477 | 843-563-3171
Dr. Gwendolyn Boyd Wright, prin. | Fax 563-5936
Other Schools – See Dorchester, Ridgeville

Dorchester Academy | 500/K-12
PO Box 901 29477 | 843-563-9511
Kimberly Brock, hdmstr. | Fax 563-4764

Saint Matthews, Calhoun, Pop. 2,093
Calhoun County SD | 1,900/PK-12
PO Box 215 29135 | 803-655-7310
James Westbury, supt. | Fax 655-7393
www.calhoun.k12.sc.us
Calhoun County HS | 500/9-12
150 Saints Ave 29135 | 803-874-3071
Sheridan Hamilton, prin. | Fax 655-5948
Ford MS | 400/6-8
PO Box 287 29135 | 803-655-7222
Carlita Davis, prin. | Fax 655-7506

Calhoun Academy | 500/PK-12
PO Box 526 29135 | 803-874-2734
Milly McLauchlin, hdmstr. | Fax 874-2734
Upward Way Christian Academy | 50/K-12
3941 Old State Rd 29135 | 803-655-9026
Shelby Neil, admin.

Saint Stephen, Berkeley, Pop. 1,749
Berkeley County SD
Supt. — See Moncks Corner
Saint Stephen MS | 300/6-8
225 Carolina Dr 29479 | 843-567-3128
Derrick Daniels, prin. | Fax 567-8162
Timberland HS | 1,000/9-12
1418 Gravel Hill Rd 29479 | 843-567-8110
Dave Barrow, prin. | Fax 567-8116

Salem, Oconee, Pop. 130
Oconee County SD
Supt. — See Walhalla
Tamassee-Salem MSHS | 200/6-12
PO Box 96 29676 | 864-944-0444
Steve Moore, prin. | Fax 944-6492

Saluda, Saluda, Pop. 2,969
Saluda SD | 2,100/PK-12
404 N Wise Rd 29138 | 864-445-8441
Pete Stone Ed.D., supt. | Fax 445-9671
www.saludak-12.org
Saluda HS | 500/9-12
160 Ivory Key Rd 29138 | 864-445-3011
Jimmy Crawford, prin. | Fax 445-3542
Saluda MS | 500/6-8
140 Ivory Key Rd 29138 | 864-445-3767
Shawn Love, prin. | Fax 445-3980

Santee, Orangeburg, Pop. 721
Orangeburg Consolidated SD 3
Supt. — See Holly Hill
Lake Marion HS | 9-12
PO Box 650 29142 | 803-854-9213
Rose Pelzer-Brower, prin. | Fax 854-5202

Seabrook, Beaufort
Beaufort County SD
Supt. — See Beaufort
Whale Branch MS | 400/6-8
2009 Trask Pkwy 29940 | 843-466-3000
Bill Payne, prin. | Fax 466-3087

Seneca, Oconee, Pop. 7,962
Oconee County SD
Supt. — See Walhalla
Hamilton Career Center | Vo/Tech
100 Vocational Dr 29672 | 864-885-5011
Michael Pearson, prin. | Fax 885-5012
Seneca HS | 1,000/9-12
100 Bobcat Rdg 29678 | 864-885-5000
Kelly Pew, prin. | Fax 885-5008
Seneca MS | 900/6-8
810 W South 4th St 29678 | 864-885-5016
Al LeRoy, prin. | Fax 885-5018

Oconee Christian Academy | 200/PK-12
150 His Way Cir 29672 | 864-882-6925
Thad Cloer, dir. | Fax 882-7217

Simpsonville, Greenville, Pop. 15,135
Greenville County SD
Supt. — See Greenville
Bryson MS | 1,300/6-8
3657 S Industrial Dr 29681 | 864-355-2100
Dr. Billie McGaha, prin. | Fax 355-2194
Hillcrest HS | 2,200/9-12
3665 S Industrial Dr 29681 | 864-355-3500
Steve Chamness, prin. | Fax 355-3382
Hillcrest MS | 1,100/6-8
510 Garrison Rd 29681 | 864-355-6100
Keith Russell, prin. | Fax 355-6120
Mauldin MS | 1,300/6-8
1190 Holland Rd 29681 | 864-355-6770
Rosia Gardner, prin. | Fax 355-6988

Greenville Classical Academy | 100/K-10
2519 Woodruff Rd 29681 | 864-329-9884
Mark Klein, hdmstr.
Southside Christian S | 1,100/PK-12
2211 Woodruff Rd 29681 | 864-234-7595
Stephen Reel Ph.D., supt. | Fax 234-7048

Six Mile, Pickens, Pop. 553

Providence Christian Academy | 100/PK-12
PO Box 10 29682 | 864-868-6896
Alice Skaar, prin. | Fax 868-6985

Spartanburg, Spartanburg, Pop. 38,379
Spartanburg SD 3
Supt. — See Glendale
Broome HS | 900/9-12
381 Cherry Hill Rd 29307 | 864-579-8040
Dr. Vernon Prosser, prin. | Fax 579-8050

Spartanburg SD 6
Supt. — See Roebuck
Fairforest MS | 800/6-8
4120 N Blackstock Rd 29301 | 864-576-1270
Dr. Shawn Foster, prin. | Fax 576-2600

Spartanburg SD 7 | 7,500/K-12
PO Box 970 29304 | 864-594-4400
Walter Tobin, supt. | Fax 594-4398
www.spart7.org
Carver JHS, 467 S Church St 29306 | 700/7-9
Charles Redmond, prin. | 864-594-4435
McCracken JHS | 800/7-9
300 Webber Rd 29307 | 864-594-4457
Jeff Stevens, prin. | Fax 596-8418
Morgan Technology Center | Vo/Tech
201 Zion Hill Rd 29307 | 864-579-2810
Wayne Chapman, prin. | Fax 579-7392
Spartanburg SHS | 1,600/10-12
500 Dupre Dr 29307 | 864-594-4410
Rodney Graves, prin. | Fax 594-6142
Whitlock JHS | 600/7-9
364 Successful Way 29303 | 864-594-4482
Virginia Jones, prin. | Fax 594-6154

Converse College | Post-Sec.
580 E Main St 29302 | 864-596-9000
Sherman College of Straight Chiropractic | Post-Sec.
PO Box 1452 29304 | 864-578-8770
South Carolina School for Deaf and Blind | Post-Sec.
355 Cedar Springs Rd 29302 | 864-577-7557
Spartanburg Christian Academy | 500/PK-12
8740 Asheville Hwy 29316 | 864-578-4238
Ken Pangel, admin. | Fax 542-1846
Spartanburg Community College | Post-Sec.
PO Box 4386 29305 | 864-591-3600
Spartanburg Day S | 500/PK-12
1701 Skylyn Dr 29307 | 864-582-7539
Christopher Dorrance, hdmstr. | Fax 948-0026
Spartanburg Methodist College | Post-Sec.
1200 Textile Rd 29301 | 800-772-7286
University of South Carolina | Post-Sec.
800 University Way 29303 | 864-503-5000
Westgate Christian S | 200/K-12
1990 Old Reidville Rd 29301 | 864-576-4953
Fred Seiber, prin. | Fax 576-7581
Wofford College | Post-Sec.
429 N Church St 29303 | 864-597-4000

Starr, Anderson, Pop. 188
Anderson SD 3
Supt. — See Iva
Starr-Iva MS | 700/6-8
1034 Rainey Rd 29684 | 864-352-6146
Carolyn Brown, prin. | Fax 352-2095

Summerton, Clarendon, Pop. 1,053
Clarendon SD 1 | 1,000/K-12
PO Box 38 29148 | 803-485-2325
Dr. Rose Wilder, supt. | Fax 485-2822
www.clarendon1.k12.sc.us
Scotts Branch HS | 300/9-12
9253 Alex Harvin Hwy 29148 | 803-478-7818
Corey Burgess, prin. | Fax 478-7659
Scott's Branch IS | 300/4-8
PO Box 67 29148 | 803-485-2043
Dr. Gwendolyn Harris, prin. | Fax 485-7012

Clarendon Hall S | 300/K-12
PO Box 609 29148 | 803-485-3550
Glenda Sternberg, prin. | Fax 485-3205

Summerville, Dorchester, Pop. 37,714
Dorchester SD 2 | 18,500/K-12
102 Green Wave Blvd 29483 | 843-873-2901
Joseph Pye, supt. | Fax 873-4053
www.dorchester2.k12.sc.us
Alston MS | 900/6-8
500 Bryan St 29483 | 843-873-3890
Sam Clark, prin. | Fax 821-3978
DuBose MS | 1,000/6-8
1000 DuBose School Rd 29483 | 843-875-7012
Kenneth Farrell, prin. | Fax 821-3995
Gregg MS | 1,200/6-8
500 Greenwave Blvd 29483 | 843-871-3150
Tom McCurry, prin. | Fax 821-3992
Rollings MS of the Arts | 600/6-8
815 S Main St 29483 | 843-873-3610
Elena Furnari, prin. | Fax 821-3985
Summerville HS | 3,200/9-12
1101 Boone Hill Rd 29483 | 843-873-6460
Roger Edwards, prin. | Fax 821-3989
Other Schools – See Ladson, North Charleston, Ridgeville

Faith Christian S | 300/PK-12
337 Farmington Rd 29483 | 843-873-8464
Rev. Doug Wolfrath, prin. | Fax 873-4288
Pinewood Prep S | 900/K-12
1114 Orangeburg Rd 29483 | 843-873-1643
Glyn Cowlishaw, prin. | Fax 821-4257

Sumter, Sumter, Pop. 39,679
Area Vocational Schools
Supt. — None
Sumter County Career Center | Vo/Tech
2612 McCrays Mill Rd 29154 | 803-481-8575
John Roveri, prin. | Fax 481-4232

Sumter SD 17 | 8,800/K-12
1109 N Pike W 29153 | 803-469-8536
Zona W. Jefferson Ph.D., supt. | Fax 469-6006
district.sumter17.k12.sc.us/
Alice Drive MS | 800/6-8
40 Miller Rd 29150 | 803-775-0821
Neil Baldwin, prin. | Fax 778-2929
Bates MS | 900/6-8
715 Estate St 29150 | 803-775-0711
Anthony Graham, prin. | Fax 775-0715
Chestnut Oaks MS | 600/6-8
1200 Oswego Hwy 29153 | 803-775-7272
Cornelius Leach, prin. | Fax 775-7601
Sumter HS | 2,400/9-12
2580 McCrays Mill Rd 29154 | 803-481-4480
Rutledge Dingle, prin. | Fax 481-4021

Sumter SD 2 | 9,100/K-12
1345 Wilson Hall Rd 29150 | 803-469-6900
Frank Baker, supt. | Fax 469-3769
www.sumter2.org
Crestwood HS | 1,400/9-12
2000 Oswego Hwy 29153 | 803-469-6200
John Huggins, prin. | Fax 469-7678
Ebenezer MS | 500/6-8
3440 Ebenezer Rd 29153 | 803-469-8571
Marlene DeWit, prin. | Fax 469-8575
Furman MS | 1,000/6-8
3400 Bethel Church Rd 29154 | 803-481-8510
Dale Wilson, prin. | Fax 481-8923
Lakewood HS | 1,200/9-12
350 Old Manning Rd 29150 | 803-506-2704
Sherril Ray, prin. | Fax 506-2708
Mayewood MS | 300/6-8
4300 E Brewington Rd 29153 | 803-495-8014
Dr. Mary Hallums, prin. | Fax 495-8016
Other Schools – See Dalzell

Central Carolina Technical College | Post-Sec.
506 N Guignard Dr 29150 | 803-778-1961
Morris College | Post-Sec.
100 W College St 29150 | 803-934-3200
St. Francis Xavier HS | 50/9-12
15 School St 29150 | 803-773-0210
Sue Lavergne, prin. | Fax 775-0119
Sumter Beauty College | Post-Sec.
921 Carolina Ave 29150 | 803-773-7311
Sumter Christian S | 400/PK-12
420 S Pike W 29150 | 803-773-1902
Ron Davis, prin. | Fax 775-1676
University of South Carolina | Post-Sec.
200 Miller Rd 29150 | 803-775-6341
Wilson Hall S | 800/PK-12
520 Wilson Hall Rd 29150 | 803-469-3475
Fred Moulton, hdmstr. | Fax 469-3477

Swansea, Lexington, Pop. 686
Lexington County SD 4 | 3,700/PK-12
607 E 5th St 29160 | 803-568-1000
Dr. Franklin Vail, supt. | Fax 568-1020
www.lexington4.net
Swansea HS | 1,000/9-12
500 E 1st St 29160 | 803-568-1100
Dr. Robert Maddox, prin. | Fax 568-1117
Other Schools – See Gaston

Taylors, Greenville, Pop. 19,619
Greenville County SD
Supt. — See Greenville
Eastside HS 1,300/9-12
1300 Brushy Creek Rd 29687 864-292-7715
John Tharp, prin. Fax 292-7328
Northwood MS 1,000/6-8
710 Ikes Rd 29687 864-355-7000
Richard Griffin, prin. Fax 355-7077

Tigerville, Greenville

North Greenville University Post-Sec.
PO Box 1892 29688 864-977-7000

Timmonsville, Florence, Pop. 2,385
Florence County SD 4 1,100/PK-12
220 N Pinckney St 29161 843-346-5391
Dr. Bertha McCants, supt. Fax 346-3145
www.florence4.k12.sc.us
Johnson MS 200/6-8
304 Kemper St 29161 843-346-4685
Ronald Bowser, prin. Fax 346-5199
Timmonsville HS 300/9-12
304 Kemper St 29161 843-346-4586
Dr. William McCall, prin. Fax 346-5416

Travelers Rest, Greenville, Pop. 4,237
Greenville County SD
Supt. — See Greenville
Lakeview MS 600/6-8
115 Wilhelm Winter St 29690 864-834-6500
Dr. Tracy Hall, prin.
Northwest MS 800/6-8
1606 Geer Hwy 29690 864-355-6900
Lee Givins, prin. Fax 355-6920
Travelers Rest HS 1,200/9-12
301 N Main St 29690 864-355-0000
Louis Lavely, prin. Fax 355-0088

Turbeville, Clarendon, Pop. 724
Clarendon SD 3 1,200/K-12
PO Box 270 29162 843-659-2188
Dr. Mary Rice-Crenshaw, supt. Fax 659-3204
www.clarendon3.org/
East Clarendon HS 300/9-12
PO Box 67 29162 843-659-2185
Brooke James, prin. Fax 659-8933
East Clarendon MS 300/6-8
PO Box 153 29162 843-659-2187
Carol Lenderman, prin. Fax 659-2192

Union, Union, Pop. 8,321
Union County SD 4,800/K-12
PO Box 907 29379 864-429-1740
Dr. Thomas White, supt. Fax 429-1745
www.union.k12.sc.us
Sims JHS 600/7-8
200 Sims Dr 29379 864-429-1755
Mickey Connolly, prin. Fax 429-1798
Union HS 1,000/9-12
1163 Lakeside Dr 29379 864-429-1750
Joe Walker, prin. Fax 429-5401
Adult Education / Lifelong Learning Adult
517 E Main St 29379 864-429-1770
Henry Sparrow, dir. Fax 429-1771
Other Schools – See Jonesville, Lockhart

University of South Carolina Post-Sec.
PO Box 729 29379 864-429-8728

Varnville, Hampton, Pop. 2,048
Hampton SD 1 2,900/PK-12
372 E Pine St 29944 803-943-4576
Dr. Terry Pruitt, supt. Fax 943-5943
www.hampton1.k12.sc.us
Hampton HS 700/9-12
115 Airport Rd 29944 803-943-3568
Greg Ackerman, prin. Fax 943-5036
North District MS 500/7-8
PO Box 368 29944 803-943-3507
Mark Dean, prin. Fax 943-4074

Wagener, Aiken, Pop. 872
Aiken County SD
Supt. — See Aiken
Corbett MS 300/6-8
10 Corbett Cir 29164 803-564-1050
Dr. Deborah Bass, prin. Fax 564-1058
Wagener-Salley HS 400/9-12
272 Main St S 29164 803-564-1100
Bryan Skipper, prin. Fax 564-1109

Walhalla, Oconee, Pop. 3,727
Oconee County SD 10,200/PK-12
PO Box 649 29691 864-886-4400
John Taylor, supt. Fax 886-4408
www.oconee.k12.sc.us
Walhalla HS 900/9-12
151 Razorback Ln 29691 864-638-4582
Evie Hughes, prin. Fax 638-4055
Walhalla MS 700/6-8
177 Razorback Ln 29691 864-638-4575
Charles Middleton, prin. Fax 638-4576
Other Schools – See Salem, Seneca, Westminster

Walterboro, Colleton, Pop. 5,548
Colleton County SD 6,300/PK-12
PO Box 290 29488 843-549-5715
Charles Gale, supt. Fax 549-2606
www.colleton.k12.sc.us
Colleton County HS 1,800/9-12
1379 Mighty Cougar Dr 29488 843-538-2904
Cliff Warren, prin. Fax 538-8151
Colleton MS 800/6-8
603 Colleton Loop 29488 843-549-2690
Shannon Stephens, prin. Fax 549-1222
Forest Circle MS 400/6-8
500 Forest Cir 29488 843-549-2361
Scott Matthews, prin. Fax 549-5061
Thunderbolt Career & Technology Center Vo/Tech
1069 Thunderbolt Dr 29488 843-538-5538
Bob McKinnon, prin. Fax 538-3009
Other Schools – See Ruffin

Colleton Prep Academy 400/K-12
PO Box 1426 29488 843-538-8959
Arthur Ellis, hdmstr. Fax 538-8260
Family Christian Academy 200/K-12
2107 Hampton St 29488 843-893-3536
Roger Quesenberry, admin. Fax 893-2174

Ware Shoals, Greenwood, Pop. 2,377
Greenwood SD 51 1,200/PK-12
25 E Main St 29692 864-456-7496
Fay Sprouse, supt. Fax 456-3578
www.gwd51.k12.sc.us
Ware Shoals JSHS 500/7-12
56 S Greenwood Ave 29692 864-456-7923
Jane Blackwell, prin. Fax 456-2959

Warrenville, Aiken
Aiken County SD
Supt. — See Aiken
Aiken County Career & Technical Center Vo/Tech
2455 Jefferson Davis Hwy 29851 803-593-7300
Patrick O'Neill, dir. Fax 593-7115
Langley-Bath-Clearwater MS 600/6-8
29 Lions Trl 29851 803-593-7260
Russell Gunter, prin. Fax 593-7119

West Columbia, Lexington, Pop. 13,413
Lexington County SD 1
Supt. — See Lexington
White Knoll MS 1,500/6-8
116 White Knoll Way 29170 803-957-4400
Nancy Turner, prin. Fax 957-5415

Lexington County SD 2 9,200/PK-12
715 9th St 29169 803-796-4708
Barry Bolen, supt. Fax 739-4067
www.lex2.org
Airport HS 1,400/9-12
1315 Boston Ave 29170 803-822-5600
Frank Jovanelly, prin. Fax 822-5665
Fulmer MS 700/6-8
1614 Walterboro St 29170 803-822-5660
Dixon Brooks, prin. Fax 822-5664
Northside MS 700/6-8
157 Cougar Dr 29169 803-739-4190
David Sims, prin. Fax 739-3188
Pine Ridge MS 500/6-8
735 Pine Ridge Dr 29172 803-755-7400
Gregg Morton, prin. Fax 755-7449
Other Schools – See Cayce

Glenforest S 100/1-12
1041 Harbor Dr 29169 803-796-7622
Gillian Barclay-Smith, admin. Fax 796-1603
Grace Christian S 400/K-12
416 Denham Ave 29169 803-794-8996
Tim Stevens, prin. Fax 739-1204

Westminster, Oconee, Pop. 2,669
Oconee County SD
Supt. — See Walhalla
West-Oak HS 900/9-12
130 Warrior Ln 29693 864-647-3065
Scott Smith, prin. Fax 647-3071
West Oak MS 500/6-8
501 Westminster Hwy 29693 864-647-3050
Paul Ricciardi, prin. Fax 647-7213

Whitmire, Newberry, Pop. 1,526
Newberry County SD
Supt. — See Newberry
Whitmire Community S 300/K-12
2597 Highway 66 29178 803-694-2320
Jim Suber, prin. Fax 694-3835

Williamston, Anderson, Pop. 3,878
Anderson SD 1 8,600/PK-12
PO Box 99 29697 864-847-7344
Dr. Wayne Fowler, supt. Fax 847-3543
www.anderson1.k12.sc.us
Palmetto HS 800/9-12
804 N Hamilton St 29697 864-847-7311
Dr. Mason Gary, prin. Fax 847-3532
Palmetto MS 800/6-8
803 N Hamilton St 29697 864-847-4333
Barry Knight, prin. Fax 847-3529
Other Schools – See Greenville, Piedmont

Area Vocational Schools
Supt. — None
Career & Technology Center Vo/Tech
702 Belton Hwy 29697 864-847-4121
Dr. Jerry Kirkley, dir. Fax 847-3539

Williston, Barnwell, Pop. 3,260
Williston SD 29 1,000/PK-12
12255 Main St 29853 803-266-7878
Alexia Clamp, supt. Fax 266-3879
www.williston.k12.sc.us
Williston-Elko HS 300/9-12
12233 Main St 29853 803-266-3110
Samuel Lax, prin. Fax 266-5489
Williston-Elko MS 300/6-8
12333 Main St 29853 803-266-3430
Dr. Eavon Hickson, prin. Fax 266-7623

Winnsboro, Fairfield, Pop. 3,612
Fairfield County SD 3,600/PK-12
PO Box 622 29180 803-635-4607
Dr. Clarence Willie, supt. Fax 635-6578
www.fairfield.k12.sc.us/
Fairfield Career & Technology Center Vo/Tech
1451 US Highway 321 N 29180 803-635-5506
Robert Sharpe, prin. Fax 635-9958
Fairfield Central HS 1,100/9-12
836 US Highway 321 Byp S 29180 803-635-1441
Nathaniel Nelson, prin. Fax 635-3997
Fairfield MS 600/7-8
728 US Highway 321 Byp S 29180 803-635-4270
Tammy Martin, prin. Fax 635-9108

Winn Academy 300/K-12
PO Box 390 29180 803-635-5494
Christopher Thoma, prin. Fax 635-4310

Woodruff, Spartanburg, Pop. 4,105
Spartanburg SD 4 3,000/PK-12
118 McEdco Rd 29388 864-476-3186
Dr. W. Rallie Liston, supt. Fax 476-8616
www.spartanburg4.org
Woodruff HS 800/9-12
710 Cross Anchor Rd 29388 864-476-7045
Karen Neal, prin. Fax 476-7224
Woodruff MS 800/6-8
205 SJ Workman Hwy 29388 864-476-3150
Denise Brown, prin. Fax 476-6036

York, York, Pop. 7,233
York SD 1 5,100/PK-12
PO Box 770 29745 803-684-9916
Russell Booker, supt. Fax 684-1903
www.york.k12.sc.us
Johnson Technical Center Vo/Tech
1010 Devinney Rd 29745 803-684-1910
Ron Roveri, prin. Fax 684-1913
York Comprehensive HS 1,000/10-12
1010 Devinney Rd 29745 803-684-2336
Diane Howell, prin. Fax 684-1932
York JHS 800/8-9
1280 Johnson Rd 29745 803-684-5008
Louvetta Dicks, prin. Fax 684-1916

Blessed Hope Baptist S 200/K-12
410 Blessed Hope Rd 29745 803-684-9819
Tommy Arrowood, prin. Fax 684-9849

SOUTH DAKOTA

SOUTH DAKOTA DEPARTMENT OF EDUCATION
700 Governors Dr, Pierre 57501
Telephone 605-773-5669
Fax 605-773-6139
Website http://www.state.sd.us/deca

Secretary of Education Dr. Rick Melmer

SOUTH DAKOTA BOARD OF EDUCATION
700 Governors Dr, Pierre 57501

President Kelly Duncan

PUBLIC, PRIVATE AND CATHOLIC SECONDARY SCHOOLS

Aberdeen, Brown, Pop. 24,098
Aberdeen SD 6-1 3,600/K-12
314 S Main St 57401 605-725-7100
Dr. Gary Harms, supt. Fax 725-7199
www.aberdeen.k12.sd.us
Central HS 1,200/9-12
2200 S Roosevelt St 57401 605-725-8100
Jason Uttermark, prin. Fax 725-8199
Holgate MS 400/6-8
2200 N Dakota St 57401 605-725-7700
Dr. Greg Aas, prin. Fax 725-7799
Simmons MS 400/6-8
1300 S 3rd St 57401 605-725-7900
Jerry Heupel, prin. Fax 725-7999

Hub Area Multi-District
640 9th Ave SW 57401 888-482-2732
John Emmett, supt. Fax 725-7899
www.hubarea.com
Hub Area Technical S Vo/Tech
640 9th Ave SW 57401 888-482-2732
John Emmett, prin. Fax 725-7899

Aberdeen Christian HS 50/9-12
PO Box 548 57402 605-226-3125
Patricia Wiens, admin. Fax 225-2873
Northern State University Post-Sec.
1200 S Jay St 57401 605-626-3011
Presentation College Post-Sec.
1500 N Main St 57401 605-225-1634
Roncalli HS 200/7-12
1400 N Dakota St 57401 605-226-2100
Mike Radke, prin. Fax 226-0616
St. Luke's Midland Regional Medical Ctr. Post-Sec.
305 S State St 57401 605-622-5230
South Dakota School Visually Handicapped Post-Sec.
423 17th Ave SE 57401 605-626-2580

Alcester, Union, Pop. 889
Alcester-Hudson SD 61-1 300/PK-12
PO Box 198 57001 605-934-1890
Jerry L. Joachim, supt. Fax 934-1936
www.alcester-hudson.k12.sd.us
Alcester-Hudson HS 100/9-12
PO Box 198 57001 605-934-1890
LeeAnn R. Haisch, prin. Fax 934-1936
Alcester-Hudson JHS 50/7-8
PO Box 198 57001 605-934-1890
LeeAnn R. Haisch, prin. Fax 934-1936

Alexandria, Hanson, Pop. 676
Hanson SD 30-1 300/PK-12
PO Box 490 57311 605-239-4387
Jeff Danielsen, supt. Fax 239-4293
www.hanson.k12.sd.us/
Hanson HS 100/9-12
PO Box 490 57311 605-239-4387
James Bridge, prin. Fax 239-4293
Hanson JHS 50/7-8
PO Box 490 57311 605-239-4387
James Bridge, prin. Fax 239-4293

Arlington, Kingsbury, Pop. 952
Arlington SD 38-1 300/K-12
PO Box 359 57212 605-983-5597
Chris Lund, supt. Fax 983-4652
www.arlington.k12.sd.us
Arlington HS 100/9-12
PO Box 359 57212 605-983-5598
Rhonda Gross, prin. Fax 983-4652
Arlington JHS 50/7-8
PO Box 359 57212 605-983-5598
Rhonda Gross, prin. Fax 983-4652

Armour, Douglas, Pop. 736
Armour SD 21-1 200/K-12
PO Box 640 57313 605-724-2153
Wallace Weatherford, supt. Fax 724-2977
www.armour.k12.sd.us/
Armour HS 100/9-12
PO Box 640 57313 605-724-2153
Brad Preheim, prin. Fax 724-2799
Armour MS 100/5-8
PO Box 640 57313 605-724-2698
Wallace Weatherford, prin. Fax 724-2799

Avon, Bon Homme, Pop. 543
Avon SD 4-1 300/PK-12
PO Box 407 57315 605-286-3291
Tom Oster, supt. Fax 286-3712
www.avon.k12.sd.us/
Avon HS 100/9-12
PO Box 407 57315 605-286-3291
Tom Culver, prin. Fax 286-3510
Avon JHS 50/7-8
PO Box 407 57315 605-286-3291
Tom Culver, prin. Fax 286-3712

Baltic, Minnehaha, Pop. 932
Baltic SD 49-1 400/PK-12
PO Box 309 57003 605-529-5464
Robert Sittig, supt. Fax 529-5443
www.baltic.k12.sd.us/
Baltic HS 100/9-12
PO Box 309 57003 605-529-5461
James Aisenbery, prin. Fax 529-5467
Baltic MS 100/6-8
PO Box 309 57003 605-529-5461
James Aisenbery, prin. Fax 529-5467

Belle Fourche, Butte, Pop. 4,675
Belle Fourche SD 9-1 1,300/PK-12
2305 13th Ave 57717 605-723-3355
William O'Dea, supt. Fax 723-3366
www.bellefourche.k12.sd.us/
Belle Fourche HS 400/9-12
2305 13th Ave 57717 605-723-3350
Steve Willard, prin. Fax 723-3357
Belle Fourche MS 400/5-8
2305 13th Ave 57717 605-723-3367
Karen Wagner, prin. Fax 723-3374

Beresford, Union, Pop. 2,027
Beresford SD 61-2 600/PK-12
209 S 4th St 57004 605-763-5012
Vince Schaefer, supt. Fax 763-2205
www.beresford.k12.sd.us/
Beresford HS 200/9-12
301 W Maple St 57004 605-763-2145
Mike Embrock, prin. Fax 763-5305
Beresford MS 100/6-8
205 W Maple St 57004 605-763-2139
Mike Limmer, prin. Fax 763-5305

Big Stone City, Grant, Pop. 570
Big Stone CSD 25-1 100/PK-8
655 Walnut St 57216 605-862-8108
Carmen Hills, supt. Fax 862-8640
www.bigstonecity.k12.sd.us
Big Stone City JHS 50/6-8
655 Walnut St 57216 605-862-8108
Carmen Hills, prin. Fax 862-8640

Bison, Perkins, Pop. 342
Bison SD 52-1 100/K-12
PO Box 9 57620 605-244-5271
Sharon Soehren, admin. Fax 244-5276
www.bison.k12.sd.us/
Bison HS 50/9-12
PO Box 9 57620 605-244-5961
Sharon Soehren, prin. Fax 244-5276
Bison JHS 50/7-8
PO Box 9 57620 605-244-5961
Sharon Soehren, prin. Fax 244-5276

Bonesteel, Gregory, Pop. 270
Bonesteel-Fairfax SD 26-5 200/PK-12
PO Box 410 57317 605-654-2314
Jack Broome, supt. Fax 654-2348
www.bonesteel-fairfax.k12.sd.us/
Bonesteel-Fairfax HS 100/9-12
PO Box 410 57317 605-654-2314
Ray Slaba, prin. Fax 654-2348
Bonesteel-Fairfax JHS 50/7-8
PO Box 410 57317 605-654-2314
Ray Slaba, prin. Fax 654-2348

Bowdle, Edmunds, Pop. 523
Bowdle SD 22-1 100/K-12
PO Box 563 57428 605-285-6272
Richard Ulrich, supt. Fax 285-6830
www.bowdle.k12.sd.us
Bowdle HS 50/9-12
PO Box 563 57428 605-285-6590
Richard Ulrich, prin. Fax 285-6830
Bowdle JHS 50/7-8
PO Box 563 57428 605-285-6590
Richard Ulrich, prin. Fax 285-6830

Box Elder, Pennington, Pop. 2,992
Douglas SD 51-1 2,500/PK-12
400 Patriot Dr 57719 605-923-0000
Dr. Loren Scheer, supt. Fax 923-0018
www.dsdk12.net
Douglas HS 700/9-12
420 Patriot Dr 57719 605-923-0030
Bud Gusso, prin. Fax 923-0031
Douglas MS 600/6-8
401 Tower Rd 57719 605-923-0050
Lee Thomas, prin. Fax 923-0051

Brandon, Minnehaha, Pop. 7,176
Brandon Valley SD 49-2 2,700/PK-12
301 S Splitrock Blvd 57005 605-582-2049
David Pappone, supt. Fax 582-7456
www.brandonvalleyschools.com
Brandon Valley HS 800/9-12
301 S Splitrock Blvd 57005 605-582-3211
Gregg Talcott, prin. Fax 582-2652
Brandon Valley MS 600/6-8
700 E Holly Blvd 57005 605-582-3214
Dan Pansch, prin. Fax 582-7206

Bridgewater, McCook, Pop. 592
Bridgewater SD 43-6 200/PK-12
PO Box 350 57319 605-729-2541
Jason Bailey, admin. Fax 729-2580
www.bridgewater.k12.sd.us/
Bridgewater HS 100/9-12
PO Box 350 57319 605-729-2541
Christena Schultz, prin. Fax 729-2580
Bridgewater MS 50/6-8
PO Box 350 57319 605-729-2541
Christena Schultz, prin. Fax 729-2580

Britton, Marshall, Pop. 1,282
Britton-Hecla SD 45-4 500/PK-12
PO Box 190 57430 605-448-2234
Donald Kirkegaard, supt. Fax 448-5994
www.britton.k12.sd.us/
Britton-Hecla HS 200/9-12
PO Box 190 57430 605-448-2234
Marcia Forrester, prin. Fax 448-5994
Britton-Hecla JHS 100/7-8
PO Box 190 57430 605-448-2234
Marcia Forrester, prin. Fax 448-5994

Brookings, Brookings, Pop. 18,715
Brookings SD 5-1 2,600/K-12
2130 8th St S 57006 605-696-4700
Orville Creighton, supt. Fax 696-4704
www.brookings.k12.sd.us/
Brookings HS 800/9-12
530 Elm Ave 57006 605-696-4100
Douglas Beste, prin. Fax 696-4128
Mickelson MS 600/6-8
1801 12th St S 57006 605-696-4500
Dan Neiles, prin. Fax 696-4506

East Central Multi-District
700 Elm Ave 57006 605-696-4754
Fran Schoenfelder, supt. Fax 696-4765
www.ecmdmulti.com
Select HS Vo/Tech
504 3rd Ave 57006 605-696-4766
Gayle Klinker, prin. Fax 696-4768

South Dakota State University Post-Sec.
PO Box 2201 57007 605-688-4151

Buffalo, Harding, Pop. 341
Harding County SD 31-1 200/K-12
PO Box 367 57720 605-375-3241
Kirby Baier, supt. Fax 375-3246
www.hardingcounty.k12.sd.us/
Harding County HS 100/9-12
PO Box 367 57720 605-375-3241
Kirby Baier, prin. Fax 375-3246
Harding County JHS 50/7-8
PO Box 367 57720 605-375-3241
Kirby Baier, prin. Fax 375-3246

Burke, Gregory, Pop. 606
Burke SD 26-2 200/K-12
PO Box 382 57523 605-775-2644
Jack Broome, supt. Fax 775-2468
Burke HS 100/9-12
PO Box 382 57523 605-775-2645
Randy DeWolf, prin. Fax 775-2468
Burke JHS 100/6-8
PO Box 382 57523 605-775-2645
Randy DeWolf, prin. Fax 775-2468

Canistota, McCook, Pop. 700
Canistota SD 43-1 300/K-12
PO Box 8 57012 605-296-3458
Wayne Wormstadt, supt. Fax 296-3158
www.canistota.k12.sd.us
Canistota HS 100/9-12
PO Box 8 57012 605-296-3458
Chad Janzen, prin. Fax 296-3158
Canistota JHS 50/7-8
PO Box 8 57012 605-296-3458
Chad Janzen, prin. Fax 296-3158

Canton, Lincoln, Pop. 3,165
Canton SD 41-1 900/PK-12
800 N Main St 57013 605-764-2706
Terry Majeres, supt. Fax 764-2700
www.canton.k12.sd.us
Canton HS 300/9-12
800 N Main St 57013 605-764-2706
Cory Strasser, prin. Fax 764-2700
Canton MS 200/6-8
800 N Main St 57013 605-764-2706
Terry Gerber, prin. Fax 764-2700

Castlewood, Hamlin, Pop. 681
Castlewood SD 28-1 300/K-12
310 E Harry St 57223 605-793-2351
Keith Fodness, supt. Fax 793-2679
www.castlewood.k12.sd.us/
Castlewood HS 100/9-12
310 E Harry St 57223 605-793-2351
Keith Fodness, prin. Fax 793-2679
Castlewood JHS 50/7-8
310 E Harry St 57223 605-793-2351
Keith Fodness, prin. Fax 793-2679

Centerville, Turner, Pop. 864
Centerville SD 60-1 300/PK-12
PO Box 100 57014 605-563-2291
Doug Voss, supt. Fax 563-2615
www.centerville.k12.sd.us
Centerville HS 100/9-12
PO Box 100 57014 605-563-2291
Roger Hansen, prin. Fax 563-2615
Centerville JHS 50/7-8
PO Box 100 57014 605-563-2291
Roger Hansen, prin. Fax 563-2615

Chamberlain, Brule, Pop. 2,259
Chamberlain SD 7-1 800/PK-12
PO Box 119 57325 605-234-4477
Tim Mitchell, supt. Fax 234-4479
www.cubs.org
Chamberlain HS 300/9-12
PO Box 119 57325 605-234-4467
Deb Johnson, prin. Fax 234-4479
Chamberlain MS 100/7-8
PO Box 119 57325 605-234-4467
Deb Johnson, prin. Fax 234-4479

Chester, Lake
Chester Area SD 39-1 400/PK-12
PO Box 159 57016 605-489-2411
Mark Greguson, supt. Fax 489-2413
www.chester.k12.sd.us
Chester HS 100/9-12
PO Box 159 57016 605-489-2411
Michael Reinhiller, prin. Fax 489-2413
Chester JHS 100/7-8
PO Box 159 57016 605-489-2411
Michael Reinhiller, prin. Fax 489-2413

Clark, Clark, Pop. 1,186
Clark SD 12-2 400/PK-12
220 N Clinton St 57225 605-532-3603
Jim Holbeck, supt. Fax 532-3600
clark.k12.sd.us/
Clark HS 100/9-12
220 N Clinton St 57225 605-532-3605
Jerry Hartley, prin. Fax 532-3600
Clark JHS 100/7-8
220 N Clinton St 57225 605-532-3605
Jerry Hartley, prin. Fax 532-3600

Clear Lake, Deuel, Pop. 1,243
Deuel SD 19-4 500/PK-12
PO Box 770 57226 605-874-2163
Dean Christensen, supt. Fax 874-8585
www.deuel.k12.sd.us/
Deuel HS 200/9-12
PO Box 770 57226 605-874-2163
Steve Benson, prin. Fax 874-8585
Deuel MS 100/6-8
PO Box 770 57226 605-874-2163
Tim Steffensen, prin. Fax 874-8585

Colman, Moody, Pop. 559
Colman-Egan SD 50-5 300/K-12
PO Box I 57017 605-534-3534
Roger Fritz, supt. Fax 534-3670
www.colman-egan.k12.sd.us
Colman-Egan HS 100/9-12
PO Box I 57017 605-534-3534
Terrance Stulken, prin. Fax 534-3670
Colman-Egan JHS 50/7-8
PO Box I 57017 605-534-3534
Terrance Stulken, prin. Fax 534-3670

Colome, Tripp, Pop. 312
Colome SD 59-1 200/K-12
PO Box 367 57528 605-842-1624
Alan Armstrong, supt. Fax 842-0783
www.colome.k12.sd.us/
Colome HS 100/9-12
PO Box 367 57528 605-842-1624
Alan Armstrong, prin. Fax 842-0783
Colome JHS 50/7-8
PO Box 367 57528 605-842-1624
Alan Armstrong, prin. Fax 842-0783

Colton, Minnehaha, Pop. 658
Tri-Valley SD 49-6 800/PK-12
46450 252nd St 57018 605-446-3538
Terry Eckstaine, supt. Fax 446-3520
www.tri-valley.k12.sd.us/
Tri-Valley HS 300/9-12
46450 252nd St 57018 605-446-3538
Tim Pflanz, prin. Fax 446-3520
Tri-Valley MS 100/7-8
46450 252nd St 57018 605-446-3538
Tim Pflanz, prin. Fax 446-3520

Conde, Spink, Pop. 171
Conde SD 56-1 100/PK-12
PO Box 10 57434 605-382-5231
Jerry McPartland, supt. Fax 382-5650
www.conde.k12.sd.us/
Conde HS 50/9-12
PO Box 10 57434 605-382-5231
Matt Pollock, prin. Fax 382-5650
Conde JHS 50/7-8
PO Box 10 57434 605-382-5231
Matt Pollock, prin. Fax 382-5650

Corsica, Douglas, Pop. 625
Corsica SD 21-2 200/PK-12
120 S Napoleon Ave 57328 605-946-5475
Vern DeGeest, supt. Fax 946-5607
www.corsica.k12.sd.us
Corsica HS 100/9-12
120 S Napoleon Ave 57328 605-946-5475
Scott Muckey, prin. Fax 946-5607
Corsica MS 50/6-8
120 S Napoleon Ave 57328 605-946-5475
Vern Degeest, prin. Fax 946-5607

Dakota Christian S 100/PK-12
37614 SD Highway 44 57328 605-243-2211
Barry Miedema, prin. Fax 243-2379

Custer, Custer, Pop. 1,991
Custer SD 16-1 1,000/PK-12
147 N 5th St 57730 605-673-3154
Dr. Tim Creal, supt. Fax 673-5607
www.csd.k12.sd.us
Custer HS 300/9-12
1645 Wild Cat Ln 57730 605-673-4473
Larry Luitjens, prin. Fax 673-4710
Custer MS 200/6-8
527 Montgomery St 57730 605-673-4540
Larry Luitjens, prin. Fax 673-4710

Dell Rapids, Minnehaha, Pop. 3,188
Dell Rapids SD 49-3 900/PK-12
1216 N Garfield Ave 57022 605-428-5473
Thomas Ludens, supt. Fax 428-5609
www.dellrapids.k12.sd.us/district
Dell Rapids HS 300/9-12
1216 N Garfield Ave 57022 605-428-5473
Bruce Olson, prin. Fax 428-5609
Dell Rapids MS 300/5-8
1216 N Garfield Ave 57022 605-428-5473
Fran Ruesink, prin. Fax 428-5609

St. Mary HS 100/7-12
812 N State Ave 57022 605-428-5591
Tom Jastram, prin. Fax 428-5377

De Smet, Kingsbury, Pop. 1,089
De Smet SD 38-2 300/K-12
PO Box 157 57231 605-854-3070
Jim Altenburg, admin. Fax 854-9138
www.desmet.k12.sd.us
De Smet HS 100/9-12
PO Box 157 57231 605-854-3423
Jim Altenburg, prin. Fax 854-9138
De Smet MS 100/6-8
PO Box 157 57231 605-854-3423
Jim Altenburg, prin. Fax 854-9138

Doland, Spink, Pop. 270
Doland SD 56-2 200/K-12
PO Box 385 57436 605-635-6302
Jerry McPartland, supt. Fax 635-6504
www.doland.k12.sd.us/
Doland HS 100/9-12
PO Box 385 57436 605-635-6241
Jim Hulscher, prin. Fax 635-6504
Doland JHS 50/7-8
PO Box 385 57436 605-635-6241
Jim Hulscher, prin. Fax 635-6504

Dupree, Ziebach, Pop. 450
Dupree SD 64-2 300/PK-12
PO Box 10 57623 605-365-5140
Dr. Chris Christensen, supt. Fax 365-5514
www.dupree.k12.sd.us/
Dupree HS 100/9-12
PO Box 10 57623 605-365-5140
Carol Veit, prin. Fax 365-5514
Dupree JHS 50/7-8
PO Box 10 57623 605-365-5140
Carol Veit, prin. Fax 365-5514

Eagle Butte, Dewey, Pop. 1,817
Eagle Butte SD 20-1 300/K-12
PO Box 260 57625 605-964-4911
Dr. Edward Slocum, supt. Fax 964-4912
Eagle Butte HS 50/9-12
PO Box 672 57625 605-964-8744
Cynthia McCrea, prin. Fax 964-8700
Eagle Butte JHS 50/7-8
PO Box 672 57625 605-964-7841
Jesse Mendoza, prin. Fax 964-1224

Si Tanka University Post-Sec.
PO Box 220 57625 605-964-8011

Edgemont, Fall River, Pop. 823
Edgemont SD 23-1 200/K-12
PO Box 29 57735 605-662-7294
Lane Ostenson, supt. Fax 662-7721
edgemont.k12.sd.us
Edgemont HS 100/9-12
PO Box 29 57735 605-662-7254
Linda Tidball, prin. Fax 662-7721
Edgemont JHS 50/7-8
PO Box 29 57735 605-662-7254
Linda Tidball, prin. Fax 662-7721

Elk Point, Union, Pop. 1,836
Elk Point-Jefferson SD 61-7 700/PK-12
PO Box 578 57025 605-356-5950
Brian Shanks, supt. Fax 356-5953
www.epj.k12.sd.us/
Elk Point-Jefferson HS 200/9-12
PO Box 578 57025 605-356-5900
Travis Aslesen, prin. Fax 356-5999
Elk Point-Jefferson MS 100/7-8
PO Box 578 57025 605-356-5900
Travis Aslesen, prin. Fax 356-5999

Elkton, Brookings, Pop. 619
Elkton SD 5-3 300/K-12
PO Box 190 57026 605-542-5361
Gordon Fuhr, supt. Fax 542-4441
elktonps.org/
Elkton HS 100/9-12
PO Box 190 57026 605-542-2541
Brian Jandahl, prin. Fax 542-4441
Elkton JHS 50/7-8
PO Box 190 57026 605-542-2541
Brian Jandahl, prin. Fax 542-4441

Ellsworth AFB, Meade, Pop. 7,017

National American University Post-Sec.
1270 Ryan St 57706 605-923-5856

Emery, Hanson, Pop. 526
Emery SD 30-2 200/PK-12
PO Box 265 57332 605-449-4271
Jason Bailey, supt. Fax 449-4270
www.emery.k12.sd.us/
Emery HS 100/9-12
PO Box 265 57332 605-449-4271
Christena Schultz, prin. Fax 449-4270
Emery JHS 50/6-8
PO Box 265 57332 605-449-4271
Christena Schultz, prin. Fax 449-4270

Estelline, Hamlin, Pop. 687
Estelline SD 28-2 200/K-12
PO Box 306 57234 605-873-2201
Chip Sundberg, supt. Fax 873-2102
www.estelline.k12.sd.us
Estelline HS 100/9-12
PO Box 306 57234 605-873-2201
Chip Sundberg, prin. Fax 873-2102

Ethan, Davison, Pop. 318
Ethan SD 17-1 200/PK-12
PO Box 169 57334 605-227-4211
Terry Mathis, supt. Fax 227-4236
www.ethan.k12.sd.us/
Ethan HS 100/9-12
PO Box 169 57334 605-227-4211
Joel Bergeson, prin. Fax 227-4236
Ethan MS 50/6-8
PO Box 169 57334 605-227-4211
Joel Bergeson, prin. Fax 227-4236

Eureka, McPherson, Pop. 988
Eureka SD 44-1 200/K-12
PO Box 10 57437 605-284-2875
Dr. Peggy Petersen, supt. Fax 284-2810
www.eureka.k12.sd.us/
Eureka HS 100/9-12
PO Box 10 57437 605-284-2521
Bo Beck, prin. Fax 284-2810
Eureka JHS 50/7-8
PO Box 10 57437 605-284-2521
Bo Beck, prin. Fax 284-2810

Faith, Meade, Pop. 474
Faith SD 46-2 200/K-12
PO Box 619 57626 605-967-2152
Mel Dutton, supt. Fax 967-2153
www.faith.k12.sd.us/
Faith HS 100/9-12
PO Box 619 57626 605-967-2152
Mel Dutton, prin. Fax 967-2153
Faith JHS 50/7-8
PO Box 619 57626 605-967-2152
Michelle Becker, prin. Fax 967-2153

Faulkton, Faulk, Pop. 703
Faulkton Area SD 24-3 300/K-12
PO Box 308 57438 605-598-6266
Joel Price, supt. Fax 598-6666
www.faulkton.k12.sd.us
Faulkton HS 100/9-12
PO Box 308 57438 605-598-6266
Craig Cassens, prin. Fax 598-6666
Faulkton JHS 50/7-8
PO Box 308 57438 605-598-6266
Craig Cassens, prin. Fax 598-6666

Flandreau, Moody, Pop. 2,327
Flandreau SD 50-3 700/K-12
600 W Community Dr 57028 605-997-3263
Rick Weber, supt. Fax 997-2457
www.flandreau.k12.sd.us
Flandreau HS 200/9-12
600 W Community Dr 57028 605-997-2455
Janna Ellingson, prin. Fax 997-2457
Flandreau MS 100/6-8
700 W Community Dr 57028 605-997-2705
Brian Relf, prin. Fax 997-2457

Florence, Codington, Pop. 297
Florence SD 14-1 200/PK-12
PO Box 66 57235 605-758-2412
Gary Leighton, supt. Fax 758-2433
www.florence.k12.sd.us/
Florence HS 100/9-12
PO Box 66 57235 605-758-2412
Gary Leighton, prin. Fax 758-2433
Florence JHS 50/7-8
PO Box 66 57235 605-758-2412
Gary Leighton, prin. Fax 758-2433

Forestburg, Sanborn
Sanborn Central SD 55-5 200/K-12
40405 SD Highway 34 57314 605-495-4183
Linda Whitney, supt. Fax 495-4185
www.sanborncentral.com/
Sanborn Central HS 100/9-12
40405 SD Highway 34 57314 605-495-4183
Linda Whitney, prin. Fax 495-4185
Sanborn Central MS 100/6-8
40405 SD Highway 34 57314 605-495-4183
Connie Vermeulen, prin. Fax 495-4185

Fort Pierre, Stanley, Pop. 2,069
Stanley County SD 57-1 500/K-12
PO Box 370 57532 605-223-7741
Larry Jaske, supt. Fax 223-7750
www.stanleycounty.k12.sd.us
Stanley County HS 200/9-12
PO Box 370 57532 605-223-7743
Brian Doherty, prin. Fax 223-7751
Stanley County MS 100/6-8
PO Box 370 57532 605-223-7743
Brian Doherty, prin. Fax 223-7751

Frederick, Brown, Pop. 243
Frederick Area SD 6-2 200/PK-12
PO Box 486 57441 605-329-2145
Randall Barondeau, supt. Fax 329-2722
www.frederickarea.k12.sd.us/
Frederick HS 100/9-12
PO Box 486 57441 605-329-2145
Randy Barondeau, prin. Fax 329-2722
Frederick JHS 50/7-8
PO Box 486 57441 605-329-2145
Randy Barondeau, prin. Fax 329-2722

Freeman, Hutchinson, Pop. 1,223
Freeman SD 33-1 400/K-12
PO Box 220 57029 605-925-4214
Don Hotchkiss, supt. Fax 925-4814
www.freeman.k12.sd.us/
Freeman HS 100/9-12
PO Box 220 57029 605-925-4214
Kim Krull, prin. Fax 925-4814
Freeman JHS 100/7-8
PO Box 220 57029 605-925-4214
Kim Krull, prin. Fax 925-4814

Freeman Academy 100/5-12
PO Box 1000 57029 605-925-4237
Nathan Epp, prin. Fax 925-4271

Garretson, Minnehaha, Pop. 1,152
Garretson SD 49-4 600/PK-12
PO Box C 57030 605-594-3451
Robert Arend, supt. Fax 594-3443
www.garretson.k12.sd.us/
Garretson HS 200/9-12
PO Box C 57030 605-594-3452
Ryan Van Zee, prin. Fax 594-3443
Garretson MS 100/6-8
PO Box C 57030 605-594-3452
Ryan Van Zee, prin. Fax 594-3443

Gayville, Yankton, Pop. 393
Gayville-Volin SD 63-1 200/K-12
PO Box 158 57031 605-267-4476
Jason Selchert, supt. Fax 267-4294
www.gayvillevolin.k12.sd.us/
Gayville-Volin HS 100/9-12
PO Box 158 57031 605-267-4476
Natasha Gault, prin. Fax 267-4294
Gayville-Volin MS 100/6-8
PO Box 158 57031 605-267-4476
Natasha Gault, prin. Fax 267-4294

Geddes, Charles Mix, Pop. 245
Geddes Community SD 11-2 100/PK-12
PO Box 197 57342 605-337-3382
Sandy Gant, admin. Fax 337-3383
www.geddes.k12.sd.us/
Geddes HS 50/9-12
PO Box 197 57342 605-337-3382
Sandy Gant, prin. Fax 337-3383
Geddes JHS 50/7-8
PO Box 197 57342 605-337-3382
Jesse Sealey, prin. Fax 337-3383

Gettysburg, Potter, Pop. 1,169
Gettysburg SD 53-1 300/K-12
100 E King Ave 57442 605-765-2436
Jeff Marlette, supt. Fax 765-2249
www.gettysburg.k12.sd.us/
Gettysburg HS 100/9-12
100 E King Ave 57442 605-765-2436
Scott Kortan, prin. Fax 765-2249
Gettysburg JHS 100/6-8
100 E King Ave 57442 605-765-2436
Scott Kortan, prin. Fax 765-2249

Gregory, Gregory, Pop. 1,186
Gregory SD 26-4 400/K-12
PO Box 438 57533 605-835-8771
David Nicholas, supt. Fax 835-8744
www.gregory.k12.sd.us/
Gregory HS 100/9-12
PO Box 438 57533 605-835-9672
Michael Dacy, prin. Fax 835-8146
Gregory MS 100/6-8
PO Box 438 57533 605-835-9672
Michael Dacy, prin. Fax 835-8146

Groton, Brown, Pop. 1,365
Groton Area SD 6-6 600/PK-12
PO Box 410 57445 605-397-2351
Laura Schuster, supt. Fax 397-8453
www.groton.k12.sd.us/
Groton HS 9-12
PO Box 410 57445 605-397-8381
Todd Sweeter, prin. Fax 397-8453
Groton JHS 7-8
PO Box 410 57445 605-397-8381
Todd Sweeter, prin. Fax 397-8453

Harrisburg, Lincoln, Pop. 1,875
Harrisburg SD 41-2 1,100/PK-12
PO Box 187 57032 605-743-2567
James Hargens, supt. Fax 743-2569
www.harrisburg.k12.sd.us
Harrisburg HS 300/9-12
PO Box 309 57032 605-743-2567
Keith Huber, prin. Fax 743-5630
Harrisburg MS 300/6-8
PO Box 309 57032 605-743-2567
Kristine Alcon, prin. Fax 743-2569

Harrold, Hughes, Pop. 206
Harrold SD 32-1 100/K-12
PO Box 160 57536 605-875-3298
Ward Thelen, supt. Fax 875-3274
www.harrold.k12.sd.us/
Harrold HS 50/9-12
PO Box 160 57536 605-875-3298
Ward Thelen, prin. Fax 875-3274
Harrold JHS 50/7-8
PO Box 160 57536 605-875-3298
Ward Thelen, prin. Fax 875-3274

Hartford, Minnehaha, Pop. 2,065
West Central SD 49-7 1,100/PK-12
PO Box 730 57033 605-528-3217
Paul Gausman, supt. Fax 528-3219
www.westcentral.k12.sd.us/
West Central HS 400/9-12
PO Box 730 57033 605-528-6236
Mark Hofer, prin. Fax 528-6217
West Central MS 300/6-8
PO Box 730 57033 605-528-3799
Guy Johnson, prin. Fax 528-3702

Hayti, Hamlin, Pop. 362
Hamlin SD 28-3 600/PK-12
44577 188th St 57241 605-783-3631
Joel Jorgenson, supt. Fax 783-3632
www.hamlin.k12.sd.us/
Hamlin HS 200/9-12
44577 188th St 57241 605-783-3644
Richard Schneider, prin. Fax 783-3360
Hamlin MS 100/7-8
44577 188th St 57241 605-783-3631
Richard Schneider, prin. Fax 783-3632

Henry, Codington, Pop. 258
Henry SD 14-2 200/K-12
PO Box 8 57243 605-532-5364
Lee Quale, supt. Fax 532-3795
www.henry.k12.sd.us/
Henry HS 100/9-12
PO Box 8 57243 605-532-5364
Lee Quale, prin. Fax 532-3795
Henry JHS 50/7-8
PO Box 8 57243 605-532-5364
Lee Quale, prin. Fax 532-5364

Herreid, Campbell, Pop. 415
Herreid SD 10-1 100/K-12
PO Box 276 57632 605-437-2263
Steve Volk, admin. Fax 437-2264
Herreid HS 50/9-12
PO Box 276 57632 605-437-2263
Steve Volk, prin. Fax 437-2264
Herreid JHS 50/6-8
PO Box 276 57632 605-437-2263
Steve Volk, prin. Fax 437-2264

Highmore, Hyde, Pop. 808
Hyde SD 34-1 300/PK-12
PO Box 416 57345 605-852-2389
Elsie Baye, supt. Fax 852-2295
Highmore HS 100/9-12
PO Box 416 57345 605-852-2275
James Jones, prin. Fax 852-2295
Highmore JHS 50/7-8
PO Box 416 57345 605-852-2275
James Jones, prin. Fax 852-2295

Hill City, Pennington, Pop. 846
Hill City SD 51-2 500/PK-12
PO Box 659 57745 605-574-3030
Mark Naugle, supt. Fax 574-3031
www.hillcity.k12.sd.us
Hill City HS 200/9-12
PO Box 659 57745 605-574-3005
Todd Satter, prin. Fax 574-3040
Hill City MS 100/6-8
PO Box 659 57745 605-574-3025
Dave Larson, prin. Fax 574-3044

Hot Springs, Fall River, Pop. 4,102
Hot Springs SD 23-2 900/PK-12
1609 University Ave 57747 605-745-4145
Vern Hagedorn, supt. Fax 745-4178
www.hssd.k12.sd.us
Hot Springs HS 300/9-12
146 N 16th St 57747 605-745-4147
Mary Weiss, prin. Fax 745-4061
Hot Springs MS 200/6-8
1609 University Ave 57747 605-745-4146
Kelly Northrup, prin. Fax 745-6387

Hoven, Potter, Pop. 436
Hoven SD 53-2 100/K-12
PO Box 128 57450 605-948-2252
Ron Jacobson, supt. Fax 948-2477
Hoven HS 50/9-12
PO Box 128 57450 605-948-2252
Ron Jacobson, prin. Fax 948-2477
Hoven JHS 50/7-8
PO Box 128 57450 605-948-2252
Ron Jacobson, prin. Fax 948-2477

Howard, Miner, Pop. 945
Howard SD 48-3 400/PK-12
500 N Section Line St 57349 605-772-5515
Mike Cullen, supt. Fax 772-5516
www.howard.k12.sd.us/default.htm
Howard HS 200/9-12
500 N Section Line St 57349 605-772-5515
Mike Cullen, prin. Fax 772-5516
Howard JHS 100/7-8
500 N Section Line St 57349 605-772-5515
Mike Cullen, prin. Fax 772-5516

Hurley, Turner, Pop. 399
Hurley SD 60-2 200/K-12
PO Box 278 57036 605-238-5221
Shane Voss, supt. Fax 238-5223
Hurley HS 50/9-12
PO Box 278 57036 605-238-5221
Shane Voss, prin. Fax 238-5223
Hurley JHS 50/7-8
PO Box 278 57036 605-238-5221
Shane Voss, prin. Fax 238-5223

Huron, Beadle, Pop. 11,086
Huron SD 2-2 2,100/K-12
PO Box 949 57350 605-353-6990
Randall Zitterkopf, supt. Fax 353-6993
www.huron.k12.sd.us
Huron HS 700/9-12
801 18th St SW 57350 605-353-8800
Terry Nebelsick, prin. Fax 353-8807
Huron MS 500/6-8
1045 18th St SW 57350 605-353-8900
Michael Taplett, prin. Fax 353-8913

James Valley Christian S 200/PK-12
1550 Dakota Ave N 57350 605-352-7737
Paula Kleinsasser, admin. Fax 352-9893

Ipswich, Edmunds, Pop. 887
Ipswich SD 22-6 400/PK-12
PO Box 306 57451 605-426-6561
Mike Steinhoff, supt. Fax 426-6029
www.ipswich.k12.sd.us/
Ipswich HS 100/9-12
PO Box 306 57451 605-426-6571
Trent Osborne, prin. Fax 426-6029
Ipswich JHS 100/7-8
PO Box 306 57451 605-426-6571
Trent Osborne, prin. Fax 426-6029

Irene, Clay, Pop. 410
Irene SD 63-2 200/PK-12
PO Box 5 57037 605-263-3311
Larry Johnke, supt. Fax 263-3316
www.irene.k12.sd.us/
Irene HS 100/9-12
PO Box 5 57037 605-263-3313
David Hutchison, prin. Fax 263-3316
Irene JHS 50/7-8
PO Box 5 57037 605-263-3313
David Hutchison, prin. Fax 263-3316

Iroquois, Kingsbury, Pop. 258
Iroquois SD 2-3 200/K-12
PO Box 98 57353 605-546-2210
Lori Wehlander, supt. Fax 546-8540
www.iroquois.k12.sd.us/
Iroquois HS 100/9-12
PO Box 98 57353 605-546-2426
Rick Soma, prin. Fax 546-8540
Iroquois MS 50/6-8
PO Box 98 57353 605-546-2426
Rick Soma, prin. Fax 546-8540

Isabel, Dewey, Pop. 237
Isabel SD 20-2 100/K-12
PO Box 267 57633 605-466-2125
Donald Kraemer, admin. Fax 466-2124
www.isabel.k12.sd.us/
Isabel HS 50/9-12
PO Box 267 57633 605-466-2125
Russell Budmayr, prin. Fax 466-2124
Isabel JHS 50/7-8
PO Box 267 57633 605-466-2125
Russell Budmayr, prin. Fax 466-2124

Northwest Area Schools Ed Co-op
PO Box 35 57633 605-466-2206
Joseph Lenz, supt. Fax 466-2207
Northwest Area Education Co-op Vo/Tech
PO Box 35 57633 605-466-2206
Erik Person, prin. Fax 466-2207

Kadoka, Jackson, Pop. 668
Kadoka SD 35-1 300/PK-12
PO Box 99 57543 605-837-2175
Mary Austad, supt. Fax 837-2176
www.kadoka.k12.sd.us/
Kadoka HS 100/7-12
PO Box 99 57543 605-837-2172
Gale Patterson, prin. Fax 837-2176

Kennebec, Lyman, Pop. 284
Lyman SD 42-1
Supt. — See Presho
Lyman MS 100/6-8
PO Box 188 57544 605-869-2213
Doug Eppard, prin. Fax 869-2283

Kimball, Brule, Pop. 693
Kimball SD 7-2 300/K-12
PO Box 479 57355 605-778-6232
Bill Thompson, supt. Fax 778-6393
www.kimball.k12.sd.us
Kimball HS 100/9-12
PO Box 479 57355 605-778-6232
Duane Noeske, prin. Fax 778-6393
Kimball JHS 50/7-8
PO Box 479 57355 605-778-6231
Duane Noeske, prin. Fax 778-6393

Kyle, Shannon, Pop. 914

Oglala Lakota College Post-Sec.
PO Box 490 57752 605-455-2321

Lake Andes, Charles Mix, Pop. 783
Andes Central SD 11-1 400/PK-12
PO Box 40 57356 605-487-7671
Janet Varejcka, supt. Fax 487-7051
www.andescentral.k12.sd.us/
Andes Central HS 100/9-12
PO Box 40 57356 605-487-7671
Rocky Brinkman, prin. Fax 487-7051
Andes Central JHS 50/7-8
PO Box 40 57356 605-487-7671
Rocky Brinkman, prin. Fax 487-7051

Lake Preston, Kingsbury, Pop. 677
Lake Preston SD 38-3 200/K-12
300 1st St NE 57249 605-847-4455
Tim Casper, supt. Fax 847-4311
www.lakepreston.k12.sd.us
Lake Preston HS 100/9-12
300 1st St NE 57249 605-847-4455
Tim Casper, prin. Fax 847-4311
Lake Preston JHS 50/7-8
300 1st St NE 57249 605-847-4455
Tim Casper, prin. Fax 847-4311

Langford, Marshall, Pop. 283
Langford SD 45-2 200/K-12
PO Box 127 57454 605-493-6454
Monte Nipp, supt. Fax 493-6447
www.langford.k12.sd.us/
Langford HS 100/9-12
PO Box 127 57454 605-493-6454
Toni Brown, prin. Fax 493-6447
Langford JHS 50/7-8
PO Box 127 57454 605-493-6454
Toni Brown, prin. Fax 493-6447

Lead, Lawrence, Pop. 2,891
Lead-Deadwood SD 40-1 900/PK-12
320 S Main St 57754 605-717-3890
Dr. Dan Leikvold, supt. Fax 717-2813
www.lead-deadwood.k12.sd.us/
Lead-Deadwood HS 300/9-12
320 S Main St 57754 605-717-3899
Nick Gottlob, prin. Fax 717-2815
Lead-Deadwood MS 200/6-8
234 S Main St 57754 605-717-3898
Nick Gottlob, prin. Fax 717-2821
Other Schools – See Nemo

Lemmon, Perkins, Pop. 1,229
Lemmon SD 52-2 300/PK-12
209 3rd St W 57638 605-374-3762
Rick Herbel, supt. Fax 374-3562
www.lemmon.k12.sd.us
Lemmon HS 100/9-12
209 3rd St W 57638 605-374-3762
Rick Herbel, prin. Fax 374-3562
Lemmon JHS 50/7-8
209 3rd St W 57638 605-374-3762
Rick Herbel, prin. Fax 374-3562

Lennox, Lincoln, Pop. 2,092
Lennox SD 41-4 1,000/PK-12
PO Box 38 57039 605-647-2202
Dr. Roger DeGroot, supt. Fax 647-2201
www.lennox.k12.sd.us
Lennox HS 300/9-12
PO Box 38 57039 605-647-2203
Tim Raabe, prin. Fax 647-6045
Lennox MS 200/6-8
PO Box 38 57039 605-647-2204
Grace Christianson, prin. Fax 647-6043

Leola, McPherson, Pop. 411
Leola SD 44-2 200/PK-12
PO Box 350 57456 605-439-3143
Jamie Hermann, supt. Fax 439-3206
www.leola.k12.sd.us/
Leola HS 100/9-12
PO Box 350 57456 605-439-3143
Jamie Hermann, prin. Fax 439-3206
Leola JHS 50/7-8
PO Box 350 57456 605-439-3143
Jamie Hermann, prin. Fax 439-3206

Mc Intosh, Corson, Pop. 302
Mc Intosh SD 15-1 200/PK-12
PO Box 80 57641 605-273-4227
Dick Schaffan, supt. Fax 273-4531
www.mcintosh.k12.sd.us/
Mc Intosh HS 50/9-12
PO Box 80 57641 605-273-4227
Dick Schaffan, prin. Fax 273-4531
Mc Intosh JHS 50/7-8
PO Box 80 57641 605-273-4227
Dick Schaffan, prin. Fax 273-4531

Mc Laughlin, Corson, Pop. 799
Mc Laughlin SD 15-2 500/PK-12
PO Box 880 57642 605-823-4484
Perry Hansen, supt. Fax 823-4886
www.mclaughlin.k12.sd.us/
Mc Laughlin HS 100/9-12
PO Box 880 57642 605-823-4484
Brian Jones, prin. Fax 823-4886
Mc Laughlin MS 100/6-8
PO Box 880 57642 605-823-4484
Brian Jones, prin. Fax 823-4886

Madison, Lake, Pop. 6,223
Madison Central SD 39-2 700/K-12
800 NE 9th St 57042 605-256-7700
Dr. Frank Palleria, supt. Fax 256-7711
www.madison.k12.sd.us
Madison HS 400/9-12
800 NE 9th St 57042 605-256-7706
Sharon Knowlton, prin. Fax 256-7711
Madison MS 300/6-8
830 NE 9th St 57042 605-256-7717
Cotton Koch, prin. Fax 256-7711

Dakota State University Post-Sec.
820 N Washington Ave 57042 605-256-5112

Marion, Turner, Pop. 833
Marion SD 60-3 200/PK-12
PO Box 207 57043 605-648-3615
Denise Fox, supt. Fax 648-3652
www.marion.k12.sd.us
Marion HS 100/9-12
PO Box 207 57043 605-648-3615
Adam Shaw, prin. Fax 648-3652
Marion JHS 50/7-8
PO Box 207 57043 605-648-3615
Adam Shaw, prin. Fax 648-3617

Martin, Bennett, Pop. 1,048
Bennett County SD 3-1 400/K-12
PO Box 580 57551 605-685-6697
Wayne Semmler, supt. Fax 685-6694
www.bennettco.k12.sd.us/
Bennett County HS 100/9-12
PO Box 580 57551 605-685-6330
Wayne Semmler, prin. Fax 685-6935
Bennett County JHS 100/7-8
PO Box 580 57551 605-685-6330
Wayne Semmler, prin. Fax 685-6935

Mellette, Spink, Pop. 227
Northwestern Area SD 56-7 300/PK-12
PO Box 45 57461 605-887-3467
Ray Sauerwein, supt. Fax 887-3101
www.northwestern.k12.sd.us
Northwestern HS 100/9-12
PO Box 45 57461 605-887-3467
Ray Sauerwein, prin. Fax 887-3101
Northwestern MS 100/6-8
PO Box 45 57461 605-887-3467
Kathy Graves, prin. Fax 887-3101

Menno, Hutchinson, Pop. 697
Menno SD 33-2 300/PK-12
PO Box 346 57045 605-387-5161
Dennis Schutt, supt. Fax 387-5171
www.menno.k12.sd.us/
Menno HS 100/9-12
PO Box 346 57045 605-387-5161
Clyde Tarrence, prin. Fax 387-5171
Menno MS 100/6-8
PO Box 346 57045 605-387-5161
Terry Quam, prin. Fax 387-5171

Midland, Haakon, Pop. 158
Midland SD 27-2 50/K-8
PO Box 226 57552 605-843-2561
Mary Austad, supt. Fax 843-2562
www.midland.k12.sd.us/
Midland JHS 50/7-8
PO Box 226 57552 605-843-2561
Mary Austad, prin. Fax 843-2562

Milbank, Grant, Pop. 3,357
Milbank SD 25-4 900/PK-12
1001 E Park Ave 57252 605-432-5579
Marlin Smart, supt. Fax 432-4137
www.milbank.k12.sd.us
Milbank HS 400/9-12
1001 E Park Ave 57252 605-432-5546
Dan Snaza, prin. Fax 432-5514
Milbank MS 200/7-8
1001 E Park Ave 57252 605-432-5510
Dan Snaza, prin. Fax 432-6610

Miller, Hand, Pop. 1,364
Miller Area SD 29-3 500/PK-12
PO Box 257 57362 605-853-2614
Michael Ruth, supt. Fax 853-3041
www.miller.k12.sd.us/
Miller HS 200/9-12
PO Box 257 57362 605-853-2455
Gerry Hunter, prin. Fax 853-3041
Miller JHS 100/7-8
PO Box 257 57362 605-853-2455
Gerry Hunter, prin. Fax 853-3041

Sunshine Bible Academy 100/K-12
400 Sunshine Dr 57362 605-853-3071
Julie Hewitt, prin. Fax 853-3072

Mission, Todd, Pop. 949
Todd County SD 66-1 2,000/PK-12
PO Box 87 57555 605-856-4457
Margo Heinert, supt. Fax 856-2449
www.tcsdk12.org/
Todd County HS 500/9-12
PO Box 726 57555 605-856-2324
Victoria Sherman, prin. Fax 856-4723
Todd County MS 400/6-8
PO Box 248 57555 605-856-2341
Peggy Diekhoff, prin. Fax 856-2032

Sinte Gleska University Post-Sec.
PO Box 105 57555 605-856-5880

Mitchell, Davison, Pop. 14,696
Mitchell SD 17-2 2,500/K-12
800 W 10th Ave 57301 605-995-3010
Joseph Graves, supt. Fax 995-3089
www.mitchell.k12.sd.us
Mitchell HS 800/9-12
920 N Capital St 57301 605-995-3034
Yvonne Palli, prin. Fax 995-3047
Mitchell MS 600/6-8
800 W 10th Ave 57301 605-995-3051
Brad Berens, prin. Fax 995-3037

Dakota Wesleyan University Post-Sec.
1200 W University Ave 57301 605-995-2600
Mitchell Christian S 200/PK-12
PO Box 1285 57301 605-996-8861
Donald Mitchell, prin. Fax 996-3642
Mitchell Technical Institute Post-Sec.
821 N Capital St 57301 605-995-3024
Queen of Peace Hospital Post-Sec.
5th & Foster 57301 605-995-2250

Mobridge, Walworth, Pop. 3,279
Mobridge SD 62-3 500/PK-12
114 10th St E 57601 605-845-7227
Terry Kraft, supt. Fax 845-3455
www.mobridge.k12.sd.us/
Mobridge HS 200/9-12
114 10th St E 57601 605-845-3460
Tim Frederick, prin. Fax 845-3455
Mobridge MS 100/6-8
114 10th St E 57601 605-845-2768
Tim Frederick, prin. Fax 845-3455

Montrose, McCook, Pop. 476
Montrose SD 43-2 200/K-12
309 S Church Ave 57048 605-363-5025
Dean Kueter, supt. Fax 363-3513
www.montroseschool.k12.sd.us/
Montrose HS 100/9-12
309 S Church Ave 57048 605-363-5025
Kenneth Greeno, prin. Fax 363-3513
Montrose JHS 50/7-8
309 S Church Ave 57048 605-363-5025
Kenneth Greeno, prin. Fax 363-3513

Mount Vernon, Davison, Pop. 461
Mount Vernon SD 17-3 300/K-12
PO Box 46 57363 605-236-5237
Patrick Mikkonen, supt. Fax 236-5604
www.mtvernon.k12.sd.us/
Mount Vernon HS 100/9-12
PO Box 46 57363 605-236-5237
Patrick Mikkonen, prin. Fax 236-5604
Mount Vernon MS 100/5-8
PO Box 46 57363 605-236-5237
Margaret Freidal, prin. Fax 236-5604

Murdo, Jones, Pop. 535
Jones County SD 37-3 200/PK-12
PO Box 109 57559 605-669-2297
Gary Knispel, supt. Fax 669-3248
www.jonesco.k12.sd.us/
Jones County HS 100/9-12
PO Box 109 57559 605-669-2258
Larry Ball, prin. Fax 669-2904
Jones County MS 50/7-8
PO Box 109 57559 605-669-2258
Larry Ball, prin. Fax 669-2904

Nemo, Lawrence
Lead-Deadwood SD 40-1
Supt. — See Lead
Box Elder Job Corps Vo/Tech
PO Box 110 57759 605-578-2371
Terry Powell, prin. Fax 578-1157

Newell, Butte, Pop. 641
Newell SD 9-2 400/K-12
PO Box 99 57760 605-456-2393
Tim McCann, supt. Fax 456-2395
www.newell.k12.sd.us
Newell HS 200/9-12
PO Box 99 57760 605-456-2393
Tim McCann, prin. Fax 456-2395
Newell MS 100/6-8
PO Box 99 57760 605-456-0102
Donavan DeBoer, prin. Fax 456-2395

New Underwood, Pennington, Pop. 653
New Underwood SD 51-3 300/K-12
PO Box 128 57761 605-754-6485
Dr. Julie Ertz, supt. Fax 754-6492
www.newunderwood.k12.sd.us
New Underwood HS 100/9-12
PO Box 128 57761 605-754-6485
Karen Fox, prin. Fax 754-6492
New Underwood JHS 50/7-8
PO Box 128 57761 605-754-6485
Karen Fox, prin. Fax 754-6492

North Sioux City, Union, Pop. 2,494
Dakota Valley SD 61-8 700/K-12
1150 Northshore Dr 57049 605-422-3800
Al Leber, supt. Fax 422-3807
www.dakotavalley.k12.sd.us/
Dakota Valley HS 200/9-12
1150 Northshore Dr 57049 605-422-3820
Jerry Rasmussen, prin. Fax 422-3827
Dakota Valley MS 100/5-8
1150 Northshore Dr 57049 605-422-3830
Harlan Halverson, prin. Fax 422-3837

Oelrichs, Fall River, Pop. 145
Oelrichs SD 23-3 100/K-12
PO Box 65 57763 605-535-2631
Gary Reder, supt. Fax 535-2046
www.oelrichs.k12.sd.us/
Oelrichs HS 50/9-12
PO Box 65 57763 605-535-2251
Dr. Don Hotalling, prin. Fax 535-2046
Oelrichs JHS 50/7-8
PO Box 65 57763 605-535-2251
Dr. Don Hotalling, prin. Fax 535-2046

Onida, Sully, Pop. 665
Agar-Blunt-Onida SD 58-3 300/K-12
PO Box 205 57564 605-258-2619
Kevin Pickner, supt. Fax 258-2361
www.abo.k12.sd.us
Sully Buttes HS 100/9-12
PO Box 205 57564 605-258-2618
Jerry Cleveland, prin. Fax 258-2361
Sully Buttes JHS 50/7-8
PO Box 205 57564 605-258-2618
Jerry Cleveland, prin. Fax 258-2361

Parker, Turner, Pop. 1,001
Parker SD 60-4 400/K-12
PO Box 517 57053 605-297-3456
Tracey Olson, supt. Fax 297-4381
parker.k12.sd.us
Parker HS 100/9-12
PO Box 517 57053 605-297-4473
Joe Meyer, prin. Fax 297-4381
Parker JHS 100/7-8
PO Box 517 57053 605-297-4473
Joe Meyer, prin. Fax 297-4381

Parkston, Hutchinson, Pop. 1,560
Parkston SD 33-3 600/K-12
102C S Chapman Dr 57366 605-928-3368
Shayne McIntosh, supt. Fax 928-7284
www.parkston.k12.sd.us
Parkston HS 200/9-12
102A S Chapman Dr 57366 605-928-3368
Joseph Kollmann, prin. Fax 928-4032
Parkston JHS 100/7-8
102A S Chapman Dr 57366 605-928-3368
Joseph Kollmann, prin. Fax 928-4032

Philip, Haakon, Pop. 756
Haakon SD 27-1 300/PK-12
PO Box 730 57567 605-859-2679
Keven Morehart, supt. Fax 859-3005
www.philip.k12.sd.us
Philip HS 100/9-12
PO Box 730 57567 605-859-2680
Jeff Rieckman, prin. Fax 859-3550
Philip MS 50/7-8
PO Box 730 57567 605-859-2680
Jeff Rieckman, prin. Fax 859-3550

Pierre, Hughes, Pop. 14,052
Pierre SD 32-2 2,600/PK-12
211 S Poplar Ave 57501 605-773-7300
John Pedersen, supt. Fax 773-7304
www.pierre.k12.sd.us
Morse MS 700/6-8
309 E Capitol Ave 57501 605-773-7330
Troy Wiebe, prin. Fax 773-7338
Riggs HS 800/9-12
1010 E Broadway Ave 57501 605-773-7350
Leroy Fugitt, prin. Fax 773-7360

Pine Ridge, Shannon, Pop. 2,596

Oglala Lakota Community College Post-Sec.
PO Box 861 57770 605-867-5857
Red Cloud Indian S 400/PK-12
100 Mission Dr 57770 605-867-5888
Fr. Paul Coelho, supt. Fax 867-2528

Plankinton, Aurora, Pop. 567
Plankinton SD 1-1 100/PK-12
PO Box 190 57368 605-942-7743
Greg East, supt. Fax 942-7453
www.plankinton.k12.sd.us
Plankinton S 100/PK-12
PO Box 190 57368 605-942-7743
Lee Ann Nussbaum, prin. Fax 942-7453

Platte, Charles Mix, Pop. 1,318
Platte Community SD 11-3 400/K-12
PO Box 140 57369 605-337-3391
Anthony Glass, supt. Fax 337-2549
www.platte.k12.sd.us/
Platte HS 100/9-12
PO Box 140 57369 605-337-3391
Steve Randall, prin. Fax 337-2549
Platte JHS 100/7-8
PO Box 140 57369 605-337-3391
Steve Randall, prin. Fax 337-2549

Pollock, Campbell, Pop. 289
Pollock SD 10-2 100/K-12
PO Box 207 57648 605-889-2831
Wayne Hanson, supt. Fax 889-2543
Pollock HS 50/9-12
PO Box 207 57648 605-889-2831
Wayne Hanson, prin. Fax 889-2543
Pollock JHS 50/7-8
PO Box 207 57648 605-889-2831
Wayne Hanson, prin. Fax 889-2543

Presho, Lyman, Pop. 628
Lyman SD 42-1 400/K-12
PO Box 1000 57568 605-895-2579
Bruce Carrier, supt. Fax 895-2216
www.lyman.k12.sd.us/
Lyman HS 100/9-12
PO Box 1000 57568 605-895-2579
Bruce Carrier, prin. Fax 895-2216
Other Schools – See Kennebec

Ramona, Lake, Pop. 185
Oldham-Ramona SD 39-5 100/PK-12
PO Box 8 57054 605-482-8244
John Bjorkman, supt. Fax 482-8282
www.oldhamramona.k12.sd.us
Oldham-Ramona HS 50/9-12
PO Box 8 57054 605-482-8244
John Bjorkman, prin. Fax 482-8282
Oldham-Ramona JHS 50/7-8
PO Box 8 57054 605-482-8244
John Bjorkman, prin. Fax 482-8282

Rapid City, Pennington, Pop. 62,167
Rapid City Area SD 51-4 12,500/K-12
300 6th St Ste 2 57701 605-394-4031
Dr. Peter Wharton, supt. Fax 394-2514
www.rcas.org
Central HS 2,300/9-12
433 N Mount Rushmore Rd 57701 605-394-4023
Mike Talley, prin. Fax 394-2537
Dakota MS 800/6-8
615 Columbus St 57701 605-394-4092
Brad Tucker, prin. Fax 394-6935
North MS 500/6-8
1501 N Maple Ave 57701 605-394-4042
Jeanne Burckhard, prin. Fax 394-6120
South MS 600/6-8
2 Indiana St 57701 605-394-4024
Larry Stevens, prin. Fax 394-5834
Southwest MS 500/6-8
4501 Park Dr 57702 605-394-6792
Gordon Kendall, prin. Fax 355-3095
Stevens HS 1,500/9-12
1200 44th St 57702 605-394-4051
John Julius, prin. Fax 394-1820
Western Dakota Technical Institute Vo/Tech
800 Mickelson Dr 57703 605-718-2400
Dr. Rich Gross, pres. Fax 394-1789
West MS 600/6-8
1003 Soo San Dr 57702 605-394-4033
Doug Foley, prin. Fax 394-1889

Black Hills Beauty College Post-Sec.
623 Saint Joseph St 57701 605-342-0697
National American University Post-Sec.
321 Kansas City St 57701 605-394-4800
Rapid City Christian HS 100/6-12
PO Box 4246 57709 605-341-3377
David Berry, admin. Fax 341-2248
Rapid City Regional Hospital Post-Sec.
353 Fairmont Blvd 57701 605-341-8100
St. Thomas More HS 200/9-12
300 Fairmont Blvd 57701 605-343-8484
Wayne Sullivan, prin. Fax 343-1315
South Dakota School Mines and Technology Post-Sec.
501 E Saint Joseph St 57701 605-394-2511
Western Dakota Technical Institute Post-Sec.
800 Mickelson Dr 57703 605-394-4034

Redfield, Spink, Pop. 2,318
Redfield SD 56-4 600/PK-12
PO Box 560 57469 605-472-4520
Randy Joyce, supt. Fax 472-4525
www.redfield.k12.sd.us
Redfield HS 200/9-12
PO Box 560 57469 605-472-4520
Rob Lewis, prin. Fax 472-4525
Redfield JHS 100/7-8
PO Box 560 57469 605-472-4520
Rob Lewis, prin. Fax 472-4525

Revillo, Grant, Pop. 141
Grant-Deuel SD 25-3 200/PK-12
16370 482nd Ave 57259 605-623-4241
Krista Atyeo-Gortmaker, supt. Fax 623-4215
www.grant-deuel.k12.sd.us/
Grant-Deuel HS 100/9-12
16370 482nd Ave 57259 605-623-4241
Brian Fox, prin. Fax 623-4215
Grant-Deuel JHS 50/7-8
16370 482nd Ave 57259 605-623-4241
Brian Fox, prin. Fax 623-4215

Roscoe, Edmunds, Pop. 297
Edmunds Central SD 22-5 100/K-12
PO Box 317 57471 605-287-4251
Lew Paulson, supt. Fax 287-4813
www.echs.k12.sd.us/
Edmunds Central HS 100/9-12
PO Box 317 57471 605-287-4251
Lew Paulson, prin. Fax 287-4813
Edmunds Central JHS 50/6-8
PO Box 317 57471 605-287-4251
Lew Paulson, prin. Fax 287-4813

Rosholt, Roberts, Pop. 439
Rosholt SD 54-4 200/PK-12
PO Box 106 57260 605-537-4283
Carolyn Eide, supt. Fax 537-4285
www.rosholt.k12.sd.us/
Rosholt HS 100/9-12
PO Box 106 57260 605-537-4278
Ron Swier, prin. Fax 537-4285
Rosholt JHS 50/7-8
PO Box 106 57260 605-537-4278
Ron Swier, prin. Fax 537-4285

Roslyn, Day, Pop. 204
Roslyn SD 18-2 200/K-12
PO Box 196 57261 605-486-4311
Marc Frankenstein, supt. Fax 486-4635
www.roslyn-eden.k12.sd.us/default.htm
Roslyn HS 100/9-12
PO Box 196 57261 605-486-4311
Marc Frankenstein, prin. Fax 486-4635
Roslyn JHS 50/7-8
PO Box 196 57261 605-486-4311
Marc Frankenstein, prin. Fax 486-4635

Rutland, Lake
Rutland SD 39-4 100/K-12
PO Box 89 57057 605-586-4352
Carl Fahrenwald, supt. Fax 586-4343
www.rutland.k12.sd.us
Rutland HS 50/9-12
PO Box 89 57057 605-586-4352
Valerie Parsley, prin. Fax 586-4343
Rutland JHS 50/7-8
PO Box 89 57057 605-586-4352
Valerie Parsley, prin. Fax 586-4343

Salem, McCook, Pop. 1,393
McCook Central SD 43-7 400/PK-12
PO Box 310 57058 605-425-2264
Dr. Carol Pistulka, supt. Fax 425-2079
www.mccookcentral.k12.sd.us/
McCook Central HS 200/9-12
PO Box 310 57058 605-425-2264
Dennis Vanoverschelde, prin. Fax 425-2079
McCook Central MS 100/5-8
PO Box 310 57058 605-425-2264
Dennis Vanoverschelde, prin. Fax 425-2079

Scotland, Bon Homme, Pop. 830
Scotland SD 4-3 300/PK-12
711 4th St 57059 605-583-2237
Bob Graham, supt. Fax 583-2239
www.scotland.k12.sd.us
Scotland HS 100/9-12
711 4th St 57059 605-583-2237
Robert Graham, prin. Fax 583-2239
Scotland MS 100/6-8
711 4th St 57059 605-583-2237
Robert Graham, prin. Fax 583-2239

Selby, Walworth, Pop. 690
Selby Area SD 62-5 200/PK-12
PO Box 324 57472 605-649-7818
Darrel McFarland, supt. Fax 649-7282
www.selby.k12.sd.us/
Selby Area HS 100/9-12
PO Box 324 57472 605-649-7818
Tony Siebrecht, prin. Fax 649-7282
Selby Area JHS 50/7-8
PO Box 324 57472 605-649-7818
Tony Siebrecht, prin. Fax 649-7282

Sioux Falls, Minnehaha, Pop. 139,517
Sioux Falls SD 49-5 19,500/PK-12
201 E 38th St 57105 605-367-7900
Dr. Pam Homan, supt. Fax 367-4637
www.sf.k12.sd.us
Axtell Park MS 700/6-8
201 N West Ave 57104 605-367-7647
Steve Cain, prin. Fax 367-8326
Edison MS 700/6-8
2101 S West Ave 57105 605-367-7643
Steve Griffith, prin. Fax 367-8457
Henry MS 1,100/6-8
2200 S 5th Ave 57105 605-367-7639
Steve Albrecht, prin. Fax 367-7693
Lincoln HS 1,900/9-12
2900 S Cliff Ave 57105 605-367-7990
Val Fox, prin. Fax 367-8492
Memorial MS 1,000/6-8
1401 S Sertoma Ave 57106 605-362-2785
Carrie Aaron, prin. Fax 362-2790
Roosevelt HS 1,900/9-12
6600 W 41st St 57106 605-362-2860
Jim Denevan, prin. Fax 362-2883
Washington HS 2,000/9-12
501 N Sycamore Ave 57110 605-367-7970
James Nold, prin. Fax 367-8494
Whittier MS 1,000/6-8
930 E 6th St 57103 605-367-7620
Dr. Diana Messick, prin. Fax 367-8357

Augustana College Post-Sec.
29th And South Smt 57197 605-274-0770
Colorado Technical University Post-Sec.
3901 W 59th St 57108 605-361-0200
Kilian Community College Post-Sec.
300 E 6th St 57103 605-221-3100
McKennan Hospital Post-Sec.
800 E 21st St 57105 605-339-8113
National American University Post-Sec.
2801 S Kiwanis Ave Ste 100 57105 605-334-5430
North American Baptist Seminary Post-Sec.
1525 S Grange Ave 57105 605-336-6588
O'Gorman HS 600/9-12
3201 S Kiwanis Ave 57105 605-336-3644
Kyle Groos, prin. Fax 336-9272
O'Gorman JHS 300/7-8
3100 W 41st St 57105 605-988-0546
Colly Broveleit, prin. Fax 336-9839
Sioux Falls Christian S 300/4-12
6120 S Charger Cir 57108 605-334-1422
Jay Woudstra, prin. Fax 334-6928
Sioux Valley Hospital Post-Sec.
PO Box 5039 57117 605-333-6424
South Dakota School for the Deaf Post-Sec.
2001 E 8th St 57103 605-367-5200
Southeast Technical Institute Post-Sec.
2320 N Career Ave 57107 800-247-0789
University of Sioux Falls Post-Sec.
1101 W 22nd St 57105 605-331-5000

Sisseton, Roberts, Pop. 2,540
Sisseton SD 54-2 1,100/K-12
516 8th Ave W 57262 605-698-7613
Dr. Stephen Schulte, supt. Fax 698-3032
www.sisseton.k12.sd.us/
Sisseton HS 300/9-12
516 8th Ave W 57262 605-698-7613
Gary Evjen, prin. Fax 698-7353
Thollehauge MS 300/5-8
516 8th Ave W 57262 605-698-7613
Craig Ebert, prin. Fax 698-7487

Sisseton Wahpeton Community College Post-Sec.
PO Box 689 57262 605-698-3966

South Shore, Codington, Pop. 260
South Shore SD 14-3 100/PK-12
PO Box 638 57263 605-756-4120
Scott Bartholomew, supt. Fax 756-4201
www.southshore.k12.sd.us/
South Shore HS 50/9-12
PO Box 638 57263 605-756-4120
Scott Bartholomew, prin. Fax 756-4201
South Shore JHS 50/7-8
PO Box 638 57263 605-756-4120
Scott Bartholomew, prin. Fax 756-4201

Spearfish, Lawrence, Pop. 9,355
Spearfish SD 40-2 1,900/PK-PK, 1-
525 E Illinois St 57783 605-717-1229
Dave Peters, supt. Fax 717-1200
www.spearfish.k12.sd.us
Spearfish HS 700/9-12
1725 N Main St 57783 605-717-1212
Steve Morford, prin. Fax 717-1211
Spearfish MS 500/6-8
1600 N Canyon St 57783 605-717-1215
Tom Riedel, prin. Fax 717-6926

Black Hills State University Post-Sec.
1200 University St 57799 605-642-6011

Stickney, Aurora, Pop. 308
Stickney SD 1-2 100/K-12
PO Box 67 57375 605-732-4221
Robert Krietlow, supt. Fax 732-4281
www.stickney.k12.sd.us/
Stickney HS 100/9-12
PO Box 67 57375 605-732-4221
Robert Krietlow, prin. Fax 732-4281
Stickney JHS 50/8-8
PO Box 67 57375 605-732-4221
Robert Krietlow, prin. Fax 732-4281

Sturgis, Meade, Pop. 6,260
Meade SD 46-1 2,700/K-12
1230 Douglas St 57785 605-347-2523
James Heinert, supt. Fax 347-0005
meade.k12.sd.us

Sturgis Brown HS | 800/9-12
12930 SD Highway 34 57785 | 605-347-2686
Jeff Simmons, prin. | Fax 347-0225
Sturgis Williams MS | 700/5-8
1425 Cedar St 57785 | 605-347-5232
Lonny Harter, prin. | Fax 720-0190

Summit, Roberts, Pop. 273
Summit SD 54-6 | 100/PK-12
PO Box 791 57266 | 605-398-6211
Bruce Johnson, supt. | Fax 398-6311
www.summit.k12.sd.us
Summit HS | 50/9-12
PO Box 791 57266 | 605-398-6211
Bruce Johnson, prin. | Fax 398-6311
Summit JHS | 50/7-8
PO Box 791 57266 | 605-398-6211
Bruce Johnson, prin. | Fax 398-6311

Tea, Lincoln, Pop. 2,455
Tea Area SD 41-5 | 700/K-12
PO Box 488 57064 | 605-498-2700
Dean Jones, supt. | Fax 498-2702
www.teaschools.k12.sd.us/
Tea HS | 200/9-12
PO Box 488 57064 | 605-498-2700
Mark Rockafellow, prin. | Fax 498-2702
Tea MS | 200/4-8
PO Box 488 57064 | 605-498-2700
Chris Fechner, prin. | Fax 498-2702

Timber Lake, Dewey, Pop. 441
Timber Lake SD 20-3 | 300/K-12
PO Box 1000 57656 | 605-865-3654
Frank Seiler, supt. | Fax 865-3294
www.tls.k12.sd.us/
Timber Lake HS | 100/9-12
PO Box 1000 57656 | 605-865-3654
Jeff Simmons, prin. | Fax 865-3294
Timber Lake MS | 100/6-8
PO Box 1000 57656 | 605-865-3654
Jeff Simmons, prin. | Fax 865-3294

Tripp, Hutchinson, Pop. 666
Tripp-Delmont SD 33-5 | 300/K-12
PO Box 430 57376 | 605-935-6766
Lynn Vlasman, supt. | Fax 935-6507
www.tridel.k12.sd.us/
Tripp-Delmont HS | 100/9-12
PO Box 430 57376 | 605-935-6766
Lynn Vlasman, prin. | Fax 935-6507
Tripp-Delmont MS | 50/6-8
PO Box 430 57376 | 605-935-6766
Lynn Vlasman, prin. | Fax 935-6507

Tulare, Spink, Pop. 202
Hitchcock-Tulare SD 56-6 | 200/K-12
PO Box 108 57476 | 605-596-4171
Scott Pudwill, supt. | Fax 596-4175
www.hitchcock-tulare.k12.sd.us/
Hitchcock-Tulare HS | 9-12
PO Box 108 57476 | 605-596-4171
Dennis Smith, prin. | Fax 596-4150
Hitchcock-Tulare JHS | 7-8
PO Box 108 57476 | 605-596-4171
Dennis Smith, prin. | Fax 596-4150

Tyndall, Bon Homme, Pop. 1,155
Bon Homme SD 4-2 | 700/PK-12
PO Box 28 57066 | 605-589-3388
Dr. Bryce Knudson, supt. | Fax 589-3468
www.bonhomme.k12.sd.us/
Bon Homme HS | 200/9-12
PO Box 28 57066 | 605-589-3387
Ed Mitzel, prin. | Fax 589-3468
Bon Homme MS | 100/6-8
PO Box 28 57066 | 605-589-3387
Ed Mitzel, prin. | Fax 589-3468

Vermillion, Clay, Pop. 9,964
Vermillion SD 13-1 | 1,300/PK-12
17 Prospect St 57069 | 605-677-7000
Dr. Mark Froke, supt. | Fax 677-7002
www.vermillion.k12.sd.us
Vermillion HS | 400/9-12
1001 E Main St 57069 | 605-677-7035
Curt Cameron, prin. | Fax 677-7042
Vermillion MS | 300/6-8
422 Princeton St 57069 | 605-677-7025
Pat Anderson, prin. | Fax 677-7028

University of South Dakota | Post-Sec.
414 E Clark St 57069 | 605-677-5011

Viborg, Turner, Pop. 799
Viborg SD 60-5 | 300/PK-12
PO Box 397 57070 | 605-766-5418
Patrick Kraning, supt. | Fax 766-5635
www.viborg.k12.sd.us/
Viborg HS | 100/9-12
PO Box 397 57070 | 605-766-5418
Pat Kraning, prin. | Fax 766-5635
Viborg JHS | 50/7-8
PO Box 397 57070 | 605-766-5418
Patrick Kraning, prin. | Fax 766-5635

Volga, Brookings, Pop. 1,442
Sioux Valley SD 5-5 | 500/PK-12
PO Box 278 57071 | 605-627-5657
Dean Johnson, supt. | Fax 627-5291
www.svschool.org
Sioux Valley HS | 200/9-12
PO Box 278 57071 | 605-627-5657
Suzanne Hegg, prin. | Fax 627-5291
Sioux Valley MS | 100/6-8
PO Box 278 57071 | 605-627-5657
Suzanne Hegg, prin. | Fax 627-5291

Wagner, Charles Mix, Pop. 1,601
Wagner Community SD 11-4 | 800/PK-12
PO Box 310 57380 | 605-384-3677
Susan Smit, supt. | Fax 384-3678
www.wagner.k12.sd.us/
Wagner HS | 200/9-12
PO Box 310 57380 | 605-384-5426
Neil Goter, prin. | Fax 384-3200
Wagner JHS | 100/7-8
PO Box 310 57380 | 605-384-5426
Steve Petry, prin. | Fax 384-3200

Wakonda, Clay, Pop. 345
Wakonda SD 13-2 | 200/PK-12
PO Box 268 57073 | 605-267-2644
Larry Johnke, supt. | Fax 267-2645
www.wakonda.k12.sd.us/
Wakonda HS | 100/9-12
PO Box 268 57073 | 605-267-2644
Dave Hutchison, prin. | Fax 267-2645
Wakonda JHS | 50/7-8
PO Box 268 57073 | 605-267-2644
Dave Hutchison, prin. | Fax 267-2645

Wakpala, Corson
Smee SD 15-3 | 300/PK-12
PO Box B 57658 | 605-845-3040
Keith McVay, supt. | Fax 845-7244
www.smee.k12.sd.us
Wakpala HS | 100/9-12
PO Box B 57658 | 605-845-3040
Francine Hall, prin. | Fax 845-7244

Wall, Pennington, Pop. 808
Wall SD 51-5 | 200/K-12
PO Box 414 57790 | 605-279-2156
Dennis Rieckman, supt. | Fax 279-2613
www.wall.k12.sd.us
Wall HS | 100/9-12
PO Box 414 57790 | 605-279-2156
Barbara Leiseth, prin. | Fax 279-2613
Wall MS | 50/6-8
PO Box 414 57790 | 605-279-2156
Barbara Leiseth, prin. | Fax 279-2613

Warner, Brown, Pop. 430
Warner SD 6-5 | 300/PK-12
PO Box 20 57479 | 605-225-6397
Kirk Easton, supt. | Fax 225-0007
www.warner.k12.sd.us/
Warner HS | 100/9-12
PO Box 20 57479 | 605-225-6194
Charles Welke, prin. | Fax 225-0007
Warner MS | 100/6-8
PO Box 20 57479 | 605-225-6194
Charles Welke, prin. | Fax 225-0007

Watertown, Codington, Pop. 20,265
Lake Area Multi-District
1311 3rd Ave NE 57201 | 605-882-6380
Julie LeVake, supt. | Fax 882-6381
www.lakeareamulti.k12.sd.us/
Lake Area Vocational S | Vo/Tech
1311 3rd Ave NE 57201 | 605-882-6380
Julie LeVake, prin. | Fax 882-6381

Watertown SD 14-4 | 3,800/PK-12
PO Box 730 57201 | 605-882-6312
Dr. Bob Mayer, supt. | Fax 882-6327
www.watertown.k12.sd.us/
Watertown HS | 1,300/9-12
200 9th St NE 57201 | 605-882-6316
Brian Field, prin. | Fax 882-6327
Watertown MS | 600/7-8
601 11th St NE 57201 | 605-882-6370
Daniel Albertsen, prin. | Fax 886-6372

Great Plains Lutheran HS | 100/9-12
1200 Luther Ln NE 57201 | 605-886-0672
Daniel Myers, prin. | Fax 882-9089
Lake Area Technical Institute | Post-Sec.
230 11th St NE 57201 | 605-882-5284
Watertown Christian S | 100/PK-12
15 12th Ave NE 57201 | 605-882-0949
Dan Relph, admin. | Fax 882-5935

Waubay, Day, Pop. 607
Waubay SD 18-3 | 200/PK-12
202 W School Rd 57273 | 605-947-4529
Al Stewart, supt. | Fax 947-4243
www.waubay.k12.sd.us/
Waubay HS | 100/9-12
202 W School Rd 57273 | 605-947-4529
Al Stewart, prin. | Fax 947-4243
Waubay JHS | 50/7-8
202 W School Rd 57273 | 605-947-4529
Al Stewart, prin. | Fax 947-4243

Waverly, Codington
Waverly SD 14-5 | 100/PK-12
319 Mary Pl, | 605-886-9174
Loren McKinney, supt. | Fax 886-6630
www.waverly.k12.sd.us
Waverly HS | 50/9-12
319 Mary Pl, | 605-886-9174
Loren McKinney, prin. | Fax 886-6630
Waverly JHS | 50/7-8
319 Mary Pl, | 605-886-9174
Laura Morrow, prin. | Fax 886-6630

Webster, Day, Pop. 1,751
Webster SD 18-4 | 500/PK-12
102 E 9th Ave 57274 | 605-345-3548
James Block, supt. | Fax 345-4421
www.webster.k12.sd.us/
Webster HS | 200/9-12
102 E 9th Ave 57274 | 605-345-4653
James Block, prin. | Fax 345-4421
Webster MS | 100/6-8
102 E 9th Ave 57274 | 605-345-4653
Craig Case, prin. | Fax 345-4421

Wessington Springs, Jerauld, Pop. 926
Wessington Springs SD 36-2 | 300/PK-12
PO Box 449 57382 | 605-539-9391
Darold Rounds, supt. | Fax 539-1029
www.wessingtonsprings.k12.sd.us
Wessington Springs HS | 100/9-12
PO Box 449 57382 | 605-539-9391
Darold J. Rounds, prin. | Fax 539-1029
Wessington Springs MS | 100/6-8
PO Box 449 57382 | 605-539-1754
Vicki Harmdierks, prin. | Fax 539-1029

White, Brookings, Pop. 499
Deubrook Area SD 5-6 | 400/K-12
PO Box 346 57276 | 605-629-1100
Kevin Keenaghan, supt. | Fax 629-3701
www.deubrook.com
Deubrook HS | 100/9-12
PO Box 346 57276 | 605-629-1101
Don Ray, prin. | Fax 629-3701
Deubrook JHS | 100/7-8
PO Box 346 57276 | 605-629-1101
Don Ray, prin. | Fax 629-3701

White Lake, Aurora, Pop. 389
White Lake SD 1-3 | 100/K-12
PO Box 246 57383 | 605-249-2251
Berle Johnson, supt. | Fax 249-2725
www.whitelake.k12.sd.us/
White Lake HS | 50/9-12
PO Box 246 57383 | 605-732-4221
Randy Hoffman, prin. | Fax 249-2725
White Lake JHS | 50/7-8
PO Box 246 57383 | 605-249-2251
Randy Hoffman, prin. | Fax 249-2725

White River, Mellette, Pop. 586
White River SD 47-1 | 400/PK-12
PO Box 273 57579 | 605-259-3311
Thomas Cameron, supt. | Fax 259-3133
www.whiteriver.k12.sd.us/
White River HS | 100/9-12
PO Box 273 57579 | 605-259-3135
Tim Hollar, prin. | Fax 259-3133
White River MS | 100/6-8
PO Box 273 57579 | 605-259-3135
David Colberg, prin. | Fax 259-3133

Willow Lake, Clark, Pop. 266
Willow Lake SD 12-3 | 200/PK-12
PO Box 170 57278 | 605-625-5945
Kevin Quimby, supt. | Fax 625-3103
www.dailypost.com/~wls
Willow Lake HS | 100/9-12
PO Box 170 57278 | 605-625-5924
Kerry Stobbs, prin. | Fax 625-3103
Willow Lake JHS | 50/7-8
PO Box 170 57278 | 605-625-5924
Kerry Stobbs, prin. | Fax 625-3103

Wilmot, Roberts, Pop. 531
Wilmot SD 54-7 | 300/PK-12
PO Box 100 57279 | 605-938-4647
Tim Graf, supt. | Fax 938-4185
www.wilmot.k12.sd.us
Wilmot HS | 100/9-12
PO Box 100 57279 | 605-938-4647
Larry Hulscher, prin. | Fax 938-4185
Wilmot JHS | 50/7-8
PO Box 100 57279 | 605-938-4647
Larry Hulscher, prin. | Fax 938-4185

Winner, Tripp, Pop. 2,917
Winner SD 59-2 | 900/K-12
PO Box 231 57580 | 605-842-8101
Mary Fisher, supt. | Fax 842-8120
www.winner.k12.sd.us
Winner HS | 300/9-12
PO Box 231 57580 | 605-842-8125
Mike Hanson, prin. | Fax 842-8121
Winner MS | 300/5-8
PO Box 231 57580 | 605-842-8150
Brian Naasz, prin. | Fax 842-8122

Wolsey, Beadle, Pop. 388
Wolsey Wessington SD 2-6 | 200/K-12
375 Ash St SE 57384 | 605-883-4221
Brian Sieh, supt. | Fax 883-4720
Wolsey Wessington HS | 100/9-12
375 Ash St SE 57384 | 605-883-4221
Brian Sieh, prin. | Fax 883-4720
Wolsey Wessington MS | 100/5-8
375 Ash St SE 57384 | 605-883-4221
Carol Rowen, prin. | Fax 883-4720

Woonsocket, Sanborn, Pop. 676
Woonsocket SD 55-4 | 200/K-12
PO Box 428 57385 | 605-796-4431
Rodrick Weber, supt. | Fax 796-4352
www.woonsocket.k12.sd.us/
Woonsocket HS | 100/9-12
PO Box 428 57385 | 605-796-4431
Rodrick Weber, prin. | Fax 796-4352

Yankton, Yankton, Pop. 13,716
Yankton SD 63-3 | 3,000/PK-12
PO Box 738 57078 | 605-665-3998
Joseph Gertsema, supt. | Fax 665-1422
www.ysd.k12.sd.us
Yankton HS | 1,000/9-12
PO Box 738 57078 | 605-665-2073
Scott Lepke, prin. | Fax 655-5948
Yankton MS | 800/6-8
PO Box 738 57078 | 605-665-2419
Wayne Kindle, prin. | Fax 665-6239

Mt. Marty College | Post-Sec.
1105 W 8th St 57078 | 605-668-1514
Sacred Heart Hospital | Post-Sec.
501 Summit St 57078 | 605-655-9371
Sacred Heart MS | 100/5-8
504 Capitol St 57078 | 605-665-1808
Linda Foos, prin. | Fax 260-9787

TENNESSEE

TENNESSEE DEPARTMENT OF EDUCATION
710 James Robertson Pkwy, Nashville 37243-1219
Telephone 615-741-2731
Fax 615-532-4791
Website http://www.state.tn.us/education

Commissioner of Education Lana Seivers

TENNESSEE BOARD OF EDUCATION
400 Deaderick St Ste 200, Nashville 37243

Chairperson B. Fielding Rolston

PUBLIC, PRIVATE AND CATHOLIC SECONDARY SCHOOLS

Adamsville, McNairy, Pop. 2,062
McNairy County SD
Supt. — See Selmer
Adamsville JSHS 600/7-12
PO Box 407 38310 731-632-3273
Brian Jackson, prin. Fax 632-3080

Afton, Greene
Greene County SD
Supt. — See Greeneville
Chuckey-Doak HS 600/9-12
365 Ripley Island Rd 37616 423-798-2636
George Frye, prin. Fax 639-5761
Chuckey Doak MS 6-8
120 Chuckey Doak Rd 37616 423-787-2038
Amy Brooks, prin. Fax 787-2096

Alamo, Crockett, Pop. 2,380
Crockett County SD 1,800/PK-12
102 N Cavalier Dr 38001 731-696-2604
Stan Black, supt. Fax 696-4734
www.ccschools.net
Crockett County HS 700/9-12
2014 Highway 88 38001 731-696-4525
Dan Black, prin. Fax 696-3124
Crockett County MS 600/6-8
497 N Cavalier Dr 38001 731-696-5583
Larry Lewis, prin. Fax 696-2034

Alcoa, Blount, Pop. 8,388
Alcoa CSD 1,400/K-12
524 Faraday St 37701 865-984-0531
Tom Shamblin, supt. Fax 984-5832
www.alcoaschools.net/
Alcoa HS 400/9-12
532 Faraday St 37701 865-982-4631
Scott Porter, prin. Fax 380-2240
Alcoa MS 500/5-8
1325 Springbrook Rd 37701 865-982-5211
James Kirk, prin. Fax 380-2533

Altamont, Grundy, Pop. 1,166
Grundy County SD 2,400/PK-12
PO Box 97 37301 931-692-3467
Phyllis Lusk, dir. Fax 692-2188
volweb.utk.edu/Schools/grundyco/grundy.index.html
Other Schools – See Coalmont

Antioch, Davidson
Davidson County SD
Supt. — See Nashville
Antioch HS 2,400/9-12
1900 Hobson Pike 37013 615-641-5400
Dr. Margaret Bess, prin. Fax 641-5422
Antioch MS 900/5-8
5050 Blue Hole Rd 37013 615-333-5642
Dr. Stephanie Kraft, prin. Fax 333-5053
Apollo MS 500/5-8
631 Richards Rd 37013 615-333-5025
James Briggs, prin. Fax 333-5029
Kennedy MS 1,000/5-8
5832 Pettus Rd 37013 615-941-7515
Dr. Barbara Ide, prin. Fax 262-6959

Ezell-Harding Christian S 900/PK-12
574 Bell Rd 37013 615-367-0532
Donald Hutchison, pres. Fax 399-8747
Jon Nave University of Cosmetology Post-Sec.
5510 Crossings Cir 37013 - -

Arlington, Shelby, Pop. 3,534
Shelby County SD
Supt. — See Memphis
Arlington HS 400/9-10
5475 Airline Rd 38002 901-867-1541
Dr. Jeff Cozzens, prin. Fax 867-1546
Arlington MS 900/6-8
5470 Lamb Rd 38002 901-867-6015
Patricia Prescott, prin. Fax 867-6080
Bolton HS 2,300/9-12
7323 Brunswick Rd 38002 901-873-8150
David Stephens, prin. Fax 829-3650
Shadowlawn MS 1,100/6-8
4734 Shadowlawn Rd 38002 901-373-2654
John McDonald, prin. Fax 373-1363

Ashland City, Cheatham, Pop. 4,550
Cheatham County SD 6,700/PK-12
102 Elizabeth St 37015 615-792-5664
Lynn E. Seifert, dir. Fax 792-2551
cheatham.k12tn.net
Cheatham County Central HS 700/9-12
1 Cub Cir 37015 615-792-5641
Fax 792-2090
Cheatham MS 700/5-8
700 Scoutview Rd 37015 615-792-2334
Robin Norris, prin. Fax 792-2337
Cheatham County Adult HS Adult
104 Elizabeth St 37015 615-746-1424
Rita Herndon, prin. Fax 746-1438
Other Schools – See Kingston Springs, Pleasant View

Athens, McMinn, Pop. 13,878
Athens CSD 1,700/PK-9
943 Crestway Dr 37303 423-745-2863
Dr. Craig Rigell, supt. Fax 745-9041
Athens JHS 500/7-9
200 Keith Ln 37303 423-745-1177
Michael Simmons, prin. Fax 745-9679

McMinn County SD 5,800/PK-12
216 N Jackson St 37303 423-745-1612
Dr. John Forgety, supt. Fax 744-1641
www.mcminn.k12.tn.us/
McMinn County HS 1,400/9-12
2215 Congress Pkwy S 37303 423-745-4142
John Grubb, prin. Fax 745-0584
McMinn Vocational Center Vo/Tech
2103 Congress Pkwy S 37303 423-746-4293
Ed McCleary, prin. Fax 744-3923
Other Schools – See Englewood

Tennessee Technology Center at Athens Post-Sec.
PO Box 848 37371 423-744-2814
Tennessee Wesleyan College Post-Sec.
PO Box 40 37371 423-745-7504

Atwood, Carroll, Pop. 982
West Carroll Special SD 1,100/K-12
1415 Highway 77 38220 731-662-4200
Eric Williams, supt. Fax 662-4250
www.wcssd.org
West Carroll JSHS 500/7-12
760 State Route 77 38220 731-662-7116
Lex Suite, prin. Fax 662-4198

Bartlett, Shelby, Pop. 43,263
Shelby County SD
Supt. — See Memphis
Appling MS 900/6-8
3700 Appling Rd 38133 901-373-1410
Odell Foster, prin. Fax 373-1360
Bartlett HS 1,900/9-12
5688 Woodlawn St 38134 901-373-2620
Mike Parnell, prin. Fax 373-2624
Elmore Park MS 700/6-8
6330 Althorne Rd 38134 901-373-2642
Marjorie Lowe, prin. Fax 373-1361

Baxter, Putnam, Pop. 1,333
Putnam County SD
Supt. — See Cookeville
Cornerstone MS 500/5-8
371 1st Ave S 38544 931-858-6601
Garry Lee, prin. Fax 858-6637
Upperman HS 500/9-12
6950 Nashville Hwy 38544 931-858-3112
Herb Leftwich, prin. Fax 858-4641

Bell Buckle, Bedford, Pop. 404

Webb S 300/6-12
PO Box 488 37020 931-389-9322
Albert Cauz, hdmstr. Fax 389-9101

Benton, Polk, Pop. 1,103
Polk County SD 2,200/PK-12
PO Box 665 37307 423-338-4506
James Jone, supt. Fax 338-2691
www.polkcountyschools.com/
Chilhowee MS 400/6-8
PO Box 188 37307 423-338-3102
Ronnie German, prin. Fax 338-3158
Polk County HS 600/9-12
PO Box 188 37307 423-338-4514
Joel Cox, prin. Fax 338-4521
Other Schools – See Copperhill

Big Sandy, Benton, Pop. 518
Benton County SD
Supt. — See Camden
Big Sandy S 400/K-12
13305 Highway 69A 38221 731-593-3221
Mike Bell, prin. Fax 593-3245

Blountville, Sullivan, Pop. 2,605
Sullivan County SD 11,800/PK-12
PO Box 306 37617 423-354-1000
Glenn Arwood, supt. Fax 354-1004
www.scde.k12.tn.us
Blountville MS 400/6-8
1651 Blountville Blvd 37617 423-354-1600
Michael Wilson, prin. Fax 354-1606
Holston MS 400/6-8
2348 Highway 75 37617 423-354-1500
Bill Miller, prin. Fax 354-1505
Sullivan Central HS 1,100/9-12
131 Shipley Ferry Rd 37617 423-354-1200
Melanie Ridon, prin. Fax 354-1206
Other Schools – See Bluff City, Bristol, Kingsport

Northeast State Tech Community College Post-Sec.
PO Box 246 37617 423-323-3191

Bluff City, Sullivan, Pop. 1,602
Sullivan County SD
Supt. — See Blountville
Bluff City MS 500/6-8
337 Carter St 37618 423-354-1801
Jack Walling, prin. Fax 354-1818
Sullivan East HS 1,000/9-12
4180 Weaver Pike 37618 423-354-1900
Angie Buckles, prin. Fax 354-1906

Bolivar, Hardeman, Pop. 5,652
Hardeman County SD 4,400/K-12
PO Box 112 38008 731-658-2510
Donald Hopper Ph.D., supt. Fax 658-2061
www.hardemancountyschools.org
Bolivar MS 500/6-8
915 Pruitt St 38008 731-658-3656
Warner Ross, prin. Fax 658-6625
Central HS 900/9-12
313 Harris St 38008 731-658-3151
Fred Kessler, prin. Fax 658-6697
Other Schools – See Middleton

Bradford, Gibson, Pop. 1,073
Bradford Special SD 600/K-12
PO Box 220 38316 731-742-3180
Bobby McCartney, supt. Fax 742-3994
www.bradfordssd.com/
Bradford JSHS 300/7-12
PO Box 70 38316 731-742-3152
Larry W. McCartney, prin. Fax 742-3088

Brentwood, Williamson, Pop. 32,426
Williamson County SD
Supt. — See Franklin
Brentwood HS 1,300/9-12
5304 Murray Ln 37027 615-472-4220
Kevin Keidel, prin. Fax 472-4241
Brentwood MS 1,000/6-8
5324 Murray Ln 37027 615-472-4250
Dr. Kay Kendrick, prin. Fax 472-4263
Ravenwood HS 1,200/9-12
1724 Wilson Pike 37027 615-472-4800
Dr. Pam Vaden, prin. Fax 472-4821
Sunset MS 6-8
200 Sunset Trl 37027 615-472-5040
Jason Pearson, prin. Fax 472-5050
Woodland MS 1,000/6-8
1500 Volunteer Pkwy 37027 615-472-4930
Priscilla Fizer, prin. Fax 472-4941

Brentwood Academy 700/6-12
219 Granny White Pike 37027 615-373-0611
Curt Masters, hdmstr. Fax 377-3709
Currey Ingram Academy 300/K-12
6544 Murray Ln 37027 615-507-3242
Kathleen Rayburn, prin. Fax 507-3170
Montessori Academy 300/PK-12
6021 Cloverland Dr 37027 615-833-3610
Eileen Bernstorf, hdmstr. Fax 833-3680

Brighton, Tipton, Pop. 2,441
Tipton County SD
Supt. — See Covington
Brighton HS 1,200/9-12
8045 Highway 51 S 38011 901-837-5800
Grant Shipley, prin. Fax 837-5829
Brighton MS 900/6-8
7785 Highway 51 S 38011 901-837-5600
John Combs, prin. Fax 837-5625

Bristol, Sullivan, Pop. 24,994
Bristol CSD 3,800/PK-12
615 Edgemont Ave 37620 423-652-9451
Steve Dixon, supt. Fax 652-9238
www.btcs.org
Tennessee HS 1,200/9-12
1112 Edgemont Ave 37620 423-652-9494
Jim Butcher, prin. Fax 652-9327
Vance MS 600/7-8
815 Edgemont Ave 37620 423-652-9449
Rigby Kind, prin. Fax 652-9297

Sullivan County SD
Supt. — See Blountville
Holston Valley MS 200/6-8
1717 Bristol Caverns Hwy 37620 423-354-1880
Jess Lockhart, prin. Fax 354-1891

Jacobs Creek Job Corps Civilian Center Post-Sec.
984 Denton Valley Rd 37620 423-878-4021
King College Post-Sec.
1350 King College Rd 37620 423-968-1187
National College Post-Sec.
1328 Highway 11W 37620 423-878-4440

Brownsville, Haywood, Pop. 10,720
Haywood County SD 3,500/PK-12
900 E Main St 38012 731-772-9613
George Chapman, supt. Fax 772-3275
www.haywood.k12.tn.us
Haywood HS 900/9-12
1175 E College St 38012 731-772-1845
Robert Mitchell, prin. Fax 772-6079
Haywood JHS 600/7-8
1201 Haralson St 38012 731-772-3265
Dontye Bradford, prin. Fax 772-3352

Bruceton, Carroll, Pop. 1,486
Hollow Rock-Bruceton Special SD 800/K-12
PO Box 135 38317 731-586-7657
Rod Sturdivant, supt. Fax 586-7419
www.hrbk12.org
Central HS 300/9-12
PO Box 135 38317 731-586-2161
Steve Wilkinson, prin. Fax 586-7419
Central MS 200/6-8
PO Box 135 38317 731-586-2161
Tim Gilmer, prin. Fax 586-7419

Byrdstown, Pickett, Pop. 875
Pickett County SD 700/K-12
141 Skyline Dr 38549 931-864-3123
Carolyn Cope, supt. Fax 864-7185
Pickett County HS 200/9-12
130 Skyline Dr 38549 931-864-3422
Paulette Dowdy, prin. Fax 864-6297

Camden, Benton, Pop. 3,736
Benton County SD 2,500/K-12
197 Briarwood St 38320 731-584-6111
Randall Robertson, supt. Fax 584-8142
www.bcos.org/index/
Benton County Career/Technical Center Vo/Tech
155 Schools Dr 38320 731-584-4492
Randy Shannon, prin. Fax 584-4493
Camden Central HS 600/9-12
115 Schools Dr 38320 731-584-7254
Bill Kee, prin. Fax 584-4221
Camden JHS 500/6-8
75 Schools Dr 38320 731-584-4518
Michelle Leonard, prin. Fax 584-4493
Benton County Adult S Adult
175 Briarwood St 38320 731-584-1372
Alvin Smothers, prin. Fax 584-3215
Other Schools – See Big Sandy

Carthage, Smith, Pop. 2,268
Smith County SD 3,100/PK-12
126 Smith Co Middle Sch Ln 37030 615-735-9625
Roger Lewis, supt. Fax 735-8271
boe.smithcounty.com/
Smith County HS 700/7-12
312 Fite Ave E 37030 615-735-9219
Jimmy Maynord, prin. Fax 735-9049
Smith County MS 400/5-8
134 Smith Co Mid School Ln 37030 615-735-8277
Ronnie Scudder, prin. Fax 735-8255
Other Schools – See Gordonsville

Cedar Hill, Robertson, Pop. 310
Robertson County SD
Supt. — See Springfield
Byrns JSHS 500/6-12
7025 Highway 41 N 37032 615-696-2251
Dr. Bill Locke, prin. Fax 696-0526

Celina, Clay, Pop. 1,369
Clay County SD 1,100/K-12
PO Box 469 38551 931-243-3310
Dr. Douglas Young, supt. Fax 243-3706
www.clay-lea.k12.tn.us/
Clay County HS 200/9-12
PO Box 40 38551 931-243-2340
Brenda Kirby, prin. Fax 243-2376
Clay County Adult HS Adult
PO Box 469 38551 931-243-5512
Anna Locke, prin. Fax 243-3706
Other Schools – See Red Boiling Springs

Centerville, Hickman, Pop. 4,002
Hickman County SD 3,800/PK-12
115 Murphree Ave 37033 931-729-3391
Dr. Jerry Nash, dir. Fax 729-3834
www.hickman.k12.tn.us
Hickman County HS 1,100/9-12
1645 Bulldog Blvd 37033 931-729-2616
Bert Mathis, prin. Fax 729-2925
Hickman County MS 500/6-8
1639 Bulldog Blvd 37033 931-729-4234
Michelle Gilbert, prin. Fax 729-5688
Other Schools – See Lyles

Chapel Hill, Marshall, Pop. 1,019
Marshall County SD
Supt. — See Lewisburg
Forrest MSHS 700/6-12
310 N Horton Pkwy 37034 931-364-7260
Mike Bishop, prin. Fax 364-2928

Charlotte, Dickson, Pop. 1,155
Dickson County SD
Supt. — See Dickson
Charlotte MS 400/6-8
250 Humphries St 37036 615-740-6060
Ray Lecomte, prin. Fax 789-7033
Creek Wood HS 900/9-12
3499 Highway 47 N 37036 615-740-6000
Janie Jones, prin. Fax 441-2868

Chattanooga, Hamilton, Pop. 154,762
Hamilton County SD 39,600/PK-12
6703 Bonny Oaks Dr 37421 423-209-8400
Dr. Jim Scales, supt. Fax 209-8601
www.hcde.org
Brainerd HS 1,100/9-12
1020 N Moore Rd 37411 423-855-2615
Frank Jones, prin. Fax 855-2651
Chattanooga HS Center for Creative Arts 500/6-12
1301 Dallas Rd 37405 423-209-5929
Gary Record, prin. Fax 209-5930
Chattanooga HS for the Arts & Sciences 700/6-12
865 E 3rd St 37403 423-209-5812
Steve Ball, prin. Fax 209-5831
Chattanooga Museum Magnet MS 300/6-8
1219 W Mississippi Ave 37405 423-209-5914
Wendy Jung, prin. Fax 209-5920
Dalewood MS 300/6-8
1300 Shallowford Rd 37411 423-493-0323
Linda Darden, prin. Fax 493-0327
East Lake Academy of Fine Arts 400/6-8
2700 E 34th St 37407 423-493-0334
Charles Joynes, prin. Fax 493-0343
East Ridge HS 900/9-12
4320 Bennett Rd 37412 423-867-6200
Mark Bean, prin. Fax 867-6220
East Ridge MS 700/6-8
4400 Bennett Rd 37412 423-867-6214
Steven Robinson, prin. Fax 867-6226
Howard HS of Academics & Technology Vo/Tech
2500 S Market St Ste 1 37408 423-209-5868
Dr. Elaine Swafford, prin. Fax 209-5869
Lookout Valley MSHS 500/6-12
350 Lookout High St 37419 423-825-7352
Lee McDade, prin. Fax 821-7951
Orchard Knob MS 400/6-8
500 N Highland Park Ave 37404 423-493-7793
Herbert McCray, prin. Fax 493-7795
Red Bank HS 1,300/9-12
640 Morrison Springs Rd 37415 423-874-1900
Gail Chuy, prin. Fax 874-1924
Red Bank MS 600/6-8
3715 Dayton Blvd 37415 423-874-1908
Robert Alford, prin. Fax 874-1938
Tyner Academy 500/9-12
6836 Tyner Rd 37421 423-855-2635
Carol Goss, prin. Fax 855-9417
Tyner Middle Academy 400/6-8
6837 Tyner Rd 37421 423-855-2648
Bob Green, prin. Fax 855-2699
Other Schools – See Harrison, Hixson, Ooltewah, Sale Creek, Signal Mountain, Soddy Daisy

Baylor S 1,000/6-12
171 Baylor School Rd 37405 423-267-8505
Bill Stacy, hdmstr. Fax 265-4276
Boyd-Buchanan S 1,000/PK-12
4626 Bonnieway Dr 37411 423-622-6177
Mary Helen Wood, prin. Fax 508-2219
Chattanooga Christian S 1,000/K-12
3354 Charger Dr 37409 423-265-6411
Don Holwerda, pres. Fax 756-4044
Chattanooga State Tech. Comm. College Post-Sec.
4501 Amnicola Hwy 37406 423-697-4400
Electronic Computer Programming College Post-Sec.
3805 Brainerd Rd 37411 423-624-0077
Girls Preparatory S 700/6-12
205 Island Ave 37405 423-634-7600
Stanley Tucker, hdmstr. Fax 634-7643
Grace Baptist Academy 900/K-12
7815 Shallowford Rd 37421 423-892-8224
David Patrick, hdmstr. Fax 892-1194
Hamilton Heights Christian Academy 100/9-12
2201 Hickory Valley Rd 37421 423-894-0597
Duke Stone, admin. Fax 894-4259
McCallie S 900/6-12
500 Dodds Ave 37404 423-624-8300
R. Kirk Walker Ph.D., prin. Fax 493-5690
Miller-Motte Technical College Post-Sec.
6020 Shallowford Rd 37421 423-510-9675
Notre Dame HS 500/9-12
2701 Vermont Ave 37404 423-624-4618
Perry Storey, prin. Fax 624-4621
Silverdale Baptist Academy 700/K-12
7236 Bonny Oaks Dr 37421 423-892-2319
Rebecca Hansard, hdmstr. Fax 648-7600
Temple Baptist Seminary Post-Sec.
1815 Union Ave 37404 423-493-4221
Tennessee Temple Academy 300/PK-12
1907 Bailey Ave 37404 423-493-4337
Constance Pearson, hdmstr. Fax 643-8360
Tennessee Temple University Post-Sec.
1815 Union Ave 37404 423-493-4100
University of Tennessee Post-Sec.
615 McCallie Ave 37403 423-425-4111

Christiana, Rutherford
Rutherford County SD
Supt. — See Murfreesboro
Christiana MS 800/6-8
4675 Shelbyville Pike 37037 615-904-3885
Dr. John Ash, prin. Fax 904-3886

Church Hill, Hawkins, Pop. 6,370
Hawkins County SD
Supt. — See Rogersville
Church Hill MS 700/6-8
PO Box 38 37642 423-357-3051
William Christian, prin. Fax 357-9873
Volunteer HS 1,100/9-12
PO Box 247 37642 423-357-3641
James Dykes, prin. Fax 357-6694

Clarkrange, Fentress
Fentress County SD
Supt. — See Jamestown
Clarkrange HS 200/9-12
5801 S York Hwy 38553 931-863-3143
William Cody, prin. Fax 863-3981

Clarksburg, Carroll, Pop. 375
South Carroll County Special SD 400/PK-12
PO Box 219 38324 731-986-4534
Diana Collins, supt. Fax 986-4562
www.rocketsonline.org/
Clarksburg S 400/PK-12
PO Box 219 38324 731-986-3165
Trey Crews, prin. Fax 986-4562

Clarksville, Montgomery, Pop. 112,878
Clarksville-Montgomery County SD 25,200/PK-12
621 Gracey Ave 37040 931-920-7808
Michael Harris, supt. Fax 648-5612
www.cmcss.net
Clarksville HS 1,400/9-12
151 Richview Rd 37043 931-648-5690
Harold Smith, prin. Fax 648-5624
Kenwood HS 1,300/9-12
251 E Pine Mountain Rd 37042 931-905-7900
Hal Bedell, prin. Fax 905-7906
Kenwood MS 1,100/6-8
241 E Pine Mountain Rd 37042 931-553-2080
Linda Medina-Griffy, prin. Fax 552-3080
New Providence MS 1,000/6-8
146 Cunningham Ln 37042 931-648-5655
Laura Barnett, prin. Fax 503-3409
Northeast HS 1,300/9-12
3701 Trenton Rd 37040 931-648-5640
Melissa Champion, prin. Fax 503-3413
Northeast MS 1,100/6-8
3703 Trenton Rd 37040 931-648-5665
Shari Salyer, prin. Fax 503-3410
Northwest HS 1,200/9-12
800 Lafayette Rd 37042 931-648-5675
Edward Stephens, prin. Fax 648-0094
Richview MS 1,000/6-8
2350 Memorial Drive Ext 37043 931-648-5620
Patrick Digby, prin. Fax 551-8111
Rossview HS 1,300/9-12
1237 Rossview Rd 37043 931-553-2070
Frank Myers, prin. Fax 503-3419
Rossview MS 1,000/6-8
2265 Cardinal Ln 37043 931-920-6150
Anna Neubauer, prin. Fax 920-6147
Adult Ed-Greenwood Complex Adult
430 Greenwood Ave 37040 931-542-5040
Betty Cook, prin.
Other Schools – See Cunningham

Austin Peay State University Post-Sec.
601 College St 37044 931-221-7011
Clarksville Academy 500/PK-12
710 N 2nd St 37040 931-647-6311
Kay Drew, hdmstr. Fax 906-0610
Draughons Junior College Post-Sec.
1860 Wilma Rudolph Blvd 37040 931-552-7600
Miller-Motte Technical College Post-Sec.
1820 Business Park Dr 37040 931-553-0071
North Central Institute Post-Sec.
168 Jack Miller Blvd 37042 931-431-9700
North Tennessee Bible Inst. & Seminary Post-Sec.
PO Box 3797 37043 931-552-1510
Queen City College Post-Sec.
1594 Fort Campbell Blvd 37042 931-645-2361
Unity Christian Academy 50/K-12
1713 Fort Campbell Blvd 37042 931-645-6003
Jacqueline Hale, prin. Fax 645-6226

Cleveland, Bradley, Pop. 38,186
Bradley County SD 9,300/K-12
800 S Lee Hwy 37311 423-476-0620
Robert Taylor, supt. Fax 476-0485
www.bradleyschools.org

Bradley Central HS 1,600/9-12
1000 S Lee Hwy 37311 423-476-0650
Johnny McDaniel, prin. Fax 476-0613
Lake Forest MS 1,000/6-8
610 Kile Lake Rd SE 37323 423-478-8821
Ritchie Stevenson, prin. Fax 478-8832
Ocoee MS 1,200/6-8
2250 N Ocoee St 37311 423-476-0630
Ron Spangler, prin. Fax 476-0588
Walker Valley HS 1,200/9-12
750 Lauderdale Mem Hwy NW 37312 423-336-1383
Danny Coggin, prin. Fax 336-1578

Cleveland CSD 4,400/K-12
4300 Mouse Creek Rd NW 37312 423-472-9571
Dr. Frederick Denning, supt. Fax 472-3390
www.clevelandschools.org
Cleveland HS 1,200/9-12
850 Raider Dr NW 37312 423-478-1113
Chuck Rockholt, prin. Fax 559-1560
Cleveland MS 1,100/6-8
3635 Georgetown Rd NW 37312 423-479-9641
Jeffrey Elliott, prin. Fax 479-9553

Academy of Beauty Arts Post-Sec.
633 Mimosa Dr NW 37312 423-476-3742
Church of God Theological Seminary Post-Sec.
PO Box 3330 37320 423-478-1131
Cleveland State Community College Post-Sec.
PO Box 3570 37320 423-472-7141
Lee University Post-Sec.
PO Box 3450 37320 423-614-8000
Tennessee Christian Academy 200/PK-12
4995 N Lee Hwy 37312 423-559-8939
Dr. R.B. Thomas, hdmstr. Fax 476-4974

Clifton, Wayne, Pop. 2,679
Wayne County SD
Supt. — See Waynesboro
Hughes S 300/K-12
PO Box A 38425 931-676-3325
Marlon Davis, prin. Fax 676-3903

Clinton, Anderson, Pop. 9,381
Anderson County SD 6,700/PK-12
101 S Main St 37716 865-463-2800
V. L. Stonecipher, supt. Fax 457-9157
www.acs.ac/
Anderson County Career & Technical Ctr Vo/Tech
140 Maverick Cir 37716 865-457-4205
Sid Spiva, prin. Fax 457-1715
Anderson County HS 1,000/9-12
130 Maverick Cir 37716 865-457-4716
Greg Deal, prin. Fax 457-3398
Clinton HS 1,200/9-12
425 Dragon Dr 37716 865-457-2611
Linda Davis, prin. Fax 457-8805
Clinton MS 700/6-8
110 N Hicks St 37716 865-457-3451
Bob Stokes, prin. Fax 457-9486
Other Schools – See Lake City, Norris, Oliver Springs

Coalfield, Morgan
Morgan County SD
Supt. — See Wartburg
Coalfield S 500/K-12
PO Box 98 37719 865-435-7332
Clay Lindsey, prin. Fax 435-2646

Coalmont, Grundy, Pop. 971
Grundy County SD
Supt. — See Altamont
Grundy County HS 700/9-12
24970 SR 108 37313 931-692-5400
Kenneth Colquette, prin. Fax 692-5403

Collegedale, Hamilton, Pop. 7,215

Collegedale SDA Academy 400/9-12
PO Box 628 37315 423-396-2124
Verle Thompson, prin. Fax 396-3363
Southern Adventist University Post-Sec.
PO Box 370 37315 423-238-2111

Collierville, Shelby, Pop. 37,564
Shelby County SD
Supt. — See Memphis
Collierville HS 2,200/9-12
1101 New Byhalia Rd 38017 901-853-3310
Dr. Timothy Setterlund, prin. Fax 853-3313
Collierville MS 1,000/6-8
146 College St 38017 901-853-3320
Ingrid Warren, prin. Fax 853-3327
Schilling Farms MS 900/6-8
935 Colbert St S 38017 901-854-2345
Sherry Phillips, prin. Fax 854-8200

St. George's Independent S Collierville 500/6-12
1880 Wolf River Blvd 38017 901-457-2000
William Taylor, hdmstr. Fax 457-2111

Collinwood, Wayne, Pop. 1,045
Wayne County SD
Supt. — See Waynesboro
Collinwood HS 400/9-12
401 N Trojan Blvd 38450 931-724-4316
Herbert Luker, prin. Fax 724-4488
Collinwood MS 300/5-8
300 4th Ave N 38450 931-724-9510
Walter Butler, prin. Fax 924-2519

Columbia, Maury, Pop. 33,777
Maury County SD 11,100/PK-12
501 W 8th St 38401 931-388-8403
Eddie Hickman, supt. Fax 840-4410
www.mauryk12.org/
Columbia Central HS 1,500/9-12
921 Lion Pkwy 38401 931-381-2222
Cindy Johnson, prin. Fax 381-6434
Cox MS 600/6-8
633 Bear Creek Pike 38401 931-840-3902
Debbie Steen, prin. Fax 840-3903
Spring Hill HS 900/9-12
1 Raider Ln 38401 931-486-2207
Richard Callahan, prin. Fax 486-3113
Whitthorne MS 1,100/6-8
915 Lion Pkwy 38401 931-388-2558
Linda Lester, prin. Fax 380-4684
Other Schools – See Culleoka, Hampshire, Mount Pleasant, Santa Fe

---

Columbia Academy 600/K-12
1101 W 7th St 38401 931-388-5363
Phillip Wright, prin. Fax 380-8506
Columbia State Community College Post-Sec.
PO Box 1315 38402 931-540-2722
Zion Christian Academy 300/K-12
6901 Old Zion Rd 38401 931-388-5731
Don Wahlman, hdmstr. Fax 388-5842

Cookeville, Putnam, Pop. 27,743
Putnam County SD 9,000/K-12
1400 E Spring St 38506 931-526-9777
Dr. Michael Martin, supt. Fax 528-6942
www.putnamcountyschools.com
Cookeville HS 2,000/9-12
2335 N Washington Ave 38501 931-520-2287
Wayne Shanks, prin. Fax 520-2268
Trace MS 900/7-8
230 Cavalier Dr 38501 931-520-2200
Linda Nash, prin. Fax 520-2204
Adult Learning Center Adult
1060B E Spring St 38501 931-528-8685
Jimmie Webber, prin. Fax 526-8133
Other Schools – See Baxter, Monterey

Daniel 1 Academy 100/4-12
1654 Burgess Falls Rd 38506 931-432-1496
Cynthia Holman, prin. Fax 432-1498
MedVance Institute Post-Sec.
1025 Highway 111 38501 931-526-3660
Middle Tennessee School of Cosmetology Post-Sec.
880 E 10th St Ste A 38501 931-526-8735
Mister Wayne's Sch of Unisex Hair Design Post-Sec.
170 S Willow Ave 38501 931-526-1478
Tennessee Technological University Post-Sec.
PO Box 5006 38505 931-372-3101

Copperhill, Polk, Pop. 482
Polk County SD
Supt. — See Benton
Copper Basin HS 300/7-12
205 Cougar Dr 37317 423-496-3291
Darren Danner, prin. Fax 496-5308

Cordova, Shelby
Memphis CSD
Supt. — See Memphis
Cordova HS 9-12
1800 Berryhill Rd 38016 901-416-4540
Ben Phillips, prin. Fax 416-4545
Cordova MS 800/5-8
900 N Sanga Rd 38018 901-416-2189
Joy Whitehead, prin. Fax 416-2191

Shelby County SD
Supt. — See Memphis
Dexter MS 600/5-8
6998 Raleigh LaGrange Rd 38018 901-373-3134
Phyllis Jones, prin.
Mt. Pisgah MS 1,100/5-8
1444 Pisgah Rd 38016 901-756-2386
John Gilmer, prin. Fax 756-2306

Evangelical Christian S 900/6-12
PO Box 1030 38088 901-754-7217
Bryan Miller, pres. Fax 754-8123
First Assembly Christian S 700/PK-12
8650 Walnut Grove Rd 38018 901-458-5543
Wendell Meadows, supt. Fax 324-3558
ITT Technical Institute Post-Sec.
7260 Goodlett Farms Pkwy 38016 901-381-0200
Mid-America Baptist Theological Seminary Post-Sec.
PO Box 2350 38088 901-751-8453
St. Benedict HS 9-12
8250 Varnavas Dr 38016 901-260-2840
George Valadie, pres. Fax 260-2850

Cornersville, Marshall, Pop. 937
Marshall County SD
Supt. — See Lewisburg
Cornersville JSHS 400/7-12
323 S Main St 37047 931-293-6505
Bob Edens, prin. Fax 293-6567

Corryton, Knox, Pop. 100
Knox County SD
Supt. — See Knoxville
Gibbs HS 1,000/9-12
7628 Tazewell Pike 37721 865-689-9130
Janice Walker, prin. Fax 689-9128

Cosby, Cocke
Cocke County SD
Supt. — See Newport
Cosby HS 400/9-12
3320 Cosby Hwy 37722 423-487-5602
Fax 487-5502

Covington, Tipton, Pop. 9,018
Tipton County SD 11,200/PK-12
PO Box 486 38019 901-476-7148
Dr. Tim Fite, supt. Fax 476-4870
www.tipton-county.com
Covington HS 900/9-12
803 S College St 38019 901-475-5876
Tom Barton, prin. Fax 476-5778
Crestview MS 800/5-8
201 Mark Walker Dr 38019 901-475-5900
James Fields, prin. Fax 475-2607
Other Schools – See Brighton, Munford

Tennessee Technology Center at Covington Post-Sec.
1600 Highway 51 S 38019 901-475-2526

Cowan, Franklin, Pop. 1,756
Franklin County SD
Supt. — See Winchester
South MS 300/7-8
601 Cumberland St W 37318 931-967-7355
Sandra Stewart, prin. Fax 967-1413

Cross Plains, Robertson, Pop. 1,517
Robertson County SD
Supt. — See Springfield
East Robertson JSHS 800/6-12
158 Kilgore Trce 37049 615-654-2191
Rick Ballard, prin. Fax 654-4563

Crossville, Cumberland, Pop. 10,424
Cumberland County SD 7,000/PK-12
368 4th St 38555 931-484-6135
Dr. Pattie Ragsdale, supt. Fax 484-6491
ccschools.k12tn.net/
Cumberland County HS 2,000/9-12
660 Stanley St 38555 931-484-6194
Janet Graham, prin. Fax 456-6872
Stone Memorial HS 9-12
2800 Cook Rd 38571 931-484-5767
Roger Eichelberger, prin.

Covenant Academy 100/PK-12
145 Interstate Dr 38555 931-707-9545
Lori Kubach, hdmstr. Fax 707-9878
Meridian Christian Academy 100/PK-12
140 Rome Rd 38555 931-484-6089
Phil Asberry, prin. Fax 484-6089
Tennessee Technology Center Crossville Post-Sec.
PO Box 2959 38557 931-484-7502

Crump, Hardin, Pop. 1,540

Tennessee Technology Center at Crump Post-Sec.
PO Box 89 38327 731-632-3393

Culleoka, Maury
Maury County SD
Supt. — See Columbia
Culleoka S 1,000/K-12
1921 Warrior Way 38451 931-987-2511
Jeff Quirk, prin. Fax 987-2594

Hopewell Church Covenant Family S 50/1-12
3886 Hopewll Church Rd 38451 931-381-2605
Charles Mangum, admin. Fax 381-8952

Cumberland Gap, Claiborne, Pop. 202
Claiborne County SD
Supt. — See Tazewell
Cumberland Gap HS 600/9-12
661 Old Jacksboro Rd 37724 423-869-9964
Troy R. Poore, prin. Fax 869-4352

Cunningham, Montgomery
Clarksville-Montgomery County SD
Supt. — See Clarksville
Montgomery Central HS 900/9-12
3955 Highway 48 37052 931-387-3201
Christy Houston, prin. Fax 387-4578
Montgomery Central MS 800/6-8
3941 Highway 48 37052 931-387-2575
Joe Nell Waters, prin. Fax 387-3391

Dandridge, Jefferson, Pop. 2,347
Jefferson County SD 7,200/PK-12
PO Box 190 37725 865-397-3194
Douglas Moody, dir. Fax 397-3301
jc-schools.net/
Jefferson County HS 2,100/9-12
115 W Dumplin Valley Rd 37725 865-397-3182
Dale Schneitman, prin. Fax 397-4121
Maury MS 600/6-8
965 Maury Cir 37725 865-397-3424
Jim Hodge, prin. Fax 397-4253
Other Schools – See Jefferson City

Covenant Christian Academy 300/PK-12
3222 Chestnut Hill School 37725 865-509-3800
Dr. Douglas Mills, hdmstr. Fax 509-3885

Dayton, Rhea, Pop. 6,443
Rhea County SD 4,000/K-12
305 California Ave 37321 423-775-7812
Dallas Smith, supt. Fax 775-7831
www.rheacounty.org
Other Schools – See Evensville, Spring City

Bryan College Post-Sec.
PO Box 7000 37321 423-775-2041
Oxford Graduate School Post-Sec.
500 Oxford Dr 37321 423-775-6596

Decatur, Meigs, Pop. 1,450
Meigs County SD 1,900/K-12
PO Box 1039 37322 423-334-5793
Robert Greene, supt. Fax 334-1462
www.meigscounty.net
Meigs County HS 600/9-12
105 Abel Ave 37322 423-334-5797
Milburn Harmon, prin. Fax 334-5798
Meigs MS 400/6-8
564 N Main St 37322 423-334-9187
Allen Roberts, prin. Fax 334-1353

Decaturville, Decatur, Pop. 846
Decatur County SD 1,600/PK-12
PO Box 369 38329 731-852-2391
Dr. Michael Price, supt. Fax 852-2960
Riverside HS 400/9-12
4250 Highway 641 S 38329 731-852-3941
Robert Myracle, prin. Fax 852-3955
Other Schools – See Parsons

Denmark, Madison
Jackson-Madison County SD
Supt. — See Jackson
West MS 400/7-8
317 Denmark Rd 38391 731-988-3810
Phinehas Hegmon, prin. Fax 988-3810

Dickson, Dickson, Pop. 12,873
Dickson County SD 8,000/PK-12
817 N Charlotte St 37055 615-446-7571
Charles Daniel, dir. Fax 441-1375
www.dicksoncountyschools.org/
Dickson County HS 1,400/9-12
509 Henslee Dr 37055 615-446-9003
Ed Littleton, prin. Fax 441-4135
Dickson MS 1,200/6-8
401 E College St 37055 615-446-2273
Johnny Chandler, prin. Fax 441-4139
Other Schools – See Charlotte, White Bluff

Tennessee Technology Center at Dickson Post-Sec.
740 Highway 46 S 37055 615-441-6220

Dover, Stewart, Pop. 1,495
Stewart County SD 1,900/PK-12
PO Box 433 37058 931-232-5176
Dr. Phillip Wallace, supt. Fax 232-5390
www.stewartcountyschools.net
Stewart County HS 600/9-12
PO Box 422 37058 931-232-5179
Chris Guynn, prin. Fax 232-3119
Stewart County MS 300/6-8
PO Box 1001 37058 931-232-9112
Jane Lancaster, prin.

Dresden, Weakley, Pop. 2,703
Weakley County SD 4,800/K-12
8319 Highway 22 Ste A 38225 731-364-2247
Richard Barber, supt. Fax 364-2662
www.weakleycountyschools.com
Dresden HS 400/9-12
7150 Highway 22 38225 731-364-2949
Charles West, prin. Fax 364-5328
Dresden MS 400/5-8
759 Linden St Ste A 38225 731-364-2407
Jeff Kelley, prin. Fax 364-5840
Weakley County Adult Learning Center Adult
8250 Highway 22 38225 731-364-5481
Julia Rich, prin. Fax 364-3580
Other Schools – See Gleason, Greenfield, Martin

Dunlap, Sequatchie, Pop. 4,681
Bledsoe County SD
Supt. — See Pikeville
Bledsoe County Vocational Center Vo/Tech
26297 US 127 37327 423-554-3293
Fax 554-3142

Sequatchie County SD 2,000/PK-12
PO Box 488 37327 423-949-3617
Johnny Cordell, supt. Fax 949-5257
Sequatchie County HS 500/9-12
PO Box 759 37327 423-949-2154
Tommy Layne, prin. Fax 949-4696
Sequatchie County MS 700/5-8
PO Box 789 37327 423-949-4149
Donald Johnson, prin. Fax 949-4140

Sequatchie Valley Preparatory Academy 50/K-12
1050 Ray Hixson Rd 37327 423-554-4677
Robert Young, admin.

Dyer, Gibson, Pop. 2,418
Gibson County SD 2,600/K-12
130 Trenton Hwy 38330 731-692-3803
Robert Galloway, dir. Fax 692-4375
www.gcssd.org
Gibson County HS 700/9-12
PO Box 190 38330 731-692-3616
B. Booth, prin. Fax 692-2123
Other Schools – See Medina

Dyersburg, Dyer, Pop. 17,466
Dyer County SD 3,200/PK-12
159 Everett Ave 38024 731-285-6712
Dr. Dwight Hedge, supt. Fax 286-6721
www.dyercs.net
Three Oaks MS 400/6-8
3200 Upper Finley Rd 38024 731-285-3100
Betty Jackson, prin. Fax 285-3360
Other Schools – See Newbern

Dyersburg CSD 3,500/K-12
PO Box 1507 38025 731-286-3600
Lloyd Ramer, supt. Fax 286-2754
www.dcs.k12tn.net/dcs/index.html
Dyersburg HS 900/9-12
125 US Highway 51 Byp W 38024 731-286-3630
Sam Miles, prin. Fax 286-2209
Dyersburg MS 900/6-8
400 Frank Maynard Dr 38024 731-286-3625
Tyles Davenport, prin. Fax 286-3624

Dyersburg State Community College Post-Sec.
1516 Lake Rd 38024 731-286-3200

Eads, Shelby

Briarcrest Christian HS 600/9-12
10103 Raleigh Lagrange Rd E 38028 901-751-6400
Bill McGee, pres. Fax 751-6402

Eagleville, Rutherford, Pop. 458
Rutherford County SD
Supt. — See Murfreesboro
Eagleville S 700/K-12
500 Highway 99 37060 615-904-6710
Ronda Holton, prin. Fax 904-6711

Eidson, Hawkins
Hawkins County SD
Supt. — See Rogersville
Clinch S 100/K-12
1010 Clinch Valley Rd 37731 423-272-3110
Linda Long, prin. Fax 272-3110

Elizabethton, Carter, Pop. 13,944
Carter County SD 6,000/PK-12
305 Academy St 37643 423-547-4000
Dallas Williams, supt. Fax 547-8338
carter.k12.tn.us
Happy Valley HS 600/9-12
121 Warpath Ln 37643 423-547-4094
Dale Campbell, prin.
Happy Valley MS 500/5-8
163 Warpath Ln 37643 423-547-4070
Carter Blevins, prin.
Unaka HS, 119 Robinson Ln 37643 400/9-12
Mickey Taylor, prin. 423-474-4100
Carter County Adult HS Adult
412 S Sycamore St 37643 423-547-4084
Paula Webster, prin.
Other Schools – See Hampton, Roan Mountain

Elizabethton CSD 2,100/PK-12
804 S Watauga Ave 37643 423-547-8000
David Roper Ed.D., supt. Fax 547-8101
www.ecschools.net
Dugger JHS 500/6-8
306 W E St 37643 423-547-8025
Regina Cates, prin. Fax 547-8021
Elizabethton HS 800/9-12
907 Jason Witten Way 37643 423-547-8015
Dr. Catherine Edwards, prin. Fax 547-8016

Tennessee Technology Center Elizabethton Post-Sec.
PO Box 789 37644 423-543-0070

Englewood, McMinn, Pop. 1,666
McMinn County SD
Supt. — See Athens
Central HS 800/9-12
145 County Road 461 37329 423-263-5541
Roger Freeman, prin. Fax 263-0399

Erin, Houston, Pop. 1,442
Houston County SD 1,400/PK-12
PO Box 209 37061 931-289-4148
Cathy Harvey, supt. Fax 289-5543
Houston County HS 400/9-12
2500 State Route 149 37061 931-289-4447
David Bell, prin.
Houston County MS 300/6-8
3460 W Main St 37061 931-289-5591
Sylvia Vinson, prin.
Houston County Adult S Adult
1214 W Main St 37061 931-289-5525
Linda McDonough, prin.

Erwin, Unicoi, Pop. 5,786
Unicoi County SD 2,200/PK-12
600 N Elm Ave 37650 423-743-1600
Denise Brown, dir. Fax 743-1615
www.unicoischools.com/
Unicoi County HS 800/8-12
700 S Mohawk Dr 37650 423-743-1632
Dr. Allen Rogers, prin. Fax 743-1636
Unicoi County Vocational S Vo/Tech
100 Okolona Dr 37650 423-743-1639
Charles Baxter, prin. Fax 743-1671

Evensville, Rhea
Rhea County SD
Supt. — See Dayton
Rhea County HS 1,400/9-12
405 Pierce Rd 37332 423-775-7821
Jerry Levengood, prin. Fax 775-7823

Fairview, Williamson, Pop. 7,190
Williamson County SD
Supt. — See Franklin
Fairview HS 600/9-12
2595 Fairview Blvd 37062 615-472-4400
Tony Donen, prin. Fax 472-4421
Fairview MS 500/6-8
7200 Cumberland Dr 37062 615-472-4430
Brian Bass, prin. Fax 472-4441

Fayetteville, Lincoln, Pop. 7,034
Fayetteville CSD 1,000/PK-9
110 Elk Ave S 37334 931-433-5542
Bill Evans, supt. Fax 433-7499
www.fcsboe.org
Fayetteville JHS 300/7-9
1800 Wilson Pkwy 37334 931-433-3158
Ron Perrin, prin. Fax 433-4611

Lincoln County SD 4,100/PK-12
206 Davidson St E 37334 931-433-3565
Dr. Wanda Shelton, supt. Fax 433-7397
www.lcdoe.org
Lincoln County SHS 1,100/10-12
1233 Huntsville Hwy 37334 931-433-6505
Jim Stewart, prin. Fax 438-1490
Ninth Grade Academy 300/9-9
900 Main Ave S 37334 931-433-6156
Sarah Wallace, prin. Fax 438-2465
Lincoln County Adult HS Adult
911 Main Ave S 37334 931-438-1489
Debbie Pardon, prin.

Fayetteville Beauty School Post-Sec.
201 Main Ave S 37334 931-433-1305

Franklin, Williamson, Pop. 53,311
Franklin Special SD 3,400/PK-8
507 New Highway 96 W 37064 615-794-6624
David Snowden Ph.D., supt. Fax 790-4716
www.fssd.org
Freedom MS 700/7-8
750 New Highway 96 W 37064 615-794-0987
Kristi Jefferson, prin. Fax 790-4742
Poplar Grove MS 5-8
2959 Del Rio Pike 37069 615-790-4721
Vanessa Garcia, prin. Fax 790-4730

Williamson County SD 23,700/PK-12
1320 W Main St Ste 202 37064 615-472-4000
Dr. Rebecca Sharber, supt. Fax 472-4190
www.wcs.edu
Centennial HS 1,400/9-12
5050 Mallory Ln 37067 615-472-4270
Dr. Terry Shrader, prin. Fax 472-4291
Franklin HS 1,700/9-12
810 Hillsboro Rd 37064 615-472-4450
Willie Dickerson, prin. Fax 472-4478
Grassland MS 1,000/6-8
2390 Hillsboro Rd 37069 615-472-4500
Dr. Susan Curtis, prin. Fax 472-4511
Middle College HS 200/9-12
108 Everbright St 37064 615-472-4670
Harold Ford, prin. Fax 472-4675
Page HS 900/9-12
6281 Arno Rd 37064 615-472-4730
Dr. Andrea Anthony, prin. Fax 472-4751
Page MS 900/6-8
6262 Arno Rd 37064 615-472-4760
Josie Jacobs, prin. Fax 472-4771
Other Schools – See Brentwood, Fairview, Thompsons Station

Battle Ground Academy 900/K-12
336 Ernest Rice Ln 37069 615-794-3501
Dr. John Griffith, hdmstr. Fax 567-8360
Franklin Christian Academy 100/7-12
PO Box 157 37065 615-599-9229
Hugh Harris, hdmstr. Fax 599-9441
Franklin Classical S 100/5-12
PO Box 1601 37065 615-595-5337
Tina Gilchrist, prin. Fax 595-5339
O'More College of Design Post-Sec.
423 S Margin St 37064 615-794-4254
Williamson Christian College Post-Sec.
200 Seaboard Ln 37067 615-771-7821

Gainesboro, Jackson, Pop. 859
Jackson County SD 1,800/K-12
711 School Dr 38562 931-268-0268
Joe D. Barlow, supt. Fax 268-3647
volweb.utk.edu/school/jackson/
Jackson County HS 500/9-12
190 Blue Devil Ln 38562 931-268-9771
Lakelan Barham, prin. Fax 268-9433
Jackson County MS 600/4-8
170 Blue Devil Ln 38562 931-268-9779
Gail Myers, prin. Fax 268-9413

Gallatin, Sumner, Pop. 26,720
Sumner County SD 24,400/PK-12
695 E Main St 37066 615-451-5200
Benny Bills, dir. Fax 451-5216
www.sumnerschools.org/
Doss MS 700/6-8
281 Big Station Camp Blvd 37066 615-206-0116
Mike Brown, prin. Fax 206-0165
Gallatin HS 1,400/9-12
700 Dan P Herron Dr 37066 615-452-2621
Rufus Lassiter, prin. Fax 451-5426
Rucker-Stewart MS 600/6-8
350 Hancock St 37066 615-452-1734
Andrew Turner, prin. Fax 451-5297
Shafer MS 600/6-8
240 Albert Gallatin Ave 37066 615-452-9100
David Hallman, prin. Fax 451-6545
Station Camp HS 900/9-12
1040 Bison Trl 37066 615-451-6551
Art Crook, prin. Fax 451-6556
Other Schools – See Hendersonville, Portland, Westmoreland, White House

---

Volunteer State Community College Post-Sec.
1480 Nashville Pike 37066 615-452-8600

Gatlinburg, Sevier, Pop. 4,426
Sevier County SD
Supt. — See Sevierville
Gatlinburg-Pittman HS 600/9-12
150 Proffitt Rd 37738 865-436-5637
Don Best, prin. Fax 436-2567

Germantown, Shelby, Pop. 37,480
Shelby County SD
Supt. — See Memphis
Germantown HS 2,100/9-12
7653 Old Poplar Pike 38138 901-756-2350
Dr. Lonnie Harris, prin. Fax 756-2356
Germantown MS 600/6-8
7925 CD Smith Rd 38138 901-756-2338
Russell Joy, prin. Fax 759-4521
Houston HS 2,100/9-12
9755 Wolf River Blvd 38139 901-756-2370
John Aitken, prin. Fax 756-2377
Houston MS 900/6-8
9400 Wolf River Blvd 38139 901-756-2366
Mike Morrison, prin. Fax 756-2346

Bodine S 100/1-12
2432 Yester Oaks Dr 38139 901-754-1800
Rene Lee, prin. Fax 751-8595

Gleason, Weakley, Pop. 1,426
Weakley County SD
Supt. — See Dresden
Gleason S 600/K-12
92-99 State Championship Dr 38229 731-648-5351
Randy Frazier, prin. Fax 648-9199

Goodlettsville, Davidson, Pop. 15,320
Davidson County SD
Supt. — See Nashville
Goodlettsville MS 500/5-8
300 S Main St 37072 615-859-8956
Sarah Moore, prin. Fax 859-8965

Miller-Motte Technical College Post-Sec.
801 Space Park N 37072 615-859-8090
Nossi College of Art Post-Sec.
907 Rivergate Pkwy Ste E6 37072 615-851-1088

Gordonsville, Smith, Pop. 1,130
Smith County SD
Supt. — See Carthage
Gordonsville HS, 104 Main St E 38563 500/7-12
Steve Armistead, prin. 615-683-8245

Gray, Washington, Pop. 1,071
Washington County SD
Supt. — See Jonesborough
Boone HS 1,200/9-12
1440 Suncrest Dr 37615 423-477-1600
Dr. Suzan Baker, prin. Fax 477-1625

Greenback, Loudon, Pop. 997
Loudon County SD
Supt. — See Loudon
Greenback S 700/K-12
400 Chilhowee Ave 37742 865-856-3028
Jerry Masingo, prin. Fax 856-5427

Greenbrier, Robertson, Pop. 6,054
Robertson County SD
Supt. — See Springfield
Greenbrier HS 800/9-12
126 Cuniff Dr 37073 615-643-4526
Gertrude Deal, prin. Fax 643-8873
Greenbrier MS 700/6-8
2450 Highway 41 S 37073 615-643-7823
Terri Simmons, prin. Fax 643-4580

Greeneville, Greene, Pop. 15,383
Greene County SD 6,500/PK-12
910 W Summer St 37743 423-639-4194
Dr. Joe Parkins, supt. Fax 639-1615
www.greenek12.org/
North Greene HS 400/9-12
4675 Old Baileyton Rd 37745 423-234-1752
Donna Waddle, prin. Fax 234-3103
South Greene HS 500/9-12
7469 Asheville Hwy 37743 423-639-3790
Cindy Bowman, prin. Fax 636-3791
Other Schools – See Afton, Mosheim

Greeneville CSD 2,600/K-12
PO Box 1420 37744 423-787-8000
Lyle Ailshie, supt. Fax 638-2540
www.gcschools.net
Greeneville HS 800/9-12
210 Tusculum Blvd 37745 423-787-8030
Jerry Ayers, prin. Fax 787-8028
Greeneville MS 600/6-8
433 E Vann Rd 37743 423-639-7841
Shelly Smith, prin. Fax 639-4112
Greenville Center for Technology Vo/Tech
1121 Hal Henard Rd 37743 423-639-0171
Jerry Renner, prin. Fax 639-0176

Greeneville Adventist Academy 100/K-10
305 Takoma Ave 37743 423-639-2011
Keith Nelson, prin. Fax 639-5002
Tusculum College Post-Sec.
PO Box 5051 37743 800-251-0256

Greenfield, Weakley, Pop. 2,084
Weakley County SD
Supt. — See Dresden
Greenfield S 600/K-12
101 N Faxon St 38230 731-235-3424
Jackie Vaughan, prin. Fax 235-3480

Halls, Lauderdale, Pop. 2,236
Lauderdale County SD
Supt. — See Ripley
Halls HS 400/9-12
800 W Tigrett St 38040 731-836-9642
Andy Pugh, prin. Fax 836-1072
Halls JHS 200/7-8
800 W Tigrett St 38040 731-836-5579
Dr. Pam Sirmans, prin. Fax 836-5579

Hampshire, Maury
Maury County SD
Supt. — See Columbia
Hampshire S 300/K-12
4235 Old State Rd 38461 931-285-2300
Stan Curtis, prin. Fax 285-2612

Hampton, Carter
Carter County SD
Supt. — See Elizabethton
Hampton HS 400/9-12
766 First Ave 37658 423-725-5200
Danny McClain, prin. Fax 725-5204

Harriman, Roane, Pop. 6,725
Roane County SD
Supt. — See Kingston
Harriman HS 300/9-12
920 N Roane St 37748 865-882-1821
Russell Jenkins, prin. Fax 882-6479
Harriman MS 300/6-8
1025 Cumberland St 37748 865-882-1727
David R. Stevens, prin. Fax 882-6285

Roane State Community College Post-Sec.
276 Patton Ln 37748 865-354-3000
Tennessee Technology Center at Harriman Post-Sec.
PO Box 1109 37748 865-882-6703

Harrison, Hamilton, Pop. 7,191
Hamilton County SD
Supt. — See Chattanooga
Brown MS 600/6-8
5716 Highway 58 37341 423-344-1439
John Stewart, prin. Fax 344-1471
Central HS 1,100/9-12
5728 Highway 58 37341 423-344-1447
Robert Sharpe, prin. Fax 344-1470

Harrogate, Claiborne, Pop. 3,985
Claiborne County SD
Supt. — See Tazewell
Livesay MS 300/5-8
PO Box 460 37752 423-869-4663
Roy Bryant, prin. Fax 869-8389

Lincoln Memorial University Post-Sec.
PO Box 2012 37752 423-869-3611
White Academy 100/5-12
Cumberland Gap Pkwy 37752 423-869-6234
Dr. Sheila Clyburn, prin. Fax 869-6425

Hartsville, Trousdale, Pop. 2,373
Trousdale County SD 1,300/K-12
103 Lock Six Rd 37074 615-374-2193
Margaret Oldham, dir. Fax 374-1108
Satterfield MS 300/6-8
210 Damascus St 37074 615-374-2748
John Kerr, prin. Fax 374-2602
Trousdale County HS 400/9-12
262 McMurry Blvd W 37074 615-374-2201
Toby Woodmore, prin. Fax 374-1120

Tennessee Technology Center Hartsville Post-Sec.
716 McMurry Blvd E 37074 615-374-2147

Henderson, Chester, Pop. 6,061
Chester County SD 2,500/PK-12
PO Box 327 38340 731-989-5134
John Pipkin, supt. Fax 989-4755
www.chestercountyschools.org
Chester County HS 700/9-12
552 E Main St 38340 731-989-8125
Troy Kilzer, prin. Fax 989-8131
Chester County JHS 400/7-8
930 E Main St 38340 731-989-8135
Ken West, prin. Fax 989-8137

Freed-Hardeman University Post-Sec.
158 E Main St 38340 731-989-6000

Hendersonville, Sumner, Pop. 44,876
Sumner County SD
Supt. — See Gallatin
Beech HS 1,200/9-12
3126 Long Hollow Pike 37075 615-824-6200
Frank Cardwell, prin. Fax 264-6553
Ellis MS 500/6-8
100 Indian Lake Rd 37075 615-264-6093
Opal Poe, prin. Fax 264-5800
Hawkins MS 500/6-8
487 Walton Ferry Rd 37075 615-824-3456
Jeff Helbig, prin. Fax 264-6003
Hendersonville HS 1,400/9-12
123 Cherokee Rd 37075 615-824-6162
Mike Shelton, prin. Fax 264-6027
Hunter MS 800/6-8
2101 New Hope Rd 37075 615-822-4720
Shelly Petty, prin. Fax 264-6036
Hyde Magnet S 500/K-12
128 Township Dr 37075 615-264-6543
Brad Schreiner, prin. Fax 264-6546
Wilson Night S Adult
102 Indian Lake Rd 37075 615-264-6085
Cynthia Horner, prin. Fax 264-6034

Pope John Paul II HS 9-12
117 Caldwell Dr 37075 615-822-2375
Hans Broekman, prin. Fax 822-6226

Hermitage, See Nashville
Davidson County SD
Supt. — See Nashville
DuPont-Tyler MS 700/5-8
431 Tyler Dr 37076 615-885-8827
Carol Cutsinger, prin. Fax 847-7322

Hixson, See Chattanooga
Hamilton County SD
Supt. — See Chattanooga
Hixson HS 1,000/9-12
5705 Middle Valley Rd 37343 423-847-4800
Eddie Gravitte, prin. Fax 847-4801
Hixson MS 600/6-8
5401 School Dr 37343 423-870-0600
Sandra Barnwell, prin. Fax 870-0623
Loftis MS 800/6-8
8611 Columbus Rd 37343 423-843-4749
Lisa Huskey, prin. Fax 843-4758

Hohenwald, Lewis, Pop. 3,791
Lewis County SD 1,900/K-12
206 S Court St 38462 931-796-3264
Benny Pace, supt. Fax 796-5127
www.lewis.k12.tn.us
Lewis County HS 600/9-12
818 W Main St 38462 931-796-4085
Allen Trull, prin. Fax 796-1172
Lewis County MS 500/6-8
207 S Court St 38462 931-796-4586
Tim Watkins, prin. Fax 796-7601

Tennessee Technology Center at Hohenwald Post-Sec.
813 W Main St 38462 931-796-5351

Humboldt, Gibson, Pop. 9,269
Humboldt CSD 1,500/K-12
1421 Osborne St Ste 6 38343 731-784-2652
Garnett Twyman, supt. Fax 784-2480
www.humboldtschools.com
Humboldt HS 400/9-12
2600 Viking Dr 38343 731-784-2781
Ron Canada, prin. Fax 784-8536
Humboldt JHS 300/7-8
1811 Ferrell St 38343 731-784-9514
Lillian Shelton, prin. Fax 784-3274

Huntingdon, Carroll, Pop. 4,186
Carroll County SD
PO Box 799 38344 731-986-4482
Charlotte Tucker, supt. Fax 986-0198
www.carrollschools.com
Carroll County Technical Center Vo/Tech
1235 Buena Vista Rd 38344 731-986-8908
John Mcadams, prin. Fax 986-3200
Adult Education Center Adult
13345 Paris St 38344 731-986-4841
Brenda Parish, prin. Fax 986-4841

Huntingdon Special SD 1,300/K-12
585 High St 38344 731-986-2222
Lynn Twyman, supt. Fax 986-4365
www.huntingdonschools.org/
Huntingdon HS 400/9-12
475 Mustang Dr 38344 731-986-8223
Mike Henson, prin. Fax 986-4031
Huntingdon MS 500/4-8
199 Browning Ave 38344 731-986-4544
Pat Dillahunty, prin. Fax 986-8689

Huntland, Franklin, Pop. 886
Franklin County SD
Supt. — See Winchester
Huntland S 700/PK-12
400 Gore St 37345 931-469-7506
Diana Spaulding, prin. Fax 469-0590

Huntsville, Scott, Pop. 1,194
Scott County SD 2,700/PK-12
PO Box 37 37756 423-663-2159
Mike Davis, supt. Fax 663-9682
www.scottcounty.net
Huntsville MS 200/6-8
3101 Baker Hwy 37756 423-663-2192
Lamance Bryant, prin. Fax 663-2967
Scott HS 800/9-12
400 Scott High Dr 37756 423-663-2801
Sharon Wilson, prin. Fax 663-2368

Tennessee Technology Center Oneida/Hunts Post-Sec.
355 Scott High Dr 37756 423-663-4900

Jacksboro, Campbell, Pop. 1,992
Campbell County SD 6,200/PK-12
PO Box 445 37757 423-562-8377
Dr. Judy Carr Blevins, supt. Fax 566-7562
www.campbell.k12.tn.us
Campbell County Comprehensive HS 1,400/9-12
150 Cougar Ln 37757 423-562-8308
Gary Seale, prin. Fax 562-2019
Jacksboro MS 500/6-8
150 Eagle Cir 37757 423-562-3773
Jamie Wheeler, prin. Fax 562-8994
Campbell County Adult HS Adult
366 Alder Springs Rd 37757 423-566-5436
Dr. Rita Goins-Claiborne, prin. Fax 562-5219
Other Schools – See Jellico, La Follette

Tennessee Technology Center at Jacksboro Post-Sec.
PO Box 419 37757 423-566-9629

Jackson, Madison, Pop. 62,099
Jackson-Madison County SD 13,400/PK-12
310 N Parkway 38305 731-664-2592
Dr. Nancy Zambito, supt. Fax 664-2502
www.jmcss.net/
Jackson Central-Merry HS 1,000/9-12
332 Lane Ave 38301 731-424-2200
Virginia Crump, prin. Fax 423-6158
Liberty Technology Magnet HS Vo/Tech
3470 Ridgecrest Road Ext 38305 731-423-9086
Johnny Reynolds, prin. Fax 424-3445
Madison Academic Magnet S 400/9-12
179 Allen Ave 38301 731-427-3501
Tommy Allen, prin. Fax 427-3587
Northeast MS 600/7-8
2665 Christmasville Rd 38305 731-422-6687
Vivian Williams, prin. Fax 423-1805
North Side HS 1,100/9-12
3066 N Highland Ave 38305 731-668-3171
Fax 661-9756
Rose Hill MS 7-8
2233 Beech Bluff Rd 38301 731-423-6170
James Shaw, prin. Fax 423-6171
South Side HS 800/9-12
84 Harts Bridge Rd 38301 731-422-9923
Jimmy Arnold, prin. Fax 423-3411
Tigrett MS 700/7-8
716 Westwood Ave 38301 731-988-3840
Nelson Piercey, prin. Fax 988-3838
Other Schools – See Denmark

Jackson Christian S 900/PK-12
832 Country Club Ln 38305 731-668-8055
Dr. Michael Weimer, pres. Fax 664-5763
Jackson State Community College Post-Sec.
2046 N Parkway 38301 731-424-3520
Lambuth University Post-Sec.
705 Lambuth Blvd 38301 731-425-2500
Lane College Post-Sec.
545 Lane Ave 38301 731-426-7500
McCollum & Ross The Hair School Post-Sec.
1433 Hollywood Dr 38301 731-427-6642
Tennessee Technology Center at Jackson Post-Sec.
2468 Technology Center Dr 38301 731-424-0691
Trinity Christian Academy 800/PK-12
130 Old Denmark Rd 38301 731-423-8924
Robbie Mason, hdmstr. Fax 427-6195
Union University Post-Sec.
1050 Union University Dr 38305 731-668-1818
University S of Jackson 1,300/PK-12
232 Mcclellan Rd 38305 731-664-0812
Steven Maloan, hdmstr. Fax 664-5046
West Tennessee Business College Post-Sec.
1186 Highway 45 Byp 38301 800-737-9822

Jamestown, Fentress, Pop. 1,865
Fentress County SD 2,300/PK-12
PO Box 963 38556 931-879-9218
Homer Linder, supt. Fax 879-4050
www.fentress.k12tn.net
Fentress County Adult HS Adult
PO Box 963 38556 931-752-8296
Gerald Huddleston, prin. Fax 752-8316
Other Schools – See Clarkrange

Jasper, Marion, Pop. 3,082
Marion County SD 4,200/PK-12
204 Betsy Pack Dr 37347 423-942-3434
Dr. Fred Taylor, supt. Fax 942-4210
www.marionschools.org/
Jasper MS 500/5-8
601 Elm Ave 37347 423-942-6251
Kim Headrick, prin. Fax 942-0141
Marion County HS 500/9-12
160 Ridley Ave 37347 423-942-5120
Sherry Prince, prin. Fax 942-5544
Other Schools – See South Pittsburg, Whitwell

Jefferson City, Jefferson, Pop. 7,931
Jefferson County SD
Supt. — See Dandridge
Jefferson MS 700/6-8
361 W Broadway Blvd 37760 865-475-6133
Amie Lambert, prin. Fax 475-8813

Carson-Newman College Post-Sec.
1646 Russell Ave 37760 865-471-4000

Jellico, Campbell, Pop. 2,514
Campbell County SD
Supt. — See Jacksboro
Jellico HS 400/9-12
141 High School Ln 37762 423-784-9455
Don Walden, prin. Fax 784-9456

Joelton, See Nashville
Davidson County SD
Supt. — See Nashville
Joelton MS 500/5-8
3500 Old Clarksville Pike 37080 615-876-5100
Mary Nollner, prin. Fax 876-1469

Johnson City, Washington, Pop. 58,718
Johnson City CSD 6,700/PK-12
PO Box 1517 37605 423-434-5200
Dr. Richard Bales, supt. Fax 434-5237
www.jcschools.org
Science Hill HS 2,400/8-12
1509 John Exum Pkwy 37604 423-232-2190
David Chupa, prin. Fax 926-1622
Science Hill Technology Center Vo/Tech
501 Liberty Bell Blvd 37604 423-232-2200
Kenneth Ralston, dir. Fax 461-1695

Washington County SD
Supt. — See Jonesborough
Boones Creek MS 400/5-8
4352 N Roan St 37615 423-283-3520
Dr. Max Williams, prin. Fax 283-3524
University S, PO Box 70632 37614 500/K-12
Deborah DeFrieze, prin. 423-929-4333

East Tennessee State University Post-Sec.
PO Box 70731 37614 423-439-1000
Emmanuel School of Religion Post-Sec.
1 Walker Dr 37601 423-926-1186
Providence Academy 500/K-12
2788 Carroll Creek Rd 37615 423-854-9819
Jerry Williams, admin. Fax 854-8958

Jonesborough, Washington, Pop. 4,550
Washington County SD 8,900/K-12
405 W College St 37659 423-753-1100
Grant Rowland, supt. Fax 753-1114
www.wcde.org
Crockett HS 1,500/9-12
684 Old State Route 34 37659 423-753-1150
Henry Marable, prin. Fax 753-1167
Jonesborough MS 500/5-8
308 Forrest Dr 37659 423-753-1190
Terry Crowe, prin. Fax 753-1570
Other Schools – See Gray, Johnson City

Kingsport, Sullivan, Pop. 44,130
Kingsport CSD 6,400/PK-12
1701 E Center St 37664 423-378-2100
Dr. Richard Kitzmiller, supt. Fax 378-2120
www.k12k.com/
Dobyns-Bennett HS 1,800/9-12
1800 Legion Dr 37664 423-378-8400
Earl Lovelace, prin. Fax 378-8535
Robinson MS 700/6-8
1517 Jessee St 37664 423-378-2200
Richard Everroad, prin. Fax 378-2220
Sevier MS 800/6-8
1200 Wateree St 37660 423-378-2450
Dr. Carolyn McPherson, prin. Fax 378-2430

Sullivan County SD
Supt. — See Blountville
Colonial Heights MS 600/6-8
415 Lebanon Rd 37663 423-354-1360
Mike Cline, prin. Fax 354-1365
Sullivan MS 200/6-8
4154 Sullivan Gardens Dr 37660 423-354-1780
Steve Thompson, prin. Fax 354-1786
Sullivan North HS 800/8-12
2533 N John B Dennis Hwy 37660 423-354-1400
Richard Carroll, prin. Fax 354-1406
Sullivan South HS 1,100/9-12
1236 Moreland Dr 37664 423-354-1300
Greg Harvey, prin. Fax 354-1306

Appalachian Christian S 50/K-12
1044 New Beason Well Rd 37660 423-288-3352
Newl Dotson, admin. Fax 288-3354

Kingston, Roane, Pop. 5,472
Roane County SD 7,400/PK-12
105 Bluff Rd 37763 865-376-5592
Dr. Toni McGriff, supt. Fax 376-1284
www.roaneschools.com/
Cherokee MS 600/6-8
200 Paint Rock Ferry Rd 37763 865-376-9281
Joan Turbyville, prin. Fax 376-8525
Midway HS 300/9-12
530 Loudon Hwy 37763 865-376-5645
Scott Mason, prin. Fax 376-8516
Roane County HS 700/9-12
540 W Cumberland St 37763 865-376-6534
Robert Dill, prin. Fax 376-8530
Other Schools – See Harriman, Oliver Springs, Rockwood, Ten Mile

Kingston Springs, Cheatham, Pop. 2,870
Cheatham County SD
Supt. — See Ashland City
Harpeth HS 600/9-12
170 E Kingston Springs Rd 37082 615-952-2811
Jenny Simpkins, prin. Fax 952-5013
Harpeth MS 600/5-8
170 Harpeth View Trl 37082 615-952-2293
Shannon Schwila, prin. Fax 952-4527

Knoxville, Knox, Pop. 180,130
Knox County SD 51,700/PK-12
912 S Gay St 37902 865-594-1800
Dr. Charles Lindsey, supt. Fax 594-1627
www.kcs.k12tn.net
Austin-East HS 800/9-12
2800 Martin Luther King Jr 37914 865-594-3792
Brian Hartsell, prin. Fax 594-1165
Bearden HS 2,000/9-12
8352 Kingston Pike 37919 865-539-7800
Barbara Jenkins, prin. Fax 539-7805
Bearden MS 1,100/6-8
1000 Francis Rd 37909 865-539-7839
Heather Karnes, prin. Fax 539-7851
Byington-Solway Technology Center Vo/Tech
2700 Byington Solway Rd 37931 865-693-3511
Clifford Davis, prin. Fax 694-7094
Cedar Bluff MS 500/6-8
707 N Cedar Bluff Rd 37923 865-539-7891
Sonya Winstead, prin. Fax 539-7792
Central HS 1,300/9-12
5321 Jacksboro Pike 37918 865-689-1400
Jon Miller, prin. Fax 689-1403
Farragut HS 2,300/9-12
11237 Kingston Pike, 865-966-9775
Mike Reynolds, prin. Fax 671-7120
Farragut MS 1,200/6-8
200 W End Ave, 865-966-9756
Dr. Dick Dalhaus, prin. Fax 671-7048
Fulton HS 1,000/9-12
2509 N Broadway St 37917 865-594-1240
Kitty Hatcher, prin. Fax 594-1228
Gresham MS 700/6-8
500 Gresham Rd 37918 865-689-1430
Donna Parker, prin. Fax 689-7437
Halls HS 1,100/9-12
4321 E Emory Rd 37938 865-922-7757
Mark Duff, prin. Fax 925-7700
Halls MS 1,000/6-8
4317 E Emory Rd 37938 865-922-7494
Doug Oliver, prin. Fax 925-7439
Holston MS 800/6-8
600 N Chilhowee Dr 37924 865-594-1300
Tom Brown, prin. Fax 594-4429
Karns HS 1,700/9-12
2710 Byington Solway Rd 37931 865-539-8670
Clifford Davis, prin. Fax 539-8679
Karns MS 1,100/6-8
2925 Gray Hendrix Rd 37931 865-539-7732
Danny Trent, prin. Fax 539-7745
Lincoln Park Tech/Trade Center Vo/Tech
535 Chickamauga Ave 37917 865-689-1454
Rick Bise, prin. Fax 689-1456
North Knox Vocational Center Vo/Tech
7411 Ledgerwood Rd 37938 865-922-7576
Fax 925-7551
Northwest MS 900/6-8
5301 Pleasant Ridge Rd 37912 865-594-1345
Kelvin McCullom, prin. Fax 594-1339
South-Doyle HS 1,300/9-12
2020 Tipton Station Rd 37920 865-577-4475
Rick Walker, prin. Fax 577-4540
South-Doyle MS 1,100/6-8
3900 Decatur Dr 37920 865-579-2133
Jeanna Swan-Cole, prin. Fax 579-2128
Vine MS 500/6-8
1807 Martin Luther King Jr 37915 865-594-4461
LaRoyce Beatty, prin. Fax 594-1702
West HS 1,400/9-12
3326 Sutherland Ave 37919 865-594-4477
Sallee Reynolds, prin. Fax 594-4486
West Valley MS 1,100/6-8
9118 George Williams Rd 37922 865-539-5145
Sheila Fuqua, prin. Fax 539-5155
Whittle Springs MS 600/6-8
2700 White Oak Ln 37917 865-594-4474
Benny Perry, prin. Fax 594-1132
Knox County Evening HS Adult
101 E 5th Ave 37917 865-594-3713
Carol Russell, prin. Fax 594-3711
Other Schools – See Corryton, Powell, Strawberry Plains

Berean Christian S 1,200/K-12
2329 Prosser Rd 37914 865-521-6054
George Waller, admin. Fax 522-5063
Christian Academy of Knoxville 1,100/PK-12
529 Academy Way 37923 865-690-4721
Scott Sandie, supt. Fax 690-4752
Fort Sanders School of Nursing Post-Sec.
9821 Cogdill Rd Ste 2 37932
Grace Christian Academy 600/K-12
5914 Beaver Ridge Rd 37931 865-691-3427
Donald Criss, hdmstr. Fax 691-1465
Huntington College of Health Sciences Post-Sec.
1204 Kenesaw Ave 37919 800-290-4226
ITT Technical Institute Post-Sec.
10208 Technology Dr 37932 865-671-2800
Johnson Bible College Post-Sec.
7900 Johnson Dr 37998 865-573-4517
Knoxville Adventist S 100/K-10
3615 Kingston Pike 37919 865-522-9929
Fax 523-7471
Knoxville Catholic HS 9-12
9245 Fox Lonas Rd 37923 865-560-0313
Richard Sompayrac Ed.D., prin. Fax 560-0314
Pellissippi State Technical Comm. Coll. Post-Sec.
PO Box 22990 37933 865-694-6400
Reuben Allen College Post-Sec.
120 Center Park Dr 37922 865-966-0400
South College Post-Sec.
3904 Lonas Dr 37909 865-251-1800
Tennessee School for the Deaf Post-Sec.
2725 Island Home Blvd 37920 865-594-6022
Tennessee School of Beauty Post-Sec.
4704 Western Ave 37921 865-588-7878
Tennessee Technology Center at Knoxville Post-Sec.
1100 Liberty St 37919 865-546-5567
University of Tennessee Post-Sec.
527 Andy Holt Tower 37996 865-974-1000
University of Tennessee Medical Center Post-Sec.
1924 Alcoa Hwy 37920 865-546-5567
Webb S of Knoxville 1,100/K-12
9800 Webb School Ln 37923 865-693-0011
Scott Hutchinson, pres. Fax 691-8057

Kodak, Sevier
Sevier County SD
Supt. — See Sevierville
Northview MS 500/5-8
3295 Douglas Dam Rd 37764 865-933-7985
Jim Davis, prin. Fax 933-7387

Lafayette, Macon, Pop. 4,177
Macon County SD 3,900/K-12
501 College St 37083 615-666-2125
Mike Prock, supt. Fax 666-7878
www.maconcountyschools.com/
Macon County HS 800/9-12
PO Box 338 37083 615-666-4320
Shawn Carter, prin. Fax 666-4757
Macon Co. JHS 700/6-8
1003 Highway 52 Byp E 37083 615-666-7545
Bobby Bransford, prin. Fax 666-9264
Other Schools – See Red Boiling Springs

La Follette, Campbell, Pop. 8,166
Campbell County SD
Supt. — See Jacksboro
La Follette MS 600/6-8
1309 E Central Ave 37766 423-562-8448
Rob Heatherly, prin. Fax 562-2107

Lake City, Anderson, Pop. 1,844
Anderson County SD
Supt. — See Clinton
Lake City MS 400/6-8
1132 S Main St 37769 865-426-2609
Paula Sellers, prin. Fax 426-9319

La Vergne, Rutherford, Pop. 25,885
Rutherford County SD
Supt. — See Murfreesboro
La Vergne HS 1,700/9-12
250 Wolverine Trl 37086 615-904-3870
Melvin Daniels, prin. Fax 904-3871
La Vergne MS 900/6-8
382 Stones River Rd 37086 615-904-3877
Dirk Ash, prin. Fax 904-3878

Lawrenceburg, Lawrence, Pop. 10,911
Lawrence County SD 6,900/PK-12
700 Mahr Ave 38464 931-762-3581
Dr. Bill Heath, supt. Fax 762-7299
www.lcss.us/
Coffman MS 400/7-8
111 Lafayette Ave 38464 931-762-6395
Bernard Fuller, prin. Fax 762-7176
Lawrence County HS 1,100/9-12
1800 Springer Rd 38464 931-762-9412
Mickey Dunn, prin. Fax 766-0761

Lawrence County Vo Ctr Vo/Tech
1906 Springer Rd 38464 931-762-6472
Mickey Dunn, prin. Fax 766-1551
Other Schools – See Loretto, Summertown

Lebanon, Wilson, Pop. 23,043
Lebanon Special SD 2,900/K-8
701 Coles Ferry Pike 37087 615-449-6060
Dr. Sharon Roberts, supt. Fax 449-5673
www.lssd.org
Baird MS 700/7-8
131 WJB Pride Ln 37087 615-444-2190
Scott Benson, prin. Fax 453-2690

Wilson County SD 12,900/PK-12
351 Stumpy Ln 37090 615-444-3282
Dr. Mike Davis, dir. Fax 449-3858
www.wcschools.com
Lebanon HS 1,600/9-12
415 Harding Dr 37087 615-444-9610
Clint Wilson, prin. Fax 443-1373
Wilson Central HS 1,500/9-12
419 Wildcat Way 37090 615-453-4600
Travis Mayfield, prin. Fax 453-4610
Wilson County Vocational Center Vo/Tech
418 Harding Dr 37087 615-444-1104
William Moss, prin. Fax 443-8745
Adult Basic Education Adult
351 Stumpy Ln 37090 615-443-8731
Bernadine Nelson, dir. Fax 453-2529
Wilson County Adult HS Adult
207 J Branham Dr 37087 615-443-7199
Pat Suddarth, lead tchr. Fax 443-2690
Other Schools – See Mount Juliet, Watertown

Cumberland University Post-Sec.
1 Cumberland Sq 37087 615-444-2562
Friendship Christian S 700/PK-12
5400 Coles Ferry Pike 37087 615-449-1573
Becky Kegley, prin. Fax 449-2769
Stylemasters Beauty Academy Post-Sec.
223 N Cumberland St 37087 615-444-4908

Lenoir City, Loudon, Pop. 7,675
Lenoir CSD 2,200/PK-12
2145 Harrison Ave 37771 865-986-8058
Wayne Miller, supt. Fax 988-6732
www.lenoircityschools.com/
Lenoir City HS 1,200/9-12
1485 Old Highway 95 37771 865-986-2072
Steve Millsaps, prin. Fax 988-2054
Lenoir City MS 300/6-8
2141 Harrison Ave 37771 865-986-2038
Chip Orr, prin. Fax 988-1964

Loudon County SD
Supt. — See Loudon
North MS 800/5-8
421 Hickory Creek Rd 37771 865-986-9944
Tim Berry, prin. Fax 988-9089

Crossroads Christian Academy 100/PK-12
1963 Martel Rd 37772 865-986-9823
Drew Guetterman, admin.

Lewisburg, Marshall, Pop. 10,790
Marshall County SD 4,800/K-12
700 Jones Cir 37091 931-359-1581
John David Pierce, supt. Fax 270-8816
www.mcs.k12.tn.us
Lewisburg MS 400/7-8
500 Tiger Blvd 37091 931-359-1265
Randy Hubbell, prin. Fax 359-4030
Marshall County HS 800/9-12
597 W Ellington Pkwy 37091 931-359-1549
Nancy Pruitt, prin. Fax 359-4784
Spot Lowe Vocational S Vo/Tech
1771 Old Columbia Rd 37091 931-359-4911
Ray Stacey, prin. Fax 359-3041
Other Schools – See Chapel Hill, Cornersville

Lexington, Henderson, Pop. 7,667
Henderson County SD 3,500/K-12
PO Box 189 38351 731-968-3661
Susan Bunch, supt. Fax 968-9457
www.henderson-lea.hc.k12tn.net/
Lexington HS 900/9-12
284 White St 38351 731-968-2961
Chuck Patton, prin. Fax 968-9399
Other Schools – See Reagan

Lexington CSD 1,000/K-8
70 Dixon St 38351 731-967-5591
Joe T. Wood, supt. Fax 967-0794
www.caywood.org
Lexington MS 300/6-8
112 Airways Dr 38351 731-968-8457
Angela Blankenship, prin. Fax 967-7130

Linden, Perry, Pop. 981
Perry County SD 1,100/K-12
333 S Mill St 37096 931-589-2102
Gil Webb, dir. Fax 589-5110
www.perryboe.com/
Linden MS 200/5-8
130 College Ave 37096 931-589-5000
Hazel Swan, prin. Fax 589-3685
Perry County HS 400/9-12
1056 Squirrel Hollow Dr 37096 931-589-2831
R. Morris, prin. Fax 589-5063

Livingston, Overton, Pop. 3,489
Overton County SD 3,300/K-12
302 Zachary St 38570 931-823-1287
Michael Gilpatrick, supt. Fax 823-4673
www.overton.k12tn.net/
Livingston Academy HS 900/9-12
120 Melvin Johnson Dr 38570 931-823-5911
Gary Ledbetter, prin. Fax 823-8626
Livingston MS 400/5-8
216 Bilbrey St 38570 931-823-5917
Rick Moles, prin. Fax 823-7549

Tennessee Technology Center Livingston Post-Sec.
740 Hi Tech Dr 38570 931-823-5525

Loretto, Lawrence, Pop. 1,710
Lawrence County SD
Supt. — See Lawrenceburg
Loretto HS 600/9-12
525 2nd Ave S 38469 931-853-4324
David Daniel, prin. Fax 853-4340

Loudon, Loudon, Pop. 4,745
Loudon County SD 5,000/PK-12
100 River Rd 37774 865-458-5411
A. Edward Headlee, dir. Fax 458-6138
k12.loudoncounty.org
Ft. Loudoun MS 400/6-8
1703 Roberts Rd 37774 865-458-2026
Sherry Smith, prin. Fax 458-6611
Loudon HS 700/9-12
1039 Mulberry St 37774 865-458-4326
John Bartlett, prin. Fax 458-0717
Other Schools – See Greenback, Lenoir City

Lyles, Hickman
Hickman County SD
Supt. — See Centerville
East Hickman MS 500/6-8
9414 E Eagle Dr 37098 931-670-4237
Julia Thomasson, prin. Fax 670-4239

Lynchburg, Moore, Pop. 5,241
Moore County SD 1,000/K-12
PO Box 219 37352 931-759-7303
Chad Moorehead, supt. Fax 759-6386
moore.k12.tn.us
Moore County JSHS 400/7-12
1502 Lynchburg Hwy 37352 931-759-4231
Stanley Bean, prin. Fax 759-6390

Motlow State Community College Post-Sec.
PO Box 8500 37352 931-393-1500

Lynnville, Giles, Pop. 339
Giles County SD
Supt. — See Pulaski
Richland MSHS 900/5-12
10610 Columbia Hwy 38472 931-527-3577
Bobbi McMasters, prin. Fax 527-3720

Mc Ewen, Humphreys, Pop. 1,480
Humphreys County SD
Supt. — See Waverly
Mc Ewen HS 300/9-12
335 Melrose St 37101 931-582-6950
Jerry Honea, prin. Fax 582-6952
McEwen JHS 200/6-8
360 Melrose St 37101 931-582-8417
T. Coleman, prin. Fax 582-8418

Mc Kenzie, Carroll, Pop. 5,363
Mc Kenzie Special SD 1,300/PK-12
114 Bell Ave 38201 731-352-2246
James Ward, supt. Fax 352-7550
www.mckenzieschools.org
Mc Kenzie HS 400/9-12
23292 Highway 22 38201 731-352-2133
Terry Howell, prin. Fax 352-1424
Mc Kenzie MS 400/5-8
80 Woodrow Ave 38201 731-352-2792
Jon Frye, prin. Fax 352-4709

Bethel College Post-Sec.
325 Cherry Ave 38201 731-352-4030
Tennessee Technology Center at Mc Kenzie Post-Sec.
PO Box 427 38201 731-352-5364

Mc Minnville, Warren, Pop. 12,060
Warren County SD 6,100/K-12
2548 Morrison St 37110 931-668-4022
Dr. Jerry Hale, dir. Fax 815-2685
www.warrenschools.com
Warren County HS 1,800/9-12
199 Pioneer Ln 37110 931-668-5858
James Bennett, prin. Fax 668-5801
Warren County MS 800/6-8
200 Caldwell St 37110 931-473-6557
Betty Wood, prin. Fax 473-2432

Georgia Career Institute Post-Sec.
755 N Chancery St 37110
Tennessee Technology Center Mc Minnville Post-Sec.
241 Vo Tech Dr 37110 931-473-5587

Madison, See Nashville
Davidson County SD
Supt. — See Nashville
Neelys Bend MS 700/5-8
1251 Neelys Bend Rd 37115 615-860-1477
Ralph Tagg, prin. Fax 612-3669

Goodpasture Christian S 1,000/PK-12
619 W Due West Ave 37115 615-868-2600
Lindsey Judd, prin. Fax 865-1766
Madison Academy 100/9-12
PO Box 6257 37116 615-865-4055
Robert Stevenson M.A., prin. Fax 865-4117
Middle Tennessee School of Anesthesia Post-Sec.
PO Box 417 37116 615-868-6503
Nashville College Post-Sec.
1556 Crestview Dr 37115 615-868-2963
Volunteer Beauty Academy Post-Sec.
1791 Gallatin Pike N 37115 615-860-4200

Madisonville, Monroe, Pop. 4,352
Monroe County SD 5,100/K-12
205 Oak Grove Rd 37354 423-442-2373
Michael Lowery, dir. Fax 442-1389
www.monroe.k12.tn.us/
Madisonville MS 500/6-8
175 Oak Grove Rd 37354 423-442-4137
Augusta Davis, prin. Fax 442-9338
Sequoyah HS 900/9-12
4128 Highway 411 37354 423-442-9230
Maurice Moser, prin. Fax 442-5520
Other Schools – See Sweetwater, Tellico Plains, Vonore

Hiwassee College Post-Sec.
225 Hiwassee College Dr 37354 423-442-2001

Manchester, Coffee, Pop. 9,497
Coffee County SD 4,300/PK-12
1343 McArthur St 37355 931-723-5150
Daniel Brigman, supt. Fax 723-5153
www.coffeecountyschools.com/
Coffee County Central HS 1,600/9-12
100 Red Raider Dr 37355 931-723-5159
Joe Pedigo, prin. Fax 723-5161
Coffee County MS 900/6-8
865 McMinnville Hwy 37355 931-723-5177
Joey Vaughn, prin. Fax 723-5180

Manchester CSD 1,300/PK-9
215 E Fort St 37355 931-728-2316
Dr. Prater Powell, supt. Fax 728-7075
www.manchestercitysch.org/
Westwood JHS 400/7-9
505 E Taylor St 37355 931-728-2071
Richie Clark, prin. Fax 728-0962

Martin, Weakley, Pop. 10,151
Weakley County SD
Supt. — See Dresden
Martin MS 500/6-8
700 Fowler Rd 38237 731-587-2346
Nate Holmes, prin. Fax 588-0529
Westview HS 600/9-12
8161 Highway 45 S 38237 731-587-4202
David Byars, prin. Fax 588-0806

University of Tennessee 38238 Post-Sec.
731-587-7000

Maryville, Blount, Pop. 25,851
Blount County SD 11,000/K-12
831 Grandview Dr 37803 865-984-1212
Alvin Hord, dir. Fax 980-1002
www.blountk12.org
Blount HS 1,600/9-12
219 County Farm Rd 37801 865-984-5500
Steve Lafon, prin. Fax 977-0153
Blount MS 800/6-8
1126 William Blount Dr 37801 865-977-5493
Alicia Lail, prin. Fax 977-1435
Carpenters MS 700/6-8
920 Huffstetler Rd 37803 865-980-1414
Rob Britt, prin. Fax 980-1404
Eagleton MS 400/6-8
2610 Cinema Dr 37804 865-982-3211
Richard Hutson, prin. Fax 982-4203
Heritage HS 1,500/9-12
3741 E Lamar Alexander Pkwy 37804 865-984-8110
Patty Mandigo, prin. Fax 984-0147
Heritage MS 800/6-8
3737 E Lamar Alexander Pkwy 37804 865-980-1300
Dr. Jesse Robinette, prin. Fax 980-1281

Maryville CSD 4,500/PK-12
833 Lawrence Ave 37803 865-982-7121
Mike Dalton, supt. Fax 977-5055
www.ci.maryville.tn.us
Maryville HS 1,400/9-12
825 Lawrence Ave 37803 865-982-1132
Ken Jarnagin, prin. Fax 983-1440
Maryville MS 700/7-8
805 Montvale Station Rd 37803 865-983-2070
Lisa McGinley, prin. Fax 977-9413

Maryville Christian S 300/PK-12
2525 Morganton Rd 37801 865-681-3205
Glenn Slater, admin. Fax 681-4086
Maryville College Post-Sec.
502 E Lamar Alexander Pkwy 37804 865-981-8000

Maynardville, Union, Pop. 1,915
Union County SD 3,100/K-12
PO Box 10 37807 865-992-5466
Charles E. Thomas, dir. Fax 992-0126
www.ucps.org/
Maynard MS 700/6-8
PO Box 669 37807 865-992-1030
Melissa Carter, prin. Fax 992-1060
Union County HS 1,000/9-12
PO Box 249 37807 865-992-5232
Linda Harrell, prin. Fax 992-5724
Union County Adult HS Adult
PO Box 609 37807 865-992-7747
Bill Robbins, prin. Fax 992-9076

Medina, Gibson, Pop. 1,290
Gibson County SD
Supt. — See Dyer
Medina MS 400/4-8
PO Box 369 38355 731-783-1962
Chad Jackson, prin. Fax 783-1964

Memphis, Shelby, Pop. 672,277
Memphis CSD 113,500/PK-12
2597 Avery Ave 38112 901-416-5300
Dr. Carol Johnson, supt. Fax 325-5578
www.mcsk12.net

Airways MS 700/6-8
2601 Ketchum Rd 38114 901-416-5006
Sharon Griffin, prin. Fax 416-5009
American Way MS 1,000/6-8
3805 American Way 38118 901-416-1250
Russell Heaston, prin.
Bellevue JHS 500/7-9
575 S Bellevue Blvd 38104 901-416-4488
Kevin Malone, prin. Fax 416-4490
Carver HS 600/9-12
1591 Pennsylvania St 38109 901-416-7594
Michele Mason, prin. Fax 416-2235
Central HS 1,300/9-12
306 S Bellevue Blvd 38104 901-416-4500
Gregory McCullough, prin. Fax 416-4506
Chickasaw JHS 600/7-9
4060 Westmont Rd 38109 901-416-8134
Dr. Willie Tobias, prin. Fax 416-8139
Colonial MS 900/6-8
4778 Sea Isle Rd 38117 901-416-8980
Marty Pettigrew, prin. Fax 416-8996
Corry MS 600/6-8
2230 Corry Rd 38106 901-416-7804
Joyce Kelly, prin. Fax 416-7863
Craigmont HS 1,400/9-12
3333 Covington Pike 38128 901-416-4312
Sherilyn Brown, prin. Fax 416-7675
Craigmont MS 1,100/6-8
3455 Covington Pike 38128 901-416-7780
Dr. Cedrick Gray, prin. Fax 416-1454
Cypress MS 500/6-8
2109 Howell Ave 38108 901-416-4524
Raymond Vasser, prin. Fax 416-4528
Diamond Academy 200/5-8
2109 Howell Ave 38108 901-416-4615
Jamal McCall, prin. Fax 416-2059
East Career & Technology Center Vo/Tech
3206 Poplar Ave 38111 901-416-6200
Dr. Charles Green, prin. Fax 416-6161
East MSHS 1,300/7-12
3206 Poplar Ave 38111 901-416-6160
Fred Curry, prin. Fax 416-6161
Fairley HS 1,300/9-12
4950 Fairley Rd 38109 901-416-8060
Clint Jackson, prin. Fax 416-8064
Fairview JHS 400/7-9
750 E Parkway S 38104 901-416-4536
Jeremiah Burks, prin. Fax 416-4539
Frayser MSHS 1,300/7-12
1530 Dellwood Ave 38127 901-416-3880
Dr. Cassandra Turner, prin. Fax 416-3894
Geeter MS 700/6-8
4649 Horn Lake Rd 38109 901-416-8157
Kenneth Pinkney, prin. Fax 416-8160
Georgian Hills JHS 700/7-9
3925 Denver St 38127 901-416-3740
Rosalind Martin, prin. Fax 416-6500
Hamilton HS 1,400/9-12
1363 E Person Ave 38106 901-416-7838
Isaac White, prin. Fax 416-7829
Hamilton MS 800/6-8
1478 Wilson St 38106 901-416-7832
Willie Rhodes, prin. Fax 416-3314
Havenview MS 900/6-8
1481 Hester Rd 38116 901-416-3093
Corey Kelly, prin. Fax 416-3092
Hickory Ridge MS 900/6-8
3920 Ridgeway Rd 38115 901-416-9337
Cedric Smith, prin. Fax 416-9210
Hillcrest HS 900/9-12
4184 Graceland Dr 38116 901-416-3104
Carolyn Shaw, prin. Fax 416-3106
Humes MS 700/6-8
659 N Manassas St 38107 901-416-3226
Michael Bates, prin. Fax 416-3228
Kansas Career & Tech Center Vo/Tech
80 W Olive Ave 38106 901-416-7300
E.C. Fields, prin. Fax 416-7315
Kingsbury Career Tech Center Vo/Tech
1328 N Graham St 38122 901-416-6000
David Johnson, prin. Fax 416-6003
Kingsbury MSHS 1,600/7-12
1270 N Graham St 38122 901-416-6060
Dr. Terrence Brown, prin. Fax 416-6054
Kirby HS 1,400/9-12
4080 Kirby Pkwy 38115 901-416-1960
Michael Smith, prin. Fax 416-1968
Kirby MS 1,100/6-8
6670 E Raines Rd 38115 901-416-1980
Jason Bolden, prin. Fax 416-0494
Lanier MS 600/6-8
817 Brownlee Rd 38116 901-416-3128
Tiffany Hardrick, prin. Fax 416-9875
Longview MS 500/5-8
1895 S Orleans St 38106 901-416-7420
Kobie Sweeton, prin. Fax 416-7381
Manassas HS 300/9-12
781 Firestone Ave 38107 901-416-3244
Dr. Gloria Williams, prin. Fax 416-3248
Melrose HS 1,200/9-12
2870 Deadrick Ave 38114 901-416-5974
Lavaugn Bridges, prin. Fax 416-5984
Messick Career & Technology Center Vo/Tech
703 S Greer St 38111 901-416-4840
Carol Miller, prin. Fax 416-4842
Middle College SHS 200/10-12
737 Union Ave 38103 901-333-5360
M. Brantley-Patterson, prin. Fax 333-5368
Mitchell Road MSHS 1,000/7-12
658 W Mitchell Rd 38109 901-789-8174
John Ware, prin. Fax 789-8176
Northside HS 1,100/9-12
1212 Vollintine Ave 38107 901-416-4582
Carolyn Currie, prin. Fax 416-4584
Oakhaven MSHS 800/7-12
3125 Ladbrook Rd 38118 901-416-2300
Marion Brewer, prin. Fax 416-2301
Overton HS 1,500/9-12
1770 Lanier Ln 38117 901-416-2136
Brett Lawson, prin. Fax 416-2135
Price Middle College 100/9-12
807 Walker Ave 38126 901-435-1765
Daphne Beasley, prin. Fax 435-1779
Raleigh-Egypt HS 1,200/9-12
3970 Voltaire Ave 38128 901-416-4108
Dr. Oscar Love, prin. Fax 416-4143
Raleigh-Egypt MS 1,200/6-8
4215 Alice Ann Dr 38128 901-416-4141
Rogenia Conley-Finnie, prin. Fax 416-4110
Ridgeway HS 1,500/9-12
2009 Ridgeway Rd 38119 901-416-8820
James Long, prin. Fax 416-2199
Ridgeway MS 1,100/6-8
6333 Quince Rd 38119 901-416-1588
Dr. Roderick Richmond, prin. Fax 416-1477
Riverview MS 600/6-8
241 Majuba Ave 38109 901-416-7340
Keith Sanders, prin. Fax 416-7343
Sheffield Career & Tech Center Vo/Tech
4350 Chuck Ave 38118 901-416-2340
John Simpson, prin. Fax 416-2394
Sheffield HS 900/9-12
4315 Sheffield Ave 38118 901-416-2370
Jimmy Holland, prin. Fax 416-2407
Sherwood MS 1,100/6-8
3480 Rhodes Ave 38111 901-416-4870
Eric Cooper, prin. Fax 416-4881
South Side HS 500/9-12
1880 Prospect St 38106 901-416-7380
Dr. Eugene Sargent, prin. Fax 416-7382
Southwest Career & Technology Center Vo/Tech
3746 Horn Lake Rd 38109 901-416-8186
Earnestine Taylor, prin. Fax 416-8188
Treadwell MSHS 800/7-12
920 N Highland St 38122 901-416-6100
Dr. John Malone, prin. Fax 416-6133
Trezevant Career & Tech Center Vo/Tech
3224 Range Line Rd 38127 901-416-3800
Milton Burchfield, prin. Fax 416-3839
Trezevant MSHS 1,400/7-12
3350 N Trezevant St 38127 901-416-3760
Willie Williams, prin. Fax 416-3761
Vance MS 500/6-8
673 Vance Ave 38126 901-416-3256
Leviticus Pointer, prin. Fax 416-3257
Walker MS 1,000/6-8
1900 E Raines Rd 38116 901-416-1030
Tonya McBride, prin. Fax 416-1075
Washington HS 600/9-12
715 S Lauderdale St 38126 901-416-7240
Alisha Kiner, prin. Fax 416-7228
Wells Academy 100/7-8
777 Firestone Ave 38107 901-416-3210
Tamika Carwell, prin. Fax 416-3205
Westside MSHS 600/7-12
3389 Dawn Dr 38127 901-416-3700
Ernestine Jackson, prin. Fax 416-3701
Westwood MSHS 600/7-12
4480 Westmont Rd 38109 901-416-8000
Tommie McCarter, prin. Fax 416-8027
Whitehaven HS 1,900/9-12
4851 Elvis Presley Blvd 38116 901-416-3000
Vincent Hunter, prin. Fax 416-3058
White Station HS 2,100/9-12
514 S Perkins Rd 38117 901-416-8880
Terry Brown, prin. Fax 416-8910
White Station MS 800/7-8
5465 Mason Rd 38120 901-416-2184
Eric Sullivan, prin. Fax 416-2187
Wooddale HS 1,600/9-12
5151 Scottsdale Ave 38118 901-416-2440
Brenda Thompson, prin. Fax 416-2476
Wooddale MS 1,400/6-8
3467 Castleman St 38118 901-416-2420
Tamala Boyd, prin. Fax 416-2426
Other Schools – See Cordova

Shelby County SD 43,100/K-12
160 S Hollywood St 38112 901-321-2500
Bobby Webb Ed.D., supt.
www.scsk12.org/
Southwind MS 1,100/6-8
7740 Lowrance Rd 38125 901-759-3000
Marcia Crouch, prin. Fax 759-3011
Other Schools – See Arlington, Bartlett, Collierville, Cordova, Germantown, Millington

---

Baptist Memorial Coll. of Health Science Post-Sec.
1003 Monroe Ave 38104 901-575-2247
Baptist Memorial Hospital Post-Sec.
350 N Humphreys Blvd #EagB2 38103
901-227-5121
Bishop Byrne HS 300/7-12
1475 E Shelby Dr 38116 901-346-3060
Dr. Donald Edwards, prin. Fax 346-9488
Christian Brothers HS 800/9-12
5900 Walnut Grove Rd 38120 901-682-7801
Br. Chris Englert, prin. Fax 682-7815
Christian Brothers University Post-Sec.
650 E Parkway S 38104 901-321-3000
Concorde Career College Post-Sec.
5100 Poplar Ave Ste 132 38137 901-761-9494
Crichton College Post-Sec.
255 N Highland St 38111 901-320-9700
Elliston Baptist Academy 200/PK-12
4179 Elliston Rd 38111 901-743-4250
Joseph Shaw, prin. Fax 743-4257
Gateway Christian S 2,000/K-12
4070 Macon Rd 38122 901-454-9958
Bryan Thompson, dir. Fax 323-0914
Harding Academy of Memphis 700/7-12
1100 Cherry Rd 38117 901-767-4949
Pamela Womack, pres. Fax 763-3424
Harding University Grad Sch of Religion Post-Sec.
1000 Cherry Rd 38117 800-680-0809
High-Tech Institute Post-Sec.
5865 Shelby Oaks Cir 38134 901-432-3800
Holy Names S 3-8
709 Keel Ave 38107 901-507-1503
Sr. Donna Banfield, prin. Fax 507-1507
Hutchison S 800/PK-12
1740 Ridgeway Rd 38119 901-761-2220
Annette Smith, hdmstr. Fax 683-3510
Immaculate Conception HS 200/9-12
1725 Central Ave 38104 901-725-2705
Betty Buchignani, prin. Fax 725-2701
Lausanne Collegiate S 700/PK-12
1381 W Massey Rd 38120 901-474-1000
Stuart McCathie, hdmstr. Fax 682-1696
Le Moyne-Owen College Post-Sec.
807 Walker Ave 38126 901-774-9090
Macon Road Baptist S 600/K-12
1082 Berclair Rd 38122 901-682-5420
Daniel Webb, hdmstr.
Margolin Hebrew Academy 300/K-12
390 S White Station Rd 38117 901-682-2400
Rochelle Kutlin, dean Fax 767-1871
Memphis Catholic HS 200/7-12
61 N McLean Blvd 38104 901-276-1221
James Pohlman, prin. Fax 725-1447
Memphis College of Art Post-Sec.
1930 Poplar Ave 38104 901-272-5100
Memphis Junior Academy 100/K-10
50 N Mendenhall Rd 38117 901-683-1061
Brian Allison, prin.
Memphis Theological Seminary Post-Sec.
168 E Parkway S 38104 901-458-8232
Memphis University S 600/7-12
6191 Park Ave 38119 901-260-1300
Ellis Haguewood, hdmstr. Fax 260-1355
Methodist Hospital Post-Sec.
1265 Union Ave 38104 901-726-8274
New Wave Hair Academy Post-Sec.
3250 Coleman Rd 38128 901-323-6100
New Wave Hair Academy Post-Sec.
804 S Highland St 38111 901-320-9283
Plaza Beauty School Post-Sec.
4682 Spottswood Ave 38117 901-761-4445
Remington College Post-Sec.
2731 Nonconnah Blvd # 160 38132 901-345-1000
Rhodes College Post-Sec.
2000 N Parkway 38112 901-843-3000
St. Agnes Academy 400/9-12
4830 Walnut Grove Rd 38117 901-767-1377
Barbara Daush, pres. Fax 682-8199
St. Mary's Episcopal S 800/PK-12
60 Perkins Ext 38117 901-537-1472
Marlene Shaw, hdmstr. Fax 682-0119
Southern College of Optometry Post-Sec.
1245 Madison Ave 38104 901-722-3200
Southern Institute of Cosmetology Post-Sec.
3099 S Perkins Rd 38118 901-363-3553
Southwest Tennessee Community College Post-Sec.
5983 Macon Cv 38134 901-333-5000
State Technical Institute Post-Sec.
5983 Macon Cv 38134 901-377-4111
Strayer University Post-Sec.
2620 Thousand Oaks Blvd 38118 901-369-0835
Strayer University Post-Sec.
6211 Shelby Oaks Dr 38134 901-383-6750
Tennessee Academy of Cosmetology Post-Sec.
7041 Stage Rd Ste 101 38133 901-382-9085
Tennessee Academy of Cosmetology Post-Sec.
7020 E Shelby Dr Ste 104 38125 901-757-4166
Tennessee Technology Center at Memphis Post-Sec.
550 Alabama Ave 38105 901-543-6100
The Beauty Institute Post-Sec.
568 Colonial Rd 38117 901-761-1888
University of Memphis 38152 Post-Sec.
901-678-2000
Univ. of Tennessee Health Science Center Post-Sec.
800 Madison Ave 38163 901-448-5500
Vatterott College Post-Sec.
2655 Dividend Dr 38132 901-761-5730
Westminster Academy 300/K-12
2500 Ridgeway Rd 38119 901-380-9192
Dr. Michael Johnson, hdmstr. Fax 405-2019
William Moore College of Technology Post-Sec.
1200 Poplar Ave 38104 901-726-1977

Middleton, Hardeman, Pop. 622
Hardeman County SD
Supt. — See Bolivar
Middleton HS 600/7-12
PO Box 477 38052 731-376-8391
Jeffery Barnes, prin. Fax 376-8391

Milan, Gibson, Pop. 7,823
Milan Special SD 2,100/PK-12
PO Box 528 38358 731-686-0844
Jerry Johnson, dir. Fax 686-8781
www.milanssd.org
Milan HS 600/9-12
7060 E Van Hook St 38358 731-686-0841
Kris Todd, prin. Fax 686-9829
Milan MS 600/5-8
4040 Middle Rd 38358 731-686-7232
Lacee Mallard, prin. Fax 723-8872

Arnold's Beauty School Post-Sec.
1179 S 2nd St 38358 731-686-7351

Milligan College, Carter

Milligan College Post-Sec.
1 Milligan College 37682 423-461-8700

Millington, Shelby, Pop. 10,306
Shelby County SD
Supt. — See Memphis

Millington HS 1,500/9-12
8057 Wilkinsville Rd 38053 901-873-8100
Nancy Norwood, prin. Fax 873-8105
Millington MS 600/6-8
4964 Cuba Millington Rd 38053 901-873-8130
Michael Lowe, prin. Fax 873-8136
Woodstock MS 700/6-8
5885 Woodstock Cuba Rd 38053 901-353-8590
Eric Linsy, prin. Fax 358-9827

Faith Heritage Christian Academy 100/K-12
PO Box 157 38083 901-872-0828
M.O. Eckel, hdmstr. Fax 872-0803

Monterey, Putnam, Pop. 2,791
Putnam County SD
Supt. — See Cookeville
Burks MS 300/5-8
300 Crossville St 38574 931-839-7641
Michael Goolsby, prin. Fax 839-6683
Monterey HS 300/9-12
710 Commercial Ave S 38574 931-839-2970
Johnny Matheney, prin. Fax 839-6070

Morristown, Hamblen, Pop. 26,187
Hamblen County SD 9,200/K-12
210 E Morris Blvd 37813 423-586-7700
Dr. Dale Lynch, supt. Fax 586-7747
www.hcboe.net
Lincoln Heights MS 500/6-8
219 Lincoln Ave 37813 423-581-3200
James D. Templin, prin. Fax 585-3763
Meadowview MS 500/6-8
1623 Meadowview Ln 37814 423-581-6360
Ron Wright, prin. Fax 585-3771
Morristown-Hamblen HS East 1,300/9-12
1 Hurricane Ln 37813 423-586-2543
Gary Johnson, prin. Fax 585-3779
Morristown-Hamblen HS West 1,300/9-12
1 Trojan Trl 37813 423-581-1600
Dr. Jeff Moorhouse, prin. Fax 585-3791
West View MS 600/6-8
1 Indian Path 37813 423-581-2407
Scott Walker, prin. Fax 585-3807
Hamblen County Adult HS Adult
376 Snyder Rd 37813 423-585-3785
Tami Morelock, prin.
Other Schools – See Whitesburg

Tennessee Technology Center Morristown Post-Sec.
821 W Louise Ave 37813 423-586-5771
Walters State Community College Post-Sec.
500 S Davy Crockett Pkwy 37813 423-585-2600

Mosheim, Greene, Pop. 1,775
Greene County SD
Supt. — See Greeneville
West Greene HS 700/9-12
275 W Greene Dr 37818 423-422-4061
Larry Bible, prin. Fax 638-3180

Mountain City, Johnson, Pop. 2,419
Johnson County SD 2,300/PK-12
211 N Church St 37683 423-727-2640
Morris Woodring, dir. Fax 727-2663
www.jocoed.k12tn.net
Johnson County HS 700/9-12
510 Fairground Ln 37683 423-727-2620
Paula Norton, prin. Fax 727-2677
Johnson County MS 400/7-8
500 Fairground Ln 37683 423-727-2600
Emogene South, prin. Fax 727-2608
Johnson County Vocational S Vo/Tech
520 Fairground Ln 37683 423-727-1860
Jim Crowder, prin. Fax 727-2693

Mount Juliet, Wilson, Pop. 18,099
Wilson County SD
Supt. — See Lebanon
Mount Juliet HS 1,400/9-12
3565 N Mount Juliet Rd 37122 615-758-5606
Mel Brown, prin. Fax 758-5645
Mount Juliet MS 1,000/6-8
1003 Woodridge Pl 37122 615-754-6688
Mlke Gwaltney, prin. Fax 754-7566
West Wilson MS 900/6-8
935 N Mount Juliet Rd 37122 615-758-5152
Wendell Marlowe, prin. Fax 758-5283

Mt. Juliet Christian Academy 600/PK-12
735 N Mount Juliet Rd 37122 615-758-2427
Kathy Kitchen, hdmstr. Fax 758-3662

Mount Pleasant, Maury, Pop. 4,452
Maury County SD
Supt. — See Columbia
Mount Pleasant JSHS 400/6-12
600 Greenwood St 38474 931-379-5583
Tommy Wolaver, prin. Fax 379-2093
Mt. Pleasant MS of Visual/Performing Art 400/6-8
410 Gray Ln 38474 931-379-1100
Elliotte Kinzer, prin. Fax 379-1108

Munford, Tipton, Pop. 5,652
Tipton County SD
Supt. — See Covington
Munford HS 1,300/9-12
1080 McLaughlin Dr 38058 901-837-5701
Darry Marshall, prin. Fax 837-5729
Munford MS 1,000/6-8
100 Education Ave 38058 901-837-1700
Glenn Turner, prin. Fax 837-5749

Murfreesboro, Rutherford, Pop. 86,793
Rutherford County SD 30,900/PK-12
2240 Southpark Dr 37128 615-893-5812
Harry Gill, supt. Fax 898-7940
www.rcs.k12.tn.us
Blackman HS 1,600/9-12
3956 Blaze Dr 37128 615-904-3850
Gail Vick, prin. Fax 904-3851
Blackman MS 900/6-8
3945 Blaze Dr 37128 615-904-3860
Will Shelton, prin. Fax 904-3861
Central MS 900/7-8
701 E Main St 37130 615-893-8262
Cary Holman, prin. Fax 898-7964
Holloway HS 100/9-12
619 S Highland Ave 37130 615-890-6004
Ivan Duggin, prin. Fax 904-7508
Oakland HS 1,400/9-12
2225 Patriot Dr 37130 615-904-3780
Butch Vaughn, prin. Fax 904-3781
Riverdale HS 1,800/9-12
802 Warrior Dr 37128 615-890-6450
Tom Nolan, prin. Fax 890-9790
Siegel HS 1,600/9-12
3300 Siegal Rd 37129 615-904-3800
Ken Nolan, prin. Fax 904-3801
Siegel MS 900/6-8
355 W Thompson Ln 37129 615-904-3830
Tom Delbridge, prin. Fax 904-3831
Rutherford Adult HS Adult
502 Memorial Blvd 37129 615-896-0876
Joe Herbert, dir.
Other Schools – See Christiana, Eagleville, La Vergne, Smyrna

---

Draughons Junior College - Murfreesboro Post-Sec.
415 Golden Bear Ct 37128 615-217-9347
Middle Tennessee Christian S 700/PK-12
100 E MTCS Rd 37129 615-893-0602
Fax 895-8815
Middle Tennessee State University Post-Sec.
1301 E Main St 37132 615-898-2300
Tennessee Technology Center Murfreesboro Post-Sec.
1303 Old Fort Pkwy 37129 615-898-8010

Nashville, Davidson, Pop. 545,915
Davidson County SD 69,100/PK-12
2601 Bransford Ave 37204 615-259-4636
Pedro E. Garcia Ed.D., supt. Fax 259-8492
www.mnps.org
Allen MS 400/5-8
500 Spence Ln 37210 615-291-6385
Ganet Johnson, prin. Fax 291-6066
Bailey MS 500/5-8
2000 Greenwood Ave 37206 615-262-6670
Jim Murrell, prin. Fax 262-6979
Bass MS 500/5-8
5200 Delaware Ave 37209 615-298-8065
Kathryn Dillard, prin. Fax 292-5548
Baxter MS 600/5-8
350 Hart Ln 37207 615-262-6710
David Martin, prin. Fax 262-6743
Bellevue MS 600/5-8
655 Colice Jeanne Rd 37221 615-662-3000
John Duckworth, prin. Fax 662-5728
Brick Church MS 600/5-8
2835 Brick Church Pike 37207 615-262-6665
Dr. Steve Chauncy, prin. Fax 262-6966
Cameron MS 600/5-8
1034 1st Ave S 37210 615-291-6365
Beverly Walker Bell, prin. Fax 291-6072
Creswell Magnet MS 5-8
3500 John Mallette Dr 37218 615-291-6515
Dr. Dorothy Gunn, prin. Fax 352-2512
Croft Design Center MS 700/5-8
482 Elysian Fields Rd 37211 615-332-0217
Barry Watkins, prin. Fax 333-5650
Dalewood MS 500/5-8
1460 Mcgavock Pike 37216 615-262-6680
Monae Fletcher, prin. Fax 291-6099
Donelson MS 700/5-8
110 Stewarts Ferry Pike 37214 615-884-4080
Paul Brunette, prin. Fax 885-8970
Early - Paideia S 300/5-8
1000 Cass St 37208 615-291-6369
Karen Bryant, prin. Fax 298-8497
East Literature Magnet S 1,000/5-12
112 Gallatin Ave 37206 615-262-6947
Frances Stewart, prin. Fax 271-1782
Ewing Park MS 400/5-8
3410 Knight Dr 37207 615-876-5115
Antionette Love, prin. Fax 501-8839
Glencliff Comprehensive HS 1,400/9-12
160 Antioch Pike 37211 615-333-5070
Dr. Lora Hall, prin. Fax 333-5003
Gra-Mar MS 600/5-8
575 Joyce Ln 37216 615-262-6685
Angela Garner, prin. Fax 353-2021
Haynes Health/Medical Science Design Ctr 400/5-8
510 W Trinity Ln 37207 615-262-6688
Robert Blankenship, prin. Fax 298-8084
Head Magnet S 500/5-8
1830 Jo Johnston Ave 37203 615-329-8160
Sharon Braden, prin. Fax 333-5646
Hill MS 500/5-8
150 Davidson Rd 37205 615-353-2020
Jud Haynie, prin. Fax 884-4028
Hillsboro Comprehensive HS 1,100/9-12
3812 Hillsboro Pike 37215 615-298-8400
Robert Lawson, prin. Fax 353-1159
Hillwood Comprehensive HS 1,600/9-12
400 Davidson Rd 37205 615-353-2025
Karl Lang, prin. Fax 298-8402
Hume-Fogg Magnet HS 900/9-12
700 Broadway 37203 615-291-6300
Paul Fleming, prin. Fax 291-6065
Hunters Lane Comprehensive HS 1,900/9-12
1150 Hunters Ln 37207 615-860-1401
Clay Myers, prin. Fax 291-6304
King Magnet JSHS 1,100/7-12
613 17th Ave N 37203 615-329-8400
Dr. Mildred Saffell-Smith, prin. Fax 501-7907
Litton MS 400/5-8
4601 Hedgewood Dr 37216 615-262-6700
Dr. Tonya Hutchinson, prin. Fax 262-6995
Maplewood Comprehensive HS 1,100/9-12
401 Walton Ln 37216 615-262-6770
Darwin Mason, prin. Fax 262-6772
McGavock Comprehensive HS 2,600/9-12
3150 Mcgavock Pike 37214 615-885-8850
Michael Tribue, prin. Fax 885-8900
McKissack MS 200/5-8
915 38th Ave N 37209 615-329-8170
Dr. Troy Journigan, prin. Fax 329-8183
McMurray MS 600/5-8
520 McMurray Dr 37211 615-333-5126
Dr. Schunn Turner, prin. Fax 333-5125
Meigs Magnet MS 600/5-8
713 Ramsey St 37206 615-271-3222
Jon Hubble, prin. Fax 271-3223
Middle College HS 10-12
120 White Bridge Pike 37209 615-353-3742
Ervin Tinnon, prin.
Moore MS 600/5-8
4425 Granny White Pike 37204 615-298-8095
Deloris Burke, prin. Fax 298-8452
Nashville S of the Arts 600/9-12
1250 Foster Ave 37243 615-291-6600
Robert Wilson, prin. Fax 271-1767
Oliver MS 300/5-8
6211 Nolensville Pike 37211 615-332-3011
Karen Lefkovitz, prin. Fax 332-3019
Overton Comprehensive HS 1,600/9-12
4820 Franklin Pike 37220 615-333-5135
Dr. Monica Dillard, prin. Fax 333-5141
Pearl-Cohn Comprehensive Magnet HS 800/9-12
904 26th Ave N 37208 615-329-8150
Marva Woods, prin. Fax 329-8192
Rose Park MS 200/5-8
1025 9th Ave S 37203 615-291-6405
Wade Jones, prin. Fax 262-6717
Stratford Comprehensive HS 1,200/9-12
1800 Stratford Ave 37216 615-242-6730
Brenda Elliott, prin. Fax 885-8929
Two Rivers MS 600/5-8
2991 Mcgavock Pike 37214 615-885-8931
William Moody, prin. Fax 333-5641
Vaught MS 300/5-8
160 Rural Ave 37209 615-353-2081
Dr. Carol Garland, prin. Fax 360-2925
West End MS 400/5-8
1625 Dr DB Todd Jr Blvd 37208 615-329-8180
Roderick Manual, prin. Fax 291-6312
Wright MS 900/5-8
180 McCall St 37211 615-333-5189
Kim Finch, prin. Fax 333-5635
Cohn Adult Learning Center Adult
4805 Park Ave 37209 615-298-8053
Bill Gemmill, prin. Fax 298-8052
Other Schools – See Antioch, Goodlettsville, Hermitage, Joelton, Madison, Old Hickory, Whites Creek

---

American Baptist College Post-Sec.
1800 Baptist World Ctr Dr 37207 615-256-1463
Aquinas College Post-Sec.
4210 Harding Rd 37205 615-297-7545
Belmont University Post-Sec.
1900 Belmont Blvd 37212 615-460-6000
Blair School of Music of Vanderbilt U. Post-Sec.
2400 Blakemore Ave 37212 615-322-7651
Christ Presbyterian Academy 900/K-12
2323A Old Hickory Blvd 37215 615-373-9550
Richard Anderson, hdmstr. Fax 370-0884
Davidson Academy 900/PK-12
1414 Old Hickory Blvd 37207 615-860-5300
Bill Chaney Ed.D., hdmstr. Fax 868-7918
Diamond Council of America Post-Sec.
3212 W End Ave Ste 202 37203 615-385-5301
Donelson Christian Academy 800/PK-12
300 Danyacrest Dr 37214 615-883-2926
Dr. Daniel Kellum, hdmstr. Fax 883-2998
Draughons Junior College Post-Sec.
340 Plus Park Blvd 37217 615-361-7555
Ensworth S 600/K-12
211 Ensworth Pl 37205 615-383-0661
William Moseley, hdmstr. Fax 269-4840
Father Ryan HS 9-12
700 Norwood Dr 37204 615-383-4200
Paul Davis, prin. Fax 383-9056
Fisk University Post-Sec.
1000 17th Ave N 37208 615-329-8500
Franklin Road Academy 1,000/PK-12
4700 Franklin Pike 37220 615-832-8845
Dr. Margaret Wade, hdmstr. Fax 834-4137
Free Will Baptist Bible College Post-Sec.
PO Box 50117 37205 800-763-9225
Harpeth Hall S 600/5-12
3801 Hobbs Rd 37215 615-297-9543
Ann Teaff, prin. Fax 297-0480
High-Tech Institute Post-Sec.
560 Royal Pkwy 37214 866-502-2627
International Academy of Design & Tech Post-Sec.
1 Bridgestone Park 37214 615-232-7384
ITT Technical Institute Post-Sec.
2845 Elm Hill Pike 37214 615-889-8700
John A. Gupton College Post-Sec.
1616 Church St 37203 615-327-3927
Lipscomb Campus S 1,400/PK-12
3901 Granny White Pike 37204 615-269-1828
Keith Nikolaus, dir. Fax 386-7633
Lipscomb University Post-Sec.
3901 Granny White Pike 37204 800-333-4358
Meharry Medical College Post-Sec.
1005 Dr DB Todd Jr Blvd 37208 615-327-6111
Montgomery Bell Academy 700/7-12
4001 Harding Rd 37205 615-298-5514
Bradford Gioia, prin. Fax 297-0271
Nashville Auto-Diesel College Post-Sec.
1524 Gallatin Ave 37206 615-226-3990

Nashville Christian S 500/K-12
7555 Sawyer Brown Rd 37221 615-356-5600
David Vester, prin. Fax 352-1324
Nashville State Technical Community Coll Post-Sec.
120 White Bridge Pike 37209 615-353-3333
National College of Business & Tech. Post-Sec.
3748 Nolensville Pike 37211 615-333-3344
New Directions Hair Academy Post-Sec.
3744 Annex Ave # A-2 37209 615-353-8333
Peabody College of Vanderbilt University Post-Sec.
PO Box 327 37203 615-322-8410
Radnor Baptist Academy 200/PK-12
3112 Nolensville Pike 37211 615-832-2004
Stephen Durham, hdmstr. Fax 833-3708
Remington College Post-Sec.
441 Donelson Pike Ste 150 37214 615-889-5520
SAE Institute Nashville Post-Sec.
7 Music Cir N 37203 615-244-5848
St. Cecilia Academy 300/9-12
4210 Harding Pike Ste 2 37205 615-298-4525
Sr. Mary Thomas, prin. Fax 783-0561
St. Thomas Hospital Post-Sec.
PO Box 380 37202 615-222-2111
Seminary Ext. Independent Study Inst. Post-Sec.
901 Commerce St Ste 500 37203 800-229-4612
Southeastern Career College Post-Sec.
2416 21st Ave S Ste 300 37212 615-269-9900
Strayer University Post-Sec.
30 Rachel Dr Ste 200 37214 615-871-2260
Tennessee School for the Blind Post-Sec.
115 Stewarts Ferry Pike 37214 615-231-7300
Tennessee State University Post-Sec.
3500 John A Merritt Blvd 37209 615-963-5000
Tennessee Technology Center at Nashville Post-Sec.
100 White Bridge Pike 37209 615-741-1241
Trevecca Nazarene University Post-Sec.
333 Murfreesboro Rd 37210 615-248-1200
University S of Nashville 1,000/K-12
2000 Edgehill Ave 37212 615-327-8000
Vincent Durnan, dir. Fax 321-0889
Vanderbilt University Post-Sec.
W End Ave 37240 615-322-7311
Volunteer Beauty Academy Post-Sec.
5666 Nolensville Pike 37211 615-331-9111
Watkins Institute-College of Art/Design Post-Sec.
2298 Metrocenter Blvd 37228 615-383-4848

Newbern, Dyer, Pop. 3,089
Dyer County SD
Supt. — See Dyersburg
Dyer County HS 1,000/9-12
1000 W Main St 38059 731-627-2229
Peggy Dodds, prin. Fax 627-2152
Northview MS 400/6-8
820 Williams St 38059 731-627-3713
Anthony Jones, prin. Fax 627-4823

Tennessee Technology Center at Newbern Post-Sec.
340 Washington St 38059 731-627-2511

Newport, Cocke, Pop. 7,299
Cocke County SD 4,700/K-12
305 Hedrick Dr 37821 423-623-7821
Larry Blazer, supt. Fax 625-3947
www.cocke-lea.cocke.k12.tn.us
Cocke County HS 1,200/9-12
216 Hedrick Dr 37821 423-623-8718
Gary Williams, prin. Fax 623-1213
Cocke County Vocational HS Vo/Tech
210 Hedrick Dr 37821 423-623-6072
Larry Williams, prin. Fax 623-6070
Other Schools – See Cosby

New Tazewell, Claiborne, Pop. 2,882
Claiborne County SD
Supt. — See Tazewell
Claiborne HS 50/9-12
815 Davis Dr 37825 423-626-3532
Steve Minton, prin. Fax 626-3555

Norris, Anderson, Pop. 1,439
Anderson County SD
Supt. — See Clinton
Norris MS 500/6-8
PO Box 980 37828 865-494-7171
Joe Forgety, prin. Fax 494-6693

Oakdale, Morgan, Pop. 239
Morgan County SD
Supt. — See Wartburg
Oakdale S 500/K-12
225 Clifty Creek Rd 37829 423-369-3885
Diana Smith, prin. Fax 369-2821

Oakland, Fayette, Pop. 2,469
Fayette County SD
Supt. — See Somerville
West JHS 400/7-9
13100 Highway 194 38060 901-465-9213
Larry Skelton, prin. Fax 465-1599

Oak Ridge, Anderson, Pop. 27,297
Oak Ridge CSD 4,400/PK-12
PO Box 6588 37831 865-425-9001
Dr. Thomas Bailey, supt. Fax 425-9070
www.ortn.edu
Jefferson MS 700/5-8
200 Fairbanks Rd 37830 865-425-9301
Bruce Lay, prin. Fax 425-9339
Oak Ridge HS 1,400/9-12
127 Providence Rd 37830 865-425-9601
Chuck Carringer, prin. Fax 425-9678
Robertsville MS 700/5-8
245 Robertsville Rd 37830 865-425-9201
Mike Baker, prin. Fax 425-9236

Old Hickory, See Nashville
Davidson County SD
Supt. — See Nashville

DuPont-Hadley MS 600/5-8
1901 Old Hickory Blvd 37138 615-847-7300
Amy Downey, prin. Fax 847-7311

Oliver Springs, Morgan, Pop. 3,275
Anderson County SD
Supt. — See Clinton
Norwood MS 300/6-8
803 E Tri County Blvd 37840 865-435-7749
Danny Richards, prin. Fax 435-5426

Roane County SD
Supt. — See Kingston
Oliver Springs HS 500/9-12
419 Kingston Ave 37840 865-435-7216
Jeffrey Woods, prin. Fax 435-6774

Oneida, Scott, Pop. 3,677
Oneida Special SD 1,300/PK-12
PO Box 4819 37841 423-569-8912
S. Henry Baggett, supt. Fax 569-2201
www.oneidaschools.org/
Oneida HS 400/9-12
372 N Main St 37841 423-569-8818
Rick Harper, prin. Fax 569-1681
Oneida MS 300/6-8
376 N Main St 37841 423-569-2475
Cheryl Butler, prin. Fax 569-5977

Ooltewah, Hamilton, Pop. 4,903
Hamilton County SD
Supt. — See Chattanooga
Hunter MS 800/6-8
5973 Hunter Rd 37363 423-344-1474
Gary Kuehn, prin. Fax 344-1485
Ooltewah HS 1,700/9-12
6123 Mountain View Rd 37363 423-238-5221
Ed Foster, prin. Fax 238-5871
Ooltewah MS 1,000/6-8
5100 Ooltewah Ringgold Rd 37363 423-238-5732
Pam Dantzler, prin. Fax 238-5735
Hamilton County Adult HS Adult
9050 Career Ln 37363 423-344-1433
Bill Warren, prin. Fax 344-1434

Paris, Henry, Pop. 9,874
Henry County SD 2,900/PK-12
217 Grove Blvd 38242 731-642-9733
Richard W. Kriesky, supt. Fax 642-8073
www.henry.k12.tn.us
Grove S 400/9-9
215 Grove Blvd 38242 731-642-4586
Greg Rockhold, prin. Fax 642-4577
Henry County HS 1,000/10-12
315 S Wilson St 38242 731-642-5232
Dawn Poole, prin. Fax 642-5240

Paris Special SD 1,500/K-8
1219 Highway 641 S 38242 731-642-9322
Paul Doyle, supt. Fax 642-9327
www.paris.k12.tn.us
Inman MS 500/6-8
400 Harrison St 38242 731-642-8131
Mike Brown, prin. Fax 642-8209

Tennessee Technology Center at Paris Post-Sec.
312 S Wilson St 38242 731-644-7365

Parsons, Decatur, Pop. 2,445
Decatur County SD
Supt. — See Decaturville
Decatur County MS 500/5-8
2740 Highway 641 S 38363 731-847-6510
Chris Villaflor, prin. Fax 847-6572

Pigeon Forge, Sevier, Pop. 5,784
Sevier County SD
Supt. — See Sevierville
Pigeon Forge HS 700/9-12
414 Tiger Dr 37863 865-774-5790
Perry Schrandt, prin. Fax 774-5798
Pigeon Forge MS 600/5-8
300 Wears Valley Rd 37863 865-453-2401
Jerry Wear, prin. Fax 453-0799

Pikeville, Bledsoe, Pop. 1,863
Bledsoe County SD 1,900/PK-12
PO Box 369 37367 423-447-2914
Clettis McDaniel, dir. Fax 447-7135
www.bledsoe.k12.tn.us/
Bledsoe County HS 500/9-12
877 Main St 37367 423-447-6851
Tommy Nipper, prin. Fax 447-6286
Bledsoe County MS 500/6-8
PO Box 147 37367 423-447-3212
Philip Kiper, prin. Fax 447-3085
Other Schools – See Dunlap

Pleasant View, Cheatham, Pop. 3,453
Cheatham County SD
Supt. — See Ashland City
Sycamore HS 800/9-12
1021 Old Clarksville Pike 37146 615-746-5013
Daniel Newton, prin. Fax 746-3653
Sycamore MS 900/5-8
1025 Old Clarksville Pike 37146 615-746-8852
Judy Bell, prin. Fax 746-5770

Portland, Sumner, Pop. 10,342
Sumner County SD
Supt. — See Gallatin
Portland HS 1,000/9-12
600 College St 37148 615-325-9201
Bob Gideon, prin. Fax 325-5302
Portland MS 900/6-8
604 S Broadway 37148 615-325-4146
Jim Butler, prin. Fax 325-5320

Highland Academy 100/9-12
211 Highland Circle Dr 37148 615-325-2036
Don Mathis, prin. Fax 325-4824

Powell, Knox, Pop. 7,534
Knox County SD
Supt. — See Knoxville
Powell HS 1,100/9-12
2136 W Emory Rd 37849 865-938-2171
Ken Dunlap, prin. Fax 947-2805
Powell MS 900/6-8
3329 W Emory Rd 37849 865-938-9008
Glenn Marquart, prin. Fax 947-4357

Pulaski, Giles, Pop. 7,917
Giles County SD 4,500/PK-12
270 Richland Dr 38478 931-363-4558
Tee Jackson, dir. Fax 363-8975
www.giles-lea.giles.k12.tn.us
Bridgeforth MS 400/6-8
1051 Bridgeforth Cir 38478 931-363-7526
J.B. Smith, prin. Fax 424-7021
Giles County HS 1,000/9-12
200 Sheila Frost Dr 38478 931-363-6532
Bobby Hastings, prin. Fax 424-7010
Other Schools – See Lynnville

Highland Christian Academy 100/K-12
1827 Mill St 38478 931-363-4144
Suzette Brewer, admin.
Martin Methodist College Post-Sec.
433 W Madison St 38478 800-727-1273
Tennessee Technology Center at Pulaski Post-Sec.
PO Box 614 38478 931-424-4014

Reagan, Henderson
Henderson County SD
Supt. — See Lexington
Scotts Hill HS 300/9-12
7871 State Route 100 38368 731-549-2900
Brian Norton, prin. Fax 549-2909

Red Boiling Springs, Macon, Pop. 1,059
Clay County SD
Supt. — See Celina
Hermitage Springs S 300/K-12
17580 Clay County Hwy 37150 615-699-2414
Donnie Cherry, prin. Fax 699-2410

Macon County SD
Supt. — See Lafayette
Red Boiling Springs JSHS 300/7-12
415 Hillcrest Dr 37150 615-699-3125
Don Jones, prin. Fax 699-3371
Tri-County Vocational Center Vo/Tech
PO Box 214 37150 615-699-2224
Jerry Spivey, prin. Fax 669-2226

Ripley, Lauderdale, Pop. 7,772
Lauderdale County SD 4,500/PK-12
PO Box 350 38063 731-635-2941
Phillip Jackson, supt. Fax 635-7985
www.lced.net
Lauderdale MS 700/6-8
309 Griggs Rd 38063 731-635-1391
Robert England, prin. Fax 635-0028
Ripley HS 900/9-12
254 S Jefferson St 38063 731-635-2642
Robert Baker, prin. Fax 635-7151
Other Schools – See Halls

Tennessee Technology Center at Ripley Post-Sec.
127 Industrial Dr 38063 731-635-3368

Roan Mountain, Carter, Pop. 1,220
Carter County SD
Supt. — See Elizabethton
Cloudland JSHS 400/7-12
476 Cloudland Dr 37687 423-772-5300
Randy Birchfield, prin. Fax 772-5309

Rockwood, Roane, Pop. 5,426
Roane County SD
Supt. — See Kingston
Rockwood HS 500/9-12
512 W Rockwood St 37854 865-354-0882
Alan Reed, prin. Fax 354-5170
Rockwood MS 400/6-8
434 W Rockwood St 37854 865-354-0931
William Thompson, prin. Fax 354-5160

Rogersville, Hawkins, Pop. 4,283
Hawkins County SD 7,400/K-12
200 N Depot St 37857 423-272-7629
Charlotte Britton, dir. Fax 272-2207
www.hawkinsschools.net
Cherokee HS 1,200/9-12
2927 Highway 66 S 37857 423-272-6507
Daffin Anderson, prin. Fax 272-6598
Rogersville MS 500/6-8
958 E Mckinney Ave 37857 423-272-7603
Dr. John Carroll, prin. Fax 272-7603
Other Schools – See Church Hill, Eidson, Surgoinsville

Rutledge, Grainger, Pop. 1,261
Grainger County SD 3,200/K-12
PO Box 38 37861 865-828-3611
E. Vernon Coffey Ed.D., supt. Fax 828-4357
www.grainger.k12.tn.us/
Rutledge HS 700/9-12
140 Pioneer Dr 37861 865-828-5291
Ron Cabbage, prin. Fax 828-4828
Rutledge MS 400/3-8
7480 Rutledge Pike 37861 865-828-5530
Stanley Roach, prin. Fax 828-5797
Grainger County Adult S Adult
PO Box 38 37861 865-828-5172
Edwin Jarnagin, prin. Fax 828-4357
Other Schools – See Washburn

Sale Creek, Hamilton
Hamilton County SD
Supt. — See Chattanooga

Sale Creek MSHS 400/6-12
211 Patterson Rd 37373 423-332-8819
Devota Barnes, prin. Fax 332-8847

Santa Fe, Maury
Maury County SD
Supt. — See Columbia
Santa Fe S 600/K-12
2629 Santa Fe Pike 38482 931-682-2172
Cathy Cook, prin. Fax 682-2606

Savannah, Hardin, Pop. 7,200
Hardin County SD 3,700/K-12
155 Guinn St 38372 731-925-3943
Bob Cromwell, supt. Fax 925-7313
www.hardin.k12.tn.us
Hardin County HS 1,100/9-12
1170 Pickwick St S 38372 731-925-3976
Bob McAdams, prin. Fax 925-7407
Hardin County MS 800/6-8
299 Lacefield Dr 38372 731-925-9037
Michael Davis, prin. Fax 925-0253

Selmer, McNairy, Pop. 4,618
McNairy County SD 4,200/K-12
170 W Court Ave 38375 731-645-3267
Charles Miskelly, supt. Fax 645-8085
www.mcnairy.org
McNairy Central HS 800/9-12
493 McNairy Central Rd 38375 731-645-3226
Cecil Stroup, prin. Fax 645-8014
Selmer MS 500/5-8
635 E Poplar Ave 38375 731-645-7977
Joel Boyd, prin. Fax 645-6377
Other Schools – See Adamsville

Styles & Profiles Beauty College Post-Sec.
119 S 2nd St 38375 731-645-9728

Sevierville, Sevier, Pop. 14,788
Sevier County SD 13,500/PK-12
226 Cedar St 37862 865-453-4671
Dr. Jack Parton, supt. Fax 522-1497
www.sevier.org
Sevier County HS 1,700/9-12
1200 Dolly Parton Pkwy 37862 865-453-5525
Toby Ward, prin. Fax 428-5867
Sevierville MS 800/6-8
520 High St 37862 865-453-0311
Jayson Nave, prin. Fax 428-2316
Whites Adult HS Adult
703 Whites School Rd 37876 865-429-1492
Curtis Clabo, prin.
Other Schools – See Gatlinburg, Kodak, Pigeon Forge, Seymour

St. Andrew's S 50/K-12
3601 Lyon Springs Rd 37862 865-429-5437
James Wood, hdmstr. Fax 429-2104

Sewanee, Franklin, Pop. 2,128

St. Andrew's-Sewanee S 300/6-12
290 Quintard Rd 37375 931-598-5651
Rev. William Wade, hdmstr. Fax 598-0039
University of the South Post-Sec.
735 University Ave 37383 931-598-1000

Seymour, Sevier, Pop. 7,026
Sevier County SD
Supt. — See Sevierville
Seymour HS 1,000/9-12
732 Boyds Creek Hwy 37865 865-577-7040
Greg Clark, prin. Fax 579-1492
Seymour MS 900/6-8
737 Boyds Creek Hwy 37865 865-579-0730
Faye Nelson, prin. Fax 579-0905

Kings Academy 400/K-12
202 Smothers Rd 37865 865-573-8321
Steve Sharp, prin. Fax 573-8323

Shelbyville, Bedford, Pop. 18,648
Bedford County SD 7,000/K-12
500 Madison St 37160 931-684-3284
Mike Bone, supt. Fax 684-1133
www.bedfordk12tn.com/
Harris MS 800/6-8
570 Eagle Blvd 37160 931-684-5195
Bill Pietkiewicz, prin. Fax 685-9455
Shelbyville Central HS 1,200/9-12
401 Eagle Blvd 37160 931-684-5672
Don Embry, prin. Fax 684-9359
Bedford Co. Adult HS and Learning Center Adult
326 E Depot St 37160 931-684-8635
Elaine Weaver, prin. Fax 684-8634
Other Schools – See Unionville, Wartrace

Tennessee Technology Center Shelbyville Post-Sec.
1405 Madison St 37160 931-685-5013

Signal Mountain, Hamilton, Pop. 7,146
Hamilton County SD
Supt. — See Chattanooga
Signal Mountain MS 300/6-8
315 Ault Rd 37377 423-886-0876
Bob Walter, prin. Fax 886-0894

Smithville, DeKalb, Pop. 4,160
DeKalb County SD 2,700/PK-12
110 S Public Sq 37166 615-597-4084
Mark Willoughby, supt. Fax 597-6326
web.dekalb.k12tn.net/
DeKalb County HS 800/9-12
1130 W Broad St 37166 615-597-4094
Kathy Hendrix, prin.
DeKalb MS, 1132 W Broad St 37166 500/6-8
Randy Jennings, prin. 615-597-7987

Smyrna, Rutherford, Pop. 33,497
Rutherford County SD
Supt. — See Murfreesboro
Rock Springs MS 800/6-8
3301 Rock Springs Rd 37167 615-904-3825
Dr. Pat Essary, prin. Fax 904-3826
Smyrna HS 1,600/9-12
100 Bulldog Dr 37167 615-904-3865
Robert Raikes, prin. Fax 904-3866
Smyrna MS 1,000/6-8
712 Hazelwood Dr 37167 615-904-3845
Dr. Linda Kennedy, prin. Fax 904-3846
Stewarts Creek MS 6-8
400 Red Hawk Blvd 37167 615-904-6700
Larry Creasy, prin. Fax 904-6701

Sneedville, Hancock, Pop. 1,317
Hancock County SD 1,000/K-12
PO Box 629 37869 423-733-2591
Mike Antrican, dir. Fax 733-8757
www.hancockcountyschools.com/
Hancock County MSHS 600/6-12
2700 Main St 37869 423-733-4611
Thomas Zachary, prin. Fax 733-1427

Soddy Daisy, Hamilton, Pop. 8,884
Hamilton County SD
Supt. — See Chattanooga
Sequoya Technology Center Vo/Tech
9517 W Ridge Trail Rd 37379 423-843-4707
Steve Holmes, prin. Fax 843-4719
Soddy Daisy HS 1,600/9-12
618 Sequoyah Rd 37379 423-332-8828
Robert Smith, prin. Fax 332-8831
Soddy Daisy MS 600/6-8
200 Turner Rd 37379 423-332-8800
Dr. Robert Jenkins, prin. Fax 332-8810

Somerville, Fayette, Pop. 2,907
Fayette County SD 3,600/PK-12
PO Box 9 38068 901-465-5260
Myles Wilson, supt. Fax 466-3725
www.fayette.k12.tn.us
East JHS 500/7-9
400 Leach Dr 38068 901-465-3151
Constance Agard, prin. Fax 465-5084
Fayette-Ware HS 600/10-12
PO Box 849 38068 901-465-9838
O. Hicks, prin. Fax 465-1377
Other Schools – See Oakland

Fayette Academy 800/K-12
PO Box 130 38068 901-465-3241
Bob Archer, prin. Fax 465-2141

South Fulton, Obion, Pop. 2,452
Obion County SD
Supt. — See Union City
South Fulton MSHS 400/6-12
1302 S Fulton Dr 38257 731-479-1441
Keith Frazier, prin. Fax 479-0586

South Pittsburg, Marion, Pop. 3,123
Marion County SD
Supt. — See Jasper
South Pittsburg JSHS 400/7-12
717 Elm Ave 37380 423-837-7561
Margie Allison, prin. Fax 837-4532

Richard CSD 300/K-12
1620 Hamilton Ave 37380 423-837-7282
Grant Barham, supt. Fax 837-0641
www.richardhardy.org
Hardy Memorial S 300/K-12
1620 Hamilton Ave 37380 423-837-7282
Dr. Bill Henry, prin. Fax 837-0641

Sparta, White, Pop. 4,766
White County SD 3,900/PK-12
136 Baker St 38583 931-836-2229
Donny Haley, supt. Fax 836-8128
www.whitecountyschools.org
White County HS 1,200/9-12
267 Allen Dr 38583 931-836-3214
Charles Dycus, prin. Fax 836-6295
White County MS 1,000/6-8
300 Turn Table Rd 38583 931-738-9238
Paul Steele, prin. Fax 738-9271
White County Vocational S Vo/Tech
275 Allen Dr 38583 931-836-8140
Tim Mackie, dir. Fax 836-2549

Spencer, Van Buren, Pop. 1,694
Van Buren County SD 800/PK-12
PO Box 98 38585 931-946-2242
Michael Martin, dir. Fax 946-2858
Van Buren County JSHS 400/6-12
PO Box 278 38585 931-946-2442
Phyllis Sullivan, prin. Fax 946-2733

Spring City, Rhea, Pop. 2,009
Rhea County SD
Supt. — See Dayton
Spring City MS 300/6-8
751 Wassom Memorial Hwy 37381 423-365-9105
Buddy Jackson, prin. Fax 365-9102

Little Village Center for Christian Educ 50/PK-12
879 Cemetery Rd 37381 423-365-7229
Patricia Schmittendorf, dir. Fax 365-9434

Springfield, Robertson, Pop. 15,916
Robertson County SD 10,000/PK-12
2121 Woodland St 37172 615-384-5588
Daniel Whitlow, supt. Fax 384-9749
www.robcoschools.org
Coopertown MS 300/6-8
3820 Highway 49 W 37172 615-382-4166
Dr. Mike Morris, prin. Fax 382-4171
Robertson County Technology Center Vo/Tech
5326 Highway 76 E 37172 615-384-2491
Linda Arms, prin. Fax 384-2491
Springfield HS 1,000/9-12
5240 Highway 76 E 37172 615-384-3516
Rick Highsmith, prin. Fax 384-0247
Springfield MS 600/6-8
715 5th Ave W 37172 615-384-4821
Shirley Whitley, prin. Fax 384-7890
Other Schools – See Cedar Hill, Cross Plains, Greenbrier, White House

Strawberry Plains, Jefferson
Knox County SD
Supt. — See Knoxville
Carter HS 900/9-12
210 N Carter School Rd 37871 865-933-3434
Cheryl Hickman, prin. Fax 932-8180
Carter MS 800/6-8
204 N Carter School Rd 37871 865-933-3426
Jewel Brock, prin. Fax 932-8170

Blue Springs Christian Academy 50/K-12
3265 Blue Springs Rd 37871 865-932-4305
June Ingram, prin.

Summertown, Lawrence
Lawrence County SD
Supt. — See Lawrenceburg
Summertown JSHS 600/7-12
PO Box 88 38483 931-964-3539
Bryan True, prin. Fax 964-3302

Sunbright, Morgan, Pop. 590
Morgan County SD
Supt. — See Wartburg
Sunbright S 600/K-12
PO Box 129 37872 423-628-2244
Rosa Dotson, prin. Fax 628-2120

Surgoinsville, Hawkins, Pop. 1,744
Hawkins County SD
Supt. — See Rogersville
Surgoinsville MS 400/5-8
1044 Main St 37873 423-345-2252
Zada Church, prin. Fax 345-3598

Tennessee Technology Center Morristown Post-Sec.
323 Phipps Bend Rd 37873 423-345-4130

Sweetwater, Monroe, Pop. 6,117
Monroe County SD
Supt. — See Madisonville
Sweetwater HS 600/9-12
414 S High St 37874 423-337-7881
David Watts, prin. Fax 337-0685

Sweetwater CSD 1,400/PK-8
PO Box 231 37874 423-337-7051
Dr. S. Keith Hickey, supt. Fax 337-6773
www.compurdy.com/scs2/
Sweetwater JHS 300/7-8
1013 Cannon Ave 37874 423-337-7336
Wayne Key, prin. Fax 337-7360

Covenant Baptist Academy 50/PK-12
PO Box 89 37874 423-337-7000
Sandy Murdock, prin. Fax 337-2328
Cross Creek Christian S 100/PK-12
501 E North St 37874 423-337-9330
Randy Nelson, pres. Fax 337-9335

Tazewell, Claiborne, Pop. 2,150
Claiborne County SD 4,100/PK-12
PO Box 179 37879 423-626-3543
Don Dobbs, supt. Fax 626-5945
www.claibornecountyschools.com
Soldiers Memorial MS 600/5-8
1510 Legion St 37879 423-626-3531
Lynn Barnard, prin. Fax 626-2151
Claiborne Adult HS Adult
PO Box 600 37879 423-626-8222
Roger Hansard, prin. Fax 626-5945
Other Schools – See Cumberland Gap, Harrogate, New Tazewell

Tellico Plains, Monroe, Pop. 930
Monroe County SD
Supt. — See Madisonville
Tellico Plains HS 500/9-12
9180 Highway 68 37385 423-253-2530
Russell Harris, prin. Fax 253-2541
Tellico Plains JHS 400/5-8
120 Old High School Rd 37385 423-253-2250
Ron Eydt, prin. Fax 253-7824

Ten Mile, Meigs
Roane County SD
Supt. — See Kingston
Midway MS 200/6-8
104 Dogtown Rd 37880 865-717-5464
Nadine Jackson, prin. Fax 376-0948

Thompsons Station, Williamson, Pop. 914
Williamson County SD
Supt. — See Franklin
Heritage MS 700/6-8
4803 Columbia Pike 37179 615-472-4540
Paula Pullian, prin. Fax 472-4553
Independence HS 700/9-12
1776 Declaration Way 37179 615-472-4600
Marilyn Webb, prin. Fax 472-4621

Tiptonville, Lake, Pop. 4,099
Lake County SD 900/PK-12
PO Box 397 38079 731-253-6601
Joey Hassell, supt. Fax 253-7111
www.lake.k12.tn.us/

Lake County HS — 200/9-12
300 Cochran St 38079 — 731-253-7733
Bret Johnson, prin. — Fax 253-7766

Trenton, Gibson, Pop. 4,577
Trenton Special SD — 1,400/PK-12
201 W 10th St 38382 — 731-855-1191
Larry Ridings, supt. — Fax 855-1414
voyager.rtd.utk.edu/~trenton/
Peabody HS — 400/9-12
2069 US Highway 45 Byp N 38382 — 731-855-2601
Tim Haney, prin. — Fax 855-1217
Trenton MS — 400/5-8
2065 US Highway 45 Byp S 38382 — 731-855-2422
Juanita Johnson, prin. — Fax 855-1826

Troy, Obion, Pop. 1,249
Obion County SD
Supt. — See Union City
Obion County Central HS — 900/9-12
528 N US Highway 51 38260 — 731-536-4688
Ray Wilson, prin. — Fax 536-0277

Tullahoma, Coffee, Pop. 18,909
Tullahoma CSD — 3,700/PK-12
510 S Jackson St 37388 — 931-454-2600
Dr. Dan Lawson, dir. — Fax 454-2642
www.tullahomacityschools.net/
East MS — 500/6-8
908 Country Club Dr 37388 — 931-454-2632
Debbie Edens, prin. — Fax 454-2660
Tullahoma HS — 1,200/9-12
1001 N Jackson St 37388 — 931-454-2620
Mike Landis, prin. — Fax 454-2662
West MS — 500/6-8
90 Hermitage Dr 37388 — 931-454-2605
Greg Carter, prin. — Fax 454-2661

Union City, Obion, Pop. 10,788
Obion County SD — 4,200/K-12
316 S 3rd St 38261 — 731-885-9743
Lonnie Grady, supt. — Fax 885-4902
www.obioncountyschools.com
Career Technology Center — Vo/Tech
1700 N 5th St 38261 — 731-885-7171
Bill Wilder, prin. — Fax 885-4734
Other Schools – See South Fulton, Troy

Union City SD — 1,400/K-12
PO Box 749 38281 — 731-885-3922
Gary Houston, supt. — Fax 885-6033
www.union-city-hs.obion.k12.tn.us/
Union City HS — 400/9-12
1305 High School Dr 38261 — 731-885-2373
Donnie Cox, prin. — Fax 885-5011
Union City MS — 300/6-8
1111 High School Dr 38261 — 731-885-2901
Dan Boykin, prin. — Fax 885-3677

Unionville, Bedford
Bedford County SD
Supt. — See Shelbyville
Community HS — 600/7-12
3470 Highway 41A N 37180 — 931-294-5125
Robert Ralston, prin. — Fax 294-5126

Vonore, Monroe, Pop. 1,383
Monroe County SD
Supt. — See Madisonville
Vonore MS — 5-8
414 Hall St 37885 — 423-884-2730
Debra Tipton, prin. — Fax 884-2731

Wartburg, Morgan, Pop. 913
Morgan County SD — 3,200/K-12
136 Flat Fork Rd 37887 — 423-346-6214
Mike Davis, dir. — Fax 346-6043
www.mcs.k12tn.net
Central HS — 400/9-12
1119 Knoxville Hwy 37887 — 423-346-6616
Dallas Davis, prin. — Fax 346-5665
Central MS — 300/6-8
146 Liberty Rd 37887 — 423-346-2800
Judy Hurst, prin. — Fax 346-2805
Morgan County Vocational Center — Vo/Tech
132 Flat Fork Rd 37887 — 423-346-6285
Mitchell Heidel, prin. — Fax 346-5857
Other Schools – See Coalfield, Oakdale, Sunbright

Wartrace, Bedford, Pop. 564
Bedford County SD
Supt. — See Shelbyville
Cascade HS — 700/6-12
1165 Bell Buckle Wartrace 37183 — 931-389-9389
Terry Looper, prin. — Fax 389-6223

Washburn, Grainger
Grainger County SD
Supt. — See Rutledge
Washburn S — 600/K-12
7925 Highway 131 37888 — 865-497-2557
Lisa Setsor, prin. — Fax 497-2934

Watertown, Wilson, Pop. 1,392
Wilson County SD
Supt. — See Lebanon
Watertown HS — 500/7-12
PO Box 67 37184 — 615-237-3434
Jeff Luttrell, prin. — Fax 237-3030

Waverly, Humphreys, Pop. 4,134
Humphreys County SD — 3,000/PK-12
2443 Highway 70 E 37185 — 931-296-2568
James Long, supt. — Fax 296-6501
www.hcss.org
Humphreys County Vocational Center — Vo/Tech
1327 Highway 70 W 37185 — 931-296-7867
Kay Webb, dir. — Fax 296-7252
Waverly Central HS — 600/9-12
1325 Highway 70 W 37185 — 931-296-3911
Richard Rawlings, prin. — Fax 296-2575
Waverly JHS — 600/4-8
520 E Main St 37185 — 931-296-4514
Andy Daniels, prin. — Fax 296-6507
Other Schools – See Mc Ewen

Waynesboro, Wayne, Pop. 2,175
Wayne County SD — 2,500/K-12
PO Box 658 38485 — 931-722-3548
Jerry Pigg, supt. — Fax 722-7579
www.wayne-lea.wayne.k12.tn.us
Wayne County HS — 400/9-12
707 S Main St 38485 — 931-722-3238
David Byrd, prin. — Fax 722-7641
Wayne County Vo Ctr — Vo/Tech
703 S Main St 38485 — 931-722-5495
Beverly Hall, prin. — Fax 722-5496
Waynesboro MS — 400/5-8
PO Box 657 38485 — 931-722-5545
Ryan Keeton, prin. — Fax 722-3953
Other Schools – See Clifton, Collinwood

Westmoreland, Sumner, Pop. 2,165
Sumner County SD
Supt. — See Gallatin
Westmoreland HS — 500/9-12
PO Box 119 37186 — 615-644-2280
Dewayne Oldham, prin. — Fax 644-3395
Westmoreland MS — 400/6-8
4128 Hawkins Dr 37186 — 615-644-3003
Danny Robinson, prin. — Fax 644-5584

White Bluff, Dickson, Pop. 2,372
Dickson County SD
Supt. — See Dickson
James MS — 300/6-8
3030 Trace Creek Rd 37187 — 615-797-3201
Louise Buchanan, prin. — Fax 797-6401

White House, Sumner, Pop. 8,723
Robertson County SD
Supt. — See Springfield
White House-Heritage JSHS — 700/6-12
220 West Dr 37188 — 615-672-0311
Kerry Baggett, prin. — Fax 672-7178

Sumner County SD
Supt. — See Gallatin
White House HS — 800/9-12
508 Tyree Springs Rd 37188 — 615-672-3761
Jeff Cordell, prin. — Fax 672-6404
White House MS — 700/6-8
2020 Highway 31 W 37188 — 615-672-4379
Jerry Apple, prin. — Fax 672-6409

Gideon Academy — 50/K-12
2948 Union Rd 37188 — 615-672-1121
Rick Dunnam, prin. — Fax 212-0123

Whitesburg, Hamblen
Hamblen County SD
Supt. — See Morristown
East Ridge MS — 600/6-8
6595 Saint Clair Rd 37891 — 423-581-3041
Marcia Carlyle, prin. — Fax 585-3763

Whites Creek, See Nashville
Davidson County SD
Supt. — See Nashville
Whites Creek Comprehensive HS — 900/9-12
7277 Old Hickory Blvd 37189 — 615-876-5132
Dr. Jamie Jenkins, prin. — Fax 321-8720

Whiteville, Hardeman, Pop. 4,489

Tennessee Technology Center Whiteville — Post-Sec.
PO Box 489 38075 — 731-254-8521

Whitwell, Marion, Pop. 1,604
Marion County SD
Supt. — See Jasper
Whitwell HS — 400/9-12
200 Tiger Trl 37397 — 423-658-5141
Wesley Green, prin. — Fax 658-0313
Whitwell MS — 400/5-8
1130 Main St 37397 — 423-658-5635
Linda Hooper, prin. — Fax 658-6949

Winchester, Franklin, Pop. 7,752
Franklin County SD — 5,800/PK-12
215 S College St 37398 — 931-967-0626
Dr. Charles Edmonds, supt. — Fax 967-7832
franklincountyschools.k12tn.net/
Franklin County HS — 1,500/9-12
833 Bypass Rd 37398 — 931-967-2821
Charlie Pike, prin. — Fax 967-6945
North MS — 500/7-8
2990 Decherd Blvd 37398 — 931-967-5323
John Butler, prin. — Fax 967-6417
Other Schools – See Cowan, Huntland

Woodbury, Cannon, Pop. 2,524
Cannon County SD — 2,100/K-12
301 W Main St Ste 100 37190 — 615-563-5752
Edward L. Diden, supt. — Fax 563-2716
www.cannoncounty.net
Cannon County HS — 700/9-12
1 Lion Dr 37190 — 615-563-2144
Kim Parsley, prin. — Fax 563-8068

TEXAS

TEXAS EDUCATION AGENCY
1701 Congress Ave, Austin 78701-1494
Telephone 512-463-9734
Fax 512-463-9838
Website http://www.tea.state.tx.us

Commissioner of Education Robert Scott

TEXAS BOARD OF EDUCATION
1701 Congress Ave, Austin 78701-1402

Chairperson Geraldine Miller

REGIONAL EDUCATION SERVICE CENTERS (RESC)

Region 1 ESC
Jack Damron, dir. 956-984-6000
1900 W Schunior St, Edinburg Fax 984-6299
www.esc1.net/

Region 2 ESC
Dr. Linda Villarreal, dir. 361-561-8400
209 N Water St Fax 883-3442
Corpus Christi 78401
www.esc2.net

Region 3 ESC
Dr. Julius Cano, dir. 361-573-0731
1905 Leary Ln, Victoria 77901 Fax 576-4804
www.esc3.net/

Region 4 ESC
Dr. William McKinney, dir. 713-462-7708
7145 W Tidwell Rd, Houston 77092 Fax 744-6514
www.esc4.net/

Region 5 ESC
Dr. R. Steve Hyden, dir. 409-838-5555
2295 Delaware St Fax 833-9755
Beaumont 77703
www.esc5.net

Region 6 ESC
Thomas Poe, dir. 936-435-8400
3332 Montgomery Rd Fax 295-1447
Huntsville 77340
www.esc6.net/

Region 7 ESC
Elizabeth Abernethy, dir. 903-988-6700
1909 N Longview St, Kilgore 75662 Fax 988-6735
www.esc7.net/

Region 8 ESC
Harvey Hohenberger, dir. 903-572-8551
PO Box 1894 Fax 575-2611
Mount Pleasant 75456
www.reg8.net/

Region 9 ESC
Anne Poplin, dir. 940-322-6928
301 Loop 11, Wichita Falls 76306 Fax 767-3836
www.esc9.net

Region 10 ESC
Dr. Jill Shugart, dir. 972-348-1700
PO Box 831300, Richardson 75083 Fax 231-3642
www.ednet10.net/

Region 11 ESC
Richard Ownby, dir. 817-740-3600
3001 North Fwy, Fort Worth 76106 Fax 740-7600
www.esc11.net

Region 12 ESC
Dr. Tom Norris, dir. 254-297-1212
PO Box 23409, Waco 76702 Fax 666-0823
www.esc12.net

Region 13 ESC
Dr. Pat Pringle, dir. 512-919-5313
5701 Springdale Rd, Austin 78723 Fax 919-5374

Region 14 ESC
Ronnie Kincaid, dir. 325-675-8600
1850 Highway 351, Abilene 79601 Fax 675-8659
www.esc14.net/

Region 15 ESC
David Smith, dir. 325-658-6571
PO Box 5199, San Angelo 76902 Fax 658-6571
www.netxv.net/

Region 16 ESC
John Bass, dir. 806-677-5000
5800 Bell St, Amarillo 79109 Fax 677-5001
www.esc16.net/

Region 17 ESC
Dr. Kyle Wargo, dir. 806-792-4000
1111 W Loop 289, Lubbock 79416 Fax 792-1523
www.esc17.net/

Region 18 ESC
Charles W. Greenawalt, dir. 432-563-2380
PO Box 60580, Midland 79711 Fax 567-3290
www.esc18.net

Region 19 ESC
Dr. James Vasquez, dir. 915-780-1919
PO Box 971127, El Paso 79997 Fax 780-6537

Region 20 ESC
Dr. Terry Smith, dir. 210-370-5200
1314 Hines, San Antonio 78208 Fax 370-5750
www.esc20.net

PUBLIC, PRIVATE AND CATHOLIC SECONDARY SCHOOLS

Abbott, Hill, Pop. 328
Abbott ISD 300/PK-12
PO Box 226 76621 254-582-9442
Terry Timmons, supt. Fax 582-5430
www.abbottisd.org
Abbott S 300/PK-12
PO Box 226 76621 254-582-3011
D. Beseda, prin. Fax 582-5430

Abernathy, Hale, Pop. 2,762
Abernathy ISD 800/PK-12
505 7th St 79311 806-298-2563
Herb Youngblood, supt. Fax 298-2400
www.abernathyisd.com
Abernathy HS 200/9-12
505 7th St 79311 806-298-2563
Gary Pugh, prin. Fax 298-4653
Abernathy JHS 200/6-8
505 7th St 79311 806-298-2563
Harold Bufe, prin. Fax 298-4775

Abilene, Taylor, Pop. 114,757
Abilene ISD 15,300/PK-12
PO Box 981 79604 325-677-1444
Dr. David Polnick, supt. Fax 794-1325
www.aisd.org
Abilene HS 2,300/9-12
2800 N 6th St 79603 325-677-1731
Terry Bull, prin. Fax 671-4127
Clack MS 700/6-8
1610 Corsicana Ave 79605 325-692-1961
Rodney Brown, prin. Fax 690-3547
Cooper HS 2,000/9-12
3639 Sayles Blvd 79605 325-691-1000
Gail Gregg, prin. Fax 690-3402
Craig MS 6-8
702 S Judge Ely Blvd 79602 325-794-4100
Jack Nall, prin.
Madison MS 900/6-8
3145 Barrow St 79605 325-692-5661
Jennifer Raney, prin. Fax 690-3584
Mann MS 600/6-8
2545 Mimosa Dr 79603 325-672-8493
Joe Alcorta, prin. Fax 671-4405
Woodson Skill Center Vo/Tech
342 Cockerell Dr 79601 325-671-4729
Elizabeth Dolton, lead tchr. Fax 671-4731
Adult Learning Center Adult
1929 S 11th St 79602 325-671-4419
Merri Lynn Rideout, dir. Fax 671-4671

Wylie ISD 2,200/PK-12
7049 Buffalo Gap Rd 79606 325-692-4353
Don Harrison, supt. Fax 695-3438
www.wylie.esc14.net
Wylie HS 900/9-12
4502 Antilley Rd 79606 325-690-1181
Terry Hagler, prin. Fax 690-0320
Wylie JHS 500/6-8
4010 Beltway S 79606 325-695-1910
Tommy Vaughn, prin. Fax 692-5786

Abilene Christian S 300/PK-12
2550 N Judge Ely Blvd 79601 325-672-9200
Billy Brant, pres. Fax 672-1262
Abilene Christian University Post-Sec.
ACU Box 29000 79699 325-674-2000
American Commercial College Post-Sec.
402 Butternut St 79602 325-672-8495
Hardin-Simmons University Post-Sec.
2200 Hickory St 79601 325-670-1000
Hendrick Medical Center Post-Sec.
1900 Pine St 79601 325-670-2201
McMurry University Post-Sec.
14th and Sayles 79697 325-793-3800
Texas College of Cosmetology Post-Sec.
117 Sayles Blvd 79605 325-677-0532

Ackerly, Dawson, Pop. 231
Sands Consolidated ISD 200/PK-12
PO Box 218 79713 432-353-4888
Wayne Blount, supt. Fax 353-4650
sands.esc17.net
Sands S 200/PK-12
PO Box 218 79713 432-353-4888
Zelda Bilbo, prin. Fax 353-4561

Addison, Dallas, Pop. 13,667

Greenhill S 1,300/PK-12
4141 Spring Valley Rd 75001 972-628-5400
Scott Griggs, hdmstr. Fax 404-8217
Sterling Health Center Post-Sec.
15070 E Beltwood Pkwy 75001 972-992-9293
Trinity Christian Academy 1,500/K-12
17001 Addison Rd 75001 972-931-8325
David Delph, admin. Fax 931-8923

Adkins, Bexar

Salem Sayers Baptist S 100/PK-12
PO Box 397 78101 210-649-1178
Bret Edwards, prin. Fax 649-3385

Adrian, Oldham, Pop. 154
Adrian ISD 100/K-12
PO Box 189 79001 806-538-6203
David Johnson, supt. Fax 538-6291
www.adrianisd.net
Adrian S 100/K-12
PO Box 189 79001 806-538-6203
David Johnson, prin. Fax 538-6291

Afton, Dickens
Patton Springs ISD 100/PK-12
PO Box 32 79220 806-689-2229
Larry McClenny, supt. Fax 689-2253
www.pattonsprings.net
Patton Springs S 100/PK-12
PO Box 32 79220 806-689-2220
Mike Norrell, prin. Fax 689-2253

Agua Dulce, Nueces, Pop. 729
Agua Dulce ISD 300/PK-12
PO Box 250 78330 361-998-2542
Paul Czerwinski, supt. Fax 998-2816
www.adisd.esc2.net
Agua Dulce JSHS 100/6-12
PO Box 250 78330 361-998-2214
Michael Gonzalez, prin. Fax 998-2994

Alamo, Hidalgo, Pop. 15,976
Pharr-San Juan-Alamo ISD
Supt. — See Pharr
Alamo MS 1,100/6-8
1819 W US Highway 83 78516 956-702-5887
Iris Guajardo, prin. Fax 702-5893
Pharr-San Juan-Alamo Memorial HS 1,900/9-12
800 S Alamo Rd 78516 956-783-3600
Orlando Noyola, prin. Fax 783-3636

Valley Christian Heritage S 100/PK-12
932 N Alamo Rd 78516 956-787-9743
Mary Rydl, prin. Fax 787-1977

Alba, Wood, Pop. 479
Alba-Golden ISD 800/PK-12
1373 County Road 2377 75410 903-768-2472
Bill Stewart, supt. Fax 768-2130
www.agisd.com
Alba-Golden JSHS 400/6-12
1373 County Road 2377 75410 903-768-2472
Dwayne Ellis, prin. Fax 768-2303

Albany, Shackelford, Pop. 1,833
Albany ISD 600/PK-12
PO Box 188 76430 325-762-3974
Shane Fields, supt. Fax 762-3876
www.albany.esc14.net
Albany JSHS 300/7-12
PO Box 188 76430 325-762-3974
Thomas W. Terrell, prin. Fax 762-3850

Aledo, Parker, Pop. 2,524
Aledo ISD 3,400/PK-12
1008 Bailey Ranch Rd 76008 817-441-8327
Don Daniel, supt. Fax 441-5144
www.aledo.k12.tx.us
Aledo HS 1,100/9-12
1000 Bailey Ranch Rd 76008 817-441-8711
Sheryl Asay, prin. Fax 441-5136
Aledo MS 600/7-8
416 S FM Road 1187 76008 817-441-5198
John Lindsay, prin. Fax 441-5133

Aledo Christian S 100/K-12
PO Box 117 76008 817-441-9062
Kay Ross, prin. Fax 441-7476

Alice, Jim Wells, Pop. 19,519
Alice ISD 5,400/K-12
2 Coyote Trl 78332 361-664-0981
Henry Herrera, supt. Fax 660-2113
www.aliceisd.net/home.asp
Adams MS 900/7-8
901 E 3rd St 78332 361-660-2055
Noel Estrada, prin. Fax 660-2094
Alice HS 1,600/9-12
1 Coyote Trl 78332 361-664-0126
Berta Longoria, prin. Fax 660-2128

Alice Christian S 50/PK-12
1200 N Stadium Rd 78332 361-668-6618

Alief, Harris
Alief ISD
Supt. — See Houston
S.O.A.R. Adult
PO Box 68 77411 281-988-3499
Beth Smith, prin. Fax 983-1698

Allen, Collin, Pop. 69,222
Allen ISD 14,000/PK-12
PO Box 13 75013 972-727-0513
Dr. Ken Helvey, supt. Fax 727-0518
www.allenisd.org
Allen SHS 3,100/10-12
300 Rivercrest Blvd 75002 972-727-0400
Steve Payne, prin. Fax 727-0515
Curtis MS 800/7-8
1530 Rivercrest Blvd 75002 972-727-0340
Becky Kennedy, prin. Fax 727-0345
Ford MS 900/7-8
630 Park Place Dr 75002 972-727-0590
Sandra McCoy-Jackson, prin. Fax 727-0596
Lowery Freshman Center 1,200/9-9
120 N Jupiter Rd 75002 972-396-6975
Steve Payne, prin. Fax 396-6981

Lovejoy ISD 900/K-12
259 Country Club Rd 75002 972-562-5077
Ted Moore, supt. Fax 562-9924
www.lovejoyisd.net/
Other Schools – See Lucas

Alpine, Brewster, Pop. 6,065
Alpine ISD 1,000/PK-12
704 W Sul Ross Ave 79830 432-837-7700
Mike Davis, supt. Fax 837-7740
www.alpine.esc18.net
Alpine HS 300/9-12
300 E Hendryx Dr 79830 432-837-7710
Verl O'Bryant, prin. Fax 837-7741
Alpine MS 300/5-8
801 Middle School Dr 79830 432-837-7720
James Angst, prin. Fax 837-7795

Sul Ross State University 79832 Post-Sec.
432-837-8032

Altair, Colorado
Rice Consolidated ISD 800/PK-12
PO Box 338 77412 979-234-3531
Michael Lanier Ph.D., supt. Fax 234-6305
www.ricecisd.org/
Rice HS 400/9-12
PO Box 338 77412 979-234-3535
Leroy Stavinoha, prin. Fax 234-5901
Other Schools – See Eagle Lake

Alto, Cherokee, Pop. 1,156
Alto ISD 700/PK-12
RR 1 Box 1000 75925 936-858-7101
Dr. Ray Despain, supt. Fax 858-2101
www.alto.esc7.net/
Alto HS 200/9-12
RR 1 Box 1000 75925 936-858-3355
Donald Patton, prin. Fax 858-4387
Alto MS 200/5-8
RR 1 Box 1000 75925 936-858-3397
Kelly West, prin. Fax 858-4579

Alton, Hidalgo, Pop. 7,057
Mission Consolidated ISD
Supt. — See Mission
Alton Memorial JHS 600/7-8
521 S Los Ebanos Rd, 956-323-5000
Sylvia Garcia, prin. Fax 323-5045

Alvarado, Johnson, Pop. 3,977
Alvarado ISD 3,500/PK-12
PO Box 387 76009 817-783-6800
Dr. Chester Juroska, supt. Fax 783-3844
www.alvaradoisd.net/
Alvarado HS 1,100/9-12
PO Box 387 76009 817-783-6940
Kenneth Estes, prin. Fax 783-6944
Alvarado JHS 500/7-8
PO Box 387 76009 817-783-6840
Melodye Broods, prin. Fax 783-6844

Alvin, Brazoria, Pop. 22,171
Alvin ISD 12,300/PK-12
301 E House St 77511 281-388-1130
Dr. Greg Smith, supt. Fax 388-0566
www.alvinisd.net/
Alvin HS 3,200/9-12
301 E House St 77511 281-331-8151
Kevon Wells, prin. Fax 331-3053
Alvin JHS 800/7-8
301 E House St 77511 281-585-8491
Deborah Roberson, prin. Fax 331-5926
Harby JHS 700/7-8
301 E House St 77511 281-585-6626
Nancy Flores, prin. Fax 388-2247
Manvel JHS 400/7-8
301 E House St 77511 281-489-8257
Trisha Upchurch, prin. Fax 489-8169
Alvin Evening S Adult
301 E House St 77511 281-331-8151
Fulvia Nolte, prin.
Other Schools – See Manvel

Alvin Community College Post-Sec.
3110 Mustang Rd 77511 281-331-6111
Living Stones Christian S 200/K-12
1407 Victory Ln 77511 281-331-0086
Jessica Cedro, admin. Fax 331-6747

Alvord, Wise, Pop. 1,309
Alvord ISD 700/K-12
PO Box 70 76225 940-427-5975
John Trice, supt. Fax 427-2313
www.alvordisd.net/
Alvord HS 200/9-12
PO Box 70 76225 940-427-9643
Carla Bullard, prin. Fax 427-9648
Alvord MS 200/6-8
PO Box 70 76225 940-427-5511
Carolyn Holloway, prin. Fax 427-2461

Amarillo, Potter, Pop. 183,021
Amarillo ISD 29,700/PK-12
7200 W Interstate 40 79106 806-326-1000
Rod Schroder, supt. Fax 354-4378
www.amaisd.org
Amarillo HS, 4225 Danbury Dr 79109 2,100/9-12
Doug Loomis, prin. 806-326-2000
Austin MS 800/6-8
1808 Wimberly Rd 79109 806-354-4450
David Vincent, prin. Fax 356-4802
Bonham MS 800/6-8
5600 SW 49th Ave 79109 806-326-3100
Curtis Crump, prin.
Bowie MS 1,100/6-8
3001 SE 12th Ave 79104 806-371-5580
Marilyn Jackson, prin. Fax 371-6015
Caprock HS, 3001 SE 34th Ave 79103 1,700/9-12
Rebecca Harrison, prin. 806-326-2200
Crockett MS, 4720 Floyd Ave 79106 700/6-8
Lynn Pulliam, prin. 806-326-3300
Fannin MS 600/6-8
4627 S Rusk St 79110 806-354-4570
Tammie Villarreal, prin. Fax 354-2304
Houston MS 900/6-8
815 S Independence St 79106 806-326-3600
David Bishop, prin.
Mann MS, 610 N Buchanan St 79107 700/6-8
Roscoe Guest, prin. 806-326-3700
Palo Duro HS, 1400 N Grant St 79107 1,900/9-12
Kevin Phillips, prin. 806-326-2400
Tascosa HS, 3921 Westlawn St 79102 2,200/9-12
Bob Daniel, prin. 806-326-2600
Travis MS, 2815 Martin Rd 79107 1,000/6-8
Jay Barrett, prin. 806-326-3800

Canyon ISD
Supt. — See Canyon
Randall HS 1,500/9-12
5800 Attebury Dr 79118 806-677-2333
Steve Williams, prin. Fax 677-2329
Westover Park JHS 800/7-8
7200 Pinnacle Dr 79119 806-677-2420
Doug Voran, prin. Fax 677-2439

Highland Park ISD 900/PK-12
PO Box 30430 79120 806-335-2823
Bill Mayfield, supt. Fax 335-3547
www.hpisd.net
Highland Park HS 200/9-12
PO Box 30430 79120 806-335-2821
Shelley Collins, prin. Fax 335-3215
Highland Park MS 200/6-8
PO Box 30430 79120 806-335-2821
Shelley Collins, prin. Fax 335-3215

River Road ISD 1,400/PK-12
9500 N US Highway 287 79108 806-381-7800
Randy Owen, supt. Fax 381-1357
www.rrisd.net
River Road HS 400/9-12
9500 N US Highway 287 79108 806-383-8867
Andy Nies, prin. Fax 381-7818
River Road MS 300/6-8
7600 Pavillard Dr 79108 806-383-8721
Richard Kelley, prin. Fax 381-7815

Amarillo College Post-Sec.
PO Box 447 79178 806-371-5000
Arbor Christian Academy 300/K-12
5000 Hollywood Rd 79118 806-355-7207
Nancy Wilcox, admin. Fax 353-8969
Bible Heritage Christian S 300/PK-12
4100 Republic Ave 79109 806-463-2427
Dennis Rawls, admin. Fax 463-2433
Exposito School of Hair Design Post-Sec.
3710 Mockingbird Ln 79109 806-355-9111
Holy Cross Catholic Academy 100/6-12
4110 S Bonham St 79110 806-355-9637
Frank Maldonado, prin. Fax 353-9520
Milan Institute Post-Sec.
7001 I-40 West 79106 806-353-3500
Milan Institute of Cosmetology Post-Sec.
2400 SE 27th Ave 79103 806-371-7600
Northwest Texas Healthcare System Post-Sec.
PO Box 1110 79105 806-354-1110
San Jacinto Christian Academy 600/PK-12
PO Box 3428 79116 806-372-2285
Christy Creacy, prin. Fax 376-6712

Amherst, Lamb, Pop. 765
Amherst ISD 200/K-12
PO Box 248 79312 806-246-3501
Byron Shelley, supt. Fax 246-3649
Amherst S 200/K-12
PO Box 248 79312 806-246-3221
Joel Rodgers, prin. Fax 246-3649

Anahuac, Chambers, Pop. 2,083
Anahuac ISD 1,500/PK-12
PO Box 369 77514 409-267-3600
Dr. Linda Kay Barnhart, supt. Fax 267-3855
www.anahuac.isd.esc4.net
Anahuac HS 400/9-12
PO Box 1560 77514 409-267-6491
Eric Humphrey, prin. Fax 267-5192
Anahuac MS 400/6-8
PO Box 849 77514 409-267-3421
Cody Abshier, prin. Fax 267-3643

Anderson, Grimes, Pop. 274
Anderson - Shiro Consolidated ISD 500/PK-12
1139 Highway 90 N 77830 936-873-2802
Fred Brent, supt. Fax 873-2673
www.ascisd.net
Anderson - Shiro JSHS 300/5-12
1139 Highway 90 N 77830 936-873-2061
Brandon Core, prin. Fax 873-2718

Andrews, Andrews, Pop. 9,391
Andrews ISD 2,900/PK-12
405 NW 3rd St 79714 432-523-3640
David Mitchell, supt. Fax 523-3343
andrews.esc18.net
Andrews HS 900/9-12
405 NW 3rd St 79714 432-523-3640
Rick Howell, prin. Fax 523-6807
Andrews MS 600/6-8
405 NW 3rd St 79714 432-523-3640
Penny Bane, prin. Fax 524-1904

Angleton, Brazoria, Pop. 18,761
Angleton ISD 6,400/PK-12
1900 N Downing Rd 77515 979-849-8594
Dr. Heath Burns, supt. Fax 849-3041
www.angletonisd.net/
Angleton HS 1,800/9-12
1201 W Henderson Rd 77515 979-849-8206
Gordon Smith, prin. Fax 864-8675
Angleton IS 1,000/7-8
1800 N Downing Rd 77515 979-849-4318
Roy Gardner, prin. Fax 849-8652

Anna, Collin, Pop. 1,750
Anna ISD 1,200/PK-12
501 S Sherley Ave 75409 972-924-3955
Dr. Joe Wardell, supt. Fax 924-3321
www.annaisd.net
Anna HS 300/9-12
501 S Sherley Ave 75409 972-924-3261
Scott Wortham, prin. Fax 924-2074
Anna MS 300/6-8
501 S Sherley Ave 75409 972-924-2380
Kevin Harris, prin. Fax 924-2856

Anson, Jones, Pop. 2,332
Anson ISD 700/PK-12
1431 Commercial Ave 79501 325-823-3671
Jay Baccus, supt. Fax 823-4444
www.ansontigers.com
Anson HS 200/9-12
1509 Commercial Ave 79501 325-823-2404
Will Brewer, prin. Fax 823-2514
Anson MS 200/6-8
1120 Avenue M 79501 325-823-2771
Harper Stewart, prin. Fax 823-3667

Anthony, El Paso, Pop. 4,072
Anthony ISD 800/PK-12
610 6th St 79821 915-886-6500
Vernon Butler, supt. Fax 886-3835
www.anthonyisd.net
Anthony HS 200/9-12
610 6th St 79821 915-886-6550
Edmond Martinez, prin. Fax 886-3875
Anthony MS 200/6-8
610 6th St 79821 915-886-6530
Dr. Terry Ann Rodriguez, prin. Fax 886-3875

Anton, Hockley, Pop. 1,172
Anton ISD 400/PK-12
PO Box 309 79313 806-997-2301
Dwayne Chenault, supt. Fax 997-2062
Anton HS 200/7-12
PO Box 309 79313 806-997-5211
Chad Elliott, prin. Fax 997-2062

Apple Springs, Trinity
Apple Springs ISD 200/PK-12
PO Box 125 75926 936-831-3344
Gregg Spivey, supt. Fax 831-2824
Apple Springs JSHS 100/6-12
PO Box 125 75926 936-831-2241
Cody Moree, prin. Fax 831-2824

Aquilla, Hill, Pop. 149
Aquilla ISD 200/PK-12
404 N Richards 76622 254-694-3770
James L. Gwaltney, supt. Fax 694-6237
www.aquillaisd.net
Aquilla S 200/PK-12
404 N Richards 76622 254-694-3770
David Edison, prin. Fax 694-6237

Aransas Pass, San Patricio, Pop. 8,877
Aransas Pass ISD 2,200/PK-12
244 W Harrison Blvd 78336 361-758-3466
Dr. Carl A. Montoya, supt. Fax 758-2962
www.apisd.org
Aransas Pass HS 500/9-12
450 S Avenue A 78336 361-758-3248
John Fitzgerald, prin. Fax 758-3251
Blunt MS 300/7-8
2103 Demory Ln 78336 361-758-2711
Bryan O'Bryant, prin. Fax 758-4690

Highland Avenue Christian S 100/K-12
1630 W Highland Ave 78336 361-758-8196
Steve Hale, prin. Fax 758-5214

Archer City, Archer, Pop. 1,859
Archer City ISD 500/PK-12
PO Box 926 76351 940-574-4536
Randel Beaver, supt. Fax 574-4051
www.esc9.net/acisd
Archer City JSHS 300/7-12
PO Box 926 76351 940-574-4713
C. Knobloch, prin. Fax 574-2636

Argyle, Denton, Pop. 2,969
Argyle ISD 1,500/PK-12
800 Eagle Dr 76226 940-464-7241
Carolyn Pierel, supt. Fax 464-7297
www.argyleisd.com
Argyle HS 500/9-12
800 Eagle Dr 76226 940-262-7777
Jeff Butts, prin. Fax 262-7783
Argyle MS 400/6-8
800 Eagle Dr 76226 940-246-2126
Chris Daniel, prin. Fax 246-2128

Liberty Christian S 1,000/PK-12
1301 S US Highway 377 76226 940-294-2000
Rodney Haire, dir. Fax 294-2045

Arlington, Tarrant, Pop. 362,805
Arlington ISD 61,400/PK-12
1203 W Pioneer Pkwy 76013 682-867-4611
Dr. Mac Bernd, supt. Fax 459-7299
www.aisd.net

Arlington HS — 2,700/9-12
818 W Park Row Dr 76013 — 682-867-8100
James Adams, prin. — Fax 801-6105
Bailey JHS — 900/7-8
2411 Winewood Ln 76013 — 682-867-0700
Jimmy Walker, prin. — Fax 801-0705
Barnett JHS — 1,000/7-8
2101 E Sublett Rd 76018 — 682-867-5000
Cindy Elwood, prin. — Fax 419-5005
Boles JHS — 800/7-8
3900 SW Green Oaks Blvd 76017 — 682-867-8000
Michelle Wilmoth, prin. — Fax 561-8005
Bowie HS — 2,600/9-12
2101 Highbank Dr 76018 — 682-867-4400
Darrell Sneed, prin. — Fax 472-4444
Carter JHS — 700/7-8
701 Tharp St 76010 — 682-867-1700
Rashel Stevens, prin. — Fax 801-1705
Ferguson JHS — 600/7-8
600 SE Green Oaks Blvd 76018 — 682-867-1600
David Tapia, prin. — Fax 472-1605
Gunn JHS — 600/7-8
3000 S Fielder Rd 76015 — 682-867-5400
Lesia Rodawalt, prin. — Fax 419-5405
Houston HS — 3,000/9-12
2000 Sam Houston Dr 76014 — 682-867-8200
Beverly McReynolds, prin. — Fax 801-4505
Hutcheson JHS — 800/7-8
2101 Browning Dr 76010 — 682-867-2400
Rose Bolden, prin. — Fax 801-2415
Lamar HS — 3,000/9-12
1400 W Lamar Blvd 76012 — 682-867-8300
Jeff Provence, prin. — Fax 801-6255
Martin HS — 3,400/9-12
4501 W Pleasant Ridge Rd 76016 — 682-867-8600
Laura Jones, prin. — Fax 561-8705
Nichols JHS — 1,000/7-8
2201 Ascension Blvd 76006 — 682-867-2600
Sandra Knox, prin. — Fax 801-2605
Ousley JHS — 700/7-8
950 Southeast Pkwy 76018 — 682-867-5700
Lora Thurston, prin. — Fax 419-5705
Seguin HS — 1,800/9-12
7001 Silo Rd 76002 — 682-867-6700
Edward Farmer, prin. — Fax 375-6705
Shackelford JHS — 700/7-8
2000 N Fielder Rd 76012 — 682-867-3600
Carolyn Galvan, prin. — Fax 801-3605
Workman JHS — 600/7-8
701 E Arbrook Blvd 76014 — 682-867-1200
David Bellile, prin. — Fax 419-1205
Young JHS — 900/7-8
3200 Woodside Dr 76016 — 682-867-3400
Mary Canon, prin. — Fax 492-3405

Mansfield ISD
Supt. — See Mansfield
Coble MS — 7-8
1200 Ballweg Rd 76002 — 817-299-6400
Darrell Douglas, prin. — Fax 453-7331
Howard MS — 1,200/7-8
7501 Calender Rd 76001 — 817-561-3828
Jimmy Neal, prin. — Fax 561-3840
Summit HS — 2,500/9-12
1071 Turner Warnell Rd 76001 — 817-473-5660
Donna Grant, prin. — Fax 473-5732
Timberview HS — 1,500/9-12
7700 S Watson Rd 76002 — 817-299-2600
Carolyn Dowler, prin. — Fax 472-2980

Arlington Baptist College — Post-Sec.
3001 W Division St 76012 — 817-461-8741
Arlington Medical Institute — Post-Sec.
2301 N Collins St Ste 100 76011 — 817-265-0706
Burton Adventist Academy — 300/PK-12
4611 Kelly Elliott Rd 76017 — 817-572-0081
Gerald Coy, prin. — Fax 561-4237
Concorde Career Institute — Post-Sec.
601 Ryan Plaza Dr Ste 200 76011 — 817-261-1594
Fellowship Academy — 200/K-12
7000 US 287 Hwy 76001 — 817-563-5913
Monica Collier, prin. — Fax 563-5427
ITT Technical Institute — Post-Sec.
551 Ryan Plaza Dr 76011 — 817-794-5100
Oakridge S — 800/PK-12
5900 W Pioneer Pkwy 76013 — 817-451-4994
Andy Broadus, hdmstr. — Fax 457-6681
Pantego Christian Academy — 700/PK-12
2201 W Park Row Dr 76013 — 817-460-3315
Steve Newby, hdmstr. — Fax 459-4687
St. Albans Episcopal S — 200/PK-12
2500 S Bowen Rd 76015 — 817-460-6071
Kathy Bonds, hdmstr. — Fax 860-8305
St. Pauls Preparatory Academy — 300/PK-12
PO Box 121234 76012 — 817-561-3500
Janice Wood, prin. — Fax 561-3408
Spurling Christian Academy — 100/K-12
1200 High Point Rd 76015 — 817-465-1122
Teri Montez, prin. — Fax 465-0609
Tarrant County Junior College — Post-Sec.
2100 Tarrant County JC Pky 76018 — 817-515-3100
University of Texas — Post-Sec.
PO Box 19111 76019 — 817-272-2011

Arp, Smith, Pop. 932
Arp ISD — 900/PK-12
PO Box 70 75750 — 903-859-8482
Toney Lowery, supt. — Fax 859-2621
www.arp.sprnet.org
Arp HS — 300/9-12
PO Box 70 75750 — 903-859-4917
Dr. Fred Zachary, prin. — Fax 859-1541
Arp JHS — 200/6-8
PO Box 70 75750 — 903-859-4936
Dwight Thomas, prin. — Fax 859-3980

Aspermont, Stonewall, Pop. 831
Aspermont ISD — 200/PK-12
PO Box 549 79502 — 940-989-3355
John Godfrey, supt. — Fax 989-3353
www.aspermont.esc14.net
Aspermont JSHS — 100/7-12
PO Box 549 79502 — 940-989-2707
Cliff Gilmore, prin. — Fax 989-3486

Athens, Henderson, Pop. 12,559
Athens ISD — 3,600/PK-12
104 Hawn St 75751 — 903-677-6900
Vance Vaughn, supt. — Fax 677-6908
www.athensisd.net
Athens HS — 1,000/9-12
708 E College St 75751 — 903-677-6920
Todd Nix, prin. — Fax 677-6925
Athens MS — 500/7-8
6800 State Highway 19 S 75751 — 903-677-3030
Annette Faulk, prin. — Fax 677-2111

Trinity Valley Community College — Post-Sec.
100 Cardinal St 75751 — 903-677-8822

Atlanta, Cass, Pop. 5,677
Atlanta ISD — 1,900/PK-12
315 N Buckner St 75551 — 903-796-4194
Gayle Stinson, supt. — Fax 796-3487
atlantaisd.com
Atlanta HS — 600/9-12
705 Rabbit Blvd 75551 — 903-796-4411
Mike White, prin. — Fax 799-1033
Atlanta MS — 400/6-8
600 High School Ln 75551 — 903-796-7928
Susan Childress, prin. — Fax 799-1021

Aubrey, Denton, Pop. 2,210
Aubrey ISD — 900/PK-12
415 Tisdell Ln 76227 — 940-365-2721
Dr. James Monaco, supt. — Fax 365-2042
www.aubreyisd.net/
Aubrey HS — 300/9-12
510 Spring Hill Rd 76227 — 940-365-2433
Jeff Mulkey, prin. — Fax 365-3271
Aubrey MS — 200/6-8
415 Tisdell Ln 76227 — 940-365-2434
Delore Jones, prin. — Fax 365-2627

Denton ISD
Supt. — See Denton
Navo MS — 6-8
1701 Navo Rd 76227 — 972-347-7500
Shaun Perry, prin. — Fax 346-2562

Austin, Travis, Pop. 690,252
Austin ISD — 79,300/PK-12
1111 W 6th St 78703 — 512-414-1700
Dr. Pascal Forgione, supt. — Fax 414-1707
www.austin.isd.tenet.edu/
Akins HS — 2,200/9-12
10701 S 1st St 78748 — 512-841-9900
Mary Alice Deike, prin. — Fax 841-9903
Anderson HS — 2,000/9-12
8403 Mesa Dr 78759 — 512-414-2538
David Kernwein, prin. — Fax 338-1293
Austin HS — 2,200/9-12
1715 W Cesar Chavez St 78703 — 512-414-2505
John Hudson, prin. — Fax 474-7935
Bailey MS — 1,100/6-8
4020 Lost Oasis Holw 78739 — 512-414-4990
Julia Fletcher, prin. — Fax 292-0898
Bedichek MS — 900/6-8
6800 Bill Hughes Rd 78745 — 512-414-3265
Gail Belcher, prin. — Fax 444-4382
Bowie HS — 2,600/9-12
4103 Slaughter Ln W 78749 — 512-414-5247
Stephen Kane, prin. — Fax 292-0527
Burnet MS — 1,000/6-8
8401 Hathaway Dr 78757 — 512-414-3225
Linda Van Horne, prin. — Fax 452-0695
Clifton Career Development S — Vo/Tech
1519 Coronado Hills Dr 78752 — 512-414-3614
Tony Dishner, prin. — Fax 323-2646
Covington MS — 900/6-8
3700 Convict Hill Rd 78749 — 512-414-3276
Karon Rilling, prin. — Fax 892-4547
Crockett HS — 1,900/9-12
5601 Manchaca Rd 78745 — 512-414-2532
Barbara Gideon, prin. — Fax 447-0489
Dobie MS — 700/6-8
1200 E Rundberg Ln 78753 — 512-414-3270
Carol Chapman, prin. — Fax 836-8411
Fulmore Magnet S — 6-8
201 E Mary St 78704 — 512-841-4916
Dr. Mary Anne Wilkenson, dir. — Fax 841-4915
Fulmore MS — 1,000/6-8
201 E Mary St 78704 — 512-414-3207
Dr. Lucio Calzada, prin. — Fax 441-3129
Health Sciences Institute of Austin — 9-12
1201 Payton Gin Rd 78758 — 512-414-2514
Mark Kincaid, prin. — Fax 832-1203
Institute of Hospitality & Culinary Arts — Vo/Tech
1211 E Oltorf St 78704 — 512-414-4491
Mark Kincaid, dir. — Fax 414-1506
International HS — 9-12
1012 Arthur Stiles Rd 78721 — 512-414-5810
Anabel Garcia, prin. — Fax 414-6819
Johnson HS — 1,600/9-12
7309 Lazy Creek Dr 78724 — 512-414-2543
Patrick Patterson, prin. — Fax 929-3955
Johnston HS — 1,000/9-12
1012 Arthur Stiles Rd 78721 — 512-414-5810
Dr. Celina Estrada-Russell, prin. — Fax 414-6819
Kealing Magnet Program — 6-8
1607 Pennsylvania Ave 78702 — 512-414-3180
Mary Ramberg, dir. — Fax 478-9133
Kealing MS — 1,300/6-8
1607 Pennsylvania Ave 78702 — 512-414-3214
Ron Gonzales, prin. — Fax 478-9133
Lamar MS — 700/6-8
6201 Wynona Ave 78757 — 512-414-3217
Mike Atchley, prin. — Fax 467-6862
Lanier HS — 1,700/9-12
1201 Payton Gin Rd 78758 — 512-414-2514
Edmund Oropez, prin. — Fax 832-1203
Liberal Arts & Science Academy — 9-12
7309 Lazy Creek Dr 78724 — 512-414-2589
Renee Sanchez, dir. — Fax 926-8407
Martin MS — 700/6-8
1601 Haskell St 78702 — 512-414-3243
Raffy Vizcaino, prin. — Fax 320-0125
McCallum Fine Arts Academy — 9-12
5600 Sunshine Dr 78756 — 512-414-7505
Lanier Bayliss, prin. — Fax 453-2599
McCallum HS — 1,600/9-12
5600 Sunshine Dr 78756 — 512-414-2519
Michael Garrison, prin. — Fax 453-2599
Mendez MS — 800/6-8
5106 Village Square Dr 78744 — 512-414-3284
Connie Barr, prin. — Fax 442-5738
Murchison MS — 1,200/6-8
3700 N Hills Dr 78731 — 512-414-3254
Donna Houser, prin. — Fax 343-1710
O'Henry MS — 800/6-8
2610 W 10th St 78703 — 512-414-3229
Peter Price, prin. — Fax 477-7428
Paredes MS — 1,300/6-8
10100 S Mary Moore Searight 78748 — 512-841-6800
Renette Bledsoe, prin. — Fax 841-7036
Pearce MS — 800/6-8
6401 N Hampton Dr 78723 — 512-414-3234
Diana Sustaita, prin. — Fax 926-6146
Porter MS — 600/6-8
2206 Prather Ln 78704 — 512-414-3236
Judy Szilagyi, prin. — Fax 441-5208
Reagan HS — 1,000/9-12
7104 Berkman Dr 78752 — 512-414-2523
Ismael Villafane, prin. — Fax 452-7089
Small MS — 1,100/6-8
4801 Monterey Oaks Blvd 78749 — 512-841-6700
Sheila Anderson, prin. — Fax 841-6703
Travis HS — 1,600/9-12
1211 E Oltorf St 78704 — 512-414-2527
Dr. Rene Garganta, prin. — Fax 707-0050
Webb MS — 700/6-8
601 E Saint Johns Ave 78752 — 512-414-3258
Charles Hunt, prin. — Fax 452-9683

Del Valle ISD
Supt. — See Del Valle
Ojeda JHS — 600/7-8
4900 McKinney Falls Pkwy 78744 — 512-386-3500
Adelaida Olivares, prin. — Fax 386-3505

Eanes ISD — 7,100/PK-12
601 Camp Craft Rd 78746 — 512-732-9001
Dr. Nola Wellman, supt. — Fax 732-9005
www.eanes.k12.tx.us
Hill Country MS — 800/6-8
1300 Walsh Tarlton Ln 78746 — 512-732-9220
Kathleen Sullivan, prin. — Fax 732-9229
Westlake HS — 2,400/9-12
4100 Westbank Dr 78746 — 512-732-9280
Linda Rawlings, prin. — Fax 732-9289
West Ridge MS — 900/6-8
9201 Scenic Bluff Dr 78733 — 512-732-9240
Karl Waggoner, prin. — Fax 732-9249

Lake Travis ISD — 5,100/PK-12
3322 Ranch Rd 620 S 78738 — 512-533-6000
Gary Ott Ed.D., supt. — Fax 533-6001
www.laketravis.txed.net
Hudson Bend MS — 500/6-8
15600 Lariat Trl 78734 — 512-533-6400
Kim Cousins, prin. — Fax 533-6401
Lake Travis HS — 1,600/9-12
3324 Ranch Road 620 S 78738 — 512-533-6100
Charles Little, prin. — Fax 533-6102
Lake Travis MS — 700/6-8
3328 Ranch Road 620 S 78738 — 512-533-6200
Kim Brents, prin. — Fax 533-6201

Leander ISD
Supt. — See Leander
Canyon Ridge MS — 6-8
12601 Country Trl 78732 — 512-434-7550
Susan Sullivan, prin. — Fax 434-7555

Pflugerville ISD
Supt. — See Pflugerville
Connally HS — 1,800/9-12
13212 N Lamar Blvd 78753 — 512-594-0800
Daniel Garcia, prin. — Fax 594-0805
Dessau MS — 900/6-8
12900 Dessau Rd 78754 — 512-594-2600
Diana Sustaita, prin. — Fax 594-2605
Westview MS — 800/6-8
1805 Scofield Ln 78727 — 512-594-2200
Ronald Gonzales, prin. — Fax 594-2205

Round Rock ISD
Supt. — See Round Rock
Canyon Vista MS — 1,000/6-8
8455 Spicewood Springs Rd 78759 — 512-464-8100
Lisa Napper, prin. — Fax 464-8210
Cedar Valley MS — 1,400/6-8
8139 Racine Trl 78717 — 512-428-2300
Jane Miller, prin. — Fax 428-2420
Deerpark MS — 1,100/6-8
8849 Anderson Mill Rd 78729 — 512-464-6600
Toni Hicks, prin. — Fax 464-6740
Grisham MS — 800/6-8
10805 School House Ln 78750 — 512-428-2650
Mary Brinkman, prin. — Fax 428-2790
McNeil HS — 2,600/9-12
5720 McNeil Dr 78729 — 512-464-6300
Cindy Doty, prin. — Fax 464-6550
Westwood HS — 2,500/9-12
12400 Mellow Meadow Dr 78750 — 512-464-4000
Rebecca Donald, prin. — Fax 464-4020

Academy of Oriental Medicine at Austin — Post-Sec.
2700 W Anderson Ln Ste 204 78757 — 512-454-1188
Allied Health Careers — Post-Sec.
5424 W Highway 290 Ste 105 78735 — 512-892-5210
A New Beginning School of Massage — Post-Sec.
2525 Wallingwood Dr # 1501 78746 — 512-306-0975
Austin Adventist Junior Academy — 100/K-10
301 W Anderson Ln 78752 — 512-459-8976
Fax 419-7868
Austin Business College — Post-Sec.
2101 S I H 35 Ste 300 78741 — 512-447-9415
Austin Christian Academy — 100/PK-12
2120 Shiloh Dr 78745 — 512-292-7848
Robert Walker, prin. — Fax 292-8889
Austin City Academy — 50/K-12
PO Box 92737 78709 — 512-288-4883
Stan Whitmore, prin. — Fax 857-0765
Austin Community College — Post-Sec.
5930 Middle Fiskville Rd 78752 — 512-223-7598
Austin Graduate School of Theology — Post-Sec.
1909 University Ave 78705 — 512-476-2772
Austin Presbyterian Theological Seminary — Post-Sec.
100 E 27th St 78705 — 512-472-6736
Austin Waldorf S — 400/K-12
8700 S View Rd 78737 — 512-288-5942
Joanne Andruscavage, admin. — Fax 301-8997
Baldwin Beauty School #5 — Post-Sec.
3005 S Lamar Blvd Ste 103 78704 — 512-441-6898
Baldwin Beauty School - North — Post-Sec.
8440 Burnet Rd 78758 — 512-458-4127
Brentwood Christian S — 700/K-12
11908 N Lamar Blvd 78753 — 512-835-5983
Marquita Moss, pres. — Fax 835-2184
Capitol City Careers — Post-Sec.
5424 W Highway 290 Ste 200 78735 — 512-892-2640
Capitol City Trade and Technical School — Post-Sec.
205 E Riverside Dr 78704 — 512-444-3257
Concordia Academy — 100/9-12
3407 Red River St 78705 — 512-248-2547
Mark Liebenow, prin. — Fax 469-0785

Concordia University Post-Sec.
3400 N I H 35 78705 512-486-2000
Culinary Academy of Austin Post-Sec.
6020 Dillard Cir Ste B 78752 512-451-5743
Diego HS 100/9-12
800 Herndon Ln 78704 512-804-1935
Pamela Jupe, prin. Fax 804-1937
Episcopal Theological Seminary of the SW Post-Sec.
PO Box 2247 78768 512-472-4133
Everest Institute Post-Sec.
9100 US Highway 290 E # 100 78754 512-928-1933
Hill Country Christian S of Austin 500/K-12
12124 Ranch Road 620 N 78750 512-331-7036
Amy Baker, dir. Fax 257-4190
Huston-Tillotson University Post-Sec.
900 Chicon St 78702 512-505-3000
Hyde Park Baptist S 800/K-12
3901 Speedway 78751 512-465-8333
Brian Littlefield, admin. Fax 371-1433
ITT Technical Institute Post-Sec.
6330 E Highway 290 Ste 150 78723 512-467-6800
Maranatha Academy 50/PK-12
8210 S 1st St 78748 512-282-4263
Katie Hart, admin. Fax 282-2426
Regents S of Austin 700/K-12
3230 Travis Country Cir 78735 512-899-8095
Roderick Gilbert, hdmstr. Fax 899-8623
St. Andrew's Episcopal S 300/9-12
5901 Southwest Pkwy 78735 512-452-5779
Lucy Nazro, hdmstr. Fax 299-9700
St. Edward's University Post-Sec.
3001 S Congress Ave 78704 512-448-8400
St. Michael's Academy 500/9-12
3000 Barton Creek Blvd 78735 512-328-2323
Sharon Scamardo, prin. Fax 328-2327
St. Stephen's Episcopal S 700/6-12
2900 Bunny Run 78746 512-327-1213
Robert Kirkpatrick, hdmstr. Fax 327-6771
Shoreline Christian S 200/PK-12
15201 Burnet Rd 78728 512-310-7358
Richard Tankersley, hdmstr. Fax 255-5955
Southern Careers Institute Post-Sec.
2301 S Congress Ave Ste 24A 78704 512-448-4795
Southwest Institute of Technology Post-Sec.
5424 W Highway 290 Ste 200 78735 512-892-2640
Texas College of Traditional Chinese Med Post-Sec.
4005 Manchaca Rd 78704 512-444-8082
Texas Culinary Academy Post-Sec.
11400 Burnet Rd Ste 2100 78758 512-837-2665
University of Texas at Austin Post-Sec.
0 the Univ of Texas 78712 512-471-3434

Avalon, Ellis
Avalon ISD 200/PK-12
PO Box 455 76623 972-627-3251
David Del Bosque, supt. Fax 627-3220
avalon.tx.schoolwebpages.com/education/
Avalon JSHS 200/PK-12
PO Box 455 76623 972-627-3251
Brenda Speer, prin. Fax 627-3220

Avery, Red River, Pop. 440
Avery ISD 400/PK-12
PO Box 97 75554 903-684-3460
Barry Bassett, supt. Fax 684-3294
avery.esc8.net/
Avery HS 100/9-12
PO Box 97 75554 903-684-3431
Robert Kelsoe, prin. Fax 684-3294
Avery MS 200/5-8
PO Box 97 75554 903-684-3079
Bill Giles, prin. Fax 684-3294

Avinger, Cass, Pop. 455
Avinger ISD 100/K-12
245 Conner 75630 903-562-1271
Douglas Carter, supt. Fax 562-1271
avinger.esc8.net/
Avinger JSHS 100/7-12
245 Conner 75630 903-562-1355
Kenny Abernathy, prin. Fax 562-1271

Avoca, Jones
Lueders-Avoca ISD
Supt. — See Lueders
Lueders-Avoca HS 50/9-12
8762 County Road 604 79503 325-773-2785
John Jensen, prin. Fax 773-3072

Axtell, McLennan
Axtell ISD 700/PK-12
308 Ottawa 76624 254-863-5301
Stanley Harris, supt. Fax 863-5651
www.axtellisd.net/
Axtell HS, 308 Ottawa 76624 200/9-12
Dale Monsey, prin. 254-863-5301
Axtell MS, 308 Ottawa 76624 100/6-8
Dale Monsey, prin. 254-863-5301

Azle, Tarrant, Pop. 10,350
Azle ISD 5,900/PK-12
300 Roe St 76020 817-444-3235
Dr. Edd Bigbee, supt. Fax 444-6866
www.azle.esc11.net
Azle HS 1,800/9-12
1200 Boyd Rd 76020 817-444-5555
Laura Bynum, prin. Fax 444-8884
Azle JHS 500/7-8
201 School St 76020 817-444-2564
Stacey Summerhill, prin. Fax 270-0880
Forte JHS 500/7-8
479 Sandy Beach Rd 76020 817-270-1133
David McClellan, prin. Fax 270-1157

Baird, Callahan, Pop. 1,680
Baird ISD 300/PK-12
PO Box 1147 79504 325-854-1400
Cliff Gardner, supt. Fax 854-2058
www.baird.esc14.net
Baird HS 100/9-12
PO Box 1147 79504 325-854-1400
Vick Orlando, prin. Fax 854-2808

Ballinger, Runnels, Pop. 4,019
Ballinger ISD 1,100/PK-12
PO Box 231 76821 325-365-3588
Scot Goen, supt. Fax 365-5920
ballinger.netxv.net/
Ballinger HS 300/9-12
PO Box 231 76821 325-365-3547
Ron Ledbetter, prin. Fax 365-5422
Ballinger JHS 200/6-8
PO Box 231 76821 325-365-3537
Mike Carter, prin. Fax 365-5420

Balmorhea, Reeves, Pop. 472
Balmorhea ISD 200/PK-12
PO Box 368 79718 432-375-2223
Mary Lou Carrasco, supt. Fax 375-2511
www.bisdbears.esc18.net
Balmorhea S 200/PK-12
PO Box 368 79718 432-375-2223
Teri Barragan, prin. Fax 375-2511

Bandera, Bandera, Pop. 1,123
Bandera ISD 2,600/PK-12
PO Box 727 78003 830-796-3313
Kevin Dyes Ed.D., supt. Fax 796-6238
www.banderaisd.net
Bandera HS 900/9-12
PO Box 727 78003 830-796-6254
Michael Nesbit, prin. Fax 796-6251
Bandera MS 600/6-8
PO Box 727 78003 830-796-6270
Gary Bitzkie, prin. Fax 796-6277

Bangs, Brown, Pop. 1,623
Bangs ISD 1,100/PK-12
PO Box 969 76823 325-752-6612
James Hartman, supt. Fax 752-6253
www.bangsisd.net
Bangs HS 300/9-12
PO Box 969 76823 325-752-6822
Dan Vera, prin. Fax 752-7028
Bangs MS 300/6-8
PO Box 969 76823 325-752-6088
Gary Hounshell, prin. Fax 752-6253

Banquete, Nueces
Banquete ISD 900/PK-12
PO Box 369 78339 361-387-2551
Jim Rumage, supt. Fax 387-7188
www.banqueteisd.esc2.net/
Banquete HS 300/9-12
PO Box 369 78339 361-387-8588
Kendall Todd, prin. Fax 767-6504
Banquete JHS 200/6-8
PO Box 369 78339 361-387-6504
Eusebio Torres, prin. Fax 387-7051

Barksdale, Edwards
Nueces Canyon Consolidated ISD 300/K-12
PO Box 118 78828 830-234-3514
Russ Perry, supt. Fax 234-3435
www.nccisd.net/
Nueces Canyon JSHS 200/7-12
PO Box 118 78828 830-234-3524
Scotty Carman, prin. Fax 234-4129

Bartlett, Bell, Pop. 1,701
Bartlett ISD 400/PK-12
PO Box 170 76511 254-527-4247
Michael Mayfield, supt. Fax 527-3340
www.bartlett.txed.net/
Bartlett HS 200/7-12
PO Box 170 76511 254-527-3351
Brenda Jirasek, prin. Fax 527-3515

Bastrop, Bastrop, Pop. 7,297
Bastrop ISD 7,700/PK-12
906 Farm St 78602 512-321-2292
Roderick Emanuel, supt. Fax 321-7469
www.bastrop.isd.tenet.edu
Bastrop HS 2,100/9-12
1614 Chambers St 78602 512-321-1151
Mike Benedict, prin. Fax 321-7502
Bastrop MS 600/7-8
709 Old Austin Hwy 78602 512-321-3911
Dr. Laurie Bauer, prin. Fax 321-1557
Other Schools – See Cedar Creek

Bay City, Matagorda, Pop. 18,323
Bay City ISD 4,200/PK-12
520 7th St 77414 979-245-5766
Richard Johnson, supt. Fax 245-3175
www.bcblackcats.net
Bay City HS 1,300/9-12
400 7th St 77414 979-245-5771
Walt Wendtland, prin. Fax 245-1220
Bay City JHS 700/7-8
1507 Sycamore Ave 77414 979-245-6345
Brandon Hood, prin. Fax 245-1419

Baytown, Harris, Pop. 68,371
Goose Creek ISD 19,300/PK-12
PO Box 30 77522 281-420-4800
Dr. Barbara Sultis, supt. Fax 420-4815
www.gccisd.net/
Baytown JHS 800/6-8
PO Box 30 77522 281-420-4560
Steve Koester, prin. Fax 420-4908
Cedar Bayou JHS 1,100/6-8
PO Box 30 77522 281-420-4570
Barbara Ardoin, prin. Fax 420-4909
Gentry JHS 800/6-8
PO Box 30 77522 281-420-4590
Tammy Edwards, prin. Fax 420-4909
Lee HS 2,500/9-12
PO Box 30 77522 281-420-4535
Bruce Davis, prin. Fax 420-4548
Mann JHS 1,000/6-8
PO Box 30 77522 281-420-4585
Jimmy Twardowski, prin. Fax 420-4664
Sterling HS 2,600/9-12
PO Box 30 77522 281-420-4500
Trey Kraemer, prin. Fax 420-4974
Stuart Career Center Vo/Tech
PO Box 30 77522 281-420-4550
Kevin Parker, dir. Fax 420-4553
School/Community Guidance Center Adult
PO Box 30 77522 281-420-4630
Michelle Verdun, prin. Fax 420-4629
Other Schools – See Highlands

Baytown Christian Academy 200/5-12
5555 N Main St 77521 281-421-4150
Dr. Carolyn Brock, hdmstr. Fax 421-4038
Lee College Post-Sec.
PO Box 818 77522 281-427-5611
San Jacinto Christian Academy 200/PK-12
301 Ilfrey St 77520 281-424-9525
Steve Weatherly, admin. Fax 424-1600

Beaumont, Jefferson, Pop. 111,799
Beaumont ISD 19,600/PK-12
3395 Harrison Ave 77706 409-899-9972
Dr. Carrol Thomas, supt. Fax 923-1025
www.beaumont.k12.tx.us
Austin MS 700/6-8
3410 Austin St 77706 409-892-0193
Dr. Aaron Covington, prin. Fax 923-5239
Central HS 1,400/9-12
88 Jaguar Dr 77702 409-981-7100
Patricia Lambert, prin. Fax 835-6233
King MS 500/6-8
1400 Avenue A 77701 409-832-4431
David Harris, prin. Fax 785-4557
Marshall MS 800/6-8
6455 Gladys Ave 77706 409-866-4174
Shannon Pier, prin. Fax 861-5211
Odom Academy 800/6-8
2550 W Virginia St 77705 409-842-3217
Tillie Hickman, prin. Fax 842-8604
Ozen HS 1,700/9-12
3443 Fannett Rd 77705 409-981-7500
James Broussard, prin. Fax 842-8501
Smith MS 300/6-8
4415 Concord Rd 77703 409-892-3811
Carol Batiste, prin. Fax 923-5365
South Park MS 500/6-8
4500 Highland Ave 77705 409-838-3941
Odis Norris, prin. Fax 785-4314
Taylor Career Center Vo/Tech
2330 North St 77702 409-835-0153
Thom Campbell-Amons, prin. Fax 785-4016
Vincent MS 900/6-8
350 Eldridge Dr 77707 409-866-1491
Randall Maxwell, prin. Fax 861-5110
West Brook HS 2,300/9-12
8750 Phelan Blvd 77706 409-981-7300
William Daniels, prin. Fax 861-1645

Hamshire-Fannett ISD
Supt. — See Hamshire
Hamshire-Fannett MS 300/7-8
11375 Dugat Rd 77705 409-794-2361
Mark Martin, prin. Fax 794-3042

Baptist Hospital of Southeast Texas Post-Sec.
PO Box 1591 77704 409-654-5351
Cathedral Christian HS 200/7-12
8200 Highway 105 77713 409-924-0500
Jon Cregor, prin. Fax 898-1506
Dolphin Technical Institute Post-Sec.
4835 Concord Rd 77703 409-892-0677
Lamar Institute of Technology Post-Sec.
855 E Lavaca St 77705 409-880-8321
Lamar University Post-Sec.
PO Box 10009 77710 409-880-7011
Monsignor Kelly Catholic HS 500/9-12
5950 Kelly Dr 77707 409-866-2351
Roger Bemis, prin. Fax 866-0917
St. Elizabeth Hospital Post-Sec.
2830 Calder St 77702 409-892-7171
Texas Careers Post-Sec.
194 Gateway St 77701 409-833-2722

Beckville, Panola, Pop. 760
Beckville ISD 500/PK-12
PO Box 37 75631 903-678-3311
Devin Tate, supt. Fax 678-2157
www.beckvilleisd.net/
Beckville JSHS 200/6-12
PO Box 37 75631 903-678-3591
Ted Reeves, prin. Fax 678-3645

Bedford, Tarrant, Pop. 48,390
Hurst-Euless-Bedford ISD 19,400/PK-12
1849 Central Dr Ste A 76022 817-283-4461
Gene Buinger Ed.D., supt. Fax 354-3311
www.hebisd.edu
Bedford JHS 900/7-9
325 Carolyn Dr 76021 817-788-3101
Pamela Wellman, prin. Fax 788-3105
Harwood JHS 900/7-9
3000 Martin Dr 76021 817-354-3360
Vicki Thurman, prin. Fax 354-3369
Technical Education Center Vo/Tech
1849 Central Dr 76022 817-354-3542
Lisa Karr, prin. Fax 354-3546
Other Schools – See Euless, Hurst

St. Vincent's Cathedral S 200/PK-10
1300 Forest Ridge Dr 76022 817-354-7979
Sharon Mayes, hdmstr. Fax 354-5073

Beeville, Bee, Pop. 13,560
Beeville ISD 3,700/PK-12
2400 N Saint Marys St 78102 361-358-7111
Dr. John Hardwick, supt. Fax 358-7837
www.beevilleisd.net/
Jones HS 1,100/9-12
1902 N Adams St 78102 361-362-6000
Roger McAdoo, prin. Fax 362-6016
Moreno JHS 600/7-8
301 N Minnesota St 78102 361-358-6262
Jean Blankenship, prin. Fax 362-6092

Coastal Bend College Post-Sec.
3800 Charco Rd 78102 361-358-2838

Bellaire, Harris, Pop. 17,206
Houston ISD
Supt. — See Houston
Bellaire HS 3,400/9-12
5100 Maple St 77401 713-295-3704
Tim Salem, prin. Fax 295-3763
Pin Oak MS 1,200/6-8
4601 Glenmont St 77401 713-295-6500
Michael McDonough, prin. Fax 295-6511

Episcopal HS 600/9-12
4650 Bissonnet St 77401 713-512-3400
Edward Becker, hdmstr. Fax 512-3603

Bellevue, Clay, Pop. 397
Bellevue ISD 200/K-12
PO Box 38 76228 940-928-2104
Dean Gilstrap, supt. Fax 928-2583
www.esc9.net/bellevue/
Bellevue JSHS 100/7-12
PO Box 38 76228 940-928-2104
Sean McBeath, prin. Fax 928-2583

Bells, Grayson, Pop. 1,270
Bells ISD 800/PK-12
PO Box 7 75414 903-965-7721
Joe D. Moore, supt. Fax 965-7036
bells.ednet10.net/

Bells HS 200/9-12
PO Box 7 75414 903-965-7315
Will Steger, prin. Fax 965-5205
Prichard JHS 100/7-8
PO Box 7 75414 903-965-4835
Sara Baker, prin. Fax 965-7036

Bellville, Austin, Pop. 4,303
Bellville ISD 2,200/PK-12
518 S Mathews St 77418 979-865-3133
John Conley, supt. Fax 865-8591
www.bellville.k12.tx.us
Bellville HS 700/9-12
518 S Mathews St 77418 979-865-3681
Jim Batson, prin. Fax 865-7080
Bellville JHS 500/6-8
518 S Mathews St 77418 979-865-5966
Laura Bailey, prin. Fax 865-7060

Faith Academy 100/PK-12
12177 Highway 36 77418 979-865-1811
Merlene Byler, admin. Fax 865-2454

Belton, Bell, Pop. 15,530
Belton ISD 5,400/PK-12
PO Box 269 76513 254-215-2000
Dr. Vivian Baker, supt. Fax 215-2001
www.bisd.net
Belton HS 2,000/9-12
600 Lake Rd 76513 254-215-2200
Kathy Cook, prin. Fax 215-2201
Belton MS 300/6-8
1704 Sparta Rd 76513 254-215-2800
Joe Peterka, prin. Fax 215-2801
Career Studies Center Vo/Tech
600 Lake Rd 76513 254-215-2260
Ken Von Gonten, prin. Fax 215-2261
Other Schools – See Temple

University of Mary Hardin-Baylor Post-Sec.
UMHB Station Box 8001 76513 254-295-8642

Benavides, Duval, Pop. 1,591
Benavides ISD 500/PK-12
PO Box P 78341 361-256-3000
Dr. Ignacio Salinas, supt. Fax 256-3005
www.benavidesisd.net/
Benavides HS 200/7-12
PO Box P 78341 361-256-3040
Olga Carrillo, prin. Fax 256-3043

Ben Bolt, Jim Wells
Ben Bolt-Palito Blanco ISD 600/PK-12
PO Box 547 78342 361-664-9904
Alberto Byington, supt. Fax 668-0446
www.bbisd.esc2.net
Ben Bolt MS 200/4-8
PO Box 547 78342 361-664-9568
Prichard Ortiz, prin. Fax 664-5235
Ben Bolt-Palito Blanco HS 200/9-12
PO Box 547 78342 361-664-9822
David Delgado, prin. Fax 664-5481

Benbrook, Tarrant, Pop. 21,922
Fort Worth ISD
Supt. — See Fort Worth
Leonard MS 900/7-8
8900 Chapin Rd 76116 817-560-5630
Richard Pritchett, prin. Fax 560-5639
Western Hills HS 1,600/9-12
3600 Boston Ave 76116 817-560-5600
Donna Jeffries, prin. Fax 560-5644

Benjamin, Knox, Pop. 239
Benjamin ISD 100/K-12
PO Box 166 79505 940-459-2231
Olivia Gloria, supt. Fax 459-2007
www.esc9.net/benjamin
Benjamin S 100/K-12
PO Box 166 79505 940-459-2231
Laura McDonald, prin. Fax 459-2007

Ben Wheeler, Van Zandt
Martins Mill ISD 500/PK-12
301 FM 1861 75754 903-479-3872
Todd Williams, supt. Fax 479-3711
www.martinsmill.esc7.net
Martins Mill HS 200/7-12
301 FM 1861 75754 903-479-3234
Todd Schneider, prin. Fax 479-3486

Big Lake, Reagan, Pop. 2,591
Reagan County ISD 800/PK-12
1111 E 12th St 76932 325-884-3705
Marshall Harrison, supt. Fax 884-3021
rcisd.esc18.net
Reagan County HS 300/9-12
1111 E 12th St 76932 325-884-3714
Ralph Traynham, prin. Fax 884-5759
Reagan County MS 200/6-8
500 N Pennsylvania Ave 76932 325-884-3728
Glenn Byrd, prin. Fax 884-2327

Big Sandy, Upshur, Pop. 1,349
Big Sandy ISD 500/PK-12
PO Box 598 75755 903-636-5222
Tonya Knowlton, supt. Fax 636-5111
www.bigsandyisd.org
Big Sandy JSHS 200/6-12
PO Box 598 75755 903-636-5287
Roger Dees, prin. Fax 636-5111

Harmony ISD 1,000/PK-12
9788 State Highway 154 W 75755 903-725-5492
Ray Miller, supt. Fax 725-6737
www.harmonyeagles.com
Harmony HS 300/9-12
9788 State Highway 154 W 75755 903-725-5495
Jed Whitaker, prin. Fax 725-7079
Harmony JHS 200/6-8
9788 State Highway 154 W 75755 903-725-5485
Perry Cowan, prin. Fax 725-7270

Big Spring, Howard, Pop. 24,253
Big Spring ISD 3,800/K-12
708 E 11th Pl 79720 432-264-3600
Michael Downes, supt. Fax 264-3646
bsisd.esc18.net/
Big Spring HS 1,100/9-12
708 E 11th Pl 79720 432-264-3641
Mike Ritchey, prin. Fax 264-4133
Big Spring JHS 600/7-8
708 E 11th Pl 79720 432-264-4135
Coby Norman, prin. Fax 264-3646

Howard College Post-Sec.
3200 Ave C 79720 432-264-3700
Howard College Post-Sec.
1001 N Birdwell Ln 79720 432-264-5000
Scenic Mountain Medical Center Post-Sec.
1601 W 11th Pl 79720 432-263-1211

Bishop, Nueces, Pop. 3,204
Bishop Consolidated ISD 1,200/PK-12
719 E 6th St 78343 361-584-3591
Christina Gutierrez, supt. Fax 584-3593
www.bishopcisd.esc2.net/
Bishop HS 300/9-12
717 E 6th St 78343 361-584-2547
Ray Garza, prin. Fax 584-2549
Luehrs JHS 200/7-8
701 E 6th St 78343 361-584-3576
Dan True, prin. Fax 584-3576

Blackwell, Nolan, Pop. 348
Blackwell Consolidated ISD 100/PK-12
PO Box 505 79506 325-282-2311
James Bible, supt. Fax 282-2027
www.blackwell.esc14.net/
Blackwell S 100/PK-12
PO Box 505 79506 325-282-2311
Gary Smith, prin. Fax 282-2027

Blanco, Blanco, Pop. 1,609
Blanco ISD 1,000/PK-12
814 11th St 78606 830-833-4414
Lynn Boyd, supt. Fax 833-2019
www.blancoisd.org/
Blanco HS 300/9-12
814 11th St 78606 830-833-4337
Tommy Bibb, prin. Fax 833-5028
Blanco MS 200/6-8
814 11th St 78606 830-833-5570
Dr. Buck Ford, prin. Fax 833-2507

Blanket, Brown, Pop. 404
Blanket ISD 200/K-12
901 Avenue H 76432 325-748-5311
Kevy Allred, supt. Fax 748-3391
blanket.netxv.net/
Blanket HS 100/9-12
901 Avenue H 76432 325-748-3341
Monty Jones, prin. Fax 748-3391

Bloomburg, Cass, Pop. 371
Bloomburg ISD 300/K-12
PO Box 156 75556 903-728-5216
Jerry Hendrick, supt. Fax 728-5399
bloomburg.esc8.net/
Bloomburg JSHS 100/7-12
PO Box 156 75556 903-728-5216
Billy Frost, prin. Fax 728-5399

Blooming Grove, Navarro, Pop. 918
Blooming Grove ISD 900/PK-12
PO Box 258 76626 903-695-2541
Michael Baldree, supt. Fax 695-2594
www.bgisd.org
Blooming Grove HS 300/9-12
PO Box 258 76626 903-695-2536
Randy O'Brien, prin. Fax 695-2594
Blooming Grove JHS 200/6-8
PO Box 258 76626 903-695-4201
Doyle Bell, prin. Fax 695-4601

Bloomington, Victoria, Pop. 1,888
Bloomington ISD 1,000/PK-12
PO Box 158 77951 361-897-1652
Dr. Suzanne Wesson, supt. Fax 897-1214
www.bisd-tx.org/
Bloomington HS 200/9-12
PO Box 158 77951 361-897-1551
Todd Deaver, prin. Fax 897-1888
Bloomington MS 200/7-8
PO Box 158 77951 361-897-2260
Todd Deaver, prin. Fax 897-3822

Blue Ridge, Collin, Pop. 939
Blue Ridge ISD 600/PK-12
10688 County Road 504 75424 972-752-5554
Jim Shurtleff, supt. Fax 752-9084
brisd.com
Blue Ridge HS 200/9-12
11020 County Road 504 75424 972-752-5707
Robin Ross, prin. Fax 752-5361
Blue Ridge S 200/5-8
318 School St 75424 972-752-4243
Andrew Seigrist, prin. Fax 752-5363

Blum, Hill, Pop. 443
Blum ISD 300/PK-12
PO Box 520 76627 254-874-5231
Jerry Kirby, supt. Fax 874-5233
www.blumisd.net
Blum JSHS 200/6-12
PO Box 520 76627 254-874-5231
Nina Wiggins, prin. Fax 874-5233

Boerne, Kendall, Pop. 8,054
Boerne ISD 5,600/PK-12
123 Johns Rd 78006 830-357-2000
Dr. John Kelly, supt. Fax 357-2009
www.boerne-isd.net
Boerne HS 1,300/10-12
1 Greyhound Ln 78006 830-357-2200
Betty Butler, prin. Fax 357-2299
Boerne MS - North 600/7-9
240 Johns Rd 78006 830-357-3100
Vicki Layer, prin. Fax 357-3199
Boerne MS - South 800/7-9
10 Cascade Caverns Rd 78015 830-357-3300
Dr. Janey Hunt, prin. Fax 357-3399

Vanguard Christian Institute 100/PK-12
43360 IH 10 W 78006 830-537-5244
Walter Tracy, prin. Fax 537-5785

Bogata, Red River, Pop. 1,314
Rivercrest ISD 700/PK-12
4100 US Highway 271 S 75417 903-632-5203
Fred Wade, supt. Fax 632-4691
www.rivercrestisd.net
Rivercrest HS 200/9-12
4220 US Highway 271 S 75417 903-632-5204
Keith Brown, prin.
Rivercrest JHS 100/6-8
4100 US Highway 271 S 75417 903-632-0878
Kelly Stansell, prin. Fax 632-4691

Boling, Wharton, Pop. 1,119
Boling ISD 900/PK-12
PO Box 160 77420 979-657-2770
Charles Butcher, supt. Fax 657-3265
www.bolingisd.net
Boling HS 300/9-12
PO Box 119 77420 979-657-2816
Keith Jedlicka, prin. Fax 657-2026
Iago JHS 200/6-8
PO Box 89 77420 979-657-2826
Bryan Blanar, prin. Fax 657-2828

Bonham, Fannin, Pop. 10,556
Bonham ISD 1,900/K-12
PO Box 490 75418 903-583-5526
Dr. Linda Gist, supt. Fax 583-8463
www.bonhamisd.org/
Bonham HS 600/9-12
1002 War Path St 75418 903-583-5567
T. Glynn Walker, prin. Fax 583-5560
Rather JHS 300/7-8
1200 N Main St 75418 903-583-7474
Karol Romans, prin. Fax 583-3713

Booker, Lipscomb, Pop. 1,330
Booker ISD 400/PK-12
PO Box 288 79005 806-658-4501
Mike Lee, supt. Fax 658-4503
Booker JSHS, PO Box 288 79005 200/5-12
Pablo De Santiago, prin. 806-658-4521

Borger, Hutchinson, Pop. 13,305
Borger ISD 2,100/PK-12
200 E 9th St 79007 806-273-6481
Clifton Stephens, supt. Fax 273-1066
www.borgerisd.net
Borger HS 800/9-12
600 W 1st St 79007 806-273-1029
Bob Callaghan, prin. Fax 273-1036
Borger MS 600/6-8
1321 S Florida St 79007 806-273-1037
Matt Ammerman, prin. Fax 273-1069

Frank Phillips College Post-Sec.
PO Box 5118 79008 806-274-5311

Bovina, Parmer, Pop. 1,804
Bovina ISD 500/PK-12
PO Box 70 79009 806-251-1336
Bill Bizzell, supt. Fax 251-1578
www.esc16.net/bovinaisd/
Bovina HS 100/9-12
PO Box 70 79009 806-251-1317
Dale Fullerton, prin. Fax 251-1002
Bovina JHS 100/6-8
PO Box 70 79009 806-251-1377
David Newhouse, prin. Fax 251-1578

Bowie, Montague, Pop. 5,543
Bowie ISD 1,700/PK-12
PO Box 1168 76230 940-872-1151
Monte Barnes, supt. Fax 872-5979
www.esc9.net/bowie/
Bowie HS 500/9-12
800 N Mill St 76230 940-872-1154
Jeff Jackson, prin. Fax 872-1299
Bowie JHS 300/6-8
501 E Tarrant St 76230 940-872-1152
Tom McEwen, prin. Fax 872-8921

Gold-Burg ISD 100/K-12
468 Prater Rd 76230 940-872-3562
Kenny Miller, supt. Fax 872-5933
www.esc9.net/gold-burg/
Gold-Burg JSHS 100/6-12
468 Prater Rd 76230 940-872-3562
Louis Clayton, prin. Fax 872-5933

Boyd, Wise, Pop. 1,300
Boyd ISD 1,000/PK-12
PO Box 92308 76023 940-433-2327
Charlie Uselton, supt. Fax 433-9569
www.boydisd.net
Boyd HS 300/9-12
PO Box 92308 76023 940-433-2327
Jack Williams, prin. Fax 433-9593
Boyd MS 200/7-8
PO Box 92308 76023 940-433-2327
Shawn Bryans, prin. Fax 433-9565

Boys Ranch, Oldham
Boys Ranch ISD 300/K-12
PO Box 219 79010 806-534-2221
Nena Mankin, supt. Fax 534-2384
www.boysranchisd.org/
Blakemore MS 100/6-8
PO Box 219 79010 806-534-2361
Mark Reasor, prin. Fax 534-0041
Boys Ranch HS 200/9-12
PO Box 219 79010 806-534-0032
Jeff Strickland, prin. Fax 534-0033

Brackettville, Kinney, Pop. 1,830
Brackett ISD 600/PK-12
PO Box 586 78832 830-563-2491
Paula Renken, supt. Fax 563-9264
www.brackett.k12.tx.us
Brackett HS 200/9-12
PO Box 586 78832 830-563-2491
Frank Taylor, prin. Fax 563-3213
Brackett JHS 100/7-8
PO Box 586 78832 830-563-2491
Frank Taylor, prin. Fax 563-9559

Brady, McCulloch, Pop. 5,345
Brady ISD 1,400/PK-12
100 W Main St 76825 325-597-2301
Steven McCarn, supt. Fax 597-3984
www.bradyisd.org
Brady HS 400/9-12
100 W Main St 76825 325-597-2491
Hector Martinez, prin. Fax 597-0182
Brady MS 300/6-8
100 W Main St 76825 325-597-8110
Eric Bierman, prin. Fax 597-4166

Brazoria, Brazoria, Pop. 2,897
Columbia-Brazoria ISD
Supt. — See West Columbia
West Brazos JHS 500/7-8
20022 N Highway 36 77422 979-799-1730
Chuck Rylander, prin. Fax 798-8000

Breckenridge, Stephens, Pop. 5,649
Breckenridge ISD 1,600/PK-12
PO Box 1738 76424 254-559-2278
Connie Martin, supt. Fax 559-2353
www.breckenridge.esc14.net
Breckenridge HS 500/9-12
500 W Lindsey St 76424 254-559-2231
Bryan Dieterich, prin. Fax 559-7485
Breckenridge JHS 200/7-8
502 W Lindsey St 76424 254-559-6581
Brent Evans, prin. Fax 559-1082

Bremond, Robertson, Pop. 896
Bremond ISD 500/PK-12
PO Box 190 76629 254-746-7145
Harold Schroeder, supt. Fax 746-7726
www.bremondisd.net
Bremond HS 100/9-12
PO Box 190 76629 254-746-7145
Harold Schroeder, prin. Fax 746-7726
Bremond MS 100/6-8
PO Box 190 76629 254-746-7145
Donna Thompson, prin. Fax 746-7726

Brenham, Washington, Pop. 14,161
Brenham ISD 4,900/PK-12
PO Box 1147 77834 979-277-6500
David Yeager, supt. Fax 277-6515
www.brenhamisd.net
Brenham HS 1,600/9-12
525 A H Ehrig Dr 77833 979-277-6570
John Dalchau, prin. Fax 277-6544
Brenham JHS 700/7-8
1200 Carlee Dr 77833 979-277-6400
Artis Edwards, prin. Fax 277-6407

Blinn College Post-Sec.
902 College Ave 77833 979-830-4000
Brenham Christian Academy 100/4-12
2111 S Blue Bell Rd 77833 979-830-8480
Diane Keller, hdmstr. Fax 830-1687

Bridge City, Orange, Pop. 8,800
Bridge City ISD 2,600/PK-12
1031 W Round Bunch Rd 77611 409-735-1602
Dr. Darrell Myers, supt. Fax 735-1694
www.esc5.net/bcisd
Bridge City HS 800/9-12
2690 Texas Ave 77611 409-735-1501
Gina Mannino, prin. Fax 735-1519
Bridge City MS 600/6-8
300 Bower Dr 77611 409-735-1513
Randy Godsy, prin. Fax 735-1517

Bridgeport, Wise, Pop. 5,659
Bridgeport ISD 2,200/PK-12
2107 15th St 76426 940-683-5124
Richard O'Hara, supt. Fax 683-4268
www.bridgeportisd.net
Bridgeport HS 700/9-12
1 Maroon Dr 76426 940-683-4064
Tom Talley, prin. Fax 683-4014
Bridgeport MS 500/6-8
702 17th St 76426 940-683-2273
Robert Haynes, prin. Fax 683-5812

Briscoe, Wheeler
Fort Elliott Consolidated ISD 200/PK-12
PO Box 138 79011 806-375-2454
Carl Baker, supt. Fax 375-2327
Ft. Elliott S 200/PK-12
PO Box 138 79011 806-375-2454
Sonya Holder, prin. Fax 375-2327

Broaddus, San Augustine, Pop. 187
Broaddus ISD 500/PK-12
PO Box 58 75929 936-872-3041
Dr. Jerry Meador, supt. Fax 872-3699
www.broaddus.esc7.net
Broaddus JSHS 200/7-12
PO Box 58 75929 936-872-3610
Shane McGown, prin. Fax 872-9020

Brock, Parker
Brock ISD 700/K-12
100 Grindstone Rd 76087 817-594-7642
Richard Tedder, supt. Fax 599-3246
www.brockisd.net
Brock HS 200/9-12
100 Grindstone Rd 76087 817-594-3492
Scott Drillette, prin. Fax 594-2509
Brock MS 200/6-8
100 Grindstone Rd 76087 817-594-3195
Dee Mills, prin. Fax 594-3191

Bronte, Coke, Pop. 981
Bronte ISD 300/PK-12
PO Box 670 76933 325-473-2511
Alan Richey, supt. Fax 473-2313
bronte.netxv.net/
Bronte JSHS 100/7-12
PO Box 670 76933 325-473-2521
Michael Bohensky, prin. Fax 473-2313

Brookeland, Sabine
Brookeland ISD 300/PK-12
RR 2 Box 18 75931 409-698-2677
Lana Comeaux, supt. Fax 698-2533
www.esc05.k12.tx.us/brookeland/
Brookeland JSHS 100/6-12
RR 2 Box 18 75931 409-698-2413
Kevin McCugh, prin. Fax 698-2891

Brookesmith, Brown
Brookesmith ISD 200/PK-12
PO Box 706 76827 325-643-3023
Tom Hall, supt. Fax 643-3378
brookesmith.netxv.net/
Brookesmith HS 100/9-12
PO Box 706 76827 325-646-3791
Bryan Swartz, prin. Fax 646-3378

Brookshire, Waller, Pop. 3,601
Royal ISD 1,700/PK-12
2520 Durkin Rd 77423 281-934-2248
Walter Fenn, supt. Fax 934-2846
www.royal.isd.esc4.net
Royal HS 400/9-12
2520 Durkin Rd 77423 281-934-2215
Nathaniel Richardson, prin. Fax 934-2866
Royal MS 400/6-8
2500 Durkin Rd 77423 281-934-2241
Martin Drayton, prin. Fax 934-2329

Brownfield, Terry, Pop. 9,173
Brownfield ISD 1,900/PK-12
601 E Tahoka Rd 79316 806-637-2591
Jerry Jones, supt. Fax 637-9208
www.brownfieldisd.net/
Brownfield HS 600/9-12
701 Cub Dr 79316 806-637-4523
Philip Timmons, prin. Fax 637-3801
Brownfield MS 400/6-8
1001 E Broadway St 79316 806-637-7521
Jerry Lawrence, prin. Fax 637-2919

Brownsboro, Henderson, Pop. 856
Brownsboro ISD 2,800/PK-12
PO Box 465 75756 903-852-3701
Elton Caldwell, supt. Fax 852-3957
www.brownsboro.k12.tx.us
Brownsboro HS 800/9-12
PO Box 465 75756 903-852-2321
Doug Williams, prin. Fax 852-5195
Brownsboro JHS 400/7-8
PO Box 465 75756 903-852-6931
Yolanda Larkin, prin. Fax 852-5238

Brownsville, Cameron, Pop. 167,493
Brownsville ISD 46,100/PK-12
1900 Price Rd 78521 956-548-8000
Hector Gonzales, supt. Fax 548-8019
www.bisd.us/
Besteiro MS 1,100/6-8
6280 Southmost Rd 78521 956-544-3900
Alma Cardenas-Rubio, prin. Fax 544-3927
Cummings MS 1,000/6-8
1800 Cummings Pl 78520 956-548-8630
Dora Sauceda, prin. Fax 548-8218
Faulk MS 1,000/6-8
2000 Roosevelt St 78521 956-548-8500
Christian Caldarera, prin. Fax 982-2894
Garcia MS 1,100/6-8
5701 FM 802 78521 956-832-6300
Dr. Oscar Cantu, prin. Fax 832-6304
Hanna HS 2,500/9-12
2615 E Price Rd 78521 956-548-7600
Yolanda Kruger, prin. Fax 548-7603
Lopez HS 2,000/9-12
3205 S Dakota Ave 78521 956-982-7400
Dawn Hall, prin. Fax 982-7499
Lucio MS 1,100/6-8
300 N Vermillion Ave 78521 956-831-4550
Rose Longoria, prin. Fax 838-2298
Oliveira MS 1,300/6-8
444 Land O Lakes Dr 78521 956-548-8530
Robert Gonzalez, prin. Fax 544-3968
Pace HS 2,400/9-12
314 W Los Ebanos Blvd 78520 956-548-7700
Jill Williams, prin. Fax 548-7710
Perkins MS 900/6-8
4750 Austin Rd 78521 956-831-8770
Victor Caballero, prin. Fax 831-8789
Porter HS 2,100/9-12
3500 International Blvd 78521 956-548-7800
Alonzo Barbosa, prin. Fax 982-2892
Rivera HS 2,500/9-12
6955 FM 802 78521 956-831-8700
Mary Tolman, prin. Fax 831-8705
Stell MS 1,300/6-8
1105 E Los Ebanos Blvd 78520 956-548-8560
Acacia Ameel, prin. Fax 548-8666
Stillman MS 6-8
2977 W Tandy Rd 78520 956-698-1000
Maricela Zarate, prin. Fax 350-3231
Vela MS 1,000/6-8
4905 Paredes Line Rd 78526 956-548-7770
Sylvia Senteno, prin. Fax 548-7780

Career Centers of Texas Post-Sec.
1900 N Expressway 78521 956-547-8200
First Baptist S 300/PK-12
1600 Boca Chica Blvd 78520 956-542-4854
Deborah Batsell, prin. Fax 542-6188
Guadalupe Regional MS 100/6-8
1214 Lincoln St 78521 956-504-5568
Cathy Thomas, prin. Fax 504-9393
Livingway Christian S 300/PK-12
PO Box 3731 78523 956-548-2223
Anne M. Moore, prin. Fax 548-1970
St. Joseph Academy 800/7-12
101 Saint Joseph Dr 78520 956-542-3581
Lucy Williams, prin. Fax 542-4748
South Texas Vocational-Technical Inst. Post-Sec.
2144 Central Blvd 78520 956-554-3515
Texas Southmost College Post-Sec.
80 Fort Brown St 78520 956-544-3879
University of Texas at Brownsville Post-Sec.
80 Fort Brown St 78520 956-544-8200
Valley Christian HS 100/9-12
PO Box 4220 78523 956-542-5222
Paul Hanson, prin. Fax 544-0038

Brownwood, Brown, Pop. 19,566
Brownwood ISD 3,500/PK-12
PO Box 730 76804 325-643-5644
Sue Jones, supt. Fax 643-5640
www.brownwoodisd.com
Brownwood HS 1,000/9-12
2100 Slayden St 76801 325-646-9549
Bill Faircloth, prin. Fax 643-1965
Brownwood MS 500/7-8
PO Box 1286 76804 325-646-9545
Bryan Allen, prin. Fax 646-3785

Central Texas Commercial College Post-Sec.
PO Box 1324 76804 325-646-0521
Howard Payne University Post-Sec.
1000 Fisk Ave 76801 325-646-2502

Bruni, Webb
Webb Consolidated ISD 300/PK-12
PO Box 206 78344 361-747-5415
Dr. David Jones, supt. Fax 747-5433
www.webb.esc1.net/
Bruni HS 100/9-12
PO Box 206 78344 361-747-5415
Steven Young, prin. Fax 747-5301
Bruni MS 100/6-8
PO Box 206 78344 361-747-5415
Humberto Javier Soliz, prin. Fax 747-5298

Bryan, Brazos, Pop. 66,306
Bryan ISD 14,000/PK-12
101 N Texas Ave 77803 979-209-1000
Michael Cargill, supt. Fax 209-1050
www.bryanisd.org
Austin MS 900/6-8
801 S Ennis St 77803 979-209-6700
Patti Moore, prin. Fax 209-6741
Bryan HS 3,400/9-12
3450 Campus Dr 77802 979-209-2400
Carol Cune, prin. Fax 209-2402
Long MS 900/6-8
1106 N Harvey Mitchell Pkwy 77803 979-209-6500
Diana Werner, prin. Fax 209-6566
Oliver HS for Human Sciences 9-12
1305 Memorial Dr 77802 979-209-2800
Judy Hughson, dean Fax 209-2809
Rayburn MS 1,200/6-8
1048 N Earl Rudder Fwy 77802 979-209-6600
Paul Hord, prin. Fax 209-6611
Adult Learning Center Adult
1700 Palasota Dr 77803 979-209-7040
Mary Blackburn, dir. Fax 209-7041

Allen Academy 300/PK-12
3201 Boonville Rd 77802 979-776-0731
Bob Meyer, prin. Fax 774-7769
Blinn College Post-Sec.
PO Box 6030 77805 979-821-0200
Brazos Christian S 200/PK-12
3000 W Villa Maria Rd 77807 979-823-1000
Robert Armstrong, hdmstr. Fax 823-1774
Charlie & Sue's School of Hair Design Post-Sec.
1711 Briarcrest Dr 77802 979-776-4375
St. Joseph Catholic S 6-12
600 S Coulter Dr 77803 979-822-6641
Mark Gherardi, prin. Fax 779-2810
St. Michael's Academy 200/PK-12
2500 S College Ave 77801 979-822-2715
Helen Spencer, prin. Fax 823-4971

Bryson, Jack, Pop. 537
Bryson ISD 300/PK-12
PO Box 309 76427 940-392-3281
Jack Coody, supt. Fax 392-2086
www.brysonisd.net
Bryson S 300/PK-12
PO Box 309 76427 940-392-2601
Jeff Decker, prin. Fax 392-2086

Buckholts, Milam, Pop. 406
Buckholts ISD 200/PK-12
PO Box 248 76518 254-593-3011
Kent Dutton, supt. Fax 593-2270
www.buckholtsisd.net
Buckholts S 200/PK-12
PO Box 248 76518 254-593-2744
Penny Coots, prin. Fax 593-2270

Buda, Hays, Pop. 3,948
Hays Consolidated ISD
Supt. — See Kyle
Barton MS 600/6-8
4950 Jack C Hays Trl 78610 512-268-1472
Judy Logan, prin. Fax 268-1610
Dahlstrom MS 600/6-8
3600 FM 967 78610 512-268-8441
Hilda Gartzke, prin. Fax 295-5346
Hays HS 1,900/9-12
4800 Jack C Hays Trl 78610 512-268-2911
Shirley Reich, prin. Fax 268-1394

Buffalo, Leon, Pop. 1,910
Buffalo ISD 800/PK-12
708 Cedar Creek Rd 75831 903-322-3765
Jack Thomason, supt. Fax 322-3091
www.buffaloisd.com
Buffalo HS 300/9-12
145 Bison Trl 75831 903-322-4243
Don Elsom, prin. Fax 322-5806
Buffalo JHS 200/6-8
355 Bison Trl 75831 903-322-4340
Lacy Freeman, prin. Fax 322-4803

Bullard, Smith, Pop. 1,562
Bullard ISD 1,700/PK-12
1426 S Houston St Ste B 75757 903-894-6639
Jim Wright, supt. Fax 894-9291
www.bullardisd.net
Bullard HS 500/9-12
PO Box 250 75757 903-894-3272
Leonard Speaker, prin. Fax 894-3051
Bullard MS 400/6-8
PO Box 250 75757 903-894-6533
Dwain Reynolds, prin. Fax 894-7592

Brook Hill S 400/PK-12
PO Box 668 75757 903-894-5000
Rod Fletcher, hdmstr. Fax 894-6332

Bulverde, Comal, Pop. 4,446

Bracken Christian S 300/PK-12
670 Old Boerne Rd 78163 830-438-3211
Craig Walker, admin. Fax 980-2327

Buna, Jasper, Pop. 2,127
Buna ISD 1,600/PK-12
PO Box 1087 77612 409-994-5101
Byron Terrier, supt. Fax 994-4808
www.bunaisd.net
Buna HS 500/9-12
PO Box 1087 77612 409-994-4811
Don Mucklerov, prin. Fax 994-4818
Buna JHS 300/6-8
PO Box 1087 77612 409-994-4860
Thomas Saunders, prin. Fax 994-4808

Burkburnett, Wichita, Pop. 10,378
Burkburnett ISD 3,600/PK-12
416 Glendale St 76354 940-569-3326
Danny Taylor, supt. Fax 569-4776
www.burkburnettisd.org
Burkburnett HS 1,000/9-12
109 W Kramer Rd 76354 940-569-1411
Del Hardaway, prin. Fax 569-1512
Burkburnett MS 800/6-8
108 S Avenue D 76354 940-569-3381
Sharon Scott, prin. Fax 569-7116

Burkeville, Newton
Burkeville ISD 300/PK-12
PO Box 218 75932 409-565-2201
Joe Gassiott, supt. Fax 565-2012
www.burkeville.com
Burkeville JSHS 100/7-12
PO Box 218 75932 409-565-4338
Hub Jordan, prin. Fax 565-2461

Burleson, Johnson, Pop. 29,613
Burleson ISD 7,500/PK-12
1160 SW Wilshire Blvd 76028 817-447-5730
Dr. Mark Jackson, supt. Fax 447-5737
www.burlesonisd.net
Burleson HS 2,200/9-12
100 Elk Dr 76028 817-447-5700
Paul Cash, prin. Fax 447-5796
Hughes MS 800/6-8
316 SW Thomas St 76028 817-447-5750
Susan Shaha, prin. Fax 447-5748
Kerr MS 1,000/6-8
517 SW Johnson Ave 76028 817-447-5810
Paul Uttley, prin. Fax 447-5742

Burnet, Burnet, Pop. 5,562
Burnet Consolidated ISD 2,300/PK-12
208 E Brier Ln 78611 512-756-2124
Jeffrey M. Hanks, supt. Fax 756-7498
www.burnet.txed.net
Burnet HS 900/9-12
1000 The Green Mile Rd 78611 512-756-6193
Craig Spinn, prin. Fax 756-4553
Burnet MS 700/6-8
1401 N Main St 78611 512-756-6182
Rich Elsasser, prin. Fax 756-7955

Burton, Washington, Pop. 367
Burton ISD 300/PK-12
PO Box 37 77835 979-289-3131
James Palmer, supt. Fax 289-3076
www.burtonisd.net
Burton JSHS 200/7-12
PO Box 499 77835 979-289-3830
Karen Steenken, prin. Fax 289-4609

Bushland, Potter
Bushland ISD 700/PK-12
PO Box 60 79012 806-359-6683
John Lemons, supt. Fax 359-6769
bushlandisd.org/
Bushland HS 9-12
PO Box 60 79012 806-359-6683
Rick Davis, prin. Fax 355-2841
Bushland MS 300/5-8
PO Box 60 79012 806-359-5418
P.J. Hanna, prin. Fax 355-2841

Byers, Clay, Pop. 530
Byers ISD 100/K-12
PO Box 286 76357 940-529-6102
Steve Wolf, supt. Fax 529-6104
www.esc9.net/byersisd/
Byers S 100/K-12
PO Box 286 76357 940-529-6101
Burt Montgomery, prin. Fax 529-6104

Bynum, Hill, Pop. 246
Bynum ISD 200/PK-12
PO Box 68 76631 254-623-4251
Polly Boyd, supt. Fax 623-4290
www.bynumisd.net/
Bynum S 200/PK-12
PO Box 68 76631 254-623-4251
Kathy Collins, prin. Fax 623-4290

Caddo Mills, Hunt, Pop. 1,211
Caddo Mills ISD 1,200/PK-12
PO Box 160 75135 903-527-6056
Vicki Payne, supt. Fax 527-4883
www.ednet10.net/caddomills/
Caddo Mills HS 400/9-12
PO Box 160 75135 903-527-3164
Brian McKamy, prin. Fax 527-4772
Caddo Mills MS 300/6-8
PO Box 160 75135 903-527-3161
Michael Powell, prin. Fax 527-2379

Caldwell, Burleson, Pop. 3,862
Caldwell ISD 1,900/PK-12
203 N Gray St 77836 979-567-9000
Randall Berryhill, supt. Fax 567-9876
www.caldwell.k12.tx.us/
Caldwell HS 600/9-12
203 N Gray St 77836 979-567-9030
John Meckel, prin. Fax 567-9032
Caldwell MS 400/6-8
203 N Gray St 77836 979-567-6270
Kim McManus, prin. Fax 567-6272

Calvert, Robertson, Pop. 1,403
Calvert ISD 200/PK-12
PO Box 7 77837 979-364-2824
Don Robbins, supt. Fax 364-2468
www.calvertisd.com/
Calvert JSHS 100/7-12
PO Box 7 77837 979-364-2845
K.L. Groholski, prin. Fax 364-2043

Cameron, Milam, Pop. 5,900
Cameron ISD 1,600/PK-12
PO Box 712 76520 254-697-3512
Maxie Morgan, supt. Fax 697-2448
www.cameronisd.net
Cameron JHS 400/6-8
PO Box 712 76520 254-697-2131
Daniel Parker, prin. Fax 605-0379
Yoe HS 500/9-12
PO Box 712 76520 254-697-3902
Clint McMahon, prin. Fax 605-0413

Campbell, Hunt, Pop. 779
Campbell ISD 300/PK-12
409 W North St 75422 903-862-3259
Strike Franklin, supt. Fax 862-2222
www.ednet10.net/campbell
Campbell JSHS 100/7-12
409 W North St 75422 903-862-3257
Earnie Phelps, prin. Fax 862-3547

Canadian, Hemphill, Pop. 2,258
Canadian ISD 600/PK-12
800 Hillside Ave 79014 806-323-5393
Frank Belcher, supt. Fax 323-8143
www.canadianisd.net
Canadian HS 200/9-12
800 Hillside Ave 79014 806-323-5373
Rick Berry, prin. Fax 323-8143
Canadian MS 100/7-8
800 Hillside Ave 79014 806-323-5351
Gary Laramore, prin. Fax 323-8791

Canton, Van Zandt, Pop. 3,591
Canton ISD 1,800/PK-12
225 W Elm St 75103 903-567-4179
Dr. Jerome Stewart, supt. Fax 567-2370
cantonisd.net
Canton HS 500/9-12
1110 W Highway 243 75103 903-567-6561
Max Callahan, prin. Fax 567-5222
Canton JHS 400/6-8
1115 S Buffalo St 75103 903-567-4329
Bruce Congleton, prin. Fax 567-1298

Canutillo, El Paso, Pop. 4,442
Canutillo ISD
Supt. — See El Paso
Alderete MS 6-8
PO Box 100 79835 915-877-6600
Annette Brigham, prin. Fax 877-6607
Canutillo MS 800/6-8
PO Box 100 79835 915-877-7900
Dr. Monica Reyes-Garcia, prin. Fax 877-7907

Canyon, Randall, Pop. 13,353
Canyon ISD 7,800/PK-12
PO Box 899 79015 806-677-2600
Mike Wartes, supt. Fax 677-2659
www.canyonisd.net
Canyon HS 900/9-12
1701 23rd St 79015 806-677-2740
Shawn Neeley, prin. Fax 677-2779
Canyon JHS 500/7-8
910 9th Ave 79015 806-677-2700
Kirk Kear, prin. Fax 677-2739
Other Schools – See Amarillo

West Texas A & M University Post-Sec.
Wtamu Box 907 79016 806-651-2000

Carmine, Fayette, Pop. 230
Round Top - Carmine ISD 200/PK-12
PO Box 385 78932 979-278-3252
Ronald Goehring, supt. Fax 278-3063
www.rtcisd.net/
Round Top - Carmine HS 100/7-12
PO Box 385 78932 979-278-3252
Mark Conley, prin. Fax 278-3063

Carrizo Springs, Dimmit, Pop. 5,681
Carrizo Springs Consolidated ISD 2,400/PK-12
300 N 7th St 78834 830-876-2473
Dr. Cecilia Moreno, supt. Fax 876-2114
www.cscisd.net
Carrizo Springs HS 700/9-12
300 N 7th St 78834 830-876-5237
Gabriel Garcia, prin. Fax 876-3052
Carrizo Springs JHS 400/7-8
300 N 7th St 78834 830-876-2496
Sofia Morones, prin. Fax 876-3655

Carrollton, Denton, Pop. 118,870
Carrollton-Farmers Branch ISD 25,400/PK-12
PO Box 115186 75011 972-968-6100
Annette T. Griffin Ed.D., supt. Fax 968-6210
www.cfbisd.edu
Blalack MS 1,100/6-8
1706 E Peters Colony Rd 75007 972-968-3500
Les Black, prin. Fax 968-3510
Creekview HS 2,200/9-12
3201 Old Denton Rd 75007 972-968-4800
Cyndi Boyd, prin. Fax 968-4810
Perry MS 1,000/6-8
1709 E Belt Line Rd 75006 972-968-4400
Joe LaPuma, prin. Fax 968-4410
Polk MS 900/6-8
2001 Kelly Blvd 75006 972-968-4600
Michelle Bailey, prin. Fax 968-4610
Smith HS 2,100/9-12
2335 N Josey Ln 75006 972-968-5200
Joe Pouncey, prin. Fax 968-5210
Turner HS 2,100/9-12
1600 S Josey Ln Bldg 1 75006 972-968-5400
Lance Campbell, prin. Fax 968-5410
Other Schools – See Dallas, Farmers Branch, Irving

Lewisville ISD
Supt. — See Flower Mound
Arbor Creek MS 800/6-8
2109 Arbor Creek Dr 75010 469-713-5971
Brad Burns, prin. Fax 350-2550
Creek Valley MS 900/6-8
4109 Creek Valley Blvd 75010 469-713-5184
Dr. Glenda Edwards, prin. Fax 395-3263
Hebron HS 2,000/9-12
4207 Plano Pkwy 75010 469-713-5183
Hugh Jones, prin. Fax 862-9095

American Heritage Academy 400/PK-12
2660 E Trinity Mills Rd 75006 972-416-5437
Robert Anderson, prin. Fax 418-5768
Carrollton Christian Academy 500/K-12
2205 E Hebron Pkwy 75010 972-242-6688
Dr. Alex Ward, hdmstr. Fax 245-0321
Prince of Peace Christian S 800/PK-12
4000 Midway Rd 75007 972-447-9887
Chris Hahn, prin. Fax 447-0877
Toni & Guy Hairdressing Academy Post-Sec.
2810 E Trinity Mills Rd 75006 972-416-8396

Carthage, Panola, Pop. 6,611
Carthage ISD 2,800/PK-12
1 Bulldog Dr 75633 903-693-3806
Reba Allison, supt. Fax 693-3650
www.carthageisd.org/
Carthage HS 800/9-12
1 Bulldog Dr 75633 903-693-2552
Jon Almeida, prin. Fax 693-9752
Carthage JHS 400/7-8
1 Bulldog Dr 75633 903-693-2751
Russell Porter, prin. Fax 693-9582

Panola College Post-Sec.
1109 W Panola St 75633 800-776-8153

Castroville, Medina, Pop. 2,936
Medina Valley ISD 1,700/PK-12
8449 FM 471 S 78009 830-931-2243
Willard Murrey, supt. Fax 931-4050
www.mvisd.com
Medina Valley HS 900/9-12
8365 FM 471 S 78009 830-931-2243
James Chase, prin. Fax 931-0371
Medina Valley MS 800/6-8
8395 FM 471 S 78009 830-931-2243
Teresa Vielma, prin. Fax 931-3258

Cayuga, Anderson
Cayuga ISD 600/PK-12
PO Box 427 75832 903-928-2102
Dr. Rick Webb, supt. Fax 928-2646
www.cayuga.esc7.net
Cayuga HS 200/9-12
PO Box 427 75832 903-928-2294
Daniel Shead, prin. Fax 928-2646
Cayuga MS 200/6-8
PO Box 427 75832 903-928-2699
Sherri McInnis, prin. Fax 928-2646

Cedar Creek, Bastrop
Bastrop ISD
Supt. — See Bastrop
Cedar Creek MS 600/7-8
125 Voss Pkwy 78612 512-332-2626
Jim Hallamek, prin. Fax 332-2631

Cedar Hill, Dallas, Pop. 41,582
Cedar Hill ISD 6,900/PK-12
PO Box 248 75106 972-291-1581
Dr. Ann Dixon, supt. Fax 291-5231
www.chisd.com
Cedar Hill SHS 1,600/10-12
PO Box 248 75106 469-272-2000
Harry Miller, prin. Fax 293-7125
Coleman MS, PO Box 248 75106 7-8
Dr. Georgetta Johnson, prin. 972-293-4505
Ninth Grade Center 9-9
PO Box 248 75106 469-272-2050
Delsenna Frazier, prin.
Permenter MS 1,300/7-8
PO Box 248 75106 972-291-5270
Joseph Showell, prin. Fax 291-5296

Northwood University Post-Sec.
1114 W FM 1382 75104 800-927-9663
Trinity Christian S 600/PK-12
1231 E Pleasant Run Rd 75104 972-291-2505
Kathleen Watts, supt. Fax 291-4739

Cedar Park, Williamson, Pop. 48,139
Leander ISD
Supt. — See Leander
Cedar Park HS 2,100/9-12
2150 Cypress Creek Rd 78613 512-435-8300
Ron Lafevers, prin. Fax 435-8305
Cedar Park MS 1,000/6-8
2100 Sunchase Blvd 78613 512-434-5025
Sandra Stewart, prin. Fax 434-7539
Henry MS 1,100/6-8
100 N Vista Ridge Pkwy 78613 512-435-4800
Dr. David Ellis, prin. Fax 435-4805
Running Brushy MS 1,000/6-8
2303 N Lakeline Blvd 78613 512-435-4700
Karin Johnson, prin. Fax 435-4705
Vista Ridge HS 1,000/9-12
200 S Vista Ridge Pkwy 78613 512-434-7300
Stu Taylor, prin. Fax 434-7305

Summit Christian Academy of Cedar Park 300/PK-12
2121 Cypress Creek Rd 78613 512-250-1369
Derek Cortez, dir. Fax 257-1851

Celeste, Hunt, Pop. 848
Celeste ISD 500/PK-12
PO Box 67 75423 903-568-4825
Collin Clark, supt. Fax 568-4495
www.celesteisd.org/
Celeste HS 200/9-12
PO Box 67 75423 903-568-4721
Ricky Beadles, prin. Fax 568-4115
Celeste JHS 100/6-8
PO Box 67 75423 903-568-4612
Lisa Lowe, prin. Fax 568-4277

Celina, Collin, Pop. 3,716
Celina ISD 1,400/PK-12
PO Box 188 75009 972-382-2751
Randy Reid, supt. Fax 382-3607
www.celina.k12.tx.us
Celina HS 400/9-12
PO Box 188 75009 972-382-2303
Jeff Oldham, prin. Fax 382-4830
Celina JHS 200/7-8
PO Box 188 75009 972-382-2373
Jerry Moore, prin. Fax 382-4258

Center, Shelby, Pop. 5,781
Center ISD 2,500/PK-12
404 Mosby St 75935 936-598-5642
Kelly Rodgers, supt. Fax 598-1515
www.centerisd.org/
Center HS 700/9-12
658 Roughrider Dr 75935 936-598-6173
Wes Kirkham, prin. Fax 598-1557
Center MS 500/6-8
302 Kennedy St 75935 936-598-5619
Heath Hagler, prin. Fax 598-1534

Center Point, Kerr
Center Point ISD 600/PK-12
PO Box 377 78010 830-634-2171
Dr. Lee Ann Ray, supt. Fax 634-2254
www.cpisd.net
Center Point HS 200/9-12
PO Box 377 78010 830-634-2244
John Scott Turner, prin. Fax 634-7430
Center Point MS 100/6-8
PO Box 377 78010 830-634-2533
John Scott Turner, prin. Fax 634-7825

Centerville, Leon, Pop. 944
Centerville ISD 700/K-12
813 S Commerce St 75833 903-536-7812
Cathy Nichols, supt. Fax 536-3133
www.centerville.k12.tx.us
Centerville JSHS 400/7-12
813 S Commerce St 75833 903-536-2935
Bob Loomis, prin. Fax 536-3133

Channelview, Harris, Pop. 30,600
Channelview ISD 6,900/PK-12
1403 Sheldon Rd 77530 281-452-8002
Tom Tasma, supt. Fax 452-8070
www.channelview.isd.esc4.net
Channelview HS 1,900/9-12
1100 Sheldon Rd 77530 281-457-7300
Dr. Laurie Bauer, prin. Fax 457-7346
Johnson JHS 1,200/7-8
15500 Proctor St 77530 281-452-8030
Cindi Ollis, prin. Fax 452-1022

Channing, Hartley, Pop. 356
Channing ISD 100/K-12
PO Box A 79018 806-235-3432
James Davis, supt. Fax 235-2609
Channing S 100/K-12
PO Box A 79018 806-235-3432
Robert McLain, prin. Fax 235-2609

Charlotte, Atascosa, Pop. 1,796
Charlotte ISD 500/PK-12
PO Box 489 78011 830-277-1431
Alfonso Obregon, supt. Fax 277-1551
charlotte.echalk.com
Charlotte HS 100/9-12
PO Box 489 78011 830-277-1432
David Carmichael, prin. Fax 277-1551
Charlotte JHS 100/6-8
PO Box 489 78011 830-277-1646
Bryan Borth, prin. Fax 277-1551

Cherokee, San Saba
Cherokee ISD 100/K-12
PO Box 100 76832 325-622-4298
Chris Perry, supt. Fax 622-4430
www.centex-edu.net/cherokee
Cherokee JSHS 100/7-12
PO Box 100 76832 325-622-4298
Shannon Jensen, prin. Fax 622-4430

Chester, Tyler, Pop. 261
Chester ISD 200/K-12
PO Box 28 75936 936-969-2211
Donald Rhodes, supt. Fax 969-2080
Chester JSHS, PO Box 28 75936 100/6-12
Donald Rhodes, prin. 936-969-2353

Chico, Wise, Pop. 1,069
Chico ISD 700/PK-12
PO Box 95 76431 940-644-2228
Thomas Ferguson, supt. Fax 644-5642
www.chicoisd.esc11.net
Chico HS 200/9-12
PO Box 95 76431 940-644-5783
Melvin Clay, prin. Fax 644-5876
Chico MS 200/6-8
PO Box 95 76431 940-644-5550
Maury Martin, prin. Fax 644-5642

Childress, Childress, Pop. 6,606
Childress ISD 1,100/PK-12
PO Box 179 79201 940-937-2501
John Wilson, supt. Fax 937-2938
www.childressisd.net/
Childress HS 300/9-12
800 Avenue J NW 79201 940-937-6131
Toby Tucker, prin. Fax 937-2039
Childress JHS 300/6-8
700 Commerce St 79201 940-937-3641
Marsha Meacham, prin. Fax 937-8427

Chillicothe, Hardeman, Pop. 736
Chillicothe ISD 200/K-12
PO Box 418 79225 940-852-5391
John Chapman, supt. Fax 852-5269
cisd-tx.net
Chillicothe JSHS 100/7-12
PO Box 550 79225 940-852-5391
John Robertson, prin. Fax 852-5465

Chilton, Falls
Chilton ISD 400/PK-12
PO Box 488 76632 254-546-1200
Benny Bobo, supt. Fax 546-1201
www.chiltonisd.org
Chilton JSHS 200/6-12
PO Box 488 76632 254-546-1200
Ray Rabroker, prin. Fax 546-1202

China, Jefferson, Pop. 1,079
Hardin-Jefferson ISD
Supt. — See Sour Lake
Henderson MS 500/6-8
PO Box 278 77613 409-981-6420
Mary Jones, prin. Fax 752-2049

China Spring, McLennan
China Spring ISD
Supt. — See Waco
China Spring HS 500/9-12
7301 N River Xing 76633 254-836-1771
Marc Faulkner, prin. Fax 836-1418
China Spring MS 300/7-8
7201 N River Xing 76633 254-836-4611
Bill Bratcher, prin. Fax 836-4777

Chireno, Nacogdoches, Pop. 408
Chireno ISD 300/K-12
PO Box 85 75937 936-362-2132
James Hockenberry, supt. Fax 362-2490
www.chirenoisd.org/
Chireno HS 100/9-12
PO Box 85 75937 936-362-2132
Bradley Durham, prin. Fax 362-9331

Christoval, Tom Green
Christoval ISD 400/K-12
PO Box 162 76935 325-896-2520
Tony Priest, supt. Fax 896-7405
www.christovalisd.org
Christoval JSHS 200/6-12
PO Box 162 76935 325-896-2355
Carl Wieburg, prin. Fax 896-2671

Cibolo, Guadalupe, Pop. 7,804
Schertz-Cibolo-Universal City ISD
Supt. — See Schertz
Dobie JHS 600/7-8
395 W Borgfeld Rd 78108 210-945-6000
Mike Wohlfarth, prin. Fax 945-6010
Steele HS 100/9-12
1300 FM 1103 78108 210-945-6500
Mary Pevoto, prin. Fax 945-6510

Cisco, Eastland, Pop. 3,833
Cisco ISD 800/PK-12
PO Box 1645 76437 254-442-3056
Hal Porter, supt. Fax 442-1412
www.ciscoisd.net/
Cisco HS 200/9-12
PO Box 1645 76437 254-442-3051
Craig Kent, prin. Fax 442-2516
Cisco JHS 200/6-8
PO Box 1645 76437 254-442-3004
Cassidy Early, prin. Fax 442-1832

Cisco Junior College Post-Sec.
101 College Hts 76437 254-442-2567

Clarendon, Donley, Pop. 2,021
Clarendon ISD 500/PK-12
PO Box 610 79226 806-874-2062
Monty Hysinger, supt. Fax 874-2579
www.clarendon.k12.tx.us/
Clarendon HS 100/9-12
PO Box 610 79226 806-874-2181
Larry Jeffers, prin. Fax 874-3428
Clarendon JHS 100/6-8
PO Box 610 79226 806-874-3232
Marvin Elam, prin. Fax 874-9748

Clarendon College Post-Sec.
PO Box 968 79226 806-874-3571

Clarksville, Red River, Pop. 3,611
Clarksville ISD 1,000/PK-12
PO Box 1016 75426 903-427-3891
Joe Oliver, supt. Fax 427-5071
www.clarksvilleisd.net/home.aspx
Cheatham MS 200/6-8
1500 W Main St 75426 903-427-3891
Pam Norwood, prin. Fax 427-4118
Clarksville HS 300/9-12
PO Box 1016 75426 903-427-3891
Chris Vaughn, prin. Fax 427-5116

Claude, Armstrong, Pop. 1,328
Claude ISD 400/PK-12
PO Box 209 79019 806-226-7331
Laura Zanchettin, supt. Fax 226-2244
www.claudeisd.net/
Claude JSHS 200/6-12
PO Box 209 79019 806-226-2191
James Kennedy, prin. Fax 226-2244

Cleburne, Johnson, Pop. 29,184
Cleburne ISD 6,400/PK-12
505 N Ridgeway Dr Ste 100 76033 817-202-1100
Robert Damron, supt. Fax 202-1460
www.cleburne.k12.tx.us/
Cleburne HS 1,500/9-12
1501 Harlin Dr 76033 817-202-1200
Justin Marchel, prin. Fax 202-1470
Cleburne MS 900/7-8
1710 Country Club Rd 76033 817-202-1500
David Diaz, prin. Fax 202-1475

Hill College Post-Sec.
PO Box 1899 76033 817-641-9887

Cleveland, Liberty, Pop. 8,032
Cleveland ISD 2,700/PK-12
316 E Dallas St 77327 281-592-8717
Kerry Cowart, supt. Fax 592-8283
www.clevelandisd.org
Cleveland HS 800/9-12
2000 E Houston St 77327 281-592-8752
Mike Ogden, prin. Fax 592-7485
Cleveland JHS 500/6-8
1600 E Houston St 77327 281-593-1148
Patricia Curry, prin. Fax 593-3400

Tarkington ISD 1,800/PK-12
2770 FM 163 Rd 77327 281-592-8781
John Kirchner, supt. Fax 592-3969
www.tarkingtonisd.net/
Tarkington HS 600/9-12
2770 FM 163 Rd 77327 281-592-7739
Robert Shaw, prin. Fax 592-0693
Tarkington MS 500/6-8
2770 FM 163 Rd 77327 281-592-7737
John Johnson, prin. Fax 592-5241

Clifton, Bosque, Pop. 3,642
Clifton ISD 1,200/PK-12
1102 Key St 76634 254-675-2827
Gregory D. Stone, supt. Fax 675-4351
www.clifton.k12.tx.us
Clifton HS 300/9-12
1101 N Avenue Q 76634 254-675-2827
Sharon Bergman, prin. Fax 675-8002
Clifton MS 300/6-8
1102 Key St 76634 254-675-2827
Billy Murrell, prin. Fax 675-2005

Clint, El Paso, Pop. 985
Clint ISD
Supt. — See El Paso
Clint HS 600/9-12
12625 Alameda Ave 79836 915-926-8000
Mark Ayala, prin. Fax 851-3895
Clint JHS 400/6-8
13100 Alameda Ave 79836 915-926-8100
Ignacio Solis, prin. Fax 851-3459

Clute, Brazoria, Pop. 10,731
Brazosport ISD 13,000/PK-12
301 W Brazoswood Dr 77531 979-730-7000
Fax 266-2409
www.brazosportisd.net
Brazoswood HS 2,600/9-12
302 W Brazoswood Dr 77531 979-730-7300
Mike Benedict, prin. Fax 266-2447
Clute IS 700/6-8
421 E Main St 77531 979-730-7230
Jay Whitehead, prin. Fax 730-7363
Other Schools – See Freeport, Lake Jackson

Clyde, Callahan, Pop. 3,673
Clyde Consolidated ISD 1,500/PK-12
PO Box 479 79510 325-893-4222
Dr. Kevin Spiller, supt. Fax 893-4024
www.clyde.esc14.net
Clyde HS 500/9-12
500 N Hays Rd 79510 325-893-2161
Terry Phillips, prin. Fax 893-2993
Clyde JHS 300/7-8
211 S 3rd St W 79510 325-893-5788
Greg Edwards, prin. Fax 893-5255

Eula ISD 500/PK-12
6040 FM 603 79510 325-529-3186
Wes Hays, supt. Fax 529-4461
www.eulaisd.us
Eula HS 200/9-12
6040 FM 603 79510 325-529-3605
Mike Bright, prin. Fax 529-5534
Eula MS 100/6-8
6040 FM 603 79510 325-529-4831
Tim Kelley, prin. Fax 529-4461

Coahoma, Howard, Pop. 915
Coahoma ISD 800/PK-12
PO Box 110 79511 432-394-4290
Jerry Johnson, supt. Fax 394-4302
www.coahomaisd.com/
Coahoma HS 300/9-12
PO Box 110 79511 432-394-4535
John Massey, prin. Fax 394-4031
Coahoma JHS 100/7-8
PO Box 110 79511 432-394-4615
Dean Richters, prin. Fax 394-4052

Coldspring, San Jacinto, Pop. 763
Coldspring-Oakhurst Consolidated ISD 1,800/PK-12
PO Box 39 77331 936-653-1115
Dr. Lynn Cummins, supt. Fax 653-2197
www.cocisd.org
Coldspring-Oakhurst HS 600/9-12
PO Box 39 77331 936-653-1140
D'Wana Bryant, prin. Fax 653-3687
Lincoln JHS 400/6-8
PO Box 39 77331 936-653-1166
Malisa Hargrove, prin. Fax 653-3688

Coleman, Coleman, Pop. 4,829
Coleman ISD 1,000/PK-12
PO Box 900 76834 325-625-3575
Royce Young, supt. Fax 625-4751
www.colemanisd.net/
Coleman HS 300/9-12
201 15th St 76834 325-625-2156
Richard Holloway, prin. Fax 625-4557
Coleman JHS 200/6-8
301 15th St 76834 325-625-3593
Paula Ringo, prin. Fax 625-3358

College Station, Brazos, Pop. 72,388
College Station ISD 8,200/PK-12
1812 Welsh Ave 77840 979-764-5400
Dr. Eddie Coulson, supt. Fax 764-5492
www.csisd.org
A & M Consolidated HS 2,300/9-12
1801 Harvey Mitchell Pkwy S 77840 979-764-5500
Ron Fox, prin. Fax 693-0212
A & M Consolidated MS 500/7-8
105 Holik St 77840 979-764-5575
Chris Scott, prin. Fax 764-5577
College Station MS 700/7-8
900 Rock Prairie Rd 77845 979-764-5545
Oliver Hadnot, prin. Fax 764-5557

Texas A&M University 77843 Post-Sec.
979-845-3211

Colleyville, Tarrant, Pop. 22,394
Grapevine-Colleyville ISD
Supt. — See Grapevine
Colleyville Heritage HS 2,300/9-12
5401 Heritage Ave 76034 817-358-4700
Becky Prentice, prin. Fax 358-4765
Colleyville MS 800/6-8
1100 Bogart Dr 76034 817-788-4400
Toni Thalkin, prin. Fax 498-9764
Heritage MS 1,000/6-8
5300 Heritage Ave 76034 817-358-4790
Pete Valamides, prin. Fax 267-9929

Covenant Christian Academy 500/PK-12
901 Cheek Sparger Rd 76034 817-281-4333
Keith Castello, hdmstr. Fax 281-4674

Collinsville, Grayson, Pop. 1,471
Collinsville ISD 600/PK-12
PO Box 49 76233 903-429-6272
Tim Wright, supt. Fax 429-6665
www.collinsvilleisd.org
Collinsville JSHS 300/7-12
PO Box 49 76233 903-429-6164
Ken Kemp, prin. Fax 429-6493

Colmesneil, Tyler, Pop. 631
Colmesneil ISD 500/K-12
PO Box 37 75938 409-837-5757
Elton Hightower, supt. Fax 837-5759
Colmesneil HS 200/9-12
PO Box 37 75938 409-837-2225
Walter McAlpin, prin. Fax 837-9107
Colmesneil MS 100/6-8
PO Box 37 75938 409-837-5272
Rodney Haught, prin. Fax 837-2307

Colorado City, Mitchell, Pop. 4,018
Colorado ISD 1,000/PK-12
PO Box 1268 79512 325-728-3721
Jim White, supt. Fax 728-8471
www.ccity.esc14.net
Colorado HS 300/9-12
1500 Lone Wolf Blvd 79512 325-728-3424
Jeremy Ross, prin. Fax 728-1083
Colorado MS 200/6-8
312 E 12th St 79512 325-728-2673
Mark Merrell, prin. Fax 728-1051
Wallace Accelerated HS 8-12
149 S State Highway 208 79512 325-728-2392
Melinda Alexander, prin.

Columbus, Colorado, Pop. 3,934
Columbus ISD 1,500/PK-12
105 Cardinal Ln 78934 979-732-5704
Randall Hoyer, supt. Fax 732-5960
www.columbusisd.org/
Columbus HS 500/9-12
103 Cardinal Ln 78934 979-732-5746
J. Pfeffer, prin. Fax 732-8862
Columbus JHS 400/6-8
702 Rampart St 78934 979-732-2891
J. Laub, prin. Fax 732-9081

Comanche, Comanche, Pop. 4,302
Comanche ISD 1,400/PK-12
1414 N Austin St 76442 325-356-2727
Rick Howard, supt. Fax 356-2312
www.comancheisd.net
Comanche HS 400/9-12
1660 N Austin St 76442 325-356-2581
Ronnie Clifton, prin. Fax 356-2658
Jeffries JHS 300/6-8
Valley Forge Dr 76442 325-356-5220
Jim Baum, prin. Fax 356-1949

Comfort, Kendall, Pop. 1,477
Comfort ISD 1,200/PK-12
PO Box 398 78013 830-995-3664
John Rouse, supt. Fax 995-2236
www.comfort.txed.net
Comfort HS 300/9-12
PO Box 280 78013 830-995-3533
Bryan Clemmons, prin. Fax 995-2261
Comfort MS 300/6-8
PO Box 187 78013 830-995-3380
Mollye Williams, prin. Fax 995-2248

Commerce, Hunt, Pop. 8,971
Commerce ISD 1,800/PK-12
PO Box 1251 75429 903-886-3755
Keith Boles, supt. Fax 886-6025
www.commerceisd.org/home.htm
Commerce HS 500/9-12
PO Box 1251 75429 903-886-3756
Trish King, prin. Fax 886-6209
Commerce MS 400/6-8
PO Box 1251 75429 903-886-3795
Mitchell Curry, prin. Fax 886-6102

Texas A&M University - Commerce Post-Sec.
PO Box 3011 75429 903-886-5102

Como, Hopkins, Pop. 645
Como-Pickton Consolidated ISD 800/PK-12
PO Box 18 75431 903-488-3671
Bryan Neal, supt. Fax 488-3133
cpisd.esc8.net/
Como-Pickton HS 200/9-12
PO Box 18 75431 903-488-3671
Jeanne Lay, prin. Fax 488-3133
Como-Pickton JHS 200/6-8
PO Box 18 75431 903-488-3671
Lydia Walden, prin. Fax 488-3133

Comstock, Val Verde
Comstock ISD 200/K-12
PO Box 905 78837 432-292-4444
Kenn Norris, supt. Fax 292-4436
Comstock S 200/K-12
PO Box 905 78837 432-292-4444
Toby Ward, prin. Fax 292-4436

Conroe, Montgomery, Pop. 47,042
Conroe ISD 35,800/PK-12
3205 W Davis St 77304 936-709-7751
Dr. Don Stockton, supt. Fax 760-7704
www.conroeisd.net/
Academy of Science & Health Professions 9-12
3200 W Davis St 77304 936-709-5731
Dr. Mary Jo Parker, hdmstr.
Academy of Science & Technology 9-12
27330 Oak Ridge School Rd 77385 936-709-7211
Dr. Ron Laugen, hdmstr. Fax 709-3299
Caney Creek HS 1,600/9-12
16840 FM 2090 Rd 77306 936-231-3330
Trish McClure, prin. Fax 231-7702
Conroe HS 2,700/9-12
3200 W Davis St 77304 936-709-5700
Mike Crowl, prin. Fax 709-5655
Moorehead JHS 1,000/7-9
16840 FM 2090 Rd 77306 936-231-2400
Sarah Sanders, prin. Fax 231-7697
Oak Ridge HS 2,300/9-12
27330 Oak Ridge School Rd 77385 832-592-5300
Tommy Johnson, prin. Fax 592-5544
Peet JHS 900/7-8
400 Sgt Ed Holcomb Blvd N 77304 936-709-3700
Curtis Null, prin. Fax 709-3828
Washington JHS 600/5-8
507 Dr Martin Luther King 77301 936-709-7400
Hartwell Brown, prin. Fax 709-7492
York JHS 1,000/6-8
27310 Oak Ridge School Rd 77385 832-592-8600
Dr. Gena Jerkins, prin. Fax 292-1520
Other Schools – See The Woodlands

Aveda Institute Post-Sec.
19241 David Memorial Dr 77385 936-539-6770
Calvary Baptist S 200/PK-12
3401 N Frazier St 77303 936-756-0743
Becky Burchett, prin. Fax 756-0764
Conroe Christian S 50/PK-12
1615 Odd Fellow St 77301 936-539-2989
Kathleen Newton, admin. Fax 539-2986
Conroe SDA S 50/PK-10
3601 S Loop 336 E 77301 936-756-5078
Carolyn Early, prin. Fax 760-4029
Covenant Christian S 300/PK-12
4503 Interstate 45 N 77304 936-890-8080
Dr. Charles Lloyd, admin. Fax 890-5343
Lifestyle Christian S 200/K-12
3993 Interstate 45 N 77304 936-756-9383
Joshua Davenport, prin. Fax 760-3003
PCAL Christian S 50/7-12
16969 Larkspur 77385 936-273-4082
Karen Parish, admin. Fax 273-4082

Converse, Bexar, Pop. 12,650
Judson ISD
Supt. — See Live Oak
Judson HS 9-10
9695 Schaefer Rd 78109 210-357-0800
Don Pittman, prin. Fax 659-8769
Judson SHS 2,100/11-12
9142 FM 78 78109 210-945-1100
Dan Pittman, prin. Fax 659-4359

Coolidge, Limestone, Pop. 882
Coolidge ISD 300/PK-12
PO Box 70 76635 254-786-2206
Dr. Chris Hulen, supt. Fax 786-4835
www.coolidge.k12.tx.us/
Coolidge HS 100/6-12
PO Box 70 76635 254-786-4822
Cynthia Pollard, prin. Fax 786-4835

Cooper, Delta, Pop. 2,185
Cooper ISD 900/PK-12
PO Box 478 75432 903-395-2111
Lynn Burton, supt. Fax 395-2117
www.cooperisd.net/
Cooper HS 300/9-12
PO Box 429 75432 903-395-0509
Chris Kiser, prin. Fax 395-2382
Cooper JHS 200/6-8
PO Box 478 75432 903-395-0509
Chris Kiser, prin. Fax 395-2382

Coppell, Dallas, Pop. 38,704
Coppell ISD 10,000/PK-12
200 S Denton Tap Rd 75019 214-496-6000
Dr. Jeff Turner, supt. Fax 496-6036
www.coppellisd.com
Coppell HS 2,900/9-12
185 W Parkway Blvd 75019 214-496-6100
Brad Hunt, prin. Fax 496-6116
Coppell MS East 700/6-8
400 Mockingbird Ln 75019 214-496-6600
Laura Springer, prin. Fax 496-6603
Coppell MS North 800/6-8
120 Natches Trce 75019 214-496-7100
Dr. Juneria Berges, prin. Fax 496-7103
Coppell MS West 800/6-8
1301 Wrangler Cir 75019 214-496-8600
Vernon Edin, prin. Fax 496-8606

Copperas Cove, Coryell, Pop. 30,643
Copperas Cove ISD 5,900/PK-12
703 W Avenue D 76522 254-547-1227
Dr. Rose Cameron, supt. Fax 547-1542
www.ccisd.com
Copperas Cove HS 2,000/9-12
400 S 25th St 76522 254-547-2535
Fax 547-9870
Copperas Cove JHS 500/6-8
702 Sunny Ave 76522 254-547-6959
Randy Troub, prin. Fax 518-2620
Lee JHS 600/6-8
1205 Courtney Ln 76522 254-542-7877
Scott Hammond, prin. Fax 542-8103

Corinth, Denton, Pop. 17,980
Denton ISD
Supt. — See Denton
Crownover MS 900/6-8
1901 Creekside Dr 76210 940-369-4700
Dianne Blair, prin. Fax 321-0502

Lake Dallas ISD
Supt. — See Lake Dallas
Lake Dallas HS 1,000/9-12
3016 Parkridge Dr 76210 940-497-4031
Dave Ketcher, prin. Fax 497-3400

Corpus Christi, Nueces, Pop. 283,474
Calallen ISD 3,900/PK-12
4205 Wildcat Dr 78410 361-242-5600
Arturo Almendarez, supt. Fax 242-5620
www.calallen.k12.tx.us
Calallen HS 1,300/9-12
4001 Wildcat Dr 78410 361-242-5626
Yvonne Marquez-Neth, prin. Fax 242-5632
Calallen MS 900/6-8
4602 Cornett Dr 78410 361-242-5672
Lynnette Felder, prin. Fax 242-5680

Corpus Christi ISD 37,800/PK-12
PO Box 110 78403 361-886-9200
D. Scott Elliff, supt. Fax 886-9109
www.corpuschristiisd.org
Baker MS 800/6-8
3445 Pecan St 78411 361-878-1420
Darla Reid, prin. Fax 878-1834
Browne MS 800/6-8
4301 Schanen Blvd 78413 361-878-1426
Donna Adams, prin. Fax 878-1836
Carroll HS 2,300/9-12
5301 Weber Rd 78411 361-806-5330
Steve Van Matre, prin. Fax 857-2548
Collegiate HS 9-12
101 Baldwin Blvd 78404 361-698-2425
Tracie Rodriguez, prin. Fax 698-2427
Cullen MS 500/6-8
5225 Greely Dr 78412 361-994-3630
Robert Templeton, prin. Fax 994-3624
Cunningham MS 600/6-8
4321 Prescott St 78416 361-878-1432
Carlos Garza, prin. Fax 878-1838
Driscoll MS 700/6-8
3501 Kenwood Dr 78408 361-886-9365
Roland Quezada, prin. Fax 886-9890
Grant MS 1,100/6-8
4350 Aaron Dr 78413 361-878-1860
Carla Rosa-Villarreal, prin. Fax 878-1871
Haas MS 500/6-8
6630 McArdle Rd 78412 361-994-3636
Deborah Scates, prin. Fax 994-3626
Hamlin MS 800/6-8
3900 Hamlin Dr 78411 361-878-1438
Debbie McAden, prin. Fax 878-1839
Kaffie MS 900/6-8
5922 Brockhampton St 78414 361-994-3600
Nancy Benson, prin. Fax 994-3604
King HS 2,400/9-12
5225 Gollihar Rd 78412 361-994-6900
Minerva Abrego, prin. Fax 994-6918
Martin MS 700/6-8
3502 Greenwood Dr 78416 361-878-1400
Defina Yzaguiere, prin. Fax 878-1841
Miller HS 1,400/9-12
1 Battlin Buc Blvd 78408 361-884-4963
Delia McLerran, prin. Fax 883-1928
Moody HS 1,900/9-12
1818 Trojan Dr 78416 361-806-5360
Conrado Garcia, prin. Fax 857-8253
Ray HS 2,100/9-12
1002 Texan Trl 78411 361-806-5300
Steven Gonzales, prin. Fax 852-6528
Seale Academy of Fine Arts 800/6-8
1707 Ayers St 78404 361-886-9359
Ada Besinaiz, prin. Fax 886-9892
South Park MS 600/6-8
3001 McArdle Rd 78415 361-878-1446
Cecilia Reynolds-Perez, prin. Fax 878-1844
Adult Learning Center Adult
3902 Morgan Ave 78405 361-886-9385
Homero Villarreal, dir. Fax 886-9387

Flour Bluff ISD 5,200/PK-12
2505 Waldron Rd 78418 361-694-9200
Dr. Julie Carbajal, supt. Fax 694-9809
www.flourbluffschools.net
Flour Bluff HS 1,600/9-12
2505 Waldron Rd 78418 361-694-9100
Eddie Chachere, prin. Fax 694-9802
Flour Bluff JHS 900/7-8
2505 Waldron Rd 78418 361-694-9300
Danny Glover, prin. Fax 694-9803

Tuloso-Midway ISD 3,500/PK-12
PO Box 10900 78460 361-903-6400
Dr. Cornelio Gonzalez, supt. Fax 241-5836
www.tmisd.esc2.net
Tuloso-Midway Academic Career Center Vo/Tech
PO Box 10900 78460 361-903-6450
Melodie McClarren, prin. Fax 289-5642
Tuloso-Midway HS 1,000/9-12
PO Box 10900 78460 361-903-6700
Ann Bartosh, prin. Fax 241-4258
Tuloso-Midway MS 800/6-8
PO Box 10900 78460 361-903-6600
Fax 241-9829

West Oso ISD 1,900/PK-12
5050 Rockford Dr 78416 361-855-5900
Dr. Crawford Helms, supt. Fax 225-8308
www.westosoisd.esc2.net
West Oso HS 500/9-12
5202 Bear Ln 78405 361-806-5960
Benito Franco, prin. Fax 299-3111
West Oso JHS 400/6-8
1115 Bloomington St 78416 361-806-5950
Gracie Stillman, prin. Fax 225-8314

Annapolis Christian Academy 200/PK-12
4420 S Staples St 78411 361-991-6004
Tim Moon, hdmstr. Fax 992-0369
Bishop Garriga MS 100/6-8
3114 Saratoga Blvd 78415 361-851-0853
Rosario Davila, prin. Fax 853-5145
Career Centers of Texas Post-Sec.
1620 S Padre Island Dr 78416 361-852-2900
Del Mar College Post-Sec.
101 Baldwin Blvd 78404 361-698-1200
Incarnate Word Academy 200/6-8
2917 Austin St 78404 361-883-0857
Adolfo Garza, prin. Fax 882-9193
Incarnate Word Academy 200/9-12
2910 S Alameda St 78404 361-883-0857
Gerald Lugaresi, prin. Fax 883-2185
Institute of Cosmetic Arts and Science Post-Sec.
1105 Airline Rd 78412 361-991-8868
John Paul II HS 9-12
3036 Saratoga Blvd 78415 361-855-5744
Ricardo Almendarez, prin. Fax 855-1343
Southern Careers Institute Post-Sec.
2422 Airline Rd 78414 361-857-5700
South Texas Barber College Post-Sec.
3917 Ayers St 78415 361-855-2297
Texas A&M University - Corpus Christi Post-Sec.
6300 Ocean Dr 78412 361-825-5700

Corrigan, Polk, Pop. 1,931
Corrigan-Camden ISD 1,100/PK-12
504 S Home St 75939 936-398-4040
Tom Bowman, supt. Fax 398-4616
www.corrigan-camdenisd.net
Corrigan-Camden HS 300/9-12
504 S Home St 75939 936-398-2543
Sherry Hughes, prin. Fax 398-2685
Corrigan-Camden JHS 200/7-8
504 S Home St 75939 936-398-2962
Ray Bostick, prin. Fax 398-4608

Corsicana, Navarro, Pop. 26,052
Corsicana ISD 5,500/PK-12
601 N 13th St 75110 903-874-7441
Don Denbow, supt. Fax 872-2100
www.cisd.org
Collins MS 800/7-8
1500 Dobbins Rd 75110 903-872-3979
Sharon McDonald, prin. Fax 874-1423
Corsicana HS 1,400/9-12
3701 W State Highway 22 75110 903-874-8211
Keith Moore, prin. Fax 874-7403

Mildred ISD 700/K-12
5475 S US Highway 287 75109 903-872-6505
Douglas Lane, supt. Fax 872-1341
www.esc12.net/mildredisd
Mildred JSHS 300/7-12
5475 S US Highway 287 75109 903-872-0392
Gerry Talley, prin. Fax 641-0356

Navarro College Post-Sec.
3200 W 7th Ave 75110 903-874-6501

Cotton Center, Hale
Cotton Center ISD 100/PK-12
PO Box 350 79021 806-879-2160
Rocky Stone, supt. Fax 879-2175
cottoncenter.esc17.net
Cotton Center S 100/PK-12
PO Box 350 79021 806-879-2176
Leslie Shaw, prin. Fax 879-2175

Cotulla, LaSalle, Pop. 3,655
Cotulla ISD 1,200/PK-12
310 N Main St 78014 830-879-3073
Elizabeth Saenz, supt. Fax 879-3609
www.cotullaisd.org
Cotulla HS 300/9-12
310 N Main St 78014 830-879-2374
Tony Gonzales, prin. Fax 879-4302
Newman MS 300/6-8
310 N Main St 78014 830-879-2224
Kim Hoff, prin. Fax 879-4357

Covington, Hill, Pop. 305
Covington ISD 300/PK-12
PO Box 67 76636 254-854-2215
Diane Innis, supt. Fax 854-2272
www.covingtonisd.org/
Covington S 300/PK-12
PO Box 67 76636 254-854-2215
Hugh Ellison, prin. Fax 854-2272

Crandall, Kaufman, Pop. 3,475
Crandall ISD 2,000/PK-12
PO Box 128 75114 972-427-8000
Dr. Larry Watson, supt. Fax 427-8001
www.crandall-isd.net
Crandall HS 600/9-12
PO Box 520 75114 972-427-8030
David Greer, prin. Fax 427-8234
Raynes MS 500/6-8
PO Box 490 75114 972-427-8080
Gail Barnes, prin. Fax 427-8031

Crane, Crane, Pop. 3,044
Crane ISD 1,000/PK-12
511 W 8th St 79731 432-558-1022
Larry Lee, supt. Fax 558-1025
www.craneisd.com
Crane HS 300/9-12
511 W 8th St 79731 432-558-1030
Carlin Grammer, prin. Fax 558-1056
Crane MS 200/6-8
511 W 8th St 79731 432-558-1040
Ted Hallford, prin. Fax 558-1046

Cranfills Gap, Bosque, Pop. 353
Cranfills Gap ISD 100/PK-12
PO Box 67 76637 254-597-2505
Dr. Carla Sigler, supt. Fax 597-0001
www.cranfillsgapisd.com/
Cranfills Gap S 100/PK-12
PO Box 67 76637 254-597-2505
Dr. Carla Sigler, prin. Fax 597-0001

Crawford, McLennan, Pop. 789
Crawford ISD 600/K-12
200 Pirate Dr 76638 254-486-2381
Kevin Noack, supt. Fax 486-2198
www.crawfordisd.net/
Crawford HS 200/9-12
200 Pirate Dr 76638 254-486-2381
Don Harris, prin. Fax 486-2198
Crawford MS 200/5-8
200 Pirate Dr 76638 254-486-2381
Jason Ray Bunting, prin. Fax 486-2198

Crockett, Houston, Pop. 7,039
Crockett ISD 1,600/PK-12
704 E Burnett Ave 75835 936-544-2125
Dr. Bill Like, supt. Fax 544-5727
www.crockettisd.net
Crockett HS 500/9-12
704 E Burnett Ave 75835 936-544-2193
Clint McLain, prin. Fax 546-0104
Crockett JHS 300/7-8
704 E Burnett Ave 75835 936-544-2149
Debra Lamb, prin. Fax 544-4164

Crosby, Harris, Pop. 1,811
Crosby ISD 4,500/PK-12
PO Box 2009 77532 281-328-9200
Dr. Don Hendrix, supt. Fax 328-9208
www.crosbyisd.org
Crosby HS 1,300/9-12
PO Box 2009 77532 281-328-9237
Deborah Frank, prin. Fax 328-9219
Crosby MS 800/7-8
PO Box 2009 77532 281-328-9264
Patricia Kay, prin. Fax 328-9356

Crosbyton, Crosby, Pop. 1,749
Crosbyton Consolidated ISD 400/PK-12
204 S Harrison St 79322 806-675-7331
Marvin Stewart, supt. Fax 675-2409
www.crosbyton.k12.tx.us
Crosbyton HS 100/9-12
204 S Harrison St 79322 806-675-7331
John-Paul Huber, prin. Fax 675-1049
Crosbyton MS 100/6-8
204 S Harrison St 79322 806-675-7331
Dennis Verkamp, prin. Fax 675-2409

Cross Plains, Callahan, Pop. 1,118
Cross Plains ISD 400/PK-12
700 N Main St 76443 254-725-6121
Jackie Tennison, supt. Fax 725-6559
www.esc14.net/schools/~cplains/default.html
Cross Plains JSHS 200/7-12
700 N Main St 76443 254-725-6121
Jimmie Cearley, prin. Fax 725-6559

Crowell, Foard, Pop. 1,062
Crowell ISD 300/PK-12
PO Box 239 79227 940-684-1403
Charles Hundley, supt. Fax 684-1616
www.crowellisd.net/
Crowell JSHS 100/7-12
PO Box 239 79227 940-684-1331
Amie Bell, prin. Fax 684-1978

Crowley, Tarrant, Pop. 9,691
Crowley ISD 11,400/PK-12
PO Box 688 76036 817-297-5800
Greg Gibson, supt. Fax 297-5805
www.crowley.k12.tx.us
Crowley 9th Grade Campus 400/9-9
1016 FM 1187 W 76036 817-297-5845
Daphne Kahn-Wiley, prin. Fax 297-5847
Crowley HS 1,200/10-12
1005 W Main St 76036 817-297-5810
Richard Crosby, prin. Fax 297-5854
Stevens MS 1,000/7-8
940 N Crowley Rd 76036 817-297-5840
Brandon Neeley, prin. Fax 297-5850
Other Schools – See Fort Worth

Nazarene Christian Academy 200/K-12
2001 E Main St 76036 817-297-7003
Sheila Meek, admin. Fax 297-1509

Crystal City, Zavala, Pop. 7,224
Crystal City ISD 1,600/PK-12
805 E Crockett St 78839 830-374-2367
Alberto Gonzales, supt. Fax 374-8004
www.ccjavs.net/
Crystal City HS 600/9-12
805 E Crockett St 78839 830-374-2341
Oscar Martinez, prin. Fax 374-8012
Fly JHS 300/7-8
805 E Crockett St 78839 830-374-2371
Ray Espinosa, prin. Fax 374-8060

Cuero, DeWitt, Pop. 6,770
Cuero ISD 2,000/PK-12
405 Park Heights Dr 77954 361-275-3832
Henry Lind, supt. Fax 275-2981
www.cueroisd.org
Cuero HS 700/9-12
920 E Broadway St 77954 361-275-6157
Michael Cavanaugh, prin. Fax 275-2430
Cuero JHS 500/6-8
608 Jr High Dr 77954 361-275-2222
Jan Reeve, prin. Fax 275-6912

Cumby, Hopkins, Pop. 637
Cumby ISD 400/PK-12
101 Sayle St 75433 903-994-2261
Bert Vandiver, supt. Fax 994-2399
cumby.esc8.net/
Cumby HS 200/7-12
101 Sayle St 75433 903-994-2260
Don Madden, prin. Fax 994-2510

Miller Grove ISD 200/K-12
7819 Farm Road 275 S 75433 903-459-3288
Steve Johnson, supt. Fax 459-3744
millergrove.esc8.net/
Miller Grove HS 100/7-12
7819 Farm Road 275 S 75433 903-459-3288
Donna George, prin. Fax 459-3744

Cushing, Nacogdoches, Pop. 653
Cushing ISD 500/PK-12
PO Box 337 75760 936-326-4890
Bob Caster, supt. Fax 326-4115
www.cushingisd.org
Cushing JSHS 200/7-12
PO Box 337 75760 936-326-4271
Michael Davis, prin. Fax 326-4131

Cypress, Harris
Cypress-Fairbanks ISD
Supt. — See Houston
Arnold MS 1,400/6-8
11111 Telge Rd 77429 281-897-4700
Susan Higgins, prin. Fax 807-8610
Carlton Vocational Center Vo/Tech
22602 Hempstead Hwy 77429 281-213-1950
Rhonda Turns, dir. Fax 213-1951
Cy-Fair HS 3,200/9-12
22602 Hempstead Hwy 77429 281-897-4600
Darlene Medford, prin. Fax 517-6530
Cypress Springs HS 3,400/9-12
7909 Fry Rd 77433 281-345-3000
Sarah Harty, prin. Fax 345-3010
Cypress Woods HS 9-12
16825 Spring Cypress Rd 77429 281-213-1727
Sue McGown, prin. Fax 213-1807
Goodson MS 1,800/6-8
17333 Huffmeister Rd 77429 281-373-2350
Phyllis Hamilton, prin. Fax 373-2355
Hamilton MS 1,400/6-8
12330 Kluge Rd 77429 281-320-7000
Teresa Hull, prin. Fax 320-7021
Spillane MS, 17500 Jarvis Rd 77429 6-8
Gary Kinninger, prin. 281-213-1645

Daingerfield, Morris, Pop. 2,470
Daingerfield-Lone Star ISD 1,500/PK-12
200 Tiger Dr 75638 903-645-2239
Mary Ann Marshall, supt. Fax 645-2137
d-lsisd.esc8.net/
Daingerfield HS 500/9-12
202 Tiger Dr 75638 903-645-3968
Michael Baysinger, prin. Fax 645-7662
Daingerfield JHS 400/6-8
200 Texas St 75638 903-645-2261
Darrel Shelton, prin. Fax 645-4010

Daisetta, Liberty, Pop. 1,090
Hull-Daisetta ISD 600/PK-12
PO Box 477 77533 936-536-6321
Steven Dozier, supt. Fax 536-6251
Hull-Daisetta HS 200/9-12
PO Box 477 77533 936-536-6321
Jay Killgo, prin. Fax 536-3839
Other Schools – See Raywood

Dalhart, Dallam, Pop. 7,146
Dalhart ISD 1,600/PK-12
315 Rock Island Ave 79022 806-244-7810
David Foote, supt. Fax 244-7822
www.dalhart.k12.tx.us
Dalhart HS 400/9-12
315 Rock Island Ave 79022 806-244-7300
David Steele, prin. Fax 244-7307
Dalhart JHS 400/6-8
315 Rock Island Ave 79022 806-244-7825
Marlin Coffman, prin. Fax 244-7835

Dallardsville, Polk
Big Sandy ISD 500/PK-12
PO Box 188 77332 936-563-1000
Kenneth Graham, supt. Fax 563-1010
www.bigsandyisd.net/
Other Schools – See Livingston

Dallas, Dallas, Pop. 1,213,825
Carrollton-Farmers Branch ISD
Supt. — See Carrollton
Long MS 1,000/6-8
2525 Frankford Rd 75287 972-968-4100
Nicoloas Lasker, prin. Fax 968-4110

Dallas ISD 147,400/PK-12
3700 Ross Ave 75204 972-925-3700
Michael Hinojosa Ed.D., supt. Fax 925-3201
www.dallasisd.org
Adams HS 2,600/9-12
2101 Millmar Dr 75228 972-502-4900
Raquel Galvan, prin. Fax 502-4901
Adamson HS 1,300/9-12
201 E 9th St 75203 972-749-1400
Rawley Sanchez, prin. Fax 749-1401
Alternative Placement Center 9-12
4949 Village Fair Dr 75224 972-925-7000
Roderick Cushing, prin. Fax 925-7001
Anderson Learning Center 700/7-8
3400 Garden Ln 75215 972-925-7900
Benita Noiel-Ashford, prin. Fax 925-7901
Atwell Law Academy 800/7-8
1303 Reynoldston Ln 75232 972-794-6400
Harnell Williams, prin. Fax 794-6401
Browne MS 1,200/7-8
3333 Sprague Dr 75233 972-502-2500
Cedric Barrett, prin. Fax 502-2501
Carter HS 1,800/9-12
1819 W Wheatland Rd 75232 214-932-5700
Gail-David Dupree, prin. Fax 932-5701
Cary MS 1,200/6-8
3978 Killion Dr 75229 972-502-7600
Santiago Camacho, prin. Fax 502-7601
Comstock MS 900/7-8
7044 Hodde St 75217 972-794-1300
Marlon Brooks, prin. Fax 794-1301
Conrad HS 9-12
7502 Fair Oaks Ave 75231 972-502-2300
Donella Perry, prin. Fax 502-2301
Dade Learning Center 50/6-8
2801 Park Row Ave 75215 972-749-3800
David Welch, prin. Fax 749-3801
Dallas Environmental Science Academy 200/7-8
3635 Greenleaf St 75212 972-794-3950
Katie Watson, prin. Fax 794-4001
Early College HS 9-12
4849 W Illinois Ave Rm W53A 75211 214-860-3614
Lucy Davila-Hakemack, prin. Fax 860-3639
Edison MS 700/7-8
2940 Singleton Blvd 75212 972-794-4100
Jimmy King, prin. Fax 794-4101
Education & Social Service Magnet HS 200/9-12
1201 E 8th St 75203 972-925-5940
Cheryl Wright, dean Fax 925-5901
Florence MS 1,100/7-8
1625 N Masters Dr 75217 972-749-6000
Bryant Joseph, prin. Fax 749-6001
Franklin MS 1,000/7-8
6920 Meadow Rd 75230 972-502-7100
Ronald Jones, prin. Fax 502-7101
Gaston MS 900/7-8
9565 Mercer Dr 75228 972-502-5400
Susie Stauss, prin. Fax 502-5401
Government Law & Law Enforcement HS 400/9-12
1201 E 8th St Ste 203 75203 972-925-5950
Robert Giesler, prin. Fax 925-6010
Greiner Exploratory Arts Academy 1,700/7-8
501 S Edgefield Ave 75208 972-925-7100
Dorothy Gomez, prin. Fax 925-7101
Health Profession Magnet HS 500/9-12
1201 E 8th St Ste 281 75203 972-925-5930
Myrtle Walker, prin. Fax 925-5901
Hillcrest HS 1,700/9-12
9924 Hillcrest Rd 75230 972-502-6800
Marty Crawford, prin. Fax 502-6801
Hill MS 800/7-8
505 Easton Rd 75218 972-502-5700
Esther Contreras, prin. Fax 502-5701
Holmes Humanities/Comm Academy 900/6-8
2001 E Kiest Blvd 75216 972-925-8500
Michael Palmer, prin. Fax 925-8501
Hood MS 1,300/7-8
7625 Hume Dr 75227 972-749-4100
Fred Davis, prin. Fax 749-4101
Hulcy MS 600/6-8
9339 S Polk St 75232 214-932-7400
Alford Tribble, prin. Fax 932-7401
Jackson Center for Learning 100/6-8
2929 Stag Rd 75241 214-932-7900
Nakia Douglass, prin. Fax 932-7901
Jefferson HS 1,700/9-12
4001 Walnut Hill Ln 75229 972-502-7300
Manuel Ontiveros, prin. Fax 502-7301
Kimball HS 1,700/9-12
3606 S Westmoreland Rd 75233 972-502-2100
Danny Stigers, prin. Fax 502-2101
Lincoln Humanities/Communications HS 1,100/9-12
2826 Hatcher St 75215 972-925-7600
Earl Jones, prin. Fax 925-7601
Longfellow Career Academy 400/7-8
5314 Boaz St 75209 972-749-5400
Rob Pipkin, prin. Fax 749-5401
Long MS 800/7-8
6116 Reiger Ave 75214 972-502-4700
Desiree Arias, prin. Fax 502-4701
Madison HS 600/9-12
3000 Mrtn Lthr King Jr Blvd 75215 972-925-2800
Marian Willard, prin. Fax 925-2801
Marsh MS 1,300/7-8
3838 Crown Shore Dr 75244 972-502-6600
Kyle Richardson, prin. Fax 502-6601
Middle College HS 100/9-12
801 Main St 75202 214-860-2356
Leicha Shaver, prin. Fax 860-2159
Molina HS 2,600/9-12
2355 Duncanville Rd 75211 972-502-1000
Patricia Dumas, prin. Fax 502-1001
Multiple Careers Magnet HS Vo/Tech
4528 Rusk Ave 75204 972-925-2200
Bill Quinones, prin. Fax 925-2201
North Dallas HS 1,800/9-12
3120 N Haskell Ave 75204 972-925-1500
Dina Townsend, prin. Fax 925-1501
Pinkston HS 1,000/9-12
2200 Dennison St 75212 972-502-2700
James Colbert, prin. Fax 502-2701
Quintanilla MS 1,100/7-8
2700 Remond Dr 75211 972-502-3200
Rodney Cooksy, prin. Fax 502-3201
Rangel Young Women's Leadership S 6-12
1718 Robert B Cullum Blvd 75210 972-749-5200
Vivian Taylor, prin. Fax 749-5201
Roosevelt HS 700/9-12
525 Bonnie View Rd 75203 972-925-6800
Fax 925-6801
Rusk MS 700/7-8
2929 Inwood Rd 75235 972-925-2000
Evangelina Kircher, prin. Fax 925-2001
Samuell HS 2,000/9-12
8928 Palisade Dr 75217 972-892-5100
Daniel Johnson, prin. Fax 892-5101
School for the Talented & Gifted 200/9-12
1201 E 8th St Ste 216 75203 972-925-5970
Michael Satarino, prin. Fax 925-6018
School of Business & Management 500/9-12
1201 E 8th St Ste 241 75203 972-925-5920
Edith Krutilek, prin. Fax 925-5901
School of Science & Engineering HS 400/9-12
1201 E 8th St 75203 972-925-5960
Charles Tuttle, prin. Fax 925-6016
Seagoville HS 1,200/9-12
15920 Seagoville Rd 75253 972-892-5900
Judie Klaus, prin. Fax 892-5901
Seagoville MS 800/7-8
950 N Woody Rd 75253 972-892-7100
Jose Cardenas, prin. Fax 892-7101

Skyline Career Development Ctr — Vo/Tech
7777 Forney Rd 75227 — 214-502-3400
Fax 502-3401
Skyline HS — 4,400/9-12
7777 Forney Rd 75227 — 972-502-3400
Leslie Williams, prin. — Fax 502-3401
Smith HS — 900/9-12
3030 Stag Rd 75241 — 214-932-7600
Dwain Govan, prin. — Fax 932-7601
South Oak Cliff HS — 1,300/9-12
3601 S Marsalis Ave 75216 — 214-932-7000
Regina Jones-Carroll, prin. — Fax 932-7001
Spence Talented/Gifted Academy — 900/6-8
4001 Capitol Ave 75204 — 972-925-2300
Mary Davies, prin. — Fax 925-2301
Spruce HS — 1,600/9-12
9733 Old Seagoville Rd 75217 — 972-892-5500
Ardis McCann, prin. — Fax 892-5501
Stockard MS — 800/7-8
2300 S Ravinia Dr 75211 — 972-794-5700
Faustino Rivas, prin. — Fax 794-5701
Storey MS — 600/7-8
3000 Maryland Ave 75216 — 972-925-8700
Cassandra Asberry, prin. — Fax 925-8701
Sunset HS — 2,100/9-12
2120 W Jefferson Blvd 75208 — 972-502-1500
Tony Tovar, prin. — Fax 502-1501
Tasby MS — 6-8
7001 Fair Oaks Ave 75231 — 972-502-1900
Paul Zevallos, prin. — Fax 502-1901
Townview Magnet Center — 9-12
1201 E 8th St 75203 — 972-925-5900
Alice Black, prin. — Fax 925-5901
Travis Academy — 200/4-8
3001 Mckinney Ave 75204 — 972-794-7500
Mari Smith, prin. — Fax 794-7501
Walker MS — 200/6-8
12532 Nuestra Dr 75230 — 972-502-6100
Eduardo Hernandez, prin. — Fax 502-6101
Washington Performing & Visual Arts HS — 700/9-12
3434 S R L Thornton Fwy 75224 — 972-925-1200
Ruth Woodward, prin. — Fax 925-1201
White HS — 2,100/9-12
4505 Ridgeside Dr 75244 — 972-502-6200
Joy Barnhart, prin. — Fax 502-6201
Wilson HS — 1,400/9-12
100 S Glasgow Dr 75214 — 972-502-4400
Ruth Vail, prin. — Fax 502-4401
Zumwalt MS — 600/6-8
2445 E Ledbetter Dr 75216 — 972-749-3600
Myrtle Dixon, prin. — Fax 749-3601
Evening Academy — Adult
7777 Forney Rd 75227 — 972-502-3458
Phillip Allen, prin. — Fax 502-3463
Manns HS — Adult
912 S Ervay St 75201 — 972-749-2200
Gene Ward, prin. — Fax 749-2201

Duncanville ISD
Supt. — See Duncanville
Kennemer MS — 7-8
7101 W Wheatland Rd 75249 — 972-708-3600
Daron Lee, prin. — Fax 708-3636

Highland Park ISD — 6,100/PK-12
7015 Westchester Dr 75205 — 214-780-3000
Dr. Cathy Bryce, supt. — Fax 780-3099
www.hpisd.org
Highland Park HS — 1,900/9-12
4220 Emerson Ave 75205 — 214-780-3700
Patrick Cates, prin. — Fax 780-3799
Highland Park MS — 900/7-8
3555 Granada Ave 75205 — 214-780-3600
Laurie Norton, prin. — Fax 780-3699

Plano ISD
Supt. — See Plano
Frankford MS — 1,200/6-8
7706 Osage Plaza Pkwy 75252 — 469-752-5200
Susan Modisette, prin. — Fax 752-5201

Richardson ISD
Supt. — See Richardson
Forest Meadow JHS — 700/7-8
9373 Whitehurst Dr 75243 — 469-593-1500
Charles Bruner, prin. — Fax 593-1461
Lake Highlands Freshman Center — 800/9-9
10200 White Rock Trl 75238 — 469-593-1300
Jayne Farmer, prin. — Fax 593-1327
Lake Highlands HS — 1,900/10-12
9449 Church Rd 75238 — 469-593-1000
Dr. Robert Iden, prin. — Fax 593-1030
Lake Highlands JHS — 700/7-8
10301 Walnut Hill Ln 75238 — 469-593-1600
Lorine Burrell, prin. — Fax 593-1606
Liberty JHS — 800/7-9
10330 Lawler Rd 75243 — 469-593-7888
Stephen Quisenberry, prin. — Fax 593-7764
Parkhill JHS — 800/7-9
16500 Shadybank Dr 75248 — 469-593-5600
Judy Marcum, prin. — Fax 593-5500
Westwood Magnet JHS — 900/7-9
7630 Arapaho Rd 75248 — 469-593-3600
Peggy Dillion, prin. — Fax 593-3508

Argosy University/Dallas — Post-Sec.
8080 Park Ln Ste 400 75231 — 214-890-9900
Art Institute of Dallas — Post-Sec.
8080 Park Ln Ste 100 75231 — 214-692-8080
ATI Career Training Center — Post-Sec.
10003 Technology Blvd W 75220 — 214-902-8191
ATI Technical Training Center — Post-Sec.
6627 Maple Ave 75235 — 214-352-2222
Aviation Institute of Maintenance — Post-Sec.
7555 Lemmon Ave 75209 — 214-333-9711
Baylor University Medical Center — Post-Sec.
3500 Gaston Ave 75246 — 214-820-2731
Bill Priest Inst. Economic Development — Post-Sec.
1402 Corinth St 75215 — 214-860-5900
Bishop Dunne HS — 600/7-12
3900 Rugged Dr 75224 — 214-339-6561
Kate Dailey, prin. — Fax 339-1438
Bishop Lynch HS — 1,100/9-12
9750 Ferguson Rd 75228 — 214-324-3607
Evelyn Grubbs, prin. — Fax 324-3600
Central Texas Commercial College — Post-Sec.
9400 N Central Expy Ste 200 75231 — 214-368-3680
Court Reporting Institute of Dallas — Post-Sec.
1341 W Mockingbird Ln # 200 75247 — 214-350-9722
Covenant S — 300/K-12
3877 Walnut Hill Ln 75229 — 214-358-5818
Kyle Queal, dir. — Fax 358-5809

Dallas Academy — 100/K-12
950 Tiffany Way 75218 — 214-324-1481
James Richardson, hdmstr. — Fax 327-8537
Dallas Baptist University — Post-Sec.
3000 Mountain Creek Pkwy 75211 — 214-333-7100
Dallas Barber and Stylist College — Post-Sec.
9357 Forest Ln 75243 — 214-360-9570
Dallas Christian College — Post-Sec.
2700 Christian Pkwy 75234 — 800-688-1029
Dallas Institute of Funeral Service — Post-Sec.
3909 S Buckner Blvd 75227 — 214-388-5466
Dallas Theological Seminary — Post-Sec.
3909 Swiss Ave 75204 — 214-824-3094
El Centro College — Post-Sec.
801 Main St 75202 — 214-860-2037
Episcopal S of Dallas — 600/5-12
4100 Merrell Rd 75229 — 214-353-5812
Rev. Stephen Swann, hdmstr. — Fax 353-5865
Everest College — Post-Sec.
6060 N Central Expy Ste 101 75206 — 214-234-4850
Fairhill S — 200/1-12
16150 Preston Rd 75248 — 972-233-1026
Jane Sego, dir. — Fax 233-8205
First Baptist Academy — 700/K-12
PO Box 868 75221 — 214-969-7861
Jake Walters, hdmstr. — Fax 969-7797
Graduate Institute of Applied Linguistic — Post-Sec.
7500 W Camp Wisdom Rd 75236 — 972-708-7340
Hockaday S — 1,000/PK-12
11600 Welch Rd 75229 — 214-363-6311
Jeanne Whitman, hdmstr. — Fax 363-0942
Interactive Learning Systems — Post-Sec.
8585 N Stemmons Fwy Ste C15 75247 — 214-637-3377
Jesuit College Preparatory S — 1,000/9-12
12345 Inwood Rd 75244 — 972-387-8700
Michael Earsing, prin. — Fax 661-9349
Jones Beauty College — Post-Sec.
10909 Webbs Chapel Rd # 129 75229 — 214-956-0088
KD Studio - Actors Conservatory — Post-Sec.
2600 N Stemmons Fwy Ste 117 75207 — 214-638-0484
Lakehill Prep S — 400/K-12
2720 Hillside Dr 75214 — 214-826-2931
Roger Perry, hdmstr. — Fax 826-4623
Lobias Murray Christian Academy — 200/K-12
330 E Ann Arbor Ave 75216 — 214-372-6466
Sharon Smith, prin. — Fax 376-6763
Lutheran HS — 300/7-12
8494 Stults Rd 75243 — 214-349-8912
Brad Krause, prin. — Fax 340-3095
Mesorah HS — 50/9-12
6921 Frankford Rd 75252 — 972-599-0031
Rabbi Avraham Kosowsky, hdmstr. — Fax 599-0033
Metropolitan Christian S — 300/PK-12
8501 Bruton Rd 75217 — 214-388-4426
MJ's Beauty Academy — Post-Sec.
3939 S Polk St Ste 505 75224 — 214-374-7500
Mountain View College — Post-Sec.
4849 W Illinois Ave 75211 — 214-860-8680
Neilson Beauty College — Post-Sec.
416 W Jefferson Blvd 75208 — 214-941-8756
Ogle School of Hair Design — Post-Sec.
6333 E Mockingbird Ln #201 75214 — 214-821-0819
Parish Episcopal S — 1,000/PK-12
4101 Sigma Rd 75244 — 972-239-8011
Gloria Snyder, hdmstr. — Fax 991-1237
Parker College of Chiropractic — Post-Sec.
2500 Walnut Hill Ln 75229 — 972-438-6932
Paul Quinn College — Post-Sec.
3837 Simpson Stuart Rd 75241 — 214-376-1000
PCI Health Training Center — Post-Sec.
8101 John W Carpenter Fwy 75247 — 214-630-0568
Presbyterian Hospital — Post-Sec.
8200 Walnut Hill Ln 75231 — 214-345-7558
Richland College — Post-Sec.
12800 Abrams Rd 75243 — 972-238-6100
St. Marks S of Texas — 800/1-12
10600 Preston Rd 75230 — 214-346-8000
Arnold Holtberg, hdmstr. — Fax 346-8002
Shelton S — 800/PK-12
15720 Hillcrest Rd 75248 — 972-774-1772
Dr. Joyce Pickering, dir. — Fax 991-3977
Southeastern Career Institute — Post-Sec.
12005 Ford Rd Ste 100 75234 — 972-385-1446
Southern Methodist University — Post-Sec.
PO Box 750181 75275 — 214-768-2000
Texas A&M Univ.-Baylor Coll. Dentistry — Post-Sec.
3302 Gaston Ave 75246 — 214-828-8100
Texas Barber Colleges & Hairstyling Sch — Post-Sec.
5148 S Lancaster Rd Ste A 75241 — 214-943-7255
The Criswell College — Post-Sec.
4010 Gaston Ave 75246 — 800-899-0012
Tyler Street Christian Academy — 200/PK-12
915 W 9th St 75208 — 214-941-9717
Dr. Karen Egger, supt. — Fax 941-0324
Ultrasound Diagnostic School — Post-Sec.
2998 N Stemmons Fwy # B 75247 — 214-638-6400
University of Texas S.W. Medical Center — Post-Sec.
5323 Harry Hines Blvd 75390 — 214-648-3111
Ursuline Academy — 800/9-12
4900 Walnut Hill Ln 75229 — 469-232-1800
Elizabeth Bourgeois, prin. — Fax 232-1836
Velma B's Beauty Academy — Post-Sec.
1511 S Ewing Ave 75216 — 214-942-1541
Wade College Dallas Market Center — Post-Sec.
PO Box 421149 75342 — 800-624-4850
Westwood College of Technology — Post-Sec.
8390 Lyndon B Johnson Fwy 75243 — 214-570-0100
White Rock Montessori — 200/PK-10
1601 Oates Dr 75228 — 214-324-5580
Sue Henry, prin. — Fax 324-5671
Winston S — 200/1-12
5707 Royal Ln 75229 — 214-691-6950
Dr. Polly Peterson, hdmstr. — Fax 691-1509
Yavneh Academy — 50/9-12
12324 Merit Dr 75251 — 214-295-3500
Donald O'Quinn, prin. — Fax 295-3505

Danbury, Brazoria, Pop. 1,667
Danbury ISD — 800/PK-12
PO Box 378 77534 — 979-922-1218
Eric Grimmett, supt. — Fax 922-8246
www.danbury.isd.esc4.net
Danbury HS — 200/9-12
PO Box 377 77534 — 979-922-1226
Christopher Kocurek, prin. — Fax 922-1051
Danbury MS — 100/7-8
PO Box 586 77534 — 979-922-1226
Christopher Kocurek, prin. — Fax 922-1051

Dawson, Navarro, Pop. 906
Dawson ISD — 500/PK-12
199 N School Ave 76639 — 254-578-1031
Hugh Ellis, supt. — Fax 578-1721
www.dawsonisd.org/
Dawson HS — 200/7-12
199 N School Ave 76639 — 254-578-1031
Ronnie Shiflet, prin. — Fax 578-1721

Dayton, Liberty, Pop. 6,622
Dayton ISD — 4,600/PK-12
PO Box 248 77535 — 936-258-2667
Greg Hayman, supt. — Fax 258-5616
www.daytonisd.net/
Dayton HS — 1,400/9-12
PO Box 248 77535 — 936-258-2510
Laurie Elliott, prin. — Fax 257-4047
Wilson JHS — 900/7-8
PO Box 248 77535 — 936-258-2309
Oran Hamilton, prin. — Fax 257-4109

Decatur, Wise, Pop. 6,031
Decatur ISD — 2,800/PK-12
501 E Collins St 76234 — 940-393-7100
Gerard Gindt Ed.D., supt. — Fax 627-3141
www.decatur.esc11.net
Decatur HS — 800/9-12
750 E Eagle Smt 76234 — 940-393-7200
Melinda Reeves, prin. — Fax 627-3669
Decatur MS — 400/7-8
1201 W Thompson St 76234 — 940-393-7300
Dr. Van Gardner, prin. — Fax 627-2497

Deer Park, Harris, Pop. 28,993
Deer Park ISD — 11,900/PK-12
203 Ivy Ave 77536 — 832-668-7000
Arnold Adair, supt. — Fax 930-1945
www.dpisd.org
Bonnette JHS — 700/6-8
5010 W Pasadena Blvd 77536 — 832-668-7700
Judy Connors, prin. — Fax 930-4756
Deer Park HS - North Campus — 1,000/9-9
402 Ivy Ave 77536 — 832-668-7300
Ernie Salazar, prin. — Fax 930-4840
Deer Park HS - South Campus — 2,600/10-12
710 W San Augustine St 77536 — 832-668-7200
Ronda Kouba, prin. — Fax 930-4894
Deer Park JHS — 800/6-8
410 E 9th St 77536 — 832-668-7500
Tiffany Regan, prin. — Fax 930-4726
Other Schools – See Pasadena

De Kalb, Bowie, Pop. 1,790
De Kalb ISD — 900/PK-12
101 Maple St 75559 — 903-667-2566
James Brewer, supt. — Fax 667-3791
www.dekalbisd.net
De Kalb HS — 300/9-12
101 Maple St 75559 — 903-667-2422
Stephanie Sparks, prin. — Fax 667-4086
De Kalb MS — 300/5-8
101 Maple St 75559 — 903-667-2834
Kim Birdsong, prin. — Fax 667-5509

De Leon, Comanche, Pop. 2,386
De Leon ISD — 700/PK-12
601 S Houston St 76444 — 254-893-5095
Dr. Randy Mohundro, supt. — Fax 893-3101
www.deleon.esc14.net
De Leon HS — 200/9-12
601 S Houston St 76444 — 254-893-6222
Mark Lewis, prin. — Fax 893-4985
Perkins MS — 200/6-8
601 S Houston St 76444 — 254-893-6111
Scott Carlisle, prin. — Fax 893-7918

Dell City, Hudspeth, Pop. 408
Dell City ISD — 100/K-12
PO Box 37 79837 — 915-964-2663
Tanya Lewis, supt. — Fax 964-2473
Dell City S — 100/K-12
PO Box 37 79837 — 915-964-2495
Tanya Lewis, prin. — Fax 964-2473

Del Rio, Val Verde, Pop. 36,020
San Felipe-Del Rio Consolidated ISD — 8,700/PK-12
PO Box 428002 78842 — 830-778-4000
Roberto Fernandez, supt. — Fax 774-9892
www.sfdr-cisd.org
Del Rio Freshman S — 800/9-9
PO Box 428002 78842 — 830-778-4400
Jorge Garza, prin. — Fax 774-9873
Del Rio HS — 1,800/10-12
PO Box 428002 78842 — 830-778-4329
Jorge Garza, prin. — Fax 774-9320
Del Rio MS — 7-8
PO Box 428002 78842 — 830-778-4530
Carlos Rios, prin. — Fax 778-4550

Amistad Christian HS — 50/9-12
901 Amistad Blvd 78840 — 830-775-0870
Virginia Craver, admin. — Fax 775-0870

Del Valle, Travis
Del Valle ISD — 7,700/PK-12
5301 Ross Rd 78617 — 512-386-3000
Bernard Blanchard, supt. — Fax 386-3015
www.del-valle.k12.tx.us
Del Valle HS — 1,800/9-12
5201 Ross Rd 78617 — 512-386-3200
Jean MacInnis, prin. — Fax 386-3205
Del Valle JHS — 600/7-8
5500 Ross Rd 78617 — 512-386-3400
Kenneth Storm, prin. — Fax 386-3405
Other Schools – See Austin

Denison, Grayson, Pop. 23,648
Denison ISD — 4,500/PK-12
1201 S Rusk Ave 75020 — 903-462-7000
Henry Scott, supt. — Fax 462-7002
denisonisd.net
Denison HS — 1,300/9-12
1901 S Mirick Ave 75020 — 903-462-7125
Cavin Boettger, prin. — Fax 462-7217
McDaniel MS — 1,100/6-8
400 S Lillis Ln 75020 — 903-462-7200
Alvis Dunlap, prin. — Fax 462-7328

Grayson County College — Post-Sec.
6101 Grayson Dr 75020 — 903-465-6030

Denton, Denton, Pop. 104,153
Denton ISD — 16,800/PK-12
1307 N Locust St 76201 — 940-369-0000
Dr. Ray Braswell, supt. — Fax 369-4982
www.dentonisd.org
Calhoun MS — 800/6-8
709 W Congress St 76201 — 940-369-2400
Anthony Sims, prin. — Fax 369-4939
Denton HS — 1,900/9-12
1007 Fulton St 76201 — 940-369-2000
Darrell Muncy, prin. — Fax 369-4953
Guyer HS — 9-12
7501 Teasley Ln 76210 — 940-369-1000
Barbara Fischer, prin. — Fax 369-4965
LaGrone Advanced Technology Complex — Vo/Tech
1504 Long Rd 76207 — 940-369-4850
Marty Thompson, dean — Fax 369-4971
McMath MS — 1,000/6-8
1900 Jason Dr 76205 — 940-369-3300
Dr. Debra Nobles, prin. — Fax 369-4946
Ryan HS — 2,300/9-12
5101 E McKinney St 76208 — 940-369-3000
Vernon Reeves, prin. — Fax 369-4960
Strickland MS — 900/6-8
324 E Windsor Dr 76209 — 940-369-4200
Kathleen Carmona, prin. — Fax 369-4950
Other Schools – See Aubrey, Corinth

Denton Calvary Academy — 200/1-12
PO Box 2414 76202 — 940-320-1944
David Brown, admin. — Fax 591-9311
International Business College — Post-Sec.
2006 W University Dr 76201 — 940-380-0024
Selwyn S — 300/PK-12
3333 W University Dr 76207 — 940-382-6771
Sandy Doerge, hdmstr. — Fax 383-0704
Texas Woman's University — Post-Sec.
PO Box 425589 76204 — 940-898-2000
University of North Texas — Post-Sec.
PO Box 305309 76203 — 940-565-2000

Denver City, Yoakum, Pop. 3,994
Denver City ISD — 1,300/PK-12
501 Mustang Dr 79323 — 806-592-5900
Dagobert Azam, supt. — Fax 592-5909
www.dcisd.org
Denver City HS — 400/9-12
601 Mustang Dr 79323 — 806-592-5950
Gary Davis, prin. — Fax 592-5959
Gravitt JHS — 300/6-8
419 Mustang Dr 79323 — 806-592-5940
Howard Wright, prin. — Fax 592-5949

De Soto, Dallas, Pop. 39,440
De Soto ISD — 7,300/PK-12
200 E Belt Line Rd, — 972-223-6666
Alton Frailey, supt. — Fax 274-8209
www.desotoisd.org
De Soto East MS — 700/6-8
601 E Belt Line Rd, — 972-223-0690
Donna Freeling, prin. — Fax 274-8156
De Soto HS Freshman Campus — 800/9-9
620 S Westmoreland Rd, — 972-274-1818
Sheila Brown, prin. — Fax 274-2501
De Soto SHS — 1,700/10-12
600 Eagle Dr, — 972-230-0726
Aubrey Todd, prin. — Fax 274-8115
De Soto West MS — 800/6-8
800 N Westmoreland Rd, — 972-230-1820
Kevin Dixon, prin. — Fax 274-8183
Other Schools – See Glenn Heights

Canterbury Episcopal S — 300/K-12
1708 N Westmoreland Rd, — 972-572-7200
Dick Cadigan, hdmstr. — Fax 572-7400

Detroit, Red River, Pop. 743
Detroit ISD — 500/PK-12
110 E Garner St 75436 — 903-674-6131
Morris Lyon, supt. — Fax 674-2478
detroitisd.esc8.net/
Detroit HS — 100/9-12
110 E Garner St 75436 — 903-674-2646
Misty Looney, prin. — Fax 674-2815
Detroit JHS — 100/6-8
110 E Garner St 75436 — 903-674-2646
Pat Travis, prin. — Fax 674-2206

Devers, Liberty, Pop. 437
Devers ISD — 200/PK-8
PO Box 488 77538 — 936-549-7135
Danny Grimes, supt. — Fax 549-7595
www.deversisd.net/
Devers JHS — 100/6-8
PO Box 488 77538 — 936-549-7135
Fax 549-7085

Devine, Medina, Pop. 4,409
Devine ISD — 1,800/PK-12
205 W College Ave 78016 — 830-851-0795
Rickey Williams, supt. — Fax 663-6706
www.devineisd.org
Devine HS — 600/9-12
1225 W Hondo Ave 78016 — 830-663-6780
Don Beck, prin. — Fax 663-6792
Devine MS — 400/6-8
400 Cardinal Dr 78016 — 830-851-0695
Lori Marek, prin. — Fax 663-6769

Deweyville, Newton, Pop. 1,218
Deweyville ISD — 800/PK-12
PO Box 408 77614 — 409-746-2731
Rick Summers, supt. — Fax 746-3360
www.esc05.k12.tx.us/dewisd/
Deweyville HS — 200/9-12
PO Box 259 77614 — 409-746-3173
Richard Sessions, prin. — Fax 746-9343
Deweyville MS — 200/6-8
PO Box 109 77614 — 409-746-2924
Darryl Dans, prin. — Fax 746-2753

D Hanis, Medina
D'Hanis ISD — 200/K-12
PO Box 307 78850 — 830-363-7216
Pam Seipp, supt. — Fax 363-7390
dhanis.tx.schoolwebpages.com
D'Hanis MSHS — 200/6-12
PO Box 307 78850 — 830-363-7216
Michael Poppell, prin. — Fax 363-7390

Diana, Upshur
New Diana ISD — 900/K-12
PO Box 26 75640 — 903-663-8000
Patrick T. Clark, supt. — Fax 663-9565
www.newdianaisd.net/
New Diana HS — 300/9-12
PO Box 26 75640 — 903-663-8001
Stevie Ford, prin. — Fax 663-2200
New Diana MS — 200/6-8
PO Box 26 75640 — 903-663-8002
Connie Robinson, prin. — Fax 663-1812

Diboll, Angelina, Pop. 5,441
Diboll ISD — 1,900/PK-12
PO Box 550 75941 — 936-829-4718
Horace Williams, supt. — Fax 829-5558
www.dibollisd.com
Diboll HS — 500/9-12
1000 Lumberjack St 75941 — 936-829-5626
Daniel Lopez, prin. — Fax 829-5708
Diboll JHS — 400/6-8
403 Dennis St 75941 — 936-829-5225
Mark Kettering, prin. — Fax 829-5848

Dickinson, Galveston, Pop. 17,898
Dickinson ISD — 7,000/PK-12
PO Box Z 77539 — 281-229-6000
Leland Williams, supt. — Fax 229-6011
www.dickinsonisd.org
Dickinson HS — 1,700/9-12
3800 Baker Dr 77539 — 281-229-6400
Michael La Touche, prin. — Fax 229-6401
McAdams JHS — 1,000/7-8
4007 Video St 77539 — 281-229-7100
Ernest Hubert, prin. — Fax 229-7101

Pine Drive Christian S — 300/PK-12
705 FM 517 Rd E 77539 — 281-534-4881
Larry Bowles, admin. — Fax 534-4318

Dilley, Frio, Pop. 4,167
Dilley ISD — 800/PK-12
245 W FM 117 78017 — 830-965-1912
Jack Seals, supt. — Fax 965-4069
dilleyisd.net
Dilley HS — 200/9-12
245 W FM 117 78017 — 830-965-1814
David Kyser, prin. — Fax 965-1276
Harper MS — 200/6-8
245 W FM 117 78017 — 830-965-2195
Nobert Rodriquez, prin. — Fax 965-2171

Dime Box, Lee
Dime Box ISD — 200/PK-12
PO Box 157 77853 — 979-884-2324
Clayton Waits, supt. — Fax 884-0106
dimebox.groupfusion.net
Dime Box S — 200/PK-12
PO Box 157 77853 — 979-884-3366
Vivian Bage, prin. — Fax 884-0106

Dimmitt, Castro, Pop. 3,981
Dimmitt ISD — 1,200/PK-12
608 W Halsell St 79027 — 806-647-3101
Charles Miller, supt. — Fax 647-5433
www.dimmittisd.net
Dimmitt HS — 300/9-12
1505 Western Cir 79027 — 806-647-3105
George Rasor, prin. — Fax 647-5795
Dimmitt MS — 400/5-8
805 W Jones St 79027 — 806-647-3108
Michael Graham, prin. — Fax 647-2996

Dodd City, Fannin, Pop. 443
Dodd City ISD — 300/PK-12
602 N Main St 75438 — 903-583-7585
Craig Reed, supt. — Fax 583-9545
doddcity.ednet10.net
Dodd City S — 300/PK-12
602 N Main St 75438 — 903-583-7585
Lesia Bridges, prin. — Fax 583-7586

Donna, Hidalgo, Pop. 15,846
Donna ISD — 12,400/PK-12
116 N 10th St 78537 — 956-464-1600
Joe Gonzalez, supt. — Fax 464-1752
www.donnaisd.net
Donna SHS — 1,700/10-12
116 N 10th St 78537 — 956-464-1700
Fernando Castillo, prin. — Fax 464-1629
Sauceda MS — 900/6-8
116 N 10th St 78537 — 956-464-1360
Nancy Castillo, prin. — Fax 464-1349
Solis MS — 800/6-8
116 N 10th St 78537 — 956-464-1650
Fax 464-1786
Todd 9th Grade Campus — 800/9-9
116 N 10th St 78537 — 956-464-1800
David C. Villarreal, prin. — Fax 464-1824
Veterans MS — 900/6-8
116 N 10th St 78537 — 956-464-1350
Jose Javier Villanueva, prin. — Fax 464-1356

Douglass, Nacogdoches
Douglass ISD — 400/PK-12
PO Box 38 75943 — 936-569-9804
Jay Hampton-Tullos, supt. — Fax 569-9446
www.douglass.esc7.net
Douglass S — 400/PK-12
PO Box 38 75943 — 936-569-9804
Eric Samford, prin. — Fax 569-9446

Dripping Springs, Hays, Pop. 1,666
Dripping Springs ISD — 3,400/PK-12
PO Box 479 78620 — 512-858-4905
Mard Herrick Ph.D., supt. — Fax 858-4232
www.dripping-springs.k12.tx.us/
Dripping Springs HS — 1,100/9-12
PO Box 479 78620 — 512-858-4612
Greg Jung, prin. — Fax 858-1656
Dripping Springs MS — 900/6-8
PO Box 479 78620 — 512-858-4902
Kim Gravell, prin. — Fax 858-7213

Driscoll, Nueces, Pop. 822
Driscoll ISD — 300/PK-8
PO Box 238 78351 — 361-387-7349
Cynthia Garcia, supt. — Fax 387-6088
www.driscollisd.esc2.net
Driscoll MS — 100/6-8
PO Box 238 78351 — 361-387-7349
Cynthia Garcia, prin. — Fax 387-6088

Dublin, Erath, Pop. 3,662
Dublin ISD — 1,300/PK-12
PO Box 169 76446 — 254-445-3341
Roy Neff, supt. — Fax 445-3345
www.dublin.k12.tx.us
Dublin HS — 400/9-12
PO Box 169 76446 — 254-445-0362
Vicky Stone, prin. — Fax 445-1706
Dublin MS — 300/6-8
PO Box 169 76446 — 254-445-2618
John Grimland, prin. — Fax 445-2607

Dumas, Moore, Pop. 13,887
Dumas ISD — 4,000/PK-12
PO Box 615 79029 — 806-935-6461
Larry Appel, supt. — Fax 935-6275
www.dumas-k12.net/
Dumas HS — 1,100/9-12
PO Box 615 79029 — 806-935-4151
Bob Callahan, prin. — Fax 934-1433
Dumas JHS — 600/7-8
PO Box 615 79029 — 806-935-4155
Danny Potter, prin. — Fax 934-1434

Duncanville, Dallas, Pop. 35,150
Duncanville ISD — 10,900/PK-12
802 S Main St 75137 — 972-708-2000
Kenneth English, supt. — Fax 708-2020
www.duncanvilleisd.org
Byrd MS — 1,000/7-8
1040 W Wheatland Rd 75116 — 972-708-3400
Gabe Trujillo, prin. — Fax 708-3434
Duncanville HS — 2,600/9-12
900 W Camp Wisdom Rd 75116 — 972-708-3700
Mike Chrietzberg, prin. — Fax 708-3737
Reed MS — 1,000/7-8
530 E Freeman St 75116 — 972-708-3500
Andre Smith, prin. — Fax 708-3535
Other Schools – See Dallas

ChristWay Academy — 100/PK-12
419 N Cedar Ridge Dr 75116 — 972-296-6525
Daryl Johnston, admin. — Fax 780-7273
Masters Academy — 50/3-12
PO Box 381174 75138 — 972-780-2616
Elderine Wyrick, dir. — Fax 283-0296
State Beauty Academy — Post-Sec.
663 Oriole Blvd 75116 — 972-298-0100

Eagle Lake, Colorado, Pop. 3,693
Rice Consolidated ISD
Supt. — See Altair
Eagle Lake JHS — 6-8
600 Johnnie D Hutchins 77434 — 979-234-3501
Mike Keenon, prin. — Fax 234-5027

Eagle Pass, Maverick, Pop. 25,571
Eagle Pass ISD — 13,500/PK-12
1420 Eidson Rd 78852 — 830-773-5181
Jesus Sanchez, supt. — Fax 773-7252
www.eaglepassisd.net
Eagle Pass HS 9th-10th Grade Campus — 1,900/9-10
1420 Eidson Rd 78852 — 830-773-2381
Rudolph Bowles, prin. — Fax 758-1795
Eagle Pass JHS — 1,000/7-8
1420 Eidson Rd 78852 — 830-758-7037
Maria Sumpter, prin. — Fax 757-1278
Eagle Pass SHS CC Winn Campus — 1,500/11-12
1420 Eidson Rd 78852 — 830-757-0828
Jesus A. Diaz-Wever, prin. — Fax 757-3268
Memorial JHS — 1,100/7-8
1420 Eidson Rd 78852 — 830-758-7053
Oscar Castillon, prin. — Fax 773-8900

SW School of Business & Tech Careers — Post-Sec.
272 Commercial St 78852 — 830-773-1373

Early, Brown, Pop. 2,774
Early ISD — 1,300/PK-12
PO Box 3315, Brownwood TX 76803 — 325-646-7934
Brett A. Koch, supt. — Fax 646-9238
www.earlyisd.net/
Early HS — 400/9-12
PO Box 3315, Brownwood TX 76803 — 325-643-4593
Wes Beck, prin. — Fax 646-4061
Early MS — 300/6-8
PO Box 3315, Brownwood TX 76803 — 325-643-5665
Randy Lancaster, prin. — Fax 646-9972

Earth, Lamb, Pop. 1,077
Springlake-Earth ISD — 400/PK-12
PO Box 130 79031 — 806-257-3310
Gary Bigham, supt. — Fax 257-3927
www.springlake-earth.org
Springlake HS — 100/9-12
PO Box 130 79031 — 806-257-3819
Robert Conkin, prin. — Fax 257-3370

East Bernard, Wharton, Pop. 2,275
East Bernard ISD — 900/PK-12
723 College St 77435 — 979-335-7519
Garland Calhoun, supt. — Fax 335-6561
www.ebisd.org/
East Bernard HS — 300/9-12
723 College St 77435 — 979-335-7519
Buck Wenglar, prin. — Fax 335-6085
East Bernard JHS — 300/5-8
723 College St 77435 — 979-335-7519
Emmett Tugwell, prin. — Fax 335-6085

Eastland, Eastland, Pop. 3,813
Eastland ISD — 1,200/PK-12
PO Box 31 76448 — 254-631-5120
Donald W. Hughes, supt. — Fax 631-5126
Eastland HS, PO Box 31 76448 — 400/9-12
Joel Lawson, prin. — 254-631-5000
Eastland MS, PO Box 31 76448 — 300/6-8
Rickie Pack, prin. — 254-631-5040

Ector, Fannin, Pop. 632
Ector ISD — 300/K-12
PO Box 128 75439 — 903-961-2355
Gary Bohannon, supt. — Fax 961-2110
ector.ednet10.net
Ector HS — 100/7-12
PO Box 128 75439 — 903-961-2076
Shannon Baker, prin. — Fax 961-2356

Edcouch, Hidalgo, Pop. 4,426
Edcouch-Elsa ISD — 5,100/PK-12
PO Box 127 78538 — 956-262-6000
Michael Sandroussi, supt. — Fax 262-6032
www.eeisd.org

Other Schools – See Elsa

Eddy, McLennan, Pop. 1,113
Bruceville-Eddy ISD 900/K-12
1 Eagle Dr 76524 254-859-5832
Richard Kilgore, supt. Fax 859-4023
www.brucevilleeddyisd.net
Bruceville-Eddy HS 200/10-12
1 Eagle Dr 76524 254-859-5848
Chris Gibbs, prin. Fax 859-5001
Bruceville-Eddy MS, 1 Eagle Dr 76524 200/7-9
Mike Hawkins, prin. 254-859-5525

Eden, Concho, Pop. 2,447
Eden Consolidated ISD 300/K-12
PO Box 988 76837 325-869-4121
Bill Alcorn, supt. Fax 869-5210
Eden JSHS 100/7-12
PO Box 988 76837 325-869-5180
Tim Siler, prin. Fax 869-5023

Edgewood, Van Zandt, Pop. 1,451
Edgewood ISD 900/PK-12
PO Box 6 75117 903-896-4332
Jack Shellnutt, supt. Fax 896-7056
www.edgewood.esc7.net
Edgewood HS 300/9-12
PO Box 6 75117 903-896-4856
Blake Cooper, prin. Fax 896-1050
Edgewood MS 200/6-8
PO Box 6 75117 903-896-1530
Terry Phillips, prin. Fax 896-7056

Edinburg, Hidalgo, Pop. 62,735
Edinburg Consolidated ISD 26,500/PK-12
PO Box 990 78540 956-289-2300
Eugenio Gutierrez, supt. Fax 383-3576
www.ecisd.us/
Barrientes MS 6-8
PO Box 990 78540 956-289-2300
Economedes HS 2,100/9-12
PO Box 990 78540 956-289-2450
Anibal Gorena, prin. Fax 385-3050
Edinburg HS 2,300/9-12
PO Box 990 78540 956-289-2400
Maria Guerra, prin. Fax 386-1225
Edinburg North HS 2,000/9-12
PO Box 990 78540 956-316-7654
Ramiro Guerra, prin. Fax 316-7712
Edinburg South MS 1,400/6-8
PO Box 990 78540 956-316-7750
Hector Gonzalez, prin. Fax 316-8817
Garza MS 1,500/6-8
PO Box 990 78540 956-316-3100
Cipriano Pena, prin. Fax 316-3109
Harwell MS 1,400/6-8
PO Box 990 78540 956-289-2440
Gilda Sanchez, prin. Fax 384-5238
Memorial MS 1,400/6-8
PO Box 990 78540 956-316-7575
Ruben Gonzalez, prin. Fax 316-7581

South Texas ISD
Supt. — See Mercedes
South Texas Business Educ &Tech Academy 700/7-12
510 S Sugar Rd 78539 956-383-1684
Magdalena Gutierrez, prin. Fax 383-8544

Rio Grande Bible Institute Post-Sec.
4300 S US Highway 281 78539 956-380-8100
University of Texas-Pan American Post-Sec.
1201 W University Dr 78539 956-381-2011

Edna, Jackson, Pop. 5,870
Edna ISD 1,500/PK-12
PO Box 919 77957 361-782-3573
Robert Wells, supt. Fax 781-1002
www.ednaisd.org
Edna HS 400/9-12
PO Box 919 77957 361-782-5255
Richard Wright, prin. Fax 781-1014
Pumphrey JHS 400/6-8
PO Box 919 77957 361-782-2351
Demetric Wells, prin. Fax 781-1025

El Campo, Wharton, Pop. 10,884
El Campo ISD 3,500/PK-12
700 W Norris St 77437 979-543-6771
Robert Mark Poole, supt. Fax 543-1670
www.ecisd.org/
El Campo HS 1,100/9-12
600 W Norris St 77437 979-543-6341
Diann Srubar, prin. Fax 543-2528
El Campo MS 800/6-8
1401 MLK Blvd 77437 979-543-6362
Rodney Montello, prin. Fax 541-5210

Eldorado, Schleicher, Pop. 1,809
Schleicher ISD 600/PK-12
PO Box W 76936 325-853-2514
Billy Collins, supt. Fax 853-2695
www.scisd.net
Eldorado HS 200/9-12
PO Box W 76936 325-853-2549
Bob Wanoreck, prin. Fax 853-2710
Eldorado MS 200/5-8
PO Box W 76936 325-853-3028
Kara Sue Garlitz, prin. Fax 853-2895

Electra, Wichita, Pop. 2,938
Electra ISD 600/PK-12
PO Box 231 76360 940-495-3683
Gary Nightingale, supt. Fax 495-3945
www.electraisd.net
Electra HS 200/9-12
400 E Roosevelt Ave 76360 940-495-2218
Nora Curry, prin. Fax 495-3303
Electra JHS 200/5-8
621 S Bailey St 76360 940-495-2533
Gene Jarvis, prin. Fax 495-4636

Elgin, Bastrop, Pop. 8,689
Elgin ISD 3,200/PK-12
PO Box 351 78621 512-281-3434
Bill Graves, supt. Fax 281-5388
www.elginisd.net
Elgin HS 1,000/9-12
PO Box 311 78621 512-281-3438
Roberto Vasquez, prin. Fax 281-9804
Elgin MS 700/6-8
902 W 2nd St 78621 512-281-3382
Ehrikka Hodge, prin. Fax 281-9781

Elkhart, Anderson, Pop. 1,260
Elkhart ISD 1,300/PK-12
301 E Parker St 75839 903-764-2952
Dr. J. Glenn Hambrick, supt. Fax 764-2466
www.elkhartisd.org/
Elkhart HS 400/9-12
301 E Parker St 75839 903-764-5161
Tim Ratcliff, prin. Fax 764-2466
Elkhart MS 300/6-8
301 E Parker St 75839 903-764-2459
Ron Mays, prin. Fax 764-2466

Slocum ISD 400/PK-12
5765 E State Highway 294 75839 903-478-3624
Fred Fulton, supt. Fax 478-3030
www.slocum.esc7.net
Slocum JSHS 200/7-12
5765 E State Highway 294 75839 903-478-3624
Cliff Lasiter, prin. Fax 478-3030

Elmaton, Matagorda
Tidehaven ISD 900/PK-12
PO Box 129 77440 361-588-6321
Tom Jones, supt. Fax 588-7109
www.tidehavenisd.com
Tidehaven HS 300/9-12
PO Box 159 77440 361-588-6810
Kathy Boyett, prin. Fax 588-6966
Tidehaven IS 200/6-8
PO Box 130 77440 361-588-6600
Debra Taska, prin. Fax 588-6600

El Paso, El Paso, Pop. 598,590
Canutillo ISD 4,600/PK-12
7965 Artcraft Rd 79932 915-877-7400
Dr. Pam Padilla, supt. Fax 877-7414
www.canutillo-isd.org
Canutillo HS 1,300/9-12
6675 S Desert Blvd 79912 915-877-7800
Max Padilla, prin. Fax 877-7807
Other Schools – See Canutillo

Clint ISD 8,500/PK-12
14521 Horizon Blvd 79928 915-926-4000
Ricardo Estrada, supt. Fax 926-4009
www.clintweb.net
East Montana MS 900/6-8
14521 Horizon Blvd 79928 915-926-5200
Mario Acosta, prin. Fax 855-0821
Horizon HS 800/9-12
14521 Horizon Blvd 79928 915-926-4200
Pam Howard, prin. Fax 852-0357
Mountain View HS 1,100/9-12
14521 Horizon Blvd 79928 915-926-5000
Edmond Martinez, prin. Fax 855-2503
Other Schools – See Clint, Horizon City

El Paso ISD 62,500/PK-12
PO Box 20100 79998 915-779-3781
Dr. Lorenzo Garcia, supt. Fax 779-6613
www.episd.org
Andress HS 1,900/9-12
5400 Sun Valley Dr 79924 915-832-8600
James Anderson, prin. Fax 757-6443
Austin HS 1,300/9-12
3500 Memphis Ave 79930 915-587-2500
Archangelo Pokluda, prin. Fax 566-7360
Bassett MS 1,000/6-8
4400 Elm St 79930 915-231-2260
Dr. Steven Lane, prin. Fax 565-1562
Bowie HS 1,300/9-12
801 S San Marcial St 79905 915-496-8200
Lionel Rubio, prin. Fax 532-1918
Burges HS 1,400/9-12
7800 Edgemere Blvd 79925 915-780-1100
Ernest Watts, prin. Fax 771-6914
Canyon Hills MS 1,000/6-8
8930 Eclipse St 79904 915-231-2240
Zack Gray, prin. Fax 757-8067
Center for Career & Technology Education Vo/Tech
1170 N Walnut St 79930 915-545-5900
Eric Winkelman, prin. Fax 544-5976
Chapin HS 1,700/9-12
7000 Dyer St 79904 915-832-6730
Dr. Carla Gonzales, prin. Fax 565-9716
Charles MS 700/6-8
4909 Trojan Dr 79924 915-849-3940
Michael Mendoza, prin. Fax 821-0505
Cordova MS 900/6-8
2231 Arizona Ave 79930 915-546-9012
Patsy Smith, prin. Fax 577-0848
Coronado HS 2,600/9-12
100 Champions Pl 79912 915-834-2460
Maria Morales, prin. Fax 587-6458
El Paso HS 1,200/9-12
800 E Schuster Ave 79902 915-496-8300
John Roskosky, prin. Fax 532-2008
Franklin HS 2,800/9-12
900 N Resler Dr 79912 915-832-6600
Carla Gasway, prin. Fax 587-4094
Guillen MS 1,000/6-8
900 S Cotton St 79901 915-496-4620
Rosa Lovelace, prin. Fax 532-1143
Henderson MS 1,100/6-8
5505 Robert Alva Ave 79905 915-887-3080
Lydia Muniz, prin. Fax 772-3425
Hornedo MS 1,800/6-8
825 E Redd Rd 79912 915-231-2200
Victoria York, prin. Fax 587-5059
Irvin HS 1,700/9-12
9465 Roanoke Dr 79924 915-587-3500
Mark Rupcich, prin. Fax 757-6450
Jefferson HS 1,200/9-12
4700 Alameda Ave 79905 915-496-8010
Samuel Villarreal, prin. Fax 532-2033
Lincoln MS 1,200/6-8
500 Mulberry Ave 79932 915-231-2180
Sandy Whitney, prin. Fax 581-1371
Magoffin MS 900/6-8
4931 Hercules Ave 79904 915-774-4040
Raul Ruiz, prin. Fax 757-7675
Morehead MS 1,200/6-8
5625 Confetti Dr 79912 915-231-2140
James Lamonica, prin. Fax 587-5355
Occupational Center Vo/Tech
5300 Warriors Dr 79932 915-587-9680
Toni Bowermaster, prin. Fax 584-2940
Richardson MS 800/6-8
11350 Loma Franklin Dr 79934 915-822-8829
Dianne Jones, prin. Fax 822-8812

Ross MS 800/6-8
6101 Hughey Cir 79925 915-887-3060
John Tanner, prin. Fax 771-6792
Silva Health Magnet HS 600/9-12
121 Val Verde St 79905 915-496-8100
Sam Villarreal, prin. Fax 533-3695
Terrace Hills MS 700/6-8
4835 Blossom Ave 79924 915-231-2120
Milton Jones, prin. Fax 759-0615
Wiggs MS 800/6-8
1300 Circle Dr 79902 915-231-2100
Jesus Teran, prin. Fax 533-2902
San Jacinto Adult Learning Center Adult
1216 Olive Ave 79901 915-533-9072
Blanca Andrade, admin. Fax 544-7163

Socorro ISD 33,100/PK-12
PO Box 292800 79929 915-937-0000
Charles Hart, supt. Fax 860-7137
www.sisd.net
Americas HS 3,000/9-12
12101 Pellicano Dr 79936 915-937-2800
Mary Ross, prin. Fax 855-6898
Clarke MS 1,200/6-8
1515 Bob Hope Dr 79936 915-937-5600
Bonnie Gonzalez, prin. Fax 857-3765
El Dorado HS 900/9-12
12401 Edgemere Blvd 79938 915-937-3200
Nora Paugh, prin. Fax 851-7820
Ensor MS 600/6-8
13600 Ryderwood Ave 79928 915-937-6000
Rosa Hood, prin. Fax 851-7590
Mission Early College HS 9-12
10700 Gateway Blvd E 79927 915-937-1201
Armando Aguirre, prin.
Montwood HS 2,700/9-12
12000 Montwood Dr 79936 915-937-2400
Juni Matthews, prin. Fax 849-2077
Montwood MS 900/6-8
11710 Pebble Hills Blvd 79936 915-937-5800
Libby Tidwell, prin. Fax 856-9909
Sanchez MS 900/6-8
321 N Rio Vista Rd 79927 915-872-7000
Clarise Jones, prin. Fax 859-6636
Slider MS 1,100/6-8
11700 School Ln 79936 915-937-5400
Mitchell Ferguson, prin. Fax 857-5804
Socorro HS 2,800/9-12
10150 Alameda Ave 79927 915-937-2000
Oscar Troncoso, prin. Fax 859-0206
Socorro MS 700/6-8
321 Bovee Rd 79927 915-937-5000
David Pena, prin. Fax 858-2672
Sun Ridge MS 600/6-8
2210 Sun Country Dr 79938 915-937-6600
Sam Hogue, prin. Fax 851-7730

Ysleta ISD 46,100/PK-12
9600 Sims Dr 79925 915-434-0000
Hector Montenegro, supt. Fax 591-4144
www.yisd.net
Bel Air HS 2,200/9-12
731 N Yarbrough Dr 79915 915-434-2000
Daniel Girard, prin. Fax 593-6110
Camino Real MS 700/6-8
9393 Alameda Ave 79907 915-434-8300
Dolores Chaparro, prin. Fax 858-3743
Del Valle HS 1,900/9-12
950 Bordeaux Dr 79907 915-434-3000
Paul Pearson, prin. Fax 858-1427
Desert View MS 600/7-8
1641 Billie Marie Dr 79936 915-434-5300
Ricardo Lopez, prin. Fax 591-9327
Eastwood HS 2,200/9-12
2430 Mcrae Blvd 79925 915-434-4000
Frank Burton, prin. Fax 594-8014
Eastwood MS 800/7-8
2612 Chaswood St 79935 915-434-4300
Malinda Carri, prin. Fax 591-9426
Hanks HS 2,400/9-12
2001 N Lee Trevino Dr 79936 915-434-5000
Dr. Eileen Wade, prin. Fax 598-4621
Hillcrest MS 600/7-8
8040 Yermoland Dr 79907 915-434-2200
Paul Covey, prin. Fax 591-9439
Indian Ridge MS 600/7-8
11201 Pebble Hills Blvd 79936 915-434-5400
Grace Martinez, prin. Fax 591-9447
Parkland HS 1,200/9-12
5932 Quail Ave 79924 915-434-6000
Miles Hume, prin. Fax 434-6291
Parkland MS 700/7-8
6045 Nova Way 79924 915-434-6300
Ruben Flores, prin. Fax 757-6608
Ranchland Hills MS 500/7-8
7615 Yuma Dr 79915 915-434-2300
Felipe de Jesus Barraza, prin. Fax 592-0036
Rio Bravo MS 400/6-8
525 Greggerson Dr 79907 915-434-8400
Michael Martinez, prin. Fax 872-0269
Riverside HS 1,500/9-12
301 Midway Dr 79915 915-434-7000
Ismael Villafane, prin. Fax 779-6983
Riverside MS 700/7-8
7615 Mimosa Ave 79915 915-434-7300
James Mesta, prin. Fax 772-7549
Valley View MS 700/7-8
8660 N Loop Dr 79907 915-434-3300
Victor Montes, prin. Fax 858-3615
Ysleta HS 1,900/9-12
8600 Alameda Ave 79907 915-434-8000
Gerard Lee, prin. Fax 858-3299
Ysleta MS 400/6-8
8691 Independence Dr 79907 915-434-8200
Irene Medina, prin. Fax 858-0261
Ysleta Community Learning Center Adult
121 Padres Dr 79907 915-434-9400
Fred Anaya, prin. Fax 858-6307

Bethel Temple Christian S 200/PK-12
6301 Alabama St 79904 915-565-2222
Marsha Hodge-Cardenas, admin. Fax 565-2223
Border Institute of Technology Post-Sec.
9611 Acer Ave 79925 915-593-7328
Business Skills Institute Post-Sec.
7850 Paseo Del Norte #216 79912 915-845-7772
Career Centers of Texas Post-Sec.
8360 Burnham Rd Ste 100 79907 915-595-1935
Cathedral HS 500/9-12
1309 N Stanton St 79902 915-532-3238
Sam Govea, prin. Fax 533-8248

Computer Career Center Post-Sec.
6101 Montana Ave 79925 915-779-8031
David L. Carrasco Job Corps Center Post-Sec.
11155 Gateway Blvd W 79935 915-594-0022
El Paso Community College Post-Sec.
PO Box 20500 79998 915-831-2000
El Paso Country Day S 200/PK-12
220 E Cliff Dr 79902 915-533-4492
Rose Ann Martinez, prin. Fax 533-9626
Faith Christian Academy 500/K-12
8960 Escobar Dr 79907 915-594-3305
Cesar Ramirez, prin. Fax 593-5474
Father Yermo HS 200/9-12
250 Washington St 79905 915-533-3185
Sr. Elia Hernandez, prin. Fax 544-0738
Immanuel Christian S 700/PK-12
1201 Hawkins Blvd 79925 915-778-6160
Donene O'Dell, admin. Fax 772-8207
International Business College Post-Sec.
5700 Cromo Dr 79912 915-842-0422
International Business College Post-Sec.
1155 N Zaragoza Rd 79907 915-859-3986
Jesus Chapel S 200/K-12
10200 Album Ave 79925 915-593-1153
Alba Wilcox, prin. Fax 593-1113
Loretto Academy 400/6-12
1300 Hardaway St 79903 915-566-8400
Abe Ramirez, prin. Fax 564-0563
North Loop Christian Academy 100/PK-12
8617 N Loop Dr 79907 915-859-9435
Mary Greenup, prin. Fax 859-3290
Patterson Institute 400/9-12
517 S Florence St 79901 915-533-8286
Hector Lachica, prin. Fax 533-5236
Pipo Academy of Hair Design Post-Sec.
3000 Pershing Dr 79903 915-565-3491
Radford S 200/PK-12
2001 Radford St 79903 915-565-2737
Dr. Irma Brooks, dir. Fax 565-2730
Tri-State Cosmetology Institute Post-Sec.
3910 Doniphan Dr Ste C 79922 915-585-8777
Tri-State Cosmetology Institute Post-Sec.
6800 Gateway Blvd E Ste 4A 79915 915-778-1741
University of Texas at El Paso Post-Sec.
500 W University Ave 79968 915-747-5000
Western Technical College Post-Sec.
9624 Plaza Cir 79927 915-760-8123
Western Technical College Post-Sec.
9451 Diana Dr 79924 915-566-9621

Elsa, Hidalgo, Pop. 6,458
Edcouch-Elsa ISD
Supt. — See Edcouch
Edcouch-Elsa HS 1,500/9-12
N Yellowjacket Dr 78543 956-262-6074
Carmen Garcia, prin. Fax 262-6060
Truan JHS 800/7-8
E 9th St 78543 956-262-6082
Fred Aguilar, prin. Fax 262-6079

Elysian Fields, Harrison
Elysian Fields ISD 1,000/PK-12
PO Box 120 75642 903-633-2420
Dr. Bob Browning, supt. Fax 633-2498
www.elysian-fields.k12.tx.us/
Elysian Fields HS 300/9-12
PO Box 120 75642 903-633-2455
Kin Bryan, prin. Fax 633-2498
Elysian Fields JHS 200/6-8
PO Box 120 75642 903-633-2306
Maynard Chapman, prin. Fax 633-2326

Emory, Rains, Pop. 1,332
Rains ISD 1,600/PK-12
PO Box 247 75440 903-473-2222
David Seago, supt. Fax 473-3053
www.rains.k12.tx.us/
Rains HS 500/9-12
PO Box 247 75440 903-473-2222
Randell Wellman, prin. Fax 473-5584
Rains JHS 400/6-8
PO Box 247 75440 903-473-2222
Denise Flagg, prin. Fax 473-5162

Ennis, Ellis, Pop. 18,735
Ennis ISD 5,500/PK-12
PO Box 1420 75120 972-875-9027
Dr. Eddie Dunn, supt. Fax 875-8667
www.ennis.k12.tx.us
Ennis HS 1,500/9-12
1405 W Lake Bardwell Dr 75119 972-875-9011
John Doslich, prin. Fax 875-7027
Ennis JHS 800/7-8
501 N Gaines St 75119 972-875-3779
Orlando Vargas, prin. Fax 875-1433

St. John S 200/K-12
701 S Paris St 75119 972-878-5411
Christopher Rebuck, prin. Fax 875-2226

Era, Cooke
Era ISD 200/K-12
PO Box 98 76238 940-665-5961
Jeremy Thompson, supt. Fax 665-5311
www.eraisd.net
Era JSHS 200/6-12
PO Box 98 76238 940-665-5961
Jerry Skelton, prin. Fax 665-5311

Euless, Tarrant, Pop. 51,226
Hurst-Euless-Bedford ISD
Supt. — See Bedford
Central JHS 800/7-9
3191 W Pipeline Rd 76040 817-354-3350
David Robbins, prin. Fax 354-3357
Euless JHS 800/7-9
306 Airport Fwy 76039 817-354-3340
Rita Wiles, prin. Fax 354-3345
Trinity SHS 2,100/10-12
500 N Industrial Blvd 76039 817-571-0271
Andy Cargile, prin. Fax 354-3322

Eustace, Henderson, Pop. 874
Eustace ISD 1,600/PK-12
PO Box 188 75124 903-425-5151
Dr. Coy Holcombe, supt. Fax 425-5147
www.eustaceisd.net/
Eustace HS 400/9-12
PO Box 188 75124 903-425-5161
Stan Sowers, prin. Fax 425-5227
Eustace MS 400/6-8
PO Box 188 75124 903-425-5171
Karyn Mullen, prin. Fax 425-5146

Evadale, Jasper, Pop. 1,422
Evadale ISD 500/PK-12
PO Box 497 77615 409-276-1337
Roy Fling, supt. Fax 276-1908
www.esc5.net/evadale/
Evadale HS 100/9-12
PO Box 497 77615 409-276-1337
Michael Nash, prin. Fax 276-1050

Evant, Coryell, Pop. 390
Evant ISD 300/PK-12
PO Box 339 76525 254-471-5536
Dr. Sid Pruitt, supt. Fax 471-5629
www.evantisd.org/
Evant HS 100/7-12
PO Box 339 76525 254-471-5536
Danny Hemphill, prin. Fax 471-5629

Everman, Tarrant, Pop. 5,733
Everman ISD 3,400/PK-12
608 Townley Dr 76140 817-568-3500
Jeri Pfeifer, supt. Fax 568-3508
www.eisd.org
Everman HS 1,100/9-12
1 Bulldog Rd 76140 817-568-3550
Kathy Culbertson, prin. Fax 568-3570
Everman JHS 700/7-8
8901 Oak Grove Rd 76140 817-568-3530
Anthony Price, prin. Fax 568-3594

Fabens, El Paso, Pop. 5,599
Fabens ISD 2,700/PK-12
PO Box 697 79838 915-764-2025
Poncho Garcia, supt. Fax 764-3115
www.fabensisd.net/
Fabens HS 800/9-12
PO Box 697 79838 915-764-2246
Robert Sepulveda, prin. Fax 764-4953
Fabens MS 600/6-8
PO Box 697 79838 915-764-7051
Luis Liano, prin. Fax 764-7263

Fairfield, Freestone, Pop. 3,508
Fairfield ISD 1,700/PK-12
615 Post Oak Rd 75840 903-389-2532
Tony Price, supt. Fax 389-7050
www.fairfield.k12.tx.us
Fairfield HS 500/9-12
631 Post Oak Rd 75840 903-389-4177
Von Wade, prin. Fax 389-5453
Fairfield JHS 600/5-8
701 Post Oak Rd 75840 903-389-4210
Elton Moore, prin. Fax 389-5454

Falfurrias, Brooks, Pop. 5,050
Brooks County ISD 1,600/PK-12
PO Box 589 78355 361-325-5681
Joe R. Trevino, supt. Fax 325-1913
www.bcisd.esc2.net
Falfurrias HS 500/9-12
PO Box 589 78355 361-325-5681
Dr. Cynthia Perez, prin. Fax 325-9284
Falfurrias JHS 400/6-8
PO Box 589 78355 361-325-5681
Juan Sandoval, prin. Fax 325-2220

Falls City, Karnes, Pop. 606
Falls City ISD 300/K-12
PO Box 399 78113 830-254-3551
Linda Bettin, supt. Fax 254-3354
www.fcisd.net/
Falls City JSHS 200/7-12
PO Box 399 78113 830-254-3551
Christy Blocker, prin. Fax 254-3354

Farmers Branch, Dallas, Pop. 26,487
Carrollton-Farmers Branch ISD
Supt. — See Carrollton
Early College HS 9-12
3939 Valley View Ln 75244 972-968-6200
Adriana Gomez, prin. Fax 968-6210
Field MS 1,100/6-8
13551 Dennis Ln 75234 972-968-3900
Dan Ford, prin. Fax 968-3910

Brookhaven College Post-Sec.
3939 Valley View Ln 75244 972-860-4700

Farmersville, Collin, Pop. 3,357
Farmersville ISD 1,300/PK-12
501A State Highway 78 N 75442 972-782-6601
Jeff Adams, supt. Fax 784-7293
www.farmersvilleisd.net/
Farmersville HS 400/9-12
499 State Highway 78 N 75442 972-548-0576
Scott Moss, prin. Fax 529-3750
Farmersville JHS 400/6-8
501 State Highway 78 N 75442 972-782-6202
Wayne Callaway, prin. Fax 782-7029

Farwell, Parmer, Pop. 1,318
Farwell ISD 500/PK-12
PO Box F 79325 806-481-3371
Larry Gregory, supt. Fax 481-9275
www.farwellschools.org
Farwell HS 100/9-12
PO Box F 79325 806-481-3351
Mike Read, prin. Fax 481-3531
Farwell JHS 100/6-8
PO Box F 79325 806-481-9260
Jimmy Mace, prin. Fax 481-9258

Fayetteville, Fayette, Pop. 272
Fayetteville ISD 200/K-12
PO Box 129 78940 979-378-4242
Roy Green, supt. Fax 378-4246
www.esc13.net/fayetteville/home.htm
Fayetteville JSHS 100/6-12
PO Box 129 78940 979-378-4242
Roy Green, prin. Fax 378-4246

Ferris, Ellis, Pop. 2,298
Ferris ISD 2,200/PK-12
PO Box 459 75125 972-544-3858
Michael Bodine, supt. Fax 544-2784
www.ferrisisd.org
Ferris HS 600/9-12
PO Box 461 75125 972-544-3737
Jana Giles, prin. Fax 544-2029
Ferris JHS 300/7-8
PO Box 459 75125 972-544-2279
Marty Renner, prin. Fax 544-2281

Fischer, Comal
Comal ISD
Supt. — See New Braunfels
Canyon Lake HS 9-12
8555 FM 32 78623 830-221-2987
Cheryl Koury, prin. Fax 885-1701

Flatonia, Fayette, Pop. 1,421
Flatonia ISD 600/PK-12
PO Box 189 78941 361-865-2941
Dr. Alice Smith, supt. Fax 865-2940
www.esc13.net/flatonia/
Flatonia HS 300/7-12
PO Box 189 78941 361-865-2941
Kathy Orsak, prin. Fax 865-2944

Florence, Williamson, Pop. 1,109
Florence ISD 1,000/PK-12
PO Box 489 76527 254-793-2850
Mike Martindale Ed.D., supt. Fax 793-3055
www.florence.k12.tx.us
Florence HS 300/9-12
PO Box 489 76527 254-793-2495
Marilyn Hill, prin. Fax 793-3784
Florence MS 200/6-8
PO Box 489 76527 254-793-2504
Sheri Hawthorn, prin. Fax 793-3054

Floresville, Wilson, Pop. 7,024
Floresville ISD 3,500/PK-12
908 10th St 78114 830-393-5300
David Vinson, supt. Fax 393-5399
www.fisd.us
Floresville HS 1,100/9-12
1000 10th St 78114 830-393-5370
Sherri Bays, prin. Fax 393-5719
Floresville MS 800/6-8
2601 B St 78114 830-393-5350
Jackie Baker, prin. Fax 393-5339

Flower Mound, Denton, Pop. 63,526
Lewisville ISD 44,100/PK-12
1800 Timber Creek Rd 75028 972-713-5200
Dr. Jerry Roy, supt. Fax 539-0239
www.lisd.net
Downing MS 600/6-8
5555 Bridlewood Blvd 75028 469-713-5962
Lisa Lingren, prin. Fax 355-7252
Flower Mound HS 2,700/9-12
3411 Peters Colony Rd 75022 469-713-5192
Jack Clark, prin. Fax 691-5826
Forestwood MS 1,100/6-8
2810 Morriss Rd 75028 469-713-5972
Dave Tickner, prin. Fax 355-6300
Lamar MS 700/6-8
4000 Timber Creek Rd 75028 469-713-5966
Mike Fields, prin. Fax 350-2050
Marcus HS 2,700/9-12
5707 Morriss Rd 75028 469-713-5196
Kevin Rogers, prin. Fax 355-7513
McKamy MS 1,000/6-8
2401 Old Settlers Rd 75022 469-713-5991
Gary Shafferman, prin. Fax 355-3404
Shadow Ridge MS 6-8
2050 Aberdeen Dr 75028 469-713-5984
Gary Goldsmith, prin. Fax 874-3865
Other Schools – See Carrollton, Highland Village, Lewisville, The Colony

Floydada, Floyd, Pop. 3,294
Floydada ISD 1,000/PK-12
226 W California St 79235 806-983-3498
Jerry Vaughn, supt. Fax 983-5739
www.floydadaisd.esc17.net
Floydada HS 300/9-12
618 Whirlwind Alley 79235 806-983-4970
Wayne Morren, prin. Fax 983-5739
Floydada JHS 200/6-8
910 S 5th St 79235 806-983-2161
Jim Bob Hobbs, prin. Fax 983-5739

Follett, Lipscomb, Pop. 414
Follett ISD 200/K-12
PO Box 28 79034 806-653-2301
Mollie Howell, supt. Fax 653-2036
www.follettisd.net
Follett S 200/K-12
PO Box 28 79034 806-653-4241
Jeff Northern, prin. Fax 653-2036

Forestburg, Montague
Forestburg ISD 200/K-12
PO Box 415 76239 940-964-2323
Dr. Fonda Huneycutt, supt. Fax 964-2531
www.nortexinfo.net/fbisd/
Forestburg S 200/K-12
PO Box 415 76239 940-964-2323
Dr. Sid Brannan, prin. Fax 964-2531

Forney, Kaufman, Pop. 10,579
Forney ISD 4,300/K-12
600 S Bois d Arc St 75126 972-564-4055
Michael Smith, supt. Fax 564-7007
www.forneyisd.net
Forney HS 1,100/9-12
800 Fm 741 75126 972-564-3890
Bobby Millicorn, prin. Fax 564-5616
Forney MS 700/7-8
1050 Windmill Farms Blvd 75126 972-564-3967
Leslie Mauk, prin. Fax 564-7022

Forsan, Howard, Pop. 221
Forsan ISD 700/K-12
PO Box A 79733 432-457-2223
Randy Johnson, supt. Fax 457-2225
forsan.esc18.net
Forsan JSHS 400/6-12
PO Box A 79733 432-457-2223
Keith Stone, prin. Fax 457-2225

Fort Davis, Jeff Davis
Fort Davis ISD 400/PK-12
PO Box 1339 79734 432-426-4440
Robert Sanford, supt. Fax 426-3841
fdisd.esc18.net/
Fort Davis JSHS 100/7-12
PO Box 1339 79734 432-426-4444
Samuel Wyatt, prin. Fax 426-4449

Fort Hancock, Hudspeth
Fort Hancock ISD 200/K-12
PO Box 98 79839 915-769-3811
Jose Franco, supt. Fax 769-3940
www.forthancockisd.net/

Fort Hancock HS 9-12
PO Box 98 79839 915-769-3867
Randy Speer, prin. Fax 769-0044
Fort Hancock MS 5-8
PO Box 98 79839 915-769-3811
Jasminka Speer, dir. Fax 769-0045

Fort Hood, Bell, Pop. 33,700
Killeen ISD
Supt. — See Killeen
Murphy MS 500/6-8
53393 Sun Dance Dr 76544 254-200-6530
Minerva Trujillo, prin. Fax 616-5245
Smith MS 500/6-8
51000 Tank Destroyer Blvd 76544 254-501-1050
Sandra Forsythe, prin. Fax 532-1247

Fort Stockton, Pecos, Pop. 7,268
Fort Stockton ISD 2,200/PK-12
101 W Division St 79735 432-336-4000
Ron Mayfield, supt. Fax 336-4008
www.fort-stockton.k12.tx.us
Fort Stockton HS 600/9-12
101 W Division St 79735 432-336-4101
Alice Duerksen, prin. Fax 336-4113
Fort Stockton MS 500/6-8
101 W Division St 79735 432-336-4131
Judy Espino, prin. Fax 336-4136

Fort Worth, Tarrant, Pop. 624,067
Castleberry ISD 3,300/PK-12
315 Churchill Rd 76114 817-252-2000
Gary S. Jones, supt. Fax 738-1062
www.castleberryisd.net
Castleberry HS 800/9-12
215 Churchill Rd 76114 817-252-2100
Laina McDonald, prin. Fax 252-2575
Marsh MS 800/6-8
415 Hagg Dr 76114 817-252-2200
Stephanie Romeo, prin. Fax 738-3454

Crowley ISD
Supt. — See Crowley
Crowley MS 1,100/7-8
3800 W Risinger Rd 76123 817-370-5650
Kathy Allen, prin. Fax 370-5656
North Crowley 9th Grade Campus 600/9-9
4630 McPherson Blvd 76123 817-297-5896
Nita Page, prin. Fax 297-5878
North Crowley HS 1,500/10-12
9100 S Hulen St 76123 817-263-1250
Trent Lovette, prin. Fax 263-1282

Eagle Mtn.-Saginaw ISD 8,700/PK-12
1200 Old Decatur Rd 76179 817-232-0880
Dr. Cole Pugh, supt. Fax 847-6124
www.emsisd.com
Boswell HS 2,300/9-12
5805 W Bailey Boswell Rd 76179 817-237-3314
Terry Houston, prin. Fax 238-8706
Creekview MS 6-8
6716 Bob Hanger St 76179 817-237-4261
Anthe Anagnostis, prin. Fax 237-2387
Highland MS 800/6-8
1001 E Bailey Boswell Rd 76131 817-847-5143
Clete Welch, prin. Fax 847-1922
Wayside MS 700/6-8
1300 Old Decatur Rd 76179 817-232-0541
Dan Jordan, prin. Fax 232-2391
Other Schools – See Saginaw

Fort Worth ISD 78,400/PK-12
100 N University Dr 76107 817-871-2000
Dr. Melody Johnson, supt. Fax 871-2112
www.fortworthisd.org
Arlington Heights HS 1,900/9-12
4501 West Fwy 76107 817-377-7200
Neta Alexander, prin. Fax 377-7266
Carter-Riverside HS 1,000/9-12
3301 Yucca Ave 76111 817-838-1500
Maria Sanchez, prin. Fax 838-1517
Daggett MS 400/6-8
1108 Carlock St 76110 817-922-6550
Rhonda Fields, prin. Fax 922-6996
Diamond Hill-Jarvis HS 900/9-12
1411 Maydell St 76106 817-740-5400
Gayla Dawson, prin. Fax 740-5402
Dunbar HS 1,200/9-12
5700 Ramey Ave 76112 817-496-7400
Ingrid Williams, prin. Fax 496-7446
Dunbar MS 700/7-8
2501 Stalcup Rd 76119 817-496-7430
Patricia Williams, prin. Fax 496-7697
Eastern Hills HS 1,600/9-12
5701 Shelton St 76112 817-496-7600
Elodia Escamilla, prin. Fax 496-7603
Elder MS 1,200/6-8
709 NW 21st St 76164 817-740-5450
Carla Westbrook, prin. Fax 740-5468
Forest Oak MS 700/6-8
3221 Pecos St 76119 817-531-6330
Gerald Batty, prin. Fax 531-4342
Handley MS 700/6-8
2801 Patino Rd 76112 817-496-7450
Lewis Washington, prin. Fax 496-7653
James MS 1,000/6-8
1101 Nashville Ave 76105 817-531-6230
Rian Townsend, prin. Fax 531-6114
Kirkpatrick MS 500/6-8
3201 Refugio Ave 76106 817-740-5350
Jorge Mendoza, prin. Fax 740-5363
McLean MS 800/6-8
3816 Stadium Dr 76109 817-922-6830
Nancy Weisskopf, prin. Fax 922-4498
Meacham MS 800/6-8
3600 Weber St 76106 817-740-5330
Manuel Cantu, prin. Fax 740-4546
Meadowbrook MS 1,100/6-8
2001 Ederville Rd S 76103 817-531-6250
Cherie Washington, prin. Fax 531-7709
Metro Opportunity S Vo/Tech
2720 Cullen St 76107 817-852-1160
Linda Ballenger, prin. Fax 852-1183
Monnig MS 700/6-8
3136 Bigham Blvd 76116 817-377-7250
Laura Stegall, prin. Fax 377-7024
Morningside MS 600/6-8
2751 Mississippi Ave 76104 817-922-6680
Andrew Chambers, prin. Fax 922-6869
North Side HS 1,600/9-12
2211 Mckinley Ave 76164 817-740-5300
Virginia Dean, prin. Fax 740-5302

Paschal HS 2,200/9-12
3001 Forest Park Blvd 76110 817-922-6600
Dr. Sharon Meng, prin. Fax 922-6661
Polytechnic HS Vo/Tech
1300 Conner Ave 76105 817-531-6200
Gary Braudaway, prin. Fax 531-6267
Riverside MS 900/6-8
1600 Bolton St 76111 817-838-1530
Daniel Scroggins, prin. Fax 838-1534
Rosemont MS 900/7-8
1501 W Seminary Dr 76115 817-922-6650
Yassmin Lee, prin. Fax 922-4491
South Hills HS 1,400/9-12
6101 Mccart Ave 76133 817-263-1600
Glynna Torres, prin. Fax 263-1607
Southwest HS 1,500/9-12
4100 Altamesa Blvd 76133 817-370-5800
Laura Williams, prin. Fax 370-5833
Stripling MS 700/6-8
2100 Clover Ln 76107 817-377-7230
Terry Mossige, prin. Fax 377-7030
Trimble Technical HS Vo/Tech
1003 W Cannon St 76104 817-871-3400
Omar Ramos, prin. Fax 871-3420
Wedgwood MS 1,000/7-8
3909 Wilkie Way 76133 817-370-5830
Linda Villarreal, prin. Fax 370-5733
Wyatt HS 1,100/9-12
2400 E Seminary Dr 76119 817-531-6300
Steven Johnson, prin. Fax 531-6326
Other Schools – See Benbrook

Keller ISD
Supt. — See Keller
Fossil Hill MS 900/7-8
3821 Staghorn Cir S 76137 817-744-3050
David Hadley, prin. Fax 847-6990
Hillwood MS 1,100/7-8
8250 Parkwood Hill Blvd 76137 817-744-3350
Jim Joros, prin. Fax 581-1810

White Settlement ISD 4,500/PK-12
401 S Cherry Ln 76108 817-367-1350
Dr. Susan Simpson, supt. Fax 367-1351
www.wsisd.com/
Ninth Grade Center 9-9
1025 West Loop 820 N 76120 817-367-1250
Mike Wallace, prin.
Other Schools – See White Settlement

All Saints' Episcopal S 800/K-12
9700 Saints Cir 76108 817-246-2413
Thaddeus Bird, hdmstr. Fax 560-5720
Bethesda Christian S 400/PK-12
4700 N Beach St 76137 817-281-6446
Vicki Vaughn, prin. Fax 281-1560
Calvary Christian Academy 400/PK-12
1401 Oakhurst Scenic Dr 76111 817-332-3351
Sue Tidwell, prin. Fax 332-4621
Career Centers of Texas Post-Sec.
2001 Beach St 76103 817-688-1132
Cassata HS 400/9-12
1400 Hemphill St 76104 817-926-1745
Nancy Martin, prin. Fax 926-3132
Christian Life Preparatory S 200/K-12
6250 South Fwy 76134 817-293-1500
Deborah Henry, admin. Fax 293-1500
College of Saint Thomas More Post-Sec.
3020 Lubbock Ave 76109 817-923-8459
Fellowship Christian Academy 100/K-12
1140 Morrison Dr 76120 817-457-2345
Angela Cuppett, supt. Fax 457-2347
Ft. Worth Adventist Jr Academy 100/PK-10
3040 Sycamore School Rd 76133 817-370-7177
Fax 370-8455
Fort Worth Beauty School Post-Sec.
6785 Camp Bowie Blvd # 100 76116 817-924-4289
Fort Worth Christian S 800/PK-12
7517 Bogart Dr 76180 817-281-6504
Brian Miller, prin. Fax 281-7063
Fort Worth Country Day S 1,100/K-12
4200 Country Day Ln 76109 817-732-7718
Evan D. Peterson, hdmstr. Fax 377-3425
Glenview Christian S 200/PK-12
4805 NE Loop 820 76137 817-281-5155
Jerome Chenausky, admin. Fax 514-0760
Harris Hospital Post-Sec.
1301 Pennsylvania Ave 76104 817-878-2106
Harvest Christian S 200/K-12
7501 Crowley Rd 76134 817-568-0021
John Winner, prin. Fax 568-1395
High Point Preparatory Academy 300/K-12
2500 E Arbrook Blvd 76104 817-394-3100
Beth Featherston, prin. Fax 394-3101
Hill S of Ft. Worth 200/2-12
4817 Odessa Ave 76133 817-923-9482
Gregory Owens, prin. Fax 923-4894
JPS Inst. for Health Career Development Post-Sec.
2400 Circle Dr 76119 817-920-7380
Key S 100/PK-12
3947 E Loop 820 S 76119 817-446-3738
Donna Mills, prin. Fax 496-3299
Lake Country Christian S 400/PK-12
8777 Boat Club Rd 76179 817-236-8703
Nancy Purtell, admin. Fax 236-1103
Nolan HS 9-12
4501 Bridge St 76103 817-457-2920
Stephen Hiner, prin. Fax 496-9775
Ogle School of Hair Design Post-Sec.
5063 Granbury Rd 76133 817-294-2950
Remington College Post-Sec.
300 E Loop 820 76112 817-451-0017
Southwest Christian Prep S 400/7-12
7001 Benbrook Lake Dr 76123 817-294-9596
Dr. Penny Armstrong, hdmstr. Fax 294-9603
Southwestern Baptist Theological Sem. Post-Sec.
PO Box 22000 76122 817-923-1921
Tarrant County Junior College Post-Sec.
5301 Campus Dr 76119 817-515-4100
Tarrant County Junior College Post-Sec.
4801 Marine Creek Pkwy 76179 817-515-7100
Temple Christian S of Ft. Worth 900/PK-12
6824 Randol Mill Rd 76120 817-457-0770
Dorothy Stringer, supt. Fax 457-0777
Texas Christian University Post-Sec.
TCU Box 297013 76129 817-257-7000
Texas Wesleyan University Post-Sec.
1201 Wesleyan St 76105 800-580-8980
Trinity Valley S 900/K-12
7500 Dutch Branch Rd 76132 817-321-0100
Gary Krahn, hdmstr. Fax 321-0105

University of N Texas Health Science Ctr Post-Sec.
3500 Camp Bowie Blvd 76107 817-735-2000
Westwood College Post-Sec.
4232 North Fwy 76137 817-685-9994

Franklin, Robertson, Pop. 1,489
Franklin ISD 1,000/PK-12
PO Box 909 77856 979-828-1900
Timothy Lowry, supt. Fax 828-1910
www.franklinisd.net/fisdwebpage/
Franklin HS 300/9-12
PO Box 909 77856 979-828-3236
Stacy Ely, prin. Fax 828-3364
Franklin MS 300/5-8
PO Box 909 77856 979-828-5434
Gerald Hancock, prin. Fax 828-3134

Frankston, Anderson, Pop. 1,233
Frankston ISD 800/PK-12
PO Box 428 75763 903-876-2556
Austin Thacker, supt. Fax 876-4558
www.frankston.esc7.net
Frankston HS 200/9-12
PO Box 428 75763 903-876-3219
Nicci Cook, prin. Fax 876-4558
Frankston MS 200/6-8
PO Box 428 75763 903-876-2215
Chris White, prin. Fax 876-4558

Fredericksburg, Gillespie, Pop. 10,432
Fredericksburg ISD 2,900/PK-12
234 Friendship Ln 78624 830-997-9551
Marc Williamson, supt. Fax 997-6164
www.fisd.org/
Fredericksburg HS 1,000/9-12
1107 S State Highway 16 78624 830-997-7551
Lynn Blackwell, prin. Fax 997-8583
Fredericksburg MS 600/6-8
110 W Travis St 78624 830-997-7657
Kevan Webb, prin. Fax 997-1927

Fredericksburg Christian S 50/K-12
1208 N Milam St 78624 830-997-9193
Linda Williams, prin.
Heritage S 200/K-12
PO Box 1217 78624 830-997-6597
Nancy Hierholzer, prin. Fax 997-4900

Freeport, Brazoria, Pop. 12,605
Brazosport ISD
Supt. — See Clute
Brazosport HS 1,100/9-12
PO Box Z 77542 979-730-7260
Gary Jones, prin. Fax 237-6310
Freeport IS 600/7-8
PO Box Z 77542 979-730-7240
Clara Sale-Davis, prin. Fax 237-6329

Freer, Duval, Pop. 3,081
Freer ISD 900/PK-12
PO Box 240 78357 361-394-6025
Edgar Camacho, supt. Fax 394-5005
www.freerisd.esc2.net
Freer HS 200/9-12
PO Box 240 78357 361-394-6717
Ramon Pulido, prin. Fax 394-5012
Freer JHS 200/6-8
PO Box 240 78357 361-394-7102
Linda Garza, prin. Fax 394-5016

Friendswood, Galveston, Pop. 33,094
Clear Creek ISD
Supt. — See League City
Brookside IS 1,300/6-8
3535 E Parkwood 77546 281-482-9710
Deanna Daws, prin. Fax 992-7858
Clear Brook HS 2,800/9-12
4607 FM 2351 Rd 77546 281-284-2100
Kristi Lamell, prin. Fax 284-2105
West Brook IS 6-8
302 W El Dorado Blvd 77546 281-284-3800
Dr. Lori Broughton, prin. Fax 284-3805

Friendswood ISD 5,600/K-12
302 Laurel Dr 77546 281-482-1267
Trish Hanks, supt. Fax 996-2513
www.fisdk12.net
Friendswood HS 1,800/9-12
702 Greenbriar Ave 77546 281-482-3413
Myrlene Kennedy, prin. Fax 996-2523
Friendswood JHS 900/7-8
402 Laurel Dr 77546 281-482-7818
Robin Lowe, prin. Fax 996-2529

Texas School of Business Post-Sec.
3208 W Parkwood Ave 77546 281-648-0880

Friona, Parmer, Pop. 3,735
Friona ISD 1,200/PK-12
909 E 11th St 79035 806-250-2747
Jim Parker, supt. Fax 250-3805
www.frionaisd.com
Friona HS 300/9-12
909 E 11th St 79035 806-250-3951
Denver Crum, prin. Fax 259-2281
Friona JHS 300/6-8
909 E 11th St 79035 806-250-2788
Kevin Wiseman, prin. Fax 250-8155

Frisco, Collin, Pop. 70,793
Frisco ISD 15,800/K-12
6942 Maple St 75034 469-633-6000
Rick Reedy, supt. Fax 633-6050
www.friscoisd.org
Clark MS 800/6-8
4600 Colby Dr 75035 469-633-4600
Mary Dowd, prin. Fax 633-4650
Frisco Centennial HS 1,400/9-12
6901 Coit Rd 75035 469-633-5600
Randy Spain, prin. Fax 633-5650
Frisco HS 1,900/9-12
6401 Parkwood Dr 75034 469-633-5500
Rick Burnett, prin. Fax 633-5550
Griffin MS 200/6-8
3703 Eldorado Pkwy 75034 469-633-4900
Elizabeth Holcomb, prin. Fax 633-4950
Liberty HS 9-12
15250 Rolater Rd 75035 469-633-5800
Mike Waldrip, prin. Fax 633-5850
Pioneer Heritage MS 800/6-8
1649 High Shoals Dr 75034 469-633-4700
Katie Kordel, prin. Fax 633-4750

Roach MS 6-8
12499 Independence Pkwy 75035 469-633-5000
Terri Gladden, prin. Fax 633-5010
Staley MS 700/6-8
6927 Stadium Ln 75034 469-633-4500
Dennis McDonald, prin. Fax 633-4550
Wakeland HS 9-12
10700 Legacy Dr 75034 469-633-5700
Mike Farish, prin. Fax 633-5750
Wester MS 1,000/6-8
12293 Shepherds Hill Ln 75035 469-633-4800
Angela Romney, prin. Fax 633-4850
Other Schools – See Plano

Legacy Christian Academy 600/PK-12
5000 Academy Dr 75034 469-633-1330
Jody Capehart, hdmstr. Fax 633-1348

Fritch, Hutchinson, Pop. 2,089
Sanford-Fritch ISD 900/PK-12
PO Box 1290 79036 806-857-3122
Daymun White, supt. Fax 857-3795
www.sanfordisd.org
Sanford-Fritch HS 300/9-12
PO Box 1290 79036 806-857-3121
Jim McClellon, prin. Fax 857-9147
Sanford-Fritch JHS 200/6-8
PO Box 1290 79036 806-857-9268
Edith Allen, prin. Fax 857-9431

Frost, Navarro, Pop. 709
Frost ISD 400/PK-12
PO Box K 76641 903-682-2711
Jim Revill, supt. Fax 682-2107
Frost JSHS 200/7-12
PO Box K 76641 903-682-2541
Gordon Lockett, prin. Fax 682-2107

Fruitvale, Van Zandt, Pop. 453
Fruitvale ISD 500/PK-12
PO Box 77 75127 903-896-1191
Stan Surratt, supt. Fax 896-1011
www.fruitvaleisd.com
Fruitvale HS 100/9-12
PO Box 77 75127 903-896-4363
Loyd Nations, prin. Fax 896-1011
Fruitvale MS 100/6-8
PO Box 77 75127 903-896-4363
Loyd Nations, prin. Fax 896-1011

Gail, Borden
Borden County ISD 200/K-12
PO Box 95 79738 806-756-4313
Jimmy Thomas, supt. Fax 756-4310
www.bcisd.net/
Borden S 200/K-12
PO Box 95 79738 806-756-4314
Bart McMeans, prin. Fax 756-4310

Gainesville, Cooke, Pop. 16,569
Callisburg ISD 1,100/PK-12
148 Dozier St 76240 940-665-0540
Dr. Charles Holloway, supt. Fax 668-2706
Callisburg HS 500/7-12
148 Dozier St 76240 940-665-0961
Skipper Waller, prin. Fax 665-2849

Gainesville ISD 2,900/PK-12
800 S Morris St 76240 940-665-4362
Charles Luke, supt. Fax 665-4473
www.gainesvilleisd.org
Gainesville HS 800/9-12
1201 S Lindsay St 76240 940-665-5528
Bill Gravitt, prin. Fax 665-7975
Gainesville JHS 400/7-8
421 N Denton St 76240 940-665-4062
Juan Lopez, prin. Fax 665-1432

North Central Texas College Post-Sec.
1525 W California St 76240 940-668-4222

Galena Park, Harris, Pop. 10,221
Galena Park ISD
Supt. — See Houston
Galena Park HS 1,700/9-12
1000 Keene St 77547 832-386-2800
Steve Kinney, prin. Fax 386-2802
Galena Park MS 1,000/6-8
400 Keene St 77547 832-386-1700
Tony Mayeux, prin. Fax 386-1738
Sheffield Career Center Vo/Tech
1001 Parkside Dr 77547 832-386-2802
Evelyn Mikel, prin. Fax 386-2851

Galveston, Galveston, Pop. 57,466
Galveston ISD 8,400/PK-12
PO Box 660 77553 409-766-5100
Lynne Cleveland, supt. Fax 766-5106
www.galveston-schools.org
Austin MS 300/6-8
1110 21st St 77550 409-765-9373
Canzetta Hollis, prin. Fax 765-5946
Ball HS 2,600/9-12
4115 Avenue O 77550 409-766-5715
Diane Reaume, prin. Fax 766-5738
Central MS 700/6-8
3014 Avenue I 77550 409-765-2101
Connie Hebert, prin. Fax 765-2141
Weis MS 800/6-8
7100 Stewart Rd 77551 409-740-5100
Dyann Polzin, prin. Fax 744-8936

Galveston College Post-Sec.
4015 Avenue Q 77550 409-763-6551
O'Connell HS 200/9-12
1320 Tremont St 77550 409-765-5534
Bill Doughty, prin. Fax 765-5536
Texas A&M at Galveston Post-Sec.
PO Box 1675 77553 409-740-4400
University of Texas Medical Branch Post-Sec.
301 University Blvd 77555 409-761-1215

Ganado, Jackson, Pop. 1,871
Ganado ISD 700/PK-12
PO Box 1200 77962 361-771-3482
Jeff Black, supt. Fax 771-2280
www.ganadoisd.org/
Ganado JSHS 300/7-12
PO Box 1200 77962 361-771-3430
Andy Bridges, prin. Fax 771-2280

Garden City, Glasscock
Glasscock County ISD 300/PK-12
PO Box 9 79739 432-354-2230
Steve Long, supt. Fax 354-2503
Glasscock County JSHS 100/7-12
PO Box 9 79739 432-354-2244
John Petree, prin. Fax 354-2503

Gardendale, Ector, Pop. 1,103

Gardendale Christian S 200/K-12
PO Box 345 79758 432-561-9024

Garland, Dallas, Pop. 216,346
Garland ISD 54,600/PK-12
PO Box 469026 75046 972-494-8201
Dr. Curtis Culwell, supt. Fax 485-4928
www.garlandisd.net
Austin Academy for Excellence MS 900/6-8
1125 Beverly Dr 75040 972-926-2620
Dr. Ann Poore, prin. Fax 926-2633
Bussey MS 900/6-8
1204 Travis St 75040 972-494-8391
Harry Farley, prin. Fax 494-8971
Classical Center at Brandenburg MS 1,100/6-8
626 Nickens Rd 75043 972-926-2630
Carra King, prin. Fax 926-2633
Garland HS 2,400/9-12
310 S Garland Ave 75040 972-494-8492
John Morris, prin. Fax 494-8415
Houston MS 700/6-8
2232 Sussex Dr 75041 972-926-2640
Don Hernandez, prin. Fax 926-2647
Hudson MS 1,200/6-8
4405 Hudson Park 75048 972-675-3070
Michelle Baker, prin. Fax 675-3077
Jackson Tech Center for Math & Science 1,100/6-8
1310 Bobbie Ln 75042 972-494-8362
David Dunphy, prin. Fax 494-8802
Lakeview Centennial HS 2,100/9-12
3505 Hayman Dr 75043 972-240-3740
Gerald Hudson, prin. Fax 240-3750
Lyles MS 1,000/6-8
4655 S Country Club Rd 75043 972-240-3720
Janice Howard, prin. Fax 240-3723
Naaman Forest HS 2,100/9-12
4843 Naaman Forest Blvd 75040 972-675-3091
Steve Baker, prin. Fax 675-3100
North Garland HS 2,300/9-12
2109 W Buckingham Rd 75042 972-675-3120
Dr. Susie Fegraeus, prin. Fax 675-3145
O'Banion MS 1,100/6-8
700 Birchwood Dr 75043 972-279-6103
John Tucci, prin. Fax 613-9532
Sellers MS 800/6-8
1009 Mars Dr 75040 972-494-8337
William Woods, prin. Fax 494-8607
South Garland HS 2,200/9-12
600 Colonel Dr 75043 972-926-2700
Charlie Rose, prin. Fax 926-2727
Webb MS 1,200/6-8
1610 Spring Creek Dr 75040 972-675-3080
Jim Lewis, prin. Fax 675-3089
Garland Evening S Adult
310 S Garland Ave 75040 972-494-8162
David Benson, prin. Fax 494-8977
Other Schools – See Rowlett, Sachse

Amberton University Post-Sec.
1700 Eastgate Dr 75041 972-279-6511
Garland Christian Academy 500/K-12
1522 Lavon Dr 75040 972-487-0043
Russell Davis, admin. Fax 276-4079
International Beauty College #3 Post-Sec.
1225 Belt Line Rd Ste 7 75040 972-530-1103
National Beauty College Post-Sec.
149 W Kingsley Rd Ste 230 75041 972-278-2020
Remington College Post-Sec.
1800 Eastgate Dr 75041 972-686-7878

Garrison, Nacogdoches, Pop. 846
Garrison ISD 700/PK-12
459 N US Highway 59 75946 936-347-7000
Arnie Kelley, supt. Fax 347-2529
www.garrisonisd.com
Garrison HS 200/9-12
459 N US Highway 59 75946 936-347-7030
Darren Webb, prin. Fax 347-2529
Garrison MS 200/6-8
459 N US Highway 59 75946 936-347-7020
Virgil Wedgeworth, prin. Fax 347-7004

Gary, Panola
Gary ISD 300/K-12
PO Box 189 75643 903-685-2291
Todd Greer, supt. Fax 685-2639
www.gary.esc7.net
Gary S 300/K-12
PO Box 189 75643 903-685-2291
Todd Greer, prin. Fax 685-2639

Gatesville, Coryell, Pop. 15,651
Gatesville ISD 2,700/PK-12
311 S Lovers Ln 76528 254-865-7251
Ricky Copp, supt. Fax 865-2279
www.gatesvilleisd.org/
Gatesville HS 800/9-12
311 S Lovers Ln 76528 254-865-8281
Michael Barr, prin. Fax 865-2293
Gatesville JHS 400/7-8
311 S Lovers Ln 76528 254-865-8271
Bobby Cole, prin. Fax 865-2252

Coryell Cosmetology College Post-Sec.
608 E Leon St 76528 254-248-1716

Georgetown, Williamson, Pop. 39,015
Georgetown ISD 8,800/PK-12
603 Lakeway Dr 78628 512-943-5000
Joe Dan Lee, supt. Fax 943-5002
www.georgetownisd.org
Benold MS 700/6-8
3407 Northwest Blvd 78628 512-943-5090
Leslie Michalik, prin. Fax 943-5099
Forbes MS 600/6-8
1911 NE Inner Loop 78626 512-943-5150
Leonard Rhoads, prin. Fax 943-5159
Georgetown HS 1,800/10-12
2211 N Austin Ave 78626 512-943-5100
Randy Weisinger, prin. Fax 943-5109

Georgetown Ninth Grade S 700/9-9
2295 S Austin Ave 78626 512-943-5130
Dwayne Lenox, prin. Fax 943-5139
Tippit MS 800/6-8
1601 Leander Rd 78628 512-943-5040
Carlos Cantu, prin. Fax 943-5049

Covenant Christian Academy 100/PK-12
1521 Northwest Blvd 78628 512-863-6946
Mary Husrt, prin. Fax 863-4756
Grace Academy of Georgetown 100/K-12
PO Box 5005 78627 512-864-9500
Nancy Donaldson, hdmstr. Fax 868-5429
Southwestern University Post-Sec.
PO Box 770 78627 512-863-6511

George West, Live Oak, Pop. 2,342
George West ISD 1,200/PK-12
913 Houston St 78022 361-449-1914
James Stansberry, supt. Fax 449-1426
www.gwisd.esc2.net/
George West HS 400/9-12
1013 Houston St 78022 361-449-1914
Cris Luna, prin. Fax 449-3128
George West JHS 200/7-8
900 Houston St 78022 361-449-1914
Pat James, prin. Fax 449-3909

Geronimo, Guadalupe
Navarro ISD
Supt. — See Seguin
Navarro JHS, PO Box 10 78115 200/7-8
Luke Morales, prin. 830-401-5550

Giddings, Lee, Pop. 5,442
Giddings ISD 1,700/PK-12
PO Box 389 78942 979-542-2854
Michael Kuhrt, supt. Fax 542-9264
www.giddings.txed.net
Giddings HS 500/9-12
PO Box 389 78942 979-542-3351
Andy Masek, prin. Fax 542-5312
Giddings MS 200/7-8
PO Box 389 78942 979-542-2057
Shane Holman, prin. Fax 542-3941

Gilmer, Upshur, Pop. 5,141
Gilmer ISD 1,800/PK-12
500 S Trinity St 75644 903-841-7400
Rick Albritton, supt. Fax 843-5279
www.gilmerisd.org
Bruce JHS 400/7-8
111 Bruce St 75645 903-843-3051
Greg Watson, prin. Fax 843-6108
Gilmer HS 700/9-12
850 Buffalo St 75644 903-843-3021
Gary Whitwell, prin. Fax 843-2171

Union Hill ISD 300/PK-12
2197 FM 2088 75644 903-762-2140
Sharon Richardson, supt. Fax 762-6845
www.uhisd.com/
Union Hill HS 200/6-12
2197 FM 2088 75644 903-762-2138
Cathy Schmidt, prin. Fax 762-6845

Gladewater, Gregg, Pop. 6,295
Gladewater ISD 2,300/PK-12
500 W Quitman Ave 75647 903-845-6991
Mike Morrison, supt. Fax 845-6994
www.gladewaterisd.com
Gladewater HS 600/9-12
2201 W Gay Ave 75647 903-845-5591
Sam Chenoweth, prin. Fax 845-3694
Gladewater MS 600/6-8
700 Melba Ave 75647 903-845-2243
James Griffin, prin. Fax 844-1738

Sabine ISD 1,300/PK-12
5424 FM 1252 W 75647 903-984-8564
Stacey Bryce, supt. Fax 984-6108
www.sabine.esc7.net
Sabine HS 400/9-12
5424 FM 1252 W 75647 903-984-8587
Eddie Shawn, prin. Fax 986-1103
Sabine MS 300/6-8
5424 FM 1252 W 75647 903-984-4767
Durwin Cooley, prin. Fax 984-8823

Union Grove ISD 500/PK-12
PO Box 1447 75647 903-845-5509
Richard Cooper, supt. Fax 845-6178
www.ungr.sprnet.org
Union Grove JSHS 200/6-12
PO Box 1447 75647 903-845-5506
Kevin Whitman, prin. Fax 845-3003

Glenn Heights, Dallas, Pop. 9,324
De Soto ISD
Supt. — See De Soto
McCowan MS 6-8
1500 Majestic Meadows Dr 75154 972-274-8090
Sissy Lowe, prin. Fax 274-8099

Glen Rose, Somervell, Pop. 2,567
Glen Rose ISD 1,600/PK-12
PO Box 2129 76043 254-898-3900
Wayne Rotan, supt. Fax 897-3651
www.grisd.net
Glen Rose HS 500/9-12
PO Box 2129 76043 254-898-3800
Tommy Corcoran, prin. Fax 897-9871
Glen Rose JHS 400/6-8
PO Box 2129 76043 254-898-3700
Shirley Craft, prin. Fax 897-4059

Godley, Johnson, Pop. 992
Godley ISD 1,300/PK-12
512 W Links Dr 76044 817-389-2536
Paul Smithson, supt. Fax 389-2543
www.godleyisd.com/
Godley HS 400/9-12
9401 N Highway 171 76044 817-389-2265
Ralph Davis, prin. Fax 389-4455
Godley MS 300/6-8
409 N Pearson St 76044 817-389-2121
David Williams, prin. Fax 389-4357

Goldthwaite, Mills, Pop. 1,824
Goldthwaite ISD 700/PK-12
PO Box 608 76844 325-648-3531
Dr. Gary Long, supt. Fax 648-2456
www.centex-edu.net/goldthwaiteisd

Goldthwaite HS 200/9-12
PO Box 608 76844 325-648-3081
Brad Jones, prin. Fax 648-2325
Goldthwaite MS, PO Box 608 76844 100/6-8
Gary Speegle, prin. 325-648-3630

Goliad, Goliad, Pop. 2,006
Goliad ISD 1,300/PK-12
PO Box 830 77963 361-645-3259
Sam Atwood, supt. Fax 645-3614
www.goliadisd.org
Goliad HS 400/9-12
PO Box 830 77963 361-645-3257
David Hill, prin. Fax 645-8039
Goliad MS 300/6-8
PO Box 830 77963 361-645-3146
Emilio Vargas, prin. Fax 645-8040

Gonzales, Gonzales, Pop. 7,514
Gonzales ISD 2,600/PK-12
926 Saint Lawrence St 78629 830-672-9551
Dr. Steven Ebell, supt. Fax 672-7159
www.gonzales.txed.net
Gonzales HS 700/9-12
1801 N Sarah DeWitt Dr 78629 830-672-7535
Ronald Bragg, prin. Fax 672-8273
Gonzales JHS 400/7-8
426 N College St 78629 830-672-8641
Tony Dominguez, prin. Fax 672-6466

Goodrich, Polk, Pop. 276
Goodrich ISD 200/K-12
PO Box 789 77335 936-365-1112
Guylene Robertson, supt. Fax 365-3518
www.goodrichisd.net
Goodrich JSHS 100/6-12
PO Box 789 77335 936-365-1121
Malissa Williams, prin. Fax 365-3518

Gordon, Palo Pinto, Pop. 465
Gordon ISD 200/K-12
PO Box 47 76453 254-693-5582
Jon Hartgraves, supt. Fax 693-5503
www.gordonisd.net
Gordon S 200/K-12
PO Box 47 76453 254-693-5342
Nelson Campbell, prin. Fax 693-5503

Goree, Knox, Pop. 288
Munday Consolidated ISD
Supt. — See Munday
Munday JHS 100/7-8
PO Box 156 76363 940-422-5233
Kristi Bufkin, prin. Fax 422-4429

Gorman, Eastland, Pop. 1,258
Gorman ISD 400/PK-12
PO Box 8 76454 254-734-3171
David Perry, supt. Fax 734-3393
www.gorman.esc14.net/
Gorman HS 200/7-12
PO Box 8 76454 254-734-2614
Ricky Panter, prin. Fax 734-3425

Graford, Palo Pinto, Pop. 602
Graford ISD 300/PK-12
400 W Division Ave 76449 940-664-3101
Chance Welch, supt. Fax 664-2123
www.grafordisd.net
Graford JSHS 200/7-12
400 W Division Ave 76449 940-664-3161
Pat Narcomey, prin. Fax 664-2026

Graham, Young, Pop. 8,715
Graham ISD 2,300/PK-12
400 3rd St 76450 940-549-0595
Beau Rees, supt. Fax 549-8656
www.grahamisd.com
Graham HS 700/9-12
1000 Brazos St 76450 940-549-4030
Delesa Styles, prin. Fax 549-4031
Graham JHS 500/6-8
1000 2nd St 76450 940-549-2002
Robert Loomis, prin. Fax 549-6991

Granbury, Hood, Pop. 7,360
Granbury ISD 5,300/PK-12
600 W Pearl St 76048 817-408-4000
William Harris, supt. Fax 408-4014
www.granbury.k12.tx.us
Acton MS 500/6-8
1300 James Rd 76049 817-408-4800
Bobby Mabery, prin. Fax 408-4849
Crossland 9th Grade Ctr. 9-9
217 N Jones St 76048 817-408-4700
Lynn Pool, prin. Fax 408-4749
Granbury MS 500/6-8
2000 Crossland Rd 76048 817-408-4850
Jimmy Dawson, prin. Fax 408-4899
Granbury SHS 1,400/10-12
2000 W Pearl St 76048 817-408-4600
Marsha Grissom, prin. Fax 408-4699

Happy Hill Farm Academy 100/K-12
3846 N Highway 144 76048 254-897-4822
Dru Pruitt, prin. Fax 897-7650

Grandfalls, Ward, Pop. 371
Grandfalls-Royalty ISD 100/PK-12
PO Box 10 79742 432-547-2266
Robert Westbrook, supt. Fax 547-2960
www.grisd.com/
Grandfalls-Royalty S 100/PK-12
PO Box 10 79742 432-547-2266
J.D. Stocks, prin. Fax 547-2960

Grand Prairie, Dallas, Pop. 144,337
Grand Prairie ISD 21,600/PK-12
PO Box 531170 75053 972-264-6141
Dr. Susan Simpson, supt. Fax 237-5440
www.gpisd.org
Adams MS 700/6-8
833 W Tarrant Rd 75050 972-262-1934
Calvin Harrison, prin. Fax 522-3099
Arnold MS 800/6-8
1204 E Marshall Dr 75051 972-642-5137
Raymond Edwards, prin. Fax 343-7499
Grand Prairie HS 9th Grade Center 800/9-9
102 High School Dr 75050 972-237-5603
Craig Spears, prin. Fax 343-6399
Grand Prairie SHS 2,000/10-12
101 Highschool Dr 75050 972-809-5711
Fax 809-5775
Jackson MS 1,000/6-8
3504 Corn Valley Rd 75052 972-264-2704
Michael Brinkley, prin. Fax 343-7599
Kennedy MS 800/6-8
2205 SE 4th St 75051 972-264-8651
Leslee Shepherd, prin. Fax 522-3699
Lee MS 800/6-8
401 E Grand Prairie Rd 75051 972-262-6785
John Lowman, prin. Fax 343-6099
Reagan MS 600/6-8
4616 Bardin Rd 75052 972-522-7300
John Walsh, prin. Fax 522-7399
South Grand Prairie HS 9th Grade Campus 9-9
305 W Warrior Trl 75052 972-264-1769
Vicki Villarreal, prin. Fax 343-7698
South Grand Prairie SHS 2,100/10-12
301 W Warrior Trl 75052 972-343-1500
Vicki Bridges, prin. Fax 642-7902
Truman MS 500/6-8
1501 Coffeyville Trl 75052 972-641-7676
Charles Lester, prin. Fax 641-8666

AIMS Academy Post-Sec.
1106 N Highway 360 #305 75050 972-988-3202
Arlington Career Institute Post-Sec.
901 E Avenue K 75050 972-647-1607
Jones Beauty College #2 Post-Sec.
311A W Pioneer Pkwy 75051 214-956-0088
Lincoln Technical Institute Post-Sec.
2501 Arkansas Ln 75052 972-660-5701
Mid Cities Barber College Post-Sec.
2345 SW 3rd St Ste 101 75051 972-642-1892
Shady Grove Christian Academy 200/PK-12
1829 W Shady Grove Rd 75050 972-790-0070
Rhonda Tuttle, admin. Fax 790-6560

Grand Saline, Van Zandt, Pop. 3,228
Grand Saline ISD 1,200/PK-12
400 Stadium Dr 75140 903-962-7546
Gerald Gilbert, supt. Fax 962-7464
www.gsisd.esc7.net
Grand Saline HS 300/9-12
500 Stadium Dr 75140 903-962-7533
Gary Redding, prin. Fax 962-7482
Grand Saline MS 300/6-8
400 Stadium Dr 75140 903-962-7537
Trevor Rogers, prin. Fax 962-7474

Grandview, Johnson, Pop. 1,567
Grandview ISD 1,100/PK-12
PO Box 310 76050 817-866-2450
Keith Scharnhorst, supt. Fax 866-3351
www.gvisd.org
Grandview HS 300/9-12
PO Box 310 76050 817-866-3320
Joe Perrin, prin. Fax 866-3351
Grandview JHS 300/6-8
PO Box 310 76050 817-866-2492
Jeff Hudson, prin. Fax 866-3912

Granger, Williamson, Pop. 1,331
Granger ISD 400/K-12
PO Box 578 76530 512-859-2613
James Bartosh, supt. Fax 859-2446
www.grangerisd.net
Granger S 400/K-12
PO Box 578 76530 512-859-2173
Chris Buerger, prin. Fax 859-2446

Grapeland, Houston, Pop. 1,421
Grapeland ISD 600/PK-12
PO Box 249 75844 936-687-4619
E. D. Sumrall, supt. Fax 687-4624
www.grapelandisd.net/
Grapeland HS 200/9-12
PO Box 249 75844 936-687-4661
Joe Young, prin. Fax 687-9739
Grapeland JHS 100/7-8
PO Box 249 75844 936-687-2351
Joe Young, prin. Fax 687-4624

Grapevine, Tarrant, Pop. 47,460
Carroll ISD 7,300/PK-12
3051 Dove Rd 76051 817-949-8282
Dr. David Faltys, supt. Fax 949-8228
www.southlakecarroll.edu
Other Schools – See Southlake

Grapevine-Colleyville ISD 13,800/PK-12
3051 Ira E Woods Ave 76051 817-251-5501
Dr. Kay Waggoner, supt. Fax 481-2907
www.gcisd-k12.org
Cross Timbers MS 800/6-8
2301 Pool Rd 76051 817-251-5320
Linda Tidmore, prin. Fax 424-4296
Grapevine HS 2,100/9-12
3223 Mustang Dr 76051 817-251-5210
Jerry Hollingsworth, prin. Fax 481-5957
Grapevine MS 800/6-8
301 Pony Pkwy 76051 817-251-5660
Tim Hughes, prin. Fax 424-1626
Other Schools – See Colleyville

Faith Christian S 500/K-12
730 E Worth St 76051 817-442-9144
Dr. Ed Smith, pres. Fax 442-9904

Greenville, Hunt, Pop. 25,637
Greenville ISD 5,000/PK-12
PO Box 1022 75403 903-457-2500
Lloyd Graham, supt. Fax 457-2504
www.greenvilleisd.com
Greenville HS 1,400/9-12
3515 Lions Lair Rd 75402 903-457-2550
Don Jefferies, prin. Fax 455-5158
Greenville MS 700/7-8
3611 Texas St 75401 903-457-2620
Mike Clyde, prin. Fax 457-2628

Greenville Christian S 300/PK-12
8420 Jack Finney Blvd 75402 903-454-1111
Julie Robinson, hdmstr. Fax 455-8470

Groesbeck, Limestone, Pop. 4,353
Groesbeck ISD 1,600/PK-12
PO Box 559 76642 254-729-4100
John Key, supt. Fax 729-5167
www.groesbeck.k12.tx.us
Groesbeck HS 500/9-12
1202 N Ellis St 76642 254-729-4101
Kent Reynolds, prin. Fax 729-5458
Groesbeck MS 400/6-8
410 Elwood Enge Dr 76642 254-729-4102
Ladena King, prin. Fax 729-8763

Groom, Carson, Pop. 587
Groom ISD 100/K-12
PO Box 598 79039 806-248-7557
Terry Stevens, supt. Fax 248-7949
www.groomisd.net
Groom S 100/K-12
PO Box 598 79039 806-248-7474
Terry Stevens, prin. Fax 248-7949

Groves, Jefferson, Pop. 15,006
Port Neches-Groves ISD
Supt. — See Port Neches
Groves MS 600/6-8
5201 Wilson St 77619 409-962-0225
Ken Cummings, prin. Fax 963-1898

Groveton, Trinity, Pop. 1,138
Centerville ISD 200/PK-12
10327 N State Highway 94 75845 936-642-1597
Craig Quincy Davis, supt. Fax 642-2810
www.centervilleisd.net/internet/
Centerville JSHS 100/7-12
10327 N State Highway 94 75845 936-642-1597
Charles Brantner, prin. Fax 642-2810

Groveton ISD 700/K-12
PO Box 728 75845 936-642-1473
Joe Driskell, supt. Fax 642-1628
www.grovetonisd.net
Groveton JSHS 300/7-12
PO Box 700 75845 936-642-1128
Johnny Rhea, prin. Fax 642-1616

Grulla, Starr, Pop. 1,613
Rio Grande City ISD
Supt. — See Rio Grande City
Grulla MS 700/6-8
PO Box 338 78548 956-487-5558
Pablo Martinez, prin. Fax 487-5633

Gruver, Hansford, Pop. 1,122
Gruver ISD 400/PK-12
PO Box 650 79040 806-733-2001
David Teal, supt. Fax 733-5416
www.gruverisd.net
Gruver HS 100/9-12
PO Box 747 79040 806-733-2477
Mike King, prin. Fax 733-2596
Gruver JHS 100/5-8
PO Box 709 79040 806-733-2081
Kevin Black, prin. Fax 733-5523

Gunter, Grayson, Pop. 1,561
Gunter ISD 800/PK-12
PO Box 109 75058 903-433-4750
R. Cohagan, supt. Fax 433-1053
www.gunterisd.org
Gunter HS 300/9-12
PO Box 109 75058 903-433-1542
Kevin Worthy, prin. Fax 433-1492
Gunter MS 200/5-8
PO Box 109 75058 903-433-1545
Diana Ferguson, prin. Fax 433-9306

Gustine, Comanche, Pop. 447
Gustine ISD 200/PK-12
503 W Main St 76455 325-667-7981
Ken Baugh, supt. Fax 667-7281
www.gustine.esc14.net/
Gustine S 200/PK-12
503 W Main St 76455 325-667-7303
Ken Baugh, prin. Fax 667-7281

Guthrie, King
Guthrie Common SD 100/PK-12
PO Box 70 79236 806-596-4466
Dan Pickering, supt. Fax 596-4519
www.guthriejags.com/
Guthrie S 100/PK-12
PO Box 70 79236 806-596-4466
Roddy Shipman, prin. Fax 596-4519

Hale Center, Hale, Pop. 2,180
Hale Center ISD 600/PK-12
PO Box 1210 79041 806-839-2451
Rick Teran, supt. Fax 839-2195
www.halecenter.esc17.net
Carr MS 200/5-8
PO Box 1210 79041 806-839-2141
Christian Rabone, prin. Fax 839-4417
Hale Center HS 200/9-12
PO Box 1210 79041 806-839-2452
Lynette Thomas, prin. Fax 839-2059

Hallettsville, Lavaca, Pop. 2,497
Hallettsville ISD 1,000/K-12
PO Box 368 77964 361-798-2242
Joseph T. Patek, supt. Fax 798-5902
www.hisdbrahmas.org
Hallettsville HS 400/9-12
200 N Ridge St 77964 361-798-2242
Lynn Cook, prin. Fax 798-9297
Hallettsville JHS 300/5-8
410 S Russell St 77964 361-798-2242
Sophie Teltschik, prin. Fax 798-3573

Sacred Heart S 300/PK-12
313 S Texana St 77964 361-798-4251
David Smolik, prin. Fax 798-4970

Hallsville, Harrison, Pop. 2,897
Hallsville ISD 3,400/PK-12
PO Box 810 75650 903-668-5990
Greg Wright, supt. Fax 668-5990
www.hisd.com
Hallsville HS 1,100/9-12
PO Box 810 75650 903-668-5990
Dr. Brian Morris, prin. Fax 668-5990
Hallsville JHS 600/7-8
PO Box 810 75650 903-668-5990
Eve Ford, prin. Fax 668-5990

Haltom City, Tarrant, Pop. 39,875
Birdville ISD 22,300/PK-12
6125 E Belknap St 76117 817-847-5700
Stephen Waddell Ed.D., supt. Fax 838-7261
www.birdville.k12.tx.us
Haltom HS 2,600/9-12
5501 Haltom Rd 76137 817-547-6000
Michael Jasso, prin. Fax 547-6352

Haltom MS 800/6-8
5000 Hires Ln 76117 817-547-4000
Susan Taylor, prin. Fax 831-5778
North Oaks MS 600/6-8
4800 Jordan Park Dr 76117 817-547-4600
Bob Koerner, prin. Fax 581-5352
Other Schools – See North Richland Hills, Richland Hills, Watauga

Hamilton, Hamilton, Pop. 2,920
Hamilton ISD 900/PK-12
PO Box 392 76531 254-386-3149
Sam Bell, supt. Fax 386-8885
www.hamilton.k12.tx.us
Hamilton HS 300/9-12
PO Box 392 76531 254-386-8167
James Hopper, prin. Fax 386-4677
Hamilton MS 200/6-8
PO Box 392 76531 254-386-8168
Brenda Smith, prin. Fax 386-8885

Hamlin, Jones, Pop. 2,018
Hamlin ISD 500/PK-12
PO Box 338 79520 325-576-2722
Tony Daniel, supt. Fax 576-2152
www.hamlin.esc14.net
Hamlin HS 100/9-12
450 SW Avenue F 79520 325-576-3625
Toby Tyler, prin. Fax 576-3926
Hamlin MS 100/6-8
250 SW Avenue F 79520 325-576-2933
Laura O'Rear, prin. Fax 576-2317

Hamshire, Jefferson
Hamshire-Fannett ISD 1,800/PK-12
PO Box 223 77622 409-243-2517
Marianne Kondo, supt. Fax 243-3437
www.hfisd.net/
Hamshire-Fannett HS 600/9-12
PO Box 223 77622 409-243-2512
Dwaine Augustine, prin. Fax 243-2518
Other Schools – See Beaumont

Happy, Swisher, Pop. 615
Happy ISD 200/K-12
PO Box 458 79042 806-558-5331
Dr. Billy Howell, supt. Fax 558-2070
www.happyisd.net
Happy HS, PO Box 458 79042 100/7-12
Cindy McCuaig, prin. 806-558-5311

Hardin, Liberty, Pop. 797
Hardin ISD 1,300/PK-12
PO Box 330 77561 936-298-2112
Craig Ringer, supt. Fax 298-9161
www.hardin.isd.esc4.net/
Hardin HS 400/9-12
PO Box 330 77561 936-298-2118
Dr. D'Ann Cathriner, prin. Fax 298-3612
Hardin MS 200/7-8
PO Box 330 77561 936-298-2054
Dr. Michael Bearden, prin. Fax 298-3264

Harker Heights, Bell, Pop. 21,337
Killeen ISD
Supt. — See Killeen
Eastern Hills MS 700/6-8
300 Indian Trl 76548 254-501-1100
Sharon Miller, prin. Fax 680-6606
Harker Heights HS 2,000/9-12
1001 E FM 2410 Rd 76548 254-501-0800
Ralph Bray, prin. Fax 698-5267
Union Grove MS 100/6-8
101 E Iowa Dr 76548 254-200-6580
Robin Champagne, prin. Fax 690-5042

Harleton, Harrison
Harleton ISD 700/PK-12
PO Box 510 75651 903-777-2372
Rickey Logan, supt. Fax 777-2406
harletonisd.net
Harleton HS 200/9-12
PO Box 710 75651 903-777-2711
Clint Coyne, prin. Fax 777-2547
Harleton JHS 200/6-8
PO Box 610 75651 903-777-3010
Craig Evers, prin. Fax 777-3009

Harlingen, Cameron, Pop. 62,318
Harlingen Consolidated ISD 17,200/PK-12
407N77 Sunshine Strip 78550 956-427-3400
Dr. Linda Wade, supt. Fax 427-3589
www.harlingen.isd.tenet.edu
Coakley MS 900/6-8
1402 S 6th St 78550 956-427-3000
Kevin Brackmeyer, prin. Fax 427-3006
Gutierrez MS 1,200/6-8
3205 Wilson Rd 78552 956-430-4400
Dr. Marsha Marchbanks, prin. Fax 430-4480
Harlingen HS 2,500/9-12
1201 Marshall St 78550 956-427-3600
Leeroy Zepeda, prin. Fax 427-3792
Harlingen HS South 2,000/9-12
1701 Dixieland Rd 78552 956-427-3800
Guadalupe Nava, prin. Fax 427-3995
Memorial MS 900/6-8
300 N 13th St 78550 956-427-3020
Alex Gonzalez, prin. Fax 427-3024
Vela MS 6-8
801 S Palm Blvd 78552 956-427-3479
Dr. Alicia Torres, prin. Fax 427-3549
Vernon MS 800/6-8
125 S 13th St 78550 956-427-3040
Gracie Gutierrez, prin. Fax 427-3046

Calvary Christian S 400/PK-10
1815 N 7th St 78550 956-425-1882
Karen Zeissel, prin. Fax 412-0324
Marine Military Academy 400/8-12
320 Iwo Jima Blvd 78550 956-423-6006
General Stephen Cheney, pres. Fax 421-9274
Texas State Technical College Post-Sec.
1901 Loop 499 78550 956-364-4001
University of Cosmetology Arts & Science Post-Sec.
913 N 13th St 78550 956-412-1212

Harper, Gillespie
Harper ISD 500/PK-12
PO Box 68 78631 830-864-4044
Pari Whitten, supt. Fax 864-4060
www.harper.txed.net/
Harper HS 200/9-12
PO Box 68 78631 830-864-4044
Chris Stevenson, prin. Fax 864-4748
Harper MS 100/6-8
PO Box 68 78631 830-864-4044
Chris Stevenson, prin. Fax 864-4748

Harrold, Wilbarger
Harrold ISD 100/K-12
PO Box 400 76364 940-886-2213
David Thweatt, supt. Fax 886-2215
www.esc9.net/harroldisd/
Harrold S 100/K-12
PO Box 400 76364 940-886-2213
Craig Templeton, prin. Fax 886-2215

Hart, Castro, Pop. 1,101
Hart ISD 300/PK-12
PO Box 490 79043 806-938-2143
Don Sanders, supt. Fax 938-2610
www.region16.net/hartisd
Hart JSHS 100/7-12
PO Box 490 79043 806-938-2141
Jay McCook, prin. Fax 938-2610

Hartley, Hartley
Hartley ISD 200/K-12
PO Box 408 79044 806-365-4458
Jimmy Hoyle, supt. Fax 365-4459
www.hartleytx.com/hartleyisd
Hartley S 200/K-12
PO Box 408 79044 806-365-4458
Rick McCarty, prin. Fax 365-4459

Haskell, Haskell, Pop. 2,782
Haskell CISD 500/PK-12
PO Box 937 79521 940-864-2602
Eddie Bland, supt. Fax 864-8096
www.haskell.esc14.net/
Haskell HS, PO Box 937 79521 200/9-12
Bryan McCulloch, prin. 940-864-8535
Other Schools – See Rochester

Paint Creek ISD 100/K-12
4485 FM 600 79521 940-864-2471
Don Ballard, supt. Fax 864-8038
www.paintcreek.esc14.net
Paint Creek S 100/K-12
4485 FM 600 79521 940-864-2471
Kristi Exum, prin. Fax 864-8038

Hawkins, Wood, Pop. 1,471
Hawkins ISD 700/PK-12
PO Box 1430 75765 903-769-2181
Dan Rose, supt. Fax 769-0505
www.hawkinsisd.org
Hawkins HS 200/9-12
PO Box 1430 75765 903-769-0571
Charles Leffall, prin. Fax 769-0573
Hawkins MS 200/6-8
PO Box 1430 75765 903-769-0552
David Ledkins, prin. Fax 769-0583

Jarvis Christian College Post-Sec.
PO Box 1470 75765 903-769-5700

Hawley, Jones, Pop. 603
Hawley ISD 800/PK-12
PO Box 440 79525 325-537-2214
Bobby Matthews, supt. Fax 537-2265
www.hawley.esc14.net
Hawley HS 200/9-12
PO Box 440 79525 325-537-2722
Larry Jones, prin. Fax 537-2265
Hawley MS 200/6-8
PO Box 440 79525 325-537-2070
Emilia Moreno, prin. Fax 537-2265

Hearne, Robertson, Pop. 4,710
Hearne ISD 1,200/PK-12
900 Wheelock St 77859 979-279-3200
David C. Deaver, supt. Fax 279-3631
www.hearne.k12.tx.us/
Hearne HS 300/9-12
1201 W Brown St 77859 979-279-2332
Norris McDaniel, prin. Fax 279-8006
Hearne JHS 200/7-8
401 Wheelock St 77859 979-279-2449
Leon Jackson, prin. Fax 279-8033

Hebbronville, Jim Hogg, Pop. 4,465
Jim Hogg County ISD 1,100/PK-12
PO Box 880 78361 361-527-3203
Pedro Lopez, supt. Fax 527-4823
www.jhcisd.net/
Hebbronville HS 300/9-12
PO Box 880 78361 361-527-3203
Fantina Garcia, prin. Fax 527-5989
Hebbronville JHS 200/6-8
PO Box 880 78361 361-527-3203
Patricia Gonzalez, prin. Fax 527-5986

Hedley, Donley, Pop. 377
Hedley ISD 200/PK-12
PO Box 69 79237 806-856-5323
Bryan Hill, supt. Fax 856-5372
Hedley S 200/PK-12
PO Box 69 79237 806-856-5323
Bryan Hill, prin. Fax 856-5372

Helotes, Bexar, Pop. 6,187
Northside ISD
Supt. — See San Antonio
O'Connor HS 3,000/9-12
12221 Leslie Rd 78023 210-397-4800
Larry Martin, prin. Fax 695-4804

Hemphill, Sabine, Pop. 1,069
Hemphill ISD 1,000/PK-12
PO Box 1950 75948 409-787-3371
Mike Terry, supt. Fax 787-4005
www.hemphill.esc7.net
Hemphill HS 300/9-12
PO Box 1950 75948 409-787-3371
Marc Griffin, prin. Fax 787-1259
Hemphill MS 300/5-8
PO Box 1950 75948 409-787-3371
C.J. O'Neal, prin. Fax 787-4005

Hempstead, Waller, Pop. 6,546
Hempstead ISD 1,400/PK-12
PO Box 1007 77445 979-826-3304
Anneta Buenger, supt. Fax 826-5510
www.hempstead.isd.esc4.net
Hempstead HS 400/9-12
PO Box 1007 77445 979-826-3331
Michael Lawson, prin. Fax 826-4779
Hempstead MS 300/6-8
PO Box 1007 77445 979-826-2530
Brenda Krchnak, prin. Fax 826-5583

Henderson, Rusk, Pop. 11,496
Henderson ISD 3,500/PK-12
PO Box 728 75653 903-657-8511
Tommy Alexander, supt. Fax 657-9271
www.hendersonisd.org/
Henderson HS 1,000/9-12
PO Box 728 75653 903-657-1483
Stacey Sullivan, prin. Fax 657-7604
Henderson MS 800/6-8
PO Box 728 75653 903-657-1491
Kelly Teems, prin. Fax 657-6499

Full Armor Christian Academy 200/PK-10
PO Box 2035 75653 903-655-8489
Stephen Scogin, prin. Fax 657-8267

Henrietta, Clay, Pop. 3,325
Henrietta ISD 1,000/PK-12
1801 E Crafton St 76365 940-538-7500
Jeff McClure, supt. Fax 538-7505
www.henrietta-isd.net
Henrietta HS 300/9-12
1700 E Crafton St 76365 940-538-7530
Jerre Gibbons, prin. Fax 538-7535
Henrietta JHS 200/6-8
308 E Gilbert St 76365 940-538-7520
Gary Parrish, prin. Fax 538-7525

Midway ISD 100/PK-12
12142 State Highway 148 S 76365 940-476-2215
Hollis Adams, supt. Fax 476-2226
www.esc9.net/midway
Midway S 100/PK-12
12142 State Highway 148 S 76365 940-476-2222
Hollis Adams, prin. Fax 476-2226

Hereford, Deaf Smith, Pop. 14,472
Hereford ISD 3,700/K-12
601 N 25 Mile Ave 79045 806-363-7600
Dr. Michael Stevens, supt. Fax 363-7699
www.herefordisd.net
Hereford HS, 200 Avenue F 79045 1,200/9-12
Richard Sauceda, prin. 806-363-7620
Hereford JHS, 704 La Plata St 79045 1,000/6-8
Amy Lopez, prin. 806-363-7630

Community Christian S 50/6-12
PO Box 487 79045 806-364-8867
Steve Louder, admin. Fax 364-0084

Hermleigh, Scurry
Hermleigh ISD 200/K-12
1026 School Ave 79526 325-863-2772
Gary Rotan, supt. Fax 863-2713
www.hermleigh.esc14.net/
Hermleigh S 200/K-12
1026 School Ave 79526 325-863-2451
Clarence Spieker, prin. Fax 863-2713

Hewitt, McLennan, Pop. 12,987
Midway ISD
Supt. — See Waco
Midway MS 900/7-8
800 N Hewitt Dr 76643 254-761-5680
Joe Kucera, prin. Fax 761-5775

Hico, Hamilton, Pop. 1,337
Hico ISD 700/PK-12
PO Box 218 76457 254-796-2181
Rod Townsend, supt. Fax 796-2446
www.hico-isd.net
Hico HS 200/9-12
PO Box 218 76457 254-796-2184
Bill Boyd, prin. Fax 796-2446
Hico JHS 200/6-8
PO Box 218 76457 254-796-2182
Shelli Stegall, prin. Fax 796-9830

Hidalgo, Hidalgo, Pop. 10,889
Hidalgo ISD 2,800/PK-12
PO Box D 78557 956-843-3100
Daniel King Ph.D., supt. Fax 843-3343
hidalgo.tx.schoolwebpages.com
Diaz JHS 700/6-8
PO Box D 78557 956-843-3140
Jose Rangel, prin. Fax 843-3198
Hidalgo HS 800/9-12
PO Box D 78557 956-843-3160
Edward Blaha, prin. Fax 843-3322

Higgins, Lipscomb, Pop. 437
Higgins ISD 100/K-12
PO Box 218 79046 806-852-2171
Hope Appel, supt. Fax 852-3502
Higgins S 100/K-12
PO Box 218 79046 806-852-2631
Hope Appel, prin. Fax 852-3502

High Island, Galveston
High Island ISD 300/K-12
PO Box 246 77623 409-286-5317
Michael Sims, supt. Fax 286-5351
www.esc05.k12.tx.us/hiisd/hiweb.html
High Island HS 100/9-12
PO Box 246 77623 409-286-5314
Audie Tackett, prin. Fax 286-2120
High Island MS 100/6-8
PO Box 246 77623 409-286-5314
Audie Tackett, prin. Fax 286-2120

Highlands, Harris, Pop. 6,632
Goose Creek ISD
Supt. — See Baytown
Highlands JHS 700/6-8
1212 E Wallisville Rd 77562 281-420-4695
Steve Herring, prin. Fax 426-4301

Chinquapin S 100/6-12
2615 E Wallisville Rd 77562 281-426-5551
Bill Heinzerling, prin. Fax 426-5553

Highland Village, Denton, Pop. 15,105
Lewisville ISD
Supt. — See Flower Mound
Briarhill MS 900/6-8
2100 Briarhill Blvd 75077 469-713-5975
Mechelle Bryson, prin. Fax 317-5953

Hillsboro, Hill, Pop. 9,000
Hillsboro ISD 1,800/PK-12
121 E Franklin St 76645 254-582-8585
Jerry Maze, supt. Fax 582-4165
www.hillsboroisd.org
Hillsboro HS 500/9-12
1600 Abbott Ave 76645 254-582-4100
David Priddy, prin. Fax 582-4108
Hillsboro JHS 200/7-8
210 E Walnut St 76645 254-582-4120
Edward Conger, prin. Fax 582-4122

Hill College Post-Sec.
PO Box 619 76645 254-582-2555

Hitchcock, Galveston, Pop. 7,193
Hitchcock ISD 1,100/PK-12
8117 Highway 6 77563 409-986-5514
Barbara Wilson, supt. Fax 986-5141
www.hitchcockisd.org
Crosby MS 300/5-8
7801 Neville Ave 77563 409-986-5528
Randy Dowdy, prin. Fax 986-9254
Hitchcock HS 400/9-12
6625 FM 2004 Rd 77563 409-986-5581
John Montelongo, prin. Fax 986-9339

Holland, Bell, Pop. 1,090
Holland ISD 500/PK-12
PO Box 217 76534 254-657-0175
Cindy Gunn, supt. Fax 657-0172
www.holland.k12.tx.us
Bowman MS 100/6-8
PO Box 217 76534 254-657-2224
Mike Mazoch, prin. Fax 657-2250
Holland HS 100/9-12
PO Box 217 76534 254-657-2523
Britt Gordon, prin. Fax 657-2250

Holliday, Archer, Pop. 1,681
Holliday ISD 900/PK-12
PO Box 689 76366 940-586-1281
Clarke Boyd, supt. Fax 586-1492
www.esc9.net/holliday
Holliday HS 300/9-12
PO Box 947 76366 940-586-1624
Kent Lemons, prin. Fax 586-9501
Holliday MS 200/6-8
PO Box 977 76366 940-586-1314
Kelly Carver, prin. Fax 586-1492

Hondo, Medina, Pop. 8,779
Hondo ISD 2,100/PK-12
PO Box 308 78861 830-426-3027
Clyde Parsons, supt. Fax 426-7683
www.hondo.k12.tx.us
Hondo HS 600/9-12
2603 Avenue H 78861 830-426-3341
Larry Carroll, prin. Fax 426-7690
McDowell JHS 500/6-8
1602 27th St S 78861 830-426-2261
Michael Neuman, prin. Fax 426-7624

Honey Grove, Fannin, Pop. 1,836
Honey Grove ISD 700/PK-12
540 6th St 75446 903-378-2264
Jan M. Cummins, supt. Fax 378-2991
www.honeygroveisd.net/
Honey Grove HS 200/9-12
540 6th St 75446 903-378-2264
Jeffry Clark, prin. Fax 378-3050
Honey Grove MS 200/6-8
540 6th St 75446 903-378-2264
Robert Milton, prin. Fax 378-2095

Hooks, Bowie, Pop. 2,924
Hooks ISD 1,100/PK-12
PO Box 39 75561 903-547-6077
Kathy Allen, supt. Fax 547-2943
www.esc8.net/hooks
Hooks HS, PO Box 1447 75561 400/9-12
Lynne Hopper, prin. 903-547-2215
Hooks JHS, PO Box 249 75561 300/5-8
Shane Krueger, prin. 903-547-2568

Horizon City, El Paso, Pop. 8,695
Clint ISD
Supt. — See El Paso
Horizon MS 600/6-8
400 N Kenazo Ave 79928 915-926-4700
Josie Perez, prin. Fax 852-9274

Houston, Harris, Pop. 2,016,582
Aldine ISD 54,900/PK-12
14910 Aldine Westfield Rd 77032 281-449-1011
Nadine Kujawa, supt. Fax 449-4291
www.aldine.k12.tx.us
Aldine MS 900/7-8
14908 Aldine Westfield Rd 77032 281-985-6580
Todd Davis, prin. Fax 985-6480
Aldine Ninth Grade S 900/9-9
10650 North Fwy 77037 281-878-6800
Janice DeBlance, prin. Fax 878-6824
Aldine SHS 2,000/10-12
11101 Airline Dr 77037 281-448-5231
Cecil Hutson, prin. Fax 878-0641
Carver HS 700/9-12
2100 S Victory Dr 77088 281-878-0310
Willie Pickens, prin. Fax 591-8579
Drew Academy 700/6-8
1910 W Little York Rd 77091 281-878-0360
Fred Walker, prin. Fax 447-4694
Eisenhower Ninth Grade S 900/9-9
3550 W Gulf Bank Rd 77088 281-878-7700
Melvin McGowen, prin. Fax 878-7736
Eisenhower SHS 2,100/10-12
7922 Antoine Dr 77088 281-878-0900
Alonzo Reynolds, prin. Fax 448-2936
Grantham Academy 1,200/7-8
13300 Chrisman Rd 77039 281-985-6590
Kenneth Hodgkinson, prin. Fax 985-6595
Hambrick MS 1,000/7-8
4600 Aldine Mail Rd 77039 281-985-6570
Holly Fisackerly, prin. Fax 442-9036
Hoffman MS 1,100/7-8
6101 W Little York Rd 77091 713-613-7670
Rhonda Johnson, prin. Fax 613-7675
MacArthur Ninth Grade S 900/9-9
12111 Gloger St 77039 281-985-7400
Therese Samperi, prin. Fax 985-7423
MacArthur SHS 1,800/10-12
4400 Aldine Mail Rd 77039 281-985-6330
Nancy Blackwell, prin. Fax 985-6294

Nimitz 9th Grade S 1,000/9-9
2425 WW Thorne Blvd 77073 281-209-8200
Tom Colwell, prin. Fax 209-8220
Nimitz SHS 1,900/10-12
2005 WW Thorne Blvd 77073 281-443-7480
Watson Wright, prin. Fax 233-4331
Plummer MS 7-8
11429 Spears Rd 77067 281-539-4000
Luis Pratts, prin. Fax 539-4017
Shotwell MS 1,000/7-8
6515 Trail Valley Way 77086 281-878-0960
Wanda Walker, prin. Fax 591-8564
Stovall MS 1,100/7-8
11201 Airline Dr 77037 281-878-0670
Raul Fonseca, prin. Fax 448-0636
Other Schools – See Humble

Alief ISD 45,500/PK-12
12302 High Star Dr 77072 281-498-8110
Louis B. Stoerner, supt. Fax 575-1923
www.aliefisd.net/
Albright MS 1,300/7-8
6315 Winkleman Rd 77083 281-983-8411
Walter Jackson, prin. Fax 983-8443
Alief MS 1,100/6-8
4415 Cook Rd 77072 281-983-8422
Maggie Cuellar, prin. Fax 983-8053
Alief Taylor HS 2,800/9-12
7555 Howell Sugar Land Rd 77083 281-988-3500
Manette Schaller, prin. Fax 561-7214
Elsik HS 2,700/10-12
12601 High Star Dr 77072 281-498-8110
Linda Graessle, prin. Fax 530-7058
Elsik Ninth Grade Center 1,500/9-9
6767 S Dairy Ashford St 77072 281-988-3239
Gregory Freeman, prin. Fax 988-3319
Hastings HS 2,700/10-12
4410 Cook Rd 77072 281-498-8110
Rhonda McWilliams, prin. Fax 561-5763
Hastings Ninth Grade Center 1,600/9-9
6750 Cook Rd 77072 281-988-3139
Gina Tomas, prin. Fax 988-3419
Holub MS 1,200/7-8
9515 S Dairy Ashford St 77099 281-983-8433
Pat Brown, prin. Fax 983-8398
Kerr HS 700/9-12
8150 Howell Sugar Land Rd 77083 281-983-8484
Pat McCutcheon, prin. Fax 983-8014
Killough MS 1,000/7-8
7600 Synott Rd 77083 281-983-8444
Luis Olivas, prin. Fax 983-8067
O'Donnell MS 1,100/6-8
14041 Alief Clodine Rd 77082 281-495-6000
Tyrone Sylvester, prin. Fax 568-5029
Olle MS 1,100/7-8
9200 Boone Rd 77099 281-983-8455
Jackie Armwood, prin. Fax 983-8077
Other Schools – See Alief

Clear Creek ISD
Supt. — See League City
Clear Horizons Early College HS 9-12
PO Box 613 77001 281-929-4657
Gale Ladehoff, prin.
Clear Lake 9th Grade Center 9-9
2903 Falcon Pass 77062 281-284-1900
Dr. Trampus Bass, prin. Fax 284-1905
Clear Lake HS 3,500/9-12
2929 Bay Area Blvd 77058 281-284-1900
Dr. Christopher Moran, prin. Fax 284-1905
Clear Lake IS 1,000/6-8
15545 El Camino Real 77062 281-488-1296
Brett Lemley, prin. Fax 488-8795
Space Center IS 1,300/6-8
17400 Saturn Ln 77058 281-284-3300
Susan Stuart, prin. Fax 284-3305

Cypress-Fairbanks ISD 78,900/PK-12
PO Box 692003 77269 281-897-4000
David Anthony Ed.D., supt. Fax 897-4125
www.cfisd.net
Aragon MS 1,600/6-8
16823 West Rd 77095 281-856-5100
Vicki McComas, prin. Fax 856-5105
Bleyl MS 1,400/6-8
10800 Mills Rd 77070 281-897-4340
Barbara Crook, prin. Fax 897-4353
Campbell MS 1,400/6-8
11415 Bobcat Rd 77064 281-897-4300
Dr. Robert Hatcher, prin. Fax 807-8634
Cook MS 1,500/6-8
9111 Wheatland Dr 77064 281-897-4400
Dr. Robert Borneman, prin. Fax 897-3850
Cypress Creek HS 2,700/9-12
9815 Grant Rd 77070 281-897-4200
Jim Wells, prin. Fax 897-4193
Cypress Falls HS 3,200/9-12
9811 Huffmeister Rd 77095 281-856-1000
Dr. Robert Worthy, prin. Fax 856-1445
Cypress Ridge HS 3,200/9-12
7900 N Eldridge Pkwy 77041 713-807-8000
Claudio Garcia, prin. Fax 807-8005
Dean MS 1,400/6-8
14104 Reo St 77040 713-460-6153
Mike Smith, prin. Fax 460-6197
Jersey Village HS 3,000/9-12
7600 Solomon St 77040 713-896-3400
Ralph Funk, prin. Fax 896-3438
Kahla MS 6-8
16212 W Little York Rd 77084 281-345-3260
Marvin Webster, prin.
Labay MS 1,400/6-8
15435 Willow River Dr 77095 281-463-5800
Dr. Cheryl Johns, prin. Fax 463-5804
Langham Creek HS 3,400/9-12
17610 FM 529 Rd 77095 281-463-5400
Tom Strother, prin. Fax 345-3509
Truitt MS 1,400/6-8
6600 Addicks Satsuma Rd 77084 281-856-1100
Robert Hull, prin. Fax 856-1104
Watkins MS 1,600/6-8
4800 Cairnvillage St 77084 281-463-5850
Diana Lewis, prin. Fax 463-5508
Other Schools – See Cypress, Katy

Fort Bend ISD
Supt. — See Sugar Land
Hodges Bend MS 1,800/6-8
16510 Bissonnet St 77083 281-634-3000
Corliss Rogers, prin. Fax 634-3028
McAuliffe MS 1,300/6-8
16650 S Post Oak Rd 77053 281-634-3360
Isaac Malbrough, prin. Fax 634-3393

Willowridge HS 1,700/9-12
16301 Chimney Rock Rd 77053 281-634-2450
Billy Polk, prin. Fax 634-2513

Galena Park ISD 20,800/PK-12
14705 Woodforest Blvd 77015 832-386-1000
Dr. Mark Henry, supt. Fax 386-1298
www.galenaparkisd.com
Cunningham MS 900/6-8
14110 Wallisville Rd 77049 832-386-4470
Thad Gittens, prin. Fax 386-4471
North Shore HS 2,300/9-10
13501 Hollypark Dr 77015 832-386-3400
John Moore, prin. Fax 386-3401
North Shore MS 1,300/6-8
120 Castlegory Rd 77015 832-386-2600
Paul Drexler, prin. Fax 386-2643
North Shore SHS 1,800/11-12
353 N Castlegory Rd 77049 832-386-4100
Kenneth Wallace, prin. Fax 386-4101
Woodland Acres MS 400/6-8
12947 Myrtle Ln 77015 832-386-4700
Michelle Chae, prin. Fax 386-4701
Other Schools – See Galena Park

Houston ISD 193,500/PK-12
4400 W 18th St 77092 713-556-6000
Dr. Abelardo Saavedra, supt. Fax 556-6006
www.houstonisd.org/
Attucks MS 900/6-8
4330 Bellfort St 77051 713-732-3670
Renaldo Wallace, prin. Fax 732-3677
Austin HS 1,800/9-12
1700 Dumble St 77023 713-924-1600
Linda M. Llorente, prin. Fax 923-3157
Black MS 700/6-8
1575 Chantilly Ln 77018 713-613-2505
Alma Sarmiento-Salman, prin. Fax 613-2533
Burbank MS 1,300/6-8
315 Berry Rd 77022 713-696-2720
Charlotte Parker, prin. Fax 696-2723
Carnegie Vanguard HS 300/9-12
10401 Scott St 77051 713-732-3694
Ramon Moss, prin. Fax 732-3692
Carter Career Center Vo/Tech
1700 Gregg St 77020 713-226-2651
Rhonda Cotton, prin. Fax 226-2666
Challenge Early College HS 200/9-12
5601 West Loop S 77081 713-664-9712
Justin Fuentes, prin. Fax 664-9780
Chavez HS 2,300/9-12
8501 Howard Dr 77017 713-641-7400
Dan DeLeon, prin. Fax 641-7408
Clifton MS 1,100/6-8
6001 Golden Forest Dr 77092 713-613-2516
Beverly Teal, prin. Fax 613-2526
Cullen MS 700/6-8
6900 Scott St 77021 713-746-8180
Ronald Mumphery, prin. Fax 746-8181
Davis HS 1,600/9-12
1101 Quitman St 77009 713-226-4900
Jaime Castaneda, prin. Fax 226-4999
Deady MS 1,200/6-8
2500 Broadway St 77012 713-845-7411
James D. Troutman, prin. Fax 845-5645
DeBakey Health Professions HS 700/9-12
3100 Shenandoah St 77021 713-741-2410
C. Deason-Collins, prin. Fax 746-5211
Dowling MS 1,700/6-8
14000 Stancliff St 77045 713-434-5600
Barrett Brooks, prin. Fax 434-5608
East Early College HS 9-12
2524 Garland St 77087 713-847-4809
Joel Castro, prin. Fax 847-4813
Edison MS 1,000/6-8
6901 Avenue I 77011 713-924-1800
George Martin, prin. Fax 924-1316
Empowerment College Preparatory HS 9-12
5655 Selinsky Rd 77048 713-732-9231
Misha Lesley, prin. Fax 732-9232
Fleming MS 600/6-8
4910 Collingsworth St 77026 713-671-4170
Maria McNeal-Sheppard, prin. Fax 671-4176
Fondren MS 900/6-8
6333 S Braeswood Blvd 77096 713-778-3360
Barbara Neal, prin. Fax 778-3362
Fonville MS 1,200/6-8
725 E Little York Rd 77076 713-696-2825
Efrain Olivo, prin. Fax 696-2829
Furr HS 1,100/9-12
520 Mercury Dr 77013 713-675-1118
Dr. Bertie Simmons, prin. Fax 671-3612
Grady MS 600/6-8
5215 San Felipe St 77056 713-625-1411
Gretchen Kasper, prin. Fax 625-1415
Gregory-Lincoln Education Center 500/6-8
1101 Taft St 77019 713-942-1400
Johnnie Jackson, prin. Fax 942-1406
Hamilton MS 1,200/6-8
139 E 20th St 77008 713-802-4725
Roger A. Bunnell, prin. Fax 802-4731
Hartman MS 1,500/6-8
7111 Westover St 77087 713-845-7435
Joseph Addison, prin. Fax 847-4706
Henry MS 1,100/6-8
10702 E Hardy Rd 77093 713-696-2650
Cynthia Banda, prin. Fax 696-2657
Hogg MS 900/6-8
1100 Merrill St 77009 713-802-4700
Imelda Medrano, prin. Fax 802-4708
Holland MS 800/6-8
1600 Gellhorn Dr 77029 713-671-3860
Brian McDonald, prin. Fax 671-3874
Houston Acad for International Studies 9-12
1515 Windbern Ave 77004 713-942-3340
Melissa Jacobs, prin. Fax 942-3346
Houston HS 2,800/9-12
9400 Irvington Blvd 77076 713-696-8970
Aida Tello, prin. Fax 696-8911
HS for Law Enforcement/Criminal Justice 700/9-12
4701 Dickson St 77007 713-867-5100
Carol Mosteit, prin. Fax 802-4600
Jackson MS 1,200/6-8
5100 Polk St 77023 713-924-1760
Ana Zamarripa, prin. Fax 924-1768
Johnston MS 1,400/6-8
10410 Manhattan Dr 77096 713-726-3616
Dave Wheat, prin. Fax 726-3622
Jones HS 1,100/9-12
7414 Saint Lo Rd 77033 713-733-1111
Adele Rogers, prin. Fax 732-3450

Jordan HS for Careers — Vo/Tech
5800 Eastex Fwy 77026 — 713-636-6900
Rever Givens, prin. — Fax 636-6917
Kashmere HS — 800/9-12
6900 Wileyvale Rd 77028 — 713-636-6400
Dr. Charlotte Parker, prin. — Fax 636-6433
Key MS — 900/6-8
4000 Kelley St 77026 — 713-636-6000
Mable Caleb, prin. — Fax 636-6008
Lamar HS — 3,400/9-12
3325 Westheimer Rd 77098 — 713-522-5960
James McSwain, prin. — Fax 535-3769
Lanier MS — 1,300/6-8
2600 Woodhead St 77098 — 713-942-1900
Julia Dimmitt, prin. — Fax 942-1907
Las Americas MS — 100/6-8
5909 Glenmont Dr 77081 — 713-661-1670
Marie Moreno, prin. — Fax 660-9259
Lee HS — 2,100/9-12
6529 Beverlyhill St 77057 — 713-787-1700
Steven Amstutz, prin. — Fax 787-1723
Long MS — 1,500/6-8
6501 Bellaire Blvd 77074 — 713-778-3380
Diana De La Rosa, prin. — Fax 778-3387
Madison HS — 2,200/9-12
13719 White Heather Dr 77045 — 713-433-9801
Gloria Legington, prin. — Fax 434-5242
Marshall MS — 1,200/6-8
1115 Noble St 77009 — 713-226-2600
Juan Gonzales, prin. — Fax 226-2605
McReynolds MS — 800/6-8
5910 Market St 77020 — 713-671-3650
Jorge Arredondo, prin. — Fax 671-3657
Milby HS — 2,200/9-12
1601 Broadway St 77012 — 713-928-7401
Richard Barajas, prin. — Fax 928-7474
Ortiz MS — 1,000/6-8
6767 Telephone Rd 77061 — 713-845-5650
Yolanda Alleman, prin. — Fax 845-5646
Performing & Visual Arts HS — 700/9-12
4001 Stanford St 77006 — 713-942-1960
Dr. Herbert Karpicke, prin. — Fax 942-1968
Pershing MS — 1,700/6-8
7000 Braes Blvd 77025 — 713-295-5240
Bryce Amos, prin. — Fax 295-5252
Reagan HS — 1,700/9-12
413 E 13th St 77008 — 713-861-5694
Connie Berger, prin. — Fax 867-0876
Revere MS — 1,200/6-8
10502 Briar Forest Dr 77042 — 713-917-3500
Kenneth Estrella, prin. — Fax 917-3505
Ryan MS — 600/6-8
2610 Elgin St 77004 — 713-942-1932
Edward Thompson, prin. — Fax 942-1943
Scarborough HS — 900/9-12
4141 Costa Rica Rd 77092 — 713-613-2200
Moses Diaz, prin. — Fax 613-2205
Sharpstown HS — 1,700/9-12
7504 Bissonnet St 77074 — 713-771-7215
David Kendler, prin. — Fax 773-6103
Sharpstown MS — 1,300/6-8
8330 Triola Ln 77036 — 713-778-3440
Jeffrey Amerson, prin. — Fax 778-3444
Sterling HS — 1,100/9-12
11625 Martindale Rd 77048 — 713-991-0510
Marcellars Mason, prin. — Fax 991-8111
Stevenson MS — 1,200/6-8
9595 Winkler Dr 77017 — 713-943-5700
Jane Crump, prin. — Fax 943-5711
Thomas MS — 900/6-8
5655 Selinsky Rd 77048 — 713-732-3500
Bill Sorrells, prin. — Fax 732-3509
Waltrip HS — 1,800/9-12
1900 W 34th St 77018 — 713-688-1361
Steven Siebenalar, prin. — Fax 957-7743
Washington HS — 1,200/9-12
119 E 39th St 77018 — 713-692-5947
Franklin Wesley, prin. — Fax 696-6657
Welch MS — 1,300/6-8
11544 S Gessner Dr 77071 — 713-778-3300
Ruby J. Andrews, prin. — Fax 995-6067
West Briar MS — 1,400/6-8
13733 Brimhurst Dr 77077 — 281-368-2140
Geoffrey Ohl, prin. — Fax 368-2194
Westbury HS — 2,200/9-12
11911 Chimney Rock Rd 77035 — 713-723-6015
Eric Coleman, prin. — Fax 726-2165
Westside HS — 2,800/9-12
14201 Briar Forest Dr 77077 — 281-920-8000
Paul Castro, prin. — Fax 920-8059
Wheatley HS — 800/9-12
4801 Providence St 77020 — 713-671-3900
Wiley Johnson, prin. — Fax 671-3951
Worthing HS — 1,200/9-12
9215 Scott St 77051 — 713-733-3433
Robert Dean, prin. — Fax 731-5537
Yates HS — 1,300/9-12
3703 Sampson St 77004 — 713-748-5400
George August, prin. — Fax 746-8206
Other Schools – See Bellaire

Katy ISD
Supt. — See Katy
Mayde Creek HS — 2,900/9-12
19202 Groeschke Rd 77084 — 281-237-3000
O.D. Tompkins, prin. — Fax 644-1715
Mayde Creek JHS — 1,300/6-8
2700 Greenhouse Rd 77084 — 281-237-3900
Richard Hull, prin. — Fax 644-1650

Klein ISD
Supt. — See Klein
Klein Forest HS — 3,400/9-12
11400 Misty Valley Dr 77066 — 832-484-4500
Bill Lakin, prin. — Fax 484-7801
Klein IS — 1,200/6-8
4710 W Mount Houston Rd 77088 — 832-249-4900
Anthony Indelicato, prin. — Fax 249-4046
Wunderlich IS — 1,400/6-8
11800 Misty Valley Dr 77066 — 832-249-5200
Patricia Crittendon, prin. — Fax 249-4050

North Forest ISD — 8,500/PK-12
PO Box 23278 77228 — 713-633-1600
James Simpson Ph.D., supt. — Fax 491-1097
www.northforestschools.org/
Elmore MS — 200/6-8
8200 Tate St 77028 — 713-672-7466
Gwenette Ferguson, prin. — Fax 671-3565
Forest Brook HS — 1,000/9-12
7525 Tidwell Rd 77016 — 713-631-7720
Ronnie Brown, prin. — Fax 635-6309

Kirby MS — 700/6-8
9706 Mesa Dr 77078 — 713-633-0670
Rubye Gilbert, prin. — Fax 636-7895
Oak Village MS — 600/6-8
6602 Winfield Rd 77050 — 281-449-6561
Charles Russell, prin. — Fax 671-7650
Smiley Career & Technology S — Vo/Tech
10726 Mesa Dr 77078 — 713-636-6753
Lance Harjo, prin. — Fax 636-8119
Smiley HS — 1,400/9-12
10725 Mesa Dr 77078 — 713-636-4300
Erroll Garrett, prin. — Fax 636-8116

Pasadena ISD
Supt. — See Pasadena
Beverly Hills IS — 1,200/6-8
11111 Beamer Rd 77089 — 713-740-0420
Alyta Harrell, prin. — Fax 740-4051
Dobie HS — 2,800/9-12
10220 Blackhawk Blvd 77089 — 713-740-0370
Steve Jamail, prin. — Fax 929-3816
Thompson IS — 1,100/6-8
11309 Sagedowne Ln 77089 — 713-740-0510
Dr. Gregory Jones, prin. — Fax 740-4083

Sheldon ISD — 4,500/PK-12
11411 C E King Pkwy 77044 — 281-727-2000
Dr. G. Steve Mills, supt. — Fax 727-2085
www.sheldonisd.com/
King HS — 1,300/9-12
8540 C E King Pkwy 77044 — 281-727-3500
Cindy Worley, prin. — Fax 459-7346
King MS — 800/7-8
8530 C E King Pkwy 77044 — 281-727-4300
Donna Ullrich, prin. — Fax 459-7452

Spring Branch ISD — 31,700/PK-12
955 Campbell Rd 77024 — 713-464-1511
Duncan Klussmann Ed.D., supt. — Fax 365-4071
www.springbranchisd.com/
Harold Guthrie Career Center — Vo/Tech
10660 Hammerly Blvd 77043 — 713-365-4610
Joe Kolenda, prin. — Fax 365-4621
Landrum MS — 700/6-8
2200 Ridgecrest Dr 77055 — 713-365-4020
Jennifer Parker, prin. — Fax 365-4040
Memorial HS — 2,200/9-12
935 Echo Ln 77024 — 713-365-5110
Stephen Shorter, prin. — Fax 365-5138
Memorial MS — 1,000/6-8
12550 Vindon Dr 77024 — 713-365-5400
Bob Price, prin. — Fax 365-5411
Northbrook HS — 2,000/9-12
1 Raider Cir 77080 — 713-365-4430
Randolph Adami, prin. — Fax 365-4416
Northbrook MS — 700/6-8
3030 Rosefield Dr 77080 — 713-329-6510
Laura Schuhmann, prin. — Fax 329-6523
Spring Branch MS — 1,000/6-8
1000 Piney Point Rd 77024 — 713-365-5500
Robert Salek, prin. — Fax 365-5515
Spring Forest MS — 900/6-8
14240 Memorial Dr 77079 — 281-560-7500
Cathryn White, prin. — Fax 560-7509
Spring Oaks MS — 800/6-8
2150 Shadowdale Dr 77043 — 713-365-4515
David Sablatura, prin. — Fax 365-4522
Spring Woods HS — 2,100/9-12
2045 Gessner Dr 77080 — 713-365-4475
Wayne Schaper, prin. — Fax 365-4474
Spring Woods MS — 800/6-8
9810 Neuens Rd 77080 — 713-365-4110
Cynthia Chai, prin. — Fax 365-4115
Stratford HS — 1,900/9-12
14555 Fern Dr 77079 — 281-560-7550
Ann Kucera, prin. — Fax 560-7578
Westchester Academy International Study — 700/6-12
901 Yorkchester Dr 77079 — 713-365-5678
Pamela Butler, dir. — Fax 365-5686

Spring ISD — 28,300/PK-12
16717 Ella Blvd 77090 — 281-586-1100
Ralph Draper, supt. — Fax 586-1134
www.springisd.org
Bammel MS — 1,500/6-8
16711 Ella Blvd 77090 — 281-586-2600
Patricia Crittendon, prin. — Fax 586-2621
Claughton MS — 1,400/6-8
3000 Spears Rd 77067 — 281-355-3101
Delic Loyde, prin. — Fax 355-3104
DeKaney HS — 9-12
22351 Imperial Valley Dr 77073 — 832-592-1600
Phil Eaton, prin.
Wells MS — 1,000/6-8
4033 Gladeridge Dr 77068 — 281-586-2630
Cornelius Phelps, prin. — Fax 586-2637
Westfield HS — 2,800/10-12
16713 Ella Blvd 77090 — 281-586-1300
Julie Guillory, prin. — Fax 587-3998
Westfield Ninth Grade Center — 1,500/9-9
16713 Ella Blvd 77090 — 832-446-1401
Eric Wiestruck, prin. — Fax 446-1402
Other Schools – See Spring

Academy of Hair Design — Post-Sec.
744 FM 1960 Rd W Ste G 77090 — 281-893-0980
Alexander-Smith Academy — 100/9-12
10255 Richmond Ave 77042 — 713-266-0920
J. David Arnold, prin. — Fax 266-8857
Alfred G. Glassell School of Art — Post-Sec.
PO Box 6826 77265 — 713-639-7500
American College of Acupuncture — Post-Sec.
9100 Park West Dr 77063 — 713-780-9777
Art Institute of Houston — Post-Sec.
1900 Yorktown St 77056 — 713-623-2040
Art Institute of Houston - Culinary — Post-Sec.
1900 Yorktown St 77056 — 800-275-4244
Astrodome Dental Career Center — Post-Sec.
2646 S Loop W Ste 415 77054 — 713-664-5300
Awty International S — 1,100/PK-12
7455 Awty School Ln 77055 — 713-686-4850
Dr. David Watson, hdmstr. — Fax 686-4956
Banff S — 200/PK-12
13726 Cutten Rd 77069 — 281-444-9326
Deborah Wasser, prin. — Fax 444-3632
Baylor College of Medicine — Post-Sec.
1 Baylor Plz 77030 — 713-798-4951
Behold! Beauty Academy — Post-Sec.
9937 Homestead Rd 77016 — 713-635-5252
Ben Taub Hospital — Post-Sec.
2525 Holly Hall St 77054 — 713-746-6400

Beren Academy — 400/PK-12
11333 Cliffwood Dr 77035 — 713-723-7170
Virginia McCracken, hdmstr. — Fax 723-8343
Bradford School of Business — Post-Sec.
4669 Southwest Fwy Ste 300 77027 — 713-629-1500
Briarwood S — 300/K-12
12207 Whittington Dr 77077 — 281-493-1070
Carole Wills, hdmstr. — Fax 493-1343
Carethers Adventist S — 100/PK-10
5878 Bellfort St 77033 — 713-733-1351
Fax 738-7283
Center for Advanced Legal Studies — Post-Sec.
3910 Kirby Dr Ste 200 77098 — 713-529-2778
Central Christian Academy — 100/K-12
2217 Bingle Rd 77055 — 713-468-3248
Scott Jacobs, admin. — Fax 468-7322
Clear Lake Christian S — 300/K-12
14325 Crescent Landing Dr 77062 — 281-488-4883
Bruce Guillot, supt. — Fax 480-3287
College of Biblical Studies — Post-Sec.
7000 Regency Square # 110 77036 — 713-785-5995
Commonwealth Institute / Funeral Service — Post-Sec.
415 Barren Springs Dr 77090 — 281-873-0262
Court Reporting Institute of Houston — Post-Sec.
13101 Northwest Fwy Ste 100 77040 — 713-996-8300
Culinary Institute — Post-Sec.
7070 Allensby St 77022 — 713-692-0077
Cypress Christian S — 600/K-12
11123 Cypress N Houston Rd 77065 — 281-469-8829
Dr. Glenn Holzman, admin. — Fax 469-6040
DeVry University — Post-Sec.
2000 West Loop S Ste 150 77027 — 713-850-0888
DeVry University — Post-Sec.
11125 Equity Dr 77041 — 713-973-3200
Duchesne Academy HS — 200/9-12
10202 Memorial Dr 77024 — 713-468-8211
Dr. Rae Flory, prin. — Fax 465-9809
Duchesne Academy MS — 200/5-8
10202 Memorial Dr 77024 — 713-468-8211
Sr. Ann Caire, prin. — Fax 465-9809
Emery/Weiner S — 400/6-12
9825 Stella Link Rd 77025 — 832-204-5900
Stuart Dow, hdmstr. — Fax 204-5910
Everest Institute — Post-Sec.
255 Northpoint Dr # 100 77060 — 281-447-7037
Everest Institute — Post-Sec.
9700 Bissonnet St Ste 1400 77036 — 713-772-4200
Everest Institute — Post-Sec.
7151 Office City Dr Ste 100 77087 — 713-645-7404
Family Christian Academy — 300/K-12
14718 Woodford Dr 77015 — 713-455-4483
Robert Anderson, prin. — Fax 450-3730
Franklin Beauty School #2 — Post-Sec.
4965 Martin Luther King 77021 — 713-645-9060
Gulf Coast Regional Blood Center — Post-Sec.
1400 La Concha Ln 77054 — 713-790-1200
Houston Baptist University — Post-Sec.
7502 Fondren Rd 77074 — 281-649-3000
Houston Christian HS — 400/9-12
2700 W Sam Houston Pkwy N 77043 — 713-580-6000
Dr. Steve Livingston, hdmstr. — Fax 580-6001
Houston Community College — Post-Sec.
PO Box 667517 77266 — 713-718-5000
Houston Graduate School of Theology — Post-Sec.
2501 Central Pkwy Ste A19 77092 — 713-942-9505
Houston Learning Academy - Galleria — 50/9-12
6108 S Rice Ave 77081 — 713-974-6658
Erik Srnka, dir. — Fax 662-2343
Houston Learning Academy - North — 50/9-12
13029 Champions Dr 77069 — 281-537-6433
Lesley bower, prin. — Fax 537-2361
Houstons Training and Education Center — Post-Sec.
7457 Harwin Dr Ste 190 77036 — 713-783-2221
Houston Training School — Post-Sec.
709 Shotwell St 77020 — 713-675-4300
Houston Training School — Post-Sec.
6630 Gulf Fwy 77087
ICC Technical Institute — Post-Sec.
3333 Fannin St Ste 203 77004 — 713-522-7799
Incarnate Word Academy — 200/9-12
609 Crawford St 77002 — 713-227-3637
Mary Getschow, prin. — Fax 227-1014
Institute of Cosmetology — Post-Sec.
7011 Harwin Dr Ste 100 77036 — 713-783-9988
Interactive Learning Systems — Post-Sec.
6200 Hillcroft St Ste 200 77081 — 713-771-5336
Interactive Learning Systems — Post-Sec.
256 N Sam Houston Pkwy E 77060 — 281-931-7717
ITT Technical Institute — Post-Sec.
2950 S Gessner Rd Ste 100 77063 — 713-952-2294
ITT Technical Institute — Post-Sec.
15621 Blue Ash Dr Ste 160 77090 — 281-873-0512
Jay's Technical Institute — Post-Sec.
9000 W Bellfort St Ste 110 77031 — 713-772-2410
Kinkaid S — 1,300/PK-12
201 Kinkaid School Dr 77024 — 713-782-1640
Donald North, hdmstr. — Fax 782-3543
Lutheran HS North — 300/9-12
1130 W 34th St 77018 — 713-880-3131
Bruce Schaller, prin. — Fax 880-5447
Lutheran South Academy — 600/K-12
12555 Ryewater Dr 77089 — 281-464-8299
Dr. Wayne Kramer, hdmstr. — Fax 464-6119
MedVance Institute — Post-Sec.
6220 W Park #180 77057 — 713-266-6594
Memorial Hall S — 100/4-12
3721 Dacoma St 77092 — 713-688-5566
Rev. George Aurich, hdmstr. — Fax 956-9751
Memorial Hospital System — Post-Sec.
7737 Southwest Fwy 77074 — 713-776-5100
Methodist Hospital — Post-Sec.
6565 Fannin St 77030 — 713-441-2599
Mt. Carmel HS — 200/9-12
6700 Mount Carmel St 77087 — 713-649-2745
Lucille Maggi, prin. — Fax 649-6851
MTI College of Business & Technology — Post-Sec.
7333 Harwin Dr # 212 77036 — 713-979-1800
MTI College of Business & Technology — Post-Sec.
7277 Regency Square Blvd 77036 — 713-974-7181
New Heights Christian Academy — 100/PK-12
1700 W 43rd St 77018 — 713-861-9101
Dr. Richard Walters, prin. — Fax 426-4525
North Harris Montgomery Comm. College — Post-Sec.
250 N Sam Houston Pkwy E 77060 — 281-260-3500
Northland Christian S — 700/PK-12
4363 Sylvanfield Dr 77014 — 281-440-1060
Cliff Kraner, prin. — Fax 440-7572
Northwest Educational Center — Post-Sec.
2910 Antoine Dr Ste B100 77092 — 713-680-2929
Oaks Adventist Christian S — 100/PK-12
11903C Tanner Rd 77041 — 713-896-0071
Catherine Pickard, prin. — Fax 896-0721

Page Parkes Center of Modeling & Acting Post-Sec.
1535 West Loop S Ste 100 77027 713-807-8200
Prairie View A&M University Post-Sec.
6436 Fannin St 77030 713-797-7000
Remington College Post-Sec.
3110 Hayes Rd 77082 281-899-1240
Rice University Post-Sec.
6100 Main St 77005 713-348-0001
St. Agnes Academy 800/9-12
9000 Bellaire Blvd 77036 713-219-5400
Sr. Jane Meyer, prin. Fax 219-5499
St. John's S 1,200/K-12
2401 Claremont Ln 77019 713-850-0222
John Allman, hdmstr. Fax 850-4089
St. Peter the Apostle MS 100/6-8
6220 La Salette St 77021 713-747-9484
Sr. Maria Goretti-Babatunde, prin. Fax 842-7055
St. Pius X HS 600/9-12
811 W Donovan St 77091 713-692-3581
Sr. Donna Pollard, prin. Fax 692-5725
St. Stephen's Episcopal S Houston 200/PK-12
1815 Sul Ross St 77098 713-821-9100
Betty Sierra, hdmstr. Fax 521-0785
St. Thomas' Episcopal S 600/K-12
4900 Jackwood St 77096 713-666-3111
Michael F. Cusack, hdmstr. Fax 668-3887
St. Thomas HS 600/9-12
4500 Memorial Dr 77007 713-864-6348
Rev. John Huber, prin. Fax 864-5750
Sanford-Brown Institute Houston Post-Sec.
10500 Forum Place Dr 77036 713-779-1110
San Jacinto College Post-Sec.
5800 Uvalde Rd 77049 281-458-4050
San Jacinto College Post-Sec.
13735 Beamer Rd 77089 281-484-1900
School of Automotive Machinists Post-Sec.
1911 Antoine Dr 77055 713-683-3817
School of the Woods 400/PK-12
1321 Wirt Rd 77055 713-686-8811
Sherry Herron, hdmstr. Fax 686-1936
Sebring Career School Post-Sec.
7060 Bissonnet St 77074 713-772-0702
Second Baptist S 1,100/PK-12
6410 Woodway Dr 77057 713-365-2310
Brett Jacobsen, supt. Fax 365-2355
Seton Catholic JHS 200/6-8
801 Roselane St 77037 281-447-2132
Patrick Clark, prin. Fax 447-1825
Shady Acres Christian S 50/1-12
7330 Vogel Rd 77088 281-999-2040
Marsha Farley, prin. Fax 999-2040
South Texas College of Law Post-Sec.
1303 San Jacinto St 77002 713-646-1510
Southwest Christian Academy 200/PK-12
7400 Eldridge Pkwy 77083 281-561-7400
Paula Thurmond, prin. Fax 240-9606
Strake Jesuit College Prep S 800/9-12
8900 Bellaire Blvd 77036 713-774-7651
Richard Nevle, prin. Fax 774-6427
Sweetwater Christian S 200/K-12
350 Century Plaza Dr 77073 281-209-9130
Reginald Nelson, admin. Fax 443-3766
Sylvia's International School of Beauty Post-Sec.
434 W Parker Rd 77091 713-697-1200
Texas Barber Colleges & Hairstyling Sch Post-Sec.
9275 Richmond Ave Ste 180 77063 713-953-0262
Texas Christian S 200/PK-12
17810 Kieth Harrow Blvd 77084 281-550-6060
Herc Palmquist, admin. Fax 550-2400
Texas Heart Institute Post-Sec.
PO Box 20345 77225 713-791-4026
Texas School of Business Post-Sec.
711 E Airtex Dr 77073 281-443-8900
Texas School of Business Southwest Post-Sec.
6363 Richmond Ave Ste 300 77057 713-975-7527
Texas Southern University Post-Sec.
3100 Cleburne St 77004 713-313-7011
Texas Woman's University Post-Sec.
6700 Fannin St 77030 713-794-2376
The Ocean Corporation Post-Sec.
10840 Rockley Rd 77099 281-530-0202
Trend Barber College Post-Sec.
8250 W Bellfort St 77071 713-721-0000
Ultrasound Diagnostic School Post-Sec.
10500 Forum Place Dr #200 77036 713-664-9632
Universal Technical Institute Post-Sec.
721 Lockhaven Dr 77073 281-443-6262
University of Houston Post-Sec.
4800 Calhoun Rd 77204 713-743-1000
University of Houston-Clear Lake Post-Sec.
2700 Bay Area Blvd 77058 281-283-7600
University of Houston-Downtown Post-Sec.
1 Main St 77002 713-221-8000
University of St. Thomas Post-Sec.
3800 Montrose Blvd 77006 713-522-7911
University of Texas Anderson Cancer Ctr. Post-Sec.
1515 Holcombe Blvd 77030 713-792-6000
University of TX Health Science Center Post-Sec.
PO Box 20036 77225 713-500-4472
University of Texas-Houston Post-Sec.
6901 Bertner Ave 77030 713-500-2100
Veterans Affairs Medical Center Post-Sec.
2002 Holcombe Blvd 77030 713-794-7100
Westbury Christian S 600/PK-12
10420 Hillcroft St 77096 713-723-8377
Robert McCloy, prin. Fax 551-8117
Westwood Aviation Institute Post-Sec.
8880 Telephone Rd 77061 800-776-7423
Westwood College - Houston South Post-Sec.
7322 Southwest Fwy Ste 1900 77074 713-777-4433

Howe, Grayson, Pop. 2,709
Howe ISD 1,000/PK-12
105 W Tutt St 75459 903-532-5518
Randy Hancock, supt. Fax 532-9378
www.howeisd.net
Howe HS 300/9-12
200 Ponderosa Rd 75459 903-532-5222
Blake Stiles, prin. Fax 532-5563
Howe MS 300/5-8
300 Beatrice St 75459 903-532-6013
Clay Wilson, prin. Fax 537-0113

Hubbard, Hill, Pop. 1,680
Hubbard ISD 500/PK-12
PO Box 218 76648 254-576-2564
Walter Padgett, supt. Fax 576-5019
www.hubbardisd.com/
Hubbard HS 100/9-12
PO Box 218 76648 254-576-2549
B.J. Paris, prin. Fax 576-2477
Hubbard MS 100/6-8
PO Box 218 76648 254-576-2758
B.J. Paris, prin. Fax 576-5017

Huffman, Harris
Huffman ISD 2,900/PK-12
24302 FM 2100 Rd 77336 281-324-1871
Douglas Killian Ph.D., supt. Fax 324-3293
www.huffmanisd.net
Hargrave HS 900/9-12
25400 Willy Ln 77336 281-324-1845
Robert Schnuriger, prin. Fax 324-3368
Huffman MS 700/6-8
3407 Huffman Eastgate Rd 77336 281-324-2598
Shirley Hitt, prin. Fax 324-2710

Hughes Springs, Cass, Pop. 1,876
Hughes Springs ISD 1,000/PK-12
PO Box 398 75656 903-639-3800
Rick Ogden, supt. Fax 639-2624
www.hsisd.net
Hughes Springs HS 300/9-12
PO Box 399 75656 903-639-3841
Terry Giddens, prin. Fax 639-3928
Hughes Springs JHS 200/6-8
PO Box 1389 75656 903-639-3812
Rex Stone, prin. Fax 639-3929

Humble, Harris, Pop. 14,803
Aldine ISD
Supt. — See Houston
Teague MS 1,200/7-8
21700 Rayford Rd 77338 281-233-4310
Michael Gallien, prin. Fax 233-4318

Humble ISD 27,800/PK-12
PO Box 2000 77347 281-641-1000
Dr. Guy M. Sconzo, supt. Fax 641-1050
www.humble.k12.tx.us
Atascocita HS 9-12
13300 Will Clayton Pkwy 77346 281-641-7500
Lawrence Kohn, prin.
Atascocita MS 1,400/6-8
18810 W Lake Houston Pkwy 77346 281-641-4600
Ron Westerfeld, prin. Fax 641-4617
Career & Technology Education Center Vo/Tech
9155 Will Clayton Pkwy 77338 281-641-7950
Bodie Wagener, prin. Fax 641-7967
Humble 9th Grade Campus 1,100/9-9
1131 Wilson Rd 77338 281-641-6000
Penne Leifer, prin. Fax 641-6017
Humble MS 1,200/6-8
11207 Will Clayton Pkwy 77346 281-641-4000
Larry Johnson, prin. Fax 641-4017
Humble SHS 3,100/10-12
1700 Wilson Rd 77338 281-641-6300
Dr. Raul Font, prin. Fax 641-6517
Timberwood MS 1,100/6-8
18450 Timber Forest Dr 77346 281-641-3800
Carol Atwood, prin. Fax 641-3817
Other Schools – See Kingwood

Christian Life Center Academy 100/PK-12
600 Charles St 77338 281-319-0077
Chelliah Soundar, admin. Fax 446-5501
Houston Learning Academy - Humble 50/9-12
5334 FM 1960 Rd E 77346 281-852-2022
Lesley Bower, prin. Fax 852-2120
Humble Christian S 300/PK-12
16202 Old Humble Rd 77396 281-441-1313
Ted Howell, admin. Fax 441-1329

Hunt, Kerr
Hunt ISD 200/PK-12
PO Box 259 78024 830-238-4893
David Kelm, supt. Fax 238-4691
www.huntisd.com
Hunt S 200/PK-12
PO Box 259 78024 830-238-4893
David Kelm, prin. Fax 238-4691

Huntington, Angelina, Pop. 2,073
Huntington ISD 1,700/PK-12
PO Box 328 75949 936-876-4287
Dr. Eric Wright, supt. Fax 876-3212
www.huntingtonisd.com/
Huntington HS 400/9-12
PO Box 328 75949 936-876-4150
Pete Jackson, prin. Fax 876-3057
Huntington MS 400/6-8
PO Box 328 75949 936-876-4722
Glenn Frank, prin. Fax 876-4009

Huntsville, Walker, Pop. 36,699
Huntsville ISD 6,700/PK-12
441 FM 2821 Rd E 77320 936-295-3421
Dr. Richard Montgomery, supt. Fax 291-3444
www.huntsville-isd.org
Huntsville HS 1,800/9-12
441 FM 2821 Rd E 77320 936-293-2626
Mike Lamb, prin. Fax 293-2670
Mance Park JHS 1,000/7-8
441 FM 2821 Rd E 77320 936-293-2755
Beth Burt, prin. Fax 293-2759

Alpha Omega Academy 300/K-12
PO Box 8419 77340 936-438-8833
Paul Davidhizar, hdmstr. Fax 438-8844
Sam Houston State University Post-Sec.
PO Box 2026 77341 936-294-1111

Hurst, Tarrant, Pop. 37,967
Hurst-Euless-Bedford ISD
Supt. — See Bedford
Bell SHS 1,900/10-12
1601 Brown Trl 76054 817-282-2551
Jim Bannister, prin. Fax 285-3200
Hurst JHS 1,000/7-9
500 Harmon Rd 76053 817-285-3220
Sherilynn Cotten, prin. Fax 285-3225

Ogle School of Hair Design Post-Sec.
720 Arcadia St Apt B 76053 817-284-9231
Tarrant County Junior College Post-Sec.
828 W Harwood Rd 76054 817-515-6100

Hutto, Williamson, Pop. 7,401
Hutto ISD 1,700/PK-12
PO Box 430 78634 512-759-3771
Dr. David Borrer, supt. Fax 759-4796
www.hutto.txed.net
Hutto HS 600/9-12
PO Box 430 78634 512-759-4700
Manuel Lunoff, prin. Fax 759-4757
Hutto MS 600/6-8
PO Box 430 78634 512-759-4541
Don Kuempel, prin. Fax 759-4753

Idalou, Lubbock, Pop. 2,046
Idalou ISD 800/PK-12
PO Box 1338 79329 806-892-2501
Jim Waller, supt. Fax 892-3204
www.idalouisd.net/
Idalou HS 200/9-12
PO Box 1558 79329 806-892-2123
Steve Bigham, prin. Fax 892-2690
Idalou MS 300/5-8
PO Box 1353 79329 806-892-2133
Steve Gunter, prin. Fax 892-2388

Imperial, Pecos
Buena Vista ISD 100/PK-12
PO Box 310 79743 432-536-2225
David Dillard, supt. Fax 536-2469
www.bvisd.esc18.net/
Buena Vista S 100/PK-12
PO Box 310 79743 432-536-2225
Letha Dulaney, prin. Fax 536-2469

Ingleside, San Patricio, Pop. 9,531
Ingleside ISD 2,300/PK-12
PO Box 1320 78362 361-776-7631
Troy Mircovich, supt. Fax 776-0267
www.inglesideisd.org
Ingleside HS 600/9-12
2807 Mustang Dr 78362 361-776-2712
Steve Snyder, prin. Fax 776-5200
Taylor JHS 300/7-8
2739 Mustang Dr 78362 361-776-2232
James Bonorden, prin. Fax 776-2192

Ingram, Kerr, Pop. 1,838
Ingram ISD 1,500/PK-12
510 College St 78025 830-367-5517
Bruce Faust, supt. Fax 367-5631
www.ingramisd.net
Ingram MS 400/6-8
510 College St 78025 830-367-4012
Jill Dworsky, prin. Fax 367-7335
Ingram-Tom Moore HS 500/9-12
510 College St 78025 830-367-4111
T.W. Carpenter, prin. Fax 367-7332

Iola, Grimes
Iola ISD 500/PK-12
PO Box 159 77861 936-394-2361
Douglas Devine, supt. Fax 394-2132
www.iolaisd.net
Iola JSHS 200/7-12
PO Box 159 77861 936-394-2361
Jeff Dyer, prin. Fax 394-4700

Iowa Park, Wichita, Pop. 6,175
Iowa Park Consolidated ISD 1,800/PK-12
PO Box 898 76367 940-592-4193
Jerry Baird, supt. Fax 592-2136
www.ipcisd.net/
George MS 400/6-8
412 E Cash St 76367 940-592-2196
Steven Moody, prin. Fax 592-2801
Iowa Park HS 600/9-12
1513 W Highway St 76367 940-592-2144
James Skeeler, prin. Fax 592-2583

Ira, Scurry
Ira ISD 200/K-12
PO Box 240 79527 325-573-2629
Dr. Larry Devitt, supt. Fax 573-5825
www.ira.esc14.net
Ira S 200/K-12
PO Box 240 79527 325-573-2628
Dr. Larry Devitt, prin. Fax 573-5825

Iraan, Pecos, Pop. 1,172
Iraan-Sheffield ISD 400/PK-12
PO Box 486 79744 432-639-2512
Kevin Allen, supt. Fax 639-2501
isisd.esc18.net
Iraan HS 100/9-12
PO Box 486 79744 432-639-2722
Benny Hernandez, prin. Fax 639-2501
Iraan JHS 100/6-8
PO Box 486 79744 432-639-2867
Lisa Slaughter, prin. Fax 639-2501

Iredell, Bosque, Pop. 380
Iredell ISD 100/PK-12
PO Box 39 76649 254-364-2411
Brian Gray, supt. Fax 364-2206
www.iredell-isd.com
Iredell S 100/PK-12
PO Box 39 76649 254-364-2411
David Mims, prin. Fax 364-2206

Irving, Dallas, Pop. 193,649
Carrollton-Farmers Branch ISD
Supt. — See Carrollton
Bush MS 600/6-8
515 Cowboys Pkwy 75063 972-968-3700
Lynda Opitz, prin. Fax 968-3710
Ranchview HS 500/9-12
8401 Valley Ranch Pkwy E 75063 972-968-5000
David Hicks, prin. Fax 968-5010

Irving ISD 31,600/PK-12
PO Box 152637 75015 972-215-5000
Jack Singley, supt. Fax 215-5201
www.irvingisd.net
Academy of Irving ISD 1,500/9-12
4601 N MacArthur Blvd 75038 972-258-5300
Robbin Wall, prin. Fax 258-5301
Austin MS 900/6-8
825 E Union Bower Rd 75061 972-721-3100
David Saenz, prin. Fax 721-3105
Bowie MS 1,000/6-8
600 E 6th St 75060 972-721-3000
Joe Moreno, prin. Fax 721-3044
Crockett MS 1,000/6-8
2431 Hancock St 75061 972-313-4700
John Rose, prin. Fax 313-4770
de Zavala MS 900/6-8
707 W Pioneer Dr 75061 972-273-8900
Sebastian Bozas, prin. Fax 273-8924

Houston MS 1,000/6-8
3033 Country Club Dr W 75038 972-261-2300
Rick Nolly, prin. Fax 261-2399
Irving HS 2,300/9-12
900 N O Connor Rd 75061 972-273-8300
Linda Kimm, prin. Fax 273-8319
Lamar MS 1,100/6-8
219 Crandall Rd 75060 972-313-4400
Rocci Malone, prin. Fax 313-4499
MacArthur HS 2,200/9-12
3700 N Macarthur Blvd 75062 972-261-2100
Cynthia Bean, prin. Fax 261-2299
Nimitz HS 2,000/9-12
100 W Oakdale Rd 75060 972-273-8600
Samuel Bean, prin. Fax 273-8610
Ratteree Career Development Center Vo/Tech
2121 S MacArthur Blvd 75060 972-313-4821
Lea Bailey, prin. Fax 313-4823
Travis MS 1,000/6-8
1600 Finley Rd 75062 972-261-2400
Terry Cooper, prin. Fax 261-2450

Cistercian Preparatory S 300/5-12
PO Box 140699 75014 469-499-5400
Fr. Peter Verhalen, hdmstr. Fax 499-5440
DeVry University Post-Sec.
4800 Regent Blvd 75063 972-929-6777
Highlands S 500/PK-12
1451 E Northgate Dr 75062 972-554-1980
Michelle Reiff, hdmstr. Fax 721-1691
High-Tech Institute Post-Sec.
4250 N Belt Line Rd 75038 972-871-2824
International Beauty College #4 Post-Sec.
2716 W Irving Blvd 75061 972-513-1176
North Lake College Post-Sec.
5001 N Macarthur Blvd 75038 972-273-3000
University of Dallas Post-Sec.
1845 E Northgate Dr 75062 972-721-5000

Italy, Ellis, Pop. 2,091
Italy ISD 700/PK-12
300 College 76651 972-483-1815
Dr. Gail Haterius, supt. Fax 483-6152
www.italyisd.org/
Italy JSHS 300/7-12
300 College 76651 972-483-7411
Don Clingenpeel, prin. Fax 483-1500

Itasca, Hill, Pop. 1,618
Itasca ISD 600/PK-12
123 N College St 76055 254-687-2922
Dr. E. Ray Freeman, supt. Fax 687-2637
www.itasca.k12.tx.us
Itasca HS 200/9-12
123 N College St 76055 254-687-2922
Glenn Pittman, prin. Fax 687-2637
Itasca MS 100/5-8
123 N College St 76055 254-687-2922
Glenn Pittman, prin. Fax 687-2637

Ivanhoe, Fannin
Sam Rayburn ISD 400/PK-12
9363 E FM 273 75447 903-664-2255
Steve Arthur, supt. Fax 664-2406
samrayburn.ednet10.net/
Rayburn JSHS 200/7-12
9363 E FM 273 75447 903-664-2165
Steve Arthur, prin. Fax 664-2406

Jacksboro, Jack, Pop. 4,610
Jacksboro ISD 1,000/PK-12
812 W Belknap St 76458 940-567-7203
Dennis Bennett, supt. Fax 567-2214
www.jacksboroisd.net/
Jacksboro HS 300/9-12
812 W Belknap St 76458 940-567-7204
Brad Burnett, prin. Fax 567-6028
Lowrance MS 200/6-8
117 N 4th St 76458 940-567-7205
Don O'Steen, prin. Fax 567-2681

Jacksonville, Cherokee, Pop. 14,395
Jacksonville ISD 4,900/PK-12
PO Box 631 75766 903-586-6511
Stuart Bird, supt. Fax 586-3133
www.jacksonvilleisd.org
Jacksonville HS 1,200/9-12
PO Box 631 75766 903-586-3661
Duane Barber, prin. Fax 586-8229
Jacksonville MS 700/7-8
PO Box 631 75766 903-586-3686
Lisa Hancock, prin. Fax 586-8071

Baptist Missionary Theological Seminary Post-Sec.
1530 E Pine St 75766 903-586-2501
Jacksonville College Post-Sec.
105 B J Albritton Dr 75766 903-586-2518
Lon Morris College Post-Sec.
800 College Ave 75766 903-589-4000

Jarrell, Williamson, Pop. 1,406
Jarrell ISD 700/PK-12
PO Box 9 76537 512-746-2124
Dr. Jamie Mattison, supt. Fax 746-2518
www.esc13.net/jarrell
Jarrell HS 200/9-12
PO Box 9 76537 512-746-4180
Freddie McFarland, prin. Fax 746-4280
Jarrell MS 100/6-8
PO Box 9 76537 512-746-4180
Julie Raby, prin. Fax 746-4280

Jasper, Jasper, Pop. 7,531
Jasper ISD 3,100/PK-12
128 Park Ln 75951 409-384-2401
Eddie Dunn Ed.D., supt. Fax 382-1084
www.jasperisd.net
Jasper HS 900/9-12
400 Bulldog Ave 75951 409-384-3242
Dr. Dean Miller, prin. Fax 382-1310
Jasper JHS 500/7-8
211 2nd St 75951 409-384-3585
Mervin Cleveland, prin. Fax 382-1160

Jayton, Kent, Pop. 472
Jayton-Girard ISD 100/PK-12
PO Box 168 79528 806-237-2991
Tim Seymore, supt. Fax 237-2670
www.jaytonjaybirds.com
Jayton S 100/PK-12
PO Box 168 79528 806-237-2991
Allen Gillespie, prin. Fax 237-2670

Jefferson, Marion, Pop. 1,992
Jefferson ISD 1,300/PK-12
1600 Martin Luther King Dr 75657 903-665-2461
Richard Cook, supt. Fax 665-7367
jeffersonisd.org/
Jefferson HS 400/9-12
1 Bulldog Dr 75657 903-665-2461
Don Prather, prin. Fax 665-2146
Jefferson JHS 300/5-8
804 N Alley St 75657 903-665-2461
John McCoy, prin. Fax 665-8914

Jefferson Christian Academy 100/9-12
3060 FM 728 75657 903-665-3973
Fax 665-5978

Jewett, Leon, Pop. 922
Leon ISD 700/PK-12
PO Box 157 75846 903-626-4532
Jay Winn, supt. Fax 626-4954
Leon HS 200/9-12
PO Box 157 75846 903-626-4444
David Jones, prin. Fax 626-5090
Leon JHS 200/6-8
PO Box 157 75846 903-626-4937
Matt Garner, prin. Fax 626-4954

Joaquin, Shelby, Pop. 946
Joaquin ISD 700/PK-12
11109 US Highway 84 E 75954 936-269-3128
Phil Worsham, supt. Fax 269-3615
www.joaquinisd.net/
Joaquin HS 200/9-12
11109 US Highway 84 E 75954 936-269-3122
Mid Johnson, prin. Fax 269-9123
Joaquin JHS 100/7-8
11109 US Highway 84 E 75954 936-269-3090
Mid Johnson, prin. Fax 269-9123

Johnson City, Blanco, Pop. 1,469
Johnson City ISD 700/PK-12
PO Box 498 78636 830-868-7410
David Shanley, supt. Fax 868-7375
www.johnsoncity.txed.net
Johnson HS 200/9-12
PO Box 498 78636 830-868-4025
A'Lann Truelock, prin. Fax 868-9244
Johnson MS 200/5-8
PO Box 498 78636 830-868-9025
Julie Storer, prin. Fax 868-7375

Jonesboro, Coryell
Jonesboro ISD 200/K-12
PO Box 125 76538 254-463-2111
Randy Savage, supt. Fax 463-2275
www.jonesboro-isd.com
Jonesboro S 200/K-12
PO Box 125 76538 254-463-2111
Larry Robinson, prin. Fax 463-2275

Joshua, Johnson, Pop. 5,500
Joshua ISD 4,500/PK-12
PO Box 40 76058 817-202-2500
Ray Dane, supt. Fax 641-2738
www.joshuaisd.org
Joshua HS 1,200/9-12
909 S Broadway St 76058 817-202-2500
Mick Cochran, prin. Fax 556-3403
Loflin MS 700/7-8
520 Stadium Dr 76058 817-202-2500
Dr. Delayne Sprinkles, prin. Fax 202-9140

Jourdanton, Atascosa, Pop. 4,235
Jourdanton ISD 1,300/PK-12
200 Zanderson Ave 78026 830-769-3548
Dr. Lana Collavo, supt. Fax 769-3272
www.jourdantonisd.net/
Jourdanton HS 300/9-12
200 Zanderson Ave 78026 830-769-2350
Keith Chapman, prin. Fax 769-3272
Jourdanton JHS 300/6-8
200 Zanderson Ave 78026 830-769-2234
Robert Rutkowski, prin. Fax 769-3272

Junction, Kimble, Pop. 2,654
Junction ISD 700/PK-12
1700 College St 76849 325-446-3580
Renee Schulze, supt. Fax 446-4413
www.junctionisd.net
Junction HS 200/9-12
1700 College St 76849 325-446-3326
Mary Murr, prin. Fax 446-8206
Junction MS 200/6-8
1700 College St 76849 325-446-2464
Melissa Hoggett, prin. Fax 446-2255

Justin, Denton, Pop. 2,938
Northwest ISD 7,500/PK-12
2001 Texan Dr 76247 817-490-6473
Dr. Karen Rue, supt. Fax 215-0170
northwest.k12.tx.us
Northwest HS 2,000/9-12
2301 Texan Dr 76247 817-215-0200
Gene Suttle, prin. Fax 215-0262
Pike MS 900/6-8
2200 Texan Dr 76247 817-215-0400
Damon Edwards, prin. Fax 215-0425
Other Schools – See Rhome, Trophy Club

Karnack, Harrison
Karnack ISD 200/PK-12
PO Box 259 75661 903-679-3117
Cozzetta Robinson, supt. Fax 679-4252
www.karnackisd.org/
Karnack JSHS 100/7-12
PO Box 259 75661 903-679-3113
Joe Chisum, prin. Fax 679-4264

Karnes City, Karnes, Pop. 3,430
Karnes City ISD 1,000/PK-12
314 N Highway 123 78118 830-780-2321
Dr. Eli Casey, supt. Fax 780-3823
www.kcisd.net
Karnes City HS 300/9-12
400 E Highway 123 78118 830-780-2321
Harold Steele, prin. Fax 780-4352
Karnes City JHS 200/6-8
410 E Highway 123 78118 830-780-2321
Ron Baker, prin. Fax 780-4382

Katy, Harris, Pop. 13,255
Cypress-Fairbanks ISD
Supt. — See Houston
Thornton MS 1,800/6-8
19802 Kieth Harrow Blvd 77449 281-856-1500
Mark McCord, prin. Fax 856-1548

Katy ISD 43,900/PK-12
PO Box 159 77492 281-396-6000
Dr. Leonard Merrell, supt. Fax 644-1800
www.katyisd.org/
Beckendorff JHS 700/6-8
8200 S Fry Rd 77494 281-237-8800
David Truitt, prin. Fax 644-1635
Beck JHS 1,100/6-8
5200 S Fry Rd 77450 281-237-3300
James Cross, prin. Fax 644-1630
Cinco Ranch HS 3,600/9-12
23440 Cinco Ranch Blvd 77494 281-237-7000
Bonnie Brasic, prin. Fax 644-1734
Cinco Ranch JHS 1,000/6-8
23420 Cinco Ranch Blvd 77494 281-237-7300
Dr. Steven Robertson, prin. Fax 644-1640
Katy HS 2,900/9-12
6331 Highway Blvd 77494 281-237-6700
Joe Kelley, prin. Fax 644-1700
Katy JHS 1,100/6-8
5350 Franz Rd 77493 281-237-6800
Scott Sheppard, prin. Fax 644-1645
McDonald JHS 1,100/6-8
3635 Lakes of Bridgewater D 77449 281-237-5300
Ed Keeney, prin. Fax 644-1655
McMeans JHS 1,200/6-8
21000 Westheimer Pkwy 77450 281-237-8000
Dr. Susan Rice, prin. Fax 644-1660
Memorial Parkway JHS 1,000/6-8
21203 Highland Knolls Dr 77450 281-237-5800
Joe Graham, prin. Fax 644-1665
Miller Career Center Vo/Tech
1734 Katyland Dr 77493 281-237-6300
Anna Webb-Storey, prin. Fax 644-1775
Morton Ranch HS 1,200/9-12
21000 Franz Rd 77449 281-237-7800
Joe Cammarata, prin. Fax 644-1746
Morton Ranch JHS 1,200/6-8
2498 N Mason Rd 77449 281-237-7400
Becky Bracewell, prin. Fax 644-1670
Opportunity Awareness Center Vo/Tech
1732 Katyland Dr 77493 281-237-6350
Dr. Patricia Bing, prin. Fax 644-1780
Seven Lakes HS 9-12
9251 S Fry Rd 77494 281-237-2800
Christie Whitbeck, prin. Fax 644-1785
Taylor HS 2,800/9-12
20700 Kingsland Blvd 77450 281-237-3100
James McDonald, prin. Fax 644-1760
West Memorial JHS 700/6-8
22311 Provincial Blvd 77450 281-237-6400
Patricia Shafer, prin. Fax 644-1675
Other Schools – See Houston

Faith West Academy 500/PK-12
2225 Porter Rd 77493 281-391-5683
Raul Hinojosa, hdmstr. Fax 391-2606
Houston Learning Academy - Katy 50/9-12
180 Applewhite Dr 77450 281-693-4151
Lawrence Ermis, prin. Fax 693-1255
Pope John XXIII HS 9-12
1800 N Grand Pkwy 77449 281-693-1000
Lynn Veazey, prin. Fax 693-1001

Kaufman, Kaufman, Pop. 7,872
Kaufman ISD 3,500/PK-12
1000 S Houston St 75142 972-932-2622
Todd Williams, supt. Fax 932-3325
www.kaufmanisd.net/
Kaufman HS 900/9-12
3205 S Houston St 75142 972-932-2811
Mark Albin, prin. Fax 932-1948
Norman JHS 500/7-8
3701 S Houston St 75142 972-932-2410
Jeri Ann Campbell, prin. Fax 932-7771

Trinity Valley Community College Post-Sec.
800 W Highway 243 75142 972-932-4309

Keene, Johnson, Pop. 5,952
Keene ISD 800/PK-12
PO Box 656 76059 817-556-9082
Kevin Sellers, supt. Fax 556-2087
www.keeneisd.org/
Keene HS 200/9-12
PO Box 656 76059 817-641-4843
Sandra Denning, prin. Fax 556-2087
Keene JHS 200/6-8
PO Box 656 76059 817-641-2931
Billie Hopps, prin. Fax 641-4035

Chisholm Trail Academy 100/9-12
PO Box 717 76059 817-641-6626
Mike Furr, prin. Fax 556-2009
Southwestern Adventist University Post-Sec.
PO Box 567 76059 817-645-3921

Keller, Tarrant, Pop. 35,706
Keller ISD 23,700/PK-12
350 Keller Pkwy 76248 817-744-1000
Dr. James Veitenheimer, supt. Fax 337-3261
www.kellerisd.net
Central HS 1,600/9-12
9450 Ray White Rd 76248 817-744-2000
David Hinson, prin. Fax 744-2252
Fossil Ridge HS 2,100/9-12
4101 Thompson Rd 76248 817-744-1700
Todd Tunnell, prin. Fax 337-3407
Indian Springs MS 700/7-8
305 Bursey Rd 76248 817-744-3200
Carrie Jackson, prin. Fax 431-4432
Keller HS 2,700/9-12
601 Pate Orr Rd N 76248 817-744-1400
Mike Kreis, prin. Fax 337-3316
Keller MS 1,000/7-8
300 College Ave 76248 817-744-2900
Debi LaMarr, prin. Fax 337-3500
Trinity Springs MS 7-8
3550 Keller Hicks Rd 76248 817-744-3500
Lindsay Anderson, prin. Fax 741-6353
Other Schools – See Fort Worth

Messiah Lutheran S 100/K-12
1308 Whitley Rd 76248 817-431-5486
Ray Maine, hdmstr. Fax 898-0365

Kemp, Kaufman, Pop. 1,258
Kemp ISD 1,700/PK-12
202 W 17th St 75143 903-498-1314
Dr. Peter Running, supt. Fax 498-1315
kemp.ednet10.net
Kemp HS 500/9-12
1 Yellow Jacket Dr 75143 903-498-1322
Mary Lyons, prin. Fax 498-1375
Kemp JHS 300/7-8
202 W 17th St 75143 903-498-1343
Amelia Hood, prin. Fax 498-1359

Kenedy, Karnes, Pop. 3,408
Kenedy ISD 800/PK-12
401 FM 719 78119 830-583-4100
Dr. Richard Irizarry, supt. Fax 583-9950
www.kenedy.isd.tenet.edu
Kenedy HS 200/9-12
401 FM 719 78119 830-583-4100
Rickey DeLeon, prin. Fax 583-9126
Kenedy MS 200/6-8
401 FM 719 78119 830-583-4100
Ricky Johnson, prin. Fax 583-9950

Kennard, Houston, Pop. 319
Kennard ISD 400/PK-12
PO Box 38 75847 936-655-2008
Gene Glover, supt. Fax 655-2327
www.kennardisd.net/
Kennard JSHS 100/7-12
PO Box 38 75847 936-655-2121
James Applewhite, prin. Fax 655-2327

Kennedale, Tarrant, Pop. 6,547
Kennedale ISD 2,900/K-12
PO Box 467 76060 817-563-8000
Gary Dugger, supt. Fax 483-3610
www.kennedale.net
Kennedale HS 900/9-12
PO Box 1208 76060 817-563-8100
Rita Whatley, prin. Fax 563-3718
Kennedale JHS 500/7-8
PO Box 489 76060 817-563-8200
Larry Westmoreland, prin. Fax 483-3655

Kerens, Navarro, Pop. 1,803
Kerens ISD 700/PK-12
PO Box 310 75144 903-396-2924
Kevin Stanford, supt. Fax 396-2334
www.kerens.k12.tx.us/
Kerens S 700/PK-12
PO Box 310 75144 903-396-2931
David Tyson, prin. Fax 396-2334

Kermit, Winkler, Pop. 5,281
Kermit ISD 1,200/PK-12
601 S Poplar St 79745 432-586-1000
Santos Lujan, supt. Fax 586-1016
www.kisd.esc18.net/
Kermit HS 300/9-12
601 S Poplar St 79745 432-586-1050
Don Humphrey, prin. Fax 586-1055
Kermit JHS 300/6-8
601 S Poplar St 79745 432-586-1040
Holly McCoy, prin. Fax 586-1045

Kerrville, Kerr, Pop. 22,010
Kerrville ISD 4,600/PK-12
1009 Barnett St 78028 830-257-2200
Dan Troxell Ph.D., supt. Fax 257-2249
www.kerrvilleisd.net
Peterson MS 800/7-8
1607 Sidney Baker St 78028 830-257-2204
Sharon Mock, prin. Fax 257-1300
Tivy HS 1,300/9-12
3250 Loop 534 78028 830-257-2212
Robert Jolly, prin. Fax 895-3575

Conlee's College of Cosmetology Post-Sec.
402 Quinlan St 78028 830-896-2380
Our Lady of the Hills Catholic HS 9-12
575 Peterson Farm Rd 78028 830-895-0501
Barry Neuberger, prin. Fax 895-3470
Schreiner University Post-Sec.
2100 Memorial Blvd 78028 800-343-4919

Kilgore, Gregg, Pop. 11,858
Kilgore ISD 3,600/PK-12
301 N Kilgore St 75662 903-984-2073
Jerry Roberts, supt. Fax 983-3212
www.kisd.org/
Kilgore HS 1,100/9-12
301 N Kilgore St 75662 903-984-5591
Robert Wheeley, prin. Fax 984-0571
Laird MS 800/6-8
301 N Kilgore St 75662 903-984-5072
Jody Clements, prin. Fax 984-6225

Kilgore College Post-Sec.
1100 Broadway Blvd 75662 903-984-8531

Killeen, Bell, Pop. 100,233
Killeen ISD 31,900/PK-12
PO Box 967 76540 254-501-0006
Dr. Jim Hawkins, supt. Fax 526-3103
www.killeenisd.org
C A T E Vo/Tech
3004 Atkinson Ave 76543 254-501-0563
Laurel Blair, prin. Fax 519-7737
Ellison HS 2,000/9-12
909 E Elms Rd 76542 254-501-0600
Marvin Rainwater, prin. Fax 501-0697
Fairway MS 600/6-8
701 Whitlow Dr 76541 254-501-1000
Teresa Daugherty, prin. Fax 519-5599
Killeen HS 1,800/9-12
500 N 38th St 76543 254-501-0400
Michael Sibberson, prin. Fax 680-2424
Liberty Hill MS 700/6-8
4500 Kit Carson Trl 76542 254-501-1370
Michael Berger, prin. Fax 953-4367
Live Oak Ridge MS 700/6-8
2600 Robinett Rd 76549 254-501-2490
Brenda Alexander, prin. Fax 554-2170
Manor MS 700/6-8
1700 S W S Young Dr 76543 254-501-1310
Floristine Gray, prin. Fax 680-7029
Nolan MS 700/6-8
505 E Jasper Dr 76541 254-501-1150
Mike Burch, prin. Fax 519-5598
Palo Alto MS 700/6-8
2301 W Elms Rd 76549 254-501-1200
Dee Levens, prin. Fax 519-5577
Rancier MS 700/6-8
3301 Hilliard Ave 76543 254-501-1250
Corbett Lawler, prin. Fax 680-6601
Shoemaker HS 2,000/9-12
3302 S Clear Creek Rd 76549 254-501-0900
Ron Gray, prin. Fax 520-1118
Other Schools – See Fort Hood, Harker Heights

American Preparatory S 100/9-12
PO Box 1800 76540 254-526-1390
Colvin Davis, dean
Central Texas College Post-Sec.
PO Box 1800 76540 254-526-1104
Killeen Adventist Junior Academy 100/PK-10
3412 Lake Rd 76543 254-699-9466
Fax 699-0519

Kingsville, Kleberg, Pop. 24,740
Kingsville ISD 4,300/PK-12
PO Box 871 78364 361-592-3387
Dr. Rudy Lopez, supt. Fax 595-7805
www.kvisd.esc2.net
King HS 1,200/9-12
PO Box 871 78364 361-592-6401
Dr. Michael McClure, prin. Fax 595-9170
Memorial MS 600/7-8
PO Box 871 78364 361-595-5771
Roel Gonzalez, prin. Fax 592-4198

Ricardo ISD 600/PK-8
138 W County Road 2160 78363 361-592-6465
Dr. Don Jones, supt. Fax 592-3101
www.ricardoisd.us
Ricardo MS 300/5-8
138 W County Road 2160 78363 361-592-6465
Karen Unterbrink, prin. Fax 593-0707

Santa Gertrudis ISD 300/PK-12
PO Box 592 78364 361-592-3937
Mary Springs, supt. Fax 592-2836
www.sgisd.esc2.net
Academy HS 200/9-12
PO Box 592 78364 361-592-0058
Mike Gonzalez, prin. Fax 592-5335

Presbyterian Pan American S 100/9-12
PO Box 1578 78364 361-592-4307
Dr. Barbara Stottlemyer, dean Fax 592-6126
Texas A&M University Post-Sec.
700 University Blvd 78363 361-593-2111

Kingwood, Harris, Pop. 37,397
Humble ISD
Supt. — See Humble
Creekwood MS 1,000/6-8
3603 W Lake Houston Pkwy 77339 281-641-4400
Walt Winicki, prin. Fax 641-4417
Kingwood 9th Grade Campus 1,100/9-9
4015 Woodland Hills Dr 77339 281-641-6600
Larry Cooper, prin. Fax 641-6617
Kingwood MS 1,000/6-8
2407 Pine Terrace Dr 77339 281-641-4200
Robert Atteberry, prin. Fax 641-4217
Kingwood SHS 2,900/10-12
2701 Kingwood Dr 77339 281-641-6900
Melissa Hayhurst, prin. Fax 641-7217
Riverwood MS 1,100/6-8
2910 High Valley Dr 77345 281-641-4800
Greg Joseph, prin. Fax 641-4817

Kingwood College Post-Sec.
20000 Kingwood Dr 77339 281-359-1600
Northeast Christian Academy 300/PK-12
1711 Hamblen Rd 77339 281-359-1090
Earl Garland, prin. Fax 359-5560

Kirbyville, Jasper, Pop. 2,029
Kirbyville Consolidated ISD 1,600/PK-12
206 E Main St 75956 409-423-7520
Dr. Joseph Burns, supt. Fax 423-2367
kirbyvillecisd.org
Kirbyville HS 500/9-12
100 E Wildcat Dr 75956 409-423-7500
Gary Fairchild, prin. Fax 423-5313
Kirbyville JHS 300/7-8
2200 S Margaret Ave 75956 409-420-0692
Micah Dyer, prin. Fax 423-6654

Klein, Harris, Pop. 12,000
Klein ISD 36,700/PK-12
7200 Spring Cypress Rd 77379 832-249-4000
Dr. Jim Cain, supt. Fax 249-4055
www.kleinisd.net
Doerre IS 1,200/6-8
18218 Theiss Mail Route Rd 77379 832-249-5700
Cecilia Saccomanno, prin. Fax 249-4054
Kleb IS 1,100/6-8
7425 Louetta Rd 77379 832-249-5500
Pam Bourgeois, prin. Fax 249-4053
Klein HS 3,400/9-12
16715 Stuebner Airline Rd 77379 832-484-4000
Larry Whitehead, prin. Fax 484-7820
Krimmel IS 6-8
7070 FM 2920 Rd 77379 832-375-7200
Scott Crowe, prin. Fax 375-7150
Strack IS 1,100/6-8
18027 Kuykendahl Rd Ste S 77379 832-249-5400
Steve Owen, prin. Fax 249-4051
Other Schools – See Houston, Spring

Knippa, Uvalde
Knippa ISD 300/PK-12
PO Box 99 78870 830-934-2176
Dr. David Rueda, supt. Fax 934-2490
www.knippa.k12.tx.us/
Knippa S, PO Box 99 78870 300/PK-12
Oscar Ontiveros, prin. 830-934-2177

Knox City, Knox, Pop. 1,083
Knox City-O'Brien Consolidated ISD 300/PK-12
606 E Main St 79529 940-657-3521
Louis Baty, supt. Fax 657-3379
www.esc9.net/knoxcity/
Knox City HS 100/9-12
606 E Main St 79529 940-658-3565
Mack Lowe, prin. Fax 658-3379
Other Schools – See O Brien

Kopperl, Bosque
Kopperl ISD 300/PK-12
PO Box 67 76652 254-889-3502
Bill Brister, supt. Fax 889-3443
Kopperl S 300/PK-12
PO Box 67 76652 254-889-3502
Ken Barrow, prin. Fax 889-3443

Kountze, Hardin, Pop. 2,153
Kountze ISD 1,400/PK-12
PO Box 460 77625 409-246-3352
Dianne Daniels, supt. Fax 246-3217
kountzeisd.org
Kountze HS 400/9-12
PO Box 460 77625 409-246-3474
Patti Carraway, prin. Fax 246-8180
Kountze MS 300/6-8
PO Box 460 77625 409-246-3551
John Ferguson, prin. Fax 246-3857

Kress, Swisher, Pop. 779
Kress ISD 200/K-12
PO Box 970 79052 806-684-2652
Doug Setliff, supt. Fax 684-2687
www.kressonline.net
Kress JSHS 100/7-12
PO Box 970 79052 806-684-2651
Leah Zeigler, prin. Fax 684-2687

Krum, Denton, Pop. 3,368
Krum ISD 1,300/PK-12
809 E McCart St 76249 940-482-6000
Troy Hamm, supt. Fax 482-3929
www.krumisd.net
Krum HS 300/9-12
809 E McCart St 76249 940-482-6000
Mike Pierson, prin. Fax 482-2997
Krum MS 300/6-8
809 E McCart St 76249 940-482-6000
John Murtell, prin. Fax 482-6299

Kyle, Hays, Pop. 17,770
Hays Consolidated ISD 9,300/PK-12
21003 I H 35 78640 512-268-2141
Dr. Kirk London, supt. Fax 268-2147
www.hayscisd.net
Chapa MS 6-8
3311 Dacy Ln 78640 512-268-8500
Lisa Islas, prin. Fax 295-7827
Lehman HS 500/9-12
1700 Lehman Rd 78640 512-268-8454
Elsa Hinojosa, prin. Fax 268-2146
Wallace MS 700/6-8
1500 W Center St 78640 512-268-2891
Brenda Agnew, prin. Fax 268-1853
Other Schools – See Buda

Ladonia, Fannin, Pop. 699
Fannindel ISD 200/PK-12
601 W Main St 75449 903-367-7251
H.L. Milton, supt. Fax 367-7252
fannindel.esc8.net/
Fannindel HS 100/6-12
601 W Main St 75449 903-367-7251
Greg Carpenter, prin. Fax 367-7252

La Feria, Cameron, Pop. 6,815
La Feria ISD 2,900/PK-12
PO Box 1159 78559 956-797-2612
Luis Garza, supt. Fax 797-3737
www.esconett.org/laferiaisd/
Green JHS 400/7-8
501 N Canal St 78559 956-797-1512
Michael Torres, prin. Fax 797-2157
La Feria HS 700/9-12
901 N Canal St 78559 956-797-1353
Rebecca Stirzaker, prin. Fax 797-9374

Lago Vista, Travis, Pop. 5,573
Lago Vista ISD 1,200/PK-12
PO Box 4929 78645 512-267-8300
Dr. Barbara Qualls, supt. Fax 267-8304
www.lagovista.txed.net/
Lago Vista HS 300/9-12
PO Box 4929 78645 512-267-8315
Donna Larkin, prin. Fax 267-8330
Lago Vista MS 300/6-8
PO Box 4929 78645 512-267-8305
Paul Bixler, prin. Fax 267-8329

La Grange, Fayette, Pop. 4,620
La Grange ISD 1,900/PK-12
PO Box 100 78945 979-968-7000
Dr. Randy Albers, supt. Fax 968-8155
www.la-grange.k12.tx.us
La Grange HS 600/9-12
PO Box 100 78945 979-968-4800
William Wagner, prin. Fax 968-6744
La Grange MS 300/7-8
PO Box 100 78945 979-968-4747
Neal Miller, prin. Fax 968-8155

Laird Hill, Rusk
Leveretts Chapel ISD 200/PK-12
PO Box 669 75666 903-834-3181
Donna Johnson, supt. Fax 834-6602
www.lcisd.esc7.net/
Other Schools – See Overton

La Joya, Hidalgo, Pop. 4,486
La Joya ISD 22,000/PK-12
201 E Expressway 83 78560 956-580-5000
Dr. Alda Benavides, supt. Fax 580-5444
www.lajoyaisd.com
Carter HS 1,600/9-10
603 N Coyote Dr 78560 956-584-4839
Mary Ann Contreras, prin. Fax 584-4848
De Zavala MS 900/6-8
603 Tabasco Rd 78560 956-580-5472
Gisela Saenz, prin. Fax 580-5494
Juarez-Lincoln HS 1,300/9-10
801 N Coyote Dr 78560 956-580-5900
Judy Solis, prin. Fax 580-5918
La Joya SHS 1,800/11-12
604 N Coyote Dr 78560 956-580-5100
Janie Vega, prin. Fax 580-5103
Schunior MS 600/6-8
200 W Expressway 83 78560 956-580-8500
Lionel Perez, prin. Fax 580-8509
Other Schools – See Mission, Palmview

Lake Dallas, Denton, Pop. 7,000
Lake Dallas ISD 3,700/PK-12
PO Box 548 75065 940-497-4039
Thomas Davenport, supt. Fax 497-3737
www.ldisd.net

Lake Dallas MS 600/7-8
PO Box 548 75065 940-497-4037
Randy Charles, prin. Fax 497-4028
Other Schools – See Corinth

Lake Jackson, Brazoria, Pop. 27,386
Brazosport ISD
Supt. — See Clute
Lake Jackson IS 900/7-8
100 Oyster Creek Dr 77566 979-730-7250
Steve Snell, prin. Fax 292-2804

Brazosport Christian S 300/PK-12
200B Willow Dr 77566 979-297-0563
Dan McDowell, admin. Fax 297-8455
Brazosport College Post-Sec.
500 College Dr 77566 979-230-3000

Lake Worth, Tarrant, Pop. 4,681
Lake Worth ISD 2,500/PK-12
6800 Telephone Rd 76135 817-306-4200
Dr. Janice Cooper, supt. Fax 237-5131
www.lwisd.org/
Collins MS 6-8
3651 Santos Dr, 817-306-4200
Howry MS 500/6-8
4000 Dakota Trl 76135 817-306-4240
Mitch McCombs, prin. Fax 237-3687
Lake Worth HS 600/9-12
4210 Boat Club Rd 76135 817-306-4230
John Hebert, prin. Fax 237-0697

La Marque, Galveston, Pop. 13,860
La Marque ISD 3,700/PK-12
PO Box 7 77568 409-938-4251
Ecomet Burley, supt. Fax 908-5012
www.la-marque.isd.tenet.edu
La Marque HS 1,100/9-12
PO Box 7 77568 409-938-4261
Travis Weatherspoon, prin. Fax 908-5036
La Marque MS 800/6-8
PO Box 7 77568 409-938-4286
Rita Goudeau, prin. Fax 908-5071

Lamesa, Dawson, Pop. 9,321
Klondike ISD 200/PK-12
2911 County Road H 79331 806-462-7334
Steve McLaren, supt. Fax 462-7333
klondike.esc17.net
Klondike S 200/PK-12
2911 County Road H 79331 806-462-7332
Steve McLaren, prin. Fax 462-7323

Lamesa ISD 2,100/PK-12
PO Box 261 79331 806-872-5461
Keith Bryant, supt. Fax 872-6220
www.lamesa.esc17.net
Lamesa HS 600/9-12
PO Box 261 79331 806-872-8385
Joe Nicks, prin. Fax 872-6608
Lamesa MS 400/6-8
PO Box 261 79331 806-872-8301
Chris Riggins, prin. Fax 872-2949

Lampasas, Lampasas, Pop. 7,465
Lampasas ISD 3,200/PK-12
207 W 8th St 76550 512-556-6224
Brant Myers Ed.D., supt. Fax 556-8711
www.lampasas.k12.tx.us
Lampasas HS 900/9-12
902 S Broad St 76550 512-556-3614
Dick Parker, prin. Fax 556-9962
Lampasas MS 600/7-8
207 E Avenue A 76550 512-556-3101
Dwain Brock, prin. Fax 556-0245

Lancaster, Dallas, Pop. 32,233
Lancaster ISD, PO Box 400 75146 3,600/PK-12
Dr. Larry Lewis, supt. 972-218-1400
www.lancasterisd.org
Lancaster HS 1,500/9-12
200 E Wintergreen Rd 75134 972-218-1800
Phillip Randall, prin. Fax 218-1834
Lancaster MS 6-8
822 W Pleasant Run Rd 75146 972-227-2418
Roosevelt Nivens, prin.

Cedar Valley College Post-Sec.
3030 N Dallas Ave 75134 972-860-8200

Laneville, Rusk
Laneville ISD 200/PK-12
PO Box 127 75667 903-863-5353
Ron Tidwell, supt. Fax 863-2736
Laneville S 200/PK-12
PO Box 127 75667 903-863-5354
Carolyn Reeves, prin. Fax 863-2376

La Porte, Harris, Pop. 33,136
La Porte ISD 7,400/PK-12
1002 San Jacinto St 77571 281-604-7000
Dr. Michael Say, supt. Fax 604-7020
www.lpisd.org
La Porte HS 2,200/9-12
1002 San Jacinto St 77571 281-604-7500
Joanne Kolius, prin. Fax 604-7503
La Porte JHS 600/7-8
1002 San Jacinto St 77571 281-604-6600
Dr. Mike Thomas, prin. Fax 604-6605
Lomax JHS 500/7-8
1002 San Jacinto St 77571 281-604-6701
Leigh Wall, prin. Fax 604-6730

La Pryor, Zavala, Pop. 1,343
La Pryor ISD 500/PK-12
PO Box 519 78872 830-365-4000
Eddie Ramirez, supt. Fax 365-4006
www.lapryor.net
La Pryor HS 200/7-12
PO Box 519 78872 830-365-4007
Victor Baron, prin. Fax 365-4026

Laredo, Webb, Pop. 208,754
Laredo ISD 24,700/PK-12
1702 Houston St 78040 956-795-3200
Daniel Garcia Ph.D., supt. Fax 795-3205
www.laredoisd.org/
Cantu Health Science Magnet S 9-12
2002 San Bernardo Ave 78040 956-795-3876
Fax 795-3875
Christen MS 1,500/6-8
2001 Santa Maria Ave 78040 956-795-3725
Guadalupe Cortez, prin. Fax 795-3732
Cigarroa HS 1,600/9-12
2600 Zacatecas St 78046 956-795-3800
Dr. Sonia Sanchez, prin. Fax 795-3814
Cigarroa MS 1,400/6-8
2600 Palo Blanco St 78046 956-795-3700
Imelda Murillo, prin. Fax 795-3711
Lamar MS 1,400/6-8
1818 N Arkansas Ave 78043 956-795-3750
Virginia Salinas, prin. Fax 795-3766
Magnet S for Engineering & Technology 9-12
2600 Zacatecas St 78046 956-795-3800
Alfredo Perez, prin. Fax 795-3814
Martin HS 1,900/9-12
2002 San Bernardo Ave 78040 956-795-3850
Blas Martinez, prin. Fax 795-3860
Memorial MS 700/6-8
2002 Marcella Ave 78040 956-795-3775
Guadalupe Perez, prin. Fax 795-3780
Nixon HS 2,200/9-12
2000 E Plum St 78043 956-795-3849
Sylvia Rios, prin. Fax 795-3844
Trevino S of Communications & Fine Arts 9-12
1701 Victoria St 78040 956-795-3325
Jose Cerda, dir. Fax 795-3330

United ISD 32,400/PK-12
201 Lindenwood Dr 78045 956-473-6201
Roberto Santos, supt. Fax 473-6415
www.uisd.net
Alexander Health & Science Magnet S 9-12
3600 E Del Mar Blvd 78041 956-473-5866
Elvira Gaona, dir. Fax 473-5998
Alexander HS 2,000/9-12
3600 E Del Mar Blvd 78041 956-473-5800
S. Alvarez del Castillo, prin. Fax 473-5999
Clark MS 800/6-8
500 W Hillside Rd 78041 956-473-7500
Dolores Barrera, prin. Fax 473-7599
Garcia MS 600/6-8
499 Pena Dr 78046 956-473-5000
Gerardo Gonzalez, prin. Fax 473-5099
Gonzalez MS 900/6-8
5208 Santa Claudia 78043 956-473-7000
Adriana Ramirez, prin. Fax 473-7099
Johnson HS 1,700/9-12
5626 Cielito Lindo 78046 956-473-5100
Oscar Perez, prin. Fax 473-5399
Lamar Bruni-Vergar MS 6-8
5910 Saint Luke 78046 956-473-6600
Annabel Rubio, prin. Fax 473-6699
Los Obispos MS 1,400/6-8
4801 S Ejido Ave 78046 956-473-7800
Armando Salazar, prin. Fax 473-1899
Trautmann MS 1,200/6-8
8501 Curly Ln 78045 956-473-7400
Raymundo Gonzalez, prin. Fax 473-7499
United Engineering Magnet HS 9-12
8800 McPherson Rd 78045 956-473-5627
David Canales, dir. Fax 473-1981
United HS 2,500/9-12
8800 McPherson Rd 78045 956-473-5600
Alberto Aleman, prin. Fax 473-1980
United MS 800/6-8
700 E Del Mar Blvd 78041 956-473-7300
Alberto Ibarra, prin. Fax 473-7399
United South HS 1,700/9-12
4001 Los Presidentes Ave 78046 956-473-5400
Roylin Wilson, prin. Fax 473-5599
United South Magnet S for Business 9-12
4001 Los Presidentes Ave 78046 956-473-5440
Maggie Martinez, dir. Fax 473-5598
United South MS 1,000/6-8
3707 Los Presidentes Ave 78046 956-473-7700
Selma Santos, prin. Fax 473-7799
Washington MS 1,000/6-8
10306 Riverbank Dr 78045 956-473-7600
David Gonzalez, prin. Fax 473-7699

Laredo Community College Post-Sec.
1 W End Washington St 78040 956-722-0521
St. Augustine HS 500/8-12
1300 Galveston St 78040 956-724-8131
Kathleen Sarmiento, prin. Fax 725-9241
Southern Careers Institute Post-Sec.
4805 Maher Ave 78041 956-723-2345
Texas A&M International University Post-Sec.
5201 University Blvd 78041 956-326-2000
Texas Careers Post-Sec.
6410 McPherson Rd 78041 956-717-5909
Trinity Christian Academy 50/PK-12
3301 Main Ave 78040 956-712-0006
Monica Calderon, prin.

La Rue, Henderson
La Poynor ISD 400/K-12
13155 US Highway 175 E, 903-876-4057
Eugene Buford, supt. Fax 876-4541
www.lapoynor.esc7.net
La Poynor HS 100/9-12
13155 US Highway 175 E, 903-876-2373
Trent Cook, prin. Fax 876-4541
La Poynor JHS 100/6-8
13155 US Highway 175 E, 903-876-1085
Lana Miller, prin. Fax 876-4541

Latexo, Houston, Pop. 275
Latexo ISD 400/K-12
PO Box 975 75849 936-544-5664
Dr. Roy H. Tucker, supt. Fax 544-5332
www.latexoisd.net
Latexo JSHS 200/7-12
PO Box 975 75849 936-544-5638
Pam Ainsworth, prin. Fax 544-8456

La Vernia, Wilson, Pop. 1,087
La Vernia ISD 2,300/PK-12
13600 US Highway 87 W 78121 830-779-2181
Dr. Tom Harvey, supt. Fax 779-2304
www.la-vernia.k12.tx.us
La Vernia HS 700/9-12
225 FM 775 78121 830-779-2181
John Burks, prin. Fax 779-3218
La Vernia JHS 400/7-8
110 D L Vest 78121 830-779-2181
Don Beck, prin. Fax 779-2728

La Villa, Hidalgo, Pop. 1,455
La Villa ISD 700/PK-12
PO Box 9 78562 956-262-4755
Dr. Norma Salaiz, supt. Fax 262-7323
La Villa HS 200/9-12
PO Box 9 78562 956-262-4715
Robert Munoz, prin. Fax 262-9798
La Villa MS 100/6-8
PO Box 9 78562 956-262-4760
Vilma Gomez, prin. Fax 262-5243

Lazbuddie, Parmer
Lazbuddie ISD 200/PK-12
PO Box 9 79053 806-965-2156
Karl Vaughn, supt. Fax 965-2892
www.lazbuddieisd.org
Lazbuddie S 200/PK-12
PO Box 9 79053 806-965-2152
John Jones, prin. Fax 965-2892

League City, Galveston, Pop. 61,490
Clear Creek ISD 32,700/PK-12
PO Box 799 77574 281-284-0000
Dr. Sandra Mossman, supt. Fax 284-0005
www.ccisd.net
Clear Creek 9th Grade Center 9-9
2451 E Main St 77573 281-284-2300
Jamey Majewski, prin. Fax 284-2305
Clear Creek HS 3,500/9-12
2305 E Main St 77573 281-284-1700
Scott Bockart, prin. Fax 284-1705
Clear Springs HS 9-12
501 Palomino St 77573 281-284-1300
Gail Love, prin.
Creekside IS 700/6-8
4320 W Main St 77573 281-284-3500
Pete Caterina, prin. Fax 284-3505
League City IS 1,100/6-8
2588 Webster St 77573 281-284-3400
Kimberly Brouillard, prin. Fax 284-3405
Victory Lakes IS 800/6-8
2880 W Walker St 77573 281-284-3700
Barry Beck, prin. Fax 284-3705
Other Schools – See Friendswood, Houston, Seabrook

Bay Area Christian S 600/K-12
4800 W Main St 77573 281-332-4814
Freddie Cullins, prin. Fax 554-5495
Devereux-Texas Treatment Network Post-Sec.
1150 Devereux Dr 77573 800-373-0011

Leakey, Real, Pop. 372
Leakey ISD 300/PK-12
PO Box 1129 78873 830-232-5595
Fred McNiel, supt. Fax 232-5535
www.leakey.k12.tx.us/
Leakey S 300/PK-12
PO Box 1129 78873 830-232-5595
Lorri Gonzalez, prin. Fax 232-5535

Leander, Williamson, Pop. 17,851
Leander ISD 19,400/PK-12
PO Box 218 78646 512-434-5000
Tom Glenn, supt. Fax 434-5387
www.leanderisd.org
Leander HS 2,000/9-12
3301 S Bagdad Rd 78641 512-435-8000
Todd Washburn, prin. Fax 435-8011
Leander MS 800/6-8
410 S West Dr 78641 512-434-7800
Sandy Trujillo, prin. Fax 434-7805
Other Schools – See Austin, Cedar Park

Lefors, Gray, Pop. 540
Lefors ISD 200/PK-12
PO Box 390 79054 806-835-2533
Gerry Nickell, supt. Fax 835-2238
www.region16.net/leforsisd/
Lefors S, PO Box 390 79054 200/PK-12
Ronnie Miller, prin. 806-835-2533

Leggett, Polk
Leggett ISD 300/PK-12
PO Box 68 77350 936-398-2804
Robert Kimball, supt. Fax 398-2078
www.leggettisd.net/
Leggett JSHS 100/7-12
PO Box 68 77350 936-398-2412
Ryan Skelton, prin. Fax 398-0889

Lenorah, Martin
Grady ISD 200/PK-12
3500 FM 829 79749 432-459-2444
John Tubb, supt. Fax 459-2729
grady.tx.schoolwebpages.com
Grady S 200/PK-12
3500 FM 829 79749 432-459-2445
Richard Gibson, prin. Fax 459-2729

Leonard, Fannin, Pop. 2,071
Leonard ISD 800/PK-12
1 Tiger Aly 75452 903-587-2318
Larry LaFavers, supt. Fax 587-2845
www.leonardisd.net
Leonard HS 200/9-12
1 Tiger Aly 75452 903-587-3556
John Kent, prin. Fax 587-8011
Leonard JHS 200/6-8
1 Tiger Aly 75452 903-587-2315
Beryl Sears, prin. Fax 587-2228

Levelland, Hockley, Pop. 12,777
Levelland ISD 2,500/PK-12
704 11th St 79336 806-894-9628
John Booth, supt. Fax 894-2583
www.levelland.isd.tenet.edu
Levelland HS 800/9-12
704 11th St 79336 806-894-8515
Leroy Mitchell, prin. Fax 894-6029
Levelland JHS 400/7-8
704 11th St 79336 806-894-6355
Mel Gierhart, prin. Fax 894-8935

South Plains College Post-Sec.
1401 College Ave 79336 806-894-9611

Lewisville, Denton, Pop. 90,348
Lewisville ISD
Supt. — See Flower Mound
Delay MS 700/6-8
136 W Purnell Rd 75057 469-713-5191
Pam Flores, prin. Fax 420-7122
Durham MS 700/6-8
2075 S Edmonds Ln 75067 469-713-5963
Alan Cassel, prin. Fax 315-9390
Hedrick MS 600/6-8
1526 Bellaire Blvd 75067 469-713-5188
Pete Taggart, prin. Fax 221-7462

Huffines MS 1,000/6-8
1440 N Valley Pkwy 75077 469-713-5990
Beth Brockman, prin. Fax 350-4950
Jackson Career Center Vo/Tech
1597 S Edmonds Ln 75067 469-713-5186
Alan Strong, prin. Fax 436-5912
Killough North HS 9-9
1301 Summit Ave 75077 469-713-5987
Andy Plunkett, prin. Fax 350-4550
Lewisville HS 2,300/9-12
1098 W Main St 75067 469-713-5190
Royce Cooper, prin. Fax 436-8658

Temple Christian Academy 300/PK-12
1010 Bellaire Blvd 75067 972-436-3480
Dr. Richard Wallace, admin. Fax 219-5639

Lexington, Lee, Pop. 1,245
Lexington ISD 1,000/PK-12
8731 N Highway 77 78947 979-773-2254
Chuck Holt, supt. Fax 773-4455
www.lexington.isd.tenet.edu
Lexington HS 300/9-12
8731 N Highway 77 78947 979-773-2255
Rebecca Otte French, prin. Fax 773-4455
Lexington MS 200/6-8
8731 N Highway 77 78947 979-773-2255
Steven Coston, prin. Fax 773-4455

Liberty, Liberty, Pop. 8,433
Liberty ISD 2,300/PK-12
1600 Grand Ave 77575 936-336-7213
Mona Chadwick, supt. Fax 336-2283
www.libertyisd.net
Liberty HS 700/9-12
2615 Jefferson Dr 77575 936-336-6483
David Taylor, prin. Fax 336-3931
Liberty MS 500/6-8
2515 Jefferson Dr 77575 936-336-3582
Bruce Lacefield, prin. Fax 336-1021

Liberty Hill, Williamson, Pop. 1,491
Liberty Hill ISD 1,400/PK-12
PO Box 68 78642 512-260-5580
Dr. Dean Andrews, supt. Fax 260-5581
www.libertyhill.txed.net
Liberty Hill HS 600/9-12
PO Box 68 78642 512-260-5500
Dalton West, prin. Fax 260-5510
Liberty Hill MS 300/7-8
PO Box 68 78642 512-515-5636
Lila West, prin. Fax 778-5937

Lindale, Smith, Pop. 4,030
Lindale ISD 3,200/PK-12
PO Box 370 75771 903-881-4001
Jane Ann Morrison, supt. Fax 882-8641
www.lindaleeagles.org
Lindale HS 900/9-12
PO Box 370 75771 903-881-4051
Jamie Holder, prin. Fax 882-2813
Lindale JHS 500/7-8
PO Box 370 75771 903-881-4150
Vicki Thrasher, prin. Fax 882-2842

Linden, Cass, Pop. 2,201
Linden-Kildare Consolidated ISD 900/PK-12
205 Kildare Rd 75563 903-756-5027
John York, supt. Fax 756-7242
www.lkcisd.net
Linden-Kildare HS 300/9-12
205 Kildare Rd 75563 903-756-7026
Hoby Holder, prin. Fax 756-8512
Linden-Kildare JHS 200/6-8
205 Kildare Rd 75563 903-756-5381
Jerry Hankins, prin. Fax 756-8832

Lindsay, Cooke, Pop. 956
Lindsay ISD 500/K-12
PO Box 145 76250 940-668-8923
Jason Ceyanes, supt. Fax 668-2662
www.esc11.net/schools/lindsay/index.htm
Lindsay HS 200/7-12
PO Box 145 76250 940-668-8474
Phillip Hall, prin. Fax 665-1637

Lingleville, Erath
Lingleville ISD 300/PK-12
PO Box 134 76461 254-968-2596
Dennis Hughes, supt. Fax 965-5821
www.lingleville.k12.tx.us/
Lingleville S 300/PK-12
PO Box 134 76461 254-968-2596
Dennis Hughes, prin. Fax 965-5821

Lipan, Hood, Pop. 488
Lipan ISD 300/PK-8
211 N Kickapoo St 76462 254-646-2266
William Stokes, supt. Fax 646-3499
Lipan JHS 7-8
211 N Kickapoo St 76462 254-646-2266
Charles Rowett, prin. Fax 646-3499

Little Elm, Denton, Pop. 18,012
Little Elm ISD 4,100/PK-12
500 Lobo Ln 75068 972-292-1847
Steve Murray, supt. Fax 294-1107
www.leisd.ws/
Lakeside JHS 600/7-8
400 Lobo Ln 75068 972-292-3200
Camille Porter, prin. Fax 292-3009
Little Elm HS 900/9-12
1900 Walker Ln 75068 972-292-1840
Gerry Talley, prin. Fax 292-3505

Littlefield, Lamb, Pop. 6,329
Littlefield ISD 1,500/PK-12
1207 E 14th St 79339 806-385-3844
Jerry Blakely, supt. Fax 385-6297
www.littlefield.k12.tx.us
Littlefield HS 400/9-12
1207 E 14th St 79339 806-385-5683
Ricky Hobbs, prin. Fax 385-3603
Littlefield JHS 400/6-8
1207 E 14th St 79339 806-385-3922
Shawn Mason, prin. Fax 385-5603

Little River, Bell, Pop. 1,512
Academy ISD 900/PK-12
704 E Main St 76554 254-982-4304
Randy Hendricks, supt. Fax 982-0023
www.academy.k12.tx.us/
Academy HS 300/9-12
602 E Main St 76554 254-982-4201
Joe Craig, prin. Fax 982-4420
Academy JHS 300/5-8
501 E Main St 76554 254-982-4620
Stephen Ash, prin. Fax 982-4776

Live Oak, Bexar, Pop. 10,942
Judson ISD 15,500/PK-12
8012 Shin Oak Dr 78233 210-945-5400
Dr. Ed Lyman, supt. Fax 945-6900
www.judsonisd.org
Other Schools – See Converse, San Antonio, Universal City

Livingston, Polk, Pop. 6,401
Big Sandy ISD
Supt. — See Dallardsville
Big Sandy S 500/PK-12
FM 1276 77351 936-563-1000
Kevin Foster, prin. Fax 563-1010

Livingston ISD 4,100/PK-12
PO Box 1297 77351 936-328-2100
Dr. Carol Ann Bonds, supt. Fax 328-2109
www.livingstonisd.com
Livingston JHS 1,000/7-9
1801 Highway 59 Loop N 77351 936-328-2120
Matthew Smith, prin. Fax 328-2139
Livingston SHS 900/10-12
1 Lions Ave 77351 936-328-2240
Jerry Ausburn, prin. Fax 328-2231

Llano, Llano, Pop. 3,348
Llano ISD 1,900/PK-12
200 E Lampasas St 78643 325-247-4747
Dennis Hill, supt. Fax 247-5623
www.llano.k12.tx.us
Llano HS 500/9-12
2509 S State Highway 16 78643 325-248-2200
Earl Jarrett, prin. Fax 247-2122
Llano JHS 400/6-8
400 E State Highway 71 E 78643 325-247-4659
Candace Hughs, prin. Fax 247-5916

Lockhart, Caldwell, Pop. 13,567
Lockhart ISD 4,500/PK-12
PO Box 120 78644 512-398-0000
Dr. John Hall, supt. Fax 398-0025
www.lockhartisd.org
Lockhart HS 900/10-12
1 Lion Country Dr 78644 512-398-0300
Larry Ramirez, prin. Fax 398-0302
Lockhart HS Freshman Campus 400/9-9
419 Bois D Arc St 78644 512-398-0170
John Henk, prin. Fax 398-0172
Lockhart JHS 1,000/6-8
1015 City Line Rd 78644 512-398-0770
Susan Brooks, prin. Fax 398-0772

Lockney, Floyd, Pop. 1,878
Lockney ISD 600/PK-12
PO Box 428 79241 806-652-2115
Phil Cotham, supt. Fax 652-2729
www.lockney.isd.tenet.edu/
Lockney HS 200/9-12
PO Box 1058 79241 806-652-3325
Dean Thompson, prin. Fax 652-4945
Lockney JHS 100/6-8
PO Box 550 79241 806-652-2236
Todd Hallmark, prin. Fax 652-4920

Lohn, McCulloch
Lohn ISD 100/PK-12
PO Box 277 76852 325-344-5749
Leon Freeman, supt. Fax 344-5789
www.centex-edu.net/lohn
Lohn S 100/PK-12
PO Box 277 76852 325-344-5749
Clay Burns, prin. Fax 344-5789

Lometa, Lampasas, Pop. 853
Lometa ISD 300/PK-12
PO Box 250 76853 512-752-3384
David Rice, supt. Fax 752-8531
www.centex-edu.net/lometa/
Lometa S 300/PK-12
PO Box 250 76853 512-752-3384
Kip Bullock, prin. Fax 752-3424

Lone Oak, Hunt, Pop. 554
Lone Oak ISD 900/PK-12
PO Box 38 75453 903-662-5427
Eddie White, supt. Fax 662-5290
loisd.echalk.com/
Lone Oak HS 300/9-12
8205 US Highway 69 S 75453 903-662-0981
Curt Hale, prin. Fax 662-0984
Lone Oak MS 300/5-8
8161 US Highway 69 S 75453 903-662-5121
Kim White, prin. Fax 662-5017

Longview, Gregg, Pop. 75,609
Longview ISD 7,600/PK-12
PO Box 3268 75606 903-381-2200
Dr. James Wilcox, supt. Fax 753-5389
www.lisd.org
Forest Park MS 500/6-8
PO Box 3268 75606 903-758-9971
Margaret Davis, prin. Fax 758-6964
Foster MS 800/6-8
PO Box 3268 75606 903-753-1692
Sedric Clark, prin. Fax 758-1571
Judson MS 500/6-8
PO Box 3268 75606 903-663-0206
Brian Kasper, prin. Fax 663-0275
Longview HS 2,200/9-12
PO Box 3268 75606 903-663-1301
James Brewer, prin. Fax 663-7180

Pine Tree ISD 4,700/PK-12
PO Box 5878 75608 903-295-5000
Lynn Whitaker, supt. Fax 295-5004
www.ptisd.org
Pine Tree JHS 800/8-9
PO Box 5878 75608 903-295-5081
Jerald Jeter, prin. Fax 295-5082
Pine Tree SHS 1,100/10-12
PO Box 5878 75608 903-295-5031
Jason Mixon, prin. Fax 295-5029

Spring Hill ISD 1,800/PK-12
3101 Spring Hill Rd 75605 903-759-4404
Wes Jones, supt. Fax 297-0141
www.springhill.esc7.net
Spring Hill HS 500/9-12
3101 Spring Hill Rd 75605 903-323-7738
Mike Gilbert, prin. Fax 323-7766
Spring Hill JHS 300/7-8
3101 Spring Hill Rd 75605 903-323-7718
David Reed, prin. Fax 323-7765

Christian Heritage S 200/K-12
2715 FM 1844 75605 903-663-4151
Connie Puryear, admin. Fax 663-4587
East Texas Christian S 200/PK-12
PO Box 8053 75607 903-757-7891
Philip Brown, prin. Fax 236-4968
Le Tourneau University Post-Sec.
PO Box 7001 75607 903-233-3000
Longview Christian S 200/K-12
2101 W Marshall Ave 75604 903-297-3501
Mark Clark, admin. Fax 663-4448
Star College of Cosmetology Post-Sec.
700 E Whaley St 75601 903-758-8611
Trinity S of Texas 300/PK-12
215 N Teague St 75601 903-753-0612
Rev. Charlene Miller, hdmstr. Fax 753-4812

Loop, Gaines
Loop ISD 100/PK-12
PO Box 917 79342 806-487-6411
Phil Mitchell, supt. Fax 487-6416
www.loopisd.net/
Loop S 100/PK-12
PO Box 917 79342 806-487-6411
Ray Conner, prin. Fax 487-6416

Loraine, Mitchell, Pop. 617
Loraine ISD 200/PK-12
PO Box 457 79532 325-737-2235
Eric Stoddard, supt. Fax 737-2019
www.loraine.esc14.net/
Loraine S 200/PK-12
PO Box 457 79532 325-737-2225
Bivian Hermosillo, prin. Fax 737-2603

Lorena, McLennan, Pop. 1,595
Lorena ISD 1,600/PK-12
PO Box 97 76655 254-857-3239
Sandra Talbert, supt. Fax 857-4533
www.lorenaisd.net
Lorena HS 500/9-12
PO Box 97 76655 254-857-4604
Randy Blanchard, prin. Fax 857-3883
Lorena MS 500/5-8
PO Box 97 76655 254-857-4621
Rusty Grimm, prin. Fax 857-3419

Lorenzo, Crosby, Pop. 1,288
Lorenzo ISD 300/PK-12
PO Box 520 79343 806-634-5591
Dick Van Hoose, supt. Fax 634-5928
lorenzo.esc17.net/
Lorenzo JSHS 100/7-12
PO Box 520 79343 806-634-5592
Joe Christian, prin. Fax 634-5788

Los Fresnos, Cameron, Pop. 5,192
Los Fresnos Consolidated ISD 8,000/PK-12
PO Box 309 78566 956-233-4407
Gonzalo Salazar, supt. Fax 233-4031
www.lfcisd.net
Liberty Memorial MS 500/6-8
PO Box 309 78566 956-233-3900
Ms. Marty Vasquez, prin. Fax 233-1074
Los Cuates MS 600/6-8
PO Box 309 78566 956-233-6250
Pablo Leal, prin. Fax 233-6265
Los Fresnos HS 2,100/9-12
PO Box 309 78566 956-233-3300
Dr. Virginia Miller, prin. Fax 233-3510
Reseca MS 700/6-8
PO Box 309 78566 956-233-6210
Jimmy McDonough, prin. Fax 233-6209

Louise, Wharton
Louise ISD 500/PK-12
PO Box 97 77455 979-648-2982
Andrew Peters, supt. Fax 648-2520
louiseisd.org
Louise JSHS 200/7-12
PO Box 97 77455 979-648-2202
Diana Blumrick, prin. Fax 648-2142

Lovelady, Houston, Pop. 611
Lovelady ISD 500/PK-12
PO Box 99 75851 936-636-7616
John Reynolds, supt. Fax 636-2212
www.loveladyisd.net
Lovelady HS 200/9-12
PO Box 250 75851 936-636-7636
Larry Hulsey, prin. Fax 636-2305

Lubbock, Lubbock, Pop. 209,737
Frenship ISD
Supt. — See Wolfforth
Terra Vista MS 6-8
1111 Upland Ave 79416 806-796-0076
Brent Lowrey, prin.

Lubbock ISD 23,500/PK-12
1628 19th St 79401 806-766-1000
Wayne Havens, supt. Fax 766-1210
www.lubbockisd.org
Alderson MS 100/6-8
219 Walnut Ave 79403 806-766-1500
George Love, prin. Fax 766-1490
Atkins MS 400/6-8
5401 Avenue U 79412 806-766-1522
Chris Huber, prin. Fax 766-2226
Cavazos MS 500/6-8
210 N University Ave 79415 806-766-6600
Mike Worth, prin. Fax 766-6627
Coronado HS 1,600/9-12
3307 Vicksburg Ave 79410 806-766-0600
Eric McKnight, prin. Fax 766-0560
Dunbar MS 500/6-8
2010 E 26th St 79404 806-766-1300
Jimmy Moore, prin. Fax 766-1320
Estacado HS 800/9-12
1504 E Itasca St 79403 806-766-1400
Paul Frazier, prin. Fax 766-1952

Evans MS 500/6-8
4211 58th St 79413 806-766-0722
Leslie Soto, prin. Fax 766-0570
Hutchinson MS 500/6-8
3102 Canton Ave 79410 806-766-0755
Dr. Samuel Ayers, prin. Fax 766-0538
Irons MS 500/6-8
5214 79th St 79424 806-766-2044
Lynn Akin, prin. Fax 766-2070
Lubbock HS 1,600/9-12
2004 19th St 79401 806-766-1444
Doyle Vogler, prin. Fax 766-1469
MacKenzie MS 400/6-8
5402 12th St 79416 806-766-0777
John Carter, prin. Fax 766-0510
Martin ATC Vo/Tech
3201 Avenue Q 79411 806-766-6651
Bill Landis, dir. Fax 766-6675
Monterey HS 1,600/9-12
3211 47th St 79413 806-766-0700
Al Griggs, prin. Fax 766-0509
Slaton MS 500/6-8
1602 32nd St 79411 806-766-1555
Shelly Bratcher, prin. Fax 766-1571
Wilson MS 400/6-8
4402 31st St 79410 806-766-0799
Cindy Wallace, prin. Fax 766-0814

Lubbock-Cooper ISD 2,200/PK-12
16302 Loop 493 79423 806-863-2282
Pat Henderson, supt. Fax 863-3130
www.lcisd.net
Lubbock-Cooper HS 600/9-12
16302 Loop 493 79423 806-863-2282
Steve Naurkal, prin. Fax 863-2877
Lubbock-Cooper JHS 400/6-8
16302 Loop 493 79423 806-863-2282
Kevin Hahn, prin. Fax 863-2654

Roosevelt ISD 1,200/PK-12
1406 County Road 3300 79403 806-842-3282
Berhl Robertson, supt. Fax 842-3266
www.roosevelt.esc17.net
Roosevelt HS 300/9-12
1406 County Road 3300 79403 806-842-3283
Ricardo Garcia, prin. Fax 842-3931
Roosevelt JHS 300/6-8
1406 County Road 3300 79403 806-842-3218
Kayla Morrison, prin. Fax 842-3337

American Commercial College Post-Sec.
2007 34th St 79411 806-747-4339
Christ the King S 300/PK-12
4011 54th St 79413 806-795-8283
Christine Wanjura, prin. Fax 795-9715
Covenant Sch. of Nursing & Allied Health Post-Sec.
2002 W Loop 289 Ste 120 79407 806-797-0955
Lubbock Christian S 400/PK-12
2604 Dover Ave 79407 806-796-8700
Peter Dahlstrom, supt. Fax 791-3569
Lubbock Christian University Post-Sec.
5601 19th St 79407 806-796-8800
Lubbock Hair Academy Post-Sec.
2844 34th St 79410 806-795-0806
Methodist Hospital Post-Sec.
3615 19th St 79410 806-792-1011
South Plains College Post-Sec.
9730 Reese Blvd 79416 806-894-9611
Texas Careers Post-Sec.
1421 9th St 79401 806-765-7051
Texas Tech University Post-Sec.
1 Texas Tech University 79409 806-742-2011
Texas Tech University Health Science Ctr Post-Sec.
79430 806-743-3111
Trinity Christian HS 300/7-12
6701 University Ave 79413 806-791-6583
David Pruett, supt. Fax 745-8641

Lucas, Collin, Pop. 3,971
Lovejoy ISD
Supt. — See Allen
Lovejoy HS 9-12
2350 Estates Pkwy, 469-742-8700
Dr. Mike Goddard, prin. Fax 742-8701
Lovejoy MS 6-8
2350 Estates Pkwy, 469-742-8700
Gavan Goodrich, prin. Fax 742-8701

Lucas Christian Academy 300/1-12
415 W Lucas Rd, 972-429-4362
Fax 429-5141

Lueders, Jones, Pop. 277
Lueders-Avoca ISD 100/PK-12
334 S McHarg St 79533 325-228-4211
Tony Reed, supt. Fax 228-4513
laisd.com
Other Schools – See Avoca

Lufkin, Angelina, Pop. 33,522
Hudson ISD 2,400/PK-12
6735 Ted Trout Dr 75904 936-875-3351
Mary Ann Whiteker, supt. Fax 875-9209
www.hudsonisd.org
Hudson HS 700/9-12
6735 Ted Trout Dr 75904 936-875-9232
Donny Webb, prin. Fax 875-9307
Hudson MS 700/5-8
6735 Ted Trout Dr 75904 936-875-9292
Stanley Tupman, prin. Fax 875-9317

Lufkin ISD 8,500/PK-12
PO Box 1407 75902 936-634-6696
Roy Knight, supt. Fax 634-8864
www.lufkinisd.org
Lufkin HS 2,300/9-12
309 S Medford Dr 75901 936-632-7721
Mark Smith, prin. Fax 632-8132
Lufkin MS 1,700/6-8
900 E Denman Ave 75901 936-630-4444
Vickie Evans, prin. Fax 632-4444

Academy of Hair Design Post-Sec.
512 S Chestnut St 75901 936-634-8440
Angelina College Post-Sec.
PO Box 1768 75902 936-639-1301

Luling, Caldwell, Pop. 5,386
Luling ISD 1,600/PK-12
212 E Bowie St 78648 830-875-3191
Mark Weisner, supt. Fax 875-3193
www.luling.txed.net
Luling HS 500/9-12
218 E Travis St 78648 830-875-2458
Chris Martinez, prin. Fax 875-2751
Luling JHS 400/6-8
214 E Bowie St 78648 830-875-2121
Brian Thompson, prin. Fax 875-5482

Lumberton, Hardin, Pop. 9,637
Lumberton ISD 3,500/PK-12
121 S Main St 77657 409-923-7580
Gus Hollomon, supt. Fax 755-7848
www.lumberton.k12.tx.us
Lumberton HS 1,000/9-12
103 S LHS Dr 77657 409-923-7890
John Valastro, prin. Fax 755-6576
Lumberton MS 500/7-8
123 S Main St 77657 409-923-7581
Robin Perez, prin. Fax 751-0641

Lyford, Willacy, Pop. 1,986
Lyford Consolidated ISD 1,600/PK-12
PO Box 220 78569 956-347-3521
Eduardo Infante, supt. Fax 347-5201
www.lyfordcisd.net
Lyford HS 400/9-12
PO Box 220 78569 956-347-3909
Isabel Solis, prin. Fax 347-5034
Lyford MS 400/6-8
PO Box 220 78569 956-347-3910
Dana Yates, prin. Fax 347-2351

Lytle, Atascosa, Pop. 2,646
Lytle ISD 1,500/PK-12
PO Box 745 78052 830-709-5100
Michelle Carroll Smith, supt. Fax 709-5104
www.lytleisd.com
Lytle HS 400/9-12
PO Box 190 78052 830-709-5105
Rosa Mares, prin. Fax 709-5107
Lytle JHS 300/6-8
PO Box 825 78052 830-709-5115
Jesse Vela, prin. Fax 709-5119

Mabank, Kaufman, Pop. 2,622
Mabank ISD 3,300/PK-12
124 E Market St 75147 903-887-9311
Dr. Russell D. Marshall, supt. Fax 887-9399
www.mabankisd.net
Mabank HS 900/9-12
124 E Market St 75147 903-887-9333
Tommy Wallis, prin. Fax 887-9303
Mabank MS 700/6-8
124 E Market St 75147 903-887-9360
Gary Jacobs, prin. Fax 887-0361
Mabank AEP Adult
124 E Market St 75147 903-880-1320
Zan Tidmore, prin. Fax 880-1324

Mc Allen, Hidalgo, Pop. 113,877
Mc Allen ISD 24,000/PK-12
2000 N 23rd St 78501 956-618-6000
Yolanda Chapa, supt. Fax 631-7206
www.mcallenisd.org/
Brown MS 900/6-8
2700 S Ware Rd 78503 956-632-8700
Yvette Cavazos, prin. Fax 632-8709
Cathey MS 900/6-8
1800 N Cynthia St 78501 956-971-4300
Joe Gonzalez, prin. Fax 632-2811
De Leon MS 1,000/6-8
4201 N 29th Ln 78504 956-632-8800
Joanetta Ellis, prin. Fax 632-8805
Fossum MS 6-8
2000 N 23rd St 78501 956-618-6000
Lincoln MS 900/6-8
1601 N 27th St 78501 956-971-4200
Rosalinda Martinez, prin. Fax 971-4273
Mc Allen HS 2,000/9-12
2021 La Vista Ave 78501 956-632-3100
Chris Beck, prin. Fax 632-3114
Memorial HS 2,000/9-12
101 E Hackberry Ave 78501 956-632-5201
Jose Saenz, prin. Fax 632-5226
Morris MS 900/6-8
1400 Trenton Rd 78504 956-618-7300
Marie Riley, prin. Fax 632-3666
Rowe HS 1,900/9-12
2101 N Ware Rd 78501 956-632-5100
Joe Puente, prin. Fax 632-8850
Travis MS 800/6-8
600 E Houston Ave 78501 956-971-4242
Trecia Munal, prin. Fax 632-8454

Sharyland ISD
Supt. — See Mission
Sharyland Worth JHS 50/7-8
5100 Dove Ave 78504 956-686-1415
David Guel, prin. Fax 668-0425

Kings Way Missionary Institute Post-Sec.
401 S 35th St 78501 956-682-6187
San Antonio College Medical Dental Asst. Post-Sec.
1500 S Jackson Rd 78503 956-630-1499
South Texas Christian Academy 100/PK-12
7001 N Ware Rd 78504 956-682-1117
Fax 682-7398
South Texas College Post-Sec.
3201 Pecan Blvd 78501 956-631-4922
South Texas Vocational-Technical Inst. Post-Sec.
2400 Daffodil Ave 78501 956-631-1107
University of Cosmetology Arts & Science Post-Sec.
PO Box 720391 78504 956-687-9444
Vanguard Institute of Technology Post-Sec.
3017 S 10th St 78503 956-787-4388

Mc Camey, Upton, Pop. 2,028
Mc Camey ISD 500/PK-12
PO Box 1069 79752 432-652-3666
Jerry Stinson, supt. Fax 652-4219
www.mcisd.esc18.net/
Mc Camey HS 200/9-12
PO Box 1069 79752 432-652-3666
Donny Wiley, prin. Fax 652-4245
Mc Camey MS 100/5-8
PO Box 1069 79752 432-652-3666
Scott Allen, prin. Fax 652-4246

Mc Gregor, McLennan, Pop. 4,940
Mc Gregor ISD 1,100/PK-12
PO Box 356 76657 254-840-2828
Kevin Houchin, supt. Fax 840-4077
www.mcgregor-isd.org
Isbill JHS 300/5-8
PO Box 356 76657 254-840-3251
Paul Miller, prin. Fax 840-4077
Mc Gregor HS 300/9-12
PO Box 356 76657 254-840-2853
James Lenamon, prin. Fax 840-4077

Mc Kinney, Collin, Pop. 73,081
Mc Kinney ISD 17,900/PK-12
1 Duvall St 75069 469-742-4000
Tom Crowe, supt. Fax 742-4071
www.mckinneyisd.net
Dowell MS 1,000/6-8
301 Ridge Rd 75070 469-742-6700
Eartha Linson, prin. Fax 742-6701
Evans MS 1,200/6-8
6998 W Eldorado Pkwy 75070 469-742-7100
Todd Young, prin. Fax 742-7101
Faubion MS 900/6-8
2000 Rollins St 75069 469-742-6900
Patty Jackson, prin. Fax 742-6901
Johnson MS 900/6-8
3400 Community Blvd 75071 469-742-4900
Dr. Melinda DeFelice, prin. Fax 742-4901
Mc Kinney Boyd HS 9-12
600 N Lake Forest Dr 75071 469-452-4900
Rick McDaniel, prin. Fax 452-4901
Mc Kinney HS 2,200/9-12
1400 Wilson Creek Pkwy 75069 469-742-5700
Donna Rother, prin. Fax 742-5701
Mc Kinney North HS 2,000/9-12
2550 Wilmeth Rd 75071 469-742-4300
Linda Theret, prin. Fax 742-4301

Faith Christian Academy 100/PK-12
115 Industrial Blvd Ste A 75069 972-562-5323
Tony Gore, dir. Fax 562-0581
International Business School Post-Sec.
1434 N Central Expy Ste 116 75070 972-548-0774
Mc Kinney Christian Academy 400/K-12
3601 Bois D Arc Rd 75071 214-544-2658
Todd Clingman, hdmstr. Fax 542-5056

Mc Lean, Gray, Pop. 764
Mc Lean ISD 200/PK-12
PO Box 90, 806-779-2301
Jimmy Hannon, supt. Fax 779-2248
Mc Lean HS 100/9-12
PO Box 90, 806-779-2571
Rhonda Patterson, prin. Fax 779-2315

Mc Leod, Cass
Mc Leod ISD 400/K-12
PO Box 350 75565 903-796-7181
Cathy May, supt. Fax 796-8443
www.mcleodisd.net
Mc Leod HS 100/9-12
PO Box 350 75565 903-796-7181
Karan Tidwell, prin. Fax 796-8443
Mc Leod MS 100/6-8
PO Box 350 75565 903-796-7181
Karan Tidwell, prin. Fax 796-8443

Madisonville, Madison, Pop. 4,250
Madisonville Consolidated ISD 2,100/PK-12
PO Box 879 77864 936-348-2797
Karen Richter, supt. Fax 348-2751
www.madisonvillecisd.org
Madisonville HS 600/9-12
PO Box 879 77864 936-348-2721
Keith Smith, prin. Fax 348-5753
Madisonville JHS 500/6-8
PO Box 819 77864 936-348-3587
James Sanders, prin. Fax 348-5603

Magnolia, Montgomery, Pop. 1,187
Magnolia ISD 9,500/PK-12
PO Box 88 77353 281-356-3571
Michael Holland, supt. Fax 356-1328
www.magnoliaisd.org
Bear Branch JHS 600/7-8
PO Box 606 77353 281-356-6088
Gerald Evans, prin. Fax 252-2060
Magnolia HS 2,600/9-12
PO Box 428 77353 281-356-3572
Jeff Springer, prin. Fax 252-2092
Magnolia JHS 900/7-8
PO Box 476 77353 281-356-1327
Mark Weatherly, prin. Fax 252-2125
Magnolia West HS 9-12
PO Box 426 77353 281-356-3571
Rob Stewart, prin. Fax 252-2560

Malakoff, Henderson, Pop. 2,370
Cross Roads ISD 600/PK-12
14434 FM 59 75148 903-489-2001
Clay Tompkins, supt. Fax 489-2527
www.crossroadsisd.org/
Cross Roads HS 200/9-12
14434 FM 59 75148 903-489-1275
Dr. Regina Davis, prin. Fax 489-0054
Cross Roads JHS 200/6-8
14434 FM 59 75148 903-489-2667
Glenda Wisenbaker, prin. Fax 489-3840

Malakoff ISD 1,200/PK-12
813 E Royall Blvd 75148 903-489-1152
Larry Hulsey, supt. Fax 489-2566
www.malakoff.esc7.net
Malakoff HS 400/9-12
15201 FM 3062 75148 903-489-1527
Randy Perry, prin. Fax 489-0971
Malakoff MS 300/6-8
106 N Cedar St 75148 903-489-0264
George Hull, prin. Fax 489-1812

Manor, Travis, Pop. 1,877
Manor ISD 3,800/PK-12
PO Box 359 78653 512-278-4000
Mark Diaz Ed.D., supt. Fax 278-4017
www.manorisd.net
Manor HS 900/9-12
PO Box 679 78653 512-278-4030
Carlton Tucker, prin. Fax 278-4033
Manor MS 800/6-8
PO Box 388 78653 512-278-4065
Don Wise, prin. Fax 278-4285

Mansfield, Tarrant, Pop. 37,976
Mansfield ISD — 22,900/PK-12
605 E Broad St 76063 — 817-473-5600
Vernon Newsom, supt. — Fax 473-5611
www.mansfieldisd.org
Barber Career Tech Center — Vo/Tech
1120 W Debbie Ln 76063 — 817-299-1900
Jerri McNair, prin. — Fax 453-6839
Brooks Wester MS — 900/7-8
1520 N Walnut Creek Dr 76063 — 817-453-7200
Scott Shafer, prin. — Fax 453-7213
Jones MS — 600/7-8
4500 E Broad St 76063 — 817-276-6200
Lamar Goree, prin. — Fax 453-7380
Mansfield HS — 2,500/9-12
3001A E Broad St 76063 — 817-473-5750
Steven Gast, prin. — Fax 473-5424
Worley MS — 900/7-8
500 Pleasant Ridge Dr 76063 — 817-473-5668
Christie Alfred, prin. — Fax 473-5623
Other Schools – See Arlington

Manvel, Brazoria, Pop. 3,287
Alvin ISD
Supt. — See Alvin
Manvel HS — 9-12
19601 Highway 6 77578 — 281-692-0700
Darrell Alexander, prin. — Fax 692-0852

Heritage Christian Academy — 100/PK-12
PO Box 848 77578 — 281-489-9746
Fax 997-7218

Marathon, Brewster
Marathon ISD — 100/PK-12
PO Box 416 79842 — 432-386-4431
Conrad Arriola, supt. — Fax 386-4395
www.marathonisd.com/
Marathon S — 100/PK-12
PO Box 416 79842 — 432-386-4431
Deborah Dannelley, prin. — Fax 386-4395

Marble Falls, Burnet, Pop. 6,745
Marble Falls ISD — 3,800/PK-12
2001 Broadway St 78654 — 830-693-4357
Dr. Ryder Warren, supt. — Fax 693-5685
www.mfisd.txed.net
Marble Falls HS — 1,100/9-12
2101 Mustang Dr 78654 — 830-693-4375
Buck Gilcrease, prin. — Fax 693-6079
Marble Falls MS — 800/6-8
1511 Pony Dr 78654 — 830-693-4439
Brandon Stiewig, prin. — Fax 693-7788

Faith Academy of Marble Falls — 200/1-12
PO Box 1240 78654 — 830-798-1333
Aaron Weast, admin. — Fax 798-1332

Marfa, Presidio, Pop. 1,978
Marfa ISD — 400/PK-12
PO Box T 79843 — 432-729-4252
Hershel Busby, supt. — Fax 729-4310
www.marfa.esc18.net
Marfa JSHS — 200/7-12
PO Box T 79843 — 432-729-4252
Telda Swinnea, prin. — Fax 729-4053

Marion, Guadalupe, Pop. 1,118
Marion ISD — 1,400/PK-12
PO Box 189 78124 — 830-914-2803
Dennis Dreyer, supt. — Fax 420-2300
www.marion.txed.net
Marion HS — 500/9-12
PO Box 189 78124 — 830-914-2803
Daryl Wendel, prin. — Fax 420-3639
Marion MS — 300/6-8
PO Box 189 78124 — 830-914-2803
Johanna Lopez, prin. — Fax 420-2300

Marlin, Falls, Pop. 6,206
Marlin ISD — 1,400/PK-12
130 Coleman St 76661 — 254-883-3585
Ray Matthews, supt. — Fax 883-6612
www.marlinisd.org
Marlin HS — 500/9-12
1400 Capps St 76661 — 254-883-2394
Rockney Terry, prin. — Fax 883-3470
Marlin MS — 300/6-8
678 Success Dr 76661 — 254-883-9241
Curtis Hurst, prin. — Fax 883-2839

Marshall, Harrison, Pop. 24,006
Marshall ISD — 5,800/PK-12
PO Box 879 75671 — 903-927-8701
Kenn Franklin, supt. — Fax 935-0203
www.marshallisd.com
Marshall HS — 1,600/9-12
1900 Maverick Dr 75670 — 903-927-8800
Richard Davis, prin. — Fax 938-7052
Marshall JHS — 900/7-8
700 W Houston St 75670 — 903-927-8830
Stephanie Richard, prin. — Fax 927-8837

East Texas Baptist University — Post-Sec.
1209 N Grove St 75670 — 903-935-7963
Texas State Technical College — Post-Sec.
2650 E End Blvd S 75672 — 903-935-1010
Wiley College — Post-Sec.
711 Wiley Ave 75670 — 903-927-3300

Mart, McLennan, Pop. 2,531
Mart ISD — 600/PK-12
PO Box 120 76664 — 254-876-2523
Leonard Williams, supt. — Fax 876-3028
www.martisd.org/
Mart HS — 200/9-12
PO Box 120 76664 — 254-876-2574
Todd Gooden, prin. — Fax 876-2575
Mart MS — 200/5-8
PO Box 120 76664 — 254-876-2762
Linda Delaney, prin. — Fax 876-2792

Martinsville, Nacogdoches
Martinsville ISD — 300/PK-12
PO Box 100 75958 — 936-564-3455
Allen D. Garner, supt. — Fax 569-0498
www.martinsville.esc7.net
Martinsville JSHS — 200/7-12
PO Box 100 75958 — 936-564-3455
Charles Farrell, prin. — Fax 569-0498

Mason, Mason, Pop. 2,211
Mason ISD — 400/PK-12
PO Box 410 76856 — 325-347-1144
Matt Underwood, supt. — Fax 347-5877
www.masonisd.net/
Mason HS — 200/9-12
PO Box 410 76856 — 325-347-1122
Casey Callahan, prin. — Fax 347-8247
Mason JHS — 5-8
PO Box 410 76856 — 325-347-1122
Pam Kruse, prin. — Fax 347-5461

Matador, Motley, Pop. 673
Motley County ISD — 200/PK-12
PO Box 310 79244 — 806-347-2676
Randy Brown, supt. — Fax 347-2871
www.motleyco.org
Motley S — 200/PK-12
PO Box 310 79244 — 806-347-2676
Marilynn Hicks, prin. — Fax 347-2871

Mathis, San Patricio, Pop. 5,462
Mathis ISD — 1,900/PK-12
PO Box 1179 78368 — 361-547-3378
Dr. Luis Baldemar Gonzalez, supt. — Fax 547-4198
www.mathisisd.esc2.net
Mathis HS — 600/9-12
PO Box 1179 78368 — 361-547-3322
Joyce St. John, prin. — Fax 547-4139
McCraw JHS — 300/7-8
PO Box 1179 78368 — 361-547-2381
Valora Ann Bartosh, prin. — Fax 547-4156

Maud, Bowie, Pop. 1,015
Maud ISD — 500/PK-12
PO Box 1028 75567 — 903-585-2219
Robert Stinnett, supt. — Fax 585-5451
www.maud.esc8.net
Maud S — 500/PK-12
PO Box 1028 75567 — 903-585-2219
Roy Crow, prin. — Fax 585-5451

May, Brown
May ISD — 300/K-12
PO Box 30 76857 — 254-259-2091
Donald Rhodes, supt. — Fax 259-3514
www.mayisd.com
May JSHS — 100/7-12
PO Box 30 76857 — 254-259-2131
Steven Howard, prin. — Fax 259-2706

Maypearl, Ellis, Pop. 876
Maypearl ISD — 900/PK-12
PO Box 40 76064 — 972-435-2116
Arvell Lynn Dehart, supt. — Fax 435-2340
maypearl.ednet10.net/
Maypearl HS — 300/9-12
PO Box 40 76064 — 972-435-2581
Kay Day, prin. — Fax 435-1701
Maypearl JHS — 200/7-8
PO Box 40 76064 — 972-435-2170
Kay Day, prin. — Fax 435-1701

Meadow, Terry, Pop. 631
Meadow ISD — 200/PK-12
400 Morehead St 79345 — 806-539-2246
Jim Kirkland, supt. — Fax 539-2529
meadow.esc17.net
Meadow HS — 200/6-12
604 4th St 79345 — 806-539-2222
Cody Carroll, prin. — Fax 539-2529

Medina, Bandera
Medina ISD — 400/K-12
PO Box 1470 78055 — 830-589-2855
Randy Moczygemba, supt. — Fax 589-7150
www.medinaisd.org
Medina HS — 200/7-12
PO Box 1470 78055 — 830-589-2851
Ross Hord, prin. — Fax 589-7150

Melissa, Collin, Pop. 2,435
Melissa ISD — 400/PK-12
1904 Cooper St 75454 — 972-837-2411
Loyd Jason Smith, supt. — Fax 837-4233
www.melissaisd.org
Melissa HS — 100/7-12
3150 Cardinal Dr 75454 — 972-837-4216
Aaron Chowning, prin. — Fax 837-4381

Memphis, Hall, Pop. 2,403
Memphis ISD — 600/PK-12
PO Box 460 79245 — 806-259-2443
Tanya Monroe, supt. — Fax 259-2515
Memphis HS — 100/9-12
PO Box 460 79245 — 806-259-2525
Dick Hutcherson, prin. — Fax 259-3026
Memphis MS — 100/6-8
PO Box 460 79245 — 806-259-3400
Patrick Shaffer, prin. — Fax 259-2051

Menard, Menard, Pop. 1,538
Menard ISD — 400/PK-12
PO Box 729 76859 — 325-396-2404
David Hutton, supt. — Fax 396-2143
Menard HS — 100/9-12
PO Box 729 76859 — 325-396-2513
Amy Bannowsky, prin. — Fax 396-2053
Menard JHS — 100/6-8
PO Box 729 76859 — 325-396-2348
Kyle Chambers, prin. — Fax 396-2761

Mercedes, Hidalgo, Pop. 14,185
Mercedes ISD — 4,500/PK-12
PO Box 419 78570 — 956-514-2000
Luis Ramos, supt. — Fax 514-2032
www.misdtx.net
Mercedes HS — 1,300/9-12
1200 Florida St 78570 — 956-514-2100
Ricardo Atkinson, prin. — Fax 514-2111
Mercedes JHS — 700/7-8
PO Box 419 78570 — 956-514-2200
David Rivera, prin. — Fax 514-2233

South Texas ISD — 2,100/7-12
100 Med High Dr 78570 — 956-565-2454
Marla Guerra Ed.D., supt. — Fax 565-9129
www.stisd.net
Science Academy of South Texas — 600/9-12
900 Med High Dr 78570 — 956-565-2454
Edward Argueta, prin. — Fax 565-9112
South Texas HS for Health Professions — 700/9-12
700 Med High Dr 78570 — 956-565-2454
Barbara Heater, prin. — Fax 565-4039

Other Schools – See Edinburg, San Benito

Meridian, Bosque, Pop. 1,527
Meridian ISD — 500/PK-12
PO Box 349 76665 — 254-435-2081
Billy Jack Henderson, supt. — Fax 435-2025
www.meridianisd.org
Meridian JSHS — 300/7-12
PO Box 349 76665 — 254-435-2723
Steve James, prin. — Fax 435-2199

Merit, Hunt
Bland ISD — 600/PK-12
PO Box 216 75458 — 903-776-2239
Bryan E. Clark, supt. — Fax 776-2240
www.blandisd.net
Bland HS — 200/9-12
PO Box 216 75458 — 903-776-2161
Brian Garner, prin. — Fax 776-2426
Bland MS — 200/5-8
PO Box 216 75458 — 903-776-2373
John Orozco, prin. — Fax 776-2853

Merkel, Taylor, Pop. 2,592
Merkel ISD — 1,300/PK-12
PO Box 430 79536 — 325-928-5813
William Hood, supt. — Fax 928-3910
www.merkel.esc14.net
Merkel HS — 400/9-12
PO Box 430 79536 — 325-928-4667
Ronny Wright, prin. — Fax 928-4684
Merkel MS — 300/6-8
PO Box 430 79536 — 325-928-5511
Joel Haragan, prin. — Fax 928-3138

Mertzon, Irion, Pop. 833
Irion County ISD — 400/PK-12
PO Box 469 76941 — 325-835-6111
Brenda Mendiola, supt. — Fax 835-2017
Irion County MSHS — 200/7-12
PO Box 469 76941 — 325-835-2881
Billy Barnett, prin. — Fax 835-2298

Mesquite, Dallas, Pop. 129,902
Mesquite ISD — 34,700/PK-12
405 E Davis St 75149 — 972-288-6411
Dr. Linda Henrie, supt. — Fax 882-7787
www.mesquiteisd.org
Agnew MS — 900/7-8
729 Wilkinson Dr 75149 — 972-882-5750
Donna Gallegos, prin. — Fax 882-5760
Berry MS — 1,100/7-8
2675 Bear Dr 75181 — 972-882-5850
Sharon Rankin, prin. — Fax 882-5888
Horn HS — 2,000/9-12
3300 E Cartwright Rd 75181 — 972-882-5200
Bruce Perkins, prin. — Fax 882-5291
Kimbrough MS — 800/7-8
3900 N Galloway Ave 75150 — 972-882-5900
Dr. Alane Malone, prin. — Fax 882-5942
McDonald MS — 1,000/7-8
2930 N Town East Blvd 75150 — 972-882-5700
Cathy Swann, prin. — Fax 882-5710
Mesquite HS — 2,400/9-12
300 E Davis St 75149 — 972-882-7800
Linda Marshall, prin. — Fax 882-7876
New MS — 900/6-8
3700 S Belt Line Rd 75181 — 972-882-5600
Ed Burns, prin. — Fax 882-5620
North Mesquite HS — 2,400/9-12
18201 Lyndon B Johnson Fwy 75150 — 972-882-7900
Susie Court, prin. — Fax 882-7908
Poteet HS — 1,700/9-12
3300 Poteet Dr 75150 — 972-882-5300
Andrew Bauer, prin. — Fax 882-5353
Vanston MS — 700/7-8
3230 Karla Dr 75150 — 972-882-5801
Sandra Bibb, prin. — Fax 882-5848
West Mesquite HS — 1,600/9-12
2500 Memorial Blvd 75149 — 972-882-7600
Keith Adams, prin. — Fax 882-7611
Wilkinson MS — 800/6-8
2100 Crest Park Dr 75149 — 972-882-5950
Ron Richardson, prin. — Fax 882-5988

Dallas Christian S — 800/K-12
1515 Republic Pkwy 75150 — 972-270-5495
Terry Harlow, pres. — Fax 270-7581
Eastfield College — Post-Sec.
3737 Motley Dr 75150 — 214-860-7002
Metroplex Beauty School — Post-Sec.
519 N Galloway Ave 75149 — 972-288-5485

Mexia, Limestone, Pop. 6,742
Mexia ISD — 2,200/PK-12
PO Box 2000 76667 — 254-562-4000
Charlene Simpson, supt. — Fax 562-4007
www.mexia.k12.tx.us/
Mexia HS — 600/9-12
PO Box 2000 76667 — 254-562-4010
Johnnie Cotton, prin. — Fax 562-2142
Mexia JHS — 500/6-8
PO Box 2000 76667 — 254-562-4020
Russ Meggs, prin. — Fax 562-5053

Miami, Roberts, Pop. 543
Miami ISD — 100/K-12
PO Box 368 79059 — 806-868-3971
Allan Dinsmore, supt. — Fax 868-3171
www.miamiisd.net
Miami S — 100/K-12
PO Box 368 79059 — 806-868-3971
Donna Gill, prin. — Fax 868-3171

Midland, Midland, Pop. 99,227
Greenwood ISD — 1,500/PK-12
2700 FM 1379 79706 — 432-685-7800
Glenn Barber, supt. — Fax 685-7804
www.greenwood.esc18.net/
Brooks MS — 200/7-8
2700 FM 1379 79706 — 432-685-7837
Byron Moreland, prin. — Fax 685-7838
Greenwood HS — 500/9-12
2700 FM 1379 79706 — 432-685-7805
Scott Knippa, prin. — Fax 685-7814

Midland ISD — 18,600/PK-12
615 W Missouri Ave 79701 — 432-689-1000
Dr. Robert E. Nicks, supt. — Fax 689-1976
www.midlandisd.net/
Abell JHS — 800/7-8
3201 Heritage Blvd 79707 — 432-689-6200
Debbie Jordan, prin. — Fax 689-6217

Alamo JHS 800/7-8
3800 Storey Ave 79703 432-689-1700
Jeff Horner, prin. Fax 689-1712
Coleman HS 200/9-12
1600 E Golf Course Rd 79701 432-689-5000
Greg McDaniel, prin. Fax 689-5016
Goddard JHS 900/7-8
2500 Haynes Dr 79705 432-689-1300
Rick Wood, prin. Fax 689-1321
Lee Freshman HS 800/9-9
1400 E Oak Ave 79705 432-689-1250
Larry Winget, prin. Fax 689-1253
Lee SHS 2,100/10-12
3500 Neely Ave 79707 432-689-1600
Patrick Jones, prin. Fax 689-1647
Midland Freshman HS 800/9-9
100 E Gist Ave 79701 432-689-1200
Elise Kail, prin. Fax 689-1209
Midland SHS 100/10-12
906 W Illinois Ave 79701 432-689-1100
Linda Jolly, prin. Fax 689-1144
San Jacinto JHS 800/7-8
1400 N N St 79701 432-689-1350
Stephanie Howard, prin. Fax 689-1385

International Business School Post-Sec.
3305 Andrews Hwy 79703 432-694-7584
Midland Christian S 1,000/PK-12
2001 Culver Dr 79705 432-694-1661
Eddie Lee, supt. Fax 694-5281
Midland College Post-Sec.
3600 N Garfield St 79705 432-685-4500
Trinity S of Midland 500/PK-12
3500 W Wadley Ave 79707 432-697-3281
Alan Barr, hdmstr. Fax 697-7403

Midlothian, Ellis, Pop. 13,188
Midlothian ISD 5,200/PK-12
100 Walter Stephenson Rd 76065 972-775-8296
Dr. J.D. Kennedy, supt. Fax 775-1757
www.midlothian-isd.net
Midlothian HS 1,700/9-12
923 S 9th St 76065 972-775-8237
James Smith, prin. Fax 775-3178
Seale MS 900/6-8
700 George Hopper Rd 76065 972-775-6145
Dee Arterburn, prin. Fax 775-1502
Walnut Grove MS 6-8
990 N Walnut Grove Rd 76065 972-775-5355
Brian Blackwell, prin. Fax 775-8127

Milano, Milam, Pop. 421
Milano ISD 400/PK-12
PO Box 145 76556 512-455-2533
Lindy Robinson, supt. Fax 455-9311
www.milanoisd.net
Milano HS 200/9-12
PO Box 145 76556 512-455-9333
Gary Birdwell, prin. Fax 455-9336
Milano JHS 100/6-8
PO Box 145 76556 512-455-6701
Clay Tarpley, prin. Fax 455-9311

Miles, Runnels, Pop. 815
Miles ISD 400/PK-12
PO Box 308 76861 325-468-2861
Robert Gibson, supt. Fax 468-2179
miles.netxv.net/index.htm
Miles JSHS 200/7-12
PO Box 308 76861 325-468-2861
Merl Brandon, prin. Fax 468-2179

Milford, Ellis, Pop. 726
Milford ISD 200/K-12
PO Box 545 76670 972-493-2911
Don Clingenpeel, supt. Fax 493-2429
www.milfordisd.org
Milford S 200/K-12
PO Box 545 76670 972-493-2921
Marilee Byrne, prin. Fax 493-4600

Millsap, Parker, Pop. 390
Millsap ISD 800/PK-12
305 Pine St 76066 940-682-3101
Bob Lee, supt. Fax 682-4476
www.millsapisd.net
Millsap HS 300/9-12
600 Bulldog Dr 76066 940-682-3182
Matt Adams, prin. Fax 682-4035
Millsap MS 200/6-8
305 Pine St 76066 940-682-3161
Zoe Hurley, prin. Fax 682-4476

Mineola, Wood, Pop. 4,994
Mineola ISD 1,600/PK-12
1000 W Loop 564 75773 903-569-2448
Mary Lookadoo, supt. Fax 569-5155
www.mineolaisd.net
Mineola HS 500/9-12
1000 W Loop 564 75773 903-569-3000
Ricky Stephens, prin. Fax 569-1930
Mineola MS 400/6-8
1000 W Loop 564 75773 903-569-5338
Bob Simmons, prin. Fax 569-5339

Mineral Wells, Palo Pinto, Pop. 16,919
Mineral Wells ISD 3,600/PK-12
906 SW 5th Ave 76067 940-325-6404
Ray M. Crass, supt. Fax 325-6378
www.mwisd.net/
Mineral Wells HS 1,000/9-12
3801 Ram Blvd 76067 940-325-4408
John Corsi, prin. Fax 325-7623
Mineral Wells JHS 500/7-8
1301 SE 14th Ave 76067 940-325-0711
Jay Walsworth, prin. Fax 328-0450

Mission, Hidalgo, Pop. 60,146
La Joya ISD
Supt. — See La Joya
Chavez MS 900/6-8
78 Showers Rd 78572 956-580-6180
Daniel Villareal, prin. Fax 580-6169
Garcia MS 900/6-8
933 Paula Dr, 956-584-0800
Alfonso Solis, prin. Fax 584-0817
Memorial MS 900/6-8
2610 N Moorefield Rd, 956-580-6087
Rolando Rios, prin. Fax 580-6084

Mission Consolidated ISD 14,500/PK-12
1201 Bryce Dr 78572 956-323-5505
Oscar Rodriguez, supt. Fax 323-5891
www.mcisd.net/
Mission HS 1,900/9-12
1201 Bryce Dr 78572 956-323-5700
Ms. San Juanita Connelly, prin. Fax 323-5890
Mission JHS 800/7-8
1201 Bryce Dr 78572 956-323-3300
Raul Sanchez, prin. Fax 323-3338
Veterans Memorial HS 1,700/9-12
1201 Bryce Dr 78572 956-323-3000
Patrick Masso, prin. Fax 323-3280
White JHS 700/7-8
1201 Bryce Dr 78572 956-323-3600
Pete Garcia, prin. Fax 323-3631
Other Schools – See Alton

Sharyland ISD 7,100/PK-12
1106 N Shary Rd 78572 956-580-5200
Scott Owings, supt. Fax 580-5225
www.sharyland.k12.tx.us/index.html
Gray JHS 1,200/7-8
1106 N Shary Rd 78572 956-580-5333
Cynthia Sandoval, prin. Fax 580-5346
Sharyland HS 2,000/9-12
1106 N Shary Rd 78572 956-580-5300
Diamantina Chapa, prin. Fax 580-5311
Other Schools – See Mc Allen

Missouri City, Fort Bend, Pop. 69,941
Fort Bend ISD
Supt. — See Sugar Land
Baines MS 6-8
9000 Sienna Ranch Rd 77459 281-634-6870
David Yaffie, prin. Fax 634-6880
Elkins HS 2,000/9-12
7007 Knights Ct 77459 281-634-2600
Barbara Whitaker, prin. Fax 634-2674
Hightower HS 2,200/9-12
3333 Hurricane Ln 77459 281-634-5240
Patricia Paquin, prin. Fax 634-5333
Lake Olympia MS 1,700/6-8
3100 Lake Olympia Pkwy 77459 281-634-3520
Kevin Shipley, prin. Fax 634-3549
Marshall HS 2,000/9-12
1220 Buffalo Run 77489 281-634-6630
Bob Banks, prin. Fax 634-6650
Missouri City MS 1,200/6-8
200 Louisiana St 77489 281-634-3440
Jerry Jones, prin. Fax 634-3473
Quail Valley MS 1,200/6-8
3019 FM 1092 Rd 77459 281-634-3600
Guillermo Mancha, prin. Fax 634-3632

Monahans, Ward, Pop. 6,325
Monahans-Wickett-Pyote ISD 1,500/PK-12
606 S Betty Ave 79756 432-943-6711
Keith Richardson, supt. Fax 943-2307
mwpisd.esc18.net
Monahans HS 600/9-12
809 S Betty Ave 79756 432-943-2519
Kellye Riley, prin. Fax 943-3327
Walker JHS 300/7-8
800 S Faye Ave 79756 432-943-4622
John Horak, prin. Fax 943-3723

Mont Belvieu, Chambers, Pop. 2,525
Barbers Hill ISD 3,000/PK-12
PO Box 1108 77580 281-576-2221
Greg Poole, supt. Fax 576-3410
www.bhisd.net/
Barbers Hill HS 900/9-12
PO Box 1108 77580 281-576-3400
Susan Haynie, prin. Fax 576-3356
Barbers Hill MS 500/7-8
PO Box 1108 77580 281-576-3351
Cindy Price, prin. Fax 576-3353

Monte Alto, Hidalgo
Monte Alto ISD 600/PK-8
25149 1st St 78538 956-262-1381
Andres Martinez, supt. Fax 262-5535
www.monte-alto.k12.tx.us
Monte Alto MS 200/6-8
25149 1st St 78538 956-262-1374
Andres Martinez, prin. Fax 262-1377

Montgomery, Montgomery, Pop. 538
Montgomery ISD 5,000/PK-12
PO Box 1475 77356 936-582-1333
Dr. Jim Gibson, supt. Fax 582-6447
www.misd.org
Montgomery HS 1,400/9-12
22825 Highway 105 W 77356 936-597-6401
Bobby Morris, prin. Fax 597-6415
Montgomery JHS 800/7-8
22627 Highway 105 W 77356 936-597-6466
Duane McFadden, prin. Fax 597-6485

Moody, McLennan, Pop. 1,393
Moody ISD 800/PK-12
107 Cora Lee Ln 76557 254-853-2172
Allen Law, supt. Fax 853-2886
www.moodyisd.org
Moody HS 200/9-12
107 Cora Lee Ln 76557 254-853-3622
Ed Husk, prin. Fax 853-3822
Moody MS 200/5-8
107 Cora Lee Ln 76557 254-853-2182
Clayton Brantley, prin. Fax 853-2886

Moran, Shackelford, Pop. 223
Moran ISD 100/PK-12
PO Box 98 76464 325-945-3101
Reggy Spencer, supt. Fax 945-2741
Moran S 100/PK-12
PO Box 98 76464 325-945-3101
Reggy Spencer, prin. Fax 945-2741

Morgan, Bosque, Pop. 518
Morgan ISD 200/PK-12
PO Box 300 76671 254-635-2311
Charles McGehee, supt. Fax 635-2224
Morgan S 200/PK-12
PO Box 300 76671 254-635-2311
Pamela Miller, prin. Fax 635-2224

Morton, Cochran, Pop. 1,962
Morton ISD 500/PK-12
500 Champion Dr 79346 806-266-5505
Fredda Schooler, supt. Fax 266-5449
www.mortonisd.net/
Morton HS 200/9-12
500 Champion Dr 79346 806-266-5524
Vicki Rice, prin. Fax 266-5780
Morton JHS 100/6-8
500 Champion Dr 79346 806-266-5505
H. Kirkland, prin. Fax 266-5739

Moulton, Lavaca, Pop. 930
Moulton ISD 300/K-12
PO Box C 77975 361-596-4609
Edward Pustka, supt. Fax 596-7578
www.moultonisd.net
Moulton JSHS 200/7-12
PO Box C 77975 361-596-4691
Tom Weeaks, prin. Fax 596-7578

Mount Enterprise, Rusk, Pop. 528
Mount Enterprise ISD 400/PK-12
301 W 3rd St N 75681 903-822-3721
Dean Evans, supt. Fax 822-3633
www.meisd.esc7.net
Mount Enterprise JSHS 200/7-12
301 W 3rd St N 75681 903-822-3721
Marty Lee, prin. Fax 822-3633

Mount Pleasant, Titus, Pop. 14,760
Chapel Hill ISD 900/PK-12
PO Box 1257 75456 903-572-8096
Marc Levesque, supt. Fax 572-1086
Chapel Hill HS 300/9-12
PO Box 1257 75456 903-572-3925
Sandi Luttrell, prin. Fax 572-9747
Chapel Hill JHS 100/7-8
PO Box 1257 75456 903-572-3925
Sandi Luttrell, prin. Fax 572-9747

Mount Pleasant ISD 5,200/PK-12
PO Box 1117 75456 903-575-2000
Terry Myers, supt. Fax 575-2014
www.mpisd.net
Mount Pleasant HS 1,300/9-12
PO Box 1117 75456 903-575-2020
David Davis, prin. Fax 575-2036
Mount Pleasant JHS 700/7-8
PO Box 1117 75456 903-575-2110
Fax 575-2117

Northeast Texas Community College Post-Sec.
PO Box 1307 75456 903-572-1911

Mount Vernon, Franklin, Pop. 2,583
Mount Vernon ISD 1,500/PK-12
PO Box 98 75457 903-537-2546
Richard Flanagan, supt. Fax 537-4784
mvisd.esc8.net/
Mount Vernon HS 500/9-12
PO Box 1139 75457 903-537-3700
David Pierce, prin. Fax 537-2536
Mount Vernon JHS 200/7-8
PO Box 1139 75457 903-537-2267
Kelly Baird, prin. Fax 537-3601

Muenster, Cooke, Pop. 1,665
Muenster ISD 600/PK-12
PO Box 608 76252 940-759-2281
David Manley, supt. Fax 759-5200
www.esc11.net/schools/Muenster/
Muenster HS 300/7-12
PO Box 608 76252 940-759-4614
Philip Newton, prin. Fax 759-2284

Sacred Heart S 300/PK-12
PO Box 588 76252 940-759-2511
Chad Riley, prin. Fax 759-4422

Muleshoe, Bailey, Pop. 4,579
Muleshoe ISD 1,500/PK-12
514 W Avenue G 79347 806-272-7400
Gene Sheets, supt. Fax 272-4120
www.muleshoeisd.net
Muleshoe HS, 514 W Avenue G 79347 400/9-12
David Jenkins, prin. 806-272-7303
Watson JHS, 514 W Avenue G 79347 300/6-8
David Dominguez, prin. 806-272-7349

Mullin, Mills, Pop. 178
Mullin ISD 100/PK-12
PO Box 128 76864 325-985-3374
C.L. Hammond, supt. Fax 985-3915
www.centex-edu.net/mullin/
Mullin HS 100/7-12
PO Box 128 76864 325-985-3374
Marion Ferguson, prin. Fax 985-3372

Mumford, Robertson
Mumford ISD 500/PK-12
PO Box 268 77867 979-279-3678
Pete Bienski, supt. Fax 279-5044
www.mumford.k12.tx.us
Mumford JSHS 200/7-12
PO Box 268 77867 979-279-3678
Pete Bienski, prin. Fax 279-5044

Munday, Knox, Pop. 1,349
Munday Consolidated ISD 500/PK-12
PO Box 300 76371 940-422-4241
Robert Dillard, supt. Fax 422-5331
www.esc9.net/munday
Munday HS 100/9-12
PO Box 300 76371 940-422-4321
David Stout, prin. Fax 422-5331
Other Schools – See Goree

Murphy, Collin, Pop. 11,026
Plano ISD
Supt. — See Plano
Murphy MS 1,000/6-8
620 N Murphy Rd 75094 469-752-7000
Bonnie Manley, prin. Fax 752-7001

Nacogdoches, Nacogdoches, Pop. 30,806
Central Heights ISD 700/PK-12
10317 US Highway 259 75965 936-564-2681
Earl W. Adams, supt. Fax 569-6889
www.centralhts.org
Central Heights JSHS 300/7-12
10317 US Highway 259 75965 936-552-3408
Andy Binford, prin. Fax 569-6889

Nacogdoches ISD 5,000/PK-12
PO Box 631521 75963 936-569-5000
Dr. Rodney Hutto, supt. Fax 569-5797
www.nacogdoches.k12.tx.us
McMichael MS 800/6-8
PO Box 631521 75963 936-552-0519
Nathan Chaddick, prin. Fax 552-0523
Moses MS 6-8
PO Box 631521 75963 936-569-5001
Steve Green, prin. Fax 569-5031
Nacogdoches HS 1,800/9-12
PO Box 631521 75963 936-564-2466
Dennis Williams, prin. Fax 560-8162

Star College of Cosmetology Post-Sec.
705 N University Dr 75961 936-462-7232
Stephen F. Austin State University Post-Sec.
PO Box 6078 75962 936-468-2011

Natalia, Medina, Pop. 1,794
Natalia ISD 1,200/PK-12
PO Box 548 78059 830-663-4416
Joey Moczygemba, supt. Fax 663-4186
Natalia HS 300/9-12
PO Box 548 78059 830-663-4417
David Bush, prin. Fax 663-6410
Natalia JHS 300/6-8
PO Box 548 78059 830-663-4027
Henry Booth, prin. Fax 663-2347

Navasota, Grimes, Pop. 7,253
Navasota ISD 2,300/PK-12
PO Box 511 77868 936-825-4200
Jennings Teel, supt. Fax 825-4297
www.navasotaisd.org
Navasota HS 800/9-12
PO Box 511 77868 936-825-4250
Brent Rumbo, prin. Fax 825-8539
Navasota JHS 700/6-8
PO Box 511 77868 936-825-4225
Cindy DeMott, prin. Fax 825-4260

Nazareth, Castro, Pop. 337
Nazareth ISD 200/K-12
PO Box 189 79063 806-945-2231
Keith Langfitt, supt. Fax 945-2431
Nazareth S 200/K-12
PO Box 189 79063 806-945-2231
Deborah Clinton, prin. Fax 945-2431

Neches, Anderson
Neches ISD 300/K-12
PO Box 310 75779 903-584-3311
Randy Snider, supt. Fax 584-3686
www.nechesisd.com
Neches JSHS 100/7-12
PO Box 310 75779 903-584-3443
Gary Godwin, prin. Fax 584-3686

Nederland, Jefferson, Pop. 16,751
Nederland ISD 5,100/PK-12
220 N 17th St 77627 409-724-2391
Beverly Gail Krohn, supt. Fax 724-4280
www.nederland.k12.tx.us
Central MS 800/5-8
220 N 17th St 77627 409-727-5765
Charles Jehlen, prin. Fax 724-4275
Nederland HS 1,500/9-12
220 N 17th St 77627 409-727-2741
Randy Lupton, prin. Fax 726-2679
Wilson MS 900/5-8
220 N 17th St 77627 409-727-6224
Stuart Kieschnick, prin. Fax 726-2699

Faris Computer School Post-Sec.
1119 Kent Ave 77627 409-722-4072

Needville, Fort Bend, Pop. 3,288
Needville ISD 2,100/PK-12
PO Box 412 77461 979-793-4308
Curtis Rhodes, supt. Fax 793-3823
www.needvilleisd.com
Needville HS 700/9-12
PO Box 412 77461 979-793-4158
Richard Janacek, prin. Fax 793-5590
Needville JHS 400/7-8
PO Box 412 77461 979-793-4250
Otis Harr, prin. Fax 793-4575

Nevada, Collin, Pop. 621
Community ISD 1,200/PK-12
PO Box 400 75173 972-853-2474
Bud Nauyokas, supt. Fax 843-2392
www.communityisd.org
Community HS 400/9-12
PO Box 400 75173 972-853-2192
Terry Sowers, prin. Fax 853-2834
Community MS 300/5-8
PO Box 400 75173 972-853-2141
John Reves, prin. Fax 843-2392

New Boston, Bowie, Pop. 4,624
New Boston ISD 1,400/PK-12
600 N McCoy Blvd 75570 903-628-2521
Gary Van Deaver Ed.D., supt. Fax 628-2235
nbisd.esc8.net/
New Boston HS 400/9-12
1 W Lion Dr 75570 903-628-6551
Roger Busse, prin. Fax 628-3695
New Boston MS 400/5-8
1215 N State Highway 8 75570 903-628-6588
Glenn Barfield, prin. Fax 628-5132

New Braunfels, Comal, Pop. 47,168
Comal ISD 10,900/PK-12
1404 N IH 35 78130 830-221-2000
Dr. Marc Walker, supt. Fax 221-2001
www.comalisd.org
Canyon HS 1,500/9-12
1510 N IH 35 78130 830-221-2400
Robert Wiegand, prin. Fax 221-2401
Canyon MS 800/6-8
2014 FM 1101 78130 830-221-2300
Patti Vlieger, prin. Fax 221-2301
Other Schools – See Fischer, Spring Branch

New Braunfels ISD 6,400/PK-12
PO Box 311688 78131 830-643-5700
Ron Reaves, supt. Fax 643-5701
www.newbraunfels.txed.net/
New Braunfels HS 1,800/9-12
2551 Loop 337 78130 830-627-6000
Robert Rodriguez, prin. Fax 627-6001
New Braunfels MS 1,000/7-8
656 S Guenther Ave 78130 830-627-6270
Dr. Demetria Cummins, prin. Fax 627-6271

New Braunfels Christian Academy 500/PK-12
995 Mission Hills Dr 78130 830-629-6222
Richard Ramirez, hdmstr. Fax 629-8049

New Caney, Montgomery, Pop. 3,000
New Caney ISD 6,900/PK-12
21580 Loop 494 77357 281-577-8600
Richard Cowan, supt. Fax 354-2639
www.newcaneyisd.org
Keefer Crossing MS 800/6-8
20350 FM 1485 Rd 77357 281-577-8840
Steve Freeman, prin. Fax 399-9859
New Caney HS 1,200/10-12
21650 Loop 494 77357 281-577-2800
John Yonker, prin. Fax 354-0186
Other Schools – See Porter

Newcastle, Young, Pop. 571
Newcastle ISD 200/PK-12
PO Box 129 76372 940-846-3551
Gordon Grubbs, supt. Fax 846-3452
esc9.net/newcastle
Newcastle HS 100/7-12
PO Box 129 76372 940-846-3531
Cathy Creel, prin. Fax 846-3452

New Deal, Lubbock, Pop. 696
New Deal ISD 700/PK-12
PO Box 280 79350 806-746-5833
Jimmy Noland, supt. Fax 746-5707
www.newdealisd.net
New Deal HS 200/9-12
PO Box 250 79350 806-746-5933
Steven McCray, prin. Fax 746-5544
New Deal MS 200/5-8
PO Box 308 79350 806-746-6633
Matt Reed, prin. Fax 746-5244

New Home, Lynn, Pop. 316
New Home ISD 200/K-12
PO Box 248 79383 806-924-7542
Leland Zant, supt. Fax 924-7520
New Home S 200/K-12
PO Box 248 79383 806-924-7543
Shane Fiedler, prin. Fax 924-7520

New London, Rusk, Pop. 991
West Rusk ISD 700/PK-12
PO Box 168 75682 903-895-4503
Will S. Jones Ed.D., supt. Fax 895-2267
www.westrusk.esc7.net
West Rusk HS 200/9-12
PO Box 168 75682 903-895-4428
Susan Brown, prin. Fax 895-2267
West Rusk JHS 100/6-8
PO Box 168 75682 903-895-4428
Susan Brown, prin. Fax 895-2267

New Summerfield, Cherokee, Pop. 1,037
New Summerfield ISD 400/PK-12
PO Box 6 75780 903-726-3306
Tony Murray, supt. Fax 726-3405
www.nsisd.sprnet.org/
New Summerfield S 400/PK-12
PO Box 6 75780 903-726-3306
Luther Taliaferro, prin. Fax 726-3405

Newton, Newton, Pop. 2,351
Newton ISD 1,300/PK-12
414 Main St 75966 409-379-8137
Gene Isabell, supt. Fax 379-2189
www.newtonisd.net
Newton HS 400/9-12
414 Main St 75966 409-379-4731
Johnny Metz, prin. Fax 379-3321
Newton MS 300/6-8
414 Main St 75966 409-379-8324
Julia House, prin. Fax 379-5082

New Waverly, Walker, Pop. 925
New Waverly ISD 900/PK-12
355 Front St 77358 936-344-6751
Dr. Clay Webb, supt. Fax 344-2438
www.new-waverly.k12.tx.us
New Waverly HS 300/9-12
355 Front St 77358 936-344-6451
Chris McKinley, prin. Fax 344-6113
New Waverly JHS 200/6-8
355 Front St 77358 936-344-2246
Truman Goodwin, prin. Fax 344-8313

Gulf Coast Trades Center Post-Sec.
PO Box 515 77358 936-344-6677

Nixon, Gonzales, Pop. 2,246
Nixon-Smiley Consolidated ISD 1,000/PK-12
PO Box 400 78140 830-582-1536
Cathy Booth Ph.D., supt. Fax 582-1920
www.esc13.net/nixon
Nixon-Smiley HS 300/9-12
PO Box 400 78140 830-582-1536
Hensley Cone, prin. Fax 582-2168
Other Schools – See Smiley

Nocona, Montague, Pop. 3,250
Nocona ISD 900/PK-12
220 Clay St 76255 940-825-3267
Vickie Gearheart, supt. Fax 825-4945
www.noconaisd.net/
Nocona HS 300/9-12
220 Clay St 76255 940-825-3264
Lynn Lierly, prin. Fax 825-7270
Nocona MS 200/6-8
220 Clay St 76255 940-825-3121
Norman Waters, prin. Fax 825-6151

Prairie Valley ISD 100/PK-12
3016 FM 103 76255 940-825-4425
W. Tucker, supt. Fax 825-4650
www.esc9.net/pvisd/
Prairie Valley JSHS 100/6-12
3016 FM 103 76255 940-825-4425
Tim West, prin. Fax 825-4650

Nordheim, DeWitt, Pop. 333
Nordheim ISD 100/PK-12
500 Broadway 78141 361-938-5211
Sonya Little, supt. Fax 938-5266
www.nordheimisd.org
Nordheim S 100/PK-12
500 Broadway 78141 361-938-5211
Sonya Little, prin. Fax 938-5266

Normangee, Leon, Pop. 763
Normangee ISD 600/PK-12
PO Box 219 77871 936-396-3111
Gary Adams, supt. Fax 396-3112
www.normangeeisd.org
Normangee JSHS 300/7-12
PO Box 219 77871 936-396-6111
Alan Andrus, prin. Fax 396-6879

North Richland Hills, Tarrant, Pop. 61,115
Birdville ISD
Supt. — See Haltom City
Birdville HS 1,900/9-12
9100 Mid Cities Blvd 76180 817-547-8000
Lane Ledbetter, prin. Fax 547-8009
North Richland MS 800/6-8
4800 Rufe Snow Dr 76180 817-547-4200
Ernie Valamides, prin. Fax 581-5372
North Ridge MS 900/6-8
7332 Douglas Ln 76180 817-547-5200
Carla Saddler-Rix, prin. Fax 581-5460
Richland HS 2,000/9-12
5201 Holiday Ln 76180 817-547-7000
Randy Cobb, prin. Fax 581-5454
Smithfield MS 800/6-8
8400 Main St 76180 817-547-5000
Jeff Russell, prin. Fax 581-5480

ATI Career Training Center Post-Sec.
6351 Boulevard 26 Ste 100 76180 817-284-1141

North Zulch, Madison
North Zulch ISD 300/PK-12
PO Box 158 77872 936-399-4151
Roy E. Gilbert, supt. Fax 399-2025
www.northzulchisd.net
North Zulch JSHS 200/7-12
PO Box 158 77872 936-399-2821
Tim Waldrip, prin. Fax 399-2038

Novice, Coleman, Pop. 135
Novice ISD 100/PK-12
PO Box 205 79538 325-625-4069
Charles Bryant, supt. Fax 625-3915
novice.netxv.net/index.html
Novice S 100/PK-12
PO Box 205 79538 325-625-4500
Heidi Gromatzky, prin. Fax 625-3915

Oakwood, Leon, Pop. 497
Oakwood ISD 200/PK-12
631 N Holly St 75855 903-545-2666
Dr. Douglas Moore, supt. Fax 545-2310
Oakwood JSHS 100/6-12
631 N Holly St 75855 903-545-2140
David Walker, prin. Fax 545-2310

O Brien, Haskell, Pop. 148
Knox City-O'Brien Consolidated ISD
Supt. — See Knox City
O'Brien MS 100/5-8
711 9th St 79539 940-658-3731
Russ Chisum, prin. Fax 658-3379

Odem, San Patricio, Pop. 2,484
Odem-Edroy ISD 1,200/PK-12
PO Box 727 78370 361-368-2561
Richard Chapa, supt. Fax 368-2879
www.oeisd.org/
Odem HS 300/9-12
PO Box 1050 78370 361-368-3401
Reymundo Gonzalez, prin. Fax 368-3781
Odem JHS 300/6-8
PO Box 1407 78370 361-368-8121
Debra Litton, prin. Fax 368-2033

Odessa, Ector, Pop. 93,546
Ector County ISD 25,200/PK-12
PO Box 3912 79760 432-334-7100
Wendell Sollis, supt. Fax 335-8984
www.ector-county.k12.tx.us/
Bonham JHS 800/7-9
PO Box 3912 79760 432-368-2811
Steve Brown, prin. Fax 362-8514
Bowie JHS 1,000/7-9
PO Box 3912 79760 432-337-8361
Karla Wright, prin. Fax 334-0879
Career Center Vo/Tech
PO Box 3912 79760 432-337-3377
Curtis Britt, prin. Fax 334-3712
Crockett JHS 900/7-9
PO Box 3912 79760 432-332-1451
Ismael Lujan, prin. Fax 332-1567
Ector JHS 1,600/7-9
PO Box 3912 79760 432-334-5269
Roy Garcia, prin. Fax 337-3472
Hood JHS 700/7-10
PO Box 3912 79760 432-362-2371
Tommie Robinson, prin. Fax 368-2221
Nimitz JHS 1,000/7-9
PO Box 3912 79760 432-366-2891
Stacy Jones, prin. Fax 368-2239
Odessa HS 2,200/9-12
PO Box 3912 79760 432-337-6655
Ron Leach, prin. Fax 332-6014
Permian HS 2,000/9-12
PO Box 3912 79760 432-366-3652
Fax 368-2209

American Commercial College Post-Sec.
5119 Twin Towers Blvd 79762 432-362-6768
Odessa College Post-Sec.
201 W University Blvd 79764 432-335-6400
University of Texas of the Permian Basin Post-Sec.
4901 E University Blvd 79762 432-552-2020

O Donnell, Lynn, Pop. 1,070
O'Donnell ISD 400/PK-12
PO Box 487, 806-428-3241
Rodney Schneider, supt. Fax 428-3395
odonnell.esc17.net
O'Donnell HS 100/9-12
PO Box 487, 806-428-3247
Clay Burns, prin. Fax 428-3759
O'Donnell JHS 100/6-8
PO Box 487, 806-428-3247
Clay Burns, prin. Fax 428-3759

Oglesby, Coryell, Pop. 458
Oglesby ISD 100/K-12
PO Box 158 76561 254-456-2271
Edna Biggerstaff, supt. Fax 456-2522
www.oglesbyisd.net
Oglesby S 100/K-12
PO Box 158 76561 254-456-2241
Joshua Carty, prin. Fax 456-2522

Olney, Young, Pop. 3,340
Olney ISD 800/PK-12
809 W Hamilton St 76374 940-564-3519
Tom Bailey, supt. Fax 564-5205
www.esc9.net/olney
Olney HS 200/9-12
704 W Grove St 76374 940-564-5637
Elaine Reno, prin. Fax 564-5733
Olney JHS 200/6-8
300 S Avenue H 76374 940-564-3517
Terry Dunlap, prin. Fax 564-8824

Olton, Lamb, Pop. 2,275
Olton ISD 700/PK-12
PO Box 388 79064 806-285-2641
Brad Lane, supt. Fax 285-2724
www.oltonisd-esc17.net/
Olton HS 200/9-12
PO Box 667 79064 806-285-2691
Bub McIver, prin. Fax 285-2724
Olton JHS 100/6-8
PO Box 509 79064 806-285-2681
Mike Wiley, prin. Fax 285-3348

Omaha, Morris, Pop. 970
Pewitt Consolidated ISD 900/PK-12
PO Box 1106 75571 903-884-2804
David Fitts, supt. Fax 884-2866
pewitt.esc8.net/
Pewitt HS 300/9-12
PO Box 1106 75571 903-884-2293
Bill Harp, prin. Fax 884-3111
Pewitt JHS 200/6-8
PO Box 1106 75571 903-884-2505
Ronnie Herron, prin. Fax 884-3111

Onalaska, Polk, Pop. 1,355
Onalaska ISD 800/PK-12
PO Box 2289 77360 936-646-1000
Kerry Cowart, supt. Fax 646-2605
www.onalaskaisd.net
Onalaska JSHS 300/7-12
PO Box 2289 77360 936-646-1020
Troy Parton, prin. Fax 646-1022

Orange, Orange, Pop. 18,052
Little Cypress-Mauriceville Cons ISD 3,800/PK-12
6586 FM 1130 77632 409-883-2232
Pauline Hargrove, supt. Fax 883-3509
www.lcmcisd.org/
Little Cypress JHS 500/6-8
6765 FM 1130 77632 409-883-2317
Keith Lindsey, prin. Fax 883-5044
Little Cypress-Mauriceville HS 1,200/9-12
7327 Highway 87 N 77632 409-886-5821
James Armstrong, prin. Fax 886-5762
Mauriceville MS 300/6-8
19952 FM 1130 77632 409-745-1958
Stacey Brister, prin. Fax 745-3383

West Orange-Cove Consolidated ISD 2,100/PK-12
PO Box 1107 77631 409-882-5500
Dr. O. Taylor Collins, supt. Fax 882-5467
www.woccisd.net
Career Center Vo/Tech
PO Box 1107 77631 409-882-5412
Mike Mason, dir. Fax 882-5573
West Orange-Stark HS 800/9-12
PO Box 1107 77631 409-882-5570
Mike Mason, prin. Fax 882-5573
West Orange-Stark MS 600/6-8
PO Box 1107 77631 409-882-5520
Anitrea Goodwin, prin. Fax 882-5545

Baptist Hospital Post-Sec.
608 Strickland Dr 77630 409-883-9361
Community Christian S 300/PK-12
3400 Martin Luther King Jr 77632 409-883-4531
Catherine Stewart, prin. Fax 883-8855
Lamar State College-Orange Post-Sec.
410 W Front St 77630 409-883-7750

Orangefield, Orange
Orangefield ISD 1,700/PK-12
PO Box 228 77639 409-735-5337
Mike Gentry, supt. Fax 735-2080
www.orangefieldisd.com/
Orangefield HS 500/9-12
PO Box 228 77639 409-735-3851
Stephen Patterson, prin. Fax 697-2301
Orangefield JHS 500/5-8
PO Box 228 77639 409-735-6737
Jacqueline Kyle, prin. Fax 792-9605

Orange Grove, Jim Wells, Pop. 1,402
Orange Grove ISD 1,500/PK-12
PO Box 534 78372 361-384-2495
Earl H. Luce, supt. Fax 384-2148
www.ogisd.esc2.net/
Orange Grove HS 500/9-12
PO Box 534 78372 361-384-2330
Bryan Henderson, prin. Fax 384-0206
Orange Grove JHS 400/6-8
PO Box 534 78372 361-384-2323
Tommy Moses, prin. Fax 384-9579

Ore City, Upshur, Pop. 1,166
Ore City ISD 900/PK-12
PO Box 100 75683 903-968-3300
Lynn Heflin, supt. Fax 968-3797
www.ocisd.net
Ore City HS 200/9-12
PO Box 100 75683 903-968-3300
Scot Wright, prin. Fax 968-8726
Ore City JHS 200/6-8
PO Box 100 75683 903-968-3300
Neil Hinson, prin. Fax 968-4913

Overton, Rusk, Pop. 2,321
Leveretts Chapel ISD
Supt. — See Laird Hill
Leveretts Chapel HS 100/9-12
8956 State Highway 42/135 N 75684 903-834-3181
Luther Cockerham, prin. Fax 834-6602

Overton ISD 500/PK-12
PO Box 130 75684 903-834-6145
Dr. Mark Stretcher, supt. Fax 834-6755
www.overtonisd.net/
Overton JSHS 200/7-12
PO Box 130 75684 903-834-6143
Jim Fenton, prin. Fax 834-6146

Ozona, Crockett, Pop. 3,181
Crockett County Consolidated SD 800/PK-12
PO Box 400 76943 325-392-5501
Abe Gott, supt. Fax 392-5177
www.ozonaschools.net
Ozona HS 300/9-12
PO Box 400 76943 325-392-5501
Dan Webb, prin. Fax 392-5177
Ozona MS 200/6-8
PO Box 400 76943 325-392-5501
J. Douglas Guynes, prin. Fax 392-5177

Paducah, Cottle, Pop. 1,363
Paducah ISD 100/PK-12
PO Box P 79248 806-492-3524
John Brinson, supt. Fax 492-2432
Paducah HS 100/9-12
810 Goodwin 79248 806-492-2009
Sally Piper, prin. Fax 492-2193

Paint Rock, Concho, Pop. 293
Paint Rock ISD 100/PK-12
PO Box 277 76866 325-732-4314
Brett Starkweather, supt. Fax 732-4384
paintrock.netxv.net/
Paint Rock S 100/PK-12
PO Box 277 76866 325-732-4314
Cindy Tribble, prin. Fax 732-4384

Palacios, Matagorda, Pop. 5,166
Palacios ISD 1,700/PK-12
1209 12th St 77465 361-972-5491
Paul Smith, supt. Fax 972-3567
www.palacios.k12.tx.us
Palacios HS 500/9-12
100 Shark Dr 77465 361-972-2571
Valerie Segovia, prin. Fax 972-6287
Palacios JHS 200/7-8
200 Shark Dr 77465 361-972-2417
Alton Perry, prin. Fax 972-6372

Palestine, Anderson, Pop. 17,912
Palestine ISD 3,100/PK-12
1600 S Loop 256 75801 903-731-8000
Jerry Mayo, supt. Fax 729-5588
www.palestine.esc7.net/
Palestine HS 900/9-12
1600 S Loop 256 75801 903-731-8005
Richard Scoggin, prin. Fax 731-9326
Palestine MS 500/6-8
233 Ben Milam Dr 75801 903-731-8008
Dr. Edd Schneider, prin. Fax 731-8010

Westwood ISD 1,800/PK-12
PO Box 260 75802 903-729-1776
Dr. Ann Griffin, supt. Fax 729-3696
www.westwoodisd.net
Westwood HS 500/9-12
PO Box 260 75802 903-729-1773
Judith Thomason, prin. Fax 729-8695
Westwood JHS 300/7-8
PO Box 260 75802 903-723-0423
Ronnie Shepperd, prin. Fax 723-6765

Palmer, Ellis, Pop. 2,074
Palmer ISD 1,100/PK-12
PO Box 790 75152 972-449-3389
Alan Oakley, supt. Fax 845-2112
www.palmer-isd.org
Palmer HS 300/9-12
PO Box 790 75152 972-449-3487
Phil Seay, prin. Fax 845-3517
Palmer MS 300/6-8
PO Box 790 75152 972-449-3319
Sherry Emerson, prin. Fax 845-3380

Palmview, Hidalgo, Pop. 4,421
La Joya ISD
Supt. — See La Joya
Richards MS 800/6-8
7005 Ann Richards Rd 78572 956-519-5710
Melba Lozano, prin. Fax 519-5726

Pampa, Gray, Pop. 16,744
Pampa ISD 3,300/PK-12
321 W Albert St 79065 806-669-4700
Barry Haenisch, supt. Fax 665-0506
www.pampaisd.net
Pampa HS 900/9-12
111 E Harvester Ave 79065 806-669-4800
Danny Seabourn, prin. Fax 669-4826
Pampa JHS 800/6-8
2401 Charles St 79065 806-669-4901
Randy Stephenson, prin. Fax 669-4742

Panhandle, Carson, Pop. 2,609
Panhandle ISD 700/PK-12
PO Box 1030 79068 806-537-3568
Gary Laramore, supt. Fax 537-5553
www.panhandleisd.net
Panhandle HS 200/9-12
PO Box 1030 79068 806-537-3897
Greg Slover, prin. Fax 537-3476
Panhandle JHS 200/6-8
PO Box 1030 79068 806-537-3541
John Strother, prin. Fax 537-5725

Pantego, Tarrant, Pop. 2,330

Ogle School of Hair Design Post-Sec.
2200 W Park Row Dr Ste 106 76013 817-277-6341

Paradise, Wise, Pop. 515
Paradise ISD 1,000/PK-12
338 School House Rd 76073 940-969-2501
Robert Criswell, supt. Fax 969-5008
www.pisd.net
Paradise HS 300/9-12
338 School House Rd 76073 940-969-2501
Shaun Barnett, prin. Fax 969-5009
Paradise MS 200/7-8
338 School House Rd 76073 940-969-2501
Scott McPherson, prin. Fax 969-5025

Paris, Lamar, Pop. 26,539
Chisum ISD 900/PK-12
3250 S Church St 75462 903-737-2830
Diane Stegall, supt. Fax 737-2831
chisum.esc8.net/
Chisum HS 300/9-12
3250 S Church St 75462 903-737-2800
Tommy Chalaire, prin. Fax 737-2801
Chisum MS 200/6-8
3250 S Church St 75462 903-737-2806
Cliff Chadwick, prin. Fax 737-2805

North Lamar ISD 3,200/PK-12
3201 Lewis Ln 75460 903-737-2000
James Dawson, supt. Fax 737-2008
www.northlamar.net
North Lamar HS 1,000/9-12
3201 Lewis Ln 75460 903-737-2011
Glen Martin, prin. Fax 737-2018
Stone MS 800/6-8
3201 Lewis Ln 75460 903-737-2041
Steve Sparks, prin. Fax 737-2089

Paris ISD 3,700/PK-12
1920 Clarksville St 75460 903-737-7473
Paul Trull, supt. Fax 737-7484
www.parisisd.net
Paris HS 900/9-12
2400 Jefferson Rd 75460 903-737-7400
Gary Preston, prin. Fax 737-7515
Travis MS 300/8-8
3270 Graham St 75460 903-737-7434
Mike Henry, prin. Fax 737-7534

Paris Junior College Post-Sec.
2400 Clarksville St 75460 903-785-7661

Pasadena, Harris, Pop. 143,852
Deer Park ISD
Supt. — See Deer Park
Deepwater JHS 700/6-8
501 Glenmore Dr 77503 832-668-7600
Stephen Harrell, prin. Fax 475-6138
Fairmont JHS 700/6-8
4911 Holly Bay Ct 77505 832-668-7800
Gay Dalton, prin. Fax 998-4456

Pasadena ISD 46,200/PK-12
1515 Cherrybrook Ln 77502 713-740-0000
Kirk Lewis, supt. Fax 475-7912
www.pasadenaisd.org
Bondy IS 1,100/6-8
5101 Keith Ave 77505 713-740-0430
Dan Connolly, prin. Fax 740-4152
Card Career & Technical Center Vo/Tech
4320 Crenshaw Rd 77504 713-740-0802
Sarah Wrobleski, dir. Fax 740-4081
Jackson IS 1,200/6-8
1020 Thomas Ave 77506 713-740-0440
Paula Sword, prin. Fax 740-4109
Miller IS 1,100/6-8
1002 Fairmont Pkwy 77504 713-740-0450
Joe Saavedra, prin. Fax 740-4106
Park View IS 1,000/6-8
3003 Dabney Dr 77502 713-740-0460
Rob Hasson, prin. Fax 740-4115
Pasadena HS 2,600/9-12
206 Shaver St 77506 713-740-0310
Chris Bolyard, prin. Fax 740-4085
Pasadena Memorial HS 1,700/9-12
4410 Crenshaw Rd 77504 713-740-0310
Billye Smith, prin. Fax 991-2450
Queens IS 1,100/6-8
1112 Queens Rd 77502 713-740-0470
Troy Jones, prin. Fax 740-4101
Rayburn HS 2,200/9-12
2121 Cherrybrook Ln 77502 713-740-0330
Troy McCarley, prin. Fax 920-8267
San Jacinto IS 900/6-8
3102 San Augustine Ave 77503 713-740-0480
Dianna Walker, prin. Fax 740-4153
Southmore IS 900/6-8
1200 Houston Ave 77502 713-740-0500
Lana Stahl, prin. Fax 740-4154
Tegeler Career Center Vo/Tech
4949 Burke Rd 77504 713-740-0410
Jean Cain, prin. Fax 740-4077
Community Evening S Adult
1838A E Sam Houston Pkwy S 77503 713-740-0298
Tom Swan, admin. Fax 740-4048
Other Schools – See Houston, South Houston

Faith Christian Academy 200/K-12
3519 Burke Rd 77504 713-943-9978
Dr. Joyce Ellis, prin. Fax 944-4416
First Baptist Christian Academy 500/PK-12
7500 Fairmont Pkwy 77505 281-991-9191
Joyce Harding, admin. Fax 991-7092
Harvest Christian Academy 200/PK-12
1117 Main St 77506 713-472-7228
Patricia Gehret, prin. Fax 472-4677
Interactive Learning Systems Post-Sec.
1001 Southmore Ave 77502 713-920-1120
Pasadena Academy Post-Sec.
2155 Red Bluff Rd 77506 713-473-1777
San Jacinto College Post-Sec.
8060 Spencer Hwy 77505 281-476-1501
Texas Chiropractic College Post-Sec.
5912 Spencer Hwy 77505 281-487-1170

Pattonville, Lamar
Prairiland ISD 1,000/PK-12
466 Farm Road 196 75468 903-652-6476
James R. Morton, supt. Fax 652-3738
www.prairiland.net
Prairiland HS 300/9-12
466 Farm Road 196 75468 903-652-5681
Jeff Ballard, prin. Fax 652-6400

Prairiland JHS 6-8
466 Farm Road 196 75468 903-652-5681
Jason Hostetler, prin.

Pearland, Brazoria, Pop. 56,790
Pearland ISD 14,200/PK-12
PO Box 7 77588 281-485-3203
Dr. Bonny Cain, supt. Fax 412-1231
www.pearlandisd.org
Dawson HS 1,100/9-12
4717 Bailey Rd 77584 281-727-1600
David Moody, prin. Fax 727-1660
Pearland East JHS 600/7-8
2315 Old Alvin Rd 77581 281-485-2481
Lonnie Leal, prin. Fax 412-1203
Pearland HS 2,800/9-12
3775 S Main St 77581 281-997-7445
Michele Staley, prin. Fax 412-1113
Pearland South JHS 700/7-8
4719 Bailey Rd 77584 281-727-1500
Fax 727-1580
Pearland West JHS 600/7-8
2337 Galveston Ave 77581 281-412-1222
Pam Wilson, prin. Fax 412-1228

Eagle Heights Christian Academy 400/PK-12
3005 Pearland Pkwy 77581 281-485-6330
John Stahl, prin. Fax 485-8682

Pearsall, Frio, Pop. 7,772
Pearsall ISD 2,300/PK-12
318 Berry Ranch Rd 78061 830-334-8001
Mario Sotelo, supt. Fax 334-8007
www.pearsall.k12.tx.us
Pearsall HS 600/9-12
1990 Maverick Dr 78061 830-334-8011
Margaret McCloskey, prin. Fax 334-5018
Pearsall JHS 500/6-8
607 E Alabama St 78061 830-334-8021
Julian Hernandez, prin. Fax 334-8025

Pecos, Reeves, Pop. 8,251
Pecos-Barstow-Toyah ISD 2,300/PK-12
PO Box 869 79772 432-447-7201
Manuel Espino, supt. Fax 447-3076
pbtisd.esc18.net/
Crockett MS 300/7-8
PO Box 869 79772 432-447-7251
Victor Tarin, prin. Fax 447-4853
Pecos HS 700/9-12
PO Box 869 79772 432-447-7222
Steve Lucas, prin. Fax 447-9055
Lamar AEP Adult
PO Box 869 79772 432-447-7265
Jimmy Dutchover, admin. Fax 445-3814

Penelope, Hill, Pop. 231
Penelope ISD 200/PK-12
PO Box 68 76676 254-533-2215
Harley Johnson, supt. Fax 533-2262
Penelope S 200/PK-12
PO Box 68 76676 254-533-2215
Gordon Vogel, prin. Fax 533-2262

Perrin, Jack
Perrin-Whitt Consolidated ISD 400/K-12
216 N Benson St 76486 940-798-3718
Darren Francis, supt. Fax 798-3071
www.pwcisd.net
Perrin JSHS 200/7-12
216 N Benson St 76486 940-798-3845
Carolyn Warterfield, prin. Fax 798-3071

Perryton, Ochiltree, Pop. 8,096
Perryton ISD 2,100/PK-12
PO Box 1048 79070 806-435-5478
Robin Adkins, supt. Fax 435-4689
www.perrytonisd.com
Perryton HS 500/9-12
PO Box 1048 79070 806-435-3633
Isabell Weynand, prin. Fax 435-2602
Perryton JHS 500/6-8
PO Box 1048 79070 806-435-3601
Sid Tanner, prin. Fax 435-3624

Petersburg, Hale, Pop. 1,255
Petersburg ISD 400/PK-12
PO Box 160 79250 806-667-3585
Joey Nichols, supt. Fax 667-3463
www.petersburgisd.net
Petersburg JSHS 200/7-12
PO Box 160 79250 806-667-3574
Dwain Milam, prin. Fax 667-3463

Petrolia, Clay, Pop. 806
Petrolia ISD 500/PK-12
PO Box 176 76377 940-524-3555
Derrith Welch, supt. Fax 524-3370
www.esc9.net/petrolia
Petrolia HS 200/9-12
PO Box 176 76377 940-524-3264
Wade Wesley, prin. Fax 524-3215
Petrolia JHS 100/6-8
PO Box 176 76377 940-524-3433
Micki Wesley, prin. Fax 524-3202

Pettus, Bee
Pettus ISD 400/PK-12
PO Box D 78146 361-375-2296
Tucker Rackley, supt. Fax 375-2295
www.pettusisd.esc2.net
Pettus HS 200/6-12
PO Box D 78146 361-375-2296
Dr. Susan Warner, prin. Fax 375-2295

Pflugerville, Travis, Pop. 27,531
Pflugerville ISD 17,500/PK-12
1401 Pecan St W 78660 512-594-0000
Charles Dupre, supt. Fax 594-0005
www.pflugervilleisd.net
Hendrickson HS 900/9-12
2905 FM 685 78660 512-594-1100
Dr. Nelson Coulter, prin. Fax 594-1105
Kelly Lane MS 6-8
18900 Falcon Pointe Blvd 78660 512-594-2800
Rachelle Warren, prin. Fax 594-2805
Park Crest MS 1,300/6-8
1500 N Railroad Ave 78660 512-594-2400
Steve Fuller, prin. Fax 594-2405
Pflugerville HS 2,100/9-12
1301 Pecan St W 78660 512-594-0500
Larry Bradley, prin. Fax 594-0505
Pflugerville MS 1,000/6-8
1600 Settlers Valley Dr 78660 512-594-2000
Mary Kimmins, prin. Fax 594-2005
Other Schools – See Austin

Pharr, Hidalgo, Pop. 58,986
Pharr-San Juan-Alamo ISD 27,200/PK-12
PO Box 1150 78577 956-702-5600
Arturo Guajardo, supt. Fax 702-5648
www.psja.k12.tx.us/
Johnson MS 1,200/6-8
500 E Sioux Rd 78577 956-702-5657
Juan Serna, prin. Fax 702-5661
Liberty MS 1,400/6-8
1212 Fir Rdg 78577 956-702-5826
Marisela Zepeda, prin. Fax 783-2820
Pharr-San Juan-Alamo North HS 2,100/9-12
500 E Nolana Loop 78577 956-783-3300
Antonio Lozano, prin. Fax 783-3307
Other Schools – See Alamo, San Juan

Valley View ISD 3,300/PK-12
RR 1 Box 122 78577 956-843-8825
Leonel Galaviz, supt. Fax 843-8688
www.valley-view-pharr.k12.tx.us
Valley View HS 800/9-12
RR 1 Box 122 78577 956-843-9222
Dr. Rosemarie Maciel, prin. Fax 843-9368
Valley View JHS 700/6-8
RR 1 Box 122 78577 956-843-2452
Ramiro Balderas, prin. Fax 843-7992

Oratory Academy 300/PK-12
1407 W Moore Rd 78577 956-781-3056
Fr. Mario Aviles, prin. Fax 702-3047
Southern Careers Institute Post-Sec.
1414 N Jackson Rd 78577 956-687-1415

Pilot Point, Denton, Pop. 4,042
Pilot Point ISD 1,400/PK-12
829 S Harrison St 76258 940-686-5221
Cloyce Purcell, supt. Fax 686-5220
www.pilotpointisd.com
Pilot Point HS 500/9-12
1300 N Washington St 76258 940-686-2189
Lori Sitzes, prin. Fax 686-5314
Pilot Point MS - J. Earl Selz Campus 300/7-8
828 S Harrison St 76258 940-686-2174
Larry Shuman, prin. Fax 686-2711

Pineland, Sabine, Pop. 916
West Sabine ISD 600/K-12
PO Box 869 75968 409-584-2655
Malcolm Nash, supt. Fax 584-2139
www.westsabine.esc7.net
West Sabine JSHS 300/7-12
PO Box 869 75968 409-584-2525
Debbie Lane, prin. Fax 584-2695

Pittsburg, Camp, Pop. 4,553
Pittsburg ISD 2,400/PK-12
PO Box 1189 75686 903-856-3628
Judy Pollan, supt. Fax 856-0269
pittsburgisd.net
Pittsburg HS 700/9-12
300 N Texas St 75686 903-856-3646
Jim Richardson, prin. Fax 855-3325
Pittsburg MS 400/7-8
313 Broach St 75686 903-856-6432
Fax 855-3357

Plains, Yoakum, Pop. 1,457
Plains ISD 500/PK-12
PO Box 479 79355 806-456-7401
James Haynes, supt. Fax 456-4325
plainsisd.esc17.net
Plains HS, PO Box 479 79355 100/9-12
Steven O'Quinn, prin. 806-456-7498
Plains MS, PO Box 479 79355 100/5-8
Michael Michaleson, prin. 806-456-7490

Plainview, Hale, Pop. 21,991
Plainview ISD 6,000/PK-12
PO Box 1540 79073 806-296-6392
Dr. Ron Miller, supt. Fax 296-4014
www.plainview.k12.tx.us
Estacado JHS 400/8-8
2500 W 20th St 79072 806-296-4165
Dr. Dana West, prin. Fax 296-4169
Plainview HS 1,500/9-12
1501 Quincy St 79072 806-296-4051
Lisa Kersh, prin. Fax 296-4069

Plainview Christian Academy 200/PK-12
310 S Ennis St 79072 806-296-6034
Brenda Williams, prin. Fax 296-0074
Wayland Baptist University Post-Sec.
1900 W 7th St 79072 806-296-5521

Plano, Collin, Pop. 250,096
Frisco ISD
Supt. — See Frisco
Fowler MS 6-8
3801 McDermott Rd 75025 469-633-5050
Donnie Wiseman, prin. Fax 633-5060

Plano ISD 52,200/PK-12
2700 W 15th St 75075 469-752-8100
Dr. Douglas Otto, supt. Fax 752-8096
www.pisd.edu
Armstrong MS 700/6-8
3805 Timberline Dr 75074 469-752-4600
Donella Chennault, prin. Fax 752-4601
Bowman MS 1,000/6-8
2501 Jupiter Rd 75074 469-752-4800
George King, prin. Fax 752-4801
Carpenter MS 1,000/6-8
1501 Cross Bend Rd 75023 469-752-5000
Shauna Koehne, prin. Fax 752-5001
Clark HS 1,300/9-10
523 W Spring Creek Pkwy 75023 469-752-7200
Stephanie Schmoker, prin. Fax 752-7201
Haggard MS 900/6-8
2401 Westside Dr 75075 469-752-5400
Julie-Anne Dean, prin. Fax 752-5401
Hendrick MS 800/6-8
7400 Red River Dr 75025 469-752-5600
Sheila Spencer, prin. Fax 752-5601
Jasper HS 2,000/9-10
6800 Archgate Dr 75024 469-752-7400
Michael Novotny, prin. Fax 752-7401
Plano East SHS 2,600/11-12
3000 Los Rios Blvd 75074 469-752-9000
Karen McDonald, prin. Fax 752-9001
Plano SHS 2,400/11-12
2200 Independence Pkwy 75075 469-752-9300
Dr. Doyle Dean, prin. Fax 752-9301
Plano West SHS 1,900/11-12
5601 W Parker Rd 75093 469-752-9600
Kathy King, prin. Fax 752-9601
Renner MS 1,200/6-8
5701 W Parker Rd 75093 469-752-5800
Mike Collinsworth, prin. Fax 752-5801
Rice MS 1,100/6-8
8500 Gifford Dr 75025 469-752-6000
Gail Stetler, prin. Fax 752-6001
Robinson MS 1,100/6-8
6701 Preston Meadow Dr 75024 469-752-6200
Kary Cooper, prin. Fax 752-6201
Schimelpfenig MS 900/6-8
2400 Maumelle Dr 75023 469-752-6400
Olga Sanchez-Grosscup, prin. Fax 752-6401
Shepton HS 1,600/9-10
5505 W Plano Pkwy 75093 469-752-7600
Burt Smith, prin. Fax 752-7601
Vines HS 1,300/9-10
1401 Highedge Dr 75075 469-752-7800
Roxanne Burleson, prin. Fax 752-7801
Williams HS 1,700/9-10
1717 17th St 75074 469-752-8300
Sara Bonser, prin. Fax 752-8301
Wilson MS 1,100/6-8
1001 Custer Rd 75075 469-752-6700
Selenda Anderson, prin. Fax 752-6701
Other Schools – See Dallas, Murphy

Bethany Christian S 100/PK-12
3300 W Parker Rd 75075 972-596-5811
Dr. Marvin Effa, prin. Fax 596-5814
Collin County Community College Post-Sec.
4800 Preston Park Blvd 75093 972-881-5790
DeVry University Post-Sec.
2301 W Plano Pkwy Ste 101 75075 972-943-8041
John Paul II HS 9-12
900 Coit Rd 75075 972-867-0005
Thomas Poore, prin. Fax 867-7557
Plano Christian Academy 100/K-12
1501 H Ave 75074 972-422-1722
Scott Harris, admin. Fax 422-5497
Prestonwood Christian Academy 1,400/PK-12
6801 W Park Blvd 75093 972-820-5300
Larry Taylor, hdmstr. Fax 820-5068

Pleasanton, Atascosa, Pop. 9,375
Pleasanton ISD 3,500/PK-12
831 Stadium Dr 78064 830-569-1200
Alton Fields, supt. Fax 569-2171
www.pisd.us
Pleasanton HS 1,000/9-12
831 Stadium Dr 78064 830-569-1250
Kenneth Whiteker, prin. Fax 569-1259
Pleasanton JHS 500/7-8
831 Stadium Dr 78064 830-569-1280
Deborah Garcia, prin. Fax 569-2514

Pollok, Angelina
Central ISD 1,700/PK-12
7622 N US Highway 69 75969 936-853-2216
Vernis Rogers, supt. Fax 853-2215
www.centralisd.com
Central HS 500/9-12
7622 N US Highway 69 75969 936-853-2167
Ronald Lindgren, prin. Fax 853-2208
Central JHS 400/6-8
7622 N US Highway 69 75969 936-853-2115
David Flowers, prin. Fax 853-2348

Ponder, Denton, Pop. 846
Ponder ISD 900/PK-12
PO Box 278 76259 940-479-8200
Bruce Yeager, supt. Fax 479-8209
www.ponderisd.net
Ponder HS 300/9-12
PO Box 278 76259 940-479-8210
Chance Allen, prin. Fax 479-8219
Ponder JHS 200/6-8
PO Box 278 76259 940-479-8220
Ted Heers, prin. Fax 479-8229

Poolville, Parker
Poolville ISD 500/K-12
PO Box 96 76487 817-594-4452
Terry Hamilton, supt. Fax 594-2651
www.poolville.net
Poolville HS 200/9-12
1001 Lone Star Rd 76487 817-599-5134
Jimmie Dobbs, prin. Fax 599-5171
Poolville JHS 100/6-8
PO Box 96 76487 817-594-4539
Bill Sanders, prin. Fax 594-0081

Port Aransas, Nueces, Pop. 3,667
Port Aransas ISD 600/PK-12
100 S Station St 78373 361-749-1205
Billy Wiggins, supt. Fax 749-1215
www.port-aransas.k12.tx.us
Brundrett MS 200/6-8
100 S Station St 78373 361-749-1209
Bob Byrd, prin. Fax 749-1218
Port Aransas HS 200/9-12
100 S Station St 78373 361-749-1206
Travis Longanecker, prin. Fax 749-1219

Port Arthur, Jefferson, Pop. 56,684
Port Arthur ISD 9,100/PK-12
PO Box 1388 77641 409-989-6244
Dr. James Weeks, supt. Fax 989-6268
www.paisd.org
Austin MS 500/6-8
2441 61st St 77640 409-736-1521
Dr. Edna Edwards, prin. Fax 736-0267
Edison MS 900/6-8
3501 12th St 77642 409-985-4311
Sharon Dozier-Davis, prin. Fax 985-6945
Memorial 9th Grade Campus 700/9-9
1023 Abe Lincoln Ave 77640 409-985-2551
Bannister Baptiste, prin. Fax 985-3376
Memorial HS 1,800/10-12
2200 Jefferson Dr 77642 409-962-8451
Raymond Polk, prin. Fax 963-3862
Stillwell Technical Center Vo/Tech
4801 9th Ave 77642 409-983-3286
Martha Harris, prin. Fax 983-2204

Academy of Hair Design Post-Sec.
3141 College St #A10 77642 409-813-3100
Lamar State College-Port Arthur Post-Sec.
PO Box 310 77641 409-983-4921
United Christian Academy 100/PK-12
2700 25th St 77640 409-985-8803
Rev. Darrell McCoy, prin. Fax 985-8804

Porter, Montgomery, Pop. 7,000
New Caney ISD
Supt. — See New Caney
New Caney 9th Grade Campus 9-9
22784 Highway 59 77365 281-354-4137
Charlotte Montgomery, prin. Fax 354-8725
White Oak MS 900/6-8
24161 Briar Berry Ln 77365 281-577-8800
Paula Burk, prin. Fax 354-5186

Port Isabel, Cameron, Pop. 5,373
Point Isabel ISD 2,500/PK-12
101 Port Rd 78578 956-943-0000
Dr. Estella Pineda, supt. Fax 943-0014
www.pi-isd.net/
Port Isabel HS 700/9-12
PO Box AH 78578 956-943-0030
Ronnie Rodriguez, prin. Fax 943-0048
Port Isabel JHS 500/6-8
PO Box AH 78578 956-943-0060
Joel Garcia, prin. Fax 943-0055

Portland, San Patricio, Pop. 16,219
Gregory-Portland ISD 4,300/PK-12
608 College St 78374 361-777-1091
Dr. Paul Clore, supt. Fax 777-1093
www.g-pisd.org
Gregory-Portland HS 1,300/9-12
4601 Wildcat Dr 78374 361-777-4251
Barbara Cade, prin. Fax 777-4272
Gregory-Portland JHS 700/7-8
4600 Wildcat Dr 78374 361-643-2552
Xavier Barrera, prin. Fax 643-3187

Port Lavaca, Calhoun, Pop. 11,696
Calhoun County ISD 4,200/PK-12
525 N Commerce St 77979 361-552-9728
Larry Nichols, supt. Fax 551-2648
www.calcoisd.org
Calhoun HS 1,100/9-12
201 Sandcrab Blvd 77979 361-552-3775
Edward Presley, prin. Fax 551-2620
Travis MS 900/6-8
705 N Nueces St 77979 361-552-3784
Scott Norris, prin. Fax 551-2692

Port Neches, Jefferson, Pop. 13,131
Port Neches-Groves ISD 4,700/PK-12
620 Avenue C 77651 409-722-4244
Dr. Lani Randall, supt. Fax 724-7864
www.pngisd.org
Port Neches-Groves HS 1,500/9-12
1401 Merriman St 77651 409-729-7644
Roy Esquivel, prin. Fax 722-7371
Port Neches MS 500/6-8
2031 Llano St 77651 409-722-8115
Marc Keith, prin. Fax 727-8342
Other Schools – See Groves

Post, Garza, Pop. 3,802
Post ISD 900/PK-12
PO Box 70 79356 806-495-3343
Marlin Marcum, supt. Fax 495-2945
www.post.k12.tx.us
Post HS 300/9-12
PO Box 70 79356 806-495-2770
John Berry, prin. Fax 495-2792
Post MS 200/6-8
PO Box 70 79356 806-495-2874
Judy Miers, prin. Fax 495-2426

Poteet, Atascosa, Pop. 3,626
Poteet ISD 1,700/PK-12
PO Box 138 78065 830-742-3567
James Henry, supt. Fax 742-3332
www.poteet.k12.tx.us
Poteet HS 500/9-12
PO Box 138 78065 830-742-3522
Andres Castillo, prin. Fax 742-8497
Poteet JHS 200/7-8
PO Box 138 78065 830-742-3571
Carveth Hall, prin. Fax 742-8495

Poth, Wilson, Pop. 2,145
Poth ISD 800/PK-12
PO Box 250 78147 830-484-3330
David Wehmeyer, supt. Fax 484-2961
www.pothisd.us
Poth HS 200/9-12
PO Box 250 78147 830-484-3322
Frank Hosek, prin. Fax 484-3304
Poth JHS 200/6-8
PO Box 250 78147 830-484-3323
Scott Caloss, prin. Fax 484-3682

Pottsboro, Grayson, Pop. 1,992
Pottsboro ISD 1,300/PK-12
PO Box 555 75076 903-786-3051
Dr. Kyle Collier, supt. Fax 786-9085
www.pottsboroisd.org/
Pottsboro HS 400/9-12
PO Box 555 75076 903-786-2470
Paul Holliday, prin. Fax 786-6349
Pottsboro MS 300/6-8
PO Box 555 75076 903-786-9702
Wendi Russell, prin. Fax 786-4902

Prairie Lea, Caldwell
Prairie Lea ISD 200/PK-12
PO Box 9 78661 512-488-2370
Jesus Lopez, supt. Fax 488-9006
Prairie Lea S 200/PK-12
PO Box 9 78661 512-488-2328
Darren Kesselus, prin. Fax 488-2425

Prairie View, Waller, Pop. 4,658

Prairie View A&M University Post-Sec.
PO Box 519 77446 936-857-3311

Premont, Jim Wells, Pop. 2,836
Premont ISD 800/PK-12
PO Box 530 78375 361-348-3915
David Garza, supt. Fax 348-2882
www.premontisd.net
Premont HS 300/9-12
PO Box B 78375 361-348-3915
Irma Johnson, prin. Fax 348-2914
Premont JHS 200/6-8
PO Box 769 78375 361-348-3915
Julie Chancler, prin. Fax 348-2751

Presidio, Presidio, Pop. 4,775
Presidio ISD 1,600/PK-12
PO Box 1401 79845 432-229-3275
Dr. Douglas Karr, supt. Fax 229-4228
www.presidio.esc18.net
Franco MS 300/6-8
PO Box 1401 79845 432-229-3113
Teresa Porras, prin. Fax 229-4087
Presidio HS 500/9-12
PO Box 1401 79845 432-229-3365
Murphy Quick, prin. Fax 229-4625

Price, Rusk
Carlisle ISD 600/PK-12
PO Box 187 75687 903-861-3801
Michael Payne, supt. Fax 861-3932
www.carl.sprnet.org/cisd2.htm
Carlisle HS 200/7-12
PO Box 187 75687 903-861-3811
Cathy Amonett, prin. Fax 861-0100

Priddy, Mills
Priddy ISD 100/K-12
PO Box 40 76870 325-966-3323
Robby Stuteville, supt. Fax 966-3380
www.centex-edu.net/priddy/
Priddy S 100/K-12
PO Box 40 76870 325-966-3323
Bob Rauch, prin. Fax 966-3380

Princeton, Collin, Pop. 4,115
Princeton ISD 2,000/PK-12
321 Panther Pkwy 75407 469-952-5400
Philip Anthony, supt. Fax 736-3505
www.princetonisd.net
Clark JHS 400/7-8
301 Panther Pkwy 75407 972-736-3503
Greg Tabor, prin. Fax 736-5903
Princeton HS 700/9-12
1000 E Princeton Dr 75407 469-952-5400
Robert Lovelady, prin. Fax 736-5902

Progreso, Hidalgo, Pop. 5,082
Progreso ISD 1,300/PK-12
PO Box 610 78579 956-565-3002
Dr. Fernando Castillo, supt. Fax 565-2128
www.progreso-isd.net/
Progreso HS 500/9-12
PO Box 610 78579 956-565-4142
Mischellene Pemelton, prin. Fax 565-6029
Thompson MS 300/5-8
PO Box 610 78579 956-565-6539
Mischellene Pemelton, prin. Fax 565-1718

Prosper, Collin, Pop. 4,207
Prosper ISD 900/PK-12
PO Box 100 75078 972-346-3316
Drew Watkins, supt. Fax 346-9247
www.prosper-isd.net
Prosper HS 400/9-12
PO Box 490 75078 972-346-2455
Mike Brown, prin. Fax 346-9246
Prosper MS 300/7-8
PO Box 100 75078 972-346-9114
Andy Baker, prin. Fax 346-9248

Quanah, Hardeman, Pop. 2,715
Quanah ISD 600/PK-12
PO Box 150 79252 940-663-2281
Terry Allen, supt. Fax 663-2875
www.qisd.net
Quanah HS 200/9-12
PO Box 150 79252 940-663-2791
Jack Campsey, prin. Fax 663-6447
Travis MS 100/7-8
PO Box 150 79252 940-663-2226
Mike Hale, prin. Fax 663-6361

Queen City, Cass, Pop. 1,591
Queen City ISD 1,100/PK-12
PO Box 128 75572 903-796-8256
Rob Barnwell, supt. Fax 796-0248
www.qcisd.net
Queen City HS 300/9-12
PO Box 128 75572 903-796-8259
Wes Kirkham, prin. Fax 796-8258
Upchurch MS 300/5-8
PO Box 128 75572 903-796-6412
Charlotte Williams, prin. Fax 796-0834

Quinlan, Hunt, Pop. 1,457
Boles ISD 500/PK-12
7071 FM 2101 75474 903-883-4464
Dr. Graham Sweeney, supt. Fax 883-4531
boles.ednet10.net
Boles HS 200/9-12
7071 FM 2101 75474 903-883-2918
Carol Brown, prin. Fax 883-4531
Boles MS 200/5-8
7071 FM 2101 75474 903-883-4464
Mikayle Moreland, prin. Fax 883-4531

Quinlan ISD 2,800/PK-12
301 E Main St 75474 903-356-3293
Larry Johnson, supt. Fax 356-2339
www.quinlanisd.net
Ford HS 900/9-12
10064 Business Highway 34 S 75474 903-356-2155
Beverly Newcomb, prin. Fax 356-3558
Thompson MS 700/6-8
423 Panther Path 75474 903-356-2154
Michael Tull, prin. Fax 356-2414

Quitman, Wood, Pop. 2,198
Quitman ISD 1,100/PK-12
1101 E Goode St 75783 903-763-5000
Bill Travis, supt. Fax 763-2710
www.quitmanisd.net/
Quitman HS 300/9-12
1101 E Goode St 75783 903-763-5000
Tony Gilbreath, prin. Fax 763-2589
Quitman JHS 200/7-8
1101 E Goode St 75783 903-763-5000
Andrea Middendorf, prin. Fax 763-2589

Ralls, Crosby, Pop. 2,122
Ralls ISD 600/PK-12
810 Avenue I 79357 806-253-2509
Deanna Logan, supt. Fax 253-2508
www.rallsisd.addr.com
Ralls HS 200/9-12
810 Avenue I 79357 806-253-2571
Deanna Logan, prin. Fax 253-2609
Ralls MS 100/6-8
810 Avenue I 79357 806-253-2549
Michael Allbright, prin. Fax 253-4031

Randolph AFB, Bexar
Randolph Field ISD 1,100/PK-12
Building 1225 78148 210-357-2300
Dr. Barbara Maddox, supt. Fax 357-2469
www.randolph-field.k12.tx.us
Randolph HS 300/9-12
Building 1225 78148 210-357-2400
Bruce Cannon, prin. Fax 357-2475
Randolph MS 200/6-8
Building 1225 78148 210-357-2400
Bruce Cannon, prin. Fax 357-2475

Ranger, Eastland, Pop. 2,535
Ranger ISD 400/PK-12
1842 E Loop 254 76470 254-647-1187
Doyle Russell, supt. Fax 647-5215
www.ranger.esc14.net
Ranger JSHS 100/6-12
1842 E Loop 254 76470 254-647-3216
John Schaefer, prin. Fax 647-1895

Ranger College Post-Sec.
1100 College Cir 76470 254-647-3234

Rankin, Upton, Pop. 725
Rankin ISD 200/PK-12
PO Box 90 79778 432-693-2461
Tena Gray, supt. Fax 693-2353
www.rankin.k12.tx.us
Rankin JSHS 100/7-12
PO Box 90 79778 432-693-2451
Paula Hill, prin. Fax 693-2453

Raymondville, Willacy, Pop. 9,483
Raymondville ISD 2,500/PK-12
1 Bearkat Blvd 78580 956-689-2471
Eloy Castaneda, supt. Fax 689-5869
www.raymondvilleisd.org/
Green MS 600/6-8
1 Bearkat Blvd 78580 956-689-2471
Joel Garcia, prin. Fax 689-5330
Raymondville HS 600/9-12
1 Bearkat Blvd 78580 956-689-2471
Norma Cavazos, prin. Fax 689-8152

Raywood, Liberty
Hull-Daisetta ISD
Supt. — See Daisetta
Hull-Daisetta JHS 200/6-8
F M 160 77582 936-536-6321
Frederick Freeman, prin. Fax 587-4093

Red Oak, Ellis, Pop. 7,171
Red Oak ISD 4,800/PK-12
PO Box 9000 75154 972-617-2941
Craig Stockstill, supt. Fax 617-4333
www.redoakisd.org
Red Oak HS 1,600/9-12
PO Box 9000 75154 972-617-3535
Bobby Stults, prin. Fax 617-4355
Red Oak JHS 800/7-8
PO Box 9000 75154 972-617-0066
Morris Watson, prin. Fax 617-4377

Ovilla Christian S 400/PK-12
3251 Ovilla Rd 75154 972-617-1177
Julie Weyand, admin. Fax 617-2275

Redwater, Bowie, Pop. 883
Redwater ISD 1,100/PK-12
PO Box 347 75573 903-671-3481
Dr. Max Thompson, supt. Fax 671-2019
redwater.esc8.net/
Redwater HS, PO Box 347 75573 400/9-12
Amy Roberts, prin. 903-671-3421
Redwater JHS 200/7-8
PO Box 347 75573 903-671-3227
Bebe Hayes, prin. Fax 671-2019

Refugio, Refugio, Pop. 2,797
Refugio ISD 500/K-12
212 W Vance St 78377 361-526-2325
W.F. Spivey, supt. Fax 526-2326
www.refugioisd.net/
Refugio JSHS 300/7-12
212 W Vance St 78377 361-526-2344
David Solomon, prin. Fax 526-1075

Rhome, Wise, Pop. 866
Northwest ISD
Supt. — See Justin
Chisholm Trail MS 300/6-8
583 FM 3433 76078 817-215-0600
Dr. Philo Waters, prin. Fax 215-0648

Rice, Ellis, Pop. 924
Rice ISD 700/PK-12
1302 SW McKinney St 75155 903-326-4287
Judith Pritchett, supt. Fax 326-4164
www.rice-isd.org
Rice JSHS 400/6-12
1400 S McKinney St 75155 903-326-4502
Tom Herrin, prin. Fax 326-5042

Richards, Grimes
Richards ISD 200/K-12
PO Box 308 77873 936-851-2364
Martey Ainsworth, supt. Fax 851-2210
Richards JSHS 100/7-12
PO Box 308 77873 936-851-2364
Marty Ainsworth, prin. Fax 851-2210

Richardson, Dallas, Pop. 99,187
Richardson ISD 32,300/PK-12
400 S Greenville Ave 75081 469-593-0000
Patti Kieker, supt. Fax 593-0402
www.risd.org
Apollo JHS 900/7-9
1600 Apollo Rd 75081 469-593-7900
Jack Noteware, prin. Fax 593-7911

Berkner HS 2,100/10-12
1600 E Spring Valley Rd 75081 469-593-7000
Ron Griffen, prin. Fax 593-7211
Pearce HS 1,500/10-12
1600 N Coit Rd 75080 469-593-5000
Karen Neal, prin. Fax 593-5169
Richardson Arts Law & Science Magnet HS 10-12
1250 W Belt Line Rd 75080 469-593-3038
Henry Hall, admin. Fax 593-3082
Richardson HS 1,500/10-12
1250 W Belt Line Rd 75080 469-593-3000
Charles Pickitt, prin. Fax 593-3010
Richardson-North JHS 800/7-9
1820 N Floyd Rd 75080 469-593-5400
Melissa Gassman, prin. Fax 593-5434
Richardson-West JHS Tech Magnet 900/7-9
1309 Holly Dr 75080 469-593-3700
Walter Kelly, prin. Fax 593-3666
Other Schools – See Dallas

Alexander S 100/8-12
409 International Pkwy 75081 972-690-9210
Andrew Cody, prin. Fax 690-9284
ATI Career Training Center Post-Sec.
1100 E Campbell Rd Ste 250 75081 214-646-8460
Canyon Creek Christian Academy 500/PK-12
2800 Custer Pkwy 75080 972-231-4890
Dr. Steve Lawrence, admin. Fax 234-8414
Compu Tech Consultants School Post-Sec.
811 S Central Expy Ste 500 75080 214-570-0404
ITT Technical Institute Post-Sec.
2101 Waterview Pkwy 75080 972-279-0500
PCI Health Training Center Post-Sec.
1300 International Pkwy 75081 214-630-0568
Richardson Adventist S 100/1-10
1201 W Belt Line Rd 75080 972-238-1183
Fax 644-3488
University of Texas at Dallas Post-Sec.
PO Box 830688 75083 972-690-2111

Richland Hills, Tarrant, Pop. 8,047
Birdville ISD
Supt. — See Haltom City
Richland MS 600/6-8
7400 Hovenkamp Ave 76118 817-547-4400
Cheri Sizemore, prin. Fax 595-5139

Richland Springs, San Saba, Pop. 340
Richland Springs ISD 200/K-12
700 US Highway 190 W 76871 325-452-3524
Travis Winn, supt. Fax 452-3230
www.rscoyotes.net
Richland Springs S 200/K-12
700 US Highway 190 W 76871 325-452-3434
Don Fowler, prin. Fax 452-3580

Richmond, Fort Bend, Pop. 13,262
Fort Bend ISD
Supt. — See Sugar Land
Bush HS 2,300/9-12
6707 FM 1464 Rd 77469 281-634-6060
Shirley Rose, prin. Fax 634-6066
Travis HS 9-12
11111 Harlem Rd 77469 281-634-7000
Jeryl Kyle, prin. Fax 634-7010

Lamar Consolidated ISD
Supt. — See Rosenberg
Briscoe JHS 1,300/6-8
4300 FM 723 Rd 77469 832-223-4000
Mike Semmler, prin. Fax 223-4001
Foster HS 1,600/9-12
4400 FM 723 Rd 77469 832-223-3800
Gene Tomas, prin. Fax 223-3801

Calvary Episcopal S 300/PK-12
1201 Austin St 77469 281-342-3161
Malcolm Smith, dir. Fax 232-9449

Riesel, McLennan, Pop. 1,004
Riesel ISD 600/PK-12
600 E Frederick St 76682 254-896-6411
Steve Clugston, supt. Fax 896-2981
www.rieselisd.org
Riesel JSHS 300/7-12
600 E Frederick St 76682 254-896-3171
David Wren, prin. Fax 896-2981

Rio Grande City, Starr, Pop. 13,651
Rio Grande City ISD 9,600/PK-12
1 S Fort Ringgold St 78582 956-716-6702
Roel Gonzalez, supt. Fax 487-8506
www.rgccisd.org/
Ringgold MS 1,400/6-8
212 Crockett St 78582 956-716-6851
Adolfo Pena, prin. Fax 716-6807
Rio Grande City 9th Grade Campus 800/9-9
1 S Fort Ringgold St 78582 956-488-6000
Joel Trigo, prin.
Rio Grande City SHS 1,500/10-12
144 N FM 3167 78582 956-488-6000
Jorge Recio, prin. Fax 488-6050
Other Schools – See Grulla

Rio Hondo, Cameron, Pop. 2,082
Rio Hondo ISD 2,200/PK-12
215 W Colorado St 78583 956-748-1000
Anneliese McMinn, supt. Fax 748-1038
www.riohondoisd.net
Rio Hondo HS 600/9-12
215 W Colorado St 78583 956-748-1200
Michell Everett, prin. Fax 748-1204
Rio Hondo JHS 500/6-8
215 W Colorado St 78583 956-748-1150
Ida Stevens, prin. Fax 748-1168

Rio Vista, Johnson, Pop. 728
Rio Vista ISD 900/PK-12
PO Box 369 76093 817-373-2241
Dr. Rock McNulty, supt. Fax 373-2076
www.rvisd.net
Rio Vista HS 300/9-12
PO Box 369 76093 817-373-2669
Andra Sparks, prin. Fax 373-3047
Rio Vista MS 200/5-8
PO Box 369 76093 817-373-2009
Gary Peacock, prin. Fax 373-3046

Rising Star, Eastland, Pop. 842
Rising Star ISD 300/PK-12
PO Box 37 76471 254-643-2717
Bill Foster, supt. Fax 643-1922
www.risingstarisd.com/
Rising Star JSHS 100/7-12
PO Box 37 76471 254-643-3521
Buddy Hale, prin. Fax 643-5408

Riviera, Kleberg
Riviera ISD 500/PK-12
203 Seahawk Dr 78379 361-296-3101
Dr. Cynthia Clary, supt. Fax 296-3108
www.rivieraisd.esc2.net
De La Paz MS 100/6-8
203 Seahawk Dr 78379 361-296-3610
Josephine Smith, prin. Fax 296-3890
Kaufer HS 200/9-12
203 Seahawk Dr 78379 361-296-3607
Brian Roberts, prin. Fax 296-3108

Roanoke, Denton, Pop. 3,518

Clariden S 200/PK-12
100 Clariden Ranch Rd 76262 682-237-0400
David Deuel, hdmstr. Fax 831-0300

Robert Lee, Coke, Pop. 1,070
Robert Lee ISD 300/PK-12
1323 W Hamilton St 76945 325-453-4555
Aaron Hood, supt. Fax 453-2326
robertlee.netxv.net/
Robert Lee HS 100/7-12
1323 W Hamilton St 76945 325-453-4557
Dwin Nanny, prin. Fax 453-2326

Robinson, McLennan, Pop. 9,062
Robinson ISD 2,100/PK-12
500 W Lyndale Ave 76706 254-662-0194
Micheal Hope, supt. Fax 662-0215
www.robinson.k12.tx.us
Robinson HS 700/9-12
500 W Lyndale Ave 76706 254-662-3840
Tim VanCleave, prin. Fax 662-4007
Robinson JHS 500/6-8
500 W Lyndale Ave 76706 254-662-3843
Barry Gann, prin. Fax 662-1845

Robstown, Nueces, Pop. 12,484
Robstown ISD 3,800/PK-12
801 N 1st St 78380 361-767-6600
Dr. Roberto E. Garcia, supt. Fax 387-6311
www.robstownisd.org/
Robstown HS 900/9-12
609 Highway 44 78380 361-387-5999
Roel Lara, prin. Fax 387-8960
Seale JHS 600/7-8
401 E Avenue G 78380 361-767-6631
Raul Garza, prin. Fax 387-0202

Roby, Fisher, Pop. 638
Roby Consolidated ISD 300/PK-12
PO Box 519 79543 325-776-2222
Wesley Hays, supt. Fax 776-2823
www.roby.esc14.net/
Roby HS 100/9-12
PO Box 519 79543 325-776-2223
Heath Dickson, prin. Fax 776-2823

Rochelle, McCulloch
Rochelle ISD 200/K-12
PO Box 167 76872 325-243-5224
Steve Butler, supt. Fax 243-5216
www.centex-edu.net/~rochelle/
Rochelle S 200/K-12
PO Box 167 76872 325-243-5224
Joe Skalak, prin. Fax 243-5216

Rochester, Haskell, Pop. 347
Haskell CISD
Supt. — See Haskell
Rochester JHS, PO Box 140 79544 7-8
Reida Penman, prin. 940-743-3260

Rockdale, Milam, Pop. 6,048
Rockdale ISD 1,900/PK-12
PO Box 632 76567 512-430-6000
Walter Pond, supt. Fax 446-3460
www.rockdaleisd.net
Rockdale HS 500/9-12
PO Box 632 76567 512-430-6140
Allen Sanders, prin. Fax 446-3512
Rockdale JHS 400/6-8
PO Box 632 76567 512-430-6100
Richard Kolek, prin. Fax 446-2597

Rockport, Aransas, Pop. 9,041
Aransas County ISD 3,400/PK-12
PO Box 907 78381 361-790-2212
P. Wayne Johnson, supt. Fax 790-2299
www.acisd.org
Rockport-Fulton HS 1,000/9-12
PO Box 907 78381 361-790-2220
Tisha Piwetz, prin. Fax 790-2206
Rockport-Fulton MS 900/6-8
PO Box 907 78381 361-790-2230
Kim James, prin. Fax 790-2030

Rocksprings, Edwards, Pop. 1,181
Rocksprings ISD 400/PK-12
PO Box 157 78880 830-683-4137
Ms. Henri Gearing, supt. Fax 683-4141
www.rockspringsisd.net
Rocksprings HS 100/9-12
PO Box 157 78880 830-683-4136
Jeff Dabney, prin. Fax 683-4141

Rockwall, Rockwall, Pop. 29,354
Rockwall ISD 10,000/PK-12
1050 Williams St 75087 972-771-0605
Dr. Gene Burton, supt. Fax 771-2637
www.rockwallisd.com
Cain MS 800/7-8
6620 FM 3097 75032 972-772-1170
Sarah Watkins, prin. Fax 772-2414
Rockwall-Heath HS 9-10
801 Laurence Dr 75032 972-772-2474
Dr. Charles Nix, prin. Fax 698-2608
Rockwall HS 2,200/10-12
901 Yellow Jacket Ln 75087 972-771-7339
Dr. Mark Le Master, prin. Fax 772-2016
Utley Freshman Center 900/9-9
1201 Townsend Dr 75087 972-771-5281
Randy Cordial, prin. Fax 772-1164
Williams MS 800/7-8
625 E FM 552 75087 972-771-8313
Billy Pringle, prin. Fax 772-2043

Heritage Christian Academy 300/PK-12
1408 S Goliad St 75087 972-772-3003
Kevin Fields, hdmstr. Fax 772-3770

Rogers, Bell, Pop. 1,102
Rogers ISD 900/PK-12
1 Eagle Dr 76569 254-642-3802
Katie Ryan, supt. Fax 642-3851
www.rogers.k12.tx.us
Rogers HS 300/9-12
1 Eagle Dr 76569 254-642-3224
Robert Chappell, prin. Fax 642-3037
Rogers MS 200/6-8
1 Eagle Dr 76569 254-642-3011
Genie Allison, prin. Fax 642-0033

Roma, Starr, Pop. 10,900
Roma ISD 6,300/PK-12
PO Box 187 78584 956-849-1377
Jesus O. Guerra, supt. Fax 849-3118
www.romaisd.com/
Roma HS 1,500/9-12
PO Box 187 78584 956-849-1333
Noe Muniz, prin. Fax 849-2655
Roma MS 900/7-8
PO Box 187 78584 956-849-1434
Teresa Ramirez, prin. Fax 849-1895

Ropesville, Hockley, Pop. 524
Ropes ISD 300/PK-12
304 Ranch Rd 79358 806-562-4031
Gary E. Lehnen, supt. Fax 562-4059
www.ropesisd.com/
Ropes S 300/PK-12
304 Ranch Rd 79358 806-562-4031
Joel Willmon, prin. Fax 562-4059

Roscoe, Nolan, Pop. 1,273
Highland ISD 200/PK-12
6625 FM 608 79545 325-766-3652
Guy Nelson, supt. Fax 766-2281
www.highland.esc14.net/
Highland S 200/PK-12
6625 FM 608 79545 325-766-3652
Duane Hyde, prin. Fax 766-3869

Roscoe ISD 300/PK-12
PO Box 579 79545 325-766-3629
Kim Alexander, supt. Fax 766-3138
www.roscoe.esc14.net
Roscoe JSHS, PO Box 10 79545 200/7-12
Frank Young, prin. 325-766-3327

Rosebud, Falls, Pop. 1,394
Rosebud-Lott ISD 900/PK-12
PO Box 638 76570 254-583-4510
Howell Wright, supt. Fax 583-2602
www.rosebudlottisd.org/
Rosebud-Lott HS 300/9-12
PO Box 638 76570 254-583-7967
Walter Key, prin. Fax 583-1130
Rosebud-Lott JHS 100/7-8
PO Box 638 76570 254-583-7967
Walter Key, prin. Fax 583-1130

Rosenberg, Fort Bend, Pop. 30,322
Lamar Consolidated ISD 18,500/PK-12
3911 Avenue I 77471 832-223-0110
Dr. Thomas Randle, supt. Fax 223-0111
www.lcisd.org
George JHS 900/7-8
4601 Airport Ave 77471 832-223-3600
Kelly Waters, prin. Fax 223-3601
Lamar Consolidated HS 1,700/9-12
4606 Mustang Ave 77471 832-223-3000
J. Walter Bevers, prin. Fax 223-3001
Lamar JHS 1,000/7-8
4814 Mustang Ave 77471 832-223-3200
Victoria Bedo, prin. Fax 223-3201
Terry HS 1,700/9-12
5500 Avenue N 77471 832-223-3400
Vera Wehring, prin. Fax 223-3401
Community Center Adult
1000 E Stadium Dr 77471 832-223-0960
Bobby Stanley, admin. Fax 223-0961
Other Schools – See Richmond

Rotan, Fisher, Pop. 1,486
Rotan ISD 400/PK-12
102 N McKinley Ave 79546 325-735-2332
Mickey Early, supt. Fax 735-2686
www.rotan.org
Rotan HS 100/9-12
102 N McKinley Ave 79546 325-735-3041
Bob Spikes, prin. Fax 735-2686
Rotan JHS 100/5-8
102 N McKinley Ave 79546 325-735-3162
Mickey Early, prin. Fax 735-2686

Round Rock, Williamson, Pop. 86,316
Round Rock ISD 36,400/PK-12
1311 Round Rock Ave 78681 512-464-5000
Jesus Chavez Ph.D., supt. Fax 464-5090
www.roundrockisd.org
Chisholm Trail MS 1,000/6-8
500 Oakridge Dr 78681 512-428-2500
Diana Negrete, prin. Fax 428-2629
Fulkes MS 700/6-8
300 W Anderson Ave 78664 512-428-3100
Nancy Guererro, prin. Fax 428-3240
Hopewell MS 1,200/6-8
1535 Gulf Way, 512-464-5200
Anthony Watson, prin. Fax 464-5349
Ridgeview MS 1,000/6-8
2000 Via Sonoma Trl 78664 512-424-8400
Jennifer Morrow, prin. Fax 424-8540
Round Rock HS 2,100/9-12
300 N Lake Creek Dr 78681 512-464-6000
Mark Gesch, prin. Fax 464-6190
Round Rock Opportunity Center Vo/Tech
931 Luther Peterson, 512-428-2900
Rene Posey, prin. Fax 428-2943
Stony Point 9th Grade Center 700/9-9
1901 Sunrise Rd 78664 512-424-8800
Albert Hernandez, prin. Fax 424-8940
Stony Point SHS 2,000/10-12
1801 Bowman Rd 78664 512-428-7000
T.J. Dilworth, prin. Fax 428-7280
Other Schools – See Austin

Round Rock Christian Academy 400/PK-12
301 N Lake Creek Dr 78681 512-255-4491
Susan Owen, prin. Fax 255-6043

Rowlett, Dallas, Pop. 53,664
Garland ISD
Supt. — See Garland
Coyle MS 1,200/6-8
4500 Skyline Dr 75088 972-475-3711
Dretha Burris, prin. Fax 412-7222
Rowlett HS 2,600/9-12
4700 Kirby Rd 75088 972-463-1712
Dr. Marlene Hammerle, prin. Fax 412-2951
Schrade MS 1,300/6-8
6201 Danridge Rd 75089 972-463-8790
Jim Thomas, prin. Fax 463-8793

Rockwall Christian Academy 300/PK-12
6005 Dalrock Rd 75088 972-412-8266
Jeanne Zakem, supt. Fax 463-3746
Rowlett Christian Academy 100/PK-12
8200 Schrade Rd 75088 972-412-7761
Dena Gregory, admin. Fax 412-2320

Roxton, Lamar, Pop. 699
Roxton ISD 200/PK-12
PO Box 307 75477 903-346-3213
Dr. Kenneth Hall, supt. Fax 346-3356
roxton.esc8.net
Roxton HS 100/7-12
PO Box 307 75477 903-346-3213
Ronnie Baker, prin. Fax 346-3356

Royse City, Rockwall, Pop. 5,589
Royse City ISD 2,400/PK-12
PO Box 479 75189 972-635-2413
Mike Harris, supt. Fax 635-7037
www.rcisd.org
Royse City HS 700/9-12
PO Box 479 75189 972-636-9991
Tony Gauntt, prin. Fax 635-2906
Royse City MS 400/6-8
PO Box 479 75189 972-635-9544
Andy Molck, prin. Fax 635-2531

Rule, Haskell, Pop. 639
Rule ISD 200/PK-12
1100 Union Ave 79547 940-997-2521
David Parr, supt. Fax 997-2446
www.rule.esc14.net
Rule S 200/PK-12
1100 Union Ave 79547 940-997-2246
Jimmy New, prin. Fax 997-2446

Runge, Karnes, Pop. 1,084
Runge ISD 300/PK-12
PO Box 158 78151 830-239-4315
Ernest Havner, supt. Fax 239-4816
www.rungeisd.org
Runge JSHS 100/7-12
PO Box 158 78151 830-239-4864
Scott Cutler, prin. Fax 239-4816

Rusk, Cherokee, Pop. 5,234
Rusk ISD 1,900/PK-12
203 E 7th St 75785 903-683-5592
Dr. James Largent, supt. Fax 683-2104
www.ruskisd.net
Rusk HS 500/9-12
203 E 7th St 75785 903-683-5401
Ricky Hassell, prin. Fax 683-6090
Rusk JHS 500/6-8
203 E 7th St 75785 903-683-2502
John Burkhalter, prin. Fax 683-4363

Sabinal, Uvalde, Pop. 1,656
Sabinal ISD 600/PK-12
PO Box 338 78881 830-988-2472
Scott Dahlin, supt. Fax 988-7151
www.sabinal.k12.tx.us
Sabinal HS 200/9-12
PO Box 338 78881 830-988-2475
Sean Johnston, prin. Fax 988-7170
Sabinal JHS 100/7-8
PO Box 338 78881 830-988-2475
Sean Johnston, prin. Fax 988-7170

Sabine Pass, Jefferson
Sabine Pass ISD 200/PK-12
PO Box 1148 77655 409-971-2321
Malcolm Nash, supt. Fax 971-2120
www.spisd.com
Sabine Pass S 200/PK-12
PO Box 1148 77655 409-971-2321
Kristi Heid, prin. Fax 971-2120

Sachse, Collin, Pop. 17,009
Garland ISD
Supt. — See Garland
Sachse HS 2,100/9-12
3901 Miles Rd 75048 972-414-7450
Steve Hammerle, prin. Fax 414-7458

Sadler, Grayson, Pop. 439
S & S Consolidated ISD 900/PK-12
PO Box 837 76264 903-564-6051
Bill Gentzel, supt. Fax 564-3492
www.sandscisd.net
S & S Consolidated HS 300/9-12
PO Box 837 76264 903-564-3768
Jay Roberts, prin. Fax 564-7308
S & S Consolidated MS 200/6-8
PO Box 837 76264 903-564-7626
Dr. Lee Yeager, prin. Fax 564-7857

Saginaw, Tarrant, Pop. 17,701
Eagle Mtn.-Saginaw ISD
Supt. — See Fort Worth
Saginaw HS 9-12
800 N Blue Mound Rd 76131 817-306-0914
Ric Canterbury, prin. Fax 306-1344

Trinity Baptist Temple Academy 100/PK-12
6045 WJ Boaz Rd 76179 817-237-4255
Woody Godbey, supt. Fax 237-5233

Saint Jo, Montague, Pop. 969
Saint Jo ISD 300/PK-12
PO Box L 76265 940-995-2668
Larry Smith, supt. Fax 995-2026
www.saintjoisd.net
Saint Jo JSHS 100/7-12
PO Box L 76265 940-995-2532
David Freeman, prin. Fax 995-2087

Salado, Bell, Pop. 1,970
Salado ISD 1,200/PK-12
PO Box 98 76571 254-947-5479
Robin Battershell, supt. Fax 947-5605
www.saladoisd.org
Salado HS 400/9-12
PO Box 98 76571 254-947-5429
Kay Matthews, prin. Fax 947-6984
Salado IS 400/5-8
PO Box 98 76571 254-947-1700
Joe Palmer, prin. Fax 947-6954

Saltillo, Hopkins
Saltillo ISD 300/PK-12
PO Box 269 75478 903-537-2386
Paul Jones, supt. Fax 537-2191
www.esc8.net/saltillo
Saltillo S 300/PK-12
PO Box 269 75478 903-537-2386
Ben Tyler, prin. Fax 537-2191

Samnorwood, Collingsworth
Samnorwood ISD 100/PK-12
PO Box 765 79077 806-256-2039
Shawn Read, supt. Fax 256-3974
www.samnorwoodisd.net/
Samnorwood S 100/PK-12
PO Box 765 79077 806-256-2039
Gerry Nickell, prin. Fax 256-3974

San Angelo, Tom Green, Pop. 88,014
Grape Creek ISD 600/PK-12
8207 US Highway 87 N 76901 325-658-7823
Frank Walter, supt. Fax 658-8719
www.grapecreek.org
Grape Creek HS 400/9-12
8207 US Highway 87 N 76901 325-653-1852
Chris duBois, prin. Fax 653-3568
Grape Creek MS 300/6-8
8207 US Highway 87 N 76901 325-655-1735
Greg Baucom, prin. Fax 657-2997

San Angelo ISD 13,400/PK-12
1621 University Ave 76904 325-947-3700
Dr. Carol Bonds, supt. Fax 947-3771
www.saisd.org
Central Freshman Campus 200/9-9
218 N Oakes St 76903 325-659-3576
Keeva Frazier, prin. Fax 659-3583
Central HS 2,300/10-12
100 Cottonwood St 76901 325-659-3400
Joe Coleman, prin. Fax 659-3413
Glenn MS 600/7-8
2201 University Ave 76904 325-947-3841
Bill Waters, prin. Fax 947-3847
Lake View HS 1,200/9-12
900 E 43rd St 76903 325-659-3500
Matt Smith, prin. Fax 653-8661
Lee MS 600/7-8
2500 Sherwood Way 76901 325-947-3871
J. D. Koehn, prin. Fax 947-3890
Lincoln MS 1,000/6-8
255 E 50th St 76903 325-659-3550
Sue Taylor, prin. Fax 659-3559

American Commercial College Post-Sec.
3177 Executive Dr 76904 325-942-6797
Angelo State University Post-Sec.
ASU Sta # 11014 76909 325-942-2041
Cornerstone Christian S 200/PK-12
1502 N Jefferson St 76901 325-655-3439
Grady Roe, admin. Fax 658-8998
Howard College Post-Sec.
3197 Executive Dr 76904 325-944-9585
Shannon West Texas Memorial Hospital Post-Sec.
120 E Harris Ave 76903 325-653-6741
Texas College of Cosmetology Post-Sec.
918 N Chadbourne St 76903 325-677-0532

San Antonio, Bexar, Pop. 1,256,509
Alamo Heights ISD 4,400/PK-12
7101 Broadway St 78209 210-824-2483
Dr. Jerry Christian, supt. Fax 822-2221
www.ahisd.net
Alamo Heights HS 1,400/9-12
6900 Broadway St 78209 210-820-8850
Dr. Linda Foster, prin. Fax 832-5777
Alamo Heights JHS 1,100/6-8
7607 N New Braunfels Ave 78209 210-824-3231
Stephanie Kershner, prin. Fax 832-5825

East Central ISD 7,900/PK-12
6634 New Sulphur Springs Rd 78263 210-648-7861
Gary Patterson, supt. Fax 648-0931
www.ecisd.net/
East Central Heritage MS 1,300/7-8
8004 New Sulphur Springs Rd 78263 210-648-4546
Stevie Gonzales, prin. Fax 648-3501
East Central HS 2,200/9-12
7173 FM 1628 78263 210-649-2951
Paul Rutledge, prin. Fax 649-3162

Edgewood ISD 10,600/PK-12
5358 W Commerce St 78237 210-444-4500
Richard Bocanegra, supt. Fax 444-4602
www.eisd.net/
Brentwood MS 700/6-8
1626 Thompson Pl 78226 210-444-7675
Gustavo Cordova, prin. Fax 444-7698
Garcia MS 600/6-8
3306 Ruiz St 78228 210-444-8075
Sharon Luce, prin. Fax 444-8098
Kennedy HS 1,600/9-12
1922 S General McMullen Dr 78226 210-444-8040
Owen J. Kelly, prin. Fax 444-8020
Memorial HS 1,200/9-12
1227 Memorial St 78228 210-444-8300
William Telford, prin. Fax 444-8336
Truman MS 500/6-8
1018 NW 34th St 78228 210-444-8425
Anne Lackner, prin. Fax 444-8448
Wrenn MS 600/6-8
627 S Acme Rd 78237 210-444-8475
Albert Snow, prin. Fax 444-8498

Fort Sam Houston ISD 1,200/PK-12
1902 Winans Rd 78234 210-368-8701
Dr. Gail E. Siller, supt. Fax 368-8741
www.fshisd.net/
Cole JSHS 400/7-12
1900 Winans Rd 78234 210-368-8730
Roland Rios, prin. Fax 368-8731

Harlandale ISD 13,300/PK-12
102 Genevieve Dr 78214 210-921-4300
Dr. Guillermo Zavala, supt. Fax 921-4334
www.harlandale.k12.tx.us
Harlandale HS 1,900/9-12
114 E Gerald Ave 78214 210-977-1300
Rey Madrigal, prin. Fax 924-2335
Harlandale MS 900/6-8
300 W Huff Ave 78214 210-921-4507
Kathryn Pena, prin. Fax 977-8764
Kingsborough MS 700/6-8
422 E Ashley Rd 78221 210-921-4428
William Hall, prin. Fax 977-9463
Leal MS 800/6-8
743 W Southcross Blvd 78211 210-921-4570
Robert Villafranca, prin. Fax 977-8764
McCollum HS 1,600/9-12
500 W Formosa Blvd 78221 210-921-4500
David Stelmazewski, prin. Fax 921-9673
Wells MS 700/6-8
422 W Hutchins Pl 78221 210-921-4774
Diana Casas, prin. Fax 923-5126

Judson ISD
Supt. — See Live Oak
Kirby MS 1,000/6-8
5441 Seguin Rd 78219 210-661-1140
Sharon Roddy, prin. Fax 662-9275
Metzger MS 1,100/6-8
7475 Binz Engleman Rd 78244 210-662-2210
Dawn Brown, prin. Fax 662-8390
Wagner HS 9-11
3000 N Foster Rd 78244 210-662-5000
Fax 662-9896
Woodlake Hills MS 1,000/6-8
6625 Woodlake Pkwy 78244 210-661-1110
Marcus Anthony, prin. Fax 666-0169

Lackland ISD 900/PK-12
2460 Kenly Ave Bldg 8265 78236 210-357-5000
Dr. David Splitek, supt. Fax 357-5050
www.lacklandisd.net/
Stacey JSHS 200/7-12
2460 Kenly Ave Bldg 8265 78236 210-357-5100
Burnie Roper, prin. Fax 357-5109

North East ISD 56,800/PK-12
8961 Tesoro Dr 78217 210-804-7000
Dr. Richard Middleton, supt. Fax 804-7017
www.neisd.net
Automotive Technology Academy Vo/Tech
3736 Perrin Central Blvd 78217 210-637-4975
David Bailey, dir. Fax 637-4992
Bradley MS 1,400/6-8
14819 Heimer Rd 78232 210-491-8300
Shelia Morse, prin. Fax 491-8314
Bush MS 1,500/6-8
1500 Evans Rd 78258 210-491-8450
Randy Hoyer, prin. Fax 491-8471
Churchill HS 2,900/9-12
12049 Blanco Rd 78216 210-442-0800
Joe Reasons, prin. Fax 442-0879
Design and Technology Academy 9-12
5110 Walzem Rd 78218 210-650-1200
Barry Lanford, dir. Fax 650-1285
Driscoll MS 1,600/6-8
17150 Jones Maltsberger Rd 78247 210-491-6450
Michael Cardona, prin. Fax 491-6467
Eisenhower MS 1,200/6-8
8231 Blanco Rd 78216 210-442-0500
Jeff Vaughan, prin. Fax 442-0537
Engineering & Technologies Academy 9-12
5110 Walzem Rd 78218 210-650-1200
Bill Sturgis, dir. Fax 650-1227
Garner MS 900/6-8
4302 Harry Wurzbach Rd 78209 210-805-5100
Donna Newman, prin. Fax 805-5138
Harris MS 6-8
5300 Knollcreek 78247 210-657-8880
Peggy Clemmons, prin. Fax 657-8892
International HS of America 500/9-12
1400 Jackson Keller Rd 78213 210-442-0404
Kristopher Wickerham, prin. Fax 442-0409
Jackson MS 900/6-8
4538 Vance Jackson Rd 78230 210-442-0550
Tom Defosset, prin. Fax 442-0580
Krueger MS 1,100/6-8
438 Lanark Dr 78218 210-650-1350
Phyllis Hickey, prin. Fax 650-1374
Lee HS 2,000/9-12
1400 Jackson Keller Rd 78213 210-442-0300
Michael Keranen, prin. Fax 442-0325
MacArthur HS 2,700/9-12
2923 E Bitters Rd 78217 210-650-1100
Bobbie Turnbo, prin. Fax 650-1195
Madison HS 3,000/9-12
5005 Stahl Rd 78247 210-637-4400
Chris Thompson, prin. Fax 637-4435
Nimitz Academy 900/6-8
5426 Blanco Rd 78216 210-442-0450
Thalia Chaney, prin. Fax 442-0489
North East School of the Arts 9-12
1400 Jackson Keller Rd 78213 210-442-2505
Judith York, dir. Fax 442-2507
Reagan HS 3,100/9-12
19000 Ronald Reagan 78258 210-482-2200
Bill Boyd, prin. Fax 482-2222
Roosevelt HS 2,400/9-12
5110 Walzem Rd 78218 210-650-1200
Carl Hall, prin. Fax 650-1291
Tejeda MS 1,200/6-8
2909 E Evans Rd 78259 210-482-2260
John Mehlbrech, prin. Fax 482-2277
White MS 1,000/6-8
7800 Midcrown Dr 78218 210-650-1400
Rick Canales, prin. Fax 650-1443
Wood MS 1,200/6-8
14800 Judson Rd 78233 210-650-1300
Kaye Fenn, prin. Fax 650-1309

Northside ISD 73,800/PK-12
5900 Evers Rd 78238 210-397-8500
Dr. John Folks, admin. Fax 706-8772
www.nisd.net
Business Careers HS 9-12
6500 Ingram Rd 78238 210-397-7070
Geri Berger, prin. Fax 706-7076
Clark HS 2,600/9-12
5150 De Zavala Rd 78249 210-397-5150
Stan Laing, prin. Fax 561-5211
Communications Arts HS 9-12
11600 W FM 471 78253 210-397-6043
James Buchanan, prin. Fax 688-6092
Connally MS 1,300/6-8
8661 Silent Sunrise 78250 210-397-1000
Linda Garcia, prin. Fax 257-1004
Health Careers HS 900/9-12
4646 Hamilton Wolfe Rd 78229 210-397-5400
Jacqueline Horras, prin. Fax 617-5423
Hobby MS 1,000/6-8
11843 Vance Jackson Rd 78230 210-397-6300
Ray Moncus, prin. Fax 690-6332
Holmes HS 2,100/9-12
6500 Ingram Rd 78238 210-397-7000
Corinne Saldana, prin. Fax 706-7030
Jay HS 3,400/9-12
7611 Marbach Rd 78227 210-397-2700
Gerardo Marquez, prin. Fax 678-2753
Jay Science and Engineering Academy 9-12
7611 Marbach Rd 78227 210-397-2773
Peggy Greff, prin.
Jones MS 1,100/6-8
1256 Pinn Rd 78227 210-397-2100
Erika Foerster, prin. Fax 678-2113
Jordan MS 1,600/6-8
1725 Richland Hills Dr 78251 210-397-6150
Jennifer Alvarez, prin. Fax 523-4876
Luna MS 1,000/6-8
200 Grosenbacher Rd N 78253 210-397-5300
Lynn Pierson, prin.
Marshall HS 2,500/9-12
8000 Lobo Ln 78240 210-397-7100
Steven Daniel, prin. Fax 706-7175
Neff MS 1,000/6-8
5227 Evers Rd 78238 210-397-4100
Sylvia Wade, prin. Fax 523-4566
Northside Vocational Transition S Vo/Tech
4711 Sid Katz Dr 78229 210-397-2401
David Lamoureux, prin. Fax 615-2411
Pease MS 900/6-8
201 Hunt Ln 78245 210-397-2950
Kevin Kearns, prin. Fax 678-2974
Rawlinson MS 1,000/6-8
14100 Vance Jackson Rd 78249 210-397-4900
Nancy Pena, prin. Fax 767-4055
Rayburn MS 800/6-8
1400 Cedarhurst Dr 78227 210-397-2150
Eric Tobias, prin. Fax 678-2181
Rudder MS 1,100/6-8
6558 Horn Blvd 78240 210-397-5000
Scott Zolinski, prin. Fax 561-5022
Stevens HS 9-12
600 N Ellison Dr 78251 210-397-6450
Harold Maldonado, prin. Fax 706-8772
Stevenson MS 1,600/6-8
8403 Tezel Rd 78254 210-397-7300
Glenda Munson, prin. Fax 706-7336
Stinson MS 1,600/6-8
13200 Skyhawk Dr 78249 210-397-3600
Willie Frantzen, prin. Fax 561-3609
Sul Ross MS 1,000/6-8
3630 Callaghan Rd 78228 210-397-6350
Deonna Dean, prin. Fax 431-6383
Taft HS 3,000/9-12
11600 W FM 471 78253 210-397-6000
Tommy Garcia, prin. Fax 688-6091
Warren HS 2,600/9-12
9411 W Military Dr 78251 210-397-4200
Patty Denham-Hill, prin. Fax 257-4246
Zachry MS 1,300/6-8
9410 Timber Path 78250 210-397-7400
Javier Martinez, prin. Fax 706-7432
Northside Evening HS Adult
6500 Ingram Rd 78238 210-397-7060
Ruben Perez, prin. Fax 706-7060
Other Schools – See Helotes

San Antonio ISD 50,700/PK-12
141 Lavaca St 78210 210-299-5500
Dr. Robert Duron, supt. Fax 299-5580
www.saisd.net
Brackenridge HS 1,900/9-12
400 Eagleland Dr 78210 210-533-8144
Linda Marsh, prin. Fax 534-9770
Burbank HS 1,300/9-12
1002 Edwards 78204 210-532-4241
Andrew Rodriguez, prin. Fax 533-4394
Connell MS 800/6-8
400 Hot Wells Blvd 78223 210-534-6511
Ruben Fernandez, prin. Fax 534-6589
Cooper MS 400/6-8
1700 Tampico St 78207 210-223-9031
Maria Saenz, prin. Fax 223-9598
Davis MS 700/6-8
4702 E Houston St 78220 210-662-8184
Charlotte Gregory, prin. Fax 662-8189
Edison HS 1,700/9-12
701 Santa Monica 78212 210-733-9147
Charles Munoz, prin. Fax 738-2408
Fox Tech HS Vo/Tech
637 N Main Ave 78205 210-226-5103
Nancy York, prin. Fax 224-8792
Harris MS 600/6-8
325 Pruitt Ave 78204 210-226-4952
Moises Ortiz, prin. Fax 226-9448
Highlands HS 2,200/9-12
3118 Elgin Ave 78210 210-333-0421
Lorna Klokkenga, prin. Fax 337-2567
Houston HS 1,100/9-12
4635 E Houston St 78220 210-661-4134
Melonie Hammons, prin. Fax 666-2915
Irving MS 1,000/6-8
1300 Delgado St 78207 210-734-2937
Anita Chavera, prin. Fax 734-0941
Jefferson HS 1,900/9-12
723 Donaldson Ave 78201 210-736-1981
David Udovich, prin. Fax 738-2406
Lanier HS 1,500/9-12
1514 W Durango Blvd 78207 210-223-2926
Beatriz Hammoudeh, prin. Fax 224-9516

Longfellow MS 800/6-8
1130 E Sunshine Dr 78228 210-433-0311
Liz Solis, prin. Fax 433-0375
Lowell MS 600/6-8
919 Thompson Pl 78226 210-223-4741
Armando Rene Gutierrez, prin. Fax 223-6248
Page MS 600/6-8
401 Berkshire Ave 78210 210-533-7331
Gary Pollock, prin. Fax 533-7369
Poe MS 900/6-8
814 Aransas Ave 78210 210-534-6331
Elizabeth Anzek, prin. Fax 534-7299
Rhodes MS 700/6-8
3000 Tampico St 78207 210-433-5092
Edward Garcia, prin. Fax 433-7299
Rogers MS 700/6-8
314 Galway St 78223 210-333-7551
Kathy Tackett, prin. Fax 333-7954
Tafolla MS 800/6-8
1303 W Durango Blvd 78207 210-227-3383
Sylvia Lopez, prin. Fax 227-7044
Twain MS 700/6-8
2411 San Pedro Ave 78212 210-732-4641
Monica Garcia, prin. Fax 738-0518
Wheatley MS 500/6-8
415 Gabriel 78202 210-227-3921
Mona Lopez, prin. Fax 227-9972
Whittier MS 800/6-8
2101 Edison Dr 78201 210-735-7181
Linda Sanchez, prin. Fax 735-0704

South San Antonio ISD 9,700/PK-12
2515 Bobcat Ln 78224 210-977-7000
Ron Durbon, supt. Fax 977-7021
www.southsanisd.net
Dwight MS 800/6-8
2454 W Southcross Blvd 78211 210-977-7300
Tommy Fonseca, prin. Fax 977-7316
Kazen MS 800/6-8
1520 Gillette Blvd 78224 210-977-7150
Steve Veazey, prin. Fax 977-7155
Shepard MS 500/6-8
5558 Ray Ellison Blvd 78242 210-623-1875
Blanca Gonzalez, prin. Fax 623-1880
South San Antonio Career Ed Vo/Tech
2615 Navajo St 78224 210-977-7350
Bob Norman, prin. Fax 977-7356
South San Antonio HS 1,700/9-12
2515 Bobcat Ln 78224 210-977-7400
Victor Ortiz, prin. Fax 977-7430
South San Antonio HS West 600/9-12
5622 Ray Ellison Blvd 78242 210-623-1800
Oswaldo Garcia, prin. Fax 623-1812
Zamora MS 6-8
2515 Bobcat Ln 78224 210-977-7000
Marcos Perez, prin. Fax 977-7021

Southside ISD 4,800/PK-12
1460 Martinez Losoya Rd 78221 210-882-1600
Fidel del Barrio Ed.D., supt. Fax 626-0101
www.southside.k12.tx.us
Southside HS 1,200/9-12
1460 Martinez Losoya Rd 78221 210-882-1606
Cynthia Trevino, prin. Fax 626-0119
Southside MS 1,200/6-8
1460 Martinez Losoya Rd 78221 210-882-1601
R. Chris Christian, prin. Fax 626-0113

Southwest ISD 9,700/PK-12
11914 Dragon Ln 78252 210-622-4300
Dr. Velma Villegas, supt. Fax 622-4301
www.swisd.net/
McAuliffe JHS 700/7-8
11914 Dragon Ln 78252 210-623-6260
Orlando Vera, prin. Fax 623-6261
Scobee JHS 800/7-8
11914 Dragon Ln 78252 210-645-7500
Patricia Escobedo, prin. Fax 645-7501
Southwest HS 2,600/9-12
11914 Dragon Ln 78252 210-622-4500
Joann Fey, prin. Fax 622-4501

Achievers Center for Education 50/6-12
5084 De Zavala Rd 78249 210-696-1033
Janet Roper, prin. Fax 696-7723
Antonian College Preparatory HS 700/9-12
6425 West Ave 78213 210-344-9265
Gilbert Saenz, prin. Fax 344-9267
Atonement Academy PK-12
15415 Red Robin Rd 78255 210-695-2944
Richard Arndt, hdmstr. Fax 695-9679
Baptist Health System Post-Sec.
215 E Quincy St 78215 210-297-1040
Baptist University of the Americas Post-Sec.
8019 S Panam Expy 78224 800-721-1396
Believers Academy 200/K-12
13714 Lookout Rd 78233 210-656-2999
Rollin Mayes, hdmstr. Fax 656-1226
Blessed Hope Academy 200/10-12
12721 Mountain Air 78249 210-697-9191
Alice Ashcraft, dir. Fax 690-9299
Cancer Therapy & Research Center Post-Sec.
7979 Wurzbach Rd 78229 210-450-5669
Career Advancement & Applied Technology Post-Sec.
9350 S Presa St 78223 210-633-1000
Career Point Institute Post-Sec.
485 Spencer Ln 78201 210-732-3000
Career Quest Post-Sec.
5430 Frdrcksburg Rd #310 78229 210-366-2701
Castle Hills First Baptist S 300/K-12
2220 NW Military Hwy 78213 210-377-8485
Jim Bazar, hdmstr. Fax 377-8473
Central Catholic HS 500/9-12
1403 N Saint Marys St 78215 210-225-6794
Pat Cunningham, admin. Fax 227-9353
Christian Academy of San Antonio 500/PK-12
325 Castroville Rd 78207 210-436-2277
Yolanda Molina, prin. Fax 436-2210
Christian Heritage S 400/PK-12
16316 San Pedro Ave 78232 210-496-1644
Jahnnette Brandt, prin. Fax 496-1993
Cornerstone Christian S 600/PK-12
4802 Vance Jackson Rd 78230 210-979-9203
Alan Hulme, admin. Fax 979-0310
Everest Institute Post-Sec.
6550 1st Park Ten Blvd 78213 210-732-7800
Ewing Educational Center 50/K-12
PO Box 290309 78280 210-732-7550
Billy G. Burchfield, prin. Fax 732-7559
Galen Health Institute School of Nursing Post-Sec.
4440 S Piedras Dr Ste 200 78228 210-733-3056

Gateway Christian S 100/PK-12
6623 Five Palms Dr 78242 210-674-5703
Roger Gaines, prin. Fax 674-6811
Hallmark Institute of Aeronautics Post-Sec.
8901 Wetmore Rd 78216 210-826-1000
Hallmark Institute of Technology Post-Sec.
10401 W IH 10 78230 210-690-9000
Harvest Academy 400/PK-12
1270 N Loop 1604 E 78232 210-496-2277
Jim Fleetwood, prin. Fax 490-3262
Healy-Murphy Center HS 200/9-12
618 Live Oak 78202 210-223-2944
Janie Whiteley, prin. Fax 224-1033
Holy Cross HS 500/6-12
426 N San Felipe Ave 78228 210-433-9395
Angel Cedillo, prin. Fax 433-1666
Incarnate Word HS 9-12
727 E Hildebrand Ave 78212 210-829-3100
B. J. Nelsen, prin. Fax 829-3120
International Bible Center Post-Sec.
2369 Benrus Blvd 78228 210-434-5541
ITT Technical Institute Post-Sec.
5700 Northwest Pkwy 78249 210-694-4612
Keystone S 400/K-12
119 E Craig Pl 78212 210-735-4022
Hugh McIntosh, hdmstr. Fax 732-4905
Laurel Ridge S 100/K-12
17720 Corporate Woods Dr 78259 210-491-9400
Fax 491-3552
Lutheran HS of San Antonio 100/9-12
18104 Babcock Rd 78255 210-694-4962
Stephen Eggold, prin. Fax 694-9150
Milan Institute Post-Sec.
6151 NW Loop 410 Ste 210 78238 210-647-5100
Milan Institute of Cosmetology Post-Sec.
5403 Walzem Rd 78218 210-656-1991
Milan Institute of Cosmetology Post-Sec.
605 SW Military Dr 78221 210-922-5900
Mims Classic Beauty College Post-Sec.
5121 Blanco Rd 78216 210-344-2041
New Life Christian Academy 200/K-12
6622 Highway 90 W 78227 210-679-6001
Anthony Jackson, prin. Fax 679-6080
Northwest Vista College Post-Sec.
3535 N Ellison Dr 78251 210-348-2001
Oblate School of Theology Post-Sec.
285 Oblate Dr 78216 210-341-1366
Our Lady of the Lake University Post-Sec.
411 SW 24th St 78207 210-434-6711
Palo Alto College Post-Sec.
1400 W Villaret Blvd 78224 210-921-5000
Providence MSHS 400/6-12
1215 N Saint Marys St 78215 210-224-6651
Sr. Antoinette Billeaud, prin. Fax 224-6214
Rainbow Hills Baptist S 300/PK-12
2255 Horal St 78227 210-674-0490
Rev. Dennis Wall, chncllr. Fax 674-3615
River City Christian S 100/K-12
5810 Blanco Rd 78216 210-384-0297
Susan Galindo, prin. Fax 384-0446
St. Anthony HS 300/9-12
3200 McCullough Ave 78212 210-832-5600
Joseph Hannon, prin. Fax 832-5615
St. Gerard HS 9-12
521 S New Braunfels Ave 78203 210-533-8061
Katheryn Stanbridge, prin. Fax 533-3697
St. Mary's Hall 900/PK-12
9401 Starcrest Dr 78217 210-483-9100
Bob Windham, hdmstr. Fax 483-9299
St. Mary's University of San Antonio Post-Sec.
1 Camino Santa Maria St 78228 210-436-3011
St. Phillip's College Post-Sec.
1801 Martin Luther King Dr 78203 210-531-3200
San Antonio Beauty College #3 Post-Sec.
4130 Naco Perrin Blvd 78217 210-654-9734
San Antonio Beauty College #4 Post-Sec.
2423 Jamar St # 2 78226 210-433-7222
San Antonio Christian HS 300/9-12
19202 Redland Rd Ste F 78259 210-340-1864
Joseph Todd Holzmann, prin. Fax 530-9624
San Antonio Christian MS 200/6-8
19202 Redland Rd Ste F 78259 210-340-1864
Dr. Thomas Erbaugh, prin. Fax 348-6030
San Antonio College Post-Sec.
1300 San Pedro Ave 78212 210-733-2000
San Antonio College Medical Dental Asst. Post-Sec.
7142 San Pedro Ave Ste 100 78216 800-840-3101
Sendero Christian Academy 400/PK-12
5408 Daughtry Dr 78238 210-543-7218
Roberto Lara, admin. Fax 543-7368
Southern Careers Institute Post-Sec.
1405 N Main Ave Ste 100 78212 210-271-0096
Sunnybrook Christian Academy 300/PK-12
1620 Pinn Rd 78227 210-674-8000
Trudie Perez, admin. Fax 673-4603
SW School of Business & Tech Careers Post-Sec.
602 W Southcross Blvd 78221 210-921-0951
SW School of Business & Tech Careers Post-Sec.
2402 San Pedro Ave 78212 210-731-8449
Texas Careers Post-Sec.
1015 Jackson-Keller Rd #102 78213 210-308-8584
TMI - The Episcopal S of Texas 300/6-12
20955 W Tejas Trl 78257 210-698-7171
Dr. James Freeman, hdmstr. Fax 698-0715
Trinity Christian Academy 200/K-12
5401 N Loop 1604 E 78247 210-653-2800
Susan Oldfield, prin. Fax 653-0303
Trinity University Post-Sec.
715 Stadium Dr 78212 210-999-7011
University Hospital Post-Sec.
4502 Medical Dr 78229 210-616-2000
University of Texas at San Antonio Post-Sec.
6900 N Loop 1604 W 78249 210-458-4011
University of Texas Health Science Ctr. Post-Sec.
7703 Floyd Curl Dr 78229 210-567-7000
University of the Incarnate Word Post-Sec.
4301 Broadway St 78209 210-829-6000
Winston S 200/K-12
8565 Ewing Halsell Dr 78229 210-615-6544
Dr. Charles Karulak, prin. Fax 615-6627

San Augustine, San Augustine, Pop. 2,465

San Augustine ISD 1,000/PK-12
702 High School Dr 75972 936-275-2306
Fax 275-9776
www.san-augustine.k12.tx.us
San Augustine HS 300/9-12
702 High School Dr 75972 936-275-9603
George Cox, prin. Fax 275-9829
San Augustine IS 200/5-8
1002 Barrett St 75972 936-275-2318
Warren Norvell, prin. Fax 275-2962

San Benito, Cameron, Pop. 24,699
San Benito Consolidated ISD 10,100/PK-12
240 N Crockett St 78586 956-361-6110
Antonio Limon, supt. Fax 361-6115
www.sbcisd.net
Cabaza MS 1,000/6-8
2901 Shafer Rd 78586 956-361-6600
William Snavely, prin. Fax 361-6608
Jordan MS 1,300/6-8
700 N McCullough St 78586 956-361-6650
Antonio Rodriguez, prin. Fax 361-6658
San Benito HS 1,600/10-12
450 S Williams Rd 78586 956-361-6500
Delia Weaver, prin. Fax 361-6508
San Benito Riverside MS 6-8
35428 Padilla St 78586 956-361-6110
Joel Wood, prin. Fax 361-6940
San Benito Veterans Memorial Academy 800/9-9
2115 N Williams Rd 78586 956-361-6000
Elaine Sandell, prin. Fax 361-6008

South Texas ISD
Supt. — See Mercedes
South Texas Acad of Medical Technology 200/9-12
151 S Helen Moore Rd 78586 956-399-4331
Harry Goette, prin. Fax 399-3570

Sanderson, Terrell, Pop. 1,128
Terrell County ISD 100/PK-12
PO Box 747 79848 432-345-2515
Gary Hamilton, supt. Fax 345-2670
www.terrell.esc18.net
Sanderson HS 100/9-12
PO Box 747 79848 432-345-2282
Gary Hamilton, prin. Fax 345-2404
Sanderson JHS 50/6-8
PO Box 747 79848 432-345-2601
Fax 345-2670

San Diego, Duval, Pop. 4,589
San Diego ISD 1,500/PK-12
609 W Labbe St 78384 361-279-3382
Luis Pizzini, supt. Fax 279-2267
www.sdisd.esc2.net
Jaime JHS 300/6-8
609 W Labbe St 78384 361-279-3382
Sam Bueno, prin. Fax 279-3139
San Diego HS 500/9-12
609 W Labbe St 78384 361-279-3544
Nora Casarez, prin. Fax 279-5098

San Elizario, El Paso, Pop. 4,385
San Elizario ISD 3,300/PK-12
PO Box 920 79849 915-872-3900
Mike Quatrini, supt. Fax 872-3903
www.seisd.net
San Elizario HS 1,000/9-12
PO Box 920 79849 915-872-3970
Joe Keith, prin. Fax 872-3971
San Elizario MS 800/6-8
PO Box 920 79849 915-872-3960
Linda Rodriguez, prin. Fax 872-3961

Sanger, Denton, Pop. 6,354
Sanger ISD 2,200/PK-12
PO Box 2399 76266 940-458-7438
Jack Biggerstaff, supt. Fax 458-5140
sisd.sangerisd.net/
Sanger HS 600/9-12
100 Indian Ln 76266 940-458-7497
Mary Edwards, prin. Fax 458-4637
Sanger MS 400/7-8
105 Berry St 76266 940-458-7916
Bob Danley, prin. Fax 458-5111

San Isidro, Starr
San Isidro ISD 300/PK-12
PO Box 10 78588 956-481-3110
Miguel Garcia, supt. Fax 481-3950
San Isidro HS 100/9-12
PO Box 10 78588 956-481-3110
Miguel Garcia, prin. Fax 481-3950

San Juan, Hidalgo, Pop. 30,773
Pharr-San Juan-Alamo ISD
Supt. — See Pharr
Austin MS 900/6-8
804 S Stewart Rd 78589 956-702-5849
Elias Hernandez, prin. Fax 702-5858
Pharr-San Juan-Alamo HS 2,300/9-12
805 Ridge Rd 78589 956-783-2200
Rene Ramirez, prin. Fax 783-2293
San Juan MS 1,200/6-8
1229 S I Rd 78589 956-783-3800
Corina Ramirez, prin. Fax 783-3811

San Marcos, Hays, Pop. 46,111
San Marcos Consolidated ISD 7,200/PK-12
PO Box 1087 78667 512-393-6700
Dr. Sylvester Perez, supt. Fax 393-6709
www.smcisd.net/
Goodnight JHS 500/7-8
1805 Peter Garza Dr 78666 512-393-6550
Steve Dow, prin. Fax 393-6560
Miller JHS 500/7-8
301 Foxtail Run 78666 512-393-6660
Jon Orozco, prin. Fax 393-6602
San Marcos HS 1,900/9-12
1301 N State Highway 123 78666 512-393-6800
Dr. Chad Kelly, prin. Fax 392-8927

Gary Job Corps Center Post-Sec.
PO Box 967 78667 512-396-6561
San Marcos Adventist Academy 50/PK-10
1523 Ranch Rd 12 78666 512-392-9475
Fax 392-2693
San Marcos Baptist Academy 300/7-12
2801 Ranch Rd 12 78666 512-753-8000
Robert Bryant, prin. Fax 753-8031
Texas State University - San Marcos Post-Sec.
601 University Dr 78666 512-245-2111

San Perlita, Willacy, Pop. 689
San Perlita ISD 200/PK-12
PO Box 37 78590 956-248-5563
Carlos Guerra, supt. Fax 248-5561
www.spisd.org
San Perlita HS 100/9-12
PO Box 37 78590 956-248-5250
Doyle Todd, prin. Fax 248-5103
San Perlita MS 50/7-8
PO Box 37 78590 956-248-5250
Doyle Todd, prin. Fax 248-5103

San Saba, San Saba, Pop. 2,615
San Saba ISD 800/PK-12
808 W Wallace St 76877 325-372-3771
Johnny Clawson, supt. Fax 372-5977
www.san-saba.net
San Saba HS 200/9-12
808 W Wallace St 76877 325-372-3786
Dave Underwood, prin. Fax 372-3478
San Saba MS 200/5-8
808 W Wallace St 76877 325-372-3200
Erbey Valdez, prin. Fax 372-5228

Santa Anna, Coleman, Pop. 1,026
Santa Anna ISD 300/K-12
701 Bowie St 76878 325-348-3136
Roger Walker, supt. Fax 348-3141
santaanna.netxv.net/
Santa Anna HS 100/7-12
701 Bowie St 76878 325-348-3137
David Robinett, prin. Fax 348-3149

Santa Fe, Galveston, Pop. 10,498
Santa Fe ISD 4,500/PK-12
PO Box 370 77510 409-925-3526
Dr. Jon Whittemore, supt. Fax 925-4002
www.sfisd.org/
Santa Fe HS 1,400/9-12
PO Box 370 77510 409-925-3526
Mike VanEssen, prin. Fax 925-0658
Santa Fe JHS 700/7-8
PO Box 370 77510 409-925-3526
Dr. Joan Bowman, prin. Fax 925-4002

Santa Maria, Cameron, Pop. 500
Santa Maria ISD 600/PK-12
PO Box 448 78592 956-565-6308
Homero Garcia, supt. Fax 565-4422
Santa Maria HS 200/9-12
PO Box 448 78592 956-565-9144
Jeffrey Wright, prin. Fax 514-1968
Santa Maria MS, PO Box 448 78592 100/6-8
David Almaguer, prin. 956-565-6309

Santa Rosa, Cameron, Pop. 2,946
Santa Rosa ISD 1,200/PK-12
PO Box 368 78593 956-636-9800
Sylvia Atkinson, supt. Fax 636-2168
www.santarosaisd.org
Nelson MS 300/6-8
PO Box 368 78593 956-636-9850
Raul Trevino, prin. Fax 636-9869
Santa Rosa HS 400/9-12
PO Box 368 78593 956-636-9830
Andres Lopez, prin. Fax 636-9846

Santo, Palo Pinto
Santo ISD 500/PK-12
PO Box 67 76472 940-769-2835
G. Gilbert, supt. Fax 769-3116
www.santoisd.net/
Santo JSHS 300/6-12
PO Box 67 76472 940-769-3847
Mike Scott, prin. Fax 769-2796

Saratoga, Hardin
West Hardin County Consolidated ISD 600/PK-12
39227 Highway 105 77585 936-274-5061
T. Brad Lane, supt. Fax 274-4321
www.esc5.net/whccisd
West Hardin HS 200/9-12
39227 Highway 105 77585 936-274-5061
Fran Bledsoe, prin. Fax 274-5671
West Hardin JHS 100/6-8
39227 Highway 105 77585 936-274-5061
Fran Bledsoe, prin. Fax 274-5671

Savoy, Fannin, Pop. 886
Savoy ISD 300/PK-12
302 W Hayes St 75479 903-965-5262
Brian Neal, supt. Fax 965-7282
www.savoyisd.org
Savoy JSHS 100/7-12
302 W Hayes St 75479 903-965-4024
Mike Smith, prin. Fax 965-5608

Schertz, Guadalupe, Pop. 26,668
Schertz-Cibolo-Universal City ISD 7,600/PK-12
1060 Elbel Rd 78154 210-945-6200
Dr. Belinda Pustka, supt. Fax 945-6252
www.scuc.txed.net
Clemens HS 2,400/9-12
1001 Elbel Rd 78154 210-945-6100
Jeff Bryan, prin. Fax 945-6171
Corbett JHS 600/7-8
301 Main 78154 210-945-6350
Jay Muennink, prin. Fax 945-6360
Other Schools – See Cibolo

Schulenburg, Fayette, Pop. 2,742
Schulenburg ISD 800/PK-12
517 North St 78956 979-743-3448
Dr. Dale Pitts, supt. Fax 743-4721
www.schulenburg.txed.net
Schulenburg HS 400/7-12
150 College St 78956 979-743-3605
Gary McNeal, prin. Fax 743-4721

Blinn College Post-Sec.
100 Ranger Dr 78956 979-743-5003

Scurry, Kaufman, Pop. 631
Scurry-Rosser ISD 800/PK-12
10705 S State Highway 34 75158 972-452-8823
Micheal French, supt. Fax 452-8586
www.scurry-rosser.com/
Scurry-Rosser HS 300/9-12
8321 S State Highway 34 75158 972-452-8823
Dan Taylor, prin. Fax 452-3694
Scurry-Rosser MS 200/5-8
10729 S State Highway 34 75158 972-452-8823
Chris Couch, prin. Fax 452-8902

Seabrook, Harris, Pop. 10,907
Clear Creek ISD
Supt. — See League City
Seabrook IS 1,100/6-8
2401 Meyer Rd 77586 281-284-3100
David Williams, prin. Fax 284-3105

Seagraves, Gaines, Pop. 2,321
Seagraves ISD 600/PK-12
PO Box 577 79359 806-387-2035
Wynn Robinson, supt. Fax 387-2451
seagraves.esc17.net/
Seagraves HS 200/9-12
PO Box 1505 79359 806-387-2520
Eric Beam, prin. Fax 387-2944
Seagraves JHS 100/6-8
PO Box 938 79359 806-387-2646
Clay Mahler, prin. Fax 387-2451

Sealy, Austin, Pop. 6,038
Sealy ISD 2,300/PK-12
939 Tiger Ln 77474 979-885-3516
Thomas Price, supt. Fax 885-6457
www.sealyisd.com
Sealy HS 700/9-12
2372 Championship Dr 77474 979-885-3515
Pamela Morris, prin. Fax 987-3398
Sealy JHS 400/6-8
939 Tiger Ln 77474 979-885-3292
Scott Kana, prin. Fax 885-6457

Blinn College Post-Sec.
3701 Outlet Center Dr 77474 979-627-7997

Seguin, Guadalupe, Pop. 24,230
Navarro ISD 1,300/PK-12
6450 N State Highway 123 78155 830-372-1930
Dee Carter, supt. Fax 372-1853
www.navarroisd.us
Navarro HS 400/9-12
6350 N State Highway 123 78155 830-372-1931
John Gary, prin. Fax 379-3135
Other Schools – See Geronimo

Seguin ISD 7,900/PK-12
1221 E Kingsbury St 78155 830-372-5771
Dr. Irene Garza, supt. Fax 379-0392
www.seguin.k12.tx.us
Barnes MS 600/7-8
1539 Joe Carrillo Blvd 78155 830-379-4717
Rey Garcia, prin. Fax 379-4239
Briesemeister MS 500/7-8
1616 W Court St 78155 830-379-0600
G. Moreno, prin. Fax 379-0615
Seguin HS 2,000/9-12
815 Lamar 78155 830-372-5770
Fax 372-9851

Lifegate Christian S 100/K-12
395 Lifegate Ln 78155 830-372-0850
Jacob Lee, prin. Fax 372-0895
Seguin Beauty College Post-Sec.
102 E Court St 78155 830-372-0935
Texas Lutheran University Post-Sec.
1000 W Court St 78155 830-372-8000

Seminole, Gaines, Pop. 5,954
Seminole ISD 2,200/PK-12
207 SW 6th St 79360 432-758-3662
Doug Harriman, supt. Fax 758-9833
www.seminole.k12.tx.us
Seminole HS 600/9-12
2100 NW Avenue D 79360 432-758-5873
Don Worth, prin. Fax 758-8146
Seminole JHS 500/6-8
601 SW Avenue B 79360 432-758-9431
Cary Moring, prin. Fax 758-5795

Seven Points, Henderson, Pop. 1,252

Lake Pointe Christian Academy 50/K-12
1724 N Tool Dr 75143 903-432-4476
Shannon Hager, admin. Fax 432-1898

Seymour, Baylor, Pop. 2,704
Seymour ISD 600/PK-12
409 W Idaho St 76380 940-889-3525
Dr. John Baker, supt. Fax 889-5340
www.esc9.net/seymourisd
Seymour HS 200/9-12
409 W Idaho St 76380 940-888-2947
John Kaufman, prin. Fax 889-1045
Seymour MS 200/5-8
409 W Idaho St 76380 940-889-4548
Dr. Greg Roach, prin. Fax 889-4962

Shallowater, Lubbock, Pop. 2,170
Shallowater ISD 1,300/PK-12
1100 Avenue K 79363 806-832-4531
Phil Warren, supt. Fax 832-4350
www.shallowaterisd.net
Shallowater HS 400/9-12
1100 Avenue K 79363 806-832-4535
Tom Johnson, prin. Fax 832-4523
Shallowater MS 300/6-8
1100 Avenue K 79363 806-832-4531
Kenny Border, prin. Fax 832-5543

Shamrock, Wheeler, Pop. 1,841
Shamrock ISD 300/K-12
100 S Illinois St 79079 806-256-3492
Ray Cogburn, supt. Fax 256-3628
www.shamrockisd.net
Shamrock HS 100/9-12
100 S Illinois St 79079 806-256-2241
Kenneth Shields, prin. Fax 256-3628

Shelbyville, Shelby
Shelbyville ISD 700/PK-12
PO Box 325 75973 936-598-2641
Dr. Ray West, supt. Fax 598-6842
www.shelbyville.k12.tx.us
Shelbyville S 700/PK-12
PO Box 325 75973 936-598-7323
Rudy Eddington, prin. Fax 598-6842

Shepherd, San Jacinto, Pop. 2,282
Shepherd ISD 1,900/PK-12
1401 S Byrd Ave 77371 936-628-3396
Jeff Dozier, supt. Fax 628-3841
www.shepherdisd.net/
Shepherd HS 500/9-12
1401 S Byrd Ave 77371 936-628-3371
Jody Cronin, prin. Fax 628-3841
Shepherd MS 500/6-8
1401 S Byrd Ave 77371 936-628-3377
Jan Page, prin. Fax 628-3841

Sherman, Grayson, Pop. 36,790
Sherman ISD 6,200/PK-12
PO Box 1176 75091 903-891-6400
Dr. Al Hambrick, supt. Fax 891-6407
www.shermanisd.net

Piner MS 1,000/7-8
402 W Pecan St 75090 903-891-6470
David Parker, prin. Fax 891-6475
Sherman HS 1,600/9-12
2201 E Lamar St 75090 903-891-6440
Thomas O'Neal, prin. Fax 891-6446

Austin College Post-Sec.
900 N Grand Ave 75090 903-813-2000
Texoma Christian S 400/PK-12
3500 W Houston St 75092 903-893-7076
Jeffrey Burley, hdmstr. Fax 891-8486

Shiner, Lavaca, Pop. 2,019
Shiner ISD 500/PK-12
PO Box 804 77984 361-594-3121
Trey Lawrence, supt. Fax 594-3925
www.shinerisd.net
Shiner JSHS 200/7-12
PO Box 804 77984 361-594-3131
David Husmann, prin. Fax 594-4295

Shiner Catholic S PK-12
PO Box 725 77984 361-594-2313
Robert Whitworth, prin. Fax 594-8599

Sidney, Comanche
Sidney ISD 100/PK-12
PO Box 190 76474 254-842-5500
Doug Bowden, supt. Fax 842-5731
www.sidney.esc14.net/
Sidney S 100/PK-12
PO Box 190 76474 254-842-5500
Aletha Patterson, prin. Fax 842-5731

Sierra Blanca, Hudspeth
Sierra Blanca ISD 200/K-12
PO Box 308 79851 915-369-3741
Henry Dyer, supt. Fax 369-2605
www.sierrablancaisd.com/
Sierra Blanca S 200/K-12
PO Box 308 79851 915-369-2781
James Lujan, prin. Fax 369-2605

Silsbee, Hardin, Pop. 6,722
Silsbee ISD 2,900/K-12
415 Highway 327 W 77656 409-385-5286
James M. McGowan, supt. Fax 385-6530
www.silsbee.k12.tx.us
Edwards-Johnson Memorial Silsbee MS 700/6-8
1140 Highway 327 E 77656 409-385-2291
Kevin Wharton, prin. Fax 386-5792
Silsbee HS 900/9-12
1575 US Highway 96 N 77656 409-385-5574
Mike Day, prin. Fax 385-9115

Silverton, Briscoe, Pop. 706
Silverton ISD 200/PK-12
PO Box 608 79257 806-823-2476
Jerry Birdsong, supt. Fax 823-2276
www.silvertonisd.net
Silverton S 200/PK-12
PO Box 608 79257 806-823-2476
Sheryl Weaver, prin. Fax 823-2276

Simms, Bowie
Simms ISD 600/PK-12
PO Box 9 75574 903-543-2219
Rex Burks, supt. Fax 543-2512
simms.esc8.net
Bowie HS 200/9-12
PO Box 9 75574 903-543-2275
Brian Gray, prin. Fax 543-2512
Bowie JHS 100/6-8
PO Box 9 75574 903-543-2275
Brian Gray, prin. Fax 543-2512

Sinton, San Patricio, Pop. 5,509
Sinton ISD 2,200/PK-12
PO Box 1337 78387 361-364-6800
Mike Roberts, supt. Fax 364-6905
www.sintonisd.net/
Sinton HS 600/9-12
400 N Pirate Blvd 78387 361-364-6652
David Patterson, prin. Fax 364-6668
Smith JHS 300/7-8
900 S San Patricio St 78387 361-364-6840
Brayde McClure, prin. Fax 364-6856

Skidmore, Bee
Skidmore-Tynan ISD 700/PK-12
PO Box 409 78389 361-287-3426
Dr. Brett Belmarez, supt. Fax 287-3442
www.stisd.esc2.net
Skidmore-Tynan HS 200/9-12
PO Box 409 78389 361-287-3426
Patricia Holubec, prin. Fax 287-0146
Skidmore-Tynan JHS 200/6-8
PO Box 409 78389 361-287-3426
Emilia Dominguez, prin. Fax 287-0714

Slaton, Lubbock, Pop. 5,727
Slaton ISD 1,300/PK-12
140 E Panhandle St 79364 806-828-6591
James Taliaferro, supt. Fax 828-5506
www.slaton.esc17.net/
Slaton HS 300/9-12
105 N 20th St 79364 806-828-5833
Chris Kennedy, prin. Fax 828-1229
Slaton JHS 300/6-8
300 W Jean St 79364 806-828-6583
Louie Spinks, prin. Fax 828-2080

Slidell, Wise
Slidell ISD 300/PK-12
PO Box 69 76267 940-466-3118
Greg Enis, supt. Fax 466-3062
www.slidellisd.net/
Slidell JSHS 100/6-12
PO Box 69 76267 940-466-3118
Jereme Dietz, prin. Fax 466-3607

Smiley, Gonzales, Pop. 482
Nixon-Smiley Consolidated ISD
Supt. — See Nixon
Nixon-Smiley MS 300/5-8
500 Anglin Rd 78159 830-587-6401
Gary Tausch, prin. Fax 587-6558

Smithville, Bastrop, Pop. 4,370
Smithville ISD 1,800/PK-12
PO Box 479 78957 512-237-2487
Gary Sage, supt. Fax 237-2775
www.smithvilleisd.org
Smithville HS 500/9-12
PO Box 479 78957 512-237-2451
Jim Manning, prin. Fax 237-5643
Smithville JHS 400/6-8
PO Box 479 78957 512-237-2407
David Edwards, prin. Fax 237-5624

Smyer, Hockley, Pop. 490
Smyer ISD 400/PK-12
PO Box 206 79367 806-234-2935
Dane A. Kerns, supt. Fax 234-2411
www.smyer-isd.org
Smyer JSHS 200/7-12
PO Box 206 79367 806-234-3871
Bruce Cunningham, prin. Fax 234-2411

Snook, Burleson, Pop. 591
Snook ISD 500/PK-12
PO Box 87 77878 979-272-8307
Larry Williams, supt. Fax 272-5041
www.snookisd.com
Snook HS 200/9-12
PO Box 87 77878 979-272-8307
Robert Reyes, prin. Fax 272-5041
Snook MS 100/6-8
PO Box 87 77878 979-272-8307
Brad Vestal, prin. Fax 272-5041

Snyder, Scurry, Pop. 10,580
Snyder ISD 2,500/PK-12
2901 37th St 79549 325-573-5401
James R. Collins, supt. Fax 573-9025
www.snyder.esc14.net
Snyder HS 700/9-12
2901 37th St 79549 325-573-6301
Larry Scott, prin. Fax 573-9500
Snyder JHS 600/6-8
2901 37th St 79549 325-573-6356
Kellye Starnes, prin. Fax 574-6024

Western Texas College Post-Sec.
6200 College Ave 79549 325-573-8511

Somerset, Bexar, Pop. 1,779
Somerset ISD 3,000/PK-12
PO Box 279 78069 866-852-9858
Mary Ellen Morin, supt. Fax 852-9860
www.somerset.k12.tx.us
Somerset HS 900/9-12
PO Box 279 78069 866-852-9861
Kathryn Oliver, prin. Fax 667-2608
Somerset JHS 700/6-8
PO Box 279 78069 866-852-9862
Saul Hinojosa, prin. Fax 448-2738

Somerville, Burleson, Pop. 1,753
Somerville ISD 700/PK-12
PO Box 997 77879 979-596-2153
Charles Camarillo, supt. Fax 596-1778
Somerville HS 200/9-12
PO Box 997 77879 979-596-1534
Sandi Belcher, prin. Fax 596-1778
Somerville JHS 200/6-8
PO Box 997 77879 979-596-1461
Susan Jackson, prin. Fax 596-2004

Sonora, Sutton, Pop. 3,008
Sonora ISD 1,000/PK-12
807 S Concho Ave 76950 325-387-6940
Doug Bawcom, supt. Fax 387-5090
www.sonoraisd.net/
Sonora HS 300/9-12
807 S Concho Ave 76950 325-387-6533
Raul Chavarria, prin. Fax 387-5348
Sonora JHS 300/5-8
807 S Concho Ave 76950 325-387-3023
John Berry, prin. Fax 387-2007

Sour Lake, Hardin, Pop. 1,716
Hardin-Jefferson ISD 2,100/PK-12
PO Box 490 77659 409-981-6400
Shannon Holmes, supt. Fax 287-2283
www.hjisd.net/
Hardin-Jefferson HS 700/9-12
PO Box 639 77659 409-981-6430
Joel Nolte, prin. Fax 287-2558
Other Schools – See China

South Houston, Harris, Pop. 16,219
Pasadena ISD
Supt. — See Pasadena
South Houston HS 2,200/9-12
3820 S Shaver St 77587 713-740-0350
Deborah Aubin, prin. Fax 740-4155
South Houston IS 1,100/6-8
900 College Ave 77587 713-740-0490
Laura Gomez, prin. Fax 740-4097

Circle J Beauty School Post-Sec.
1611 Spencer Hwy Ste E 77587 713-946-5055

Southlake, Tarrant, Pop. 24,902
Carroll ISD
Supt. — See Grapevine
Carroll HS 1,200/9-10
800 N White Chapel Blvd 76092 817-949-5600
Rick Westfall, prin. Fax 949-5656
Carroll MS 600/7-8
1101 E Dove Rd 76092 817-949-5400
Kenneth Anderson, prin. Fax 949-5454
Carroll SHS 1,100/11-12
1501 W Southlake Blvd 76092 817-949-5800
Dr. Danniel Presley, prin. Fax 949-5858
Dawson MS 700/7-8
400 S Kimball Ave 76092 817-949-5500
Trudie Jackson, prin. Fax 949-5555

Southland, Garza
Southland ISD 200/K-12
190 Eighth St 79364 806-996-5599
Toby Miller, supt. Fax 996-5342
www.southlandisd.net
Southland S 200/K-12
190 Eighth St 79364 806-996-5339
Brad Ellison, prin. Fax 996-5595

Spearman, Hansford, Pop. 2,924
Spearman ISD 800/PK-12
403 E 11th Ave 79081 806-659-3233
Rodney Sumner, supt. Fax 659-2079
www.spearmanisd.com
Spearman HS 200/9-12
403 E 11th Ave 79081 806-659-2584
Bill Belger, prin. Fax 659-3824
Spearman JHS 200/6-8
505 Townsend St 79081 806-659-2563
Shane Whiteley, prin. Fax 659-3933

Splendora, Montgomery, Pop. 1,394
Splendora ISD 3,200/PK-12
23419 FM 2090 Rd 77372 281-689-3129
Billy Bowman, supt. Fax 689-7509
www.splendoraisd.org/
Splendora HS 800/9-12
23747 FM 2090 Rd 77372 281-689-8008
David Parker, prin. Fax 689-8675
Splendora JHS 500/7-8
23411 FM 2090 Rd 77372 281-689-6343
Will Gollihar, prin. Fax 689-8702

Spring, Harris, Pop. 37,100
Klein ISD
Supt. — See Klein
Hildebrandt IS 1,600/6-8
22800 Hildebrandt Rd 77389 832-249-5100
Joffrey Jones, prin. Fax 249-4048
Klein Collins HS 2,800/9-12
20811 Ella Blvd 77388 832-484-5500
Randy Kirk, prin. Fax 484-7811
Klein Oak HS 2,100/9-12
22603 Northcrest Dr 77389 832-484-5000
Kelly Schumacher, prin. Fax 484-7831
Schindewolf IS 1,300/6-8
20903 Ella Blvd 77388 832-249-5900
Debbie Hamilton, prin. Fax 249-4066

Spring ISD
Supt. — See Houston
Bailey MS 6-8
3377 James Leo Dr 77373 832-446-4201
Veronica Vijil, prin. Fax 288-5043
Dueitt MS 1,100/6-8
1 Eagle Xing 77373 281-355-3100
Kelly Ingram, prin. Fax 249-2210
Spring HS 3,200/9-12
19428 Interstate 45 77373 281-353-3465
Gloria Marshall, prin. Fax 355-2112
Twin Creeks MS 1,400/6-8
27100 Cypresswood Dr 77373 281-355-3130
Charlie Rooke, prin. Fax 249-2240

Legacy Preparatory Christian Academy 50/PK-10
2930 Rayford Rd 77386 281-362-1029
Audra May, dir.
Success Institute of Business Post-Sec.
16120 Stuebner Airline #104 77379 713-682-2262

Spring Branch, Comal
Comal ISD
Supt. — See New Braunfels
Smithson Valley HS 2,200/9-12
14001 State Highway 46 W 78070 830-885-1000
Chris Trotter, prin. Fax 885-1001
Smithson Valley MS 500/6-8
6101 FM 311 78070 830-885-1200
Link Fuller, prin. Fax 885-1201
Spring Branch MS 700/6-8
21053 State Highway 46 W 78070 830-885-1150
Jo Beth Jimerson, prin. Fax 885-1151

Springtown, Parker, Pop. 2,639
Springtown ISD 3,400/PK-12
101 E 2nd St 76082 817-220-7243
Lonnie Seipp, supt. Fax 523-5766
www.springtownisd.net
Springtown HS 1,100/9-12
915 W Highway 199 76082 817-220-3888
Mike Kelley, prin. Fax 523-5290
Springtown MS 600/7-8
500 Po Jo Dr 76082 817-220-7455
Mark Wilson, prin. Fax 220-2395

Spur, Dickens, Pop. 1,027
Spur ISD 300/PK-12
PO Box 250 79370 806-271-3272
Bobby Azam, supt. Fax 271-4575
www.spurbulldogs.com/
Spur MSHS 100/6-12
PO Box 250 79370 806-271-3385
Kevin Brendle, prin. Fax 271-4575

Spurger, Tyler
Spurger ISD 500/PK-12
PO Box 38 77660 409-429-3464
Angela M. Matterson, supt. Fax 429-3770
www.spurger.k12.tx.us
Spurger HS 200/7-12
PO Box 38 77660 409-429-3464
Summer Carter, prin. Fax 429-3770

Stafford, Fort Bend, Pop. 19,227
Stafford Municipal SD 2,500/PK-12
1625 Staffordshire Rd 77477 281-261-9200
H.D. Chambers, supt. Fax 261-9249
www.stafford.msd.esc4.net
Stafford HS 800/9-12
1625 Staffordshire Rd 77477 281-261-9239
Carolyn Williams, prin. Fax 261-9347
Stafford MS 500/7-8
1625 Staffordshire Rd 77477 281-261-9215
Dr. Phyllis Tyler, prin. Fax 261-9349

Houston Learning Academy - Stafford 50/9-12
3964 Bluebonnet Dr 77477 281-240-6060
Diana Monn, prin. Fax 240-0022

Stamford, Jones, Pop. 3,253
Stamford ISD 700/PK-12
507 S Orient St 79553 325-773-2705
Dr. Arthur Casey, supt. Fax 773-5684
www.stamford.esc14.net
Stamford HS 200/9-12
507 S Orient St 79553 325-773-2701
Fax 773-4015
Stamford MS 200/6-8
507 S Orient St 79553 325-773-2651
Fax 773-4052

Stanton, Martin, Pop. 2,262
Stanton ISD 800/PK-12
PO Box 730 79782 432-756-2244
David Carr, supt. Fax 756-2052
www.esc18.net/stanton/stanton.htm
Stanton HS 200/9-12
PO Box 730 79782 432-756-3326
Mark Cotton, prin. Fax 756-2052
Stanton MS 200/6-8
PO Box 730 79782 432-756-2544
Timothy Outlaw, prin. Fax 756-2052

Star, Mills
Star ISD 100/K-12
PO Box 838 76880 325-948-3661
Roger Hashem, supt. Fax 948-3398
www.centex-edu.net/star
Star S 100/K-12
PO Box 838 76880 325-948-3661
Bryan Lee, prin. Fax 948-3398

Stephenville, Erath, Pop. 15,948
Huckabay ISD 200/K-12
200 County Road 421 76401 254-968-8476
Cheryl Floyd, supt. Fax 965-3740
www.huckabay.k12.tx.us
Huckabay S 200/K-12
200 County Road 421 76401 254-968-5274
Christopher Morrow, prin. Fax 965-3140

Stephenville ISD 3,400/PK-12
2655 W Overhill Dr 76401 254-968-7990
Dr. Darrell Floyd, supt. Fax 968-5942
www.sville.us
Stephenville HS 1,100/9-12
2650 W Overhill Dr 76401 254-968-4141
Travis Stilwell, prin. Fax 968-4897
Stephenville JHS 500/7-8
2798 W Frey St 76401 254-968-6967
Paul Henderson, prin. Fax 965-7018

Stephenville Beauty College Post-Sec.
951 S Lillian St 76401 254-968-2111
Tarleton State University Post-Sec.
PO Box T0030 76402 254-968-9000

Sterling City, Sterling, Pop. 1,013
Sterling City ISD 300/K-12
PO Box 786 76951 325-378-4781
Ronnie Krejci, supt. Fax 378-2283
sterlingcity.netxv.net
Sterling City HS 100/9-12
PO Box 786 76951 325-378-5821
Sharla Arp, prin. Fax 378-2087
Sterling City JHS 100/6-8
PO Box 786 76951 325-378-5821
Glenn Coles, prin. Fax 378-2283

Stinnett, Hutchinson, Pop. 1,860
Plemons-Stinnett-Phillips Cons ISD 700/PK-12
PO Box 3440 79083 806-878-2858
Bill Wiggins, supt. Fax 878-3585
www.pspcisd.net
West Texas HS 200/9-12
PO Box 3440 79083 806-878-2456
Steven Scott, prin. Fax 878-2456
West Texas MS 100/6-8
PO Box 3440 79083 806-878-2247
Kevin Freriks, prin. Fax 878-3434

Stockdale, Wilson, Pop. 1,579
Stockdale ISD 700/K-12
PO Box 7 78160 830-996-3551
Reece Blincoe, supt. Fax 996-1071
www.stockdale.k12.tx.us
Stockdale HS 200/9-12
PO Box 7 78160 830-996-3103
Sandy Lynn, prin. Fax 996-1071
Stockdale JHS 200/6-8
PO Box 7 78160 830-996-3153
Roxanne Seidel, prin. Fax 996-1071

Stratford, Sherman, Pop. 1,923
Stratford ISD 600/PK-12
PO Box 108 79084 806-366-3300
Tim Gilliland, supt. Fax 366-3304
www.stratfordisd.net
Stratford HS 200/9-12
PO Box 108 79084 806-366-3330
Steve Haynes, prin. Fax 366-3304
Stratford JHS 200/5-8
PO Box 108 79084 806-366-3320
Clint Seward, prin. Fax 366-3304

Strawn, Palo Pinto, Pop. 758
Strawn ISD 200/K-12
PO Box 428 76475 254-672-5313
Andrew Lindsey, supt. Fax 672-5662
Strawn S 200/K-12
PO Box 428 76475 254-672-5776
Melanie Cormack, prin. Fax 672-5662

Sudan, Lamb, Pop. 1,040
Sudan ISD 400/K-12
PO Box 249 79371 806-227-2431
Hollis Lowrance, supt. Fax 227-2146
www.sudanisd.net
Sudan JSHS 100/8-12
PO Box 249 79371 806-227-2336
Ronald Beard, prin. Fax 227-2146

Sugar Land, Fort Bend, Pop. 75,754
Fort Bend ISD 61,900/PK-12
16431 Lexington Blvd 77479 281-634-1000
Dr. Timothy Jenney, supt. Fax 634-1700
www.fortbend.k12.tx.us
Austin HS 2,700/9-12
3434 Pheasant Creek Dr 77478 281-634-2000
Mike Leach, prin. Fax 634-2074
Clements HS 2,300/9-12
4200 Elkins Rd 77479 281-634-2150
Kevin Moran, prin. Fax 634-2168
Dulles HS 2,400/9-12
550 Dulles Ave 77478 281-634-5600
Lance Hindt, prin. Fax 634-5681
Dulles MS 1,500/6-8
500 Dulles Ave 77478 281-634-5750
Michael Heinzen, prin. Fax 634-5781
First Colony MS 1,200/6-8
3225 Austin Pkwy 77479 281-634-3240
Lee Crews, prin. Fax 634-3267
Fort Settlement MS 1,100/6-8
5440 Elkins Rd 77479 281-634-6440
Karon Crockett, prin. Fax 634-6456
Garcia MS 1,600/6-8
18550 Old Richmond Rd 77478 281-634-3160
Viretta West, prin. Fax 634-3207
Kempner HS 2,500/9-12
14777 Voss Rd 77478 281-634-2300
Dr. James May, prin. Fax 634-2378
Sartartia MS 1,100/6-8
8125 Homeward Way 77479 281-634-6310
Dr. Sara Thurman, prin. Fax 634-6373
Sugar Land MS 1,500/6-8
321 7th St 77478 281-634-3080
Lisa Padron, prin. Fax 634-3108
Technical Education Center Vo/Tech
540 Dulles Ave 77478 281-634-5671
Kennith Kendziora, admin. Fax 634-5700
Other Schools – See Houston, Missouri City, Richmond

Ft. Bend Baptist Academy 200/6-8
1250 7th St 77478 281-263-9191
Ronald Bell, prin. Fax 242-7195
Ft. Bend Baptist Academy 300/9-12
1250 7th St 77478 281-263-9175
David Hook, prin. Fax 263-9148
Grand Parkway Christian Academy 100/PK-10
16425 Old Richmond Rd 77478 281-495-1814
Karen Bowen, prin. Fax 495-1831

Sulphur Bluff, Hopkins
Sulphur Bluff ISD 200/PK-12
PO Box 30 75481 903-945-2460
Mark Keahey, supt. Fax 945-2459
www.sulphurbluffschool.net
Sulphur Bluff HS 100/7-12
PO Box 30 75481 903-945-2460
Gwen Crutcher, prin. Fax 945-2459

Sulphur Springs, Hopkins, Pop. 15,228
North Hopkins ISD 400/PK-12
1994 Farm Road 71 W 75482 903-945-2192
Tom Long, supt. Fax 945-2531
www.northhopkins.net/
North Hopkins JSHS 200/7-12
1994 Farm Road 71 W 75482 903-945-2192
Brian Bymaster, prin. Fax 945-2531

Sulphur Springs ISD 4,100/PK-12
631 Connally St 75482 903-885-2153
Patsy Bolton, supt. Fax 439-6162
www.ssisd.net/
Sulphur Springs HS 1,100/9-12
1200 Connally St 75482 903-885-2158
Chuck King, prin. Fax 439-6116
Sulphur Springs MS 900/6-8
829 Bell St 75482 903-885-7741
Glenn Wilson, prin. Fax 439-6126

Sundown, Hockley, Pop. 1,540
Sundown ISD 600/PK-12
PO Box 1110 79372 806-229-3021
Mike Motheral, supt. Fax 229-2004
www.sundownisd.com
Sundown HS 100/9-12
PO Box 1110 79372 806-229-2511
Jack Gaskins, prin. Fax 229-2004
Sundown JHS 100/6-8
PO Box 1110 79372 806-229-4691
Eddie Carter, prin. Fax 229-2004

Sunnyvale, Dallas, Pop. 3,817

Grace Fellowship Christian S 100/K-12
3052 N Belt Line Rd 75182 972-226-4499
Edris Carr, prin. Fax 226-0242

Sunray, Moore, Pop. 1,942
Sunray ISD 500/PK-12
PO Box 240 79086 806-948-4411
Michael Brown, supt. Fax 948-5274
Sunray HS 100/9-12
PO Box 240 79086 806-948-5515
Judy Stewart, prin. Fax 948-5399
Sunray MS 200/5-8
PO Box 240 79086 806-948-4444
Sid Whiteley, prin. Fax 948-4208

Sweeny, Matagorda, Pop. 3,622
Sweeny ISD 2,100/PK-12
1310 N Elm St 77480 979-491-8000
Randy Miksch, supt. Fax 491-8030
www.sweeny.isd.esc4.net/
Sweeny HS 600/9-12
1310 N Elm St 77480 979-491-8100
Michael Heinroth, prin. Fax 491-8171
Sweeny JHS 500/6-8
1310 N Elm St 77480 979-491-8200
Raymond Washington, prin. Fax 491-8274

Sweetwater, Nolan, Pop. 10,694
Sweetwater ISD 2,000/PK-12
207 Musgrove St 79556 325-235-8601
Ronny Beard, supt. Fax 235-5561
www.esc14.net/sweetwaterisd/sisd.htm
Sweetwater HS 600/9-12
1205 Ragland St 79556 325-235-4371
Chris Wigington, prin. Fax 235-4861
Sweetwater MS 500/6-8
305 Lamar St 79556 325-236-6303
Kent Ruffin, prin. Fax 236-6941

Texas State Technical College Post-Sec.
300 Homer K Taylor Dr 79556 325-235-7300

Taft, San Patricio, Pop. 3,429
Taft ISD 1,500/PK-12
400 College St 78390 361-528-2636
Don Madden, supt. Fax 528-2223
www.taftisd.net
Taft HS 300/9-12
502 Rincon Rd 78390 361-528-2636
Dr. Charles Climer, prin. Fax 528-3918
Taft JHS 300/6-8
727 McIntyre Ave 78390 361-528-2636
Ricardo Trevino, prin. Fax 528-5477

Tahoka, Lynn, Pop. 2,730
Tahoka ISD 700/PK-12
PO Box 1230 79373 806-561-4105
Jimmy Parker, supt. Fax 561-4160
www.tahoka.esc17.net
Tahoka HS 200/9-12
PO Box 1500 79373 806-561-4538
Troy Hinds, prin. Fax 561-6082
Tahoka MS 100/7-8
PO Box 1500 79373 806-561-4538
Tom Thomas, prin. Fax 561-6082

Tatum, Rusk, Pop. 1,188
Tatum ISD 1,200/PK-12
PO Box 808 75691 903-947-6482
Dee Hartt Ed.D., supt. Fax 947-3295
www.tatumisd.org/
Tatum HS 400/9-12
PO Box 808 75691 903-947-6486
Debbie Maxey, prin. Fax 947-6206
Tatum MS 200/7-8
PO Box 808 75691 903-947-6487
Bob Garcia, prin. Fax 947-2322

Taylor, Williamson, Pop. 15,014
Taylor ISD 2,900/PK-12
602 W 12th St 76574 512-365-1391
Bruce Scott Ed.D., supt. Fax 365-3800
www.taylorisd.org
Taylor HS 900/9-12
3101 N Main St 76574 512-365-1291
Kim Mason, prin. Fax 365-9334
Taylor MS 700/6-8
304 Carlos Parker Blvd NW 76574 512-365-8591
Ester Allgower, prin. Fax 365-8589

Teague, Freestone, Pop. 4,630
Teague ISD 1,100/PK-12
420 N 10th Ave 75860 254-739-3071
Ned Burns, supt. Fax 739-5223
www.teagueisd.org/
Teague HS 400/9-12
420 N 10th Ave 75860 254-739-2532
Darrell Evans, prin. Fax 739-2724
Teague JHS 200/7-8
420 N 10th Ave 75860 254-739-3011
Donnie Osborn, prin. Fax 739-5896

Temple, Bell, Pop. 55,447
Belton ISD
Supt. — See Belton
Lake Belton MS 300/6-8
8818 Tarver Dr 76502 254-215-2900
Suzy McKinney, prin. Fax 215-2901

Temple ISD 8,200/PK-12
PO Box 788 76503 254-215-8473
Beto Gonzalez, supt. Fax 215-6783
www.tisd.org
Bonham MS 500/6-8
4600 Midway Dr 76502 254-215-6600
Judy Hundley, prin. Fax 215-6634
Lamar MS 600/6-8
2120 N 1st St 76501 254-215-6444
Jennifer Mathesen, prin. Fax 215-6483
Temple HS 2,100/9-12
415 N 31st St 76504 254-215-7000
J. J. Villarreal, prin. Fax 899-2926
Travis MS 700/6-8
1500 S 19th St 76504 254-215-6300
Eddy McNamara, prin. Fax 215-6352

Central Texas Beauty College Post-Sec.
2010 S 57th St 76504 254-773-9911
Central Texas Christian S 500/PK-12
4141 W FM 93 76502 254-939-5700
Ed Thomas, supt. Fax 939-5733
Holy Trinity Catholic HS 100/9-12
418 N 11th St 76501 254-771-0787
Robin Couvillon, prin. Fax 771-2285
Scott & White Memorial Hospital & Clinic Post-Sec.
2401 S 31st St 76508 254-724-5177
Temple College Post-Sec.
2600 S 1st St 76504 254-298-8300

Tenaha, Shelby, Pop. 1,100
Tenaha ISD 400/PK-12
PO Box 318 75974 936-248-5000
Don Fallin, supt. Fax 248-3902
www.tenahaisd.com/
Tenaha HS 100/9-12
PO Box 318 75974 936-248-5000
Tom Jones, prin. Fax 248-4009
Tenaha MS 100/6-8
PO Box 318 75974 936-248-5000
Martha Boren, prin. Fax 248-3902

Terlingua, Brewster
Terlingua Common SD 200/PK-12
PO Box 256 79852 432-371-2281
Kathy Killingsworth, supt. Fax 371-2245
Big Bend HS 100/9-12
PO Box 256 79852 432-371-2281
Kathy Killingsworth, prin. Fax 371-2245

Terrell, Kaufman, Pop. 17,665
Terrell ISD 4,200/PK-12
700 N Catherine St 75160 972-563-7504
Walt Davis, supt. Fax 563-1406
www.terrellisd.com/
Furlough MS 600/7-8
1351 Colquitt Rd 75160 972-563-7501
Danielle Banz, prin. Fax 563-5721
Terrell HS 1,100/9-12
400 Poetry Rd 75160 972-563-7525
Bob Densmore, prin. Fax 563-6318

Poetry Community Christian S 200/K-12
18688 FM 986 75160 972-563-7227
Anne Puidk Horan, admin. Fax 563-0025
Southwestern Christian College Post-Sec.
PO Box 10 75160 972-524-3341

Texarkana, Bowie, Pop. 35,746
Liberty-Eylau ISD 2,700/PK-12
2901 Leopard Dr 75501 903-832-1535
Scott Niven, supt. Fax 838-9444
www.leisd.net
Liberty-Eylau HS 700/9-12
2905 Leopard Dr 75501 903-832-1535
Lewis Lincoln, prin. Fax 831-6113
Liberty-Eylau MS 800/5-8
5555 Leopard Dr 75501 903-838-5555
Christy Tidwell, prin. Fax 832-6700

Pleasant Grove ISD 2,000/PK-12
8500 N Kings Hwy 75503 903-831-4086
Margaret Davis, supt. Fax 831-4435
www.pgisd.net
Pleasant Grove HS 600/9-12
5406 McKnight Rd 75503 903-832-8005
Jason Marshall, prin. Fax 832-5381
Pleasant Grove MS 600/5-8
5605 Cooks Ln 75503 903-831-4295
Jeanie Davis, prin. Fax 831-5501

Red Lick ISD 400/K-8
3511 N FM 2148 75503 903-838-8230
Dr. Richard Hervey, supt. Fax 831-6134
www.redlickisd.com
Red Lick MS 100/6-8
3511 N FM 2148 75503 903-838-8230
Phyllis Deese, prin. Fax 831-6134

Texarkana ISD 5,800/PK-12
4241 Summerhill Rd 75503 903-794-3651
F. Larry Sullivan Ed.D., supt. Fax 792-2632
www.txkisd.net
Texas HS 1,500/9-12
2112 Kennedy Ln 75503 903-794-3891
Paul Norton, prin. Fax 792-8971
Texas MS 1,300/6-8
2100 College Dr 75503 903-793-5631
George Moore, prin. Fax 792-2935

Career Academy Post-Sec.
32 Oaklawn Vlg 75501 903-832-1021
Texarkana College Post-Sec.
2500 N Robison Rd 75501 903-838-4541
Texas A&M University - Texarkana Post-Sec.
PO Box 5518 75505 903-223-3000
Wadley Regional Medical Center Post-Sec.
1000 Pine St 75501 903-798-8000

Texas City, Galveston, Pop. 44,274
Texas City ISD 5,800/PK-12
PO Box 1150 77592 409-942-2713
Richard Ettredge, supt. Fax 942-2655
www.texascity.isd.tenet.edu
Blocker MS 1,000/7-8
500 14th Ave N 77590 409-942-2756
R. Carter, prin. Fax 942-2755
Texas City HS 1,500/9-12
1800 9th Ave N 77590 409-942-2645
Mike Rhodes, prin. Fax 942-2672

College of the Mainland Post-Sec.
1200 N Amburn Rd 77591 409-938-1211
Living Word Christian S 50/K-10
2121 6th St N 77590 409-692-5844
Jeanette Huwe, prin. Fax 948-2977

Texline, Dallam, Pop. 514
Texline ISD 100/K-12
PO Box 60 79087 806-362-4667
Gary Laramore, supt. Fax 362-4538
www.texlineisd.net
Texline S 100/K-12
PO Box 60 79087 806-362-4284
Ken Rosser, prin. Fax 362-4538

The Colony, Denton, Pop. 37,972
Lewisville ISD
Supt. — See Flower Mound
Griffin MS 700/6-8
5105 N Colony Blvd 75056 469-713-5973
Cynthia Williams, prin. Fax 350-2950
Lakeview MS 900/6-8
4300 Keys Dr 75056 469-713-5974
Dr. Steve Nauman, prin. Fax 350-3150
The Colony HS 2,000/9-12
4301 Blair Oaks Dr 75056 469-713-5178
Becky MacDonald, prin. Fax 625-9015

The Woodlands, Montgomery, Pop. 63,000
Conroe ISD
Supt. — See Conroe
Knox JHS 1,200/7-8
12104 Sawmill Rd 77380 832-592-8400
Gale Drummond, prin. Fax 592-8410
McCullough JHS 7-8
3800 S Panther Creek Dr 77381 832-592-5100
Chris McCord, prin. Fax 592-5116
The Woodlands College Park HS 9-12
3701 College Park Dr 77384 936-709-3000
Mark Murrell, prin. Fax 709-3019
The Woodlands HS 1,400/9-9
10010 Branch Crossing Dr 77382 832-592-8200
Marguerite Weatherall, prin. Fax 592-8202
The Woodlands SHS 2,400/10-12
6101 Research Forest Dr 77381 936-273-4837
Dr. Gregg Colschen, prin. Fax 273-8599

Cooper S 1,000/PK-12
1 John Cooper Dr 77381 281-367-0900
Michael Maher, hdmstr. Fax 292-9201
Woodlands Christian Academy 400/PK-12
5800 Academy Way 77384 936-273-2555
Julie Ambler, hdmstr. Fax 271-3115

Thorndale, Milam, Pop. 1,330
Thorndale ISD 500/K-12
PO Box 870 76577 512-898-2538
Gene Solis, supt. Fax 898-5356
www.thorndale.txed.net/
Thorndale HS 200/9-12
PO Box 870 76577 512-898-2321
Davis Denny, prin. Fax 898-5558
Thorndale MS 100/6-8
PO Box 870 76577 512-898-2670
Heather Klotz, prin. Fax 898-5505

Thrall, Williamson, Pop. 847
Thrall ISD 400/K-12
201 S Bounds St 76578 512-898-0062
Keith Brown, supt. Fax 898-5349
www.thrallisd.com
Thrall MSHS 200/6-12
201 S Bounds St 76578 512-898-5193
Mac Edwards, prin. Fax 898-2132

Three Rivers, Live Oak, Pop. 1,764
Three Rivers ISD 600/PK-12
108 N School Rd 78071 361-786-3626
Mac Johanson, supt. Fax 786-2555
www.trisd.esc2.net
Three Rivers HS 200/9-12
108 N School Rd 78071 361-786-3531
Kenneth Rohrbach, prin. Fax 786-3533
Three Rivers MS 200/6-8
108 N School Rd 78071 361-786-3803
Hortensia Brooks, prin. Fax 786-2555

Throckmorton, Throckmorton, Pop. 789
Throckmorton ISD 200/PK-12
210 College St 76483 940-849-2411
Scott Hogue, supt. Fax 849-3345
www.esc9.net/tisd
Throckmorton HS 100/9-12
210 College St 76483 940-849-2421
John Powers, prin. Fax 849-3345

Tilden, McMullen
McMullen County ISD 200/PK-12
PO Box 359 78072 361-274-3315
Frank Franklin, supt. Fax 274-3665
www.mcisd.us
McMullen County S 200/PK-12
PO Box 359 78072 361-274-3371
Dr. Jay Smith, prin. Fax 274-3580

Timpson, Shelby, Pop. 1,144
Timpson ISD 600/PK-12
PO Box 370 75975 936-254-2463
Dr. Leland Moore, supt. Fax 254-3878
www.timpson.k12.tx.us
Timpson HS 200/9-12
PO Box 370 75975 936-254-3125
Kelly Parker, prin. Fax 254-3263
Timpson MS 100/6-8
PO Box 370 75975 936-254-2078
Calvin Smith, prin. Fax 254-2355

Tivoli, Refugio
Austwell-Tivoli ISD 200/K-12
207 Redfish St 77990 361-286-3212
Dr. Antonio Aguirre, supt. Fax 286-3637
www.atisd.net
Austwell-Tivoli JSHS 100/7-12
207 Redfish St 77990 361-286-3582
Tracy Gleghorn, prin. Fax 286-3637

Tolar, Hood, Pop. 643
Tolar ISD 600/PK-12
PO Box 368 76476 254-835-4718
Jack Davis, supt. Fax 835-4704
www.tolar.esc11.net
Tolar HS 200/9-12
PO Box 368 76476 254-835-4316
Bruce Gibbs, prin. Fax 835-4237
Tolar JHS 100/6-8
PO Box 368 76476 254-835-5207
Harold Roan, prin. Fax 835-5208

Tomball, Harris, Pop. 9,938
Tomball ISD 8,800/PK-12
221 W Main St 77375 281-357-3100
John Neubauer, supt. Fax 357-3128
www.tomballisd.net
Tomball HS 2,600/9-12
30330 Quinn Rd 77375 281-357-3220
Gary Moss, prin. Fax 357-3248
Tomball JHS 600/7-8
30403 Quinn Rd 77375 281-357-3000
Dan Johnson, prin. Fax 357-3027
Willow Wood JHS 800/7-8
11770 Gregson Rd 77377 281-357-3030
Dr. Kate Caffery, prin. Fax 357-3044

Concordia Lutheran HS 400/9-12
700 E Main St 77375 281-351-2547
Joel Bode, prin. Fax 255-8806
Rosehill Christian S 300/PK-12
19830 FM 2920 Rd 77377 281-351-8114
Dean Unsicker, admin. Fax 516-3418

Tom Bean, Grayson, Pop. 995
Tom Bean ISD 800/K-12
PO Box 128 75489 903-546-6076
Dr. Jerry Stout, supt. Fax 546-6104
www.tombean-isd.org
Tom Bean HS 300/9-12
PO Box 128 75489 903-546-6319
Roger Ellis, prin. Fax 546-6319
Tom Bean MS 200/6-8
PO Box 128 75489 903-546-6161
Charlie Williams, prin. Fax 546-6161

Tornillo, El Paso
Tornillo ISD 1,200/PK-12
PO Box 170 79853 915-764-2366
Paul Vranish, supt. Fax 764-2120
www.tisd.us/
Tornillo HS 300/9-12
PO Box 170 79853 915-764-2040
Ray Cobos, prin. Fax 764-3482
Tornillo JHS 200/7-8
PO Box 170 79853 915-764-5701
Ruth Lara, prin. Fax 764-2020

Trent, Taylor, Pop. 313
Trent ISD 100/PK-12
PO Box 105 79561 325-862-6400
Greg Priddy, supt. Fax 862-6448
www.esc14.net/data/trent.pdf
Trent S 100/PK-12
PO Box 105 79561 325-862-6125
Greg Priddy, prin. Fax 862-6448

Trenton, Fannin, Pop. 703
Trenton ISD 600/PK-12
PO Box 5 75490 903-989-2245
Jerry Don Cook, supt. Fax 989-2767
www.trentonisd.com
Trenton HS 200/9-12
PO Box 5 75490 903-989-2242
Rick Foreman, prin. Fax 989-2767
Trenton MS 100/6-8
PO Box 5 75490 903-989-2243
Rick Largent, prin. Fax 989-5173

Trinidad, Henderson, Pop. 1,147
Trinidad ISD 300/PK-12
PO Box 329 75163 903-778-2673
David Atkeisson, supt. Fax 778-4120
www.trinidadisd.com
Trinidad S 300/PK-12
PO Box 329 75163 903-778-2415
Corey Jenkins, prin. Fax 778-4120

Trinity, Trinity, Pop. 2,780
Trinity ISD 1,200/PK-12
PO Box 752 75862 936-594-3569
Dr. Douglas E. Moore, supt. Fax 594-8425
www.trinity.k12.tx.us
Trinity HS 300/9-12
PO Box 752 75862 936-594-3560
Jeremy Glenn, prin. Fax 594-2162
Trinity JHS 300/6-8
PO Box 752 75862 936-594-2321
Jeremy Glenn, prin. Fax 594-2162

Trophy Club, Denton, Pop. 7,334
Northwest ISD
Supt. — See Justin
Medlin MS 600/6-8
601 Parkview Dr 76262 817-215-0500
Robin Ellis, prin. Fax 215-0548

Troup, Smith, Pop. 2,052
Troup ISD 1,000/PK-12
PO Box 578 75789 903-842-3067
Marvin Beaty, supt. Fax 842-4563
www.troupisd.org
Troup HS 300/9-12
PO Box 578 75789 903-842-3065
Derek Driver, prin. Fax 842-4563
Troup MS 200/6-8
PO Box 578 75789 903-842-3081
Ava Johnson, prin. Fax 842-4563

Troy, Bell, Pop. 1,365
Troy ISD 1,200/PK-12
PO Box 409 76579 254-938-2595
Kerry Hansen, supt. Fax 938-7323
www.troyisd.org
Troy HS 400/9-12
PO Box 409 76579 254-938-2561
Wayne Cooper, prin. Fax 938-2328
Troy MS 300/6-8
PO Box 409 76579 254-938-2543
Jimmy Cox, prin. Fax 938-2880

Tulia, Swisher, Pop. 4,714
Tulia ISD 1,100/PK-12
702 NW 8th St 79088 806-995-4591
Dr. Ken Miller, supt. Fax 995-3169
www.tuliaisd.net
Tulia HS 400/9-12
501 Hornet Pl 79088 806-995-2759
Dennis Holt, prin. Fax 995-4413
Tulia JHS 200/6-8
421 NE 3rd St 79088 806-995-4842
Johnny Lara, prin. Fax 995-4498

Turkey, Hall, Pop. 492
Turkey-Quitaque ISD 300/K-12
PO Box 397 79261 806-455-1411
Jerry Smith, supt. Fax 455-1718
Valley S 300/K-12
PO Box 397 79261 806-455-1411
Jon Davidson, prin. Fax 455-1718

Tuscola, Taylor, Pop. 714
Jim Ned Consolidated ISD 1,000/PK-12
PO Box 9 79562 325-554-7500
Kent LeFevre, supt. Fax 554-7740
www.jimned.esc14.net/
Jim Ned HS 300/9-12
PO Box 9 79562 325-554-7755
Paul Lippe, prin. Fax 554-7550
Jim Ned MS 200/6-8
PO Box 9 79562 325-554-7870
Bob Easterling, prin. Fax 554-7750

Tyler, Smith, Pop. 91,936
Chapel Hill ISD 3,100/PK-12
11134 County Road 2249 75707 903-566-2441
Joe Stubblefield, supt. Fax 566-8469
www.chapelhillisd.org
Chapel Hill HS 900/9-12
13172 State Highway 64 E 75707 903-566-2311
Lamond Dean, prin. Fax 566-5343
Chapel Hill MS 700/6-8
13174 State Highway 64 E 75707 903-566-1491
Lisa McCreary, prin. Fax 566-6441

Tyler ISD 17,500/PK-12
PO Box 2035 75710 903-262-1000
Dr. David Simmons, supt. Fax 262-1178
www.tylerisd.org
Boulter Creative Arts Magnet S 500/6-8
2926 Garden Valley Rd 75702 903-262-1390
Vanessa Choice, prin. Fax 262-1392
Dogan MS 600/6-8
2621 N Border Ave 75702 903-262-1450
Onella Brown, prin. Fax 262-1451
Hogg MS 600/6-8
920 S Broadway Ave 75701 903-262-1500
Jo Ann Burns, prin. Fax 262-1501
Hubbard MS 900/6-8
1300 Hubbard Dr 75703 903-262-1560
Tammy VanSchoubroek, prin. Fax 262-1566
Lee HS 2,500/9-12
411 E Southeast Loop 323 75701 903-262-2625
Roger McAdoo, prin. Fax 262-2630
Moore MST Magnet MS 800/6-8
1200 S Tipton Ave 75701 903-262-1640
Claude Lane, prin. Fax 262-1641
Stewart MS 500/6-8
2800 W Shaw St 75701 903-262-1710
Debra Robertson, prin. Fax 262-1711
Tyler HS 1,900/9-12
1120 N Northwest Loop 323 75702 903-262-2850
Michael McFarland, prin. Fax 262-2852

All Saints Episcopal S 700/PK-12
2695 S Southwest Loop 323 75701 903-579-6000
Art Burke, hdmstr. Fax 579-6002
Bishop Gorman MSHS 400/6-12
1405 E Southeast Loop 323 75701 903-561-2424
Jim Franz, prin. Fax 561-2645
Careers Unlimited Post-Sec.
335 S Bonner Ave 75702 903-593-4424
Christian Heritage S 200/K-12
961 County Road 1143 75704 903-593-2702
James Kilkenny, hdmstr. Fax 531-2226
East Texas Christian Academy 200/PK-12
1797 Shiloh Rd 75703 903-561-8642
Scott Fossey, pres. Fax 561-9620
Good Shepherd Reformed Episcopal S 200/PK-12
2525 Old Jacksonville Rd 75701 903-592-4045
Fr. Walter Banek, hdmstr. Fax 596-7149

Grace Community S 500/6-12
3001 University Blvd 75701 903-566-5661
John Ferguson, admin. Fax 566-5639
King's Academy Christian S 50/K-12
714 Shelley Dr 75701 903-534-9992
Mitch Rhodes, admin. Fax 534-9555
Star College of Cosmetology Post-Sec.
520 E Front St 75702 903-596-7860
Texas College Post-Sec.
2404 N Grand Ave 75702 903-593-8311
Tyler Junior College Post-Sec.
PO Box 9020 75711 903-510-2200
University of Texas at Tyler Post-Sec.
3900 University Blvd 75701 800-888-9537

Universal City, Bexar, Pop. 16,653
Judson ISD
Supt. — See Live Oak
Kitty Hawk MS 1,300/6-8
840 Old Cimarron Trl 78148 210-945-1220
Yvonne Anglada, prin. Fax 659-0687

First Baptist Academy 400/PK-12
1401 Pat Booker Rd 78148 210-658-5331
Cissy Stubblefield, admin. Fax 658-7024

Utopia, Uvalde
Utopia ISD 200/K-12
PO Box 880 78884 830-966-1928
John Walts, supt. Fax 966-6162
www.utopiaisd.net
Utopia S 200/K-12
PO Box 880 78884 830-966-3339
James D. Phillips, prin. Fax 966-6162

Uvalde, Uvalde, Pop. 16,441
Uvalde Consolidated ISD 5,100/PK-12
PO Box 1909 78802 830-278-6655
Dr. Wendell Brown, supt. Fax 591-4909
www.ucisd.net
Uvalde HS 1,400/9-12
PO Box 1909 78802 830-591-2950
Hal Harrell, prin. Fax 591-2961
Uvalde JHS 800/7-8
PO Box 1909 78802 830-591-2980
Kenneth Mueller, prin. Fax 591-2975

Southwest Texas Junior College Post-Sec.
2401 Garner Field Rd 78801 830-278-4401
SW School of Business & Tech Careers Post-Sec.
122 W North St 78801

Valentine, Jeff Davis, Pop. 193
Valentine ISD 100/PK-12
PO Box 188 79854 432-467-2671
George Elliott, supt. Fax 467-2004
valentineisd.esc18.net
Valentine S 100/PK-12
PO Box 188 79854 432-467-2671
Maria Williams, prin. Fax 467-2004

Valera, Coleman
Panther Creek Consolidated ISD 200/PK-12
129 Private Road 3421 76884 325-357-4506
Dan Harris, supt. Fax 357-4470
www.panthercountry.net/
Panther Creek JSHS 100/6-12
129 Private Road 3421 76884 325-357-4449
David Low, prin. Fax 357-4470

Valley Mills, Bosque, Pop. 1,145
Valley Mills ISD 600/PK-12
PO Box 518 76689 254-932-5210
Dr. John Spies, supt. Fax 932-6601
www.vmisd.net
Valley Mills HS 200/9-12
PO Box 518 76689 254-932-5251
Randy Anderson, prin. Fax 932-6601
Valley Mills JHS 100/7-8
PO Box 518 76689 254-932-5251
Randy Anderson, prin. Fax 932-6601

Valley View, Cooke, Pop. 808
Valley View ISD 600/K-12
200 Newton St 76272 940-726-3659
Kathy Garrison, supt. Fax 726-3614
www.vvisd.net
Valley View HS 200/9-12
200 Newton St 76272 940-726-3522
Clay Montgomery, prin. Fax 726-3862
Valley View MS 200/5-8
200 Newton St 76272 940-726-3244
Matthew Chalmers, prin. Fax 726-3862

Van, Van Zandt, Pop. 2,574
Van ISD 2,100/PK-12
PO Box 697 75790 903-963-8328
Joddie Witte, supt. Fax 963-3904
www.van.sprnet.org
Van HS 700/9-12
PO Box 697 75790 903-963-8623
Keith Murphy, prin. Fax 963-5591
Van JHS 500/6-8
PO Box 697 75790 903-963-8321
Don Dunn, prin. Fax 963-3277

Van Alstyne, Grayson, Pop. 2,760
Van Alstyne ISD 1,400/PK-12
PO Box 518 75495 903-482-8802
Dr. Allen Seay, supt. Fax 482-6086
www.vanalstyneisd.org
Van Alstyne HS 400/9-12
2001 N Waco St 75495 903-482-8803
John Williamson, prin. Fax 482-8885
Van Alstyne JHS 200/7-8
PO Box 699 75495 903-482-8804
Jim Martin, prin. Fax 482-9234

Vanderbilt, Jackson
Industrial ISD 1,000/PK-12
PO Box 369 77991 361-284-3226
Anthony Williams, supt. Fax 284-3349
www.iisd1.org
Industrial HS 300/9-12
PO Box 399 77991 361-284-3226
Jim Green, prin. Fax 284-3328
Industrial JHS 200/6-8
PO Box 367 77991 361-284-3226
Monte Althaus, prin. Fax 284-3049

Van Horn, Culberson, Pop. 2,157
Culberson County-Allamore ISD 600/PK-12
PO Box 899 79855 432-283-2245
Anne E. Pemberton, supt. Fax 283-9062
www.ccaisd.net/
Van Horn HS 200/9-12
PO Box 899 79855 432-283-2245
Merle Dunn, prin. Fax 283-9062
Van Horn JHS 100/6-8
PO Box 899 79855 432-283-2245
Charles Mohler, prin. Fax 283-9062

Van Vleck, Matagorda, Pop. 1,534
Van Vleck ISD 1,000/PK-12
142 S 4th St 77482 979-245-8518
Dr. Juan Antonio Jasso, supt. Fax 245-1214
www.vvisd.org
Herman MS 200/6-8
719 1st St 77482 979-245-6401
John O'Brien, prin. Fax 245-8538
Van Vleck HS 300/9-12
133 S 4th St 77482 979-245-4664
Larry Meche, prin. Fax 244-3485

Vega, Oldham, Pop. 898
Vega ISD 300/K-12
PO Box 190 79092 806-267-2123
Steve Hopper, supt. Fax 267-2146
www.region16.net/vegaisd
Vega HS 200/7-12
PO Box 190 79092 806-267-2126
Ashley Hartsell, prin. Fax 267-2146

Venus, Johnson, Pop. 2,229
Venus ISD 1,800/PK-12
PO Box 364 76084 972-366-3448
Elizabeth Treadway, supt. Fax 366-8742
www.venusisd.net/
Venus HS 500/9-12
PO Box 364 76084 972-366-8815
Robert White, prin. Fax 366-8919
Venus MS 400/6-8
PO Box 364 76084 972-366-3358
Jill Bottelberghe, prin. Fax 366-1740

Veribest, Tom Green
Veribest ISD 200/PK-12
PO Box 475 76886 325-655-4912
Jeffrey Brasher, supt. Fax 655-3355
veribest.netxv.net/
Veribest HS 100/6-12
PO Box 475 76886 325-655-2851
Ken Newman, prin. Fax 655-3355

Vernon, Wilbarger, Pop. 11,077
Northside ISD 200/K-12
18040 US Highway 283 76384 940-552-2551
Ed Donahue, supt. Fax 553-4919
www.esc9.net/northside
Northside S 200/K-12
18040 US Highway 283 76384 940-552-2551
Ed Donahue, prin. Fax 553-4919

Vernon ISD 2,200/PK-12
1713 Wilbarger St 76384 940-553-1900
Tom Woody, supt. Fax 553-3802
vernonisd.org/
Vernon HS 600/9-12
2102 Yucca Ln 76384 940-553-3377
Kenny Railsback, prin. Fax 553-4531
Vernon MS 500/6-8
2200 Yamparika St 76384 940-552-6231
William Belew, prin. Fax 552-0504

Vernon College Post-Sec.
4400 College Dr 76384 940-552-6291

Victoria, Victoria, Pop. 61,790
Victoria ISD 14,000/PK-12
PO Box 1759 77902 361-576-3131
Bob Moore, supt. Fax 788-9643
www.visd.com
Crain MS 1,000/6-8
PO Box 1759 77902 361-573-7453
Lisa Blundell, prin. Fax 788-9566
Howell MS 1,000/6-8
PO Box 1759 77902 361-578-1561
Debbie Crick, prin. Fax 788-9547
Memorial HS 2,500/10-12
PO Box 1759 77902 361-575-7451
Dr. Michael Maples, prin. Fax 788-9701
Memorial HS Stroman Campus 1,200/9-9
PO Box 1759 77902 361-578-2711
Richard LaFavers, prin. Fax 788-9800
Profit Magnet HS 200/9-12
PO Box 1759 77902 361-788-9650
Fax 788-9649
Victoria Career Development S Vo/Tech
PO Box 1759 77902 361-788-9288
Lauri Voss, prin. Fax 788-9656
Welder Magnet MS 1,000/6-8
PO Box 1759 77902 361-575-4553
Calvin Singleton, prin. Fax 788-9629

Citizens Medical Center Post-Sec.
2701 Hospital Dr 77901 361-573-9181
Devereux-Texas Treatment Network Post-Sec.
120 David Wade Dr 77902 800-383-5000
Faith Academy 100/PK-12
PO Box 4824 77903 361-573-2484
Dr. Chris Royael, admin. Fax 573-5058
St. Joseph HS 400/9-12
110 E Red River St 77901 361-573-2446
William McArdle, prin. Fax 573-4221
Texas Vocational School Post-Sec.
1921 E Red River St 77901 361-575-4768
University of Houston-Victoria Post-Sec.
3007 N Ben Wilson St 77901 361-570-4848
Victoria Beauty College Post-Sec.
1508 N Laurent St 77901 361-575-4526
Victoria College Post-Sec.
2200 E Red River St 77901 361-573-3291

Vidor, Orange, Pop. 11,290
Vidor ISD 5,200/PK-12
120 E Bolivar St 77662 409-951-8714
Robert E. Madding, supt. Fax 769-0093
www.vidor.k12.tx.us
Vidor HS 1,400/9-12
500 Orange St 77662 409-769-5418
Dr. Lynn Hancock, prin. Fax 769-6767
Vidor JHS 800/7-8
945 N Tram Rd 77662 409-951-8970
Debra Jordan, prin. Fax 769-6754

Waco, McLennan, Pop. 120,465
Bosqueville ISD 500/PK-12
7636 Rock Creek Rd 76708 254-757-3113
Stephanie Kucera, supt. Fax 752-4909
www.bosqueville.k12.tx.us
Bosqueville JSHS 200/7-12
7636 Rock Creek Rd 76708 254-757-3113
Gregg McCarthy, prin. Fax 752-0326

China Spring ISD 1,800/PK-12
6301 Sylvia St 76708 254-836-1115
George Kazanas, supt. Fax 836-0559
www.chinaspringisd.net
Other Schools – See China Spring

Connally ISD 2,700/PK-12
200 Cadet Way 76705 254-296-6460
Bruce Shores, supt. Fax 412-5530
www.connally.org/
Connally HS 700/9-12
900 N Lacy Dr 76705 254-296-6700
Joe Crownover, prin. Fax 412-5549
Connally JHS 400/7-8
100 Hancock Dr 76705 254-296-7700
Keith Pate, prin. Fax 829-2354

La Vega ISD 2,600/PK-12
3100 Bellmead Dr 76705 254-799-4963
Dr. Monte Geren, supt. Fax 799-8642
www.lavegaisd.org
La Vega HS 600/9-12
555 N Loop 340 76705 254-799-4951
Jerry Brem, prin. Fax 799-0720
La Vega JHS George Dixon Campus 400/7-8
4401 Orchard Ln 76705 254-799-2428
Bryant Adams, prin. Fax 799-8943

Midway ISD 6,000/PK-12
1205 Foundation Dr 76712 254-761-5610
Jim Boyle Ed.D., supt. Fax 666-7785
www.midwayisd.org/
Midway HS 1,900/9-12
8200 Mars Dr 76712 254-761-5650
Sharron Zachry, prin. Fax 761-5770
Other Schools – See Hewitt

Waco ISD 15,500/PK-12
PO Box 27 76703 254-755-9463
Dr. Roland Hernandez, supt. Fax 755-9690
www.wacoisd.org
Brazos MS 300/6-8
2415 Cumberland Ave 76707 254-754-5491
Fax 750-3576
Carver Academy 600/6-8
1601 J J Flewellen Rd 76704 254-757-0787
Pamela Correa, prin. Fax 750-3442
Chavez MS 400/6-8
700 S 15th St 76706 254-750-3736
Alfredo Loredo, prin. Fax 750-3739
Lake Air MS 600/6-8
4601 Cobbs Dr 76710 254-772-1910
Dr. Louise Powell, prin. Fax 741-4945
Moore Academy 700/9-12
500 N University Parks Dr 76701 254-753-6486
Dr. Debra Bishop, prin. Fax 750-3464
Tennyson MS 500/6-8
6100 Tennyson Dr 76710 254-772-1440
Robin Wilson, prin. Fax 741-4970
University HS 1,100/9-12
2600 Bagby Ave 76711 254-756-1843
Nolan Correa, prin. Fax 750-3709
University MS 500/6-8
1820 Irving Lee St 76711 254-753-1533
Raul Moreno, prin. Fax 750-3486
Waco HS 1,800/9-12
2020 N 42nd St 76710 254-776-1150
Dr. Heliodoro Torres Sanchez, prin. Fax 741-4815
Wiley MS 300/6-8
1030 E Live Oak St 76704 254-752-9691
Kermit Ward, prin. Fax 750-3434

Baylor University Post-Sec.
Po Box 97008 76798 254-710-1011
Hillcrest Baptist Medical Center Post-Sec.
3000 Herring Ave 76708 254-756-8551
McLennan Community College Post-Sec.
1400 College Dr 76708 254-299-8000
Reicher Catholic HS 9-12
2102 N 23rd St 76708 254-752-8349
Arlene Anderson Jones, prin. Fax 752-8408
Texas Christian Academy 300/PK-12
4600 Sanger Ave 76710 254-772-5474
Albert Beck, hdmstr. Fax 772-4485
Texas State Technical College Post-Sec.
3801 Campus Dr 76705 254-799-3611
Vanguard College Preparatory S 200/7-12
2517 Mount Carmel Dr 76710 254-772-8111
Bill Borg, hdmstr. Fax 772-8263

Waelder, Gonzales, Pop. 1,009
Waelder ISD 200/K-12
PO Box 247 78959 830-788-7161
Dave Plymale, supt. Fax 788-7429
Waelder JSHS 100/6-12
PO Box 247 78959 830-788-7151
L.D. Johnson, prin. Fax 788-7323

Wall, Tom Green
Wall ISD 900/K-12
PO Box 259 76957 325-651-7790
Walter Holik, supt. Fax 651-5081
www.wall.netxv.net
Miles Vocational Training Vo/Tech
PO Box 259 76957 325-651-7521
Russell Dacy, prin. Fax 651-9419
Wall HS 300/9-12
PO Box 259 76957 325-651-7521
Russell Dacy, prin. Fax 651-9419
Wall MS 200/6-8
PO Box 259 76957 325-651-7648
Ryan Snowden, prin. Fax 651-9664

Waller, Waller, Pop. 1,998
Waller ISD 4,900/PK-12
2214 Waller St 77484 936-931-3685
Richard McReavy, supt. Fax 372-5576
www.waller.isd.esc4.net/

Waller HS — 1,400/9-12
20950 Fields Store Rd 77484 — 936-372-3654
Kelly Baehren, prin. — Fax 372-4114
Waller JHS — 800/7-8
2402 Waller St 77484 — 936-931-1353
Troy Mooney, prin. — Fax 931-4044

Wallis, Austin, Pop. 1,271
Brazos ISD — 800/PK-12
PO Box 819 77485 — 979-478-6551
Dr. Mike Bergman, supt. — Fax 478-6413
www.brazosisd.net/
Brazos HS — 300/9-12
PO Box 458 77485 — 979-478-6000
Lyle Ebner, prin. — Fax 478-6002
Brazos MS — 200/6-8
PO Box 879 77485 — 979-478-6411
Jackie Ellis, prin. — Fax 478-6042

Walnut Springs, Bosque, Pop. 805
Walnut Springs ISD — 300/PK-12
PO Box 63 76690 — 254-797-2133
Randy Edwards, supt. — Fax 797-2191
Walnut Springs S — 300/PK-12
PO Box 63 76690 — 254-797-2132
Peggy Chapman, prin. — Fax 797-2191

Warren, Tyler
Warren ISD — 1,100/PK-12
PO Box 69 77664 — 409-547-2241
Mike Pate, supt. — Fax 547-3405
Warren HS — 300/9-12
PO Box 190 77664 — 409-547-2243
James Swinney, prin. — Fax 547-0214
Warren JHS — 300/6-8
PO Box 205 77664 — 409-547-2246
Ernestine Mitchell, prin. — Fax 547-2740

Waskom, Harrison, Pop. 2,129
Waskom ISD — 800/PK-12
PO Box 748 75692 — 903-687-3361
Jimmy E. Cox, supt. — Fax 687-3253
www.waskomisd.net
Waskom HS — 200/9-12
PO Box 748 75692 — 903-687-3361
Rick Baker, prin. — Fax 687-3372
Waskom MS — 200/6-8
PO Box 748 75692 — 903-687-3361
Penny Champion, prin. — Fax 687-3372

Watauga, Tarrant, Pop. 23,548
Birdville ISD
Supt. — See Haltom City
Watauga MS — 700/6-8
6300 Maurie Dr 76148 — 817-547-4800
Fax 581-5369

Harvest Christian Academy — 300/K-12
7200 Denton Hwy 76148 — 817-485-1660
William Pevey, hdmstr. — Fax 514-6279

Water Valley, Tom Green
Water Valley ISD — 300/PK-12
PO Box 250 76958 — 325-484-2478
David Howard, supt. — Fax 484-3359
www.watervalley.netxv.net
Water Valley JSHS — 100/7-12
PO Box 250 76958 — 325-484-2424
Jason Powers, prin. — Fax 484-3359

Waxahachie, Ellis, Pop. 25,454
Waxahachie ISD — 6,000/PK-12
411 N Gibson St 75165 — 972-923-4631
Dr. James E. Wilcox, supt. — Fax 923-4759
www.wisd.org
Waxahachie HS — 1,400/10-12
1000 N Highway 77 75165 — 972-923-4600
David Nix, prin. — Fax 923-4617
Waxahachie JHS — 1,000/7-8
2401 Brown St 75165 — 972-923-4680
Robert Woodhouse, prin. — Fax 923-4687
Waxahatchie 9th Grade Academy — 500/9-9
275 Indian Dr 75165 — 972-923-4780
John Aune, prin. — Fax 923-4782

Southwestern Assemblies of God Univ. — Post-Sec.
1200 Sycamore St 75165 — 972-937-4010
Waxahachie Preparatory Academy — 200/K-12
PO Box P 75168 — 972-937-0440
John Cullen, prin. — Fax 937-5033

Weatherford, Parker, Pop. 23,315
Peaster ISD — 1,000/PK-12
3602 Harwell Lake Rd 76088 — 817-341-5000
Philip Bledsoe, supt. — Fax 341-5003
www.peaster.net
Peaster HS — 300/9-12
3600 Harwell Lake Rd 76088 — 817-341-5000
Ed Daugherty, prin. — Fax 341-5027
Peaster MS — 200/6-8
8512 FM Road 920 76088 — 817-341-5000
Jeff Perkins, prin. — Fax 341-5052

Weatherford ISD — 7,000/PK-12
1100 Longhorn Dr 76086 — 817-598-2800
Dr. Deborah Cron, supt. — Fax 598-2835
www.weatherfordisd.com
Hall MS — 600/7-8
902 Charles St 76086 — 817-598-2822
Michelle Howard-Schwind, prin. — Fax 598-2854
Ninth Grade Center — 600/9-9
1007 S Main St 76086 — 817-598-2847
Charles Carroll, prin. — Fax 598-2928
Tison MS — 500/7-8
102 Meadowview Rd 76087 — 817-598-2960
Debbie Bradley, prin. — Fax 598-2963
Weatherford HS — 1,500/10-12
2121 Bethel Rd 76087 — 817-598-2858
Dr. Chip Evans, prin. — Fax 598-2881

Weatherford Christian S — 200/PK-12
111 E Columbia St 76086 — 817-596-7807
Van Gravitt, hdmstr. — Fax 596-0529
Weatherford College — Post-Sec.
225 College Park Dr 76086 — 817-594-5471

Webster, Harris, Pop. 8,852

ITT Technical Institute — Post-Sec.
1001 Magnolia St 77598 — 281-316-4700

Weimar, Colorado, Pop. 2,016
Weimar ISD — 600/PK-12
506 W Main St 78962 — 979-725-9504
Mike Wallace Ed.D., supt. — Fax 725-8737
www.weimarisd.org/
Weimar HS — 200/9-12
506 W Main St 78962 — 979-725-9504
Dr. Mike Laird, prin. — Fax 725-8737
Weimar JHS — 100/6-8
101 N West St 78962 — 979-725-9515
Nancy Schapp, prin. — Fax 725-8383

Welch, Dawson
Dawson ISD — 200/PK-12
PO Box 180 79377 — 806-489-7461
Lindsey Wallace, supt. — Fax 489-7463
Dawson S — 200/PK-12
PO Box 180 79377 — 806-489-7461
Marva Hogue, prin. — Fax 489-7463

Wellington, Collingsworth, Pop. 2,090
Wellington ISD — 500/PK-12
609 15th St 79095 — 806-447-2512
Carl Taylor, supt. — Fax 447-5124
www.wellingtonisd.net
Wellington HS — 100/9-12
811 15th St 79095 — 806-447-2527
Tim Webb, prin. — Fax 447-9012
Wellington JHS — 100/6-8
1504 Amarillo St 79095 — 806-447-5726
Don Hinsley, prin. — Fax 447-5089

Wellman, Terry, Pop. 201
Wellman-Union ISD — 200/K-12
PO Box 69 79378 — 806-637-4910
Leslie Vann, supt. — Fax 637-2585
wellman.esc17.net
Wellman-Union HS — 100/6-12
PO Box 129 79378 — 806-637-4619
Russell Schaub, prin. — Fax 637-2585

Wells, Cherokee, Pop. 792
Wells ISD — 300/PK-12
PO Box 469 75976 — 936-867-4466
Dale Morton, supt. — Fax 867-4466
www.wells.esc7.net
Wells HS — 100/9-12
PO Box 469 75976 — 936-867-4400
Bradley Hines, prin. — Fax 867-4466

Weslaco, Hidalgo, Pop. 31,442
Weslaco ISD — 15,300/PK-12
PO Box 266 78599 — 956-969-6500
Richard Rivera, supt. — Fax 969-2664
www.wisd.us
Central MS — 900/6-8
503 E 6th St 78596 — 956-969-6710
Lauren Arce, prin. — Fax 969-0779
Cuellar MS — 700/6-8
1201 S Bridge Ave 78596 — 956-969-6720
Mario Hernandez, prin. — Fax 973-9797
Garza MS — 1,000/6-8
1111 W Sugar Cane Dr 78596 — 956-969-6774
Daniel Budimir, prin. — Fax 447-0484
Hoge MS — 800/6-8
2302 N International Blvd 78596 — 956-969-6730
Patricia Munoz, prin. — Fax 514-0903
Weslaco East HS — 1,700/9-12
810 S Pleasantview Dr 78596 — 956-969-6950
Sue Peterson, prin. — Fax 968-8693
Weslaco HS — 2,100/9-12
1005 W Pike Blvd 78596 — 956-969-6700
Isidoro Nieto, prin. — Fax 968-8008

Advanced Barber College and Hair Design — Post-Sec.
2818 S International Blvd 78596 — 956-969-0341
South Texas Vocational-Technical Inst. — Post-Sec.
2419 E Hagger Ave 78596 — 956-969-1564
Valley Grande Academy — 100/9-12
PO Box 1126 78599 — 956-968-0573
Pam Bickell, prin. — Fax 968-9814

West, McLennan, Pop. 2,711
West ISD — 1,500/PK-12
801 N Reagan St 76691 — 254-826-7500
Rob Hart Ed.D., supt. — Fax 826-7503
www.westisd.net
West HS — 500/9-12
801 N Reagan St 76691 — 254-826-7510
Phyllis Ramsey, prin. — Fax 826-7514
West MS — 300/6-8
801 N Reagan St 76691 — 254-826-7520
Grady Fulbright, prin. — Fax 826-7524

Westbrook, Mitchell, Pop. 196
Westbrook ISD — 200/PK-12
PO Box 99 79565 — 325-644-2311
Todd Burleson, supt. — Fax 644-5101
www.westbrookisd.com
Westbrook S — 200/PK-12
PO Box 99 79565 — 325-644-2311
Doc Rowell, prin. — Fax 644-5101

West Columbia, Brazoria, Pop. 4,240
Columbia-Brazoria ISD — 2,900/PK-12
PO Box 158 77486 — 979-345-5147
Carol Bertholf, supt. — Fax 345-4890
www.cbisd.com
Columbia HS — 800/9-12
PO Box 158 77486 — 979-345-5147
Steve Galloway, prin. — Fax 345-6785
Other Schools – See Brazoria

Columbia Christian S — 100/PK-12
725 W Brazos Ave 77486 — 979-345-2434
Kenneth Canion, prin. — Fax 345-5134

Wharton, Wharton, Pop. 9,374
Wharton ISD — 2,500/PK-12
2100 N Fulton St 77488 — 979-532-6201
Don Hillis, supt. — Fax 532-6228
www.wharton.isd.tenet.edu/
Wharton HS — 700/9-12
1 Tiger Ave 77488 — 979-532-6800
Don Jennings, prin. — Fax 532-6807
Wharton JHS — 400/7-8
1120 N Rusk St 77488 — 979-532-6840
Larry Boyette, prin. — Fax 532-6849

Wharton County Junior College — Post-Sec.
911 E Boling Hwy 77488 — 979-532-4560

Wheeler, Wheeler, Pop. 1,217
Wheeler ISD — 400/PK-12
PO Box 1010 79096 — 806-826-5241
Paul Mahler, supt. — Fax 826-3118
Wheeler S, PO Box 1010 79096 — 400/PK-12
Toby Tucker, prin. — 806-826-5534

White Deer, Carson, Pop. 1,071
White Deer ISD — 400/K-12
PO Box 517 79097 — 806-883-2311
Danny Ferrell, supt. — Fax 883-2321
www.pan-tex.net/wdisd
White Deer HS — 100/9-12
PO Box 247 79097 — 806-883-6411
Bryan Hanna, prin. — Fax 883-5029

Whiteface, Cochran, Pop. 407
Whiteface Consolidated ISD — 400/PK-12
PO Box 7 79379 — 806-287-1154
Elbert Wuthrich, supt. — Fax 287-1131
www.whiteface.k12.tx.us
Whiteface JSHS — 200/7-12
PO Box 67 79379 — 806-287-1104
James German, prin. — Fax 287-1131

Whitehouse, Smith, Pop. 7,122
Whitehouse ISD — 4,100/PK-12
106 Wildcat Dr 75791 — 903-839-5500
Dennis Miller, supt. — Fax 839-5515
www.whitehouseisd.org
Whitehouse HS, 901 E Main St 75791 — 1,200/9-12
Tony Black, prin. — 903-839-5551
Whitehouse JHS — 600/7-8
108 Wildcat Dr 75791 — 903-839-5590
David Smith, prin.

White Oak, Gregg, Pop. 6,130
White Oak ISD — 1,300/PK-12
200 S White Oak Rd 75693 — 903-291-2000
Jack R. Hale, supt. — Fax 291-2222
isd.woccn.org/
White Oak HS — 400/9-12
200 S White Oak Rd 75693 — 903-291-2000
Don Noll, prin. — Fax 291-2034
White Oak MS — 300/6-8
200 S White Oak Rd 75693 — 903-291-2050
Ronnie Hinkle, prin. — Fax 291-2035

Whitesboro, Grayson, Pop. 4,001
Whitesboro ISD — 1,600/PK-12
115 4th St 76273 — 903-564-4200
Ray Lea, supt. — Fax 564-9303
www.whitesboroisd.org
Whitesboro HS — 500/9-12
1 Bearcat Dr 76273 — 903-564-4208
Rendell Cole, prin. — Fax 564-4288
Whitesboro MS — 400/6-8
600 4th St 76273 — 903-564-4240
Patty Mitchell, prin. — Fax 564-5939

White Settlement, Tarrant, Pop. 15,736
White Settlement ISD
Supt. — See Fort Worth
Brewer HS — 800/10-12
1000 S Cherry Ln 76108 — 817-367-1200
Julio Toro, prin. — Fax 367-1242
Brewer MS — 700/7-8
1000 S Cherry Ln 76108 — 817-367-1267
Christie Beaty, prin. — Fax 367-1268

Whitewright, Grayson, Pop. 1,780
Whitewright ISD — 800/PK-12
PO Box 888 75491 — 903-364-2155
Robert O'Connor, supt. — Fax 364-2839
Whitewright HS — 300/9-12
PO Box 888 75491 — 903-364-2535
Wade Stanford, prin. — Fax 364-2579
Whitewright MS — 200/6-8
PO Box 888 75491 — 903-364-2151
Bobby Worthy, prin. — Fax 364-5263

Whitharral, Hockley
Whitharral ISD — 200/K-12
PO Box 225 79380 — 806-299-1184
Ed Sharp, supt. — Fax 299-1257
www.whitharral.k12.tx.us/
Whitharral S — 200/K-12
PO Box 225 79380 — 806-299-1135
Carla Kristinek, prin. — Fax 299-1257

Whitney, Hill, Pop. 2,049
Whitney ISD — 1,600/PK-12
PO Box 518 76692 — 254-694-2254
Lee Coffman, supt. — Fax 694-2064
www.whitney.k12.tx.us
Whitney HS — 500/9-12
PO Box 518 76692 — 254-694-3457
Curt Haley, prin. — Fax 694-4206
Whitney JHS, PO Box 518 76692 — 400/6-8
Wayne Redding, prin. — 254-694-3446

Wichita Falls, Wichita, Pop. 99,846
City View ISD — 1,100/PK-12
1025 City View Dr 76306 — 940-855-4042
Michael Smith, supt. — Fax 851-8889
www.cityview-isd.net/
City View JSHS — 400/7-12
1600 City View Dr 76306 — 940-855-7511
Steve Harris, prin. — Fax 851-5027

Wichita Falls ISD — 14,100/PK-12
PO Box 97533 76307 — 940-720-3273
Dr. Dawson Orr, supt. — Fax 720-3167
www.wfisd.net
Barwise JHS — 600/7-8
3807 Kemp Blvd 76308 — 940-720-3035
Linda Muehlberger, prin. — Fax 692-2372
Carrigan Vocational Center — Vo/Tech
1609 Blonde St 76301 — 940-720-3224
Rhonda Hall, prin. — Fax 720-3368
Hirschi HS — 900/9-12
3106 Borton St 76306 — 940-716-2800
Wanda Jackson, prin. — Fax 716-2835
Kirby JHS — 500/7-8
1715 Loop 11 76306 — 940-716-2900
Dee Palmore, prin. — Fax 716-2915
McNiel JHS — 700/7-8
4712 Barnett Rd 76310 — 940-720-3030
Carol English, prin. — Fax 720-3032
Rider HS — 1,700/9-12
4611 Cypress Ave 76310 — 940-720-3000
Nat Lunn, prin. — Fax 720-3002

Wichita Falls HS 1,500/9-12
2149 Avenue H 76309 940-720-3177
Dr. Robert Mobley, prin. Fax 767-4248
Zundelowitz JHS 400/7-8
1706 Polk St 76309 940-720-3170
Chad Brewster, prin. Fax 720-3172

Agape Christian S 100/K-12
5600 Burkburnett Rd 76306 940-851-6727
John Meade, prin. Fax 851-6592
American Commercial College Post-Sec.
4317 Barnett Rd 76310 940-691-0454
Midwestern State University Post-Sec.
3410 Taft Blvd 76308 940-397-4000
Notre Dame S 300/PK-12
2821 Lansing Blvd 76309 940-692-6041
Cindy Huckabee, prin. Fax 692-2811
United Regional Health Care System Post-Sec.
1600 11th St 76301 940-764-3187

Willis, Montgomery, Pop. 4,172
Willis ISD 5,000/PK-12
204 W Rogers St 77378 936-856-1200
Dr. Brian Zemlicka, supt. Fax 856-5182
wisd.willis.k12.tx.us
Brabham MS 600/6-8
10000 FM 830 Rd 77318 936-890-2312
Sheryl Burlison, prin. Fax 856-2910
Lucas MS 500/6-8
1304 N Campbell St 77378 936-856-1274
Tiffany Forester, prin. Fax 856-1065
Willis HS 1,400/9-12
1201 FM 830 Rd 77378 936-856-1250
Tim Patton, prin. Fax 856-3391

Willow Park, Parker, Pop. 3,463

Trinity Christian Academy 400/PK-12
4954 E Interstate 20 Svc Rd 76087 817-441-7901
Dr. Marsha Barber, admin. Fax 441-7912

Wills Point, Van Zandt, Pop. 3,855
Wills Point ISD 2,700/PK-12
338 W North Commerce St 75169 903-873-3161
William Stewart, supt. Fax 873-2462
willspoint.ednet10.net
Wills Point HS 800/9-12
1800 W South Commerce St 75169 903-873-2371
Jim Lamb, prin. Fax 873-6008
Wills Point JHS 400/7-8
200 Tiger Dr 75169 903-873-4924
Thomas Harp, prin. Fax 873-4873

Wilson, Lynn, Pop. 501
Wilson ISD 200/PK-12
PO Box 9 79381 806-628-6271
Mike Jones, supt. Fax 628-6441
wilson.esc17.net/
Wilson S 200/PK-12
PO Box 9 79381 806-628-6261
Mike Jones, prin. Fax 628-6441

Wimberley, Hays, Pop. 2,712
Wimberley ISD 1,900/PK-12
14401 Ranch Rd 12 78676 512-847-2414
Dr. Marian Strauss, supt. Fax 847-2142
www.wimberley.txed.net/
Wimberley HS 700/9-12
100 Carney Ln 78676 512-847-5729
Dwain York, prin. Fax 847-7269
Wimberley JHS 500/6-8
200 Texan Blvd 78676 512-847-2181
Dee Howard, prin. Fax 847-7897

Windthorst, Archer, Pop. 443
Windthorst ISD 500/PK-12
PO Box 190 76389 940-423-6688
Don Windham, supt. Fax 423-6505
Windthorst JSHS 200/7-12
PO Box 190 76389 940-423-6680
Lonnie Hise, prin. Fax 423-6505

Wink, Winkler, Pop. 883
Wink-Loving ISD 300/PK-12
PO Box 637 79789 432-527-3880
John Benham, supt. Fax 527-3505
wlisd.esc18.net
Wink JSHS 200/7-12
PO Box 637 79789 432-527-3880
Danny Carrillo, prin. Fax 527-3505

Winnie, Chambers, Pop. 2,238
East Chambers ISD 1,200/PK-12
1955 State Highway 124 77665 409-296-6100
Scott Campbell, supt. Fax 296-3528
www.eastchambers.net
East Chambers HS 300/9-12
234 E Buccaneer Dr 77665 409-296-6100
Steve Franzen, prin. Fax 296-9596
East Chambers JHS 200/7-8
1931 State Highway 124 77665 409-296-6100
Lou Ann Rainey, prin. Fax 296-2724

Winnsboro, Wood, Pop. 3,794
Winnsboro ISD 1,500/PK-12
207 E Pine St 75494 903-342-3737
Dr. Mark Bosold, supt. Fax 342-3380
www.winnsboroisd.org
Memorial MS 400/5-8
505 S Chestnut St 75494 903-342-5711
Nan Saucier, prin. Fax 342-6689
Winnsboro HS 400/9-12
409 Newsome St 75494 903-342-3641
Susan Morton, prin. Fax 342-3645

Winona, Smith, Pop. 605
Winona ISD 900/PK-12
PO Box 218 75792 903-939-4001
Rodney Fausett, supt. Fax 877-9387
www.winonaisd.org
Winona HS 300/9-12
PO Box 218 75792 903-939-4100
Leland Hand, prin. Fax 877-2451
Winona MS 200/6-8
PO Box 218 75792 903-939-4040
Oscar Rendon, prin. Fax 877-9150

Winters, Runnels, Pop. 2,728
Winters ISD 700/PK-12
603 N Heights St 79567 325-754-5574
David Hutton, supt. Fax 754-5374
www.wintersisd.net/
Winters HS 200/9-12
603 N Heights St 79567 325-754-5516
Susan Sharp, prin. Fax 754-5085
Winters JHS 100/7-8
603 N Heights St 79567 325-754-5518
Chad Wright, prin. Fax 754-5085

Woden, Nacogdoches
Woden ISD 900/PK-12
PO Box 100 75978 936-564-2073
L. Wayne Mason, supt. Fax 564-1250
www.woden.esc7.net/
Woden HS 300/9-12
PO Box 100 75978 936-564-7903
Mike King, prin. Fax 462-4962
Woden JHS, PO Box 100 75978 200/6-8
Keith Lowery, prin. 936-564-2481

Wolfe City, Hunt, Pop. 1,647
Wolfe City ISD 600/PK-12
PO Box L 75496 903-496-2283
Rick Loesch, supt. Fax 496-7905
www.wcisd.net
Wolfe City HS 200/9-12
505 W Dallas St 75496 903-496-2891
Chris Sheets, prin. Fax 496-7124
Wolfe City MS 100/6-8
505 W Dallas St 75496 903-496-7333
Chris Sheets, prin. Fax 496-7905

Wolfforth, Lubbock, Pop. 2,942
Frenship ISD 4,600/PK-12
PO Box 100 79382 806-866-9541
John R. Thomas, supt. Fax 866-4135
www.frenship.us
Frenship HS 1,400/9-12
PO Box 100 79382 806-866-4440
Kim Spicer, prin. Fax 866-9370
Frenship MS 800/6-8
PO Box 100 79382 806-866-4464
Jerry Jerabek, prin. Fax 866-2181
Other Schools – See Lubbock

Woodsboro, Refugio, Pop. 1,626
Woodsboro ISD 500/PK-12
PO Box 770 78393 361-543-4518
Steven Self, supt. Fax 543-4856
www.wisd.net
Woodsboro HS 100/9-12
PO Box 770 78393 361-543-4521
Brian Hicks, prin. Fax 543-5140
Woodsboro JHS, PO Box 770 78393 100/7-8
Mary Vickery, prin. 361-543-4622

Woodson, Throckmorton, Pop. 259
Woodson ISD 100/PK-12
PO Box 287 76491 940-345-6528
Dan Bellah, supt. Fax 345-6549
www.esc9.net/woodson/
Woodson S 100/PK-12
PO Box 287 76491 940-345-6521
Gordon Thomas, prin. Fax 345-6549

Woodville, Tyler, Pop. 2,313
Woodville ISD 1,400/PK-12
505 N Charlton St 75979 409-283-3752
Glen Conner, supt. Fax 283-7962
www.esc05.k12.tx.us/woodville
Woodville HS 400/9-12
505 N Charlton St 75979 409-283-3714
Roschelle Springfield, prin. Fax 331-3427
Woodville MS 400/6-8
505 N Charlton St 75979 409-283-7109
Jim Stricklan, prin. Fax 331-3418

Wortham, Freestone, Pop. 1,089
Wortham ISD 400/PK-12
PO Box 247 76693 254-765-3080
Albert Armer, supt. Fax 765-3473
www.worthamisd.org
Wortham HS 100/9-12
PO Box 247 76693 254-765-3094
Lynn Jantzen, prin. Fax 765-3473
Wortham MS 100/6-8
PO Box 247 76693 254-765-3094
Lynn Jantzen, prin. Fax 765-3473

Wylie, Dallas, Pop. 29,061
Wylie ISD 7,800/PK-12
PO Box 490 75098 972-429-3000
Dr. H. John Fuller, supt. Fax 442-5368
www.wylieisd.net
Burnett JHS 500/7-8
PO Box 490 75098 972-429-3200
Mike Williams, prin. Fax 429-7999
McMillan JHS 700/7-8
PO Box 490 75098 972-429-3225
Jon Peters, prin. Fax 941-6372
Wylie HS 1,900/9-12
PO Box 490 75098 972-429-3100
Gary Brown, prin. Fax 429-3077

Wylie Preparatory Academy 100/1-12
PO Box 2273 75098 972-442-1388
Julie Calhoun, admin. Fax 429-3568

Yantis, Wood, Pop. 359
Yantis ISD 400/PK-12
105 W Oak St 75497 903-383-2463
Harold Cowley, supt. Fax 383-7620
www.yantisisd.net
Yantis HS 200/6-12
105 W Oak St 75497 903-383-2463
Kevin White, prin. Fax 383-3075

Yoakum, Lavaca, Pop. 5,720
Yoakum ISD 1,600/PK-12
PO Box 737 77995 361-293-3162
Michael Poynor, supt. Fax 293-6678
www.yoakumisd.net/
Yoakum HS 500/9-12
PO Box 737 77995 361-293-3442
Chris Kvinta, prin. Fax 293-2145
Yoakum JHS 300/6-8
PO Box 737 77995 361-293-3111
Pat Brewer, prin. Fax 293-5787

Yorktown, DeWitt, Pop. 2,265
Yorktown ISD 700/PK-12
PO Box 487 78164 361-564-2252
Deborah Kneese, supt. Fax 564-2254
www.yisd.org
Yorktown HS 200/9-12
PO Box 487 78164 361-564-2252
Jose Ramos, prin. Fax 564-2274
Yorktown JHS 200/6-8
PO Box 487 78164 361-564-2252
Sylvia Hernandez, prin. Fax 564-2289

Zapata, Zapata, Pop. 7,119
Zapata County ISD 3,400/PK-12
PO Box 158 78076 956-765-6546
Romeo Rodriguez, supt. Fax 765-8350
www.zcisd.org
Zapata HS 800/9-12
PO Box 3750 78076 956-765-0280
Janie Rodriguez, prin. Fax 765-0274
Zapata MS 700/6-8
PO Box 3636 78076 956-765-6542
Suzette Barrera, prin. Fax 765-9204

Zavalla, Angelina, Pop. 656
Zavalla ISD 500/PK-12
PO Box 45 75980 936-897-2271
Dr. Kathy Ray, supt. Fax 897-2674
www.zavalla.esc7.net
Zavalla JSHS 200/6-12
PO Box 45 75980 936-897-2301
Clark Bynum, prin. Fax 897-2674

Zephyr, Brown
Zephyr ISD 200/K-12
11625 County Road 281 76890 325-739-5331
David Whisenhunt, supt. Fax 739-2126
Zephyr JSHS 100/7-12
11625 County Road 281 76890 325-739-5331
Gary Bufe, prin. Fax 739-2126

UTAH

UTAH OFFICE OF EDUCATION
PO Box 144200, Salt Lake City 84114-4200
Telephone 801-538-7500
Fax 801-538-7768
Website http://www.usoe.k12.ut.us

Superintendent of Public Instruction Patti Harrington

UTAH BOARD OF EDUCATION
250 E 500 S, Salt Lake City 84111-3284

REGIONAL SERVICE CENTERS (RSC)

Central Utah Educational Services
Glen Taylor, dir. 435-896-4469
195 E 500 N, Richfield 84701 Fax 896-4767

Northeastern Utah Educational Services
Duke Mossman, dir. 435-654-1921
755 S Main St, Heber City 84032 Fax 654-2403

Southeast Educational Service Center
Thomas Roush, dir. 435-637-1173
685 E 200 S, Price 84501 Fax 637-1178
Southwest Educational Development Ctr
Randy Johnson, dir. 435-586-2865
520 W 800 S, Cedar City 84720 Fax 586-2868

PUBLIC, PRIVATE AND CATHOLIC SECONDARY SCHOOLS

Alpine, Utah, Pop. 9,063
Alpine SD
Supt. — See American Fork
Timberline MS 1,000/7-9
500 W Canyon Crest Rd 84004 801-763-7005
Terry Hill, prin. Fax 763-7045

Altamont, Duchesne, Pop. 183
Duchesne SD
Supt. — See Duchesne
Altamont JSHS 200/7-12
PO Box 130 84001 435-738-1345
Mary Ellen Kettle, prin. Fax 738-1370

American Fork, Utah, Pop. 21,372
Alpine SD 52,800/K-12
575 N 100 E 84003 801-756-8400
Dr. Vernon Henshaw, supt. Fax 756-8516
www.alpine.k12.ut.us/
American Fork JHS 1,500/7-9
20 W 1120 N 84003 801-756-8543
Theron Murphy, prin. Fax 756-8407
American Fork SHS 1,500/10-12
510 N 600 E 84003 801-756-8547
Carolyn Merrill, prin. Fax 756-8575
Other Schools – See Alpine, Highland, Lehi, Lindon, Orem, Pleasant Grove

Beaver, Beaver, Pop. 2,558
Beaver SD 1,500/K-12
PO Box 31 84713 435-438-2291
Ray Terry, supt. Fax 438-5898
www.beaver.k12.ut.us
Beaver JSHS 400/7-12
PO Box 71 84713 435-438-2301
David Green, prin. Fax 438-1519
Other Schools – See Milford

Bicknell, Wayne, Pop. 335
Wayne SD 500/K-12
PO Box 127 84715 435-425-3813
Jessie Pace, supt. Fax 425-3806
www.wayne.k12.ut.us
Wayne HS 200/9-12
PO Box 217 84715 435-425-3411
Charles Nelson, prin. Fax 425-3480
Wayne MS 100/6-8
PO Box 128 84715 435-425-3421
Mary Bray, lead tchr. Fax 425-3130

Big Water, Kane, Pop. 415
Kane SD
Supt. — See Kanab
Big Water HS 50/7-12
PO Box 410126 84741 435-675-5821
Gary Young, prin. Fax 675-5821

Blanding, San Juan, Pop. 3,135
San Juan SD 3,000/K-12
200 N Main St 84511 435-678-1200
Dr. Douglas Wright, supt. Fax 678-1204
www.sanjuanschools.org/
Lyman MS 300/6-8
535 N 100 E 84511 435-678-1398
Chas DeWitt, prin. Fax 678-1399
San Juan HS 400/9-12
311 N 100 E 84511 435-678-1301
Bob Peterson, prin. Fax 678-1396
Other Schools – See Montezuma Creek, Monticello, Monument Valley

Bountiful, Davis, Pop. 41,085
Davis SD
Supt. — See Farmington
Bountiful JHS 700/7-9
30 W 400 N 84010 801-402-6000
Steve Lindsay, prin. Fax 402-6001
Bountiful SHS 1,300/10-12
695 Orchard Dr 84010 801-402-3900
Ryck Astle, prin. Fax 402-3901
Millcreek JHS 600/7-9
245 E 1000 S 84010 801-402-6200
David Tanner, prin. Fax 402-6201
Mueller Park JHS 700/7-9
955 Mueller Park Rd 84010 801-402-6300
Dr. Doug Beer, prin. Fax 402-6301
South Davis JHS 900/7-9
298 W 2600 S 84010 801-402-6400
Bryan Nielsen, prin. Fax 402-6401
Viewmont SHS 1,800/10-12
120 W 1000 N 84010 801-402-4200
Scott Tennis, prin. Fax 402-4201

Brigham City, Box Elder, Pop. 18,355
Box Elder SD 10,200/K-12
960 S Main St 84302 435-734-4800
Martell Menlove, supt. Fax 734-4833
www.besd.net
Box Elder MS 1,000/8-9
18 S 500 E 84302 435-734-4880
Scott Hunsaker, prin. Fax 734-4885
Box Elder SHS 1,400/10-12
380 S 600 W 84302 435-734-4840
Darrell Eddington, prin. Fax 734-4846
Young Alternative HS Adult
230 W 200 S 84302 435-734-4834
Steve Chadaz, prin. Fax 734-4860
Other Schools – See Garland, Grouse Creek, Park Valley

Northridge Learning Center 100/K-12
44 S Main St 84302 435-734-2550
Dixie Evans, dir. Fax 723-3903

Castle Dale, Emery, Pop. 1,615
Emery County SD
Supt. — See Huntington
Emery SHS 500/10-12
PO Box 499 84513 435-381-2689
Gwen Callahan, prin. Fax 381-5370

Cedar City, Iron, Pop. 23,983
Iron SD 6,200/K-12
2077 W Royal Hunte Dr 84720 435-586-2804
James Johnson, supt. Fax 586-2815
www.iron.k12.ut.us
Canyon View HS 1,000/9-12
166 W 1925 N 84720 435-586-2813
Jennifer Wood, prin. Fax 586-2849
Canyon View MS 6-8
1865 N Main St 84720 435-586-2830
Conrad Aitken, prin. Fax 586-2837
Cedar HS 900/9-12
703 W 600 S 84720 435-586-2820
Kevin Garrett, prin. Fax 586-2826
Cedar MS 500/6-8
2215 W Royal Hunte Dr 84720 435-586-2810
Kendall Benson, prin. Fax 586-2829
Adult HS/Southwest Education Academy Adult
510 W 800 S 84720 435-586-2870
Dennis Heaton, prin. Fax 586-2815
Other Schools – See Parowan

Southern Utah University Post-Sec.
351 W Center St 84720 435-586-7715
Southwest Applied Technology College Post-Sec.
510 W 800 S 84720 435-586-2899

Centerville, Davis, Pop. 14,898
Davis SD
Supt. — See Farmington
Centerville JHS 1,000/7-9
625 S Main St 84014 801-402-6100
Aaron Hogge, prin. Fax 402-6101

Clearfield, Davis, Pop. 27,413
Davis SD
Supt. — See Farmington
Clearfield SHS 2,100/10-12
931 S 1000 E 84015 801-402-8200
Mike Timothy, prin. Fax 402-8336
North Davis JHS 900/7-9
835 S State St 84015 801-402-6500
Curtis Stromberg, prin. Fax 402-6501

Certified Careers Institute Post-Sec.
775 S 2000 E 84015 801-774-9900

Coalville, Summit, Pop. 1,451
North Summit SD 1,000/PK-12
PO Box 497 84017 435-336-5654
Steven Carlsen, supt. Fax 336-2401
www.nsummit.k12.ut.us
North Summit HS 300/9-12
PO Box 497 84017 435-336-5656
Jerre Holmes, prin. Fax 336-0309
North Summit MS 300/5-8
PO Box 497 84017 435-336-5678
Lloyd Marchant, prin. Fax 336-4474

Cottonwood Heights, Salt Lake, Pop. 27,500
Jordan SD
Supt. — See Sandy
Brighton SHS 2,000/10-12
2220 Bengal Blvd, 801-256-5200
Rebecca Laney, prin. Fax 256-5270

Delta, Millard, Pop. 3,106
Millard SD 3,000/K-12
285 E 450 N 84624 435-864-1000
David Taylor, supt. Fax 864-5684
www.millard.k12.ut.us
Delta HS 600/9-12
50 W 300 N 84624 435-864-5610
Dean Fowles, prin. Fax 864-5619
Delta MS 500/6-8
251 E 300 N 84624 435-864-5660
David Styler, prin. Fax 864-5669
Delta Tech Ctr Vo/Tech
305 E 200 N 84624 435-864-5710
LaVoy Starley, prin. Fax 864-5719
Other Schools – See Fillmore

Draper, Salt Lake, Pop. 35,119

Ameritech College Post-Sec.
12257 Business Park Dr #108 84020 801-816-1444
Juan Diego Catholic HS 700/9-12
300 E 11800 S 84020 801-984-7602
Gabriel Colosimo, prin. Fax 984-7601
Oxford Learning Source 50/PK-12
1259 Draper Pkwy 84020 801-501-0228
Millicent Jacobson, dir. Fax 501-0296
Pine Ridge Academy 50/7-12
PO Box 909 84020 801-562-1717
Lisa Wisham, dir. Fax 572-8220
St. John the Baptist MS 300/6-8
300 E 11800 S 84020 801-984-7613
Nikki Ward, prin. Fax 984-7649

Duchesne, Duchesne, Pop. 1,481
Duchesne SD — 3,900/K-12
PO Box 446 84021 — 435-738-1240
John Aland, supt. — Fax 738-1254
www.dcsd.org
Duchesne JSHS — 300/7-12
PO Box 330 84021 — 435-738-1260
Stan Young, prin. — Fax 738-1285
Other Schools – See Altamont, Roosevelt, Tabiona

Dugway, Tooele, Pop. 1,761
Tooele County SD
Supt. — See Tooele
Dugway JSHS — 100/7-12
5020 5th St 84022 — 435-831-4566
Karen Swenson, prin. — Fax 831-4951

Eden, Weber
Weber SD
Supt. — See Ogden
Snowcrest JHS — 400/7-9
2755 N Highway 162 84310 — 801-476-5360
Velden Wardle, prin. — Fax 476-5399

Enterprise, Washington, Pop. 1,419
Washington County SD
Supt. — See Saint George
Enterprise JSHS — 400/7-12
PO Box 460 84725 — 435-878-2248
Russell Holmes, prin. — Fax 878-2479

Ephraim, Sanpete, Pop. 4,977
South Sanpete SD
Supt. — See Manti
Ephraim MS — 400/6-8
555 S 100 E 84627 — 435-283-4037
Kent Larsen, prin. — Fax 283-4885

Snow College — Post-Sec.
150 College Ave 84627 — 435-283-7000

Escalante, Garfield, Pop. 744
Garfield SD
Supt. — See Panguitch
Escalante HS — 100/7-12
PO Box 228 84726 — 435-826-4205
Angie Alvey, prin. — Fax 826-4231

Eureka, Juab, Pop. 793
Tintic SD — 300/PK-12
PO Box 210 84628 — 435-433-6363
Ron Barlow, supt. — Fax 433-6643
www.tintic.k12.ut.us
Tintic JSHS — 100/7-12
PO Box 230 84628 — 435-433-6939
Gordon Grimstead, prin. — Fax 433-6845
Other Schools – See Trout Creek

Farmington, Davis, Pop. 14,357
Davis SD — 58,500/PK-12
PO Box 588 84025 — 801-402-0588
Dr. W. Bryan Bowles, supt. — Fax 402-5261
www.davis.k12.ut.us
Farmington JHS — 1,100/7-9
150 S 200 W 84025 — 801-402-6900
Bill Fullmer, prin. — Fax 402-6901
Other Schools – See Bountiful, Centerville, Clearfield, Kaysville, Layton, Sunset, Syracuse, West Point, Woods Cross

Ferron, Emery, Pop. 1,571
Emery County SD
Supt. — See Huntington
San Rafael JHS — 300/7-9
PO Box 790 84523 — 435-384-2335
Garth Johnson, prin. — Fax 384-3354

Fillmore, Millard, Pop. 2,178
Millard SD
Supt. — See Delta
Fillmore MS — 300/5-8
435 S 500 W 84631 — 435-743-5660
Kerry Watson, prin. — Fax 743-5669
Millard HS — 300/9-12
200 W Eagle Ave 84631 — 435-743-5610
Dennis Alldredge, prin. — Fax 743-5619

Garland, Box Elder, Pop. 1,982
Box Elder SD
Supt. — See Brigham City
Bear River MS — 700/8-9
300 E 1500 S 84312 — 435-257-2540
Calvin Bingham, prin. — Fax 257-3945
Bear River SHS — 1,000/10-12
1450 S Main St 84312 — 435-257-2500
Gary Allen, prin. — Fax 257-3899

Grantsville, Tooele, Pop. 7,494
Tooele County SD
Supt. — See Tooele
Grantsville HS — 900/9-12
155 Cowboy Dr 84029 — 435-884-4500
Travis McCluskey, prin. — Fax 884-4502
Grantsville JHS — 500/7-8
318 S Hale St 84029 — 435-884-4510
Keith Davis, prin. — Fax 884-4513

Green River, Emery, Pop. 952
Emery County SD
Supt. — See Huntington
Green River JSHS — 100/7-12
PO Box 450 84525 — 435-564-3461
Nolan Johnson, prin. — Fax 564-3508

Grouse Creek, Box Elder
Box Elder SD
Supt. — See Brigham City
Grouse Creek S — 50/K-10
1 W Buckaroo Blvd 84313 — 435-747-7321
Duane Runyan, prin. — Fax 747-7182

Gunnison, Sanpete, Pop. 2,700
South Sanpete SD
Supt. — See Manti
Gunnison Valley HS — 300/9-12
PO Box 460 84634 — 435-528-7256
Kirk Anderson, prin. — Fax 528-3556
Gunnison Valley MS — 200/6-8
PO Box 1090 84634 — 435-528-5337
Alan Peterson, prin. — Fax 528-5397

Harrisville, Weber, Pop. 5,020
Weber SD
Supt. — See Ogden
Orion JHS — 700/7-9
370 W 2000 N 84404 — 801-452-4700
Steve Elsnab, prin. — Fax 452-4777

Heber City, Wasatch, Pop. 5,299
Wasatch SD — 4,200/K-12
101 E 200 N 84032 — 435-654-0280
Terry Shoemaker, supt. — Fax 654-4714
www.wasatch.edu/
Wasatch HS — 900/10-12
64 E 600 S 84032 — 435-654-0640
Paul Sweat, prin. — Fax 654-3011
Wasatch Mountain JHS — 600/8-9
200 E 800 S 84032 — 435-654-0550
James Judd, prin. — Fax 654-0622

Helper, Carbon, Pop. 1,878
Carbon SD
Supt. — See Price
Helper JHS — 200/7-9
130 Uintah St 84526 — 435-472-5441
Tom Montoya, prin. — Fax 472-3502

Northridge Learning Center — 100/K-12
202 S Main St 84526 — 435-472-0870
Dixie Evans, prin. — Fax 472-0806

Herriman, Salt Lake, Pop. 11,226
Jordan SD
Supt. — See Sandy
Fort Herriman MS — 7-9
14058 Mirabella Dr, — 801-412-2450
Michael Sirois, prin. — Fax 412-2460

Highland, Utah, Pop. 13,350
Alpine SD
Supt. — See American Fork
Lone Peak SHS — 1,800/10-12
10189 N 4800 W 84003 — 801-763-7050
Kenneth Koop, prin. — Fax 763-7064
Mountain Ridge JHS — 1,200/7-9
5525 W 10400 N 84003 — 801-763-7010
Paula Fugal, prin. — Fax 763-7018

Huntington, Emery, Pop. 2,062
Emery County SD — 2,400/K-12
PO Box 120 84528 — 435-687-9846
Kirk Sitterud, supt. — Fax 687-9849
www.emery.k12.ut.us
Canyon View JHS — 200/7-9
PO Box 250 84528 — 435-687-2265
Larry Davis, prin. — Fax 687-9546
Other Schools – See Castle Dale, Ferron, Green River

Hurricane, Washington, Pop. 10,989
Washington County SD
Supt. — See Saint George
Hurricane MS — 800/6-8
395 N 200 W 84737 — 435-635-4634
Richard Holmes, prin. — Fax 635-4663
Hurricane SHS — 800/10-12
345 W Tiger Blvd 84737 — 435-635-3280
Dr. Roy Hoyt, prin. — Fax 635-3719

Hyrum, Cache, Pop. 6,061
Cache SD
Supt. — See Logan
Mountain Crest SHS — 1,400/10-12
255 S 800 E 84319 — 435-245-6093
Jack Robinson, prin. — Fax 245-3818
South Cache JHS — 1,000/8-9
10 S 400 W 84319 — 435-245-6433
Teri Cutler, prin. — Fax 245-6662

Junction, Piute, Pop. 167
Piute SD — 300/PK-12
PO Box 69 84740 — 435-577-2912
Dr. Lewis S. Mullins, supt. — Fax 577-2561
Piute JSHS — 100/7-12
550 N 100 W 84740 — 435-577-2881
Scott Bagley, prin. — Fax 577-2512

Kamas, Summit, Pop. 1,502
South Summit SD — 1,300/PK-12
375 E 300 S 84036 — 435-783-4301
Timothy Smith, supt. — Fax 783-4501
www.ssummit.k12.ut.us/
South Summit HS — 400/9-12
45 S 300 E 84036 — 435-783-4313
Gary Twitchell, prin. — Fax 783-4765
South Summit MS — 300/6-8
355 E 300 S 84036 — 435-783-4341
Barry Walker, prin. — Fax 783-2787

Kanab, Kane, Pop. 3,516
Kane SD — 1,200/K-12
746 S 175 E 84741 — 435-644-2555
Robert Johnson, supt. — Fax 644-2509
www.kane.k12.ut.us
Kanab HS — 200/9-12
59 Cowboy Dr 84741 — 435-644-5821
Doug Jacobs, prin. — Fax 644-5242
Kanab MS — 100/7-8
690 Cowboy Way 84741 — 435-644-5800
Doug Jacobs, prin. — Fax 644-5121
Other Schools – See Big Water, Lake Powell, Orderville

Abundant Life Academy — 50/7-12
220 W 300 N 84741 — 435-215-1550
Rod Quamberg, prin. — Fax 644-8294

Kaysville, Davis, Pop. 22,510
Davis SD
Supt. — See Farmington
Davis SHS — 2,300/10-12
325 S Main St 84037 — 801-402-8800
Rulon Homer, prin. — Fax 402-8801
Fairfield JHS — 1,100/7-9
951 N Fairfield Rd 84037 — 801-402-7000
Steve Davis, prin. — Fax 402-7001
Kaysville JHS — 1,200/7-9
100 E 350 S 84037 — 801-402-7200
Dr. Ken Hadlock, prin. — Fax 402-7201

Davis Applied Technology College — Post-Sec.
550 E 300 S 84037 — 801-593-2500

Kearns, Salt Lake, Pop. 34,900
Granite SD
Supt. — See Salt Lake City
Jefferson JHS — 1,200/7-9
5850 S 5600 W 84118 — 801-646-5194
Karl Moody, prin. — Fax 646-5195
Kearns JHS — 1,000/7-9
4040 Sams Blvd 84118 — 801-646-5204
Kandace Barber, prin. — Fax 646-5206
Kearns SHS — 1,900/10-12
5525 Cougar Ln 84118 — 801-646-5380
Stephen Hess, prin. — Fax 646-5392

Koosharem, Sevier, Pop. 288

Sorenson's Ranch S — 100/7-12
PO Box 440219 84744 — 435-638-7318
Shane Sorenson, dir. — Fax 638-7582

Lake Powell, San Juan, Pop. 15
Kane SD
Supt. — See Kanab
Lake Powell HS — 50/7-12
PO Box 4345 84533 — 435-684-2268
Gordon Miller, prin. — Fax 684-3821

Laketown, Rich, Pop. 184
Rich SD
Supt. — See Randolph
Rich MS — 100/6-8
PO Box 129 84038 — 435-946-3359
Kip Motta, prin. — Fax 946-3366

La Verkin, Washington, Pop. 4,105

Cross Creek Academy — 400/6-12
150 N State St 84745 — 435-635-6016
Andrea Gardner, admin. — Fax 635-1099

Layton, Davis, Pop. 61,782
Davis SD
Supt. — See Farmington
Central Davis JHS — 1,000/7-9
663 Church St 84041 — 801-402-7100
Karyn Bertelsen, prin. — Fax 402-7101
Layton SHS — 1,700/10-12
440 Wasatch Dr 84041 — 801-402-4800
Paul Smith, prin. — Fax 402-4801
North Layton JHS — 1,100/7-9
1100 W 2000 N 84041 — 801-402-6600
David Turner, prin. — Fax 402-6601
Northridge SHS — 2,100/10-12
2430 N Hill Field Rd 84041 — 801-402-8500
Dr. Steve Hill, prin. — Fax 402-8501

Fran Brown College of Beauty — Post-Sec.
521 W 600 N 84041 — 801-546-6166
Layton Christian Academy — 500/PK-12
2352 E Highway 193 84040 — 801-771-7141
Greg Miller, admin. — Fax 771-0170
Northridge Learning Center — 200/K-12
2405 N Hillfield Rd 84041 — 801-776-4532
Dixie Dorius Evans, dir. — Fax 776-0638

Lehi, Utah, Pop. 31,730
Alpine SD
Supt. — See American Fork
Lehi JHS — 1,000/7-9
700 Cedar Hollow Rd 84043 — 801-768-7010
Kevin Cox, prin. — Fax 768-7016
Lehi SHS — 1,500/10-12
180 N 500 E 84043 — 801-768-7000
Chuck Bearce, prin. — Fax 768-7007
Willow Creek MS — 1,000/7-9
2275 W 300 N 84043 — 801-766-5273
Fred Openshaw, prin. — Fax 766-5168

Lindon, Utah, Pop. 9,679
Alpine SD
Supt. — See American Fork
Oak Canyon JHS — 1,500/7-9
111 S 725 E 84042 — 801-785-8760
David Smith, prin. — Fax 785-8768

Loa, Wayne, Pop. 498

Aspen Ranch S — 100/8-12
PO Box 369 84747 — 435-836-2080
Lisa Lewis, prin. — Fax 836-2088

Logan, Cache, Pop. 47,357
Cache SD — 13,200/K-12
2063 N 1200 E 84341 — 435-752-3925
Dr. Steven Norton, supt. — Fax 753-2168
www.cache.k12.ut.us/
Other Schools – See Hyrum, Richmond, Smithfield

Logan CSD 5,900/K-12
101 W Center St 84321 435-755-2300
Marshal Garrett, supt. Fax 755-2311
www.lcsd.logan.k12.ut.us
Logan HS 1,600/9-12
162 W 100 S 84321 435-755-2380
Pat Hansen, prin. Fax 755-2387
Mt. Logan MS 1,300/6-8
875 N 200 E 84321 435-755-2370
Dan Johnson, prin. Fax 755-2370

Bridgerland Applied Technology Center Post-Sec.
1301 N 600 W 84321 435-753-6780
New Horizons Beauty College Post-Sec.
550 N Main St Ste 115 84321 435-753-9779
Stevens Henager College Post-Sec.
755 Main St 84321 435-713-4777
Utah State University 84322 Post-Sec.
435-797-1000

Magna, Salt Lake, Pop. 17,829
Granite SD
Supt. — See Salt Lake City
Brockbank JHS 1,100/7-9
2935 S 8560 W 84044 801-646-5134
Terri VanWinkle, prin. Fax 646-5135
Cyprus SHS 1,400/10-12
8623 W 3000 S 84044 801-646-5300
Mark Manning, prin. Fax 646-5303
Matheson JHS 1,000/7-9
3650 Montclair St 84044 801-646-5290
Marijean Woolf, prin. Fax 646-5299

Vista S 50/7-12
PO Box 69 84044 801-250-9762
Ron Crossman, prin. Fax 250-8483

Manila, Daggett, Pop. 304
Daggett SD 200/K-12
PO Box 249 84046 435-784-3174
Bruce Northcott, supt. Fax 784-3549
www.dsdf.org
Manila JSHS 100/7-12
PO Box 249 84046 435-784-3174
Bruce Northcott, prin. Fax 784-3271

Manti, Sanpete, Pop. 3,185
South Sanpete SD 2,700/PK-12
39 S Main St 84642 435-835-2261
Don Hill, supt. Fax 835-2265
www.ssanpete.k12.ut.us
Manti HS 500/9-12
100 W 500 N 84642 435-835-2281
Ralph Squire, prin. Fax 835-2285
Other Schools – See Ephraim, Gunnison

Mapleton, Utah, Pop. 5,972
Nebo SD
Supt. — See Spanish Fork
Mapleton JHS, 362 E 1200 N 84664 7-8
Suzanne Kimball, prin. 801-489-2892

Midvale, Salt Lake, Pop. 27,170
Jordan SD
Supt. — See Sandy
Hillcrest SHS 1,700/10-12
7350 S 900 E 84047 801-256-5400
Sue Malone, prin. Fax 256-5488
Midvale MS 700/7-9
7852 Pioneer St 84047 801-412-2150
Paula Logan, prin. Fax 412-2190

Kendall's Academy of Beauty Arts/Science Post-Sec.
7353 S 900 E 84047 801-561-5610

Milford, Beaver, Pop. 1,437
Beaver SD
Supt. — See Beaver
Milford JSHS 200/7-12
PO Box 159 84751 435-387-2751
John Nielsen, prin. Fax 387-2494

Moab, Grand, Pop. 4,807
Grand SD 1,400/PK-12
264 S 400 E 84532 435-259-5317
Ron Ferguson, supt. Fax 259-6212
www.grand.k12.ut.us
Grand County HS 500/9-12
608 S 400 E 84532 435-259-8931
Tom Brown, prin. Fax 259-4191
Grand County MS 200/7-8
439 S 100 E 84532 435-259-7158
Melinda Snow, prin. Fax 259-6221

Monroe, Sevier, Pop. 1,831
Sevier SD
Supt. — See Richfield
South Sevier HS 400/9-12
430 W 100 S 84754 435-527-4651
Bruce Douglas, prin. Fax 527-4653
South Sevier MS 300/6-8
300 E Center St 84754 435-527-4607
William Jolley, prin. Fax 527-4636

Montezuma Creek, San Juan, Pop. 345
San Juan SD
Supt. — See Blanding, UT
Whitehorse HS 300/7-12
PO Box 660 84534 435-678-1209
John Fahey, prin. Fax 678-1854

Monticello, San Juan, Pop. 1,913
San Juan SD
Supt. — See Blanding, UT
Monticello JSHS 300/7-12
PO Box 69 84535 435-587-1130
Scott Shakespeare, prin. Fax 587-1150

Monument Valley, San Juan
San Juan SD
Supt. — See Blanding, UT
Monument Valley JSHS 200/7-12
PO Box 360008 84536 435-678-1208
Patricia Seltzer, prin. Fax 678-1258

Morgan, Morgan, Pop. 2,932
Morgan SD 2,000/K-12
PO Box 530 84050 801-829-3411
Ronald Wolff, supt. Fax 829-3531
www.morgan.k12.ut.us
Morgan HS 700/9-12
PO Box 917 84050 801-829-3418
Ken Adams, prin. Fax 829-6553
Morgan MS 600/5-8
PO Box 470 84050 801-829-3467
Tom McFarland, prin. Fax 829-0645

Moroni, Sanpete, Pop. 1,276
North Sanpete SD
Supt. — See Mount Pleasant
North Sanpete MS 400/7-8
PO Box 307 84646 435-436-8206
Randy Shelley, prin. Fax 436-8208

Mount Pleasant, Sanpete, Pop. 2,703
North Sanpete SD 2,300/PK-12
220 E 700 S 84647 435-462-2485
Courtney Syme, supt. Fax 462-2480
www.nsanpete.k12.ut.us
North Sanpete HS 700/9-12
390 E 700 S 84647 435-462-2452
John Ericksen, prin. Fax 462-3112
Other Schools – See Moroni

Wasatch Academy 200/9-12
120 S 100 W 84647 435-462-1400
Joseph Loftin, hdmstr. Fax 462-1450

Murray, Salt Lake, Pop. 44,555
Murray CSD 6,400/K-12
147 E 5065 S 84107 801-264-7400
Richard Tranter, supt. Fax 264-7456
www.murrayschools.org/
Hillcrest JHS 800/7-9
126 E 5300 S 84107 801-264-7442
David Dunn, prin. Fax 264-4820
Murray SHS 1,500/10-12
5440 S State St 84107 801-264-7460
Scott Bushnell, prin. Fax 264-7499
Riverview JHS 800/7-9
751 Tripp Ln 84123 801-264-7446
Shauna Ballou, prin. Fax 264-7458

Cameo College of Essential Beauty Post-Sec.
124 E 5770 S 84107 801-484-6173
Eagle Gate College Post-Sec.
5588 Green St 84123 801-268-9271
ITT Technical Institute Post-Sec.
920 Levoy Dr 84123 801-263-3313
Mt. Vernon Academy 50/K-12
184 E Vine St 84107 801-266-5521
Nancy Woodward, prin. Fax 269-8080
Stevens Henager College Post-Sec.
383 W Vine St 84123 801-262-7600

Nephi, Juab, Pop. 5,045
Juab SD 2,000/K-12
346 E 600 N 84648 435-623-1940
Kirk Wright, supt. Fax 623-1941
www.juab.ut.proschoolweb.com/
Juab HS 600/9-12
802 N 650 E 84648 435-623-1764
M. Richard Durbin, prin. Fax 623-1772
Juab JHS 300/7-8
555 E 800 N 84648 435-623-1541
Ken Rowley, prin. Fax 623-4995

Oakley, Summit, Pop. 1,228

Oakley S 100/9-12
PO Box 357 84055 435-783-5001
James Meyer, dir. Fax 783-5010

Ogden, Weber, Pop. 78,309
Ogden City SD 10,300/K-12
1950 Monroe Blvd 84401 801-737-7300
Noel Zabriskie, supt. Fax 627-7654
www.ogdensd.org
Highland MS 800/6-8
325 Gramercy Ave 84404 801-737-7700
Tim Peters, prin. Fax 625-8860
Lomond HS 1,400/9-12
800 Jackson Ave 84404 801-737-7900
Ben Smith, prin. Fax 625-1138
Mound Fort MS 600/6-8
1400 Mound Fort Dr 84404 801-737-7800
Kevin Kuykendall, prin. Fax 625-8993
Mt. Ogden MS 900/6-8
3260 Harrison Blvd 84403 801-737-8600
Trevor Wilson, prin. Fax 627-7641
Ogden HS 1,600/9-12
2828 Harrison Blvd 84403 801-737-8673
Sondra Jolovich-Motes, prin. Fax 392-7338
Adult Education S Adult
1950 Monroe Blvd 84401 801-737-7458
Dr. Donna Corby, prin.

Weber SD 28,200/K-12
5320 S 500 E 84405 801-476-7500
Michael Jacobsen, supt. Fax 476-8139
www.weber.k12.ut.us/
Bonneville SHS 1,300/10-12
251 E 4800 S 84405 801-452-4050
Leslie Meyer, prin. Fax 452-4099
North Ogden JHS 800/7-9
575 E 2900 N 84414 801-452-4800
Dale Pfister, prin. Fax 452-4849
South Ogden JHS 800/7-9
4300 Madison Ave 84403 801-452-4460
Bill Grilz, prin. Fax 452-4499
Wahlquist JHS 900/7-9
1033 N 1200 W 84404 801-452-4640
Ray Long, prin. Fax 452-4679
Weber SHS 1,800/10-12
430 W Weber High Dr 84414 801-476-3700
Alan Stokes, prin. Fax 476-3799
Other Schools – See Eden, Harrisville, Plain City, Roy, Washington Tr, West Haven

---

Ogden-Weber Applied Technology College Post-Sec.
200 N Washington Blvd 84404 801-627-8300
St. Joseph's HS 200/9-12
1790 Lake St 84401 801-394-1515
Louise Price, prin. Fax 394-6428
Stacey's Hands of Champions Beauty Coll Post-Sec.
3721 S 250 W 84405 801-394-5718
Stevens Henager College Post-Sec.
PO Box 9428 84409 801-394-7791
Utah Schools for the Deaf and the Blind Post-Sec.
742 Harrison Blvd 84404 801-629-4700
Weber State University Post-Sec.
1001 University Cir 84408 801-626-6000

Orderville, Kane, Pop. 586
Kane SD
Supt. — See Kanab
Valley HS 200/7-12
PO Box 128 84758 435-648-2278
Jim Wood, prin. Fax 648-2366

Orem, Utah, Pop. 89,713
Alpine SD
Supt. — See American Fork
Canyon View JHS 1,200/7-9
625 E 950 N 84097 801-227-8748
Amelia Schwartz, prin. Fax 227-8706
Lakeridge JHS 1,200/7-9
951 S 400 W 84058 801-227-8752
Garrick Peterson, prin. Fax 227-2490
Mountain View SHS 1,500/10-12
665 W Center St 84057 801-227-8759
Rick Clark, prin. Fax 227-8764
Orem JHS 1,000/7-9
765 N 600 W 84057 801-227-8756
Steven Stewart, prin. Fax 227-8796
Orem SHS 1,300/10-12
175 S 400 E 84097 801-227-8765
Jane Lindhout, prin. Fax 227-8774
Timpanogos SHS 1,500/10-12
1450 N 200 E 84057 801-223-3120
Brad Kendall, prin. Fax 223-3134

Careers Unlimited Post-Sec.
University Mall # I-163 84097 801-687-1271
Evan's Hairstyling College Post-Sec.
798 W 400 N 84057 801-224-6034
Mountainland Applied Technology College Post-Sec.
987 S Geneva Rd 84058 801-863-7662
Provo Canyon S 200/7-12
1350 E 750 N 84097 801-227-2100
Nicholas Pakidko, prin. Fax 227-2184
Stevens Henager College Post-Sec.
1476 Sandhill Rd 84058 801-375-5455
Utah Valley State College Post-Sec.
800 W University Pkwy 84058 801-222-8000

Panguitch, Garfield, Pop. 1,477
Garfield SD 1,000/K-12
PO Box 398 84759 435-676-8821
Dr. George Park, supt. Fax 676-8266
www.garfield.k12.ut.us
Panguitch HS 100/9-12
PO Box 393 84759 435-676-8805
Betty Ann Rember, prin. Fax 676-8521
Panguitch MS 100/7-8
PO Box 393 84759 435-676-8225
Betty Ann Rember, prin. Fax 676-2518
Other Schools – See Escalante, Tropic

Park City, Summit, Pop. 8,066
Park City SD 3,300/K-12
2700 Kearns Blvd 84060 435-645-5600
Dave Adamson, supt. Fax 645-5609
www.parkcity.k12.ut.us
Park City SHS 900/10-12
1750 Kearns Blvd 84060 435-645-5650
Hilary Hays, prin. Fax 645-5658
Treasure Mountain International S 200/8-9
2530 Kearns Blvd 84060 435-645-5640
Bob O'Connor, prin. Fax 645-5644

Park Valley, Box Elder
Box Elder SD
Supt. — See Brigham City
Park Valley S 50/K-10
788 Education Dr 84329 435-871-4411
Brian Anderson, prin. Fax 871-4444

Parowan, Iron, Pop. 2,532
Iron SD
Supt. — See Cedar City
Parowan HS 400/7-12
168 N Main St 84761 435-477-3366
Scott Doubek, prin. Fax 477-3743

Payson, Utah, Pop. 16,442
Nebo SD
Supt. — See Spanish Fork
Mt. Nebo JHS 500/7-8
851 W 450 S 84651 801-465-6040
Kaye Isakson, prin. Fax 465-6045
Payson JHS 1,100/8-9
1025 S Highway 91 84651 801-465-6015
Clark Clayson, prin. Fax 465-6023

Payson SHS 1,500/10-12
1050 S Main St 84651 801-465-6025
John Penrod, prin. Fax 465-6067

Plain City, Weber, Pop. 4,320
Weber SD
Supt. — See Ogden
Fremont SHS 1,800/10-12
1900 N 4700 W 84404 801-452-4000
Jeff Meyer, prin. Fax 452-4049

Pleasant Grove, Utah, Pop. 29,376
Alpine SD
Supt. — See American Fork
Pleasant Grove JHS 1,300/7-9
810 N 100 E 84062 801-785-8707
Blaine Edman, prin. Fax 785-8743
Pleasant Grove SHS 1,700/10-12
700 E 200 S 84062 801-785-8700
Jess Christen, prin. Fax 785-8744

Price, Carbon, Pop. 8,081
Carbon SD 3,300/K-12
PO Box 1438 84501 435-637-1732
Dr. David A. Armstrong, supt. Fax 637-9417
www.carbon.k12.ut.us
Carbon SHS 700/10-12
750 E 400 N 84501 435-637-2463
Robert Cox, prin. Fax 637-4127
Mont Harmon JHS 600/7-9
60 W 400 N 84501 435-637-0510
Kerry Jensen, prin. Fax 637-6074
Other Schools – See Helper

College of Eastern Utah Post-Sec.
451 E 400 N 84501 435-637-2120
Southeast Applied Technology College Post-Sec.
375 S Carbon Ave 84501 435-613-1438

Provo, Utah, Pop. 113,459
Provo CSD 12,200/K-12
280 W 940 N 84604 801-374-4800
Dr. Randall J. Merrill, supt. Fax 374-4808
www.provo.edu
Centennial MS 800/7-8
305 E 2320 N 84604 801-374-4621
Mitch Swenson, prin. Fax 374-4626
Dixon MS 700/7-8
750 W 200 N 84601 801-374-4980
Rosanna Ungerman, prin. Fax 374-4884
Provo HS 1,900/9-12
1125 N University Ave 84604 801-373-6550
Sam Ray, prin. Fax 374-4880
Timpview HS 1,700/9-12
3570 Timpview Dr 84604 801-221-9720
George Bayles, prin. Fax 224-4210
Center for High School Studies Adult
243 E 2320 N 84604 801-374-4840
Anita Craven, coord. Fax 374-4816

American Inst. of Medical-Dental Tech. Post-Sec.
1675 N Freedom Blvd 84604 801-377-2900
Brigham Young University 84602 Post-Sec.
801-378-5000
Dallas Roberts Academy of Hair Design Post-Sec.
1700 N State St Ste 18 84604 801-375-1501
Discovery Academy 100/7-12
105 N 500 W 84601 801-374-2121
Jonathan Jones, prin. Fax 373-4451
Heritage S 50/7-12
5600 Heritage School Dr 84604 801-226-4621
Bruce Knowlton, prin. Fax 226-4630
Meridian S 200/PK-12
931 E 300 N 84606 801-374-5480
David H. Hennessey Ph.D., hdmstr. Fax 374-5491
Provo College Post-Sec.
1450 W 820 N 84601 801-375-1861
Utah Valley Regional Medical Center Post-Sec.
1034 N 500 W 84604 801-373-7850
Von Curtis Academy of Hair Design Post-Sec.
480 N 900 E 84606 801-374-5111

Randolph, Rich, Pop. 472
Rich SD 400/K-12
PO Box 67 84064 435-793-2135
Dale Lamborn, supt. Fax 793-2136
www.rich.k12.ut.us
Rich HS 100/9-12
PO Box 278 84064 435-793-2365
Rick Larsen, prin. Fax 793-2375
Other Schools – See Laketown

Richfield, Sevier, Pop. 7,044
Sevier SD 4,300/PK-12
180 E 600 N 84701 435-896-8214
Brent Thorne, supt. Fax 896-8804
www.sevier.k12.ut.us
Red Hills MS 500/6-8
400 S 600 W 84701 435-896-6421
Brent Gubler, prin. Fax 896-6423
Richfield HS 700/9-12
510 W 100 S 84701 435-896-8247
Randall Brown, prin. Fax 896-8246
Other Schools – See Monroe, Salina

Richmond, Cache, Pop. 1,849
Cache SD
Supt. — See Logan
North Cache JHS 1,000/8-9
157 W 600 S 84333 435-258-2452
Larry Larson, prin. Fax 258-5437

Riverdale, Weber, Pop. 7,934

Christian Heritage S 600/PK-12
5101 S 1050 W 84405 801-393-4475
Mike Hoff, prin. Fax 621-8452

Riverton, Salt Lake, Pop. 32,089
Jordan SD
Supt. — See Sandy
Oquirrh Hills MS 1,200/7-9
12949 S 2700 W 84065 801-412-2350
G. Norma Villar, prin. Fax 412-2370
Riverton SHS 2,400/10-12
12476 S 2700 W 84065 801-256-5800
Stephen Park, prin. Fax 256-5880
South Hills MS 1,500/7-9
13508 S 4000 W 84065 801-412-2400
Janette Milano, prin. Fax 412-2430

Roosevelt, Duchesne, Pop. 4,553
Duchesne SD
Supt. — See Duchesne
Roosevelt JHS 400/7-8
265 N 300 W Ste 425-1 84066 435-725-4585
David Brotherson, prin. Fax 725-4622
Union HS 800/9-12
135 N Union St Ste 124-3 84066 435-725-4525
Brent Feldsted, prin. Fax 725-4576

Uintah SD
Supt. — See Vernal
West JHS 200/6-9
RR 2 Box 2466 84066 435-722-4563
Deborah Clarke, prin. Fax 722-4565

Uintah Basin Applied Technology College Post-Sec.
1100 E Lagoon St 84066 435-722-4523

Roy, Weber, Pop. 35,229
Weber SD
Supt. — See Ogden
Roy JHS 900/7-9
5400 S 2100 W 84067 801-476-5260
Sue Sweet, prin. Fax 476-5299
Roy SHS 1,400/10-12
2150 W 4800 S 84067 801-476-3600
Lee Dickemore, prin. Fax 476-3699
Sand Ridge JHS 800/7-9
2075 W 4600 S 84067 801-476-5320
N. James Shaw, prin. Fax 476-5359

Saint George, Washington, Pop. 56,382
Washington County SD 21,100/K-12
121 W Tabernacle St 84770 435-673-3553
Max Rose Ph.D., supt. Fax 673-3216
www.washk12.org/
Dixie MS 900/7-9
825 S 100 E 84770 435-628-0441
Jim McKim, prin. Fax 674-6467
Dixie SHS 1,100/10-12
350 E 700 S 84770 435-673-4682
Larry Bergeson, prin. Fax 673-2384
Millcreek SHS 200/10-12
2410 E Riverside Dr 84790 435-628-2462
Terry Ogborn, prin. Fax 628-8206
Pine View MS 900/8-9
2145 E 130 N 84790 435-628-7915
Mike Stephenson, prin. Fax 634-0470
Pine View SHS 1,200/10-12
2850 E 750 N 84790 435-628-5255
Rick Palmer, prin. Fax 628-0327
Snow Canyon MS 800/8-9
1215 Lava Flow Dr 84770 435-674-6474
Rusty Taylor, prin. Fax 628-3289
Snow Canyon SHS 1,100/10-12
1385 Lava Flow Dr 84770 435-634-1967
Warren Brooks, prin. Fax 634-1130
Other Schools – See Enterprise, Hurricane

Calvary Chapel Christian S 50/K-12
3922 S Pioneer Rd 84790 435-634-8309
Penny Frank, admin. Fax 674-4908
Cinnamon Hills S 100/6-12
770 E Saint George Blvd 84770 435-674-0984
Fax 674-4628
Dixie State College of Utah Post-Sec.
225 S 700 E 84770 435-652-7500
Evan's Hairstyling College Post-Sec.
955 E Tabernacle St 84770 435-673-6128
Hairitage Hair Academy Post-Sec.
900 S Bluff St Ste 9 84770 435-673-5233
Hatch Academy 50/K-12
PO Box 910400 84791 435-673-6474
Brent Arnold, dir. Fax 673-5339
Sun Hawk Academy 100/7-12
948 N 1300 W 84770 435-656-3211
Brent Arnold, prin. Fax 656-3213

Salina, Sevier, Pop. 2,382
Sevier SD
Supt. — See Richfield
North Sevier HS 300/9-12
350 W 400 N 84654 435-529-3717
Steve Camp, prin. Fax 529-7910
North Sevier MS 200/6-8
135 N 100 W 84654 435-529-3841
Jill Porter, prin. Fax 529-7377

Salt Lake City, Salt Lake, Pop. 178,097
Granite SD 65,900/PK-12
2500 S State St 84115 801-646-5000
Dr. Stephen Ronnenkamp, supt. Fax 646-4128
www.granite.k12.ut.us
Bennion JHS 1,000/7-9
6055 S 2700 W 84118 801-646-5114
Dr. Mary Rhodes, prin. Fax 646-5119
Bonneville JHS 900/7-9
5330 S 1600 E 84117 801-646-5124
Joel Dunning, prin. Fax 646-5127
Churchill JHS 700/7-9
3450 Oakview Dr 84124 801-646-5144
Bryce Hollbrook, prin. Fax 646-5147
Cottonwood SHS 1,500/10-12
5715 S 1300 E 84121 801-646-5264
Garrett Muse, prin. Fax 646-5266
Eisenhower JHS 1,200/7-9
4351 S Redwood Rd 84123 801-646-5154
Nancy Jadallah, prin. Fax 646-5156
Evergreen JHS 800/7-9
3401 S 2000 E 84109 801-646-5164
Mark Grant, prin. Fax 646-5165
Granite Park JHS 600/7-9
3031 S 200 E 84115 801-646-5174
John Anderson, prin. Fax 646-5175
Granite SHS 900/10-12
3305 S 500 E 84106 801-646-5340
Carole Harris, prin. Fax 646-5353
Granite Technical Institute Vo/Tech
2500 S State St 84115 801-646-4350
James Taylor, prin. Fax 646-4347
Olympus JHS 800/7-9
2217 Murray Holladay Rd 84117 801-646-5224
Eric Bergman, prin. Fax 646-5227
Olympus SHS 1,400/10-12
4055 S 2300 E 84124 801-646-5400
Paul Hansen, prin. Fax 646-5403
Skyline SHS 1,500/10-12
3251 E 3760 S 84109 801-646-5420
Kathy Clark, prin. Fax 646-5422
Taylorsville SHS 1,900/10-12
5225 S Redwood Rd 84123 801-646-5455
Jerry Haslam, prin. Fax 646-5457
Wasatch JHS 900/7-9
3450 Oakview Dr 84124 801-646-5244
Doug Bingham, prin. Fax 646-5246
Granite Peaks Adult & Comm Education Adult
2500 S State St 84115 801-646-4666
Dr. Claudia Thorum, prin. Fax 646-4667
Other Schools – See Kearns, Magna, West Valley

Jordan SD
Supt. — See Sandy
Butler MS 1,100/7-9
7530 S 2700 E 84121 801-412-2250
Marsha Morgan, prin. Fax 412-2277

Salt Lake City SD 23,300/K-12
440 E 100 S 84111 801-578-8599
Dr. McKell Withers, supt. Fax 578-8248
www.slc.k12.ut.us
Bryant MS 600/7-8
40 S 800 E 84102 801-578-8118
Francis Battle, prin. Fax 578-8125
Clayton MS 600/7-8
1471 S 1800 E 84108 801-481-4810
Rosemary Baron, prin. Fax 481-4884
East HS 2,000/9-12
840 S 1300 E 84102 801-583-1661
Dr. Robyn Roberts, prin. Fax 584-2927
Glendale MS 600/7-8
1400 Goodwin Ave 84116 801-974-8319
Ernie Nix, prin. Fax 974-8356
Highland HS 1,800/9-12
2166 S 1700 E 84106 801-484-4343
Paul Schulte, prin. Fax 481-4893
Hillside MS 600/7-8
2375 Garfield Ave 84108 801-481-4828
Jane Larson, prin. Fax 481-4831
Northwest MS 800/7-8
1730 W 1700 N 84116 801-578-8547
Cherrie Brinlee, prin. Fax 578-8558
West HS 2,100/9-12
241 N 300 W 84103 801-578-8500
Margery Parker, prin. Fax 578-8516

Anchor Christian Academy 100/K-12
1880 E 5600 S 84121 801-272-9405
Randall Love, prin.
California College for Health Sciences Post-Sec.
5295 Commerce Dr 84107 800-221-7374
Certified Careers Institute Post-Sec.
1385 W 2200 S Ste 100 84119 801-973-7008
Hairitage College of Beauty Post-Sec.
5414 S 900 E 84117 801-266-4693
Intermountain Christian S 300/PK-12
6515 Lion Ln 84121 801-942-8811
Karen Dahl, prin. Fax 942-8813
Judge Memorial Catholic HS 900/9-12
650 S 1100 E 84102 801-363-8895
James Hamburge, prin. Fax 521-3920
Kendall's Academy of Beauty Arts/Science Post-Sec.
2230 S 700 E 84106 801-486-0101
L.D.S. Business College Post-Sec.
95 North 300 West 84101 801-524-8100
Myotherapy College of Utah Post-Sec.
2120 S 1300 E Ste 102 84106 801-484-7624
Odyssey House S 50/8-12
607 E 200 S 84102 801-578-8613
James Anderson, prin. Fax 578-8613
Oxford Learning Source 50/PK-12
2290 E 4500 S 84117 801-942-4449
Millicent Jacobsen, dir. Fax 495-2992
Realms of Inquiry S 100/PK-12
1140 S 900 E 84105 801-467-5911
Laurie Bragg, hdmstr. Fax 467-5932
Rowland Hall-St. Marks ES 900/PK-12
720 Guardsman Way 84108 801-355-7485
Deborah Mohrman, prin. Fax 363-5521
Rowland Hall-St. Marks HS 9-12
843 Lincoln St 84102 801-355-7494
Lee Thompsen, prin. Fax 355-0474
Rowland Hall-St. Marks MS 6-8
970 E 800 S 84102 801-355-0272
Stephen Bennhoff, prin. Fax 359-8318
Salt Lake Community College Post-Sec.
PO Box 30808 84130 801-957-4111
Salt Lake Lutheran HS 100/9-12
4020 S 900 E 84124 801-266-6676
Charles Gebhardt, prin. Fax 266-1953
Skin Works School of Advanced Skin Care Post-Sec.
2121 Nowell Cir 84115 801-530-0001

Tooele Applied Technology College — Post-Sec.
1655 E 3300 S 84106 — 801-493-8700
University of Utah — Post-Sec.
1460 E 201 S 84112 — 801-581-7200
Valley Christian S — 100/K-12
3818 W 4700 S 84118 — 801-968-8107
Kevin Bowles, prin. — Fax 968-8182
Veterans Affairs Medical Center — Post-Sec.
500 Foothill Dr 84148 — 801-582-1565
Western Governors University — Post-Sec.
4001 S 700 E Ste 700 84107 — 801-274-3280
Westminster College — Post-Sec.
1840 S 1300 E 84105 — 801-484-7651
Woodland Hills S — 200/7-12
5858 S 900 E 84121 — 801-266-1262
Joyce Hansen, prin. — Fax 266-5876

Sandy, Salt Lake, Pop. 89,664
Jordan SD — 74,800/K-12
9361 S 300 E 84070 — 801-567-8100
Barry Newbold Ed.D., supt. — Fax 567-8064
www.jordandistrict.org/
Albion MS — 1,100/7-9
2755 Newcastle Dr 84093 — 801-412-2700
Larry Odom, prin. — Fax 412-2720
Alta SHS — 2,400/10-12
11055 S 1000 E 84094 — 801-256-5000
Mont Winderberg, prin. — Fax 256-5081
Crescent View MS — 1,400/7-9
11150 S 300 E 84070 — 801-412-2750
Gregory Leavitt, prin. — Fax 412-2780
Eastmont MS — 1,000/7-9
10100 S 1300 E 84094 — 801-412-2000
Janice Sterzer, prin. — Fax 412-2040
Indian Hills MS — 1,200/7-9
1180 Sanders Rd 84094 — 801-412-2550
Floyd Stensrud, prin. — Fax 412-2580
Jordan Applied Technology Center — Vo/Tech
825 E 9085 S 84094 — 801-256-2700
Ronald Sing, prin. — Fax 256-5710
Jordan SHS — 2,000/10-12
95 Beetdigger Blvd 84070 — 801-256-5500
Robert Dowdle, prin. — Fax 256-5556
Mt. Jordan MS — 700/7-9
9360 S 300 E 84070 — 801-412-2050
Misty Saurez, prin. — Fax 412-2055
Union MS — 1,000/7-9
615 E 8000 S 84070 — 801-412-2200
Mary Anderson, prin. — Fax 412-2227
Southpointe HS — Adult
825 E 9085 S 84094 — 801-256-5740
Dr. Ronald Sing, prin. — Fax 256-5779
Other Schools – See Cottonwood Heights, Herriman, Midvale, Riverton, Salt Lake City, South Jordan, West Jordan

---

Francois D. Hair Design Academy — Post-Sec.
111 W 9000 S 84070 — 801-561-2244
Oxford Learning Source — 50/PK-12
1842 E 9400 S 84093 — 801-942-4449
Millicent Jacobsen, dir. — Fax 495-2992
Waterford S — 1,000/PK-12
1480 E 9400 S 84093 — 801-572-1780
Nancy Heuston, hdmstr. — Fax 572-1787

Smithfield, Cache, Pop. 7,589
Cache SD
Supt. — See Logan
Sky View SHS — 1,500/10-12
520 S 250 E 84335 — 435-563-6273
Dee Ashcroft, prin. — Fax 563-9534

South Jordan, Salt Lake, Pop. 40,209
Jordan SD
Supt. — See Sandy
Bingham SHS — 2,200/10-12
2160 W Miners Mile 84095 — 801-256-5100
Jolene Jolley, prin. — Fax 256-5151
Elk Ridge MS — 1,300/7-9
3659 W 9800 S 84095 — 801-412-2800
Raymond Jenson, prin. — Fax 412-2830
South Jordan MS — 1,400/7-9
10245 S 2700 W 84095 — 801-412-2900
Diana Kline, prin. — Fax 412-2930

Spanish Fork, Utah, Pop. 26,606
Nebo SD — 22,100/PK-12
350 S Main St 84660 — 801-354-7400
Chris Sorensen, supt. — Fax 798-4010
www.nebo.edu
Diamond Fork JHS — 700/7-8
50 N 900 E 84660 — 801-798-4052
Steve Dudley, prin. — Fax 798-4098
Spanish Fork JHS — 1,300/8-9
600 S 820 E 84660 — 801-798-4075
John DeGraffenried, prin. — Fax 798-4097
Spanish Fork SHS — 1,800/10-12
99 N 300 W 84660 — 801-798-4060
Dave McKee, prin. — Fax 798-0483
Other Schools – See Mapleton, Payson, Springville

New Haven S — 50/7-12
2152 E 7200 S 84660 — 801-794-1218
Laurie Laird, prin. — Fax 794-9558

Springville, Utah, Pop. 25,309
Nebo SD
Supt. — See Spanish Fork
Springville JHS — 1,100/8-9
165 S 700 E 84663 — 801-489-2880
Everett Kelepolo, prin. — Fax 489-2838
Springville SHS — 1,500/10-12
1205 E 900 S 84663 — 801-489-2870
Ann Anderson, prin. — Fax 489-2806
Nebo Learning Center — Adult
570 S Main St 84663 — 801-489-2833
Dave Harlan, prin. — Fax 489-2829

Sunset, Davis, Pop. 4,947
Davis SD
Supt. — See Farmington
Sunset JHS — 1,000/7-9
1610 N 250 W 84015 — 801-402-6700
Dr. James Schmidt, prin. — Fax 402-6701

Syracuse, Davis, Pop. 17,938
Davis SD
Supt. — See Farmington
Syracuse JHS — 1,000/7-9
1450 S 2000 W 84075 — 801-402-6800
Dr. Robin Bowden, prin. — Fax 402-6801

Island View S — 100/7-12
2650 W 2700 S 84075 — 801-773-0200
Jan Whimpey, prin. — Fax 773-0208

Tabiona, Duchesne, Pop. 154
Duchesne SD
Supt. — See Duchesne
Tabiona HS — 100/7-12
PO Box 470 84072 — 435-738-1320
Robert Park, prin. — Fax 738-1332

Tooele, Tooele, Pop. 28,369
Tooele County SD — 10,600/K-12
92 Lodestone Way 84074 — 435-833-1900
Michael Johnsen, supt. — Fax 833-1912
www.tooele.k12.ut.us
Johnsen JHS — 7-8
2152 N 400 W 84074 — 435-833-1900
Hal Strain, prin. — Fax 843-3816
Tooele HS — 1,700/9-12
301 W Vine St 84074 — 435-833-1978
Kendall Topham, prin. — Fax 833-1984
Tooele JHS — 1,000/7-8
412 W Vine St 84074 — 435-833-1921
Larry Abraham, prin. — Fax 833-1923
Tooele Valley HS — 50/9-12
Tooele Army Depot Bldg S110 84074 — 435-833-1928
Terry Linares, prin. — Fax 833-1929
Other Schools – See Dugway, Grantsville, Wendover

Tropic, Garfield, Pop. 463
Garfield SD
Supt. — See Panguitch
Bryce Valley HS — 100/7-12
PO Box 70 84776 — 435-679-8835
Earl Slack, prin. — Fax 679-8539

Trout Creek, Juab
Tintic SD
Supt. — See Eureka
West Desert JSHS — 50/7-12
PO Box 440 84083 — 435-693-3112
Edgar Alder, prin. — Fax 693-3109

Vernal, Uintah, Pop. 7,960
Uintah SD — 5,600/PK-12
635 W 200 S 84078 — 435-781-3100
Charles Nelson Ed.D., supt. — Fax 781-3107
www.uintah.net/
Uintah SHS — 1,100/10-12
1880 W 500 N 84078 — 435-781-3110
Robert Stearmer, prin. — Fax 781-3117
Vernal JHS — 800/8-9
161 N 1000 W 84078 — 435-781-3130
Kent Bunderson, prin. — Fax 781-3134
Other Schools – See Roosevelt

Washington Tr, Weber, Pop. 8,701
Weber SD
Supt. — See Ogden
Bell JHS — 600/7-9
165 W 5100 S 84405 — 801-452-4600
Corey Jenkins, prin. — Fax 452-4639

Wendover, Tooele, Pop. 1,620
Tooele County SD
Supt. — See Tooele
Wendover JSHS — 200/7-12
PO Box 610 84083 — 435-665-2343
John Barrus, prin. — Fax 665-7706

West Haven, Weber, Pop. 5,558
Weber SD
Supt. — See Ogden
Rocky Mountain JHS — 900/7-9
4350 W 4800 S 84401 — 801-476-5220
Craig Jessop, prin. — Fax 476-5259

West Jordan, Salt Lake, Pop. 91,444
Jordan SD
Supt. — See Sandy
Copper Hills SHS — 1,900/10-12
5445 New Bingham Hwy 84088 — 801-256-5300
Mary Bailey, prin. — Fax 256-5393
Jensen MS — 1,000/7-9
8105 S 3200 W 84088 — 801-412-2850
Joanne Ackerman, prin. — Fax 412-2875
Jordan Applied Technology Center — Vo/Tech
9301 Wights Fort Rd 84088 — 801-256-5900
Todd Quamberg, prin. — Fax 256-5930
Sunset Ridge MS — 7-9
6881 W 8200 S 84088 — 801-412-2475
Catherine Jensen, prin. — Fax 412-2490
West Hills MS — 1,600/7-9
8270 Grizzly Way 84088 — 801-412-2300
Kim Baker, prin. — Fax 412-2327
West Jordan MS — 1,100/7-9
7550 S 1700 W 84084 — 801-412-2100
Joanne Mattes, prin. — Fax 412-2140
West Jordan SHS — 2,000/10-12
8136 S 2700 W 84088 — 801-256-5600
Paul Argyle, prin. — Fax 256-5670

Copperhills Youth Center — 50/6-12
5899 Rivendell Dr 84088 — 801-304-7171
Seema Mehta, prin. — Fax 561-3393
Hawthorne Academy — 50/9-12
1323 W 7900 S 84088 — 801-255-3651
Kraig Munsert, dir. — Fax 255-3957
Utah Career College — Post-Sec.
1902 W 7800 S 84088 — 801-304-4224
West Ridge Academy — 100/6-12
5500 Bagley Park Rd 84088 — 801-282-1034
Paul Keene, prin. — Fax 282-1009

West Point, Davis, Pop. 7,650
Davis SD
Supt. — See Farmington
West Point JHS — 1,100/7-9
2775 W 550 N 84015 — 801-402-8100
Dr. Jane Muna, prin. — Fax 402-8101

West Valley, Salt Lake, Pop. 111,254
Granite SD
Supt. — See Salt Lake City
Granger SHS — 1,500/10-12
3690 S 3600 W 84119 — 801-646-5320
Arthur Cox, prin. — Fax 646-5322
Hunter JHS — 1,000/7-9
6131 Wending Ln 84128 — 801-646-5184
Mary Anne Stevens, prin. — Fax 646-5185
Hunter SHS — 2,100/10-12
4200 S 5600 W 84120 — 801-646-5360
Maile Loo, prin. — Fax 646-5374
Kennedy JHS — 1,200/7-9
4495 S 4800 W 84120 — 801-646-5214
Dr. Howard Sagers, prin. — Fax 646-5215
Valley JHS — 900/7-9
4195 S 3200 W 84119 — 801-646-5234
Bill Kenley, prin. — Fax 646-5235
West Lake JHS — 1,100/7-9
3400 S 3450 W 84119 — 801-646-5254
Dave Rettie, prin. — Fax 646-5259

Mountain West College — Post-Sec.
3280 W 3500 S 84119 — 801-840-4800
Premier Hair Academy — Post-Sec.
4062 S 4000 W 84120 — 801-966-8414

Woods Cross, Davis, Pop. 8,019
Davis SD
Supt. — See Farmington
Woods Cross SHS — 1,200/10-12
2200 S 600 W 84010 — 801-402-4500
Vickie Ingram, prin. — Fax 402-4501

Benchmark S — 50/8-12
592 W 1350 S 84010 — 801-299-5300
Michelle Brown, dir. — Fax 296-2163

VERMONT

VERMONT DEPARTMENT OF EDUCATION
120 State St, Montpelier 05620-0002
Telephone 802-828-3135
Fax 802-828-3140
Website http://www.state.vt.us/educ/

Commissioner of Education Richard Cate

VERMONT BOARD OF EDUCATION
120 State St, Montpelier 05620-0002

Chairperson Tom James

PUBLIC, PRIVATE AND CATHOLIC SECONDARY SCHOOLS

Arlington, Bennington, Pop. 1,311
Battenkill Valley Supervisory Union 400/K-12
530 E Arlington Rd Ste A 05250 802-375-9744
Charles F. Sweetman, supt. Fax 375-2368
Arlington Memorial HS 300/6-12
529 E Arlington Rd 05250 802-375-2589
Kerry Czismesia, prin. Fax 375-1547

Ascutney, Windsor
Windsor Southeast Supervisory Union
Supt. — See Windsor
Weathersfield MS 200/4-8
PO Box 279 05030 802-674-5400
Mario Bevacqua, prin. Fax 674-9963

Barre, Washington, Pop. 9,128
Barre Supervisory Union 2,900/PK-12
120 Ayers St 05641 802-476-5011
Michele Fagan Ed.D., supt. Fax 476-4944
Barre Technical Center Vo/Tech
155 Ayers St 05641 802-476-6237
Robert Phillips, dir. Fax 476-4045
Spaulding HS 900/9-12
155 Ayers St 05641 802-476-4811
Cynthia Donlon, prin. Fax 479-4535

Washington Central Supervisory Union 1,600/PK-12
22 E View Ln 05641 802-229-0553
Robbe Brook, supt. Fax 229-2761
www.wcsuonline.org
Other Schools – See Montpelier

Central Vermont SDA S 50/K-12
317 Vine St 05641 802-479-0868
Sherrie Wall, prin. Fax 479-4311

Bellows Falls, Windham, Pop. 3,019
Windham Northeast Supervisory Union 1,300/K-12
8A Atkinson St 05101 802-463-9958
Johanna Harpster, supt. Fax 463-9705
www.wnesu.org
Bellows Falls MS 300/5-8
11-17 School St 05101 802-463-4366
Marcy Henry, prin. Fax 463-9738
Bellows Falls Union HS 400/9-12
RR 5 S 05101 802-463-3944
Christopher Hodsden, prin. Fax 463-9322

Bennington, Bennington, Pop. 9,532
Southwest Vermont Supervisory Union 3,500/K-12
246 S Stream Rd 05201 802-447-7501
Wesley L. Knapp, supt. Fax 447-0475
www.svsu.org
Mt. Anthony Union HS 1,200/9-12
301 Park St 05201 802-447-7511
Suzanne Maguire, prin. Fax 442-1260
Mt. Anthony Union MS 600/7-8
747 East Rd 05201 802-447-7541
Warren Roaf, prin. Fax 442-1262
SW VT Career Development Center Vo/Tech
321 Park St 05201 802-447-0220
Donna Oyama, prin. Fax 442-1745

Bennington College Post-Sec.
1 College Dr 05201 800-833-6845
Bennington Regional Day Program Post-Sec.
05201 802-258-9535
Bennington S, 192 Fairview St 05201 100/6-12
Jeffrey LaBonte, prin. 802-447-1557
Grace Christian S 200/PK-12
104 Kocher Dr 05201 802-447-2233
Joyce Lloyd, admin. Fax 442-8403
Southern Vermont College Post-Sec.
982 Mansion Dr 05201 802-442-5427

Bethel, Windsor
Windsor Northwest Supervisory Union 700/PK-12
PO Box 37 05032 802-234-5364
Timothy Mock, supt. Fax 234-6730
Whitcomb JSHS 200/7-12
273 Pleasant St 05032 802-234-9966
Andrew West, prin. Fax 234-5779
Other Schools – See Rochester

Bradford, Orange, Pop. 824
Orange East Supervisory Union 1,300/K-12
PO Box 396 05033 802-222-5216
Wendy Hovey, supt. Fax 222-4451
www.orangeeast.k12.vt.us/
Oxbow HS 500/7-12
36 Oxbow Dr 05033 802-222-5214
Charles Brown, prin. Fax 222-5847
River Bend Career & Tech Center Vo/Tech
PO Box 618 05033 802-222-5212
Ted Guilemette, dir. Fax 222-4621

Brandon, Rutland, Pop. 1,902
Rutland Northeast Supervisory Union 1,900/PK-12
49 Court Dr 05733 802-247-5757
William Mathis, supt. Fax 247-5548
www.rnesu.k12.vt.us/
Otter Valley Union JSHS 700/7-12
2997 Franklin St 05733 802-247-6833
Dana Cole-Levesque, prin. Fax 247-4627

Brattleboro, Windham, Pop. 8,612
Windham Southeast Supervisory Union 2,900/K-12
53 Green St 05301 802-254-3731
Ron Stahley, supt. Fax 254-3733
www.wssu.k12.vt.us
Brattleboro Area MS 300/7-8
109 Sunny Acres St 05301 802-451-3500
Ingrid Chrisco, prin. Fax 451-3502
Brattleboro Union HS 1,100/9-12
131 Fairground Rd 05301 802-451-3400
James Day, prin. Fax 451-3935
Windham Regional Career Center Vo/Tech
131 Fairground Rd 05301 802-257-7335
Dr. Ed Bouquillon, prin. Fax 257-3079

Austine School for the Deaf Post-Sec.
60 Austine Dr 05301 802-258-9522
School for International Training Post-Sec.
PO Box 676 05302 802-257-7751
The William Center Post-Sec.
60 Austine Dr 05301 802-258-9537

Bristol, Addison, Pop. 1,841
Addison Northeast Supervisory Union 1,900/K-12
10 Orchard Terrace Park 05443 802-453-3657
Evelyn Howard, supt. Fax 453-2029
www.mtabe.k12.vt.us
Mt. Abraham Union JSHS 28 900/7-12
7 Airport Dr 05443 802-453-2333
Paulette Bogan, prin. Fax 453-4359

Burlington, Chittenden, Pop. 38,531
Burlington SD 3,600/PK-12
150 Colchester Ave 05401 802-865-5332
Jeanne Collins, supt. Fax 864-8501
www.bsdvt.org/
Burlington HS 1,200/9-12
52 Institute Rd, 802-864-8411
Amy Mellencamp, prin. Fax 864-8408
Burlington Technical Center Vo/Tech
52 Institute Rd, 802-864-8426
Mark Aliquo, dir. Fax 864-8521
Edmunds MS 400/6-8
275 Main St 05401 802-864-8486
Bonnie Johnson-Aten, prin. Fax 864-2218
Hunt MS 500/6-8
1364 North Ave, 802-864-8469
Linda Carroll, prin. Fax 864-8467

Burlington College Post-Sec.
95 North Ave 05401 802-862-9616
Champlain College Post-Sec.
PO Box 670 05402 802-860-2700
Fletcher Allen Health Care Post-Sec.
111 Colchester Ave 05401 802-847-5133
Rock Point S 50/9-12
1 Rock Point Rd, 802-863-1104
John Rouleau, hdmstr. Fax 863-6628
University of Vermont Post-Sec.
194 S Prospect St 05401 802-656-3131

Cabot, Washington, Pop. 247
Washington NE Supervisory Union
Supt. — See Plainfield
Cabot S 200/PK-12
PO Box 98 05647 802-563-2289
Dr. Frank Mellaci, prin. Fax 563-2022

Canaan, Essex
Essex North Supervisory Union 300/K-12
PO Box 100 05903 802-266-3330
Daniel French, supt. Fax 266-7085
www.essexnorth.org/
Canaan S 300/K-12
99 School St 05903 802-266-8910
Christopher Masson, prin. Fax 266-7068

Castleton, Rutland
Addison-Rutland Supervisory Union
Supt. — See Fair Haven
Castleton Village S 100/7-8
PO Box 68 05735 802-468-2203
Albert J. Rousse, prin. Fax 468-5131

Castleton State College 05735 Post-Sec.
800-639-8521

Charlotte, Chittenden

Lake Champlain Waldorf HS 100/9-12
735 Ferry Rd 05445 802-425-6195
Stephan Vdoviak, admin. Fax 425-6207

Chelsea, Orange
Orange-Windsor Supervisory Union
Supt. — See South Royalton
Chelsea S 200/K-12
6 School St 05038 802-685-4551
Karl Stein, prin. Fax 685-3310

Chester, Windsor, Pop. 1,057
Windsor Southwest Supervisory Union 1,100/K-12
89 VT Route 103 S 05143 802-875-3365
Edward Brown, supt. Fax 875-3313
www.wswsu.org/
Green Mountain Union JSHS 400/7-12
716 VT Route 103 S 05143 802-875-2146
Carol Gilbert, prin. Fax 875-3183

Colchester, Chittenden
Colchester SD 2,400/PK-12
PO Box 27 05446 802-658-4047
Armando Vilaseca, supt. Fax 863-4774
www.colchester.k12.vt.us
Colchester HS 800/9-12
PO Box 900 05446 802-658-1570
Amy Minor, prin. Fax 864-0450
Colchester MS 600/6-8
PO Box 30 05446 802-655-1772
John Barone, prin. Fax 655-4495

St. Michael's College Post-Sec.
1 Winooski Park # 7 05439 802-654-2000

Concord, Essex
Essex-Caledonia Supervisory Union 600/PK-12
PO Box 255 05824 802-695-3373
Stephen Sanborn, supt. Fax 695-1334
Concord S 300/PK-12
173 School St 05824 802-695-2550
Phyllis Perkins, prin. Fax 695-3311

Craftsbury Common, Orleans
Orleans Southwest Supervisory Union
Supt. — See Hardwick
Craftsbury Academy 100/7-12
PO Box 73, 802-586-2541
Chris Young, prin. Fax 586-7524

Sterling College Post-Sec.
PO Box 72 05827 802-586-7711

Derby, Orleans, Pop. 725
Orleans-Essex North Supervisory Union
Supt. — See Newport
North Country Union JHS 300/7-8
57 Jr High Dr 05829 802-766-2276
Nicole Larose, prin. Fax 766-2287

Dorset, Bennington

Long Trail S 200/6-12
1045 Kirby Hollow Rd 05251 802-867-5717
David Wilson, hdmstr. Fax 867-4525

Duxbury, See Waterbury
Washington West Supervisory Union
Supt. — See Waitsfield
Crossett Brook MS 300/5-8
5672 VT Route 100 05676 802-244-6100
Kenneth Page, prin. Fax 244-6899

East Burke, Caledonia

Burke Mountain Academy 100/8-12
PO Box 78 05832 802-626-5607
Kirk Dwyer, hdmstr. Fax 626-3784

Enosburg Falls, Franklin, Pop. 1,473
Franklin Northeast Supervisory Union
Supt. — See Richford
Cold Hollow Career Center Vo/Tech
PO Box 530 05450 802-933-4003
Arthur Liskowsky, dir. Fax 933-2431
Enosburg Falls HS 300/9-12
PO Box 417 05450 802-933-7777
Edward Grossman, prin. Fax 933-5375
Enosburg Falls MS 100/6-8
PO Box 417 05450 802-933-7777
Jay Nichols, prin. Fax 933-5375

Essex Junction, Chittenden, Pop. 8,841
Chittenden Central Supervisory Union 2,900/PK-12
21 New England Dr 05452 802-879-5579
Michael Deweese, supt. Fax 878-1370
www.ejhs.k12.vt.us/ccsu/
Center for Technology/Essex Vo/Tech
3 Educational Dr 05452 802-879-5562
Kathy Finck, prin. Fax 879-5593
Essex Junction HS 1,600/9-12
2 Educational Dr 05452 802-879-7121
Robert Reardon, prin. Fax 879-5503
Lawton MS 400/6-8
104 Maple St 05452 802-878-1388
Laurie Singer, prin. Fax 879-8175

Essex Town SD 1,400/PK-8
58 Founders Rd 05452 802-878-8168
Jim Fitzpatrick, supt. Fax 878-5190
www.etsdvt.org
Essex MS 500/6-8
60 Founders Rd 05452 802-879-7173
Ned Kirsch, prin. Fax 879-1363

Essex Technical Center Post-Sec.
3 Educational Dr 05452
New England Culinary Institute Post-Sec.
5 Franklin St 05452 802-872-3400

Fairfax, Franklin
Franklin West Supervisory Union 800/PK-12
PO Box 108 05454 802-849-2283
Armando Vilaseca, supt. Fax 849-2865
Bellows Free Academy PK-12
75 Hunt St 05454 802-849-6711
D. Scott Lang, prin. Fax 849-6711

Fair Haven, Rutland, Pop. 2,432
Addison-Rutland Supervisory Union 1,700/PK-12
49 Main St 05743 802-265-4905
Ronald C. Ryan, supt. Fax 265-2158
Fair Haven Union HS 600/9-12
33 Mechanic St 05743 802-265-4966
Felice Clauder, prin. Fax 265-3602
Other Schools – See Castleton

Hardwick, Caledonia
Orleans Southwest Supervisory Union 1,200/K-12
PO Box 338 05843 802-472-6531
Mark Andrews, supt. Fax 472-6250
ossu35.tripod.com/index.htm
Hazen Union JSHS 400/7-12
PO Box 368 05843 802-472-6511
Elaine Laine, prin. Fax 472-3327
Other Schools – See Craftsbury Common

Hinesburg, Chittenden
Chittendon South Supervisory Union
Supt. — See Shelburne
Champlain Valley Union HS 15 1,300/9-12
369 CVU Rd 05461 802-482-7100
Sean McMannon, prin. Fax 482-7108

Hyde Park, Lamoille, Pop. 426
Lamoille North Supervisory Union 1,900/PK-12
95 Cricket Hill Rd 05655 802-888-3142
Terry D. Bailey Ed.D., supt. Fax 888-7908
Green Mountain Technology & Career Ctr Vo/Tech
PO Box 600 05655 802-888-4447
Joe Teagarden, prin. Fax 888-7838
Lamoille Union HS 600/9-12
736 VT 15 W 05655 802-888-4261
Sharon Fortune, prin. Fax 888-2997
Lamoille Union MS 300/7-8
736 VT 15 W 05655 802-851-1300
Chris Hindes, prin. Fax 851-1397

Jericho, Chittenden, Pop. 1,405
Chittenden East Supervisory Union
Supt. — See Richmond
Browns River MS 500/5-8
20 River Rd 05465 802-899-3711
Nancy Guyette, prin. Fax 899-4281
Mt. Mansfield Union HS 1,100/9-12
211 Browns Trace Rd 05465 802-899-4690
Jennifer Botzojorns, prin. Fax 899-2904

Johnson, Lamoille, Pop. 1,410

Johnson State College Post-Sec.
337 College Hl 05656 802-635-2356

Ludlow, Windsor, Pop. 1,037
Rutland Windsor Supervisory Union 500/K-12
8 High St 05149 802-228-2541
Dr. Frank Perotti, supt. Fax 228-8359
www.rwsu.org/
Black River JSHS 200/7-12
43 Main St 05149 802-228-4721
James Frail, prin. Fax 228-7233

Lyndon Center, Caledonia

Lyndon Institute 700/9-12
PO Box 127 05850 802-626-3357
Richard Hilton, prin. Fax 626-9164

Lyndonville, Caledonia, Pop. 1,222

Lyndon State College Post-Sec.
PO Box 919 05851 802-626-6200

Manchester, Bennington, Pop. 723

Burr and Burton Academy 700/9-12
PO Box 498 05254 802-362-1775
Charles Scranton, hdmstr. Fax 362-0574

Marlboro, Windham

Marlboro College Post-Sec.
PO Box A 05344 802-257-4333

Middlebury, Addison, Pop. 6,007
Addison Central Supervisory Union 2,000/PK-12
49 Charles Ave 05753 802-382-1274
William Lee Sease, supt. Fax 388-0024
www.acsu.k12.vt.us/
Hannaford Career Center Vo/Tech
51 Charles Ave 05753 802-382-1012
D. Lynn Coale, prin. Fax 388-2591
Middlebury Union HS 700/9-12
73 Charles Ave 05753 802-382-1500
William Lawson, prin. Fax 382-1101
Middlebury Union MS 300/7-8
48 Deerfield Ln 05753 802-382-1600
Inga Duktig, prin. Fax 382-1215

Middlebury College 05753 Post-Sec.
802-443-5000

Milton, Chittenden, Pop. 1,557
Milton Town SD 1,900/PK-12
42 Herrick Ave 05468 802-893-3210
Holden Waterman, supt. Fax 893-3213
www.mtsd-vt.org
Milton HS 500/9-12
17 Rebecca Lander Dr 05468 802-893-3230
Anne Blake, prin. Fax 893-3247
Milton JHS 300/7-8
17 Rebecca Lander Dr 05468 802-893-3230
Laurie Hodgdon, prin. Fax 893-3247

Montpelier, Washington, Pop. 8,003
Montpelier SD 1,000/K-12
58 Barre St 05602 802-223-9796
John Everitt, supt. Fax 223-9795
www.mpsvt.org
Main Street MS 300/6-8
170 Main St 05602 802-223-3404
Pamela Arnold, prin. Fax 223-9220
Montpelier HS 400/9-12
5 High School Dr 05602 802-225-8000
Peter Evans, prin. Fax 223-9227

Washington Central Supervisory Union
Supt. — See Barre
Union 32 JSHS 900/7-12
930 Gallison Hill Rd 05602 802-229-0321
Keith Gerritt, prin. Fax 223-7411

New England Culinary Institute Post-Sec.
56 College St 05602 802-223-6324
Union Institute & University Post-Sec.
36 College St 05602 802-828-8740
Woodbury College Post-Sec.
660 Elm St 05602 802-229-0516

Morrisville, Lamoille, Pop. 2,057
Lamoille South Supervisory Union 1,700/K-12
PO Box 340 05661 802-888-4541
Alice Angney, supt. Fax 888-6710
Peoples Academy 400/9-12
202 Copley Ave 05661 802-888-4600
Otho Thompson, prin. Fax 888-6726
Peoples Academy MS 200/6-8
202 Copley Ave 05661 802-888-1402
Leslie Beatson, prin. Fax 888-6488
Other Schools – See Stowe

Newport, Orleans, Pop. 5,207
Orleans-Essex North Supervisory Union 3,000/K-12
338 Highland Ave Ste 4 05855 802-334-5847
Robert Kern, supt. Fax 334-6528
www.northcountryschools.org
North Country Career Center Vo/Tech
PO Box 705 05855 802-334-5469
Robert Fitts, prin. Fax 334-3492
North Country Union HS 1,000/9-12
209 Veterans Ave 05855 802-334-7921
William Rivard, prin. Fax 334-1618
Other Schools – See Derby

United Christian Academy 100/K-12
65 School St 05855 802-334-3112
Dr. Richard O'Hara, hdmstr. Fax 334-2305

North Clarendon, Rutland
Rutland South Supervisory Union 1,100/K-12
PO Box 87 05759 802-775-3264
Walter Goetz, supt. Fax 775-8063
www.rssu.org/
Mill River Union JSHS 700/7-12
PO Box 6 05759 802-775-1925
Cynthia Hinrichsen, prin. Fax 775-6447

Northfield, Washington, Pop. 3,157
Washington South Supervisory Union 800/PK-12
37 Cross St 05663 802-485-7755
David Bickford, supt. Fax 485-3348
wssu.org
Northfield MSHS 500/6-12
37 Cross St Ste 2 05663 802-485-4500
Tom Marshall, prin. Fax 485-4440

Norwich University Post-Sec.
158 Harmon Dr 05663 800-468-6679

Orleans, Orleans, Pop. 847
Orleans Central Supervisory Union 1,100/K-12
PO Box 207 05860 802-754-6945
Ronald D. Paquette Ed.D., supt. Fax 754-2781
www.ocsu.org/
Lake Region Union HS 24 400/9-12
317 Lake Region Rd 05860 802-754-6521
Steve Urgensen, prin. Fax 754-2780

Plainfield, Washington
Washington NE Supervisory Union 700/PK-12
6328 US Route 2 05667 802-426-3245
George Burlison, supt. Fax 426-3801
Twinfield Union S 500/PK-12
106 Nasmith Brook Rd 05667 802-426-3213
Owen Bradley, prin. Fax 426-4085
Other Schools – See Cabot

Goddard College Post-Sec.
123 Pitkin Rd 05667 802-454-8311

Poultney, Rutland, Pop. 1,556
Rutland Southwest Supervisory Union 700/PK-12
168 York St 05764 802-287-5286
Cheryl Chedester, supt. Fax 287-2284
www.rswsu.org
Poultney HS 300/7-12
154 E Main St 05764 802-287-5861
Jean Oakman, prin. Fax 287-2304

Green Mountain College Post-Sec.
1 College Cir 05764 802-287-8000

Proctor, Rutland
Rutland Central Supervisory Union
Supt. — See Rutland
Proctor JSHS 200/7-12
4 Park St 05765 802-459-3353
Christopher J. Sousa, prin. Fax 459-6323

Putney, Windham

Landmark College Post-Sec.
River Rd S 05346 802-387-4767
Putney S 200/9-12
418 Houghton Brook Rd 05346 802-387-5566
Brian Morgan, dir. Fax 387-6259

Randolph, Orange
Orange Southwest Supervisory Union 1,100/K-12
24 Central St 05060 802-728-5052
Brent Kay, supt. Fax 728-4844
www.orangesw.k12.vt.us/
Randolph TCC Vo/Tech
17 Forest St 05060 802-728-9595
Bill Sugarman, prin. Fax 728-9596
Randolph Union JSHS 600/7-12
15 Forest St 05060 802-728-3397
John Holmes, prin. Fax 728-6703

Randolph Center, Orange

Vermont Technical College Post-Sec.
PO Box 500 05061 802-728-1000

Richford, Franklin, Pop. 1,417
Franklin Northeast Supervisory Union 1,700/K-12
PO Box 130 05476 802-848-7661
Edward Schuler, supt. Fax 848-3531
Richford JSHS 200/7-12
1 Corliss Hts 05476 802-848-7416
Dale Guertin, prin. Fax 848-3210
Other Schools – See Enosburg Falls

Richmond, Chittenden
Chittenden East Supervisory Union 3,000/K-12
PO Box 282 05477 802-434-2128
James Massingham, supt. Fax 434-2196
www.cesu.k12.vt.us
Camels Hump MS 400/5-8
173 School St 05477 802-434-2188
Mark Carbone, prin. Fax 434-2192
Other Schools – See Jericho

Rochester, Windsor
Windsor Northwest Supervisory Union
Supt. — See Bethel
Rochester S 200/K-12
222 S Main St 05767 802-767-3161
Bob Gray, prin. Fax 767-1130

Rutland, Rutland, Pop. 17,046

Rutland Central Supervisory Union 1,100/PK-12
257 S Main St 05701 802-775-4342
Karen White, supt. Fax 775-7319
www.rcsu.org
Other Schools – See Proctor, West Rutland

Rutland City SD 2,800/K-12
6 Church St 05701 802-773-1900
Mary Moran, supt. Fax 773-1927
rutlandhs.k12.vt.us

Rutland HS 1,100/9-12
22 Stratton Rd 05701 802-773-1955
Peter Folaros, prin. Fax 770-1020

Rutland MS 400/7-8
65 Library Ave 05701 802-773-1960
Wilfred Cunningham, prin. Fax 773-1914

Stafford Tech Ctr Vo/Tech
8 Stratton Rd 05701 802-773-1990
Lyle Jepson, prin. Fax 770-1066

College of Saint Joseph Post-Sec.
71 Clement Rd 05701 802-773-5900

Mt. St. Joseph Academy 200/9-12
127 Convent Ave 05701 802-775-0151
Paolo Zancanaro, prin. Fax 775-0424

Rutland Area Christian S 100/PK-12
112 Lincoln Ave 05701 802-775-0709
Ron Comfort, hdmstr. Fax 786-0111

Rutland Regional Medical Center Post-Sec.
160 Allen St 05701 802-775-7111

Saint Albans, Franklin, Pop. 7,565

Franklin Central Supervisory Union 3,000/PK-12
28 Catherine St 05478 802-524-2600
Marilyn Grunewald, supt. Fax 524-1540
www.sover.net/~fcsu/

Bellows Free Academy 1,200/9-12
71 S Main St 05478 802-527-6555
Ned Caron, prin. Fax 527-6402

Northwest Technical Center Vo/Tech
71 S Main St 05478 802-527-0614
Ned Caron, prin. Fax 527-6469

DLI Distance Learning International Post-Sec.
PO Box 846 05478 800-489-4114

Saint Johnsbury, Caledonia, Pop. 6,424

St. Johnsbury Academy 900/9-12
PO Box 906 05819 802-748-8171
Thomas Lovett, hdmstr. Fax 748-5463

Saxtons River, Windham, Pop. 496

Vermont Academy 300/9-12
PO Box 500 05154 802-869-6200
James Mooney, prin. Fax 869-6242

Sharon, Windsor

Sharon Academy, PO Box 207 05065 100/6-12
Michael Livingston, prin. 802-763-2531

Shelburne, Chittenden

Chittendon South Supervisory Union 4,400/PK-12
5420 Shelburne Rd Ste 300 05482 802-383-1234
Bob Mason, admin. Fax 383-1242
www.cssu.org/
Other Schools – See Hinesburg

South Burlington, Chittenden, Pop. 16,993

South Burlington SD 2,600/K-12
550 Dorset St 05403 802-652-7250
David Young, supt. Fax 652-7257
www.sbschools.net

South Burlington HS 1,000/9-12
550 Dorset St 05403 802-652-7000
Patrick Burke, prin. Fax 652-7006

Tuttle MS 600/6-8
500 Dorset St 05403 802-652-7100
Joseph O'Brien, prin. Fax 652-7152

O'Briens Training Center Post-Sec.
1475 Shelburne Rd 05403 802-658-9591

Rice Memorial HS 400/9-12
99 Proctor Ave 05403 802-862-6521
Fr. Bernard Bourgeois, prin. Fax 864-9931

South Duxbury, Washington

Washington West Supervisory Union
Supt. — See Waitsfield

Harwood Union HS 700/7-12
458 VT Route 100 05660 802-244-5186
Duane Pierson, prin. Fax 882-1199

South Royalton, Windsor

Orange-Windsor Supervisory Union 1,100/PK-12
3590 VT Route 14 05068 802-763-8840
Stephen Metcalf, supt. Fax 763-3235

South Royalton S 500/PK-12
223 S Windsor St 05068 802-763-8844
Shaun Pickett, prin. Fax 763-3233
Other Schools – See Chelsea

Vermont Law School Post-Sec.
PO Box 96 05068 802-763-8303

Springfield, Windsor, Pop. 4,207

Springfield SD 1,500/K-12
60 Park St 05156 802-885-5141
Rose Rooth, supt. Fax 885-8169
www.springfield.k12.vt.us

Riverside MS 300/6-8
13 Fairground Rd 05156 802-885-8490
Judy Pullinen, prin. Fax 885-8442

River Valley Technical Center Vo/Tech
307 South St 05156 802-885-8300
Carl Mock, prin. Fax 885-8454

Springfield HS 600/9-12
303 South St 05156 802-885-7900
Dr. Judson Bolles, prin. Fax 885-4459

Stowe, Lamoille, Pop. 500

Lamoille South Supervisory Union
Supt. — See Morrisville

Stowe HS 200/9-12
413 Barrows Rd 05672 802-253-7229
Richard Kraemer, prin. Fax 253-6911

Stowe MS 200/6-8
413 Barrows Rd 05672 802-253-6913
Nancy Shiok, prin. Fax 253-5314

Stratton Mountain, Windham, Pop. 50

Stratton Mountain S 100/7-12
7 World Cup Cir 05155 802-297-1886
Christopher Kaltsas, prin. Fax 297-0020

Swanton, Franklin, Pop. 2,573

Franklin Northwest Supervisory Union 2,300/K-12
100 Robin Hood Dr 05488 802-868-4967
John McCarthy, supt. Fax 868-4265
www.fnwsu.org

Missisquoi Valley Union MSHS 1,000/7-12
100 Thunderbird Dr 05488 802-868-7311
Chaunce Benedict, prin. Fax 868-3129

Thetford, Orange

Thetford Academy, PO Box 190 05074 400/7-12
Martha Rich, prin. 802-785-4805

Townshend, Windham

Windham Central Supervisory Union 1,000/K-12
1219 Vt Route 30 05353 802-365-9510
James Peters, supt. Fax 365-7934
www.wcsu.k12.vt.us

Leland-Gray Union HS 400/7-12
PO Box 128 05353 802-365-7355
Lloyd Szulborski, prin. Fax 365-4126

Vergennes, Addison, Pop. 2,763

Addison Northwest Supervisory Union 1,300/K-12
48 Green St Ste 1 05491 802-877-3332
Thomas F. O'Brien, supt. Fax 877-3628
www.anwsu.org

Vergennes Union JHS 300/7-9
50 Monkton Rd 05491 802-877-2938
Peter Reynolds, prin. Fax 877-2558

Vergennes Union SHS 300/10-12
50 Monkton Rd 05491 802-877-2938
Edwin Webbley, prin. Fax 877-2558

Waitsfield, Washington

Washington West Supervisory Union 2,000/PK-12
1673 Main St Ste A 05673 802-496-2272
Robert McNamara, supt. Fax 496-6515
www.harwood.org
Other Schools – See Duxbury, South Duxbury

Green Mountain Valley S 100/9-12
271 Moulton Rd 05673 802-496-2150
David Gavett, prin.

Waterbury, Washington, Pop. 1,683

Community College of Vermont Post-Sec.
PO Box 120 05676 802-241-3535

Wells River, Orange, Pop. 342

Blue Mountain SD 400/PK-12
2420 Route 302 05081 802-757-2766
Dr. Gordon Schnare, supt. Fax 757-2790
www.bmuschool.org

Blue Mountain Union S 21 400/PK-12
2420 Route 302 05081 802-757-2711
Carol Curtis, prin. Fax 757-3894

West Rutland, Rutland, Pop. 2,246

Rutland Central Supervisory Union
Supt. — See Rutland

West Rutland S 400/PK-12
713 Main St 05777 802-438-2288
Joseph Bowen, prin. Fax 438-5708

White River Junction, Windsor, Pop. 2,521

Hartford SD 1,900/PK-12
73 Highland Ave 05001 802-295-8600
Donald LaPlante, supt. Fax 295-8602
www.hartfordschools.net/

Hartford Area Career & Technology Center Vo/Tech
1 Gifford Rd 05001 802-295-8630
Michael Redington, prin. Fax 295-8631

Hartford HS 800/9-12
37 Highland Ave 05001 802-295-8620
Joseph Collea, prin. Fax 295-8611

Hartford Memorial MS 400/6-8
245 Highland Ave 05001 802-295-8640
John Grant, prin. Fax 295-8602

Mid-Vermont Christian S 100/PK-12
399 W Gilson Ave 05001 802-295-6800
Robert Bracy, hdmstr. Fax 295-3748

Williamstown, Orange

Orange North Supervisory Union 800/PK-12
111 Brush Hill Rd 05679 802-433-5818
Douglas R. Shiok, supt. Fax 433-5825

Williamstown MSHS 300/6-12
120 Hebert Rd 05679 802-433-5350
Kathleen Morris-Kortz, prin. Fax 433-1037

Williston, Chittenden

Pine Ridge S 100/9-12
9505 Williston Rd 05495 802-434-2161
Douglas Dague, hdmstr. Fax 434-5512

Vermont College of Cosmetology Post-Sec.
400 Cornerstone Dr Ste 220 05495 802-863-4666

Williston Regional Day Program Post-Sec.
195 Central School Dr 05495 802-879-4787

Wilmington, Windham

Windham Southwest Supervisory Union 800/PK-12
211 Route 9 W 05363 802-464-1300
M. Wright, supt. Fax 464-1303

Twin Valley HS 300/9-12
1 School St 05363 802-464-5255
Frank Spencer, prin. Fax 464-5903

Windsor, Windsor, Pop. 3,714

Windsor Southeast Supervisory Union 1,300/K-12
105 Main St Ste 200 05089 802-674-2144
Fax 674-6357

Windsor JSHS 400/7-12
19 Ascutney St 05089 802-674-6344
Henry Rupertsberger, prin. Fax 674-9802
Other Schools – See Ascutney

Winooski, Chittenden, Pop. 6,353

Winooski SD 800/PK-12
60 Normand St 05404 802-655-0485
Bruce Chattman, supt. Fax 655-7602
www.winooski.k12.vt.us

Winooski HS 200/9-12
80 Normand St 05404 802-655-3531
Steve Perkins, prin. Fax 655-6538

Winooski MS 200/6-8
80 Normand St 05404 802-655-3530
Mary Woodruff, prin. Fax 655-6538

Woodstock, Windsor, Pop. 961

Windsor Central Supervisory Union 1,200/PK-12
496 Woodstock Rd Ste 2 05091 802-457-1213
Meg Gallagher, supt. Fax 457-2989
www.wcsu.net/

Woodstock Union HS 400/9-12
496 Woodstock Rd Ste 1 05091 802-457-1317
Greg Schillinger, prin. Fax 457-1850

Woodstock Union MS 200/7-8
496 Woodstock Rd Ste 1 05091 802-457-1330
Dana Peterson, prin. Fax 457-5048

VIRGINIA

VIRGINIA DEPARTMENT OF EDUCATION
PO Box 2120, Richmond 23218-2120
Telephone 804-225-2020
Fax 804-371-2099
Website http://www.pen.k12.va.us

Superintendent of Public Instruction Dr. Billy Cannaday

VIRGINIA BOARD OF EDUCATION
PO Box 2120, Richmond 23218-2120

President Dr. Mark Emblidge

PUBLIC, PRIVATE AND CATHOLIC SECONDARY SCHOOLS

Abingdon, Washington, Pop. 7,925
Regional Academic Governors SD
Supt. — See Richmond
Holton Governor's S 10-12
PO Box 1987 24212 276-619-4326
Danny Dixon, dir. Fax 619-4328

Washington County SD 7,400/PK-12
812 Thompson Dr 24210 276-739-3003
Dr. Alan Lee, supt. Fax 623-4137
www.wcs.k12.va.us
Abingdon HS 1,000/9-12
705 Thompson Dr 24210 276-739-3200
Jeff Noe, prin. Fax 628-1897
Neff Center for Science & Tech Vo/Tech
255 Stanley St 24210 276-739-3101
Douglas Sparks, prin. Fax 623-4126
Stanley MS 700/6-8
297 Stanley St 24210 276-739-3300
Kathy Laster, prin. Fax 676-1945
Washington County Technical S Vo/Tech
850 Thompson Dr 24210 276-739-3140
Douglas Sparks, prin. Fax 623-4197
Other Schools – See Bristol, Damascus, Glade Spring

Virginia Highlands Community College Post-Sec.
PO Box 828 24212 276-676-5484
Washington County Adult Skill Center Post-Sec.
848 Thompson Dr 24210 276-676-1948

Accomac, Accomack, Pop. 545
Accomack County SD 5,200/K-12
PO Box 330 23301 757-787-5754
W. Richard Bull, supt. Fax 787-2951
sbo.accomack.k12.va.us
Other Schools – See Chincoteague, Oak Hall, Onley, Tangier

Afton, Nelson

Afton Christian S 100/K-12
9357 Critzers Shop Rd 22920 540-456-6853
Debbie Beaver, hdmstr. Fax 456-6236

Alberta, Brunswick, Pop. 303

Southside Virginia Community College Post-Sec.
109 Campus Dr 23821 434-949-1000

Aldie, Loudoun
Loudoun County SD
Supt. — See Ashburn
Mercer MS 600/6-8
42149 Greenstone Dr 20105 703-444-8060
Frederic Gauriloff, prin. Fax 444-8068

Alexandria, Alexandria, Pop. 135,337
Alexandria CSD 10,100/K-12
2000 N Beauregard St 22311 703-824-6600
Rebecca Perry, supt. Fax 824-6699
www.acps.k12.va.us
Hammond MS 1,300/6-8
4646 Seminary Rd 22304 703-461-4100
Randolph Mitchell, prin. Fax 461-4111
Howard 9th Grade Ctr 9-9
3801 W Braddock Rd 22302 703-824-6750
Grace Taylor, prin. Fax 824-6781
Washington MS 1,100/6-8
1005 Mount Vernon Ave 22301 703-706-4500
Keisha Boggan, prin. Fax 706-4507
Williams HS 2,100/10-12
3330 King St 22302 703-824-6800
Mel Riddile, prin. Fax 824-6826

Fairfax County SD
Supt. — See Falls Church
Edison HS 1,900/9-12
5801 Franconia Rd 22310 703-924-8000
Gregory Croghan, prin. Fax 924-8097
Glasgow MS 1,100/6-8
4101 Fairfax Pkwy 22312 703-813-8700
Deirdre Lavery, prin. Fax 813-8797
Hayfield JSHS 4,100/7-12
7630 Telegraph Rd 22315 703-924-7400
Bill Oehrlein, prin. Fax 924-7497
Holmes MS 800/6-8
6525 Montrose St Ste 1 22312 703-658-5900
Roberto Pamas, prin. Fax 658-5997
Jefferson Science & Tech HS 1,700/9-12
6560 Braddock Rd 22312 703-750-8300
Dr. Evan Glazer, prin. Fax 750-5010
Landmark Career Academy Vo/Tech
5801 Duke St 22304 703-658-6451
Jan McKee, prin. Fax 658-6497
Mt. Vernon HS 1,800/9-12
8515 Old Mount Vernon Rd 22309 703-619-3100
Nardos King, prin. Fax 619-3197
Pulley Career Center Vo/Tech
6500 Quander Rd 22307 703-718-2700
Fax 718-2797
Sandburg MS 1,200/7-8
8428 Fort Hunt Rd 22308 703-799-6100
Wendy Eaton, prin. Fax 799-6197
Twain MS 1,100/7-8
4700 Franconia Rd 22310 703-313-3700
Carol Robinson, prin. Fax 313-3797
West Potomac HS 2,100/9-12
6500 Quander Rd 22307 703-718-2500
Rima Vesilind, prin. Fax 718-2597
Whitman MS 1,000/7-8
2500 Parkers Ln 22306 703-660-2400
Otha Davis, prin. Fax 660-2497

Alexandria Friends S 50/9-12
25 S Quaker Ln 22314 703-461-7222
William Stewart, hdmstr. Fax 461-7003
Bishop Ireton HS 800/9-12
201 Cambridge Rd 22314 703-751-7606
Rev. Matthew Hillyard, prin. Fax 212-8173
Episcopal HS 400/9-12
1200 N Quaker Ln 22302 703-933-3000
F. Robertson Hershey, hdmstr. Fax 933-3017
Northern Virginia Community College Post-Sec.
3001 N Beauregard St 22311 703-845-6200
Protestant Episcopal Theologcl. Seminary Post-Sec.
3737 Seminary Rd 22304 703-370-6600
St. Stephen's & St. Agnes S 300/6-8
4401 W Braddock Rd 22304 703-212-2741
Joan Holden, hdmstr. Fax 751-7142
St. Stephen's & St. Agnes S 500/9-12
1000 Saint Stephens Rd 22304 703-751-2700
Joan Holden, hdmstr. Fax 751-7142
TESST Electronic School Post-Sec.
6315 Bren Mar Dr 22312 703-354-1005

Altavista, Campbell, Pop. 3,385
Campbell County SD
Supt. — See Rustburg
Altavista JSHS 800/6-12
904 Bedford Ave 24517 434-369-4768
Clayton Stanley, prin. Fax 369-5191

Amelia Court House, Amelia
Amelia County SD 1,800/PK-12
8701 Otterburn Rd Ste 101 23002 804-561-2621
Dr. David M. Gangel, supt. Fax 561-3057
eclipse.achs.amelia.k12.va.us/public/
Amelia County HS 600/9-12
8500 Otterburn Rd 23002 804-561-2101
Karl Leap, prin. Fax 561-4567
Amelia County MS 400/6-8
8740 Otterburn Rd 23002 804-561-4422
Dr. Teresa Lee, prin. Fax 561-6525

Amherst, Amherst, Pop. 2,225
Amherst County SD 4,700/K-12
PO Box 1257 24521 434-946-9387
John Walker Ed.D., supt. Fax 946-9346
www.amherst.k12.va.us
Amherst County HS 1,500/9-12
139 Lancer Ln 24521 434-946-2898
Ernie Guill, prin. Fax 946-2263
Amherst MS 500/6-8
165 Gordons Fairgrounds Rd 24521 434-946-0691
Christie Cundiff, prin. Fax 946-0258
Other Schools – See Madison Heights

Annandale, Fairfax, Pop. 55,800
Fairfax County SD
Supt. — See Falls Church
Annandale HS 2,500/9-12
4700 Medford Dr 22003 703-642-4100
John Ponton, prin. Fax 642-4197
Poe MS 1,200/6-8
7000 Cindy Ln 22003 703-813-3800
Sonya Swansbrough, prin. Fax 813-3897

Northern Virginia Community College Post-Sec.
4001 Wakefield Chapel Rd 22003 703-323-3000
Springfield Beauty Academy Post-Sec.
4223 Annandale Rd 22003 703-256-5662

Appalachia, Wise, Pop. 1,771
Wise County SD
Supt. — See Wise
Appalachia HS 300/8-12
205 Lee St 24216 276-565-0214
Buzz Akeridge, prin. Fax 565-0922

Appomattox, Appomattox, Pop. 1,729
Appomattox County SD 2,300/PK-12
PO Box 548 24522 434-352-8251
Dr. Walter Krug, supt. Fax 352-0883
www.appomattox.k12.va.us
Appomattox HS 700/9-12
198 Evergreen Ave 24522 434-352-7146
Dr. Greg Wheeler, prin. Fax 352-0822
Appomattox MS 500/6-8
2020 Church St 24522 434-352-8257
Jeff Garrett, prin. Fax 352-5621

Arlington, Arlington, Pop. 189,927
Arlington County SD 18,800/PK-12
1426 N Quincy St 22207 703-228-6000
Dr. Robert G. Smith, supt. Fax 228-6188
www.arlington.k12.va.us
Gunston MS 700/6-8
2700 S Lang St 22206 703-228-6900
Margaret Gill, prin. Fax 519-9183
Jefferson MS 700/6-8
125 S Old Glebe Rd 22204 703-228-5900
Sharon Monde, prin. Fax 979-3744
Kenmore MS 800/6-8
200 S Carlin Springs Rd 22204 703-228-6800
Dr. John Word, prin. Fax 998-3069
Swanson MS 700/6-8
5800 Washington Blvd 22205 703-228-5500
Chrystal Forrester, prin. Fax 536-2775
Tech Ed & Career Center Vo/Tech
816 S Walter Reed Dr 22204 703-228-5800
Dr. Gerald Caputo, prin. Fax 228-5815
Wakefield HS 1,700/9-12
4901 S Chesterfield Rd 22206 703-228-6700
Doris Jackson, prin. Fax 575-8832
Washington-Lee HS 1,800/9-12
1300 N Quincy St 22201 703-228-6200
Gregg Robertson, prin. Fax 524-9814
Williamsburg MS 1,000/6-8
3600 N Harrison St 22207 703-228-5450
Kathleen Francis, prin. Fax 536-2870
Yorktown HS 1,800/9-12
5201 28th St N 22207 703-228-5400
Dr. Raymond Pasi, prin. Fax 228-5409
HS Continuation - Arlington Mill Adult
4975 Columbia Pike 22204 703-228-5350
Barbara Thompson, prin. Fax 575-8666
HS Continuation - Langston Adult
2121 N Culpeper St 22207 703-228-5295
Cleveland James, prin. Fax 807-0614

ACT College Post-Sec.
1100 Wilson Blvd Ste M780 22209 703-527-6660
Argosy University/Washington DC Post-Sec.
1550 Wilson Blvd Ste 600 22209 703-526-5800
Art Institute of Washington Post-Sec.
1820 Fort Myer Dr 22209 703-358-9550
Bishop Denis J. O'Connell HS 9-12
6600 Little Falls Rd 22213 703-237-1400
Dick Martin, prin. Fax 237-1412
DeVry University Post-Sec.
2341 Jefferson Davis Hwy 22202 866-338-7932
DeVry University Post-Sec.
2450 Crystal Dr 22202 703-415-0600
Graham Webb Intl. Academy of Hair Post-Sec.
1621 N Kent St # 1617LL 22209 703-243-9322
Marymount University Post-Sec.
2807 N Glebe Rd 22207 703-522-5600
University of Management and Technology Post-Sec.
1901 Fort Myer Dr Ste 700 22209 703-516-0035

Ashburn, Loudoun, Pop. 3,393
Loudoun County SD 43,500/PK-12
21000 Education Ct 20148 571-252-1000
Dr. Edgar Hatrick, supt. Fax 252-1669
www.loudoun.k12.va.us
Briar Woods HS 9-12
22525 Belmont Ridge Rd 20148 703-957-4400
Edward Starzenski, prin. Fax 542-5923
Broad Run HS 1,700/9-12
21670 Ashburn Rd 20147 703-771-6620
Dr. Edgar Markley, prin. Fax 771-6636
Eagle Ridge MS 600/6-8
42901 Waxpool Rd 20148 571-252-2140
Janice Koslowski, prin. Fax 779-8977
Farmwell Station MS 1,100/6-8
44281 Gloucester Pkwy 20147 703-771-6491
Sherryl Loya, prin. Fax 771-6495
Stone Bridge HS 1,800/9-12
43100 Hay Rd 20147 571-252-2200
James Person, prin. Fax 252-2201
Other Schools – See Aldie, Hamilton, Leesburg, Purcellville, South Riding, Sterling

---

Christian Fellowship S 400/PK-12
21673 Beaumeade Cir Ste 600 20147 703-729-5968
Kevin Jeter, hdmstr. Fax 729-6635
Strayer University Post-Sec.
45150 Russell Branch Pkwy 20147 703-729-8800

Ashland, Hanover, Pop. 6,996
Hanover County SD 18,300/K-12
200 Berkley St 23005 804-365-4500
Dr. Stewart Roberson, supt. Fax 365-4680
www.hcps.us
Henry HS 1,600/9-12
12449 W Patrick Henry Rd 23005 804-365-8000
Dr. Jeffrey Crook, prin. Fax 365-8027
Liberty MS 1,100/6-8
13496 Liberty School Rd 23005 804-365-8060
Donald E. Latham, prin. Fax 365-8061
Other Schools – See Mechanicsville

Randolph-Macon College Post-Sec.
PO Box 5005 23005 804-752-7200

Bassett, Henry, Pop. 1,579
Henry County SD
Supt. — See Collinsville
Bassett HS 1,300/9-12
85 Riverside Dr 24055 276-629-1731
A. Dean Randall, prin. Fax 629-9329

Bastian, Bland
Bland County SD 900/K-12
361 Bears Trl 24314 276-688-3361
Don Hodock, supt. Fax 688-4659
www.bland.k12.va.us
Other Schools – See Bland, Rocky Gap

Bealeton, Fauquier
Fauquier County SD
Supt. — See Warrenton
Cedar-Lee MS 700/6-8
11138 Marsh Rd 22712 540-439-3207
Steven Parker, prin. Fax 439-2051
Liberty HS 1,700/9-12
6300 Independence Ave 22712 540-439-6300
Roger Lee, prin. Fax 439-3397

Bedford, Bedford, Pop. 6,211
Bedford County SD 10,900/K-12
PO Box 748 24523 540-586-1045
Dr. James Blevins, supt. Fax 586-7703
www.bedford.k12.va.us
Bedford MS 500/7-8
503 Longwood Ave 24523 540-586-7735
Rhetta Watkins, prin. Fax 586-4957
Bedford Science and Technology Center Vo/Tech
600 Edmund St 24523 540-586-3933
Dr. Fred Conner, prin. Fax 586-7711
Liberty HS 1,000/9-12
100 Minute Man Dr 24523 540-586-2541
Dr. Cherie Whitehurst, prin. Fax 586-7720
Other Schools – See Forest, Moneta

Ben Hur, Lee
Lee County SD
Supt. — See Jonesville
Lee County Career & Technical Center Vo/Tech
PO Box 100 24218 276-346-1960
Randal A. Ingle, prin. Fax 346-2831

Berryville, Clarke, Pop. 3,157
Clarke County SD 2,200/PK-12
309 W Main St 22611 540-955-6100
Dr. Eleanor Smalley, supt. Fax 955-6109
www.clarke.k12.va.us
Clarke County HS 700/9-12
240 Westwood Rd 22611 540-955-6130
Francis Ball, prin. Fax 955-6139
Johnson-Williams MS 500/6-8
200 Swan Ave 22611 540-955-6160
Evan Robb, prin. Fax 955-6169

Big Stone Gap, Wise, Pop. 5,854
Wise County SD
Supt. — See Wise
Powell Valley HS 500/9-12
1 Avenue of Champions 24219 276-523-1290
David Lee, prin. Fax 523-6804
Powell Valley MS 600/5-8
3137 2nd Ave E 24219 276-523-0195
David Dowdy, prin. Fax 523-4762

Mountain Empire Community College Post-Sec.
3441 Mountain Empire Rd 24219 276-523-2400

Blacksburg, Montgomery, Pop. 39,130
Montgomery County SD
Supt. — See Christiansburg
Blacksburg HS 1,200/9-12
520 Patrick Henry Dr 24060 540-951-5706
Michael Hurst, prin. Fax 951-5714
Blacksburg MS 900/6-8
3109 Prices Fork Rd 24060 540-951-5800
G. Daniel Knott, prin. Fax 951-5808

Dayspring Christian Academy 200/K-12
PO Box 909 24063 540-552-7777
William Hampton, admin. Fax 552-7778
Virginia College of Osteopathic Medicine Post-Sec.
2265 Kraft Dr 24060 540-231-4000
Virginia Polytechnic Inst. & State Univ. Post-Sec.
24061 540-231-6000

Blackstone, Nottoway, Pop. 3,558

Kenston Forest S 400/PK-12
75 Ridge Rd 23824 434-292-7218
James Milroy, hdmstr. Fax 292-7455

Bland, Bland
Bland County SD
Supt. — See Bastian
Bland HS 200/8-12
31 Rocket Dr 24315 276-688-3621
Kevin Siers, prin. Fax 688-4451

Bluefield, Tazewell, Pop. 4,989
Tazewell County SD
Supt. — See Tazewell
Graham HS 500/9-12
210 Valleydale St 24605 276-326-1235
John O'Neal, prin. Fax 326-1128
Graham MS 400/6-8
1 Academic Cir 24605 276-326-1101
Kathy Tabor, prin. Fax 322-1409

Bluefield College Post-Sec.
3000 College Dr 24605 276-326-3682
National College Post-Sec.
100 Logan St 24605 276-326-3621

Bowling Green, Caroline, Pop. 995
Caroline County SD 3,900/PK-12
16221 Richmond Tpke 22427 804-633-5088
Stanley O. Jones, supt. Fax 633-5563
www.caroline.k12.va.us
Other Schools – See Milford

Boydton, Mecklenburg, Pop. 466
Mecklenburg County SD 4,700/PK-12
PO Box 190 23917 434-738-6111
Dr. Frank J. Polakiewicz, supt. Fax 738-6679
www.meck.k12.va.us
Other Schools – See Skipwith, South Hill

Bridgewater, Rockingham, Pop. 5,413
Rockingham County SD
Supt. — See Harrisonburg
Ashby HS 1,100/9-12
800 N Main St 22812 540-828-2008
Steven Walk, prin. Fax 828-4764

Bridgewater College Post-Sec.
402 E College St 22812 540-828-8000

Bristol, Bristol, Pop. 17,335
Bristol CSD 2,300/K-12
222 Oak St 24201 276-821-5600
Dr. Douglas Arnold, supt. Fax 821-5601
www.bvps.org/
Virginia HS 700/9-12
1200 Long Crescent Dr 24201 276-821-5858
Ina Danko, prin. Fax 821-5851
Virginia MS 600/6-8
501 Piedmont Ave 24201 276-821-5660
Gary Ritchie, prin. Fax 821-5661

Washington County SD
Supt. — See Abingdon
Battle HS 600/9-12
21264 Battle Hill Dr 24202 276-642-5300
Judy Wilson, prin. Fax 645-2386
Wallace MS 500/6-8
13077 Wallace Pike 24202 276-642-5400
Dr. Fred Keller, prin. Fax 645-2365

Graham Bible College Post-Sec.
PO Box 1630 24203 423-968-4201
Virginia Intermont College Post-Sec.
1013 Moore St 24201 276-669-6101

Bristow, Prince William
Prince William County SD
Supt. — See Manassas
Marsteller MS 1,400/6-8
14000 Sudley Manor Dr 20136 703-393-7608
Roberta Knetter, prin. Fax 530-6327

Broadway, Rockingham, Pop. 2,460
Rockingham County SD
Supt. — See Harrisonburg
Broadway HS 1,000/9-12
269 Gobbler Dr 22815 540-896-7081
Dr. Stephen Leaman, prin. Fax 896-2640
Hillyard MS 800/6-8
226 Hawks Hill Dr 22815 540-896-8961
Douglas Alderfer, prin. Fax 896-6641

Buchanan, Botetourt, Pop. 1,236
Botetourt County SD
Supt. — See Fincastle
James River HS 500/9-12
9906 Springwood Rd 24066 540-254-1121
James Talbott, prin. Fax 254-2765

Buckingham, Buckingham, Pop. 370
Buckingham County SD 2,200/K-12
PO Box 24 23921 434-969-6100
Larry A. Massie, supt. Fax 969-1176
www.bchs.k12.va.us
Buckingham County HS 700/9-12
78 Knights Rd 23921 434-969-6160
Claude Morris, prin. Fax 969-3209
Buckingham County MS 600/6-8
1184 High School Rd 23921 434-983-2102
Nancy Sherrill, prin. Fax 983-1002

Buena Vista, Buena Vista, Pop. 6,437
Buena Vista CSD 1,100/K-12
2329 Chestnut Ave Ste A 24416 540-261-2129
Dr. Rebecca Gates, supt. Fax 261-2967
www.buena-vista.k12.va.us
McCluer HS 300/9-12
100 Bradford Dr 24416 540-261-2128
Haywood Hand, prin. Fax 261-1828
McCluer MS 300/5-8
2329 Chestnut Ave 24416 540-261-7340
Lori Teague, prin. Fax 261-3292

Southern Virginia University Post-Sec.
1 University Hill Dr 24416 540-261-8400

Burke, Fairfax, Pop. 57,700
Fairfax County SD
Supt. — See Falls Church
Lake Braddock JSHS 3,900/7-12
9200 Burke Lake Rd 22015 703-426-1000
Linda Burke, prin. Fax 426-1093

Carson, Prince George
Jointly Operated Vo Tech SD
Supt. — None
Rowanty Vocational Tech Center Vo/Tech
20000 Rowanty Rd 23830 434-246-5741
Tom Cope, prin. Fax 246-5721

Castlewood, Russell, Pop. 3,036
Russell County SD
Supt. — See Lebanon
Castlewood HS 400/8-12
304 Blue Devil Cir 24224 276-762-9449
Scotty Fletcher, prin. Fax 762-9418

Centreville, Fairfax, Pop. 56,700
Fairfax County SD
Supt. — See Falls Church
Stone MS 1,100/7-8
5500 Sully Park Dr 20120 703-631-5500
Kenneth Gaudreault, prin. Fax 631-5598

Chantilly, Fairfax, Pop. 44,300
Fairfax County SD
Supt. — See Falls Church
Chantilly HS 2,800/9-12
4201 Stringfellow Rd 20151 703-222-8100
James Kacur, prin. Fax 222-8197
Franklin MS 1,100/7-8
3300 Lees Corner Rd 20151 703-904-5100
Sharon Eisenberg, prin. Fax 904-5197
Rocky Run MS 800/7-8
4400 Stringfellow Rd 20151 703-802-7700
Dan Parris, prin. Fax 802-7797
Westfield HS 3,200/9-12
4700 Stonecroft Blvd 20151 703-488-6300
Tim Thomas, prin. Fax 488-6397

Charles City, Charles City
Charles City County SD 900/K-12
10910 Courthouse Rd 23030 804-652-4612
Dr. Janet Crawley, supt. Fax 829-6723
208.31.123.10/
Charles City County HS 300/9-12
10039 Courthouse Rd 23030 804-829-9249
Pamela Boyd, prin. Fax 829-2644
Charles City County MS 200/6-8
10035 Courthouse Rd 23030 804-829-9252
Tanya Roane, prin. Fax 829-2363

Charlotte Court House, Charlotte, Pop. 446
Charlotte County SD 2,300/PK-12
PO Box 790 23923 434-542-5151
Melody Hackney, supt. Fax 542-4261
www.ccps.k12.va.us
Central MS 500/6-8
PO Box 748 23923 434-542-4536
Bonita Hamlett, prin. Fax 542-4630
Randolph-Henry HS 700/9-12
PO Box 668 23923 434-542-4111
Gloria Talbott, prin. Fax 542-4114

Charlottesville, Charlottesville, Pop. 40,437
Albemarle County SD 12,300/K-12
401 McIntire Rd 22902 434-972-4055
Dr. Pamela Moran, supt. Fax 296-5869
www.k12albemarle.org/
Albemarle HS 1,700/9-12
2775 Hydraulic Rd 22901 434-975-9300
Dr. Matthew Haas, prin. Fax 974-4335
Burley MS 400/6-8
901 Rose Hill Dr 22903 434-295-5101
Marcha Howard, prin. Fax 984-4975
Jouett MS 600/6-8
210 Lambs Ln 22901 434-975-9320
Kathryn Baylor, prin. Fax 975-9322
Monticello HS 1,200/9-12
1400 Independence Way 22902 434-244-3100
John W. Haun, prin. Fax 244-3104
Sutherland MS 700/6-8
2801 Powell Creek Dr 22911 434-975-0599
David Rogers, prin. Fax 975-0852
Walton MS 600/6-8
4217 Red Hill Rd 22903 434-977-5615
Eric D. Johnson, prin. Fax 296-6648
Other Schools – See Crozet

Charlottesville CSD 4,400/PK-12
1562 Dairy Rd 22903 434-245-2400
Rosa Atkins, supt. Fax 245-2603
www.ccs.k12.va.us
Buford MS 600/7-8
617 9th St SW 22903 434-245-2411
Timothy J. Flynn, prin. Fax 245-2611
Charlottesville HS 1,300/9-12
1400 Melbourne Rd 22901 434-245-2410
Kenneth H. Leatherwood, prin. Fax 245-2610

Jointly Operated Vo Tech SD
Supt. — None
Charlottsville-Albemarle Tech Center Vo/Tech
1000 Rio Rd E 22901 434-973-4461
Joseph Johnson, dir. Fax 973-4876

Albemarle Christian Academy 100/PK-12
PO Box 6839 22906 434-973-6571
Jeff Cale, prin. Fax 974-6799
Covenant S 700/PK-12
175 Hickory St 22902 434-220-7329
Dr. Ronald Sykes, hdmstr. Fax 220-7320
Miller S of Albemarle 200/8-12
1000 Samuel Miller Loop 22903 434-823-4805
Lindsay Barnes, hdmstr. Fax 823-6617
National College Post-Sec.
1819 Emmet St N 22901 434-295-0136
Piedmont Virginia Community College Post-Sec.
501 College Dr 22902 434-977-3900
RSHT Training Center Post-Sec.
702 Charlton Ave Ste A 22903 434-245-0400
St. Anne's Belfield S 800/PK-12
2132 Ivy Rd 22903 434-296-5106
David Lourie, hdmstr. Fax 979-1486
Tandem Friends S 200/5-12
279 Tandem Ln 22902 434-296-1303
Paul Perkinson, hdmstr. Fax 296-1886
University of Virginia Post-Sec.
PO Box 400160 22904 434-924-0311
Virginia School of Massage Post-Sec.
2008 Morton Dr 22903 434-293-4031

Chatham, Pittsylvania, Pop. 1,298
Pittsylvania County SD 9,300/PK-12
PO Box 232 24531 434-432-2761
James McDaniel, supt. Fax 432-9560
www.pcs.k12.va.us
Chatham HS 700/9-12
100 Chatham Cavalier Cir 24531 434-432-8305
Stephen Welch, prin. Fax 432-8351
Chatham MS 500/6-8
11650 US Highway 29 24531 434-432-2169
Danny Bowman, prin.
Pittsylvania Career Tech Vo/Tech
11700 U S Highway 29 24531 434-432-9416
Jimmie Tickle, prin. Fax 432-0516
Other Schools – See Dry Fork, Gretna, Ringgold

Chatham Hall S 100/9-12
800 Chatham Hall Cir 24531 434-432-2941
Dr. Gary Fountain, prin. Fax 432-1002
Hargrave Military Academy 400/7-12
200 Military Dr 24531 434-432-2481
Wheeler Baker, pres. Fax 432-3129

Chesapeake, Chesapeake, Pop. 218,968
Chesapeake CSD 40,200/K-12
PO Box 16496 23328 757-547-0165
Dr. W. Randolph Nichols, supt. Fax 547-0196
eclipse.cps.k12.va.us
Chesapeake Center Science & Tech Vo/Tech
1617 Cedar Rd 23322 757-547-0134
William Joe, prin. Fax 547-2391
Crestwood MS 700/6-8
1420 Great Bridge Blvd 23320 757-494-7560
Jacqueline Tate, prin. Fax 494-7599
Deep Creek HS 2,000/9-12
2900 Margaret Booker Dr 23323 757-558-5302
Nathan Hardee, prin. Fax 558-5305
Deep Creek MS 600/6-8
1955 Deal Dr 23323 757-558-5321
J. Coppage-Miller, prin. Fax 558-5320
Grassfield HS 9-12
2007 Grizzly Trail 23323 757-547-2095
Carolyn Bernard, prin.
Great Bridge HS 2,300/9-12
301 Hanbury Rd W 23322 757-482-5191
Dr. Janet Andrejco, prin. Fax 482-5559
Great Bridge MS 1,400/6-8
441 Battlefield Blvd S 23322 757-482-5128
Beverly Oliver, prin. Fax 482-0210
Greenbrier MS 900/6-8
1016 Greenbrier Pkwy 23320 757-548-5309
Michelle Porter, prin. Fax 548-8921
Hickory HS 2,500/9-12
1996 Hawk Blvd 23322 757-421-4295
Dr. Woodley Koonce, prin. Fax 421-2190
Hickory MS 1,900/6-8
1997 Hawk Blvd 23322 757-421-0468
Dr. Jean Infantino, prin. Fax 421-0475
Indian River HS 1,900/9-12
1969 Braves Trl 23325 757-578-7000
James Frye, prin. Fax 578-7004
Indian River MS 900/6-8
2300 Old Greenbrier Rd 23325 757-578-7030
Naomi Epps, prin. Fax 578-7036
Jolliff MS 800/6-8
1021 Jolliff Rd 23321 757-465-5246
Dr. Lee Fowler, prin. Fax 465-1646
Owens MS 1,100/6-8
1997 Horseback Run 23323 757-558-5382
John Sykes, prin. Fax 558-5386
Smith HS 2,200/9-12
1994 Tiger Dr 23320 757-548-0696
Paul Joseph, prin. Fax 548-0531
Smith MS 1,100/6-8
2500 Rodgers St 23324 757-494-7590
Dr. Linda Scott, prin. Fax 494-7680
Western Branch HS 2,200/9-12
1968 Bruin Pl 23321 757-638-7900
Arthur Brandriff, prin. Fax 638-7904
Western Branch MS 1,000/6-8
4201 Hawksley Dr 23321 757-638-7920
Craig Jones, prin. Fax 638-7926

Atlantic Shores Christian S 400/7-12
1217 Centerville Tpke N 23320 757-479-9598
Keith Hall, admin. Fax 479-5311
Greenbrier Christian Academy 700/PK-12
311 Kempsville Rd 23320 757-547-9595
Dr. Ron White, supt. Fax 547-9569
Sentara School of Health Professions Post-Sec.
1441 Crossways Blvd Ste 105 23320 757-388-2900
StoneBridge S 500/PK-12
PO Box 9247 23321 757-488-2214
Dr. Jim Arcieri, hdmstr. Fax 465-7637
Strayer University Post-Sec.
700 Independence Pkwy # 400 23320 757-382-9900
Tidewater Adventist Academy 100/K-12
1136 Centerville Tpke N 23320 757-479-0002
Donna Steen, prin. Fax 479-0008
Tidewater Community College Post-Sec.
1428 Cedar Rd 23322 757-547-9271
Tidewater Tech Post-Sec.
932 Ventures Way 23320 757-549-2121

Chester, Chesterfield, Pop. 14,986
Chesterfield County SD
Supt. — See Chesterfield
Carver MS 1,300/6-8
3800 Cougar Trl 23831 804-524-3620
Donald Ashburn, prin. Fax 520-0189
Chesterfield Community HS 300/9-12
12400 Branders Bridge Rd 23831 804-768-6156
Jamie Accashian, prin. Fax 768-6171
Chester MS 900/6-8
3900 W Hundred Rd 23831 804-768-6145
Brent Thomas, prin. Fax 768-6152
Dale HS 2,200/9-12
3626 W Hundred Rd 23831 804-768-6245
Robert Stansberry, prin. Fax 768-6256

Evangel Christian S 200/PK-12
16801 Harrow Gate Rd 23831 804-526-5941
Ada Dowdy, prin. Fax 526-3582
John Tyler Community College Post-Sec.
13101 Jefferson Davis Hwy 23831 800-522-3490

Chesterfield, Chesterfield
Chesterfield County SD 56,100/PK-12
PO Box 10 23832 804-748-1405
Dr. Marcus Newsome, supt. Fax 796-7178
www.chesterfield.k12.va.us
Bird HS 1,800/9-12
10301 Courthouse Rd 23832 804-768-6110
Joseph Tylus, prin. Fax 768-6117
Chesterfield Technical Center Vo/Tech
10101 Courthouse Rd 23832 804-768-6160
Michael Rose, prin. Fax 768-6164
Cosby HS 9-12
10101 Courthouse Rd 23832 804-768-6160
Brenda Mayo, prin.
Other Schools – See Chester, Ettrick, Matoaca, Midlothian, Richmond

---

Richmond Christian S 500/K-12
6511 Belmont Rd 23832 804-276-3193
Stanford Stone, admin. Fax 276-9106

Chilhowie, Smyth, Pop. 1,787
Smyth County SD
Supt. — See Marion
Chilhowie HS 400/9-12
PO Box 2280 24319 276-646-8966
Stephen D. Reedy, prin. Fax 646-5951
Chilhowie MS 400/6-8
PO Box 5018 24319 276-646-3942
Sue Tilson, prin. Fax 646-0210

Chincoteague, Accomack, Pop. 4,416
Accomack County SD
Supt. — See Accomac
Chincoteague HS 400/6-12
4586 Main St 23336 757-336-6166
Warren Holland, prin. Fax 336-1902

Christchurch, Middlesex

Christchurch S 200/8-12
49 Seahorse Ln 23031 804-758-2306
John Byers, hdmstr. Fax 758-0721

Christiansburg, Montgomery, Pop. 17,926
Montgomery County SD 9,500/PK-12
200 Junkin St 24073 540-382-5100
Dr. Tiffany Anderson, supt. Fax 381-6127
www.mcps.org
Christiansburg HS 1,000/9-12
100 Independence Blvd 24073 540-382-5178
Rhonda Poindexter, prin. Fax 381-6525
Christiansburg MS 800/6-8
1205 Buffalo Dr 24073 540-394-2180
Annette Perkins, prin. Fax 394-2197
Other Schools – See Blacksburg, Elliston, Riner, Shawsville

Clifton, Fairfax, Pop. 206
Fairfax County SD
Supt. — See Falls Church
Centreville HS 2,200/9-12
6001 Union Mill Rd 20124 703-802-5400
Mike Campbell, prin. Fax 802-5497
Liberty MS 1,100/7-8
6801 Union Mill Rd 20124 703-988-8100
Peggy Kelly, prin. Fax 988-8197

Clifton Forge, Clifton Forge, Pop. 4,077
Regional Academic Governors SD
Supt. — See Richmond
Jackson River Governor's HS 11-12
PO Box 1000 24422 540-863-2841
Dr. Susan Rollinson, dir. Fax 863-2915

Dabney S. Lancaster Community College Post-Sec.
PO Box 1000 24422 540-863-2800

Clinchco, Dickenson, Pop. 413
Dickenson County SD
Supt. — See Clintwood
Dickenson County Career Center Vo/Tech
335 Vocational Dr 24226 276-835-9384
Brian Baker, prin. Fax 835-9386

Clinchport, Scott, Pop. 75
Scott County SD
Supt. — See Gate City
Rye Cove HS 300/8-12
RR 4 24244 276-940-2701
James Meade, prin. Fax 940-2277

Clintwood, Dickenson, Pop. 1,518
Dickenson County SD 2,500/PK-12
PO Box 1127 24228 276-926-4643
Damon Rasnick, supt. Fax 926-6374
www.dickenson.k12.va.us
Clintwood HS 300/9-12
PO Box 577 24228 276-926-8400
Bill Castle, prin. Fax 926-6154
Other Schools – See Clinchco, Haysi, Nora

Cloverdale, Botetourt, Pop. 1,689
Botetourt County SD
Supt. — See Fincastle
Read Mountain MS 700/6-8
182 Orchard Hill Dr 24077 540-966-8655
Julie Baker, prin. Fax 966-8656

Coeburn, Wise, Pop. 1,982
Wise County SD
Supt. — See Wise
Coeburn HS 400/9-12
PO Box 2036 24230 276-395-3389
Dante Lee, prin. Fax 395-5167
Coeburn MS 400/5-8
PO Box 670 24230 276-395-2135
Haydee Robinson, prin. Fax 395-5453

Flatwoods Civilian Conservation Center Post-Sec.
2803 Dungannon Rd 24230 276-395-3384

Collinsville, Henry, Pop. 7,280
Henry County SD 5,200/PK-12
PO Box 8958 24078 276-634-4700
Dr. Sharon D. Dodson, supt. Fax 638-2925
www.henry.k12.va.us
Fieldale-Collinsville MS 6-8
645 Miles Rd 24078 276-647-3841
Moriah Dollarhite, prin. Fax 647-4090
Other Schools – See Bassett, Martinsville, Ridgeway

Regional Academic Governors SD
Supt. — See Richmond
Piedmont Governor's S for Math/Sci/Tech 11-12
PO Box 728 24078 276-632-5079
Brian Pace, prin. Fax 632-5380

Colonial Beach, Westmoreland, Pop. 3,515
Colonial Beach SD 600/K-12
16 Irving Ave N 22443 804-224-0906
Dr. Alice Howard, supt. Fax 224-8357
www.cbschools.net
Colonial Beach HS 200/8-12
100 1st St 22443 804-224-7166
Clint Runyan, prin. Fax 224-7465

Monroe Bay Christian Academy 100/PK-12
PO Box 208 22443 804-224-9375
James Maxey, dir. Fax 224-6517

Colonial Heights, Colonial Heights, Pop. 17,567
Colonial Heights CSD 2,900/K-12
512 Boulevard 23834 804-524-3400
Dr. Joseph O. Cox, supt. Fax 526-4524
www.colonialhts.net
Colonial Heights HS 900/9-12
3600 Conduit Rd 23834 804-524-3405
John Keeler, prin. Fax 520-7222
Colonial Heights MS 700/6-8
500 Conduit Rd 23834 804-524-3420
Roger Green, prin. Fax 526-9288

Living Word Christian S 100/PK-12
1221 Boulevard 23834 804-520-8276
Linda Thomas, prin. Fax 520-8273

Council, Buchanan
Buchanan County SD
Supt. — See Grundy
Council HS 200/8-12
HC 4 Box 230 24260 276-859-2627
Karen Taylor, prin. Fax 859-6227

Courtland, Southampton, Pop. 1,251
Southampton County SD 2,800/PK-12
PO Box 96 23837 757-653-2692
Charles Turner, supt. Fax 653-9422
www.southampton.k12.va.us/
Southampton HS 900/9-12
23350 Southampton Pkwy 23837 757-653-2751
Allene Atkinson, prin. Fax 653-0414
Southampton MS 700/6-8
23450 Southampton Pkwy 23837 757-653-9250
Angela Goodloe, prin. Fax 653-7251
Southampton Technical Career Center Vo/Tech
23350 Southampton Pkwy 23837 757-653-9170
Linda Adams, admin. Fax 653-9404

Southampton Academy 400/PK-12
26495 Old Plank Rd 23837 757-653-2512
Craig Jones, hdmstr. Fax 653-0011

Covington, Covington, Pop. 6,205
Alleghany County SD 2,900/PK-12
110 Rosedale Ave Ste A 24426 540-965-1800
Robert P. Grimesey, supt. Fax 965-1804
www.alleghany.k12.va.us/
Alleghany HS 800/9-12
210 Mountaineer Dr 24426 540-863-1700
R. Kenneth Higgins, prin. Fax 863-1705
Clifton MS 600/6-8
1000 Riverview Farm Rd 24426 540-863-1726
Brenda Siple, prin. Fax 863-1731

Covington CSD 800/PK-12
340 E Walnut St 24426 540-965-1400
Edward Graham, supt. Fax 965-1404
www.covington.k12.va.us/
Covington JSHS 400/8-12
530 S Lexington Ave 24426 540-965-1410
Ruth Fuhrman, prin.

Jointly Operated Vo Tech SD
Supt. — None
Jackson River Tech Center | Vo/Tech
105 E Country Club Ln 24426 | 540-862-1308
Thomas Beirne, prin. | Fax 862-3592

Crewe, Nottoway, Pop. 2,291
Nottoway County SD
Supt. — See Nottoway
Nottoway HS | 700/9-12
5267 Old Nottoway Rd 23930 | 434-292-5373
Anne Stinson, prin. | Fax 292-3021
Nottoway MS | 400/7-8
5279 Old Nottoway Rd 23930 | 434-292-5375
George Smith, prin. | Fax 292-7479

Crozet, Albemarle, Pop. 2,256
Albemarle County SD
Supt. — See Charlottesville
Henley MS | 700/6-8
5880 Rockfish Gap Tpke 22932 | 434-823-4393
Dr. Anne Coughlin, prin. | Fax 823-2711
Western Albemarle HS | 1,100/9-12
5941 Rockfish Gap Tpke 22932 | 434-823-8700
Chris Dyer, prin. | Fax 823-8711

Crozier, Goochland

Salem Christian S | 100/PK-10
1701 Cardwell Rd 23039 | 804-784-4174
Norman Brooking, admin. | Fax 784-0432

Culpeper, Culpeper, Pop. 12,047
Culpeper County SD | 6,400/K-12
450 Radio Ln 22701 | 540-825-3677
Dr. David A. Cox, supt. | Fax 829-2111
www.culpeperschools.org
Binns MS | 800/6-8
205 E Grandview Ave 22701 | 540-825-6894
Sherri Harkness, prin. | Fax 829-9926
Culpeper County HS | 1,900/9-12
14240 Achievement Dr 22701 | 540-825-8310
Jeff Dietz, prin. | Fax 829-6615
Culpeper County MS | 800/6-8
14300 Achievement Dr 22701 | 540-825-4140
William W. Zierden, prin. | Fax 825-7543

Cumberland, Cumberland
Cumberland County SD | 1,500/PK-12
PO Box 170 23040 | 804-492-4212
James Thornton, supt. | Fax 492-4818
www.cucps.k12.va.us
Cumberland HS | 400/9-12
PO Box 140 23040 | 804-492-4808
Larry Bryan, prin. | Fax 492-3138
Cumberland MS | 400/6-8
PO Box 184 23040 | 804-492-9627
Alvin Beasley, prin. | Fax 492-9326

Daleville, Botetourt, Pop. 1,163
Botetourt County SD
Supt. — See Fincastle
Lord Botetourt HS | 1,100/9-12
1435 Roanoke Rd 24083 | 540-992-1261
Alan Brenner, prin. | Fax 992-8381

Damascus, Washington, Pop. 1,083
Washington County SD
Supt. — See Abingdon
Damascus MS | 200/6-8
32101 Government Rd 24236 | 276-739-4100
Janet Lester, prin. | Fax 475-4032
Holston HS | 300/9-12
21308 Monroe Rd 24236 | 276-739-4000
Jimmy King, prin. | Fax 475-4024

Danville, Danville, Pop. 46,143
Danville CSD | 7,100/PK-12
PO Box 9600 24543 | 434-799-6400
Sue Davis Ed.D., supt. | Fax 799-5267
web.dps.k12.va.us
Bonner MS | 700/6-8
300 Apollo Ave 24540 | 434-799-6446
Dr. J. David Cochran, prin. | Fax 797-8867
Galileo Magnet HS | 300/9-12
230 S Ridge St 24541 | 434-773-8186
Wilfred Lawrence, prin. | Fax 773-8188
Gibson MS | 500/6-8
1215 Industrial Ave 24541 | 434-799-6426
John Thacker, prin. | Fax 797-8857
Washington HS | 1,900/9-12
701 Broad St 24541 | 434-799-6410
Dr. Ron Sieber, prin. | Fax 799-5251
Westwood MS | 500/6-8
500 Apollo Ave 24540 | 434-797-8860
Wanda Fields, prin. | Fax 797-8874

Averett University | Post-Sec.
420 W Main St 24541 | 434-791-5600
Danville Community College | Post-Sec.
1008 S Main St 24541 | 434-797-2222
Danville Regional Medical Center | Post-Sec.
142 S Main St 24541 | 434-799-4510
National College | Post-Sec.
336 Old Riverside Dr 24541 | 434-793-6822
Westover Christian Academy | 500/PK-12
5665 Riverside Dr 24541 | 434-822-0800
Violet Long, admin. | Fax 822-0441

Dayton, Rockingham, Pop. 1,345
Rockingham County SD
Supt. — See Harrisonburg
Pence MS | 800/6-8
375 Bowman Rd 22821 | 540-879-2535
Mary Shifflett, prin. | Fax 879-2179

Dendron, Surry, Pop. 294
Surry County SD
Supt. — See Surry
Jackson MS | 300/5-8
4255 New Design Rd 23839 | 757-267-2810
Carol Butler, prin. | Fax 267-0809
Surry County HS | 400/9-12
1675 Hollybush Rd 23839 | 757-267-2211
Rita Holmes, prin. | Fax 267-2978

Dinwiddie, Dinwiddie
Dinwiddie County SD | 4,500/K-12
PO Box 7 23841 | 804-469-4190
Dr. Charles Maranzano, supt. | Fax 469-4197
www.dinwiddie.k12.va.us
Dinwiddie County HS | 1,400/9-12
PO Box 299 23841 | 804-469-4280
Barbara T. Pittman, prin.
Dinwiddie County MS | 1,200/6-8
PO Box 340 23841 | 804-469-4380
Alfred Cappellanti, prin.

Dry Fork, Pittsylvania
Pittsylvania County SD
Supt. — See Chatham
Tunstall HS, 100 Trojan Cir 24549 | 900/9-12
Hattie Hairston, prin. | 434-724-7111
Tunstall MS | 600/6-8
1160 Tunstall High Rd 24549 | 434-724-7086
Rebecca Stevens, prin. | Fax 724-7907

Dublin, Pulaski, Pop. 2,208
Pulaski County SD
Supt. — See Pulaski
Dublin MS | 600/6-8
650 Giles Ave 24084 | 540-643-0367
Robin Keener, prin. | Fax 674-0813
Pulaski County HS | 1,500/9-12
5414 Cougar Trail Rd 24084 | 540-643-0747
Rodney Reedy, prin. | Fax 674-4722

New River Community College | Post-Sec.
PO Box 1127 24084 | 540-674-3600

Dumfries, Prince William, Pop. 4,816
Prince William County SD
Supt. — See Manassas
Potomac HS | 1,500/9-12
3401 Panther Pride Dr 22026 | 703-441-4200
Rodger Jones, prin. | Fax 441-4497
Potomac MS | 6-8
3130 Panther Pride Dr 22026 | 703-221-4996
Benita Stephens, prin.

Eastville, Northampton, Pop. 198
Northampton County SD
Supt. — See Machipongo
Northampton HS | 600/9-12
PO Box 38 23347 | 757-678-8040
Andrea Price, prin. | Fax 678-5244

Elkton, Rockingham, Pop. 2,606
Rockingham County SD
Supt. — See Harrisonburg
Elkton MS | 300/6-8
21063 Blue and Gold Dr 22827 | 540-298-1228
Ramona Pence, prin. | Fax 298-0029

Elliston, Montgomery, Pop. 1,243
Montgomery County SD
Supt. — See Christiansburg
Eastern Montgomery HS | 300/9-12
4695 Crosier Rd 24087 | 540-268-3010
Nelson Simpkins, prin. | Fax 268-3012

Emory, Washington, Pop. 2,248

Emory & Henry College | Post-Sec.
PO Box 10 24327 | 276-944-4121

Emporia, Emporia, Pop. 5,587
Greensville County SD | 2,600/PK-12
105 Ruffin St 23847 | 434-634-3748
Dr. Philip Worrell, supt. | Fax 634-3495
www.greensville.k12.va.us/
Greensville County HS | 800/9-12
403 Harding St 23847 | 434-634-2195
Dr. Alvera Parrish, prin.
Wyatt MS, 206 Slagles Lake Rd 23847 | 400/7-8
Ann Wade, prin. | 434-634-5159

Ettrick, Chesterfield, Pop. 5,290
Chesterfield County SD
Supt. — See Chesterfield
Matoaca HS | 1,500/9-12
6001 Hickory Rd 23803 | 804-590-3108
Stephen Cunningham, prin. | Fax 590-3022

Ewing, Lee
Lee County SD
Supt. — See Jonesville
Walker HS | 400/8-12
PO Box 39 24248 | 276-445-4111
Terry Welch, prin. | Fax 445-3046

Exmore, Northampton, Pop. 1,393

Broadwater Academy | 500/PK-12
PO Box 546 23350 | 757-442-9041
Kendall Berry, prin. | Fax 442-9615

Fairfax, Fairfax, Pop. 21,963
Fairfax County SD
Supt. — See Falls Church
Fairfax HS | 2,100/9-12
3500 Old Lee Hwy 22030 | 703-219-2200
Scott Brabrand, prin. | Fax 219-2297
Frost MS | 1,100/7-8
4101 Pickett Rd 22032 | 703-426-5700
Marti Jo Jackson, prin. | Fax 426-5797
Lanier MS | 1,000/7-8
3710 Bevan Dr 22030 | 703-934-2400
Scott Poole, prin. | Fax 934-2497
Robinson JSHS | 4,300/7-12
5035 Sideburn Rd 22032 | 703-426-2100
Dan Meier, prin. | Fax 426-2197
Woodson HS | 2,000/9-12
9525 Main St 22031 | 703-503-4600
Robert Elliott, prin. | Fax 503-4697

George Mason University | Post-Sec.
4400 University Dr 22030 | 703-993-2400
Northern Virginia Christian Academy | 200/K-12
11000 Berry St 22030 | 703-273-0803
Greg Slater, prin. | Fax 273-0805

Paul VI HS | 1,100/9-12
10675 Lee Hwy 22030 | 703-352-0925
Ginny Colwell, prin. | Fax 273-9845
Reformed Theological Seminary | Post-Sec.
12500 Fair Lakes Cir # 325 22033 | 703-222-7871
Trinity Christian S | 500/1-12
11204 Braddock Rd 22030 | 703-273-8787
David Vanderpoel Ph.D., hdmstr. | Fax 352-8522
Way of Faith Christian Academy | 200/K-12
8800 Arlington Blvd 22031 | 703-573-7221
Ellen Blackwell, dir. | Fax 573-7248

Fairfield, Rockbridge
Rockbridge County SD
Supt. — See Lexington
Rockbridge MS | 200/6-8
PO Box 328 24435 | 540-348-5445
John Morris, prin. | Fax 348-1016

Falls Church, Falls Church, Pop. 10,781
Fairfax County SD | 161,900/K-12
8115 Gatehouse Rd 22042 | 703-423-1000
Jack Dale, supt. | Fax 423-1007
www.fcps.edu
Davis Career Center | Vo/Tech
7731 Leesburg Pike 22043 | 703-714-5600
Aaron Engley, admin. | Fax 714-5697
Falls Church HS | 1,400/9-12
7521 Jaguar Trl 22042 | 703-207-4000
Janice Lloyd, prin. | Fax 207-4097
Jackson MS | 1,100/7-8
3020 Gallows Rd 22042 | 703-204-8100
Carol Robinson, prin. | Fax 204-8197
Longfellow MS | 1,100/7-8
2000 Westmoreland St 22043 | 703-533-2600
Vince Lynch, prin. | Fax 533-2697
Marshall HS | 1,400/9-12
7731 Leesburg Pike 22043 | 703-714-5400
Jay Pearson, prin. | Fax 714-5497
Stuart HS | 1,500/9-12
3301 Peace Valley Ln 22044 | 703-824-3900
Pamela Jones, prin. | Fax 824-3997
Other Schools – See Alexandria, Annandale, Burke, Centreville, Chantilly, Clifton, Fairfax, Herndon, Lorton, Mc Lean, Reston, Springfield, Vienna

Falls Church CSD | 1,600/K-12
803 W Broad St Ste 300 22046 | 703-248-5600
Lois Berlin, supt. | Fax 248-5613
www.fccps.org/
Mason HS | 700/8-12
7124 Leesburg Pike 22043 | 703-248-5550
Robert Snee, prin. | Fax 248-5533

Child Development Ctr. of Northern VA | Post-Sec.
111 N Cherry St 22046
Fairfax Hospital | Post-Sec.
3300 Gallows Rd 22042 | 703-698-3371
Potomac Academy of Hair Design | Post-Sec.
350 S Washington St 22046 | 703-532-5050
Stratford University | Post-Sec.
7777 Leesburg Pike Ste 100S 22043 | 703-821-8570

Falmouth, Stafford, Pop. 3,541
Stafford County SD
Supt. — See Stafford
Drew MS | 900/6-8
501 Cambridge St 22405 | 540-371-1415
Joseph Soldan, prin. | Fax 371-1447
Gayle MS | 1,100/6-8
100 Panther Dr 22406 | 540-373-0383
Donald Upperco, prin. | Fax 373-8856
Stafford HS | 2,100/9-12
33 Stafford Indians Ln 22405 | 540-371-7200
Tricia Jacobs, prin. | Fax 371-2389

Farmville, Prince Edward, Pop. 6,876
Prince Edward County SD | 2,700/K-12
35 Eagle Dr 23901 | 434-315-2100
Dr. Margaret Blackmon, supt. | Fax 392-1911
www.pecps.k12.va.us
Prince Edward County HS | 900/9-12
35 Eagle Dr 23901 | 434-315-2130
Odessa Pride, prin. | Fax 392-1901
Prince Edward MS | 900/5-8
35 Eagle Dr 23901 | 434-315-2120
Rodney Kane, prin. | Fax 392-4286

Fuqua S | 500/PK-12
PO Box 328 23901 | 434-392-4131
Ruth Murphy, pres. | Fax 392-5062
Longwood University | Post-Sec.
201 High St 23909 | 434-395-2000
New Life Christian Academy | 100/PK-12
9 Mahan Rd 23901 | 434-392-6236
Dr. Betty Weaver, admin. | Fax 392-4462

Ferrum, Franklin, Pop. 1,514

Ferrum College | Post-Sec.
PO Box 1000 24088 | 800-868-9797

Fincastle, Botetourt, Pop. 358
Botetourt County SD | 4,800/PK-12
143 Poor Farm Rd 24090 | 540-473-8263
Dr. Anthony Brads, supt. | Fax 473-8298
www.bcps.k12.va.us
Botetourt Technical Education Center | Vo/Tech
253 Poor Farm Rd 24090 | 540-473-8216
Chester Adams, prin. | Fax 473-8376
Central Academy MS | 400/6-8
367 Poor Farm Rd 24090 | 540-473-8333
Vaneta McAlexander, prin. | Fax 473-8398
Other Schools – See Buchanan, Cloverdale, Daleville

Fishersville, Augusta, Pop. 3,230
Augusta County SD | 10,700/K-12
6 John Lewis Rd 22939 | 540-245-5100
Gary McQuain, supt. | Fax 245-5115
www.augusta.k12.va.us
Wilson Memorial HS | 700/9-12
189 Hornet Rd 22939 | 540-886-4286
Doug Shifflett, prin. | Fax 886-4611

Wilson MS 6-8
232 Hornet Rd 22939 540-245-5185
Donald Curtis, prin. Fax 245-5189
Other Schools – See Fort Defiance, Staunton, Stuarts Draft, Swoope

Jointly Operated Vo Tech SD
Supt. — None
Valley Vocational Tech Center Vo/Tech
49 Hornet Rd 22939 540-245-5002
Darla Miller, prin. Fax 885-0407

Regional Academic Governors SD
Supt. — See Richmond
Shenandoah Valley Governor's S 11-12
49 Hornet Rd 22939 540-245-5088
Linda Cauley, dir. Fax 886-6476

Augusta Medical Center Post-Sec.
PO Box 1000 22939 540-332-4539
Woodrow Wilson Rehabilitation Center Post-Sec.
PO Box 1500 22939 540-332-7265

Floyd, Floyd, Pop. 434
Floyd County SD 2,100/K-12
140 Harris Hart Rd NE 24091 540-745-9400
Terry E. Arbogast Ed.D., supt. Fax 745-9496
www.floyd.k12.va.us
Floyd County HS 800/8-12
721 Baker St 24091 540-745-9450
Barry Hollandsworth, prin. Fax 745-9481

Forest, Bedford, Pop. 5,624
Bedford County SD
Supt. — See Bedford
Forest MS 1,000/6-8
100 Ashwood Dr 24551 434-525-6630
Michelle Morgan, prin. Fax 525-1284
Jefferson Forest HS 1,300/9-12
1 Cavalier Cir 24551 434-525-2674
Anthony Francis, prin. Fax 525-0106

Timberlake Christian Schools 300/PK-12
202 Horizon Dr 24551 434-237-5943
Dr. Randl Spear, supt. Fax 239-3319

Fork Union, Fluvanna
Fluvanna County SD
Supt. — See Palmyra
Fluvanna MS 800/6-8
9172 James Madison Hwy 23055 434-842-2222
Kathi Driver, prin. Fax 842-5150

Fork Union Military Academy 500/6-12
PO Box 278 23055 434-842-3212
John Jackson, prin. Fax 842-4300

Fort Defiance, Augusta
Augusta County SD
Supt. — See Fishersville
Fort Defiance HS 900/9-12
195 Fort Defiance Rd 24437 540-245-5050
Larry Landes, prin. Fax 245-5054
Stewart MS 900/6-8
118 Fort Defiance Rd 24437 540-245-5046
Bill Roberts, prin. Fax 245-5049

Franklin, Franklin, Pop. 8,594
Franklin CSD 1,400/PK-12
207 W 2nd Ave 23851 757-569-8111
Dr. Alline Farmer, supt. Fax 516-1015
www.franklincity.k12.va.us
Franklin HS 400/9-12
310 Crescent Dr 23851 757-562-5187
Samuel Jones, prin. Fax 562-3656
King MS 400/6-8
501 Charles St 23851 757-562-4631
Jo Ann Murray, prin. Fax 562-0231

Paul D. Camp Community College Post-Sec.
100 N College Dr 23851 757-569-6700

Fredericksburg, Fredericksburg, Pop. 20,732
Fredericksburg CSD 1,700/K-12
817 Princess Anne St 22401 540-372-1130
Dale Sander, supt. Fax 372-1111
www.cityschools.com
Monroe HS 800/9-12
2300 Washington Ave 22401 540-372-1100
Daryl Chesley, prin. Fax 373-8643
Walker-Grant MS 400/6-8
1 Learning Ln 22401 540-372-1145
Dennis Keffer, prin. Fax 891-5449

Regional Academic Governors SD
Supt. — See Richmond
Commonwealth Governor's HS 9-12
12301 Spotswood Furnace Rd 22407 540-548-1278
Dr. David Baker, dir. Fax 548-1736

Spotsylvania County SD 22,100/PK-12
8020 River Stone Dr 22407 540-834-2500
Dr. Jerry Hill, supt. Fax 834-2556
www.spotsylvania.k12.va.us
Battlefield MS 700/6-8
11120 Leavells Rd 22407 540-786-4400
Sheila Smith, prin. Fax 786-7109
Chancellor HS 1,200/9-12
6300 Harrison Rd 22407 540-786-2606
Jacqueline Bass-Fortune, prin. Fax 786-1176
Chancellor MS 800/6-8
6320 Harrison Rd 22407 540-786-8099
Shirley Eye, prin. Fax 785-9392
Freedom MS 900/6-8
7315 Smith Station Rd 22407 540-548-1030
Alan Jacobs, prin. Fax 786-0782
Massaponax HS 1,700/9-12
8201 Jefferson Davis Hwy 22407 540-710-0419
Joseph Rodkey, prin. Fax 710-1596
Riverbend HS 1,500/9-12
12301 Spotswood Furnace Rd 22407 540-548-4051
Steven Fitch, prin. Fax 548-2964
Other Schools – See Spotsylvania

Stafford County SD
Supt. — See Stafford
Dixon-Smith MS 6-8
503 Deacon Rd 22405 540-899-0860
Steve Trant, prin. Fax 899-0881

Career Training Solutions Post-Sec.
100 Riverside Pkwy Ste 123 22406 540-373-2200
Fredericksburg Academy 500/PK-12
10800 Academy Dr 22408 540-898-0020
Robert Graves, hdmstr. Fax 898-8951
Fredericksburg Christian HS 300/9-12
9400 Thornton Rolling Rd 22408 540-371-3852
Sharon E. Roper, prin. Fax 371-4121
Fredericksburg Christian MS 300/4-8
2231 Jefferson Davis Hwy 22401 540-373-5357
Warren Aldrich, prin. Fax 899-6211
Mary Washington Hospital Post-Sec.
1001 Sam Perry Blvd 22401 540-899-1565
South Stafford Christian S 50/K-12
15 Pine Rd 22405 540-371-1886
Rev. Dan Bayman, admin.
University of Mary Washington Post-Sec.
1301 College Ave 22401 540-654-1000

Front Royal, Warren, Pop. 14,499
Warren County SD 5,200/K-12
210 N Commerce Ave 22630 540-635-2171
Pamela McInnis, supt. Fax 636-4195
www.wcps.k12.va.us
Warren County HS 1,100/10-12
240 Luray Ave 22630 540-635-4144
Melinda Calhoun, prin. Fax 635-2009
Warren County JHS 900/8-9
155 Westminster Dr 22630 540-636-3199
Andrew Keller, prin. Fax 636-3244

Christendom College Post-Sec.
134 Christendom Dr 22630 540-636-2900
Notre Dame Grad Sch of Christendom Coll. Post-Sec.
134 Christendom Dr 22630 800-877-5456
Randolph-Macon Academy 400/6-12
200 Academy Dr 22630 540-636-5200
Henry Hobgood, pres. Fax 636-5344
Riverfront Christian S 200/PK-10
55 E Strasburg Rd 22630 540-635-8202
Cindy Martin, admin. Fax 636-4418
Royal Christian Academy 100/PK-12
1111 N Shenandoah Ave 22630 540-636-7940
Frank Kane, prin. Fax 636-7213

Gainesville, Prince William
Prince William County SD
Supt. — See Manassas
Bull Run MS 1,300/6-8
6308 Catharpin Rd 20155 703-753-9969
William Bixby, prin. Fax 753-9610

Galax, Galax, Pop. 6,676
Galax CSD 1,300/K-12
223 Long St 24333 276-236-2911
Samuel Cook, supt. Fax 236-5776
www.gcps.k12.va.us/
Galax JSHS 400/8-12
200 Maroon Tide Dr 24333 276-236-2991
William Sturgill, prin. Fax 236-8011

Gate City, Scott, Pop. 2,072
Scott County SD 3,600/K-12
261 E Jackson St 24251 276-386-6118
James Scott, supt. Fax 386-2684
scott.k12.va.us/
Gate City HS 400/10-12
127 Beech St 24251 276-386-7522
Michael Brickey, prin. Fax 386-2695
Gate City MS 500/7-9
125 Beech St 24251 276-386-6065
John Ferguson, prin. Fax 386-2556
Scott County Career & Technical Center Vo/Tech
150 Broadwater Ave 24251 276-386-6515
Ralph Quesinberry, prin. Fax 386-2852
Other Schools – See Clinchport, Nickelsville

Glade Spring, Washington, Pop. 1,537
Washington County SD
Supt. — See Abingdon
Glade Spring MS 300/6-8
33474 Stagecoach Rd 24340 276-739-3800
Sharon Rainey, prin. Fax 429-4211
Henry HS 500/9-12
31437 Hillman Hwy 24340 276-739-3700
Keith Perrigan, prin. Fax 944-2125

Glen Allen, Henrico, Pop. 9,010
Henrico County SD
Supt. — See Richmond
Center for Information Technology 9-12
4801 Twin Hickory Rd 23059 804-364-8000
Aaron Spence, prin.
Deep Run HS 1,400/9-12
4801 Twin Hickory Rd 23059 804-364-8000
Dr. Aaron C. Spence, prin. Fax 364-0887
Hungary Creek MS 900/6-8
4909 Francistown Rd 23060 804-527-2640
Elizabeth Armbruster, prin.
Short Pump MS 1,100/6-8
4701 Pouncey Tract Rd 23059 804-360-0800
Dr. Mark E. Chamberlain, prin. Fax 360-0808

ECPI Technical College Post-Sec.
4305 Cox Rd 23060 804-934-0100

Gloucester, Gloucester
Gloucester County SD 6,100/PK-12
6489 Main St 23061 804-693-5300
Dr. Howard B. Kiser, supt. Fax 693-1426
gets.gc.k12.va.us/
Gloucester HS, 6680 Short Ln 23061 2,000/9-12
Dr. Layton Beverage, prin. 804-693-2526
Page MS 600/6-8
5628 George Washington Mem 23061 804-693-2540
Dr. Barbara Anderson, prin. Fax 693-6595

Peasley MS 900/6-8
2885 Hickory Fork Rd 23061 804-693-1499
Bryan Hartley, prin. Fax 693-1497

Gloucester Point, Gloucester, Pop. 8,509

College of William and Mary Post-Sec.
PO Box 1346 23062 804-642-7000

Goochland, Goochland
Goochland County SD 2,200/K-12
PO Box 169 23063 804-556-5316
Frank E. Morgan, supt. Fax 556-3847
www.glnd.k12.va.us
Goochland HS 900/8-12
3250 River Rd W 23063 804-556-5322
Jon Bennett, prin. Fax 556-6485

Gretna, Pittsylvania, Pop. 1,222
Pittsylvania County SD
Supt. — See Chatham
Gretna HS, PO Box 398 24557 700/9-12
Deborah D. Powell, prin. 434-656-2246
Gretna MS, 201 Coffey St 24557 600/6-8
Vera F. Glass, prin. 434-656-2217

Grundy, Buchanan, Pop. 1,004
Buchanan County SD 3,600/PK-12
PO Box 833 24614 276-935-4551
Tommy P. Justus, supt. Fax 935-6091
www.buc.k12.va.us
Buchanan County Tech & Career Center Vo/Tech
Slate Creek Rd 24614 276-935-4541
Sandra Cook, prin. Fax 935-4682
Grundy HS 500/9-12
RR 5 Box 23 24614 276-935-2106
Leslie Horne, prin. Fax 935-8602
Other Schools – See Council, Hurley, Pilgrims Knob

Appalachian School of Law Post-Sec.
PO Box 2825 24614 800-895-7411

Halifax, Halifax, Pop. 1,293
Halifax County SD 4,100/K-12
PO Box 1849 24558 434-476-2171
Paul D. Stapleton, supt. Fax 476-1858
www.halifax.k12.va.us
Halifax County Career Center Vo/Tech
PO Box 1849 24558 434-476-5515
Charles Lowery, prin. Fax 476-5527
Other Schools – See South Boston

Hamilton, Loudoun, Pop. 718
Loudoun County SD
Supt. — See Ashburn
Harmony IS 1,000/8-9
38174 W Colonial Hwy 20158 540-338-0800
Sherron Gladden, prin. Fax 338-0805

Catholic Distance University Post-Sec.
120 E Colonial Hwy 20158 540-338-2700

Hampden Sydney, Prince Edward, Pop. 1,240

Hampden-Sydney College Post-Sec.
PO Box 667 23943 800-755-0733

Hampton, Hampton, Pop. 145,579
Hampton CSD 22,300/PK-12
1 Franklin St 23669 757-727-2000
Dr. Patrick Russo, supt. Fax 727-2002
www.sbo.hampton.k12.va.us
Bethel HS 2,100/9-12
1067 Big Bethel Rd 23666 757-825-4400
John Bailey, prin. Fax 825-4464
Davis MS 1,100/6-8
1435 Todds Ln 23666 757-825-4520
David Leech, prin. Fax 825-4533
Eaton MS 900/6-8
2108 Cunningham Dr 23666 757-825-4540
Raymond Haynes, prin. Fax 825-4551
Hampton HS 1,600/9-12
1491 W Queen St 23669 757-825-4430
Myra Chambers, prin. Fax 825-4711
Jones Magnet MS 600/6-8
1819 Nickerson Blvd 23663 757-850-7900
Dr. Catherine Worley, prin. Fax 850-5395
Kecoughtan HS 1,900/9-12
522 Woodland Rd 23669 757-850-5000
Arnold Baker, prin. Fax 850-5153
Lindsay MS 1,000/6-8
1636 Briarfield Rd 23661 757-825-4560
Tamara Cooper, prin. Fax 825-4839
New Horizons Regional Education Center Vo/Tech
520 Butler Farm Rd 23666 757-766-1100
J. Joseph Johnson, prin. Fax 766-3591
Phoebus HS 1,400/9-12
100 Ireland St 23663 757-727-1000
Robert Johnson, prin. Fax 727-0981
Spratley MS 800/6-8
339 Woodland Rd 23669 757-850-5032
Rashard Wright, prin. Fax 850-5186
Syms MS 1,200/6-8
170 Fox Hill Rd 23669 757-850-5050
John Caggiano, prin. Fax 850-5413

Jointly Operated Vo Tech SD
Supt. — None
New Horizons Reg Ed Ctr - Butler Farm Vo/Tech
520 Butler Farm Rd 23666 757-874-4444
Kelley Brown Wood, prin.

Regional Academic Governors SD
Supt. — See Richmond
New Horizons Governor's S Science/Tech. 11-12
520 Butler Farm Rd 23666 757-766-1100
Dr. Donna Poland, dir. Fax 766-3591

Crescent Cosmetology University Post-Sec.
34 Holloway Dr 23666 757-826-4609
Faith Outreach Education Center 100/PK-12
3105 W Mercury Blvd 23666 757-838-8949
Crystal Caskie, prin. Fax 838-4434

Hampton Christian HS 300/7-12
2419 N Armistead Ave 23666 757-838-7427
Frank Carvell, supt. Fax 827-8067
Hampton University 23669 Post-Sec.
757-727-5000
Riverside Academy Post-Sec.
2244 Executive Dr 23666 757-315-3683
Thomas Nelson Community College Post-Sec.
PO Box 9407 23670 757-825-2700
Virginia School for the Deaf and Blind Post-Sec.
700 Shell Rd 23661 757-247-2058
Virginia School of Hair Design Post-Sec.
101 W Queens Way 23669 757-722-0211

Harrisonburg, Harrisonburg, Pop. 40,438
Harrisonburg CSD 4,200/K-12
317 S Main St 22801 540-434-9916
Donald Ford, supt. Fax 434-5196
www.harrisonburg.k12.va.us
Harrisonburg HS 1,300/9-12
1001 Garbers Church Rd 22801 540-433-2651
Irene Reynolds, prin. Fax 433-3595
Harrison MS 900/6-8
1311 W Market St 22801 540-434-1949
Elisabeth Dunnenberger, prin. Fax 434-4052

Jointly Operated Vo Tech SD
Supt. — None
Massanutten Tech Center Vo/Tech
325 Pleasant Valley Rd 22801 540-434-5961
Marshall Price, prin. Fax 434-1402

Rockingham County SD 11,200/PK-12
100 Mount Clinton Pike 22802 540-564-3200
Dr. Carol Fenn, supt. Fax 564-3241
www.rockingham.k12.va.us/
Other Schools – See Bridgewater, Broadway, Dayton, Elkton, Penn Laird

---

Eastern Mennonite HS 300/6-12
801 Parkwood Dr 22802 540-432-4500
Paul Leaman, prin. Fax 432-4528
Eastern Mennonite University Post-Sec.
1200 Park Rd 22802 540-432-4000
Good Shepherd S 200/PK-12
342 Neff Ave 22801 540-564-1744
Steve McClay, prin. Fax 564-2480
James Madison University Post-Sec.
800 S Main St 22807 540-568-6211
National College Post-Sec.
1515 Country Club Rd 22802 540-432-0943
Rockingham Memorial Hospital Post-Sec.
235 Cantrell Ave 22801 540-564-5407

Haymarket, Prince William, Pop. 1,083
Prince William County SD
Supt. — See Manassas
Battlefield HS 1,100/9-12
15000 Graduation Dr 20169 571-261-4400
Amy Ethridge-Conti, prin. Fax 261-3719

Haysi, Dickenson, Pop. 181
Dickenson County SD
Supt. — See Clintwood
Haysi HS 300/9-12
PO Box G 24256 276-865-5126
Larry Compton, prin. Fax 865-5240

Heathsville, Northumberland
Northumberland County SD
Supt. — See Lottsburg
Northumberland HS 400/9-12
PO Box 40 22473 804-580-5192
Larry Shumaker, prin.
Northumberland MS 300/6-8
PO Box 100 22473 804-580-5753
Robert Bailey, prin.

Herndon, Fairfax, Pop. 21,965
Fairfax County SD
Supt. — See Falls Church
Carson MS 1,100/7-8
13618 McLearen Rd 20171 703-925-3600
August Frattali, prin. Fax 925-3697
Herndon HS 2,300/9-12
700 Bennett St 20170 703-810-2200
Frances Ivey, prin. Fax 810-2262
Herndon MS 1,200/7-8
901 Locust St 20170 703-904-4800
Frank Jenkins, prin. Fax 904-4897

AKS Massage School Post-Sec.
462 Herndon Pkwy Ste 208 20170 703-464-0333

Highland Springs, Henrico, Pop. 13,823
Henrico County SD
Supt. — See Richmond
Center for Engineering 9-12
15 S Oak Ave 23075 804-328-4000
Albert Ciarochi, prin.
Highland Springs HS 1,800/9-12
15 S Oak Ave 23075 804-328-4000
Albert M. Ciarochi, prin. Fax 328-4013
Highland Springs Technical Center Vo/Tech
100 Tech Dr 23075 804-328-4075
Thomas Collier, prin. Fax 328-4074
Adult Education Center Adult
201 E Nine Mile Rd 23075 804-328-4095
Elaine Callahan, prin.

Hillsville, Carroll, Pop. 2,716
Carroll County SD 3,900/K-12
605 Pine St Ste 9 24343 276-728-3191
Oliver McBride, supt. Fax 728-3195
www.ccpsd.k12.va.us
Carroll County HS 800/10-12
100 Cavs Ln 24343 276-728-2125
Robbie Patton, prin. Fax 728-9067
Carroll County IS 700/8-9
1036 N Main St 24343 276-728-2382
Dr. Kevin Harris, prin. Fax 728-4089

New Life Christian S International 50/7-12
PO Box 1268 24343 276-730-0706
Leon Goad, admin. Fax 730-0705

Honaker, Russell, Pop. 921
Russell County SD
Supt. — See Lebanon
Honaker HS 500/8-12
PO Box 764 24260 276-873-6363
Tony Bush, prin. Fax 873-7252

Hopewell, Hopewell, Pop. 22,690
Hopewell CSD 3,900/K-12
103 N 12th Ave 23860 804-541-6400
Dr. Winston Odom, supt. Fax 541-6401
www.hopewell.k12.va.us
Hopewell HS 1,100/9-12
400 S Mesa Dr 23860 804-541-6402
Gayle Keith, prin. Fax 541-6403
Woodson MS 1,000/6-8
1000 Winston Churchill Dr 23860 804-541-6404
Cheryl Webb, prin. Fax 541-6405

Hot Springs, Bath
Bath County SD
Supt. — See Warm Springs
Bath County HS 300/8-12
464 Charger Ln 24445 540-839-2431
Pete Pitard, prin. Fax 839-3290

Hurley, Buchanan
Buchanan County SD
Supt. — See Grundy
Hurley HS 300/8-12
6339 Hurley Rd 24620 276-566-8334
Richie T. Blankenship, prin. Fax 566-7127

Hurt, Pittsylvania, Pop. 1,245

Faith Christian Academy 100/PK-12
PO Box 670 24563 434-324-8276
Lisa Moore, prin. Fax 324-8279

Independence, Grayson, Pop. 921
Grayson County SD 2,100/K-12
PO Box 888 24348 276-773-2832
Elizabeth Thomas, supt. Fax 773-2939
www.grayson.k12.va.us
Fries MS, PO Box 155 24348 6-8
Ellen Forbes-Copenhaver, prin. 276-744-7548
Grayson County Career & Technical Center Vo/Tech
PO Box 707 24348 276-773-2951
Angela Lawson, prin. Fax 773-2396
Grayson County HS 700/9-12
PO Box 828 24348 276-773-2131
Diane Haynes, prin. Fax 773-2682
Independence MS 400/6-8
PO Box 155 24348 276-773-3020
Bobby Cheeks, prin. Fax 773-0479
Other Schools – See Whitetop

Isle of Wight, Isle of Wight

Isle of Wight Academy 500/PK-12
PO Box 105 23397 757-357-3866
Benjamin Vaughan, hdmstr. Fax 357-6886

Jetersville, Amelia
Jointly Operated Vo Tech SD
Supt. — None
Amelia-Nottoway Vo Tech Ctr Vo/Tech
148 Votech Rd 23083 434-645-7854
Jack Raines, prin. Fax 645-1044

Nottoway County SD
Supt. — See Nottoway
Piedmont Alternative S Vo/Tech
128 Votech Rd 23083 434-645-7471
Fax 645-1044

Jonesville, Lee, Pop. 980
Lee County SD 3,500/PK-12
5 Park St 24263 276-346-2107
Fred Marion, supt. Fax 346-0307
www.leectysch.com/
Jonesville MS 300/6-8
RR 1 Box 104H 24263 276-346-1011
Connie Daugherty, prin. Fax 346-1411
Lee HS 800/9-12
RR 2 Box 3145 24263 276-346-0173
Ronald Earley, prin. Fax 346-4032
Other Schools – See Ben Hur, Ewing, Pennington Gap

Kenbridge, Lunenburg, Pop. 1,319
Lunenburg County SD 1,800/PK-12
1009 Main St 23944 434-676-2467
Wayne Staples, supt. Fax 676-1000
Other Schools – See Victoria

Keysville, Charlotte, Pop. 782
Regional Academic Governors SD
Supt. — See Richmond
Governor's S of Southside VA 11-12
200 Daniel Rd 23947 434-736-0616
Catherine Cottrell, dir. Fax 736-0719

Southside Virginia Community College Post-Sec.
200 Daniel Rd 23947 434-736-2018

Kilmarnock, Lancaster, Pop. 1,215
Lancaster County SD 1,500/PK-12
PO Box 2000 22482 804-435-3183
Randolph H. Latimore Ed.D., supt. Fax 435-3309
www.lcs.k12.va.us
Lancaster MS, 191 School St 22482 500/4-8
Craig Kauffman, prin. 804-435-1681
Other Schools – See Lancaster

King and Queen Court House, King and Queen
King & Queen County SD 800/K-12
PO Box 97 23085 804-785-5981
Fax 785-5686
www.kqps.net
Central HS 300/8-12
17024 The Trl 23085 804-785-6102
Veronica Simms, prin. Fax 785-5129

King George, King George
King George County SD 3,300/K-12
PO Box 1239 22485 540-775-5833
Dr. Candace Brown, supt. Fax 775-2165
www.kgcs.k12.va.us
King George HS 1,000/9-12
8246 Dahlgren Rd 22485 540-775-3055
Todd Satterwhite, prin. Fax 775-5345
King George MS 500/7-8
8562 Dahlgren Rd 22485 540-775-2331
Seidh Ashshaheed, prin. Fax 775-0263

King William, King William
King William County SD 1,900/PK-12
PO Box 185 23086 804-769-3434
Dr. Brenda Cowlbeck, supt. Fax 769-3312
www.kwcps.k12.va.us
Hamilton-Holmes MS 500/6-8
18444 King William Rd 23086 804-769-3316
Stacey B. Johnson, prin.
King William HS, 80 Cavalier Dr 23086 600/9-12
Charles Clare, prin. 804-769-2708

Lancaster, Lancaster
Lancaster County SD
Supt. — See Kilmarnock
Lancaster HS, PO Box 790 22503 500/9-12
Sandra Spears, prin. 804-462-5177

Lawrenceville, Brunswick, Pop. 1,157
Brunswick County SD 1,800/PK-12
1718 Farmers Field Rd 23868 434-848-3138
Dr. Oliver Spencer, supt. Fax 848-4001
www.brun.k12.va.us
Brunswick SHS 500/9-12
2171 Lawrenceville Plank Rd 23868 434-848-2716
Lawrence Whiting, prin. Fax 848-6303
Russell MS 300/6-8
19400 Christanna Hwy 23868 434-848-2132
Sandra King, prin. Fax 848-6201

Brunswick Academy 500/PK-12
2100 Planters Rd 23868 434-848-2220
Jean Grizzard, hdmstr. Fax 848-4729
St. Paul's College Post-Sec.
406 Windsor Ave 23868 434-848-3111

Lebanon, Russell, Pop. 3,225
Russell County SD 3,700/K-12
PO Box 8 24266 276-889-6500
Lorraine Turner, supt. Fax 889-6508
www.russell.k12.va.us
Lebanon HS 600/9-12
PO Box 217 24266 276-889-6539
Nelson Dodi, prin. Fax 889-0622
Lebanon MS 6-8
PO Box 577 24266 276-889-6548
Joey Long, prin. Fax 889-4262
Russell County Career & Technology Ctr Vo/Tech
PO Box 849 24266 276-889-6550
Brian Hooker, prin. Fax 889-4470
Other Schools – See Castlewood, Honaker

Leesburg, Loudoun, Pop. 36,269
Loudoun County SD
Supt. — See Ashburn
Belmont Ridge MS 1,100/6-8
19045 Upper Belmont Pl 20176 571-252-2220
Theresa N. Redd, prin. Fax 669-1455
Harper Park MS 700/6-8
701 Potomac Station Dr NE 20176 703-779-8860
William Shipp, prin. Fax 779-8867
Heritage HS 1,300/9-12
520 Evergreen Mill Rd SE 20175 703-669-1400
Margaret Huckaby, prin. Fax 669-1410
Loudoun County HS 1,200/9-12
415 Dry Mill Rd SW 20175 703-771-6580
William Oblas, prin. Fax 771-6595
Monroe Technology Center Vo/Tech
715 Childrens Center Rd SW 20175 703-771-6560
Wagner B. Grier, prin. Fax 771-6563
Simpson MS 800/6-8
490 Evergreen Mill Rd SE 20175 703-771-6640
John Bannister, prin. Fax 771-6643
Smart's Mill MS 800/6-8
850 N King St 20176 703-669-1480
Eric L. Steward, prin. Fax 669-1485

Lexington, Lexington, Pop. 6,776
Lexington CSD 500/K-8
300A White St 24450 540-463-7146
Dr. Daniel Lyons, supt. Fax 464-5230
www.lexedu.org/
Lylburn-Downing MS 200/6-8
302 Diamond St 24450 540-463-3532
Richard Dowd, prin.

Rockbridge County SD 2,900/K-12
1972 Big Spring Dr 24450 540-463-7386
John Burks, supt. Fax 463-7823
www.rcs.rang.k12.va.us
Maury River MS 400/6-8
600 Waddell St 24450 540-463-3129
Lena Beason, prin. Fax 464-4838
Rockbridge County HS 1,100/9-12
143 Greenhouse Rd 24450 540-463-5555
Jennifer Weaver, prin. Fax 463-6152
Other Schools – See Fairfield

Virginia Military Institute 24450 Post-Sec.
540-464-7000
Washington & Lee University 24450 Post-Sec.
540-463-8400

Locust Grove, Orange
Orange County SD
Supt. — See Orange
Locust Grove MS 500/6-8
31208 Constitution Hwy 22508 540-661-4550
Martha Roby, prin. Fax 661-4447

Germanna Community College Post-Sec.
2130 Germanna Hwy 22508 540-727-3000

Locust Hill, Middlesex
Middlesex County SD
Supt. — See Saluda
St. Clare Walker MS 400/6-8
PO Box 9 23092 804-758-2561
Joe Fears, prin. Fax 758-0834

Lorton, Fairfax, Pop. 15,385
Fairfax County SD
Supt. — See Falls Church
South County JSHS 7-12
8501 Silverbrook Rd 22079 703-446-1600
Dale Rumberger, prin. Fax 446-1697

Lottsburg, Northumberland
Northumberland County SD 1,500/PK-12
2172 Northumberland Hwy 22511 804-529-6134
Clint Stables, supt. Fax 529-6449
Other Schools – See Heathsville

Lovingston, Nelson
Nelson County SD 2,000/PK-12
PO Box 276 22949 434-263-7100
Dr. Roger Dale Collins, supt. Fax 263-7115
www.nelson.k12.va.us
Nelson County HS 700/9-12
6919 Thomas Nelson Hwy 22949 434-263-8317
Emma Wardlaw, prin. Fax 263-5987
Nelson MS 500/6-8
6925 Thomas Nelson Hwy 22949 434-263-4801
Jody Ray, prin. Fax 263-4483

Luray, Page, Pop. 4,865
Page County SD 3,600/PK-12
735 W Main St 22835 540-743-6533
Dr. Randall W. Thomas, supt. Fax 743-7784
www.pagecounty.k12.va.us
Luray HS, 14 Luray Ave 22835 600/8-12
David Ponn, prin. 540-743-3800
Page County Technical Ctr Vo/Tech
525 Middleburg Rd 22835 540-778-7282
Philip Secrist, prin.
Other Schools – See Shenandoah

Lynchburg, Lynchburg, Pop. 66,973
Campbell County SD
Supt. — See Rustburg
Brookville HS 1,000/9-12
100 Laxton Rd 24502 434-239-2636
James Whorley, prin. Fax 239-6706
Brookville MS 700/6-8
320 Bee Dr 24502 434-239-9267
Robert Bailey, prin. Fax 237-8974

Lynchburg CSD 8,600/PK-12
PO Box 1599 24505 434-522-3700
Dr. Paul McKendrick, supt. Fax 846-1500
www.lynchburg.org
Central VA Governor's S Science & Tech. 11-12
3020 Wards Ferry Rd 24502 434-582-1104
Dr. Thomas Morgan, prin. Fax 239-4140
Dunbar MS for Innovation 600/6-8
1200 Polk St 24504 434-522-3740
Brian Wray, prin. Fax 522-3727
Glass HS 1,600/9-12
2111 Memorial Ave 24501 434-522-3712
Susan Morrison, prin. Fax 522-3741
Heritage HS 1,100/9-12
3020 Wards Ferry Rd 24502 434-582-1147
Mark Miear, prin. Fax 582-1137
Linkhorne MS 700/6-8
2525 Linkhorne Dr 24503 434-384-5150
Robert Kerns, prin. Fax 384-2810
Sandusky MS 600/6-8
805 Chinook Pl 24502 434-582-1120
James E. Sales, prin. Fax 582-1183
Adult Learning Center Adult
1015 Miller Park Sq 24501 434-522-2319
Linda Cole, prin. Fax 522-2320

Centra Health Post-Sec.
1920 Atherholt Rd 24501 434-947-4705
Central Virginia Community College Post-Sec.
3506 Wards Rd 24502 434-832-7600
Holy Cross S PK-12
2125 Langhorne Rd 24501 434-847-5436
John Jones, prin. Fax 847-4156
Liberty Christian Academy 1,200/PK-12
100 Mountain View Rd 24502 434-832-2000
Harvey Klamm, supt. Fax 832-2027
Liberty University Post-Sec.
PO Box 20000 24506 434-582-2000
Lynchburg College Post-Sec.
1501 Lakeside Dr 24501 434-544-8100
Lynchburg General Hosp School of Nursing Post-Sec.
1901 Tate Springs Rd 24501 434-947-3070
Miller-Motte Technical College Post-Sec.
1011 Creekside Ln 24502 877-333-6622
National College Post-Sec.
104 Candlewood Ct 24502 434-239-3500
Ralph's Virginia School of Cosmetology Post-Sec.
3225 Old Forest Rd Ste 5 24501 434-385-7722
Randolph College Post-Sec.
2500 Rivermont Ave 24503 434-947-8000
Virginia Episcopal S 200/9-12
PO Box 408 24505 434-385-3600
Dr. Philip Hadley, hdmstr. Fax 385-3603
Virginia University of Lynchburg Post-Sec.
2058 Garfield Ave 24501 434-528-5276

Machipongo, Northampton
Northampton County SD 2,000/K-12
7207 Young St 23405 757-678-5151
Dr. Richard Bowmaster, supt. Fax 678-7267
www.ncps.k12.va.us
Northampton MS 500/6-8
7247 Young St 23405 757-678-8070
Irma Berry, prin. Fax 678-7645
TECH Center Vo/Tech
7207 Young St 23405 757-678-8004
Dr. David van de Graaff, prin. Fax 678-7267
Other Schools – See Eastville

Mc Lean, Fairfax, Pop. 39,100
Fairfax County SD
Supt. — See Falls Church
Cooper MS 1,000/7-8
977 Balls Hill Rd 22101 703-442-5800
Arlene Randall, prin. Fax 442-5897
Langley HS 2,000/9-12
6520 Georgetown Pike 22101 703-287-2700
William Clendaniel, prin. Fax 287-2797
Mc Lean HS 1,700/9-12
1633 Davidson Rd 22101 703-714-5700
Paul Wardinski, prin. Fax 714-5797

Keller Graduate School Post-Sec.
1751 Pinnacle Dr Ste 250 22102 703-556-9669
Madeira S 300/9-12
8328 Georgetown Pike 22102 703-556-8200
Dr. Elisabeth Griffith, hdmstr. Fax 893-3289
Oakcrest HS 6-12
850 Balls Hill Rd 22101 703-790-5450
Ellen Cavanagh, prin. Fax 790-5380
Potomac S 900/K-12
PO Box 430 22101 703-356-4101
Geoffrey Jones, hdmstr. Fax 883-9031

Madison, Madison, Pop. 213
Madison County SD 1,800/K-12
PO Box 647 22727 540-948-3780
Dr. Brenda Tanner, supt. Fax 948-6988
www.madisonschools.k12.va.us
Madison County HS 600/9-12
68 Mountaineer Ln 22727 540-948-3785
Mike Sisler, prin. Fax 948-4425
Wetsel MS 500/6-8
186 Mountaineer Ln 22727 540-948-3783
Robert Otto, prin. Fax 948-4809

Madison Heights, Amherst, Pop. 11,700
Amherst County SD
Supt. — See Amherst
Monelison MS 700/6-8
257 Trojan Rd 24572 434-846-1307
Kathleen M. Pierce, prin. Fax 846-5318

Manassas, Manassas, Pop. 37,569
Manassas CSD 6,700/K-12
9000 Tudor Ln 20110 703-257-8808
Dr. Sidney Zullinger, supt. Fax 257-8807
www.manassas.k12.va.us
Metz JHS 1,500/6-8
9700 Fairview Ave 20110 703-257-8600
Melissa Saunders, prin. Fax 257-8615
Osbourn HS 2,000/9-12
9005 Tudor Ln 20110 703-257-8500
John Conti, prin. Fax 530-0937

Prince William County SD 65,800/PK-12
PO Box 389 20108 703-791-7200
Steven Walts Ph.D., supt. Fax 791-7309
www.pwcs.edu
Benton MS 1,100/6-8
7411 Hoadly Rd 20112 703-791-0727
Linda Leibert, prin. Fax 791-0977
Jackson HS 2,400/9-12
8820 Rixlew Ln 20109 703-365-2900
David Huckestein, prin. Fax 365-6895
Osbourn Park HS 2,700/9-12
8909 Euclid Ave 20111 703-365-6500
Timothy Healey, prin. Fax 365-6798
Parkside MS 1,200/6-8
8602 Mathis Ave 20110 703-361-3106
Marie Bowe-Quick Ed.D., prin. Fax 361-8993
Saunders MS 1,200/6-8
13557 Spriggs Rd 20112 703-670-9188
Pat Puttre, prin. Fax 670-3078
Stonewall MS 1,000/6-8
10100 Lomond Dr 20109 703-361-3185
John G. Miller, prin. Fax 368-1266
Other Schools – See Bristow, Dumfries, Gainesville, Haymarket, Nokesville, Triangle, Woodbridge

---

American Military University Post-Sec.
10110 Battleview Pkwy # 200 20109 703-330-5398
ECPI College of Technology Post-Sec.
10021 Balls Ford Rd # 100 20109 703-330-5300
Emmanuel Christian S 300/PK-12
8302 Spruce St 20111 703-369-3950
David Culpepper, hdmstr. Fax 330-9285
Heritage Institute Post-Sec.
8255 Shoppers Sq 20111 703-361-7775
Northern Virginia Community College Post-Sec.
6901 Sudley Rd 20109 703-368-0184
Seton S 400/7-12
9314 Maple St 20110 703-368-3220
Anne Carroll, prin. Fax 393-1199
Strayer University Post-Sec.
9990 Battleview Pkwy 20109 703-330-8400
University of Northern Virginia Post-Sec.
10021 Balls Ford Rd 20109 703-392-0771

Manassas Park, Manassas Park, Pop. 11,622
Manassas Park CSD 2,400/PK-12
1 Park Center Ct Ste A 20111 703-335-8850
Dr. Thomas DeBolt, supt. Fax 361-4583
www.mpark.net
Manassas Park HS 600/9-12
8200 Euclid Ave 20111 703-361-9131
Tracy Shaver, prin. Fax 330-1218
Manassas Park MS 500/6-8
8202 Euclid Ave 20111 703-361-1510
Elizabeth Purcell, prin. Fax 331-3538

Marion, Smyth, Pop. 6,164
Smyth County SD 5,100/PK-12
121 Bagley Cir Ste 300 24354 276-783-3791
Jim R. Sullivan, supt. Fax 783-3291
www.scsb.org
Marion HS 800/9-12
848 Stage St 24354 276-783-4731
Dale Holt, prin. Fax 783-4117
Marion MS 600/6-8
134 Wilden St 24354 276-783-4466
Kyle Rhodes, prin. Fax 783-4952

Smyth Career & Technology Center Vo/Tech
147 Fox Valley Rd 24354 276-646-8117
Edward L. Worley, prin. Fax 646-4009
Other Schools – See Chilhowie, Saltville

Blue Ridge Job Corps Center Post-Sec.
245 W Main St 24354 276-783-7221

Marshall, Fauquier
Fauquier County SD
Supt. — See Warrenton
Marshall MS 600/6-8
PO Box 117 20116 540-364-1551
Christine Moschetti, prin. Fax 364-4699

Fresta Valley Christian S 300/PK-12
6428 Wilson Rd 20115 540-364-1929
Kevin Worsham, admin. Fax 364-4603

Martinsville, Martinsville, Pop. 14,925
Henry County SD
Supt. — See Collinsville
Laurel Park MS 6-8
280 Laurel Park Ave 24112 276-632-7216
Florence Simpson, prin. Fax 632-4865
Center for Community Learning Adult
340 Ridgedale Dr 24112 276-638-1668
Lynn Fitzgibbons, prin. Fax 638-3942

Martinsville CSD 2,000/PK-12
202 Cleveland Ave 24112 276-403-5820
Dr. Scott Kizner, supt. Fax 403-5830
www.martinsville.k12.va.us/
Martinsville HS 800/9-12
351 Commonwealth Blvd E 24112 276-632-9755
Thomas Fitzgibbons, prin. Fax 632-1516
Martinsville MS 600/6-8
201 Brown St 24112 276-403-5737
Christine McNair, prin. Fax 638-4140

Carlisle S 400/PK-12
PO Box 5388 24115 276-632-7288
Simon Owen-Williams, prin. Fax 632-9545
National College Post-Sec.
10 Church St 24114 276-632-5621
Patrick Henry Community College Post-Sec.
PO Box 5311 24115 276-638-8777

Mathews, Mathews
Mathews County SD 1,300/K-12
PO Box 369 23109 804-725-3909
David J. Holleran Ed.D., supt. Fax 725-3951
www.mathews.k12.va.us
Hunter MS 400/5-8
PO Box 339 23109 804-725-2434
Dino A. Papas, prin. Fax 725-2337
Mathews HS 400/9-12
PO Box 38 23109 804-725-3702
David Malechek, prin. Fax 725-5778

Matoaca, Chesterfield
Chesterfield County SD
Supt. — See Chesterfield
Matoaca MS 900/6-8
20300 Halloway Ave 23803 804-590-3130
Jeff McGee, prin. Fax 590-3136

Max Meadows, Wythe
Wythe County SD
Supt. — See Wytheville
Ft. Chiswell HS 500/9-12
1 Pioneer Trl 24360 276-637-3437
Brett Booher, prin. Fax 637-6316
Ft. Chiswell MS 400/6-8
101 Pioneer Trl 24360 276-637-4400
Rebecca James, prin. Fax 637-4452

Mechanicsville, Hanover, Pop. 22,027
Hanover County SD
Supt. — See Ashland
Atlee HS 1,400/9-12
9414 Atlee Station Rd 23116 804-723-2100
Vincent L. D'Agostino, prin. Fax 723-2131
Chickahominy MS 1,200/6-8
9450 Atlee Station Rd 23116 804-723-2160
Debbie Arco, prin. Fax 723-2191
Hanover HS 1,200/9-12
10307 Chamberlayne Rd 23116 804-723-3700
Dr. George Sadler, prin. Fax 723-3759
Jackson MS 1,200/6-8
8021 Lee Davis Rd 23111 804-723-2260
Dr. Robert Staley, prin. Fax 723-2261
Lee-Davis HS 1,500/9-12
7052 Mechanicsville Tpke 23111 804-723-2200
Stanley B. Jones, prin. Fax 723-2202
Oak Knoll MS 900/6-8
10295 Chamberlayne Rd 23116 804-365-4740
Caroline Harris, prin. Fax 365-4741

Melfa, Accomack, Pop. 448

Eastern Shore Community College Post-Sec.
29300 Lankford Hwy 23410 757-787-5900

Middleburg, Loudoun, Pop. 880

Foxcroft S 200/9-12
PO Box 5555 20118 540-687-5555
Mary Leipheimer, prin. Fax 687-8061
Notre Dame Academy 300/9-12
35321 Notre Dame Ln 20117 540-687-5581
John Borley, prin. Fax 687-3103

Middletown, Frederick, Pop. 1,098

Lord Fairfax Community College Post-Sec.
173 Skirmisher Ln 22645 800-906-5322

Midlothian, Chesterfield
Chesterfield County SD
Supt. — See Chesterfield
Bailey Bridge MS 1,600/6-8
12501 Bailey Bridge Rd 23112 804-739-6200
Donald Skeen, prin. Fax 739-6211

Clover Hill HS 2,100/9-12
13900 Hull Street Rd 23112 804-739-6230
Deborah Marks, prin. Fax 739-6239
James River HS 2,000/9-12
3700 James River Rd 23113 804-378-2420
John Titus, prin. Fax 379-2695
Manchester HS 2,500/9-12
12601 Bailey Bridge Rd 23112 804-739-6275
Pete Koste, prin. Fax 739-6340
Midlothian HS 1,600/9-12
401 Charter Colony Pkwy 23114 804-378-2440
Christine Wilson, prin. Fax 378-2450
Midlothian MS 1,500/6-8
13501 Midlothian Tpke 23113 804-378-2460
Patrick Stanfield, prin. Fax 378-7556
Robious MS 1,100/6-8
2701 Robious Crossing Dr 23113 804-378-2510
Jeff Ellick, prin. Fax 378-2519
Swift Creek MS 1,500/6-8
3700 Old Hundred Rd S 23112 804-739-6315
Mary Robinson, prin. Fax 739-6322

Empire Beauty School Post-Sec.
10807 Hull Street Rd 23112 800-575-5983
Heritage Christian Academy 100/6-12
10700 Academy Dr 23112 804-745-2387
Clarinda Cole, prin. Fax 745-8178

Milford, Caroline
Caroline County SD
Supt. — See Bowling Green
Caroline HS 1,100/9-12
19155 Rogers Clark Blvd 22514 804-633-9886
Jeff Wick, prin. Fax 633-2435
Caroline MS 900/6-8
13325 Devils Three Jump Rd 22514 804-633-6561
Harold Pellegreen, prin. Fax 633-9014

Mineral, Louisa, Pop. 459
Louisa County SD 4,400/PK-12
PO Box 7 23117 540-894-5115
Dr. David Melton, supt. Fax 894-0252
www.lcps.k12.va.us
Louisa HS 1,400/9-12
PO Box 328 23117 540-894-5436
Michael Wills, prin. Fax 894-0534
Louisa MS 1,100/6-8
PO Box 448 23117 540-894-5457
Thomas Schott, prin. Fax 894-5096

Moneta, Bedford
Bedford County SD
Supt. — See Bedford
Staunton River HS 1,100/9-12
1095 Golden Eagle Dr 24121 540-297-7151
Michael Kelly, prin. Fax 297-4514
Staunton River MS 800/6-8
1293 Golden Eagle Dr 24121 540-297-4152
Linwood Roberts, prin. Fax 297-4076

Monterey, Highland, Pop. 149
Highland County SD 300/PK-12
PO Box 250 24465 540-468-2240
Gary Blair, supt. Fax 468-2940
Highland JSHS, PO Box 430 24465 200/6-12
Randolph Hooke, prin. 540-468-2129

Montross, Westmoreland, Pop. 305
Westmoreland County SD 1,900/PK-12
141 Opal Ln 22520 804-493-8018
A. Elaine Fogliani, supt. Fax 493-9323
www.wmlcps.org/
Montross MS 500/6-8
8884 Menokin Rd 22520 804-493-9818
Richie Hopkins, prin. Fax 493-0918
Washington & Lee HS 600/9-12
16380 Kings Hwy 22520 804-493-8015
Chastine Williams, prin. Fax 493-0243

Mount Jackson, Shenandoah, Pop. 1,766
Regional Academic Governors SD
Supt. — See Richmond
Massanutten Governor's S 11-12
6375 Main St 22842 540-477-3226
Dr. Catherine Glenn, prin.

Shenandoah County SD
Supt. — See Woodstock
Triplett Vo-Tech, 6375 Main St 22842 Vo/Tech
Lee Sterner, prin. 540-477-3161

Mouth of Wilson, Grayson

Oak Hill Academy 200/8-12
2635 Oak Hill Rd 24363 276-579-2619
Dr. Michael Groves, pres. Fax 579-4722

Narrows, Giles, Pop. 2,150
Giles County SD
Supt. — See Pearisburg
Narrows HS 300/8-12
1 Green Wave Ln 24124 540-726-2384
Robert N. Stump, prin. Fax 726-2775

Naruna, Campbell
Campbell County SD
Supt. — See Rustburg
Campbell JSHS 600/6-12
PO Box 7 24576 434-376-2015
Robert Arnold, prin. Fax 376-5859

New Castle, Craig, Pop. 175
Craig County SD 700/K-12
PO Box 245 24127 540-864-5191
Dr. Katherine Rodgers, supt. Fax 864-6885
www.craig.k12.va.us/
Craig County MSHS 400/6-12
RR 3 Box 1007 24127 540-864-5185
Tracy Poff, prin. Fax 864-5636

Newington, Fairfax, Pop. 17,965

Strayer University Post-Sec.
PO Box 487 22122 703-339-1850

New Kent, New Kent
New Kent County SD 2,600/K-12
PO Box 110 23124 804-966-9650
J. Roy Geiger, supt. Fax 966-9879
www.nkcps.k12.va.us
New Kent County HS 800/9-12
PO Box 130 23124 804-966-9671
Yvonne Jones, prin. Fax 966-2773
New Kent County MS 700/6-8
PO Box 190 23124 804-966-9655
Howard Ormond, prin. Fax 966-2703

New Market, Shenandoah, Pop. 1,831

Shenandoah Valley Academy 200/9-12
234 W Lee Hwy 22844 540-740-3161
Dr. Dale Twomley, prin. Fax 740-3336

Newport News, Newport News, Pop. 179,899
Jointly Operated Vo Tech SD
Supt. — None
New Horizons Regional Ed Ctr - Woodside Vo/Tech
13400 Woodside Ln 23608 757-874-4444
Roger Tomlinson, prin. Fax 872-8951

Newport News CSD 31,900/PK-12
12465 Warwick Blvd 23606 757-591-4500
Dr. Marcus J. Newsome, supt. Fax 599-8270
www.sbo.nn.k12.va.us
Achievable Dream MSHS 200/6-12
3401 Orcutt Ave 23607 757-283-7820
Timothy Sweeney, prin.
Aviation Academy Vo/Tech
902B Bland Blvd 23602 757-886-2745
John Hutchinson, dir. Fax 877-5647
Crittenden MS 1,200/6-8
6158 Jefferson Ave 23605 757-591-4900
Stephanie Bourgeois, prin. Fax 838-8261
Denbigh HS 1,900/9-12
259 Denbigh Blvd 23608 757-886-7700
Michael Evans, prin. Fax 872-6542
Dozier MS 1,000/6-8
432 Industrial Park Dr 23608 757-888-3300
Felicia Barnett, prin. Fax 887-3662
Gildersleeve MS 1,300/6-8
1 Minton Dr 23606 757-591-4862
Susan Tilley, prin. Fax 596-2059
Heritage HS 1,700/9-12
5800 Marshall Ave 23605 757-928-6100
Michael Nichols, prin. Fax 247-9058
Hines MS 1,300/6-8
561 McLawhorne Dr 23601 757-591-4878
Benjamin A. Hogan, prin. Fax 591-0119
Huntington MS 900/6-8
3401 Orcutt Ave 23607 757-928-6846
Michele D. Mitchell, prin. Fax 245-8451
Menchville HS 2,100/9-12
275 Menchville Rd 23602 757-886-7722
Robert Surry, prin. Fax 875-0648
Passage MS 1,200/6-8
400 Atkinson Way 23608 757-886-7600
Kipp Rogers, prin. Fax 886-7661
Reservoir MS 600/6-8
15638 Warwick Blvd 23608 757-888-3310
Angela Seiders, prin. Fax 888-2066
Warwick HS 2,000/9-12
51 Copeland Ln 23601 757-591-4700
Varinda Robinson, prin. Fax 596-7415
Washington MS 6-8
3700 Chestnut Ave 23607 757-928-6860
Deborah L. Fields, prin. Fax 247-1119
Woodside HS 1,900/9-12
13450 Woodside Ln 23608 757-886-7530
Stephanie Hautz, prin. Fax 877-0480

Apprentice Sch. - Northrop Grumman Post-Sec.
4101 Washington Ave 23607 757-880-3717
Christopher Newport University Post-Sec.
1 University Pl 23606 757-594-7000
Denbigh Baptist Christian S 500/PK-12
13010 Mitchell Point Rd 23602 757-249-2654
Wayne Embry, admin. Fax 249-9480
ECPI College of Technology Post-Sec.
1001 Omni Blvd Ste 100 23606 757-838-9191
Hampton Roads Academy 500/6-12
739 Academy Ln 23602 757-884-9100
Thomas Harvey, hdmstr. Fax 884-9137
Kee Business College Post-Sec.
803 Diligence Dr 23606 757-873-1111
Medical Careers Institute Post-Sec.
1001 Omni Blvd Ste 200 23606 757-873-2423
Peninsula Catholic HS 8-12
600 Harpersville Rd 23601 757-596-7247
Rebecca Henle, prin. Fax 591-9718
Riverside School of Health Careers Post-Sec.
316 Main St 23601 757-240-2200
Tidewater Tech Post-Sec.
616 Denbigh Blvd 23608 757-874-2121

Nickelsville, Scott, Pop. 435
Scott County SD
Supt. — See Gate City
Twin Springs HS 300/8-12
RR 1 24271 276-479-2185
Michael V. Lane, prin. Fax 479-3103

Nokesville, Prince William
Prince William County SD
Supt. — See Manassas
Brentsville District HS 1,100/9-12
12109 Aden Rd 20181 703-594-2161
Alexander Carter, prin. Fax 594-2365

Nora, Dickenson
Dickenson County SD
Supt. — See Clintwood
Ervinton JSHS 200/8-12
153 Rebel Dr 24272 276-835-8604
Rodney Compton, prin. Fax 835-1242

Norfolk, Norfolk, Pop. 231,954
Norfolk CSD 36,100/PK-12
PO Box 1357 23501 757-628-3830
Dr. Stephen Jones, supt. Fax 628-3820
www.nps.k12.va.us/
Azalea Gardens MS 800/6-8
7721 Azalea Garden Rd 23518 757-531-3000
Sharon Byrdsong, prin. Fax 531-3013
Blair MS 1,200/6-8
730 Spotswood Ave 23517 757-628-2400
Sarah Bell-McKown, prin. Fax 628-2422
Coronado S Vo/Tech
1025 Widgeon Rd 23513 757-852-4630
Yvette Williams, admin. Fax 852-4632
Granby HS 2,200/9-12
7101 Granby St 23505 757-451-4110
Edward L. Daughtrey, prin. Fax 451-4118
Lafayette-Winona MS 1,000/6-8
1701 Alsace Ave 23509 757-628-2477
Cassandra Goodwyn, prin. Fax 628-2486
Lake Taylor HS 1,500/9-12
1384 Kempsville Rd 23502 757-892-3200
Clifton Harrison, prin. Fax 892-3210
Lake Taylor MS 1,100/6-8
1380 Kempsville Rd 23502 757-892-3230
Inez Blount-Mason, prin. Fax 892-3240
Madison Career Center Vo/Tech
3700 Bowdens Ferry Rd 23508 757-628-3417
Dr. Julia Avery Muse, prin. Fax 628-3406
Maury HS 1,900/9-12
322 Shirley Ave 23517 757-628-3344
Michael J. Caprio, prin. Fax 628-3359
Norfolk Technical Vocational Center Vo/Tech
1330 N Military Hwy 23502 757-892-3300
William Davis, prin. Fax 892-3305
Northside MS 1,200/6-8
8720 Granby St 23503 757-531-3150
Dr. Andrea Tottossy, prin. Fax 531-3144
Norview HS 1,700/9-12
6501 Chesapeake Blvd 23513 757-852-4500
Marjorie Stealey, prin. Fax 852-4511
Norview MS 1,100/6-8
6325 Sewells Point Rd 23513 757-852-4600
Dr. Joseph Melvin, prin. Fax 852-4590
Rosemont MS 800/6-8
1330 Branch Rd 23513 757-852-4610
Jeanne Kruger, prin. Fax 852-4615
Ruffner Academy 1,100/6-8
610 May Ave 23504 757-628-2466
Kenyetta Goshen, prin. Fax 628-2465
School of International Studies 300/6-8
7620 Shirland Ave 23505 757-451-4133
Lynnell Gibson, prin. Fax 451-4136
Washington HS 1,400/9-12
1111 Park Ave 23504 757-628-3575
Cynthia J. Watson, prin. Fax 628-3566

Regional Academic Governors SD
Supt. — See Richmond
Governor's S for the Arts 9-12
Old Dominion University 23529 757-451-4711
Leon Hughes, dir. Fax 451-4715

Calvary Christian S 300/PK-12
2331 E Little Creek Rd 23518 757-480-4400
Olivia Dabney, admin. Fax 480-5689
De Paul Medical Center Post-Sec.
150 Kingsley Ln 23505 757-489-5120
Eastern Virginia Medical School Post-Sec.
PO Box 1980 23501 757-446-5600
Ghent Beauty Academy Post-Sec.
2811 Lafayette Blvd 23509 757-855-2103
ITT Technical Institute Post-Sec.
500 Granby St #3A 23510 757-466-1260
Norfolk Academy 1,200/1-12
1585 Wesleyan Dr 23502 757-461-6236
Dennis G. Manning, hdmstr. Fax 455-3181
Norfolk Christian HS 200/9-12
255 Thole St 23505 757-423-5770
Dirk Mroczek, hdmstr. Fax 440-5388
Norfolk Christian MS 200/6-8
255 Thole St 23505 757-423-5770
Adrian Rowland, prin. Fax 440-5388
Norfolk Collegiate S 400/6-12
7336 Granby St 23505 757-480-2885
William King, hdmstr. Fax 588-8655
Norfolk Skills Center Post-Sec.
922 W 21st St 23517 757-628-3300
Norfolk State University Post-Sec.
700 Park Ave 23504 757-823-8600
Old Dominion University Post-Sec.
1 Old Dominion Univ 23529 757-683-3000
Tidewater Community College Post-Sec.
121 College Pl 23510 757-822-1030
Tidewater Tech Post-Sec.
7020 N Military Hwy 23518 757-853-2121
Virginia Wesleyan College Post-Sec.
1584 Wesleyan Dr 23502 757-455-3200
Wards Corner Beauty Academy Post-Sec.
7525 Tidewater Dr Ste 45 23505 757-583-3300

Norton, Norton, Pop. 3,677
Norton CSD 700/PK-12
22 10th St NW 24273 276-679-2330
Dr. Lee Brannon, supt. Fax 679-4315
www.nortoncityschools.org/
Burton HS 300/8-12
109 11th St SW 24273 276-679-2554
Scott Keith, prin. Fax 679-2664

Nottoway, Nottoway
Nottoway County SD 2,300/K-12
10321 E Colonial Hwy 23955 434-645-9596
Dr. Gwen E. Edwards, supt. Fax 645-1266
www.nottowayschools.org
Other Schools – See Crewe, Jetersville

Oak Hall, Accomack
Accomack County SD
Supt. — See Accomac
Arcadia HS 700/9-12
PO Box 69 23416 757-824-5613
Alma Brim, prin. Fax 824-0767

Arcadia MS 600/6-8
PO Box 220 23416 757-824-4862
Eddie Lawrence, prin. Fax 824-6618
Badger Technical Center North Vo/Tech
PO Box 69 23416 757-824-4659
Alma Brim, prin. Fax 824-0767

Oakton, Fairfax, Pop. 24,610

Flint Hill S 900/PK-12
3320 Jermantown Rd 22124 703-584-2300
John Thomas, hdmstr. Fax 584-2417

Onley, Accomack, Pop. 496
Accomack County SD
Supt. — See Accomac
Badger Technical Center South Vo/Tech
26350B Lankford Hwy 23418 757-787-4514
Dennis Custis, prin. Fax 787-2194
Nandua HS 700/9-12
26350 Lankford Hwy 23418 757-787-4514
Dennis Custis, prin. Fax 787-2194
Nandua MS 600/6-8
20330 Warrior Dr 23418 757-787-7037
Jessie Duncill, prin. Fax 787-8807

Orange, Orange, Pop. 4,429
Orange County SD 4,300/K-12
200 Dailey Dr 22960 540-661-4550
William Crawford, supt. Fax 661-4599
www.ocss-va.org
Orange County HS 1,300/9-12
201 Selma Rd 22960 540-661-4300
Gene Kotulka, prin. Fax 661-4299
Prospect Heights MS 500/6-8
202 Dailey Dr 22960 540-661-4400
Chuck Winkler, prin. Fax 661-4399
Other Schools – See Locust Grove

Palmyra, Fluvanna
Fluvanna County SD 3,400/K-12
PO Box 419 22963 434-589-8208
Thomas W.D. Smith, supt. Fax 589-2248
www.fluco.org
Fluvanna County HS 1,000/9-12
3717 Central Plains Rd 22963 434-589-3666
James Barlow, prin. Fax 589-3137
Other Schools – See Fork Union

Regional Academic Governors SD
Supt. — See Richmond
Blue Ridge Governor's HS 100/9-12
PO Box 419 22963 434-589-8208
Marc Carraway, dir. Fax 589-2248

Pearisburg, Giles, Pop. 2,768
Giles County SD 2,500/K-12
151 School Rd 24134 540-921-1421
Dr. Terry Arbogast, supt. Fax 921-1424
sbo.gilesk12.org/
Giles County Technology Center Vo/Tech
PO Box 479 24134 540-921-1166
Forest Fowler, prin. Fax 921-3906
Giles HS 700/8-12
1825 Wenonah Ave 24134 540-921-1711
Gregory A. Brown, prin. Fax 921-3861
Other Schools – See Narrows

Pennington Gap, Lee, Pop. 1,753
Lee County SD
Supt. — See Jonesville
Pennington MS 300/6-8
201 Middle School Dr 24277 276-546-1453
Harry Reasor, prin. Fax 546-3515

Penn Laird, Rockingham
Rockingham County SD
Supt. — See Harrisonburg
Montevideo MS 700/6-8
7648 McGaheysville Rd 22846 540-289-3401
Robert Scott, prin. Fax 289-3601
Spotswood HS 1,200/9-12
368 Blazer Dr 22846 540-289-3100
Tim Woodward, prin. Fax 289-3301

Petersburg, Petersburg, Pop. 32,604
Petersburg CSD 4,900/PK-12
255 E South Blvd 23805 804-732-0510
Edwin Betts, supt. Fax 732-0514
www.petersburg.k12.va.us/home.asp
Johns MS 700/6-8
3101 Homestead Dr 23805 804-862-7020
Paul Britt, prin. Fax 862-5434
Peabody MS 600/6-8
725 Wesley St 23803 804-862-7075
Dr. Virginia Berry, prin. Fax 733-6091
Petersburg HS 1,600/9-12
3101 Johnson Rd 23805 804-861-4884
Alicia Fields, prin. Fax 862-7188

Regional Academic Governors SD
Supt. — See Richmond
Appomattox Reg. Governor's S Arts/Tech 9-12
512 W Washington St 23803 804-722-0200
Dr. James Ruffa, dir. Fax 722-0201

Restoration Military Academy 100/PK-12
PO Box 2489 23804 804-862-9571
Sonya Brown, dir. Fax 526-4613
Richard Bland College Post-Sec.
11301 Johnson Rd 23805 804-862-6100
Rock Church Academy 100/K-10
2301 County Dr 23803 804-733-3973
Kristen Davis, prin. Fax 733-3093
Southside Regional Medical Center Post-Sec.
801 S Adams St 23803 804-862-5800
Virginia State University Post-Sec.
1 Hayden Dr 23806 804-524-5000

Pilgrims Knob, Buchanan
Buchanan County SD
Supt. — See Grundy
Twin Valley HS 300/8-12
PO Box 190 24634 276-259-7818
Janie West, prin. Fax 259-6147

Pocahontas, Tazewell, Pop. 432
Tazewell County SD
Supt. — See Tazewell
Pocahontas JSHS 200/6-12
PO Box 308 24635 276-945-5988
Chris Stacy, prin. Fax 945-2722

Poquoson, Poquoson, Pop. 11,811
Poquoson CSD 2,600/PK-12
PO Box 2068 23662 757-868-3055
Dr. Jonathan Lewis, supt. Fax 868-3107
www.sbo.poquoson.k12.va.us
Poquoson HS 900/9-12
51 Odd Rd 23662 757-868-7123
Donald Bock, prin. Fax 868-3141
Poquoson MS 600/6-8
985 Poquoson Ave 23662 757-868-6031
Ken Crum, prin. Fax 868-4220

Portsmouth, Portsmouth, Pop. 100,169
Portsmouth CSD 12,200/PK-12
PO Box 998 23705 757-393-8751
Dr. David C. Stuckwisch, supt. Fax 393-5236
www.pps.k12.va.us
Churchland HS 1,800/9-12
4301 Cedar Ln 23703 757-686-2500
Dr. Susan Bechtol, prin. Fax 686-2504
Churchland MS 800/7-8
4051 River Shore Rd 23703 757-686-2512
Dr. Karen Giacometti, prin. Fax 686-2515
Cradock MS 400/7-8
21 Alden Ave 23702 757-393-8788
Dr. Eric Fischer, prin. Fax 393-5020
Norcom HS 1,200/9-12
1801 London Blvd 23704 757-393-5442
Lynn Briley, prin. Fax 393-5449
Waters MS 500/7-8
600 Roosevelt Blvd 23701 757-558-2813
Fax 485-2829
Wilson HS 1,300/9-12
1401 Elmhurst Ln 23701 757-465-2907
Timothy Johnson, prin. Fax 405-1335
EXCEL Campus Adult
1401 Elmhurst Ln 23701 757-465-2958
Dr. Rosalynn Sanderlin, prin. Fax 465-2913

Alliance Christian S 300/PK-12
5809 Portsmouth Blvd 23701 757-488-5552
Duane Ranard, admin. Fax 488-3192
Hicks Academy of Beauty Culture Post-Sec.
904 Loudoun Ave 23707 757-399-2400
Portsmouth Christian S 800/PK-12
3214 Elliott Ave 23702 757-393-0725
Bruce Devers, admin. Fax 397-7487
Tidewater Community College Post-Sec.
State Route 135 23703 757-484-2121

Pound, Wise, Pop. 1,087
Wise County SD
Supt. — See Wise
Pound HS 300/9-12
11531 Wildcat Dr 24279 276-796-4432
Marcia Shortt, prin. Fax 796-5983

Powhatan, Powhatan
Powhatan County SD 4,200/K-12
2320 Skaggs Rd 23139 804-598-5700
Margaret Meara, supt. Fax 598-5705
www.powhatan.k12.va.us
Powhatan HS 1,300/9-12
1800 Judes Ferry Rd 23139 804-598-5710
Richard Cole, prin. Fax 598-0036
Powhatan JHS 700/7-8
4135 Old Buckingham Rd 23139 804-598-5782
Richard Stewart, prin.
Powhatan Vo-Tech Vo/Tech
1800 Judes Ferry Rd 23139 804-598-5700
Kathryn Garrett, prin.

Blessed Sacrament S 500/PK-12
2501 Academy Rd 23139 804-598-4211
Dr. Lou Hopewell, pres. Fax 598-1053

Prince George, Prince George
Prince George County SD 6,200/PK-12
PO Box 400 23875 804-733-2700
Dr. R. Francis Moore, supt. Fax 733-2737
pgs.k12.va.us
Clements JHS 1,100/8-9
7800 Laurel Spring Rd 23875 804-733-2730
Peter Fisher, prin. Fax 733-3783
Prince George SHS 1,300/10-12
7801 Laurel Spring Rd 23875 804-733-2720
Dave Clark, prin. Fax 861-4530

Pulaski, Pulaski, Pop. 9,088
Pulaski County SD 4,900/PK-12
202 N Washington Ave 24301 540-643-0200
Donald E. Stowers Ed.D., supt. Fax 980-4147
www.pcva.us
Pulaski MS 600/6-8
500 Pico Ter 24301 540-643-0767
Joseph Reed, prin. Fax 980-8571
Other Schools – See Dublin

Regional Academic Governors SD
Supt. — See Richmond
SW VA Governor's S Science Math & Tech 11-12
100 Northwood Dr 24301 540-643-0637
Margaret Duncan, dir. Fax 994-5841

Purcellville, Loudoun, Pop. 4,680
Loudoun County SD
Supt. — See Ashburn
Blue Ridge MS 1,000/6-8
551 E A St 20132 540-338-6820
Roberta Griffith, prin. Fax 338-6823
Loudoun Valley HS 1,300/9-12
340 N Maple Ave 20132 540-338-6800
Susan Ross, prin. Fax 338-6815

Patrick Henry College Post-Sec.
1 Patrick Henry Cir 20132 540-338-1776

Quicksburg, Shenandoah
Shenandoah County SD
Supt. — See Woodstock
Jackson HS, 150 Stonewall Ln 22847 500/9-12
Karen Whetzel, prin. 540-477-2732
North Fork MS 400/6-8
1018 Caverns Rd 22847 540-477-2953
David Hinegardner, prin.

Radford, Radford, Pop. 14,575
Radford CSD 1,500/PK-12
PO Box 3698 24143 540-731-3647
Dr. Chuck Bishop, supt. Fax 731-4419
www.rcps.org/
Dalton IS 200/7-8
60 Dalton Dr 24141 540-731-3651
Walter Smith, prin. Fax 731-5033
Radford HS 500/9-12
50 Dalton Dr 24141 540-731-3649
Mark Lineburg, prin. Fax 731-4427

Radford University Post-Sec.
PO Box 6903 24142 540-831-5000

Reston, Fairfax, Pop. 58,200
Fairfax County SD
Supt. — See Falls Church
Hughes MS 900/7-8
11401 Ridge Heights Rd 20191 703-715-3600
Deborah Jackson, prin. Fax 715-3697
South Lakes HS 1,600/9-12
11400 S Lakes Dr 20191 703-715-4500
Bruce Butler, prin. Fax 715-4597

Richlands, Tazewell, Pop. 4,116
Tazewell County SD
Supt. — See Tazewell
Richlands HS 800/9-12
138 Tornado Aly 24641 276-964-4602
Karen A. Webb, prin. Fax 963-1049
Richlands MS 700/6-8
185 Learning Ln 24641 276-963-5370
Lynn Lawson, prin. Fax 963-0210

Southwest Virginia Community College Post-Sec.
PO Box SVCC 24641 276-964-2555

Richmond, Richmond, Pop. 193,777
Chesterfield County SD
Supt. — See Chesterfield
Falling Creek MS 1,200/6-8
4724 Hopkins Rd 23234 804-743-3640
Sarah Fraher, prin. Fax 743-3644
Manchester MS 1,500/6-8
7401 Hull Street Rd 23235 804-674-1385
Carolyn Tisdale, prin. Fax 674-1394
Meadowbrook HS 1,700/9-12
4901 Cogbill Rd 23234 804-743-3675
C.W. Fletcher, prin. Fax 743-3686
Monacan HS 1,700/9-12
11501 Smoketree Dr 23236 804-378-2480
David Sovine, prin. Fax 378-2489
Providence MS 1,000/6-8
900 Starlight Ln 23235 804-674-1355
Harold Saunders, prin. Fax 674-1361
Salem Church MS 1,100/6-8
9700 Salem Church Rd 23237 804-768-6225
Kenneth Butta, prin. Fax 768-6230

Henrico County SD 46,100/K-12
PO Box 23120 23223 804-652-3600
Fred Morton, supt. Fax 652-3856
www.henrico.k12.va.us
Brookland MS 1,200/6-8
9200 Lydell Dr 23228 804-261-5000
Dallas Dance, prin. Fax 261-5003
Byrd MS 1,000/6-8
9400 Quioccasin Rd 23238 804-750-2630
Anne Poates, prin. Fax 750-2629
Center for Communications 9-12
7053 Messer Rd 23231 804-226-8700
Tracie Omohundro, prin.
Center for Foreign Language Immersion 9-12
2910 N Parham Rd 23294 804-527-4600
Gwen Miller, prin.
Center for Science Mathematics & Tech 9-12
2101 Pump Rd 23238 804-750-2600
Terry Moore, prin.
Center for the Arts 9-12
302 Azalea Ave 23227 804-228-2718
William Parker, prin.
Center for the Humanities 9-12
8301 Hungary Spring Rd 23228 804-756-3000
Robert Tyson, prin.
Ctr for Leadership Govt & Global Studies 9-12
8701 Three Chopt Rd 23229 804-673-3700
Edward Pruden, prin.
Fairfield MS 1,300/6-8
5121 Nine Mile Rd 23223 804-328-4020
Deborah Jones, prin. Fax 328-4031
Freeman HS 1,700/9-12
8701 Three Chopt Rd 23229 804-673-3700
Dr. Edward Pruden, prin. Fax 673-3713
Godwin HS 2,100/9-12
2101 Pump Rd 23238 804-750-2600
David Myers, prin. Fax 750-2611
Henrico HS 1,500/9-12
302 Azalea Ave 23227 804-228-2700
William H. Parker, prin. Fax 228-2715
Hermitage HS 2,300/9-12
8301 Hungary Spring Rd 23228 804-756-3000
Robert B. Tyson, prin. Fax 672-1501
Hermitage Technical Center Vo/Tech
8301 Hungary Spring Rd 23228 804-756-3020
Johnnie Collie, prin. Fax 756-3025
Moody MS 1,000/6-8
7800 Woodman Rd 23228 804-261-5015
E. Earl Binns, prin. Fax 261-5024
Mount Vernon MS 100/6-8
7850 Carousel Ln 23294 804-527-4660
Ronald Rodriguez, prin. Fax 527-4665
New Bridge S 200/3-8
5915 Nine Mile Rd 23223 804-328-6125
Dr. Hope George, prin. Fax 328-5502

Pocahontas MS 900/6-8
12000 Three Chopt Ln 23233 804-364-0830
Raymond E. Honeycutt, prin.
Rolfe MS 1,400/6-8
6901 Messer Rd 23231 804-226-8730
A. Katrise Perera, prin. Fax 226-8739
Tuckahoe MS 1,200/6-8
9000 Three Chopt Rd 23229 804-673-3720
Dr. Kurt E. Hulett, prin. Fax 673-3731
Tucker HS 1,400/9-12
2910 N Parham Rd 23294 804-527-4600
Gwen E. Miller, prin. Fax 527-4618
Varina HS 1,800/9-12
7053 Messer Rd 23231 804-226-8700
Tracie Omohundro, prin. Fax 226-8706
Wilder MS 1,000/6-8
6900 Wilkinson Rd 23227 804-515-1100
Christie Forrest, prin. Fax 515-1110
Other Schools – See Glen Allen, Highland Springs

Regional Academic Governors SD 100/9-12
PO Box 2120 23218 804-225-2884
www.doe.virginia.gov/VDOE/Instruction/Govschools/
Governor's S for Gov & Intl Studies 9-12
1000 N Lombardy St 23220 804-354-6800
Doug Hunt, dir. Fax 354-6939
Other Schools – See Abingdon, Clifton Forge, Collinsville, Fishersville, Fredericksburg, Hampton, Keysville, Mount Jackson, Norfolk, Palmyra, Petersburg, Pulaski, Roanoke, Tappahannock, Warrenton

Richmond CSD 24,100/PK-12
301 N 9th St 23219 804-780-7700
Deborah Jewell-Sherman Ed.D., supt. Fax 780-4122
www.richmond.k12.va.us
Armstrong HS 1,300/9-12
2300 Cool Ln 23223 804-780-4449
Dimitric Roseboro, prin. Fax 780-4485
Binford MS 500/6-8
1701 Floyd Ave 23220 804-780-6231
Juanita Nicholson Ed.D., prin. Fax 780-6057
Boushall MS 800/6-8
3400 Hopkins Rd 23234 804-780-5016
Sheron Carter-Gunter, prin. Fax 780-5396
Brown MS 700/6-8
6300 Jahnke Rd 23225 804-319-3013
Colleen Boyd, prin. Fax 319-3009
Chandler MS 500/6-8
201 E Brookland Park Blvd 23222 804-780-4332
Denise Lewis, prin. Fax 780-4423
Elkhardt MS 500/6-8
6300 Hull Street Rd 23224 804-745-3600
Eric Jones, prin. Fax 674-5518
Franklin Military Academy 200/9-12
701 N 37th St 23223 804-780-8526
Sterling Stokes, prin. Fax 780-8054
Henderson MS 600/6-8
4319 Old Brook Rd 23227 804-780-8288
Dionne Ward, prin. Fax 228-5357
Hill MS 500/6-8
3400 Patterson Ave 23221 804-780-6107
Michael Kight, prin. Fax 780-8754
Huguenot HS 1,200/9-12
7945 Forest Hill Ave 23225 804-320-7967
Cynthia Gentry, prin. Fax 560-9103
Jefferson HS 700/9-12
4100 W Grace St 23230 804-780-6028
Barbara Ulschmid, prin. Fax 780-6295
King MS 900/6-8
1000 Mosby St 23223 804-780-8011
Aaron L. Dixon, prin. Fax 780-5590
Marshall HS 900/9-12
4225 Old Brook Rd 23227 804-780-6052
Beverly Britt, prin. Fax 780-4991
Open HS 200/9-12
600 S Pine St 23220 804-780-4661
Priscilla Green, prin. Fax 780-4865
Richmond Community HS 200/9-12
5800 Patterson Ave 23226 804-285-1015
Howard Hopkins Ed.D., prin. Fax 282-1303
Richmond Technical Center North Vo/Tech
2015 Seddon Way 23230 804-780-6272
N. Mauricee Holmes, prin. Fax 780-6040
Richmond Technical Center South Vo/Tech
2020 Westwood Ave 23230 804-780-6237
N. Mauricee Holmes, prin. Fax 780-6061
Thompson MS 700/6-8
7825 Forest Hill Ave 23225 804-272-7554
Thomas H. Beatty Ed.D., prin. Fax 560-5115
Wythe HS 1,100/9-12
4314 Crutchfield St 23225 804-780-5037
A. Parker Land, prin. Fax 780-5043
Adult Career Development Center Adult
119 W Leigh St 23220 804-780-4388
Martha Suber, prin. Fax 780-8184

Banner Christian S 200/K-12
PO Box 74010 23236 804-276-5200
Patricia Burkett, hdmstr. Fax 276-7620
Baptist Theological Seminary Post-Sec.
3400 Brook Rd 23227 888-345-2877
Benedictine HS 300/9-12
304 N Sheppard St 23221 804-342-1300
John McGinty, hdmstr. Fax 355-2407
Beta Tech Post-Sec.
7914 Midlothian Tpke 23235 804-330-0111
Beta Tech West Post-Sec.
7001 W Broad St 23294 804-672-2300
Braxton School Post-Sec.
3600 W Broad St Ste 190 23230 804-353-4458
Bryant & Stratton College Post-Sec.
8141 Hull Street Rd 23235 804-745-2444
Buford Academy Post-Sec.
PO Box 26665 23261
Collegiate S 1,500/K-12
103 N Mooreland Rd 23229 804-740-7077
Keith Evans, hdmstr. Fax 741-9797
East End Christian Academy 50/PK-12
3294 Britton Rd 23231 804-795-9266
Daniel Helland, admin. Fax 795-2222
ECPI Technical College Post-Sec.
800 Moorefield Park Dr 23236 804-330-5533
Grove Avenue Baptist Christian S 200/PK-12
8701 Ridge Rd 23229 804-741-2860
Clay Fogler, admin. Fax 754-8534
ITT Technical Institute Post-Sec.
300 Gateway Centre Pkwy 23235 804-330-4992
J. Sargeant Reynolds Community College Post-Sec.
PO Box 85622 23285 804-371-3000
Medical Careers Institute Post-Sec.
800 Moorefield Park Dr #302 23236 804-521-0400
New Community S 100/6-12
4211 Hermitage Rd 23227 804-266-2494
Julia Ann Greenwood, hdmstr. Fax 264-3281
Richmond Adventist Academy 100/K-12
3809 Patterson Ave 23221 804-353-0036
Sandra Maddox, prin. Fax 358-8797
RSHT Training Center Post-Sec.
1601 Willow Lawn Dr Ste 320 23230 804-288-1000
Rudlin Torah Academy 100/K-12
12285 Patterson Ave 23238 804-784-9050
Rabbi Hal Klestzick, prin. Fax 784-9005
St. Catherine's S 800/PK-12
6001 Grove Ave 23226 804-288-2804
Auguste Bannard, prin. Fax 285-8169
St. Christopher's S 900/PK-12
711 Saint Christophers Rd 23226 804-282-3185
Charles Stillwell, hdmstr. Fax 285-3914
St. Gertrude HS 300/9-12
3215 Stuart Ave 23221 804-358-9114
Susan Walker, prin. Fax 355-5682
St. Mary's Hospital Post-Sec.
5801 Bremo Rd 23226 804-285-2011
Steward S 600/K-12
11600 Gayton Rd 23238 804-740-3394
Kenneth H. Seward, prin. Fax 740-1464
Trinity Episcopal HS 400/8-12
3850 Pittaway Dr 23235 804-272-5864
Dr. Thomas Aycock, hdmstr. Fax 323-1335
Union Theological Sem. & Presbyterian Post-Sec.
3401 Brook Rd 23227 800-229-2990
University of Richmond 23173 Post-Sec.
804-289-8000
Victory Christian Academy 200/K-12
8491 Chamberlayne Rd 23227 804-262-8256
Andrea Cassidy, prin. Fax 553-1905
Virginia Commonwealth University Post-Sec.
901 W Franklin St 23284 804-828-0100
Virginia Home for Boys Post-Sec.
8716 W Broad St 23294
Virginia School of Technology Post-Sec.
9210 Arboretum Pkwy Ste 100 23236 804-323-1020
Virginia Union University Post-Sec.
1500 N Lombardy St 23220 804-257-5600
Yeshiva of Virginia 100/9-12
6801 Patterson Ave 23226 804-288-7610
Rabbi Chaim Chait, prin. Fax 784-9005

Ridgeway, Henry, Pop. 798
Henry County SD
Supt. — See Collinsville
Magna Vista HS 1,200/9-12
701 Magna Vista School Rd 24148 276-956-3147
Gracie Agnew, prin. Fax 956-1401

Riner, Montgomery
Montgomery County SD
Supt. — See Christiansburg
Auburn HS 300/9-12
4163 Riner Rd 24149 540-382-5160
Carl Pauli, prin. Fax 381-6110
Auburn MS 300/6-8
4069 Riner Rd 24149 540-382-5165
Guylene Wood-Setzer, prin. Fax 381-6562

Ringgold, Pittsylvania
Pittsylvania County SD
Supt. — See Chatham
Dan River HS 700/9-12
100 Wildcat Circle 24586 434-822-7081
Martin E. Ringstaff, prin.
Dan River MS 500/6-8
5875 Kentuck Rd 24586 434-822-6027
Sherri Crumpton, prin. Fax 822-6548

Roanoke, Roanoke, Pop. 92,631
Regional Academic Governors SD
Supt. — See Richmond
Roanoke Valley Governor's S Science/Tech 9-12
2104 Grandin Rd SW 24015 540-853-2116
Dr. Scott Watson, dir. Fax 853-1056

Roanoke CSD 13,600/PK-12
PO Box 13145 24031 540-853-2381
Marvin Thompson, supt. Fax 853-2951
www.rcps.info
Addison Aerospace Magnet MS 500/6-8
1220 5th St NW 24016 540-853-2681
Robert Johnson, prin. Fax 853-2842
Breckinridge MS 500/6-8
3901 Williamson Rd NW 24012 540-853-2251
Asia Jones, prin. Fax 853-6505
Fleming HS 1,500/9-12
3649 Ferncliff Ave NW 24017 540-853-2781
Susan Willis, prin. Fax 563-1984
Henry HS 1,800/9-12
2102 Grandin Rd SW 24015 540-853-2255
Dr. Jeffrey Crook, prin. Fax 853-1575
Jackson MS 500/6-8
1004 Montrose Ave SE 24013 540-853-6040
Stephanie Hogan, prin. Fax 853-6027
Madison MS 500/6-8
1160 Overland Rd SW 24015 540-853-2351
Debra Dietrich, prin. Fax 853-1050
Ruffner MS 600/6-8
3601 Ferncliff Ave NW 24017 540-853-2605
Mark Hairston, prin. Fax 853-1350
Wilson MS 500/6-8
1813 Carter Rd SW 24015 540-853-2358
Connie Ratcliffe, prin. Fax 853-2004
Roanoke County SD 14,500/K-12
5937 Cove Rd 24019 540-562-3700
Dr. Lorraine Lange, supt. Fax 562-3994
www.rcs.k12.va.us
Cave Spring HS 800/9-12
3712 Chaparral Dr 24018 540-772-7550
Steve Spangler, prin. Fax 772-2107
Cave Spring MS 600/6-8
4880 Brambleton Ave 24018 540-772-7560
Steven Boyer, prin. Fax 772-2195
Hidden Valley HS 1,100/9-12
5000 Titan Trl 24018 540-776-7320
Rhonda Stegall, prin. Fax 776-7322
Hidden Valley MS 900/6-8
4902 Hidden Valley School 24018 540-772-7570
Ken Nicely, prin. Fax 772-7519
Northside HS 1,000/9-12
6758 Northside High School 24019 540-561-8155
Frank Dent, prin. Fax 561-8160
Northside MS 700/6-8
6810 Northside High School 24019 540-561-8145
Lori Wimbush, prin. Fax 561-8152
Other Schools – See Salem, Vinton

BarPalma Beauty Careers Academy Post-Sec.
3535 Franklin Rd SW Ste D 24014 540-343-0153
Carilion Health Systems Post-Sec.
PO Box 13727 24036 540-981-7347
ECPI Technical College Post-Sec.
5234 Airport Rd NW 24012 540-563-8080
Faith Christian S 200/K-12
4873 Brambleton Ave Ste A 24018 540-769-5200
Samuel Cox, admin. Fax 769-6030
Hollins University Post-Sec.
PO Box 9707 24020 540-362-6000
Jefferson College of Health Sciences Post-Sec.
PO Box 13186 24031 540-985-8483
National College Post-Sec.
PO Box 6400 24017 540-986-1800
North Cross S 500/PK-12
4254 Colonial Ave 24018 540-989-6641
Paul Stellato, hdmstr. Fax 989-7299
Parkway Christian Academy 200/PK-12
3230 King St NE 24012 540-982-2400
Troy Dixon, prin. Fax 982-0128
Roanoke Catholic S 600/PK-12
621 N Jefferson St 24016 540-982-3532
Ray Correia, pres. Fax 345-0785
Roanoke Valley Christian S 300/K-12
PO Box 7010 24019 540-366-2432
Rick Brown, admin. Fax 366-9719
TAP Center for Employment Training Post-Sec.
108 N Jefferson St Ste 303 24016 540-767-6222
Virginia Western Community College Post-Sec.
PO Box 14007 24038 540-857-7311

Rocky Gap, Bland
Bland County SD
Supt. — See Bastian
Rocky Gap HS 200/8-12
PO Box 9 24366 276-928-1100
Robert Morehead, prin. Fax 928-1988

Rocky Mount, Franklin, Pop. 4,568
Franklin County SD 7,300/PK-12
25 Bernard Rd 24151 540-483-5138
Dr. Charles Lackey, supt. Fax 483-5806
www.frco.k12.va.us
Franklin County HS 2,200/9-12
700 Tanyard Rd 24151 540-483-0221
Debora Decker, prin. Fax 483-5306
Franklin MS West 900/7-8
225 Middle School Rd 24151 540-483-5105
Derrick Scarborough, prin. Fax 483-5501
Gereau CATCE Vo/Tech
150 Technology Dr 24151 540-483-5446
Kevin Bezy, prin. Fax 483-5788

Christian Heritage Academy 200/PK-12
625 Glennwood Dr 24151 540-483-5855
Ed Roller, admin. Fax 483-9355

Rosedale, Russell

Anchors Academy 100/K-12
PO Box 500 24280 276-880-9013
Patricia Owen, admin. Fax 859-2233

Rural Retreat, Wythe, Pop. 1,354
Wythe County SD
Supt. — See Wytheville
Rural Retreat HS 300/9-12
321 E Buck Ave 24368 276-686-4143
Michael Neal, prin. Fax 686-4601
Rural Retreat MS 200/6-8
321 E Buck Ave 24368 276-686-5200
Marion Haga, prin. Fax 686-4944

Rustburg, Campbell
Campbell County SD 8,800/K-12
PO Box 99 24588 434-332-3458
Dr. George Nolley, supt. Fax 528-1655
www.campbell.k12.va.us
Campbell Technical Center Vo/Tech
194 Dennis Riddle Dr 24588 434-821-6213
Robert Ashwell, prin. Fax 821-2808
Rustburg HS 900/9-12
PO Box 830 24588 434-332-5171
Denton Sisk, prin. Fax 332-1187
Rustburg MS 900/5-8
PO Box 130 24588 434-332-5141
Haywood McCrickard, prin. Fax 332-2058
Other Schools – See Altavista, Lynchburg, Naruna

Clearview Christian S 100/PK-12
PO Box 386 24588 434-845-0637
Terry Cook, admin. Fax 845-4778

Ruther Glen, Caroline

Carmel Christian Academy 100/PK-12
PO Box 605 22546 804-448-3288
Jan Carneal, admin. Fax 448-3146

Ladysmith Baptist Academy 100/PK-10
18290 Jefferson Davis Hwy 22546 804-448-3860
Joe Farnitano, prin. Fax 448-5806

Saint George, Greene

Blue Ridge S 200/9-12
273 Mayo Dr, 434-985-2811
David Bouton Ph.D., hdmstr. Fax 985-7215

Saint Paul, Wise, Pop. 969
Wise County SD
Supt. — See Wise
Saint Paul HS 200/8-12
PO Box 976 24283 276-762-5221
Walt Padgett, prin. Fax 762-5580

Salem, Salem, Pop. 24,654
Roanoke County SD
Supt. — See Roanoke
Burton Technical Center Vo/Tech
1760 Roanoke Blvd 24153 540-857-5000
Andrew McClung, prin. Fax 857-5061
Glenvar HS 600/9-12
4549 Malus Dr 24153 540-387-6536
Joseph Hafey, prin. Fax 387-6347
Glenvar MS 500/6-8
4555 Malus Dr 24153 540-387-6322
Juliette Meyers, prin. Fax 387-6283

Salem CSD 3,900/PK-12
510 S College Ave 24153 540-389-0130
Dr. H. Alan Seibert, supt. Fax 389-4135
www.salem.k12.va.us
Lewis MS 1,000/6-8
616 S College Ave 24153 540-387-2513
Jerome Campbell, prin. Fax 389-8914
Salem HS 1,300/9-12
400 Spartan Dr 24153 540-387-2437
Caleb Hall, prin. Fax 387-2543

National College Post-Sec.
1813 E Main St 24153 540-986-1800
Roanoke College Post-Sec.
221 College Ln 24153 540-375-2500

Saltville, Smyth, Pop. 2,267
Smyth County SD
Supt. — See Marion
Northwood HS 300/9-12
PO Box Y 24370 276-496-7751
Steven Johnston, prin. Fax 496-3216
Northwood MS 300/6-8
156 Long Hollow Rd 24370 276-624-3341
Jeffrey Comer, prin. Fax 624-3535

Saluda, Middlesex
Middlesex County SD 1,300/PK-12
PO Box 205 23149 804-758-2277
Harriet Dawson, supt. Fax 758-3727
www.mcps.k12.va.us/
Middlesex HS 400/9-12
PO Box 206 23149 804-758-2132
Chris Valdrighi, prin. Fax 758-2786
Other Schools – See Locust Hill

Rappahannock Community College Post-Sec.
12745 College Dr 23149 804-758-6700

Sandston, Henrico, Pop. 3,630

New Bridge Academy 100/K-10
5701 Elko Rd 23150 804-737-7833
Katherine Muller, admin. Fax 737-1181

Shawsville, Montgomery, Pop. 1,260
Montgomery County SD
Supt. — See Christiansburg
Shawsville MS 300/6-8
4179 Oldtown Rd 24162 540-268-2262
Rebecca Kahila, prin. Fax 268-1868

Shenandoah, Page, Pop. 1,870
Page County SD
Supt. — See Luray
Page County HS 700/8-12
5550 US Highway 340 22849 540-652-8712
Dr. Morgan Phenix, prin.

Skipwith, Mecklenburg
Mecklenburg County SD
Supt. — See Boydton
Bluestone HS 800/9-12
6825 Skipwith Rd 23968 434-372-5177
Lindell Palmer, prin. Fax 372-5217
Bluestone MS 600/6-8
250 Middle School Rd 23968 434-372-3266
Mona Rainey, prin. Fax 372-3362

Smithfield, Isle of Wight, Pop. 6,840
Isle of Wight County SD 4,400/PK-12
820 W Main St 23430 757-357-4393
Michael W. McPherson Ed.D., supt. Fax 357-0849
www.iwcs.k12.va.us
Smithfield HS 1,100/9-12
14171 Turner Dr 23430 757-357-3108
Rebecca Mercer, prin. Fax 357-7253
Smithfield MS 600/7-8
14175 Turner Dr 23430 757-365-4100
Dr. Garett Smith, prin. Fax 365-4222
Other Schools – See Windsor

James River Christian Academy 200/PK-12
14353 Benns Church Blvd 23430 757-357-3707
Ray Owens, admin. Fax 365-4195

South Boston, Halifax, Pop. 8,115
Halifax County SD
Supt. — See Halifax
Halifax HS 1,600/9-12
PO Box 310 24592 434-572-4977
Albert Randolph, prin. Fax 572-2675
Halifax MS 1,000/6-8
1011 Middle School Cir 24592 434-572-4100
Gail Bosiger, prin. Fax 572-4106

South Hill, Mecklenburg, Pop. 4,607
Mecklenburg County SD
Supt. — See Boydton
Park View HS 700/9-12
205 Park View Cir 23970 434-447-3435
George Taylor, prin. Fax 447-7876
Park View MS 600/6-8
365 Dockery Rd 23970 434-447-3761
Michelle Mateka, prin. Fax 447-4920

South Riding, See Fairfax
Loudoun County SD
Supt. — See Ashburn
Freedom HS 9-12
25450 Riding Center Dr 20152 703-957-4300
Christine M. Forester, prin. Fax 542-2086

Spotsylvania, Spotsylvania
Spotsylvania County SD
Supt. — See Fredericksburg
Courtland HS 1,300/9-12
6701 Smith Station Rd 22553 540-898-4445
Michael Bedwell, prin. Fax 898-4458
Ni River MS 800/6-8
11632 Catharpin Rd 22553 540-785-3990
Stephen Covert, prin. Fax 785-0658
Post Oak MS 6-8
6959 Courthouse Rd, 540-582-7517
Keith Wolfe, prin. Fax 582-7510
Spotsylvania HS 1,200/9-12
6975 Courthouse Rd, 540-582-3882
Rusty Davis, prin. Fax 582-3890
Spotsylvania MS 900/6-8
8801 Courthouse Rd 22553 540-582-6341
Mark Beckett, prin. Fax 582-3207
Spotsylvania Vocational Ctr Vo/Tech
6713 Smith Station Rd 22553 540-898-2655
Lee Browning, prin. Fax 891-1784
Thornburg MS 800/6-8
6929 N Roxbury Mill Rd, 540-582-7600
Kirk Tower, prin. Fax 582-7606

Springfield, Fairfax, Pop. 23,706
Fairfax County SD
Supt. — See Falls Church
Irving MS 1,200/7-8
8100 Old Keene Mill Rd 22152 703-912-4500
Danny Little, prin. Fax 912-4597
Key MS 1,000/7-8
6402 Franconia Rd 22150 703-313-3900
Penny Myers, prin. Fax 313-3997
Lee HS 2,100/9-12
6540 Franconia Rd 22150 703-924-8300
Donald Thurston, prin. Fax 924-8397
West Springfield HS 2,200/9-12
6100 Rolling Rd 22152 703-913-3800
David Smith, prin. Fax 913-3897

Accotink Academy Post-Sec.
8519 Tuttle Rd 22152
Word of Life Christian Academy 400/PK-12
5225 Backlick Rd 22151 703-354-4222
Michael Burroughs, admin. Fax 750-1306

Stafford, Stafford
Stafford County SD 25,500/PK-12
31 Stafford Ave 22554 540-658-6000
David Sawyer, supt. Fax 658-5963
www.pen.k12.va.us/Div/Stafford/
Brooke Point HS 1,900/9-12
1700 Courthouse Rd 22554 540-658-6080
Cynthia Holder, prin. Fax 658-6072
Colonial Forge HS 1,900/9-12
550 Courthouse Rd 22554 540-658-6115
Dr. Lisa Martin, prin. Fax 658-6120
Mountain View HS 9-12
2135 Mountain View Rd, 540-658-6840
James Stemple, prin. Fax 658-6860
North Stafford HS 2,000/9-12
839 Garrisonville Rd 22554 540-658-6150
Thomas Nichols, prin. Fax 658-6158
Poole MS 1,100/6-8
800 Eustace Rd 22554 540-658-6190
Mary Grace McGraw, prin. Fax 658-6176
Stafford MS 1,100/6-8
101 Spartan Dr 22554 540-658-6210
Steven Butters, prin. Fax 658-6204
Thompson MS 1,100/6-8
75 Walpole St 22554 540-658-6420
Gwendolyn Payne, prin. Fax 658-6430
Wright MS 800/6-8
100 Wood Dr, 540-658-6240
William Boatwright, prin. Fax 658-6238
Other Schools – See Falmouth, Fredericksburg

Grace Preparatory S 100/1-12
200 Onville Rd, 540-657-4500
Kristine Lisech, admin.

Stanardsville, Greene, Pop. 501
Greene County SD 2,700/PK-12
PO Box 1140 22973 434-985-5254
Raymond Dingledine, supt. Fax 985-4686
www.greenecountyschools.com
Greene County Technical Education Center Vo/Tech
PO Box 510 22973 434-985-5239
Harry Daniel, prin. Fax 985-2071
Monroe HS 800/9-12
254 Monroe Dr 22973 434-985-5273
Mike Jamerson, prin. Fax 985-1461
Monroe MS 600/6-8
148 Monroe Dr 22973 434-985-5240
Deborah DuPell, prin. Fax 985-1359

Staunton, Staunton, Pop. 23,337
Augusta County SD
Supt. — See Fishersville
Beverley Manor MS 800/6-8
58 Cedar Green Rd 24401 540-886-5806
Nancy Miller, prin. Fax 886-4019
Riverheads HS 500/9-12
19 Howardsville Rd 24401 540-337-1921
P. Steve Barnett, prin. Fax 337-0258

Staunton CSD 2,700/K-12
PO Box 900 24402 540-332-3920
Harry Lunsford, supt. Fax 332-3924
www.staunton.k12.va.us
Lee HS, 1200 N Coalter St 24401 800/9-12
J. Clay Chandler, prin. 540-332-3926
Shelburne MS 600/6-8
300 Grubert Ave 24401 540-332-3930
Dori Walk, prin.

Grace Christian HS 100/7-12
19 S Market St 24401 540-886-9109
Debbie Harper, admin. Fax 886-5958
Guardian Angel Academy 200/K-12
300 Churchville Ave 24401 540-887-5900
Dan Dolan, prin. Fax 887-5905
Mary Baldwin College 24401 Post-Sec.
800-468-2262
Richards Jr Academy 100/K-10
414 Sterling St 24401 540-886-4984
Steve Wilson, prin. Fax 886-7087
Staunton School of Cosmetology Post-Sec.
PO Box 2385 24402 540-885-0808
Stuart Hall 200/6-12
PO Box 210 24402 540-885-0356
Mark Eastham, hdmstr. Fax 886-2275
Virginia School for the Deaf and Blind Post-Sec.
24401

Stephens City, Frederick, Pop. 1,247
Frederick County SD
Supt. — See Winchester
Aylor MS 1,000/6-8
901 Aylor Rd 22655 540-869-3736
Donald Williams, prin. Fax 867-2756
Sherando HS 1,300/9-12
185 S Warrior Dr 22655 540-869-0060
John Nelson, prin. Fax 869-5183

Shenandoah Valley Christian Academy 300/PK-12
PO Box 1360 22655 540-869-4600
Robert Quinn, supt. Fax 869-4662

Sterling, Loudoun, Pop. 20,512
Loudoun County SD
Supt. — See Ashburn
Dominion HS 1,000/9-12
21326 Augusta Dr 20164 703-444-8025
Dr. W. John Brewer, prin. Fax 444-8035
Park View HS 1,300/9-12
400 W Laurel Ave 20164 703-444-7500
Dr. Virginia Minshew, prin. Fax 444-7421
Potomac Falls HS 1,400/9-12
46400 Algonkian Pkwy 20165 703-444-7542
David Spage, prin. Fax 444-7526
River Bend MS 1,100/6-8
46240 Algonkian Pkwy 20165 703-444-7574
Bennett P. Lacy, prin. Fax 444-7578
Seneca Ridge MS 900/6-8
98 Seneca Ridge Dr 20164 703-444-7480
Mark McDermott, prin. Fax 444-7567
Sterling MS 900/6-8
201 W Holly Ave 20164 703-444-7490
Michael Williams, prin. Fax 444-7492

Faith Christian S 100/PK-12
21393 Potomac View Rd # 100 20164 703-430-0499
Randy Luckette, hdmstr. Fax 430-4235
Northern Virginia Community College Post-Sec.
1000 Harry Flood Byrd Hwy 20164 703-323-3000

Strasburg, Shenandoah, Pop. 4,269
Shenandoah County SD
Supt. — See Woodstock
Signal Knob MS 500/6-8
687 Sandy Hook Rd 22657 540-465-3422
Charles Everett, prin.
Strasburg HS, 250 Ram Dr 22657 600/9-12
Mike Dorman, prin. 540-465-5195

Stuart, Patrick, Pop. 925
Patrick County SD 2,600/K-12
PO Box 346 24171 276-694-3163
Judy Lacks, supt. Fax 694-3170
www.patrick-county.org
Patrick County HS 1,000/8-12
215 Cougar Ln 24171 276-694-7137
E.G. Bradshaw, prin. Fax 694-6997

Stuarts Draft, Augusta, Pop. 5,087
Augusta County SD
Supt. — See Fishersville
Stuarts Draft HS 800/9-12
1028 Augusta Farms Rd 24477 540-946-7600
T. Nate Collins, prin. Fax 946-7605
Stuarts Draft MS 900/6-8
1088 Augusta Farms Rd 24477 540-946-7611
Betsy Agee, prin. Fax 946-7613

Suffolk, Suffolk, Pop. 78,994
Jointly Operated Vo Tech SD
Supt. — None
Pruden Center for Industry/Technology Vo/Tech
4169 Pruden Blvd 23434 757-539-7407
Peggy Wade, prin.

Suffolk CSD 13,700/PK-12
PO Box 1549 23439 757-925-6750
Dr. Milton Liverman, supt. Fax 925-6751
www.sps.k12.va.us
Forest Glen MS 500/6-8
200 Forest Glen Dr 23434 757-925-5550
Melvin Bradshaw, prin. Fax 925-5557
Kennedy MS 800/6-8
2325 E Washington St 23434 757-925-5560
Vivian Covington, prin. Fax 925-5594
King's Fork HS 1,300/9-12
351 Kings Fork Rd 23434 757-923-5240
Daniel Ward, prin.

King's Fork MS 1,200/6-8
350 Kings Fork Rd 23434 757-925-5750
Talmadge Darden, prin. Fax 925-5754
Lakeland HS 1,300/9-12
214 Kenyon Rd 23434 757-925-5530
Thomas Whitley, prin. Fax 925-5599
Nansemond River HS 1,300/9-12
3301 Nansemond Pkwy 23434 757-538-5420
T. McLemore, prin. Fax 538-5430
Yeates MS 900/6-8
4901 Bennetts Pasture Rd 23435 757-538-5400
Daniel O'Leary, prin. Fax 538-5416

Nansemond-Suffolk Academy 1,000/PK-12
3373 Pruden Blvd 23434 757-539-8789
Shane Foster, hdmstr. Fax 539-3465
Suffolk Beauty Academy Post-Sec.
860 Portsmouth Blvd 23434 757-934-0656

Surry, Surry, Pop. 254
Surry County SD 1,100/PK-12
PO Box 317 23883 757-294-5229
Dr. Marion Wilkins, supt. Fax 294-5263
www.surryschools.net/
Other Schools – See Dendron

Sussex, Sussex
Sussex County SD 1,300/K-12
PO Box 1368 23884 434-246-1099
Charles H. Harris, supt. Fax 246-8214
www.sussex.k12.va.us/
Sussex Central HS 400/9-12
PO Box 1307 23884 434-246-6051
Arthur Jarrett, prin. Fax 246-5503
Sussex Central MS 400/6-8
PO Box 1387 23884 434-246-2251
Nancy Coner, prin. Fax 246-8912

Sweet Briar, Amherst

Sweet Briar College 24595 Post-Sec.
434-381-6100

Swoope, Augusta
Augusta County SD
Supt. — See Fishersville
Buffalo Gap HS 600/9-12
1800 Buffalo Gap Hwy 24479 540-337-6021
William Deardorff, prin. Fax 337-6236

Tangier, Accomack, Pop. 694
Accomack County SD
Supt. — See Accomac
Tangier S 100/K-12
PO Box 245 23440 757-891-2234
Nina Pruitt, prin. Fax 891-2572

Tappahannock, Essex, Pop. 2,155
Essex County SD 1,600/PK-12
PO Box 756 22560 804-443-4366
Thomas Saville, supt. Fax 443-4498
www.essex.k12.va.us
Essex HS 500/9-12
PO Box 1006 22560 804-443-4301
Lawrence Lenz, prin. Fax 443-4272
Essex MS 500/5-8
PO Box 609 22560 804-443-3040
Wanda Wallace-Durham, prin. Fax 445-1079

Regional Academic Governors SD
Supt. — See Richmond
Chesapeake Bay Governor's S 10-12
PO Box 756 22560 804-443-0267
Patricia Griffin, dir. Fax 443-4498

St. Margaret's S 200/8-12
PO Box 158 22560 804-443-3357
Margaret Broad, hdmstr. Fax 443-1832

Tazewell, Tazewell, Pop. 4,404
Tazewell County SD 6,900/PK-12
PO Box 927 24651 276-988-5511
Dr. Brenda B. Lawson, supt. Fax 988-6765
tazewell.k12.va.us
Tazewell County Career Technical Center Vo/Tech
100 Advantage Dr 24651 276-988-2529
Dr. Charles Grindstaff, prin. Fax 988-5494
Tazewell HS 600/9-12
627 E Fincastle St 24651 276-988-6502
B. Keith Hovis, prin. Fax 988-3263
Tazewell MS 500/6-8
100 Bull Dog Ave 24651 276-988-6513
Kristina Welch, prin. Fax 988-6514
Other Schools – See Bluefield, Pocahontas, Richlands

Toano, James City
Williamsburg-James City County SD
Supt. — See Williamsburg
Toano MS 800/6-8
7817 Richmond Rd 23168 757-566-4251
Lynda Poller, prin. Fax 566-3006

Triangle, Prince William, Pop. 4,740
Prince William County SD
Supt. — See Manassas
Graham Park MS 1,300/6-8
3613 Graham Park Rd 22172 703-221-2118
Gary Anderson, prin. Fax 221-1079

Calvary Christian S 200/PK-12
4345 Inn St 22172 703-221-2016
John Wallace, admin. Fax 221-7698

Victoria, Lunenburg, Pop. 1,789
Lunenburg County SD
Supt. — See Kenbridge
Central HS 600/9-12
131 K V Rd 23974 434-696-2137
Sarah Nicholas, prin. Fax 696-1322
Lunenburg MS 400/6-8
583 Tomlinson Rd 23974 434-696-2161
Nancy Chappell, prin. Fax 696-2162

Vienna, Fairfax, Pop. 14,842
Fairfax County SD
Supt. — See Falls Church
Kilmer MS 1,000/7-8
8100 Wolftrap Rd 22182 703-846-8800
Deborah Hernandez, prin. Fax 846-8897
Madison HS 1,800/9-12
2500 James Madison Dr 22181 703-319-2300
Mark Merrell, prin. Fax 319-2397
Oakton HS 2,400/9-12
2900 Sutton Rd 22181 703-319-2700
John Banbury, prin. Fax 319-2797
Thoreau MS 700/7-8
2505 Cedar Ln 22180 703-846-8000
Mark Greenfelder, prin. Fax 846-8097

Fairfax Christian S 300/PK-12
1624 Hunter Mill Rd 22182 703-759-5100
Jo Thoburn, admin. Fax 759-2143
Gibbs College - Northern Virginia Post-Sec.
1980 Gallows Rd 22182 703-556-8888

Vinton, Roanoke, Pop. 7,734
Roanoke County SD
Supt. — See Roanoke
Byrd HS 1,100/9-12
2902 E Washington Ave 24179 540-890-3090
Richard Turner, prin. Fax 890-7568
Byrd MS 1,000/6-8
2910 E Washington Ave 24179 540-890-1035
Janet Womack, prin. Fax 890-0703
Roanoke County Central MS 6-8
100 Highland Rd 24179 540-857-5004
Becky Rowe, prin. Fax 857-5066

Virginia Beach, Virginia Beach, Pop. 438,415
Virginia Beach CSD 75,500/PK-12
PO Box 6038 23456 757-263-1000
Dr. James Merrill, supt. Fax 263-1397
www.vbschools.com/
Advanced Technology Center Vo/Tech
1800 College Cres, 757-468-8960
Michael Taylor, dir. Fax 468-4235
Bayside HS 2,200/9-12
4960 Haygood Rd 23455 757-473-5050
Kay Thomas, prin. Fax 473-5123
Bayside MS 1,300/6-8
965 Newtown Rd 23462 757-473-5080
Dr. Barbara Cooper, prin. Fax 473-5185
Brandon MS 1,400/6-8
1700 Pope St 23464 757-366-4545
Dr. Catherine S. Rogers, prin. Fax 366-4550
Corporate Landing MS 1,700/6-8
1597 Corporate Landing Pkwy 23454 757-437-6199
Rodney J. Burnsworth, prin. Fax 437-6487
Cox HS 2,100/9-12
2425 Shorehaven Dr 23454 757-496-6767
Dr. Brian K. Matney, prin. Fax 496-6731
First Colonial HS 2,100/9-12
1272 Mill Dam Rd 23454 757-496-6711
Dale Holt, prin. Fax 496-6719
Great Neck MS 1,200/6-8
1848 N Great Neck Rd 23454 757-496-6770
Dr. John Smith, prin. Fax 496-6774
Green Run HS 1,800/9-12
1700 Dahlia Dr, 757-431-4040
George Parker, prin. Fax 431-4153
Independence MS 1,500/6-8
1370 Dunstan Ln 23455 757-460-7500
Peggy W. Peebles, prin. Fax 460-0508
Kellam HS 2,500/9-12
2323 Holland Rd, 757-427-3232
Bruce Biehl, prin. Fax 427-6265
Kemps Landing Magnet MS 600/6-8
4722 Jericho Rd 23462 757-473-5665
Randi Reigel-Riesbeck, prin. Fax 473-5106
Kempsville HS 2,000/9-12
5194 Chief Trl 23464 757-474-8400
Shea Paisley, prin. Fax 474-8404
Kempsville MS 1,100/6-8
860 Churchill Dr 23464 757-474-8444
Dr. James Smith, prin. Fax 474-8449
Landstown HS 2,200/9-12
2001 Concert Dr 23456 757-468-3800
Brian Baxter, prin. Fax 468-1860
Landstown MS 1,600/6-8
2204 Recreation Dr 23456 757-430-2412
Timothy Albert, prin. Fax 430-3247
Larkspur MS 1,900/6-8
4696 Princess Anne Rd 23462 757-474-8525
Dr. Dianne Cunningham, prin. Fax 474-8598
Lynnhaven MS 1,300/6-8
1250 Bayne Dr 23454 757-496-6790
Dr. Michael D. Kelly, prin. Fax 496-6793
Ocean Lakes HS 2,400/9-12
885 Schumann Dr 23454 757-721-4110
Cheryl Askew, prin. Fax 721-4309
Plaza MS 1,200/6-8
3080 S Lynnhaven Rd 23452 757-431-4060
Andrea Warren, prin. Fax 431-5331
Princess Anne MS 1,600/6-8
2509 Seaboard Rd 23456 757-427-5325
Lauralee Grim, prin. Fax 430-0972
Princess Anne HS 2,200/9-12
4400 Virginia Beach Blvd 23462 757-473-5000
Patricia Griffin, prin. Fax 473-5004
Salem HS 2,000/9-12
1993 Sundevil Dr 23464 757-474-8484
Donald Robertson, prin. Fax 474-0100
Salem MS 1,300/6-8
2380 Lynnhaven Pkwy 23464 757-474-8411
Dr. Eugene Soltner, prin. Fax 474-8467
Tallwood HS 2,100/9-12
1668 Kempsville Rd 23464 757-474-8555
Jobynia Caldwell, prin. Fax 479-5534
Technical & Career Education Center Vo/Tech
2925 N Landing Rd 23456 757-427-5300
David Swanger, prin. Fax 427-5558
Virginia Beach MS 800/6-8
600 25th St 23451 757-437-4892
Rita Simpson, prin. Fax 437-4708

Adult Learning Center Adult
4160 Virginia Beach Blvd 23452 757-306-0991
Bonnie Mizenko, dir. Fax 306-0999

Advanced Technology Institute Post-Sec.
5700 Southern Blvd # 100 23462 757-490-1241
Atlantic University Post-Sec.
215 67th St 23451 800-428-1512
Aviation Institute of Maintenance Post-Sec.
1429 Miller Store Rd 23455 757-363-2121
Bishop Sullivan Catholic HS 500/9-12
4552 Princess Anne Rd 23462 757-467-2881
Dennis Price, prin. Fax 467-0284
Bryant & Stratton College Post-Sec.
301 Centre Pointe Dr 23462 757-499-7900
Cape Henry Collegiate S 1,000/PK-12
1320 Mill Dam Rd 23454 757-481-2446
Dr. John P. Lewis, prin. Fax 481-9194
Coastal Christian Academy 50/PK-12
640 Kempsville Rd 23464 757-495-5200
Rev. Anne Giminez, prin. Fax 467-5298
ECPI College of Technology Post-Sec.
5555 Greenwich Rd Ste 300 23462 757-671-7171
Kings Grant Day S 100/PK-12
873 Little Neck Rd 23452 757-431-9744
Sharon Clark, admin. Fax 431-9472
Medical Careers Institute Post-Sec.
5501 Greenwich Rd 23462 757-497-8400
Regent University Post-Sec.
1000 Regent University Dr 23464 757-226-4000
Rudy & Kelly Academy of Hair & Nails Post-Sec.
5606 Princess Anne Rd 23462 757-473-0994
Tidewater Community College Post-Sec.
1700 College Cres, 757-468-6348
Tidewater Tech Post-Sec.
2697 Dean Dr Ste 100 23452 757-340-2121
Virginia Beach Friends S 200/PK-12
1537 Laskin Rd 23451 757-428-7534
Jonathan K. Alden, hdmstr. Fax 428-7511
Virginia Career Institute Post-Sec.
100 Constitution Dr Ste 101 23462 757-499-5447
World College Post-Sec.
5193 Shore Dr Ste 105 23455 757-464-4600

Wakefield, Sussex, Pop. 971

Tidewater Academy 300/PK-12
PO Box 536 23888 757-899-5401
Rodney Taylor, hdmstr. Fax 899-2521

Warm Springs, Bath
Bath County SD 800/K-12
PO Box 67 24484 540-839-2722
Dr. K. David Smith, supt. Fax 839-3040
www.bath.k12.va.us
Other Schools – See Hot Springs

Warrenton, Fauquier, Pop. 8,635
Fauquier County SD 10,700/PK-12
320 Hospital Dr Ste 40 20186 540-351-1000
Dr. J. David Martin, supt. Fax 347-1026
www.fcps1.org
Auburn MS 500/6-8
7270 Riley Rd 20187 540-428-3750
Jim Angelo, prin. Fax 428-3760
Fauquier HS 1,700/9-12
705 Waterloo Rd 20186 540-347-6100
Roger Sites, prin. Fax 347-6110
Taylor MS 400/6-8
350 E Shirley Ave 20186 540-347-6140
Ruth Nelson, prin. Fax 347-6145
Warrenton MS 400/6-8
244 Waterloo St 20186 540-347-6160
Wallicia Gill, prin. Fax 347-6169
Other Schools – See Bealeton, Marshall

Regional Academic Governors SD
Supt. — See Richmond
Mountain Vista Governor's S 9-12
6480 College St 20187 540-347-6237
Dr. Rosanne Williamson, prin. Fax 347-6215

Fireside Christian S 100/PK-12
4295 Aiken Dr 20187 540-349-4989
Karen Morris, prin. Fax 349-3177
Highland S 500/PK-12
597 Broadview Ave 20186 540-878-2700
Hank Berg, prin. Fax 878-2731

Warsaw, Richmond, Pop. 1,366
Jointly Operated Vo Tech SD
Supt. — None
Northern Neck Technical Center Vo/Tech
PO Box 787 22572 804-333-4940
Harold Randolph Long, prin. Fax 333-0538

Richmond County SD 1,200/K-12
PO Box 1507 22572 804-333-3681
Robert Luttrell, supt. Fax 333-5586
www.richmond-county.k12.va.us/
Rappahannock HS 400/9-12
PO Box 550 22572 804-333-3551
Jack Cooley, prin. Fax 333-5186
Richmond County IS 300/6-8
PO Box 519 22572 804-333-3560
Daniel Bowling, prin. Fax 333-5387

Rappahannock Community College Post-Sec.
52 Campus Dr 22572 804-333-6700

Washington, Rappahannock, Pop. 182
Rappahannock County SD 1,000/K-12
6 School House Rd 22747 540-987-8773
Robert Chappell, supt. Fax 987-8896
www.rappahannock.k12.va.us
Rappahannock County HS 400/8-12
12576 Lee Hwy 22747 540-987-8575
Roger Mello, prin. Fax 987-9331

Waynesboro, Waynesboro, Pop. 21,269
Waynesboro CSD 3,000/K-12
301 Pine Ave 22980 540-946-4600
Dr. Robin Crowder, supt. Fax 946-4608
www.waynesboro.k12.va.us

Collins MS, 1625 Ivy St 22980 700/6-8
Julie Zook, prin. 540-946-4635
Waynesboro HS 900/9-12
1200 W Main St 22980 540-946-4616
Sue Wright, prin.

Fishburne Military S 200/8-12
PO Box 988 22980 540-946-7700
William Alexander, supt. Fax 946-7702

West Point, King William, Pop. 3,013
West Point SD 800/K-12
PO Box T 23181 804-843-4368
Dr. Jane Massey Redd, supt. Fax 843-4421
www.wpps.k12.va.us
West Point HS 300/9-12
2700 Mattaponi Ave 23181 804-843-3630
Mark Dorsey, prin. Fax 843-3406
West Point MS 200/6-8
1040 Thompson Ave 23181 804-843-3630
Todd Perelli, prin. Fax 843-3406

Weyers Cave, Augusta

Blue Ridge Community College Post-Sec.
PO Box 80 24486 540-234-9261

Whitetop, Grayson
Grayson County SD
Supt. — See Independence
Mt. Rogers S 100/K-12
11337 Highlands Pkwy 24292 276-388-3489
Judy Greear, prin. Fax 388-3103

Williamsburg, Williamsburg, Pop. 11,751
Williamsburg-James City County SD 9,400/K-12
101 Mounts Bay Rd Bldg D 23185 757-253-6777
Gary Mathews, supt. Fax 229-3027
www.wjcc.k12.va.us/
Berkeley MS 900/6-8
1118 Ironbound Rd 23188 757-229-8051
Sammy Fudge, prin. Fax 229-6133
Blair MS 600/6-8
117 Ironbound Rd 23185 757-229-1341
Byron Bishop, prin. Fax 229-7057
Jamestown HS 1,500/9-12
3751 John Tyler Hwy 23185 757-259-3600
Chuck Wagner, prin. Fax 259-3759
LaFayette HS 1,500/9-12
4460 Longhill Rd 23188 757-565-0373
Anita Swinton, prin. Fax 565-4268
Other Schools – See Toano

York County SD
Supt. — See Yorktown
Bruton HS 700/9-12
185 E Rochambeau Dr 23188 757-220-4050
Catherine Jones Ed.D., prin. Fax 220-4090
Queens Lake MS 500/6-8
124 W Queens Dr 23185 757-220-4080
Kendra Crump Ed.D., prin. Fax 220-4074
School of the Arts 9-12
185 E Rochambeau Dr 23188 757-220-4095
Sonya Fischer, prin.

College of William and Mary Post-Sec.
PO Box 8795 23187 757-221-4000
Walsingham Academy Upper S 300/8-12
PO Box 8702 23187 757-229-6026
Peter Bender, prin. Fax 259-1401
Williamsburg Christian Academy 300/PK-12
101 School House Ln 23188 757-220-1978
Gwendolyn Martin, prin. Fax 741-4009

Winchester, Winchester, Pop. 25,119
Frederick County SD 11,700/K-12
1415 Amherst St 22601 540-662-3888
Patricia Taylor, supt. Fax 722-2788
www.frederick.k12.va.us
Byrd MS 6-8
134 Rosa Ln 22602 540-662-0500
Mark Whittle, prin. Fax 662-7790
Frederick County MS 800/6-8
441 Linden Dr 22601 540-667-4233
Sharon Riggleman, prin. Fax 667-2392
Howard Center Vo/Tech
156 Dowell J Cir 22602 540-722-2134
Charlotte Casey, dir. Fax 662-9112
Millbrook HS 1,000/9-12
251 First Woods Dr 22603 540-545-2800
Carolyn Butler, prin. Fax 545-7962

Wood HS 1,300/9-12
161 Apple Pie Ridge Rd 22603 540-667-5226
Joseph Salyer, prin. Fax 667-3154
Wood MS 1,200/6-8
1313 Amherst St 22601 540-667-7500
Teresa Miller, prin. Fax 667-7500
Other Schools – See Stephens City

Winchester CSD 3,400/K-12
PO Box 551 22604 540-667-4253
Dennis Kellison, supt. Fax 722-3583
www.wps.k12.va.us
Handley HS 1,100/9-12
PO Box 910 22604 540-662-3471
Doug Joyner, prin. Fax 722-6722
Morgan MS 900/5-8
48 S Purcell Ave 22601 540-667-7171
Adam Burket, prin. Fax 723-8897

Crossroads Christian Academy 100/K-12
PO Box 4339 22604 540-722-8660
Greg Roberts, prin. Fax 722-8667
Grafton School Post-Sec.
PO Box 2500 22604 540-542-0200
Mountain View Christian Academy 300/K-12
153 Narrow Ln 22602 540-868-1231
Minta Hardman, admin. Fax 869-8976
Shenandoah University Post-Sec.
1460 University Dr 22601 540-665-4500
Winchester Memorial Hospital Post-Sec.
PO Box 3340 22604 540-722-8000

Windsor, Isle of Wight, Pop. 2,429
Isle of Wight County SD
Supt. — See Smithfield
Windsor HS 500/9-12
24 Church St 23487 757-242-6172
William Owen, prin. Fax 242-4948
Windsor MS 400/6-8
23320 N Court St 23487 757-242-3229
Calvin Bullock, prin. Fax 242-3405

Wise, Wise, Pop. 3,282
Wise County SD 6,900/PK-12
PO Box 1217 24293 276-328-8017
Dr. Gregory Killough, supt. Fax 328-3350
www.wise.k12.va.us
Addington MS 500/5-8
PO Box 977 24293 276-328-8821
James Bryant, prin. Fax 328-2044
Kelly HS 500/9-12
PO Box 796 24293 276-328-8015
Charles Collins, prin. Fax 328-8316
Wise County Career-Technical Center Vo/Tech
PO Box 1218 24293 276-328-6113
Larry Hamilton, prin. Fax 328-4443
Other Schools – See Appalachia, Big Stone Gap, Coeburn, Pound, Saint Paul

---

University of Virginia College at Wise Post-Sec.
1 College Ave 24293 276-328-0100
Wise County Christian S 100/PK-12
PO Box 3297 24293 276-328-3297
Gary Hill, prin. Fax 328-3248

Woodberry Forest, Madison

Woodberry Forest S 400/9-12
PO Box 10 22989 540-672-3900
Dennis Campbell, hdmstr. Fax 672-0928

Woodbridge, Prince William, Pop. 33,300
Prince William County SD
Supt. — See Manassas
Beville MS 1,200/6-8
4901 Dale Blvd 22193 703-878-2593
Dominick Graziano, prin. Fax 730-1274
Forest Park HS 2,500/9-12
15721 Forest Park Dr 22193 703-583-3200
Eric Brent, prin. Fax 583-6867
Freedom HS 1,000/9-12
15201 Neabsco Mills Rd 22191 703-583-1405
Inez Bryant, prin. Fax 583-2394
Gar-Field HS 2,600/9-12
14000 Smoketown Rd 22192 703-730-7000
Roger Dallek, prin. Fax 730-7197
Godwin MS 1,200/6-8
14800 Darbydale Ave 22193 703-670-6166
William Reid, prin. Fax 670-9888

Hylton HS 2,400/9-12
14051 Spriggs Rd 22193 703-580-4000
Carolyn Custard, prin. Fax 580-4299
Lake Ridge MS 1,000/6-8
12350 Mohican Rd 22192 703-494-5154
Jo Fitzgerald, prin. Fax 494-8246
Lynn MS 1,200/6-8
1650 Prince William Pkwy 22191 703-494-5157
John Thomas Payne, prin. Fax 491-5141
Rippon MS 1,200/6-8
15101 Blackburn Rd 22191 703-491-2171
Shelia Coleman, prin. Fax 491-2487
Woodbridge HS 2,500/9-12
3001 Old Bridge Rd 22192 703-497-8000
Alan Ross, prin. Fax 497-8117
Woodbridge MS 1,100/6-8
2201 York Dr 22191 703-494-3181
Skyles Calhoun, prin. Fax 491-1441

Northern Virginia Community College Post-Sec.
15200 Neabsco Mills Rd 22191 703-670-2191
Richard Milburn High School Post-Sec.
3421 Commission Ct Ste 201 22192 703-494-0147

Woodstock, Shenandoah, Pop. 4,229
Shenandoah County SD 5,900/K-12
600 N Main St Ste 200 22664 540-459-6222
H.D. Northern, supt. Fax 459-6707
shenandoah.va.schoolwebpages.com
Central HS, 1147 Susan Ave 22664 700/9-12
Mike McCormick, prin. 540-459-2161
Muhlenberg MS 600/6-8
1251 Susan Ave 22664 540-459-2941
Gina Stetter, prin.
Other Schools – See Mount Jackson, Quicksburg, Strasburg

Massanutten Military Academy 100/6-12
614 S Main St 22664 540-459-2167
Roy Zinser, pres. Fax 459-5421

Wytheville, Wythe, Pop. 8,038
Wythe County SD 4,200/K-12
1570 W Reservoir St 24382 276-228-5411
Dr. Albert Armentrout, supt. Fax 228-9192
wcps.wythe.k12.va.us
Scott Memorial MS 400/6-8
950 S 7th St 24382 276-228-2851
Sidney Crockett, prin. Fax 228-8261
Wythe Co. Technical Center Vo/Tech
1505 W Spiller St 24382 276-228-5481
Debbie Stone, prin. Fax 228-8254
Wythe HS 500/9-12
1 Maroon Way 24382 276-228-3157
Ricky Skeens, prin. Fax 228-4124
Other Schools – See Max Meadows, Rural Retreat

Wytheville Community College Post-Sec.
1000 E Main St 24382 276-223-4700

Yorktown, York
York County SD 12,300/K-12
302 Dare Rd 23692 757-898-0300
Steve Staples, supt. Fax 890-0771
www.yorkcountyschools.org
Grafton HS 1,300/9-12
403 Grafton Dr 23692 757-898-0530
Stephanie Guy, prin. Fax 898-0533
Grafton MS 1,000/6-8
405 Grafton Dr 23692 757-898-0525
Edward Holler Ed.D., prin. Fax 898-0534
Tabb HS 1,300/9-12
4431 Big Bethel Rd 23693 757-867-7400
Laura Abel, prin. Fax 867-7414
Tabb MS 900/6-8
300 Yorktown Rd 23693 757-898-0320
Susan Rhew, prin. Fax 867-7425
York HS 1,000/9-12
9300 George Washington Mem 23692 757-898-0354
Royce Hart, prin. Fax 898-8235
Yorktown MS 700/6-8
11201 George Washington Mem 23692 757-898-0360
Michael Cataldo, prin. Fax 898-0412
Other Schools – See Williamsburg

Summit Christian Academy 100/7-12
4209 Big Bethel Rd 23693 757-867-7005
Marilyn Lane, prin. Fax 867-8590

WASHINGTON

WASHINGTON DEPARTMENT OF EDUCATION
PO Box 47200, Olympia 98504-7200
Telephone 360-725-6000
Fax 360-753-6712
Website http://www.k12.wa.us

Superintendent of Public Instruction Terry Bergeson

WASHINGTON BOARD OF EDUCATION
PO Box 47206, Olympia 98504-7206

President Mary Jean Ryan

EDUCATIONAL SERVICE DISTRICTS (ESD)

North Central ESD 171
Dr. Richard McBride, supt. 509-665-2610
PO Box 1847, Wenatchee 98807 Fax 662-9027
www.ncesd.org
Northwest ESD 189
Dr. Gerald Jenkins, supt. 360-299-4000
1601 R Ave, Anacortes 98221 Fax 299-4070
www.esd189.org
ESD 113
Dr. Bill Keim, supt. 360-464-6700
601 McPhee Rd SW Fax 464-6900
Olympia 98502
www.esd113.k12.wa.us
Olympic ESD 114
Dr. Walt Bigby, supt. 360-479-0993
105 National Ave N Fax 478-6869
Bremerton 98312
www.oesd.wednet.edu
ESD 123
Bruce Hawkins, supt. 509-547-8441
3918 W Court St, Pasco 99301 Fax 544-5795
www.esd123.org
Puget Sound ESD
Dr. Monte Bridges, supt. 800-664-4549
800 Oakesdale Ave SW Fax 917-7777
Renton 98057
www.psesd.org
ESD 101
Dr. Terry Munther, supt. 509-789-3800
4202 S Regal St, Spokane 99223 Fax 789-3780
www.esd101.net
ESD 112
Dr. Twyla Barnes, supt. 360-750-7500
2500 NE 65th Ave Fax 750-9706
Vancouver 98661
www.esd112.org
ESD 105
Dr. Jane Gutting, supt. 509-575-2885
33 S 2nd Ave, Yakima 98902 Fax 575-2918
www.esd105.wednet.edu

PUBLIC, PRIVATE AND CATHOLIC SECONDARY SCHOOLS

Aberdeen, Grays Harbor, Pop. 16,358
Aberdeen SD 5 3,700/PK-12
216 N G St 98520 360-538-2000
Martin Kay, supt. Fax 538-2014
www.asd5.org
Aberdeen HS 1,000/9-12
414 N I St 98520 360-538-2040
David Tobin, prin. Fax 538-2046
Miller JHS 600/7-8
100 E Lindstrom St 98520 360-538-2100
Dennis Eygabroad, prin. Fax 538-2106

Wishkah Valley SD 117 200/K-12
4640 Wishkah Rd 98520 360-532-3128
Tom Manke, supt. Fax 533-4638
www.wishkah.org
Wishkah Valley S 200/K-12
4640 Wishkah Rd 98520 360-532-3128
Joel Tyndell, prin. Fax 533-4638

Grays Harbor College Post-Sec.
1620 Edward P Smith Dr 98520 360-532-9020

Adna, Lewis
Adna SD 226 600/PK-12
PO Box 118 98522 360-748-0362
Edward J. Rothlin, supt. Fax 748-9217
www.adna.k12.wa.us
Adna JSHS 300/6-12
PO Box 148 98522 360-748-0315
Richard DuBois, prin. Fax 748-1625

Amanda Park, Grays Harbor
Lake Quinault SD 97 200/K-12
PO Box 38 98526 360-288-2260
John Jones, supt. Fax 288-2732
www.quinault.k12.wa.us/
Lake Quinault HS 100/9-12
PO Box 38 98526 360-288-2414
Beth Daneker, prin. Fax 288-2209

Amboy, Clark
Battle Ground SD 119
Supt. — See Brush Prairie
Amboy MS 600/5-8
22115 NE Chelatchie Rd 98601 360-885-6050
Shayla Ebner, prin. Fax 885-6055

Anacortes, Skagit, Pop. 16,083
Anacortes SD 103 2,900/K-12
2200 M Ave 98221 360-293-1200
Chris Borgen, supt. Fax 293-1222
www.asd103.org/
Anacortes HS 900/9-12
1600 20th St 98221 360-293-2166
Donna Zickuhr, prin. Fax 293-0744
Anacortes MS 500/7-8
2200 M Ave 98221 360-293-1230
Susan Willet, prin. Fax 293-1231

Arlington, Snohomish, Pop. 15,277
Arlington SD 16 5,100/PK-12
315 N French Ave 98223 360-618-6200
Linda Byrnes, supt. Fax 618-6221
www.asd.wednet.edu
Arlington HS 1,600/9-12
18821 Crown Ridge Blvd 98223 360-618-6300
Kurt Criscione, prin. Fax 618-6310
Haller MS 6-8
600 E 1st St 98223 360-618-6400
Eric DeJong, prin. Fax 618-6402
Post MS 800/6-8
1220 E 5th St 98223 360-435-3458
Brian Beckley, prin. Fax 435-1242

Lakewood SD 306
Supt. — See Marysville
Lakewood HS 800/9-12
17023 11th Ave NE 98223 360-652-4505
Kevin Allen, prin. Fax 652-4507

Academy Northwest / Family Academy 300/K-12
23420 Jordan Rd 98223 360-435-9423
Diana McAlister, admin.
Arlington Christian S 100/PK-12
PO Box 3337 98223 360-652-2988
Ruth Graber, admin. Fax 652-2921
Masters Touch Christian S 100/K-12
135 S French Ave 98223 360-403-8351
Mark Brown, prin. Fax 403-4821

Asotin, Asotin, Pop. 1,124
Asotin-Anatone SD 420 600/K-12
PO Box 489 99402 509-243-1100
Greg Godwin, supt. Fax 243-4251
www.aasd.wednet.edu/index.htm
Asotin JSHS 300/7-12
PO Box 489 99402 509-243-4151
Dale Bonfield, prin. Fax 243-4090

Auburn, King, Pop. 47,086
Auburn SD 408 13,700/K-12
915 4th St NE 98002 253-931-4900
Linda Cowan, supt. Fax 931-8006
www.auburn.wednet.edu
Auburn HS 2,500/9-12
800 4th St NE 98002 253-931-4880
Paul Harvey, prin. Fax 931-4701
Auburn Mountainview HS 9-12
28900 124th Ave SE 98092 253-804-4539
Bob Odman, prin.
Auburn Riverside HS 1,900/9-12
501 Oravetz Rd SE 98092 253-804-5154
Bruce Phillips, prin.
Cascade MS 700/6-8
1015 24th St NE 98002 253-931-4995
Dennis Grad, prin. Fax 833-7580
Mt. Baker MS, 620 37th St SE 98002 800/6-8
Louanne Decker, prin. 253-804-4555
Olympic MS 800/6-8
1825 K St SE 98002 253-931-4966
Paul Douglas, prin. Fax 939-2753
Rainier MS 900/6-8
30620 116th Ave SE 98092 253-931-4843
Ben Talbert, prin.

Federal Way SD 210
Supt. — See Federal Way
Jefferson HS 1,900/9-12
4248 S 288th St 98001 253-945-5600
Mark Marshall, prin. Fax 945-5656
Kilo MS 900/6-8
4400 S 308th St 98001 253-945-4700
Debbie Brewer, prin. Fax 945-4747
Sequoyah MS 6-8
3425 S 360th St 98001 253-945-3670
Mark Demick, prin. Fax 945-3699

Auburn Adventist Academy 400/9-12
5000 Auburn Way S 98092 253-939-5000
Keith Hallam, prin. Fax 351-9806
Green River Community College Post-Sec.
12401 SE 320th St 98092 253-833-9111
Northwest Aviation College Post-Sec.
506 23rd St NE 98002 253-854-4960
Ranier Christian HS 100/9-12
19830 SE 328th Pl 98092 253-735-1413
Ted Madden, prin. Fax 887-8234

Bainbridge Island, Kitsap, Pop. 21,951
Bainbridge Island SD 303 4,100/K-12
8489 Madison Ave NE 98110 206-842-4714
Dr. Ken Crawford, supt. Fax 842-2928
www.bainbridge.wednet.edu
Bainbridge HS 1,500/9-12
9330 NE High Sch Rd 98110 206-842-2634
Brent Peterson, prin. Fax 780-1260
Eagle Harbor HS 100/9-12
9530 NE High Sch Rd 98110 206-780-1646
Catherine Camp, prin. Fax 855-0511
Woodward MS 600/7-8
9125 Sportsman Club Rd NE 98110 206-842-4787
Mary O'Neill, prin. Fax 780-4525

Battle Ground, Clark, Pop. 13,237
Battle Ground SD 119
Supt. — See Brush Prairie
Battle Ground HS 2,100/9-12
PO Box 200 98604 360-885-6500
Tim Lexow, prin. Fax 687-6590
Lewisville MS 800/6-8
406 NW 5th Ave 98604 360-885-6350
Linda Allen, prin. Fax 885-6355
Maple Grove MS 700/5-8
12500 NE 199th St 98604 360-885-6700
Bill Penrose, prin. Fax 885-6701

Columbia Adventist Academy 100/9-12
11100 NE 189th St 98604 360-687-3161
Gary Brown, prin. Fax 687-9856

Belfair, Mason
North Mason SD 403 2,200/K-12
71 E Campus Dr 98528 360-277-2300
Thomas J. Kelly, supt. Fax 277-2320
www.nmsd.wednet.edu/
Hawkins MS 400/7-8
300 E Campus Dr 98528 360-277-2302
Josh Joslin, prin. Fax 277-2324

North Mason HS 800/9-12
200 E Campus Dr 98528 360-277-2303
Ted Jansen, prin. Fax 277-2323

Bellevue, King, Pop. 117,137
Bellevue SD 405 15,500/PK-12
PO Box 90010 98009 425-456-4000
Dr. Michael Riley, supt. Fax 456-4176
www.bsd405.org
Bellevue HS 1,400/9-12
10416 Wolverine Way 98004 425-456-7000
Michael Bacigalupi, prin. Fax 456-7005
Chinook MS 800/6-8
2001 98th Ave NE 98004 425-456-6300
Frank Atkinson, prin. Fax 456-6304
Highland MS 500/6-8
15027 Bel Red Rd 98007 425-456-6400
David Wellington, prin. Fax 456-6499
Interlake HS 800/9-12
16245 NE 24th St 98008 425-456-7200
Sharon Collins, prin. Fax 456-7215
International S 500/6-12
445 128th Ave SE 98005 425-456-6500
Peter Bang-Knudsen, prin. Fax 456-6565
Newport HS 1,400/9-12
4333 Factoria Blvd SE 98006 425-456-7400
Patricia Siegwarth, prin. Fax 456-7530
Odle MS 700/6-8
14401 NE 8th St 98007 425-456-6600
Laurie Harvey, prin. Fax 456-6616
Sammamish HS 1,200/9-12
100 140th Ave SE 98005 425-456-7600
Laura Bang-Knudsen, prin. Fax 456-7630
Tillicum MS 600/6-8
16020 SE 16th St 98008 425-456-6700
Tom Duenwald, prin. Fax 456-6770
Tyee MS 800/6-8
13630 SE Allen Rd 98006 425-456-6800
Jerry Schaefer, prin. Fax 456-6859

Bellevue Community College Post-Sec.
3000 Landerholm Cir SE 98007 425-564-1000
Bellvue Beauty School Post-Sec.
14045 NE 20th St 98007 425-643-0270
City University Post-Sec.
11900 NE 1st St 98005 425-637-1010
Dartmoor S 100/1-12
13401 Bel Red Rd 98005 425-603-1975
Celeste Duncan, hdmstr. Fax 603-0038
DeVry University Post-Sec.
500 108th Ave NE Ste 320 98004 425-455-2242
Eastside Catholic HS 500/9-12
11650 SE 60th St 98006 425-644-7737
Greg Marsh, prin. Fax 644-8127
Forest Ridge HS 400/5-12
4800 139th Ave SE 98006 425-641-0700
Alycia Allen, prin. Fax 643-3881

Bellingham, Whatcom, Pop. 74,547
Bellingham SD 501 10,600/PK-12
1306 Dupont St 98225 360-676-6400
Ken Vedra, supt. Fax 676-2793
www.bham.wednet.edu
Bellingham HS 1,100/9-12
2020 Cornwall Ave 98225 360-676-6575
Steve Clarke, prin. Fax 647-6803
Fairhaven MS 600/6-8
110 Parkridge Rd 98225 360-676-6450
Deirdre O'Neill, prin. Fax 647-6887
Kulshan MS 600/6-8
1250 Kenoyer Dr, 360-676-4886
Gordon Grissom, prin. Fax 647-6892
Sehome HS 1,100/9-12
2700 Bill Mcdonald Pkwy 98225 360-676-6481
Phyllis Textor, prin. Fax 647-6819
Shuksan MS 600/6-8
2713 Alderwood Ave 98225 360-676-6454
Andrew Mark, prin. Fax 647-6879
Squalicum HS 1,300/9-12
3773 E McLeod Rd 98226 360-676-6471
Dr. David Engle, prin. Fax 676-6561
Whatcom MS 700/6-8
810 Halleck St 98225 360-676-6460
Jeffrey Coulter, prin. Fax 647-6899

Meridian SD 505 1,500/K-12
214 W Laurel Rd 98226 360-398-7111
Dr. Burton Dickerson, supt. Fax 398-8966
www.meridian.wednet.edu
Meridian HS 500/9-12
194 W Laurel Rd 98226 360-398-8111
David Shockley, prin. Fax 398-7720
Other Schools – See Lynden

Bellingham Beauty School Post-Sec.
4192 Meridian St 98226 360-734-1090
Bellingham Technical College Post-Sec.
3028 Lindbergh Ave 98225 360-738-0221
Northwest Indian College Post-Sec.
2522 Kwina Rd 98226 360-676-2772
Western Washington University Post-Sec.
516 High St 98225 360-650-3000
Whatcom Community College Post-Sec.
237 W Kellogg Rd 98226 360-676-2170

Benton City, Benton, Pop. 2,971
Kiona-Benton City SD 52 1,400/PK-12
1107 Grace 99320 509-588-2000
Gary Henderson, supt. Fax 588-5580
www.owt.com/kibe/
Kiona-Benton City HS 500/9-12
1107 Grace 99320 509-588-2140
Rick Linehan, prin. Fax 588-2651
Kiona-Benton City MS 400/6-8
1107 Grace 99320 509-588-2040
Vance Wing, prin. Fax 588-2905

Bickleton, Klickitat
Bickleton SD 203 100/K-12
PO Box 10 99322 509-896-5473
Ric Palmer, supt. Fax 896-2071
Bickleton S 100/K-12
PO Box 10 99322 509-896-5473
Ric Palmer, prin. Fax 896-2071

Blaine, Whatcom, Pop. 4,330
Blaine SD 503 2,200/PK-12
765 H St 98230 360-332-5881
Ron Spanjer, supt. Fax 332-7568
www.blaine.k12.wa.us
Blaine HS 700/9-12
1055 H St 98230 360-332-6045
Dan Newell, prin. Fax 332-7568
Blaine MS 500/6-8
975 H St 98230 360-332-8226
Darren Benson, prin. Fax 332-7568

Bonney Lake, Pierce, Pop. 14,611
Sumner SD 320
Supt. — See Sumner
Bonney Lake HS 9-12
10920 199th Avenue Ct E, 253-891-5725
Linda Masteller, prin. Fax 891-5797
Lakeridge MS 400/6-8
5909 Myers Rd E, 253-891-5100
Steve Fulkerson, prin. Fax 891-5145
Mountain View MS 500/6-8
10921 199th Avenue Ct E, 253-891-5200
Laurie Dent-Cleveland, prin. Fax 891-5245

Bothell, King, Pop. 30,916
Northshore SD 417 19,700/PK-12
3330 Monte Villa Pkwy 98021 425-489-6000
Karen Forys Ph.D., supt. Fax 489-6005
www.nsd.org
Bothell SHS 1,600/10-12
18125 92nd Ave NE 98011 425-489-6100
Bob Stewart, prin. Fax 489-6179
Canyon Park JHS 900/7-9
23723 23rd Ave SE 98021 425-489-6476
Sharon Lehwalder, prin. Fax 402-5549
Northshore JHS 900/7-9
12101 NE 160th St 98011 425-489-6411
Gretchen Schaefer, prin. Fax 402-7653
Skyview JHS 900/7-9
21404 35th Ave SE 98021 425-489-6040
Mike Anderson, prin. Fax 402-5217
Other Schools – See Kenmore, Woodinville

Bastyr University Post-Sec.
14500 Juanita Dr NE 98028 425-823-1300
Cedar Park Christian S 1,300/PK-12
16300 112th Ave NE 98011 425-488-9778
Clint Behrends, supt. Fax 483-5765
Mars Hill Graduate School Post-Sec.
2525 220th St SE Ste 100 98021 425-415-0505

Bremerton, Kitsap, Pop. 37,828
Bremerton SD 100-C 4,600/PK-12
134 Marion Ave N 98312 360-478-5151
Dr. Elizabeth M. Hyde, supt. Fax 478-6082
www.bremertonschools.org
Bremerton Freshman Academy 9-9
1300 E 30th St 98310 360-478-5104
Aaron Leavell, prin. Fax 478-0787
Bremerton HS 1,200/10-12
1500 13th St 98337 360-478-6033
Aaron Leavell, prin. Fax 478-5061
Mountain View MS Sheridan Campus 8-8
1300 E 30th St 98310 360-478-5025
Jerry Willson, prin. Fax 478-6070
West Sound Technical Skills Center Vo/Tech
101 National Ave N 98312 360-478-5083
Kathrin Carr, dir. Fax 478-5090

Central Kitsap SD 401
Supt. — See Silverdale
Fairview JHS 800/7-9
8107 Central Valley Rd NW 98311 360-662-2600
Kathy Wales, prin. Fax 662-2601
Olympic HS 1,100/10-12
7070 Stampede Blvd NW 98311 360-662-2700
Robert Barnes, prin. Fax 662-2701

Everest College Post-Sec.
155 Washington Ave Ste 200 98337 360-473-1120
Kings West S 400/K-12
4012 Chico Way NW 98312 360-377-7700
Dr. Eric Rasmussen, supt. Fax 377-7795
Olympic College Post-Sec.
1600 Chester Ave 98337 360-792-6050

Brewster, Okanogan, Pop. 2,140
Brewster SD 111 800/PK-12
PO Box 97 98812 509-689-3418
Dan Farrell, supt. Fax 689-2892
www.brewster.wednet.edu
Brewster JSHS 300/7-12
PO Box 97 98812 509-689-3449
Randy Phillips, prin. Fax 689-2580

Bridgeport, Douglas, Pop. 2,043
Bridgeport SD 75 500/PK-12
PO Box 1060 98813 509-686-5656
Gene Schmidt, supt. Fax 686-2221
www.bridgeport.wednet.edu
Bridgeport HS 100/9-12
PO Box 1090 98813 509-686-8770
Scott Sattler, prin. Fax 686-9622
Bridgeport MS 100/6-8
PO Box 1060 98813 509-686-9501
Diane Hull, prin. Fax 686-4052

Brier, Snohomish, Pop. 6,344
Edmonds SD 15
Supt. — See Lynnwood
Brier Terrace MS 700/7-8
22200 Brier Rd 98036 425-431-7834
Kevin Allen, prin. Fax 431-7836

Brush Prairie, Clark, Pop. 2,650
Battle Ground SD 119 11,500/K-12
11104 NE 149th St 98606 360-885-5300
Shonny Bria Ph.D., supt. Fax 885-5310
www.bgsd.k12.wa.us/
Other Schools – See Amboy, Battle Ground, Vancouver

Hockinson SD 98 2,000/K-12
17912 NE 159th St 98606 360-448-6400
Delcine Mesa-Johnson, supt. Fax 448-6409
www.hock.k12.wa.us/
Hockinson HS 400/9-12
16818 NE 159th St 98606 360-448-6450
Sandra Yager, prin. Fax 448-6459
Hockinson MS 600/6-8
15916 NE 182nd Ave 98606 360-448-6440
Peter Rosenkranz, prin. Fax 448-6449

Buckley, Pierce, Pop. 4,473
White River SD 416 2,600/K-12
PO Box 2050 98321 360-829-0600
Tom Lockyer, supt. Fax 829-3843
www.whiteriver.wednet.edu
White River HS 9-12
PO Box 1683 98321 360-829-3352
Michael Hagadone, prin. Fax 829-3351
White River MS 500/6-8
PO Box 2180 98321 360-829-3353
Teresa Sinay, prin. Fax 829-3364
Other Schools – See Wilkeson

Rainier School, PO Box 600 98321 Post-Sec.

Burbank, Walla Walla, Pop. 1,745
Columbia SD 400 1,000/PK-12
755 Maple St 99323 509-547-2136
Ben Small, supt. Fax 546-0603
www.cbvcp.com/columbiasd
Columbia HS 300/9-12
787 Maple St 99323 509-545-8573
Kyle Miller, prin. Fax 545-6553
Columbia MS 300/6-8
835 Maple St 99323 509-545-8571
Mike Taylor, prin. Fax 547-4277

Burien, King, Pop. 30,737
Highline SD 401 14,700/K-12
PO Box 66100 98166 206-433-0111
John Welch, supt. Fax 433-2351
www.hsd401.org
Highline HS 1,500/9-12
225 S 152nd St 98148 206-433-2511
Michael Fosberg, prin. Fax 433-2235
Pugent Sound Skills Center Vo/Tech
18010 8th Ave S 98148 206-433-2524
Dr. Sue Shields, prin. Fax 433-2405
Sylvester MS 700/7-8
16222 Sylvester Rd SW 98166 206-433-2401
Vicki Fisher, prin. Fax 433-2530
Other Schools – See Des Moines, SeaTac, Seattle

Kennedy Memorial HS 900/9-12
140 S 140th St 98168 206-246-0500
Michael L. Prato, prin. Fax 242-0831

Burlington, Skagit, Pop. 8,247
Burlington-Edison SD 100 3,700/K-12
927 E Fairhaven Ave 98233 360-757-3311
Richard Jones, supt. Fax 755-9198
www.be.wednet.edu/
Burlington-Edison HS 1,100/9-12
301 N Burlington Blvd 98233 360-757-4074
Beth VanderVeen, prin. Fax 757-3350

Skagit Adventist S 200/PK-12
530 N Section St 98233 360-755-9261
Ken Knudsen, admin. Fax 755-9931

Camas, Clark, Pop. 16,671
Camas SD 117 4,600/K-12
1919 NE Ione St 98607 360-833-5400
Dr. Mike Nerland, supt. Fax 833-5401
www.camas.wednet.edu/
Camas HS 1,500/9-12
26900 SE 15th St 98607 360-833-5750
Richard Zimmerman, prin. Fax 833-5751
Liberty MS 6-8
1612 NE Garfield St 98607 360-833-5850
Marilyn Boerke, prin. Fax 833-5851
Skyridge MS 800/6-8
5220 NW Parker St 98607 360-833-5800
Ann Perrin, prin. Fax 833-5801

Carnation, King, Pop. 1,828
Riverview SD 407 2,900/K-12
32240 NE 50th St 98014 425-844-4500
Conrad Robertson, supt. Fax 844-4502
www.riverview.wednet.edu
Tolt MS 700/6-8
3740 Tolt Ave 98014 425-844-4600
Janet Gavigan, prin. Fax 844-4602
Other Schools – See Duvall

Carson, Skamania
Stevenson-Carson SD 303
Supt. — See Stevenson
Wind River MS 100/7-8
441 Hot Springs Ave 98610 509-427-8952
Kathleen Browning, prin. Fax 427-8614

Cashmere, Chelan, Pop. 2,985
Cashmere SD 222 1,500/PK-12
210 S Division St 98815 509-782-3355
Glenn Johnson, supt. Fax 782-4747
www.cashmere.wednet.edu

Cashmere HS — 500/9-12
329 Tigner Rd 98815 — 509-782-2914
Tony Boyle, prin. — Fax 782-2891
Cashmere MS — 500/5-8
300 Tigner Rd 98815 — 509-782-2001
Rolf Oxos, prin. — Fax 782-2547

Castle Rock, Cowlitz, Pop. 2,104
Castle Rock SD 401 — 1,300/PK-12
600 Huntington Ave S 98611 — 360-501-2940
Richard Wilde, supt. — Fax 501-3140
www.castlerock.wednet.edu
Castle Rock HS — 500/9-12
5180 Westside Hwy 98611 — 360-501-2930
Henry Karnotski, prin. — Fax 501-2999
Castle Rock MS — 300/7-8
615 Front Ave SW 98611 — 360-501-2920
Bryan Keatley, prin. — Fax 501-3125

Cathlamet, Wahkiakum, Pop. 547
Wahkiakum SD 200 — 500/K-12
PO Box 398 98612 — 360-795-3971
Bob Garrett, supt. — Fax 795-0545
Wahkiakum HS — 200/9-12
PO Box 398 98612 — 360-795-3271
Loren Davis, prin. — Fax 795-0545
Wahkiakum MS — 100/6-8
PO Box 398 98612 — 360-795-3261
Theresa Libby, prin. — Fax 795-3205

Centralia, Lewis, Pop. 15,404
Centralia SD 401 — 3,400/K-12
PO Box 610 98531 — 360-330-7600
Dr. Doug Kernutt, supt. — Fax 330-7604
www.centralia.wednet.edu
Centralia HS — 1,100/9-12
813 Eshom Rd 98531 — 360-330-7605
Tom Boehme, prin. — Fax 330-7616
Centralia MS — 500/7-8
901 Johnson Rd 98531 — 360-330-7619
Steve Warren, prin. — Fax 330-7622

Centralia College — Post-Sec.
600 Centralia College Blvd 98531 — 360-736-9391

Chattaroy, Spokane
Riverside SD 416 — 1,800/PK-12
34515 N Newport Hwy 99003 — 509-464-8201
Galen Hansen, supt. — Fax 464-8206
www.riversidesd.org
Riverside HS — 600/9-12
4120 E Deer Park Milan Rd 99003 — 509-464-8550
John McCoy, prin. — Fax 464-8556
Riverside MS — 500/6-8
3814 E Deer Park Milan Rd 99003 — 509-464-8450
Gerald Califano, prin. — Fax 464-8447

Chehalis, Lewis, Pop. 7,205
Chehalis SD 302 — 2,900/K-12
310 SW 16th St 98532 — 360-807-7200
Dr. Greg Kirsch, supt. — Fax 748-8899
www.chehalis.k12.wa.us
Chehalis MS — 600/6-8
1060 SW 20th St 98532 — 360-807-7230
James Budgett, prin. — Fax 740-1849
West HS — 900/9-12
342 SW 16th St 98532 — 360-807-7235
Dr. Linda Smith, prin. — Fax 748-3664

Lewis County Adventist S — 100/PK-10
2104 S Scheuber Rd 98532 — 360-748-3213
Dan Baker, prin. — Fax 748-6399

Chelan, Chelan, Pop. 3,684
Lake Chelan SD 129 — 1,300/K-12
PO Box 369 98816 — 509-682-3515
Dr. Jim Busey, supt. — Fax 682-5842
www.chelanschools.org
Chelan HS — 400/9-12
PO Box 369 98816 — 509-682-4061
Barry DePaoli, prin. — Fax 682-5001
Chelan MS — 300/6-8
PO Box 369 98816 — 509-682-4073
Barry DePaoli, prin. — Fax 682-5001

Cheney, Spokane, Pop. 10,356
Cheney SD 360 — 3,400/PK-12
520 4th St 99004 — 509-559-4599
Michael Dunn, supt. — Fax 559-4508
www.cheneysd.org
Cheney HS — 1,100/9-12
460 N 6th St 99004 — 509-559-4000
Thomas Gresch, prin. — Fax 559-4005
Cheney MS — 800/6-8
2716 N 6th St 99004 — 509-559-4400
Erika Burden, prin. — Fax 559-4479

Eastern Washington University 99004 — Post-Sec.
509-359-6200

Chewelah, Stevens, Pop. 2,285
Chewelah SD 36 — 1,100/K-12
PO Box 47 99109 — 509-935-8671
Marcus Morgan, supt. — Fax 935-8605
www.chewelah.k12.wa.us
Jenkins HS — 400/9-12
PO Box 138 99109 — 509-935-8671
John Polm, prin. — Fax 935-9206
Jenkins MS — 300/6-8
PO Box 1099 99109 — 509-935-8671
C. Jean Homer, prin. — Fax 935-4404

Chimacum, Jefferson
Chimacum SD 49 — 1,300/PK-12
PO Box 278 98325 — 360-385-3922
Mike Blair, supt. — Fax 732-4336
www.csd49.org
Chimacum HS — 400/9-12
PO Box 278 98325 — 360-732-4481
Whitney Meissner, prin. — Fax 732-7359
Chimacum MS — 300/6-8
PO Box 278 98325 — 360-732-4219
Whitney Meissner, prin. — Fax 732-6859

Clallam Bay, Clallam
Cape Flattery SD 401
Supt. — See Sekiu
Clallam Bay S — 200/K-12
PO Box 337 98326 — 360-963-2324
Phil Fournier, prin. — Fax 963-2228

Clarkston, Asotin, Pop. 7,304
Clarkston SD J 250-185 — 2,700/K-12
PO Box 70 99403 — 509-758-2531
Pete Lewis, supt. — Fax 758-3326
www.csdk12.org
Adams HS — 800/9-12
PO Box 370 99403 — 509-758-5591
Van Cummings, prin. — Fax 758-2831
Lincoln MS — 400/7-8
1945 4th Ave 99403 — 509-758-5506
Dan LejaMeyer, prin. — Fax 758-7838

Cle Elum, Kittitas, Pop. 1,796
Cle Elum-Roslyn SD 404 — 1,000/K-12
2690 State Route 903 98922 — 509-649-4850
Mark Flatau, supt. — Fax 649-2404
Cle Elum-Roslyn HS — 300/9-12
2692 State Route 903 98922 — 509-649-4900
Boyd Keyser, prin. — Fax 649-3563
Strom MS — 200/6-8
2694 State Route 903 98922 — 509-649-4800
Kim Headrick, prin. — Fax 649-3634

Clyde Hill, King, Pop. 2,943

Bellevue Christian JSHS — 500/7-12
1601 98th Ave NE 98004 — 425-454-4028
Bill Safstrom, prin. — Fax 454-4418

Colbert, Spokane

Northwest Christian S — 300/7-12
5104 E Bernhill Rd 99005 — 509-238-4005
Jack Hancock, hdmstr. — Fax 238-2242

Colfax, Whitman, Pop. 2,780
Colfax SD 300 — 700/K-12
1110 N Morton St 99111 — 509-397-3042
Michael Morgan, supt. — Fax 397-5835
www.colfax.k12.wa.us
Colfax HS — 300/9-12
1110 N Morton St 99111 — 509-397-4368
Gary Weitz, prin. — Fax 397-2414

College Place, Walla Walla, Pop. 8,945
College Place SD 250 — 800/K-8
107 SE 2nd St 99324 — 509-525-4827
Timothy Payne, supt. — Fax 525-3741
www.cpps.org
Sager MS — 200/7-8
1755 S College Ave 99324 — 509-525-5300
Jeff Peterson, prin. — Fax 525-5305

Walla Walla College — Post-Sec.
204 S College Ave 99324 — 509-527-2615
Walla Walla Valley Academy — 200/9-12
300 SW Academy Way 99324 — 509-525-1050
John M. Deming, prin. — Fax 525-1056

Colton, Whitman, Pop. 366
Colton SD 306 — 200/K-12
706 Union St 99113 — 509-229-3385
C. Foley, supt. — Fax 229-3374
www.colton.k12.wa.us/
Colton S, 706 Union St 99113 — 200/K-12
Nate Smith, prin. — 509-229-3386

Colville, Stevens, Pop. 5,029
Colville SD 115 — 1,900/K-12
217 S Hofstetter St 99114 — 509-684-7850
Ken Emmil, supt. — Fax 684-7855
www.colsd.org
Colville HS — 700/9-12
154 Highway 20 E 99114 — 509-684-7800
Kevin Knight, prin. — Fax 684-7809
Colville JHS — 300/7-8
990 S Cedar St 99114 — 509-684-7820
Paul Dumas, prin. — Fax 684-7825

Colville Valley Junior Academy — 50/K-10
139 E Cedar Loop 99114 — 509-684-6830
Laurie Hosey, prin. — Fax 684-1084

Concrete, Skagit, Pop. 800
Concrete SD 11 — 800/K-12
45389 Airport Way 98237 — 360-853-8141
Barbara Hawkings, supt. — Fax 853-7521
www.concrete.k12.wa.us
Concrete HS — 200/9-12
7830 S Superior Ave 98237 — 360-853-8143
Don Beazizo, prin. — Fax 853-8110
Concrete MS — 100/7-8
45389 Airport Way 98237 — 360-853-8116
Don Beazizo, prin. — Fax 853-7521

Connell, Franklin, Pop. 2,980
North Franklin SD J 51-162 — 1,900/K-12
PO Box 829 99326 — 509-234-2021
Michael Kirby, supt. — Fax 234-9200
www.nfsd.k12.wa.us
Connell HS — 500/9-12
PO Box 829 99326 — 509-234-2911
Pat Ena, prin. — Fax 234-9226
Olds JHS — 300/7-8
PO Box 829 99326 — 509-234-3931
Mary Nipper, prin. — Fax 234-8171

Cosmopolis, Grays Harbor, Pop. 1,646
North River SD 200 — 100/K-12
2867 N River Rd 98537 — 360-532-3079
David Pickering, supt. — Fax 532-1738
www.nr.k12.wa.us/
North River S — 100/K-12
2867 N River Rd 98537 — 360-532-3079
David Pickering, prin. — Fax 532-1738

Coulee City, Grant, Pop. 637
Coulee-Hartline SD 151 — 200/K-12
PO Box 428 99115 — 509-632-8642
Dr. Edward Fisk, supt. — Fax 632-5166
www.achsd.org
Other Schools – See Hartline

Coulee Dam, Okanogan, Pop. 1,080
Grand Coulee Dam SD 301J — 800/K-12
110 Stevens Ave 99116 — 509-633-2143
Jeff Loe, supt. — Fax 633-2530
www.gcdsd.org
Lake Roosevelt HS — 300/9-12
500 Civic Way 99116 — 509-633-1442
Karl Miller, prin. — Fax 633-0356
Other Schools – See Grand Coulee

Coupeville, Island, Pop. 1,813
Coupeville SD 204 — 1,100/K-12
2 S Main St 98239 — 360-678-4522
Bill Myhr, supt. — Fax 678-4834
pride.coup.wednet.edu
Coupeville HS — 400/9-12
501 S Main St 98239 — 360-678-4409
Sheldon Rosenkrance, prin. — Fax 678-0540
Coupeville MS — 300/6-8
501 S Main St 98239 — 360-678-4409
David Ebersole, prin. — Fax 678-0540

Covington, King, Pop. 16,610
Kent SD 415
Supt. — See Kent
Cedar Heights MS — 900/7-8
19640 SE 272nd St 98042 — 253-373-7620
Angela Grutko, prin. — Fax 373-7628
Kentwood SHS — 2,300/9-12
25800 164th Ave SE 98042 — 253-373-7680
Doug Hostetter, prin. — Fax 373-7326
Mattson MS — 700/7-8
16400 SE 251st St 98042 — 253-373-7670
Steve Beck, prin. — Fax 373-7673

Tahoma SD 409
Supt. — See Maple Valley
Tahoma SHS — 1,500/10-12
18200 SE 240th St 98042 — 425-413-6200
Terry Duty, prin. — Fax 413-6333

Cowiche, Yakima
Highland SD 203 — 1,100/K-12
PO Box 38 98923 — 509-678-4173
Gary Masten, supt. — Fax 678-4177
www.highland.wednet.edu/
Highland HS — 300/10-12
PO Box 38 98923 — 509-678-4161
Greg George, prin. — Fax 678-4140
Highland JHS — 200/7-9
PO Box 38 98923 — 509-678-7200
Trevor Greene, prin. — Fax 678-4006

Creston, Lincoln, Pop. 231
Creston SD 73 — 100/K-12
PO Box 17 99117 — 509-636-2721
Michael Crowell, supt. — Fax 636-2910
www.creston.wednet.edu
Creston JSHS — 100/7-12
PO Box 17 99117 — 509-636-2721
Michael Crowell, prin. — Fax 636-2910

Curlew, Ferry
Curlew SD 50 — 200/K-12
PO Box 370 99118 — 509-779-4931
Steve McCullough, supt. — Fax 779-4938
www.curlew.wednet.edu/default.htm
Curlew S — 200/K-12
PO Box 370 99118 — 509-779-4931
Brett Simpson, prin. — Fax 779-4938

Cusick, Pend Oreille, Pop. 221
Cusick SD 59 — 300/K-12
305 Monumental Rd 99119 — 509-445-1125
Dan Read, supt. — Fax 445-1598
www.cusick.wednet.edu/
Cusick JSHS — 100/7-12
305 Monumental Rd 99119 — 509-445-1125
Kathy Christiansen, prin. — Fax 445-1598

Darrington, Snohomish, Pop. 1,333
Darrington SD 330 — 500/K-12
PO Box 27 98241 — 360-436-1323
Larry Johnson, supt. — Fax 436-2045
www.dsd.k12.wa.us
Darrington MSHS — 200/7-12
PO Box 27 98241 — 360-436-1140
Dave Holmer, prin. — Fax 436-1089

Davenport, Lincoln, Pop. 1,726
Davenport SD 207 — 500/PK-12
801 7th St 99122 — 509-725-1481
Candi Stoner, supt. — Fax 725-2260
www.davenport.wednet.edu/
Davenport JSHS — 200/7-12
801 7th St 99122 — 509-725-4021
Mike Perry, prin. — Fax 725-2260

Dayton, Columbia, Pop. 2,703
Dayton SD 2 — 600/PK-12
609 S 2nd St 99328 — 509-382-2543
Richard Stewart, supt. — Fax 382-2081
www.dayton.wednet.edu/
Dayton HS — 200/9-12
614 S 3rd St 99328 — 509-382-4775
Jude Cornaggia, prin. — Fax 382-2081

Dayton MS — 100/7-8
609 S 2nd St 99328 — 509-382-2522
Katie Leid, prin. — Fax 381-2081

Deer Park, Spokane, Pop. 3,105

Deer Park SD 414 — 1,900/K-12
PO Box 490 99006 — 509-464-5500
Mick Miller, supt. — Fax 464-5510
www.dpsd.org
Deer Park HS — 600/9-12
PO Box 550 99006 — 509-464-5900
Trip Goodall, prin. — Fax 464-5910
Deer Park MS — 500/6-8
PO Box 882 99006 — 509-464-5800
Brent Seedall, prin. — Fax 464-5810

Deming, Whatcom

Mt. Baker SD 507 — 2,400/K-12
PO Box 95 98244 — 360-383-2000
Dr. Richard Gantman, supt. — Fax 383-2009
www.mtbaker.wednet.edu
Mt. Baker HS — 700/9-12
PO Box 95 98244 — 360-383-2015
Steve King, prin. — Fax 383-2029
Mt. Baker JHS — 400/7-8
PO Box 95 98244 — 360-383-2030
Charles Burleigh, prin. — Fax 383-2039

Des Moines, King, Pop. 28,767

Highline SD 401
Supt. — See Burien
Mount Rainier HS — 1,300/9-12
22450 19th Ave S 98198 — 206-631-7000
Toni Pace, prin. — Fax 433-2423
Pacific MS — 700/7-8
22705 24th Ave S 98198 — 206-433-2581
Cecilia Beaman, prin. — Fax 433-2451

Evergreen Lutheran HS — 100/9-12
2021 S 260th St 98198 — 253-946-4488
Greg Thiesfeldt, prin. — Fax 529-9475
Highline Community College — Post-Sec.
PO Box 98000 98198 — 206-878-3710

Duvall, King, Pop. 5,710

Riverview SD 407
Supt. — See Carnation
Cedarcrest HS — 800/9-12
29000 NE 150th St 98019 — 425-844-4800
Clarence Lavarias, prin. — Fax 844-4802

Easton, Kittitas

Easton SD 28 — 100/PK-12
PO Box 8 98925 — 509-656-2317
Suellen White, supt. — Fax 656-2585
www.easton.wednet.edu
Easton S — 100/PK-12
PO Box 8 98925 — 509-656-2317
Suellen White, prin. — Fax 656-2585

Eastsound, San Juan

Orcas Island SD 137 — 500/K-12
557 School Rd 98245 — 360-376-2284
Dr. Jeff Van Handel, supt. — Fax 376-2283
www.orcasislandschools.org
Orcas Island HS — 200/9-12
715 School Rd 98245 — 360-376-2287
Barbara Kline, prin. — Fax 376-6078
Orcas Island MS — 100/7-8
715 School Rd 98245 — 360-376-2287
Barbara Kline, prin. — Fax 376-6078

Orcas Christian Day S — 100/1-12
PO Box 669 98245 — 360-376-6683
Fax 376-7642

East Wenatchee, Douglas, Pop. 8,819

Eastmont SD 206 — 4,700/K-12
460 9th St NE 98802 — 509-884-7169
Tom Pickett, supt. — Fax 884-4210
www.eastmont206.com/distoff/main/
Eastmont JHS — 900/8-9
905 8th St NE 98802 — 509-884-2407
John Westerman, prin. — Fax 884-1988
Eastmont SHS — 1,300/10-12
955 3rd St NE 98802 — 509-884-6665
Mark Marney, prin. — Fax 884-8805
Other Schools – See Wenatchee

Eatonville, Pierce, Pop. 2,328

Eatonville SD 404 — 2,200/K-12
PO Box 698 98328 — 360-879-1000
Raymond F. Arment, supt. — Fax 879-1086
cruiser.eatonville.wednet.edu/
Eatonville HS — 700/9-12
PO Box 699 98328 — 360-879-1200
Garth Steedman, prin. — Fax 879-1284
Eatonville MS — 500/6-8
PO Box 910 98328 — 360-879-1400
Ken Andersen, prin. — Fax 879-1480

Edgewood, Pierce, Pop. 9,718

Puyallup SD 3
Supt. — See Puyallup
Edgemont JHS — 400/7-9
2300 110th Ave E 98372 — 253-841-8727
Krista Bates, prin. — Fax 840-8883

Edmonds, Snohomish, Pop. 39,937

Edmonds SD 15
Supt. — See Lynnwood
Edmonds-Woodway HS — 1,800/9-12
7600 212th St SW 98026 — 425-431-7900
Michelle Trifunovic, prin. — Fax 431-7929

Edwall, Lincoln

Christian Heritage S — 100/K-12
PO Box 118 99008 — 509-236-2224
Marty Klein, admin. — Fax 236-2224

Ellensburg, Kittitas, Pop. 16,914

Ellensburg SD 401 — 2,800/K-12
1300 E 3rd Ave 98926 — 509-925-8000
John Glenewinkel, supt. — Fax 925-8025
wonders.eburg.wednet.edu/
Ellensburg HS — 900/9-12
1203 E Capitol Ave 98926 — 509-925-8300
Jeff Ellersick, prin. — Fax 925-8305
Morgan MS — 700/6-8
400 E 1st Ave 98926 — 509-925-8200
Gary Ristine, prin. — Fax 925-8202

Central Washington University — Post-Sec.
400 E University Way 98926 — 509-963-1111

Elma, Grays Harbor, Pop. 3,164

Elma SD 68 — 1,900/K-12
1235 Monte Elma Rd 98541 — 360-482-2822
Howard King, supt. — Fax 482-2092
www.elma.wednet.edu
Elma HS — 700/9-12
1235 Monte Elma Rd 98541 — 360-482-3121
Deborah Parriott, prin. — Fax 482-1200
Elma MS — 400/6-8
1235 Monte Elma Rd 98541 — 360-482-2237
Greg Scroggins, prin. — Fax 482-4872

Mary M. Knight SD 311 — 200/PK-12
2987 W Matlock Brady Rd 98541 — 360-426-6767
Carol Ersland, supt. — Fax 427-5516
mary.wa.schoolwebpages.com
Knight JSHS — 100/7-12
2987 W Matlock Brady Rd 98541 — 360-426-6767
Carol Ersland, prin. — Fax 427-5516

Endicott, Whitman, Pop. 322

Endicott SD 308 — 100/K-8
308 School Dr 99125 — 509-657-3523
Rick Winters, supt. — Fax 657-3521
www.sje.wednet.edu
Endicott-St. John MS — 100/7-8
308 School Dr 99125 — 509-657-3523
Suzanne Schmick, prin. — Fax 657-3521

Entiat, Chelan, Pop. 999

Entiat SD 127 — 400/K-12
2650 Entiat Way 98822 — 509-784-1800
Dennis Chambers, supt. — Fax 784-2986
www.entiatschools.org
Entiat JSHS — 200/7-12
2650 Entiat Way 98822 — 509-784-1911
Miles Caples, prin. — Fax 784-2986

Enumclaw, King, Pop. 10,896

Enumclaw SD 216 — 4,500/K-12
2929 McDougall Ave 98022 — 360-802-7100
Arthur Jarvis, supt. — Fax 802-7123
www.enumclaw.wednet.edu/
Enumclaw HS — 1,700/9-12
226 Semanski St 98022 — 360-802-7669
David Dorn, prin. — Fax 802-7676
Enumclaw MS — 600/6-8
550 Semanski St 98022 — 360-802-7150
Steve Rabb, prin. — Fax 802-7224
Thunder Mountain MS — 600/6-8
42018 264th Ave SE 98022 — 360-802-7492
Darin Adams, prin. — Fax 802-7500

Ephrata, Grant, Pop. 7,178

Ephrata SD 165 — 2,100/K-12
499 C St NW 98823 — 509-754-2474
Dr. Jerry Simon, supt. — Fax 754-4712
www.ephrataschools.org
Ephrata HS — 700/9-12
333 4th Ave NW 98823 — 509-754-2043
Dan Martell, prin. — Fax 754-5285
Ephrata MS, 384 A St SE 98823 — 400/7-8
Rick Allstot, prin. — 509-754-4659

New Life Christian S — 100/PK-12
911 E Division Ave 98823 — 509-754-5558
Joseph Johnson, admin. — Fax 754-3540

Everett, Snohomish, Pop. 96,604

Everett SD 2 — 17,600/PK-12
PO Box 2098, — 425-385-4000
Carol Whitehead Ed.D., supt. — Fax 385-4012
www.everett.k12.wa.us
Cascade HS — 1,800/9-12
801 E Casino Rd 98203 — 425-385-6000
Cathy Woods, prin. — Fax 385-6002
Eisenhower MS — 800/6-8
10200 25th Ave SE 98208 — 425-385-7500
Joyce Brossoit, prin. — Fax 385-7502
Everett HS — 1,600/9-12
2416 Colby Ave 98201 — 425-385-4400
Catherine Matthews, prin. — Fax 385-4402
Evergreen MS — 900/6-8
7621 Beverly Ln 98203 — 425-385-5700
Joyce Stewart, prin. — Fax 385-5702
Gateway MS — 900/6-8
15404 Silver Firs Dr 98208 — 425-385-6600
Eldon Allen, prin. — Fax 385-6602
North MS — 600/6-8
2514 Rainier Ave 98201 — 425-385-4800
Kelly Shepherd, prin. — Fax 385-4802
Other Schools – See Mill Creek

Lake Stevens SD 4
Supt. — See Lake Stevens
Lake Stevens MS — 800/6-8
1031 91st Ave SE 98205 — 425-335-1544
John Gebert, prin. — Fax 335-1564

Mukilteo SD 6 — 14,200/K-12
9401 Sharon Dr 98204 — 425-356-1274
Marci Larsen, supt. — Fax 356-1310
www.mukilteo.wednet.edu
Explorer MS — 800/6-8
9600 Sharon Dr 98204 — 425-356-1240
Ali Williams, prin. — Fax 356-1288
Mariner HS — 2,100/9-12
200 120th St SW 98204 — 425-356-1700
Brent Kline, prin. — Fax 356-1717
Sno-Isle Vo Skills Ctr — Vo/Tech
9001 Airport Rd 98204 — 425-348-2220
Steve Burch, prin. — Fax 356-2201
Voyager MS — 800/6-8
11711 4th Ave W 98204 — 425-356-1730
Wes Bailey, prin. — Fax 290-3747
Other Schools – See Mukilteo

Archbishop Thomas Murphy HS — 300/9-12
12911 39th Ave SE 98208 — 425-379-6363
Dr. Kristine Smith, prin. — Fax 385-2875
Cedar Park Christian S — 300/PK-12
13000 21st Dr SE 98208 — 425-337-6992
Curt Frunz, prin. — Fax 357-9399
Everest College — Post-Sec.
906 SE Evrtt Mall Way #600 98208 — 425-789-7960
Everett Community College — Post-Sec.
2000 Tower St 98201 — 425-388-9100
ITT Technical Institute — Post-Sec.
1615 75th St SW Ste 220 98203 — 425-583-0200
Milan Institute of Cosmetology — Post-Sec.
607 SE Everett Mall Way #5 98208 — 425-353-8193
Montessori S of Snohomish County — 200/PK-12
1804 Puget Dr 98203 — 425-355-1311
Kathleen Gunnell, admin.
Puget Sound Christian College — Post-Sec.
PO Box 13108 98206 — 425-257-3090
Western Pacific Truck School — Post-Sec.
9901 Evergreen Way 98204 — 425-486-7117

Everson, Whatcom, Pop. 2,067

Nooksack Valley SD 506 — 1,700/PK-12
3326 E Badger Rd 98247 — 360-988-4754
Mark Johnson, supt. — Fax 988-8983
www.nooksackschools.org
Nooksack Valley HS — 600/9-12
3326 E Badger Rd 98247 — 360-988-2641
Robert Prosch, prin. — Fax 988-7058
Nooksack Valley MS — 500/6-8
404 W Columbia St 98247 — 360-966-7561
Cindy Stockwell, prin. — Fax 966-7805

Fall City, King, Pop. 1,582

Snoqualmie Valley SD 410
Supt. — See Snoqualmie
Chief Kanim MS — 500/6-8
PO Box 639 98024 — 425-831-8225
Kirk Dunckel, prin. — Fax 831-8290

Federal Way, King, Pop. 83,088

Federal Way SD 210 — 22,500/PK-12
31405 18th Ave S 98003 — 253-945-2000
Tom Murphy, supt. — Fax 945-2001
www.fwps.org
Beamer HS — 1,500/9-12
35999 16th Ave S 98003 — 253-945-2570
Joshua Garcia, prin. — Fax 945-2599
Decatur HS — 1,700/9-12
2800 SW 320th St 98023 — 253-945-5200
Tom Leacy, prin. — Fax 945-5252
Federal Way HS — 1,600/9-12
30611 16th Ave S 98003 — 253-945-5400
Lisa Griebel, prin. — Fax 945-5454
Illahee MS — 1,000/6-8
36001 1st Ave S 98003 — 253-945-4600
Stacy Lucas, prin. — Fax 945-4646
Lakota MS — 700/6-8
1415 SW 314th St 98023 — 253-945-4800
Pam Tuggle, prin. — Fax 945-4848
Sacajawea MS — 800/6-8
1101 S Dash Point Rd 98003 — 253-945-4900
Randy Kaczor, prin. — Fax 945-4949
Saghalie MS — 700/6-8
33914 19th Ave SW 98023 — 253-945-5000
Damon Hunter, prin. — Fax 945-5050
Truman HS — Adult
31455 28th Ave S 98003 — 253-945-5800
Stuart Crisman, prin. — Fax 945-5858
Other Schools – See Auburn, Kent

DeVry University — Post-Sec.
3600 S 344th Way 98001 — 253-943-2800
Gene Juarez Academy of Beauty — Post-Sec.
2222 S 314th St 98003 — 253-839-6483
Life Academy of Puget Sound — 100/K-12
414 SW 312th St 98023 — 253-839-7378
Sue Austin, admin. — Fax 839-1031

Ferndale, Whatcom, Pop. 9,977

Ferndale SD 502 — 4,900/PK-12
PO Box 698 98248 — 360-383-9200
Dr. Roger Lehnert, supt. — Fax 383-9201
www.ferndale.wednet.edu
Ferndale HS — 1,500/9-12
PO Box 428 98248 — 360-383-9240
Dawn Fairchild, prin. — Fax 383-9242
Horizon MS — 400/7-8
PO Box 1769 98248 — 360-383-9850
David Hutchinson, prin. — Fax 383-9852
Vista MS — 400/7-8
PO Box 1328 98248 — 360-383-9370
Mary Kanikeberg, prin. — Fax 383-9372
Windward HS — 9-12
PO Box 428 98248 — 360-383-9150
Jill Iwasaki, prin. — Fax 383-9152

Forks, Clallam, Pop. 3,192
Quillayute Valley SD 402 1,300/PK-12
411 S Spartan Ave 98331 360-374-6262
Frank Walter, supt. Fax 374-6990
www.forks.wednet.edu
Forks HS 300/9-12
261 S Spartan Ave 98331 360-374-6262
Raymond Marshall, prin. Fax 374-9657
Forks MS 300/6-8
121 S Spartan Ave 98331 360-374-6262
Raymond Marshall, prin. Fax 374-2362

Friday Harbor, San Juan, Pop. 2,096
San Juan Island SD 149 900/K-12
PO Box 458 98250 360-378-4133
Michael D. Soltman, supt. Fax 378-6276
www.sjisd.wednet.edu
Friday Harbor HS 300/9-12
PO Box 458 98250 360-378-5215
Patricia Scott, prin. Fax 378-2647
Friday Harbor MS 200/6-8
PO Box 458 98250 360-378-5214
Ann Spratt, prin. Fax 378-9750

Garfield, Whitman, Pop. 632
Garfield SD 302 100/PK-8
PO Box 398 99130 509-635-1331
Bill LaMunyan, supt. Fax 635-1332
www.garpal.wednet.edu
Garfield-Palouse MS 50/6-8
PO Box 398 99130 509-635-1331
Bill LaMunyan, prin. Fax 635-1332

Gig Harbor, Pierce, Pop. 6,620
Peninsula SD 401 9,700/PK-12
14015 62nd Ave NW 98332 253-530-1000
Terry Bouck, supt. Fax 530-1010
www.peninsula.wednet.edu
Gig Harbor HS 1,700/9-12
5101 Rosedale St NW 98335 253-530-1400
Greg Schellenberg, prin. Fax 530-1420
Goodman MS 600/6-8
3701 38th Ave NW 98335 253-530-1600
Doris Bolender, prin. Fax 858-5515
Harbor Ridge MS 600/6-8
9010 Prentice Ave 98332 253-530-1900
Connie West, prin. Fax 530-1920
Kopachuck MS 600/6-8
10414 56th St NW 98335 253-530-4100
David Colombini, prin. Fax 265-8810
Peninsula HS 1,500/9-12
14105 Purdy Dr NW 98332 253-857-3530
Grant Hosford, prin. Fax 857-8133
Other Schools – See Lakebay

Glenwood, Klickitat
Glenwood SD 401 50/K-12
PO Box 12 98619 509-364-3595
Shane Couch, supt. Fax 364-3689
www.glenwood.k12.wa.us/schoolinfo.HTM
Glenwood S 50/K-12
PO Box 12 98619 509-364-3565
Calvin McRae, prin. Fax 364-3689

Goldendale, Klickitat, Pop. 3,713
Goldendale SD 404 1,100/K-12
603 S Roosevelt Ave 98620 509-773-5177
Dr. Marie Phillips, supt. Fax 773-6028
www.golden.wednet.edu
Goldendale HS 400/9-12
525 E Simcoe Dr 98620 509-773-5846
Mike Lindhe, prin. Fax 773-6900
Goldendale MS 400/5-8
520 E Collins St 98620 509-773-4323
Dave Barta, prin. Fax 773-4579

Goldendale Christian S 50/PK-12
PO Box 603 98620 509-773-0232
Roxanne Garland, admin. Fax 733-3615

Graham, Pierce
Bethel SD 403
Supt. — See Spanaway
Cougar Mountain JHS 900/7-9
5108 260th St E 98338 253-683-8000
Cliff Anderson, prin. Fax 683-8098
Frontier JHS 900/7-9
22110 108th Ave E 98338 253-683-8300
Tom Mitchell, prin. Fax 683-8398
Graham-Kapowsin HS 10-12
22100 108th Ave E 98338 253-683-6100
Jennifer Bethman, prin. Fax 683-6198

Grand Coulee, Grant, Pop. 925
Grand Coulee Dam SD 301J
Supt. — See Coulee Dam
Grand Coulee Dam MS 200/5-8
PO Box J 99133 509-633-1520
Dawn Millard, prin. Fax 633-2257

Grandview, Yakima, Pop. 8,908
Grandview SD 200 3,100/K-12
913 W 2nd St 98930 509-882-8500
Kevin Chase, supt. Fax 882-2029
www.grandview.wednet.edu
Grandview HS 800/9-12
1601 W 5th St 98930 509-882-8750
Arcella Hall, prin. Fax 882-8739
Grandview MS 700/6-8
1401 W 2nd St 98930 509-882-8600
Matt Mallery, prin. Fax 882-8665

Granger, Yakima, Pop. 2,836
Granger SD 204 1,200/PK-12
701 E Ave 98932 509-854-1515
Timothy J. Dunn, supt. Fax 854-1126
www.gsd.wednet.edu
Granger HS 300/9-12
315 Mentzer Ave 98932 509-854-1115
Richard Esparza, prin. Fax 854-2757
Granger MS 400/5-8
501 Bailey Ave 98932 509-854-1003
Lisa Rosberg, prin. Fax 854-1083

Granite Falls, Snohomish, Pop. 2,863
Granite Falls SD 332 2,400/K-12
307 N Alder St 98252 360-691-7717
Joel Thaut, supt. Fax 691-4459
www.gfalls.wednet.edu
Granite Falls HS 700/9-12
405 N Alder St 98252 360-691-7713
Eric Cahan, prin. Fax 691-3704
Granite Falls MS 600/6-8
205 N Alder St 98252 360-691-7710
Dr. Richard Panagos, prin. Fax 691-3726

Harrington, Lincoln, Pop. 420
Harrington SD 204 100/K-12
PO Box 204 99134 509-253-4331
Randy Behrens, supt. Fax 456-6306
www.harrsd.k12.wa.us
Harrington HS 100/7-12
PO Box 204 99134 509-253-4331
Randy Behrens, prin. Fax 456-6306

Hartline, Grant, Pop. 142
Coulee-Hartline SD 151
Supt. — See Coulee City
Almira/Coulee-Hartline HS 100/9-12
PO Box 98 99135 509-639-2611
Terry Cosentino, prin. Fax 639-2353

Hoquiam, Grays Harbor, Pop. 9,030
Hoquiam SD 28 2,000/K-12
305 Simpson Ave 98550 360-538-8200
Mike Parker, supt. Fax 538-8202
www.hoquiam.k12.wa.us
Hoquiam HS 700/9-12
501 W Emerson Ave 98550 360-538-8210
Mark VandenHazel, prin. Fax 538-8212
Hoquiam MS 400/7-8
200 Spencer St 98550 360-538-8220
Tony Miles, prin. Fax 538-8222

Hunters, Stevens
Columbia SD 206 200/PK-12
PO Box 7 99137 509-722-3311
B. Paul Turner, supt. Fax 722-3310
www.columbia206.k12.wa.us/
Columbia S 200/PK-12
PO Box 7 99137 509-722-3311
Chuck Wyborney, prin. Fax 722-3310

Ilwaco, Pacific, Pop. 981
Ocean Beach SD 101
Supt. — See Long Beach
Ilwaco JSHS 200/7-12
PO Box F 98624 360-642-3731
Lisa Nelson, prin. Fax 642-1224

Inchelium, Ferry, Pop. 393
Inchelium SD 70 100/K-12
PO Box 285 99138 509-722-6181
Ron Washington, supt. Fax 722-6192
www.inchelium.wednet.edu
Inchelium S 100/K-12
PO Box 285 99138 509-722-6181
Virginia Elkington, prin. Fax 722-6192

Ione, Pend Oreille, Pop. 500
Selkirk SD 70
Supt. — See Metaline Falls
Selkirk JSHS 200/7-12
10372 Highway 31 99139 509-446-3505
Larry Reed, prin. Fax 446-2408

Issaquah, King, Pop. 17,059
Issaquah SD 411 14,000/PK-12
565 NW Holly St 98027 425-837-7000
Steve Rasmussen, supt. Fax 837-7005
www.issaquah.wednet.edu
Beaver Lake MS 1,000/6-8
25025 SE 32nd St 98029 425-837-4150
Josh Almy, prin. Fax 837-4195
Issaquah HS 1,200/10-12
700 2nd Ave SE 98027 425-837-6000
Paula Phelps, prin. Fax 837-6078
Issaquah MS 900/6-8
400 1st Ave SE 98027 425-837-6800
Corrine DeRosa, prin. Fax 837-6855
Pacific Cascade Freshman Campus 9-9
24635 SE Issaquah Fall City 98029 425-837-5900
Dana Bailey, prin. Fax 837-5910
Pine Lake MS 900/6-8
3200 228th Ave SE 98075 425-837-5700
Roy Adler, prin. Fax 837-5762
Skyline HS 1,200/10-12
1122 228th Ave SE 98075 425-837-7700
Lisa Hechtman, prin. Fax 837-7705
Other Schools – See Renton

Trinity Lutheran College Post-Sec.
4221 228th Ave SE 98029 425-392-0400

Joyce, Clallam
Crescent SD 313 100/K-12
PO Box 20 98343 360-928-3311
Tom Anderson, supt. Fax 928-3066
www.crescent.wednet.edu
Crescent JSHS 100/7-12
PO Box 20 98343 360-928-3311
Tom Anderson, prin. Fax 928-3066

Kahlotus, Franklin, Pop. 231
Kahlotus SD 56 100/K-12
PO Box 69 99335 509-282-3338
Fax 282-3339
Kahlotus JSHS 50/7-12
PO Box 69 99335 509-282-3338
Ron Hopkins, prin. Fax 282-3339

Kalama, Cowlitz, Pop. 1,938
Kalama SD 402 1,000/K-12
548 China Garden Rd 98625 360-673-5282
James Sutton, supt. Fax 673-5228
www.kalama.k12.wa.us
Kalama JSHS 600/6-12
548 China Garden Rd 98625 360-673-5212
Mike Hamilton, prin. Fax 673-1280

Kelso, Cowlitz, Pop. 11,854
Kelso SD 458 5,300/PK-12
601 Crawford St 98626 360-501-1900
Glenys Hill, supt. Fax 501-1902
www.kelso.wednet.edu
Coweeman MS 700/6-8
2000 Allen St 98626 360-501-1750
Randy Heath, prin. Fax 501-1782
Huntington JHS 700/6-8
500 Redpath St 98626 360-501-1700
Elaine Cockrell, prin. Fax 501-1723
Kelso HS 1,800/9-12
1904 Allen St 98626 360-501-1800
Adele Marshall, prin. Fax 501-1843

Three Rivers Christian S 100/7-12
PO Box 33 98626 360-636-1600
Wayne Hayes, admin. Fax 577-5955

Kenmore, King, Pop. 19,564
Northshore SD 417
Supt. — See Bothell
Inglemoor SHS 1,900/10-12
15500 Simonds Rd NE 98028 425-489-6500
Vicki Sherwood, prin. Fax 489-6593
Kenmore JHS 800/7-9
20323 66th Ave NE 98028 425-489-6211
Tim Gordon, prin. Fax 402-5314

Kennewick, Benton, Pop. 60,997
Finley SD 53 1,000/PK-12
224606 E Game Farm Rd 99337 509-586-3217
Suzanne Feeney, supt. Fax 586-4408
www.finleysd.org
Finley MS 300/6-8
37208 S Finley Rd 99337 509-586-7561
Rod Bryson, prin. Fax 582-8452
River View HS 300/9-12
36509 S Lemon Dr 99337 509-582-2158
Russell Hill, prin. Fax 586-9297

Kennewick SD 17 14,100/K-12
524 S Auburn St 99336 509-222-5000
Marlis Lindbloom, supt. Fax 222-5050
www.ksd.org
Desert Hills MS 900/6-8
6011 W 10th Pl 99338 509-222-6600
Steve Jones, prin. Fax 222-6601
Highlands MS 800/6-8
425 S Tweedt St 99336 509-222-6700
Scott Parker, prin. Fax 222-6701
Horse Heaven Hills MS 900/6-8
3500 S Vancouver St 99337 509-222-6800
Susan Denslow, prin. Fax 222-6801
Kamiakin HS 1,600/9-12
600 N Arthur St 99336 509-222-7000
Chris Chelin, prin. Fax 222-7001
Kennewick HS 1,600/9-12
500 S Dayton St 99336 509-222-7100
Jack Anderson, prin. Fax 222-7101
Park MS 800/6-8
1011 W 10th Ave 99336 509-222-6900
Rob Phillips, prin. Fax 222-6901
Southridge HS 1,400/9-12
3520 Southridge Blvd 99338 509-222-7200
Ron Williamson, prin. Fax 222-7201
Tri-Tech Vocational Skills Center Vo/Tech
5929 W Metaline Ave 99336 509-222-7300
Gerry Ringwood, prin. Fax 222-7301

Kent, King, Pop. 81,800
Federal Way SD 210
Supt. — See Federal Way
Totem MS 800/6-8
26630 40th Ave S 98032 253-945-5100
Jeanette Crute-Bullock, prin. Fax 945-5151

Kent SD 415 27,100/K-12
12033 SE 256th St 98030 253-373-7000
Dr. Barbara Grohe, supt. Fax 373-7231
www.kent.k12.wa.us
Kentlake SHS 2,000/9-12
21401 SE 300th St 98042 253-373-4900
Diana Pratt, prin. Fax 373-4908
Kent-Meridian SHS 1,900/9-12
10020 SE 256th St, 253-373-7405
Tim Sherry, prin. Fax 373-7411
Kentridge SHS 2,200/9-12
12430 SE 208th St 98031 253-373-7345
Mike Albrecht, prin. Fax 373-7363
Meridian MS 800/7-8
23480 120th Ave SE 98031 253-373-7383
Doug Boushey, prin. Fax 373-7395
Mill Creek MS 7-8
620 Central Ave N 98032 253-373-7446
Dennis Duffy, prin. Fax 373-7478
Sequoia MS 500/7-8
11000 SE 264th St, 253-373-7542
Beverlie Duff, prin. Fax 373-7554
Other Schools – See Covington, Renton

Rainier Christian MS 100/7-8
26201 180th Ave SE 98042 253-639-7715
Ed Parr, admin. Fax 639-3184

Kettle Falls, Stevens, Pop. 1,588
Kettle Falls SD 212 900/K-12
PO Box 458 99141 509-738-6625
Greg Goodnight, supt. Fax 738-6375
www.kettlefalls.wednet.edu/

Kettle Falls HS 300/9-12
PO Box 458 99141 509-738-6388
James Hill, prin. Fax 738-2670
Kettle Falls MS 300/5-8
PO Box 458 99141 509-738-6014
Tom Graham, prin. Fax 738-2401

Kingston, Kitsap, Pop. 1,270
North Kitsap SD 400
Supt. — See Poulsbo
Kingston HS 9-12
26201 Siyaya Ave NE 98346 360-394-2623
Christy Cole, prin.
Kingston MS 800/6-8
9000 NE West Kingston Rd 98346 360-394-4900
Susan Wistrand, prin. Fax 394-4901

Kirkland, King, Pop. 45,814
Lake Washington SD 414
Supt. — See Redmond
B E S T HS 200/9-12
10903 NE 53rd St 98033 425-828-3289
Gayle Cudworth, prin. Fax 828-3293
Environmental S 100/6-9
8040 NE 132nd St 98034 425-825-1411
Cindy Duenas, prin. Fax 825-0921
Finn Hill JHS 500/7-9
8040 NE 132nd St 98034 425-821-6544
Victor Scarpelli, prin. Fax 814-2955
Futures S, 10601 NE 132nd Pl 98034 100/9-12
Gary Moed, prin. 425-823-7635
International S 400/7-12
11133 NE 65th St 98033 425-889-6880
Cindy Duenas, prin. Fax 889-6881
Juanita SHS 1,100/10-12
10601 NE 132nd St 98034 425-823-7600
Gary Moed, prin. Fax 823-7637
Kamiakin JHS 700/7-9
14111 132nd Ave NE 98034 425-823-6750
Joe Joss, prin. Fax 823-2921
Kirkland JHS 500/7-9
430 18th Ave 98033 425-822-6224
Deborah McCarson, prin. Fax 889-1589
Lake Washington SHS 1,100/10-12
12033 NE 80th St 98033 425-828-3371
Brad Malloy, prin. Fax 828-3390
Northstar JHS 100/7-9
11822 NE 75th St 98033 425-828-3360
Gayle Cudworth, prin. Fax 828-3364

Eastside Preparatory S 100/6-12
10635 NE 38th Pl 98033 425-822-5668
Dr. Terry Macaluso, prin. Fax 822-5648
Lake Washington Technical College Post-Sec.
11605 132nd Ave NE 98034 425-739-8100
Northwest University Post-Sec.
PO Box 579 98083 425-822-8266
Puget Sound Adventist Academy 100/9-12
5320 108th Ave NE 98033 425-822-7554
Doug White, prin. Fax 828-0856

Kittitas, Kittitas, Pop. 1,133
Kittitas SD 403 600/K-12
PO Box 599 98934 509-968-3115
Jerry Harding, supt. Fax 968-4730
www.kittitas.wednet.edu
Kittitas HS 300/6-12
PO Box 1079 98934 509-968-3902
Monty Sabin, prin. Fax 968-3370

Klickitat, Klickitat
Klickitat SD 402 100/K-12
PO Box 37 98628 509-369-4145
Jerry Lynch, supt. Fax 369-3422
www.klickitat.wednet.edu/
Klickitat JSHS 100/7-12
PO Box 37 98628 509-369-4145
Kevin Davis, prin. Fax 369-3422

La Center, Clark, Pop. 1,873
La Center SD 101 1,400/K-12
PO Box 1840 98629 360-263-2131
Mark Mansell, supt. Fax 263-1140
www.lacenterschools.org
La Center HS 400/9-12
PO Box 1780 98629 360-263-1700
Dave Holmes, prin. Fax 263-1705
La Center MS 300/6-8
PO Box 1750 98629 360-263-2136
David Cooke, prin. Fax 263-5936

Lacey, Thurston, Pop. 33,368
North Thurston SD 3 13,100/PK-12
305 College St NE 98516 360-412-4400
Dr. James Koval, supt. Fax 412-4410
www.nthurston.k12.wa.us
Chinook MS 700/7-8
4301 6th Ave NE 98516 360-412-4760
Monica Sweet, prin. Fax 412-4769
Komachin MS 800/7-8
3650 College St SE 98503 360-412-4740
Julie Phipps, prin. Fax 412-4749
Nisqually MS 600/7-8
8100 Steilacoom Rd SE 98503 360-412-4770
Karen Owen, prin. Fax 493-2756
North Thurston HS 1,500/9-12
600 Sleater Kinney Rd NE 98506 360-412-4800
Steve Rood, prin. Fax 412-4819
River Ridge HS 1,200/9-12
350 River Ridge Dr SE 98513 360-412-4820
Karen Remy-Anderson, prin. Fax 412-4839
Timberline HS 1,300/9-12
6120 Mullen Rd SE 98503 360-412-4860
Dave Lehnis, prin. Fax 412-4879

Northwest Christian HS 200/9-12
4710 Park Center Ave NE 98516 360-491-2966
Al Lynch, prin. Fax 491-3086

St. Martin's University Post-Sec.
5300 Pacific Ave SE 98503 360-491-4700

La Conner, Skagit, Pop. 784
La Conner SD 311 600/K-12
PO Box 2103 98257 360-466-3171
Tim Bruce, supt. Fax 466-3523
lcsd.wednet.edu/index.htm
La Conner HS, PO Box 2103 98257 200/9-12
Kurt Schonberg, prin. 360-466-3173
La Conner MS, PO Box 2103 98257 200/6-8
K. C. Knudson, prin. 360-466-4113

La Crosse, Whitman, Pop. 355
LaCrosse SD 126 100/K-12
111 Hill Ave 99143 509-549-3591
Gary Wargo, supt. Fax 549-3529
www.lax.wednet.edu
LaCrosse JSHS 50/6-12
111 Hill Ave 99143 509-549-3592
Doug Curtis, prin. Fax 549-3529

Lakebay, Pierce
Peninsula SD 401
Supt. — See Gig Harbor
Key Peninsula MS 600/6-8
5510 Key Peninsula Hwy N 98349 253-530-4200
Sharon Shaffer, prin. Fax 530-4220

Lake Stevens, Snohomish, Pop. 7,558
Lake Stevens SD 4 7,400/PK-12
12309 22nd St NE 98258 425-335-1500
David Burgess, supt. Fax 335-1549
www.lkstevens.wednet.edu
Lake Stevens HS 2,100/9-12
2908 113th Ave NE 98258 425-335-1515
Ken Collins, prin. Fax 335-1524
North Lake MS 900/6-8
2202 123rd Ave NE 98258 425-335-1530
Gary Taber, prin. Fax 335-1576
Other Schools – See Everett

Lakewood, Snohomish, Pop. 57,671
Clover Park SD 400 12,000/PK-12
10903 Gravelly Lake Dr SW 98499 253-583-5000
Dr. Al Cohen, supt. Fax 583-5198
www.cloverpark.k12.wa.us/
Clover Park HS 1,400/9-12
11023 Gravelly Lake Dr SW 98499 253-583-5500
John Seaton, prin. Fax 583-5508
Hudtloff MS 700/6-8
7702 Phillips Rd SW 98498 253-583-5400
Moureen David, prin. Fax 583-5408
Lakes HS 1,400/9-12
10320 Farwest Dr SW 98498 253-583-5550
Brian Laubach, prin. Fax 583-5558
Lochburn MS 700/6-8
5431 Steilacoom Blvd SW 98499 253-583-5420
Helen Wilson, prin. Fax 583-5428
Mann MS 600/6-8
11509 Holden Rd SW 98498 253-583-5440
Ron Banner, prin. Fax 583-5448
Woodbrook MS 700/6-8
14920 Spring St SW 98439 253-583-5460
Nancy LaChapelle, prin. Fax 583-5468

Clover Park Technical College Post-Sec.
4500 Steilacoom Blvd SW 98499 253-589-5800
Pierce College Post-Sec.
9401 Farwest Dr SW 98498 253-964-6500

Lamont, Whitman, Pop. 99
Lamont SD 264 50/6-8
602 Main St 99017 509-257-2463
Mark Stedman, supt. Fax 257-2316
Lamont MS 50/6-8
602 Main St 99017 509-257-2463
Joseph Whipple, prin. Fax 257-2316

Langley, Island, Pop. 1,018
South Whidbey SD 206 2,000/K-12
PO Box 346 98260 360-221-6100
Fred McCarthy, supt. Fax 221-3835
www.sw.wednet.edu
Langley MS 500/6-8
PO Box 370 98260 360-221-5100
Rod Merrell, prin. Fax 221-8545
South Whidbey HS 700/9-12
PO Box 390 98260 360-221-4300
Mike Johnson, prin. Fax 221-5797

Leavenworth, Chelan, Pop. 2,206
Cascade SD 228 1,400/PK-12
330 Evans St 98826 509-548-5885
Rob Clark, supt. Fax 548-6149
www.cascade.wednet.edu/
Cascade HS 500/9-12
10190 Chumstick Hwy 98826 509-548-5277
Bill Wadlington, prin. Fax 548-7458
Icicle River MS 300/6-8
10195 Titus Rd 98826 509-548-4042
Kenny Renner-Singer, prin. Fax 548-6646

Upper Valley Christian S 100/K-12
111 Ski Hill Dr 98826 509-548-5292
John Bangsund, admin. Fax 548-5293

Lind, Adams, Pop. 576
Lind SD 158 200/PK-12
PO Box 340 99341 509-677-3481
David Thomas, supt. Fax 677-3463
www.lind.k12.wa.us
Lind JSHS 100/7-12
PO Box 340 99341 509-677-3408
John McGregor, prin. Fax 677-3420

Long Beach, Pacific, Pop. 1,386
Ocean Beach SD 101 500/K-12
PO Box 778 98631 360-642-3739
Rainer Houser, supt. Fax 642-1298
www.ocean.k12.wa.us
Other Schools – See Ilwaco

Longview, Cowlitz, Pop. 36,137
Longview SD 122 7,400/PK-12
2715 Lilac St 98632 360-575-7000
Dr. Nicholas Seaver, supt. Fax 575-7022
www.longview.k12.wa.us
Cascade MS, 2821 Parkview Dr 98632 900/6-8
Bruce Holway, prin. 360-577-2703
Long HS 1,100/9-12
2903 Nichols Blvd 98632 360-575-7225
Rolland Johnson, prin. Fax 577-2828
Monticello MS, 1225 28th Ave 98632 900/6-8
Bill Marshall, prin. 360-575-7050
Morris HS, 1602 Mark Morris Ct 98632 1,100/9-12
Chris Fritsch, prin. 360-575-7770
Mt. Solo MS, 5300 Mt Solo Rd 98632 6-8
Lori Cournyer, prin. 360-577-2800

Lower Columbia College Post-Sec.
PO Box 3010 98632 360-577-2300
Stylemasters College of Hair Design Post-Sec.
1224 Commerce Ave 98632 360-636-2720

Lopez Island, San Juan
Lopez Island SD 144 300/K-12
86 School Rd 98261 360-468-2202
Bill Evans, supt. Fax 468-2212
www.lopez.k12.wa.us
Lopez Island MSHS 200/6-12
86 School Rd 98261 360-468-2219
Roland MacNichol, prin.

Lyle, Klickitat
Lyle SD 406 400/K-12
PO Box 368 98635 509-365-2191
Martin Huffman, supt. Fax 365-5000
Lyle HS 100/9-12
PO Box 368 98635 509-365-2211
Phil Williams, prin. Fax 365-2665
Lyle MS 100/7-8
PO Box 368 98635 509-365-2211
Phil Williams, prin. Fax 365-2665

Lynden, Whatcom, Pop. 10,697
Lynden SD 504 2,700/K-12
1203 Bradley Rd 98264 360-354-4443
Dennis L. Carlson Ed.D., supt. Fax 354-7662
www.lynden.wednet.edu
Lynden HS 900/9-12
1201 Bradley Rd 98264 360-354-4401
Jeff Baglio, prin. Fax 354-0991
Lynden MS 600/6-8
516 Main St 98264 360-354-2952
Kris Petersen, prin. Fax 354-6631

Meridian SD 505
Supt. — See Bellingham
Meridian MS 400/6-8
861 Ten Mile Rd 98264 360-398-2291
Gerald Sanderson, prin. Fax 398-8131

Cornerstone Christian S 100/1-12
8872 Northwood Rd 98264 360-318-0663
Otto Bouwman, prin. Fax 318-8175
Lynden Christian HS 500/9-12
515 Drayton St 98264 360-354-3221
Keith Lambert, prin. Fax 354-1047
Lynden Christian MS 300/5-8
503 Lyncs Dr 98264 360-354-3358
Aaron Bishop, prin. Fax 354-6690

Lynnwood, Snohomish, Pop. 33,504
Edmonds SD 15 19,900/PK-12
20420 68th Ave W 98036 425-431-7000
Nick Brossoit Ed.D., supt. Fax 431-7182
www.edmonds.wednet.edu
Alderwood MS 700/7-8
20000 28th Ave W 98036 425-431-7579
Mike VanOrden, prin. Fax 431-7580
College Place MS 700/7-8
7501 208th St SW 98036 425-431-7451
Thea Gardner, prin. Fax 431-7449
Lynnwood HS 1,400/9-12
3001 184th St SW 98037 425-431-7520
David Golden, prin. Fax 431-7527
Meadowdale HS 1,600/9-12
6002 168th St SW 98037 425-431-7650
Dale Cote, prin. Fax 431-7655
Meadowdale MS 700/7-8
6500 168th St SW 98037 425-431-7707
Christine Avery, prin. Fax 431-7714
Other Schools – See Brier, Edmonds, Mountlake Terrace

Edmonds Community College Post-Sec.
20000 68th Ave W 98036 425-640-1500

Mabton, Yakima, Pop. 2,038
Mabton SD 120 900/K-12
PO Box 37 98935 509-894-4852
Sandra Pasiero-Davis, supt. Fax 894-4769
www.mabton.wednet.edu
Mabton JSHS 400/7-12
PO Box 38 98935 509-894-4951
Jay Tyus, prin. Fax 894-4761

Mansfield, Douglas, Pop. 331
Mansfield SD 207 100/PK-12
PO Box 188 98830 509-683-1012
Larry Keller, supt. Fax 683-1281
www.mansfield.wednet.edu/
Mansfield S 100/PK-12
PO Box 188 98830 509-683-1012
Larry Keller, prin. Fax 683-1281

Manson, Chelan
Manson SD 19 600/PK-12
PO Box A 98831 509-687-3140
Steve McKenna, supt. Fax 687-9877
www.manson.org
Manson JSHS 300/7-12
PO Box A 98831 509-687-9585
Marsha Hanson, prin. Fax 687-6109

Maple Valley, King, Pop. 15,153
Tahoma SD 409 6,600/K-12
25720 Maple Valley Black Di 98038 425-413-3400
Mike Maryanski, supt. Fax 413-3455
www.tahoma.wednet.edu
Other Schools – See Covington, Ravensdale

Marysville, Snohomish, Pop. 29,889
Lakewood SD 306 2,600/PK-12
17110 16th Dr NE 98271 360-652-4500
Larry Francois, supt. Fax 652-4502
www.lwsd.wednet.edu
Lakewood MS 600/6-8
16800 16th Dr NE 98271 360-652-4510
Crystal Knight, prin. Fax 652-4512
Other Schools – See Arlington

Marysville SD 25 10,700/PK-12
4220 80th St NE 98270 360-653-7058
Dr. Larry Nyland, supt. Fax 653-5717
www.msvl.k12.wa.us
Cedarcrest MS 1,000/6-8
6400 88th St NE 98270 360-653-0850
Susan Bell, prin. Fax 658-9699
Marysville JHS 1,000/8-9
1605 7th St 98270 360-653-0610
Judy Albertson, prin. Fax 659-2780
Marysville-Pilchuck SHS 2,100/10-12
5611 108th St NE 98271 360-653-0600
Tracy Suchan Toothaker, prin. Fax 659-1364

Grace Academy 400/PK-12
8521 67th Ave NE 98270 360-659-8517
Timothy Lugg, prin. Fax 653-5899

Mattawa, Grant, Pop. 3,287
Wahluke SD 73 1,500/PK-12
PO Box 907 99349 509-932-4565
Gary Greene, supt. Fax 932-4571
www.wsd73.wednet.edu
Schott MS 400/5-8
PO Box 907 99349 509-932-4455
R. Christopher Rust, prin. Fax 932-4282
Sentinel Technical Center Vo/Tech
PO Box 907 99349 509-932-3133
Dale Hedman, prin. Fax 932-3320
Wahluke HS 400/9-12
PO Box 907 99349 509-932-4477
Dale Hedman, prin. Fax 932-4241

Mead, Spokane
Mead SD 354 8,700/K-12
12828 N Newport Hwy 99021 509-465-6000
Thomas Rockefeller, supt. Fax 465-6020
www.mead.k12.wa.us
Mountainside MS 600/7-8
12509 N Market St 99021 509-465-7400
Craig Busch, prin. Fax 465-7420
Mount Spokane HS 1,400/9-12
6015 E Mt Spokane Park Dr 99021 509-465-7200
John Hook, prin. Fax 465-7220
Other Schools – See Spokane

Medical Lake, Spokane, Pop. 4,190
Medical Lake SD 326 2,300/PK-12
PO Box 128 99022 509-565-3100
Dr. Pam Veltri, supt. Fax 565-3102
www.mlsd.org/
Medical Lake HS 700/9-12
PO Box 128 99022 509-565-3200
John McSmith, prin. Fax 565-3201
Medical Lake MS 300/7-8
PO Box 128 99022 509-565-3300
Mike Dahmen, prin. Fax 565-3301

Lakeland Village School Post-Sec.
PO Box 200 99022

Mercer Island, King, Pop. 22,862
Mercer Island SD 400 4,100/K-12
4160 86th Ave SE 98040 206-236-3330
Dr. Cynthia Sickman Simms, supt. Fax 236-3333
www.misd.k12.wa.us
Islander MS 1,000/6-8
8225 SE 72nd St 98040 206-236-3400
Sharon Gillaspie, prin. Fax 236-3408
Mercer Island HS 1,500/9-12
9100 SE 42nd St 98040 206-236-3345
John Harrison, prin. Fax 236-3358

ETC Preparatory Academy 100/K-12
8005 SE 28th St Ste 102 98040 206-236-1095
Meredith Atkins, dir. Fax 236-0998
Northwest Yeshiva HS 100/9-12
5017 90th Ave SE 98040 206-232-5272
Rabbi Bernie Fox, hdmstr. Fax 232-2711

Metaline Falls, Pend Oreille, Pop. 232
Selkirk SD 70 300/PK-12
PO Box 129 99153 509-446-2951
Nancy Lotze, supt. Fax 446-2929
www.selkirk.k12.wa.us
Other Schools – See Ione

Mill Creek, Snohomish, Pop. 13,501
Everett SD 2
Supt. — See Everett
Heatherwood MS 800/6-8
1419 Trillium Blvd SE 98012 425-385-6300
Janet Gillingham, prin. Fax 385-6302

Jackson HS 1,700/9-12
1508 136th St SE 98012 425-385-7000
Terry Cheshire, prin. Fax 385-7002

Monroe, Snohomish, Pop. 15,653
Monroe SD 103 5,200/K-12
200 E Fremont St 98272 360-794-7777
Dr. Ken Hoover, supt. Fax 794-3029
www.monroe.wednet.edu
Monroe HS 1,300/9-12
17001 Tester Rd 98272 360-863-4000
John Lombardi, prin. Fax 805-0528
Monroe MS 500/6-8
351 Short Columbia St 98272 360-794-3020
Linda Boyle, prin. Fax 805-3233
Park Place MS 500/6-8
1408 W Main St 98272 360-794-3010
JoAnn Carbonetti, prin. Fax 794-7833
Other Schools – See Snohomish

Montesano, Grays Harbor, Pop. 3,399
Montesano SD 66 1,300/PK-12
302 N Church St 98563 360-249-3942
Dr. Marti Harruff, supt. Fax 249-3391
www.monte.wednet.edu
Montesano JSHS 700/7-12
303 N Church St 98563 360-249-4041
Robert Corley, prin. Fax 249-4459
Community Education Adult
302 N Church St 98563 360-249-5781
Judy Thompson, coord. Fax 249-3391

Morton, Lewis, Pop. 1,083
Morton SD 214 400/K-12
PO Box H 98356 360-496-5300
John Flaherty, supt. Fax 586-3208
www.morton.wednet.edu
Morton JSHS 300/6-12
PO Box F 98356 360-496-5137
Joshua Brooks, prin. Fax 496-6035

Moses Lake, Grant, Pop. 16,793
Moses Lake SD 161 6,900/K-12
920 W Ivy Ave 98837 509-766-2650
Steven Chestnut, supt. Fax 766-2678
www.moseslakeschools.org
Chief Moses MS 800/6-8
1111 E Nelson Rd 98837 509-766-2661
Mark Johnson, prin. Fax 766-2680
Frontier MS 700/6-8
517 W 3rd Ave 98837 509-766-2662
Chris Lupo, prin. Fax 766-2663
Moses Lake HS 1,800/9-12
803 Sharon Ave E 98837 509-766-2666
Dave Balcom, prin. Fax 766-2682

Big Bend Community College Post-Sec.
7662 Chanute St NE 98837 509-762-5351
Moses Lake Christian Academy 300/PK-12
1475 Nelson Rd NE Ste A 98837 509-765-9704
LeAnne Parton, admin. Fax 765-3698

Mossyrock, Lewis, Pop. 504
Mossyrock SD 206 600/K-12
PO Box 478 98564 360-983-3181
Dr. Karen Ernest, supt. Fax 983-8111
viking.mossyrock.k12.wa.us
Mossyrock HS 200/9-12
PO Box 454 98564 360-983-3183
Jim Forrest, prin. Fax 983-3188
Mossyrock JHS 100/7-8
PO Box 454 98564 360-983-3183
Jim Forrest, prin. Fax 983-3188

Mountlake Terrace, Snohomish, Pop. 20,251
Edmonds SD 15
Supt. — See Lynnwood
Mountlake Terrace HS 1,700/9-12
21801 44th Ave W 98043 425-431-7776
Greg Schwab, prin. Fax 431-7771

North Sound Christian HS 200/7-12
23607 54th Ave W 98043 425-774-7773
Debbie Schindler, admin. Fax 774-3218

Mount Vernon, Skagit, Pop. 29,271
Mount Vernon SD 320 5,700/K-12
124 E Lawrence St 98273 360-428-6110
Carl Bruner, supt. Fax 428-6172
www.mv.k12.wa.us
LaVenture MS 400/7-8
1200 N Laventure Rd 98273 360-428-6116
Tara Dowd, prin. Fax 428-6189
Mount Baker MS 500/7-8
2310 E Section St 98274 360-428-6127
Beth Ashley, prin. Fax 428-6155
Mount Vernon HS 1,800/9-12
314 N 9th St 98273 360-428-6100
David Anderson, prin. Fax 428-6152

Mt. Vernon Beauty School Post-Sec.
615 S 1st St 98273 360-336-6553
Mt. Vernon Christian S 300/PK-12
820 W Blackburn Rd 98273 360-424-9157
Patrick DeJong, prin. Fax 424-9256
Skagit Valley College Post-Sec.
2405 E College Way 98273 360-416-7600

Mukilteo, Snohomish, Pop. 19,857
Mukilteo SD 6
Supt. — See Everett
Harbour Pointe MS 900/6-8
5000 Harbour Pointe Blvd 98275 425-356-6658
Nikki Cannon, prin. Fax 356-6660
Kamiak HS 2,200/9-12
10801 Harbour Pointe Blvd 98275 425-356-6620
Keith Rittel, prin. Fax 356-6635

Olympic View MS 800/6-8
2602 Mukilteo Speedway 98275 425-356-1308
Nancy Coogan, prin. Fax 356-1332

Naches, Yakima, Pop. 681
Naches Valley SD JT3 1,600/K-12
PO Box 99 98937 509-653-2220
Duane Lyons, supt. Fax 653-1211
www.naches.wednet.edu
Naches Valley HS 500/9-12
PO Box 159 98937 509-653-2342
Rich Rouleau, prin. Fax 653-2921
Naches Valley MS 500/5-8
PO Box 39 98937 509-653-2725
Todd Hilmes, prin. Fax 653-2729

Nile Christian S / Hope Academy 50/K-12
370 Flying H Loop 98937 509-658-2990
Bruce Gillespie, prin. Fax 658-2009

Napavine, Lewis, Pop. 1,449
Napavine SD 14 700/PK-12
PO Box 840 98565 360-262-3303
George Crawford, supt. Fax 262-9737
www.napa.k12.wa.us
Napavine JSHS 300/7-12
PO Box 357 98565 360-262-3301
Douglas Skinner, prin. Fax 262-9541

Naselle, Pacific
Naselle-Grays River Valley SD 155 300/K-12
793 State Route 4 98638 360-484-7123
Alan Bennett, supt. Fax 484-3191
www.naselle.wednet.edu
Naselle-Grays River Valley S 200/K-12
793 State Route 4 98638 360-484-7121
Karen Wirkkala, prin. Fax 484-3191

Neah Bay, Clallam, Pop. 916
Cape Flattery SD 401
Supt. — See Sekiu
Neah Bay S 300/K-12
PO Box 86 98357 360-645-2221
Ann Renker, prin. Fax 645-2574

Newman Lake, Spokane
East Valley SD 361
Supt. — See Spokane
Mountain View MS 500/6-8
6011 N Chase Rd 99025 509-226-1379
Jim McAdam, prin. Fax 226-3082

Newport, Pend Oreille, Pop. 2,157
Newport SD 56-415 1,200/PK-12
PO Box 70 99156 509-447-3167
Teresa von Marbod, supt. Fax 447-2553
www.newport.wednet.edu
Halstead MS 400/5-8
PO Box 70 99156 509-447-2426
Janet Burcham, prin. Fax 447-4914
Newport HS 400/9-12
PO Box 70 99156 509-447-2481
Steve McCoy, prin. Fax 447-4354

Nine Mile Falls, Spokane
Nine Mile Falls SD 325 1,600/PK-12
10110 W Charles Rd 99026 509-340-4300
Michael Green, supt. Fax 340-4301
www.9mile.org
Lakeside HS 600/9-12
5909 Highway 291 99026 509-340-4200
Mark St. Clair, prin. Fax 340-4201
Lakeside MS 400/6-8
6169 Highway 291 99026 509-340-4100
Jeff Baerwald, prin. Fax 340-4101

Northport, Stevens, Pop. 338
Northport SD 211 200/K-12
PO Box 1280 99157 509-732-4441
Patsy Guglielmino, supt. Fax 732-6606
www.northportschools.org
Northport HS 100/9-12
PO Box 1280 99157 509-732-4430
Patsy Guglielmino, prin. Fax 233-2815

Oakesdale, Whitman, Pop. 395
Oakesdale SD 324 100/K-12
PO Box 228 99158 509-285-5296
Steven Deal, supt. Fax 285-5121
www.oakesdale.wednet.edu
Oakesdale HS 100/9-12
PO Box 228 99158 509-285-5296
Karl Ostheller, prin. Fax 285-5121

Oak Harbor, Island, Pop. 22,327
Oak Harbor SD 201 5,800/PK-12
350 S Oak Harbor St 98277 360-279-5000
Dr. Rick Schulte, supt. Fax 279-5070
www.ohsd.net
North Whidbey MS 600/6-8
67 NE Izett St 98277 360-279-5500
Dale Leach, prin. Fax 675-1420
Oak Harbor HS 1,800/9-12
950 NW 2nd Ave 98277 360-279-5400
Dwight Lundstrom, prin. Fax 679-4846
Oak Harbor MS 700/6-8
150 SW 6th Ave 98277 360-279-5300
Peggy Ellis, prin. Fax 279-5399

Oakville, Grays Harbor, Pop. 688
Oakville SD 400 200/K-12
PO Box H 98568 360-273-0171
Brian Metke, supt. Fax 273-6724
Oakville HS 100/9-12
PO Box H 98568 360-273-5947
Kevin Acuff, prin. Fax 273-8229
Oakville MS 4-8
PO Box H 98568 360-273-5947
Tom Phimister, prin. Fax 273-8229

Ocean Shores, Grays Harbor, Pop. 4,467
North Beach SD 64 700/K-12
PO Box 159 98569 360-289-2447
Stanley Pinnick, supt. Fax 289-2492
www.northbeach.k12.wa.us
North Beach HS 200/9-12
PO Box 969 98569 360-289-3888
Roger Lee, prin. Fax 289-0996
North Beach MS 100/7-8
PO Box 969 98569 360-289-2666
Roger Lee, prin. Fax 289-0996

Odessa, Lincoln, Pop. 942
Odessa SD 105-157-166 J 200/K-12
PO Box 248 99159 509-982-2668
Douglas L. Johnson, supt. Fax 982-0163
www.odessa.wednet.edu/
Odessa JSHS 200/6-12
PO Box 248 99159 509-982-2111
Ken C. Schutz, prin. Fax 982-0163

Okanogan, Okanogan, Pop. 2,398
Okanogan SD 105 1,000/K-12
PO Box 592 98840 509-422-3629
Dr. Richard Johnson, supt. Fax 422-1525
www.oksd.wednet.edu
Okanogan HS 300/9-12
PO Box 592 98840 509-422-3770
Bob Shacklett, prin. Fax 422-4457
Okanogan MS 200/6-8
PO Box 592 98840 509-422-2680
Brett Baum, prin. Fax 422-0068

Olympia, Thurston, Pop. 44,114
Olympia SD 111 9,000/K-12
1113 Legion Way SE 98501 360-596-6100
Bill Lahmann, supt. Fax 596-6111
osd.wednet.edu
Capital HS 1,500/9-12
2707 Conger Ave NW 98502 360-596-8000
Nancy Faaren, prin. Fax 596-8001
Jefferson MS 500/6-8
2200 Conger Ave NW 98502 360-596-3200
Michael Cimino, prin. Fax 596-3201
Marshall MS 400/6-8
3939 20th Ave NW 98502 360-596-7600
Kevin Evoy, prin. Fax 596-7601
Olympia HS 1,800/9-12
1302 North St SE 98501 360-596-7000
Matt Grant, prin. Fax 596-7001
Reeves MS 400/6-8
2200 Quince St NE 98506 360-596-3400
Martha Roth, prin. Fax 596-3401
Washington MS 700/6-8
3100 Cain Rd SE 98501 360-596-3000
Joni Wolpert, prin. Fax 596-3001

Tumwater SD 33
Supt. — See Tumwater
West Black Hills HS 1,000/9-12
7741 Littlerock Rd SW 98512 360-709-7800
Jim Hainer, prin. Fax 709-7802

Evergreen State College Post-Sec.
2700 Evergreen Pkwy NW 98505 360-866-6000
Gospel Outreach Christian S 100/1-12
1925 S Bay Rd NE 98506 360-786-0070
David Hill, prin. Fax 357-1417
Nova S 100/6-8
2020 22nd Ave SE 98501 360-491-7097
Lisa Iverson, admin. Fax 491-0775
Olympia Christian S 100/PK-10
1416 26th Ave NE 98506 360-352-1831
Anita McKown, prin. Fax 352-1195

Omak, Okanogan, Pop. 4,755
Omak SD 19 1,500/PK-12
PO Box 833 98841 509-826-0320
R. Robert Risinger, supt. Fax 826-7689
www.omaksd.wednet.edu
Omak HS 500/9-12
PO Box 833 98841 509-826-5150
John Belcher, prin. Fax 826-8515
Omak MS 300/7-8
PO Box 833 98841 509-826-2320
John Belcher, prin. Fax 826-7696

Wenatchee Valley College Post-Sec.
PO Box 2058 98841 509-422-7805

Onalaska, Lewis
Onalaska SD 300 800/PK-12
540 Carlisle Ave 98570 360-978-4111
Dale McDaniel, supt. Fax 978-4185
www.onysd.wednet.edu
Onalaska HS 300/9-12
540 Carlisle Ave 98570 360-978-4111
Bill Huizinga, prin. Fax 978-5040

Oroville, Okanogan, Pop. 1,599
Oroville SD 410 700/PK-12
816 Juniper St 98844 509-476-2281
Dr. Ernie Bartelson, supt. Fax 476-2190
www.oroville.wednet.edu/
Oroville JSHS 300/7-12
816 Juniper St 98844 509-476-3612
Steve Quick, prin. Fax 476-3224

Orting, Pierce, Pop. 4,789
Orting SD 344 2,000/K-12
120 Washington Ave N 98360 360-893-6500
Jeff Davis, supt. Fax 893-2300
www.orting.wednet.edu
Orting HS 600/9-12
320 Washington Ave N 98360 360-893-2246
Gerald Black, prin. Fax 893-5701
Orting MS 500/6-8
121 Whitesell St NE 98360 360-893-3565
Patrick Kelly, prin. Fax 893-2919

Othello, Adams, Pop. 6,221
Othello SD 147-163-55 3,200/K-12
615 E Juniper St 99344 509-488-2659
George Juarez, supt. Fax 488-5876
www.othello.wednet.edu
McFarland JHS 500/7-8
790 S 10th Ave 99344 509-488-3326
Dennis Adams, prin. Fax 488-4844
Othello HS 800/9-12
340 S 7th Ave 99344 509-488-3351
Matt Stevens, prin. Fax 488-4600

Palouse, Whitman, Pop. 945
Palouse SD 301 200/PK-12
600 E Alder St 99161 509-878-1921
Bev Fox, supt. Fax 878-1948
www.garpal.wednet.edu
Garfield-Palouse HS 100/9-12
600 E Alder St 99161 509-878-1921
Bev Fox, prin. Fax 878-1675

Pasco, Franklin, Pop. 46,494
Pasco SD 1 11,000/K-12
1215 W Lewis St 99301 509-543-6700
Saundra L. Hill, supt. Fax 546-2685
www.pasco.wednet.edu
McLoughlin MS 900/6-8
2803 N Road 88 99301 509-547-4542
Michelle Whitney, prin. Fax 543-6797
Ochoa MS 800/6-8
1801 E Sheppard St 99301 509-543-6742
Jackie Ramirez, prin. Fax 543-6744
Pasco HS 2,800/9-12
1108 N 10th Ave 99301 509-547-5581
Raul Sital, prin. Fax 546-2684
Stevens MS 700/6-8
1120 N 10th Ave 99301 509-543-6798
Robert Elizondo, prin. Fax 546-2854

Clare's Beauty College Post-Sec.
104 N 4th Ave 99301 509-547-8871
Columbia Basin College Post-Sec.
2600 N 20th Ave 99301 509-547-0511
Kingspoint Christian S 100/PK-12
7900 W Court St 99301 509-547-6498
Georgia Perkins, admin. Fax 547-6788
Tri Cities Preparatory S 100/9-12
9612 Saint Thomas Dr 99301 509-546-2465
Steve Potter, prin. Fax 546-2490
Tri-City Junior Academy 100/K-10
4115 W Henry St 99301 509-547-8092
Anthony Oucharek, prin. Fax 547-8516

Pateros, Okanogan, Pop. 624
Pateros SD 122 200/K-12
PO Box 98 98846 509-923-2751
Lawrence Keller, supt. Fax 923-2283
www.pateros.org
Pateros S 200/K-12
PO Box 98 98846 509-923-2343
Laura Christian, prin. Fax 923-2283

Pe Ell, Lewis, Pop. 680
Pe Ell SD 301 300/K-12
PO Box 368 98572 360-291-3244
Scott Fenter, supt. Fax 291-3823
Pe Ell S 300/K-12
PO Box 368 98572 360-291-3244
F. Patrick Meehan, prin. Fax 291-3823

Pomeroy, Garfield, Pop. 1,480
Pomeroy SD 110 400/K-12
PO Box 950 99347 509-843-3393
James Kowalkowski, supt. Fax 843-3046
www.psd.wednet.edu
Pomeroy JSHS 200/7-12
PO Box 950 99347 509-843-1331
Kim Spacek, prin. Fax 843-8245

Port Angeles, Clallam, Pop. 18,927
Port Angeles SD 121 4,700/K-12
216 E 4th St 98362 360-457-8575
Gary D. Cohn, supt. Fax 457-4649
www.portangelesschools.org/
North Olympic Peninsula Skills Center Vo/Tech
905 W 9th St 98363 360-565-1533
Jacob Jackson, prin. Fax 417-9068
Port Angeles HS 1,500/9-12
304 E Park Ave 98362 360-452-7602
Scott Harker, prin. Fax 452-0256
Roosevelt MS 500/6-8
106 Monroe Rd 98362 360-452-8973
Diane Metcalf, prin. Fax 452-4011
Stevens MS 600/6-8
1139 W 14th St 98363 360-452-5590
Charles Lisk, prin. Fax 457-5709

Olympic Christian S 200/PK-12
43 OBrien Rd 98362 360-457-4640
Brian Clark, prin. Fax 457-4612
Peninsula College Post-Sec.
1502 E Lauridsen Blvd 98362 360-452-9277

Port Hadlock, Jefferson, Pop. 2,742

Northwest School of Wooden Boatbuilding Post-Sec.
42 N Water St 98339 360-385-4948

Port Orchard, Kitsap, Pop. 7,986
South Kitsap SD 402 11,000/K-12
1962 Hoover Ave SE 98366 360-874-7000
Dr. Beverly Cheney, supt. Fax 874-7068
www.skitsap.wednet.edu
Cedar Heights JHS 900/7-9
2220 Pottery Ave 98366 360-874-6020
Andrew Cain, prin. Fax 874-6420
Sedgewick JHS 1,000/7-9
8995 SE Sedgwick Rd 98366 360-874-6090
Jay Villars, prin. Fax 874-6430
South Kitsap SHS 2,500/10-12
425 Mitchell Ave 98366 360-874-5600
Jerry Holsten, prin. Fax 874-5892
Whitman JHS 1,000/7-9
1887 Madrona Dr SE 98366 360-874-6160
Brian Carlson, prin. Fax 874-6440

Burley Christian S 100/PK-12
14687 Olympic Dr SE 98367 253-851-8619
Dennis Myers, admin. Fax 857-0093
South Kitsap Christian S 100/PK-12
1780 Lincoln Ave SE 98366 360-876-5595
Sandy Jennings, admin. Fax 876-2206

Port Townsend, Jefferson, Pop. 9,001
Port Townsend SD 50 1,500/K-12
450 Fir St 98368 360-379-4502
Thomas Opstad, supt. Fax 385-3617
www.ptsd.wednet.edu
Blue Heron MS 400/6-8
3939 San Juan Ave 98368 360-379-4540
Mark Decker, prin. Fax 379-4548
Port Townsend HS 600/9-12
1500 Van Ness St 98368 360-379-4520
Carrie Ehrhardt, prin. Fax 379-4505

Poulsbo, Kitsap, Pop. 7,593
North Kitsap SD 400 6,800/PK-12
18360 Caldart Ave NE 98370 360-779-8704
Dr. Eugene Medina, supt. Fax 697-3175
www.nkschools.org
North Kitsap HS 1,500/9-12
1780 NE Hostmark St 98370 360-779-4408
Kathy Prasch, prin. Fax 598-8406
Poulsbo MS 800/6-8
2003 NE Hostmark St 98370 360-779-4453
Matt Vandeleur, prin. Fax 598-1041
Other Schools – See Kingston

Northwest College of Art Post-Sec.
16301 Creative Dr NE 98370 360-779-9993

Prescott, Walla Walla, Pop. 327
Prescott SD 402-37 300/K-12
PO Box 65 99348 509-849-2216
Scott Harris, supt. Fax 849-2800
www.prescott.k12.wa.us/
Prescott JSHS, PO Box 65 99348 100/7-12
Ron Woodruff, prin. 509-849-2215

Prosser, Benton, Pop. 5,140
Prosser SD 116 2,800/K-12
823 Park Ave 99350 509-786-3323
Dr. Ray Tolcacher, supt. Fax 786-2062
www.prosserschools.org/
Housel MS 700/6-8
2001 Highland Dr 99350 509-786-1732
Steven Ellis, prin. Fax 786-2814
Prosser HS 800/9-12
1203 Prosser Ave 99350 509-786-1224
Kevin Lusk, prin. Fax 786-4227

Pullman, Whitman, Pop. 25,262
Pullman SD 267 2,300/K-12
240 SE Dexter St 99163 509-332-3581
Paul Sturm, supt. Fax 334-0375
www.psd267.wednet.edu
Lincoln MS 500/6-8
315 SE Crestview St 99163 509-334-3411
Bill Motsenbocker, prin. Fax 334-9678
Pullman HS 700/9-12
510 NW Larry St 99163 509-332-1551
Jason Thompson, prin. Fax 332-6868

Pullman Christian S 100/K-12
345 SW Kimball Dr 99163 509-332-3545
Sherri Goetze, prin. Fax 332-5433
Washington State University Post-Sec.
1 SE Stadium Way 99164 509-335-3564

Puyallup, Pierce, Pop. 35,861
Puyallup SD 3 19,800/PK-12
PO Box 370 98371 253-841-1301
Dr. Tony Apostle, supt. Fax 840-8959
www.puyallup.k12.wa.us
Aylen JHS 900/7-9
101 15th St SW 98371 253-841-8723
Christine Moloney, prin. Fax 840-8856
Ballou JHS 900/7-9
9916 136th St E 98373 253-841-8725
Sandra Jacobson, prin. Fax 840-8819
Emerald Ridge SHS 1,500/10-12
12405 184th St E 98374 253-435-6300
Brian Lowney, prin. Fax 435-6310
Ferrucci JHS 800/7-9
3213 Wildwood Park Dr 98374 253-841-8756
Ailene Baxter, prin. Fax 840-8855
Kalles JHS 900/7-9
515 3rd St SE 98372 253-841-8729
Mario Casello, prin. Fax 841-6414
Puyallup SHS 1,600/10-12
105 7th St SW 98371 253-841-8711
Mike Joyner, prin. Fax 841-8624
Rogers SHS 1,500/10-12
12801 86th Ave E 98373 253-841-8717
Scott Brittain, prin. Fax 840-8802
Stahl JHS 1,100/7-9
9610 168th Street Ct E 98375 253-840-8881
John Bustad, prin. Fax 840-8992
Other Schools – See Edgewood

BJ's Beauty & Barber College Post-Sec.
12020 Meridian E Ste K 98373 253-848-1595
Cascade Christian JSHS 500/7-12
811 21st St SE 98372 253-445-9706
Terry Broberg, prin. Fax 445-0859
Pierce College Post-Sec.
1601 39th Ave SE 98374 253-840-8470

Quilcene, Jefferson
Quilcene SD 48 300/K-12
PO Box 40 98376 360-765-3363
David Andersen, supt. Fax 765-4183
www.quilcene.wednet.edu
Quilcene S 300/K-12
PO Box 40 98376 360-765-3363
David Andersen, prin. Fax 765-4183

Quincy, Grant, Pop. 5,568
Quincy SD 144-101 2,400/K-12
119 J St SW 98848 509-787-4571
Roger Fox, supt. Fax 787-4336
www.qsd.wednet.edu
Quincy HS 600/9-12
16 6th Ave SE 98848 509-787-3501
Chris McKnight, prin. Fax 787-8989
Quincy High Tech HS Vo/Tech
404 1st Ave SW 98848 509-787-1678
Garry Stidman, prin. Fax 787-1680
Quincy JHS 400/7-8
417 C St SE 98848 509-787-4435
Scott Ramsey, prin. Fax 787-8949

Rainier, Thurston, Pop. 1,649
Rainier SD 307 900/K-12
PO Box 98 98576 360-446-2207
Dennis Friedrich, supt. Fax 446-2918
www.rainier.wednet.edu
Rainier HS 300/9-12
PO Box 98 98576 360-446-2205
Jennifer Shaw, prin. Fax 446-2208
Rainier MS, PO Box 98 98576 100/7-8
Paulette Johnson, prin. 360-446-2206

Randle, Lewis
White Pass SD 303 600/PK-12
PO Box 188 98377 360-497-3791
Brian Talbott, supt. Fax 497-2560
www.wpsd.wednet.edu
White Pass JSHS 400/7-12
516 Silverbrook Rd 98377 360-497-5816
Karen Larsen, prin. Fax 497-7773

Ravensdale, King, Pop. 3,778
Tahoma SD 409
Supt. — See Maple Valley
Tahoma JHS 1,100/8-9
25600 SE Summit-Landsburg R 98051
425-413-5600
Rob Morrow, prin. Fax 413-5500

Raymond, Pacific, Pop. 2,995
Raymond SD 116 500/K-12
1016 Commercial St 98577 360-942-3415
Stephen A. Holland, supt. Fax 942-3416
www.raymond.k12.wa.us
Raymond JSHS 300/7-12
1016 Commercial St 98577 360-942-2474
Ron Bell, prin. Fax 942-2504

Willapa Valley SD 160 300/K-12
22 Viking Way 98577 360-942-5855
Dr. Paula Akerlund, supt. Fax 942-3216
www.willapa.wednet.edu
Menlo MS, 22 Viking Way 98577 6-8
Rob Friese, prin. 360-942-2006
Willapa Valley HS 200/9-12
22 Viking Way 98577 360-942-2006
Rob Friese, prin.

Reardan, Spokane, Pop. 610
Reardan-Edwall SD 9 500/K-12
PO Box 225 99029 509-796-2701
Doug Asbjornsen, supt. Fax 796-4954
www.reardan.net
Reardan JSHS, PO Box 225 99029 200/7-12
Gene Nelson, prin. 509-796-2711

Redmond, King, Pop. 47,579
Lake Washington SD 414 23,400/K-12
PO Box 97039 98073 425-702-3200
Dr. Don Saul, supt. Fax 702-3213
www.lwsd.org
Eastlake SHS 1,300/10-12
400 228th Ave NE 98074 425-836-6600
Rondel Hardie, prin. Fax 836-6609
Evergreen JHS 800/7-9
6900 208th Ave NE 98053 425-868-2600
Jan Olson, prin. Fax 868-2613
Inglewood JHS 1,100/7-9
24120 NE 8th St 98074 425-836-7280
Tim Stonich, prin. Fax 868-0628
Redmond JHS 900/7-9
10055 166th Ave NE 98052 425-885-7034
Prato Barone, prin. Fax 556-9806
Redmond SHS 1,400/10-12
17272 NE 104th St 98052 425-498-7130
Jane Todd, prin. Fax 498-7169
Rose Hill JHS 600/7-9
13505 NE 75th St 98052 425-881-2079
Jay Ellis, prin. Fax 556-0629
Stella Schola S 100/6-8
13505 NE 75th St 98052 425-558-0842
Jay Ellis, prin. Fax 556-0629
Other Schools – See Kirkland

Bear Creek S 700/K-12
8905 208th Ave NE 98053 425-898-1720
Karen Beman, hdmstr. Fax 898-1430
DigiPen Institute of Technology Post-Sec.
5001 150th Ave NE 98052 425-558-0299
Overlake S 500/5-12
20301 NE 108th St 98053 425-868-1000
Dr. Francisco Grijalva, hdmstr. Fax 868-6770

Renton, King, Pop. 55,817
Issaquah SD 411
Supt. — See Issaquah
Liberty HS 1,300/9-12
16655 SE 136th St 98059 425-837-4800
Mike Deletis, prin. Fax 837-4905
Maywood MS 900/6-8
14490 168th Ave SE 98059 425-837-6900
Patrick Murphy, prin. Fax 837-6910

Kent SD 415
Supt. — See Kent
Meeker MS 700/7-8
12600 SE 192nd St 98058 253-373-7284
Jeff Pelzel, prin. Fax 373-7560
Northwood MS 700/7-8
17007 SE 184th St 98058 253-373-7780
Colleen Nelson, prin. Fax 373-7788

Renton SD 403 12,800/K-12
300 SW 7th St 98057 425-204-2340
Dr. Mary Alice Heuschel, supt. Fax 204-2456
www.renton.wednet.edu
Hazen HS 1,300/9-12
1101 Hoquiam Ave NE 98059 425-204-4200
Sue Beeson, prin. Fax 204-4220
Lindbergh HS 1,200/9-12
16426 128th Ave SE 98058 425-204-3200
Tres Genger, prin. Fax 204-3220
McKnight MS 1,100/6-8
1200 Edmonds Ave NE 98056 425-204-3600
Mary Merritt, prin. Fax 204-3680
Nelson MS 1,100/6-8
2403 Jones Ave S 98055 425-204-3000
Dr. James Noddings, prin. Fax 204-3079
Renton HS 1,000/9-12
400 S 2nd St 98057 425-204-3400
Kathryn Hutchinson, prin. Fax 204-3412
Other Schools – See Seattle

Everest College Post-Sec.
981 Powell Ave SW Ste 200 98057 425-255-3281
Pima Medical Institute Post-Sec.
555 S Renton Village Pl 98057 425-228-9600
Renton Technical College Post-Sec.
3000 NE 4th St 98056 425-235-2352

Republic, Ferry, Pop. 988
Republic SD 309 400/K-12
30306 E Highway 20 99166 509-775-3173
Dan Chaplik, supt. Fax 775-3712
www.republic.wednet.edu
Republic HS 200/9-12
30306 E Highway 20 99166 509-775-3171
Nancy Giddings, prin. Fax 775-1098
Republic JHS 7-8
30306 E Highway 20 99166 509-775-3171
Shawn Anderson, prin. Fax 775-1098

Richland, Benton, Pop. 44,317
Richland SD 400 9,200/K-12
615 Snow Ave 99352 509-967-6000
Dr. Richard Semler, supt. Fax 942-2401
www.rsd.edu
Carmichael MS 800/6-8
620 Thayer Dr 99352 509-942-2468
Tim Praino, prin. Fax 942-2471
Chief Joseph MS 800/6-8
504 Wilson St, 509-942-2487
Jon Lobdell, prin. Fax 942-2492
Hanford HS 1,300/9-12
450 Hanford St, 509-371-2600
Todd Baddley, prin. Fax 371-2601
Richland HS 2,000/9-12
930 Long Ave 99352 509-942-2500
Sergio Fossa, prin. Fax 942-2512
Other Schools – See West Richland

Liberty Christian S of the Tri-Cities 500/PK-12
2200 Williams Blvd, 509-946-0602
Leonard Edlung, admin. Fax 943-5623

Ridgefield, Clark, Pop. 2,869
Ridgefield SD 122 1,900/K-12
2724 S Hillhurst Rd 98642 360-619-1300
John Simpson, supt. Fax 619-1397
www.ridge.k12.wa.us
Ridgefield HS 600/9-12
2630 S Hillhurst Rd 98642 360-619-1320
John Kniseley, prin. Fax 619-1395
View Ridge MS 300/7-8
510 Pioneer St 98642 360-619-1400
Gary Dietderich, prin. Fax 619-1459

Ritzville, Adams, Pop. 1,721
Ritzville SD 160-67 400/PK-12
209 E Wellsandt Rd 99169 509-659-1660
Dwight Remick, supt. Fax 659-0927
www.ritzville.wednet.edu
Ritzville HS 100/9-12
209 E Wellsandt Rd 99169 509-659-1720
David Funk, prin. Fax 659-5140

Rochester, Thurston, Pop. 1,250
Rochester SD 401 2,000/K-12
PO Box 457 98579 360-273-5536
James Anderson, supt. Fax 273-5547
www.rochester.wednet.edu/
Rochester HS 600/9-12
19800 Carper Rd SW 98579 360-273-5534
Greg McDaniel, prin. Fax 273-2570
Rochester MS 500/6-8
PO Box 398 98579 360-273-5958
Will Maus, prin. Fax 273-2045

Rockford, Spokane, Pop. 494
Freeman SD 358 600/K-12
15001 S Jackson Rd 99030 509-291-3695
Sergio Hernandez, supt. Fax 291-3636
www.freemansd.org
Freeman HS 300/9-12
14626 S Jackson Rd 99030 509-291-3721
Patrick Kane, prin. Fax 291-7337
Freeman MS 6-8
14917 S Jackson Rd 99030 509-291-7301
Jim Straw, prin. Fax 291-7339

Rosalia, Whitman, Pop. 600
Rosalia SD 320 300/K-12
916 S Josephine Ave 99170 509-523-3061
Dr. Thomas Crowley, supt. Fax 523-3861
www.rosalia.wednet.edu
Rosalia S 300/K-12
916 S Josephine Ave 99170 509-523-3061
Darrell Kuhn, prin. Fax 523-3861

Royal City, Grant, Pop. 1,952
Royal SD 160 1,400/K-12
PO Box 486 99357 509-346-2222
Rosemarie Search, supt. Fax 346-8746
www.royal.wednet.edu/
Royal HS 400/9-12
PO Box 486 99357 509-346-2256
Jack Hill, prin. Fax 346-9739
Royal MS 300/6-8
PO Box 486 99357 509-346-2268
David Jaderlund, prin. Fax 346-2269

Saint John, Whitman, Pop. 552
St. John SD 322 100/PK-12
301 W Nob Hill St 99171 509-648-3336
Rick Winters, supt. Fax 648-3451
www.sje.wednet.edu/index.html
St. John-Endicott HS 100/9-12
301 W Nob Hill St 99171 509-648-3336
Rob Roettger, prin.

SeaTac, King, Pop. 25,081
Highline SD 401
Supt. — See Burien
Academy of Citizenship & Empowerment HS 1,200/9-12
4424 S 188th St 98188 206-433-2342
Stacy Spector, prin. Fax 998-7238
Chinook MS 600/7-8
18650 42nd Ave S 98188 206-433-2231
Evie Livingston, prin. Fax 433-2308
Global Connections HS 9-12
4424 S 188th St 98188 206-433-2343
Rick Harwood, prin. Fax 433-2227
Odyssey HS 9-12
4424 S 188th St 98188 206-433-2344
Joan Ferrigno, prin. Fax 988-7239

Christian Faith S 400/K-12
21024 24th Ave S 98198 206-878-6036
Dr. Natalie Ellington, prin. Fax 878-3610
Seattle Christian S 700/K-12
18301 Military Rd S 98188 206-246-8241
Gloria Hunter, supt. Fax 246-9066

Seattle, King, Pop. 573,911
Highline SD 401
Supt. — See Burien
Arts and Academics Academy 9-12
830 SW 116th St 98146 206-433-2311
Victor Anderson, prin. Fax 433-2488
Aviation HS 9-12
6770 E Marginal Way S 98108 206-716-0006
Reba Gilman, prin. Fax 716-0020
Cascade MS 600/7-8
11212 10th Ave SW 98146 206-433-2551
Fax 433-2296
Health Sciences & Human Services HS 9-12
830 SW 116th St 98146 206-433-2311
Paula Montgomery, prin. Fax 433-2488
Technology Communications/Engineering S 9-12
830 SW 116th St 98146 206-433-2311
Eric Hong, prin. Fax 433-2488

Renton SD 403
Supt. — See Renton
Dimmitt MS 900/6-8
12320 80th Ave S 98178 425-204-2800
Dan Sakaue, prin. Fax 204-2812

Seattle SD 1 45,400/PK-12
PO Box 34165 98124 206-252-0000
Raj Manhas, supt. Fax 252-0102
www.seattleschools.org
Ballard HS 1,600/9-12
1418 NW 65th St 98117 206-252-1000
Phil Brockman, prin. Fax 252-1001
Center S 300/9-12
305 Harrison St 98109 206-252-9850
Brian Vance, prin. Fax 252-9851
Cleveland HS 800/9-12
5950 Delridge Way SW 98106 206-252-7800
Donna Marshall, prin. Fax 252-7801
Denny MS 700/6-8
8402 30th Ave SW 98126 206-252-9000
Jeff Clarke, prin. Fax 252-9001
Eckstein MS 1,200/6-8
3003 NE 75th St 98115 206-252-5010
Marnie Campbell, prin. Fax 252-5011
Franklin HS 1,500/9-12
3013 S Mount Baker Blvd 98144 206-252-6150
Jennifer Wiley, prin. Fax 252-6151
Garfield HS at Lincoln 1,600/9-12
4400 Interlake Ave N 98103 206-252-2270
Ted Howard, prin. Fax 252-2271
Hale HS 1,100/9-12
10750 30th Ave NE 98125 206-252-3680
Lisa Hechtman, prin. Fax 262-3681
Hamilton International MS 800/6-8
1610 N 41st St 98103 206-252-5810
Terry Acena, prin. Fax 252-5811
Ingraham HS 1,200/9-12
1819 N 135th St 98133 206-252-3880
Martin Floe, prin. Fax 252-3881

Kurose MS 700/6-8
3928 S Graham St 98118 206-252-7700
Bi Hoa Caldwell, prin. Fax 252-7701
Madison MS 900/6-8
3429 45th Ave SW 98116 206-252-9200
Jill Hudson, prin. Fax 252-9201
McClure MS 600/6-8
1915 1st Ave W 98119 206-252-1900
Kathy Bledsoe, prin. Fax 252-1901
Meany MS 500/6-8
301 21st Ave E 98112 206-252-2500
Princess Shareef, prin. Fax 252-2501
Mercer MS 800/6-8
1600 S Columbian Way 98108 206-252-8000
Andhra Lutz, prin. Fax 252-8001
Rainier Beach HS 500/9-12
8815 Seward Park Ave S 98118 206-252-6350
Robert Gary, prin. Fax 252-6351
Roosevelt HS 1,600/9-12
1410 NE 66th St 98115 206-252-4810
Dick Campbell, prin. Fax 252-4811
Sealth HS 900/9-12
2600 SW Thistle St 98126 206-252-8550
John Boyd, prin. Fax 252-8551
Washington MS 1,000/6-8
2101 S Jackson St 98144 206-252-2600
Jon Halfaker, prin. Fax 252-2601
West Seattle HS 1,200/9-12
3000 California Ave SW 98116 206-252-8800
Susan Derse, prin. Fax 252-8801
Whitman MS 1,100/6-8
9201 15th Ave NW 98117 206-252-1200
Robert Kogane, prin. Fax 252-1201
Seattle Evening HS Adult
520 NE Ravenna Blvd 98115 206-252-4680
Marella Francois, prin. Fax 252-4681

Antioch University Post-Sec.
2326 6th Ave 98121 206-441-5352
Argosy University/Seattle Post-Sec.
2601A Elliott Ave 98121 206-283-4500
Art Institute of Seattle Post-Sec.
2323 Elliott Ave 98121 206-448-0900
Bakke Graduate University of Ministry Post-Sec.
1013 8th Ave 98104 206-264-9100
Billings MS 100/6-8
7217 Woodlawn Ave NE 98115 206-547-4614
Ted Kalmus, hdmstr. Fax 545-8505
Bishop Blanchet HS 1,100/9-12
8200 Wallingford Ave N 98103 206-527-7711
Kent Hickey, prin. Fax 527-7712
Bush S 600/K-12
3400 E Harrison St 98112 206-322-7978
Frank Magusin, hdmstr. Fax 860-3876
Cornish College of the Arts Post-Sec.
1000 Lenora St 98121 206-726-5151
Divers Institute of Technology Post-Sec.
PO Box 70667 98127 206-783-5542
Gene Juarez Academy of Beauty Post-Sec.
10715 8th Ave NE 98125 206-365-6900
Greenwood Academy of Hair Design Post-Sec.
8501 Greenwood Ave N 98103 206-782-0220
Holy Names Academy 600/9-12
728 21st Ave E 98112 206-323-4272
Elizabeth Swift, prin. Fax 323-5254
Lakeside MS 300/5-8
13510 1st Ave NE 98125 206-368-3630
Bernie Noe, hdmstr. Fax 440-2777
Lakeside Upper S 500/9-12
14050 1st Ave NE 98125 206-368-3600
Bernie Noe, hdmstr.
Menachem Mendel Seattle Cheder 100/PK-12
4541 19th Ave NE 98105 206-523-9766
Rabbi Charytan, prin. Fax 524-6105
Northgate Christian Academy 50/K-12
10510 Stone Ave N 98133 206-525-5699
North Seattle Community College Post-Sec.
9600 College Way N 98103 206-527-3600
Northwest S 500/6-12
1415 Summit Ave 98122 206-682-7309
Ellen Taussig, hdmstr. Fax 467-7353
O'Dea HS 500/9-12
802 Terry Ave 98104 206-622-6596
Br. Dominic Murray, prin. Fax 340-4110
Photographic Center Northwest Post-Sec.
900 12th Ave 98122 206-720-7222
Pima Medical Institute Post-Sec.
9709 3rd Ave NE Ste 400 98115 206-322-6100
Pima Medical Institute Post-Sec.
9709 3rd Ave NE Ste 400 98115 206-322-6100
Seattle Academy of Arts & Sciences 200/6-8
1432 15th Ave 98122 206-323-6880
Jean Orvis, dir. Fax 323-6881
Seattle Academy of Arts & Sciences 300/9-12
1201 E Union St 98122 206-323-6600
Jean Orvis, dir. Fax 323-6618
Seattle Central Community College Post-Sec.
1701 Broadway 98122 206-587-3800
Seattle Girls' S 100/5-8
PO Box 22576 98122 206-709-2228
Marja Brandon, hdmstr. Fax 329-1580
Seattle Institute of Oriental Medicine Post-Sec.
916 NE 65th St # B 98115 206-517-4541
Seattle Lutheran HS 100/9-12
4141 41st Ave SW 98116 206-937-7722
Jeff Norton, prin. Fax 937-6781
Seattle Pacific University Post-Sec.
3307 3rd Ave W 98119 206-281-2000
Seattle Preparatory S 700/9-12
2400 11th Ave E 98102 206-324-0400
Rev. Michael Tyrrell, prin. Fax 577-2198
Seattle University Post-Sec.
901 12th Ave 98122 206-296-6000
Seattle University School of Law Post-Sec.
901 12th Ave 98122 206-398-4200

Sha'arei Binah Jewish Girls HS 9-12
5224 Wilson Ave S 98118 206-760-0200
Rivka Goldberg, prin.
South Seattle Community College Post-Sec.
6000 16th Ave SW 98106 206-764-5300
University of Washington 98195 Post-Sec.
206-543-2100
University Prep Academy 400/6-12
8000 25th Ave NE 98115 206-525-2714
Erica Hamlin, hdmstr. Fax 525-9659
Wolf HS 50/9-12
160 John St 98109 206-522-2644
Carol Oliver, coord. Fax 522-2631

Sedro Woolley, Skagit, Pop. 7,506
Sedro Woolley SD 101 4,500/K-12
801 Trail Rd 98284 360-855-3500
Mark Venn, supt. Fax 855-3574
www.swsd.k12.wa.us
Cascade MS 700/7-8
201 N Township St 98284 360-855-3520
Michelle Kuss-Cybula, prin. Fax 855-3521
Sedro Woolley HS 1,200/9-12
1235 3rd St 98284 360-855-3510
Mike Schweigert, prin. Fax 855-3517

Sekiu, Clallam
Cape Flattery SD 401 500/K-12
PO Box 109 98381 360-963-2329
Gene Laes, supt. Fax 963-2373
www.capeflattery.wednet.edu
Other Schools – See Clallam Bay, Neah Bay

Selah, Yakima, Pop. 6,875
Selah SD 119 3,500/K-12
105 W Bartlett Ave 98942 509-697-0706
Dr. Larry Parsons, supt. Fax 697-0823
www.selah.k12.wa.us
Selah HS 700/10-12
801 N 1st St 98942 509-697-0800
Joe Jones, prin. Fax 697-0811
Selah JHS 600/8-9
411 N 1st St 98942 509-697-0500
Marc Gallaway, prin. Fax 697-0696

Sequim, Clallam, Pop. 5,162
Sequim SD 323 2,900/K-12
503 N Sequim Ave 98382 360-582-3260
Bill Bentley, supt. Fax 683-6303
www.sequim.k12.wa.us/
Sequim HS 1,000/9-12
601 N Sequim Ave 98382 360-582-3600
Shawn Langston, prin. Fax 681-8688
Sequim MS 700/6-8
301 W Hendrickson Rd 98382 360-582-3500
Brian Jones, prin. Fax 582-9486

Shelton, Mason, Pop. 9,065
Pioneer SD 402 800/PK-8
611 E Agate Rd 98584 360-426-9115
Daniel Winter, supt. Fax 426-1036
www.psd402.org
Pioneer MS 400/4-8
611 E Agate Rd 98584 360-426-8291
Bill Lanning, prin. Fax 426-1036

Shelton SD 309 3,600/PK-12
700 S 1st St 98584 360-426-1687
Joan Zook, supt. Fax 427-8610
www.sheltonschools.org
Oakland Bay JHS 800/8-9
3301 N Shelton Springs Rd 98584 360-426-7991
Sheryal Balding, prin. Fax 427-2940
Shelton HS 1,100/9-12
3737 N Shelton Springs Rd 98584 360-426-4471
Wanda Berndtson, prin. Fax 427-6141
Choice HS Adult
807 W Pine St 98584 360-426-7664
Gordy Hansen, prin. Fax 462-1203

Mason County Christian S 200/PK-12
470 E Eagle Ridge Dr 98584 360-426-7616
David Roller, supt. Fax 426-6582

Shoreline, King, Pop. 52,024
Shoreline SD 412 9,600/PK-12
18560 1st Ave NE 98155 206-367-6111
Sue Walker, supt. Fax 361-4204
www.shorelineschools.org
Einstein MS 800/7-8
19343 3rd Ave NW 98177 206-368-4730
Bill Dunbar, prin. Fax 368-4735
Kellogg MS 700/7-8
16045 25th Ave NE 98155 206-368-4783
Lori Longo, prin. Fax 368-4780
Shorecrest HS 1,500/9-12
15343 25th Ave NE 98155 206-361-4286
Pat Hegarty, prin. Fax 361-4284
Shorewood HS 1,800/9-12
17300 Fremont Ave N 98133 206-361-4372
John Green, prin. Fax 368-4711

King's JSHS 600/7-12
19303 Fremont Ave N 98133 206-546-7245
Randy Hibbard, prin. Fax 546-7214
Shoreline Christian S 300/PK-12
2400 NE 147th St 98155 206-364-7777
Timothy Visser, prin. Fax 364-0349
Shoreline Community College Post-Sec.
16101 Greenwood Ave N 98133 206-546-4101

Silverdale, Kitsap, Pop. 7,660
Central Kitsap SD 401 11,400/K-12
PO Box 8 98383 360-662-1610
Gregory Lynch, supt. Fax 662-1611
www.cksd.wednet.edu
Career & Technical Education Vo/Tech
PO Box 8 98383 360-662-1800
Katharine Gleysteen, dir. Fax 662-1801

Central Kitsap HS 1,300/10-12
PO Box 8 98383 360-662-2400
John Cervinsky, prin. Fax 662-2401
Central Kitsap JHS 1,000/7-9
PO Box 8 98383 360-662-2300
Franklyn MacKenzie, prin. Fax 662-2301
Klahowya Secondary S 1,000/7-12
PO Box 8 98383 360-662-4000
Ryan Stevens, prin. Fax 662-4001
Ridgetop JHS 900/7-9
PO Box 8 98383 360-662-2900
Brent Anderson, prin. Fax 662-2901
Other Schools – See Bremerton

Skykomish, King, Pop. 207
Skykomish SD 404 100/K-12
PO Box 325 98288 360-677-2623
Desiree L. Gould, supt. Fax 677-2418
Skykomish JSHS 50/7-12
PO Box 325 98288 360-677-2623
Desiree L. Gould, prin. Fax 677-2418

Snohomish, Snohomish, Pop. 8,720
Monroe SD 103
Supt. — See Monroe
Hidden River MS 200/6-8
9224 Paradise Lake Rd 98296 360-863-4100
Steve Shurtleff, prin. Fax 668-5222

Snohomish SD 201 8,200/K-12
1601 Avenue D 98290 360-563-7300
William Mester Ph.D., supt. Fax 563-7373
www.sno.wednet.edu
Centennial MS 700/7-8
3000 S Machias Rd 98290 360-563-4525
Scott Peacock, prin. Fax 563-4585
Snohomish Freshman Campus 50/9-9
601 Glen Ave 98290 360-563-4300
Beth Porter, prin. Fax 563-4360
Snohomish SHS 2,000/10-12
1316 5th St 98290 360-563-4000
Diana Plumis, prin. Fax 563-4183
Valley View MS 800/7-8
14308 Broadway Ave 98296 360-563-4225
Nancy Rhoades, prin. Fax 563-4236

Peaceful Glen Christian S 100/PK-12
PO Box 710 98291 360-563-0131
Kathleen Biehl, dir.

Snoqualmie, King, Pop. 6,082
Snoqualmie Valley SD 410 5,000/PK-12
PO Box 400 98065 425-831-8000
Joel Aune, supt. Fax 831-8040
www.snoqualmie.k12.wa.us
Mount Si HS 1,300/9-12
8651 Meadowbrook Way SE 98065 425-831-8100
Randy Taylor, prin. Fax 831-8222
Snoqualmie MS 600/6-8
9200 Railroad Ave SE 98065 425-831-8450
Ruth Moen, prin. Fax 831-8440
Other Schools – See Fall City

Soap Lake, Grant, Pop. 1,844
Soap Lake SD 156 400/PK-12
PO Box 158 98851 509-246-1822
John Adkins, supt. Fax 246-0669
Soap Lake HS 100/9-12
PO Box 878 98851 509-246-1201
Dan Andrews, prin. Fax 246-0669
Soap Lake MS, PO Box 878 98851 100/6-8
Dan Andrews, prin. 509-246-1201

South Bend, Pacific, Pop. 1,831
South Bend SD 118 500/PK-12
PO Box 437 98586 360-875-6041
Mike Morris, supt. Fax 875-6062
www.southbend.wednet.edu/
South Bend JSHS 200/7-12
PO Box 437 98586 360-875-5707
Michael Rogers, prin. Fax 875-6036

Spanaway, Pierce, Pop. 15,001
Bethel SD 403 17,500/PK-12
516 176th St E 98387 253-683-6000
Tom Seigel, supt. Fax 683-6059
www.bethelsd.org
Bethel JHS 900/7-9
22001 38th Ave E 98387 253-683-7200
Paul Rempfer, prin. Fax 683-7298
Bethel SHS 2,000/10-12
22215 38th Ave E 98387 253-683-7000
Wanda Riley, prin. Fax 683-7098
Cedarcrest JHS 900/7-9
19120 13th Avenue Ct E 98387 253-683-7500
Cheryl Barnett, prin. Fax 683-7598
Spanaway Lake SHS 1,800/10-12
1305 168th St E 98387 253-683-5600
Michelle Ledbetter, prin. Fax 683-5698
Other Schools – See Graham, Tacoma

Spangle, Spokane, Pop. 234
Liberty SD 362 500/K-12
29818 S North Pine Creek Rd 99031 509-245-3223
Duane Reidenbach, supt. Fax 245-3288
www.liberty.wednet.edu/
Liberty HS 200/9-12
6404 E Spangle Waverly Rd 99031 509-245-3229
Steve Boosinger, prin. Fax 245-3205

Upper Columbia Academy 300/9-12
3025 E Spangle Waverly Rd 99031 509-245-3600
Jeff Bovee, prin. Fax 245-3643

Spokane, Spokane, Pop. 196,818
East Valley SD 361 4,300/K-12
12325 E Grace Ave 99216 509-924-1830
Christine Burgess, supt. Fax 927-9500
www.evsd.org

East Valley HS 1,400/9-12
15711 E Wellesley Ave 99216 509-927-3200
Jeffrey Miller, prin. Fax 921-6830
East Valley MS 600/6-8
4920 N Progress Rd 99216 509-924-9383
Doris Hoffman, prin. Fax 927-3214
Other Schools – See Newman Lake

Mead SD 354
Supt. — See Mead
Mead HS 1,600/9-12
302 W Hastings Rd 99218 509-465-7000
Ken Russell, prin. Fax 465-7020
Northwood MS 700/7-8
13120 N Pittsburg St 99208 509-465-7500
Dave Stenersen, prin. Fax 465-7520

Spokane SD 81 30,600/PK-12
200 N Bernard St 99201 509-354-5900
Brian L. Benzel Ph.D., supt. Fax 354-5965
www.spokaneschools.org
Chase MS 900/7-8
4747 E 37th Ave 99223 509-354-5000
John Andes, prin. Fax 354-5100
Ferris HS 1,800/9-12
3020 E 37th Ave 99223 509-354-6000
Erik Ohlund, prin. Fax 354-6161
Garry MS 700/7-8
725 E Joseph Ave 99208 509-354-5200
Brenda Meenach, prin. Fax 354-5212
Glover MS 800/7-8
2404 W Longfellow Ave 99205 509-354-5400
Roberta Kramer, prin. Fax 354-5399
Lewis & Clark HS 2,000/9-12
521 W 4th Ave 99204 509-354-7000
Jon Swett, prin. Fax 354-6969
North Central HS 1,600/9-12
1600 N Howard St 99205 509-354-6300
Steven Gering, prin. Fax 354-6303
Rogers HS 1,700/9-12
1622 E Wellesley Ave 99207 509-354-6600
Carol Meyer, prin. Fax 354-6665
Sacajawea MS 900/7-8
401 E 33rd Ave 99203 509-354-5500
Paula Ronhaar, prin. Fax 354-5505
Salk MS 800/7-8
6411 N Alberta St 99208 509-354-5600
Mark Gorman, prin. Fax 354-5542
Shadle Park HS 1,700/9-12
4327 N Ash St 99205 509-354-6700
Herb Rotchford, prin. Fax 354-6710
Shaw MS 700/7-8
4106 N Cook St 99207 509-354-5800
Christine Lynch, prin. Fax 354-5899
Spokane Area Professional Tech Skill Ctr Vo/Tech
4141 N Regal St 99207 509-354-7470
Don Howell, prin. Fax 354-7474

West Valley SD 363 3,500/PK-12
PO Box 11739 99211 509-924-2150
Dr. Polly Crowley, supt. Fax 922-5295
www.wvsd.com
Centennial MS 500/6-8
915 N Ella Rd 99212 509-922-5482
Pam Francis, prin. Fax 891-9520
Spokane Valley HS 100/9-12
2011 N Hutchinson Rd 99212 509-922-5475
Larry Bush, prin. Fax 922-5477
West Valley City MS 200/5-8
8920 E Valleyway Ave 99212 509-921-2836
Tom Moore, prin. Fax 921-2849
West Valley HS 900/9-12
8301 E Buckeye Ave 99212 509-922-5488
Gary Neal, prin. Fax 928-3676

All Saints MS 200/5-8
1428 E 33rd Ave 99203 509-624-5712
Katherine Hicks, prin. Fax 624-7752
Apollo College Post-Sec.
10102 E Knox Ave 99206 509-532-8888
Cornerstone Christian Academy 100/K-12
1801 E 29th Ave 99203 509-835-1235
Christina Hilderbrand, admin.
Glen Dow Academy of Hair Design Post-Sec.
309 W Riverside Ave 99201 509-624-3244
Gonzaga Preparatory S 9-12
1224 E Euclid Ave 99207 509-483-8511
Rev. Kevin Connell, prin. Fax 483-3124
Gonzaga University Post-Sec.
502 E Boone Ave 99258 509-328-4220
Gonzaga University 99258 Post-Sec.
509-323-5546
Holy Family Hospital Post-Sec.
5633 N Lidgerwood St 99208 509-482-2450
Inland Northwest HVAC Training Center Post-Sec.
811 E Sprague Ave Ste 6 99202 509-747-8810
Intercollegiate Center/Nursing Education Post-Sec.
2917 W Fort Gorge Wright Dr 99204 509-324-7360
Oaks-A Classical Christian Academy 300/K-12
4224 E 4th Ave 99202 509-536-5955
Bruce Williams, prin. Fax 536-7877
Sacred Heart Medical Center Post-Sec.
101 W 8th Ave 99204 509-455-3040
St. George's S 400/K-12
2929 W Waikiki Rd 99208 509-466-1636
Mo Copeland, hdmstr. Fax 467-3258
Spokane Community College Post-Sec.
1810 N Greene St 99217 509-533-7000
Spokane Falls Community College Post-Sec.
3410 W Fort George Wright 99224 509-533-3500
Spokane Junior Academy 100/K-10
1888 N Wright Dr 99224 509-325-1985
Donald Bryan, prin. Fax 324-8904
Whitworth College Post-Sec.
300 W Hawthorne Rd 99251 800-533-4668

Spokane Valley, Spokane
Central Valley SD 356 11,500/PK-12
19307 E Cataldo Ave, 509-228-5400
Mike Pearson, supt. Fax 228-5439
www.cvsd.org
Bowdish MS 600/6-8
2109 S Skipworth Rd, 509-228-4700
Dave Bouge, prin. Fax 228-4714
Central Valley HS 1,700/9-12
821 S Sullivan Rd, 509-228-5100
Mike Hittle, prin. Fax 228-5109
Evergreen MS 600/6-8
14221 E 16th Ave, 509-228-4780
Dave Feldhusen, prin. Fax 228-4789
Greenacres MS 600/6-8
17409 E Sprague Ave, 509-228-4860
Vern DiGiovanni, prin. Fax 228-4869
Horizon MS 500/6-8
3915 S Pines Rd, 509-228-4940
Denis Rusca, prin. Fax 228-4983
North Pines MS 500/6-8
701 N Pines Rd, 509-228-5020
Gordon Grassi, prin. Fax 228-5029
University HS 1,800/9-12
12420 E 32nd Ave, 509-228-5240
Daryl Hart, prin. Fax 228-5249

ITT Technical Institute Post-Sec.
13518 E Indiana Ave, 509-926-2900
Valley Christian S 600/K-12
10212 E 9th Ave, 509-924-9131
Derick Tabish, admin. Fax 924-2971

Sprague, Lincoln, Pop. 489
Sprague SD 8 100/K-12
PO Box 305 99032 509-257-2591
Mark Stedman, supt. Fax 257-2539
www.sprague.wednet.edu
Sprague HS, PO Box 305 99032 50/9-12
Patrick Whipple, prin. 509-257-2511

Springdale, Stevens, Pop. 287
Mary Walker SD 207 500/PK-12
PO Box 159 99173 509-258-4534
Kevin Jacka, supt. Fax 258-4707
www.marywalker.org/
Springdale MS 100/7-8
PO Box 159 99173 509-258-7357
Cheryl Henjum, prin. Fax 258-7756
Walker HS 200/9-12
PO Box 159 99173 509-258-4533
Matthew Cobb, prin. Fax 258-4555

Stanwood, Snohomish, Pop. 5,068
Stanwood-Camano SD 401 5,400/K-12
26920 Pioneer Hwy 98292 360-629-1200
Dr. Jean Shumate, supt. Fax 629-1242
www.stanwood.wednet.edu
Port Susan MS 800/6-8
7506 267th St NW 98292 360-629-1360
Cinco Delgado, prin. Fax 629-1365
Stanwood HS 1,700/9-12
7400 272nd St NW 98292 360-629-1300
Christine Gruver, prin. Fax 629-1310
Stanwood MS 600/6-8
9405 271st St NW 98292 360-629-1350
Barbara Marsh, prin. Fax 629-1354

Steilacoom, Pierce, Pop. 6,140
Steilacoom Historical SD 1 2,100/K-12
510 Chambers St 98388 253-983-2200
Dr. Arthur Himmler, supt. Fax 584-7198
www.steilacoom.k12.wa.us
Pioneer MS 500/6-8
511 Chambers St 98388 253-983-2400
Dan Luce, prin. Fax 589-4892
Steilacoom HS 700/9-12
54 Sentinel Dr 98388 253-983-2300
Janice McCrimmon, prin. Fax 584-6255

Stevenson, Skamania, Pop. 1,256
Stevenson-Carson SD 303 1,000/K-12
PO Box 850 98648 509-427-5674
Jim Saltness, supt. Fax 427-4028
www.scsd.k12.wa.us
Stevenson HS 400/9-12
PO Box 850 98648 509-427-5631
Brian Howe, prin. Fax 427-5639
Other Schools – See Carson

Sultan, Snohomish, Pop. 3,943
Sultan SD 311 2,200/K-12
514 4th St 98294 360-793-9800
Al Robinson, supt. Fax 793-9890
www.sultan.k12.wa.us
Sultan HS 600/9-12
13715 310th Ave SE 98294 360-793-9860
Dave Harrington, prin. Fax 793-9864
Sultan MS 600/6-8
301 High Ave 98294 360-793-9850
Robin Briganti, prin. Fax 793-9859

Sumner, Pierce, Pop. 9,298
Dieringer SD 343 1,100/K-8
1320 178th Ave E, 253-862-2537
Dr. Judy Neumeier-Martinson, supt. Fax 862-8472
www.dieringer.wednet.edu
North Tapps MS 400/6-8
20029 12th St E, 253-862-2776
Pat Keaton, prin. Fax 862-2587

Sumner SD 320 6,700/K-12
1202 Wood Ave 98390 253-891-6000
Dr. Gil Mendoza, supt. Fax 891-6097
www.sumner.wednet.edu
Sumner HS 1,800/9-12
1707 Main St 98390 253-891-5500
Bill Gaines, prin. Fax 891-5585
Sumner MS 500/6-8
1508 Willow St 98390 253-891-5000
Chuck Eychaner, prin. Fax 891-5045
Other Schools – See Bonney Lake

Sunnyside, Yakima, Pop. 14,426
Sunnyside SD 201 5,100/K-12
1110 S 6th St 98944 509-836-6532
Dr. Richard D. Cole, supt. Fax 837-0535
www.sunnyside.wednet.edu
Harrison MS 900/6-8
810 S 16th St 98944 509-837-3601
Janie Hernandez, prin. Fax 837-0450
Sierra Vista MS, 916 N 16th St 98944 6-8
Doug Rogers, prin. 509-836-6532
Sunnyside HS 1,400/9-12
1801 E Edison Ave 98944 509-837-2601
Brian Hart, prin. Fax 837-0494

Professional Beauty School Post-Sec.
214 S 6th St 98944 509-837-4040
Sunnyside Christian HS 100/9-12
1820 Sheller Rd 98944 509-837-8995
Dean Wagenaar, prin. Fax 837-8895

Tacoma, Pierce, Pop. 195,898
Bethel SD 403
Supt. — See Spanaway
Spanaway JHS 900/7-9
15701 B St E 98445 253-683-5400
Roger Samples, prin. Fax 683-5498

Fife SD 417 3,100/K-12
5802 20th St E 98424 253-517-1000
Dr. Stephen D. McCammon, supt. Fax 517-1055
www.fifeschools.com
Columbia JHS 600/8-9
2901 54th Ave E 98424 253-517-1600
J. Nelson, prin. Fax 517-1605
Fife SHS 800/10-12
5616 20th St E 98424 253-517-1100
John McCrossin, prin. Fax 517-1105

Franklin Pierce SD 402 7,800/PK-12
315 129th St S 98444 253-298-3000
Frank Hewins, supt. Fax 298-3015
www.fp.k12.wa.us
Ford MS 1,000/6-8
1602 104th St E 98445 253-298-3600
Gary Benson, prin. Fax 298-3615
Keithley MS 800/6-8
12324 12th Ave S 98444 253-298-4300
Joyce Knowles, prin. Fax 298-4315
Pierce HS 1,300/9-12
11002 18th Ave E 98445 253-298-3800
Jennifer Shaw, prin. Fax 298-3815
Washington HS 1,100/9-12
12420 Ainsworth Ave S 98444 253-298-4700
James Hester, prin. Fax 298-4715

Tacoma SD 10 30,700/PK-12
PO Box 1357 98401 253-571-1000
Dr. Charles Milligan, supt. Fax 571-2550
www.tacomaschools.org/
Baker MS 700/6-8
8320 S I St 98408 253-571-5000
Harold H. Wright, prin. Fax 571-5090
Foss HS 1,800/9-12
2112 S Tyler St 98405 253-571-7300
Don Herbert, prin. Fax 571-7466
Gault MS 400/6-8
1115 E Division Ln 98404 253-571-1405
Delores Beason, prin. Fax 571-1478
Giaudrone MS 700/6-8
4902 S Alaska St 98408 253-571-5811
Gaile McLaurin, prin. Fax 571-5812
Gray MS 700/6-8
3109 S 60th St 98409 253-571-1860
Yvonne Bullock, prin. Fax 571-1890
Hunt MS 600/6-8
6501 S 10th St 98465 253-571-2335
Katherine Boyd, prin. Fax 571-2351
Lee MS 600/6-8
602 N Sprague Ave 98403 253-571-1395
Harjeet Sandhu, prin. Fax 571-1466
Lincoln HS 1,600/9-12
6229 S Tyler St 98409 253-571-2000
Patrick Erwin, prin. Fax 571-6789
Mason MS 800/6-8
3901 N 28th St 98407 253-571-2256
Patrice Sulkosky, prin. Fax 571-2294
McIlvaigh MS 500/6-8
1801 E 56th St 98404 253-571-2080
Daniel Dizon, prin. Fax 571-2179
Meeker MS 700/6-8
4402 Nassau Ave NE 98422 253-571-1377
Adrian Hartness, prin. Fax 571-1266
Mount Tahoma HS 1,800/9-12
4634 S 74th St 98409 253-571-3800
Greg Eisnaugle, prin. Fax 571-3801
School of the Arts 300/9-12
1818 Tacoma Ave S 98402 253-571-7900
Jonathan Ketler, dir. Fax 571-7901
Stadium HS 1,600/9-12
111 N E St 98403 253-571-3100
Jonathan Kellett, prin. Fax 571-3101
Stewart MS 600/6-8
5010 Pacific Ave 98408 253-571-2085
Krestin Bahr, prin. Fax 571-2134
Truman MS 700/6-8
5801 N 35th St 98407 253-571-2245
Patricia Robinson, prin. Fax 571-2293
Wilson HS 1,600/9-12
1202 N Orchard St 98406 253-571-6000
Dan Besett, prin. Fax 571-6162

Bates Technical College Post-Sec.
1101 Yakima Ave 98405 253-680-7000

Bellarmine Prep S — 1,000/9-12
2300 S Washington St 98405 — 253-752-7701
Chris Gavin, prin. — Fax 756-3887
BJ's Beauty & Barber College — Post-Sec.
5239 S Tacoma Way 98409 — 253-473-4320
Covenant HS — 100/9-12
620 S Shirley St 98465 — 253-759-9570
Richard Hannula, prin. — Fax 752-5992
Crown College — Post-Sec.
8739 S Hosmer St 98444 — 253-531-3123
Everest College — Post-Sec.
2156 Pacific Ave 98402 — 253-207-4000
Faith Evangelical Lutheran Seminary — Post-Sec.
3504 N Pearl St 98407 — 253-752-2020
Life Christian S — 1,100/PK-12
1717 S Union Ave 98405 — 253-756-5317
Ross Hjelseth, hdmstr. — Fax 761-9798
Mount Rainier Lutheran HS — 100/9-12
7306 Waller Rd E 98443 — 253-284-4433
Dr. Robert Malzahn, dir. — Fax 284-4435
Northwest Baptist Seminary — Post-Sec.
4301 N Stevens St 98407 — 253-759-6104
Pacific Lutheran University — Post-Sec.
12180 Park Ave S 98447 — 253-531-6900
Tacoma Baptist S — 400/PK-12
2052 S 64th St 98409 — 253-475-7226
Robert White, admin. — Fax 471-9949
Tacoma Community College — Post-Sec.
6501 S 19th St 98466 — 253-566-5000
University of Puget Sound — Post-Sec.
1500 N Warner St 98416 — 253-879-3100
Western Pacific Truck School — Post-Sec.
11020 S Tacoma Way 98499 — 253-581-6494
Wright S — 500/PK-12
827 N Tacoma Ave 98403 — 253-272-2216
Rick Clarke, hdmstr. — Fax 572-3616

Taholah, Grays Harbor, Pop. 788
Taholah SD 77 — 200/PK-12
PO Box 249 98587 — 360-276-4729
Robert Boyle, supt. — Fax 276-4370
www.taholah.k12.wa.us/
Taholah S — 200/PK-12
PO Box 249 98587 — 360-276-4514
Brian Freeman, prin. — Fax 276-4370

Tekoa, Whitman, Pop. 772
Tekoa SD 265 — 200/PK-12
PO Box 869 99033 — 509-284-3281
Wayne Massie, supt. — Fax 284-2045
www.tekoa.wednet.edu
Tekoa JSHS — 100/7-12
PO Box 869 99033 — 509-284-3401
Wayne Roellich, prin. — Fax 284-5802

Tenino, Thurston, Pop. 1,584
Tenino SD 402 — 1,400/PK-12
PO Box 4024 98589 — 360-264-3400
Dr. Steven Smedley, supt. — Fax 264-3438
www.tenino.k12.wa.us
Tenino HS — 500/9-12
PO Box 4024 98589 — 360-264-3500
Jeff Johnson, prin. — Fax 264-3538
Tenino MS — 300/6-8
PO Box 4024 98589 — 360-264-3600
Tony Howard, prin. — Fax 264-3638

Thorp, Kittitas
Thorp SD 400 — 200/K-12
PO Box 150 98946 — 509-964-2107
Dr. Virginia Erion, supt. — Fax 964-2313
www.thorp.wednet.edu
Thorp S — 200/K-12
PO Box 150 98946 — 509-964-2107
Dr. Virginia Erion, prin. — Fax 964-2313

Toledo, Lewis, Pop. 676
Toledo SD 237 — 1,000/PK-12
PO Box 469 98591 — 360-864-6325
Sharon Bower, supt. — Fax 864-6326
www.toledo.k12.wa.us
Toledo HS — 300/9-12
PO Box 820 98591 — 360-864-2391
Shawn Corrigan, prin. — Fax 864-2396
Toledo MS — 200/6-8
PO Box 668 98591 — 360-864-2395
Bill Waag, prin. — Fax 864-8147

Tonasket, Okanogan, Pop. 970
Tonasket SD 404 — 1,100/PK-12
35 Highway 20 98855 — 509-486-2126
Randall Hauff, supt. — Fax 486-1263
www.tonasket.wednet.edu
Tonasket HS — 400/9-12
35 Highway 20 98855 — 509-486-2161
Jeff Hardesty, prin. — Fax 486-4382
Tonasket MS — 300/6-8
35 Highway 20 98855 — 509-486-2147
Ed Morgan, prin. — Fax 486-1576

Toppenish, Yakima, Pop. 9,207
Toppenish SD 202 — 3,200/K-12
306 Bolin Dr 98948 — 509-865-4455
Steve Myers, supt. — Fax 865-2067
www.toppenish.wednet.edu/
Toppenish HS — 700/9-12
141 Ward Rd 98948 — 509-865-3370
Walt Wegener, prin. — Fax 865-3244
Toppenish MS — 800/6-8
104 Goldendale Ave 98948 — 509-865-2730
Leonor de Maldonado, prin. — Fax 865-7503

Heritage University — Post-Sec.
3240 Fort Rd 98948 — 509-865-8500

Touchet, Walla Walla
Touchet SD 300 — 300/K-12
PO Box 135 99360 — 509-394-2352
Dan McDonald, supt. — Fax 394-2952
www.touchet.org/
Touchet S — 300/K-12
PO Box 135 99360 — 509-394-2352
Jim Greene, prin. — Fax 394-2952

Toutle, Cowlitz
Toutle Lake SD 130 — 600/K-12
5050 Spirit Lake Hwy 98649 — 360-274-6182
Scott Grabenhorst, supt. — Fax 274-7608
www.toutlesd.k12.wa.us
Toutle Lake JSHS — 300/7-12
5050 Spirit Lake Hwy 98649 — 360-274-6132
Larry Hearst, prin. — Fax 274-7608

Trout Lake, Klickitat
Trout Lake SD R-400 — 200/K-12
PO Box 488 98650 — 509-395-2571
Doug Dearden, supt. — Fax 395-2399
www.troutlake.k12.wa.us/default.htm
Trout Lake JSHS — 100/5-12
PO Box 488 98650 — 509-395-2571
Doug Dearden, prin. — Fax 395-2399

Tukwila, King, Pop. 16,969
Tukwila SD 406 — 2,600/K-12
4640 S 144th St 98168 — 206-901-8000
Dr. James Quezon Hammond, supt. — Fax 901-8016
www.tukwila.wednet.edu
Foster HS — 700/9-12
4242 S 144th St 98168 — 206-901-7900
George Ilgenfritz, prin. — Fax 901-7907
Showalter MS — 600/6-8
4628 S 144th St 98168 — 206-901-7800
Brett Christopher, prin. — Fax 901-7807

ITT Technical Institute — Post-Sec.
12720 Gateway Dr S Ste 100 98168 — 206-244-3300

Tumwater, Thurston, Pop. 13,331
Tumwater SD 33 — 6,000/K-12
419 Linwood Ave SW 98512 — 360-709-7000
Terry Borden, supt. — Fax 709-7002
www.tumwater.k12.wa.us
Bush MS — 500/7-8
2120 83rd Ave SW 98512 — 360-709-7400
Linda O'Shaughnessy, prin. — Fax 709-7402
New Market Vocational Skills Center — Vo/Tech
7299 New Market St SW 98501 — 360-570-4500
Joe Kinerk, prin. — Fax 570-4502
Tumwater HS — 1,100/9-12
700 Israel Rd SW 98501 — 360-709-7600
Scott Seaman, prin. — Fax 709-7602
Tumwater MS — 500/7-8
6335 Littlerock Rd SW 98512 — 360-709-7500
Jon Wilcox, prin. — Fax 709-7502
Other Schools – See Olympia

South Puget Sound Community College — Post-Sec.
2011 Mottman Rd SW 98512 — 360-754-7711

Union Gap, Yakima, Pop. 5,707

La Salle HS — 200/9-12
3000 Lightning Way 98903 — 509-225-2900
Br. James Joost, prin. — Fax 225-2950

University Place, Pierce, Pop. 30,425
University Place SD 83 — 5,300/K-12
3717 Grandview Dr W 98466 — 253-566-5600
Patricia Banks, supt. — Fax 566-5607
www.upsd.wednet.edu
Curtis JHS — 1,000/8-9
8901 40th St W 98466 — 253-566-5670
Jeff Chamberlin, prin. — Fax 566-5644
Curtis SHS — 1,300/10-12
8425 40th St W 98466 — 253-566-5710
David Hammond, prin. — Fax 566-5626

Wright Academy — 700/PK-12
7723 Chambers Creek Rd W 98467 — 253-620-8300
Robert Camner, prin. — Fax 620-8431

Vancouver, Clark, Pop. 157,493
Battle Ground SD 119
Supt. — See Brush Prairie
Laurin MS — 500/5-8
13601 NE 97th Ave 98662 — 360-885-5200
JoDee McMillen, prin. — Fax 885-5201
Pleasant Valley MS — 500/5-8
14320 NE 50th Ave 98686 — 360-885-5500
Ward Holcomb, prin. — Fax 885-5510
Prairie HS — 1,500/9-12
11500 NE 117th Ave 98662 — 360-885-5000
Jason Perrins, prin. — Fax 885-5050

Evergreen SD 114 — 24,500/PK-12
PO Box 8910 98668 — 360-604-4000
John Deeder, supt. — Fax 892-5307
www.egreen.wednet.edu
Cascade MS — 800/6-8
13900 NE 18th St 98684 — 360-604-3600
Gary Price, prin. — Fax 604-3602
Clark County Vocational Skills Center — Vo/Tech
12200 NE 28th St 98682 — 360-604-1050
Dennis Kampe, prin. — Fax 604-1052
Covington MS — 900/6-8
11200 NE Rosewood Ave 98662 — 360-604-6300
Byron Molle, prin. — Fax 604-6302
Evergreen HS — 2,300/9-12
14300 NE 18th St 98684 — 360-604-3700
Roland Brosius, prin. — Fax 604-3702
Frontier MS — 1,000/6-8
7600 NE 166th Ave 98682 — 360-604-3200
Lisa Wagner, prin. — Fax 604-3202
Heritage HS — 2,300/9-12
7825 NE 130th Ave 98682 — 360-604-3400
Ann Sosky, prin. — Fax 604-3402
Mountain View HS — 2,200/9-12
1500 SE Blairmont Dr 98683 — 360-604-6100
Mike Meloy, prin. — Fax 604-6102
Pacific MS — 1,000/6-8
2017 NE 172nd Ave 98684 — 360-604-6500
Kathy Stellfox, prin. — Fax 604-6502
Shahala MS — 900/6-8
601 SE 192nd Ave 98683 — 360-604-3800
Renee Bernazzani, prin. — Fax 604-3802
Wy' East MS — 1,000/6-8
1112 SE 136th Ave 98683 — 360-604-6400
Gary Tichenor, prin. — Fax 604-6402

Vancouver SD 37 — 22,100/PK-12
PO Box 8937 98668 — 360-313-1000
John Erickson Ph.D., supt. — Fax 313-1001
www.vansd.org
Alki MS — 800/6-8
1800 NW Bliss Rd 98685 — 360-313-3200
Curtis Smith, prin. — Fax 313-3201
Columbia River HS — 1,300/9-12
800 NW 99th St 98665 — 360-313-3900
Christina Iremonger, prin. — Fax 313-3901
Discovery MS — 800/6-8
800 E 40th St 98663 — 360-313-3300
Chris Olsen, prin. — Fax 313-3301
Fir Grove Childrens Center — 100/K-12
2920 Falk Rd 98661 — 360-313-1800
Daniel Bettis, prin. — Fax 313-1801
Ft. Vancouver HS — 1,600/9-12
5700 E 18th St 98661 — 360-313-4000
Jeff Snell, prin. — Fax 313-4001
Gaiser MS — 900/6-8
3000 NE 99th St 98665 — 360-313-3400
Betty Roberts, prin. — Fax 313-3401
Hudson's Bay HS — 1,600/9-12
1206 E Reserve St 98661 — 360-313-4400
Bill Oman, prin. — Fax 313-4401
Jefferson MS — 600/6-8
3000 NW 119th St 98685 — 360-313-3700
Marianne Thompson, prin. — Fax 313-3701
Lee MS — 900/6-8
8500 NW 9th Ave 98665 — 360-313-3500
Susan Cone, prin. — Fax 313-3501
McLoughlin MS — 900/6-8
5802 MacArthur Blvd 98661 — 360-313-3600
Richard Reeves, prin. — Fax 313-3601
School of Arts & Academics — 500/6-12
3101 Main St 98663 — 360-313-4600
James O'Banion, prin. — Fax 313-4601
Skyview HS — 1,900/9-12
1300 NW 139th St 98685 — 360-313-4200
Kym Tyelyn-Carlson, prin. — Fax 313-4201

Clark College — Post-Sec.
1800 E McLoughlin Blvd 98663 — 360-992-2000
E. Fries School of Piano Tuning & Tech. — Post-Sec.
2510 E Evergreen Blvd 98661 — 360-693-1511
International Air & Hospitality Academy — Post-Sec.
2901 E Mill Plain Blvd 98661 — 360-695-2500
Kings Way Christian S — 500/PK-10
3300 NE 78th St 98665 — 360-574-1613
Steve Jensen, prin. — Fax 573-5895
New Generation Christian S — 100/PK-12
PO Box 820289 98682 — 360-944-3905
Dave Webb, prin. — Fax 254-5567
Phagans' Orchards Beauty School — Post-Sec.
10411 NE 4th Plain Blvd 109 98662 — 360-254-9519
Vancouver Christian HS — 100/9-12
PO Box 87625 98687 — 360-735-7915
Roger Miller, admin. — Fax 735-8049
Washington State School for the Blind — Post-Sec.
2214 E 13th St 98661
Washington State School for the Deaf — Post-Sec.
611 Grand Blvd 98661
Western Business College — Post-Sec.
120 NE 136th Ave Ste 130 98684 — 360-254-3282

Vashon, King
Vashon Island SD 402 — 1,500/PK-12
18850 103rd Ave SW 98070 — 206-408-8100
Dr. Mimi Walker, supt. — Fax 463-6262
www.vashonsd.org
McMurray MS — 400/6-8
9329 SW Cemetery Rd 98070 — 206-463-9168
Greg Allison, prin. — Fax 463-9707
Vashon Island HS — 500/9-12
20120 Vashon Hwy SW 98070 — 206-463-9171
Susan Hanson, prin. — Fax 463-1944

Waitsburg, Walla Walla, Pop. 1,224
Waitsburg SD 401-100 — 400/K-12
PO Box 217 99361 — 509-337-6301
Dr. Carol Clarke, supt. — Fax 337-6042
www.waitsburgsd.org
Preston Hall MS — 100/6-8
PO Box 217 99361 — 509-337-9474
Dr. Ben Christensen, prin. — Fax 337-6170
Waitsburg HS — 100/9-12
PO Box 217 99361 — 509-337-6351
Ken Beasley, prin. — Fax 337-6551

Walla Walla, Walla Walla, Pop. 30,989
Walla Walla SD 140 — 5,700/K-12
364 S Park St 99362 — 509-527-3000
Dr. Richard Carter, supt. — Fax 529-7713
www.wwps.org
Garrison MS — 600/6-8
906 Chase Ave 99362 — 509-527-3040
Jim Sporleder, prin. — Fax 527-3048
Pioneer MS — 600/6-8
450 Bridge St 99362 — 509-527-3050
Dana Jones, prin. — Fax 526-5212
Walla Walla HS — 1,900/9-12
800 Abbott Rd 99362 — 509-527-3020
Darcy Weisner, prin. — Fax 527-3034

DeSales HS — 300/6-12
919 E Sumach St 99362 — 509-525-3030
John Lesko, prin. — Fax 527-0361

Walla Walla Community College — Post-Sec.
500 Tausick Way 99362 — 509-527-4283
Whitman College — Post-Sec.
345 Boyer Ave 99362 — 509-527-5111

Wapato, Yakima, Pop. 4,619
Wapato SD 207 — 3,400/K-12
PO Box 38 98951 — 509-877-4181
Art Edgerly, supt. — Fax 877-6077
www.wapato.k12.wa.us/
Wapato HS — 800/9-12
PO Box 38 98951 — 509-877-3138
Bob Anacker, prin. — Fax 877-4334
Wapato MS — 800/6-8
PO Box 38 98951 — 509-877-2173
Kelly Garza, prin. — Fax 877-6232

Warden, Grant, Pop. 2,635
Warden SD 146-161 — 1,000/PK-12
101 W Beck Way 98857 — 509-349-2366
Sandra Sheldon, supt. — Fax 349-2367
www.warden.wednet.edu
Warden HS — 300/9-12
101 W Beck Way 98857 — 509-349-2581
Leonard Lusk, prin. — Fax 349-2531
Warden MS — 200/6-8
101 W Beck Way 98857 — 509-349-2581
Mike Villarreal, prin. — Fax 349-2531

Washougal, Clark, Pop. 10,732
Washougal SD 112-6 — 2,800/K-12
4855 Evergreen Way 98671 — 360-954-3000
Teresa Baldwin, supt. — Fax 835-7776
www.washougal.k12.wa.us
Canyon Creek MS — 200/6-8
9731 Washougal River Rd 98671 — 360-954-3500
Sandi Christensen, prin. — Fax 837-1500
Jemtegaard MS — 400/6-8
35300 SE Evergreen Hwy 98671 — 360-954-3400
Doug Bright, prin. — Fax 835-9145
Washougal HS — 900/9-12
1201 39th St 98671 — 360-954-3100
Missy Hallead, prin. — Fax 835-3968
Washougal Community Education — Adult
4855 Evergreen Way 98671 — 360-954-3838
Jan Storm, prin. — Fax 335-0320

Washtucna, Adams, Pop. 258
Washtucna SD 109-43 — 100/K-12
PO Box 688 99371 — 509-646-3237
Chris Gregory, supt. — Fax 646-3249
Washtucna S — 100/K-12
100 School St 99371 — 509-646-3401
Glenn Martin, prin. — Fax 646-3249

Waterville, Douglas, Pop. 1,155
Waterville SD 209 — 300/K-12
PO Box 490 98858 — 509-745-8584
Mark Heid, supt. — Fax 745-9073
www.waterville.wednet.edu/
Waterville JSHS — 200/7-12
PO Box 490 98858 — 509-745-8583
Mark Heid, prin. — Fax 745-9073

Wellpinit, Stevens
Wellpinit SD 49 — 400/K-12
PO Box 390 99040 — 509-258-4535
Tim Ames, supt. — Fax 258-7378
www.wellpinit.wednet.edu
Wellpinit HS — 100/9-12
PO Box 390 99040 — 509-258-4535
Terry Bartolino, prin. — Fax 258-7378
Wellpinit MS — 100/6-8
PO Box 390 99040 — 509-258-4535
Terry Bartolino, prin. — Fax 258-7378
Other Schools – See White Swan

Wenatchee, Chelan, Pop. 29,374
Eastmont SD 206
Supt. — See East Wenatchee
North Central Washington Skills Center — Vo/Tech
327 E Penny Rd Ste D 98801 — 509-662-8827
John Linder, prin. — Fax 662-5993

Wenatchee SD 246 — 7,200/K-12
PO Box 1767 98807 — 509-663-8161
Brian Flones, supt. — Fax 663-3082
home.wsd.wednet.edu
Foothills MS, 1410 Maple St 98801 — 600/6-8
John Waldren, prin. — 509-664-8961
Orchard MS — 500/6-8
1024 Orchard Ave 98801 — 509-662-7745
Mike Hopkins, prin. — Fax 663-8042
Pioneer MS — 600/6-8
1620 Russell St 98801 — 509-663-7171
Mark Helm, prin. — Fax 663-0453
Wenatchee HS — 2,000/9-12
1101 Millerdale Ave 98801 — 509-663-8117
Michele Wadeikis, prin. — Fax 663-2573

Academy of Hair Design — Post-Sec.
208 S Wenatchee Ave 98801 — 509-662-9082
Cascade Christian Academy — 200/K-12
600 N Western Ave 98801 — 509-662-2723
Mark Witas, prin. — Fax 662-5892
River Academy — 100/PK-12
PO Box 4485 98807 — 509-665-2415
Fax 662-9235
SkillSource Office & Technology Center — Post-Sec.
234 N Mission St 98801 — 509-665-0313
Wenatchee Valley College — Post-Sec.
1300 5th St 98801 — 509-682-6800

Westport, Grays Harbor, Pop. 2,402
Ocosta SD 172 — 700/PK-12
2580 S Montesano St 98595 — 360-268-9125
Gail Sackman, supt. — Fax 268-2540
www.ocosta.k12.wa.us/
Ocosta JSHS — 400/7-12
2580 S Montesano St 98595 — 360-268-9125
Mike Church, prin. — Fax 268-0908

West Richland, Benton, Pop. 9,907
Richland SD 400
Supt. — See Richland
Enterprise MS — 6-8
5200 Paradise Dr 99353 — 509-967-6200
Mary McConnell, prin. — Fax 967-5685

White Salmon, Klickitat, Pop. 2,280
White Salmon Valley SD 405-17 — 1,200/K-12
PO Box 157 98672 — 509-493-1500
Dale Palmer, supt. — Fax 493-2275
schools.gorge.net/whitesalmon
Columbia HS — 400/9-12
PO Box 1339 98672 — 509-493-1970
Malcolm Dennis, prin. — Fax 493-4182
Henkle MS — 300/5-8
PO Box 1309 98672 — 509-493-1502
Rick George, prin. — Fax 493-3385

White Swan, Yakima, Pop. 2,669
Mount Adams SD 209 — 1,000/PK-12
PO Box 578 98952 — 509-874-2611
Mary Hall Ed.D., supt. — Fax 874-2960
www.mtadams.wednet.edu
Mount Adams MS — 200/7-8
PO Box 578 98952 — 509-874-2324
Henry Strom, prin. — Fax 874-2646
White Swan HS — 300/9-12
PO Box 578 98952 — 509-874-2324
Bob Johnson, prin. — Fax 874-2646

Wellpinit SD 49
Supt. — See Wellpinit
Wellpinit Alliance HS - Ft Simcoe — 100/11-12
40 Abella Lane 98952 — 509-874-2007
Chris Schott, dir. — Fax 874-2004

Wilbur, Lincoln, Pop. 901
Wilbur SD 200 — 200/K-12
PO Box 1090 99185 — 509-647-2221
Steve Gaub, supt. — Fax 647-2509
www.wilbur.wednet.edu/
Wilbur JSHS — 100/7-12
PO Box 1090 99185 — 509-647-5602
Tom Johnson, prin. — Fax 647-2509

Wilkeson, Pierce, Pop. 405
White River SD 416
Supt. — See Buckley
Glacier MS — 6-8
PO Box 1976, — 360-829-3395
Andy McGrath, prin. — Fax 829-3391

Wilson Creek, Grant, Pop. 242
Wilson Creek SD 167-202 — 100/K-12
PO Box 46 98860 — 509-345-2541
Linda McKay, supt. — Fax 345-2288
www.wilsoncreek.org
Wilson Creek JSHS — 100/7-12
PO Box 46 98860 — 509-345-2541
Keith Jensen, prin. — Fax 345-2288

Winlock, Lewis, Pop. 1,209
Winlock SD 232 — 700/PK-12
311 NW Fir St 98596 — 360-785-3582
Richard Conley, supt. — Fax 785-3583
Winlock HS — 200/9-12
241 N Military Rd 98596 — 360-785-3537
John Stemkoski, prin. — Fax 785-3538
Winlock MS — 200/6-8
241 N Military Rd 98596 — 360-785-3046
Marshall Mayer, prin. — Fax 785-3047

Winthrop, Okanogan, Pop. 359
Methow Valley SD 350 — 600/PK-12
18 Twin Lakes Rd 98862 — 509-996-9205
Dr. Louis Gates, supt. — Fax 996-9208
www.methow.org
Liberty Bell JSHS — 300/7-12
18 Twin Lakes Rd 98862 — 509-996-2215
Deborah Dekalb, prin.

Wishram, Klickitat
Wishram SD 94 — 100/PK-12
PO Box 8 98673 — 509-748-2551
Duane Grams, supt. — Fax 748-2127
Wishram S — 100/PK-12
PO Box 8 98673 — 509-748-2551
Duane Grams, prin. — Fax 748-2127

Woodinville, King, Pop. 9,889
Northshore SD 417
Supt. — See Bothell
Leota JHS — 700/7-9
19301 168th Ave NE 98072 — 425-402-5400
Bruce DuBois, prin. — Fax 402-5412
Timbercrest JHS — 700/7-9
19115 215th Way NE, — 425-806-7000
Larry Little, prin. — Fax 806-7011
Woodinville SHS — 1,400/10-12
19819 136th Ave NE 98072 — 425-489-6700
Vicki Puckett, prin. — Fax 489-6787

Chrysalis S — 300/K-12
14241 NE Woodinville Duvall 98072 — 425-481-2228
Karen Fogle, dir. — Fax 486-8107
Kirkland Beauty School — Post-Sec.
17311 140th Ave NE 98072 — 425-487-0437

Woodland, Cowlitz, Pop. 4,336
Woodland SD 404 — 2,000/PK-12
800 3rd St 98674 — 360-225-9451
Dr. William Hundley, supt. — Fax 225-8956
www.woodland.wednet.edu
Woodland HS — 600/9-12
757 Park St 98674 — 360-225-8201
John Shoup, prin. — Fax 225-8814
Woodland MS — 300/7-8
755 Park St 98674 — 360-225-9416
Cari Thomson Ph.D., prin. — Fax 225-6725

West Coast Training — Post-Sec.
PO Box 970 98674 — 360-225-6787

Yakima, Yakima, Pop. 81,214
East Valley SD 90 — 2,500/K-12
2002 Beaudry Rd 98901 — 509-573-7300
John J. Schieche, supt. — Fax 573-7340
www.evsd90.wednet.edu
East Valley Central MS — 400/7-8
2010 Beaudry Rd 98901 — 509-573-7500
Jeri Young, prin. — Fax 573-7540
East Valley HS — 800/9-12
1900 Beaudry Rd 98901 — 509-573-7400
Mark Hummel, prin. — Fax 573-7440

West Valley SD 208 — 4,700/K-12
8902 Zier Rd 98908 — 509-972-6000
Dr. Peter Ansingh, supt. — Fax 972-6001
www.wvsd208.org
West Valley JHS — 800/8-9
7505 Zier Rd 98908 — 509-966-5800
Jim Berndt, prin. — Fax 972-5801
West Valley SHS — 1,100/10-12
9206 Zier Rd 98908 — 509-972-5900
Jean Seibert, prin. — Fax 972-5901

Yakima SD 7 — 14,300/PK-12
104 N 4th Ave 98902 — 509-573-7000
Benjamin Soria, supt. — Fax 573-7181
www.yakimaschools.org/
Davis HS — 1,700/9-12
212 S 6th Ave 98902 — 509-573-2500
Ben Ramirez, prin. — Fax 573-2525
Eisenhower HS — 1,800/9-12
702 S 40th Ave 98908 — 509-573-2600
Stacey Locke, prin. — Fax 573-2626
Franklin MS — 800/6-8
410 S 19th Ave 98902 — 509-573-2100
Bill Hilton, prin. — Fax 573-2121
Lewis & Clark MS — 700/6-8
1114 W Pierce St 98902 — 509-573-2200
Lois Betzing, prin. — Fax 573-2222
Washington MS — 700/6-8
510 S 9th St 98901 — 509-573-2300
Lorenzo Alvarado, prin. — Fax 573-2323
Wilson MS — 800/6-8
902 S 44th Ave 98908 — 509-573-2400
Ernesto Araiza, prin. — Fax 573-2424
Yakima Valley Technical Skills Center — Vo/Tech
1116 S 15th Ave 98902 — 509-573-5000
Craig Dwight, dir. — Fax 573-5023

McAuliffe Academy — 500/K-12
402 E Yakima Ave Ste 1100 98901 — 509-575-4989
Glen Blomgren, dir. — Fax 575-4976
Perry Technical Institute — Post-Sec.
2011 W Washington Ave 98903 — 509-453-0374
Professional Beauty School — Post-Sec.
PO Box 9243 98909 — 509-877-6443
Riverside Christian S — 500/PK-12
721 Keys Rd 98901 — 509-965-2602
Rick Van Beek, supt. — Fax 966-7031
Yakima Adventist Christian S — 100/K-10
1200 City Reservoir Rd 98908 — 509-966-1933
Patrick Frey, prin. — Fax 966-3907
Yakima Valley Community College — Post-Sec.
PO Box 22520 98907 — 509-574-4600

Yelm, Thurston, Pop. 4,543
Yelm Community SD 2 — 4,400/PK-12
PO Box 476 98597 — 360-458-1900
Dr. Alan Burke, supt. — Fax 458-6178
www.ycs.wednet.edu
Ridgeline MS — 7-9
PO Box 476 98597 — 360-458-1100
John Johnson, prin. — Fax 400-1256
Yelm HS — 1,000/10-12
PO Box 476 98597 — 360-458-7777
Pete Diklich, prin. — Fax 458-6198
Yelm MS — 800/7-9
PO Box 476 98597 — 360-458-3600
Lorene Rang, prin. — Fax 458-6122

Zillah, Yakima, Pop. 2,599
Zillah SD 205 — 1,300/PK-12
1301 Cutler Way 98953 — 509-829-5911
Kevin McKay, supt. — Fax 829-6290
www.zillahschools.org/
Zillah HS — 400/9-12
1602 2nd Ave 98953 — 509-829-5565
Mike Torres, prin. — Fax 829-5285
Zillah MS — 200/7-8
1301 Cutler Way 98953 — 509-829-5511
Michael Harrington, prin. — Fax 829-6290

WEST VIRGINIA

WEST VIRGINIA DEPARTMENT OF EDUCATION
1900 Kanawha Blvd E Rm 358, Charleston 25305-0330
Telephone 304-558-2681
Fax 304-558-0048
Website wvde.state.wv.us

State Superintendent of Schools Steve Paine

WEST VIRGINIA BOARD OF EDUCATION
1900 Kanawha Blvd E Rm 358, Charleston 25305-0330

President Delores Cook

REGIONAL EDUCATION SERVICE AGENCIES (RESA)

RESA I
Keith Butcher, dir. 304-256-4712
400 Neville St, Beckley 25801 Fax 256-4683
resa1.k12.wv.us/
RESA II
Rick Powell, dir. 304-529-6205
2001 McCoy Rd, Huntington 25701 Fax 529-6209
resa2.k12.wv.us/
RESA III
Charles Nichols, dir. 304-766-7655
501 22nd St, Dunbar 25064 Fax 766-7915
resa3.k12.wv.us
RESA IV
Elmer Pritt, dir., 404 Old Main Dr 304-872-6440
Summersville 26651 Fax 872-6442
resa4.k12.wv.us/
RESA V
Ron Nichols, dir. 304-485-6513
2507 9th Ave, Parkersburg 26101 Fax 485-6515
resa5.k12.wv.us/
RESA VII
Gabriel Devono, dir. 304-624-6554
1201 N 15th St, Clarksburg 26301 Fax 624-5223
resa7.k12.wv.us/
RESA VIII
John Hough, dir., 109 S College St 304-267-3595
Martinsburg 25401 Fax 267-3599
resa8.k12.wv.us/
RESA VI
Nick Zervos, dir. 304-243-0440
30 G C and P Rd, Wheeling 26003 Fax 243-0443
resa6.k12.wv.us/

PUBLIC, PRIVATE AND CATHOLIC SECONDARY SCHOOLS

Ansted, Fayette, Pop. 1,604
Fayette County SD
Supt. — See Fayetteville
Ansted MS 200/5-8
PO Box 766 25812 304-658-5170
Chris Pinnick, prin. Fax 658-5170

Ashton, Mason
Mason County SD
Supt. — See Point Pleasant
Hannan JSHS 300/7-12
6770 Ashton Upland Rd 25503 304-576-2571
Tom McNeely, prin. Fax 743-4513

Athens, Mercer, Pop. 1,182

Concord University 24712 Post-Sec.
304-384-3115

Avondale, McDowell
McDowell County SD
Supt. — See Welch
Sandy River MS 300/6-8
PO Box 419 24811 304-938-2407
William Campbell, prin. Fax 938-2418

Baker, Hardy
Hardy County SD
Supt. — See Moorefield
East Hardy HS 200/9-12
PO Box 120 26801 304-897-5948
David Jones, prin. Fax 897-6261
East Hardy MS 300/5-8
PO Box 260 26801 304-897-5970
Rebecca Brill, prin. Fax 897-6653

Barboursville, Cabell, Pop. 3,185
Cabell County SD
Supt. — See Huntington
Barboursville MS 800/6-8
1400 Central Ave 25504 304-733-3003
Jerry Lake, prin. Fax 733-3009

Covenant S 200/K-12
5800 US Route 60 E 25504 304-736-0000
H. Keener Fry, hdmstr. Fax 736-5213

Beaver, Raleigh, Pop. 1,244

Victory Baptist Academy 100/K-12
PO Box 549 25813 304-255-4535
David Robinson, prin.

Beckley, Raleigh, Pop. 16,936
Raleigh County SD 11,400/PK-12
105 Adair St 25801 304-256-4500
Charlotte Hutchens Ed.D., supt. Fax 256-4707
boe.rale.k12.wv.us
Academy of Careers and Technology Vo/Tech
390 Stanaford Rd 25801 304-256-4615
Glenn Smith, prin. Fax 256-4674
Beckley-Stratton MS 700/6-8
401 Grey Flats Rd 25801 304-256-4616
Judy Thomas, prin. Fax 256-4616
Park MS 400/6-8
212 Park Ave 25801 304-256-4586
Joe Wright, prin. Fax 256-4709
Wilson HS 1,300/9-12
400 Stanaford Rd 25801 304-256-4646
Bob Maynard, prin. Fax 256-4642
Other Schools – See Coal City, Glen Daniel, Shady Spring, Sophia

---

Beckley Beauty Academy Post-Sec.
109 S Fayette St 25801 304-253-8326
Mountain State University Post-Sec.
PO Box 9003 25802 304-253-7351
New River Community & Technical College Post-Sec.
167 Dye Dr 25801 304-255-5812
Trinity Christian Academy 100/PK-12
PO Box 1123 25802 304-254-9600
J.S. Peterson, admin. Fax 254-9655
Valley College of Technology Post-Sec.
713 S Oakwood Ave 25801 304-252-9547
Veterans Administration Hospital Post-Sec.
200 Veterans Ave 25801 304-255-2121

Belington, Barbour, Pop. 1,814
Barbour County SD
Supt. — See Philippi
Belington MS 200/6-8
RR 2 Box 343 26250 304-823-1281
H. Moke Post, prin. Fax 823-2403

Belle, Kanawha, Pop. 1,187
Kanawha County SD
Supt. — See Charleston
DuPont MS 400/6-8
1 Panther Dr 25015 304-348-1978
David Miller, prin. Fax 949-1793
Riverside HS 1,200/9-12
1 Warrior Way 25015 304-348-1996
Paula Potter, prin. Fax 348-1921

Belmont, Pleasants, Pop. 1,009
Pleasants County SD
Supt. — See Saint Marys
Pleasants County MS 400/5-8
510 Riverview Dr 26134 304-665-2415
Mike Wells, prin. Fax 665-2451

Berkeley Springs, Morgan, Pop. 756
Morgan County SD 2,500/PK-12
247 Harrison Ave 25411 304-258-2430
David Temple, supt. Fax 258-9146
www.morganschools.net
Berkeley Springs HS 600/9-12
149 Concord Ave 25411 304-258-2876
George Ward, prin. Fax 258-5058
Warm Springs MS 600/6-8
1415 Fairfax St 25411 304-258-1500
Gene Brock, prin. Fax 258-4600
Other Schools – See Paw Paw

Berkeley Springs SDA S 50/K-10
3606 Valley Rd 25411 304-258-3581
Fax 258-8344

Bethany, Brooke, Pop. 985

Bethany College 26032 Post-Sec.
304-829-7000

Blacksville, Monongalia, Pop. 172
Monongalia County SD
Supt. — See Morgantown
Clay-Battelle JSHS 400/7-12
PO Box A 26521 304-432-8208
Karen Church, prin. Fax 432-8189

Bluefield, Mercer, Pop. 11,119
Mercer County SD
Supt. — See Princeton
Bluefield HS 700/9-12
535 W Cumberland Rd 24701 304-325-9116
Joe Turner, prin. Fax 325-0529
Bluefield MS 600/6-8
2002 Stadium Dr 24701 304-325-2481
Todd Browning, prin. Fax 325-2156

Bluefield Regional Medical Center Post-Sec.
500 Cherry St 24701 304-327-1701
Bluefield State College Post-Sec.
219 Rock St 24701 304-327-4000
Valley View SDA S 50/K-12
PO Box 6312 24701 304-325-8679
Rosalie Stockil, prin.

Bradley, Raleigh, Pop. 2,144

Appalachian Bible College Post-Sec.
PO Box ABC 25818 800-678-9222

Branchland, Lincoln
Lincoln County SD
Supt. — See Hamlin
Guyan Valley MS 200/6-8
700 State Route 10 25506 304-824-3235
Kevin Prichard, prin. Fax 824-3459

Bridgeport, Harrison, Pop. 7,486
Harrison County SD
Supt. — See Clarksburg
Bridgeport HS 800/9-12
515 Johnson Ave 26330 304-842-3693
Mike DeFazio, prin. Fax 842-6288
Bridgeport MS 700/6-8
413 Johnson Ave 26330 304-842-6251
Carole Crawford, prin. Fax 842-6275

West Virginia Junior College Post-Sec.
176 Thompson Dr 26330 304-842-4007

Buckeye, Pocahontas
Pocahontas County SD
Supt. — See Marlinton
Marlinton MS 200/5-8
RR 2 Box 52S 24924 304-799-6773
Cyrus Lester, prin. Fax 799-7278

Buckhannon, Upshur, Pop. 5,687
Upshur County SD 3,700/K-12
102 Smithfield St 26201 304-472-5480
Dr. Charles Chandler, supt. Fax 472-0258
boe.upsh.k12.wv.us
Buckhannon-Upshur HS 1,100/9-12
50 B U Dr 26201 304-472-3720
Donald Swisher, prin. Fax 472-0772
Buckhannon-Upshur MS 900/6-8
RR 6 Box 303 26201 304-472-1520
Renee Warner, prin. Fax 472-6864
Eberle Tech Ctr Vo/Tech
RR 5 Box 2 26201 304-472-1259
Mike Cutright, prin. Fax 472-3418

West Virginia Wesleyan College — Post-Sec.
59 College Ave 26201 — 304-473-8000

Buffalo, Putnam, Pop. 1,204
Putnam County SD
Supt. — See Winfield
Buffalo HS — 300/9-12
3317 Buffalo Rd 25033 — 304-937-2661
Richard Grim, prin. — Fax 937-3470

Bunker Hill, Berkeley
Berkeley County SD
Supt. — See Martinsburg
Musselman MS — 1,100/6-8
105 Pride Ave 25413 — 304-229-1965
James Holland, prin. — Fax 229-1967

Cameron, Marshall, Pop. 1,142
Marshall County SD
Supt. — See Moundsville
Cameron JSHS — 400/7-12
61 Maple Ave 26033 — 304-686-3336
Jack Cain, prin. — Fax 686-3510

Capon Bridge, Hampshire, Pop. 214
Hampshire County SD
Supt. — See Romney
Capon Bridge MS — 400/6-8
PO Box 147 26711 — 304-856-2534
Jeff Meadows, prin. — Fax 856-3192

Center Point, Doddridge

Mountain State Academy — 100/K-12
PO Box 10 26339 — 304-266-7794
Fax 659-2666

Ceredo, Wayne, Pop. 1,631
Wayne County SD
Supt. — See Wayne
Ceredo-Kenova MS — 300/6-8
PO Box 705 25507 — 304-453-3588
Barry Scragg, prin. — Fax 453-4420

Chapmanville, Logan, Pop. 1,145
Logan County SD
Supt. — See Logan
Chapmanville HS — 500/9-12
200 Vance St 25508 — 304-855-4522
Terry M. Elkins, prin. — Fax 855-1911
Chapmanville MS — 600/5-8
300 Vance St 25508 — 304-855-8378
Martina Mills, prin. — Fax 855-1307

Charleston, Kanawha, Pop. 51,176
Kanawha County SD — 27,700/PK-12
200 Elizabeth St 25311 — 304-348-7732
Ronald Duerring Ed.D., supt. — Fax 348-7735
kcs.kana.k12.wv.us/
Adams MS — 800/6-8
2002 Presidential Dr 25314 — 304-348-6652
Thomas Kidd, prin. — Fax 348-6592
Capital HS — 1,300/9-12
1500 Greenbrier St 25311 — 304-348-6500
Clinton Giles, prin. — Fax 348-6509
Carver Career Center — Vo/Tech
4799 Midland Dr 25306 — 304-348-1965
James Casdorph, prin. — Fax 348-1938
Garnet Career Center — Vo/Tech
422 Dickinson St 25301 — 304-348-6195
Sharon Miller, prin. — Fax 348-6198
Jackson MS — 600/6-8
812 Park Ave 25302 — 304-348-6123
George Aulenbacher, prin. — Fax 348-1999
Mann MS — 400/6-8
4300 Maccorkle Ave SE 25304 — 304-348-1971
James Blackwell, prin. — Fax 348-6591
Sissonville HS — 600/9-12
6100 Sissonville Dr 25312 — 304-348-1954
Calvin McKinney, prin. — Fax 348-6565
Tyler MS — 6-8
4277 Washington St W 25313 — 304-348-6133
Wayman Wilson, prin. — Fax 348-6690
Washington HS — 1,000/9-12
1522 Tennis Club Rd 25314 — 304-348-7729
James Vickers, prin. — Fax 344-4947
Other Schools – See Belle, Clendenin, Cross Lanes, Dunbar, East Bank, Elkview, Nitro, Saint Albans, Sissonville, South Charleston

---

Carver Career and Tech Education Center — Post-Sec.
4799 Midland Dr 25306 — 304-348-1965
Charleston Catholic HS — 500/6-12
1033 Virginia St E 25301 — 304-342-8415
Debra Sullivan, prin. — Fax 342-1259
Charleston School of Beauty Culture — Post-Sec.
210 Capitol St 25301 — 304-346-9603
Cross Lanes Christian S — 300/K-12
5330 Floradale Dr 25313 — 304-776-5020
Steve Adams, admin. — Fax 776-5074
Fairhaven Christian S — 100/K-12
689 Fairhaven Dr 25306 — 304-925-5954
Jimmy McMillan, prin. — Fax 720-8403
Garnet Career Center — Post-Sec.
422 Dickinson St 25301 — 304-348-6195
University of Charleston — Post-Sec.
2300 Maccorkle Ave SE 25304 — 304-357-4800
West Virginia Junior College — Post-Sec.
1000 Virginia St E 25301 — 304-345-2820

Charles Town, Jefferson, Pop. 3,704
Jefferson County SD — 7,700/PK-12
PO Box 987 25414 — 304-725-9741
Dr. Steven Nichols, supt. — Fax 725-6487
boe.jeff.k12.wv.us
Charles Town MS — 900/6-8
193 High St 25414 — 304-725-7821
Charles Hampton, prin. — Fax 728-7526
Other Schools – See Harpers Ferry, Shenandoah Junction, Shepherdstown

---

American Public University — Post-Sec.
111 W Congress St 25414 — 877-468-6268

Charmco, Greenbrier
Greenbrier County SD
Supt. — See Lewisburg
Greenbrier West HS — 300/9-12
PO Box 325 25958 — 304-438-6191
Randy Auvil, prin. — Fax 438-9189

Clarksburg, Harrison, Pop. 16,439
Harrison County SD — 10,500/PK-12
PO Box 1370 26302 — 304-624-3300
Carl Friebel Ed.D., supt. — Fax 624-3361
www.harcoboe.com
Byrd HS — 800/9-12
1 Eagle Way 26301 — 304-624-2453
Leon Pilewski, prin. — Fax 624-3211
Irving MS — 700/6-8
443 Lee Ave 26301 — 304-624-3271
Douglas Hogue, prin. — Fax 624-3388
Liberty HS — 600/9-12
1 Mountaineer Dr 26301 — 304-624-3264
Dennis Zahradnik, prin. — Fax 623-3159
Mountaineer MS — 6-8
2 Mountaineer Dr 26301 — 304-624-3300
Pamela Leggett, prin.
United Technical Ctr — Vo/Tech
RR 3 Box 43C 26301 — 304-624-3280
Joan Smith, prin. — Fax 622-6138
Other Schools – See Bridgeport, Lost Creek, Lumberport, Shinnston

---

Clarksburg Beauty Academy — Post-Sec.
120 S 3rd St 26301 — 304-624-6475
Emmanuel Christian S — 100/PK-12
1318 N 16th St 26301 — 304-624-6125
Daryl Van Norman, prin. — Fax 624-5349
Notre Dame HS — 100/7-12
127 E Pike St 26301 — 304-623-1026
Dr. Carroll Morrison, prin. — Fax 623-1026
United Hospital Center — Post-Sec.
PO Box 2308 26302 — 304-624-2332

Clay, Clay, Pop. 580
Clay County SD — 2,100/PK-12
PO Box 120 25043 — 304-587-4266
Larry Gillespie, supt. — Fax 587-4181
www.claycountyschools.org
Clay County HS — 600/9-12
1 Panther Dr 25043 — 304-587-4226
Phillip Dobbins, prin. — Fax 587-7698
Clay County MS — 500/6-8
PO Box 489 25043 — 304-587-2343
Joe Paxton, prin. — Fax 587-2759

Clear Fork, Wyoming
Wyoming County SD
Supt. — See Pineville
Westside HS — 600/9-12
HC 65 Box 275 24822 — 304-682-8965
Deborah Marsh, prin. — Fax 682-6273

Clendenin, Kanawha, Pop. 1,056
Kanawha County SD
Supt. — See Charleston
Hoover HS — 700/9-12
275 Elk River Rd S 25045 — 304-965-3394
Roy Jones, prin. — Fax 965-1871

Coal City, Raleigh, Pop. 1,876
Raleigh County SD
Supt. — See Beckley
Independence HS — 700/9-12
PO Box 1595 25823 — 304-683-3228
Bob Meadows, prin. — Fax 683-4393

Cowen, Webster, Pop. 506
Webster County SD
Supt. — See Webster Springs
Glade MS — 300/5-8
25 Mill St 26206 — 304-226-5353
Stephen White, prin. — Fax 226-3666

Craigsville, Nicholas, Pop. 1,955
Nicholas County SD
Supt. — See Summersville
Nicholas County Career and Technical Ctr — Vo/Tech
215 Milam Addition Rd 26205 — 304-742-5416
Vicki Nutter, prin. — Fax 742-3953

Crawley, Greenbrier
Greenbrier County SD
Supt. — See Lewisburg
Western Greenbrier MS — 200/6-8
HC 40 Box 14 24931 — 304-392-6446
Mark Keaton, prin. — Fax 392-6785

Cross Lanes, Kanawha, Pop. 10,878
Kanawha County SD
Supt. — See Charleston
Jackson MS — 700/6-8
5445 Big Tyler Rd 25313 — 304-776-3310
Lisa Woo, prin. — Fax 776-3305

Everest Institute — Post-Sec.
5514 Big Tyler Rd 25313 — 304-776-6290

Crum, Wayne
Wayne County SD
Supt. — See Wayne
Crum MS — 100/6-8
PO Box 9 25669 — 304-393-3200
Jim Fletcher, prin. — Fax 393-4429

Danville, Boone, Pop. 540
Boone County SD
Supt. — See Madison
Boone County Career & Tech Ctr — Vo/Tech
3505 Daniel Boone Pkwy 25053 — 304-369-4585
Keith Phipps, prin. — Fax 369-3692

Boone County Career Center — Post-Sec.
3505 Daniel Boone Pkwy # B 25053 — 304-369-4585

Delbarton, Mingo, Pop. 442
Mingo County SD
Supt. — See Williamson
Burch HS — 300/9-12
RR 2 Box 521A 25670 — 304-475-2700
Jada Hunter, prin. — Fax 475-5106
Mingo Career & Technical Center — Vo/Tech
RR 2 Box 52A 25670 — 304-475-3347
Thomas Hoffman, prin. — Fax 475-3797

Regional Christian S — 100/PK-12
PO Box 236 25670 — 304-475-3468
Michael Edds, hdmstr. — Fax 475-5287

Dunbar, Kanawha, Pop. 7,740
Kanawha County SD
Supt. — See Charleston
Dunbar MS — 400/6-8
325 27th St 25064 — 304-766-0363
Lynda Gilkeson, prin. — Fax 766-0365
Franklin Career & Tech Ed — Vo/Tech
500 28th St 25064 — 304-766-0369
John Baird, prin. — Fax 766-0371

Dunmore, Pocahontas
Pocahontas County SD
Supt. — See Marlinton
Pocahontas County HS — 400/9-12
RR 1 Box 133A 24934 — 304-799-6565
Thomas Sanders, prin. — Fax 799-6893

East Bank, Kanawha, Pop. 896
Kanawha County SD
Supt. — See Charleston
East Bank MS — 500/6-8
PO Box 897 25067 — 304-595-2311
Candy Strader, prin. — Fax 595-4676

Eleanor, Putnam, Pop. 1,491
Putnam County SD
Supt. — See Winfield
Putnam County Technical Center — Vo/Tech
RR 62 Box 640 25070 — 304-586-3494
Robert Manley, prin. — Fax 586-4467
Washington MS — 300/6-8
PO Box 660 25070 — 304-586-2875
Joann Stewart, prin. — Fax 586-3037

Elizabeth, Wirt, Pop. 972
Wirt County SD — 1,000/PK-12
PO Box 189 26143 — 304-275-4279
Dan Metz, supt. — Fax 275-4581
boe.wirt.k12.wv.us/
Wirt County HS — 300/9-12
PO Box 219 26143 — 304-275-4241
Kenneth Heiney, prin. — Fax 275-3271
Wirt County MS — 300/5-8
PO Box 699 26143 — 304-275-3977
J. D. Hoover, prin. — Fax 275-4257

Elkins, Randolph, Pop. 7,109
Randolph County SD — 4,400/PK-12
40 11th St 26241 — 304-636-9150
Susan Hinzman, supt. — Fax 636-9157
boe.rand.k12.wv.us
Elkins HS — 900/9-12
100 Kennedy Dr 26241 — 304-636-9170
Thomas Pritt, prin. — Fax 636-9168
Elkins MS — 800/6-8
308 Robert E Lee Ave 26241 — 304-636-9176
David Roth, prin. — Fax 636-9178
Randolph Technical Center — Vo/Tech
200 Kennedy Dr 26241 — 304-636-9195
Don Johnson, prin. — Fax 636-9169
Other Schools – See Harman, Mill Creek, Pickens

Davis & Elkins College — Post-Sec.
100 Campus Dr 26241 — 304-637-1900
Highland Adventist S — 50/K-12
205 Wilson St 26241 — 304-636-0811
Fax 636-0811

Elkview, Kanawha, Pop. 1,047
Kanawha County SD
Supt. — See Charleston
Elkview MS — 800/6-8
5090 Elk River Rd 25071 — 304-348-1947
Rick Messinger, prin. — Fax 348-6590

Elk Valley Christian S — 200/PK-12
5110 Elk River Rd 25071 — 304-965-7063
Barbara Hamm, prin. — Fax 965-7064

Ellenboro, Ritchie, Pop. 372
Ritchie County SD
Supt. — See Harrisville
Ritchie County HS — 500/9-12
107 Ritchie Co School Rd 26346 — 304-869-3526
April Haught, prin. — Fax 869-3526
Ritchie County MS — 400/6-8
105 Ritchie Co School Rd 26346 — 304-869-3512
Michael Dotson, prin. — Fax 869-3512

Fairmont, Marion, Pop. 19,049
Marion County SD — 8,100/PK-12
200 Gaston Ave 26554 — 304-367-2100
Dr. James Phares, supt. — Fax 367-2111
www.marionboe.com/index.asp?process=schools
East Fairmont HS — 900/9-12
1993 Airport Rd 26554 — 304-367-2140
David Nuzum, prin. — Fax 367-2180
East Fairmont JHS — 400/7-8
1 Orion Ln 26554 — 304-367-2123
Christine Miller, prin. — Fax 367-2179
Fairmont HS — 800/9-12
1 Loop Park Dr 26554 — 304-367-2150
Chad Norman, prin. — Fax 366-5980

Miller JHS 400/7-8
2 Pennsylvania Ave 26554 304-367-2147
Rockie DeLorenzo, prin. Fax 367-2169
Marion County Adult & Community Educ. Adult
601 Locust Ave 26554 304-363-7323
Roman Prezioso, prin. Fax 366-2483
Other Schools – See Fairview, Farmington, Mannington, Monongah

Calvary Christian S 100/K-12
28 Fellowship Dr 26554 304-363-8008
David West, prin.
Fairmont State University Post-Sec.
1201 Locust Ave 26554 304-367-4000

Fairview, Marion, Pop. 436
Marion County SD
Supt. — See Fairmont
Fairview MS, 17 Jesses Run Rd 26570 200/5-8
Steve Rodriguez, prin. 304-449-1312

Farmington, Marion, Pop. 387
Marion County SD
Supt. — See Fairmont
Marion County Technical Center Vo/Tech
2 N Marion Dr 26571 304-986-3590
Roger Perdue, prin. Fax 986-3440
North Marion HS 900/9-12
1 N Marion Dr 26571 304-986-3063
Judd Ashcraft, prin. Fax 986-3086

Fayetteville, Fayette, Pop. 2,657
Fayette County SD 6,100/PK-12
111 Fayette Ave 25840 304-574-1176
Chris Perkins, supt. Fax 574-3643
boe.faye.k12.wv.us
Fayetteville HS 300/7-12
515 W Maple Ave 25840 304-574-0560
Bryan Parsons, prin. Fax 574-0118
Other Schools – See Ansted, Hico, Lookout, Meadow Bridge, Mount Hope, Oak Hill, Smithers

Follansbee, Brooke, Pop. 2,971
Brooke County SD
Supt. — See Wellsburg
Follansbee MS 600/5-8
Main and Mark Ave 26037 304-527-1942
Joe Starcher, prin. Fax 527-1954

Fort Gay, Wayne, Pop. 818
Wayne County SD
Supt. — See Wayne
Fort Gay MS 300/6-8
PO Box 460 25514 304-648-5404
Donita Webb, prin. Fax 648-7082
Tolsia HS 500/9-12
1 Rebel Dr 25514 304-648-5566
L. Matthew Stanley, prin. Fax 648-5447

Franklin, Pendleton, Pop. 824
Pendleton County SD 1,200/PK-12
PO Box 888 26807 304-358-2207
Doug Lambert, supt. Fax 358-2936
pendletoncountyschools.com/
Pendleton County MSHS 500/7-12
PO Box 40 26807 304-358-2573
Charles Hedrick, prin. Fax 358-7701

Gilbert, Mingo, Pop. 399
Mingo County SD
Supt. — See Williamson
Gilbert HS 400/7-12
PO Box 366 25621 304-664-8197
Daniel Dean, prin. Fax 664-8249

Glen Dale, Marshall, Pop. 1,475
Marshall County SD
Supt. — See Moundsville
Marshall HS 1,400/9-12
1300 Wheeling Ave 26038 304-843-4444
Thomas Wood, prin. Fax 843-4419

Glen Daniel, Raleigh
Raleigh County SD
Supt. — See Beckley
Liberty HS 600/9-12
PO Box 265 25844 304-934-5307
Clyde Stepp, prin. Fax 934-5307
Trap Hill MS 500/6-8
665 Coal River Rd 25844 304-934-5392
Marsha Smith, prin. Fax 934-5393

Glenville, Gilmer, Pop. 1,482
Gilmer County SD 1,000/PK-12
201 N Court St 26351 304-462-7386
Edward Toman, supt. Fax 462-5103
gilmercountyschools.org/
Gilmer County JSHS 500/7-12
300 Pine St 26351 304-462-7960
Robert Daquilante, prin. Fax 462-7059

Glenville State College Post-Sec.
200 High St 26351 304-462-7361

Grafton, Taylor, Pop. 5,407
Taylor County SD 2,200/PK-12
1 Prospect St 26354 304-265-2497
Jane Reynolds, supt. Fax 265-2508
www.wvonline.com/taylorcounty
Grafton HS 700/9-12
400 Riverside Dr 26354 304-265-3046
Orville Wright, prin. Fax 265-2156
Taylor County MS 700/5-8
RR 2 Box 148A 26354 304-265-0722
James Reneau, prin. Fax 265-4623
Taylor County Vo Ctr Vo/Tech
115 Luby St 26354 304-265-1050
Mary Tucker, prin. Fax 265-1058

Grantsville, Calhoun, Pop. 546
Calhoun County SD
Supt. — See Mount Zion

Calhoun Gilmer Career Center Vo/Tech
5236 E Little Kanawha Hwy 26147 304-354-6151
John Bennett, dir. Fax 354-6154

Hambleton, Tucker, Pop. 250
Tucker County SD
Supt. — See Parsons
Tucker County Career Center Vo/Tech
RR 1 Box 152 26269 304-478-3111
Joe Michael, prin.
Tucker County HS 300/9-12
RR 1 Box 152 26269 304-478-2651
David Dilly, prin. Fax 478-4357

Hamlin, Lincoln, Pop. 1,100
Lincoln County SD 1,900/PK-12
10 Marland Ave 25523 304-824-3033
Anne Seaver, supt. Fax 824-7947
boe.linc.k12.wv.us/
Lincoln HS 9-12
81 Lincoln Panther Way 25523 304-824-6000
Dana Snyder, prin.
Other Schools – See Branchland, Harts

Harman, Randolph, Pop. 126
Randolph County SD
Supt. — See Elkins
Harman S 200/K-12
PO Box 130 26270 304-227-4114
Debbie Schmidlen, prin. Fax 227-3610

Harpers Ferry, Jefferson, Pop. 313
Jefferson County SD
Supt. — See Charles Town
Harpers Ferry MS 500/6-8
1710 W Washington St 25425 304-535-6357
Joseph Spurgas, prin. Fax 535-6986

Harpers Ferry Job Corps Post-Sec.
146 Buffalo Dr 25425 304-728-5772

Harrisville, Ritchie, Pop. 1,861
Ritchie County SD 1,600/PK-12
134 S Penn Ave 26362 304-643-2991
Dr. Richard Butler, supt. Fax 643-2994
Other Schools – See Ellenboro

Harts, Lincoln, Pop. 2,332
Lincoln County SD
Supt. — See Hamlin
Harts IS 100/4-8
RR 1 Box 130 25524 304-855-4881
Peggy Adkins, prin. Fax 855-7945

Hedgesville, Berkeley, Pop. 244
Berkeley County SD
Supt. — See Martinsburg
Hedgesville HS 1,500/9-12
109 Ridge Rd N 25427 304-754-3354
Don Dellinger, prin. Fax 754-7445
Hedgesville MS 600/6-8
334 Schoolhouse Dr 25427 304-754-3313
Charles Scott, prin. Fax 754-6613

Hico, Fayette
Fayette County SD
Supt. — See Fayetteville
Midland Trail HS 300/9-12
PO Box 89 25854 304-658-5184
Diane Blume, prin. Fax 658-5185

Hilltop, Fayette, Pop. 250

Mountainview Christian S 200/PK-12
2 Mountain View Rd 25855 304-465-0502
Rev. Rudell Bloomfield, hdmstr. Fax 465-5484

Hinton, Summers, Pop. 2,696
Summers County SD 1,600/PK-12
116 Main St 25951 304-466-6000
Vicki Hinerman, supt. Fax 466-6008
boe.summ.k12.wv.us
Summers County HS 500/9-12
HC 74 Box 11A 25951 304-466-6040
Garrett Crowder, prin. Fax 466-6044
Summers MS 400/6-8
400 Temple St 25951 304-466-6030
Kitrick Durnan, prin. Fax 466-2271

Hundred, Wetzel, Pop. 335
Wetzel County SD
Supt. — See New Martinsville
Hundred HS 100/9-12
PO Box 830 26575 304-775-5221
Samuel M. Snyder, prin. Fax 775-2922

Huntington, Cabell, Pop. 49,198
Cabell County SD 12,100/PK-12
2850 5th Ave 25702 304-528-5000
William Smith, supt. Fax 528-5080
boe.cabe.k12.wv.us
Beverly Hills MS 500/6-8
2901 Saltwell Rd 25705 304-528-5102
Gary Cook, prin. Fax 528-5197
Cabell County Career Technology Center Vo/Tech
1035 Norway Ave 25705 304-528-5106
Brenda Tanner, prin. Fax 528-5110
Cammack MS 400/6-8
200 10th Ave 25701 304-528-5116
Mary Freeman, prin. Fax 528-5199
Enslow MS 300/6-8
2613 Collis Ave 25702 304-528-5121
Georgia Thornton, prin. Fax 528-5097
Huntington HS 1,600/9-12
1 Highlander Way 25701 304-528-6400
Greg Webb, prin. Fax 528-6422
West MS 200/6-8
1001 Jefferson Ave 25704 304-528-5180
Joe Brison, prin. Fax 528-5215
Other Schools – See Barboursville, Milton, Ona

Wayne County SD
Supt. — See Wayne
Spring Valley HS 1,100/9-12
1 Timberwolfe Dr 25704 304-429-1699
Paula Staley, prin. Fax 429-7315
Vinson MS 300/6-8
3851 Piedmont Rd 25704 304-429-1641
Tammy Brumfield, prin. Fax 429-6162

Cabell Huntington Hospital Post-Sec.
1340 Hal Greer Blvd 25701 304-526-2111
Grace Christian S 400/PK-12
1111 Adams Ave 25704 304-522-8635
Dr. Dan Brokke, admin. Fax 522-3240
Huntington Junior College Post-Sec.
900 5th Ave 25701 304-697-7550
Huntington School of Beauty Culture Post-Sec.
5185 US Route 60 Ste 115 25705 304-736-6289
Marshall University Post-Sec.
400 Hal Greer Blvd 25755 304-696-3170
St. Joseph Central HS 100/7-12
600 13th St 25701 304-525-5096
Patrick Finneran, prin. Fax 525-0781
St. Mary's Medical Center Post-Sec.
2900 1st Ave 25702 304-526-1270

Hurricane, Putnam, Pop. 5,968
Putnam County SD
Supt. — See Winfield
Hurricane HS 1,000/9-12
3350 Teays Valley Rd 25526 304-562-3991
Roger Hart, prin. Fax 562-5460
Hurricane MS 800/6-8
518 Midland Trl 25526 304-562-9271
Greg LeMaster, prin. Fax 562-7163

Calvary Baptist Academy 100/K-12
3655 Teays Valley Rd 25526 304-757-6768
Milton Thompson, prin. Fax 757-6777

Iaeger, McDowell, Pop. 314
McDowell County SD
Supt. — See Welch
Iaeger HS 500/9-12
PO Box 779 24844 304-938-2431
Doug Addair, prin. Fax 938-5158

Institute, Kanawha

WV State Community & Technical College Post-Sec.
PO Box 1000 25112 304-766-3118
West Virginia State University Post-Sec.
PO Box 1000 25112 304-766-3000

Inwood, Berkeley, Pop. 1,360
Berkeley County SD
Supt. — See Martinsburg
Musselman HS 1,300/9-12
126 Excellence Way 25428 304-229-1950
Ronald Stephens, prin. Fax 229-1959

Kenova, Wayne, Pop. 3,391
Wayne County SD
Supt. — See Wayne
Buffalo MS 400/6-8
298 Buffalo Creek Rd 25530 304-429-6062
John Waugaman, prin. Fax 429-7245

Keyser, Mineral, Pop. 5,410
Mineral County SD 4,500/PK-12
1 Baker Pl 26726 304-788-4200
Skip Hackworth, supt. Fax 788-4204
boe.mine.k12.wv.us/
Keyser HS 800/9-12
1 Tornado Way 26726 304-788-4230
Charles Wimer, prin. Fax 788-4234
Mineral County Technical Center Vo/Tech
600 S Water St 26726 304-788-4240
Alan Whetzel, prin. Fax 788-4243
Other Schools – See Ridgeley

Potomac State College of West Virginia U Post-Sec.
101 Fort Ave Bldg 1 26726 304-788-6800

Kingwood, Preston, Pop. 2,926
Preston County SD 4,600/K-12
PO Box 566 26537 304-329-0580
John Lofink, supt. Fax 329-0720
www.prestonboe.com
Central Preston MS 300/6-8
100 E High St 26537 304-329-0033
Thomas Strahin, prin. Fax 329-2389
Preston HS 1,400/9-12
400 Preston Dr 26537 304-329-0400
Douglas Riley, prin. Fax 329-3899
Other Schools – See Masontown, Tunnelton

Integrity Christian S 50/K-12
PO Box 457 26537 304-329-2498
Teresa Lewis, prin. Fax 329-2498

Le Roy, Jackson
Jackson County SD
Supt. — See Ripley
Roane-Jackson Tech Ctr Vo/Tech
4800 Spencer Rd 25252 304-372-7335
Dennis Carpenter, prin. Fax 372-7336

Lewisburg, Greenbrier, Pop. 3,595
Greenbrier County SD 4,300/PK-12
202 Chestnut St 24901 304-647-6470
John Curry, supt. Fax 647-6490
boe.gree.k12.wv.us/
Greenbrier East HS 800/9-12
1 Spartan Ln 24901 304-647-6464
Jeff Bryant, prin. Fax 645-2698
Other Schools – See Charmco, Crawley, Ronceverte

Greenbrier Adventist Junior Academy 50/K-10
235 N Court St 24901 304-647-9750

West Virginia Sch./Osteopathic Medicine Post-Sec.
400 N Lee St 24901 304-645-6270

Lindside, Monroe
Monroe County SD
Supt. — See Union
Monroe County Technical Center Vo/Tech
RR 1 Box 97 24951 304-753-9971
Paul Lovett, dir. Fax 753-9792
Monroe HS 600/9-12
RR 1 Box 97-1A 24951 304-753-5182
Christine Parker, prin. Fax 753-5184

Logan, Logan, Pop. 1,547
Logan County SD 6,000/PK-12
PO Box 477 25601 304-792-2060
David Godby, supt. Fax 752-3711
lc2.boe.loga.k12.wv.us/
Logan HS 700/9-12
1 Wildcat Way 25601 304-752-6606
Robert Lucas, prin. Fax 752-6614
Logan MS 900/5-8
14 Wildcat Way 25601 304-752-1804
Ernestine Sutherland, prin. Fax 752-0207
Willis Vo-Tech Center Vo/Tech
PO Box 1747 25601 304-752-4687
Clarence Elkins, prin. Fax 752-2943
Other Schools – See Chapmanville, Man

Lookout, Fayette
Fayette County SD
Supt. — See Fayetteville
Nuttall MS 200/5-8
PO Box 130 25868 304-574-0429
Susan Maddox, prin. Fax 574-0491

Lost Creek, Harrison, Pop. 497
Harrison County SD
Supt. — See Clarksburg
South Harrison HS 400/9-12
RR 1 Box 58 26385 304-745-3315
Philip Brown, prin. Fax 745-4292
South Harrison MS 300/6-8
RR 1 Box 58B 26385 304-745-5582
Phil Brown, prin. Fax 745-5587

Lumberport, Harrison, Pop. 969
Harrison County SD
Supt. — See Clarksburg
Lumberport MS 500/6-8
PO Box 309 26386 304-584-4090
Anthony Fratto, prin. Fax 584-4602

Mc Mechen, Marshall, Pop. 2,019

Bishop Donahue Memorial HS 100/9-12
325 Logan St 26040 304-233-3850
Daniel Angalich, prin. Fax 233-8677

Madison, Boone, Pop. 2,634
Boone County SD 4,500/PK-12
69 Avenue B 25130 304-369-3131
Steve Pauley, supt. Fax 369-6789
www.boonecountyboe.org
Madison MS 600/6-8
404 Riverside Dr W 25130 304-369-4464
Gary Bell, prin. Fax 369-5800
Scott HS 700/9-12
1 Skyhawk Pl 25130 304-369-3011
Leonard Bolton, prin. Fax 369-6564
Other Schools – See Danville, Seth, Van

Man, Logan, Pop. 716
Logan County SD
Supt. — See Logan
Man HS 400/9-12
800 E McDonald Ave 25635 304-583-6521
Sandy Manning, prin. Fax 583-6566

Mannington, Marion, Pop. 2,080
Marion County SD
Supt. — See Fairmont
Mannington MS 400/5-8
113 Clarksburg St 26582 304-986-1050
Mike Call, prin.

Marlinton, Pocahontas, Pop. 1,247
Pocahontas County SD 1,400/PK-12
926 5th Ave 24954 304-799-4505
Dr. Patrick Law, supt. Fax 799-4499
boe.poca.k12.wv.us
Other Schools – See Buckeye, Dunmore

Martinsburg, Berkeley, Pop. 15,996
Berkeley County SD 14,600/PK-12
401 S Queen St 25401 304-267-3500
Manny Arvon, supt. Fax 267-3524
boe.berk.k12.wv.us
Martinsburg HS 1,500/9-12
701 S Queen St 25401 304-267-3530
Kenneth Pack, prin. Fax 267-3536
Martinsburg North MS 700/6-8
250 East Rd, 304-267-3540
David Rudy, prin. Fax 264-5066
Martinsburg South MS 800/6-8
Bulldog Blvd 25401 304-267-3545
David Rogers, prin. Fax 264-5062
Rumsey Technical Institute Vo/Tech
3274 Hedgesville Rd, 304-754-7925
Vicki Jenkins, dir. Fax 754-7933
Spring Mills MS 500/6-8
255 Campus Dr, 304-274-5030
Marc Arvon, prin. Fax 274-3598
Other Schools – See Bunker Hill, Hedgesville, Inwood

Blue Ridge Community & Technical College Post-Sec.
400 W Stephen St 25401 304-260-4380
Faith Christian Academy 300/PK-12
138 Greensburg Rd, 304-263-0011
Eric Kerns, admin. Fax 267-0638
International Beauty School Post-Sec.
201 W King St 25401 304-263-4929
Martinsburg Christian Academy 200/PK-12
2247 Williamsport Pike, 304-267-6368
Dr. Craig Bush, prin. Fax 263-0287
Valley College of Technology Post-Sec.
287 Aikens Ctr, 304-263-0979

Mason, Mason, Pop. 1,052
Mason County SD
Supt. — See Point Pleasant
Wahama JSHS 500/7-12
PO Box 348 25260 304-773-5539
Tim Click, prin. Fax 773-5216

Masontown, Preston, Pop. 649
Preston County SD
Supt. — See Kingwood
West Preston MS 200/6-8
PO Box 70 26542 304-864-5221
Karen Finamore, prin. Fax 864-5298

Matewan, Mingo, Pop. 501
Mingo County SD
Supt. — See Williamson
Matewan HS 200/9-12
100 Tiger Ln 25678 304-426-6555
Marcella Charles, prin. Fax 426-6292
Matewan MS 200/5-8
PO Box 535 25678 304-426-8569
Fax 426-4480

Meadow Bridge, Fayette, Pop. 310
Fayette County SD
Supt. — See Fayetteville
Meadow Bridge JSHS 300/7-12
PO Box 10 25976 304-484-7917
Al Martine, prin. Fax 484-7921

Middlebourne, Tyler, Pop. 853
Tyler County SD 1,600/PK-12
PO Box 25 26149 304-758-2145
Jeff Hoover, supt. Fax 758-4566
Other Schools – See Sistersville

Mill Creek, Randolph, Pop. 658
Randolph County SD
Supt. — See Elkins
Tygarts Valley JSHS 600/6-12
PO Box 68 26280 304-335-4575
Wilbert Smith, prin. Fax 335-6963

Milton, Cabell, Pop. 2,262
Cabell County SD
Supt. — See Huntington
Milton MS 700/6-8
1302 W Main St 25541 304-743-7308
Dan Gleason, prin. Fax 743-7324

Monongah, Marion, Pop. 912
Marion County SD
Supt. — See Fairmont
Monongah MS, 1 Camden Rd 26554 300/5-8
James Pulice, prin. 304-367-2164

Montcalm, Mercer, Pop. 1,023
Mercer County SD
Supt. — See Princeton
Montcalm HS 400/7-12
PO Box 330 24737 304-589-3719
Brenda Ash, prin. Fax 589-7140

Montgomery, Fayette, Pop. 2,030

West Virginia University Inst of Tech. Post-Sec.
405 Fayette Pike 25136 304-442-3071

Moorefield, Hardy, Pop. 2,408
Hardy County SD 2,000/PK-12
510 Ashby St 26836 304-530-2348
Ronald Whetzel, supt. Fax 530-2340
www.hardycountyschools.com/
Moorefield HS 400/9-12
401 N Main St 26836 304-530-6034
Douglas Hines, prin. Fax 530-7569
Moorefield MS 500/5-8
303 Caledonia Dr 26836 304-434-3000
Patrick McGregor, prin. Fax 434-3003
Other Schools – See Baker

Morgantown, Monongalia, Pop. 28,292
Monongalia County SD 9,100/PK-12
13 S High St 26501 304-291-9210
Frank Devono, supt. Fax 291-3015
boe.mono.k12.wv.us
Cheat Lake MS 600/5-8
160 Crosby Rd 26508 304-594-1165
Joanne Hines, prin. Fax 594-1677
Monongalia County Tech Education Center Vo/Tech
1000 Mississippi St 26501 304-291-9240
John George, prin. Fax 291-9247
Morgantown HS 1,600/9-12
109 Wilson Ave 26501 304-291-9260
Robert DeSantis, prin. Fax 291-9263
South MS 800/6-8
500 E Parkway Dr 26501 304-291-9340
Dennis Gallon, prin. Fax 291-9306
Suncrest MS 400/6-8
360 Baldwin St 26505 304-291-9335
James Napolillo, prin. Fax 284-9362
University HS 1,300/9-12
991 Price St 26505 304-291-9270
James Forst, prin. Fax 291-9248
Westwood MS 500/6-8
670 River Rd 26501 304-291-9300
Leonard Haney, prin. Fax 284-9368
Adult Basic Education Adult
1000 Mississippi St 26501 304-291-9240
Johnnie Hamilton, prin. Fax 291-9247
Other Schools – See Blacksville

Monongalia County Tech Education Center Post-Sec.
1000 Mississippi St 26501 304-291-9240
Morgantown Beauty College Post-Sec.
276 Walnut St 26505 304-292-8475
Trinity Christian S 300/PK-12
200 Trinity Way 26505 304-291-4659
Michael Staud, supt. Fax 291-4660
West Virginia Junior College Post-Sec.
148 Willey St 26505 304-296-8282
West Virginia University Post-Sec.
PO Box 6001 26506 304-293-0111
West Virginia University Hospital Post-Sec.
PO Box 8150 26506 304-598-4000

Moundsville, Marshall, Pop. 9,567
Marshall County SD 5,200/PK-12
PO Box 578 26041 304-843-4400
Alfred Renzella, supt. Fax 843-4409
boe.mars.k12.wv.us
Moundsville JHS 400/7-8
223 Tomlinson Ave 26041 304-843-4440
M. Jan Madden, prin. Fax 843-4446
Other Schools – See Cameron, Glen Dale, Wheeling

Mount Gay Shamrock, Logan, Pop. 3,377

Southern WV Community & Technical Coll. Post-Sec.
PO Box 2900 25637 304-792-7160

Mount Hope, Fayette, Pop. 1,411
Fayette County SD
Supt. — See Fayetteville
Mount Hope MSHS 400/5-12
110 High School Dr 25880 304-877-2121
David Null, prin. Fax 877-6354

Mount Zion, Calhoun
Calhoun County SD 1,200/PK-12
HC 89 Box 119 26151 304-354-7011
Ron Blankenship, supt. Fax 354-7420
boe.calh.k12.wv.us
Calhoun County MSHS 700/5-12
HC 89 Box 118 26151 304-354-6148
Karen Kirby, prin. Fax 354-7382
Other Schools – See Grantsville

Mullens, Wyoming, Pop. 1,653
Wyoming County SD
Supt. — See Pineville
Mullens MS 200/5-8
801 Moran Ave 25882 304-294-5757
Stephen Kirby, prin. Fax 294-5762

New Cumberland, Hancock, Pop. 1,043
Hancock County SD 4,300/PK-12
PO Box 1300 26047 304-564-3411
Danny Kaser, supt. Fax 564-3990
www.hancockschools.org
Oak Glen HS 600/9-12
195 Golden Bear Dr 26047 304-564-3500
Wayne Neely, prin. Fax 387-2079
Oak Glen MS 700/5-8
39 Golden Bear Dr 26047 304-387-2363
Donna Popovich, prin.
Rockefeller Career Center Vo/Tech
95 Rockyside Rd 26047 304-564-3337
George Danford, dir. Fax 564-4058
Other Schools – See Weirton

New Martinsville, Wetzel, Pop. 5,791
Wetzel County SD 3,100/PK-12
333 Foundry St 26155 304-455-2441
Paul E. Barcus Ed.D., supt. Fax 455-3446
www.wetzelcountyschools.com
Magnolia HS 500/9-12
601 Maple Ave 26155 304-455-1990
Timothy Haught, prin. Fax 455-5536
Other Schools – See Hundred, Paden City, Pine Grove

New Richmond, Wyoming
Wyoming County SD
Supt. — See Pineville
Wyoming East HS 600/9-12
PO Box 390 24867 304-294-5200
Barry Wayne Smith, prin. Fax 294-5900

Nitro, Kanawha, Pop. 6,750
Kanawha County SD
Supt. — See Charleston
Nitro HS 800/9-12
1301 Park Ave 25143 304-755-4321
Paul McClanahan, prin. Fax 755-4345

Nutter Fort Stonewood, Harrison, Pop. 1,800

West Virginia Business College Post-Sec.
116 Pennsylvania Ave 26301 304-624-7695

Oak Hill, Fayette, Pop. 7,312
Fayette County SD
Supt. — See Fayetteville
Collins MS 800/5-8
601 Jones Ave 25901 304-469-3711
David Perry, prin. Fax 465-1352
Fayette Institute of Technology Vo/Tech
300 Oyler Ave 25901 304-469-2911
Barry Crist, prin. Fax 469-6963
Oak Hill HS 700/9-12
350 W Oyler Ave 25901 304-469-3551
Fred McLain, prin. Fax 465-1769

Oceana, Wyoming, Pop. 1,478
Wyoming County SD
Supt. — See Pineville
Oceana MS 300/5-8
HC 65 Box 520 24870 304-682-6296
Jim Hopkins, prin. Fax 682-6330

Omar, Logan

Beth Haven Christian S 100/PK-12
PO Box 620 25638 304-946-4447

Ona, Cabell
Cabell County SD
Supt. — See Huntington
Cabell Midland HS 1,800/9-12
2300 US Route 60 25545 304-743-7400
Dr. Karen Oldham, prin. Fax 743-7577

Paden City, Wetzel, Pop. 2,737
Wetzel County SD
Supt. — See New Martinsville
Paden City HS 200/7-12
201 N 4th Ave 26159 304-337-2266
Warren Grace, prin. Fax 337-2290

Parkersburg, Wood, Pop. 32,020
Wood County SD 13,700/PK-12
1210 13th St 26101 304-420-9663
William Niday, supt. Fax 420-9513
www.netassoc.net/wcboe/
Blennerhassett JHS 700/7-9
444 Jewell Rd 26101 304-863-3356
Steve Angel, prin. Fax 863-3357
Caperton Center for Applied Tech Vo/Tech
300 Campus Dr 26104 304-424-8365
Joe Smith, prin. Fax 424-8366
Edison JHS 700/7-9
1201 Hillcrest St 26101 304-420-9525
Jean Mewshaw, prin. Fax 420-9527
Hamilton JHS 600/7-9
3501 Cadillac Dr 26104 304-420-9547
Mike Windland, prin. Fax 420-9567
Parkersburg SHS 1,400/10-12
2101 Dudley Ave 26101 304-420-9595
Ralph Board, prin. Fax 420-9604
Parkersburg South SHS 1,300/10-12
1511 Blizzard Dr 26101 304-420-9610
Tom Eschbacher, prin. Fax 420-9607
Van Devender JHS 400/7-9
918 31st St 26104 304-420-9645
Steve Taylor, prin. Fax 420-9647
Wood County Technical Center Vo/Tech
1515 Blizzard Dr 26101 304-420-9501
Doug Kiger, prin. Fax 485-1048
Other Schools – See Vienna, Williamstown

Camden Clark Memorial Hospital Post-Sec.
800 Garfield Ave 26101 304-424-2204
Mountain State College Post-Sec.
1508 Spring St 26101 304-485-5487
Parkersburg Catholic HS 7-12
3201 Fairview Ave 26104 304-485-6341
Marie Held, prin. Fax 485-4697
Parkersburg Christian S 100/K-12
1093 Core Rd 26104 304-485-6654
Jason Dodge, prin. Fax 428-4444
Valley Beauty School Post-Sec.
707 Market St 26101 304-422-2226
West Virginia University at Parkersburg Post-Sec.
300 Campus Dr 26104 304-424-8000

Parsons, Tucker, Pop. 1,400
Tucker County SD 1,200/PK-12
501 Chestnut St 26287 304-478-2771
Rick Hicks, supt. Fax 478-3422
www.tuckercountyschools.com
Other Schools – See Hambleton

Paw Paw, Morgan, Pop. 507
Morgan County SD
Supt. — See Berkeley Springs
Paw Paw JSHS 100/7-12
36 Pirate Cir 25434 304-947-7425
Michelle Fleming, prin. Fax 947-5513

Petersburg, Grant, Pop. 2,634
Grant County SD 2,000/PK-12
204 Jefferson Ave 26847 304-257-1011
Dr. Marsha Carr-Lambert, supt. Fax 257-2453
www.grantcountyschools.com
Petersburg JSHS 800/7-12
207 Jefferson Ave 26847 304-257-1444
Dennis Albright, prin. Fax 257-5243
South Branch Career & Technical Center Vo/Tech
401 Pierpont St 26847 304-257-1331
Robert Sisk, dir. Fax 257-2270

Peterstown, Monroe, Pop. 497
Monroe County SD
Supt. — See Union
Peterstown MS 300/5-8
36 College Dr 24963 304-753-4322
Lisa Canterbury, prin. Fax 772-4322

Philippi, Barbour, Pop. 2,826
Barbour County SD 2,600/PK-12
105 S Railroad St 26416 304-457-3030
DeEdra Lundeen, supt. Fax 457-3559
www.wvschools.com/barbourcountyschools/
Barbour County Vocational Center Vo/Tech
25 Horseshoe Dr 26416 304-457-4807
Fax 457-3009
Barbour HS 800/9-12
1 Horseshoe Dr 26416 304-457-1360
Garry Tenney, prin. Fax 457-2658
Philippi MS 300/6-8
RR 3 Box 40 26416 304-457-2999
James Sprouse, prin. Fax 457-2561
Other Schools – See Belington

Alderson-Broaddus College 26416 Post-Sec.
304-457-1700

Pickens, Randolph
Randolph County SD
Supt. — See Elkins
Pickens S 50/K-12
1 Panther Pl 26230 304-924-5525
Diane Butler, prin. Fax 924-6460

Pine Grove, Wetzel, Pop. 543
Wetzel County SD
Supt. — See New Martinsville
Valley HS 200/9-12
1 Lumberjack Ln 26419 304-889-3151
Tammy Wells, prin. Fax 889-2534

Pineville, Wyoming, Pop. 676
Wyoming County SD 4,200/PK-12
PO Box 69 24874 304-732-6262
Frank Blackwell, supt. Fax 732-7226
boe.wyom.k12.wv.us/
Pineville MS 300/5-8
PO Box 470 24874 304-732-6442
Deirdre Cline, prin. Fax 732-6737
Wyoming County Career & Technical Center Vo/Tech
HC 72 Box 200 24874 304-732-8050
Glennis Paul McNair, prin. Fax 732-8332
Other Schools – See Clear Fork, Mullens, New Richmond, Oceana

Pipestem, Summers

Pipestem Christian Academy 100/K-12
PO Box 49 25979 304-466-2413
Jeff Schuman, prin. Fax 466-2413

Poca, Putnam, Pop. 1,028
Putnam County SD
Supt. — See Winfield
Poca HS 500/9-12
RR 1 Box 5B 25159 304-755-5001
Vic Donalson, prin. Fax 755-5009
Poca MS 400/6-8
PO Box 647 25159 304-755-7343
Dale Eggleton, prin. Fax 755-8930

Point Pleasant, Mason, Pop. 4,481
Mason County SD 4,000/PK-12
1200 Main St 25550 304-675-4540
Dr. Larry Parsons, supt. Fax 675-7226
boe.maso.k12.wv.us/
Mason County Career Center Vo/Tech
Ohio River Rd 25550 304-675-3039
Pam Abston, dir. Fax 675-3413
Point Pleasant HS 700/9-12
RR 1 Box 4 25550 304-675-1350
Roger Keefer, prin. Fax 675-7480
Point Pleasant MS 400/7-8
2312 Jackson Ave 25550 304-675-3820
Rita Cooper, prin. Fax 675-7950
Other Schools – See Ashton, Mason

Christ Academy, PO Box 224 25550 50/PK-12
Michael Langona, admin. 304-675-1559

Princeton, Mercer, Pop. 6,222
Mercer County SD 9,200/PK-12
1403 Honaker Ave 24740 304-487-1551
Deborah Akers Ed.D., supt. Fax 425-5844
boe.merc.k12.wv.us/
Mercer County Technical Education Ctr Vo/Tech
1397 Stafford Dr 24740 304-425-9551
William Sherwood, prin. Fax 425-0833
Pikeview HS 600/9-12
3566 Eads Mill Rd 24740 304-384-7586
Ben Disibbio, prin. Fax 384-7901
Princeton HS 1,000/9-12
1321 Stafford Dr 24740 304-425-8101
Dr. Stephen Akers, prin. Fax 425-2823
Princeton MS 600/6-8
300 N Johnston St 24740 304-425-7517
Danny Buckner, prin. Fax 487-2250
Other Schools – See Bluefield, Montcalm

Mercer Christian Academy 200/K-12
314 Oakvale Rd Ste A 24740 304-487-1603
Bob Brooks, admin. Fax 431-2514
Valley College of Technology Post-Sec.
616 Harrison St 24740 304-425-2323

Prosperity, Raleigh, Pop. 1,322

Greater Beckley Christian S 200/PK-12
PO Box 670 25909 304-255-1571
John O'Neal, admin. Fax 255-2675

Rainelle, Greenbrier, Pop. 1,511

Rainelle Christian Academy 100/K-12
PO Box 784 25962 304-438-8874
Milburn Pack, admin. Fax 438-8874

Ravenswood, Jackson, Pop. 3,991
Jackson County SD
Supt. — See Ripley
Ravenswood HS 500/9-12
100 Plaza Dr 26164 304-273-9301
Kent Kennedy, prin. Fax 273-9556
Ravenswood MS 400/6-8
409 Sycamore St 26164 304-273-5480
Gary Higginbotham, prin. Fax 273-5746

Heritage Christian Academy 100/K-12
PO Box 427 26164 304-273-9463
John Henry, prin. Fax 868-2229

Richwood, Nicholas, Pop. 2,369
Nicholas County SD
Supt. — See Summersville
Richwood HS 300/10-12
1 Valley Ave 26261 304-846-2591
Bill Hutchinson, prin. Fax 846-2684
Richwood MS 400/7-9
2 Valley Ave 26261 304-846-2638
Mark Skaggs, prin. Fax 846-2639

Ridgeley, Mineral, Pop. 709
Mineral County SD
Supt. — See Keyser
Frankfort HS 600/9-12
RR 3 Box 169 26753 304-726-4767
Joseph Riley, prin. Fax 726-8597
Frankfort MS 600/5-8
RR 3 Box 170 26753 304-726-4341
Susan Ray, prin. Fax 726-4339

Ripley, Jackson, Pop. 3,266
Jackson County SD 5,000/PK-12
PO Box 770 25271 304-372-7300
Blaine Hess, supt. Fax 372-7312
boe.jack.k12.wv.us
Ripley HS 900/9-12
2 School St 25271 304-372-7355
Todd Layhew, prin. Fax 372-7334
Ripley MS 700/6-8
RR 2 Box 75A 25271 304-372-7350
Gail Varney, prin. Fax 372-7332
Other Schools – See Le Roy, Ravenswood

Romney, Hampshire, Pop. 1,975
Hampshire County SD 3,600/PK-12
46 S High St 26757 304-822-3528
Cynthia Kolsun, supt. Fax 822-5382
boe.hamp.k12.wv.us/Schools.htm
Hampshire HS 1,100/9-12
HC 63 Box 1970 26757 304-822-5016
Bill Cottrill, prin. Fax 822-5760
Romney MS 500/6-8
111 School St 26757 304-822-5014
John Watson, prin. Fax 822-5744
Other Schools – See Capon Bridge

West Virginia Schools/Deaf and Blind Post-Sec.
26757

Ronceverte, Greenbrier, Pop. 1,544
Greenbrier County SD
Supt. — See Lewisburg
Eastern Greenbrier MS 600/6-8
RR 1 Box 150 24970 304-647-6498
Doug Clemons, prin. Fax 647-3087

Seneca Trail Christian Academy 100/K-12
RR 2 Box 269 24970 304-647-4878
Cynthia Dillon, prin. Fax 647-4051

Saint Albans, Kanawha, Pop. 11,167
Kanawha County SD
Supt. — See Charleston
Hayes MS 500/6-8
830 Strawberry Rd 25177 304-722-0222
Scott Monty, prin. Fax 722-0247
McKinley JHS 300/6-8
3000 Kanawha Ter 25177 304-722-0218
David Gillispie, prin. Fax 722-0246
Saint Albans HS 1,000/9-12
2100 Kanawha Ter 25177 304-722-0212
Dr. Tom Williams, prin. Fax 722-0211

Mountaineer Beauty College Post-Sec.
PO Box 547 25177 304-727-9999

Saint Marys, Pleasants, Pop. 1,979
Pleasants County SD 1,400/PK-12
PO Box 210 26170 304-684-2215
Dr. Joe Super, supt. Fax 684-3569
boe.plea.k12.wv.us
Mid-Ohio Technical Institute Vo/Tech
PO Box 29 26170 304-684-2464
Rick Coffman, prin. Fax 684-2544
Saint Marys HS 400/9-12
1002 2nd St 26170 304-684-2421
Bruce Martin, prin. Fax 684-3859
Other Schools – See Belmont

Salem, Harrison, Pop. 1,976

Salem International University Post-Sec.
PO Box 500 26426 304-782-5011

Scott Depot, Putnam

Teays Valley Christian S 300/K-12
4373 Teays Valley Rd 25560 304-757-9550
Jack Davis, prin. Fax 757-0529

Seth, Boone
Boone County SD
Supt. — See Madison
Sherman HS 400/9-12
PO Box AB 25181 304-837-3301
Fax 837-7529
Sherman JHS 300/7-8
PO Box AA 25181 304-837-3694
David Price, prin. Fax 837-7603

Shady Spring, Raleigh, Pop. 1,929
Raleigh County SD
Supt. — See Beckley
Shady Spring HS 700/9-12
PO Box 2001 25918 304-256-4647
Danny Moye, prin. Fax 256-4711
Shady Spring MS 600/6-8
500 Flat Top Rd 25918 304-256-4570
Gary Nichols, prin. Fax 256-4612

Shenandoah Junction, Jefferson
Jefferson County SD
Supt. — See Charles Town
Jefferson HS 9th Grade Campus 600/9-9
1209 Shenandoah Junction Rd 25442
Ralph Dinges, prin. 304-728-4518
Jefferson HS 1,600/10-12
4141 Flowing Springs Rd 25442 304-725-8491
Fax 728-6590

Shepherdstown, Jefferson, Pop. 1,158
Jefferson County SD
Supt. — See Charles Town
Shepherdstown MS 500/6-8
54 Minden St 25443 304-876-6120
Judy Marcus, prin. Fax 876-1826

Shepherd University — Post-Sec.
PO Box 3210 25443 — 304-876-5000

Shinnston, Harrison, Pop. 2,240
Harrison County SD
Supt. — See Clarksburg
Lincoln HS — 700/9-12
100 Jerry Toth Dr 26431 — 304-592-2248
Brad Underwood, prin. — Fax 592-3415

Sissonville, Kanawha, Pop. 4,290
Kanawha County SD
Supt. — See Charleston
Sissonville MS — 500/6-8
8316 Old Mill Rd 25320 — 304-348-1993
Fax 348-6594

Sistersville, Tyler, Pop. 1,512
Tyler County SD
Supt. — See Middlebourne
Tyler Consolidated HS — 500/9-12
1993 Silver Knight Dr 26175 — 304-758-9000
Sandra Weese, prin. — Fax 758-9006
Tyler Consolidated MS — 400/6-8
1993 Silver Knight Dr 26175 — 304-758-9000
Norris Stombock, prin. — Fax 758-9006

Smithers, Fayette, Pop. 858
Fayette County SD
Supt. — See Fayetteville
Valley MSHS — 200/6-12
PO Box 459 25186 — 304-442-8284
H. Ray Londeree, prin. — Fax 442-5865

Sophia, Raleigh, Pop. 1,260
Raleigh County SD
Supt. — See Beckley
Independence MS — 600/6-8
PO Box 1171 25921 — 304-683-4542
Terry Poe, prin. — Fax 683-4552

South Charleston, Kanawha, Pop. 12,700
Kanawha County SD
Supt. — See Charleston
South Charleston HS — 1,100/9-12
1 Eagle Way 25309 — 304-766-0352
William Walton, prin. — Fax 768-4663
South Charleston MS — 400/6-8
400 3rd Ave 25303 — 304-348-1919
Henry Graves, prin. — Fax 744-4869

Spencer, Roane, Pop. 2,258
Roane County SD — 2,600/PK-12
PO Box 609 25276 — 304-927-6400
Stephen Goffreda, supt. — Fax 927-6402
www.roanecountyschools.com/
Roane County HS — 700/9-12
1 Raider Way 25276 — 304-927-6420
David Tupper, prin. — Fax 927-6404
Spencer MS — 500/5-8
102 Chapman Ave 25276 — 304-927-6415
William Chapman, prin. — Fax 927-6416

Summersville, Nicholas, Pop. 3,369
Nicholas County SD — 4,200/PK-12
400 Old Main Dr 26651 — 304-872-3611
Luther Baker, supt. — Fax 872-4626
boe.nich.k12.wv.us
Nicholas County SHS — 600/10-12
30 Grizzley Ln 26651 — 304-872-2141
Pat Metheney, prin. — Fax 872-3026
Summersville MS — 700/7-9
40 Grizzley Ln 26651 — 304-872-5092
Freddy Amick, prin. — Fax 872-6314
Other Schools – See Craigsville, Richwood

New Life Christian Academy — 200/PK-12
899 Broad St 26651 — 304-872-1148
Margaret Campbell, prin. — Fax 872-7477

Sutton, Braxton, Pop. 993
Braxton County SD — 2,500/PK-12
411 N Hill Rd 26601 — 304-765-7101
Carolyn Long, supt. — Fax 765-7148
boe.brax.k12.wv.us/
Braxton County HS — 800/9-12
200 Jerry Burton Dr 26601 — 304-765-7331
James Lambert, prin. — Fax 765-7976
Braxton County MS — 800/5-8
100 Carter Braxton Dr 26601 — 304-765-2644
Denver Drake, prin. — Fax 765-2696

Tunnelton, Preston, Pop. 346
Preston County SD
Supt. — See Kingwood
South Preston MS — 200/6-8
PO Box 400 26444 — 304-568-2331
Darrell Martin, prin. — Fax 568-2759

Union, Monroe, Pop. 550
Monroe County SD — 2,000/PK-12
PO Box 330 24983 — 304-772-3094
Dr. Lyn Guy, supt. — Fax 772-5020
www.monroecountyschoolswv.org
Other Schools – See Lindside, Peterstown

Upperglade, Webster
Webster County SD
Supt. — See Webster Springs
Webster County HS — 500/9-12
1 Highlander Dr 26266 — 304-226-5772
Paula Varney, prin. — Fax 226-5792

Van, Boone
Boone County SD
Supt. — See Madison
Van JSHS — 300/6-12
PO Box 100 25206 — 304-245-8237
Fax 245-8695

Vienna, Wood, Pop. 10,770
Wood County SD
Supt. — See Parkersburg
Jackson JHS — 600/7-9
1601 34th St 26105 — 304-420-9551
Richard Summers, prin. — Fax 295-9954

Ohio Valley University — Post-Sec.
1 Campus View Dr 26105 — 877-446-8668

War, McDowell, Pop. 692
McDowell County SD
Supt. — See Welch
Big Creek HS — 300/9-12
PO Box 790 24892 — 304-875-2287
Steven Tucker, prin. — Fax 875-4208

Wayne, Wayne, Pop. 1,154
Wayne County SD — 7,500/PK-12
PO Box 70 25570 — 304-272-5116
Gary Adkins, supt. — Fax 272-6500
boe.wayn.k12.wv.us/
Wayne HS — 600/9-12
100 Pioneer Rd 25570 — 304-272-5639
Dr. Kevin Smith, prin. — Fax 272-6439
Wayne MS — 600/6-8
200 Pioneer Rd 25570 — 304-272-3227
Loren Perry, prin. — Fax 272-5811
Other Schools – See Ceredo, Crum, Fort Gay, Huntington, Kenova

Webster Springs, Webster, Pop. 836
Webster County SD — 1,600/PK-12
315 S Main St 26288 — 304-847-5638
Kay Carpenter, supt. — Fax 847-2538
boe.webs.k12.wv.us/
Other Schools – See Cowen, Upperglade

Weirton, Hancock, Pop. 19,544
Hancock County SD
Supt. — See New Cumberland
Weir HS — 700/9-12
100 Red Rider Rd 26062 — 304-748-7600
Marty Hudek, prin. — Fax 748-7602
Weir MS — 700/5-8
125 Sinclair Ave 26062 — 304-748-6080
Dawn Petrovich, prin. — Fax 748-0847

Madonna HS — 100/9-12
150 Michael Ave 26062 — 304-723-0545
Dr. Cathy Sistilli, prin. — Fax 723-0564
West Virginia Northern Community College — Post-Sec.
150 Park Ave 26062 — 304-723-2210

Welch, McDowell, Pop. 2,371
McDowell County SD — 3,900/PK-12
30 Central Ave 24801 — 304-436-8441
Suzette Cook, supt. — Fax 436-4008
boe.mcdo.k12.wv.us
McDowell County Vocational Tech Ctr — Vo/Tech
PO Box V 24801 — 304-436-3488
Roger Smith, prin. — Fax 436-8063
Mount View HS — 500/9-12
950 Mount View Rd 24801 — 304-436-2939
Eric Carder, prin. — Fax 436-4714
Mount View MS — 300/7-8
960 Mount View Rd 24801 — 304-436-4657
Eric Carder, prin. — Fax 436-3472
Adult Learning Center — Adult
PO Box 556 24801 — 304-436-6580
Everett Sparks, coord. — Fax 436-6580
Other Schools – See Avondale, Iaeger, War

Wellsburg, Brooke, Pop. 2,727
Brooke County SD — 3,400/K-12
1201 Pleasant Ave 26070 — 304-737-3481
Mary Hervey DeGarmo, supt. — Fax 737-3480
bhs.broo.k12.wv.us/Brk-Schs/
Brooke HS — 1,100/9-12
Bruin Dr 26070 — 304-527-1410
Joyce Rea, prin. — Fax 527-3604
Wellsburg MS — 500/5-8
1447 Main St 26070 — 304-737-2922
Toni Ann Shute, prin. — Fax 737-2976
Other Schools – See Follansbee

West Liberty, Ohio, Pop. 1,203

West Liberty State College — Post-Sec.
PO Box 295 26074 — 304-336-5000

Weston, Lewis, Pop. 4,241
Lewis County SD — 2,700/PK-12
239 Court Ave 26452 — 304-269-8300
Dr. Joseph L. Mace, supt. — Fax 269-8305
boe.lewi.k12.wv.us/
Bland MS — 900/5-8
358 Court Ave 26452 — 304-269-8325
Grace Talhammer, prin. — Fax 269-8310
Lewis County HS — 800/9-12
205 Minuteman Dr 26452 — 304-269-8315
Timothy Derico, prin. — Fax 269-8319

West Union, Doddridge, Pop. 808
Doddridge County SD — 1,300/PK-12
104 Sistersville Pike 26456 — 304-873-2300
Janice Michels, supt. — Fax 873-2210
Doddridge County HS — 400/9-12
201 Stuart St 26456 — 304-873-2521
Bonnie Allman, prin. — Fax 873-1873
Doddridge County MS — 400/5-8
RR 2 Box 35C 26456 — 304-873-2390
Betsy Yeager, prin. — Fax 873-2541

Wheeling, Ohio, Pop. 29,639
Marshall County SD
Supt. — See Moundsville
Sherrard JHS — 300/7-8
1000 Fairmont Pike 26003 — 304-233-3331
Marily McWhorler, prin. — Fax 233-6418

Ohio County SD — 5,300/K-12
2203 National Rd 26003 — 304-243-0300
Lawrence Miller, supt. — Fax 243-0328
wphs.ohio.k12.wv.us/ocbe/
Bridge Street MS — 400/6-8
19 Junior Ave 26003 — 304-243-0381
Amy Minch, prin. — Fax 243-0385
Triadelphia MS — 500/6-8
1636 National Rd 26003 — 304-243-0387
Richard Dunlevy, prin. — Fax 243-0392
Wheeling MS — 200/6-8
3500 Chapline St 26003 — 304-243-0425
Patrick Riddle, prin. — Fax 243-0426
Wheeling Park HS — 1,800/9-12
1976 Park View Rd 26003 — 304-243-0400
Christine Carder, prin. — Fax 243-0449

Central Catholic HS — 400/9-12
75 14th St 26003 — 304-233-1660
Dr. Joseph Viglietta, prin. — Fax 233-3187
Linsly S — 400/5-12
60 Knox Ln 26003 — 304-233-3260
Reno Diorio, prin. — Fax 232-1975
Mt. de Chantal Visitation Academy — 200/PK-12
410 Washington Ave 26003 — 304-233-3771
Dr. Becky Johnen, prin. — Fax 233-8598
Ohio Valley Medical Center — Post-Sec.
2000 Eoff St 26003 — 304-234-8294
Scott College of Cosmetology — Post-Sec.
1502 Market St 26003 — 304-232-7798
Speiro Academy — 50/K-12
135 Stewarts Hill Rd 26003 — 304-243-0001
Susan Olinda Cline, prin. — Fax 845-4047
West Virginia Business College — Post-Sec.
1052 Main St 26003 — 304-232-0361
West Virginia Northern Community College — Post-Sec.
1704 Market St 26003 — 304-233-5900
Wheeling Hospital — Post-Sec.
1 Medical Park 26003 — 304-243-3000
Wheeling Jesuit University — Post-Sec.
316 Washington Ave 26003 — 304-243-2000

Williamson, Mingo, Pop. 3,181
Mingo County SD — 4,500/PK-12
RR 2 Box 310 25661 — 304-235-3333
Dwight Dials, supt. — Fax 235-3410
boe.ming.k12.wv.us
Tug Valley HS — 400/9-12
555 Panther Ave 25661 — 304-235-2266
Thomas Newsome, prin. — Fax 235-2636
Williamson HS — 200/9-12
801 Alderson St 25661 — 304-235-2518
Jeffrey Marion Reynolds, prin. — Fax 235-6590
Williamson MS — 200/5-8
801 Alderson St 25661 — 304-235-3430
Raymond Clagg, prin. — Fax 235-5567
Other Schools – See Delbarton, Gilbert, Matewan

Southern WV Community & Technical Coll. — Post-Sec.
25661 — 304-235-2800

Williamstown, Wood, Pop. 2,955
Wood County SD
Supt. — See Parkersburg
Williamstown JSHS — 700/7-12
219 W 5th St 26187 — 304-375-6151
Jack Mental, prin. — Fax 375-6194

Winfield, Putnam, Pop. 2,011
Putnam County SD — 8,900/PK-12
9 Courthouse Dr 25213 — 304-586-0500
Harold Hatfiled, supt. — Fax 586-0553
www.putnamschools.com
Winfield HS — 800/9-12
3022 Winfield Rd 25213 — 304-586-3279
William Hughes, prin. — Fax 586-3601
Winfield MS — 700/6-8
3280 Winfield Rd 25213 — 304-586-3072
Clarence Woodworth, prin. — Fax 586-0920
Other Schools – See Buffalo, Eleanor, Hurricane, Poca

WISCONSIN

WISCONSIN DEPARTMENT PUBLIC INSTRUCTION

PO Box 7841, Madison 53707-7841
Telephone 608-266-3390
Fax 608-267-1052
Website http://www.dpi.state.wi.us

Superintendent of Public Instruction Elizabeth Burmaster

COOPERATIVE EDUCATIONAL SERVICE AGENCIES (CESA)

CESA 1
Timothy Gavigan, admin. 262-787-9500
19601 W Bluemound Rd Fax 787-9501
Brookfield 53045
www.cesa1.k12.wi.us

CESA 2
Gary Albrecht, admin. 608-758-6232
448 E High St, Milton 53563 Fax 868-4864
www.cesa2.k12.wi.us

CESA 3
Gary Rooney, admin. 608-822-3276
1300 Industrial Dr Fax 822-3760
Fennimore 53809
www.cesa3.k12.wi.us

CESA 4
Jerry Freimark, admin. 608-786-4800
923 E Garland St Fax 786-4801
West Salem 54669
www.cesa4.k12.wi.us

CESA 5
Don Stevens, admin. 608-742-8811
PO Box 564, Portage 53901 Fax 742-2384
www.cesa5.k12.wi.us

CESA 6
Joan Wade, admin. 920-233-2372
PO Box 2568, Oshkosh 54903 Fax 424-3478
www.cesa6.k12.wi.us

CESA 7
Carol Gerhardt, admin. 920-492-5960
595 Baeten Rd, Green Bay 54304 Fax 492-5965
www.cesa7.k12.wi.us

CESA 8
Bob Kellogg, admin. 920-855-2114
PO Box 320, Gillett 54124 Fax 855-2299
www.cesa8.k12.wi.us

CESA 9
Jerome Fiene, admin. 715-453-2141
PO Box 449, Tomahawk 54487 Fax 453-7519
www.cesa9.k12.wi.us

CESA 10
Larry D. Annett, admin. 715-723-0341
725 W Park Ave Fax 720-2070
Chippewa Falls 54729
www.cesa10.k12.wi.us

CESA 11
Robert Rykal, admin. 715-986-2020
225 Ostermann Dr Fax 986-2040
Turtle Lake 54889
www.cesa11.k12.wi.us

CESA 12
Fred Schlichting, admin. 715-682-2363
618 Beaser Ave, Ashland 54806 Fax 682-7244
www.cesa12.k12.wi.us

PUBLIC, PRIVATE AND CATHOLIC SECONDARY SCHOOLS

Abbotsford, Clark, Pop. 1,901
Abbotsford SD 600/PK-12
PO Box 70 54405 715-223-6715
Reed Welsh, supt. Fax 223-4239
www.abbotsford.k12.wi.us
Abbotsford JSHS 400/6-12
PO Box 70 54405 715-223-2386
Jerry Zanotelli, prin. Fax 223-4239

Adams, Adams, Pop. 1,781
Adams-Friendship Area SD
Supt. — See Friendship
Adams-Friendship HS 700/9-12
1109 E North St 53910 608-339-3921
Tim Hodkiewicz, prin. Fax 339-2569
Adams-Friendship MS 500/6-8
420 N Main St 53910 608-339-4064
Garret Gould, prin. Fax 339-2434

Albany, Green, Pop. 1,133
Albany SD 400/PK-12
PO Box 349 53502 608-862-3225
Stephen Guenther, supt. Fax 862-3230
www.albany.k12.wi.us
Albany HS 100/9-12
PO Box 349 53502 608-862-3135
Susan McGuire, prin. Fax 862-3230
Albany MS 100/6-8
PO Box 349 53502 608-862-3135
Susan McGuire, prin. Fax 862-3230

Algoma, Kewaunee, Pop. 3,197
Algoma SD 200/PK-12
1715 Division St 54201 920-487-7001
Ronald Welch, supt. Fax 487-7016
www.alghs.k12.wi.us
Algoma S 200/PK-12
1715 Division St 54201 920-487-7010
William Bush, prin. Fax 487-7015

Alma, Buffalo, Pop. 899
Alma SD 300/PK-12
S1618 State Road 35 54610 608-685-4416
Steven Sedlmayr, supt. Fax 685-4446
www.alma.k12.wi.us
Alma HS 100/9-12
S1618 State Road 35 54610 608-685-4416
Bert Plucker, prin. Fax 685-4446

Alma Center, Jackson, Pop. 449
Alma Center-Humbird-Merrillan SD 600/PK-12
PO Box 308 54611 715-964-8271
Robert Lambert, supt. Fax 964-1005
www.achm.k12.wi.us
Lincoln HS 200/9-12
PO Box 308 54611 715-964-5311
Jeffrey Arzt, prin. Fax 964-1005
Lincoln JHS 100/7-8
PO Box 308 54611 715-964-5311
Jeffrey Arzt, prin. Fax 964-1005

Almond, Portage, Pop. 431
Almond-Bancroft SD 500/PK-12
1336 Elm St 54909 715-366-2941
Joe Garza, admin. Fax 366-2940
www.abschools.k12.wi.us
Almond-Bancroft JSHS 300/6-12
1336 Elm St 54909 715-366-2941
Jeff Rykal, prin. Fax 366-2943

Altoona, Eau Claire, Pop. 6,448
Altoona SD 1,400/PK-12
1903 Bartlett Ave 54720 715-839-6032
Gregory Fahrman, supt. Fax 839-6066
www.altoona.k12.wi.us
Altoona HS 400/9-12
711 7th St W 54720 715-839-6031
Jeff Pepowski, prin. Fax 839-6028
Altoona MS 400/5-8
1903 Bartlett Ave 54720 715-839-6030
Jack Wagener, prin. Fax 839-6099

Otter Creek Christian Academy 50/1-10
919 10th St W 54720 715-834-1782
Richard Bauer, prin.

Amery, Polk, Pop. 2,868
Amery SD 1,800/PK-12
543 Minneapolis Ave S 54001 715-268-9771
Stephen Schiell, supt. Fax 268-7300
www.amerysd.k12.wi.us
Amery HS 600/9-12
555 Minneapolis Ave S 54001 715-268-9771
Shawn Doerfler, prin. Fax 268-7792
Amery MS 400/6-8
501 Minneapolis Ave S 54001 715-268-9771
Thomas Bensen, prin. Fax 268-4967

Amherst, Portage, Pop. 973
Tomorrow River SD 900/PK-12
357 N Main St 54406 715-824-5521
John Haugen, supt. Fax 824-7177
www.amherst.k12.wi.us
Amherst HS 300/9-12
357 N Main St 54406 715-824-5522
Peter Sippel, prin. Fax 824-5454
Amherst MS 200/6-8
357 N Main St 54406 715-824-5522
Michael Toelle, prin. Fax 824-5454

Antigo, Langlade, Pop. 8,282
Antigo SD 2,700/PK-12
120 S Dorr St 54409 715-627-4355
Roxann Bornemann, supt. Fax 623-3279
www.antigo.k12.wi.us/
Antigo HS 1,000/9-12
1900 10th Ave 54409 715-623-7611
Thomas Zamzow, prin. Fax 623-7624
Antigo MS 600/6-8
815 7th Ave 54409 715-623-4173
Douglas Knol, prin. Fax 627-4982

Appleton, Outagamie, Pop. 70,217
Appleton Area SD 13,600/PK-12
PO Box 2019 54912 920-832-6161
Lee Allinger, supt. Fax 832-1725
www.aasd.k12.wi.us
Appleton East HS 1,600/9-12
2121 E Emmers Dr 54915 920-832-6212
Ben Vogel, prin. Fax 832-4880
Appleton North HS 1,800/9-12
5000 N Ballard Rd 54913 920-832-4300
Barry O'Connor, prin. Fax 832-4301
Appleton West HS 1,500/9-12
610 N Badger Ave 54914 920-832-6219
Greg Hartjes, prin. Fax 832-4198
Einstein MS 500/7-8
324 E Florida Ave 54911 920-832-6240
James Huggins, prin. Fax 832-6164
Madison MS 700/7-8
2020 S Carpenter St 54915 920-832-6276
Chris VanderHeyden, prin. Fax 832-6337
Roosevelt MS 400/7-8
318 E Brewster St 54911 920-832-6294
Al Brant, prin. Fax 832-4605
Wilson MS 500/7-8
225 N Badger Ave 54914 920-832-6226
John Magas, prin. Fax 832-4857

Fox Valley Lutheran HS 600/9-12
5300 N Meade St 54913 920-739-4441
Paul Hartwig, prin. Fax 739-4418
Fox Valley Technical College Post-Sec.
PO Box 2277 54912 920-735-5600
Gill-Tech Academy of Hair Design Post-Sec.
230 S McCarthy Rd 54914 920-739-8684
Lawrence University Post-Sec.
PO Box 599 54912 920-832-7000
St. Elizabeth Hospital Post-Sec.
1506 S Oneida St 54915 920-738-2015
St. Joseph MS 500/6-8
2626 N Oneida St 54911 920-730-8849
Brad Norcross, prin. Fax 730-4147
Xavier HS 500/9-12
1600 W Prospect Ave 54914 920-733-6632
Matt Reynebeau, prin. Fax 733-5513

Arcadia, Trempealeau, Pop. 2,348
Arcadia SD 900/PK-12
756 Raider Dr 54612 608-323-3315
Jon Turnell, supt. Fax 323-2256
www.arcadia.k12.wi.us/
Arcadia HS 300/9-12
756 Raider Dr 54612 608-323-3334
Louie Ferguson, prin. Fax 323-2256

Argyle, Lafayette, Pop. 784
Argyle SD 400/PK-12
PO Box 256 53504 608-543-3318
Michael Manning, supt. Fax 543-3868
www.argyle.k12.wi.us
Argyle MSHS 200/6-12
PO Box 256 53504 608-543-3318
Gerry Benish, prin. Fax 543-3868

Ashland, Ashland, Pop. 8,306
Ashland SD 2,300/PK-12
2000 Beaser Ave 54806 715-682-7080
Kenneth Kasinski, supt. Fax 682-7097
www.ashland.k12.wi.us
Ashland HS 800/9-12
1900 Beaser Ave 54806 715-682-7089
Steve Gromala, prin. Fax 682-2075
Ashland MS 500/6-8
203 11th St E 54806 715-682-7087
Thomas Gaudreau, prin. Fax 682-7944

Northland College Post-Sec.
1411 Ellis Ave 54806 715-682-1699

Athens, Marathon, Pop. 1,045
Athens SD 500/PK-12
PO Box F 54411 715-257-7511
Frank Harrington, supt. Fax 257-7502
www.athens.k12.wi.us
Athens HS 200/9-12
PO Box F 54411 715-257-7511
Timothy Micke, prin. Fax 257-7651
Athens MS 100/6-8
PO Box F 54411 715-257-7511
Timothy Micke, prin. Fax 257-7651

Auburndale, Wood, Pop. 728
Auburndale SD 800/PK-12
PO Box 139 54412 715-652-2117
John Timmerman, supt. Fax 652-2836
www.aubschools.com
Auburndale JSHS 400/7-12
PO Box 190 54412 715-652-2115
Kevin Yeske, prin. Fax 652-6322

Augusta, Eau Claire, Pop. 1,370
Augusta SD 600/PK-12
E19320 Bartig Rd 54722 715-286-3300
Stephen LaFave, supt. Fax 286-3336
www.augusta.k12.wi.us
Augusta JSHS 300/6-12
E19320 Bartig Rd 54722 715-286-3352
Judy Dekan, dean Fax 286-3393

Baldwin, Saint Croix, Pop. 3,509
Baldwin-Woodville Area SD 1,500/PK-12
550 US Highway 12 54002 715-684-3411
Russell J. Helland, supt. Fax 684-3168
www.bwsd.k12.wi.us/
Baldwin-Woodville HS 500/9-12
1000 13th Ave 54002 715-684-3321
Eric Russell, prin. Fax 684-5160
Other Schools – See Woodville

Balsam Lake, Polk, Pop. 1,026
Unity SD 1,100/PK-12
PO Box 307 54810 715-825-3515
Brandon Robinson, supt. Fax 825-3517
www.unity.k12.wi.us/
Unity HS 400/9-12
PO Box 307 54810 715-825-2131
William Alleva, prin. Fax 825-4430
Unity MS 300/6-8
PO Box 307 54810 715-825-2101
Elizabeth Jorgensen, prin. Fax 825-4410

Bangor, LaCrosse, Pop. 1,375
Bangor SD 600/K-12
PO Box 99 54614 608-486-2331
Roger Foegen, supt. Fax 486-4587
www.bangor.k12.wi.us
Bangor MSHS 400/6-12
PO Box 99 54614 608-486-2331
Don Addington, prin. Fax 486-4587

Baraboo, Sauk, Pop. 10,927
Baraboo SD 2,800/PK-12
101 2nd Ave 53913 608-355-3950
Lance Alwin, supt. Fax 355-3960
www.baraboo.k12.wi.us
Baraboo HS 1,000/9-12
1201 Draper St 53913 608-355-3940
Machell Schwarz, prin. Fax 355-3962
Young MS 700/6-8
1531 Draper St 53913 608-355-3930
Robert Meicher, prin. Fax 355-3998

University of Wisconsin Baraboo/Sauk Co. Post-Sec.
1006 Connie Rd 53913 608-355-5230

Barneveld, Iowa, Pop. 1,148
Barneveld SD 400/K-12
PO Box 98 53507 608-924-4711
Joe Bertone, supt. Fax 924-1646
www.barneveld.k12.wi.us
Barneveld MSHS 200/6-12
PO Box 98 53507 608-924-4711
Kevin Knudson, prin. Fax 924-1646

Barron, Barron, Pop. 3,151
Barron Area SD 1,400/PK-12
100 W River Ave 54812 715-537-5612
Monti Hallberg, supt. Fax 637-5161
www.barron.k12.wi.us/
Barron HS 500/9-12
1050 E Woodland Ave 54812 715-537-5627
Kirk Haugestuen, prin. Fax 637-1603
Riverview MS 300/6-8
135 W River Ave 54812 715-537-5641
John Gevens, prin. Fax 637-5373

Bayfield, Bayfield, Pop. 602
Bayfield SD 500/PK-12
PO Box 5001 54814 715-779-3201
Fax 779-5268
www.bayfield.k12.wi.us
Bayfield HS 200/9-12
PO Box 5001 54814 715-779-3201
Robert Kent, prin. Fax 779-5226
Bayfield MS 100/6-8
PO Box 5001 54814 715-779-3201
Michael J. Malyuk, prin. Fax 779-5226

Beaver Dam, Dodge, Pop. 15,153
Beaver Dam SD 3,200/K-12
705 McKinley St 53916 920-885-7300
Donald Childs, supt. Fax 885-7305
www.beaverdam.k12.wi.us
Beaver Dam HS 1,100/9-12
500 Gould St 53916 920-885-7313
Chris Ligocki, prin. Fax 885-7317
Beaver Dam MS 700/6-8
108 4th St 53916 920-885-7365
Richard Brouillard, prin. Fax 885-7415

Moraine Park Technical College Post-Sec.
700 Gould St 53916 920-887-1101
Wayland Academy 200/9-12
101 N University Ave 53916 920-885-3373
Robert Esten, pres. Fax 887-3373

Belleville, Dane, Pop. 2,114
Belleville SD 900/PK-12
625 W Church St 53508 608-424-3315
Dr. Randy Freese, supt. Fax 424-3486
www.belleville.k12.wi.us/
Belleville HS 300/9-12
635 W Church St 53508 608-424-1902
Rick Conroy, prin. Fax 424-3692
Belleville MS 200/7-8
625 W Church St 53508 608-424-1902
Rick Conroy, prin. Fax 424-3692

Belmont, Lafayette, Pop. 894
Belmont Community SD 300/K-12
PO Box 348 53510 608-762-5131
Johannus Benkers, supt. Fax 762-5129
www.belmont.k12.wi.us
Belmont JSHS 200/7-12
PO Box 348 53510 608-762-5131
Ken Hasenmueller, prin. Fax 762-5129

Beloit, Rock, Pop. 35,621
Beloit SD 7,000/PK-12
1633 Keeler Ave 53511 608-361-4000
Lowell Holtz, supt. Fax 361-4122
www.sdb.k12.wi.us
Aldrich MS 700/6-8
1859 Northgate Dr 53511 608-361-3605
Walter James, prin. Fax 361-3620
McNeel MS 800/6-8
1524 Frederick St 53511 608-361-3800
Mark Day, prin. Fax 361-3820
Memorial HS 2,100/9-12
1225 4th St 53511 608-361-3005
Carlton Jenkins, prin. Fax 361-3080

Beloit Turner SD 1,300/PK-12
1237 E Inman Pkwy 53511 608-364-6372
Charles Melvin, supt. Fax 364-6373
www.fjturner.k12.wi.us
Turner HS 400/9-12
1231 E Inman Pkwy 53511 608-364-6370
Dennis McCarthy, prin. Fax 365-4768
Turner MS 300/6-8
1237 E Inman Pkwy 53511 608-364-6367
Randall McClellan, prin. Fax 364-6369

Beloit College Post-Sec.
700 College St 53511 608-363-2000
Rock County Christian HS 100/6-12
916 Bushnell St 53511 608-365-7378
Tim Befus, admin. Fax 365-7382

Benton, Lafayette, Pop. 979
Benton SD 50/PK-12
PO Box 7 53803 608-759-4002
Gary Neis, admin. Fax 759-3805
www.benton.k12.wi.us
Benton JSHS 50/7-12
PO Box 7 53803 608-759-4002
Gary Neis, prin. Fax 759-3805

Berlin, Green Lake, Pop. 5,213
Berlin Area SD 1,600/PK-12
295 E Marquette St 54923 920-361-2004
Jerry Runice, supt. Fax 361-2170
www.berlin.k12.wi.us
Berlin HS 600/9-12
222 Memorial Dr 54923 920-361-2000
Robert Eidahl, prin. Fax 361-2005
Berlin MS 400/6-8
289 E Huron St 54923 920-361-2441
Diane Toraason, prin. Fax 361-2945

Birchwood, Washburn, Pop. 537
Birchwood SD 100/PK-12
300 S Wilson St 54817 715-354-3471
Frank Helquist, supt. Fax 354-3469
www.birchwood.k12.wi.us/
Birchwood HS 100/9-12
300 S Wilson St 54817 715-354-3471
Jeff Stanley, prin. Fax 354-3469

Black River Falls, Jackson, Pop. 3,485
Black River Falls SD 1,400/PK-12
301 N 4th St 54615 715-284-4357
Fax 284-7064
www.brf.org
Black River Falls HS 700/9-12
1200 Pierce St 54615 715-284-4324
Robert Lecheler, prin. Fax 284-7626
Black River Falls MS 400/6-8
1202 Pierce St 54615 715-284-5315
David Roou, prin. Fax 284-0364

Blair, Trempealeau, Pop. 1,261
Blair-Taylor SD 600/PK-12
PO Box 125 54616 608-989-2881
Guy Leavitt, supt. Fax 989-2451
btsd.k12.wi.us
Blair-Taylor MSHS 300/7-12
PO Box 107 54616 608-989-2525
Jeff Eide, prin. Fax 989-9161

Blanchardville, Lafayette, Pop. 774
Pecatonica Area SD 500/PK-12
PO Box 117 53516 608-523-4248
Nancy Hendrickson, supt. Fax 523-4286
www.pecatonica.k12.wi.us
Pecatonica JSHS 200/7-12
PO Box 117 53516 608-523-4285
David McSherry, prin. Fax 523-4286

Bloomer, Chippewa, Pop. 3,280
Bloomer SD 1,100/PK-12
1310 17th Ave 54724 715-568-2800
Douglas Martin, supt. Fax 568-5315
www.bloomer.k12.wi.us
Bloomer HS 400/9-12
1310 17th Ave 54724 715-568-5300
Brent Ashland, prin. Fax 568-5304
Bloomer MS 200/6-8
600 Jackson St 54724 715-568-1025
Barry Kamrath, prin. Fax 568-3687

Bloomington, Grant, Pop. 688
River Ridge SD
Supt. — See Patch Grove
River Ridge MS 200/5-8
PO Box 97 53804 608-994-2711
Michael Murphy, prin. Fax 994-2714

Bonduel, Shawano, Pop. 1,390
Bonduel SD 900/PK-12
PO Box 310 54107 715-758-4860
Peter Behnke, supt. Fax 758-4869
www.bonduel.k12.wi.us
Bonduel HS 300/9-12
PO Box 310 54107 715-758-4850
Gary Berger, prin. Fax 758-4859
Bonduel MS 200/6-8
PO Box 310 54107 715-758-4840
Connie Rutledge, prin. Fax 758-4849

Boscobel, Grant, Pop. 3,373
Boscobel Area SD 900/PK-12
1110 Park St 53805 608-375-4164
Dr. Stephen Smith, supt. Fax 375-2378
www.boscobel.k12.wi.us
Boscobel HS 300/9-12
300 Brindley St 53805 608-375-4161
William Mercer, prin. Fax 375-2640
Boscobel MS 200/7-8
300 Brindley St 53805 608-375-4161
William Mercer, prin. Fax 375-2640

Bowler, Shawano, Pop. 336
Bowler SD 500/PK-12
PO Box 8 54416 715-793-4307
Scott Peterson, supt. Fax 793-1302
www.bowler.k12.wi.us
Bowler JSHS 200/7-12
PO Box 8 54416 715-793-4301
Barry Wolff, dean Fax 793-1302

Boyceville, Dunn, Pop. 1,034
Boyceville Community SD 700/PK-12
1003 Tiffany St 54725 715-643-4311
Dennis Rettke, supt. Fax 643-3127
www.boyceville.k12.wi.us
Boyceville MSHS 300/7-12
1003 Tiffany St 54725 715-643-4321
William Fisher, prin. Fax 643-2209

Brillion, Calumet, Pop. 2,910
Brillion SD 800/PK-12
315 S Main St 54110 920-756-2368
Dominick Madison, supt. Fax 756-3705
www.brillion.k12.wi.us
Brillion HS 300/9-12
W1101 County Road HR 54110 920-756-9238
Paul Nistler, prin. Fax 756-9427
Brillion MS 200/6-8
315 S Main St 54110 920-756-2166
Ann Hatch, prin. Fax 756-3705

Brodhead, Green, Pop. 3,068
Brodhead SD 1,200/PK-12
2501 W 5th Ave 53520 608-897-2141
Charles J. Deery, supt. Fax 897-2770
www.brodhead.k12.wi.us
Brodhead HS 400/9-12
2501 W 5th Ave 53520 608-897-2155
Leonard Lueck, prin. Fax 897-3026
Brodhead MS 300/6-8
2100 W 9th Ave 53520 608-897-2184
Charles Urness, prin. Fax 897-2789

Brookfield, Waukesha, Pop. 39,656
Elmbrook SD 7,600/PK-12
PO Box 1830 53008 262-781-3030
Matthew Gibson, supt. Fax 783-0983
www.elmbrook.k12.wi.us
Central HS 1,400/9-12
16900 Gebhardt Rd 53005 262-785-3910
Don La Bonte, prin. Fax 785-3993
East HS 1,400/9-12
3305 Lilly Rd 53005 262-781-3500
Brett Bowers, prin. Fax 790-5445
Wisconsin Hills MS 900/6-8
18700 W Wisconsin Ave 53045 262-785-3960
Robyn Martino, prin. Fax 785-3967
Other Schools – See Elm Grove

Brookfield Academy 700/PK-12
PO Box 907 53008 262-783-3200
Dr. Robert Solsrud, hdmstr. Fax 783-3213
Ottawa University Post-Sec.
245 S Executive Dr Ste 110 53005 262-879-0200

Brown Deer, Milwaukee, Pop. 11,611
Brown Deer SD 1,800/PK-12
8200 N 60th St 53223 414-371-6750
Bruce Connolly, supt. Fax 371-6751
www.bdsd.k12.wi.us
Brown Deer HS 700/9-12
8060 N 60th St 53223 414-371-7000
James Piatt, prin. Fax 371-7001
Brown Deer MS 600/5-8
5757 W Dean Rd 53223 414-371-6900
Blake Peuse, prin. Fax 371-6901

Bruce, Rusk, Pop. 731
Bruce SD 600/PK-12
104 W Washington Ave 54819 715-868-2533
Debra Brown, supt. Fax 868-2534
www.bruce.k12.wi.us
Bruce HS 200/9-12
104 W Washington Ave 54819 715-868-2585
Larry Villiard, prin. Fax 868-2534
Bruce MS 100/7-8
104 W Washington Ave 54819 715-868-2585
Larry Villiard, prin. Fax 868-2534

Brussels, Door
Southern Door SD 1,300/PK-12
2073 County Road DK 54204 920-825-7311
Joseph Innis, supt. Fax 825-7311
www.southerndoor.k12.wi.us
Southern Door HS 400/9-12
2073 County Road DK 54204 920-825-7333
Lois Mahaffey, prin. Fax 825-7081
Southern Door MS 300/6-8
2073 County Road DK 54204 920-825-7321
Gary Langenberg, prin. Fax 825-7692

Burlington, Racine, Pop. 11,148
Burlington Area SD 3,600/K-12
100 N Kane St 53105 262-763-0210
Ronald Jandura, supt. Fax 763-0215
www.basd.k12.wi.us
Burlington HS 1,400/9-12
400 Mc Canna Pkwy 53105 262-763-0200
Barbara Kopack-Hill, prin. Fax 763-0216
Karcher MS 600/7-8
225 Robert St 53105 262-763-0190
Mark Sheldon, prin. Fax 767-5580

Catholic Central HS 200/9-12
148 McHenry St 53105 262-763-1510
Ralph Lynch, prin. Fax 763-1509

Butternut, Ashland, Pop. 387
Butternut SD 100/PK-12
PO Box 247 54514 715-769-3434
Bruce LaRose, supt. Fax 769-3712
www.butternut.k12.wi.us
Butternut S 100/PK-12
PO Box 247 54514 715-769-3434
Bruce LaRose, prin. Fax 769-3712

Cadott, Chippewa, Pop. 1,313
Cadott Community SD 900/PK-12
PO Box 310 54727 715-289-3795
Guy Habeck, supt. Fax 289-3748
www.cadott.k12.wi.us
Cadott HS 300/9-12
PO Box 310 54727 715-289-4211
Matthew McDonough, prin. Fax 289-3085
Cadott JHS 100/7-8
PO Box 310 54727 715-289-4211
Matthew McDonough, prin. Fax 289-3085

Cambria, Columbia, Pop. 789
Cambria-Friesland SD 500/PK-12
410 E Edgewater St 53923 920-348-5548
Tony Hinden, supt. Fax 348-5119
www.cf.k12.wi.us
Cambria-Friesland MSHS 300/6-12
410 E Edgewater St 53923 920-348-5135
Rick Hammes, prin. Fax 348-5119

Cambridge, Dane, Pop. 1,227
Cambridge SD 1,000/PK-12
403 Blue Jay Way 53523 608-423-4345
Ronald Dayton, supt. Fax 423-9869
www.cambridge.k12.wi.us
Cambridge HS 300/9-12
403 Blue Jay Way 53523 608-423-3262
Robert Rosen, prin. Fax 423-9598
Nikolay MS 200/6-8
211 South St 53523 608-423-7335
George Smith, prin. Fax 423-4499

Cameron, Barron, Pop. 1,655
Cameron SD 900/PK-12
PO Box 378 54822 715-458-4560
Randal Braun, supt. Fax 458-4822
www.cameron.k12.wi.us
Cameron HS 300/9-12
PO Box 378 54822 715-458-4510
Joseph Leschisin, prin. Fax 458-4236
Cameron MS 300/5-8
PO Box 378 54822 715-458-4563
Thomas Spanel, prin. Fax 458-3436

Campbellsport, Fond du Lac, Pop. 1,930
Campbellsport SD 1,500/PK-12
114 W Sheboygan St 53010 920-533-8381
Dan Olson, supt. Fax 533-5726
www.csd.k12.wi.us
Campbellsport HS 500/9-12
114 W Sheboygan St 53010 920-533-4811
Tom Hercules, prin. Fax 533-3521
Campbellsport JHS 200/7-8
114 W Sheboygan St 53010 920-533-3411
Michael Maxson, prin. Fax 533-5726

Casco, Kewaunee, Pop. 564
Luxemburg-Casco SD
Supt. — See Luxemburg
Luxemburg-Casco MS 300/7-8
619 Church Ave 54205 920-837-2205
John LeClair, prin. Fax 837-7517

Cashton, Monroe, Pop. 1,018
Cashton SD 500/PK-12
PO Box 129 54619 608-654-5131
Norbert Resheske, supt. Fax 654-5136
www.cashton.k12.wi.us
Cashton JSHS 300/7-12
PO Box 129 54619 608-654-5131
Bradford Saron, prin. Fax 654-5136

Cassville, Grant, Pop. 1,045
Cassville SD 300/PK-12
715 E Amelia St 53806 608-725-5116
Joe Zydowsky, supt. Fax 725-2353
www.cassvillesd.k12.wi.us
Cassville JSHS 200/7-12
715 E Amelia St 53806 608-725-5116
Joe Zydowsky, prin. Fax 725-2353

Cazenovia, Richland, Pop. 338
Weston SD 400/PK-12
E2511A County Rd S 53924 608-986-2151
John Klang, supt. Fax 986-2205
www.weston.k12.wi.us
Weston HS 100/9-12
E2511A County Rd S 53924 608-986-2151
John Klang, prin. Fax 986-2205
Weston MS 100/6-8
E2511A County Rd S 53924 608-986-2151
John Klang, prin. Fax 986-2205

Cedarburg, Ozaukee, Pop. 11,298
Cedarburg SD 3,100/K-12
W68N611 Evergreen Blvd 53012 262-376-6100
Dr. Daryl Herrick, supt. Fax 376-6110
www.cedarburg.k12.wi.us
Cedarburg HS 1,200/9-12
W68N611 Evergreen Blvd 53012 262-376-6200
Robert Kobylski, prin. Fax 376-6210
Webster MS 700/6-8
W75N624 Wauwatosa Rd 53012 262-376-6500
Robert Klimpke, prin. Fax 376-6510

Cedar Grove, Sheboygan, Pop. 2,012
Cedar Grove-Belgium Area SD 1,000/PK-12
321 N 2nd St 53013 920-668-8686
Michael Salkowski, supt. Fax 668-8605
www.cedargrovebelgium.k12.wi.us/
Cedar Grove-Belgium HS 300/9-12
321 N 2nd St 53013 920-668-8686
John Hocking, prin. Fax 668-8605
Cedar Grove-Belgium MS 300/5-8
321 N 2nd St 53013 920-668-8518
Jeanne Courneene, prin. Fax 668-8566

Chetek, Barron, Pop. 2,150
Chetek SD 1,000/K-12
1001 Knapp St 54728 715-924-2226
Al Brown, supt. Fax 924-2376
www.chetek.k12.wi.us/
Chetek HS 400/9-12
1001 Knapp St 54728 715-924-3137
Ed Harris, prin. Fax 924-2921
Chetek MS 200/6-8
1001 Knapp St 54728 715-924-3136
Bryan Yenter, prin. Fax 924-2921

Chilton, Calumet, Pop. 3,617
Chilton SD 1,200/PK-12
530 W Main St 53014 920-849-8109
Steve Patz, supt. Fax 849-4539
www.chilton.k12.wi.us
Chilton HS 500/9-12
530 W Main St 53014 920-849-2358
Timothy Schaid, prin. Fax 849-3998
Chilton MS 400/5-8
421 Court St 53014 920-849-9152
Robert Knadle, prin. Fax 849-7210

Chippewa Falls, Chippewa, Pop. 13,374
Chippewa Falls Area SD 4,500/PK-12
1130 Miles St 54729 715-726-2417
Michael Schoch, supt. Fax 726-2781
cfsd.chipfalls.k12.wi.us
Chippewa Falls HS 1,500/9-12
735 Terrill St 54729 715-726-2406
James Sauter, prin. Fax 726-2792
Chippewa Falls MS 1,100/6-8
750 Tropicana Blvd 54729 715-726-2400
Janet Etmund, prin. Fax 726-2789

McDonell Central HS 200/9-12
1316 Bel Air Blvd 54729 715-723-9126
John Flanagan, prin. Fax 723-1501
Notre Dame MS 200/6-8
22 S Prairie St 54729 715-723-4777
Adam Zenner, prin. Fax 723-3353

Clayton, Polk, Pop. 584
Clayton SD 400/PK-12
PO Box 130 54004 715-948-2163
Cathleen Shimon, supt. Fax 948-2362
www.claytonsd.k12.wi.us
Clayton HS 100/9-12
PO Box 130 54004 715-948-2163
Cathleen Shimon, prin. Fax 948-2362
Clayton MS 100/6-8
PO Box 130 54004 715-948-2163
Cathleen Shimon, prin. Fax 948-2362

Clear Lake, Polk, Pop. 1,077
Clear Lake SD 500/PK-12
1101 3rd St SW 54005 715-263-2114
Mark Heyerdahl, supt. Fax 263-2933
www.clearlake.k12.wi.us
Clear Lake HS 200/9-12
1101 3rd St SW 54005 715-263-2113
Wayne Whitwam, prin. Fax 263-3550
Clear Lake JHS 100/7-8
1101 3rd St SW 54005 715-263-2113
Wayne Whitwam, prin. Fax 263-3550

Cleveland, Manitowoc, Pop. 1,401

Lakeshore Technical College Post-Sec.
1290 North Ave 53015 920-693-8213

Clinton, Rock, Pop. 3,124
Clinton Community SD 1,200/PK-12
PO Box 566 53525 608-676-5482
Rebecca Nodorft, supt. Fax 676-4444
www.clinton.k12.wi.us
Clinton HS 400/9-12
PO Box 566 53525 608-676-2223
Marc Eckmann, prin. Fax 676-4444
Clinton MS 400/5-8
PO Box 559 53525 608-676-2275
Carol Langley, prin. Fax 676-5176

Clintonville, Waupaca, Pop. 4,399
Clintonville SD 1,300/PK-12
45 W Green Tree Rd 54929 715-823-7215
Tom O'Toole, supt. Fax 823-1315
www.clintonville.k12.wi.us
Clintonville HS 600/9-12
64 W Green Tree Rd 54929 715-823-7215
Garrett Rogowski, prin. Fax 823-1481
Clintonville MS 400/5-8
255 N Main St 54929 715-823-7215
Tom Dechant, prin. Fax 823-1443

Colby, Clark, Pop. 1,664
Colby SD 900/PK-12
PO Box 139 54421 715-223-2301
J. Terry Downen, supt. Fax 223-4539
www.colby.k12.wi.us
Colby HS 400/9-12
PO Box 110 54421 715-223-2338
Nancy Marcott, prin. Fax 223-4388
Colby MS 200/5-8
PO Box 110 54421 715-223-8869
James Hagen, prin. Fax 223-6754

Coleman, Marinette, Pop. 706
Coleman SD 800/PK-12
PO Box 259 54112 920-897-4011
Les Larmour, supt. Fax 897-2015
www.coleman.k12.wi.us
Coleman HS 300/9-12
PO Box 259 54112 920-897-2291
Kelly Casper, prin. Fax 897-2015

Faith Christian S 100/K-12
233 W Main St 54112 920-897-3380
Eric Schindler, admin. Fax 897-4880

Colfax, Dunn, Pop. 1,070
Colfax SD 800/PK-12
601 University Ave 54730 715-962-3773
Dennis Geissler, supt. Fax 962-4024
www.colfax.k12.wi.us/
Colfax HS 200/9-12
601 University Ave 54730 715-962-3155
John Dachel, prin. Fax 962-4024

Columbus, Columbia, Pop. 5,101
Columbus SD 1,100/PK-12
200 W School St 53925 920-623-5950
Mark Jansen, supt. Fax 623-5958
www.columbus.k12.wi.us
Columbus HS 400/9-12
1164 Farnham St 53925 920-623-5956
Connie Valenza, prin. Fax 623-5959
Columbus MS 400/4-8
400 S Dickason Blvd 53925 920-623-5954
Doug Waitrovich, prin. Fax 623-5742

Wisconsin Academy 100/9-12
N2355 Du Borg Rd Bldg 1 53925 920-623-3300
Derral Reeve, prin. Fax 623-3318

Cornell, Chippewa, Pop. 1,392
Cornell SD 500/PK-12
PO Box 517 54732 715-239-6577
Paul M. Schley, supt. Fax 239-6467
www.cornell.k12.wi.us
Cornell JSHS 300/7-12
PO Box 517 54732 715-239-6464
David Elliott, prin. Fax 239-6467

Crandon, Forest, Pop. 1,867
Crandon SD 900/PK-12
9750 US Highway 8 W 54520 715-478-3339
Dr. Richard Peters, supt. Fax 478-5130
www.crandon.k12.wi.us
Crandon HS 300/9-12
9750 US Highway 8 W 54520 715-478-3583
John Gruber, prin. Fax 478-5570
Crandon MS 200/6-8
9750 US Highway 8 W 54520 715-478-3713
Glen Pfeifer, prin. Fax 478-5570

Crivitz, Marinette, Pop. 1,030
Crivitz SD 800/PK-12
PO Box 130 54114 715-854-2721
Charles Poches, supt. Fax 854-3755
www.crivitz.k12.wi.us
Crivitz HS 300/9-12
PO Box 130 54114 715-854-2721
Vic Gehm, prin. Fax 854-3755
Crivitz MS 100/7-8
PO Box 130 54114 715-854-2721
Eugene Chapman, prin. Fax 854-2050

Cross Plains, Dane, Pop. 3,418
Middleton-Cross Plains Area SD
Supt. — See Middleton
Glacier Creek MS 600/6-8
2800 Military Rd 53528 608-829-9420
Tim Keeler, prin. Fax 798-5425

Cuba City, Grant, Pop. 2,104
Cuba City SD 700/PK-12
101 N School St 53807 608-744-2847
Sam McGrew, supt. Fax 744-2324
www.cubacity.k12.wi.us

Cuba City HS | 300/9-12
101 N School St 53807 | 608-744-8888
Tim Hazen, prin. | Fax 744-2324

Cudahy, Milwaukee, Pop. 18,316
Cudahy SD | 2,900/PK-12
2915 E Ramsey Ave 53110 | 414-294-7400
James Heiden, supt. | Fax 769-2319
www.cudahy.k12.wi.us/
Cudahy HS | 900/9-12
4950 S Lake Dr 53110 | 414-294-2700
Kay Marks, prin. | Fax 769-2379
Cudahy MS | 400/7-8
5530 S Barland Ave 53110 | 414-294-2830
Gene Bibis, prin. | Fax 489-3010

Cumberland, Barron, Pop. 2,242
Cumberland SD | 200/PK-12
1010 8th Ave 54829 | 715-822-5124
Donald Groth, supt. | Fax 822-5136
www.cumberland.k12.wi.us/
Cumberland HS | 100/9-12
1000 8th Ave 54829 | 715-822-5121
Ritchie Narges, prin. | Fax 822-5138
Cumberland MS | 50/5-8
980 8th Ave 54829 | 715-822-5122
Jim Sciacca, prin. | Fax 822-5132

Darlington, Lafayette, Pop. 2,341
Darlington Community SD | 800/PK-12
11630 Center Hill Rd 53530 | 608-776-2006
Joseph Galle, supt. | Fax 776-3407
www.darlington.k12.wi.us
Darlington HS | 300/9-12
11838 Center Hill Rd 53530 | 608-776-4001
Dan Myers, prin. | Fax 776-2378

Deerfield, Dane, Pop. 2,202
Deerfield Community SD | 700/PK-12
300 Simonson Blvd 53531 | 608-764-5431
Michelle Jensen, supt. | Fax 764-5433
www.deerfield.k12.wi.us
Deerfield HS | 200/9-12
300 Simonson Blvd 53531 | 608-764-5431
David Podmolik, prin. | Fax 764-5433
Deerfield MS | 100/7-8
300 Simonson Blvd 53531 | 608-764-5431
David Podmolik, prin. | Fax 764-5433

De Forest, Dane, Pop. 6,262
De Forest Area SD | 3,200/PK-12
520 E Holum St 53532 | 608-842-6500
Jon Bales, supt. | Fax 842-6576
www.deforest.k12.wi.us
De Forest Area HS | 1,000/9-12
815 Jefferson St 53532 | 608-842-6600
Tim Onsager, prin. | Fax 842-6615
De Forest Area MS | 1,000/5-8
404 Yorktown Rd 53532 | 608-842-6000
Ann Higgins, prin. | Fax 842-6015

Delafield, Waukesha, Pop. 6,767

St. Johns Northwestern Military Academy | 300/7-12
1101 Genesee St 53018 | 262-646-7111
Jack Albert, pres. | Fax 646-4796

Delavan, Walworth, Pop. 8,370
Delavan-Darien SD | 2,600/K-12
324 Beloit St 53115 | 262-728-2642
James Sorensen, supt. | Fax 728-5954
www.ddschools.org
Delavan-Darien HS | 900/9-12
150 Cumming St 53115 | 262-728-2642
Mike Cipriano, prin. | Fax 728-9713
Phoenix MS | 600/6-8
414 Beloit St 53115 | 262-728-2642
Deborah Bissett, prin. | Fax 728-0359

Wisconsin School for the Deaf | Post-Sec.
309 W Walworth Ave 53115

Denmark, Brown, Pop. 1,990
Denmark SD | 1,600/PK-12
450 N Wall St 54208 | 920-863-4000
Tony Klaubauf, supt. | Fax 863-4015
www.denmark.k12.wi.us
Denmark HS | 500/9-12
450 N Wall St 54208 | 920-863-4200
Kevin Kilstofte, prin. | Fax 863-8856
Denmark MS | 400/6-8
450 N Wall St 54208 | 920-863-4100
Dyan Pasono, prin. | Fax 863-3184

De Pere, Brown, Pop. 23,375
De Pere SD | 3,400/PK-12
1700 Chicago St 54115 | 920-337-1032
Benjamin Villarruel, supt. | Fax 337-1033
www.depere.k12.wi.us
De Pere HS | 1,100/9-12
1700 Chicago St 54115 | 920-337-1020
Annette Brace, prin. | Fax 337-1041
De Pere MS | 500/7-8
700 Swan Rd 54115 | 920-337-1024
Tammy Woulf, prin. | Fax 337-1049

West De Pere SD | 2,100/PK-12
930 Oak St 54115 | 920-337-1393
Lanny J. Tibaldo, supt. | Fax 337-1398
www.wdpsd.com
West De Pere HS | 700/9-12
665 Grant St 54115 | 920-338-5200
Russell Gerke, prin. | Fax 338-5310
West De Pere MS | 600/5-8
1177 S 9th St 54115 | 920-337-1099
James Finley, prin. | Fax 337-1380

St. Norbert College | Post-Sec.
100 Grant St 54115 | 800-236-4878

De Soto, Vernon, Pop. 369
De Soto Area SD | 600/PK-12
615 Main St 54624 | 608-648-0102
Michael Davis, supt. | Fax 648-3959
www.desoto.k12.wi.us
De Soto HS | 200/9-12
615 Main St 54624 | 608-648-0100
Martin Kirchhof, prin. | Fax 648-0117
De Soto MS | 100/6-8
615 Main St 54624 | 608-648-0104
Martin Kirchhof, prin. | Fax 648-0117

Dodgeville, Iowa, Pop. 4,840
Dodgeville SD | 1,300/PK-12
400 N Johnson St 53533 | 608-935-3307
Diane Messer, supt. | Fax 935-3021
www.dsd.k12.wi.us/
Dodgeville HS | 400/9-12
912 W Chapel St 53533 | 608-935-3307
Jeff Athey, prin. | Fax 935-9540
Dodgeville MS | 300/6-8
951 W Chapel St 53533 | 608-935-3307
Mitch Wainwright, prin. | Fax 935-9643

Dousman, Waukesha, Pop. 1,885
Kettle Moraine SD
Supt. — See Wales
Kettle Moraine MS | 1,000/6-8
301 E Ottawa Ave 53118 | 262-965-6500
Ryan Krohn, prin. | Fax 965-6506

Drummond, Bayfield
Drummond Area SD | 500/PK-12
PO Box 40 54832 | 715-739-6669
Henry Lamkin, supt. | Fax 739-6345
www.dasd.k12.wi.us
Drummond HS | 200/9-12
PO Box 40 54832 | 715-739-6231
Ellen Nelson, prin. | Fax 739-6345
Drummond MS | 100/7-8
PO Box 40 54832 | 715-739-6231
Ellen Nelson, prin. | Fax 739-6345

Dunbar, Marinette

Northland Baptist Bible College | Post-Sec.
W10085 Pike Plains Rd 54119 | 715-324-6900

Durand, Pepin, Pop. 1,898
Durand SD | 700/PK-12
604 7th Ave E 54736 | 715-672-8919
Jerry Walters, supt. | Fax 672-8900
www.durand.k12.wi.us
Durand JSHS | 400/7-12
604 7th Ave E 54736 | 715-672-8917
Bill Clouse, prin. | Fax 672-8930

St. Mary S | 100/4-8
901 W Prospect St 54736 | 715-672-5617
Bernard Huettl, prin. | Fax 672-3931

Eagle River, Vilas, Pop. 1,608
Northland Pines SD | 1,400/PK-12
1800 Pleasure Island Rd 54521 | 715-479-6487
Mike Richie, supt. | Fax 479-7633
www.npsd.k12.wi.us/
Northland Pines HS | 600/9-12
1800 Pleasure Island Rd 54521 | 715-479-4473
Pat Sullivan, prin. | Fax 479-5808
Northland Pines MS | 400/6-8
1700 Pleasure Island Rd 54521 | 715-479-6479
Jacqueline Coghlan, prin. | Fax 479-7303

East Troy, Walworth, Pop. 4,224
East Troy Community SD | 1,700/K-12
2043 Division St 53120 | 262-642-6710
Robert Spence, supt. | Fax 642-6712
www.easttroy.k12.wi.us
East Troy HS | 600/9-12
3128 Graydon Ave 53120 | 262-642-6760
Rick Penniston, prin. | Fax 642-6776
East Troy MS | 400/6-8
3143 Graydon Ave 53120 | 262-642-6740
Michael Willeman, prin. | Fax 642-6743

Eau Claire, Eau Claire, Pop. 62,570
Eau Claire Area SD | 10,100/PK-12
500 Main St 54701 | 715-852-3000
Dr. William Klaus, supt. | Fax 852-3004
www.ecasd.k12.wi.us
Delong MS | 900/6-8
2000 Vine St 54703 | 715-852-4900
Dr. Deb Hansen, prin. | Fax 852-4904
Memorial HS | 1,800/9-12
2225 Keith St 54701 | 715-852-6300
Tim Leibham, prin. | Fax 852-6304
North HS | 1,600/9-12
1801 Piedmont Rd 54703 | 715-852-6600
Dave Valk, prin. | Fax 852-6604
Northstar MS | 600/6-8
2711 Abbe Hill Dr 54703 | 715-852-5100
Tom Fiedler, prin. | Fax 852-5104
South MS | 900/6-8
2115 Mitscher Ave 54701 | 715-852-5200
John Wallace, prin. | Fax 852-5204

Chippewa Valley Technical College | Post-Sec.
620 W Clairemont Ave 54701 | 715-833-6200
Eau Claire Academy | 100/3-12
PO Box 1168 54702 | 715-834-6681
Laurie Van Beek, prin. | Fax 834-9954
Immanuel Lutheran College HS | 100/9-12
501 Grover Rd 54701 | 715-836-6621
Jeffrey Schierenbeck, prin. | Fax 836-6634
Professional Hair Design Academy | Post-Sec.
3408 Mall Dr 54701 | 715-835-2345
Regis HS | 9-12
2100 Fenwick Ave 54701 | 715-830-2271
Bill Uelmen, prin. | Fax 830-5461
Regis MS | 100/7-8
2100 Fenwick Ave 54701 | 715-830-2272
William Uelmen, prin. | Fax 830-5461
Sacred Heart Hospital | Post-Sec.
900 W Clairemont Ave 54701 | 715-839-4131
University of Wisconsin | Post-Sec.
PO Box 4004 54702 | 715-836-2637

Edgar, Marathon, Pop. 1,327
Edgar SD | 600/PK-12
PO Box 196 54426 | 715-352-2351
Mark Lacke, supt. | Fax 352-3198
www.edgar.k12.wi.us/edgar/
Edgar HS | 200/9-12
PO Box 196 54426 | 715-352-2352
Bob Houts, prin. | Fax 352-3198
Edgar MS | 100/6-8
PO Box 198 54426 | 715-352-2727
Lisa Witt, prin. | Fax 352-3022

Edgerton, Rock, Pop. 5,102
Edgerton SD | 1,800/PK-12
200 Elm High Dr 53534 | 608-884-9402
Dr. Norman Fjelstad, supt. | Fax 884-9327
www.edgerton.k12.wi.us
Edgerton HS | 600/9-12
200 Elm High Dr 53534 | 608-884-9402
James Halberg, prin. | Fax 884-7969
Edgerton MS | 500/6-8
300 Elm High Dr 53534 | 608-884-9402
Jerry Roth, prin. | Fax 884-2279

Oaklawn Academy | 200/6-8
432 Liguori Rd 53534 | 608-884-3425
Javier Valenzuela, prin. | Fax 884-8175

Elcho, Langlade
Elcho SD | 400/PK-12
PO Box 800 54428 | 715-275-3205
Christopher Thomalla, supt. | Fax 275-4388
www.elcho.k12.wi.us
Elcho HS | 100/9-12
PO Box 800 54428 | 715-275-3707
Don Peterson, prin. | Fax 275-4388

Elkhart Lake, Sheboygan, Pop. 1,068
Elkhart Lake - Glenbeulah SD | 600/PK-12
PO Box K 53020 | 920-876-3381
Jerry Smith, supt. | Fax 876-3511
www.elgs.com/
Elkhart Lake - Glenbeulah HS | 200/9-12
PO Box K 53020 | 920-876-3381
John Quella, prin. | Fax 876-3511
Elkhart Lake - Glenbeulah MS | 200/5-8
PO Box 518 53020 | 920-876-3307
Ann Buechel Haack, prin. | Fax 876-3105

Elkhorn, Walworth, Pop. 9,021
Elkhorn Area SD | 2,700/K-12
3 N Jackson St 53121 | 262-723-3160
Gregory Wescott, supt. | Fax 723-4652
www.elkhorn.k12.wi.us
Elkhorn Area HS | 900/9-12
482 E Geneva St 53121 | 262-723-4920
Gary Baumann, prin. | Fax 723-8092
Elkhorn Area MS | 700/6-8
627 E Court St 53121 | 262-723-6800
John Gendron, prin. | Fax 723-4967

Gateway Technical College | Post-Sec.
400 County Road H 53121 | 262-741-8200

Elk Mound, Dunn, Pop. 815
Elk Mound Area SD | 900/PK-12
405 University St 54739 | 715-879-5066
Ronald Walsh, supt. | Fax 879-5846
www.elkmound.k12.wi.us
Elk Mound HS | 300/9-12
405 University St 54739 | 715-879-5521
Paul Weber, prin. | Fax 879-5846
Elk Mound MS | 200/5-8
302 University St 54739 | 715-879-5595
Eric Wright, prin. | Fax 879-5846

Ellsworth, Pierce, Pop. 3,060
Ellsworth Community SD | 1,700/PK-12
PO Box 1500 54011 | 715-273-3900
Dan Kaler, supt. | Fax 273-5775
www.ellsworth.k12.wi.us
Ellsworth HS | 600/9-12
PO Box 1500 54011 | 715-273-3904
Charles Buckel, prin. | Fax 273-6824
Ellsworth MS | 400/5-8
PO Box 1500 54011 | 715-273-3908
Steve Broton, prin. | Fax 273-6834

Elm Grove, Waukesha, Pop. 6,182
Elmbrook SD
Supt. — See Brookfield
Pilgrim Park MS | 900/6-8
1500 Pilgrim Pkwy 53122 | 262-785-3920
Don Galster, prin. | Fax 785-3933

Elmwood, Pierce, Pop. 796
Elmwood SD | 300/PK-12
213 S Scott St 54740 | 715-639-2711
Barry Rose, supt. | Fax 639-3110
www.elmwood.k12.wi.us
Elmwood HS | 100/9-12
213 S Scott St 54740 | 715-639-2721
Barry Rose, prin. | Fax 639-3110
Elmwood MS | 7-8
213 S Scott St 54740 | 715-639-2721
Shawn Madden, prin. | Fax 639-3110

Elroy, Juneau, Pop. 1,527
Royall SD | 600/PK-12
PO Box 125 53929 | 608-462-2600
Scott A. Sarnow, supt. | Fax 462-2618
www.royall.k12.wi.us

Royall MSHS 400/6-12
PO Box 125 53929 608-462-2602
Kyle Luedtke, prin. Fax 462-2604

Evansville, Rock, Pop. 4,658
Evansville Community SD 1,700/PK-12
340 Fair St 53536 608-882-5224
Heidi Carvin, supt. Fax 882-6564
www.evansville.k12.wi.us
Evansville HS 500/9-12
640 S 5th St 53536 608-882-4600
Jamie Gillespie, prin. Fax 882-6157
McKenna MS 400/6-8
307 S 1st St 53536 608-882-4780
Robert Flaherty, prin. Fax 882-5744

Fall Creek, Eau Claire, Pop. 1,213
Fall Creek SD 800/PK-12
336 E Hoover Ave 54742 715-877-2123
Dr. Craig Hitchens, supt. Fax 877-2911
www.fallcreek.k12.wi.us
Fall Creek HS 300/9-12
336 E Hoover Ave 54742 715-877-2809
Brian Schulner, prin. Fax 877-2911
Fall Creek MS 200/6-8
336 E Hoover Ave 54742 715-877-2511
Brian Schulner, prin. Fax 877-2911

Fall River, Columbia, Pop. 1,280
Fall River SD 500/PK-12
PO Box 116 53932 920-484-3333
Heidi A. Schmidt, supt. Fax 484-3600
www.fallriver.k12.wi.us
Fall River HS 200/6-12
PO Box 116 53932 920-484-3333
Bradley Johnsrud, prin. Fax 484-3600

Fennimore, Grant, Pop. 2,357
Fennimore Community SD 800/PK-12
1397 9th St 53809 608-822-3243
Richard Feutz, supt. Fax 822-3250
www.fennimore.k12.wi.us
Fennimore JSHS 400/7-12
510 7th St 53809 608-822-3245
Dan Bredeson, prin. Fax 822-3247

Southwest Wisconsin Technical College Post-Sec.
1800 Bronson Blvd 53809 608-822-3262

Fish Creek, Door
Gibraltar Area SD 600/PK-12
3924 State Highway 42 54212 920-868-3284
Stephen Seyfer, supt. Fax 868-2714
www.gibraltar.k12.wi.us
Gibraltar HS 200/9-12
3924 State Highway 42 54212 920-868-3284
Kirk Knutson, prin. Fax 868-2714
Gibraltar MS 100/6-8
3924 State Highway 42 54212 920-868-3284
Kirk Knutson, prin. Fax 868-2714

Fitchburg, Dane, Pop. 22,040
Verona Area SD
Supt. — See Verona
Savanna Oaks MS 400/6-8
5890 Lacy Rd 53711 608-845-4000
Stephanie Edwards, prin. Fax 845-4020

Florence, Florence
Florence SD 700/PK-12
PO Box 440 54121 715-528-3217
Jan Dooley, supt. Fax 528-5338
www.florence.k12.wi.us
Florence HS 200/9-12
PO Box 440 54121 715-528-3215
Brandon Jerue, admin. Fax 528-5330
Florence MS 200/6-8
PO Box 440 54121 715-528-3215
Brandon Jerue, admin. Fax 528-5338

Fond du Lac, Fond du Lac, Pop. 42,435
Fond du Lac SD 7,100/K-12
72 W 9th St 54935 920-929-2900
Gregory R. Maass Ph.D., supt. Fax 929-6804
www.fonddulac.k12.wi.us
Fond du Lac HS 2,400/9-12
801 Campus Dr 54935 920-929-2740
Mary Fran Merwin, prin. Fax 929-6964
Sabish MS 600/6-8
100 N Peters Ave 54935 920-929-2800
Kelly Noble, prin. Fax 929-2807
Theisen MS 600/6-8
525 E Pioneer Rd 54935 920-929-2850
Kim Pahlow, prin. Fax 929-2854
Woodworth MS 500/6-8
101 Morningside Dr 54935 920-929-6900
Steven Hill, prin. Fax 929-6944

FACES MS 300/3-8
PO Box 2138 54936 920-921-9610
Susan Zackerl, prin. Fax 921-0457
Fond du Lac Christian S 100/K-12
720 Rienzi Rd 54935 920-924-2177
Matthew Bro, prin. Fax 322-9459
Marian College of Fond du Lac Post-Sec.
45 S National Ave 54935 920-923-7600
Moraine Park Technical College Post-Sec.
235 N National Ave 54935 920-922-8611
St. Mary Springs HS 200/9-12
255 County Road K 54935 920-921-4870
Tom Wonderling, prin. Fax 921-2786
University of Wisconsin Center Post-Sec.
400 University Dr 54935 920-929-3606
Winnebago Lutheran Academy 300/9-12
475 E Merrill Ave 54935 920-921-4930
Randall Westphal, prin. Fax 921-4280

Fort Atkinson, Jefferson, Pop. 11,949
Fort Atkinson SD 2,700/PK-12
201 Park St 53538 920-563-7807
James Fitzpatrick, supt. Fax 563-7809
www.fortschools.org
Fort Atkinson HS 900/9-12
925 Lexington Blvd 53538 920-563-7811
Jeff Zaspel, prin. Fax 563-7810
Fort Atkinson MS 600/6-8
310 S 4th St E 53538 920-563-7833
Robert Abbott, prin. Fax 563-7838

Fountain City, Buffalo, Pop. 1,026
Cochrane-Fountain City SD 700/PK-12
S2770 State Road 35 54629 608-687-7771
Gordy Geurink, supt. Fax 687-3312
www.cfc.k12.wi.us
Cochrane-Fountain City JSHS 300/7-12
S2770 State Road 35 54629 608-687-4391
Sally Peterson, prin. Fax 687-6412

Franklin, Milwaukee, Pop. 33,263
Franklin SD 4,000/K-12
8255 W Forest Hill Ave 53132 414-529-8220
Steve Patz, supt. Fax 529-8230
www.franklin.k12.wi.us
Forest Park MS 600/7-8
8225 W Forest Hill Ave 53132 414-529-8250
Matthew Lesar, prin. Fax 529-8249
Franklin HS 1,400/9-12
8222 S 51st St 53132 414-423-4640
Michael Cady, prin. Fax 421-0558

Frederic, Polk, Pop. 1,233
Frederic SD 600/PK-12
1437 Clam Falls Dr 54837 715-327-5630
Gerald Tischer, supt. Fax 327-5609
www.frederic.k12.wi.us/
Frederic JSHS 300/7-12
1437 Clam Falls Dr 54837 715-327-4223
Raymond Draxler, prin. Fax 327-8655

Fredonia, Ozaukee, Pop. 2,192
Northern Ozaukee SD 800/PK-12
401 Highland Dr 53021 262-692-2489
William Harbron, supt. Fax 692-6257
www.nosd.edu
Ozaukee HS 300/9-12
401 Highland Dr 53021 262-692-2453
Kevin Parker, prin. Fax 692-6257
Ozaukee MS 200/5-8
401 Highland Dr 53021 262-692-2463
Pam Warner, prin. Fax 692-2313

Freedom, Outagamie
Freedom Area SD 1,500/PK-12
PO Box 1008 54131 920-788-7944
Lois Cuff, supt. Fax 788-7949
www.freedomschools.k12.wi.us
Freedom HS 500/9-12
PO Box 1003 54131 920-788-7940
Dannette Arndt, prin. Fax 788-7700
Freedom MS 300/6-8
PO Box 1002 54131 920-788-7945
Ken Fisher, prin. Fax 788-7701

Friendship, Adams, Pop. 766
Adams-Friendship Area SD 2,000/PK-12
201 W 6th St 53934 608-339-3213
Steven Lavallee, supt. Fax 339-6213
www.af.k12.wi.us/pages/index.cfm
Other Schools – See Adams

Galesville, Trempealeau, Pop. 1,462
Galesville-Ettrick-Trempealeau SD 200/PK-12
PO Box 4000 54630 608-582-2291
Craig Gerlach, supt. Fax 582-4263
www.getschools.k12.wi.us
Coulee Region HS 9-12
16935 N Main St 54630 608-582-2200
Chuck Forster, prin. Fax 582-4263
Gale-Ettrick-Tremp HS 100/9-12
PO Box 4000 54630 608-582-2291
Chuck Forster, prin. Fax 582-4263
Other Schools – See Trempealeau

Genoa City, Walworth, Pop. 2,742
Genoa City J2 SD 50/K-8
PO Box 250 53128 262-279-1051
Bill Lehner, supt. Fax 279-1052
Brookwood MS 50/5-8
PO Box 250 53128 262-279-1053
Kellie Bohn, prin. Fax 279-1052

Germantown, Washington, Pop. 19,245
Germantown SD 3,700/PK-12
N104W13840 Donges Bay Rd 53022 262-253-3900
Victor Rossetti, supt. Fax 251-6999
www.germantown.k12.wi.us
Germantown HS 1,300/9-12
W180N11501 River Ln 53022 262-253-3400
Jim Blackburn, prin. Fax 253-3494
Kennedy MS 900/6-8
W160N11836 Crusader Ct 53022 262-253-3450
Steven Bold, prin. Fax 253-3499

Gillett, Oconto, Pop. 1,188
Gillett SD 800/PK-12
PO Box 227 54124 920-855-2137
Stuart Rivard, supt. Fax 855-1557
www.gillett.k12.wi.us
Gillett HS 300/9-12
PO Box 227 54124 920-855-2137
Sam Santacroce, prin. Fax 855-6600
Gillett MS 200/6-8
PO Box 227 54124 920-855-2137
Sam Santacroce, prin. Fax 855-6600

Gilman, Taylor, Pop. 460
Gilman SD 500/PK-12
325 N 5th Ave 54433 715-447-8216
Drew Johnson, supt. Fax 447-8731
www.gilman.k12.wi.us
Gilman JSHS 200/7-12
325 N 5th Ave 54433 715-447-8211
Dawn Randall, prin. Fax 447-8731

Gilmanton, Buffalo
Gilmanton SD 200/PK-12
PO Box 28 54743 715-946-3158
William Perry, supt. Fax 946-3474
www.ghs.k12.wi.us
Gilmanton JSHS 100/7-12
PO Box 28 54743 715-946-3158
William Perry, prin. Fax 946-3474

Glendale, Milwaukee, Pop. 12,880
Glendale-River Hills SD 1,000/PK-8
2600 W Mill Rd 53209 414-351-7170
Larry Smalley, supt. Fax 434-0109
www.glendale.k12.wi.us
Glen Hills MS 500/5-8
2600 W Mill Rd 53209 414-351-7160
Larry Smalley, prin. Fax 351-8100

Nicolet UNHSD 500/9-12
6701 N Jean Nicolet Rd 53217 414-351-7520
Dr. Elliott Moeser, supt. Fax 351-7526
nicolet.k12.wi.us/
Nicolet Union HS 500/9-12
6701 N Jean Nicolet Rd 53217 414-351-1700
Dr. Elliott Moeser, prin. Fax 351-7526

Glenwood City, Saint Croix, Pop. 1,225
Glenwood City SD 800/K-12
850 Maple St 54013 715-265-4757
Timothy J. Emholtz, supt. Fax 265-4214
www.gcsd.k12.wi.us/
Glenwood City HS 300/9-12
850 Maple St 54013 715-265-4266
Timothy Johnson, prin. Fax 265-7129
Glenwood City JHS 100/7-8
850 Maple St 54013 715-265-4266
Timothy Johnson, prin.

Glidden, Ashland
Glidden SD 100/PK-12
RR 1 Box 1 54527 715-264-2141
Mark W. Luoma, supt. Fax 264-3413
www.glidden.k12.wi.us
Glidden S 100/PK-12
RR 1 Box 1 54527 715-264-2141
Mark Luoma, prin. Fax 264-3413

Goodman, Marinette
Goodman-Armstrong Creek SD 200/PK-12
PO Box 160 54125 715-336-2575
Jeff Reeder, supt. Fax 336-2576
www.goodman.k12.wi.us
Goodman JSHS 100/7-12
PO Box 160 54125 715-336-2575
Jeff Reeder, prin. Fax 336-2576

Grafton, Ozaukee, Pop. 11,625
Grafton SD 2,000/PK-12
1900 Washington St 53024 262-376-5400
Jeffrey Pechura, supt. Fax 376-5599
www.grafton.k12.wi.us/
Grafton HS 800/9-12
1950 Washington St 53024 262-376-5500
Ken McCormick, prin. Fax 376-5510
Long MS 500/6-8
700 Hickory St 53024 262-376-5800
Tom Engel, prin. Fax 376-5810

Granton, Clark, Pop. 402
Granton Area SD 300/K-12
217 N Main St 54436 715-238-7292
Rick Rehm, supt. Fax 238-7288
www.granton.k12.wi.us/
Granton HS 100/9-12
217 N Main St 54436 715-238-7175
Craig Anderson, prin. Fax 238-7827

Grantsburg, Burnett, Pop. 1,397
Grantsburg SD 1,000/PK-12
480 E James Ave 54840 715-463-5499
Joni Burgin, supt. Fax 463-2534
www.gk12.net/
Grantsburg HS 300/9-12
480 E James Ave 54840 715-463-2531
Jeff Bush, prin. Fax 463-5068
Grantsburg MS 400/4-8
480 E James Ave 54840 715-463-2455
Brad Jones, prin. Fax 463-3209

Gratiot, Lafayette, Pop. 247
Black Hawk SD
Supt. — See South Wayne
Black Hawk MS 100/5-8
PO Box 457 53541 608-922-6457
Kevin Shetler, prin. Fax 922-3376

Green Bay, Brown, Pop. 101,203
Ashwaubenon SD 3,100/PK-12
1055 Griffiths Ln 54304 920-492-2900
Sue Alberti, supt. Fax 492-2911
www.ashwaubenon.k12.wi.us
Ashwaubenon HS 1,100/9-12
2391 S Ridge Rd 54304 920-492-2950
Mark Sheedy, prin. Fax 492-2912
Parkview MS 800/6-8
955 Willard Dr 54304 920-492-2940
Brian Nelsen, prin. Fax 492-2944

Green Bay Area SD — 20,300/PK-12
PO Box 23387 54305 — 920-448-2000
Daniel Nerad, supt. — Fax 448-3562
www.greenbay.k12.wi.us
East HS — 1,500/9-12
1415 E Walnut St 54301 — 920-448-2090
Ed Dorff, prin. — Fax 448-2166
Edison MS — 1,200/6-8
442 Alpine Dr 54302 — 920-391-2450
Rodney Bohm, prin. — Fax 391-2531
Franklin MS — 800/6-8
1234 W Mason St 54303 — 920-492-2670
Matthew Weller, prin. — Fax 492-5563
Lombardi MS — 900/6-8
1520 S Point Rd 54313 — 920-492-2625
Nancy Croy, prin. — Fax 492-5564
Preble HS — 2,200/9-12
2222 Deckner Ave 54302 — 920-391-2400
Christopher Wagner, prin. — Fax 391-2530
Southwest HS — 1,400/9-12
1331 Packerland Dr 54304 — 920-492-2650
Bryan Davis, prin. — Fax 492-5561
Washington MS — 1,000/6-8
314 S Baird St 54301 — 920-448-2095
Amy Bindas, prin. — Fax 448-3551
West HS — 1,300/9-12
966 Shawano Ave 54303 — 920-492-2600
Luke Valitchka, prin. — Fax 492-2641

Howard-Suamico SD — 4,800/K-12
2700 Lineville Rd 54313 — 920-662-7878
Damian LaCroix, supt. — Fax 662-9777
www.hssd.k12.wi.us
Bay Port HS — 1,500/9-12
2710 Lineville Rd 54313 — 920-662-7000
Michael Frieder, prin. — Fax 662-7291
Bay View MS — 800/7-8
1217 Cardinal Ln 54313 — 920-662-8196
Steve Meyers, prin. — Fax 662-7979

Bay City Baptist S — 100/PK-12
1840 Bond St 54303 — 920-499-5561
Ray Anderson, prin. — Fax 499-5619
Bellin College of Nursing — Post-Sec.
PO Box 23400 54305 — 920-433-5803
Bellin Hospital — Post-Sec.
PO Box 23400 54305 — 920-433-3497
Martin's College of Cosmetology — Post-Sec.
2575 W Mason St 54303 — 920-494-1430
Northeastern Wisconsin Lutheran HS — 100/9-12
1311 S Robinson Ave 54311 — 920-469-6810
Stephen Siekmann, prin. — Fax 469-2200
Northeast Wisconsin Technical College — Post-Sec.
PO Box 19042 54307 — 920-498-5400
Notre Dame De La Baie Academy — 700/9-12
610 Maryhill Dr 54303 — 920-429-6100
Dr. Mark Schmidt, prin. — Fax 429-6140
St. Vincent Hospital — Post-Sec.
PO Box 13508 54307 — 920-433-8155
University of Wisconsin — Post-Sec.
2420 Nicolet Dr 54311 — 920-465-2000
Wisconsin College of Cosmetology — Post-Sec.
2960 Allied St 54304 — 920-336-8888

Greendale, Milwaukee, Pop. 13,860
Greendale SD — 2,400/PK-12
5900 S 51st St 53129 — 414-423-2700
William Hughes, supt. — Fax 423-2723
www.greendale.k12.wi.us
Greendale HS — 900/9-12
6801 Southway 53129 — 414-423-0110
Steven Lodes, prin. — Fax 423-1667
Greendale MS — 600/6-8
6800 Schoolway 53129 — 414-423-2800
Wendy Dzurick, prin. — Fax 423-2806

Martin Luther HS — 400/9-12
5201 S 76th St 53129 — 414-421-4000
Carl Eisman, admin. — Fax 421-4071

Greenfield, Milwaukee, Pop. 35,753
Greenfield SD — 3,300/PK-12
8500 W Chapman Ave 53228 — 414-529-9090
Louis Birchbauer, supt. — Fax 529-9478
www.greenfield.k12.wi.us
Greenfield HS — 1,200/9-12
4800 S 60th St 53220 — 414-281-6200
John Thomsen, prin. — Fax 281-8860
Greenfield MS — 700/6-8
3200 W Barnard Ave 53221 — 414-282-4700
Todd Bugnacki, prin. — Fax 282-1017

Whitnall SD — 2,500/PK-12
5000 S 116th St 53228 — 414-525-8400
Karen Petric, supt. — Fax 525-8401
www.whitnall.com
Whitnall HS — 900/9-12
5000 S 116th St 53228 — 414-525-8500
Joel Eul, prin. — Fax 525-8501
Whitnall MS — 600/6-8
5025 S 116th St 53228 — 414-525-8650
Fred Wendt, prin. — Fax 525-8651

Green Lake, Green Lake, Pop. 1,125
Green Lake SD — 400/PK-12
PO Box 369 54941 — 920-294-6411
Nancy Burns, supt. — Fax 294-6589
www.greenlakeschools.com
Green Lake JSHS — 200/7-12
PO Box 369 54941 — 920-294-6411
E. Jon Tracy, prin. — Fax 294-6589

Greenville, Outagamie
Hortonville SD
Supt. — See Hortonville
Greenville MS — 400/6-8
N1450 Fawn Ridge Dr 54942 — 920-757-7140
Bruce Carew, prin. — Fax 757-7141

Greenwood, Clark, Pop. 1,082
Greenwood SD — 500/PK-12
306 W Central Ave 54437 — 715-267-6101
Marsha Hochhalter, supt. — Fax 267-6113
www.greenwood.k12.wi.us/
Greenwood MSHS — 200/7-12
306 W Central Ave 54437 — 715-267-6101
David Schaller, prin. — Fax 267-6113

Gresham, Shawano, Pop. 585
Gresham SD — 300/PK-12
501 Schabow St 54128 — 715-787-3211
Fax 787-3951
Gresham HS — 100/9-12
501 Schabow St 54128 — 715-787-3211
Fax 787-3951

Hales Corners, Milwaukee, Pop. 7,535

Hales Corners Lutheran MS — 100/6-8
12300 W Janesville Rd 53130 — 414-529-6702
Albert Amling, prin. — Fax 529-6710
Sacred Heart School of Theology — Post-Sec.
PO Box 429 53130 — 414-425-8300

Hammond, Saint Croix, Pop. 1,695
St. Croix Central SD — 1,000/PK-12
PO Box 118 54015 — 715-796-2256
Dan Woll, supt. — Fax 796-2460
www.scc.k12.wi.us
St. Croix HS — 400/9-12
1751 Broadway St 54015 — 715-796-5383
Glenn Webb, prin. — Fax 796-5662
St. Croix MS — 200/7-8
PO Box 118 54015 — 715-796-2256
Scott Woodington, prin. — Fax 796-2460

Hartford, Washington, Pop. 13,017
Hartford J1 SD — 1,600/PK-8
675 E Rossman St 53027 — 262-673-3155
Dr. Mark Smits, admin. — Fax 673-3548
www.hartfordjt1.k12.wi.us
Central MS — 500/6-8
1100 Cedar St 53027 — 262-673-8040
Wayne Thuecks, prin. — Fax 673-7596

Hartford UNHSD — 1,700/9-12
805 Cedar St 53027 — 262-670-3200
Michael Kremer Ph.D., supt. — Fax 673-8384
www.huhs.org
Hartford Union HS — 1,700/9-12
805 Cedar St 53027 — 262-670-3200
Mary Koehl, prin. — Fax 673-8384

Hartland, Waukesha, Pop. 8,672
Arrowhead UNHSD — 2,400/9-12
700 North Ave 53029 — 262-369-3611
David Lodes Ph.D., supt. — Fax 367-7406
www.arrowheadschools.org
Arrowhead Union HS - North Campus — 1,100/11-12
800 North Ave 53029 — 262-369-3612
Bonnie Laugerman Ed.D., prin. — Fax 369-0996
Arrowhead Union HS - South Campus — 1,200/9-10
700 North Ave 53029 — 262-369-3611
Gregg Wieczorek, prin. — Fax 367-4693

Hartland-Lakeside J3 SD — 1,300/PK-8
800 N Shore Dr 53029 — 262-369-6700
Glenn Schilling, supt. — Fax 369-6755
www.hartlake.org
North Shore MS — 400/6-8
800 N Shore Dr 53029 — 262-369-6767
Dale Fisher, prin. — Fax 369-6766

University Lake S — 300/PK-12
PO Box 290 53029 — 262-367-6011
Bradley Ashley, hdmstr. — Fax 367-3146

Hayward, Sawyer, Pop. 2,293
Hayward Community SD — 2,000/PK-12
PO Box 860 54843 — 715-634-2619
Michael Cox, supt. — Fax 634-3560
www.hayward.k12.wi.us
Hayward HS — 700/9-12
PO Box 860 54843 — 715-634-2619
Tom Kuklinski, prin. — Fax 634-2761
Hayward MS — 500/6-8
PO Box 860 54843 — 715-634-2619
Jane Gillis, prin. — Fax 634-9953

Lac Courte Oreilles Ojibwa Comm College — Post-Sec.
13466 W Trepania Rd 54843 — 715-634-4790
Northern Lights Christian Academy — 50/K-12
PO Box 757 54843 — 715-634-5040
Sandra Warner, admin. — Fax 634-7878

Hazel Green, Grant, Pop. 1,205
Southwestern Wisconsin SD — 600/PK-12
PO Box 368 53811 — 608-854-2261
James Egan, supt. — Fax 854-2305
www.swsd.k12.wi.us
Southwestern Wisconsin HS — 200/9-12
PO Box 368 53811 — 608-854-2261
Darren Sirianni, prin. — Fax 854-2315

Highland, Iowa, Pop. 817
Highland SD — 300/PK-12
PO Box 2850 53543 — 608-929-4525
David Romstad, supt. — Fax 929-4527
www.highland.k12.wi.us
Highland HS — 200/5-12
1030 Cardinal Dr 53543 — 608-929-4525
David Romstad, prin. — Fax 929-4527

Hilbert, Calumet, Pop. 1,087
Hilbert SD — 500/PK-12
PO Box 390 54129 — 920-853-3558
Anthony Sweere, supt. — Fax 853-7030
www.hilbert.k12.wi.us
Hilbert HS — 200/9-12
PO Box 390 54129 — 920-853-3558
Anthony Sweere, prin. — Fax 853-7030
Hilbert MS — 100/7-8
PO Box 390 54129 — 920-853-3558
Martha Albers, prin. — Fax 853-7030

Hillsboro, Vernon, Pop. 1,303
Hillsboro SD — 200/PK-12
PO Box 526 54634 — 608-489-2221
Ron Benish, supt. — Fax 489-2811
www.hillsboro.k12.wi.us
Hillsboro JSHS — 100/7-12
PO Box 526 54634 — 608-489-2221
Greg Zimmerman, prin. — Fax 489-2811

Holcombe, Chippewa
Lake Holcombe SD — 500/PK-12
27331 262nd Ave 54745 — 715-595-4241
Tom Goulet, supt. — Fax 595-6383
lakeholcombe.k12.wi.us
Holcombe HS — 200/9-12
27331 262nd Ave 54745 — 715-595-4241
Mark Porter, prin. — Fax 595-6383

Holmen, LaCrosse, Pop. 7,446
Holmen SD — 3,100/PK-12
PO Box 580 54636 — 608-526-6610
Fred Frick, supt. — Fax 526-1333
www.holmen.k12.wi.us
Holmen HS — 900/9-12
PO Box 430 54636 — 608-526-3372
Bernie Ferry, prin. — Fax 526-9446
Holmen MS — 700/6-8
PO Box 490 54636 — 608-526-3391
Roger Kordus, prin. — Fax 526-6716

Horicon, Dodge, Pop. 3,604
Horicon SD — 900/PK-12
611 Mill St 53032 — 920-485-2898
James A. McCartney, supt. — Fax 485-3601
www.horicon.k12.wi.us
Horicon HS — 400/9-12
841 Gray St 53032 — 920-485-4441
Jeffrey Higgins, prin. — Fax 485-3244
Van Brunt MS — 200/6-8
611 Mill St 53032 — 920-485-4423
Scott Miller, prin. — Fax 485-4318

Mountain Top Christian Academy — 50/PK-12
W3941 State Road 33 53032 — 920-485-6630
Stacey Nummerdor, prin.

Hortonville, Outagamie, Pop. 2,630
Hortonville SD — 2,900/PK-12
PO Box 70 54944 — 920-779-7900
Gregory Joseph, supt. — Fax 779-7903
www.hasd.org
Hortonville HS — 1,100/9-12
PO Box 220 54944 — 920-779-7933
Bob McIntosh, prin. — Fax 779-7935
Hortonville MS — 400/6-8
PO Box 70 54944 — 920-779-7922
John Brattlund, prin. — Fax 779-7923
Other Schools – See Greenville

Howards Grove, Sheboygan, Pop. 3,034
Howards Grove SD — 1,000/K-12
403 Audubon Rd 53083 — 920-565-4454
John Eickholt, supt. — Fax 565-4461
Howards Grove HS — 300/9-12
401 Audubon Rd 53083 — 920-565-4450
Mark Holzman, prin. — Fax 565-4451
Howards Grove MS — 300/5-8
506 Kennedy Ave 53083 — 920-565-4452
Andy Hansen, prin. — Fax 565-4460

Hudson, Saint Croix, Pop. 11,367
Hudson SD — 4,800/PK-12
1401 Vine St 54016 — 715-377-3700
Mary Bowen-Eggebraaten, supt. — Fax 377-3701
www.hudson.k12.wi.us
Hudson HS — 1,500/9-12
1501 Vine St 54016 — 715-377-3800
Ed Lucas, prin. — Fax 377-3801
Hudson MS — 1,100/6-8
1300 Carmichael Rd 54016 — 715-377-3820
Dan Koch, prin. — Fax 377-3821

Hurley, Iron, Pop. 1,678
Hurley SD — 400/PK-12
5503 W Range View Dr 54534 — 715-561-4900
Christopher Patritto, supt. — Fax 561-4953
www.hurley.k12.wi.us
Hurley S — 400/PK-12
5503 W Range View Dr 54534 — 715-561-4900
Jeffrey Gulan, prin. — Fax 561-4157

Hustisford, Dodge, Pop. 1,106
Hustisford SD — 400/PK-12
PO Box 326 53034 — 920-349-8109
Ed Van Ravenstein, supt. — Fax 349-3716
www.hustisford.k12.wi.us
Hustisford JSHS — 200/7-12
PO Box 326 53034 — 920-349-3261
Jeremy Biehl, prin. — Fax 349-8495

Independence, Trempealeau, Pop. 1,246
Independence SD — 300/PK-12
23786 Indee Blvd 54747 — 715-985-3172
Dave Laehn, supt. — Fax 985-2303
www.indps.k12.wi.us
Independence HS — 100/9-12
23786 Indee Blvd 54747 — 715-985-3172
Dave Laehn, prin. — Fax 985-2303

Iola, Waupaca, Pop. 1,232
Iola-Scandinavia SD — 800/PK-12
450 Division St 54945 — 715-445-2411
Joseph Price, supt. — Fax 445-4468
www.iola.k12.wi.us/

Iola-Scandinavia JSHS 400/7-12
540 S Jackson St 54945 715-445-2411
Sara Anderson, prin. Fax 445-5119

Jackson, Washington, Pop. 6,036

Kettle Moraine Lutheran HS 400/9-12
3399 Division Rd 53037 262-677-4051
Stephen Granberg, prin. Fax 677-4290
Living Word Lutheran HS 50/9-12
2230 Living Word Ln 53037 262-677-9353
Dr. Cary Stelmachowicz, dir. Fax 677-8357

Janesville, Rock, Pop. 61,962

Janesville SD 10,500/PK-12
527 S Franklin St, 608-743-5000
Thomas Evert, supt. Fax 743-5110
www.janesville.k12.wi.us/sdj
Craig HS 1,800/9-12
401 S Randall Ave 53545 608-743-5200
Michael Kuehne, prin. Fax 743-5150
Edison MS 800/6-8
1649 S Chatham St 53546 608-743-5900
Steve Sperry, prin. Fax 743-5910
Franklin MS 700/6-8
450 N Crosby Ave, 608-743-6000
Kim Ehrhardt, prin. Fax 743-6010
Marshall MS 1,000/6-8
25 S Pontiac Dr 53545 608-743-6200
Steven Salerno, prin. Fax 743-6210
Parker HS 1,800/9-12
3125 Mineral Point Ave, 608-743-5600
Dale Carlson, prin. Fax 743-5550

Blackhawk Technical College Post-Sec.
PO Box 5009 53547 608-758-6900
Oakhill Christian S 100/K-12
1650 S Oakhill Ave 53546 608-754-2759
Charlene Meiklejohn, admin. Fax 754-2159
University of Wisconsin Center Post-Sec.
2909 Kellogg Ave 53546 608-755-2823
WI School for Visually Handicapped Post-Sec.
1700 W State St 53546 608-758-6100

Jefferson, Jefferson, Pop. 7,592

Jefferson SD 1,800/PK-12
206 S Taft Ave 53549 920-675-1000
Michael Swartz, supt. Fax 675-1020
www.jefferson.k12.wi.us
Jefferson HS 600/9-12
700 W Milwaukee St 53549 920-675-1100
Richard Lovett, prin. Fax 675-1120
Jefferson MS 400/6-8
501 S Taft Ave 53549 920-675-1300
Mark Rollefson, prin. Fax 675-1320

St. Coletta School, RR 1 Box 43 53549 Post-Sec.

Johnson Creek, Jefferson, Pop. 2,024

Johnson Creek SD 500/PK-12
PO Box 39 53038 920-699-2811
Michael Garvey Ph.D., supt. Fax 699-2801
www.johnsoncreek.k12.wi.us/
Johnson Creek HS 200/7-12
PO Box 39 53038 920-699-3481
Eric Ranzen, prin. Fax 699-3566

Juda, Green

Juda SD 300/PK-12
N2385 Spring St 53550 608-934-5251
Gary Scheuerell, supt. Fax 934-5254
www.juda.k12.wi.us
Juda HS 100/9-12
N2385 Spring St 53550 608-934-5251
Gary Scheuerell, prin. Fax 934-5254

Juneau, Dodge, Pop. 2,587

Dodgeland SD 800/PK-12
401 S Western Ave 53039 920-386-4404
Joseph G. Reed, supt. Fax 386-4498
www.dodgeland.k12.wi.us
Dodgeland HS 300/9-12
401 S Western Ave 53039 920-386-4404
Steven Schiller, prin. Fax 386-2601
Dodgeland MS 200/6-8
401 S Western Ave 53039 920-386-4404
Michelle Weidemann, prin. Fax 386-2601

Kansasville, Racine

Providence Catholic S - West Campus 5-8
1714 240th Ave 53139 262-878-2713
Wilson Shierk, prin.

Kaukauna, Outagamie, Pop. 14,656

Kaukauna Area SD 3,800/PK-12
112 Main Ave 54130 920-766-6100
Lloyd McCabe, supt. Fax 766-6104
www.kaukauna.k12.wi.us
Kaukauna HS 1,300/9-12
1701 County Road CE 54130 920-766-6113
Joe Lewis, prin. Fax 766-6157
River View MS 800/6-8
101 Oak St 54130 920-766-6111
Mark Elworthy, prin. Fax 766-6109

Holy Cross S 100/3-8
220 Doty St 54130 920-766-0186
Elizabeth Watson, prin. Fax 759-2428

Kenosha, Kenosha, Pop. 95,240

Kenosha SD 20,100/PK-12
PO Box 340 53141 262-653-6320
R. Scott Pierce, supt. Fax 653-7672
www.kusd.edu/
Bradford HS 2,100/9-12
3700 Washington Rd 53144 262-653-6200
Sue Savaglio-Jarvis, prin. Fax 653-5948
Bullen MS 800/6-8
2804 39th Ave 53144 262-597-4460
Kim Fischer, prin. Fax 597-4487
Indian Trail Academy 1,100/9-12
6800 60th St 53144 262-653-0317
Richard Aiello, prin. Fax 653-9956
Lakeview Technology Academy Vo/Tech
9449 88th Ave 53158 262-947-8155
William Hittman, prin. Fax 947-8159
Lance MS 1,000/6-8
4515 80th St 53142 262-942-2240
Bethany Ormseth, prin. Fax 942-2184
Lincoln MS 900/6-8
6729 18th Ave 53143 262-653-6296
Margaret Modory, prin. Fax 653-5966
Mahone MS 800/6-8
6900 60th St 53144 262-605-8100
Brian Edwards, prin. Fax 605-6851
McKinley MS 600/6-8
5710 32nd Ave 53144 262-653-6367
Sharon Miller, prin. Fax 653-6089
Reuther Central HS 700/9-12
913 57th St 53140 262-653-6160
Daniel Tenuta, prin. Fax 653-6281
Tremper HS 2,400/9-12
8560 26th Ave 53143 262-942-2200
Ken Dopke, prin. Fax 942-2187
Washington MS 600/6-8
811 Washington Rd 53140 262-653-6291
Elizabeth Sabo, prin. Fax 653-6056

Carthage College Post-Sec.
2001 Alford Park Dr 53140 262-551-8500
Christian Life S 800/PK-12
10700 75th St 53142 262-694-3900
Paul Blount, admin. Fax 694-3312
Gateway Technical College Post-Sec.
3520 30th Ave 53144 262-564-2200
St. Joseph HS 300/7-12
2401 69th St 53143 262-654-8651
Robert Freund, prin. Fax 654-1615
University of Wisconsin Post-Sec.
PO Box 2000 53141 262-595-2345

Keshena, Menominee, Pop. 685

Menominee Indian SD 900/K-12
PO Box 1330 54135 715-799-3824
Wendell Waukau, supt. Fax 799-4659
www.misd.k12.wi.us
Menominee Indian HS 400/9-12
PO Box 850 54135 715-799-3846
Charles Raasch, prin. Fax 799-5558
Other Schools – See Neopit

College of Menominee Nation Post-Sec.
PO Box 1179 54135 715-799-5600

Kewaskum, Washington, Pop. 3,607

Kewaskum SD 1,800/PK-12
PO Box 37 53040 262-626-8427
Michael Krumm, supt. Fax 626-2961
www.kewaskumschools.org
Kewaskum HS 700/9-12
PO Box 426 53040 262-626-8427
Christine Horbas, prin. Fax 626-4214
Kewaskum MS 400/6-8
PO Box 432 53040 262-626-8427
Ken Soerens, prin. Fax 626-4214

Kewaunee, Kewaunee, Pop. 2,877

Kewaunee SD 800/PK-12
915 2nd St 54216 920-388-3230
Barbara Lundgren, supt. Fax 388-5174
www.kewaunee.k12.wi.us
Kewaunee HS 400/9-12
911 3rd St 54216 920-388-2951
Michael Holtz, prin. Fax 388-5165
Kewaunee MS 5-8
921 3rd St 54216 920-388-2458
Marge Weichelt, prin. Fax 388-5696

Kiel, Manitowoc, Pop. 3,507

Kiel Area SD 1,300/PK-12
PO Box 201 53042 920-894-2266
Jerry Schutz, supt. Fax 894-5100
www.kiel.k12.wi.us/
Kiel HS 500/9-12
210 Raider Hts 53042 920-894-2263
Dario Talerico, prin. Fax 894-5101
Kiel MS 400/5-8
PO Box 197 53042 920-894-2264
David Slosser, prin. Fax 894-5121

Kieler, Grant

Holy Ghost/Immaculate Conception S 50/4-8
PO Box 129 53812 608-568-7220
Beverly Florence, prin. Fax 568-3811

Kimberly, Outagamie, Pop. 6,230

Kimberly Area SD 3,100/PK-12
217 E Kimberly Ave 54136 920-788-7900
Dr. Mel Lightner, supt. Fax 788-7919
www.kimberly.k12.wi.us
Gerritts MS 600/7-8
545 S John St 54136 920-788-7905
Cathy Clarksen, prin. Fax 788-7914
Kimberly HS 1,100/9-12
W2662 Kennedy Ave 54136 920-687-3024
Michael Rietveld, prin. Fax 687-3029

Kohler, Sheboygan, Pop. 1,991

Kohler SD 500/PK-12
333 Upper Rd 53044 920-459-2920
Jeffrey Dickert, supt. Fax 459-2930
www.kohler.k12.wi.us
Kohler JSHS 200/7-12
333 Upper Rd 53044 920-459-2921
Lance Northey, prin. Fax 459-2930

La Crosse, LaCrosse, Pop. 50,287

La Crosse SD 6,800/PK-12
807 East Ave S 54601 608-789-7600
Gerald Kember, supt. Fax 789-7960
www.lacrosseschools.com/
Central HS 1,400/9-12
1801 Losey Blvd S 54601 608-789-7900
Thomas Barth, prin. Fax 789-7931
Lincoln MS 400/6-8
510 9th St S 54601 608-789-7780
Larry Myhra, prin. Fax 789-7181
Logan HS 1,000/9-12
1500 Ranger Dr 54603 608-789-7700
Scott Mihalovic, prin. Fax 789-7711
Logan MS 600/6-8
1450 Avon St 54603 608-789-7740
Troy Harcey, prin. Fax 789-7754
Longfellow MS 600/6-8
1900 Denton St 54601 608-789-7670
Penny Reedy, prin. Fax 789-7975

Aquinas HS 400/9-12
315 11th St S 54601 608-784-0287
Patrick Burkhart, prin. Fax 782-8851
Aquinas MS South Campus 200/7-8
315 11th St S 54601 608-784-0156
Patricia Kosmatka, prin. Fax 784-0229
Gunderson Medical Foundation Post-Sec.
1836 South Ave 54601 608-782-7300
Scientific College of Beauty/Barbering Post-Sec.
326 Pearl St 54601 608-784-4702
University of Wisconsin - LaCrosse Post-Sec.
1725 State St 54601 608-785-8000
Viterbo University Post-Sec.
815 9th St S 54601 608-796-3000
Western Wisconsin Technical College Post-Sec.
PO Box 908 54602 608-785-9200

Ladysmith, Rusk, Pop. 3,789

Ladysmith-Hawkins SD 900/PK-12
1700 Edgewood Ave E 54848 715-532-5277
James Schuchardt, supt. Fax 532-7445
www.lhsd.k12.wi.us/
Ladysmith HS 300/9-12
1700 Edgewood Ave E 54848 715-532-5531
Robert King, prin. Fax 532-5961
Ladysmith MS 200/6-8
115 E 6th St S 54848 715-532-5252
Kurt Lindau, prin. Fax 532-7455

La Farge, Vernon, Pop. 799

La Farge SD 200/PK-12
301 W Adams St 54639 608-625-0103
Al Szepi, admin. Fax 625-0118
www.lafarge.k12.wi.us/
La Farge HS 100/9-12
301 W Adams St 54639 608-625-2400
Jack Sulik, prin. Fax 625-0152
La Farge MS 50/6-8
301 W Adams St 54639 608-625-2400
Jack Sulik, prin. Fax 625-0152

Lake Geneva, Walworth, Pop. 8,223

Lake Geneva J1 SD 1,800/K-8
208 E South St 53147 262-348-1000
James Gottinger, supt. Fax 248-9704
www.lakegenevaschools.com
Lake Geneva MS 700/6-8
600 N Bloomfield Rd 53147 262-348-3000
Donna Jaeger, prin. Fax 348-3092

Lake Geneva-Genoa City UHSD 1,300/9-12
208 E South St 53147 262-348-1000
James Gottinger, supt. Fax 248-9704
www.lakegenevaschools.com
Badger HS 1,300/9-12
220 E South St 53147 262-348-2000
Steve McNeal, prin. Fax 248-6178

Lake Mills, Jefferson, Pop. 5,241

Lake Mills Area SD 1,200/PK-12
120 E Lake Park Pl 53551 920-648-2215
Dean Sanders, supt. Fax 648-5795
www.lakemills.k12.wi.us
Lake Mills HS 400/9-12
615 Catlin Dr 53551 920-648-2355
Robert Gilpatrick, prin. Fax 648-2357
Lake Mills MS 300/6-8
318 College St 53551 920-648-2358
Doris Thompson, prin. Fax 648-8928

Lakeside Lutheran HS 400/9-12
231 Woodland Beach Rd 53551 920-648-2321
James Grasby, prin. Fax 648-5625

Lancaster, Grant, Pop. 3,977

Lancaster Community SD 1,100/PK-12
925 W Maple St 53813 608-723-2175
Robert Wagner, supt. Fax 723-6397
www.lancastersd.k12.wi.us
Lancaster HS 400/9-12
806 E Elm St 53813 608-723-2173
Gary Swanstrom, prin. Fax 723-2441
Lancaster MS 200/6-8
802 E Elm St 53813 608-723-6425
Mark Uppena, prin. Fax 723-6731

Land O Lakes, Vilas

Conserve S 600/9-12
5400 N Black Oak Lake Rd 54540 715-547-1300
Stefan Anderson, hdmstr. Fax 547-1386

Laona, Forest

Laona SD 300/PK-12
PO Box 100 54541 715-674-2143
Storm Carroll, supt. Fax 674-5904
www.laona.k12.wi.us

Laona JSHS 100/7-12
PO Box 100 54541 715-674-2143
James Hansen, prin. Fax 674-5904

Lena, Oconto, Pop. 501
Lena SD 500/PK-12
304 E Main St 54139 920-829-5244
Robert Werley, supt. Fax 829-5122
www.lena.k12.wi.us
Lena HS 200/9-12
304 E Main St 54139 920-829-5244
David Honish, prin. Fax 829-5122
Lena MS 100/6-8
304 E Main St 54139 920-829-5244
David Honish, prin. Fax 829-5122

Little Chute, Outagamie, Pop. 10,870
Little Chute Area SD 1,600/PK-12
325 Meulemans St Ste A 54140 920-788-7605
David Botz, supt. Fax 788-7603
www.littlechute.k12.wi.us
Little Chute HS 600/9-12
1402 Freedom Rd 54140 920-788-7600
Daniel Valentyn, prin. Fax 788-7841
Little Chute MS 300/6-8
325 Meulemans St 54140 920-788-7607
Lori Van Handel, prin. Fax 788-7603

Livingston, Iowa, Pop. 581
Iowa-Grant SD 900/PK-12
498 County Road IG 53554 608-943-6311
Terrance Slack, supt. Fax 943-8438
www.igs.k12.wi.us
Iowa-Grant HS 300/9-12
462 County Road IG 53554 608-943-6312
Mitch Munson, prin. Fax 943-8707

Lodi, Columbia, Pop. 3,030
Lodi SD 1,600/PK-12
115 School St 53555 608-592-3851
Michael Shimshak, supt. Fax 592-3852
www.lodi.k12.wi.us
Lodi HS 500/9-12
1100 Sauk St 53555 608-592-3853
Laura Love, prin. Fax 592-1045
Lodi MS 400/6-8
900 Sauk St 53555 608-592-3854
David Dyb, prin. Fax 592-1035

Lomira, Dodge, Pop. 2,410
Lomira SD 1,000/K-12
1030 4th St 53048 920-269-4396
Jeffrey McCartney, admin. Fax 269-4996
www.lomira.k12.wi.us/
Lomira HS 400/9-12
1030 4th St 53048 920-269-4396
Shannon Stein, prin. Fax 269-4996
Lomira JHS 200/6-8
1030 4th St 53048 920-269-4396
Robert Lloyd, prin. Fax 269-4996

Loyal, Clark, Pop. 1,282
Loyal SD 600/PK-12
PO Box 10 54446 715-255-8552
Graeme Williams, supt. Fax 255-8553
www.loyal.k12.wi.us
Loyal HS 200/9-12
PO Box 10 54446 715-255-8511
Walter Leipart, prin. Fax 255-8553
Loyal JHS 100/7-8
PO Box 10 54446 715-255-8511
Walter Leipart, prin. Fax 255-8553

Luck, Polk, Pop. 1,209
Luck SD 600/K-12
810 S 7th St 54853 715-472-2151
Rick Palmer, supt. Fax 472-2159
www.lucksd.k12.wi.us
Luck JSHS 300/7-12
810 S 7th St 54853 715-472-2152
Mark Gobler, prin. Fax 472-2159

Luxemburg, Kewaunee, Pop. 2,211
Luxemburg-Casco SD 1,900/PK-12
PO Box 70 54217 920-845-2391
Patrick Saunders, supt. Fax 845-5871
www.luxcasco.k12.wi.us/
Luxemburg-Casco HS 700/9-12
PO Box 410 54217 920-845-2336
Steve Okoniewski, prin. Fax 845-2280
Other Schools – See Casco

Mc Farland, Dane, Pop. 5,724
Mc Farland SD 2,000/PK-12
5101 Farwell St 53558 608-838-3169
Scott Brown, admin. Fax 838-3074
www.mcfarland.k12.wi.us
Indian Mound MS 500/6-8
6330 Exchange St 53558 608-838-8980
Roberta Felker, prin. Fax 838-4588
Mc Farland HS 600/9-12
5103 Farwell St 53558 608-838-3166
James Hickey, prin. Fax 838-4562

Madison, Dane, Pop. 221,551
Madison Metro SD 24,500/PK-12
545 W Dayton St 53703 608-663-1879
Art Rainwater, supt. Fax 204-0341
www.madison.k12.wi.us
Black Hawk MS 400/6-8
1402 Wyoming Way 53704 608-204-4360
Mary Kelley, prin. Fax 204-0368
Cherokee Heights MS 600/6-8
4301 Cherokee Dr 53711 608-204-1240
Karen Seno, prin. Fax 204-0378
East HS 2,000/9-12
2222 E Washington Ave 53704 608-204-1600
Alan Harris, prin. Fax 204-0388
Hamilton MS 700/6-8
4801 Waukesha St 53705 608-204-4620
Henry Schmelz, prin. Fax 204-0417
Jefferson MS 500/6-8
101 S Gammon Rd 53717 608-663-6403
John Burmaster, prin. Fax 442-2193
LaFollette HS 1,800/9-12
702 Pflaum Rd 53716 608-204-3600
Joe Gothard, prin. Fax 204-0435
Memorial HS 2,300/9-12
201 S Gammon Rd 53717 608-663-5990
Bruce Dahmen, prin. Fax 442-2197
O'Keeffe MS 400/6-8
510 S Thornton Ave 53703 608-204-6820
Kay Enright, prin. Fax 204-0561
Sennett MS 600/6-8
502 Pflaum Rd 53716 608-204-1920
Colleen Lodholz, prin. Fax 204-0495
Sherman MS 600/6-8
1610 Ruskin St 53704 608-204-2100
Michael Hernandez, prin. Fax 204-0501
Spring Harbor MS 200/6-8
1110 Spring Harbor Dr 53705 608-204-1100
Gail Anderson, prin. Fax 204-0509
Toki MS 600/6-8
5606 Russett Rd 53711 608-204-4740
Nicole Schaefer, prin. Fax 204-0523
West HS 2,100/9-12
30 Ash St 53726 608-204-4100
Ed Holmes, prin. Fax 204-0529
Whitehorse MS 400/6-8
218 Schenk St 53714 608-204-4480
Anne Nolan, prin. Fax 204-0538

Abundant Life Christian S 300/K-12
4901 E Buckeye Rd 53716 608-221-1520
Bill Zehner, admin. Fax 221-8572
Edgewood College Post-Sec.
1000 Edgewood College Dr 53711 800-444-4861
Edgewood HS 600/9-12
2219 Monroe St 53711 608-257-1023
Robert Growney, prin. Fax 257-9133
Herzing College Post-Sec.
5218 E Terrace Dr 53718 608-249-6611
Madison Area Technical College Post-Sec.
3550 Anderson St 53704 608-246-6282
Madison Cosmetology College Post-Sec.
310 Westgate Mall 53711 608-271-4206
Madison Media Institute Post-Sec.
2702 Agriculture Dr 53718 608-663-2000
Martin's College of Cosmetology Post-Sec.
6414 Odana Rd 53719 608-270-0188
St. Ambose Academy 7-12
602 Everglade Dr 53717 608-827-5863
John Gillett, prin.
University of Wisconsin Post-Sec.
716 Langdon St 53706 608-262-1234
WSLH School of Cytotechnology Post-Sec.
465 Henry Mall 53706 608-262-3524

Manawa, Waupaca, Pop. 1,333
Manawa SD 1,000/PK-12
800 Beech St 54949 920-596-2525
Larry Brown, supt. Fax 596-5308
www.manawa.k12.wi.us
Little Wolf HS 400/9-12
515 E 4th St 54949 920-596-2524
Duane Braun, prin. Fax 596-2655
Manawa MS 300/5-8
800 Beech St 54949 920-596-2551
Larry Brown, prin. Fax 596-5320

Manitowoc, Manitowoc, Pop. 33,917
Manitowoc SD 5,300/PK-12
PO Box 1657 54221 920-683-4777
Mark Swanson, supt. Fax 686-4780
www.mpsd.k12.wi.us
Lincoln SHS 1,400/10-12
1433 S 8th St 54220 920-683-4861
Keith Shaw, prin. Fax 683-4845
Washington JHS 600/7-9
2101 Division St 54220 920-683-4757
Kathleen Lemberger, prin. Fax 683-7989
Wilson JHS 600/7-9
1201 N 11th St 54220 920-683-4759
Darlene Wotachek, prin. Fax 683-7988

Manitowoc Lutheran HS 300/9-12
4045 Lancer Cir 54220 920-682-0215
Dennis Steinbrenner, prin. Fax 682-2363
Martin's College of Cosmetology Post-Sec.
1034 S 18th St 54220 920-684-3028
Roncalli HS 300/9-12
2000 Mirro Dr 54220 920-682-8801
Tim Olson, prin. Fax 686-8110
St. Francis Cabrini MS 200/6-8
2109 Marshall St 54220 920-683-6884
James Clark, prin. Fax 683-6882
Silver Lake College Post-Sec.
2406 S Alverno Rd 54220 920-684-6691
University of Wisconsin Center Post-Sec.
705 Viebahn St 54220 920-683-4707

Maple, Douglas
Maple SD 1,300/K-12
PO Box 188 54854 715-363-2431
Gregg Lundberg, supt. Fax 363-2191
www.maple.k12.wi.us
Northwestern HS 400/9-12
PO Box 188 54854 715-363-2434
Steve High, prin. Fax 363-2523
Other Schools – See Poplar

Marathon, Marathon, Pop. 1,642
Marathon City SD 700/PK-12
PO Box 37 54448 715-443-2228
Donald Viegut, supt. Fax 443-2611
www.marathon.k12.wi.us
Marathon HS 300/9-12
PO Box 37 54448 715-443-2226
David Beranek, prin. Fax 443-2611

Marinette, Marinette, Pop. 11,275
Marinette SD 2,300/K-12
2139 Pierce Ave 54143 715-735-1406
Dr. Nancy Hipskind, supt. Fax 732-7930
www.marinette.k12.wi.us
Marinette HS 800/9-12
2135 Pierce Ave 54143 715-732-7920
Corry Lambie, prin. Fax 732-7929
Marinette MS 700/5-8
1011 Water St 54143 715-732-7900
Adam DeWitt, prin. Fax 732-7939

Holy Family S 100/5-8
1200 Main St 54143 715-735-7174
Fax 735-7146
Northeast Wisconsin Technical College Post-Sec.
1601 University Dr 54143 715-735-9361
St. Thomas Aquinas Academy 100/9-12
1200 Main St 54143 715-735-7481
Fax 735-7146
University of Wisconsin-Marinette Post-Sec.
750 W Bay Shore St 54143 715-735-7470

Marion, Waupaca, Pop. 1,241
Marion SD 600/PK-12
1001 N Main St 54950 715-754-2511
Earl Knitt, supt. Fax 754-4508
www.marion.k12.wi.us
Marion JSHS 300/7-12
105 School St 54950 715-754-5273
Keary Mattson, prin. Fax 754-1350

Markesan, Green Lake, Pop. 1,349
Markesan SD 800/PK-12
PO Box 248 53946 920-398-2373
Susan Alexander, supt. Fax 398-3281
www.markesan.k12.wi.us
Markesan HS 300/9-12
PO Box 248 53946 920-398-2373
Pamela Waite, prin. Fax 398-3281
Markesan MS 100/7-8
PO Box 248 53946 920-398-2373
Pamela Waite, prin. Fax 398-3281

Marshall, Dane, Pop. 3,561
Marshall SD 900/PK-12
PO Box 76 53559 608-655-3466
Barb Sramek, supt. Fax 655-4481
www.marshall.k12.wi.us
Marshall HS 200/9-12
PO Box 76 53559 608-655-1310
Dennis Riley, prin. Fax 655-3046
Marshall MS 100/7-8
PO Box 76 53559 608-655-1571
Mark Mueller, prin. Fax 655-1591

Marshfield, Wood, Pop. 18,796
Marshfield SD 4,000/PK-12
1010 E 4th St 54449 715-387-1101
Bruce King, supt. Fax 387-0133
www.marshfield.k12.wi.us/
Marshfield HS 1,400/9-12
1401 E Becker Rd 54449 715-387-8464
John Blankush, prin. Fax 384-3589
Marshfield MS 700/7-8
900 E 4th St 54449 715-387-1249
David Schoepke, prin. Fax 384-9269

Columbus HS 100/9-12
710 S Columbus Ave 54449 715-387-1177
Barbara Billings, prin. Fax 384-4535
Columbus MS 100/6-8
710 S Columbus Ave 54449 715-387-1177
Barbara Billings, prin. Fax 384-4535
Marshfield Clinic/St. Josephs Hospital Post-Sec.
1000 N Oak Ave 54449 715-387-7440
Mid-State Technical College Post-Sec.
2600 W 5th St 54449 715-387-2538
St. Joseph Hospital/Marshfield Clinic Post-Sec.
611 Saint Joseph Ave 54449 715-387-1713
Univ. of Wisconsin - Marshfield/Wood Co. Post-Sec.
2000 W 5th St 54449 715-389-6530

Mauston, Juneau, Pop. 4,291
Mauston SD 1,600/PK-12
510 Grayside Ave 53948 608-847-5451
Bruce Anderson, supt. Fax 847-4635
www.mauston.k12.wi.us
Mauston HS 600/9-12
800 Grayside Ave 53948 608-847-4410
William Bomber, prin. Fax 847-4802
Olson MS 400/6-8
508 Grayside Ave 53948 608-847-6603
Tom Reisenauer, prin. Fax 847-4925

Mayville, Dodge, Pop. 5,055
Mayville SD 1,100/PK-12
234 N John St 53050 920-387-7963
Ronald Bieri, supt. Fax 387-7979
www.mayville.k12.wi.us
Mayville HS 500/9-12
500 N Clark St 53050 920-387-7960
Lee Zarnott, prin. Fax 387-7977
Mayville MS 400/3-8
445 N Henninger St 53050 920-387-7970
Robert Clark, prin. Fax 387-7974

Mazomanie, Dane, Pop. 1,528
Wisconsin Heights SD 1,000/PK-12
10173 US Highway 14 53560 608-767-2595
Larry Black, supt. Fax 767-3579
www.wisheights.k12.wi.us
Wisconsin Heights HS 400/9-12
10173 US Highway 14 53560 608-767-2586
Vince Breunig, prin. Fax 767-2062
Wisconsin Heights MS 300/6-8
10173 US Highway 14 53560 608-767-2596
Patricia Larson, prin. Fax 767-3579

Medford, Taylor, Pop. 4,189
Medford Area SD 2,200/PK-12
124 W State St 54451 715-748-4620
Steve Russ, supt. Fax 748-6839
www.medford.k12.wi.us
Medford HS 800/9-12
1015 W Broadway Ave 54451 715-748-5951
Jill Schafer, prin. Fax 748-6438
Medford MS 600/5-8
509 Clark St 54451 715-748-2516
Al Leonard, prin. Fax 748-1213

Mellen, Ashland, Pop. 808
Mellen SD 300/PK-12
PO Box 500 54546 715-274-3601
Jeffrey Ehrhardt, supt. Fax 274-3715
www.mellen.k12.wi.us
Mellen HS 100/9-12
PO Box 500 54546 715-274-3601
Thomas Kriesel, prin. Fax 274-3715

Melrose, Jackson, Pop. 516
Melrose-Mindoro SD 700/PK-12
N181 State Road 108 54642 608-488-2201
Ron Perry, supt. Fax 488-2805
www.mel-min.k12.wi.us
Melrose-Mindoro HS 200/9-12
N181 State Road 108 54642 608-488-2201
Del DeBerg, prin. Fax 488-2805

Menasha, Winnebago, Pop. 16,306
Menasha JSD 3,600/PK-12
PO Box 360 54952 920-967-1400
Keith Fuchs, supt. Fax 751-5038
www.mjsd.k12.wi.us
Maplewood MS 800/6-8
1600 Midway Rd 54952 920-967-1600
Bev Sturke, prin. Fax 832-5837
Menasha HS 1,100/9-12
420 7th St 54952 920-967-1800
Lawrence Haase, prin. Fax 751-5223

Seton Catholic MS 200/6-8
312 Nicolet Blvd 54952 920-727-0279
Monica Bausom, prin. Fax 727-1215
University of Wisconsin Center Post-Sec.
1478 Midway Rd 54952 920-832-2620

Menomonee Falls, Waukesha, Pop. 34,125
Menomonee Falls SD 4,500/K-12
N84W16579 Menomonee Ave 53051 262-255-8440
Dr. Keith Marty, supt. Fax 255-8461
www.sdmf.k12.wi.us
Menomonee Falls HS 1,200/10-12
W142N8101 Merrimac Dr 53051 262-255-8444
William C. Hintz, prin. Fax 255-8377
North JHS 800/8-9
N88W16750 Garfield Dr 53051 262-255-8450
Barbara Tays, prin. Fax 255-8475

Bethlehem Lutheran S - South 100/5-8
N84W15252 Menomonee Ave 53051 262-251-3120
Daryl Weber, prin. Fax 251-4679
Calvary Baptist S 300/K-12
N84W19049 Menomonee Ave 53051 262-251-0328
Steven Lafferty, admin. Fax 250-0624
Falls Baptist Academy 200/K-12
N69W12703 Appleton Ave 53051 262-251-7051
John Flanders, admin. Fax 251-7043

Menomonie, Dunn, Pop. 15,244
Menomonie Area SD 3,200/PK-12
215 Pine Ave NE 54751 715-232-1642
Jesse Harness, supt. Fax 232-1317
msd.k12.wi.us
Menomonie HS 1,200/9-12
1715 5th St W 54751 715-232-2606
Tom Schmelzle, prin. Fax 232-2629
Menomonie MS 700/6-8
920 21st St SE 54751 715-232-1673
Dudley Markham, prin. Fax 232-5486

University of Wisconsin Post-Sec.
124 Bowman Hall 54751 715-232-1123

Mequon, Ozaukee, Pop. 23,820
Mequon-Thiensville SD 3,700/PK-12
5000 W Mequon Rd 53092 262-238-8503
Robert J. Slotterback, supt. Fax 238-8520
www.mtsd.k12.wi.us
Homestead HS 1,600/9-12
5000 W Mequon Rd 53092 262-238-5646
Mark Roherty, prin. Fax 238-5633
Lake Shore MS 400/6-8
11036 N Range Line Rd 53092 262-238-7613
Carolyn Wilson, prin. Fax 238-7650
Steffen MS 500/6-8
6633 W Steffen Dr 53092 262-238-4706
Deborah Anderson, prin. Fax 238-4740

Concordia University Post-Sec.
12800 N Lake Shore Dr 53097 262-243-5700
Lumen Christi MS 300/4-8
11300 N Saint James Ln 53092 262-242-7960
Richard Goeden, prin. Fax 512-8986
Milwaukee Area Technical College Post-Sec.
5555 W Highland Rd 53092 262-238-2200

Mercer, Iron
Mercer SD 200/PK-12
2690 W Margaret St 54547 715-476-2154
Ron Vaughn, supt. Fax 476-2587
www.mercer.k12.wi.us
Mercer S 200/PK-12
2690 W Margaret St 54547 715-476-2154
Ron Vaughn, prin. Fax 476-2587

Merrill, Lincoln, Pop. 10,145
Merrill Area SD 3,100/PK-12
1111 N Sales St 54452 715-536-4581
Sally Sarnstrom, supt. Fax 536-1788
www.maps.k12.wi.us
Merrill HS 1,200/9-12
1201 N Sales St 54452 715-536-4594
Shannon Murray, prin. Fax 536-5504
Prairie River MS 700/6-8
106 N Polk St 54452 715-536-9593
Gerald Beyer, prin. Fax 536-6378

Merton, Waukesha, Pop. 2,643
Merton Community SD 900/PK-8
PO Box 15 53056 262-538-1130
Mark Flynn, supt. Fax 538-4978
www.merton.k12.wi.us
Merton IS 500/4-8
PO Box 15 53056 262-538-1130
Jon Wagner, prin. Fax 538-4978

Middleton, Dane, Pop. 15,816
Middleton-Cross Plains Area SD 5,600/PK-12
7106 South Ave 53562 608-829-9000
William Reis, supt. Fax 836-1536
www.mcpasd.k12.wi.us
Kromrey MS 700/6-8
7009 Donna Dr 53562 608-829-9530
Mike Nummerdor, prin. Fax 831-8388
Middleton HS 1,800/9-12
2100 Bristol St 53562 608-829-9660
Denise Herrmann, prin. Fax 831-1995
Other Schools – See Cross Plains

Milton, Rock, Pop. 5,464
Milton SD 3,000/PK-12
430 E High St Ste 2 53563 608-868-9200
Peg Ekedahl, supt. Fax 868-9215
www.milton.k12.wi.us
Milton HS 1,000/9-12
114 W High St 53563 608-868-9300
Randy Refsland, prin. Fax 868-9399
Milton MS 500/7-8
20 E Madison Ave 53563 608-868-9350
Bob Parker, prin. Fax 868-9269

Milwaukee, Milwaukee, Pop. 578,887
Fox Point Bayside SD 1,000/PK-8
7300 N Lombardy Rd 53217 414-247-4167
Gary W. Petersen, supt. Fax 351-7164
www.foxbay.k12.wi.us
Bayside MS 400/5-8
601 E Ellsworth Ln 53217 414-247-4201
John Roubik, prin. Fax 247-8963

Milwaukee SD 73,200/PK-12
PO Box 2181 53201 414-475-8393
William Andrekopoulos, supt. Fax 475-8595
www.milwaukee.k12.wi.us
Bay View HS 1,700/9-12
2751 S Lenox St 53207 414-294-2400
Barbara Goss, prin. Fax 294-2415
Bell MS 800/6-8
6506 W Warnimont Ave 53220 414-604-7800
Suzanne Kirby, prin. Fax 604-7815
Bradley Tech & Trade HS Vo/Tech
700 S 4th St 53204 414-212-2400
Edward Kovochich, prin. Fax 212-2415
Burroughs MS 800/6-8
6700 N 80th St 53223 414-393-3500
Darrell Williams, prin. Fax 393-3515
Custer HS 1,200/9-12
5075 N Sherman Blvd 53209 414-393-4900
Kathy Bonds, prin. Fax 393-4915
Edison MS 500/6-8
5372 N 37th St 53209 414-616-5400
Jennie Dorsey, prin. Fax 616-5415
Foster & Williams HS 9-12
4141 N 64th St 53216 414-393-3800
Charles Marks, prin.
Grand Ave MS 700/6-8
2430 W Wisconsin Ave 53233 414-934-4200
Minnie Polliam-Novy, prin. Fax 934-4215
Hamilton HS 2,100/9-12
6215 W Warnimont Ave 53220 414-327-9300
Myron Cain, prin. Fax 327-9315
King HS 1,500/9-12
1801 W Olive St 53209 414-267-0700
Greg Willis, prin. Fax 267-0715
Lincoln MS of the Arts 800/6-8
820 E Knapp St 53202 414-212-3300
Debra Ortiz, prin. Fax 212-3315
Madison HS 1,600/9-12
8135 W Florist Ave 53218 414-393-6100
Mary Bowie, prin. Fax 393-6262
Marshall HS 1,100/9-12
4141 N 64th St 53216 414-393-2300
Paul Armour, prin. Fax 393-2315
Marshall Montessori HS 9-12
4141 N 64th St 53216 414-393-2566
Phillip Dosmann, prin.
Milwaukee Education Center MS 700/6-8
227 W Pleasant St 53212 414-212-2900
Jessie Rodriguez, prin. Fax 212-2967
Milwaukee HS of the Arts 1,000/9-12
2300 W Highland Ave 53233 414-934-7000
Eugene Humphrey, prin. Fax 934-7015
Milwaukee S of Languages 800/6-10
8400 W Burleigh St 53222 414-393-5700
Grace Thomsen, prin. Fax 393-5715
Morse MS 1,100/6-8
4601 N 84th St 53225 414-616-5800
Rogers Onick, prin. Fax 616-5815
Muir MS 600/6-8
5496 N 72nd St 53218 414-393-3100
D. Rose Coppins, prin. Fax 393-3115
Pulaski HS 1,600/9-12
2500 W Oklahoma Ave 53215 414-902-8900
Ada Rivera, prin. Fax 902-8915

Reagan HS 9-12
4965 S 20th St 53221 414-304-6100
Julia D'Amato, prin. Fax 304-6115
Riverside HS 1,600/9-12
1615 E Locust St 53211 414-906-4900
Daniel Donder, prin. Fax 906-4915
Roosevelt MS 800/6-8
800 W Walnut St 53205 414-267-8800
Tom Matthews, prin. Fax 267-8815
Scott for the Health Sciences MS 800/6-8
1017 N 12th St 53233 414-934-4000
Willie Hickman, prin. Fax 934-4015
South Division HS 1,600/9-12
1515 W Lapham Blvd 53204 414-902-8300
Mark Kuxhause, prin. Fax 902-8315
Vincent HS 1,600/9-12
7501 N Granville Rd 53224 262-236-1200
Gloria Erkins, prin. Fax 236-1254
Washington HS of Expeditonary Lrng 9-12
2525 N Sherman Blvd 53210 414-875-2892
Greg Ogunbowale, prin. Fax 875-5915
Washington HS of Info Technology 1,000/9-12
2525 N Sherman Blvd 53210 414-875-5900
Winnifred Aitch, prin. Fax 875-5915
Washington HS of Law-Ed-Public Service 9-12
2525 N Sherman Blvd 53210 414-875-6056
Amita Antao, prin. Fax 875-5915

Alverno College Post-Sec.
PO Box 343922 53234 414-382-6000
Atlas Preparatory Academy 600/K-10
2911 S 32nd St 53215 414-385-0771
Michelle Lukacs, prin. Fax 385-0773
Aurora Health Care Post-Sec.
3000 W Montana St 53215 414-647-3000
Believers in Christ Christian Academy 300/PK-12
4065 N 25th St 53209 414-444-1146
Candace Covington, prin. Fax 444-5378
Blood Center of SE Wisconsin Post-Sec.
1701 W Wisconsin Ave 53233 414-937-6338
Bryant & Stratton College Post-Sec.
310 W Wisconsin Ave 53203 414-276-5200
Bufkin Academy 100/PK-12
827 N 34th St 53208 414-934-8885
Texas Bufkin, admin. Fax 934-8886
Cardinal Stritch University Post-Sec.
6801 N Yates Rd 53217 414-410-4000
Columbia College of Nursing Post-Sec.
2121 E Newport Ave 53211 414-961-3530
Columbia Hospital Post-Sec.
2025 E Newport Ave 53211 414-961-3800
Destiny HS 100/9-12
7210 N 76th St 53223 414-353-4430
Steven Robertson, prin. Fax 353-4450
DeVry University Post-Sec.
100 E Wsconsin Ave #2550 53202 414-278-7677
Divine Savior-Holy Angels HS 600/9-12
4257 N 100th St 53222 414-466-3706
Sr. Virginia Honish, prin. Fax 466-0590
Early View Academy of Excellence 300/PK-10
7132 W Good Hope Rd 53223 414-431-0001
Annie Oliver, prin. Fax 431-0046
Froedtert Memorial Lutheran Hospital Post-Sec.
PO Box 26099 53226 414-259-2606
Heritage Christian S 700/PK-12
1300 S 109th St 53214 414-259-1231
Thomas Wittkamper, supt. Fax 257-2548
Holy Redeemer Christian Academy 400/PK-12
3500 W Mother Daniels Way 53209 414-466-1800
Alton Townsel, admin. Fax 466-4930
Holy Wisdom Academy West Campus 100/4-8
3344 S 16th St 53215 414-383-3453
Richard Mason, prin. Fax 672-2645
Hope MS 100/5-8
510 E Burleigh St 53212 414-264-6284
Patrick Hurley, prin. Fax 264-6278
Hope S 100/9-12
3215 N Dr Martin L King Dr 53212 414-264-4476
Tommie Myles, admin. Fax 264-4592
ITT Technical Institute Post-Sec.
6300 W Layton Ave 53220 414-282-9494
Lakeside School of Massage Therapy Post-Sec.
1726 N 1st St 53212 414-372-4345
Marquette University Post-Sec.
PO Box 1881 53201 414-288-7700
Marquette University HS 1,000/9-12
3401 W Wisconsin Ave 53208 414-933-7220
Fr. John Belmonte, prin. Fax 937-8588
Medical College of Wisconsin Post-Sec.
PO Box 26509 53226 414-456-8296
Messmer HS 500/9-12
742 W Capitol Dr 53206 414-264-5440
Jeff Monday, prin. Fax 264-0672
Milwaukee Area Technical College Post-Sec.
700 W State St 53233 414-297-6600
Milwaukee Institute of Art & Design Post-Sec.
273 E Erie St 53202 414-291-8070
Milwaukee Lutheran HS 800/9-12
9700 W Grantosa Dr 53222 414-461-6000
Paul Bahr, prin. Fax 461-2733
Milwaukee School of Engineering Post-Sec.
1025 N Broadway 53202 414-277-7300
Milwaukee SDA S 50/1-10
10900 W Mill Rd 53225 414-353-3520
Alberto Torres, admin. Fax 353-1451
Mohammed S 200/PK-12
317 W Wright St 53212 414-263-6772
Basimah Abdullah, admin. Fax 263-6852
Mt. Mary College Post-Sec.
2900 N Menomonee River Pkwy 53222
414-258-4810
Nativity Jesuit MS 100/6-8
1515 S 29th St 53215 414-645-1060
Rosarios Sanchez, prin. Fax 645-0505
Noach S 100/K-12
222 E Burleigh St 53212 414-265-5343
Dr. Brenda Noach-Ewing, admin. Fax 265-2736

Notre Dame MS 100/5-8
1420 W Scott St 53204 414-671-3000
Mary Garcia-Velez, prin. Fax 671-3170
Pius XI HS 1,400/9-12
135 N 76th St 53213 414-290-7000
Melissa Skrade, prin. Fax 290-7001
Prince of Peace S 200/PK-K, 6-8
1646 S 22nd St 53204 414-645-4922
Donna Schmidt, prin. Fax 645-8918
St. Aemilian Lakeside S 100/1-10
8901 W Capitol Dr 53222 414-463-1880
Tami Trulock, prin. Fax 463-2770
St. Francis Hospital Post-Sec.
3237 S 16th St 53215 414-647-5106
St. Joan Antida HS 300/9-12
1341 N Cass St 53202 414-272-8423
Sioux Henzig, prin. Fax 272-3135
St. Luke's Medical Center Post-Sec.
2900 W Oklahoma Ave 53215 414-649-7500
St. Rafael the Archangel S - South 100/5-8
2251 S 31st St 53215 414-645-1300
Carolyn Ettlie, prin. Fax 645-1415
Salam S 400/PK-10
4707 S 13th St 53221 414-282-0504
Dr. Abdul-Mun'im Jitmoud, admin. Fax 282-6959
Thomas More HS 600/9-12
2601 E Morgan Ave 53207 414-481-8370
James Griswold, prin. Fax 481-3382
Torah Academy 50/9-12
6789 N Green Bay Ave 53209 414-352-6789
Sara Rauch, prin. Fax 352-6646
University of Wisconsin Post-Sec.
PO Box 413 53201 414-229-1122
University S 1,100/PK-12
2100 W Fairy Chasm Rd 53217 414-352-6000
Ward Ghory, hdmstr. Fax 352-8076
Vici Beauty School Post-Sec.
11010 W Hampton Ave 53225 414-464-5002
Wisconsin Conservatory of Music Post-Sec.
1584 N Prospect Ave 53202 414-276-5760
Wisconsin Institute for Torah Study 100/9-12
3288 N Lake Dr 53211 414-963-9317
Earl Lebakken, prin. Fax 963-1415
Wisconsin Lutheran College Post-Sec.
8800 W Bluemound Rd 53226 414-443-8800
Wisconsin Lutheran HS 900/9-12
330 Glenview Ave 53213 414-453-4567
Ned Goede, prin. Fax 453-3001
WI School of Professional Psychology Post-Sec.
9120 W Hampton Ave Ste 212 53225 414-464-9777
Zablocki VA Medical Center Post-Sec.
5000 W National Ave 53295 414-384-2000

Mineral Point, Iowa, Pop. 2,495
Mineral Point SD 800/PK-12
705 Ross St 53565 608-987-3924
Terry Hemann, supt. Fax 987-3766
www.mp.k12.wi.us
Mineral Point HS 300/9-12
705 Ross St 53565 608-987-2321
Ted Evans, prin. Fax 987-3766
Mineral Point MS 200/6-8
705 Ross St 53565 608-987-2371
Ted Evans, prin. Fax 987-3766

Minocqua, Oneida
Lakeland UNHSD 1,000/9-12
9573 State Highway 70 54548 715-358-8480
Michael Dailey, supt. Fax 356-1892
www.luhs.k12.wi.us
Lakeland HS 1,000/9-12
9573 State Highway 70 54548 715-356-5252
Todd Kleinhans, prin. Fax 356-1892

Minong, Washburn, Pop. 578
Northwood SD 500/PK-12
N14463 Highway 53 54859 715-466-2297
Donald Anderson, supt. Fax 466-5149
northwood.k12.wi.us/
Northwood S 500/PK-12
N14463 Highway 53 54859 715-466-2297
Clendon Gustafson, prin. Fax 466-5149

Mishicot, Manitowoc, Pop. 1,413
Mishicot SD 1,100/PK-12
PO Box 280 54228 920-755-4633
Stephen Cromell, supt. Fax 755-2390
www.mishicot.k12.wi.us
Mishicot HS 400/9-12
PO Box 280 54228 920-755-4633
Deborah Knox, prin. Fax 755-2390
Mishicot MS 300/6-8
PO Box 280 54228 920-755-4633
Colleen Timm, prin. Fax 755-2390

Mondovi, Buffalo, Pop. 2,618
Mondovi SD 1,100/PK-12
337 N Jackson St 54755 715-926-3684
Cheryl Gullicksrud, supt. Fax 926-3617
www.mondovi.k12.wi.us/
Mondovi HS 300/9-12
337 N Jackson St 54755 715-926-3656
Mike Bruning, prin. Fax 926-3617
Mondovi MS 300/6-8
337 N Jackson St 54755 715-926-3457
Michael Erickson, prin. Fax 926-3617

Monona, Dane, Pop. 7,716
Monona Grove SD 2,800/PK-12
5301 Monona Dr 53716 608-221-7660
Gary Schumacher, supt. Fax 221-7688
www.mononagrove.org
Monona Grove HS 900/9-12
4400 Monona Dr 53716 608-221-7666
Paul Brost, prin. Fax 221-7690
Winnequah MS 700/6-8
800 Greenway Rd 53716 608-221-7676
Patti McGinnis, prin. Fax 221-7694

Monroe, Green, Pop. 10,563
Monroe SD 2,500/PK-12
925 16th Ave Ste 3 53566 608-328-7171
Craig Jefson, supt. Fax 328-7214
www.monroeschools.com
Monroe HS 800/9-12
1600 26th St 53566 608-328-7117
Mark Burandt, prin. Fax 328-7230
Monroe MS 600/6-8
1510 13th St 53566 608-328-7120
William Van Meer, prin. Fax 328-7224

Four Seasons Salon and Day Spa School Post-Sec.
128 W 8th St Ste 8 53566 608-325-4007

Montello, Marquette, Pop. 1,483
Montello SD 800/PK-12
222 Forest Ln 53949 608-297-7617
Randy Guttenberg, supt. Fax 297-7726
www.montello.k12.wi.us
Montello JSHS 400/7-12
222 Forest Ln 53949 608-297-2126
Jeffrey Holmes, prin. Fax 297-7726

Monticello, Green, Pop. 1,132
Monticello SD 400/PK-12
334 S Main St 53570 608-938-4194
Karen Ballin, supt. Fax 938-1062
www.monticello.k12.wi.us/
Monticello HS 100/9-12
334 S Main St 53570 608-938-4194
Kenneth Colle, prin. Fax 938-1062
Monticello MS 100/6-8
334 S Main St 53570 608-938-4194
Kenneth Colle, prin. Fax 938-1062

Mosinee, Marathon, Pop. 3,996
Mosinee SD 2,100/PK-12
591 W State Highway 153 54455 715-693-2530
Jerry L. Rosso, supt. Fax 693-7272
www.mosineeschools.org
Mosinee HS 700/9-12
1000 High St 54455 715-693-2550
James Debroux, prin. Fax 693-1152
Mosinee MS 800/4-8
700 High St 54455 715-693-3660
Ronald Mueller, prin. Fax 693-6655

Northland Lutheran HS 100/9-12
2107 Tower Rd 54455 715-359-3400
Rick Grundman, prin. Fax 241-9203
WI Valley Lutheran HS 50/9-12
601 Maple Ridge Rd 54455 715-693-2693
Jim Rawlings, prin. Fax 693-5962

Mount Calvary, Fond du Lac, Pop. 935

St. Lawrence Seminary HS 200/9-12
301 Church St 53057 920-753-7500
David Bartel, dean Fax 753-7507

Mount Horeb, Dane, Pop. 6,188
Mount Horeb Area SD 2,100/PK-12
1304 E Lincoln St 53572 608-437-2400
Wayne Anderson, supt. Fax 437-5597
www.mhasd.k12.wi.us
Mount Horeb HS 600/9-12
305 S 8th St 53572 608-437-2400
Michael Garrow, prin. Fax 437-4926
Mount Horeb MS 500/6-8
900 E Garfield St 53572 608-437-2400
Jeff Rasmussen, prin. Fax 437-6227

Mukwonago, Waukesha, Pop. 6,857
Mukwonago SD 4,900/K-12
423 Division St 53149 262-363-6300
Paul Strobel, supt. Fax 363-6272
www.mukwonago.k12.wi.us
Mukwonago HS 1,800/9-12
605 W School Rd 53149 262-363-6200
Dale Henry, prin. Fax 363-6239
Park View MS 800/7-8
930 N Rochester St 53149 262-363-6292
Mark Doome, prin. Fax 363-6320

Norris SD 100/7-12
W247S10395 Center Dr 53149 262-662-5911
Sara Trampf, supt. Fax 662-5502
www.norriscenter.org/
Norris JSHS 100/7-12
W247S10395 Center Dr 53149 262-662-5911
Sara Trampf, prin. Fax 662-5502

Muscoda, Grant, Pop. 1,408
Riverdale SD 800/PK-12
PO Box 66 53573 608-739-3832
Duane Bark, supt. Fax 739-3751
www.riverdale.k12.wi.us/
Riverdale HS 300/9-12
PO Box 66 53573 608-739-3116
John Willey, prin. Fax 739-4486
Riverdale MS 200/6-8
800 N 6th St 53573 608-739-3101
Sharon Ennis, prin. Fax 739-9118

Muskego, Waukesha, Pop. 22,872
Muskego-Norway SD 4,800/PK-12
S87W18763 Woods Rd 53150 262-679-5400
Richard Drury, supt. Fax 679-5790
www.mnsd.k12.wi.us
Bay Lane MS 700/5-8
S75W16399 Hilltop Dr 53150 414-422-0430
Bonnie Murphy, prin. Fax 422-2204
Lake Denoon MS 800/5-8
W216S10586 Crowbar Dr 53150 262-662-1454
Ryan Oertel, prin. Fax 662-1588
Muskego HS 1,700/9-12
W183S8750 Racine Ave 53150 262-679-2300
Dennis Bussen, prin. Fax 679-3534

Nashotah, Waukesha, Pop. 1,378

Nashotah House Post-Sec.
2777 Mission Rd 53058 262-646-6500

Necedah, Juneau, Pop. 878
Necedah Area SD 700/K-12
1801 S Main St 54646 608-565-2256
Charles Krupa, supt. Fax 565-3201
www.necedah.k12.wi.us
Necedah MSHS 400/7-12
1801 S Main St 54646 608-565-2256
Peggy Saylor, prin. Fax 565-7044

Neenah, Winnebago, Pop. 24,596
Neenah SD 6,200/PK-12
410 S Commercial St 54956 920-751-6800
James Wiswall, supt. Fax 751-6809
www.neenah.k12.wi.us
Mann MS 600/6-8
1021 Oak St 54956 920-751-6940
Jon Fleming, prin. Fax 751-7099
Neenah HS 2,100/9-12
1275 Tullar Rd 54956 920-751-6900
Mark Duerwaechter, prin. Fax 751-7011
Shattuck MS 900/6-8
600 Elm St 54956 920-751-6850
Jon Fleming, prin. Fax 751-6899

St. Mary Central HS 300/9-12
1050 Zephyr Dr 54956 920-722-7796
Sr. Rochelle Kerkhof, prin. Fax 722-5940
Theda Clark Regional Medical Center Post-Sec.
130 2nd St 54956 920-729-2004

Neillsville, Clark, Pop. 2,694
Neillsville SD 1,200/PK-12
614 E 5th St 54456 715-743-3323
John Gaier, supt. Fax 743-8718
www.neillsville.k12.wi.us
Neillsville HS 400/9-12
401 Center St 54456 715-743-8738
Allen Mohr, prin. Fax 743-8714
Neillsville MS 300/6-8
504 E 5th St 54456 715-743-8712
Tim Rueth, prin. Fax 743-8715

Nekoosa, Wood, Pop. 2,585
Nekoosa SD 1,400/K-12
600 S Section St 54457 715-886-8000
Wayne Johnson, supt. Fax 886-8012
www.nekoosa.k12.wi.us/
Alexander MS 500/4-8
540 Birch St 54457 715-886-8040
Barbara Sparish, prin. Fax 886-8097
Nekoosa HS 500/9-12
500 Cedar St 54457 715-886-8060
Robb Jensen, prin. Fax 886-8087

Neopit, Menominee, Pop. 615
Menominee Indian SD
Supt. — See Keshena
Menominee Indian MS 200/6-8
PO Box 9 54150 715-756-2324
Faith Gagnon, prin. Fax 756-2496

Neosho, Dodge, Pop. 579

Lake Country Victory Christian HS 50/9-12
PO Box 46 53059 920-625-3995
Bruce Dickman, prin. Fax 625-3995

New Auburn, Chippewa, Pop. 547
New Auburn SD 300/PK-12
PO Box 110 54757 715-237-2202
Howard Hanson, supt. Fax 237-2350
www.newauburn.k12.wi.us
New Auburn JSHS 200/7-12
PO Box 110 54757 715-237-2505
Brian Henning, prin. Fax 237-2350

New Berlin, Waukesha, Pop. 38,547
New Berlin SD 3,300/PK-12
4333 S Sunnyslope Rd 53151 262-789-6220
James Benfield, supt. Fax 786-0512
www.nbps.k12.wi.us
Eisenhower MSHS 800/7-12
4333 S Sunnyslope Rd 53151 262-789-6300
Michael Fesenmaier, prin. Fax 789-3313
New Berlin West MSHS 800/7-12
18695 W Cleveland Ave 53146 262-789-6400
David LaBorde, prin. Fax 789-6442

New Glarus, Green, Pop. 2,058
New Glarus SD 800/PK-12
PO Box 7 53574 608-527-2410
Barbara Thompson, supt. Fax 527-5101
www.ngsd.k12.wi.us
New Glarus MSHS 400/6-12
PO Box 7 53574 608-527-2410
Jason Tadlock, prin. Fax 527-5101

New Holstein, Calumet, Pop. 3,200
New Holstein SD 1,100/PK-12
1715 Plymouth St 53061 920-898-5115
Joseph Wieser, supt. Fax 898-4112
nhsd.k12.wi.us
New Holstein HS 500/9-12
1715 Plymouth St 53061 920-898-4256
Kathy Kops, prin. Fax 898-4112
New Holstein MS 200/6-8
2226 Park Ave 53061 920-898-4208
Rick Amundson, prin. Fax 898-9152

New Lisbon, Juneau, Pop. 2,464
New Lisbon SD 700/PK-12
500 S Forest St 53950 608-562-3700
Ed Dombrowski, supt. Fax 562-5333
www.newlisbon.k12.wi.us

New Lisbon JSHS 300/7-12
500 S Forest St 53950 608-562-3700
Linda Hanson, prin. Fax 562-5333

New London, Waupaca, Pop. 6,926
New London SD 2,500/PK-12
901 W Washington St 54961 920-982-8530
Bill Fitzpatrick, supt. Fax 982-8551
www.newlondon.k12.wi.us
New London HS 900/9-12
1700 Klatt Rd 54961 920-982-8420
Joe Pomrening, prin. Fax 982-8440
New London MS 600/6-8
1000 W Washington St 54961 920-982-8532
Andy Jones, prin. Fax 982-8605

Starr Academy 100/7-12
E7475 Rawhide Rd 54961 920-982-6100
Daniel Birr, admin. Fax 982-7283

New Richmond, Saint Croix, Pop. 7,726
New Richmond SD 2,600/K-12
701 E 11th St 54017 715-243-7411
Maurice Veilleux, supt. Fax 246-3638
www.newrichmond.k12.wi.us
New Richmond HS 800/9-12
701 E 11th St 54017 715-243-7451
Jeffrey Moberg, prin. Fax 243-7464
New Richmond MS 600/6-8
701 E 11th St 54017 715-243-7471
Fax 246-0580

Wisconsin Indianhead Technical College Post-Sec.
1019 S Knowles Ave 54017 715-246-6561

Niagara, Marinette, Pop. 1,805
Niagara SD 200/K-12
700 Jefferson Ave 54151 715-251-1330
Peter Kososki, supt. Fax 251-4544
www.niagara.k12.wi.us
Niagara S 200/K-12
700 Jefferson Ave 54151 715-251-4541
Peter Kososki, prin. Fax 251-3715

North Fond du Lac, Fond du Lac, Pop. 5,024
North Fond Du Lac SD 800/PK-12
225 McKinley St 54937 920-929-3750
James Sebert, supt. Fax 929-3696
www.nfdl.k12.wi.us
Allen MS 200/6-8
305 Mckinley St 54937 920-929-3754
Aaron Sadoff, prin. Fax 929-3747
Mann HS 300/9-12
325 Mckinley St 54937 920-929-3740
Samantha McGill, prin. Fax 929-3664

Oak Creek, Milwaukee, Pop. 32,312
Oak Creek-Franklin SD 5,200/PK-12
7630 S 10th St 53154 414-768-5886
Sara Larsen, supt. Fax 768-6172
www.oakcreek.k12.wi.us
Oak Creek East MS 600/6-8
9330 S Shepard Ave 53154 414-768-6260
Peter DeRubeis, prin. Fax 768-6293
Oak Creek HS 1,800/9-12
340 E Puetz Rd 53154 414-768-6210
Paul Sigler, prin. Fax 768-6130
Oak Creek West MS 600/6-8
8401 S 13th St 53154 414-768-6250
Donald Kreuser, prin. Fax 768-6296

Milwaukee Area Technical College Post-Sec.
6665 S Howell Ave 53154 414-762-2500
Parkway Christian Academy 200/K-12
10940 S Nicholson Rd 53154 414-571-2684
Theresa Tamel, admin. Fax 571-2690

Oakfield, Fond du Lac, Pop. 1,021
Oakfield SD 500/PK-12
PO Box 99 53065 920-583-3146
Joseph Heinzelman, supt. Fax 583-4033
www.oakfield.k12.wi.us/
Oakfield HS 200/9-12
PO Box 39 53065 920-583-3141
Paul Dix, prin. Fax 583-4673
Oakfield MS 100/6-8
PO Box 69 53065 920-583-4117
Paul Dix, prin. Fax 583-3820

Oconomowoc, Waukesha, Pop. 13,711
Oconomowoc Area SD 4,000/PK-12
W360N7077 Brown St 53066 262-560-1115
Patricia Neudecker, supt. Fax 474-7595
www.oasd.k12.wi.us
Oconomowoc HS 1,500/9-12
641 E Forest St 53066 262-560-3100
Joseph C. Moylan, prin. Fax 567-8960
Oconomowoc MS 600/7-8
623 Summit Ave 53066 262-560-4300
Christine Maas, prin. Fax 567-1618

Lake Country Lutheran HS 200/9-12
1101 S Silver Lake St 53066 262-569-6500
Mark Bahr, prin. Fax 567-4324

Oconto, Oconto, Pop. 4,564
Oconto SD 1,200/PK-12
400 Michigan Ave 54153 920-834-7800
Dr. Sara L. Croney, supt. Fax 834-9884
www.oconto.k12.wi.us
Oconto HS 400/9-12
1717 Superior Ave 54153 920-834-7812
Bill Slough, prin. Fax 834-7804
Oconto MS 400/5-8
400 Michigan Ave 54153 920-834-7806
Jeffrey Werner, prin. Fax 834-7810

Oconto Falls, Oconto, Pop. 2,729
Oconto Falls SD 2,000/PK-12
200 N Farm Rd 54154 920-848-4471
David Polashek, supt. Fax 848-4474
www.ocontofalls.k12.wi.us
Oconto Falls HS 600/9-12
PO Box 988 54154 920-848-4467
Bruce Russell, prin. Fax 846-4444
Washington MS 400/6-8
102 S Washington St 54154 920-846-4463
Tom Menor, prin. Fax 846-4453

Omro, Winnebago, Pop. 3,282
Omro SD 1,300/PK-12
455 Fox Trl 54963 920-685-5666
Paul Amundson, admin. Fax 685-5757
www.omro.k12.wi.us/
Omro HS 400/9-12
455 Fox Trl 54963 920-685-7405
Bret Steffen, prin. Fax 685-7040
Omro MS, 455 Fox Trl 54963 300/6-8
Paul Williams, prin. 920-685-7403

Onalaska, LaCrosse, Pop. 15,701
Onalaska SD 2,800/K-12
PO Box 429 54650 608-781-9700
John Burnett, supt. Fax 781-9712
www.onalaska.k12.wi.us
Onalaska HS 900/9-12
700 Hilltopper Pl 54650 608-783-4561
Peter Woerpel, prin. Fax 783-0102
Onalaska MS 700/6-8
711 Quincy St 54650 608-783-5366
Roger Fruit, prin. Fax 781-8030

Luther HS 300/9-12
PO Box 129 54650 608-783-5435
Paul Wichmann, prin. Fax 783-4758

Ontario, Vernon, Pop. 481
Norwalk-Ontario-Wilton SD 700/PK-12
PO Box 130 54651 608-337-4403
Kelly Burhop, supt. Fax 337-4348
www.now.k12.wi.us/
Brookwood JSHS 300/7-12
PO Box 130 54651 608-337-4401
Brad Pettit, prin. Fax 337-4348

Oostburg, Sheboygan, Pop. 2,772
Oostburg SD 900/PK-12
PO Box 700100 53070 920-564-2346
Brian Hanes, supt. Fax 564-6138
oostburg.k12.wi.us
Oostburg HS 300/9-12
PO Box 700100 53070 920-564-2346
Scott Greupink, prin. Fax 564-6138
Oostburg MS, PO Box 700100 53070 200/6-8
Steve Harder, prin. 920-564-2383

Oregon, Dane, Pop. 8,493
Oregon SD 2,200/K-12
200 N Main St 53575 608-835-4091
Brian Busler, supt. Fax 835-9509
www.oregon.k12.wi.us
Oregon HS 800/9-12
456 N Perry Pkwy 53575 608-835-4301
Chris Ligocki, prin. Fax 835-7894
Oregon MS 300/7-8
601 Pleasant Oak Dr 53575 608-835-4801
Kyle Cherry, prin. Fax 835-3849

Orfordville, Rock, Pop. 1,336
Parkview SD 1,100/PK-12
PO Box 250 53576 608-879-2717
Gary Reineck, supt. Fax 879-2732
www.parkview.k12.wi.us
Parkview HS 300/9-12
PO Box 247 53576 608-879-2994
Chris Nelson, prin. Fax 879-2732
Parkview JHS 200/7-8
PO Box 247 53576 608-879-2994
John Abrahamson, prin. Fax 879-2732

Osceola, Polk, Pop. 2,685
Osceola SD 1,800/PK-12
PO Box 128 54020 715-294-4140
Roger Kumlien, supt. Fax 294-2428
www.osceola.k12.wi.us
Osceola HS 600/9-12
PO Box 128 54020 715-294-2127
Michael McMartin, prin. Fax 755-2068
Osceola MS, PO Box 128 54020 400/6-8
Rebecca Styles, prin. 715-294-4180

Oshkosh, Winnebago, Pop. 63,485
Oshkosh Area SD 9,700/PK-12
PO Box 3048 54903 920-424-0160
Dr. Ronald Heilmann, supt. Fax 424-0466
www.oshkosh.k12.wi.us
Merrill MS 500/6-8
108 W New York Ave 54901 920-424-0177
Christine Fabian, prin. Fax 424-7512
Oshkosh North HS 1,400/9-12
1100 W Smith Ave 54901 920-424-7000
Dennis Remington, prin. Fax 424-4054
Oshkosh West HS 1,900/9-12
375 N Eagle St 54902 920-424-4090
Peter Cernohous, prin. Fax 424-4950
South Park MS 400/6-8
1551 Delaware St 54902 920-424-0431
Lisa McLaughlin, prin. Fax 424-7513
Stanley MS 500/6-8
915 Hazel St 54901 920-424-0442
Marceline Peters-Felice, prin. Fax 424-7515
Tipler MS 400/6-8
325 S Eagle St 54902 920-424-0320
Ann Schultz, prin. Fax 424-7514
Traeger MS 600/6-8
3000 W 20th Ave 54904 920-424-0065
Jeanne Koepke, prin. Fax 424-7511

Fox Valley Technical College Post-Sec.
150 N Campbell Rd 54902 920-735-5600
Lourdes HS 200/9-12
110 N Sawyer St 54902 920-235-5670
Sr. Michelle Wronkowski, prin. Fax 235-7453
Mercy Medical Center Post-Sec.
PO Box 3370 54903 920-233-5110
Oshkosh Christian S 300/K-12
3450 Vinland St 54901 920-231-9704
Todd Benson, admin. Fax 231-9804
St. John Neumann S 100/6-8
110 N Sawyer St 54902 920-426-6421
Nancy Crowley, prin. Fax 235-7453
University of Wisconsin Post-Sec.
800 Algoma Blvd 54901 920-424-0200

Osseo, Trempealeau, Pop. 1,661
Osseo-Fairchild SD 1,000/PK-12
PO Box 130 54758 715-597-3141
Kerry Jacobson, supt. Fax 597-3606
www.ofsd.k12.wi.us
Osseo-Fairchild HS 300/9-12
PO Box 130 54758 715-597-3141
Steve Glocke, prin. Fax 597-3647
Osseo MS 300/6-8
PO Box 130 54758 715-597-3141
Steve Glocke, prin. Fax 597-3647

Owen, Clark, Pop. 914
Owen-Withee SD 600/PK-12
PO Box 417 54460 715-229-2151
James Friesen, supt. Fax 229-4322
www.owen-withee.k12.wi.us
Owen-Withee HS 200/9-12
PO Box 417 54460 715-229-2151
Dan Taft, prin. Fax 229-4322
Owen-Withee JHS 100/7-8
PO Box 417 54460 715-229-2151
Dan Taft, prin. Fax 229-4322

Palmyra, Jefferson, Pop. 1,763
Palmyra-Eagle Area SD 1,100/PK-12
PO Box 901 53156 262-495-7101
Bruce Gunderson, supt. Fax 495-7151
www.palmyra.k12.wi.us
Palmyra-Eagle HS 400/9-12
PO Box 901 53156 262-495-7101
Bruce Gunderson, prin. Fax 495-7146
Palmyra-Eagle MS 200/7-8
PO Box 901 53156 262-495-7101
Tim Kooi, prin. Fax 495-7146

Pardeeville, Columbia, Pop. 2,125
Pardeeville Area SD 800/PK-12
120 Oak St 53954 608-429-3666
Wayne Edwards, supt. Fax 429-2277
www.pardeeville.k12.wi.us
Pardeeville HS 300/9-12
120 Oak St 53954 608-429-2153
Paul Peterson, prin. Fax 429-2277
Pardeeville MS 200/6-8
120 Oak St 53954 608-429-2153
Tonya Broyles-Brouillard, prin. Fax 429-2277

Park Falls, Price, Pop. 2,464
Park Falls SD 700/PK-12
420 2nd Ave N 54552 715-762-4343
Dennis Dervetski, admin. Fax 762-5469
www.cardinalcountry.net
Park Falls HS 300/9-12
400 9th St N 54552 715-762-2474
Cindy Greenwood, prin. Fax 762-5674
Park Falls MS 200/6-8
420 2nd Ave N 54552 715-762-3815
Michael Plemon, prin. Fax 762-5469

Patch Grove, Grant, Pop. 169
River Ridge SD 600/PK-12
PO Box 78 53817 608-994-2715
Michael Murphy, supt. Fax 994-2891
www.rrsd.k12.wi.us
River Ridge HS 200/9-12
PO Box 78 53817 608-994-3719
Rod Lewis, prin. Fax 994-2891
Other Schools – See Bloomington

Pembine, Marinette
Beecher-Dunbar-Pembine SD 300/PK-12
PO Box 247 54156 715-324-5314
Robert R. Berndt, supt. Fax 324-5282
www.pembine.k12.wi.us/
Pembine JSHS 100/7-12
PO Box 247 54156 715-324-5314
Robert F. Berndt, prin. Fax 324-5282

Pepin, Pepin, Pop. 925
Pepin Area SD 300/PK-12
PO Box 128 54759 715-442-2391
Bruce A. Quinton, supt. Fax 442-3607
Pepin HS 100/9-12
PO Box 128 54759 715-442-2391
Bruce Quinton, prin. Fax 442-3607

Peshtigo, Marinette, Pop. 3,346
Peshtigo SD 1,200/PK-12
341 N Emery Ave 54157 715-582-3677
Kim Eparvier, supt. Fax 582-3850
www.peshtigo.k12.wi.us
Peshtigo MSHS 600/7-12
380 Green St 54157 715-582-3711
Stephen Motkowski, prin. Fax 582-0740

Pewaukee, Waukesha, Pop. 21,388
Pewaukee SD 2,200/PK-12
404 Lake St 53072 262-691-2100
JoAnn Sternke, supt. Fax 691-1052
www.pewaukee.k12.wi.us
Clark MS 400/7-8
472 Lake St 53072 262-691-2100
Randy Daul, prin. Fax 695-5004

Pewaukee HS 700/9-12
510 Lake St 53072 262-691-2100
Marty Van Hulle, prin. Fax 695-5006

Trinity Academy 200/K-12
W225N3131 Duplainville Rd 53072 262-695-2933
Robin Mitchell, admin. Fax 695-2934
Waukesha County Technical College Post-Sec.
800 Main St 53072 262-691-5566

Phelps, Vilas
Phelps SD 200/K-12
4451 Old School Rd 54554 715-545-2724
Richard Parks, supt. Fax 545-3728
www.phelps.k12.wi.us
Phelps HS 100/9-12
4451 Old School Rd 54554 715-545-2724
Jason Pertile, prin. Fax 545-3728

Phillips, Price, Pop. 1,499
Phillips SD 900/PK-12
PO Box 70 54555 715-339-2141
Jerry Trochinski, supt. Fax 339-2144
www.phillips.k12.wi.us/
Phillips HS 400/9-12
PO Box 70 54555 715-339-2141
Colin Hoogland, prin. Fax 339-2144
Phillips MS 200/6-8
PO Box 70 54555 715-339-3393
Dale Houdek, prin. Fax 339-6783

Pittsville, Wood, Pop. 847
Pittsville SD 700/PK-12
5459 Elementary Ave Ste 2 54466 715-884-6694
Mary Peterson, supt. Fax 884-5218
www.pittsville.k12.wi.us
Pittsville HS 300/9-12
5407 1st Ave 54466 715-884-6412
John Olig, prin. Fax 884-2870

Plainfield, Waushara, Pop. 899
Tri-County Area SD 500/PK-12
PO Box 67 54966 715-335-6366
Tony Marinack, supt. Fax 335-6365
www.penguin.tricounty.k12.wi.us
Tri-County HS 300/7-12
PO Box 67 54966 715-335-6366
Larry Mancl, prin. Fax 335-6322

Platteville, Grant, Pop. 9,854
Platteville SD 1,500/PK-12
780 N 2nd St 53818 608-342-4000
Dean Isaacson, supt. Fax 342-4412
www.platteville.k12.wi.us
Platteville HS 500/9-12
710 E Madison St 53818 608-342-4020
Jeffrey Jacobson, prin. Fax 342-4427
Platteville MS 400/5-8
40 E Madison St 53818 608-342-4010
David Allen, prin. Fax 342-4497

University of Wisconsin Post-Sec.
1 University Plz 53818 608-342-1200

Plum City, Pierce, Pop. 576
Plum City SD 300/K-12
907 Main St 54761 715-647-2591
Todd Leroy, supt. Fax 647-3015
www.plumcity.k12.wi.us
Plum City JSHS 200/6-12
907 Main St 54761 715-647-2591
Paul Churchill, prin. Fax 647-3015

Plymouth, Sheboygan, Pop. 8,217
Plymouth SD 2,400/PK-12
125 S Highland Ave 53073 920-892-2661
Clark Reinke, supt. Fax 892-6366
www.plymouth.k12.wi.us
Plymouth HS 900/9-12
125 S Highland Ave 53073 920-893-6911
Dan Mella, prin. Fax 892-6366
Riverview MS 600/6-8
300 Riverside Cir 53073 920-892-4353
Tom Malmstadt, prin. Fax 892-5072

Poplar, Douglas, Pop. 591
Maple SD
Supt. — See Maple
Northwestern MS 300/6-8
PO Box 46 54864 715-364-2218
Ken Bartelt, prin. Fax 364-2540

Portage, Columbia, Pop. 10,035
Portage Community SD 2,500/PK-12
904 De Witt St 53901 608-742-4879
Daniel Pulsfus, supt. Fax 742-4950
www.portage.k12.wi.us
Portage HS 800/9-12
301 E Collins St 53901 608-742-8545
Karin Exo, prin. Fax 742-0617
Portage JHS 400/7-8
2505 New Pinery Rd 53901 608-742-2165
Wayne Bartels, prin. Fax 742-6987

Port Edwards, Wood, Pop. 1,797
Port Edwards SD 500/K-12
801 2nd St 54469 715-887-9000
Mike Alexander, supt. Fax 887-9040
www.pesd.k12.wi.us
Edwards HS 200/9-12
801 2nd St 54469 715-887-9000
Steve Lutzke, prin. Fax 887-9040
Edwards MS 200/5-8
801 2nd St 54469 715-887-9000
Steve Lutzke, prin. Fax 887-9040

Port Washington, Ozaukee, Pop. 10,892
Port Washington-Saukville SD 2,700/PK-12
100 W Monroe St 53074 262-268-6000
Michael Weber Ph.D., supt. Fax 268-6020
www.pwssd.k12.wi.us
Jefferson MS 800/5-8
1403 N Holden St 53074 262-268-6100
Arlan Galarowicz, prin. Fax 268-6120
Port Washington HS 900/9-12
427 W Jackson St 53074 262-268-5500
Duane Woelfel, prin. Fax 268-5520

Port Washington Catholic MS 100/5-8
1802 N Wisconsin St 53074 262-284-2682
Lee Kaschinska, prin. Fax 284-4168

Port Wing, Bayfield
South Shore SD 200/PK-12
PO Box 40 54865 715-774-3500
Marc Christianson, supt. Fax 774-3569
www.sshore.k12.wi.us
South Shore JSHS 100/7-12
PO Box 40 54865 715-774-3361
Marc Christianson, prin. Fax 774-3569

Potosi, Grant, Pop. 728
Potosi SD 400/PK-12
128 US Highway 61 N 53820 608-763-2162
Dr. Steven Lozeau, supt. Fax 763-2035
www.potosisd.k12.wi.us
Potosi HS 200/9-12
128 US Highway 61 N 53820 608-763-2161
Terry Mengel, prin. Fax 763-2035
Potosi MS 100/6-8
128 US Highway 61 N 53820 608-763-2162
Terry Mengel, prin. Fax 763-2035

Poynette, Columbia, Pop. 2,563
Poynette SD 1,100/PK-12
PO Box 10 53955 608-635-4347
Barbara Wolfe, supt. Fax 635-9200
www.poynette.k12.wi.us
Poynette HS 300/9-12
PO Box 10 53955 608-635-4347
Craig McCallum, prin. Fax 635-9201
Poynette MS 300/6-8
PO Box 10 53955 608-635-4347
Brian Sutton, prin. Fax 635-9233

Prairie du Chien, Crawford, Pop. 5,880
Prairie du Chien Area SD 1,200/PK-12
420 S Wacouta Ave 53821 608-326-8451
James P. O'Meara, supt. Fax 326-0000
www.pdc.k12.wi.us
Bluff View IS 500/3-8
1901 E Wells St 53821 608-326-0503
Joan Wick, prin. Fax 326-5364
Prairie du Chien HS 500/9-12
800 E Crawford St 53821 608-326-8437
Andy Banasik, prin. Fax 326-2333

St. John Nepomucene MS 6-8
720 S Wacouta Ave 53821 608-326-4400
Kathleen Schwartz, prin. Fax 326-4876

Prairie du Sac, Sauk, Pop. 3,547
Sauk Prairie SD
Supt. — See Sauk City
Sauk Prairie HS 900/9-12
105 9th St 53578 608-643-5900
Chris Grinde, prin. Fax 643-5419

Prairie Farm, Barron, Pop. 508
Prairie Farm SD 300/K-12
630 River Ave S 54762 715-455-1683
Dr. Donald E. Hauck, supt. Fax 455-1056
www.prairiefarm.k12.wi.us
Prairie Farm HS 100/9-12
630 River Ave S 54762 715-455-1861
Jim Boebel, prin. Fax 455-1056
Prairie Farm MS 100/6-8
630 River Ave S 54762 715-455-1841
Jim Boebel, prin. Fax 455-1056

Prentice, Price, Pop. 563
Prentice SD 400/PK-12
PO Box 110 54556 715-428-2811
Gregory Krause, supt. Fax 428-2815
www.prentice.k12.wi.us
Prentice HS 200/9-12
PO Box 110 54556 715-428-2811
Randall Bergman, prin. Fax 428-2815

Prescott, Pierce, Pop. 4,009
Prescott SD 1,000/PK-12
1220 Saint Croix St 54021 715-262-5782
Roger Hulne, supt. Fax 262-5091
www.prescott.k12.wi.us
Prescott HS 400/9-12
1220 Saint Croix St 54021 715-262-5010
Steven Shaw, prin. Fax 262-5091
Prescott MS 200/6-8
125 Elm St N 54021 715-262-5389
Lyle Nolt, prin. Fax 262-5091

Princeton, Green Lake, Pop. 1,463
Princeton SD 400/K-12
PO Box 147 54968 920-295-6571
Robert Beaver, supt. Fax 295-4778
www.princeton.k12.wi.us/
Princeton S 400/K-12
PO Box 147 54968 920-295-6571
Jean Rigden, prin. Fax 295-4778

Pulaski, Brown, Pop. 3,540
Pulaski Community SD 3,600/PK-12
PO Box 36 54162 920-822-6000
Dr. Kristine Martin, supt. Fax 822-6005
www.pulaski.k12.wi.us/index.htm
Pulaski Community MS 900/6-8
911 S Saint Augustine St 54162 920-822-6500
William Derricks, prin. Fax 822-6505
Pulaski HS 1,100/9-12
1040 S Saint Augustine St 54162 920-822-6700
Glenn Schlender, prin. Fax 822-6707

Racine, Racine, Pop. 79,392
Racine USD 19,500/PK-12
2220 Northwestern Ave 53404 262-635-5600
Thomas Hicks Ph.D., supt. Fax 631-7121
www.racine.k12.wi.us
Case HS 2,100/9-12
7345 Washington Ave 53406 262-619-4200
Tom Sager, prin. Fax 619-4259
Gilmore MS 800/6-8
2330 Northwestern Ave 53404 262-619-4260
Richard Larson, prin. Fax 619-4272
Horlick HS 2,100/9-12
2119 Rapids Dr 53404 262-619-4300
Nola Starling-Ratliff, prin. Fax 619-4390
Jerstad-Agerholm MS 800/6-8
3601 Lasalle St 53402 262-664-6075
Brian Colbert, prin. Fax 664-6120
Mitchell MS 900/6-8
2701 Drexel Ave 53403 262-664-6400
Robert Wilhelmi, prin. Fax 664-6444
Park HS 2,300/9-12
1901 12th St 53403 262-619-4400
Dan Thielen, prin. Fax 619-4490
Starbuck MS 800/6-8
1516 Ohio St 53405 262-664-6500
Sandy Brand, prin. Fax 664-6510
Walden III MSHS 300/6-12
1012 Center St 53403 262-664-6250
Robert Holzem, prin. Fax 664-6255

All Saints Healthcare System Post-Sec.
1320 Wisconsin Ave 53403 262-636-2846
Gateway Technical College Post-Sec.
1001 Main St 53403 262-619-6200
Lutheran HS 200/9-12
251 Luedtke Ave 53405 262-637-6538
Randy Baganz, prin. Fax 637-6601
Midwest College of Oriental Medicine Post-Sec.
6232 Bankers Rd 53403 262-554-2010
Prairie S 700/PK-12
4050 Lighthouse Dr 53402 262-260-3845
Wm. Mark Murphy, hdmstr. Fax 260-3790
St. Catherine HS 400/9-12
1200 Park Ave 53403 262-632-2785
Jeffrey Johnson, prin. Fax 632-5144
San Juan Diego MS 6-8
1101 Douglas Ave 53402 262-619-0402
Michael Frontier, pres.

Randolph, Columbia, Pop. 1,820
Randolph SD 500/PK-12
110 Meadowood Dr 53956 920-326-2427
Jerry Hopfensperger, supt. Fax 326-2439
www.randolph.k12.wi.us
Randolph HS 200/9-12
110 Meadowood Dr 53956 920-326-2425
Thomas Erdman, prin. Fax 326-2430

Random Lake, Sheboygan, Pop. 1,585
Random Lake SD 800/PK-12
605 Random Lake Rd 53075 920-994-4342
Joseph Gassert, supt. Fax 994-4820
www.randomlake.k12.wi.us
Random Lake HS 400/9-12
605 Random Lake Rd 53075 920-994-9193
Keith Hilts, prin. Fax 994-4820
Random Lake MS 200/5-8
605 Random Lake Rd 53075 920-994-2498
David Farnham, prin. Fax 994-4820

Reedsburg, Sauk, Pop. 8,497
Reedsburg SD 2,500/PK-12
501 K St 53959 608-524-2401
Thomas Benson, supt. Fax 524-6818
www.rsd.k12.wi.us
Reedsburg Area HS 900/9-12
1100 S Albert Ave 53959 608-524-4327
Rob Taylor, prin. Fax 524-1373
Webb MS 500/6-8
707 N Webb Ave 53959 608-524-2328
Casey Campbell, prin. Fax 524-1161

Reedsville, Manitowoc, Pop. 1,162
Reedsville SD 700/PK-12
PO Box 340 54230 920-754-4341
Robert Scrivner, supt. Fax 754-4344
www.reedsville.k12.wi.us
Reedsville HS 300/9-12
PO Box 340 54230 920-754-4341
Tony Butturini, prin. Fax 754-4344
Reedsville MS 100/7-8
PO Box 340 54230 920-754-4345
Pat Popp, prin. Fax 754-4577

Rhinelander, Oneida, Pop. 7,889
Rhinelander SD 2,200/K-12
665 Coolidge Ave Ste B 54501 715-365-9700
Dr. Roger G. Erdahl, supt. Fax 365-9719
www.rhinelander.k12.wi.us
Rhinelander HS 1,100/9-12
665 Coolidge Ave 54501 715-365-9500
Michael Werbowsky, prin. Fax 365-9568
Williams MS 600/6-8
915 Acacia Ln 54501 715-365-9220
Paul Johnson, prin. Fax 369-7562

Nicolet Area Technical College Post-Sec.
PO Box 518 54501 715-365-4410

Rib Lake, Taylor, Pop. 858
Rib Lake SD 500/PK-12
PO Box 278 54470 715-427-3222
Dan Boxx, supt. Fax 427-3221
www.riblake.k12.wi.us
Rib Lake HS 200/9-12
PO Box 278 54470 715-427-3220
Rick Cardey, prin. Fax 427-5022

Rib Lake MS 100/6-8
PO Box 278 54470 715-427-5446
Rick Cardey, prin. Fax 427-3221

Rice Lake, Barron, Pop. 8,361
Rice Lake Area SD 2,500/PK-12
700 Augusta St 54868 715-234-9007
Paul Vine, supt. Fax 234-4552
www.ricelake.k12.wi.us
Rice Lake HS 800/9-12
30 S Wisconsin Ave 54868 715-234-2181
Larry Zeman, prin. Fax 234-6679
Rice Lake MS 500/6-8
204 Cameron Rd 54868 715-234-8156
Steve Sirek, prin. Fax 234-9439

Univ. of Wisconsin Center-Barron County Post-Sec.
1800 College Dr 54868 715-234-8176

Richfield, Washington
Richfield J1 SD 400/PK-8
3117 Holly Hill Rd 53076 262-628-1032
Craig Baker, supt. Fax 628-3013
www.richfield.k12.wi.us
Richfield ES 300/3-8
3117 Holly Hill Rd 53076 262-628-1032
Craig Baker, prin. Fax 628-3013

Richland Center, Richland, Pop. 5,177
Ithaca SD 400/K-12
24615 State Hwy 58 53581 608-585-2512
Kristine Blakeley, supt. Fax 585-2505
www.ithaca.k12.wi.us/
Ithaca HS 100/9-12
24615 State Hwy 58 53581 608-585-2311
Kristine Blakeley, prin. Fax 585-2505
Ithaca MS 100/6-8
24615 State Hwy 58 53581 608-585-2311
Kristine Blakeley, prin. Fax 585-2505

Richland SD 1,400/PK-12
26220 Executive Ln Ste A 53581 608-647-6106
Rachel Schultz, supt. Fax 647-8454
www.richland.k12.wi.us
Richland Center HS 500/9-12
23200 Hornet High Rd 53581 608-647-6131
John Cler, prin. Fax 647-8734
Richland MS 300/6-8
1801 State Hwy 80 S 53581 608-647-6381
David Guy, prin. Fax 647-4735

Eagle S 100/PK-12
26700 Fellowship Ln 53581 608-647-7226
Erwin Holmes, admin. Fax 647-5669
University of Wisconsin Center Post-Sec.
1200 US Hwy 14 W 53581 608-647-6186

Rio, Columbia, Pop. 998
Rio Community SD 500/PK-12
411 Church St 53960 920-992-3141
Mark McGuire, supt. Fax 992-3157
www.rio.k12.wi.us
Rio MSHS 300/6-12
411 Church St 53960 920-992-3141
Mark McGuire, prin. Fax 992-3157

Ripon, Fond du Lac, Pop. 7,268
Ripon SD 1,700/PK-12
PO Box 991 54971 920-748-4600
Richard N. Zimman, supt. Fax 748-2715
www.ripon.k12.wi.us
Ripon HS 600/9-12
PO Box 991 54971 920-748-4616
Dan Tjernagel, prin. Fax 748-4622
Ripon MS 400/6-8
PO Box 991 54971 920-748-4638
Melanie Oppor, prin. Fax 748-4653

Ripon College Post-Sec.
PO Box 248 54971 920-748-8115

River Falls, Pierce, Pop. 13,254
River Falls SD 2,900/PK-12
852 E Division St 54022 715-425-1800
Boyd McLarty, supt. Fax 425-1804
www.rfsd.k12.wi.us
Meyer MS 700/6-8
230 N 9th St 54022 715-425-1820
Michael Johnson, prin. Fax 425-1823
River Falls HS 1,000/9-12
818 Cemetery Rd 54022 715-425-1830
Dr. Elaine Baumann, prin. Fax 425-1827

University of Wisconsin Post-Sec.
410 S 3rd St 54022 715-425-3911

Rosendale, Fond du Lac, Pop. 1,035
Rosendale-Brandon SD 900/PK-12
300 W Wisconsin St 54974 920-872-2851
Gary Hansen, supt. Fax 872-2647
www.rbsd.k12.wi.us
Laconia HS 300/9-12
301 W Division St 54974 920-872-2161
Wayne Weber, prin. Fax 872-2777
Rosendale IS 200/4-8
200 S Main St 54974 920-872-2126
John Hokenson, prin. Fax 872-2061

Rosholt, Portage, Pop. 483
Rosholt SD 700/PK-12
PO Box 310 54473 715-677-4542
Kenneth Camlek, supt. Fax 677-3543
www.rosholt.k12.wi.us
Rosholt HS 300/9-12
PO Box 310 54473 715-677-4541
James Grygleski, prin. Fax 677-6767
Rosholt MS 200/6-8
PO Box 310 54473 715-677-4541
James Grygleski, prin. Fax 677-6767

Saint Croix Falls, Polk, Pop. 2,052
St. Croix Falls SD 1,100/PK-12
PO Box 130 54024 715-483-9823
Glenn Martin, supt. Fax 483-3695
www.scf.k12.wi.us
St. Croix Falls HS 300/9-12
PO Box 130 54024 715-483-9823
Pete Nusbaum, prin. Fax 483-3695
St. Croix Falls MS 400/5-8
PO Box 130 54024 715-483-9823
Kathleen Willow, prin. Fax 483-3695

Valley Christian S 50/PK-12
1263 State Road 35 54024 715-483-9126
Ron Brace, admin. Fax 483-5679

Saint Francis, Milwaukee, Pop. 8,809
St. Francis SD 1,000/PK-12
4225 S Lake Dr 53235 414-747-3900
Carol Topinka, supt. Fax 482-7198
www.stfrancisschools.org
Deer Creek IS 200/4-8
3680 S Kinnickinnic Ave 53235 414-482-8400
Terry Balster, prin. Fax 482-8406
Saint Francis HS 600/9-12
4225 S Lake Dr 53235 414-747-3600
Dr. Gerald Luecht, prin. Fax 747-3605

St. Francis Seminary Post-Sec.
3257 S Lake Dr 53235 414-747-6400

Salem, Kenosha
Central-Westosha UNHSD 1,200/9-12
PO Box 38 53168 262-843-4211
Doug Potter, supt. Fax 843-4069
www.westosha.k12.wi.us
Central HS 1,200/9-12
PO Box 38 53168 262-843-1987
Barb Sonnenberg, prin. Fax 843-4069

Salem SD 1,100/K-8
PO Box 160 53168 262-843-2356
David Milz, supt. Fax 843-4138
www.salem.k12.wi.us
Salem MS, PO Box 160 53168 400/6-8
Eileen Bruton, prin. 262-843-2356

Sauk City, Sauk, Pop. 3,006
Sauk Prairie SD 2,600/PK-12
213 Maple St 53583 608-643-5990
Craig Bender, supt. Fax 643-6216
www.saukpr.k12.wi.us
Sauk Prairie MS 700/6-8
207 Maple St 53583 608-643-5500
Ellen Paul, prin. Fax 643-5503
Other Schools – See Prairie du Sac

Schofield, Marathon, Pop. 2,160
D.C. Everest Area SD 5,300/PK-12
6300 Alderson St 54476 715-359-4221
Kristine Gilmore, supt. Fax 359-2056
www.dce.k12.wi.us
D.C. Everest HS 1,300/10-12
6500 Alderson St 54476 715-359-6561
Thomas Johanson, prin. Fax 355-7220
D.C. Everest JHS 900/8-9
1000 Machmueller St 54476 715-359-0511
Steven Pophal, prin. Fax 359-9395

Seneca, Crawford
Seneca SD 300/PK-12
PO Box 34 54654 608-734-3411
Richard Burby, supt. Fax 734-3430
www.seneca.k12.wi.us
Seneca HS 100/9-12
PO Box 34 54654 608-734-3411
Richard Burby, prin. Fax 734-3430
Seneca JHS 100/5-8
PO Box 34 54654 608-734-3411
Richard Burby, prin. Fax 734-3430

Seymour, Outagamie, Pop. 3,432
Seymour Community SD 2,400/PK-12
10 Circle Dr 54165 920-833-2304
William Loasching, supt. Fax 833-6037
www.seymour.k12.wi.us/
Seymour HS 800/9-12
10 Circle Dr 54165 920-833-2306
Michael Flaherty, prin. Fax 833-7608
Seymour MS 500/6-8
10 Circle Dr 54165 920-833-7199
Robert Battisti, prin. Fax 833-9376

Shawano, Shawano, Pop. 8,441
Shawano-Gresham SD 2,600/PK-12
218 County Road B 54166 715-526-3194
Todd Carlson, supt. Fax 526-6072
www.ssd.k12.wi.us/
Shawano Community HS 1,000/9-12
220 County Road B 54166 715-526-2175
Todd Stiede, prin. Fax 524-8414
Shawano Community MS 700/5-8
1050 S Union St 54166 715-526-2192
Daniel Labby, prin. Fax 526-5037

East Central WI Lutheran HS 100/9-12
PO Box 542 54166 715-524-5301
Paul Weismantel, prin. Fax 524-4876

Sheboygan, Sheboygan, Pop. 48,872
Sheboygan Area SD 10,200/PK-12
830 Virginia Ave 53081 920-459-3511
Joseph Sheehan Ph.D., supt. Fax 459-6487
www.sheboygan.k12.wi.us
Farnsworth MS 700/6-8
1017 Union Ave 53081 920-459-3655
David Williams, prin. Fax 459-3660
Mann MS 700/6-8
2820 Union Ave 53081 920-459-3666
Russ Groblewski, prin. Fax 459-3669
North HS 1,700/9-12
1042 School Ave 53083 920-459-3600
Rick Schultz, prin. Fax 459-3601
South HS 1,500/9-12
3128 S 12th St 53081 920-459-3637
Lee Benish, prin. Fax 459-6733
Urban MS 800/6-8
1226 North Ave 53083 920-459-3680
Susan Nennig, prin. Fax 459-4065

Lakeland College Post-Sec.
PO Box 359 53082 920-565-2111
Sheboygan Area Lutheran HS 200/9-12
3323 University Dr 53081 920-452-3323
Allen Holzheimer, prin. Fax 452-1310
Sheboygan County Christian HS 200/9-12
929 Greenfield Ave 53081 920-458-9981
Wayne Dykstra, prin. Fax 458-9957
University of Wisconsin Center Post-Sec.
1 University Dr 53081 920-459-3733

Sheboygan Falls, Sheboygan, Pop. 7,527
Sheboygan Falls SD 1,700/PK-12
220 Amherst Ave 53085 920-467-7893
Fax 467-7899
www.sheboyganfalls.k12.wi.us
Sheboygan Falls HS 600/9-12
220 Amherst Ave 53085 920-467-7890
Scott Sabol, prin. Fax 467-7825
Sheboygan Falls MS 500/5-8
101 School St 53085 920-467-7880
Meloney Markofski, prin. Fax 467-7885

Shell Lake, Washburn, Pop. 1,372
Shell Lake SD 500/K-12
271 Highway 63 S 54871 715-468-7816
Gerald Gauderman, supt. Fax 468-7812
www.shelllake.k12.wi.us
Shell Lake JSHS 300/7-12
271 Highway 63 S 54871 715-468-7814
Terry Reynolds, prin.

Wisconsin Indianhead Technical College Post-Sec.
505 Pine Ridge Dr 54871 715-468-2815

Shiocton, Outagamie, Pop. 920
Shiocton SD 800/PK-12
PO Box 68 54170 920-986-3351
Dave Moscinski, supt. Fax 986-3291
www.shiocton.k12.wi.us
Shiocton HS 300/8-12
PO Box 68 54170 920-986-3351
Kelly Zeinert, prin. Fax 986-3291

Shorewood, Milwaukee, Pop. 13,192
Shorewood SD 2,100/PK-12
1701 E Capitol Dr 53211 414-963-6901
Blane McCann, supt. Fax 963-6904
www.shorewoodschools.org
Shorewood HS 700/9-12
1701 E Capitol Dr 53211 414-963-6921
Rick Monroe, prin. Fax 961-2819
Shorewood IS 300/7-8
3830 N Morris Blvd 53211 414-963-6951
Roxanne Hanney, prin. Fax 963-6946

Shullsburg, Lafayette, Pop. 1,198
Shullsburg SD 400/PK-12
444 N Judgement St 53586 608-965-4427
Loras Kruser, admin. Fax 965-3794
www.shullsburg.k12.wi.us
Shullsburg HS 100/9-12
444 N Judgement St 53586 608-965-4427
Loras Kruser, prin. Fax 965-3794
Shullsburg JHS 100/6-8
444 N Judgement St 53586 608-965-4427
Loras Kruser, prin. Fax 965-3794

Siren, Burnett, Pop. 1,015
Siren SD 400/PK-12
PO Box 29 54872 715-349-2290
Scott Johnson, supt. Fax 349-7476
www.siren.k12.wi.us
Siren HS 200/9-12
PO Box 29 54872 715-349-2277
Joseph Zirngibl, prin. Fax 349-7476

Slinger, Washington, Pop. 4,358
Slinger SD 2,800/PK-12
207 Polk St 53086 262-644-9615
Robert Reynolds, supt. Fax 644-7514
www.slinger.k12.wi.us
Slinger HS 900/9-12
209 Polk St 53086 262-644-5261
Vic Erickson, prin. Fax 644-0479
Slinger MS 700/6-8
521 Olympic Dr 53086 262-644-5226
Patricia Harmann, prin. Fax 644-7353

Soldiers Grove, Crawford, Pop. 614
North Crawford SD 500/PK-12
47050 County Road X 54655 608-735-4318
Daniel Davies, supt. Fax 735-4317
www.northcrawford.com/
North Crawford HS 200/9-12
47050 County Road X 54655 608-735-4311
Daniel Davies, prin. Fax 624-6269

Solon Springs, Douglas, Pop. 577
Solon Springs SD 300/PK-12
8993 E Baldwin Ave 54873 715-378-2263
Gary Frankiewicz, supt. Fax 378-2073
eyrie.solonk12.net/school/
Solon Springs S 300/PK-12
8993 E Baldwin Ave 54873 715-378-2263
Gary Frankiewicz, prin. Fax 378-2073

Somers, Kenosha

Shoreland Lutheran HS 300/9-12
PO Box 295 53171 262-859-2595
Jeffery Wiechman, prin. Fax 859-2783

Somerset, Saint Croix, Pop. 2,539
Somerset SD 1,500/PK-12
PO Box 100 54025 715-247-3313
Randal Rosburg, supt. Fax 247-5588
www.somerset.k12.wi.us
Somerset HS 400/9-12
PO Box 100 54025 715-247-3355
Lynn Rieck-Hudnall, prin. Fax 247-3864
Somerset MS 400/5-8
PO Box 100 54025 715-247-4400
Richard Lange, prin. Fax 247-4437

South Milwaukee, Milwaukee, Pop. 20,849
South Milwaukee SD 3,500/PK-12
901 15th Ave 53172 414-766-5000
David Ewald, supt. Fax 766-5005
www.sdsm.k12.wi.us/
South Milwaukee HS 1,200/9-12
801 15th Ave 53172 414-766-5100
Dr. Gary Kiltz, prin. Fax 766-5131
South Milwaukee MS 700/6-8
1001 15th Ave 53172 414-766-5800
Mike Connor, prin. Fax 766-5803

Calvary Academy 50/5-12
2200 9th Ave 53172 414-571-1522
Carlton Weisheim, prin. Fax 571-5242

South Wayne, Lafayette, Pop. 473
Black Hawk SD 500/PK-12
PO Box 303 53587 608-439-5400
Kevin Shetler, supt. Fax 439-1022
www.blackhawk.k12.wi.us
Black Hawk HS 200/9-12
PO Box 303 53587 608-439-5371
Jerry Mortimer, prin. Fax 439-1022
Other Schools – See Gratiot

Sparta, Monroe, Pop. 8,827
Sparta Area SD 2,300/PK-12
506 N Black River St 54656 608-269-3151
John Hendricks, supt. Fax 269-6428
www.spartan.org
Sparta HS 800/9-12
506 N Black River St 54656 608-269-2107
William Tourdot, prin. Fax 269-7165
Sparta Meadowview MS 600/6-8
506 N Black River St 54656 608-269-2185
Cheri Kulland, prin. Fax 366-3404

Sparta Area Christian S 50/PK-12
413 Osborne Dr 54656 608-269-0358
Tom Lago, admin. Fax 269-0358

Spencer, Marathon, Pop. 1,833
Spencer SD 800/PK-12
300 School St 54479 715-659-5347
David Wessel, supt. Fax 659-5470
www.spencer.k12.wi.us
Spencer HS 300/9-12
300 School St 54479 715-659-4211
Harry Toufar, prin. Fax 659-5470

Spooner, Washburn, Pop. 2,670
Spooner Area SD 1,400/PK-12
500 College St 54801 715-635-2171
Dr. Donald Haack, supt. Fax 635-7174
www.spooner.k12.wi.us
Spooner HS 500/9-12
500 College St 54801 715-635-2172
Robert Kinderman, prin. Fax 635-7074
Spooner MS 400/5-8
500 College St 54801 715-635-2173
Lynnea Lake, prin. Fax 635-7074

Spring Green, Sauk, Pop. 1,436
River Valley SD 1,400/PK-12
660 W Daley St 53588 608-588-2551
Jamie Benson, supt. Fax 588-2558
www.rvschools.org
River Valley HS 600/9-12
660 Varsity Blvd 53588 608-588-2554
Kim Kaukl, prin. Fax 588-2827
River Valley MS 300/6-8
660 W Daley St 53588 608-588-2556
Roger Hoffman, prin. Fax 588-2026

Spring Valley, Pierce, Pop. 1,283
Spring Valley SD 600/K-12
PO Box 249 54767 715-778-5551
David A. Wellington, supt. Fax 778-4761
www.springvalley.k12.wi.us
Spring Valley MSHS 300/7-12
PO Box 249 54767 715-778-5554
Gretchen Cipriano, prin. Fax 778-5556

Stanley, Chippewa, Pop. 3,304
Stanley-Boyd Area SD 1,000/PK-12
507 E 1st Ave 54768 715-644-5534
James Jones, supt. Fax 644-5584
www.stanleyboyd.k12.wi.us
Stanley-Boyd HS 400/9-12
507 E 1st Ave 54768 715-644-5534
Mark Carlson, prin. Fax 644-6701
Stanley-Boyd MS 200/6-8
507 E 1st Ave 54768 715-644-5715
Patrick Marion, prin. Fax 644-5584

Stevens Point, Portage, Pop. 24,298
Stevens Point Area SD 4,900/PK-12
1900 Polk St 54481 715-345-5444
Bette Lang Ed.D., supt. Fax 345-7302
www.wisp.k12.wi.us
Franklin JHS 800/7-9
2000 Polk St 54481 715-345-5413
Connie Negaard, prin. Fax 345-5696
Jacobs JHS 900/7-9
2400 Main St 54481 715-345-5422
Fax 345-7340
Stevens Point Area SHS 1,800/10-12
1201 Northpoint Dr 54481 715-345-5400
Mike Devine, prin. Fax 345-5408

Mid-State Technical College Post-Sec.
933 Michigan Ave 54481 715-344-3063
Pacelli HS 200/9-12
1301 Maria Dr 54481 715-341-2442
Br. Roger Betzold, prin. Fax 341-6779
St. Peter MS 200/6-8
708 1st St 54481 715-344-1890
Ellen Lopas, prin. Fax 342-2005
Stevens Point Christian Academy 100/K-12
801 US Highway 10 W 54481 715-341-3275
Heidi Uitenbroek, prin. Fax 341-3023
University of Wisconsin Post-Sec.
2100 Main St 54481 715-346-0123

Stockbridge, Calumet, Pop. 676
Stockbridge SD 300/PK-12
PO Box 188 53088 920-439-1782
LeRoy Kopecky, supt. Fax 439-1150
www.stockbridge.k12.wi.us/
Stockbridge HS 100/9-12
PO Box 188 53088 920-439-1159
Kenneth Kappell, prin. Fax 439-1150
Stockbridge MS 100/6-8
PO Box 188 53088 920-439-1158
Kenneth Kappell, prin. Fax 439-1150

Stoughton, Dane, Pop. 12,646
Stoughton Area SD 3,500/PK-12
320 North St 53589 608-877-5001
Myron Palomba, supt. Fax 877-5008
www.stoughton.k12.wi.us
River Bluff MS 600/7-8
235 N Forrest St 53589 608-877-5501
Richard Pertzborn, prin. Fax 877-5508
Stoughton HS 1,200/9-12
600 Lincoln Ave 53589 608-877-5601
Jerry Movrich, prin. Fax 877-5619

Stratford, Marathon, Pop. 1,515
Stratford SD 800/PK-12
PO Box 7 54484 715-687-3130
Scott Winch, supt. Fax 687-4074
www.stratford.k12.wi.us
Stratford JSHS 400/7-12
PO Box 7 54484 715-687-4311
Paul Rozak, prin. Fax 687-4652

Strum, Trempealeau, Pop. 971
Eleva-Strum SD 700/PK-12
W23597 US Highway 10 54770 715-695-2696
Kenneth Rogers Ph.D., admin. Fax 695-3519
www.esschools.k12.wi.us/
Eleva-Strum MSHS 300/7-12
W23597 US Highway 10 54770 715-695-2696
Mark Gruen, prin. Fax 695-3938

Sturgeon Bay, Door, Pop. 9,180
Sevastopol SD 600/PK-12
4550 State Highway 57 54235 920-743-6282
Ann Smejkal, supt. Fax 743-4009
www.sevastopol.k12.wi.us
Sevastopol HS 300/9-12
4550 State Highway 57 54235 920-743-6282
Ron Shefchik, prin. Fax 743-4009
Sevastopol JHS 100/7-8
4550 State Highway 57 54235 920-743-6282
Ron Shefchik, prin. Fax 743-4009

Sturgeon Bay SD 1,300/PK-12
1230 Michigan St 54235 920-746-2800
Joe Stutting, supt. Fax 746-3888
www.sturbay.k12.wi.us
Sturgeon Bay HS 500/9-12
1230 Michigan St 54235 920-746-2800
Robert Nickel, prin. Fax 746-3888
Walker MS 300/6-8
19 N 14th Ave 54235 920-746-2810
Randy Watermolen, prin. Fax 746-3885

Northeast Wisconsin Technical College Post-Sec.
229 N 14th Ave 54235 920-743-2207

Sun Prairie, Dane, Pop. 25,392
Sun Prairie Area SD 5,500/PK-12
501 S Bird St 53590 608-834-6500
Tim Culver, supt. Fax 837-9311
www.spasd.k12.wi.us
Marsh MS 600/6-8
1351 Columbus St 53590 608-834-7600
Clark Luessman, prin. Fax 834-7692
Prairie View MS 600/6-8
400 N Thompson Rd 53590 608-834-7800
Nancy Hery, prin. Fax 834-7892
Sun Prairie HS 1,600/9-12
220 Kroncke Dr 53590 608-834-6700
Paul Keats, prin. Fax 834-6792

Diesel Truck Driver Training School Post-Sec.
7190 Elder Ln 53590 608-837-7800

Superior, Douglas, Pop. 26,779
Superior SD 4,800/PK-12
3025 Tower Ave 54880 715-394-8700
Jay Mitchell, supt. Fax 394-8708
www.superior.k12.wi.us
Superior HS 1,600/9-12
2600 Catlin Ave 54880 715-394-8720
Kent Bergum, prin. Fax 394-8760
Superior MS 1,100/6-8
3626 Hammond Ave 54880 715-394-8740
Richard Flaherty, prin. Fax 395-8483

Maranatha Academy 100/PK-12
4916 S State Road 35 54880 715-399-8757
Rosemary Niebauer, admin. Fax 399-0496
University of Wisconsin Post-Sec.
PO Box 2000 54880 715-394-8101

Suring, Oconto, Pop. 563
Suring SD 500/PK-12
PO Box 158 54174 920-842-2178
Todd Carlson, supt. Fax 842-4570
www.suring.k12.wi.us
Suring HS 200/9-12
PO Box 158 54174 920-842-2182
Robert Ray, prin. Fax 842-4570

Sussex, Waukesha, Pop. 9,812
Hamilton SD 3,900/K-12
W220N6151 Town Line Rd 53089 262-246-1973
Dr. Kathleen Cooke, supt. Fax 246-6552
www.hamiltondist.k12.wi.us/
Hamilton HS 1,200/9-12
W220N6151 Town Line Rd 53089 262-246-6471
Candis Morgan, prin. Fax 246-1885
Templeton MS 900/6-8
N59W22490 Silver Spring Dr 53089 262-246-6477
Patricia Polczynski, prin. Fax 246-0465

Richmond SD 400/PK-8
N56W26530 Richmond Rd 53089 262-538-1360
George Zimmer, supt. Fax 538-1572
www.richmond.k12.wi.us
Richmond MS 200/5-8
N56W26530 Richmond Rd 53089 262-538-1360
George Zimmer, prin. Fax 538-1572

Thorp, Clark, Pop. 1,554
Thorp SD 600/PK-12
PO Box 449 54771 715-669-5401
Barkley Anderson, admin. Fax 669-5403
www.thorp.k12.wi.us/
Thorp HS 200/9-12
PO Box 449 54771 715-669-5401
James Montgomery, prin. Fax 669-5403

Three Lakes, Oneida
Three Lakes SD 700/PK-12
6930 W School St 54562 715-546-3496
George Karling, supt. Fax 546-8125
www.threelakessd.k12.wi.us
Three Lakes HS 300/9-12
6930 W School St 54562 715-546-3321
William Greb, prin. Fax 546-2828
Three Lakes JHS 100/7-8
6930 W School St 54562 715-546-3321
William Greb, prin. Fax 546-2828

Tigerton, Shawano, Pop. 744
Tigerton SD 400/PK-12
PO Box 10 54486 715-535-4000
Nicholas Alioto, admin. Fax 535-3215
www.tigerton.k12.wi.us
Tigerton MSHS 200/6-12
PO Box 40 54486 715-535-4000
Donald Aanonsen, prin. Fax 535-1355

Tomah, Monroe, Pop. 8,620
Tomah Area SD 3,000/PK-12
129 W Clifton St 54660 608-374-7004
Robert T. Fasbender, supt. Fax 372-5087
www.tomah.k12.wi.us
Tomah HS 1,100/9-12
901 Lincoln Ave 54660 608-374-7358
Marlon Mee, prin. Fax 374-7290
Tomah MS 600/6-8
612 Hollister Ave 54660 608-374-7882
Cindy Zahrte, prin. Fax 374-7303

Tomahawk, Lincoln, Pop. 3,829
Tomahawk SD 1,600/PK-12
1048 E King Rd 54487 715-453-5551
Allan Prosser, supt. Fax 453-1855
www.tomahawk.k12.wi.us
Tomahawk HS 600/9-12
1048 E King Rd 54487 715-453-2106
Scott Swenty, prin. Fax 453-1437
Tomahawk MS 400/6-8
1048 E King Rd 54487 715-453-5371
Tom Freude, prin. Fax 453-9630

Tony, Rusk, Pop. 97
Flambeau SD 300/PK-12
PO Box 86 54563 715-532-3183
William Pfalzgraf, supt. Fax 532-5405
www.flambeau.k12.wi.us
Flambeau S 300/PK-12
PO Box 86 54563 715-532-3183
Linda Michek, prin. Fax 532-5405

Trempealeau, Trempealeau, Pop. 1,459
Galesville-Ettrick-Trempealeau SD
Supt. — See Galesville
Gale-Ettrick-Tremp MS 50/7-8
PO Box 277 54661 608-534-6391
Paul Uhren, prin. Fax 534-6395

Turtle Lake, Barron, Pop. 1,008
Turtle Lake SD 500/PK-12
205 Oak St 54889 715-986-2597
Charles Dunlop, supt. Fax 986-2444
www.cesa11.k12.wi.us/turtle-lake
Turtle Lake HS 200/9-12
205 Oak St 54889 715-986-4470
Wayne Olson, prin. Fax 986-2444

Two Rivers, Manitowoc, Pop. 12,144
Two Rivers SD 1,900/PK-12
4521 Lincoln Ave 54241 920-793-4560
Randy Fredrikson, supt. Fax 793-4014
www.trschools.k12.wi.us
Clarke MS 500/6-8
4608 Bellevue Pl 54241 920-794-1614
Stanley Phelps, prin. Fax 793-1819
Two Rivers HS 700/9-12
4519 Lincoln Ave 54241 920-793-2291
Ridge Schott, prin. Fax 793-5068

Union Grove, Racine, Pop. 4,614
Union Grove UNHSD 700/9-12
3433 S Colony Ave 53182 262-878-4427
David Magar, supt. Fax 878-3291
www.ug.k12.wi.us
Union Grove HS 700/9-12
3433 S Colony Ave 53182 262-878-2434
Alan Mollerskov, prin. Fax 878-4056

Union Grove Christian S 200/PK-12
PO Box 87 53182 262-878-1264
Lee Morey, prin. Fax 878-2085

Valders, Manitowoc, Pop. 995
Valders Area SD 1,100/PK-12
138 Wilson St 54245 920-775-9500
Thomas Hughes, supt. Fax 775-9509
www.valders.k12.wi.us
Valders HS 400/9-12
201 W Wilson St 54245 920-775-9530
Richard Druschke, prin. Fax 775-9509
Valders MS 400/5-8
138 Jefferson St 54245 920-775-9520
Derrick Krey, prin. Fax 775-9509

Verona, Dane, Pop. 10,166
Verona Area SD 3,700/PK-12
700 N Main St 53593 608-845-4300
Dean Gorrell, supt. Fax 845-4321
www.verona.k12.wi.us
Badger Ridge MS 500/6-8
740 N Main St 53593 608-845-4100
David Jennings, prin. Fax 845-4120
Verona Area HS 1,400/9-12
300 Richard St 53593 608-845-4400
Kelly Meyers, prin. Fax 845-4420
Other Schools – See Fitchburg

Viola, Richland, Pop. 659
Kickapoo Area SD 500/PK-12
S6520 State Highway 131 54664 608-627-0102
Thomas Simonson, supt. Fax 627-0118
www.kickapoo.k12.wi.us
Kickapoo MSHS 300/6-12
S6520 State Highway 131 54664 608-627-0100
Keith Rocklewitz, prin. Fax 627-0132

Viroqua, Vernon, Pop. 4,424
Viroqua Area SD 1,200/PK-12
115 N Education Ave 54665 608-637-1186
David Johnston, supt. Fax 637-8554
www.viroqua.k12.wi.us
Viroqua HS 400/9-12
100 Blackhawk Dr 54665 608-637-3191
Katherine Klos, prin. Fax 637-8034
Viroqua MS 300/5-8
100 Blackhawk Dr 54665 608-637-3171
Katherine Klos, prin. Fax 637-1589

Cornerstone Christian Academy 100/PK-12
S3656 US Highway 14 54665 608-634-4102
Craig Skrede, admin. Fax 634-4162

Wabeno, Forest
Wabeno Area SD 600/PK-12
PO Box 460 54566 715-473-2592
Kimberly Odekirk, supt. Fax 473-5201
www.wabeno.k12.wi.us
Wabeno JSHS 300/7-12
PO Box 460 54566 715-473-5122
Timothy Brauer, prin. Fax 473-3406

Wales, Waukesha, Pop. 2,610
Kettle Moraine SD 4,400/PK-12
563 A J Allen Cir 53183 262-968-6330
Patricia Deklotz, supt. Fax 968-6391
www.kmsd.edu/
Kettle Moraine HS 1,500/9-12
349 N Oak Crest Dr 53183 262-968-6200
Tanya Kotlowski, prin. Fax 968-6217
Other Schools – See Dousman

Walworth, Walworth, Pop. 2,682
Big Foot UNHSD 600/9-12
PO Box 99 53184 262-275-2116
Thomas Nykl, supt. Fax 275-5117
www.bigfoot.k12.wi.us
Big Foot Union HS 600/9-12
PO Box 99 53184 262-275-2116
Michael Hinske, prin. Fax 275-5117

Washburn, Bayfield, Pop. 2,281
Washburn SD 700/PK-12
PO Box 730 54891 715-373-6187
Gerald Eichman, supt. Fax 373-5877
www.washburn.k12.wi.us
Dupont MS 100/7-8
PO Box 730 54891 715-373-6188
Todd Lindstrom, prin. Fax 373-0535
Washburn HS 300/9-12
PO Box 730 54891 715-373-6188
Todd Lindstrom, prin. Fax 373-0535

Washington Island, Door
Washington SD 100/K-12
888 Main Rd 54246 920-847-2507
Susan Churchill-Chastan, supt. Fax 847-2865
www.island.k12.wi.us
Washington Island HS 50/9-12
888 Main Rd 54246 920-847-2507
Susan Churchill-Chastan, prin. Fax 847-2865

Waterford, Racine, Pop. 4,828
Waterford J1 SD 1,500/K-8
819 W Main St 53185 262-514-8250
Gwen O'Cull, supt. Fax 514-8251
www.waterford.k12.wi.us
Fox River MS 400/7-8
921 W Main St 53185 262-514-8240
Darlene Markle, prin. Fax 514-8241

Waterford UNHSD 100/9-12
507 W Main St 53185 262-534-9059
Keith Brandstetter, supt. Fax 534-6871
www.waterforduhs.k12.wi.us
Waterford Union HS 100/9-12
100 Field Dr 53185 262-534-3189
Erik Blake, prin. Fax 534-4971

Waterloo, Jefferson, Pop. 3,282
Waterloo SD 800/PK-12
813 N Monroe St 53594 920-478-3633
Connie L. Schiestl, supt. Fax 478-3821
waterloo.k12.wi.us
Waterloo HS 300/9-12
865 N Monroe St 53594 920-478-2171
Brad Donner, prin. Fax 478-9539
Waterloo MS 100/5-8
865 N Monroe St 53594 920-478-2696
Ann Kox, prin. Fax 478-3987

Watertown, Jefferson, Pop. 22,816
Watertown Unified SD 3,700/PK-12
111 Dodge St 53094 920-262-1460
Douglas W. Keiser Ph.D., supt. Fax 262-1469
www.watertown.k12.wi.us
Riverside MS 800/6-8
131 Hall St 53094 920-262-1480
Kent Jacobson, prin. Fax 262-1468
Watertown HS 1,400/9-12
825 Endevour Dr 53098 920-262-7500
Scott Bostwick, prin. Fax 262-7545

Luther Preparatory S 400/9-12
1300 Western Ave 53094 920-261-4352
Rev. Mark Schroeder, prin. Fax 262-8118
Madison Area Technical College Post-Sec.
1300 W Main St 53098 920-261-3303
Maranatha Baptist Bible College Post-Sec.
745 W Main St 53094 920-261-9300

Waukesha, Waukesha, Pop. 67,658
Waukesha SD 12,900/PK-12
222 Maple Ave 53186 262-970-1000
David S. Schmidt, supt. Fax 970-1021
www.waukesha.k12.wi.us
Butler MS 700/7-8
310 N Hine Ave 53188 262-970-2900
Michael Bralick, prin. Fax 970-2920
Central MS 600/7-8
400 N Grand Ave 53186 262-970-3100
Jeff Copson, prin. Fax 970-3120
Horning MS 600/7-8
2000 Wolf Rd 53186 262-970-3300
Dana Monogue, prin. Fax 970-3320
North HS 1,300/9-12
2222 Michigan Ave 53188 262-970-3500
Ryan Champeau, prin. Fax 970-3520
South HS 1,500/9-12
401 E Roberta Ave 53186 262-970-3705
Mark Hansen, prin. Fax 970-3720
West HS 1,500/9-12
3301 Saylesville Rd 53189 262-970-3900
Doug Straus, prin. Fax 970-3920

Carroll College Post-Sec.
100 N East Ave 53186 262-547-1211
Catholic Memorial HS 800/9-12
601 E College Ave 53186 262-542-7101
Dr. Kathleen Cepelka, prin. Fax 542-1633
Keller Graduate School Post-Sec.
20935 Swenson Dr Ste 450 53186 262-798-9889
St. Joseph MS 200/6-8
818 N East Ave 53186 262-896-2930
Kathy Rempe, prin. Fax 896-2935
University of Wisconsin Waukesha Post-Sec.
1500 N University Dr 53188 262-521-5200
Waukesha Christian Academy 100/K-12
PO Box 31 53187 262-542-7766
Rev. Glen Teasdale, admin. Fax 542-4171

Waunakee, Dane, Pop. 10,360
Waunakee Community SD 3,100/PK-12
101 School Dr 53597 608-849-2000
Chuck Pursell, supt. Fax 849-9746
www.waunakee.k12.wi.us
Waunakee HS 1,000/9-12
100 School Dr 53597 608-849-2100
Brian Kersten, prin. Fax 849-2164
Waunakee MS 500/7-8
1001 South St 53597 608-849-2060
Shelley Weiss, prin. Fax 849-2088

Madison Country Day S 300/PK-12
5606 River Rd 53597 608-850-6000
Adam de Pencier, admin. Fax 850-6006

Waupaca, Waupaca, Pop. 5,877
Waupaca SD 2,300/K-12
515 School St 54981 715-258-4121
David Poeschl, supt. Fax 258-4125
www.wsd.waupaca.k12.wi.us
Waupaca HS 800/9-12
E2325 King Rd 54981 715-258-4131
John Erspamer, prin. Fax 258-4135
Waupaca MS 600/6-8
1149 Shoemaker Rd 54981 715-258-4140
Wayne Verdon, prin. Fax 256-5681

Waupun, Dodge, Pop. 10,558
Waupun SD 2,200/PK-12
950 Wilcox St 53963 920-324-9341
John Zegers, supt. Fax 324-2630
www.waupun.k12.wi.us
Waupun HS 700/9-12
801 E Lincoln St 53963 920-324-5591
Jeff Finstad, prin. Fax 324-6980
Waupun MS 500/6-8
451 E Spring St 53963 920-324-9322
Delnice Hill, prin. Fax 324-2929

Central Wisconsin Christian HS 200/6-12
301 Fox Lake Rd 53963 920-324-4233
Ron Halma, prin. Fax 324-5036

Wausau, Marathon, Pop. 37,292
Wausau SD 8,700/PK-12
PO Box 359 54402 715-261-0505
Stephen Murley, supt. Fax 261-2503
www.wausau.k12.wi.us
Mann MS 900/6-8
3101 N 13th St 54403 715-261-0725
Ty Becker, prin. Fax 261-2035
Muir MS 1,100/6-8
1400 Stewart Ave 54401 715-261-0100
Dean Hess, prin. Fax 261-2461
Wausau East HS 1,300/9-12
2607 N 18th St 54403 715-261-0650
Bradley Peck, prin. Fax 261-3600
Wausau West HS 1,700/9-12
1200 W Wausau Ave 54401 715-261-0850
Joy Trollop, prin. Fax 261-3260

Faith Christian Academy 100/K-12
E1045 County Road J 54403 715-842-0797
Teresa Stine, admin. Fax 842-0797
Newman Catholic HS 200/9-12
1130 W Bridge St 54401 715-845-8274
Lawrence Theiss, prin. Fax 842-1302
Newman Catholic MS at St. Matthew 200/6-8
225 S 28th Ave 54401 715-842-4857
Tina Meyer, prin. Fax 845-2937
Northcentral Technical College Post-Sec.
1000 W Campus Dr 54401 715-675-3331
State College of Beauty Culture Post-Sec.
1930 Grand Ave 54403 715-849-5368
University of Wisconsin Marathon County Post-Sec.
518 S 7th Ave 54401 715-845-9602
Wausau Hospital Center Post-Sec.
333 Pine Ridge Blvd 54401 715-847-2117

Wausaukee, Marinette, Pop. 551
Wausaukee SD 700/PK-12
PO Box 258 54177 715-856-5153
Robert Werley, supt. Fax 856-6592
www.wausaukee.k12.wi.us
Wausaukee HS 200/9-12
PO Box 258 54177 715-856-5151
Pamela Beach, prin. Fax 856-6592
Wausaukee JHS 100/7-8
PO Box 258 54177 715-856-5151
Pamela Beach, prin. Fax 856-6592

Wautoma, Waushara, Pop. 2,103
Wautoma Area SD 1,500/PK-12
PO Box 870 54982 920-787-7112
Jeff Kasuboski, supt. Fax 787-1389
www.wautoma.k12.wi.us
Parkside MS 500/4-8
PO Box 870 54982 920-787-4577
Tom Rheinheimer, prin. Fax 787-7336
Wautoma HS 500/9-12
PO Box 870 54982 920-787-3354
Carl Guden, prin. Fax 787-1513

Wauwatosa, Milwaukee, Pop. 45,014
Wauwatosa SD 6,400/PK-12
12121 W North Ave 53226 414-773-1000
Phil Ertl, supt. Fax 773-1019
www.wauwatosaschools.org
East HS 1,200/9-12
7500 Milwaukee Ave 53213 414-773-2000
Nick Hughes, prin. Fax 773-2020
Longfellow MS 800/6-8
7600 W North Ave 53213 414-773-2400
Dennis Mahony, prin. Fax 773-2420
West HS 700/9-12
11400 W Center St 53222 414-773-3000
Kristin Bowers, prin. Fax 773-3020
Whitman MS 600/6-8
11100 W Center St 53222 414-773-2600
Jeff Keranen, prin. Fax 773-2620

Wauzeka, Crawford, Pop. 765
Wauzeka-Steuben SD 200/PK-12
301 E Main St 53826 608-875-5311
Glen Denk, supt. Fax 875-5100
www.wauzeka.k12.wi.us
Wauzeka-Steuben S 200/PK-12
301 E Main St 53826 608-875-5311
Glen Denk, prin. Fax 875-5100

Webster, Burnett, Pop. 683
Webster SD 600/PK-12
PO Box 9 54893 715-866-4391
Jim Erickson, supt. Fax 866-4283
www.webster.k12.wi.us
Webster HS 200/7-12
7564 Alder St W 54893 715-866-4281
Tim Widiker, prin. Fax 866-4377

West Allis, Milwaukee, Pop. 58,798
West Allis SD 8,700/PK-12
9333 W Lincoln Ave 53227 414-604-3000
Kurt Wachholz, supt. Fax 546-5795
www.wawm.k12.wi.us
Central HS 1,700/9-12
8516 W Lincoln Ave 53227 414-604-3110
Jeff Nelson, prin. Fax 546-5536
Hale HS 1,400/9-12
11601 W Lincoln Ave 53227 414-604-3210
Kathleen MacDonald, prin. Fax 546-5734
Wright MS 800/7-8
9501 W Cleveland Ave 53227 414-604-3410
Joan Delaney, prin. Fax 546-5785
Other Schools – See West Milwaukee

Grace Christian Academy 200/PK-12
8420 W Beloit Rd 53227 414-327-4200
Cynthia Hummitzsch, admin. Fax 327-4386
Milwaukee Area Technical College Post-Sec.
1200 S 71st St 53214 414-476-3040

West Bend, Washington, Pop. 29,549
West Bend SD 6,400/K-12
735 S Main St 53095 262-335-5435
Dr. Patricia Herdrich, supt. Fax 335-5470
www.west-bend.k12.wi.us
Badger MS 500/6-8
710 S Main St 53095 262-335-5456
Ted Neitzke, prin. Fax 335-6187
East HS 1,300/9-12
1305 E Decorah Rd 53095 262-335-5532
Cassandra Schug, prin. Fax 335-8242
Silverbrook MS 600/6-8
120 N Silverbrook Dr 53095 262-335-5499
Jean Broadwater, prin. Fax 335-5610
West HS 1,200/9-12
1305 E Decorah Rd 53095 262-335-5587
Patrick Gardon, prin. Fax 335-8251

Moraine Park Technical College Post-Sec.
2151 N Main St 53090 262-334-3413
University of Wisconsin Center Post-Sec.
400 S University Dr 53095 262-335-5201

Westby, Vernon, Pop. 2,142
Westby Area SD 1,000/PK-12
206 West Ave S 54667 608-634-0101
Roy Green, supt. Fax 634-0118
westby.k12.wi.us
Westby HS 400/9-12
206 West Ave S 54667 608-634-3101
Ken Manning, prin. Fax 634-0123
Westby MS 300/5-8
206 West Ave S 54667 608-634-0200
Clarice Nestingen, prin. Fax 634-0218

Westfield, Marquette, Pop. 1,211
Westfield SD 1,300/PK-12
N7046 County Road CH 53964 608-296-2107
Roger Schmidt, supt. Fax 296-2938
www.westfield.k12.wi.us
Pioneer Westfield HS 400/9-12
N7046 County Road CH 53964 608-296-2141
Julia Ferris, prin. Fax 296-2293
Pioneer Westfield MS 200/7-8
N7046 County Road CH 53964 608-296-4721
Susan Porfilio, prin. Fax 296-4232

West Milwaukee, Milwaukee, Pop. 4,012
West Allis SD
Supt. — See West Allis
West Milwaukee MS 500/7-8
5104 W Greenfield Ave 53214 414-604-3310
Jeffrey Borland, prin. Fax 389-3815

West Salem, LaCrosse, Pop. 4,709
West Salem SD 1,600/PK-12
405 E Hamlin St 54669 608-786-0700
Eugene Ertz, supt. Fax 786-2960
www.wsalem.k12.wi.us
West Salem HS 500/9-12
405 E Hamlin St 54669 608-786-1220
Troy Gunderson, prin. Fax 786-1273
West Salem MS 400/6-8
450 N Mark St 54669 608-786-2090
Dean Buchanan, prin. Fax 786-1081

Coulee Region Christian S 200/PK-12
230 W Garland St 54669 608-786-3004
Marliss Katsma, supt. Fax 786-3005

Weyauwega, Waupaca, Pop. 1,772
Weyauwega-Fremont SD 1,100/PK-12
PO Box 580 54983 920-867-2148
F. James Harlan, supt. Fax 867-2510
www.wegafremont.k12.wi.us
Weyauwega HS 400/9-12
PO Box 580 54983 920-867-3191
Scott Bleck, prin. Fax 867-2510
Weyauwega MS 300/6-8
PO Box 580 54983 920-867-2148
Scott Bleck, prin. Fax 867-2510

Weyerhaeuser, Rusk, Pop. 331
Weyerhaeuser Area SD 200/K-12
402 N 2nd St 54895 715-353-2254
Barbara Lorkowski, supt. Fax 353-2288
www.fwsd.k12.wi.us
Weyerhaeuser HS 100/9-12
402 N 2nd St 54895 715-353-2254
Todd Solberg, prin. Fax 353-2288

Whitefish Bay, Milwaukee, Pop. 13,508
Whitefish Bay SD 2,200/PK-12
1200 E Fairmount Ave 53217 414-963-3921
James Rickabaugh, supt. Fax 963-3959
www.wfbschools.com
Whitefish Bay HS 700/9-12
1200 E Fairmount Ave 53217 414-963-3928
William Henkle, prin. Fax 963-3870
Whitefish Bay MS 500/6-8
1144 E Henry Clay St 53217 414-963-6800
Lisa Gies, prin. Fax 963-6808

Dominican HS 300/9-12
120 E Silver Spring Dr 53217 414-332-1170
Eamonn O'Keeffe, prin. Fax 332-4101

Whitehall, Trempealeau, Pop. 1,628
Whitehall SD 800/PK-12
PO Box 37 54773 715-538-4374
Michael Beighley, supt. Fax 538-4639
www.whitehallsd.k12.wi.us
Whitehall HS 200/9-12
PO Box 37 54773 715-538-4364
Susan Speltz, prin. Fax 538-4639
Whitehall MS 200/6-8
PO Box 37 54773 715-538-4364
Susan Speltz, prin. Fax 538-4639

White Lake, Langlade, Pop. 335
White Lake SD 200/K-12
PO Box 67 54491 715-882-8421
Doug Druse, supt. Fax 882-2914
www.whitelake.k12.wi.us
White Lake JSHS 100/7-12
PO Box 67 54491 715-882-2361
Doug Druse, prin. Fax 882-2914

Whitewater, Walworth, Pop. 14,311
Whitewater USD 2,000/K-12
419 S Elizabeth St 53190 262-472-8700
Leslie Steinhaus, supt. Fax 472-8710
www.wwusd.org
Whitewater HS 700/9-12
534 S Elizabeth St 53190 262-472-8100
Vance Dalzin, prin. Fax 472-8181
Whitewater MS 500/6-8
401 S Elizabeth St 53190 262-472-8300
Eric Runez, prin. Fax 472-8310

University of Wisconsin Post-Sec.
800 W Main St 53190 262-472-1234

Wild Rose, Waushara, Pop. 756
Wild Rose SD 700/PK-12
PO Box 276 54984 920-622-4203
Claude Olson, supt. Fax 622-4604
www.wildrose.k12.wi.us
Wild Rose MSHS 400/6-12
PO Box 276 54984 920-622-4201
Charles Schuessler, prin. Fax 622-4801

Williams Bay, Walworth, Pop. 2,668
Williams Bay SD 500/K-12
PO Box 259 53191 262-245-1575
Frederic C. Vorlop, supt. Fax 245-5877
www.williamsbay.k12.wi.us
Williams Bay HS 200/9-12
PO Box 259 53191 262-245-6224
Dan Bice, prin. Fax 245-5877
Williams Bay JHS 100/7-8
PO Box 259 53191 262-245-6224
Dan Bice, prin. Fax 245-5877

Faith Christian S 200/PK-12
PO Box 1230 53191 262-245-9404
Ted Caucutt, admin. Fax 245-0128

Wilmot, Kenosha
Wilmot UNHSD 1,100/9-12
PO Box 8 53192 262-862-2351
William Heitman, supt. Fax 862-6413
www.wilmothighschool.com
Wilmot HS 1,100/9-12
PO Box 8 53192 262-862-2351
Carl Breitlow, prin. Fax 862-6929

Winneconne, Winnebago, Pop. 2,445
Winneconne Community SD 1,600/PK-12
PO Box 5000 54986 920-582-5802
Robert Reinke, supt. Fax 582-5816
www.winneconne.k12.wi.us
Winneconne HS 500/9-12
PO Box 5000 54986 920-582-5810
James Smasal, prin. Fax 582-5813
Winneconne MS 400/6-8
PO Box 5000 54986 920-582-5800
Peggy Larson, prin. Fax 582-5812

Winter, Sawyer, Pop. 352
Winter SD 400/PK-12
PO Box 310 54896 715-266-3301
Stu Waller, admin. Fax 266-2216
www.winterk12.net/
Winter HS 100/9-12
PO Box 310 54896 715-266-3301
Timothy Kief, prin. Fax 266-2216
Winter MS 100/6-8
PO Box 310 54896 715-266-6701
Timothy Kief, prin. Fax 266-2216

Wisconsin Dells, Columbia, Pop. 2,559
Wisconsin Dells SD 1,700/PK-12
811 County Road H 53965 608-254-7769
Charles Whitsell, supt. Fax 254-8058
www.sdwd.k12.wi.us
Spring Hill MS 400/6-8
300 Vine St 53965 608-253-2468
Dan Wenkman, prin. Fax 254-6397
Wisconsin Dells HS 600/9-12
520 Race St 53965 608-253-1461
Randy Kuhnau, prin. Fax 254-6288

Wisconsin Rapids, Wood, Pop. 17,621
Wisconsin Rapids SD 5,400/PK-12
510 Peach St 54494 715-422-6000
Robert Crist, supt. Fax 422-6070
www.wrps.org
East JHS 800/7-9
311 Lincoln St 54494 715-422-6114
Kathi Stebbins-Hintz, prin. Fax 422-6270
Lincoln SHS 1,400/10-12
1801 16th St S 54494 715-423-1520
Thomas Mancuso, prin. Fax 422-6097
West JHS 600/7-9
1921 27th Ave S 54495 715-422-6200
Tracy Ginter, prin. Fax 422-6187

Assumption HS 200/9-12
445 Chestnut St 54494 715-422-0910
Thomas Reichenbacher, prin. Fax 422-0912
Assumption MS 100/7-8
440 Mead St 54494 715-422-0950
Joan Bond, prin. Fax 422-0955
Community Christian Academy 100/K-12
550 Center St 54494 715-423-0770
Cheryl Ver Hulst, admin. Fax 423-0779
Mid-State Technical College Post-Sec.
500 32nd St N 54494 715-422-5300

Wittenberg, Shawano, Pop. 1,123
Wittenberg-Birnamwood SD 1,300/K-12
400 W Grand Ave 54499 715-253-2213
David Bardo, supt. Fax 253-3588
www.wittbirn.k12.wi.us/
Wittenberg-Birnamwood HS 500/9-12
400 W Grand Ave 54499 715-253-2211
Craig Kaney, prin. Fax 253-3588

Wonewoc, Juneau, Pop. 802
Wonewoc-Union Center SD 400/PK-12
PO Box 368 53968 608-464-3165
Arthur Keenan, supt. Fax 464-3325
www.theclasslist.com/wcschools
Wonewoc HS 200/9-12
PO Box 368 53968 608-464-3165
Michelle Noll, prin. Fax 464-3325
Wonewoc JHS 100/7-8
PO Box 368 53968 608-464-3165
Michelle Noll, prin. Fax 464-3325

Woodville, Saint Croix, Pop. 1,276
Baldwin-Woodville Area SD
Supt. — See Baldwin
Viking MS 400/5-8
500 Southside Dr 54028 715-698-2456
Henry Dupuis, prin. Fax 698-3315

Wrightstown, Brown, Pop. 2,248
Wrightstown Community SD 1,100/K-12
PO Box 128 54180 920-532-5551
Carla Buboltz, supt. Fax 532-4664
www.wrightstown.k12.wi.us
Wrightstown HS 400/9-12
PO Box 128 54180 920-532-0525
Scott Thompson, prin. Fax 532-0860
Wrightstown MS 400/5-8
PO Box 128 54180 920-532-5553
Rich Schenkus, prin. Fax 532-3869

WYOMING

WYOMING DEPARTMENT OF EDUCATION
2300 Capitol Ave, Cheyenne 82001
Telephone 307-777-7673
Fax 307-777-6234
Website http://www.k12.wy.us

Superintendent of Public Instruction Jim McBride

WYOMING BOARD OF EDUCATION
2300 Capitol Ave, Cheyenne 82001

Chairperson Michelle Sullivan

BOARDS OF COOPERATIVE EDUCATIONAL SERVICES (BOCES)

Carbon Co. Higher Education Center BOCES
Joan Evans, dir. 307-328-9204
705 Rodeo St, Rawlins 82301 Fax 324-3338
www.cchec.org
Central Wyoming BOCES 307-577-0253
, 970 N Glenn Rd, Casper 82601 Fax 261-6109
Douglas BOCES
Connie Woehl, dir. 307-358-5622
203 N 6th St, Douglas 82633 Fax 358-5629
Fremont County BOCES
Sandy Barton, dir. 307-856-2028
320 W Main St, Riverton 82501 Fax 856-4058
www.fcboces.org

Mountain View & Lyman BOCES
Lana Hillstead, dir. 307-782-6401
PO Box 130, Mountain View 82939 Fax 782-7410
Northeast Wyoming BOCES
Julie Cudmore, dir. 307-682-0231
410 N Miller Ave, Gillette 82716 Fax 686-7628
www.new-boces.k12.wy.us/
Northwest Wyoming BOCES
Carolyn Connor, dir. 307-864-2171
PO Box 112, Thermopolis 82443 Fax 864-9463
www.nwboces.com/

Oyster Ridge BOCES
Michael Clark Ph.D., dir. 307-877-6958
PO Box 423, Kemmerer 83101 Fax 828-9040
www.kemmereroutreach.com
Region V BOCES
Dr. Dennis Donohue, dir. 307-733-8210
PO Box 240, Wilson 83014 Fax 733-8462
Sweetwater BOCES
Bernadine Craft Ph.D., dir. 307-382-1607
PO Box 428, Rock Springs 82902 Fax 382-1875
www.wwcc.wy.edu/boces/
Uinta BOCES
Michael Williams, dir. 307-789-5742
1013 W Cheyenne Dr Unit A Fax 789-7975
Evanston 82930

PUBLIC, PRIVATE AND CATHOLIC SECONDARY SCHOOLS

Afton, Lincoln, Pop. 1,831
Lincoln County SD 2 2,500/K-12
PO Box 219 83110 307-885-3811
Jon Abrams, supt. Fax 885-9562
www.lcsd2.org
Star Valley HS 700/9-12
PO Box 8000 83110 307-885-7847
Shannon Harris, prin. Fax 885-3299
Star Valley MS 400/7-8
PO Box 8001 83110 307-885-5208
Kem Cazier, prin. Fax 885-0472
Other Schools – See Cokeville

Baggs, Carbon, Pop. 354
Carbon County SD 1
Supt. — See Rawlins
Little Snake River Valley S 200/K-12
PO Box 9 82321 307-383-2185
Rick Newton, prin. Fax 383-2184

Basin, Big Horn, Pop. 1,224
Big Horn County SD 4 400/PK-12
PO Box 151 82410 307-568-2684
Ray Yoder, supt. Fax 568-2654
www.bgh4.k12.wy.us/
Riverside HS 100/9-12
PO Box 151 82410 307-568-2416
Tony Anson, prin. Fax 568-2415
Other Schools – See Manderson

Big Horn, Sheridan
Sheridan County SD 1
Supt. — See Ranchester
Big Horn HS 100/9-12
PO Box 490 82833 307-674-8190
George Mirich, prin. Fax 672-5306
Big Horn MS 100/6-8
PO Box 490 82833 307-674-8190
George Mirich, prin. Fax 672-5306

Big Piney, Sublette, Pop. 455
Sublette County SD 9 600/K-12
PO Box 769 83113 307-276-3322
B. Shelley, supt. Fax 276-3731
Big Piney HS 200/9-12
PO Box 769 83113 307-276-3324
Terry Statton, prin. Fax 276-3480
Big Piney MS, PO Box 769 83113 100/6-8
Gerry Chase, prin. 307-276-3315

Buffalo, Johnson, Pop. 4,290
Johnson County SD 1 1,100/K-12
601 W Lott St 82834 307-684-9571
Rod Kessler, supt. Fax 684-5182
www.jcsd1.k12.wy.us
Buffalo HS 400/9-12
326 S Burritt Ave 82834 307-684-2269
Kelly Hornby, prin. Fax 684-9481
Clear Creek MS 300/5-8
58 N Adams Ave 82834 307-684-5594
Troy Stone, prin. Fax 684-9096
Other Schools – See Kaycee

Burlington, Big Horn, Pop. 248
Big Horn County SD 1
Supt. — See Cowley
Burlington HS 100/9-12
PO Box 9 82411 307-762-3334
George Risberg, prin. Fax 762-3604
Burlington JHS 100/7-8
PO Box 9 82411 307-762-3334
George Risberg, prin. Fax 762-3604

Burns, Laramie, Pop. 310
Laramie County SD 2
Supt. — See Pine Bluffs
Burns JSHS 200/7-12
PO Box 160 82053 307-245-4100
Mike Brownawell, prin. Fax 547-3583

Byron, Big Horn, Pop. 548
Big Horn County SD 1
Supt. — See Cowley
Rocky Mountain HS 100/9-12
PO Box 176 82412 307-548-2723
Tim Winland, prin. Fax 548-6452

Casper, Natrona, Pop. 51,738
Natrona County SD 1 11,400/PK-12
970 N Glenn Rd 82601 307-577-0200
Jim Lowham Ed.D., supt. Fax 577-4422
www.natronaschools.org/
Casper Classical Academy 100/6-9
970 1/2 N Glenn Rd 82601 307-261-6181
Marie Puryear, prin. Fax 261-6184
Centennial JHS 800/6-9
1421 Waterford St 82609 307-577-4600
Valerie Braughton, prin. Fax 233-2891
CY JHS 600/6-9
2211 Essex Ave 82604 307-577-4474
Dean Braughton, prin. Fax 233-2683
Frontier MS 6-8
900 S Beverly St 82609 307-577-4400
Verba Echols, prin. Fax 233-2274
Morgan JHS 900/6-9
1440 S Elm St 82601 307-577-4440
Walter Wilcox, prin. Fax 233-2411
Natrona County SHS 1,400/10-12
930 S Elm St 82601 307-577-0330
Dean Kelly, prin. Fax 233-1507
Walsh HS 1,300/9-12
3500 E 12th St 82609 307-233-2000
Brad Diller, prin. Fax 233-2066
Other Schools – See Midwest

Casper College Post-Sec.
125 College Dr 82601 307-268-2110
Paradise Valley Christian S 100/PK-12
3041 Paradise Dr 82604 307-234-2450
C. Jeanne Boyd, admin. Fax 577-0763
Sage Technical School Post-Sec.
2368 Oil Dr 82604 307-234-0242
Wyoming School for the Deaf Post-Sec.
539 Payne Ave 82609

Cheyenne, Laramie, Pop. 55,731
Laramie County SD 1 12,500/K-12
2810 House Ave 82001 307-771-2100
Dan Stephan, supt. Fax 771-2364
www.laramie1.k12.wy.us
Carey JHS 1,100/7-9
1780 E Pershing Blvd 82001 307-771-2580
Evelyn Abbott, prin. Fax 771-2578
Central SHS 1,200/10-12
5500 Education Dr 82009 307-771-2680
Rick Porter, prin. Fax 771-2699
East SHS 1,500/10-12
2800 E Pershing Blvd 82001 307-771-2663
Sam Mirich, prin. Fax 771-2679
Johnson JHS 900/7-9
1236 W Allison Rd 82007 307-771-2640
Alice Hunter, prin. Fax 771-2660
McCormick JHS 1,200/7-9
6000 Education Dr 82009 307-771-2650
Jeff Conine, prin. Fax 771-2661

Cheeks Intl Academy of Beauty Culture Post-Sec.
207 W 18th St 82001 307-637-8700
Laramie County Community College Post-Sec.
1400 E College Dr 82007 307-778-5222
St. Mary S 300/PK-12
112 E 24th St 82001 307-638-9268
Carol Ricken, prin. Fax 635-2847

Chugwater, Platte, Pop. 231
Platte County SD 1
Supt. — See Wheatland
Chugwater HS 50/9-12
500 5th St 82210 307-422-3501
George Kopf, prin. Fax 422-3433
Chugwater JHS 50/7-8
1150 Pine 82210 307-422-3501
George Kopf, prin. Fax 422-3433

Clearmont, Sheridan, Pop. 117
Sheridan County SD 3 100/PK-12
PO Box 125 82835 307-758-4412
John Baule, supt. Fax 758-4444
Arvada-Clearmont HS 50/9-12
PO Box 125 82835 307-758-4412
Charles Auzqui, prin. Fax 758-4444
Arvada-Clearmont JHS 50/7-8
PO Box 125 82835 307-758-4412
Charles Auzqui, prin. Fax 758-4444

Cody, Park, Pop. 9,100
Park County SD 6 2,200/K-12
919 Cody Ave 82414 307-587-4253
Bryan Monteith, supt. Fax 527-5762
www.park6.org/
Cody HS 800/9-12
919 Cody Ave 82414 307-587-4251
Dave Treick, prin. Fax 587-9369
Cody MS 500/6-8
919 Cody Ave 82414 307-587-4273
Larry Gerber, prin. Fax 587-3547

West Park Hospital Post-Sec.
707 Sheridan Ave 82414 307-527-7501

Cokeville, Lincoln, Pop. 492
Lincoln County SD 2
Supt. — See Afton

Cokeville JSHS 100/7-12
PO Box 220 83114 307-279-3273
Keith Harris, prin. Fax 279-3221

Cowley, Big Horn, Pop. 582
Big Horn County SD 1 600/PK-12
PO Box 688 82420 307-548-2254
Kevin Mitchell, supt. Fax 548-7610
bighorn1.bgh1.k12.wy.us/
Other Schools – See Burlington, Byron, Deaver

Dayton, Sheridan, Pop. 717
Sheridan County SD 1
Supt. — See Ranchester
Tongue River HS 200/9-12
PO Box 408 82836 307-655-2236
Don White, prin. Fax 655-9798

Deaver, Big Horn, Pop. 177
Big Horn County SD 1
Supt. — See Cowley
Rocky Mountain MS 100/6-8
PO Box 185 82421 307-664-2252
Teresa Staab, prin. Fax 664-2314

Diamondville, Lincoln, Pop. 695
Lincoln County SD 1 600/K-12
PO Box 335 83116 307-877-9095
Gene Carmody, supt. Fax 877-9638
www.lcsd1.k12.wy.us
Other Schools – See Kemmerer

Douglas, Converse, Pop. 5,581
Converse County SD 1 1,600/K-12
615 Hamilton St 82633 307-358-2942
Dan Espeland, supt. Fax 358-3934
www.ccsd1.k12.wy.us
Douglas HS 600/9-12
615 Hamilton St 82633 307-358-2940
John Weigel, prin. Fax 358-2737
Douglas MS 400/6-8
615 Hamilton St 82633 307-358-9771
Fred George, prin. Fax 358-5315

Dubois, Fremont, Pop. 991
Fremont County SD 2 200/K-12
PO Box 188 82513 307-455-2323
Susan Kinneman, supt. Fax 455-2178
rams.fremont2.k12.wy.us/
Dubois HS 100/9-12
PO Box 188 82513 307-455-2279
Brad Moon, prin. Fax 455-2178

Encampment, Carbon, Pop. 462
Carbon County SD 2
Supt. — See Saratoga
Encampment S 100/K-12
PO Box 277 82325 307-327-5442
Mike Erickson, prin. Fax 327-5142

Ethete, Fremont, Pop. 1,059
Fremont County SD 14 600/PK-12
638 Blue Sky Hwy 82520 307-332-3904
Michelle Hoffman, supt. Fax 332-7567
www.fremont14.k12.wy.us
Wyoming Indian HS 100/9-12
636 Blue Sky Hwy 82520 307-332-9765
Phil Garhart, prin. Fax 335-7739
Wyoming Indian MS 200/6-8
535 Ethete Rd 82520 307-332-2992
Pam Frederick, prin. Fax 335-7318

Evanston, Uinta, Pop. 11,459
Uinta County SD 1 2,900/K-12
PO Box 6002 82931 307-789-7571
Dennis Wilson, supt. Fax 789-6225
www.uinta1.k12.wy.us
Davis MS 300/6-8
PO Box 6002 82931 307-789-8096
Jim Harrell, prin. Fax 789-3386
Evanston HS 900/9-12
PO Box 6002 82931 307-789-0757
Jeffrey Harrah, prin. Fax 789-7447
Evanston MS 300/6-8
PO Box 6002 82931 307-789-5499
Monique Flickinger, prin. Fax 789-7972

Farson, Sweetwater
Sweetwater County SD 1
Supt. — See Rock Springs
Farson-Eden HS 100/9-12
PO Box 400 82932 307-273-9301
Gregory Lasley, prin. Fax 273-9313
Farson-Eden MS 50/6-8
PO Box 400 82932 307-273-9301
Gregory Lasley, prin. Fax 273-9313

Fort Washakie, Fremont, Pop. 1,334
Fremont County SD 21 300/PK-8
90 Ethete Rd 82514 307-332-3648
Patricia Baker-Benally, supt. Fax 332-7267
Fort Washakie MS 100/7-8
90 Ethete Rd 82514 307-332-2380
Mike Helenbolt, prin. Fax 332-3597

Gillette, Campbell, Pop. 22,685
Campbell County SD 1 7,200/K-12
PO Box 3033 82717 307-682-5171
Dr. Richard Strahorn, supt. Fax 682-6619
www.ccsd.k12.wy.us
Campbell County HS 1,500/10-12
1000 Camel Dr 82716 307-682-7247
Larry Steiger, prin. Fax 687-0032
Sage Valley JHS 700/7-9
1000 W Lakeway Rd 82718 307-682-2225
Alex Ayers, prin. Fax 687-7614
Twin Spruce JHS 800/7-9
100 E 7th St 82716 307-682-3144
Dave Foreman, prin. Fax 686-1969
Other Schools – See Wright

Heritage Christian S 100/PK-12
510 Wall Street Ct 82718 307-686-1392
Brent Potthoff, admin. Fax 682-6515
Northern Wyoming Community College Post-Sec.
300 W Sinclair St 82718 307-686-0254

Glendo, Platte, Pop. 229
Platte County SD 1
Supt. — See Wheatland
Glendo HS 50/9-12
305 Paige St 82213 307-735-4471
Stanetta Twiford, prin. Fax 735-4220
Glendo JHS 50/7-8
305 Paige St 82213 307-735-4471
Stanetta Twiford, prin. Fax 735-4220

Glenrock, Converse, Pop. 2,351
Converse County SD 2 600/K-12
PO Box 1300 82637 307-436-5331
Kirk Hughes, supt. Fax 436-8235
www.cnv2.k12.wy.us/
Glenrock HS 200/9-12
PO Box 1300 82637 307-436-9201
Christopher Gray, prin. Fax 436-8517
Glenrock MS 100/5-8
PO Box 1300 82637 307-436-9258
Tobey Cass, prin. Fax 436-7507

Green River, Sweetwater, Pop. 11,787
Sweetwater County SD 2 2,400/K-12
320 Monroe Ave 82935 307-872-5500
Barbara VanMatre, supt. Fax 872-5518
www.sw2.k12.wy.us
Expedition Academy 100/10-12
351 Monroe Ave 82935 307-872-4800
Harry Petty, prin. Fax 872-4797
Green River HS 800/9-12
1615 Hitching Post Dr 82935 307-872-4747
Brad Madison, prin. Fax 872-4758
Lincoln MS 400/7-8
350 Monroe Ave 82935 307-872-4400
Clay Cates, prin. Fax 872-4477

Greybull, Big Horn, Pop. 1,752
Big Horn County SD 3 500/PK-12
636 14th Ave N 82426 307-765-4756
Craig Sorensen, supt. Fax 765-4617
Greybull HS 200/9-12
600 N 6th St 82426 307-765-2537
Fax 765-2870
Greybull MS 100/6-8
640 8th Ave N 82426 307-765-4492
Kris Cundall, prin. Fax 765-2833

Guernsey, Platte, Pop. 1,118
Platte County SD 2 200/K-12
PO Box 189 82214 307-836-2735
Dave Barker, supt. Fax 836-2450
www.plt2.k12.wy.us
Guernsey-Sunrise HS 100/9-12
PO Box 189 82214 307-836-2745
Ken Griffith, prin. Fax 836-2729
Guernsey-Sunrise JHS 100/7-8
PO Box 189 82214 307-836-2745
Ken Griffith, prin. Fax 836-2729

Hanna, Carbon, Pop. 863
Carbon County SD 2
Supt. — See Saratoga
Hanna-Elk Mountain-Medicine Bow JSHS 100/7-12
PO Box 810 82327 307-325-6545
Brad Barlow, prin. Fax 325-9223

Hulett, Crook, Pop. 429
Crook County SD 1
Supt. — See Sundance
Hulett S 100/K-12
PO Box 127 82720 307-467-5231
Fax 467-5280

Jackson, Teton, Pop. 9,038
Teton County SD 1 2,300/K-12
PO Box 568 83001 307-733-2704
Pam Shea, supt. Fax 733-6443
www.tcsd.org/
Jackson Hole HS 700/9-12
PO Box 568 83025 307-732-3700
Dr. Gary Elliott, prin. Fax 732-3720
Jackson Hole MS 500/6-8
PO Box 568 83025 307-733-4234
Jean Coldsmith, prin. Fax 733-4254
Summit HS 100/9-12
PO Box 568 83025 307-733-9116
Jim Rooks, prin. Fax 739-8922

Kaycee, Johnson, Pop. 273
Johnson County SD 1
Supt. — See Buffalo
Kaycee JSHS 50/7-12
PO Box 6 82639 307-738-2323
Lana Latta, prin. Fax 738-2496

Kemmerer, Lincoln, Pop. 2,560
Lincoln County SD 1
Supt. — See Diamondville
Kemmerer HS 200/9-12
1525 3rd West Ave 83101 307-877-6991
Orlen Zempel, prin. Fax 877-4117
Kemmerer MS 200/5-8
1310 Antelope St 83101 307-877-2286
Gene Carmody, prin. Fax 877-3365

Lander, Fremont, Pop. 6,898
Fremont County SD 1 1,800/K-12
400 Baldwin Creek Rd 82520 307-332-4711
Paige Fenton-Hughes, supt. Fax 332-6671
www.fcsd1.com
Lander Valley HS 600/9-12
350 Baldwin Creek Rd 82520 307-332-4433
Shaun Nicklas, prin. Fax 332-2861

Starrett JHS 300/7-8
863 Sweetwater St 82520 307-332-4040
Brian Janish, prin. Fax 332-0435

Wyoming State Training School Post-Sec.
8204 Wyoming Highway 789 82520 307-332-5302

Laramie, Albany, Pop. 26,050
Albany County SD 1 3,500/PK-12
1948 E Grand Ave 82070 307-721-4400
Dr. Brian Recht, supt. Fax 721-4408
www.ac1.k12.wy.us
Laramie JHS 700/7-9
1355 N 22nd St 82072 307-721-4430
Steve Hoff, prin. Fax 721-4435
Laramie SHS 700/10-12
1275 N 11th St 82072 307-721-4420
Kim Sorenson, prin. Fax 721-4419
Other Schools – See Rock River

University of Wyoming Post-Sec.
PO Box 3435 82071 307-766-1121
Wyoming Technical Institute Post-Sec.
4373 N 3rd St 82072 307-742-3776

Lingle, Goshen, Pop. 490
Goshen County SD 1
Supt. — See Torrington
Lingle-Ft. Laramie HS 100/9-12
PO Box 379 82223 307-837-2296
Ty Flock, prin. Fax 837-3025
Lingle-Fort Laramie MS 100/6-8
PO Box 379 82223 307-837-2283
Ty Flock, prin. Fax 837-2057

Lovell, Big Horn, Pop. 2,277
Big Horn County SD 2 700/K-12
502 Hampshire Ave 82431 307-548-2259
Dan Coe, supt. Fax 548-7555
www.bgh2.k12.wy.us/
Lovell HS 200/9-12
502 Hampshire Ave 82431 307-548-2256
Scott O'Tremba, prin. Fax 548-9452
Lovell MS 100/6-8
325 W 9th St 82431 307-548-6553
Sherie Monk, prin. Fax 548-6136

Lusk, Niobrara, Pop. 1,348
Niobrara County SD 1 200/K-12
PO Box 629 82225 307-334-3793
Richard Luchsinger, supt. Fax 334-0126
www.lusk.k12.wy.us/
Niobrara County HS 100/9-12
PO Box 1050 82225 307-334-3320
Joe Tully, prin. Fax 334-2331

Lyman, Uinta, Pop. 1,937
Uinta County SD 6 600/K-12
PO Box 1090 82937 307-786-4100
Randy Hillstead, supt. Fax 787-3241
www.uinta6.k12.wy.us/
Lyman HS 200/9-12
PO Box 1090 82937 307-787-6197
Todd Limoges, prin. Fax 787-6193
Lyman MS, PO Box 1090 82937 200/6-8
Christy Campbell, prin. 307-786-4608

Manderson, Big Horn, Pop. 101
Big Horn County SD 4
Supt. — See Basin
Cloud Peak MS 100/6-8
PO Box 97 82432 307-568-2846
Becky Allred, prin. Fax 568-3885

Meeteetse, Park, Pop. 347
Park County SD 16 100/K-12
PO Box 218 82433 307-868-2501
Robert Lewandowski, supt. Fax 868-9264
www.park16.k12.wy.us/
Meeteetse S 100/K-12
PO Box 218 82433 307-868-2501
Rick Edwards, prin. Fax 868-9264

Midwest, Natrona, Pop. 431
Natrona County SD 1
Supt. — See Casper
Midwest S 200/PK-12
PO Box 368 82643 307-437-6545
Bruce Youngquist, prin. Fax 437-6820

Moorcroft, Crook, Pop. 845
Crook County SD 1
Supt. — See Sundance
Moorcroft JSHS 200/7-12
PO Box 129 82721 307-756-3446
John Cook, prin. Fax 756-3724

Mountain View, Uinta, Pop. 1,163
Uinta County SD 4 600/K-12
PO Box 130 82939 307-782-3377
Jack Cozort, supt. Fax 782-6879
www.uinta4.k12.wy.us/
Mountain View HS 200/9-12
PO Box 130 82939 307-782-6340
Jeffrey Newton, prin. Fax 782-6967
Mountain View MS 100/6-8
PO Box 130 82939 307-782-6338
Kim Dolezal, prin. Fax 782-6876

Newcastle, Weston, Pop. 3,221
Weston County SD 1 800/K-12
116 Casper Ave 82701 307-746-4451
Brad LaCroix, supt. Fax 746-3289
www.weston1.k12.wy.us
Newcastle HS 300/9-12
116 Casper Ave 82701 307-746-2713
Tracy Ragland, prin. Fax 746-2350
Newcastle MS 200/6-8
116 Casper Ave 82701 307-746-2746
Scott Shoop, prin. Fax 746-4983

Pavillion, Fremont, Pop. 164
Fremont County SD 6 — 400/PK-12
PO Box 10 82523 — 307-856-7970
Diana Clapp, supt. — Fax 856-3385
www.fre6.k12.wy.us/
Wind River MSHS — 200/6-12
PO Box 10 82523 — 307-856-6327
Troy Lurz, prin. — Fax 856-4248

Pine Bluffs, Laramie, Pop. 1,162
Laramie County SD 2 — 900/K-12
PO Box 489 82082 — 307-245-4050
Margie Simineo, supt. — Fax 245-3561
web.lrm2.k12.wy.us/
Pine Bluffs JSHS — 200/7-12
PO Box 520 82082 — 307-245-4000
John Binning, prin. — Fax 245-3144
Other Schools – See Burns

Pinedale, Sublette, Pop. 1,658
Sublette County SD 1 — 700/K-12
PO Box 549 82941 — 307-367-2139
Charles Grove, supt. — Fax 367-4626
www.pinedaleschools.org/
Pinedale HS — 200/9-12
PO Box 549 82941 — 307-367-2137
Richard Kennedy, prin. — Fax 367-2611
Pinedale MS — 200/6-8
PO Box 549 82941 — 307-367-2821
Mike Vassallo, prin. — Fax 367-4217

Powell, Park, Pop. 5,288
Park County SD 1 — 1,600/K-12
160 N Evarts St 82435 — 307-754-2215
Jerry Maurer, supt. — Fax 754-4273
www.park1.k12.wy.us/
Powell HS — 500/9-12
160 N Evarts St 82435 — 307-754-2287
Bill Schwan, prin. — Fax 754-5996
Powell MS — 400/6-8
160 N Evarts St 82435 — 307-754-5716
Jason Sleep, prin. — Fax 754-2507

Northwest College — Post-Sec.
231 W 6th St 82435 — 307-754-6000

Ranchester, Sheridan, Pop. 717
Sheridan County SD 1 — 900/K-12
PO Box 819 82839 — 307-655-9541
Sue Belish, supt. — Fax 655-9477
www.sheridan.k12.wy.us/
Tongue River MS — 100/6-8
PO Box 879 82839 — 307-655-9533
Terry Myers, prin. — Fax 655-9894
Other Schools – See Big Horn, Dayton

Rawlins, Carbon, Pop. 8,658
Carbon County SD 1 — 1,700/K-12
PO Box 160 82301 — 307-328-9200
Peggy Sanders, supt. — Fax 328-9258
www-rawlins.crb1.k12.wy.us/
Rawlins HS — 400/9-12
1401 Colorado St 82301 — 307-328-9280
Shane Odgen, prin. — Fax 328-9286
Rawlins MS — 300/6-8
1500 Harshman St 82301 — 307-328-9205
Traci Blaize, prin. — Fax 328-9226
Other Schools – See Baggs

Riverton, Fremont, Pop. 9,430
Fremont County SD 25 — 2,400/K-12
121 N 5th St W 82501 — 307-856-9407
Craig Beck, supt. — Fax 856-3390
www.fremont25.k12.wy.us
Riverton HS — 800/9-12
121 N 5th St W 82501 — 307-856-9491
JoAnne Flanagan, prin. — Fax 856-2333
Riverton MS — 600/6-8
121 N 5th St W 82501 — 307-856-9443
Cheryl Mowry, prin. — Fax 857-1695

Central Wyoming College — Post-Sec.
2660 Peck Ave 82501 — 307-855-2000

Rock River, Albany, Pop. 214
Albany County SD 1
Supt. — See Laramie
Rock River S — 50/K-12
PO Box 128 82083 — 307-378-2271
Heather Moro, prin. — Fax 378-2505

Rock Springs, Sweetwater, Pop. 18,772
Sweetwater County SD 1 — 4,200/K-12
PO Box 1089 82902 — 307-352-3400
Paul Grube, supt. — Fax 352-3411
www.sweetwater1.org/
Rock Springs East JHS — 700/7-8
PO Box 1089 82902 — 307-352-3474
Dr. LaWana Sweet, prin. — Fax 352-3482
Rock Springs HS — 1,100/9-12
PO Box 1089 82902 — 307-352-3440
Dr. Randal Wendling, prin. — Fax 352-3446
Other Schools – See Farson, Wamsutter

Columbia Commonwealth University — Post-Sec.
327 N St 82901 — 800-552-5522
Western Wyoming Community College — Post-Sec.
2500 College Dr 82901 — 307-382-1600

Saratoga, Carbon, Pop. 1,714
Carbon County SD 2 — 500/K-12
PO Box 1530 82331 — 307-326-5271
Robert Gates, supt. — Fax 326-8089
www.crb2.k12.wy.us
Saratoga MSHS — 100/7-12
PO Box 1710 82331 — 307-326-5246
Larry Uhling, prin. — Fax 326-9607
Other Schools – See Encampment, Hanna

Sheridan, Sheridan, Pop. 16,333
Sheridan County SD 2 — 2,300/K-12
PO Box 919 82801 — 307-674-7405
Craig Dougherty, supt. — Fax 674-5041
www.scsd2.com/
Sheridan HS — 900/9-12
1056 Long Dr 82801 — 307-672-2495
Dirlene Wheeler, prin. — Fax 672-8071
Sheridan JHS — 6-8
500 Lewis St 82801 — 307-674-6545
Scott Stults, prin. — Fax 672-5311

Sheridan College — Post-Sec.
PO Box 1500 82801 — 307-674-6446

Shoshoni, Fremont, Pop. 659
Fremont County SD 24 — 300/PK-12
112 W 3rd St 82649 — 307-876-2583
Tammy Cox, supt. — Fax 876-2469
www.f24.k12.wy.us
Shoshoni HS — 100/9-12
112 W 3rd St 82649 — 307-876-2576
Aaron Carr, prin. — Fax 876-9325
Shoshoni JHS — 50/7-8
112 W 3rd St 82649 — 307-876-2576
Aaron Carr, prin. — Fax 876-9325

Sundance, Crook, Pop. 1,184
Crook County SD 1 — 800/K-12
PO Box 830 82729 — 307-283-2299
Lon Streib, supt. — Fax 283-1810
www.crooknet.k12.wy.us
Sundance JSHS — 100/7-12
PO Box 850 82729 — 307-283-1007
Fax 283-2300
Other Schools – See Hulett, Moorcroft

Ten Sleep, Washakie, Pop. 315
Washakie County SD 2 — 100/K-12
PO Box 105 82442 — 307-366-2223
Jerry Erdahl, supt. — Fax 366-2304
Ten Sleep HS — 50/9-12
PO Box 105 82442 — 307-366-2233
Mike Sharum, prin. — Fax 366-2304
Ten Sleep MS — 50/6-8
PO Box 105 82442 — 307-366-2233
Mike Sharum, prin. — Fax 366-2304

Thermopolis, Hot Springs, Pop. 2,905
Hot Springs County SD 1 — 700/K-12
415 Springview St 82443 — 307-864-6515
John Balow, supt. — Fax 864-6615
www.hotsprings.k12.wy.us
Hot Springs County HS — 200/9-12
415 Springview St 82443 — 307-864-6511
Steve Sexton, prin. — Fax 864-6611
Thermopolis MS — 200/6-8
415 Springview St 82443 — 307-864-6551
Jodie Cameron, prin. — Fax 864-6508

Torrington, Goshen, Pop. 5,533
Goshen County SD 1 — 1,900/K-12
2602 W E St 82240 — 307-532-2171
Ray Schulte, supt. — Fax 532-7085
www.goshen.k12.wy.us
Torrington HS — 400/9-12
2400 W C St 82240 — 307-532-7101
Marty Wood, prin. — Fax 532-2696
Torrington MS — 300/6-8
626 W 25th Ave 82240 — 307-532-7014
Marvin Haiman, prin. — Fax 532-8402
Other Schools – See Lingle, Yoder

Eastern Wyoming College — Post-Sec.
3200 W C St 82240 — 307-532-8200
St. Joseph's S — 100/PK-12
PO Box 1117 82240 — 307-532-4197
Travis Lenz, prin. — Fax 532-8405

Upton, Weston, Pop. 857
Weston County SD 7 — 200/K-12
PO Box 470 82730 — 307-468-2461
Troy Claycomb, supt. — Fax 468-2797
bobcat.weston7.k12.wy.us
Upton HS — 100/9-12
PO Box 470 82730 — 307-468-2361
Gary Glodt, prin. — Fax 468-2459
Upton MS — 100/6-8
PO Box 470 82730 — 307-468-9331
Clark Coberly, prin. — Fax 468-2832

Wamsutter, Sweetwater, Pop. 265
Sweetwater County SD 1
Supt. — See Rock Springs
Desert MS — 50/6-8
PO Box 10 82336 — 307-324-7811
Richard Freudenberg, prin. — Fax 324-4824

Wheatland, Platte, Pop. 3,464
Platte County SD 1 — 1,200/K-12
1350 Oak St 82201 — 307-322-5480
Stuart Nelson, supt. — Fax 322-2084
www.platte1.k12.wy.us/
Wheatland HS — 300/9-12
1350 Oak St 82201 — 307-322-2075
Maureen Ryff, prin. — Fax 322-9739
Wheatland MS — 200/6-8
1350 Oak St 82201 — 307-322-1550
Steven Loyd, prin. — Fax 322-1560
Other Schools – See Chugwater, Glendo

Worland, Washakie, Pop. 4,967
Washakie County SD 1 — 1,300/K-12
1900 Howell Ave 82401 — 307-347-9286
Mike Hejtmanek, supt. — Fax 347-8116
whs.1wyo.net/
Worland HS — 400/9-12
801 S 17th St 82401 — 307-347-2412
Hal Johnson, prin. — Fax 347-8549
Worland MS — 300/6-8
2150 Howell Ave 82401 — 307-347-3233
Richard Schaal, prin. — Fax 347-3710

Wright, Campbell, Pop. 1,425
Campbell County SD 1
Supt. — See Gillette
Wright JSHS — 200/7-12
PO Box 490 82732 — 307-464-0140
Kirby Eisenhauer, prin. — Fax 464-0154

Yoder, Goshen, Pop. 163
Goshen County SD 1
Supt. — See Torrington
Southeast HS — 100/9-12
PO Box 160 82244 — 307-532-7176
Brian Grasmick, prin. — Fax 532-5771
Southeast JHS — 50/7-8
PO Box 160 82244 — 307-532-7176
Brian Grasmick, prin. — Fax 532-5771

CHARTER SCHOOLS

School	Address	City,State	Zip code	Telephone	Fax	Grade	Contact
Alaska							
Academy Charter S	801 E Artic Ave	Palmer, AK	99645	907-746-2358	746-2368	K-8	Barbara Gerard
Anvil City Science Academy	PO Box 131	Nome, AK	99762-0131	907-443-6207	443-5144	5-8	Todd Hindman
Aquarian Charter S	1705 W 32nd Ave	Anchorage, AK	99517-2002	907-742-4900	742-4919	K-6	Susan Forbes
Aurora Borealis Charter S	705 Frontage Rd Ste A	Kenai, AK	99611-7740	907-283-0292	283-0293	K-8	Larry Nauta
Career Education Center	725 26th Ave Ste 202	Fairbanks, AK	99701-7000	907-479-4061	479-0230	11-12	Annie Keep-Barnes
Chinook Charter S	3002 International St	Fairbanks, AK	99701-7391	907-452-5020	452-5048	K-8	Barbara Smith
Delta Cyber S	PO Box 1672	Delta Junction, AK	99737-1672	907-895-1043	895-5198	K-12	Michael Opp
Eagle Academy Charter S	10901 Mausel St Ste 101	Eagle River, AK	99577-8065	907-742-3025	742-3035	K-6	Mary Meade
Family Partnership Charter S	401 E Fireweed Ln Ste 101	Anchorage, AK	99503-2100	907-742-3700	742-3710	K-12	Reed Whitmore
Fireweed Academy	PO Box 474	Homer, AK	99603-0474	907-235-9728	235-8561	3-6	Kiki Abrahamson
Frontier Charter S	400 W Northern Lights Blvd	Anchorage, AK	99503	907-742-1180	742-1188	K-12	Tim Scott
Galena Interior Learning Academy	PO Box 359	Galena, AK	99741-0359	907-656-2053	656-2107	9-12	Harry White
Highland Tech Charter S	5530 E Northern Lights Blvd	Anchorage, AK	99504-3135	907-742-1700	742-1711	7-12	Mark Standley
Juneau Community Charter S	10014 Crazy Horse Dr	Juneau, AK	99801-8529	907-586-2526	586-3543	K-6	Carol Valentine
Kaleidoscope S	549 N Forest Dr	Kenai, AK	99611-7410	907-283-0804	283-3786	K-4	Mick Wykis
Ketchikan Charter S	410 Schoenbar Rd	Ketchikan, AK	99901-6218	907-225-8568	247-8568	K-8	Margaret Spink
Kokrine Charter S	601 Loftus Rd	Fairbanks, AK	99709-3430	907-474-0958	479-2104	7-12	Eleanor Laughlin
Midnight Sun Family Learning Center	7362 W Parks Hwy Ste 714	Wasilla, AK	99654	907-357-3733	373-6786	K-12	George Hronkin
Soldotna Montessori Charter S	162 E Park Ave	Soldotna, AK	99669-7552	907-260-9221	260-9032	K-6	Mary Jo Sanders
Star of the North Secondary S	2945 Monk Ct	North Pole, AK	99705-6129	907-490-9025	490-9021	7-12	Annie Keep-Barnes
Twindly-Bridge Charter S	230 E Paulson Ave Ste 76	Wasilla, AK	99654	907-376-6680	746-6683	K-12	Greg Miller
Winterberry Charter S	508 W 2nd Ave	Anchorage, AK	99501-2208	907-742-4980	742-4985	K-6	Shanna Mall
Arizona							
AAEC - Paradise Valley	17811 N 32nd St	Phoenix, AZ	85032-1201	602-569-1101	569-6372	9-12	Dennis Gray
AAEC - Red Mountain	2165 N Power Rd	Mesa, AZ	85215-2971	480-833-8899	833-1266	9-12	Linda LaFontain
AAEC - SMCC Campus	7050 S 24th St	Phoenix, AZ	85042-5806	602-243-8004	243-8001	9-12	Dr. William Torres Conley
Academic & Personal Excellence HS	2859 E Elvira Rd	Tucson, AZ	85706-7126	520-889-4246	889-5812	6-12	Jim Parks
Academy Adventures PS	3902 N Flowing Wells Rd	Tucson, AZ	85705-2403	520-407-1200	407-1201	K-4	
Academy of Arizona - Main	2100 W Indian School Rd	Phoenix, AZ	85015-4907	602-274-0422	274-0543	K-8	Diana Likes
Academy of Arizona North Campus	13002 N 33rd Ave	Phoenix, AZ	85029-1208	602-843-0681	843-2092	K-6	Diana Likes
Academy of Building Industries	1547 E Lipan Blvd	Fort Mohave, AZ	86426-6031	928-788-2601	788-2610	9-12	Jean Thomas
Academy of Excellence	425 N 36th St	Phoenix, AZ	85008-6303	602-389-4271	389-4278	K-8	Eula Dean
Academy of Excellence - Central AZ	340 W Vah Ki Inn Rd	Coolidge, AZ	85228-3734	520-723-4773	723-4773	K-8	Zedna Grubbs
Academy of Hope	PO Box 435	Ash Fork, AZ	86320-0435	928-637-2487	637-2499	K-12	Terra Chesnutt
Academy of Math & Science	1557 W Prince Rd	Tucson, AZ	85705-3023	520-293-2676	888-1732	K-12	Tatyana Chayka
Academy of Tucson ES	9209 E Wrightstown Rd	Tucson, AZ	85715-5514	520-886-6076	886-6575	K-5	Caroline Martin
Academy of Tucson HS	10720 E 22nd St	Tucson, AZ	85748-7029	520-733-0096	733-0097	9-12	Susan Pearson
Academy of Tucson MS	2300 N Tanque Verde Loop Rd	Tucson, AZ	85749-9786	520-749-1413	749-2824	6-8	Laurie Ocampo
Academy With Community Partners	433 N Hall	Mesa, AZ	85203-7407	480-833-0068	833-8966	9-12	Margaret Williamson
Accelerated Learning Center	4101 E Shea Blvd	Phoenix, AZ	85028-3525	602-485-0309	485-9356	9-12	Frank Canady
Accelerated Learning Center Laboratory	5245 N Camino De Oeste	Tucson, AZ	85745-8925	520-743-2256	743-2417	K-12	David Jones
Accelerated Learning Charter S	320 S Main St	Cottonwood, AZ	86326-3905	928-634-0650	634-0672	K-8	Susan Glendening
ACCLAIM Charter S	5350 W Indian School Rd	Phoenix, AZ	85031-2607	623-691-0919	691-6091	K-8	Melanie Powers
ACE Charter HS	1901 N Stone Ave	Tucson, AZ	85705-5642	520-623-5843	791-9893	9-12	Kathleen Bibby
A Child's View S	2846 W Drexel Rd Ste 100	Tucson, AZ	85746	520-578-2075	578-2076	K-5	Morris Shaw
Acorn Montessori Charter S	8556 E Loos Dr	Prescott Valley, AZ	86314-6455	928-772-5778	775-8654	K-6	Cynthia Puplava
Adventure Academy	323 N Gilbert Rd	Mesa, AZ	85203	928-830-5088		5-7	
Adventure S	1950 E Placita Sin Nombre	Tucson, AZ	85718-2092	520-296-0656	721-4472	K-4	Maryann Penczar
Ahwatukee Foothills Prep S	10210 S 50th Pl	Phoenix, AZ	85044-5209	480-763-5101	763-5107	1-8	Eddilu Hoedebeck
All Aboard Charter S	5827 N 35th Ave	Phoenix, AZ	85017-1915	602-433-0500	973-8208	K-2	Rhonda Newton
Allsports Academy	8570 E 22nd St	Tucson, AZ	85710-6522	520-731-2150	731-2160	5-9	Moses Montoya
Alta Vista Charter HS	5040 S Campbell Ave	Tucson, AZ	85706-1510	520-294-4922	294-4933	9-12	Alicia Alvarez
American Heritage Academy	2030 E Cherry St	Cottonwood, AZ	86326-6963	928-634-2144	634-9053	K-12	Steve Anderson
American Heritage Academy	675 W Sunland Dr	Camp Verde, AZ	86322-7059	928-567-0462	567-0464	K-2	Michael Pospisil
Amerischools Academy	1333 W Camelback Rd	Phoenix, AZ	85013-2106	602-532-0100	532-9964	K-12	Dr. Reginald Barr
Amerischools Academy	1150 N Country Club Rd	Tucson, AZ	85716-3942	520-620-1100	322-5351	K-12	Greg Gaines
Amerischools Academy - Yuma	2098 S 3rd Ave	Yuma, AZ	85364-6425	928-329-1100	329-9177	K-8	Dea Bermudez
Amerischools College Prep Academy	7444 E Broadway Blvd	Tucson, AZ	85710-1411	520-722-1200	624-4376	K-12	Charlene Mendoza
Apache Trail HS	945 W Apache Trl	Apache Junction, AZ	85220-5409	480-288-0337	288-0340	9-12	Giles Glithero
Apex Academy	945 W Apache Trl	Apache Junction, AZ	85220-5409	480-288-0337	288-0340	K-8	Bill Coats
Arizona Academy of Science & Technology	PO Box 13606	Phoenix, AZ	85002-3606	602-253-1199	595-8693	K-12	Joan Miller
AZ Call-A-Teen Center of Excellence	649 N 6th Ave	Phoenix, AZ	85003-1659	602-252-6721	252-2952	9-12	Pam Smith
Arizona Charter Academy	PO Box 1929	Surprise, AZ	85378-1929	623-974-4959	974-4840	K-12	Heather Henderson
AZ Conservatory for Arts & Academics	2820 W Kelton Ln	Phoenix, AZ	85053-3028	602-266-4278	266-7827	6-12	Joann Garrett
Arizona School for the Arts	1313 N 2nd St	Phoenix, AZ	85004	602-257-1444	252-7795	6-12	Dr. Leah Roberts
Arizona Upgrade Academy	327 S 15th St	Cottonwood, AZ	86326-3432	928-634-3722	634-3695	5-8	Allen Smithson
Arizona Virtual Academy	4495 S Palo Verde Rd	Tucson, AZ	85714	520-623-1483	623-1803	K-12	Mary Gifford
Arts Academy at Estrella Mountain	2504 S 91st Ave	Tolleson, AZ	85353-8921	623-474-2120	936-5337	K-8	Bill Bressler
Arts Academy at South Mountain	4039 E Raymond St	Phoenix, AZ	85040-1930	602-437-3947	426-1342	K-8	Mike Epperson
Avalon S at San Marcos	1045 S San Marcos Dr	Apache Junction, AZ	85220-6337	480-373-9575	373-9600	K-8	Mathew Reese
Az-Tec HS	2330 W 28th St	Yuma, AZ	85364-6954	928-314-1900	726-2826	9-12	Linda Munk
Aztlan Academy	3376 S 6th Ave	South Tucson, AZ	85713-6139	520-844-0650	844-1602	6-12	Judy Bisignano
BASIS S - Tucson	3825 E 2nd St	Tucson, AZ	85716-4368	520-326-6367	326-6359	5-12	Carolyn McGarvey
Basis Scottsdale	9128 E San Salvador Dr	Scottsdale, AZ	85258	480-451-7500	451-4555	5-12	Diane Moser
Beginning Academy	3067 N Campbell Ave	Tucson, AZ	85719-2816	520-299-6259	299-6880	K-5	Betsy Sales
Belle Affeld Beloved Humanities Academy	PO Box 5554	Lake Montezuma, AZ	86342-5554	928-567-4475	567-4636	4-12	J'Anne Affeld
Benchmark ES	4120 E Acoma Dr	Phoenix, AZ	85032-4753	602-765-3582	765-1932	K-6	Barbara Darroch
Berean Academy	4699 E Highway 90	Sierra Vista, AZ	85635-2437	520-459-4113	459-4121	K-12	Mark Bennett
Bradley Academy of Excellence	200 N Dysart Rd	Avondale, AZ	85323-2418	623-932-9902	932-9904	K-8	Tanya Burston
Bright Beginnings S	400 N Andersen Blvd	Chandler, AZ	85224-8273	480-821-1404	821-1463	K-8	Karen Edris
Bright Ideas Charter S - Van Buren	2720 S Dorsey Ln	Tempe, AZ	85282-2708	602-275-3400	275-3558	K-8	Beth Brantley
Burke Basic S	131 E Southern Ave	Mesa, AZ	85210-5355	480-964-4602	964-6566	K-8	Glen Gaddie
Calli Olin Academy	5757 E Pima St	Tucson, AZ	85712-5609	520-883-5051		9-12	Theresa Carino
Calli Ollin Academy	200 N Stone Ave Fl 3	Tucson, AZ	85701	520-882-3029	882-3041	9-12	Magdalena Verdugo
Cambridge Academy East	9412 E Brown Rd	Mesa, AZ	85207-4338	480-641-2828	325-2365	K-6	Linda Gonzalez
Camelback Academy	7634 W Camelback Rd	Glendale, AZ	85303-5627	623-247-2204	247-1113	K-6	Karen Kordon
Canyon Rose Academy	3686 W Orange Grove Rd	Tucson, AZ	85741	520-514-5112	797-8868	9-12	Lisa Cothrun
Carden of Tucson S	5260 N Royal Palm Dr	Tucson, AZ	85705-1148	520-293-6661	408-7366	K-8	Bette Jeppson
Carden Traditional S of Glendale	4744 W Grovers Ave	Glendale, AZ	85308-3453	602-439-5026	547-2841	K-8	Timothy Smith
Carden Traditional S of Surprise	15688 W Acoma Dr	Surprise, AZ	85379-5652	623-556-2179	547-2806	K-8	Kristy Faux
Career Success HS	3816 N 27th Ave	Phoenix, AZ	85017-4703	602-285-5525	285-0026	9-12	Raymond Pacheco
Career Success HS - Cave Creek	PO Box 7010	Cave Creek, AZ	85327-7010	480-575-0075	575-0061	9-12	Maureen Racz
Career Success HS - Copper Square	301 W Roosevelt St	Phoenix, AZ	85003-1324	602-393-4200	393-4205	9-12	Kathy Scott
Career Success S - Glendale	8632 W Northern Ave Bldg 3	Glendale, AZ	85305	602-285-5525	285-0026	9-12	Sonia Gonzales
Career Success S - Sage Campus	3120 N 32nd St	Phoenix, AZ	85018-6202	602-955-0355	508-0682	K-12	Kathy Randall
Casa Verde Charter HS	1362 N Casa Grande Ave	Casa Grande, AZ	85222-2648	520-876-0661	876-0667	9-12	Anna McCauley
CASY Country Day S 1	7214 E Jenan Dr	Scottsdale, AZ	85260-5416	480-951-3190	998-4029	K-5	Bill Thompson
CASY Country Day S 2	9350 E Cactus Rd	Scottsdale, AZ	85260-5020	480-661-1930	314-7306	K-5	Bill Thompson
CASY South Valley Academy	2033 E Southern Ave	Phoenix, AZ	85040-3344	602-276-2818	276-2492	K-8	Bill Thompson
Center for Academic Success #1	650 E Wilcox Dr	Sierra Vista, AZ	85635-2534	520-458-4200	458-6396	9-12	Phillip Hirales
Center for Academic Success #2	510 N G Ave	Douglas, AZ	85607-2822	520-364-2616	805-0973	9-12	Stephen Huff
Center for Academic Success #3	1415 F Ave	Douglas, AZ	85607-1655	520-805-1558	805-1549	K-8	Stephen Huff
Center for Academic Success #5	800 Taylor Dr	Sierra Vista, AZ	85635-1050	520-459-7259	458-1409	K-5	Linda Denno
Center for Creative Education Charter S	215 S Main St	Cottonwood, AZ	86326-3908	928-634-3288	634-9781	K-6	Mary Ann Green
Center for Educational Excellence	1700 E Elliot Rd Ste 9	Tempe, AZ	85284-1631	480-632-1940	632-1398	K-8	Stacey Cochran
Challenge Charter S	5801 W Greenbriar Dr	Glendale, AZ	85308-3847	602-938-5411	938-5393	K-6	Gregory Miller
Challenger Basic S	1315 N Greenfield Rd	Gilbert, AZ	85234-2813	480-830-1750	830-1763	K-6	Brad Tobin
Chandler Preparatory Academy	2020 N Arizona Ave	Chandler, AZ	85225	480-899-9181	855-7789	7-8	Helen Hayes
Chavez MS	3376 S 6th Ave	Tucson, AZ	85713-6139	520-573-1500	573-1600	6-8	Sr. Judy Bisignano
Children Reaching for the Sky Prep	1844 S Alvernon Way	Tucson, AZ	85711-5607	520-790-8400	620-6570	K-6	Lee Griffin
Childrens Success Academy	PO Box 11368	Tucson, AZ	85734-1368	520-799-8403	799-8427	K-8	Nanci Aiken

School	Address	City,State	Zip code	Telephone	Fax	Grade	Contact
City HS	PO Box 2608	Tucson, AZ	85702-2608	520-623-7223	547-0680	9-12	Carolyn Brennan
Civano Charter S	10673 E Mira Ln	Tucson, AZ	85747-5983	520-731-3466	731-3477	K-6	Connie Erickson
Collegiate HS	PO Box 6502	Yuma, AZ	85366-6502	928-317-3113	317-0828	6-12	Rick Ogston
Compass HS	8250 E 22nd St	Tucson, AZ	85710	520-296-4070	296-4103	9-12	John Ferguson
Coolidge HS Success Center	450 N Arizona Blvd	Coolidge, AZ	85228-4108	520-723-2112	723-2150	9-12	Susan Price
Copper Canyon Academy	7785 W Peoria Ave	Peoria, AZ	85345-5922	623-930-1734	930-8709	K-6	Jinny Ludwig
Cornerstone Charter S	7107 N Black Canyon Hwy	Phoenix, AZ	85021-7619	602-595-2198	242-2398	9-12	George Smith
Country Gardens Charter S	6301 W Alta Vista Rd	Laveen, AZ	85339	602-237-3741	237-3892	K-12	Goldie Burge
Crittenton Youth Academy	715 W Mariposa St	Phoenix, AZ	85013	602-274-7318	274-7549	6-12	Dan Johnston
Crown Charter S	PO Box 363	Litchfield Park, AZ	85340-0363	623-535-9300	535-5410	K-6	James Shade
Daisy Early Learning	2255 W Ina Rd	Tucson, AZ	85741-2650	520-219-6700	219-6701		Nuray Tugrul
Deer Valley Academy	18424 N 51st Ave	Glendale, AZ	85308	623-445-4915	445-4915	9-12	Barbara Daggett
Desert Heights Charter S	5821 W Beverly Ln	Glendale, AZ	85306-1801	602-896-2900	467-9540	K-8	Mark Giles
Desert Hills HS	1515 S Val Vista Dr	Gilbert, AZ	85296-3854	480-813-1151	813-1161	9-12	Art Madden
Desert Marigold S	6210 S 28th St	Phoenix, AZ	85042-4715	602-243-6909	243-6933	K-8	Amy Bird
Desert Mosaic S	5757 W Ajo Hwy	Tucson, AZ	85735-9334	520-578-2022	578-0834	K-12	Lynn Spoon
Desert Pointe Academy	7785 W Peoria Ave	Peoria, AZ	85345-5922	623-930-1734	930-8709	7-12	Jinny Ludwig
Desert Rose Academy	326 W Fort Lowell Rd	Tucson, AZ	85705-3816	520-696-0819	797-8868	9-12	
Desert Sky Community S	122 N Craycroft Rd	Tucson, AZ	85711-3238	520-745-3888	745-5110	K-3	
Desert Springs Academy	3833 E 2nd St	Tucson, AZ	85716-4368	520-321-1709	321-9316	K-8	Lydia Capara
Desert Star Community S	55 Rojo Dr	Sedona, AZ	86351-9326	928-282-0171	284-9565	K-6	
Desert Technology HS	3155 Maricopa Ave	Lk Havasu Cty, AZ	86406-8635	928-453-3383	453-3886	9-12	Leon Buttler
Desert View Academy	2363 S Kennedy Ln	Yuma, AZ	85365-2416	928-314-1102	314-1086	K-5	Rick Ogston
Destiny Community S	PO Box 3320	Gilbert, AZ	85299-3320	480-325-8950	539-0147	K-8	Wendy Noble
Destiny S	22 Prickly Pear Dr	Globe, AZ	85501	928-425-0925		K-12	Nancy McLendon
DINE Southwest HS	HC 63 Box 303	Winslow, AZ	86047-9424	928-657-3272	657-3272	9-12	Cheryl Chischillie
Discovery Plus Academy	PO Box 549	Pima, AZ	85543-0549	928-485-2498	485-2508	K-6	Donna Bolinger
Dobson Academy	PO Box 6070	Chandler, AZ	85246-6070	480-855-6325	855-6323	K-8	George Ellis
Doby MS	8632 W Northern Ave	Glendale, AZ	85305	623-878-8059	878-8175	5-8	Sharon Foster
Downtown Arts Academy	210 E Broadway Blvd	Tucson, AZ	85701-2014	520-882-9144	792-0668	K-9	Frank Dipietro
Dragonfleye Charter S	10202 N 19th Ave	Phoenix, AZ	85021-1910	602-944-4322	944-1450	K-9	Gail Battistella
E.A.G.L.E. Academy	423 S Colorado Rd	Golden Valley, AZ	86413-9203	928-565-3430	565-3454	K-12	Mary Stuart
Eagle's Aerie S	17019 S Greenfield Rd	Gilbert, AZ	85295-1900	480-988-3212	988-3280	K-12	Tim Peak
Eastpointe HS	8495 E Broadway Blvd	Tucson, AZ	85710-4009	520-731-8180	731-8179	9-12	Todd Brown
East Valley Academy	1858 E Brown Rd	Mesa, AZ	85203	480-610-1711	421-0183	K-6	Janet Stoeppelman
East Valley HS	7420 E Main St	Mesa, AZ	85207-8306	480-981-2008	641-4473	9-12	Kathy Tolman
E-cadamie	417 N 16th St	Phoenix, AZ	85006-3710	602-416-6400	416-6393	9-12	Arturo Ortiz
Edge Charter S-Child & Family Resources	2555 E 1st St	Tucson, AZ	85716	520-881-8940	325-8780	9-12	Reese Millen
Edge Charter S - Himmel Park	2555 E 1st St	Tucson, AZ	85716	520-881-1389	881-0852	9-12	Reese Millen
Edge Charter S - Northwest	2555 E 1st St	Tucson, AZ	85716	520-877-9179	877-9225	9-12	Cathy Sivilli
Edge Charter S - Sahuarita	15500 S Sahuarita Park Rd	Sahuarita, AZ	85629	520-393-1690	881-1689	9-12	Reese Millen
Educational Opportunity Center	3810 W 16th St	Yuma, AZ	85364-4107	928-329-0990	783-0886	9-12	Brian Grossenburg
EduPreneurship Student Center	1201 N 85th Pl	Scottsdale, AZ	85257	480-990-2475	990-0378	K-8	Carol Ann Sammans
EduPreneurship Student Center	2632 W Augusta Ave	Phoenix, AZ	85051-6732	602-973-8998	973-5510	K-8	Carol Ann Sammans
Edu-Prize S	580 W Melody Ave	Gilbert, AZ	85233-1418	480-813-9537	813-6742	K-8	Lynn Robershotte
E-Institute at Acoma	15688 W Acoma Dr	Surprise, AZ	85379-5652	623-556-2179	556-2806	9-12	Scott Maxwell
E-Institute at Union Hills	3515 W Union Hills Dr	Glendale, AZ	85308	602-843-3891	843-4375	9-12	John Cortez
El Dorado HS	2200 N Arizona Ave Ste 17	Chandler, AZ	85225-3452	480-726-9536	726-9543	9-12	Ramona Gonzales
Enterprise Academy	415 W Grant St	Phoenix, AZ	85003-2431	602-254-1844	254-1533	K-6	Shane Stuckey
Esperanza Community Collegial Academy	2507 E Bell Rd	Phoenix, AZ	85032-2413	602-996-1125	996-4238	9-12	Pamela Cullen
Estrella HS	510 N Central Ave	Avondale, AZ	85323-1909	623-932-6561	932-1263	9-12	William Horton
Excalibur Charter S	10839 E Apache Trl Ste 113	Apache Junction, AZ	85220-3415	480-373-9575	373-9600	K-12	Jeffrey Parker
Excel Education Center	2229 E Spruce Ave	Flagstaff, AZ	86004-5011	928-214-7442	214-7256	9-12	Michael Gerdes
Excel Education Center - Chino Valley	1985 N Road 1 W	Chino Valley, AZ	86323-7600	928-636-1444	636-1414	9-12	Katie Reynolds
Excel Education Center - Cottonwood	1229 E Cherry St	Cottonwood, AZ	86326-3458	928-634-2065	639-2952	9-12	Sharon Ackerman
Excel Education Center - Fort Mohave	1385 E Gemini St	Fort Mohave, AZ	86426-8326	928-758-5472	758-2821	9-12	Don Coe
Excel Education Center - Prescott	1040 Whipple St Ste 401	Prescott, AZ	86305-3405	928-541-1701	778-5766	6-12	Brenda Clark
Excel Education Center - San Carlos	PO Box 729	Peridot, AZ	85542-0729	928-475-2292	475-2441	9-12	Larry Beaver
Excel Education Centers-Prescott Valley	7515 E Long Look Dr	Prescott Valley, AZ	86314-5507	928-775-6681	775-6691	9-12	Mark Gorman
Excel Education Center - Williams Campus	790 E Rodeo Rd	Williams, AZ	86046-9653	928-635-3998	635-3999	9-12	Michael Gerdes
Flagstaff Arts and Leadership Academy	3100 N Fort Valley Rd	Flagstaff, AZ	86001	928-779-7223	779-7041	9-12	Kirk Quitter
Flagstaff Junior Academy	306 W Cedar Ave	Flagstaff, AZ	86001-1413	928-774-6007	774-7268	PK-8	Dulcie Ambrose
Foothills Academy	7191 E Ashler Hills Dr	Scottsdale, AZ	85266-9300	480-488-5583	488-6902	6-12	Donald Senneville
Fountain Hills Charter S	15055 N Fountain Hills Blvd	Fountain Hills, AZ	85268-2330	480-837-0046	837-0024	K-8	Michael Bashaw
4 Winds Academy	725 E Main	Springerville, AZ	85938	928-333-1060	333-2926	K-8	Steve Chavez
Franklin Arts Academies - Liberty	3015 S Power Rd	Mesa, AZ	85212-3000	480-830-3444	830-4335	K-6	Ted North
Franklin Arts Academy	862 E Elliot Rd	Gilbert, AZ	85234-6912	480-325-6100	807-1630	K-6	Dana Rodgers
Franklin Arts Academy - Gold	2929 E McKellips Rd	Mesa, AZ	85213-3128	480-924-1500	924-0552	K-8	Jason Lobik
Franklin Charter S	320 E Warner Rd	Gilbert, AZ	85296-2976	480-632-0722	632-8716	K-6	Terry Nicoll
Franklin Charter S	21151 S Crismon Rd	Queen Creek, AZ	85242-8957	480-987-0722	987-3517	K-8	Jack McLeod
Franklin Charter S	2345 N Horne	Mesa, AZ	85203-1823	480-649-0712	649-8716	K-5	Debra Stoddard
Franklin HS	5646 E Main St	Mesa, AZ	85205	480-985-6112	807-1630	9-12	Matt Williams
Franklin Phonetic S	6116 E State Route 69	Prescott Valley, AZ	86314-2806	928-775-6747	775-6740	K-8	Cindy Franklin
Freire Freedom S	300 E University Blvd	Tucson, AZ	85705	520-624-7552	624-7518	6-8	JoAnn Groh
Friendly House Academia Del Pueblo S	201 E Durango St	Phoenix, AZ	85004-2913	602-258-4353	416-7375	K-8	Ximena Doyle
GateWay Early College HS	108 N 40th St	Phoenix, AZ	85034-1795	602-286-8759	286-8752	9-12	Yvonne Watterson
GEM Charter S	1704 N Center St	Mesa, AZ	85201-2223	480-833-2622	833-2655	K-6	Nelleke van Savooyen
Genesis Academy	640 N 1st Ave	Phoenix, AZ	85003-1515	602-223-4200	223-4210	9-12	Karen Callahan
Gila Preparatory Academy	1976 W Thatcher Blvd	Safford, AZ	85546-3318	928-348-8688	348-8877	6-12	Kathy Maxwell
Glenn Academy	5625 S 51st Ave	Laveen, AZ	85339-6300	623-247-4100	247-4101	9-12	Jeffrey DeMatte
Grand Canyon College Prep Charter S	7541 S Willow Dr	Tempe, AZ	85283-5032	480-233-3622	491-7096	6-12	David Gordon
Great Expectations Academy	1466 W Camino Antigua	Sahuarita, AZ	85629-9720	520-399-2121	399-2123	K-8	Beth Phillips
Guerrero MS	2797 N Introspect Dr	Tucson, AZ	85745-9454	520-807-2836	623-9679	3-8	Carmen Campuzano
Ha:San Prep & Leadership Charter S	1333 E 10th St	Tucson, AZ	85719-5808	520-882-8826	882-8651	6-12	Michael Norris
Happy Valley S	7140 W Happy Valley Rd	Peoria, AZ	85383-3255	623-376-2900	655-7870	K-8	Glen Gaddie
Harvest Preparatory Academy	PO Box 6826	Yuma, AZ	85366-6826	928-783-6266	783-4543	K-12	Deborah Ybarra
Hayes Memorial Applied Learning Ctr	PO Box 10899	Bapchule, AZ	85221-0899	520-315-5100	315-5115	9-12	Richard Stoner
Hearn Academy	17606 N 7th Ave	Phoenix, AZ	85023-1567	602-896-9160	896-1997	K-8	Jane Vert
Heritage Academy	32 S Center St	Mesa, AZ	85210-1306	480-969-5641	969-6972	7-12	Earl Taylor
Heritage ES	13419 W Ocotillo Rd	Glendale, AZ	85307-3220	623-935-1931	935-1931	K-8	Aaron Robinson
Hermosa Montessori Charter S	12051 E Fort Lowell Rd	Tucson, AZ	85749-9702	520-749-5518	749-6087	K-8	Sheila Stolov
Higgins Institute	1805 E Elliot Rd Ste 112	Tempe, AZ	85284-1746	480-413-0829	413-9365	K-8	Martha Wallace
Highland Free S	510 S Highland Ave	Tucson, AZ	85719-6427	520-623-0104	903-1318	K-5	Nicholas Sofka
Hope HS	9040 W Campbell Ave	Phoenix, AZ	85037-1408	623-772-8013		9-12	Jef Heredia
Hope HS Online	1717 W Northern Ave	Phoenix, AZ	85021	602-674-5555	943-9700	9-12	Barbara Day
Horizon Community Learning Center	16233 S 48th St	Phoenix, AZ	85048-0801	480-659-3000	659-3022	K-12	Lawrence Pieratt
Horizons Back-to-Basics S	749 E Baseline Rd	Phoenix, AZ	85042-6414	602-304-1763	323-9704	K-8	Jorge Vega
Humanities and Science Institute	1105 E Broadway Rd	Tempe, AZ	85282-1505	480-317-5900	529-4999	9-12	Ana Kennedy
Humanities & Sciences Institute	5201 N 7th St	Phoenix, AZ	85014-2802	602-650-1333	650-1881	9-12	Sue Durkin
Imagine Charter S at Bell Canyon	18052 N Black Canyon Hwy	Phoenix, AZ	85053-1715	602-547-7920	547-7923	K-6	Susan Scorza
Imagine Charter S at Cortez Park	3535 W Dunlap Ave	Phoenix, AZ	85051-5303	602-589-9840	589-9841	K-8	Freddie Villalon
Imagine Charter S at East Mesa	9701 E Southern Ave	Mesa, AZ	85209-3769	480-355-6830	355-6840	K-9	Sheri Ruttinger
Imagine Charter S at Rosefield	12050 N Bullard Ave	Surprise, AZ	85379-6325	623-344-4300	344-4310	K-8	Thomas Shearer
Imagine Charter S at Sierra Vista	1000 E Wilcox Dr	Sierra Vista, AZ	85635-2622	520-224-2500	224-2511	K-8	Ken King
Imagine Charter S at West Gilbert	2061 S Gilbert Rd	Gilbert, AZ	85295-4620	480-855-2700	855-2701	K-8	Linda Horner
Integrity Education Centre	1290 N Scottsdale Rd #123	Tempe, AZ	85281	480-731-4829	394-0711	K-12	Holly Mullan
Intelli School - Glendale	13806 N 51st Ave	Glendale, AZ	85306-4834	602-564-7210	564-7211	9-12	Janet Jorgensen
Intelli School - Main	4629 E Chandler Blvd	Phoenix, AZ	85048	602-564-7300	564-7301	9-12	Jonathan Owen
Intelli School - Metro Center	3101 W Peoria Ave Ste B305	Phoenix, AZ	85029-5210	602-564-7240	564-7241	9-12	Jennifer Lowing
Intelli School - Paradise Valley	1107 E Bell Rd Ste 109A	Phoenix, AZ	85022	602-564-7280	564-7281	9-12	Timothy Howard
International Commerce Institute	5201 N 7th St	Phoenix, AZ	85014-2802	602-650-1116	650-1881	11-12	Sue Durkin
International Commerce Institute - Tempe	1105 E Broadway Rd	Tempe, AZ	85282-1505	480-317-5900	829-4999	7-12	Michael Curd
International Commerce Institute-Tsaile	Dine College - Bldg AJ	Tsaile, AZ	86556	800-762-0010	650-1777	7-12	Arthur Ben
International Studies Academy	4744 W Grovers Ave	Glendale, AZ	85308-3453	602-547-8806	547-2841	7-12	Timothy Smith
Jefferson Academy of Advanced Learning	40 S 11th St	Show Low, AZ	85901-6001	928-537-5432	537-0440	K-12	Sandy Stewart
Jefferson HS	5625 S 51st Dr	Laveen, AZ	85339	623-247-4100	247-4101	9-12	Helen Fortune
JWJ Academy	367 N 21st Ave	Phoenix, AZ	85009-4525	602-258-6060	258-6195	K-12	Walter Tilford
Kachina Country Day S	6602 E Malcomb Dr	Paradise Valley, AZ	85253-5318	480-951-0745	951-1267	PK-6	Janece Kline
Kachina Country Day S - North Campus	10460 N 56th St	Scottsdale, AZ	85253-1133	480-348-1333	348-1454	K-8	Steve Prahcharov
Kestrel HS	PO Box 11028	Prescott, AZ	86304-1028	928-541-1090	541-9939	9-12	Stephen Myers
Keystone Montessori Charter S	1025 E Liberty Ln	Phoenix, AZ	85048-8462	480-460-7312	283-8402	1-8	Sherri Sampson
Khalsa Montessori S	2536 N 3rd St	Phoenix, AZ	85004-1308	602-252-3759	252-5224	K-8	Satwant Khalsa
Khalsa Montessori S	3701 E River Rd	Tucson, AZ	85718-6633	520-529-3611	615-0625	K-8	Nirvair Khalsa
Kingman Academy of Learning HS	2299 E Beverly Ave	Kingman, AZ	86409-0736	928-681-2900	681-2424	9-12	Jeff Martin
Kingman Academy of Learning IS	2299 E Beverly Ave	Kingman, AZ	86409-0736	928-681-3200	681-3202	3-5	Debbie Padilla
Kingman Academy of Learning MS	2299 E Beverly Ave	Kingman, AZ	86409-0736	928-692-5265	692-3444	6-8	Dawn Day
Kingman Academy of Learning PS	2299 E Beverly Ave	Kingman, AZ	86409-0736	928-718-2500	718-2505	K-2	Trudi Bradley

School	Address	City,State	Zip code	Telephone	Fax	Grade	Contact
Lake Havasu Charter S	1055 Empire Dr	Lk Havasu Cty, AZ	86404	928-505-5427	505-3533	K-12	Patty Hauchrog
Lake Havasu Charter S	2700 Jamaica Blvd S	Lk Havasu Cty, AZ	86406-7711	928-505-5427	505-3533	K-6	Patty Hauchrog
La Paloma Academy	2050 N Wilmot Rd	Tucson, AZ	85712-3039	520-721-4205	721-4263	K-10	Jackie Trujillo
La Paloma Academy - Lakeside	8140 E Golflinks Rd	Tucson, AZ	85730-1229	520-733-7373	733-7392	K-8	Randy Musgrove
La Paloma Academy - Midtown	225 N Country Club Rd	Tucson, AZ	85716-5233	520-325-5566	325-6622	K-6	Austin Thies
La Puerta HS	1951 W Camelback Rd	Phoenix, AZ	85015	623-878-8059	878-8175	9-12	Sharon Foster
Leading Edge Academy	459 N Gilbert Rd Ste A146	Gilbert, AZ	85234-4773	480-250-4515	632-7151	K-10	Victoria Hallam
Leading Edge Academy	326 E Guadalupe Rd	Gilbert, AZ	85234-4659	480-545-8011		9-12	Ron Body
Leading Edge Academy	4815 W Hunt Hwy	Queen Creek, AZ	85242-3271	480-655-6787	632-7151	K-8	Laura Newcomb
Learning Crossroads Basic Academy	1130 W 23rd St	Tempe, AZ	85282-1810	480-446-9288	449-9565	K-12	Robin Cubley
Learning Foundation & Performing Arts S	1120 S Gilbert Rd	Gilbert, AZ	85296	480-635-1900	635-1906	K-12	
Learning Foundation Performing Arts S	851 N Stapley Dr	Mesa, AZ	85203	480-834-6202	834-6210	K-12	Lori Graham
Learning Institute	5312 N 12th St	Phoenix, AZ	85014	602-241-7876	241-7886	7-12	Catherine Gerber
Legacy S	7464 E Main St	Mesa, AZ	85207-8306	480-981-1500	641-4473	K-10	Kathy Tolman
Legacy Traditional S	1150 W Grove Pkwy	Tempe, AZ	85283	480-262-8522	204-1051	K-6	Aaron Hale
Liberty HS	PO Box 2343	Globe, AZ	85502-2343	928-402-8024	402-8358	9-12	Sara Macdonald Ph.D.
Liberty Traditional Charter S	4027 N 45th Ave	Phoenix, AZ	85031-2840	602-442-8791	353-9270	K-8	Bonnie Knauel
Lifelong Learning Academy	3295 W Orange Grove Rd	Tucson, AZ	85741-2937	520-219-4383	544-0220	K-6	Mary Lou Klem
Life Skills Center of Arizona	8123 N 35th Ave	Phoenix, AZ	85051	602-242-6400	242-6823	9-12	William Flake
Luz Academy of Tucson	2797 N Introspect Dr	Tucson, AZ	85745-9454	520-882-6216	623-9291	9-12	Alfred Montes
Madison Preparatory S	5815 S Mcclintock Dr	Tempe, AZ	85283-3227	480-345-2306	345-0059	7-12	David Batchelder
Masada Charter S	PO Box 2277	Colorado City, AZ	86021-2277	928-875-2525	875-2526	K-9	Le Anne Timpson
Maya HS	3660 W Glendale Ave	Phoenix, AZ	85051-8335	602-242-3442	242-5255	9-12	Ricardo Borunda
Mesa Arts Academy	221 W 6th Ave	Mesa, AZ	85210-2446	480-844-3965	844-0205	K-8	Susan Douglas
Metropolitan Arts Institute	1700 N 7th Ave	Phoenix, AZ	85007	602-258-9500	258-9504	9-12	Matthew Baker
Mexicayotl Charter S	850 N Morley Ave	Nogales, AZ	85621-2924	520-287-6790	287-0037	K-12	Baltizar Garcia
Midtown HS	7318 W Lynwood St	Phoenix, AZ	85035-4542	623-936-8682	936-8559	9-12	John White
Midtown PS	4735 N 19th Ave	Phoenix, AZ	85015-3725	602-265-5133	604-2337	K-3	Judy White
Milestones Charter S	4707 E Robert E Lee St	Phoenix, AZ	85032-9529	602-404-1009	404-5456	K-5	Tara Cabardo
Mingus Mountain Academy	3071 N Robert Rd	Prescott Valley, AZ	86314	602-335-2072	335-2071	6-12	Cynthia Hancock
Mingus Springs Charter S	PO Box 827	Chino Valley, AZ	86323-0827	928-636-4766	636-5149	K-8	Adrienne Leckliter
Mission Academy HS	1118 W Glendale Ave	Phoenix, AZ	85021-8635	602-944-2097		8-10	
Mission Charter S	7000 N Central Ave	Phoenix, AZ	85020-4817	602-943-4986	943-5936	1-7	Jane Shaw
Mission Montessori Academy	12990 E Shea Blvd	Scottsdale, AZ	85259-5305	480-860-4330	657-3715	K-6	Betty Matthews
Mohave Accelerated Learning Center	PO Box 21288	Bullhead City, AZ	86439-1288	928-704-9345	704-4977	K-12	Vickie Christensen
Montage Academy	32619 N Scottsdale Rd	Scottsdale, AZ	85262	480-990-8763	488-0241	K-8	Esperanza Vega
Montessori Academy	2928 N 67th Pl	Scottsdale, AZ	85251-6002	480-945-1121	874-2928	K-8	Julianne Lewis
Montessori Charter S of Flagstaff	850 N Locust St	Flagstaff, AZ	86001-3343	928-226-1212	774-0337	K-8	Marina Smith
Montessori Childrens House	2400 W Datsi St	Camp Verde, AZ	86322-8412	928-567-1878	567-2107	K-K	Janet Taylor
Montessori Day Charter S - Mountainside	9215 N 14th St	Phoenix, AZ	85020-2713	602-943-7672	395-0271	K-8	Pat Freeman
Montessori Day Charter S - Tempe	1700 W Warner Rd	Chandler, AZ	85224-2676	480-730-8886	730-9072	K-8	Colleen Ortega
Montessori de Santa Cruz Charter S	PO Box 4706	Tubac, AZ	85646-4706	520-398-0536	398-0776	K-6	Lisa Harrison
Montessori Education Centre Charter S	2834 E Southern Ave	Mesa, AZ	85204-5517	480-926-8375	503-0515	K-9	Tamara Whiting
Montessori Education Ctr - Charter S N	815 N Gilbert Rd	Mesa, AZ	85203-5805	480-964-1381	668-5457	K-8	Tammy Whiting
Montessori House Charter S	2415 N Terrace Cir	Mesa, AZ	85203-1220	480-464-2800	464-2836	K-6	Sheryl Richardson
Montessori S at Anthem	42302 N Vision Way Ste 110	Phoenix, AZ	85086-1467	623-551-5083	551-5679	K-8	Debra Slagle
Montessori Schoolhouse	1301 E Fort Lowell Rd	Tucson, AZ	85719-2239	520-622-8668	622-2067	K-K	Regine Ebner
Montessori Schoolhouse	1301 E Fort Lowell Rd	Tucson, AZ	85719-2239	520-319-8668	881-4096	1-5	Michael Ebner
Montezuma MS	5040 S Price Rd	Tempe, AZ	85282-7445	480-831-6057	831-6095	6-8	Abelardo Batista
Morningstar Academy	1150 W Superstition Blvd	Apache Junction, AZ	85220-4043	480-671-5673	671-5675	K-6	Carol Kennedy
Mountain English Spanish Academy	2300 E 6th Ave	Flagstaff, AZ	86004-4247	928-773-4088	773-4086	6-8	Ana Archuleta
Mountain Oak Charter S	124 N Virginia St	Prescott, AZ	86301-3224	928-541-7700	445-1301	K-8	Cynthia Roe
Mountain Rose Academy	3686 W Orange Grove Rd	Tucson, AZ	85741	520-930-9373	797-8868	9-12	Catherine Kinghorn
Mountain S	311 W Cattle Drive Trl	Flagstaff, AZ	86001-7060	928-779-2392	773-3246	PK-5	Renee Fauset
New Horizon S for the Performing Arts	446 E Broadway Rd	Mesa, AZ	85204-2020	480-655-7444	655-8220	K-6	Jim Wyler
New Samaritan HS	1455 S Stapley Dr	Mesa, AZ	85204	480-833-7470	833-7480	9-12	Brian Miller
New School for the Arts	1216 E Apache Blvd	Tempe, AZ	85281-6005	480-481-9235	970-6625	9-12	Katy Cardenas
New School for the Arts MS	1112 E Apache Blvd	Tempe, AZ	85281-5822	480-446-7177	446-7309	7-8	Katy Cardenas
Newton Montessori & Charter S	PO Box 2166	Camp Verde, AZ	86322-2166	928-567-2363	567-5374	PK-5	Shirley Sullivan
New Visions Academy	PO Box 1539	Cottonwood, AZ	86326-1539	928-634-7320	634-7494	9-12	Ann Jenkins
New Visions Academy - St. John's Campus	PO Box 791	Saint Johns, AZ	85936-0791	928-337-3268	337-3383	9-12	Joey Grant
New West S	98 N Oak Dr	Benson, AZ	85602-7732	520-586-1976	586-1655	K-3	Hank Payton
New West S	98 N Oak Dr	Benson, AZ	85602-7732	520-586-1976	586-1655	4-12	Hank Payton
New World Educational Center Charter S	1313 N 2nd St Ste 200	Phoenix, AZ	85004-1701	602-238-9577	238-9210	K-12	Frank Garcia
New World Education Center	4710 E Baseline Rd	Mesa, AZ	85206-4602	480-807-2800	807-2916	K-12	Frank Garcia
NFL YET College Prep Academy	4848 S 2nd St	Phoenix, AZ	85040-2122	602-305-7788	243-7788	7-12	Raul Ruiz
Northern AZ Academy for Career Dev.	PO Box 125	Taylor, AZ	85939-0125	928-536-4222	536-4441	9-12	Kathy Doucette-Edwards
Northern AZ Academy for Career Dev.	502 Airport Rd	Winslow, AZ	86047-5400	928-289-3329	289-4485	9-12	Tamara Pogue
Northland Preparatory Academy	3300 E Sparrow Ave	Flagstaff, AZ	86004-6703	928-214-8776	214-8778	7-12	Ted Briggs
North Pointe Academy	4941 W Union Hills Dr	Glendale, AZ	85308-1486	602-896-1166	896-1164	K-6	Audey Rogus
North Pointe Preparatory S	10215 N 43rd Ave	Phoenix, AZ	85051-1025	623-209-0017	209-0021	7-12	Dr. Todd Herberg
North Star Charter S	10720 W Indian School Rd	Phoenix, AZ	85037	623-907-2661	907-2501	9-12	Aldine Dickens
Nosotros Academy	440 N Grande Ave	Tucson, AZ	85745-2703	520-624-1023	624-7999	6-12	Paul Felix
Oasis HS	8632 W Northern Ave	Glendale, AZ	85305-1308	623-878-8059	878-8175	9-12	Sharon Foster
Ocotillo HS	2616 E Greenway Rd	Phoenix, AZ	85032-4320	602-765-8470	765-8471	9-12	Gabriel Trujillo
Old Pueblo Children's Academy	450 N Pantano Rd	Tucson, AZ	85710-2309	520-296-1600	298-0558	K-8	Ronda McCarthy
Ombudsman Learning Center - East	3943 E Thomas Rd	Phoenix, AZ	85018-7511	602-840-2997	840-1402	7-12	Janice Zagorniak
Ombudsman Learning Center - Metro	4220 W Northern Ave	Phoenix, AZ	85051	602-840-1402	842-6157	6-12	Janice Zagorniak
Ombudsman Learning Center - Northeast	3242 E Bell Rd	Phoenix, AZ	85032-2727	602-485-9872	367-0367	6-12	Janice Zagorniak
Ombudsman Learning Center - Northwest	9516 W Peoria Ave	Peoria, AZ	85345	602-840-2997	840-1402	6-12	Janice Zagorniak
Ombudsman Learning Center - West	3618 W Bell Rd	Glendale, AZ	85308	602-840-2997	840-1402	6-12	Janice Zagorniak
Omega Academy	1951 W Camelback Rd	Phoenix, AZ	85015	602-269-1007	269-1073	K-4	Carmen Gulley
Omega Alpha Academy	1402 N San Antonio Ave	Douglas, AZ	85607-2434	520-805-1261	805-1272	K-12	Dennis Gordon
Omega Alpha Academy S	35 E Wilcox Dr	Sierra Vista, AZ	85635-2521	520-452-7965	452-7966	K-12	Steve Carvalho
PACE Preparatory Academy	155 S Montezuma Castle Hwy	Camp Verde, AZ	86322	928-567-1805		6-12	Kate Pagle
PACE Preparatory Academy	6287 E Copper Hill Dr	Prescott Valley, AZ	86314-2906	928-775-9675	775-9673	9-12	Richard Thelander
Pan-American Charter ES	3001 W Indian School Rd	Phoenix, AZ	85017	602-266-3989	266-3979	K-6	Marta Pasos
Paradise Education Center	15533 W Paradise Ln	Surprise, AZ	85374-5851	623-975-2646	975-2841	K-8	Jeffrey Sloggett
Paramount Academy	11039 W Olive Ave	Peoria, AZ	85345-9200	623-977-0614	977-0615	K-8	Douglas Williams
Park View MS	8300 E Dana Dr	Prescott Valley, AZ	86314-8183	928-775-5115	775-6253	6-8	Mary Bruhn
Patagonia Community Montessori S	PO Box 1008	Patagonia, AZ	85624-1008	520-394-9530	394-2864	PK-8	Paisley McGuire
Pathfinder Academy	2542 N 76th Pl	Mesa, AZ	85207-1252	480-986-7071	986-9858	K-12	Susan Stradling
Patriot Academy	19011 E San Tan Blvd	Queen Creek, AZ	85242	480-279-4780	807-1290	K-8	Jay Brown
Paulden ES	24850 N Naples St	Paulden, AZ	86334	928-583-0455	636-4568	K-6	Kay Deliman
Payson Center for Success	PO Box 919	Payson, AZ	85547-0919	928-472-2011	472-2039	9-12	Kathe Ketchem
Peak S	2016 N 1st St Ste A	Flagstaff, AZ	86004	928-779-0771	779-0774	K-8	Paula Drossman
Peoria Accelerated HS	8885 W Peoria Ave	Peoria, AZ	85345-6442	623-979-0031	979-0113	9-12	Marcus Englund
Peoria Horizons Charter S	11820 N 81st Ave	Peoria, AZ	85345-5736	623-990-7223	990-0936	K-6	Beth Eliason
Phoenix Advantage Charter S	3738 N 16th St	Phoenix, AZ	85016-5915	602-263-8777	263-8822	K-8	Mary Haluska
Pillar Academy of Business & Finance	1589 Plantation Rd	Mohave Valley, AZ	86440	928-346-3925	346-3930	9-12	Marv Lamer
Pima Partnership S	1346 N Stone Ave	Tucson, AZ	85705-7338	520-326-2528	326-2527	9-12	John Powers
Pima Vocational HS	97 E Congress St	Tucson, AZ	85701	520-903-0102	903-0753	9-12	Gloria Proo
Pine Forest Charter S	1120 W Kaibab Ln	Flagstaff, AZ	86001-6217	928-779-9880	779-9792	K-6	Michael Heffernan
Pinnacle - Day Star Academy	2030 N 36th St	Phoenix, AZ	85008-3027	602-275-3852	275-5685	K-12	Stacey Boyd
Pinnacle - Freedom Academy	15014 N 56th St Ste 1	Scottsdale, AZ	85254-2407	602-424-0771	424-0773	K-8	Linda Hoffman
Pinnacle HS - Casa Grande	409 W McMurray Blvd	Casa Grande, AZ	85222-2314	520-423-2380	423-2383	9-12	Mel Logue
Pinnacle HS - Chandler	900 E Pecos Rd	Chandler, AZ	85225	480-633-9222	633-8666	K-12	Maria Gunter
Pinnacle HS - Mesa	151 N Centennial Way	Mesa, AZ	85201-6734	480-668-5003	668-5005	9-12	Ric Borom
Pinnacle HS - Nogales	2055 N Grand Ave	Nogales, AZ	85621-1038	520-281-5109	281-5132	9-12	Locha Partida
Pinnacle HS - Tempe E	1712 E Guadalupe Rd Ste 101	Tempe, AZ	85283-3983	480-785-7776	785-7778	9-12	Michael Williams
Pinnacle HS - Tempe W	2224 W Southern Ave Ste 2	Tempe, AZ	85282-4345	602-414-0950	414-0927	9-12	Michael Matwick
Pinnacle Pointe Academy	6753 W Pinnacle Peak Rd	Glendale, AZ	85310-5301	623-537-3535	537-4433	K-4	Ian Hodor
Pinnacle Virtual HS	4700 S McClintock Dr	Tempe, AZ	85282	480-755-8222	755-8111	7-12	Michael Matwick
PPEP TEC - Arnold Learning Center	4140 W Ina Rd Ste 118	Tucson, AZ	85741-2236	520-579-8560	579-8566	9-12	Rebecca Edmonds
PPEP TEC - Borjorquez Learning Center	203 Bisbee Rd	Bisbee, AZ	85603-1122	520-741-4370	741-4369	9-12	Rebecca Edmonds
PPEP TEC - Chavez Learning Center	1233 N Main St	San Luis, AZ	85349	928-627-8550	627-8980	9-12	Rebecca Edmonds
PPEP TEC - Eugene Lopez Learning Center	158 W Maley St	Willcox, AZ	85643-2130	520-741-4370	741-4369	9-12	Rebecca Edmonds
PPEP TEC - Fernandez Learning Center	1840 E Benson Hwy	Tucson, AZ	85714-1770	520-889-8276	741-4369	9-12	Rebecca Edmonds
PPEP TEC - Paul Learning Center	220 E Florence Blvd	Casa Grande, AZ	85222-4031	520-836-6549	836-0290	9-12	Rebecca Edmonds
PPEP TEC - Pena Learning Center	725 N Central Ave Ste 113	Avondale, AZ	85323-1660	623-925-2161	925-1035	9-12	Rebecca Edmonds
PPEP TEC - Powell Learning Center	4116 Avenida Cochise Ste F	Sierra Vista, AZ	85635-5843	520-458-8205	458-8293	9-12	Rebecca Edmonds
PPEP TEC - Raul H. Castro Learning Ctr	530 E 12th St	Douglas, AZ	85607-1925	520-364-4405	364-1405	9-12	Rebecca Edmonds
PPEP Tec - Robles Junction	10451 S Sasabe Hwy	Tucson, AZ	85736-1254	520-822-3064	822-5070	9-12	Rebecca Edmonds
PPEP TEC - Soltero Learning Center	8677 E Golf Links Rd	Tucson, AZ	85730-1315	520-290-9167	290-9220	9-12	Rebecca Edmonds
PPEP TEC - Yepez Learning Center	115 N Columbia Ave	Somerton, AZ	85350	928-627-9648	627-9197	9-12	Rebecca Edmonds
Precision Academy	7318 W Lynwood St	Phoenix, AZ	85035-4542	623-936-8682	936-8559	10-12	Dr. Caroline White
Precision Academy System Charter S	3906 E Broadway Rd	Phoenix, AZ	85040	602-453-3661	453-3667	9-12	Daniel Martinez

School	Address	City,State	Zip code	Telephone	Fax	Grade	Contact
Premier Charter HS	7544 W Indian School Rd	Phoenix, AZ	85033	623-245-1500	245-1506	9-12	Elisha Madden
Prescott Valley S	9500 E Lorna Ln	Prescott Valley, AZ	86314-2324	928-772-8744	775-4457	K-12	Jennifer Mraz
Presidio S	1695 E Fort Lowell Rd	Tucson, AZ	85719-2319	520-881-5222	881-5522	K-12	Terry Garza
Primavera Technical Learning Center	3029 N Alma School Rd	Chandler, AZ	85224	480-456-6678	820-2168	9-12	Damian Creamer
Rawlins ES	PO Box 13606	Phoenix, AZ	85002-3606	623-332-5478	595-8693	K-5	Sarah Rollins
RCB HS - Phoenix	6049 N 43rd Ave	Phoenix, AZ	85019-1638	602-973-6018	589-1349	9-12	Mark Hebert
Redwood Elementary Academy	9510 N 75th Ave	Peoria, AZ	85345-6621	623-878-0986	776-7956	K-8	Ronald Palmer
Renaissance Academy - Anasazi Campus	PO Box 2741	Pinetop, AZ	85935-2741	928-367-3074	367-5307	9-12	Brad Call
Renaissance Academy - Heber/Overgaard	PO Box 2741	Pinetop, AZ	85935-2741	928-587-2906		K-12	Steve Chavez
Renaissance Academy - John Reeder Campus	411 N 18th Pl	Show Low, AZ	85901-5218	928-532-0195	532-0243	K-8	Steve Chavez
Renaissance Academy - Malpais Campus	1223 E Main St	Springerville, AZ	85938	928-333-1554	333-1555	7-12	Brian Struble
Renaissance Academy - St. Johns Campus	645 W Cleveland	Saint Johns, AZ	85936	928-337-4508	337-3176	1-8	Daniel Mikeworth
Rimrock Public HS	PO Box 248	Rimrock, AZ	86335-0248	928-567-9213	567-9304	9-12	Kathleen McCabe
Romero HS	3005 E Fillmore St	Phoenix, AZ	85008-6120	602-850-2600	850-2615	9-11	Dr. Jane Juliano
SABIS International	1903 E Roeser Rd	Phoenix, AZ	85040-3341	602-305-8865	323-5526	K-12	Graeg Lehmunn
Sandoval Preparatory HS	3830 N 67th Ave	Phoenix, AZ	85033-4036	623-845-0781	849-2840	9-12	David Moore
San Pedro Valley HS	197 E 7th St	Benson, AZ	85602-6629	520-586-8901	586-6189	9-12	Shad Housley
Satori Charter S	3727 N 1st Ave	Tucson, AZ	85719-1609	520-293-7555	293-7020	K-8	Phyllis Gold
Scholars' Academy	PO Box 3475	Quartzsite, AZ	85359-3475	928-927-9420	927-9425	9-12	Steve McClenning
School for Integrated Academics & Tech	518 S 3rd St	Phoenix, AZ	85004-2506	602-258-3927	258-3985	9-12	Geraldine Baumann
School for Integrated Academics & Tech	901 S Campbell Ave	Tucson, AZ	85719-6519	520-791-3016	791-3582	9-12	David Gerber
Sedona Charter S	165 Kachina Dr	Sedona, AZ	86336-4303	928-204-6464	204-6486	K-8	Alice Madar
SEES Charter S	1290 N Scottsdale Rd	Tempe, AZ	85281	480-481-5051	481-5047	9-12	Thea Yockus
Self Development Charter S	1709 N Greenfield Rd	Mesa, AZ	85205-3103	480-641-2640	641-2678	K-8	Anjum Majeed
Sequoia Charter S	1460 S Horne	Mesa, AZ	85204-5760	480-649-7737	649-0711	K-12	Jay Twitchell
Sequoia Choice S - AZ Distance Learning	1460 S Horne	Mesa, AZ	85204-5760	480-655-7005	655-7911	K-12	Linda Harless
Sequoia Ranch S	PO Box 399	Mayer, AZ	86333-0399	928-632-9851	632-9852	K-12	Michael Pospisil
Sequoia S for Deaf & Hard of Hearing	1460 S Horne	Mesa, AZ	85204-5760	480-649-7737	649-0711	K-12	Curt Radford
Sequoia School - Sequoia Village S	982 Full House Ln	Show Low, AZ	85901-4042	928-537-1208	537-4275	K-12	Tony Rhineheart
Shelby S	PO Box 31570	Mesa, AZ	85275-1570	480-478-4706	478-0861	K-10	Nicole Kamp
Sierra Oaks S	650 W Linda Vista Rd	Oracle, AZ	85623-6039	520-896-3100	896-3101	1-8	Paula Jensen
Sierra Summit Achievement S	PO Box 1360	Hereford, AZ	85615-1360	520-803-0508	803-0877	8-12	Siamak Khadjenoury
Skyline JHS	17667 N 91st Ave	Peoria, AZ	85382-3019	623-875-3175	875-9261	6-8	Brian Shipman
Skyline Ranch S	1084 San Tan Hills Dr	Queen Creek, AZ	85243-3489	480-888-7520	868-2302	K-8	G. Meko
Skyline Technical HS	15220 S 50th St Ste 109	Phoenix, AZ	85044-9132	480-763-8425	763-8427	9-12	Ronda Owens
Skyline West HS	17667 N 91st Ave	Peoria, AZ	85382-3019	623-875-3175	875-9261	9-12	Brian Shipman
Skyview S	125 S Rush St	Prescott, AZ	86303-4432	928-776-1730	776-1742	K-8	John Hurley
Solon Academy	2716 N Dobson Rd	Chandler, AZ	85224	480-782-1082	782-1089	K-6	Kevin Sieling
Solon Academy of Arts & Sciences	1375 N McClintock Dr	Chandler, AZ	85226-1304	480-899-7717	899-7793	4-12	Kevin Sieling
Sonoran Desert S	4448 E Main St Ste 7	Mesa, AZ	85205-7916	480-396-5463	396-4980	9-12	Patricia Dalman
Sonoran Science Academy	2255 W Ina Rd	Tucson, AZ	85741-2650	520-797-9836	572-0586	3-12	Ercan Aydogdu
Sonoran Science Academy - Phoenix	4837 E McDowell Rd	Phoenix, AZ	85008-4225	602-244-9855	244-9856	K-8	Mehmet Argin
Southern Arizona Community HS	2470 N Tucson Blvd	Tucson, AZ	85716-2469	520-319-6113	319-6115	9-12	Abelardo Cubillas
Southgate Academy	850 W Valencia Rd	Tucson, AZ	85706-7619	520-741-7900	741-7901	K-12	Sherry Matyjasik
South Pointe HS	8325 S Central Ave	Phoenix, AZ	85042-6576	602-243-0600	243-0800	9-12	Larry McGill
South Ridge HS	1122 S 67th Ave	Phoenix, AZ	85043-4417	602-953-2933	953-0831	9-12	Kerry Clark
Southside Community S	2701 S Campbell Ave	Tucson, AZ	85713-5080	520-623-7102	623-7125	K-8	Janet Dougherty
STAR Charter S	145 Leupp Rd	Flagstaff, AZ	86004-8501	928-606-7419	606-9965	K-8	Mark Sorenson
Starshine Academy	2801 N 31st St	Phoenix, AZ	85008-1126	602-957-9557	956-0065	K-12	Patricia Adams
STARS Prep Academy - Scottsdale	5334 E Thunderbird Rd	Scottsdale, AZ	85254-3655	602-393-6500	393-6501	K-12	Jeff Maynard
Star Valley S	HC 4 Box 4N	Star Valley, AZ	85541-8712	928-468-1401	468-1402	9-12	Russell Koch
Stellar Prep	8632 W Northern Ave	Glendale, AZ	85305-1308	623-878-8059	878-8175	K-4	Sharon Foster
Stepping Stones Academy	35812 N 7th St	Phoenix, AZ	85086-7410	623-465-4910	587-8514	K-8	Ann Marie Short
Student Choice HS	1833 N Scottsdale Rd	Tempe, AZ	85281-1563	480-947-9511	947-9624	9-12	Peggy Lynam
Sturgeon MS	1951 W Camelback Rd	Phoenix, AZ	85015	602-269-1007	269-1073	5-8	Carmen Gulley
Summit ES	1313 N 2nd St	Phoenix, AZ	85004	602-252-7727	252-7729	K-6	Carolyn Sawyer
Summit HS	728 E Mcdowell Rd	Phoenix, AZ	85006-2592	602-258-8959	258-8953	9-12	Mike Little
Sunnyside Charter & Montessori S	PO Box 2166	Camp Verde, AZ	86322-2166	928-567-2363	567-5374	6-9	Dowling Campbell
Sun Valley HS	1143 S Lindsay Rd	Mesa, AZ	85204-6298	480-497-4800	497-1314	9-12	Joe Procopio
Superior S	PO Box 1929	Surprise, AZ	85378-1929	623-875-5975	875-5985	9-12	Tina Davis
TAG S	10129 E Speedway Blvd	Tucson, AZ	85748-1921	520-296-0006	296-0046	K-8	Ron Hom
Teacher Preparation Charter HS	640 N 1st Ave	Phoenix, AZ	85003-1515	602-223-4100	223-4110	9-12	Leticia Ruiz
Telesis Preparatory Academy	2598 Starlite Ln	Lk Havasu Cty, AZ	86403-4946	928-855-8661	855-9302	K-12	Sandra Breece
Tempe Accelerated HS	5040 S Price Rd	Tempe, AZ	85282-7445	480-831-6057	831-6095	9-12	Abelardo Batista
Tempe Preparatory Academy	1251 E Southern Ave	Tempe, AZ	85282-5605	480-839-3402	755-0546	7-12	Ronald Bergez
Tertulia: A Learning Community	812 S 6th Ave	Phoenix, AZ	85003-2528	602-262-2200	262-2570	K-4	Gabriella Ketcham
Tertulia: A Learning Community #2	812 S 6th Ave	Phoenix, AZ	85003-2528	602-262-2200	262-2570	5-8	Juan Sierra
Toltecali Academy	200 N Stone Ave	Tucson, AZ	85701-1208	520-807-7923	807-7827	9-12	Yolanda Carr
Transformational Learning Centers	PO Box 5310	Tucson, AZ	85703-0310	520-628-1404	628-1394	K-12	Tina Giberti
Tri-City College Prep HS	5522 Side Rd	Prescott, AZ	86301-8483	928-777-0403	777-0402	9-12	Dr. Mary Ellen Halvorson
Triumphant Learning Center	201 E Main St	Safford, AZ	85546-2051	928-348-8422	348-8423	K-8	Robin Dutt
Tucson Accelerated HS	7820 E Wrightstown Rd	Tucson, AZ	85715-4339	520-722-4721	722-4785	9-12	Shannon Hughes
Tucson Country Day S	9239 E Wrightstown Rd	Tucson, AZ	85715-5514	520-296-0883	290-1521	K-8	Richard Cooper
Tucson International Academy	1625 W Valencia Rd Ste 109	Tucson, AZ	85746-6022	520-792-3255	792-3245	K-10	Dr. Jennifer Herrera
Tucson International Academy	1230 E Broadway Blvd	Tucson, AZ	85719-5821	520-792-3255	792-3245	K-10	Dr. Jennifer Herrera
Tucson Preparatory S	1525 N Oracle Rd	Tucson, AZ	85705	520-622-4185	622-4755	9-12	Jody Sullivan
Tucson Urban League Academy	2305 S Park Ave	Tucson, AZ	85713-3644	520-622-3651	622-4767	6-12	Charles Monroe
Vah-ki MS	PO Box 10885	Bapchule, AZ	85221-0885	480-403-8580	315-2017	5-8	Beverly Crawford
Vail HS	9040 S Rita Rd Ste 1270	Tucson, AZ	85747-9192	520-382-3200	382-3226	9-12	Dennis Barger
Valley Academy - Charter S	1520 W Rose Garden Ln	Phoenix, AZ	85027-3529	623-516-7747	516-2703	K-8	Sharon Malone
Ventana Academic S	PO Box 1589	Cave Creek, AZ	85327-1589	480-488-9362	488-2079	K-8	Helen Shoulders
Venture Academy	2940 W Bethany Home Rd	Phoenix, AZ	85017-1615	602-943-1317	943-0280	K-8	Fred Bennett
Veritas Preparatory Academy	2131 E Lincoln Dr	Phoenix, AZ	85016-1122	602-263-1128	263-7997	7-12	Andrew Ellison
Victory HS West Campus	PO Box 8374	Phoenix, AZ	85066-8374	602-243-7583	243-7563	9-12	Shirley Branham
Villa Montessori - Phoenix	4535 N 28th St	Phoenix, AZ	85016-4998	602-955-2210	381-4017	K-8	Margo O'Neill
Vision Charter S	PO Box 23455	Tucson, AZ	85734-3455	520-444-0241	741-8123	9-12	Dr. Wilma Soroosh
Visions Unlimited Academy	1275 E Barney Ln	Benson, AZ	85602-7955	520-586-8691	586-3074	K-8	Richard Valentine
Webster Basic S	7301 E Baseline Rd	Mesa, AZ	85209-4907	480-986-2335	354-3490	K-6	Kelly Wade
Westland S	4141 N 67th Ave	Phoenix, AZ	85033-3314	623-247-6456	247-6520	K-12	Kathryn Couch
West Phoenix HS	3835 W Thomas Rd	Phoenix, AZ	85019-4434	602-269-1110	269-1112	9-12	Robert Villa
Westwind Preparatory Academy	2045 W Northern Ave	Phoenix, AZ	85021-5157	602-864-7731	864-7720	7-12	Debra Slagle
Wildcat S	5660 S 12th Ave	Tucson, AZ	85706-3102	520-294-5473	294-5475	6-7	
Willow Creek Charter S	2100 Willow Creek Rd	Prescott, AZ	86301-5391	928-776-1212	776-0009	K-8	Terese Soto
Woods HS	3160 N 33rd Ave	Phoenix, AZ	85017-4817	602-385-4490	864-7720	9-12	Lee Dillenbeck
YCFA Achieve Academy	10401 Highway 89A	Prescott Valley, AZ	86314	928-775-8000	775-8064	4-12	James Wojcik
Young Scholars Academy	1501 Valencia Rd	Bullhead City, AZ	86426-5218	928-704-1100	704-1177	K-8	Tonnie Smith
Youngtown Charter S	13226 N 113th Ave	Youngtown, AZ	85363-1026	623-974-0331	815-8902	K-8	Jacob Duran

Arkansas

School	Address	City,State	Zip code	Telephone	Fax	Grade	Contact
Academic Center of Excellence	112 N School St	Osceola, AR	72370-2413	870-563-2150	622-1025	4-8	Ellouise Tubbs
Academics Plus Charter S	900 Edgewood Dr	Maumelle, AR	72113-6275	501-851-3333	851-2599	3-12	Dr. Mona Briggs
Academy of Technology	PO Box 160	Vilonia, AR	72173-0160	501-796-2018	796-4322	K-12	Sue Farris
Arise Charter S	PO Box 880	Monticello, AR	71657-0880	870-367-6600	367-6395	4-8	Lorenza Simmons
Benton County School of the Arts	2005 S 12th St	Rogers, AR	72758-6307	479-636-2272	636-5447	K-8	Gary Moore
Blytheville Charter S	415 Tennessee St	Blytheville, AR	72315-2170	870-763-7191	762-0172	7-12	Ann Lewis
Cabot Academic Center for Excellence	404 N 2nd St	Cabot, AR	72023-2540	501-843-3138		7-12	Michele Evans
Focus Learning Academy	707 Robins St Ste 100	Conway, AR	72034-6516	501-513-9352	513-9353	K-5	Vivian Harris
Haas Hall Academy	13370 Rheas Mill Rd	Farmington, AR	72730-9625	479-267-4805	267-4862	10-12	Dr. Martin Schoppmeyer
Imboden Area Charter S	PO Box 297	Imboden, AR	72434-0297	870-869-3015	869-3016	K-6	Judy Warren
KIPP: Delta College Preparatory S	215 Cherry St	Helena, AR	72342	870-753-9444	753-9450	5-8	Scott Shirey
Lisa Academy	21 Corporate Hill Dr	Little Rock, AR	72205-4537	501-227-4942	227-4952	6-12	Birol Furat
Mountain Home HS Career Academies	500 Bomber Blvd	Mountain Home, AR	72653-4628	870-425-1215		9-12	Susan Bergman
Raider Open Door Academy	4109 Race St	Jonesboro, AR	72401-7650	870-910-7800	910-7852	5-8	Nicole Covey
Ridgeroad Charter MS	4601 Ridge Rd	No Little Rock, AR	72116-7264	501-771-8155	771-8159	7-8	Lenisha Broadway

California

School	Address	City,State	Zip code	Telephone	Fax	Grade	Contact
Abraxis Charter HS	PO Box 2587	Santa Rosa, CA	95405-0587	707-568-4492	576-0866	9-12	Carley Moore
Academia Avance	PO Box 42095	Los Angeles, CA	90042-0095	213-447-4561	652-0994	6-12	Ricardo Mireles
Academia Semillas del Pueblo	4736 Huntington Dr S	Los Angeles, CA	90032-1942	323-225-4549	987-1240	K-8	Marcos Aguilar
Academic/Vocational Charter Institute	112 Diamond Dr	Watsonville, CA	95076-3184	831-786-2100	786-2318	11-12	Lee Takemoto
Academy for Academic Excellence	17500 Mana Rd	Apple Valley, CA	92307-2181	760-946-5414	946-5343	K-12	Gordon Soholt
Academy for Career Education Charter S	801 Olive St	Wheatland, CA	95692-9787	530-633-3113	633-3106	9-12	Claudia O'Leary
Accelerated Achievement Academy	1031 N State St	Ukiah, CA	95482-3413	707-463-7080	463-7085	4-12	Dr. Kimberly Logan
Accelerated Charter S	119 E 37th St	Los Angeles, CA	90011-2603	323-235-6343	235-6346	K-5	Jonathan Williams
Accelerated S	4000 S Main St	Los Angeles, CA	90037	323-235-6343	235-6346	K-8	Kevin Sved

School	Address	City,State	Zip code	Telephone	Fax	Grade	Contact
Achieve Charter S of Paradise	771 Elliott Rd	Paradise, CA	95969-3913	530-872-4100	872-4105	K-5	Casey Taylor
Acorns to Oaks Charter S	PO Box 639	Anderson, CA	96007-0639	530-365-1055	347-4996	K-8	Debra Clark
Alameda Community Learning Center	210 Central Ave	Alameda, CA	94501-3246	510-521-7123	521-7350	7-12	Paul Bentz
Alexander Science Center	3737 S Figueroa St	Los Angeles, CA	90007-4366	213-744-7409	746-7443	K-5	Brenda Rogers
Alianza Charter S	115 Casserly Rd	Watsonville, CA	95076-9740	831-728-6333	728-6947	K-6	Michael Jones
All Tribes American Indian Charter S	34320 Valley Center Rd	Valley Center, CA	92082-6046	760-749-5982	749-4153	6-9	Mary Ann Donohue
Alvarado Academy Charter S	26247 Ellis St	Madera, CA	93638-0813	760-533-6441	945-4090	K-6	Dr. Nicolas Retana
Alvina S	295 W Saginaw Ave	Caruthers, CA	93609-9710	559-864-9411	864-1808	K-8	Paul Cannon
American Indian Academy	1300 Murray Rd	Mc Kinleyville, CA	95519-3503	707-825-2428	825-2034	9-12	Chris Hartley
American Indian Charter HS	3626 35th Ave	Oakland, CA	94619-1402	510-482-6000	482-6002	9-12	Carey Blakely
American Indian Charter S	3637 Magee Ave	Oakland, CA	94619-1427	510-482-6000	482-6002	6-9	Dr. Ben Chavis
Americas Choice HS	5241 J St	Sacramento, CA	95819-3941	916-277-6545	277-6560	9-12	Beate Martinez
Anderson New Technology HS	2098 North St	Anderson, CA	96007-3477	530-365-3100	365-2957	9-12	Pat Allison
Animo-De La Hoya S	5156 Whittier Blvd	Los Angeles, CA	90022-3932	323-780-1952	780-1953	9-12	Kris Terry
Animo Inglewood Charter HS	3425 W Manchester Blvd	Inglewood, CA	90305-2101	323-565-2100		9-12	Annette Gonzalez
Animo Leadership Charter HS	1071 W Arbor Vitae St	Inglewood, CA	90301	310-216-3277	216-3947	9-11	Julio Murcia
Animo South L.A. HS	11100 S Western Ave	Los Angeles, CA	90047-4845	323-779-0544	392-8752	9-12	John Newsom
Animo Venice HS	841 California Ave	Venice, CA	90291-3411	310-925-7201	392-8752	9-12	Tommy Chang
Annenberg HS	4000 S Main St	Los Angeles, CA	90037	323-235-6343	235-6346	9-12	Manuel Arellano
Antelope Valley Desert Montessori S	44514 20th St W	Lancaster, CA	93534-2715	661-949-0691	949-0691	K-8	Leslie Barrett
Antelope Valley Learning Academy	3145 Rancho Vista Blvd	Palmdale, CA	93551	661-942-2550	940-4427	K-8	Maria Meneses-Trejo Ph.D.
Antelope View Charter S	3243 Center Court Ln	Antelope, CA	95843-9111	916-339-4690	339-4693	6-12	Mary Navarro
Antioch Charter Academy	3325 Hacienda Way	Antioch, CA	94509	925-755-7311	755-7313	K-8	Debbie Hobin
Archway Academy Charter S	108 Campus Way	Modesto, CA	95350-5803	209-558-4415	558-4453	9-12	Bob Vizzolini
Arroyo Vista Charter S	2491 School House Rd	Chula Vista, CA	91915-2534	619-656-9676	656-1858	K-6	Patricia Roth
Arts & Ethics Academy	3360 Coffey Ln Ste A2	Santa Rosa, CA	95403-1995	707-527-6810	546-2882	9-12	Dyan Foster
Arundel ES	200 Arundel Rd	San Carlos, CA	94070-1999	650-508-7311	508-7314	K-4	Allison Liner
ASA Charter S	2050 Pacific St	San Bernardino, CA	92404-6179	909-388-1255	388-1257	K-12	Patricia Campbell
Audeo Charter S	10170 Huennekens St	San Diego, CA	92121-2964	858-678-2050	552-9394	6-12	Tim Tuter
Aveson Global Leadership Acadmey	PO Box 434	Pasadena, CA	91102-0434	626-797-1440	628-3399	6-12	Kate Bean
Aveson School of Leaders	PO Box 434	Pasadena, CA	91102	626-797-1440	628-3399	K-5	Kate Bean
Banks Charter S	PO Box 80	Pala, CA	92059-0080	760-742-3300	742-3102	K-5	
Bay Area S of Enterprise	2750 Todd St	Alameda, CA	94501-7250	510-748-4314	748-4326	9-12	Page Tompkins
Bay Area Technology S	1920 Telegraph Ave	Oakland, CA	94612-2202	510-645-9932	645-9934	6-12	Oscar Yildiz
Bayshore Prep Charter S	100 N Rancho Santa Fe Rd	San Marcos, CA	92069	760-597-0847	597-0275	K-12	Carolyn Lucia
Bellevue-Sante Fe Charter S	1401 San Luis Bay Dr	San Luis Obispo, CA	93405-8007	805-595-7169	595-9013	K-6	Brian Getz
Berkley Maynard Academy	6200 San Pablo Ave	Oakland, CA	94608-2228	510-658-2900	251-1670	K-5	Kristyn Klei
Bitney Springs Charter HS	12338 McCourtney Rd	Grass Valley, CA	95949-9756	530-477-1235	272-1091	9-12	Marshall Goldberg
Blue Oak Charter S	PO Box 6220	Chico, CA	95927-6220	530-879-7483	879-7490	K-8	Stephen Work
Bowling Green Charter ES	4211 Turnbridge Dr	Sacramento, CA	95823-1999	916-433-5426	433-5429	K-6	John Ginn
Bright Star Secondary Academy	2636 S Mansfield Ave	Los Angeles, CA	90016-3512	323-954-9957	954-6415	8-12	Jeff Hilger
Brittan Acres S	2000 Belle Ave	San Carlos, CA	94070-3798	650-508-7307	508-7310	K-4	Kenneth Gallegos
Buckingham Magnet Charter S	188 Bella Vista Rd Ste B	Vacaville, CA	95687-3719	707-453-7300	453-7303	K-12	Bob Hampton
Bullis Charter S	102 W Portola Ave	Los Altos, CA	94022-1210	650-947-4939	947-4989	K-6	Wanny Hersey
Cali Calmecac Charter S	9491 Starr Rd	Windsor, CA	95492-9460	707-837-7747	837-7752	K-8	Ginger Dale
California Academy for Liberal Studies	700 Wilshire Blvd	Los Angeles, CA	90017	213-239-0063	239-9008	9-12	Darryl Adams
California Academy for Liberal Studies	3838 Eagle Rock Blvd	Los Angeles, CA	90065-3638	323-254-4427	254-4099	6-8	Nick Orlando
California College Prep Academy	6200 San Pablo Ave	Oakland, CA	94608-2228	510-658-2900	251-1670	6-12	Michael Prada
California Military Institute	227 N D St Ste C	Perris, CA	92570-1946	951-443-2774	657-3085	7-12	Richard Wallis
California Montessori Project-Amer Rvr	6838 Kermit Ln	Fair Oaks, CA	95628	916-864-0081	864-0084	K-8	Deanna Gardner
California Montessori Project-Capitol	2700 L St	Sacramento, CA	95816	916-325-0910	325-0912	K-8	Bernie Evangelista
California Montessori Project-Elk Grove	8828 Elk Grove Blvd	Elk Grove, CA	95624	916-714-9699	714-9703	K-8	Deirdre Slamkowski
California Montessori Project-Shingl Spr	4645 Buckeye Rd	Shingle Springs, CA	95682	530-672-3095	672-3097	K-8	Kim Zawilski
California Virtual Academy	2360 Shasta Way	Simi Valley, CA	93065	805-581-0202	581-0330	K-12	James Konantz
Camino Nuevo Charter Academy	635 S Harvard Blvd	Los Angeles, CA	90005-2511	213-736-5542	736-5664	PK-8	Kendra Kecker
Camino Nuevo Charter HS	3500 W Temple St	Los Angeles, CA	90004-3620	213-736-5542	736-5664	9-12	Steve Seaford
Camptonville Academy	848 Gold Flat Rd Ste 3	Nevada City, CA	95959-3201	530-478-9458	478-9629	K-12	Janis Jablecki
Canyon Charter ES	421 Entrada Dr	Santa Monica, CA	90402-1303	310-454-7510	454-7543	K-5	Carol Henderson
Capistrano Connections Academy	1211 Puerta Del Sol Ste 220	San Clemente, CA	92673-6357	949-492-9131	492-9140	K-12	Dr. Jean Swenk
Capitol Heights Academy	2520 33rd St	Sacramento, CA	95817-1943	916-739-8520	739-8529	K-8	Robert Spencer
Career Academy at Piner-Olivet	3450 Coffey Ln	Santa Rosa, CA	95403-1919	707-522-3320	522-3101	7-12	Karen Ricketts
Casa Ramona Academy for Technology	1524 W 7th St	San Bernardino, CA	92411-2599	909-889-0011	381-2871	K-12	Esther Ramos Estrada
Castle Rock Charter S	301 W Washington Blvd	Crescent City, CA	95531	707-464-0390	464-9606	K-12	Dennis Burns
Celerity Nascent Charter	3417 W Jefferson Blvd	Los Angeles, CA	90018-3235	323-732-6613	733-2977	K-8	Grace Canada
Centennial College Preparatory Academy	2079 Saturn Ave	Huntington Park, CA	90255-3635	323-826-9616		4-6	Maribel Galan
Center for Advanced Research Technology	2555 Clovis Ave	Clovis, CA	93612-3901	559-248-7400	248-7423	11-12	Susan Fisher
Central California Connections Academy	523 E Grangeville Blvd	Hanford, CA	93230	559-696-1490	740-0867	7-12	Robert Hudson
Central City Value S	221 N Westmoreland Ave	Los Angeles, CA	90004-4815	323-981-7149	981-0162	9-12	David Doyle
Central Valley Home School	1776 6th Avenue Dr	Kingsburg, CA	93631-1701	559-897-6740	897-6872	K-8	Stephen Powers Ph.D.
Century Academy for Excellence	2404 W 85th St	Inglewood, CA	90305	805-642-2000	258-0740	6-8	Dr. Giselle Wilson Edman
Century Community Charter S	901 Maple St	Inglewood, CA	90301-3823	310-412-2286	412-4085	6-8	Teri Delahousie Norris
Challenge Charter High S	PO Box 581	Oroville, CA	95965-0581	530-538-2359	538-2374	9-12	Walt Gess
Charter Alternative Academy	6832 Avenue 280	Visalia, CA	93277-9429	559-730-7491	730-7490	7-12	Rudy Soleno
Charter Community S and Home Study Acad	6767 Green Valley Rd	Placerville, CA	95667-8984	530-295-2259	642-0492	K-12	David Publicover
Charter HS of Arts Multimedia/Performing	6952 Van Nuys Blvd	Van Nuys, CA	91405-3984	818-994-4744	994-0099	9-12	Norman Isaacs
Charter Home School Academy	31411 Road 160	Visalia, CA	93292-9019	559-730-7916	735-8060	K-8	Christine Fischer
Charter S of Morgan Hill	9530 Monterey Rd	Morgan Hill, CA	95037-9356	408-463-0618	462-0267	K-7	Paige Cisewski
Charter S of San Diego	10170 Huennekens St	San Diego, CA	92121-2964	858-678-2020	552-6660	7-12	Mary Bixby
Chavez Dual Language Immersion Charter S	1102 E Yanonali St	Santa Barbara, CA	93103-2704	805-966-7392	966-7243	K-6	Eva Neuer
Chico Country Day S	102 W 11th St	Chico, CA	95928-6006	530-895-2650	895-9159	K-8	Paul Weber
Childrens Community Charter S	6830 Pentz Rd	Paradise, CA	95969-2902	530-877-2227	872-1396	K-8	Bruce Crist
Children's Conservation Academy	3910 University Ave	San Diego, CA	92105	619-501-0349		K-6	Nicole Decatur
CHIME Charter MS	22280 Devonshire St	Chatsworth, CA	91311-2736	818-998-6794	998-0121	6-8	Jennifer Lockwood
CHIME Charter S	19722 Collier St	Woodland Hills, CA	91364-3618	818-346-5100	346-5120	K-5	Jennifer Herschbein
Choice 2000 On-Line S	11 S D St	Perris, CA	92570-2126	951-940-5700	940-5706	9-12	Dr. Cynthia Cartwright
Choices Charter S	3425 Arden Way	Sacramento, CA	95825-2018	916-575-2830	575-1935	7-12	Marie Pflugrath
Chrysalis Charter S	PO Box 993310	Redding, CA	96099-3310	530-225-0318	225-0319	K-8	Paul Krafel
Chula Vista Learning Community Charter S	590 K St	Chula Vista, CA	91911-1118	619-426-2885	426-3048	K-6	Dr. Jorge Ramirez
Circle of Independent Learning	4700 Calaveras Ave	Fremont, CA	94538-1124	510-797-0100	797-0118	K-12	Mary Musgrove
City Arts Academy	611 S 35th St	San Diego, CA	92113-2717	619-238-5233		K-K	Cheryl Bloom
City Arts & Technology HS	301 De Montfort Ave	San Francisco, CA	94112-1733	415-841-2200	585-3009	9-12	Josh Brankman
City Life Downtown Charter S	1501 Wilshire Blvd	Los Angeles, CA	90017-2205	213-989-2267	989-6814	6-12	Jacki Breger
Classical Academy	2950 Bear Valley Pkwy S	Escondido, CA	92025-7446	760-546-0101	739-8289	K-8	Robert Goode
Classical Academy HS	2950 Bear Valley Pkwy S	Escondido, CA	92025-7446	760-480-9845	546-0413	9-12	Mark Reardon
Clear View Charter S	455 Windrose Way	Chula Vista, CA	91910-7400	619-498-3000	498-3007	K-6	Sherrol Stogsdill-Posey
Coastal Academy Charter	4183 Avenida de la Plata	Oceanside, CA	92056-6002	760-631-4020	739-4027	K-8	Robert Goode
Coastal Grove Charter S	PO Box 510	Arcata, CA	95518-0510	707-825-8804		K-8	Bettina Eipper
College Ready Academy #6	1729 W Martin Luther King	Los Angeles, CA	90062	323-293-9169	293-0427	9-12	Ena Lavan
College Ready Academy HS #4	644 W 17th St	Los Angeles, CA	90015-3400	323-309-8952		9-12	Emilio Pack
College Ready Academy HS #5	644 W 17th St	Los Angeles, CA	90015-3400	323-309-8952		9-12	Dean Morello
College Ready Academy HS #7	6501 112th St	Los Angeles, CA	90047	213-804-2548	943-4931	9-12	Raul Carranza Ed.D.
College Ready Academy MS #2	603 E 115th St	Los Angeles, CA	90059-2322			6-8	Joy May-Harris
Collins Charter S at Cherry Valley	1001 Cherry St	Petaluma, CA	94952-2065	707-778-4740	778-4839	K-8	Karen McGahey
Community Charter MS	919 8th St	San Fernando, CA	91340-1312	818-837-4420	837-1420	6-9	Fidel Ramirez
Community Charter S	16945 Sherman Way	Van Nuys, CA	91406-3614	818-774-9888	837-1420	9-11	Daniele Assael
Community Harvest Charter S	3202 W Adams Blvd	Los Angeles, CA	90018-1832	323-373-2000	373-9922	6-12	Charletta Johnson
Connecting Waters Charter S	219 N Reinway Ave	Waterford, CA	95386	209-874-9463	874-9531	K-12	Sherri Nelson
Connections Charter S	17555 Tuolumne Rd	Tuolumne, CA	95379-9701	209-928-4228	928-1422	7-9	Michael Gibson
Conservatory of Vocal/Instrumental Arts	6454 Valley View Rd	Oakland, CA	94611-1229	510-339-2961		K-8	Dr. Valerie Abad
Constellation Charter MS	PO Box 2130	Long Beach, CA	90801-2130	562-435-7181	435-3981	6-8	Daphne Ching-Jackson
Cornerstone Prep Charter MS	2232 Lincoln Blvd	Venice, CA	90291-3953	310-636-2774	636-2775	6-8	Daniel Davis
Cornerstone Prep S	7651 S Central Ave	Los Angeles, CA	90001-2945	323-581-4495	581-4214	K-8	Stephan Bean
Corona Charter S	12953 Branford St	Pacoima, CA	91331-4303	818-834-5805	834-8075	6-8	Yvette Berg
Cortez Hill Academy	201 A St	San Diego, CA	92101-4003	619-338-9206	338-0448	9-12	Michael Hazelton
Creative Arts Charter S	1601 Turk St	San Francisco, CA	94115-4527	415-749-3647	749-3649	K-8	Stephen Good
Creative Connections Arts Academy	7201 Arutas Dr	North Highlands, CA	95660-2809	916-566-1870	331-2959	K-8	Joe Breault
Crenshaw Arts-Tech Charter HS	2941 W 70th St	Los Angeles, CA	90043-4420	323-778-7700	778-7712	9-12	Patricia Smith
Crescendo Charter Academy	13000 Van Ness Ave	Gardena, CA	90249-1726	323-329-1300	329-9300	K-5	Reginald Brunson
Crescendo Charter ES	4900 S Western Ave	Los Angeles, CA	90062-2326	323-295-9495	295-0845	K-5	John Allen
Crescent View Charter HS	3502 N Blackstone Ave	Fresno, CA	93726	559-222-8439	222-8430	9-12	Demitri Gonos
Cross Cultural Environmental Leadership	682 Schofield Rd	San Francisco, CA	94129-1198	415-642-5822		K-12	Cristina Valdez
Crossroads Charter S	1766 N 10th Ave	Hanford, CA	93230	559-585-7295	585-7298	K-12	Laurie Blue
Crosswalk Charter S	12061 Jacaranda Ave Ste 5	Hesperia, CA	92345-4962	760-949-8002	947-9648	5-12	Chala Salisbury
Culture & Language Academy of Success	100 E Nutwood St	Inglewood, CA	90301-2343	310-680-7100	680-7103	K-8	Janis Bucknor
Cypress Charter HS	2039 Merrill St	Santa Cruz, CA	95062-4176	831-477-0302	477-7659	9-12	Les Forster
Darnall E-Charter S	6020 Hughes St	San Diego, CA	92115-6520	619-582-1822	287-4732	K-6	Cinda Doughty
Dehesa Charter S	1441 Montiel Rd	Escondido, CA	92026	760-743-7880	743-7919	K-12	Terri Novacek

School	Address	City,State	Zip code	Telephone	Fax	Grade	Contact
Delta Charter ES	2773 Clicker Ct	West Sacramento, CA	95691	916-995-1335	405-3944	K-6	Debra Daniels
Delta Charter HS	31400 S Koster Rd	Tracy, CA	95304-8824	209-830-6363	830-9324	9-12	Mary Vink
Delta Charter S	343 Soquel Ave	Santa Cruz, CA	95062-2305	831-477-5213	479-6173	9-12	Mary Gaukel
Delta View District-wide Charter S	1201 Lacey Blvd	Hanford, CA	93230-9306	559-582-3122	582-3139	K-8	Bernie Hanlon
Denair Charter Academy	3460 Lester Rd	Denair, CA	95316-9502	209-634-0917	669-9282	K-12	Alex Marshall
Desert Sands Charter HS	3030 E Palmdale Blvd Ste G	Palmdale, CA	93550	661-272-0044	944-4857	9-12	Mary Gil
Diamond Mountain Charter HS	55 S Weatherlow St	Susanville, CA	96130	530-257-5566	257-5851	9-12	Brett Mitchell
Discovery Charter S	1100 Camino Biscay	Chula Vista, CA	91910-7737	619-656-0797	656-3899	K-6	Michael Cole
Discovery Charter S	12550 Van Nuys Blvd	Pacoima, CA	91331-1354	818-897-1187	897-1295	9-12	Matthew Macarah
Discovery Charter S	51 E Beverly Pl	Tracy, CA	95376-3191	209-831-5240	831-5243	5-8	Virginia Stewart
Discovery Charter S	4021 Teale Ave	San Jose, CA	95117	408-243-9800	243-9810	K-8	Stephen Fiss
Dixon Montessori Charter S	180 S 1st St Ste 6	Dixon, CA	95620	707-678-8953	678-4285	K-6	Carolyn Pfister
Downtown College Preparatory	1460 The Alameda	San Jose, CA	95126-2652	408-271-1730	271-1734	9-12	Jennifer Andaluz
Downtown Value S	950 W Washington Blvd	Los Angeles, CA	90015-3312	213-748-8868	748-8062	K-8	Gerry Jacoby
Eagle Peak Montessori S	800 Hutchinson Rd	Walnut Creek, CA	94598-4505	925-946-0994	946-9409	K-6	Michelle Hammons
Eagles Peak Charter S	981 Vale Terrace Dr	Vista, CA	92084-5213	866-806-3200	630-5323	K-12	Kathleen Hermsmyer
East Bay Conservation Corps Charter S	1021 3rd St	Oakland, CA	94607-2507	510-992-7819	992-7950	9-12	Kate Mahar
East Bay Conservation Corps Charter S	1086 Alcatraz Ave	Oakland, CA	94608-1265	510-420-3701	420-3703	K-5	Carolyn Gramstorff
East Oakland Leadership Academy	2614 Seminary Ave	Oakland, CA	94605-1570	510-562-5238	562-5239	6-8	Laura Armstrong
East Palo Alto Charter S	1286 Runnymede St	East Palo Alto, CA	94303-1332	650-614-9100	614-9183	K-8	Allie Leslie
Eastside Campus Westside Prep Charter S	6469 Guthrie St	North Highlands, CA	95660-3944	916-566-1860	339-2033	7-8	Ken Gammelgard
EcoAcademy HS - Central LA	1403 S Union Ave	Los Angeles, CA	90015-3205	213-389-3103	389-3105	9-12	
Edison-Bethune Charter Academy	1616 S Fruit Ave	Fresno, CA	93706-2819	559-457-2530	498-0711	K-6	Felicia Treadwell
Edison-Brentwood Academy	2086 Clarke Ave	East Palo Alto, CA	94303-1916	650-329-2881	329-2877	K-3	Dianne Witwer
Edison Charter Academy	3531 22nd St	San Francisco, CA	94114-3405	415-970-3330	285-0527	K-8	Margaret Quillen
Edison McNair Academy	2033 Pulgas Ave	East Palo Alto, CA	94303-2025	650-329-2888	327-9163	4-8	Doug Harrell
Education for Change	9860 Sunnyside St	Oakland, CA	94603-2750	510-904-6300	904-6733	K-5	Michael Scott
Education for Change - E Oakland Charter	1700 28th Ave	Oakland, CA	94601-2455	510-904-6400	904-6763	K-3	Susan Sperber
Education for Change - Upper ES	1700 28th Ave	Oakland, CA	94601	510-904-6440	904-6761	4-5	Fernando Yanez
Eel River Charter S	PO Box 218	Covelo, CA	95428-0218	707-983-6946	983-6197	K-8	Betty Tuttle
Einstein Academy	3035 Ash St	San Diego, CA	92102-1718	619-795-1190	795-1180	K-8	Luci Fowers
EJE Academy Charter ES	191 E Chase Ave	El Cajon, CA	92020	619-401-4150	401-4151	K-3	Delia Pacheco
Elk Grove Charter S	5900 Bamford Dr	Sacramento, CA	95823-4607	916-714-1653	428-8307	1-12	Christy Moustris
El Rancho Charter MS	181 S Del Giorgio Rd	Anaheim, CA	92808-1399	714-997-6238	281-8791	7-8	John Besta
El Sol Science & Arts Charter Academy	1010 N Broadway	Santa Ana, CA	92701-3408	714-543-0023	543-0026	K-8	Monique Davis
Emerson Parkside Academy	2625 Josie Ave	Long Beach, CA	90815-1511	562-420-2631	420-7642	K-5	Mark Andreatta
Environmental Charter HS	4234 W 147th St	Lawndale, CA	90260-1602	310-676-3107	676-3981	9-12	Joanna Paul
Envision Academy for Arts & Technology	967 Stanford Ave	Emeryville, CA	94608	510-596-8901	596-8905	9-12	Alcine Mumby
e-Scholar Charter S	20 Antelope Blvd	Red Bluff, CA	96080	530-527-0188	527-0273	K-12	Harold Vietti
Escondido Charter HS	1868 E Valley Pkwy	Escondido, CA	92027-2525	760-737-3154	738-8996	9-12	Denny Snyder
Escuela Popular/Ctr Training & Careers	467 N White Rd	San Jose, CA	95127	408-275-7193	275-7192	K-12	Patricia Reguerin
Etna Academy of Arts	PO Box 490	Etna, CA	96027-0490	530-467-3320	467-3465	7-8	James Pindell
Evergreen Charter S	PO Box 992418	Redding, CA	96099-2418	530-247-1800	247-1824	K-6	Connie Champp
Excel Charter Academy	2635 Pasadena Ave	Los Angeles, CA	90031	323-222-5010	222-5148	6-8	Patricia Mora
Excelsior Education Center Charter S	12217 Spring Valley Pkwy	Victorville, CA	92395	760-245-4448	245-4009	7-12	Charles Gehrke
Explorer ES	2230 Truxtun Rd	San Diego, CA	92106	619-398-8600	398-8601	K-5	Jill Green
FAME Public Charter S	39899 Balentine Dr	Newark, CA	94560	510-687-9111	687-9145	K-12	Maram Alaiwat
Fammatre Charter ES	2800 New Jersey Ave	San Jose, CA	95124-1556	408-377-5480	377-8751	K-5	Midge Jambor
Fanno Academy	401 S 45th St	San Diego, CA	92113	619-269-9929		K-6	Kadumu Moyenda
Farnham Charter ES	15711 Woodard Rd	San Jose, CA	95124-2668	408-377-3321	377-7237	K-5	Maureen Ricketts
Feaster Charter S	670 Flower St	Chula Vista, CA	91910-1399	619-422-8397	422-4780	K-6	Erik Latoni
Fenton Avenue Charter S	11828 Gain St	Sylmar, CA	91342-7130	818-896-7482	890-9986	PK-5	Irene Sumida
Finch S	451 S Villa Ave	Willows, CA	95988-2964	530-934-6320	934-6325	K-12	Ann Lambert
Five Keys Charter S	70 Oak Grove St	San Francisco, CA	94107-1019	415-734-3310	734-3314	9-12	Sheryl Corke
Folsom Community Charter S	101 Dean Way	Folsom, CA	95630-2801	916-817-8499	817-8860	K-8	Wayne Edney
Forest Charter S	224 Church St	Nevada City, CA	95959-2505	530-265-4823	265-5037	K-12	Sandy McDivitt
Forestville Academy	6321 Hwy 116	Forestville, CA	95436-9606	707-887-2279	887-1037	K-8	Robert Borbe
4 Winds Charter S	2345 Fair St	Chico, CA	95928-6749	530-879-7411	879-7414	K-12	Terri Tozier
Fremont Charter S	1120 W 22nd St	Merced, CA	95340-3540	209-385-6627	385-6301	K-5	Dalinda Saich
Freshwater Charter S	75 Greenwood Heights Dr	Eureka, CA	95503-9441	707-442-2969	442-9527	K-8	Thom McMahon
Fresno Preparatory Academy	3355 E Shields Ave	Fresno, CA	93726-6906	559-222-3840	222-3540	9-12	Bill Realin
Frontier Charter S	6691 Silverthorne Cir	Sacramento, CA	95842-2699	916-566-1840	344-8932	7-8	Ellen Giffin
Fuenta Nueva Charter S	1435 Buttermilk Ln	Arcata, CA	95521	707-822-3348		K-5	Beth Wylie
Futures HS	3701 Stephen Dr	North Highlands, CA	95660-4532	916-286-1900	263-6059	7-12	Anjam Kahn
Gabriela Charter S	631 S Commonwealth Ave	Los Angeles, CA	90005-4003	213-487-0839	487-0894	K-5	Susan Gurman
Garfield Charter S	3600 Middlefield Rd	Menlo Park, CA	94025-3010	650-369-3759	367-4358	K-8	Alex Hunt
GARR Academy of Math & Entrepreneurial	5101 S Western Ave	Los Angeles, CA	90062	323-294-2008	295-3936	K-5	Doris Sims Ph.D.
Gates ES	23882 Landisview Ave	Lake Forest, CA	92630-5199	949-837-2260	837-5013	K-6	Yvonne Estling
Gateway HS	1430 Scott St	San Francisco, CA	94115-3510	415-749-3600	749-2716	9-12	Peter Thorp
Gateway to College	4800 Magnolia Ave	Riverside, CA	92506	951-222-8931	222-8975	9-12	Jill Marks
Genesis S	5601 47th Ave	Sacramento, CA	95824-4031	916-433-5300	433-5372	7-12	Judy Billingsley
Gertz-Ressler HS-College Ready HS 1	2023 S Union Ave	Los Angeles, CA	90007-1326	213-745-8141	745-8142	9-12	Howard Lappin
Giraffe Charter ES	436 S Alexandria Ave	Los Angeles, CA	90020-2703	213-614-1745	614-2046	K-1	Jill Wells
Glacier Charter HS	41267 Highway 41	Oakhurst, CA	93644-9403	559-642-1422	642-1592	9-12	Michael Cox
Global Youth Charter HS	3243 Center Court Ln	Antelope, CA	95843	916-339-4680	339-4684	9-12	Addie Ellis
Golden Valley Charter	2421 Portola Rd Ste C	Ventura, CA	93003-8048	805-642-3435	642-3468	K-12	Terri Adams
Golden Valley Charter S	6838 Kermit Ln	Fair Oaks, CA	95628	916-962-3104	962-3107	K-8	Debi Lenny
Gold Oak Arts Charter S	3171 Pleasant Valley Rd	Placerville, CA	95667-9299	530-626-3157	626-3159	4-8	Sylvia Shannon
Gold Rush Charter S	14673 Mono Way	Sonora, CA	95370-9220	209-533-8644	588-9988	K-12	Kathleen Hanson
Gompers Charter S	1005 47th St	San Diego, CA	92102-3699	619-263-2171		6-9	Vince Riveroll
Gorman Learning Center	1826 Orange Tree Ln	Redlands, CA	92374-2821	909-307-6312	793-5964	K-12	Waldo Burford
Granada Hills HS	10535 Zelzah Ave	Granada Hills, CA	91344-5999	818-360-2361	363-9504	9-12	Brian Bauer
Grant Community Outreach Center	5800 Skvarla Ave	Mc Clellan AFB, CA	95652-2418	916-286-5170	640-0227	K-12	Lorissa Gonchar
Grass Valley Charter S	342 S School St	Grass Valley, CA	95945-6699	530-273-8723	271-0557	K-8	Stephen Burns
Grayson Charter S	301 Howard Rd	Westley, CA	95387	209-894-3762	894-3393	K-5	Arturo Duran
Greater San Diego Academy	13881 Campo Rd	Jamul, CA	91935	619-669-3050	669-3066	K-12	Gail Levine
Grizzly ChalleNGe Charter S	PO Box 3209	San Luis Obispo, CA	93403-3209	805-782-6882	594-6341	10-12	Paul Piette
Grove Charter HS	200 Nevada St	Redlands, CA	92373-5385	909-798-7831	307-6464	9-12	Michael Waski
Guajome Park Academy	2000 N Santa Fe Ave	Vista, CA	92083-1534	760-631-6077	631-3411	6-12	Penny Harrison
Guidance Charter S	1125 E Palmdale Blvd Ste B	Palmdale, CA	93550	661-272-1701	272-1728	K-8	Kamal Al-Khatib
Hallmark Charter S	2551 9th St	Sanger, CA	93657	559-875-1372	875-3573	K-12	Alfred Sanchez
Hart-Ransom Academic Charter S	3920 Shoemake Ave	Modesto, CA	95358-8577	209-523-0401	523-1064	K-8	Sherry Smith
Hawthorne Math Science & Tech S	4467 W Broadway	Hawthorne, CA	90250-3819	310-973-8620	973-8167	9-12	David Morrow
Hearthstone Charter S	2120B Robinson St	Oroville, CA	95965-4937	530-532-5848	532-5847	K-12	Kim Guzzetti
Heather S	2757 Melendy Dr	San Carlos, CA	94070-3604	650-508-7303	508-7306	K-4	Pam Jasso
Helix HS	7323 University Ave	La Mesa, CA	91941-6092	619-466-4194	462-9257	9-12	Dr. Douglas Smith
Heritage Charter S	1855 E Valley Pkwy	Escondido, CA	92027-2517	760-737-3154	738-8996	K-8	Dennis Snyder
Heritage College Ready HS	603 E 115th St	Los Angeles, CA	90059-2322	323-754-2364		9-12	Doc Ervin
Heritage Peak Charter S	3600 Madison Ave Ste 59	North Highlands, CA	95660	866-992-9033	338-4770	K-12	Paul Keefer
Heritage S	PO Box 296000	Phelan, CA	92329-6000	760-868-2422	868-0589	K-8	John Garner
Hickman Charter S	13306 4th St	Hickman, CA	95323-9634	209-874-9070	874-1457	K-8	Patricia Golding
Hickman ES	13306 4th St	Hickman, CA	95323-9634	209-874-1816	874-3721	K-5	Christine Linder
Hickman MS	13306 4th St	Hickman, CA	95323-9634	209-874-1816	874-3721	6-8	Robert Loretelli
High Desert Academy	15411 Village Dr	Victorville, CA	92394-1912	760-843-7445	245-9541	7-12	Anthony Chambers
High Tech High Media Art	2230 Truxtun Rd	San Diego, CA	92106	619-398-8620	224-1198	9-12	Ted Cuevas
High Tech HS Bayshore	890 Broadway St	Redwood City, CA	94063	650-381-0100	591-5446	9-12	Joe Feldman
High Tech HS Chula Vista	1501 Magdalena Ave	Chula Vista, CA	91913	619-838-2308	243-5050	9-12	Colleen Warwick
High Tech HS - LA	17111 Victory Blvd	Van Nuys, CA	91406-5455	818-881-2640	881-1754	9-12	Marsha Rybin
High Tech HS North County	San Marcos Blvd & Discovery	San Marcos, CA	92069	760-560-6249		9-12	Nicole Hinostro
High Tech International HS	2855 Farragut Rd	San Diego, CA	92106	619-398-4900	758-1960	9-12	Kelly Wilson
High Tech Middle Media Arts	2230 Truxtun Rd	San Diego, CA	92106	619-398-8640	758-9568	6-8	Nicole Hinostro
High Tech MS	2359 Truxtun Rd	San Diego, CA	92106	619-814-5060	814-5088	6-8	Laura McBain
Holly Drive Leadership Academy	4999 Holly Dr	San Diego, CA	92113-2046	619-266-7333	266-7330	K-8	Alysia Smith
Holt College Prep Academy	3201 Morada Ln	Stockton, CA	95212-3110	209-955-1477	955-1472	6-12	Gretchen Salvetti
HomeTech Charter S	7126 Skyway	Paradise, CA	95969	530-872-1171	872-1172	K-12	Sue Gioia
Horizon Charter S	PO Box 489000	Lincoln, CA	95648-9000	916-408-5260	408-5223	K-12	Luanne Boone
Huerta Learning Academy	1936 Courtland Ave	Oakland, CA	94601-4614	510-533-9790	533-9794	K-8	Kenneth Reed
Huntington Park College Ready Academy	2071 Saturn Ave	Huntington Park, CA	90255-3635	323-923-1588	923-1589	9-12	Laura Galvan
Iftin Charter S	6605 University Ave	San Diego, CA	92115	619-265-2411		K-6	Abdulkadir Mohamed
Imagine Academy Charter S	16651A Rinaldi St	Granada Hills, CA	91344-3632	818-368-1557	368-1935	6-12	Diane Fresh
Impact Academy of Arts & Technology	1515 Webster St	Oakland, CA	94612	510-596-8901		9-12	Jennifer Davis Wickens
Inland Leaders Charter S	13456 Bryant St	Yucaipa, CA	92399	909-844-5772	363-8545	K-6	Michael Gordon Ed.D.
Institute of Business & Law	6650 Inglewood Ave	Stockton, CA	95207-3861	209-933-7475	472-7841	9-12	Bill Parks
Integrity Charter S	125 Palm Ave	National City, CA	91950-1719	619-474-5643	474-5643	K-6	Sandra Dominguez
International S of Monterey	1720 Yosemite St	Seaside, CA	93955	831-583-2165	899-7653	K-7	Chrissie Jahn
Island S	7799 21st Ave	Lemoore, CA	93245-9694	559-924-6424	924-0247	K-8	Tom Bates
Ivy Academia	6221 Fallbrook Ave	Woodland Hills, CA	91367-1602	818-348-8190	332-4136	K-12	Eugene Selivanov

School	Address	City,State	Zip code	Telephone	Fax	Grade	Contact
Jacobs High Tech HS	2861 Womble Rd	San Diego, CA	92106-6025	619-243-5000	243-5050	9-12	Ben Daley
Jacoby Creek S	1617 Old Arcata Rd	Bayside, CA	95524-9324	707-822-4896	822-4898	K-8	Eric Grantz
Jardin De la Infancia	307 E 7th St	Los Angeles, CA	90014-2209	213-614-1745	614-2046	K-1	Alice Callaghan
Johnson JHS	1300 Stroud Ave	Kingsburg, CA	93631-1000	559-897-1091	897-6867	7-8	Laurie Goodman
Jordan MS	22250 Elkwood St	Canoga Park, CA	91304-5501	818-468-3637	709-3961	6-8	Myranda Marsh
Journey S	23431 Knollwood	Aliso Viejo, CA	92656-4240	949-448-7232	448-7256	K-5	Tim Connolly
Julian Charter S	PO Box 1780	Julian, CA	92036-1780	866-853-0003	765-3849	K-12	Jennifer Cauzza
Junior Space Exploration Academy	2722 Adeline St	Oakland, CA	94607	510-832-7827		6-8	Wilhelmina Santa Maria
Keiller Leadership Academy	7270 Lisbon St	San Diego, CA	92114-3007	619-263-9266	262-2217	6-8	Patricia Ladd
Keith B. Kenny Charter S	3525 Martin Luther King Blv	Sacramento, CA	95817	916-277-6500	277-6513	K-6	David Ermshar
Kenter Canyon Charter S	645 N Kenter Ave	Los Angeles, CA	90049-1999	310-472-5918	472-9738	K-5	Terry Moren
Kern Workforce 2000 Academy Charter	5801 Sundale Ave	Bakersfield, CA	93309-2924	661-827-3224	827-3320	9-12	Fuchsia Ward
Keyes To Learning Charter S	PO Box 519	Keyes, CA	95328-0519	209-634-6467	669-7121	K-9	Lee Ann Stangl
Kid Street Learning Center	PO Box 6784	Santa Rosa, CA	95406-0784	707-525-9223	525-9432	K-6	Linda Conklin
King Chavez Academy of Excellence	735 Cesar E Chavez Pkwy	San Diego, CA	92113-1118	619-232-2825	232-2943	K-8	Toni Smith
King/Chavez Arts Academy	415 31st St	San Diego, CA	92102-4236	619-525-7320		3-5	Roxanne Rojas
King/Chavez Athletics Academy	415 31st St	San Diego, CA	92102-4236	619-525-7320		3-5	Dr. Brian French
King/Chavez Preparatory Academy	415 31st St	San Diego, CA	92102-4236	619-525-7320		6-6	Elena Bolanos
King/Chavez Primary Academy	415 31st St	San Diego, CA	92102-4236	619-525-7320		K-2	Irisbelle de Blanco
King City Arts Charter S	519 Broadway St	King City, CA	93930-3230	831-385-3246	385-6310	K-1	Bob Bilek
Kings River-Hardwick S	10300 Excelsior Ave	Hanford, CA	93230-9794	559-584-4475	585-1422	K-8	Leslie Ford
KIPP Academy Fresno	2445 W Dakota Ave	Fresno, CA	93705-2611	559-233-5477	432-9793	5-8	Chi Tschang
KIPP Academy of Opportunity	7019 S Van Ness Ave	Los Angeles, CA	90047-1659	323-778-0125	778-0162	5-8	Mikelle Willis
KIPP Adelante Preparatory S	1475 6th Ave Fl 2	San Diego, CA	92101	619-233-3242	233-3212	5-8	Kelly Wright
KIPP Bayview Academy	1060 Key Ave	San Francisco, CA	94124-3563	415-467-2522	467-9522	5-8	Molly Wood
KIPP Heartwood Academy	1250 S King Rd	San Jose, CA	95122-2146	408-928-2400	928-2401	5-8	Sehba Zhumkhawala
KIPP King Collegiate HS	2005 Via Barrett	San Lorenzo, CA	94580-1315			9-12	Jason Singer
KIPP LA College Prep S	1855 N Main St	Los Angeles, CA	90031-3227	323-223-5477	223-5410	5-8	Carolyn Ruff
KIPP San Francisco Bay Academy	1430 Scott St	San Francisco, CA	94115-3510	415-440-4306	440-4308	5-8	Lydia Glassie
KIPP Summit Academy	2005 Via Barrett	San Lorenzo, CA	94580-1315	510-798-9434		5-8	Cathy Cowan
Klamath River Early College of Redwoods	PO Box 849	Klamath, CA	95548-0849	707-482-1737	482-1738	9-12	Geneva Wiki
LACC Charter HS - East	1020 S Fickett St	Los Angeles, CA	90023-1410	323-526-1460	526-1453	9-12	
LACC Charter HS - South Central	2824 S Main St	Los Angeles, CA	90007-3334	213-749-3601	745-8890	9-12	Noel Trout
LA Educ Achievement Partnership HS	20920 Knapp St	Chatsworth, CA	91311-5906	818-709-4282	709-3961	9-12	Aviva Ebner
LA International Charter S	15355 Morrison St	Sherman Oaks, CA	91403-1514	323-257-1499	729-9684	9-12	Ben Maurer
Lake County International Charter S	PO Box 984	Middletown, CA	95461-0984	707-987-3063	825-9344	K-8	Karl Reichman
Lakeview Charter Academy	1445 Celis St	San Fernando, CA	91340-3207	818-837-9190	837-0520	6-8	Edward Vandenberg
Lammersville Charter S	16555 Von Sosten Rd	Tracy, CA	95304-7220	209-836-7225	835-1113	K-8	Bill Lebo
Language Academy	4500 Roosevelt Ave	Sacramento, CA	95820-4546	916-277-7137	277-7141	K-7	Martha Quadros
Larchmont Charter S	815 N El Centro Ave	Los Angeles, CA	90038-3805	323-836-0860	656-1467	K-6	Alice Horevitz
La Sierra HS	1735 E Houston Ave	Visalia, CA	93292-2349	559-733-6963	733-6845	9-12	Dr. Lorene Valentino
Latino College Preparatory Academy	14271 Story Rd	San Jose, CA	95127-3823	408-729-2283	285-5324	9-12	Jess Barajas
La Vida Charter S	16201 N Highway 101	Willits, CA	95490-8724	707-459-6344	459-6377	K-12	Ann Kelly
Leadership Academy	400 Mansell St	San Francisco, CA	94134-1829	415-841-8910	841-8925	9-12	Greg Peters
Leadership Public S - Campbell	1980 Hamilton Ave	San Jose, CA	95125	415-695-0669	358-4513	9-12	Joe Pacheco
Leadership Public S - Hayward	28000 Calaroga Ave	Hayward, CA	94545-4600	510-300-1340	372-0396	9-12	Brian Greenberg
Leadership Public S Richmond	715 Chanslor Ave	Richmond, CA	94801-3533	510-235-4522	588-4593	9-12	John Harris
Leadership Public S - San Jose	1881 Cunningham Ave	San Jose, CA	95122	408-937-2700	937-2705	9-12	Larry Vilaubi
Learner-Centered S	PO Box 1521	Antioch, CA	94509-0152	925-755-1252	755-7527	K-9	Debbie Hobin
Learning Choice Academy	PO Box 531588	San Diego, CA	92153-1588	858-536-8388		K-12	Kathy Bass
Learning for Life Charter S	330 Reservation Rd Ste F	Marina, CA	93933-3286	831-582-9820	582-9825	7-12	Cindy Dotson
Lemoore University Charter S	100 Vine St	Lemoore, CA	93245-3418	559-924-6890	924-6839	5-8	Crescenciano Camarena
Lennox Math Science & Tech Academy	10319 Firmona Ave	Lennox, CA	90304-1419	310-680-5600	671-5029	9-12	Armando Mena
Life Learning Academy	651 8th St Bldg 229	San Francisco, CA	94130-1901	415-397-8957	397-9274	9-12	Teri Delane
Lifeline Learning Charter S	357 E Palmer St	Compton, CA	90221-2610	310-605-2510	764-4890	7-12	Paula DeGroat
Lighthouse Community Charter HS	1600 Broadway	Oakland, CA	94612	510-271-8403	271-8803	7-12	Stephen Sexton
Lighthouse Community Charter S	345 12th St	Oakland, CA	94607-4217	510-271-8801	271-8803	K-6	Melissa Barnes Dholakia
Lincoln ES	1900 Mariposa St	Kingsburg, CA	93631-2044	559-897-5141	897-3537	2-4	Jennifer DuPras
Linscott Charter S	220 Elm St	Watsonville, CA	95076-5025	831-728-6301	761-5478	K-8	Robin Higbee
Literacy First Charter S	799 E Washington Ave	El Cajon, CA	92020-5327	619-579-7232	579-5730	K-8	Debbie Beyer
Live Oak Charter S	100 Gnoss Concourse	Petaluma, CA	94952	707-762-9020	762-9019	K-12	Will Stapp
Livermore Valley Charter S	543 Sonoma Ave	Livermore, CA	94550-4045	925-443-1690	443-1692	K-8	Tina Morris
Long Valley Charter S	PO Box 7	Doyle, CA	96109-0007	530-827-2395	827-3562	K-12	J. D. Lietaker
Los Angeles Academy of Arts & Enterprise	600 S La Fayette Park Pl	Los Angeles, CA	90057	213-487-0600	487-0500	6-12	Sabrina Bow
Los Angeles Leadership Academy	668 S Catalina St	Los Angeles, CA	90005-1708	213-381-8484	381-8489	6-12	Roger Lowenstein
Los Feliz Charter S for the Arts	1265 N Fairfax Ave	West Hollywood, CA	90046-5205	323-656-2810	656-2812	K-6	Karin Newlin
Lucerne Valley Career Academy	8560 Aliento Rd	Lucerne Valley, CA	92356	760-248-6800	248-3330	9-12	Michael Talerico
Lugo Academy	6410 Rita Ave	Huntington Park, CA	90255-4126	323-585-1153	585-1283	K-5	
MAAC Community Charter S	1385 3rd Ave	Chula Vista, CA	91911-4302	619-476-0749	476-0913	9-12	Joe Lara
MACSA Academica Calmecac	660 Sinclair Dr	San Jose, CA	95116-3464	408-937-3702	929-1025	9-12	Adolfo Reyes
MACSA El Portal Leadership Academy	240 Swanston Ln	Gilroy, CA	95020-4548	408-846-1715	846-1815	9-12	Noemi Reyes
Magnolia Science Academy	18238 Sherman Way	Reseda, CA	91335-4550	818-609-0507	609-0534	6-12	Engin Eryilmaz
Mammoth Olympic Academy	PO Box 3509	Mammoth Lakes, CA	93546-3509	760-934-7636	934-7510	9-12	Jim Barnes
Manzanita Charter MS	3200 Barrett Ave	Richmond, CA	94804-1718	510-232-3300	232-0009	6-8	Kristin Kirkman
Mare Island Technology Academy HS	2 Positive Pl	Vallejo, CA	94589-1825	707-552-6482	552-0288	6-12	Louise Santiago
Maria Montessori Charter Academy	3175 Sunset Blvd Ste 104	Rocklin, CA	95677	916-630-1510	624-7305	K-8	Brent Boothby
Marin S of Arts & Technology	1850 Ignacio Blvd	Novato, CA	94949	415-883-7390	883-7353	9-12	Stewart Fox
Marquez Charter S	16821 Marquez Ave	Pacific Plsds, CA	90272-3294	310-454-4019	573-1532	K-5	Phillip Hollis
Marysville Charter Academy for the Arts	1917 B St	Marysville, CA	95901	530-749-6157	741-7892	7-12	John Pimentel
Math and Science S - MASS	5156 Whittier Blvd	Los Angeles, CA	90022-3932	323-859-2920	859-2924	9-12	Derrick Chau Ph.D.
Mattole Valley Charter S	PO Box 39	Honeydew, CA	95545-0039	707-629-3634	629-3649	K-12	Richard Graey
McGill School of Success	3025 Fir St	San Diego, CA	92102-1123	619-239-0632	239-1318	K-2	Deborah Huggins
Memorial Academy Charter S	2850 Logan Ave	San Diego, CA	92113-2412	619-525-7400	525-7498	6-9	Marco Curiel
Merkin MS	2023 S Union Ave	Los Angeles, CA	90007-1326	213-748-0141		6-8	Donna Jacobson
Metropolitan Arts & Tech HS	1550 Treat Ave	San Francisco, CA	94110-5234	415-550-5920	206-1444	9-12	Kenny Purser
Met Sacramento Charter HS	810 V St	Sacramento, CA	95818-1330	916-264-4700	264-4701	9-12	Beth Kay
Mid Valley Alternative Charter S	9895 7th Ave	Hanford, CA	93230-8802	559-583-1149	582-7565	K-8	Charlotte Meade
Milagro Charter ES	1855 N Main St	Los Angeles, CA	90031-3227	323-223-1786	223-8593	K-5	Sacsha Robinett
Millsmont Academy	3200 62nd Ave	Oakland, CA	94605-1614	510-638-9445	638-0744	K-12	Diana Adams
Modoc Charter S	214 W 1st St	Alturas, CA	96101-3903	530-233-3861	233-3864	K-12	John Calzia
Mojave River Academy	PO Box 386	Oro Grande, CA	92368-0386	760-245-9260	245-1339	K-12	Joseph Andreasen
Momentum MS	6365 Lake Atlin Ave	San Diego, CA	92119-3206	619-644-1300	644-1600	6-7	Adnan Doyuran
Monarch Academy	1445 101st Ave	Oakland, CA	94603-3207	510-568-3101	655-1222	K-5	Tatiana Epanchin-Troyan
Monarch Learning Center	PO Box 992418	Redding, CA	96099-2418	530-247-7307	243-4819	K-8	Krista Sterrett
Montague Street School	13000 Montague St	Pacoima, CA	91331-4193	818-899-0215	834-9782	PK-5	Rebeca Rodriguez
Monterey County Home Charter S	PO Box 80851	Salinas, CA	93912-0851	831-755-0331	755-0837	K-12	Mary Sgheiza
Mountain Home Charter S	41267 Highway 41	Oakhurst, CA	93644-9403	559-642-1422	642-1592	K-8	Michael Cox
Mountain Oaks S	PO Box 1209	San Andreas, CA	95249-1209	209-754-0532	754-3556	K-12	Richard Anderson
Mountain View Montessori Charter S	15579 8th St	Victorville, CA	92395-3360	760-843-3303	843-1074	K-6	Geraldine Terranova
Mueller Charter S	715 I St	Chula Vista, CA	91910-5199	619-422-6192	422-0356	K-8	Dr. Kevin Riley
Muir Charter S	9845 Horn Rd	Sacramento, CA	95827	916-366-7319		9-12	Buzz Breedlove
Multicultural Learning Center	7510 DeSoto Ave	Canoga Park, CA	91303-1430	818-716-5783	716-1085	K-6	Toby Bornstein
Museum Charter S	211 Maple St	San Diego, CA	92103-6527	619-236-8712	236-8906	3-9	Phil Beaumont
Napa Valley Language Academy	2700 Kilburn Ave	Napa, CA	94558-5623	707-253-3678	259-8427	K-6	Deborah Wallace
Natomas Charter S	4600 Blackrock Dr	Sacramento, CA	95835-1250	916-928-5353	928-5333	K-12	Charlie Leo
Natomas-Pacific Pathways Prep	3700 Del Paso Rd Bldg N	Sacramento, CA	95834	916-739-7270	567-5540	9-12	Tom Rutter
Nevada City Charter	750 Hoover Ln	Nevada City, CA	95959-2910	530-265-1885	265-1889	K-8	Mike McGarr
Nevada City S for the Arts	13032 Bitney Springs Rd # 8	Nevada City, CA	95959	530-273-7736	273-1378	K-8	Holly Pettitt
Nevada County Academy of Learning	112 Nevada City Hwy	Nevada City, CA	95959-3117	530-478-6400	478-6410	K-12	Dawn Bateman
NEW Academy of Science & Arts	379 S Loma Ave	Los Angeles, CA	90017	213-413-9183	413-9187	K-5	Fausto Barragan
N.E.W. Canoga Park ES	21425 Cohasset St	Canoga Park, CA	91303-1450	818-887-6945	483-7848	K-5	Edward Fiszer
New City S	1230 Pine Ave	Long Beach, CA	90813-3123	562-436-0689	436-7475	K-8	Ted Hamory
New Designs S	3756 Santa Rosalia Dr Ste 5	Los Angeles, CA	90008	323-293-7009	293-7130	6-12	Yaw Audtwun
New Jerusalem Charter S	31400 S Koster Rd	Tracy, CA	95304-9543	209-830-6870	830-9707	K-8	David Thoming
New Millennium Institute of Education	830 Fresno S Ste 400	Fresno, CA	93706	559-497-9331	497-9109	7-12	Dolphas Trotter
New Technology HS	1400 Dickson St	Sacramento, CA	95822-3437	916-433-2839	433-2840	9-12	Paula M. Hanzel
New West Charter MS	11625 W Pico Blvd	Los Angeles, CA	90064-2908	310-943-5444	231-3399	6-8	Dr. Sharon Weir
Northcoast Charter S	269 Big Lagoon Park Rd	Trinidad, CA	95570-9622	707-822-0861	822-0878	K-12	Jean Bazemore
North Oakland Community Charter S	1000 42nd St	Emeryville, CA	94608-3621	510-655-0540	655-1222	K-5	Francisco Gutierrez
North Woods Discovery S	14732 Bass Dr	Redding, CA	96003-7303	530-275-5480	275-5416	K-8	John Husome
Nova Academy	2130 E 4th St Ste 200	Santa Ana, CA	92705-3818	714-543-5437	543-5463	7-12	Renee Lancaster
Novato Charter S	940 C St	Novato, CA	94949-5060	415-883-4254	883-1859	K-8	Rachel Bishop
Nubia Leadership Academy	6134 Benson Ave	San Diego, CA	92114-4204	619-262-0050	262-4215	K-6	Myrion Doakes
Nuview Bridge Early College HS	30401 Reservoir Ave	Nuevo, CA	92567-9361	951-928-8498	928-0186	9-12	Rebecca Mashatt
Oakdale Charter S	1235 E D St	Oakdale, CA	95361-3223	209-848-4361	848-4363	9-12	Hector Sanchez
Oakland Charter Academy	3001 International Blvd	Oakland, CA	94601-2203	510-532-6751	532-6753	6-8	Jorge Lopez
Oakland Military Institute	2405 W 14th St	Oakland, CA	94607-5005	510-267-3900	286-3935	6-12	Bruce Holaday

School	Address	City,State	Zip code	Telephone	Fax	Grade	Contact
Oakland S for the Arts	1800 San Pablo Ave	Oakland, CA	94612-1545	510-873-8800	873-8816	9-12	Saul Drevitch
Oakland Unity HS	6038 Brann St	Oakland, CA	94605-1544	510-635-7170	635-3830	9-12	Jane Searight
Oasis Charter Academy	11988 Hesperia Rd Ste B	Hesperia, CA	92345-1851	760-947-0006	947-0008	7-12	Cynthia Ferguson
Oasis Charter HS	285 17th St	Oakland, CA	94612-4123	510-251-8103		9-12	Hugo Arabia
Oasis Charter S	PO Box 720	Salinas, CA	93902-0720	831-424-9003	424-9005	K-6	Jane Roberts
Ocean Charter School	12606 Culver Blvd	Los Angeles, CA	90066-6506	310-827-5511	827-2012	K-8	Alex Metcalf
Oceanside S of Business and Technology	320 N Horne St	Oceanside, CA	92054-2810	760-231-1512	231-8249	9-12	Rocky Chavez
Odyssey Charter S	725 W Altadena Dr	Altadena, CA	91001-4103	626-229-0993	229-0586	K-8	Franca Campopiano
O'Farrell Community S	6130 Skyline Dr	San Diego, CA	92114-5620	619-263-3009	263-4339	6-8	Byron King
Olive Grove Charter S	PO Box 208	Los Olivos, CA	93441-0208	805-693-5933	688-4885	K-12	Jesse Leyva
Open Charter Magnet S	5540 W 77th St	Los Angeles, CA	90045-3214	310-568-0735	568-0904	K-5	Robert Burke
Oportunities Unlimited	10513 S Vermont Ave	Los Angeles, CA	90044-3021	323-241-1100	789-6518	9-12	A. Marcoulas
Opportunities for Learning Charter S	18259 Soledad Canyon Rd	Santa Clarita, CA	91387-3532	661-424-1337	424-1129	7-12	Bill Toomey
Options for Youth	2627 Alta Arden Expy	Sacramento, CA	95825-1306	916-971-3175	971-3186		
Options for Youth	5720 Watt Ave	North Highlands, CA	95660-4752	916-338-2375	338-2417	7-12	Chris Timpson
Options for Youth	11088 Olson Dr	Rancho Cordova, CA	95670	916-631-8113	631-8121		
Options for Youth Charter S	1701 W Verdugo Ave	Burbank, CA	91506-2147			K-12	Ellen Harris
Options for Youth Charter S	6110 Fair Oaks Blvd Ste E	Carmichael, CA	95608-4826	916-485-5155	485-5484	K-12	Christopher Timpson
Options for Youth-San Gabriel Charter S	609 Las Tunas Dr	San Gabriel, CA	91776	626-282-0390		K-12	Mary Jensen
Options for Youth - Upland	310 N Mountain Ave	Upland, CA	91786-5115	909-946-0500		K-12	
Options for Youth Victor Valley Charter	15048 Bear Valley Rd	Victorville, CA	92395	760-241-8300		K-12	Kathy Lento
Orange County Arts Academy	825 N Broadway	Santa Ana, CA	92701-3423	714-558-2787	558-2775	K-8	Claudine Dumais
Orange County HS of the Arts	1010 N Main St	Santa Ana, CA	92701-3602	714-560-0900	664-0463	7-12	Barbara O'Connor
Orchard View Charter S	700 Watertrough Rd	Sebastopol, CA	95472-3917	707-823-4709	823-6187	K-12	Carol Rogers
Our Community S	16514 Nordhoff St	North Hills, CA	91343	818-920-5285	920-5383	K-6	Chris Ferris
Pacifica Community Charter S	3754 Dunn Dr	Los Angeles, CA	90034-5805	310-845-9405	845-9402	K-8	Janette Kiso
Pacific Coast Charter S	PO Box 50010	Watsonville, CA	95077-5010	831-761-6021	786-2192	K-12	Vicki Carr
Pacific Collegiate Charter S	PO Box 1701	Santa Cruz, CA	95061-1701	831-479-7785	427-5254	7-12	Andrew Goldenkrantz
Pacific Community Charter S	PO Box 984	Point Arena, CA	95468-0984	707-882-4131	882-4132	K-12	Yoland Highhouse
Pacific View Charter S	3355 Mission Ave Ste 139	Oceanside, CA	92058-1333	760-757-0161	435-2666	K-12	Gina Campbell
Pacific View Charter S	2937 Moore Ave	Eureka, CA	95501-3316	707-269-9490	269-9491	K-12	Ron Flenner
Pacoima Charter S	11016 Norris Ave	Pacoima, CA	91331-2598	818-899-0201	890-3812	K-5	Irene Smerigan
Palisades Charter ES	800 Via De La Paz	Pacific Plsds, CA	90272-3617	310-454-3700	459-5627	K-5	Tami Weiser
Palisades Charter HS	15777 Bowdoin St	Pacific Plsds, CA	90272-3586	310-454-0611	454-6076	9-12	Dr. Gloria Martinez
Paradise Charter MS	6473 Clark Rd	Paradise, CA	95969-3501	530-872-7277	872-2924	6-8	Chris Reid
Paradise Charter Network	622 Pearson Rd	Paradise, CA	95969-5133	530-872-6440	872-9708	7-12	Carol Mooney
Paradise Charter S	3361 California Ave	Modesto, CA	95358	209-524-0184	524-0363	K-8	Rusty Wynn
Para Los Ninos Charter S	1617 E 7th St	Los Angeles, CA	90021-1207	213-239-6605	239-9821	K-5	Norma Silva
Pasadena Rosebud Academy	2561 Fair Oaks Ave	Altadena, CA	91001	626-395-0699		K-1	Shawn Brumfield Ed.D.
Pathways Charter S	607 Bobelaine Dr	Santa Rosa, CA	95405-6604	707-573-6117	573-6122	K-12	Karri Smith
Peabody Charter S	3018 Calle Noguera	Santa Barbara, CA	93105-2899	805-563-1172	569-7042	K-6	Kate Ford
Phillips-Edison Charter S	1210 Shetler Ave	Napa, CA	94559-4205	707-253-3481	259-8425	K-6	Debra Brown
Phoenix Academy	PO Box 4925	San Rafael, CA	94913-4925	415-491-0581	491-0981	9-12	Lisa Schwartz
Pine Mountain Learning Center	PO Box 876	Lebec, CA	93243-0876	661-248-6247		K-6	Mary Griffin
Piner-Olivet Charter S	2707 Francisco Ave	Santa Rosa, CA	95403-1869	707-522-3310	522-3317	7-8	Diana Drew-Ingham
Pioneer MS	101 W Pioneer Way	Hanford, CA	93230-9489	559-584-0112	584-0118	6-8	Rich Callaghan
Pioneer Technical Center	28123 Avenue 14	Madera, CA	93638-4905	559-664-1600	673-5569	9-12	Steve Carney
Pioneer Union ES	8810 14th Ave	Hanford, CA	93230-9680	559-584-8831	584-1422	K-5	Lisa Horne
Plumas Charter S	2288 E Main St	Quincy, CA	95971-9660	530-283-3851	283-3841	K-12	Kent Frid
Plumas Lake Charter S	2743 Plumas School Rd	Marysville, CA	95901	530-743-4428	743-1408	K-12	Joe Hendrix
Port of Los Angeles HS	250 W 5th St	San Pedro, CA	90731-3304	310-832-9201	514-1568	9-12	Dr. Marie Collins
Preuss S	9500 Gilman Dr	La Jolla, CA	92093	858-658-7400	658-0988	6-12	Dr. Doris Alvarez
Price Charter MS	2650 New Jersey Ave	San Jose, CA	95124-1520	408-377-2532	377-7406	6-8	Debra Negrete
P.R.I.D.E. Charter S	3804 Ocean View Blvd	San Diego, CA	92113	619-264-8764	262-3238	9-11	Sharon Whitehurst-Payne
Primary Charter S	51 E Beverly Pl	Tracy, CA	95376	209-831-5240	831-5094	K-4	Virginia Stewart
Promise Charter S	730 45th St	San Diego, CA	92102-3619	619-262-5083		K-7	Olivia Flores
Provisional Accelerated Learning Academy	PO Box 7100	San Bernardino, CA	92411-0100	909-887-7002	887-8942	9-12	Dr. Mildred Henry
Public Safety Academy	1494 E Art Townsend Dr	San Bernardino, CA	92408	909-382-2211	382-2202	6-12	Michael Dickinson
Puente Charter S	501 S Boyle Ave	Los Angeles, CA	90033-3816	323-780-0076	780-0359	K-K	Jerome Greening
Quail Lake Environmental Charter S	4087 N Quail Lake Dr	Clovis, CA	93619-4646	559-292-1273	292-1276	K-8	Chris Stilson
Rainbow Advanced Institute for Learning	5253 5th St	Fallbrook, CA	92028-9795	760-728-4305	728-7712	6-12	Paul Cartas
Redding S of the Arts	2200 Eureka Way	Redding, CA	96001-0337	530-247-6933	245-2633	K-8	Jean Hatch
Redwood Academy of Ukiah	PO Box 1383	Ukiah, CA	95482-1383	707-467-0500	467-4942	7-12	Dr. Kimberly Logan
Reems Academy of Technology & Art	8425 Macarthur Blvd	Oakland, CA	94605-3553	510-729-6635	562-9539	K-8	Lisa Blair
Rehoboth Charter Academy	9191 Colorado Ave	Riverside, CA	92503-2636	951-683-0553	687-2622	K-6	Toya Y. Flakes
Renaissance Arts Academy	1800 Colorado Blvd	Los Angeles, CA	90041-1340	323-259-5700	259-5718	6-12	P. K. Candaux
Revere Charter MS	1450 Allenford Ave	Los Angeles, CA	90049-3614	310-451-5789	576-7957	6-8	Art Cooper
Rhythms of the Village Charter HS	3126 Glenrose Ave	Altadena, CA	91101	626-798-4732	798-3987	9-12	Marilyn Chukwurah
Richmond College Prep K-5 Charter S	PO Box 2814	Richmond, CA	94802	510-234-1200	234-3399		Peppina Chang
Ridgecrest Charter S	325 S Downs St	Ridgecrest, CA	93555-4531	760-375-1010	375-7766	K-8	Don Beene
Rincon Valley Charter S	1000 Yulupa Ave	Santa Rosa, CA	95405	707-539-3410	537-1791	7-8	Matt Reno
River Oak Charter S	555 Leslie St	Ukiah, CA	95482-5507	707-467-1855	467-1857	K-8	David Taxis
River Oaks Charter S	1801 Pyrenees Ave	Stockton, CA	95210-5207	209-956-8100	956-8102	K-8	Kat Mathers
River S Charter	2447 Old Sonoma Rd	Napa, CA	94558-6006	707-253-6813	258-2800	6-8	Linda Inlay
Riverside Preparatory S	PO Box 455	Oro Grande, CA	92368	760-245-9260	245-1339	K-12	Joseph Andreasen
River Springs Charter S	43466 Business Park Dr	Temecula, CA	92590	951-252-8800	252-8801	K-12	Dr. Kathleen Hermsmeyer
River Valley Charter HS	9707 1/2 Marilla Dr	Lakeside, CA	92040-2807	619-390-2579	390-2581	7-12	William Wellhouse
Rocketship One Public S	405 S 10th St	San Jose, CA	95112	408-286-3330	286-3301	K-5	Preston Smith
Roosevelt Community Learning Center	31191 Road 180	Visalia, CA	93292-9585	559-592-9160	592-2927	K-12	Klara East
Roosevelt ES	1185 10th Ave	Kingsburg, CA	93631-2100	559-897-5193	897-6865	5-6	Ruben Diaz
Rosa Parks Academy	1930 S D St	Stockton, CA	95206	209-944-5590	465-2690	K-5	Dr. Mary Welch
Roseland Charter S	1777 West Ave	Santa Rosa, CA	95407-7449	707-546-7050	546-0434	7-8	Rima Meechan
Roseland University Preparatory S	100 Sebastopol Rd	Santa Rosa, CA	95407-6928	707-566-9990	566-9992	9-12	Amy Jones-Kerr
Russian River Charter S	PO Box 139	Guerneville, CA	95446-0139	707-887-8790	887-8759	7-12	Carol Miller
Sacramento HS	2315 34th St	Sacramento, CA	95817-1299	916-277-6200	277-6370	9-12	Aaron Thornsberry
Sacramento River Discovery Center	PO Box 1298	Red Bluff, CA	96080-1298	530-529-1650	529-1694	6-12	Larry Newman
St. Hope Public School 7	5201 Strawberry Ln	Sacramento, CA	95820-4815	916-649-7850	277-7039	K-7	Marianna Harris
San Carlos Charter Learning Center	750 Dartmouth Ave Ste 1	San Carlos, CA	94070-1768	650-508-7343	508-7341	K-8	Paula Hunter
San Diego Cooperative Charter S	2850 6th Ave	San Diego, CA	92103	619-574-0694	574-0861	K-8	Dr. Wendy Ranck-Buhr
Sanger Academy Charter S	2207 9th St	Sanger, CA	93657-2711	559-875-5562	875-8045	K-8	Ken Garcia
San Jacinto Valley Academy	480 N San Jacinto Ave	San Jacinto, CA	92583-2729	951-654-6113	654-5083	K-9	
San Jose Conservation Corps Charter S	2650 Senter Rd	San Jose, CA	95111	408-283-6521	288-6521	9-12	Donna Howe
San Jose-Edison Charter S	2021 W Alwood St	West Covina, CA	91790-3259	626-856-1693		K-8	Dr. Denise Patton
San Lorenzo Valley USD Charter S	325 Marion Ave	Ben Lomond, CA	95005-9403	831-336-1827	336-9657	K-12	Eric Schoffstall
Santa Ana Arts Academy	825 N Broadway	Santa Ana, CA	92701-3423	714-240-9636		K-6	Ralph Opacic
Santa Barbara Charter S	6100 Stow Canyon Rd	Goleta, CA	93117-1705	805-967-6522	967-6382	K-8	Bev Abrams
Santa Monica Blvd Community Charter S	1022 N Van Ness Ave	Los Angeles, CA	90038-3252	323-469-0971	462-4093	K-5	Vahe Markarian
Santa Rosa Accelerated Charter	4650 Badger Rd	Santa Rosa, CA	95409-2633	707-528-5255	528-5644	5-6	Matt Marshall
Santa Rosa Charter S	1835A W Steele Ln	Santa Rosa, CA	95403	707-547-2480	547-2482	K-8	LaDonna Moore
Santa Ynez Valley Charter S	PO Box 59	Santa Ynez, CA	93460-0059	805-693-1755	693-1765	K-8	Mary Ann Cooley
Santiago Charter MS	515 N Rancho Santiago Blvd	Orange, CA	92869-2724	714-997-6366	532-4758	7-8	Mary Henry
Sartorette Charter ES	3850 Woodford Dr	San Jose, CA	95124-3799	408-264-4380	264-1758	K-5	Richard Wendell
School of Arts & Enterprise	300 W 2nd St	Pomona, CA	91766-1634	909-622-0699	620-1018	9-12	Lucille Berger
School of Unlimited Learning	2336 Calaveras St	Fresno, CA	93721-1104	559-498-8543	642-1592	7-12	Alma Kowalski
Sebastopol Independent Charter S	PO Box 1170	Sebastopol, CA	95473-1170	707-824-9700	824-1432	K-8	Susan Olson
Sedona Charter Academy	16519 Victor St	Victorville, CA	92395	760-245-3222	245-3774	K-12	Steve Meremess
Sequoia Charter S	21445 Centre Pointe Pkwy	Santa Clarita, CA	91350-2684	661-259-0033	286-2120	9-12	Lori Andrews
Serna Charter S	19 S Central Ave	Lodi, CA	95240-2901	209-331-7809	331-7997	K-6	Michael Gillespie
Shasta Secondary Home S	1401 Gold St	Redding, CA	96001-1937	530-245-2600	245-2611	6-12	Lynn Peebles
Shearer Charter S	1590 Elm St	Napa, CA	94559-3924	707-253-3508	253-3847	K-5	Lisa Miri
Shenandoah HS	6540 Koki Ln	El Dorado, CA	95623-4328	530-622-6212	622-1071	9-12	Valerie Lott
Sherman Oaks Community Charter S	1800 Fruitdale Ave Ste C	San Jose, CA	95128-4976	408-795-1140	341-7180	K-6	Julie Henderson
Sierra Charter S	1931 N Fine Ave	Fresno, CA	93727-1510	559-490-4290	490-4292	K-12	Lisa Marasco
Six Rivers Charter HS	1720 M St	Arcata, CA	95521-5741	707-825-2428	825-2034	9-12	Chris Hartley
Sixth Street Prep S	15579 8th St	Victorville, CA	92395-3399	760-241-0962	241-0967	K-6	Linda Mikels
Soledad Enrichment Action Charter S	222 N Virgil Ave	Los Angeles, CA	90004-3622	213-480-4200	480-4199	9-12	Cesar Calderon
Somis Academy	950 Flynn Rd	Camarillo, CA	93012	805-987-1188	987-1108	9-12	Carol Andersen
Sonoma Charter S	17202 Sonoma Hwy	Sonoma, CA	95476-3667	707-935-4232	935-4207	K-8	Nora Flood
South Sutter Charter S	2452 El Centro Blvd	East Nicolaus, CA	95659-9748	866-934-4327	295-3583	K-12	Michael Talerico
Stella Middle Charter Academy	2636 S Mansfield Ave	Los Angeles, CA	90016-3512	323-954-9957	954-6415	5-8	Jeff Hilger
Stellar Charter School	PO Box 992418	Redding, CA	96099-2418	530-245-7730	225-2249	K-12	Cindy Anderson
Summit Charter Academy	2036 E Hatch Rd	Modesto, CA	95351-5142	209-538-8082	538-1670	K-8	Kara Backman
Summit Charter S	PO Box 130	Mammoth Lakes, CA	93546-0130	760-934-0031	934-1443	K-12	Joseph Garrett
Summit Leadership Academy	PO Box 401606	Hesperia, CA	92340-1606	760-949-9202	949-9257	9-12	Karen Adams
Summit Preparatory HS	260 James Ave	Redwood City, CA	94062-5123	650-839-8967		9-12	Diane Tavenner
SunRidge Charter S	487 Watertrough Rd	Sebastopol, CA	95472-3911	707-824-2844	824-0861	K-7	Mark Rice
Sunset Charter S	1755 S Crystal Ave	Fresno, CA	93706-2797	559-457-3310	495-1334	K-7	Alicia Estigoy

School	Address	City,State	Zip code	Telephone	Fax	Grade	Contact
Sun Valley Charter S	2102 Main St	Ramona, CA	92065-2528	760-788-8008	788-8616	9-12	David Tarr
Synergy Charter S	1010 E 34th St	Los Angeles, CA	90011-2527	323-233-8559	931-3298	K-5	Randy Palisoc
Temecula Preparatory S	35777 Abelia St	Winchester, CA	92596-8450	951-926-6776	926-6797	K-12	Dianne McClenahan
Temecula Valley Charter S	35755 Abelia St	Winchester, CA	92596-8450	951-294-6775	294-6780	K-8	Jo Ann Burnett
The New S	127 W Elder St	Fallbrook, CA	92028-2853	760-451-3639	451-3422	K-6	Sue Miller-Hurst
Thomas Charter S	1902 Howard Rd	Madera, CA	93637-5123	559-674-8922	674-8955	K-6	Roger Leach
Tierra Linda MS	750 Dartmouth Ave Ste 3	San Carlos, CA	94070-1768	650-508-7343	508-7341	5-8	Lesley Martin
Tierra Pacifica Charter S	2008 17th Ave	Santa Cruz, CA	95062-1808	831-462-9404	477-0936	K-8	Linda Lambdin
Todays Fresh Start Charter S	4514 Crenshaw Blvd	Los Angeles, CA	90043-1221	323-293-9826	293-9202	K-5	Dr. Jeanette Parker
Topanga ES	141 N Topanga Canyon Blvd	Topanga, CA	90290-3831	310-455-3711	455-3517	K-6	Liam Joyce
Tree of Life Montessori S	PO Box 966	Ukiah, CA	95482-0966	707-462-0913	462-0914	1-8	Celeste Beck
Trillium Charter S	1464 Spear Ave	Arcata, CA	95521-4882	707-822-4721	822-7054	K-5	Marianne Keller
Tubman Village S	6880 Mohawk St	San Diego, CA	92115-1728	619-668-8635	668-2480	K-8	Catherine Pope
Twin Ridges Home Study Charter S	PO Box 529	North San Juan, CA	95960-0529	530-292-3305	292-1918	K-8	Terry Juhl
Twin Rivers Charter S	840 Cooper Ave	Yuba City, CA	95991-3849	530-755-2872	673-1847	K-8	Theresa Johansen
Union Hill Charter S	10879 Bartlett Dr	Grass Valley, CA	95945-8730	530-273-0647	273-5626	K-8	Eileen Barker
University Charter S	3313 Coffee Rd	Modesto, CA	95355-1534	209-544-8722	544-8864	K-6	Laura Mifflin
University Preparatory Charter Academy	3030 75th Ave	Oakland, CA	94605-2906	510-569-7880	569-7905	9-10	Isaac Haqq
University Preparatory S	2200 Eureka Way	Redding, CA	96001-0337	530-245-2790	245-2610	6-12	Erin Stuart
Univ Preparation S of Channel Islands	550 Temple Ave	Camarillo, CA	93010-4833	805-482-4608	388-5814	PK-7	Linda Ngarupe
Urbani Institute for Language	640 N San Joaquin St	Stockton, CA	95202-2030	209-933-7370	933-7371	4-8	Antonia Jimenez
Valley Business HS	108 Campus Way	Modesto, CA	95350-5803	209-558-4407	558-4453	9-12	Bob Vizzolini
Valley Oak Charter S	PO Box 878	Ojai, CA	93024-0878	805-640-4421	646-4700	K-10	Laura Fulmer
Valley Oaks Charter S	3501 Chester Ave	Bakersfield, CA	93301-1629	661-633-5288	633-5287	K-12	
Vantage Point Charter S	10862 Spenceville Rd	Penn Valley, CA	95946-9625	530-432-5312	432-8744	K-12	Shane Carnahan
Vaughn Next Century Learning Center	13330 Vaughn St	San Fernando, CA	91340-2216	818-896-7461	834-9036	PK-12	Yvonne Chan
Venture Academy	2829 Transworld Dr	Stockton, CA	95206-3950	209-468-5940	468-9000	K-12	Kathleen Focacci
View Park Accelerated MS	5749 Crenshaw Blvd	Los Angeles, CA	90043-2409	323-293-0448	931-5504	6-8	Brian Taylor
View Park Prep. Accelerated Charter S	3751 W 54th St	Los Angeles, CA	90043-2356	323-245-2660	245-2660	K-5	Bruce King
View Park Prep Accelerated HS	5701 Crenshaw Blvd	Los Angeles, CA	90043-2409	323-293-0448		9-12	Robert Schwartz
Village Charter S	5146 Old Redwood Hwy	Santa Rosa, CA	95403-1276	707-591-9262	591-9275	K-6	Jeanna Ruppel
Visalia Charter Independent Study	909 W Murray Ave	Visalia, CA	93291-4825	559-735-8055	622-3170	7-12	Missy Yavasile
Visions in Education Charter S	4800 Manzanita Ave	Carmichael, CA	95608-0825	916-971-7037	971-5590	K-12	Vince Candido
Washington Charter S	45768 Portola Ave	Palm Desert, CA	92260-4861	760-862-4350	862-4356	K-5	Allan Lehmann
Washington ES	1501 Ellis St	Kingsburg, CA	93631-1896	559-897-2955	897-6863	K-1	Ruben Diaz
Watsonville Charter S of the Arts	115 Casserly Rd	Watsonville, CA	95076-8645	831-728-8123	728-6286	K-8	Sue Forson
Watts Learning Center	310 W 95th St	Los Angeles, CA	90003-4012	323-754-9900	754-0935	K-5	Katherine Nelson
WEB DuBois Charter S	302 Fresno St Ste 205	Fresno, CA	93706-3641	559-499-0799	442-5811	9-12	Alicia Taylor
West Charter S	5350 Faught Rd	Santa Rosa, CA	95403-1205	707-524-2741	524-2782	K-8	Pam Carpenter
Westlake Charter S	3201 E River Dr Ste 101	Sacramento, CA	95833	916-567-5760		K-3	Kim Pablo
West Oakland Community S	955 12th St	Oakland, CA	94607-3233	510-465-9627	465-8071	6-8	Akiyu Hatano
West Park Charter Academy	2695 S Valentine Ave	Fresno, CA	93706-9042	559-485-0727	485-0682	K-12	Liz Hammond
Westside Preparatory Charter S	6537 W 2nd St	Rio Linda, CA	95673-3231	916-566-1990	991-5842	7-8	Shannon Brown
Westwood Charter S	2050 Selby Ave	Los Angeles, CA	90025-6397	310-474-7788	475-1295	K-5	Judy Utvich
Westwood Charter S	PO Box 56	Westwood, CA	96137-0056	877-256-2994	256-2964	K-12	Henry Bietz
Wheatland Charter Academy	123 Beale Hwy	Beale Afb, CA	95903	530-788-2097	788-2631	K-12	Mike Reid
White Oaks ES	1901 White Oak Way	San Carlos, CA	94070-4799	650-508-7317	508-7320	K-4	Betty Casey
Whitmore Charter S	PO Box 307	Ceres, CA	95307-0307	209-556-1073	538-7931	K-12	Paula Smith
Wilder's Preparatory Academy Charter S	830 N La Brea Ave	Inglewood, CA	90302-2206	310-671-5578	671-2424	K-8	Raymond Wilder
Willits Charter S	7 S Marin St	Willits, CA	95490	707-459-5506	459-5576	6-12	Sally Rulison
Willow Creek Academy	PO Box 366	Sausalito, CA	94966-0366	415-331-7530	331-5524	K-8	Carol Cooper
Wilson College Prep S	400 105th Ave	Oakland, CA	94603-2968	510-635-7737	635-7727	6-12	Adrian Kirk
Woodland Star Charter S	17811 Arnold Dr	Sonoma, CA	95476-4019	707-996-3849	996-4369	K-8	Chip Romer
Woodson Charter S	3333 N Bond Ave	Fresno, CA	93726-5712	559-229-3529	229-0459	7-12	Alicia Taylor
Youth Employment Partnership	2300 International Blvd	Oakland, CA	94601-1019	510-533-3447	533-3469	9-12	Michelle Clark
Youth Opportunities HS - Watts	1827 E 103rd St	Los Angeles, CA	90002-2928	323-249-7845	249-1170	9-12	
Yuba City Charter S	990 Klamath Ln Ste 15	Yuba City, CA	95993-8979	530-822-9031	674-1322	K-12	Sandi Lininger
Yuba County Career Prep Charter S	1104 E St	Marysville, CA	95901-4825	530-741-6025	741-6032	K-12	Carol Holtz
Yuba River Charter S	13026 Bitney Springs Rd # 3	Nevada City, CA	95959	530-272-8078	272-1952	K-8	Caleb Buckley

Colorado

School	Address	City,State	Zip code	Telephone	Fax	Grade	Contact
Academy at High Point	PO Box 440245	Aurora, CO	80044-0245	303-217-5152	217-5153	PK-8	Pat Leger
Academy Charter S	1551 Prairie Hawk Dr	Castle Rock, CO	80109-7900	303-660-4881	660-6385	K-8	Kindra Nelson
Academy of Charter S	11800 Lowell Blvd	Westminster, CO	80031-5097	303-289-8088	289-8087	K-12	John Kaufman
Academy of Urban Learning Charter S	835 E 18th Ave	Denver, CO	80218-1024	303-282-0900	282-0902	9-12	Mark Koester
Ace Community Challenge Charter S	948 Santa Fe Dr	Denver, CO	80204-3937	303-436-9588	436-0919	8-10	Eloy Chavez
Alta Vista Charter ES	PO Box 449	Lamar, CO	81052-0449	719-336-2154	336-0170	K-6	Talara Coen
American Academy	8600 Park Meadows Dr	Lonetree, CO	80124	303-873-7395	873-7398	K-8	Roberta Harrell
Aspen Community Charter S	PO Box 336	Woody Creek, CO	81656-0336	970-923-4646	923-7380	K-8	Skye Skinner
Aurora Academy Charter S	10251 E 1st Ave	Aurora, CO	80010-4308	303-367-5983	367-5820	K-8	Stephen Garretson
Banning Lewis Ranch Academy	7094 Cottonwood Tree Dr	Colorado Spgs, CO	80927-5000	719-570-0075		K-8	Kim Davis
Battle Rock Charter S	11247 Road G	Cortez, CO	81321-9546	970-565-3237	564-1140	K-8	Matt Linsey-Paek
Belle Creek Charter S	9290 E 107th Ave	Henderson, CO	80640-8964	303-468-0160	468-0164	K-8	Irene German
Blair Edison Charter S	4905 Cathay St	Denver, CO	80249-8376	303-371-9570	371-8348	K-8	Kathleen Garvey
Boulder Prep Charter HS	PO Box 4249	Boulder, CO	80306-4249	303-545-6186	545-6187	9-12	Bruce Blodgett
Brighton Charter S	1931 E Bridge St	Brighton, CO	80601	303-655-0773	655-9155	9-12	Chris McCandless
Bromley East Charter S	356 Longspur Dr	Brighton, CO	80601-8700	720-685-3297	685-9513	K-8	Bob Bair
Carbondale Community Charter S	PO Box 365	Carbondale, CO	81623-0365	970-963-9647	704-0501	K-8	Leslie Emerson
Carbon Valley Charter S	4040 Coriolis Way	Frederick, CO	80504-5449	303-774-9555	774-9592	K-8	Chad Auer
Cardinal Community Academy	3101 County Road 65	Keenesburg, CO	80643-8604	303-732-9312	732-9314	K-6	Gary Wilson
Challenges Choices & Images Charter S	1537 Alton St	Aurora, CO	80010-1712	303-341-7554	340-2404	K-12	Carolyn Jones
Challenge to Excellence Charter S	16995 Carlson Dr	Parker, CO	80134-8000	303-841-9816	840-3246	K-8	Donna Mitchell
Chavez Academy	2500 W 18th St	Pueblo, CO	81003-1152	719-295-1623	295-1625	K-8	Dr. Lawrence Hernandez
Cherry Creek Charter Academy	6260 S Dayton St	Englewood, CO	80111-5203	303-779-8988	779-8817	K-8	Donna Fitzgerald
Cheyenne Mountain Charter Academy	1832 S Wahsatch Ave	Colorado Spgs, CO	80906-2341	719-471-1999	471-4949	K-8	Colin Mullaney
CIVA Charter S	225 S Union Blvd	Colorado Spgs, CO	80910	719-633-1306	633-1691	9-11	Randy Zimmerman
Classical Academy Central	1655 Springcrest Rd	Colorado Spgs, CO	80920-1545	719-265-9766	265-1751	K-6	Don Stump
Classical Academy East	8650 Scarborough Dr	Colorado Spgs, CO	80920-7532	719-282-1181	282-3226	K-8	Diana Burditt
Classical Academy North	975 Stout Rd	Colorado Spgs, CO	80921-3801	719-484-0081	484-0087	K-12	Mark Hyatt
Cole College Prep Charter S	3240 Humboldt St	Denver, CO	80205-3934	303-293-2653	293-2666	7-8	Richard Harrison
Collegiate Academy of Colorado	8420 Sangre De Cristo Rd	Littleton, CO	80127-4201	303-972-7433	932-0695	K-12	Dr. William Eggers
Colorado Charter HS	1175 Osage St Ste 100	Denver, CO	80204-3445	303-892-8475	825-3011	9-12	Cyndi Bush-Luna
Colorado Distance & Electronic Learning	4700 E Bromley Ln Ste 205	Brighton, CO	80601-7821	303-637-9234	637-9273	K-9	Gary Goodnight
Colorado Springs Charter Academy	2577 N Chelton Rd	Colorado Spgs, CO	80909	719-636-2722	636-2726	K-8	Martha Huddleston
Colorado Virtual Academy	11990 Grant St Ste 402	Northglenn, CO	80233-1136	303-255-4650	255-7044	K-12	Stephen Martin
Community Leadership Academy	6880 Holly St	Commerce City, CO	80022-2536	303-288-2711	288-2714	K-8	Dana Frazee
Community Prep Charter S	332 E Willamette Ave	Colorado Spgs, CO	80903-1116	719-227-8836	227-8897	9-12	Vicki Leaf
Compass Montessori Charter S	10399 W 44th Ave	Wheat Ridge, CO	80033-2701	303-420-8288	420-0139	PK-6	Dirk Angevine
Compass Montessori Charter S	4441 Salvia St	Golden, CO	80403-1698	303-271-1977	271-1984	PK-12	Katy Myers
Connect Charter S	104 E 7th St	Pueblo, CO	81003-4109	719-542-0224	583-9799	6-8	Judy Mikulas
Core Knowledge Charter S	11661 N Pine Dr	Parker, CO	80138-8022	303-840-7070	840-9785	K-8	Teri Aplin
Corridor Community Academy	420 7th St	Bennett, CO	80102-8124	303-644-5180	644-4918	K-6	Rachel Murphy
Crestone Charter S	PO Box 400	Crestone, CO	81131-0400	719-256-4907	256-4908	K-12	Kathryn Brady
Crown Pointe Academy	7281 Irving St	Westminster, CO	80030-4907	303-428-1882	428-1938	K-6	Barbara Ridenour
Da Vinci Academy	1335 Bridle Oaks Ln	Colorado Spgs, CO	80921-3621	719-234-5400	234-5499	K-5	Pat Iagulli
DCS Montessori Charter S	311 Castle Pines Pkwy	Castle Rock, CO	80108-8101	303-387-5625	387-5626	PK-6	Bill Zajic
Deep River Charter S	2813 Patterson Rd	Grand Junction, CO	81506-6065	970-255-8565	255-8568	K-12	Larry Beissel
Denver Arts & Technology Academy	3752 Tennyson St	Denver, CO	80212-1914	720-855-7504	855-7529	K-8	Christina Burton
Denver S of Science and Technology	2000 Valentia St	Denver, CO	80238-2785	303-320-5570	377-5101	9-12	Bill Kurtz
Eagle County Charter Academy	1105 Miller Ranch Rd	Edwards, CO	81632	970-926-0656	926-0786	K-8	Jay Cerny
Elbert County Charter S	PO Box 1490	Elizabeth, CO	80107-1490	303-646-2636	646-2635	K-12	Merlin Holmes
Emerson-Edison Charter Academy	4220 E Pikes Peak Ave	Colorado Spgs, CO	80909-6728	719-570-7822	570-7824	6-8	Casey Tencick
Excel Academy	11500 W 84th Ave	Arvada, CO	80005-5272	303-467-2295	467-2291	K-8	Dr. Holly Hensey
EXCEL Charter S	215 E 12th St	Durango, CO	81301-5206	970-259-0203	385-1180	6-12	Jule Scoglund
Flagstaff Academy	1841 Lefthand Cir	Longmont, CO	80501	303-651-7900	200-8846	K-8	Jere Pearcy
Free Horizon Montessori S	581 Conference Pl	Golden, CO	80401-5615	303-231-9801	231-9983	PK-6	Jamie Boarman
Frontier Academy Charter S	2560 W 29th St	Greeley, CO	80631-8507	970-330-1780	330-4334	K-6	Rebecca Dougherty
Frontier Academy Charter S	6530 W 16th St	Greeley, CO	80634-8675	970-339-9153	339-5631	7-12	Harlan Ptomey
Frontier Charter Academy	PO Box 418	Calhan, CO	80808-0418	719-347-3156	347-3054	K-8	Candy Putch
Georgetown Community S	PO Box 74	Georgetown, CO	80444-0074	303-569-3277	569-2761	PK-6	Dr. Mike Holmes
GLOBE Charter S	2132 E Bijou St	Colorado Spgs, CO	80909-5904	719-630-0577	630-0395	K-12	Marty Caldwell
Guffey Community Charter S	PO Box 147	Guffey, CO	80820-0147	719-689-2093	689-3407	K-8	Pam Moore
Highline Academy	7808 Cherry Creek South Dr	Denver, CO	80231	720-449-0317	449-0328	K-8	Alyssa Whitehead-Bust
Hope Co-Op Academy	6728 Lakeside Cir	Littleton, CO	80125-9616	303-324-2100	471-1756	K-12	Heather O'Mara
Horizons Alternative S	4545 Sioux Dr	Boulder, CO	80303-3732	303-447-5580	499-9680	K-8	Sonny Zinn
Huerta Preparatory HS	2500 W 18th St	Pueblo, CO	81003-1152	719-583-1030	583-1031	9-12	Gloria Guerrero

School	Address	City,State	Zip code	Telephone	Fax	Grade	Contact
Indian Peaks Charter S	PO Box 1819	Granby, CO	80446-1819	970-887-3805	887-3829	K-6	Polly Gallagher
Irwin Charter ES	5525 Astrozon Blvd	Colorado Spgs, CO	80916-4226	719-884-0987	884-0992	K-5	Elizabeth Berg
Irwin Charter HS	5525 Astrozon Blvd	Colorado Spgs, CO	80916-4226	719-576-8055	576-8071	9-12	Kim Will
Irwin Charter MS	5525 Astrozon Blvd	Colorado Spgs, CO	80916-4226	719-591-2122	591-9993	6-8	Elizabeth Richard
Jefferson Academy	9955 Yarrow St	Broomfield, CO	80021-4048	303-887-1992	887-2435	7-12	Tammy Stringari
Jefferson Academy	9955 Yarrow St	Broomfield, CO	80021-4048	303-438-1011	438-1046	K-6	Mike Munier
Justice HS	1777 6th St	Boulder, CO	80302-5814	303-441-1695	441-1695	9-12	Tijani Cole
KIPP Sunshine Peak Academy	375 S Tejon St	Denver, CO	80223-1961	303-623-5772	623-0410	5-8	Richard Barrett
Knowledge Quest Academy	110 Centennial Dr Ste B	Milliken, CO	80543-3215	970-587-5742	587-5750	K-8	Dr. Robert Arkfeld
Lake George Charter S	PO Box 420	Lake George, CO	80827-0420	719-748-3911	748-8151	PK-6	Kay Lynn Waddell
Liberty Common S	1725 Sharp Point Dr	Fort Collins, CO	80525-4424	970-482-9800	482-8007	K-9	Russ Spicer
Life Skills Center of Colorado Springs	1810 Eastlake Blvd	Colorado Spgs, CO	80910-3422	719-471-0684	471-4392	9-12	Charles Holt
Life Skills Center of Denver	1000 Cherokee St	Denver, CO	80204-4039	720-889-2898	889-2897	9-12	Santiago Lopez
Lincoln Academy	6980 Pierce St	Arvada, CO	80003-3646	303-467-5363	467-5367	PK-8	Mary Ann Mahoney
Littleton Charter Academy	1200 W Mineral Ave	Littleton, CO	80120-4536	303-798-5252	798-0298	K-8	Jan Johnson-Pote
Littleton Prep Charter S	5151 S Federal Blvd	Littleton, CO	80123-2975	303-734-1995	734-3620	K-8	Kim Ash
Lotus S for Excellence	9202 E Severn Pl Bldg 901	Denver, CO	80230	303-360-0052	360-0071	6-12	Varol Gurler
Madison Charter Academy	660 Syracuse St	Colorado Spgs, CO	80911-2546	719-391-3977	391-1744	K-6	Dr. Anne Shineman
Marble Charter S	412 W Main St	Marble, CO	81623-9396	970-963-9550	963-8435	K-10	Wendy Boland
Montessori Peaks Academy	9904 W Capri Ave	Littleton, CO	80123-3535	303-972-2627	933-4182	PK-6	Char Weaver
Monument Academy	1890 Willow Park Way	Monument, CO	80132-9041	719-481-1950	481-1948	K-12	Mike AuClaire
Mountain View Core Knowledge S	890 Field Ave	Canon City, CO	81212-9250	719-275-1980	275-1998	K-8	Manuel Calderson
New America S	1005 Wadsworth Blvd	Lakewood, CO	80214-4201	303-894-3171		9-12	Jon Berninzoni
New America S	11700 Irma Dr	Northglenn, CO	80233	303-991-0130	991-0135	9-12	Paulette Schoeder
New America S	9125 E 7th Pl	Denver, CO	80230-7111	303-320-9854		9-12	Scott Mader
New Vision Charter S	2366 E 1st St	Loveland, CO	80537-5906	970-593-6827		K-6	Dennis Corash
Northeast Academy	4895 Peoria St	Denver, CO	80239-2847	303-307-8837	307-8867	K-8	Naomi Bradford
Northern CO Academy of Arts & Knowledge	PO Box 311	Fort Collins, CO	80522-0311	970-402-7365		K-6	
North Routt Charter S	54200 County Road 62	Clark, CO	80428	970-871-6062	871-6067	K-8	Colleen Poole
North Star Academy	16700 Keystone Blvd	Parker, CO	80134-3544	720-851-7827	851-0976	K-6	Cynthia Haws
Odyssey Charter S	8750 E 28th Ave	Denver, CO	80238-2609	303-316-3944	316-4016	K-8	Nelson Chase
Paradox Valley Charter S	PO Box 420	Paradox, CO	81429-0420	970-859-7236	859-7236	K-8	Renee Owen
Passage Charter S	703 S 9th St	Montrose, CO	81401-4409	970-249-8066	249-3497	7-12	Corinne Vogenthaler
Peak to Peak Charter S	800 Merlin Dr	Lafayette, CO	80026-2146	303-453-4600	453-4613	K-12	Anthony Fontana
Pikes Peak S of Expeditionary Learning	5450 Meridian Rd	Peyton, CO	80831-7773	719-683-9544	683-3475	K-8	Don Knapp
Pinnacle Charter S	1001 W 84th Ave	Federal Heights, CO	80260-4717	303-450-3985	255-6305	K-12	Dr. William Wiener
Pioneer Charter S	3230 E 38th Ave	Denver, CO	80205-3726	303-329-8412	424-4785	PK-6	Dorothy Ward
Pioneer S for Expeditionary Learning	2745 Minnesota Dr	Fort Collins, CO	80525-4767	970-206-0714	206-0738	7-12	Celeste Di Lorio
Platte River Academy	4085 Lark Sparrow St	Highlands Ranch, CO	80126-5209	303-221-1070	221-1069	K-8	Dr. Gary Stueven
Prairie Creeks Charter S	PO Box 889	Strasburg, CO	80136-0889	303-622-6328	622-6327	9-12	Jeremy David
PS 1 Charter S	1062 Delaware St	Denver, CO	80204-4033	303-575-6690	575-6661	6-12	Liz Aybar
Pueblo S for the Arts & Sciences	1745 Acero Ave	Pueblo, CO	81004-2645	719-549-2737	549-2659	K-8	Cheryl Gomez
Ridge View Academy	28101A E Quincy Ave	Watkins, CO	80137	303-214-1139	766-2151	6-12	John Fry
Ridgeview Classical S	1800 S Lemay Ave	Fort Collins, CO	80525-1240	970-494-4620	494-4625	9-12	Dr. Terrence Moore
Rocky Mountain Academy of Evergreen	PO Box 3162	Evergreen, CO	80437-3162	303-670-1070	670-1253	K-8	Jere Pearcy
Rocky Mountain Classical Academy	1710 Piros Dr	Colorado Spgs, CO	80915	719-622-8000	622-8004	K-8	Tina Leone
Rocky Mountain Deaf S	1921 Youngfield St	Golden, CO	80401	303-984-5749	984-7290	PK-5	Janet Cerney
Roosevelt Edison Charter S	205 Byron Dr	Colorado Spgs, CO	80910-2599	719-637-0311	380-0176	K-5	Dr. Precious Broadnax
Ross Montessori Charter S	407 Merrill Ave	Carbondale, CO	81623-1643	970-963-7199	963-7342	K-8	Mark Grice
Shivers Academy of Art - Science & Tech	2573 Airport Rd	Colorado Spgs, CO	80910-3119	719-473-6566	473-6601	9-12	Wanda Cousar
Skyland Community HS	3240 Humboldt St	Denver, CO	80205-3934	303-388-4759	388-2470	9-12	Allen Smith
Southwest Early College Charter S	3001 S Federal Blvd	Denver, CO	80236-2711	303-935-5473	935-5591	9-12	Chris Gerboth
Southwest Open Charter S	PO Box DD	Cortez, CO	81321-0870	970-565-1150	565-8770	9-12	Judy Hite
STAR Academy	PO Box 10018	Colorado Spgs, CO	80932-1018	719-321-4434		K-5	Charles Chisholm
Stargate Charter S	3951 Cottonwood Lakes Blvd	Thornton, CO	80241-2187	303-450-3936	450-3941	K-8	Patricia Crone
Summit MS	PO Box 3125	Boulder, CO	80307-3125	303-499-9511	499-0215	6-8	David Finell
Swallows Charter Academy	278 S Mcculloch Blvd	Pueblo West, CO	81007-2844	719-547-1627	547-2509	K-8	Eva Chamberlin
21st Century Charter S	525 E Costilla St	Colorado Spgs, CO	80903-3764	719-570-7575	475-0831	K-8	Mike AuClaire
Twin Peaks Charter Academy	820 Main St	Longmont, CO	80501	720-652-8201	774-9855	K-8	B.J. Buchmann
Union Colony Prep S	2000 Clubhouse Dr	Greeley, CO	80634-3643	970-348-2800	348-2830	7-12	Pat Gilliam
University Schools	6525 W 18th St	Greeley, CO	80634-8674	970-330-2221	506-7070	K-12	Greg Pierson
Ute Creek Secondary Academy	1198 Boston Ave	Longmont, CO	80501-5856	303-774-0066	774-8291	9-12	Jay Ritter
Vista Charter S	PO Box 10000	Montrose, CO	81402-9701	970-249-4470	252-3354	10-12	Coni Wilson
West Denver Prep Charter S	PO Box 19484	Denver, CO	80219-0484	303-573-2017	935-5004	6-8	
Wilson Academy	8300 W 94th Ave	Westminster, CO	80021-4590	303-431-3694	423-4388	K-8	Tim Matlick
Windsor Charter Academy	680 Academy Ct	Windsor, CO	80550-3101	970-674-5020	674-5017	K-8	Lyn Tausan
Wyatt-Edison Charter S	3620 Franklin St	Denver, CO	80205-3325	303-292-5515	292-5111	K-8	Kay Frunzi
Youth & Family Academy Charter S	1920 Valley Dr	Pueblo, CO	81008-1764	719-549-7653	542-1335	7-12	Darryl Vaughn

Connecticut

School	Address	City,State	Zip code	Telephone	Fax	Grade	Contact
Amistad Academy	407 James St	New Haven, CT	06513-3016	203-773-0390	773-0364	5-8	Matt Taylor
Bridge Academy	410 Kossuth St	Bridgeport, CT	06608	203-336-9999	336-9852	7-12	Timothy Dutton
Common Ground HS	358 Springside Ave	New Haven, CT	06515-1024	203-389-4333	389-7458	9-12	Oliver Barton
Cross Cultural Academy	237 Hamilton St	Hartford, CT	06106	860-951-7880	951-7891	5-6	Lynette Harper
Elm City College Preparatory S	240 Greene St	New Haven, CT	06511-6934	203-498-0702	498-0712	K-6	Marc Michaelson
Explorations Charter S	71 Spencer St	Winsted, CT	06098	860-738-9070	738-9092	10-12	Gail Srebnik
Highville Mustard Seed Charter S	130 Leeder Hill Dr	Hamden, CT	06517-2730	203-287-0528	287-0693	PK-8	Lawrence DiPalma
Integrated Day Charter S	68 Thermos Ave	Norwich, CT	06360	860-892-1900	892-1902	PK-8	Rosemarie Rose
Interdistrict S for Arts & Communication	190 Governor Winthrop Blvd	New London, CT	06320	860-447-1003	447-0470	6-8	Ruth Cole-Chu
Jumoke Academy	250 Blue Hills Ave	Hartford, CT	06112-1836	860-527-0575	525-7758	K-7	Michael Sharpe
New Beginnings Family Academy	184 Garden St	Bridgeport, CT	06605-1213	203-384-2897	384-2898	K-7	Lori Motta
Odyssey Community S	579 Middle Tpke W	Manchester, CT	06040-2728	860-645-1234	533-0324	4-8	Elaine Stancliffe
Park City Prep Charter S	510 Barnum Ave	Bridgeport, CT	06608	203-953-3766	953-3771	6-8	Bruce Ravage
Side by Side Community S	10 Chestnut St	Norwalk, CT	06854-2928	203-857-0306	838-2666	PK-8	Matthew Nittoly
Stamford Academy	229 North St	Stamford, CT	06901-1112	203-324-6300	324-6310	9-12	Michael McGuire
Trailblazers Academy	PO Box 359	Stamford, CT	06904-0359	203-977-5690	977-5688	6-8	Craig Baker

Delaware

School	Address	City,State	Zip code	Telephone	Fax	Grade	Contact
Academy of Dover Charter S	104 Saulsbury Rd	Dover, DE	19904-2705	302-674-0684	674-3894	K-6	Leonard Litzi
Campus Community HS	350 Pear St	Dover, DE	19904-3016	302-736-0403	736-5330	9-12	Heidi Greene
Campus Community S	21 N Bradford St	Dover, DE	19904-3101	302-736-3300	736-3390	K-8	Trish Hermance
Charter S of Wilmington	100 N DuPont Rd	Wilmington, DE	19807-3199	302-651-2727	652-1246	9-12	Ronald Russo
Delaware Military Academy	112 Middleboro Rd	Wilmington, DE	19804-1621	302-998-0745	998-3521	9-12	Robert Chester
East Side Charter S	3000 N Claymont St	Wilmington, DE	19802-2807	302-762-5834	762-3864	K-7	Will Robinson
Edison Charter S	2200 N Locust St	Wilmington, DE	19802-4429	302-778-1101	778-2232	K-8	Charles Hughes
Family Foundations Academy	1101 Delaware St	New Castle, DE	19720-6033	302-324-8901	324-8908	1-3	Dr. Tennell Brewington
Kuumba Academy Charter S	519 N Market St	Wilmington, DE	19801-3004	302-472-6450	472-6452	K-8	Dr. Sondra Shippen
Marion T. Academy Charter S	1121 Thatcher St	Wilmington, DE	19802-5135	302-575-1190	575-1425	K-8	John Taylor
MOT Charter S	1156 Levels Rd	Middletown, DE	19709-9078	302-376-5125	376-5120	K-8	Linda Jennings
Moyer Academy	97 Vandever Ave	Wilmington, DE	19802-4219	302-428-9500	428-9506	6-9	Theopalis Gregory
Newark Charter S	2001 Patriot Way	Newark, DE	19711-1809	302-369-2001	368-3460	5-8	Greg Meece
Odyssey Charter S	3821 Lancaster Pike	Wilmington, DE	19805-1512	302-994-6490	994-6915	K-2	Anthony Skoutelas
Pencader Business & Finance Charter HS	170 Lukens Dr	New Castle, DE	19720-2727	302-472-0794	472-0796	9-10	Dave Jones
Positive Outcomes Charter S	193 S Dupont Hwy	Camden, DE	19934-1310	302-697-8805	697-8813	7-12	Edward Emmett
Providence Creek Academy Charter S	PO Box 265	Clayton, DE	19938-0265	302-653-6276	653-7850	K-8	Charles Taylor
Sussex Academy of Arts and Sciences	21777 Sussex Pines Rd	Georgetown, DE	19947-3901	302-856-3636	856-3376	6-8	Patricia Oliphant Ed.D.

District Of Columbia

School	Address	City,State	Zip code	Telephone	Fax	Grade	Contact
Amos II Charter S	1351 Nicholson St NW	Washington, DC	20011-2813	202-723-5136	723-5139	PK-K	Toosdhi Tucker
Amos Public Charter S	1300 Allison St NW	Washington, DC	20011-4441	202-723-4100	723-6867	PK-5	Kyle Williams
Angelou Charter S	1851 9th St NW	Washington, DC	20001-4133	202-939-9080	939-9084	10-12	Eugene Pinkard
Arts & Technology Academy	5300 Blaine St NE	Washington, DC	20019-6665	202-398-6811	388-8467	PK-6	Errick Greene
Associates for Renewal in Education	45 P St NW	Washington, DC	20001-1133	202-483-9424	667-5299	8-12	Patricia Barr
Bethune Charter S	5413 16th St NW	Washington, DC	20011-3618	202-723-5800	723-5820	PK-4	D. Maurice Rawles
Bethune Charter S	253 42nd St NE	Washington, DC	20019-3405	202-397-3044	397-3046	PK-K	D. Maurice Rawles
Business & Finance Academy	5500 Eads St NE	Washington, DC	20019-6720	202-724-4512		9-12	Virgil Smith
Butler Bilingual Charter S	5 Thomas Cir NW	Washington, DC	20005	202-332-6565	332-1073	PK-5	Ibis Villegas
Capital City Public Charter S	3047 15th St NW	Washington, DC	20009-4211	202-387-0309	387-7074	PK-8	Karen Dresden
Chavez Public Policy Charter HS	3701 Hayes St NE	Washington, DC	20019-1702	202-387-6980	387-7808	6-12	Lisa Raymond
Childrens Studio Public Charter S	1301 V St NW	Washington, DC	20009-4413	202-387-6148	986-0792	PK-6	Tracie Jenkins
City Lights Charter S	62 T St NE	Washington, DC	20002-1577	202-832-4366	832-3654	9-12	Michelle Codrington
DC Bilingual Public Charter S	1420 Columbia Rd NW	Washington, DC	20009	202-332-4200	745-2562	PK-1	Alison Auerbach
DC Preparatory Academy	701 Edgewood St NE	Washington, DC	20017-3341	202-882-5700	882-5701	4-8	Natalie Butler
Eagle Academy Public Charter S	770 M St SE	Washington, DC	20003	202-544-2646	544-0187	PK-K	Cassandra Pinkney
Friendship Charter S - Blow-Pierce	725 19th St NE	Washington, DC	20002-4713	202-572-1070	399-6157	6-8	Ralph Neal

School	Address	City,State	Zip code	Telephone	Fax	Grade	Contact
Friendship Charter S - Chamberlain	1345 Potomac Ave SE	Washington, DC	20003-4411	202-547-5800	547-4554	K-5	James Shepherd
Friendship Collegiate Academy	4095 Minnesota Ave NE	Washington, DC	20019-3541	202-396-5500	396-8229	9-12	Brian Beck
Friendship Public Charter S - Woodridge	2959 Carlton Ave NE	Washington, DC	20018-2615	202-635-6500	635-6481	PK-7	Mary Dunnock
Haynes Public Charter S	3029 14th St NW	Washington, DC	20009-6820	202-667-4446	667-8811	PK-3	Jennifer Niles
Health & Human Services Academy	1700 E Capitol St NE	Washington, DC	20003-1622	202-698-4571		9-12	Faye Dixon
Hyde Leadership Public Charter S	101 T St NE	Washington, DC	20002-1519	202-529-4400	529-4500	K-12	Dr. Jacqueline Frierson
Ideal Academy Charter S	100 Peabody St NW Fl 2	Washington, DC	20011-2219	202-723-6798	723-6799	PK-8	George Rutherford Ph.D.
IDEA Public Charter HS	1027 45th St NE	Washington, DC	20019-3802	202-399-4750	399-4387	7-12	Charlotte Blount-Luis
Jordan Public Charter S	100 Peabody St NW	Washington, DC	20011	202-554-0922		5-8	Sherilyn Reid
JOS-ARZ Academy Public Charter S	220 Taylor St NE	Washington, DC	20017-1009	202-269-6004	269-6005	9-12	Marlind Boxley
Kamit Institute Magnificent Achievers	100 Peabody St NW	Washington, DC	20011	202-723-7886	723-0239	7-12	Saungktakhu Richey
KIPP DC/KEY Academy	770 M St SE	Washington, DC	20003	202-543-6595	543-6594	5-8	Sarah Hayes
Latin American Montessori Bilingual S	1375 Missouri Ave NW	Washington, DC	20011-1807	202-726-6200		PK-PK	Cristina Encinas
Marriott Public Hospitality S	410 8th St NW	Washington, DC	20004	202-737-9122	737-7363	9-12	Lorraine Gibbs
Meridian Public Charter S	1328 Florida Ave NW	Washington, DC	20009	202-387-9830	387-7605	PK-8	Robinette Breedlove
Milburn Public Charter Alt. HS	100 Peabody St NW Fl 1	Washington, DC	20011-2212	202-829-7045		9-12	Richard Johnson
Milburn Public Charter Alt. HS	1027 45th St NE	Washington, DC	20019-3802	202-397-8010		9-12	Dr. Thomas Simpson
New S for Enterprise & Development	1920 Bladensburg Rd NE	Washington, DC	20002-1812	202-526-0161	526-8349	9-12	Vivian Carson
Next Step Public Charter S	1419 Columbia Rd NW	Washington, DC	20009-4705	202-319-2249	332-0398	9-12	Susan Evans
Options Public Charter S	1375 E St NE	Washington, DC	20002	202-547-1028	547-1272	5-8	Ronald Nicholas
Pre-Engineering SWSC	1301 New Jersey Ave NW	Washington, DC	20001-1227	202-673-7233		9-12	Gertrude Turner Wills
Rand Technology Center	33 Riggs Rd NE	Washington, DC	20011-2463	202-723-4010	723-4013	PK-8	Leroy Swain
Roots Public Charter S	6222 N Capitol St NW	Washington, DC	20011-1408	202-882-5155	882-5157	PK-K	Dr. Bernida Thompson
Roots Public Charter S	115 Kennedy St NW	Washington, DC	20011-5260	202-882-8073	882-8075	K-8	Dr. Bernida Thompson
Rosario International Public Charter S	1100 Harvard St NW	Washington, DC	20009-5356	202-797-4700	232-6442	10-12	Sonia Gutierrez
SABIS International Charter S	3022 Chestnut St NW	Washington, DC	20015-1408	202-363-1118		K-12	Louis Steadwell
St. Coletta of Greater Washington	1901 Independence Ave SE	Washington, DC	20003-1733	202-350-8680	350-8699	PK-12	Janice Corazza
Sasha Bruce Public Charter S	745 8th St SE	Washington, DC	20003-2802	202-675-9354	675-0225	6-12	Harold Thomas
School for Arts in Learning	1100 16th St NW	Washington, DC	20036-4802	202-296-9100	261-0200	K-5	Reem Labib
School Within School at Peabody	425 C St NE	Washington, DC	20002-5817	202-698-3283		PK-K	John Burst
SEED Public Charter S	4300 C St SE	Washington, DC	20019-4100	202-248-7773	248-3021	7-12	John Ciccone
Southeast Academy of Excellence	645 Milwaukee Pl SE	Washington, DC	20032-2606	202-562-1980	562-6380	K-8	Nadia Casseus
Stokes Charter S	3220 16th St NW	Washington, DC	20010-3356	202-265-7237	265-4656	K-6	Patricia Crain deGalarce
Techworld Public Charter S	401 M St SW Ste 2718	Washington, DC	20024	202-488-1845		9-9	Daanen Strachan
Tree of Life Community Charter S	2315 18th Pl NE	Washington, DC	20018-3610	202-832-1108	832-1113	PK-8	Patricia Williams
Tri-Community Charter S	3700 N Capitol St NW	Washington, DC	20011-8400	202-882-1930	882-1936	PK-5	Joyce Bowles
Two Rivers Public Charter S	1830 Constitution Ave NE	Washington, DC	20002-6628	202-546-4477	546-0869	PK-5	Jessica Wodatch
Urban Family Institute	1300 Allison St NW	Washington, DC	20011-4441	202-234-5437		K-10	Kent Amos
Washington Academy Charter S	3000 Pennsylvania Ave SE	Washington, DC	20020-3718	202-583-2222	583-2235	1-7	Jackie Gartrell
Washington Charter S for Technical Arts	1346 Florida Ave NW	Washington, DC	20009	202-232-6090	232-6382	9-12	Richard Jackson
Washington MST Public Charter HS	1920 Bladensburg Rd NE	Washington, DC	20002-1812	202-636-8011	636-3495	9-12	Floyd Gilmore
Washington Very Special Arts Charter S	1100 16th St NW	Washington, DC	20036-4802	202-296-9100	261-0200	PK-2	Lawrence Ricco
World Charter S of Washington	595 1/2 3rd St NW	Washington, DC	20001	202-269-4800		PK-K	Dorothy Goodman
WVSA Auto Arts Academy Public Charter S	1100 16th St NW	Washington, DC	20036-4802	202-296-9100		9-10	Curtiss Brazil
Young America Works Charter S	6015 Chillum Pl NE	Washington, DC	20011-1501	202-722-9295	722-9293	9-12	Nadine Evans

Florida

School	Address	City,State	Zip code	Telephone	Fax	Grade	Contact
Academy at the Farm	9500 Alex Lange Way	Dade City, FL	33525-8213	352-588-9737	588-0508	K-8	Dr. Michael Rom
Academy Da Vinci	1380 Pinehurst Rd	Dunedin, FL	34698-5407	727-298-2778	298-2780	K-5	Dawn Wilson
Academy for International Studies	757 Lighthouse Dr	No Palm Beach, FL	33408-4741	561-776-1130	776-0975	6-6	Kendall Artusi
Academy for Positive Learning Charter S	128 N C St	Lake Worth, FL	33460-3232	561-585-6104	585-7849	K-8	Renatta Adan-Espinoza
Academy of Arts & Minds	3138 Commodore Plz	Miami, FL	33133	305-448-1100	448-9737	9-12	Alex Tamargo
Academy of Environmental Science	12695 W Fort Island Trl	Crystal River, FL	34429-5290	352-795-8793	794-0065	10-12	Ben Stofcheck
ACE Charter S	710 E Bella Vista St	Lakeland, FL	33805-3009	863-686-3189	682-1348	PK-PK	Susan Snover
Achievement Academy - Bartow	695 E Summerlin St	Bartow, FL	33830-4848	863-533-0690	534-0798	PK-PK	Paula Sullivan
Achievement Academy - Lakeland	716 E Bella Vista St	Lakeland, FL	33805-3009	863-683-6504	688-9292	PK-PK	Paula Sullivan
Achievement Academy - Winter Haven	2221 28th St NW	Winter Haven, FL	33881	863-965-7586	968-5016	PK-PK	Paula Sullivan
Advanced Technology Center	1770 Technology Blvd	Daytona Beach, FL	32117-7149	386-506-4100		11-12	Dr. Michelle McCraney
Alachua Learning Center	PO Box 1389	Alachua, FL	32616-1389	386-418-2080	418-4116	1-8	Tom Allin
Alee Academy Charter S	755 S Central Ave	Umatilla, FL	32784-9504	352-669-1280	669-1282	9-12	Jennings Neeld
Anderson Academy	2708 N Central Ave	Tampa, FL	33602-1602	813-273-6767	225-1639	K-3	Jeanette Collins
Apalachicola Bay Charter S	350 Fred Meyer St	Apalachicola, FL	32320-2502	850-653-1222	653-1857	K-7	Don Hungerford
APPLE S	3425 New Jersey Rd	Lakeland, FL	33803-4225	863-619-7170	644-5882	K-8	Beth Nave
Archimedean Academy	12425 SW 72nd St	Miami, FL	33183-2513	305-640-6278	993-1328	K-5	Pat Booth
Archimedean Middle Conservatory	12425 SW 72nd St	Miami, FL	33183-2513	305-640-6278	675-8448	6-8	Vasiliki Moysidis
ASPIRA De Hostos Charter S	1 NE 19th St	Miami, FL	33132	305-576-1512	576-0810	6-8	Fernando Lopez
ASPIRA South Youth Leadership	14112 SW 288th St	Leisure City, FL	33033-1864	305-246-1111	246-1433	6-8	Aymet Chaples
ASPIRA Youth Leadership	13300 Memorial Hwy	North Miami, FL	33161-3940	305-893-8050	891-6055	6-8	Iliana Pena
Athenian Academy of Pasco	3118 Seven Springs Blvd	New Port Richey, FL	34655-3340	727-372-0200	376-1916	K-5	Susan Dahn
Athenian Academy	2817 Saint Marks Dr	Dunedin, FL	34698-1920	727-298-2718	298-2719	K-5	Lemonia Poumakis
Aventura Charter ES	3333 NE 188th St	Aventura, FL	33180-2933	305-466-1499	466-1339	K-8	Dr. Katherine Murphy
Balere Language Academy	10600 Caribbean Blvd	Cutler Bay, FL	33189-1361	305-232-9797	232-4535	K-8	Rocka Malik
Bay Haven Charter Academy	2501 Hawks Landing Blvd	Panama City, FL	32405-6658	850-248-3500	248-3514	K-8	Dr. Tim Kitts
Believers Academy	5840 Corporate Way Ste 100	West Palm Beach, FL	33407-2040	561-340-2507	340-2510	9-12	Lori Dyer
Bellalago Charter Academy	3651 Pleasant Hill Rd	Kissimmee, FL	34746-2935	407-933-1690	933-2143	K-12	Cecile Diez
Berkley Accelerated MS	5316 Berkley Rd	Auburndale, FL	33823-8493	863-968-2400	968-2411	6-8	Jill Bolender
Berkley ES	5240 Berkley Rd	Auburndale, FL	33823-8491	863-968-5024	968-5026	PK-5	Randy Borland
Beulah Academy	5805 Beulah Church Rd	Pensacola, FL	32526-4222	850-944-2822		6-8	Sherry Bailey
Big Pine Key Neighborhood S	PO Box 432131	Big Pine Key, FL	33043-2131	305-872-1266	872-1265	PK-3	
Boca Raton Charter S	414 NW 35th St	Boca Raton, FL	33431-5708	561-750-0437	750-7880	K-5	Deborah Nash-Utterback
Bonita Springs Charter S	25380 Bernwood Dr	Bonita Springs, FL	34135-7850	239-992-6932	992-7359	K-8	Deborah Tracy
Bradenton Charter S	2615 26th St W	Holmes Beach, FL	34217	941-739-6100	752-3250	3-8	Richard Donnelly
Bright Futures International	757 Lighthouse Dr	No Palm Beach, FL	33408-4741	561-776-1130	776-0975	K-5	Kendall Artusi
Broward Community Charter S	201 N University Dr	Coral Springs, FL	33071-7323	954-341-0082	341-0024	K-8	Jay Drag
Broward Community Charter S West	11401 NW 56th Dr	Coral Springs, FL	33076-3122	954-227-5133	227-0433	K-5	Jay Drag
Byrneville Charter S	1600 Byrneville Rd	Century, FL	32535-3640	850-256-6350	256-6357	K-5	Dee Wolfe-Sullivan
Campus Charter S	3805 Curtis Blvd	Port Saint John, FL	32927-3942	321-633-8234	633-8234	K-4	Pamela Dodd
Canoe Creek Charter S	3600 Canoe Creek Rd	Saint Cloud, FL	34772-9132	407-891-7320	891-7730	PK-8	Barbara Hernandez
Cape Coral Charter S	76 Mid Cape Ter	Cape Coral, FL	33991-2008	239-995-0904	995-0369	K-5	Patricia Duffy
Capstone Academy	4901 W Fairfield Dr	Pensacola, FL	32506-4111	850-455-7754		K-5	Charles Thomas
Caring & Sharing Charter S	PO Box 5936	Gainesville, FL	32627-5936	352-372-1004	372-0894	K-5	Dr. Simon Johnson
Central Charter S	4525 N State Road 7	Laud Lakes, FL	33319-5855	954-735-6295	735-6232	K-6	Tracy Nessl
Central City Academy	3916 E Hillsborough Ave	Tampa, FL	33610-4542	813-239-9827	239-9268	K-5	Wayne Quin
Central FL Speech & Hearing Charter S	710 E Bella Vista St	Lakeland, FL	33805-3009	863-686-3189	682-1348	PK-PK	Sue Snover
Chain of Lakes Collegiate HS	999 Avenue H NE	Winter Haven, FL	33881-4256	863-298-6800	298-6800	11-12	Bridget Fetter
Chancellor Charter S	1395 S State Rd 7	N Lauderdale, FL	33068-4023	954-973-8900	974-5588	K-8	LaMarr Moses
Chancellor Charter S at Lantana	600 S East Coast Ave	Lantana, FL	33462-4577	561-585-1189	585-1166	K-5	Laura Mardyks
Chancellor Charter S at Weston	2500 Glades Cir	Weston, FL	33327-2253	954-659-3600	659-3620	K-5	Susan Messing
Charter S at National Deaf Academy	19650 US Highway 441	Mount Dora, FL	32757-6959	352-735-9500	735-4939	PK-12	Rebecca Hilding
Charter S at Waterstone	855 Waterstone Way	Homestead, FL	33033-5941	305-248-6206	248-6208	K-8	Dr. Cristina Cruz
Charter S Institute Annex	5420 N State Road 7	Fort Lauderdale, FL	33319-2922	954-486-1640	486-4549	K-6	Dr. Joseph Valbrun
Charter S Institute Training	520 NW 5th St	Hallandale, FL	33009-3314	954-454-5348	454-2463	K-6	Dr. Joseph Valbrun
Charter S of Boynton Beach	801 N Congress Ave Ste 529	Boynton Beach, FL	33426-3365	561-738-2380	738-2378	K-5	Wayne Owens
Charter S of Excellence	1217 SE 3rd Ave	Fort Lauderdale, FL	33316-1905	954-522-2997	522-3159	K-6	Lisa Castro
Chautauqua Learn & Serve Charter S	1118 Magnolia Ave	Panama City, FL	32401-2815	850-785-5056	785-5071		Cynthia McCauley
Chiles Academy	1250 Reed Canal Rd Ste A	Port Orange, FL	32129-9106	386-322-6102		6-12	Anne Ferguson
Choices in Learning Charter S	893 E State Road 434	Longwood, FL	32750-5306	407-331-8477	331-5075	K-6	Shannon McCutcheon
City of Cape Coral Charter MS	3507 Oasis Blvd	Cape Coral, FL	33914-4914	239-945-1999		6-8	Chris Terrill
City of Cape Coral Charter North ES	2817 SW 3rd Ln	Cape Coral, FL	33991-1151	239-283-4511		K-5	Dr. Lee Bush
City of Cape Coral Charter South ES	3415 Oasis Blvd	Cape Coral, FL	33914	239-542-1577	549-7662	K-5	Steven Hook
City of Coral Springs Charter S	3205 N University Dr	Coral Springs, FL	33065-4115	954-340-4100	340-4111	6-12	Billie Miller
City of Pembroke Pines Charter HS	17189 Sheridan St	Pembroke Pines, FL	33331-1934	954-538-3700	538-3714	9-12	Peter Bayer
City of Pembroke Pines Charter MS West	18500 Pembroke Rd	Pembroke Pines, FL	33029-6108	954-443-4847	447-1691	6-8	Devarn Flowers
City of Pembroke Pines Charter S East	10801 Pembroke Rd	Pembroke Pines, FL	33025-1707	954-443-4800	443-4811	K-5	Sean Chance
City of Pembroke Pines Charter S West	1680 SW 184th Ave	Pembroke Pines, FL	33029-6120	954-450-6990	443-4820	K-5	Devarn Flowers
City of Pembroke Pines ES - Central	12350 Sheridan St	Pembroke Pines, FL	33026-3813	954-322-3330	322-3383	K-5	Kenneth Bass
City of Pembroke Pines MS - Central	12350 Sheridan St	Pembroke Pines, FL	33026-3813	954-322-3300	322-3383	6-8	Kenneth Bass
COAST Charter S	48 Shell Island Rd	Saint Marks, FL	32355	850-925-6344	925-6396	K-8	Susan Flournoy
Compass Middle Charter S	550 E Clower St	Bartow, FL	33830-6403	863-519-8701	519-8704	6-8	Harry Williams
Cooperative Charter S	1743-51 NW 54th St	Miami, FL	33161	305-693-2541	693-2543	K-5	Dr. John Johnson
Coral Reef Montessori Academy	10853 SW 216th St	Cutler Bay, FL	33170-3146	305-255-0064	255-4085	K-8	Juliet King
Countryside Montessori Academy	5852 Ehren Cutoff	Land O Lakes, FL	34639-3428	813-996-0991	996-0993	1-6	Jean Audino
Crossroad Academy Charter S	1500 Strong Rd Ste 1	Quincy, FL	32351	850-875-9626	875-1403	K-8	Millie Forehand
Daniels Charter S	2201 SW 42nd Ave	West Park, FL	33023-3456	954-894-2826	895-5357	K-5	Richard Garrick
Dayspring Academy ES	8911 Timber Oaks Ave	Port Richey, FL	34668-2426	727-862-8600	868-5175	K-5	Suzanne Chase
Dayspring Academy MS	9509 Palm Ave	Port Richey, FL	34668-4647	727-847-9003	848-8774	6-8	Suzanne Chase

School	Address	City,State	Zip code	Telephone	Fax	Grade	Contact
DayStar Academy of Excellence	970 N Seacrest Blvd	Boynton Beach, FL	33435-4702	561-369-2323	369-2642	K-5	Doris Bennett
Delray Beach Academy	PO Box 1388	Boynton Beach, FL	33425-1388	561-736-8828		6-8	Joe Green
Delray Youth Vocational Charter S	601 N Congress Ave Ste 110	Delray Beach, FL	33445-4625	561-266-2206	266-2208	9-12	Dr. Frank Little
DeSoto HS	PO Box 358604	Gainesville, FL	32635-8604	352-745-6890		9-12	Mary Malo
Discovery Academy at Lake Alfred	1000 N Buena Vista Dr	Lake Alfred, FL	33850-2031	863-295-5955	295-5978	6-8	Carol Fulks
Doctors Charter S of Miami Shores	11301 NW 5th Ave	Miami Shores, FL	33168-3343	305-754-2381	751-5833	6-12	Marjorie Wessel
Doral Academy	2450 NW 97th Ave	Miami, FL	33172-2308	305-597-9999	591-2669	K-5	Ileana Gomez
Doral Academy HS	11100 NW 27th St	Miami, FL	33172-5001	305-597-9950	477-6762	9-12	Frank Jimenez
Doral Academy MS	2601 NW 112th Ave	Miami, FL	33172-1804	305-591-0020	591-9251	6-8	Ofelia Alvarez
Doral Performing Arts Academy	2601 NW 112th Ave	Miami, FL	33172-1804	305-591-0020	591-9251	9-12	Eleonora Cuesta
Downtown Academy of Technical Arts	101 SE 3rd Ave	Fort Lauderdale, FL	33301-1920	954-767-0403	767-1011	6-8	Jim DiSebastian
Downtown Miami Charter S	305 NW 3rd Ave	Miami, FL	33128-1606	305-579-2112	579-2115	K-6	Paul Thompson
Eagle Academy	3020 NW 33rd Ave	Laud Lakes, FL	33311-1106	954-343-9960	343-9970	6-8	Dewanda Chambers
Eagles Nest ES	1840 NE 41st St	Pompano Beach, FL	33064-6071	954-942-3318	942-3179	K-5	John Grant
Eagles Nest MS	1840 NE 41st St	Pompano Beach, FL	33064-6071	954-942-3318	942-3179	6-8	John Grant
Early Beginnings Academy-Civic Center	1411 NW 14th Ave	Miami, FL	33125-1616	305-325-1080	325-1044	PK-K	Leigh Kapps
Early Beginnings Academy-North Shore	985 NW 91st St	Miami, FL	33150-2350	305-835-9006	696-1688	PK-K	Carol Byrd
Early Beginnings West	3117 SW 13th Ct	Fort Lauderdale, FL	33312-2714	954-584-7178	584-3151	PK-K	Ana Pardo
Easter Seals Charter S	2219 S Woodland Blvd	De Land, FL	32720-8628	386-736-9849		PK-K	Dr. Robert Carlton
Easter Seals Charter S	1219 Dunn Ave	Daytona Beach, FL	32114-2405	386-255-4568		PK-K	Dr. Robert Carlton
Educational Horizons Charter S	1281 S Wickham Rd	West Melbourne, FL	32904-2450	321-729-0786	951-8005	1-5	Aileen Tapp
Ed Venture Charter S	117 E Coast Ave	Lantana, FL	33462-5316	561-582-1454	547-9682	10-12	Barbara Fitz
Einstein Montessori Charter S	5650 King St	Cocoa, FL	32926-2351	321-631-9876	752-6572	3-8	Pam Juhr
Einstein Montessori S	5930 SW Archer Rd	Gainesville, FL	32608-4702	352-335-4321	335-1575	2-8	Zach Osbrach
Emerald Coast Marine Institute	207 4th St SE	Ft Walton Bch, FL	32548-5636	850-244-2711	244-2171	6-12	Bernard Williams
Escambia Charter S	PO Box 1147	Gonzalez, FL	32560-1147	850-937-0500	968-5605	9-12	Stan Callender
Everglades Preparatory Academy	183 S Lake Ave	Pahokee, FL	33476-1803	561-924-3002	924-3013	9-12	Antoine Russell
Excel Academy Charter S	6001 NW 8th Ave	Miami, FL	33127-1005	305-751-6770	751-6771	K-5	Ralph Brantley
Excelsior Charter S of Broward	10046 W McNab Rd	Tamarac, FL	33321-1894	954-726-5227	726-5228	K-5	Raul Baez
Explorer S	475 S John Rodes Blvd	West Melbourne, FL	32904	321-733-1917	733-0748	K-8	Ruben Rosario
Expressions Learning Arts Academy	5408 SW 13th St	Gainesville, FL	32608-5038	352-373-5223	373-6327	K-5	Cheryl Valantis
Fair Babson Park ES	815 N Scenic Hwy	Babson Park, FL	33827-9795	863-678-4664	678-4669	K-5	Ken Hensen
First Coast Technical Institute	2980 Collins Ave	Saint Augustine, FL	32084-1919	904-824-4401	824-6750		Chris Cothron
Florida Intercultural Academy	1704 Buchanan St	Hollywood, FL	33020-4030	954-924-8006		K-5	Dr. Gwendolyn Purcell
Florida International Academy	7630 Biscayne Blvd	Miami, FL	33138	305-758-6912	758-6985	6-8	Sonia Mitchell
Florida SIA Tech at Gainesville	5301 NE 40th Ter	Gainesville, FL	32609-1670	352-371-4424	371-4426	9-12	Tina Bullock
Foundation Charter S	1325 George Jenkins Blvd	Lakeland, FL	33815-1367	863-682-8111	687-8205	6-12	Emory Welch
Foundation Middle Academy	2426 Remington Blvd	Kissimmee, FL	34744-8467	407-697-1020	697-1021	6-8	Diane Beatty
Four Corners Charter S	9100 Teacher Ln	Davenport, FL	33897-6212	407-787-4300	787-4301	PK-8	Dr. Walter Thomas
Gainer S	4000 W Fairfield Dr	Pensacola, FL	32505-4733	850-439-3888	439-3898	9-12	Dr. Ulysees Hughes
Gallagher Neighborhood S	3300 Schoolhouse Rd	Saint Cloud, FL	34773-6009	407-957-3570	957-6023	K-8	
Gateway Charter HS	12770 Gateway Blvd	Fort Myers, FL	33913-8654	239-768-3350	768-3874	9-12	Joseph Roles
Gateway Charter S	12850 Commonwealth Dr	Fort Myers, FL	33913-8039	239-768-5048	768-5710	K-8	Dr. Deborah Nauss
Genesis Preparatory S	207 NW 23rd Ave	Gainesville, FL	32609-3604	352-379-1188	379-1142	K-3	Charmaine Henry
Gibson Charter S	450 SW 4th St	Miami, FL	33130-1410	305-324-1335	324-1343	PK-8	Charles Bethel
Glades Academy	1200 E Main St	Pahokee, FL	33476-1102	561-924-9402	924-9279	K-5	Dr. Don Zumpano
Good Schools for all Leadership Academy	40 NW 4th Ave	Delray Beach, FL	33444-2626	561-278-3533	278-3633	K-8	Valarie Thompson
Goodwill Academy	3105 N Tamiami Trl	Sarasota, FL	34234-5859	941-915-9508		9-12	Darleen Zimmerman
G-STAR School of the Arts	2065 Prairie Rd	West Palm Beach, FL	33406	561-967-2023	963-8975	9-10	Reno Boffice
Guided Path Academy	1199 Lantana Rd	Lantana, FL	33462-1514	561-588-2800	588-0870	K-5	Evelyn Francis
Gulfstream Goodwill Career Academy	269 NE 14th St	Boca Raton, FL	33432-1821	561-367-1067	367-1372	9-12	Dee Naukana
Gulfstream Goodwill LIFE Academy	3800 S Congress Ave Ste 12	Boynton Beach, FL	33426-8424	561-259-1000	259-1004	9-12	Gloria Zimmerman
Gulfstream Goodwill Transition Academy	950 N Congress Ave	Riviera Beach, FL	33404-6400	561-863-1297	863-1373	9-12	Gloria Zimmerman
Harris Pyramid S of Learning	PO Box 2881	Pensacola, FL	32513-2881	850-432-2273	432-4624	K-5	Celestine Lewis
Hartridge Academy	1400 US Highway 92	Winter Haven, FL	33881-8137	863-956-4434	956-3267	K-5	Debra Richards
Healthy Learning Academy	2101 NW 39th Ave	Gainesville, FL	32609	352-372-2573		K-2	Bettianne Ford
Hoggetowne MS	3930 NE 15th St	Gainesville, FL	32609-2007	352-367-4369	376-3345	6-8	Kristine Santos
Hollywood Academy of Arts & Science	1720 Harrison St	Hollywood, FL	33020	954-925-6404	925-8123	K-5	Leslie Brown
Hope Charter S	1450 Daniels Rd	Winter Garden, FL	34787-4376	407-656-4673	656-6094	K-6	Crystal Yoakum
Hope Preparatory Academy	3916 E Hillsborough Ave	Tampa, FL	33610-4542	813-236-1462	232-9680	K-5	Celeste Kellar
IMAGINE S	2580 Metrocentre Blvd	West Palm Beach, FL	33407	561-683-6200	683-7783	K-5	Alphonso Milligan
Immokalee Charter S	402 W Main St	Immokalee, FL	34142-3933	239-658-3560		K-4	Maria Jimenez
Indian River Charter HS	6055 College Ln	Vero Beach, FL	32966-1093	772-567-6600	567-2288	9-12	Cynthia Aversa
Inlet Grove Community HS	7071 Garden Rd	Riviera Beach, FL	33404-4906	561-881-4600	881-4668	9-12	Emma Banks
International Studies Charter HS	396 Alhambra Cir	Coral Gables, FL	33134	305-442-7449	442-7729	9-12	Victor Lopez
Island S	PO Box 1090	Boca Grande, FL	33921-1090	941-964-8016	964-8017	K-5	Rosa Ramos
Island Village Montessori North S	3975 Fruitville Rd	Sarasota, FL	34232-1614	941-954-4999	342-6502	K-5	Kym Elder
Island Village Montessori S	2001 Pinebrook Rd	Venice, FL	34292-1560	941-484-4999	484-2150	K-6	Kym Elder
Jackson Preparatory S	546 Mary Esther Cut Off NW	Ft Walton Bch, FL	32548	850-833-3321	833-3292	PK-8	Dr. Samantha Dawson
JFK Medical Center Charter S	4696 Davis Rd	Lake Worth, FL	33461-5204	561-868-6100	963-4697	K-5	Chuck Shaw
Keys Gate Charter S	2000 SE 28th Ave	Homestead, FL	33035-2102	305-230-1616	230-1347	K-8	Robin Sandler
Kids Community College	10544 Lake St Charles Blvd	Riverview, FL	33569	813-671-1440	671-1245	K-2	Jeff Baker
King Academy	4180 NE 15th St	Gainesville, FL	32609-2011	352-376-4014	376-3345	1-5	Naomi Williams
Kissimmee Charter Academy	2850 Bill Beck Blvd	Kissimmee, FL	34744-4073	407-847-1400	847-1401	PK-6	Jo Ann Kandrac
Lake Eola Charter S	135 N Magnolia Ave	Orlando, FL	32801-2301	407-246-0900	246-6334	K-8	Ronnie Denoia
Lakeland Montessori Schoolhouse	PO Box 7521	Lakeland, FL	33807-7521	863-413-0003	413-0006	PK-3	Josie Zinninger
Lakeside Academy	716 S Main St	Belle Glade, FL	33430-4202	561-993-5000	993-5001	K-5	Barbara Litinski
Language Academy	4125 US Highway 19	New Port Richey, FL	34652-5948	727-847-9300	847-9315	5-8	Joyce Nunn
Lawrence Academy	777 W Palm Dr	Florida City, FL	33034-3223	305-247-4800	247-4895	6-8	Dr. Keitha Burnett
Leadership Academy West	2030 S Congress Ave	West Palm Beach, FL	33406-7602	561-434-0996	434-0575	9-12	Nicole Bret
Learning Academy	2312 N Stewart St	Milton, FL	32570	850-983-3495	983-8098	6-12	Chad White
Learning Gate Charter S	16215 Hanna Rd	Lutz, FL	33549-5701	813-948-4190	948-7587	K-7	Patricia Girard
Lee Charter Academy	3637 Dr M L King Blvd	Fort Myers, FL	33916	239-334-2235	334-2241	K-8	Dr. Shirley Chapman
Liberty City Charter S	8700 NW 5th Ave	Miami, FL	33150-2407	305-751-2700	751-1316	K-6	Katrina Wilson-Davis
LIFE Academy	940D Tarpon St	Fort Myers, FL	33916	239-334-4434	334-4439	9-12	Lynn Pottorf
Life Skills	6000 N Federal Hwy	Fort Lauderdale, FL	33308-2226	954-764-1665	764-1655	9-12	Laurel Moorehead
Life Skills Center	407 E Memorial Blvd	Lakeland, FL	33801-1768	863-683-6279	802-3547	9-12	Viesta Skipper
Life Skills Center	2360 W Oakland Park Blvd	Oakland Park, FL	33311-1410	754-625-6447	625-6409	9-12	Laurel Moorehead
Life Skills Center	4901 Central Ave	St Petersburg, FL	33710-8239	727-322-1758		9-12	Bonnie Solinsky
Life Skills Center	3637 Dr Martin Luther King	Fort Myers, FL	33916	239-332-3484	332-3446	9-12	Dr. Victor Hall
Life Skills Center Miami-Dade County	3535 NW 7th St	Miami, FL	33125	305-643-9111	643-9141	9-12	Jose Filpo
Life Skills Center of Palm Beach County	600 N Congress Ave Ste 560	Delray Beach, FL	33445-3463	561-279-1354	266-9274	9-12	Mary Delsignore
Life Skills Center Opa Locka	3400 NW 135th St	Opa Locka, FL	33054-4708	305-685-1415	685-1614	9-12	Erik Rashad
Life Skills S	4010 N Nebraska Ave	Tampa, FL	33603-4324	813-314-2154		9-12	Nicole Williams
Literacy/Leadership Technology Academy	6771 Madison Ave	Tampa, FL	33619-6836	813-793-3042	793-3043	6-8	Curt Miller
Littles Charter S	5829 Corporate Way Flr 2	West Palm Beach, FL	33407	561-689-9970	682-1342	K-8	Rev. Richard Scott
L'Ouverture HS	777 E Atlantic Ave Ste 242	Delray Beach, FL	33483	561-495-9991	495-1877	9-12	Joseph Bemadel
Love to Learn Education Center	125 NW 23rd Ave Ste 3	Gainesville, FL	32609-3681	352-381-1900	381-8080	1-5	Dr. Lavetta Palmer
Manatee County Juvenile Justice	14470 Harllee Rd	Bradenton, FL	34205	941-747-3011	714-7333	9-12	Harry Reif
Manatee S for the Arts	700 Haben Blvd	Palmetto, FL	34221-4173	941-721-6800	721-6805	6-12	Bill Jones
Manatee S of Arts/Science	3700 32nd St W	Bradenton, FL	34205-2708	941-755-5012	755-7934	PK-5	Miriam Jolly
Marco Island Charter MS	1401 Trinidad Ave	Marco Island, FL	34145-3949	239-389-4818	389-4921	6-8	George Abounder
Marion Charter S	39 Cedar Rd	Ocala, FL	34472-8331	352-687-2100	687-2700	K-5	Gina Evers
Mater Academy	7700 NW 98th St	Hialeah Gardens, FL	33016-2403	305-698-9900	698-3822	K-8	Kim Guilarte
Mater Academy Charter HS	7901 NW 103rd St	Hialeah Gardens, FL	33016-2419	305-828-1886	828-6175	9-10	Judith Marty
Mater Academy Charter MS	7901 NW 103rd St	Hialeah Gardens, FL	33016-2419	305-828-1886	828-6175	6-8	Kenneth Feria
Mater Academy East Charter S	450 SW 4th St	Miami, FL	33130-1410	305-324-4667	324-6580	K-9	Beatriz Riera
Mater Academy Lakes HS	5875 NW 163rd St	Miami Lakes, FL	33014-5618	305-512-9775	512-3708	9-12	Rene Rovirosa
Mater Academy Lakes MS	5875 NW 163rd St	Miami Lakes, FL	33014-5618	305-512-9775	512-3708	6-8	Jennifer Share
Mater Gardens Academy	9010 NW 178th Ln	Miami, FL	33018-6548	305-512-9775	512-3708	K-8	Lourdes Isla-Marrero
Mater Performing Arts Academy	7901 NW 103rd St	Hialeah Gardens, FL	33016-2419	305-828-1886	828-6175	9-12	Christine McGuinn
Mc Intosh Area Charter S	PO Box 769	Mc Intosh, FL	32664-0769	352-591-9797	591-9747	K-2	Shirley Lane
McKeel Academy of Applied Tech	1810 W Parker St	Lakeland, FL	33815-1243	863-499-2818	284-4383	6-12	Harold Maready
McKeel ES	411 N Florida Ave	Lakeland, FL	33801-4803	863-499-1287	688-1607	K-5	Judith Morris
MESTA Charter S	PO Box 580038	Orlando, FL	32858-0038	407-298-6378		6-8	Elaine Morris
Metropolitan Ministries Charter S	2002 N Florida Ave	Tampa, FL	33602-2204	813-209-1003	209-1234	K-5	Bonnie Guertin
Miami Childrens Museum Charter S	980 MacArthur Cswy	Miami, FL	33132-1604	305-329-3758	329-3767	K-5	Maria Greer
Miami Community Charter S	101 S Redland Rd	Florida City, FL	33034-4630	305-245-2552	245-2527	K-6	Jila Rezaie
Micanopy Area Cooperative S	PO Box 386	Micanopy, FL	32667-0386	352-466-0990	466-4090	K-5	Carl Landry
Micanopy MS	PO Box 109	Micanopy, FL	32667-0109	352-466-1090	466-1030	6-8	Dr. Edward Daleuski
Milburn Academy	2400 S Ridgewood Ave Ste 20	South Daytona, FL	32119-3073	386-304-0086		9-12	Sam Smith
Milburn Academy	7545 Little Rd	New Port Richey, FL	34654-5522	727-859-9323	859-0834	9-12	Krista Morton
Milburn Academy	2207 Industrial Blvd	Sarasota, FL	34234-3119	941-355-0835	953-9014	9-12	Melanie Dunham
Milburn Academy	3830 Evans Ave	Fort Myers, FL	33901	239-278-4774	278-0470	9-12	Patricia Lightner
Milburn Academy	6210 17th Ave W	Bradenton, FL	34209-7838	941-761-4393	761-2992	9-12	Edna Bailey
Milestones Community S	31600 Camp Challenge Rd	Sorrento, FL	32776-9558	352-385-0390	383-0744	K-8	Karen Gray
Minneola ES	300 E Pearl St	Minneola, FL	34715-9001	352-394-2600	394-2079	PK-5	Sandra Reaves

School	Address	City,State	Zip code	Telephone	Fax	Grade	Contact
Montessori Academy Northern Palm Beach	9482 MacArthur Blvd	Palm Bch Gdns, FL	33403-1102	561-514-5289	514-5291	K-5	Virginia Smith
Montessori Academy of Early Enrichment	2925 10th Ave N Ste 108	Palm Springs, FL	33461-3054	561-649-0004	649-0964	K-3	Jean Ranck
Montessori Charter ES	1127 United St	Key West, FL	33040-3330	305-294-4910	294-1404	1-5	Judy Dunlap
Montessori Island Charter S	92295 Old State Rd	Tavernier, FL	33070	305-852-3482	852-2432	K-5	Kelly Astin
Mount Pleasant Standard Base MS	1906 N Rome Ave	Tampa, FL	33607-4424	813-253-0053	253-0182	6-8	Yolanda Waitress
Nap Ford Community Charter S	648 W Livingston St	Orlando, FL	32801-1418	407-245-8711	245-8712	K-3	Jeraldine Perkins
New Dimensions HS	4900 Pleasant Hill Rd	Kissimmee, FL	34759	407-870-9949	870-8976	9-12	Jacqueline Dodge
New Hope Charter S	108 NW 3rd Ave	Chiefland, FL	32626-0841	352-490-6690	490-5288	9-10	Kim Martin
Noahs Ark International Charter S	21 W 22nd St	Riviera Beach, FL	33404-5509	561-848-7575	844-9563	K-5	Erika Hadden
North Broward Academy of Excellence	957 SW 71st Ave	N Lauderdale, FL	33068-2313	954-718-5032		K-4	Michael Hoffman
North Broward Academy of Excellence MS	8200 SW 17th St	N Lauderdale, FL	33068-4101	954-718-2211	764-1655	6-8	Michael Hoffman
North County Charter S	11 N Willow St	Fellsmere, FL	32948-5330	772-571-0153	571-8489	1-5	Dori Miller
North Dade Community Charter S	13850 NW 26th Ave	Opa Locka, FL	33054-4078	305-687-2325	687-0098	K-5	Valerie Goram-Kinnon
Northeast Academy	1750 NE 168th St	North Miami, FL	33162-3021	305-948-1247		K-5	Terry Maus
North Lauderdale Academy HS	7101 Kimberly Blvd	N Lauderdale, FL	33068-2388	954-720-0299	722-1508	9-12	Rosbin Ivery
NorthStar Charter HS	14681 Riviera Pointe Dr	Orlando, FL	32828-7404	407-273-1188	277-3340	9-10	Kelly Young
Oakwood Academy	7145 Babcock St SE	Palm Bay, FL	32909-5462	321-723-0150	723-0650	K-12	Tresa Vernon
Oasis ES	3415 Oasis Blvd	Cape Coral, FL	33914	239-542-1577		K-5	Dr. Patrick Mark
Oasis Enrichment Academy	PO Box 602	Gainesville, FL	32602-0602	352-692-3773	692-3774	6-8	Sharla Head-Jones
Odyssey Charter S	1755 Eldron Blvd SE	Palm Bay, FL	32909-6832	321-733-0442	733-1178	K-6	Irving Rashkover
Okaloosa Academy	81 Roberts Blvd	Ft Walton Bch, FL	32547-5118	850-864-3133	834-4305	6-12	Margaret Walton
Okaloosa Academy	2053 S Ferdon Blvd	Crestview, FL	32536-8424	850-689-7688	689-0799	6-12	Ron Panucci
One Room S House Project	4180 NE 15th St	Gainesville, FL	32609-2011	352-376-4014	376-3345	K-5	Neil Drake
Opportunity Charter S	202 13th Ave E	Bradenton, FL	34208-3246	941-714-7260	714-7333	9-12	Joe Kinnan
Origins Montessori Charter S	26 Willow Dr	Orlando, FL	32807-3220	321-235-3739	235-3509	K-8	Julie Sanborn
Osprey ES	720 Roy Wall Blvd	Rockledge, FL	32955-6212	877-258-0060		K-5	Debra Halstead
Our Children's Academy	555 Burns Ave	Lake Wales, FL	33853-3335	863-679-3338	679-3944	PK-2	Sharon McManus
OWC Collegiate HS	100 College Blvd E	Niceville, FL	32578-1347	850-678-5111	729-4950	10-12	Dr. Jill White
Oxford Academy of Miami	10870 SW 113th Pl	Miami, FL	33176-3227	305-598-4494	598-4475	K-5	Dr. Pauline Young
PAL Academy Charter S	202 13th Ave E	Bradenton, FL	34208-3246	941-714-7260	714-7333	1-8	Joe Kinnan
Palm Bay Academy	1465 Baytree Dr NE	Palm Bay, FL	32905-3950	321-984-2710	984-0799	K-6	Madhu Longani
Palm Bay Community Charter S	1350 Wyoming Dr SE	Palm Bay, FL	32909-5757	321-409-4500	409-4501	K-8	Pamela Franco
Palm Beach Academy for Learning	6201 S Military Trl	Lake Worth, FL	33463-7288	561-649-7505	732-3397	K-12	Joann Huprich
Palm Beach Maritime Academy	7719 S Dixie Hwy	West Palm Beach, FL	33405-4817	561-547-3775	540-5177	K-8	Marie Turchiaro
Palm Beach S for Autism	1199 Lantana Rd Ste 16	Lantana, FL	33462	561-582-1645	582-1699	PK-PK	Nancy Frank
Paragon Academy of Technology	2210 Pierce St	Hollywood, FL	33020-4414	954-925-0155	925-0209	6-8	Dr. Steven Montes
Paragon ES	3311 N Andrews Ave	Pompano Beach, FL	33064	954-943-0471	943-0473	K-5	Ardonnis Lumpkin
Parks Charter S	713 W Palm Dr	Florida City, FL	33034-3223	305-246-3336	246-3340	K-8	Marva de Silva
Parks Community S	430 NW 9th St	Homestead, FL	33030	305-379-4905		K-6	Michael Banks
Parkway Academy	7451 Riviera Blvd	Miramar, FL	33023	954-961-2911	961-2451	9-12	Dr. Clarissa Scott
Passport S	5221 Curry Ford Rd	Orlando, FL	32812-8741	407-658-9900		K-8	Dr. Osvaldo Garcia
Pathways Academy	101 State St W	Jacksonville, FL	32202-3099	904-633-8125		9-12	Maureen Martin
PCC Collegiate HS	3425 Winter Lake Rd	Lakeland, FL	33803-9765	863-669-2322	669-2330	11-12	Joy Browne
Pensacola Beach ES	900 Via De Luna Dr	Pensacola Beach, FL	32561-2262	850-934-4020	934-4040	K-5	Jeff Castleberry
Pepin Academy	3916 E Hillsborough Ave	Tampa, FL	33610-4542	813-237-1239	236-1195	6-12	Monica Patton
Pinecrest Academy	15130 SW 80th St	Miami, FL	33193-1302	305-386-0800	386-6298	K-5	Victoria Larrauri
Pinecrest Academy MS	14301 SW 42nd St	Miami, FL	33175-7832	305-207-1027	207-1897	6-8	Maria Nunez
Pinecrest Preparatory Academy	14301 SW 42nd St	Miami, FL	33175-7832	305-207-1027	207-1897	K-5	Susie Dopico
Pinellas Preparatory Academy	403 1st Ave SW	Largo, FL	33770-3437	727-581-9550	581-9590	4-8	Curtis Fuller
Plato Academy	401 S Old Coachman Rd	Clearwater, FL	33765-4410	727-793-2400		K-5	Steve Christopoulos
Pompano Charter MS	3311 N Andrews Ave	Pompano Beach, FL	33064	954-943-0471	943-0473	6-8	Ardonnis Lumpkin
Potentials Charter S	1201 Australian Ave	Riviera Beach, FL	33404-6635	561-842-3213	863-4352	PK-5	Rosie Portera
Potentials South Charter S	701 NW 35th St	Boca Raton, FL	33431	561-395-2012	395-4607	PK-5	Rosie Portera
Prince Academy	1006 N 50th St	Tampa, FL	33619	813-741-3191	741-2424	K-6	Carmen Marichal
Princeton House Charter S	720 W Princeton St	Orlando, FL	32804-5214	407-523-7121	523-7187	K-6	Carol Tucker
Quest MS	3916 E Hillsborough Ave	Tampa, FL	33610-4542	813-239-2092	232-9680	6-8	JoAnn Shaw
Rays of Hope Charter S	1780 W Airport Blvd	Sanford, FL	32771-4091	407-322-5010	322-8003	6-8	Carolyn Flanagan
RCMA Wimauma Academy	18240 US Highway 301 S	Wimauma, FL	33598-4307	813-672-5159	633-6119	K-8	Daniel Oceguera
Reading Edge Academy	2975 Enterprise Rd	De Bary, FL	32713-2708	386-668-8911		K-5	Margaret Comardo
ReBirth Academy Charter S	1924 E Comanche Ave	Tampa, FL	33610-8226	813-239-1321	239-2702	K-5	K.C. Williams
Renaissance Elementary Charter S	8360 NW 33rd St	Miami, FL	33122-1938	305-591-2225	591-2984	K-8	Ana Cordal
Renaissance Learning Center	5800 Corporate Way	West Palm Beach, FL	33407-2004	561-640-0270	640-0272	K-5	Debra Johnson
Richardson Montessori S	6815 N Rome Ave	Tampa, FL	33604-5839	813-930-2988	930-2929	K-6	Tommie Lee Brumfield
Ridgeview Global Studies Academy	1000 Dunson Rd	Davenport, FL	33896-8383	863-419-3171	419-3172	PK-5	Ralph Frier
Rio Grande Charter S	2210 S Rio Grande Ave	Orlando, FL	32805-5262	407-649-9122	649-8151	K-5	Barbara McLean-Smith
River's Edge Charter S	4400 Dixie Hwy NE	Palm Bay, FL	32905-4334	321-729-0500	729-0744	K-12	Ralph Garbart
Riviera Beach Maritime Academy	251 W 11th St	Riviera Beach, FL	33404-7534	561-841-7600		9-12	Joseph Powlis
Round Lake ES	31333 Round Lake Rd	Mount Dora, FL	32757-9599	352-385-4399	735-1860	K-5	Dale Moxley
Royal Palm Charter S	7145 Babcock St SE	Palm Bay, FL	32909-5462	321-723-0650	723-0650	K-2	Carolyn Thon
Sagan Academy	4610 E Hanna Ave	Tampa, FL	33610-2521	813-612-4433	862-0220	6-7	Kelly Browning
St. Mary's Pre S Children with Autism	5325 Greenwood Ave Ste 101	West Palm Beach, FL	33407-2452	561-840-6681		PK-PK	Nancy Frank
Saint Peter's Academy	4250 38th Ave	Vero Beach, FL	32967-1711	772-562-1963	562-8920	K-5	Ruth Jefferson
St. Petersburg Collegiate HS	PO Box 13489	St Petersburg, FL	33733-3489	727-341-4610		10-12	Linda Benware
Sarasota Community S for Excellence	1751 Dr Martin Luther King	Sarasota, FL	34234	941-373-9755		K-5	Pauline Hodges
Sarasota Military Academy	801 Orange Ave	Sarasota, FL	34236-4116	941-926-1700	926-1701	9-12	Dan Kennedy
Sarasota S of Arts/Sciences	645 Central Ave	Sarasota, FL	34236-4016	941-330-1855	330-1835	6-8	Pepar Anspaugh
Sarasota Suncoast Academy	133 McIntosh Rd	Sarasota, FL	34232-1934	941-342-4966	343-9632	K-4	Steve Crump
Sawgrass MS	716 Roy Wall Blvd	Rockledge, FL	32955-6212	877-258-0060	264-9995	6-8	Jeanette Karvis
School of Arts & Sciences	3208 Thomasville Rd	Tallahassee, FL	32308-7904	850-386-6566	386-8183	K-8	Deborah Powers
School of Integrated Academics and Tech	4811 Payne Stewart Dr	Jacksonville, FL	32209-9208	904-360-8200	768-8618	9-12	Michael LaRoche
School of Success Academy	6974 Wilson Blvd	Jacksonville, FL	32210-3663	904-573-0880	573-0889	6-8	Genell Mills
Sculptor Charter S	1301 Armstrong Dr	Titusville, FL	32780-7907	321-264-9991	264-9995	PK-8	Pat O'Sullivan
Seagull Academy for Independent Living	1801 12th Ave S	Lake Worth, FL	33461-5771	561-540-8110	540-8331	9-Adu	Bob Estreicher
Seaside Neighborhood S	PO Box 4610	Santa Rsa Bch, FL	32459-4610	850-231-0396	231-4725	6-8	Cathy Brubaker
Sebastian Charter JHS	782 Wave St	Sebastian, FL	32958-5049	772-388-8838	388-8815	6-8	Donna Dittman
SIATech	12350 SW 285th St	Homestead, FL	33033-1251	305-258-9477	258-9584	9-12	Marjorie Lopez
SIATech	3050 NW 183rd St	Miami Gardens, FL	33056-3536	305-624-1144	624-9172	9-12	Marjorie Lopez
Six Mile Charter Academy	6851 Lancer Ave	Fort Myers, FL	33912-4334	239-768-9375	225-2477	K-8	Jennifer Topper
Smart S Charter HS	3020 NW 33rd Ave	Laud Lakes, FL	33311-1106	954-343-9965	343-9970	9-12	Robert Martin
Smart School Charter MS	3698 NW 15th St	Lauderhill, FL	33311-4133	954-321-6777	321-7760	6-8	Chandra Glen-Phillips
Sojourner Truth HS	4951 Richard St Ste C	Jacksonville, FL	32207	904-448-5151	448-5159	9-11	Leslie Harris
Somerset Academy	12425 SW 53rd St	Miramar, FL	33027-5493	305-829-2406	829-4477	K-8	Shannine Sadesky-Hunt
Somerset Academy	20801 Johnson St	Pembroke Pines, FL	33029-1916	954-442-0233	442-0813	K-5	Anthony Taibi
Somerset Academy	18491 SW 134th Ave	Miami, FL	33177-2923	305-969-6074	969-6077	K-8	Suzette Ruiz
Somerset Academy Charter HS	SW 117th Ave & 232nd St	Miami, FL	33170	305-597-9950	477-6762	9-12	Jose Baca
Somerset Academy Davie	3788 SW 64th Ave	Davie, FL	33314-2417	954-584-5528	584-5598	K-5	Dina Miller
Somerset Academy MSHS	20803 Johnson St	Pembroke Pines, FL	33029-1916	954-442-0233	442-1762	7-12	Bernardo Montero
South McKeel ES	2222 Edgewood Dr S	Lakeland, FL	33803-3631	863-510-0044	510-0021	K-5	Julie Grice
South Tech Academy	1300 SW 30th Ave	Boynton Beach, FL	33426-9018	561-369-7004	369-7024	9-12	James Kidd
Spanish Academy Charter S	447 NW Spanish River Blvd	Boca Raton, FL	33431-4613	561-338-5700	338-5704	K-4	Judith Smith
Spiral Tech Charter S	12400 SW 72nd St	Miami, FL	33183-2514	305-273-0474	273-0242	K-5	Gisela Batan
Spirit City Academy	285 NW 199th St	Miami Gardens, FL	33169-2920	305-614-0451	652-7377	K-5	Cecilia Honeywood
Spring Creek ES	44440 Spring Creek Rd	Paisley, FL	32767-9063	352-669-3275	669-3762	PK-5	Robert Curry
STAR Charter S	225 Avenue B NW	Winter Haven, FL	33881-4529	863-299-0063	299-2343	9-12	Wanda Jackson
Steele/Collins Charter MS	428 W Tennessee St	Tallahassee, FL	32301-1026	850-681-1929	224-1663	6-8	Mary Henry
Stepping Stones Charter S	4400 Dixie Hwy NE	Palm Bay, FL	32905-4334	321-729-0500	729-0744	K-4	Scott Infante
Student Leadership Academy	200 Field Ave E	Venice, FL	34285-3936	941-485-5551	485-2694	6-8	Vickie Marble
Summit Charter S	1250 N Maitland Ave	Maitland, FL	32751-4305	407-599-4001	599-4004	K-6	Alan Smolowe
Suncoast S for Innovative Studies	1300 S Tuttle Ave	Sarasota, FL	34239-2603	941-952-5277	952-5087	K-8	Phil Blankenship
Sunrise Community Charter S	7100 W Oakland Park Blvd	Sunrise, FL	33313-1015	954-747-1550	747-1650	K-12	Lucy Thomas
Sunshine Academy	7130 Pembroke Rd	Miramar, FL	33023-2690	786-210-8324	962-1264	K-8	Ann-Marie Manzano
Sunshine Academy	14550 NE 6th Ave	North Miami, FL	33161-2357	305-947-3650	947-3609	K-8	Alcira Manzano
Sunshine ES	2210 Pierce St	Hollywood, FL	33020-4414	954-925-0155	925-0209	K-5	Dr. Steven Montes
Survivors Charter S	1310 N Congress Ave	West Palm Beach, FL	33409	561-712-1800	712-0360	10-12	Randy Stafford
Survivors Charter S of Boynton Beach	1325 Gateway Blvd	Boynton Beach, FL	33426-8304	561-731-1800	375-6242	9-12	Marc Flamer
Tampa Bay Academy	12012 Boyette Rd	Riverview, FL	33569-5631	813-677-6700	677-5467	K-12	Joanne Nelson
Tampa Charter S	5429 Beaumont Center Blvd	Tampa, FL	33634	813-887-3800	885-9626	3-8	Sheila Thomley
Tapestry Park Charter S	410 Lyndell Ln	Panama City, FL	32407	850-249-2144	249-2149	K-5	Antonius Barnes
Terrace Community Charter S	PO Box 16325	Tampa, FL	33687-6325	813-987-6555	987-6565	5-8	Gary Hocevar
Touchdowns4Life Charter S	10044 W McNab Rd	Tamarac, FL	33321-1894	954-726-8785	726-9590	6-8	Wayne Neunie
Transitional Learning Academy	1411 NW 14th Ave	Miami, FL	33125-1616	305-325-1080	325-1044	8-12	Pamela Miller
Trinity S for Children	2402 W Osborne Ave	Tampa, FL	33603-1434	813-874-2402	874-2412	K-5	Madeline O'Dea
Trinity Upper S	4807 N Armenia Ave	Tampa, FL	33603-1427	813-874-2402	874-2412	6-8	Madeline O'Dea
UCP Charter S	3305 S Orange Ave	Orlando, FL	32806-6125	407-852-3333	852-3301	PK-5	Ilene Wilkins
UCP Child Development Center	448 W Donegan Ave	Kissimmee, FL	34741-2335	407-932-3445	932-3480	PK-PK	Heather Miller
UCP Seminole Child Development	3590 N Highway 17/92	Lake Mary, FL	32746	407-322-6222	322-5596	PK-K	Marife Gomez
USF Charter S at Mosi	11801 USF Bull Run Dr	Tampa, FL	33617-5103	813-974-3831	974-1280	K-8	L. Rylene Stein

School	Address	City,State	Zip code	Telephone	Fax	Grade	Contact
Village of Excellence Academy	8718 N 46th St	Temple Terrace, FL	33617-6002	813-988-8632	983-0683	K-3	Cametra Edwards
Villages Charter ES	420 Village Campus Cir	Lady Lake, FL	32162-7169	352-259-7700	259-7707	K-2	Leanne Yerk
Villages Charter HS	251 Buffalo Trl	Lady Lake, FL	32162-7176	352-259-3777	259-6802	9-11	Michael Kelly
Villages Charter MS	450 Village Campus Cir	Lady Lake, FL	32162-7169	352-259-0044	753-1113	6-8	Pam Roberts
Villages Charter S	521 Old School Rd	Lady Lake, FL	32162-7170	352-259-2300	259-2056	3-5	Leanne Yerk
Walton Academy	389 Dorsey Ave	Defuniak Spgs, FL	32435-3013	850-892-3999	892-7854	6-12	Jerry White
Walton Academy of the Performing Arts	PO Box 7578	Tampa, FL	33673-7578	813-231-9272	231-9271	K-5	Tanika Walton
Wayman Academy of the Arts	1176 Labelle St	Jacksonville, FL	32205-6487	904-695-9995	695-9992	K-5	Tracy Hay
Wells Charter S	2426 Remington Blvd	Kissimmee, FL	34744-8467	407-697-1020	697-1021	PK-5	Diane Beatty
Western Academy Charter S	500 Royal Plaza Rd Ste F	Ryl Palm Bch, FL	33411-7688	561-792-4123	792-9905	K-8	Linda Terranova
Westminister Academy	830 29th St	Orlando, FL	32805	407-841-6560	841-7311	K-12	Elizabeth Addeo
West Orange Co. Charter ES	PO Box 949	Orlando, FL	32802-0949	407-654-2039	654-3039	K-5	Nina Kuhn
Whispering Winds Charter S	12390 NW Old Fannin Rd	Chiefland, FL	32626-8115	352-490-5799	490-7242	K-8	Dr. Suzanne Cornell
Wiener S of Opportunity	20000 NW 47th Ave	Miami Gardens, FL	33055	305-623-9631	623-9621	K-5	Jeanine del Valle
Wiener S of Opportunity	11025 SW 84th St	Miami, FL	33173-3804	305-279-3064	279-3294	K-5	Lissa Gonzalez
WINGS Academy	PO Box 48367	Sarasota, FL	34230-5367	941-351-7267	358-6957	6-8	Anthon Francis
Youth Co-Op Charter S	12051 W Okeechobee Rd	Hialeah Gardens, FL	33018-2933	305-819-8855	819-8455	K-8	Maritza Aragon

Georgia

School	Address	City,State	Zip code	Telephone	Fax	Grade	Contact
Academy of Lithonia	3235 Evans Mill Rd	Lithonia, GA	30038-3012	678-526-9655		K-6	Denise Hentz
Achieve Academy	1335 Kimberly Rd SW	Atlanta, GA	30331-4617	404-472-3065	472-3069		David Morgan
Adairsville ES	122 King St	Adairsville, GA	30103-2300	770-606-5840	773-7755	K-5	Melissa Zerafoss
Addison ES	3055 Ebenezer Rd	Marietta, GA	30066-4542	770-578-2700	578-2702	PK-5	Genie Byrd
Amana Academy	1565 Holcomb Bridge Rd	Roswell, GA	30076-2517	678-795-1080		K-8	Shereen Salam
Atlanta Charter MS	820 Essie Ave SE	Atlanta, GA	30316-2425	678-904-0051	904-0052	6-8	Christopher Morse
Baconton Community Charter S	260 E Walton St	Baconton, GA	31716-7706	229-787-9999	787-0077	PK-12	Lynn Pinson
Bishop Hall Charter S	1815 E Clay St	Thomasville, GA	31792-4736	229-227-1397	225-1093	9-12	Rich Johnson
Central Educational Center	PO Box 280	Newnan, GA	30264-0280	678-423-2000	423-2008	9-12	Mark Whitlock
Chamblee Charter HS	3688 Chamblee Dunwoody Rd	Chamblee, GA	30341-2185	678-676-6902	676-6910	9-12	Rochelle Lowery
Charter Conservatory Liberal Arts/Tech.	149 Northside Dr E	Statesboro, GA	30458-1089	912-764-5888		3-12	Dr. Kathy Harwood
Chesnut Charter ES	4576 N Peachtree Rd	Dunwoody, GA	30338-5892	678-676-7102	676-7110	PK-5	Sonja Alexander
Cloverleaf ES	PO Box 564	Cartersville, GA	30120-0564	770-606-5847	606-3842	K-5	Susan Stephens
DeKalb Academy of Tech & Environment	1833 Stone Mtn Lithonia Rd	Lithonia, GA	30058	770-484-5865	484-6296	K-12	Maury Wills
DeKalb PATH Academy	3007 Hermance Dr NE	Atlanta, GA	30319-2627	404-846-3242	846-3243	5-8	Suttiwan Cox
Drew Charter S	301 E Lake Blvd SE	Atlanta, GA	30317-3152	404-687-0001	687-0480	K-8	Dr. Nicholas Stapleton
Druid Hills HS	1798 Haygood Dr NE	Atlanta, GA	30307-1119	678-874-6302	874-6310	9-12	Everett Patrick
Dunwoody Springs ES	8100 Roberts Dr	Atlanta, GA	30350-4120	770-673-4060	673-4064	PK-5	Donna Bennett
Eastvalley ES	2570 Lower Roswell Rd	Marietta, GA	30068-3698	770-578-7214	578-7216	K-5	Althea Singletary
Ellis S	220 E 49th St	Savannah, GA	31405-2299	912-201-5470	201-5473	PK-8	Charles Wooten
Emerson ES	54 7th St	Emerson, GA	30137-2219	770-606-5848	606-3847	K-5	Denise Welker
Fargo Charter S	PO Box 267	Fargo, GA	31631-0267	912-637-5466	637-5242	K-3	Danny Ellis
Fulton Science Academy	1675 Hembree Rd	Alpharetta, GA	30004-2083	770-753-4141	753-4948	6-8	
Futral Road ES	180 Futral Rd	Griffin, GA	30224-7454	770-229-3735	233-6001	K-5	Larry Jones
Green Acres ES	2000 Gober Ave SE	Smyrna, GA	30080-1111	678-842-6905	842-6907	PK-5	David Pearce
Hapeville Charter MS	3535 S Fulton Ave	Hapeville, GA	30354-1701	404-767-7730	767-7706	6-8	
International Community Charter	3260 Covington Hwy	Decatur, GA	30032-1121	404-499-8969	499-8968	K-5	Bill Moon
Jenkins-White Charter ES	800 15th Ave	Augusta, GA	30901-4145	706-737-7320	731-7651	K-5	Marva Tutt Gibson
Kennesaw Charter S	1370 Lockhart Dr NW	Kennesaw, GA	30144-7047	678-290-9628	290-9628	K-5	Shawn Black
KidsPeace S of Georgia	101 Kidspeace Dr	Bowdon, GA	30108-3447	770-437-7200		7-12	Scott Merritt
Kingsley ES	2051 Brendon Dr	Dunwoody, GA	30338-4599	678-874-8902	874-8910	PK-5	Karen Graham
Kingston ES	240 Hardin Bridge Rd	Kingston, GA	30145-2668	770-606-5850	336-5591	K-5	LaDonna Turrentine
KIPP South Fulton	1286 Washington Ave	East Point, GA	30344-3537	678-278-0160	278-0165	5-8	
KIPP WAYS Academy	80 Joseph E Lowery Blvd NW	Atlanta, GA	30314-3421	404-475-1941		5-8	David Jernigan
Lewis Academy of Excellence	6390 Church St	Riverdale, GA	30274-1624	770-909-6697	909-6699	9-12	Dr. Patricia Lewis
Mercer MS	201 Rommel Ave	Savannah, GA	31408-1636	912-965-6700	965-6719	6-8	Gloria Dukes
Mission Road ES	1100 Mission Rd SW	Cartersville, GA	30120-5779	770-606-5863	606-3862	K-5	Nancy Summey
Mt. Bethel ES	1210 Johnson Ferry Rd	Marietta, GA	30068-2719	770-578-7248	578-7250	PK-5	Robin Lattizori
Neighborhood Charter S	688 Grant St SE	Atlanta, GA	30315-1420	404-624-6226		K-5	Dr. Jackie Rosswurm
Odyssey Charter S	1485 Highway 34 E Ste B1	Newnan, GA	30265-6409	678-423-5155		K-5	Andy Geeter
Oglethorpe Charter S	707 Stiles Ave	Savannah, GA	31415-5324	912-201-5075	201-5077	6-8	Kevin Wall
Peachtree Charter MS	4664 N Peachtree Rd	Atlanta, GA	30338-5898	678-676-7702	676-7710	6-8	Steve Donahue
Pine Log ES	3370 Pine Log Rd NE	Rydal, GA	30171-1234	770-606-5864	606-3866	K-5	Cathy Strickland
Rainbow ES	2801 Kelley Chapel Rd	Decatur, GA	30034-2299	678-874-1702	874-1710	PK-5	Annette Sanders-Roberts
School for Integrated Academics & Tech.	239 W Lake Ave NW	Atlanta, GA	30314-1803	404-799-9101	799-5388	9-12	Monica Bomengen
Sedalia Park ES	2230 Lower Roswell Rd	Marietta, GA	30068-3359	770-509-5162	509-5342	K-5	Dr. Patricia Thomas
Spalding Drive ES	130 W Spalding Dr NE	Atlanta, GA	30328-1999	770-551-5880	673-4090	PK-5	Christine Young
Talbot Co. Charter Alternative Academy	PO Box 515	Talbotton, GA	31827-0515	706-665-3620	665-8099	9-12	Jerome Harris
Taliaferro County S	557 Broad St NW	Crawfordville, GA	30631-2918	706-456-2575	456-2689	K-12	Algie Arbee
Taylorsville ES	1502 Old Alabama Rd	Taylorsville, GA	30178-1505	770-606-5867	606-2056	K-5	Bernadette Dipetta
TEACH Charter HS	4100 Old Milton Pkwy Ste 10	Alpharetta, GA	30005	770-475-3223		9-12	Ali Ozer
Tech HS	1043 Memorial Dr SE	Atlanta, GA	30316-1473	678-904-5091	904-5095	9-12	Elisa Falco
Technical Career Academy N.E. Georgia	PO Box 80571	Athens, GA	30608-0571	706-369-5871	425-3114	10-12	Reginald Woods
Unidos Dual Language Charter S	4475 Hendrix Dr	Forest Park, GA	30297-1244	404-361-3494	362-2498	K-2	Dell Perry
University Community Academy	953 Ralph D Abernathy SW	Atlanta, GA	30310	404-753-4050	215-3481	K-8	Dr. James Harris
Walton HS	1590 Bill Murdock Rd	Marietta, GA	30062-5999	770-578-3225	578-3227	9-12	Dr. Tom Higgins
White ES	1395 Cass White Rd NE	White, GA	30184-2600	770-606-5869	606-3876	K-5	Avis King
Woodland ES	1130 Spalding Dr	Atlanta, GA	30350-5013	770-551-5890	673-4091	PK-5	Noris Price

Hawaii

School	Address	City,State	Zip code	Telephone	Fax	Grade	Contact
Connections New Century Charter S	174 Kamehameha Ave	Hilo, HI	96720	808-961-3664	961-2665	K-8	John Thatcher
Education Laboratory	1776 University Ave	Honolulu, HI	96822	808-956-7833	956-7260	K-12	Peter Estomago
Hakipuu Learning Center	PO Box 1159	Kaneohe, HI	96744-1159	808-235-9155	235-9160	7-12	Charlene Hoe
Halau Ku Mana Charter S	3737 Manoa Rd	Honolulu, HI	96822	808-988-8995	988-8999	6-12	Keola Nakanishi
Halau Lokahi Charter S	401 Waiakamilo Rd Unit 1A	Honolulu, HI	96817	808-832-3594	842-9800	K-12	Laara Allbrett
Hawaii Academy of Arts & Science	PO Box 1494	Pahoa, HI	96778-1494	808-965-3730	965-3733	K-12	Steve Hirakami
Innovations Public Charter S	76-147A Royal Poinciana Dr	Kailua Kona, HI	96740	808-327-6205	327-6209	1-6	Barbara Woerner
Kanuikapono Charter S	PO Box 12	Anahola, HI	96703-0012	808-822-9032	822-8321	K-12	Ku'uipo Torio
Kanu O Ka 'Aina New Century Charter S	PO Box 398	Kamuela, HI	96743-0398	808-887-8144	887-8146	K-12	Dr. Ku Kahakalau
Ka 'Umeke Ka'eo Public Charter S	222 Desha Ave	Hilo, HI	96720-4815	808-933-3482	933-3488	K-6	Albert Nahale-A
Ka Waihona O Ka Na'auao Charter S	89-195 Farrington Hwy	Waianae, HI	96792-4102	808-620-9030	620-9036	K-6	Alvin Parker
Ke Ana La'ahana Public Charter S	1500 Kalanianaole Ave	Hilo, HI	96720-4914	808-961-6228	961-6229	7-12	
Ke Kula Ni'ihau Kekaha Public Charter S	PO Box 129	Kekaha, HI	96752-0129	808-337-0481	337-1289	PK-12	Haunani Seward
Ke Kula O Kamakau Lab S	45-037 Kaneohe Bay Dr	Kaneohe, HI	96744-2417	808-235-9175	235-9173	K-12	Marci Sarsona
Ke Kula 'O Nawahiokalani'opu'u Charter S	PO Box 506	Keaau, HI	96749-0506	808-982-4260	966-7821	K-6	Kauanoe Kamana
Kihei Charter S	300 Ohukai Rd Unit 214	Kihei, HI	96753	808-875-0700	874-6745	K-12	Mark Christiano
Kualapu'u Charter ES	PO Box 260	Kualapuu, HI	96757-0260	808-567-6900	567-6906	K-6	Lydia Trinidad
Kua O Ka La Public Charter S	PO Box 1413	Pahoa, HI	96778-1413	808-965-5098	965-9618	6-11	Susan Osborne
Kula Aupuni Niihau A Kahelelani Aloha	PO Box 690390	Makaweli, HI	96769-0390	808-338-0055	338-0550	K-12	Hinaleimoana Wong
Lanikai ES	140 Alala Rd	Kailua, HI	96734-3199	808-266-7844	266-7848	PK-6	Frederick Birkett
Na Wai Ola Charter S	RR 4 Box 2249	Pahoa, HI	96778-9703	808-968-1275	968-8011	K-12	Libby Oshiyama
Thompson Academy	629 Pohukaina St Ste 3	Honolulu, HI	96813-5004	808-441-8000	586-3640	K-12	Diana Oshiro
Volcano S of Arts & Sciences	PO Box 845	Volcano, HI	96785-0845	808-985-9800	985-9898	K-8	Dr. David Rizor
Voyager Charter S	670 Auahi St Ste A5	Honolulu, HI	96813-5166	808-521-9770	521-9772	K-8	Susan Lee Deuber
Wai'alae ES	1045 19th Ave	Honolulu, HI	96816-4699	808-733-4880	733-4886	K-5	Wendy Lagareta
Waimea Charter MS	67-1229 Mamalahoa Hwy	Kamuela, HI	96743-8429	808-887-6090	887-6087	6-8	Albert Campbell
Waters of Life Charter S	16-643 Kipimana St Ste 11	Keaau, HI	96749	808-966-6175	982-7863	K-12	Katheryn Shay
West Hawaii Explorations Academy	73-4460 Queen Kaahumanu Hwy	Kailua Kona, HI	96740	808-327-4751	327-4750	7-12	Heather Nakakura

Idaho

School	Address	City,State	Zip code	Telephone	Fax	Grade	Contact
Academy	240 E Maple St	Pocatello, ID	83201-4647	208-232-1447	232-1448	K-8	Rafael Baca
ANSER Charter S	1187 W River St	Boise, ID	83702-7048	208-426-9840	426-9863	K-7	Dr. Suzanne Gregg
Coeur D'Alene Charter Academy	4904 N Duncan Dr	Coeur d Alene, ID	83815-8329	208-676-1667	676-8667	6-12	Dan Nicklay
Compass Charter S	2511 W Cherry Ln	Meridian, ID	83642-1135	208-855-2802	855-4868	K-7	Kelly Trudeau
Falcon Ridge Charter S	PO Box 326	Kuna, ID	83634-0326	208-922-9228	922-4198	K-8	Gerald Chouinard
Garden City Community Charter S	PO Box 573	Boise, ID	83701-0573	208-703-2666	216-0254	K-8	Linda Vermette
Hidden Springs Charter S	5480 W Hidden Springs Dr	Hidden Springs, ID	83714-9402	208-229-4727	229-4747	K-9	Luigi Yannotta
Idaho Arts Charter S	PO Box 114	Nampa, ID	83653-0114	208-463-4324	468-0572	K-12	Jackie Collins
Idaho Distance Education Academy	PO Box 339	Bovill, ID	83806-0339	208-826-3029	877-3360	K-12	Shauna Kron
Idaho Leadership Academy	PO Box 59	Pingree, ID	83262-0059	208-684-9696	684-9404	9-12	Cameron Baxter
Idaho Virtual Academy	PO Box 191099	Boise, ID	83719-1099	208-332-3559	322-3688	K-9	Cody Claver
Inspire Virtual Charter S	404 S 8th St Ste 310	Boise, ID	83702-7133	208-332-4002	332-4008	K-12	Dr. Dallas Taylor
Liberty Charter S	PO Box 1901	Nampa, ID	83653-1901	208-466-7952	466-7961	K-12	Becky Stallcop
McKenna Charter HS	1993 E 8th N Ste 105	Mountain Home, ID	83647-2333	208-580-2449	580-2450	9-12	Larry Slade
Meridian Charter HS	3800 N Locust Grove Rd	Meridian, ID	83646-5510	208-288-2928	288-5685	9-12	Christian Housel
Meridian Medical Arts Charter HS	1789 E Leighfield Dr	Meridian, ID	83646-2692	208-855-4075		9-12	Craig Miller

School	Address	City,State	Zip code	Telephone	Fax	Grade	Contact
Moscow Charter S	1723 E F St	Moscow, ID	83843-9571	208-883-3195	892-3855	K-6	Trish Bechtel
North Star Charter S	PO Box 877	Eagle, ID	83616-0877	208-939-9600	939-6090	K-8	Phyllis Smith
Pocatello Community Charter S	995 S Arthur Ave	Pocatello, ID	83204-3400	208-478-2522	478-2622	K-8	Dr. Martha Martin
Rolling Hills Charter S	12781 W Ashcreek St	Boise, ID	83713-2088	208-375-1176	377-3969	K-8	Dr. Caroline Mauer
Sandpoint Charter S	614 S Madison Ave	Sandpoint, ID	83864-8724	208-255-7771	263-9441	7-8	Alan Millar
Taylors Crossing Charter S	PO Box 2434	Idaho Falls, ID	83403-2434	208-552-0397	529-2755	K-12	Gail Harding-Thomas
Upper Carmen Charter S	508 Carmen Creek Rd	Carmen, ID	83462	208-756-4590		K-3	Sue Smith
Victory Charter S	PO Box 3454	Nampa, ID	83653-3454	208-442-9400	442-9401	K-7	Dr. Marianne Saunders
White Pine Charter S	2959 John Adams Pkwy	Ammon, ID	83406	208-522-4432	522-4452	K-8	Peggy Sharp

Illinois

School	Address	City,State	Zip code	Telephone	Fax	Grade	Contact
ACE Technical Charter HS	5410 S State St	Chicago, IL	60609-6382	773-548-8705	548-8706	9-12	Geri Harston
ACT Charter S	4319 W Washington Blvd	Chicago, IL	60624-2232	773-626-4200	626-4268	6-12	Terri Milsap
Addams Alternative HS	1814 S Union Ave	Chicago, IL	60616-1045	312-563-1748	563-1756	9-12	
Albizu Campos HS	2739 W Division St	Chicago, IL	60622-2854	773-342-8022	342-6609	9-12	Lourdes Lugo
Aspira - Antonia Pantoja Alternative HS	3121 N Pulaski Rd	Chicago, IL	60641-5447	773-427-0759	427-0872	9-12	Nelson Rivera
ASPIRA at Haugan MS	3729 W Leland Ave	Chicago, IL	60625-5706	773-252-0970	267-3568	6-8	Norma Quintano
ASPIRA - Mirta Ramirez	2435 N Western Ave	Chicago, IL	60647-2028	773-252-0990	252-0994	9-12	Patricia Munoz
Association House - El Cuarto Ano HS	1116 N Kedzie Ave	Chicago, IL	60651-4152	773-772-7170	772-8671	9-12	Harriet Sadauskas
Austin Business & Entrepreneurship S	231 N Pine Ave	Chicago, IL	60644-2333	773-534-6316	534-6313	9-12	Stefan Fisher
Austin Career Education Center	5352 W Chicago Ave	Chicago, IL	60651-2857	773-626-6988	626-2641	9-12	Judy Vojta
Bronzeville Blue Gargoyle S	220 W 45th Pl	Chicago, IL	60609-3903	773-538-0242	538-0164	9-12	LaShaun Jackson
Bronzeville Lighthouse Charter S	8 W Root St	Chicago, IL	60609-2931	773-535-1757	535-1459	K-5	April Knox
Catalyst Charter S	1616 S Spaulding Ave	Chicago, IL	60623-2653	773-534-1753		K-8	Michael Neis
Chicago Choir Academy	3737 S Paulina St	Chicago, IL	60609-2047	773-890-4720	890-4773	4-8	Krystal Muldrow
Chicago International Charter S - Avalon	1501 E 83rd Pl	Chicago, IL	60619-6501	773-721-3076	731-0142	K-5	Anthony Chambers
Chicago International Charter S Basil	1816 W Garfield Blvd	Chicago, IL	60609	773-778-9455	778-9456	PK-8	Gloria Hall
Chicago International Charter S Bucktown	2235 N Hamilton Ave	Chicago, IL	60647-3360	773-645-3321	645-3327	K-8	Turon Ivy
Chicago International Charter S Longwood	1309 W 95th St	Chicago, IL	60643	773-238-5330	238-5350	K-12	Robert Lang
Chicago International Charter S Prairie	11530 S Prairie Ave	Chicago, IL	60628-5612	773-928-0480	928-6971	K-8	Aisha Strong
Chicago International Charter S W Belden	2245 N McVicker Ave	Chicago, IL	60639	773-637-9430	637-9791	K-8	Margaret O'Brien
Chicago Intl Charter S Northtown	3900 W Peterson Ave Ste 1	Chicago, IL	60659-3162	773-478-3655	478-6029	9-12	Loren Stillwell
Chicago Intl Charter S Ralph Ellison	8101 S Honore St	Chicago, IL	60620-4564	312-455-7890	535-8096	9-10	Dr. Eboni Wilson
Chicago Intl Charter S Washington Park	6105 S Michigan Ave	Chicago, IL	60637	773-324-3300	324-3302	K-8	Pamela Creed
Chicago Intl Charter S Wrightwood	8130 S California Ave	Chicago, IL	60652-2716	773-434-4575	434-2026	K-6	Tarsa Stovall
Chicago Math and Science Academy	1709 W Lunt Ave	Chicago, IL	60626-3212	773-761-8960	761-8961	6-12	Salim Ucan
Chicago Virtual Charter S	1 E Jackson Blvd	Chicago, IL	60604-2201	312-362-7680	535-8096	K-8	Sharon Hayes
Community Services West - ASA	4651 W Madison St	Chicago, IL	60644-3646	773-921-1315	921-8324	9-12	Gladys Simpson
Community Youth Development Institute	7836 S Union Ave	Chicago, IL	60620-2409	773-224-2273	224-2214		Elfreda Austin
De Las Casas Charter S	1641 W 16th St	Chicago, IL	60608-2039	312-432-3224	432-1066	K-8	Joseph Dolan
Donoghue Charter S	707 E 37th St	Chicago, IL	60653-1406	773-729-5300	729-5290	PK-4	Nicole Woodard-Iliev
DuSable Leadership Academy	4934 S Wabash Ave	Chicago, IL	60615	773-535-1170	535-1912	9-10	Dr. Loretta Young-Wright
Erie Charter S	2510 W Cortez St	Chicago, IL	60622-3422	773-486-7161	486-7234	K-2	Linda Ponce de Leon
Fort Bowman Academy Charter S	2734 Calvin Blvd	Cahokia, IL	62206-2707	618-332-7404	332-7561	K-12	Beth Peeples
Fuentes Charter S	2845 W Barry Ave	Chicago, IL	60618-7015	312-279-9826	279-9852	K-8	Thomas Denneen
Galapagos Charter S	3814 W Iowa St	Chicago, IL	60651-3708	773-384-9400	384-4866	K-5	Michael Lane
Houston Alternative HS	9035 S Langley Ave	Chicago, IL	60619	773-723-9631	723-9022	9-12	Lisa Williams
Howard Area Alternative HS	7647 N Paulina St	Chicago, IL	60626-1017	773-381-0366	338-7693	9-12	Benjamin Churchill
KIPP Ascend Charter S	715 S Kildare Ave	Chicago, IL	60624-3564	773-533-1770	533-1784	5-8	Jim O'Conner
Latino Youth Alternative HS	2001 S California Ave	Chicago, IL	60608	773-648-2130		9-12	Guadalupe Martinez
LEARN Charter S	1132 S Homan Ave	Chicago, IL	60624-4344	773-826-6330	826-0015	PK-8	Courtney Francis
Legacy Charter S	4217 W 18th St	Chicago, IL	60623-2325	773-542-1640	542-1699	PK-3	Lisa Kenner
Lincoln Charter S	300 4th St	Venice, IL	62090-1015	618-874-7792	874-3682	9-12	Precious Afolayan
Locke Charter Academy	3141 W Jackson Blvd	Chicago, IL	60612-2729	773-265-7230	265-7258	PK-8	Lennie Jones
Lozano Leadership Academy	2570 S Blue Island Ave	Chicago, IL	60608-4817	773-890-0055	890-1537	9-12	Juan Salgado
Mandela Alternative HS	7105 S Ridgeland Ave	Chicago, IL	60649-2320	773-643-4011	643-3258	9-12	Pa Joof
McKinley Lakeside Campus	2929 S Wabash Ave	Chicago, IL	60616	773-949-5010	949-5015	9-12	George Jones
Namaste S	3540 S Hermitage Ave	Chicago, IL	60609-1217	773-715-9558	376-6495	K-3	Allison Slade
Noble Street Charter S	1010 N Noble St	Chicago, IL	60622	773-862-1449	278-0421	9-12	William Olsen
North Kenwood/Oakland Charter S	1119 E 46th St	Chicago, IL	60653-4403	773-536-2399	536-2435	PK-8	Stacy Beardsley
North Lawndale College Prep Charter HS	1616 S Spaulding Ave	Chicago, IL	60623-2653	773-542-1490	542-1492	9-12	Robert Karpinski
Octavio Paz Charter S	2401 W Congress Pkwy	Chicago, IL	60612-3534	312-432-1170	432-1180	4-8	Dan Goodwin
Octavio Paz Charter S - Washtenaw	2651 W 23rd St	Chicago, IL	60608-3609	773-890-1054		K-3	Vanessa McNorton
Passages Charter S	1447 W Montrose Ave	Chicago, IL	60613-1348	773-549-1052	549-1210	PK-5	Dr. Sally Ewing
Perspectives Charter S	1930 S Archer Ave	Chicago, IL	60616-6505	312-225-7400	225-7411	6-12	Kim Day
Perspectives Charter S Calumet Campus	8131 S May St	Chicago, IL	60620-3007	773-538-6100		7-9	Tamara Davis
Prairie Crossing Charter S	1571 Jones Point Rd	Grayslake, IL	60030-3536	847-543-9722	543-9744	K-8	Myron Dagley
Pritzker College Prep Campus	4131 W Cortland St	Chicago, IL	60639-4923	773-862-1449	278-0421	9-12	Pablo Sierra
Prologue Alternative HS	640 W Irving Park Rd	Chicago, IL	60613-3106	773-935-9925	665-8357	9-12	Pa Joof
Providence Englewood Charter S	6515 S Ashland Ave	Chicago, IL	60636-3003	773-535-9060	535-8096	K-5	Paul Adams
Rauner College Prep Campus	1337 W Ohio St	Chicago, IL	60622-6430	773-862-1449	278-0421	9-12	Eric Thomas
Robertson Charter S	2240 E Geddes Ave	Decatur, IL	62526-5127	217-428-7072	428-9214	K-3	Cordell Ingram
Rufino Tamayo Charter S	5135 S California Ave	Chicago, IL	60632-2124	773-434-6355	434-5036	K-8	Dawn Delgado
Shabazz International Charter S	7823 S Ellis Ave	Chicago, IL	60619-3213	773-651-1221	651-0302	K-8	Dr. Elaine Mosley
Simon Academy	3348 S Kedzie Ave	Chicago, IL	60623-5114	773-890-3129	847-2855	9-12	Cecilia Arroyo
SIU Charter S of East St. Louis	601 James R Thompson Blvd	E Saint Louis, IL	62201	618-482-8370	482-8372	9-12	Anthony Neal
Sizemore Academy of B Shabazz	1540 W 84th St	Chicago, IL	60620-3918	773-779-5666	779-5668	6-8	Soyini Walton
Springfield Ball Charter S	2530 E Ash St	Springfield, IL	62703-5600	217-525-3275	525-3316	PK-8	Nicole Gales
Tomorrows Builders Charter S	PO Box 6126	E Saint Louis, IL	62202-6126	618-874-1671	874-8451	9-12	Keith Willis
Truman Middle College HS	1145 W Wilson Ave	Chicago, IL	60640-5691	773-907-4840	907-4844	9-12	Tom O'Hale
University of Chicago Charter S Woodlawn	6420 S University Ave	Chicago, IL	60637	773-535-6797		6-9	Barbara Crock
Urban Prep Academy Charter S	6130 S Wolcott Ave	Chicago, IL	60636-2100	773-535-9678	755-1050	9-12	Tim King
Westside Holistic Alternative HS	5443 W Huron St	Chicago, IL	60644-1105	773-626-9744	626-9745	9-12	Dr. Romana Smith
West Town Academy Alternative HS	2039 W Fulton St	Chicago, IL	60612	312-563-9044	563-9672	9-12	Keisha Johnson
Young Womens Leadership S	2641 S Calumet Ave	Chicago, IL	60616-2901	312-949-9400	949-9142	7-12	Margaret Small
Youth Connection Leadership Academy	3424 S State St Fl 2	Chicago, IL	60616-5000	312-225-4668	225-4862	9-12	Doris Franklin
Youth Connection-Sullivan House Alt HS	8164 S South Chicago Ave	Chicago, IL	60617-1041	773-978-8680	375-1482	9-12	Dr. Thomas Gattuso

Indiana

School	Address	City,State	Zip code	Telephone	Fax	Grade	Contact
Bowman Leadership Academy	975 W 6th Ave	Gary, IN	46402-1708	219-226-3355		K-9	Vito Bianco
Brown Charter Academy	3600 N German Church Rd	Indianapolis, IN	46235-8504	317-891-0730		K-8	Thelma Wyatt
Campagna Academy Charter S	7403 Cline Ave	Schererville, IN	46375-2645	219-322-8614	322-8436	9-12	Amy Rosen
Challenge Foundation Academy	3960 Meadows Dr	Indianapolis, IN	46205-3114	317-231-0010		K-12	Donna Birdsong
Charter School of the Dunes	860 N Lake St	Gary, IN	46403-1070	219-939-9690	939-9031	K-8	William Ignatowski
Christel House Academy	2717 S East St	Indianapolis, IN	46225-2104	317-783-4690	783-4693	K-8	Carey Dahncke
Community Montessori S	4102 Saint Joseph Rd	New Albany, IN	47150-9750	812-948-1000		PK-8	Barbara Burke-Fondren
Decatur Discovery Academy	5125 Decatur Blvd	Indianapolis, IN	46241	317-856-0900		9-12	Kevin Leineweber
East Chicago Urban Enterprise Academy	1402 E Chicago Ave	East Chicago, IN	46312-3587	219-392-3650		K-5	Charlotte Jackson
Flanner House ES	2424 Dr Mrtn Lthr Kng Jr St	Indianapolis, IN	46208	317-925-4231	923-9632	K-7	Frances Malone
Flanner House Higher Learning Inc.	2424 Dr Mrtn Lthr Kng Jr St	Indianapolis, IN	46208	317-925-4231		9-12	Cynthia Diamond
Galileo Charter S	855 N 12th St	Richmond, IN	47374-2477	765-983-3709		K-3	Kevin Handley
Gary Lighthouse Charter S	3201 Pierce St	Gary, IN	46408-1100	219-880-1762		K-12	Karen Poplawski
Goodwill Education Initiatives II S	1635 W Michigan St	Indianapolis, IN	46222-3852	317-524-4501		K-12	Scott Bess
Herron Charter S	PO Box 8	Indianapolis, IN	46206-0008	317-231-0010		9-12	Dr. Rex Bolinger
Hope Academy	8102 Clearvista Pkwy	Indianapolis, IN	46256-1661	317-572-9356		K-12	Dr. Michelle Thompson
Indianapolis Lighthouse Charter S	1780 Sloan Ave	Indianapolis, IN	46203-3640	317-351-1534		K-12	Dr. Douglas Thaman
Irvington Community S	6705 Julian Ave	Indianapolis, IN	46219-6642	317-357-5359	357-9752	K-9	Timothy Ehrgott
Johnson Academy	7908 S Anthony Blvd	Fort Wayne, IN	46816-2504	260-441-8727	441-9357	K-8	Steve Bollier
Joshua Academy	867 Walnut St	Evansville, IN	47713	812-424-9498	401-6300	K-5	Pam Decker
KIPP Indianapolis College Prep	PO Box 18615	Indianapolis, IN	46218-0615	317-637-9780		K-12	Omotayo Ola-Niyi
KIPP Lead College Prep Charter	150 W 15th Ave	Gary, IN	46407-1219	219-979-9236		K-12	April Goble
Lawrence Early College HS	7250 E 7th St	Indianapolis, IN	46256	317-423-8320		K-12	Dr. Walter Bourke
Montessori Academy @ Geist	6633 W 900 N	Mc Cordsville, IN	46055-9761	317-335-3456		K-12	Cynthia Thompson
New Community S	710 North St	Lafayette, IN	47901-1158	765-420-9617	464-1999	K-7	Daniel Beaver
Options Charter S	PO Box 3790	Carmel, IN	46082-3790	317-815-2098	846-3806	9-12	Kevin Davis
Options Charter S - Noblesville	9945 Cumberland Pointe Blvd	Noblesville, IN	46060	317-773-8659		K-12	Kevin Davis
Rural Community S	PO Box 85	Graysville, IN	47852-0085	812-382-4500		K-8	Susie Pierce
Signature S	610 Main St	Evansville, IN	47708-1618	812-421-1820	421-9189	9-12	Vicki Snyder
Southeast Neighborhood S of Excellence	1601 Barth Ave	Indianapolis, IN	46203-2743	317-423-0204		K-12	Dr. J.C. Lasmanis
Tindley Accelerated S	3960 Meadows Dr	Indianapolis, IN	46205-3114	317-545-1745		6-12	Marcus Robinson
21st Century Charter S	2540 N Capitol Ave Ste 101	Indianapolis, IN	46208-5682	317-536-1027		K-12	Kevin Teasley
Veritas Academy	PO Box 10028	South Bend, IN	46680-0028	574-287-3230	287-2643	K-8	Angela Piazza
West Gary Lighthouse Charter S	725 Clark Rd	Gary, IN	46406-1822	219-977-9583		PK-5	Kim Sia

School	Address	City,State	Zip code	Telephone	Fax	Grade	Contact
Iowa							
Buffalo Ridge Charter S	4440 US Highway 71	Sioux Rapids, IA	50585-2030	712-283-2571	283-2285	1-6	Kevin Teno
Elma ES	PO Box 298	Elma, IA	50628-0298	641-393-2280		PK-6	Robert Hughes
Hartley-Melvin-Sanborn Charter HS	300 N 8th Ave W	Hartley, IA	51346-1074	712-928-3406	928-2152	9-12	Mark Petersen
Iowa Central Charter HS	PO Box 49	Burnside, IA	50521-0049	515-359-2235	359-2236	11-12	Mike Jorgensen
Lincoln Fundamental ES	318 E 7th St	Davenport, IA	52803-5597	563-324-0497	322-7503	PK-5	Jeff Womack
Northeast Iowa Charter HS	PO Box 54	Maynard, IA	50655-0054	563-637-2283	637-2294	11-12	Todd Abrahamson
Prescott ES	1151 White St	Dubuque, IA	52001-5005	563-552-4200	552-4201	PK-5	Christine McCarron
Storm Lake/Iowa Central/Buena Vista HS	621 Tornado Dr	Storm Lake, IA	50588-2277	712-732-8065		9-12	Michale Hanna
Kansas							
Alcott Charter ES	500 N Forest Ave	Chanute, KS	66720-1721	620-432-2530	431-7498	1-5	Jim Goracke
Alternative Learning Ctr at Enterprise	108 N Factory	Enterprise, KS	67441-9104	785-263-8330	493-0770	9-12	Larry Patrick
Basehor-Linwood Virtual Charter S	2108 N 155th St	Basehor, KS	66007-9395	913-724-1727	724-4518	K-12	Brenda DeGroot
Complete HS Maize	11411 W 49th St N	Maize, KS	67101	316-722-4790	729-0621	9-12	Teresa Ott
Cornerstone Alternative HS	720 E 7th St	Galena, KS	66739-1704	620-783-4499	783-1718	9-12	Tony Simmons
Delia Charter S	PO Box 99	Delia, KS	66418-0099	785-771-3470	771-3461	PK-8	Pam Sumner
Elkhart Cyber S	PO Box 999	Elkhart, KS	67950-0999	620-697-1166	697-2607	K-12	Sherri Hurn
Greeley County Charter S	400 W Lawrence St	Tribune, KS	67879-9636	620-376-4265	376-2465	K-12	Dale Herl
Haysville Charter S	130 Stewart Ave	Haysville, KS	67060-1602	316-554-2305		K-12	Mark Foster
Hope Street Academy Charter S	1900 SW Hope St	Topeka, KS	66604-3557	785-438-4280	271-3684	1-12	William Bagshaw
Hutchinson Cyber Charter S	100 W 27th Ave	Hutchinson, KS	67502-3424	620-665-4670		K-12	Rod Rathbun
Learning Center of Harper	1014 Central St	Harper, KS	67058-1309	620-896-2447	896-2479	9-12	Emily Ximinez
McPherson Alternative Center	1600 E Euclid St	Mc Pherson, KS	67460-3899	620-241-9507	241-9509	K-12	Karen Meats
New Beginnings Academy	411 S Central Ave	Chanute, KS	66720-2323	620-432-2503	432-2506	9-12	Kent Wire
Peoria Street Charter S	PO Box 1270	Louisburg, KS	66053-1270	913-837-3458	837-3458	9-12	John Brooks
Pleasantview Academy	5013 S Dean Rd	Hutchinson, KS	67501-9123	620-662-5516	662-5031	PK-12	Brian Boston
Productivity Academy	123 N Oak St	Pratt, KS	67124-1846	620-672-4555	672-4558	9-12	Bill Harris
Reno County Academies	1 E 9th Ave	Hutchinson, KS	67501	620-665-4125	665-4143	1-12	Don Thomas
Smoky Valley Virtual Charter S	1/2 Viking Blvd	Lindsborg, KS	67456	785-227-4254	227-2982	7-12	Marla Elmquist
Sterling Academy	125 W Cooper St	Sterling, KS	67579-2500	620-278-4215	278-4375	K-6	Judith Best
21st Century Learning Academy	PO Box 124	Mullinville, KS	67109-0124	620-548-2289	548-2389	K-12	John Jones
West Franklin Charter S	1966 California Rd	Pomona, KS	66076	785-746-5440	746-5748	K-12	Robert Allen
Yoder Charter S	PO Box 78	Yoder, KS	67585-0078	620-465-2605	465-2307	K-8	Deleon Martens
Louisiana							
Audubon Charter S	428 Broadway St	New Orleans, LA	70118-3514	504-862-5135	866-1691	PK-8	Janice Dupuy
Avoyelles Charter S	201 Longfellow Rd	Mansura, LA	71350-4292	318-240-8285	253-8453	K-12	Julie Durand
Behrman S	715 Opelousas Ave	New Orleans, LA	70114-2499	504-324-7030	309-8174	PK-8	Rene Carter
Belle Chase Academy	100 5th St	Belle Chasse, LA	70037-1002	504-433-5850	433-5590	K-8	Jane Fitzgerald Dye
Capdau Charter S	3821 Franklin Ave	New Orleans, LA	70122-6099	504-942-3634		PK-9	Shannon Verrett
Children's Charter S	900 McClung St	Baton Rouge, LA	70802-8129	225-387-9273	387-9272	PK-5	Stephen Ketcham
Community S for Apprenticeship Learning	1555 Madison Ave	Baton Rouge, LA	70802-3460	225-336-1410	336-1414	6-8	Dujan Johnson
Delhi Charter S	6940 Highway 17	Delhi, LA	71232-7021	318-878-0433	878-0434	K-12	Vicki Russell
Easton HS	3019 Canal St	New Orleans, LA	70119-6305	504-324-7400	827-4545	9-12	Alexina Medley
Einstein Charter S	5100 Cannes St	New Orleans, LA	70129-1203	504-324-7450		K-8	Alice Midkiff
Eisenhower ES	3700 Tall Pines Dr	New Orleans, LA	70131-8499	504-398-7125	398-7129	K-8	Cynthia Bernard
Fischer ES	1801 L B Landry Ave	New Orleans, LA	70114-6166	504-304-3976	363-1013	PK-8	Dahme Bolden
Franklin HS	2001 Leon C Simon Dr	New Orleans, LA	70122-3525	504-286-2600	286-2642	9-12	Carol Christian
Glencoe Charter S	4491 Highway 83	Franklin, LA	70538-7500	337-923-6900	923-0982	K-8	Michael Toney Parrie
Green Charter S	2319 Valence St	New Orleans, LA	70115-5959	504-896-4086	896-4147	K-8	Anthony Recasner
Harte ES	5300 Berkley Dr	New Orleans, LA	70131-7204	504-398-7101	398-7103	K-8	Anna Faye Marciante
Haynes Charter ES	356 East Blvd	Baton Rouge, LA	70802-5914	225-346-0067	346-0069	PK-5	Maurice Haynes
Hynes Charter S	719 S Carrolton	New Orleans, LA	70115	504-324-7160		PK-4	Michelle Douglas
Hynes S	821 General Pershing St	New Orleans, LA	70115-2731	504-483-6100	309-4161	5-8	Michelle Douglas
International School	1400 Camp St	New Orleans, LA	70130-4208	504-464-7488	488-3555	K-6	Sean Wilson
Jefferson Community Charter S	3528 Montford St	Jefferson, LA	70121-1824	504-836-0808	828-6888	6-8	Glenn Gennaro
Karr HS	3332 Huntlee Dr	New Orleans, LA	70131-7046	504-398-7115	398-7118	9-12	John Hiser
King Charter S for Science & Tech	PO Box 742417	New Orleans, LA	70174-2417	504-891-6924		PK-8	Doris Hicks
KIPP Believe College Prep S	1607 S Carrollton Ave	New Orleans, LA	70118-2825	504-312-2420		5-8	Adam Meinig
Lafayette Academy	2727 S Carrollton Ave	New Orleans, LA	70118-4387	504-861-8370		K-7	Eileen Williams
Lafayette Charter HS	516 E Pinhook Rd	Lafayette, LA	70501-8610	337-261-8981	235-6187	9-12	Kenneth Douet
Lake Forest Charter S	12000 Hayne Blvd	New Orleans, LA	70128-1127	504-299-2929		K-7	Mardele Early
Louisiana S for Agricultural Sciences	5303 Highway 115	Bunkie, LA	71322-4301	318-346-2762	346-4479	8-12	Jude Pitre
Lusher Charter S	5624 Freret St	New Orleans, LA	70115-6547	504-304-3960		6-11	Kathleen Riedlinger
Lusher Charter S	7315 Willow St	New Orleans, LA	70118	504-862-5110	309-4171	K-5	Kathy Reidlinger
McDonogh 15 S	721 Saint Philip St	New Orleans, LA	70116-2795	504-202-2004		PK-8	Gary Robichaux
McDonogh 32 S	800 De Armas St	New Orleans, LA	70114-4414	504-363-1057	363-1060	K-8	Kecia Wright
Milestone/Sabis Charter S	5951 Patton St	New Orleans, LA	70115-3232	504-894-0557		K-8	Janice Watson
Moton ES	1501 Abundance St	New Orleans, LA	70126	504-430-3143	942-3616	PK-6	Paulette Bruno
Nelson Charter S	1111 Milan St	New Orleans, LA	70115-2760	504-942-3670	309-8072	PK-8	Ava Lee
New Orleans Free S	3601 Camp St	New Orleans, LA	70115-2537	504-656-6763		PK-8	Easter James
New Orleans Science and Math HS	5625 Loyola Ave	New Orleans, LA	70115-5014	504-483-1832		9-12	Barbara McPhee
New Vision Learning Academy	507 Swayze St	Monroe, LA	71201-8130	318-338-9995	338-9987	PK-6	Rev. Andrew Mansfield
Priestley Charter S	1607 S Carrollton Ave	New Orleans, LA	70118-2825	504-324-7200	862-5199	9-12	Michelle Biagas
Singleton Charter S	2220 Oretha C Haley Blvd	New Orleans, LA	70113	504-568-3466		PK-8	Melrose Biagas
Tubman S	2013 General Meyer Ave	New Orleans, LA	70114-1533	504-363-1064	363-1067	K-8	Patsy Gearing
Tureaud ES	2021 Pauger St	New Orleans, LA	70116-1533	504-330-0205	330-0206	K-5	Perretta Mitchell
Walker HS	2832 General Meyer Ave	New Orleans, LA	70114-3097	504-363-1072	363-1085	9-12	Mary Laurie
Wicker S	2011 Bienville St	New Orleans, LA	70112-3397	504-571-1023	330-0196	K-8	Ella Lewis
Wright Charter S	1426 Napoleon Ave	New Orleans, LA	70115-3980	504-304-3915	896-4095	K-8	Sharon Clark
Maryland							
Chesapeake Science Point Charter S	1321 Mercedes Dr	Hanover, MD	21076	410-684-2886	684-2883	6-8	Judith Henry
City Neighbors Charter S	4301 Raspe Ave	Baltimore, MD	21206-1913	410-325-2627		PK-8	Michael Chalupa
ConneXions Leadership Academy	2801 N Dukeland St	Baltimore, MD	21216-2801	410-984-1418	669-4418	6-12	Dana Polson
Crossroads S	802 S Caroline St	Baltimore, MD	21231-3332	410-685-0295		6-8	Mark Conrad
Excel Academy	6251 Ammendale Rd	Beltsville, MD	20705-1267	240-264-8190		K-12	Deborah Moore
Green S	335 W 27th St	Baltimore, MD	21211-3004	410-483-5784		K-5	Kate Primm
Inner Harbor East Academy	200 N Central Ave	Baltimore, MD	21202-5005	410-276-0306		K-12	Maria Dent
KIPP Harbor Academy Charter S	135 Stepney Ln	Edgewater, MD	21037-1432	410-956-5075	956-5074	5-6	Jallon Brown
KIPP Ujima Village Academy	4701 Greenspring Ave	Baltimore, MD	21209-4704	410-545-3669	664-6865	K-5	Shayna Hammond
Maryland Academy of Technology & Math	4701 Greenspring Ave	Baltimore, MD	21209	410-262-6072	461-6850	8-12	Rebekah Ghosh
Monocacy Valley Montessori S	217 Dill Ave	Frederick, MD	21701-4905	301-668-5013	668-5015	K-6	Bettejane Weiss
Northwood Appold S	4417 Loch Raven Blvd	Baltimore, MD	21218-1554	410-323-6712		K-2	Virginia Richardson
Patterson Park S	27 N Lakewood Ave	Baltimore, MD	21224-1155	410-558-1230		PK-8	Jennifer Schmidberger
Potomac Charter S	12788 Old Fort Rd Ste C	Fort Washington, MD	20744-2881	301-292-7888		K-12	Johnnie Searcy
Southwest Charter S	31 S Schroeder St	Baltimore, MD	21223-2559	443-980-9016		PK-8	Turi Nillson
Turning Point Academy	7800 Good Luck Rd	Lanham Seabrook, MD	20706-3505	301-552-0164		K-12	Dr. Kenneth Jones
Massachusetts							
Academy of Pacific Rim Charter S	1 Westinghouse Plz	Hyde Park, MA	02136-2059	617-361-0050	361-0045	6-12	Dimitry Anselme
Academy of Strategic Learning	9 Water St	Amesbury, MA	01913	978-388-8037	388-8073	7-12	Donna Georges
Advanced Math & Science Academy	201 Forest St	Marlborough, MA	01752-3012	508-597-2400	597-2499	6-8	Julia Sigalovsky
Atlantis Charter S	37 Park St	Fall River, MA	02721-1712	508-672-3537	672-2474	K-8	Fernando Goulart
Banneker Charter S	21 Notre Dame Ave	Cambridge, MA	02140-2505	617-497-7771	497-4223	K-8	Lenora Jennings
Barnstable Horace Mann Charter S	730 Osterville-W Barnstable	Marstons Mills, MA	02648	508-420-2272	420-0185	5-6	Kara Peterson
Berkshire Arts & Technology Charter S	PO Box 267	Adams, MA	01220-0267	413-743-7311	743-7327	6-11	Ellen Ennis
Boston Collegiate Charter S	11 Mayhew St	Dorchester, MA	02125-1628	617-265-1172	265-1176	5-12	Tobey Jackson
Boston Day & Evening Academy	20 Kearsarge Ave	Roxbury, MA	02119-2318	617-635-6789	635-6380	9-12	Margaret Maccini
Boston Preparatory Charter S	1286 Hyde Park Ave	Hyde Park, MA	02136-2714	617-333-6688	333-6689	6-8	Howard Mccue
Boston Renaissance Charter S	250 Stuart St	Boston, MA	02116-5435	617-357-0900	338-2647	K-6	Roger F. Harris
Brooke Charter S	190 Cummins Hwy	Roslindale, MA	02131-3722	617-325-7977	325-2260	K-8	Jon C. Clark
Cape Cod Lighthouse Charter S	225 Route 6A	Orleans, MA	02653	508-240-2800	240-3583	6-8	Paul Niles
Champion Charter S	20 Union St	Brockton, MA	02301	508-894-4377	894-4380	9-12	Virginia Warn
City on a Hill Charter S	320 Huntington Ave	Boston, MA	02115-5018	617-262-9838	262-9064	9-12	Erica Jamison
Codman Academy	637 Washington St	Dorchester, MA	02124-3510	617-287-0700	287-9064	9-12	Meg Campbell
Community Charter S of Cambridge	245 Bent St	Cambridge, MA	02141-2001	617-354-0047	354-3624	7-9	Paula Evans
Community Day Charter S	190 Hampshire St	Lawrence, MA	01840	978-682-6628	681-5838	K-8	Sheila Balboni
Conservatory Lab Charter S	25 Arlington St	Brighton, MA	02135-2124	617-254-8904	254-8909	K-5	Mark Jacobson
Excel Academy Charter S	1150 Saratoga St	East Boston, MA	02128-1228	617-561-1371	561-1378	7-8	Yutaka Tamura
Foster Charter S	10 New Bond St	Worcester, MA	01606	508-854-8400	595-0370	K-12	Robert Harrington
Four Rivers Charter S	248 Colrain Rd	Greenfield, MA	01301-9701	413-775-4577	775-4578	7-11	Edward Blatchford

School	Address	City,State	Zip code	Telephone	Fax	Grade	Contact
Foxboro Regional Charter S	131 Central St	Foxboro, MA	02035-2458	508-543-2508	543-7982	K-12	Mark Logan
Franklin Classical Charter S	201 Main St	Franklin, MA	02038-1933	508-541-3434	541-5396	K-8	Kevin O'Malley
Health Careers Academy	360 Huntington Ave	Boston, MA	02115-5005	617-373-8576	373-7850	9-12	Albert Holland
Hilltown Cooperative Charter S	PO Box 147	Haydenville, MA	01039-0147	413-268-3421	268-3185	K-8	Daniel Klatz
Hill View Montessori S	PO Box 1545	Haverhill, MA	01831-2145	978-521-2616	521-2656	K-8	Peg Roberts
Holyoke Community Charter S	2200 Northampton St	Holyoke, MA	01040-3430	413-533-0111	536-5444	K-8	Zandrina Atherley
Hughes Academy	91 School St	Springfield, MA	01105-1316	413-747-5200	747-4528	K-8	Marlina Duncan
Innovation Academy Charter S	40 Brick Kiln Rd	Chelmsford, MA	01824-3222	978-970-0100	970-3522	5-8	Walter Landberg
King Charter S of Excellence	694 State St	Springfield, MA	01109	413-209-5787		K-2	Allan Katz
Kipp Academy Lynn Charter S	25 Bessom St	Lynn, MA	01902-1204	781-598-1609	598-1629	5-7	Joshua Zoia
Lawrence Family Development Charter S	34 West St	Lawrence, MA	01841-3426	978-689-9863	689-8133	K-8	Connie Tarsook
Lowell Community Charter S	206 Jackson St	Lowell, MA	01852-2106	978-323-0800	970-0715	K-8	Elizabeth Torosian
Lowell Middlesex Academy Charter S	33 Kearney Sq	Lowell, MA	01852-1901	978-656-3165	459-0546	9-12	Margaret McDevitt
Marblehead Community Charter S	17 Lime St	Marblehead, MA	01945-2530	781-631-0777	631-0500	4-8	Thomas Commeret
Marstons Mills East Horace Mann Charter	760 Osterville-W Barnstable	Marstons Mills, MA	02648	508-420-1100	420-1486	K-4	Edward Deusser
Martha's Vineyard Charter S	PO Box 1150	West Tisbury, MA	02575-1150	508-693-9900	696-9008	K-12	Robert Moore
MATCH Charter HS	1001 Commonwealth Ave	Boston, MA	02215-1308	617-232-0300	232-2838	9-12	Jorge Miranda
McAuliffe Regional Charter S	25 Clinton St	Framingham, MA	01702-6702	508-879-9000	879-1066	6-8	Daniel Barcan
Mystic Valley Regional Charter S	770 Salem St	Malden, MA	02148-4415	781-388-0222	321-5688	K-12	Anthony Biegler
Neighborhood House Charter S	21 Queen St	Dorchester, MA	02122-2509	617-825-0703	825-1829	PK-8	Kevin Andrews
New Bedford Global Learning Charter S	455 County St	New Bedford, MA	02740-5194	508-991-7000	991-4127	5-12	Paul Fay
New Leadership Charter S	180 Ashland Ave	Springfield, MA	01119-2704	413-782-9111	782-9991	6-12	Douglas Greer
North Central Essential Charter S	1 Oak Hill Rd	Fitchburg, MA	01420	978-345-2701	345-9127	7-12	Patricia May
Parker Charter Essential S	49 Antietam St	Ayer, MA	01434-5230	978-772-3293	772-3295	7-12	Teriann Schrader
Phoenix Charter Academy	47 Clark Ave	Chelsea, MA	02150	617-276-4670	599-4252	9-12	Beth Anderson
Pioneer Valley Performing Arts Charter S	15 Mulligan Dr	South Hadley, MA	01075-7511	413-552-1580	552-1594	7-12	Robert Brick
Prospect Hill Academy Charter S	15 Webster Ave	Somerville, MA	02143-3311	617-284-7800	284-7940	K-12	Nanzetta Merriman
Rising Tide Charter S	6 Resnik Rd	Plymouth, MA	02360-4873	508-747-2620	830-9441	5-8	Jill Crafts
River Valley Charter S	2 Perry Way	Newburyport, MA	01950-4001	978-465-0065	465-0119	K-8	Dr. Dale Bishop
SABIS International Charter S	160 Joan St	Springfield, MA	01129-1530	413-783-2600	783-2555	K-12	Maretta Thomsen
Salem Academy Charter S	PO Box 8014	Salem, MA	01971-8014	978-744-2105	744-7246	6-9	Rachel Hunt
Seven Hills Charter S	51 Gage St	Worcester, MA	01605-3014	508-799-7500	753-7318	K-8	Krista Piazza
Smith Leadership Academy Charter S	23 Leonard St	Boston, MA	02122-2718	617-474-7950	474-7957	6-8	Karmala Sherwood
South Shore Charter S	100 Longwater Cir	Norwell, MA	02061-1650	781-982-4202	982-4201	K-12	Thomas Gorsuch
Sturgis Charter S	427 Main St	Hyannis, MA	02601-3905	508-778-1782	771-6785	9-12	Eric Hieser
Uphams Corner Charter S	7 Elkins St	Boston, MA	02127-1601	617-268-4695	268-5604	5-8	Edward Cook

Michigan

School	Address	City,State	Zip code	Telephone	Fax	Grade	Contact
Abney Academy	1435 Fulton St E	Grand Rapids, MI	49503-3853	616-454-5541	454-5598	K-5	Tamasha James
Academic and Career Education Academy	884 E Isabella Rd	Midland, MI	48640-8326	989-631-5202	631-4541	9-12	Jeff McNeal
Academic Transitional Academy	1520 Michigan Rd	Port Huron, MI	48060-4750	810-364-3449	364-3347	9-10	Pete Spencer
Academy for Technology & Enterprise	2102 Weiss St	Saginaw, MI	48602-5049	989-399-6150	399-6165	11-12	Julie Walker
Academy of Business and Technology	19625 Wood St	Melvindale, MI	48122-2201	313-382-3422	382-3906	6-12	John Kirk
Academy of Business and Technology ES	5277 Calhoun St	Dearborn, MI	48126-3203	313-581-2223	581-2247	K-5	Paul Merritt
Academy of Detroit - West	16418 W Mcnichols Rd	Detroit, MI	48235-3354	313-272-5473	272-4823	K-1	Mae Alexander
Academy of Detroit West - Redford	23749 Elmira	Redford, MI	48239-1405	313-387-9238	387-9261	2-6	Delores Snorton
Academy of Flint	4100 W Coldwater Rd	Flint, MI	48504-1102	810-789-9484	789-9483	K-8	Verdell Duncan
Academy of Inkster	28612 Avondale St	Inkster, MI	48141-1642	734-641-1312	641-1317	9-12	Raymond J. Alvarado
Academy of Lathrup Village	27700 Southfield Rd	Southfield, MI	48076-7901	248-569-0089	569-4944	K-8	Joe Moody
Academy of Michigan	20820 Greenfield Rd	Oak Park, MI	48237-3051	248-968-0440	968-0622	9-12	LaGuardia Summers
Academy of Oak Park	21700 Marlow St	Oak Park, MI	48237-2604	248-547-2323	547-2515	K-5	Rashid Fai'Sal
Academy of Oak Park	21300 Mendota Ave	Ferndale, MI	48220-2164	248-586-9358	586-9362	6-12	Barbara Easley
Academy of Southfield	18330 George Washington Dr	Southfield, MI	48075-2785	248-557-6121	557-2915	K-8	Carolyn Mosley
Academy of Warren	13943 E 8 Mile Rd	Warren, MI	48089	586-552-8010	552-8014	K-8	Jerry Parker
Academy of Waterford	3000 Sashabaw Rd	Waterford, MI	48329-4040	248-674-1649	674-3173	K-8	Bradley Gibbs
Academy of Westland	300 S Henry Ruff Rd	Westland, MI	48186-5087	734-722-1465	722-8025	K-8	Christopher Lindsay
Advanced Technology Academy	7265 Calhoun St	Dearborn, MI	48126-1492	313-582-4500	582-9407	K-12	Barry Hawthorne
A.G.B.U. Alex & Marie Manoogian S	22001 Northwestern Hwy	Southfield, MI	48075-4001	248-569-2988	569-1346	K-12	H. Torossian
Aisha Shule/W.E.B. Dubois Prep Academy	20119 Wisconsin St	Detroit, MI	48221-1132	313-345-6050	345-1059	K-12	Imani Humphrey
Allen Academy	8666 Quincy St	Detroit, MI	48204-2306	313-898-6444	898-6555	K-12	Tim Green
American Montessori Academy	14800 Middlebelt Rd	Livonia, MI	48154-4031	734-525-7100	525-8952	K-5	Amy Pogorzelski
Ann Arbor Learning Community	3980 Research Park Dr	Ann Arbor, MI	48108-2220	734-477-0340	929-6505	K-8	Jennifer Taylor
Arbor Academy	55 Arbor St	Battle Creek, MI	49015-2903	269-963-5851	964-2643	K-6	Paul Doersam
Arts Academy in the Woods	32101 Caroline	Fraser, MI	48026-3209	586-294-0391	294-0617	9-12	Kay Dyer
Arts & Technology Academy of Pontiac	48980 Woodward Ave	Pontiac, MI	48342-5034	248-452-9309	452-9312	K-8	Sadie Mahone
Battle Creek Area Learning Center	15 Arbor St	Battle Creek, MI	49015-2903	269-565-4782	565-4784	10-12	Charles Crider
Bay-Arenac Community HS	1608 Hudson St	Essexville, MI	48732-1387	989-893-8811	895-7749	9-12	Ryan Donlan
Bay County Public School Academy	1110 State St	Bay City, MI	48706-3699	989-684-6484	684-6202	PK-8	Alicia Kubacki
Benton Harbor Charter S	455 Riverview Dr	Benton Harbor, MI	49022-5015	269-925-3807	927-3673	PK-8	Cynthia Jack
Bingham Arts Academy	555 S 5th Ave	Alpena, MI	49707-2744	989-358-2500	358-2503	PK-7	Ron Miller
Black River Public S	491 Columbia Ave	Holland, MI	49423-4838	616-355-0055	355-0057	1-12	David Angerer
Blue Water Learning Academy	5202 Taft Rd	Algonac, MI	48001-4701	810-794-8067	794-8888	7-12	James Lenore
Bradford Academy	24218 Garner St	Southfield, MI	48033-2900	248-351-0000	356-4770	K-7	Fred Borowski
Bridge Academy	9600 Buffalo St	Hamtramck, MI	48212-3323	313-887-8100	887-8101	K-8	Naji Jaber
Bruce Academy	5555 Conner St	Detroit, MI	48213	313-656-2610	924-0095	7-12	Talbert Allen
Bruce Academy	3500 John R St	Detroit, MI	48201-2402	313-494-3259	831-8202	5-12	Edythe Friley
Bruce Academy	330 Glendale St	Highland Park, MI	48203-3277	313-852-7506	852-7566	5-12	Douglas Gabriel
Bruce Academy	609 E Grand Blvd	Detroit, MI	48207-3543	313-656-2600	568-6116	5-12	Vickie Brent
Bruce Academy	4707 Saint Antoine St	Detroit, MI	48201-1427	313-656-2632	568-6116	5-12	Vickie Brent
Bruce Academy	15225 Mayfield St	Detroit, MI	48205	313-656-2600	568-6116	5-12	Vickie Brent
Bruce Academy	1200 Alter Rd	Detroit, MI	48215-2833	313-656-2600	568-6116	5-12	Vickie Brent
Bruce Academy	2629 Lenox St	Detroit, MI	48215-2667	313-656-2600	568-6116	5-12	Vickie Brent
Burton Glen Charter Academy	4171 E Atherton Rd	Burton, MI	48519-1435	810-744-2300	744-2400	PK-8	Donald Hammond
Business Entrepreneurship Sci & Tech S	200 Highland St	Highland Park, MI	48203-3405	313-869-1000	868-1741	K-6	Delria Crippen
Byron Center Charter S	9930 Burlingame Ave SW	Byron Center, MI	49315-8631	616-878-4852	878-7196	PK-12	Tom Kruzel
Canton Charter Academy	49100 Ford Rd	Canton, MI	48187-5415	734-453-9517	453-9551	K-8	Claudia Williamson
Capitol Area Academy	5525 S Pennsylvania Ave	Lansing, MI	48911-4091	517-882-1400	882-0400	K-8	Michael Haggen
Carleton Academy	2001 W Hallett Rd	Hillsdale, MI	49242-1959	517-437-2000	437-2919	K-12	Colleen Gadwood
Carver Academy	14510 2nd Ave	Highland Park, MI	48203-5715	313-865-6024	865-6658	K-8	Marcie Wade
Casa Richard Academy	2635 Howard St	Detroit, MI	48216-2058	313-963-7757	963-7768	9-12	Angela Johnson
CASMAN Alternative Academy	225 9th St	Manistee, MI	49660-3109	231-723-4981	723-1555	7-12	Cameron Clark
Center Academy	310 W Oakley St	Flint, MI	48503-3915	810-341-6944	341-6949	K-8	Elizabeth Jordan
Center for Literacy & Creativity	18401 W McNichols Rd	Detroit, MI	48219-4113	313-537-9400	537-9410	K-8	Deborah Holt-Foster
Central Academy	2459 S Industrial Hwy	Ann Arbor, MI	48104-6129	734-822-1110	822-1101	PK-12	Luay Shalabi
Chandler Park Academy - Kelly	20100 Kelly Rd	Harper Woods, MI	48225-1201	313-839-9886	839-3221	K-7	Vivian Jackson
Chandler Park Academy - Philip	4901 Haverhill St	Detroit, MI	48224-3559	313-884-8830	884-9130	8-8	Darah Griffin
Chandler Woods Charter Academy	6895 Samrick Ave NE	Belmont, MI	49306-8844	616-866-6000	866-6001	K-8	Fred Slade
Chatfield S	231 Lake Dr	Lapeer, MI	48446-1661	810-667-8970	667-8983	K-6	Betty McCauley
Chavez Academy	8126 W Vernor Hwy	Detroit, MI	48209-1524	313-843-9440	297-6948	K-5	Cheri Wasiel
Chavez HS	1761 Waterman St	Detroit, MI	48209	313-551-0611	551-0552	9-12	Christopher Silva
Chavez MS	6782 Goldsmith St	Detroit, MI	48209-2089	313-842-0006	842-0167	6-8	Rick Guerra
Cherry Hill School of Performing Arts	28500 Avondale St	Inkster, MI	48141	734-722-2811	641-9439	K-12	J. Perkins
Cole Academy	1915 W Mount Hope Ave	Lansing, MI	48910-2434	517-372-0038	372-1446	K-5	James Henderson
Commonwealth Cmmnty Development Acad.	13477 Eureka St	Detroit, MI	48212-1754	313-366-9470	366-9471	K-6	Cullian Hill
Concord Academy - Antrim	5055 Corey Rd	Mancelona, MI	49659-9467	231-584-2080	584-2082	K-12	K. Loyer Schanski
Concord Academy - Boyne	401 E Dietz Rd	Boyne City, MI	49712-9653	231-582-0194	582-4214	K-12	Larry Kubovchick
Concord Academy-Petoskey	2468 Atkins Rd	Petoskey, MI	49770-9003	231-439-6800	439-6803	K-12	Benjamin Jankens
Conner Creek Academy	28111 Imperial Dr	Warren, MI	48093-4281	586-575-9500	575-9483	K-12	Demetria Wesley
Conner Creek Academy East	16911 Eastland St	Roseville, MI	48066-2078	586-779-8055	498-8734	K-12	Charles Meredith
Consortium College Preparatory HS	1250 Rosa Parks Blvd	Detroit, MI	48216-1950	313-964-2339	964-3922	7-12	Rod Atkins
Countryside Charter S	4800 Meadowbrook Rd	Benton Harbor, MI	49022-9629	269-944-3319	944-3724	K-12	Paul Marazita
Covenant House Life Skills Ctr Central	2959 Martin Luther King Jr	Detroit, MI	48208	313-898-8816	898-8861	9-12	Antoinette Cunningham
Covenant House Life Skills Ctr East	7600 Goethe St	Detroit, MI	48214-1762	313-922-8901	922-8903	9-12	Derrick Bryant
Covenant House Life Skills Ctr West	5668 Baker St	Detroit, MI	48209-2169	313-554-8130	554-8140	9-12	Tracye Davis
Creative Learning Academy of Science	540 Lang Rd	Beaverton, MI	48612-8101	989-435-8252	435-4187	K-8	Shelly Patton
Creative Montessori Academy	15100 Northline Rd	Southgate, MI	48195-2408	734-284-5600	281-2637	K-8	Rochelle Cochran
Creative Technologies Academy	350 Pine St	Cedar Springs, MI	49319-8680	616-696-4905	696-4920	K-12	Lexie Coxon
Crescent Academy	17570 W 12 Mile Rd	Southfield, MI	48076-1905	248-423-4581	423-1027	K-8	Rose Marie Trotter
Crockett Academy	4851 14th St	Detroit, MI	48208-2204	313-896-6078	896-1363	K-12	Mary Lou Van Antwerp
Cross Creek Charter Academy	7701 Kalamazoo Ave SE	Byron Center, MI	49315-9320	616-656-4000	656-4001	PK-8	Joe Nieuwkoop
Crossroads Charter Academy	215 N State St	Big Rapids, MI	49307-1444	231-796-9041	796-9790	K-12	David Vander Goot
da Vinci Institute	559 Murphy Dr	Jackson, MI	49202-1622	517-780-9980	780-9747	K-8	Kimberly Norton
da Vinci Institute	2255 Emmons Rd	Jackson, MI	49201-8335	517-796-0031	796-0320	9-12	Sandy Maxson
Dearborn Academy	19310 Ford Rd Ste 2	Dearborn, MI	48128-2403	313-982-1300	982-9087	K-8	Cynthia Leaman
Detroit Academy of Arts & Sciences	2985 E Jefferson Ave	Detroit, MI	48207-4288	313-259-1744	259-8393	K-5	Stan Bowman
Detroit Academy of Arts & Sciences	2260 Medbury St	Detroit, MI	48211-2718	313-923-0281	923-0437	6-12	Thomas Goodley

School	Address	City,State	Zip code	Telephone	Fax	Grade	Contact
Detroit Community ES	12675 Burt Rd	Detroit, MI	48223-3314	313-537-6717	537-0558	K-6	Mary Loenhardi
Detroit Community HS	12675 Burt Rd	Detroit, MI	48223-3314	313-537-3570	537-6904	9-12	Bart Eddy
Detroit Edison Academy	1903 Wilkins St	Detroit, MI	48207-2112	313-833-1100	833-8653	K-8	Ralph Bland
Detroit Enterprise Academy	11224 Kercheval St	Detroit, MI	48214-3323	313-823-5799	823-0342	K-6	Candace Rogers
Detroit Merit Academy	1091 Alter Rd	Detroit, MI	48215-2861	313-331-3328	331-3278	K-8	Heidi Benser
Detroit Premier Academy	7781 Asbury Park	Detroit, MI	48228-3685	313-945-1472	945-1744	K-7	Von Glass
Discovery Arts & Technology Academy	27355 Woodfield Rd	Inkster, MI	48141	313-827-0762	827-0763	K-5	Claude Tiller
Discovery S	PO Box 1070	Fennville, MI	49408-1070	269-561-2191	561-2302	K-8	Bruce Foerch
Dove Academy of Detroit	8210 Rolyat St	Detroit, MI	48234-3358	313-366-9110	366-9130	K-6	Frank Nardelli
Drew Academy	50 W Josephine St	Ecorse, MI	48229-1748	313-383-7501	383-7502	K-7	Dan Henry
Eagle Crest Charter Academy	11950 Riley St	Holland, MI	49424-8553	616-786-2400	786-4692	K-8	Daniel Harris
Eastern Washtenaw Multicultural Academy	5550 Platt Rd	Ann Arbor, MI	48108-9762	734-677-0732	677-0740	K-10	John Nordlinger
Eaton Academy	21450 Universal Ave	Eastpointe, MI	48021-2969	586-777-1519	777-1527	K-12	Holly Davis-Webster
Edison-Oakland Academy	22111 Woodward Ave	Ferndale, MI	48220-1812	248-582-8191	582-8196	K-6	Gail Georgette Parks
El-Hajj Malik El-Shabazz Academy	1028 W Barnes Ave	Lansing, MI	48910-1377	517-267-8474	484-0095	PK-6	Dr. Eugene L. Cain
Ellis Academy	18977 Schaefer Hwy	Detroit, MI	48235-1762	313-927-5395	927-5376	K-8	Theo Overton
Endeavor Charter Academy	380 Helmer Rd N	Battle Creek, MI	49037	269-962-9300	962-9393	K-8	Russ Ainslee
Excel Charter Academy	4201 Breton Rd SE	Grand Rapids, MI	49512-3857	616-281-9339	281-6707	K-8	William Knoester
Ford Academy	PO Box 1148	Dearborn, MI	48121-1148	313-982-6200	982-6195	9-12	Cora Christmas
Forten Academy	5690 Cecil St	Detroit, MI	48210-1964	313-897-2203	897-2206	6-12	Cameron Owens
Fortis Academy	3875 Golfside Dr	Ypsilanti, MI	48197-3726	734-572-3623	572-5792	K-7	Chris Thompson
Frontier International Academy	2619 Florian St	Hamtramck, MI	48212-3452	313-887-7500	887-7501	6-12	Harun Rashid
Gateway Middle HS	311 State St SE	Grand Rapids, MI	49503-4312	616-458-9646	458-9647	7-12	Meg Hackett Carrier
Gaudior Academy	27100 Avondale St	Inkster, MI	48141-1816	313-792-9444	792-9445	PK-8	Rosemarie Gonzales
Gist Academy - South	4825 Dancy St	Westland, MI	48186-5148	734-721-5515	721-9129	K-4	Tina Hatcher
Gist Academy	28955 Rosewood St	Inkster, MI	48141-1656	734-728-4813	722-5111	5-8	June Hearn
Grand Blanc Academy	5135 E Hill Rd	Grand Blanc, MI	48439-7637	810-953-3140	953-3165	K-8	Zel Seidenberg
Grand Rapids Child Discovery Center	640 5th St NW	Grand Rapids, MI	49504-5107	616-459-0330	732-4437	K-5	Susan Lukaart
Grand Traverse Academy	1245 Hammond Rd E	Traverse City, MI	49686-9000	231-995-0665	995-0880	K-12	Kaye Mentley
Grattan Academic HS	9481 Jordan Rd	Greenville, MI	48838-9437	616-754-9360	754-9363	6-12	Catherine Browers
Grattan Academy	12047 Old Belding Rd NE	Belding, MI	48809-9367	616-691-8999	691-9857	K-5	Elizabeth Witt-Kreiner
Great Lakes Academy	46312 Woodward Ave	Pontiac, MI	48342-5006	248-334-6434	334-6457	K-6	Debra Seay
Great Oaks Academy	1075 E Gardenia Ave	Madison Heights, MI	48071-3433	586-427-4540	427-4541	K-7	Elise Seitz
Hamtramck Academy	11420 Conant St	Hamtramck, MI	48212-3134	313-368-7312	368-7376	K-7	S. Glenn
Hanley International Academy	3056 Hanley St	Hamtramck, MI	48212-3572	313-872-9080	872-9113	K-3	Carolyn Glover
Hanley International Academy	2609 Poland St	Hamtramck, MI	48212-3459	313-875-8888	875-8889	4-6	Carolyn Glover
Health Careers Academy of St. Clair Co.	PO Box 1500	Marysville, MI	48040-8000	810-364-8990	364-8139	11-12	Patrick Yanik
HEART Academy	19800 Anita St	Harper Woods, MI	48225-1109	313-882-4631	882-4761	9-12	Sandra Robinson
Hillsdale Preparatory S	160 Mechanic Rd Ste 170	Hillsdale, MI	49242	517-437-4625	437-3830	K-6	James Rowen
Holly Academy	820 Academy Rd	Holly, MI	48442-1546	248-634-5554	634-5564	K-8	Julie Kildee
Honey Creek Community S	PO Box 1406	Ann Arbor, MI	48106-1406	734-994-2636	994-2341	K-8	Dr. Sarena Shivers
Hope Academy	10100 Grand River Ave	Detroit, MI	48204-2042	313-934-0054	934-0074	K-6	Veneda Fox Sanders
Hope of Detroit Academy	4443 N Campbell St	Detroit, MI	48210-2520	313-897-8720	897-5142	K-8	Anthony Hubbard
Horizons Community HS	1585 36th St SW	Wyoming, MI	49509	616-530-7535	249-7661	9-12	Teriena Schwartz
Hospitality Academy of St. Clair County	PO Box 1500	Marysville, MI	48040-8000	810-364-8990	364-8139	11-12	Patrick Yanik
Huron Academy	11401 Metropolitan Pkwy	Sterling Hts, MI	48312-2937	586-446-9170	446-9173	K-8	Rhonda Filippi
Industrial Technology Academy	PO Box 1500	Marysville, MI	48040-8000	810-364-8990	364-8139	11-12	Patrick Yanick
Information Technology Academy	PO Box 1500	Marysville, MI	48040-8000	810-364-8990	364-8139	11-12	Patrick Yanick
International Academy of Flint	2820 S Saginaw St	Flint, MI	48503-5708	810-251-5151	251-5154	K-12	Traci Cormier
Island City Academy	6421 S Clinton Trl	Eaton Rapids, MI	48827-9698	517-663-0111	663-0167	K-8	Thomas Ackerson
Jackson Arts & Technology Academy	500 Griswold St	Jackson, MI	49203-4062	517-796-0080	796-0104	K-7	Lezlie Bowles
JKL Bahweting Charter S	1301 Marquette Ave	Sault S Marie, MI	49783-9533	906-635-5055	635-3805	K-8	Nick Oshelski
Joy Preparatory Academy	1129 Oakman Blvd	Detroit, MI	48238-2950	313-867-7828	867-7831	K-2	Michael Jackson
Joy Preparatory Academy	15055 Dexter Ave	Detroit, MI	48238-2124	313-340-0023	340-0678	3-8	Frances Gardulescu
Kalamazoo Advantage Academy	121 W South St	Kalamazoo, MI	49007-4865	269-345-7850	345-7851	K-8	Frank Sebastian
Kensington Woods HS	3700 Cleary Dr	Howell, MI	48843-6614	517-545-0828	545-7588	9-12	James Perry
Keystone Academy	47925 Bemis Rd	Belleville, MI	48111-9760	734-697-9470	697-9471	K-8	Kay Murray
King Education Center	16827 Appoline St	Detroit, MI	48235-4205	313-341-4944	341-7014	K-6	Constance Price
Knapp Charter Academy	1759 Leffingwell Ave NE	Grand Rapids, MI	49525-4531	616-364-1100	364-9780	K-8	Jami Hoeksema
Lakeshore Public Academy	PO Box 9	Hart, MI	49420-0009	231-873-8199	873-8196	K-12	Robert Doty
Landmark Academy	4800 Lapeer Rd	Kimball, MI	48074-1517	810-982-7210	982-0679	K-8	Nancy Gardner
Laurus Academy	24590 Lahser Rd	Southfield, MI	48033-6040	248-799-8401	799-8404	K-7	Raul Calderon
Life Skills Center	3100 E Jefferson Ave	Detroit, MI	48207-4221	313-567-3235	567-8554	9-12	Nathaniel King
Life Skills Center of Pontiac	142 Auburn Ave	Pontiac, MI	48342-3008	248-322-1163	322-1164	9-12	Olatunji Bolden
Linden Charter Academy	3244 N Linden Rd	Flint, MI	48504-1753	810-720-0515	720-0626	K-8	Linda Cain-Smith
Lundy Academy	950 Selden St	Detroit, MI	48201-2234	313-831-4961	831-4964	6-12	Carlitta Cabell
Macomb Academy	39092 Garfield Rd	Clinton Twp, MI	48038	586-228-2201	228-2210	12-12	Betty Yee
Madison Academy	1291 E Maple Ave	Burton, MI	48529-1503	810-744-9100	743-1796	K-7	Kenneth Maurey
Marshall Academy	18203 Homer Rd	Marshall, MI	49068-8718	269-781-6330	781-8749	K-9	Pam Gerten
Merritt Academy	59900 Havenridge Rd	New Haven, MI	48048-1915	586-749-6000	749-8582	K-9	Dan Schluckbier
Metro Charter Academy	34800 Ecorse Rd	Romulus, MI	48174-1642	734-641-3200	641-6530	K-8	Andrew Cook
Michigan Health Academy	5845 Auburn St	Detroit, MI	48228-3905	313-982-9422	982-9415	9-12	Anthony Jackson
Michigan Technical Academy	19940 Mansfield St	Detroit, MI	48235-2332	313-272-1649	272-1849	3-5	Susan Williams
Michigan Technical Academy	19900 Evergreen Rd	Detroit, MI	48219-2044	313-538-4927	538-8396	K-2	Brendolyn McClain
Michigan Technical Academy	19780 Meyers Rd	Detroit, MI	48235-1229	313-864-0595	864-2271	6-8	James Abercrombie
Michigan Technical Academy HS	23750 Elmira	Redford, MI	48239	313-537-9312		9-12	Reid Perry
Midland Acad Advanced & Creative Studies	4653 E Bailey Bridge Rd	Midland, MI	48640-8542	989-496-2404	496-2466	K-12	Kathryn Shick
Mid-Michigan Leadership Academy	730 W Maple St	Lansing, MI	48906-5086	517-485-5379	485-5892	K-8	Mark Eitrem
Morey Charter S	380 W Blanchard Rd	Shepherd, MI	48883-9552	989-866-6739	866-6737	PK-12	Greg Vander Goot
Mt. Clemens Montessori Academy	1070 Hampton Rd	Mount Clemens, MI	48043-2955	586-465-5545	465-2283	PK-5	Genie P'Sachoulias
Muskegon Technical Academy	2900 E Apple Ave	Muskegon, MI	49442-4504	231-777-3682	767-8488	5-12	Barbara Stellard
Nataki Talibah S of Detroit	19176 Northrop St	Detroit, MI	48219-1857	313-531-3720	531-3779	K-8	Carmen N'Namdi
New Bedford Academy	6315 Secor Rd	Lambertville, MI	48144-9411	734-854-5437	854-1573	K-8	Greg Sauter
New Beginnings Academy	211 E Michigan Ave	Ypsilanti, MI	48198-5677	734-481-9001	544-2706	K-5	Wayne Millette
New Branches S	256 Alger St SE	Grand Rapids, MI	49507-3409	616-243-4763	243-0305	K-6	Pamela Duffy
New City Academy	2130 W Holmes Rd Ste B	Lansing, MI	48910	517-272-3000	272-3544	K-8	Duane Shepherd
Northpointe Academy	53 Candler St	Highland Park, MI	48203-2827	313-868-2916	868-0443	K-8	Sharon Taylor
Northridge Academy	5306 North St	Flint, MI	48505-2927	810-785-8811	785-9844	K-8	Nat Burtley
North Saginaw Charter Academy	2332 Trautner Dr	Saginaw, MI	48604-9593	989-249-5400	249-5800	K-8	Tonya Reed
North Star Academy	PO Box 577	Ishpeming, MI	49849	906-226-0156	226-0167	9-12	Mary St. Clair
North Star Academy - Polaris MS	PO Box 577	Marquette, MI	49855-0577	906-226-0156	226-0167	7-8	Deborah White
Northwest Academy	115 W Hurlbut St	Charlevoix, MI	49720-1510	231-547-9000	547-9464	K-12	Cindy Romero
Nsoroma Institute	22180 Parklawn St	Oak Park, MI	48237-2674	248-541-2548	541-2594	K-8	Malik Yakini
Oakland Academy	6325 Oakland Dr	Portage, MI	49024	269-324-8951	324-8974	K-6	Melissa Dahlinger
Oakland International Academy	6111 Miller St	Detroit, MI	48211-1552	313-347-0246		6-12	Adnan Aabed
Oakland International Academy	4001 Miller St	Detroit, MI	48211-1554	313-923-0790	923-0927	K-5	James Honey
Ojibwe Charter S	11507 W Industrial Dr	Brimley, MI	49715-9087	906-248-2530	248-2532	K-10	Ralph Crosslin
Old Redford Academy ES	17195 Redford St	Detroit, MI	48219-3259	313-532-7510	543-2055	PK-6	Tiffany Crayton
Old Redford Academy MS	7000 W Outer Dr	Detroit, MI	48235-3166	313-653-3888	653-4855	7-8	Rosalind Bratwaite
Old Redford Academy Prep HS	8001 W Outer Dr	Detroit, MI	48235-3293	313-543-3080	543-3129	9-12	Danielle Jackson
Outlook Academy	310 Thomas St	Allegan, MI	49010-9158	269-686-8227	686-7036	5-10	Mike Hagerty
Pansophia Academy	52 Abbott Ave	Coldwater, MI	49036-1430	517-279-4686	279-0089	K-12	Tom Dove
Paragon Charter Academy	3750 McCain Rd	Jackson, MI	49201-7675	517-750-9500	750-9501	K-8	Kathy J. Watson
Paramount Charter Academy	3624 S Westnedge Ave	Kalamazoo, MI	49008-2969	269-553-6400	553-6401	K-8	Sharon Lockett-Gibson
Plymouth Educational Center S	1460 E Forest Ave	Detroit, MI	48207-1000	313-831-3280	831-5766	PK-8	Phyllis A. Ross
Pontiac Academy of Excellence	196 Oakland Ave	Pontiac, MI	48343	248-745-9420	745-9485	K-12	Todd Evans
Powell Academy	4800 Coplin St	Detroit, MI	48215-2109	313-823-5791	823-3410	K-8	D. Badger
Presque Isle Academy	PO Box 731	Onaway, MI	49765-0731	989-733-6708	733-6701	9-12	Rick Bongard
Prevail Academy	353 Cass Ave	Mount Clemens, MI	48043-2112	586-783-0173	783-0179	K-7	Catherine Witt
Public Safety Academy	PO Box 1500	Marysville, MI	48040-8000	810-364-8990	364-8139	11-12	Patrick Yanik
Reh Academy	2201 Owen St	Saginaw, MI	48601-3466	989-753-2349	753-1819	K-8	Diane Hofman
Renaissance Public S Academy	2797 S Isabella Rd	Mount Pleasant, MI	48858-2067	989-773-9889	772-4503	K-8	David Krause
Richfield Public School Academy	3807 N Center Rd	Flint, MI	48506-2642	810-736-1281	736-2326	K-8	Gareth Volz
Ridge Park Charter Academy	4120 Camelot Ridge Dr SE	Grand Rapids, MI	49546-2432	616-222-0093	222-0138	K-8	David King
Riverside Academy	7124 Miller Rd	Dearborn, MI	48126-1918	313-586-0200	586-0201	K-5	Eman Radha
Riverside Academy	6409 Schaefer Rd	Dearborn, MI	48126-2212	313-945-6504	945-1976	6-12	Albert Harp
Ross Charter Academy	8525 Cole Dr	Warren, MI	48093-5239	586-575-9418	575-9876	K-8	Thomas Smith
Ross Hill Academy	3111 Elmwood St	Detroit, MI	48207-2418	313-922-8088	922-2015	K-7	Nellie Williams
Ross Hill Junior Academy	317 Harper Ave	Detroit, MI	48202-3500	313-875-2207	875-9462	8-12	Nellie Williams
Saginaw County Transition Academy	919 Veterans Memorial Pkwy	Saginaw, MI	48601-1432	989-752-6176	752-6280	7-12	William Pagel
Saginaw Learn to Earn Academy	PO Box 5679	Saginaw, MI	48603-0679	989-399-7400	399-7484	10-12	Richard Beck
Saginaw Preparatory Academy	5173 Lodge St	Saginaw, MI	48601-6829	989-752-9600	752-9618	PK-6	Pamela Williams
St. Clair County Academy of Style	PO Box 1500	Marysville, MI	48040-8000	810-364-8990	364-8139	11-12	Patrick Yanik
St. Clair County Intervention Academy	PO Box 1500	Marysville, MI	48040-8000	810-364-8990	364-7474	6-12	Denice Lapish
St. Clair County Learning Academy	PO Box 1500	Marysville, MI	48040-8000	810-364-8990	364-7474	6-12	Denice Lapish
Sankofa Shule Public S Academy	4817 Bristol St	Lansing, MI	48910-6125	517-394-4023	394-4544	K-8	Saleef Kafajouffe
South Arbor Charter Academy	8200 Carpenter Rd	Ypsilanti, MI	48197-9800	734-528-2821	528-2829	K-8	Timothy DiLaura

School	Address	City,State	Zip code	Telephone	Fax	Grade	Contact
Star International Academy	24425 Hass St	Dearborn Hts, MI	48127-3275	313-724-8990	724-8994	K-12	Anita Hassan
Stockwell Academy	9758 E Highland Rd	Howell, MI	48843-9098	810-632-2200	632-2201	K-8	Shelley Stockwell
Summit Academy	30100 Olmstead Rd	Flat Rock, MI	48134-9619	734-379-6810	379-6745	K-8	Erin Avery
Summit Academy HS	18601 Middlebelt Rd	Romulus, MI	48174	734-955-1730	955-1737	9-12	Jason Hamstra
Summit Academy MS	18601 Middlebelt Rd	Romulus, MI	48174	734-955-1712	955-1729	6-8	Sally Emerson
Summit Academy North	28697 Sibley Rd	Romulus, MI	48174-9736	734-789-1428	789-1431	K-5	Marie Maci
Sunrise Educational Center	686 Aulerich Rd	East Tawas, MI	48730	989-362-2945	362-7968	K-8	Julie Bather
Three Oaks Public School Academy	1212 Kingsley St	Muskegon, MI	49442-4025	231-767-3365	777-9815	PK-10	Sheila Pantlind
Threshold Academy	PO Box 113	Greenville, MI	48838-0113	616-761-2296	761-2298	K-6	Mary Boots
Timberland Charter Academy	2574 McLaughlin Ave	Muskegon, MI	49442-4439	231-767-9700	767-9710	K-8	Juanita Preston
Timbuktu Academy of Science & Technology	10800 E Canfield St	Detroit, MI	48214-1601	313-823-6000	823-9748	K-8	Ife Kilimanjaro
Toussaint Academy	2450 S Beatrice St	Detroit, MI	48217-1631	313-383-1485	383-6532	K-8	Cynthia Moore
Traverse Bay Community S	7224 Supply Rd	Traverse City, MI	49686-9400	231-947-7474	947-7667	K-8	Mark Child
Trillium Academy	15740 Rancho Rd	Taylor, MI	48180	734-374-8222	374-5025	K-9	Angela Romanowski
Triumph Academy	3000 Vivian Rd	Monroe, MI	48162-8600	734-240-2610	240-2785	K-7	Tim Lenahan
Tri-Valley Academy of Arts and Academics	2140 Valley St	Muskegon, MI	49444-1261	231-722-7118	727-0042	PK-8	Jaronique Benjamin
Universal Academy	4612 Lonyo St	Detroit, MI	48210-2105	313-581-5006	581-5514	K-12	Nawal Hamadeh
Universal Learning Academy	22579 Ann Arbor Trl	Dearborn Hts, MI	48127-2507	313-724-8060	724-8082	K-3	Halim Ahmed
University Preparatory Academy ES	957 Holden St	Detroit, MI	48202-3443	313-874-9800		K-5	Doug Ross
University Preparatory Academy HS	600 Antoinette St	Detroit, MI	48202-3457	313-874-4340	874-4510	9-12	Doug Ross
University Preparatory Academy MS	5310 Saint Antoine St	Detroit, MI	48202-4131	313-831-0100	831-4197	6-8	Doug Ross
Vanderbilt Charter Academy	301 W 16th St	Holland, MI	49423-3329	616-820-5050	820-5051	K-8	Ivan J. Kraker
Vanguard Charter Academy	1620 52nd St SW	Wyoming, MI	49519-9629	616-538-3630	538-3646	K-8	Kim Blaszak
Victory Academy Charter S	855 Jefferson St	Ypsilanti, MI	48197-5209	734-485-7040	485-9102	K-5	Kevin Whelan
Vista Charter Academy	711 32nd St SE	Grand Rapids, MI	49548-2307	616-246-6920	246-6930	K-8	Joe Grandy
Voyageur Academy	4321 Military St	Detroit, MI	48210-2451	313-361-4180	361-4770	K-6	Rod Adkins
Walden Green Day S	17771 W Spring Lake Rd	Spring Lake, MI	49456-1447	616-842-4523	842-4522	K-8	Tom Hicks
Walker Charter Academy	1801 3 Mile Rd NW	Grand Rapids, MI	49544-1445	616-785-2700	785-0894	K-8	Steve Bagley
Walton Charter Academy	744 E Walton Blvd	Pontiac, MI	48340-1361	248-371-9300	371-1642	K-8	April Butler
Warrendale Charter Academy	19400 Sawyer St	Detroit, MI	48228-3330	313-240-4200	240-4203	K-8	Brigitte Brown
Washtenaw Technical Middle College	PO Box D-1	Ann Arbor, MI	48106-1610	734-973-3410	973-3464	10-12	Lee Schleicher
Wavecrest Career Academy	633 Apple Ave	Holland, MI	49423-5434	616-393-7662	393-7633	9-12	Cynthia McCartney
Wells Academy	281 S Fair Ave	Benton Harbor, MI	49022-7219	269-926-2885		K-6	P. Renene Price
West MI Acad. Environmental Science	4463 Leonard St NW	Grand Rapids, MI	49534-2138	616-791-7320	791-1446	K-12	Laura Otten
West Michigan Acad of Arts & Academics	17350 Hazel St	Spring Lake, MI	49456-1222	616-844-9961	844-9941	PK-8	Floyd Strandberg
Weston Technical Academy	22930 Chippewa St	Detroit, MI	48219-1161	313-387-6038	387-6180	K-12	Fiona Hinds
West Village Academy	3530 Westwood St	Dearborn, MI	48124-3100	313-274-9200	274-0062	K-5	Brett Heflin
West Village Academy - North Campus	9331 Grandville Ave	Detroit, MI	48228-1798	313-835-8410	835-8427	6-8	Ghassan Taha
White Pine Academy	PO Box 495	Leslie, MI	49251-0495	517-589-8961	589-9194	K-8	Jared Vickers
Winans Academy of Performing Arts ES	9740 McKinney St	Detroit, MI	48224-2503	313-640-4611		K-5	R. Hayward
Winans Academy Performing Arts HS	7616 E Nevada St	Detroit, MI	48234	313-365-5578	365-5684	9-12	H. McKee
Winans Academy Performing Arts MS	7616 E Nevada St	Detroit, MI	48234	313-365-5578	365-5684	6-8	R. Hayward
Windemere Park Charter Academy	3100 W Saginaw St	Lansing, MI	48917-2307	517-327-0700	327-0800	K-8	Jeffrey Whipple
Windover HS	32 S Homer Rd	Midland, MI	48640-8383	989-832-0852	839-7699	9-12	Terrie Kaiser
Woodland Park Academy	2083 E Grand Blanc Rd	Grand Blanc, MI	48439-8112	810-695-4710	695-1658	K-8	Michele Baskin
Woodmont Academy	25175 Code Rd	Southfield, MI	48033-5805	248-352-1805	352-1810	K-6	Ronald Newton
Woodward Academy	951 E Lafayette St	Detroit, MI	48207-2999	313-961-2108	961-1625	K-8	Georgia Hubbard
YMCA Service Learning Academy	21605 W 7 Mile Rd	Detroit, MI	48219-1810	313-541-7619	541-7656	K-8	Eylastine Green-Roberts

Minnesota

School	Address	City,State	Zip code	Telephone	Fax	Grade	Contact
Abdulle Academy	PO Box 1052	Rochester, MN	55903-1052	507-252-5995		K-8	Farhan Hussein
Academia Cesar Chavez	1800 Ames Ave	Saint Paul, MN	55119-4898	651-778-2940	778-2942	K-12	Ramona de Rosales
Academy of Biosciences	4056 Central Ave NE	Columbia Hts, MN	55421-2916	763-571-5039		5-12	Mari Bergerson
Achieve Language Academy	2169 Stillwater Ave E	Saint Paul, MN	55119-3552	651-738-4875	738-8268	K-5	Mary Apuli
Agricultural & Food Sciences Academy	100 Vadnais Blvd	Saint Paul, MN	55127-4036	651-209-3910	209-3911	9-12	Becky Meyer
Artech Charter S	PO Box 349	Northfield, MN	55057-0349	507-663-8806	663-8802	6-12	Timothy Goodwin
Ascension Academy Charter S	1704 Dupont Ave N	Minneapolis, MN	55411-3219	612-465-8121	465-8125	9-12	Mary Taylor
Augsburg Fairview Academy /Health Career	1326 Energy Park Dr	Saint Paul, MN	55108-5202	612-333-1614		9-12	Dr. William Spira
Aurora Charter S	2520 Minnehaha Ave	Minneapolis, MN	55404-4118	612-870-3891	870-4287	K-3	Cheryl Avina
Avalon Charter S	1745 University Ave W	Saint Paul, MN	55104	651-649-5495	649-5462	9-12	Carrie Bakken
Beacon Academy	12325 Highway 55	Plymouth, MN	55441-4750	763-546-9999	593-9382	K-5	Jordan Ford
Beacon Preparatory S	12325 Highway 55	Plymouth, MN	55441-4750	763-546-9999	593-9382	6-8	Robert Schreck
Birch Grove Community S	PO Box 2242	Tofte, MN	55615-2242	218-663-0170		K-5	Lisa Hoff
Bluesky Online Charter S	33 Wentworth Ave E Ste 300	Saint Paul, MN	55118-3433	651-642-0888	642-0435	7-12	Tom Ellis
Bluffview Montessori S	1321 Gilmore Ave	Winona, MN	55987-2459	507-452-2807	452-6869	K-8	Mary Hallman
Cedar Riverside Community Charter S	1610 S 6th St Ste 100	Minneapolis, MN	55454	612-339-5767	339-2951	K-8	Shelton Rucker
City Academy	958 Jessie St	Saint Paul, MN	55130-4058	651-298-4624	292-6511	9-12	Milo Cutter
Community of Peace Academy	471 Magnolia Ave E	Saint Paul, MN	55130-3849	651-776-5151	771-4841	K-12	Karen Rusthoven
Concordia Creative Learning Academy	1355 Pierce Butler Rte #100	Saint Paul, MN	55104	651-649-5795	649-5799	K-6	Mary Donaldson
Crosslake Community S	PO Box 1079	Crosslake, MN	56442-1079	218-692-5437	692-5437	K-6	David Skogen
Cyber Village Academy	1336 Energy Park Dr Ste 2	Saint Paul, MN	55108-6110	651-523-7170	523-7113	4-8	Bob Bilyk
Cygnus Academy	440 Pierce St	Anoka, MN	55303-1604	763-998-4624		6-12	Virginia Heesch
Dakota Academy	1301 Riverwood Dr	Burnsville, MN	55337-1547	952-736-1000		6-12	Faith Crump
Dakota Area Community Charter S	220 Golden Rule Rd	Dakota, MN	55925-7103	507-643-6869	643-6953	K-5	Darin Shepardson
Discovery Public S	126 8th St NW	Faribault, MN	55021-4241	507-331-5423	331-2618	7-12	Steve Darkow
Dugsi Academy	1821 University Ave W	Saint Paul, MN	55104	651-642-0667	642-0668	K-5	Mohamed Osman
Duluth Edison Charter S	1750 Kenwood Ave	Duluth, MN	55811-2224	218-728-9556	728-2075	K-12	Bonnie Jorgenson
Eagle Ridge Academy Charter S	7255 Flying Cloud Dr	Eden Prairie, MN	55344-3549	952-746-7760	746-7765	6-12	Judy Ingeson
E.C.H.O. Charter S	PO Box 158	Echo, MN	56237-0158	507-925-4143	925-4165	K-8	Larry Schueler
Eci' Nompa Woonspe' Charter S	PO Box 10	Morton, MN	56270-0010	507-697-9055	697-9065	K-12	Tim Blue
Edvisions Off Campus S	501 Main St	Henderson, MN	56044	507-248-3738		9-12	Keven Kroehler
El Colegio Charter S	4137 Bloomington Ave	Minneapolis, MN	55407-3332	612-728-5728	728-5790	9-12	David Greenberg
Emily Charter S	PO Box 40	Emily, MN	56447-0040	218-763-3401	763-4401	K-6	Virginia Brannan
Excell Academy for Higher Learning	6510 Zane Ave N	Brooklyn Park, MN	55429	763-533-0500	533-0508	PK-3	Sabrina Williams
Face to Face Academy	1165 Arcade St	Saint Paul, MN	55106-2615	651-772-5555	772-5566	8-12	Mary Planten-Krell
Four Directions Charter S	1113 W Broadway Ave	Minneapolis, MN	55411-2505	612-588-0183	588-1844	9-12	Ronald Buckanaga
Fraser Academy	1601 Laurel Ave	Minneapolis, MN	55403-1205	612-465-8600	465-8603	K-5	Linda Silrum
Friendship Acad of Fine Arts Charter S	310 E 38th St	Minneapolis, MN	55409	612-879-6703	879-6707	K-4	Ethel Norwood
Great Expectations S	PO Box 310	Grand Marais, MN	55604-0310	218-387-9322	387-9344	K-8	Peter James
Great River Education Center	400 Great Oak Dr Ste 108	Waite Park, MN	56387-2512	320-258-3117	258-3118	7-12	Alonzo Symalla
Great River S	1326 Energy Park Dr	Saint Paul, MN	55108-5202	651-305-2780	305-2781	7-12	Ben Moudry
Green Isle Community S	PO Box 277	Green Isle, MN	55338-0277	507-326-7144	326-5434	K-6	Kristen Kinzler
Harbor City International S	332 W Michigan St Ste 300	Duluth, MN	55802-1644	218-722-7574	625-6068	9-12	Chris Hazleton
Heart of the Earth S	1209 4th St SE	Minneapolis, MN	55414-2084	612-331-8862	331-1747	K-12	Joel Pourier
Higher Ground Academy	1381 Marshall Ave	Saint Paul, MN	55104-6353	651-645-1000	645-2100	K-12	Bill Wilson
High School for Recording Arts	550 Vandalia St	Saint Paul, MN	55114	651-287-0890	287-0891	9-12	David Ellis
Hmong Academy	1515 Brewster St	Saint Paul, MN	55108-2612	612-209-8002	209-8003	9-12	Christianna Hang
Hope Community Academy	720 Payne Ave	Saint Paul, MN	55130-4127	651-796-4500	796-4599	K-6	MayChy Vu
Jennings Experiential HS	1919 University Ave W	Saint Paul, MN	55104	651-649-5403	649-5490	9-12	Bill Zimneiwicz
Kaleidoscope Charter S	21755 129th Ave N	Rogers, MN	55374-4639	763-428-1890	428-1691	K-8	Michelle Strait
La Crescent Montessori Academy	28 S Oak St	La Crescent, MN	55947-1332	507-895-4054	895-4064	K-7	
Lafayette Public Charter S	PO Box 125	Lafayette, MN	56054-0125	507-228-8943	228-2509	K-8	Andrea Harder
Lakes Area Charter S	601 W Nokomis St	Osakis, MN	56360-8203	320-859-5302	859-5342	7-12	Dennis Johnson
Lakes International Language Academy	246 11th Ave SE	Forest Lake, MN	55025	651-464-0771	464-4429	K-4	Cameron Hedlund
Lake Superior HS	5215 Rice Lake Rd	Duluth, MN	55803-8422	218-529-2468	279-3628	7-12	Mike Degen
Liberty HS	308 Northtown Dr NE	Blaine, MN	55434-1039	763-786-4799		9-12	Gary Knox
Lighthouse Academy of Nations	2600 E 26th St	Minneapolis, MN	55406-1201	612-722-2555	722-2274	9-12	Phil Lederman
Loveworks Academy for Arts	2225 Zenith Ave N	Golden Valley, MN	55422-3852	952-522-6830	522-6840	K-8	Patrice Dorral
Main Street S of Performing Arts	1320 Mainstreet	Hopkins, MN	55343-7497	952-224-1342	224-2955	9-12	Karen Charles
Math & Science Academy	8430 Woodbury Xing	Woodbury, MN	55125-9433	651-353-2317	578-7532	6-12	Paul Simone
Metro Deaf Charter S	265 W Lafayette Frontage Rd	Saint Paul, MN	55107-1628	651-224-3995	222-0939	K-8	Dyan Sherwood
Milroy Area Charter S	PO Box 129	Milroy, MN	56263-0129	507-336-2563	336-2568	K-4	Dan Deitte
Minneapolis Academy Charter S	5011 31st Ave S	Minneapolis, MN	55417-1405	612-455-1340	455-1345	5-8	Leon Cooper
Minnesota International MS	277 12th Ave N	Minneapolis, MN	55401-1026	612-821-6470	821-6477	5-8	Abdirashid Warsame
Minnesota Internship Center	1313 5th St SE Ste 208C	Minneapolis, MN	55414-4515	612-379-3900	379-3914	9-12	Kevin Byrne
Minnesota New Country S	PO Box 488	Henderson, MN	56044-0488	507-248-3353	248-3604	7-12	
Minnesota North Star Academy	1669 Arcade St	Saint Paul, MN	55106-1041	651-771-2000	771-2200	9-12	Jack Busenbark
Minnesota Online HS	1313 5th St SE	Minneapolis, MN	55414	612-227-8499		9-12	Julie Williams
Minnesota Transitions Charter S	2872 26th Ave S	Minneapolis, MN	55406-1529	612-722-9013	722-0013	K-12	Patty Brostrom
Naytahwaush Community S	PO Box 9	Naytahwaush, MN	56566-0009	218-935-5025	935-5263	K-6	John Eggers
Nerstrand Charter S	PO Box 156	Nerstrand, MN	55053-0156	507-333-6850	333-6870	K-5	Lauren Satrom
New Century Charter S	PO Box 484	Hutchinson, MN	55350-0484	320-234-3660	234-3668	7-12	Dave Conrad
New City S	229 13th Ave NE	Minneapolis, MN	55413-1117	612-623-3309	623-3319	K-6	Terrance Russ
New Discoveries Montessori Academy	126 N High Dr NE	Hutchinson, MN	55350-1249	320-583-1877		K-6	Allan Hoffman
New Heights Charter S	614 Mulberry St W	Stillwater, MN	55082-4858	651-439-1962	439-0716	K-12	Thomas Kearney
New Millenium Academy	1203 Bryant Ave N	Minneapolis, MN	55411-4087	612-377-6260	377-6261	K-8	Neng Heur

School	Address	City,State	Zip code	Telephone	Fax	Grade	Contact
New Spirit S	260 Edmund Ave	Saint Paul, MN	55103-1783	651-225-9177	225-2990	K-8	Walter Stull
New Visions Charter S	1800 2nd St NE	Minneapolis, MN	55418-4306	612-706-5566	706-5599	K-8	Bob DeBoer
Northern Lights Community S	PO Box 2829	Warba, MN	55793-2829	218-492-4400	492-4402	6-12	David Hagman
North Lakes Academy	255b 7th Ave NW	Forest Lake, MN	55025-1157	651-982-2773	464-6409	6-9	Jackie Saunders
North Shore Community S	5926 Ryan Rd	Duluth, MN	55804-9672	218-525-0663	525-0024	K-6	Sheri Camper
Northwest Passage HS	11288 Robinson Dr NW	Coon Rapids, MN	55433-3762	763-862-9223	862-9250	9-12	James Steckart
Nova Classical Academy	1668 Montreal Ave	Saint Paul, MN	55116-2469	651-227-8622	699-5959	K-12	John Greving
Odyssey Charter S	6201 Noble Ave N	Brooklyn Park, MN	55429-2483	763-971-8200	549-2380	K-9	Jim Redfield
PACT Charter S	7250 E Ramsey Pkwy	Ramsey, MN	55303-6902	763-712-4200	712-4201	K-12	Daniel DeBruyn
Paideia Academy Charter S	7200 147th St W	Apple Valley, MN	55124-9008	952-807-3713		K-8	Laura Jones
Partnership Academy	305 E 77th St Ste B	Minneapolis, MN	55423	612-866-3630	866-3640	K-7	Lisa Ladue
Pillager Area Charter S	PO Box 130	Pillager, MN	56473-0130	218-746-3875	746-3876	9-12	Mark Wolhart
Prairie Creek Community S	27695 Denmark Ave	Northfield, MN	55057-5333	507-645-9640	645-8234	K-5	Caroline Jones
Prairie Seeds Academy	2201 Girard Ave N	Minneapolis, MN	55411-2548	612-302-8555	302-9041	K-8	Ger Cha Yang
Recovery S of Southern MN	1225 Lincoln Ave	Owatonna, MN	55060-4029	507-214-2057		9-12	Lisa Orke
Ridgeway Community S	35564 County Road 12	Houston, MN	55943-4006	507-454-9566	454-9567	K-6	Jodi Dansingburg
RiverBend Academy	110 N 6th St	Mankato, MN	56001-4443	507-387-5524	387-5680	7-12	Beth Hannafin-Johnson
River Heights Charter S	60 Marie Ave E	West Saint Paul, MN	55118	651-457-7427	554-7611	9-12	Jill Wohlman
Riverway Learning Community Charter S	PO Box 43	Minnesota City, MN	55959-0043	507-689-2844	689-2834	PK-12	Laura Krause
Rochester Off Campus Charter HS	2364 Valleyhigh Dr NW	Rochester, MN	55901-7641	507-282-3325	282-0976	9-12	Jay Martini
Sage Academy Charter S	3900 85th Ave N	Brooklyn Park, MN	55443-1908	763-315-4020	315-4028	9-12	Diane Scholten
Saint Croix Preparatory Academy	216 Myrtle St W	Stillwater, MN	55082-4805	651-379-3160	379-3165	K-9	Jon Gutierrez
Saint Paul Conservatory Performing Art	75 5th St W	Saint Paul, MN	55102	651-290-2225	290-9000	9-12	Terry Tofte
Schoolcraft Learning Community S	PO Box 1685	Bemidji, MN	56619-1685	218-586-3284	586-3285	K-8	Scott Anderson
Seed Academy/Harvest Prep S	1300 Olson Memorial Hwy	Minneapolis, MN	55411	612-381-9743	377-2999	PK-6	Eric Mahmoud
Seven Hills Classical Academy	8600 Bloomington Ave	Bloomington, MN	55425-1920	952-426-6000	426-6020	K-8	Margaret O'Brien
Skills for Tomorrow HS	547 Wheeler St N	Saint Paul, MN	55104-3078	651-647-6000	645-2388	9-12	Claude Maddox
Sobriety HS	2233 University Ave W	Saint Paul, MN	55114	651-773-8378	748-5290	9-12	Lyle Taipale Ed.D.
Sojourner Truth Academy	3820 Emerson Ave N	Minneapolis, MN	55412-2039	612-588-3599	588-0217	K-8	Julie Guy
Soul Academy Charter S	333 S 12th St	Minneapolis, MN	55404-1496	612-872-0800	872-0814	K-4	Gilbert Hale
Southside Family Charter S	2123 Clinton Ave	Minneapolis, MN	55404-2650	612-872-8322	872-0612	K-8	Eliza Goodwin
Spectrum HS	605 6th St NW	Elk River, MN	55330	763-241-8703		9-12	Vanessa Spark
Stride Academy	1025 18th St N	Saint Cloud, MN	56303-1205	320-230-5340	253-0006	K-6	Dale Beutel
Studio Academy	415 16th St SW	Rochester, MN	55902-2125	507-529-1662	529-1643	10-12	Eric Holsen
Swan River Montessori Charter S	500 Maple St	Paynesville, MN	56362	763-271-7926	295-0075	K-6	Sandra Morrow
Tarek Ibn Ziyad Academy	4100 66th St E	Inver Grove, MN	55076-2230	651-457-7072	457-7190	K-5	Asad Zaman
TEAM Academy	501 Elm Ave E	Waseca, MN	56093-3360	507-835-1048		K-6	Chris Hering
Treknorth HS	2518 Hannah Ave NW	Bemidji, MN	56601-2110	218-444-1888	444-1893	7-12	Dan McKeon
Trio Wolf Creek Distance Learning	13750 Lake Blvd	Lindstrom, MN	55045-9361	651-213-2017	257-0576	4-12	Tracy Quarnstrom
Twin Cities Academy Charter S	426 Osceola Ave S	Saint Paul, MN	55102-3535	651-205-4797	205-4799	6-12	Liz Wynne
Twin Cities German Immersion S	1399 Eustis St	Saint Paul, MN	55108-1548	651-492-7106	789-0107	K-8	Mary Watkins
Twin Cities International ES	277 12th Ave N	Minneapolis, MN	55401-1026	612-821-6470	821-6477	K-4	Randal Eckart
Ubah Medical Academy Charter S	277 12th Ave N	Minneapolis, MN	55401-1026	612-600-7833	821-6477	9-12	Denny Hartman
Urban Academy Charter S	133 7th St E	Saint Paul, MN	55101	651-215-9419	215-9571	K-6	Mongsher Ly
Vessey Leadership S	33 Wentworth Ave E Ste 100	Saint Paul, MN	55118-3432	651-206-2980		9-12	Doug Trenda
Voyageurs Expeditionary HS	PO Box 727	Bemidji, MN	56619-0727	218-444-3130	444-3126	9-12	Karen Baldwin
Watershed HS	2344 Nicollet Ave Ste 200	Minneapolis, MN	55404-3373	612-871-4363	871-1004	9-12	Scott Cole
Woodson Institute for Excellence	2620 Russell Ave N	Minneapolis, MN	55411-1725	612-522-4022	522-4012	K-6	LaTanya Washington
World Learner Charter S	112050 Hundertmark Rd	Chaska, MN	55318-2817	952-368-7398	368-6094	K-6	Randi Shapiro
Worthington Area Language Academy	PO Box 185	Bigelow, MN	56117-0185	507-683-2004	683-2013	K-6	Randy Haley
Yankton Country S	PO Box 406	Balaton, MN	56115-0406	507-734-2677	734-2678	9-12	Cynthia Duus
Yinghua Academy	1355 Pierce Butler Rte	Saint Paul, MN	55104-1359	651-494-8666		K-4	Betsy Lueth

Mississippi

School	Address	City,State	Zip code	Telephone	Fax	Grade	Contact
Hayes Cooper Center	500 N Martin Luther King Jr	Merigold, MS	38759-9632	662-748-2734	748-2735	PK-6	Beverly Hardy

Missouri

School	Address	City,State	Zip code	Telephone	Fax	Grade	Contact
Academie Lafayette S	6903 Oak St	Kansas City, MO	64113-2530	816-361-7735	361-5788	K-8	Gerry Lukaska
Academy of Kansas City	2015 E 72nd St	Kansas City, MO	64132-1756	816-523-4707	523-5449	K-8	Vonnelle Middleton
Allen Village S	706 W 42nd St	Kansas City, MO	64111-3120	816-931-0177	561-4640	K-8	Phyllis Washington
Alta Vista Charter S	1722 Holly St	Kansas City, MO	64108-2217	816-471-2582	471-2139	9-12	Eduardo Mendez
Banneker Charter Academy Technology	8310 Holmes Rd	Kansas City, MO	64131-2254	816-926-9110	926-0115	K-8	Dr. Marion Brown
Bosco Education Center	531 Garfield Ave	Kansas City, MO	64124-1513	816-691-2915	691-2927	9-12	Bill Elliott
Brookside Charter Academy	5220 Troost Ave	Kansas City, MO	64110-2546	816-531-2192	756-3055	K-6	Millie Krna
Confluence Academy-Old North St. Louis	3017 N 13th St	Saint Louis, MO	63107-3924	314-241-1110	241-1115	K-7	William Polite
Confluence Academy-South City Campus	4235 S Compton Ave	Saint Louis, MO	63111-1129	314-832-8600		K-8	Sharon Traylor
Confluence Academy-Walnut Park Campus	5421 Thekla Ave	Saint Louis, MO	63120-2513	314-383-8900		K-7	Vanessa Garry
Construction Careers Center	1224 Grattan St	Saint Louis, MO	63104-2922	314-588-9991	588-1982	9-12	Dr. Michael Musick
Genesis S	3800 E 44th St	Kansas City, MO	64130-2183	816-921-0775	921-4268	6-9	Alan Dubois
Hedgeman Lyle Academy	1509 Washington Ave #800S	Saint Louis, MO	63103	314-436-1345	436-3746	K-9	D'Anne Tombs-Shelton
Hogan Preparatory Academy	1221 E Meyer Blvd	Kansas City, MO	64131-1207	816-444-3464	363-0473	9-12	Bernard Williams
Lamb ES	1000 Charlotte St	Kansas City, MO	64106-3051	816-221-0043	221-0937	K-6	
Lift for Life Academy	1731 S Broadway	Saint Louis, MO	63104-4050	314-436-2337	231-1299	6-8	Katrice Noble
Paideia Academy	5223 N 20th St	Saint Louis, MO	63107-1138	314-534-1085	531-0815	K-8	James Gant
Parks ES	3715 Wyoming St	Kansas City, MO	64111-3945	816-753-6700	753-3436	K-5	Kajuan Cummings
St. Louis Charter S	5279 Fyler Ave	Saint Louis, MO	63139-1300	314-645-9600	645-9700	K-8	Tracy Garrett
Scuola Vita Nuova	544 Wabash Ave	Kansas City, MO	64124-1747	816-231-5788	231-5181	K-8	Nicole King
Thomas Academy	201 E Armour Blvd	Kansas City, MO	64111-1205	816-531-7144	753-8856	K-8	Leah Martisko
Tolbert Community Academy	3400 Paseo Blvd	Kansas City, MO	64109-2429	816-561-0114	561-1015	K-8	Vivian Roper
University Academy	6801 Holmes Rd	Kansas City, MO	64131-1382	816-412-5900	412-0322	K-12	Cheri Shannon
Urban Community Leadership Academy	1524 Paseo Blvd	Kansas City, MO	64108-1622	816-483-8035	483-8998	5-9	Joyce McGautha

Nevada

School	Address	City,State	Zip code	Telephone	Fax	Grade	Contact
Academy for Career Education	2800 Vassar St	Reno, NV	89502-3214	775-324-3900	324-3901	10-12	Silvia Marin
Agassi Academy	1201 W Lake Mead Blvd	Las Vegas, NV	89106-2411	702-948-6000	948-6002	K-12	Roy Parker
Bailey Charter ES	1090 Bresson Ave	Reno, NV	89502-2625	775-323-6767	323-6799	K-6	Carl Meibergen
Carson Montessori S	2263 Mouton Dr	Carson City, NV	89706-0446	775-887-9500	887-9502	K-6	George Barnes
Coral Academy of Science	1350 E 9th St	Reno, NV	89512-2904	775-323-2332	323-2366	K-12	Ben Karaduman
Explore Knowledge Academy	4801 S Sandhill Rd	Las Vegas, NV	89121-6020	702-870-5032	870-5032	K-12	Dr. Joan Sando
High Desert Montessori Charter S	2590 Orovada St	Reno, NV	89512-2119	775-624-2800	624-2801	PK-8	Carol Andrew
I Can Do Anything Charter HS	1195 Corporate Blvd Ste C	Reno, NV	89502-2363	775-857-1544	857-6825	9-12	Jill Wells
Innovations International Charter S	1600 E Oakey Blvd	Las Vegas, NV	89104-3334	702-216-4337	216-4353	K-12	Dr. Connie Malin
Keystone Academy Charter HS	PO Box 7750	Sandy Valley, NV	89019	702-723-1966	723-1967	9-12	Al Oppegard
Mariposa Academy of Language & Learning	3875 Glen St	Reno, NV	89502-4803	775-826-4040	826-4030	K-6	Aida Tadeo
Nevada State HS	1125 Nevada State Dr	Henderson, NV	89002-9455	702-992-2017	566-5793	11-12	Dr. Wendi Hawk
Odyssey Charter S	2251 S Jones Blvd	Las Vegas, NV	89146	702-257-0578	259-7793	K-12	Dr. Craig Butz
One Hundred Academy of Excellence	2341 Comstock Dr	North Las Vegas, NV	89032-3512	702-636-2551	636-9475	K-12	Juan Henderson
Rainshadow Community Charter HS	434 Washington St	Reno, NV	89503-4323	775-322-5566	322-5509	9-12	Carol White Ed.D.
Sierra Crest Academy	PO Box 2439	Minden, NV	89423-2439	775-783-9002	552-9815	K-12	David Brackett
Sierra Nevada Academy	13880 Stead Blvd	Reno, NV	89506-1579	775-677-4500	677-4441	K-8	Kim Regan-Goatley
Silver State HS	3719 N Carson St	Carson City, NV	89706-1934	775-883-7900	883-9130	9-12	Steve Knight
Team A Charter HS	981 Bible Way	Reno, NV	89502-2122	775-323-8555	323-8557	9-12	Judy Kroshus

New Hampshire

School	Address	City,State	Zip code	Telephone	Fax	Grade	Contact
Academy for Science & Design	20 University Dr	Nashua, NH	03063-1323	603-577-6600		7-12	Michael Fishbein
Cocheco Arts and Technology Academy	37A Province Ln	Barrington, NH	03825-3937	603-664-9671	664-9679	9-12	Deborah Byrne
Equestrian Academy Charter S	PO Box 808	Rochester, NH	03866-0808	603-335-6900	224-8366	9-12	Susan Hollins
Franklin Career Academy Charter S	PO Box 70	Franklin, NH	03235-0070	603-934-9200	934-9206	7-12	Walter Anacki
Great Bay eLearning Charter S	56 Linden St	Exeter, NH	03833-4104	603-775-8638	775-8988	8-12	Cheryl McDonough
New Heights Charter Academy	27 Wallace Rd	Goffstown, NH	03045-1824	603-497-4841	497-5257	9-12	Mark Roth
North Country Charter Academy	260 Cottage St Ste A	Littleton, NH	03561-4137	603-444-1535	444-9843	7-12	Lisa Lavoie
Seacoast Charter S	PO Box 892	Exeter, NH	03833-0892	603-772-5019	772-5019	3-6	Emily Hamilton

New Jersey

School	Address	City,State	Zip code	Telephone	Fax	Grade	Contact
Academy Charter HS	1725 Main St	South Belmar, NJ	07719-3051	732-681-8377	681-8375	9-12	Mary Jo McKinley
Bergen Arts and Science Charter S	200 MacArthur Ave	Garfield, NJ	07026	201-880-6256	621-4409	K-8	Bekir Duz
Burch Charter S of Excellence	3003 Washington St 3rd Fl	Newark, NJ	07102	973-643-0300	624-1265	K-1	Veronica Ray
Camden Academy Charter HS	879 Beideman Ave	Camden, NJ	08105-4227	856-365-1000	365-1005	9-9	Dr. Joseph Conway
Camden's Pride Charter S	879 Beideman Ave	Camden, NJ	08105-4227	856-365-1000	365-1005	K-4	Rebecca Brinkman
Camden's Promise Charter S	879 Beideman Ave	Camden, NJ	08105-4227	856-365-1000	365-1005	5-8	Dr. Joe Conway
Central Jersey Arts Charter S	35 Watchung Ave	Plainfield, NJ	07060-1207	908-753-0030	753-0032	K-5	Dennis Cruz
Central Jersey College Prep Charter S	1001 Finnegan Ln	North Brunswick, NJ	08902-1056	732-821-4671	821-4675	7-12	Eric Altunkaya
ChARTer-TECHnical HS	413 New Rd	Somers Point, NJ	08244-2143	609-926-7458	926-8472	9-12	Janice Strigh

School	Address	City,State	Zip code	Telephone	Fax	Grade	Contact
Classical Academy Charter S of Clifton	20 Valley Rd	Clifton, NJ	07013-1030	973-278-7707	278-7720	6-8	Vincent DeRosa
Community Charter S of Paterson	32 Spruce St	Paterson, NJ	07501	973-413-1600	413-1640	K-3	Robert Guarasci
CREATE Charter S	164 Lembeck Ave	Jersey City, NJ	07305-3803	201-413-1500	413-1800	9-12	Stephen S. Lipski
Discovery Charter S	303 Washington St	Newark, NJ	07102	973-623-0222	623-0024	4-8	Irene Hall
D.U.E. Season Charter S	1000 Atlantic Ave Ste 524	Camden, NJ	08104	856-225-0511	668-2196	K-12	Dr. Doris Carpenter
East Orange Community Charter S	99 Washington St	East Orange, NJ	07017-1006	973-996-0400	996-0398	K-4	Harvin Dash
Elysian Charter S	301 Garden St Ste 5	Hoboken, NJ	07030-5895	201-876-0102	876-9576	K-6	Carol Stock
Englewood on the Palisades Charter S	65 W Demarest Ave	Englewood, NJ	07631-2316	201-569-9765	568-9576	K-5	Anthony Barckett
Environment Comm Opportunity Charter S	817 Carpenter St	Camden, NJ	08102-1132	856-963-2627	963-2628	K-12	Antoinette Dendtler
Fisher S of Advanced Studies	31 Chancery Ln	Trenton, NJ	08618-4805	609-656-1444	656-0999	6-12	G. Dallas Dixon
Foundation Academy Charter S	PO Box 180	Trenton, NJ	08601-0180	609-920-9200	920-9205	5-8	Ronald Brady
Freedom Academy Charter S	1400 Collings Rd	Camden, NJ	08104-3113	856-962-0766	962-0769	5-7	Ruth Green-Brown
Galloway Community Charter S	112 S New York Rd	Galloway, NJ	08205-9608	609-652-7118	652-3640	K-6	Deborah Nataloni
Golden Door Charter S	180 9th St	Jersey City, NJ	07302-1703	201-795-4400	795-3308	K-8	Brian Stiles
Gray Charter S	55 Liberty St	Newark, NJ	07102-4815	973-824-6661	824-2296	K-8	Verna Gray
Greater Brunswick Charter S	429B Joyce Kilmer Ave	New Brunswick, NJ	08901-3322	732-448-1052	448-1055	K-9	Rick Pressler
Greater Newark Charter S	72 Central Ave	Newark, NJ	07102-1905	973-242-3543	242-5792	5-8	Peter Turnamian
Hoboken Charter S	4th & Garden St 3rd Floor	Hoboken, NJ	07030	201-963-0222	963-0880	PK-12	Donald DePascale
Hope Academy Charter S	700 Grand Ave	Asbury Park, NJ	07712-6629	732-988-4227	988-9218	K-8	Alexis Harris
International Charter S of Trenton	105 Grand St	Trenton, NJ	08611-2417	609-394-3111	394-3116	K-5	Melissa Benford
Jersey City Community Charter S	128 Danforth Ave	Jersey City, NJ	07305-2626	201-433-2288	433-5803	K-8	Carletta Martin-Goldston
Lady Liberty Academy Charter S	PO Box 180	Newark, NJ	07101-0180	973-623-9005	623-4088	K-8	Fiona Thomas
LEAP Academy University Charter S	549 Cooper St	Camden, NJ	08102-1210	856-614-0400	342-7190	K-9	Gloria Hancock
Learning Community Charter S	1 Canal St	Jersey City, NJ	07302-4330	201-332-0900	332-4981	K-5	Susan Grierson
Liberty Academy Charter S	211 Sherman Ave	Jersey City, NJ	07307-2040	201-217-6771	217-6772	K-8	Dr. Walter Uszenski
Mercer Arts Charter S	207 Laurel Cir	Princeton, NJ	08540-2719	609-921-7698	921-0563	9-12	Barbara Taylor
New Horizons Community Charter S	45 Hayes St	Newark, NJ	07103-3019	973-848-0400	596-0984	K-5	Andre Hollis
North Star Academy Charter S	10 Washington Pl	Newark, NJ	07102-3106	973-642-0101	642-5800	5-12	Carol Lejnieks
Oceanside Charter S	1750 Bacharach Blvd	Atlantic City, NJ	08401-4308	609-348-3485	348-5951	PK-8	Jeanine Middleton
PACE Charter School of Hamilton	1949 Hamilton Ave	Hamilton, NJ	08619-3736	609-587-2288	587-8483	K-3	Michael Mikitish
Paterson Charter S Science & Tech	69-75 Lehigh Ave	Paterson, NJ	07503-1728	973-247-0600	247-9924	6-9	Frank Kosar
PleasanTech Academy Charter S	535 Mrtn Luther King Jr Ave	Pleasantville, NJ	08232	609-383-1717	484-1085	K-8	Diane Osbourne
Pride Academy Charter S	PO Box 3745	Newark, NJ	07103-0745	973-991-2410	350-9989	5-8	Amanda Hayes
Princeton Charter S	100 Bunn Dr	Princeton, NJ	08540-2821	609-924-0575	924-7183	K-8	Charles Marsee
Queen City Academy Charter S	815 W 7th St	Plainfield, NJ	07063-1449	908-753-4700	753-4816	K-8	Dr. Char Stanko
Red Bank Charter S	58 Oakland St	Red Bank, NJ	07701-1104	732-450-9799	936-1923	K-8	Meredith Pennotti
Ridge & Valley Charter S	1234 State Route 94	Blairstown, NJ	07825-4115	908-362-1114	362-6680	K-8	David Wyllie
Sanford Charter S	15 James St	Newark, NJ	07102-2001	973-297-0048	297-0700	K-5	Fredricka Bey
Schomburg Charter S	508 Grand St	Jersey City, NJ	07302-4103	201-451-7770	451-1770	K-5	Dr. Harry Dissinger
Soaring Heights Charter S	1 Romar Ave	Jersey City, NJ	07305-1713	201-434-4800	434-7474	K-8	Claudia Zuorick
Sussex Co. Charter S for Technology	105 N Church Rd	Sparta, NJ	07871-3203	973-383-6700	383-2901	7-8	Jill Ekel
TEAM Academy Charter S	85 Custer Ave	Newark, NJ	07112-2511	973-705-8326	556-1238	5-8	Ryan Hill
Teaneck Community Charter S	1650 Palisade Ave	Teaneck, NJ	07666-3610	201-833-9600	833-9225	K-8	Dr. Rex Shaw
Thomas Charter S	370 S 7th St	Newark, NJ	07103-2047	973-621-0060	621-0061	K-7	Lynette Charles
Treat Academy Charter S	443 Clifton Ave	Newark, NJ	07104-1339	973-482-8811	482-7681	K-5	Michael Pallante
Trenton Community Charter S	349 W State St	Trenton, NJ	08618-5705	609-394-0068	695-0193	K-8	Jerri Morrison
Union County TEAMS Charter S	515 W 4th St	Plainfield, NJ	07060-4225	908-754-9043	754-7790	K-12	Sheila Thorpe
Unity Charter S	340 Speedwell Ave	Morristown, NJ	07960-2938	973-292-1808	267-9288	K-8	Rob Agree
University Academy Charter HS	275 W Side Ave	Jersey City, NJ	07305-1130	201-200-3200	200-3262	9-12	John Marquet
University Heights Charter S	74 Hartford St	Newark, NJ	07103-2832	973-623-1965	623-8511	K-12	Linda Woodson
Varisco-Rogers Charter S	PO Box 180	Newark, NJ	07101-0180	973-242-5690	242-3469	6-8	Anne Heyward
Village Charter S	101 Sullivan Way	Trenton, NJ	08628-3425	609-695-0110	695-1880	K-5	Aisha Thomas-Johnson

New Mexico

School	Address	City,State	Zip code	Telephone	Fax	Grade	Contact
Academia De Lengua Y Cultura	PO Box 9087	Albuquerque, NM	87119-9087	505-563-4242	563-4260	6-8	Colleen Adolph
Academy for Tech & Classics	PO Box 8646	Santa Fe, NM	87504-8646	505-473-4282	473-4292	7-12	Ruth La Blanc
Albuquerque Charter Vocational HS	1011 Lamberton Pl NE	Albuquerque, NM	87107-1641	505-341-0888	341-0749	9-12	Geri Romero-Roybal
Albuquerque Institute of Math & Science	PO Box 20141	Albuquerque, NM	87154-0141	505-314-7272		9-12	Kathy Sandoval
Albuquerque Talent Development Charter S	4019 Silvery Minnow Pl NW	Albuquerque, NM	87120-4741	505-385-2404	821-2554	9-12	Dr. Vickey Lester
Alma D Arte Charter HS	PO Box 10	Las Cruces, NM	88004-0010	505-541-0145	541-0146	9-12	Catherine Martinez
Amistad Charter S	PO Box 168	Amistad, NM	88410-0168	505-633-2283	633-3383	K-6	Bruce Delaney
Anansi Charter S	PO Box 1709	El Prado, NM	87529-1709	505-776-2256	776-5561	K-2	Michele Hunt
Bataan Charter S	PO Box 1454	Tijeras, NM	87059-1454	505-321-5123		9-12	Shelby Tallchief
Biehl Charter HS	8300 Phoenix Ave NE	Albuquerque, NM	87110-3700	505-299-9409	299-9493	9-12	Tony Monfiletto
Bridge Academy	PO Box 1119	Las Vegas, NM	87701-1119	505-425-3302	425-3309	9-12	Carole Winkel
Bunche Academy	1718 Yale Blvd SE	Albuquerque, NM	87106-4136	505-292-0100	292-0109	K-8	Jasper Matthews
Career Academy Charter S	4500 Bogan Ave NE	Albuquerque, NM	87109-2215	505-252-3250		10-12	Glee Hare
Carinos De Los Ninos S	PO Box 1078	San Juan Pueblo, NM	87566-1078	505-852-3119		K-6	Victoria Garcia
Charter S 37	73 Los Hornos	Lamy, NM	87540-9666	505-466-7426		9-12	Jody Drew
Chavez Community S	1718 Yale Blvd SE	Albuquerque, NM	87106-4136	505-877-0558	877-4991	9-12	Caryl Thomas
Cottonwood Valley Charter S	PO Box 1829	Socorro, NM	87801-1829	505-838-2026	838-2420	K-8	Mary Nutt
Creative Education Prep Institute #1	PO Box 50880	Albuquerque, NM	87181-0880	505-314-2374	314-2377	9-12	Tom Crespin
Creative Education Prep Institute #2	69 Hotel Cir NE	Albuquerque, NM	87123-1202	505-237-2374	237-2380	9-12	Anna Zamora
Deming Cesar Chavez Charter HS	PO Box 1755	Deming, NM	88031-1755	505-265-3717	265-5412	9-12	Arlene Trujillo
Duncan Charter S	5201 Central Ave NW	Albuquerque, NM	87105	505-268-3274	268-3276	6-8	Jesus Moncada
East Mountain HS	PO Box 340	Sandia Park, NM	87047-0340	505-281-7400	281-4173	9-12	Danielle Johnston
Espanola Military Academy	PO Box 100	Espanola, NM	87532-0100	505-747-3317	747-6084	6-12	Benito Chavez
Gutierrez MS	PO Box 1437	Roswell, NM	88202-1437	505-347-9703	347-9707	6-8	Joe Andreis
Horizon Academy - South	3713 Isleta Blvd SW	Albuquerque, NM	87105	505-873-4100	873-4200	K-6	Jennifer Joyce
Horizon Academy - West	1900 Atrisco Dr NW	Albuquerque, NM	87120-1146	505-998-0459	998-0463	K-6	Amie Duran
Jefferson Montessori Academy	PO Box 2184	Carlsbad, NM	88221-2184	505-887-9380	887-9391	K-12	Deb Glass
Kennedy HS	1511 Central Ave NE	Albuquerque, NM	87106-4408	505-923-3024	242-7444	9-12	Greta Roskom
La Academia de Esperanza	5200 Sequoia Rd NW	Albuquerque, NM	87120-1208	505-764-5500	764-5501	7-8	Steve Woods
La Academia Dolores Huerta	1480 N Main St	Las Cruces, NM	88001-1106	505-526-2984	523-2924	6-8	Dr. Luis Quinones
La Luz del Monte Learning Center	10301 Candelaria Rd NE	Albuquerque, NM	87112-1504	505-296-7677	296-0510	6-8	Dr. Dalene Juarez
La Promesa Early Learning Center	518 1st St NW	Albuquerque, NM	87102-2304	505-268-3275	242-7365	K-3	Dr. Analee Maestas
La Resolana Learning Academy	1718 Yale Blvd SE	Albuquerque, NM	87106-4136	505-765-5517		6-8	Justina Montoya
Learning Community Charter S	4575 San Mateo Blvd NE	Albuquerque, NM	87109	505-332-3200	342-5955	6-12	Viola Martinez
Leopold Charter S	PO Box 770	Silver City, NM	88062-0770	505-590-5906		9-12	Jerry Boswell
Lindrith Area Heritage Charter S	PO Box 166	Lindrith, NM	87029-0166	505-774-6669		K-6	Peggy Gibson
Los Puentes Charter S	1106 Griegos Rd NW	Albuquerque, NM	87107-3751	505-342-5959	342-5955	8-12	Ellen Moore
Middle College HS	200 College Rd Ste 9	Gallup, NM	87301	505-863-7551	863-7627	10-12	Wally Feldman
Monte Del Sol	PO Box 4068	Santa Fe, NM	87502-4068	505-982-5225	982-5321	7-12	Tony Gerlicz
Montessori ES	3821 Singer Blvd NE	Albuquerque, NM	87109-5804	505-796-0149	796-0147	K-6	Mary Jane Besante
Montessori of the Rio Grande Charter S	1650 Gabaldon Dr NW	Albuquerque, NM	87104-2761	505-842-5993	242-2907	K-5	Dr. Bonnie Dodge
Moreno Valley HS	PO Box 1037	Angel Fire, NM	87710-1037	505-377-3100	377-7263	9-12	Dr. Damon Cathey
Mosaic Academy	101 Ute Ave	Aztec, NM	87410-2381	505-334-6364		K-8	Bonnie Braden
Mountain Mahogany Community S	5014 4th St NW	Albuquerque, NM	87107-3908	505-341-1424		K-5	Dr. Kay Birukoff
Native American Community Academy	1100 Cardenas Dr SE	Albuquerque, NM	87108-4809	505-266-0992	266-2905	6-7	Kara Bobroff
North Albuquerque Coop Community ES	4261 Balloon Park Rd NE	Albuquerque, NM	87109-5802	505-344-0746	342-3955	K-6	Shelly Cherrin
North Valley Academy	7939 4th St NW	Albuquerque, NM	87114-1008	505-998-0501	998-0505	K-8	Jerald Snider
Nuestros Valores Charter S	1021 Isleta Blvd SW	Albuquerque, NM	87105-3934	505-873-7758	873-3567	9-12	Monica Sanchez
Public Academy for Performing Arts	4665 Indian School Rd NE	Albuquerque, NM	87110-3918	505-262-4888	262-4893	6-12	Katy Harvey
Red River Valley Charter S	PO Box 742	Red River, NM	87558-0742	505-754-6117	754-3258	K-8	Karen Phillips
Rio Gallinas S	1300 Mineral Hill Rte	Las Vegas, NM	87701-9842	505-454-8687	454-6055	4-8	Cindy McLeod
Roots & Wings Community S	PO Box 1152	El Prado, NM	87529-1152	505-586-2076	586-2087	6-12	Margaret Bartlett
San Diego Riverside S	PO Box 99	Jemez Pueblo, NM	87024-0099	505-834-7419	834-9167	K-8	Eugene Johnson
School for Integrated Academics & Tech	1500 Indian School Rd NW	Albuquerque, NM	87104-2306	505-242-6640	242-6872	9-12	Kelly Callahan
Simms MS	PO Box 359	Alamogordo, NM	88311-0359	505-437-4011	437-4012	6-8	Ron Forbis
South Valley Academy	3426 Blake Rd SW	Albuquerque, NM	87105-5009	505-452-3132	452-3133	9-12	Alan Marks
Southwest Primary Learning Center	10301 Candelaria Rd NE	Albuquerque, NM	87112-1504	505-385-1389	296-0510	K-6	Scott Glasrud
Southwest Secondary Learning Center	10301 Candelaria Rd NE	Albuquerque, NM	87112-1504	505-296-7677	296-0510	7-12	Deb Young
Taos Charter S	PO Box 3009	Ranchos de Taos, NM	87557-3009	505-751-7222	751-7546	K-8	Nancy O'Bryan
Turqoise Trail ES	13a San Marcos Loop	Santa Fe, NM	87508-8627	505-467-1700	474-7862	K-6	Sandra Davis
Twenty-First Century Public Academy	3100 Menaul Blvd NE	Albuquerque, NM	87107-1835	505-254-0280	254-8507	6-8	Donna Eldredge
Village Academy	PO Box 1247	Placitas, NM	87043-1247	505-867-9094		6-8	Pamela Engstrom
Vistas Grande HS	PO Box 1152	El Prado, NM	87529-1152	505-586-2285	770-8681	9-12	Todd Wynward
Walatowa Charter HS	PO Box 60	Jemez Pueblo, NM	87024-0060	505-834-0443	834-0449	9-12	Tony Archuleta
YouthBuild Trade & Technology HS	1718 Yale Blvd SE	Albuquerque, NM	87106-4136	505-765-5517	765-5925	9-12	Van Sanders

New York

School	Address	City,State	Zip code	Telephone	Fax	Grade	Contact
Achievement Academy Charter S	42 S Dove St	Albany, NY	12202-1253	518-533-1601		5-8	Nala Woodard
Achievement First Bushwick Charter S	84 Schaefer St	Brooklyn, NY	11207-1024	718-774-0906		K-12	Lizette Suxo
Achievement First Charter S	557 Pennsylvania Ave	Brooklyn, NY	11207-5727	718-485-4924	342-5194	K-2	Denniston Reid
Achievement First Crown Heights Charter	790 E New York Ave	Brooklyn, NY	11203-1212	718-774-0762	774-0830	K-12	Orpheus Williams

School	Address	City,State	Zip code	Telephone	Fax	Grade	Contact
Achievement First Endeavor Charter S	850 Kent Ave	Brooklyn, NY	11205-2702	718-744-0906		5-8	Eric Redwine
Albany Community Charter S	42 S Dove St	Albany, NY	12202-1253	518-433-1500	433-1501	K-1	S. Neal Currie
Albany Prep Charter S	250 Central Ave	Albany, NY	12206-2610	518-694-5005		5-8	
Amber Charter S	220 E 106th St	New York, NY	10029-4007	212-534-9667	534-6225	K-6	Evelyn Marzan
Ark Community Charter S	762 River St	Troy, NY	12180-1231	518-274-6312		K-5	Mary Streck
Beginning With Children Charter S	11 Bartlett St	Brooklyn, NY	11206-5001	718-388-8847	388-8936	K-8	Cynthia Bailey
Brighter Choice Charter S	250 Central Ave	Albany, NY	12206-2639	518-694-4100		K-3	Melissa Jarvis-Cedeno
Bronx Charter for Better Learning	3740 Baychester Ave	Bronx, NY	10466-5031	718-655-6660	655-5555	1-4	Ted Swartz
Bronx Charter S for Children	388 Willis Ave	Bronx, NY	10454-1303	718-402-3300	402-3258	K-5	Karen Drezner
Bronx Charter S for Excellence	1960 Benedict Ave	Bronx, NY	10462-4402	718-828-7301	828-7302	K-8	Marc Etienne
Bronx Charter S for the Arts	950 Longfellow Ave	Bronx, NY	10474-4809	718-893-1042	893-7910	K-6	Xanthe Jory
Bronx Lighthouse Charter S	1001 Intervale Ave	Bronx, NY	10459-3151	718-860-4340	860-4125	K-4	Jeffrey Tsang
Bronx Preparatory Charter S	3872 3rd Ave	Bronx, NY	10457-8222	718-294-0841	294-2381	5-12	Kristin Jordan
Brooklyn Charter S	545 Willoughby Ave	Brooklyn, NY	11206-6815	718-302-2085	302-2426	K-5	Omigbade Escayg
Brooklyn Excelsior Charter S	856 Quincy St	Brooklyn, NY	11221-3612	718-246-5681	246-5864	K-8	Irwin Kurz
Buffalo Academy of Science Charter S	15 Jewett Pkwy	Buffalo, NY	14214-2319	716-446-5681	446-5682	7-12	Levent Kaya
Buffalo United Charter S	325 Manhattan Ave	Buffalo, NY	14214-1809	716-835-9862		K-8	Gary Bell
Charter S for Applied Technologies	2303 Kenmore Ave	Buffalo, NY	14207-1311	716-876-6724		K-10	J. Efrain Martinez
Charter S of Educational Excellence	260 Warburton Ave	Yonkers, NY	10701-2226	914-476-5070		K-5	Migda Agosto
Child Dev. Center / Hamptons Charter S	110 Stephen Hands Pat	East Hampton, NY	11937	631-324-0207		K-5	Cindy Golden-Allentuck
Community Charter S	404 Edison Ave	Buffalo, NY	14215-2936	716-833-5967		K-8	Karen D'Aurizio
Community Partnership Charter S	241 Emerson Pl	Brooklyn, NY	11205-3808	718-399-1495	399-2149	K-5	Melanie Bryon
Community Roots Charter S	51 Saint Edwards St	Brooklyn, NY	11205-2932	212-437-8356		K-5	Allison Keil
Democracy Prep Charter S	222 W 134th St	New York, NY	10030-3002	212-281-1248	283-4202	6-12	Seth Andrew
East NY Preparatory Charter S	400 Ashford St	Brooklyn, NY	11207-3801	718-277-0213	484-0787	K-5	Sheila Joseph
Elmwood Village Charter S	124 Elmwood Ave	Buffalo, NY	14201	716-886-4581		K-4	John Sheffield
Enterprise Charter S	275 Oak St	Buffalo, NY	14203	716-855-2114		K-8	Jill Norton
Excellence Charter S	225 Patchen Ave	Brooklyn, NY	11233-1529	718-638-1830	638-2548	K-5	Jabali Sawicki
Explore Charter S	15 Snyder Ave	Brooklyn, NY	11226-4020	718-703-4484	703-8550	K-8	Morton Ballen
Family Life Academy Charter S	14 W 170th St	Bronx, NY	10452-3227	718-410-8100	410-8800	K-5	Marilyn Calo
Future Leaders Institute	134 W 122nd St	New York, NY	10027-5501	212-678-2868	666-2749	K-8	Gianna Cassetta
Genesee Community Charter S	657 East Ave	Rochester, NY	14607-2101	585-271-4552		K-5	Lisa Wing
Girls Preparatory Charter S	333 E 4th St	New York, NY	10009-6912	212-388-0241	388-1086	K-2	Miriam Raccah
Global Concepts Charter S	1001 Ridge Rd	Buffalo, NY	14218-1755	716-821-1903		K-5	Lawrence Jungberg
Grand Concourse Charter S	116 E 169th St	Bronx, NY	10452-7704	718-590-1300	590-1065	K-4	Ira Victor
Harbor Science & Arts Charter S	1 E 104th St	New York, NY	10029	212-427-2244	360-7429	1-8	Joanne Hunt
Harlem Childrens Zone Charter S	35 E 125th St	New York, NY	10035-1816	212-534-0700	234-2340	K-12	Doreen Land
Harlem Childrens Zone Charter S	220 W 121st St	New York, NY	10027-6217	212-534-0700	234-2340	K-12	Lyn Pinder
Harlem Day Charter S	240 E 123rd St	New York, NY	10035	212-876-9953	876-9926	K-5	Anne Burns
Harlem Link Charter S	134 W 122nd St	New York, NY	10027-5501	646-472-7998		K-8	Steven Evangelista
Harlem Success Charter S	34 W 118th St	New York, NY	10026-1904	212-763-8092		K-8	Iris Nelson
Harlem Village Academy Charter S	244 W 144th St	New York, NY	10030-1202	646-548-9570	548-9576	5-12	Nick Timpone
Hellenic Classical Charter S	646 5th Ave	Brooklyn, NY	11215-5401	718-499-0957	499-0959	K-8	Joseph Martucci
Hyde Leadership Charter S	730 Bryant Ave	Bronx, NY	10474-6006	212-437-8366		K-6	Joanne Gonbourn
Icahn Charter S	1525 Brook Ave	Bronx, NY	10457-8005	718-716-8105	716-6716	K-7	Jeffrey Litt
International Charter S of Schenectady	901 Draper Ave	Rotterdam, NY	12306-3039	518-344-5107		K-12	Christi Seiple-Cole
International Leadership Charter S	2900 Exterior St	Bronx, NY	10463	212-437-8361		9-12	Elaine Lopez
Johnson Charter S	1 Dudley Hts	Albany, NY	12210-2601	518-432-4300	432-4311	K-4	Lillian Turner
King Center Charter S	938 Genesee St	Buffalo, NY	14211-3025	716-891-7912		K-4	Dr. Claity Massey
KIPP Academy Charter S	250 E 156th St	Bronx, NY	10451-4796	718-665-3555	585-7982	5-8	Quinton Vance
KIPP A.M.P. Charter S	1224 Park Pl	Brooklyn, NY	11213-2703	718-309-0799		5-6	Ky Adderley
KIPP Infinity Charter S	625 W 133rd St	New York, NY	10027-7303	212-694-5786	694-5769	5-6	Joseph Negron
KIPP Sankofa Charter S	140 Central Park Plz	Buffalo, NY	14214-2235	716-446-5708		5-8	April Jayes
KIPP S.T.A.R College Prep Charter S	433 W 123rd St	New York, NY	10027-5002	212-769-7615	769-7601	5-8	Maggie Shefa
KIPP Tech Valley Charter S	1 Dudley Hts	Albany, NY	12210-2601	518-694-9494	694-9411	5-5	Dan Ceaser
Leadership Village Academy Charter S	315 E 113th St	New York, NY	10029-2207	212-369-3319		5-6	Deborah Kenny
Lindsay Wildcat Academy Charter S	17 Battery Pl	New York, NY	10004	212-209-6036	635-3874	8-12	Ronald Tabano
Manhattan Charter S	100 Attorney St	New York, NY	10002-3405	212-533-2743	533-2820	K-2	James Manly
Maria de Hostos Charter S	938 Clifford Ave	Rochester, NY	14621-4808	585-544-6170		K-6	Miriam Vazquez
Merrick Academy-Queens Public Charter S	20701 Jamaica Ave	Queens Village, NY	11428-1544	718-479-3753	479-8108	K-6	Alma Alston
New Covenant Charter S	50 Lark St	Albany, NY	12210-1518	518-463-3912	626-9916	PK-8	Elizabeth Ahearn
New Heights Academy Charter S	1818 Amsterdam Ave	New York, NY	10031-1715	646-271-7563		5-12	Stacy Winitt
NY Center for Autism Charter S	433 E 100th St	New York, NY	10029-6606	212-860-2580	860-2960	K-9	
Niagara Charter S	2077 Lockport Rd	Niagara Falls, NY	14304-1109	716-297-4520	297-4617	K-4	Karen Brown
Opportunity Charter S	240 W 113th St	New York, NY	10026-3306	212-283-0670	283-1138	6-12	Betty Marsella
Oracle Charter S	888 Delaware Ave	Buffalo, NY	14209-2008	716-362-3188	362-3187	7-9	Julia Forsberg
Our World Neighborhood Charter S	3612 35th Ave	Astoria, NY	11106-1227	718-392-3405	392-2840	K-8	Brian Ferguson
Peninsula Prep Academy Charter S	1045 Nameoke St	Far Rockaway, NY	11691-4906	718-471-7220	471-7385	K-5	Judith Tyler
Pinnacle Charter S	115 Ash St	Buffalo, NY	14204-1452	716-842-1244		K-8	Heidi Rotella
ReadNet Bronx Charter S	429 E 148th St	Bronx, NY	10455-4128	718-292-3474	292-2904	K-4	
Renaissance Charter S	3559 81st St	Jackson Heights, NY	11372-5033	718-803-0060	803-3785	K-12	Monte Joffee
Riverhead Charter S	3685 Middle Country Rd	Calverton, NY	11933-1807	631-369-5252		K-5	Robert Pinckney
Roosevelt Childrens Academy Charter S	105 Pleasant Ave	Roosevelt, NY	11575-2126	516-867-6202	867-6206	K-4	Roxanne Ashley
Ross Global Academy Charter S	52 Chambers St	New York, NY	10007	646-613-8303	613-9081	K-12	Mark English
Sisulu-Walker Childrens Academy	125 W 115th St	New York, NY	10026-2908	212-663-8216	866-5793	K-8	Karen Jones
South Bronx Charter S	383 E 139th St	Bronx, NY	10454-2603	718-401-9216	401-9219	K-5	Evelyn Hey
South Bronx Classical Charter S	977 Fox St	Bronx, NY	10459-3320	646-479-5134		K-5	Monalisa Kalina
South Buffalo Charter S	2219 S Park Ave	Buffalo, NY	14220	716-826-7213		K-8	Dr. Cederick Ellis
Southside Academy Charter S	800 S Wilbur Ave	Syracuse, NY	13204-2732	315-476-3019		K-8	Greg Speranza
Syracuse Academy of Science Charter S	1001 Park Ave	Syracuse, NY	13204-2125	315-428-8997	428-9109	7-12	Hakki Karaman
Tapestry Charter S	40 North St	Buffalo, NY	14202-1106	716-332-0754		K-6	Joy Pepper
THINK Collegiate Charter S	1084 Lenox Rd	Brooklyn, NY	11212-1930	718-919-7701	302-4641	5-12	Brett Peiser
True North Rochester Prep Charter S	630 Brooks Ave	Rochester, NY	14619-2255	585-436-8629	436-5985	5-8	Stacey Shells
Tubman Charter S	3565 3rd Ave	Bronx, NY	10456-3403	718-537-9912	537-9858	K-8	Gwen Stephens
UFT Elementary Charter S	300 Wyona St	Brooklyn, NY	11207-3522	718-922-0438	922-0543	K-6	Rita Danis
Urban Choice Charter S	545 Humboldt St	Rochester, NY	14610-1221	585-288-5702	654-9882	K-12	Brian Schmidt
Western NY Maritime Charter S	266 Genesee St	Buffalo, NY	14204-1453	716-842-6289	842-4241	9-12	Richard Middaugh
Westminster Community Charter S	24 Westminster Ave	Buffalo, NY	14215-1614	716-816-3450	838-7458	K-8	Dr. Yvonne Regan
Williamsburg Charter S	424 Leonard St	Brooklyn, NY	11222-3908	718-782-9830	782-9834	9-12	Eddie Melendez
Williamsburg Collegiate Charter S	157 Wilson St	Brooklyn, NY	11211-7706	718-302-4018	302-4161	5-6	Julie Trott

North Carolina

School	Address	City,State	Zip code	Telephone	Fax	Grade	Contact
Academy of Moore County	105 Turner St	Southern Pines, NC	28387-7054	910-693-7924	693-7925	K-8	Bill Moore
Alpha Academy	PO Box 35476	Fayetteville, NC	28303-0476	910-223-7711	678-9011	K-8	Eugene Slocum
American Renaissance Charter S	111 Cooper St	Statesville, NC	28677-5855	704-924-8870	873-1398	K-5	Sharon Molleur
American Renaissance MS	217 S Center St	Statesville, NC	28677-5806	704-878-6009	878-9350	6-8	Stephen Gay
Arapahoe Charter S	9005 NC Highway 306 S	Arapahoe, NC	28510-9699	252-249-2599	249-1316	K-8	Grady Simpson
Arts Based ES	1380 N Martin Luther King	Winston Salem, NC	27101	336-748-4116		K-5	Robin Hollis
ArtSpace Charter S	2030 US 70 Hwy	Swannanoa, NC	28778-8211	828-298-2787	298-6221	K-8	Dr. Tony Horning
Baker Charter HS	PO Box 2415	Raleigh, NC	27602-2415	919-856-5929	857-9298	9-12	Marti Wilson
Bethany Community MS	181 Bethany Rd	Reidsville, NC	27320-7464	336-951-2500	951-0087	6-8	Edward Mise
Bethel Hill Charter S	401 Bethel Hill School Rd	Roxboro, NC	27574-7503	336-599-2823	599-9299	K-6	John Betterton
Brevard Academy	299 Andante Ln	Brevard, NC	28712-9125	828-885-2665	862-3497	K-8	Albert Evans
Bridges Charter S	2587 Pleasant Ridge Rd	State Road, NC	28676-9318	336-874-2721	874-3804	K-8	Paul Welborn
Cape Fear Center for Inquiry	3131 Randall Pkwy Ste B	Wilmington, NC	28403	910-362-0000	362-0048	K-8	Dr. Lisa Griffin
Cape Lookout Marine Science HS	1108 Bridges St	Morehead City, NC	28557-3799	252-726-1601	726-5245	9-12	Susan Smith
Carolina International S	PO Box 366	Harrisburg, NC	28075-0366	704-455-3847	455-4672	K-8	Dr. Richard Beall
Carter Community S	1305 W Club Blvd	Durham, NC	27705-3513	919-416-9025	416-9815	K-8	Gail Taylor
Casa Esperanza Montessori S	2600 Sumner Blvd Ste 130	Raleigh, NC	27616-5146	919-855-9811	855-9813	PK-6	Janice Bonham West
Central Park S for Children	724 Foster St	Durham, NC	27701-2111	919-682-1200	683-1261	K-5	Carolyn Kirkland
Charter Day S	7055 Bacons Way NE	Leland, NC	28451-7960	910-655-1214	655-1549	K-7	Mark Cramer
Chatham Charter	PO Box 245	Siler City, NC	27344-0245	919-742-4550	742-2518	K-8	Ronald Joyce
Children's Community S	PO Box 2059	Davidson, NC	28036-2059	704-896-6262	896-2025	K-5	Joy K. Warner
Childrens Village Academy	PO Box 2206	Kinston, NC	28502-2206	252-939-1958	939-1242	K-6	Gloria Carr-Battle
CIS Academy	118 W 3rd St	Pembroke, NC	28372	910-521-1669	521-1670	6-8	Ronald Bryant
Clover Garden S	2454 Altmhaw Union Ridge Rd	Burlington, NC	27217	336-586-9440	586-9477	K-12	Dr. David Pugh
Community Charter S	510 S Torrence St	Charlotte, NC	28204-3160	704-377-3180	377-3182	K-5	Dennis LaCaria
Community Partners Charter HS	PO Box 100	Holly Springs, NC	27540-0100	919-567-9955	567-9956	9-12	Caroll Reed
Crosscreek Charter S	PO Box 1075	Louisburg, NC	27549-1075	919-497-3198	497-0232	K-8	S. McFarland
Crossnore Academy	PO Box 309	Crossnore, NC	28616-0309	828-733-5241	737-7915	K-12	Sharon Wise
Crossroads Charter HS	5500 N Tryon St	Charlotte, NC	28213-7120	704-597-5100	597-3941	9-12	Kenneth Simmons
Delany New S	PO Box 16161	Asheville, NC	28816-0161	828-236-9441	236-9442	K-8	Buffy Fowler
Dillard Academy	PO Box 1188	Goldsboro, NC	27533-1188	919-581-0128	581-0122	K-4	Hilda Hicks
Downtown MS	280 S Liberty St	Winston Salem, NC	27101-5211	336-748-3838	748-3359	5-8	Amanda Davis Gane
East Wake Academy	400 NMC Dr	Zebulon, NC	27597-2759	919-404-0444	404-2377	K-12	Brandon Smith
Evergreen Community Charter S	50 Bell Rd	Asheville, NC	28805-1538	828-298-2173	298-2269	K-8	Dr. Jackie Williams

School	Address	City,State	Zip code	Telephone	Fax	Grade	Contact
Exploris MS	207 E Hargett St	Raleigh, NC	27601-1437	919-821-3168	836-9768	6-8	Kevin Piacenza
Forsyth Academy	5426 Shattalon Dr	Winston Salem, NC	27106-1919	336-922-1121	922-1033	K-8	Dorothy Heath
Franklin Academy I & II	604 S Franklin St	Wake Forest, NC	27587-2276	919-554-4911	554-2340	K-12	Denise Kent
Gaston College Preparatory S	PO Box 1292	Gaston, NC	27832-1292	252-308-6932	308-6936	5-10	Caleb Dolan
Grandfather Academy	PO Box 2260	Banner Elk, NC	28604-2260	828-898-3868	898-3849	K-12	Doug Herman
Gray Stone Day S	PO Box 960	Misenheimer, NC	28109-0960	704-463-0567	463-0569	9-12	Helen Nance
Greensboro Academy	4049 Battleground Ave	Greensboro, NC	27410-8410	336-286-8404	286-8403	K-8	Rudy Swofford
Guilford Preparatory Charter S	900 16th St	Greensboro, NC	27405-4810	336-954-1344	954-1341	K-9	Dr. John von Rohr
Haliwa-Saponi Tribal S	130 Haliwa Saponi Trl	Hollister, NC	27844-9390	252-257-5853	257-1093	K-12	Goode Walter
Healthy Start Academy	807 W Chapel Hill St	Durham, NC	27701-3112	919-956-5599	688-9027	K-8	Dietrich Danner
Highland Charter S	PO Box 1653	Gastonia, NC	28053-1653	704-852-8518	866-6341	K-2	Sherida Lewis Stevens
Hope Elementary Charter S	1116 N Blount St	Raleigh, NC	27604-1302	919-834-0941	834-9338	K-5	Robbie Graham
Howard S	1004 Herring Ave E	Wilson, NC	27893-3311	252-293-4150	293-4151	K-8	Dr. Jo Anne Woodard
Imani Institute Charter MS	201 N Church St	Greensboro, NC	27401-2941	336-333-9484	333-9454	6-8	Bethel Smith
Jefferson Classical Academy	2527 US 221A Hwy	Mooresboro, NC	28114-7698	828-657-9998	657-9012	6-12	Joseph Maimone
Joy Charter S	1955 W Cornwallis Rd	Durham, NC	27705-5707	919-493-6056	402-4263	K-8	Dr. Les Stein
Kennedy Charter S	PO Box 472527	Charlotte, NC	28247-2527	704-688-2939	688-2962	6-12	Stacey Rose
Kestrel Heights S	2119 Chapel Hill Rd	Durham, NC	27707-1405	919-403-9194	490-8658	6-12	Tim Dugan
Kinston Charter Academy	2000 Martin L King Jr Blvd	Kinston, NC	28501	252-522-0210	527-6878	K-8	Walter Anderson
Lake Norman Charter S	12820 Church St	Huntersville, NC	28078-4223	704-948-8600	948-8778	5-8	Ben Putman
Laurinburg Homework Center	PO Box 929	Laurinburg, NC	28353-0929	910-277-8010	277-8019	8-12	Annie Cureton
Learning Center	945 Connahetta St	Murphy, NC	28906-3524	828-835-7240	835-9471	K-5	Mary Jo Dyre
Lincoln Charter S	133 Eagle Nest Rd	Lincolnton, NC	28092-7383	704-736-9888	736-1166	K-12	Keith Hain
Magellan Charter S	9400 Forum Dr	Raleigh, NC	27615-2971	919-844-0277	844-3882	4-8	Mary Griffin
Metrolina Regional Scholars Academy	7000 Endhaven Ln	Charlotte, NC	28277-2370	704-503-1112	503-1183	K-8	Dr. Marie Peine
Millennium Charter Academy	500 Old Springs Rd	Mount Airy, NC	27030-3034	336-789-7570	789-8445	K-7	Kirby McCrary
Mountain Community S	613 Glover St	Hendersonville, NC	28792-5451	828-696-8480	696-8451	K-8	Chadwick Hamby
Mountain Discovery Charter S	PO Box 1879	Bryson City, NC	28713-1879	828-488-1222	488-0526	K-8	Chantelle Carroll
New Century HS	PO Box 10	Saxapahaw, NC	27340-0010	336-376-1122	376-6995	9-12	Dr. Marcia Hugh
New Dimensions S	PO Box 2248	Morganton, NC	28680-2248	828-437-5753	437-2980	K-5	Pamela Shue
Omuteko Gwamaziima S	PO Box 52072	Durham, NC	27717-2072	919-687-0870	680-2573	K-8	Bernitha Jenkins
Orange County Charter	920 Corporate Dr	Hillsborough, NC	27278-8557	919-644-6272	644-6275	K-8	David Christenbury
PACE Academy	1713 Legion Rd	Chapel Hill, NC	27517-2359	919-933-7699	967-9905	9-12	Rhonda R. Franklin
Phoenix Academy	4020 Meeting Way St	High Point, NC	27265-8233	336-869-0079	869-3399	K-8	Kim Norcross
Piedmont Community S	PO Box 3706	Gastonia, NC	28054-0020	704-853-2428	853-3689	K-12	Courtney Madden
PreEminent Charter S	3815 Rock Quarry Rd	Raleigh, NC	27610-5123	919-235-0511	235-0514	K-8	Dr. Les Stein
Provisions Academy	PO Box 5437	Sanford, NC	27331-5437	919-775-7800	775-7722	6-12	Dr. Sadie Jordan
Quality Education Academy	5012D Lansing Dr	Winston Salem, NC	27105	336-744-0804	744-2523	3-9	Simon Johnson
Queens Grant Community S	6400 Matthews Mint Hill Rd	Mint Hill, NC	28227-9323	704-573-6611	573-0995	K-8	Christy Morrin
Quest Academy	9650 Strickland Rd Ste 175	Raleigh, NC	27615-2082	919-841-0441	841-0443	K-8	Dr. Charles Watson
Raleigh Charter HS	1111 Haynes St	Raleigh, NC	27604	919-715-1155	839-1766	9-12	Dr. Thomas Humble
Research Triangle Academy	2418 Ellis Rd	Durham, NC	27703-5543	919-957-7108	957-9698	K-8	Terri Gullick
River Mill Academy	PO Box 1450	Graham, NC	27253-1450	336-229-0909	229-9975	K-12	Kristen Shattuck
Rocky Mount Prep S	3334 Bishop Rd	Battleboro, NC	27809-9039	252-443-9923	443-9932	K-12	Michael Pratt
Roxboro Community S	115 Lake Dr	Roxboro, NC	27573	336-597-0020		K-12	Samuel Kennington
Sandhills Theatre Arts Renaissance S	140 Southern Dunes Dr	Vass, NC	28394-9218	910-695-1004	695-7322	K-8	David Jackson
Socrates Academy	8310 McAlpine Park Dr	Charlotte, NC	28211-6247	704-366-1115	366-1585	K-5	Janis Dellinger-Holt
SPARC Academy	PO Box 37518	Raleigh, NC	27627-7518	919-835-2000	835-2009	PK-8	Jackie Mburu
Sterling Montessori Academy	202 Treybrooke Dr	Morrisville, NC	27560-9300	919-462-8889	462-8890	K-8	Mike Jordan
Success Institute	1424 Rickert St	Statesville, NC	28677-6856	704-881-0441	881-0870	K-8	Tenna Williams
Sugar Creek Charter S	4101 N Tryon St	Charlotte, NC	28206-2066	704-509-5470	921-1004	K-8	Cheryl Ellis
Summit Charter S	PO Box 1339	Cashiers, NC	28717-1339	828-743-5755	743-9157	K-8	Dr. Patrici Ingraham
Tiller S	1950 US Highway 70 E	Beaufort, NC	28516-7836	252-728-1995	728-3711	K-8	Rita Bowman
Torchlight Academy	3211 Bramer Dr	Raleigh, NC	27604	919-850-9960	850-9961	K-5	Dr. Cynthia McQueen
Two Rivers Community S	1018 Archie Carroll Rd	Boone, NC	28608-0001	828-262-5411	262-5412	K-12	Steve Oates
Union Academy	675 N Martin Luther Jr Blvd	Monroe, NC	28110	704-283-8883	283-8823	K-8	Ken Templeton
Vance Charter S	1227 Dabney Dr	Henderson, NC	27536-3558	252-431-0440	436-0688	K-8	Dr. John von Rohr
Washington Montessori S	500 Avon Ctr	Washington, NC	27889-3851	252-946-1977	946-5938	K-8	Stacey Shepherd
Woods Charter S	PO Box 5008	Chapel Hill, NC	27514-5001	919-960-8353	960-0133	K-12	Simon King
Woodson S of Challenge	437 Goldfloss St	Winston Salem, NC	27127-3125	336-723-6838	723-6425	K-12	Ruth Hopkins

Ohio

School	Address	City,State	Zip code	Telephone	Fax	Grade	Contact
A+ Arts Academy	270 S Napoleon Ave	Columbus, OH	43213-4235	614-338-0767	338-0787	6-8	Carolyn Berkley
Academic Acceleration Academy	1990 Jefferson Ave	Columbus, OH	43211-2175	614-298-4742			
Academy of Arts & Humanities	1400 Tod Ave NW	Warren, OH	44485	330-399-6882	399-6884	3-6	
Academy of Arts & Sciences	201 W Erie Ave	Lorain, OH	44052-1641	440-244-0156	244-3935	K-12	
Academy of Business & Technology	1462 Woodland Ave	Toledo, OH	43607-3977	419-242-7508	242-7550	K-8	Linda Ransey
Academy of Cleveland	9114 Miles Park Ave	Cleveland, OH	44105-5106	216-271-0237	271-0361	K-6	Linda Harris
Academy of Columbus	4656 Heaton Rd	Columbus, OH	43229-6612	614-433-7510	433-7515	K-8	
Academy of Dayton	4095 Little Richmond Rd	Dayton, OH	45427-3310	937-567-1072	567-1075	K-4	Daisy Edwards
Akron Digital Academy	335 S Main St	Akron, OH	44308-1203	330-237-2200	237-2204	K-12	William Romano
Allen Academy III	299 Knightsbridge Dr	Hamilton, OH	45011-3166	513-868-2900	868-0498	K-7	Aleta Benson
Allen Academy II	400 E 2nd St	Dayton, OH	45402-1724	937-586-9756	586-9764	K-8	Michelle Thomas
Allen Academy	700 Heck Ave	Dayton, OH	45408-2641	937-586-9815	586-0271	K-8	Kim Cockrell
Allen Preparatory S	1034 Superior Ave	Dayton, OH	45402-5953	937-567-9124	567-9129	K-12	Yolanda Clark
Alliance Academy of Cincinnati	1712 Duck Creek Rd	Cincinnati, OH	45207-1644	513-751-5555	751-5072	K-8	Mary Cann
Alliance Academy of Toledo	1501 Monroe St Ste 2	Toledo, OH	43604-5752	419-418-5155	418-5160	K-12	Letha Ferguson
Alternative Education Academy	1830 Adams St	Toledo, OH	43604-4428			K-12	
Amanda-Clearcreek Community S	414 N School St	Amanda, OH	43102	740-969-7254	969-7620	K-K	James Dick
Apex Academy	16005 Terrace Rd	East Cleveland, OH	44112-2001	216-451-1725	451-1765	K-8	Michael Ward
Arise Academy	1 Elizabeth Pl	Dayton, OH	45408-1445	937-853-0560	853-0623	K-12	
Arts Academy	4125 Leavitt Rd	Lorain, OH	44053-2341	440-960-0470	960-0475	K-12	Alexis Rainbow
Arts & College Preparatory Academy	2002 S Hamilton Rd	Columbus, OH	43232	614-986-9974	986-9976	9-12	Paula Lasley
Arts and Science Academy	1400 Tod Ave NW	Warren, OH	44485	330-399-6882	399-6884	K-2	
Arts and Science Prep Academy	1140 Euclid Ave	Cleveland, OH	44115-1603	216-926-6641		K-12	
Aspire Academy	4526 Ridge Ave SE	Canton, OH	44707-1118	330-484-8010		6-8	
Aurora Academy	541 Utah St	Toledo, OH	43605-2299	419-693-6841	693-4799	K-8	Cindy Wilson
Autism Academy of Learning	219 Page St	Toledo, OH	43620-1430	419-865-7487	865-8360	K-12	Mona Qaimari
Bennett Venture Academy	5130 Bennett Rd	Toledo, OH	43612-3422	419-269-2247	269-2257	K-8	Judith Pesa
Bridges Community Academy	190 Saint Francis Ave	Tiffin, OH	44883	419-455-9295	455-9296	K-12	
Buckeye On-Line School for Success	519 Broadway St	East Liverpool, OH	43920-3137	330-385-1987	385-4535	K-12	Randall Calhoun
Canton Academy	1356 Stark Ave SW	Canton, OH	44706-1766	330-454-2205	438-2768	9-12	Linda Betz
Canton Arts Academy	3408 13th St SW	Canton, OH	44710-2208	330-454-2254	454-2273	3-8	Minerva Spanner-Morrow
Canton Digital Academy	3408 13th St SW	Canton, OH	44710-2208	330-454-2418	454-2249	K-12	Minerva Spanner-Morrow
Cardinal Digital Academy	5362 State Route 183 NE	Magnolia, OH	44643-8481	330-866-9371	866-2490	K-12	
Cardington Lincoln Digital Academy	121 Nichols St	Cardington, OH	43315-1121	419-560-7246	864-3143	K-12	
Carver Preparatory S	2283 Sunbury Rd	Columbus, OH	43219-3528	614-509-2440	509-2460	K-8	William Fowles
CASTLE	1729 Superior Ave E	Cleveland, OH	44114	216-443-5400	443-9017	9-12	Rolando Peterson
CCAcademy HS	33 N High St Ste 400	Columbus, OH	43215	614-324-1492	324-1060	9-12	
Center for Student Achievement	450 Vaughn St	Jackson, OH	45640-1944	740-286-6442		K-12	Philip Karl
Chase Academy for Communication Arts	1533 Cleveland Ave	Columbus, OH	43211-2743	614-297-7014	297-6042	K-8	Celia Jones
Cincinnati College Prep Academy	1425 Linn St	Cincinnati, OH	45214-2605	513-684-0777	684-8888	K-8	Guyton Mathews
Cincinnati Prep & Fitness Academy	9208 Daly Rd	Cincinnati, OH	45231-3610	513-587-6280	587-6299	K-8	Myrrha Hawkins-Pammer
Citizens' Academy	1827 Ansel Rd	Cleveland, OH	44106-4107	216-791-4195	791-3013	K-8	Monyka Price
City Day Community S Inc.	318 S Main St	Dayton, OH	45402-2716	937-223-8130	223-8136	K-8	Roseda Goff
Cleveland Art & Social Science Academy	1140 Euclid Ave	Cleveland, OH	44115-1603	216-357-2953	589-0583	K-12	Gavita Haynes
Cleveland Entrepreneurship S	540 E 105th St	Cleveland, OH	44108	216-456-2080		6-12	Marshall Emerson
Cleveland Lighthouse Charter S	1701 E 12th St	Cleveland, OH	44114	216-523-1133	523-1134	K-12	Niloy Gangopadhyay
Columbus Arts & Tech Academy	2255 Kimberly Pkwy E	Columbus, OH	43232-7210	614-577-0900	888-0300	K-12	Dawn Linden
Columbus Humanities	1729 Northland Mall	Columbus, OH	43229	614-261-7200	261-7612	K-8	
Columbus Prep & Fitness Academy	1160 Watkins Rd	Columbus, OH	43207-2606	614-301-4856	491-4180	K-8	Lynn Hursey
Columbus Preparatory Academy	3330 Chippewa St	Columbus, OH	43204-1653	614-275-3600	275-3601	K-7	Leticia Wincko
Coshocton Opportunity S	724 Walnut St	Coshocton, OH	43812-1620	740-622-5547	622-6573	9-12	
Crittenton Community S	1418 E Broad St	Columbus, OH	43205	614-251-0103	372-2416	6-9	Misha Boyer
Cupe Community S	1132 Windsor Ave	Columbus, OH	43211-2836	614-294-3020	279-3680	K-12	Estella Stephens
Dayton Academy	4401 Dayton Liberty Rd	Dayton, OH	45418-1903	937-262-4080	262-4091	K-8	Emory Wyckoff
Dayton Tech Design HS	329 Abbey Ave	Dayton, OH	45417-2102	937-542-6000	542-6001	10-12	
Dayton View Academy	1416 W Riverview Ave	Dayton, OH	45402-6217	937-567-9426	567-9446	K-8	Amy Doerman
Dohn Community HS	608 E McMillan St	Cincinnati, OH	45206-1926	513-281-6100	281-6103	9-12	Robert Suess
Dunbar Academy	331 14th St	Toledo, OH	43604-5402	419-244-4202	244-4205	K-6	Thomas Williams
Eagle Academy	2014 Consaul St	Toledo, OH	43605-1412	419-691-4876	691-5184	K-7	Terrence Franklin
Eagle Heights Academy	1833 Market St	Youngstown, OH	44507-1137	330-742-9090	742-9595	K-8	Barbara Murphy
Eagle Learning Center HS	5721 Seaman St	Oregon, OH	43616-2631	419-436-4162		9-12	
East Canton Digital Academy	310 Browning Ct N	East Canton, OH	44730-1248	330-488-0316	488-4001	7-12	Christopher Corbi
East End Community Heritage S	PO Box 9889	Cincinnati, OH	45209-0889	513-281-3900	281-0818	K-12	Janice Glaspie
East End Community S	111 Xenia Ave	Dayton, OH	45410-1523	937-222-7355	222-7316	K-6	Scott Ervin

School	Address	City,State	Zip code	Telephone	Fax	Grade	Contact
East Muskingum Academy	13505 John Glenn School Rd	New Concord, OH	43762-9702	740-826-7641	826-7194	7-12	
Edge Academy	92 N Union St	Akron, OH	44304-1347	330-535-4581	535-5074	K-5	Lori Grimaldi
Education Alternatives Community S	21100 Southgate Park Blvd	Maple Heights, OH	44137	216-332-9360	332-9375	K-12	
Electronic Classroom of Tomorrow	3700 S High St Ste 95	Columbus, OH	43207-4083	614-492-8884	492-8894	K-12	Jeffrey Forster
Elgin Digital Academy	4616 Larue Prospect Rd W	Marion, OH	43302-8859	740-382-1101		K-12	Paula Everett
Elyria Community S	300 Abbe Rd N	Elyria, OH	44035-3724	440-366-5225	366-6280	K-9	Lee Henderson
Emerson Academy of Dayton	501 Hickory St	Dayton, OH	45410-1232	937-223-2889	223-3757	K-7	Barbara Wagner
Englewood Peace Academy	1120 Horace St	Toledo, OH	43606-4737	419-243-7260	243-7268	K-8	Mark Sholl
Fairborn Digital Academy	700 Black Ln	Fairborn, OH	45324-5844	937-879-0511	879-8160	K-12	Robert Grimshaw
FCI Academy	2177 Mock Rd	Columbus, OH	43219-1258	614-471-4527	471-4943	K-12	
Findlay Digital Academy	1200 Broad Ave	Findlay, OH	45840-2653	419-425-3598	425-3588	9-12	Lawrence Grove
Focus Learning Academy East	4480 Refugee Rd	Columbus, OH	43232	614-269-0150	501-9470	9-12	Naim Sanders
Focus Learning Academy North	4807 Evanswood Dr	Columbus, OH	43229	614-310-0430	501-9470	9-12	Deshannon Butler
Focus Learning Academy Southwest	190 Southwood Ave	Columbus, OH	43207-1133	614-545-2000	501-9470	9-12	Robert Ater
Fox Academy	2238 Jefferson Ave	Toledo, OH	43604-7120	419-720-4500	720-4502	7-12	Earl Apgar
Foxfire Center for Student Success	PO Box 1818	Zanesville, OH	43702-1818	740-453-4509	455-4084	9-12	
Franklin Local Digital Academy	360 Cedar St	Duncan Falls, OH	43734	740-674-5094	674-5214	K-12	Sharon McDermott
Garvey Academy	13830 Euclid Ave Ste 2	Cleveland, OH	44112	216-451-7995	451-7998	6-9	Ross Cockfield
Glass City Academy	2275 Collingwood Blvd	Toledo, OH	43620	419-720-6311	720-6315	11-12	
Goal Digital Academy	PO Box 216	Edison, OH	43320-0216	419-946-1903	947-9551	K-12	Laura Chervenak
Graham Digital Academy	370 E Main St	Saint Paris, OH	43072-9200	937-663-4123	663-4670	K-12	Marcia Ward
Graham S	3950 Indianola Ave	Columbus, OH	43214-3158	614-262-1111	262-5878	9-12	Eileen Meers
Greater Achievement Community S	3443 E 93rd St	Cleveland, OH	44104-5252	216-341-8138	341-8530	K-11	Phyllis Alford
Greater Heights Academy	1970 S Taylor Rd	Cleveland Hts, OH	44118-2100	216-320-1720	320-2952	K-11	Karen Gazis
Great Western Academy	310 N Wilson Rd	Columbus, OH	43204-6221	614-276-1028	276-1049	K-8	Amy Buttke
Groveport Community S	4485 S Hamilton Rd	Groveport, OH	43125-9334	614-574-4100	574-4107	K-8	
Hamilton County Math & Science S	7601 Harrison Ave	Mount Healthy, OH	45231-3107	513-728-8620	728-8623	K-5	Dwan Moore
Hamilton Local Digital Academy	1055 Rathmell Rd	Columbus, OH	43207-4742	614-554-5598	491-8323	K-12	William Morrison
Harmony Community S	1580 Summit Rd	Cincinnati, OH	45237-1904	513-921-5260	921-2020	6-12	Deland McCullough
Harvard Avenue Community S	12000 Harvard Ave	Cleveland, OH	44105-5444	216-283-5100	283-5762	K-8	
Heir Force Community S	PO Box 180	Lima, OH	45802-0180	419-228-9241	228-1555	K-8	Judith Steiner
Hope Academy Broadway Campus	3398 E 55th St	Cleveland, OH	44127-1691	216-271-7747	271-6438	K-8	Lydia Harris
Hope Academy-Brown Street Campus E	1035 Clay St	Akron, OH	44301-1517	330-785-0180	785-0681	K-8	Wendy Rydarowicz
Hope Academy Canton Campus	1379 Garfield Ave SW	Canton, OH	44706-5200	330-454-3128	454-3145	K-8	Tony Townsend
Hope Academy Cathedral Campus	10615 Lamontier Ave	Cleveland, OH	44104-4847	216-721-6909	721-1565	K-8	Lynda Carn-Farkas
Hope Academy Chapelside Campus	3845 E 131st St	Cleveland, OH	44120-4661	216-283-6589	283-3087	K-12	Victoria Dorsey
Hope Academy - Cuyahoga Campus	12913 Bennington Ave	Cleveland, OH	44135-3761	216-251-5450	251-6410	K-8	Sharon Durant
Hope Academy East Campus	15720 Kipling Ave	Cleveland, OH	44110-3105	216-383-1214		K-12	Lynnette Stevens
Hope Academy HS	3121 Euclid Ave	Cleveland, OH	44115-2507	216-431-4927	431-8017	9-12	Reginald Ray
Hope Academy Lincoln Park	2421 W 11th St	Cleveland, OH	44113-4401	216-263-7008	263-7007	K-8	Ray Terry
Hope Academy Northcoast Campus	4310 E 71st St	Cleveland, OH	44105-5759	216-429-0232	429-0249	K-8	Muata Niamke
Hope Academy Northwest	1441 W 116th St	Cleveland, OH	44102-2301	216-226-6800	226-6805	K-12	Edna West
Hope Academy University Campus	107 S Arlington St	Akron, OH	44306-1328	330-535-7728	535-7864	K-12	Kenan Bishop
Horizon Science Academy	545 Odlin Ave	Dayton, OH	45405-2743	937-277-1177	277-3090	K-12	Kemal Kaman
Horizon Science Academy	630 S Reynolds Rd	Toledo, OH	43615-6314	419-535-0524	535-0525	5-8	Mustafa Yazici
Horizon Science Academy	1055 Laidlaw Ave	Cincinnati, OH	45237-5005	513-242-0099	275-4597	K-12	
Horizon Science Academy	425 Jefferson Ave	Toledo, OH	43604	419-244-5710	244-5721	K-12	Fatih Unlu Ph.D.
Horizon Science Academy	1329 Bethel Rd	Columbus, OH	43220-2611	614-846-7616	846-7696	5-12	Aydin Kara
Horizon Science Academy	6000 S Marginal Rd	Cleveland, OH	44103-1042	216-432-3660	432-3670	6-12	David Disli
Horizon Science Academy Cleveland MS	6100 S Marginal Rd	Cleveland, OH	44103-1043	216-432-9940	432-9941	5-8	Ugur Zengince
Horizon Science Academy - Denison	1700 Denison Ave	Cleveland, OH	44109-2945	216-739-9911	739-9913	K-12	Sagnak Murat
IMAC HS	856 W Cook Rd	Mansfield, OH	44907-5012	419-525-6411	525-0082	9-12	Harold Dean
Imani Learning Academy	728 Parkside Blvd	Toledo, OH	43607-3858	419-535-7078	535-5915	K-8	Randel Grieser
Intergenerational S	12200 Fairhill Rd	Cleveland, OH	44120	216-721-0120	721-0126	K-8	Dr. Cathy Whitehouse
International Academy of Columbus	1201 Schrock Rd	Columbus, OH	43229-1117	614-844-5539	844-5857	K-10	Mouhamed Tarazi
International College Prep Academy	244 Southern Ave	Cincinnati, OH	45219-3023	513-224-1141	241-6059	K-12	
ISUS Institute	140 N Keowee St	Dayton, OH	45402-1309	937-223-2323	223-9303	9-12	Gary Cross
James Leadership Academy	120 Knox Ave	Dayton, OH	45427-1723	937-835-3580	835-3576	9-12	Kecia Williams
Kent Digital Academy	321 N Depeyster St	Kent, OH	44240-2514	330-676-7610	676-7686	K-12	Joe Giancola
Kessler S	118 E Wood St	Youngstown, OH	44503-1625	330-746-3095	746-4272	K-8	Lydia Brown-Payton
King Academy Community S	933 Bank St	Cincinnati, OH	45214-2103	513-421-7519	421-5768	K-8	Andrea Martinez
Lake Erie Academy	2740 W Central Ave	Toledo, OH	43606-3452	419-475-3786	475-6048	K-8	Beverly Baker
Lakewood City Academy	1470 Warren Rd	Lakewood, OH	44107-3918	216-529-4037	227-5975	K-12	Terrilynn Bornino
Lakewood Digital Academy	PO Box 70	Hebron, OH	43025-0070	740-928-5878	928-3152	K-12	Jay Gault
Lancaster Digital Academy	111 S Broad St	Lancaster, OH	43130	740-687-7364	687-7303	K-12	Stephen St. Clair
Lancaster Fairfield Community S	320 E Locust St	Lancaster, OH	43130-4437	740-687-7177	687-7178	7-12	Jeffrey Graf
Legacy Academy for Leaders & Arts	1812 Oak Hill Ave	Youngstown, OH	44507-1053	330-747-1620	747-1753	K-8	Joyce Baldwin
Life Skills Center of Akron	80 W Bowery St	Akron, OH	44308	330-376-8700	376-6700	9-12	Joseph Cole
Life Skills Center of Canton	1100 Cleveland Ave NW	Canton, OH	44702-1816	330-456-4490		9-12	Scott McClain
Life Skills Center of Cincinnati	2612 Gilbert Ave	Cincinnati, OH	45206-1205	513-475-0222	475-0444	9-12	Kevin Jamison
Life Skills Center of Cleveland	4600 Carnegie Ave	Cleveland, OH	44103	216-431-7571	431-7652	9-12	Yolanda Eiland
Life Skills Center of Dayton	1721 N Main St	Dayton, OH	45405-4143	937-274-2841	274-2873	9-12	James Brown
Life Skills Center of Elyria	2015 W River Rd N	Elyria, OH	44035-2309	440-324-1755	324-1723	9-12	Deb Gurich
Life Skills Center of Hamilton County	7710 Reading Rd	Cincinnati, OH	45237	513-821-6695	821-8755	9-12	Arnez Booker
Life Skills Center of Lake Erie	9200 Madison Ave	Cleveland, OH	44102-2719	216-631-1090		9-12	Joseph Czerwien
Life Skills Center of North Akron	1458 Brittain Rd	Akron, OH	44310-3641	330-633-5990	633-7005	9-12	Beth Ferguson
Life Skills Center of Northeast OH	12201 Larchmere Blvd	Shaker Heights, OH	44120-1101	216-421-7587	421-8189	9-12	David Pannell
Life Skills Center of Northern Columbus	1900 E Dublin Granville Rd	Columbus, OH	43229	614-891-9041		9-12	Tami Augustine
Life Skills Center of SE Columbus	2400 S Hamilton Rd	Columbus, OH	43232-4963	614-863-9175	863-9185	9-12	Andrew Pasquinilli
Life Skills Center of Springfield	1637 Selma Rd	Springfield, OH	45505-4245	937-322-2940	322-2944	9-12	Edward Haskins
Life Skills Center of Summit County	2168 Romig Rd	Akron, OH	44320-3879	330-745-3678	753-1506	9-12	Lashawn Terrel
Life Skills Center of Toledo	1830 Adams St	Toledo, OH	43604-4428	419-241-5504	241-9176	9-12	Jon Marie Strode
Life Skills Center of Trumbull County	458 Franklin St SE	Warren, OH	44483-5715	330-392-0231	392-0253	9-12	Kerry Jupina
Life Skills Center of Youngstown	3405 Market St	Youngstown, OH	44507-2009	330-743-6698	743-6702	9-12	Jeremy Batchelor
Lighthouse Academy ES	1585 Frederick Blvd Ste 100	Akron, OH	44320	330-836-6370	836-6351	K-5	Judith Schueller
Lighthouse Community S	6100 Desmond St	Cincinnati, OH	45227-1897	513-561-7888	561-7818	6-12	Daniel Trujillo
Like Skills Center	631 S Breiel St	Middletown, OH	45042	513-423-1800	423-1818	9-12	Charles Hall
Lion of Judah Academy	1254 E 74th St	Cleveland, OH	44103-1904	216-214-5425	881-9201	K-8	
London Digital Academy	60 S Walnut St	London, OH	43140-1246	740-852-5700	852-3078	K-12	Jeffrey Thompson
Lorain Academy for Gifted Students	307 W 7th St	Lorain, OH	44052-1813	440-244-0855	244-0857	K-9	Richard Hronek
Lorain Community MS	300 Broadway	Lorain, OH	44052	440-242-2023	204-2134	5-9	Jeannine Wolfe
Lorain Community S	201 W Erie Ave	Lorain, OH	44052-1641	440-204-2130	204-2134	K-9	Melisa Munitz
Lorain Digital Academy	3301 Meister Rd	Lorain, OH	44053-1134	440-282-4087	282-4088	K-12	Fred Dull
Madison Community ES	2015 W 95th St	Cleveland, OH	44102-3727	216-651-5212	651-9040	K-4	Kathryn Delzani
Mahoning Unlimited S	100 Debartolo Pl Ste 115	Youngstown, OH	44512-7019	330-965-7828	965-7902	K-12	
Mahoning Valley Opportunity S	496 Glenwood Ave Ste 112	Youngstown, OH	44502	330-240-7527		9-12	Ronald Schulay
Main Street Automotive Magnet S	440 Hunter Ave	Dayton, OH	45404-1564	937-222-2725	222-3952	7-12	
Main Street Education Center	407 E Main St	Louisville, OH	44641-1419	330-875-9591	875-7674	PK-K	Sherry Unger
Mansfield Community S	455 Park Ave W	Mansfield, OH	44906-3117	419-522-4578	522-3563	K-8	Bethany Young
Mansfield Elective Academy	445 Bowman St	Mansfield, OH	44903-1201	419-247-4475	247-3392	K-8	Sophia Speelman
Mansfield Enhancement Academy	215 N Trimble Rd	Mansfield, OH	44906-2630	419-525-0105	525-0106	9-12	
Mansfield Preparatory Academy	3333 Chippewa St	Columbus, OH	43204-1654	440-244-0156	244-3935	K-12	
Marion City Digital Academy	910 E Church St	Marion, OH	43302-4396	740-223-4417	223-4569	K-12	Raymond Haines
Massillon Digital Academy	207 Oak Ave SE	Massillon, OH	44646-6790	330-830-3900	830-0953	K-12	
Meadows Choice Community S	1853 South Ave	Toledo, OH	43609	419-385-5730	385-5781	1-8	Ellin Bick
Miamisburg Digital HS	540 Park Ave	Miamisburg, OH	45342-2854	937-866-3381	865-5250	9-12	
Middletown Fitness & Prep Academy	800 2nd Ave	Middletown, OH	45044-4294	513-424-6110	424-6121	K-8	Michelle Spencer
Millenium Community ES	1850 Bostwick Rd	Columbus, OH	43227-3301	614-255-5585	255-5580	K-6	
Miree Fundamental Academy	1660 Sternblock Ln	Cincinnati, OH	45237-3805	513-351-8034	366-3395	K-8	Pauline Olverson
MODEL Community S	1615 Holland Rd	Maumee, OH	43537-1622	419-897-4400	897-4403	K-12	Mary Walters
Montessori Renaissance Experience	PO Box 8457	Columbus, OH	43201-0457	614-262-6510	299-1169	K-6	Cynthia Frazier
Moraine Community S	5656 Springboro Pike	Dayton, OH	45449-2806	937-294-4522	294-4545	K-12	
Mound Street Health Careers Academy	354 Mound St	Dayton, OH	45402-8325	937-223-3041	223-5867	9-12	Sue Garretson
Mound Street IT Careers Academy	354 Mound St	Dayton, OH	45402-8325	937-223-3041	223-5867	9-12	Sue Garretson
Mound Street Military Careers Academy	354 Mound St	Dayton, OH	45402-8325	937-223-3041	223-5867	9-12	Susan Garretson
Newark Digital Academy	255 Woods Ave	Newark, OH	43055-4436	740-328-2022	328-2270	K-12	
New Choices Community S	601 S Keowee St	Dayton, OH	45410-1168	937-224-8201	224-8209	7-12	Gary Hardman
New City S	1516 Salem Ave	Dayton, OH	45406-4943	937-277-7155	277-7017	1-12	
New Day Academy	8566 Barbara Dr	Mentor, OH	44060-1917	216-797-1602	797-1604	K-12	
NIA University Community S	7243 Eastlawn Dr	Cincinnati, OH	45237-3515	513-373-9337	631-1615	7-12	
Noble Academy - Cleveland	1200 E 200th St	Euclid, OH	44117-1111	216-486-8866	486-2846	K-7	
Noble Academy - Columbus	1345 Bethel Rd	Upper Arlington, OH	43220	614-457-2231	457-5064	K-12	
North Dayton S of Science & Discovery	3901 Turner Rd	Dayton, OH	45415-3654	937-278-6671	278-6964	K-8	Bert Seard
Northland Prep & Fitness ES	1875 Morse Rd	Columbus, OH	43229-6603	614-318-0600	318-0610	K-8	Shawn Gibbs
Nu Bethel Center of Excellence	1120 Germantown St	Dayton, OH	45408-1465	937-275-0433	275-0890	K-6	Victoria Elliott
Oakstone Community S	5747 Cleveland Ave	Columbus, OH	43231-2831	614-865-9643	865-9649	K-12	Susan Bone
Ohio Connections Academy	2727 Madison Rd	Cincinnati, OH	45209	513-533-3230	533-3260	K-12	Raymond Lambert

School	Address	City,State	Zip code	Telephone	Fax	Grade	Contact
Ohio Virtual Academy	1655 Holland Rd Ste F	Maumee, OH	43537-1656	419-482-0948	482-0954	K-12	Susan Stagner
Old Brooklyn Community MS	4430 State Rd	Cleveland, OH	44109	216-351-0280	661-5975	5-9	Amy Mobley
Old Brooklyn Community S	4430 State Rd	Cleveland, OH	44109	216-661-7888	661-5975	K-4	Cherie Kaiser
Omega S of Excellence	1821 Emerson Ave	Dayton, OH	45406-4802	937-278-2372	278-0267	K-8	Angela Wycoff
Orion Academy	1798 Queen City Ave	Cincinnati, OH	45214-1427	513-251-6000	251-3851	K-7	Dennis McNeal
Outreach Academy for Children	3326 Broadview Rd	Cleveland, OH	44109-3316	216-661-6655	635-1883	K-12	Mary Wideman-Blake
P.A.C.E. S	4753 Reading Rd	Cincinnati, OH	45237-6107	513-751-7223	482-3322	K-12	
Par - Excellence Academy	96 Maholm St	Newark, OH	43055-3994	740-344-7279	344-7272	PK-6	Dr. Nora Noble
Parma Community S	7667 Day Dr Fl 1	Parma, OH	44129	440-888-5490	888-5890	K-8	Linda Geyer
Pathway S of Discovery	173 Avondale Dr	Dayton, OH	45404-2123	937-235-5498	235-5569	K-8	Susan Kyllo
Performing Arts S	425 Jefferson Ave	Toledo, OH	43604	419-243-4752	259-9129	7-12	
Perrysburg Digital Academy	140 E Indiana Ave	Perrysburg, OH	43551-2261	419-874-9131	872-8820	K-12	
Peterson Entrepreneurial HS	1 Elizabeth Pl	Dayton, OH	45408-1445	937-853-0560	853-0623	9-12	William Peterson
Phillips Academy	3648 Victory Ave	Toledo, OH	43607-2564	419-534-4272	534-4276	K-8	
Phoenix Academy Community S	2238 Jefferson Ave	Toledo, OH	43604-7120	419-720-4500		7-12	Earl Apgar
Phoenix Community Learning Center	7030 Reading Rd Ste 350	Cincinnati, OH	45237-1756	513-351-5801	351-5809	K-8	Dr. Glenda D. Brown
Phoenix Village Academy	1881 E 71st St	Cleveland, OH	44103-4005	216-426-8601	426-9528	K-12	
Phoenix Village Academy	4265 Northfield Rd	Highland Hills, OH	44128-2811			K-12	
Phoenix Village Academy	442 Bell St	Akron, OH	44307-2306			K-3	
Pinnacle Academy	840 E 222nd St	Euclid, OH	44123-3317	216-731-0127	731-0688	K-8	Virginia Barkhurst
Pleasant Community Digital S	1107 Owens Rd W	Marion, OH	43302-8421	740-389-4476	389-6985	K-12	
Powell Leadership Academy	834 Randolph St	Dayton, OH	45408-1749	937-263-3937	263-0432	K-12	Lorraine Renee Clemons
Premier Academy of Ohio	1185 Noe Bixby Rd	Columbus, OH	43213-3530	614-501-3820		7-12	
Project Rebuild Community HS	1500 Superior Ave NE	Canton, OH	44705-1956	330-452-8414	452-8452	9-12	Joseph Cole
Pschtecin S	985 Mediterranean Ave	Columbus, OH	43229-2541	614-985-3428	985-3115	8-12	
Puritas Community S	15204 Puritas Ave	Cleveland, OH	44135-2716	216-688-0680	688-0609	K-9	Donald Disantis
Quaker Digital Academy	248 Front Ave SW	New Phila, OH	44663-2150	330-364-0600	364-9310	K-12	Steve Eckert
Quest Academy Community S	190 E 8th St	Lima, OH	45804	419-227-7730	227-7515	K-7	Oscar Marshall
Ridgedale Community S	3103 Hillman Ford Rd	Morral, OH	43337-9302	740-382-6065	383-6538	K-12	
Rittman Academy	75 N Main St	Rittman, OH	44270-1440	330-927-7401		K-12	Brett Lanz
Riverside Academy	3280 River Rd	Cincinnati, OH	45204-1214	513-921-7777	921-7704	K-8	Roger Conners
River Valley Digital Academy	197 Brocklesby Rd	Caledonia, OH	43314-9501	740-725-5401	725-5499	K-12	
Schnee HS	2222 Issaquah St	Cuyahoga Falls, OH	44221-3704	330-922-1966		9-12	
Scholarts Preparatory S	400 E Town St Ste G30	Columbus, OH	43215-4755	614-224-1610	221-8842	K-12	
Sciotoville S	224 Marshall St	Sciotoville, OH	45662-5549	740-776-6777	776-6812	5-12	Rodney Walker
South Scioto Academy	707 E Jenkins Ave	Columbus, OH	43207-1318	614-445-7684		K-4	
Southwest Licking Digital Academy	927 South St Ste A	Pataskala, OH	43062	740-927-3941	927-4648	K-12	
Springfield Academy of Excellence	623 S Center St	Springfield, OH	45506-2209	937-325-0962		K-6	Edna Chapman
Springfield Prep & Fitness S	1615 Selma Rd	Springfield, OH	45505-4245	937-323-6250	323-6252	K-8	Thomas Zaboski
Stambaugh Charter Academy	2420 Donald Ave	Youngstown, OH	44509-1306	330-792-4806		K-5	Todd Avis
Stockyard Community ES	3200 W 65th St	Cleveland, OH	44102-5510	216-651-5209		K-6	Audrey Petsche
Summit Academy Akron	88 Kent St	Akron, OH	44305-2544	330-253-7441	253-7457	1-8	
Summit Academy - Canton	2400 Cleveland Ave NW	Canton, OH	44709-3613	330-453-8547	453-8924	1-12	
Summit Academy Cincinnati	3066 Madison Rd	Cincinnati, OH	45209-1723	513-321-0561	321-0795	1-8	
Summit Academy Columbus	1855 E Dublin Granville Rd	Columbus, OH	43229	614-880-0714	880-0732	1-8	
Summit Academy Creative Arts	864 E Market St	Akron, OH	44305-2424	330-434-2343	434-5295	8-12	Trina Holloway
Summit Academy Dayton	1407 E 3rd St	Dayton, OH	45403-1818	937-223-3154	223-3229	K-12	
Summit Academy Lorain	1949 Broadway	Lorain, OH	44052-3626	440-245-5440	245-2545	8-12	
Summit Academy Lorain	2140 E 36th St	Lorain, OH	44055-2756	440-277-4110	277-4112	1-8	
Summit Academy - Middletown	7 S Marshall Rd	Middletown, OH	45044-5375	513-420-9767	727-1520	1-8	Edward Lemmert
Summit Academy Toledo	3891 Martha Ave	Toledo, OH	43612-1250	419-476-0784	476-0763	1-8	
Summit Academy Warren	2106 Arbor Ave SE	Warren, OH	44484-5296	330-369-4233	369-4299	K-5	
Summit Academy - Xenia	870 S Detroit St	Xenia, OH	45385-5510	937-372-5210	372-5250	1-8	
Summit Academy - Youngstown	1400 Oak Hill Ave	Youngstown, OH	44507-1018	330-747-0950	747-0957	8-12	Kathleen Mioni
Summit Academy Youngstown	144 N Schenley Ave	Youngstown, OH	44509-2041	330-259-0421	259-0424	K-5	
T.C.P. World Academy	6000 Ridge Ave	Cincinnati, OH	45213-1624	513-531-9500	531-2406	K-6	Karen French
Tech Con Institute HS	2075 Shiloh Springs Rd	Trotwood, OH	45426	937-854-4000	854-4004	9-12	
Tiffin City Digital Academy	244 S Monroe St	Tiffin, OH	44883-2906	419-448-5671	448-5202	K-12	
Toledo Academy of Learning	301 Collingwood Blvd	Toledo, OH	43604-8624	419-255-0253	255-0279	K-12	Judith Miller
Toledo Accelerated Academy	2913 S Republic Blvd	Toledo, OH	43615-1911	419-539-7173	539-7174	6-12	Bernard Crawford
Toledo S for the Arts	333 14th St	Toledo, OH	43604	419-246-8732	244-3979	6-12	Howard Walters
Tomorrow Center	PO Box 216	Edison, OH	43320-0216	419-946-1903	947-9551	K-12	Lane Warner
TRECA Digital Academy	1713 Marion Mount Gilead Rd	Marion, OH	43302	740-389-4798	389-6695	K-12	Mike Carder
Trotwood Fitness & Prep Academy	3100 Shiloh Springs Rd	Trotwood, OH	45426-2247	937-854-4100	854-1177	K-8	Jeffrey Neely
Upper Arlington Community S	1950 N Mallway Dr	Upper Arlington, OH	43221-4326	614-487-5200	487-5238	11-12	Kip Greenhill
Upper Arlington IB HS	1650 Ridgeview Rd	Upper Arlington, OH	43221-2997	614-487-5200	487-5238	11-12	Kip Greenhill
Urbana Community S	711 Wood St	Urbana, OH	43078-1498	937-653-1478	652-3845	K-12	David Yocum
Urban Youth Academy	1408 Clifton Ave	Springfield, OH	45505-3728	937-360-5169	322-2977	7-12	
Veritas/Cesar Chavez Academy	1812 Central Pkwy	Cincinnati, OH	45214-2304	513-651-9624	651-9629	K-12	
Victory Academy of Toledo	3319 Nebraska Ave	Toledo, OH	43607-2819	419-534-2304	534-2379	K-8	
Virtual Community S of Ohio	6100 Channingway Blvd	Columbus, OH	43232	614-501-9473	501-9470	K-12	Jim McCord
Virtual Schoolhouse	736 Lakeview Rd	Cleveland, OH	44108-2608	216-541-2048	541-2018	K-12	
V L T Academy	1100 Sycamore St	Cincinnati, OH	45202-1321	513-421-1129		K-12	
Warren County Virtual Community S	320 E Silver St	Lebanon, OH	45036	513-695-2567	695-2961	9-12	
Washington Park Community S	4000 Washington Park Blvd	Newburgh Hts, OH	44105-3248	216-271-6055	271-6099	K-8	Robert Horrocks
W.E.B. DuBois S	1812 Central Pkwy	Cincinnati, OH	45214-2304	513-702-3057	651-9629	K-12	
Weems S	2280 Professor Ave	Cleveland, OH	44113-4467	216-771-6799	771-6884	K-8	
Wells Community Academy	1180 Slosson St	Akron, OH	44320-2730	330-867-1085	867-1074	K-5	
West Central Learning Academy	650 E Edwards St	Lima, OH	45801-3724	419-227-9252	227-2511	7-12	
Westpark Community MS	3326 Broadview Rd	Cleveland, OH	44109-3316	216-688-0271	688-0273	5-9	Karil Sako
Westpark Community S	16210 Lorain Ave	Cleveland, OH	44111-5521	216-688-0271	688-0273	K-4	Macey Baldizzi
Westside Academy	147 E New England Ave	Worthington, OH	43085-3750	614-272-9392		K-8	Heather O'Bannon
Whitehall Prep & Fitness S	3474 E Livingston Ave	Columbus, OH	43227-2219	614-314-6301		K-8	Chad Monahan
Wickliffe Progressive Community S	2405 Wickliffe Rd	Upper Arlington, OH	43221-1833	614-487-5150	487-5161	K-5	Fred Burton
Wildwood Environmental Academy	1546 Dartford Rd	Maumee, OH	43537-1374	419-868-9885	868-9981	K-8	Cheryl Chester
Winterfield Venture Academy	286 Wenz Rd	Toledo, OH	43615	419-531-3285	531-3637	K-7	Hobart Johnson
Woods Community S	PO Box 9843	Columbus, OH	43209-0843	614-252-3630		K-4	Carol Rivers
Wright ECC	306 E Whittier Ave	Fairborn, OH	45324-5313	937-548-0063		K-K	
Youngstown Academy of Excellence	1408 Rigby St	Youngstown, OH	44506-1617	330-746-3970	746-3965	K-12	
Youngstown Community ES	50 Essex St	Youngstown, OH	44502-1838	330-746-2240	746-6618	K-6	Mary Dunn
YouthBuild Columbus Comm S	1183 Essex Ave	Columbus, OH	43201-2925	614-291-0805	291-0890	9-12	Derek Steward
Zenith Academy	8210 Havens Rd	Blacklick, OH	43004-8630	614-419-6753		K-9	

Oklahoma

School	Address	City,State	Zip code	Telephone	Fax	Grade	Contact
ASTEC Charter S	2401 NW 23rd St	Oklahoma City, OK	73107	405-947-6274	947-0035	6-12	Dr. Freda Deskin
Brown Community S	3 S Cincinnati Ave	Tulsa, OK	74103-2400	918-425-1407		K-5	Deborah Brown
Dove Science Academy	919 NW 23rd St	Oklahoma City, OK	73106-5691	405-524-9762	524-9471	6-12	Yalcin White
DOVE Science Academy	280 S Memorial Dr	Tulsa, OK	74112-2202	918-834-3936	834-3352	6-12	Zekeruya Yuksel
Garvey S	1537 NE 24th St	Oklahoma City, OK	73111-3212	405-427-7616	425-4632	K-5	Dr. Kevin McPherson
Harding Charter Preparatory HS	3333 N Shartel Ave	Oklahoma City, OK	73118-7277	405-528-0562	556-5063	9-12	Richard Caram
Harding Fine Arts Center	PO Box 18895	Oklahoma City, OK	73154-0895	405-702-4322	601-0904	9-10	Sherry Rowan Ph.D.
Independence Charter MS	3232 NW 65th St	Oklahoma City, OK	73116-3512	405-841-3132	841-3134	6-8	Vana Baker
KIPP S	1901 NE 13th St	Oklahoma City, OK	73117-3613	405-425-4622	231-2003	5-8	Tracy McDaniel
KIPP Tulsa Academy	1661 E Virgin St	Tulsa, OK	74106-5552	918-925-1580	925-1590	5-8	Millard House
Santa Fe South HS	301 SE 38th St	Oklahoma City, OK	73129-3099	405-632-3062	634-7077	9-12	Chris Brewster
Santa Fe South MS	4712 S Santa Fe Ave	Oklahoma City, OK	73109-7545	405-409-7706		7-8	Mike Figueroa
SeeWorth Academy	12600 N Kelley Ave	Oklahoma City, OK	73131-1869	405-475-8565		3-12	
Tulsa S of Arts and Sciences	5155 E 51st St Ste 200	Tulsa, OK	74135-7458	918-828-7727	828-7747	9-12	Pat Lubas
Wesley Academy	2240 NE 19th St	Oklahoma City, OK	73111-1708	405-427-6800	425-4614	9-12	Dr. Elton Matthews
Western Village ES	1508 NW 106th St	Oklahoma City, OK	73114-5299	405-751-1774	752-6833	PK-5	Margaret Brinson

Oregon

School	Address	City,State	Zip code	Telephone	Fax	Grade	Contact
Armadillo Technical Institute	PO Box 1560	Phoenix, OR	97535-1560	541-535-3287		6-12	Mike Warner
Arthur Academy	13717 SE Division St	Portland, OR	97236-2841	503-252-3753	761-4143	K-4	Charles Arthur
Arts & Technology Charter S	8633 SW Main St	Wilsonville, OR	97070-8650	503-673-7020	673-7001	9-10	Mike Tannenbaum
Baker Charter S	999 Locust St NE	Salem, OR	97301-0954	503-364-4042	566-6929	K-3	Tracy Moisan
Ballston Community Charter S	9015 De Jong Rd	Amity, OR	97101-9518	503-843-2537		K-12	Jeff Clabaugh
Bethany Charter S	11824 Hazelgreen Rd NE	Silverton, OR	97381-9611	503-873-4300	873-0143	K-8	Kathy Frank
Blue Mountain Charter S	76132 Blue Mtn School Rd	Cottage Grove, OR	97424	541-942-7764	942-7597	K-12	Lesley Stine
Camas Valley S	PO Box 57	Camas Valley, OR	97416-0057	541-445-2131	445-2041	K-12	Vince Swagerty
Cascade Heights Charter S	13515 SE Rusk Rd	Milwaukie, OR	97222-3212	503-701-0009		K-6	Holly Denman
Center for Advanced Learning	1484 NW Civic Dr	Gresham, OR	97030-5564	503-667-4978		11-12	Bill Lesh
Childs Way Charter S	37895 Row River Rd	Culp Creek, OR	97427	541-946-1821	946-2007	6-10	Mike Kerns
City View Charter S	1771 SE Minter Bridge Rd	Hillsboro, OR	97123-5160	503-844-9424		1-6	Pamela Grant
Clackamas Middle College HS	19729 Highway 213	Oregon City, OR	97045-4190	503-518-5900	518-5928	9-12	Tim King

School	Address	City,State	Zip code	Telephone	Fax	Grade	Contact
Clackamas Web Academy	19721 Highway 213	Oregon City, OR	97045-4190	503-518-5900	518-5904	1-12	Tim King
CM2 Opal S	4015 SW Canyon Rd	Portland, OR	97221-2759	503-471-9902	223-6600	PK-4	Lynette Engstrom
Columbia County Education Campus	474 N 16th St	Saint Helens, OR	97051-1340	503-366-3207	397-2723	7-12	Colleen Grogan
Days Creek Charter S	PO Box 10	Days Creek, OR	97429-0010	541-825-3296	825-3052	6-12	Laurie Newton
Deschutes Edge Charter S	2105 W Antler Ave	Redmond, OR	97756-9398	541-923-4840		6-8	Carrie Carpenter
Douglas Avenue Charter S	PO Box 195	Gervais, OR	97026-0195	503-792-3803	792-3770	9-12	Chuck Borberg
Eddyville Charter S	PO Box 68	Eddyville, OR	97343-0068	541-875-2942	875-2491	K-12	Don McDonald
Emerson Charter S	105 NW Park Ave	Portland, OR	97209-3315	503-525-6124	223-4875	K-5	Tara O'Neil
Four Rivers Community S	2232 SW 4th Ave	Ontario, OR	97914-1850	541-889-3715		K-5	Chelle Robins
Goodall Environmental MS	2805 Lansing Ave NE	Salem, OR	97301-8555	503-399-3215	399-4070	6-8	Mike Weddle
Howard Street Charter S	710 Howard St SE	Salem, OR	97302-3098	503-399-3408	375-7861	6-8	Alan Ball
International S of the Cascades	2105 W Antler Ave	Redmond, OR	97756-9398	541-923-4840	923-4846	9-12	Donna Howard
Ione S	PO Box 167	Ione, OR	97843-0167	541-422-7131	422-7555	K-12	Bryn Browning
Kings Valley Charter S	38840 Kings Valley Hwy	Philomath, OR	97370-9750	541-929-2134	929-8179	K-8	Mark Hazelton
Leadership & Entrepreneurship Charter HS	8111 NE Holman St	Portland, OR	97218-4021	503-254-2537	252-9560	9-12	Reese Lord
Lighthouse S	93670 Viking Ln	North Bend, OR	97459	541-751-1649		K-6	Alane Jennings
Lincoln City Career Tech HS	801 SW Highway 101 Ste 404	Lincoln City, OR	97367-2752	541-996-5534	265-8507	9-12	Marie Jones
Lourdes Charter S	39059 Jordan Rd	Scio, OR	97374-9330	503-394-3340		K-8	Linda Duman
Luckiamute Valley Charter S	12975 Kings Valley Hwy	Monmouth, OR	97361-9525	503-838-1933		K-8	Dan Austin
Milwaukie Academy of the Arts	11300 SE 23rd Ave	Milwaukie, OR	97222-7753	503-353-5851	353-5845	9-12	Bill Maher
MITCH Charter S	PO Box 230575	Tigard, OR	97281-0575	503-639-5757		K-8	Debi Lorence
MITCH Sherwood Charter S	PO Box 1342	Sherwood, OR	97140-1342	503-925-8007		K-3	Fred Puhl
Mosier Community S	PO Box 307	Mosier, OR	97040-0307	541-478-3321	478-2536	K-6	Carole Schmidt
Multisensory Learning Academy	402 NE 172nd Ave	Portland, OR	97230-6442	503-261-0202	261-9099	K-5	Terri Amacher
Network Charter S	45 W Broadway Ste 201	Eugene, OR	97401-3046	541-344-1229		7-12	Mary Leighton
New Urban HS	1905 SE Oak Grove Blvd	Milwaukie, OR	97267-2621	503-353-5925	353-5928	9-12	Tim King
Nixyaawi Community S	PO Box 638	Pendleton, OR	97801-0638	541-966-2643		9-12	Anna Tester
North Columbia Academy	28168 Old Rainier Rd	Rainier, OR	97048-3017	503-556-5041	556-2203	9-12	Kristin Carrico
Optimum Learning Environments Charter S	7905 June Reid Pl NE	Keizer, OR	97303-2559	503-399-5548	399-2647	1-5	Gary Etchemendy
Oregon City Service Learning Academy	PO Box 2110	Oregon City, OR	97045-5010	503-785-8445		9-12	Melanie Schaffer
Oregon Coast Technology S	1913 Meade St	North Bend, OR	97459-3432	541-756-8307	756-1313	6-12	James Moyer
Oregon Connections Academy	38875 NW 1st Ave	Scio, OR	97374-9501	503-394-4315		K-12	Jim Thomas
Oregon Virtual S	520 NW Wall St Ste 230	Bend, OR	97701	541-383-6027		9-12	Peter Miller
Paisley Charter S	PO Box 97	Paisley, OR	97636-0097	541-943-3111	943-3129	K-12	Mark Jeffery
Phoenix S of Roseburg	3131 NE Diamond Lake Blvd	Roseburg, OR	97470-3632	541-673-3036	957-5906	7-12	Ron Breyne
Portland Arthur Academy	7507 SE Yamhill St	Portland, OR	97215-2282	503-252-3936		K-2	Charles Arthur
REALMS	1501 NE Neff Rd	Bend, OR	97701-6149	541-322-5323	322-5473	6-8	Roger White
Resource Link Charter S	PO Box 509	Coos Bay, OR	97420-0102	541-267-1499	266-7314	5-12	Lesli Gieselman
Reynolds Arthur Academy	123 SE 21st St	Troutdale, OR	97060-3300	503-465-8882	465-8883	K-5	Peggy Concillo
Riddle Education Center	PO Box 45	Riddle, OR	97469-0045	541-874-3101		7-12	Dave Gianotti
Ridgeline Montessori	2855 Lincoln St	Eugene, OR	97405	541-681-9662	681-4394	K-8	Cindy Bass
Sand Ridge Charter S	30581 Sodaville Mtn Home Rd	Lebanon, OR	97355-9008	541-258-2416		K-12	Mary Northern
SEI Academy Charter S	3920 N Kerby Ave	Portland, OR	97227-1255	503-249-1721	249-1955	6-8	Linda Harris
Sheridan Japanese S	PO Box 446	Sheridan, OR	97378-0446	503-843-3400	843-7438	4-12	Laura Siering
Siletz Valley S	PO Box 247	Siletz, OR	97380-0247	541-444-1100	444-2368	K-12	Van Peters
South Columbia Family S	52181 SW EM Watts Rd	Scappoose, OR	97056-2602	503-543-7077	543-7087	1-12	Anita Ott
Springwater Environmental Sciences S	PO Box 3010	Oregon City, OR	97045-0301	503-655-2065		K-4	Deb Odell
Sweet Home Charter S	1825 Long St	Sweet Home, OR	97386-2322	541-367-1833	258-1898	1-4	Jay Jackson
Technology Learning Center	475 Bridge St	Vernonia, OR	97064-1215	503-429-5891	429-7049	9-12	Kenneth Cox
Three Rivers Charter S	4975 Willamette Falls Dr	West Linn, OR	97068-3348	503-723-6019	723-6407	4-8	Katherine Holtgraves
Trillium Charter S	5420 N Interstate Ave	Portland, OR	97217-4569	503-285-3833	281-3937	K-12	
Upper Chetco Charter S	99603 N Bank Chetco River	Brookings, OR	97415	541-412-9072	412-9047	2-6	
Village S	2855 Lincoln St	Eugene, OR	97405	541-345-7285	242-6874	K-8	Martha Collins
West Lane Technology Learning Center	24936 Fir Grove Ln	Elmira, OR	97437-9751	541-935-2101		9-12	Donna Garner
West Side Dual Language Charter S	3685 Belmont Dr	Hood River, OR	97031-8763	541-386-1535	387-5059	K-5	Dan Patton
Willamette Leadership Academy	87230 Central Rd	Eugene, OR	97402-9208	541-935-4205		6-12	Roger McClelland
Woodburn Arthur Academy	575 Gatch St	Woodburn, OR	97071-4927	503-981-5746	761-4143	K-2	Charles Arthur

Pennsylvania

School	Address	City,State	Zip code	Telephone	Fax	Grade	Contact
Academy Charter S	900 Agnew Rd	Pittsburgh, PA	15227-3902	412-885-5200		K-12	William Styche
Achievement House Charter S	1021 W Lancaster Ave	Bryn Mawr, PA	19010	610-527-0143		K-12	Wallace Wallace
Ad Prima Charter S	124 Bryn Mawr Ave	Bala Cynwyd, PA	19004-3013	610-617-9121		K-8	Dr. June Brown
Agora Cyber Charter S	124 Bryn Mawr Ave	Bala Cynwyd, PA	19004-3013	610-617-9121		K-12	Dr. June Brown
Allen Preparatory Charter S	5151 Warren St	Philadelphia, PA	19131-4441	215-878-1544	878-8171	5-8	Lawrence F. Jones
Alliance For Progress Charter S	1821 Cecil B Moore Ave	Philadelphia, PA	19121-3135	215-232-4892	232-4893	K-5	Stacey E. Hill
Architecture & Design Charter HS	675 Sansom St	Philadelphia, PA	19106-3300	215-351-2900	351-9458	9-12	Dr. Peter Kountz
Attucks Youth Build Charter S	605 S Duke St	York, PA	17401-3111	717-848-3610	843-3914	12-12	Floyd Goff
Avon Grove Charter S	110 State Rd	West Grove, PA	19390-8908	484-667-5000		K-6	Dr. Kevin Brady
Bear Creek Community Charter S	2000 Bear Creek Blvd	Wilkes Barre, PA	18702-9684	570-820-4070		K-6	Dr. Janice Solkov
Beaver Area Academic Charter S	Gypsy Glen Rd	Beaver, PA	15009	724-774-0250		9-12	Brian White
Belmont Charter S	4030 Brown St	Philadelphia, PA	19104-4899	215-790-1294		K-6	Alice Lunsford
Bracetti Academy Charter S	2501 Kensington Ave	Philadelphia, PA	19125-1321	215-291-4436	291-4985	6-10	Angela Villani
Brown Charter S	279 Boas St	Harrisburg, PA	17102-2940	717-232-7696	236-3829	K-8	Rae L. Talley
Bucks County Montessori Charter S	8931 New Falls Rd	Levittown, PA	19054	215-547-5230	547-5032	K-6	John Funston
Byers Charter S	1911 Arch St	Philadelphia, PA	19103-1403	215-972-1700	972-1701	K-3	Salome Thomas-EL
Career Connections Charter HS	4412 Butler St	Pittsburgh, PA	15201-3012	412-682-1816	682-6559	9-11	Dr. Theresa Henderson
Center for Student Learning Charter S	134 Yardley Ave	Fallsington, PA	19054-1119	215-428-4100		6-12	Michelle Hunter
Central Pennsylvania Digital Charter S	1500 4th Ave	Altoona, PA	16602-3616	814-940-6989		K-12	Dr. Janette Kelly
Centre Learning Community Charter S	2643 W College Ave	State College, PA	16801-2604	814-861-7980	861-8030	5-8	Kosta Dussias
Chester Community Charter S	214 E 5th St	Chester, PA	19013-4510	610-447-0400	876-5716	K-6	Steven Lee
Chester Co. Family Academy	323 E Gay St Ste B7	West Chester, PA	19380	610-696-5910	696-6324	K-2	Lorraine Anderson
City Charter HS	717 Liberty Ave	Pittsburgh, PA	15222	412-690-2489		9-10	Maxine Klimasara
Clemente Charter S	136 S 4th St	Allentown, PA	18102	610-439-5181	435-4731	6-12	Carlos Lopez
Collegium Charter S	535 James Hance Ct	Exton, PA	19341-2560	610-903-1300	903-1317	K-12	Bill Winters
Columbus Charter S	916 Christian St	Philadelphia, PA	19147-3808	215-925-7400	925-7491	K-4	Rosemary Dougherty
Commonwealth Connections Charter S	5010 E Trindle Rd	Mechanicsburg, PA	17050	717-605-8900		K-8	Earl Grier
Community Academy of Philadelphia	1100 E Erie Ave	Philadelphia, PA	19124-5424	215-533-6700		K-12	Joe Proietta
DeHostos Charter S	4322 N 5th St	Philadelphia, PA	19140-2302	215-455-2300	455-6312	K-K,	Evelyn Lebron
Delaware Valley Charter HS	5201 Old York Rd	Philadelphia, PA	19141-2995	215-455-2550		9-12	Ava Greene Bedden
Discovery Charter S	5070 Parkside Ave Unit 6200	Philadelphia, PA	19131-4750	215-879-8182		K-6	Jacquelyn Kelley
Evergreen Community Charter S	PO Box 523	Mountainhome, PA	18342-0523	570-595-6355	595-6038	6-12	Jill Shoesmith
Family Charter S	907 N 41st St	Philadelphia, PA	19104-1278	215-790-1294		K-4	Alice Lunsford
Fell Charter S	777 Main St	Simpson, PA	18407-1236	570-282-5199		K-6	Debi Zischke
First Philadelphia Charter S	4300 Tacony St	Philadelphia, PA	19124-4134	215-743-3100		K-3	Stacy Cruise-Clark
Folk Arts-Cultural Treasures Charter S	1118 Market St	Philadelphia, PA	19107-3601	215-569-2600		K-8	Neeta Patel
Forbes Charter S	PO Box 197	Lincoln Univ, PA	19352-0197	484-368-2575		K-3	Dr. Lenetta Lee
Franklin Towne Charter HS	PO Box 310	Philadelphia, PA	19105-0310	215-289-5000	535-8910	9-12	Joseph Venditti
Freire Charter S	2027 Chestnut St	Philadelphia, PA	19103	215-557-8555	557-9051	8-12	Dr. Kelly Davenport
GECAC Community Charter S	1446 E Lake Rd	Erie, PA	16507-1936	814-461-9600	461-0226	K-7	Gregory Myers
Germantown Settlement Charter S	4811 Germantown Ave	Philadelphia, PA	19144-3014	215-713-0855	713-0553	5-8	Cynthia Hart
Graystone Academy Charter S	139 Modena Rd	Coatesville, PA	19320-4036	610-383-4311		K-6	Dr. Linda Portlock
Green Woods Charter S	8480 Hagys Mill Rd	Philadelphia, PA	19128-1938	215-482-6337	482-9135	K-6	Deborah Binder
Hope Charter S	2116 E Haines St	Philadelphia, PA	19138-2600	215-336-2730		9-12	Richard L. Chapman
Imani Education Circle Charter S	5612 Greene St Fl 2	Philadelphia, PA	19144	215-713-9240		K-8	Dr. Francine Fulton
Imhotep Institute Charter HS	2101 W Godfrey Ave	Philadelphia, PA	19138-2597	215-438-4140	438-4160	9-12	M. Christine Wiggins
Independence Charter S	105 S 7th St	Philadelphia, PA	19106	215-238-8000	238-1998	K-4	Jurate Krokys
Infinity Charter S	51 Banks St Ste 1	Penbrook, PA	17103-2067	717-238-1880		K-6	Nancy Hall
Keystone Education Center Charter S	425 S Good Hope Rd	Greenville, PA	16125-8629	724-588-2511	588-2545	6-12	Mike Gentile
Khepera Charter S	144 Carpenter Ln	Philadelphia, PA	19119-2563	215-843-3527		K-8	Lenee Johnson
KIPP Academy Charter S	2709 N Broad St	Philadelphia, PA	19132-2722	215-227-1728		5-5	Marc Mannella
La Academia Charter S	30 N Ann St	Lancaster, PA	17602-3063	717-295-7763	399-6456	6-12	Dr. Maritza Robert
Laboratory Charter S	124 Bryn Mawr Ave	Bala Cynwyd, PA	19004-3013	610-617-9121	660-8416	K-8	Dr. June Hairston-Brown
Leadership Learning Partners Charter S	1425 N 2nd St	Philadelphia, PA	19122-3801	215-739-2007	739-2606	K-6	Dr. Ruthie Green-Brown
Lehigh Valley Academy	1560 Valley Center Pkwy	Bethlehem, PA	18017	610-866-9660		K-12	Susan Mauser
Lehigh Valley Charter HS	675 E Broad St	Bethlehem, PA	18018-6332	610-868-2971		9-12	Dr. Thomas Lubben
Lincoln Charter S	559 W King St	York, PA	17401-3776	717-699-1573	846-4031	K-5	Erin Holman
Lincoln Park Performing Arts Charter S	652 Midland Ave	Midland, PA	15059-1433	724-643-9004	643-0769	K-12	Dr. Nick Trombetta
Manchester Academic Charter S	1214 Liverpool St	Pittsburgh, PA	15233-1309	412-322-0585	322-2176	K-8	Vasilios A. Scoumis
Maritime Academy Charter S	3020 Market St	Philadelphia, PA	19104-2801	215-387-7066		5-8	Dr. Ann Gillis Waiters
MAST Community Charter S	1800 Byberry Rd	Philadelphia, PA	19116-3012	215-348-1100		K-12	Richard Trzaska
Mastery Charter HS	35 S 4th St	Philadelphia, PA	19106-2710	215-922-1902	922-1903	9-10	Scott H. Gordon
Math Civics & Sciences Charter S	447 N Broad St	Philadelphia, PA	19123	215-923-4880	923-4859	1-12	Veronica Joyner
Midwestern Regional Virtual Charter S	453 Maple St	Grove City, PA	16127-2399	724-458-6700	458-5083	K-12	Angelo Pezzuolo
Montessori Regional Charter S	2910 Sterrettania Rd	Erie, PA	16506-2646	814-833-7771	833-1838	K-6	Anthony Pirrello
Morris Charter S	2600 W Thompson St	Philadelphia, PA	19121-4699	215-684-5087	684-8881	K-8	Ruth King
Multi-Cultural Academy Charter S	4666 N 15th St	Philadelphia, PA	19140-1109	215-457-6666	457-2982	9-12	Dr. Vuong Thuy

School	Address	City,State	Zip code	Telephone	Fax	Grade	Contact
New Foundations Charter S	8001 Torresdale Ave	Philadelphia, PA	19136-2917	215-624-8100		K-8	Paul Stadelberger
New Media Technology Charter S	7800 Ogontz Ave	Philadelphia, PA	19150-1408	267-286-6900		9-12	Dr. Ina Walker
Nittany Valley Charter S	1612 Norma St	State College, PA	16801-6228	814-867-3842	231-0795	1-8	Carolyn Maroncelli
Northside Urban Pathways Charter S	914 Penn Ave	Pittsburgh, PA	15222	412-392-4601	392-4602	6-12	Linda Clautti
Northwood Academy	4621 Castor Ave	Philadelphia, PA	19124-3097	215-289-5606	676-8340	K-6	Brien Gardiner
Nueva Esperanza Academy Charter HS	301 W Hunting Park Ave	Philadelphia, PA	19140-2625	215-457-3667	457-4381	9-12	David Rossi
Penn Charter S	3000 W School House Ln	Philadelphia, PA	19144-5412	215-844-3460	843-3939	K-12	Earl Ball
Pennsylvania Cyber Charter S	900 Midland Ave	Midland, PA	15059-1529	724-643-1180	643-1181	K-12	Dr. Nick Trombetta
Pennsylvania Distance Learning Charter S	23 N Front St	Harrisburg, PA	17101	717-232-3220		K-12	Dr. James Hoover
Pennsylvania Leadership Charter S	1332 Enterprise Dr	West Chester, PA	19380	610-701-3333		K-12	Dr. James Hanak
PA Learners Online Regional S	475 Waterfront Dr E	Homestead, PA	15120-1144	412-394-5733		K-12	Dr. David Martin
Pennsylvania Virtual Charter S	1 W Main St Ste 400	Norristown, PA	19401-4766	610-275-8501	275-1719	K-5	Joanne Jones Barnett
People for People Charter S	800 N Broad St	Philadelphia, PA	19130-2202	215-763-7060	235-6435	K-5	Andre Williams
Perseus House Charter S of Excellence	2931 Harvard Rd	Erie, PA	16508-1220	814-459-3954		7-12	Dr. John Linden
Philadelphia Academy Charter S	11000 Roosevelt Blvd	Philadelphia, PA	19116	215-676-8320	676-8340	K-8	Brien Gardner
Philadelphia Electrical & Tech Charter S	1420 Chestnut St	Philadelphia, PA	19102-2505	267-514-1823	514-1834	9-10	Michael Nemitz
Philadelphia Harambee Inst Charter S	640 N 66th St	Philadelphia, PA	19151	215-472-8770	472-9611	K-8	John Skief
Philadelphia Montessori Charter S	2227 Island Rd	Philadelphia, PA	19142-1009	215-365-4011	365-4367	PK-3	Kathleen Dzura
Philadelphia Performing Arts Charter S	2600 S Broad St	Philadelphia, PA	19145-4616	215-551-4000	551-1113	K-7	Angela Corosanite
Pocono Mountain Charter S	16 Carriage Sq	Tobyhanna, PA	18466-8979	570-894-5108		K-12	Dennis Bloom
Preparatory Charter S	1928 Point Breeze Ave	Philadelphia, PA	19145-2612	215-334-6144	334-6147	9-12	John Badagliacco
Propel Charter S - East	1611 Monroeville Ave	Turtle Creek, PA	15145-1652	412-823-0347		K-6	Jeremy Resnick
Propel Charter S - Homestead	129 E 10th Ave	Homestead, PA	15120	412-464-2604		K-8	George Fitch
Propel Charter S - Mc Keesport	413 Shaw Ave	Mc Keesport, PA	15132-3036	412-678-7215		K-6	
Propel Charter S - Montour	24 S 18th St	Pittsburgh, PA	15203	412-325-7305		K-6	
Raising Horizons Quest Charter S	4960 Master St	Philadelphia, PA	19131-4521	215-477-6672	477-6674	K-6	Martha Russell
RAPAH-Edison Charter S	120 S Whitfield St	Pittsburgh, PA	15206-3806	412-362-8818		K-2	Alecia Gibbs
Renaissance Academy - Edison Charter S	40 Pine Crest Ave	Phoenixville, PA	19460-2955	610-983-4080	983-4096	K-12	Gina Guarino-Buli
Renaissance Advantage Charter S	1712 S 56th St	Philadelphia, PA	19143-5308	215-724-2343	724-2374	K-8	Bill Williams
Renaissance Charter S	7500 Germantown Ave Ste I	Philadelphia, PA	19119-1678	215-753-0390	753-0615	6-8	A. Donald Lepore
Ridgeview Academy Charter S	1133 Village Way	Latrobe, PA	15650-5201	724-537-9110	537-9114	1-12	Sherri L. Holler
Sankofa Academy	446 W Gay St	West Chester, PA	19380-2851	610-696-0333		5-12	Dr. LaMont McKim
School Lane Charter S	2400 Bristol Pike	Bensalem, PA	19020-5293	215-245-6055	245-6058	K-8	Karen Schade
Souderton Charter S Collaborative	110 E Broad St	Souderton, PA	18964-1276	215-721-4560	721-4071	K-7	Jennifer Arevalo
Spectrum Charter S	4369 Northern Pike	Monroeville, PA	15146-2807	412-374-8130	374-9629	9-12	Michelle Johnson
Sugar Valley Rural Charter S	PO Box 104	Loganton, PA	17747-0104	570-725-7822	725-7825	K-12	Logan Coney
SUSQ-Cyber Charter S	90 Lawton Ln	Milton, PA	17847-9756	570-523-1155	523-0674	9-12	James Street
Sylvan Heights Science Charter S	915 S 13th St	Harrisburg, PA	17104-3402	717-232-9220	232-9221	K-4	Dr. Kevin Moran
Tidioute Community Charter S	241 Main St	Tidioute, PA	16351-1299	814-484-3550	484-3977	K-12	David Craig
Tuscarora Blended Learning Charter S	2527 US Highway 522 S	Mc Veytown, PA	17051-9434	814-542-2501		K-12	Tony Payne
21st Century Cyber Charter S	455 Boot Rd	Downingtown, PA	19335-3043	484-237-5206		6-12	Jon Marsh
Universal Institute Charter S	801 S 15th St	Philadelphia, PA	19146-2215	215-732-7988	732-8066	K-8	John Walker
Urban League of Pittsburgh Charter S	327 N Negley Ave	Pittsburgh, PA	15206-2851	412-361-1008	361-1042	K-5	Dr. Gail Edwards
Village Charter S of Chester-Upland	200 Commerce Dr	Chester, PA	19014-3203	610-494-2100		PK-12	Harry Hill
Vitalistic Therapeutic Charter S	902 4th Ave	Bethlehem, PA	18018-3702	610-861-7570		K-3	Naomi H. Grossman
Wakisha Charter S	1209 Vine St	Philadelphia, PA	19107-1111	267-256-0950	256-0953	6-8	Denise Johnson
West Oak Lane Charter S	7115 Stenton Ave	Philadelphia, PA	19138-1136	215-927-7995	927-7980	K-5	Donnamaria Parker
West Philadelphia Achievement Charter S	111 N 49th St	Philadelphia, PA	19139-2718	215-476-6471	476-6470	K-5	Stacey Gill-Phillips
Widener Partnership Charter S	1 University Pl	Chester, PA	19013-5700	610-497-7399		K-5	Dr. Annette Anderson
Wissahickon Charter S	4700 Wissahickon Ave	Philadelphia, PA	19144	267-338-1020		K-5	Julie Carroll
Wonderland Charter S	2112 Sandy Dr	State College, PA	16803-2282	814-234-5886		K-K	Harold Ohnmeis
World Communications Charter S	512 S Broad St	Philadelphia, PA	19146-1695	215-735-3197	735-3824	6-12	Dr. Martin Ryder
Young Scholars Charter S	1415 N Broad St	Philadelphia, PA	19122	215-232-9727	232-4542	6-8	C. Lars Beck
Young Scholars of Central PA Charter S	3020 Research Dr	State College, PA	16801-2782	814-237-9727		K-5	Bulent Tarman
Youth Build Charter S	1231 N Broad St	Philadelphia, PA	19122	215-627-8671	763-5774	9-12	Simran Sidhu
Rhode Island							
BEACON Charter S	320 Main St	Woonsocket, RI	02895-3138	401-671-6261	671-6264	9-12	Robert Pilkington
Blackstone Academy	334 Pleasant St	Pawtucket, RI	02860-5273	401-726-1750	726-1753	9-12	Carolyn Sheehan
Compass S	537 Old North Rd	Kingston, RI	02881-1220	401-783-8322	788-8326	K-8	Allen Zipke
Construction Career Academy	4 Sharpe Dr	Cranston, RI	02920-4410	401-270-8692	270-8697	9-12	Dr. Michael Silva
Cuffee S	459 Promenade St	Providence, RI	02908-5601	401-453-2626	453-4964	K-8	David Bourns
CVS Highlander Charter S	45 Greeley St	Providence, RI	02904-2214	401-277-2600	277-2603	K-8	Jim Donahue
International Charter S	334 Pleasant St	Pawtucket, RI	02860-5273	401-721-0824	721-0976	K-5	Julie Nora
Kingston Hill Academy	850 Stony Fort Rd	Saunderstown, RI	02874-1003	401-783-8282	783-5656	K-6	Daniel Parker
Learning Community S	21 Lincoln Ave	Central Falls, RI	02863-2012	401-722-9998	722-0990	K-3	Sarah Friedman
Textron/Chamber of Commerce Academy	130 Broadway	Providence, RI	02903-3003	401-456-1738	521-0653	9-12	Lawrence DeSalvatore
Times 2 Academy	50 Fillmore St	Providence, RI	02908-3105	401-272-5094	272-0555	K-12	Dr. Stanley Thompson
South Carolina							
Academy for Teaching and Learning	109 Hinton St	Chester, SC	29706-2022	803-385-6334	385-6335	PK-8	Robyn Welborn
Aiken Academy	10612 Augusta Rd	Belton, SC	29627-9246	864-243-3443	243-5743	1-8	Glynda Caddell
Boykin Academy	4851 Rivers Ave	N Charleston, SC	29406-6502	843-744-8882	744-8885	K-12	Dee Gathers
Brashier Middle College HS	404 Vardry St	Greenville, SC	29601-3308	864-232-2112	232-2390	9-12	Michael Sinclair
Bridgewater Academy	316 Bush Dr	Myrtle Beach, SC	29579-7314	843-236-3689	236-4921	K-8	Carol Merrill
Carolina School for Inquiry	7405 Fairfield Rd Ste A	Columbia, SC	29203	803-691-1250	691-1247	K-5	Victoria Dixon-Mokeba
Charleston Development Academy	PO Box 20518	Charleston, SC	29413-0518	843-722-2689	722-2694	K-6	Cecelia Gordon Rogers
Children's Attention Home	PO Box 2912	Rock Hill, SC	29732-4912	803-328-8871	324-0437	K-8	Dr. Carey Harper
CHOiCES	PO Box 15386	Florence, SC	29506-0386	843-664-8993	664-8881	5-8	Ralph Porter
Discovery S of Lancaster	PO Box 130	Lancaster, SC	29721-0130	803-285-8430	416-8907	K-5	Tom McDuffie
East Cooper Montessori Charter S	188 Civitas St	Mount Pleasant, SC	29464-2669	843-216-2883	216-8880	1-8	Jody Swanigan
Fox Creek HS	PO Box 6430	North Augusta, SC	29861-6430	803-613-9435	613-1533	9-12	Dr. Tim Murph
Fuller Normal Charter S	901 Anderson Rd	Greenville, SC	29601-4103	864-271-3698	272-0241	K-5	Brenda Humbert
Greenville Technical Charter HS	PO Box 5616	Greenville, SC	29606-5616	864-250-8845	250-8846	9-12	W. Fred Crawford
James Island Charter HS	1000 Fort Johnson Rd	Charleston, SC	29412-8898	843-762-2754	762-5228	9-12	Robert Bohnstengel
Langston Charter MS	288 Rocky Creek Rd	Greenville, SC	29615-6145	864-286-9700	286-9699	6-8	Gregory Abel
Lloyd Kennedy Charter S	PO Box 418	Aiken, SC	29802-0418	803-644-4824	641-1155	9-12	Keisha Lloyd-Kennedy
Lloyd Kennedy Charter S	PO Box 418	Aiken, SC	29802-0418	803-644-4824	641-1155	5-8	Keisha Lloyd-Kennedy
Meyer Center for Special Children	1132 Rutherford Rd	Greenville, SC	29609-3927	864-250-0005	250-0028	PK-2	Louise Anthony
Midlands Math & Business Academy	PO Box 4487	Columbia, SC	29240-4487	803-799-5101	799-5318	4-8	Michelle Spradley
Midland Valley Preparatory S	2432 Jefferson Davis Hwy	Graniteville, SC	29829-3828	803-594-1028	594-0511	K-8	Lilian Thomas-Wilson
MLD Learning Academy	PO Box 136	Bishopville, SC	29010-0136	803-428-3350	484-1822	4-8	Benita Robinson
Murray Hill Academy	3795 Spruill Ave	N Charleston, SC	29405-7149	843-745-9540	308-9340		Reginald Flenory
Orange Grove ES	1225 Orange Branch Rd	Charleston, SC	29407-3300	843-763-1520	769-2245	K-4	Larry Dicenzo
Palmetto Youth Academy	1209 N Douglas St	Florence, SC	29501-0600	843-679-7070	679-7046	3-6	Yvonne Burgess
Phoenix Charter HS	PO Box 170	Alcolu, SC	29001-0170	803-505-6800	505-6801	9-12	Anne Darby
Richland One Middle College S	316 S Beltline Blvd	Columbia, SC	29205	803-738-7114	738-7117	11-12	Audrey Breland
Wohali Academy	PO Box 1005	Travelers Rest, SC	29690-1005	864-834-8013	834-6977	K-12	Laura Blackmore
Youth Academy Charter S	PO Box 174	Kingstree, SC	29556-0174	843-355-5424	355-5753	7-12	Cheryl West
YouthBuild Charleston Charter S	7555 Spartan Blvd N	N Charleston, SC	29420-8820	843-207-8308	552-1684	9-12	Annette Goodwin
Tennessee							
Circles of Success Charter S	867 S Parkway E	Memphis, TN	38106-5605	901-322-7978	322-7993	K-4	Sheri Catron
City University S of Liberal Arts	1500 Dunn Ave	Memphis, TN	38106-7318	901-368-9890	368-9894	9-10	Van Snyder
KIPP Academy	123 Douglas Ave	Nashville, TN	37207-5155	615-226-4484	226-4401	5-8	Randy Dowell
Memphis Academy of Health Sciences	3925 Chelsea Avenue Ext	Memphis, TN	38108-2612	901-382-1441	382-1944	6-8	Curtis Weathers
Memphis Academy of Science & Engineering	20 Dudley St	Memphis, TN	38103	901-448-6273	448-8850	6-10	Tommie Henderson
Memphis Business Academy	3333 Old Brownsville Rd	Memphis, TN	38134-8419	901-380-8176	380-8179	6-8	Anthony Anderson
Promise Academy	1635 Georgian Dr	Memphis, TN	38127-4312	901-358-7752	358-7753	K-4	Dr. Blakely Wallace
Smithson-Craighead Academy	3307 Brick Church Pike	Nashville, TN	37207-2301	615-228-9886	228-9799	PK-4	Janelle Glover
Southern Avenue Charter S	3310 Kimball Ave	Memphis, TN	38111	901-743-7335	743-7677	K-3	George Knox
STAR Academy Charter S	3260 James Rd	Memphis, TN	38128-5351	901-387-5050	387-0798	K-3	Dr. Kia Young
Stax Music Academy Charter S	910 E McLemore Ave	Memphis, TN	38106-3338	901-942-7627	507-1460	6-12	David Hill
Yo Academy Charter S	2140 S 3rd St	Memphis, TN	38109-7734	901-947-1207		9-12	Dr. Marie Milam
Texas							
A+ Academy	10327 Rylie Rd	Dallas, TX	75217-8240	972-557-5578	557-5807	PK-12	Brenton White
Academy of Accelerated Learning	6025 Chimney Rock Rd	Houston, TX	77081-4011	713-773-4766	666-2532	PK-5	Joyce Bethany
Academy of Accelerated Learning	6025 Chimney Rock Rd	Houston, TX	77081-4011	713-645-0336	640-2435	PK-5	Joyce Bethany
Academy of Beaumont	2600 Girolamo St	Beaumont, TX	77703-4800	409-833-1600	833-1612	PK-8	Cynthia Solomon
Academy of Careers & Technologies	6812 Bandera Rd Ste 112	San Antonio, TX	78238-1368	210-226-7568	572-5321	9-12	Pamela Bradley White
Academy of Dallas	1030 Oak Park Dr	Dallas, TX	75232-1238	214-371-9600	371-1053	PK-8	Conrad Hargest
Accelerated Interdisciplinary Academy	PO Box 20589	Houston, TX	77225-0589	713-283-6298	283-6190	PK-5	Dr. David Fuller
Accelerated Interdisciplinary Academy	1730 N Northwest Loop 323	Tyler, TX	75702	903-526-1730	526-3334	PK-6	Connie Isabell

School	Address	City,State	Zip code	Telephone	Fax	Grade	Contact
Accelerated Intermediate Academy	PO Box 20589	Houston, TX	77225-0589	713-283-6298	283-6190	PK-8	Dr. David Fuller
Accelerated Learning Center	721 Omaha Dr	Corpus Christi, TX	78408-2839	361-887-7766	887-6035	PK-12	Maria Garza
Advantage Academy of Waxahachie	701 W Highway 287 Byp	Waxahachie, TX	75165-5163	972-937-9851	937-9876	K-12	Dr. Liz Matteson
Alief Montessori Community S	4215 H St	Houston, TX	77072-5380	281-530-9406	530-2233	PK-5	Nancy Chieu
Allen Charter	5220 Nomas St	Dallas, TX	75212-3229	972-794-5100	794-5101	PK-5	Connie Hovseth
Alpha Charter S	701 W State St	Garland, TX	75040-6310	972-272-2173	205-9050	K-12	
Ambassadors Preparatory Academy	2724 61st St Ste B	Galveston, TX	77551	409-762-6795	762-3903	K-5	Dr. Patricia Williams
American Academy of Excellence Charter S	PO Box 52877	Houston, TX	77052-2877	713-283-9235	571-9726	9-12	Jean LaGrone
American Youth Works Charter S	216 E 4th St	Austin, TX	78701-3610	512-236-6100	472-1189	9-12	Dr. Carole Lewis
American Youth Works Charter S	1901 E Ben White Blvd	Austin, TX	78741-7840	512-744-1900	916-4708	9-12	Kim Bookman
Amigos Por Vida-Friends for Life Charter	5500 El Camino Del Rey St	Houston, TX	77081	713-399-9945	349-0671	PK-6	Carlos Villagrana
Annunciation Home	3610 Shell Rd	Georgetown, TX	78628	512-864-7755	931-2406	6-12	Kathy Uplinger
Arlington Classics Academy	2111 Roosevelt Dr	Arlington, TX	76013-5920	817-274-2008	274-8768	K-8	Ken Simon
Austin Can Academy Charter S	2406 Rosewood Ave	Austin, TX	78702-2408	512-477-4226	931-8034	9-12	Charles Long
Austin Discovery S	PO Box 4356	Austin, TX	78765-4356	512-674-0700	407-8373	K-5	Kelly McRee
Austin S	621 W Euclid Ave	San Antonio, TX	78212-5128	210-226-5441	226-6192	PK-8	Maribel Rodriguez
Azleway Charter S	15892 County Road 26	Tyler, TX	75707-2728	903-566-8444	566-2053	K-12	Tom Evans
Banneker-McNair Math/Science Academy	4924 Griggs Rd	Houston, TX	77021-3251	713-748-2262	440-6767	PK-3	Donna Williams
Bay Area Charter MS	PO Box 2126	League City, TX	77574-2126	281-316-0001	316-0018	6-8	Dr. Rosalind Perez
Bay Area Charter S	2600 Humble Dr	El Lago, TX	77586-5900	281-326-4555	326-4888	PK-8	Kris Wessale
Benji's Special Education Academy	2903 Jensen Dr	Houston, TX	77026-6019	713-229-0560	224-6724	PK-12	
Bexar County Academy	1485 Hillcrest Dr	San Antonio, TX	78228-3900	210-432-8600	432-1195	PK-8	Dr. Keyshar Breedlove
Big Springs Charter S	PO Box 399	Leakey, TX	78873-0399	830-232-7101	232-4279	5-12	Deanna Kilpatrick
Brazos River Charter S	PO Box 949	Nemo, TX	76070-0949	254-898-9226	898-2297	8-12	Mike Thames
Brazos S for Inquiry & Creativity	301 York St	Houston, TX	77003			PK-8	Barbara Rueban
Brazos S for Inquiry & Creativity	8787 N Houston Rosslyn Rd	Houston, TX	77088-6430	713-983-6877	983-7036	PK-6	Sally Wickers
Brazos S for Inquiry & Creativity	802 Autumn Cir	College Station, TX	77840-7816	979-268-8884	268-8882	PK-12	Linda Page
Brazos S for Inquiry & Creativity	4637 Gano St	Houston, TX	77009-3457	713-222-8400	222-8409	PK-8	Barbara Rueban
Briarmeadow Charter S	3601 Dunvale Rd	Houston, TX	77063-5707	713-458-5500	458-5506	PK-8	Lynn Barnes
Bright Ideas Charter S	2507 Central Fwy E	Wichita Falls, TX	76302-5802	940-767-1561	767-1904	K-12	Lynda Plummer
Briscoe ES	2015 S Flores St	San Antonio, TX	78204-1990	210-222-8782	222-0822	PK-6	Julie Benavides
Brooks Academy of Science & Engineering	9350 S Presa St	San Antonio, TX	78223-4733	210-633-9006	633-9990	6-12	Rufus Samkin
Brown-Fellowship Charter School	6901 S Westmoreland Rd	Dallas, TX	75237-2431	972-709-4700	709-6605	PK-6	Paula Brown
Burch Charter S	5703 Blanco Rd	San Antonio, TX	78216-6616	210-431-9881	432-8467	4-6	Valerie Walker
Burnham Wood Charter S	7310 Bishop Flores Dr	El Paso, TX	79912-1429	915-584-9499	585-8814	PK-3	Alison Ford
Cameron S	3635 Belgium Ln	San Antonio, TX	78219-2500	210-224-0310	224-2954	PK-8	Carolyn McClure
Career Plus Learning Academy	1122 S WW White Rd	San Antonio, TX	78220-3424	210-333-8389	225-2448	6-12	Charles R. Hayes
Carroll S	463 Holmgreen Rd	San Antonio, TX	78220-3319	210-333-1130	333-1133	PK-8	Nikki Foley-Demby
Cedar Crest Charter S	3500 S Interstate 35	Belton, TX	76513-9498	254-939-4094	939-4046	K-12	Dr. Susan Perez
Cedar Ridge Charter S	PO Box 214	Lometa, TX	76853-0214	512-752-3142	752-3239	PK-12	Robin Beauregard
Cedars International Academy	1320 E 51st St	Austin, TX	78723-3037	512-419-1551	419-1581	K-7	Dr. Donna Williams
Children First Academy of Dallas	1638 E Ann Arbor Ave	Dallas, TX	75216-6335	214-371-2545	371-4682	PK-7	
Children First Academy of Houston	7803 Little York Rd	Houston, TX	77016-2436	713-491-9030	491-9032	PK-7	
Children of the Sun Charter S	5324 E US Highway 83 Ste 2	Rio Grande City, TX	78582	956-488-8883	488-0889	PK-12	Augie Pena
Children of the Sun Charter S	1205 S 7th St	Raymondville, TX	78580	956-689-3300	292-0371	PK-12	Alejandro Perez
Coastal Bend Youth City S	PO Box 268	Driscoll, TX	78351-0268	361-387-4513	387-0995	5-12	Sally Irvine
Comquest Academy	207 Peach St	Tomball, TX	77375-4733	281-516-0611	516-0993	9-12	
Copeland ES	1826 Basse Rd	San Antonio, TX	78213-4606	210-431-9881	253-2198	K-6	Betty Carnevale
Cornerstone Academy	9016 Westview Dr	Houston, TX	77055-4602	713-365-5766	365-5787	6-8	Jill Wright
Corpus Christi Academy	800 Ayers St	Corpus Christi, TX	78404	361-225-4240	225-4021	9-12	Joe Martinez
Corpus Christi Montessori Charter S	3530 Gollihar Rd	Corpus Christi, TX	78415-2759	361-852-0707	852-0640	1-5	Virginia Wallace
Crossroad Community Education Center	5830 Van Fleet St	Houston, TX	77033-2036	713-645-9122	645-9121	9-12	Andrea Williams
Crosstimbers Academy	PO Box 1327	Weatherford, TX	76086-1327	817-594-6220	594-6227	9-12	Mike Thames
Crutch's - Life Support Center	7115 Clarewood Dr	Houston, TX	77036-4401	713-779-9990	779-3047	6-12	Debra Gaddis
Cumberland Academy	8225 S Broadway Ave	Tyler, TX	75703-5494	903-581-2890	581-1476	K-6	James Moyers
Dallas Can! Academy	325 W 12th St Ste 175	Dallas, TX	75208	214-943-2244	946-4427	9-12	Laura Rodriguez
Dallas Can! Academy Charter S	4621 Ross Ave	Dallas, TX	75204-4994	214-824-4226	841-7951	9-12	Keith Lott
Dallas Community Charter S	722 Tenison Memorial Dr	Dallas, TX	75223-1138	214-824-8950	827-7683	PK-3	Terrybeth Ford
DaVinci S for Science and the Arts	7310 Bishop Flores Dr	El Paso, TX	79912-1429	915-584-4024	581-9840	4-7	Debbie Crinzi
DePelchin - Elkins Campus	4950 Memorial Dr	Houston, TX	77007	713-730-2335	802-7629	K-12	John Merriwether
DePelchin - Richmond Campus	710 S 7th St	Richmond, TX	77469	281-342-4906		2-12	John Merriwether
Destiny Honors Academy	1001 E Veterans Mem Ste 301	Killeen, TX	76541	254-200-2465	519-7672	K-8	James Bivins
Dominion Academy	1102 Pinemont Dr	Houston, TX	77018	713-476-9800	476-9707	6-8	Shinell Terrance-Clark
Draw Academy	3920 Stoney Brook Dr	Houston, TX	77063-6406	713-706-3729	706-3711	PK-8	Lisa Newton
Eagle Academy of Abilene	3161 S 23rd St Ste 4	Abilene, TX	79605-5861	325-698-8111	695-5620	PK-12	Jerry Kiser
Eagle Academy of Austin	1701 W Ben White Blvd #100A	Austin, TX	78704	512-444-8442	444-1266	9-12	Joseph Riggs
Eagle Academy of Beaumont	209 N 11th St	Beaumont, TX	77702-2213	409-835-4303	835-2882	6-12	Shawn Williams
Eagle Academy of Brownsville	955 Paredes Line Rd	Brownsville, TX	78521-2659	956-550-0890	554-0809	6-12	Norma Sorola
Eagle Academy of Del Rio	4300 E Highway 90	Del Rio, TX	78840-8878	830-298-2100	298-2122	6-12	Lupe Sotelo
Eagle Academy of Fort Worth	6411 Camp Bowie Blvd Ste B	Fort Worth, TX	76116-5449	817-731-2028	731-2129	6-12	
Eagle Academy of Laredo	1720 E Hillside Rd	Laredo, TX	78041-3336	956-723-7788	753-6101	6-12	
Eagle Academy of Lindale	17141 State Highway 110 N	Lindale, TX	75771-5933	903-881-9940	882-0183	K-12	Brad Crain
Eagle Academy of Lubbock	3501 50th St Ste 200	Lubbock, TX	79413-4043	806-763-1518	763-9310	6-12	Michael Griffin
Eagle Academy of Midland	2500 W Illinois Ave	Midland, TX	79701-6339	432-682-0384	682-0897	6-12	Molly Jasso
Eagle Academy of Pharr	200 E Expressway 83 Ste C	Pharr, TX	78577-6506	956-781-8800	781-7464	6-12	Cleo Hinojosa
Eagle Academy of San Antonio	3622 Fredericksburg Rd	San Antonio, TX	78201-3841	210-434-6090	434-7578	6-12	
Eagle Academy of Trinity	219 Bette St	Trinity, TX	75862-7208	936-594-1427	594-1395	6-12	Herschel Brannen
Eagle Academy of Tyler	2235 W Gentry Pkwy	Tyler, TX	75702-2809	903-592-5222	592-0324	6-12	Laqueta Timmons
Eagle Academy of Waco	1601 Washington Ave	Waco, TX	76701-1134	254-752-0441	752-0445	6-12	Butch Jackson
Eagle Advantage Charter S	4010 Joseph Hardin Dr	Dallas, TX	75236-1508	214-467-9101	467-9131	K-12	Dr. Allen Beck
East Fort Worth Montessori Academy	501 Oakland Blvd	Fort Worth, TX	76103-1014	817-496-3003	496-3004	PK-3	Joyce Brown
East Texas Charter HS	2402 Alpine Rd	Longview, TX	75601-3407	903-753-9400	753-0285	9-12	Terry Lapic
Eastwood Academy	1315 Dumble St	Houston, TX	77023-1902	713-924-1697	924-1715	9-12	Rogelio Lopez
Eden Park Academy	6215 Manchaca Rd Bldg D	Austin, TX	78745-4927	512-383-0613	383-0665	K-8	Lisa Robinson
Education and Training Center	6944 S Sunbelt Dr	San Antonio, TX	78218-3335	210-804-1786	804-1469	9-12	Barbara Hawkins
Education Center at Little Elm	100 E Park St Ste A	Little Elm, TX	75068-5129	972-292-3562	292-3563	K-12	Dr. Lisa Ashmore
Education Center at The Colony	5201 S Colony Blvd Ste 550	The Colony, TX	75056	972-370-3562	370-3563	K-12	Donica Hill
Education Center International Academy	2422 N Jupiter Rd	Garland, TX	75044-7347	972-530-6157	530-8635	K-12	Ula Davis
Ehrhart S of Fine Arts & Athletics	PO Box 7733	Beaumont, TX	77726-7733	409-839-8200	839-8242	PK-8	T. Chris Comick
El Paso Academy	11000 Argal Ct	El Paso, TX	79935-3712	915-590-8589	590-0052	9-12	Charles Gonzalez
El Paso Academy West	11000 Argal Ct	El Paso, TX	79935-3712	915-845-7997	845-7522	9-12	Carol Gardner
El Paso School of Excellence	1599 George Dieter Dr # 501	El Paso, TX	79936	915-595-1599	595-3100	PK-5	Judy Jimenez
El Paso School of Excellence	1605 George Dieter Dr # 501	El Paso, TX	79936	915-598-1755	598-8188	6-12	J.L. Lewis
Encino S	PO Box 106	Encino, TX	78353-0106	361-568-3375	568-3625	PK-8	Roberto Gonzalez
Energized for Excellence Academy	6201 Bissonnet St	Houston, TX	77081-6809	713-773-3600	773-3630	PK-8	Lois Bullock
Erath Excels! Academy	2900 W Washington St Ste 12	Stephenville, TX	76401	254-965-8883	965-8654	9-12	
Evolution Academy Charter S	1100 Business Pkwy	Richardson, TX	75081-5025	972-907-3755	907-3765	9-12	Cynthia Jones Trigg
Faith Family Academy of Oak Cliff	300 W Kiest Blvd	Dallas, TX	75224	214-375-7682	375-7681	PK-12	Sonja Jackson
Focus Learning Academy	135 W Wintergreen Rd	De Soto, TX	75115	972-283-1414	709-1111	K-6	Linus Walton
Fort Worth Academy of Fine Arts	3901 S Hulen St	Fort Worth, TX	76109-3321	817-924-1482	926-9932	K-12	John Shreve
Fort Worth Can! Academy	4301 Campus Dr	Fort Worth, TX	76119-5535	817-431-4226	531-0443	9-12	Cynthia Miles
Fort Worth Can! Academy	5508 Black Oak Ln	River Oaks, TX	76114	817-735-1515	735-1465	9-12	Gary Applewhite
Frontier Academy	2800 S Dakota Ave	Brownsville, TX	78521-6133	956-541-2002		K-2	Roberta Harris
Frontier College Prep S	2800 S Dakota Ave	Brownsville, TX	78521-6133	956-541-2002		6-8	Ernesto Cantu
Fruit of Excellence	109 Alum Creek Dr	Paige, TX	78659	512-303-5550	303-7028	PK-12	Roslyn Martin
Galaviz Academy	5206 Airline Dr	Houston, TX	77022-1902	713-694-6027	694-0419	9-12	Luis Cano
Garza-Gonzales Charter S	4129 Greenwood Dr	Corpus Christi, TX	78416-1841	361-881-9988	881-9994	PK-12	Adolfo Chapa
Gates S	510 Morningview Dr	San Antonio, TX	78220-3299	210-333-3621	333-3644	PK-8	Debbie Grady
Gateway Academy	1230 Townlake Dr	Laredo, TX	78041	956-722-0747	722-0767	9-12	Frances Johnson
Gateway Charter Academy	6103 Houston School Rd	Dallas, TX	75241-2516	214-375-2039	375-1842	PK-12	Lester Singleton
GCCLR Institute of Technology	4129 Greenwood Dr	Corpus Christi, TX	78416-1841	361-881-9988	881-9994	PK-12	Adolfo Chapa
Gervin Academy	6944 S Sunbelt Dr	San Antonio, TX	78218-3335	210-804-1786	804-1469	PK-3	Barbara Hawkins
Girls & Boys Prep Academy	8415 W Bellfort St	Houston, TX	77071-2205	713-270-5994	270-1302	5-12	Kimya McKinney
Girls & Boys Prep Academy	8415 W Bellfort St	Houston, TX	77071-2205	713-270-2006	270-2046	PK-4	Vonda Washington
Golden Rule Charter S	2602 W Illinois Ave	Dallas, TX	75233	214-333-9330	330-9325	PK-12	Martha Delgado
Guardian Angel Performance Academy	2361 Austin Hwy Ste 101	San Antonio, TX	78218	210-648-2229		6-8	Jacquelyn Darby
Gulf Shores HS	11300 S Post Oak Rd Ste 1	Houston, TX	77035	713-723-3494	723-3513	9-12	Tiffany Taylor
Gulf Shores MS	11300 S Post Oak Rd Ste 1	Houston, TX	77035	713-723-3494	723-3513	7-8	Linda Johnson
Harllee ES	1216 E 8th St	Dallas, TX	75203-2500	972-925-6500	925-6501	PK-5	Yolunda Wilson
Harmony ES	5435 S Braeswood Blvd	Houston, TX	77096-4001	713-541-3030	541-3032	K-5	Ozgur Ozer
Harmony Science Academy	555 SW Loop 410	San Antonio, TX	78227-5303	210-674-7788	674-7766	K-8	Ali Tekin
Harmony Science Academy	5651 Westcreek Dr	Fort Worth, TX	76133	817-263-0700	263-0705	K-12	Tevfik Eski
Harmony Science Academy	5435 S Braeswood Blvd	Houston, TX	77096-4001	713-729-4400	729-6600	6-12	Kadir Almus
Harmony Science Academy	11800 Stonehollow Dr # 100	Austin, TX	78758	512-821-1700	821-1702	K-5	Robert Johnson
Harmony Science Academy	11995 Forestgate Dr	Dallas, TX	75243	972-234-9993	234-9994	PK-12	Nihat Guvercin
Harmony Science Academy - Austin	930 E Rundberg Ln	Austin, TX	78753-4826	512-835-7900	835-7901	6-12	Kaan Camuz
Hawkins HS	1826 Basse Rd	San Antonio, TX	78213-4606	210-461-9881	253-2197	9-12	Ernesto Velazquez

School	Address	City,State	Zip code	Telephone	Fax	Grade	Contact
Hawthorne S	115 W Josephine St	San Antonio, TX	78212-4125	210-733-1321	733-1495	PK-8	G. Rodriguez-Pollock
Heritage Champions Academy of Huntsville	2407 Sam Houston Ave	Huntsville, TX	77340-5862	936-293-8096	259-9203	6-12	Pam Bouldin
Higgs Carter King Gifted & Talented S	PO Box 18854	San Antonio, TX	78218-0854	210-735-2341	733-6434	PK-12	Claudette Yarbrough
Highland Heights ES	865 Paul Quinn St	Houston, TX	77091-4154	713-696-2920	696-2922	PK-5	Kettisha Jones
Hill Country Youth Ranch	3484 Highway 27 W	Ingram, TX	78025	830-367-2611	367-2626	1-8	Maria De La Cruz
Horizon Montessori S	220 N Main St	Mc Allen, TX	78501	956-380-1101	380-5110	PK-5	Chrissy Urias
Houston Alternative Prep Charter S	17300 El Camino Real	Houston, TX	77058	713-524-6905	524-6344	PK-12	Dr. Lucille Abney
Houston Can! Academy - Hobby	9020 Gulf Fwy	Houston, TX	77017-7007	832-379-4226	944-6736	9-12	Ledy Garza
Houston Can! Academy - Main	2301 Main St	Houston, TX	77002-9101	713-659-4226	651-1493	9-12	Tiffany Abrams
Houston Gateway Academy	3400 Evergreen Dr	Houston, TX	77087-3715	713-649-3092	649-8165	K-8	Fransico Penning
Houston Heights HS	1125 Lawrence St	Houston, TX	77008-6651	713-868-9797	868-9750	8-12	Richard Mik
Houston Heights Learning Academy	902 W 8th St	Houston, TX	77007-1408	713-869-9453	869-0785	PK-5	Yvette East
I Am That I Am Academy	4720 Lynnacre Dr	Dallas, TX	75211-7911	214-372-6838	372-6871	4-12	Walter Parker
IDEA Academy	401 S 1st St	Donna, TX	78537-3055	956-464-0203	464-4137	PK-5	Paula Garcia
IDEA College Prep S	401 S 1st St	Donna, TX	78537-3055	956-464-0203	464-8532	6-12	Jeremy Beard
Inspired Vision Academy I	10327 Rylie Rd	Dallas, TX	75217-8240	214-391-7964	391-7954	PK-6	Lana Sprayberry-King
Inspired Vision Academy II	10327 Rylie Rd	Dallas, TX	75217-8240	972-285-5758	285-0061	PK-8	Tony Rorie
Jackson Academy	5400 Griggs Rd	Houston, TX	77021-3757	713-845-2451	643-9850	9-12	A. Jackson
Jamie's House Charter S	PO Box 681183	Houston, TX	77268-1183	281-866-9777	880-9919	6-12	Jewel Teagle
Jubilee Academic Center	4434 Roland Rd	San Antonio, TX	78222-2830	210-333-6227	337-2357	PK-12	Daniel Amador
Kaleidoscope Charter S	5909 Glenmont Dr	Houston, TX	77081	713-661-1670	660-9259	6-8	Marie Moreno
Kandy Stripe Academy	5310 Southlea St	Houston, TX	77033-1727	713-734-4909	731-2780	PK-8	Kaye Anderson
Kelley Charter S	802 Oblate Dr	San Antonio, TX	78216-7330	210-431-9881	432-8467	K-3	Alma Garza
King S	3501 Martin Luther King Dr	San Antonio, TX	78220-2325	210-223-8621	223-6907	PK-8	Dr. Derrick Thomas
KIPP 3D Academy	4610 E Crosstimbers St	Houston, TX	77016-6337	713-636-6082	328-0178	6-8	Dan Caesar
KIPP Academy Charter	10711 Kipp Way Dr	Houston, TX	77099-2675	832-328-1051	328-0178	6-12	Elliott Witney
KIPP Aspire Academy	1401 West Ave Ste 3	San Antonio, TX	78201	210-735-7300	735-7305	5-7	Mark Larson
KIPP Austin College Prep S	8509 FM 969	Austin, TX	78724	512-637-6870		5-8	Jill Kolasinski
KIPP Liberation S	10711 Kipp Way Dr	Houston, TX	77099-2675	832-633-1857		5-6	Tori Dugar
KIPP NE Lower S	4610 E Crosstimbers St	Houston, TX	77016-6337	713-636-6082	328-0178	PK-5	Claudia Macias
KIPP Spirit S	10711 Kipp Way Dr	Houston, TX	77099-2675	713-731-1235		5-6	Stephanie Wilkins
KIPP SW Lower S	10711 Kipp Way Dr	Houston, TX	77099-2675	832-328-1051	328-0178	PK-5	Aaron Brenner
KIPP Truth Academy	3200 S Lancaster Rd # 230A	Dallas, TX	75216	214-375-8326	375-2990	5-8	Steven Colmus
Kozmetsky S	PO Box 19454	Austin, TX	78760-9454	512-439-9298	232-9177	PK-12	Georgia Johnson
La Academia de Estrellas	125 Sunset Ave	Dallas, TX	75208-4516	214-946-8908		K-5	Lorraine Mantei
La Amistad Love & Learning Academy	6600 Sanford Rd	Houston, TX	77096-5548	713-988-1100	988-1471	PK-5	
La Escuela de las Americas	2300 W Commerce St Ste 200	San Antonio, TX	78207-3840	210-978-0562	978-0547	PK-5	Rene Gallegoes
Landmark S	101 Brushy Creek Rd	Palestine, TX	75803-8619	903-729-4208	729-1389	9-12	James Bivins
Laurel Ridge	17720 Corporate Woods Dr	San Antonio, TX	78259	210-491-9400	491-3552	PK-12	Athena Caroselli
Lawson Institute	3826 Wheeler St	Houston, TX	77004-2604	713-225-1551	225-1561	6-8	Lloyd Choice
Lee Academy	4327 E Lancaster Ave	Fort Worth, TX	76103-3224	817-534-5595	534-3813	9-12	Artie Jackson
Legacy HS	601 S Washington St	Kaufman, TX	75142-2407	972-962-0306	962-2265	9-12	Mike Anderson
Life S - Oak Cliff	4400 S R L Thornton Fwy	Dallas, TX	75224-5110	214-376-8208	376-8209	K-12	J. Wood
Life S - Red Oak	777 S Interstate 35 E	Red Oak, TX	75154	214-376-8200	617-5767	K-8	Joseph Mena
Lighthouse Charter S	2718 Frontier Dr	San Antonio, TX	78227-4069	210-674-4100	674-4108	K-7	Joyce Williams
Mainland Preparatory Academy	319 Newman Rd	La Marque, TX	77568-3440	409-934-9100	934-9130	PK-8	Wilma Green
Mann MS	2123 W Huisache Ave	San Antonio, TX	78201-4809	210-732-4851	732-7999	6-8	Linda Nance
Massieu Academy	823 N Center St	Arlington, TX	76011-5859	817-460-0396	460-4762	PK-12	Bobby Dunivan
Mayes Institute	5807 Calhoun Rd	Houston, TX	77021	713-747-5629	747-5683	K-8	Beatrice Mayes
McCullough Academy of Excellence	1605 Kramer Ln	Austin, TX	78758	512-977-9200	977-9206	K-5	Wilretta Collins
Medical Center Charter S	1920 N Braeswood Blvd	Houston, TX	77030-3711	713-791-9980	791-9594	PK-8	James McKey
Medical Center Charter S Southwest	10420 Mullins Dr	Houston, TX	77096-4927	713-726-0223		PK-6	William Heard
Meridell Achievement Center	12550 W State Highway 29	Liberty Hill, TX	78642	512-528-2145	515-5875	K-12	Kathy Uplinger
Methodist Children's Home	1111 Herring Ave	Waco, TX	76708	254-753-0181	755-7609	PK-12	Jeff Rhodes
Metro Charter Academy	500 Houston St	Arlington, TX	76011-7429	817-226-1261	226-1758	PK-12	Lasonia Russell
Meyerpark Charter S	PO Box 35616	Houston, TX	77235-5616	713-729-9712	729-9720	K-5	Julia Hutcherson
Midland Academy Charter S	500 N Baird St	Midland, TX	79701-4704	432-686-0003	686-0845	K-12	Wade Cherry
Mid-Valley Academy	200 N 17th St	Mc Allen, TX	78501-4743	956-618-2303	618-2323	9-12	Martin Perez
Mid-Valley Academy	103 E 2nd St	Mercedes, TX	78570-2701	956-618-2303	618-2323	9-12	Adolfo Huerta
Milburn Academy - Amarillo	4106 SW 51st Ave	Amarillo, TX	79109-6132	806-463-2284	463-2331	9-12	Bill Flowers
Milburn Academy - Beaumont	1310 Pennsylvania St Ste C	Beaumont, TX	77701	409-833-7757	833-7767	9-12	Luther J. Thompson
Milburn Academy-Corpus Christi	3875 S Staples St	Corpus Christi, TX	78411-2347	361-225-4424	225-4945	9-12	Su Cline
Milburn Academy - Ector County	2525 N Grandview Ave # 600	Odessa, TX	79761	432-550-7833	550-7884	9-12	David Cavitt
Milburn Academy - Fort Worth	6777 Camp Bowie Blvd St 300	Fort Worth, TX	76116	817-731-7627	731-7628	9-12	Calvin H. Lawrence
Milburn Academy - Houston	713 E Airtex Dr Bldg B	Houston, TX	77073-6032	281-443-3111	443-3116	9-12	G. Lopez
Milburn Academy - Killeen	1001 E Veterans Mem # 301C	Killeen, TX	76541	254-634-4444	634-4044	9-12	Rose Thompson
Milburn Academy - Lubbock	4902 34th St Ste 10	Lubbock, TX	79410-2342	806-740-0811	740-0804	9-12	Starlette Gill
Milburn Academy - Midland	3306 Andrews Hwy	Midland, TX	79703-5131	432-522-7200	522-5201	9-12	Camal Dakil
Miller S	207 Lincolnshire Dr	San Antonio, TX	78220-3114	210-333-0521	333-0563	PK-8	Sandra Booker
Miracle Farm	10802 FM 2621	Brenham, TX	77833	979-836-0901	277-0939	6-12	Donnie Wilson
National Elite Gymnastics	PO Box 7667	Austin, TX	78713-7667	512-288-9722	288-4633	6-12	Carola Garcia-Lemke
Nelms Charter HS	20625 Clay Rd	Katy, TX	77449-5593	281-398-8031	398-8032	9-12	Vincente Fuentez
Nelms Charter MS	20625 Clay Rd	Katy, TX	77449-5593	281-398-8031	398-8032	5-8	Wendy Wolski
Nelms Charter S - Northwest	1346 Wilkins St	Hempstead, TX	77445	979-826-8302	826-2135	K-12	Robert Guercio
Newcomer Charter HS	6529 Beverlyhill St	Houston, TX	77057-6406	713-787-1700	787-1723	11-12	Monico Rivas
New Directions Charter S	1201 Austin Hwy Ste 200	San Antonio, TX	78209	210-828-2161	826-9962	9-12	Sue Eakle
New Frontiers Charter	4018 S Presa St	San Antonio, TX	78223-1005	210-533-3655	533-5077	K-8	Jesse Sandoz,
Ney Charter S	PO Box 311268	New Braunfels, TX	78131-1268	830-629-6571	608-1262	4-12	Gwendolyn Rehling
North Hills S	606 E Royal Ln	Irving, TX	75039-3503	972-501-0645	501-9439	K-12	Cheryl Huisman
North Houston HS for Business	455 W Parker Rd	Houston, TX	77091-3202	713-691-3123	691-2511	9-12	
North Houston Multi-Language Academy	455 W Parker Rd	Houston, TX	77091-3202	713-691-3123	691-2511	1-5	Avernia Waddle
Northwest Preparatory S	4705 Lyons Ave	Houston, TX	77020-4306	713-635-8270	688-0884	PK-5	Erik Singleton
Northwest Preparatory S	4712 New Orleans St	Houston, TX	77020	713-491-9220	688-0884	6-8	Steve Roberts
Nova Academy	PO Box 170127	Dallas, TX	75217-0127	214-381-3422	381-3499	PK-6	Antonio Williamson
Nova Charter S Southeast	PO Box 170127	Dallas, TX	75217-0127	214-309-9030	398-6363	PK-6	John Carson
Now College Prep Charter S	10711 Kipp Way Dr	Houston, TX	77099-2675	832-328-1051	328-0178	K-5	Korbin Johnson
NYOS Charter S	8007 Gessner Dr	Austin, TX	78753-6507	512-835-6601	835-6692	PK-3	Linda Whatley
NYOS Charter S	12301 N Lamar Blvd	Austin, TX	78753-1320	512-836-7620	583-6973	K-12	Teresa Elliott
Oaks Treatment Center	PO Box 7667	Austin, TX	78713-7667	512-464-0400	464-0486	1-12	Holly Engleman
Odyssey Academy	901 13th St	Galveston, TX	77550-6109	409-750-9289	750-9356	PK-8	Henry James Amparan
Omega Academic Center	4434 Roland Rd	San Antonio, TX	78222-2830	210-922-0132	923-2788	6-12	Thomas Baldwin
One Stop Multiservice Charter S	4737 S Sugar Rd	Edinburg, TX	78539	956-380-6616	292-0371	PK-12	George Banda
One Stop Multiservice Charter S	615 S International Blvd	Weslaco, TX	78596	956-969-2600	969-1191	PK-12	Anival Henrichson
One-Stop Multiservice Charter S	101 1st Blvd	Mission, TX	78572	956-519-2227	687-6062	PK-12	Martin Perez
Osborne ES	800 Ringold St	Houston, TX	77088-6337	281-405-2525	405-2528	PK-5	Jacqueline Parnell
Outreach Word Academy	PO Box 4873	Victoria, TX	77903-4873	361-579-6922	573-5788	PK-12	Oliver Burbridge
Panola Charter S	PO Box 610	Carthage, TX	75633-0610	903-693-6355	693-6391	8-12	Mark Thornton
Paradigm Accelerated S	PO Box 160	Dublin, TX	76446-0160	254-445-4844	445-4907	7-12	Ronald Johnson
Paso Del Norte Academy Charter S	711 N Mesa St	El Paso, TX	79902-3925	915-532-7216	532-2251	9-12	Arturo Peralta
Paso Del Norte Academy - Ysleta	400 S Zaragoza Rd Ste 230	El Paso, TX	79907	915-532-7216	532-2251	9-12	Maria Baquera
Pathfinder Camp	20800 FM 150 W	Driftwood, TX	78619	512-858-4258	464-0486	6-12	Carola Garcia-Lemke
Pathways 3H Ranch	PO Box 230	Mountain Home, TX	78058-0230	830-866-3701	866-3705	6-12	Sally Arnold
Peak Academy	4605 Live Oak St	Dallas, TX	75204	214-821-7325	370-3972	K-12	Dawn Osborne
Peak Advantage	4536 Bryan St	Dallas, TX	75204	214-276-5200		6-12	Jacqueline Ray
Pegasus Campus	PO Box 577	Lockhart, TX	78644-0577	512-376-2101	398-2731	K-12	Margaret Riddle
Pegasus Charter HS	604 N Akard St Ste 203	Dallas, TX	75201	214-740-9991	740-9799	4-12	Virginia Hart
Pfeiffer S	4551 Dietrich Rd	San Antonio, TX	78219-2899	210-661-3121	661-8087	PK-8	Anita O'Neal
Phoenix Charter S	8501 Jack Finney Blvd	Greenville, TX	75402-3018	903-454-7153	454-7806	PK-12	Vickie Glasscock
Pineywoods Community Academy	2515 E Lufkin Ave	Lufkin, TX	75901-5133	936-634-5515	634-5518	K-8	John Malloy
Pinnacle S	6550 Camp Bowie Blvd	Fort Worth, TX	76116	817-735-8527	735-1910	K-9	Lorrie Renfro
Pleasant Hill Academy	1305 Benson St	Houston, TX	77020-4099	713-224-3232	224-0060	PK-5	Mildred Nicks
Porter S	PO Box 2025	Wimberley, TX	78676-6925	512-847-6867	847-0737	9-12	Dr. Yana Bland
Por Vida Academy	1135 Mission Rd	San Antonio, TX	78210-4505	210-532-8816	534-0795	9-12	Steve Langseth
Positive Solutions Charter S	1325 N Flores St	San Antonio, TX	78212	210-299-1025	299-1052	9-12	Pamela Solitaire
Positive Solutions Charter S	623 Mary Lake Dr	Bryan, TX	77801	979-822-9988	822-9988	7-12	Pamela Solitaire
Preschool Academy	1826 Basse Rd	San Antonio, TX	78213-4606	210-431-9881	432-8467	PK-PK	Susan Norris
Project Chrysalis MS	4528 Leeland St	Houston, TX	77023-3047	713-924-1700	924-1704	6-8	Jose Covarrubia
Pro-Vision Charter S	4422 Balkin St	Houston, TX	77021-4104	713-748-0031	748-0037	5-8	Alphonso Fulton
Quest Academy	14001 N 29th St	Mc Allen, TX	78504	956-287-1003		K-2	Sharon Chapman
Quest Academy	111 N Beckley Ave	Dallas, TX	75203	214-946-5157	946-5150	6-10	Julie Gilmour
Quest College Prep S	14001 N 29th St	Mc Allen, TX	78504	956-287-1003		6-8	Scott Hollinger
Radiance Academy of Learning	2845 Thousand Oaks Dr	San Antonio, TX	78232-4107	210-545-4415	545-4478	9-12	
Radiance Academy of Learning	2235 Thousand Oaks Dr #130	San Antonio, TX	78232	210-404-9650	404-1271	PK-12	Daniel Martinez
Radiance Academy of Learning	709 Kings Way	Del Rio, TX	78840-2029	830-774-5755	719-5090	6-8	Francisco Longoria
Radiance Academy of Learning West Lake	1305 SW Loop 410 Ste 210	San Antonio, TX	78227-1671	210-670-8800	670-0903	PK-12	Francisco Longoria
Ramirez Charter S	702 Avenue T	Lubbock, TX	79401-2303	806-766-1833	766-1825	K-6	Stace McEwin
Ranch Academy	3120 VZ County Road 2318	Canton, TX	75103-4671	903-479-3601	479-1161	6-12	Richard Boardman

School	Address	City,State	Zip code	Telephone	Fax	Grade	Contact
Rapoport Academy	2000 J J Flewellen Rd	Waco, TX	76704-1642	254-799-4191	799-4525	PK-4	Dr. Nancy Grayson
Rapoport Academy Preparatory S	2000 J J Flewellen Rd	Waco, TX	76704-1642	254-867-6000	867-6005	9-9	Dr. Nancy Grayson
Rapoport Academy - Quinn Campus	2000 J J Flewellen Rd	Waco, TX	76704-1642	254-754-8000	754-8009	5-8	Dr. Nancy Grayson
Raven S	PO Box 515	New Waverly, TX	77358-0515	936-344-6677	344-7236	9-12	Sandi Belcher
Reach Charter S	520 Mercury Dr	Houston, TX	77013-5217	713-675-1118		11-12	Bertie Simmons
Rhodes S	13518 Mobile St	Houston, TX	77015-4418	281-224-5873	453-6321	PK-5	Michelle Bonton
Richland Collegiate HS	12800 Abrams Rd	Dallas, TX	75243-2199	972-761-6888	761-6890	11-12	Kristyn Edney
Ripley House Charter S	4410 Navigation Blvd	Houston, TX	77011-1036	713-315-6480	547-8201	K-5	Cynthia Patton
Rise Academy	PO Box 5171	Lubbock, TX	79408-5171	806-744-0430		PK-6	Richard Baumgartner
Riverside Park ES	202 School St	San Antonio, TX	78210-3940	210-534-6951	534-6987	PK-5	Beatrice Aleman
Saenz Charter JHS	1830 Basse Rd	San Antonio, TX	78213	210-431-9881	435-8096	7-8	Ernesto Velazquez
SAILL Charter S	PO Box 141909	Austin, TX	78714-1909	512-282-7161	280-9428	K-12	Jamie Judd-Wall
St. Anthony Academy	3732 Myrtle St	Dallas, TX	75215-3849	214-421-3645	421-7416	PK-8	David Ray
St. Johns Academy	2019 Crawford St	Houston, TX	77002-9002	713-659-3237		PK-K	Robin Owens
St. Marys Academy Charter S	PO Box 279	Beeville, TX	78104-0279	361-358-5601	358-5704	K-8	Stan Simonson
San Antonio Can Academy	502 E Southcross Blvd	San Antonio, TX	78214-2044	210-923-1226	928-3366	9-12	Veronica Hernandez
San Antonio Preparatory Academy	8308 Fredericksburg Rd	San Antonio, TX	78229-3316	210-593-0111	614-7199	K-12	Raul Garcia
San Antonio S for Inquiry & Creativity	4618 San Pedro Ave	San Antonio, TX	78212-1411	210-738-0020	738-0033	K-12	Tony Espinar
San Antonio Technology Academy	6655 First Park Ten Blvd	San Antonio, TX	78213	210-527-9250	225-7282	9-12	Henry Egeolu
Sanchez HS	6001 Gulf Fwy	Houston, TX	77023	713-926-1112	926-1346	9-12	Roberto Lopez
Sanchez HS	436 S Main Ave	San Antonio, TX	78204-1131	210-270-8567	886-0816	8-12	Wendell Beene
San Marcos Treatment Center	120 Bert Brown St	San Marcos, TX	78666	512-396-8500	754-3883	5-12	Catherine Toohey
School of Liberal Arts & Science	PO Box 5129	Dallas, TX	75208-9129	214-941-4881	941-4866	PK-10	Linda Gromowsky
School of Science and Technology	1450 NE Loop 410	San Antonio, TX	78209-1543	210-804-0222	822-3422	6-8	Mark Namver
Seashore Learning Center	14493 S Padre Island Dr	Corpus Christi, TX	78418	361-949-1222	949-6762	PK-7	Dr. Jan Loveless
Sentry Technology Prep S	508 E Elizabeth St	Brownsville, TX	78520	956-542-3363	292-0371	PK-12	Elsa Haman
SER-Ninos Charter S	5815 Alder Dr	Houston, TX	77081-2708	713-667-6145	667-0645	PK-8	Charmaine Constantine
Settlement Home	PO Box 7667	Austin, TX	78713-7667	512-836-2150	836-2159	6-12	Carola Garcia-Lemke
Shekinah Radiance Academy	5130 Casey St	La Marque, TX	77568-2707	409-935-8773	935-4426	PK-12	Dr. A. Breedlove
Shekinah Radiance Academy	6663 Walzem Rd	San Antonio, TX	78239-3612	210-967-6933	967-6280	PK-12	Ray Garcia
Shekinah Radiance Academy	13069 N IH 35	San Antonio, TX	78233-2615	210-590-0838	590-0856	PK-6	Dorothy Scott
Shekinah Radiance Academy	5203 Pearsall Rd	San Antonio, TX	78242	210-623-3030	623-3046	PK-12	Javier Arredondo
South Plains Academy	4008 Avenue R	Lubbock, TX	79412-1603	806-744-0330	741-1089	9-12	Leticia Flores
Southwest ES	3333 Bering Dr Ste 200	Houston, TX	77057-6703	713-784-6345	974-3137	PK-3	Ken Goeddeke
Southwest HS	3333 Bering Dr Ste 200	Houston, TX	77057-6703	713-954-9528	953-0119	9-12	Ken Goeddeke
Southwest MS	3333 Bering Dr Ste 200	Houston, TX	77057-6703	713-954-9528	953-0119	6-8	Ken Goeddeke
Southwest Preparatory S NE Campus	1258 Austin Hwy Ste 220	San Antonio, TX	78209	210-829-8017	829-8514	9-12	Ana Ramirez
Southwest Preparatory S NW Campus	4550 NW Loop 410 Ste 111	San Antonio, TX	78229-5169	210-432-2634	432-5482	9-12	Richard Joyer
Southwest Preparatory S SE Campus	735 S WW White Rd	San Antonio, TX	78220-2524	210-333-1403	333-3024	9-12	Otis Spears
Star Charter S	1901 Fleischer Dr	Austin, TX	78728-5704	512-989-2672	989-3150	1-12	Rollie Ford
Stepping Stones Charter S	11250 S Wilcrest Dr	Houston, TX	77099-4313	281-988-9855	988-9894	K-6	William Clark
Storm ES	435 Brady Blvd	San Antonio, TX	78207-8099	210-224-7321	224-1998	PK-5	Angela Dominguez
Summit Academy	1220 W Presidio St	Fort Worth, TX	76102-4512	817-336-5134	336-2573	K-12	Dr. Terry Antoine
Tafolla Charter S	PO Box 1709	Uvalde, TX	78802-1709	830-278-1297	591-1465	PK-12	Jorge Botello
Technology Education Charter HS	116 W 5th St	Weslaco, TX	78596-6008	956-668-7761	969-8614	9-12	Alim Ansari
Tekoa Academy	326 Thomas Blvd	Port Arthur, TX	77640-5242	409-982-5400	982-8498	PK-9	Paula Richardson
Temple Education Center	1400 E Avenue B	Temple, TX	76501-4710	254-778-8682	778-8690	PK-12	Rick Haley
Texans Can! Academy at Paul Quinn	3837 Simpson Stuart Rd	Dallas, TX	75241-4331	214-371-6226	372-2294	9-12	Mene Khepera
Texans Can! S at Carrollton/Farmers	2720 Hollandale Ln	Farmers Branch, TX	75234-2035	972-243-2178	243-2669	9-12	Eric Brown
Texas Empowerment Academy	3613 Bluestein Dr	Austin, TX	78721-2900	512-494-0760	494-0199	5-12	David Nowlin
Texas NeuroRehabilitation Center	PO Box 7667	Austin, TX	78713-7667	512-444-4835	462-6709	K-12	Holly Engleman
Texas Preparatory S	900 Bugg Ln Ste 110A	San Marcos, TX	78666-8004	512-805-7737	805-7739	PK-8	Mark Terry
Texas Serenity Academy	8612 Trippie St	Dallas, TX	75241			K-12	Edward Watson
Texas Serenity Academy	16673 Interstate 45 N	Willis, TX	77318	936-334-8700	334-8700	6-12	Edward Watson
Texas Virtual Academy at Southwest	3333 Bering Dr Ste 200	Houston, TX	77057-6703	713-784-6345	972-3137	3-6	Ken Goeddeke
Transformative Charter Academy	807 N 8th St	Killeen, TX	76541-4818	254-628-8989	628-8981	9-12	Claudette Morgan-Scott
Treetops School International	12500 S Pipeline Rd	Euless, TX	76040-5853	817-283-1771	684-0892	K-12	Lou Blanchard
Trinity Basin Prep S	PO Box 5129	Dallas, TX	75208-9129	214-942-6501	942-8864	PK-8	Janice Chancelor
Trinity Charter S	5638 Medical Center Dr	Katy, TX	77494-6325	281-392-7505	392-7560	1-12	Amanda Broussard
Trinity Charter S	650 Scarbourough	Canyon Lake, TX	78133-4529	830-964-4390	964-4391	1-12	Debi Christensen
Trinity Charter S	4601 N Interstate 35	Denton, TX	76207-3419	940-484-8232	484-1385	1-12	Mary Littlepage
Trinity Charter S	5517 S Alameda St	Corpus Christi, TX	78412	361-994-1214	994-0555	1-12	Brayde McClure
TSU/HISD Lab S	3805 Burkett St	Houston, TX	77004-4621	713-747-1760	747-0672	K-5	Phyllis Tyler
Two Dimensions Preparatory Academy	12121 Veterans Memorial # 9	Houston, TX	77067	281-440-8853	440-4233	PK-5	Daisy Simpson
Two Dimensions Preparatory Academy	901 E 10th Ave	Corsicana, TX	75110	281-872-2988	872-2858	PK-8	Karen Williams
Two Dimensions Preparatory Academy	12121 Veterans Memorial # 9	Houston, TX	77067	281-987-7300	987-7306	PK-8	Sally Wickers
Universal Academy	2616 N MacArthur Blvd	Irving, TX	75062-5401	972-255-1800	255-6122	PK-12	
Universal Academy - Flower Mound	2143 N Stemmons Fwy	Lewisville, TX	75077	214-513-1608		PK-12	Janice Blackmon
University Charter S	2200 E 6th St	Austin, TX	78702-3457	512-471-4363	499-4240	PK-5	Dr. Edwin Sharpe
University of Houston Charter S of Tech	3855 Holman St	Houston, TX	77204-6056	713-743-9107	743-9121	K-5	Carolyn Black
University S	1404 W Walnut Hill Ln	Irving, TX	75038-3009	972-753-6165	550-1425	6-12	Dr. Olga Korobovskaya
Valenzuela Leadership Academy	2300 W Commerce St Ste 200	San Antonio, TX	78207-3840	210-978-0500	978-0547	6-8	Francis Teran
Vanguard Academy	1200 E Kelly Ave	Pharr, TX	78577-5033	956-283-1700	702-2180	PK-8	Narciso Garcia
Varnett Charter S	PO Box 1457	Houston, TX	77251-1457	713-723-4699	723-5853	PK-5	Kelvin Williamson
Varnett Charter S - East	PO Box 1457	Houston, TX	77251-1457	713-637-6574	637-8319	PK-5	Lennon Phillips
Varnett Charter S - Northeast	PO Box 1457	Houston, TX	77251-1457	713-631-4396	491-3597	PK-5	Dora Morrow
Vista Academy of Mission	1203 St Claire Blvd	Mission, TX	78572-6601	956-424-9290	424-7661	6-12	Dina Acededo
Waco Charter S	615 N 25th St	Waco, TX	76707-3443	254-754-8169	754-7389	K-5	Valerie Ovalle
Waxahachie Faith Family Academy	701 Ovilla Rd	Waxahachie, TX	75167-9430	972-938-3996	937-5806	PK-12	Mary Plasket Ozuna
Wesley ES	800 Dillard St	Houston, TX	77091-2301	713-696-2860	696-2866	PK-5	Dr. Kimberly Agnew
West Houston Charter S	5618 11th St	Katy, TX	77493-1971	281-391-5003	391-5010	K-8	Shannon Clark
Westlake Academy	2600 Ottinger Rd	Westlake, TX	76262	817-490-5757	490-5758	K-12	Barbara Brizuela
White Memorial HS	PO Box 2126	League City, TX	77574-2126	281-316-0001	316-0018	9-12	Dr. Rosalind Perez
Williams Charter MS	6100 Knox St	Houston, TX	77091-4143	713-696-2600	696-2604	6-8	Delesa O'Dell-Thomas
Winfree Academy Charter S	1661 Gateway Blvd	Richardson, TX	75080	972-234-9855	234-9975	9-12	Brenda Cupps
Winfree Academy Charter S	1250 William D Tate Ste 100	Grapevine, TX	76051	817-481-5803	329-6307	9-12	Paulette Gillespie
Winfree Academy Charter S	6221 Riverside Dr Ste 110	Irving, TX	75039-3529	972-251-2010	251-4301	9-12	Brenda Cupps
Winfree Academy Charter S	341 Bennett Ln	Lewisville, TX	75057-4801	214-222-2200	222-0201	9-12	Lisa Ehrke
Winfree Academy Charter S	6311 Boulevard 26	N Richlnd Hls, TX	76180	817-590-2240	590-8724	9-12	Paulette Gillespie
Wood Charter S at Afton Oaks	3201 Cherry Ridge Ste C315	San Antonio, TX	78230	210-499-0351	403-3058	5-12	Susie Mariano
Wood Charter S at Huebner Road	3201 Cherry Ridge Ste C315	San Antonio, TX	78230	210-798-0350	690-4139	6-12	Joe Inman
Wood Charter S at St. Francis	3201 Cherry Ridge Ste C315	San Antonio, TX	78230	210-923-1421	921-4948	5-12	George Pena
Yes College Preparatory S	2000 Preston St	Richmond, TX	77469-2623	281-238-8000	238-8098	6-12	Robert Lundin
Yes College Preparatory S	3401 Hardy St	Houston, TX	77009-5928	713-208-1519	910-2350	6-6	Bill Durbin
Yes College Preparatory S - East End	353 Crenshaw Rd	Houston, TX	77034-1543	713-333-2931	333-2935	6-12	Luz Navarro
Young Learners Charter S	3333 Bering Dr Ste 200	Houston, TX	77057-6703	713-784-6345	974-3137	PK-PK	Ken Goeddeke
Young Scholars Academy of Excellence	1809 Louisiana St	Houston, TX	77002-8013	713-654-1400	654-1401	PK-4	Anella Coleman
Yzaguirre S for Success	2255 N Coria St	Brownsville, TX	78520	713-644-2340	644-5397	PK-12	Adriana Tamez
Yzaguirre S for Success	355 W Elizabeth St	Brownsville, TX	78520	956-542-2404	542-2667	PK-5	Janis Sotherden
Zoe Learning Academy	5430 Miller Ave	Fort Worth, TX	76119	817-535-5655	531-6310	PK-6	Charles Polk
Zoe Learning Academy	3505 Alice St	Houston, TX	77021-4867	713-748-4228	748-7833	PK-6	Linda Ware
Utah							
Academy of Math Engineering & Science	5715 S 1300 E	Salt Lake City, UT	84121-1023	801-278-9460	277-3527	9-12	Al Church
American Leadership Academy	898 W 1100 S	Spanish Fork, UT	84660-5654	801-794-2226	794-2130	K-12	Rob Muhlestein
American Preparatory Academy	12892 Pony Express Rd	Draper, UT	84020-9273	801-553-8500	576-9300	K-9	Carolyn Sharette
Beehive Science & Tech Academy	3098 Highland Dr Ste 100	Salt Lake City, UT	84106-6004	801-322-2782	322-2783	7-9	Zack Kiyma
CBA Center	305 E 200 N	Delta, UT	84624-8405	435-864-5695	864-5711	9-12	Mike Louder
Channing Hall Charter S	314 Manilla Dr	Draper, UT	84020-5111	801-305-4250		K-8	Deena Pyle
City Academy	555 E 200 S	Salt Lake City, UT	84102-2007	801-596-8489	521-4181	7-12	Sonja Woodbury
DaVinci Academy of Science and the Arts	2033 Grant Ave	Ogden, UT	84401-0409	801-409-0700	866-1311	9-12	Lewis Reese
East Hollywood HS	2185 S 3600 W	West Valley, UT	84119-1121	801-886-8181	972-9585	9-12	Eric Lindsay
Edison Charter S - North	180 E 2600 N	North Logan, UT	84341-1551	435-787-2820	787-0299	K-8	Scott Jackson
Edison Charter S - South	1275 W 2350 S	Logan, UT	84321-6181	435-752-0123	787-4350	K-7	Eldon Budge
Entheos Academy	4702 W 6200 S	Kearns, UT	84118-6702	801-860-4195		K-8	Michael Farley
Fast Forward Charter S	875 W 1400 N	Logan, UT	84321-6804	435-713-4255	753-9615	9-12	Stephanie Sorenson
Freedom Academy	1958 S 950 E	Provo, UT	84606-6200	801-437-3100	437-3149	K-8	Lynne Herring
Hancock Charter S	125 N 100 E	Pleasant Grove, UT	84062-2355	801-796-5646	785-4934	K-8	Julie Adamic
Intech Collegiate HS	2801 Old Main Hl	Logan, UT	84321	435-797-8337	797-3939	9-10	Steve Zsiray
Itineris Early College HS	9301 Wights Fort Rd	West Jordan, UT	84088-8850	801-256-5970	256-5992	9-12	Stephen Jolley
Lakeview Academy	1304 Redwood Rd	Saratoga Sprngs, UT	84045-4734	801-766-9888		K-8	Arnie Adler
Legacy Preparatory Academy	PO Box 1253	Bountiful, UT	84011-1253	801-897-5604	994-6853	K-9	Elizabeth Hatch
Liberty Academy	1195 Elk Ridge Dr	Salem, UT	84653-5521	801-465-4434	465-7808	K-8	Lisa Denning
Lincoln Academy	PO Box 546	American Fork, UT	84003-0546	801-756-2039	785-2109	K-9	Mark Dennison
Moab Community S	358 E 300 S	Moab, UT	84532-2624	435-259-2277	259-6652	K-8	Rosie O'Connor
Monticello Academy	PO Box 70806	West Valley, UT	84170-0806	801-955-5141		K-8	Walt Hackford

School	Address	City,State	Zip code	Telephone	Fax	Grade	Contact
Mountainville Academy	195 S Main St	Alpine, UT	84004-1630	801-756-9805	756-9823	K-8	Wade Glathar
Navigator Pointe Academy	6844 Navigator Dr	West Jordan, UT	84084-4405	801-840-1210	840-1236	K-8	Judy Farris
North Davis Preparatory Academy	1765 W Hill Field Rd	Layton, UT	84041-7323	801-547-1809	547-1649	K-6	Deborah Gomberg
Northern Utah Academy	PO Box 248	Roy, UT	84067-0248	801-402-5920	402-5921	9-12	Rob Stillwell
Northern Utah Academy	550 E 300 S	Kaysville, UT	84037	801-402-5922	402-5921	9-12	Rob Stillwell
North Star Academy	2920 W 14010 S	Bluffdale, UT	84065-5331	801-302-9579	302-9578	K-9	Mark Johnson
Odyssey Charter S	738 Quality Dr	American Fork, UT	84003-3309	801-492-8105	763-8743	K-8	Nymna Brooks
Ogden Preparatory Academy	2221 Grant Ave	Ogden, UT	84401-1405	801-627-2066	394-2267	K-4	Kathleen Thornburg
Ogden Preparatory Academy	215 E 22nd St	Ogden, UT	84401-2646	801-627-3066	395-2267	5-8	Kathleen Thornburg
Paradigm HS	4881 Cave Peak Dr	Riverton, UT	84096-1792	801-446-6365	273-5707	9-12	Celia Johnson
Pinnacle Canyon Academy	210 N 600 E	Price, UT	84501-2613	435-613-8102	613-8105	K-10	Roberta Hardy
Ranches Academy	7789 Tawny Owl Cir	Eagle Mountain, UT	84005-4308	801-789-4000	789-4001	K-8	Darren Beck
Reagan Academy	1143 W Center St	Springville, UT	84663-3028	801-489-7828	491-2829	K-8	Warren Shenk
Renaissance Academy	3435 N 1120 E	Lehi, UT	84043-6538	801-768-4202		K-8	Grant Flygare
Salt Lake Arts Academy	844 S 200 E	Salt Lake City, UT	84111-4203	801-531-1173	531-7726	5-8	Amy Wadsworth
Soldier Hollow S	PO Box 779	Midway, UT	84049-0779	435-654-1347	654-1349	K-7	Charles Weber
Spectrum Academy	837 Foxboro Dr	North Salt Lake, UT	84054-6037	801-965-0791		K-8	Melissa Aubrey-Harper
Success Academy	351 W Center St	Cedar City, UT	84720-2470	435-865-8790	865-8795	9-12	Vickie Wilson
Success Academy	225 S 700 E	Saint George, UT	84770-3875	435-652-7830	656-4149	10-10	Vickie Wilson
Success S	4122 Carriage Sq Ste 2B	Taylorsville, UT	84119-5569	801-964-4258	964-4259	7-12	Diane Austin
Summit Academy	1285 E 13200 S	Draper, UT	84020	801-572-4166	572-4169	K-7	Jill Neff
Syracuse Arts Academy	3000 W Antelope Dr	Syracuse, UT	84075	801-779-2066		K-6	Jan Whimpey
Timpanogos Academy	55 S 100 E	Lindon, UT	84042-2058	801-785-4979	785-9690	K-8	Errol Porter
Tuacahn HS for the Performing Arts	1100 Tuacahn	Ivins, UT	84738-6088	435-652-3201	652-3306	9-12	Bill Fowler
Uintah River HS	PO Box 235	Fort Duchesne, UT	84026-0235	435-726-4088	722-0811	9-12	Kathleen Chegup
Utah County Academy of Sciences	940 W 800 S	Orem, UT	84058-5915	801-225-8227	225-2214	10-12	Clark Baron
Walden S of Liberal Arts	250 W 500 N	Provo, UT	84601-2819	801-374-1545	374-3397	6-8	Diana West
Wasatch Peak Academy	414 Cutler Dr	North Salt Lake, UT	84054-2951	801-936-3066	936-0887	K-6	Vivian Powell
Washington Academy	3138 S 1420 E	Saint George, UT	84790-7041	435-669-2139	986-9656	K-8	Tiffany White
Webster Academy	205 E 400 S	Orem, UT	84058-6311	801-426-6624		K-6	Sharon Moss

Virginia

School	Address	City,State	Zip code	Telephone	Fax	Grade	Contact
Hampton Harbour Academy	23 Semple Farm Rd	Hampton, VA	23666-1456	757-766-5313	766-5319	6-8	Andrea James
Murray Charter HS	1200 Forest St	Charlottesville, VA	22903-5264	434-296-3090	979-6479	9-12	Dr. Vicki Crews-Miller
York River Academy	9300 George Washington Mem	Yorktown, VA	23692	757-898-0516	890-1045	9-10	Walter Cross

Washington

School	Address	City,State	Zip code	Telephone	Fax	Grade	Contact
5/12 Learning Community	3230 85th St S	Lakewood, WA	98499-8814	253-583-5418	583-5348	5-12	Lisa Boyd

Wisconsin

School	Address	City,State	Zip code	Telephone	Fax	Grade	Contact
Academic Center HS	601 University Ave	Colfax, WI	54730-9773	715-962-3676	962-4024	9-12	Dennis Geissler
Academy of Learning & Leadership	1530 W Center St	Milwaukee, WI	53206-2101	414-372-3942	372-8260	K-8	M. Camille Mortimore
A L A S	971 W Windlake Ave	Milwaukee, WI	53204-3822	414-902-7300	902-7315	9-12	Linda Peters
A L B A	1515 W Lapham Blvd	Milwaukee, WI	53204-3236	414-902-8323	902-8424	K-5	Brenda Martinez
Alliance Charter S	215 E Forest Ave	Neenah, WI	54956-2765	920-751-6970	751-6861	K-5	
Alliance S	234 W Galena St	Milwaukee, WI	53212-3955	414-227-2550		9-12	Tina Owen
ALPS Charter S	108 W New York Ave	Oshkosh, WI	54901-3760	920-424-0349	424-7596	4-8	Shelly Muza
Appleton Central Alternative HS	PO Box 2019	Appleton, WI	54912-2019	920-832-6136	993-7074	9-12	Nichole Schweitzer
Appleton Community Learning Center	PO Box 2019	Appleton, WI	54912-2019	920-997-1497	993-7074	7-8	Nichole Schweitzer
Appleton eSchool	2121 E Emmers Dr	Appleton, WI	54915-3802	920-997-1399	832-1741	9-12	Connie Radtke
Appleton Montessori Charter S	2725 E Forest St	Appleton, WI	54915-3332	920-832-6265	832-6199	1-6	Dom Ferrito
Argyle Land Ethic Academy	PO Box 256	Argyle, WI	53504-0256	608-543-3318	543-3868	11-12	Gerry Benish
Ascend Academy	PO Box 40	Drummond, WI	54832-0040	715-739-6669	739-6345	7-12	Al Gillberg
Audubon Technology & Communication Ctr	3300 S 39th St	Milwaukee, WI	53215-4019	414-902-7800	902-7815	6-8	Katrice Cotton
Aurora Weier HS	2669 N Richards St	Milwaukee, WI	53212-2850	414-562-8398	562-8494	9-12	Luis Baez
Barron County Learning Center	1725 S Main St	Rice Lake, WI	54868-2915	715-736-3464	234-4552	9-12	Paul Vine
Beaver Dam Charter S	400 E Burnett St	Beaver Dam, WI	53916-1902	920-885-7423	885-7429	7-12	Martha Hyke
Brompton S	7951 36th Ave	Kenosha, WI	53142-2119	262-942-2191	942-2194	K-5	Patricia Jones
Bruce - Guadalupe Community S	1028 S 9th St	Milwaukee, WI	53204-1335	414-643-6441	649-9022	K-8	Pascual Rodriquez
Capitol West Academy	3939 W 88th St	Milwaukee, WI	53222-2748	414-465-1302	465-1319	PK-4	Donna Niccolai-Weber
C.A.R.E. Charter S	2000 Polk St	Stevens Point, WI	54481-5876	715-345-5620	345-5696	7-9	Connie Negaard
Carter S of Excellence	2001 W Vliet St	Milwaukee, WI	53205-1943	414-933-4044	933-4958	PK-5	Lorraine Carter
CASTLE Charter S	1700 Klatt Rd	New London, WI	54961-8603	920-982-8420	982-8440	7-12	Joe Pemrening
Central Cities HS	1801 16th St S	Wisc Rapids, WI	54494-5499	715-423-1520		11-12	Thomas Mancuso
Central City Cyberschool	4301 N 44th St	Milwaukee, WI	53216-1473	414-444-2330	444-2435	1-8	Christine Faltz
Chippewa Valley Montessori Charter S	400 Cameron St	Eau Claire, WI	54703-5101	715-852-6950	852-3504	K-5	Dr. Holly Hart
Chippewa Valley Technology Charter S	400 Cameron St	Eau Claire, WI	54703-5101	715-852-3101	852-6304	9-12	Dr. Holly Hart
CITIES - Project HS	700 W Michigan St	Milwaukee, WI	53233	414-344-8480	347-0110	9-11	Daniel Grego
Clark County Alternative Charter S	501 Hewett St	Neillsville, WI	54456	715-743-7443		9-12	Kelly Timmons
Classical Charter S	3310 N Durkee St	Appleton, WI	54911-1215	920-832-4968	997-1390	K-8	Constance Ford
Community HS	1017 N 12th St	Milwaukee, WI	53233-1307	414-212-3122	212-3114	9-10	Roxane Mayeur
Comprehensive Learning Center	258 E Gage St	Richland Center, WI	53581	608-647-9177	647-7293	9-12	Fred Flasher
Connects Learning Center	6201 S Barland Ave	Cudahy, WI	53110-2951	414-766-5100	766-5005	9-12	Dr. Gary Kiltz
CORE Charter S	W2662 Kennedy Ave	Kimberly, WI	54136-2339	920-687-3024	687-3029	9-12	Julie Holbrook
Core Knowledge Charter S	740 N Main St	Verona, WI	53593-1153	608-845-4130	845-4961	K-8	Bob McNallie
Coulee Montessori Charter S	1307 Hayes St	La Crosse, WI	54603-1949	608-789-7760	789-7080	K-6	Harvey Witzenburg
Crandon Alternative Resource S	9750 US Highway 8 W	Crandon, WI	54520-8499	715-478-3713	478-5570	7-12	John Gruber
Deerfield Charter HS	300 Simonson Blvd	Deerfield, WI	53531-9543	608-764-5431	764-5433	9-12	Barb Callahan
Denmark Empowerment Charter S	450 N Wall St	Denmark, WI	54208-9416	920-863-4031	863-5526	K-12	Steve Pasono
Dimensions of Learning Academy	6218 25th Ave	Kenosha, WI	53143-4370	262-605-6849	605-1234	K-8	Diana Pearson
DLH Academy	7151 N 86th St	Milwaukee, WI	53224-4861	414-358-3542	760-4364	K-12	Barbara Horton
Downtown Institute of Arts and Letters	227 W Pleasant St	Milwaukee, WI	53212-3941	414-248-9717		9-12	Lynette Jackson
Downtown Montessori Academy	2319 E Kenwood Blvd	Milwaukee, WI	53211-3315	414-332-8214	332-8215	K-K	Virginia Flynn
DuBois HS	8135 W Florist Ave	Milwaukee, WI	53218-1745	414-393-2580	393-2585	9-12	Larry Miller
EAA Charter S	1225 N Oakwood Rd	Oshkosh, WI	54904-8456	920-424-0315	424-7591	3-3	Kirby Schultz
Eagleville Charter S	S101W34511 County Road LO	Eagle, WI	53119-1860	262-363-6258	594-5495	1-5	Jodi Gebhard
East HS	405 Washington Ave	Oshkosh, WI	54901-5043	920-424-0160	232-0676	7-12	Jeff Walters
Environmental Education Charter S	1225 N Oakwood Rd	Oshkosh, WI	54904-8456	920-424-0315	424-7591	4-5	Kirby Schultz
Expressions School of the Arts	5496 N 72nd St	Milwaukee, WI	53218-2820	414-393-3100		9-12	Leslie Seib
Fairview S	6500 W Knncknnic River Pkwy	Milwaukee, WI	53219	414-546-7700	546-7715	PK-8	Jacqueline Scudder
Fifth Dimension	PO Box 76	Marshall, WI	53559-0076	608-655-1310	655-3046	11-12	Barb Seramek
Flambeau Charter S	PO Box 86	Tony, WI	54563-0086	715-532-5559	532-5405	11-12	Linda Michek
Foster ES	305 W Foster St	Appleton, WI	54915-1515	920-832-6288	832-4831	K-6	Judith Baseman
Fox River Academy	1000 S Mason St	Appleton, WI	54914-5457	920-932-6260	993-7060	3-6	Tom Marquette
Fox River Academy	2020 S Carpenter St	Appleton, WI	54915-4833	920-832-6276	832-6337	7-8	Chris VanderHeyden
Fritsche MS	2969 S Howell Ave	Milwaukee, WI	53207-2083	414-294-1000	294-1015	6-8	Robin Kitzrow
Genesis HS	1011 W Center St	Milwaukee, WI	53206-3299	414-267-5003	267-4915	9-10	Kathelyne Dye
Grantsburg Virtual S	480 E James Ave	Grantsburg, WI	54840-7959	715-463-5165	463-5068	9-12	Stanley Marczak
HACIL	PO Box 860	Hayward, WI	54843-0860	715-865-3107	934-8080	K-12	Kathryn Hexum
Highland Community S	3030 W Highland Blvd	Milwaukee, WI	53208-3246	414-342-1412	342-1408	PK-3	Kathy Ronco
Hmong American Peace Academy	1418 S Layton Blvd	Milwaukee, WI	53215-1923	414-383-4944	383-4950	K-10	Chris Her-Xiong
Honey Creek Continuous Progess ES	6701 W Eden Pl	Milwaukee, WI	53220-1335	414-604-7900	604-7915	PK-5	Gitanjali Chawla
Humboldt Park ES	3230 S Adams Ave	Milwaukee, WI	53207-2700	414-294-1700	294-1715	PK-5	Kristi Cole
IDEAL Charter S	4965 S 20th St	Milwaukee, WI	53221-2860	414-304-6200	304-6215	K-8	Barbara Ernest
Inland Seas S of Expedition	631 N 19th St	Milwaukee, WI	53233-2152	414-933-9713	431-0018	9-12	William Nimke
IQ Academy of Wisconsin	222 Maple Ave	Waukesha, WI	53186-4725	262-970-1074	970-1020	9-12	Kristine Diener
Janesville Academy for Intl Studies	31 W Milwaukee St	Janesville, WI	53548-2911	608-314-1180	314-1180	9-12	Donna Behn
Jefferson S for the Arts	1800 East Ave	Stevens Point, WI	54481-3799	715-345-5418	345-7352	K-6	Dave Lockett
Journeys Charter S	405 Washington Ave	Oshkosh, WI	54901-5043	920-232-0673	232-0676	7-12	Jeff Walters
Juneau County Charter S	N11003 17th Ave	Necedah, WI	54646-7618	608-565-7494	565-7559	7-12	Michele Yates-Wickus
Kiel eSchool	PO Box 201	Kiel, WI	53042-0201	920-894-2266	894-5100	7-12	Sue Steiner
Kilbourn Academy	520 Race St	Wisconsin Dells, WI	53965-1824	608-253-1461	254-6288	9-12	Randy Kuhnau
Kosciuszko Montessori MS	971 W Windlake Ave	Milwaukee, WI	53204-3822	414-902-7200	902-7215	6-8	Cheryl Clancy
La Causa S	PO Box 04188	Milwaukee, WI	53204-0188	414-902-1660	902-1676	K-5	Elma Radtke
LaCrossroads Charter HS	1500 Ranger Dr	La Crosse, WI	54603-2713	608-789-7700	789-7711	9-12	Doug Leclair
Lafayette County Community Charter S	1300 Industrial Dr	Fennimore, WI	53809-9702	608-822-3276		9-12	Gary Baxter
Lakeshore Alternative S	915 2nd St	Kewaunee, WI	54216-1619	920-388-4558	388-5174	11-12	Dawn Madland
Lakeview Montessori S	506 N Black River St	Sparta, WI	54656-1548	608-269-6144	366-3522	PK-3	Mike Roddick
Lalich Charter S	5503 W Range View Dr	Hurley, WI	54534-9000	715-561-4900	561-4157	6-12	Elizabeth Jorgensen
Laurel HS	100 Blackhawk Dr	Viroqua, WI	54665-1399	608-637-8486	637-8034	9-12	Renee Baker
LEARN Charter S	304 E Main St	Lena, WI	54139-9488	920-829-5703		9-12	Robert Werley
LIFT Charter S	PO Box 70	Clinton, WI	53525-0070	608-676-2211	676-5717	K-1	Denise Wellnitz
Lodi Charter S	1100 Sauk St	Lodi, WI	53555-1446	608-592-3853	592-1045	8-12	Kim Amidon
Lucas Charter S	N5639 200th St	Menomonie, WI	54751	715-232-1790	232-2026	9-12	Lynne Maslowski
Maasai Institute	4744 N 39th St	Milwaukee, WI	53209-5862	414-288-1691	755-7815		Janis McCollum

School	Address	City,State	Zip code	Telephone	Fax	Grade	Contact
Magellan Charter S	225 N Badger Ave	Appleton, WI	54914-3832	920-832-6226	832-4857	7-8	Lisa Eastman
Malcolm X Academy	2760 N 1st St	Milwaukee, WI	53212-2402	414-267-8600	267-8615	6-8	Lonnie Anderson
Mauston Alternative Resource	508 Grayside Ave	Mauston, WI	53948-1921	608-847-6603	847-4925	6-8	Tom Reisenauer
McDill Academies	2516 School St	Stevens Point, WI	54481-6100	715-345-5420	345-7345	K-6	Dennis Raabe
McKinley Center	2926 Blaine St	Stevens Point, WI	54481-4799	715-345-5421	345-7350	PK-6	John Blader
McKinley Charter MS	2340 Mohr Ave	Racine, WI	53405-2645	262-664-6150	664-6196	6-8	Lori Sue Pelk
McKinley Charter S	1266 McKinley Rd	Eau Claire, WI	54703-2220	715-839-2831		6-12	Dr. Holly Hart
Meeme LEADS Charter S	12121 County Road XX	Newton, WI	53063-9732	920-693-8255	693-8730	PK-4	Chad Ramminger
Milwaukee Academy of Aviation	4141 N 64th St	Milwaukee, WI	53216-1149	414-875-6400		9-12	Dura Hale
Milwaukee Academy of Science	2000 W Kilbourn Ave	Milwaukee, WI	53233-1625	414-933-0302	933-1914	K-7	Tracey Sparrow
Milwaukee Career Exploration Center	7000 N 60th St	Milwaukee, WI	53223	414-342-6232			William McMurtrey
Milwaukee College Prep S	2449 N 36th St	Milwaukee, WI	53210-3040	414-445-8020	445-8167	K-12	Robert Rauh
Milwaukee Leadership Training Center	2360 N 52nd St	Milwaukee, WI	53210-2701	414-874-8588	874-8515	K-12	Maria Dixon
Milwaukee Learning Lab	6506 W Warnimont Ave	Milwaukee, WI	53220-1344	414-604-7940		9-12	David Coyle
Milwaukee S of Entrepreneurship	6914 W Appleton Ave	Milwaukee, WI	53216-2732	414-438-5200	438-5208	9-12	John Polczynski
Monona Grove Alternative HS	5104 Gordon Ave	Monona, WI	53716-2718	608-223-1895		9-12	Paul Brost
Monroe Alternative Charter S	1220 16th Ave	Monroe, WI	53566-2047	608-328-7227	328-7826	6-12	Dan Bauer
Monroe Independent Virtual Charter S	801 32nd Ave	Monroe, WI	53566-1900	608-328-7299	328-7288	6-12	Dan Bauer
New Century Charter S	401 W Verona Ave	Verona, WI	53593-1318	608-845-4900	845-4720	K-5	Tim Bubon
New Horizons Charter S	120 S 14th Ave	Wausau, WI	54401-4217	715-261-0150	261-2461	7-9	Julie Sprague
New Horizons for Learning	1701 E Capitol Dr	Shorewood, WI	53211-1911	414-963-6933	963-6933	11-12	Richard Monroe
Next Door Charter S	2545 N 29th St	Milwaukee, WI	53210-3155	414-562-2929	562-1979	PK-K	Sharon Schulz
Northern Star S	5075 N Sherman Blvd	Milwaukee, WI	53209-5246	414-393-5000	393-5015	6-8	Valerie Benton-Davis
Northwoods Community Secondary S	511 S Pelham St	Rhinelander, WI	54501-3316	715-365-9720		6-12	Janet Bontz
Nuestro Mundo Community S	4201 Buckeye Rd	Madison, WI	53716-1648	608-204-1076	204-0364	K-1	Gary Zehrbach
Oconto Falls Alternative Learning Site	320 E Central Ave	Oconto Falls, WI	54154-1456	920-848-4455	848-3899	10-12	Becky James
Odyssey Charter S	2037 N Elinor St	Appleton, WI	54914-2255	920-832-6250	832-4389	3-6	Val Dreier
Odyssey-Magellan MS	305 W Foster St	Appleton, WI	54915-1515	920-832-6226	832-4389	5-8	James Donnellan
Paideia Charter School Academy	5821 10th Ave	Kenosha, WI	53140-4008	262-658-4540	658-4583	6-8	Ellen Becker
Parkview Charter S	422 Highway 11 W	Footville, WI	53537	608-879-2994	876-4185	10-12	Tracy Walczak
Passage Middle S	9501 W Watertown Plank Rd	Milwaukee, WI	53226-3552	414-476-2122			Christy Johnson
Philip Alternative Charter S	621 W College Ave	Waukesha, WI	53186	262-970-4355	970-4380	7-12	James Haessly
Portage Academy of Achievement	117 W Franklin St	Portage, WI	53901-1755	608-742-1409		9-12	Karen Exo
Preparatory School for Global Leadership	1916 N 4th St	Milwaukee, WI	53212-3612	414-264-3380	264-4450	6-7	Angela Dye
Professional Learning Institute	4965 S 20th St	Milwaukee, WI	53221-2860	414-304-6180	304-6188	9-10	Theresa Erbe
Project Change Alt Recovery Charter Schl	111 E Main St	Waukesha, WI	53186-5016	262-524-8677	524-8653	9-12	James Haessly
REAL Charter S	5915 Erie St	Racine, WI	53402-1925	262-664-8100	664-8110	6-12	Robert Holzem
Renaissance Charter Alternative Academy	211 N Fremont St	River Falls, WI	54022-2148	715-425-7645	425-7671	9-12	Donna Hill
Renaissance S for the Arts	610 N Badger Ave	Appleton, WI	54914-3405	920-832-5708	832-4198	9-12	Greg Hartjes
River Crossings Charter S	191 E Slifer St	Portage, WI	53901-1297	608-742-3764		7-8	Wayne Bartels
River Falls Public Montessori Academy	439 W Maple St	River Falls, WI	54022	715-425-7645	425-7671	K-5	Charles Eaton
Rock River Charter S	31 W Milwaukee St	Janesville, WI	53548-2911	608-752-8273	752-8430	9-12	Marge Hollenbeck
Roosevelt IDEA	2200 Wisconsin Ave	Plover, WI	54467-2981	715-345-5425	345-7347	K-6	Pam Bork
Rural Virtual Academy	124 W State St	Medford, WI	54451-1760	715-748-4620	748-6839	K-8	Charlie Heckel
School for Early Develpmnt & Achievmnt	2020 W Wells St	Milwaukee, WI	53233-2720	414-937-2024	937-2021	K-12	Mary Beth Minkley
School of Humanities	1011 W Center St	Milwaukee, WI	53206-3262	414-267-5000	267-4915	9-10	
School of Technology & Arts	1111 7th St S	La Crosse, WI	54601-5474	608-789-7695	789-7030	K-5	Nancy Matchett
School of Technology & Arts II	1900 Denton St	La Crosse, WI	54601-5816	608-789-7695	789-7030	6-8	Penny Reedy
Siefert ES	1547 N 14th St	Milwaukee, WI	53205-2109	414-935-1500	935-1515	PK-5	Janel Howard-Hawkins
Soset Charter S	PO Box 125	Blair, WI	54616-0125	608-989-9835	989-2451	3-6	Connie Biedron
Spalding Academy	PO Box 2019	Appleton, WI	54912-2019	920-832-6136	993-7074	7-12	Nichole Schweitzer
Sparta Area Independent Learning	506 N Black River St	Sparta, WI	54656-1548	608-366-3491	366-3455	K-12	William Tourdot
Sparta Charter Preschool	506 N Black River St	Sparta, WI	54656-1548	608-269-3151	366-3473	PK-PK	Tarry Hall
Sparta High Point S	506 N Black River St	Sparta, WI	54656-1548	608-366-3456		9-12	Mathew Toetz
Synectics Charter S	1859 Northgate Dr	Beloit, WI	53511-2667	608-361-3632	361-3620	6-8	Margaret Thomas
Tenor High S	840 N Jackson St	Milwaukee, WI	53202-3807	414-431-4371	431-4376	9-12	Jan Druetzler-Katz
Tesla Engineering Charter S	2121 E Emmers Dr	Appleton, WI	54915-3802	920-997-1399	832-4880	9-12	Becky Walker
Time 4 Learning Charter S	5900 S 51st St	Greendale, WI	53129-2634	414-423-2750	423-0592		Theresa A. West
Transitional Skills Center	850 Maple St	Glenwood City, WI	54013-4346	715-265-4266	265-7129	10-12	Timothy Johnson
Trevor Accelerated Program	26325 Wilmot Rd	Trevor, WI	53179-9701	262-862-2356	862-9226	PK-K	Jayme Donaldson
Truth Institute	1011 W Center St	Milwaukee, WI	53206-3262	414-267-4978	267-4915	9-10	
21st Century Prep S	1220 Mound Ave	Racine, WI	53404	262-598-0026	598-0031	K-4	K. Michele Clarke
Urban League Academy	3814 W North Ave	Milwaukee, WI	53208-1351	414-615-3915	444-2291	PK-8	Barbara Fisher
Valley New S	10 E College Ave Ste 225	Appleton, WI	54911-5688	920-993-7037	832-1725	7-12	Todd Gray
Veritas HS	3025 W Oklahoma Ave	Milwaukee, WI	53215-4347	414-389-5575	389-5576	9-12	Marcia Spector
Vernon County Area Better Futures HS	100 Blackhawk Dr	Viroqua, WI	54665-1399	608-637-3191	637-8034	10-12	Kathrine Klos
Waadookodaading S	PO Box 860	Hayward, WI	54843-0860	715-634-2619		K-4	Cathy Begay
Walker International MS	1712 S 32nd St	Milwaukee, WI	53215-2104	414-902-7500	902-7515	6-8	Hector LaBoy
Walworth County Education Alternative HS	400 County Road H	Elkhorn, WI	53121-2035	262-741-8138	741-8131	11-12	Jerry Hawver
Washington Service Learning Center	3500 Prais St	Stevens Point, WI	54481-2298	715-345-5426	345-7353	K-6	William Carlson
Waukesha Academy of Health Professions	401 E Roberta Ave	Waukesha, WI	53186-6637	262-970-3771	970-3720	9-12	Linda Farina
Waupaca County Charter S	PO Box 457	Weyauwega, WI	54983-0457	920-867-4744		6-12	Michele Wickus
Waupun Alternative HS	801 E Lincoln St	Waupun, WI	53963-1753	920-324-5591	324-6980	9-12	Jeff Finstad
Wausau Area Montessori Charter S	3101 N 13th St	Wausau, WI	54403-2317	715-261-0795	261-2035	1-5	Kurt Weyers
W.E.B. DuBois HS	4141 N 64th St	Milwaukee, WI	53216-1198	414-393-2580	393-2585	9-12	Larry Miller
Westside Academy I	1945 N 31st St	Milwaukee, WI	53208-1902	414-934-5000	934-5015	PK-3	James Sonnenberg
Westside Academy II	1940 N 36th St	Milwaukee, WI	53208-1927	414-934-4400	934-4415	4-8	James Sonnenberg
Whittier ES	4382 S 3rd St	Milwaukee, WI	53207-4999	414-294-1400	294-1415	PK-5	Peggy Mystrow
Wildlands Research Charter S	E19320 Bartig Rd	Augusta, WI	54722-7501	715-877-2292	877-2234	6-12	Paul Tweed
Wilmot Bright Horizons	PO Box 68	Wilmot, WI	53192-0068	262-862-6461	862-7301	K-K	Teresa Curley
Wings Academy	1501 S Layton Blvd	Milwaukee, WI	53215-1924	414-431-1356	431-1358	3-12	Dani LaPorte
Wisconsin Career Academy	4801 S 2nd St	Milwaukee, WI	53207-5919	414-483-2117	483-2152	6-12	Tarik Celik
Wisconsin Connections Academy	PO Box 2019	Appleton, WI	54912-2019	920-832-4800	832-6284	K-8	Nichole Schweitzer
Wisconsin Rivers Community Charter S	1201 Northpoint Dr	Stevens Point, WI	54481-1114	715-345-5504		10-12	Mike Devine
Wisconsin Virtual Academy	401 Highland Dr	Fredonia, WI	53021-9491	262-692-3988	692-3952	K-8	Daniel Hanrahan
Woodlands S	5510 W Blue Mound Rd	Milwaukee, WI	53208-3012	414-475-1600	475-9575	K-6	Maureen Sullivan
Wright Charter MS	1717 Fish Hatchery Rd	Madison, WI	53713-1244	608-204-1340	204-0547	6-8	Nancy Evans
YMCA Young Leaders Academy	1350 W North Ave	Milwaukee, WI	53205-1264	414-374-9400	374-9459	K-12	Ronn Johnson

Wyoming

School	Address	City,State	Zip code	Telephone	Fax	Grade	Contact
Arapaho Charter HS	445 Little Wind Rvr Bottom	Arapahoe, WY	82510	307-856-9333	856-2440	9-12	Gail Ridgely
Fort Washakie Charter HS	90 Ethete Rd	Fort Washakie, WY	82514	307-332-2380	332-7267	9-12	Shad Hamilton

BUREAU OF INDIAN AFFAIRS SCHOOLS

BUREAU OF INDIAN AFFAIRS
1849 C St NW, Washington, DC 20240-0001
Telephone 202-208-6123
Fax 208-3312
Website http://www.oiep.bia.edu/

BUREAU OF INDIAN AFFAIRS SCHOOLS

Agency/School	Address	City,State	Zip code	Telephone	Fax	Grade	Enr	Superintendent/Principal
Billings Area Office	**316 N 26th St**	**Billings, MT**	**59101**	**406-247-7953**	**247-7965**	**K-12**		
Blackfeet Dormitory	PO Box 880	Browning, MT	59417-0880	406-338-7441	338-5732	1-12		
Northern Cheyenne Tribal S of Busby	PO Box 150	Busby, MT	59016-0150	406-592-3733	592-3645	K-12		
St. Stephens Indian S	PO Box 345	Saint Stephens, WY	82524-0345	307-856-4147	856-3742	K-12		
Cheyenne River Agency	**PO Box 2020**	**Eagle Butte, SD**	**57625-2020**	**605-964-8722**	**964-1155**	**K-12**		Dr. Cherie Farlee
Cheyenne-Eagle Butte S	PO Box 672	Eagle Butte, SD	57625-0672	605-964-8777	964-8776	K-12		

Agency/School	Address	City,State	Zip code	Telephone	Fax	Grade	Enr	Superintendent/Principal
Pierre Indian Learning Center	3001 E Sully Ave	Pierre, SD	57501	605-224-8661	224-8465	K-8		Darrell Jeanotte
Takini S	HC 77 Box 537	Howes, SD	57748-9511	605-538-4399	538-4315	K-12		Larry Mendoza
Tiospaye Topa S	PO Box 300	Ridgeview, SD	57652-0300	605-733-2290	733-2299	K-12		Don Farlee
Chinle Agency	**PO Box 6003**	**Chinle, AZ**	**86503-6003**	**928-674-5131**	**674-5134**	**K-12**		**Dr. Rena Yazzie**
Black Mesa Community S	PO Box 97	Pinon, AZ	86510-0097	928-674-3632	659-8187	K-8		Marie Rose
Chinle Boarding S	PO Box 70	Many Farms, AZ	86538-3070	928-781-6221	781-6376	K-8		Gregory Morring
Cottonwood Day S	Navajo Route 4	Chinle, AZ	86503	928-725-3256	725-3255	K-8		Esther Frejo
Jeehdeez'a Academy	PO Box 1073	Pinon, AZ	86510-1073	928-725-3308	725-3306	K-5		Jim Davis
Lukachukai Community S	Navajo Route 13	Lukachukai, AZ	86507	928-787-4400	787-2311	K-8		Herbert Harvey
Many Farms HS	PO Box 307	Many Farms, AZ	86538-3307	928-781-6226	781-6355	9-12		Brian Dillon
Nazlini Community S	HC 58 Box 35	Ganado, AZ	86505-9704	928-755-6125	755-3729	K-8		Ronald Arias
Pinon Community S	PO Box 159	Pinon, AZ	86510-0159	928-725-3234	725-3232	K-12		Phillip Belone
Rock Point Community S	Highway 191	Rock Point, AZ	86545	928-659-4221	659-4235	K-12		Peter Belleto
Rough Rock Community S	HC 61 Box 5050PTT	Chinle, AZ	86503	928-728-3501	728-3564	K-12		Dr. Charles Monty Roessel
Crow Creek/Lower Brule/Agency	**PO Box 139**	**Fort Thompson, SD**	**57339-0139**	**605-473-5531**	**473-9217**	**K-12**		**Dan Shroyer**
Crow Creek Reservation HS	PO Box 12	Stephan, SD	57346-0012	605-852-2455	852-2140	6-12		Joe Ashley
Crow Creek Sioux Tribal ES	PO Box 469	Fort Thompson, SD	57339-0469	605-245-2373	245-2310	K-5		Robyn Thompson
Enemy Swim S	13495 446th Ave	Waubay, SD	57273-5318	605-947-4605	947-4188	K-8		Sherry Johnson
Lower Brule Day S	PO Box 245	Lower Brule, SD	57548-0245	605-473-5382	473-0214	PK-6		Richard Baysinger
Lower Brule HS	PO Box 245	Lower Brule, SD	57548-0245	605-473-5510	473-5207	7-12		Neil Russell
Tiospa Zina Tribal S	PO Box 719	Agency Village, SD	57262-0719	605-698-3954	698-6556	K-12		Ron Campbell
Eastern Navajo Agency	**PO Box 328**	**Crownpoint, NM**	**87313-0328**	**505-786-6151**	**786-6112**	**K-12**	4,500	**Geraldine Thomason**
Alamo Navajo S	PO Box 907	Magdalena, NM	87825-0907	505-854-2635	854-2545	K-12		Alfonso Garcia
Baca Community S	PO Box 509	Prewitt, NM	87045-0509	505-876-2769	876-2310	K-4		Timothy Nelson
Bread Springs Day S	PO Box 1117	Gallup, NM	87305-1117	505-778-5665	778-5692	K-3		Carl Granfors
Chi-Chil Tah/Jones Ranch S	PO Box 278	Vanderwagen, NM	87326-0278	505-778-5574	778-5575	K-8		Judy Quesenberry
Dibe Yazhi Habitiin Olta S	PO Box 679	Crownpoint, NM	87313-0679	505-786-5237	786-7078	K-8		Dr. Robert Gross
Dzilth-Na-O-Dith-Hle Comm. S	35 Rd 7585 Ste 5003	Bloomfield, NM	87413	505-632-1697	632-8563	K-12		June Gann
Huerfano Dormitory	PO Box 639	Bloomfield, NM	87413-0639	505-325-3411	327-3591	K-12		Dwane Robinson
Lake Valley Navajo S	PO Box 748	Crownpoint, NM	87313-0748	505-786-6392	786-5956	K-8		Pauline Villegas
Mariano Lake Community S	PO Box 498	Crownpoint, NM	87313-0498	505-786-5265	786-5203	K-6		Sylvia Largo
NaNeel Zhiin Ji'olta S	HC 79 Box 9	Cuba, NM	87013-9701	505-731-2272	731-2252	K-8		Kenneth Toledo
Ojo Encino S	HC 79 Box 7	Cuba, NM	87013-9701	505-731-2333	731-2361	K-8		Theresa Kedelty
Pueblo Pintado Community S	HC 79 Box 80	Cuba, NM	87013-9600	505-655-3341	655-3342	K-8		Notah Benally
T'iists'oozi Bi'olta S	PO Box 178	Crownpoint, NM	87313-0178	505-786-6159	786-6163	K-8		Virginia Jumbo
To'Hajiilee Ji'Olta S	PO Box 438	Canoncito, NM	87026	505-831-6426	831-4914	K-12		Jane Pitts
Tse'ii'ahi' Community S	PO Box 828	Crownpoint, NM	87313-0828	505-786-5389	786-5635	K-4		Rebecca Vesely
Wingate HS	PO Box 2	Fort Wingate, NM	87316-0002	505-488-6400	488-6444	9-12		Mary Ann Sherman
Wingate S	PO Box 1	Fort Wingate, NM	87316-0001	505-488-6300	488-6312	K-8		Dianne Owens
Fort Apache Agency	**PO Box 920**	**Whiteriver, AZ**	**85941-0920**	**928-338-5442**	**338-1944**	**K-12**		**Kevin Skenandore**
Cibecue Community S	PO Box 80068	Cibecue, AZ	85911-0068	928-332-2480	332-2341	K-12		Linda Roma
Kennedy S, John F.	PO Box 130	Whiteriver, AZ	85941-0130	928-338-4593	338-4592	K-8		Michael Bragiel
Roosevelt JHS, Theodore	PO Box 567	Fort Apache, AZ	85926-0567	928-338-4464	338-1009	6-8		Wil Numkena
Fort Defiance Agency	**PO Box 110**	**Fort Defiance, AZ**	**86504-0110**	**928-729-7255**	**729-7286**	**K-12**		**Jacqueline Wade**
Ch'ooshgai Community S	PO Box 321	Tohatchi, NM	87325-0321	505-733-2719	733-2703	K-8		Johanson Phillips
Crystal Boarding S		Navajo, NM	87328	505-777-2385	777-2648	K-6		
Dilcon Community S	HC 63 Box G	Winslow, AZ	86047-9414	928-657-3485	657-3213	K-8		
Greasewood Springs Community S	HC 58 Box 60	Ganado, AZ	86505-9706	928-654-3383	654-3384	K-8		Arlene Tuchawena
Hunters Point Boarding S	PO Box 99	Saint Michaels, AZ	86511-0099	928-871-4439	871-4435	K-5		Cindy G. Joe
Kin Dah Lichi'i Olta	PO Box 800	Ganado, AZ	86505-0800	928-755-3707	755-3448	K-6		Ora James
Pine Springs Day S	PO Box 4198	Houck, AZ	86506-4198	928-871-4311	871-4341	K-4		Lou Ann M. Jones
Seba Dalkai Boarding S	HC 63 Box H	Winslow, AZ	86047-9415	928-657-3208	657-3224	K-8		
Tiiyaatin Residential Hall	1100 W Buffalo St	Holbrook, AZ	86025-2330	928-524-6222	524-2231	9-12		Maye Bigboy
Wide Ruins Community S	PO Box 309	Chambers, AZ	86502-0309	928-652-3251	652-3252	K-6		James Byrnes
Winslow Residential Hall	600 N Alfred Ave	Winslow, AZ	86047-3130	928-289-4483	289-2821	7-12		Mike K. James
Hopi Agency	**PO Box 568**	**Keams Canyon, AZ**	**86034-0568**	**928-738-2262**	**738-5139**	**K-12**		**Jimmy Hastings**
First Mesa ES	PO Box 750	Polacca, AZ	86042-0750	928-737-2581	738-5139	K-6		Bruce Steele
Havasupai S	PO Box 40	Supai, AZ	86435-0040	928-448-2901	448-2551	K-8		Virginia Velasquez
Hopi Day S	PO Box 42	Kykotsmovi, AZ	86039-0042	928-734-2468	734-2470	K-6		Dr. John Thomas
Hopi JSHS	PO Box 337	Keams Canyon, AZ	86034-0337	928-738-5111	738-5333	7-12	700	Dr. Paul Reynolds
Hotevilla-Bacavi Community S	PO Box 48	Hotevilla, AZ	86030-0048	928-734-2462	734-2225	K-8		Alma Sinquah
Keams Canyon ES	PO Box 397	Keams Canyon, AZ	86034-0397	928-738-2385	738-5519	K-6		Michael Krug
Moencopi Day S	PO Box 185	Tuba City, AZ	86045-0185	928-283-5361	283-4662	K-6		Joel Longie
Second Mesa Day S	PO Box 98	Second Mesa, AZ	86043-0098	928-737-2571	737-2565	K-6		Donald Harvey
Minneapolis Agency	**1 Federal Dr Rm 550**	**Fort Snelling, MN**	**55111-4008**	**612-725-4591**	**713-4438**	**K-12**		**Bill Walters**
Bug-O-Nay-Ge-Shig S	15353 Silver Eagle Dr NW	Bena, MN	56626-1012	218-665-3000	665-3024	K-12		Michelle Johnson
Circle of Life S	PO Box 447	White Earth, MN	56591-0447	218-983-4180	983-3767	K-12		Mitch Vogt
Circle of Nations Indian Boarding S	832 8th St N	Wahpeton, ND	58075-3642	701-642-3796	642-5880	4-8		David Keehn
Flandreau Indian S	1005 S Mountain Chief Dr #1	Flandreau, SD	57028	605-997-3773	997-2601	9-12		Betty Belkham
Fond du Lac Ojibwe S	105 University Rd	Cloquet, MN	55720-8520	218-878-7571	878-7573	K-12		Rae Villebran
Hannahville Indian S	N14911 Hannahville Road B 1	Wilson, MI	49896-9612	906-466-2952	466-2556	K-12	200	William Boda
Lac Courte Oreilles Ojibwa S	8875 N Round Lake School Rd	Hayward, WI	54843	715-634-8924	634-6058	K-12		Craig Euneau
Lumsden Bahweting Anishinabe S, J.K.	1301 Marquette Ave	Sault S Marie, MI	49783-9533	906-635-5055	635-3805	K-8	400	Nick Oshleski
Menominee Tribal S	PO Box 39	Neopit, WI	54150-0039	715-756-2354	756-2364	K-8		Alan Coldwell
Meskwaki Settlement S	1605 305th St	Tama, IA	52339	641-484-4990	484-3264	K-12		Jerry Stephens
Nay Ah Shing S	43651 Oodena Dr	Onamia, MN	56359-2320	320-532-4695	532-4675	K-12		Eric North
Oneida Nation ES	PO Box 365	Oneida, WI	54155-0365	920-869-1676	869-1684	K-12		Sharon Mousseau
Navajo Co. Special Services Consortium	**PO Box 668**	**Holbrook, AZ**	**86025-0668**	**928-524-2123**	**524-6367**	**K-12**	**50**	**Betty Walch**
Rainbow Accomodation	PO Box 668	Holbrook, AZ	86025-0668	928-524-1821	524-6367	K-12	50	Autumn Hanson
Northern Navajo Agency	**PO Box 3239**	**Shiprock, NM**	**87420-3239**	**505-368-3400**	**368-3409**	**K-12**		**Dr. Joel Longie**
Aneth Community S	PO Box 600	Montezuma Creek, UT	84534-0600	435-651-3271	651-3272	K-6		Clayton Michael Aaron
Atsa'biya'a'zh Community S	PO Box 1809	Shiprock, NM	87420-1809	505-368-2084	368-2100	K-6		Melissa Culler
Aztec Dormitory	1600 Lydia Rippey Rd	Aztec, NM	87410-1662	505-334-6565	334-8630	9-12		John Nolan
Beclabito Day S	PO Box 1200	Shiprock, NM	87420-1200	928-656-3555		K-4		Daniel Sosnowski
Cove Day S	PO Box 2000	Red Valley, AZ	86544-2000	928-653-4457	653-4415	K-6		Perfilliea Charlie
Navajo Prep S	1220 W Apache St	Farmington, NM	87401-3886	505-326-6571	326-2155	9-12		Betty O'Jaye
Nenahnezad Community S	PO Box 337	Fruitland, NM	87416-0337	505-598-6922	598-0970	K-6		Sylvia Ashley
Red Rock Day S	PO Box 2007	Red Valley, AZ	86544-2007	928-653-4456	653-5711	K-8		Susanna Gaddy
Sanostee Day S	PO Box 159	Sanostee, NM	87461-0159	505-723-2476	723-2425	K-3		Jeannie Haskie
Shiprock Alternative Dormitory Program	PO Box 1809	Shiprock, NM	87420-1809	505-368-2074	368-5102	9-12		Johnny Anderson
Shiprock Northwest HS	PO Box 1809	Shiprock, NM	87420-1809	505-368-2070	368-5102	9-12		Rick Hover
T'iisNazbas Community S	PO Box 102	Teec Nos Pos, AZ	86514-0102	928-656-3252	656-3486	K-8		Delphina John
Tohaali' Community S	PO Box 9857	Newcomb, NM	87455-9857	505-789-3201	789-3202	K-8		Delores Bitsilly
Northern Pueblos Agency	**PO Box 4269**	**Espanola, NM**	**87533-4269**	**505-753-1465**	**753-1475**	**K-12**		
Jicarilla Dormitory	PO Box 1009	Dulce, NM	87528-1009	505-759-3101	759-3338	1-12		
Ohkay Owingeh Community S	PO Box 1077	San Juan Pueblo, NM	87566-1077	505-852-2154	852-4305	K-8		Alfred Garcia
San Ildefonso S	36 Tunyo Po	Santa Fe, NM	87506-7258	505-455-2366	455-2155	K-6		
Santa Clara S	PO Box 2183	Espanola, NM	87532-2183	505-753-4406	753-8866	K-6		
Santa Fe Indian S	PO Box 5340	Santa Fe, NM	87502-5340	505-989-6300	989-6317	7-12		
Taos S	PO Box X	Taos, NM	87571-1189	505-758-3652	758-1566	K-8		
Te Tsu Geh Oweenge S	RR 42 Box 2	Santa Fe, NM	87506-8368	505-982-1516	982-2331	K-6		
Oklahoma Education Office	**200 NW 4th St Ste 4049**	**Oklahoma City, OK**	**73102-3072**	**405-605-6051**	**605-6057**	**K-12**		**Joy Martin**
Carter Seminary	2400 Chickasaw Blvd	Ardmore, OK	73401-1347	580-223-8547	223-6325	1-12		Mike Abla
Eufaula Dormitory	Swadley Dr	Eufaula, OK	74432	918-689-2522	689-2438	1-12		Greg Anderson
Jones Academy	HC 74 Box 102-5	Hartshorne, OK	74547-9717	918-297-2518	297-2364	1-12		Brad Spears
Kickapoo Nation S	PO Box 106	Powhattan, KS	66527-0106	785-474-3550	474-3530	K-12		Pat McAfee
Riverside Indian S	RR 1	Anadarko, OK	73005	405-247-6673	247-5529	4-12		Don Sims
Sequoyah HS	PO Box 948	Tahlequah, OK	74465-0948	918-456-0631	456-0634	9-12		Gina Stanley
Pacific Regional Office	**2800 Cottage Way Ste W2820**	**Sacramento, CA**	**95825-1886**	**916-978-6000**	**978-6056**	**K-12**	1,100	
Duckwater Shoshone S	PO Box 140068	Duckwater, NV	89314-0068	775-863-0180	863-0199	K-8		Keith Honnaker
Noli S	PO Box 500	San Jacinto, CA	92581	951-654-5596	654-4198	6-12		Donovan Post
Pyramid Lake HS	PO Box 256	Nixon, NV	89424-0256	775-574-1016	574-1037	7-12		Randy Melendez
Sherman Indian HS	9010 Magnolia Ave	Riverside, CA	92503-3972	951-276-6332	276-6336	9-12		Don Sims
Papago - Pima Agency	**HC 1 Box 8600**	**Sells, AZ**	**85634-9743**	**520-361-3510**	**361-3514**	**K-12**		**Lester Hudson**
Blackwater Community S	RR 1 Box 95	Coolidge, AZ	85228-9681	520-215-5859	215-5862	K-2	100	Jacquelyn Power
Casa Blanca S	PO Box 10940	Bapchule, AZ	85221-0940	520-315-3489	315-3504	K-4		Patty Cook
Gila Crossing S	PO Box 10	Laveen, AZ	85339-0010	520-550-4834	550-4252	K-8		Katie Stevens
Salt River HS	10005 E Osborn Rd	Scottsdale, AZ	85256-4019	480-362-2000	362-2090	7-12		Mike McCarthy
Salt River S	10000 E McDowell Rd	Scottsdale, AZ	85256-5201	480-850-2900	850-7600	K-6		Jacque Bradley
San Simon S	HC 1 Box 8292	Sells, AZ	85634-9711	520-362-2231	362-2405	K-8		Frank Rogers
Santa Rosa Boarding S	HC 01 Box 8400	Sells, AZ	85634	520-361-2276	361-2511	K-8		Keith Seaman
Santa Rosa Ranch S	HC 01 Box 7570	Sells, AZ	85634	520-383-2359	383-3960	K-8		Delbert Ortiz
Tohono O'Odham HS	HC 01 Box 8513	Sells, AZ	85634	520-362-2400	362-2256	9-12		William Reese

Agency/School	Address	City,State	Zip code	Telephone	Fax	Grade	Enr	Superintendent/Principal
Pine Ridge Agency	**PO Box 333**	**Pine Ridge, SD**	**57770-0333**	**605-867-1306**	**867-5610**	**K-12**		**Norma Tibbitts**
American Horse S	PO Box 660	Allen, SD	57714-0660	605-455-6750	455-2249	K-8		Gloria Kitsopoulas
Crazy Horse S	PO Box 260	Wanblee, SD	57577-0260	605-455-6800	462-6510	K-12		Donald Standing Elk
Little Wound S	PO Box 500	Kyle, SD	57752-0500	605-455-6175	455-2703	K-12		Linda Hunter
Loneman S	PO Box 50	Oglala, SD	57764-0050	605-455-6882	867-5109	K-8		Deborah Bordeaux
Pine Ridge S	PO Box 1202	Pine Ridge, SD	57770-1202	605-455-6500	867-5482	K-12		Melvin Sierra
Porcupine S	PO Box 180	Porcupine, SD	57772-0180	605-455-6450	867-5480	K-8		Thomas Raymond
Wounded Knee S	PO Box 350	Manderson, SD	57756-0350	605-455-6363	867-2051	K-8		Chris Bordeaux
Portland Area Office	**911 NE 11th Ave**	**Portland, OR**	**97232**	**503-872-2743**	**231-6219**	**PK-12**		**John Reimer**
Chemawa Indian S	3700 Chemawa Rd NE	Salem, OR	97305-1199	503-399-5721	399-5870	9-12		
Chief Leschi S	5625 52nd St E	Puyallup, WA	98371-3610	253-445-3003	445-2350	K-12		
Couer D'Alene Tribal S	PO Box 338	Desmet, ID	83824-0338	208-686-5126	686-5080	K-8		
Lummi HS	2530 Kwina Rd	Bellingham, WA	98226-9278	360-384-2330	380-1464	9-12		
Lummi Tribal S	2530 Kwina Rd	Bellingham, WA	98226-9278	360-384-2293	384-2334	K-8		
Muckleshoot Tribal S	39015 172nd Ave SE	Auburn, WA	98092-9763	253-931-6709	939-2922	K-12		
Paschal Sherman Indian S	25 Mission Rd Ste A	Omak, WA	98841-9455	509-422-7590	422-7539	K-9		
Quileute Tribal S	PO Box 39	La Push, WA	98350-0039	360-374-5602	374-9608	K-12		
Shoshone Bannock S	PO Box 790	Fort Hall, ID	83203-0790	208-238-4200	238-2628	K-8		
Two Eagle River S	PO Box 160	Pablo, MT	59855-0160	406-675-0292	675-0294	K-8		
Wa He Lut Indian S	11110 Conine Ave SE	Olympia, WA	98513-9603	360-456-1311	456-1319	K-8		
Yakima Tribal S	PO Box 151	Toppenish, WA	98948-0151	509-865-5121	865-6092	7-12		
Rosebud Agency	**PO Box 669**	**Mission, SD**	**57555-0669**	**605-856-4478**	**856-4487**	**K-12**		**Neva Sherwood**
Marty Indian S	PO Box 187	Marty, SD	57361-0187	605-384-2212	384-5933	K-12		Russell Leonard
St. Francis Indian S	PO Box 379	Saint Francis, SD	57572-0379	605-747-2299	747-2379	K-12		Larry Parker
Sicangu Owaye Oti	PO Box 669	Mission, SD	57555-0669	605-856-4486	856-4490	1-12		Nancy Hernandez
South & Eastern States Agency	**545 Marriott Dr Ste 720**	**Nashville, TN**	**37214-5081**	**615-564-6630**	**564-6631**	**PK-12**		
Ahafachkee S	HC 61 Box 40	Clewiston, FL	33440-9771	863-983-6348	983-6535	K-12		Terry Porter
Bogue Chitto S	13241 Highway 491 N	Philadelphia, MS	39350-5463	601-389-1000	389-1002	K-8		Evelyn Terrell
Cherokee Central JSHS	PO Box 134	Cherokee, NC	28719-0134	828-497-5511	497-4372	7-12		Arlin Middleton
Cherokee Central S	PO Box 134	Cherokee, NC	28719-0134	828-497-9130	497-4351	K-8		Charlee Easton
Chitimacha Day S	3613 Chitimacha Trl	Jeanerette, LA	70544-8317	337-923-9960	923-7346	K-8		Tanya Rosamond
Choctaw Central HS	150 Recreation Rd	Choctaw, MS	39350-7180	601-663-7777	656-7077	9-12		Greg Carlyle
Choctaw Central MS	150 Recreation Rd	Choctaw, MS	39350	601-656-8938	656-1558	7-8		Roger McLeod
Conehatta S	851 Tushka Rd	Conehatta, MS	39057-2804	601-775-8254	775-9229	K-8		Charles Hull
Indian Island S	1 River St	Old Town, ME	04468	207-827-4285	827-3599	PK-8		Linda McLeod
Indian Township S	13 School Dr	Princeton, ME	04668-5000	207-796-2362	796-2726	PK-8		Ralph Shannon
Miccosukee Indian S	PO Box 440021	Miami, FL	33144-0021	305-894-2364	894-2365	K-12		Tom Albano
Pearl River ES	470 Industrial Rd	Choctaw, MS	39350-4256	601-656-9051	656-9054	K-6		David McCullom
Rafferty S, Beatrice	22 Bayview Dr	Pleasant Point, ME	04667-4111	207-853-6085	853-2483	PK-8		Mike Chadwick
Red Water S	555 Red Water Rd	Carthage, MS	39051-9103	601-267-8500	267-5193	K-8		Bobbie Boone
Standing Pine ES	538 Highway 487 E	Carthage, MS	39051-6031	601-267-9225	267-9129	K-6		Jackie Harpole
Tucker S	126 E Tucker Cir	Philadelphia, MS	39350-8351	601-656-8775	656-9341	K-8		Joe Wood
Southern Pueblos Agency	**PO Box 26567**	**Albuquerque, NM**	**87125-6567**	**505-563-3690**	**563-3078**	**K-12**	**2,800**	**Bartholomew Stevens**
Isleta ES	PO Box 550	Isleta, NM	87022-0550	505-869-2321	869-1625	K-6		Joe Robledo
Jemez Day S	PO Box 139	Jemez Pueblo, NM	87024-0139	505-834-7304	834-7081	K-6		Freddie Cardenas
Laguna ES	PO Box 191	Laguna, NM	87026-0191	505-552-9200	552-7294	K-5		Brenda Kofahl
Laguna MS	PO Box 268	Laguna, NM	87026-0268	505-552-9091	552-6466	6-8		Yolanda Batrez
Mescalero Apache S	PO Box 230	Mescalero, NM	88340-0230	505-464-4470	464-4822	K-12	100	Charles Harrison
Pine Hill S	PO Box 220	Pinehill, NM	87357-0220	505-775-3243	775-3241	K-12		Sam Alonza
San Felipe Pueblo S	PO Box 4343	San Felipe Pb, NM	87001-4343	505-867-3364	867-6253	K-7		James Whitman
Sky City Community S	PO Box 349	Pueblo of Acoma, NM	87034-0349	505-552-6671	552-6672	K-8		Richard Jaramillo
T'siya S, Zia	1000 Borrego Canyon Rd	Zia Pueblo, NM	87053-6104	505-867-3553	867-5079	K-8		Pauline Panama
Standing Rock Agency	**PO Box E**	**Fort Yates, ND**	**58538-0523**	**701-854-3497**	**854-7280**	**K-12**		
Jamerson S, Theodore	3315 University Dr	Bismarck, ND	58504-7565	701-255-3285	530-0601	K-8		Francis Azure
Little Eagle S	PO Box 26	Little Eagle, SD	57639-0026	605-823-4235	823-2292	K-8		
Rock Creek Grant S	PO Box 127	Bullhead, SD	57621-0127	605-823-4971	823-4350	K-8		
Tate Topa Tribal S	PO Box 199	Fort Totten, ND	58335-0199	701-766-1470	766-4766	K-8		Dean Dauphinais
Turtle Mountain Education Line Office	**PO Box 30**	**Belcourt, ND**	**58316-0030**	**701-477-3463**	**477-9364**	**PK-12**		**Rose-Marie Davis**
Dunseith Day S	PO Box 759	Dunseith, ND	58329-0759	701-263-4636	263-4200	K-8		Yvonne St. Claire
Mandaree S	PO Box 488	Mandaree, ND	58757-0488	701-759-3311	759-3493	K-12		Carolyn Bluestone
Ojibwa Indian S	PO Box 600	Belcourt, ND	58316-0600	701-477-3108	477-3760	K-8		Michael Blue
Trenton S	PO Box 239	Trenton, ND	58853-0239	701-774-8221	774-8040	PK-12	100	Michael O'Brien
Turtle Mountain ES	PO Box 440	Belcourt, ND	58316-0440	701-477-6471	477-8835	K-5		Dave Gourneau
Turtle Mountain HS	PO Box 440	Belcourt, ND	58316-0440	701-477-6471	477-8821	9-12		Rosemary Jaros
Turtle Mountain MS	PO Box 440	Belcourt, ND	58316-0440	701-477-6471	477-3973	6-8		Louis Dauphinais
Twin Buttes S	7997 7A St NW	Halliday, ND	58636-4004	701-938-4396	938-4398	K-8	50	Chad Dahlen
White Shield S	2 2nd Ave W	Roseglen, ND	58775-6009	701-743-4355	743-4501	K-12		Ioane Schmidt
Western Navajo Agency	**PO Box 746**	**Tuba City, AZ**	**86045-0746**	**928-283-2218**	**283-2286**	**K-12**		**Joe Frazier**
Chilchinbeto Community S	PO Box 740	Kayenta, AZ	86033-0740	928-697-3800	697-3448	K-8		Leonard Eltsosie
Dennehotso Boarding S	PO Box 2570	Dennehotso, AZ	86535-2570	928-658-3201	658-3221	K-8		James Brown
Greyhills Academy HS	PO Box 160	Tuba City, AZ	86045-0160	928-283-6271	283-6604	9-12		Andrew Tan
Kaibito Boarding S	PO Box 1420	Kaibito, AZ	86053-1420	928-673-3480	673-3489	K-8		Richard Harjo
Kayenta Community S	PO Box 188	Kayenta, AZ	86033-0188	928-697-3439	697-3490	K-8		Velma Eisenberger
KinLani Bordertown Dormitory	901 N Kinlani Dr	Flagstaff, AZ	86001-1585	928-774-5270	774-5270	9-12		James Kimery
Leupp S	HC 61 Box D	Winslow, AZ	86047-9313	928-686-6211	686-6216	K-12		Emma Yazzie
Little Singer Community S	HC 61 Box 310	Winslow, AZ	86047	928-526-6680	526-8894	K-6		Lucinda Godinez
Naa Tsis 'Aan Community S	PO Box 10010	Tonalea, AZ	86044-5010	928-672-2335	672-2609	K-8		Mary Rule
Richfield Residential Hall	PO Box 638	Richfield, UT	84701-0638	435-896-5101	896-6157	9-12		Boyd Kiesel
Rocky Ridge Boarding S	PO Box 299	Kykotsmovi, AZ	86039-0299	928-725-3650	725-3655	K-8		Bart Moore
Shonto Preparatory S	PO Box 7900	Shonto, AZ	86054-7900	928-672-2652	672-2849	K-12	500	Eugene Thomas
Tonalea Day S	PO Box 39	Tonalea, AZ	86044-0039	928-283-6325	283-6326	K-8		Gregory Mooring
Tuba City Boarding S	PO Box 187	Tuba City, AZ	86045-0187	928-283-2330	283-2348	K-8		Don Coffland

DEPARTMENT OF DEFENSE DEPENDENT SCHOOLS

DEPT. OF DEFENSE DEPENDENT SCHOOLS
4040 Fairfax Dr Fl 9, Arlington, VA 22203
Telephone 703-696-4247
Website http://www.odedodea.edu

DEPARTMENT OF DEFENSE DEPENDENT SCHOOLS

District/School	Address	City,State	Zip code	Telephone	Fax	Grade	Enr	Superintendent/Principal
Fort Campbell Dependent SD	**77 Texas Ave**	**Fort Campbell, KY**	**42223-5127**	**270-439-1927**	**439-3179**	**PK-12**	**4,900**	**Martha Brown**
Barkley ES	4720 Polk Rd	Fort Campbell, KY	42223-1900	270-439-3795	439-1901	PK-5		Madeline Haller
Fort Campbell HS	1101 Bastogne Ave	Fort Campbell, KY	42223-5133	931-431-5056	431-9386	9-12		Dave Witte
Jackson ES	675 Mississippi Ave	Fort Campbell, KY	42223-5353	931-431-6211	431-4453	PK-5		Susan Ahart
Lincoln ES	4718 Polk Rd	Fort Campbell, KY	42223-1400	270-439-3794	439-2335	PK-5		Sandy Meacham
Lucas ES, Andre	2115 Airborne St	Fort Campbell, KY	42223-5382	931-431-7711	431-5842	PK-5		James Walker
Mahaffey MS	585 S Carolina Ave	Fort Campbell, KY	42223-5134	270-439-3792	439-3472	6-8		Hugh McKinnon
Marshall ES	75 Texas Ave	Fort Campbell, KY	42223-5135	270-439-3793	439-4382	PK-5		Dr. Suzanne Jones
Wassom MS	3066 Forest Rd	Fort Campbell, KY	42223-5272	270-439-3791	439-0671	6-8		Elaine Gallivan
Fort Knox Community SD	**281 Fayette Ave**	**Fort Knox, KY**	**40121-6201**	**502-624-2345**	**624-4256**	**PK-12**	**3,300**	**Todd Curkendall**
Fort Knox HS	107 Missouri St	Fort Knox, KY	40121-6812	502-624-3697	624-6171	9-12		Sarah Turner
Kingsolver ES	411 Eisenhower Ave	Fort Knox, KY	40121-5137	502-624-8650	624-3969	PK-3		Peggy Fink
Macdonald IS	128 McCracken St	Fort Knox, KY	40121-2706	502-624-5650	624-2108	4-6		Youlanda Washington
Mudge ES	190 S Paquette St	Fort Knox, KY	40121-2278	502-624-8345	624-3969	PK-3		Anne Campbell
Pierce ES	174 Maine St	Fort Knox, KY	40121-2290	502-624-7449	624-5274	PK-3		Joe Medley
Scott MS	266 Mississippi St	Fort Knox, KY	40121-6814	502-624-2236	624-5433	7-8		Floyd Hines
Van Voorhis ES	120 Folger St	Fort Knox, KY	40121-6086	502-624-5854	624-7267	PK-3		Dr. Jo Blease

District/School	Address	City,State	Zip code	Telephone	Fax	Grade	Enr	Superintendent/Principal
Walker IS	114 Conroy Ave	Fort Knox, KY	40121-2276	502-624-7835	624-6759	4-6		David Reed
Georgia / Alabama Dependent SD	**7441 Custer Rd Bldg 2670**	**Fort Benning, GA**	**31905**	**706-545-7276**	**545-8227**	**PK-8**	**2,600**	**Dr. Dell McMullen**
Dexter ES, Herbert J.	99 Yeager Ave	Fort Benning, GA	31905-9699	706-545-3424	545-7877	PK-5		Melissa Klopfer
Faith MS, Don C.	1375 Ingersoll St	Fort Benning, GA	31905-7200	706-545-5524		6-8		Dr. Julio Gonzalez
Fort Rucker ES	PO Box 620279	Fort Rucker, AL	36362-0279	334-598-4408	598-6784	2-6		Barbara Doherty
Fort Rucker PS	PO Box 620279	Fort Rucker, AL	36362-0279	334-598-4473	598-5534	PK-2		Deborah Patton
Loyd ES, Frank R.	5701 Santa Fe Rd	Fort Benning, GA	31905	706-544-8964	544-8972	PK-5		Julita Martinez
Maxwell AFB ES	800 Magnolia Blvd	Maxwell AFB, AL	36113	334-953-7804	953-4339	PK-6		Melissa Hayes
McBride ES, Morris R.	700 Custer Rd	Fort Benning, GA	31905-7402	706-544-9411	544-9299	PK-5		Phyllis Parker
Robins AFB ES	895 11th St	Robins AFB, GA	31098	478-926-5003	926-5745	PK-6		Bill Rose
Stowers ES, Freddie	7791 Stowers Dr	Fort Benning, GA	31905-3130	706-544-2312	544-2349	PK-5		Angie McPherson
White ES, Edward A.	300 1st Division Rd	Fort Benning, GA	31905-6627	706-545-4623	545-5469	PK-5		Dr. Tommy Lee
Wilson ES, Richard G.	112 Lavoie Ave	Fort Benning, GA	31905-7523	706-545-5723	545-9505	PK-5		Del Hicks
NY/VA Domestic Dependent School System	**3308 John Quick Rd Ste 201**	**Quantico, VA**	**22134**	**703-784-2319**	**784-3100**	**PK-12**	**1,200**	**Lawanna Mangleburg**
Ashurst ES	4320 Dulaney Rd	Quantico, VA	22134-2248	703-221-4108	784-2694	PK-3		Janice Weiss
Burrows ES, W.W.	3308 John Quick Rd	Quantico, VA	22134-1702	703-640-6118	704-1353	4-5		Dr. William Ramos
Dahlgren S	193 Sampson Rd	Dahlgren, VA	22448	540-653-8822	653-4591	PK-8		Steve Hovanic
Quantico MSHS	3307 Purvis Rd	Quantico, VA	22134-2198	703-784-0303	784-4851	6-12		Charlie Winters
Russell ES, John H.	3301 Purvis Rd	Quantico, VA	22134-2199	703-221-4161	784-4870	PK-3		Randall Ekanger
West Point ES	705A Barry Rd	West Point, NY	10996-1196	845-938-2313	938-3352	PK-4		Ed Drozdowski
West Point MS	705 Barry Rd	West Point, NY	10996	845-938-2923	938-2568	5-8		Michael Hollier
North Carolina Dependent SD	**PO Box 70089**	**Fort Bragg, NC**	**28307-0089**	**910-907-0200**	**907-1405**	**PK-9**		**Thomas Hager**
Albritton JHS	PO Box 70089	Fort Bragg, NC	28307-0089	910-907-0201	432-4072	7-9		Mike Thornburg
Bitz IS	15 Florida Ave	Camp Lejeune, NC	28547	910-451-2575	451-1475	3-5		Dr. Rick Scroggs
Bowley ES	PO Box 70089	Fort Bragg, NC	28307-0089	910-907-0202	907-3513	PK-4		Dr. Susan Walters
Brewster MS	1290 Stone St Bldg 883	Camp Lejeune, NC	28547-2500	910-451-2561	451-2600	6-8		Eric Steimel
Butner ES	PO Box 70089	Fort Bragg, NC	28307-0089	910-907-0203	432-8400	PK-4		Dr. Mary Brigham
Camp Lejeune HS	835 Stone St	Camp Lejeune, NC	28547-2520	910-451-2451	451-3130	9-12		Daniel Osgood
Delalio ES	1500 Curtis Rd	Jacksonville, NC	28540-3406	910-449-0601	449-0677	PK-5		Carol Perry
Devers ES	PO Box 70089	Fort Bragg, NC	28307-0089	910-907-0204	396-7374	PK-4		Ginny Breece
Holbrook ES	PO Box 70089	Fort Bragg, NC	28307-0089	910-907-0205	432-8385	PK-4		Priscilla Joiner
Irwin IS	PO Box 70089	Fort Bragg, NC	28307-0089	910-907-0206	907-1247	5-6		Rob Richardson
Johnson PS	2027 Stone St	Camp Lejeune, NC	28547	910-451-2431	451-2433	K-1		Dr. Janet Kinney
McNair ES	PO Box 70089	Fort Bragg, NC	28307-0089	910-907-0207	432-8386	PK-4		
Murray ES	PO Box 70089	Fort Bragg, NC	28307-0089	910-907-0208	907-0506	PK-4		Charles Council
Pope ES	PO Box 70089	Fort Bragg, NC	28307-0089	910-907-0209	907-0901	PK-4		Dr. Bob Kirkpatrick
Tarawa Terrace II ES	84 Iwo Jima Blvd	Tarawa Terrace, NC	28543-1231	910-450-1635	450-1637	PK-5		Elizabeth Thomas
Tarawa Terrace I PS	60 Tarawa Blvd	Jacksonville, NC	28543-1153	910-450-1662	450-1661	K-1		Linda Hawes
South Carolina / Fort Stewart SD	**376 Davis Ave**	**Fort Stewart, GA**	**31315-1033**	**912-369-6691**	**876-8417**	**PK-6**	**1,600**	**Dr. Joseph Guiendon**
Bolden ES, Charles Frank	1523 Laurel Bay Blvd	Beaufort, SC	29906-3675	843-846-6112	846-9283	3-6		Dr. Jacque Taton-Saunders
Brittin ES	2772 Hero Rd	Fort Stewart, GA	31315-1713	912-368-3324	368-7515	K-6		Dr. Fordyce Stone
Diamond ES	482 Davis Ave	Fort Stewart, GA	31315	912-876-5797	876-8350	PK-6		Norman Heitzman
Elliott ES, Middleton Stuart	1635 Albacore St	Beaufort, SC	29906-3570	843-846-6982	846-6720	PK-2		Barbara Hazzard
Galer ES, Robert Edward	1516 Cardinal Ln	Beaufort, SC	29906-3486	843-846-6100	846-1860	PK-2		Noel Tillman
Hood Street ES	5615 Hood St	Columbia, SC	29206-5360	803-787-8266	782-8863	2-3		Dr. Thelma Gibson
Pierce Terrace ES	5715 Adams Ct	Columbia, SC	29206-5379	803-782-1772	738-8895	PK-1		Mr. Jan Long
Pinckney ES, Charles C.	5900 Chesnut Rd	Columbia, SC	29206-5365	803-787-6815	790-2169	4-6		Carol Kress

CATHOLIC SCHOOL SUPERINTENDENTS

NATIONAL CATHOLIC EDUCATIONAL ASSOC.
1077 30th St NW Ste 100, Washington, DC 20007-3816
Telephone 202-337-6232
Fax 333-6706
Website ncea.org

CATHOLIC SCHOOL SUPERINTENDENTS

Archdiocese/Diocese	Address	City,State	Zip code	Telephone	Fax	Grade	Enr	Superintendent
Diocese of Albany	40 N Main Ave	Albany, NY	12203	518-453-6666	453-6667	PK-12	8,800	Sr. Mary Jane Herb
Diocese of Alexandria	PO Box 7417	Alexandria, LA	71306-0417	318-445-2401	448-6121	PK-12	3,000	Sr. Ann Lacour
Diocese of Allentown	2145 Madison Ave	Bethlehem, PA	18017	610-866-0581	867-8702	PK-12	15,500	Philip J. Fromuth
Diocese of Altoona-Johnstown	126A Logan Blvd	Hollidaysburg, PA	16648-2698	814-693-1401	695-8894	PK-12	5,400	Sr. Donna Leiden
Diocese of Amarillo	1800 N Spring St	Amarillo, TX	79107-7252	806-383-2243	383-8452	PK-12	800	Bernice Noggler
Archdiocese of Anchorage	225 Cordova St	Anchorage, AK	99501-2409	907-297-7790	279-7707	PK-12	300	Sr. Ann Fallon
Diocese of Arlington	200 N Glebe Rd Ste 600	Arlington, VA	22203-3728	703-841-2519	524-8670	PK-12	15,700	Dr. Timothy McNiff
Archdiocese of Atlanta	680 W Peachtree St NW	Atlanta, GA	30308-1931	404-888-7833	885-7430	PK-12	9,200	Diane Starkovich
Diocese of Austin	1625 Rutherford Ln	Austin, TX	78754	512-873-7771	873-8338	PK-12	4,100	Dr. Ned Vanders
Diocese of Baker	PO Box 5999	Bend, OR	97708-5999	541-388-4004	388-2566	PK-8	500	Roger Richmond
Archdiocese of Baltimore	320 Cathedral St	Baltimore, MD	21201	410-547-5515	547-5566	PK-12	33,500	Dr. Ronald Valenti
Diocese of Baton Rouge	PO Box 2028	Baton Rouge, LA	70821-2028	225-336-8735	336-8711	PK-12	15,600	Sr. Mary Michaeline
Diocese of Beaumont	PO Box 3948	Beaumont, TX	77704-3948	409-838-0451	838-4511	PK-12	1,700	George A. Pressey
Diocese of Belleville	2620 Lebanon Ave	Belleville, IL	62221	618-235-9601	235-7115	PK-12	7,500	Thomas Posnanski
Diocese of Biloxi	1790 Popps Ferry Rd	Biloxi, MS	39532-2118	228-702-2130	702-2135	PK-12	3,500	Dr. Mike Ladner
Diocese of Birmingham	PO Box 12047	Birmingham, AL	35202-2047	205-838-8303	838-8330	PK-12	6,300	Sr. Mary Leanne Welch
Diocese of Bismarck	PO Box 1137	Bismarck, ND	58502-1137	701-222-3035	222-0269	PK-12	2,300	Betty Greff
Diocese of Boise	303 S Federal Way	Boise, ID	83705-5925	208-342-1311	342-0224	PK-12	3,100	Dan Makley
Diocese of Boston	2200 Dorchester Ave	Boston, MA	02124-5607	617-298-6555	298-6622	PK-12	44,800	Sr. Kathleen Fitz Simons
Diocese of Bridgeport	238 Jewett Ave	Bridgeport, CT	06606-2892	203-416-1375	372-1961	PK-12	12,200	Dr. Margaret Dames
Diocese of Brooklyn	PO Box 159013	Brooklyn, NY	11215-9013	718-965-7300	965-7323	PK-12	55,800	Dr. Thomas Chadzutko
Diocese of Brownsville	700 Virgen de San Juan	San Juan, TX	78589	956-787-8571	784-5081	PK-12	3,700	Sr. Marcella Ewers
Diocese of Buffalo	795 Main St	Buffalo, NY	14203-1250	716-847-5501	847-5593	PK-12	22,500	Diane Vigrass
Diocese of Burlington	PO Box 489	Burlington, VT	05402-0489	802-658-6110	658-6112	PK-12	3,000	Sr. Marie Kelly
Diocese of Camden	631 Market St	Camden, NJ	08102-1103	856-756-7900	756-0225	PK-12	17,300	Sr. Dawn Gear
Diocese of Charleston	1662 Ingram Rd	Charleston, SC	29407-4242	843-402-9115	402-7724	PK-12	7,400	Sr. Julia Hutchison
Diocese of Charlotte	1123 S Church St	Charlotte, NC	28203-4003	704-370-3270	370-3292	PK-12	6,700	Linda L. Cherry
Diocese of Cheyenne	2121 Capitol Ave	Cheyenne, WY	82001	307-638-1530	637-7936	PK-12	1,000	Gary Catalano
Archdiocese of Chicago	PO Box 1979	Chicago, IL	60690-1979	312-751-5200	751-5295	PK-12	95,700	Dr. Nicholas Wolsonovich
Archdiocese of Cincinnati	100 E 8th St Fl 8	Cincinnati, OH	45202-2150	513-421-3131	421-6271	PK-12	48,100	Br. Joseph Kamis
Diocese of Cleveland	1404 E 9th St	Cleveland, OH	44114	216-696-6525	579-9655	PK-12	51,700	Margaret Lyons
Diocese of Colorado Springs	228 N Cascade Ave	Colorado Spgs, CO	80903-1324	719-636-2345	866-6453	PK-12	1,800	Michelle Maher
Diocese of Columbus	197 E Gay St Ste 300	Columbus, OH	43215-3229	614-221-5829	241-2563	PK-12	18,100	Lucia McQuaide
Diocese of Corpus Christi	PO Box 2620	Corpus Christi, TX	78403-2620	361-882-6191	814-1831	PK-12	2,600	Rene Gonzalez
Diocese of Covington	PO Box 15550	Covington, KY	41015-0550	859-392-1530	392-1537	K-12	11,800	Dr. Lawrence Bowman
Diocese of Crookston	1200 Memorial Dr	Crookston, MN	56716	218-281-4533	281-5991	PK-12	1,400	Sr. Pat Murphy
Diocese of Dallas	PO Box 190507	Dallas, TX	75219-0507	214-528-2360	522-1753	PK-12	13,600	Charles LeBlanc Ed.D.
Diocese of Davenport	2706 N Gaines St	Davenport, IA	52804-1998	563-324-1911	324-5811	PK-12	4,400	Mary Wieser
Archdiocese of Denver	1300 S Steele St	Denver, CO	80210-2599	303-715-3200	715-2042	PK-12	13,300	Richard Thompson
Diocese of Des Moines	601 Grand Ave	Des Moines, IA	50309-2501	515-237-5013	237-5070	PK-12	5,200	Luvern Gubbels Ed.D.
Archdiocese of Detroit	305 Michigan Ave Ste 600	Detroit, MI	48226-2625	313-237-5775	237-5857	PK-12	36,500	Sr. Mary Gehringer
Diocese of Dodge City	910 Central Ave	Dodge City, KS	67801-4905	620-227-1513	227-1570	PK-8	1,100	Ann Depperschmidt
Archdiocese of Dubuque	1229 Mount Loretta Ave	Dubuque, IA	52003-8787	563-556-2580	556-5464	PK-12	12,600	Dr. Jeff Henderson
Diocese of Duluth	2830 E 4th St	Duluth, MN	55812-1501	218-724-9111	724-1056	PK-8	1,600	Cynthia Zook
Diocese of El Paso	499 Saint Matthews St	El Paso, TX	79907-4214	915-872-8426	872-8434	PK-12	4,500	Sr. Elizabeth Swartz
Diocese of Erie	PO Box 10397	Erie, PA	16514-0397	814-824-1241	824-1239	PK-12	10,800	Patricia McLaughlin
Diocese of Evansville	PO Box 4169	Evansville, IN	47724-0169	812-424-5536	421-1334	PK-12	7,300	Phyllis Bussing Ph.D.
Diocese of Fairbanks	1316 Peger Rd	Fairbanks, AK	99709-5168	907-374-9500	374-9580	K-12	200	Rose Anne Sample
Diocese of Fall River	423 Highland Ave	Fall River, MA	02720-3718	508-678-2828	674-4218	PK-12	7,400	Dr. George A. Milot
Diocese of Fargo	5201 Bishops Blvd S Ste A	Fargo, ND	58104-7605	701-356-7900	356-7994	PK-12	1,900	Thomas Frei
Diocese of Fort Worth	800 W Loop 820 S	Fort Worth, TX	76108-2936	817-560-3300	244-8839	PK-12	5,600	Donald Miller

Archdiocese/Diocese	Address	City,State	Zip code	Telephone	Fax	Grade	Enr	Superintendent
Diocese of Fresno	1510 N Fresno St	Fresno, CA	93703-3711	559-488-7420	488-7422	PK-12	6,800	Richard Sexton
Diocese of Ft. Wayne-South Bend	PO Box 390	Fort Wayne, IN	46801-0390	260-422-4611	426-3077	PK-12	13,300	Rev. Stephen Kempinger
Diocese of Gallup	PO Box 1338	Gallup, NM	87305-1338	505-863-4406	863-8150	PK-12	1,700	Sr. Rene Backe
Diocese of Galveston-Houston	2403 Holcombe Blvd	Houston, TX	77021-2023	713-741-8704	741-7379	PK-12	17,000	Sally Landram
Diocese of Gary	9292 Broadway	Merrillville, IN	46410-7088	219-769-9292	738-9034	K-12	7,700	Kim Pryzbylski Ph.D.
Diocese of Gaylord	611 W North St	Gaylord, MI	49735-8349	989-732-5147	705-3589	PK-12	3,500	Michael Buell
Diocese of Grand Island	PO Box 996	Grand Island, NE	68802-0996	308-382-6565	382-6569	PK-12	1,400	Rev. Thomas Ryan
Diocese of Grand Rapids	600 Burton St SE	Grand Rapids, MI	49507-3202	616-243-0491	243-1442	PK-12	8,800	Bernard Stanko Ed.D.
Diocese of Great Falls-Billings	PO Box 31158	Billings, MT	59107-1158	406-252-9595	252-9875	PK-12	2,700	Sr. Jean Dawson
Diocese of Green Bay	PO Box 23825	Green Bay, WI	54305-3825	920-437-7531	437-0694	PK-12	12,700	Leland Nagel
Diocese of Greensburg	723 E Pittsburgh St	Greensburg, PA	15601-2697	724-837-0901	837-0857	PK-12	4,100	Trent Bocan
Diocese of Harrisburg	PO Box 3553	Harrisburg, PA	17105-3553	717-657-4804	657-3790	PK-12	12,900	Sr. Sue Ann Steves
Archdiocese of Hartford	467 Bloomfield Ave	Bloomfield, CT	06002-2903	860-242-4362	242-8683	PK-12	19,300	Dr. Dale Hoyt
Diocese of Helena	PO Box 1729	Helena, MT	59624-1729	406-594-1461	327-8537	PK-12	1,200	Patrick Haggarty
Diocese of Honolulu	6301 Pali Hwy	Kaneohe, HI	96744-5224	808-263-8844	262-6126	PK-12	10,800	Carmen Himenes Ed.D.
Diocese of Houma-Thibodaux	PO Box 505	Schriever, LA	70395-0505	985-850-3113	850-3225	PK-12	5,700	Sr. Immaculata Paisant
Archdiocese of Indianapolis	PO Box 1410	Indianapolis, IN	46206-1410	317-236-1430	261-3364	PK-12	22,700	Ron Costello
Diocese of Jackson	PO Box 2248	Jackson, MS	39225-2248	601-969-2742	960-8469	PK-12	4,000	Sr. Deborah Hughes
Diocese of Jefferson City	PO Box 104900	Jefferson City, MO	65110-4900	573-635-9127	635-2286	PK-12	7,600	Donald F. Novotney
Diocese of Joliet	402 S Independence Blvd	Romeoville, IL	60446-2264	815-838-2181	838-2182	PK-12	22,900	Sr. Helen Kormelink
Diocese of Juneau	415 6th St Ste 300	Juneau, AK	99801-1091	907-225-7400	247-0041	PK-6	100	
Diocese of Kalamazoo	215 N Westnedge Ave	Kalamazoo, MI	49007-3718	269-349-8714	349-6440	PK-12	3,700	Margaret Erich
Archdiocese of Kansas City	12615 Parallel Ave	Kansas City, KS	66109-3748	913-721-1570	721-5598	PK-12	15,000	Dr. Kathleen O'Hara
Diocese of Kansas City-Saint Joseph	PO Box 419037	Kansas City, MO	64141-6037	816-756-1850	756-1571	PK-12	11,900	Dr. Patricia Clune
Diocese of Knoxville	PO Box 11127	Knoxville, TN	37939-1127	865-584-3307	584-4319	PK-12	3,000	Dr. Sherry Morgan
Diocese of La Crosse	PO Box 4004	La Crosse, WI	54602-4004	608-788-7707	788-7709	PK-12	8,900	Diana Roberts
Diocese of Lafayette	2300 S 9th St	Lafayette, IN	47909-2400	765-474-6644	474-3403	PK-12	4,500	Marie Williams
Diocese of Lafayette	1408 Carmel Dr	Lafayette, LA	70501-5215	337-261-5529	261-5572	PK-12	14,000	Anna Larriviere
Diocese of Lake Charles	411 Iris St	Lake Charles, LA	70601-5234	337-439-7426	439-7428	PK-12	2,900	Mary Ann Moses
Diocese of Lansing	300 W Ottawa St	Lansing, MI	48933-1577	517-342-2482	342-2515	PK-12	10,500	Sr. Dorita Wotiska
Diocese of Laredo	1901 Corpus Christi St	Laredo, TX	78043-3308	956-753-5208	753-5203	K-12	2,000	Dr. Rosa Maria Vida
Diocese of Las Cruces	1280 Med Park Dr	Las Cruces, NM	88005-3239	505-523-7577	524-3874	PK-8	500	Tomas Lucero
Diocese of Las Vegas	PO Box 18316	Las Vegas, NV	89114-8316	702-697-5918	735-8941	K-12	3,600	Richard Facciolo Ed.D.
Diocese of Lexington	1310 W Main St	Lexington, KY	40508-2048	859-253-1993	255-1134	K-12	4,200	
Diocese of Lincoln	PO Box 80328	Lincoln, NE	68501-0328	402-488-2040	488-6525	K-12	7,000	Rev. John Perkinton
Diocese of Little Rock	PO Box 7565	Little Rock, AR	72217-7565	501-664-0340	603-0518	K-12	6,800	Vernell Bowen M.Ed.
Archdiocese of Los Angeles	3424 Wilshire Blvd	Los Angeles, CA	90010-2241	213-637-7300	637-6140	PK-12	88,400	Nancy Coonis
Archdiocese of Louisville	1935 Lewiston Dr	Louisville, KY	40216-2523	502-448-8581	448-5518	PK-12	20,100	Leisa Speer
Diocese of Lubbock	4620 4th St	Lubbock, TX	79416-4726	806-792-3943	792-8109	PK-9	400	Leo Cottenoir
Diocese of Madison	PO Box 44983	Madison, WI	53744-4983	608-821-3180	821-3181	PK-12	7,700	James Silver Ed.D.
Diocese of Manchester	PO Box 310	Manchester, NH	03105-0310	603-669-3100	669-0377	PK-12	9,200	Mary Moran
Diocese of Marquette	PO Box 1000	Marquette, MI	49855-1000	906-227-9127	225-0437	PK-8	1,500	Gloria Kalbfleisch
Diocese of Memphis	5825 Shelby Oaks Dr	Memphis, TN	38134-7316	901-373-1219	373-1223	PK-12	6,500	Dr. Mary McDonald
Diocese of Metuchen	146 Metlars Ln	Piscataway, NJ	08854	732-562-1990	562-1016	PK-12	15,100	Ellen Ayoub
Archdiocese of Miami	9401 Biscayne Blvd	Miami Shores, FL	33138-2970	305-762-1076	762-1115	PK-12	33,000	Br. Richard DeMaria
Archdiocese of Milwaukee	PO Box 070912	Milwaukee, WI	53207-0912	414-769-3300	769-3408	PK-12	32,900	John Augustine
Diocese of Mobile	PO Box 129	Mobile, AL	36601-0129	251-438-4611	438-4612	PK-12	5,800	Gwen Byrd
Diocese of Monterey	485 Church St	Monterey, CA	93940-3207	831-373-1608	373-0173	PK-12	4,700	Jack Marchi Ph.D.
Diocese of Nashville	30 White Bridge Rd	Nashville, TN	37205-1401	615-352-7218	353-7972	PK-12	4,200	Dr. Therese Williams
Archdiocese of Newark	PO Box 9500	Newark, NJ	07104-0500	973-497-4260	497-4249	PK-12	41,000	Rev. Kevin Hanbury Ed.D.
Archdiocese of New Orleans	7887 Walmsley Ave	New Orleans, LA	70125-3496	504-866-7916	861-6260	PK-12	41,400	Rev. William Maestri
Diocese of New Ulm	1400 6th St N	New Ulm, MN	56073-2057	507-359-2966	354-3667	PK-12	2,700	Wayne Pelzel
Archdiocese of New York	1011 1st Ave Fl 6	New York, NY	10022-4112	212-371-1000	317-9236	PK-12	84,700	Dr. Catherine Hickey
Diocese of Norwich	43 Perkins Ave	Norwich, CT	06360-3643	860-887-4086	887-9371	PK-12	6,000	Sr. Joan O'Connor
Diocese of Oakland	3014 Lakeshore Ave	Oakland, CA	94610-3615	510-628-2154	451-5331	PK-12	19,100	Mark DeMarco
Diocese of Ogdensburg	PO Box 369	Ogdensburg, NY	13669-0369	315-393-2920	393-8977	PK-12	1,700	Sr. Ellen Coughlin
Archdiocese of Oklahoma City	PO Box 32180	Oklahoma City, OK	73123-0380	405-721-5651	709-2811	PK-12	4,900	Sr. Catherine Powers
Archdiocese of Omaha	PO Box 4130	Omaha, NE	68104-0130	402-554-8493	827-3792	PK-12	19,800	Fr. James Gilg
Diocese of Orange	PO Box 14195	Orange, CA	92863-1595	714-282-3055	282-5059	PK-12	16,900	Rev. Gerald Horan
Diocese of Orlando	PO Box 1800	Orlando, FL	32802-1800	407-246-4900	246-4940	PK-12	14,000	Dr. Harry Purpur
Diocese of Owensboro	600 Locust St	Owensboro, KY	42301-2130	270-683-1545	683-6883	K-12	3,400	Jim Mattingly
Diocese of Palm Beach	9995 N Military Trl	West Palm Beach, FL	33410	561-775-9547	775-9545	PK-12	7,000	Sr. Joan Dawson
Diocese of Paterson	777 Valley Rd	Clifton, NJ	07013-2297	973-777-8818	779-0083	PK-12	15,200	Dr. Frank Petrucelli
Diocese of Pensacola-Tallahassee	11 N B St	Pensacola, FL	32501-4601	850-435-3500	436-6424	PK-12	2,700	Susan Jones Mueller
Diocese of Peoria	412 NE Madison Ave	Peoria, IL	61603-3720	309-671-1579	671-1595	PK-12	12,900	Br. William Dygert
Archdiocese of Philadelphia	222 N 17th St	Philadelphia, PA	19103-1295	215-587-3700	587-5644	PK-12	94,800	Dr. Thomas F. O'Brien
Diocese of Phoenix	400 E Monroe St	Phoenix, AZ	85004-2336	602-354-2345	354-2436	PK-12	13,200	MaryBeth Mueller
Diocese of Pittsburgh	111 Blvd Of The Allies	Pittsburgh, PA	15222-1618	412-456-3090	456-3098	PK-12	23,500	Dr. Robert Paserba
Archdiocese of Portland	2838 E Burnside St	Portland, OR	97214-1895	503-233-8300	236-3683	PK-12	13,200	Robert Mizia
Diocese of Portland	PO Box 11559	Portland, ME	04104-7559	207-773-6471	773-0182	PK-12	4,700	Sr. Rosemary Donohue
Diocese of Providence	1 Cathedral Sq	Providence, RI	02903-3695	401-278-4550	278-4596	PK-12	16,800	Sheila Durante
Diocese of Pueblo	1001 N Grand Ave	Pueblo, CO	81003-2979	719-544-9861	544-5202	PK-12	1,100	Sr. Betty Werner
Diocese of Raleigh	715 Nazareth St	Raleigh, NC	27606-2187	919-821-9749	821-8140	PK-12	6,800	Dr. Michael Fedewa
Diocese of Rapid City	300 Fairmont Blvd	Rapid City, SD	57701-5423	605-343-8484	343-1315	K-12	1,200	Barb Honeycutt
Diocese of Reno	290 S Arlington Ave Ste 200	Reno, NV	89501-1713	775-326-9430	348-8619	PK-12	700	Kitty Bergin
Diocese of Richmond	811 S Cathedral Pl Ste A	Richmond, VA	23220	804-359-5661	358-9159	PK-12	9,800	John Elcesser
Diocese of Rochester	1150 Buffalo Rd	Rochester, NY	14624-1890	585-328-3228	328-3149	PK-12	12,900	Sr. Elaine Poitras Ph.D.
Diocese of Rockford	PO Box 7044	Rockford, IL	61125-7044	815-399-4300	399-6278	PK-12	15,700	Sr. Patricia Downey
Diocese of Rockville Center	PO Box 9023	Rockville Ctr, NY	11571-9023	516-678-5800	678-7362	PK-12	31,700	Sr. Joanne Callahan
Diocese of Sacramento	2110 Broadway	Sacramento, CA	95818-2518	916-733-0110	733-0120	PK-12	15,700	Domenic Puglisi
Diocese of Saginaw	5800 Weiss St	Saginaw, MI	48603-2762	989-799-7910	797-6645	PK-12	3,900	Barbara Davis
Diocese of St. Augustine	11625 Saint Augustine Rd	Jacksonville, FL	32258	904-262-3200	596-1042	PK-12	9,100	Patricia Tierney
Diocese of St. Cloud	305 7th Ave N Ste 201	Saint Cloud, MN	56303-3633	320-251-0111	251-0259	PK-12	6,000	Linda Kaiser
Archdiocese of St. Louis	20 Archbishop May Dr	Saint Louis, MO	63119-5738	314-792-7300	792-7350	PK-12	46,800	George Henry
Archdiocese of St. Paul	328 Kellogg Blvd W	Saint Paul, MN	55102-1900	651-291-4498	290-1628	PK-12	35,000	Dr. Lori Glynn
Diocese of St. Petersburg	PO Box 40200	St Petersburg, FL	33743-0200	727-347-5539	374-0209	PK-12	11,500	Br. John Cummings Ed.D.
Diocese of Salina	PO Box 825	Salina, KS	67402-0825	785-827-8746	827-6133	PK-12	2,700	Dr. Nick Compagnone
Diocese of Salt Lake City	27 C St	Salt Lake City, UT	84103-2302	801-328-8641	328-9680	PK-12	5,600	Sr. Catherine Kamphaus
Diocese of San Angelo	499 Saint Matthews St	El Paso, TX	79907	325-651-7500	651-6688	PK-8	600	Sr. Elizabeth Ann Swartz
Archdiocese of San Antonio	2718 W Woodlawn Ave	San Antonio, TX	78228-5195	210-734-2620	734-9112	PK-12	12,900	Sr. Carla Marie Lusch
Diocese of San Bernardino	1201 E Highland Ave	San Bernardino, CA	92404-4607	909-475-5437	475-5477	PK-12	8,000	Sr. Sara Kane
Diocese of San Diego	PO Box 85728	San Diego, CA	92186-5728	858-490-8241	490-8272	PK-12	15,600	Stevan Laaperi
Archdiocese of San Francisco	1 Peter Yorke Way	San Francisco, CA	94109-6602	415-614-5660	614-5664	PK-12	25,900	Maureen Huntington
Diocese of San Jose	900 Lafayette St Ste 301	Santa Clara, CA	95050-4966	408-983-0185	983-0192	PK-12	15,900	Marian Stuckey
Archdiocese of Santa Fe	4000 Saint Josephs Pl NW	Albuquerque, NM	87120-1714	505-831-8173	831-8107	PK-12	5,400	Sr. Mary Klersey M.P.
Diocese of Santa Rosa	PO Box 6654	Santa Rosa, CA	95406-0654	707-566-3311	566-3382	PK-12	4,700	Dr. John Collins
Diocese of Savannah	601 E Liberty St	Savannah, GA	31401-5118	912-201-4121	201-4101	K-12	6,300	Sr. Rose Mary Collins
Diocese of Scranton	300 Wyoming Ave	Scranton, PA	18503-1243	570-207-2251	207-2261	PK-12	8,900	Joseph Casciano
Archdiocese of Seattle	710 9th Ave	Seattle, WA	98104-2017	206-382-4861	654-4651	PK-12	21,000	Sr. Joyce M. Cox Ph.D.
Diocese of Shreveport	3500 Fairfield Ave	Shreveport, LA	71104-4108	318-219-7253	868-5057	PK-12	2,100	Sr. Carol Shively
Diocese of Sioux City	PO Box 3379	Sioux City, IA	51102-3379	712-255-7933	233-7598	PK-12	6,000	Kevin Vickery
Diocese of Sioux Falls	523 N Duluth Ave	Sioux Falls, SD	57104-2714	605-988-3766	988-3795	PK-12	4,600	
Diocese of Spokane	PO Box 1453	Spokane, WA	99210-1453	509-358-7330	358-7302	PK-12	3,700	Duane Schafer Ph.D.
Diocese of Springfield-Cape Girardeau	601 S Jefferson Ave	Springfield, MO	65806-3107	417-866-0841	866-1140	PK-12	4,600	Leon Witt
Diocese of Springfield	PO Box 3187	Springfield, IL	62708-3187	217-698-8500	698-8620	PK-12	12,000	Jean Johnson
Diocese of Springfield	PO Box 1730	Springfield, MA	01102-1730	413-452-0830	452-0555	PK-12	6,800	Sr. M. Andrea Ciszewski
Diocese of Steubenville	PO Box 969	Steubenville, OH	43952-5969	740-282-3631	282-3327	PK-12	2,800	Dr. Peter Chila
Diocese of Stockton	1105 N Lincoln St	Stockton, CA	95203-2410	209-466-0636	941-9722	PK-12	4,600	Sr. Marian Clare Valenteen
Diocese of Superior	PO Box 280	Haugen, WI	54841-0280	715-234-5044	234-5241	PK-8	2,700	Peggy Schoenfuss
Diocese of Syracuse	PO Box 511	Syracuse, NY	13201-0511	315-470-1450	470-1470	PK-12	8,900	Michael Colabufo
Diocese of Toledo	PO Box 985	Toledo, OH	43697-0985	419-244-6711	255-8269	PK-12	23,900	Jack Altenburger
Diocese of Trenton	PO Box 5147	Trenton, NJ	08638-0147	609-406-7400	406-7416	PK-12	21,400	Judith Caviston Ed.D.
Diocese of Tucson	PO Box 31	Tucson, AZ	85702-0031	520-792-3410	838-2589	PK-12	7,000	Sr. Rosa Maria Ruiz
Diocese of Tulsa	820 S Boulder Ave	Tulsa, OK	74119-1624	918-582-9177	582-1851	PK-12	3,800	Todd Goldsmith
Diocese of Tyler	1015 E Southeast Loop 323	Tyler, TX	75701-9656	903-534-1077	534-1370	PK-12	700	Dr. C. Charles LeBlanc
Diocese of Venice	1000 Pinebrook Rd	Venice, FL	34285-6426	941-484-9543	484-1121	PK-12	5,300	Rosemary Bratton
Diocese of Victoria	PO Box 4070	Victoria, TX	77903-4070	361-573-0828	573-5725	PK-12	2,200	Sr. Gloria Cain
Archdiocese of Washington DC	5001 Eastern Ave	Hyattsville, MD	20782	301-853-4518	853-7670	PK-12	29,600	Patricia O'Neill Ph.D.
Diocese of Wheeling-Charleston	PO Box 230	Wheeling, WV	26003-0010	304-232-0444	233-8551	PK-12	6,000	John Yelenic
Diocese of Wichita	424 N Broadway St	Wichita, KS	67202-2310	316-269-3950	269-2486	PK-12	9,300	Bob Voboril
Diocese of Wilmington	1626 N Union St	Wilmington, DE	19806-2540	302-573-3133	573-6945	PK-12	12,300	Catherine Weaver
Diocese of Winona	PO Box 588	Winona, MN	55987-0588	507-454-4643	454-8106	PK-12	5,300	P.J. Thompson
Diocese of Worcester	49 Elm St	Worcester, MA	01609-2514	508-929-4317	929-4386	PK-12	9,600	Stephen Perla
Diocese of Yakima	5301 Tieton Dr Ste B	Yakima, WA	98908-3479	509-965-7110	966-0596	PK-12	1,800	Dr. Robert Glennen
Diocese of Youngstown	144 W Wood St	Youngstown, OH	44503-1081	330-744-8451	744-5099	K-12	11,100	Dr. Michael Skube

LUTHERAN SCHOOL SUPERINTENDENTS

LUTHERAN CHURCH MISSOURI SYNOD
1333 S Kirkwood Rd, Saint Louis, MO 63122-7295
Telephone 314-965-9000
Fax 822-8307
Website http://www.lcms.org

LUTHERAN SCHOOL SUPERINTENDENTS

Region	Address	City,State	Zip code	Telephone	Fax	Superintendent
Atlantic	171 White Plains Rd	Bronxville, NY	10708-1923	914-337-5700	337-7471	Dr. David Benke
California-Nevada-Hawaii	2772 Constitution Dr Ste A	Livermore, CA	94551-7571	925-245-4000	245-1107	
Central Illinois	1850 N Grand Ave W	Springfield, IL	62702-1626	217-793-1802	793-1822	Rev. David Bueltmann
Eastern	5111 Main St	Williamsville, NY	14221-5203	716-634-5111	634-5452	Dr. John Brunner
English	33100 Freedom Rd	Farmington, MI	48336-4030	248-476-0039	476-0188	Rev. David Stechholz
Florida-Georgia	7207 Monetary Dr	Orlando, FL	32809-5753	407-857-5556	857-5665	Mark Brink
Indiana	1145 Barr St	Fort Wayne, IN	46802-3135	800-837-1145	423-1514	Daniel May
Iowa East	1100 Blairs Ferry Rd	Marion, IA	52302-3093	319-373-2112	373-9827	Dr. Gary Arp
Iowa West	PO Box 1155	Fort Dodge, IA	50501-1155	515-576-7666	576-2323	Bob Riggert
Kansas	1000 SW 10th Ave	Topeka, KS	66604-1104	785-357-4441	357-5071	Jim Bradshaw
Michigan	3773 Geddes Rd	Ann Arbor, MI	48105-3028	734-665-3791	665-0255	Rev. C. William Hoesman
Mid-South	1675 Wynne Rd	Cordova, TN	38016-4905	901-373-1343	373-4826	Rev. Kenneth Lampe
Minnesota North	PO Box 604	Brainerd, MN	56401-0604	218-829-1781	829-0037	Rev. Donald Fondow
Minnesota South	14301 Grand Ave	Burnsville, MN	55306-5790	952-435-2550	435-2581	Dr. Lane Seitz
Missouri	660 Mason Ridge Center Dr	Saint Louis, MO	63141-8557	314-317-4550	317-4574	Dennis Gehrke
Montana	30 Broadwater Ave	Billings, MT	59101-1826	406-259-2908	259-1305	Rev. Terry Forke
Nebraska	PO Box 407	Seward, NE	68434-0407	888-643-2961	643-2990	Rev. Russ Sommerfeld
New England	400 Wilbraham Rd	Springfield, MA	01109-2723	413-783-0131	783-0909	Rev. James Keurulainen
New Jersey	1168 Springfield Ave	Mountainside, NJ	07092-2906	908-233-8111	233-3883	Rev. William Klettke
North Dakota	PO Box 9029	Fargo, ND	58106-9029	877-526-7633	293-9022	Rev. Larry Harvala
Northern Illinois	2301 S Wolf Rd	Hillside, IL	60162-2211	708-449-3020	449-3026	
Northwest	1700 NE Knott St	Portland, OR	97212-3301	503-288-8383	284-2785	Dr. Warren Schumacher
North Wisconsin	PO Box 8064	Wausau, WI	54402-8064	715-845-8241	845-3836	Bob Whipky
Ohio	PO Box 38277	Olmsted Falls, OH	44138-0277	440-235-2297	235-1970	Gordon Stuckert
Oklahoma	1232 SW 89th St	Oklahoma City, OK	73139	405-912-5847	912-5829	Rev. Paul Hartman
Pacific Southwest	1540 Concordia	Irvine, CA	92612-3203	949-854-3232	854-8140	Rachel Klitzing
Rocky Mountain	14334 E Evans Ave	Aurora, CO	80014-1408	303-695-8001	695-4047	Paul Albers
SELC	4850 S Lake Dr	Cudahy, WI	53110-1743	414-481-8286	481-0736	Rev. Carl Krueger
South Dakota	PO Box 89110	Sioux Falls, SD	57109-9110	605-361-1514	361-7959	David Schwan
Southeastern	6315 Grovedale Dr	Alexandria, VA	22310-2501	703-971-9371	922-6047	Dr. Jon Diefenthaler
Southern	PO Box 8396	New Orleans, LA	70182-8396	504-282-2632	283-4885	Rev. Kurtis Schultz
Southern Illinois	2408 Lebanon Ave	Belleville, IL	62221-2529	618-234-4767	234-4830	
South Wisconsin	8100 W Capitol Dr	Milwaukee, WI	53222-1981	414-464-8100	464-0602	Gary Janetzke
Texas	7900 E Highway 290	Austin, TX	78724-2402	512-926-4272	926-1006	Dr. William Hinz
Wyoming	2400 S Hickory St	Casper, WY	82604-3471	307-265-9000	234-6629	Rev. Richard Boche

GENERAL CONFERENCE OF SEVENTH-DAY ADVENTISTS SUPERINTENDENTS

NORTH AMERICAN DIV. OFFICE OF EDUCATION
12501 Old Columbia Pike, Silver Spring, MD 20904-6601
Telephone 301-680-6440
Fax 680-6463
Website http://www.nadeducation.adventist.org

GENERAL CONFERENCE OF SEVENTH-DAY ADVENTISTS SUPERINTENDENTS

Conference	Address	City,State	Zip code	Telephone	Fax	Superintendent
Atlantic Union	**PO Box 1189**	**South Lancaster, MA**	**01561-1189**	**978-368-8333**	**368-7948**	**Astrid Thomassian**
Greater New York Conference	PO Box 5029	Manhasset, NY	11030-5029	516-627-9350	627-9272	David Cadavero
New York Conference	4930 W Seneca Tpke	Syracuse, NY	13215-2225	315-469-6921	469-6924	Stan Rouse M.A.
Northeastern Conference	11550 Merrick Blvd	Jamaica, NY	11434-1852	718-291-8006	739-5133	Pollyanna Barnes Ph.D.
Northern New England Conference	91 Allen Ave	Portland, ME	04103-3710	207-797-3760	797-2851	Trudy Wright M.A.
Southern New England Conference	PO Box 1169	South Lancaster, MA	01561-1169	978-365-4551	365-3838	
Columbia Union Conference	**5427 Twin Knolls Rd**	**Columbia, MD**	**21045-3200**	**410-997-3414**	**997-7420**	**Hamlet Canosa**
Allegheny East Conference	PO Box 266	Pine Forge, PA	19548-0266	610-326-4610	326-3946	James Willis M.Ed.
Allegheny West Conference	1339 E Broad St	Columbus, OH	43205-1588	614-252-5271	252-3246	Jerome Hurst B.S.
Chesapeake Conference	6600 Martin Rd	Columbia, MD	21044-3999	410-995-1910	995-1434	Carole Smith Ed.D.
Mountain View Conference	1400 Liberty St	Parkersburg, WV	26101-4124	304-422-4581	422-4582	
New Jersey Conference	2160 US Highway 1	Trenton, NJ	08648-4489	609-392-7131	396-9273	J. Wayne Hancock Ed.D.
Ohio Conference	PO Box 1230	Mount Vernon, OH	43050-8230	740-397-4665	397-1648	E. Jay Colburn
Pennsylvania Conference	720 Museum Rd	Reading, PA	19611-1429	610-374-8331	374-9331	Vaughn Jennings
Potomac Conference	606 Greenville Ave	Staunton, VA	24401-4881	540-886-0771	886-5734	Larry D. Marsh M.Ed.
Lake Union Conference	**PO Box C**	**Berrien Springs, MI**	**49103-0904**	**269-473-8200**	**473-8209**	**Gary Randolph**
Illinois Conference	619 Plainfield Rd Ste 200	Willowbrook, IL	60527	630-734-0920	734-0929	James Martz
Indiana Conference	PO Box 1950	Carmel, IN	46082-1950	317-844-6201	571-9281	Mark Haynal M.A.
Lake Region Conference	8517 S State St	Chicago, IL	60619-5697	773-846-2661	846-5309	Edward Woods
Michigan Conference	PO Box 19009	Lansing, MI	48901-9009	517-316-1500	316-1501	Duane Roush M.A.
Wisconsin Conference	3505 US Highway 151	Sun Prairie, WI	53590-9701	608-241-5235	837-9421	Kenneth Kirkham M.A.
Mid-America Union Conference	**PO Box 6128**	**Lincoln, NE**	**68506-0128**	**402-484-3000**	**483-4453**	**Ronald Russell M.Ed.**
Central States Conference	3301 Parallel Pkwy	Kansas City, KS	66104-4354	913-371-1071	371-1609	Desiree Bryant M.A.
Dakota Conference	PO Box 520	Pierre, SD	57501-0520	605-224-8868	224-7886	Leonard Quaile
Iowa-Missouri Conference	PO Box 65665	West Des Moines, IA	50265-0665	515-223-3556	223-5692	Gary Rouse M.A.
Kansas-Nebraska Conference	3440 SW Urish Rd	Topeka, KS	66614-4601	785-478-4726	478-1000	Chuck Castle M.A.
Minnesota Conference	7384 Kirkwood Ct	Maple Grove, MN	55369-5200	763-424-8923	424-9576	Pamela Consuegra M.A.
Rocky Mountain Conference	2520 S Downing St	Denver, CO	80210-5818	303-733-3771	733-1843	Lonnie Hetterle B.A.
North Pacific Union Conference	**5709 N 20th St**	**Ridgefield, WA**	**98642-7724**	**360-857-7000**	**857-7001**	**Alan Hurlbert M.Ed.**
Alaska Conference	6100 OMalley Rd	Anchorage, AK	99507-6958	907-346-1004	346-3279	John Kriegelstein M.Ed.
Idaho Conference	7777 W Fairview Ave	Boise, ID	83704-8418	208-375-7524	375-7526	Paulette Jackson
Montana Conference	175 Canyon View Rd	Bozeman, MT	59715-0607	406-587-3101	587-1598	Archie Harris
Oregon Conference	19800 Oatfield Rd	Gladstone, OR	97027-2546	503-850-3500	654-5657	John Gatchet
Upper Columbia Conference	505 S College Ave Ste 1	College Place, WA	99324	509-838-2761	838-4882	Keith Waters M.S.
Washington Conference	3254 SW 323rd St	Federal Way, WA	98023	253-681-6008	681-6009	Lon Gruesbeck M.A.
Pacific Union Conference	**PO Box 5005**	**Westlake Vlg, CA**	**91359-5005**	**805-413-7314**	**413-7319**	**Dr. Kelly Bock**

Conference	Address	City,State	Zip code	Telephone	Fax	Superintendent
Arizona Conference	PO Box 12340	Scottsdale, AZ	85267-2340	480-991-6777	991-4833	Ivan E. Weiss M.A.
Central California Conference	PO Box 770	Clovis, CA	93613-0770	559-347-3000	347-3120	Vern Biloff M.A.
Hawaii Conference	2728 Pali Hwy	Honolulu, HI	96817-1428	808-595-7591	595-2345	Teryl D. Loeffler M.Ed.
Nevada-Utah Conference	PO Box 10730	Reno, NV	89510-0730	775-322-6929	954-0005	Larry Unterseher
Northern California Conference	PO Box 23165	Pleasant Hill, CA	94523-0165	925-685-4300	685-2014	Berit VonPohle
Southeastern California Conference	PO Box 8050	Riverside, CA	92515-8050	951-509-2200	509-2390	Donald Dudley
Southern California Conference	PO Box 969	Glendale, CA	91209-0969	818-546-8400	546-8454	Richard Carey
Southern Union Conference	**PO Box 849**	**Decatur, GA**	**30031-0849**	**404-299-1832**	**299-9726**	**Conrad Gill M.A.**
Carolina Conference	PO Box 560339	Charlotte, NC	28256-0339	704-596-3200	596-5775	Robert Crux
Florida Conference	PO Box 2626	Winter Park, FL	32790-2626	407-644-5000	644-7550	Jim Epperson Ed.D.
Georgia-Cumberland Conference	PO Box 12000	Calhoun, GA	30703-7001	706-629-7951	526-3684	Cynthia Gettys Ph.D.
Gulf States Conference	PO Box 240249	Montgomery, AL	36124-0249	334-272-7493	272-7987	Leslie Louis M.A.
Kentucky-Tennessee Conference	PO Box 1088	Goodlettsville, TN	37070-1088	615-859-1391	859-2120	Larry Boughman Ph.D.
South Atlantic Conference	PO Box 92447	Atlanta, GA	30314-0447	404-792-0535	792-7817	Pennie Lister-Archie
South Central Conference	715 Youngs Ln	Nashville, TN	37207-4898	615-226-6500	262-9141	Gilbert Cooper
Southeastern Conference	1701 Robie Ave	Mount Dora, FL	32757	352-735-3142	735-3562	Elisa Young
Southwestern Union Conference	**PO Box 4000**	**Burleson, TX**	**76097-1630**	**817-295-0476**	**447-2443**	**Doug Walker M.A.**
Arkansas-Louisiana Conference	PO Box 31000	Shreveport, LA	71130-1000	318-631-6240	631-6247	Don Hevener M.A.
Oklahoma Conference	PO Box 32098	Oklahoma City, OK	73123-0298	405-721-6110	721-7594	Jack Francisco M.A.
Southwest Region Conference	PO Box 226289	Dallas, TX	75222-6289	214-943-4491	946-2528	Frank Jones
Texas Conference	PO Box 800	Alvarado, TX	76009-0800	817-790-2255	783-2697	Bonnie Eder Ed.D.
Texico Conference	PO Box 1366	Corrales, NM	87048-1366	505-244-1611	244-1811	Chuck Workman M.A.

Patterson's
SCHOOLS CLASSIFIED

Part II

POST-SECONDARY SCHOOLS

HOW TO USE PATTERSON'S SCHOOLS CLASSIFIED

Patterson's SCHOOLS CLASSIFIED contains the broadest assortment of post-secondary schools available in any single directory. More than 7,000 post-secondary schools, accredited by the organizations shown below, are classified by school type and academic discipline.

The basic listing for the School Classification contains the school name, mailing address, contact person and phone number needed for supplementary information or registration details. Many of the listings are in larger type or contain additional descriptive material supplied by the school. The student should interpret the added emphasis as an indication of the school's desire to attract qualified students. Listings are arranged alphabetically within each classification, first by state and then by school name.

In addition to our regular editorial work, each school has been contacted within the past twelve months to verify names, addresses, academic subjects covered and degrees offered. The contributions of the responding schools is sincerely appreciated.

11 Institutional Accrediting Organizations

Accrediting Association of Bible Colleges
Accrediting Commission of Career Schools/Colleges of Technology
Accrediting Council for Independent Colleges and Schools
Association of Advanced Rabbinical & Talmudic Schools
Association of Theological Schools in the USA & Canada
Middle States Association of Colleges & Schools
New England Association of Schools & Colleges
North Central Association of Colleges & Schools
Northwest Association of Schools & Colleges
Southern Association of Colleges & Schools
Western Association of Schools & Colleges

40 Professional and Specialized Accrediting Organizations

Accreditation Board for Engineering & Technology
Accrediting Bureau of Health Education Schools
Accrediting Commission on Education for Health Services Administration
Accrediting Council on Education in Journalism & Mass Communication
American Association of Family and Consumer Sciences
American Bar Association
American Board of Funeral Service Education
American Council for Construction Education
American Council on Pharmaceutical Education
American Dental Association
American Dietetic Association
American Institute of Certified Planners
American Library Association
American Optometric Association
American Osteopathic Association
American Physical Therapy Association
American Podiatric Medical Association
American Psychological Association
American Society of Landscape Architects
American Speech-Language-Hearing Association
American Veterinary Medical Association
Association of American Law Schools
Association to Advance Collegiate Schools of Business
Computer Science Accreditation Commission
Council for Accreditation of Counseling & Related Educational Programs
Council on Chiropractic Education
Council on Education for Public Health
Council on Occupational Education
Council on Rehabilitation Education
Council on Social Work Education
Foundation for Interior Design Education Research
Liaison Committee on Medical Education
National Architectural Accrediting Board
National Association of Schools of Art & Design
National Association of Schools of Music
National Association of Schools of Public Affairs & Administration
National Council for Accreditation of Teacher Education
National League for Nursing
National Recreation & Park Association
Society of American Foresters

SCHOOL CLASSIFICATIONS

If you are interested in a particular type of school, such as a **Career School** or a **Community** or **Junior College**, go directly to that classification and you will find a listing of accredited schools.

If you are looking for a particular school by name go to the index where you will find an alphabetical listing of the schools contained in this book along with the state abbreviation and classification code. Refer to page 953 for an explanation of how the index works.

ACADEMIC CLASSIFICATIONS

Academic Classifications cover the major areas of study selected by more than 90% of secondary students. Once the student has selected a major, reference to that classification will direct him to an appropriate selection of schools.

Academic Classifications offered by a relatively small number of schools, such as **Architecture** and **Engineering** are intended to be complete at the Baccalaureate level. However, to list every school under every possible classification would make the directory so large as to be a disservice to the student. **Music**, for example, is taught in one form or another by virtually every school. **Music** listings include all schools approved by the National Association of Schools of Music. They do not, however, include all of the schools that offer degrees in music. The reader should recognize that the omission of a school from such disciplines as **Music**, **Liberal Arts and Sciences** or **Business and Management** is not a failure in editorial content but, an effort to reduce redundancy.

Inclusion in Academic Classifications of schools below the Baccalaureate Degree is progressively more selective. For a broader selection, the student may choose to contact schools from a School Classification.

COMMINGLED SCHOOLS IN ACADEMIC CLASSIFICATIONS

A special feature of this book is the commingling of colleges, community and junior colleges and career schools in Academic Classifications. The student considering further education is exposed to a wide range of educational opportunities without the need for multiple directories. In all cases listings for schools which offer less than a Baccalaureate Degree are identified by a symbol to the left of the school name to help the reader quickly identify the highest degree, diploma or certificate offered. See page 681.

GUIDE TO EDITORIAL STYLE

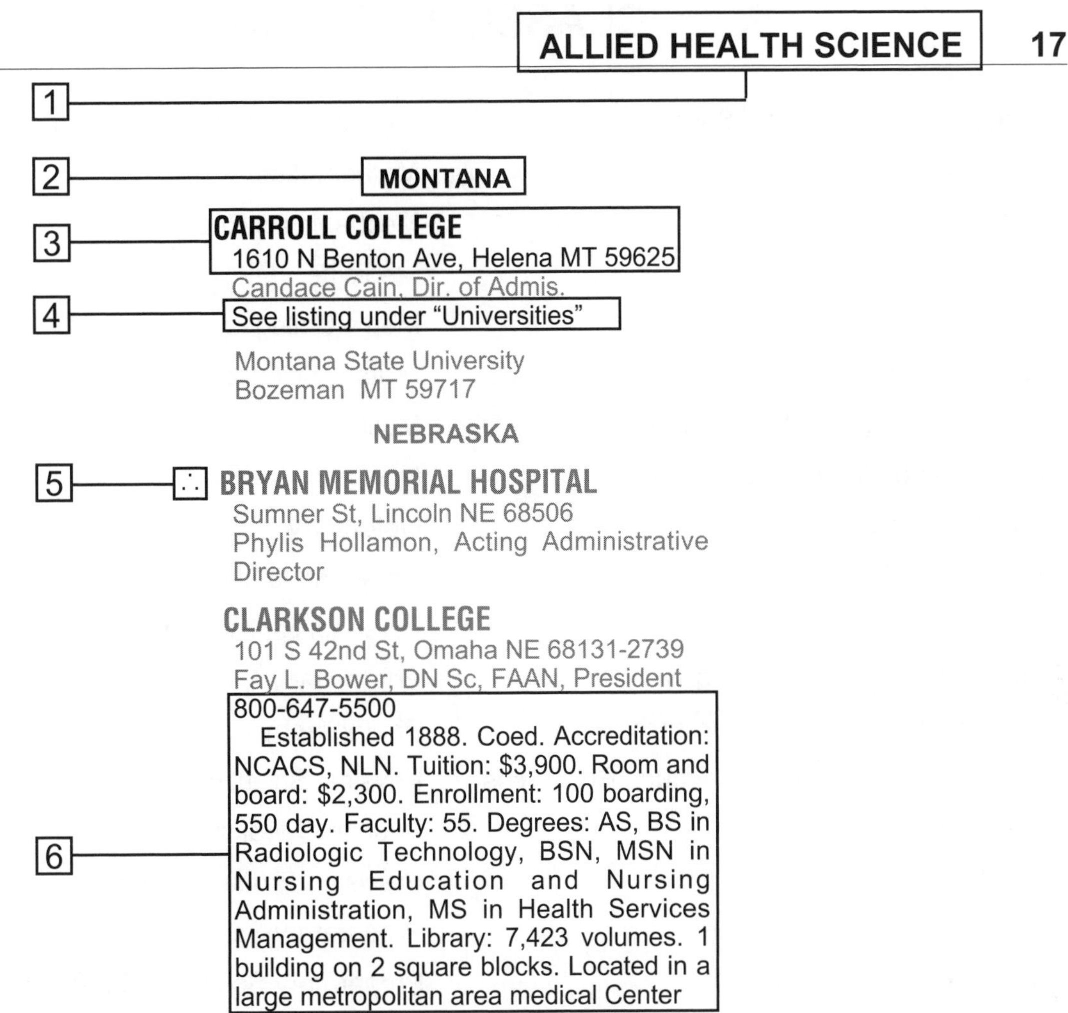

1. Classification and page number.
2. State (in alphabetical sequence within each classification).
3. School name and address (in alphabetical sequence within each state).
4. Cross reference line (to direct the reader's attention to a school's larger listing in a different classification).
5. School type code (identifies school type if below the baccalaureate degree in academic classifications).
   - · Community and Junior Colleges
   - : Career Schools
   - ∴ Teaching Hospitals
   - : : Preparatory Schools
   - ·:· Handicapped Schools
   - ::: Home Study Schools
6. Supplemental information provided by the school.

CLASSIFICATIONS

Aeronautics, Aviation and Space
Agriculture
Allied Health Science
Architecture
Art
Biological Science
Business - Administrative Support
Business and Management
Career Schools
Chiropractic Medicine
Communications
Community and Junior Colleges
Computer and Information Science
Conservation & Renewable Natural Resources
Construction Trades
Dentistry
Engineering
Engineering Technology
Ethnic Studies
Fashion Art
Graduate Schools
Handicapped, Schools for the
Home Economics
Home Study and Correspondence
Interior Design
Landscape Architecture
Law
Letters
Liberal Arts and Sciences
Library Science
Marketing and Distribution
Master of Business Administration
Mathematics
Mechanics & Repairers
Medicine
Men's Colleges
Military Science
Music
Nursing
Optometry
Osteopathic Medicine
Personal & Miscellaneous Services
Pharmacy
Photography
Physical Science
Podiatric Medicine
Precision Production Trades
Preparatory Schools for Boys
Preparatory Schools - Coeducational
Preparatory Schools for Girls
Protective Services
Psychology
Public Health
Social Science
Speech and Drama
Study Abroad
Summer Sessions
Teacher Education
Theological Studies & Religious Vocations
Universities and Colleges
Veterinary Medicine
Women's Colleges
Women's Studies

AERONAUTICS, AVIATION AND SPACE

ALABAMA

CALHOUN COMMUNITY COLLEGE
PO Box 2216, Decatur AL 35609-2216
M. Wayne Tosh, Registrar
256-306-2500 Fax: 256-306-2941
Website: www.calhoun.edu
E-mail: rls@calhoun.edu
See listing under "Community and Junior Colleges"

ALASKA

University of Alaska Anchorage
PO Box 141629, Anchorage AK 99514-1629
Cecile Mitchell, Director of Enrollment Services
907-786-1480 Fax: 907-786-4888
Website: www.uaa.alaska.edu/
E-mail: enroll@uaa.alaska.edu

ARIZONA

Embry-Riddle Aeronautical University
Arizona Campus
3700 Willow Creek Rd, Prescott AZ 86301-3720
William Thompson, Director of Admissions
800-888-3728 Fax: 928-777-6613
Website: www.embryriddle.edu
E-mail: pradmit@erau.edu

CALIFORNIA

Orange Coast College
PO Box 5005, Costa Mesa CA 92628-5005
Kristin Clark, Director of Admissions
714-432-5773 Fax: 714-432-5736
Website: www.orangecoastcollege.edu
E-mail: kclark@cccd.edu

San Diego Christian College
2100 Greenfield Dr, El Cajon CA 92019-1157
Rene Inman, Director of Admissions
800-676-2242 Fax: 619-590-1739
Website: www.sdcc.edu
E-mail: admissions@sdcc.edu

San Joaquin Valley College
Fresno Aviation Campus
4985 E Anderson Ave, Fresno CA 93727-1501
Joseph Holt, Director of Admissions
559-453-0123 Fax: 559-651-4864
Website: www.sjvc.edu
E-mail: josephh@sjvc.edu

COLORADO

Colorado Northwestern Community College
500 Kennedy Dr, Rangely CO 81648-3502
Tresa England, Director of Student Services
800-562-1105 Fax: 970-675-3343
Website: www.cncc.edu
E-mail: tresa.england@cncc.edu

FLORIDA

DELTA CONNECTION ACADEMY
2700 Flightline Ave, Sanford FL 32773-9683
Ron Lewis, Director of Admissions
407-430-4174 Fax: 407-330-0448
Website: www.deltaconnectionacademy.com
E-mail: info@deltaconnectionacademy.com

Embry-Riddle Aeronautical University
Daytona Beach Campus
PO Box 11767, Daytona Beach FL 32120-1767
C. Richard Clarke, Director of Admissions
800-862-2416 Fax: 386-226-7070
Website: www.embryriddle.edu
E-mail: dbadmit@erau.edu

EVERGLADES UNIVERSITY (MAIN CAMPUS)
5002 T-Rex Ave Suite 100, Boca Raton FL 33431
Kristi Mollis, President
888-772-6077 Fax: 561-912-1191
Website: www.evergladesuniversity.edu
E-mail: admissions-boca@evergladesuniversity.edu
See listing under "Universities"

EVERGLADES UNIVERSITY
Orlando Campus (Branch Campus)
887 E Altamonte Dr, Altamonte Springs FL 32701
Linda Volz, Vice President
866-289-1078 Fax: 407-482-9801
Website: www.evergladesuniversity.edu
E-mail: admissions-orl@evergladesuniversity.edu
See listing under "Universities"

EVERGLADES UNIVERSITY
Sarasota Campus (Branch Campus)
6001 Lake Osprey Dr, Suite 110, Sarasota FL 34240
Brad Brewer, Vice President
866-907-2262 Fax: 941-907-6634
Website: www.evergladesuniversity.edu
E-mail: admissions-sar@evergladesuniversity.edu
See listing under "Universities"

Florida Air Academy
1950 S Academy Dr, Melbourne FL 32901-4396
Colonel James Dwight, President
321-723-3211 ext. 30041 Fax: 321-676-0422
Website: www.flair.com
E-mail: tderegnaucourt@flair.com

GEORGE T. BAKER AVIATION SCHOOL
3275 NW 42nd Ave, Miami FL 33142-5626
Sean E. Gallagan, Principal
305-871-3143 Fax: 305-871-5840
Website: www.bakeraviation.edu
E-mail: gtba@dadeschools.net

Lynn University
3601 N Military Trl, Boca Raton FL 33431-5598
Director of Admissions
561-237-7900 Fax: 561-237-7100
Website: www.lynn.edu
E-mail: admission@lynn.edu

NATIONAL AVIATION ACADEMY
6225 Ulmerton Rd, Clearwater FL 33760
Karen Acker, Registrar
727-531-2080 or 800-659-2080 Fax: 727-535-8727
Website: www.naa.edu
E-mail: admissions@naa.edu

PELICAN FLIGHT TRAINING CENTER
1601 SW 75th Ave, Pembroke Pines FL 33023
Meg Fensome, Vice President
954-966-9750 Fax: 954-985-8271
Website: www.pelican-airways.com
E-mail: pelicanftc@pelican-airways.com

Phoenix East Aviation, Inc.
Daytona Beach
561 Pearl Harbor Dr, Daytona Beach FL 32114-3845
Pat Cobleigh, Director of Admissions
386-258-0703 or 800-868-4359 Fax: 386-254-6842
Website: pea.com
E-mail: patc@pea.com
See listing under "Career Schools"

IOWA

Iowa Lakes Community College
300 S 18th St, Estherville IA 51334-2721
Anne Stansbury, Asst. Director of Admissions
712-362-7945 Fax: 712-362-8363
Website: www.iowalakes.edu
E-mail: info@iowalakes.edu

KENTUCKY

Morehead State University
Morehead KY 40351-1689
Jeffrey Liles, Enrollment Services
800-585-6781 Fax: 606-783-5038
Website: www.moreheadstate.edu
E-mail: admissions@moreheadstate.edu

LOUISIANA

VORTEX HELICOPTERS
PO Box 9789, New Iberia LA 70562-9789
Mary Sheeran, Vice President
228-864-7357 Fax: 228-864-5850
Website: www.vortex-helicopters.com
E-mail: vortexheli@earthlink.net

MASSACHUSETTS

Boston University
121 Bay State Rd, Boston MA 02215
Kelly Walter, Executive Director of Admissions
617-353-2300 Fax: 617-353-9695
Website: web.bu.edu
E-mail: admissions@bu.edu

Massachusetts Institute of Technology
77 Massachusetts Ave, Cambridge MA 02139-4307
617-253-1000 Fax: 617-253-4016
Website: my.mit.edu
E-mail: admissions@mit.edu

North Shore Community College
1 Ferncroft Rd, Danvers MA 01923-4093
Jennifer Kirk, Director of Admissions & Recruitment Outreach
978-762-4000 Fax: 978-762-4015
Website: www.northshore.edu
E-mail: jkirk@northshore.edu

Worcester Polytechnic Institute
100 Institute Rd, Worcester MA 01609-2280
Edward J. Connor, Director of Admissions
508-831-5286 Fax: 508-831-5875
Website: admissions.wpi.edu
E-mail: admissions@wpi.edu

MICHIGAN

Delta College
University Center MI 48710-0001
Duff Zube, Director of Admissions
989-686-9093 Fax: 989-667-2202
Website: www.delta.edu
E-mail: admit@delta.edu

Northwestern Michigan College
1701 E Front St, Traverse City MI 49686-3061
Jim Bensley, Director of Admissions
800-748-0566 Fax: 231-995-1339
Website: www.nmc.edu
E-mail: jbensley@nmc.edu

MINNESOTA

Academy College
1101 E 78th St, Bloomington MN 55420-1402
Tracey Schantz, Director of Admissions
952-851-0066 Fax: 952-851-0094

University of Minnesota
2900 University Ave, Crookston MN 56716-5001
218-281-6510 Fax: 218-281-8575
Website:
admissions.umcrookston.edu/requirements/apply.htm
E-mail: info@umcrookston.edu

NEW JERSEY

Teterboro School of Aeronautics
80 Moonachie Ave, Teterboro NJ 07608-1003
Richard Ciasulli, Director of Admissions
201-288-6300 Fax: 201-288-5609
Website: www.teterboroschool.com
E-mail: teterboroschool@nj.rr.com

NEW YORK

Dowling College
150 Idle Hour Blvd, Oakdale NY 11769-1999
Diane Kazanecki-Kempter, Contact
631-244-3000 Fax: 631-244-1059
Website: www.dowling.edu
E-mail: admissions@dowling.edu

VAUGHN COLLEGE OF AERONAUTICS AND TECHNOLOGY
8601 23rd Ave, Flushing NY 11369-1037
Vincent Papandrea, Director of Admissions
800-776-2376 Fax: 718-429-0671
Website: www.vaughn.edu
E-mail: admitme@vaughn.edu

Established 1932. Private. Coed. Accreditation: MSACS, ABET. Tuition: $13,400. Fees: $280. Enrollment: 842 full-time, 284 part-time. Faculty: 59. Student-faculty ratio: 11:1. Degrees: BS, AAS, AOS. Library: 62,000 vols. Offering bachelor and associate degrees in airport management, aviation maintenance, flight training, electronic technology, engineering, general management, mechatronic engineering, pre-engineering and computerized design/animated graphics. Hands-on training. Extensive career development services and financial aid available.

NORTH DAKOTA

Williston State College
PO Box 1326, Williston ND 58802-1326
Penny Soiseth, Associate Director Enrollment Services
701-774-4200 Fax: 701-774-4544
Website: www.wsc.nodak.edu
E-mail: penny.soiseth@wsc.nodak.edu

OHIO

The Ohio State University
Department of Aerospace Engineering
328 Bolz Hall, 2036 Neil Avenue Mall
Columbus OH 43210
614-292-2691 Fax: 614-292-8290
Website: aerospace.eng.ohio-state.edu
E-mail: haritonidis.1@osu.edu

The Ohio State University, Department of Aviation
Aviation Building, 164 W 19th Ave
Columbus OH 43210
614-292-2405, Fax: 614-292-1014
Website: aviation.osu.edu/
E-mail: aviation@osu.edu

University of Dayton
300 College Park, Dayton OH 45469-1300
Robert F. Durkle, Director of Admission
800-837-7433 Fax: 937-229-4729
Website: admission.udayton.edu
E-mail: admission@udayton.edu

OKLAHOMA

Oklahoma State University
Stillwater OK 74078
Steven K. Marks, Department Head
405-744-6275
Website: www.okstate.edu
E-mail: steve.marks@okstate.edu

SPARTAN COLLEGE OF AERONAUTICS AND TECHNOLOGY
8820 E Pine St, Tulsa OK 74115-5802
Director of Admissions
800-331-1204 Fax: 918-831-8609
Website: www.spartan.edu
E-mail: spartan@mail.spartan.edu

Established 1928. Coed. Accredited member school: ACCSCT. Providing Technical training and education in Avionics, Aviation Maintenance; Nondestructive Testing and Quality Control. Complete flight training program. Offering Diplomas, Associate of Applied Science and Bachelor of Science in Aviation Technology Management.

PENNSYLVANIA

Community College of Allegheny County
Allegheny Campus: 808 Ridge Ave, Pittsburgh PA 15212 Admissions: 412.237.2700
Boyce Campus: 595 Beatty Rd, Monroeville PA 15146 Admissions: 724.325.6614
North Campus: 8701 Perry Highway, Pittsburgh PA 15237 Admissions: 412.369.3600
South Campus: 1750 Clairton Rd, West Mifflin PA 15122 Admissions: 412-469-4301
Website: www.ccac.edu

Community College of Beaver County
1 Campus Dr, Monaca PA 15061-2566
724-775-8561 Fax: 724-775-4687
Website: www.ccbc.edu
E-mail: admissions@ccbc.edu

PIA SCHOOL OF SPECIALIZED TECHNOLOGY
(Pittsburgh Institute of Aeronautics)
PO Box 10897, Pittsburgh PA 15236-0897
Vincent J. Mezza, Director of Admissions
800-444-1440 Fax: 412-466-0513
Website: www.pia.edu
E-mail: admissions@pia.edu
Established in 1929. Coed. Accredited Member School: ACCSCT. Providing technical training in Aviation Maintenance, Aviation Electronics and Electronic Systems (Associate in Specialized Technology Degree). Financial aid to those who qualify. Scholarship match program. Ongoing placement assistance. Varsity sports in bowling and golf, member of WPCC and PCAA.

TENNESSEE

NORTH CENTRAL INSTITUTE
168 Jack Miller Blvd, Clarksville TN 37042-4810
Dr. John McCurdy, President
931-431-9700 Fax: 931-431-9771
Website: www.nci.edu
E-mail: admissions@nci.edu
Established 1988. Private. Coed. Accreditation: Accrediting Commission of the Council on Occupational Education. Student-faculty ratio: 20:1. Degrees: AAS in Aviation Technology - concentrations in Flight, Maintenance, or Operations/Air Traffic Control. FAA part 147 Aviation Maintenance Technician Program enables students to become FAA Certified Airframe/Powerplant Technicians. Our Credit Inventory Evaluation Service turns military training into college credit. Financial Aid and Veterans benefits to those who qualify.

TEXAS

AVIATION INSTITUTE OF MAINTENANCE
7555 Lemmon Ave, Dallas TX 75209-3017
James Cooper, School Director
214-333-9711 Fax: 214-333-9185
Website: www.aviationmaintenance.edu
E-mail: directoramd@aviationmaintenance.edu

Hallmark Institute of Aeronautics
Aeronautics Campus-Aviation Technology
8901 Wetmore Rd, San Antonio TX 78216-4229
Joe Fisher, President
210-826-1000 Fax: 210-826-3707
Website: www.hallmarkinstitute.edu
E-mail: sross@hallmarkinstitute.edu

University of Texas at Arlington
Box 19111, Arlington TX 76019-0111
Hans Gatterdam, Director of Admission
817-272-6287 Fax: 817-272-3435
Website: www.uta.edu
E-mail: admissions@uta.edu

VIRGINIA

AVIATION INSTITUTE OF MAINTENANCE
1429 Miller Store Rd, Virginia Beach VA 23455-3324
Michael Huffman, Director
757-363-2121 Fax: 757-363-2044
Website: www.aviationmaintenance.edu
E-mail: directoramn@tidetech.com

WASHINGTON

Everett Community College
2000 Tower St, Everett WA 98201
Christine Kerlin, Associate Dean
425-388-9100 Fax: 425-388-9173
Website: www.everettcc.edu
E-mail: ckerlin@everettcc.edu

WEST VIRGINIA

Fairmont State University
1201 Locust Ave, Fairmont WV 26554-2470
Steve Leadman, Director of Admissions
304-367-4892 or 800-641-5678 Fax: 304-367-4789
Website: www.fairmontstate.edu
E-mail: admit@fairmontstate.edu

WISCONSIN

Blackhawk Technical College
PO Box 5009, Janesville WI 53547-5009
Gregg Bosak, Administration, Community Information
608-757-7769 Fax: 608-757-7740
Website: www.blackhawk.edu
E-mail: gbosak@blackhawk.edu

AGRICULTURE

ALABAMA

CALHOUN COMMUNITY COLLEGE
PO Box 2216, Decatur AL 35609-2216
M. Wayne Tosh, Registrar
256-306-2500 Fax: 256-306-2941
Website: www.calhoun.edu
E-mail: jfd@calhoun.edu

CALIFORNIA

Butte College
3536 Butte Campus Dr, Oroville CA 95965-8399
Carole Gish, Director of Admissions
530-895-2511 Fax: 530-879-4313
Website: www.butte.edu
E-mail: admissions@butte.edu

COLORADO

NORTHEASTERN JUNIOR COLLEGE
100 College Ave, Sterling CO 80751-2399
Dr. Lance Bolton, Chief Administrative Officer
Tina Joyce, Director of Admissions
970-521-7000 or 970-521-6752 Fax: 970-521-6801
Website: www.njc.edu
E-mail: tina.joyce@njc.edu

San Juan Basin Technical College
PO Box 970, Cortez CO 81321-0970
Shannon South, Vice President
970-565-8457 Fax: 970-565-8450
Website: www.sjbtc.edu
E-mail: info@sjbtc.edu

GEORGIA

North Georgia Technical College
434 Meeks Ave, Blairsville GA 30512-2983
Admissions
706-439-6300 Fax: 706-439-6301
Website: www.northgatech.edu
E-mail: info@northgatech.edu

North Georgia Technical College
Clarkesville Campus
PO Box 65, Clarkesville GA 30523-0002
Admissions
706-754-7700 Fax: 706-754-7777
Website: www.northgatech.edu
E-mail: info@northgatech.edu

IDAHO

Brigham Young University - Idaho
120 Kimball Bldg, Rexburg ID 83460-1615
Rob Garrett, Director of Admissions
208-496-1020 Fax: 208-496-1220
Website: www.byui.edu
E-mail: admissions@byui.edu

University of Idaho
Moscow ID 83844-4253
Lloyd Scott, Director of New Student Services
208-885-6163 Fax: 208-885-4477
Website: www.uidaho.edu
E-mail: nss@uidaho.edu

IOWA

Iowa Lakes Community College
3200 College Dr, Emmetsburg IA 50536-1055
Anne Stansbury, Asst. Director of Admissions
712-852-5212 Fax: 712-362-8363
Website: www.iowalakes.edu
E-mail: info@iowalakes.edu

KANSAS

COLBY COMMUNITY COLLEGE
1255 S Range Ave, Colby KS 67701-4099
Director of Admissions
888-634-9350 or 785-460-4690 Fax: 785-460-4691
Website: www.colbycc.edu
E-mail: admissions@colbycc.edu

KENTUCKY

Bluegrass Community and Technical College
Oswald Building
470 Cooper Drive, Lexington KY 40506-0235
Shelbie Hugle, Director of Admissions
859-246-6200 Fax: 859-246-4664
Website: www.bluegrass.kctcs.edu
E-mail: bctc_info@kctcs.edu
Equine Studies.

Morehead State University
Morehead KY 40351-1689
Jeffrey Liles, Enrollment Services
800-585-6781 Fax: 606-783-5038
Website: www.moreheadstate.edu
E-mail: admissions@moreheadstate.edu

MASSACHUSETTS

North Shore Community College
1 Ferncroft Rd, Danvers MA 01923-4093
Jennifer Kirk, Director of Admissions & Recruitment Outreach
978-762-4000 Fax: 978-762-4015
Website: www.northshore.edu
E-mail: jkirk@northshore.edu

MINNESOTA

Ridgewater College-Willmar Campus
PO Box 1097, Willmar MN 56201-1097
Sally Kerfeld, Director of Admissions
800-722-1151 Fax: 320-222-5212
Website: www.ridgewater.edu
E-mail: sally.kerfeld@ridgewater.edu

University of Minnesota
2900 University Ave, Crookston MN 56716-5001
218-281-6510 Fax: 218-281-8575
Website:
admissions.umcrookston.edu/requirements/apply.htm
E-mail: info@umcrookston.edu

MISSOURI

Northwest Missouri State University
800 University Dr, Maryville MO 64468-6001
Beverly Schenkel, Dean of Enrollment Management
660-562-1562 Fax: 660-562-1121
Website: www.nwmissouri.edu
E-mail: admissions@nwmissouri.edu

Truman State University
100 E Normal, Kirksville MO 63501
Office of Admission
660-785-4114 Fax: 660-785-7456
Website: admissions.truman.edu
E-mail: admissions@truman.edu

NEVADA

GREAT BASIN COLLEGE
1500 College Pkwy, Elko NV 89801-5032
Julie G. Byrnes, Director of Enrollment Management
775-753-2271 Fax: 775-753-2311
Website: www.gbcnv.edu
E-mail: julieb@gwmail.gbcnv.edu
See listing under "Universities"

NEW JERSEY

Bergen Community College
400 Paramus Rd, Paramus NJ 07652
Julian Gomez, Asst. Director of Admissions
201-447-7100 Fax: 201-444-7036
Website: www.bergen.edu
E-mail: jgomez@bergen.edu

NEW YORK

SUNY College of Technology
Alfred NY 14802
Deborah J. Goodrich, Associate VP Enrollment Mgmt.
800-4AL-FRED Fax: 607-587-4299
Website: www.alfredstate.edu
E-mail: admissions@alfredstate.edu

NORTH CAROLINA

James Sprunt Community College
PO Box 398, Kenansville NC 28349-0398
Lea Grady, Admissions
910-296-2500 Fax: 910-296-1636
Website: www.jamessprunt.edu

NORTH DAKOTA

Dickinson State University
Dickinson ND 58601-4896
Steve Glasser, Director of Enrollment Services
800-279-4295 Fax: 701-483-2409
Website: www.dickinsonstate.edu
E-mail: dsu.hawks@dickinsonstate.edu

Williston State College
PO Box 1326, Williston ND 58802-1326
Penny Soiseth, Associate Director Enrollment Services
701-774-4200 Fax: 701-774-4544
Website: www.wsc.nodak.edu
E-mail: penny.soiseth@wsc.nodak.edu

OHIO

The Ohio State University
College of Food, Agriculture, and Environmental Sciences
Agricultural Admin Bldg, 2120 Fyffe Rd
Columbus OH 43210
614-292-6891 Fax: 614-292-1218
Website: cfaes.osu.edu

Owens Community College
3200 Bright Rd, Findlay OH 45840
William J. Ivoska PhD., Vice President of Student Services
567-429-3500 Fax: 567-423-0246
Website: www.owens.edu
E-mail: admissions@owens.edu

Owens Community College
PO Box 10000, Toledo OH 43699-1947
William J. Ivoska, Ph.D, Vice President of Student Services
567-661-7000 Fax: 567-661-7607
Website: www.owens.edu
E-mail: admissions@owens.edu

OKLAHOMA

Oklahoma State University
Stillwater OK 74078
Edwin Miller, Assoc. Dean
405-744-5398
Website: www.okstate.edu
E-mail: ed.miller@okstate.edu

OREGON

Linn-Benton Community College
6500 Pacific Blvd SW, Albany OR 97321-3774
Christine Baker, Outreach Coordinator
541-917-4811 Fax: 541-917-4868
Website: www.linnbenton.edu
E-mail: admissions@linnbenton.edu

PENNSYLVANIA

Community College of Allegheny County
Allegheny Campus: 808 Ridge Ave, Pittsburgh PA 15212 Admissions: 412.237.2700
Boyce Campus: 595 Beatty Rd, Monroeville PA 15146 Admissions: 724.325.6614
North Campus: 8701 Perry Highway, Pittsburgh PA 15237 Admissions: 412.369.3600
South Campus: 1750 Clairton Rd, West Mifflin PA 15122 Admissions: 412-469-4301
Website: www.ccac.edu

Delaware Valley College
700 E Butler Ave, Doylestown PA 18901-2697
Stephen W. Zenko, Director of Admissions
800-2DE-LVAL Fax: 215-230-2968
Website: www.delval.edu
E-mail: stephenzenko@delval.edu

SOUTH DAKOTA

Western Dakota Technical Institute
800 Mickelson Dr, Rapid City SD 57703-4018
Jill Elder, Admissions Coordinator
605-394-4034 Fax: 605-394-2204
Website: www.wdt.edu
E-mail: jill.elder@wdt.edu

TENNESSEE

Austin Peay State University
601 College St, Clarksville TN 37044-0002
931-221-7011 Fax: 931-221-6168
Website: www.apsu.edu
E-mail: admissions@apsu.edu

TEXAS

Abilene Christian University
ACU Box 29000, Abilene TX 79699-0001
325-674-2000 Fax: 325-674-2202
Website: www.acu.edu
E-mail: info@admissions.acu.edu

Lubbock Christian University
5601 19th St, Lubbock TX 79407-2099
Stan Scott, Director of Admissions
806-796-8800 Fax: 806-720-7162
Website: www.lcu.edu
E-mail: stan.scott@lcu.edu

Weatherford College
225 College Park Dr, Weatherford TX 76086
Dr. Joe Birmingham, President
800-287-5471 Fax: 817-598-6205
Website: www.wc.edu
E-mail: willingham@wc.edu

WASHINGTON

Walla Walla Community College
500 Tausick Way, Walla Walla WA 99362-9270
Jerry Kjack, Director
509-527-4283 or 877-992-9922 Fax: 509-527-4572
Website: www.wwcc.edu
E-mail: jerry.kjack@wwcc.edu
See listing under "Community and Junior Colleges"

WISCONSIN

Wisconsin Indianhead Technical College
505 Pine Ridge Dr, Shell Lake WI 54871
Randy Deli, Dean
800-243-9482 Fax: 715-468-2819
Website: www.witc.edu
E-mail: randy.deli@witc.edu

WYOMING

University of Wyoming
Admissions Office
Dept 3435, Laramie WY 82071-3435
Brooke Culver, Contact
800-342-5996 Fax: 307-766-4042
Website: www.uwyo.edu
E-mail: why-wyo@uwyo.edu

GUAM

University of Guam
UOG Station, Mangilao GU 96923
Deborah Leon Guerrero, Registrar
671-735-2201 or 671-735-2208 Fax: 671-735-2203
Website: www.uog.edu
E-mail: admitme@uog9.uog.edu

ALLIED HEALTH SCIENCE

ALABAMA

Alabama A & M University
PO Box 908, Normal AL 35762
Antonio Boyle, Director of Admissions
256-372-5245

Auburn University
Auburn AL 36849
334-844-4000

Auburn University at Montgomery
PO Box 244023, Montgomery AL 36124
334-244-3000

Baptist Medical Center
301 Brown Springs Rd, Montgomery AL 36117
334-273-4400

Bessemer State Technical College
PO Box 308, Bessemer AL 35021-0308
205-428-6391

CALHOUN COMMUNITY COLLEGE
PO Box 2216, Decatur AL 35609-2216
M. Wayne Tosh, Registrar
256-306-2500 Fax: 256-306-2941
Website: www.calhoun.edu
E-mail: aww@calhoun.edu

Carraway Methodist Medical Center
1600 Carraway Blvd, Birmingham AL 35234-2804
205-226-6000

Gadsden State Community College
PO Box 227, Gadsden AL 35902-0227
256-549-8200

George C. Wallace Community College - Dothan
1141 Wallace Dr, Dothan AL 36303
334-983-3521

George C. Wallace State Community College
PO Box 2530, Selma AL 36702-2530
Mrs. Donitha J. Griffin, Dean of Students
334-876-9295 Fax: 334-876-9300
Website: www.wccs.edu
E-mail: dgriffin@wccs.edu

Herzing College
280 W Valley Ave, Homewood AL 35209-4816
Kim Conway, Director of Admissions
205-916-2800 Fax: 205-916-2807
Website: www.herzing.edu/birmingham
E-mail: info@bhm.herzing.edu

Jacksonville State University
700 Pelham Rd N, Jacksonville AL 36265-1602
256-782-5000

James H. Faulkner State Community College
1900 S US Highway 31, Bay Minette AL 36507-2619
334-580-2100

Jefferson State Community College
2601 Carson Rd, Birmingham AL 35215-3098
205-853-1200

Lurleen B. Wallace Community College
PO Box 1418, Andalusia AL 36420-1418
Judy Hall, Director of Student Services
334-222-6591 ext. 2271

The Robert B Adams/LabCorp CLS Program
543 S Hull St, Montgomery AL 36104-4609
334-263-5745

Samford University
800 Lakeshore Dr, Birmingham AL 35229-0002
205-726-3673

Shelton State Community College
9500 Old Greensboro Rd
Tuscaloosa AL 35405-8522
205-759-1541

Southern Union State Community College
1701 Lafayette Pkwy, Opelika AL 36801-3113
334-745-6437

South University
5355 Vaughn Rd, Montgomery AL 36116-1120
334-395-8800

Trenholm State Technical College
Trenholm Campus
1225 Air Base Blvd, Montgomery AL 36108-3199
Dr. Anthony Molina, President
334-420-4200 Fax: 334-420-4206
Website: www.trenholmtech.cc.al.us
E-mail: molinaa@trenholmtech.cc.al.us

Troy University
Troy AL 36082-0001
Jim Hutto, Dean of Enrollment Management
334-670-3175

Tuskegee University
Tuskegee Institute AL 36088
334-727-8011

University of Alabama
Box 870118, Tuscaloosa AL 35487
Dr. Lisa B. Harris, Director of Admissions
205-348-5666

University of Alabama at Birmingham
Univ Sta, Birmingham AL 35294-0001
205-934-4011

University of Alabama Hospital
619 19th St S, Birmingham AL 35249-0001
205-934-5490

University of Alabama in Huntsville
PO Box 1247, Huntsville AL 35899-0001
Nikki Willis, Assoc. Director for Recruiting Program and Events
1-800-UAH-CALL Fax: 256-824-6073
Website: www.uah.edu
E-mail: willisn@uah.edu

University of Montevallo
Station 6030, Montevallo AL 35115
205-665-6030

University of South Alabama
307 University Blvd N, Mobile AL 36688-3053
Melissa Haab, Director of Admissions
251-460-6141 Fax: 251-460-7876
Website: www.southalabama.edu
E-mail: admiss@usouthal.edu

Wallace State Community College - Hanceville
PO Box 2000, Hanceville AL 35077-2000
256-352-8000

ALASKA

University of Alaska Anchorage
PO Box 141629, Anchorage AK 99514-1629
Cecile Mitchell, Director of Enrollment Services
907-786-1480 Fax: 907-786-4888
Website: www.uaa.alaska.edu/
E-mail: enroll@uaa.alaska.edu

University of Alaska Southeast
11120 Glacier Hwy, Juneau AK 99801-8625
Paul Kraft, Dean of Students/Enrollment Management
907-796-6000

ARIZONA

Apollo College
630 W Southern Ave, Mesa AZ 85210-5005
480-831-6585 Fax: 480-827-0022

Apollo College
8503 N 27th Ave, Phoenix AZ 85051-4063
602-864-1571 Fax: 602-864-8207

Apollo College
2701 W Bethany Home Rd, Phoenix AZ 85017-1705
602-433-1333 Fax: 602-433-1414

Apollo College
3550 N Oracle Rd, Tucson AZ 85705
520-888-5885 Fax: 520-887-3005

ARIZONA SCHOOL OF HEALTH SCIENCES A.T. STILL UNIVERSITY
5850 E Still Circle, Mesa AZ 85206
Admissions Counselor
866-626-2878 or 480-219-6000 Fax: 480-219-6100
Website: www.atsu.edu
E-mail: info@ashs.edu

Arizona State University
PO Box 870112, Tempe AZ 85287-0112
480-965-9011

Bryman School
2250 W Peoria Ave Ste A100, Phoenix AZ 85029
602-274-4300

Carondelet Saint Marys Hospital
1601 W Saint Marys Rd, Tucson AZ 85745-2623
520-622-5833

GateWay Community College
108 N 40th St, Phoenix AZ 85034-1795
Cathy Gibson, Director of Admissions & Records
602-286-8052

International Institute of the Americas
925 S Gilbert Rd Ste 201, Mesa AZ 85204-4440
Todd Olehausen, Director
480-545-8755 Fax: 480-926-1371
Website: www.iia.edu
E-mail: tolehausen@iia.edu

International Institute of the Americas
6049 N 43rd Ave, Phoenix AZ 85019-1600
John Pechota, Director of Admissions
602-242-6265 Fax: 602-589-1353
Website: www.iia.edu
E-mail: jpechota@iia.edu

International Institute of the Americas
5441 E 22nd St, Tucson AZ 85710
Leigh Anne Pechota, Director
520-748-9799 Fax: 520-748-9355
Website: www.iia.edu
E-mail: lpechota@iia.edu

Long Technical College
Phoenix Campus
13450 N Black Canyon Hwy Ste 104
Phoenix AZ 85029-6323
602-548-1955

Northern Arizona University
PO Box 4084, Flagstaff AZ 86011-0001
520-523-9011

Phoenix College
1202 W Thomas Rd, Phoenix AZ 85013-4234
602-264-2492

Pima Community College
4905 E Broadway Blvd, Tucson AZ 85709-1010
Wendy Kilgore, Ph.D., Director of Admissions
520-206-4500 Fax: 520-206-4790
Website: www.pima.edu
E-mail: infocenter@pima.edu

PIMA MEDICAL INSTITUTE
957 S Dobson Rd, Mesa AZ 85202-2903
Christopher Luebke, Director
480-644-0267 Fax: 480-649-5249
Website: www.pmi.edu
E-mail: asc@pmi.edu

Pima Medical Institute
3350 E Grant Rd, Tucson AZ 85716-2800
520-326-1600

University of Arizona
Tucson AZ 85721-0040
Paul Kohn, Director of Admissions
520-621-3237

University of Phoenix
4615 E Elwood St, Phoenix AZ 85040-1908
480-966-9577

Walter Boswell Memorial Hospital
10401 W Thunderbird Blvd, Sun City AZ 85351-3004
623-977-7211

ARKANSAS

Arkansas State University
PO Box 1630, State University AR 72467-1630
870-972-2100

Arkansas State University - Beebe
PO Box 1000, Beebe AR 72012-1000
501-882-6452

Arkansas Tech University
215 W O St, Russellville AR 72801-2222
479-968-0389

Arkansas Valley Technical Institute
PO Box 506, Ozark AR 72949-0506
479-667-2117

Black River Technical College
PO Box 468, Pocahontas AR 72455-0468
870-892-4565

Central Arkansas Radiation Therapy Institute
PO Box 55050, Little Rock AR 72215-5050
501-664-8573

Cotton Boll Technical Institute
PO Box 36, Burdette AR 72321-0036
Brenda Morris, Supervisor of Instruction
870-763-1486

Harding University
900 E Center Ave, Searcy AR 72149
501-279-4000

National Park Community College
101 College Dr
Hot Springs National Park AR 71913-9173
501-760-4222

North Arkansas College
1515 Pioneer Ridge Dr, Harrison AR 72601
870-743-3000

Northwest Arkansas Community College
1 College Dr, Bentonville AR 72712-5091
479-636-9222

Northwest Technical Institute
709 S Old Missouri Rd, Springdale AR 72764
Charles L. Kelley, President
479-751-8824 Fax: 479-751-7780
Website: www.nti.tec.ar.us
E-mail: info@nit.tec.ar.us

Ouachita Baptist University
410 Ouachita St, Arkadelphia AR 71998-0001
David Goodman, Director of Admissions
870-245-5110

Phillips Community College of the University of Arkansas
PO Box 785, Helena AR 72342-0785
Dr. Steven Murray, Chancellor
Lynn Boone, Vice Chancellor for Student Services / Registrar
870-338-6474 Fax: 870-338-7542
Website: www.pccua.edu
E-mail: lboone@pccua.edu

Pulaski Technical College
3000 W Scenic Dr, North Little Rock AR 72118-3347
Clark Atkins, Director of Admissions
501-771-1000

St. Vincent Infirmary Medical Center
2 Saint Vincent Cir, Little Rock AR 72205-5402
501-660-3910

South Arkansas Community College
PO Box 7010, El Dorado AR 71731-7010
870-862-8131

University of Arkansas at Fayetteville
1 University of Arkansas, Fayetteville AR 72701-1201
479-575-2000

University of Arkansas at Fort Smith
PO Box 3649, Fort Smith AR 72913-3649
479-788-7000

University of Arkansas at Little Rock
2801 S University Ave, Little Rock AR 72204-1000
501-569-3000

University of Arkansas at Pine Bluff
1200 University Dr, Pine Bluff AR 71601-2799
870-543-8000

University of Arkansas Community College at Hope
PO Box 140, Hope AR 71802-0140
Laura Massey, Health Professions Division Chair
870-777-5722 Fax: 870-722-6630
Website: www.uacch.edu
E-mail: lmassey@uacch.edu

University of Central Arkansas
201 Donaghey Ave, Conway AR 72035-5003
501-450-5000

CALIFORNIA

American Career College
4021 Rosewood Ave, Los Angeles CA 90004-6818
Rita Totten, Campus Director
323-383-2862

American College of Health Professions
700 E Redlands Blvd #U227
Redlands CA 92373-6109
Admissions
909-307-6022

AMERICAN COLLEGE OF MEDICAL TECHNOLOGY
555 W Redondo Beach Blvd #100
Gardena CA 90248
Scott Jacobus, Contact
310-324-1000 Fax: 310-515-3944
Website: www.acmt.ac
E-mail: info@acmt.ac

American River College
4700 College Oak Dr, Sacramento CA 95841-4286
916-484-8011

Associated Technical College
1670 Wilshire Blvd, Los Angeles CA 90017-1690
Samuel Romano, Director of Admissions
213-353-1845 Fax: 213-413-4864
Website: www.associatedtechcollege.com
E-mail: decatc@earthlink.net

Bakersfield College
1801 Panorama Dr, Bakersfield CA 93305-1299
661-395-4301

Butte College
3536 Butte Campus Dr, Oroville CA 95965-8399
Carole Gish, Director of Admissions
530-895-2511 Fax: 530-879-4313
Website: www.butte.edu
E-mail: admissions@butte.edu

Cabrillo College
6500 Soquel Dr, Aptos CA 95003-3194
831-479-6100

CALIFORNIA COLLEGE SAN DIEGO
2820 Camino Del Rio S # 300, San Diego CA 92108
Randy Wolford, Director of Admissions
619-295-5785 Fax: 619-295-5762
Website: www.cc-sd.edu
E-mail: rwolford@cc-sd.edu

CALIFORNIA HEALING ARTS COLLEGE
12217 Santa Monica Blvd, Los Angeles CA 90025
310-826-7622 Fax: 310-826-4913
Website: www.chac.edu

California Polytechnic State University
San Luis Obispo CA 93407
805-756-1111

California State Polytechnic University
3801 W Temple Ave, Pomona CA 91768-2557
909-869-2000

California State University-Chico
Chico CA 95929-0001
530-898-6116

California State University-Dominguez Hills
1000 E Victoria St, Carson CA 90747-0001
310-243-3300

California State University-East Bay
25800 Carlos Bee Blvd, Hayward CA 94542-3001
510-885-3000

California State University-Fresno
Fresno CA 93740-0001
559-278-4240

California State University-Fullerton
PO Box 34080
Fullerton CA 92634
714-278-2011

California State University-Long Beach
1250 N Bellflower Blvd, Long Beach CA 90840-0006
562-985-4111

California State University-Los Angeles
5151 State University Dr, Los Angeles CA 90032
323-343-3000

California State University-Northridge
18111 Nordhoff St, Northridge CA 91330-0001
818-677-1200

California State University-Sacramento
6000 J St, Sacramento CA 95819-2605
916-278-6011

California State University-San Bernadino
5500 University Pkwy
San Bernardino CA 92407-2393
Olivia Rosas, Director of Admissions
909-537-5188 Fax: 909-537-7034
Website: www.csusb.edu
E-mail: orosas@csusb.edu

Canada College
4200 Farm Hill Blvd, Redwood City CA 94061-1099
Marilyn McBride, Dean

Center of Employment Training
701 Vine St, San Jose CA 95110
Luis Aguilar, Contact
408-287-7924

Cerritos College
11110 Alondra Blvd, Norwalk CA 90650-6296
562-860-2451

Chabot College
25555 Hesperian Blvd, Hayward CA 94545-2400
Judy Young, Director of Admissions
510-723-6600 Fax: 510-723-7510
Website: www.chabotcollege.edu
E-mail: ccarcom@clpccd.cc.ca.us

Chaffey College
5885 Haven Ave, Alta Loma CA 91737-9400
909-941-2358

Chapman University
One University Drive, Orange CA 92866-1099
Michael Drummy, Assistant Vice President for Enrollment
Services and Chief Admission Officer
714-997-6411 or 888-CUAPPLY Fax: 714-997-6713
Website: www.chapman.edu
E-mail: admit@chapman.edu

Charles R. Drew University of Medicine & Science
1621 E 120th St, Los Angeles CA 90059
323-563-4800

Citrus College
1000 W Foothill Blvd, Glendora CA 91741-1885
626-963-0323

City College of San Francisco
50 Phelan Ave, San Francisco CA 94112-1821
415-239-3000

College of Alameda
555 Atlantic Ave, Alameda CA 94501-2109
510-522-7221

COLLEGE OF INFORMATION TECHNOLOGY
2701 E Chapman Ave Ste 101, Fullerton CA 92831
Mohammad Qamaruddin, Director
714-879-5100 Fax: 714-879-2272
Website: www.collegeofit.com
E-mail: mqamar@collegeofit.com

College of Marin
835 College Ave, Kentfield CA 94904-2590
415-457-8811

College of San Mateo
1700 W Hillsdale Blvd, San Mateo CA 94402-3784
650-574-6161

College of the Desert
43500 Monterey Ave, Palm Desert CA 92260-9399
760-346-8041

Concorde Career College
12412 Victory Blvd, North Hollywood CA 91606-3134
Guy Lopatin, Director of Admissions
818-766-8151

Concorde Career College
201 E Airport Dr #A, San Bernardino CA 92408
Rosie Brownlee, Director of Admissions
909-884-8891

Concorde Career Institute
12951 Euclid St Ste 101
Garden Grove CA 92840-9201
Craig McVey, Director of Admissions
714-703-1900

Contra Costa College
2600 Mission Bell Dr, San Pablo CA 94806-3195
510-235-7800

Cosumnes River College
8401 Center Pkwy, Sacramento CA 95823-5799
916-691-7344

Crafton Hills College
11711 Sand Canyon Rd, Yucaipa CA 92399-1799
Dr. Luis S. Gomez, President
909-389-3200

Cypress College
9200 Valley View St, Cypress CA 90630-5897
714-484-7000

DeAnza College
21250 Stevens Creek Blvd
Cupertino CA 95014-5793
408-864-5678

Diablo Valley College
321 Golf Club Rd, Pleasant Hill CA 94523-1544
925-685-1230

Dominican University of California
50 Acacia Ave, San Rafael CA 94901-2298
Office of Admissions
888-323-6762 Fax: 415-485-3214
Website: www.dominican.edu
E-mail: enroll@dominican.edu

East Los Angeles College
1301 Avenida Cesar Chavez
Monterey Park CA 91754-6001
323-265-8650

East Los Angeles Occupational Center
2100 Marengo St, Los Angeles CA 90033-1321
323-223-1283

Eisenhower Memorial Hospital
39000 Bob Hope Dr, Rancho Mirage CA 92270-3221
760-340-3911

El Camino College
16007 Crenshaw Blvd, Torrance CA 90506-0002
310-660-3670

EMPEROR'S COLLEGE OF TRADITIONAL ORIENTAL MEDICINE
1807 Wilshire Blvd Ste B
Santa Monica CA 90403-5678
Mary Good, Director of Admissions
310-453-8300 Fax: 310-829-3838
Website: www.emperors.edu
E-mail: mary@emperors.edu

Everest College
2215 W Mission Rd, Alhambra CA 91803-1310
626-979-4970

Everest College
511 N Brookhurst St Ste 300
Anaheim CA 92801-5229
714-953-6500

Everest College
22336 Main St, Hayward CA 94541
H. Albizo, President
510-582-9500

Everest College
3460 Wilshire Blvd Ste 500
Los Angeles CA 90010-2223
213-388-9950

Everest College
18040 Sherman Way #400, Reseda CA 91335-4631
Lani Townsend, School President
818-774-0550

Everest College
217 Club Center Dr Ste A, San Bernardino CA 92408
909-777-3300

Everest College
814 Mission St Ste 500
San Francisco CA 94103-3038
415-777-2500

Everest College
1245 S Winchester Blvd #102, San Jose CA 95128
408-246-4171

Everst College
1045 W Redondo Beach Blvd #275
Gardena CA 90247
310-527-7105

FIVE BRANCHES INSTITUTE
3031 Tisch Way Ste 605, San Jose CA 95128
Eleonor Mendelson, Director of Admissions
408-260-0208 Fax: 408-261-3166
Website: www.fivebranches.edu
E-mail: sicampus@fivebrances.edu

FIVE BRANCHES INSTITUTE
College of Traditional Chinese Medicine
200 7th Ave, Santa Cruz CA 95062-4668
Eleonor Mendelson, Admissions
831-476-9424 Fax: 831-476-8928
Website: www.fivebranches.edu
E-mail: tcm@fivebranches.edu

Fremont College
18000 Studebaker Rd Suite 900, Cerritos CA 90703
Mark Buch, President & COO
562-809-5100 Fax: 562-809-7100
Website: www.fremont.edu
E-mail: senon.lee@fremont.edu

FRESNO CITY COLLEGE
1101 E University Ave, Fresno CA 93741-0002
Dayann Dietrich, Contact
559-442-8241 Fax: 559-237-4232
Website: www.fresnocitycollege.com
E-mail: fcc.admissions@scccd.com

Grossmont College
8800 Grossmont College Dr, El Cajon CA 92020-1798
619-644-7000

Haciende LaPuente Valley Adult Education
14101 Nelson Ave, La Puente CA 91746
626-934-2800

Health Staff Training Institute
1505 E 17th St Ste 122, Santa Ana CA 92705-8520
714-543-9828

Loma Linda University
Loma Linda CA 92350-0001
Richard Weismeyer, Director
800-422-4558

Los Angeles City College
855 N Vermont Ave, Los Angeles CA 90029-3588
323-953-4000

Los Angeles County College of Nursing and Allied Health
1200 N State St, Los Angeles CA 90033-1029
323-226-4911

Los Angeles Valley College
5800 Fulton Ave, Van Nuys CA 91401-4062
818-947-2600

Loyola Marymount University
7900 Loyola Blvd, Los Angeles CA 90045-2699
310-338-2700

Maric College
9055 Balboa Ave, San Diego CA 92123
Geraldine Rorrison, Director of Admissions
858-279-4500 Fax: 858-279-4885
Website: www.mariccollege.edu
E-mail: grorrison@mariccollege.edu

MARIC COLLEGE
722 W March Ln, Stockton CA 95207-6216
John Bermudez, Director of Admissions
209-462-8777 Fax: 209-462-3219
Website: www.mariccollege.edu
E-mail: jbermudez@mariccollege.edu

Merced College
3600 M St, Merced CA 95348-2898
209-384-6000

Merritt College
12500 Campus Dr, Oakland CA 94619-3196
510-531-4911

Modesto Junior College
435 College Ave, Modesto CA 95350-5800
209-575-6498

Monterey Peninsula College
980 Fremont Ave, Monterey CA 93940-4799
831-645-1376

Moorpark College
7075 Campus Rd, Moorpark CA 93021-1695
805-378-1400

Mt. San Antonio College
1100 N Grand Ave, Walnut CA 91789-1399
909-594-5611

MTI BUSINESS COLLEGE OF STOCKTON
6006 N El Dorado St, Stockton CA 95207-4349
Steven Brenner, Director
888-302-2009 Fax: 209-474-8705
Website: www.mtistockton.com
E-mail: mtistockton@comcast.net
Established 1968. Accredited: ACCSCT. Family owned/operated 36 years.

MTI College
5221 Madison Ave, Sacramento CA 95841-3003
Marije Miller, Director of Admissions
916-339-1500 Fax: 916-339-0305
Website: www.mticollege.edu
E-mail: mmiller@mticollege.edu

MUELLER COLLEGE OF HOLISTIC STUDIES
4607 Park Blvd, San Diego CA 92116
David Taylor, Registrar
619-291-9811 Fax: 619-543-1113
Website: www.mueller.edu
E-mail: info@mueller.edu

Napa State Hospital
2100 Napa Vallejo Hwy, Napa CA 94558-6293
707-253-5428

Napa Valley College
2277 Napa Vallejo Hwy, Napa CA 94558-6236
707-253-3076

Notre Dame de Namur University
1500 Ralston Ave, Belmont CA 94002-1997
Martin Bednarek, Director of Admissions
800-263-0545

Ohlone College
PO Box 3909, Fremont CA 94539-0390
510-659-6000

Olive View/UCLA Medical Centers
14445 Olive View Dr, Sylmar CA 91342-1438
818-364-4224

Orange Coast College
PO Box 5005, Costa Mesa CA 92628-5005
Kristin Clark, Director of Admissions
714-432-5773 Fax: 714-432-5736
Website: www.orangecoastcollege.edu
E-mail: kclark@cccd.edu

Oxnard College
4000 S Rose Ave, Oxnard CA 93033-6699
805-986-5800

PACIFIC COLLEGE OF ORIENTAL MEDICINE
7445 Mission Valley Rd #105, San Diego CA 92108
619-574-6909 Fax: 619-574-6641
Website: www.pacificcollege.edu
E-mail: admissions-sd@pacificcollege.edu

Palomar College
1140 W Mission Rd, San Marcos CA 92069-1415
760-744-1150

Pasadena City College
1570 E Colorado Blvd, Pasadena CA 91106-2041
626-585-7123

Patton State Hospital
3102 E Highland Ave, Patton CA 92369
909-425-7297

Pepperdine University
24255 Pacific Coast Hwy, Malibu CA 90263-0002
310-456-4000

Redwoods Community College
7351 Tompkins Hill Rd, Eureka CA 95501-9300
707-476-4100

Sacramento City College
3835 Freeport Blvd, Sacramento CA 95822-1386
916-558-2111

Sacramento Medical Foundation Blood Bank
1625 Stockton Blvd, Sacramento CA 95816-7053
916-456-1500

ST. FRANCIS CAREER COLLEGE
3630 E Imperial Hwy, Lynwood CA 90262-2636
Petra Arredondo-Rios, Director of Enrollment
310-603-1830 Fax: 310-763-3987
E-mail: marilynoverby@dochs.org

St. Joseph Hospital
1100 Stewart Dr, Orange CA 92868
714-771-8111

SAMRA UNIVERSITY OF ORIENTAL MEDICINE
3000 S Robertson Blvd 4 Fl
Los Angeles CA 90034-3158
Simon Song, Director of Operations
310-202-6444 Fax: 310-202-6007
Website: www.samra.edu
E-mail: admissions@samra.edu

San Bernardino Valley College
701 S Mount Vernon Ave
San Bernardino CA 92410-2798
Kay Ragan, Ed.D., Director of Admissions
909-888-6511 Fax: 909-889-4988
Website: www.valleycollege.edu
E-mail: kragan@sbccd.cc.ca.us

San Diego Mesa College
7250 Mesa College Dr, San Diego CA 92111-4996
858-627-2600

San Diego State University
5500 Campanile Dr, San Diego CA 92182-0002
619-594-5200

San Francisco State University
1600 Holloway Ave, San Francisco CA 94132-1722
415-338-1111

San Joaquin Valley College
201 New Stine Rd, Bakersfield CA 93309-2659
Jaime Delgado, Enrollment Services Director
661-834-1026 Fax: 559-651-4864
Website: www.sjvc.edu
E-mail: jaime.delgado@sjvc.edu

San Joaquin Valley College
295 E Sierra Ave, Fresno CA 93710-3616
Nora Twarynski, Enrollment Services Director
559-448-8282 Fax: 559-651-4864
Website: www.sjvc.edu
E-mail: nora.twarynski@sjvc.edu

San Joaquin Valley College
1700 McHenry Village Way Suite 6
Modesto CA 95350
Joseph Holt, Director of Admissions
209-527-7582 Fax: 559-651-4864
Website: www.sjvc.edu
E-mail: josephh@sjvc.edu

San Joaquin Valley College
11050 Olson Dr, Rancho Cordova CA 95670
Joseph Holt, Director of Admissions
559-651-2500 Fax: 559-651-4864
Website: www.sjvc.edu
E-mail: joseph.holt@sjvc.edu

San Joaquin Valley College
8400 W Mineral King Ave, Visalia CA 93291-9283
Susie Topjian, Enrollment Services Director
559-651-2500 Fax: 559-651-4864
Website: www.sjvc.edu
E-mail: susiet@sjvc.edu

San Jose City College
2100 Moorpark Ave, San Jose CA 95128-2797
408-298-2181

San Jose State University
1 Washington Sq, San Jose CA 95192-0001
408-924-1000

Santa Ana College
1530 W 17th St, Santa Ana CA 92706-3398
714-564-6000

Santa Barbara City College
721 Cliff Dr, Santa Barbara CA 93109-2394
Patricia E. Canning, Coordinator, School Relations
805-965-0581 ext. 2201

Santa Monica College
1900 Pico Blvd, Santa Monica CA 90405-1644
310-434-4000

Santa Rosa Junior College
1501 Mendocino Ave, Santa Rosa CA 95401-4395
Renee LoPilato, Dean of Admissions
707-527-4011

Simi Valley Adult Education
1880 Blackstock Ave, Simi Valley CA 93065
805-579-6200

Simpson University
2211 College View Dr, Redding CA 96003-8606
Jim Herberger, Director of Admissions
888-9-SIMPSON Fax: 530-226-4861
Website: www.simpsonuniversity.edu
E-mail: admissions@simpsonuniversity.edu
See listing under "Universities"

Skyline College
3300 College Dr, San Bruno CA 94066-1698
650-738-4100

Sonoma State University
1801 E Cotati Ave, Rohnert Park CA 94928-3609
Louis T. Levy, Senior Director Enrollment Services
707-664-2880

SOUTH BAYLO UNIVERSITY
School of Acupuncture & Oriental Medicine
1126 N Brookhurst St, Anaheim CA 92801
Seung W. Lee, Director of Admissions
714-533-1495 Fax: 714-533-6040
Website: www.southbaylo.edu
E-mail: swl@southbaylo.edu

Southwestern College
900 Otay Lakes Rd, Chula Vista CA 91910-7297
619-421-6700

Stanford University
520 Lasuen Mall Union 232, Stanford CA 94305-3005
650-723-2300

Taft College
29 Emmons Park Dr, Taft CA 93268-2317
661-763-7700

Uni Health America/Glendale Memorial Hospital
1420 S Central Ave, Glendale CA 91204-2508
818-502-2334

University of California
110 Sproul Hall, Berkeley CA 94720-5804
510-642-6000

University of California
1 Shields Ave, Davis CA 95616
530-752-1011

University of California
Irvine CA 92697-0001
949-824-5011

University of California
Parnassus and 3rd Ave
San Francisco CA 94143-0001
415-476-9000

University of California Los Angeles
Center for the Health Sciences
10833 Le Conte Ave, Los Angeles CA 90095-3075
310-825-5654

University of California Medical Center
200 W Arbor Dr #H-910C, San Diego CA 92103-1911
619-543-6654

University of Redlands
PO Box 3080, Redlands CA 92373-0999
909-793-2121

University of Southern California
Univ Park, Los Angeles CA 90089-0001
213-740-2311

University of the Pacific
3601 Pacific Ave, Stockton CA 95211-0197
209-946-2011

∴ Veterans Affairs Medical Center
3350 La Jolla Village Dr, San Diego CA 92161-0002
858-552-8585

· Victor Valley Community College
18422 Bear Valley Rd, Victorville CA 92395-5849
760-245-4271

· Western Career College
2157 Country Hills Dr, Antioch CA 94509-7435
Dr. Tim Gienapp, Executive Director
925-522-7777
Website: www.westerncollege.edu

· Western Career College
7301 Greenback Ln Bldg A, Citrus Heights CA 95621
Jim Murphy, Executive Director
916-722-8200 Fax: 916-722-6883
Website: www.westerncollege.edu

· Western Career College
6001 Shellmound St, Suite 145, Emeryville CA 94608
Dr. Paul Dancy, Contact
510-601-0133 Fax: 510-601-0793
Website: www.westerncollege.edu

· Western Career College
380 Civic Dr Ste 300, Pleasant Hill CA 94523-1984
LaShawn Wells, Executive Director
925-609-6650 Fax: 926-609-6666
Website: www.westerncollege.edu

· Western Career College
8909 Folsom Blvd, Sacramento CA 95826-3203
Sue Smith, Executive Director
916-361-5100 Fax: 916-361-6666
Website: www.westerncollege.edu

· Western Career College
6201 San Ignacio Ave, San Jose CA 95119
Steve Ashab, Executive Director
408-360-0840 Fax: 408-360-0848
Website: www.westerncollege.edu

· Western Career College
15555 E 14th St Ste 500, San Leandro CA 94578
Dawn Matthews, Executive Director
510-276-3888 Fax: 510-276-3653
Website: www.westerncollege.edu

· Western Career College
1313 W Robinhood Dr Ste B, Stockton CA 95207
Dave Semrau, Executive Director
209-956-1240 Fax: 209-956-1244
Website: www.westerncollege.edu

Western University of Health Sciences
College of Allied Health Professions
309 E 2nd St, Pomona CA 91766-1854
Kathryn Ford, Director
909-469-5335

· West Los Angeles College
4800 Freshman Dr, Culver City CA 90230-3519
310-287-4200

∴ West Los Angeles VA Medical Center
Wilshire & Sawtelle Blvds, Los Angeles CA 90073
310-824-3132

· West Valley College
14000 Fruitvale Ave, Saratoga CA 95070-5697
408-867-2200

Whittier College
PO Box 634, Whittier CA 90608-0634
Kieron Miller, Director of Admissions
562-907-4200 Fax: 562-907-4870
Website: www.whittier.edu
E-mail: kmiller@whittier.edu

· Yuba College
2088 N Beale Rd, Marysville CA 95901-7699
Connie Elder, Registrar
530-741-6989

COLORADO

Adams State College
Alamosa CO 81102
Matt Gallegos, Director of Admissions
800-824-6494

· Aims Community College
PO Box 69, Greeley CO 80632-0069
970-330-8008

· Arapahoe Community College
5900 S Sante Fe Dr, Littleton CO 80160
Linda Comeaux, Contact
303-797-5997

· Bel-Rea Institute of Animal Technology
1681 S Dayton St, Denver CO 80247-3048
Paulette Kaufman, Administrator
303-751-8700 Fax: 303-751-9969
Website: www.bel-rea.com
E-mail: admissions@bel-rea.com

· Blair College
1815 Jet Wing Dr, Colorado Springs CO 80916-2300
719-638-6580

∴ **THE COLORADO CENTER FOR MEDICAL LABORATORY SCIENCE**
1719 E 19th Ave, Denver CO 80218
Karen Myers, Director
303-839-6485 Fax: 303-869-1720
Website: www.medlabed.org
E-mail: medlabed@coloradohealth.org

· Colorado Northwestern Community College
500 Kennedy Dr, Rangely CO 81648-3502
Tresa England, Director of Student Services
800-562-1105 Fax: 970-675-3343
Website: www.cncc.edu
E-mail: tresa.england@cncc.edu

COLORADO SCHOOL OF TRADITIONAL CHINESE MEDICINE
1441 York St Ste 202, Denver CO 80206
David DiBrigida, Administrative Director
303-329-6355 Fax: 303-388-8165
Website: www.cstcm.edu
E-mail: admin@cstcm.edu

Colorado State University
1062 Campus Delivery, Fort Collins CO 80523
970-491-1101

∴ Columbia HealthOne
501 E Hampden, Englewood CO 80113
303-788-6484

· Community College of Denver
PO Box 173363, Denver CO 80217-3363
303-556-2600

: Concorde Career College
111 N Havana St, Aurora CO 80010-4314
Kevin McNeil, Director of Admissions
303-861-1151

Denver Seminary
6399 S Santa Fe Dr, Littleton CO 80120
Robert Jones, VP Student Services
303-762-6982 Fax: 303-783-3122
Website: denverseminary.edu
E-mail: robert.jones@denverseminary.edu

: Emily Griffith Opportunity School
1250 Welton St, Denver CO 80204-2124
720-423-4700

: Everest College
Aurora Campus
14280 E Jewell Ave, Aurora CO 80012-5692
John Heckman, Director of Admissions
303-367-2757 Fax: 303-745-6245
Website: www.cci.edu

∴ HealthONE North Suburban Medical Center
9191 Grant St, Thornton CO 80229-4361
303-451-7800

: Heritage College
12 Lakeside Ln, Denver CO 80212-7413
Jennifer Sprague, Director
303-477-7240 Fax: 303-477-7276
Website: www.heritage-education.com
E-mail: info@heritage-education.com
See listing under "Career Schools"

: IntelliTec College
772 Horizon Dr, Grand Junction CO 81506-3907
Jennifer Daniels, Contact
970-245-8101 Fax: 970-243-8074
Website: www.intelliteccollege.edu
E-mail: admgj@intelliteccollege.edu

: IntelliTec College
3673 Parker Blvd Ste 250, Pueblo CO 81008
Crystal Barajas, Director of Admissions
719-542-3181 Fax: 719-242-0068
Website: www.intelliteccollege.edu
E-mail: admpbl@intelliteccollege.edu

: Kaplan College
500 E 84th Ave Suite W200
Thornton CO 80229-5316
Michael Como, Director of Admissions
800-848-0550 Fax: 303-295-0102
Website: www.kaplancollege.com
E-mail: admissions-045@kaplan.edu

Mesa State College
1100 North Ave, Grand Junction CO 81501
970-248-1020

· Morgan Community College
17800 County Road 20, Fort Morgan CO 80701
Judy Beckmann, Director of Student Support
800-622-0216

Naropa University
2130 Arapahoe Ave, Boulder CO 80302-6697
303-546-3572

: Pickens Technical Center
500 Airport Blvd, Aurora CO 80011-9307
303-344-4910

· Pikes Peak Community College
5675 S Academy Blvd
Colorado Springs CO 80906-5498
719-576-7711

: **PIMA MEDICAL INSTITUTE**
1701 W 72nd Ave Ste 130, Denver CO 80221-2727
Sue Anderson, Director
303-426-1800 Fax: 303-430-4048
Website: www.pimamedical.com
E-mail: denverpima@aol.com

· Pueblo Community College
900 W Orman Ave, Pueblo CO 81004-1499
719-549-3200

· Red Rocks Community College
13300 W 6th Ave, Lakewood CO 80228-1255
303-988-6160

Regis University
3333 Regis Blvd, Denver CO 80221-1099
303-458-4900

∴ Tri-County Health Nutrition Services
7000 E Blleview Ave #301
Englewood CO 80111-1628
303-220-9200

University of Colorado
Boulder CO 80309-0001
303-492-1411

University of Colorado at Denver and Health Sciences Center
Health Sciences Program
4200 E 9th Ave Box C245, Denver CO 80262
Phoebe Lindsey Barton, Ph.D., Director

University of Northern Colorado
Greeley CO 80639
Vincent Scalia, Dean / Health & Human Sciences
970-351-2877

· Westwood College - Denver North
7350 Broadway, Denver CO 80221-3610
303-426-7000

CONNECTICUT

: Branford Hall Career Institute
1 Summit Pl, Branford CT 06405
800-959-7599
Website: www.branfordhall.com

: Branford Hall Career Institute
35 N Main St, Southington CT 06489-2577
860-276-0600
Website: www.branfordhall.com

: Branford Hall Career Institute
995 Day Hill Rd, Windsor CT 06095-1722
860-683-4900
Website: www.branfordhall.com

· Briarwood College
2279 Mount Vernon Rd, Southington CT 06489-1057
860-628-4751

· Capital Community College
950 Main St, Hartford CT 06103-1211
860-906-5000

: Connecticut Center for Massage Therapy
1154 Poquonnock Rd, Groton CT 06340
Susan Scoboria, Contact
877-295-2268 Fax: 860-446-9410
Website: www.ccmt.edu
E-mail: info@ccmt.edu

: Connecticut Center for Massage Therapy
75 Kitts Ln, Newington CT 06111-3954
Wendy Dorsey, Director of Admissions
877-282-2268 Fax: 860-667-4566
Website: www.ccmt.edu
E-mail: info@ccmt.edu

: Connecticut Center for Massage Therapy
25 Sylvan Rd S, Westport CT 06880-4619
Glen Vigorito, Contact
877-292-2268 Fax: 203-221-0144
Website: www.ccmt.edu
E-mail: info@ccmt.edu

∴ Connecticut Childrens Medical Center
282 Washington St, Hartford CT 06106
Rich Janis, Team Leader
860-545-8514

∴ Connecticut Childrens Medical Center
170 Ridge Rd, Wethersfield CT 06109-1044
860-545-8551

Fairfield University
1073 N Benson Rd, Fairfield CT 06824-5171
203-254-4000

: Fox Institute of Business
99 South St, West Hartford CT 06110-1922
860-947-2299

· Gateway Community College
60 Sargent Dr, New Haven CT 06511-5918
203-789-7071

· Goodwin College
745 Burnside Ave, East Hartford CT 06108-2777
Daniel Noonan, Director of Enrollment and Student Services
860-528-4111

· Housatonic Community College
900 Lafayette Blvd, Bridgeport CT 06604
203-332-5000

· Manchester Community College
PO Box 1046, Manchester CT 06045-1046
860-647-6000

· Middlesex Community College
100 Training Hill Rd, Middletown CT 06457-4889
Mensimah Shabazz, Director of Admissions
860-343-5800 Fax: 860-344-3055
Website: www.mxcc.commnet.edu
E-mail: mshabazz@mxcc.commnet.edu

· Naugatuck Valley Community College
750 Chase Pkwy, Waterbury CT 06708-3089
203-575-8040

· Northwestern Connecticut Community-Technical College
2 Park Pl, Winsted CT 06098-1706
860-738-6300

: Porter and Chester Institute
138 Weymouth Rd, Enfield CT 06082
860-741-2561

: Porter and Chester Institute
670 Lordship Blvd, Stratford CT 06615-7158
Mark Breslin, Director of Admissions
203-375-4463

: Porter and Chester Institute
320 Sylvan Lake Rd, Watertown CT 06779-1459
Jack Burke, Executive Director
860-274-9294

: Porter and Chester Institute
125 Silas Deane Hwy, Wethersfield CT 06109-1255
860-529-2519

Prince Regional Vocational Technical School
500 Brookfield St, Hartford CT 06106
860-246-8594

Quinebaug Valley Community College
742 Upper Maple St, Danielson CT 06239-1440
860-774-1160

Quinnipiac University
275 Mount Carmel Ave, Hamden CT 06518-1905
Joan Isaac Mohr, VP & Dean of Admissions
203-582-8600

Ridley-Lowell Business & Technical Inst
PO Box 652, New London CT 06320-0652
Kimberly L. Mayer, Director
860-443-7441

Sacred Heart University
5151 Park Ave, Fairfield CT 06825-1023
203-371-7999

St. Joseph College
1678 Asylum Ave, West Hartford CT 06117-2791
860-232-4571

St. Mary's Hospital
56 Franklin St, Waterbury CT 06706-1281
203-574-6300

St. Vincent's College
2800 Main St, Bridgeport CT 06606-4292
Director of Admissions
203-576-5513

Southern Connecticut State University
501 Crescent St, New Haven CT 06515-1355
203-392-5200

Stamford Hospital
PO Box 9317, Stamford CT 06904-9317
Dorothy Saia, MA, RT, Program Director
203-276-7877

Stone Academy
1315 Dixwell Ave, Hamden CT 06514-4155
Jeanna LaBella, Director of Admissions
203-288-7474

Tunxis Community College
271 Scott Swamp Rd, Farmington CT 06032-3187
860-677-7701

University of Bridgeport
126 Park Ave, Bridgeport CT 06604-5620
Barbara L. Maryak, Dean of Admissions
203-576-4552

University of Connecticut
Storrs CT 06269-0001
860-486-2000

University of Hartford
200 Bloomfield Ave, West Hartford CT 06117-1599
860-768-4100

University of New Haven
300 Boston Post Rd, West Haven CT 06516
Director of Undergraduate Admissions
203-932-7319

Western Connecticut State University
181 White St, Danbury CT 06810-6826
203-837-8200

Windham Regional Vocational Technical School
210 Birch St, Willimantic CT 06226-2108
860-456-3789

Yale-New Haven Hospital
20 York St, New Haven CT 06504
203-785-5074

Yale University
38 Hillhouse Ave, New Haven CT 06511
203-432-4771

DELAWARE

Bayhealth Medical Center
640 S State St, Dover DE 19901-3530
302-674-7001

Christiana Care Health Services
PO Box 1668, Wilmington DE 19899-1668
302-428-2571

Delaware State University
1200 N DuPont Hwy, Dover DE 19901-2275
302-857-6060

Delaware Technical & Community College
PO Box 610, Georgetown DE 19947-0610
302-856-5400

Delaware Technical & Community College
333 N Shipley St, Wilmington DE 19801-2499
302-571-5474

University of Delaware
Newark DE 19711
302-831-2000

Wesley College
120 N State St, Dover DE 19901-3876
302-736-2300 Fax: 302-736-2301
Website: www.wesley.edu

Wilmington College
320 N DuPont Hwy, New Castle DE 19720-6491
302-328-9401

DISTRICT OF COLUMBIA

Gallaudet University
800 Florida Ave NE, Washington DC 20002-3695
Charity Reedy Hines, Director of Admissions
202-651-5750 Fax: 202-651-5744
Website: www.gallaudet.edu
E-mail: admissions.office@gallaudet.edu

Georgetown University
37th and O St NW, Washington DC 20057-0001
202-687-0100

George Washington University
2035 H St NW, Washington DC 20052-0002
202-994-1000

Howard University
2400 6th St NW, Washington DC 20059-0002
202-806-6100

University of the District of Columbia
4200 Connecticut Ave NW
Washington DC 20008-1174
LaVerne M. Hill-Flanagan, Director of Admissions
202-274-5100

FLORIDA

ACUPUNCTURE & MASSAGE COLLEGE
10506 N Kendall Dr, Miami FL 33176
Joe Calareso, Admissions Director
305-595-9500 Fax: 305-595-2622
Website: www.amcollege.edu
E-mail: admissions@amcollege.edu

ATLANTIC INSTITUTE OF ORIENTAL MEDICINE
100 E Broward Blvd Ste 100
Fort Lauderdale FL 33301-3510
Prof. Yan Cheng, Academic Dean
954-763-9840 Fax: 954-763-9844
Website: www.atom.edu
E-mail: dean@atom.edu

Barry University
11300 NE 2nd Ave, Miami Shores FL 33161-6695
800-695-2279

BAYFRONT MEDICAL CENTER
School of Medical Technology
701 6th St S, Saint Petersburg FL 33701-4891
727-893-6604 Fax: 727-893-6977
Website: www.bayfront.org
E-mail: maria.duynslager@bayfront.org

Bay Medical Center
615 N Bonita Ave, Panama City FL 32401
Sherry Tindall, Director of Education, Training, & Research
800-422-2418

Bethune-Cookman College
640 Dr Mary McLeod Bethune Blvd
Daytona Beach FL 32114-3099
Edwin Coffie, Director of Admissions
800-448-0228

Brevard Community College
1519 Clearlake Rd, Cocoa FL 32922-6597
321-632-1111

Broward Community College
225 E Las Olas Blvd, Fort Lauderdale FL 33301-2298
954-475-6500

Central Florida Community College
PO Box 1388, Ocala FL 34478-1388
352-854-2322

Central Florida Institute
30522 US Highway 19 N, Palm Harbor FL 34684
727-786-4707

Charlotte Technical Center
18150 Murdock Cir, Port Charlotte FL 33948
Carolyn Gorton, Assistant Principal
941-255-7500

City College
2000 W Commercial Blvd, Fort Lauderdale FL 33309
Mercedes Segal, Director of Admissions
954-492-5353 Fax: 954-491-1965
Website: www.citycollege.edu

COMPU-MED VOCATIONAL CAREERS
2900 W 12th Ave Ste 3, Hialeah FL 33012-4861
Mayra Rodriguez, President
305-888-9200 Fax: 305-888-3614
Website: www.compumedschool.com
E-mail: compumed44@aol.com

COMPU-MED VOCATIONAL CAREERS
9738 SW 24th St, Miami FL 33165-7513
Mayra Rodriguez, President
305-553-2898 Fax: 305-553-7423
Website: www.compumedschools.com
E-mail: compumed44@aol.com

Daytona Beach Community College
PO Box 2811, Daytona Beach FL 32120-2811
Tom LoBasso, Dean of Enrollment/Development
386-255-8131

D.G. Erwin Technical Center
2010 E Hillsborough Ave, Tampa FL 33610-8299
813-231-1800

Edison College
PO Box 60210, Fort Myers FL 33906-6210
Billee Silva, Director Student Development
239-489-9054

EVERGLADES UNIVERSITY (MAIN CAMPUS)
5002 T-Rex Ave Suite 100, Boca Raton FL 33431
Kristi Mollis, President
888-772-6077 Fax: 561-912-1191
Website: www.evergladesuniversity.edu
E-mail: admissions-boca@evergladesuniversity.edu
See listing under "Universities"

EVERGLADES UNIVERSITY
Orlando Campus (Branch Campus)
887 E Altamonte Dr, Altamonte Springs FL 32701
Linda Volz, Vice President
866-289-1078 Fax: 407-482-9801
Website: www.evergladesuniversity.edu
E-mail: admissions-orl@evergladesuniversity.edu
See listing under "Universities"

EVERGLADES UNIVERSITY
Sarasota Campus (Branch Campus)
6001 Lake Osprey Dr, Suite 110, Sarasota FL 34240
Brad Brewer, Vice President
866-907-2262 Fax: 941-907-6634
Website: www.evergladesuniversity.edu
E-mail: admissions-sar@evergladesuniversity.edu
See listing under "Universities"

First Coast Technical Institute
2980 Collins Ave, Saint Augustine FL 32084-1919
904-829-1010

Florida A&M University
Tallahassee FL 32307
850-599-3000

Florida Atlantic University
PO Box 3091, Boca Raton FL 33431-0991
800-299-4328

FLORIDA CAREER INSTITUTE
5925 Imperial Pkwy Ste 200, Mulberry FL 33860
863-646-1400
Website: www.floridacareerinstitute.com
E-mail: swadhwa@edaff.com

Florida Community College
North Campus
4501 Capper Rd, Jacksonville FL 32218-4436
904-766-6500

FLORIDA HOSPITAL COLLEGE OF HEALTH SCIENCES
671 Winyah Dr, Orlando FL 32803
Office of Enrollment Services
800-500-7747 or 407-303-8192 Fax: 407-303-5626
Website: www.fhchs.edu
E-mail: samantha.lopez@fhchs.edu or yvonne.l.williams@fhchs.edu

Established in 1992. Private. Coed. Accreditation. Commission on Colleges of the Southern Association of Colleges and Schools, 1866 Southern Lane, Decatur, GA 30033-4097. 404-679-4500. Tuition: $255 per credit hour (matriculation & program fees additional). Room only: $3,200 (2 trimesters). Enrollment: 635 full-time, 870 part-time. Faculty: 64. Degrees: BS, AS, and Certificates. Professional Programs: Diagnostic Medical Sonography, Health Sciences, Nuclear Medicine Technology, Nursing, Occupational Therapy Assistant, Pre-Professional Studies, Radiography. Professional programs are accredited by their respective accrediting bodies. The College provides state-of-the-art learning labs where students hone their skills before entering the clinical arena. Small class sizes allow instructors to know students on an individual basis. Graduates continue to outscore the national averages on licensure and credentialing examinations. Job outlook for careers in healthcare is excellent. College housing and financial aid is available for qualified students.

FLORIDA INSTITUTE OF ULTRASOUND, INC.
8800 University Pkwy Ste A4
Pensacola FL 32514-4913
Polly Brown, Administrative Assistant
850-478-7300 Fax: 850-478-3727
Website: www.fiuonline.net
E-mail: fiupcola@aol.com

Florida International University
Tamiami Trl, Miami FL 33199-0001
305-348-2000

Florida Metropolitan University-Brandon
3924 Coconut Palm Dr, Tampa FL 33619-1354
Marty Baca, Director of Admissions
877-338-0068 (Toll Free)

Florida Metropolitan University
Melbourne Campus
2401 N Harbor City Blvd, Melbourne FL 32935
321-253-2929

Florida Metropolitan University
Orlando College - North
5421 Diplomat Cir, Orlando FL 32810-5601
Charlene Donnelly, Director of Admissions
800-628-5870

Florida Metropolitan University
Orlando South
9200 Southpark Center Loop, Orlando FL 32819
Annette Cloin, Contact
407-851-2525

Florida Metropolitan University
Pinellas Campus
2471 N McMullen Booth Rd
Clearwater FL 33759-1359
Sandra Williams, Director of Admissions
800-353-3687

Florida Metropolitan University
Tampa Campus
3319 W Hillsborough Ave, Tampa FL 33614-5801
Donnie Broughton, Director of Admissions
813-879-6000

Florida National College
Hialeah Campus
4425 W 20th Ave, Hialeah FL 33012
Jorge Afonso, Campus Dean
305-821-3333 ext. 1022 Fax: 305-362-0595
Website: www.fnc.edu
E-mail: omarsnc@fnc.edu

Florida National College
South Campus
11865 SW 26th St, Miami FL 33175
Jon Beisenherz, Campus Dean
305-266-9999
Website: www.fnc.edu
E-mail: omarsnc@fnc.edu

Florida Southern College
Athletic Training
111 Lake Hollingsworth Dr, Lakeland FL 33801-5607
Robert B. Palmer, V.P., Dean of Enrollment Management
863-680-4131

Gulf Coast Community College
5230 W Highway 98, Panama City FL 32401-1058
850-769-1551

Heritage Institute
6811 Palisades Park Ct, Fort Myers FL 33912
Eva Hutson, Director
239-936-5822 Fax: 239-225-9117
Website: www.heritage-education.com
E-mail: info@heritage-education.com
See listing under "Career Schools"

Heritage Institute
4130 N Salisbury Rd Suite 1100
Jacksonville FL 32216
Sonnie Willingham, Director
904-332-0910 Fax: 904-332-0920
Website: www.heritage-education.com
E-mail: info@heritage-education.com
See listing under "Career Schools"

HERZING COLLEGE
1595 S Semoran Blvd #1501
Winter Park FL 32792-5509
Kathy Nagle, Director of Admissions
407-478-0500 Fax: 407-478-0501
Website: www.herzing.edu
E-mail: info@orl.herzing.edu

Hillsborough Community College
1404 Tech Blvd, Tampa FL 33619-7865
813-253-7000

Indian River Community College
3209 Virginia Ave, Fort Pierce FL 34981-5596
772-462-4700

James Haley Veteran's Hospital
13000 Bruce B Downs Blvd, Tampa FL 33612-4745
813-972-2000

Jones College
5353 Arlington Expy, Jacksonville FL 32211-5588
Dorothy D. Jones, Chief Executive Officer
904-743-1122 Fax: 904-744-4446
Website: www.jones.edu
E-mail: fmccaffe@jones.edu

Keiser College
1800 Business Park Blvd, Daytona Beach FL 32114
Matt McEnany, Vice President
386-274-5060

Keiser College
900 S Babcock St, Melbourne FL 32901-1461
321-255-2255

Keiser University
1500 NW 49th St, Fort Lauderdale FL 33309-3700
Anne O'Connell, Director Community Relations
954-776-4456

Key College
225 E Dania Beach Blvd #130
Dania Beach FL 33004
Ronald Dooley, President
954-923-4440 Fax: 954-923-9226
Website: www.keycollege.edu
E-mail: admissions@keycollege.edu

Lake City Community College
149 SE College Pl, Lake City FL 32025
386-752-1822

Lake Technical Center
2001 Kurt St, Eustis FL 32726-6164
352-589-2250

Lincoln College of Technology
2410 Metrocentre Blvd
West Palm Beach FL 33407-3105
Don Cunningham, Vice President of Admissions
561-688-2001 Fax: 561-842-9503
Website: www.lincolncollegeoftechnology.com
E-mail: dcunningham@lincolntech.com

Lindsey Hopkins Technical Education Center
750 NW 20th St, Miami FL 33127-4618
305-324-6070

Lively Area Vocational Technical School
500 Appleyard Dr, Tallahassee FL 32304-2810
850-487-7555

Lorenzo Walker Institute of Technology
3702 Estey Ave, Naples FL 34104-4405
239-430-6900

Manatee Technical Institute East Campus
5520 Lakewood Ranch Blvd, Bradenton FL 34211
Carla Brokaw, Director of Admissions
941-752-8100

Marion County School of Radiologic Technology
1014 SW 7th Rd, Ocala FL 34471
352-671-7200

Medical Career Center
19 W Garden St, Pensacola FL 32502-5678
850-436-8444

Miami-Dade College
300 NE 2nd Ave, Miami FL 33132-2296
305-237-3316

National School of Technology
111 NW 183rd St Ste 200, Miami FL 33169-4538
305-949-9500

North Technical Education Center
7071 Garden Rd, Riviera Beach FL 33404-4906
561-881-4600

Nova Southeastern University
3301 College Ave, Davie FL 33314-7796
954-262-7300

Orange Technical Education Center - Orlando Tech
301 W Amelia St, Orlando FL 32801-1122
407-246-7060

Orange Technical Education Centers-Winter Park Tech
901 W Webster Ave, Winter Park FL 32789-3049
Diane Culpepper, Director
407-622-2900

Pasco-Hernando Community College
10230 Ridge Rd, New Port Richey FL 34654-5129
727-847-2727

Pensacola Junior College
1000 College Blvd, Pensacola FL 32504-8998
850-484-1000

Pinellas Technical Education Center
901 34th St S, Saint Petersburg FL 33711-2209
727-893-2500

Polk Community College
999 Avenue H NE, Winter Haven FL 33881-4299
863-297-1000

Professional Training Center
13926 SW 47th St, Miami FL 33175
Maria Rizo, Admission Director
305-220-4120

Radiation Therapy Services, Inc.
1419 SE 8th Terrace, Cape Coral FL 33990
Donald E. Moody, Program Director
239-772-3202

Robert Morgan Educational Center
18180 SW 122nd Ave, Miami FL 33177-2407
Antonio Martinez, Principal
305-253-9920

Rollins College
1000 Holt Ave, Winter Park FL 32789
407-646-2000

ROSS MEDICAL EDUCATION CENTER
6847 Taft St, Hollywood FL 33024
954-963-0043 Fax: 954-963-0211

St. Luke's Hospital/Mayo Clinic
4201 Belfort Rd, Jacksonville FL 32216-1431
904-296-3733

St. Petersburg College
PO Box 13489, Saint Petersburg FL 33733-3489
727-341-3600

SANFORD BROWN INSTITUTE
1201 W Cypress Creek Rd, Fort Lauderdale FL 33309
Todd Oxendine, Director of Admissions
954-308-7400 Fax: 954-375-6900
Website: www.sbftlaud.com
E-mail: toxendine@sbftlaud.com

Sanford Brown Institute
5701 E Hillsborough Ave #1417, Tampa FL 33610
Patricia Meredith, President
813-621-0072

Santa Fe Community College
3000 NW 83rd St, Gainesville FL 32606-6200
Jackson N. Sasser, President
352-395-5787

Sarasota County Technical Institute
4748 Beneva Rd, Sarasota FL 34233-1798
Wm. A. Storms Jr., Director
941-924-1365 ext. 325

Sarasota Memorial Hospital
1700 S Tamiami Trl, Sarasota FL 34239-3555
941-917-1080

Seminole Community College
100 Weldon Blvd, Sanford FL 32773-6199
407-328-4722

Sheridan Vocational-Technical Center
5400 Sheridan St, Hollywood FL 33021-3399
Rosa Lee, Guidance Director
754-321-5400

South Florida Community College
600 W College Dr, Avon Park FL 33825-9356
863-453-6661

South University
1760 N Congress Ave
West Palm Beach FL 33409-5178
Steven A. Schwab, President
561-697-9200

SOUTHWEST FLORIDA COLLEGE
1685 Medical Ln, Fort Myers FL 33907-1157
866-SWFC-NOW or 239-939-4766 Fax: 239-936-4040
Website: www.swfc.edu
E-mail: studentinfo@swfc.edu

Stetson University
421 N Woodland Boulevard, De Land FL 32720-3761
386-822-7000

Tallahassee Community College
444 Appleyard Dr, Tallahassee FL 32304-2895
850-201-8595

Tampa General Hospital
School of Medical Technology
PO Box 1289, Tampa FL 33601-1289
Laura Ferguson, Education Coordinator
813-844-7985

Tom P. Haney Technical Center
3016 Highway 77, Panama City FL 32405-5004
850-747-5500

Traviss Technical Center
3225 Winter Lake Rd, Lakeland FL 33803-9709
863-499-2700

University of Central Florida
PO Box 160111, Orlando FL 32816
407-823-3000

University of Florida
PO Box 114000, Gainesville FL 32611-4000
352-392-3261

University of Miami
PO Box 248006, Coral Gables FL 33124-8006
305-284-2211

University of North Florida
4567 Saint Johns Bluff Rd S
Jacksonville FL 32224-2645
904-620-1000

University of South Florida
4202 E Fowler Ave, Tampa FL 33620-6900
J. Robert Spatig, Director of Admissions
877-USF-BULL Fax: 813-974-9689
Website: www.usf.edu
E-mail: admissions@admin.usf.edu
See listing under "Universities"

University of West Florida
11000 University Pkwy, Pensacola FL 32514-5750
850-474-2000

Valencia Community College
PO Box 3028, Orlando FL 32802-3028
407-299-5000

West Boca Medical Center
21644 State Road 7, Boca Raton FL 33428-1899
561-488-8000

William T. McFatter Technical Center
6500 Nova Dr, Davie FL 33317-7405
954-370-8324

GEORGIA

Albany Technical College
1704 S Slappey Blvd, Albany GA 31701
229-430-3500

Armstrong Atlantic State University
11935 Abercorn St, Savannah GA 31419-1997
Kim West, Asst. Dean and Registrar Enrollment Services
912-927-5277 Fax: 912-921-5462
Website: www.armstrong.edu
E-mail: admissions@mail.armstrong.edu

Athens Technical College
800 Highway 29 N, Athens GA 30601-1546
706-355-5000

Atlanta Technical College
1560 Metropolitan Pkwy SW, Atlanta GA 30310-4499
404-756-3700

Augusta Technical College
3116 Deans Bridge Rd, Augusta GA 30906-3399
706-771-4000

Brenau University
500 Washington St SE, Gainesville GA 30501
800-252-5119

Central Georgia Technical College
3300 Macon Tech Dr, Macon GA 31206-3628
478-757-3501

Chattahoochee Technical College
980 S Cobb Dr SE, Marietta GA 30060-3300
770-528-4465

Clark Atlanta University
223 James Brawley Dr SW, Atlanta GA 30314
404-880-8000

Clayton State University
5900 N Lee St, Morrow GA 30260
770-961-3500

Coastal Georgia Community College
3700 Altama Ave, Brunswick GA 31520-3632
912-264-7235

Columbus State University
4225 University Ave, Columbus GA 31907-5645
706-568-2001

Columbus Technical College
928 Manchester Expressway
Columbus GA 31904-6577
706-649-1837

Coosa Valley Technical Institute
1 Maurice Culberson Dr SW, Rome GA 30161
706-295-6927

Dalton State College
650 College Dr, Dalton GA 30720
706-272-4436

Darton College
2400 Gillionville Rd, Albany GA 31707-3098
229-430-6000

DeKalb Technical College
495 N Indian Creek Dr, Clarkston GA 30021-2397
Terry Richardson, Director of Admissions
404-297-9522 Fax: 404-294-6496
Website: www.dekalbtech.edu
E-mail: richardt@dekalbtech.edu

Emory University
200B Jones Center, Atlanta GA 30322
404-727-6123

EVEREST INSTITUTE
1706 Northeast Expy, Atlanta GA 30329
Director of Admissions
404-327-8787 Fax: 404-327-8980
Website: www.everest-institute.com

Fort Valley State University
1005 State University Dr, Fort Valley GA 31030-3298
478-825-6307

Georgia Southern University
PO Box 8024, Statesboro GA 30460
Admissions Office
912-681-5532

Georgia State University
PO Box 4009, Atlanta GA 30302-4009
404-651-2365

Grady Health System
PO Box 26189, Atlanta GA 30303-0001
404-616-4252

Griffin Technical College
501 Varsity Rd, Griffin GA 30223-2042
770-228-7366

Gupton-Jones College of Funeral Service
5141 Snapfinger Woods Dr, Decatur GA 30035-4022
Patty S. Hutcheson, President
770-593-2257 Fax: 770-593-1891
Website: www.gupton-jones.edu
E-mail: gjcfs@mindspring.com

Gwinnett Technical College
5150 Sugarloaf Pkwy, Lawrenceville GA 30043-5702
770-962-7580

Heart of Georgia Area Technical Institute
560 Pinehill Rd, Dublin GA 31021-1253
478-275-6590

Lanier Technical College
2990 Landrum Education Dr
Oakwood GA 30566-3405
Michael C. Marlowe, Director of Admissions
770-531-6328

Life University
1269 Barclay Cir SE, Marietta GA 30060-2903
Dr. Deborah E. Heairlston, Director of New Student Development
770-426-2884 Fax: 770-426-2895
Website: www.life.edu
E-mail: admissions@life.edu

Macon State College
100 College Station Dr, Macon GA 31206-5145
478-471-2800

Medical College of Georgia
1120 15th St, Augusta GA 30912-0004
706-721-2725

Medix School
2108 Cobb Pkwy SE, Smyrna GA 30080-7630
Berhan Bayleygn, Director of Admissions
770-980-0002
Website: www.medixschool.com

Middle Georgia College
1100 2nd St SE, Cochran GA 31014-1564
478-934-6221

MIDDLE GEORGIA TECHNICAL COLLEGE
80 Cohen Walker Dr, Warner Robins GA 31088-2729
Dr. Ivan Allen, President
478-988-6800 Fax: 478-988-6835
Website: www.middlegatech.edu
E-mail: aparham@middlegatech.edu

Moultrie Technical College
800 Veterans Pkwy N, Moultrie GA 31788
229-891-7000

North Georgia College & State University
Dahlonega GA 30597-0001
706-864-1400

North Georgia Technical College
434 Meeks Ave, Blairsville GA 30512-2983
Admissions
706-439-6300 Fax: 706-439-6301
Website: www.northgatech.edu
E-mail: info@northgatech.edu

North Georgia Technical College
8989 Highway 17, Toccoa GA 30577
706-779-8100 Fax: 706-779-8130
Website: www.northgatech.edu
E-mail: info@northgatech.edu

North Georgia Technical College
Clarkesville Campus
PO Box 65, Clarkesville GA 30523-0002
Admissions
706-754-7700 Fax: 706-754-7777
Website: www.northgatech.edu
E-mail: info@northgatech.edu

North Metro Technical College
5198 Ross Rd SE, Acworth GA 30102-3129
Missy Cusack, Director of Admissions
770-975-4000 Fax: 770-975-4142
Website: www.northmetrotech.edu
E-mail: info@northmetrotech.edu

Northwestern Technical College
265 Bicentennial Trl, Rock Spring GA 30739-2306
Dr. Ray Brooks, President
Greg Cross, Vice President for Student Services
706-764-3518

Ogeechee Technical College
1 Joseph E Kennedy Blvd
Statesboro GA 30458-3199
912-681-5500

Okefenokee Technical College
1701 Carswell Ave, Waycross GA 31503-4016
912-287-6584

Savannah Technical College
5717 White Bluff Rd, Savannah GA 31405-5521
912-351-6362

Southern Regional Medical Center
11 Upper Riverdale Rd SW
Riverdale GA 30274-2615
770-991-8053

Southwest Georgia Technical College
15689 US Highway 19 N, Thomasville GA 31792
229-225-5096

Swainsboro Technical College
346 Kite Rd, Swainsboro GA 30401-5700
478-289-2200

Thomas University
1501 Millpond Rd, Thomasville GA 31792-7478
Darla M. Glass, Director of Student Affairs
229-226-1621

University Hospital Health System
1350 Walton Way, Augusta GA 30901-2629
706-722-9011

University of Georgia
Athens GA 30602-0001
706-542-3000

Valdosta State University
N Patterson St, Valdosta GA 31698-0001
229-333-5952

Valdosta Technical College
4089 Val Tech Rd, Valdosta GA 31602-0928
Amanda Leavy, Admissions Coordinator
229-333-2100 Fax: 229-249-4980
Website: www.valdostatech.edu
E-mail: aleavy@valdostatech.edu

West Central Technical College
4600 Timber Ridge Dr, Douglasville GA 30135-1225
770-947-7200

West Georgia Technical College
303 Fort Dr, La Grange GA 30240-5901
706-845-4323

HAWAII

Heald College, Honolulu
1500 Kapiolani Blvd, Honolulu HI 96814-3732
Wendy N. Nishimura, Director of Admissions
808-955-1500 or 800-940-0530 Fax: 808-955-6964
Website: www.heald.edu
E-mail: wendy_nishimura@heald.edu

Kapiolani Community College
4303 Diamond Head Rd, Honolulu HI 96816-4496
808-734-9111

University of Hawaii at Manoa
2444 Dole St, Honolulu HI 96822-2302
808-956-5280

IDAHO

Apollo College Boise
1200 N Liberty St, Boise ID 83704-8742
208-377-8080

Boise State University
1910 University Dr, Boise ID 83725-0399
208-426-1011

Brigham Young University - Idaho
120 Kimball Bldg, Rexburg ID 83460-1615
Rob Garrett, Director of Admissions
208-496-1020 Fax: 208-496-1220
Website: www.byui.edu
E-mail: admissions@byui.edu

College of Southern Idaho
PO Box 1238, Twin Falls ID 83303-1238
208-733-9554

Eastern Idaho Technical College
1600 S 25th E, Idaho Falls ID 83404
208-524-3000

Idaho State University
PO Box 8270, Pocatello ID 83209-0001
208-282-0211

St. Alphonsus Regional Medical Center
1055 N Curtis Rd, Boise ID 83706-1309
208-378-2000

ILLINOIS

ADVOCATE ILLINOIS MASONIC
School of Radiologic Technology
836 W Wellington Ave, Chicago IL 60657
Philis George, Director
773-296-8950 Fax: 773-296-8960
Website: www.advocatehealth.com
E-mail: IMMCSRT@advocatehealth.com

Aurora University
347 S Gladstone Ave, Aurora IL 60506-4892
Carol R. Dunn, Ed.D., Vice President for Enrollment
800-742-5281 Fax: 630-844-5535
Website: www.aurora.edu
E-mail: admission@aurora.edu

Benedictine University
5700 College Rd, Lisle IL 60532-0900
630-829-6300 or 888-829-6363 Fax: 630-829-6301
Website: www.ben.edu
E-mail: admissions@ben.edu
See listing under "Universities"

Black Hawk College
6600 34th Ave, Moline IL 61265-5899
309-796-5000

BLOOMINGTON-NORMAL SCHOOL OF RADIOGRAPHY
900 Franklin Ave, Normal IL 61761-4604
Beth Kuhfuss, MS, RT (R) ARRT, Program Director
309-452-2834 Fax: 309-392-2835
Website: www.bnradiography.com

Bradley University
1501 W Bradley Ave, Peoria IL 61625-0002
800-447-6460

Carl Sandburg College
2232 S Lake Storey Rd, Galesburg IL 61401-9576
309-344-2518

Central Medical Education
550 E Washington St, West Chicago IL 60185-2200
630-682-1600

CHICAGO SCHOOL OF MASSAGE THERAPY
17 N State St Fl 5, Chicago IL 60602-3047
Shaun McFarland, Director of Admissions
312-753-7900 Fax: 312-753-7901
Website: www.csmt.com
E-mail: pjb@csmt.com

Chicago State University
9501 S King Dr, Chicago IL 60628-1598
773-995-2000

College of DuPage
425 Fawell Blvd, Glen Ellyn IL 60137-6708
630-942-2800

College of Lake County
19351 W Washington St, Grayslake IL 60030-1148
847-223-6601

College of Office Technology
1520 W Division St, Chicago IL 60622
Bill Bolton, Director of Admissions
773-278-0042 Fax: 773-278-0143
Website: www.cot.edu
E-mail: bbolton@cotedu.com

Dominican University
7900 Division St, River Forest IL 60305-1066
708-366-2490

Eastern Illinois University
600 Lincoln Ave, Charleston IL 61920-3099
217-581-5000

Elgin Community College
1700 Spartan Dr, Elgin IL 60123-7193
847-214-7385

Governors State University
1 University Pkwy, University Park IL 60466-0975
708-534-5000

Harry S. Truman College
1145 W Wilson Ave, Chicago IL 60640-5691
773-878-1700

Illinois Central College
1 College Dr, Peoria IL 61635-0002
309-694-5011

Illinois Institute of Technology
3300 S Federal St, Chicago IL 60616-3793
Brent Benner, Director of Admissions
312-567-3000

ILLINOIS SCHOOL OF HEALTH CAREERS
11 E Adams St Ste 200, Chicago IL 60603
Jeffrey L. Jarmes, Executive Director
312-913-1230 Fax: 312-913-1113
Website: www.ishc.edu
E-mail: jjarmes@ishc.edu

Illinois State University
Normal IL 61790-0001
309-438-2111

Illinois Valley Community College
815 N Orlando Smith St, Oglesby IL 61348-9692
815-224-2720

Ingalls Memorial Hospital
1 Ingalls Dr, Harvey IL 60426-3558
708-333-2300

John A. Logan College
700 Logan College Rd, Carterville IL 62918
Terry Crain, Associate Dean Student Services
618-985-3741

Kankakee Community College
100 College Dr, Kankakee IL 60901
815-802-8100

Kaskaskia College
27210 College Rd, Centralia IL 62801-7878
Tyra Taylor, Dean of Enrollment Management and Retention Services
618-545-3000 Fax: 618-532-1990
Website: www.kaskaskia.edu
E-mail: ttaylor@kaskaskia.edu

Kennedy-King College
6800 S Wentworth Ave, Chicago IL 60621-3798
773-602-5000

Kishwaukee College
21193 Malta Rd, Malta IL 60150-9699
815-825-2086

Lake Land College
5001 Lake Land Blvd, Mattoon IL 61938-9366
217-234-5253

Lewis & Clark Community College
5800 Godfrey Rd, Godfrey IL 62035-2426
618-466-3411

Lincoln Land Community College
5250 Shepherd Rd, Springfield IL 62703-5408
217-786-2200

Loyola University of Chicago
820 N Michigan Ave, Chicago IL 60611-2103
312-915-6000

Malcolm X College
1900 W Van Buren St, Chicago IL 60612-3197
312-850-7031

Midstate College
411 W Northmoor Rd, Peoria IL 61614-3595
309-692-4092

MIDWEST COLLEGE OF ORIENTAL MEDICINE
4334 N Hazel St Ste 206, Chicago IL 60613-1429
Kelly Westerlund, Contact
800-593-2320 Fax: 262-554-7475
Website: www.acupuncture.edu
E-mail: mwcadmissions@yahoo.com

Midwestern University
555 31st St, Downers Grove IL 60515-1235
Raelene Brower, Director of Admissions
630-969-4400

Moraine Valley Community College
10900 S 88th Ave, Palos Hills IL 60465-0937
708-974-4300

Morton College
3801 S Central Ave, Cicero IL 60804-4398
708-656-8000

National-Louis University
5202 Old Orchard Rd Ste 300, Skokie IL 60077-4409
224-233-2000

Northern Illinois University
DeKalb IL 60115
815-753-1000

Northwestern Business College
7725 S Harlem Ave, Bridgeview IL 60455-1318
800-682-9113

Northwestern Business College
4829 N Lipps Ave, Chicago IL 60630-2298
Mark Sliz, Director of Admissions
773-777-4220

Northwestern University
1801 Hinman Ave, Evanston IL 60208-1260
847-491-3741

Oakton Community College
1600 E Golf Rd, Des Plaines IL 60016-1256
David Cole, Director of Enrollment Management
847-635-1600

Olivet Nazarene University
1 University Ave
Bourbonnais IL 60914
815-939-5011

Olney Central College
305 N West St, Olney IL 62450-1099
618-395-7777

Parkland College
2400 W Bradley Ave, Champaign IL 61821-1899
Mike Henry, Contact
217-351-2208

Prairie State College
202 S Halsted St, Chicago Heights IL 60411-8226
708-709-3500

Robert Morris College
401 S State St, Chicago IL 60605-1229
312-935-6800

Rockford Memorial Hospital
2400 N Rockton Ave, Rockford IL 61103-3681
815-971-5000

Rock Valley College
3301 N Mulford Rd, Rockford IL 61114-5699
815-654-4250

Roosevelt University
430 S Michigan Ave, Chicago IL 60605
Gwen E. Kanelos, Asst. Vice President for Enrollment Services
877-APPLY-RU Fax: 312-341-4216
Website: www.roosevelt.edu
E-mail: applyru@roosevelt.edu

Rosalind Franklin University of Medicine and Science
3333 Green Bay Rd, North Chicago IL 60064-3037
847-578-3000

Rush University
College Admission Services
600 S Paulina St #440, Chicago IL 60612-3806
Hicela Castruita, Director
312-942-7100

St. Anthony Medical Center
5666 E State St, Rockford IL 61108-2472
815-226-2000

St. Augustine College
1333 W Argyle St, Chicago IL 60640-3593
773-878-8756

St. John's Hospital
800 E Carpenter St, Springfield IL 62769-0002
217-544-6464

St. Xavier University
3700 W 103rd St, Chicago IL 60655-3199
773-298-3000

Sanford-Brown College
1101 Eastport Plaza Dr, Collinsville IL 62234-6108
Connie Frazier, Director of Admissions
618-344-5600
Website: www.sanford-brown.edu
E-mail: cfrazier@sbc-collinsville.com

Sauk Valley Community College
173 IL Route 2, Dixon IL 61021
815-288-5511

School of the Art Institute of Chicago
Art Therapy Program
37 S Wabash Ave, Chicago IL 60603-3002
800-232-7242

Southeastern Illinois College
3575 College Rd, Harrisburg IL 62946-4925
618-252-6376

Southern Illinois University
Carbondale IL 62901-4400
618-453-2121

Southern Illinois University Edwardsville
Edwardsville IL 62026-0001
618-650-3705

South Suburban College of Cook County
15800 State St, South Holland IL 60473
Jane Ellen Stocker, Dean of Enrollment Services
708-596-2000

Southwestern Illinois College
2500 Carlyle Ave, Belleville IL 62221-5899
618-235-2700

Trinity College of Nursing & Health Sciences
2122 25th Ave, Rock Island IL 61201-5317
Joanne Cunningham, Director of Admissions
309-779-7700 Fax: 309-799-7748
Website: www.trinitycollegeqc.edu
E-mail: con@trinityqc.com

Trinity International University
2065 Half Day Rd, Deerfield IL 60015-1241
847-945-8800 Fax: 847-317-8097
Website: www.tiu.edu
E-mail: tcadmissions@tiu.edu

Triton College
2000 5th Ave, River Grove IL 60171-1995
Jeffery Cooks, Director, Admission Services
708-456-0300 ext. 3130 Fax: 708-583-3147
Website: www.triton.edu
E-mail: triton@triton.edu
See listing under "Community and Junior Colleges"

University of Chicago Hospital/Roosevelt University
5841 S Maryland Ave, Chicago IL 60637-1463
773-702-6240

University of Illinois
901 W Illinois St, Urbana IL 61801
217-333-1000

University of Illinois at Chicago
PO Box 5220, Chicago IL 60680-5220
312-996-3000

University of Illinois at Springfield
One University Plaza, Springfield IL 62794
217-206-4847

Waubonsee Community College
Route 47 at Waubonsee Dr, Sugar Grove IL 60554
630-466-7900

Western Illinois University
1 University Cir, Macomb IL 61455-1390
309-295-1414

Westwood College
8501 W Higgins Rd Ste 500, Chicago IL 60631
Tash Uray, Director of Admissions
773-380-6800 Fax: 773-714-0828
Website: www.westwood.edu
E-mail: turay@westwood.edu

Wilbur Wright College North
4300 N Narragansett Ave, Chicago IL 60634-1591
773-777-7900

William Rainey Harper College
1200 W Algonquin Rd, Palatine IL 60067-7373
847-925-6000

INDIANA

Ancilla Domini College
Donaldson IN 46513
Erin Alonzo, Director of Admissions
574-936-8898 Fax: 574-935-1773
Website: www.ancilla.edu
E-mail: erin.alonzo@ancilla.edu

Anderson University
1100 E 5th St, Anderson IN 46012-3495
765-649-9071

Ball State University
2000 W University Ave, Muncie IN 47306-0002
765-285-5555

Bloomington Hospital
PO Box 1149, Bloomington IN 47402-1149
812-336-6821

BROWN MACKIE COLLEGE - FORT WAYNE
3000 E Coliseum Blvd, Fort Wayne IN 46805
Daniel Summer, Campus President
260-484-4400 Fax: 260-484-2678
Website: www.brownmackie.edu

BROWN MACKIE COLLEGE - SOUTH BEND
1030 E Jefferson Blvd, South Bend IN 46617-3123
Connie Adelman, Campus President
574-237-0774 Fax: 574-237-3585
Website: www.brownmackie.edu

Butler University
4600 Sunset Ave, Indianapolis IN 46208-3443
317-940-8000

Columbus Regional Hospital
2400 17th St, Columbus IN 47201-5360
812-376-5439

Community College of Indiana - Valparaiso
3100 Ivy Tech Dr, Valparaiso IN 46383
219-464-8514

Fort Wayne School of Radiography
700 Broadway, Fort Wayne IN 46802-1402
Ann Lewis, Program Director
260-425-3990

Franklin College
101 Branigin Blvd, Franklin IN 46131
Jacqueline S. Acosta, Director of Admissions
800-852-0232 Fax: 317-738-8274
Website: www.franklincollege.edu
E-mail: admissions@franklincollege.edu

Hancock Memorial Hospital
801 N State St, Greenfield IN 46140-1270
317-462-0457

Indiana Business College
550 E Washington St, Indianapolis IN 46204
317-264-5656

Indiana State University
Terre Haute IN 47809-0001
Richard Toomey, Director of Admissions
812-237-6311

Indiana University
300 N Jordan Ave, Bloomington IN 47405-1106
812-855-4848

Indiana University at South Bend
PO Box 7111, South Bend IN 46634-7111
574-237-4111

Indiana University Northwest
3400 Broadway, Gary IN 46408-1101
219-980-6500

Indiana University-Purdue University at Fort Wayne
2101 E Coliseum Blvd, Fort Wayne IN 46805-1445
260-481-6100

Indiana University-Purdue University at Indianapolis
355 Lansing St, Indianapolis IN 46202-2815
317-274-5555

Indiana University School of Allied Health Sciences
1140 W Michigan St, Indianapolis IN 46202-5119
317-274-4702

Indiana Vocational Technical College
PO Box 1763, Indianapolis IN 46206-1763
317-921-4882

Indiana Wesleyan University
4201 S Washington St, Marion IN 46953-4974
765-674-6901

International Business College
5699 Coventry Ln, Fort Wayne IN 46804
260-459-4500 Fax: 260-436-1896
Website: www.ibcfortwayne.edu
E-mail: skinzer@ibcfortwayne.edu

International Business College
7205 Shadeland Station Way
Indianapolis IN 46256-3954
317-841-6400

Ivy Tech Community College - North Central
220 Dean Johnson Blvd, South Bend IN 46601-3415
Pam Decker, Director of Admissions
574-289-7001 Fax: 574-236-7177
Website: www.ivytech.edu
E-mail: pdecker@ivytech.edu

Ivy Tech Community College of Indiana - Columbus
4475 Central Ave, Columbus IN 47203-1868
812-372-9925

Ivy Tech Community College of Indiana - East Central
4301 S Cowan Rd, Muncie IN 47302-9448
765-289-2291

Ivy Tech Community College of Indiana - Kokomo
PO Box 1373, Kokomo IN 46903-1373
765-459-0561

Ivy Tech Community College of Indiana - Lafayette
PO Box 6299, Lafayette IN 47903-6299
765-772-9100

Ivy Tech Community College of Indiana - Northeast
3800 N Anthony Blvd, Fort Wayne IN 46805-1430
260-482-9171

Ivy Tech Community College of Indiana - Northwest
1440 E 35th Ave, Gary IN 46409-1401
219-981-1111

Ivy Tech Community College of Indiana - Richmond
2325 Chester Blvd, Richmond IN 47374-1220
765-966-2656

Ivy Tech Community College of Indiana - Southeast
590 Ivy Tech Dr, Madison IN 47250
812-265-2580

Ivy Tech Community College of Indiana - Southern Indiana
8204 Highway 311, Sellersburg IN 47172-1829
812-246-3301

Ivy Tech Community College of Indiana - Southwest
3501 N 1st Ave, Evansville IN 47710-3319
812-426-2865

Ivy Tech Community College Wabash Valley
8000 S Education Dr, Terre Haute IN 47802
812-299-1121

Ivy Tech State College
104 W 53rd St, Anderson IN 46013
765-643-7133

King's Daughter's Hospital
PO Box 447, Madison IN 47250-0447
812-265-5211

Lakeshore Medical Laboratory Training Programs
402 Franklin St, Michigan City IN 46360-3327
Gina Watson, MT (ASCP), Program Director
219-872-7032

Marian College
3200 Cold Spring Rd, Indianapolis IN 46222-1997
317-955-6000

Methodist Hospital/Clarian Health Partners
PO Box 1367, Indianapolis IN 46206-1367
317-929-5900

Porter Memorial Hospital
814 LaPorte Ave, Valparaiso IN 46383-5898
Bridget Burge, B.S., R.T., Program Director
219-465-4883

Professional Careers Institute
7302 Woodland Dr, Indianapolis IN 46278-1736
317-299-6001

Purdue University
2200 169th St, Hammond IN 46323
219-989-2993

Purdue University
1401 S US Highway 421, Westville IN 46391-9542
219-785-5200

Reid Hospital & Health Care Services
1401 Chester Blvd, Richmond IN 47374-1908
765-983-3167

St. Francis Hospital Center
1600 Albany St, Beech Grove IN 46107-1593
317-783-8220

St. Joseph Hospital & Health Center
1907 W Sycamore St, Kokomo IN 46901-4197
765-452-5611

St. Margaret Hospital
5454 S Hohman Ave, Hammond IN 46320-1931
219-932-2300

University of Evansville
1800 Lincoln Ave, Evansville IN 47722-0001
Don Vos, Dean of Admission
800-423-8633 Fax: 812-488-4076
Website: www.evansville.edu
E-mail: admission@evansville.edu

University of Indianapolis
1400 E Hanna Ave, Indianapolis IN 46227-3697
317-788-3368

University of St. Francis
2701 Spring St, Fort Wayne IN 46808-3994
Matthew P. Nettleton, Director of Admissions
260-434-3279

University of Southern Indiana
8600 University Blvd, Evansville IN 47712-3591
812-464-8600

Vincennes University
1002 N 1st St, Vincennes IN 47591-1504
Chris M. Crews, Director of Admission
812-888-4313

Welborn Baptist Hospital
401 SE 6th St, Evansville IN 47713-1299
812-426-8264

IOWA

Allen College
1825 Logan Ave, Waterloo IA 50703-1999
319-226-2000

Briar Cliff University
PO Box 2100, Sioux City IA 51104-0100
Sharisue Wilcoxon, VP for Enrollment Management
712-279-5200 Fax: 712-279-1632
Website: www.briarcliff.edu
E-mail: admissions@briarcliff.edu

Clarke College
1550 Clarke Dr, Dubuque IA 52001-3198
Andy Schroeder, Director of Admissions
800-383-2345 Fax: 563-584-8666
Website: www.clarke.edu
E-mail: andy.schroeder@clarke.edu

Covenant Medical Center
3421 W 9th St, Waterloo IA 50702-5401
319-272-7296

Des Moines Area Community College
Ankeny Campus
2006 S Ankeny Blvd, Ankeny IA 50023-8995
515-964-6200

Des Moines University - Osteopathic Medical Center
3200 Grand Ave, Des Moines IA 50312-4198
Jodi Cahalan, Dean, College of Health Sciences
515-271-1650
Website: www.dmu.edu
E-mail: dmuadmit@dmu.edu

Graceland University
1 University Place, Lamoni IA 50140
Greg Sutherland, Interim Vice President for Enrollment and Dean of Admissions
641-784-5196 Fax: 641-784-5480
Website: www.admissions.graceland.edu
E-mail: admissions@graceland.edu

Hamilton College
7009 Nordic Dr, Cedar Falls IA 50613
Connie Reidy, Campus President
319-277-0220 Fax: 319-363-3812
Website: www.hamiltonia.edu
E-mail: coreidy@hamiltoncf.com

Hamilton College
3165 Edgewood Pkwy SW, Cedar Rapids IA 52404
Susan Spivey, Campus President
319-363-0481 Fax: 319-363-3812
Website: www.hamiltonia.edu
E-mail: sspivey@hamiltonia.edu

Hamilton College
1751 Madison Ave Ste 750, Council Bluffs IA 51503
Michael Zawisky, Executive Director
712-328-4212
Website: www.hamiltonia.edu
E-mail: mzawisky@hamiltonia.edu

Hamilton College
2570 4th St SW, Mason City IA 50401-4665
Joe Albers, Executive Director
641-423-2530 Fax: 641-423-7512
Website: www.hamiltonia.edu
E-mail: jalbers@hamiltonia.edu

Hamilton College
4655 121st St, Urbandale IA 50323-2311
Colleen McDermott, Campus President
515-727-2100 Fax: 515-727-2115
Website: www.hamiltonia.edu
E-mail: cmcdermott@hamiltonia.edu

Hamilton Technical College
1011 E 53rd St, Davenport IA 52807-2653
Mark Christy, Director
563-386-3570 Fax: 563-386-6756
Website: www.hamiltontechcollege.com
E-mail: mchristy@hamiltontechcollege.com
See listing under "Career Schools"

Hawkeye Community College
1501 E Orange Rd, Waterloo IA 50704
Molly Quinn, Director of Admissions
800-670-4769

Indian Hills Community College
525 Grandview Ave, Ottumwa IA 52501-1398
641-683-5111

Iowa Central Community College
330 Avenue M, Fort Dodge IA 50501-5798
515-576-7201

Iowa Lakes Community College
1900 Grand Ave, Suite 8, Spencer IA 51301
Anne Stansbury, Assistant Director of Admissions
712-262-7141 Fax: 712-262-4047
Website: www.iowalakes.edu
E-mail: info@iowalakes.edu

Iowa Methodist Medical Center
1200 Pleasant St, Des Moines IA 50309-1453
515-241-6201

Iowa State University
Ames IA 50011-0001
515-294-4111

Iowa Western Community College
2700 College Rd, Council Bluffs IA 51503-0567
800-432-5852

Jennie Edmundson Memorial Hospital
933 E Pierce St, Council Bluffs IA 51503-4652
712-328-6239

Kaplan University
1801 E Kimberly Rd #1, Davenport IA 52807-2095
563-355-3500

Kirkwood Community College
PO Box 2068, Cedar Rapids IA 52406-2068
319-398-5411

Marshalltown Community College
3700 S Center St, Marshalltown IA 50158-4760
641-752-7106

MERCY COLLEGE OF HEALTH SCIENCES
928 6th Ave, Des Moines IA 50309-1225
Susan Rhoades, Dean Enrollment & Student Services
515-643-3180 Fax: 515-643-6698
Website: www.mchs.edu
E-mail: srhoades@mercydesmoines.org

Mercy Medical Center - Sioux City
801 5th St, Sioux City IA 51101-1399
712-279-2018

Mercy-St. Luke's Hospital
1026 A Ave NE, Cedar Rapids IA 52402-5098
319-369-7204

Northeast Iowa Community College
PO Box 400, Calmar IA 52132-0400
563-562-3263

Northeast Iowa Community College
RR 1, Peosta IA 52068
563-556-5110

North Iowa Area Community College
500 College Dr, Mason City IA 50401-7213
641-423-1264

North Iowa Mercy Health Center
1000 4th St SW, Mason City IA 50401
641-422-7722

PALMER COLLEGE OF CHIROPRACTIC
Davenport Campus
1000 Brady St, Davenport IA 52803-5287
800-722-3648 or 563-884-5656 Fax: 563-884-5414
Website: www.palmer.edu
E-mail: pcadmit@palmer.edu

St. Ambrose University
518 W Locust St, Davenport IA 52803-2898
563-333-6000

St. Luke's College
2720 Stone Park Blvd, Sioux City IA 51104-3734
712-279-3149

Scott Community College
500 Belmont Rd, Riverdale IA 52722-6804
563-441-4000

Southeastern Community College
PO Box 180, West Burlington IA 52655
319-752-2731

University of Iowa
107 Calvin Hall, Iowa City IA 52242-1315
319-335-3500

University of Northern Iowa
Cedar Falls IA 50614-0001
319-273-2311

Wartburg College
PO Box 1003, Waverly IA 50677-0903
Brent Matthias, Interim Director of Admissions
319-352-8200

Western Iowa Tech Community College
PO Box 5199, Sioux City IA 51102-5199
Dr. Carolyn Rants, Dean of Students
712-274-6400

KANSAS

Barton County Community College
245 NE 30th Rd, Great Bend KS 67530-9107
Mary Anne Clark, Associate Dean
800-748-7594

COLBY COMMUNITY COLLEGE
1255 S Range Ave, Colby KS 67701-4099
Director of Admissions
888-634-9350 or 785-460-4690 Fax: 785-460-4691
Website: www.colbycc.edu
E-mail: admissions@colbycc.edu

Emporia State University
1200 Commercial St, Emporia KS 66801-5087
620-343-1200

Flint Hills Technical College
3301 W 18th Ave, Emporia KS 66801-5957
Lisa Kirmer, Dean of Student Services
620-343-4600 Fax: 620-343-4610
Website: www.fhtc.net
E-mail: lkirmer@fhtc.net

Fort Hays State University
600 Park St, Hays KS 67601-4099
785-628-4000

Independence Community College
PO Box 708, Independence KS 67301-0708
Dr. Terry Hetrick, President
800-842-6063 Fax: 620-331-5344
Website: www.indycc.edu
E-mail: admissions@indycc.edu

Johnson County Community College
12345 College Blvd, Overland Park KS 66210-1299
913-469-3803 Fax: 913-469-2524
Website: www.jccc.edu
E-mail: jcccadmissions@jccc.edu

Kansas State University
Manhattan KS 66506
785-532-6250

Labette Community College
200 S 14th St, Parsons KS 67357-9966
Tammy Fuentez, Director of Admissions
620-421-6700 Fax: 620-421-2309
Website: www.labette.edu
E-mail: tammyf@labette.edu

Newman University
3100 W McCormick St, Wichita KS 67213
Jann Reusser, Admissions Recruitment Coordinator
316-942-4291 ext. 2144

Pittsburg State University
1701 S Broadway St, Pittsburg KS 66762-7500
620-231-7000

Salina Area Vocational Technical School
2562 Centennial Rd, Salina KS 67401
785-309-3100

Seward County Community College
PO Box 1137, Liberal KS 67905-1137
620-629-2710

Tabor College
400 S Jefferson St, Hillsboro KS 67063-1758
Rusty Allen, Dean of Enrollment Management
800-822-6799 Fax: 620-947-6276
Website: www.tabor.edu
E-mail: admissions@tabor.edu
See listing under "Universities"

University of Kansas
Lawrence KS 66045-0001
Alan Cerveny, Director of Admissions

University of Kansas Medical Center
3901 Rainbow Blvd, Kansas City KS 66160-0001
Lydia Wingate, Dean
913-588-5000

Washburn University
1700 SW College Ave, Topeka KS 66621-0001
785-231-1010

Wichita Area Technical College
324 N Emporia St, Wichita KS 67202-2512
316-833-4664

Wichita State University
1845 N Fairmount St, Wichita KS 67260-0124
Gina Crabtree, Director of Admissions
316-978-3085

KENTUCKY

Ashland Community and Technical College
1400 College Dr, Ashland KY 41101-3683
606-329-2999

Berea College
Berea KY 40404-0001
859-985-3000

Bluegrass Community and Technical College
Oswald Building
470 Cooper Drive, Lexington KY 40506-0235
Shelbie Hugle, Director of Admissions
859-246-6200 Fax: 859-246-4664
Website: www.bluegrass.kctcs.edu
E-mail: bctc_info@kctcs.edu

Bowling Green Technical College
1845 Loop Ave, Bowling Green KY 42101-3601
270-746-7461

Brown Cancer Center
529 S Jackson St, Louisville KY 40202-3229
502-588-6905

Brown Mackie College - Louisville
3605 Fern Valley Rd, Louisville KY 40219-1916
Mark Donahue, Director of Admissions
502-968-7191 Fax: 502-357-9956
Website: www.brownmackie.edu
E-mail: mdonahue@brownmackie.edu

BROWN MACKIE COLLEGE
Northern Kentucky Campus
309 Buttermilk Pike, Fort Mitchell KY 41017-2191
Joanne Dellefield, Director of Admissions
859-341-5627 Fax: 859-341-6483
Website: www.brownmackie.edu
E-mail: jdellefield@brownmackie.edu

Central Kentucky Technical College
308 Vo Tech Rd, Lexington KY 40511
Dr. Michael Krause, Dean of Student Affairs
859-246-2400

Cumberland Technical College Rockcastle County
PO Box 275, Mount Vernon KY 40456-0275
606-256-4346

Daymar College
4400 Breckenridge Ln #415, Louisville KY 40218
Shawn McDaniel, Director of Admissions
502-495-1040 Fax: 502-495-1518
Website: www.daymarcollege.com

Daymar College
3361 Buckland Sq, Owensboro KY 42301-5830
Vickie McDougal Director of Admissions
800-960-4090 Fax: 270-685-4090
Website: www.daymarcollege.com

Eastern Kentucky University
521 Lancaster Ave, Richmond KY 40475-3102
859-622-1000

Elizabethtown Technical College
620 College Street Rd, Elizabethtown KY 42701
270-766-5133

Henderson Community College
2660 S Green St, Henderson KY 42420-4699
270-827-1867

Jefferson Community & Technical College
109 E Broadway, Louisville KY 40202-2000
502-584-0181

Jefferson Technical College
727 W Chestnut St, Louisville KY 40203-2036
502-213-4290

Lindsey Wilson College
210 Lindsey Wilson St, Columbia KY 42728-1223
270-384-8100

Madisonville Community College
2000 College Dr, Madisonville KY 42431-9199
270-821-2250

Mayo Technical College
513 3rd St, Paintsville KY 41240-1032
606-789-5321

Maysville Community College
1401 Dixie Hwy, Park Hills KY 41011-2816

Midway College
512 E Stephens St, Midway KY 40347-1120
800-755-0031

Morehead State University
Morehead KY 40351-1689
Jeffrey Liles, Enrollment Services
800-585-6781 Fax: 606-783-5038
Website: www.moreheadstate.edu
E-mail: admissions@moreheadstate.edu

Murray State University
Murray KY 42071
Phil Bryan, Director of Admissions
270-762-3011

National College
115 E Lexington Ave, Danville KY 40422-1517
Gloria Walls, Director of Admissions
859-236-6991 Fax: 859-236-1063
Website: www.national-college.edu
E-mail: info@national-college.edu

National College
7627 Ewing Blvd, Florence KY 41042-1812
Doug Dedeker, Director of Admissions
859-525-6510 Fax: 859-525-8961
Website: www.national-college.edu
E-mail: info@national-college.edu

National College
2376 Sir Barton Way, Lexington KY 40509
Terry Fisher, Director of Admissions
859-253-0621 Fax: 859-254-7664
Website: www.national-college.edu
E-mail: info@national-college.edu

National College
4205 Dixie Hwy, Louisville KY 40216
Ted Scharre, Director of Admissions
502-447-7634 Fax: 502-447-7665
Website: www.national-college.edu
E-mail: info@national-college.edu

National College
50 National College Blvd, Pikeville KY 41501
Janet Head, Director of Admissions
606-478-7200 Fax: 606-478-7209
Website: www.national-college.edu
E-mail: info@national-college.edu

National College
125 S Killarney Ln, Richmond KY 40475
Keeley Gadd, Director of Admissions
859-623-8956 Fax: 859-623-8956
Website: www.national-college.edu
E-mail: info@national-college.edu

Northern Kentucky University
Newport KY 41099-0001
859-572-5100

Owensboro Community & Technical College
1501 Frederica St, Owensboro KY 42301-4806
270-687-7255

Owensboro Community and Technical College
4800 New Hartford Rd, Owensboro KY 42303-1899
270-686-4400

Owensboro Mercy Health System
811 E Parrish Ave, Owensboro KY 42303-3258
270-688-2100

Pathology and Cytology Laboratories
290 Big Run Rd, Lexington KY 40503-2934
859-278-9513

Pikeville Medical Center
911 S Bypass Rd, Pikeville KY 41501-1595
606-437-3500

Rowan Technical College
609 Viking Dr, Morehead KY 40351-8320
606-783-1538

ST. ELIZABETH MEDICAL CENTER
School of Medical Technology
1 Medical Village Dr, Edgewood KY 41017-3441
Beth Warning, MS, MT(ASCP), Program Director
859-301-2170 Fax: 859-301-5560
Website: www.stelizabeth.com
E-mail: bwarning@stelizabeth.com

St. Joseph's Hospital
1 Saint Joseph Dr, Lexington KY 40504-3754
859-278-3436

Somerset Community College
808 Monticello St, Somerset KY 42501-2936
606-679-8501

Southeast Kentucky Community and Technical College
300 College Rd, Cumberland KY 40823-1031
606-589-2145

Spalding University
851 S 4th St, Louisville KY 40203-2188
502-585-9911

Spencerian College
1575 Winchester Rd, Lexington KY 40505
Victor Lamoin Adcock II, Director of Admissions
800-456-3253
E-mail: ladcock@spencerian.edu

Spencerian College
4627 Dixie Hwy, Louisville KY 40216
Kathleen Belanger, Director of Admissions
502-447-1000 Fax: 502-447-4574
Website: www.spencerian.edu
E-mail: kbelanger@spencerian.edu

University of Kentucky
Lexington KY 40506-0001
Don Witt, Director of Admissions
859-257-9000

University of Kentucky Chandler Medical Center
103 Administration Plz A311
Lexington KY 40536-0001
859-323-5126

University of Louisville
2301 S 3rd St, Louisville KY 40292-2001
502-852-5555

Western Kentucky University
1 Big Red Way, Bowling Green KY 42101
270-745-0111

West Kentucky Community and Technical College
PO Box 7380, Paducah KY 42002-7380
270-554-9200

LOUISIANA

Baton Rouge General Medical Center
PO Box 2511, Baton Rouge LA 70821-2511
225-387-7767

Bossier Parish Community College
6220 E Texas St, Bossier City LA 71111
318-678-6000

Delgado Community College
615 City Park Ave, New Orleans LA 70119
Gwen A. Boutte, Director of Admissions
504-483-4410

Grambling State University
PO Box 864, Grambling LA 71245
318-274-3811

Lafayette General Medical Center
PO Box 52009, Lafayette LA 70505-2009
337-261-7381

Lake Charles Memorial Hospital
1701 Oak Park Blvd, Lake Charles LA 70601-8911
337-494-3200

Louisiana State University
1100 Florida Ave, New Orleans LA 70119-2714
504-948-8530

Louisiana State University
1 University Pl, Shreveport LA 71115-2301
318-797-5000

Louisiana State University and A & M College
Louisiana State Univ, Baton Rouge LA 70803-0001
225-578-3202

Louisiana State University at Eunice
PO Box 1129, Eunice LA 70535-1129
Ron Ryder, Registrar
337-457-7311 Fax: 337-550-1306
Website: www.lsue.edu
E-mail: rryder@lsue.edu

Louisiana State University Health Sciences Center
433 Bolivar St, New Orleans LA 70112-2223
504-568-4808

Louisiana Technical College
Lafayette Campus
1101 Bertrand Dr, Lafayette LA 70506-4909
Gen M. Bienvenu, Director of Admissions
337-262-5962

Louisiana Technical College
West Jefferson Campus
475 Manhattan Blvd, Harvey LA 70058-4441
504-361-6464

Louisiana Tech University
PO Box 3168, Ruston LA 71272-0001
318-257-0211

Loyola University New Orleans
6363 Saint Charles Ave, New Orleans LA 70118-6143
504-865-2011

McNeese State University
4100 Ryan St, Lake Charles LA 70605-4510
337-475-5000

Medical Center of Louisiana - Charity Campus
1541 Tulane Ave, New Orleans LA 70112-2821
504-568-2311

Nicholls State University
PO Box 2004, Thibodaux LA 70310-0001
985-446-8111

North Oaks Medical Center
15790 Medical Arts Dr, Hammond LA 70403-1436
985-543-6600

Northwestern State University
Natchitoches LA 71497-0001
Jana Lucky, Director of Enrollment Services
318-357-4503

Ochsner School of Allied Health Sciences
1516 Jefferson Hwy, New Orleans LA 70121-2429
504-842-3267

Our Lady of Holy Cross College
4123 Woodland Dr, New Orleans LA 70131-7399
Office of Enrollment Services
504-394-7744 Fax: 504-391-2421
Website: www.olhcc.edu

Our Lady of the Lake College
7434 Perkins Rd, Baton Rouge LA 70808
Marvell Nesmith, Director of Admissions
225-768-1700

Overton Brooks VA Medical Center
510 E Stoner Ave, Shreveport LA 71101-4243
318-424-6037

Rapides Regional Medical Center
PO Box 30101, Alexandria LA 71301
318-473-3150

St. Francis Medical Center
PO Box 1901, Monroe LA 71210-1901
318-327-4141

St. Patrick's Hospital
524 S Ryan St, Lake Charles LA 70601-5799
337-491-7730

Southeastern Louisiana University
PO Box 784, Hammond LA 70404-0784
985-549-2000

Southern University A&M College
Southern University, Baton Rouge LA 70813-0001
225-771-4500

Southern University at Shreveport
3050 M L King Dr, Shreveport LA 71107
318-674-3300

Touro Infirmary
1401 Foucher St, New Orleans LA 70115-3593
504-897-8244

Tulane University
6823 Saint Charles Ave, New Orleans LA 70118-5698
504-865-4000

University Medical Center
2390 W Congress St, Lafayette LA 70506-4298
337-261-6004

University of Louisiana at Lafayette
PO Box 42210, Lafayette LA 70504
337-482-6278

University of Louisiana at Monroe
700 University Ave, Monroe LA 71209-9001
318-342-1000

University of New Orleans
New Orleans LA 70148-0001
504-280-6000

MAINE

Beal College
99 Farm Rd, Bangor ME 04401-6831
207-947-4591

Central Maine Community College
1250 Turner St, Auburn ME 04210-6498
Walter Clark, Director of Admissions
207-755-5100

Central Maine Medical Center
70 Middle St, Lewiston ME 04240
207-795-2840

Eastern Maine Community College
354 Hogan Rd, Bangor ME 04401-4206
207-974-4600

Eastern Maine Medical Center
489 State St, Bangor ME 04401-6674
207-973-7051

HUSSON COLLEGE
One College Cir, Bangor ME 04401-2999
800-477-4723 or 207-941-7100 Fax: 207-941-7935
Website: www.husson.edu
E-mail: admit@husson.edu
M.S. in Physical Therapy & Occupational Therapy.
See listing under "Universities"

Kennebec Valley Community College
92 Western Ave, Fairfield ME 04937-1337
Kathy Moore, Director of Admissions
207-453-5035

Maine Medical Center
School of Surgical Technology
SMTC Fort Rd, South Portland ME 04106
Maureen Bien, RN, Program Director
207-767-9589

Mercy Hospital
144 State St, Portland ME 04101-3795
207-879-3000

St. Joseph's College of Maine
278 Whites Bridge Rd, Standish ME 04084-5263
Vincent Kloskowski, Dean of Admissions
800-338-7057 Fax: 207-893-7862
Website: www.sjcme.edu
E-mail: admission@sjcme.edu

Southern Maine Community College
2 Fort Rd, South Portland ME 04106-1698
Dr. James Ortiz, President
Scott MacDonald, Director of Financial Aid
207-741-5500 Fax: 207-741-5671
Website: www.smccme.edu
E-mail: oharmon@maine.rr.com

University of Maine
46 University Dr, Augusta ME 04330
207-621-3000

University of Maine
Orono ME 04469-0001
207-581-1110

University of Maine at Presque Isle
181 Main St, Presque Isle ME 04769-2844
207-768-9532

University of New England
11 Hills Beach Rd, Biddeford ME 04005-9526
207-283-0171

University of Southern Maine
PO Box 9300, Portland ME 04104-9300
207-780-4141

MARYLAND

Allegany College of Maryland
12401 Willowbrook Rd, Cumberland MD 21502-2596
301-784-5000

Baltimore City Community College
2901 Liberty Heights Ave, Baltimore MD 21215
Scheherazade Foreman, Director of Admissions
410-462-8000

Carroll Community College
1601 Washington Rd, Westminster MD 21157-6913
410-386-8000

Cecil College
One Seahawk Dr, North East MD 21901
Sandra S. Rajaski, Registrar & Director of Admissions
410-287-1000 Fax: 410-287-1001
Website: www.cecil.edu
E-mail: srajaski@cecil.edu

Chesapeake College
PO Box 8, Wye Mills MD 21679-0008
410-822-5400

Columbia Union College
7600 Flower Ave, Takoma Park MD 20912-7794
301-891-4000

The Community College of Baltimore County
Catonsville Campus
800 S Rolling Rd, Catonsville MD 21228-5317
Diane Drake, Director of Admissions
410-455-4555

Community College of Baltimore County
Essex Campus
7201 Rossville Blvd, Baltimore MD 21237-3898
Marcia Amaimo, Director of Admissions
410-780-6363

Coppin State University
2500 W North Ave, Baltimore MD 21216-3698
410-951-3000

Frederick Community College
7932 Opossumtown Pike, Frederick MD 21702-2097
Welcome and Registration Center
301-846-2430

Greater Baltimore Medical Center
6701 N Charles St, Baltimore MD 21204-6881
410-828-2121

Hagerstown Community College
11400 Robinwood Dr, Hagerstown MD 21742-6590
Dr. Daniel E. Bock, Assistant Director of Admissions
301-790-2800 Fax: 301-791-9165
Website: www.hagerstowncc.edu
E-mail: bockd@hagerstowncc.edu

Harford Community College
401 Thomas Run Rd, Bel Air MD 21015-1696
410-836-4000

Holy Cross Hospital
1500 Forest Glen Rd, Silver Spring MD 20910-1484
301-905-1216

Johns Hopkins University
600 N Wolfe St, Baltimore MD 21287-0005
410-955-3182

Johns Hopkins University
3400 N Charles St, Baltimore MD 21218-2680
410-516-8000

Kaplan College
Hagerstown Campus
18618 Crestwood Dr, Hagerstown MD 21742-2797
W. Christopher Motz, President
Steve Shinham, Director of Admissions
800-422-2670 Fax: 301-739-0474
Website: www.hagerstownbusinesscol.edu

Loyola College
4501 N Charles St, Baltimore MD 21210-2694
410-617-2000

Maryland General Hospital
827 Linden Ave, Baltimore MD 21201-4606
410-995-8600

MEDIX SCHOOL
700 York Rd, Towson MD 21204-2503
Lisa Harper, Director of Admissions
410-337-5155 Fax: 410-337-5104
Website: www.medixschooltowson.edu
E-mail: admissions@medixsch.com

Mercy Hospital
301 Saint Paul St, Baltimore MD 21202-2147
410-332-9202

Montgomery College
51 Mannakee St, Rockville MD 20850-1199
301-279-5000

Morgan State University
1700 E Cold Spring Ln, Baltimore MD 21251-0002
443-885-3000

Salisbury University
1101 Camden Ave, Salisbury MD 21801-6837
410-543-6000

Sodexho Marriott Healthcare Mid-Atlantic
9801 Washingtonian Blvd
Gaithersburg MD 20878-5355
301-987-4127

Towson State University
8000 York Rd, Towson MD 21252-0002
410-830-2000

University of Maryland
520 W Lombard St, Baltimore MD 21201
410-706-3100

University of Maryland
1000 Hilltop Cir, Baltimore MD 21250-0001
410-455-1000

University of Maryland
College Park MD 20742-0001
301-405-1000

University of Maryland Eastern Shore
Princess Anne MD 21853
Edwina Morse, Director of Admissions
410-651-6410

Villa Julie College
1525 Greenspring Valley Rd
Stevenson MD 21153-0641
Mark Hergan, V.P. Enrollment Services
410-486-7001

Washington Adventist Hospital
7600 Carroll Ave, Takoma Park MD 20912
301-891-7600

Wor-Wic Community College
32000 Campus Dr, Salisbury MD 21804-1485
410-334-2800

MASSACHUSETTS

Anna Maria College
50 Sunset Ln, Paxton MA 01612
Timothy M. Donahue, Director of Recruitment and Admissions
508-849-3360 Fax: 508-849-3362
Website: www.annamaria.edu
E-mail: admissions@annamaria.edu

Assumption College
500 Salisbury St, Worcester MA 01609-1294
Kathleen Murphy, Dean of Enrollment
508-767-7000 Fax: 508-799-4412
Website: www.assumption.edu
E-mail: admiss@assumption.edu

Bay Path College
588 Longmeadow St, Longmeadow MA 01106-2292
Lisa Casassa, Director of Admissions
413-565-1331

Bay State College
122 Commonwealth Ave, Boston MA 02116-2901
Craig Pfannenstiehl, President
617-217-9000 Fax: 617-536-1735

Becker College
Campuses in Worcester and Leicester, MA
61 Sever St, Worcester MA 01609-2165
Karen Schedin, Dean of Admissions
508-791-9241 Fax: 508-890-1500
Website: www.becker.edu
E-mail: admissions@becker.edu
See listing under "Universities"

Berklee College of Music
1140 Boylston St, Boston MA 02215-3693
Suzanne Hanser, Chair Music Therapy Dept.
617-266-1400

Berkshire Medical Center
725 North St, Pittsfield MA 01201-4124
413-447-2144

Beth Israel Healthcare
330 Brookline Ave, Boston MA 02215-5400
617-667-2539

Boston University
121 Bay State Rd, Boston MA 02215
Kelly Walter, Executive Director of Admissions
617-353-2300 Fax: 617-353-9695
Website: web.bu.edu
E-mail: admissions@bu.edu

Brandeis University
415 South St, Waltham MA 02453-2700
781-736-3500

Bridgewater State College
Bridgewater MA 02325-0001
508-697-1237

Brigham and Women's Hospital
75 Francis St, Boston MA 02115-6110
617-732-7493

Bristol Community College
777 Elsbree St, Fall River MA 02720-7395
Rodney S. Clark, Director of Admissions
508-678-2811 ext. 2516, 2179 Fax: 508-730-3265
Website: www.bristol.mass.edu
E-mail: admissions@bristol.mass.edu

Bunker Hill Community College
250 Rutherford Ave, Boston MA 02129-2925
617-228-2000

Cape Cod Community College
2240 Iyannough Rd, West Barnstable MA 02668
508-362-2131

Caritas Laboure College
2120 Dorchester Ave, Dorchester MA 02124-5698
617-296-8300

Children's Hospital
300 Longwood Ave, Boston MA 02115-5737
617-355-6433

C.H. McCann Technical School
70 Hodges Cross Road, North Adams MA 01247
Patricia E. Durkee, Admissions
413-663-5383

Endicott College
376 Hale St, Beverly MA 01915-2098
978-927-0585

Fisher College
118 Beacon St, Boston MA 02116-1501
Stephen Carter, Director of Admissions
800-446-1226

Fitchburg State College
160 Pearl St, Fitchburg MA 01420-2697
978-345-2151

Framingham State College
PO Box 9101, Framingham MA 01704-0101
508-620-1220

Greenfield Community College
1 College Dr, Greenfield MA 01301-9739
413-775-1000

Holyoke Community College
303 Homestead Ave, Holyoke MA 01040-1099
413-538-7000

Lasell College
1844 Commonwealth Ave, Newton MA 02466-2716
617-243-2225

Lesley University
29 Everett St, Cambridge MA 02138-2790
Jane Raley, Director of Admissions
617-349-8800

Massachusetts Bay Community College
50 Oakland St, Wellesley MA 02481-5307
781-239-3000

Massachusetts College of Pharmacy and Health Sciences
179 Longwood Ave, Boston MA 02115-5896
Kathleen B. Houghton, Director of Admissions
617-732-2850

Massachusetts Institute of Technology
77 Massachusetts Ave, Cambridge MA 02139-4307
617-253-1000 Fax: 617-253-4016
Website: my.mit.edu
E-mail: admissions@mit.edu

MGH Institute of Health Professions
36 1st Ave, Boston MA 02129-4557
Michael Bonanno, Manager of Admissions
617-726-3140

Middlesex Community College
Springs Rd, Bedford MA 01730-1114
Darcy Orellana, Director of Admissions
800-818-3434

Middlesex Community College
33 Kearney Sq, Lowell MA 01852-1987
Darcy Orellana, Director of Admissions
800-818-3434

Mt. Ida College
777 Dedham St, Newton Center MA 02459-3323
617-969-7000

Mt. Wachusett Community College
444 Green St, Gardner MA 01440
Karin Schedin, Director of Admissions
978-632-6600 ext. 110

Newbury College
129 Fisher Ave, Brookline MA 02445-5796
Salvadore Liberto, Vice President of Enrollment
617-730-7000 Fax: 617-731-9618
Website: www.newbury.edu
E-mail: info@newbury.edu
See listing under "Universities"

Northeastern University
360 Huntington Ave, Boston MA 02115-5000
617-373-2000

NORTHERN ESSEX COMMUNITY COLLEGE
100 Elliott St, Haverhill MA 01830
Nora B. Sheridan, Director of Admission
978-556-3700
Website: www.NECC.Mass.edu
E-mail: nsheridan@necc.mass.edu

North Shore Community College
1 Ferncroft Rd, Danvers MA 01923-4093
Jennifer Kirk, Director of Admissions & Recruitment Outreach
978-762-4000 Fax: 978-762-4015
Website: www.northshore.edu
E-mail: jkirk@northshore.edu

Quincy College
34 Coddington St, Quincy MA 02169-4501
617-984-1600

Quinsigamond Community College
670 W Boylston St, Worcester MA 01606-2092
508-853-2300

St. Luke's Hospital
101 Page St, New Bedford MA 02740-3464
508-997-1525

Salem State College
352 Lafayette St, Salem MA 01970-5353
978-741-6000

Salter School
184 W Boylston St Ste 1
West Boylston MA 01583-1700
508-853-1074

Simmons College
300 Fenway, Boston MA 02115-5898
617-521-2000

Sodexho Marriott Services
200 5th Ave, Waltham MA 02451-8779
800-926-7429

Southeastern Technical Institute
250 Foundry St, South Easton MA 02375-1780
Beverly A. Pusateri, Director
508-238-1860 Fax: 508-230-1558
Website: ti.sersd.org
E-mail: bpusateri@sersd.org

Springfield College
263 Alden St, Springfield MA 01109-3788
Mary DeAngelo, Director of Admissions
800-343-1257

Springfield Technical Community College
1 Armory Sq, Springfield MA 01105-1296
Andrea Lucy-Allen, Director of Admissions
413-755-4202

Tufts University
520 Boston Ave, Medford MA 02155-5555
617-628-5000

University of Massachusetts
Amherst MA 01003
413-545-0111

University of Massachusetts at Worcester
55 Lake Ave N, Worcester MA 01655-0001
508-856-8989

University of Massachusetts Boston
100 William T Morrissey Blvd, Boston MA 02125-3393
Liliana Mickle, Director of Undergraduate Admissions
617-287-6000

University of Massachusetts Dartmouth
Old Westport Rd, North Dartmouth MA 02747-2300
Steven T. Briggs, Director of Admissions
508-999-8605 Fax: 508-999-8755
Website: explore.umassd.edu
E-mail: sbriggs@umassd.edu

University of Massachusetts Lowell
1 University Ave, Lowell MA 01854-2893
978-934-4000

∴ Veterans Administration Medical Center
150 S Huntington Ave, Boston MA 02130-4817
617-232-9500

Worcester State College
486 Chandler St, Worcester MA 01602-2597
508-929-8000

MICHIGAN

· Alpena Community College
666 Johnson St, Alpena MI 49707-1495
989-356-9021

Andrews University
Berrien Springs MI 49104-0001
Randall Graves, Director of Recruitment Services
800-253-2874

Baker College of Auburn Hills
1500 University Dr, Auburn Hills MI 48326-2642
248-340-0600

Baker College of Cadillac
9600 E 13th St, Cadillac MI 49601-9574
Mike Tisdale, Director of Admissions
231-876-3100

Baker College of Clinton Township
34950 Little Mack Ave
Clinton Township MI 48035-4701
586-791-6610

Baker College of Flint
1050 W Bristol Rd, Flint MI 48507-5508
810-767-4000

Baker College of Jackson
2800 Springport Rd, Jackson MI 49202-1230
Kelli Hoban, Director of Admissions
517-789-6123

Baker College of Muskegon
1903 Marquette Ave, Muskegon MI 49442-1453
231-726-4904

Baker College of Owosso
1020 S Washington St, Owosso MI 48867-4400
989-729-3300

Baker College of Port Huron
3403 Lapeer Rd, Port Huron MI 48060-2597
Dan Kenny, Director of Admissions
888-262-2442

: **CARNEGIE INSTITUTE**
550 Stephenson Hwy Ste 100, Troy MI 48083-1159
Gloria J. McEachern, President
248-589-1078 Fax: 248-589-1631
Website: www.carnegie-institute.edu
E-mail: info@carnegie-institute.edu

Central Michigan University
100 Warriner Hall, Mount Pleasant MI 48859-0001
989-774-4000

· Charles S. Mott Community College
1401 E Court St, Flint MI 48503-6208
810-762-0200

· Charles Stewart Mott Community College
2100 W Thompson Rd, Fenton MI 48430
810-762-0200

Davenport University
4123 W Main St, Kalamazoo MI 49006-2748
Debra Burley, Director of Admissions
269-552-3308

Davenport University
5300 Bay Rd, Saginaw MI 48604
989-799-7800

Davenport University - Central Region
3555 E Patrick Rd, Midland MI 48642-5891
989-835-5588

· Delta College
University Center MI 48710-0001
Duff Zube, Director of Admissions
989-686-9093 Fax: 989-667-2202
Website: www.delta.edu
E-mail: admit@delta.edu

: Detroit Business Institute
23077 Greenfield Rd #LL28
Southfield MI 48075-3751
Greg Mitchell, Director of Admissions
248-552-6300 Fax: 248-552-7300
Website: www.dbisouthfield.com
E-mail: info@dbisouthfield.com

: Detroit Business Institute - Downriver
19100 Fort St, Riverview MI 48193
Theresa Hernandez, Director of Admissions
734-479-0660 Fax: 734-479-0738
Website: www.dbidownriver.com
E-mail: info@dbidownriver.com

∴ Detroit Health Department
1151 Taylor St, Detroit MI 48202
313-876-4090

∴ DMC University Laboratories
4201 Saint Antoine St, Detroit MI 48201-2153
313-745-3053

Eastern Michigan University
Ypsilanti MI 48197
800-GO-TO-EMU

: Everest Institute
5177 W Main St, Kalamazoo MI 49009
Susan Smith, Director of Admission
269-381-9616 Fax: 269-381-2513
Website: www.everest-institute.com
E-mail: susans@cci.edu

∴ Grace Hospital
6071 W Outer Dr, Detroit MI 48235-2679
313-966-3525

· Grand Rapids Community College
143 Bostwick Ave NE, Grand Rapids MI 49503-3201
616-234-4000

Grand Valley State University
1 Campus Dr, Allendale MI 49401-9403
Jodi Chycinski, Director of Admissions
616-331-6611 Fax: 616-331-2000
Website: www.gvsu.edu
E-mail: go2gvsu@gvsu.edu

· Great Lakes College
3930 Traxler Ct, Bay City MI 48706-9286
989-686-1572

· Great Lakes College
1231 Cleaver Rd, Caro MI 48723-9376
989-673-5857

∴ Harper Hospital
3990 John R St, Detroit MI 48201-2018
313-745-9375

· Henry Ford Community College
5101 Evergreen Rd, Dearborn MI 48128-2407
313-845-9615

∴ Henry Ford Hospital
2799 W Grand Blvd, Detroit MI 48202-2689
313-876-1257

Hope College
PO Box 9000, Holland MI 49422-9000
616-395-7000

∴ Hurley Medical Center
701 W 8th Ave, Flint MI 48503-1261
810-257-9237

· Jackson Community College
2111 Emmons Rd, Jackson MI 49201-8399
517-796-8425

· Kalamazoo Valley Community College
PO Box 4070, Kalamazoo MI 49003-4070
Marilyn Schlack, President
269-372-5000

· Kellogg Community College
450 North Ave, Battle Creek MI 49017-3397
269-965-3931

· Lake Michigan College
2755 E Napier Ave, Benton Harbor MI 49022-1899
269-927-8100

Lake Superior State University
650 W Easterday Ave
Sault Sainte Marie MI 49783-1637
Susan Camp, Director of Admissions
888-800-LSSU Fax: 906-635-6696
Website: www.lssu.edu
E-mail: admissions@lssu.edu
See listing under "Universities"

· Lansing Community College
419 N Capitol Ave, Lansing MI 48933-1293
517-483-1620

· **MACOMB COMMUNITY COLLEGE**
44575 Garfield Rd, Clinton Township MI 48038-1139
Information Center
586-445-7999
Website: www.macomb.edu
E-mail: answer@macomb.edu

· **MACOMB COMMUNITY COLLEGE**
14500 E 12 Mile Rd, Warren MI 48088-3896
Information Center
586-445-7999
Website: www.macomb.edu
E-mail: answer@macomb.edu

Madonna University
36600 Schoolcraft Rd, Livonia MI 48150-1173
734-432-5300

∴ Marquette General Hospital
420 W Magnetic St, Marquette MI 49855-2794
906-225-3434

Michigan State University
250 Administration Bldg, East Lansing MI 48824
517-355-1855

· Mid-Michigan Community College
1375 S Clare Ave, Harrison MI 48625-9447
989-386-6622

· Monroe County Community College
1555 S Raisinville Rd, Monroe MI 48161-9047
734-242-7300

∴ Munson Medical Center
1105 6th St, Traverse City MI 49684-2386
231-935-6501

· Muskegon Community College
221 S Quarterline Rd, Muskegon MI 49442-1493
231-773-9131

Northern Michigan University
1401 Presque Isle Ave, Marquette MI 49855-5301
906-227-1000

· Northwestern Michigan College
1701 E Front St, Traverse City MI 49686-3061
Jim Bensley, Director of Admissions
800-748-0566 Fax: 231-995-1339
Website: www.nmc.edu
E-mail: jbensley@nmc.edu

· Oakland Community College
27055 Orchard Lake Rd, Farmington Hills MI 48334
248-522-3400

· Oakland Community College
7350 Cooley Lake Rd, Waterford MI 48327-4187
248-942-3100

∴ Oakland County Health Division
1200 N Telegraph Rd, Pontiac MI 48341
248-858-1832

Oakland University
2200 N Squirrel Rd, Rochester MI 48309
Eleanor L. Reynolds, Assistant Vice President & Director of Admissions
248-370-2100
Website: www.oakland.edu
E-mail: ouinfo@oakland.edu

∴ Oakwood - Hospital Annapolis Center
33155 Annapolis St, Wayne MI 48184-2405
734-467-4000

: **OLYMPIA CAREER TRAINING INSTITUTE**
1750 Woodworth St NE
Grand Rapids MI 49525-2301
Bobbi Blok, Director of Admissions
616-364-8464 Fax: 616-364-5454
Website: www.cci.edu
E-mail: rblok@cci.edu

∴ Port Huron Hospital
1001 Kearney St, Port Huron MI 48060-3531
810-987-5000

∴ Providence Hospital
16001 W 9 Mile Rd, Southfield MI 48075-4854
248-424-3000

Saginaw Valley State University
7400 Bay Rd, University Center MI 48710-0001
989-790-4000

∴ St. John's Hospital
22101 Moross Rd, Detroit MI 48236-2172
313-343-7531

∴ St. Mary's Medical Center
800 S Washington Ave, Saginaw MI 48601
989-776-8176

· Schoolcraft College
18600 Haggerty Rd, Livonia MI 48152-2696
734-462-4400

∴ Spectrum Health
100 Michigan St NE, Grand Rapids MI 49503-2551
616-391-1605

University of Detroit-Mercy
PO Box 19900, Detroit MI 48219-0900
313-993-1000

University of Michigan-Ann Arbor
1220 Student Activities Bldg, Ann Arbor MI 48109
734-764-1817

University of Michigan-Flint
303 E Kearsley St, Flint MI 48502-1950
810-762-3000

· Washtenaw Community College
PO Box D-1, Ann Arbor MI 48106-1610
734-973-3300

· Wayne County Community College
801 W Fort St, Detroit MI 48226-3095
313-496-2500

Wayne State University
5980 Cass Ave, Detroit MI 48202-3489
313-577-2424

Western Michigan University
Kalamazoo MI 49008
269-387-1000

∴ William Beaumont Hospital
3601 W 13 Mile Rd, Royal Oak MI 48073-6769
248-551-0681

MINNESOTA

· Alexandria Technical College
1601 Jefferson St, Alexandria MN 56308-3707
320-762-0221

· Anoka Technical College
1355 Highway 10, Anoka MN 55303
763-576-4700

ARGOSY UNIVERSITY / TWIN CITIES
(formerly Medical Institute of Minnesota)
1515 Central Pkwy, Eagan MN 55121-1756
O. Jeanne Stoneking, Director of Admissions
651-846-2882 Fax: 651-994-7956
Website: www.argosyu.edu
E-mail: tcadmissions@argosyu.edu

Augsburg College
2211 Riverside Ave, Minneapolis MN 55454-1350
612-330-1000

· Central Lakes College
501 W College Dr, Brainerd MN 56401-3900
218-855-8000

College of Saint Benedict
37 College Ave S, Saint Joseph MN 56374-2099
320-363-5011

College of St. Catherine
2004 Randolph Ave, Saint Paul MN 55105-1789
651-690-6000

College of Saint Scholastica
1200 Kenwood Ave, Duluth MN 55811-4199
Brian Dalton, V.P. of Enrollment Management
800-447-5444

Concordia College
901 8th St S, Moorhead MN 56562-0002
Scott Ellingson, Director of Admissions
218-299-3004

· Dakota County Technical College
1300 145th St E, Rosemount MN 55068-2999
800-548-5502

· Duluth Business University
4724 Mike Colalillo Dr, Duluth MN 55807-2723
Bonnie Kupczynski, Director
800-777-8406 Fax: 218-628-2127
Website: www.dbumn.edu
E-mail: info@dbumn.edu

· Globe College
7166 10th St N, Oakdale MN 55128
Mike Hughes, Campus Director
651-730-5100 Fax: 651-730-5151
Website: www.globecollege.edu
E-mail: admissions@globecollege.edu

Gustavus Adolphus College
800 W College Ave, Saint Peter MN 56082-1485
Mark H. Anderson, Dean of Admission
800-GUSTAVUS Fax: 507-933-7474
Website: www.gustavus.edu
E-mail: admission@gustavus.edu

Health System Minnesota/Methodist Hospital
6500 Excelsior Blvd, Saint Louis Park MN 55426-4700
952-993-3601

Hennepin County Medical Center
701 Park Ave, Minneapolis MN 55415-1829
612-347-2352

Hennepin Technical College
9000 Brooklyn Blvd, Brooklyn Park MN 55445-2320
952-995-1300

Hibbing Community College
1515 E 25th St, Hibbing MN 55746-3300
Holly Bigelow, Director of Enrollment
800-224-4HCC or 218-262-7200 Fax: 218-262-6717
Website: www.hibbing.edu
E-mail: admissions@hibbing.edu

High-Tech Institute
5100 Gamble Dr Ste 200
Saint Louis Park MN 55416-1521
Jeri Prochaska, Director of Admissions
763-560-9700 Fax: 952-545-6149
Website: www.hightechinstitute.edu
E-mail: jprochaska@hightechinstitute.edu

Lake Superior College
2101 Trinity Rd, Duluth MN 55811-3399
218-733-7600

Mayo School of Health Sciences
200 1st Ave SW, Rochester MN 55905-0001
507-284-3678

Minneapolis Business College
1711 County Road B W, Roseville MN 55113-4036
651-636-7406

Minneapolis Community and Technical College
1501 Hennepin Ave, Minneapolis MN 55403-1779
Dena Russell, Director of Admissions
612-659-6282

Minneapolis VA Medical Center
1 Veterans Dr, Minneapolis MN 55417-2300
612-725-2000

Minnesota School of Business
5910 Shingle Creek Pkwy #200
Brooklyn Center MN 55430-2319
763-566-7777

Minnesota School of Business
1401 W 76th St Ste 500, Richfield MN 55423-3846
612-861-2000

Minnesota State College - Southeast Technical
Red Wing Campus
308 Pioneer Rd, Red Wing MN 55066
Al DuCett, Director of Admissions
877-853-8324 Fax: 507-453-2715
Website: www.southeastmn.edu
E-mail: aducett@southeastmn.edu
70+ degrees, diplomas & certificates (15+ online) in Business & Office Careers, Musical Instrument Repair, Physical Health, Transportation, Technology, and Trades.

Minnesota State College - Southeast Technical
Winona Campus
PO Box 409, 1250 Homer Rd, Winona MN 55987
Al DuCett, Director of Admissions
877-853-8324 Fax: 507-453-2715
Website: www.southeastmn.edu
E-mail: aducett@southeastmn.edu
70+ degrees, diplomas & certificates (15+ online) in Business & Office Careers, Musical Instrument Repair, Physical Health, Transportation, Technology, and Trades.

Minnesota State Community and Technical College
1900 28th Ave S, Moorhead MN 56560-4899
Laurie McKeever, Director of Admissions
800-426-5603

Minnesota State Community and Technical College
Fergus Falls
1414 College Way, Fergus Falls MN 56537-1009
218-739-7500

Minnesota State University Mankato
228 Wiecking Center, Mankato MN 56001
507-389-1866

Minnesota State University Moorhead
1104 7th Ave S, Moorhead MN 56563-0002
Regina Monson, Director of Admissions
218-477-2161 Fax: 218-477-4374
Website: go.mnstate.edu
E-mail: dragon@mnstate.edu

Minnesota West Community and Technical College
Granite Falls Campus
1593 11th Ave, Granite Falls MN 56241-1061
Becky Weber, Contact
800-657-3247

Normandale Community College
9700 France Ave S, Bloomington MN 55431-4399
Rick Smith, Director of Admissions
952-832-6000

North Hennepin Community College
7411 85th Ave N, Brooklyn Park MN 55445-2299
763-424-0702

Northland Community and Technical College
2022 Central Ave NE
East Grand Forks MN 56721-2702
Elizabeth McMahon, Allied Health Division Chair
800-451-3441 Fax: 218-773-4502
Website: www.northlandcollege.edu
E-mail: admissions@northlandcollege.edu

North Memorial Medical Center
3300 Oakdale Ave N, Minneapolis MN 55422-2900
763-520-5200

Northwest Technical College
905 Grant Ave SE, Bemidji MN 56601
Richard Lehmann, Admissions
800-942-8324

Rasmussen College
7905 Golden Triangle Dr Ste 100
Eden Prairie MN 55344-7220
952-545-2000

Rice Memorial Hospital
School of Radiologic Technology
301 Becker Ave SW, Willmar MN 56201-3395
Luther Linn RT, Program Director
320-231-4553

Ridgewater College-Hutchinson Campus
2 Century Ave SE, Hutchinson MN 55350-3100
Dawn Bjork, Counselor
800-722-1151 Fax: 320-234-8506
Website: www.ridgewater.edu
E-mail: dawn.bjork@ridgewater.edu

Ridgewater College-Willmar Campus
PO Box 1097, Willmar MN 56201-1097
Sally Kerfeld, Director of Admissions
800-722-1151 Fax: 320-222-5212
Website: www.ridgewater.edu
E-mail: sally.kerfeld@ridgewater.edu

Riverland Community College
1900 8th Ave NW, Austin MN 55912-1400
Dani Heiny, Director of Admissions
800-247-5039

Riverland Community College
Albert Lea Campus
2200 Riverland Dr, Albert Lea MN 56007
Dani Heiny, Director of Admissions
800-333-2584

Riverland Technical College
1225 3rd St SW, Faribault MN 55021-5720
800-422-0391

Rochester Community & Technical College
851 30th Ave SE, Rochester MN 55904-4999
507-285-7210

St. Cloud Hospital
1406 6th Ave N, Saint Cloud MN 56303-1901
320-255-5666

St. Cloud State University
720 4th Ave S, Saint Cloud MN 56301-4442
877-654-7278

St. Cloud Technical College
1540 Northway Dr, Saint Cloud MN 56303-1240
Jodi Elness, Director of Enrollment Management
800-222-1009 Fax: 320-308-5981
Website: www.sctc.edu
E-mail: jelness@sctc.edu

St. Mary's Hospital/Mayo Medical Center
1216 2nd St NW, Rochester MN 55901-0322
507-255-5221

St. Mary's University of Minnesota
700 Terrace Hts Ste 2, Winona MN 55987-1321
507-452-4430

St. Paul College
A Community & Technical College
235 Marshall Ave, Saint Paul MN 55102-1800
651-221-1300

South Central College
1920 Lee Blvd, North Mankato MN 56003-2508
507-389-7200

Sr. Rosalind Gefre Schools of Massage
416 S Front St, Mankato MN 56001
Mary Pegram, Director of Admissions
507-344-0220 Fax: 507-344-0204
Website: www.sisterrosalind.org
E-mail: mankatocampus@sisterrosalind.org

Sr. Rosalind Gefre Schools of Massage
300 Elton Hills Dr NW, Rochester MN 55901
Steve King, Director of Admissions
507-286-8608 Fax: 507-282-2893
Website: www.sisterrosalind.org
E-mail: rochestercampus@sisterrosalind.org

Sr. Rosalind Gefre Schools of Massage
1007 Industrial Dr S, Sauk Rapids MN 56379
Anita Figallo, Director of Admissions
320-259-6185 Fax: 320-259-6173
Website: www.sisterrosalind.org
E-mail: saukrapidscampus@sisterrosalind.org

Sr. Rosalind Gefre Schools of Massage
149 Thompson Ave Ste 150
West Saint Paul MN 55118
Jen Maudel, Director of Admissions
651-554-3010 Fax: 651-554-7608
Website: www.sisterrosalind.org
E-mail: stpaulcampus@sisterrosalind.org

University of Minnesota
2900 University Ave, Crookston MN 56716-5001
218-281-6510 Fax: 218-281-8575
Website:
admissions.umcrookston.edu/requirements/apply.htm
E-mail: info@umcrookston.edu

University of Minnesota
10 University Dr, Duluth MN 55812-2496
Beth Esselstrom, Director of Admissions
218-726-7171

University of Minnesota
231 Pillsbury Dr SE, Minneapolis MN 55455-0230
612-625-2008

MISSISSIPPI

Alcorn State University
PO Box 359, Lorman MS 39096
601-877-6147

Copiah-Lincoln Community College
PO Box 457, Wesson MS 39191-0457
601-643-5101

Delta State University
Hwy 8 W, Cleveland MS 38733
662-846-3000

Forrest General Hospital
6051 U S Highway 49, Hattiesburg MS 39401-7225
601-288-4201

Hattiesburg Radiology Group
5000 W 4th St, Hattiesburg MS 39402-1077
601-288-4241

Hinds Community College
PO Box 1100, Raymond MS 39154
601-857-5261

Itawamba Community College
602 W Hill St, Fulton MS 38843
662-862-8000

Jackson State University
1440 J.R. Lynch St, Jackson MS 39217
Stephanie Chatman, Director of Admissions
601-979-2100

Jones County Junior College
900 S Court St, Ellisville MS 39437-3999
601-477-4000

Meridian Community College
910 Highway 19 N, Meridian MS 39307-5801
601-483-8241

Mississippi Baptist Medical Center
1225 N State St, Jackson MS 39202-2002
601-968-5130

Mississippi Delta Community College
PO Box 668, Moorhead MS 38761-0668
662-246-6322

Mississippi Gulf Coast Community College
PO Box 609, Perkinston MS 39573
601-928-5211

Mississippi State University
PO Box J, Mississippi State MS 39762-5509
662-325-2323

Mississippi University for Women
1100 College St Unit W1613, Columbus MS 39701
Terri Heath, Director of Admissions
877-GO-2-THEW

Northeast Mississippi Community College
101 Cunningham Blvd, Booneville MS 38829-1726
662-728-7751

North Mississippi Medical Center
830 S Gloster St, Tupelo MS 38801-4934
662-841-3136

Northwest Mississippi Community College
4975 Highway 51 N, Senatobia MS 38668
662-562-3200

Pearl River Community College
Station A, Poplarville MS 39470
601-795-6801

St. Dominic-Jackson Memorial Hospital
969 Lakeland Dr, Jackson MS 39216-4602
601-364-6935

Southwest Mississippi Regional Medical Center
PO Box 1307, Mc Comb MS 39649-1307
601-249-1807

University of Mississippi
University MS 38677
662-232-7226

University of Mississippi Medical Center
2500 N State St, Jackson MS 39216-4500
601-984-1010

University of Southern Mississippi
PO Box 5165, Hattiesburg MS 39406-1000
601-266-5000

William Carey College
498 Tuscan Ave, Hattiesburg MS 39401-5461
800-962-5991

MISSOURI

ALLIED COLLEGE - NORTH
13723 Riverport Dr Ste 103
Maryland Heights MO 63043
Heidi Wind, Campus President
866-501-1291 Fax: 314-739-5133
Website: www.alliedcollege.edu

ARAMARK Healthcare Support Services SW
1000 Carondelet Dr, Kansas City MO 64114-4673
816-943-2146

Avila University
11901 Wornall Rd, Kansas City MO 64145-1698
Patricia Harper, Director of Admissions
816-942-8400

Cape Girardeau Career & Technology Center
1080 S Silver Springs Rd
Cape Girardeau MO 63703-7511
573-334-0826

Central Institute for the Deaf
818 S Euclid Ave, Saint Louis MO 63110-1594
314-652-3200

Central Methodist University
411 Central Methodist Sq, Fayette MO 65248-1198
Larry Anderson, Director of Admissions
660-248-6247 Fax: 660-248-1872
Website: www.centralmethodist.edu
E-mail: landerso@centralmethodist.edu

Central Missouri State University
Warrensburg MO 64093-8888
Charles Petentler, Associate Director of Admissions
800-956-0177

College of the Ozarks
Point Lookout MO 65726
417-334-6411

Concorde Career College
3239 Broadway St, Kansas City MO 64111-2407
Steve Koberlein, Director of Admissions
816-531-5223

Cox College of Nursing & Health Sciences
1423 N Jefferson Ave, Springfield MO 65802-1917
417-269-3401

DVA Medical Center
1 Jefferson Barracks Rd, Saint Louis MO 63125-4181
314-894-6631

East Central College
1964 Prairie Dell Rd, Union MO 63084
Karen Wieda, Registrar
636-583-5195 ext. 2220 Fax: 636-583-1897
Website: www.eastcentral.edu
E-mail: wiedaks@eastcentral.edu

EVEREST COLLEGE
1010 W Sunshine St, Springfield MO 65807-2446
Melanie Exter, Contact
417-864-7220 or 800-475-2699 Fax: 417-866-3335
Website: www.everest-college.com
E-mail: mexter@cci.edu

Fontbonne University
6800 Wydown Blvd, Saint Louis MO 63105-3098
314-889-1419

Hannibal Area Vocational Technical School
4550 McMasters Ave, Hannibal MO 63401-2242
Harold D. Ward, Director
573-221-4430

Heritage College
1200 E 104th St Ste 300, Kansas City MO 64131
Larry Cartmill, Director
816-942-5474 Fax: 816-942-5405
Website: www.heritage-education.com
E-mail: info@heritage-education.com
See listing under "Career Schools"

IHM Health Studies Center
3663 Lindell Blvd, Saint Louis MO 63108
314-768-1000

Lindenwood University
209 S Kingshighway St
Saint Charles MO 63301-1695
Sheryl Guffey, Director of Admissions
636-949-2000 Fax: 636-949-4989
Website: www.lindenwood.edu

Linn State Technical College
1 Technology Dr, Linn MO 65051-9606
Becky Dunn, Admissions
800-743-8324 Fax: 573-897-5026
Website: www.linnstate.edu
E-mail: admissions@linnstate.edu

Mineral Area Regional Medical Center
1212 Weber Rd, Farmington MO 63640-3309
573-756-4581

Missouri College
10121 Manchester Rd, Saint Louis MO 63122-1525
Erin Cunningham, Director of Admissions
314-821-7700

Missouri Southern State University - Joplin
3950 Newman Rd, Joplin MO 64801-1512
417-625-9300

Missouri State University
901 S National Ave, Springfield MO 65897
417-836-5000

Missouri Western State College
4525 Downs Dr, Saint Joseph MO 64507-2294
800-662-7041

Nichols Career Center
605 Union St, Jefferson City MO 65101-2814
573-659-3100

North Kansas City Hospital
2800 Clay Edwards Dr
North Kansas City MO 64116-3220
816-691-2000

Northwest Missouri State University
800 University Dr, Maryville MO 64468-6001
Beverly Schenkel, Dean of Enrollment Management
660-562-1562 Fax: 660-562-1121
Website: www.nwmissouri.edu
E-mail: admissions@nwmissouri.edu

Ozarks Technical Community College
1001 E Chestnut Expressway
Springfield MO 65802-3625
Delvan Mitchell, Director of Admissions
417-447-7500 Fax: 417-447-6925
Website: www.otc.edu
E-mail: admissions@otc.edu

Penn Valley Community College
3201 SW Traffic Way, Kansas City MO 64111
816-759-4000

Research Medical Center
2316 E Meyer Blvd, Kansas City MO 64132-1199
816-276-4101

Rockhurst University
1100 Rockhurst Rd, Kansas City MO 64110-2561
Mark Kopenski, VP of Enrollment Management
816-501-4000

St. Charles Community College
4601 Mid Rivers Mall Dr, Cottleville MO 63376
Kathy Brockgreitens-Gober, Director of Admissions
636-922-8000 Fax: 636-922-8236
Website: www.stchas.edu
E-mail: adm-reg@stchas.edu

St. John's Mercy Medical Center
615 S New Ballas Rd, Saint Louis MO 63141-8277
314-569-6182

St. John's Regional Health Center
1235 E Cherokee St, Springfield MO 65804-2263
417-885-2845

St. John's Regional Medical Center
2727 Mc Clelland Blvd, Joplin MO 64804-1694
417-781-2727

St. Louis Community College
11333 Big Bend Rd, Kirkwood MO 63122-5799
314-984-7500

St. Louis Community College
5600 Oakland Ave, Saint Louis MO 63110-1316
314-644-9100

St. Louis Community College at Florissant Valley
3400 Pershall Rd, Saint Louis MO 63135-1408
Janice Evans, Chair, Enrollment Management
314-595-4368

St. Louis University
221 N Grand Blvd, Saint Louis MO 63103-2097
314-977-2222

Saint Luke's College
8320 Ward Parkway Suite 300
Kansas City MO 64114
Josh Richards Asst. Director of Admissions
816-932-2367

Sanford-Brown College
1345 Smizer Mill Rd, Fenton MO 63026
Kevin Frank, Director of HS Admissions
636-651-1600

Southeast Missouri Hospital
College of Nursing and Health Sciences
2001 William St #2, Cape Girardeau MO 63703-5815
Don Pugh, Registrar
573-334-6825

Southeast Missouri State University
1 University Plz, Cape Girardeau MO 63701-4710
573-651-2000

State Fair Community College
3201 W 16th St, Sedalia MO 65301-2199
Director of Admissions
660-530-5833 Fax: 660-596-7472
Website: www.sfccmo.edu
E-mail: mparris@sfccmo.edu

Stephens College
PO Box 2121, Columbia MO 65215-0001
David Adams, Dean of Enrollment Management
573-442-2211 Fax: 573-876-7237
Website: www.stephens.edu
E-mail: dadams@stephens.edu

Three Rivers Community College
2080 Three Rivers Blvd, Poplar Bluff MO 63901
573-840-9605

Truman Medical Center
2301 Holmes St, Kansas City MO 64108-2677
816-556-3153

Truman State University
100 E Normal, Kirksville MO 63501
Office of Admission
660-785-4114 Fax: 660-785-7456
Website: admissions.truman.edu
E-mail: admissions@truman.edu

University of Missouri
228 Jesse Hall, Columbia MO 65211-0001
573-882-2121

University of Missouri
5100 Rockhill Rd, Kansas City MO 64110-2446
816-235-1000

Washington University in St. Louis
1 Brookings Dr, Saint Louis MO 63130-4899
314-935-5000

William Jewell College
500 College Hill, Liberty MO 64068-1896
Dr. Rick Winslow, VP Enrollment Management and Student Affairs
800-753-7009 Fax: 816-415-5040
Website: www.jewell.edu
E-mail: winslowr@william.jewell.edu

MONTANA

Benefits Health Care-West Campus
PO Box 5013, Great Falls MT 59403-5013
406-727-3333

Carroll College
1601 N Benton Ave, Helena MT 59625-0002
Dr. Thomas J. Trebon, President
Cynthia Thornquist, Director of Admissions & Enrollment Operations
406-447-4384 Fax: 406-447-4533
Website: www.carroll.edu
E-mail: admission@carroll.edu

Flathead Valley Community College
777 Grandview Dr, Kalispell MT 59901-2622
406-756-3846

Montana State University - Billings
1500 University Dr, Billings MT 59101-0252
Karen Everett, Director
800-565-MSUB

Montana State University - Bozeman
103 Culbertson Hall, Bozeman MT 59715-5072
406-994-2452

Montana State University
Great Falls College of Technology
2100 16th Ave S, Great Falls MT 59405-4909
406-771-4300

Rocky Mountain College
1511 Poly Dr, Billings MT 59102-1796
Bonnie Knapp, Director of Admissions
800-877-6259

St. Patrick Hospital
PO Box 4587, Missoula MT 59806-4587
406-543-7271

St. Vincent's Hospital & Health Center
PO Box 35200, Billings MT 59107
406-657-7102

Salish Kootenai College
PO Box 70, Pablo MT 59855
Jackie Moran, Admissions/Transfers
406-275-4866

NEBRASKA

Bishop Clarkson Memorial Hospital
4350 Dewey Ave, Omaha NE 68105-1017
402-552-3203

Central Community College-Hastings Campus
PO Box 1024, Hastings NE 68902-1024
Bob Glenn, Director of Admissions
402-463-9811 Fax: 402-562-1201
Website: www.cccneb.edu
E-mail: rglenn@cccneb.edu

Clarkson College
101 S 42nd St, Omaha NE 68131-2715
Sara Bonney, Director of Admissions
800-647-5500 Fax: 402-552-6057
Website: www.clarksoncollege.edu
E-mail: admiss@clarksoncollege.edu

College of Saint Mary
7000 Mercy Rd, Omaha NE 68106
Lorin Werth,V.P. for Enrollment
800-926-5534

Creighton University
2500 California Plz, Omaha NE 68178-0001
402-280-2700

Hamilton College
3350 N 90th St, Omaha NE 68134-4710
402-572-8500

Immanuel Medical Center
6901 N 72nd St, Omaha NE 68122-1709
402-572-2270

Mary Lanning Memorial Hospital
715 N Saint Joseph Ave, Hastings NE 68901-4497
402-463-4521

Metropolitan Community College
PO Box 3777, Omaha NE 68103-0777
Becky Nicks, Director of Admissions
402-449-8400 Fax: 402-457-2616
Website: www.mccnab.edu
E-mail: bnicks@mccnab.edu

Nebraska Methodist College
720 N 87th St, Omaha NE 68114
Deann Sterner, Director of Admissions
402-354-7200

Nebraska Wesleyan University
5000 Saint Paul Ave, Lincoln NE 68504-2794
Patricia Karthauser, V.P. for University Enrollment
402-466-2371 Fax: 402-465-2177
Website: www.nebrwesleyan.edu
E-mail: admissions@nebrwesleyan.edu

Northeast Community College
PO Box 469, Norfolk NE 68702-0469
402-371-2020

Regional West Medical Center
4021 Avenue B, Scottsbluff NE 69361-4695
308-635-3711

Southeast Community College
8800 O St, Lincoln NE 68520-1299
402-437-2500

Union College
3800 S 48th St, Lincoln NE 68506-4300
Buell Fogg, V.P. for Enrollment Services
800-228-4600

University of Nebraska
14th & R Sts, Lincoln NE 68588
402-472-7211

University of Nebraska at Kearney
905 W 25th St, Kearney NE 68849-0001
Dusty Newton, Director of Admissions
800-KEARNEY Fax: 308-865-8987
Website: www.unk.edu
E-mail: admissionsug@unk.edu

University of Nebraska at Omaha
60th and Dodge St, Omaha NE 68182-0001
402-554-2800

University of Nebraska Medical Center
985150 Nebraska Medical Center
Omaha NE 68198-5150
800-626-8431

NEVADA

Associated Pathologist Laboratories
4230 Burnham Ave, Las Vegas NV 89119-5408
702-733-7866

Career College of Northern Nevada
1195-A Corporate Blvd, Reno NV 89502-2331
Nathan Clark, Director
775-856-2266 Fax: 775-856-0935
Website: www.ccnn.edu
E-mail: lgoldhammer@ccnn4u.com
See listing under "Career Schools"

Community College of Southern Nevada
3200 E Cheyenne Ave
North Las Vegas NV 89030-4228
702-651-4536

GREAT BASIN COLLEGE
1500 College Pkwy, Elko NV 89801-5032
Julie G. Byrnes, Director of Enrollment Management
775-753-2271 Fax: 775-753-2311
Website: www.gbcnv.edu
E-mail: julieb@gwmail.gbcnv.edu
See listing under "Universities"

Heritage College
3315 Spring Mountain Rd, Las Vegas NV 89102
Mimi Ritenour, Director of Admissions
702-368-2338

Truckee Meadows Community College
7000 Dandini Blvd, Reno NV 89512-3999
Rita Huneycutt, Interim President
775-673-7000

University of Nevada
Reno NV 89557-0001
775-784-1110

University of Nevada Las Vegas
4505 S Maryland Pkwy, Las Vegas NV 89154-9901
800-334-8658

NEW HAMPSHIRE

Keene State College
229 Main St, Keene NH 03435-0002
603-358-2276

New Hampshire Community Technical College
1 College Dr, Claremont NH 03743
Charles Kusselow, Admissions Counselor
603-542-7744

New Hampshire Community Technical College
1066 Front St, Manchester NH 03102-8528
Jacquie Poirier, Director of Admissions
603-668-6706 Fax: 603-668-5354
Website: www.manchester.nhctc.edu
E-mail: jpoirier@nhctc.edu

New Hampshire Technical Institute
11 Institute Dr, Concord NH 03301-7400
603-271-6484

Plymouth State University
17 High St, MSC #44, Bagley House
Plymouth NH 03264-1595
603-535-5000

University of New Hampshire
Durham NH 03824
603-862-1234

NEW JERSEY

Atlantic Cape Community College
5100 Black Horse Pike
Mays Landing NJ 08330-2699
Linda McLeod, Assistant Director of College Recruitment
609-343-5000 Fax: 609-343-4921
Website: www.atlantic.edu
E-mail: accadmit@atlantic.edu
See listing under "Community and Junior Colleges"

Atlantic County Vocational Technical School
5080 Atlantic Ave, Mays Landing NJ 08330-2022
609-625-2249

BERDAN INSTITUTE
201 Willowbrook Blvd, Wayne NJ 07470-7041
David Dahlke, Director of Admissions
973-837-1818 Fax: 973-837-1840
Website: www.berdaninstitute.com
E-mail: info@berdaninstitute.com

Bergen Community College
400 Paramus Rd, Paramus NJ 07652
Julian Gomez, Asst. Director of Admissions
201-447-7100 Fax: 201-444-7036
Website: www.bergen.edu
E-mail: jgomez@bergen.edu

BEST CARE TRAINING INSTITUTE
68 S Harrison St, East Orange NJ 07017
Florence Brown, RN, MSN, APNC, Contact
973-673-3900 Fax: 973-673-0597
Website: www.bestcarehealth.com
E-mail: fbrown3260@aol.com

Burdette Tomlin Memorial Hospital
2 Stone Harbor Blvd
Cape May Court House NJ 08210-2171
609-463-2180

Burlington County College
County Route 530, Pemberton NJ 08068
609-894-9311

Burlington County Institute of Technology - Adult Education
695 Woodlane Rd, Mount Holly NJ 08060-3813
Dr. Fred Laier, Contact
609-267-4226

Camden County College
PO Box 200, Blackwood NJ 08012-0200
856-227-7200

THE CHUBB INSTITUTE
40 Journal Sq, Jersey City NJ 07306-4097
Valerie Yancey, Campus President
201-876-3800 Fax: 201-656-2091
Website: www.chubbinstitute.edu
E-mail: vyancey@chubbinstitute.edu

College of New Jersey
PO Box 7718, Ewing NJ 08628-0718
609-771-1855

College of Saint Elizabeth
2 Convent Rd, Morristown NJ 07960-6923
973-292-4000

Cooper Hospital/University Medical Center
1 Cooper Plz #217, Camden NJ 08103-1461
Joan D'Antonio, Director
856-342-2416

County College of Morris
214 Center Grove Rd, Randolph NJ 07869-2086
973-328-5000

Cumberland County College
PO Box 1500, Vineland NJ 08362-1500
856-691-8600

Cumberland County Technical Education Center
601 Bridgeton Ave, Bridgeton NJ 08302-4810
856-451-9000

Dover Business College
15 E Blackwell St, Dover NJ 07801-4643
973-285-8400

Dover Business College
East 81 Route 4 W, Paramus NJ 07652
201-843-8500

Elizabeth General Medical Center School
925 E Jersey St, Elizabeth NJ 07201-2789
908-965-7390

Englewood Hospital & Medical Center
350 Engle St, Englewood NJ 07631-1898
201-894-3002

Essex County College
303 University Ave, Newark NJ 07102-1798
973-877-3000

Fairleigh Dickinson University
1000 River Rd, Teaneck NJ 07666-1996
201-692-2000

Felician College
262 S Main St, Lodi NJ 07644-2198
201-559-6000

Gloucester County College
1400 Tanyard Rd, Sewell NJ 08080
856-468-5000

Gloucester Township Technical School
343 Berlin Cross Keys Rd, Sicklerville NJ 08081-4000
Gayle Butler, Director of Admissions
856-767-7002

Hackensack Univ Medical Center
30 Prospect Ave, Hackensack NJ 07601-1991
201-996-2000

Helene Fuld Medical Center
750 Brunswick Ave, Trenton NJ 08638-4174
609-394-3174

HoHoKus School of Business & Medical Sciences
10 S Franklin Tpke, Ramsey NJ 07446-2546
Thomas Eastwick, Director
201-327-8877 Fax: 201-327-9054
Website: www.hohokus.edu
E-mail: tomeastwick@aol.com

Hohokus School - RETS Nutley
103 Park Ave, Nutley NJ 07110-3505
Thomas Eastwick, President
973-661-0600 Fax: 973-661-2954
Website: www.rets-institute.com
E-mail: admissions@rets-institute.com

HUDSON AREA SCHOOL OF RADIOLOGIC TECHNOLOGY
176 Palisade Ave, Jersey City NJ 07306
Kenneth Lee, D.H.S., R.T. (R)(M)
201-795-8246 Fax: 201-795-5818
Website: www.christhospital.org
E-mail: lleclaire@christhospital.org

Hudson County Community College
25 Journal Sq, Jersey City NJ 07306
201-656-2020

The Institute for Health Education
7 Spielman Rd, Fairfield NJ 07004-3403
973-808-1666

Jersey Shore Medical Center
1945 State Route 33, Neptune City NJ 07753-4889
732-776-4603

Kean University
1000 Morris Ave, Union NJ 07083-7133
908-527-2000

MCELLIS TRAINING INSTITUTE
800 Broad St, Newark NJ 07102
Sharon Bradbury, Assistant Director
973-643-6917 Fax: 973-643-6973
E-mail: mcellisinstitute@aol.com

Middlesex County College
2600 Woodbridge Ave, Edison NJ 08837-3675
732-548-6000

Monmouth Medical Center
300 2nd Ave, Long Branch NJ 07740-6395
John A. Mihok, MT Program Director
732-222-5200

Montclair State University
Montclair State University, Montclair NJ 07043-1624
973-655-4000

Morristown Memorial Hospital
100 Madison Ave, Morristown NJ 07960-6095
973-971-5177

Mountainside Hospital
1 Bay Ave, Montclair NJ 07042-4898
973-429-6850

MUHLENBERG REGIONAL MEDICAL CENTER
Harold B. & Dorothy A. Snyder Schools of Nursing, Medical Imaging & Therapeutic Sciences
Plainfield, NJ 07061
Jane Vatsky, Director of Admissions
908-668-2400 Fax: 908-226-4568
Website: www.muhlenbergschools.org
E-mail: ssonmits@solarishs.org
See listing under "Nursing"

New Jersey City University
2039 John F Kennedy Blvd
Jersey City NJ 07305-1588
Carmen Panlilio, Asst. V.P. for Admissions and Financial Aid
201-200-3234 Fax: 201-200-2044
Website: www.njcu.edu
E-mail: admissions@njcu.edu

Ocean County College
College Dr, Toms River NJ 08754
732-255-0400

Pascack Valley Hospital
250 Old Hook Rd, Westwood NJ 07675-3181
201-358-3010

Passaic Co. Community College
1 College Blvd, Paterson NJ 07505
973-684-6800

Raritan Valley Community College
PO Box 3300, Somerville NJ 08876-1265
908-526-1200

RICHARD STOCKTON COLLEGE OF NEW JERSEY
PO Box 195, Pomona NJ 08240
John Iacovelli, Dean of Enrollment Management
866-RSC-2885 Fax: 609-626-5541
Website: www.stockton.edu
E-mail: admissions@stockton.edu
Stockton College is a comprehensive liberal arts, coed institution founded in 1969. Advance Pre-Professional Degree Options: 7-yr BS/MD with UMDNJ; NJ Dental School; NJ Medical School, Robert Wood Johnson Medical, School of Osteopathic Medicine; NY College of Podiatric Medicine, Pennsylvania College of Podiatric Medicine, SUNY College of Optometry. Pharmacy doctorate program with Rutgers University. 5-yr Engineering with NJIT and Rutgers University. Dual BA/MA in Criminal Justice. 5-yr BS/MS in Computational Science. BS/MS in Nursing. Doctorate of Physical Therapy. Additional Programs: Forensic Science, Pre-Law, Pre-Occupational Therapy, and Pre-Veterinary.

Rutgers-The State University of New Jersey
New Brunswick Campus
35 College Ave, New Brunswick NJ 08901
732-932-4636

St. Barnabas Medical Center
94 Old Short Hills Rd, Livingston NJ 07039-5668
973-533-5628

St. Francis Medical Center
601 Hamilton Ave, Trenton NJ 08629-1986
609-599-5000

Shore Memorial Hospital
Shore Rd, Somers Point NJ 08244
609-653-3545

STAR TECHNICAL INSTITUTE
3003 English Creek Ave Suite 212
Egg Harbor Township NJ 08234-4880
George Z. Negrete, Director
609-407-2999 Fax: 609-646-9472
Website: www.startechnicalinstitute.com
E-mail: info@stareggharbor.com

Sussex County Community College
1 College Hill, Newton NJ 07860
973-300-2100

UMDNJ-University of Medicine and Dentistry of New Jersey
65 Bergen St, Newark NJ 07107-3001
973-972-4300

Union County College
1033 Springfield Ave, Cranford NJ 07016-1528
908-709-7000

Valley Hospital
223 N Van Dien Ave, Ridgewood NJ 07450-2736
201-447-8002

Warren County Community College
475 State Route 57 W, Washington NJ 07882-4343
908-835-9222

West Jersey Health System
1000 Atlantic Ave, Camden NJ 08104-1595
856-342-4600

William Paterson University
300 Pompton Rd, Wayne NJ 07470-2103
973-720-2000

NEW MEXICO

Albuquerque TVI Community College
525 Buena Vista Dr SE, Albuquerque NM 87106-4096
Jane Campbell, Registrar
505-224-3061

Apollo College
1001 Menaul Blvd NE Ste C, Albuquerque NM 87107
800-368-7246 Fax: 505-254-1101

Clovis Community College
417 Schepps Blvd, Clovis NM 88101-8381
505-769-2811

Eastern New Mexico University
Portales NM 88130
800-367-3668

Eastern New Mexico University-Roswell
PO Box 6000, Roswell NM 88202-6000
505-624-7000

International Institute of the Americas
4201 Central Ave NW Suite J
Albuquerque NM 87105-1649
Ed Sigman, Director
505-880-2877 Fax: 505-352-0199
Website: www.iia.edu
E-mail: esigman@iia.edu

New Mexico State University
2400 Scenic Dr, Alamogordo NM 88310-3722
505-439-3600

New Mexico State University
PO Box 30001, Las Cruces NM 88003-8001
505-646-0111

New Mexico State University
Dona Ana Branch Community College
PO Box 30001, Las Cruces NM 88003-8001
505-527-7500

Northern New Mexico College
921 Paseo de Onate, Espanola NM 87532
505-747-2100

Pima Medical Institute
2201 San Pedro Dr NE, Albuquerque NM 87110-4155
505-881-1234

San Juan College
4601 College Blvd, Farmington NM 87402-4699
505-326-3311

Southwestern Indian Polytechnic Institute
PO Box 10146, Albuquerque NM 87184-0146
505-346-2347

University of New Mexico
1 University Campus, Albuquerque NM 87131-0001
505-277-0111

University of New Mexico
200 College Rd, Gallup NM 87301-5603
505-863-7500

NEW YORK

Adelphi University
Garden City NY 11530
516-877-3100

Advanced Software Analysis Institute of Business and Computer Technology
151 Lawrence St Ste 2, Brooklyn NY 11201-5208
718-522-9073

ALBANY COLLEGE OF PHARMACY
106 New Scotland Ave, Albany NY 12208-3492
Carly Connors, Director of Admissions
888-203-8010 Fax: 518-694-7322
Website: www.acp.edu
E-mail: admissions@acp.edu

ARNOT-OGDEN MEDICAL CENTER
School of Radiologic Technology
600 Roe Ave, Elmira NY 14905-1629
Ellen Richards, BS RT (R) Director
607-737-4289 Fax: 607-737-4116
Website: www.arnotheath.org
E-mail: erichards@aomc.org

Bellevue Hospital Center
462 1st Ave, New York NY 10016-9198
212-561-4132

Bronx Lebanon Hospital Center
1650 Grand Concourse, Bronx NY 10457-7697
718-518-1800

Brooklyn Hospital
121 DeKalb Ave, Brooklyn NY 11201-5493
718-250-8005

Broome Community College
907 Upper Front St, Binghamton NY 13905
Anthony S. Fiorelli, Director of Admissions
607-778-5001 Fax: 607-778-5442
Website: www.sunybroome.edu
E-mail: fiorelli_a@sunybroome.edu

Bryant & Stratton College
1259 Central Ave, Albany NY 12205
518-437-1802

Bryant & Stratton College
465 Main St Ste 400, Buffalo NY 14203-1713
716-884-9120

Bryant & Stratton College
150 Bellwood Dr, Rochester NY 14606
585-720-0660

Bryant & Stratton College
1225 Jeffson Rd, Rochester NY 14623
585-292-5627

Bryant & Stratton College
953 James St, Syracuse NY 13203-2502
315-472-6603

CAREER INSTITUTE OF HEALTH & TECHNOLOGY
340 Flatbush Avenue Ext, Brooklyn NY 11201
Mary Miller, Contact
718-422-1212 Fax: 718-422-1222
Website: www.careerinstitute.edu
E-mail: admissions@careerinstitute.edu

CAREER INSTITUTE OF HEALTH & TECHNOLOGY
200 Garden City Plz, Garden City NY 11530
Mary Miller, Contact
516-877-1225 Fax: 516-877-1959
Website: www.careerinstitute.edu
E-mail: admissions@careerinstitute.edu

CAREER INSTITUTE OF HEALTH & TECHNOLOGY
9525 Queens Blvd Ste 600, Rego Park NY 11374
Mary Miller, Contact
718-897-4868 Fax: 718-897-4863
Website: www.careerinstitute.edu
E-mail: admissions@careerinstitute.edu

Central Suffolk Hospital
1300 Roanoke Ave, Riverhead NY 11901-2058
631-548-6000

Champlain Valley Physicians Hospital
75 Beekman St, Plattsburgh NY 12901
518-561-2000

THE CHUBB INSTITUTE
498 7th Ave, New York NY 10018
James Cruz, Director of Admissions
212-659-2116 Fax: 212-659-2175
Website: www.chubbinstitute.edu
E-mail: jamescruz@chubbinstitute.edu

Clinton Community College
136 Clinton Point Dr, Plattsburgh NY 12901-6002
Robert C. Wood, Assoc. Dean for Enrollment
518-562-4200

College of New Rochelle
29 Castle Pl, New Rochelle NY 10805-2339
914-654-5000

College of Saint Rose
432 Western Ave, Albany NY 12203-1419
Maryelizabeth Amico, Asst V.P. for Undergraduate Admissions
518-454-5150 Fax: 518-454-2013
Website: www.strose.edu
E-mail: admit@strose.edu

Columbia University
168th & Broadway, New York NY 10032
212-305-5756

Cornell University
410 Thurston Ave, Ithaca NY 14850-2432
607-255-2000

County University School of Dental & Oral Surgery
630 W 168th St, New York NY 10032

CUNY Borough of Manhattan Community College
199 Chambers St, New York NY 10007-1044
212-346-8800

CUNY Bronx Community College
W 181st and University Ave, Bronx NY 10453-2895
718-289-5100

CUNY Brooklyn College
2900 Bedford Ave, Brooklyn NY 11210-2814
718-951-5000

CUNY City College
Convent Ave at 138th St, New York NY 10031
Celia Lloyd, Interim Director of Admissions
212-650-6977

CUNY College of Staten Island
2800 Victory Blvd, Staten Island NY 10314-6600
718-982-2000

CUNY Hunter College
695 Park Ave, New York NY 10021
Aaron Gibbs, Assistant Director of Recruitment
212-650-3946 Fax: 212-650-3336
Website: www.hunter.cuny.edu
E-mail: aaron.gibbs@hunter.cuny.edu

CUNY Lehman College
250 Bedford Park Blvd W, Bronx NY 10468-1527
718-960-8000

CUNY Queens College
6530 Kissena Blvd, Flushing NY 11367-1575
718-997-5000

CUNY York College
9420 Guy R Brewer Blvd, Jamaica NY 11451-0001
718-262-2000

Daemen College
4380 Main St, Amherst NY 14226-3592
Donna Shaffner, Director of Admissions
800-462-7652 Fax: 716-839-8229
Website: www.daemen.edu/admissions
E-mail: admissions@daemen.edu

Dutchess Community College
53 Pendell Rd, Poughkeepsie NY 12601-1512
845-431-8000

D'Youville College
320 Porter Ave, Buffalo NY 14201-1084
716-829-7600

Erie Community College
City Campus
121 Ellicott St, Buffalo NY 14203-2698
716-842-2770

Erie Community College North
6205 Main St, Williamsville NY 14221-8402
716-634-0800

Erie Community College South
4041 Southwestern Blvd
Orchard Park NY 14127-2199
716-648-5400

Farmingdale SUNY
2350 Broadhollow Rd, Farmingdale NY 11735
631-420-2200

FAXTON-ST. LUKE'S HEALTHCARE SCHOOL OF MEDICAL RADIOGRAPHY
PO Box 479, Utica NY 13503-0479
Rosemary Morin, MS, RTR, Director
315-624-6136 Fax: 315-624-4787
Website: mvnhealth.com
E-mail: valesand@mvnhealth.com

Genesee Community College
1 College Rd, Batavia NY 14020-9703
585-343-0055

Glens Falls Hospital
100 Park St, Glens Falls NY 12801-4447
518-792-3151

Gloden Hall Health Care Center
Golden Hill Dr, Kingston NY 12401
845-339-4540

Herkimer County Community College
100 Reservoir Rd, Herkimer NY 13350-1545
888-464-4222

Hochstim School of Radiography
PO Box 9007, Oceanside NY 11572-9007
516-763-2030

Hofstra University
100 Hofstra University, Hempstead NY 11549-1000
516-463-6600

Hostos Community College - CUNY
500 Grand Concourse, Bronx NY 10451-5323
Roland Velez, Director of Admissions
718-518-4406

Institute of Allied Medical Professions
405 Park Ave, New York NY 10022-4405
212-758-1410

Interboro Institute
450 W 56th St, New York NY 10019
212-399-0091

Ithaca College
953 Danby Rd, Ithaca NY 14850-7002
607-274-3011

Keuka College
PO Box 98, Keuka Park NY 14478-0098
315-536-4411

LaGuardia Community College / CUNY
31-10 Thompson Ave, Long Island City NY 11101
718-482-7200

Le Moyne College
1419 Salt Springs Rd, Syracuse NY 13214-1301
800-333-4733

Long Island College Hospital School of Nursing
339 Hicks St, Brooklyn NY 11201
718-780-1000

Long Island University-Brooklyn Campus
1 University Plz, Brooklyn NY 11201-5372
718-488-1000

Long Island University-C. W. Post Campus
720 Northern Blvd, Brookville NY 11548-1300
Joanne Graziano, Executive Director of Admissions
516-299-2900 Fax: 516-299-2137
Website: www.liu.edu/cwpost
E-mail: enroll@cwpost.liu.edu

Manhattan College
4513 Manhattan College Pkwy
Riverdale NY 10471-4099
Dr. William Merriman, Dean of Education
718-862-7200

Maria College of Albany
700 New Scotland Ave, Albany NY 12208-1715
518-438-3111

Marymount College at Fordham University
100 Marymount Ave, Tarrytown NY 10591-3796
914-631-3200

Memorial Sloan Kettering Cancer Center
1275 York Ave, New York NY 10065
212-639-6561

Mercy College
555 Broadway, Dobbs Ferry NY 10522-1189
Kathleen Jackson, Director of Admissions
800-MERCY-NY

Mercy Medical Center
PO Box 9024, Rockville Centre NY 11571-9024
516-705-2525

Mohawk Valley Community College
1101 Sherman Dr, Utica NY 13501-5394
315-792-5400

Molloy College
1000 Hempstead Ave
Rockville Centre NY 11570-1100
Marguerite Lane, Director of Admissions
516-678-5000 ext. 6291 Fax: 516-256-2247
Website: www.molloy.edu
E-mail: admissions@molloy.edu
See listing under "Universities"

Monroe Community College
1000 E Henrietta Rd, Rochester NY 14623-5701
585-292-2000

Montefiore Medical Center
111 E 210th St, Bronx NY 10467-2490
718-920-4001

Mount Sinai School of Medicine of New York University
Box 1022, 1 Gustave L Levy Place
New York NY 10029
212-241-6546

Nassau Community College
1 Education Dr, Garden City NY 11530-6719
516-572-7501

Nazareth College of Rochester
4245 East Ave, Rochester NY 14618-3790
585-389-2525

New York City College of Technology CUNY
300 Jay St, Brooklyn NY 11201-1909
Joe Lento, Director of Admissions
718-260-5000

NEW YORK COLLEGE OF HEALTH PROFESSIONS
6801 Jericho Tpke, Syosset NY 11791
Mary Rodas, Associate Director of Admissions
800-9-CAREER Fax: 516-364-0989
Website: www.nycollege.edu
E-mail: admissions@nycollege.edu

NEW YORK EYE & EAR INFIRMARY / ORTHOPTIC PROGRAM
310 E 14th St, New York NY 10003-4201
Sara Shippman, Chief Orthoptist
212-979-4375 Fax: 212-979-4564
Website: www.nyee.edu
E-mail: sshippman@nyee.edu

New York Institute of Technology
PO Box 8000, Old Westbury NY 11568-8000
516-686-7516

New York Medical College
Valhalla NY 10595
914-594-4000

New York Methodist Hospital
Clinical Laboratory Science/School of Medical Technology
506 6th St, Brooklyn NY 11215-3609
Adrienne Arso-Paez, Program Director
718-780-3706

New York Presbyterian Hospital
525 E 68th St, New York NY 10065
212-746-4000

NEW YORK SCHOOL FOR MEDICAL AND DENTAL ASSISTANTS
33-10 Queens Blvd, Long Island City NY 11101-2327
Donna Stirber-Gamelin, Executive Director of Admissions
718-793-2330 Fax: 718-793-0619
Website: www.nysmda.com
E-mail: info@nysmda.com

New York University
70 Washington Sq S, New York NY 10012-1019
212-998-1212

New York University Medical Center
550 1st Ave, New York NY 10016-6481
212-263-5111

North Country Community College
School of Health Professions
23 Santanoni, Saranac Lake NY 12983-2046
Edwin Trathen, Assistant to the President for Enrollment Services
1-888-TRY-NCCC ext. 686

Northport VA Medical Center
79 Middleville Rd, Northport NY 11768-2200
631-261-4400

Onondaga Community College
4941 Onondaga Rd, Syracuse NY 13215-2001
315-498-2622

Ridley-Lowell Business & Technical Institute
116 Front St, Binghamton NY 13905-3102
David Lounsbury, Executive Director
607-724-2941 Fax: 607-724-0799
Website: www.ridley.edu
E-mail: info@ridley.edu

Rochester General Hospital
1425 Portland Ave, Rochester NY 14621-3095
585-338-4430

Rochester Institute of Technology
1 Lomb Memorial Dr, Rochester NY 14623-5603
585-475-2411

Russell Sage College
45 Ferry St, Troy NY 12180-4115
518-244-2000

Russell Sage Graduate School
45 Ferry St, Troy NY 12180-4115
518-244-2264

St. Elizabeth College of Nursing
2215 Genesee St, Utica NY 13501-5930
315-798-8125

St. James Mercy Hospital
411 Canisteo St, Hornell NY 14843-2197
607-324-3900

St. John's University
8000 Utopia Pkwy, Queens NY 11439
Office of Admission
877-STJ-5550 ext. 101 Fax: 718-990-2096
Website: www.stjohns.edu/learnmore
E-mail: admhelp@stjohns.edu
See listing under "Universities"

St. Joseph's College
245 Clinton Ave, Brooklyn NY 11205-3688
Theresa LaRocca Meyer, V.P. for Enrollment Management
718-636-6800 Fax: 718-636-8303
Website: www.sjcny.edu
E-mail: tlaroccameyer@sjcny.edu

St. Vincent's Hospital & Medical Center
153 W 11th St, New York NY 10011-8397
212-604-7500

St. Vincent's Medical Center
355 Bard Ave, Staten Island NY 10310-1699

Samaritan Medical Center
830 Washington St, Watertown NY 13601-4034
315-785-4000

Sarah Lawrence College
1 Meadway, Bronxville NY 10708
914-337-0700

Sisters of Charity Medical Center - Bayley Seton Campus
75 Vanderbilt Ave, Staten Island NY 10304-3850
718-818-6470

SUNY Adirondack Community College
640 Bay Rd, Queensbury NY 12804
Sarah Jane Linehan, Director of Enrollment Management
518-743-2264

SUNY at Albany
1400 Washington Ave, Albany NY 12222-1000
Thomas Flemming, Associate Director of Admissions
518-442-5435

SUNY at Stony Brook
Stony Brook NY 11794-0001
631-689-6000

SUNY Canton - College of Technology
34 Cornell Dr, Canton NY 13617-1037
315-386-7011

SUNY College at Brockport
350 New Campus Dr, Brockport NY 14420-2997
Bernard S. Valento, Director of Undergraduate Admissions
585-395-2751 Fax: 585-395-5452
Website: www.brockport.edu
E-mail: admit@brockport.edu

SUNY College at Buffalo
1300 Elmwood Ave, Buffalo NY 14222-1004
716-878-4000

SUNY College at Cortland
PO Box 2000, Cortland NY 13045-0900
Mark Yacavone, Assistant Director
607-753-4711

SUNY College at Fredonia
Fredonia NY 14063
716-673-3111

SUNY College at Geneseo
1 College Cir, Geneseo NY 14454-1401
585-245-5211

SUNY College at New Paltz
1 Hawk Dr, New Paltz NY 12561
845-257-2121

SUNY College at Oneonta
Oneonta NY 13820
607-436-3500

SUNY College at Plattsburgh
Plattsburgh NY 12901
518-564-2000

SUNY College of Agriculture & Technology
107 Schenectady Ave, Cobleskill NY 12043
Clayton A. Smith, Director of Admissions
800-295-8988

SUNY College of Agriculture & Technology
Morrisville NY 13408
Thomas Ver Dow, Dean of Enrollment Management
800-258-0111

SUNY College of Technology
Alfred NY 14802
Deborah J. Goodrich, Associate VP Enrollment Mgmt.
800-4AL-FRED Fax: 607-587-4299
Website: www.alfredstate.edu
E-mail: admissions@alfredstate.edu

SUNY Educational Opportunity Center
465 Washington St, Buffalo NY 14203-1707
716-849-6725

SUNY Health Science Center
450 Clarkson Ave, Brooklyn NY 11203-2056
718-270-1000

SUNY Hudson Valley Community College
80 Vandenburgh Ave, Troy NY 12180-6025
Jack Mahoney, Director of Admissions
518-629-HVCC (629-4822)

SUNY Institute of Technology Utica/Rome
PO Box 3050, Utica NY 13504-3050
315-792-7100

SUNY Niagara County Community College
3111 Saunders Settlement Rd
Sanborn NY 14132-9487
Kathleen Saunders, Director of Admissions
716-614-6200 Fax: 716-614-6820
Website: www.niagaracc.suny.edu
E-mail: admissions@niagaracc.suny.edu

SUNY Orange County Community College
115 South St, Middletown NY 10940-6437
Margot St. Lawrence, Director of Admissions
845-341-4030 Fax: 845-342-8662
Website: www.sunyorange.edu
E-mail: apply@sunyorange.edu
See listing under "Community and Junior Colleges"

SUNY Rockland Community College
145 College Rd, Suffern NY 10901-3611
Charles Connolly, Coordinator of Admissions & Recruitment
845-574-4000

SUNY Suffolk County Community College
Crooked Hill Rd, Brentwood NY 11717-1017
Andrea Bhella, Contact
631-851-6276

SUNY Suffolk County Community College
533 College Rd, Selden NY 11784-2851
631-451-4110

SUNY Sullivan County Community College
112 College Rd, Loch Sheldrake NY 12759-5151
Sari Rosenheck, Director of Admissions
845-434-5750 Fax: 845-434-0923
Website: www.sullivan.suny.edu
E-mail: admissions@sullivan.suny.edu
Student Housing on Campus.

SUNY Upstate Medical University
750 E Adams St, Syracuse NY 13210
315-464-5540

SWEDISH INSTITUTE
College of Health Sciences
226 W 26th St, New York NY 10001-6700
Tamica Ward, Director of Admissions
212-924-5900 ext. 125 Fax: 212-924-7600
Website: www.swedishinstitute.edu
E-mail: admissions@swedishinstitute.edu

Established 1916. Private. Coed. Degrees: Associate in Occupational Studies in Massage Therapy. Master of Science in Acupuncture. Focused program in massage therapy features Western & Eastern approaches. Can be completed in 16 months full-time. The Master of Science in Acupuncture focuses on classical Chinese Acupuncture. Full time students can complete the degree in three years.

Syracuse University
Syracuse NY 13244-0001
315-443-1870

Teachers College of Columbia University
525 W 120th St, New York NY 10027-6625
212-678-3000

Touro College
27 W 23rd St Ste 33, New York NY 10010-4202
212-463-0400

Trocaire College
360 Choate Ave, Buffalo NY 14220-2003
Paul B. Hurley, Ph.D., President
716-826-1200

United Health Services Hospital
33-57 Harrison St, Johnson City NY 13790-2174
607-763-6000

University of Rochester
Wallis Hall, Rochester NY 14627
585-275-2121

Utica School of Commerce
201 Bleecker St, Utica NY 13501-2280
Bruce Davis, Director of Marketing
315-733-2307 Fax: 315-733-9281
Website: www.uscny.edu
E-mail: admissions@uscny.edu

Veterans Affairs Medical Center
130 W Kingsbridge Rd, Bronx NY 10468-3992
718-579-1640

Wagner College
One Campus Rd, Staten Island NY 10301
Leigh Ann DePascale, Director of Admissions
718-390-3411

Weill Medical College of Cornell University
1300 York Ave, New York NY 10065
212-746-5454

Westchester Community College
75 Grasslands Rd, Valhalla NY 10595-1693
914-785-6600

Westchester County Medical Center
Grasslands Rd, Valhalla NY 10595
914-285-7276

Winthrop University Hospital
259 1st St, Mineola NY 11501-3987
516-663-2201

Woman's Christian Association Hospital
207 Foote Ave, Jamestown NY 14701-7077
716-664-8110

Wood Tobe-Coburn School
8 E 40th St, New York NY 10016-0102
212-686-9040

NORTH CAROLINA

Alamance Community College
PO Box 8000, Graham NC 27253-8000
336-578-2002

Appalachian State University
ASU Station, Boone NC 28608-0001
828-262-2000

Asheville Buncombe Technical Community College
340 Victoria Rd, Asheville NC 28801-4897
828-254-1921

Beaufort County Community College
PO Box 1069, Washington NC 27889
252-946-6194

Bennett College
900 E Washington St, Greensboro NC 27401-3298
336-273-4431

Brevard College
One Brevard College Dr, Brevard NC 28712
Joretta Nelson, Vice President Enrollment Management
828-883-8292 Fax: 828-884-3790
Website: www.brevard.edu
E-mail: admissions@brevard.edu

Brunswick Community College
PO Box 30, Supply NC 28462-0030
910-755-7300

CABARRUS COLLEGE OF HEALTH SCIENCES
401 Medical Park Dr, Concord NC 28025
Mark Ellison, Director of Admissions
704-783-1556 Fax: 704-783-2077
Website: www.cabarruscollege.edu
E-mail: admissions@cabarruscollege.edu
See listing under "Universities"

Caldwell Community College and Technical Institute
2855 Hickory Blvd, Hudson NC 28638
828-726-2200

Cape Fear Community College
411 N Front St, Wilmington NC 28401-3910
910-251-5100

Carolinas College of Health Sciences
PO Box 32861, Charlotte NC 28232-2861
Elizabeth West, Admissions Officer
704-355-5043

Carteret Community College
Dept. of Respiratory Care & Radiography
3505 Arendell St, Morehead City NC 28557-2989
Rick Hill, Beth Belcher, Counselors
252-247-4142 ext. 153

Catawba College
2300 W Innes St, Salisbury NC 28144-2488
Dr. L. Russell Watjen, Ph.D., V.P. & Dean of Admissions
704-637-4402 Fax: 704-637-4222
Website: www.catawba.edu
E-mail: admission@catawba.edu

Catawba Valley Community College
2550 US Highway 70 SE, Hickory NC 28602-8302
828-327-7000

Central Carolina Community College
1105 Kelly Dr, Sanford NC 27330-9000
Preston Sellers, Dean
919-775-5401

Central Piedmont Community College
PO Box 35009, Charlotte NC 28235-5009
704-330-2722

Chowan University
One University Pl, Murfreesboro NC 27855
Chad Holt, Dean of Admissions
800-488-4101 Fax: 252-398-1190
Website: www.chowan.edu
E-mail: holtc@chowan.edu

Cleveland Community College
137 S Post Rd, Shelby NC 28152-6205
704-484-4000

Coastal Carolina Community College
444 Western Blvd, Jacksonville NC 28546-6899
910-455-1221

Davidson County Community College
PO Box 1287, Lexington NC 27293-1287
336-249-8186

Duke University
Durham NC 27706-8001
919-684-8111

· Durham Technical Community College
1637 E Lawson St, Durham NC 27703-5023
919-686-3333

East Carolina University
Belk 302C, Greenville NC 27858
Dr. Harold P. Jones, Dean

· Edgecombe Community College
2009 W Wilson St, Tarboro NC 27886-9361
Thomas B. Anderson, VP of Student Services
252-823-5166

· Fayetteville Technical Community College
PO Box 35236, Fayetteville NC 28303-0236
910-678-8400

· Forsyth Technical Community College
2100 Silas Creek Pkwy
Winston Salem NC 27103-5150
336-723-0371

· Gaston College
201 Highway 321 S, Dallas NC 28034-1499
704-922-6200

· Guilford Technical Community College
PO Box 309, Jamestown NC 27282-0309
336-334-4822

· Haywood Community College
185 Freedlander Dr, Clyde NC 28721
Debbie Rowland, Coordinator of Admissions
828-627-4500 Fax: 828-627-4513
Website: www.haywood.edu
E-mail: drowland@haywood.edu

High Point University
933 Montlieu Ave, High Point NC 27262-3598
336-841-9000

· James Sprunt Community College
PO Box 398, Kenansville NC 28349-0398
Lea Grady, Admissions
910-296-2500 Fax: 910-296-1636
Website: www.jamessprunt.edu

· Johnston Community College
PO Box 2350, Smithfield NC 27577-2350
919-934-3051

· King's College
322 Lamar Ave, Charlotte NC 28204-2493
704-372-0266

· Lenoir Community College
PO Box 188, Kinston NC 28502-0188
252-527-6223

∴ Lenoir Memorial Hospital
100 Airport Rd, Kinston NC 28501-1604
252-522-7797

Lenoir-Rhyne College
7th Ave and 8th St, Hickory NC 28603
828-328-1741

· Martin Community College
1161 Kehukee Park Rd, Williamston NC 27892-8307
252-792-1521

Meredith College
3800 Hillsborough St, Raleigh NC 27607-5298
Heidi L. Fletcher, Director of Admissions
919-760-8581

Methodist College
5400 Ramsey St, Fayetteville NC 28311-1498
910-630-7000

· Miller-Motte Technical College
5000 Market St, Wilmington NC 28405-3430
800-784-2110

· Mitchell Community College
500 W Broad St, Statesville NC 28677-5264
704-878-3200

· Montgomery Community College
1011 Page St, Troy NC 27371-8387
910-576-6222

∴ Moses H. Cone Memorial Hospital
1200 N Elm St, Greensboro NC 27401-1020
336-574-7881

· Nash Community College
PO Box 7488, Rocky Mount NC 27804-0488
252-443-4011

∴ New Hanover Regional Medical Center
2131 S 17th St, Wilmington NC 28401-7407
910-343-7074

North Carolina A&T State University
1601 E Market St, Greensboro NC 27411
Lee Young, AVC Enrollment
336-334-7500

North Carolina Central University
PO Box 19617, Durham NC 27707-0022
919-560-6100

North Carolina State University
PO Box 7001, Raleigh NC 27695-0001
919-515-2011

· Pitt Community College
PO Box 7007, Greenville NC 27835-7007
252-321-4200

∴ Presbyterian Hospital
PO Box 33549, Charlotte NC 28233-3549
Michael P. Smith, Director of Admissions
704-384-4141

Queens University of Charlotte
1900 Selwyn Ave, Charlotte NC 28274-0002
704-337-2212

· Robeson Community College
PO Box 1420, Lumberton NC 28359
Judith Revels, Director of Admissions
910-738-7101

· Rockingham Community College
PO Box 38, Wentworth NC 27375-0038
336-342-4261

· Rowan-Cabarrus Community College
PO Box 1595, Salisbury NC 28145-1595
704-637-0760

Salem College
Winston Salem NC 27108
Dana Evans, Dean of Admissions/Fin. Aid
800-32-SALEM Fax: 336-917-5572
Website: www.salem.edu
E-mail: admissions@salem.edu
See listing under "Women's Colleges"

· Sandhills Community College
3395 Airport Rd, Pinehurst NC 28374
910-692-6185

· South College
29 Turtle Creek Dr, Asheville NC 28803
Robert Davis, Dean of Academic Affairs
828-277-5521 Fax: 828-277-6151
Website: southcollegenc.com
E-mail: bdavis@southcollegenc.com

· South Piedmont Community College
PO Box 126, Polkton NC 28135-0126
Joy Pope, Contact
704-272-5338
Website: www.spcc.edu
E-mail: jpope@spcc.edu

· Southwestern Community College
447 College Dr, Sylva NC 28779-8581
828-586-4091

· Stanly Community College
141 College Dr, Albemarle NC 28001-6418
704-982-0121

University of North Carolina
Chapel Hill NC 27599-0001
919-962-2211

University of North Carolina
9201 University City Blvd, Charlotte NC 28223
704-547-2000

University of North Carolina
601 S College Rd, Wilmington NC 28403-3201
910-962-3000

University of North Carolina at Greensboro
1000 Spring Garden St, Greensboro NC 27412-0001
336-334-5243

∴ University of North Carolina Hospitals
101 Manning Dr, Chapel Hill NC 27514-4220
919-966-5111

· Vance-Granville Community College
PO Box 917, Henderson NC 27536-0917
252-492-2061

Wake Forest University
Medical Center Blvd, Winston Salem NC 27157-0001
336-748-4424

· Wake Technical Community College
9101 Fayetteville Rd, Raleigh NC 27603-5696
Dr. Robert E. Ireland, Director of Admissions
919-662-3357

· Wayne Community College
PO Box 8002, Goldsboro NC 27533-8002
Kathy Garner, Public Information Officer
919-735-5151

Western Carolina University
University Dr, Cullowhee NC 28723-9646
828-227-7211

· Western Piedmont Community College
1001 Burkemont Ave, Morganton NC 28655-4511
828-438-6000

∴ Wilkes Regional Medical Center
School of Radiologic Technology
PO Box 609, North Wilkesboro NC 28659-0609
336-651-8431

Winston-Salem State University
601 S Mrtn Lther King Jr Dr
Winston Salem NC 27110-0003
336-750-2000

NORTH DAKOTA

· Bismarck State College
PO Box 5587, Bismarck ND 58506
701-224-5400

Dickinson State University
Dickinson ND 58601-4896
Steve Glasser, Director of Enrollment Services
800-279-4295 Fax: 701-483-2409
Website: www.dickinsonstate.edu
E-mail: dsu.hawks@dickinsonstate.edu

∴ Medcenter One Health System
222 N 7th St, Bismarck ND 58501-4436
701-222-5413

Minot State University
500 University Ave W, Minot ND 58707-0002
Dennis Parisien, Enrollment Services Rep.
800-777-0750 ext. 3350

Minot State University-Bottineau Campus
105 Simrall Blvd, Bottineau ND 58318-1159
Paula Berg, Associate Dean of Student Affairs
800-542-6866 Fax: 701-228-5499
Website: www.misu-b.nodak.edu
E-mail: paula.berg@misu.nodak.edu

· North Dakota State College of Science
800 6th St N, Wahpeton ND 58076
701-671-1130

North Dakota State University
Fargo ND 58105
701-237-7211

∴ St. Alexius Medical Center
PO Box 5510, Bismarck ND 58506-5510
701-224-7600

: Sr. Rosalind Gefre Schools of Massage
3101 39th St SW Ste E, Fargo ND 58104
Annie Thorseth, Director of Admissions
701-297-5993 Fax: 701-297-5994
Website: www.sisterrosalind.org
E-mail: fargocampus@sisterrosalind.org

∴ Trinity Medical Center
3 Burdick Expy, Minot ND 58701
701-857-5000

· Turtle Mountain Community College
PO Box 340, Belcourt ND 58316-0340
701-477-7862

· United Tribes Technical College
3315 University Dr, Bismarck ND 58504-7596
701-255-3285

University of Mary
7500 University Dr, Bismarck ND 58504-9652
701-255-7500

University of North Dakota
Box 8193 University Station, Grand Forks ND 58203
701-777-2011

· Williston State College
PO Box 1326, Williston ND 58802-1326
Penny Soiseth, Associate Director Enrollment Services
701-774-4200 Fax: 701-774-4544
Website: www.wsc.nodak.edu
E-mail: penny.soiseth@wsc.nodak.edu

OHIO

∴ Akron General Medical Center
400 Wabash Ave, Akron OH 44307-2463
330-846-6548

: Akron Institute
1600 S Arlington St Ste 100, Akron OH 44306
330-724-1600

∴ Arthur James Cancer Hospital
300 W 10th Ave, Columbus OH 43210
614-293-5485

∴ Aultman Hospital
2600 6th St SW, Canton OH 44710-1799
330-438-6241

Baldwin-Wallace College
275 Eastland Rd, Berea OH 44017-2088
440-826-2900

· Belmont Technical College
120 Fox Shannon Pl, Saint Clairsville OH 43950-8751
740-695-9500

Bluffton University
1 University Dr, Bluffton OH 45817
419-358-3000

Bowling Green State University
110 McFall Center, Bowling Green OH 43403-0001
866-CHOOSE-BGSU

· Bradford School
2469 Stelzer Rd, Columbus OH 43219-3129
Raeann Lee, Director of Admissions
614-416-6200

· Brown Mackie College - Akron
755 White Pond Dr Ste 101, Akron OH 44320-4221
330-733-8766

· Brown Mackie College - Cincinnati
1011 Glendale Milford Rd, Cincinnati OH 45215-1107
Robin Krout, President
513-771-2424 Fax: 513-771-3413
Website: www.brownmackie.edu
E-mail: rkrout@brownmackie.edu

Capital University
2199 E Main St, Columbus OH 43209-2394
614-236-6011

Case Western Reserve University
10900 Euclid Ave, Cleveland OH 44106
216-368-2000

· Central Ohio Technical College
1179 University Dr, Newark OH 43055-1767
740-366-9222

∴ Children's Hospital & Medical Center
1 Perkins Sq, Akron OH 44308-1062
330-379-8293

∴ Christ Hospital
2139 Auburn Ave, Cincinnati OH 45219-2989
513-369-2201

· Cincinnati State Technical & Community College
3520 Central Pkwy, Cincinnati OH 45223-2612
513-569-1500

· Clark State Community College
570 E Leffel Ln, Springfield OH 45505-4749
937-325-0691

: Cleveland Clinic Foundation
9500 Euclid Ave, Cleveland OH 44195-0001
216-445-5719

Cleveland State University
2121 Euclid Ave RW 204, Cleveland OH 44115
Dr. Richard Arndt, Dean of Undergraduate Recruitment and College Partnerships
888-CSU-OHIO Fax: 216-687-9210
Website: www.csuohio.edu
E-mail: admissions@csuohio.edu

∴ Cleveland Veterans Affairs Medical Center
10701 East Blvd, Cleveland OH 44106-1702
216-421-3028

: Collins Career Center
11627 State Route 243, Chesapeake OH 45619-7962
740-867-6641

· Columbus State Community College
550 E Spring St, Columbus OH 43215-1786
Ken Conner, Director of Admissions
614-287-3669

∴ **COOPERATIVE MEDICAL TECHNOLOGY PROGRAM OF AKRON**
1 Perkins Sq, Akron OH 44308-1062
Sharon K. Shriber, MBA, Program Director
330-543-8720 Fax: 330-543-6303
Website: www.akronchildrens.org
E-mail: sshriber@chmca.org

· Cuyahoga Community College
25444 Harvard Rd, Highland Hills OH 44122-6202
216-987-2019

Davis College
4747 Monroe St, Toledo OH 43623-4389
Dana Stern, Admissions Director
419-473-2700 Fax: 419-473-2472
Website: www.daviscollege.edu
E-mail: learn@daviscollege.edu

Franciscan University of Steubenville
University Blvd, Steubenville OH 43952
Margaret J. Weber, Director of Admissions
800-783-6220 or 740-283-6226 Fax: 740-284-5456
Website: www.admissions.edu
E-mail: mweber@franciscan.edu

∴ Good Samaritan Hospital
375 Dixmyth Ave, Cincinnati OH 45220-2489
513-872-1983

Hocking College
3301 Hocking Pkwy, Nelsonville OH 45764-9704
Diane K. Wolf, Assistant Director of Admissions Information
800-282-4163

· James A. Rhodes State College
4240 Campus Dr, Lima OH 45804-3597
419-995-8000

· Jefferson Community College
4000 Sunset Blvd, Steubenville OH 43952-3598
740-264-5591

Kent State University
PO Box 5190, Kent OH 44242-0001
Paul Deutsch, Director of Admissions
330-672-2444

Kettering College of Medical Arts
3737 Southern Blvd, Kettering OH 45429-1299
David Lofthouse, Director of Enrollment Services
800-433-5262

: Knox County Career Center
306 Martinsburg Rd, Mount Vernon OH 43050-4225
740-397-5820

· Lakeland Community College
7700 Clocktower Dr, Kirtland OH 44094-5198
Tracey Cooper, Director of Admissions
440-953-7100

Marietta College
215 5th St, Marietta OH 45750-4047
740-376-4600

∴ Marion General Hospital
1000 McKinley Park Dr, Marion OH 43302
740-383-8700

· Marion Technical College
1467 Mount Vernon Ave, Marion OH 43302-5628
Joel Liles, Director of Admissions
740-389-4636

: Medina County Career Center
1101 W Liberty St, Medina OH 44256-1346
330-725-8461

∴ Memorial Hospital
401 Matthew St, Marietta OH 45750-1635
740-374-1412

∴ Meridia Health System
17325 Euclid Ave, Cleveland OH 44112-1209
440-446-8260

∴ MetroHealth Medical Center
2500 Metrohealth Dr, Cleveland OH 44109-1900
216-459-5700

· Miami-Jacobs Career College
110 N Patterson Blvd, Dayton OH 45402
Sean Kuhn, Regional Director of Admissions
937-222-7337

Miami University
E High St, Oxford OH 45056
513-529-2531

∴ Miami Valley Hospital
1 Wyoming St, Dayton OH 45409-2722
937-223-6192

∴ Middletown Regional Hospital
105 McKnight Dr, Middletown OH 45044-4898
513-420-5100

Mount Carmel College of Nursing
127 S Davis Ave, Columbus OH 43222-1504
800-556-6972

· North Central State College
PO Box 698, Mansfield OH 44901-0698
Troy Shutler, Director of Admissions
419-755-4800

Notre Dame College
4545 College Rd, Cleveland OH 44121-4293
216-381-1680

: **OHIO INSTITUTE OF HEALTH CAREERS**
631 Griswold Rd, Elyria OH 44035
866-636-4734
Website: www.ohioinstituteofhealthcareers.edu

· Ohio Institute of Photography & Technology
2029 Edgefield Rd, Dayton OH 45439-1917
Robert A. Martin, Executive Director
937-294-6155

The Ohio State University
School of Allied Medical Professions
Atwell Hall, 453 W 10th Ave, Columbus OH 43210
614-292-1706 Fax: 614-292-0210
Website: amp.osu.edu
E-mail: studentaffairs@osu.edu

∴ Ohio State University Hospitals
450 W 10th Ave, Columbus OH 43210-1240
614-293-5555

Ohio University
Chillicothe Campus
PO Box 629, Chillicothe OH 45601
Student Services
740-774-7200 Fax: 740-774-7295
Website: www.ohiou.edu/chillicothe/

· **OHIO VALLEY COLLEGE OF TECHNOLOGY**
16808 St. Clair Ave, PO Box 7000
East Liverpool OH 43920
Scott S. Rogers, Director
330-385-1070 Fax: 330-385-4606
Website: www.ovct.edu
E-mail: info@ovct.edu

· Owens Community College
3200 Bright Rd, Findlay OH 45840
William J. Ivoska PhD., Vice President of Student Services
567-429-3500 Fax: 567-423-0246
Website: www.owens.edu
E-mail: admissions@owens.edu

· Owens Community College
PO Box 10000, Toledo OH 43699-1947
William J. Ivoska, Ph.D, Vice President of Student Services
567-661-7000 Fax: 567-661-7607
Website: www.owens.edu
E-mail: admissions@owens.edu

∴ Parma Community General Hospital
7007 Powers Blvd, Parma OH 44129-5495
440-743-3000

: **PROFESSIONAL SKILLS INSTITUTE**
20 Arco Dr, Toledo OH 43607-2901
Daniel A. Finch, Chairman/CEO
419-531-9610 Fax: 419-531-4732
Website: www.proskills.com
E-mail: admissions@proskills.com

∴ Riverside Hospital
3404 W Sylvania Ave, Toledo OH 43623-4467
419-729-6059

∴ St. Charles Hospital
2600 Navarre Ave, Oregon OH 43616-3286
419-698-7341

∴ St. Elizabeth Hospital
PO Box 1790, Youngstown OH 44501-1790
330-746-7211

∴ St. Luke's Medical Center
2351 E 22nd St, Cleveland OH 44115-3111
216-368-7000

Shawnee State University
940 2nd St, Portsmouth OH 45662-4344
740-354-3205

· Sinclair Community College
444 W 3rd St, Dayton OH 45402-1460
Director of Admissions
937-512-3000 Fax: 937-512-2393
Website: www.sinclair.edu
E-mail: admit@sinclair.edu

· Southern State Community College
100 Hobart Rd, Hillsboro OH 45133-9488
937-393-3431

∴ Southwest General Hospital
18697 Bagley Rd, Cleveland OH 44130-3497
440-816-6801

· Stark State College of Technology
6200 Frank Ave NW, Canton OH 44720-7228
330-494-6170

∴ Timken Mercy Medical Center
1320 Mercy Dr NW, Canton OH 44708-2641
330-489-1001

∴ University Hospital of Cleveland
11100 Euclid Ave, Cleveland OH 44106-1736
216-844-7565

University of Akron
381 Buchtel Mall, Akron OH 44304-1584
330-972-7111

University of Cincinnati
2700 Clifton Ave, Cincinnati OH 45220-2873
513-556-6000

· University of Cincinnati
College of Allied Health Sciences
PO Box 670394, Cincinnati OH 45267-0394
Gilbert Hageman, Associate Dean
513-558-7495

University of Findlay
1000 N Main St, Findlay OH 45840-3695
419-422-8313

University of Rio Grande
School for Medical Lab Technicians
General Delivery, Rio Grande OH 45674-9999
Ron Cheadle, Program Director
740-245-5353 ext. 7301

University of Toledo
2801 W Bancroft St, Toledo OH 43606-3390
419-530-4636

University of Toledo
College of Health and Human Services
3000 Arlington Ave, Toledo OH 43614-2595
419-383-4000 Fax: 419-383-2800
Website: www.hsc.utoledo.edu
E-mail: admissions@meduohio.edu

Ursuline College
2550 Lander Rd, Cleveland OH 44124-4398
Sarah E. Sundermeier, Director of Admissions
888-URSULINE Toll Free Fax: 440-684-6138
Website: www.admission.ursuline.edu
E-mail: admission@ursuline.edu

· Washington State Community College
710 Colegate Dr, Marietta OH 45750-9225
740-374-8716

∴ Western Reserve Care System
345 Oak Hill Ave, Youngstown OH 44502-1894
330-747-0777

Wright State University
3640 Colonel Glenn Hwy, Dayton OH 45435-0002
937-775-3333

Xavier University
3800 Victory Pkwy, Cincinnati OH 45207-1092
513-745-3000

Youngstown State University
Sweeney Welcome Ctr, One University Plz
Youngstown OH 44555-0002
Sue Davis, Contact
877-GO-TO-YSU

· Zane State College
1555 Newark Rd, Zanesville OH 43701-2694
740-454-2501

OKLAHOMA

Bacone College
2299 Old Bacone Rd, Muskogee OK 74403-1568
Jerrett Phillips, Director of Admissions
918-781-7340

∴ Comanche Co. Memorial Hospital
PO Box 129, Lawton OK 73502-0129
580-355-8620

East Central University
1100 E 14th St
Ada OK 74820-6999
Pamla Armstrong, Director of Admissions
580-332-8000

: Great Plains Area Vocational Technical School
4500 SW Lee Blvd, Lawton OK 73505-8304
580-355-6371

: Heritage College
7100 S I-35 Service Rd Suite 7118
Oklahoma City OK 73149
Cheryl Morris, Director
405-631-3399 Fax: 405-631-6711
Website: www.heritage-education.com
E-mail: info@heritage-education.com
See listing under "Career Schools"

: Indian Meridian Vocational Technical School
1312 S Sangre Rd, Stillwater OK 74074-1899
405-377-3333

Langston University
PO Box 907, Langston OK 73050-0907
405-466-2231

∴ Muskogee General Hospital
300 Rockefeller Dr, Muskogee OK 74401-5075
918-682-5501

· Northeastern Oklahoma A & M College
200 I St NE, Miami OK 74354-6434
Linda Oldham Barns, Director of Admissions
800-234-3409

Northeastern State University
600 N Grand Ave, Tahlequah OK 74464-2301
918-456-5511

· Oklahoma City Community College
7777 S May Ave, Oklahoma City OK 73159-4419
405-682-1611

: **OKLAHOMA HEALTH ACADEMY**
2865 E Skelly Dr Ste 224, Tulsa OK 74105
Stephanie Holderman, Director of Admissions
918-748-9900 Fax: 918-748-9937
E-mail: stephanieh@oklahomahealthacademy.org

Oklahoma State University
Stillwater OK 74078
Pamela Hathorn, Coordinator
405-744-6243
Website: www.okstate.edu
E-mail: pamela.hathorn@okstate.edu

· Oklahoma State University-Okmulgee
1801 E 4th St, Okmulgee OK 74447-3901
Cary Fox, Director of Admissions
800-722-4471

: O. T. Autry Area Vocational Technical Center
1201 W Willow Rd, Enid OK 73703-2506
580-242-2750

Platt College
3801 S Sheridan Rd, Tulsa OK 74145-1111
Angie Morelock, Director of Admissions
918-663-9000 Fax: 918-622-1240
Website: www.plattcollege.org
E-mail: angiem@plattcollege.org

· Rose State College
6420 SE 15th St, Midwest City OK 73110-2799
405-733-7300

∴ St. Francis Hospital
6161 S Yale Ave, Tulsa OK 74136-1992
918-494-1370

∴ St. Mary's Hospital
305 S 5th St, Enid OK 73701-5899
580-233-6100

· Seminole State College
PO Box 351, Seminole OK 74818-0351
405-382-9950

Southwestern Oklahoma State University
100 Campus Dr, Weatherford OK 73096-3098
580-772-6611

⁚ Tulsa County Area Vocational Technical District 18
3420 S Memorial Dr, Tulsa OK 74145-1340
918-627-7200

⁚ Tuttle Vocational Technical Center
12777 N Rockwell Ave
Oklahoma City OK 73142-2710
405-722-7799

∴ University Hospital of Oklahoma City
PO Box 26307, Oklahoma City OK 73126-0307
405-271-4000

University of Central Oklahoma
100 N University Dr, Edmond OK 73034-5209
405-974-2000

University of Oklahoma Health Sciences
1000 Stanton L Young Blvd
Oklahoma City OK 73190
405-271-4000

University of Tulsa
600 S College Ave, Tulsa OK 74104-3126
Earl Johnson, Dean of Admission
918-631-2307 Fax: 918-631-5003
Website: www.utulsa.edu
E-mail: admission@utulsa.edu

∴ Valley View Regional Hospital
430 N Monte Vista St, Ada OK 74820-4657
580-332-2323

· Vatterott College - Tulsa
4343 S 118th East Ave, Tulsa OK 74146
Tim Maloukis, Director of Admissions
918-835-8288 Fax: 918-836-9698
Website: www.vatterott-college.com
E-mail: tim.maloukis@vatterott-college.com

OREGON

Apollo College
2004 Lloyd Ctr Fl 3, Portland OR 97232-1309
503-761-6100 Fax: 503-761-3351

· Blue Mountain Community College
PO Box 100, Pendleton OR 97801-1000
541-276-1260

· Central Oregon Community College
2600 NW College Way, Bend OR 97701-5933
Alicia Moore, Director of Admissions and Records
541-383-7500

· Chemeketa Community College
PO Box 14007, Salem OR 97309-7070
Kay Carnegie, Dean
503-399-5058

⁚ Concorde Career Institute
1827 NE 44th Ave, Portland OR 97213-1443
Rick Stillman, Director of Admissions
503-281-4181

· Lane Community College
4000 E 30th Ave, Eugene OR 97405-0640
541-747-4501

· Linn-Benton Community College
6500 Pacific Blvd SW, Albany OR 97321-3774
Christine Baker, Outreach Coordinator
541-917-4811 Fax: 541-917-4868
Website: www.linnbenton.edu
E-mail: admissions@linnbenton.edu

· Mt. Hood Community College
26000 SE Stark St, Gresham OR 97030-3300
503-491-6422

OREGON COLLEGE OF ORIENTAL MEDICINE
10525 SE Cherry Blossom Dr, Portland OR 97216
Nicola Moll, Admissions Coordinator
503-253-3443 Fax: 503-253-2701
Website: www.ocom.edu
E-mail: admissions@ocom.edu

Oregon Health & Science University
3181 SW Sam Jackson Park Rd
Portland OR 97239-3079
503-494-7800

Oregon Institute of Technology
3201 Campus Dr, Klamath Falls OR 97601-8801
541-885-1000

Oregon State University
Corvallis OR 97333-9800
541-737-0123

PACIFIC UNIVERSITY
2043 College Way, Forest Grove OR 97116-1797
Karen M. Dunston, Executive Director of Admissions
800-677-6712 Fax: 503-352-2975
Website: www.pacific.edu
E-mail: admissions@pacific.edu

· Portland Community College
PO Box 19000, Portland OR 97280-0990
Dennis Bailey-Fougnier, Director of Admissions
503-977-4519

Portland State University
PO Box 751, Portland OR 97207-0751
503-725-3000

· Rogue Community College
3345 Redwood Hwy, Grants Pass OR 97527-9298
Claudia Sullivan, Director of Enrollment Services
541-956-7500 Fax: 541-471-3585
Website: www.roguecc.edu
E-mail: csullivan@roguecc.edu
See listing under "Community and Junior Colleges"

∴ St. Vincent Hospital & Medical Center
9205 SW Barnes Rd, Portland OR 97225-6603
503-216-3031

University of Oregon
1217 University of Oregon, Eugene OR 97403
541-346-1000

University of Portland
5000 N Willamette Blvd, Portland OR 97203-5798
Jason McDonald, Dean of Admissions
503-943-7911 Fax: 503-943-7315
Website: www.up.edu
E-mail: mcdonaja@up.edu

∴ Veterans Administration Medical Center
PO Box 1034, Portland OR 97207-1034
503-220-8262

Western Oregon University
345 Monmouth Ave N, Monmouth OR 97361-1314
David McDonald, Dean, Admission, Retention & Enrollment Management
877-877-1593

Willamette University
900 State St, Salem OR 97301-3931
503-370-6300

PENNSYLVANIA

∴ Abington Memorial Hospital
1200 Old York Rd, Abington PA 19001-3788
215-576-2000

∴ Albert Einstein Medical Center
5501 Old York Rd, Philadelphia PA 19141-3098
Christine Szymkowski, Interim Program Director
215-456-7010

∴ Allegheny Valley Hospital
1301 Carlisle St, Natrona Heights PA 15065-1152
724-226-7000

∴ Altoona Hospital
620 Howard Ave, Altoona PA 16601-4899
814-946-2223

∴ ARAMARK Healthcare Support Services
1101 Market St 12th Fl, Philadelphia PA 19107-2934
610-687-8600

∴ Armstrong County Memorial Hospital
1 Nolte Dr, Kittanning PA 16201-7199
724-543-8404

· Berks Technical Institute
2205 Ridgewood Rd, Wyomissing PA 19610-1168
Elizabeth Wade, Director of Admissions
610-372-1722 Fax: 610-376-4684
Website: www.berkstech.com

Bloomsburg University of Pennsylvania
400 E 2nd St, Bloomsburg PA 17815-1399
570-389-4000

∴ Bradford Regional Medical Center
School of Radiography
116 Interstate Pkwy, Bradford PA 16701-1036
S. Gregoire, Program Director
814-362-8292

· Bradford School
125 W Station Square Dr, Pittsburgh PA 15219
Director of Admissions
412-391-6710

∴ Brandywine Hospital
School of Nursing
201 Reeceville Rd, Coatesville PA 19320-1536

· Butler County Community College
PO Box 1203, Butler PA 16003-1203
724-287-8711

California University of Pennsylvania
250 University Ave, California PA 15419-1394
724-938-4000

· Career Training Academy
4314 Old William Penn Highway Ste 103
Monroeville PA 15146
Gina Hudac, Admissions Representitive
412-372-3900 Fax: 412-373-4262
Website: www.careerta.edu
E-mail: admissions2@careerta.edu

· Career Training Academy
950 5th Ave, New Kensington PA 15068-6308
John Reddy, Director
Tyna Putignano, Director of Admissions
724-337-1000 Fax: 724-335-7140
Website: www.careerta.edu
E-mail: admissions@careerta.edu
See listing under "Career Schools"

· Career Training Academy
1500 Northway Mall, Pittsburgh PA 15237
Anna Bartolini, Director North Hills Branch Campus
412-367-4000 Fax: 412-369-7223
Website: www.careerta.edu
E-mail: admissions3@careerta.edu

Cedar Crest College
100 College Dr, Allentown PA 18104-6196
Judith A. Neyhart, Vice President Enrollment
800-360-1222

∴ **CENTER FOR EMERGENCY MEDICINE**
Western PA
230 McKee Pl #500, Pittsburgh PA 15213-4912
Thomas E. Platt, Program Director
412-647-4665 Fax: 412-647-4670
Website: www.centerem.com

Central Pennsylvania College
College Hill & Valley Rds, Summerdale PA 17093
Katie Borrelli, Admissions Director
800-759-2727 Fax: 717-728-2505
Website: www.centralpenn.edu
E-mail: katie.borrelli@centralpenn.edu

Chatham College
Woodland Rd, Pittsburgh PA 15232-2826
412-365-1100

Clarion University of Pennsylvania
840 Wood St, Clarion PA 16214-1232
William Bailey, Dean of Enrollment Management
814-393-2306 Fax: 814-393-2030
Website: www.clarion.edu
E-mail: admissions@clarion.edu

∴ Clearfield Hospital
PO Box 992, Clearfield PA 16830-0992
814-768-2496

College Misericordia
301 Lake St, Dallas PA 18612-1008
Admissions
570-674-6400

· Community College of Allegheny County
Allegheny Campus: 808 Ridge Ave, Pittsburgh PA 15212 Admissions: 412.237.2700
Boyce Campus: 595 Beatty Rd, Monroeville PA 15146 Admissions: 724.325.6614
North Campus: 8701 Perry Highway, Pittsburgh PA 15237 Admissions: 412.369.3600
South Campus: 1750 Clairton Rd, West Mifflin PA 15122 Admissions: 412-469-4301
Website: www.ccac.edu

· Community College of Beaver County
1 Campus Dr, Monaca PA 15061-2566
724-775-8561 Fax: 724-775-4687
Website: www.ccbc.edu
E-mail: admissions@ccbc.edu

· Community College of Philadelphia
1700 Spring Garden St, Philadelphia PA 19130-3936
215-751-8010

∴ **CONEMAUGH VALLEY MEMORIAL HOSPITAL**
1086 Franklin St, Johnstown PA 15905-4398
Louise Pugliese, Director
814-534-9844 Fax: 814-534-3354
Website: www.conemaugh.org
E-mail: lpuglie@conemaugh.org
Programs include: Program for Surgical Technology; School of Radiologic Technology; School of Histotechnology; Program for Emergency Medicine Paramedic; and Medical Technologist Program.

· Delaware County Community College
901 Media Line Rd, Media PA 19063-1094
610-359-5000

⁚ **DELAWARE VALLEY ACADEMY OF MEDICAL & DENTAL ASSISTANTS**
3330 Grant Ave, Philadelphia PA 19114-2600
Glenn Goldsmith, Director
215-676-1200
Website: delawarevalleyacademy.com
E-mail: delvalacad@aol.com

DeSales University
2755 Station Ave, Center Valley PA 18034-9565
610-282-1100 Fax: 610-282-2342
Website: www.desales.edu

∴ Divine Providence Hospital
1100 Grampian Blvd, Williamsport PA 17701-1995
570-326-8101

· Douglas Education Center
130 7th St, Monessen PA 15062-1097
Sherry Lee Walters, Director of Enrollment Services
800-413-6013 Fax: 724-684-7463
Website: www.douglas-school.com
E-mail: swalters@douglas-school.com

Drexel University
3141 Chestnut St, Philadelphia PA 19104-2875
Dana R. Davies, Director of Undergraduate Enrollment
800-2-DREXEL

· Duffs Business Institute
100 Forbes Ave Ste 1200, Pittsburgh PA 15222-1320
412-261-4520

Duquesne University
600 Forbes Ave, Pittsburgh PA 15282-0001
Paul-James Cukanna, Director of Admissions
412-396-5000

East Stroudsburg University of PA
200 Prospect St
East Stroudsburg PA 18301
570-424-3211

Edinboro University of Pennsylvania
Edinboro PA 16444-0001
814-732-2000

Elizabethtown College
1 Alpha Dr, Elizabethtown PA 17022-2298
717-361-1000

Gannon University
109 University Sq, Erie PA 16541-0001
Christopher Tremblay, Director of Admissions
800-GANNON-U

∴ Geisinger Medical Center
100 N Academy Ave, Danville PA 17822-9800
570-271-5200

⁚ Greater Johnstown Area Vocational Technical School
445 Schoolhouse Rd, Johnstown PA 15904-2927
814-266-6073

Gwynedd-Mercy College
1325 Sumneytown Pike, Gwynedd Valley PA 19437
Dennis Murphy, V.P. Enrollment Management
800-DIAL-GMC

· Harcum College
750 Montgomery Ave, Bryn Mawr PA 19010-3476
610-525-4100

· Harrisburg Area Community College
1 HACC Dr, Harrisburg PA 17110-2999
717-780-2300

Holy Family University
9801 Frankford Avenue, Philadelphia PA 19114
Lauren Campbell, Director of Admissions
215-637-3050 Fax: 215-281-1022
Website: www.holyfamily.edu
E-mail: admissions@holyfamily.edu

∴ Holy Spirit Hospital
505 N 21st St, Camp Hill PA 17011-2288
717-763-2106

ICM School of Business and Medical Careers
10 Wood St, Pittsburgh PA 15222-1931
Maureen McBride, Assistant Director of Admissions
800-441-5222

Indiana University of Pennsylvania
Indiana PA 15705-0001
724-357-2100

INTERNATIONAL ACADEMY OF ADVANCED REFLEXOLOGY & MEDICAL REFLEXOLOGY CLINIC
1701 Snyder Rd, Green Lane PA 18054
Professor L.J. Telepo, President
215-234-0307 or 267-377-5128 Fax: 267-377-5128
Website: www.reflexology.net
E-mail: postsecondary@reflexology.net
Established 1987. Private. Coed. Tuition: $1,850 for Program. Student-faculty ratio: 20:1. Diploma Offered. Access the Student Handbook table of contents page for all official government codes which gives you your permissions and restrictions, especially under "Medical Services". We are located in beautiful Green Lane Park, see Website for more information. This program is entitled under Medical Reflexology.

INTERNATIONAL ACADEMY OF ADVANCED REFLEXOLOGY & MEDICAL REFLEXOLOGY CLINIC
1177 6th St, Whitehall PA 18052
Professor L.J. Telepo, President
215-234-0307 or 267-377-5128 Fax: 267-329-8008
Website: www.reflexology.net
E-mail: postsecondary@reflexology.net
See listing under "Allied Health Science"

Johnson College
3427 N Main Ave, Scranton PA 18508-1495
Dr. Ann L. Pipinski, President & CEO
Melissa Ide, Director of Enrollment Management
800-2WE-WORK or 570-342-6404 ext. 125
Fax: 570-348-2181
Website: www.johnson.edu
E-mail: admit@johnson.edu

Juniata College
1700 Moore St, Huntingdon PA 16652-2196
Michelle Bartol, Dean of Enrollment
877-JUNIATA Fax: 814-641-3100
Website: www.juniata.edu
E-mail: admissions@juniata.edu

Kaplan Career Institute
5650 Derry St, Harrisburg PA 17111-3571
Roy Hawkins, Director
717-564-4112

KEYSTONE TECHNICAL INSTITUTE
2301 Academy Dr, Harrisburg PA 17112-1012
Tom Bogush, Director of Admissions
717-545-4747 Fax: 717-901-9090
Website: www.acadcampus.com
E-mail: educdir@acadcampus.com
Established 1980. Private. Coed. Accreditation: ACCSCT. Enrollment: 210 full-time, 50 part-time. Faculty: 15. Student-faculty ratio: 20:1. Degrees offered: Occupational Associate Degrees (AST/ASB). Library: 2,000 volumes. 1 building on 8 acres. Combined classroom; real world lab experience and externships for career training in Medical Assistant, Dental Assistant, Massage Therapy, Paralegal, Culinary Arts, Child Care, Computers.

King's College
133 N River St, Wilkes Barre PA 18711-0801
Michelle Lawrence-Schmude, Dean of Admission
570-208-5900 Fax: 570-208-5971
Website: www.kings.edu
E-mail: admissions@kings.edu

Lancaster General College of Nursing and Health Sciences
410 N Lime St, Lancaster PA 17602-2337
Elma Hess, Director of Admissions
717-544-4902 Fax: 717-544-5970
Website: www.lancastergeneralcollege.org
E-mail: elhess@lancastergeneral.org

Lankenau Hospital
100 E Lancaster Ave, Wynnewood PA 19096-3498
610-526-3019

Latrobe Area Hospital
101 W 2nd Ave, Latrobe PA 15650-1068
724-537-1001

Lehigh Carbon Community College
4525 Education Park Dr
Schnecksville PA 18078-2502
610-799-1134

Lehigh Valley College
2809 E Saucon Valley Rd
Center Valley PA 18034-8447
Sam Jarvis, Director of Marketing
800-227-9109 Fax: 610-791-7810
Website: www.lehighvalley.edu
E-mail: joshua.padron@lehighvalley.edu

Lehigh Valley Hospital & Health Network
Center for Education
PO Box 7017, Allentown PA 18105-7017
610-402-2556

Lincoln University
Lincoln University PA 19352
Michael C. Taylor, Director of Admissions
800-790-0191

Lock Haven University
Lock Haven PA 17745
James C. Reeser, Dean of Admissions
570-893-2027

Luzerne County Community College
1333 S Prospect St, Nanticoke PA 18634-3899
800-377-5222 ext. 337

Manor College
700 Fox Chase Rd, Jenkintown PA 19046-4118
215-885-2360

Mansfield University of Pennsylvania
Academy St, Mansfield PA 16933
570-662-4000

Marywood University
2300 Adams Ave, Scranton PA 18509-1598
570-348-6211

Medical Center of Beaver County
1000 Dutch Ridge Rd, Beaver PA 15009-9700
724-728-7000

Medical College Hospitals
60 Township Line Rd, Elkins Park PA 19027-2220
215-663-6150

Mercyhurst College
501 E 38th St, Erie PA 16546-0001
800-825-1926

Messiah College
1 S College Ave, Grantham PA 17027
717-766-2511

Millersville University of Pennsylvania
PO Box 1002, Millersville PA 17551-0302
717-872-3024

Milton S. Hershey Medical Center Hospital
PO Box 850, Hershey PA 17033-0850
717-531-8803

Monsour Medical Center
70 Lincoln Hwy E, Jeannette PA 15644-3185
724-527-0600

Montgomery County Community College
340 DeKalb Pike, Blue Bell PA 19422-1400
215-641-6300

MOUNT ALOYSIUS COLLEGE
7373 Admiral Peary Hwy, Cresson PA 16630-1999
Frank C. Crouse Jr., Vice President for Enrollment Management
814-886-6383 or 888-823-2220 Fax: 814-886-6441
Website: www.mtaloy.edu
E-mail: admissions@mtaloy.edu

Nazareth Hospital
2601 Holme Ave, Philadelphia PA 19152-2096
215-335-6000

Neumann College
1 Neumann Dr, Aston PA 19014-1298
Dennis Murphy, Director of Admissions
610-459-0905 Fax: 610-558-5652
Website: www.neumann.edu
E-mail: neumann@neumann.edu

Northampton Co. Area Community College
3835 Green Pond Rd, Bethlehem PA 18020-7599
610-861-5300

Northwest Medical Center
100 Fairfield Dr, Seneca PA 16346
814-677-1711

Pennsylvania College of Technology
1 College Ave, Williamsport PA 17701
570-326-3761

Pennsylvania Hospital
800 Spruce St, Philadelphia PA 19107-6192
215-829-3312

Pennsylvania State Milton S Hershey Medical Center
College of Medicine
500 University Dr Box 850, Hershey PA 17033
717-534-8521

Pennsylvania State University
Hazelton Campus, Hazleton PA 18201
570-450-3000

Pennsylvania State University
3550 7th St Rd, New Kensington PA 15068-1765
Patricia K. Brady, Director of Admissions
724-334-5466

Pennsylvania State University
200 University Dr, Schuylkill Haven PA 17972-2202
570-385-6000

Pennsylvania State University
201 Shields Bldg PO Box 300
University Park PA 16802-3000
814-865-4700

Philadelphia University
4201 Henry Ave, Philadelphia PA 19144-5409
215-951-2700

Point Park University
St. Francis Medical Center
201 Wood St, Pittsburgh PA 15222-1912
412-392-3879

Reading Area Community College
PO Box 1706, Reading PA 19603-1706
David J. Adams, Director of Admissions
610-607-6224

Reading Hospital & Medical Center
PO Box 16052, Reading PA 19612-6052
610-378-6664

Robert Morris University
6001 University Blvd, Coraopolis PA 15108
412-262-8200

Robert Packer Hospital
1 Guthrie Sq, Sayre PA 18840-1698
570-888-6666

Sacred Heart Hospital
421 W Chew St, Allentown PA 18102-3490
610-776-4745

St. Francis University
PO Box 600, Loretto PA 15940-0600
814-472-3000

St. Joseph's Hospital
PO Box 316, Reading PA 19603-0316
610-378-2000

Seton Hill University
Greensburg PA 15601-1599
Mary Kay Cooper, Director of Admissions and Adult Student Services
800-826-6234

Sewickley Valley Hospital
700 Blackburn Rd, Sewickley PA 15143-1454
412-741-6600

Shadyside Hospital
5230 Centre Ave, Pittsburgh PA 15232-1381
412-622-2010

Sharon Regional Health System
School of Radiography
740 E State St, Sharon PA 16146-3395
Sherry A. Masotto, Program Director
724-983-5603

Slippery Rock University
14 Maltby Dr, Slippery Rock PA 16057-1326
724-738-9000

Somerset Community Hospital
225 S Center Ave, Somerset PA 15501-2088
814-443-5221

South Hills School of Business & Technology
480 Waupelani Dr, State College PA 16801-4516
Maralyn Mazza, Director
888-282-7427

Temple University
Broad St & Montgomery Ave, Philadelphia PA 19122
215-204-7000

Temple University
3307 N Broad St, Philadelphia PA 19140-5101
215-787-7000

Thiel College
75 College Ave, Greenville PA 16125-2181
724-589-2000

Thomas Jefferson University
111 S 11th St, Philadelphia PA 19107-4824
215-955-6000

University Health Center
300 Halket St, Pittsburgh PA 15213-3108
412-641-4664

University of Pittsburgh
4200 5th Ave, Pittsburgh PA 15260-3583
412-624-4141

University of Pittsburgh at Johnstown
450 Schoolhouse Rd, Johnstown PA 15904-2990
814-269-7000

University of Scranton
800 Linden St, Scranton PA 18510-4501
570-941-7400

UPMC SCHOOL OF MEDICAL IMAGING
3434 Forbes Ave Murdoch Bldg Ste 206
Pittsburgh PA 15213-2582
Denise Csonka Lake, Program Director
412-647-3528 Fax: 412-647-3713
Website: www.schoolofmedicalimaging.upmc.com
E-mail: laked@upmc.edu

Washington & Jefferson College
60 S Lincoln St, Washington PA 15301-4801
Alton E. Newell, Vice President for Enrollment
724-223-6025 Fax: 724-223-6534
Website: www.washjeff.edu
E-mail: admission@washjeff.edu

West Chester University of Pennsylvania
S High St, West Chester PA 19383-0001
610-436-1000

Western School of Health & Business Careers
421 7th Ave, Pittsburgh PA 15219-1907
Michael Joyce, Director of Admissions
800-333-6607

Westmoreland County Community College
145 Pavilion Ln, Youngwood PA 15697
724-925-4000

Widener University
1 University Pl, Chester PA 19013-5792
Edwin Wright, Dean of Admissions
610-499-4000 Fax: 610-499-4676
Website: www.widener.edu
E-mail: admissions.office@widener.edu

Wilkes Barre General Hospital
575 N River St, Wilkes Barre PA 18764-0001
570-829-8111

Williamsport Hospital
777 Rural Ave, Williamsport PA 17701-3191
570-326-8101

York College of Pennsylvania
PO Box 15199, York PA 17405-7199
717-846-7788

York Hospital
1001 S George St, York PA 17403-3645
717-851-2942

RHODE ISLAND

Community College of Rhode Island
Knight Campus
400 East Ave, Warwick RI 02886-1805
Elizabeth A. Mancini, Assistant Dean of Enrollment Services
401-825-2003

MTTI - MOTORING TECHNICAL TRAINING INSTITUTE
54 Water St, East Providence RI 02914-5022
Sharon Ring, Program Director
401-434-4840 or 866-454-6884 Fax: 401-434-9540
Website: www.mtti.edu
E-mail: info@mtti.edu

New England Institute of Technology
2500 Post Rd, Warwick RI 02886-2244
Michael Kwiatkowski, Director of Admissions
401-739-5000 Fax: 401-738-5122
Website: www.neit.edu
E-mail: eflynn@neit.edu

Rhode Island Hospital
593 Eddy St, Providence RI 02903-4923
401-444-5123

St. Joseph's Hospital
200 High Service Ave
North Providence RI 02904-5199
401-456-3050

University of Rhode Island
Kingston RI 02881
401-874-1000

Women & Infants Hospital
101 Dudley St, Providence RI 02905-2499
401-274-1100

SOUTH CAROLINA

Aiken Technical College
PO Box 696, Aiken SC 29802-0796
803-593-9231

Anderson Memorial Hospital
800 N Fant St, Anderson SC 29621-5708
864-261-1109

Baptist Medical Center
1519 Marion St, Columbia SC 29201-2910
803-771-5042

Charleston Southern University
PO Box 118087, Charleston SC 29423-8087
Cheryl Burton, Director of Admissions
800-947-7474

Clemson University
105 Sikes Hall, Clemson SC 29634
864-656-2287

Florence-Darlington Technical College
PO Box 100548, Florence SC 29501-0548
843-661-8324

Forrest Junior College
601 E River St, Anderson SC 29624-2405
Pamela Johnson, MBA, President
864-225-7653 Fax: 864-261-7471
Website: www.forrestcollege.edu
E-mail: info@forrestcollege.edu
Medical Assisting, Nurse Assisting.
See listing under "Community and Junior Colleges"

Greenville Technical College
PO Box 5616, Greenville SC 29606-5616
Carolyn Watkins, Dean of Admissions
800-723-0673 (US) or 800-922-1183 (SC)
Website: www.greenvilletech.com

Horry-Georgetown Technical College
PO Box 261966, Conway SC 29528-6066
843-349-5277

McLeod Regional Medical Center
555 E Cheves St, Florence SC 29506-2606
843-667-2297

Medical University of South Carolina
PO Box 250402, Charleston SC 29425
843-792-2300

Midlands Technical College
PO Box 2408, Columbia SC 29202-2408
803-738-8324

Orangeburg-Calhoun Technical College
3250 Saint Matthews Rd NE
Orangeburg SC 29118-8299
803-536-0311

Piedmont Technical College
PO Box 1467, Greenwood SC 29648-1467
864-941-8324

South Carolina State University
PO Box 7127, Orangeburg SC 29117-0001
Lillian M. Adderson, Director of Admissions
803-536-7185

South University
9 Science Court, Columbia SC 29203
Trish Wade, Contact
803-799-9082 Fax: 803-799-9038
Website: www.southuniversity.edu
E-mail: twade@southuniversity.edu

Spartanburg Community College
PO Box 4386, Spartanburg SC 29305-4386
Nancy Garmroth, Dean of Admissions & Financial Aid
864-592-4810 Fax: 864-592-4945
Website: sccsc.edu

Tri-County Tech College
PO Box 587, Pendleton SC 29670-0587
864-646-8361

Trident Technical College
PO Box 118067, Charleston SC 29423-8067
843-574-6111

University of South Carolina
Columbia SC 29208-0001
803-777-7700

Winthrop University
701 W Oakland Ave, Rock Hill SC 29733-0001
803-323-2211

York Technical College
452 Anderson Rd S, Rock Hill SC 29730-7318
803-327-8000

SOUTH DAKOTA

Colorado Technical University
3901 W 59th St, Sioux Falls SD 57108
605-361-0200

Dakota State University
820 N Washington Ave, Madison SD 57042-1799
605-256-5112

Lake Area Technical Institute
230 11th St NE, Watertown SD 57201
605-882-5284

McKennan Hospital
800 E 21st St, Sioux Falls SD 57105-1096
605-339-8113

Mitchell Technical Institute
821 N Capital St, Mitchell SD 57301-2002
Allen Dvorak, Director of Admissions
800-952-0042

Mt. Marty College
1105 W 8th St, Yankton SD 57078-3724
605-668-1514

Presentation College
1500 N Main St, Aberdeen SD 57401-1280
JoEllen Lindner, VP for Enrollment
605-229-8492 Fax: 605-229-8425
Website: www.presentation.edu
E-mail: admit@presentation.edu

Queen of Peace Hospital
5th & Foster, Mitchell SD 57301
605-995-2250

Rapid City Regional Hospital
353 Fairmont Blvd, Rapid City SD 57701-7375
605-341-8100

Sacred Heart Hospital
501 Summit St, Yankton SD 57078-3855
605-655-9371

St. Luke's Midland Regional Medical Center
305 S State St, Aberdeen SD 57401-4590
605-622-5230

Sioux Valley Hospital
PO Box 5039, Sioux Falls SD 57117-5039
605-333-6424

South Dakota State University
PO Box 2201, Brookings SD 57007-0001
605-688-4151

Southeast Technical Institute
2320 N Career Ave, Sioux Falls SD 57107
Tracy Noldner, Supervisor Student/Instructional Services
800-247-0789

University of South Dakota
414 E Clark St, Vermillion SD 57069-2307
605-677-5011

Western Dakota Technical Institute
800 Mickelson Dr, Rapid City SD 57703-4018
Jill Elder, Admissions Coordinator
605-394-4034 Fax: 605-394-2204
Website: www.wdt.edu
E-mail: jill.elder@wdt.edu

TENNESSEE

Austin Peay State University
601 College St, Clarksville TN 37044-0002
931-221-7011 Fax: 931-221-6168
Website: www.apsu.edu
E-mail: admissions@apsu.edu

Baptist Memorial College of Health Science
1003 Monroe Ave, Memphis TN 38104-3104
Office of Admissions
866-575-2247

Baptist Memorial Hospital
350 N Humphreys Blvd #EaglBld2
Memphis TN 38120-2177
901-227-5121

Carson-Newman College
1646 Russell Ave, Jefferson City TN 37760
865-471-4000

Chattanooga State Technical Community College
4501 Amnicola Hwy, Chattanooga TN 37406-1018
423-697-4400

Cleveland State Community College
PO Box 3570, Cleveland TN 37320-3570
423-472-7141

Columbia State Community College
PO Box 1315, Columbia TN 38402-1315
931-540-2722

DRAUGHONS JUNIOR COLLEGE - MURFREESBORO
415 Golden Bear Ct, Murfreesboro TN 37128
615-217-9347 Fax: 615-217-9348
Website: www.draughons.org

East Tennessee State University
PO Box 70623, Johnson City TN 37614
Dr. Wilsie Bishop, Dean of Public & Allied Health
423-439-4243

Jackson State Community College
2046 N Parkway, Jackson TN 38301-3797
731-424-3520

Lincoln Memorial University
PO Box 2012, Harrogate TN 37752
423-869-3611

Lipscomb University
3901 Granny White Pike, Nashville TN 37204-3951
Ricky Holaway, Director of Admissions
800-333-4358 ext. 1776 Fax: 615-269-1804
Website: www.lipscomb.edu
E-mail: admissions@lipscomb.edu

MEDVANCE INSTITUTE
1025 Highway 111, Cookeville TN 38501-4305
Shirley Cole, Campus Director
866-86-GO-MED or 931-526-3660 Fax: 931-372-2603
Website: www.medvance.edu

Methodist Hospital
1265 Union Ave, Memphis TN 38104-3415
901-726-8274

MIDDLE TENNESSEE SCHOOL OF ANESTHESIA
PO Box 417, Madison TN 37116-6414
Mary E. DeVasher, Dean
615-868-6503 Fax: 615-868-9885
Website: www.mtsa.edu
E-mail: ikey@mtsa.edu

Middle Tennessee State University
1301 E Main St, Murfreesboro TN 37132-0001
615-898-2300

Miller-Motte Technical College
1820 Business Park Dr, Clarksville TN 37040-6023
Lisa Teague, Director of Admissions
931-553-0071 Fax: 931-552-2916
Website: www.miller-motte.com
E-mail: lteague@miller-motte.com

MILLER-MOTTE TECHNICAL COLLEGE
801 Space Park N, Goodlettsville TN 37072
Kevin Suhr, Campus Administrator
615-859-8090 Fax: 615-859-9634
Website: www.miller-motte.com
E-mail: ksuhr@miller-motte.com

Nashville State Technical Community College
120 White Bridge Pike, Nashville TN 37209-4515
615-353-3333

National College
1328 Highway 11W, Bristol TN 37620
Becky Wild, Director of Admissions
423-878-4440 Fax: 423-793-1060
Website: www.national-college.edu
E-mail: info@national-college.edu

National College of Business & Technology
3748 Nolensville Pike, Nashville TN 37211-3322
Lynda Dandridge, Director of Admissions
615-333-3344 Fax: 615-333-3429
Website: www.national-college.edu
E-mail: info@national-college.edu

Northeast State Technical Community College
PO Box 246, Blountville TN 37617-0246
423-323-3191

Roane State Community College
276 Patton Ln, Harriman TN 37748-8664
865-354-3000

St. Thomas Hospital
PO Box 380, Nashville TN 37202-0380
615-222-2111

Southwest Tennessee Community College
5983 Macon Cove, Memphis TN 38134
Vanessa R. Dowdy, Director of Admissions
901-333-5000 Fax: 901-333-4523
Website: www.southwest.tn.edu
E-mail: vdowdy@southwest.tn.edu

Tennessee State University
3500 John A Merritt Blvd, Nashville TN 37209-1561
John Cade, Dean of Admissions & Records
615-963-5101 Fax: 615-963-2930
Website: www.tnstate.edu
E-mail: jcade@tnstate.edu

Tennessee Technological University
PO Box 5006, Cookeville TN 38505-0001
931-372-3101

Tennessee Technology Center at Knoxville
1100 Liberty St, Knoxville TN 37919-2327
Marilyn Canady, Coordinator of Student Services
865-546-5567

Tennessee Technology Center at Livingston
740 Hi Tech Dr, Livingston TN 38570
931-823-5525

Tennessee Technology Center at Memphis
550 Alabama Ave, Memphis TN 38105-3604
901-543-6100

Trevecca Nazarene University
333 Murfreesboro Rd, Nashville TN 37210-2834
615-248-1200

University of Memphis
Memphis TN 38152-0001
901-678-2000

University of Tennessee
615 McCallie Ave, Chattanooga TN 37403-2504
Yancy Freeman, Director of Admissions
423-425-4111 Fax: 423-425-4157
Website: www.utc.edu
E-mail: Yancy-Freeman@utc.edu

University of Tennessee
527 Andy Holt Tower, Knoxville TN 37996-0001
865-974-1000

University of Tennessee
Martin TN 38238-0001
731-587-7000

University of Tennessee Health Science Center
800 Madison Ave, Memphis TN 38163-0002
901-448-5500

University of Tennessee Medical Center
1924 Alcoa Hwy, Knoxville TN 37920
865-544-6404

Vanderbilt University
W End Ave, Nashville TN 37240-0001
615-322-7311

Volunteer State Community College
1480 Nashville Pike, Gallatin TN 37066-3188
615-452-8600

Walters State Community College
500 S Davy Crockett Pkwy
Morristown TN 37813-6899
423-585-2600

TEXAS

Abilene Christian University
ACU Box 29000, Abilene TX 79699-0001
325-674-2000 Fax: 325-674-2202
Website: www.acu.edu
E-mail: info@admissions.acu.edu

ACADEMY OF ORIENTAL MEDICINE AT AUSTIN
2700 W Anderson Ln Ste 204, Austin TX 78757
Amy Scott, Admissions Director
512-492-3017 Fax: 512-454-7001
Website: www.aoma.edu
E-mail: info@aoma.edu

· Alvin Community College
3110 Mustang Rd, Alvin TX 77511-4807
281-756-3531

· Amarillo College
PO Box 447, Amarillo TX 79178-0001
806-371-5000

· Angelina College
PO Box 1768, Lufkin TX 75902-1768
Judith M. Cutting, Director of Admissions/Registration
936-639-1301

: ATI Career Training Center
6351 Boulevard 26 Ste 100
North Richland Hills TX 76180
817-284-1141
Website: www.aticareertraining.edu

∴ Baptist Health System
215 E Quincy St, San Antonio TX 78215
210-297-1040

∴ Baptist Hospital
608 Strickland Dr, Orange TX 77630-4717
409-883-9361

∴ Baptist Hospital of Southeast Texas
PO Box 1591, Beaumont TX 77704-1591
409-654-5351

Baylor College of Medicine
1 Baylor Plz, Houston TX 77030-3498
713-798-4951

Baylor University
Po Box 97008, Waco TX 76798-7008
254-710-1011

Baylor University Medical Center
3500 Gaston Ave, Dallas TX 75246-2088
214-820-2731

∴ Ben Taub Hospital
2525 Holly Hall St, Houston TX 77054-4124
713-746-6400

· Blinn College
902 College Ave, Brenham TX 77833-4098
Dennis K. Crowson, Registrar
979-830-4000

: Bradford School of Business
4669 Southwest Freeway Ste 300, Houston TX 77027
713-629-1500

∴ CANCER THERAPY & RESEARCH CENTER
School of Medical Dosimetry
7979 Wurzbach Rd, San Antonio TX 78229-4427
Melissa Blough, Ph.D., DABR, School Director
210-450-5669 Fax: 210-616-5682
Website: www.ctrc.net
E-mail: mblough@ctrc.net

: Career Centers of Texas - El Paso
8360 Burnham Rd Ste 100, El Paso TX 79907-1526
Barbara Martinez, Director of Admissions
915-595-1935 Fax: 915-595-6619
Website: www.careercenters.edu
E-mail: bmartinez@cct-ep.com

· Central Texas College
PO Box 1800, Killeen TX 76540-1800
Lillian Kroeger, Director of Admissions
254-526-1104

· Cisco Junior College
101 College Hts, Cisco TX 76437
254-442-2567

∴ Citizens Medical Center
2701 Hospital Dr, Victoria TX 77901-5748
361-573-9181

· Coastal Bend College
3800 Charco Rd, Beeville TX 78102-2197
361-358-2838

· College of the Mainland
1200 N Amburn Rd, Texas City TX 77591-2499
409-938-1211

· Collin County Community College
4800 Preston Park Blvd, Plano TX 75093
972-881-5790

· COVENANT SCHOOL OF NURSING AND ALLIED HEALTH
2002 W Loop 289 Ste 120, Lubbock TX 79407-7701
Admissions
806-797-0955 Fax: 806-793-0720
Website: www.covenantson.com
E-mail: admissionscsn@covhs.org

· Del Mar College
101 Baldwin Blvd, Corpus Christi TX 78404-3894
361-698-1200

· El Centro College
801 Main St, Dallas TX 75202-3698
214-860-2037

· El Paso Community College
PO Box 20500, El Paso TX 79998-0500
915-831-2000

· Galveston College
4015 Avenue Q, Galveston TX 77550-7496
Brian Lowery, Registrar
409-763-6551 Fax: 409-944-1501
Website: www.gc.edu
E-mail: blowery@gc.edu

· Grayson County College
6101 Grayson Dr, Denison TX 75020
903-465-6030

∴ Gulf Coast Regional Blood Center
1400 La Concha Ln, Houston TX 77054-1887
713-790-1200

· Hallmark Institute of Technology - Technology Campus
10401 W IH 10, San Antonio TX 78230-1736
Joe Fisher, President
210-690-9000 Fax: 210-697-8225
Website: www.hallmarkinstitute.com
E-mail: sross@hallmarkinstitute.com
Electronics Engineering Technology, Business Office Administration, Computer Network Systems Technology, & Medical Assistant.

∴ Harris Hospital
1301 Pennsylvania Ave, Fort Worth TX 76104-2190
817-878-2106

∴ Hendrick Medical Center
1900 Pine St, Abilene TX 79601
325-670-2201

∴ Hillcrest Baptist Medical Center
3000 Herring Ave, Waco TX 76708-3299
254-756-8551

· Houston Community College
PO Box 667517, Houston TX 77266-7517
713-718-2000

· Howard College
3197 Executive Dr, San Angelo TX 76904-6801
LeAnne Byrd, Contact
325-944-9585

∴ JPS Institute for Health Career Development
2400 Circle Dr, Fort Worth TX 76119
Byron D. Lancaster, Marketing Coordinator
817-920-7380

· Kilgore College
1100 Broadway Blvd, Kilgore TX 75662-3299
Ray McLeod, Director, Marketing & Enrollment
903-984-8531

: Kingwood College
20000 Kingwood Dr, Kingwood TX 77339-3801
Isaac Williams, Director of Enrollment Management
281-312-1600

Lamar University
PO Box 10009, Beaumont TX 77710-0009
409-880-8845

· Laredo Community College
1 W End Washington St, Laredo TX 78040-4348
956-722-0521

· Lee College
PO Box 818, Baytown TX 77522-0818
Dr. Dennis Dressler, Director of Admissions
281-427-5611

· McLennan Community College
1400 College Dr, Waco TX 76708-1498
Dr. Bridget Moore, Director, Health Sciences
254-299-8000 Fax: 254-299-8854
Website: www.mclennan.edu
E-mail: bmoore@mclennan.edu

∴ Memorial Hospital System
7737 SW Freeway, Houston TX 77074
713-776-5100

∴ METHODIST HOSPITAL
6565 Fannin St, B154, Houston TX 77030-2707
Judy Jobe, MT (ASCP), Program Director
713-441-2599 Fax: 713-793-7408
E-mail: jjobe@tmh.tmc.edu

∴ Methodist Hospital
3615 19th St, Lubbock TX 79410-1209
806-792-1011

· Midland College
3600 N Garfield St, Midland TX 79705-6397
432-685-4500

Midwestern State University
3410 Taft Blvd, Wichita Falls TX 76308-2096
940-397-4000

· Navarro College
3200 W 7th Ave, Corsicana TX 75110-4899
903-874-6501

· North Central Texas College
1525 W California St, Gainesville TX 76240-4636
Michelle Winters, Registrar
940-668-3315

: Northwest Texas Healthcare System
PO Box 1110, Amarillo TX 79105
806-354-1110

· Odessa College
201 W University Blvd, Odessa TX 79764-7127
432-335-6400

Our Lady of the Lake University
411 SW 24th St, San Antonio TX 78207-4666
Mary Kay Cooper, Dean of Enrollment
210-434-6711

Prairie View A&M University
PO Box 519, Prairie View TX 77446
936-857-3311

∴ Presbyterian Hospital
8200 Walnut Hill Ln, Dallas TX 75231-4402
214-345-7558

· Remington College - Fort Worth Campus
300 E Loop 820, Fort Worth TX 76112-1280
Director of Recruitment
817-451-0017 Fax: 817-496-1257
Website: www.remingtoncollege.edu
E-mail: lynn.wey@remingtoncollege.edu

∴ St. Elizabeth Hospital
2830 Calder St, Beaumont TX 77702-1892
409-892-7171

· St. Phillip's College
1801 Martin Luther King Dr
San Antonio TX 78203-2098
210-531-3200

Sam Houston State University
PO Box 2026, Huntsville TX 77341
936-294-1111

· San Antonio College
1300 San Pedro Ave, San Antonio TX 78212-4299
210-733-2000

: SAN ANTONIO COLLEGE OF MEDICAL AND DENTAL ASSISTANTS
7142 San Pedro Ave Ste 100, San Antonio TX 78216
Carig Czubati, Director of Admissions
210-733-0777 Fax: 210-735-2431
Website: www.sacmda.com
E-mail: cczubati@sac-mda.com

· San Jacinto College
8060 Spencer Hwy, Pasadena TX 77505-5998
281-476-1501

∴ Scenic Mountain Medical Center
1601 W 11th Pl, Big Spring TX 79720-4198
432-263-1211

∴ Scott & White Memorial Hospital and Clinic
2401 S 31st St, Temple TX 76508-0002
Janet Duben-Engelkirk Ed.D., MT(ASCP), Program Director
254-724-5177

∴ Shannon West Texas Memorial Hospital
120 E Harris Ave, San Angelo TX 76903-5904
325-653-6741

Southern Methodist University
PO Box 750181, Dallas TX 75275-0181
Ron Moss, Dean of Admission
214-768-2058

· South Plains College - Reese Campus
9730 Reese Blvd, Lubbock TX 79416
Kimbra Quinn, Director of New Student Relations
806-894-9611 ext. 2113

Stephen F. Austin State University
PO Box 6078, Nacogdoches TX 75962-0001
936-468-2011

Tarleton State University
PO Box T0030, Stephenville TX 76402
254-968-9000

· Tarrant County Junior College
Northeast Campus
828 W Harwood Rd, Hurst TX 76054-3299
Cathie J. Jackson, Director of Admissions and Records
817-515-6100

· Temple College
2600 S 1st St, Temple TX 76504-7435
Toni Borras, Director of Admissions & Records
254-298-8808 Fax: 254-298-8288
Website: www.templejc.edu
E-mail: admissionsrecords@templejc.edu

Texas A&M University
College Station TX 77843-0001
979-845-3211

Texas A&M University
700 University Blvd, Kingsville TX 78363
361-593-2111

Texas A&M University - Corpus Christi
6300 Ocean Dr, Corpus Christi TX 78412-5503
361-825-5700

: TEXAS CAREERS
1015 Jackson-Keller Rd #102
San Antonio TX 78213-3752
Laura Bledsoe, Campus President
210-308-8584 Fax: 210-308-8985
Website: www.texascareers.com
E-mail: lbledsoe@texascareers.com

Texas Christian University
TCU Box 297013, Fort Worth TX 76129
817-257-7000

TEXAS COLLEGE OF TRADITIONAL CHINESE MEDICINE
4005 Manchaca Rd, Austin TX 78704
Admissions Coordinator
512-444-8082 Fax: 512-444-6345
Website: www.tctcm.edu
E-mail: info@texastcm.edu

∴ Texas Heart Institute
PO Box 20345, Houston TX 77225-0345
713-791-4026

Texas Southern University
3100 Cleburne St, Houston TX 77004-4583
713-313-7011

· Texas Southmost College
80 Fort Brown St, Brownsville TX 78520-4993
956-544-3879

· Texas State Technical College
1901 N Loop 499, Harlingen TX 78550
956-364-4001

Texas State University - San Marcos
601 University Dr, San Marcos TX 78666-4685
512-245-2111

Texas Tech University Health Science Center
Lubbock TX 79430
806-743-3111

Texas Woman's University
PO Box 425589, Denton TX 76204-5589
Erma Nieto-Brecht, Director of Admissions
866-809-6130 Fax: 940-898-3081
Website: www.twu.edu
E-mail: admissions@twu.edu

Texas Woman's University
6700 Fannin St, Houston TX 77030-2343
Erma Nieto-Brecht, Director of Admissions
866-809-6130 Fax: 940-898-3081
Website: www.twu.edu
E-mail: admissions@twu.edu

Trinity Valley Community College
100 Cardinal St, Athens TX 75751
903-677-8822

Tyler Junior College
PO Box 9020, Tyler TX 75711-9020
Joan Jones, Interim Dean
800-687-5680
Website: www.tjc.edu
E-mail: jjon@tjc.edu
See listing under "Community and Junior Colleges"

United Regional Health Care System
Medical Technology Program
1600 11th St, Wichita Falls TX 76301
Gwen Morman, MS, MT(ASCP), Program Director
940-764-3187

University Hospital
4502 Medical Dr, San Antonio TX 78229-4492
210-616-2000

University of Houston
122 E Cullen Bldg, Houston TX 77204-2023
Office of Admission
713-743-9595
Website: www.uh.edu
E-mail: admissions@uh.edu

University of Houston-Clear Lake
2700 Bay Area Blvd, Houston TX 77058-1025
281-283-2500

University of North Texas
PO Box 305309, Denton TX 76203-5309
940-565-2000

University of Texas at Arlington
Box 19111, Arlington TX 76019-0111
Hans Gatterdam, Director of Admission
817-272-6287 Fax: 817-272-3435
Website: www.uta.edu
E-mail: admissions@uta.edu

University of Texas at Austin
0 the Univ of Texas, Austin TX 78712
512-471-3434

University of Texas at Dallas
PO Box 830688, Richardson TX 75083-0688
972-690-2111

University of Texas at El Paso
500 W University Ave, El Paso TX 79968-8900
915-747-5000

University of Texas at Tyler
3900 University Blvd, Tyler TX 75701-6622
Jim Hutto, Dean Enrollment Management
800-888-9537

University of Texas Health Science Center
PO Box 20036, Houston TX 77225-0036
713-500-4472

University of Texas Health Science Center
7703 Floyd Curl Dr, San Antonio TX 78229
210-567-7000

UNIVERSITY OF TEXAS M.D. ANDERSON CANCER CENTER
1515 Holcombe Blvd, Houston TX 77030-4009
Anne Bettinger, Academic Recruiter
713-745-1205 Fax: 713-792-0800
Website: www.mdanderson.org/healthsciences
E-mail: ambettin@mdanderson.org

The University of Texas Medical Branch
301 University Blvd, Galveston TX 77555-0802
409-772-1215

University of Texas-Pan American
1201 W University Dr, Edinburg TX 78539-2909
956-381-2011

University of Texas Southwestern Medical Center
5323 Harry Hines Blvd, Dallas TX 75390-7208
214-648-3111

University of the Incarnate Word
4301 Broadway St, San Antonio TX 78209-6318
210-829-6000

Veterans Affairs Medical Center
2002 Holcombe Blvd, Houston TX 77030-4211
713-794-7100

Victoria College
2200 E Red River St, Victoria TX 77901-4494
361-573-3291

Wadley Regional Medical Center
1000 Pine St, Texarkana TX 75501-5170
903-798-8000

Weatherford College
225 College Park Dr, Weatherford TX 76086
Dr. Joe Birmingham, President
800-287-5471 Fax: 817-598-6205
Website: www.wc.edu
E-mail: willingham@wc.edu

Western Technical College
9624 Plaza Cir, El Paso TX 79927-2105
Bill Terrell, Chief Administrative Officer
915-760-8123
Website: www.wtc-ep.edu
E-mail: bterrell@wtc-ep.edu

Western Technical College
9451 Diana Dr, El Paso TX 79924-6936
Bill Terrell, Chief Administrative Officer
915-566-9621 Fax: 915-565-9903
Website: www.wtc-ep.edu
E-mail: bterrell@wtc-ep.edu

West Texas A & M University
WTAMU Box 907, Canyon TX 79016-0001
806-651-2000

Wharton County Junior College
911 E Boling Hwy, Wharton TX 77488-3298
979-532-4560

UTAH

American Institute of Medical-Dental Technology
1675 N Freedom Blvd, Provo UT 84604-2540
801-377-2900

Brigham Young University
Provo UT 84602-0001
801-378-5000

California College for Health Sciences
5295 Commerce Dr, Salt Lake City UT 84107
800-221-7374

L.D.S. BUSINESS COLLEGE
95 North 300 West, Salt Lake City UT 84101-3500
Kathleen Howe, Assistant Director of Admissions
801-524-8145 Fax: 801-524-1900
Website: www.ldsbc.edu
E-mail: admissions@ldsbc.edu
See listing under "Career Schools"

Provo College
1450 W 820 N, Provo UT 84601-1305
801-375-1861

Salt Lake Community College
PO Box 30808, Salt Lake City UT 84130-0808
801-957-4111

Stevens Henager College
755 Main St, Logan UT 84321
Josh Swayne, Executive Director
435-713-4777
Website: www.stevenshenager.edu

Stevens Henager College
PO Box 9428, Ogden UT 84409-0428
Cindy Williams, Director of Admissions
801-394-7791 Fax: 801-621-0866
Website: www.stevenshenager.edu
E-mail: shcogden@yahoo.com

University of Utah
1460 E 201 S, Salt Lake City UT 84112
801-581-7200

Utah Career College
1902 W 7800 S, West Jordan UT 84088-4021
Denice Dunker, Director of Admissions
801-304-4224

Utah State University
Logan UT 84322-0001
435-797-1000

Utah Valley Regional Medical Center
1034 N 500 W, Provo UT 84604-3380
801-373-7850

Veterans Affairs Medical Center
500 Foothill Dr, Salt Lake City UT 84148-0001
801-582-1565

Weber State University
1001 University Cir, Ogden UT 84408
801-626-6000

VERMONT

Champlain College
PO Box 670, Burlington VT 05402-0670
802-860-2727

FLETCHER ALLEN HEALTH CARE SCHOOL OF CYTOTECHNOLOGY
111 Colchester Ave, Burlington VT 05401-1473
Sandra Giroux, Program Director
802-847-5133 Fax: 802-847-3632
Website: www.fahc.org/cytoschool
E-mail: sandra.giroux@vtmednet.org

Rutland Regional Medical Center
160 Allen St, Rutland VT 05701-4595
802-775-7111

University of Vermont
194 S Prospect St, Burlington VT 05401-3518
802-656-3131

VIRGINIA

ACT COLLEGE
1100 Wilson Blvd Suite M780, Arlington VA 22209
Robert Boderman, EVP of Operations
703-527-6660 Fax: 703-527-6688
Website: www.actcollege.edu
E-mail: rboderman@actcollege.edu

AUGUSTA MEDICAL CENTER
School of Clinical Laboratory Science
PO Box 1000, Fishersville VA 22939-1000
Bernadette Bekken, Program Director
540-332-4539 Fax: 540-332-4543
Website: www.augustamed.com/cls
E-mail: bbekken@augustamed.com

Bryant & Stratton College
8141 Hull St Rd, Richmond VA 23235-6411
David K. Mayle, Director of Admissions
804-745-2444 Fax: 804-745-6884
Website: www.bryantstratton.edu
E-mail: dkmayle@bryantstratton.edu

Bryant & Stratton College
301 Centre Pointe Dr, Virginia Beach VA 23462-4417
Tracy Nannery, Director
757-499-7900

Carilion Health Systems
PO Box 13727, Roanoke VA 24036-3727
540-981-7347

Centra Health
1920 Atherholt Rd, Lynchburg VA 24501-1120
804-947-4705

Central Virginia Community College
3506 Wards Rd, Lynchburg VA 24502-2498
804-832-7600

De Paul Medical Center
150 Kingsley Ln, Norfolk VA 23505-4650
757-489-5120

ECPI College of Technology
5555 Greenwich Rd Ste 300
Virginia Beach VA 23462-6542
757-671-7171 Fax: 757-671-8661
Website: www.ecpi.edu

Fairfax Hospital
3300 Gallows Rd, Falls Church VA 22042-3300
703-698-3371

Hampton University
Hampton VA 23669
757-727-5000

Heritage Institute
8255 Shoppers Square, Manassas VA 20111-2176
Tess Anderson, Director
703-361-7775 Fax: 703-335-9987
Website: www.heritage-education.com
E-mail: info@heritage-education.com
See listing under "Career Schools"

James Madison University
800 S Main St, Harrisonburg VA 22807-0002
540-568-6211

Jefferson College of Health Sciences
Formerly Community Hospital
PO Box 13186, Roanoke VA 24031-3186
Judith McKeon, Director of Admissions
540-985-8483

J. Sargeant Reynolds Community College
PO Box 85622, Richmond VA 23285-5622
804-371-3000

Longwood University
201 High St, Farmville VA 23909-1801
804-395-2000

Mary Baldwin College
Staunton VA 24401
Lisa A. Branson, Executive Director of Admissions and Financial Aid
800-468-2262 Fax: 540-887-7292
Website: www.mbc.edu
E-mail: admit@mbc.edu

Mary Washington Hospital
1001 Sam Perry Blvd, Fredericksburg VA 22401-3354
Marcia R. Floyd, Education Director
540-899-1565

Mountain Empire Community College
3441 Mountain Empire Rd
Big Stone Gap VA 24219-0700
276-523-2400

National College
100 Logan St, Bluefield VA 24605
Tonya Elmore, Director of Admissions
276-326-3621 Fax: 276-322-5731
Website: www.national-college.edu
E-mail: info@national-college.edu

National College
1819 Emmet St N, Charlottesville VA 22901-2812
434-295-0136 Fax: 434-979-8061
Website: www.national-college.edu
E-mail: info@national-college.edu

National College
336 Old Riverside Dr, Danville VA 24541
Jeff Moore, Director of Admissions
434-793-6822 Fax: 434-793-3634
Website: www.national-college.edu
E-mail: info@national-college.edu

National College
1515 Country Club Rd, Harrisonburg VA 22802
Kathy Sours, Director of Admissions
540-432-0943 Fax: 540-432-1133
Website: www.national-college.edu
E-mail: info@national-college.edu

National College
104 Candlewood Ct, Lynchburg VA 24502-2653
Nancy Fortune, Director of Admissions
434-239-3500 Fax: 434-239-3948
Website: www.national-college.edu
E-mail: info@national-college.edu

National College
1813 E Main St, Salem VA 24153-4598
Ron Smith, Director of Admissions
540-986-1800 Fax: 540-444-4195
Website: www.national-college.edu
E-mail: info@national-college.edu

Norfolk State University
700 Park Ave, Norfolk VA 23504
Michelle Marable, Director of Admissions
757-823-8600

Old Dominion University
1 Old Dominion University, Norfolk VA 23529-1000
757-683-3000

Radford University
PO Box 6903, Radford VA 24142
David W. Kraus, Director of Admissions
800-890-4265 Fax: 540-831-5038
Website: www.radford.edu
E-mail: ruadmiss@radford.edu

Riverside School of Health Careers
316 Main St, Newport News VA 23601
Tracey Hiller, Recruitment Coordinator
757-240-2200 Fax: 757-240-2225
Website: www.riversideonline.com/rshc
E-mail: tracey.hiller@rivhs.com

Roanoke College
221 College Ln, Salem VA 24153-3794
James A. Pennix, Director of Admissions
540-375-2500 Fax: 540-375-2267
Website: www.roanoke.edu
E-mail: pennix@roanoke.edu

Rockingham Memorial Hospital
School of Medical Technology
235 Cantrell Ave, Harrisonburg VA 22801-3293
Randall Vandevander, Program Director
540-564-5407

St. Mary's Hospital
5801 Bremo Rd, Richmond VA 23226-1900
804-285-2011

Sentara School of Health Professions
1441 Crossways Blvd Suite 105
Chesapeake VA 23320
Shelly Vinson, Director
757-388-2900 Fax: 757-388-2905
Website: www.sentara.com/healthprofessions
E-mail: healthprofessions@sentara.com

Shenandoah University
1460 University Dr, Winchester VA 22601-5195
Michael D. Carpenter, Director of Admissions
800-432-2266

Southside Regional Medical Center
801 S Adams St, Petersburg VA 23803-5133
Tonia Little, Director of Admissions
804-862-5800 Fax: 804-862-5937
Website: www.srmcnursing.org
E-mail: tlittle@chs.net

Southwest Virginia Community College
PO Box SVCC, Richlands VA 24641-1101
276-964-2555

Thomas Nelson Community College
PO Box 9407, Hampton VA 23670-0407
757-825-2700

Tidewater Community College
State Route 135, Portsmouth VA 23703
757-484-2121

TIDEWATER TECH
7020 N Military Hwy, Norfolk VA 23518-4833
Laura Silva, Director of Admissions
757-853-2121 Fax: 757-852-9017
Website: www.tidewatertech.edu
E-mail: admdirttn@tidewatertech.edu

University of Virginia
PO Box 400160, Charlottesville VA 22904
804-924-0311

Virginia Commonwealth University
901 W Franklin St, Richmond VA 23284
804-828-0100

Virginia Polytechnic Institute & State University
Blacksburg VA 24061
540-231-6000

Virginia State University
1 Hayden Dr, Petersburg VA 23806-0001
804-524-5000

Virginia Western Community College
PO Box 14007, Roanoke VA 24038-4007
540-857-7311

Winchester Memorial Hospital
PO Box 3340, Winchester VA 22604-2540
540-722-8000

Wytheville Community College
1000 E Main St, Wytheville VA 24382-3308
276-223-4700

WASHINGTON

Apollo College
10102 E Knox Ave, Spokane WA 99206-4146
509-532-8888 Fax: 509-533-5983

Bastyr University
14500 Juanita Dr NE, Bothell WA 98028-4966
425-823-1300

BATES TECHNICAL COLLEGE
1101 S Yakima Ave, Tacoma WA 98405-4895
David Borofsky, President
253-680-7000 Fax: 253-680-7101
Website: www.bates.ctc.edu
E-mail: info@bates.ctc.edu

Bellevue Community College
3000 Landerholm Cir SE, Bellevue WA 98007-6484
425-564-1000

Bellingham Technical College
3028 Lindbergh Ave, Bellingham WA 98225-1599
360-738-0221

Central Washington University
400 E University Way, Ellensburg WA 98926
William Swain, Director of Admissions
509-963-3001

Clark College
1800 E McLoughlin Blvd, Vancouver WA 98663-3598
360-992-2000

Clover Park Technical College
4500 Steilacoom Blvd SW
Lakewood WA 98499-4098
Dr. Sharon McGavick, President
253-589-5678

Eastern Washington University
Cheney WA 99004
509-359-6200

Everett Community College
2000 Tower St, Everett WA 98201
Christine Kerlin, Associate Dean
425-388-9100 Fax: 425-388-9173
Website: www.everettcc.edu
E-mail: ckerlin@everettcc.edu

Green River Community College
12401 SE 320th St, Auburn WA 98092-3622
253-833-9111

Highline Community College
PO Box 98000, Des Moines WA 98198-9800
206-878-3710

Holy Family Hospital
5633 N Lidgerwood St, Spokane WA 99208-1224
509-482-2450

Lake Washington Technical College
11605 132nd Ave NE, Kirkland WA 98034-8505
James B. West, Director of Admissions
425-739-8100 Fax: 425-739-8110
Website: www.lwtc.ctc.edu

North Seattle Community College
9600 College Way N, Seattle WA 98103-3599
206-527-3790
Website: www.northseattle.edu
E-mail: nsccinfo@sccd.ctc.edu

Pierce College Fort Steilacoom
9401 Farwest Dr SW, Lakewood WA 98498-1999
Cherilyn Williams, Communications Coordinator
253-964-6435

Pima Medical Institute
555 S Renton Village Pl Ste 400, Renton WA 98057
425-228-9600

PIMA MEDICAL INSTITUTE
9709 3rd Ave NE Ste 400, Seattle WA 98115
George Borchers, Campus Director
206-322-6100 Fax: 206-324-1985
Website: www.pmi.edu
E-mail: spima@pmi.edu

Pima Medical Institute
9709 3rd Ave NE Ste 400, Seattle WA 98115
206-322-6100

RENTON TECHNICAL COLLEGE
3000 NE 4th St, Renton WA 98056-4195
Becky Riverman, Registrar
425-235-2352 or 425-235-5840 Fax: 425-235-7832
Website: www.RTC.edu
E-mail: dgrant@RTC.edu

Sacred Heart Medical Center
101 W 8th Ave, Spokane WA 99204-2307
509-455-3040

Seattle Pacific University
3307 3rd Ave W, Seattle WA 98119-1997
206-281-2000

Seattle University
901 12th Ave, Seattle WA 98122
206-296-6000

SHORELINE COMMUNITY COLLEGE
16101 Greenwood Ave N, Shoreline WA 98133-5696
Chris Melton, Acting Registrar
206-546-4581 Fax: 206-546-5835
Website: www.shoreline.edu

South Puget Sound Community College
2011 Mottman Rd SW, Tumwater WA 98512-6292
360-754-7711

Spokane Community College
1810 N Greene St, Spokane WA 99217-5399
509-533-7000

Tacoma Community College
6501 S 19th St, Tacoma WA 98466
253-566-5000

University of Puget Sound
1500 N Warner St, Tacoma WA 98416-0005
253-879-3100

University of Washington
Seattle WA 98195-0001
206-543-2100

Walla Walla Community College
500 Tausick Way, Walla Walla WA 99362-9270
Marilyn Galusha, Director
509-527-4240 or 877-992-9922 Fax: 509-527-3667
Website: www.wwcc.edu
E-mail: marilyn.galusha@wwcc.edu
See listing under "Community and Junior Colleges"

Washington State University
1 SE Stadium Way, Pullman WA 99164-0001
509-335-3564

Wenatchee Valley College
1300 5th St, Wenatchee WA 98801-1799
Marco Azurdia, Dean, Student Development
509-682-6805

Western Washington University
516 High St, Bellingham WA 98225-5996
360-650-3000

Yakima Valley Community College
PO Box 22520, Yakima WA 98907
509-574-4600

WEST VIRGINIA

Bluefield Regional Medical Center
500 Cherry St, Bluefield WV 24701-3390
304-327-1701

Bluefield State College
219 Rock St, Bluefield WV 24701-2198
304-327-4000

Blue Ridge Community and Technical College
400 W Stephen St, Martinsburg WV 25401
Leslie See, Director of Enrollment
304-260-4380 Fax: 304-260-1752
Website: www.blueridgectc.edu
E-mail: lsee@blueridgectc.edu

Cabell Huntington Hospital
1340 Hal Greer Blvd, Huntington WV 25701-0195
304-526-2111

Camden Clark Memorial Hospital
800 Garfield Ave, Parkersburg WV 26101-5378
304-424-2204

Carver Career and Tech Education Center
4799 Midland Dr, Charleston WV 25306-6353
304-348-1965

Fairmont State University
1201 Locust Ave, Fairmont WV 26554-2470
Steve Leadman, Director of Admissions
304-367-4003 or 800-641-5678 Fax: 304-367-4789
Website: www.fairmontstate.edu
E-mail: admit@fairmontstate.edu

Marshall University
400 Hal Greer Blvd, Huntington WV 25755-0003
304-696-3170

Mountain State College
1508 Spring St, Parkersburg WV 26101-3993
Judith Sutton, Director
304-485-5487 Fax: 304-485-3524
Website: www.mountainstate.org
E-mail: admin@mountainstate.org
See listing under "Career Schools"

Mountain State University
Box 9003, Beckley WV 25802-9003
Tony England, Director of Admissions
866-FOR-MSU1 or 304-929-INFO Fax: 304-253-5072
Website: www.mountainstate.edu
E-mail: gomsu@mountainstate.edu
See listing under "Universities"

Ohio Valley Medical Center
2000 Eoff St, Wheeling WV 26003-3870
304-234-8294

St. Mary's Medical Center
2900 1st Ave, Huntington WV 25702-1272
Dr. Sheila Kyle, VP Schools of Nursing & Health Professions
304-526-1270

Southern West Virginia Community & Technical College
PO Box 2900, Mount Gay WV 25637
304-792-7160

United Hospital Center
PO Box 2308, Clarksburg WV 26302-2308
304-624-2332

Veterans Administration Hospital
200 Veterans Ave, Beckley WV 25801-6444
304-255-2121

West Liberty State College
PO Box 295, West Liberty WV 26074
304-336-5000

West Virginia Junior College
176 Thompson Dr, Bridgeport WV 26330
Kathryn Stanley, Director of Admissions
304-842-4007 Fax: 304-842-8191
Website: www.wvjcinfo.net
E-mail: kstanley@wvjcinfo.net

West Virginia Northern Community College
1704 Market St, Wheeling WV 26003-3643
304-233-5900

West Virginia State University
PO Box 1000, Institute WV 25112-1000
304-766-3000

West Virginia University
PO Box 6001, Morgantown WV 26506-6001
304-293-0111

West Virginia University Hospital
PO Box 8150, Morgantown WV 26506-8150
304-598-4000

West Virginia University Institute of Technology
405 Fayette Pike, Montgomery WV 25136-2436
304-442-3071

West Virginia Wesleyan College
59 College Ave, Buckhannon WV 26201-2699
Robert N. Skinner II, Director of Admission
800-722-9933

Wheeling Hospital
1 Medical Park, Wheeling WV 26003-6300
304-243-3000

Wheeling Jesuit University
316 Washington Ave, Wheeling WV 26003-6295
304-243-2000

WISCONSIN

All Saints Healthcare System
1320 Wisconsin Ave, Racine WI 53403-1978
262-636-2846

Aurora Health Care
3000 W Montana St, Milwaukee WI 53215-3686
414-647-3000

BELLIN HOSPITAL
PO Box 23400, Green Bay WI 54305-3400
Randy Griswold, Program Director
920-433-3497 Fax: 920-433-5811
Website: www.bellin.org
E-mail: rcgris@bellin.org

Blackhawk Technical College
PO Box 5009, Janesville WI 53547-5009
Gregg Bosak, Administration, Community Information
608-757-7769 Fax: 608-757-7740
Website: www.blackhawk.edu
E-mail: gbosak@blackhawk.edu

∴ Blood Center of SE Wisconsin
1701 W Wisconsin Ave, Milwaukee WI 53233-2113
414-937-6338

· Bryant & Stratton College
310 W Wisconsin Ave Suite 500, Milwaukee WI 53203
Kathryn Cotey, Director of Admissions
414-276-5200

· Chippewa Valley Technical College
620 W Clairemont Ave, Eau Claire WI 54701-6162
Admissions Office
715-833-6246

∴ Columbia Hospital
2025 E Newport Ave, Milwaukee WI 53211-2990
414-961-3800

Concordia University
12800 N Lake Shore Dr, Mequon WI 53097-2402
262-243-5700

· Fox Valley Technical College
PO Box 2277, Appleton WI 54912-2277
Bob Burdick, Registrar
920-735-5600

∴ Froedtert Memorial Lutheran Hospital
PO Box 26099, Milwaukee WI 53226-0099
414-259-2606

· Gateway Technical College
3520 30th Ave, Kenosha WI 53144-1690
Zina Haywood, Director of Admissions
262-564-2200

∴ Gunderson Medical Foundation
1836 South Ave, La Crosse WI 54601-5429
608-782-7300

· Lakeshore Technical College
1290 North Ave, Cleveland WI 53015-1414
Information Fulfillment Specialist
888-GOTOLTC Fax: 920-693-3561
Website: www.gotoltc.edu
E-mail: info@gotoltc.edu

· Madison Area Technical College
3550 Anderson St, Madison WI 53704-2599
608-246-6282

Marquette University
PO Box 1881, Milwaukee WI 53201-1881
Robert Blust, Director of Admissions
414-288-7302 Fax: 414-288-3764
Website: www.mu.edu
E-mail: admissions@marquette.edu

: **MARSHFIELD CLINIC/ST. JOSEPH'S HOSPITAL**
1000 N Oak Ave, Marshfield WI 54449
Julie J. Seehafer, MS, MT(ASCP)SH
Director, Laboratory Education
715-387-7440 Fax: 715-387-7121
Website: www.marshfieldlaboratories.org
E-mail: seehafer.julie@marshfieldclinic.org (Office)

∴ Mercy Medical Center
PO Box 3370, Oshkosh WI 54903-3370
920-233-5110

· Mid-State Technical College
500 32nd St N, Wisconsin Rapids WI 54494-5512
715-423-5300

MIDWEST COLLEGE OF ORIENTAL MEDICINE
6232 Bankers Rd, Racine WI 53403-9747
Kelly Westerlund, Contact
800-593-2320 Fax: 262-554-7475
Website: www.acupuncture.edu
E-mail: mwcadmissions@yahoo.com

· Milwaukee Area Technical College
700 W State St, Milwaukee WI 53233-1419
414-297-6600

Milwaukee School of Engineering
1025 N Broadway, Milwaukee WI 53202-3109
414-277-7300

· Moraine Park Technical College
235 N National Ave, Fond du Lac WI 54935
920-922-8611

Mount Mary College
2900 N Menomonee River Pkwy
Milwaukee WI 53222-4597
414-256-1219

· Northcentral Technical College
1000 W Campus Dr, Wausau WI 54401-1880
Carolyn Michalski, Director of Admissions
715-675-3331

· Northeast Wisconsin Technical College
PO Box 19042, Green Bay WI 54307-9042
800-422-NWTC

∴ Sacred Heart Hospital
900 W Clairemont Ave, Eau Claire WI 54701-5105
715-839-4131

∴ St. Elizabeth Hospital
1506 S Oneida St, Appleton WI 54915-1396
920-738-2015

∴ St. Francis Hospital
3237 S 16th St, Milwaukee WI 53215-4592
414-647-5106

∴ St. Joseph Hospital/Marshfield Clinic
611 Saint Joseph Ave, Marshfield WI 54449-1898
715-387-1713

∴ St. Luke's Medical Center
2900 W Oklahoma Ave, Milwaukee WI 53215-4330
414-649-7500

St. Norbert College
100 Grant St, De Pere WI 54115
Brian Studebaker, Director of Admission
800-236-4878 Fax: 920-403-4072
Website: www.snc.edu
E-mail: admit@snc.edu

∴ St. Vincent Hospital
PO Box 13508, Green Bay WI 54307-3508
920-433-8155

∴ Theda Clark Regional Medical Center
130 2nd St, Neenah WI 54956-2883
920-729-2004

University of Wisconsin
PO Box 4004, Eau Claire WI 54702
715-836-2637

University of Wisconsin
716 Langdon St, Madison WI 53706-1481
608-262-1234

University of Wisconsin
PO Box 413, Milwaukee WI 53201-0413
414-229-1122

University of Wisconsin
410 S 3rd St, River Falls WI 54022
715-425-3911

University of Wisconsin
2100 Main St, Stevens Point WI 54481-3871
715-346-0123

University of Wisconsin Green Bay
2420 Nicolet Dr, Green Bay WI 54311-7003
Pamela Harvey-Jacobs, Interim Director of Admissions
920-465-2111

University of Wisconsin in La Crosse
115 Graff Main Hall, La Crosse WI 54601
Tim Lewis, Director of Admissions
608-785-8939

University of Wisconsin - Oshkosh
800 Algoma Blvd, Oshkosh WI 54901-8602
920-424-0202

University of Wisconsin-Stout
124 Bowman Hall, Menomonie WI 54751-2662
715-232-1123

University of Wisconsin - Whitewater
800 W Main St, Whitewater WI 53190-1791
262-472-1234

Viterbo University
815 9th St S, La Crosse WI 54601-8802
608-796-3000

· Waukesha County Technical College
800 Main St, Pewaukee WI 53072-4601
262-691-5566

∴ Wausau Hospital Center
333 Pine Ridge Blvd, Wausau WI 54401-4187
715-847-2117

· Western Wisconsin Technical College
PO Box 908, La Crosse WI 54602-0908
608-785-9200

· Wisconsin Indianhead Technical College
1019 S Knowles Ave, New Richmond WI 54017-1738
715-246-6561

WSLH SCHOOL OF CYTOTECHNOLOGY
465 Henry Mall, Madison WI 53706
Michele Smith, Education Coordinator
608-262-3524 Fax: 608-265-6294
Website: www.slh.wisc.edu/cytology/index.html
E-mail: msmith27@wisc.edu

∴ Zablocki VA Medical Center
5000 W National Ave, Milwaukee WI 53295-0001
414-384-2000

WYOMING

· Casper College
125 College Dr, Casper WY 82601-4699
307-268-2110

· Laramie County Community College
1400 E College Dr, Cheyenne WY 82007-3204
Jenny Hargett, Director of Admissions
307-778-5222 Fax: 307-778-1350
Website: www.lccc.wy.edu
E-mail: learnmore@lccc.wy.edu

· Sheridan College
PO Box 1500, Sheridan WY 82801-1500
307-674-6446

University of Wyoming
Admissions Office
Dept 3435, Laramie WY 82071-3435
Brooke Culver, Contact
800-342-5996 Fax: 307-766-4042
Website: www.uwyo.edu
E-mail: why-wyo@uwyo.edu

· Western Wyoming Community College
2500 College Dr, Rock Springs WY 82901-5802
Laurie Watkins, Director of Admissions
307-382-1600

∴ West Park Hospital
707 Sheridan Ave, Cody WY 82414-3409
307-527-7501

GUAM

· Guam Community College
PO Box 23069, G.M.F. GU 96921-0307
Virginia Charfauros Tudela, Ph.D., Registrar
671-735-5531

PUERTO RICO

: EDIC College
PO Box 9120, Caguas PR 00726-9120
Virginia Cartagena, Director of Admissions
787-744-8519 Fax: 787-743-0855
Website: www.ediccollege.com
E-mail: edic@coqui.net

· Huertas Junior College
PO Box 8429, Caguas PR 00726-8429
787-746-1400

· Humacao Community College
PO Box 9139, Humacao PR 00792
787-852-1430

Inter American University of Puerto Rico
PO Box 191293, Hato Rey PR 00919
787-250-1912

Inter American University of Puerto Rico
PO Box 5100, San German PR 00683
787-264-1912

: **PONCE PARAMEDICAL COLLEGE**
1213 Calle Acacia Villa Flores, Ponce PR 00716-2901
Alberto Aristizabal, President
787-848-1589 Fax: 787-259-0169
Website: www.popac.edu
E-mail: ppcadmin@popac.edu

Pontifical Catholic University of Puerto Rico
2250 Ave Las Americas, Ponce PR 00717-0777
787-841-2000

Universidad Adventista de las Antillas
PO Box 118, Mayaguez PR 00681
Evelyn Del Valle Rivera, Director of Admissions
787-834-9595

Universidad Central Del Caribe
PO Box 60327, Bayamon PR 00960-6032
787-798-3001

· Universidad del Este
PO Box 2010, Carolina PR 00984
787-257-7373

Universidad Metropolitana
PO Box 21150, San Juan PR 00928-1150
787-766-1717

University of Puerto Rico
PO Box 365067, San Juan PR 00936-5067
787-758-2525

University of the Sacred Heart
PO Box 12383, Santurce PR 00914
787-728-1515

ARCHITECTURE

ALASKA

University of Alaska Anchorage
PO Box 141629, Anchorage AK 99514-1629
Cecile Mitchell, Director of Enrollment Services
907-786-1480 Fax: 907-786-4888
Website: www.uaa.alaska.edu/
E-mail: enroll@uaa.alaska.edu

ARKANSAS

Northwest Technical Institute
709 S Old Missouri Rd, Springdale AR 72764
Charles L. Kelley, President
479-751-8824 Fax: 479-751-7780
Website: www.nti.tec.ar.us
E-mail: info@nit.tec.ar.us

CALIFORNIA

American Film Institute
AFI Conservatory
2021 N Western Ave, Los Angeles CA 90027
Danielle McVickers, Admissions Manager
323-856-7740 Fax: 323-856-7720
Website: www.afi.com
E-mail: dmcvickers@afi.com
Production Design.

California College of the Arts
1111 Eighth St, San Francisco CA 94107
Robynne Royster, Director of Admission
800-447-1-ART or 415-703-9523 Fax: 415-703-9539
Website: www.cca.edu
E-mail: enroll@cca.edu

Chabot College
25555 Hesperian Blvd, Hayward CA 94545-2400
Judy Young, Director of Admissions
510-723-6600 Fax: 510-723-7510
Website: www.chabotcollege.edu
E-mail: ccarcom@clpccd.cc.ca.us

Orange Coast College
PO Box 5005, Costa Mesa CA 92628-5005
Kristin Clark, Director of Admissions
714-432-5773 Fax: 714-432-5736
Website: www.orangecoastcollege.edu
E-mail: kclark@cccd.edu

SOUTHERN CALIFORNIA INSTITUTE OF ARCHITECTURE
960 E 3rd St, Los Angeles CA 90013-1822
J.J. Jackman, Director of Admissions
213-613-2200 ext 321 Fax: 213-613-2260
Website: www.sciarc.edu
E-mail: admissions@sciarc.edu
Established 1972. Coed. Accreditation: NAAB, WASC. Tuition: $10,180/sem. Enrollment: 450. Faculty: 80. Student-faculty ratio: 15:1. Degrees offered: BArch, 3 yr MArch, 2 yr MArch, 2 Post-Grad degrees. Library: 30,000 volumes. Founded as a radical alternative to the conventional system of arch education; only architecture-focused academic library in Southern California; dark room; CNC facilities, print center, wood & metal shop all on premises; located in downtown LA.

FLORIDA

Lincoln College of Technology
2410 Metrocentre Blvd
West Palm Beach FL 33407-3105
Don Cunningham, Vice President of Admissions
561-688-2001 Fax: 561-842-9503
Website: www.lincolncollegeoftechnology.com
E-mail: dcunningham@lincolntech.com

University of South Florida
4202 E Fowler Ave, Tampa FL 33620-6900
J. Robert Spatig, Director of Admissions
877-USF-BULL Fax: 813-974-9689
Website: www.usf.edu
E-mail: admissions@admin.usf.edu
See listing under "Universities"

IDAHO

University of Idaho
Moscow ID 83844-4253
Lloyd Scott, Director of New Student Services
208-885-6163 Fax: 208-885-4477
Website: www.uidaho.edu
E-mail: nss@uidaho.edu

ILLINOIS

Columbia College Chicago
600 S Michigan Ave, Chicago IL 60605-1996
Murphy Monroe, Executive Director of Admissions
312-344-7130 Fax: 312-344-8024
Website: www.colum.edu
E-mail: admissions@colum.edu

IOWA

Iowa Lakes Community College
300 S 18th St, Estherville IA 51334-2721
Anne Stansbury, Asst. Director of Admissions
712-362-7945 Fax: 712-362-8363
Website: www.iowalakes.edu
E-mail: info@iowalakes.edu

KENTUCKY

Bluegrass Community and Technical College
Oswald Building
470 Cooper Drive, Lexington KY 40506-0235
Shelbie Hugle, Director of Admissions
859-246-6200 Fax: 859-246-4664
Website: www.bluegrass.kctcs.edu
E-mail: bctc_info@kctcs.edu

Louisville Technical Institute
3901 Atkinson Square Dr, Louisville KY 40218
Kevin Woods, Director of Admissions
800-844-6528 Fax: 502-456-2341
Website: www.louisvilletech.com
E-mail: kwoods@louisvilletech.com

Spencerian College
1575 Winchester Rd, Lexington KY 40505
Victor Lamoin Adcock II, Director of Admissions
800-456-3253
E-mail: ladcock@spencerian.edu

MAINE

Southern Maine Community College
2 Fort Rd, South Portland ME 04106-1698
Dr. James Ortiz, President
Scott MacDonald, Director of Financial Aid
207-741-5500 Fax: 207-741-5671
Website: www.smccme.edu
E-mail: oharmon@maine.rr.com

MASSACHUSETTS

Benjamin Franklin Institute of Technology
41 Berkeley St, Boston MA 02116-6307
Norman Kraft, Dean of Enrollment
617-423-4630 ext. 121 Fax: 617-482-3706
Website: www.bfit.edu
E-mail: admissions@bfit.edu

Massachusetts Institute of Technology
77 Massachusetts Ave, Cambridge MA 02139-4307
617-253-1000 Fax: 617-253-4016
Website: my.mit.edu
E-mail: admissions@mit.edu

MICHIGAN

ITT TECHNICAL INSTITUTE
4020 Sparks Dr SE, Grand Rapids MI 49546-6192
Dennis Hormel, Director
616-956-1060 Fax: 616-956-5606
Website: www.itt-tech.edu
E-mail: dhormel@itt-tech.edu

Lawrence Technological University
21000 W 10 Mile Rd, Southfield MI 48075-1058
Jane Rohrback, Director of Admissions
800-225-5588 Fax: 248-204-2228
Website: www.ltu.edu
E-mail: admissions@ltu.edu
See listing under "Universities"

MINNESOTA

Dunwoody College of Technology
818 Dunwoody Blvd, Minneapolis MN 55403-1192
John Slama, Vice President Enrollment Management
800-292-4625 or 612-374-5800 Fax: 612-374-4128
Website: www.dunwoody.edu
E-mail: jslama@dunwoody.edu
See listing under "Career Schools"

MISSOURI

Ranken Technical College
4431 Finney Ave, Saint Louis MO 63113-2898
Admissions Office
314-371-0233 Fax: 314-371-0241
Website: www.ranken.edu
E-mail: admissions@ranken.edu

NEW YORK

College of Saint Rose
432 Western Ave, Albany NY 12203-1419
Maryelizabeth Amico, Asst V.P. for Undergraduate Admissions
518-454-5150 Fax: 518-454-2013
Website: www.strose.edu
E-mail: admit@strose.edu

ISLAND DRAFTING & TECHNICAL INSTITUTE
128 Broadway (Route 110), Amityville NY 11701-2704
James G. DiLiberto, President
631-691-8733 Fax: 631-691-8738
Website: www.idti.edu
E-mail: info@idti.edu

Pratt Institute
200 Willoughby Ave, Brooklyn NY 11205-3899
Heidi Metcalf, Director of Admissions
718-636-3600 Fax: 718-636-3670
Website: www.pratt.edu
E-mail: hmetcalf@pratt.edu

SUNY College of Technology
Alfred NY 14802
Deborah J. Goodrich, Associate VP Enrollment Mgmt.
800-4AL-FRED Fax: 607-587-4299
Website: www.alfredstate.edu
E-mail: admissions@alfredstate.edu

SUNY Orange County Community College
115 South St, Middletown NY 10940-6437
Margot St. Lawrence, Director of Admissions
845-341-4030 Fax: 845-342-8662
Website: www.sunyorange.edu
E-mail: apply@sunyorange.edu
See listing under "Community and Junior Colleges"

NORTH CAROLINA

ART INSTITUTE OF CHARLOTTE
2110 Water Ridge Pkwy, Charlotte NC 28217
Pamela Notemyer, Director of Admissions
800-872-4417 Fax: 704-357-1133
Website: www.artinstitutes.edu/charlotte
E-mail: admin@aii.edu
See listing under "Career Schools"

OHIO

The Ohio State University
Austin E. Knowlton School of Architecture
Knowlton Arch Bldg, 275 W Woodruff Ave
Columbus OH 43210
614-292-1012 Fax: 614-292-7106
Website: knowlton.osu.edu
E-mail: ugadvisor@knowlton.osu.edu

OKLAHOMA

Oklahoma State University
Stillwater OK 74078
J. Randall Seitsinger, Department Head
405-744-6043
Website: www.okstate.edu
E-mail: randy.seitsinger@okstate.edu

PENNSYLVANIA

Community College of Allegheny County
Allegheny Campus: 808 Ridge Ave, Pittsburgh PA 15212 Admissions: 412.237.2700
Boyce Campus: 595 Beatty Rd, Monroeville PA 15146 Admissions: 724.325.6614
North Campus: 8701 Perry Highway, Pittsburgh PA 15237 Admissions: 412.369.3600
South Campus: 1750 Clairton Rd, West Mifflin PA 15122 Admissions: 412-469-4301
Website: www.ccac.edu

Johnson College
3427 N Main Ave, Scranton PA 18508-1495
Dr. Ann L. Pipinski, President & CEO
Melissa Ide, Director of Enrollment Management
800-2WE-WORK or 570-342-6404 ext. 125
Fax: 570-348-2181
Website: www.johnson.edu
E-mail: admit@johnson.edu

TEXAS

Abilene Christian University
ACU Box 29000, Abilene TX 79699-0001
325-674-2000 Fax: 325-674-2202
Website: www.acu.edu
E-mail: info@admissions.acu.edu

ITT TECHNICAL INSTITUTE
2950 S Gessner Rd Ste 100, Houston TX 77063-3751
Jennifer Gomez, Director of Recruitment
713-952-2294 Fax: 713-952-2393
Website: www.itt-tech.edu
E-mail: jgomez@itt-tech.edu

University of Houston
122 E Cullen Bldg, Houston TX 77204-2023
Office of Admission
713-743-9595
Website: www.uh.edu
E-mail: admissions@uh.edu

University of Texas at Arlington
Box 19111, Arlington TX 76019-0111
Hans Gatterdam, Director of Admission
817-272-6287 Fax: 817-272-3435
Website: www.uta.edu
E-mail: admissions@uta.edu

VERMONT

NORWICH UNIVERSITY
158 Harmon Dr, Northfield VT 05663
Arthur Schaller, Division Head
800-468-6679 Fax: 802-485-2624
Website: www.norwich.edu
E-mail: schaller@norwich.edu

WISCONSIN

Herzing College
5218 E Terrace Dr, Madison WI 53718-8340
Donald Madelung, President
800-582-1227 Fax: 608-249-8593
Website: www.herzing.edu
E-mail: info@msn.herzing.edu
See listing under "Universities"

ALABAMA

CALHOUN COMMUNITY COLLEGE
PO Box 2216, Decatur AL 35609-2216
M. Wayne Tosh, Registrar
256-306-2500 Fax: 256-306-2941
Website: www.calhoun.edu
E-mail: aprater@calhoun.edu

Judson College
302 Bibb St, Marion AL 36756
Michael Scotto, Director of Admissions
800-447-9472 Fax: 334-683-5147
Website: www.judson.edu
E-mail: admissions@judson.edu

University of Alabama in Huntsville
PO Box 1247, Huntsville AL 35899-0001
Nikki Willis, Assoc. Director for Recruiting Program and Events
1-800-UAH-CALL Fax: 256-824-6073
Website: www.uah.edu
E-mail: willisn@uah.edu

University of South Alabama
307 University Blvd N, Mobile AL 36688-3053
Melissa Haab, Director of Admissions
251-460-6141 Fax: 251-460-7876
Website: www.southalabama.edu
E-mail: admiss@usouthal.edu

ALASKA

University of Alaska Anchorage
PO Box 141629, Anchorage AK 99514-1629
Cecile Mitchell, Director of Enrollment Services
907-786-1480 Fax: 907-786-4888
Website: www.uaa.alaska.edu/
E-mail: enroll@uaa.alaska.edu

ARIZONA

Collins College: A School of Design and Technology
(Formerly Al Collins Graphic Design School)
1140 S Priest Dr, Tempe AZ 85281-5240
Toby Craver, Director of National Admissions
800-876-7070 Fax: 480-829-0183
Website: www.collinscollege.edu

The Conservatory of Recording Arts & Sciences
2300 E Broadway Rd, Tempe AZ 85282-1707
Tonya Visconti, Director of Admissions
800-562-6383 or 480-858-9400 Fax: 480-829-1332
Website: cras.org
E-mail: info@cras.org
See listing under "Music"

ARKANSAS

Williams Baptist College
PO Box 3737, Walnut Ridge AR 72476-3737
Angela Flippo, Vice President for Enrollment Management
800-722-4434 Fax: 870-759-4163
Website: www.williamsbaptistcollege.com
E-mail: admissions@wbcoll.edu

CALIFORNIA

American Film Institute
AFI Conservatory
2021 N Western Ave, Los Angeles CA 90027
Danielle McVickers, Admissions Manager
323-856-7740 Fax: 323-856-7720
Website: www.afi.com
E-mail: dmcvickers@afi.com
Production Design.

ART CENTER COLLEGE OF DESIGN
1700 Lida St, Pasadena CA 91103-1999
Kit Baron, V.P. Admissions
626-396-2373 Fax: 626-795-0578
Website: www.artcenter.edu
E-mail: admissions@artcenter.edu

Established 1930. Private. Coed. Accreditation: WASC, NASAD. Tuition: $26,310. Enrollment: 1,400. Faculty: 425. Student-faculty ratio: 9:1. Degrees: BFA, BS, MFA, MA, MS. Library: 65,000 volumes. Specialized programs in advertising, illustration, industrial design, film, photography, graphic design, fine arts. Emphasis on preparation for professional specialty through both skill and concept development and intense exposure to professional projects.

Butte College
3536 Butte Campus Dr, Oroville CA 95965-8399
Carole Gish, Director of Admissions
530-895-2511 Fax: 530-879-4313
Website: www.butte.edu
E-mail: admissions@butte.edu

California College of the Arts
1111 Eighth St, San Francisco CA 94107
Robynne Royster, Director of Admission
800-447-1-ART or 415-703-9523 Fax: 415-703-9539
Website: www.cca.edu
E-mail: enroll@cca.edu

California State University-San Bernadino
5500 University Pkwy
San Bernardino CA 92407-2393
Olivia Rosas, Director of Admissions
909-537-5188 Fax: 909-537-7034
Website: www.csusb.edu
E-mail: orosas@csusb.edu

Chabot College
25555 Hesperian Blvd, Hayward CA 94545-2400
Judy Young, Director of Admissions
510-723-6600 Fax: 510-723-7510
Website: www.chabotcollege.edu
E-mail: ccarcom@clpccd.cc.ca.us

Chapman University
One University Drive, Orange CA 92866-1099
Michael Drummy, Assistant Vice President for Enrollment
Services and Chief Admission Officer
714-997-6411 or 888-CUAPPLY Fax: 714-997-6713
Website: www.chapman.edu
E-mail: admit@chapman.edu

Cogswell College
1175 Bordeaux Dr, Sunnyvale CA 94089-1210
Dr. Valarie Brown, Dean of Enrollment Management
800-264-7955 or 408-541-0100 Fax: 408-747-0764
Website: www.cogswell.edu
E-mail: info@cogswell.edu
See listing under "Universities"

Concordia University
1530 Concordia, Irvine CA 92612-3203
Lori McDonald, Executive Director of Enrollment Services
800-229-1200 or 949-854-8002 Fax: 949-854-6894
Website: www.cui.edu
E-mail: admission@cui.edu

FIDM/THE FASHION INSTITUTE OF DESIGN & MERCHANDISING
919 S Grand Ave, Los Angeles CA 90015-1421
Director of Admissions
213-624-1201 or 800-624-1200 Fax: 213-624-4799
Website: www.fidm.edu
E-mail: info@fidm.com
See listing under "Community and Junior Colleges"

IDYLLWILD ARTS ACADEMY
PO Box 38, Idyllwild CA 92549-0038
Karen Porter, Dean of Admission
951-659-2171 ext. 2223 Fax: 951-659-5463
Website: www.idyllwildarts.org
E-mail: admission@idyllwildarts.org

John F. Kennedy University
100 Ellinwood Way, Pleasant Hill CA 94523-4817
800-696-5358
Website: www.jfku.edu

Orange Coast College
PO Box 5005, Costa Mesa CA 92628-5005
Kristin Clark, Director of Admissions
714-432-5773 Fax: 714-432-5736
Website: www.orangecoastcollege.edu
E-mail: kclark@cccd.edu

PLATT (MEDIA ARTS) COLLEGE - SAN DIEGO
6250 El Cajon Blvd, San Diego CA 92115
Al Medro, Vice President
619-265-0107 or 866-752-8826 Fax: 619-308-0570
Website: www.platt.edu
E-mail: info@platt.edu

Point Loma Nazarene University
3900 Lomaland Dr, San Diego CA 92106-2810
Chip Killingsworth, Director of Undergraduate Admissions
800-733-7770 Fax: 619-849-2601
Website: www.pointloma.edu
E-mail: admissions@pointloma.edu

SAN FRANCISCO ART INSTITUTE
800 Chestnut St, San Francisco CA 94133
800-345-SFAI Fax: 415-749-4503
Website: www.sfai.edu
E-mail: admissions@sfai.edu

Founded in 1871, SFAI offers one of the most innovative and interdisciplinary environments in higher education. Through its School of Studio Practice, SFAI offers accredited Bachelor of Fine Arts (BFA), Master of Fine Arts (MFA), Summer Master of Fine Arts (SMFA), and Post-Baccalaureate (PB) programs. SFAI's School of Studio Practice centers on the development of the artist's vision and consists of the departments of: Design+Technology, Film, New Genres, Painting, Photography, Printmaking, and Sculpture. At SFAI students become part of an educational environment that sees experimentation as necessary for independent and collaborative invention. The School of Interdisciplinary Studies is the complementary other half of SFAI, offering three areas of study: History and Theory of Contemporary Art (BA, MA); Urban Studies (BA, MA); and Exhibition and Museum Studies (MA). Together the two schools provide an inclusive model to address contemporary art and culture. The BFA, MFA, and PB programs are at their core interdisciplinary, and students can take courses in any department. The Summer MFA program has the same rigor as the Academic Year MFA program, yet is designed for those who choose an alternate academic schedule. The Post-Baccalaureate program is an excellent way to prepare for entrance into an MFA program or to enhance skills and knowledge. SFAI's faculty is comprised of active artists, scholars, writers, and curators. Dean of Academic Affairs is renowned curator and critic Okwui Enwezor. Dean of Graduate Studies is artist and filmmaker Renee Green. Director of Exhibitions and Public Programs is curator Hou Hanru. Visiting artists and scholars play a significant role in education at SFAI, with recent visitors including Matthew Barney, William Kentridge, Raqs Media Collective, and others. All students have 24-hour access to the SFAI campus, SFAI's main campus includes painting, photography, sculture, and printmaking studios, postproduction facilities, and the first high-definition video research lab in the Bay Area. The Diego Rivera Gallery, an open-air amphitheater, and a 250-seat theater are also available to students for exhibiting and screening work. SFAI's library collection includes more than 26,000 volumes with emphasis on modern and contemporary art, over 200 current periodicals, and an extensive image, video, and audio archive available only to SFAI students. The 62,000 square-foot Graduate Center includes a digital lab, film and sound studios, darkrooms, a woodshop, and a gallery for student work. SFAI has rolling application deadlines, and there are competitive and need-based scholarships available to undergraduates, a fellowship program for graduate students, and community college scholarships for transfer students. Visit the SFAI website for specific application requirements.

Western Career College
6001 Shellmound St, Suite 145, Emeryville CA 94608
Dr. Paul Dancy, Contact
510-601-0133 Fax: 510-601-0793
Website: www.westerncollege.edu

Western Career College
380 Civic Dr Ste 300, Pleasant Hill CA 94523-1984
LaShawn Wells, Executive Director
925-609-6650 Fax: 926-609-6666
Website: www.westerncollege.edu

Western Career College
6201 San Ignacio Ave, San Jose CA 95119
Steve Ashab, Executive Director
408-360-0840 Fax: 408-360-0848
Website: www.westerncollege.edu

Whittier College
PO Box 634, Whittier CA 90608-0634
Kieron Miller, Director of Admissions
562-907-4200 Fax: 562-907-4870
Website: www.whittier.edu
E-mail: kmiller@whittier.edu

COLORADO

ROCKY MOUNTAIN COLLEGE OF ART & DESIGN
1600 Pierce St, Denver CO 80214
Angela Carlson, Director of Admissions
800-888-2787 Fax: 303-759-4970
Website: www.rmcad.edu
E-mail: admissions@rmcad.edu

CONNECTICUT

Albertus Magnus College
700 Prospect St, New Haven CT 06511-1189
Richard Lolatte, Dean of Admission
203-773-8501 or 800-578-9160 Fax: 203-773-5248
Website: www.albertus.edu
E-mail: admissions@albertus.edu

HARTT COMMUNITY DIVISION
200 Bloomfield Ave, West Hartford CT 06117
Alana Seddon, Interim Director
860-768-7768 Fax: 860-768-4777
Website: www.hartford.edu/hartt/community
E-mail: harttcomm@hartford.edu

DISTRICT OF COLUMBIA

CORCORAN COLLEGE OF ART AND DESIGN
500 17th St NW, Washington DC 20006-4804
Elizabeth Paladino, Director of Admission
202-639-1814 or 888-CORCORAN Fax: 202-639-1830
Website: www.corcoran.edu
E-mail: admissions@corcoran.org

FLORIDA

Florida State University
600 W College Ave, Tallahassee FL 32306-1096
Janice V. Finney, Director of Admissions
850-644-2525 Fax: 850-644-0197
Website: admissions.fsu.edu
E-mail: admissions@admin.fsu.edu

INTERNATIONAL ACADEMY OF DESIGN AND TECHNOLOGY
5959 Lake Ellenor Dr, Orlando FL 32809-4633
Dr. John Dietrich, VP of Admissions
877-753-0007 Fax: 407-888-4006
Website: www.iadt.edu
E-mail: info@iadt.edu

Lynn University
3601 N Military Trl, Boca Raton FL 33431-5598
Director of Admissions
561-237-7900 Fax: 561-237-7100
Website: www.lynn.edu
E-mail: admission@lynn.edu

University of South Florida
4202 E Fowler Ave, Tampa FL 33620-6900
J. Robert Spatig, Director of Admissions
877-USF-BULL Fax: 813-974-9689
Website: www.usf.edu
E-mail: admissions@admin.usf.edu
See listing under "Universities"

GEORGIA

Kennesaw State University
1000 Chastain Rd NW, Kennesaw GA 30144-5591
Joseph Meeks, Dean of the School of the Arts
770-423-6742
Website: www.kennesaw.edu

Portfolio Center
125 Bennett St NW, Atlanta GA 30309-1268
Catherine Menes, Admissions Department
404-351-5055 ext. 26 Fax: 404-355-8838
Website: www.portfoliocenter.com
E-mail: catherine@portfoliocenter.com

IDAHO

Brigham Young University - Idaho
120 Kimball Bldg, Rexburg ID 83460-1615
Rob Garrett, Director of Admissions
208-496-1020 Fax: 208-496-1220
Website: www.byui.edu
E-mail: admissions@byui.edu

University of Idaho
Moscow ID 83844-4253
Lloyd Scott, Director of New Student Services
208-885-6163 Fax: 208-885-4477
Website: www.uidaho.edu
E-mail: nss@uidaho.edu

ILLINOIS

American Academy of Art
332 S Michigan Ave Fl 3, Chicago IL 60604-4302
Stuart Rosenbloom, Director of Admissions
312-461-0600 Fax: 312-294-9570
Website: www.aaart.edu
E-mail: info@aaart.edu

Columbia College Chicago
600 S Michigan Ave, Chicago IL 60605-1996
Murphy Monroe, Executive Director of Admissions
312-344-7130 Fax: 312-344-8024
Website: www.colum.edu
E-mail: admissions@colum.edu

CONCORDIA UNIVERSITY
7400 Augusta St, River Forest IL 60305-1402
708-209-3100 Fax: 708-209-3176
Website: www.cuchicago.edu
E-mail: admission@cuchicago.edu

HARRINGTON COLLEGE OF DESIGN
200 W Madison St, Chicago IL 60606-3433
Wendi Franczyk, VP of Admissions
877-939-4975 Fax: 312-697-8032
Website: www.harringtoncollege.com
E-mail: wfranczyk@harringtoncollege.com
See listing under "Universities"

INDIANA

Ancilla Domini College
Donaldson IN 46513
Erin Alonzo, Director of Admissions
574-936-8898 Fax: 574-935-1773
Website: www.ancilla.edu
E-mail: erin.alonzo@ancilla.edu

International Business College
5699 Coventry Ln, Fort Wayne IN 46804
260-459-4500 Fax: 260-436-1896
Website: www.ibcfortwayne.edu
E-mail: skinzer@ibcfortwayne.edu

Ivy Tech Community College - North Central
220 Dean Johnson Blvd, South Bend IN 46601-3415
Pam Decker, Director of Admissions
574-289-7001 Fax: 574-236-7177
Website: www.ivytech.edu
E-mail: pdecker@ivytech.edu

Oakland City University
138 N Lucretia St, Oakland City IN 47660
Brian J. Baker, Director of Admissions
800-737-5125 Fax: 812-749-1433
Website: www.oak.edu
E-mail: bbaker@oak.edu
See listing under "Universities"

University of Evansville
1800 Lincoln Ave, Evansville IN 47722-0001
Don Vos, Dean of Admission
800-423-8633 Fax: 812-488-4076
Website: www.evansville.edu
E-mail: admission@evansville.edu

IOWA

Briar Cliff University
PO Box 2100, Sioux City IA 51104-0100
Sharisue Wilcoxon, VP for Enrollment Management
712-279-5200 Fax: 712-279-1632
Website: www.briarcliff.edu
E-mail: admissions@briarcliff.edu

Clarke College
1550 Clarke Dr, Dubuque IA 52001-3198
Andy Schroeder, Director of Admissions
800-383-2345 Fax: 563-584-8666
Website: www.clarke.edu
E-mail: andy.schroeder@clarke.edu

Graceland University
1 University Place, Lamoni IA 50140
Greg Sutherland, Interim Vice President for Enrollment and Dean of Admissions
641-784-5196 Fax: 641-784-5480
Website: www.admissions.graceland.edu
E-mail: admissions@graceland.edu

Iowa Lakes Community College
300 S 18th St, Estherville IA 51334-2721
Anne Stansbury, Asst. Director of Admissions
712-362-7945 Fax: 712-362-8363
Website: www.iowalakes.edu
E-mail: info@iowalakes.edu

KANSAS

Flint Hills Technical College
3301 W 18th Ave, Emporia KS 66801-5957
Lisa Kirmer, Dean of Student Services
620-343-4600 Fax: 620-343-4610
Website: www.fhtc.net
E-mail: lkirmer@fhtc.net

KENTUCKY

Bluegrass Community and Technical College
Oswald Building
470 Cooper Drive, Lexington KY 40506-0235
Shelbie Hugle, Director of Admissions
859-246-6200 Fax: 859-246-4664
Website: www.bluegrass.kctcs.edu
E-mail: bctc_info@kctcs.edu

Louisville Technical Institute
3901 Atkinson Square Dr, Louisville KY 40218
Kevin Woods, Director of Admissions
800-844-6528 Fax: 502-456-2341
Website: www.louisvilletech.com
E-mail: kwoods@louisvilletech.com

Morehead State University
Morehead KY 40351-1689
Jeffrey Liles, Enrollment Services
800-585-6781 Fax: 606-783-5038
Website: www.moreheadstate.edu
E-mail: admissions@moreheadstate.edu

Spencerian College
1575 Winchester Rd, Lexington KY 40505
Victor Lamoin Adcock II, Director of Admissions
800-456-3253
E-mail: ladcock@spencerian.edu

MAINE

HEARTWOOD COLLEGE OF ART
123 York St, Kennebunk ME 04043
Berri Kramer, President
207-985-0985 Fax: 207-985-6333
Website: www.heartwoodcollegeofart.org
E-mail: hca@heartwoodcollegeofart.org

Established 1992. Private. Coed. Tuition: $10,400. Enrollment: 30 full-time, 20 part-time. Faculty: 20. Student-faculty ratio: 6:1. Small art college on the coast of Maine, offering an Associate and a Bachelor's degree in Fine Arts; Design and Crafts; and Photography. Studio facilities include ceramics, jewelry, photography, painting & drawing, printmaking, book arts, lampworking, and weaving. Inspirational faculty, studios, and location.

MARYLAND

Cecil College
One Seahawk Dr, North East MD 21901
Sandra S. Rajaski, Registrar & Director of Admissions
410-287-1000 Fax: 410-287-1001
Website: www.cecil.edu
E-mail: srajaski@cecil.edu

Hagerstown Community College
11400 Robinwood Dr, Hagerstown MD 21742-6590
Dr. Daniel E. Bock, Assistant Director of Admissions
301-790-2800 Fax: 301-791-9165
Website: www.hagerstowncc.edu
E-mail: bockd@hagerstowncc.edu

Kaplan College
Hagerstown Campus
18618 Crestwood Dr, Hagerstown MD 21742-2797
W. Christopher Motz, President
Steve Shinham, Director of Admissions
800-422-2670 Fax: 301-739-0474
Website: www.hagerstownbusinesscol.edu

MASSACHUSETTS

Anna Maria College
50 Sunset Ln, Paxton MA 01612
Timothy M. Donahue, Director of Recruitment and Admissions
508-849-3360 Fax: 508-849-3362
Website: www.annamaria.edu
E-mail: admissions@annamaria.edu

The Art Institute of Boston at Lesley University
700 Beacon St, Boston MA 02215-2598
Office of Admission
617-585-6710 Fax: 617-585-6720
Website: www.aiboston.edu
E-mail: admissions@aiboston.edu

Assumption College
500 Salisbury St, Worcester MA 01609-1294
Kathleen Murphy, Dean of Enrollment
508-767-7000 Fax: 508-799-4412
Website: www.assumption.edu
E-mail: admiss@assumption.edu

Boston University
121 Bay State Rd, Boston MA 02215
Kelly Walter, Executive Director of Admissions
617-353-2300 Fax: 617-353-9695
Website: web.bu.edu
E-mail: admissions@bu.edu

Bristol Community College
777 Elsbree St, Fall River MA 02720-7395
Rodney S. Clark, Director of Admissions
508-678-2811 ext. 2516, 2179 Fax: 508-730-3265
Website: www.bristol.mass.edu
E-mail: admissions@bristol.mass.edu

CENTER FOR DIGITAL IMAGING ARTS AT BOSTON UNIVERSITY
282 Moody St, Waltham MA 02453
800-808-2342

Gordon College
255 Grapevine Rd, Wenham MA 01984-1899
Barbara R. Layne, Associate Vice President, Enrollment
866-464-6736 Fax: 978-867-4682
Website: www.gordon.edu
E-mail: admissions@gordon.edu

Montserrat College of Art
PO Box 26, 23 Essex St, Beverly MA 01915-0026
Jessica Sarin-Perry, Dean of Admissions and Enrollment Management
800-836-0487 ext 1153 Fax: 978-921-4241
Website: www.montserrat.edu
E-mail: admiss@montserrat.edu

Newbury College
129 Fisher Ave, Brookline MA 02445-5796
Salvadore Liberto, Vice President of Enrollment
617-730-7000 Fax: 617-731-9618
Website: www.newbury.edu
E-mail: info@newbury.edu
See listing under "Universities"

School of the Museum of Fine Arts, Boston
230 The Fenway, Boston MA 02115-5534
Office of Admissions
617-369-3626 or 800-643-6078 Fax: 617-369-4264
Website: www.smfa.edu
E-mail: admissions@smfa.edu
See listing under "Universities"

Smith College
Northampton MA 01063-0001
Debra Shaver, Director of Admissions
800-383-3232 Fax: 413-585-2527
Website: www.smith.edu
E-mail: admission@smith.edu

University of Massachusetts Dartmouth
Old Westport Rd, North Dartmouth MA 02747-2300
Steven T. Briggs, Director of Admissions
508-999-8605 Fax: 508-999-8755
Website: explore.umassd.edu
E-mail: sbriggs@umassd.edu

MICHIGAN

Alma College
614 W Superior St, Alma MI 48801-1599
Evan Montague, Director of Admissions
800-321-ALMA Fax: 989-463-7057
Website: www.alma.edu
E-mail: admissions@alma.edu

College for Creative Studies
201 E Kirby St, Detroit MI 48202-4048
Julie Hingelberg, Dean of Enrollment Services
313-664-7425
Website: www.ccscad.edu

Concordia University
4090 Geddes Rd, Ann Arbor MI 48105-2797
Gary Neumann, Director of Admissions
734-995-7300 Fax: 734-995-4610
Website: www.cuaa.edu
E-mail: admissions@cuaa.edu

CRANBROOK ACADEMY OF ART
PO Box 801, Bloomfield Hills MI 48303-0801
Katharine Willman, Dean of Admissions
248-645-3300 Fax: 248-646-0046
Website: www.cranbrookart.edu
E-mail: caaadmissions@cranbrook.edu
Graduate Only, Visual Arts and Architecture

Delta College
University Center MI 48710-0001
Duff Zube, Director of Admissions
989-686-9093 Fax: 989-667-2202
Website: www.delta.edu
E-mail: admit@delta.edu

Grand Valley State University
1 Campus Dr, Allendale MI 49401-9403
Jodi Chycinski, Director of Admissions
616-331-6611 Fax: 616-331-2000
Website: www.gvsu.edu
E-mail: go2gvsu@gvsu.edu

HILLSDALE COLLEGE
33 E College St, Hillsdale MI 49242-1298
Professor Sam Knecht, Director
517-607-2269 Fax: 517-607-2657
Website: www.hillsdale.edu
E-mail: sam.knecht@hillsdale.edu

Interlochen Arts Academy
PO Box 199, Interlochen MI 49643-0199
231-276-7472
Website: www.interlochen.org
E-mail: admissions@interlochen.org

Kendall College of Art & Design
17 Fountain St NW, Grand Rapids MI 49503-3002
Dr. Oliver H. Evans, President
800-676-2787 or 616-451-2787 Fax: 616-831-9689
Website: www.kcad.edu
E-mail: brittons@ferris.edu

Lawrence Technological University
21000 W 10 Mile Rd, Southfield MI 48075-1058
Jane Rohrback, Director of Admissions
800-225-5588 Fax: 248-204-2228
Website: www.ltu.edu
E-mail: admissions@ltu.edu
See listing under "Universities"

MACOMB COMMUNITY COLLEGE
44575 Garfield Rd, Clinton Township MI 48038-1139
Information Center
586-445-7999
Website: www.macomb.edu
E-mail: answer@macomb.edu

MACOMB COMMUNITY COLLEGE
14500 E 12 Mile Rd, Warren MI 48088-3896
Information Center
586-445-7999
Website: www.macomb.edu
E-mail: answer@macomb.edu

MINNESOTA

Academy College
1101 E 78th St, Bloomington MN 55420-1402
Tracey Schantz, Director of Admissions
952-851-0066 Fax: 952-851-0094

Bethany Lutheran College
700 Luther Dr, Mankato MN 56001
Don Westphal, Dean of Admissions
507-344-7000 Fax: 507-344-7376
Website: www.blc.edu
E-mail: admiss@blc.edu

Carleton College
1 N College St, Northfield MN 55057-4044
800-995-2275 or 507-646-4190 Fax: 507-646-4526
Website: www.carleton.edu
E-mail: admissions@acs.carleton.edu

Minneapolis College of Art & Design
2501 Stevens Ave, Minneapolis MN 55404-4347
Admissions Office
800-874-6223 or 612-874-3760 Fax: 612-874-3701
Website: www.mcad.edu
E-mail: admissions@mcad.edu

Minnesota State University Moorhead
1104 7th Ave S, Moorhead MN 56563-0002
Regina Monson, Director of Admissions
218-477-2161 Fax: 218-477-4374
Website: go.mnstate.edu
E-mail: dragon@mnstate.edu

Pillsbury Baptist Bible College
315 S Grove Ave, Owatonna MN 55060-3097
Susanne Martin, Admissions Coordinator
507-451-2710 Fax: 507-451-0156
Website: www.pillsbury.edu
E-mail: admissions@pillsbury.edu

MISSISSIPPI

Tougaloo College
500 W County Line Rd, Tougaloo MS 39174-9799
Juno Leggette Jacobs, Director of Admissions
601-977-7768 Fax: 601-977-4501
Website: www.tougaloo.edu
E-mail: jjacobs@tougaloo.edu

MISSOURI

Columbia College
1001 Rogers St, Columbia MO 65216-0001
Regina Morin, Director of Admissions
573-875-7352 Fax: 573-875-7506
Website: www.ccis.edu
E-mail: admissions@ccis.edu

Hickey College
940 Westport Plz, Saint Louis MO 63146-3127
Christopher A. Gearin, President
800-777-1544 or 314-434-2212 Fax: 314-434-1974
Website: www.hickeycollege.edu
E-mail: admin@hickeycollege.edu

Northwest Missouri State University
800 University Dr, Maryville MO 64468-6001
Beverly Schenkel, Dean of Enrollment Management
660-562-1562 Fax: 660-562-1121
Website: www.nwmissouri.edu
E-mail: admissions@nwmissouri.edu

St. Charles Community College
4601 Mid Rivers Mall Dr, Cottleville MO 63376
Kathy Brockgreitens-Gober, Director of Admissions
636-922-8000 Fax: 636-922-8236
Website: www.stchas.edu
E-mail: adm-reg@stchas.edu

State Fair Community College
3201 W 16th St, Sedalia MO 65301-2199
Director of Admissions
660-530-5833 Fax: 660-596-7472
Website: www.sfccmo.edu
E-mail: mparris@sfccmo.edu

Truman State University
100 E Normal, Kirksville MO 63501
Office of Admission
660-785-4114 Fax: 660-785-7456
Website: admissions.truman.edu
E-mail: admissions@truman.edu

University of Missouri
1 University Blvd, Saint Louis MO 63121-4499
Dr. Mark Burkholder, Dean-College of Arts & Sciences
314-516-5501 Fax: 314-516-5415
Website: www.umsl.edu
E-mail: admissions@umsl.edu

Webster University
470 E Lockwood Ave, Saint Louis MO 63119-3194
Peter Sargent, Dean, College of Fine Arts
314-968-7006 Fax: 314-968-7139
Website: www.webster.edu
E-mail: langtk@webster.edu
See listing under "Universities"

William Woods University
1 University Ave, Fulton MO 65251-1098
Jimmy Clay, Director of Admissions
573-642-2251 Fax: 573-592-1146
Website: www.williamwoods.edu
E-mail: admissions@williamwoods.edu
See listing under "Universities"

NEBRASKA

University of Nebraska at Kearney
905 W 25th St, Kearney NE 68849-0001
Dusty Newton, Director of Admissions
800-KEARNEY Fax: 308-865-8987
Website: www.unk.edu
E-mail: admissionsug@unk.edu

NEW JERSEY

Bergen Community College
400 Paramus Rd, Paramus NJ 07652
Julian Gomez, Asst. Director of Admissions
201-447-7100 Fax: 201-444-7036
Website: www.bergen.edu
E-mail: jgomez@bergen.edu

New Jersey City University
2039 John F Kennedy Blvd
Jersey City NJ 07305-1588
Carmen Panlilio, Asst. V.P. for Admissions and Financial Aid
201-200-3234 Fax: 201-200-2044
Website: www.njcu.edu
E-mail: admissions@njcu.edu

Ramapo College of New Jersey
505 Ramapo Valley Rd, Mahwah NJ 07430-1623
Director of Admissions
201-684-7300 or 201-684-7301 Fax: 201-684-7964
Website: www.ramapo.edu
E-mail: admissions@ramapo.edu

RICHARD STOCKTON COLLEGE OF NEW JERSEY

PO Box 195, Pomona NJ 08240
John Iacovelli, Dean of Enrollment Management
866-RSC-2885 Fax: 609-626-5541
Website: www.stockton.edu
E-mail: admissions@stockton.edu

Stockton College is a comprehensive liberal arts, coed institution founded in 1969. Advance Pre-Professional Degree Options: 7-yr BS/MD with UMDNJ; NJ Dental School; NJ Medical School, Robert Wood Johnson Medical, School of Osteopathic Medicine; NY College of Podiatric Medicine, Pennsylvania College of Podiatric Medicine, SUNY College of Optometry. Pharmacy doctorate program with Rutgers University. 5-yr Engineering with NJIT and Rutgers University. Dual BA/MA in Criminal Justice. 5-yr BS/MS in Computational Science. BS/MS in Nursing. Doctorate of Physical Therapy. Additional Programs: Forensic Science, Pre-Law, Pre-Occupational Therapy, and Pre-Veterinary.

NEW MEXICO

Institute of American Indian Arts
83 A Van Nu Po, Santa Fe NM 87508-1300
John Gritts, Director of Admissions, Records & Enrollment
505-424-2330 Fax: 505-424-4500
Website: www.iaia.edu
E-mail: recruitment@iaia.edu

NEW YORK

College of Saint Rose
432 Western Ave, Albany NY 12203-1419
Maryelizabeth Amico, Asst V.P. for Undergraduate Admissions
518-454-5150 Fax: 518-454-2013
Website: www.strose.edu
E-mail: admit@strose.edu

CUNY Hunter College
695 Park Ave, New York NY 10021
Aaron Gibbs, Assistant Director of Recruitment
212-650-3946 Fax: 212-650-3336
Website: www.hunter.cuny.edu
E-mail: aaron.gibbs@hunter.cuny.edu

Daemen College
4380 Main St, Amherst NY 14226-3592
Donna Shaffner, Director of Admissions
800-462-7652 Fax: 716-839-8229
Website: www.daemen.edu/admissions
E-mail: admissions@daemen.edu

Dowling College
150 Idle Hour Blvd, Oakdale NY 11769-1999
Diane Kazanecki-Kempter, Contact
631-244-3000 Fax: 631-244-1059
Website: www.dowling.edu
E-mail: admissions@dowling.edu

Long Island University-C. W. Post Campus
720 Northern Blvd, Brookville NY 11548-1300
Joanne Graziano, Executive Director of Admissions
516-299-2900 Fax: 516-299-2137
Website: www.liu.edu/cwpost
E-mail: enroll@cwpost.liu.edu

Marymount Manhattan College
221 E 71st St, New York NY 10021-4501
Jim Rogers, Dean of Admissions
800-MARYMOUNT Fax: 212-517-0448
Website: www.mmm.edu
E-mail: admissions@mmm.edu

Molloy College
1000 Hempstead Ave
Rockville Centre NY 11570-1100
Marguerite Lane, Director of Admissions
516-678-5000 ext. 6291 Fax: 516-256-2247
Website: www.molloy.edu
E-mail: admissions@molloy.edu
See listing under "Universities"

NEW YORK SCHOOL OF INTERIOR DESIGN

170 E 70th St, New York NY 10021-5110
David Sprouls, Director of Admissions
800-33-NYSID or 212-472-1500 Fax: 212-472-1867
Website: www.nysid.edu
E-mail: admissions@nysid.edu

Established 1916. Private. Coed. College devoted to Interior Design education. Tuition: $21,450 per year. Fees: $145. Enrollment: 750. Faculty: 95. Accreditation: NASAD, FIDER. Four programs offered: Master of Fine Arts, 4-year Bachelor degree, 2-year Associate degree, 1-year non-degree Basic Interior Design. Located in Manhattan's historic Upper East Side near center of interior design industry. Faculty consists of Designers, Architects and Artists.

Pratt Institute
200 Willoughby Ave, Brooklyn NY 11205-3899
Heidi Metcalf, Director of Admissions
718-636-3600 Fax: 718-636-3670
Website: www.pratt.edu
E-mail: hmetcalf@pratt.edu

PURCHASE COLLEGE STATE UNIVERSITY OF NEW YORK (SUNY)

735 Anderson Hill Rd, Purchase NY 10577-1400
Stephanie McCaine, Director of Admissions
914-251-6300 Fax: 914-251-6314
Website: www.purchase.edu
E-mail: admisn@purchase.edu
See listing under "Universities"

Roberts Wesleyan College
2301 Westside Dr, Rochester NY 14624-1997
Office of Admissions
585-594-6400 Fax: 585-594-6371
Website: www.roberts.edu
E-mail: admissions@roberts.edu

SUNY College at Brockport
350 New Campus Dr, Brockport NY 14420-2997
Bernard S. Valento, Director of Undergraduate Admissions
585-395-2751 Fax: 585-395-5452
Website: www.brockport.edu
E-mail: admit@brockport.edu

SUNY Orange County Community College
115 South St, Middletown NY 10940-6437
Margot St. Lawrence, Director of Admissions
845-341-4030 Fax: 845-342-8662
Website: www.sunyorange.edu
E-mail: apply@sunyorange.edu
See listing under "Community and Junior Colleges"

SUNY Sullivan County Community College
112 College Rd, Loch Sheldrake NY 12759-5151
Sari Rosenheck, Director of Admissions
845-434-5750 Fax: 845-434-0923
Website: www.sullivan.suny.edu
E-mail: admissions@sullivan.suny.edu
Student Housing on Campus.

NORTH CAROLINA

Haywood Community College
185 Freedlander Dr, Clyde NC 28721
Debbie Rowland, Coordinator of Admissions
828-627-4500 Fax: 828-627-4513
Website: www.haywood.edu
E-mail: drowland@haywood.edu

Peace College
15 E Peace St, Raleigh NC 27604-1194
Laura C. Bingham, President
800-PEACE-47 Fax: 919-508-2306
Website: www.peace.edu
E-mail: admissions@peace.edu

Salem College
Winston Salem NC 27108
Dana Evans, Dean of Admissions/Fin. Aid
800-32-SALEM Fax: 336-917-5572
Website: www.salem.edu
E-mail: admissions@salem.edu
See listing under "Women's Colleges"

SCHOOL OF COMMUNICATION ARTS

3000 Wakefield Crossing Dr, Raleigh NC 27614-7076
Debra Ann Hooper, Director and VP
919-981-0972 Fax: 919-981-0946
Website: www.higherdigital.com
E-mail: school@higherdigital.com

NORTH DAKOTA

Dickinson State University
Dickinson ND 58601-4896
Steve Glasser, Director of Enrollment Services
800-279-4295 Fax: 701-483-2409
Website: www.dickinsonstate.edu
E-mail: dsu.hawks@dickinsonstate.edu

OHIO

ART ACADEMY OF CINCINNATI

1212 Jackson St, Cincinnati OH 45202
Gregory Allgire Smith, President
John Wadell, Director of Admissions
513-562-6262 Fax: 513-562-8778
Website: www.artacademy.edu
E-mail: admissions@artacademy.edu

Established 1887. Private. Coed. Accreditation: NCACS, NASAD. Tuition: $19,990. Student Activities Fee: $350. Enrollment: 150. Faculty: 14. Student-Faculty ratio: 10-1. Degrees: BFA in Fine Arts, Communications Arts, Art History. AS in Graphic Design. MA in Art Education (summer program). Financial Aid and Scholarships available.

THE ART INSTITUTE OF CINCINNATI

1171 E Kemper Rd, Cincinnati OH 45246
Cyndi Mendell, Director of Admissions
513-751-1206 Fax: 513-751-1209
Website: www.theartinstituteofcincinnati.com
E-mail: aic@theartinstituteofcincinnati.com

Established 1976. Two year design college. Small classes, individual instruction. Faculty: 7 (professional designers). Limited enrollment of 75. Accreditation: ACCSCT. First year, art foundation; Second year, integrates illustration, design with computers - a computer on each table. Associate degree offered.

Cleveland State University
2121 Euclid Ave RW 204, Cleveland OH 44115
Dr. Richard Arndt, Dean of Undergraduate Recruitment and College Partnerships
888-CSU-OHIO Fax: 216-687-9210
Website: www.csuohio.edu
E-mail: admissions@csuohio.edu

Davis College
4747 Monroe St, Toledo OH 43623-4389
Dana Stern, Admissions Director
419-473-2700 Fax: 419-473-2472
Website: www.daviscollege.edu
E-mail: learn@daviscollege.edu

The Ohio State University
Department of Art
Hopkins Hall, 128 N Oval Mall, Columbus OH 43210
Sergio Soave, Department Chair
614-292-5072 Fax: 614-292-1674
Website: art.osu.edu
E-mail: soave.1@osu.edu

Owens Community College
3200 Bright Rd, Findlay OH 45840
William J. Ivoska PhD., Vice President of Student Services
567-429-3500 Fax: 567-423-0246
Website: www.owens.edu
E-mail: admissions@owens.edu

Owens Community College
PO Box 10000, Toledo OH 43699-1947
William J. Ivoska, Ph.D, Vice President of Student Services
567-661-7000 Fax: 567-661-7607
Website: www.owens.edu
E-mail: admissions@owens.edu

the school of advertising art
1725 E David Rd, Kettering OH 45440-1612
Jessica Kantner, Director of Admissions
877-300-9326 Fax: 937-294-5869
Website: www.saacollege.com
E-mail: jessica@saacollege.com

University of Dayton
300 College Park, Dayton OH 45469-1300
Robert F. Durkle, Director of Admission
800-837-7433 Fax: 937-229-4729
Website: admission.udayton.edu
E-mail: admission@udayton.edu

Ursuline College
2550 Lander Rd, Cleveland OH 44124-4398
Sarah E. Sundermeier, Director of Admissions
888-URSULINE Toll Free Fax: 440-684-6138
Website: www.admission.ursuline.edu
E-mail: admission@ursuline.edu

OKLAHOMA

Oklahoma State University
Stillwater OK 74078
Nicholas Bormann, Department Head
405-744-6016
Website: www.okstate.edu
E-mail: nborman@okstate.edu

OREGON

Marylhurst University
17600 Pacific Hwy (Hwy 43)
Marylhurst OR 97036-0261
Director of Admissions
800-634-9982 ext. 6268 Fax: 503-635-6585
Website: www.marylhurst.edu
E-mail: studentinfo@marylhurst.edu

OREGON COLLEGE OF ART & CRAFT
8245 SW Barnes Rd, Portland OR 97225-6399
Debrah Spencer, Interim Director of Admissions
503-297-5544 or 800-390-0632 Fax: 503-297-9651
Website: www.ocac.edu
E-mail: admissions@ocac.edu

PACIFIC NORTHWEST COLLEGE OF ART
1241 NW Johnson St, Portland OR 97209-3023
Chris Sweet, Director of Admissions
503-821-8972 Fax: 503-821-8978
Website: www.pnca.edu
E-mail: admissions@pnca.edu

PENNSYLVANIA

Antonelli Institute - Art & Photography
300 Montgomery Ave, Erdenheim PA 19038-8242
Dr. Thomas Treacy, President
215-836-2222 or 800-722-7871 Fax: 215-836-2794
Website: www.antonelli.edu
E-mail: admissions@antonelli.edu

Art Institute of Philadelphia
1622 Chestnut St, Philadelphia PA 19103-5119
Larry McHugh, Director of Admissions
800-275-2474 Fax: 215-405-6399
Website: www.artinstitutes.edu/philadelphia
E-mail: aiphinfo@aii.edu

ART INSTITUTE OF PITTSBURGH
420 Boulevard Of The Allies, Pittsburgh PA 15219
Jeffrey Bucklew, Director of Admissions
800-275-2470 Fax: 412-263-6667
Website: www.aip.aii.edu
E-mail: pahughes@aii.edu
See listing under "Universities"

Community College of Allegheny County
Allegheny Campus: 808 Ridge Ave, Pittsburgh PA 15212 Admissions: 412.237.2700
Boyce Campus: 595 Beatty Rd, Monroeville PA 15146 Admissions: 724.325.6614
North Campus: 8701 Perry Highway, Pittsburgh PA 15237 Admissions: 412.369.3600
South Campus: 1750 Clairton Rd, West Mifflin PA 15122 Admissions: 412-469-4301
Website: www.ccac.edu

Douglas Education Center
130 7th St, Monessen PA 15062-1097
Sherry Lee Walters, Director of Enrollment Services
800-413-6013 Fax: 724-684-7463
Website: www.douglas-school.com
E-mail: swalters@douglas-school.com

Holy Family University
9801 Frankford Avenue, Philadelphia PA 19114
Lauren Campbell, Director of Admissions
215-637-3050 Fax: 215-281-1022
Website: www.holyfamily.edu
E-mail: admissions@holyfamily.edu

HUSSIAN SCHOOL OF ART
1118 Market St, Philadelphia PA 19107-3679
Lynne Wartman, Director of Admissions
215-981-0900 Fax: 215-864-9115
Website: www.hussianart.edu
E-mail: info@hussianart.edu

Juniata College
1700 Moore St, Huntingdon PA 16652-2196
Michelle Bartol, Dean of Enrollment
877-JUNIATA Fax: 814-641-3100
Website: www.juniata.edu
E-mail: admissions@juniata.edu

Lehigh Valley College
2809 E Saucon Valley Rd
Center Valley PA 18034-8447
Sam Jarvis, Director of Marketing
800-227-9109 Fax: 610-791-7810
Website: www.lehighvalley.edu
E-mail: joshua.padron@lehighvalley.edu

PENNSYLVANIA COLLEGE OF ART AND DESIGN
PO Box 59, Lancaster PA 17608-0059
Susan Matson, Director of Enrollment Management
717-396-7833 Fax: 717-396-1339
Website: www.pcad.edu
E-mail: admissions@pcad.edu

Washington & Jefferson College
60 S Lincoln St, Washington PA 15301-4801
Alton E. Newell, Vice President for Enrollment
724-223-6025 Fax: 724-223-6534
Website: www.washjeff.edu
E-mail: admission@washjeff.edu

SOUTH CAROLINA

Erskine College & Seminary
PO Box 176, Due West SC 29639
Bart Walker, Director of Admissions
864-379-8838 Fax: 864-379-3048
Website: www.erskine.edu
E-mail: admissions@erskine.edu

North Greenville University
PO Box 1892, Tigerville SC 29688-1892
Jim Craft, Art Department
Website: www.ngu.edu
See listing under "Universities"

TENNESSEE

Austin Peay State University
601 College St, Clarksville TN 37044-0002
931-221-7011 Fax: 931-221-6168
Website: www.apsu.edu
E-mail: admissions@apsu.edu

Lipscomb University
3901 Granny White Pike, Nashville TN 37204-3951
Ricky Holaway, Director of Admissions
800-333-4358 ext. 1776 Fax: 615-269-1804
Website: www.lipscomb.edu
E-mail: admissions@lipscomb.edu

O'More College of Design
423 S Margin St, Franklin TN 37064-2816
Dr. K. Mark Hilliard, President
Chris Lee, Director of Enrollment Management
615-794-4254 Fax: 615-790-1662
Website: www.omorecollege.edu
E-mail: clee@omorecollege.edu

Tennessee State University
3500 John A Merritt Blvd, Nashville TN 37209-1561
John Cade, Dean of Admissions & Records
615-963-5101 Fax: 615-963-2930
Website: www.tnstate.edu
E-mail: jcade@tnstate.edu

University of Tennessee
615 McCallie Ave, Chattanooga TN 37403-2504
Yancy Freeman, Director of Admissions
423-425-4111 Fax: 423-425-4157
Website: www.utc.edu
E-mail: Yancy-Freeman@utc.edu

Watkins College of Art and Design
and The Watkins Film School
2298 Metrocenter Blvd, Nashville TN 37228-1306
615-383-4848 or 866-887-6395 Fax: 615-383-4849
Website: www.watkins.edu
E-mail: admissions@watkins.edu

TEXAS

Abilene Christian University
ACU Box 29000, Abilene TX 79699-0001
325-674-2000 Fax: 325-674-2202
Website: www.acu.edu
E-mail: info@admissions.acu.edu

Remington College - Fort Worth Campus
300 E Loop 820, Fort Worth TX 76112-1280
Director of Recruitment
817-451-0017 Fax: 817-496-1257
Website: www.remingtoncollege.edu
E-mail: lynn.wey@remingtoncollege.edu

Texas Woman's University
PO Box 425589, Denton TX 76204-5589
Erma Nieto-Brecht, Director of Admissions
866-809-6130 Fax: 940-898-3081
Website: www.twu.edu
E-mail: admissions@twu.edu

University of Houston
122 E Cullen Bldg, Houston TX 77204-2023
Office of Admission
713-743-9595
Website: www.uh.edu
E-mail: admissions@uh.edu

University of Texas at Arlington
Box 19111, Arlington TX 76019-0111
Hans Gatterdam, Director of Admission
817-272-6287 Fax: 817-272-3435
Website: www.uta.edu
E-mail: admissions@uta.edu

VERMONT

Green Mountain College
1 College Cir, Poultney VT 05764-1199
Sandra Bartholomew, Ph.D., Dean of Enrollment Management
802-287-8000 Fax: 802-287-8099
Website: www.greenmtn.edu
E-mail: bartholomews@greenmtn.edu

VIRGINIA

Gibbs College - Northern Virginia
1980 Gallows Rd, Vienna VA 22182-3913
Everson Travers, Director of Admissions
703-556-8888 Fax: 703-556-0953
Website: www.gibbsva.edu
E-mail: etravers@gibbsva.edu

Mary Baldwin College
Staunton VA 24401
Lisa A. Branson, Executive Director of Admissions and Financial Aid
800-468-2262 Fax: 540-887-7292
Website: www.mbc.edu
E-mail: admit@mbc.edu

Radford University
PO Box 6903, Radford VA 24142
David W. Kraus, Director of Admissions
800-890-4265 Fax: 540-831-5038
Website: www.radford.edu
E-mail: ruadmiss@radford.edu

Randolph College
2500 Rivermont Ave, Lynchburg VA 24503
Patricia LeDonne, Director of Admissions
434-947-8100 Fax: 434-947-8996
Website: www.randolphcollege.edu
E-mail: admissions@randolphcollege.edu

WEST VIRGINIA

Davis & Elkins College
100 Campus Dr, Elkins WV 26241-3996
Renee Heckel, Director of Enrollment Management
800-624-3157 Fax: 304-637-1800
Website: www.davisandelkins.edu
E-mail: admiss@davisandelkins.edu

Fairmont State University
1201 Locust Ave, Fairmont WV 26554-2470
Steve Leadman, Director of Admissions
304-367-4892 or 800-641-5678 Fax: 304-367-4789
Website: www.fairmontstate.edu
E-mail: admit@fairmontstate.edu

WISCONSIN

Alverno College
PO Box 343922, Milwaukee WI 53234-3922
Dianna Gaebler, Director of Admissions
414-382-6100 Fax: 414-382-6354
Website: www.alverno.edu
E-mail: admissions@alverno.edu

Herzing College
5218 E Terrace Dr, Madison WI 53718-8340
Donald Madelung, President
800-582-1227 Fax: 608-249-8593
Website: www.herzing.edu
E-mail: info@msn.herzing.edu
See listing under "Universities"

MADISON MEDIA INSTITUTE
College of Media Arts
2702 Agriculture Dr, Madison WI 53718-6787
Steve Hutchings, Director of Admissions
800-236-4997 or 608-663-2000 Fax: 608-442-0141
Website: www.madisonmedia.edu
E-mail: mmi@madisonmedia.com

St. Norbert College
100 Grant St, De Pere WI 54115
Brian Studebaker, Director of Admission
800-236-4878 Fax: 920-403-4072
Website: www.snc.edu
E-mail: admit@snc.edu

WYOMING

University of Wyoming
Admissions Office
Dept 3435, Laramie WY 82071-3435
Brooke Culver, Contact
800-342-5996 Fax: 307-766-4042
Website: www.uwyo.edu
E-mail: why-wyo@uwyo.edu

GUAM

University of Guam
UOG Station, Mangilao GU 96923
Deborah Leon Guerrero, Registrar
671-735-2201 or 671-735-2208 Fax: 671-735-2203
Website: www.uog.edu
E-mail: admitme@uog9.uog.edu

BIOLOGICAL SCIENCE

ALABAMA

CALHOUN COMMUNITY COLLEGE
PO Box 2216, Decatur AL 35609-2216
M. Wayne Tosh, Registrar
256-306-2500 Fax: 256-306-2941
Website: www.calhoun.edu
E-mail: jfd@calhoun.edu

Judson College
302 Bibb St, Marion AL 36756
Michael Scotto, Director of Admissions
800-447-9472 Fax: 334-683-5147
Website: www.judson.edu
E-mail: admissions@judson.edu

University of Alabama in Huntsville
PO Box 1247, Huntsville AL 35899-0001
Nikki Willis, Assoc. Director for Recruiting Program and Events
1-800-UAH-CALL Fax: 256-824-6073
Website: www.uah.edu
E-mail: willisn@uah.edu

University of South Alabama
307 University Blvd N, Mobile AL 36688-3053
Melissa Haab, Director of Admissions
251-460-6141 Fax: 251-460-7876
Website: www.southalabama.edu
E-mail: admiss@usouthal.edu

ALASKA

University of Alaska Anchorage
PO Box 141629, Anchorage AK 99514-1629
Cecile Mitchell, Director of Enrollment Services
907-786-1480 Fax: 907-786-4888
Website: www.uaa.alaska.edu/
E-mail: enroll@uaa.alaska.edu

ARIZONA

Pima Community College
4905 E Broadway Blvd, Tucson AZ 85709-1010
Wendy Kilgore, Ph.D., Director of Admissions
520-206-4500 Fax: 520-206-4790
Website: www.pima.edu
E-mail: infocenter@pima.edu

ARKANSAS

Williams Baptist College
PO Box 3737, Walnut Ridge AR 72476-3737
Angela Flippo, Vice President for Enrollment Management
800-722-4434 Fax: 870-759-4163
Website: www.williamsbaptistcollege.com
E-mail: admissions@wbcoll.edu

CALIFORNIA

Butte College
3536 Butte Campus Dr, Oroville CA 95965-8399
Carole Gish, Director of Admissions
530-895-2511 Fax: 530-879-4313
Website: www.butte.edu
E-mail: admissions@butte.edu

California State University-San Bernadino
5500 University Pkwy
San Bernardino CA 92407-2393
Olivia Rosas, Director of Admissions
909-537-5188 Fax: 909-537-7034
Website: www.csusb.edu
E-mail: orosas@csusb.edu

Chapman University
One University Drive, Orange CA 92866-1099
Michael Drummy, Assistant Vice President for Enrollment
Services and Chief Admission Officer
714-997-6411 or 888-CUAPPLY Fax: 714-997-6713
Website: www.chapman.edu
E-mail: admit@chapman.edu

Cleveland Chiropractic College - Los Angeles Campus
590 N Vermont Ave, Los Angeles CA 90004-2196
Teresa Moore, Director of Admissions
800-466-CCLA (2252) or 323-906-2031
Fax: 323-906-2094
Website: www.cleveland.edu
E-mail: la.admissions@cleveland.edu

Concordia University
1530 Concordia, Irvine CA 92612-3203
Lori McDonald, Executive Director of Enrollment Services
800-229-1200 or 949-854-8002 Fax: 949-854-6894
Website: www.cui.edu
E-mail: admission@cui.edu

Dominican University of California
50 Acacia Ave, San Rafael CA 94901-2298
Office of Admissions
888-323-6762 Fax: 415-485-3214
Website: www.dominican.edu
E-mail: enroll@dominican.edu

FRESNO CITY COLLEGE
1101 E University Ave, Fresno CA 93741-0002
Dayann Dietrich, Contact
559-442-8241 Fax: 559-237-4232
Website: www.fresnocitycollege.com
E-mail: fcc.admissions@scccd.com

New College School of Law
50 Fell St, San Francisco CA 94102-5206
Sharon Pittman, Dean of Admissions
415-241-1300 Fax: 415-241-9525
Website: www.newcollege.edu
E-mail: spittman@newcollege.edu or lawadmissions@newcollege.edu

Orange Coast College
PO Box 5005, Costa Mesa CA 92628-5005
Kristin Clark, Director of Admissions
714-432-5773 Fax: 714-432-5736
Website: www.orangecoastcollege.edu
E-mail: kclark@cccd.edu

Point Loma Nazarene University
3900 Lomaland Dr, San Diego CA 92106-2810
Chip Killingsworth, Director of Undergraduate Admissions
800-733-7770 Fax: 619-849-2601
Website: www.pointloma.edu
E-mail: admissions@pointloma.edu

San Bernardino Valley College
701 S Mount Vernon Ave
San Bernardino CA 92410-2798
Kay Ragan, Ed.D., Director of Admissions
909-888-6511 Fax: 909-889-4988
Website: www.valleycollege.edu
E-mail: kragan@sbccd.cc.ca.us

San Diego Christian College
2100 Greenfield Dr, El Cajon CA 92019-1157
Rene Inman, Director of Admissions
800-676-2242 Fax: 619-590-1739
Website: www.sdcc.edu
E-mail: admissions@sdcc.edu

Simpson University
2211 College View Dr, Redding CA 96003-8606
Jim Herberger, Director of Admissions
888-9-SIMPSON Fax: 530-226-4861
Website: www.simpsonuniversity.edu
E-mail: admissions@simpsonuniversity.edu
See listing under "Universities"

Whittier College
PO Box 634, Whittier CA 90608-0634
Kieron Miller, Director of Admissions
562-907-4200 Fax: 562-907-4870
Website: www.whittier.edu
E-mail: kmiller@whittier.edu

COLORADO

Colorado Christian University
8787 W Alameda Ave, Lakewood CO 80226
Sean Kadel, Director of Admissions
800-44-FAITH Fax: 303-963-3201
Website: www.ccu.edu
E-mail: admissions@ccu.edu

CONNECTICUT

Albertus Magnus College
700 Prospect St, New Haven CT 06511-1189
Richard Lolatte, Dean of Admission
203-773-8501 or 800-578-9160 Fax: 203-773-5248
Website: www.albertus.edu
E-mail: admissions@albertus.edu

DELAWARE

Wesley College
120 N State St, Dover DE 19901-3876
302-736-2300 Fax: 302-736-2301
Website: www.wesley.edu

DISTRICT OF COLUMBIA

Gallaudet University
800 Florida Ave NE, Washington DC 20002-3695
Charity Reedy Hines, Director of Admissions
202-651-5750 Fax: 202-651-5744
Website: www.gallaudet.edu
E-mail: admissions.office@gallaudet.edu

FLORIDA

Florida State University
600 W College Ave, Tallahassee FL 32306-1096
Janice V. Finney, Director of Admissions
850-644-2525 Fax: 850-644-0197
Website: admissions.fsu.edu
E-mail: admissions@admin.fsu.edu

Lynn University
3601 N Military Trl, Boca Raton FL 33431-5598
Director of Admissions
561-237-7900 Fax: 561-237-7100
Website: www.lynn.edu
E-mail: admission@lynn.edu

St. Thomas University
16401 NW 37th Ave, Miami Gardens FL 33054
Dr. Edward Ajhar, Contact
800-367-9010 or 305-628-6546 Fax: 305-628-6591
Website: www.stu.edu
E-mail: signup@stu.edu

University of South Florida
4202 E Fowler Ave, Tampa FL 33620-6900
J. Robert Spatig, Director of Admissions
877-USF-BULL Fax: 813-974-9689
Website: www.usf.edu
E-mail: admissions@admin.usf.edu
See listing under "Universities"

GEORGIA

Armstrong Atlantic State University
11935 Abercorn St, Savannah GA 31419-1997
Kim West, Asst. Dean and Registrar Enrollment Services
912-927-5277 Fax: 912-921-5462
Website: www.armstrong.edu
E-mail: admissions@mail.armstrong.edu

Kennesaw State University
1000 Chastain Rd NW, Kennesaw GA 30144-5591
Laurence Peterson, Dean of College of Science and Mathematics
770-423-6160
Website: www.kennesaw.edu

Life University
1269 Barclay Cir SE, Marietta GA 30060-2903
Dr. Deborah E. Heairlston, Director of New Student Development
770-426-2884 Fax: 770-426-2895
Website: www.life.edu
E-mail: admissions@life.edu

TOCCOA FALLS COLLEGE
PO Box 800899, Toccoa Falls GA 30598
888-785-5624 Fax: 706-282-6012
Website: www.tfc.edu
E-mail: admissions@tfc.edu

IDAHO

Brigham Young University - Idaho
120 Kimball Bldg, Rexburg ID 83460-1615
Rob Garrett, Director of Admissions
208-496-1020 Fax: 208-496-1220
Website: www.byui.edu
E-mail: admissions@byui.edu

Lewis-Clark State College
500 8th Ave, Lewiston ID 83501-2698
Diane Douglas, Ph.D., Registrar/Director of Admissions
800-933-5272 Fax: 208-792-2429
Website: www.lcsc.edu
E-mail: admissions@lcsc.edu

University of Idaho
Moscow ID 83844-4253
Lloyd Scott, Director of New Student Services
208-885-6163 Fax: 208-885-4477
Website: www.uidaho.edu
E-mail: nss@uidaho.edu

ILLINOIS

Aurora University
347 S Gladstone Ave, Aurora IL 60506-4892
Carol R. Dunn, Ed.D., Vice President for Enrollment
800-742-5281 Fax: 630-844-5535
Website: www.aurora.edu
E-mail: admission@aurora.edu

Benedictine University
5700 College Rd, Lisle IL 60532-0900
630-829-6300 or 888-829-6363 Fax: 630-829-6301
Website: www.ben.edu
E-mail: admissions@ben.edu
See listing under "Universities"

CONCORDIA UNIVERSITY
7400 Augusta St, River Forest IL 60305-1402
708-209-3100 Fax: 708-209-3176
Website: www.cuchicago.edu
E-mail: admission@cuchicago.edu

National University of Health Sciences
200 E Roosevelt Rd, Lombard IL 60148-4583
Dr. James Winterstein, President
800-826-6285 Fax: 630-889-6554
Website: www.nuhs.edu
E-mail: admissions@nuhs.edu

Roosevelt University
430 S Michigan Ave, Chicago IL 60605
Gwen E. Kanelos, Asst. Vice President for Enrollment Services
877-APPLY-RU Fax: 312-341-4216
Website: www.roosevelt.edu
E-mail: applyru@roosevelt.edu

Trinity International University
2065 Half Day Rd, Deerfield IL 60015-1241
847-945-8800 Fax: 847-317-8097
Website: www.tiu.edu
E-mail: tcadmissions@tiu.edu

INDIANA

Ancilla Domini College
Donaldson IN 46513
Erin Alonzo, Director of Admissions
574-936-8898 Fax: 574-935-1773
Website: www.ancilla.edu
E-mail: erin.alonzo@ancilla.edu

Franklin College
101 Branigin Blvd, Franklin IN 46131
Jacqueline S. Acosta, Director of Admissions
800-852-0232 Fax: 317-738-8274
Website: www.franklincollege.edu
E-mail: admissions@franklincollege.edu

Ivy Tech Community College - North Central
220 Dean Johnson Blvd, South Bend IN 46601-3415
Pam Decker, Director of Admissions
574-289-7001 Fax: 574-236-7177
Website: www.ivytech.edu
E-mail: pdecker@ivytech.edu

Oakland City University
138 N Lucretia St, Oakland City IN 47660
Brian J. Baker, Director of Admissions
800-737-5125 Fax: 812-749-1433
Website: www.oak.edu
E-mail: bbaker@oak.edu
See listing under "Universities"

Rose-Hulman Institute of Technology
5500 Wabash Ave, Terre Haute IN 47803-3920
James A. Goecker, Dean of Admissions
812-877-8213 Fax: 812-877-8941
Website: www.rose-hulman.edu
E-mail: admissions@rose-hulman.edu

University of Evansville
1800 Lincoln Ave, Evansville IN 47722-0001
Don Vos, Dean of Admission
800-423-8633 Fax: 812-488-4076
Website: www.evansville.edu
E-mail: admission@evansville.edu

IOWA

Briar Cliff University
PO Box 2100, Sioux City IA 51104-0100
Sharisue Wilcoxon, VP for Enrollment Management
712-279-5200 Fax: 712-279-1632
Website: www.briarcliff.edu
E-mail: admissions@briarcliff.edu

Clarke College
1550 Clarke Dr, Dubuque IA 52001-3198
Andy Schroeder, Director of Admissions
800-383-2345 Fax: 563-584-8666
Website: www.clarke.edu
E-mail: andy.schroeder@clarke.edu

Graceland University
1 University Place, Lamoni IA 50140
Greg Sutherland, Interim Vice President for Enrollment and Dean of Admissions
641-784-5196 Fax: 641-784-5480
Website: www.admissions.graceland.edu
E-mail: admissions@graceland.edu

Iowa Lakes Community College
300 S 18th St, Estherville IA 51334-2721
Anne Stansbury, Asst. Director of Admissions
712-362-7945 Fax: 712-362-8363
Website: www.iowalakes.edu
E-mail: info@iowalakes.edu

PALMER COLLEGE OF CHIROPRACTIC
Davenport Campus
1000 Brady St, Davenport IA 52803-5287
800-722-3648 or 563-884-5656 Fax: 563-884-5414
Website: www.palmer.edu
E-mail: pcadmit@palmer.edu

Waldorf College
106 S 6th St, Forest City IA 50436-1713
Dr. Linda Hoopes, Vice President of Admission and Marketing
800-292-1903 or 641-585-8112 Fax: 641-585-8125
Website: www.waldorf.edu
E-mail: hoopesl@waldorf.edu
See listing under "Universities"

KANSAS

COLBY COMMUNITY COLLEGE
1255 S Range Ave, Colby KS 67701-4099
Director of Admissions
888-634-9350 or 785-460-4690 Fax: 785-460-4691
Website: www.colbycc.edu
E-mail: admissions@colbycc.edu

Independence Community College
PO Box 708, Independence KS 67301-0708
Dr. Terry Hetrick, President
800-842-6063 Fax: 620-331-5344
Website: www.indycc.edu
E-mail: admissions@indycc.edu

Tabor College
400 S Jefferson St, Hillsboro KS 67063-1758
Rusty Allen, Dean of Enrollment Management
800-822-6799 Fax: 620-947-6276
Website: www.tabor.edu
E-mail: admissions@tabor.edu
See listing under "Universities"

KENTUCKY

Bluegrass Community and Technical College
Oswald Building
470 Cooper Drive, Lexington KY 40506-0235
Shelbie Hugle, Director of Admissions
859-246-6200 Fax: 859-246-4664
Website: www.bluegrass.kctcs.edu
E-mail: bctc_info@kctcs.edu

Morehead State University
Morehead KY 40351-1689
Jeffrey Liles, Enrollment Services
800-585-6781 Fax: 606-783-5038
Website: www.moreheadstate.edu
E-mail: admissions@moreheadstate.edu

Transylvania University
300 N Broadway, Lexington KY 40508-1776
859-233-8242 Fax: 859-233-8797
Website: www.transy.edu
E-mail: admissions@transy.edu

LOUISIANA

Louisiana State University at Alexandria
8100 Highway 71 S, Alexandria LA 71302-9121
Dr. Thomas Armstrong, Director of Admissions
318-445-3672 Fax: 318-473-6418
Website: www.lsua.edu

Our Lady of Holy Cross College
4123 Woodland Dr, New Orleans LA 70131-7399
Office of Enrollment Services
504-394-7744 Fax: 504-391-2421
Website: www.olhcc.edu

MAINE

HUSSON COLLEGE
One College Cir, Bangor ME 04401-2999
Jane Goodwin, Director of Admissions
800-4HU-SSON or 207-941-7100 Fax: 207-941-7935
Website: www.husson.edu
E-mail: admit@husson.edu
See listing under "Universities"

St. Joseph's College of Maine
278 Whites Bridge Rd, Standish ME 04084-5263
Vincent Kloskowski, Dean of Admissions
800-338-7057 Fax: 207-893-7862
Website: www.sjcme.edu
E-mail: admission@sjcme.edu

MARYLAND

Cecil College
One Seahawk Dr, North East MD 21901
Sandra S. Rajaski, Registrar & Director of Admissions
410-287-1000 Fax: 410-287-1001
Website: www.cecil.edu
E-mail: srajaski@cecil.edu

Hagerstown Community College
11400 Robinwood Dr, Hagerstown MD 21742-6590
Dr. Daniel E. Bock, Assistant Director of Admissions
301-790-2800 Fax: 301-791-9165
Website: www.hagerstowncc.edu
E-mail: bockd@hagerstowncc.edu

MASSACHUSETTS

Assumption College
500 Salisbury St, Worcester MA 01609-1294
Kathleen Murphy, Dean of Enrollment
508-767-7000 Fax: 508-799-4412
Website: www.assumption.edu
E-mail: admiss@assumption.edu

Boston University
121 Bay State Rd, Boston MA 02215
Kelly Walter, Executive Director of Admissions
617-353-2300 Fax: 617-353-9695
Website: web.bu.edu
E-mail: admissions@bu.edu

Gordon College
255 Grapevine Rd, Wenham MA 01984-1899
Barbara R. Layne, Associate Vice President, Enrollment
866-464-6736 Fax: 978-867-4682
Website: www.gordon.edu
E-mail: admissions@gordon.edu

Massachusetts Institute of Technology
77 Massachusetts Ave, Cambridge MA 02139-4307
617-253-1000 Fax: 617-253-4016
Website: my.mit.edu
E-mail: admissions@mit.edu

Smith College
Northampton MA 01063-0001
Debra Shaver, Director of Admissions
800-383-3232 Fax: 413-585-2527
Website: www.smith.edu
E-mail: admission@smith.edu

University of Massachusetts Dartmouth
Old Westport Rd, North Dartmouth MA 02747-2300
Steven T. Briggs, Director of Admissions
508-999-8605 Fax: 508-999-8755
Website: explore.umassd.edu
E-mail: sbriggs@umassd.edu

Worcester Polytechnic Institute
100 Institute Rd, Worcester MA 01609-2280
Edward J. Connor, Director of Admissions
508-831-5286 Fax: 508-831-5875
Website: admissions.wpi.edu
E-mail: admissions@wpi.edu

MICHIGAN

Alma College
614 W Superior St, Alma MI 48801-1599
Evan Montague, Director of Admissions
800-321-ALMA Fax: 989-463-7057
Website: www.alma.edu
E-mail: admissions@alma.edu

Concordia University
4090 Geddes Rd, Ann Arbor MI 48105-2797
Gary Neumann, Director of Admissions
734-995-7300 Fax: 734-995-4610
Website: www.cuaa.edu
E-mail: admissions@cuaa.edu

Delta College
University Center MI 48710-0001
Duff Zube, Director of Admissions
989-686-9093 Fax: 989-667-2202
Website: www.delta.edu
E-mail: admit@delta.edu

Grand Valley State University
1 Campus Dr, Allendale MI 49401-9403
Jodi Chycinski, Director of Admissions
616-331-6611 Fax: 616-331-2000
Website: www.gvsu.edu
E-mail: go2gvsu@gvsu.edu

HILLSDALE COLLEGE
33 E College St, Hillsdale MI 49242-1298
Dr. Francis Steiner, Chairperson
517-607-2399 Fax: 517-607-2399
Website: www.hillsdale.edu
E-mail: fxs@hillsdale.edu

Lake Superior State University
650 W Easterday Ave
Sault Sainte Marie MI 49783-1637
Susan Camp, Director of Admissions
888-800-LSSU Fax: 906-635-6696
Website: www.lssu.edu
E-mail: admissions@lssu.edu
See listing under "Universities"

MACOMB COMMUNITY COLLEGE
44575 Garfield Rd, Clinton Township MI 48038-1139
Information Center
586-445-7999
Website: www.macomb.edu
E-mail: answer@macomb.edu

MACOMB COMMUNITY COLLEGE
14500 E 12 Mile Rd, Warren MI 48088-3896
Information Center
586-445-7999
Website: www.macomb.edu
E-mail: answer@macomb.edu

Northwestern Michigan College
1701 E Front St, Traverse City MI 49686-3061
Jim Bensley, Director of Admissions
800-748-0566 Fax: 231-995-1339
Website: www.nmc.edu
E-mail: jbensley@nmc.edu

Oakland University
2200 N Squirrel Rd, Rochester MI 48309
Eleanor L. Reynolds, Assistant Vice President & Director of Admissions
248-370-2100
Website: www.oakland.edu
E-mail: ouinfo@oakland.edu

MINNESOTA

Bethany Lutheran College
700 Luther Dr, Mankato MN 56001
Don Westphal, Dean of Admissions
507-344-7000 Fax: 507-344-7376
Website: www.blc.edu
E-mail: admiss@blc.edu

Carleton College
1 N College St, Northfield MN 55057-4044
800-995-2275 or 507-646-4190 Fax: 507-646-4526
Website: www.carleton.edu
E-mail: admissions@acs.carleton.edu

Crown College
8700 College View Dr, Saint Bonifacius MN 55375
Mitch Fisk, Director of Admissions
952-446-4142 Fax: 952-446-4149
Website: www.crown.edu
E-mail: johnsonj@crown.edu

Gustavus Adolphus College
800 W College Ave, Saint Peter MN 56082-1485
Mark H. Anderson, Dean of Admission
800-GUSTAVUS Fax: 507-933-7474
Website: www.gustavus.edu
E-mail: admission@gustavus.edu

Minnesota State University Moorhead
1104 7th Ave S, Moorhead MN 56563-0002
Regina Monson, Director of Admissions
218-477-2161 Fax: 218-477-4374
Website: go.mnstate.edu
E-mail: dragon@mnstate.edu

Northwestern Health Sciences University
Northwestern College of Chiropractic Admissions Office
2501 W 84th St, Minneapolis MN 55431
Dr. Mark Zeigler, President
Bill Kuehl, Director of Admissions
952-888-4777 ext. 409 Fax: 952-881-3028
Website: www.nwhealth.edu
E-mail: admit@nwhealth.edu

Pillsbury Baptist Bible College
315 S Grove Ave, Owatonna MN 55060-3097
Susanne Martin, Admissions Coordinator
507-451-2710 Fax: 507-451-0156
Website: www.pillsbury.edu
E-mail: admissions@pillsbury.edu

University of Minnesota
2900 University Ave, Crookston MN 56716-5001
218-281-6510 Fax: 218-281-8575
Website:
admissions.umcrookston.edu/requirements/apply.htm
E-mail: info@umcrookston.edu

MISSISSIPPI

Tougaloo College
500 W County Line Rd, Tougaloo MS 39174-9799
Juno Leggette Jacobs, Director of Admissions
601-977-7768 Fax: 601-977-4501
Website: www.tougaloo.edu
E-mail: jjacobs@tougaloo.edu

MISSOURI

Central Methodist University
411 Central Methodist Sq, Fayette MO 65248-1198
Larry Anderson, Director of Admissions
660-248-6247 Fax: 660-248-1872
Website: www.centralmethodist.edu
E-mail: landerso@centralmethodist.edu

Cleveland Chiropractic College - Kansas City Campus
6401 Rockhill Rd, Kansas City MO 64131-1122
Melissa Denton, Director of Admissions
800-467-CCKC (2252) or 816-501-0100
Fax: 816-501-0205
Website: www.cleveland.edu
E-mail: kc.admissions@cleveland.edu

East Central College
1964 Prairie Dell Rd, Union MO 63084
Karen Wieda, Registrar
636-583-5195 ext. 2220 Fax: 636-583-1897
Website: www.eastcentral.edu
E-mail: wiedaks@eastcentral.edu

Lindenwood University
209 S Kingshighway St
Saint Charles MO 63301-1695
Sheryl Guffey, Director of Admissions
636-949-2000 Fax: 636-949-4989
Website: www.lindenwood.edu

Northwest Missouri State University
800 University Dr, Maryville MO 64468-6001
Beverly Schenkel, Dean of Enrollment Management
660-562-1562 Fax: 660-562-1121
Website: www.nwmissouri.edu
E-mail: admissions@nwmissouri.edu

Stephens College
PO Box 2121, Columbia MO 65215-0001
David Adams, Dean of Enrollment Management
573-442-2211 Fax: 573-876-7237
Website: www.stephens.edu
E-mail: dadams@stephens.edu

Truman State University
100 E Normal, Kirksville MO 63501
Office of Admission
660-785-4114 Fax: 660-785-7456
Website: admissions.truman.edu
E-mail: admissions@truman.edu

University of Missouri
1 University Blvd, Saint Louis MO 63121-4499
Dr. Mark Burkholder, Dean-College of Arts & Sciences
314-516-5458 Fax: 314-516-6759
Website: www.umsl.edu
E-mail: admissions@umsl.edu

Webster University
470 E Lockwood Ave, Saint Louis MO 63119-3194
Dr. Ron Gaddis, Chairman, Biological Sciences
314-968-7160 Fax: 314-968-7194
Website: www.webster.edu
E-mail: rgaddis@webster.edu
See listing under "Universities"

William Jewell College
500 College Hill, Liberty MO 64068-1896
Dr. Rick Winslow, VP Enrollment Management and Student Affairs
800-753-7009 Fax: 816-415-5040
Website: www.jewell.edu
E-mail: winslowr@william.jewell.edu

William Woods University
1 University Ave, Fulton MO 65251-1098
Jimmy Clay, Director of Admissions
573-642-2251 Fax: 573-592-1146
Website: www.williamwoods.edu
E-mail: admissions@williamwoods.edu
See listing under "Universities"

MONTANA

Carroll College
1601 N Benton Ave, Helena MT 59625-0002
Dr. Thomas J. Trebon, President
Cynthia Thornquist, Director of Admissions & Enrollment Operations
406-447-4384 Fax: 406-447-4533
Website: www.carroll.edu
E-mail: admission@carroll.edu

NEBRASKA

Midland Lutheran College
900 N Clarkson St, Fremont NE 68025-4200
Todd Hansen, Associate Director of Admissions
402-941-6501 Fax: 402-941-6513
Website: www.mlc.edu
E-mail: admissions@mlc.edu

Nebraska Wesleyan University
5000 Saint Paul Ave, Lincoln NE 68504-2794
Patricia Karthauser, V.P. for University Enrollment
402-466-2371 Fax: 402-465-2177
Website: www.nebrwesleyan.edu
E-mail: admissions@nebrwesleyan.edu

University of Nebraska at Kearney
905 W 25th St, Kearney NE 68849-0001
Dusty Newton, Director of Admissions
800-KEARNEY Fax: 308-865-8987
Website: www.unk.edu
E-mail: admissionsug@unk.edu

NEW JERSEY

New Jersey City University
2039 John F Kennedy Blvd
Jersey City NJ 07305-1588
Carmen Panlilio, Asst. V.P. for Admissions and Financial Aid
201-200-3234 Fax: 201-200-2044
Website: www.njcu.edu
E-mail: admissions@njcu.edu

Ramapo College of New Jersey
505 Ramapo Valley Rd, Mahwah NJ 07430-1623
Director of Admissions
201-684-7300 or 201-684-7301 Fax: 201-684-7964
Website: www.ramapo.edu
E-mail: admissions@ramapo.edu

RICHARD STOCKTON COLLEGE OF NEW JERSEY

PO Box 195, Pomona NJ 08240
John Iacovelli, Dean of Enrollment Management
866-RSC-2885 Fax: 609-626-5541
Website: www.stockton.edu
E-mail: admissions@stockton.edu

Stockton College is a comprehensive liberal arts, co-ed institution founded in 1969. Advance Pre-Professional Degree Options: 7-yr BS/MD with UMDNJ; NJ Dental School; NJ Medical School, Robert Wood Johnson Medical, School of Osteopathic Medicine; NY College of Podiatric Medicine, Pennsylvania College of Podiatric Medicine, SUNY College of Optometry. Pharmacy doctorate program with Rutgers University. 5-yr Engineering with NJIT and Rutgers University. Dual BA/MA in Criminal Justice. 5-yr BS/MS in Computational Science. BS/MS in Nursing. Doctorate of Physical Therapy. Additional Programs: Forensic Science, Pre-Law, Pre-Occupational Therapy, and Pre-Veterinary.

NEW MEXICO

College of the Southwest
6610 N Lovington Hwy, Hobbs NM 88240-9129
Dr. Steve Hill, Dean of Recuitment
505-392-6561 Fax: 505-392-6006
Website: www.csw.edu
E-mail: shill@csw.edu

New Mexico Military Institute
101 W College Blvd, Roswell NM 88201-5173
LTC. Steven D. Klein, VP, Enrollment & Marketing
800-421-5376 or 505-624-8050 Fax: 505-624-8058
Website: www.nmmi.edu
E-mail: admissions@nmmi.edu
See listing under "Community and Junior Colleges"

New Mexico State University
1500 N 3rd St, Grants NM 87020-2025
Irene Lutz, Director of Admissions
505-287-7981 Fax: 505-287-2329
Website: www.grants.nmsu.edu
E-mail: ilutz@nmsu.edu

NEW YORK

ALBANY COLLEGE OF PHARMACY

106 New Scotland Ave, Albany NY 12208-3492
Carly Connors, Director of Admissions
888-203-8010 Fax: 518-694-7322
Website: www.acp.edu
E-mail: admissions@acp.edu

College of Saint Rose
432 Western Ave, Albany NY 12203-1419
Maryelizabeth Amico, Asst V.P. for Undergraduate Admissions
518-454-5150 Fax: 518-454-2013
Website: www.strose.edu
E-mail: admit@strose.edu

CUNY Hunter College
695 Park Ave, New York NY 10021
Aaron Gibbs, Assistant Director of Recruitment
212-650-3946 Fax: 212-650-3336
Website: www.hunter.cuny.edu
E-mail: aaron.gibbs@hunter.cuny.edu

Daemen College
4380 Main St, Amherst NY 14226-3592
Donna Shaffner, Director of Admissions
800-462-7652 Fax: 716-839-8229
Website: www.daemen.edu/admissions
E-mail: admissions@daemen.edu

Dowling College
150 Idle Hour Blvd, Oakdale NY 11769-1999
Diane Kazanecki-Kempter, Contact
631-244-3000 Fax: 631-244-1059
Website: www.dowling.edu
E-mail: admissions@dowling.edu

Iona College
715 North Ave, New Rochelle NY 10801-1890
Kevin Cavanagh, Assistant V.P. for College Admissions
914-633-2502 Fax: 914-637-2778
Website: www.iona.edu

Long Island University-C. W. Post Campus
720 Northern Blvd, Brookville NY 11548-1300
Joanne Graziano, Executive Director of Admissions
516-299-2900 Fax: 516-299-2137
Website: www.liu.edu/cwpost
E-mail: enroll@cwpost.liu.edu

Marymount Manhattan College
221 E 71st St, New York NY 10021-4501
Jim Rogers, Dean of Admissions
800-MARYMOUNT Fax: 212-517-0448
Website: www.mmm.edu
E-mail: admissions@mmm.edu

Molloy College
1000 Hempstead Ave
Rockville Centre NY 11570-1100
Marguerite Lane, Director of Admissions
516-678-5000 ext. 6291 Fax: 516-256-2247
Website: www.molloy.edu
E-mail: admissions@molloy.edu
See listing under "Universities"

PURCHASE COLLEGE STATE UNIVERSITY OF NEW YORK (SUNY)

735 Anderson Hill Rd, Purchase NY 10577-1400
Stephanie McCaine, Director of Admissions
914-251-6300 Fax: 914-251-6314
Website: www.purchase.edu
E-mail: admisn@purchase.edu
See listing under "Universities"

Roberts Wesleyan College
2301 Westside Dr, Rochester NY 14624-1997
Office of Admissions
585-594-6400 Fax: 585-594-6371
Website: www.roberts.edu
E-mail: admissions@roberts.edu

St. John's University
8000 Utopia Pkwy, Queens NY 11439
Office of Admission
877-STJ-5550 ext. 101 Fax: 718-990-2096
Website: www.stjohns.edu/learnmore
E-mail: admhelp@stjohns.edu
See listing under "Universities"

St. Joseph's College
245 Clinton Ave, Brooklyn NY 11205-3688
Theresa LaRocca Meyer, V.P. for Enrollment Management
718-636-6800 Fax: 718-636-8303
Website: www.sjcny.edu
E-mail: tlaroccameyer@sjcny.edu

Siena College
515 Loudonville Rd, Loudonville NY 12211-1462
Heather Renault, Director of Admissions
518-783-2300 Fax: 518-783-2436
Website: www.siena.edu
E-mail: hrenault@siena.edu

SUNY College at Brockport
350 New Campus Dr, Brockport NY 14420-2997
Bernard S. Valento, Director of Undergraduate Admissions
585-395-2751 Fax: 585-395-5452
Website: www.brockport.edu
E-mail: admit@brockport.edu

SUNY College of Technology
Alfred NY 14802
Deborah J. Goodrich, Associate VP Enrollment Mgmt.
800-4AL-FRED Fax: 607-587-4299
Website: www.alfredstate.edu
E-mail: admissions@alfredstate.edu

SUNY Orange County Community College
115 South St, Middletown NY 10940-6437
Margot St. Lawrence, Director of Admissions
845-341-4030 Fax: 845-342-8662
Website: www.sunyorange.edu
E-mail: apply@sunyorange.edu
See listing under "Community and Junior Colleges"

SUNY Sullivan County Community College
112 College Rd, Loch Sheldrake NY 12759-5151
Sari Rosenheck, Director of Admissions
845-434-5750 Fax: 845-434-0923
Website: www.sullivan.suny.edu
E-mail: admissions@sullivan.suny.edu
Student Housing on Campus.

Wells College
PO Box 500, Aurora NY 13026
Susan Sloan, Director of Admissions
800-952-9355 Fax: 315-364-3227
Website: www.wells.edu
E-mail: ssloan@wells.edu

NORTH CAROLINA

Catawba College
2300 W Innes St, Salisbury NC 28144-2488
Dr. L. Russell Watjen, Ph.D., V.P. & Dean of Admissions
704-637-4402 Fax: 704-637-4222
Website: www.catawba.edu
E-mail: admission@catawba.edu

Chowan University
One University Pl, Murfreesboro NC 27855
Chad Holt, Dean of Admissions
800-488-4101 Fax: 252-398-1190
Website: www.chowan.edu
E-mail: holtc@chowan.edu

Peace College
15 E Peace St, Raleigh NC 27604-1194
Laura C. Bingham, President
800-PEACE-47 Fax: 919-508-2306
Website: www.peace.edu
E-mail: admissions@peace.edu

Salem College
Winston Salem NC 27108
Dana Evans, Dean of Admissions/Fin. Aid
800-32-SALEM Fax: 336-917-5572
Website: www.salem.edu
E-mail: admissions@salem.edu
See listing under "Women's Colleges"

NORTH DAKOTA

Dickinson State University
Dickinson ND 58601-4896
Steve Glasser, Director of Enrollment Services
800-279-4295 Fax: 701-483-2409
Website: www.dickinsonstate.edu
E-mail: dsu.hawks@dickinsonstate.edu

Valley City State University
101 College St SW, Valley City ND 58072-4024
Dan Klein, Director of Enrollment Services
800-532-8641 ext. 7101 Fax: 701-845-7299
Website: www.vcsu.edu
E-mail: enrollment.services@vcsu.edu
See listing under "Universities"

OHIO

Cleveland State University
2121 Euclid Ave RW 204, Cleveland OH 44115
Dr. Richard Arndt, Dean of Undergraduate Recruitment and College Partnerships
888-CSU-OHIO Fax: 216-687-9210
Website: www.csuohio.edu
E-mail: admissions@csuohio.edu

Franciscan University of Steubenville
University Blvd, Steubenville OH 43952
Margaret J. Weber, Director of Admissions
800-783-6220 or 740-283-6226 Fax: 740-284-5456
Website: www.admissions.edu
E-mail: mweber@franciscan.edu

OHIO NORTHERN UNIVERSITY

525 S Main St, Ada OH 45810-1555
Terry Keiser, Chair of Biological Sciences Dept.
419-772-2325
Website: www.onu.edu
E-mail: admissions-ug@onu.edu
See listing under "Universities"

The Ohio State University
College of Biological Sciences
Biological Sciences Bldg, 484 W 12th Ave
Columbus OH 43210
614-292-8772
Website: www.biosci.ohio-state.edu

OHIO WESLEYAN UNIVERSITY

61 S Sandusky St, Delaware OH 43015-2398
Director of Admission
740-368-3020 Fax: 740-368-3314
Website: www.owu.edu
E-mail: owuadmit@owu.edu

Owens Community College
3200 Bright Rd, Findlay OH 45840
William J. Ivoska PhD., Vice President of Student Services
567-429-3500 Fax: 567-423-0246
Website: www.owens.edu
E-mail: admissions@owens.edu

Owens Community College
PO Box 10000, Toledo OH 43699-1947
William J. Ivoska, Ph.D, Vice President of Student Services
567-661-7000 Fax: 567-661-7607
Website: www.owens.edu
E-mail: admissions@owens.edu

University of Dayton
300 College Park, Dayton OH 45469-1300
Robert F. Durkle, Director of Admission
800-837-7433 Fax: 937-229-4729
Website: admission.udayton.edu
E-mail: admission@udayton.edu

Ursuline College
2550 Lander Rd, Cleveland OH 44124-4398
Sarah E. Sundermeier, Director of Admissions
888-URSULINE Toll Free Fax: 440-684-6138
Website: www.admission.ursuline.edu
E-mail: admission@ursuline.edu

OKLAHOMA

Oklahoma State University
Stillwater OK 74078
James Shaw, Department Head
405-744-5555
Website: www.okstate.edu
E-mail: shawjh@okstate.edu

University of Tulsa
600 S College Ave, Tulsa OK 74104-3126
Earl Johnson, Dean of Admission
918-631-2307 Fax: 918-631-5003
Website: www.utulsa.edu
E-mail: admission@utulsa.edu

OREGON

Cascade College
9101 E Burnside St, Portland OR 97216-1599
Jim Murphy, Director of Enrollment Management
800-550-7678 Fax: 503-257-1222
Website: www.cascade.edu
E-mail: admissions@cascade.edu

Concordia University
2811 NE Holman St, Portland OR 97211-6099
Bobi Swan, Director of Admissions
503-288-9371 Fax: 503-280-8531
Website: www.cu-portland.edu
E-mail: cu-admissions@cu-portland.edu

Linn-Benton Community College
6500 Pacific Blvd SW, Albany OR 97321-3774
Christine Baker, Outreach Coordinator
541-917-4811 Fax: 541-917-4868
Website: www.linnbenton.edu
E-mail: admissions@linnbenton.edu

Warner Pacific College
2219 SE 68th Ave, Portland OR 97215-4026
Shannon Mackey, Director of Admissions
503-517-1000 Fax: 503-517-1352
Website: www.warnerpacific.edu
E-mail: admissions@warnerpacific.edu

PENNSYLVANIA

Clarion University of Pennsylvania
840 Wood St, Clarion PA 16214-1232
William Bailey, Dean of Enrollment Management
814-393-2306 Fax: 814-393-2030
Website: www.clarion.edu
E-mail: admissions@clarion.edu

Community College of Allegheny County
Allegheny Campus: 808 Ridge Ave, Pittsburgh PA 15212 Admissions: 412.237.2700
Boyce Campus: 595 Beatty Rd, Monroeville PA 15146 Admissions: 724.325.6614
North Campus: 8701 Perry Highway, Pittsburgh PA 15237 Admissions: 412.369.3600
South Campus: 1750 Clairton Rd, West Mifflin PA 15122 Admissions: 412-469-4301
Website: www.ccac.edu

Delaware Valley College
700 E Butler Ave, Doylestown PA 18901-2697
Stephen W. Zenko, Director of Admissions
800-2DE-LVAL Fax: 215-230-2968
Website: www.delval.edu
E-mail: stephenzenko@delval.edu

DeSales University
2755 Station Ave, Center Valley PA 18034-9565
610-282-1100 Fax: 610-282-2342
Website: www.desales.edu

Holy Family University
9801 Frankford Avenue, Philadelphia PA 19114
Lauren Campbell, Director of Admissions
215-637-3050 Fax: 215-281-1022
Website: www.holyfamily.edu
E-mail: admissions@holyfamily.edu

Juniata College
1700 Moore St, Huntingdon PA 16652-2196
Michelle Bartol, Dean of Enrollment
877-JUNIATA Fax: 814-641-3100
Website: www.juniata.edu
E-mail: admissions@juniata.edu

King's College
133 N River St, Wilkes Barre PA 18711-0801
Michelle Lawrence-Schmude, Dean of Admission
570-208-5900 Fax: 570-208-5971
Website: www.kings.edu
E-mail: admissions@kings.edu

MOUNT ALOYSIUS COLLEGE

7373 Admiral Peary Hwy, Cresson PA 16630-1999
Frank C. Crouse Jr., Vice President for Enrollment Management
814-886-6383 or 888-823-2220 Fax: 814-886-6441
Website: www.mtaloy.edu
E-mail: admissions@mtaloy.edu

Neumann College
1 Neumann Dr, Aston PA 19014-1298
Dennis Murphy, Director of Admissions
610-459-0905 Fax: 610-558-5652
Website: www.neumann.edu
E-mail: neumann@neumann.edu

Washington & Jefferson College
60 S Lincoln St, Washington PA 15301-4801
Alton E. Newell, Vice President for Enrollment
724-223-6025 Fax: 724-223-6534
Website: www.washjeff.edu
E-mail: admission@washjeff.edu

Widener University
1 University Pl, Chester PA 19013-5792
Edwin Wright, Dean of Admissions
610-499-4000 Fax: 610-499-4676
Website: www.widener.edu
E-mail: admissions.office@widener.edu

SOUTH CAROLINA

Bob Jones University
1700 Wade Hampton Blvd
Greenville SC 29614-0001
David Christ, Director of Admissions
800-BJ-AND-ME Fax: 800-2-FAX-BJU
Website: www.bju.edu
E-mail: admissions@bju.edu
See listing under "Universities"

Coastal Carolina University
PO Box 261954, Conway SC 29528-6054
Office of Admissions
800-277-7000 Fax: 843-349-2127
Website: www.coastal.edu
E-mail: admissions@coastal.edu

Erskine College & Seminary
PO Box 176, Due West SC 29639
Bart Walker, Director of Admissions
864-379-8838 Fax: 864-379-3048
Website: www.erskine.edu
E-mail: admissions@erskine.edu

Limestone College
1115 College Dr, Gaffney SC 29340-3799
Chris Phenicie, V.P. for Enrollment
864-489-7151 Fax: 864-488-8206
Website: www.limestone.edu
E-mail: cphenicie@limestone.edu

North Greenville University
PO Box 1892, Tigerville SC 29688-1892
Website: www.ngu.edu
See listing under "Universities"

University of South Carolina - Upstate
800 University Way, Spartanburg SC 29303-4932
Donette Stewart, Assistant VC for Enrollment Services
864-503-5246 Fax: 864-503-5727
Website: www.uscupstate.edu
E-mail: dstewart@uscupstate.edu
See listing under "Universities"

SOUTH DAKOTA

Presentation College
1500 N Main St, Aberdeen SD 57401-1280
JoEllen Lindner, VP for Enrollment
605-229-8492 Fax: 605-229-8425
Website: www.presentation.edu
E-mail: admit@presentation.edu

TENNESSEE

Austin Peay State University
601 College St, Clarksville TN 37044-0002
931-221-7011 Fax: 931-221-6168
Website: www.apsu.edu
E-mail: admissions@apsu.edu

Crichton College
255 N Highland St, Memphis TN 38111-4745
Shelly Luttrell, Dean of Admissions
901-320-9797 Fax: 901-320-9791
Website: www.crichton.edu
E-mail: admissions@crichton.edu

Free Will Baptist Bible College
3606 W End Ave, Nashville TN 37205
Ryan Lewis, Director of Recruitment
800-76-FWBBC Fax: 615-269-6028
Website: www.fwbbc.edu
E-mail: recruit@fwbbc.edu

Lipscomb University
3901 Granny White Pike, Nashville TN 37204-3951
Ricky Holaway, Director of Admissions
800-333-4358 ext. 1776 Fax: 615-269-1804
Website: www.lipscomb.edu
E-mail: admissions@lipscomb.edu

Southwest Tennessee Community College
5983 Macon Cove, Memphis TN 38134
Vanessa R. Dowdy, Director of Admissions
901-333-5000 Fax: 901-333-4523
Website: www.southwest.tn.edu
E-mail: vdowdy@southwest.tn.edu

Tennessee State University
3500 John A Merritt Blvd, Nashville TN 37209-1561
John Cade, Dean of Admissions & Records
615-963-5101 Fax: 615-963-2930
Website: www.tnstate.edu
E-mail: jcade@tnstate.edu

University of Tennessee
615 McCallie Ave, Chattanooga TN 37403-2504
Yancy Freeman, Director of Admissions
423-425-4111 Fax: 423-425-4157
Website: www.utc.edu
E-mail: Yancy-Freeman@utc.edu

TEXAS

Abilene Christian University
ACU Box 29000, Abilene TX 79699-0001
325-674-2000 Fax: 325-674-2202
Website: www.acu.edu
E-mail: info@admissions.acu.edu

Galveston College
4015 Avenue Q, Galveston TX 77550-7496
Brian Lowery, Registrar
409-763-6551 Fax: 409-944-1501
Website: www.gc.edu
E-mail: blowery@gc.edu

Lubbock Christian University
5601 19th St, Lubbock TX 79407-2099
Stan Scott, Director of Admissions
806-796-8800 Fax: 806-720-7162
Website: www.lcu.edu
E-mail: stan.scott@lcu.edu

Parker College of Chiropractic
2500 Walnut Hill Ln, Dallas TX 75229-5609
Andrea Robles, Asst. Director of Admissions
972-438-6932 Fax: 214-902-2413
Website: www.parkercc.edu
E-mail: admissions@parkercc.edu

Temple College
2600 S 1st St, Temple TX 76504-7435
Toni Borras, Director of Admissions & Records
254-298-8808 Fax: 254-298-8288
Website: www.templejc.edu
E-mail: admissionsrecords@templejc.edu

Texas Woman's University
PO Box 425589, Denton TX 76204-5589
Erma Nieto-Brecht, Director of Admissions
866-809-6130 Fax: 940-898-3081
Website: www.twu.edu
E-mail: admissions@twu.edu

Tyler Junior College
PO Box 9020, Tyler TX 75711-9020
Joan Jones, Interim Dean
800-687-5680
Website: www.tjc.edu
E-mail: jjon@tjc.edu
See listing under "Community and Junior Colleges"

University of Dallas
1845 E Northgate Dr, Irving TX 75062-4736
Curt Eley, Dean
972-721-5000 Fax: 972-721-5017
Website: www.udallas.edu
E-mail: ugadmis@udallas.edu

University of Houston
122 E Cullen Bldg, Houston TX 77204-2023
Office of Admission
713-743-9595
Website: www.uh.edu
E-mail: admissions@uh.edu

University of Texas at Arlington
Box 19111, Arlington TX 76019-0111
Hans Gatterdam, Director of Admission
817-272-6287 Fax: 817-272-3435
Website: www.uta.edu
E-mail: admissions@uta.edu

Weatherford College
225 College Park Dr, Weatherford TX 76086
Dr. Joe Birmingham, President
800-287-5471 Fax: 817-598-6205
Website: www.wc.edu
E-mail: willingham@wc.edu

VERMONT

NORWICH UNIVERSITY

158 Harmon Dr, Northfield VT 05663
Dr. Eduardo Hernandez, Department Head
800-468-6679 Fax: 802-485-2333
Website: www.norwich.edu
E-mail: ehernand@norwich.edu
See listing under "Universities"

VIRGINIA

Mary Baldwin College
Staunton VA 24401
Lisa A. Branson, Executive Director of Admissions and Financial Aid
800-468-2262 Fax: 540-887-7292
Website: www.mbc.edu
E-mail: admit@mbc.edu

Radford University
PO Box 6903, Radford VA 24142
David W. Kraus, Director of Admissions
800-890-4265 Fax: 540-831-5038
Website: www.radford.edu
E-mail: ruadmiss@radford.edu

Randolph College
2500 Rivermont Ave, Lynchburg VA 24503
Patricia LeDonne, Director of Admissions
434-947-8100 Fax: 434-947-8996
Website: www.randolphcollege.edu
E-mail: admissions@randolphcollege.edu

Roanoke College
221 College Ln, Salem VA 24153-3794
James A. Pennix, Director of Admissions
540-375-2500 Fax: 540-375-2267
Website: www.roanoke.edu
E-mail: pennix@roanoke.edu

University of Mary Washington
1301 College Ave, Fredericksburg VA 22401-5300
Dr. Martin A. Wilder, Jr., Director of Admissions
540-654-2000 Fax: 540-654-1857
Website: www.umw.edu
E-mail: admit@umw.edu

WEST VIRGINIA

Davis & Elkins College
100 Campus Dr, Elkins WV 26241-3996
Renee Heckel, Director of Enrollment Management
800-624-3157 Fax: 304-637-1800
Website: www.davisandelkins.edu
E-mail: admiss@davisandelkins.edu

Fairmont State University
1201 Locust Ave, Fairmont WV 26554-2470
Steve Leadman, Director of Admissions
304-367-4642 or 800-641-5678 Fax: 304-367-4789
Website: www.fairmontstate.edu
E-mail: admit@fairmontstate.edu

Mountain State University
Box 9003, Beckley WV 25802-9003
Tony England, Director of Admissions
866-FOR-MSU1 or 304-929-INFO Fax: 304-253-5072
Website: www.mountainstate.edu
E-mail: gomsu@mountainstate.edu
See listing under "Universities"

WISCONSIN

Alverno College
PO Box 343922, Milwaukee WI 53234-3922
Dianna Gaebler, Director of Admissions
414-382-6100 Fax: 414-382-6354
Website: www.alverno.edu
E-mail: admissions@alverno.edu

Lakeland College
PO Box 359, Sheboygan WI 53082-0359
Nathan Dehne, Director of Admission
920-565-1100 Fax: 920-565-1215
Website: www.lakeland.edu
E-mail: admissions@lakeland.edu

Marquette University
PO Box 1881, Milwaukee WI 53201-1881
Robert Blust, Director of Admissions
414-288-7302 Fax: 414-288-3764
Website: www.mu.edu
E-mail: admissions@marquette.edu

St. Norbert College
100 Grant St, De Pere WI 54115
Brian Studebaker, Director of Admission
800-236-4878 Fax: 920-403-4072
Website: www.snc.edu
E-mail: admit@snc.edu

WYOMING

Laramie County Community College
1400 E College Dr, Cheyenne WY 82007-3204
Jenny Hargett, Director of Admissions
307-778-5222 Fax: 307-778-1350
Website: www.lccc.wy.edu
E-mail: learnmore@lccc.wy.edu

University of Wyoming
Admissions Office
Dept 3435, Laramie WY 82071-3435
Brooke Culver, Contact
800-342-5996 Fax: 307-766-4042
Website: www.uwyo.edu
E-mail: why-wyo@uwyo.edu

GUAM

University of Guam
UOG Station, Mangilao GU 96923
Deborah Leon Guerrero, Registrar
671-735-2201 or 671-735-2208 Fax: 671-735-2203
Website: www.uog.edu
E-mail: admitme@uog9.uog.edu

BUSINESS - ADMINISTRATIVE SUPPORT

ALABAMA

Herzing College
280 W Valley Ave, Homewood AL 35209-4816
Kim Conway, Director of Admissions
205-916-2800 Fax: 205-916-2807
Website: www.herzing.edu/birmingham
E-mail: info@bhm.herzing.edu

Trenholm State Technical College
Trenholm Campus
1225 Air Base Blvd, Montgomery AL 36108-3199
Dr. Anthony Molina, President
334-420-4200 Fax: 334-420-4206
Website: www.trenholmtech.cc.al.us
E-mail: molinaa@trenholmtech.cc.al.us

ALASKA

University of Alaska Anchorage
PO Box 141629, Anchorage AK 99514-1629
Cecile Mitchell, Director of Enrollment Services
907-786-1480 Fax: 907-786-4888
Website: www.uaa.alaska.edu/
E-mail: enroll@uaa.alaska.edu

ARIZONA

Apollo College
630 W Southern Ave, Mesa AZ 85210-5005
480-831-6585 Fax: 480-827-0022

Apollo College
8503 N 27th Ave, Phoenix AZ 85051-4063
602-864-1571 Fax: 602-864-8207

Apollo College
2701 W Bethany Home Rd, Phoenix AZ 85017-1705
602-433-1333 Fax: 602-433-1414

Apollo College
3550 N Oracle Rd, Tucson AZ 85705
520-888-5885 Fax: 520-887-3005

International Institute of the Americas
925 S Gilbert Rd Ste 201, Mesa AZ 85204-4440
Todd Olehausen, Director
480-545-8755 Fax: 480-926-1371
Website: www.iia.edu
E-mail: tolehausen@iia.edu

International Institute of the Americas
6049 N 43rd Ave, Phoenix AZ 85019-1600
John Pechota, Director of Admissions
602-242-6265 Fax: 602-589-1353
Website: www.iia.edu
E-mail: jpechota@iia.edu

International Institute of the Americas
5441 E 22nd St, Tucson AZ 85710
Leigh Anne Pechota, Director
520-748-9799 Fax: 520-748-9355
Website: www.iia.edu
E-mail: lpechota@iia.edu

Pima Community College
4905 E Broadway Blvd, Tucson AZ 85709-1010
Wendy Kilgore, Ph.D., Director of Admissions
520-206-4500 Fax: 520-206-4790
Website: www.pima.edu
E-mail: infocenter@pima.edu

ARKANSAS

Northwest Technical Institute
709 S Old Missouri Rd, Springdale AR 72764
Charles L. Kelley, President
479-751-8824 Fax: 479-751-7780
Website: www.nti.tec.ar.us
E-mail: info@nit.tec.ar.us

Phillips Community College of the University of Arkansas
PO Box 785, Helena AR 72342-0785
Dr. Steven Murray, Chancellor
Lynn Boone, Vice Chancellor for Student Services / Registrar
870-338-6474 Fax: 870-338-7542
Website: www.pccua.edu
E-mail: lboone@pccua.edu

CALIFORNIA

Butte College
3536 Butte Campus Dr, Oroville CA 95965-8399
Carole Gish, Director of Admissions
530-895-2511 Fax: 530-879-4313
Website: www.butte.edu
E-mail: admissions@butte.edu

Chabot College
25555 Hesperian Blvd, Hayward CA 94545-2400
Judy Young, Director of Admissions
510-723-6600 Fax: 510-723-7510
Website: www.chabotcollege.edu
E-mail: ccarcom@clpccd.cc.ca.us

FRESNO CITY COLLEGE
1101 E University Ave, Fresno CA 93741-0002
Dayann Dietrich, Contact
559-442-8241 Fax: 559-237-4232
Website: www.fresnocitycollege.com
E-mail: fcc.admissions@scccd.com

HEALD COLLEGE, MILPITAS
341 Great Mall Pkwy, Milpitas CA 95035-8008
Sharon Kitko, Director's Assistant
408-934-4900 Fax: 408-934-7777
Website: www.heald.edu

MARIC COLLEGE
14355 Roscoe Blvd, Panorama City CA 91402-4222
Linda King, Contact
818-672-3000 Fax: 818-672-8919
Website: www.mariccollege.edu
E-mail: lking@mariccollege.edu

MTI BUSINESS COLLEGE OF STOCKTON
6006 N El Dorado St, Stockton CA 95207-4349
Steven Brenner, Director
888-302-2009 Fax: 209-474-8705
Website: www.mtistockton.com
E-mail: mtistockton@comcast.net
Established 1968. Accredited: ACCSCT. Family owned/operated 36 years.

MTI College
5221 Madison Ave, Sacramento CA 95841-3003
Marije Miller, Director of Admissions
916-339-1500 Fax: 916-339-0305
Website: www.mticollege.edu
E-mail: mmiller@mticollege.edu

Orange Coast College
PO Box 5005, Costa Mesa CA 92628-5005
Kristin Clark, Director of Admissions
714-432-5773 Fax: 714-432-5736
Website: www.orangecoastcollege.edu
E-mail: kclark@cccd.edu

Point Loma Nazarene University
3900 Lomaland Dr, San Diego CA 92106-2810
Chip Killingsworth, Director of Undergraduate Admissions
800-733-7770 Fax: 619-849-2601
Website: www.pointloma.edu
E-mail: admissions@pointloma.edu

San Bernardino Valley College
701 S Mount Vernon Ave
San Bernardino CA 92410-2798
Kay Ragan, Ed.D., Director of Admissions
909-888-6511 Fax: 909-889-4988
Website: www.valleycollege.edu
E-mail: kragan@sbccd.cc.ca.us

San Joaquin Valley College
201 New Stine Rd, Bakersfield CA 93309-2659
Jaime Delgado, Enrollment Services Director
661-834-1026 Fax: 559-651-4864
Website: www.sjvc.edu
E-mail: jaime.delgado@sjvc.edu

San Joaquin Valley College
295 E Sierra Ave, Fresno CA 93710-3616
Nora Twarynski, Enrollment Services Director
559-448-8282 Fax: 559-651-4864
Website: www.sjvc.edu
E-mail: nora.twarynski@sjvc.edu

San Joaquin Valley College
1700 McHenry Village Way Suite 6
Modesto CA 95350
Joseph Holt, Director of Admissions
209-527-7582 Fax: 559-651-4864
Website: www.sjvc.edu
E-mail: josephh@sjvc.edu

San Joaquin Valley College
11050 Olson Dr, Rancho Cordova CA 95670
Joseph Holt, Director of Admissions
559-651-2500 Fax: 559-651-4864
Website: www.sjvc.edu
E-mail: joseph.holt@sjvc.edu

San Joaquin Valley College
10641 Church St, Rancho Cucamonga CA 91730
Ramon Abreu, Enrollment Services Director
909-948-7582 Fax: 559-651-4864
Website: www.sjvc.edu
E-mail: ramon.abreu@sjvc.edu

San Joaquin Valley College
8400 W Mineral King Ave, Visalia CA 93291-9283
Susie Topjian, Enrollment Services Director
559-651-2500 Fax: 559-651-4864
Website: www.sjvc.edu
E-mail: susiet@sjvc.edu

COLORADO

Colorado Northwestern Community College
500 Kennedy Dr, Rangely CO 81648-3502
Tresa England, Director of Student Services
800-562-1105 Fax: 970-675-3343
Website: www.cncc.edu
E-mail: tresa.england@cncc.edu

Everest College
Aurora Campus
14280 E Jewell Ave, Aurora CO 80012-5692
John Heckman, Director of Admissions
303-367-2757 Fax: 303-745-6245
Website: www.cci.edu

IntelliTec College
772 Horizon Dr, Grand Junction CO 81506-3907
Jennifer Daniels, Contact
970-245-8101 Fax: 970-243-8074
Website: www.intelliteccollege.edu
E-mail: admgj@intelliteccollege.edu

IntelliTec College
3673 Parker Blvd Ste 250, Pueblo CO 81008
Crystal Barajas, Director of Admissions
719-542-3181 Fax: 719-242-0068
Website: www.intelliteccollege.edu
E-mail: admpbl@intelliteccollege.edu

San Juan Basin Technical College
PO Box 970, Cortez CO 81321-0970
Shannon South, Vice President
970-565-8457 Fax: 970-565-8450
Website: www.sjbtc.edu
E-mail: info@sjbtc.edu

CONNECTICUT

Middlesex Community College
100 Training Hill Rd, Middletown CT 06457-4889
Mensimah Shabazz, Director of Admissions
860-343-5800 Fax: 860-344-3055
Website: www.mxcc.commnet.edu
E-mail: mshabazz@mxcc.commnet.edu

DELAWARE

Goldey-Beacom College
4701 Limestone Rd, Wilmington DE 19808-1993
Stacey Schwartz, Assistant Director of Admissions
302-998-8814 Fax: 302-996-5408
Website: www.gbc.edu
E-mail: admissions@gbc.edu

FLORIDA

City College
2000 W Commercial Blvd, Fort Lauderdale FL 33309
Mercedes Segal, Director of Admissions
954-492-5353 Fax: 954-491-1965
Website: www.citycollege.edu

Florida National College
Hialeah Campus
4425 W 20th Ave, Hialeah FL 33012
Jorge Afonso, Campus Dean
305-821-3333 ext. 1022 Fax: 305-362-0595
Website: www.fnc.edu
E-mail: omarsnc@fnc.edu

Florida National College
South Campus
11865 SW 26th St, Miami FL 33175
Jon Beisenherz, Campus Dean
305-266-9999
Website: www.fnc.edu
E-mail: omarsnc@fnc.edu

Florida State University
600 W College Ave, Tallahassee FL 32306-1096
Janice V. Finney, Director of Admissions
850-644-2525 Fax: 850-644-0197
Website: admissions.fsu.edu
E-mail: admissions@admin.fsu.edu

Jones College
5353 Arlington Expy, Jacksonville FL 32211-5588
Dorothy D. Jones, Chief Executive Officer
904-743-1122 Fax: 904-744-4446
Website: www.jones.edu
E-mail: fmccaffe@jones.edu

Jones College
11430 N Kendall Dr Ste 200, Miami FL 33176
Patricia Carbonell, Contact
305-275-9996 Fax: 305-743-4446
Website: www.jones.edu
E-mail: pcarbone@jones.edu

Key College
225 E Dania Beach Blvd #130
Dania Beach FL 33004
Ronald Dooley, President
954-923-4440 Fax: 954-923-9226
Website: www.keycollege.edu
E-mail: admissions@keycollege.edu

Lincoln College of Technology
2410 Metrocentre Blvd
West Palm Beach FL 33407-3105
Don Cunningham, Vice President of Admissions
561-688-2001 Fax: 561-842-9503
Website: www.lincolncollegeoftechnology.com
E-mail: dcunningham@lincolntech.com

SOUTHWEST FLORIDA COLLEGE
1685 Medical Ln, Fort Myers FL 33907-1157
866-SWFC-NOW or 239-939-4766 Fax: 239-936-4040
Website: www.swfc.edu
E-mail: studentinfo@swfc.edu

GEORGIA

Kennesaw State University
1000 Chastain Rd NW, Kennesaw GA 30144-5591
Timothy Mescon, Dean of College of Business
770-423-6425
Website: www.kennesaw.edu

Medix School
2108 Cobb Pkwy SE, Smyrna GA 30080-7630
Berhan Bayleygn, Director of Admissions
770-980-0002
Website: www.medixschool.com

North Georgia Technical College
434 Meeks Ave, Blairsville GA 30512-2983
Admissions
706-439-6300 Fax: 706-439-6301
Website: www.northgatech.edu
E-mail: info@northgatech.edu

North Georgia Technical College
8989 Highway 17, Toccoa GA 30577
706-779-8100 Fax: 706-779-8130
Website: www.northgatech.edu
E-mail: info@northgatech.edu

North Georgia Technical College
Clarkesville Campus
PO Box 65, Clarkesville GA 30523-0002
Admissions
706-754-7700 Fax: 706-754-7777
Website: www.northgatech.edu
E-mail: info@northgatech.edu

North Metro Technical College
5198 Ross Rd SE, Acworth GA 30102-3129
Missy Cusack, Director of Admissions
770-975-4000 Fax: 770-975-4142
Website: www.northmetrotech.edu
E-mail: info@northmetrotech.edu

TOCCOA FALLS COLLEGE
PO Box 800899, Toccoa Falls GA 30598
888-785-5624 Fax: 706-282-6012
Website: www.tfc.edu
E-mail: admissions@tfc.edu

IDAHO

Brigham Young University - Idaho
120 Kimball Bldg, Rexburg ID 83460-1615
Rob Garrett, Director of Admissions
208-496-1020 Fax: 208-496-1220
Website: www.byui.edu
E-mail: admissions@byui.edu

ILLINOIS

Aurora University
347 S Gladstone Ave, Aurora IL 60506-4892
Carol R. Dunn, Ed.D., Vice President for Enrollment
800-742-5281 Fax: 630-844-5535
Website: www.aurora.edu
E-mail: admission@aurora.edu

College of Office Technology
1520 W Division St, Chicago IL 60622
Bill Bolton, Director of Admissions
773-278-0042 Fax: 773-278-0143
Website: www.cot.edu
E-mail: bbolton@cotedu.com

Kaskaskia College
27210 College Rd, Centralia IL 62801-7878
Tyra Taylor, Dean of Enrollment Management and Retention Services
618-545-3000 Fax: 618-532-1990
Website: www.kaskaskia.edu
E-mail: ttaylor@kaskaskia.edu

Sanford-Brown College
1101 Eastport Plaza Dr, Collinsville IL 62234-6108
Connie Frazier, Director of Admissions
618-344-5600
Website: www.sanford-brown.edu
E-mail: cfrazier@sbc-collinsville.com

SPANISH COALITION FOR JOBS
2011 W Pershing Rd, Chicago IL 60609
Henrietta Barcelo, Recruitment & Publicity Coordinator
773-247-0707 Fax: 773-247-3924
Website: www.scj-usa.org
E-mail: hbarcelo@scj-usa.org

INDIANA

Ancilla Domini College
Donaldson IN 46513
Erin Alonzo, Director of Admissions
574-936-8898 Fax: 574-935-1773
Website: www.ancilla.edu
E-mail: erin.alonzo@ancilla.edu

BROWN MACKIE COLLEGE - FORT WAYNE
3000 E Coliseum Blvd, Fort Wayne IN 46805
Daniel Summer, Campus President
260-484-4400 Fax: 260-484-2678
Website: www.brownmackie.edu

BROWN MACKIE COLLEGE - SOUTH BEND
1030 E Jefferson Blvd, South Bend IN 46617-3123
Connie Adelman, Campus President
574-237-0774 Fax: 574-237-3585
Website: www.brownmackie.edu

International Business College
5699 Coventry Ln, Fort Wayne IN 46804
260-459-4500 Fax: 260-436-1896
Website: www.ibcfortwayne.edu
E-mail: skinzer@ibcfortwayne.edu

Ivy Tech Community College - North Central
220 Dean Johnson Blvd, South Bend IN 46601-3415
Pam Decker, Director of Admissions
574-289-7001 Fax: 574-236-7177
Website: www.ivytech.edu
E-mail: pdecker@ivytech.edu

Oakland City University
138 N Lucretia St, Oakland City IN 47660
Brian J. Baker, Director of Admissions
800-737-5125 Fax: 812-749-1433
Website: www.oak.edu
E-mail: bbaker@oak.edu
See listing under "Universities"

IOWA

AIB College of Business
2500 Fleur Dr, Des Moines IA 50321-1799
800-444-1921 Fax: 515-244-6773
Website: www.aib.edu
E-mail: admissions@aib.edu

Hamilton College
7009 Nordic Dr, Cedar Falls IA 50613
Connie Reidy, Campus President
319-277-0220 Fax: 319-363-3812
Website: www.hamiltonia.edu
E-mail: coreidy@hamiltoncf.com

Hamilton College
3165 Edgewood Pkwy SW, Cedar Rapids IA 52404
Susan Spivey, Campus President
319-363-0481 Fax: 319-363-3812
Website: www.hamiltonia.edu
E-mail: sspivey@hamiltonia.edu

Hamilton College
1751 Madison Ave Ste 750, Council Bluffs IA 51503
Michael Zawisky, Executive Director
712-328-4212
Website: www.hamiltonia.edu
E-mail: mzawisky@hamiltonia.edu

Hamilton College
2570 4th St SW, Mason City IA 50401-4665
Joe Albers, Executive Director
641-423-2530 Fax: 641-423-7512
Website: www.hamiltonia.edu
E-mail: jalbers@hamiltonia.edu

Hamilton College
4655 121st St, Urbandale IA 50323-2311
Colleen McDermott, Campus President
515-727-2100 Fax: 515-727-2115
Website: www.hamiltonia.edu
E-mail: cmcdermott@hamiltonia.edu

Iowa Lakes Community College
3200 College Dr, Emmetsburg IA 50536-1055
Anne Stansbury, Asst. Director of Admissions
712-852-5212 Fax: 712-362-8363
Website: www.iowalakes.edu
E-mail: info@iowalakes.edu

Iowa Lakes Community College
300 S 18th St, Estherville IA 51334-2721
Anne Stansbury, Asst. Director of Admissions
712-362-7945 Fax: 712-362-8363
Website: www.iowalakes.edu
E-mail: info@iowalakes.edu

Iowa Lakes Community College
1900 Grand Ave, Suite 8, Spencer IA 51301
Anne Stansbury, Assistant Director of Admissions
712-262-7141 Fax: 712-262-4047
Website: www.iowalakes.edu
E-mail: info@iowalakes.edu

Northwest Iowa Community College
603 W Park St, Sheldon IA 51201-1046
Lisa Story, Director of Enrollment Management
712-324-5061 Fax: 712-324-4136
Website: www.nwicc.edu
E-mail: lstory@nwicc.edu

KANSAS

COLBY COMMUNITY COLLEGE
1255 S Range Ave, Colby KS 67701-4099
Director of Admissions
888-634-9350 or 785-460-4690 Fax: 785-460-4691
Website: www.colbycc.edu
E-mail: admissions@colbycc.edu

Flint Hills Technical College
3301 W 18th Ave, Emporia KS 66801-5957
Lisa Kirmer, Dean of Student Services
620-343-4600 Fax: 620-343-4610
Website: www.fhtc.net
E-mail: lkirmer@fhtc.net

Labette Community College
200 S 14th St, Parsons KS 67357-9966
Tammy Fuentez, Director of Admissions
620-421-6700 Fax: 620-421-2309
Website: www.labette.edu
E-mail: tammyf@labette.edu

PINNACLE CAREER INSTITUTE
1601 W 23rd St Ste 200, Lawrence KS 66046-2703
Lisa Allen, Admissions Representative
785-841-9640 Fax: 785-841-4854
Website: www.pcitraining.edu
E-mail: lallen@pcitraining.edu

Tabor College
400 S Jefferson St, Hillsboro KS 67063-1758
Rusty Allen, Dean of Enrollment Management
800-822-6799 Fax: 620-947-6276
Website: www.tabor.edu
E-mail: admissions@tabor.edu
See listing under "Universities"

KENTUCKY

BECKFIELD COLLEGE
16 Spiral Drive, Florence KY 41042
Leah Boerger, Contact
859-371-9393 Fax: 859-371-5096
Website: www.beckfield.edu
E-mail: lboerger@beckfield.edu

Brown Mackie College - Louisville
3605 Fern Valley Rd, Louisville KY 40219-1916
Mark Donahue, Director of Admissions
502-968-7191 Fax: 502-357-9956
Website: www.brownmackie.edu
E-mail: mdonahue@brownmackie.edu

BROWN MACKIE COLLEGE
Northern Kentucky Campus
309 Buttermilk Pike, Fort Mitchell KY 41017-2191
Joanne Dellefield, Director of Admissions
859-341-5627 Fax: 859-341-6483
Website: www.brownmackie.edu
E-mail: jdellefield@brownmackie.edu

Daymar College
3361 Buckland Sq, Owensboro KY 42301-5830
Vickie McDougal Director of Admissions
800-960-4090 Fax: 270-685-4090
Website: www.daymarcollege.com

Morehead State University
Morehead KY 40351-1689
Jeffrey Liles, Enrollment Services
800-585-6781 Fax: 606-783-5038
Website: www.moreheadstate.edu
E-mail: admissions@moreheadstate.edu

National College
115 E Lexington Ave, Danville KY 40422-1517
Gloria Walls, Director of Admissions
859-236-6991 Fax: 859-236-1063
Website: www.national-college.edu
E-mail: info@national-college.edu

National College
7627 Ewing Blvd, Florence KY 41042-1812
Doug Dedeker, Director of Admissions
859-525-6510 Fax: 859-525-8961
Website: www.national-college.edu
E-mail: info@national-college.edu

National College
2376 Sir Barton Way, Lexington KY 40509
Terry Fisher, Director of Admissions
859-253-0621 Fax: 859-254-7664
Website: www.national-college.edu
E-mail: info@national-college.edu

National College
4205 Dixie Hwy, Louisville KY 40216
Ted Scharre, Director of Admissions
502-447-7634 Fax: 502-447-7665
Website: www.national-college.edu
E-mail: info@national-college.edu

National College
50 National College Blvd, Pikeville KY 41501
Janet Head, Director of Admissions
606-478-7200 Fax: 606-478-7209
Website: www.national-college.edu
E-mail: info@national-college.edu

National College
125 S Killarney Ln, Richmond KY 40475
Keeley Gadd, Director of Admissions
859-623-8956 Fax: 859-623-8956
Website: www.national-college.edu
E-mail: info@national-college.edu

Spencerian College
4627 Dixie Hwy, Louisville KY 40216
Kathleen Belanger, Director of Admissions
502-447-1000 Fax: 502-447-4574
Website: www.spencerian.edu
E-mail: kbelanger@spencerian.edu

LOUISIANA

HERZING COLLEGE
2400 Veterans Memorial Blvd #410
Kenner LA 70062-4715
Genny Bordelon, Director of Admissions
504-733-0074 Fax: 504-733-0020
Website: www.herzing.edu
E-mail: info@nor.herzing.edu

Louisiana State University at Eunice
PO Box 1129, Eunice LA 70535-1129
Ron Ryder, Registrar
337-457-7311 Fax: 337-550-1306
Website: www.lsue.edu
E-mail: rryder@lsue.edu

MAINE

St. Joseph's College of Maine
278 Whites Bridge Rd, Standish ME 04084-5263
Vincent Kloskowski, Dean of Admissions
800-338-7057 Fax: 207-893-7862
Website: www.sjcme.edu
E-mail: admission@sjcme.edu

Southern Maine Community College
2 Fort Rd, South Portland ME 04106-1698
Dr. James Ortiz, President
Scott MacDonald, Director of Financial Aid
207-741-5500 Fax: 207-741-5671
Website: www.smccme.edu
E-mail: oharmon@maine.rr.com

MARYLAND

Cecil College
One Seahawk Dr, North East MD 21901
Sandra S. Rajaski, Registrar & Director of Admissions
410-287-1000 Fax: 410-287-1001
Website: www.cecil.edu
E-mail: srajaski@cecil.edu

Hagerstown Community College
11400 Robinwood Dr, Hagerstown MD 21742-6590
Dr. Daniel E. Bock, Assistant Director of Admissions
301-790-2800 Fax: 301-791-9165
Website: www.hagerstowncc.edu
E-mail: bockd@hagerstowncc.edu

Kaplan College
Hagerstown Campus
18618 Crestwood Dr, Hagerstown MD 21742-2797
W. Christopher Motz, President
Steve Shinham, Director of Admissions
800-422-2670 Fax: 301-739-0474
Website: www.hagerstownbusinesscol.edu

MASSACHUSETTS

Bay State College
122 Commonwealth Ave, Boston MA 02116-2901
Craig Pfannenstiehl, President
617-217-9000 Fax: 617-536-1735

Newbury College
129 Fisher Ave, Brookline MA 02445-5796
Salvadore Liberto, Vice President of Enrollment
617-730-7000 Fax: 617-731-9618
Website: www.newbury.edu
E-mail: info@newbury.edu
See listing under "Universities"

North Shore Community College
1 Ferncroft Rd, Danvers MA 01923-4093
Jennifer Kirk, Director of Admissions & Recruitment Outreach
978-762-4000 Fax: 978-762-4015
Website: www.northshore.edu
E-mail: jkirk@northshore.edu

Southeastern Technical Institute
250 Foundry St, South Easton MA 02375-1780
Beverly A. Pusateri, Director
508-238-1860 Fax: 508-230-1558
Website: ti.sersd.org
E-mail: bpusateri@sersd.org

MICHIGAN

CARNEGIE INSTITUTE
550 Stephenson Hwy Ste 100, Troy MI 48083-1159
Gloria J. McEachern, President
248-589-1078 Fax: 248-589-1631
Website: www.carnegie-institute.edu
E-mail: info@carnegie-institute.edu

Delta College
University Center MI 48710-0001
Duff Zube, Director of Admissions
989-686-9093 Fax: 989-667-2202
Website: www.delta.edu
E-mail: admit@delta.edu

Detroit Business Institute
23077 Greenfield Rd #LL28
Southfield MI 48075-3751
Greg Mitchell, Director of Admissions
248-552-6300 Fax: 248-552-7300
Website: www.dbisouthfield.com
E-mail: info@dbisouthfield.com

Detroit Business Institute - Downriver
19100 Fort St, Riverview MI 48193
Theresa Hernandez, Director of Admissions
734-479-0660 Fax: 734-479-0738
Website: www.dbidownriver.com
E-mail: info@dbidownriver.com

Everest Institute
5177 W Main St, Kalamazoo MI 49009
Susan Smith, Director of Admission
269-381-9616 Fax: 269-381-2513
Website: www.everest-institute.com
E-mail: susans@cci.edu

MACOMB COMMUNITY COLLEGE
44575 Garfield Rd, Clinton Township MI 48038-1139
Information Center
586-445-7999
Website: www.macomb.edu
E-mail: answer@macomb.edu

MACOMB COMMUNITY COLLEGE
14500 E 12 Mile Rd, Warren MI 48088-3896
Information Center
586-445-7999
Website: www.macomb.edu
E-mail: answer@macomb.edu

Northwestern Michigan College
1701 E Front St, Traverse City MI 49686-3061
Jim Bensley, Director of Admissions
800-748-0566 Fax: 231-995-1339
Website: www.nmc.edu
E-mail: jbensley@nmc.edu

MINNESOTA

Academy College
1101 E 78th St, Bloomington MN 55420-1402
Tracey Schantz, Director of Admissions
952-851-0066 Fax: 952-851-0094

Duluth Business University
4724 Mike Colalillo Dr, Duluth MN 55807-2723
Bonnie Kupczynski, Director
800-777-8406 Fax: 218-628-2127
Website: www.dbumn.edu
E-mail: info@dbumn.edu

Globe College
7166 10th St N, Oakdale MN 55128
Mike Hughes, Campus Director
651-730-5100 Fax: 651-730-5151
Website: www.globecollege.edu
E-mail: admissions@globecollege.edu

Hibbing Community College
1515 E 25th St, Hibbing MN 55746-3300
Holly Bigelow, Director of Enrollment
800-224-4HCC or 218-262-7200 Fax: 218-262-6717
Website: www.hibbing.edu
E-mail: admissions@hibbing.edu

Inver Hills Community College
2500 80th St E, Inver Grove Heights MN 55076
651-450-8500 Fax: 651-450-8679
Website: www.inverhills.edu

Minnesota State College - Southeast Technical
Red Wing Campus
308 Pioneer Rd, Red Wing MN 55066
Al DuCett, Director of Admissions
877-853-8324 Fax: 507-453-2715
Website: www.southeastmn.edu
E-mail: aducett@southeastmn.edu
70+ degrees, diplomas & certificates (15+ online) in Business & Office Careers, Musical Instrument Repair, Physical Health, Transportation, Technology, and Trades.

Minnesota State College - Southeast Technical
Winona Campus
PO Box 409, 1250 Homer Rd, Winona MN 55987
Al DuCett, Director of Admissions
877-853-8324 Fax: 507-453-2715
Website: www.southeastmn.edu
E-mail: aducett@southeastmn.edu
70+ degrees, diplomas & certificates (15+ online) in Business & Office Careers, Musical Instrument Repair, Physical Health, Transportation, Technology, and Trades.

Minnesota State University Moorhead
1104 7th Ave S, Moorhead MN 56563-0002
Regina Monson, Director of Admissions
218-477-2161 Fax: 218-477-4374
Website: go.mnstate.edu
E-mail: dragon@mnstate.edu

Northland Community and Technical College
2022 Central Ave NE
East Grand Forks MN 56721-2702
Deb Riely, Business Program Chair
800-451-3441 Fax: 218-773-4502
Website: www.northlandcollege.edu
E-mail: admissions@northlandcollege.edu

Pillsbury Baptist Bible College
315 S Grove Ave, Owatonna MN 55060-3097
Susanne Martin, Admissions Coordinator
507-451-2710 Fax: 507-451-0156
Website: www.pillsbury.edu
E-mail: admissions@pillsbury.edu

Ridgewater College-Hutchinson Campus
2 Century Ave SE, Hutchinson MN 55350-3100
Dawn Bjork, Counselor
800-722-1151 Fax: 320-234-8506
Website: www.ridgewater.edu
E-mail: dawn.bjork@ridgewater.edu

Ridgewater College-Willmar Campus
PO Box 1097, Willmar MN 56201-1097
Sally Kerfeld, Director of Admissions
800-722-1151 Fax: 320-222-5212
Website: www.ridgewater.edu
E-mail: sally.kerfeld@ridgewater.edu

St. Cloud Technical College
1540 Northway Dr, Saint Cloud MN 56303-1240
Jodi Elness, Director of Enrollment Management
800-222-1009 Fax: 320-308-5981
Website: www.sctc.edu
E-mail: jelness@sctc.edu

University of Minnesota
2900 University Ave, Crookston MN 56716-5001
218-281-6510 Fax: 218-281-8575
Website:
admissions.umcrookston.edu/requirements/apply.htm
E-mail: info@umcrookston.edu

MISSOURI

East Central College
1964 Prairie Dell Rd, Union MO 63084
Karen Wieda, Registrar
636-583-5195 ext. 2220 Fax: 636-583-1897
Website: www.eastcentral.edu
E-mail: wiedaks@eastcentral.edu

EVEREST COLLEGE
1010 W Sunshine St, Springfield MO 65807-2446
Melanie Exter, Contact
417-864-7220 or 800-475-2699 Fax: 417-866-3335
Website: www.everest-college.com
E-mail: mexter@cci.edu

Hickey College
940 Westport Plz, Saint Louis MO 63146-3127
Christopher A. Gearin, President
800-777-1544 or 314-434-2212 Fax: 314-434-1974
Website: www.hickeycollege.edu
E-mail: admin@hickeycollege.edu

Northwest Missouri State University
800 University Dr, Maryville MO 64468-6001
Beverly Schenkel, Dean of Enrollment Management
660-562-1562 Fax: 660-562-1121
Website: www.nwmissouri.edu
E-mail: admissions@nwmissouri.edu

St. Charles Community College
4601 Mid Rivers Mall Dr, Cottleville MO 63376
Kathy Brockgreitens-Gober, Director of Admissions
636-922-8000 Fax: 636-922-8236
Website: www.stchas.edu
E-mail: adm-reg@stchas.edu

State Fair Community College
3201 W 16th St, Sedalia MO 65301-2199
Director of Admissions
660-530-5833 Fax: 660-596-7472
Website: www.sfccmo.edu
E-mail: mparris@sfccmo.edu

NEBRASKA

Metropolitan Community College
PO Box 3777, Omaha NE 68103-0777
Becky Nicks, Director of Admissions
402-449-8400 Fax: 402-457-2616
Website: www.mccnab.edu
E-mail: bnicks@mccnab.edu

Midland Lutheran College
900 N Clarkson St, Fremont NE 68025-4200
Todd Hansen, Associate Director of Admissions
402-941-6501 Fax: 402-941-6513
Website: www.mlc.edu
E-mail: admissions@mlc.edu

University of Nebraska at Kearney
905 W 25th St, Kearney NE 68849-0001
Dusty Newton, Director of Admissions
800-KEARNEY Fax: 308-865-8987
Website: www.unk.edu
E-mail: admissionsug@unk.edu

NEVADA

Career College of Northern Nevada
1195-A Corporate Blvd, Reno NV 89502-2331
Nathan Clark, Director
775-856-2266 Fax: 775-856-0935
Website: www.ccnn.edu
E-mail: lgoldhammer@ccnn4u.com
See listing under "Career Schools"

GREAT BASIN COLLEGE
1500 College Pkwy, Elko NV 89801-5032
Julie G. Byrnes, Director of Enrollment Management
775-753-2271 Fax: 775-753-2311
Website: www.gbcnv.edu
E-mail: julieb@gwmail.gbcnv.edu
See listing under "Universities"

Morrison University
10315 Professional Circle Suite 201
Reno NV 89521-4826
Charles Timinsky, Director of Enrollment
775-850-0700 Fax: 775-850-0711
Website: www.morrisonuniversity.com

NEW HAMPSHIRE

New Hampshire Community Technical College
1066 Front St, Manchester NH 03102-8528
Jacquie Poirier, Director of Admissions
603-668-6706 Fax: 603-668-5354
Website: www.manchester.nhctc.edu
E-mail: jpoirier@nhctc.edu

NEW JERSEY

Atlantic Cape Community College
5100 Black Horse Pike
Mays Landing NJ 08330-2699
Linda McLeod, Assistant Director of College Recruitment
609-343-5000 Fax: 609-343-4921
Website: www.atlantic.edu
E-mail: accadmit@atlantic.edu
See listing under "Community and Junior Colleges"

Bergen Community College
400 Paramus Rd, Paramus NJ 07652
Julian Gomez, Asst. Director of Admissions
201-447-7100 Fax: 201-444-7036
Website: www.bergen.edu
E-mail: jgomez@bergen.edu

HoHoKus School of Business & Medical Sciences
10 S Franklin Tpke, Ramsey NJ 07446-2546
Thomas Eastwick, Director
201-327-8877 Fax: 201-327-9054
Website: www.hohokus.edu
E-mail: tomeastwick@aol.com

Hohokus School - RETS Nutley
103 Park Ave, Nutley NJ 07110-3505
Thomas Eastwick, President
973-661-0600 Fax: 973-661-2954
Website: www.rets-institute.com
E-mail: admissions@rets-institute.com

NEW MEXICO

Apollo College
1001 Menaul Blvd NE Ste C, Albuquerque NM 87107
800-368-7246 Fax: 505-254-1101

International Institute of the Americas
4201 Central Ave NW Suite J
Albuquerque NM 87105-1649
Ed Sigman, Director
505-880-2877 Fax: 505-352-0199
Website: www.iia.edu
E-mail: esigman@iia.edu

New Mexico State University
1500 N 3rd St, Grants NM 87020-2025
Irene Lutz, Director of Admissions
505-287-7981 Fax: 505-287-2329
Website: www.grants.nmsu.edu
E-mail: ilutz@nmsu.edu

NEW YORK

Briarcliffe College
1055 Stewart Ave, Bethpage NY 11714-3545
Theresa Donohue, Director of Admissions
516-918-3600 Fax: 516-470-6020
Website: www.briarcliffe.edu

Broome Community College
907 Upper Front St, Binghamton NY 13905
Anthony S. Fiorelli, Director of Admissions
607-778-5001 Fax: 607-778-5442
Website: www.sunybroome.edu
E-mail: fiorelli_a@sunybroome.edu

CAREER INSTITUTE OF HEALTH & TECHNOLOGY
340 Flatbush Avenue Ext, Brooklyn NY 11201
Mary Miller, Contact
718-422-1212 Fax: 718-422-1222
Website: www.careerinstitute.edu
E-mail: admissions@careerinstitute.edu

CAREER INSTITUTE OF HEALTH & TECHNOLOGY
200 Garden City Plz, Garden City NY 11530
Mary Miller, Contact
516-877-1225 Fax: 516-877-1959
Website: www.careerinstitute.edu
E-mail: admissions@careerinstitute.edu

CAREER INSTITUTE OF HEALTH & TECHNOLOGY
9525 Queens Blvd Ste 600, Rego Park NY 11374
Mary Miller, Contact
718-897-4868 Fax: 718-897-4863
Website: www.careerinstitute.edu
E-mail: admissions@careerinstitute.edu

Hilbert College
5200 S Park Ave, Hamburg NY 14075-1597
Timothy Lee, Director of Admissions
716-649-7900 Fax: 716-649-0702
Website: www.hilbert.edu
E-mail: tlee@hilbert.edu

KATHARINE GIBBS SCHOOL
320 S Service Rd, Melville NY 11747-3201
Derrick Ruffin, VP of Admissions
516-370-3510 Fax: 516-293-1763
Website: www.gibbslongisland.com
E-mail: druffin@gibbsmelville.com

LONG ISLAND BUSINESS INSTITUTE
136-18 39 Ave, Flushing NY 11354
Donna E. McCullough, President
718-939-5100 Fax: 718-989-9235
Website: www.libi.edu
E-mail: dwang@libi.edu

Private. Coed. Accreditation: ACICS. Approvals. National Court Reporting Association, NY State Board of Regents. Tuition: $325.00 per credit hour. Fees: $50.00 application fee. Enrollment: 850. Faculty: 25. Student-faculty ratio: 12:1. Associate of Occupational Studies degree offered in Court Reporting, Office Technology with Medical Office, Business Management, Accounting. Diploma programs in Office Technology, Medical Insurance & Billing, Court Reporting.

Monroe College
2501 Jerome Ave, Bronx NY 10468-4305
Evan Jerome, Director of Admissions
718-933-6700 Fax: 718-364-3552
Website: www.monroecollege.edu
E-mail: ejerome@monroecollege.edu

Olean Business Institute
301 N Union St, Olean NY 14760-2691
Carl English, Director of Admissions
716-372-7978 Fax: 716-372-2120
Website: www.obi.edu
E-mail: cenglish@obi.edu

Ridley-Lowell Business & Technical Institute
116 Front St, Binghamton NY 13905-3102
David Lounsbury, Executive Director
607-724-2941 Fax: 607-724-0799
Website: www.ridley.edu
E-mail: info@ridley.edu

SUNY Niagara County Community College
3111 Saunders Settlement Rd
Sanborn NY 14132-9487
Kathleen Saunders, Director of Admissions
716-614-6200 Fax: 716-614-6820
Website: www.niagaracc.suny.edu
E-mail: admissions@niagaracc.suny.edu

SUNY Orange County Community College
115 South St, Middletown NY 10940-6437
Margot St. Lawrence, Director of Admissions
845-341-4030 Fax: 845-342-8662
Website: www.sunyorange.edu
E-mail: apply@sunyorange.edu
See listing under "Community and Junior Colleges"

SUNY Sullivan County Community College
112 College Rd, Loch Sheldrake NY 12759-5151
Sari Rosenheck, Director of Admissions
845-434-5750 Fax: 845-434-0923
Website: www.sullivan.suny.edu
E-mail: admissions@sullivan.suny.edu
Student Housing on Campus.

Utica School of Commerce
201 Bleecker St, Utica NY 13501-2280
Bruce Davis, Director of Marketing
315-733-2307 Fax: 315-733-9281
Website: www.uscny.edu
E-mail: admissions@uscny.edu

NORTH CAROLINA

Brevard College
One Brevard College Dr, Brevard NC 28712
Joretta Nelson, Vice President Enrollment Management
828-883-8292 Fax: 828-884-3790
Website: www.brevard.edu
E-mail: admissions@brevard.edu

Chowan University
One University Pl, Murfreesboro NC 27855
Chad Holt, Dean of Admissions
800-488-4101 Fax: 252-398-1190
Website: www.chowan.edu
E-mail: holtc@chowan.edu

Haywood Community College
185 Freedlander Dr, Clyde NC 28721
Debbie Rowland, Coordinator of Admissions
828-627-4500 Fax: 828-627-4513
Website: www.haywood.edu
E-mail: drowland@haywood.edu

James Sprunt Community College
PO Box 398, Kenansville NC 28349-0398
Lea Grady, Admissions
910-296-2500 Fax: 910-296-1636
Website: www.jamessprunt.edu

Mayland Community College
PO Box 547, Spruce Pine NC 28777-0547
Cathy B. Morrison, Director of Enrollment Management
828-765-7351 Fax: 828-765-0728
Website: www.mayland.edu
E-mail: cmorrison@mayland.edu

South Piedmont Community College
PO Box 126, Polkton NC 28135-0126
John Curtis, Contact
704-272-5324 Fax: 704-272-8904
Website: www.spcc.edu
E-mail: jcurtis@spcc.edu

NORTH DAKOTA

AAKERS COLLEGE
4012 19th Ave S, Fargo ND 58103-7196
Elizabeth Largent, Director
701-277-3889 Fax: 701-277-5604
Website: www.aakers.edu
E-mail: blargent@aakers.edu

Dickinson State University
Dickinson ND 58601-4896
Steve Glasser, Director of Enrollment Services
800-279-4295 Fax: 701-483-2409
Website: www.dickinsonstate.edu
E-mail: dsu.hawks@dickinsonstate.edu

Minot State University-Bottineau Campus
105 Simrall Blvd, Bottineau ND 58318-1159
Paula Berg, Associate Dean of Student Affairs
800-542-6866 Fax: 701-228-5499
Website: www.misu-b.nodak.edu
E-mail: paula.berg@misu.nodak.edu

Williston State College
PO Box 1326, Williston ND 58802-1326
Penny Soiseth, Associate Director Enrollment Services
701-774-4200 Fax: 701-774-4544
Website: www.wsc.nodak.edu
E-mail: penny.soiseth@wsc.nodak.edu

OHIO

ACADEMY OF COURT REPORTING
2044 Euclid Ave, Cleveland OH 44115-2282
Sheila Woods, Director of Admissions
216-861-3222 Fax: 216-861-4517
Website: www.acr.edu
E-mail: woods.sheila@acr.edu

Brown Mackie College - Cincinnati
1011 Glendale Milford Rd, Cincinnati OH 45215-1107
Robin Krout, President
513-771-2424 Fax: 513-771-3413
Website: www.brownmackie.edu
E-mail: rkrout@brownmackie.edu

Davis College
4747 Monroe St, Toledo OH 43623-4389
Dana Stern, Admissions Director
419-473-2700 Fax: 419-473-2472
Website: www.daviscollege.edu
E-mail: learn@daviscollege.edu

Ohio University
Chillicothe Campus
PO Box 629, Chillicothe OH 45601
Student Services
740-774-7200 Fax: 740-774-7295
Website: www.ohiou.edu/chillicothe/

OHIO VALLEY COLLEGE OF TECHNOLOGY
16808 St. Clair Ave, PO Box 7000
East Liverpool OH 43920
Scott S. Rogers, Director
330-385-1070 Fax: 330-385-4606
Website: www.ovct.edu
E-mail: info@ovct.edu

Owens Community College
3200 Bright Rd, Findlay OH 45840
William J. Ivoska PhD., Vice President of Student Services
567-429-3500 Fax: 567-423-0246
Website: www.owens.edu
E-mail: admissions@owens.edu

Owens Community College
PO Box 10000, Toledo OH 43699-1947
William J. Ivoska, Ph.D, Vice President of Student Services
567-661-7000 Fax: 567-661-7607
Website: www.owens.edu
E-mail: admissions@owens.edu

Sinclair Community College
444 W 3rd St, Dayton OH 45402-1460
Director of Admissions
937-512-3000 Fax: 937-512-2393
Website: www.sinclair.edu
E-mail: admit@sinclair.edu

OKLAHOMA

CAREER POINT INSTITUTE
3138 S Garnett Rd, Tulsa OK 74146-1933
Brad Oakley, Director of Admissions
918-627-8074 Fax: 918-627-4007
E-mail: tadmdir@career-point.org

OREGON

Linn-Benton Community College
6500 Pacific Blvd SW, Albany OR 97321-3774
Christine Baker, Outreach Coordinator
541-917-4811 Fax: 541-917-4868
Website: www.linnbenton.edu
E-mail: admissions@linnbenton.edu

Rogue Community College
3345 Redwood Hwy, Grants Pass OR 97527-9298
Claudia Sullivan, Director of Enrollment Services
541-956-7500 Fax: 541-471-3585
Website: www.roguecc.edu
E-mail: csullivan@roguecc.edu
See listing under "Community and Junior Colleges"

PENNSYLVANIA

Berks Technical Institute
2205 Ridgewood Rd, Wyomissing PA 19610-1168
Elizabeth Wade, Director of Admissions
610-372-1722 Fax: 610-376-4684
Website: www.berkstech.com

Career Training Academy
4314 Old William Penn Highway Ste 103
Monroeville PA 15146
Gina Hudac, Admissions Representitive
412-372-3900 Fax: 412-373-4262
Website: www.careerta.edu
E-mail: admissions2@careerta.edu

Career Training Academy
950 5th Ave, New Kensington PA 15068-6308
John Reddy, Director
Tyna Putignano, Director of Admissions
724-337-1000 Fax: 724-335-7140
Website: www.careerta.edu
E-mail: admissions@careerta.edu
See listing under "Career Schools"

Career Training Academy
1500 Northway Mall, Pittsburgh PA 15237
Anna Bartolini, Director North Hills Branch Campus
412-367-4000 Fax: 412-369-7223
Website: www.careerta.edu
E-mail: admissions3@careerta.edu

Community College of Allegheny County
Allegheny Campus: 808 Ridge Ave, Pittsburgh PA 15212 Admissions: 412.237.2700
Boyce Campus: 595 Beatty Rd, Monroeville PA 15146 Admissions: 724.325.6614
North Campus: 8701 Perry Highway, Pittsburgh PA 15237 Admissions: 412.369.3600
South Campus: 1750 Clairton Rd, West Mifflin PA 15122 Admissions: 412-469-4301
Website: www.ccac.edu

Community College of Beaver County
1 Campus Dr, Monaca PA 15061-2566
724-775-8561 Fax: 724-775-4687
Website: www.ccbc.edu
E-mail: admissions@ccbc.edu

Douglas Education Center
130 7th St, Monessen PA 15062-1097
Sherry Lee Walters, Director of Enrollment Services
800-413-6013 Fax: 724-684-7463
Website: www.douglas-school.com
E-mail: swalters@douglas-school.com

Erie Business Center
246 W 9th St, Erie PA 16501-1392
Donna Perino, Director
814-456-7504 Fax: 814-456-6015
Website: www.eriebc.edu
E-mail: perinod@eriebc.edu

KEYSTONE TECHNICAL INSTITUTE
2301 Academy Dr, Harrisburg PA 17112-1012
Tom Bogush, Director of Admissions
717-545-4747 Fax: 717-901-9090
Website: www.acadcampus.com
E-mail: educdir@acadcampus.com
Established 1980. Private. Coed. Accreditation: ACCSCT. Enrollment: 210 full-time, 50 part-time. Faculty: 15. Student-faculty ratio: 20:1. Degrees offered: Occupational Associate Degrees (AST/ASB). Library: 2,000 volumes. 1 building on 8 acres. Combined classroom; real world lab experience and externships for career training in Medical Assistant, Dental Assistant, Massage Therapy, Paralegal, Culinary Arts, Child Care, Computers.

Lancaster Bible College
901 Eden Rd, Lancaster PA 17601-5036
Joanne M. Roper, Associate VP for Admissions
866-LBC-4YOU or 717-560-8271 Fax: 717-560-8213
Website: www.lbc.edu
E-mail: admissions@lbc.edu
See listing under "Theological Studies & Religious Vocations"

RHODE ISLAND

MTTI - MOTORING TECHNICAL TRAINING INSTITUTE
54 Water St, East Providence RI 02914-5022
Sharon Ring, Program Director
401-434-4840 or 866-454-6884 Fax: 401-434-9540
Website: www.mtti.edu
E-mail: info@mtti.edu

New England Institute of Technology
2500 Post Rd, Warwick RI 02886-2244
Michael Kwiatkowski, Director of Admissions
401-739-5000 Fax: 401-738-5122
Website: www.neit.edu
E-mail: eflynn@neit.edu

SOUTH CAROLINA

Forrest Junior College
601 E River St, Anderson SC 29624-2405
Pamela Johnson, MBA, President
864-225-7653 Fax: 864-261-7471
Website: www.forrestcollege.edu
E-mail: info@forrestcollege.edu
Bookeeper, Admininstrative Asst.
See listing under "Community and Junior Colleges"

Spartanburg Community College
PO Box 4386, Spartanburg SC 29305-4386
Nancy Garmroth, Dean of Admissions & Financial Aid
864-592-4810 Fax: 864-592-4945
Website: sccsc.edu

SOUTH DAKOTA

NATIONAL AMERICAN UNIVERSITY
321 Kansas City St, Rapid City SD 57701-3692
Angela G. Beck, Director of Enrollment Management
605-394-4800 Fax: 605-394-4871
Website: www.rapid.national.edu
E-mail: rcadmissions@national.edu

Presentation College
1500 N Main St, Aberdeen SD 57401-1280
JoEllen Lindner, VP for Enrollment
605-229-8492 Fax: 605-229-8425
Website: www.presentation.edu
E-mail: admit@presentation.edu

Western Dakota Technical Institute
800 Mickelson Dr, Rapid City SD 57703-4018
Jill Elder, Admissions Coordinator
605-394-4034 Fax: 605-394-2204
Website: www.wdt.edu
E-mail: jill.elder@wdt.edu

TENNESSEE

Austin Peay State University
601 College St, Clarksville TN 37044-0002
931-221-7011 Fax: 931-221-6168
Website: www.apsu.edu
E-mail: admissions@apsu.edu

Lipscomb University
3901 Granny White Pike, Nashville TN 37204-3951
Ricky Holaway, Director of Admissions
800-333-4358 ext. 1776 Fax: 615-269-1804
Website: www.lipscomb.edu
E-mail: admissions@lipscomb.edu

Miller-Motte Technical College
1820 Business Park Dr, Clarksville TN 37040-6023
Lisa Teague, Director of Admissions
931-553-0071 Fax: 931-552-2916
Website: www.miller-motte.com
E-mail: lteague@miller-motte.com

National College
1328 Highway 11W, Bristol TN 37620
Becky Wild, Director of Admissions
423-878-4440 Fax: 423-793-1060
Website: www.national-college.edu
E-mail: info@national-college.edu

National College of Business & Technology
3748 Nolensville Pike, Nashville TN 37211-3322
Lynda Dandridge, Director of Admissions
615-333-3344 Fax: 615-333-3429
Website: www.national-college.edu
E-mail: info@national-college.edu

Southwest Tennessee Community College
5983 Macon Cove, Memphis TN 38134
Vanessa R. Dowdy, Director of Admissions
901-333-5000 Fax: 901-333-4523
Website: www.southwest.tn.edu
E-mail: vdowdy@southwest.tn.edu

Tennessee State University
3500 John A Merritt Blvd, Nashville TN 37209-1561
John Cade, Dean of Admissions & Records
615-963-5101 Fax: 615-963-2930
Website: www.tnstate.edu
E-mail: jcade@tnstate.edu

University of Tennessee
615 McCallie Ave, Chattanooga TN 37403-2504
Yancy Freeman, Director of Admissions
423-425-4111 Fax: 423-425-4157
Website: www.utc.edu
E-mail: Yancy-Freeman@utc.edu

TEXAS

American Commercial College
2007 34th St, Lubbock TX 79411-1899
Michael Otto, Director
806-747-4339 Fax: 806-765-9838
Website: www.acc-careers.com
E-mail: mjotto@acc-careers.com

American Commercial College
5119 Twin Towers Blvd, Odessa TX 79762-5504
Donna Duree, Director
432-362-6768 Fax: 432-550-0556
Website: www.acc-careers.com
E-mail: americancc@acc-careers.com

COURT REPORTING INSTITUTE OF DALLAS
1341 W Mockingbird Ln Ste 200 East
Dallas TX 75247
Cindy Smith, Director
214-350-9722 Fax: 214-631-0143
Website: www.crid.com
E-mail: csmith@crid.com

COURT REPORTING INSTITUTE OF HOUSTON
13101 Northwest Fwy Ste 100, Houston TX 77040
Cindy Smith, Director
713-996-8300 Fax: 713-996-8360
Website: www.crid.com
E-mail: csmith@crid.com

Galveston College
4015 Avenue Q, Galveston TX 77550-7496
Brian Lowery, Registrar
409-763-6551 Fax: 409-944-1501
Website: www.gc.edu
E-mail: blowery@gc.edu

Hallmark Institute of Technology - Technology Campus
10401 W IH 10, San Antonio TX 78230-1736
Joe Fisher, President
210-690-9000 Fax: 210-697-8225
Website: www.hallmarkinstitute.com
E-mail: sross@hallmarkinstitute.com
Electronics Engineering Technology, Business Office Administration, Computer Network Systems Technology, & Medical Assistant.

ITT Technical Institute
6330 E Highway 290 Ste 150, Austin TX 78723-1035
Willard Real, Director of Admissions
512-467-6800 Fax: 512-467-6677
Website: www.itt-tech.edu
E-mail: wreal@itt-tech.edu

Lubbock Christian University
5601 19th St, Lubbock TX 79407-2099
Stan Scott, Director of Admissions
806-796-8800 Fax: 806-720-7162
Website: www.lcu.edu
E-mail: stan.scott@lcu.edu

McLennan Community College
1400 College Dr, Waco TX 76708-1498
Linda Stanford, Director, Business Programs
254-299-8000 Fax: 254-299-8854
Website: www.mclennan.edu
E-mail: lstanford@mclennan.edu

Remington College - Fort Worth Campus
300 E Loop 820, Fort Worth TX 76112-1280
Director of Recruitment
817-451-0017 Fax: 817-496-1257
Website: www.remingtoncollege.edu
E-mail: lynn.wey@remingtoncollege.edu

Temple College
2600 S 1st St, Temple TX 76504-7435
Toni Borras, Director of Admissions & Records
254-298-8808 Fax: 254-298-8288
Website: www.templejc.edu
E-mail: admissionsrecords@templejc.edu

Tyler Junior College
PO Box 9020, Tyler TX 75711-9020
Joan Jones, Interim Dean
800-687-5680
Website: www.tjc.edu
E-mail: jjon@tjc.edu
See listing under "Community and Junior Colleges"

University of Houston
122 E Cullen Bldg, Houston TX 77204-2023
Office of Admission
713-743-9595
Website: www.uh.edu
E-mail: admissions@uh.edu

Weatherford College
225 College Park Dr, Weatherford TX 76086
Dr. Joe Birmingham, President
800-287-5471 Fax: 817-598-6205
Website: www.wc.edu
E-mail: willingham@wc.edu

UTAH

L.D.S. BUSINESS COLLEGE
95 North 300 West, Salt Lake City UT 84101-3500
Kathleen Howe, Assistant Director of Admissions
801-524-8145 Fax: 801-524-1900
Website: www.ldsbc.edu
E-mail: admissions@ldsbc.edu
See listing under "Career Schools"

Stevens Henager College
PO Box 9428, Ogden UT 84409-0428
Cindy Williams, Director of Admissions
801-394-7791 Fax: 801-621-0866
Website: www.stevenshenager.edu
E-mail: shcogden@yahoo.com

VIRGINIA

Bryant & Stratton College
8141 Hull St Rd, Richmond VA 23235-6411
David K. Mayle, Director of Admissions
804-745-2444 Fax: 804-745-6884
Website: www.bryantstratton.edu
E-mail: dkmayle@bryantstratton.edu

ECPI College of Technology
5555 Greenwich Rd Ste 300
Virginia Beach VA 23462-6542
757-671-7171 Fax: 757-671-8661
Website: www.ecpi.edu

Gibbs College - Northern Virginia
1980 Gallows Rd, Vienna VA 22182-3913
Everson Travers, Director of Admissions
703-556-8888 Fax: 703-556-0953
Website: www.gibbsva.edu
E-mail: etravers@gibbsva.edu

National College
100 Logan St, Bluefield VA 24605
Tonya Elmore, Director of Admissions
276-326-3621 Fax: 276-322-5731
Website: www.national-college.edu
E-mail: info@national-college.edu

National College
1819 Emmet St N, Charlottesville VA 22901-2812
434-295-0136 Fax: 434-979-8061
Website: www.national-college.edu
E-mail: info@national-college.edu

National College
336 Old Riverside Dr, Danville VA 24541
Jeff Moore, Director of Admissions
434-793-6822 Fax: 434-793-3634
Website: www.national-college.edu
E-mail: info@national-college.edu

National College
1515 Country Club Rd, Harrisonburg VA 22802
Kathy Sours, Director of Admissions
540-432-0943 Fax: 540-432-1133
Website: www.national-college.edu
E-mail: info@national-college.edu

National College
104 Candlewood Ct, Lynchburg VA 24502-2653
Nancy Fortune, Director of Admissions
434-239-3500 Fax: 434-239-3948
Website: www.national-college.edu
E-mail: info@national-college.edu

National College
10 Church St, Martinsville VA 24114
Barbara Rakes, Director of Admissions
276-632-5621 Fax: 276-632-7915
Website: www.national-college.edu
E-mail: info@national-college.edu

National College
1813 E Main St, Salem VA 24153-4598
Ron Smith, Director of Admissions
540-986-1800 Fax: 540-444-4195
Website: www.national-college.edu
E-mail: info@national-college.edu

Radford University
PO Box 6903, Radford VA 24142
David W. Kraus, Director of Admissions
800-890-4265 Fax: 540-831-5038
Website: www.radford.edu
E-mail: ruadmiss@radford.edu

Southside Virginia Community College
109 Campus Dr, Alberta VA 23821-2930
Ronald E. Mattox, Dean of Admissions
434-949-1014 Fax: 434-949-7863
Website: www.sv.vccs.edu
E-mail: ronald.mattox@sv.vccs.edu

Southside Virginia Community College
200 Daniel Rd, Keysville VA 23947
Ronald E. Mattox, Dean of Admissions
434-736-2018 Fax: 434-736-2082
Website: www.sv.vccs.edu
E-mail: ronald.mattox@sv.vccs.edu

VIRGINIA CAREER INSTITUTE
100 Constitution Dr Ste 101
Virginia Beach VA 23462-6758
Andy Tysinger, School Director
757-499-5447 Fax: 757-473-5735
Website: www.virginiacareerinstitute.edu
E-mail: atysinger@success.edu

WASHINGTON

Apollo College
10102 E Knox Ave, Spokane WA 99206-4146
509-532-8888 Fax: 509-533-5983

Everett Community College
2000 Tower St, Everett WA 98201
Christine Kerlin, Associate Dean
425-388-9100 Fax: 425-388-9173
Website: www.everettcc.edu
E-mail: ckerlin@everettcc.edu

SHORELINE COMMUNITY COLLEGE
16101 Greenwood Ave N, Shoreline WA 98133-5696
Chris Melton, Acting Registrar
206-546-4581 Fax: 206-546-5835
Website: www.shoreline.edu

Walla Walla Community College
500 Tausick Way, Walla Walla WA 99362-9270
Dan Biagi, Director
509-527-4283 or 877-992-9922 Fax: 509-527-4480
Website: www.wwcc.edu
E-mail: dan.biagi@wwcc.edu
See listing under "Community and Junior Colleges"

WEST VIRGINIA

Davis & Elkins College
100 Campus Dr, Elkins WV 26241-3996
Renee Heckel, Director of Enrollment Management
800-624-3157 Fax: 304-637-1800
Website: www.davisandelkins.edu
E-mail: admiss@davisandelkins.edu

Mountain State College
1508 Spring St, Parkersburg WV 26101-3993
Judith Sutton, Director
304-485-5487 Fax: 304-485-3524
Website: www.mountainstate.org
E-mail: admin@mountainstate.org
See listing under "Career Schools"

Mountain State University
Box 9003, Beckley WV 25802-9003
Tony England, Director of Admissions
866-FOR-MSU1 or 304-929-INFO Fax: 304-253-5072
Website: www.mountainstate.edu
E-mail: gomsu@mountainstate.edu
See listing under "Universities"

West Virginia Junior College
176 Thompson Dr, Bridgeport WV 26330
Kathryn Stanley, Director of Admissions
304-842-4007 Fax: 304-842-8191
Website: www.wvjcinfo.net
E-mail: kstanley@wvjcinfo.net

WISCONSIN

Blackhawk Technical College
PO Box 5009, Janesville WI 53547-5009
Gregg Bosak, Administration, Community Information
608-757-7769 Fax: 608-757-7740
Website: www.blackhawk.edu
E-mail: gbosak@blackhawk.edu

Wisconsin Indianhead Technical College
505 Pine Ridge Dr, Shell Lake WI 54871
Laura Wassenaar, Dean
800-243-9482 Fax: 715-468-2819
Website: www.witc.edu
E-mail: laura.wassenaar@witc.edu

WYOMING

Laramie County Community College
1400 E College Dr, Cheyenne WY 82007-3204
Jenny Hargett, Director of Admissions
307-778-5222 Fax: 307-778-1350
Website: www.lccc.wy.edu
E-mail: learnmore@lccc.wy.edu

University of Wyoming
Admissions Office
Dept 3435, Laramie WY 82071-3435
Brooke Culver, Contact
800-342-5996 Fax: 307-766-4042
Website: www.uwyo.edu
E-mail: why-wyo@uwyo.edu

PUERTO RICO

EDIC College
PO Box 9120, Caguas PR 00726-9120
Virginia Cartagena, Director of Admissions
787-744-8519 Fax: 787-743-0855
Website: www.ediccollege.com
E-mail: edic@coqui.net

PONCE PARAMEDICAL COLLEGE
1213 Calle Acacia Villa Flores, Ponce PR 00716-2901
Alberto Aristizabal, President
787-848-1589 Fax: 787-259-0169
Website: www.popac.edu
E-mail: ppcadmin@popac.edu

BUSINESS AND MANAGEMENT

ALABAMA

Alabama A & M University
PO Box 908, Normal AL 35762
Antonio Boyle, Director of Admissions
256-372-5245

Auburn University
Auburn AL 36849
334-844-4000

Auburn University at Montgomery
PO Box 244023, Montgomery AL 36124
334-244-3000

Bishop State Community College - Four Campuses
351 N Broad St, Mobile AL 36603-5898
Dr. Terry Hazzard, Dean of Students
251-690-6801 Fax: 251-690-6446
Website: www.bishop.edu
E-mail: thazzard@bishop.edu

CALHOUN COMMUNITY COLLEGE
PO Box 2216, Decatur AL 35609-2216
M. Wayne Tosh, Registrar
256-306-2500 Fax: 256-306-2941
Website: www.calhoun.edu
E-mail: sla@calhoun.edu

Faulkner University
5345 Atlanta Hwy, Montgomery AL 36109-3398
Keith Mock, Director of Admissions
800-879-9816 ext. 7200

George C. Wallace State Community College
PO Box 2530, Selma AL 36702-2530
Mrs. Donitha J. Griffin, Dean of Students
334-876-9295 Fax: 334-876-9300
Website: www.wccs.edu
E-mail: dgriffin@wccs.edu

Herzing College
280 W Valley Ave, Homewood AL 35209-4816
Kim Conway, Director of Admissions
205-916-2800 Fax: 205-916-2807
Website: www.herzing.edu/birmingham
E-mail: info@bhm.herzing.edu

Huntingdon College
1500 E Fairview Ave, Montgomery AL 36106-2148
334-833-4222

Judson College
302 Bibb St, Marion AL 36756
Michael Scotto, Director of Admissions
800-447-9472 Fax: 334-683-5147
Website: www.judson.edu
E-mail: admissions@judson.edu

Oakwood College
Oakwood Rd NW, Huntsville AL 35896-0001
256-726-7000

Samford University
800 Lakeshore Dr, Birmingham AL 35229-0002
205-726-3673

Spring Hill College
4000 Dauphin St, Mobile AL 36608-1791
334-460-4000

Stillman College
PO Box 1430, Tuscaloosa AL 35403-1430
205-349-4240

Talladega College
627 Battle St W, Talladega AL 35160-2354
256-362-0206

Troy University
Troy AL 36082-0001
Jim Hutto, Dean of Enrollment Management
334-670-3175

Troy University Dothan
PO Box 8368, Dothan AL 36304-0368
334-983-6556

University of Alabama
Box 870118, Tuscaloosa AL 35487
Dr. Lisa B. Harris, Director of Admissions
205-348-5666

University of Alabama at Birmingham
Univ Sta, Birmingham AL 35294-0001
205-934-4011

University of Alabama in Huntsville
PO Box 1247, Huntsville AL 35899-0001
Nikki Willis, Assoc. Director for Recruiting Program and Events
1-800-UAH-CALL Fax: 256-824-6073
Website: www.uah.edu
E-mail: willisn@uah.edu

University of Mobile
5735 College Pkwy, Mobile AL 36613
800-946-7267

University of Montevallo
Station 6030, Montevallo AL 35115
205-665-6030

University of South Alabama
307 University Blvd N, Mobile AL 36688-3053
Melissa Haab, Director of Admissions
251-460-6141 Fax: 251-460-7876
Website: www.southalabama.edu
E-mail: admiss@usouthal.edu

University of West Alabama
Hwy 11, Livingston AL 35470
205-652-3400

ALASKA

Sheldon Jackson College
801 Lincoln St, Sitka AK 99835-7651
800-478-4556

University of Alaska Anchorage
PO Box 141629, Anchorage AK 99514-1629
Cecile Mitchell, Director of Enrollment Services
907-786-1480 Fax: 907-786-4888
Website: www.uaa.alaska.edu/
E-mail: enroll@uaa.alaska.edu

University of Alaska Fairbanks
PO Box 757480, Fairbanks AK 99775
907-474-7581

University of Alaska Southeast
11120 Glacier Hwy, Juneau AK 99801-8625
Paul Kraft, Dean of Students/Enrollment Management
907-796-6000

ARIZONA

Apollo College
8503 N 27th Ave, Phoenix AZ 85051-4063
602-864-1571 Fax: 602-864-8207

Apollo College
3550 N Oracle Rd, Tucson AZ 85705
520-888-5885 Fax: 520-887-3005

Arizona State University
PO Box 870112, Tempe AZ 85287-0112
480-965-9011

Arizona State University West
PO Box 37110, Phoenix AZ 85069-7110
602-543-5500

Embry-Riddle Aeronautical University
Arizona Campus
3700 Willow Creek Rd, Prescott AZ 86301-3720
William Thompson, Director of Admissions
800-888-3728 Fax: 928-777-6613
Website: www.embryriddle.edu
E-mail: pradmit@erau.edu

International Institute of the Americas
925 S Gilbert Rd Ste 201, Mesa AZ 85204-4440
Todd Olehausen, Director
480-545-8755 Fax: 480-926-1371
Website: www.iia.edu
E-mail: tolehausen@iia.edu

International Institute of the Americas
6049 N 43rd Ave, Phoenix AZ 85019-1600
John Pechota, Director of Admissions
602-242-6265 Fax: 602-589-1353
Website: www.iia.edu
E-mail: jpechota@iia.edu

International Institute of the Americas
5441 E 22nd St, Tucson AZ 85710
Leigh Anne Pechota, Director
520-748-9799 Fax: 520-748-9355
Website: www.iia.edu
E-mail: lpechota@iia.edu

Northern Arizona University
PO Box 4084, Flagstaff AZ 86011-0001
520-523-9011

Pima Community College
4905 E Broadway Blvd, Tucson AZ 85709-1010
Wendy Kilgore, Ph.D., Director of Admissions
520-206-4500 Fax: 520-206-4790
Website: www.pima.edu
E-mail: infocenter@pima.edu

Southwestern College
2625 E Cactus Rd, Phoenix AZ 85032-7097
Admissions/Financial Aid Office
800-247-2697

Thunderbird, The Garvin School of International Management
15249 N 59th Ave, Glendale AZ 85306-3236
Judy Johnson, Associate VP of Admissions & Financial Aid
800-848-9084 or 602-978-7100 Fax: 602-439-5432
Website: www.thunderbird.edu
E-mail: johnsonj@thunderbird.edu

University of Arizona
Tucson AZ 85721-0040
Paul Kohn, Director of Admissions
520-621-3237

University of Phoenix
4615 E Elwood St, Phoenix AZ 85040-1908
480-966-9577

ARKANSAS

Arkansas State University
PO Box 1630, State University AR 72467-1630
870-972-2100

Hendrix College
1600 Washington Ave, Conway AR 72032-3080
501-329-6811

John Brown University
2000 W University St, Siloam Springs AR 72761-2121
877-JBU-INFO

Lyon College
PO Box 2317, Batesville AR 72503-2317
Dan Rutledge, Director of Admissions
870-793-9813

Ouachita Baptist University
410 Ouachita St, Arkadelphia AR 71998-0001
David Goodman, Director of Admissions
870-245-5110

Phillips Community College of the University of Arkansas
PO Box 785, Helena AR 72342-0785
Dr. Steven Murray, Chancellor
Lynn Boone, Vice Chancellor for Student Services / Registrar
870-338-6474 Fax: 870-338-7542
Website: www.pccua.edu
E-mail: lboone@pccua.edu

Southern Arkansas University
100 E University, Magnolia AR 71753
870-235-4000

University of Arkansas at Fayetteville
1 University of Arkansas, Fayetteville AR 72701-1201
479-575-2000

University of Arkansas at Little Rock
2801 S University Ave, Little Rock AR 72204-1000
501-569-3000

University of Arkansas at Monticello
PO Box 3600, Monticello AR 71656
870-367-6811

University of Arkansas at Pine Bluff
1200 University Dr, Pine Bluff AR 71601-2799
870-543-8000

University of Arkansas Community College at Hope
PO Box 140, Hope AR 71802-0140
Willie Buck, Business Technology Division Chair
870-777-5722 Fax: 870-722-6630
Website: www.uacch.edu
E-mail: wbuck@uacch.edu

University of Central Arkansas
201 Donaghey Ave, Conway AR 72035-5003
501-450-5000

University of the Ozarks
415 N College Ave, Clarksville AR 72830-2880
Jim Decker, Director of Admissions
479-979-1000

Williams Baptist College
PO Box 3737, Walnut Ridge AR 72476-3737
Angela Flippo, Vice President for Enrollment Management
800-722-4434 Fax: 870-759-4163
Website: www.williamsbaptistcollege.com
E-mail: admissions@wbcoll.edu

CALIFORNIA

Antioch University
801 Garden St Ste 101
Santa Barbara CA 93101-1581
Ankara McPherson, Director of Admissions
805-962-8179

Antioch University Southern California
400 Corporate Pointe, Culver City CA 90230-7615
Admissions Office
800-7-ANTIOCH Fax: 310-821-6032
E-mail: admissions@antiochla.edu
Master of Arts in Organizational Management.

Azusa Pacific University
901 E Alosta Ave, Azusa CA 91702
626-969-3434

Biola University
13800 Biola Ave, La Mirada CA 90639-0001
562-903-4752

Butte College
3536 Butte Campus Dr, Oroville CA 95965-8399
Carole Gish, Director of Admissions
530-895-2511 Fax: 530-879-4313
Website: www.butte.edu
E-mail: admissions@butte.edu

California Baptist University
8432 Magnolia Ave, Riverside CA 92504-3297
951-689-5771

CALIFORNIA COAST UNIVERSITY

700 N Main St, Santa Ana CA 92701
Admissions Office: 888-CCU-UNIV or 714-547-9625
Fax: 714-547-5777
Dr. Thomas Neal, President
Dr. Cynthia Teeple, Academic Vice President
Website: www.calcoast.edu
E-mail: info@calcoast.edu

Established 1973. Proprietary. Coed. Accreditation: California Coast University holds accreditation through the Accrediting Commission of the Distance Education and Training Council (DETC). The DETC is an educational association located in Washington, D.C. Founded in 1926, it is the standard setting agency for distance education institutions. Approval: Bureau for Private Post-secondary and Vocational Education - State of California, charter member California Association of State Approved Colleges & Universities, member Association for Adult & Continuing Education, member The Alliance for Private Post Secondary Academic Institutions.

Tuition: $2,805-$12,070. California Coast University has selected the SLM Corporation, commonly known as Sallie Mae, to help the university provide financing for its students. Sallie Mae is the nation's leading provider of education funding. Sallie Mae also allows students to borrow additional loan amounts to cover additional expenses, such as textbooks, equipment, or living expenses.

Enrollment: 30,000. California Coast University is approved by the California State Approving Agency to enroll veterans or other eligible persons under Title 38, U.S. Code. California Coast University holds a Memorandum of Understanding with Defense Activity for Non-Traditional Education Support (DANTES) as an external degree provider.

A private college offering off-campus independent study programs in the traditional areas of business administration, management, psychology, education. Admissions: enroll year round, requires official transcripts, letters of recommendation, detailed curriculum vita or occupational history.

Process: evaluation of prior academic work followed by analysis of occupational history, including participation in workshops, seminars, training programs, specialized projects for credit. Credit is demonstrated by accelerated learning guides or study guides.

Residency: All course work may be completed off campus, utilizing correspondence methods. Interest free loans available to students.

California Polytechnic State University
San Luis Obispo CA 93407
805-756-1111

California State Polytechnic University
3801 W Temple Ave, Pomona CA 91768-2557
909-869-2000

California State University-Bakersfield
9001 Stockdale Hwy, Bakersfield CA 93311-1022
661-664-2011

California State University-Chico
Chico CA 95929-0001
530-898-6116

California State University-East Bay
25800 Carlos Bee Blvd, Hayward CA 94542-3001
510-885-3000

California State University-Fresno
Fresno CA 93740-0001
559-278-4240

California State University-Fullerton
PO Box 34080
Fullerton CA 92634
714-278-2011

California State University-Long Beach
1250 N Bellflower Blvd, Long Beach CA 90840-0006
562-985-4111

California State University-Los Angeles
5151 State University Dr, Los Angeles CA 90032
323-343-3000

California State University-Northridge
18111 Nordhoff St, Northridge CA 91330-0001
818-677-1200

California State University-Sacramento
6000 J St, Sacramento CA 95819-2605
916-278-6011

California State University-San Bernadino
5500 University Pkwy
San Bernardino CA 92407-2393
Olivia Rosas, Director of Admissions
909-537-5188 Fax: 909-537-7034
Website: www.csusb.edu
E-mail: orosas@csusb.edu

California State University-Stanislaus
801 W Monte Vista Ave, Turlock CA 95382-0256
Lisa Bernardo, Director of Admissions
209-667-3507

Chapman University
One University Drive, Orange CA 92866-1099
Michael Drummy, Assistant Vice President for Enrollment
Services and Chief Admission Officer
714-997-6411 or 888-CUAPPLY Fax: 714-997-6713
Website: www.chapman.edu
E-mail: admit@chapman.edu

CONCORDIA UNIVERSITY

1530 Concordia, Irvine CA 92612-3203
Lori McDonald, Executive Director of Enrollment Services
800-229-1200 or 949-854-8002 Fax: 949-854-6894
Website: www.cui.edu
E-mail: admission@cui.edu

Dominican University of California
50 Acacia Ave, San Rafael CA 94901-2298
Office of Admissions
888-323-6762 Fax: 415-485-3214
Website: www.dominican.edu
E-mail: enroll@dominican.edu

FASHION CAREERS COLLEGE

1923 Morena Blvd, San Diego CA 92110-3555
Silvana Carelli, Director of Enrollment
619-275-4700 Fax: 619-275-0635
Website: www.fashioncareerscollege.com
E-mail: info@fashioncareerscollege.com

Established 1979. Private. Coed. Accreditation: ACICS. Tuition: $16,900 per year for Fashion Business & Technology. $16,900 per year for Fashion Design & Technology program, day or evening program (tuition includes required books & certain supplies). Registration Fee: $25. Enrollment: 120 full-time. Faculty: 15. Student-faculty ratio: 10:1. Degree & Certificate programs. Library: 850 volumes. Theoretical and practical training gives students a relevant and comprehensive education in Fashion Business & Technology and Fashion Design & Technology. Placement assistance and internships available.

Fielding Graduate University
School of Human and Organization Development
2112 Santa Barbara St
Santa Barbara CA 93105-3538
DeAnne Taylor, Director of Admissions
805-687-1099 Fax: 805-687-9793
Website: www.fielding.edu
E-mail: admission@fielding.edu

Fremont College
18000 Studebaker Rd Suite 900, Cerritos CA 90703
Mark Buch, President & COO
562-809-5100 Fax: 562-809-7100
Website: www.fremont.edu
E-mail: senon.lee@fremont.edu

FRESNO CITY COLLEGE

1101 E University Ave, Fresno CA 93741-0002
Dayann Dietrich, Contact
559-442-8241 Fax: 559-237-4232
Website: www.fresnocitycollege.com
E-mail: fcc.admissions@scccd.com

Fresno Pacific University
1717 S Chestnut Ave, Fresno CA 93702-4798
559-453-2000

GEMOLOGICAL INSTITUTE OF AMERICA

The Robert Mouawad Campus
5345 Armada Dr, Carlsbad CA 92008-4602
Jason Drake, Admissions Manager
800-421-7250 ext. 4001 or 760-603-4001
Fax: 760-603-4003
Website: www.gia.edu
E-mail: eduinfo@gia.edu

Established 1931. Nonprofit. Private. Coed. Accreditation: ACCSCT and DETC. Diplomas: Graduate Gemologist, Graduate Jeweler, Graduate Jeweler Gemologist, Jewelry Business Management, Applied Jewelry Arts. Degree: BBA (Bachelor of Business Administration). Financial aid. Classes begin year round.

See listing under "Home Study and Correspondence"

Holy Names University
3500 Mountain Blvd, Oakland CA 94619-1699
Dr. Hoffman-Marr, Director of Admissions
510-436-1010

Humboldt State University
1 Harpst St, Arcata CA 95521-8299
707-826-3011

ITT Technical Institute
12669 Encinitas Ave, Sylmar CA 91342-3664
Kelly Christensen, Director of Admissions
818-364-5151 Fax: 818-364-5150
Website: www.itt-tech.edu
E-mail: kchristensen@itt-tech.edu

John F. Kennedy University
100 Ellinwood Way, Pleasant Hill CA 94523-4817
800-696-5358
Website: www.jfku.edu

La Sierra University
4500 Riverwalk Pkwy, Riverside CA 92505
Bobby Brown, Director of Admissions
800-874-5587

Loyola Marymount University
7900 Loyola Blvd, Los Angeles CA 90045-2699
310-338-2700

Maric College
9055 Balboa Ave, San Diego CA 92123
Geraldine Rorrison, Director of Admissions
858-279-4500 Fax: 858-279-4885
Website: www.mariccollege.edu
E-mail: grorrison@mariccollege.edu

Menlo College
1000 El Camino Real, Atherton CA 94027-4300
650-688-3753

MTI College
5221 Madison Ave, Sacramento CA 95841-3003
Marije Miller, Director of Admissions
916-339-1500 Fax: 916-339-0305
Website: www.mticollege.edu
E-mail: mmiller@mticollege.edu

Mt. St. Mary's College
12001 Chalon Rd, Los Angeles CA 90049-1599
310-954-4000

National University
11255 N Torrey Pines Rd, La Jolla CA 92037-1011
858-642-8000

Northwestern Polytechnic University
47671 Westinghouse Dr, Fremont CA 94539
Paul Jensen, Contact
510-657-5913 Fax: 510-657-8975
Website: www.npu.edu
E-mail: npuadm@npu.edu

Notre Dame de Namur University
1500 Ralston Ave, Belmont CA 94002-1997
Martin Bednarek, Director of Admissions
800-263-0545

Orange Coast College
PO Box 5005, Costa Mesa CA 92628-5005
Kristin Clark, Director of Admissions
714-432-5773 Fax: 714-432-5736
Website: www.orangecoastcollege.edu
E-mail: kclark@cccd.edu

Pacific States University
1516 S Western Ave, Los Angeles CA 90006
Dr. Brandon Kim, Associate University Dean
323-731-2383 Fax: 323-731-7276
Website: www.psuca.edu
E-mail: admissions@psuca.edu
See listing under "Universities"

Pacific Union College
1 Angwin Ave, Angwin CA 94508-9797
707-965-6311

Point Loma Nazarene University
3900 Lomaland Dr, San Diego CA 92106-2810
Chip Killingsworth, Director of Undergraduate Admissions
800-733-7770 Fax: 619-849-2601
Website: www.pointloma.edu
E-mail: admissions@pointloma.edu

San Bernardino Valley College
701 S Mount Vernon Ave
San Bernardino CA 92410-2798
Kay Ragan, Ed.D., Director of Admissions
909-888-6511 Fax: 909-889-4988
Website: www.valleycollege.edu
E-mail: kragan@sbccd.cc.ca.us

San Diego Christian College
2100 Greenfield Dr, El Cajon CA 92019-1157
Rene Inman, Director of Admissions
800-676-2242 Fax: 619-590-1739
Website: www.sdcc.edu
E-mail: admissions@sdcc.edu

San Diego State University
5500 Campanile Dr, San Diego CA 92182-0002
619-594-5200

San Francisco State University
1600 Holloway Ave, San Francisco CA 94132-1722
415-338-1111

San Joaquin Valley College
201 New Stine Rd, Bakersfield CA 93309-2659
Jaime Delgado, Enrollment Services Director
661-834-1026 Fax: 559-651-4864
Website: www.sjvc.edu
E-mail: jaime.delgado@sjvc.edu

San Joaquin Valley College
295 E Sierra Ave, Fresno CA 93710-3616
Nora Twarynski, Enrollment Services Director
559-448-8282 Fax: 559-651-4864
Website: www.sjvc.edu
E-mail: nora.twarynski@sjvc.edu

San Joaquin Valley College
1700 McHenry Village Way Suite 6
Modesto CA 95350
Joseph Holt, Director of Admissions
209-527-7582 Fax: 559-651-4864
Website: www.sjvc.edu
E-mail: josephh@sjvc.edu

San Joaquin Valley College
11050 Olson Dr, Rancho Cordova CA 95670
Joseph Holt, Director of Admissions
559-651-2500 Fax: 559-651-4864
Website: www.sjvc.edu
E-mail: joseph.holt@sjvc.edu

San Joaquin Valley College
10641 Church St, Rancho Cucamonga CA 91730
Ramon Abreu, Enrollment Services Director
909-948-7582 Fax: 559-651-4864
Website: www.sjvc.edu
E-mail: ramon.abreu@sjvc.edu

San Joaquin Valley College
8400 W Mineral King Ave, Visalia CA 93291-9283
Susie Topjian, Enrollment Services Director
559-651-2500 Fax: 559-651-4864
Website: www.sjvc.edu
E-mail: susiet@sjvc.edu

San Jose State University
1 Washington Sq, San Jose CA 95192-0001
408-924-1000

Santa Clara University
500 El Camino Real, Santa Clara CA 95053-0001
408-554-4000

Simpson University
2211 College View Dr, Redding CA 96003-8606
Jim Herberger, Director of Admissions
888-9-SIMPSON Fax: 530-226-4861
Website: www.simpsonuniversity.edu
E-mail: admissions@simpsonuniversity.edu
See listing under "Universities"

Sonoma State University
1801 E Cotati Ave, Rohnert Park CA 94928-3609
Louis T. Levy, Senior Director Enrollment Services
707-664-2880

Stanford University
520 Lasuen Mall Union 232, Stanford CA 94305-3005
650-723-2300

University of California
110 Sproul Hall, Berkeley CA 94720-5804
510-642-6000

University of California
1 Shields Ave, Davis CA 95616
530-752-1011

University of California
Irvine CA 92697-0001
949-824-5011

University of California
Los Angeles CA 90095-0001
310-825-4321

University of California
900 University Ave, Riverside CA 92521-0001
951-827-1012

University of California-Santa Cruz
Santa Cruz CA 95064
831-459-0111

University of Judaism
15600 Mulholland Dr, Los Angeles CA 90077-1599
Bryan Pisetsky, Director of Undergraduate Admissions
310-476-9777

University of La Verne
1950 3rd St, La Verne CA 91750-4443
800-876-4858

University of San Diego
5998 Alcala Park, San Diego CA 92110-2492
Admissions
619-260-4506

University of San Francisco
2130 Fulton St, San Francisco CA 94117-1050
415-422-5555

University of Southern California
Univ Park, Los Angeles CA 90089-0001
213-740-2311

University of the Pacific
3601 Pacific Ave, Stockton CA 95211-0197
209-946-2011

Vanguard University of Southern California
55 Fair Dr, Costa Mesa CA 92626-6597
714-556-3610

Whittier College
PO Box 634, Whittier CA 90608-0634
Kieron Miller, Director of Admissions
562-907-4200 Fax: 562-907-4870
Website: www.whittier.edu
E-mail: kmiller@whittier.edu

COLORADO

Adams State College
Alamosa CO 81102
Matt Gallegos, Director of Admissions
800-824-6494

Colorado Christian University
8787 W Alameda Ave, Lakewood CO 80226
Sean Kadel, Director of Admissions
800-44-FAITH Fax: 303-963-3201
Website: www.ccu.edu
E-mail: admissions@ccu.edu

Colorado Northwestern Community College
500 Kennedy Dr, Rangely CO 81648-3502
Tresa England, Director of Student Services
800-562-1105 Fax: 970-675-3343
Website: www.cncc.edu
E-mail: tresa.england@cncc.edu

Colorado State University
1062 Campus Delivery, Fort Collins CO 80523
970-491-1101

Colorado State University - Pueblo
2200 Bonforte Blvd, Pueblo CO 81001-4990
719-549-2461

Community College of Aurora
16000 E Centretech Pkwy, Aurora CO 80011-9036
Kristen Cusack, Director of Admissions and Records
303-360-4700 Fax: 303-361-7432
Website: www.ccaurora.edu
E-mail: enrollment@ccaurora.edu

Everest College
Aurora Campus
14280 E Jewell Ave, Aurora CO 80012-5692
John Heckman, Director of Admissions
303-367-2757 Fax: 303-745-6245
Website: www.cci.edu

Fort Lewis College
1000 Rim Dr, Durango CO 81301-3999
970-247-7010

Mesa State College
1100 North Ave, Grand Junction CO 81501
970-248-1020

Metropolitan State College
PO Box 173362, Campus Box 13
Denver CO 80217-3362
303-556-3245

National American University
5125 N Academy Blvd
Colorado Springs CO 80918-4001
Jeanne Liepe, Campus Director
719-277-0588

National American University
1325 S Colorado Blvd #100, Denver CO 80222-3308
Nathan Larson, Regional President
303-758-6700

NORTHEASTERN JUNIOR COLLEGE
100 College Ave, Sterling CO 80751-2399
Dr. Lance Bolton, Chief Administrative Officer
Tina Joyce, Director of Admissions
970-521-7000 or 970-521-6752 Fax: 970-521-6801
Website: www.njc.edu
E-mail: tina.joyce@njc.edu

Regis University
3333 Regis Blvd, Denver CO 80221-1099
303-458-4900

San Juan Basin Technical College
PO Box 970, Cortez CO 81321-0970
Shannon South, Vice President
970-565-8457 Fax: 970-565-8450
Website: www.sjbtc.edu
E-mail: info@sjbtc.edu

University of Colorado
Boulder CO 80309-0001
303-492-1411

University of Colorado
1420 Austin Bluffs Pkwy
Colorado Springs CO 80918-3735
719-262-3000

University of Colorado at Denver and Health Sciences Center
Downtown Denver Campus
PO Box 173364, Denver CO 80217-3364
303-556-5800

University of Denver
2199 S University Blvd, Denver CO 80208-0001
303-871-2000

UNIVERSITY OF DENVER UNIVERSITY COLLEGE
2211 S Josephine St, Denver CO 80208
Dr. Denise Pearson, Assistant Dean of Academics
303-871-3354 Fax: 303-871-4047
Website: www.universitycollege.du.edu
E-mail: ucolinfo@du.edu

University of Northern Colorado
Greeley CO 80639
Robert Lynch, Dean
970-351-2764

Western State College of Colorado
Gunnison CO 81231-0001
Director of Admissions
800-876-5309

CONNECTICUT

Albertus Magnus College
700 Prospect St, New Haven CT 06511-1189
Richard Lolatte, Dean of Admission
203-773-8501 or 800-578-9160 Fax: 203-773-5248
Website: www.albertus.edu
E-mail: admissions@albertus.edu

Eastern Connecticut State University
83 Windham St, Willimantic CT 06226-2295
860-456-5000

Fairfield University
1073 N Benson Rd, Fairfield CT 06824-5171
203-254-4000

INTERNATIONAL COLLEGE OF HOSPITALITY MANAGEMENT
1760 Mapleton Ave, Suffield CT 06078
Jolie Swanson, Director of Admissions
860-668-3515 Fax: 860-668-7369
Website: www.ichm.edu
E-mail: admissions@ichm.edu

Middlesex Community College
100 Training Hill Rd, Middletown CT 06457-4889
Mensimah Shabazz, Director of Admissions
860-343-5800 Fax: 860-344-3055
Website: www.mxcc.commnet.edu
E-mail: mshabazz@mxcc.commnet.edu

Post University
800 Country Club Rd, Waterbury CT 06708-3240
Sandra M. Fernandes, Associate Director of Admissions
Will Johnson, Associate Director of Admissions
203-596-4520

Quinnipiac University
275 Mount Carmel Ave, Hamden CT 06518-1905
Joan Isaac Mohr, VP & Dean of Admissions
203-582-8600

St. Joseph College
1678 Asylum Ave, West Hartford CT 06117-2791
860-232-4571

UNITED STATES COAST GUARD ACADEMY
15 Mohegan Ave, New London CT 06320-8131
Captain Susan D. Bibeau, Contact
800-883-8724 Fax: 860-701-6700
Website: www.uscga.edu
E-mail: admissions@uscga.edu

University of Bridgeport
126 Park Ave, Bridgeport CT 06604-5620
Barbara L. Maryak, Dean of Admissions
203-576-4552

University of Connecticut
Storrs CT 06269-0001
860-486-2000

University of Hartford
200 Bloomfield Ave, West Hartford CT 06117-1599
860-768-4100

University of New Haven
300 Boston Post Rd, West Haven CT 06516
Director of Undergraduate Admissions
203-932-7319

Yale University
38 Hillhouse Ave, New Haven CT 06511
203-432-4771

DELAWARE

Goldey-Beacom College
4701 Limestone Rd, Wilmington DE 19808-1993
Stacey Schwartz, Assistant Director of Admissions
302-998-8814 Fax: 302-996-5408
Website: www.gbc.edu
E-mail: admissions@gbc.edu

University of Delaware
Newark DE 19711
302-831-2000

Wesley College
120 N State St, Dover DE 19901-3876
302-736-2300 Fax: 302-736-2301
Website: www.wesley.edu

DISTRICT OF COLUMBIA

American University
4400 Massachusetts Ave NW
Washington DC 20016-8200
202-885-1000

Gallaudet University
800 Florida Ave NE, Washington DC 20002-3695
Charity Reedy Hines, Director of Admissions
202-651-5750 Fax: 202-651-5744
Website: www.gallaudet.edu
E-mail: admissions.office@gallaudet.edu

Georgetown University
37th and O St NW, Washington DC 20057-0001
202-687-0100

George Washington University
2035 H St NW, Washington DC 20052-0002
202-994-1000

Howard University
2400 6th St NW, Washington DC 20059-0002
202-806-6100

Potomac College
4000 Chesapeake St NW, Washington DC 20016
Florence Tate, President
202-686-0876 Fax: 202-686-0818
Website: www.potomac.edu
E-mail: ftate@potomac.edu

SOUTHEASTERN UNIVERSITY
501 I St SW, Washington DC 20024-2788
Sean Jamieson, Director of Admissions
202-478-8210 Fax: 202-488-8093
Website: www.seu.edu
E-mail: admissions@admin.seu.edu

Trinity University
125 Michigan Ave NE, Washington DC 20017-1090
202-884-9000

University of the District of Columbia
4200 Connecticut Ave NW
Washington DC 20008-1174
LaVerne M. Hill-Flanagan, Director of Admissions
202-274-5100

FLORIDA

Barry University
11300 NE 2nd Ave, Miami Shores FL 33161-6695
800-695-2279

Bethune-Cookman College
640 Dr Mary McLeod Bethune Blvd
Daytona Beach FL 32114-3099
Edwin Coffie, Director of Admissions
800-448-0228

CARLOS ALBIZU UNIVERSITY
2173 NW 99th Ave, Miami FL 33172-2209
Carlos Alicea, Director of Admissions, Recruitment & Outreach
305-593-1223 ext. 137 Fax: 305-593-1854
Website: www.mia.albizu.edu
E-mail: admissions@albizu.edu

City College
2000 W Commercial Blvd, Fort Lauderdale FL 33309
Mercedes Segal, Director of Admissions
954-492-5353 Fax: 954-491-1965
Website: www.citycollege.edu

Clearwater Christian College
3400 Gulf To Bay Blvd, Clearwater FL 33759-4595
727-726-1153

Eckerd College
4200 54th Ave S, Saint Petersburg FL 33711
727-867-1166

Embry-Riddle Aeronautical University
Daytona Beach Campus
PO Box 11767, Daytona Beach FL 32120-1767
C. Richard Clarke, Director of Admissions
800-862-2416 Fax: 386-226-7070
Website: www.embryriddle.edu
E-mail: dbadmit@erau.edu

EVERGLADES UNIVERSITY (MAIN CAMPUS)
5002 T-Rex Ave Suite 100, Boca Raton FL 33431
Kristi Mollis, President
888-772-6077 Fax: 561-912-1191
Website: www.evergladesuniversity.edu
E-mail: admissions-boca@evergladesuniversity.edu
See listing under "Universities"

EVERGLADES UNIVERSITY
Orlando Campus (Branch Campus)
887 E Altamonte Dr, Altamonte Springs FL 32701
Linda Volz, Vice President
866-289-1078 Fax: 407-482-9801
Website: www.evergladesuniversity.edu
E-mail: admissions-orl@evergladesuniversity.edu
See listing under "Universities"

EVERGLADES UNIVERSITY
Sarasota Campus (Branch Campus)
6001 Lake Osprey Dr, Suite 110, Sarasota FL 34240
Brad Brewer, Vice President
866-907-2262 Fax: 941-907-6634
Website: www.evergladesuniversity.edu
E-mail: admissions-sar@evergladesuniversity.edu
See listing under "Universities"

Flagler College
PO Box 1027, Saint Augustine FL 32085-1027
904-829-6481

Florida A&M University
Tallahassee FL 32307
850-599-3000

Florida Atlantic University
PO Box 3091, Boca Raton FL 33431-0991
800-299-4328

Florida International University
Tamiami Trl, Miami FL 33199-0001
305-348-2000

Florida Southern College
111 Lake Hollingsworth Dr, Lakeland FL 33801-5607
Robert B. Palmer, V.P., Dean of Enrollment Management
863-680-4131

Florida State University
600 W College Ave, Tallahassee FL 32306-1096
Janice V. Finney, Director of Admissions
850-644-2525 Fax: 850-644-0197
Website: admissions.fsu.edu
E-mail: admissions@admin.fsu.edu

HERZING COLLEGE
1595 S Semoran Blvd #1501
Winter Park FL 32792-5509
Kathy Nagle, Director of Admissions
407-478-0500 Fax: 407-478-0501
Website: www.herzing.edu
E-mail: info@orl.herzing.edu

Jones College
5353 Arlington Expy, Jacksonville FL 32211-5588
Dorothy D. Jones, Chief Executive Officer
904-743-1122 Fax: 904-744-4446
Website: www.jones.edu
E-mail: fmccaffe@jones.edu

Jones College
11430 N Kendall Dr Ste 200, Miami FL 33176
Patricia Carbonell, Contact
305-275-9996 Fax: 305-743-4446
Website: www.jones.edu
E-mail: pcarbone@jones.edu

Lynn University
3601 N Military Trl, Boca Raton FL 33431-5598
Director of Admissions
561-237-7900 Fax: 561-237-7100
Website: www.lynn.edu
E-mail: admission@lynn.edu

Northwood University
2600 N Military Trl, West Palm Beach FL 33409-2999
Jack Letvinchuk, Director of Admissions
800-458-8325 Fax: 561-640-3328
Website: www.northwood.edu
E-mail: fladmit@northwood.edu

Palm Beach Atlantic University
PO Box 24708, West Palm Beach FL 33416-4708
561-803-2000

Rollins College
1000 Holt Ave, Winter Park FL 32789
407-646-2000

Saint Leo University
PO Box 6665, Saint Leo FL 33574
Director of Admissions
800-334-5532

St. Thomas University
16401 NW 37th Ave, Miami Gardens FL 33054
Dr. Ted Abernathy, Contact
800-367-9010 or 305-628-6546 Fax: 305-628-6591
Website: www.stu.edu
E-mail: signup@stu.edu

SOUTHWEST FLORIDA COLLEGE
1685 Medical Ln, Fort Myers FL 33907-1157
866-SWFC-NOW or 239-939-4766 Fax: 239-936-4040
Website: www.swfc.edu
E-mail: studentinfo@swfc.edu

Stetson University
421 N Woodland Boulevard, De Land FL 32720-3761
386-822-7000

University of Central Florida
PO Box 160111, Orlando FL 32816
407-823-3000

University of Florida
PO Box 114000, Gainesville FL 32611-4000
352-392-3261

University of Miami
PO Box 248006, Coral Gables FL 33124-8006
305-284-2211

University of North Florida
4567 Saint Johns Bluff Rd S
Jacksonville FL 32224-2645
904-620-1000

University of South Florida
4202 E Fowler Ave, Tampa FL 33620-6900
J. Robert Spatig, Director of Admissions
877-USF-BULL Fax: 813-974-9689
Website: www.usf.edu
E-mail: admissions@admin.usf.edu
See listing under "Universities"

University of West Florida
11000 University Pkwy, Pensacola FL 32514-5750
850-474-2000

Warner Southern College
5301 US Highway 27 S, Lake Wales FL 33859-8725
863-638-1426

GEORGIA

American InterContinental University
3330 Peachtree Rd NE, Atlanta GA 30326-1016
404-965-5700

American InterContinental University
6600 Peachtree Dunwoody Rd
500 Embassy Row, Atlanta GA 30328
404-965-6500

Augusta State University
2500 Walton Way, Augusta GA 30904-4562
706-737-1400

Brewton-Parker College
Highway 280, Mount Vernon GA 30445
800-342-1087

Clark Atlanta University
223 James Brawley Dr SW, Atlanta GA 30314
404-880-8000

Clayton State University
5900 N Lee St, Morrow GA 30260
770-961-3500

DeVry University - Decatur Campus
250 N Arcadia Ave, Decatur GA 30030
Eric Stafford, Director of Admissions
404-292-7900 Fax: 404-292-7011
Website: www.devry.edu
E-mail: estafford@admin.atl.devry.edu

Emory University
200B Jones Center, Atlanta GA 30322
404-727-6123

Georgia College and State University
231 W Hancock St, Milledgeville GA 31061-3371
478-445-5350

Georgia Institute of Technology
225 North Ave NW, Atlanta GA 30332-0002
404-894-2000

Georgia Southern University
PO Box 8024, Statesboro GA 30460
Admissions Office
912-681-5532

Georgia State University
PO Box 4009, Atlanta GA 30302-4009
404-651-2365

Kennesaw State University
1000 Chastain Rd NW, Kennesaw GA 30144-5591
Timothy Mescon, Dean of College of Business
770-423-6425
Website: www.kennesaw.edu

LaGrange College
601 Broad St, LaGrange GA 30240-2955
Andy Geeter, Director of Admission
800-593-2885

Life University
1269 Barclay Cir SE, Marietta GA 30060-2903
Dr. Deborah E. Heairlston, Director of New Student Development
770-426-2884 Fax: 770-426-2895
Website: www.life.edu
E-mail: admissions@life.edu

Mercer University in Atlanta
3001 Mercer University Dr, Atlanta GA 30341-4155
678-547-6000

Mercer University in Macon
1400 Coleman Ave, Macon GA 31207-0003
John P. Cole, Sr. Assoc. V.P. for Admissions
478-301-2650

North Georgia College & State University
Dahlonega GA 30597-0001
706-864-1400

North Georgia Technical College
434 Meeks Ave, Blairsville GA 30512-2983
Admissions
706-439-6300 Fax: 706-439-6301
Website: www.northgatech.edu
E-mail: info@northgatech.edu

North Georgia Technical College
8989 Highway 17, Toccoa GA 30577
706-779-8100 Fax: 706-779-8130
Website: www.northgatech.edu
E-mail: info@northgatech.edu

North Georgia Technical College
Clarkesville Campus
PO Box 65, Clarkesville GA 30523-0002
Admissions
706-754-7700 Fax: 706-754-7777
Website: www.northgatech.edu
E-mail: info@northgatech.edu

North Metro Technical College
5198 Ross Rd SE, Acworth GA 30102-3129
Missy Cusack, Director of Admissions
770-975-4000 Fax: 770-975-4142
Website: www.northmetrotech.edu
E-mail: info@northmetrotech.edu

Oglethorpe University
4484 Peachtree Rd NE, Atlanta GA 30319-2797
Kelly Gosnell, Director of Admission
404-261-1441

Paine College
1235 15th St, Augusta GA 30901-3182
800-476-7703

Piedmont College
PO Box 10, Demorest GA 30535-0010
800-277-7020

Savannah State University
3219 College St, Savannah GA 31404-5255
912-356-2187

Thomas University
1501 Millpond Rd, Thomasville GA 31792-7478
Darla M. Glass, Director of Student Affairs
229-226-1621

TOCCOA FALLS COLLEGE
PO Box 800899, Toccoa Falls GA 30598
888-785-5624 Fax: 706-282-6012
Website: www.tfc.edu
E-mail: admissions@tfc.edu

University of Georgia
Athens GA 30602-0001
706-542-3000

University of West Georgia
Carrollton GA 30118-0001
770-836-6500

Valdosta State University
N Patterson St, Valdosta GA 31698-0001
229-333-5952

Valdosta Technical College
4089 Val Tech Rd, Valdosta GA 31602-0928
Amanda Leavy, Admissions Coordinator
229-333-2100 Fax: 229-249-4980
Website: www.valdostatech.edu
E-mail: aleavy@valdostatech.edu

HAWAII

Brigham Young University
55-220 Kulanui St, Laie HI 96762-1293
808-293-3211

Chaminade University of Honolulu
3140 Waialae Ave, Honolulu HI 96816-1510
Joy Bouey, Dean of Enrollment Management
808-739-4619

Hawaii Pacific University
45-045 Kamehameha Hwy, Kaneohe HI 96744-5297
808-235-3641

Heald College, Honolulu
1500 Kapiolani Blvd, Honolulu HI 96814-3732
Wendy N. Nishimura, Director of Admissions
808-955-1500 or 800-940-0530 Fax: 808-955-6964
Website: www.heald.edu
E-mail: wendy_nishimura@heald.edu

Kauai Community College
3-1901 Kaumualii Hwy, Lihue HI 96766-9500
808-245-8225 Fax: 808-245-8297
Website: kauai.hawaii.edu
E-mail: arkauai@hawaii.edu

University of Hawaii at Manoa
2444 Dole St, Honolulu HI 96822-2302
808-956-5280

IDAHO

Boise State University
1910 University Dr, Boise ID 83725-0399
208-426-1011

Brigham Young University - Idaho
120 Kimball Bldg, Rexburg ID 83460-1615
Rob Garrett, Director of Admissions
208-496-1020 Fax: 208-496-1220
Website: www.byui.edu
E-mail: admissions@byui.edu

Idaho State University
PO Box 8270, Pocatello ID 83209-0001
208-282-0211

Lewis-Clark State College
500 8th Ave, Lewiston ID 83501-2698
Diane Douglas, Ph.D., Registrar/Director of Admissions
800-933-5272 Fax: 208-792-2429
Website: www.lcsc.edu
E-mail: admissions@lcsc.edu

University of Idaho
Moscow ID 83844-4253
Lloyd Scott, Director of New Student Services
208-885-6163 Fax: 208-885-4477
Website: www.uidaho.edu
E-mail: nss@uidaho.edu

ILLINOIS

AMERICAN INTERCONTINENTAL UNIVERSITY ONLINE
5550 Prairie Stone Parkway Suite 400
Hoffman Estates IL 60192
Admissions Department
877-701-3800
Website: www.aiuonline.edu
E-mail: info@aiuonline.edu

ARGOSY UNIVERSITY/CHICAGO
350 N Orleans St, Merchandise Mart
Chicago IL 60654
Jamal Scott, Director of Admissions
800-626-4123 Fax: 312-777-7750
Website: www.argosyu.edu
E-mail: jscott@argosyu.edu

Augustana College
639 38th St, Rock Island IL 61201-2296
309-794-7000

Aurora University
347 S Gladstone Ave, Aurora IL 60506-4892
Carol R. Dunn, Ed.D., Vice President for Enrollment
800-742-5281 Fax: 630-844-5535
Website: www.aurora.edu
E-mail: admission@aurora.edu

Benedictine University
5700 College Rd, Lisle IL 60532-0900
630-829-6300 or 888-829-6363 Fax: 630-829-6301
Website: www.ben.edu
E-mail: admissions@ben.edu
See listing under "Universities"

Bradley University
1501 W Bradley Ave, Peoria IL 61625-0002
800-447-6460

Columbia College Chicago
600 S Michigan Ave, Chicago IL 60605-1996
Murphy Monroe, Executive Director of Admissions
312-344-7130 Fax: 312-344-8024
Website: www.colum.edu
E-mail: admissions@colum.edu

CONCORDIA UNIVERSITY
7400 Augusta St, River Forest IL 60305-1402
708-209-3100 Fax: 708-209-3176
Website: www.cuchicago.edu
E-mail: admission@cuchicago.edu

De Paul University
1 E Jackson Blvd, Chicago IL 60604-2287
Carlene Klaas, Director of Admissions
312-362-8000

Eastern Illinois University
600 Lincoln Ave, Charleston IL 61920-3099
217-581-5000

Elmhurst College
190 S Prospect Ave, Elmhurst IL 60126-3296
630-279-4100

Eureka College
300 E College Ave, Eureka IL 61530-1500
309-467-3721

Greenville College
315 E College Ave, Greenville IL 62246-1199
618-664-1840

Illinois College
1101 W College Ave, Jacksonville IL 62650-2299
217-245-3000

Illinois Institute of Technology
Chicago-Kent College of Law
565 W Adams St, Chicago IL 60661-3601
Nicole Vilches, Assistant Dean for Admissions
312-906-5000 Fax: 312-906-5274
Website: www.kentlaw.edu
E-mail: admit@kentlaw.edu

Illinois State University
Normal IL 61790-0001
309-438-2111

Illinois Wesleyan University
PO Box 2900, Bloomington IL 61702-2900
Dr. David Marvin & Dr. David Willis, Co-Chairpersons
309-556-3171

International Academy of Design and Technology
1 N State St #500, Chicago IL 60602-3300
Cecily Arroyo, Director of Admissions
888-803-0111 Fax: 312-541-3929
Website: www.iadtchicago.edu
E-mail: carroyo@iadtchicago.com

Kaskaskia College
27210 College Rd, Centralia IL 62801-7878
Tyra Taylor, Dean of Enrollment Management and Retention Services
618-545-3000 Fax: 618-532-1990
Website: www.kaskaskia.edu
E-mail: ttaylor@kaskaskia.edu

Kendall College
900 N North Branch St, Chicago IL 60622
Office of Admissions
800-569-8179 Fax: 312-752-2021
Website: www.kendall.edu
E-mail: admissions@kendall.edu

Lewis University
One University Parkway, Romeoville IL 60446
800-897-9000

Loyola University - Mundelein College
6525 N Sheridan Rd, Chicago IL 60626-5311
773-262-8100

Loyola University of Chicago
820 N Michigan Ave, Chicago IL 60611-2103
312-915-6000

MacCormac College
29 E Madison St, Chicago IL 60602-4405
David F. Grassi, Admissions Counselor
312-922-1884 ext. 101 Fax: 312-922-4328
Website: www.maccormac.edu
E-mail: dgrassi@maccormac.edu

MacMurray College
447 E College Ave, Jacksonville IL 62650-2590
217-479-7000

Millikin University
1184 W Main St, Decatur IL 62522-2084
Lin Stoner, Dean of Admission
800-373-7733

Monmouth College
700 E Broadway, Monmouth IL 61462-1963
309-457-2131

National-Louis University
5202 Old Orchard Rd Ste 300, Skokie IL 60077-4409
224-233-2000

North Central College
30 N Brainard St, Naperville IL 60540-4690
Martha Stolze, Director of Admissions
630-637-5800

NORTHEASTERN ILLINOIS UNIVERSITY
5500 N Saint Louis Ave, Chicago IL 60625-4699
Varkey Titus, Dean
773-442-4050 Fax: 773-442-4020
Website: www.neiu.edu
E-mail: v-titus@neiu.edu

Northern Illinois University
DeKalb IL 60115
815-753-1000

Northwestern University
1801 Hinman Ave, Evanston IL 60208-1260
847-491-3741

Olivet Nazarene University
1 University Ave
Bourbonnais IL 60914
815-939-5011

Principia College
Elsah IL 62028-9799
618-374-2131

Quincy University
1800 College Ave, Quincy IL 62301-2670
217-222-8020

Rockford College
5050 E State St, Rockford IL 61108-2393
William Laffey, Director of Admission
800-892-2984

Roosevelt University
430 S Michigan Ave, Chicago IL 60605
Gwen E. Kanelos, Asst. Vice President for Enrollment Services
877-APPLY-RU Fax: 312-341-4216
Website: www.roosevelt.edu
E-mail: applyru@roosevelt.edu

Southern Illinois University
Carbondale IL 62901-4400
618-453-2121

Southern Illinois University Edwardsville
Edwardsville IL 62026-0001
618-650-3705

Trinity Christian College
6601 W College Dr, Palos Heights IL 60463-0929
Joshua Lenarz, Director of Admissions
708-597-3000

Trinity International University
2065 Half Day Rd, Deerfield IL 60015-1241
847-945-8800 Fax: 847-317-8097
Website: www.tiu.edu
E-mail: tcadmissions@tiu.edu

Triton College
2000 5th Ave, River Grove IL 60171-1995
Jeffery Cooks, Director, Admission Services
708-456-0300 ext. 3130 Fax: 708-583-3147
Website: www.triton.edu
E-mail: triton@triton.edu
See listing under "Community and Junior Colleges"

University of Chicago
5801 S Ellis Ave, Chicago IL 60637-1476
773-702-1234

University of Illinois
901 W Illinois St, Urbana IL 61801
217-333-1000

University of Illinois at Chicago
PO Box 5220, Chicago IL 60680-5220
312-996-3000

University of Illinois at Springfield
One University Plaza, Springfield IL 62794
217-206-4847

University of St. Francis
500 Wilcox St, Joliet IL 60435
800-735-7500

Western Illinois University
1 University Cir, Macomb IL 61455-1390
309-295-1414

INDIANA

Ancilla Domini College
Donaldson IN 46513
Erin Alonzo, Director of Admissions
574-936-8898 Fax: 574-935-1773
Website: www.ancilla.edu
E-mail: erin.alonzo@ancilla.edu

Ball State University
2000 W University Ave, Muncie IN 47306-0002
765-285-5555

Bethel College
1001 W McKinley Ave, Mishawaka IN 46545-5591
Office of Admissions
574-257-3339

BROWN MACKIE COLLEGE - FORT WAYNE
3000 E Coliseum Blvd, Fort Wayne IN 46805
Daniel Summer, Campus President
260-484-4400 Fax: 260-484-2678
Website: www.brownmackie.edu

BROWN MACKIE COLLEGE - SOUTH BEND
1030 E Jefferson Blvd, South Bend IN 46617-3123
Connie Adelman, Campus President
574-237-0774 Fax: 574-237-3585
Website: www.brownmackie.edu

Butler University
4600 Sunset Ave, Indianapolis IN 46208-3443
317-940-8000

Calumet College of St. Joseph
2400 New York Ave, Whiting IN 46394-2195
219-473-7770

Franklin College
101 Branigin Blvd, Franklin IN 46131
Jacqueline S. Acosta, Director of Admissions
800-852-0232 Fax: 317-738-8274
Website: www.franklincollege.edu
E-mail: admissions@franklincollege.edu

Goshen College
1700 S Main St, Goshen IN 46526-4794
574-535-7000

Grace College
200 Seminary Dr, Winona Lake IN 46590-1224
800-54-GRACE

Hanover College
PO Box 108, Hanover IN 47243-0108
William D. Preble, Dean of Admission
800-213-2178

Huntington College
2303 College Ave, Huntington IN 46750-1299
260-356-6000

Indiana State University
Terre Haute IN 47809-0001
Richard Toomey, Director of Admissions
812-237-6311

Indiana University
300 N Jordan Ave, Bloomington IN 47405-1106
812-855-4848

Indiana University at South Bend
PO Box 7111, South Bend IN 46634-7111
574-237-4111

Indiana University Northwest
3400 Broadway, Gary IN 46408-1101
219-980-6500

Indiana University-Purdue University at Fort Wayne
2101 E Coliseum Blvd, Fort Wayne IN 46805-1445
260-481-6100

Indiana University Southeast
4201 Grant Line Rd, New Albany IN 47150-2158
812-941-2000

Indiana Wesleyan University
4201 S Washington St, Marion IN 46953-4974
765-674-6901

International Business College
5699 Coventry Ln, Fort Wayne IN 46804
260-459-4500 Fax: 260-436-1896
Website: www.ibcfortwayne.edu
E-mail: skinzer@ibcfortwayne.edu

Ivy Tech Community College - North Central
220 Dean Johnson Blvd, South Bend IN 46601-3415
Pam Decker, Director of Admissions
574-289-7001 Fax: 574-236-7177
Website: www.ivytech.edu
E-mail: pdecker@ivytech.edu

Manchester College
604 E College Ave, North Manchester IN 46962-1276
260-982-5000

Marian College
3200 Cold Spring Rd, Indianapolis IN 46222-1997
317-955-6000

Oakland City University
138 N Lucretia St, Oakland City IN 47660
Brian J. Baker, Director of Admissions
800-737-5125 Fax: 812-749-1433
Website: www.oak.edu
E-mail: bbaker@oak.edu
See listing under "Universities"

Purdue University
2200 169th St, Hammond IN 46323
219-989-2993

Purdue University
1401 S US Highway 421, Westville IN 46391-9542
219-785-5200

St. Mary-of-the-Woods College
Saint Mary of the Woods IN 47876
James P. Malley, Jr., Director of Admission
800-926-7692

St. Mary's College
46 Madeliva, Notre Dame IN 46556
574-284-4000

Taylor University
500 W Reade Ave, Upland IN 46989-1002
765-998-2751

University of Evansville
1800 Lincoln Ave, Evansville IN 47722-0001
Don Vos, Dean of Admission
800-423-8633 Fax: 812-488-4076
Website: www.evansville.edu
E-mail: admission@evansville.edu

University of Indianapolis
1400 E Hanna Ave, Indianapolis IN 46227-3697
317-788-3368

University of Notre Dame
220 Main Building, Notre Dame IN 46556
574-631-5000

University of Southern Indiana
8600 University Blvd, Evansville IN 47712-3591
812-464-8600

Valparaiso University
Valparaiso IN 46383
219-464-5000

IOWA

AIB College of Business
2500 Fleur Dr, Des Moines IA 50321-1799
800-444-1921 Fax: 515-244-6773
Website: www.aib.edu
E-mail: admissions@aib.edu

Briar Cliff University
PO Box 2100, Sioux City IA 51104-0100
Sharisue Wilcoxon, VP for Enrollment Management
712-279-5200 Fax: 712-279-1632
Website: www.briarcliff.edu
E-mail: admissions@briarcliff.edu

Buena Vista University
610 W 4th St, Storm Lake IA 50588-1798
712-749-2235

Clarke College
1550 Clarke Dr, Dubuque IA 52001-3198
Andy Schroeder, Director of Admissions
800-383-2345 Fax: 563-584-8666
Website: www.clarke.edu
E-mail: andy.schroeder@clarke.edu

Coe College
1220 1st Ave NE, Cedar Rapids IA 52402-5092
319-399-8000

Dordt College
498 4th Ave NE, Sioux Center IA 51250-1697
Quentin Van Essen, Executive Director of Admissions
800-343-6738

Drake University
2507 University Ave, Des Moines IA 50311-4505
Laura Linn, Director of Admissions
515-271-2011

Graceland University
1 University Place, Lamoni IA 50140
Greg Sutherland, Interim Vice President for Enrollment and Dean of Admissions
641-784-5196 Fax: 641-784-5480
Website: www.admissions.graceland.edu
E-mail: admissions@graceland.edu

Grand View College
1200 Grandview Ave, Des Moines IA 50316-1599
515-263-2800

Hamilton College
3165 Edgewood Pkwy SW, Cedar Rapids IA 52404
Susan Spivey, Campus President
319-363-0481 Fax: 319-363-3812
Website: www.hamiltonia.edu
E-mail: sspivey@hamiltonia.edu

Hamilton College
4655 121st St, Urbandale IA 50323-2311
Colleen McDermott, Campus President
515-727-2100 Fax: 515-727-2115
Website: www.hamiltonia.edu
E-mail: cmcdermott@hamiltonia.edu

Iowa Lakes Community College
3200 College Dr, Emmetsburg IA 50536-1055
Anne Stansbury, Asst. Director of Admissions
712-852-5212 Fax: 712-362-8363
Website: www.iowalakes.edu
E-mail: info@iowalakes.edu

Iowa Lakes Community College
300 S 18th St, Estherville IA 51334-2721
Anne Stansbury, Asst. Director of Admissions
712-362-7945 Fax: 712-362-8363
Website: www.iowalakes.edu
E-mail: info@iowalakes.edu

Iowa Lakes Community College
1900 Grand Ave, Suite 8, Spencer IA 51301
Anne Stansbury, Assistant Director of Admissions
712-262-7141 Fax: 712-262-4047
Website: www.iowalakes.edu
E-mail: info@iowalakes.edu

Iowa State University
Ames IA 50011-0001
515-294-4111

Loras College
1450 Alta Vista St, Dubuque IA 52001-4399
Tim Hauber, Director of Admissions
800-245-6727

Luther College
700 College Dr, Decorah IA 52101-1045
563-387-2000

Morningside College
1501 Morningside Ave, Sioux City IA 51106-1717
712-274-5000

Mount Mercy College
1330 Elmhurst Dr NE, Cedar Rapids IA 52402-4797
Jim Krystofiak, Dean of Admission
800-248-4504

Northwestern College
101 7th St SW, Orange City IA 51041-1996
712-737-7000

Northwest Iowa Community College
603 W Park St, Sheldon IA 51201-1046
Lisa Story, Director of Enrollment Management
712-324-5061 Fax: 712-324-4136
Website: www.nwicc.edu
E-mail: lstory@nwicc.edu

University of Iowa
107 Calvin Hall, Iowa City IA 52242-1315
319-335-3500

University of Northern Iowa
Cedar Falls IA 50614-0001
319-273-2311

Upper Iowa University
PO Box 1857, Fayette IA 52142-1857
563-425-5200

Waldorf College
106 S 6th St, Forest City IA 50436-1713
Dr. Linda Hoopes, Vice President of Admission and Marketing
800-292-1903 or 641-585-8112 Fax: 641-585-8125
Website: www.waldorf.edu
E-mail: hoopesl@waldorf.edu
See listing under "Universities"

Wartburg College
PO Box 1003, Waverly IA 50677-0903
Brent Matthias, Interim Director of Admissions
319-352-8200

KANSAS

Benedictine College
1020 N 2nd St, Atchison KS 66002-1499
913-367-5340

Bethany College
421 N 1st St, Lindsborg KS 67456-1897
785-227-3311

COLBY COMMUNITY COLLEGE
1255 S Range Ave, Colby KS 67701-4099
Director of Admissions
888-634-9350 or 785-460-4690 Fax: 785-460-4691
Website: www.colbycc.edu
E-mail: admissions@colbycc.edu

Emporia State University
1200 Commercial St, Emporia KS 66801-5087
620-343-1200

Fort Hays State University
600 Park St, Hays KS 67601-4099
785-628-4000

Independence Community College
PO Box 708, Independence KS 67301-0708
Dr. Terry Hetrick, President
800-842-6063 Fax: 620-331-5344
Website: www.indycc.edu
E-mail: admissions@indycc.edu

Kansas State University
Manhattan KS 66506
785-532-6250

McPherson College
PO Box 1402, Mc Pherson KS 67460-1402
620-241-0731

Newman University
3100 W McCormick St, Wichita KS 67213
Jann Reusser, Admissions Recruitment Coordinator
316-942-4291 ext. 2144

Ottawa University
1001 S Cedar St, Ottawa KS 66067-3399
785-242-5200

Pittsburg State University
1701 S Broadway St, Pittsburg KS 66762-7500
620-231-7000

Southwestern College
100 College St, Winfield KS 67156-2499
620-229-6000

Tabor College
400 S Jefferson St, Hillsboro KS 67063-1758
Rusty Allen, Dean of Enrollment Management
800-822-6799 Fax: 620-947-6276
Website: www.tabor.edu
E-mail: admissions@tabor.edu
See listing under "Universities"

University of Kansas
Lawrence KS 66045-0001
Tom, Sarowski, Dean

University of Saint Mary
4100 S 4th St, Leavenworth KS 66048-5023
913-682-5151

Wichita State University
1845 N Fairmount St, Wichita KS 67260-0124
Gina Crabtree, Director of Admissions
316-978-3085

KENTUCKY

Alice Lloyd College
100 Purpose Rd, Pippa Passes KY 41844-9005
John Mills, Director of Admissions
888-280-4252

Asbury College
1 Macklem Dr, Wilmore KY 40390-1198
859-858-3511

Bellarmine University
2001 Newburg Rd, Louisville KY 40205-1877
502-452-8000

Bluegrass Community and Technical College
Oswald Building
470 Cooper Drive, Lexington KY 40506-0235
Shelbie Hugle, Director of Admissions
859-246-6200 Fax: 859-246-4664
Website: www.bluegrass.kctcs.edu
E-mail: bctc_info@kctcs.edu

Brescia University
717 Frederica St, Owensboro KY 42301-3023
Sr. Mary Austin Blank, OSB, Director of Admissions
877-BRESCIA

Brown Mackie College - Louisville
3605 Fern Valley Rd, Louisville KY 40219-1916
Mark Donahue, Director of Admissions
502-968-7191 Fax: 502-357-9956
Website: www.brownmackie.edu
E-mail: mdonahue@brownmackie.edu

BROWN MACKIE COLLEGE
Northern Kentucky Campus
309 Buttermilk Pike, Fort Mitchell KY 41017-2191
Joanne Dellefield, Director of Admissions
859-341-5627 Fax: 859-341-6483
Website: www.brownmackie.edu
E-mail: jdellefield@brownmackie.edu

Campbellsville University
1 University Dr, Campbellsville KY 42718-2799
Scott Necessary, Coordinator of Undergraduate Admissions
270-789-5000

Daymar College
3361 Buckland Sq, Owensboro KY 42301-5830
Vickie McDougal Director of Admissions
800-960-4090 Fax: 270-685-4090
Website: www.daymarcollege.com

Kentucky Wesleyan College
3000 Frederica St, Owensboro KY 42301-6055
800-999-0592

Morehead State University
Morehead KY 40351-1689
Jeffrey Liles, Enrollment Services
800-585-6781 Fax: 606-783-5038
Website: www.moreheadstate.edu
E-mail: admissions@moreheadstate.edu

Murray State University
Murray KY 42071
Phil Bryan, Director of Admissions
270-762-3011

National College
115 E Lexington Ave, Danville KY 40422-1517
Gloria Walls, Director of Admissions
859-236-6991 Fax: 859-236-1063
Website: www.national-college.edu
E-mail: info@national-college.edu

National College
7627 Ewing Blvd, Florence KY 41042-1812
Doug Dedeker, Director of Admissions
859-525-6510 Fax: 859-525-8961
Website: www.national-college.edu
E-mail: info@national-college.edu

National College
2376 Sir Barton Way, Lexington KY 40509
Terry Fisher, Director of Admissions
859-253-0621 Fax: 859-254-7664
Website: www.national-college.edu
E-mail: info@national-college.edu

National College
4205 Dixie Hwy, Louisville KY 40216
Ted Scharre, Director of Admissions
502-447-7634 Fax: 502-447-7665
Website: www.national-college.edu
E-mail: info@national-college.edu

National College
50 National College Blvd, Pikeville KY 41501
Janet Head, Director of Admissions
606-478-7200 Fax: 606-478-7209
Website: www.national-college.edu
E-mail: info@national-college.edu

National College
125 S Killarney Ln, Richmond KY 40475
Keeley Gadd, Director of Admissions
859-623-8956 Fax: 859-623-8956
Website: www.national-college.edu
E-mail: info@national-college.edu

Northern Kentucky University
Newport KY 41099-0001
859-572-5100

Pikeville College
147 Sycamore St, Pikeville KY 41501
606-218-5250

Spalding University
851 S 4th St, Louisville KY 40203-2188
502-585-9911

Transylvania University
300 N Broadway, Lexington KY 40508-1776
859-233-8242 Fax: 859-233-8797
Website: www.transy.edu
E-mail: admissions@transy.edu

Union College
310 College St, Barbourville KY 40906-1499
Joretta Nelson, Vice President for Enrollment Management
800-489-8646

University of Kentucky
Lexington KY 40506-0001
Don Witt, Director of Admissions
859-257-9000

University of Louisville
2301 S 3rd St, Louisville KY 40292-2001
502-852-5555

Western Kentucky University
1 Big Red Way, Bowling Green KY 42101
270-745-0111

LOUISIANA

Centenary College of Louisiana
PO Box 41188, Shreveport LA 71134-1188
318-869-5011

Dillard University
2601 Gentilly Blvd, New Orleans LA 70122-3097
Linda G. Nash, Director of Admissions

Grambling State University
PO Box 864, Grambling LA 71245
318-274-3811

Louisiana College
PO Box 566, Pineville LA 71359-0001
318-487-7259

Louisiana State University
1 University Pl, Shreveport LA 71115-2301
318-797-5000

Louisiana State University and A & M College
Louisiana State Univ, Baton Rouge LA 70803-0001
225-578-3202

Louisiana State University at Alexandria
8100 Highway 71 S, Alexandria LA 71302-9121
Dr. Thomas Armstrong, Director of Admissions
318-445-3672 Fax: 318-473-6418
Website: www.lsua.edu

Louisiana Tech University
PO Box 3168, Ruston LA 71272-0001
318-257-0211

Loyola University New Orleans
6363 Saint Charles Ave, New Orleans LA 70118-6143
504-865-2011

McNeese State University
4100 Ryan St, Lake Charles LA 70605-4510
337-475-5000

Nicholls State University
PO Box 2004, Thibodaux LA 70310-0001
985-446-8111

Northwestern State University
Natchitoches LA 71497-0001
Jana Lucky, Director of Enrollment Services
318-357-4503

Our Lady of Holy Cross College
4123 Woodland Dr, New Orleans LA 70131-7399
Office of Enrollment Services
504-394-7744 Fax: 504-391-2421
Website: www.olhcc.edu

Southeastern Louisiana University
PO Box 784, Hammond LA 70404-0784
985-549-2000

Tulane University
6823 Saint Charles Ave, New Orleans LA 70118-5698
504-865-4000

University of Louisiana at Lafayette
PO Box 43570, Lafayette LA 70504
337-482-6087

University of Louisiana at Monroe
700 University Ave, Monroe LA 71209-9001
318-342-1000

University of New Orleans
New Orleans LA 70148-0001
504-280-6000

MAINE

HUSSON COLLEGE
One College Cir, Bangor ME 04401-2999
Jane Goodwin, Director of Admissions
800-4HU-SSON or 207-941-7100 Fax: 207-941-7935
Website: www.husson.edu
E-mail: admit@husson.edu
See listing under "Universities"

St. Joseph's College of Maine
278 Whites Bridge Rd, Standish ME 04084-5263
Vincent Kloskowski, Dean of Admissions
800-338-7057 Fax: 207-893-7862
Website: www.sjcme.edu
E-mail: admission@sjcme.edu

Southern Maine Community College
2 Fort Rd, South Portland ME 04106-1698
Dr. James Ortiz, President
Scott MacDonald, Director of Financial Aid
207-741-5500 Fax: 207-741-5671
Website: www.smccme.edu
E-mail: oharmon@maine.rr.com

Thomas College
180 W River Rd, Waterville ME 04901-5097
207-859-1111

University of Maine
246 Main St, Farmington ME 04938
Sharon M. Oliver, Director of Admissions
207-778-7000

University of Maine
Orono ME 04469-0001
207-581-1110

University of Maine at Fort Kent
23 University Dr, Fort Kent ME 04743
888-TRY-UMFK

University of Southern Maine
PO Box 9300, Portland ME 04104-9300
207-780-4141

Westbrook College
716 Stevens Ave, Portland ME 04103-2693
207-797-7261

MARYLAND

BALTIMORE INTERNATIONAL COLLEGE
17 Commerce St, Baltimore MD 21202-3230
Kristin Ciarlo, Director of Admissions
410-752-4710 ext. 120 Fax: 410-752-3730
Website: www.bic.edu
E-mail: admissions@bic.edu
See listing under "Universities"

Cecil College
One Seahawk Dr, North East MD 21901
Sandra S. Rajaski, Registrar & Director of Admissions
410-287-1000 Fax: 410-287-1001
Website: www.cecil.edu
E-mail: srajaski@cecil.edu

Frostburg State University
Frostburg MD 21532-1001
301-687-4000

Goucher College
1021 Dulaney Valley Rd, Baltimore MD 21204-2780
410-337-6000

Griggs University
PO Box 4437, Silver Spring MD 20914-4437
Joan Wilson, Director of Admissions
301-680-6570 Fax: 301-680-6583
Website: www.griggs.edu
E-mail: registrar@griggs.edu

Hagerstown Community College
11400 Robinwood Dr, Hagerstown MD 21742-6590
Dr. Daniel E. Bock, Assistant Director of Admissions
301-790-2800 Fax: 301-791-9165
Website: www.hagerstowncc.edu
E-mail: bockd@hagerstowncc.edu

Kaplan College
Hagerstown Campus
18618 Crestwood Dr, Hagerstown MD 21742-2797
W. Christopher Motz, President
Steve Shinham, Director of Admissions
800-422-2670 Fax: 301-739-0474
Website: www.hagerstownbusinesscol.edu

Loyola College
4501 N Charles St, Baltimore MD 21210-2694
410-617-2000

Morgan State University
1700 E Cold Spring Ln, Baltimore MD 21251-0002
443-885-3000

Mt. St. Mary's University
16300 Old Emmitsburg Rd
Emmitsburg MD 21727-7799
301-447-6122

Salisbury University
1101 Camden Ave, Salisbury MD 21801-6837
410-543-6000

Towson State University
8000 York Rd, Towson MD 21252-0002
410-830-2000

University of Baltimore
1420 N Charles St, Baltimore MD 21201-5779
410-837-4200

University of Maryland
College Park MD 20742-0001
301-405-1000

University of Maryland Eastern Shore
Princess Anne MD 21853
Edwina Morse, Director of Admissions
410-651-6410

Villa Julie College
1525 Greenspring Valley Rd
Stevenson MD 21153-0641
Mark Hergan, V.P. Enrollment Services
410-486-7001

MASSACHUSETTS

American International College
1000 State St, Springfield MA 01109-3155
Peter Miller, Dean of Admissions
413-737-7000

Anna Maria College
50 Sunset Ln, Paxton MA 01612
Timothy M. Donahue, Director of Recruitment and Admissions
508-849-3360 Fax: 508-849-3362
Website: www.annamaria.edu
E-mail: admissions@annamaria.edu

Assumption College
500 Salisbury St, Worcester MA 01609-1294
Kathleen Murphy, Dean of Enrollment
508-767-7000 Fax: 508-799-4412
Website: www.assumption.edu
E-mail: admiss@assumption.edu

Atlantic Union College
PO Box 1000, South Lancaster MA 01561-1000
Office of Enrollment Services
800-282-2030

Babson College
PO Box 57310, Babson Park MA 02457-0310
781-235-1200

Bay State College
122 Commonwealth Ave, Boston MA 02116-2901
Craig Pfannenstiehl, President
617-217-9000 Fax: 617-536-1735

Becker College
Campuses in Worcester and Leicester, MA
61 Sever St, Worcester MA 01609-2165
Karen Schedin, Dean of Admissions
508-791-9241 Fax: 508-890-1500
Website: www.becker.edu
E-mail: admissions@becker.edu
See listing under "Universities"

Bentley College
175 Forest St, Waltham MA 02452-4705
781-891-2000

Boston College
140 Commonwealth Ave
Chestnut Hill MA 02467-3800
617-552-8000

Boston University
121 Bay State Rd, Boston MA 02215
Kelly Walter, Executive Director of Admissions
617-353-2300 Fax: 617-353-9695
Website: web.bu.edu
E-mail: admissions@bu.edu

Bristol Community College
777 Elsbree St, Fall River MA 02720-7395
Rodney S. Clark, Director of Admissions
508-678-2811 ext. 2516, 2179 Fax: 508-730-3265
Website: www.bristol.mass.edu
E-mail: admissions@bristol.mass.edu

Clark University
950 Main St, Worcester MA 01610-1473
508-793-7711

Curry College
1071 Blue Hill Ave, Milton MA 02186-2395
Bruce Weckworth, Director of Admissions
617-333-2210

Elms College
291 Springfield St, Chicopee MA 01013-2839
800-255-3567

Fisher College
118 Beacon St, Boston MA 02116-1501
Stephen Carter, Director of Admissions
800-446-1226

Gordon College
255 Grapevine Rd, Wenham MA 01984-1899
Barbara R. Layne, Associate Vice President, Enrollment
866-464-6736 Fax: 978-867-4682
Website: www.gordon.edu
E-mail: admissions@gordon.edu

Harvard University
8 Garden St, Cambridge MA 02138-3630
617-495-1000

Lasell College
1844 Commonwealth Ave, Newton MA 02466-2716
617-243-2225

Lesley University
29 Everett St, Cambridge MA 02138-2790
Jane Raley, Director of Admissions
617-349-8800

Massachusetts College of Liberal Arts
375 Church St, North Adams MA 01247-4100
413-662-5311

Massachusetts Institute of Technology
77 Massachusetts Ave, Cambridge MA 02139-4307
617-253-1000 Fax: 617-253-4016
Website: my.mit.edu
E-mail: admissions@mit.edu

Merrimack College
315 Turnpike St, North Andover MA 01845-5800
978-683-7111

Mt. Ida College
777 Dedham St, Newton Center MA 02459-3323
617-969-7000

THE NATIONAL GRADUATE SCHOOL OF QUALITY SYSTEMS MANAGEMENT
186 Jones Rd, Falmouth MA 02540-2908
Virginia C. Petisce, VP Enrollment Management
508-457-1313 Fax: 508-457-5347
Website: www.ngs.edu
E-mail: vpetisce@ngs.edu

Newbury College
129 Fisher Ave, Brookline MA 02445-5796
Salvadore Liberto, Vice President of Enrollment
617-730-7000 Fax: 617-731-9618
Website: www.newbury.edu
E-mail: info@newbury.edu
See listing under "Universities"

Nichols College
Dudley MA 01571-5000
Kimberly A. Kossuth, Director of Admissions
508-943-1560

Northeastern University
360 Huntington Ave, Boston MA 02115-5000
617-373-2000

NORTHERN ESSEX COMMUNITY COLLEGE
100 Elliott St, Haverhill MA 01830
Nora B. Sheridan, Director of Admission
978-556-3700
Website: www.NECC.Mass.edu
E-mail: nsheridan@necc.mass.edu

North Shore Community College
1 Ferncroft Rd, Danvers MA 01923-4093
Jennifer Kirk, Director of Admissions & Recruitment Outreach
978-762-4000 Fax: 978-762-4015
Website: www.northshore.edu
E-mail: jkirk@northshore.edu

Pine Manor College
400 Heath St, Chestnut Hill MA 02467-2332
Bill Nichols, Dean of Admission
617-731-7167

Regis College
235 Wellesley St, Weston MA 02493-1571
781-768-2000

Salem State College
352 Lafayette St, Salem MA 01970-5353
978-741-6000

Springfield College
263 Alden St, Springfield MA 01109-3788
Mary DeAngelo, Director of Admissions
800-343-1257

Stonehill College
320 Washington St, Easton MA 02357-5610
508-565-1373

Suffolk University
8 Ashburton Pl, Boston MA 02108-2770
617-573-8460

University of Massachusetts
Amherst MA 01003
413-545-0111

University of Massachusetts Boston
100 William T Morrissey Blvd, Boston MA 02125-3393
Liliana Mickle, Director of Undergraduate Admissions
617-287-6000

University of Massachusetts Dartmouth
Old Westport Rd, North Dartmouth MA 02747-2300
Steven T. Briggs, Director of Admissions
508-999-8605 Fax: 508-999-8755
Website: explore.umassd.edu
E-mail: sbriggs@umassd.edu

University of Massachusetts Lowell
1 University Ave, Lowell MA 01854-2893
978-934-4000

Western New England College
1215 Wilbraham Rd, Springfield MA 01119-2655
413-782-1321

Westfield State College
PO Box 1630, Westfield MA 01086
Michelle Mattie, Associate Dean, Admission and Enrollment Services
413-572-5300

Worcester Polytechnic Institute
100 Institute Rd, Worcester MA 01609-2280
Edward J. Connor, Director of Admissions
508-831-5286 Fax: 508-831-5875
Website: admissions.wpi.edu
E-mail: admissions@wpi.edu

Worcester State College
486 Chandler St, Worcester MA 01602-2597
508-929-8000

MICHIGAN

Albion College
611 E Porter St, Albion MI 49224-1831
800-858-6770

Alma College
614 W Superior St, Alma MI 48801-1599
Evan Montague, Director of Admissions
800-321-ALMA Fax: 989-463-7057
Website: www.alma.edu
E-mail: admissions@alma.edu

Andrews University
Berrien Springs MI 49104-0001
Randall Graves, Director of Recruitment Services
800-253-2874

Aquinas College
1607 Robinson Rd SE, Grand Rapids MI 49506-1799
Paula Meehan, Dean of Admissions
616-732-4460

Baker College of Cadillac
9600 E 13th St, Cadillac MI 49601-9574
Mike Tisdale, Director of Admissions
231-876-3100

Baker College of Clinton Township
34950 Little Mack Ave
Clinton Township MI 48035-4701
586-791-6610

Baker College of Flint
1050 W Bristol Rd, Flint MI 48507-5508
810-767-4000

Baker College of Jackson
2800 Springport Rd, Jackson MI 49202-1230
Kelli Hoban, Director of Admissions
517-789-6123

Baker College of Muskegon
1903 Marquette Ave, Muskegon MI 49442-1453
231-726-4904

Baker College of Owosso
1020 S Washington St, Owosso MI 48867-4400
989-729-3300

Baker College of Port Huron
3403 Lapeer Rd, Port Huron MI 48060-2597
Dan Kenny, Director of Admissions
888-262-2442

Calvin College
3201 Burton St SE, Grand Rapids MI 49546-4388
800-688-0122

Central Michigan University
100 Warriner Hall, Mount Pleasant MI 48859-0001
989-774-4000

Cleary University - Washtenaw Campus
3601 Plymouth Rd, Ann Arbor MI 48105-2659
734-332-4477

Concordia University
4090 Geddes Rd, Ann Arbor MI 48105-2797
Gary Neumann, Director of Admissions
734-995-7300 Fax: 734-995-4610
Website: www.cuaa.edu
E-mail: admissions@cuaa.edu

Davenport University
6191 Kraft Ave SE, Grand Rapids MI 49512
866-383-3548
Website: www.explore.davenport.edu

Delta College
University Center MI 48710-0001
Duff Zube, Director of Admissions
989-686-9093 Fax: 989-667-2202
Website: www.delta.edu
E-mail: admit@delta.edu

Eastern Michigan University
Ypsilanti MI 48197
800-GO-TO-EMU

Ferris State University
901 S State St, Big Rapids MI 49307-2295
231-591-2000

Grand Valley State University
1 Campus Dr, Allendale MI 49401-9403
Jodi Chycinski, Director of Admissions
616-331-6611 Fax: 616-331-2000
Website: www.gvsu.edu
E-mail: go2gvsu@gvsu.edu

HILLSDALE COLLEGE
33 E College St, Hillsdale MI 49242-1298
Dr. David Paas, Director
517-607-2547 Fax: 517-437-3923
Website: www.hillsdale.edu

ITT TECHNICAL INSTITUTE
4020 Sparks Dr SE, Grand Rapids MI 49546-6192
Dennis Hormel, Director
616-956-1060 Fax: 616-956-5606
Website: www.itt-tech.edu
E-mail: dhormel@itt-tech.edu

Lake Superior State University
650 W Easterday Ave
Sault Sainte Marie MI 49783-1637
Susan Camp, Director of Admissions
888-800-LSSU Fax: 906-635-6696
Website: www.lssu.edu
E-mail: admissions@lssu.edu
See listing under "Universities"

Lawrence Technological University
21000 W 10 Mile Rd, Southfield MI 48075-1058
Jane Rohrback, Director of Admissions
800-225-5588 Fax: 248-204-2228
Website: www.ltu.edu
E-mail: admissions@ltu.edu
See listing under "Universities"

MACOMB COMMUNITY COLLEGE
44575 Garfield Rd, Clinton Township MI 48038-1139
Information Center
586-445-7999
Website: www.macomb.edu
E-mail: answer@macomb.edu

MACOMB COMMUNITY COLLEGE
14500 E 12 Mile Rd, Warren MI 48088-3896
Information Center
586-445-7999
Website: www.macomb.edu
E-mail: answer@macomb.edu

Michigan State University
250 Administration Bldg, East Lansing MI 48824
517-355-1855

Michigan Technological University
1400 Townsend Dr, Houghton MI 49931-1200
Nancy Rehling, Director of Admissions
906-487-2335

Northern Michigan University
1401 Presque Isle Ave, Marquette MI 49855-5301
906-227-1000

Northwestern Michigan College
1701 E Front St, Traverse City MI 49686-3061
Jim Bensley, Director of Admissions
800-748-0566 Fax: 231-995-1339
Website: www.nmc.edu
E-mail: jbensley@nmc.edu

Northwood University
4000 Whiting Dr, Midland MI 48640
Daniel F. Toland, Dean of Admissions
800-457-7878 Fax: 989-837-4490
Website: www.northwood.edu
E-mail: miadmit@northwood.edu

Oakland University
2200 N Squirrel Rd, Rochester MI 48309
Eleanor L. Reynolds, Assistant Vice President & Director of Admissions
248-370-2100
Website: www.oakland.edu
E-mail: ouinfo@oakland.edu

Olivet College
300 S Main St, Olivet MI 49076-9724
269-749-7000

Saginaw Valley State University
7400 Bay Rd, University Center MI 48710-0001
989-790-4000

University of Detroit-Mercy
PO Box 19900, Detroit MI 48219-0900
313-993-1000

University of Michigan-Ann Arbor
1220 Student Activities Bldg, Ann Arbor MI 48109
734-764-1817

University of Michigan-Dearborn
4901 Evergreen Rd, Dearborn MI 48128-1491
The Office of Admissions & Orientation
313-593-5100

University of Michigan-Flint
303 E Kearsley St, Flint MI 48502-1950
810-762-3000

Wayne State University
5980 Cass Ave, Detroit MI 48202-3489
313-577-2424

Western Michigan University
Kalamazoo MI 49008
269-387-1000

MINNESOTA

Academy College
1101 E 78th St, Bloomington MN 55420-1402
Tracey Schantz, Director of Admissions
952-851-0066 Fax: 952-851-0094

ARGOSY UNIVERSITY / TWIN CITIES
1515 Central Pkwy, Eagan MN 55121-1756
O. Jeanne Stoneking, Director of Admissions
651-846-2882 Fax: 651-994-7956
Website: www.argosyu.edu
E-mail: tcadmissions@argosyu.edu

Augsburg College
2211 Riverside Ave, Minneapolis MN 55454-1350
612-330-1000

Bethany Lutheran College
700 Luther Dr, Mankato MN 56001
Don Westphal, Dean of Admissions
507-344-7000 Fax: 507-344-7376
Website: www.blc.edu
E-mail: admiss@blc.edu

Bethel College
3900 Bethel Dr, Saint Paul MN 55112-6999
651-638-6400

College of Saint Benedict
37 College Ave S, Saint Joseph MN 56374-2099
320-363-5011

College of St. Catherine
2004 Randolph Ave, Saint Paul MN 55105-1789
651-690-6000

College of Saint Scholastica
1200 Kenwood Ave, Duluth MN 55811-4199
Brian Dalton, V.P. of Enrollment Management
800-447-5444

Concordia College
901 8th St S, Moorhead MN 56562-0002
Scott Ellingson, Director of Admissions
218-299-3004

Concordia University-Saint Paul
275 Syndicate St N, Saint Paul MN 55104-5494
651-641-8278

Crown College
8700 College View Dr, Saint Bonifacius MN 55375
Mitch Fisk, Director of Admissions
952-446-4142 Fax: 952-446-4149
Website: www.crown.edu
E-mail: johnsonj@crown.edu

Duluth Business University
4724 Mike Colalillo Dr, Duluth MN 55807-2723
Bonnie Kupczynski, Director
800-777-8406 Fax: 218-628-2127
Website: www.dbumn.edu
E-mail: info@dbumn.edu

Dunwoody College of Technology
818 Dunwoody Blvd, Minneapolis MN 55403-1192
John Slama, Vice President Enrollment Management
800-292-4625 or 612-374-5800 Fax: 612-374-4128
Website: www.dunwoody.edu
E-mail: jslama@dunwoody.edu
See listing under "Career Schools"

Globe College
7166 10th St N, Oakdale MN 55128
Mike Hughes, Campus Director
651-730-5100 Fax: 651-730-5151
Website: www.globecollege.edu
E-mail: admissions@globecollege.edu

Gustavus Adolphus College
800 W College Ave, Saint Peter MN 56082-1485
Mark H. Anderson, Dean of Admission
800-GUSTAVUS Fax: 507-933-7474
Website: www.gustavus.edu
E-mail: admission@gustavus.edu

Hamline University
1536 Hewitt Ave, Saint Paul MN 55104-1284
651-523-2800

Hibbing Community College
1515 E 25th St, Hibbing MN 55746-3300
Holly Bigelow, Director of Enrollment
800-224-4HCC or 218-262-7200 Fax: 218-262-6717
Website: www.hibbing.edu
E-mail: admissions@hibbing.edu

Inver Hills Community College
2500 80th St E, Inver Grove Heights MN 55076
651-450-8500 Fax: 651-450-8679
Website: www.inverhills.edu

McNally Smith College of Music
19 Exchange St East, St. Paul MN 55101
Debbie Sandridge, Director of Admissions
800-594-9500 Fax: 651-291-0366
Website: www.mcnallysmith.edu
E-mail: dsandridge@mcnallysmith.edu
See listing under "Universities"

Minnesota State College - Southeast Technical
Red Wing Campus
308 Pioneer Rd, Red Wing MN 55066
Al DuCett, Director of Admissions
877-853-8324 Fax: 507-453-2715
Website: www.southeastmn.edu
E-mail: aducett@southeastmn.edu
70+ degrees, diplomas & certificates (15+ online) in Business & Office Careers, Musical Instrument Repair, Physical Health, Transportation, Technology, and Trades.

Minnesota State College - Southeast Technical
Winona Campus
PO Box 409, 1250 Homer Rd, Winona MN 55987
Al DuCett, Director of Admissions
877-853-8324 Fax: 507-453-2715
Website: www.southeastmn.edu
E-mail: aducett@southeastmn.edu
70+ degrees, diplomas & certificates (15+ online) in Business & Office Careers, Musical Instrument Repair, Physical Health, Transportation, Technology, and Trades.

Minnesota State University Mankato
228 Wiecking Center, Mankato MN 56001
507-389-1866

Minnesota State University Moorhead
1104 7th Ave S, Moorhead MN 56563-0002
Regina Monson, Director of Admissions
218-477-2161 Fax: 218-477-4374
Website: go.mnstate.edu
E-mail: dragon@mnstate.edu

National American University
1550 W Highway 36, Roseville MN 55113
Matthew Mottl, Director of Admissions
651-644-1265

Northland Community and Technical College
2022 Central Ave NE
East Grand Forks MN 56721-2702
Deb Riely, Business Program Chair
800-451-3441 Fax: 218-773-4502
Website: www.northlandcollege.edu
E-mail: admissions@northlandcollege.edu

Pillsbury Baptist Bible College
315 S Grove Ave, Owatonna MN 55060-3097
Susanne Martin, Admissions Coordinator
507-451-2710 Fax: 507-451-0156
Website: www.pillsbury.edu
E-mail: admissions@pillsbury.edu

Ridgewater College-Hutchinson Campus
2 Century Ave SE, Hutchinson MN 55350-3100
Dawn Bjork, Counselor
800-722-1151 Fax: 320-234-8506
Website: www.ridgewater.edu
E-mail: dawn.bjork@ridgewater.edu

Ridgewater College-Willmar Campus
PO Box 1097, Willmar MN 56201-1097
Sally Kerfeld, Director of Admissions
800-722-1151 Fax: 320-222-5212
Website: www.ridgewater.edu
E-mail: sally.kerfeld@ridgewater.edu

St. Cloud State University
720 4th Ave S, Saint Cloud MN 56301-4442
877-654-7278

St. Mary's University of Minnesota
700 Terrace Hts Ste 2, Winona MN 55987-1321
507-452-4430

Southwest Minnesota State University
1501 State St, Marshall MN 56258-1598
507-537-7678

University of Minnesota
2900 University Ave, Crookston MN 56716-5001
218-281-6510 Fax: 218-281-8575
Website: admissions.umcrookston.edu/requirements/apply.htm
E-mail: info@umcrookston.edu

University of Minnesota
10 University Dr, Duluth MN 55812-2496
Beth Esselstrom, Director of Admissions
218-726-7171

University of Minnesota
231 Pillsbury Dr SE, Minneapolis MN 55455-0230
612-625-2008

University of Minnesota - Morris
600 E 4th St, Morris MN 56267-2132
Rodney Oto, Director
800-992-8863

Winona State University
PO Box 5838, Winona MN 55987-0838
507-457-5000

MISSISSIPPI

Belhaven College
1500 Peachtree St, Jackson MS 39202-1789
601-968-5927

Delta State University
Hwy 8 W, Cleveland MS 38733
662-846-3000

Jackson State University
1440 J.R. Lynch St, Jackson MS 39217
Stephanie Chatman, Director of Admissions
601-979-2100

Millsaps College
PO Box 15495, Jackson MS 39210
601-974-1000

Mississippi College
PO Box 4086, Clinton MS 39058-0001
601-925-3000

Mississippi State University
PO Box J, Mississippi State MS 39762-5509
662-325-2323

Mississippi University for Women
1100 College St Unit W1613, Columbus MS 39701
Terri Heath, Director of Admissions
877-GO-2-THEW

Mississippi Valley State University
14000 Highway 82 W Box 7222
Itta Bena MS 38941-1401
Office of Admissions
662-254-3347

Tougaloo College
500 W County Line Rd, Tougaloo MS 39174-9799
Juno Leggette Jacobs, Director of Admissions
601-977-7768 Fax: 601-977-4501
Website: www.tougaloo.edu
E-mail: jjacobs@tougaloo.edu

University of Mississippi
University MS 38677
662-232-7226

University of Southern Mississippi
PO Box 5165, Hattiesburg MS 39406-1000
601-266-5000

MISSOURI

Central Methodist University
411 Central Methodist Sq, Fayette MO 65248-1198
Larry Anderson, Director of Admissions
660-248-6247 Fax: 660-248-1872
Website: www.centralmethodist.edu
E-mail: landerso@centralmethodist.edu

Central Missouri State University
Warrensburg MO 64093-8888
Charles Petentler, Associate Director of Admissions
800-956-0177

College of the Ozarks
Point Lookout MO 65726
417-334-6411

Columbia College
1001 Rogers St, Columbia MO 65216-0001
Regina Morin, Director of Admissions
573-875-7352 Fax: 573-875-7506
Website: www.ccis.edu
E-mail: admissions@ccis.edu

Culver-Stockton College
1 College Hl, Canton MO 63435-1299
Betty Smith, Director of Enrollment Services
800-537-1883

Drury University
900 N Benton Ave, Springfield MO 65802-3791
417-873-7879

East Central College
1964 Prairie Dell Rd, Union MO 63084
Karen Wieda, Registrar
636-583-5195 ext. 2220 Fax: 636-583-1897
Website: www.eastcentral.edu
E-mail: wiedaks@eastcentral.edu

EVEREST COLLEGE
1010 W Sunshine St, Springfield MO 65807-2446
Melanie Exter, Contact
417-864-7220 or 800-475-2699 Fax: 417-866-3335
Website: www.everest-college.com
E-mail: mexter@cci.edu

Harris-Stowe State University
3026 Laclede Ave, Saint Louis MO 63103-2199
LaShanda R. Boone, Director of Admissions
314-340-3300 Fax: 314-340-3555
Website: www.hssu.edu
E-mail: admissions@hssu.edu

Hickey College
940 Westport Plz, Saint Louis MO 63146-3127
Christopher A. Gearin, President
800-777-1544 or 314-434-2212 Fax: 314-434-1974
Website: www.hickeycollege.edu
E-mail: admin@hickeycollege.edu

Lindenwood University
209 S Kingshighway St
Saint Charles MO 63301-1695
Sheryl Guffey, Director of Admissions
636-949-2000 Fax: 636-949-4989
Website: www.lindenwood.edu

Missouri Southern State University - Joplin
3950 Newman Rd, Joplin MO 64801-1512
417-625-9300

Missouri State University
901 S National Ave, Springfield MO 65897
417-836-5000

Missouri Valley College
500 E College St, Marshall MO 65340-3197
John R. Campbell, Division Dean
660-831-4165

Missouri Western State College
4525 Downs Dr, Saint Joseph MO 64507-2294
800-662-7041

Northwest Missouri State University
800 University Dr, Maryville MO 64468-6001
Beverly Schenkel, Dean of Enrollment Management
660-562-1562 Fax: 660-562-1121
Website: www.nwmissouri.edu
E-mail: admissions@nwmissouri.edu

Park University
8700 NW River Park Dr, Parkville MO 64152-3795
816-741-2000

Rockhurst University
1100 Rockhurst Rd, Kansas City MO 64110-2561
Mark Kopenski, VP of Enrollment Management
816-501-4000

St. Charles Community College
4601 Mid Rivers Mall Dr, Cottleville MO 63376
Kathy Brockgreitens-Gober, Director of Admissions
636-922-8000 Fax: 636-922-8236
Website: www.stchas.edu
E-mail: adm-reg@stchas.edu

St. Louis University
221 N Grand Blvd, Saint Louis MO 63103-2097
314-977-2222

Southeast Missouri State University
1 University Plz, Cape Girardeau MO 63701-4710
573-651-2000

Southwest Baptist University
1600 University Ave, Bolivar MO 65613-2597
417-328-5281

State Fair Community College
3201 W 16th St, Sedalia MO 65301-2199
Director of Admissions
660-530-5833 Fax: 660-596-7472
Website: www.sfccmo.edu
E-mail: mparris@sfccmo.edu

Stephens College
PO Box 2121, Columbia MO 65215-0001
David Adams, Dean of Enrollment Management
573-442-2211 Fax: 573-876-7237
Website: www.stephens.edu
E-mail: dadams@stephens.edu

Truman State University
100 E Normal, Kirksville MO 63501
Office of Admission
660-785-4114 Fax: 660-785-7456
Website: admissions.truman.edu
E-mail: admissions@truman.edu

University of Missouri
228 Jesse Hall, Columbia MO 65211-0001
573-882-2121

University of Missouri
5100 Rockhill Rd, Kansas City MO 64110-2446
816-235-1000

University of Missouri
102 Parker, Rolla MO 65409
Lynn Stichnote, Director of Admission
573-341-4164

University of Missouri
1 University Blvd, Saint Louis MO 63121-4499
Dr. Keith Womer, Dean-College of Business
314-516-5888 Fax: 314-516-6420
Website: www.umsl.edu
E-mail: admissions@umsl.edu

Washington University in St. Louis
1 Brookings Dr, Saint Louis MO 63130-4899
314-935-5000

Webster University
470 E Lockwood Ave, Saint Louis MO 63119-3194
Dr. Benjamin Akande, Dean School of Business and Management
314-961-2660 ext. 5950 Fax: 314-968-7077
Website: www.webster.edu
E-mail: mtaylor@webster.edu
See listing under "Universities"

Westminister College
501 Westminster Ave, Fulton MO 65251-1299
573-642-3361

William Jewell College
500 College Hill, Liberty MO 64068-1896
Dr. Rick Winslow, VP Enrollment Management and Student Affairs
800-753-7009 Fax: 816-415-5040
Website: www.jewell.edu
E-mail: winslowr@william.jewell.edu

William Woods University
1 University Ave, Fulton MO 65251-1098
Jimmy Clay, Director of Admissions
573-642-2251 Fax: 573-592-1146
Website: www.williamwoods.edu
E-mail: admissions@williamwoods.edu
See listing under "Universities"

MONTANA

Carroll College
1601 N Benton Ave, Helena MT 59625-0002
Dr. Thomas J. Trebon, President
Cynthia Thornquist, Director of Admissions & Enrollment Operations
406-447-4384 Fax: 406-447-4533
Website: www.carroll.edu
E-mail: admission@carroll.edu

Montana State University - Billings
1500 University Dr, Billings MT 59101-0252
Karen Everett, Director
800-565-MSUB

Montana State University - Bozeman
103 Culbertson Hall, Bozeman MT 59715-5072
406-994-2452

Montana Tech of the University of Montana
1300 W Park St, Butte MT 59701-8997
800-445-TECH

Rocky Mountain College
1511 Poly Dr, Billings MT 59102-1796
Bonnie Knapp, Director of Admissions
800-877-6259

University of Montana
Missoula MT 59812-0001
406-243-0211

NEBRASKA

Bellevue University
1000 Galvin Rd S, Bellevue NE 68005-3098
Doug Frost, Dean of College of Business

Chadron State College
1000 Main St, Chadron NE 69337-2690
308-432-6000

College of Saint Mary
7000 Mercy Rd, Omaha NE 68106
Lorin Werth,V.P. for Enrollment
800-926-5534

Creighton University
2500 California Plz, Omaha NE 68178-0001
402-280-2700

Dana College
2848 College Dr, Blair NE 68008-1099
Duane A. Heffelfinger, Dean of Enrollment Management
800-444-3262

Metropolitan Community College
PO Box 3777, Omaha NE 68103-0777
Becky Nicks, Director of Admissions
402-449-8400 Fax: 402-457-2616
Website: www.mccnab.edu
E-mail: bnicks@mccnab.edu

Midland Lutheran College
900 N Clarkson St, Fremont NE 68025-4200
Todd Hansen, Associate Director of Admissions
402-941-6501 Fax: 402-941-6513
Website: www.mlc.edu
E-mail: admissions@mlc.edu

Nebraska Wesleyan University
5000 Saint Paul Ave, Lincoln NE 68504-2794
Patricia Karthauser, V.P. for University Enrollment
402-466-2371 Fax: 402-465-2177
Website: www.nebrwesleyan.edu
E-mail: admissions@nebrwesleyan.edu

Peru State College
PO Box 10, Peru NE 68421-0010
Office of Admissions
800-742-4412

Union College
3800 S 48th St, Lincoln NE 68506-4300
Buell Fogg, V.P. for Enrollment Services
800-228-4600

University of Nebraska
14th & R Sts, Lincoln NE 68588
402-472-7211

University of Nebraska at Kearney
905 W 25th St, Kearney NE 68849-0001
Dusty Newton, Director of Admissions
800-KEARNEY Fax: 308-865-8987
Website: www.unk.edu
E-mail: admissionsug@unk.edu

University of Nebraska at Omaha
60th and Dodge St, Omaha NE 68182-0001
402-554-2800

NEVADA

Career College of Northern Nevada
1195-A Corporate Blvd, Reno NV 89502-2331
Nathan Clark, Director
775-856-2266 Fax: 775-856-0935
Website: www.ccnn.edu
E-mail: lgoldhammer@ccnn4u.com
See listing under "Career Schools"

GREAT BASIN COLLEGE
1500 College Pkwy, Elko NV 89801-5032
Julie G. Byrnes, Director of Enrollment Management
775-753-2271 Fax: 775-753-2311
Website: www.gbcnv.edu
E-mail: julieb@gwmail.gbcnv.edu
See listing under "Universities"

Morrison University
10315 Professional Circle Suite 201
Reno NV 89521-4826
Charles Timinsky, Director of Enrollment
775-850-0700 Fax: 775-850-0711
Website: www.morrisonuniversity.com

University of Nevada
Reno NV 89557-0001
775-784-1110

University of Nevada Las Vegas
4505 S Maryland Pkwy, Las Vegas NV 89154-9901
800-334-8658

NEW HAMPSHIRE

Antioch University New England
40 Avon St, Keene NH 03431-3516
David Caruso, President
Leatrice A. Oram, Director of Admissions
603-357-6265 Fax: 603-357-0718
Website: www.antiochne.edu
E-mail: admissions@antiochne.edu

Daniel Webster College
20 University Dr, Nashua NH 03063-1323
Paul LaBarre, Director of Enrollment Services
603-577-6600

Dartmouth College
Hanover NH 03755
603-646-1110

Franklin Pierce College
20 College Rd, Rindge NH 03461
800-437-0048

New England College
98 Bridge St, Henniker NH 03242
603-428-2211

New Hampshire Community Technical College
1066 Front St, Manchester NH 03102-8528
Jacquie Poirier, Director of Admissions
603-668-6706 Fax: 603-668-5354
Website: www.manchester.nhctc.edu
E-mail: jpoirier@nhctc.edu

Rivier College
420 S Main St, Nashua NH 03060-5086
David Boisvert, Director of Undergraduate Admissions
603-897-8507

St. Anselm College
100 Saint Anselms Dr, Manchester NH 03102-1310
603-641-7000

Southern New Hampshire University
2500 N River Rd, Hooksett NH 03106-1045
Steve Soba, Director of Admissions
603-645-9611 Fax: 603-645-9693
Website: www.snhu.edu
E-mail: s.soba@snhu.edu

University of New Hampshire
Durham NH 03824
603-862-1234

NEW JERSEY

Atlantic Cape Community College
5100 Black Horse Pike
Mays Landing NJ 08330-2699
Linda McLeod, Assistant Director of College Recruitment
609-343-5000 Fax: 609-343-4921
Website: www.atlantic.edu
E-mail: accadmit@atlantic.edu
See listing under "Community and Junior Colleges"

Bergen Community College
400 Paramus Rd, Paramus NJ 07652
Julian Gomez, Asst. Director of Admissions
201-447-7100 Fax: 201-444-7036
Website: www.bergen.edu
E-mail: jgomez@bergen.edu

Bloomfield College
467 Franklin St, Bloomfield NJ 07003
973-748-9000

Caldwell College
9 Ryerson Ave, Caldwell NJ 07006-6195
973-618-3000

Centenary College
400 Jefferson St, Hackettstown NJ 07840-2100
Glenna Warren, Director of Admissions
908-852-1400

College of New Jersey
PO Box 7718, Ewing NJ 08628-0718
609-771-1855

Fairleigh Dickinson University
285 Madison Ave, Madison NJ 07940-1099
800-338-8803

Felician College
262 S Main St, Lodi NJ 07644-2198
201-559-6000

HoHoKus School of Business & Medical Sciences
10 S Franklin Tpke, Ramsey NJ 07446-2546
Thomas Eastwick, Director
201-327-8877 Fax: 201-327-9054
Website: www.hohokus.edu
E-mail: tomeastwick@aol.com

Hohokus School - RETS Nutley
103 Park Ave, Nutley NJ 07110-3505
Thomas Eastwick, President
973-661-0600 Fax: 973-661-2954
Website: www.rets-institute.com
E-mail: admissions@rets-institute.com

Monmouth University
400 Cedar Ave, West Long Branch NJ 07764-1890
732-571-3400

Montclair State University
Montclair State University, Montclair NJ 07043-1624
973-655-4000

New Jersey City University
2039 John F Kennedy Blvd
Jersey City NJ 07305-1588
Carmen Panlilio, Asst. V.P. for Admissions and Financial Aid
201-200-3234 Fax: 201-200-2044
Website: www.njcu.edu
E-mail: admissions@njcu.edu

New Jersey Institute of Technology
University Heights, Newark NJ 07102
973-596-3000

Ramapo College of New Jersey
505 Ramapo Valley Rd, Mahwah NJ 07430-1623
Director of Admissions
201-684-7300 or 201-684-7301 Fax: 201-684-7964
Website: www.ramapo.edu
E-mail: admissions@ramapo.edu

RICHARD STOCKTON COLLEGE OF NEW JERSEY
PO Box 195, Pomona NJ 08240
John Iacovelli, Dean of Enrollment Management
866-RSC-2885 Fax: 609-626-5541
Website: www.stockton.edu
E-mail: admissions@stockton.edu
See listing under "Universities"

Rider University
2083 Lawrenceville Rd, Lawrenceville NJ 08648-3099
Susan Christian, Director of Admissions
609-896-5042

Rowan University
201 Mullica Hill Rd, Glassboro NJ 08028-1700
856-256-4000

Rutgers-The State University of New Jersey
Camden Campus
311 N 5th St, Camden NJ 08102-1405
856-225-6026

Rutgers-The State University of New Jersey
Newark Campus
Newark NJ 07102
973-353-5568

Rutgers-The State University of New Jersey
New Brunswick Campus
35 College Ave, New Brunswick NJ 08901
732-932-4636

St. Peter's College
Hudson Terrace, Englewood Cliffs NJ 07632
201-568-7730

St. Peter's College
2627 John F Kennedy Blvd, Jersey City NJ 07306
888-SPC-9933

Seton Hall University
400 S Orange Ave, South Orange NJ 07079-2697
973-761-9000

Thomas Edison State College
101 W State St, Trenton NJ 08608-1101
609-984-1100

NEW MEXICO

College of the Southwest
6610 N Lovington Hwy, Hobbs NM 88240-9129
Dr. Steve Hill, Dean of Recuitment
505-392-6561 Fax: 505-392-6006
Website: www.csw.edu
E-mail: shill@csw.edu

Eastern New Mexico University
Portales NM 88130
800-367-3668

International Institute of the Americas
4201 Central Ave NW Suite J
Albuquerque NM 87105-1649
Ed Sigman, Director
505-880-2877 Fax: 505-352-0199
Website: www.iia.edu
E-mail: esigman@iia.edu

National American University
4775 Indian Sch Rd NE #200
Albuquerque NM 87110-3976
505-265-7517

National American University
1601 Rio Rancho Dr SE #200
Rio Rancho NM 87124-1093
505-891-1111

New Mexico Highlands University
PO Box 9000, Las Vegas NM 87701
Margaret Young, Contact
505-454-3115

New Mexico State University
1500 N 3rd St, Grants NM 87020-2025
Irene Lutz, Director of Admissions
505-287-7981 Fax: 505-287-2329
Website: www.grants.nmsu.edu
E-mail: ilutz@nmsu.edu

New Mexico State University
PO Box 30001, Las Cruces NM 88003-8001
505-646-0111

University of New Mexico
1 University Campus, Albuquerque NM 87131-0001
505-277-0111

NEW YORK

Adelphi University
Garden City NY 11530
516-877-3100

Alfred University
1 Saxson Dr, Alfred NY 14802
607-871-2111

Briarcliffe College
1055 Stewart Ave, Bethpage NY 11714-3545
Theresa Donohue, Director of Admissions
516-918-3600 Fax: 516-470-6020
Website: www.briarcliffe.edu

Broome Community College
907 Upper Front St, Binghamton NY 13905
Anthony S. Fiorelli, Director of Admissions
607-778-5001 Fax: 607-778-5442
Website: www.sunybroome.edu
E-mail: fiorelli_a@sunybroome.edu

Canisius College
2001 Main St, Buffalo NY 14208-1098
716-883-7000

Cazenovia College
Cazenovia NY 13035-1084
Robert Croot, Dean of Admissions & Financial Aid
800-654-3210

Clarkson University
PO Box 5500, Potsdam NY 13699
315-268-6400

College of New Rochelle
29 Castle Pl, New Rochelle NY 10805-2339
914-654-5000

College of Saint Rose
432 Western Ave, Albany NY 12203-1419
Maryelizabeth Amico, Asst V.P. for Undergraduate Admissions
518-454-5150 Fax: 518-454-2013
Website: www.strose.edu
E-mail: admit@strose.edu

Columbia University
2960 Broadway, New York NY 10027-6900
212-854-1754

Cornell University
410 Thurston Ave, Ithaca NY 14850-2432
607-255-2000

CULINARY ACADEMY OF NEW YORK
154 W 14th St, New York NY 10011-7307
Harold Kaplan, Contact
212-675-6655 Fax: 212-463-9194
Website: www.culinaryacademy.edu
E-mail: hkaplan@culinaryacademy.edu

CUNY Bernard M. Baruch College
17 Lexington Ave, New York NY 10010-5518
212-802-2000

CUNY City College
Convent Ave at 138th St, New York NY 10031
Celia Lloyd, Interim Director of Admissions
212-650-6977

CUNY York College
9420 Guy R Brewer Blvd, Jamaica NY 11451-0001
718-262-2000

Daemen College
4380 Main St, Amherst NY 14226-3592
Donna Shaffner, Director of Admissions
800-462-7652 Fax: 716-839-8229
Website: www.daemen.edu/admissions
E-mail: admissions@daemen.edu

Dominican College of Blauvelt
470 Western Hwy, Orangeburg NY 10962-1210
845-359-7800

Dowling College
150 Idle Hour Blvd, Oakdale NY 11769-1999
Diane Kazanecki-Kempter, Contact
631-244-3000 Fax: 631-244-1059
Website: www.dowling.edu
E-mail: admissions@dowling.edu

D'Youville College
320 Porter Ave, Buffalo NY 14201-1084
716-829-7600

Elmira College
1 Park Pl, Elmira NY 14901-2099
Gary Fallis, Dean of Admissions
607-735-1724

Excelsior College
7 Columbia Cir, Albany NY 12203-5156
518-464-8500

Farmingdale SUNY
2350 Broadhollow Rd, Farmingdale NY 11735
631-420-2200

FIVE TOWNS COLLEGE
305 N Service Rd, Dix Hills NY 11746-5871
631-424-7000 ext. 2110 Fax: 631-656-2172
Website: www.fivetowns.edu
E-mail: admissions@ftc.edu
See listing under "Universities"

Fordham University
441 E Fordham Rd, Bronx NY 10458-9993
John W. Buckley, Dean of Admissions
718-817-4000

Hilbert College
5200 S Park Ave, Hamburg NY 14075-1597
Timothy Lee, Director of Admissions
716-649-7900 Fax: 716-649-0702
Website: www.hilbert.edu
E-mail: tlee@hilbert.edu

Hofstra University
100 Hofstra University, Hempstead NY 11549-1000
516-463-6600

Houghton College
PO Box 128, Houghton NY 14744-0128
585-567-9200

Iona College
715 North Ave, New Rochelle NY 10801-1890
Kevin Cavanagh, Assistant V.P. for College Admissions
914-633-2502 Fax: 914-637-2778
Website: www.iona.edu

Ithaca College
953 Danby Rd, Ithaca NY 14850-7002
607-274-3011

Keuka College
PO Box 98, Keuka Park NY 14478-0098
315-536-4411

LABORATORY INSTITUTE OF MERCHANDISING
12 E 53rd St, New York NY 10022-5268
Kristina Gibson, Director of Admissions
800-677-1323 or 212-752-1530 Fax: 212-750-3432
Website: www.limcollege.edu
E-mail: admissions@limcollege.edu
See listing under "Universities"

Le Moyne College
1419 Salt Springs Rd, Syracuse NY 13214-1301
800-333-4733

Long Island University
121 Speonk Riverhead Rd, Riverhead NY 11901
631-287-8010

Long Island University-C. W. Post Campus
720 Northern Blvd, Brookville NY 11548-1300
Joanne Graziano, Executive Director of Admissions
516-299-2900 Fax: 516-299-2137
Website: www.liu.edu/cwpost
E-mail: enroll@cwpost.liu.edu

Manhattan College
4513 Manhattan College Pkwy
Riverdale NY 10471-4099
Dr. James Suarez, Dean of Business
718-862-7200

Manhattanville College
2900 Purchase St, Purchase NY 10577-2132
914-694-2200

Marist College
3399 North Rd, Poughkeepsie NY 12601
Jay E. Murray, Director of Admissions
845-575-3000

Marymount College at Fordham University
100 Marymount Ave, Tarrytown NY 10591-3796
914-631-3200

Marymount Manhattan College
221 E 71st St, New York NY 10021-4501
Jim Rogers, Dean of Admissions
800-MARYMOUNT Fax: 212-517-0448
Website: www.mmm.edu
E-mail: admissions@mmm.edu

Medaille College
18 Agassiz Cir, Buffalo NY 14214-2695
716-884-3281

Mercy College
555 Broadway, Dobbs Ferry NY 10522-1189
Kathleen Jackson, Director of Admissions
800-MERCY-NY

Molloy College
1000 Hempstead Ave
Rockville Centre NY 11570-1100
Marguerite Lane, Director of Admissions
516-678-5000 ext. 6291 Fax: 516-256-2247
Website: www.molloy.edu
E-mail: admissions@molloy.edu
See listing under "Universities"

Monroe College
2501 Jerome Ave, Bronx NY 10468-4305
Evan Jerome, Director of Admissions
718-933-6700 Fax: 718-364-3552
Website: www.monroecollege.edu
E-mail: ejerome@monroecollege.edu

Mt. St. Mary College
330 Powell Ave, Newburgh NY 12550-3494
845-561-0800

Nazareth College of Rochester
4245 East Ave, Rochester NY 14618-3790
585-389-2525

New York Institute of Technology
PO Box 8000, Old Westbury NY 11568-8000
516-686-7516

New York University
70 Washington Sq S, New York NY 10012-1019
212-998-1212

Niagara University
PO Box 2011, Niagara University NY 14109-2011
George Pachter, Dean of Admissions & Records
800-462-2111

Nyack College
1 South Blvd
Nyack NY 10960-3698
845-358-1710

Olean Business Institute
301 N Union St, Olean NY 14760-2691
Carl English, Director of Admissions
716-372-7978 Fax: 716-372-2120
Website: www.obi.edu
E-mail: cenglish@obi.edu

Pace University
1 Pace Plz, New York NY 10038-1502
212-346-1200

Polytechnic University
6 Metrotech Ctr, Brooklyn NY 11201-3840
718-260-3600

Rensselaer Polytechnic Institute
110 8th St, Troy NY 12180-3590
518-276-6000

Roberts Wesleyan College
2301 Westside Dr, Rochester NY 14624-1997
Office of Admissions
585-594-6400 Fax: 585-594-6371
Website: www.roberts.edu
E-mail: admissions@roberts.edu

Rochester Institute of Technology
1 Lomb Memorial Dr, Rochester NY 14623-5603
585-475-2411

Russell Sage College
45 Ferry St, Troy NY 12180-4115
518-244-2000

St. Bonaventure University
Saint Bonaventure NY 14778-9999
585-375-2000

St. John Fisher College
3690 East Ave, Rochester NY 14618-3597
585-385-8000

St. John's University
8000 Utopia Pkwy, Queens NY 11439
Office of Admission
877-STJ-5550 ext. 101 Fax: 718-990-2096
Website: www.stjohns.edu/learnmore
E-mail: admhelp@stjohns.edu
See listing under "Universities"

St. Joseph's College
245 Clinton Ave, Brooklyn NY 11205-3688
Theresa LaRocca Meyer, V.P. for Enrollment Management
718-636-6800 Fax: 718-636-8303
Website: www.sjcny.edu
E-mail: tlaroccameyer@sjcny.edu

St. Joseph's College
155 W Roe Blvd, Patchogue NY 11772
631-447-3200

Siena College
515 Loudonville Rd, Loudonville NY 12211-1462
Heather Renault, Director of Admissions
518-783-2300 Fax: 518-783-2436
Website: www.siena.edu
E-mail: hrenault@siena.edu

Skidmore College
815 N Broadway, Saratoga Springs NY 12866-1698
518-580-5000

SUNY at Albany
1400 Washington Ave, Albany NY 12222-1000
Thomas Flemming, Associate Director of Admissions
518-442-5435

SUNY at Binghamton
PO Box 6001, Binghamton NY 13902-6001
607-777-2000

SUNY College at Brockport
350 New Campus Dr, Brockport NY 14420-2997
Bernard S. Valento, Director of Undergraduate Admissions
585-395-2751 Fax: 585-395-5452
Website: www.brockport.edu
E-mail: admit@brockport.edu

SUNY College at Old Westbury
PO Box 210, Old Westbury NY 11568-0210
516-876-3000

SUNY College of Agriculture & Technology
107 Schenectady Ave, Cobleskill NY 12043
Clayton A. Smith, Director of Admissions
800-295-8988

SUNY College of Technology
Alfred NY 14802
Deborah J. Goodrich, Associate VP Enrollment Mgmt.
800-4AL-FRED Fax: 607-587-4299
Website: www.alfredstate.edu
E-mail: admissions@alfredstate.edu

SUNY Institute of Technology Utica/Rome
PO Box 3050, Utica NY 13504-3050
315-792-7100

SUNY Niagara County Community College
3111 Saunders Settlement Rd
Sanborn NY 14132-9487
Kathleen Saunders, Director of Admissions
716-614-6200 Fax: 716-614-6820
Website: www.niagaracc.suny.edu
E-mail: admissions@niagaracc.suny.edu

SUNY Orange County Community College
115 South St, Middletown NY 10940-6437
Margot St. Lawrence, Director of Admissions
845-341-4030 Fax: 845-342-8662
Website: www.sunyorange.edu
E-mail: apply@sunyorange.edu
See listing under "Community and Junior Colleges"

SUNY Sullivan County Community College
112 College Rd, Loch Sheldrake NY 12759-5151
Sari Rosenheck, Director of Admissions
845-434-5750 Fax: 845-434-0923
Website: www.sullivan.suny.edu
E-mail: admissions@sullivan.suny.edu
Student Housing on Campus.

Syracuse University
Syracuse NY 13244-0001
315-443-1870

United States Military Academy West Point
646 Swift Rd, West Point NY 10996-1905
Colonel Michael L. Jones, Director of Admissions
845-938-4041 Fax: 845-938-8121
Website: admissions.usma.edu
E-mail: admissions@usma.edu

University at Buffalo, The State University of New York
15 Capen Hall, Buffalo NY 14260-1660
Patricia G. Armstrong, Director of Admissions
888-UB-ADMIT

University of Rochester
Wallis Hall, Rochester NY 14627
585-275-2121

Utica College
1600 Burrstone Rd, Utica NY 13502-4857
315-792-3111

Utica School of Commerce
201 Bleecker St, Utica NY 13501-2280
Bruce Davis, Director of Marketing
315-733-2307 Fax: 315-733-9281
Website: www.uscny.edu
E-mail: admissions@uscny.edu

VAUGHN COLLEGE OF AERONAUTICS AND TECHNOLOGY
8601 23rd Ave, Flushing NY 11369-1037
Vincent Papandrea, Director of Admissions
800-776-2376 Fax: 718-429-0671
Website: www.vaughn.edu
E-mail: admitme@vaughn.edu

Established 1932. Private. Coed. Accreditation: MSACS, ABET. Tuition: $13,400. Fees: $280. Enrollment: 842 full-time, 284 part-time. Faculty: 59. Student-faculty ratio: 11:1. Degrees: BS, AAS, AOS. Library: 62,000 vols. Offering bachelor and associate degrees in airport management, aviation maintenance, flight training, electronic technology, engineering, general management, mechatronic engineering, pre-engineering and computerized design/animated graphics. Hands-on training. Extensive career development services and financial aid available.

Wagner College
One Campus Rd, Staten Island NY 10301
Leigh Ann DePascale, Director of Admissions
718-390-3411

NORTH CAROLINA

Appalachian State University
ASU Station, Boone NC 28608-0001
828-262-2000

Barton College
PO Box 5000, Wilson NC 27893
252-399-6300

Belmont Abbey College
100 Belmont Mount Holly Rd
Belmont NC 28012-1802
888-222-0110

Brevard College
One Brevard College Dr, Brevard NC 28712
Joretta Nelson, Vice President Enrollment Management
828-883-8292 Fax: 828-884-3790
Website: www.brevard.edu
E-mail: admissions@brevard.edu

Campbell University
PO Box 546, Buies Creek NC 27506-0546
Herbert V. Kerner, Jr., Director of Admissions
800-334-4111

Catawba College
2300 W Innes St, Salisbury NC 28144-2488
Dr. L. Russell Watjen, Ph.D., V.P. & Dean of Admissions
704-637-4402 Fax: 704-637-4222
Website: www.catawba.edu
E-mail: admission@catawba.edu

Chowan University
One University Pl, Murfreesboro NC 27855
Chad Holt, Dean of Admissions
800-488-4101 Fax: 252-398-1190
Website: www.chowan.edu
E-mail: holtc@chowan.edu

Duke University
Durham NC 27706-8001
919-684-8111

East Carolina University
General Classroom Bldg. 3119, Greenville NC 27858
Dr. Ernest B. Uhr, Dean

Gardner-Webb University
PO Box 817, Boiling Springs NC 28017
704-406-2361

Greensboro College
815 W Market St, Greensboro NC 27401-1875
336-272-7102

Guilford College
5800 W Friendly Ave, Greensboro NC 27410-4173
Randy Doss, Dean of Enrollment
336-316-2100

Haywood Community College
185 Freedlander Dr, Clyde NC 28721
Debbie Rowland, Coordinator of Admissions
828-627-4500 Fax: 828-627-4513
Website: www.haywood.edu
E-mail: drowland@haywood.edu

High Point University
933 Montlieu Ave, High Point NC 27262-3598
336-841-9000

James Sprunt Community College
PO Box 398, Kenansville NC 28349-0398
Lea Grady, Admissions
910-296-2500 Fax: 910-296-1636
Website: www.jamessprunt.edu

JOHN WESLEY COLLEGE
2314 N Centennial St, High Point NC 27265-3197
Greg Workman, Admissions Officer
336-889-2262 ext. 127 Fax: 336-889-2261
Website: www.johnwesley.edu
E-mail: admissions@johnwesley.edu
See listing under "Theological Studies & Religious Vocations"

Lees-McRae College
PO Box 128, Banner Elk NC 28604-0128
Walt Crutchfield, Dean of Admissions
800-280-4562

Livingstone College
701 W Monroe St, Salisbury NC 28144-5298
704-797-1000

Mars Hill College
Mars Hill NC 28754
Chad Holt, Dean of Enrollment
866-MHC-4-YOU

Mayland Community College
PO Box 547, Spruce Pine NC 28777-0547
Cathy B. Morrison, Director of Enrollment Management
828-765-7351 Fax: 828-765-0728
Website: www.mayland.edu
E-mail: cmorrison@mayland.edu

Meredith College
3800 Hillsborough St, Raleigh NC 27607-5298
Heidi L. Fletcher, Director of Admissions
919-760-8581

Methodist College
5400 Ramsey St, Fayetteville NC 28311-1498
910-630-7000

Montreat College
PO Box 1267, Montreat NC 28757-1267
800-622-6968

Mt. Olive College
634 Henderson St, Mount Olive NC 28365
Tim Woodard, Director of Admissions
919-658-2502

North Carolina A&T State University
1601 E Market St, Greensboro NC 27411
Lee Young, AVC Enrollment
336-334-7500

North Carolina State University
PO Box 7001, Raleigh NC 27695-0001
919-515-2011

North Carolina Wesleyan College
3400 N Wesleyan Blvd, Rocky Mount NC 27804-8677
252-985-5100

Peace College
15 E Peace St, Raleigh NC 27604-1194
Laura C. Bingham, President
800-PEACE-47 Fax: 919-508-2306
Website: www.peace.edu
E-mail: admissions@peace.edu

Pfeiffer University
PO Box 960, Misenheimer NC 28109-0960
704-463-1360

Queens University of Charlotte
1900 Selwyn Ave, Charlotte NC 28274-0002
704-337-2212

St. Andrews Presbyterian College
1700 Dogwood Mile St, Laurinburg NC 28352-5521
Glenn Batten, Vice President for Enrollment
910-277-5554

Salem College
Winston Salem NC 27108
Dana Evans, Dean of Admissions/Fin. Aid
800-32-SALEM Fax: 336-917-5572
Website: www.salem.edu
E-mail: admissions@salem.edu
See listing under "Women's Colleges"

South College
29 Turtle Creek Dr, Asheville NC 28803
Robert Davis, Dean of Academic Affairs
828-277-5521 Fax: 828-277-6151
Website: southcollegenc.com
E-mail: bdavis@southcollegenc.com

South Piedmont Community College
PO Box 126, Polkton NC 28135-0126
John Curtis, Contact
704-272-5324 Fax: 704-272-8904
Website: www.spcc.edu
E-mail: jcurtis@spcc.edu

University of North Carolina
Chapel Hill NC 27599-0001
919-962-2211

University of North Carolina
9201 University City Blvd, Charlotte NC 28223
704-547-2000

University of North Carolina
601 S College Rd, Wilmington NC 28403-3201
910-962-3000

University of North Carolina at Greensboro
1000 Spring Garden St, Greensboro NC 27412-0001
336-334-5243

University of North Carolina at Pembroke
PO Box 1510, Pembroke NC 28372-1510
910-521-6000

Wake Forest University
PO Box 7305, Winston Salem NC 27109-7305
336-759-5000

Warren Wilson College
PO Box 9000, Asheville NC 28815-9000
Richard Blomgren, Dean of Admissions
828-298-3325

Western Carolina University
University Dr, Cullowhee NC 28723-9646
828-227-7211

Winston-Salem State University
601 S Mrtn Lther King Jr Dr
Winston Salem NC 27110-0003
336-750-2000

NORTH DAKOTA

Dickinson State University
Dickinson ND 58601-4896
Steve Glasser, Director of Enrollment Services
800-279-4295 Fax: 701-483-2409
Website: www.dickinsonstate.edu
E-mail: dsu.hawks@dickinsonstate.edu

Jamestown College
6000 College Ln, Jamestown ND 58405-0002
701-252-3467

Mayville State University
330 3rd St NE, Mayville ND 58257-1299
Dr. Ray Gerszewski, Vice President Student Affairs
800-437-4104 Fax: 701-788-4748
Website: www.mayvillestate.edu
E-mail: admit@mayvillestate.edu

Minot State University
500 University Ave W, Minot ND 58707-0002
Dennis Parisien, Enrollment Services Rep.
800-777-0750 ext. 3350

University of Mary
7500 University Dr, Bismarck ND 58504-9652
701-255-7500

University of North Dakota
Box 8193 University Station, Grand Forks ND 58203
701-777-2011

Valley City State University
101 College St SW, Valley City ND 58072-4024
Dan Klein, Director of Enrollment Services
800-532-8641 ext. 7101 Fax: 701-845-7299
Website: www.vcsu.edu
E-mail: enrollment.services@vcsu.edu
See listing under "Universities"

Williston State College
PO Box 1326, Williston ND 58802-1326
Penny Soiseth, Associate Director Enrollment Services
701-774-4200 Fax: 701-774-4544
Website: www.wsc.nodak.edu
E-mail: penny.soiseth@wsc.nodak.edu

OHIO

Baldwin-Wallace College
275 Eastland Rd, Berea OH 44017-2088
440-826-2900

Bowling Green State University
110 McFall Center, Bowling Green OH 43403-0001
866-CHOOSE-BGSU

Brown Mackie College - Cincinnati
1011 Glendale Milford Rd, Cincinnati OH 45215-1107
Robin Krout, President
513-771-2424 Fax: 513-771-3413
Website: www.brownmackie.edu
E-mail: rkrout@brownmackie.edu

Capital University
2199 E Main St, Columbus OH 43209-2394
614-236-6011

Case Western Reserve University
10900 Euclid Ave, Cleveland OH 44106
216-368-2000

Cleveland State University
2121 Euclid Ave RW 204, Cleveland OH 44115
Dr. Richard Arndt, Dean of Undergraduate Recruitment and College Partnerships
888-CSU-OHIO Fax: 216-687-9210
Website: www.csuohio.edu
E-mail: admissions@csuohio.edu

College of Wooster
Wooster OH 44691-2363
Paul J. Deutsch, Dean of Admissions
800-877-9905

Davis College
4747 Monroe St, Toledo OH 43623-4389
Dana Stern, Admissions Director
419-473-2700 Fax: 419-473-2472
Website: www.daviscollege.edu
E-mail: learn@daviscollege.edu

Defiance College
701 N Clinton St, Defiance OH 43512-1695
419-784-4010

Franciscan University of Steubenville
University Blvd, Steubenville OH 43952
Margaret J. Weber, Director of Admissions
800-783-6220 or 740-283-6226 Fax: 740-284-5456
Website: www.admissions.edu
E-mail: mweber@franciscan.edu

Franklin University
201 S Grant Ave, Columbus OH 43215-5399
614-341-6300

Heidelberg College
310 E Market St, Tiffin OH 44883-2462
418-448-2000

Hiram College
PO Box 96, Hiram OH 44234-0096
800-362-5280

John Carroll University
20700 N Park Blvd, Cleveland OH 44118-4581
216-397-1886

Kent State University
PO Box 5190, Kent OH 44242-0001
Paul Deutsch, Director of Admissions
330-672-2444

Lake Erie College
391 W Washington St, Painesville OH 44077-3389
440-352-3361

Malone College
515 25th St NW, Canton OH 44709-3897
John Chopka, Dean of Admissions
330-471-8100

Marietta College
215 5th St, Marietta OH 45750-4047
740-376-4600

Miami University
E High St, Oxford OH 45056
513-529-2531

Mt. Union College
1972 Clark Ave, Alliance OH 44601-3929
Vincent Heslop, Director of Admissions
800-334-6682

Mount Vernon Nazarene University
800 Martinsburg Rd, Mount Vernon OH 43050-9509
Timothy Eades, Director of Admissions
866-462-6868

MYERS UNIVERSITY
3921 Chester Ave, Cleveland OH 44114-4624
Ronald G. Brown, Vice President for Enrollment Management
216-432-8992 Fax: 216-361-9274
Website: www.myers.edu
E-mail: rgbrown@myers.edu

Notre Dame College
4545 College Rd, Cleveland OH 44121-4293
216-381-1680

Ohio Dominican University
1216 Sunbury Rd, Columbus OH 43219-2099
614-253-2741

OHIO NORTHERN UNIVERSITY
525 S Main St, Ada OH 45810-1555
James Fenton, Dean
419-772-2070
Website: www.onu.edu
See listing under "Universities"

The Ohio State University
Fisher College of Business
Schoenbaum Hall, 210 W Woodruff Ave
Columbus OH 43210
614-292-2715 Fax: 614-292-5735
Website: fisher.osu.edu
E-mail: fisherundergrad@cob.osu.edu

Ohio State University-Lima Campus
4240 Campus Dr, Lima OH 45804-3576
Garlene Smithson, Dir. Enrollment Services
419-995-8396

Ohio University
Chillicothe Campus
PO Box 629, Chillicothe OH 45601
Student Services
740-774-7200 Fax: 740-774-7295
Website: www.ohiou.edu/chillicothe/

Ohio University - Zanesville Branch
1425 Newark Rd, Zanesville OH 43701-2695
740-588-1439

OHIO WESLEYAN UNIVERSITY
61 S Sandusky St, Delaware OH 43015-2398
Director of Admission
740-368-3020 Fax: 740-368-3314
Website: www.owu.edu
E-mail: owuadmit@owu.edu

Owens Community College
3200 Bright Rd, Findlay OH 45840
William J. Ivoska PhD., Vice President of Student Services
567-429-3500 Fax: 567-423-0246
Website: www.owens.edu
E-mail: admissions@owens.edu

Owens Community College
PO Box 10000, Toledo OH 43699-1947
William J. Ivoska, Ph.D, Vice President of Student Services
567-661-7000 Fax: 567-661-7607
Website: www.owens.edu
E-mail: admissions@owens.edu

Shawnee State University
940 2nd St, Portsmouth OH 45662-4344
740-354-3205

Sinclair Community College
444 W 3rd St, Dayton OH 45402-1460
Director of Admissions
937-512-3000 Fax: 937-512-2393
Website: www.sinclair.edu
E-mail: admit@sinclair.edu

University of Akron
381 Buchtel Mall, Akron OH 44304-1584
330-972-7111

University of Cincinnati
2700 Clifton Ave, Cincinnati OH 45220-2873
513-556-6000

University of Dayton
300 College Park, Dayton OH 45469-1300
Robert F. Durkle, Director of Admission
800-837-7433 Fax: 937-229-4729
Website: admission.udayton.edu
E-mail: admission@udayton.edu

University of Findlay
1000 N Main St, Findlay OH 45840-3695
419-422-8313

University of Northwestern Ohio
1441 N Cable Rd, Lima OH 45805-1498
Rick Morrison, Director of Admissions
419-998-3120

University of Rio Grande
General Delivery, Rio Grande OH 45674-9999
Dr. George Ulrich, Dean
740-245-5353 ext. 7287

University of Toledo
2801 W Bancroft St, Toledo OH 43606-3390
419-530-4636

Urbana University
579 College Way, Urbana OH 43078
937-484-1301

Ursuline College
2550 Lander Rd, Cleveland OH 44124-4398
Sarah E. Sundermeier, Director of Admissions
888-URSULINE Toll Free Fax: 440-684-6138
Website: www.admission.ursuline.edu
E-mail: admission@ursuline.edu

Wilmington College
1870 Quaker Way, Wilmington OH 45177
937-382-6661

Wittenberg University
PO Box 720, Springfield OH 45501-0720
937-327-6231

Wright State University
3640 Colonel Glenn Hwy, Dayton OH 45435-0002
937-775-3333

Xavier University
3800 Victory Pkwy, Cincinnati OH 45207-1092
513-745-3000

Youngstown State University
Sweeney Welcome Ctr, One University Plz
Youngstown OH 44555-0002
Sue Davis, Contact
877-GO-TO-YSU

OKLAHOMA

Bacone College
2299 Old Bacone Rd, Muskogee OK 74403-1568
Jerrett Phillips, Director of Admissions
918-781-7340

Cameron University
2800 W Gore Blvd, Lawton OK 73505-6377
580-581-2200

Mid-America Christian University
3500 SW 119th St, Oklahoma City OK 73170-4504
Haley Hope, Director of Admissions
405-691-3800 Fax: 405-692-3165
Website: www.macu.edu
E-mail: info@macu.edu

Oklahoma Christian University
PO Box 11000, Oklahoma City OK 73136-1100
405-425-5000

Oklahoma City University
2501 N Blackwelder Ave
Oklahoma City OK 73106-1493
Shery Boyles, Director of Admissions
405-521-5050

Oklahoma Panhandle State University
PO Box 430, Goodwell OK 73939-0430
580-349-2611

Oklahoma State University
Stillwater OK 74078
Ken Eastman, Department Head
405-744-5201
Website: www.okstate.edu
E-mail: ken.eastman@okstate.edu

Oklahoma Wesleyan University
2201 Silver Lake Rd, Bartlesville OK 74006-6299
918-333-6151

Oral Roberts University
7777 S Lewis Ave, Tulsa OK 74171-0001
Chris Belcher, Director of Undergraduate Admissions
800-678-8876

Rogers State University - Claremore Campus
1701 W Will Rogers Blvd, Claremore OK 74017-3259
Joe Wiley, President
918-343-7777

Southwestern Oklahoma State University
100 Campus Dr, Weatherford OK 73096-3098
580-772-6611

SPARTAN COLLEGE OF AERONAUTICS AND TECHNOLOGY
8820 E Pine St, Tulsa OK 74115-5802
Director of Admissions
800-331-1204 Fax: 918-831-8609
Website: www.spartan.edu
E-mail: spartan@mail.spartan.edu
Established 1928. Coed. Accredited member school: ACCSCT. Providing Technical training and education in Avionics, Aviation Maintenance; Nondestructive Testing and Quality Control. Complete flight training program. Offering Diplomas, Associate of Applied Science and Bachelor of Science in Aviation Technology Management.

University of Oklahoma at Norman
660 Parrington Oval, Norman OK 73019-3070
405-325-0311

University of Tulsa
600 S College Ave, Tulsa OK 74104-3126
Earl Johnson, Dean of Admission
918-631-2307 Fax: 918-631-5003
Website: www.utulsa.edu
E-mail: admission@utulsa.edu

OREGON

Cascade College
9101 E Burnside St, Portland OR 97216-1599
Jim Murphy, Director of Enrollment Management
800-550-7678 Fax: 503-257-1222
Website: www.cascade.edu
E-mail: admissions@cascade.edu

Concordia University
2811 NE Holman St, Portland OR 97211-6099
Bobi Swan, Director of Admissions
503-288-9371 Fax: 503-280-8531
Website: www.cu-portland.edu
E-mail: cu-admissions@cu-portland.edu

Corban College
5000 Deer Park Dr SE, Salem OR 97317-9330
503-581-8600

Linn-Benton Community College
6500 Pacific Blvd SW, Albany OR 97321-3774
Christine Baker, Outreach Coordinator
541-917-4811 Fax: 541-917-4868
Website: www.linnbenton.edu
E-mail: admissions@linnbenton.edu

Marylhurst University
17600 Pacific Hwy (Hwy 43)
Marylhurst OR 97036-0261
Director of Admissions
800-634-9982 ext. 6268 Fax: 503-635-6585
Website: www.marylhurst.edu
E-mail: studentinfo@marylhurst.edu

Oregon Institute of Technology
3201 Campus Dr, Klamath Falls OR 97601-8801
541-885-1000

Oregon State University
Corvallis OR 97333-9800
541-737-0123

PACIFIC UNIVERSITY
2043 College Way, Forest Grove OR 97116-1797
Karen M. Dunston, Executive Director of Admissions
800-677-6712 Fax: 503-352-2975
Website: www.pacific.edu
E-mail: admissions@pacific.edu

Portland State University
PO Box 751, Portland OR 97207-0751
503-725-3000

Southern Oregon University
1250 Siskiyou Blvd, Ashland OR 97520-5010
541-552-7672

University of Oregon
1217 University of Oregon, Eugene OR 97403
541-346-1000

University of Portland
5000 N Willamette Blvd, Portland OR 97203-5798
Jason McDonald, Dean of Admissions
503-943-7911 Fax: 503-943-7315
Website: www.up.edu
E-mail: mcdonaja@up.edu

Warner Pacific College
2219 SE 68th Ave, Portland OR 97215-4026
Shannon Mackey, Director of Admissions
503-517-1000 Fax: 503-517-1352
Website: www.warnerpacific.edu
E-mail: admissions@warnerpacific.edu

Western Oregon University
345 Monmouth Ave N, Monmouth OR 97361-1314
David McDonald, Dean, Admission, Retention & Enrollment Management
877-877-1593

Willamette University
900 State St, Salem OR 97301-3931
503-370-6300

PENNSYLVANIA

Albright College
PO Box 15234, Reading PA 19612-5234
800-252-1856

Alvernia College
400 Saint Bernardine St, Reading PA 19607
610-796-8200

Arcadia University
450 S Easton Rd, Glenside PA 19038-3295
Dennis Nostrand, VP for Enrollment Management
877-ARCADIA (877-272-2342)

ART INSTITUTE OF PITTSBURGH
420 Boulevard Of The Allies, Pittsburgh PA 15219
Jeffrey Bucklew, Director of Admissions
800-275-2470 Fax: 412-263-6667
Website: www.aip.aii.edu
E-mail: pahughes@aii.edu
See listing under "Universities"

Berks Technical Institute
2205 Ridgewood Rd, Wyomissing PA 19610-1168
Elizabeth Wade, Director of Admissions
610-372-1722 Fax: 610-376-4684
Website: www.berkstech.com

Bloomsburg University of Pennsylvania
400 E 2nd St, Bloomsburg PA 17815-1399
570-389-4000

Cabrini College
610 King of Prussia Rd, Radnor PA 19087-3698
Mark T. Osborn, VP for Enrollment Management
610-902-8100

California University of Pennsylvania
250 University Ave, California PA 15419-1394
724-938-4000

Carlow University
3333 5th Ave, Pittsburgh PA 15213-3165
412-578-6000

Carnegie Mellon University
5000 Forbes Ave, Pittsburgh PA 15213-3890
412-268-2000

Cedar Crest College
100 College Dr, Allentown PA 18104-6196
Judith A. Neyhart, Vice President Enrollment
800-360-1222

Central Pennsylvania College
College Hill & Valley Rds, Summerdale PA 17093
Katie Borrelli, Admissions Director
800-759-2727 Fax: 717-728-2505
Website: www.centralpenn.edu
E-mail: katie.borrelli@centralpenn.edu

Chatham College
Woodland Rd, Pittsburgh PA 15232-2826
412-365-1100

Chestnut Hill College
9601 Germantown Ave, Philadelphia PA 19118-2693
Jodie King, Director of Admissions
215-248-7001

Clarion University of Pennsylvania
840 Wood St, Clarion PA 16214-1232
William Bailey, Dean of Enrollment Management
814-393-2306 Fax: 814-393-2030
Website: www.clarion.edu
E-mail: admissions@clarion.edu

College Misericordia
301 Lake St, Dallas PA 18612-1008
Admissions
570-674-6400

Community College of Allegheny County
Allegheny Campus: 808 Ridge Ave, Pittsburgh PA 15212 Admissions: 412.237.2700
Boyce Campus: 595 Beatty Rd, Monroeville PA 15146 Admissions: 724.325.6614
North Campus: 8701 Perry Highway, Pittsburgh PA 15237 Admissions: 412.369.3600
South Campus: 1750 Clairton Rd, West Mifflin PA 15122 Admissions: 412-469-4301
Website: www.ccac.edu

Community College of Beaver County
1 Campus Dr, Monaca PA 15061-2566
724-775-8561 Fax: 724-775-4687
Website: www.ccbc.edu
E-mail: admissions@ccbc.edu

Delaware Valley College
700 E Butler Ave, Doylestown PA 18901-2697
Stephen W. Zenko, Director of Admissions
800-2DE-LVAL Fax: 215-230-2968
Website: www.delval.edu
E-mail: stephenzenko@delval.edu

DeSales University
2755 Station Ave, Center Valley PA 18034-9565
610-282-1100 Fax: 610-282-2342
Website: www.desales.edu

Douglas Education Center
130 7th St, Monessen PA 15062-1097
Sherry Lee Walters, Director of Enrollment Services
800-413-6013 Fax: 724-684-7463
Website: www.douglas-school.com
E-mail: swalters@douglas-school.com

Drexel University
3141 Chestnut St, Philadelphia PA 19104-2875
Dana R. Davies, Director of Undergraduate Enrollment
800-2-DREXEL

Duquesne University
600 Forbes Ave, Pittsburgh PA 15282-0001
Paul-James Cukanna, Director of Admissions
412-396-5000

Eastern University
1300 Eagle Rd, Saint Davids PA 19087-3696
610-341-5800

Edinboro University of Pennsylvania
Edinboro PA 16444-0001
814-732-2000

Elizabethtown College
1 Alpha Dr, Elizabethtown PA 17022-2298
717-361-1000

Erie Business Center
246 W 9th St, Erie PA 16501-1392
Donna Perino, Director
814-456-7504 Fax: 814-456-6015
Website: www.eriebc.edu
E-mail: perinod@eriebc.edu

Gannon University
109 University Sq, Erie PA 16541-0001
Christopher Tremblay, Director of Admissions
800-GANNON-U

Geneva College
3200 College Ave, Beaver Falls PA 15010-3599
724-846-5100

Gettysburg College
300 N Washington St, Gettysburg PA 17325-1483
Gail Sweezey, Director of Admissions
717-337-6100

Gwynedd-Mercy College
1325 Sumneytown Pike, Gwynedd Valley PA 19437
Dennis Murphy, V.P. Enrollment Management
800-DIAL-GMC

Holy Family University
9801 Frankford Avenue, Philadelphia PA 19114
Lauren Campbell, Director of Admissions
215-637-3050 Fax: 215-281-1022
Website: www.holyfamily.edu
E-mail: admissions@holyfamily.edu

Immaculata University
Immaculata PA 19345
Women's College Office of Admissions
610-647-4400

Juniata College
1700 Moore St, Huntingdon PA 16652-2196
Michelle Bartol, Dean of Enrollment
877-JUNIATA Fax: 814-641-3100
Website: www.juniata.edu
E-mail: admissions@juniata.edu

King's College
133 N River St, Wilkes Barre PA 18711-0801
Michelle Lawrence-Schmude, Dean of Admission
570-208-5900 Fax: 570-208-5971
Website: www.kings.edu
E-mail: admissions@kings.edu

La Roche College
9000 Babcock Blvd, Pittsburgh PA 15237-5898
Thomas Hassett, Director of Admissions
412-536-1272

La Salle University
1900 W Olney Ave, Philadelphia PA 19141-1199
Robert Voss, Dean of Admissions
215-951-1500

Lebanon Valley College
101 N College Ave, Annville PA 17003-1400
William Brown, Dean of Admissions & Financial Aid
866-LVC-4ADM

Lehigh University
27 Memorial Dr West, Bethlehem PA 18015-3094
Eric Kaplan, Dean of Admissions
610-758-3100

Lehigh Valley College
2809 E Saucon Valley Rd
Center Valley PA 18034-8447
Sam Jarvis, Director of Marketing
800-227-9109 Fax: 610-791-7810
Website: www.lehighvalley.edu
E-mail: joshua.padron@lehighvalley.edu

Lincoln University
Lincoln University PA 19352
Michael C. Taylor, Director of Admissions
800-790-0191

Lock Haven University
Lock Haven PA 17745
James C. Reeser, Dean of Admissions
570-893-2027

Lycoming College
700 College Pl, Williamsport PA 17701-5192
570-321-4000

Marywood University
2300 Adams Ave, Scranton PA 18509-1598
570-348-6211

Mercyhurst College
501 E 38th St, Erie PA 16546-0001
800-825-1926

Messiah College
1 S College Ave, Grantham PA 17027
717-766-2511

Millersville University of Pennsylvania
PO Box 1002, Millersville PA 17551-0302
717-872-3024

MOUNT ALOYSIUS COLLEGE
7373 Admiral Peary Hwy, Cresson PA 16630-1999
Frank C. Crouse Jr., Vice President for Enrollment Management
814-886-6383 or 888-823-2220 Fax: 814-886-6441
Website: www.mtaloy.edu
E-mail: admissions@mtaloy.edu

Muhlenberg College
2400 W Chew St, Allentown PA 18104-5586
610-821-3100

Neumann College
1 Neumann Dr, Aston PA 19014-1298
Dennis Murphy, Director of Admissions
610-459-0905 Fax: 610-558-5652
Website: www.neumann.edu
E-mail: neumann@neumann.edu

Pennsylvania College of Technology
1 College Ave, Williamsport PA 17701
570-326-3761

Pennsylvania State University
Broadhead Rd, Monaca PA 15061
724-773-3500

Pennsylvania State University
3550 7th St Rd, New Kensington PA 15068-1765
Patricia K. Brady, Director of Admissions
724-334-5466

Pennsylvania State University
201 Shields Bldg PO Box 300
University Park PA 16802-3000
814-865-4700

Point Park University
201 Wood St, Pittsburgh PA 15222-1984
Philip Clarke, Associate Director of Admissions
412-392-3430

THE RESTAURANT SCHOOL AT WALNUT HILL COLLEGE
4207 Walnut St, Philadelphia PA 19104-5296
Karl D. Becker, Admissions Director
215-222-4200 ext. 3011 Fax: 215-222-4219
Website: www.walnuthillcollege.edu
E-mail: info@walnuthillcollege.edu

Robert Morris College
600 5th Ave, Pittsburgh PA 15219-3010
412-227-6800

Robert Morris University
6001 University Blvd, Coraopolis PA 15108
412-262-8200

Rosemont College
1400 Montgomery Ave, Rosemont PA 19010-1699
Ms. Rennie Andrews, Director of Admissions
610-526-2966

St. Vincent College
300 Fraser Purchase Rd, Latrobe PA 15650-2690
724-539-9761

Seton Hill University
Greensburg PA 15601-1599
Mary Kay Cooper, Director of Admissions and Adult Student Services
800-826-6234

Shippensburg University
1871 Old Main Dr, Shippensburg PA 17257-2299
717-477-7447

Slippery Rock University
14 Maltby Dr, Slippery Rock PA 16057-1326
724-738-9000

Susquehanna University
514 University Ave, Selinsgrove PA 17870-1164
570-374-0101

Temple University
Broad St & Montgomery Ave, Philadelphia PA 19122
215-204-7000

Temple University Ambler
Ambler PA 19002
David Kaiser, Contact
215-283-1674

Thiel College
75 College Ave, Greenville PA 16125-2181
724-589-2000

University of Pennsylvania
3400 Spruce St, Philadelphia PA 19104-4274
215-898-5000

University of Pittsburgh
150 Finoli Dr, Greensburg PA 15601
Brandi S. Darr, Director of Admissions and Financial Aid
724-836-9880

University of Pittsburgh
4200 5th Ave, Pittsburgh PA 15260-3583
412-624-4141

University of Pittsburgh at Bradford
300 Campus Dr, Bradford PA 16701-2812
Alexander Nazemetz, Director of Admissions
814-362-7555

University of Scranton
800 Linden St, Scranton PA 18510-4501
570-941-7400

Villanova University
800 E Lancaster Ave, Villanova PA 19085
610-519-4500

Washington & Jefferson College
60 S Lincoln St, Washington PA 15301-4801
Alton E. Newell, Vice President for Enrollment
724-223-6025 Fax: 724-223-6534
Website: www.washjeff.edu
E-mail: admission@washjeff.edu

Waynesburg College
51 W College St, Waynesburg PA 15370-1222
Robin L. Moore, Dean of Admissions
800-225-7393

West Chester University of Pennsylvania
S High St, West Chester PA 19383-0001
610-436-1000

Westminster College
New Wilmington PA 16172-0001
Doug Swartz, Director of Admissions
724-946-7100

Widener University
1 University Pl, Chester PA 19013-5792
Edwin Wright, Dean of Admissions
610-499-4000 Fax: 610-499-4676
Website: www.widener.edu
E-mail: admissions.office@widener.edu

Wilkes University
170 S Franklin St, Wilkes Barre PA 18766-0001
570-408-5000

York College of Pennsylvania
PO Box 15199, York PA 17405-7199
717-846-7788

RHODE ISLAND

Bryant University
1150 Douglas Pike, Smithfield RI 02917-1287
401-232-6000

New England Institute of Technology
2500 Post Rd, Warwick RI 02886-2244
Michael Kwiatkowski, Director of Admissions
401-739-5000 Fax: 401-738-5122
Website: www.neit.edu
E-mail: eflynn@neit.edu

Providence College
549 River Ave, Providence RI 02918-0002
401-865-1000

Rhode Island College
600 Mount Pleasant Ave, Providence RI 02908-1924
401-456-8000

Salve Regina University
100 Ochre Point Ave, Newport RI 02840-4192
401-847-6650

University of Rhode Island
Kingston RI 02881
401-874-1000

SOUTH CAROLINA

Benedict College
1600 Harden St, Columbia SC 29204-1086
Phyllis L. Thompson, Director of Admissions
803-253-5143

Charleston Southern University
PO Box 118087, Charleston SC 29423-8087
Cheryl Burton, Director of Admissions
800-947-7474

The Citadel
171 Moultrie St, Charleston SC 29409-0002
843-953-5000

Clemson University
105 Sikes Hall, Clemson SC 29634
864-656-2287

Coastal Carolina University
PO Box 261954, Conway SC 29528-6054
Office of Admissions
800-277-7000 Fax: 843-349-2127
Website: www.coastal.edu
E-mail: admissions@coastal.edu

College of Charleston
66 George St, Charleston SC 29424-1407
Suzette Stille, Admissions
843-953-5670

Columbia College
1301 Columbia College Dr, Columbia SC 29203-5998
Elizabeth G. Quackenbush, Director of Admissions
803-786-3871

Columbia International University
PO Box 3122, Columbia SC 29230-3122
Michelle MacGregor, Director of University Admissions
800-777-2227 Fax: 803-786-4209
Website: www.ciu.edu
E-mail: yesciu@ciu.edu
See listing under "Theological Studies & Religious Vocations"

Erskine College & Seminary
PO Box 176, Due West SC 29639
Bart Walker, Director of Admissions
864-379-8838 Fax: 864-379-3048
Website: www.erskine.edu
E-mail: admissions@erskine.edu

Forrest Junior College
601 E River St, Anderson SC 29624-2405
Pamela Johnson, MBA, President
864-225-7653 Fax: 864-261-7471
Website: www.forrestcollege.edu
E-mail: info@forrestcollege.edu
Accounting, Office Systems Tech, Childcare Mgt.
See listing under "Community and Junior Colleges"

Francis Marion University
PO Box 100547, Florence SC 29501-0547
843-661-1362

Furman University
3300 Poinsett Hwy, Greenville SC 29613-0002
864-294-2000

Greenville Technical College
PO Box 5616, Greenville SC 29606-5616
Carolyn Watkins, Dean of Admissions
800-723-0673 (US) or 800-922-1183 (SC)
Website: www.greenvilletech.com

Lander University
320 Stanley Ave, Greenwood SC 29649-2099
Jonathan Reece, Director of Admissions
888-4-LANDER

Limestone College
1115 College Dr, Gaffney SC 29340-3799
Chris Phenicie, V.P. for Enrollment
864-489-7151 Fax: 864-488-8206
Website: www.limestone.edu
E-mail: cphenicie@limestone.edu

North Greenville University
PO Box 1892, Tigerville SC 29688-1892
Dr. Ralph Johnson, Dean
Website: www.ngu.edu
See listing under "Universities"

Presbyterian College
503 S Broad St, Clinton SC 29325
Richard Dana Paul, Dean of Admissions
800-476-7272

South Carolina State University
PO Box 7127, Orangeburg SC 29117-0001
Lillian M. Adderson, Director of Admissions
803-536-7185

Southern Wesleyan University
PO Box 1020, Central SC 29630-1020
864-644-5000

South University
9 Science Court, Columbia SC 29203
Trish Wade, Contact
803-799-9082 Fax: 803-799-9038
Website: www.southuniversity.edu
E-mail: twade@southuniversity.edu

Spartanburg Community College
PO Box 4386, Spartanburg SC 29305-4386
Nancy Garmroth, Dean of Admissions & Financial Aid
864-592-4810 Fax: 864-592-4945
Website: sccsc.edu

University of South Carolina
Columbia SC 29208-0001
803-777-7700

University of South Carolina - Upstate
800 University Way, Spartanburg SC 29303-4932
Donette Stewart, Assistant VC for Enrollment Services
864-503-5246 Fax: 864-503-5727
Website: www.uscupstate.edu
E-mail: dstewart@uscupstate.edu
See listing under "Universities"

Voorhees College
Voorhees Rd, Denmark SC 29042
803-793-3351

Winthrop University
701 W Oakland Ave, Rock Hill SC 29733-0001
803-323-2211

Wofford College
429 N Church St, Spartanburg SC 29303-3663
864-597-4000

SOUTH DAKOTA

Dakota State University
820 N Washington Ave, Madison SD 57042-1799
605-256-5112

Dakota Wesleyan University
1200 W University Ave, Mitchell SD 57301
605-995-2600

Mt. Marty College
1105 W 8th St, Yankton SD 57078-3724
605-668-1514

National American University
1270 Ryan St - 28 MSS/DPE, Ellsworth AFB SD 57706
605-923-5856

NATIONAL AMERICAN UNIVERSITY
321 Kansas City St, Rapid City SD 57701-3692
Angela G. Beck, Director of Enrollment Management
605-394-4800 Fax: 605-394-4871
Website: www.rapid.national.edu
E-mail: rcadmissions@national.edu

National American University
2801 S Kiwanis Ave Ste 100
Sioux Falls SD 57105-4293
605-334-5430

Northern State University
1200 S Jay St, Aberdeen SD 57401-7198
605-626-3011

Presentation College
1500 N Main St, Aberdeen SD 57401-1280
JoEllen Lindner, VP for Enrollment
605-229-8492 Fax: 605-229-8425
Website: www.presentation.edu
E-mail: admit@presentation.edu

South Dakota State University
PO Box 2201, Brookings SD 57007-0001
605-688-4151

University of South Dakota
414 E Clark St, Vermillion SD 57069-2307
605-677-5011

Western Dakota Technical Institute
800 Mickelson Dr, Rapid City SD 57703-4018
Jill Elder, Admissions Coordinator
605-394-4034 Fax: 605-394-2204
Website: www.wdt.edu
E-mail: jill.elder@wdt.edu

TENNESSEE

Aquinas College
4210 Harding Rd, Nashville TN 37205
Diane C. LeJeune, Director of Admissions
615-297-7545 ext. 460 Fax: 615-279-3893
Website: www.aquinascollege.edu
E-mail: lejeuned@aquinascollege.edu

Austin Peay State University
601 College St, Clarksville TN 37044-0002
931-221-7011 Fax: 931-221-6168
Website: www.apsu.edu
E-mail: admissions@apsu.edu

Belmont University
1900 Belmont Blvd, Nashville TN 37212-3757
615-460-6000

Bryan College
PO Box 7000, Dayton TN 37321-7000
423-775-2041

Carson-Newman College
1646 Russell Ave, Jefferson City TN 37760
865-471-4000

Christian Brothers University
650 E Parkway S, Memphis TN 38104-5568
901-321-3000

Crichton College
255 N Highland St, Memphis TN 38111-4745
Shelly Luttrell, Dean of Admissions
901-320-9797 Fax: 901-320-9791
Website: www.crichton.edu
E-mail: admissions@crichton.edu

East Tennessee State University
PO Box 70699, Johnson City TN 37614
Dr. Linda Garceau, Dean of Business
423-439-5489

Fisk University
1000 17th Ave N, Nashville TN 37208-3051
William Carter, Director of Admissions
615-329-8766

Freed-Hardeman University
158 E Main St, Henderson TN 38340-2398
731-989-6000

Free Will Baptist Bible College
3606 W End Ave, Nashville TN 37205
Ryan Lewis, Director of Recruitment
800-76-FWBBC Fax: 615-269-6028
Website: www.fwbbc.edu
E-mail: recruit@fwbbc.edu

Lee University
PO Box 3450, Cleveland TN 37320-3450
Evaline Echols, Chairperson - Department of Business
800-533-9930

Le Moyne-Owen College
807 Walker Ave, Memphis TN 38126-6595
901-774-9090

Lincoln Memorial University
PO Box 2012, Harrogate TN 37752
423-869-3611

Lipscomb University
3901 Granny White Pike, Nashville TN 37204-3951
Ricky Holaway, Director of Admissions
800-333-4358 ext. 1776 Fax: 615-269-1804
Website: www.lipscomb.edu
E-mail: admissions@lipscomb.edu

Maryville College
502 E Lamar Alexander Pkwy
Maryville TN 37804-5919
865-981-8000

Middle Tennessee State University
1301 E Main St, Murfreesboro TN 37132-0001
615-898-2300

National College
1328 Highway 11W, Bristol TN 37620
Becky Wild, Director of Admissions
423-878-4440 Fax: 423-793-1060
Website: www.national-college.edu
E-mail: info@national-college.edu

National College of Business & Technology
3748 Nolensville Pike, Nashville TN 37211-3322
Lynda Dandridge, Director of Admissions
615-333-3344 Fax: 615-333-3429
Website: www.national-college.edu
E-mail: info@national-college.edu

Rhodes College
2000 N Parkway, Memphis TN 38112-1624
901-843-3000

Southwest Tennessee Community College
5983 Macon Cove, Memphis TN 38134
Vanessa R. Dowdy, Director of Admissions
901-333-5000 Fax: 901-333-4523
Website: www.southwest.tn.edu
E-mail: vdowdy@southwest.tn.edu

Tennessee State University
3500 John A Merritt Blvd, Nashville TN 37209-1561
John Cade, Dean of Admissions & Records
615-963-5101 Fax: 615-963-2930
Website: www.tnstate.edu
E-mail: jcade@tnstate.edu

Tennessee Technological University
PO Box 5006, Cookeville TN 38505-0001
931-372-3101

Tennessee Temple University
1815 Union Ave, Chattanooga TN 37404-3587
423-493-4100

Trevecca Nazarene University
333 Murfreesboro Rd, Nashville TN 37210-2834
615-248-1200

Tusculum College
PO Box 5051, Greeneville TN 37743
Melissa Ripley, Associate Director of Admissions
800-729-0256

Union University
1050 Union University Dr, Jackson TN 38305
731-668-1818

University of Memphis
Memphis TN 38152-0001
901-678-2000

University of Tennessee
615 McCallie Ave, Chattanooga TN 37403-2504
Yancy Freeman, Director of Admissions
423-425-4111 Fax: 423-425-4157
Website: www.utc.edu
E-mail: Yancy-Freeman@utc.edu

University of Tennessee
527 Andy Holt Tower, Knoxville TN 37996-0001
865-974-1000

University of Tennessee
Martin TN 38238-0001
731-587-7000

Vanderbilt University
W End Ave, Nashville TN 37240-0001
615-322-7311

TEXAS

Abilene Christian University
ACU Box 29000, Abilene TX 79699-0001
325-674-2000 Fax: 325-674-2202
Website: www.acu.edu
E-mail: info@admissions.acu.edu

Angelo State University
ASU Station 11014, San Angelo TX 76909
Bonnie Stennett, Coordinator of Recruiting
800-946-8627

Austin College
900 N Grand Ave, Sherman TX 75090-4400
903-813-2000

Baylor University
Po Box 97008, Waco TX 76798-7008
254-710-1011

Concordia University
3400 N I H 35, Austin TX 78705-2702
512-486-2000

East Texas Baptist University
1209 N Grove St, Marshall TX 75670-1498
903-935-7963

Galveston College
4015 Avenue Q, Galveston TX 77550-7496
Brian Lowery, Registrar
409-763-6551 Fax: 409-944-1501
Website: www.gc.edu
E-mail: blowery@gc.edu

Hallmark Institute of Technology - Technology Campus
10401 W IH 10, San Antonio TX 78230-1736
Joe Fisher, President
210-690-9000 Fax: 210-697-8225
Website: www.hallmarkinstitute.com
E-mail: sross@hallmarkinstitute.com
Electronics Engineering Technology, Business Office Administration, Computer Network Systems Technology, & Medical Assistant.

Lamar University
PO Box 10009, Beaumont TX 77710-0009
409-880-8622

Le Tourneau University
PO Box 7001, Longview TX 75607-7001
903-233-3000

Lubbock Christian University
5601 19th St, Lubbock TX 79407-2099
Stan Scott, Director of Admissions
806-796-8800 Fax: 806-720-7162
Website: www.lcu.edu
E-mail: stan.scott@lcu.edu

McLennan Community College
1400 College Dr, Waco TX 76708-1498
Annette Bigham, Program Director, Business Programs
254-299-8000 Fax: 254-299-8964
Website: www.mclennan.edu
E-mail: abigham@mclennan.edu

Midwestern State University
3410 Taft Blvd, Wichita Falls TX 76308-2096
940-397-4000

Northwood University
1114 W FM 1382, Cedar Hill TX 75104-1204
Sylvia Correa, Director of Admissions
800-927-WOOD Fax: 972-291-3824
Website: www.northwood.edu
E-mail: ray@northwood.edu

Our Lady of the Lake University
411 SW 24th St, San Antonio TX 78207-4666
Mary Kay Cooper, Dean of Enrollment
210-434-6711

Prairie View A&M University
PO Box 519, Prairie View TX 77446
936-857-3311

Remington College - Fort Worth Campus
300 E Loop 820, Fort Worth TX 76112-1280
Director of Recruitment
817-451-0017 Fax: 817-496-1257
Website: www.remingtoncollege.edu
E-mail: lynn.wey@remingtoncollege.edu

St. Edward's University
3001 S Congress Ave, Austin TX 78704-6489
512-448-8400

St. Mary's University of San Antonio
1 Camino Santa Maria St
San Antonio TX 78228-8500
210-436-3011

Sam Houston State University
PO Box 2026, Huntsville TX 77341
936-294-1111

Schreiner University
2100 Memorial Blvd, Kerrville TX 78028-5697
Todd D. Brown, Director of Admissions
800-343-4919

Southern Methodist University
PO Box 750181, Dallas TX 75275-0181
Ron Moss, Dean of Admission
214-768-2058

Stephen F. Austin State University
PO Box 6078, Nacogdoches TX 75962-0001
936-468-2011

Temple College
2600 S 1st St, Temple TX 76504-7435
Toni Borras, Director of Admissions & Records
254-298-8808 Fax: 254-298-8288
Website: www.templejc.edu
E-mail: admissionsrecords@templejc.edu

Texas A&M University
College Station TX 77843-0001
979-845-3211

Texas A&M University
700 University Blvd, Kingsville TX 78363
361-593-2111

Texas A&M University - Commerce
PO Box 3011, Commerce TX 75429
903-886-5102

Texas A&M University - Corpus Christi
6300 Ocean Dr, Corpus Christi TX 78412-5503
361-825-5700

Texas Christian University
TCU Box 297013, Fort Worth TX 76129
817-257-7000

Texas Lutheran University
1000 W Court St, Seguin TX 78155-5978
830-372-8000

Texas Southern University
3100 Cleburne St, Houston TX 77004-4583
713-313-7011

Texas State University - San Marcos
601 University Dr, San Marcos TX 78666-4685
512-245-2111

Texas Tech University
1 Texas Tech University, Lubbock TX 79409-0001
806-742-2011

Texas Wesleyan University
1201 Wesleyan St, Fort Worth TX 76105-1536
Stephanie Boatner, Director of Freshman Admission
800-580-8980

Texas Woman's University
PO Box 425589, Denton TX 76204-5589
Erma Nieto-Brecht, Director of Admissions
866-809-6130 Fax: 940-898-3081
Website: www.twu.edu
E-mail: admissions@twu.edu

Trinity University
715 Stadium Dr, San Antonio TX 78212-7200
210-999-7011

Tyler Junior College
PO Box 9020, Tyler TX 75711-9020
Joan Jones, Interim Dean
800-687-5680
Website: www.tjc.edu
E-mail: jjon@tjc.edu
See listing under "Community and Junior Colleges"

University of Dallas
1845 E Northgate Dr, Irving TX 75062-4736
Curt Eley, Dean
972-721-5000 Fax: 972-721-5017
Website: www.udallas.edu
E-mail: ugadmis@udallas.edu

University of Houston
122 E Cullen Bldg, Houston TX 77204-2023
Office of Admission
713-743-9595
Website: www.uh.edu
E-mail: admissions@uh.edu

University of Houston-Clear Lake
2700 Bay Area Blvd, Houston TX 77058-1025
281-283-2500

University of Houston-Downtown
1 Main St, Houston TX 77002-1014
713-221-8000

University of North Texas
PO Box 305309, Denton TX 76203-5309
940-565-2000

University of St. Thomas
3800 Montrose Blvd, Houston TX 77006-4626
Eduardo Prieto, Director of Admissions
713-522-7911

University of Texas at Arlington
Box 19111, Arlington TX 76019-0111
Hans Gatterdam, Director of Admission
817-272-6287 Fax: 817-272-3435
Website: www.uta.edu
E-mail: admissions@uta.edu

University of Texas at Austin
0 the Univ of Texas, Austin TX 78712
512-471-3434

University of Texas at Dallas
PO Box 830688, Richardson TX 75083-0688
972-690-2111

University of Texas at El Paso
500 W University Ave, El Paso TX 79968-8900
915-747-5000

University of Texas at San Antonio
6900 N Loop 1604 W, San Antonio TX 78249-1130
210-458-4011

University of Texas at Tyler
3900 University Blvd, Tyler TX 75701-6622
Jim Hutto, Dean Enrollment Management
800-888-9537

University of Texas-Pan American
1201 W University Dr, Edinburg TX 78539-2909
956-381-2011

University of the Incarnate Word
4301 Broadway St, San Antonio TX 78209-6318
210-829-6000

Wade College
Dallas Market Center
PO Box 421149, Dallas TX 75342
Harry Davros, President
800-624-4850 or 214-637-3530 Fax: 214-637-0827
Website: www.wadecollege.edu
E-mail: admissions@wadecollege.edu
See listing under "Community and Junior Colleges"

Weatherford College
225 College Park Dr, Weatherford TX 76086
Dr. Joe Birmingham, President
800-287-5471 Fax: 817-598-6205
Website: www.wc.edu
E-mail: willingham@wc.edu

West Texas A & M University
WTAMU Box 907, Canyon TX 79016-0001
806-651-2000

UTAH

Brigham Young University
Provo UT 84602-0001
801-378-5000

ITT TECHNICAL INSTITUTE

920 Levoy Dr, Murray UT 84123-2500
Gary Wood, Director of Recruitment
801-263-3313 Fax: 801-263-3497
Website: www.itt-tech.edu
E-mail: gwood@itt-tech.edu

Southern Utah University
351 W Center St, Cedar City UT 84720-2470
Carl Templin, Dean
435-586-5401

Stevens Henager College
755 Main St, Logan UT 84321
Josh Swayne, Executive Director
435-713-4777
Website: www.stevenshenager.edu

Stevens Henager College
PO Box 9428, Ogden UT 84409-0428
Cindy Williams, Director of Admissions
801-394-7791 Fax: 801-621-0866
Website: www.stevenshenager.edu
E-mail: shcogden@yahoo.com

University of Utah
1460 E 201 S, Salt Lake City UT 84112
801-581-7200

Utah State University
Logan UT 84322-0001
435-797-1000

Weber State University
1001 University Cir, Ogden UT 84408
801-626-6000

Westminster College
1840 S 1300 E, Salt Lake City UT 84105-3617
801-832-2200

VERMONT

Castleton State College
Castleton VT 05735
William Allen Jr., Dean of Enrollment
800-639-8521

College of St. Joseph
71 Clement Rd, Rutland VT 05701-3899
802-773-5900

Goddard College
121 Pitkin Rd, Plainfield VT 05667
802-454-8311

Green Mountain College
1 College Cir, Poultney VT 05764-1199
Sandra Bartholomew, Ph.D., Dean of Enrollment Management
802-287-8000 Fax: 802-287-8099
Website: www.greenmtn.edu
E-mail: bartholomews@greenmtn.edu

NEW ENGLAND CULINARY INSTITUTE

56 College St, Montpelier VT 05602
Sheri Gilmore, Director of Admissions
877-223-6324 Fax: 802-225-3280
Website: www.neci.edu
E-mail: Admissions@neci.edu

Established in 1980. Private. Coed. Accreditation: ACCSCT. Located in Vermont. Tuition: $22,455. Room and board: $6,060. Low student:teacher ratio. Associate's and Bachelor's degrees in Hospitality and Restaurant Management. The Associate's degree is a 15-month program that utilizes a hands-on method of teaching to prepare students for management careers in the rapidly growing food service industry. The Bachelor's degree is an 15-month program (beyond the Associate's or other qualifying educational credits) designed to develop management and entreprenuerial skills of those seeking top-of-the house and hospitality management careers. Both programs include a 6-month, paid internship following the residency period.

NORWICH UNIVERSITY

158 Harmon Dr, Northfield VT 05663
Dr. Frank Vanecek, Division Head
800-468-6679 Fax: 802-485-2087
Website: www.norwich.edu
E-mail: vanecek@norwich.edu
See listing under "Universities"

Saint Michael's College
One Winooski Park, Colchester VT 05439-0001
Jacqueline Murphy, Director
802-654-3000

Southern Vermont College
982 Mansion Dr, Bennington VT 05201-6002
Joel Wincowski, Director of Admissions
800-378-2782 Fax: 802-447-4695
Website: www.svc.edu
E-mail: admis@svc.edu

University of Vermont
194 S Prospect St, Burlington VT 05401-3518
802-656-3131

VIRGINIA

Averett University
420 W Main St, Danville VA 24541-3692
434-791-5600

Bluefield College
3000 College Dr, Bluefield VA 24605-1799
276-326-3682

Bridgewater College
402 E College St, Bridgewater VA 22812-1599
540-828-8000

Bryant & Stratton College
8141 Hull St Rd, Richmond VA 23235-6411
David K. Mayle, Director of Admissions
804-745-2444 Fax: 804-745-6884
Website: www.bryantstratton.edu
E-mail: dkmayle@bryantstratton.edu

Christopher Newport University
1 University Pl, Newport News VA 23606
757-594-7000

College of William and Mary
PO Box 8795, Williamsburg VA 23187-8795
757-221-4000

Eastern Mennonite University
1200 Park Rd, Harrisonburg VA 22802-2404
540-432-4000

Emory & Henry College
PO Box 947, Emory VA 24327-0947
276-944-4121

Ferrum College
PO Box 1000, Ferrum VA 24088-9001
Gilda Q. Woods, Director of Admissions
800-868-9797

George Mason University
4400 University Dr, Fairfax VA 22030-4444
Eddie Tallent, Director of Admissions
703-993-2400

Gibbs College - Northern Virginia
1980 Gallows Rd, Vienna VA 22182-3913
Everson Travers, Director of Admissions
703-556-8888 Fax: 703-556-0953
Website: www.gibbsva.edu
E-mail: etravers@gibbsva.edu

James Madison University
800 S Main St, Harrisonburg VA 22807-0002
540-568-6211

Liberty University
PO Box 20000, Lynchburg VA 24506-8001
804-582-2000

Longwood University
201 High St, Farmville VA 23909-1801
804-395-2000

Lynchburg College
1501 Lakeside Dr, Lynchburg VA 24501-3199
804-544-8100

Mary Baldwin College
Staunton VA 24401
Lisa A. Branson, Executive Director of Admissions and Financial Aid
800-468-2262 Fax: 540-887-7292
Website: www.mbc.edu
E-mail: admit@mbc.edu

Marymount University
2807 N Glebe Rd, Arlington VA 22207-4299
Michael Canfield, Director of Admissions
800-548-7638 Fax: 703-522-0348
Website: www.marymount.edu
E-mail: admissions@marymount.edu

National College
100 Logan St, Bluefield VA 24605
Tonya Elmore, Director of Admissions
276-326-3621 Fax: 276-322-5731
Website: www.national-college.edu
E-mail: info@national-college.edu

National College
1819 Emmet St N, Charlottesville VA 22901-2812
434-295-0136 Fax: 434-979-8061
Website: www.national-college.edu
E-mail: info@national-college.edu

National College
336 Old Riverside Dr, Danville VA 24541
Jeff Moore, Director of Admissions
434-793-6822 Fax: 434-793-3634
Website: www.national-college.edu
E-mail: info@national-college.edu

National College
1515 Country Club Rd, Harrisonburg VA 22802
Kathy Sours, Director of Admissions
540-432-0943 Fax: 540-432-1133
Website: www.national-college.edu
E-mail: info@national-college.edu

National College
104 Candlewood Ct, Lynchburg VA 24502-2653
Nancy Fortune, Director of Admissions
434-239-3500 Fax: 434-239-3948
Website: www.national-college.edu
E-mail: info@national-college.edu

National College
10 Church St, Martinsville VA 24114
Barbara Rakes, Director of Admissions
276-632-5621 Fax: 276-632-7915
Website: www.national-college.edu
E-mail: info@national-college.edu

National College
1813 E Main St, Salem VA 24153-4598
Ron Smith, Director of Admissions
540-986-1800 Fax: 540-444-4195
Website: www.national-college.edu
E-mail: info@national-college.edu

Norfolk State University
700 Park Ave, Norfolk VA 23504
Michelle Marable, Director of Admissions
757-823-8600

Old Dominion University
1 Old Dominion University, Norfolk VA 23529-1000
757-683-3000

Radford University
PO Box 6903, Radford VA 24142
David W. Kraus, Director of Admissions
800-890-4265 Fax: 540-831-5038
Website: www.radford.edu
E-mail: ruadmiss@radford.edu

Randolph College
2500 Rivermont Ave, Lynchburg VA 24503
Patricia LeDonne, Director of Admissions
434-947-8100 Fax: 434-947-8996
Website: www.randolphcollege.edu
E-mail: admissions@randolphcollege.edu

Randolph-Macon College
PO Box 5005, Ashland VA 23005-5505
804-752-7200

Roanoke College
221 College Ln, Salem VA 24153-3794
James A. Pennix, Director of Admissions
540-375-2500 Fax: 540-375-2267
Website: www.roanoke.edu
E-mail: pennix@roanoke.edu

Shenandoah University
1460 University Dr, Winchester VA 22601-5195
Michael D. Carpenter, Director of Admissions
800-432-2266

Southside Virginia Community College
109 Campus Dr, Alberta VA 23821-2930
Ronald E. Mattox, Dean of Admissions
434-949-1014 Fax: 434-949-7863
Website: www.sv.vccs.edu
E-mail: ronald.mattox@sv.vccs.edu

Southside Virginia Community College
200 Daniel Rd, Keysville VA 23947
Ronald E. Mattox, Dean of Admissions
434-736-2018 Fax: 434-736-2082
Website: www.sv.vccs.edu
E-mail: ronald.mattox@sv.vccs.edu

Stratford University
7777 Leesburg Pike #100 South
Falls Church VA 22043
Keith Evans, Contact
703-821-8570 Fax: 703-734-5335
Website: www.stratford.edu
E-mail: admissions@stratford.edu

UNIVERSITY OF MANAGEMENT AND TECHNOLOGY
1901 Fort Myer Dr Ste 700, Arlington VA 22209
703-516-0035 Fax: 703-516-0985
Website: www.umtweb.edu
E-mail: info@umtweb.edu

University of Mary Washington
1301 College Ave, Fredericksburg VA 22401-5300
Dr. Martin A. Wilder, Jr., Director of Admissions
540-654-2000 Fax: 540-654-1857
Website: www.umw.edu
E-mail: admit@umw.edu

University of Richmond
Richmond VA 23173
804-289-8000

University of Virginia
PO Box 400160, Charlottesville VA 22904
804-924-0311

University of Virginia College at Wise
1 College Ave, Wise VA 24293
276-328-0100

Virginia Commonwealth University
901 W Franklin St, Richmond VA 23284
804-828-0100

Virginia Intermont College
1013 Moore St, Bristol VA 24201-4225
540-669-6101

Virginia Military Institute
Lexington VA 24450
540-464-7000

Virginia Polytechnic Institute & State University
Blacksburg VA 24061
540-231-6000

Virginia Wesleyan College
1584 Wesleyan Dr, Norfolk VA 23502-5599
757-455-3200

Washington & Lee University
Lexington VA 24450
540-463-8400

WASHINGTON

Antioch University
2326 6th Ave, Seattle WA 98121
Pam Smith Mentz, Director of Enrollment Services
888-268-4477

Central Washington University
400 E University Way, Ellensburg WA 98926
William Swain, Director of Admissions
509-963-3001

City University
11900 NE 1st St, Bellevue WA 98005-3030
800-426-5596

CROWN COLLEGE
8739 S Hosmer St, Tacoma WA 98444-1836
John Wabel, CEO
253-531-3123 Fax: 253-531-3521
Website: www.crowncollege.edu
E-mail: jwabel@crowncollege.edu

Eastern Washington University
Cheney WA 99004
509-359-6200

Everett Community College
2000 Tower St, Everett WA 98201
Christine Kerlin, Associate Dean
425-388-9100 Fax: 425-388-9173
Website: www.everettcc.edu
E-mail: ckerlin@everettcc.edu

Gonzaga University
502 E Boone Ave, Spokane WA 99258-0102
Julie McCulloh, Dean of Admission
800-322-2584

Heritage University
3240 Fort Rd, Toppenish WA 98948-9599
509-865-8500

Pacific Lutheran University
12180 Park Ave S, Tacoma WA 98447-0014
David E. Gunovich, Director of Admissions
253-535-7151

St. Martin's University
5300 Pacific Ave SE, Lacey WA 98503-1297
360-491-4700

Seattle Pacific University
3307 3rd Ave W, Seattle WA 98119-1997
206-281-2000

Seattle University
901 12th Ave, Seattle WA 98122
206-296-6000

SHORELINE COMMUNITY COLLEGE
16101 Greenwood Ave N, Shoreline WA 98133-5696
Chris Melton, Acting Registrar
206-546-4581 Fax: 206-546-5835
Website: www.shoreline.edu

University of Puget Sound
1500 N Warner St, Tacoma WA 98416-0005
253-879-3100

University of Washington
Seattle WA 98195-0001
206-543-2100

Walla Walla College
204 S College Ave, College Place WA 99324-1198
509-527-2615

Walla Walla Community College
500 Tausick Way, Walla Walla WA 99362-9270
Dan Biagi, Director
509-527-4283 or 877-471-9292 Fax: 509-527-4480
Website: www.wwcc.edu
E-mail: dan.biagi@wwcc.edu
See listing under "Community and Junior Colleges"

Washington State University
1 SE Stadium Way, Pullman WA 99164-0001
509-335-3564

Western Washington University
516 High St, Bellingham WA 98225-5996
360-650-3000

Whitworth College
300 W Hawthorne Rd, Spokane WA 99251-0001
Fred Pfursich, Dean of Admissions & Financial Aid
800-533-4668

WEST VIRGINIA

Alderson-Broaddus College
Philippi WV 26416
Eric A. Ruf, Director of Admissions
800-263-1549

Blue Ridge Community and Technical College
400 W Stephen St, Martinsburg WV 25401
Leslie See, Director of Enrollment
304-260-4380 Fax: 304-260-1752
Website: www.blueridgectc.edu
E-mail: lsee@blueridgectc.edu

Concord University
Athens WV 24712
Michael Curry, Vice President of Financial Aid & Admissions
888-384-5249

Davis & Elkins College
100 Campus Dr, Elkins WV 26241-3996
Renee Heckel, Director of Enrollment Management
800-624-3157 Fax: 304-637-1800
Website: www.davisandelkins.edu
E-mail: admiss@davisandelkins.edu

Fairmont State University
1201 Locust Ave, Fairmont WV 26554-2470
Steve Leadman, Director of Admissions
304-367-4261 or 800-641-5678 Fax: 304-367-4789
Website: www.fairmontstate.edu
E-mail: admit@fairmontstate.edu

Glenville State College
200 High St, Glenville WV 26351-1200
304-462-4128

Marshall University
400 Hal Greer Blvd, Huntington WV 25755-0003
304-696-3170

Mountain State University
Box 9003, Beckley WV 25802-9003
Tony England, Director of Admissions
866-FOR-MSU1 or 304-929-INFO Fax: 304-253-5072
Website: www.mountainstate.edu
E-mail: gomsu@mountainstate.edu
See listing under "Universities"

Shepherd University
PO Box 3210
Shepherdstown WV 25443
304-876-5000

University of Charleston
2300 MacCorkle Ave SE, Charleston WV 25304-1099
304-357-4800

West Virginia Junior College
176 Thompson Dr, Bridgeport WV 26330
Kathryn Stanley, Director of Admissions
304-842-4007 Fax: 304-842-8191
Website: www.wvjcinfo.net
E-mail: kstanley@wvjcinfo.net

West Virginia State University
PO Box 1000, Institute WV 25112-1000
304-766-3000

West Virginia University
PO Box 6001, Morgantown WV 26506-6001
304-293-0111

West Virginia Wesleyan College
59 College Ave, Buckhannon WV 26201-2699
Robert N. Skinner II, Director of Admission
800-722-9933

Wheeling Jesuit University
316 Washington Ave, Wheeling WV 26003-6295
304-243-2000

WISCONSIN

Alverno College
PO Box 343922, Milwaukee WI 53234-3922
Dianna Gaebler, Director of Admissions
414-382-6100 Fax: 414-382-6354
Website: www.alverno.edu
E-mail: admissions@alverno.edu

Beloit College
700 College St, Beloit WI 53511-5596
Jeffrey L. Adams, Professor and Chair
608-363-2327

Blackhawk Technical College
PO Box 5009, Janesville WI 53547-5009
Gregg Bosak, Administration, Community Information
608-757-7769 Fax: 608-757-7740
Website: www.blackhawk.edu
E-mail: gbosak@blackhawk.edu

Cardinal Stritch University
6801 N Yates Rd, Milwaukee WI 53217-3985
414-410-4000

Carroll College
100 N East Ave, Waukesha WI 53186-5593
James Wiseman, Dean of Admissions
800-CARROLL

Carthage College
2001 Alford Park Dr, Kenosha WI 53140-1994
262-551-6000

Concordia University
12800 N Lake Shore Dr, Mequon WI 53097-2402
262-243-5700

Edgewood College
1000 Edgewood College Dr, Madison WI 53711
608-663-4861

Herzing College
5218 E Terrace Dr, Madison WI 53718-8340
Donald Madelung, President
800-582-1227 Fax: 608-249-8593
Website: www.herzing.edu
E-mail: info@msn.herzing.edu
See listing under "Universities"

Lakeland College
PO Box 359, Sheboygan WI 53082-0359
Nathan Dehne, Director of Admission
920-565-1100 Fax: 920-565-1215
Website: www.lakeland.edu
E-mail: admissions@lakeland.edu

Marquette University
PO Box 1881, Milwaukee WI 53201-1881
Robert Blust, Director of Admissions
414-288-7302 Fax: 414-288-3764
Website: www.mu.edu
E-mail: admissions@marquette.edu

Mount Mary College
2900 N Menomonee River Pkwy
Milwaukee WI 53222-4597
414-256-1219

Ripon College
PO Box 248, Ripon WI 54971-0248
920-748-8115

St. Norbert College
100 Grant St, De Pere WI 54115
Brian Studebaker, Director of Admission
800-236-4878 Fax: 920-403-4072
Website: www.snc.edu
E-mail: admit@snc.edu

Silver Lake College
2406 S Alverno Rd, Manitowoc WI 54220-9319
920-684-6691

University of Wisconsin
PO Box 4004, Eau Claire WI 54702
715-836-2637

University of Wisconsin
PO Box 2000, Kenosha WI 53141-2000
262-595-2345

University of Wisconsin
716 Langdon St, Madison WI 53706-1481
608-262-1234

University of Wisconsin
PO Box 413, Milwaukee WI 53201-0413
414-229-1122

University of Wisconsin
1 University Plz, Platteville WI 53818-3001
Angela Udelhofen, Recruitment Manager
608-342-1200

University of Wisconsin
410 S 3rd St, River Falls WI 54022
715-425-3911

University of Wisconsin
PO Box 2000, Superior WI 54880
715-394-8101

University of Wisconsin Green Bay
2420 Nicolet Dr, Green Bay WI 54311-7003
Pamela Harvey-Jacobs, Interim Director of Admissions
920-465-2111

University of Wisconsin in La Crosse
115 Graff Main Hall, La Crosse WI 54601
Tim Lewis, Director of Admissions
608-785-8939

University of Wisconsin - Oshkosh
800 Algoma Blvd, Oshkosh WI 54901-8602
920-424-0202

University of Wisconsin-Stout
124 Bowman Hall, Menomonie WI 54751-2662
715-232-1123

University of Wisconsin - Whitewater
800 W Main St, Whitewater WI 53190-1791
262-472-1234

Viterbo University
815 9th St S, La Crosse WI 54601-8802
608-796-3000

Wisconsin Indianhead Technical College
505 Pine Ridge Dr, Shell Lake WI 54871
Laura Wassenaar, Dean
800-243-9482 Fax: 715-468-2819
Website: www.witc.edu
E-mail: laura.wassenaar@witc.edu

WYOMING

Laramie County Community College
1400 E College Dr, Cheyenne WY 82007-3204
Jenny Hargett, Director of Admissions
307-778-5222 Fax: 307-778-1350
Website: www.lccc.wy.edu
E-mail: learnmore@lccc.wy.edu

University of Wyoming
Admissions Office
Dept 3435, Laramie WY 82071-3435
Brooke Culver, Contact
800-342-5996 Fax: 307-766-4042
Website: www.uwyo.edu
E-mail: why-wyo@uwyo.edu

GUAM

University of Guam
UOG Station, Mangilao GU 96923
Deborah Leon Guerrero, Registrar
671-735-2201 or 671-735-2208 Fax: 671-735-2203
Website: www.uog.edu
E-mail: admitme@uog9.uog.edu

PUERTO RICO

Pontifical Catholic University of Puerto Rico
2250 Ave Las Americas, Ponce PR 00717-0777
787-841-2000

Universidad Adventista de las Antillas
PO Box 118, Mayaguez PR 00681
Evelyn Del Valle Rivera, Director of Admissions
787-834-9595

University of Puerto Rico
R Ave Antonio R Barcelo, Cayey PR 00736-5534
787-738-2161

University of Puerto Rico
CUH Station Rd 908 Bo Tejas, Humacao PR 00791
787-850-0000

University of Puerto Rico
PO Box 9020, Mayaguez PR 00681
787-832-4040

University of Puerto Rico
PO Box 23303, Rio Piedras PR 00931-3303
787-764-0000

University of Puerto Rico at Arecibo
PO Box 4010, Arecibo PR 00614
787-815-0000

University of Puerto Rico at Ponce
PO Box 7186, Ponce PR 00732-7186
787-844-8181

University of Puerto Rico
Bayamón University College
Carretera 174, Km 2.8, Bayamón PR 00959
787-786-2885

:CAREER SCHOOLS

ALABAMA

Alabama State College of Barber Styling
9480 Parkway E, Birmingham AL 35215
205-836-2404

Baptist Medical Center
301 Brown Springs Rd, Montgomery AL 36117
334-273-4400

Bishop State Community College-Carver
414 Stanton Rd, Mobile AL 36617-2313
Mrs. M.O. Taylor, Contact
251-473-8692

Bishop State Community College-Southwest Campus
925 Dauphin Island Pkwy, Mobile AL 36605-3299
334-479-0003

Blue Cliff School of Therapeutic Massage
2970 Cottage Hill Rd Ste 175, Mobile AL 36606-4749
251-665-9900

CAPPS College
3590 Pleasant Valley Rd, Mobile AL 36609
334-473-1393

Carraway Methodist Medical Center
1600 Carraway Blvd, Birmingham AL 35234-2804
205-226-6000

DCH Regional Medical Center
809 University Blvd E, Tuscaloosa AL 35401-2071
205-759-7177

Flowers Hospital
School of Surgical Technology
PO Box 6907, Dothan AL 36302
334-793-5000

Gadsden Business College
3225 Rainbow Dr Ste 246
Rainbow City AL 35906-5821
256-442-2805

Gadsden Business College of Anniston
1809 Hillyer Robinson Pkwy Ste B
Anniston AL 36207
Randy Kerr, President
256-831-3838

Gaither Beauty College
414 E Willow St, Scottsboro AL 35768
256-259-1001

Huntsville Hospital
101 Sivley Rd SW, Huntsville AL 35801-4470
256-533-8123

Jefferson Davis Community College
PO Box 1119, Atmore AL 36504-1119
334-368-8118

Montgomery Job Corps Center
1145 Air Base Blvd, Montgomery AL 36108
334-262-8883

Remington College
828 Downtowner Loop W, Mobile AL 36609-5519
334-343-8200

Southeast Alabama Medical Center
PO Box 6987, Dothan AL 36302
334-793-8100

Southeastern School of Cosmetology
26B Phillips Dr, Midfield AL 35228
205-925-0011

Trenholm State Technical College
Trenholm Campus
1225 Air Base Blvd, Montgomery AL 36108-3199
Dr. Anthony Molina, President
334-420-4200 Fax: 334-420-4206
Website: www.trenholmtech.cc.al.us
E-mail: molinaa@trenholmtech.cc.al.us

Virginia College
2800 Bob Wallace Ave SW #A
Huntsville AL 35805-4164
256-533-7387

ALASKA

Alaska Vocational Technical School
PO Box 889, Seward AK 99664
907-224-4159

Career Academy
1415 E Tudor Rd, Anchorage AK 99507-1033
907-563-7575

University of Alaska Anchorage
PO Box 141629, Anchorage AK 99514-1629
Cecile Mitchell, Director of Enrollment Services
907-786-1480 Fax: 907-786-4888
Website: www.uaa.alaska.edu/
E-mail: enroll@uaa.alaska.edu

ARIZONA

American Institute of Technology
440 S 54th Ave, Phoenix AZ 85043-4729
602-233-2222

Apollo College
630 W Southern Ave, Mesa AZ 85210-5005
480-831-6585 Fax: 480-827-0022

Apollo College
8503 N 27th Ave, Phoenix AZ 85051-4063
602-864-1571 Fax: 602-864-8207

Apollo College
2701 W Bethany Home Rd, Phoenix AZ 85017-1705
602-433-1333 Fax: 602-433-1414

Apollo College
3550 N Oracle Rd, Tucson AZ 85705
520-888-5885 Fax: 520-887-3005

Arizona Academy of Beauty
5631 E Speedway Blvd, Tucson AZ 85712
520-885-4120

Arizona Academy of Beauty - North
4066 N Oracle Rd, Tucson AZ 85705
520-888-0170

Arizona Automotive Institute
6829 N 46th Ave, Glendale AZ 85301-3597
623-934-7273

Arizona College of Allied Health
4425 W Olive Ave Ste 300, Glendale AZ 85302-3843
602-222-9300

Art Institute of Phoenix
2233 W Dunlap Ave, Phoenix AZ 85021-2859
602-331-7500

Artistic Beauty College
2978 N Alma School Rd Ste 3, Chandler AZ 85224
480-855-7901

Artistic Beauty College
1790 E Route 66, Flagstaff AZ 86004
928-774-7146

Artistic Beauty College
10820 N 43rd Ave, Glendale AZ 85304
623-937-2749

Artistic Beauty College
2727 W Glendale Ave Ste 200
Phoenix AZ 85051-8412
623-939-8364

Artistic Beauty College
410 W Goodwin St, Prescott AZ 86303
928-778-5064

Artistic Beauty College
7730 E McDowell Rd, Scottsdale AZ 85257
480-949-7557

Artistic Beauty College
3030 E Speedway Blvd, Tucson AZ 85716
520-327-6544

Bryman School
2250 W Peoria Ave Ste A100, Phoenix AZ 85029
602-274-4300

Carsten Institute of Hair and Beauty
3345 S Rural Rd, Tempe AZ 85282
480-491-0449

Chaparral College
4585 E Speedway Blvd #204, Tucson AZ 85712-5311
Scott Rhude, President
520-327-6866

Charles of Italy Beauty College
1987 McCulloch Blvd #205
Lake Havasu City AZ 86403
928-453-6666

CollegeAmerica
1800 S Milton Rd, Flagstaff AZ 86001
Joshua Swayne, Executive Director
928-526-0763

CollegeAmerica
6533 N Black Canyon Hwy, Phoenix AZ 85015
Daryl Goldberg, Executive Director
602-246-3041

Collins College: A School of Design and Technology
(Formerly Al Collins Graphic Design School)
1140 S Priest Dr, Tempe AZ 85281-5240
Toby Craver, Director of National Admissions
800-876-7070 Fax: 480-829-0183
Website: www.collinscollege.edu

Conservatory of Recording Arts & Sciences
1205 N Fiesta Blvd, Gilbert AZ 85233
Tonya Visconti, Director of Admissions
480-858-9400 Fax: 480-829-1332
Website: www.audiorecordingschool.com
E-mail: info@cras.org

The Conservatory of Recording Arts & Sciences
2300 E Broadway Rd, Tempe AZ 85282-1707
Tonya Visconti, Director of Admissions
800-562-6383 or 480-858-9400 Fax: 480-829-1332
Website: cras.org
E-mail: info@cras.org
See listing under "Music"

Desert Institute of the Healing Arts
639 N 6th Ave, Tucson AZ 85705-8330
David Shahan, Director of Admissions
520-733-8098

DeVoe College of Beauty
750 Bartow Dr, Sierra Vista AZ 85635
520-458-8660

Earl's Academy of Beauty
2111 S Alma School Rd #21, Mesa AZ 85210
480-897-1688

Everest College
10400 N 25th Ave Suite 190, Phoenix AZ 85021-1610
Melissa Agee, Director of Admissions
602-942-4141

GOLF ACADEMY OF ARIZONA
670 N Arizona Ave Ste 13, Chandler AZ 85225-6742
Paul Zagnoni, President
800-342-7342 Fax: 480-905-8705
Website: www.sdgagolf.com
E-mail: sdga@sdgagolf.com

HDS TRUCK DRIVING INSTITUTE
PO Box 17600, Tucson AZ 85731
Robert Knapp, School Director
520-721-5825 Fax: 520-798-3247
Website: www.hdsdrivers.com
E-mail: bob_knapp@hdsdrivers.com

INTERNATIONAL ACADEMY OF BEAUTY
4812 S Mill Ave, Tempe AZ 85282-6730
480-964-8675 Fax: 480-964-5528
Website: www.intlacademy.biz
E-mail: intltempe@intlacademy.biz

INTERNATIONAL ACADEMY OF HAIR DESIGN
3350 N Arizona Ave Ste 4, Chandler AZ 85225
480-820-9422 Fax: 480-820-9348
Website: www.intlacademy.biz
E-mail: intlchandler@intlacademy.biz

ITT Technical Institute
5005 S Wendler Dr, Tempe AZ 85282
602-437-7500

ITT Technical Institute
1455 W River Rd, Tucson AZ 85704-5829
520-408-7488

LAMSON COLLEGE
1126 N Scottsdale Rd Ste 17, Tempe AZ 85281
Miguel Sanchez, Director of Admissions
480-898-7000 Fax: 480-967-6645
Website: www.lamsoncollege.com
E-mail: msanchez@lamsoncollege.com

Long Technical College
4646 E Van Buren St Ste 350
Phoenix AZ 85008-6952
Michael Meckstroth, Director of Admissions
602-252-2171

Long Technical College
Phoenix Campus
13450 N Black Canyon Hwy Ste 104
Phoenix AZ 85029-6323
602-548-1955

Maricopa Beauty College
515 W Western Ave, Avondale AZ 85323
623-932-4414

MOTORCYCLE MECHANICS INSTITUTE
2844 W Deer Valley Rd, Phoenix AZ 85027-2399
Rodney Thompson, Director of Admissions
800-528-7995 Fax: 623-581-2871
Website: www.uticorp.com
E-mail: mmi@crl.com

Established 1971. Comprehensive technical training in all aspects of motorcycle and personal watercraft repair. Endorsed and equipped by Harley-Davidson, Honda, Yamaha, Suzuki, Kawasaki, and BMW. Classes are scheduled 5-hours per day in the morning, afternoon, or evening. Accredited member school: ACCSCT. A graduate placement department is available to assist students in finding full-time employment in the motorcycle industry. Manufacturers' assist with placement through promotional campaigns to their dealership network. Housing coordinator works with local apartment complexes to find housing while in school. Job advisor will assist with local employment while in school. Financial aid available to those who qualify. VA and Agency assistance where applicable.

PIMA MEDICAL INSTITUTE
957 S Dobson Rd, Mesa AZ 85202-2903
Christopher Luebke, Director
480-644-0267 Fax: 480-649-5249
Website: www.pmi.edu
E-mail: asc@pmi.edu

Pima Medical Institute
3350 E Grant Rd, Tucson AZ 85716-2800
520-326-1600

Quantum Helicopters
2401 S Heliport Way, Chandler AZ 85286
480-814-8118

RainStar University
8370 E Via de Ventura, Scottsdale AZ 85258
Ranay Yarian, Director of Community & Student Relations
480-423-0375 ext 1

Refrigeration School
4210 E Washington St, Phoenix AZ 85034-1894
Crystal Otts, Admissions Manager
602-275-7133 Fax: 602-267-4805
Website: www.refrigerationschool.com
E-mail: crystal@rsiaz.edu

Roberto-Venn Guitar Making School
4011 S 16th St, Phoenix AZ 85040-1314
Ann Fountain, Admissions Director
602-243-1179

Safford College of Beauty Culture
1550 W Thatcher Blvd, Safford AZ 85546
928-428-0331

Scott Cole Academy
7201 E Camelback Rd Ste 100, Scottsdale AZ 85251
480-994-4222

Scottsdale Culinary Institute
8100 E Camelback Rd, Scottsdale AZ 85251-2729
Admissions Department
480-990-3773

SOUTHWEST INSTITUTE OF HEALING ARTS
1100 E Apache Blvd, Tempe AZ 85281
Admissions
480-994-9244 Fax: 480-994-3228
Website: www.swiha.org
E-mail: doyourdream@swiha.org

Tucson College
7310 E 22nd St, Tucson AZ 85710
Rebecca Montgomery, Director of Admissions
520-296-3261

Universal Technical Institute
10695 W Pierce St, Avondale AZ 85323-7946
John Palumbo, Director of Admissions
623-245-4600 Fax: 623-245-4603
Website: www.uticorp.com

University of Advancing Technology
2625 W Baseline Rd, Tempe AZ 85283
Lary Dougherty, Director of Admissions
800-658-5744

ARKANSAS

American Professional Institute
103 S Avalon St, West Memphis AR 72301

Arkadelphia Beauty College
2708 Pine St, Arkadelphia AR 71923
870-246-6726

Arkansas Aviation Technologies Center
2350 W Old Farmington Rd, Fayetteville AR 72701
479-444-3058

Arkansas Beauty School
5108 Baseline Rd, Little Rock AR 72209
501-562-5673

Arkansas Beauty School - Conway
1061 Markham St, Conway AR 72032-4309
501-329-8303

Arkansas Career Training Institute
105 Reserve St, Hot Springs National Park AR 71901
501-624-4411

Arkansas College of Barbering and Hair Design
200 E Washington Ave, North Little Rock AR 72114
501-376-9696

Arkansas State University
Searcy Campus
PO Box 909, Searcy AR 72145-0909
501-207-4000

Arkansas Valley Technical Institute
PO Box 506, Ozark AR 72949-0506
479-667-2117

Arthur's Beauty College
2600 John Harden Dr, Jacksonville AR 72076
501-982-8987

Baptist Schools of Allied Health
11900 Colonel Glenn Rd, Little Rock AR 72210-2820
501-202-7415

Bee-Jay's Hairstyling Academy
130 W Main St, Batesville AR 72501
870-793-3898

Bee-Jay's Hairstyling Academy
1907 Hinson Loop Rd, Little Rock AR 72212
501-224-2442

Black River Technical College
PO Box 468, Pocahontas AR 72455-0468
870-892-4565

Blytheville Academy of Cosmetology
100 E Main St, Blytheville AR 72315
870-763-6326

Cass Civilian Conservation Job Corps Center
21424 N Highway 23, Ozark AR 72949
479-667-3686

Central Arkansas Radiation Therapy Institute
PO Box 55050, Little Rock AR 72215-5050
501-664-8573

Cotton Boll Technical Institute
PO Box 36, Burdette AR 72321-0036
Brenda Morris, Supervisor of Instruction
870-763-1486

Crowley's Ridge Technical Institute
1620 New Castle Rd, Forrest City AR 72335
870-633-5411

Delta Technical Institute
PO Box 280, Marked Tree AR 72365-0280
Keith Steele, President
870-358-2117

Eastern College of Health Vocations
6423 Forbing Rd, Little Rock AR 72209-3535
501-568-0211

Eaton Beauty Stylist College
814 W 7th St, Little Rock AR 72201
501-375-0211

Fayetteville Beauty College
2167 W 6th St, Fayetteville AR 72701
479-442-5181

Forest Echoes Technical Institute
1326 Highway 82W, Crossett AR 71635
870-364-6414

Hot Springs Beauty College
100 Cones Rd, Hot Springs AR 71901
501-624-0203

ITT Technical Institute
4520 S University Ave, Little Rock AR 72204-7739
501-565-5550

Jefferson Regional Medical Center
1515 W 42nd Ave, Pine Bluff AR 71603-7055
870-541-7269

Lee's School of Cosmetology
2700 W Pershing Blvd
North Little Rock AR 72114-3800
501-758-2800

Leon's Hair Training Academy
200 Holcomb St, Springdale AR 72764-4403
479-756-6060

Marsha Kay Beauty College
408 Highway 201 N, Mountain Home AR 72653
870-425-7575

Mellie's Beauty College
311 S 16th St, Fort Smith AR 72901
479-782-5059

New Tyler Barber College
1221 Bishop Lindsey Ave, North Little Rock AR 72114
501-375-0377

Northwest Technical Institute
709 S Old Missouri Rd, Springdale AR 72764
Charles L. Kelley, President
479-751-8824 Fax: 479-751-7780
Website: www.nti.tec.ar.us
E-mail: info@nit.tec.ar.us

Ozarka College
PO Box 10, Melbourne AR 72556-0010
870-368-7371

Phillips Community College of the University of Arkansas
PO Box 785, Helena AR 72342-0785
Dr. Steven Murray, Chancellor
Lynn Boone, Vice Chancellor for Student Services / Registrar
870-338-6474 Fax: 870-338-7542
Website: www.pccua.edu
E-mail: lboone@pccua.edu

Professional Cosmetology Education Center
PO Box 429, Camden AR 71701
870-836-5481

Pulaski Technical College
3000 W Scenic Dr, North Little Rock AR 72118-3347
Clark Atkins, Director of Admissions
501-771-1000

Remington College
19 Remington Rd, Little Rock AR 72204
501-312-0007

Searcy Beauty College
1004 S Main St, Searcy AR 72143
501-268-6300

Southeast Arkansas College
1900 S Hazel St, Pine Bluff AR 71603-3900
870-543-5900

Southern Institute of Cosmetology
103 S Avalon St, West Memphis AR 72301
870-735-2800

University of Arkansas Community College at Morrilton
1537 University Blvd, Morrilton AR 72110
Susan Dewey, Admissions Counselor
800-264-1094

University of Arkansas - Monticello
College of Technology - Crossett
1326 Highway 52 W, Crossett AR 71635-4853
870-364-6414

Velvatex College of Beauty Culture
1520 Dr Martin Luther King, Little Rock AR 72202
501-372-9678

CALIFORNIA

Academy Education Services
3151 W 5th St Ste E101, Oxnard CA 93030
805-984-2511

Academy Pacific Travel College
1777 Vine St #30, Hollywood CA 90028-5218
323-462-3211

Adcon Technical Institute
12440 Firestone Blvd Ste 2001, Norwalk CA 90650
562-864-0506

Adcon Technical Institute
17821 17th St Ste 120, Tustin CA 92780
714-730-7080

Adrian's Beauty College of Turlock
2412 McHenry Ave, Modesto CA 95350
209-632-2233

Advanced College
13180 Paramount Blvd, South Gate CA 90280
562-408-6969

ADVANCED TRAINING ASSOCIATES
1810 Gillespie Way Ste 4, El Cajon CA 92020-0918
Joann Ferrera-Zakarin, President
800-720-2125 Fax: 619-596-4526
Website: www.advancedtraining.edu
E-mail: joann@advancedtraining.edu

Alameda Beauty College
2318 Central Ave, Alameda CA 94501
510-523-1050

Alhambra Beauty College
PO Box 7494, Alhambra CA 91802
626-282-6433

American Academy of Dramatic Arts - Los Angeles
1336 N LaBrea Ave, Hollywood CA 90028
Dan Justin, Director of Admissions
800-222-2867 Fax: 323-464-1250
Website: www.aada.org
E-mail: admissions-ca@aada.org

American Beauty College
16512 Bellflower Blvd, Bellflower CA 90706
562-866-0728

American Career College
1200 N Magnolia Ave, Anaheim CA 92801
714-952-9066

American Career College
4021 Rosewood Ave, Los Angeles CA 90004-6818
Rita Totten, Campus Director
323-383-2862

American College of California
760 Market St Ste 1009
San Francisco CA 94102-2305
Sherris Goodwin, Director
415-677-9717

American College of Health Professions
700 E Redlands Blvd #U227
Redlands CA 92373-6109
Admissions
909-307-6022

AMERICAN COLLEGE OF MEDICAL TECHNOLOGY
555 W Redondo Beach Blvd #100
Gardena CA 90248
Scott Jacobus, Contact
310-324-1000 Fax: 310-515-3944
Website: www.acmt.ac
E-mail: info@acmt.ac

Arrowhead Regional Medical Center
400 N Pepper Ave, Colton CA 92324
909-580-1000

The Art Institute of California
2900 31st St, Santa Monica CA 90405
310-752-4700

The Art Institute of California - San Diego
7650 Mission Valley Rd, San Diego CA 92108
Jesus Moreno, Director of Admissions
858-598-1200

Asian American International Beauty College
7871 Westminster Blvd, Westminster CA 92683-4043
Le Nguyen, General Manager
714-891-0508

Associated Technical College
1670 Wilshire Blvd, Los Angeles CA 90017-1690
Samuel Romano, Director of Admissions
213-353-1845 Fax: 213-413-4864
Website: www.associatedtechcollege.com
E-mail: decatc@earthlink.net

Associated Technical College
1445 6th Ave, San Diego CA 92101-3204
619-234-2181

Avalon Beauty College
504 N Milpas St, Santa Barbara CA 93103
805-966-1931

Avance Beauty College
750 Beyer Way Ste B, San Diego CA 92154
619-575-1511

Aviation & Electronic School of America
PO Box 1810, Colfax CA 95713
800-345-2742

Bay Vista College of Beauty
1520 E Plaza Blvd, National City CA 91950
619-474-6607

Brooks Institute of Photography
801 Alston Rd, Santa Barbara CA 93108-2399
Inge B. Kautzmann, Director of Admissions
805-966-3888 ext. 217 or 218

Brownson Technical School
1110 S Technology Cir Ste D
Anaheim CA 92805-6316
William D. Brown, Director
714-774-9443

BRYAN COLLEGE
2317 Gold Meadow Way, Gold River CA 95670-4443
Nora Wilkinson, Director of Admissions
866-649-2400 Fax: 916-641-8649
Website: www.ntcollege.com
E-mail: studentinfo@ntcollege.com

Bryan College
2333 Beverly Blvd, Los Angeles CA 90057-2209
213-484-8850

California Beauty College
1115 15th St, Modesto CA 95354
209-524-5184

California Career School
1100 Technology Cir, Anaheim CA 92805-6329
A. Charles Emanuele, Director
714-635-6585

California College of Communication
762 Sunset Glen Dr Ste 2, San Jose CA 95123
408-374-5066

CALIFORNIA COLLEGE SAN DIEGO
2820 Camino Del Rio S # 300, San Diego CA 92108
Randy Wolford, Director of Admissions
619-295-5785 Fax: 619-295-5762
Website: www.cc-sd.edu
E-mail: rwolford@cc-sd.edu

CALIFORNIA COSMETOLOGY COLLEGE
955 Monroe St, Santa Clara CA 95050-4808
408-247-2200 Fax: 408-247-9730
E-mail: admin@calcosmetcollege.com

California Culinary Academy
625 Polk St, San Francisco CA 94102
Barry Gordon, President
Nancy Seyfert, V.P. of Admissions
800-BAY-CHEF

CALIFORNIA DESIGN COLLEGE
3440 Wilshire Blvd 10th Floor
Los Angeles CA 90010-2102
Gregory J. Marick, President
213-251-3636 Fax: 213-385-3545
Website: www.aicdc.artinstitutes.edu

California Hair Design Academy
8011 University Ave #A-2, La Mesa CA 91941
619-461-8600

CALIFORNIA HEALING ARTS COLLEGE
12217 Santa Monica Blvd, Los Angeles CA 90025
310-826-7622 Fax: 310-826-4913
Website: www.chac.edu

California Institute of Locksmithing
(Friedman College)
14719 1/2 Oxnard St, Van Nuys CA 91411-3122
J. Corey Friedman, President
877-LOCK-411

California Learning Center
6812 Pacific Blvd, Huntington Park CA 90255-4197
323-581-0600

California Maritime Academy
200 Maritime Academy Dr, Vallejo CA 94590
707-654-1000

California School of Culinary Arts
521 E Green St, Pasadena CA 91101
Sandra Stevens, Director of Admissions
626-403-8490

CAREER ACADEMY OF BEAUTY
663 N Euclid St, Anaheim CA 92801
Dayna Pattison, Director
714-776-8400
Website: beautycareers.com
E-mail: info@beautycareers.com

Career Academy of Beauty
12471 Valley View St, Garden Grove CA 92845
714-897-3010

CAREER COLLEGE OF AMERICA
5612 Imperial Hwy, South Gate CA 90280
Avi Paladino, Director of Operations
562-861-8702 Fax: 562-869-7013
Website: www.careercolleges.edu
E-mail: avin@careercolleges.edu

CEI
20700 Avalon Blvd Ste 210, Carson CA 90746-3734
310-532-6328

CEI
4900 Rivergrade Rd Ste E210
Irwindale CA 91706-1438
626-338-8886

CEI
25381 Commercentre Dr #200
Lake Forest CA 92630-8858
949-472-4192

CEI
3699 Wilshire Blvd Fl 4, Los Angeles CA 90010-2719
213-351-2000

CEI
980 Corporate Center Dr, Pomona CA 91768-2643
909-865-9008

CEI
1635 Spruce St, Riverside CA 92507-2494
951-276-1704

CEI
1050 Los Vallecitos Blvd
San Marcos CA 92069-1469
760-471-9300

Center of Employment Training
701 Vine St, San Jose CA 95110
Luis Aguilar, Contact
408-287-7924

Central California School of Continuing Education
271 Ott St Ste 23, Corona CA 92882-7104
951-549-0693

Central California School of Continuing Education
3195 McMillan Ave Ste F
San Luis Obispo CA 93401-6739
805-543-9123

Chase College
3580 Wilshire Blvd 4th Flr, Los Angeles CA 90010
213-365-1999

Children's Hospital of Los Angeles
4650 W Sunset Blvd, Los Angeles CA 90027-6062
323-669-2301

City College of San Francisco
50 Phelan Ave, San Francisco CA 94112-1821
415-239-3000

City of Hope Medical Center
1500 Duarte Rd, Duarte CA 91010-3000
626-359-8111

Clarita Career College
27125 Sierra Hwy Ste 329
Canyon Country CA 91351-5488
Julie Ha, Director
661-252-1864

Coachella Valley Technical Skills Center
35325 Date Palm Dr Ste 101
Cathedral City CA 92234
760-328-5554

COBA ACADEMY
102 N Glassell St, Orange CA 92866-1407
Roger N. Williams, Owner
714-633-5950 Fax: 714-633-5950
Website: www.coba.edu
E-mail: info@coba.edu

COLBURN SCHOOL
200 S Grand Ave, Los Angeles CA 90012-3007
Kathleen Tesar, Director of Admissions and Student Affairs
213-621-2200 Fax: 213-621-2110
Website: www.colburnschool.edu
E-mail: admissions@colburnschool.edu

Colleen O'Hara's Beauty Academy
109 W 4th St Floor 2, Santa Ana CA 92701
714-568-5399

College of Automotive Management
3000 W MacArthur Blvd Fl 3
Santa Ana CA 92704-6916
Eric Andersen, President
714-755-6894

COLLEGE OF CAREER TRAINING
7220 Fair Oaks Blvd Ste A, Carmichael CA 95608
916-481-9001 Fax: 916-481-9002
Website: www.collegeofcareertraining.com
E-mail: sima84344@aol.com

COLLEGE OF INFORMATION TECHNOLOGY
2701 E Chapman Ave Ste 101, Fullerton CA 92831
Mohammad Qamaruddin, Director
714-879-5100 Fax: 714-879-2272
Website: www.collegeofit.com
E-mail: mqamar@collegeofit.com

Columbia College Hollywood
18618 Oxnard St, Tarzana CA 91356-1411
Carmen Munoz & Jennifer Corinna, Admissions Coordinators
800-785-0585 Fax: 818-345-9053
Website: www.columbiacollege.edu
E-mail: admissions@columbiacollege.edu

Community Business College
3800 McHenry Ave, Modesto CA 95356
209-529-3648

Computer Tutor Business & Technical Institute
4306 Sisk Rd, Modesto CA 95356
209-545-5200

Concorde Career Institute
4393 Imperial Ave Suite 100, San Diego CA 92113
Denise Galvez, Director of Admissions
619-688-0800

CULINARY INSTITUTE OF AMERICA AT GREYSTONE
2555 Main St, Saint Helena CA 94574-9504
800-888-7850 Fax: 845-451-1078
Website: www.ciaprochef.com
E-mail: ciaprochef@culinary.edu

Cynthia's Beauty Academy
4130 Gage Ave, Bell CA 90201
323-560-2207

Daniel Freeman Memorial Hospital
333 N Prairie Ave, Inglewood CA 90301-4514
310-674-7050

Desert Career College
67501 E Palm Canyon Dr #C
Cathedral City CA 92234-5452
760-864-1356

Design School of Cosemetology
715 24th St Ste E, El Paso de Robles CA 93446
805-237-8575

East Los Angeles Occupational Center
2100 Marengo St, Los Angeles CA 90033-1321
323-223-1283

Edgewood College of California
4930 Earle Ave, Rosemead CA 91770
626-291-5000

Elegance International
1622 Highland Ave, Hollywood CA 90028
323-871-8318

Elegante Beauty College
200 N San Fernando Blvd, Burbank CA 91502
818-954-8894

Elegante Beauty College
1600 S Azusa Ave Unit 244
City of Industry CA 91748-1674
626-965-2532

Elegante Beauty College
23635 El Toro Rd Ste K, Lake Forest CA 92630
949-586-4900

Elegante Beauty College
24741 Alessandro Blvd
Moreno Valley CA 92553-3941
Rita Calafatello, Office Manager
951-247-2047

Elite Progressive School of Cosmetology
5522 Garfield Ave, Sacramento CA 95841
916-338-1885

Emergency Medical Sciences Training Institute
1801 E March Ln Ste 260, Stockton CA 95210
209-461-5550

Empire College School of Business & Law
3035 Cleveland Ave, Santa Rosa CA 95403
Roy O. Hurd, President
707-546-4000

Escuelas Leicester
1940 S Figueroa St, Los Angeles CA 90007
213-746-7666

Estes Institute Cosmetology Arts & Sciences
324 E Main St, Visalia CA 93291
559-733-3617

Everest College
2215 W Mission Rd, Alhambra CA 91803-1310
626-979-4970

Everest College
511 N Brookhurst St Ste 300
Anaheim CA 92801-5229
714-953-6500

Everest College
12801 Crossroads Pkwy S
city of Industry CA 91746-3412
562-908-2500

Everest College
22336 Main St, Hayward CA 94541
H. Albizo, President
510-582-9500

Everest College
3460 Wilshire Blvd Ste 500
Los Angeles CA 90010-2223
213-388-9950

Everest College
3000 S Robertson Blvd, Los Angeles CA 90034-3158
310-840-5777

Everest College
1460 S Milliken Ave, Ontario CA 91761-2338
909-984-5027

Everest College
18040 Sherman Way #400, Reseda CA 91335-4631
Lani Townsend, School President
818-774-0550

Everest College
217 Club Center Dr Ste A, San Bernardino CA 92408
909-777-3300

Everest College
814 Mission St Ste 500
San Francisco CA 94103-3038
415-777-2500

Everest College
1245 S Winchester Blvd #102, San Jose CA 95128
408-246-4171

Everst College
1045 W Redondo Beach Blvd #275
Gardena CA 90247
310-527-7105

Executive 2000
2041 Business Center Dr Ste 107, Irvine CA 92612
949-794-9090

FASHION CAREERS COLLEGE
1923 Morena Blvd, San Diego CA 92110-3555
Silvana Carelli, Director of Enrollment
619-275-4700 Fax: 619-275-0635
Website: www.fashioncareerscollege.com
E-mail: info@fashioncareerscollege.com

Established 1979. Private. Coed. Accreditation: ACICS. Tuition: $16,900 per year for Fashion Business & Technology. $16,900 per year for Fashion Design & Technology program, day or evening program (tuition includes required books & certain supplies). Registration Fee: $25. Enrollment: 120 full-time. Faculty: 15. Student-faculty ratio: 10:1. Degree & Certificate programs. Library: 850 volumes. Theoretical and practical training gives students a relevant and comprehensive education in Fashion Business & Technology and Fashion Design & Technology. Placement assistance and internships available.

Federico College of Hairstyling
1515 Sports Dr, Sacramento CA 95834-1905
916-929-4242

FIDM/The Fashion Institute of Design & Merchandising
17590 Gillette Ave, Irvine CA 92614
Director of Admissions
949-851-6200 or 888-974-3436 Fax: 949-851-6808
Website: www.fidm.edu
E-mail: info@fidm.com
See listing under "Community and Junior Colleges"

FIDM/The Fashion Institute of Design & Merchandising
919 S Grand Ave, Los Angeles CA 90015-1421
Director of Admissions
213-624-1201 or 800-624-1200 Fax: 213-624-4799
Website: www.fidm.edu
E-mail: info@fidm.com
See listing under "Community and Junior Colleges"

FIDM/The Fashion Institute of Design & Merchandising
1010 2nd Ave, San Diego CA 92101-4903
Director of Admissions
619-235-2049 or 800-243-3436 Fax: 619-232-4322
Website: www.fidm.edu
E-mail: info@fidm.com
See listing under "Community and Junior Colleges"

FIDM/The Fashion Institute of Design & Merchandising
55 Stockton St, San Francisco CA 94108-5829
Director of Admissions
415-675-5200 or 800-422-3436 Fax: 415-296-7299
Website: www.fidm.edu
E-mail: info@fidm.com
See listing under "Community and Junior Colleges"

Four-D College
1020 E Washington St, Colton CA 92324-4187
909-783-9331

Franklin Career College
1274 Slater Cir, Ontario CA 91761-1522
909-937-9007

Frederick and Charles Beauty College
831 F St, Eureka CA 95501
707-443-2733

Fremont College
18000 Studebaker Rd Suite 900, Cerritos CA 90703
Mark Buch, President & COO
562-809-5100 Fax: 562-809-7100
Website: www.fremont.edu
E-mail: senon.lee@fremont.edu

Galen College Medical & Dental Assts.
1325 N Wishon Ave, Fresno CA 93728-2348
559-264-9726

Galen College of Medical & Dental Assistants
1604 Ford Ave Ste 10, Modesto CA 95350-4655
209-527-5084

Gemological Institute of America
600 Corporate Pointe Ste 100, Culver City CA 90230
310-670-2100

GEMOLOGICAL INSTITUTE OF AMERICA
The Robert Mouawad Campus
5345 Armada Dr, Carlsbad CA 92008-4602
Jason Drake, Admissions Manager
800-421-7250 ext. 4001 or 760-603-4001
Fax: 760-603-4003
Website: www.gia.edu
E-mail: eduinfo@gia.edu

Established 1931. Nonprofit. Private. Coed. Accreditation: ACCSCT and DETC. Diplomas: Graduate Gemologist, Graduate Jeweler, Graduate Jeweler Gemologist, Jewelry Business Management, Applied Jewelry Arts. Degree: BBA (Bachelor of Business Administration). Financial aid. Classes begin year round.
See listing under "Home Study and Correspondence"

Glendale Career College
1015 Grandview Ave, Glendale CA 91201
818-243-1131

GOLF ACADEMY OF SAN DIEGO
1910 Shadowridge Dr Ste 111, Vista CA 92083-9007
Paul Zagnoni, President
800-342-7342 Fax: 480-905-8705
Website: www.sdgagolf.com
E-mail: sdga@sdgagolf.com

Haciende LaPuente Valley Adult Education
14101 Nelson Ave, La Puente CA 91746
626-934-2800

Hair Masters University of Beauty
208 W Highland Ave, San Bernardino CA 92405
909-882-2987

Heald College, Concord
5130 Commercial Cir, Concord CA 94520
925-827-1300

Heald College, Fresno
255 W Bullard Ave, Fresno CA 93704-1706
Chris Souza, Director of Admissions
559-438-4222

Heald College, Hayward
25500 Industrial Blvd., Hayward CA 94545-1552
Ken Gardner, Director of Admissions
510-783-2100

Heald College Rancho Cordova
2910 Prospect Park Dr
Rancho Cordova CA 95670-6005
Donald Ed Hardenbrook, Regional Director
916-638-1616

HEALD COLLEGE, ROSEVILLE
7 Sierra Gate Plz, Roseville CA 95678-6602
Guy Adams, Executive Director of Campus Operations
916-789-8600 Fax: 916-789-8616
Website: www.heald.edu
E-mail: guy_adams@heald.edu

Heald College, Salinas
1450 N Main St, Salinas CA 93906-5100
831-443-1700

Heald College, San Francisco
350 Mission St, San Francisco CA 94105-2206
415-808-3000

Heald College, Stockton
1605 E March Ln, Stockton CA 95210-6632
209-477-1114

Health Staff Training Institute
1505 E 17th St Ste 122, Santa Ana CA 92705-8520
714-543-9828

High-Tech Institute
9738 Lincoln Village Dr, Sacramento CA 95827-3302
866-502-2627

Hilltop Beauty School
6317 Mission St, Daly City CA 94014
650-756-2720

Huntington College of Dental Technology
14848 Monroe St, Midway City CA 92655
Patrick Vu, President

Huntington Memorial Hospital
100 W California Blvd, Pasadena CA 91105-3097
626-397-5000

ICDC College
6330 Pacific Blvd Ste 200, Huntington Park CA 90255
323-655-9100

ICDC College
5422 W Sunset Blvd, Los Angeles CA 90027-5614
323-468-0404

ICDC College
14434 Sherman Way, Van Nuys CA 91405
818-787-0007

Image School of Cosmetology
13070 Palm Dr, Desert Hot Springs CA 92240
760-251-5373

Image School of Cosmetology
2627 W Florida Ave, Hemet CA 92545
951-766-5759

Inland Technical Skills Center
101 E Redlands Blvd Ste 247, Redlands CA 92373

Institute for Business and Technology
2400 Walsh Ave, Santa Clara CA 95051-1303
408-727-1060

Institute of Computer Technology
3200 Wilshire Blvd, Los Angeles CA 90010-1308
Director of Admissions
213-381-3333

Institute of Network Technology
2525 Cherry Ave Ste 110, Signal Hill CA 90755-2054
562-424-9200

Institute of Technology - Clovis Campus
564 W Herndon Ave, Clovis CA 93612
Joseph Haydock, Director of Admissions
559-297-4500

Institute of Technology - Modesto Campus
5737 Stoddard Rd, Modesto CA 95356
Richard Dyer, Director of Admissions
209-545-3100

Institute of Technology - Sacramento
3695 Bleckely St, Mather CA 95655
916-363-4300

Institute of Technology - Sacramento Campus
3695 Bleckely St, Mather CA 95655
Gib Linzman, Director of Admissions
916-363-4300

Integrated Digital Technologies
2555 E Colorado Blvd Ste 200, Pasadena CA 91107
Juan Rodriguez, CEO
626-585-6300

Intercoast Colleges
401 S Glenoaks Blvd Ste 211, Burbank CA 91502
818-500-8400

INTERNATIONAL CHRISTIAN EDUCATION COLLEGE
Early Childhood Education
3807 Wilshire Blvd Ste 730
Los Angeles CA 90010-3108
Dr. Charles Chong Y. Lee, President
213-368-0316 Fax: 213-368-0318
E-mail: icec@sbcglobal.net

International Professional School of Body Work
1366 Hornblend St, San Diego CA 92109-4227
858-272-4142

International School of Cosmetology
13613 Hawthorne Blvd, Hawthorne CA 90250-5809
Mary Costello, President
310-973-7774

ITT Technical Institute
16916 S Harlan Rd, Lathrop CA 95330-8737
Donald Fraser, Director
209-858-0077

ITT Technical Institute
650 W Cienega Ave, San Dimas CA 91773
909-971-2300

ITT Technical Institute
12669 Encinitas Ave, Sylmar CA 91342-3664
Kelly Christensen, Director of Admissions
818-364-5151 Fax: 818-364-5150
Website: www.itt-tech.edu
E-mail: kchristensen@itt-tech.edu

ITT Technical Institute
20050 S Vermont Ave, Torrance CA 90502
310-380-1555

Ivory Dental Technology College
16600 Harbor Blvd Ste I
Fountain Valley CA 92708-1363
714-899-8382

James Albert School of Cosmetology
281 E 17th St, Costa Mesa CA 92627
949-642-0606

Je Boutique College of Beauty
1073 E Main St, El Cajon CA 92021
619-442-3407

John Wesley International Barber and Beauty College
717 Pine Ave, Long Beach CA 90813
562-435-7060

Kaiser Permanente Medical Center
901 Nevin Ave, Richmond CA 94801
510-307-2412

Kensington College
2428 N Grand Ave Ste D, Santa Ana CA 92705
714-542-8086

Kim Anh Academy of Beauty
12141 Brookhurst St Ste 101
Garden Grove CA 92840-2816
714-896-9847

Lake College
2655 Bechelli Ln, Redding CA 96002
530-224-7227

Lake Forest Beauty College
23600 Rockfield Blvd Ste 3C, Lake Forest CA 92630
949-951-8883

Lancaster Beauty School
44646 10th St W, Lancaster CA 93534
661-948-1672

Liberty Training Institute
2706 Wilshire Blvd, Los Angeles CA 90057
213-383-9545

Lola Beauty College
11883 Valley View St, Garden Grove CA 92845
714-894-3366

Los Amigos Research & Education Institute
PO Box 3500, Downey CA 90242
562-401-8111

Los Angeles County College of
Nursing and Allied Health
1200 N State St, Los Angeles CA 90033-1029
323-226-4911

Los Angeles County Harbor-UCLA Medical Center
1000 W Carson St, Torrance CA 90502-2004
310-533-2101

Lyle's Bakersfield College of Beauty
2935 F St, Bakersfield CA 93301
661-327-9784

Lyle's College of Beauty
6735 N 1st St Ste 112, Fresno CA 93710
559-431-6060

Lyle's Fresno College of Beauty
3125 W Shaw Ave, Fresno CA 93711
559-222-6060

Lytle's Redwood Empire Beauty College
186 Wikiup Dr, Santa Rosa CA 95403
707-545-8490

Madera Beauty College
325 N Gateway Dr, Madera CA 93637
559-673-9201

MAKE-UP DESIGNORY
129 S San Fernando Blvd, Burbank CA 91502
Tate Holland, School Director
818-729-9420 Fax: 818-729-9971
Website: www.mud.edu
E-mail: tate@mud.edu

Manchester Beauty College
3756 N Blackstone Ave, Fresno CA 93726
559-224-4242

Maric College
1914 Wible Rd, Bakersfield CA 93304
866-574-5550

Maric College
6180 Laurel Canyon Blvd Ste 101
North Hollywood CA 91606-3249
818-763-2563

MARIC COLLEGE
14355 Roscoe Blvd, Panorama City CA 91402-4222
Linda King, Contact
818-672-3000 Fax: 818-672-8919
Website: www.mariccollege.edu
E-mail: lking@mariccollege.edu

Maric College
5172 Kiernan Ct, Salida CA 95358-9083
Willie Triplett, Director of Admissions
209-543-7000

Maric College
9055 Balboa Ave, San Diego CA 92123
Geraldine Rorrison, Director of Admissions
858-279-4500 Fax: 858-279-4885
Website: www.mariccollege.edu
E-mail: grorrison@mariccollege.edu

MARIC COLLEGE
722 W March Ln, Stockton CA 95207-6216
John Bermudez, Director of Admissions
209-462-8777 Fax: 209-462-3219
Website: www.mariccollege.edu
E-mail: jbermudez@mariccollege.edu

Maric College
2022 University Dr, Vista CA 92083-7736
Jann Underwood, Executive Director
760-630-1555

Maric College East County
6160 Mission Gorge Rd #108
San Diego CA 92120-3425
619-282-9000

Maric College - Sacremento Campus
4330 Watt Ave Ste 400, Sacramento CA 95821-5512
Charlie Reese, Director of Admissions
916-649-8168

Marinello School of Beauty
240 S Market St, Inglewood CA 90301
310-674-8100

Marinello School of Beauty
1241 S Soto St Ste 101, Los Angeles CA 90023
213-627-5561

Marinello School of Beauty
6111 Wilshire Blvd, Los Angeles CA 90048
323-938-2005

Marinello School of Beauty
2700 Colorado Blvd Ste 266, Los Angeles CA 90041
323-254-6226

Marinello School of Beauty
6219 Laurel Canyon Blvd, North Hollywood CA 91606
818-980-1300

Marinello School of Beauty
940 N Mountain Ave, Ontario CA 91762
909-984-5884

Marinello School of Beauty
18442 Sherman Way, Reseda CA 91335
818-881-2521

Marinello School of Beauty
721 W 2nd St Ste E, San Bernardino CA 92410
909-884-8747

Marinello School of Beauty
7550 Miramar Rd Ste 440, San Diego CA 92126
858-547-9260

Marinello School of Beauty
118 Plaza Dr, West Covina CA 91790
626-962-1021

Marinello School of Beauty
6538 Greenleaf Ave, Whittier CA 90601
562-698-0068

MARTINEZ ADULT EDUCATION
600 F St, Martinez CA 94553
Registrar
925-228-3276 Fax: 925-228-6989
Website: www.martinez-ed.org
E-mail: mae@martinez-ed.org

MCed Career College
School of Business & Technology
2002 N Gateway Blvd, Fresno CA 93727-1620
559-456-0623

Medical Institute
5170 Santa Monica Blvd #300
Los Angeles CA 90029
323-663-2700

Milan Institute
915 17th St, Bakersfield CA 93301
Patrick Taylor, Director
661-325-8900

Milan Institute
731 W Shaw Ave, Clovis CA 93612
Susan Hutchison, Director
559-323-2800

Milan Institute
45-691 Monroe St Ste 2, Indio CA 92201
Monty Jordan, Director
760-347-5000

Milan Institute of Cosmetology
934 Missouri St, Fairfield CA 94533
Karen Keden, Director
707-425-2288

Milan Institute of Cosmetology
3328 S Fairway, Visalia CA 93277
Patrick Taylor, Director
559-735-3829

Mills - Peninsula Health Services
1783 El Camino Real, Burlingame CA 94010-3282
650-696-5678

Miss Marty's School of Beauty & Hairstyling
1087 Mission St, San Francisco CA 94103
415-227-4240

Modern Beauty Academy
699 S C St, Oxnard CA 93030
805-483-4994

Modern Technology School
16560 Harbor Blvd, Fountain Valley CA 92708-1362
714-418-9100

Moler Barber College
3815 Telegraph Ave, Oakland CA 94609-2419
510-652-4177

Montebello Beauty College
2201 W Whittier Blvd, Montebello CA 90640
323-727-7851

Moro Beauty College
124 N Brand Blvd, Glendale CA 91203
818-246-7376

Mount Sierra College
101 E Huntington Dr, Monrovia CA 91016
Vaughn Hartunian, President & CEO
626-873-2100

MTI BUSINESS COLLEGE OF STOCKTON
6006 N El Dorado St, Stockton CA 95207-4349
Steven Brenner, Director
888-302-2009 Fax: 209-474-8705
Website: www.mtistockton.com
E-mail: mtistockton@comcast.net
Established 1968. Accredited: ACCSCT. Family owned/operated 36 years.

MUELLER COLLEGE OF HOLISTIC STUDIES
4607 Park Blvd, San Diego CA 92116
David Taylor, Registrar
619-291-9811 Fax: 619-543-1113
Website: www.mueller.edu
E-mail: info@mueller.edu

MUSICIANS INSTITUTE
1655 N McCadden Pl, Hollywood CA 90028
Steve Lunn, Director of Admissions
323-462-1384 Fax: 323-462-6978
Website: www.mi.edu
E-mail: admissions@mi.edu

My-Le's Beauty College
5972 Stockton Blvd, Sacramento CA 95824
916-422-0223

National Career Education
6060 Sunrise Vista Dr #3000
Citrus Heights CA 95610

National Institute of Technology
2161 Technology Pl, Long Beach CA 90810-3800
Therese El Khoury, Director of Admissions
562-437-0501

National Polytechnic College
2465 W Whittier Blvd # 201, Montebello CA 90640
323-728-9636

NATIONAL POLYTECHNIC COLLEGE OF ENGINEERING & OCEANEERING
272 S Fries Ave, Wilmington CA 90744-6399
Tony Rodriguez, Director of Admissions
800-432-DIVE (3483) Fax: 310-952-8582
Website: www.natpoly.edu
E-mail: trodriguez@natpoly.edu

Newberry School of Beauty
16860 Devonshire St, Granada Hills CA 91344
Deanna L. Jacobsen, CEO
818-366-3211

Newbridge College
425 E Colorado St, Glendale CA 91205
714-550-8000

Newbridge College
3799 E Burnett St, Long Beach CA 90815
562-498-4500

Newbridge College
583 Monterey Pass Rd
Monterey Park CA 91754-2416
626-576-2444

Newbridge College
1840 E 17th St Ste 140, Santa Ana CA 92705-8605
714-550-8000

Newschool of Architecture and Design
1249 F St, San Diego CA 92101-6634
Gilbert D. Cooke, AIA, Dean
Barbara Wingate, Director of Admissions
619-235-4100 ext. 123

Nick Harris Detective Academy
(Friedman College)
14721 Oxnard St, Van Nuys CA 91411
J. Corey Friedman, President
800-245-9007

North Adrian's Beauty College
124 Floyd Ave, Modesto CA 95350
209-526-2040

North American Computer Consultants
570 W Stocker St Unit 311, Glendale CA 91202-2237
818-500-7227

Northwest College of Medical & Dental Assistants
221 N Brand Blvd, Glendale CA 91203-2609
818-242-0205

Northwest College of Medical & Dental Assistants
530 E Union St, Pasadena CA 91101-1744
626-796-5815

Northwest College of Medical & Dental Assistants
134 W Holt Ave, Pomona CA 91768-3101
909-623-1552

Northwest College of Medical & Dental Assistants
2121 W Garvey Ave N, West Covina CA 91790-2051
626-960-5046

NORTHWEST LINEMAN COLLEGE
2009 Challenger Ave, Oroville CA 95965
Leann Day, Manager of Marketing & Communications
530-534-7260 Fax: 530-534-7087
Website: www.lineman.edu
E-mail: nlc@lineman.edu

NTMA Training Center of Southern California
14926 Bloomfield Ave, Norwalk CA 90650-6099
Gina Marinello, Campus Director
562-404-4295

NTMA Training Center of Southern California
1717 S Grove Ave, Ontario CA 91761
909-947-9363

NTMA Training Center of Southern California
13230 Firestone Blvd Ste A
Santa Fe Springs CA 90670
562-404-4295

Occupational Training Services
8799 Balboa Ave Ste 100, San Diego CA 92123
858-560-0411

Oceanside College of Beauty
1575 S Coast Hwy, Oceanside CA 92054
760-757-6161

Oxman College
375 3rd Ave, San Francisco CA 94118
415-751-6461

Pacific College
3160 Redhill Ave, Costa Mesa CA 92626
714-662-4402

Palladium Technical Academy
10507 Valley Blvd Ste 806, El Monte CA 91731
626-444-0880

Palomar Institute of Cosmetology
355 Via Vera Cruz Ste 3, San Marcos CA 92078
760-744-7900

Paramount School of Beauty
8527 Alondra Blvd Ste 129, Paramount CA 90723
714-998-7461

Paris Beauty College
1655 Willow Pass Rd, Concord CA 94520-2611
925-685-7600

Paul Mitchell The School
1534 Adams Ave, Costa Mesa CA 92626
714-546-8786

Pima Medical Institute - Chula Vista
780 Bay Blvd Ste 101, Chula Vista CA 91910
619-425-3200

PLATT (MEDIA ARTS) COLLEGE - SAN DIEGO
6250 El Cajon Blvd, San Diego CA 92115
Al Medro, Vice President
619-265-0107 or 866-752-8826 Fax: 619-308-0570
Website: www.platt.edu
E-mail: info@platt.edu

Platt College
7755 Center Ave Ste 400
Huntington Beach CA 92647-9114
714-373-3240

Platt College Los Angeles
1000 S Fremont Ave Building A-9 West
Alhambra CA 91803
Pamela Ramirez, Director of Admissions
626-300-5444

Platt College Ontario
3700 Inland Empire Blvd #400
Ontario CA 91764-4907
Joe Blackman, Campus President
909-941-9410

Porterville Development Center
PO Box 2000, Porterville CA 93258
559-782-2753

Poway Academy of Hair Design
13266 Poway Rd, Poway CA 92064
858-748-1490

Precision Technical Institute
9342 Tech Center Suite 600, Sacramento CA 95826
916-366-3431

Premiere Career College
12901 Ramona Blvd Ste D, Irwindale CA 91706-3746
626-814-2080

Professional Career Institute
17215 Studebaker Rd Ste 310, Cerritos CA 90703
562-916-5055

PROFESSIONAL GOLFERS CAREER COLLEGE
26109 Ynez Rd, Temecula CA 92591-6013
Dr. Tim Somerville, President
800-877-4380 Fax: 951-719-1643
Website: www.golfcollege.edu
E-mail: admin@golfcollege.edu

Professional Institute of Beauty
10801 Valley Mall, El Monte CA 91731
626-443-9401

Public Health Foundation Enterprises
12781 Schabarum Ave, Irwindale CA 91706
626-856-6376

Richard's Beauty College
200 N Euclid Ave, Ontario CA 91762-3513
909-988-7584

Rosemead Beauty School
8531 Valley Blvd, Rosemead CA 91770
626-286-2147

ROYALE COLLEGE OF BEAUTY
27485 Commerce Center Dr
Temecula CA 92590-2525
951-676-0833 Fax: 951-676-0653
Website: www.beautyschools.com
E-mail: roylcoll@aol.com

Sage College
12125 Day St Ste L, Moreno Valley CA 92557-6720
951-781-2727

ST. FRANCIS CAREER COLLEGE
3630 E Imperial Hwy, Lynwood CA 90262-2636
Petra Arredondo-Rios, Director of Enrollment
310-603-1830 Fax: 310-763-3987
E-mail: marilynoverby@dochs.org

St. John's Regional Medical Center
1600 N Rose Ave, Oxnard CA 93030-3723
805-988-2500

San Fernando Beauty Academy
8700 Van Nuys Blvd, Panorama City CA 91402
Jorge Luna, Admissions
818-894-9550

San Joaquin General Hospital
PO Box 1020, Stockton CA 95201-3120
209-468-6600

San Joaquin Valley College
201 New Stine Rd, Bakersfield CA 93309-2659
Jaime Delgado, Enrollment Services Director
661-834-1026 Fax: 559-651-4864
Website: www.sjvc.edu
E-mail: jaime.delgado@sjvc.edu

San Joaquin Valley College
295 E Sierra Ave, Fresno CA 93710-3616
Nora Twarynski, Enrollment Services Director
559-448-8282 Fax: 559-651-4864
Website: www.sjvc.edu
E-mail: nora.twarynski@sjvc.edu

San Joaquin Valley College
1700 McHenry Village Way Suite 6
Modesto CA 95350
Joseph Holt, Director of Admissions
209-527-7582 Fax: 559-651-4864
Website: www.sjvc.edu
E-mail: josephh@sjvc.edu

San Joaquin Valley College
11050 Olson Dr, Rancho Cordova CA 95670
Joseph Holt, Director of Admissions
559-651-2500 Fax: 559-651-4864
Website: www.sjvc.edu
E-mail: joseph.holt@sjvc.edu

San Joaquin Valley College
10641 Church St, Rancho Cucamonga CA 91730
Ramon Abreu, Enrollment Services Director
909-948-7582 Fax: 559-651-4864
Website: www.sjvc.edu
E-mail: ramon.abreu@sjvc.edu

San Joaquin Valley College
8400 W Mineral King Ave, Visalia CA 93291-9283
Susie Topjian, Enrollment Services Director
559-651-2500 Fax: 559-651-4864
Website: www.sjvc.edu
E-mail: susiet@sjvc.edu

San Joaquin Valley College
Fresno Aviation Campus
4985 E Anderson Ave, Fresno CA 93727-1501
Joseph Holt, Director of Admissions
559-453-0123 Fax: 559-651-4864
Website: www.sjvc.edu
E-mail: josephh@sjvc.edu

Santa Barbara Business College
211 S Real Rd, Bakersfield CA 93309-2139
661-835-1100

Santa Barbara Business College
5266 Hollister Ave, Santa Barbara CA 93111-4026
805-967-9677

Santa Barbara Business College
303 Plaza Dr, Santa Maria CA 93454-6943
805-922-8256

Santa Barbara Cottage & General Hospital
PO Box 689, Santa Barbara CA 93102-0689
805-569-7290

Scripps Memorial Hospital
9888 Genesee Ave, La Jolla CA 92037-1200
858-457-6100

Sequoia Institute
200 Whitney Pl, Fremont CA 94539-7655
510-490-6900

Sierra Academy of Aeronautics
550 Airway Blvd, Livermore CA 94551-9533
800-243-6300

Sierra College of Beauty
1340 W 18th St, Merced CA 95340
209-723-2989

Sierra Valley Business College
4747 N 1st St # D, Fresno CA 93726-0563
559-222-0947

Simi Valley Adult Education
1880 Blackstock Ave, Simi Valley CA 93065
805-579-6200

Sonoma College
1304 Southpoint Blvd Ste 280, Petaluma CA 94954
800-437-9474

Sonoma College - San Francisco
301 Howard St Ste 510, San Francisco CA 94105
888-649-7801

South Coast College
2011 W Chapman Ave, Orange CA 92868-2616
Kevin J. Magner, Director of Admissions
800-33-STENO

Southern California Institute of Technology
1900 W Crescent Ave, Anaheim CA 92801-3801
714-520-5552

Southern California Regional Occupational Center
2300 Crenshaw Blvd, Torrance CA 90501
310-224-4220

SUTECH School of Voc/Tech Training
PO Box 23098, Los Angeles CA 90023-0098
Oswaldo Forero, Director
323-262-3210

Thanh Le College School of Cosmetology
12875 Chapman Ave, Garden Grove CA 92840-4100
714-971-5844

TRAVEL UNIVERSITY INTERNATIONAL
3870 Murphy Canyon Rd Suite #310
San Diego CA 92123-4403
Nancy Chappie, President
858-292-9755 Fax: 858-292-8008
Website: www.traveluniversity.edu
E-mail: travel@traveluniversity.edu

Truck Driving Academy
5711 Florin Perkins Rd, Sacramento CA 95828-1034
916-381-2285

Tulare Beauty College
1400 W Inyo Ave, Tulare CA 93274
559-688-2901

United Beauty College
10229 Lower Azusa Rd, Temple City CA 91780-4027
626-433-1371

United Truck & Car Driving School
2425 Camino Del Rio S, San Diego CA 92108
619-296-2020

Universal College of Beauty
718 W Compton Blvd, Compton CA 90220
310-635-6969

Universal College of Beauty
8619 S Vermont Ave, Los Angeles CA 90044
323-750-5750

Universal College of Beauty
3419 W 43rd Pl, Los Angeles CA 90008
323-298-0045

Universal Technical Institute
9494 Haven Ave
Rancho Cucamonga CA 91730-5843
909-484-1929

Universal Technical Institute
4100 Duckhorn Dr, Sacramento CA 95834-2588
877-884-2254

Universal Training Center
3875 Atlantic Ave, Highland CA 92346
909-864-1918

VICTOR VALLEY BEAUTY COLLEGE
16515 Mojave Dr, Victorville CA 92395-3821
Irma Silva, Director
760-245-2522 Fax: 760-245-5681
Website: www.victorvalleybeautycollege.com

Virginia School Center
1033 S Broadway, Los Angeles CA 90015
Sara Cristi, Director
213-747-8292

West Coast Ultrasound Institute
291 S La Cienega Blvd # 500, Beverly Hills CA 90211
310-289-5123

Westech College
3491 Concours, Ontario CA 91764-4988
909-980-4474

Western Career College
2157 Country Hills Dr, Antioch CA 94509-7435
Dr. Tim Gienapp, Executive Director
925-522-7777
Website: www.westerncollege.edu

Western Career College
7301 Greenback Ln Bldg A, Citrus Heights CA 95621
Jim Murphy, Executive Director
916-722-8200 Fax: 916-722-6883
Website: www.westerncollege.edu

Western Career College
6001 Shellmound St, Suite 145, Emeryville CA 94608
Dr. Paul Dancy, Contact
510-601-0133 Fax: 510-601-0793
Website: www.westerncollege.edu

Western Career College
380 Civic Dr Ste 300, Pleasant Hill CA 94523-1984
LaShawn Wells, Executive Director
925-609-6650 Fax: 926-609-6666
Website: www.westerncollege.edu

Western Career College
8909 Folsom Blvd, Sacramento CA 95826-3203
Sue Smith, Executive Director
916-361-5100 Fax: 916-361-6666
Website: www.westerncollege.edu

Western Career College
6201 San Ignacio Ave, San Jose CA 95119
Steve Ashab, Executive Director
408-360-0840 Fax: 408-360-0848
Website: www.westerncollege.edu

Western Career College
15555 E 14th St Ste 500, San Leandro CA 94578
Dawn Matthews, Executive Director
510-276-3888 Fax: 510-276-3653
Website: www.westerncollege.edu

Western Career College
1313 W Robinhood Dr Ste B, Stockton CA 95207
Dave Semrau, Executive Director
209-956-1240 Fax: 209-956-1244
Website: www.westerncollege.edu

Western Pacific Truck School
2316 Nickerson Dr, Modesto CA 95358-9483
Ruben Ramirez, Campus Manager
800-333-1233

Western Pacific Truck School
8720 Fruitridge Rd, Sacramento CA 95826-9740
Sean Day, Campus Manager
800-333-1233

Western Pacific Truck School
1002 N Broadway Ave, Stockton CA 95205-3928
Ray VerSteeg, Campus Manager
800-333-1233

Westwood College
1551 S Douglass Rd, Anaheim CA 92806
714-704-2727

Westwood College - Inland Empire
20 W 7th St, Upland CA 91786
909-931-7500

Westwood College of Aviation Technology
8911 Aviation Blvd, Inglewood CA 90301-2904
800-597-8690

Westwood College
South Bay Campus
19700 S Vermont Ave Ste 100
Torrance CA 90502-1148
310-965-0888

Wyotech
980 Riverside Pkwy, West Sacramento CA 95605
Steve Coffee, Director of Admissions
916-376-8888

COLORADO

Academy of Beauty Culture
2992 North Ave, Grand Junction CO 81504
970-245-5570

Art Institute of Colorado
1200 Lincoln St, Denver CO 80203-2172
David Zorn, President
Brian A. Parker, Director of Admissions
800-275-2420

Artistic Beauty College
3811 E 120th Ave, Thornton CO 80233-1659
303-451-5808

Artistic Beauty College
3049 W 74th Ave Ste A, Westminster CO 80030
303-428-5100

Bel-Rea Institute of Animal Technology
1681 S Dayton St, Denver CO 80247-3048
Paulette Kaufman, Administrator
303-751-8700 Fax: 303-751-9969
Website: www.bel-rea.com
E-mail: admissions@bel-rea.com

BOULDER COLLEGE OF MASSAGE THERAPY
6255 Longbow Dr, Boulder CO 80301-3295
Admissions Department
303-530-2100 Fax: 303-530-2204
Website: www.bcmt.org
E-mail: admissions@bcmt.org

Cambridge College
350 Blackhawk St, Aurora CO 80011-8754
Sandi Parks, Campus President
303-338-9700

Centura-St. Anthony Hospital
4231 W 16th Ave, Denver CO 80204-1335
303-629-4350

Cheeks International Academy of Beauty Culture
2925 S College Ave Unit 9, Fort Collins CO 80525
970-226-1416

Cheeks International Academy of Beauty Culture
2547 11th Ave Ste B, Greeley CO 80631
970-352-4500

CollegeAmerica - Colorado
Main Campus
1385 S Colorado Blvd 5th Floor
Denver CO 80222-3304
Barbara Thomas, President
303-691-9756

THE COLORADO CENTER FOR MEDICAL LABORATORY SCIENCE
1719 E 19th Ave, Denver CO 80218
Karen Myers, Director
303-839-6485 Fax: 303-869-1720
Website: www.medlabed.org
E-mail: medlabed@coloradohealth.org

COLORADO INSTITUTE OF TAXIDERMY
708 Royal Gorge Blvd, Canon City CO 81212
Jerry Vinnola, President
719-276-2883 Fax: 719-276-3187
Website: www.coloradotaxidermyschool.com
E-mail: cotaxidermy@amigo.net

Colorado School of Healing Arts
7655 W Mississippi #100, Lakewood CO 80226-4332
Victoria Steere, Director
303-986-2320

Colorado School of Trades
1575 Hoyt St, Lakewood CO 80215-2996
Patti O'Shea, Contact
303-233-4697

Cortiva Institute - Colorado
390 Interlocken Crescent Ste 450
Broomfield CO 80021-8039
303-996-5050

Denver Academy of Court Reporting
9051 Harlan St Ste 20, Westminster CO 80031-2943
Charles W. Jarstfer, President
800-574-2087

Denver Automotive & Diesel College
PO Box 9366, Denver CO 80209
Joseph R. Chalupa, College Director
800-347-3232

Denver Health Medical Center
660 Bannock St, Denver CO 80204
303-436-6611

Durango Air Service
1340 Airport Rd, Durango CO 81303-6791
Don Watkins, Contact
970-247-5535

Emily Griffith Opportunity School
1250 Welton St, Denver CO 80204-2124
720-423-4700

Everest College
Aurora Campus
14280 E Jewell Ave, Aurora CO 80012-5692
John Heckman, Director of Admissions
303-367-2757 Fax: 303-745-6245
Website: www.cci.edu

Glenwood Beauty Academy
51241 Highway 6 Ste 1, Glenwood Springs CO 81601
970-945-0485

Hair Dynamics Education Center
6464 S College Ave, Fort Collins CO 80525
970-223-9943

HERITAGE COLLEGE
12 Lakeside Ln, Denver CO 80212-7413
Jennifer Sprague, Director
303-477-7240 Fax: 303-477-7276
Website: www.heritage-education.com
E-mail: info@heritage-education.com

Accredited Member School: ACCSCT. Providing quality education in Esthetics, Therapeutic Massage, Personal Training, Pharmacy Technician and X-Ray Medical Technician. Financial aid available to those who qualify.

Institute of Business & Medical Careers
1609 Oakridge Dr Ste 102
Fort Collins CO 80525-5563
Steve Steele, Director of Operations
970-223-2669

IntelliTec College
2315 E Pikes Peak Ave
Colorado Springs CO 80909-6096
Michael Castellano, Contact
719-632-7626 Fax: 719-632-7451
Website: www.intelliteccollege.edu
E-mail: admcs@intelliteccollege.edu

IntelliTec College
772 Horizon Dr, Grand Junction CO 81506-3907
Jennifer Daniels, Contact
970-245-8101 Fax: 970-243-8074
Website: www.intelliteccollege.edu
E-mail: admgj@intelliteccollege.edu

IntelliTec College
3673 Parker Blvd Ste 250, Pueblo CO 81008
Crystal Barajas, Director of Admissions
719-542-3181 Fax: 719-242-0068
Website: www.intelliteccollege.edu
E-mail: admpbl@intelliteccollege.edu

International Beauty Academy
5705 N Academy Blvd, Colorado Springs CO 80918
719-597-1413

Johnson & Wales University
7150 Montview Blvd, Denver CO 80220-1866
Kim Ostrowski, Director of Admissions
303-256-9300

Kaplan College
500 E 84th Ave Suite W200
Thornton CO 80229-5316
Michael Como, Director of Admissions
800-848-0550 Fax: 303-295-0102
Website: www.kaplancollege.com
E-mail: admissions-045@kaplan.edu

Memorial Hospital
1400 E Boulder St, Colorado Springs CO 80909-5599
719-365-6819

Misers Inspection and Training
1825 W Baker Ave, Englewood CO 80110
Eric Peters, Training Coordinator
303-922-8821

Misers Inspection and Training Inc
2401 S Raritan St, Englewood CO 80110
Eric Peters, Training Coordinator
303-761-8860

MJM Institute of Cosmetology
1048 Independent Ave #A113
Grand Junction CO 81505
970-241-9060

Ohio Center for Broadcasting - Colorado
1310 Wadsworth Blvd Ste 100, Lakewood CO 80214
303-937-7070

Parks College
9065 Grant St, Denver CO 80229-4339
303-457-2757

Parkview Medical Center
400 W 16th St, Pueblo CO 81003-2745
719-584-4573

Penrose-St. Francis Health System
2215 N Cascade Ave
Colorado Springs CO 80907-6736
719-776-5111

PHLEBOTOMY LEARNING CENTER
1780 S Bellaire St Ste 780, Denver CO 80222
Matthew Kurtz, Owner
303-584-0575 Fax: 303-756-0066
Website: www.plcofdenver.com
E-mail: mkurtz@plcofdenver.com

Pickens Technical Center
500 Airport Blvd, Aurora CO 80011-9307
303-344-4910

PIMA MEDICAL INSTITUTE
1701 W 72nd Ave Ste 130, Denver CO 80221-2727
Sue Anderson, Director
303-426-1800 Fax: 303-430-4048
Website: www.pimamedical.com
E-mail: denverpima@aol.com

Platt College
3100 S Parker Rd, Aurora CO 80014-3141
Jerald B. Sirbu, President
303-369-5151

Remington College
6050 Erin Park Dr #250
Colorado Springs CO 80918-3401
719-532-1234

ROLF INSTITUTE OF STRUCTURAL INTEGRATION
5055 Chaparral Ct Ste 103, Boulder CO 80301
Jim Jones, Director of Education
303-449-5903 Fax: 303-449-5978
Website: www.rolf.org
E-mail: jjones@rolf.org

San Juan Basin Technical College
PO Box 970, Cortez CO 81321-0970
Shannon South, Vice President
970-565-8457 Fax: 970-565-8450
Website: www.sjbtc.edu
E-mail: info@sjbtc.edu

TONI & GUY HAIRDRESSING ACADEMY
332 Main St, Colorado Springs CO 80911
Lynn Whitesides, Director
719-390-9898 Fax: 719-390-0977
Website: www.toniguyco.com
E-mail: whitesides@tigics.com

Westwood College - Denver North
7350 Broadway, Denver CO 80221-3610
303-426-7000

Westwood College - Denver South
Health Careers Division
3150 S Sheridan Blvd, Denver CO 80227
303-934-2790

Westwood College of Aviation Technology
10851 W 120th Ave, Broomfield CO 80021-3465
Mike Foss, President / Director
Laura Goldhammer, Regional Director of Admissions
800-888-3995

XENON INTERNATIONAL
2231 S Peoria St, Aurora CO 80014
Connie Voss, Director
303-752-1560 Fax: 303-752-0218
Website: www.xenonintl.com
E-mail: cvoss@xenonintl.com

CONNECTICUT

ALLEN INSTITUTE CENTER FOR INNOVATIVE LEARNING
PO Box 100, Hebron CT 06248
Dan Spada, Director of Marketing and Communication
866-666-6910 Fax: 860-859-4159
Website: www.thealleninstitute.org
E-mail: dspada@eastersealsct.org

American Academy of Cosmetology
109 South St, Danbury CT 06810-8039
Melissa Diacri, Director of Admissions
203-744-0900

Baran Institute of Technology
PO Box 807, East Windsor CT 06088
860-627-4300

Branford Hall Career Institute
1 Summit Pl, Branford CT 06405
800-959-7599
Website: www.branfordhall.com

Branford Hall Career Institute
35 N Main St, Southington CT 06489-2577
860-276-0600
Website: www.branfordhall.com

Branford Hall Career Institute
995 Day Hill Rd, Windsor CT 06095-1722
860-683-4900
Website: www.branfordhall.com

Bridgeport Hospital
267 Grant St, Bridgeport CT 06610-2870
203-384-3464

Bridgeport Hospital School of Nursing
200 Mill Hill Ave, Bridgeport CT 06610
Yolanda Torres, Contact
203-384-3022

Brio Academy of Cosmetology
1231 E Main St, Meriden CT 06450
203-237-6683

Butler Business School
2710 North Ave, Bridgeport CT 06604-2383
203-333-3601

Connecticut Center for Massage Therapy
1154 Poquonnock Rd, Groton CT 06340
Susan Scoboria, Contact
877-295-2268 Fax: 860-446-9410
Website: www.ccmt.edu
E-mail: info@ccmt.edu

Connecticut Center for Massage Therapy
75 Kitts Ln, Newington CT 06111-3954
Wendy Dorsey, Director of Admissions
877-282-2268 Fax: 860-667-4566
Website: www.ccmt.edu
E-mail: info@ccmt.edu

Connecticut Center for Massage Therapy
25 Sylvan Rd S, Westport CT 06880-4619
Glen Vigorito, Contact
877-292-2268 Fax: 203-221-0144
Website: www.ccmt.edu
E-mail: info@ccmt.edu

Connecticut Childrens Medical Center
282 Washington St, Hartford CT 06106
Rich Janis, Team Leader
860-545-8514

CONNECTICUT CULINARY INSTITUTE
85 Sigourney St, Hartford CT 06105
Tina Merullo, Director of Admissions
860-895-6100 or 800-76-CHEFS (762-4337)
Fax: 860-895-6157
Website: www.ctculinary.edu
E-mail: tmerullo@ctculinary.edu

Established 1987. Private. Coed. Accreditation: ACCSCT. Tuition: $15,000 - $24,000. Fees vary. Federal Financial Aid, private payment plans, and scholarships available (for qualified applicants).

Enrollment: 500 full time, 150 part time. Faculty: 30 (includes full & part time). Student-Professional Chef/Instructor ratio 15:1, allowing for extensive individualized attention. Classes are predominantly "hands-on".

Three programs offered year round. Advanced Culinary Arts Program: 60 weeks/full-time days and 90 weeks/part-time evenings; 60.5 credit hours including 660-hour paid externship. Pastry & Baking Program: 35 weeks/full-time days and 47 weeks/part-time evenings; 36 credit hours. Advanced Italian Culinary Arts Program: 60 weeks/full-time days; 60.5 credit hours. Opportunity to study abroad in Italy for 15 weeks.

Advanced Culinary Arts Program includes International Cuisines and American Regional Cuisine, Foundation Skills, Business and Nutrition, Pastry & Baking, Special Diets, Garde Manger, Facilities and Career Planning.

Admissions requirements: A minimum of High School Diploma or GED, plus $100 registration/application fee. No prior culinary experience required.

Student housing available. Located in the "Hub" of scenic and Historic New England; close to NYC, Boston, Cape Cod, Newport, New Hampshire & Vermont. Enjoy the "bonus" pleasures of: hiking, biking, camping, boating, fishing, skiing, and sports, historical tours, and some of the best restaurants in the country!

Outstanding employment placement (state and national): restaurants, hotels, country clubs, private clubs, private estates, caterers, pastry shops, bed & breakfasts, country inns, resorts, cruise ships, casinos, schools and universities, retirement communities, industrial cafeterias, hospital dining services. Some students start their own businesses.

Connecticut Culinary Institute
1760 Mapleton Ave, Suffield CT 06078
Tina Merullo, Director of Admissions
860-668-3500 or 866-67-CHEFS Fax: 860-668-3518
Website: www.ctculinary.edu
E-mail: tmerullo@ctculinary.edu
See listing under "Career Schools"

Connecticut Institute of Hair Design
1681 Meriden Rd, Wolcott CT 06716
203-879-4247

Danbury Hospital
24 Hospital Ave, Danbury CT 06810-6099
203-797-7210

Eli Whitney Regional Vocational Technical School
71 Jones Rd, Hamden CT 06514
203-397-4037

Fox Institute of Business
99 South St, West Hartford CT 06110-1922
860-947-2299

Gal Mar Academy of Hairdressing, Skin & Nails, LLC
97 Washington Ave Ste 8, North Haven CT 06473
203-281-4477

Gibbs College
10 Norden Pl, Norwalk CT 06855-1436
Anthony Reich, Director of Admissions
800-845-5333

Goodwin Institute
1315 Dixwell Ave, Hamden CT 06514-4125
800-889-3282

Goodwin Institute Business School
101 Pierpont Rd, Waterbury CT 06705-3823
203-756-5500

Hartford Conservatory
834 Asylum Ave, Hartford CT 06105-2807
Lynn Tracey, Director of Admissions
860-246-2588

Hartford Hospital
PO Box 5037, Hartford CT 06102-5037
860-545-2100

Industrial Management and Training
233 Mill St, Waterbury CT 06706-1211
203-753-7910

INTERNATIONAL COLLEGE OF HOSPITALITY MANAGEMENT
1760 Mapleton Ave, Suffield CT 06078
Jolie Swanson, Director of Admissions
860-668-3515 Fax: 860-668-7369
Website: www.ichm.edu
E-mail: admissions@ichm.edu

Leon Institute of Hair Design
111 Wall St, Bridgeport CT 06604
203-333-1465

New England Technical Institute
109 Sanford St, Hamden CT 06514
203-287-7300

New England Technical Institute
200 John Downey Dr, New Britain CT 06051-2904
Robert Dockendorff, Director of Education
860-225-8641

New England Technical Institute
8 Progress Dr, Shelton CT 06484
203-929-0592

New England Tractor Trailer Training
PO Box 326, Somers CT 06071-0326
860-749-0711

Norwalk Hospital
24 Stevens St, Norwalk CT 06850-3852
203-852-2211

Porter and Chester Institute
138 Weymouth Rd, Enfield CT 06082
860-741-2561

Porter and Chester Institute
670 Lordship Blvd, Stratford CT 06615-7158
Mark Breslin, Director of Admissions
203-375-4463

Porter and Chester Institute
320 Sylvan Lake Rd, Watertown CT 06779-1459
Jack Burke, Executive Director
860-274-9294

Porter and Chester Institute
125 Silas Deane Hwy, Wethersfield CT 06109-1255
860-529-2519

Porter and Chester Institute of Branford
221 W Main St, Branford CT 06405-4022
203-315-1060

Prince Regional Vocational Technical School
500 Brookfield St, Hartford CT 06106
860-246-8594

Ridley-Lowell Business & Technical Inst
PO Box 652, New London CT 06320-0652
Kimberly L. Mayer, Director
860-443-7441

Sawyer School
1125 Dixwell Ave, Hamden CT 06514-4735
203-865-2900

Sawyer School
141 Washington St, Hartford CT 06106
860-568-1554

∴ Stamford Hospital
PO Box 9317, Stamford CT 06904-9317
Dorothy Saia, MA, RT, Program Director
203-276-7877

Stone Academy
1315 Dixwell Ave, Hamden CT 06514-4155
Jeanna LaBella, Director of Admissions
203-288-7474

Windham Community Memorial Hospital
112 Mansfield Ave, Willimantic CT 06226-2041
860-456-6800

Windham Regional Vocational Technical School
210 Birch St, Willimantic CT 06226-2108
860-456-3789

DELAWARE

∴ Beebe Medical Center School of Nursing
424 Savannah Rd, Lewes DE 19958-1462
Connie E. Bushey, Director
302-645-3251

Dawn Training Centre
3700 Lancaster Pike, Wilmington DE 19805-1511
Hollis C. Anglin, President
302-633-9075

Deep Muscle Therapy School
5341 Limestone Rd, Wilmington DE 19808
Patricia Draper, LMT, Director
302-234-8525

National Massage Therapy Institute
Route 113 Box 144D, Dagsboro DE 19939
800-264-9835

Schilling-Douglas School of Hair Design
70 Amstel Ave, Newark DE 19711
302-737-5100

Star Technical Institute
655 S Bay Rd Ste 562, Dover DE 19901
302-736-6111

DISTRICT OF COLUMBIA

Bennett Beauty Institute
700 Monroe St NE, Washington DC 20017
202-526-1400

Dudley Beauty College
2031 Rhode Island Ave NE, Washington DC 20018
202-269-3666

Levine School of Music
2801 Upton St NW, Washington DC 20008-3829
202-686-8000

NATIONAL CONSERVATORY OF DRAMATIC ARTS
1556 Wisconsin Ave NW
Washington DC 20007-2758
Nan Kyle Ficca, Vice President
202-333-2202 Fax: 202-333-1753
Website: theconservatory.org
E-mail: ncdadrama@aol.com

Walter Reed Medical Center
6825 16th St NW, Washington DC 20307-0002
202-782-6104

Washington Hospital Center
110 Irving St NW, Washington DC 20010-2975
202-877-6101

FLORIDA

Academy for Practical Nursing & Health Occupations
5154 Okeechobee Blvd #201
West Palm Beach FL 33417
561-683-1400

Academy of Healing Arts Massage & Facial Skin Care
3141 S Military Trl, Lake Worth FL 33463
561-965-4686

Advanced/Basic Hair Design Training Center
2088 N Courtenay Pkwy, Merritt Island FL 32953
321-452-8490

Advance Science Institute
3750 W 12th Ave, Hialeah FL 33012
305-827-5452

Americare School of Nursing
7275 Estapona Circle, Fern Park FL 32730
407-673-7406

Ari Ben Aviator
3800 Saint Lucie Blvd, Fort Pierce FL 34946-9022
772-466-4822

Art Institute of Fort Lauderdale
1799 SE 17th St, Fort Lauderdale FL 33316-3013
Eileen Northrop, V.P./Director of Admissions
800-275-7603

ASM BEAUTY WORLD ACADEMY
6423 Stirling Rd, Davie FL 33314
Leticia Milazzo, Assistant School Director
877-678-9532 or 954-321-8411 Fax: 954-321-8683
Website: www.asmbeautyworld.com
E-mail: asm60@bellsouth.net

· ATI Career Training Center
2890 W Cypress Creek Rd, Fort Lauderdale FL 33309
954-973-4760

· ATI Career Training Center
7265 NW 25th St, Miami FL 33122
305-573-1600

· ATI Career Training Center
3501 Powerline Rd, Oakland Park FL 33309-5916
Michael Ackerman, Executive Director
954-563-5899

Atlantic Technical Center
4700 Coconut Creek Pkwy, Margate FL 33063-3999
954-977-2000

Audio Recording Technology Institute
4525 Vineland Rd Ste 201B, Orlando FL 32811
407-423-2784

Baptist/St. Vincent's Health System
1800 Barrs St, Jacksonville FL 32204-4799
904-387-7300

Baptist Medical Centers
800 Prudential Dr, Jacksonville FL 32207-8203
904-393-2001

∴ **BAYFRONT MEDICAL CENTER**
School of Medical Technology
701 6th St S, Saint Petersburg FL 33701-4891
727-893-6604 Fax: 727-893-6977
Website: www.bayfront.org
E-mail: maria.duynslager@bayfront.org

Beauty and Barber Academy
5505 Manatee Ave W, Bradenton FL 34209
941-761-4400

Beauty Schools of America
1060 W 49th St, Hialeah FL 33012
305-362-9003

Beauty Schools of America
1176 SW 67th Ave, Miami FL 33144

BENE'S INTERNATIONAL SCHOOL OF BEAUTY, BARBER, AND MASSAGE
7127 US Highway 19
New Port Richey FL 34652-1638
Patricia Martin, Contact
727-848-8415 Fax: 727-846-0269
Website: www.isbschool.com
E-mail: isbschool@aol.com

Bethesda Memorial Hospital
2815 S Seacrest Blvd
Boynton Beach FL 33435-7995
561-737-7733

Bradford-Union Area Vo-Tech Center
609 N Orange St, Starke FL 32091
904-966-6760

Cape Coral Beauty School
1214 SE 47th St, Cape Coral FL 33904
239-549-1819

Career Training Institute
3318 Edgewater Dr, Orlando FL 32804
407-884-1816

Central Florida Blood Bank
8669 Commodity Cir, Orlando FL 32819-9054
407-849-6100

Central Florida College
1573 W Fairbanks Ave #100
Winter Park FL 32789-4679
407-843-9828

· Central Florida Institute
30522 US Highway 19 N, Palm Harbor FL 34684
727-786-4707

CHAPMAN SCHOOL OF SEAMANSHIP
4343 SE Saint Lucie Blvd, Stuart FL 34997-6898
Bruce Robertson, Registrar
800-225-2841 Fax: 772-283-2019
Website: www.chapman.org
E-mail: info@chapman.org

Charlotte Technical Center
18150 Murdock Cir, Port Charlotte FL 33948
Carolyn Gorton, Assistant Principal
941-255-7500

· City College
853 Semoran Blvd Ste 200, Casselberry FL 32707
Dr. Diane Owens, Executive Director
407-831-9816

COLLEGE OF BUSINESS & TECHNOLOGY
8991 SW 107th Ave #200, Miami FL 33176-1412
Luis Llerena, Executive Director
305-273-4499 Fax: 305-596-3835
Website: www.cbt.edu
E-mail: admissions@cbt.edu

COMPU-MED VOCATIONAL CAREERS
2900 W 12th Ave Ste 3, Hialeah FL 33012-4861
Mayra Rodriguez, President
305-888-9200 Fax: 305-888-3614
Website: www.compumedschool.com
E-mail: compumed44@aol.com

COMPU-MED VOCATIONAL CAREERS
9738 SW 24th St, Miami FL 33165-7513
Mayra Rodriguez, President
305-553-2898 Fax: 305-553-7423
Website: www.compumedschools.com
E-mail: compumed44@aol.com

Coral Ridge Nurse's Assistant Training School
2740 E Oakland Park Blvd
Fort Lauderdale FL 33306-1626
E. Mais, Director
954-561-2022

Core Institute
223 W Carolina St, Tallahassee FL 32301
866-830-0108

Darlyne McGee's Academy of Cosmetology
1975 Palm Bay Rd NE Ste 106, Palm Bay FL 32905
321-951-0595

DELTA CONNECTION ACADEMY
2700 Flightline Ave, Sanford FL 32773-9683
Ron Lewis, Director of Admissions
407-430-4174 Fax: 407-330-0448
Website: www.deltaconnectionacademy.com
E-mail: info@deltaconnectionacademy.com

D.G. Erwin Technical Center
2010 E Hillsborough Ave, Tampa FL 33610-8299
813-231-1800

Educating Hands School of Massage
120 SW 8th St, Miami FL 33130
305-285-6991

EduTech Centers
2262 S Falkenburg Rd, Riverview FL 33569
Nannette Worlinsky, Admissions Director
800-485-0717

EduTech Centers Inc.
410 Park Place Blvd, Clearwater FL 33759-3924
Nancy O'Donnell-Kenny, Executive Director
727-724-1037

The English Center
3501 SW 28th St, Miami FL 33133
305-445-7731

Euro Hair Design Institute
5995 University Blvd W #3
Jacksonville FL 32216-4933
904-731-4766

FAA Center for Management Development
4500 Palm Coast Pkwy SE
Palm Coast FL 32137-8011
386-446-7136

Fashion Focus Hair Academy
2184 Gulf Gate Dr, Sarasota FL 34231-4813
941-921-4877

First Coast Technical Institute
2980 Collins Ave, Saint Augustine FL 32084-1919
904-829-1010

FlightSafety International
PO Box 2708, Vero Beach FL 32961-2708
772-564-7600

Florida Barber Academy
3269 N Federal Hwy, Pompano Beach FL 33064
954-781-6066

Florida Blood Services
10100 Dr Mrtn Lthr King St
Saint Petersburg FL 33716
727-568-5433

· Florida Career College
1321 SW 107th Ave Ste 201B, Miami FL 33174-2521
305-553-6065

· **FLORIDA CAREER COLLEGE**
7891 Pines Blvd, Pembroke Pines FL 33024-6916
Michael Schwam, Executive Director
954-965-7272 Fax: 954-983-2707
Website: www.careercollege.edu
E-mail: mschwam@careercollege.edu

FLORIDA CAREER INSTITUTE
5925 Imperial Pkwy Ste 200, Mulberry FL 33860
863-646-1400
Website: www.floridacareerinstitute.com
E-mail: swadhwa@edaff.com

· Florida College of Natural Health
616 67th Street Circle East, Bradenton FL 34208
Wayne Dawson, Campus Director
941-954-8999

· Florida College of Natural Health
2600 Lake Lucien Dr Suite 140, Maitland FL 32751
Steve Richards, Campus Director
800-393-7337

· Florida College of Natural Health
7925 NW 12th St Ste 201, Miami FL 33126-1821
800-599-9599

Florida College of Natural Health
2001 W Sample Rd Ste 100
Pompano Beach FL 33064-1342
954-975-6400

Florida Education Institute
5818 SW 8th St, West Miami FL 33144
305-444-1515

Florida Institute of Animal Arts
3776 Howell Branch Rd, Winter Park FL 32792
407-657-8088

FLORIDA INSTITUTE OF ULTRASOUND, INC.
8800 University Pkwy Ste A4
Pensacola FL 32514-4913
Polly Brown, Administrative Assistant
850-478-7300 Fax: 850-478-3727
Website: www.fiuonline.net
E-mail: fiupcola@aol.com

Florida Keys Community College
5901 College Rd, Key West FL 33040-4397
Cheryl Malsheimer, Director of Admissions & Records
305-296-9081 ext. 495

Florida Metropolitan University-Brandon
3924 Coconut Palm Dr, Tampa FL 33619-1354
Marty Baca, Director of Admissions
877-338-0068 (Toll Free)

Florida Metropolitan University
Pinellas Campus
2471 N McMullen Booth Rd
Clearwater FL 33759-1359
Sandra Williams, Director of Admissions
800-353-3687

Florida School of Massage
6421 SW 13th St, Gainesville FL 32608
352-378-7891

Florida Technical College
298 Havendale Blvd, Auburndale FL 33823-4508
Sandra Herndon, Dean
863-967-8822

Florida Technical College
8711 Lone Star Rd, Jacksonville FL 32211-5123
Joseph Rogalski, Director of Admissions
904-724-2229

Fort Pierce Beauty Academy
3028 S US 1, Fort Pierce FL 34982
772-464-4885

Full Sail - Real World Education
3300 University Blvd, Winter Park FL 32792
407-679-0100

George Stone Vocational Technical Center
2400 Longleaf Dr, Pensacola FL 32526-8901
850-941-6200

GEORGE T. BAKER AVIATION SCHOOL
3275 NW 42nd Ave, Miami FL 33142-5626
Sean E. Gallagan, Principal
305-871-3143 Fax: 305-871-5840
Website: www.bakeraviation.edu
E-mail: gtba@dadeschools.net

GOLF ACADEMY OF THE SOUTH
1200 E Altamonte Dr #1010
Altamonte Springs FL 32701-5050
Paul Zagoni, President
800-342-SDGA Fax: 480-905-8705
Website: www.sdgagolf.com
E-mail: sdga@sdgagolf.com

Gulf Coast College
3910 N US Highway 301 Ste 200
Tampa FL 33619-1283
813-620-1446

Halifax Medical Center
PO Box 2830, Daytona Beach FL 32120-2830
386-254-4065

HARRY WENDELSTEDT UMPIRE SCHOOL
88 S Saint Andrews Dr
Ormond Beach FL 32174-3857
Harry Wendelstedt, President
386-672-4879 Fax: 386-672-3212
Website: www.umpireschool.com
E-mail: umpsch@aol.com

Helicopter Adventures
365 Golden Knights Blvd, Titusville FL 32780
321-385-2919

HENRY W. BREWSTER TECHNICAL CENTER
2222 N Tampa St, Tampa FL 33602-2196
William Cade, Department Head/Counselor
813-276-5464 Fax: 813-276-5756
Website: www.brewstertech.org

HERITAGE INSTITUTE
6811 Palisades Park Ct, Fort Myers FL 33912
Eva Hutson, Director
239-936-5822 Fax: 239-225-9117
Website: www.heritage-education.com
E-mail: info@heritage-education.com

Accredited Member School: ACCSCT. Providing quality education in Esthetics, Therapeutic Massage, Personal Training and X-Ray Medical Technician. Financial aid available to those who qualify.

HERITAGE INSTITUTE
4130 N Salisbury Rd Suite 1100
Jacksonville FL 32216
Sonnie Willingham, Director
904-332-0910 Fax: 904-332-0920
Website: www.heritage-education.com
E-mail: info@heritage-education.com

Accredited Member School: ACCSCT. Providing quality education in Esthetics, Massage Therapy and X-Ray Medical Technician. Financial aid available to those who qualify.

HERZING COLLEGE
1595 S Semoran Blvd #1501
Winter Park FL 32792-5509
Kathy Nagle, Director of Admissions
407-478-0500 Fax: 407-478-0501
Website: www.herzing.edu
E-mail: info@orl.herzing.edu

High-Tech Institute
3710 Maguire Blvd, Orlando FL 32803-3013
407-893-7400

Hope Career Institute
3714 W Oakland Park Blvd
Lauderdale Lakes FL 33311
954-741-0088

Humanities Center Institute of Allied Health
4045 Park Blvd, Pinellas Park FL 33781-3634
727-541-5200

International Academy
2550 S Ridgewood Ave
South Daytona FL 32119-3536
Tracy Franchina, Contact
386-767-4600

International Academy of Design & Technology
5104 Eisenhower Blvd, Tampa FL 33634-6313
Richard Costa, V.P. of Admissions and Marketing
813-880-8092

INTERNATIONAL ACADEMY OF DESIGN AND TECHNOLOGY
5959 Lake Ellenor Dr, Orlando FL 32809-4633
Dr. John Dietrich, VP of Admissions
877-753-0007 Fax: 407-888-4006
Website: www.iadt.edu
E-mail: info@iadt.edu

International Training Careers
7360 Coral Way, Miami FL 33155
305-263-9696

ITT Technical Institute
4809 Memorial Hwy, Tampa FL 33634-7515
813-885-2244

Jackson Memorial Medical Center
1611 NW 12th Ave, Miami FL 33136-1096
305-585-6754

Keiser Career College
6812 Forest Hill Blvd Ste D1, Greenacres FL 33413
561-433-2330

Keiser Career College
17395 NW 59th Ave, Hialeah FL 33015
305-820-5003

Keiser Career College
9468 S US 1, Port Saint Lucie FL 34652
727-398-9990

Key College
225 E Dania Beach Blvd #130
Dania Beach FL 33004
Ronald Dooley, President
954-923-4440 Fax: 954-923-9226
Website: www.keycollege.edu
E-mail: admissions@keycollege.edu

La Belle Beauty Academy
2960 SW 8th St, Miami FL 33135
305-649-4899

La Belle Beauty School
775 W 49th St Ste 5, Hialeah FL 33012
305-558-0562

Lakeland Regional Medical Center
1324 Lakeland Hills Blvd, Lakeland FL 33805-4500
863-687-1100

Lake Technical Center
2001 Kurt St, Eustis FL 32726-6164
352-589-2250

Le Cordon Bleu College of Culinary Arts
3221 Enterprise Way, Miramar FL 33025
954-438-8882

Lee County High Tech Center North
360 Santa Barbara Blvd N, Cape Coral FL 33993
239-574-4440

Lee County High Technical Center Central
3800 Michigan Ave, Fort Myers FL 33916-2299
239-334-4544

Lincoln College of Technology
2410 Metrocentre Blvd
West Palm Beach FL 33407-3105
Don Cunningham, Vice President of Admissions
561-688-2001 Fax: 561-842-9503
Website: www.lincolncollegeoftechnology.com
E-mail: dcunningham@lincolntech.com

Lindsey Hopkins Technical Education Center
750 NW 20th St, Miami FL 33127-4618
305-324-6070

Lively Area Vocational Technical Center
3290 Capital Cir SW, Tallahassee FL 32310
850-488-2460

Lively Area Vocational Technical School
500 Appleyard Dr, Tallahassee FL 32304-2810
850-487-7555

LORAINE'S ACADEMY
1012 58th St N, Saint Petersburg FL 33710-6391
Kathryn B. Alvarez, Vice President
727-347-4247 Fax: 727-347-6491
Website: www.lorainesacademy.edu

Lorenzo Walker Institute of Technology
614 S 5th St, Immokalee FL 34142

Lorenzo Walker Institute of Technology
3702 Estey Ave, Naples FL 34104-4405
239-430-6900

Manatee Technical Institute
5603 34th St W, Bradenton FL 34210-3509
Aurea Martinez, Director of Admissions
941-751-7900

Manatee Technical Institute East Campus
5520 Lakewood Ranch Blvd, Bradenton FL 34211
Carla Brokaw, Director of Admissions
941-752-8100

Manhattan Beauty School
2317 E Fletcher Ave, Tampa FL 33612-9405
813-264-3535

Manhattan Hairstyling Academy
1906 W Platt St, Tampa FL 33606-1709
813-837-2525

Manhattan Hairstyling Academy
3244 Lithia Pinecrest #103, Valrico FL 33594
813-655-4545

Margate School of Beauty
5281 Coconut Creek Pkwy, Margate FL 33063
954-972-9630

Marion County School of Radiologic Technology
1014 SW 7th Rd, Ocala FL 34471
352-671-7200

Medical Career Center
19 W Garden St, Pensacola FL 32502-5678
850-436-8444

Medical Career Institute of South Florida
802 S Dixie Hwy, Lake Worth FL 33460
561-493-5022

Melbourne Beauty School
686 N Wickham Rd, Melbourne FL 32935
321-259-0001

Miami Ad School
955 Alton Rd, Miami Beach FL 33139-5203
Pippa Seichrist, President
305-538-3193

Miami Job Corps Center
3050 NW 183rd St, Miami Gardens FL 33056-3536
Janet Perales, Business Community Liaison
305-626-7800

Miami Lakes Educational Center
5780 NW 158th St, Hialeah FL 33014-6785
305-557-1100

MOTORCYCLE MECHANICS & MARINE MECHANICS INSTITUTES
9751 Delegates Dr, Orlando FL 32837-8351
Karen Duncan, Director of Admissions
800-342-9253 Fax: 407-240-4104
Website: www.uticorp.com
E-mail: mmi@crl.com

Established 1971. Comprehensive technical training in all aspects of motorcycle and personal watercraft repair. Endorsed and equipped by Harley-Davidson, Honda, Mercury Marine, Yamaha, Suzuki, and Kawasaki. Classes are scheduled 5-hours per day in the morning, afternoon, or evening. Accredited member school: ACCSCT. A graduate placement department is available to assist students in finding full-time employment in the motorcycle industry. Manufacturers' assist with placement through promotional campaigns to their dealership network. Housing coordinator works with local apartment complexes to find housing while in school. Job advisor will assist with local employment while in school. Financial aid available to those who qualify. VA and Agency assistance where applicable.

Mt. Sinai Medical Center
4300 Alton Rd, Miami Beach FL 33140-2800
305-674-2222

NATIONAL AVIATION ACADEMY
6225 Ulmerton Rd, Clearwater FL 33760
Karen Acker, Registrar
727-531-2080 or 800-659-2080 Fax: 727-535-8727
Website: www.naa.edu
E-mail: admissions@naa.edu

NATIONAL HEAVY EQUIPMENT OPERATOR SCHOOL
PO Box 65789, Orange Park FL 32065
Larry Lark, Director
904-272-4000 Fax: 904-272-6702
Website: www.earthmoverschool.com
E-mail: heinforequests@nationaltrainingschools.com

National School of Technology
4410 W 16th Ave Ste 52, Hialeah FL 33012-7193
305-558-9500

National School of Technology
111 NW 183rd St Ste 200, Miami FL 33169-4538
305-949-9500

National School of Technology
9020 SW 137th Ave, Miami FL 33186
305-386-9900

New Concept Massage & Beauty School
2022 SW 1st St, Miami FL 33135
305-642-3020

New Professions Technical Institute
4000 W Flagler St, Coral Gables FL 33134
Maria Z. Faughaner, Contact
305-461-2223

Normandy Beauty School of Jacksonville
5373 Lenox Ave, Jacksonville FL 32205
904-786-6250

North Florida Cosmetology Institute
2424 Allen Rd, Tallahassee FL 32312
850-878-5269

North Florida Institute
560 Wells Rd, Orange Park FL 32073-2999
904-269-7086

North Technical Education Center
7071 Garden Rd, Riviera Beach FL 33404-4906
561-881-4600

Nouvelle Institute
500 W 49th St 2nd Floor, Hialeah FL 33012
305-557-3017

Nouvelle Institute
3271 NW 7th St Ste 106, Miami FL 33125
305-643-3360

Okaloosa Applied Technical Center
1976 Lewis Turner Blvd
Fort Walton Beach FL 32547-1217
850-833-3500

Orange Technical Education Center
Mid-Florida Technical Institute
2900 W Oak Ridge Rd, Orlando FL 32809-3701
407-855-5880

Orange Technical Education Center - Orlando Tech
301 W Amelia St, Orlando FL 32801-1122
407-246-7060

Orange Technical Education Centers-Winter Park Tech
901 W Webster Ave, Winter Park FL 32789-3049
Diane Culpepper, Director
407-622-2900

Orange Technical Education Center
Westside Technical Center
955 E Story Rd, Winter Garden FL 34787-3798
407-905-2001

PC Professor
7056 Beracasa Way, Boca Raton FL 33433
561-750-7879

PC PROFESSOR
600 N Hiatus Rd Ste 105, Pembroke Pines FL 33026
954-704-4444 Fax: 954-704-2222
Website: www.pcprofessor.edu
E-mail: train@pcprofessor.com

PC Professor
6080 Okeechobee Blvd, West Palm Beach FL 33417
561-684-3333

PELICAN FLIGHT TRAINING CENTER
1601 SW 75th Ave, Pembroke Pines FL 33023
Meg Fensome, Vice President
954-966-9750 Fax: 954-985-8271
Website: www.pelican-airways.com
E-mail: pelicanftc@pelican-airways.com

PHOENIX EAST AVIATION, INC.
Daytona Beach
561 Pearl Harbor Dr
Daytona Beach FL 32114
386-258-0703 or 800-868-4359, Fax: 386-258-8609
Website: pea.com
E-mail: patc@pea.com
Spence Edwards, President
Accredited by ACCET

Established 1972. Private. Coed. Accreditation: FAA approved, FAR Part 141 and FAR Part 61. Tuition, Room and board vary. Enrollment fee: $50. Enrollment: 250 full-time, 50 part-time. Faculty: 55 Flight Instructors. Student-faculty ratio: 5:1. Degrees: FAA Pilot Certificates - Private, Commercial, Instrument, Multi CFI, CFII, MEI, ATP. Phoenix East Aviation offers a wide variety of teaching programs from professional pilot courses to airline transport pilot. In addition, Phoenix East Aviation has developed advanced programs to enhance the training of the student and meet the needs of the industry. The reputation for quality is enhanced by its Florida location, which provides an excellent environment for the training of career pilots. Students are exposed to every facet of professional training with year-round flying conditions.

Pinellas Technical Education Center
6100 154th Ave N, Clearwater FL 33760-2140
727-538-7167

Pinellas Technical Education Center
901 34th St S, Saint Petersburg FL 33711-2209
727-893-2500

Port St. Lucie Beauty Academy
7644 S US 1, Port Saint Lucie FL 34983
772-340-3540

Poynter Institute for Media Studies
801 3rd St S, Saint Petersburg FL 33701-4920
727-821-9494

The Praxis Institute
4162 W 12th Ave, Hialeah FL 33012
Rebecca Alfie, Executive Director
305-556-1424

The Praxis Institute
1850 SW 8th St, Miami FL 33135
Rebecca Alfie, Executive Director
305-642-4104

Professional Training Center
13926 SW 47th St, Miami FL 33175
Maria Rizo, Admission Director
305-220-4120

Radford M. Locklin Technical Center
5330 Berryhill Rd, Milton FL 32570-8015
850-983-5700

Radiation Therapy Services, Inc.
1419 SE 8th Terrace, Cape Coral FL 33990
Donald E. Moody, Program Director
239-772-3202

Remington College
7011 A C Skinner Pky Suite 140
Jacksonville FL 32256-6953
Bobby Johns, Director of Student Recruitment
904-296-3435

Remington College
8550 Ulmerton Rd Ste 100, Largo FL 33771
727-532-1999

Remington College, Tampa Campus
2410 E Busch Blvd, Tampa FL 33612-8410
Director of Recruitment
813-935-5700

Ridge Vocational-Technical Center
7700 State Rd 544, Winter Haven FL 33881-9518
863-419-3060

Riverside Hairstyling Academy
3530 Beach Blvd, Jacksonville FL 32207
904-398-0502

Robert Morgan Educational Center
18180 SW 122nd Ave, Miami FL 33177-2407
Antonio Martinez, Principal
305-253-9920

ROSS MEDICAL EDUCATION CENTER
6847 Taft St, Hollywood FL 33024
954-963-0043 Fax: 954-963-0211

Ross Medical Education Center
2601 S Military Trl Ste 29
West Palm Beach FL 33415-7512
561-433-1288

Sanford-Brown Inst
10255 Fortune Pkwy Ste 501
Jacksonville FL 32256-3520
904-363-6221

SANFORD BROWN INSTITUTE
1201 W Cypress Creek Rd, Fort Lauderdale FL 33309
Todd Oxendine, Director of Admissions
954-308-7400 Fax: 954-375-6900
Website: www.sbftlaud.com
E-mail: toxendine@sbftlaud.com

Sanford Brown Institute
5701 E Hillsborough Ave #1417, Tampa FL 33610
Patricia Meredith, President
813-621-0072

Sarasota County Technical Institute
4748 Beneva Rd, Sarasota FL 34233-1798
Wm. A. Storms Jr., Director
941-924-1365 ext. 325

Sarasota School of Massage Therapy
1932 Ringling Blvd, Sarasota FL 34236-5919
941-957-0577

The School of Health Careers
3190 N State Road 7, Lauderdale Lakes FL 33319
954-777-0083

Shands Jacksonville Medical Center
655 W 8th St, Jacksonville FL 32209-6511
904-244-0411

Sheridan Vocational-Technical Center
5400 Sheridan St, Hollywood FL 33021-3399
Rosa Lee, Guidance Director
754-321-5400

Southeastern School of Neuromuscular and Massage Therapy
9424 Baymeadows Rd Suite 200
Jacksonville FL 32256
904-448-9499

South Florida Institute of Technology
720 NW 27th Ave, Miami FL 33125
305-649-2050

Space Coast Health Institute
1070 S Wickham Rd, West Melbourne FL 32904
321-729-9000

Star Academy for Pet Stylists
2201 SE Indian St Unit C6, Stuart FL 34997
Curtis, Chief Administrative Officer
772-221-9330

Stenotype Institute Court Reporting School
3986 Boulevard Center Dr Bldg. 1200 #200
Jacksonville FL 32207-2819
904-246-7466

Suncoast II - The Tampa Bay School of Health
2005 Pan Am Cir Ste 100, Tampa FL 33607-2380
813-287-1099

SUNSTATE ACADEMY OF HAIR DESIGN
2525 Drew St, Clearwater FL 33765-2818
727-538-3827 Fax: 727-539-6118
Website: www.sunstate.edu
E-mail: information@sunstate.edu

SUNSTATE ACADEMY OF HAIR DESIGN
2418 Colonial Blvd, Fort Myers FL 33907-1415
Debbie Rodriguez, Campus Director
239-278-1311 Fax: 239-278-1432
Website: www.sunstate.edu
E-mail: drodriguez@sunstate.edu

Suwannee-Hamilton Technical Center
415 Pinewood Dr SW, Live Oak FL 32064-4099
Dianne Westcott, Principal
386-364-2750

Tallahassee Memorial Hospital
1300 Miccosukee Rd, Tallahassee FL 32308-5037
850-681-5385

Tampa General Hospital
School of Medical Technology
PO Box 1289, Tampa FL 33601-1289
Laura Ferguson, Education Coordinator
813-844-7985

Taylor Technical Institute
3233 S Byron Butler Pkwy, Perry FL 32348
850-838-2545

Technical Career Institute
7757 W Flagler St Ste 23, Miami FL 33144
305-863-1818

Technical Education Center - Osceola
501 Simpson Rd, Kissimmee FL 34744-4459
407-344-5080

Tom P. Haney Technical Center
3016 Highway 77, Panama City FL 32405-5004
850-747-5500

Traviss Technical Center
3225 Winter Lake Rd, Lakeland FL 33803-9709
863-499-2700

TULSA WELDING SCHOOL
3500 Southside Blvd, Jacksonville FL 32216-4634
Roger Hess, President
877-935-3529 Fax: 904-646-9956
Website: www.weldingschool.com
E-mail: tws@ionet.net

Universal Technical Institute
2202 W Taft Vineland Rd, Orlando FL 32837
321-281-9810

Washington Holmes Technical Center
757 Hoyt St, Chipley FL 32428-1618
850-638-1180

William T. McFatter Technical Center
6500 Nova Dr, Davie FL 33317-7405
954-370-8324

Withlacoochee Technical Institute
1201 W Main St, Inverness FL 34450-4696
352-726-2430

Youth Co-op Training Institute
12051 W Okeechobee Rd
Hialeah Gardens FL 33018
305-819-8855

GEORGIA

Albany Technical College
1704 S Slappey Blvd, Albany GA 31701
229-430-3500

Altamaha Technical College
1777 W Cherry St, Jesup GA 31545-0612
Karla Eubanks, Associate VP of Student Services
912-427-5800

AMERICAN PROFESSIONAL INSTITUTE
1990 Riverside Dr, Macon GA 31201-1370
Arthur Cuff, Executive Director
478-314-4444 Fax: 478-314-4449
Website: www.api.edu
E-mail: scapers@api.edu

Appalachian Technical College
100 Campus Dr, Jasper GA 30143
706-253-4500

Arnold/Padrick's University of Cosmetology
4971 Courtney Dr, Forest Park GA 30297
404-361-5641

Atlanta Job Corps Center
239 W Lake Ave NW, Atlanta GA 30314-1894
404-794-9512

Atlanta Medical Center
303 Parkway Dr NE, Atlanta GA 30312
404-265-4203

Atlanta School of Massage
2 Dunwoody Park, Atlanta GA 30338-6704
Admissions Department
770-454-7167 ext. 120

Atlanta Technical College
1560 Metropolitan Pkwy SW, Atlanta GA 30310-4499
404-756-3700

Aviation Institute of Maintenance
500 Briscoe Blvd, Lawrenceville GA 30045-6707
Gene Love, School Director
770-377-5600

Beauty College of America
1171 Main St, Forest Park GA 30297
404-361-4098

Brown College of Court Reporting & Medical Transcription
1740 Peachtree St NW, Atlanta GA 30309-2335
Lynette Eggers, President
404-876-1227

CAREER EDUCATION INSTITUTE
5675 Jimmy Carter Blvd #100, Norcross GA 30071
Myra Hadley, Executive Director
678-966-9411 Fax: 678-966-9687
Website: www.ceitraining.com
E-mail: mhadley@ceitraining.com

Central Georgia Technical College
3300 Macon Tech Dr, Macon GA 31206-3628
478-757-3501

Central Georgia Technical College
54 GA Highway 22 W, Milledgeville GA 31061

Cobb Beauty College
3096 Cherokee St, Kennesaw GA 30144
770-424-6915

Coosa Valley Technical College
1151 Highway 53 Spur SW, Calhoun GA 30701

Coosa Valley Technical College
466 Brock Rd, Rockmart GA 30153

Coosa Valley Technical Institute
1 Maurice Culberson Dr SW, Rome GA 30161
706-295-6927

The Creative Circus
812 Lambert Dr, Atlanta GA 30324
Benita Van Winkle, Director of Admission
800-728-1590 ext. 111 or 103

DeKalb Medical Center
2701 N Decatur Rd, Decatur GA 30033-5918
404-501-5206

East Central Technical College
667 Perry House Rd, Fitzgerald GA 31750-8806
229-468-2000

Empire Beauty College
1455 Pleasant Hill Rd #105, Lawrenceville GA 30044
800-575-5983

Empire Beauty School
4719 Ashford-Dunwoody Rd #205
Dunwoody GA 30338
800-575-5983

Empire Beauty School
425 Ernest Barrett Pkwy Suite H-2
Kennesaw GA 30144
800-575-5983

ETI Career Institute
9500 S Main St, Jonesboro GA 30236
770-477-2799

Everest Institute
101 Marietta St NW Suite 600, Atlanta GA 30303
Sonya Jabriel, Director of Admissions
404-525-1111

EVEREST INSTITUTE
1706 Northeast Expy, Atlanta GA 30329
Director of Admissions
404-327-8787 Fax: 404-327-8980
Website: www.everest-institute.com

Everest Institute
6431 Tara Blvd, Jonesboro GA 30236-1214
770-603-0000

Everest Institute
1600 Terrell Rd Suite G, Marietta GA 30067
770-303-7997

Fayette Beauty Academy
386 Glynn St N, Fayetteville GA 30214
770-461-4669

Flint River Technical College
1533 Highway 19 S, Thomaston GA 30286-4752
706-646-6144

Georgia Aviation Technical College
71 Airport Rd, Eastman GA 31023
Donna Rogers, Admissions Specialist
478-374-6402

Georgia Career Institute
1820 Highway 20 Ste 200, Conyers GA 30013
770-922-7653

GEORGIA DRIVING ACADEMY
1449 V F W Dr SW, Conyers GA 30012-5237
Brad Barber, President
770-918-8501 Fax: 770-918-8770
Website: www.gadrivingacademy.com
E-mail: bbarber651@aol.com

Georgia Institute of Cosmetology
3531 Atlanta Hwy, Athens GA 30606-3152
706-549-6003

Georgia Institute of Cosmetology
2803 Wrightsboro Rd, Augusta GA 30909

Georgia Medical Institute
1750 Beaver Ruin Rd Ste 500, Norcross GA 30093
770-921-1085

Griffin Technical College
501 Varsity Rd, Griffin GA 30223-2042
770-228-7366

Gwinnett College of Business
4230 Lwrncvll Hwy NW #11, Lilburn GA 30047
770-381-7200

Heart of Georgia Area Technical Institute
560 Pinehill Rd, Dublin GA 31021-1253
478-275-6590

Herzing College
3393 Peachtree Rd NE, Atlanta GA 30326
Richard Hinton, Director of Admissions
404-816-4533

High-Tech Institute
1090 Northchase Pky Ste 150, Marietta GA 30067
770-988-9877

Interactive College of Technology
5303 New Peachtree Rd, Chamblee GA 30341-2818
Troy Maloveri, Contact
770-216-2960

Interactive College of Technology
2323 Browns Bridge Rd, Gainesville GA 30504
678-450-0550

Interactive College of Technology
1580 Southlake Pkwy Ste C, Morrow GA 30260
770-960-1298

International City Beauty College
1859 Watson Blvd, Warner Robins GA 31093
478-923-0915

INTERNATIONAL SCHOOL OF SKIN AND NAILCARE
5600 Roswell Rd NE, Atlanta GA 30342-1150
Alan R. Shinall, Operations Manager
404-843-1005 Fax: 404-843-1007
Website: www.skin-nails.com
E-mail: issn@skin-nails.com

Iverson Business School
500 Pinnacle Ct, Norcross GA 30071
770-446-1333

Javelin Technical Training Center
4501 Circle 75 Ste C-3180, Atlanta GA 30339
770-859-9779

Javelin Technical Training Center
1396 Southlake Plaza Dr, Morrow GA 30260
770-968-9155

Lanier Technical College
7745 Majors Rd, Cumming GA 30041-7050
Gary Bush, Director of Student Services / Placement
770-781-6770

Le Cordon Bleu College of Culinary Arts
1957 Lakeside Pkwy Ste 515, Tucker GA 30084
770-938-4711

Medical Center
PO Box 951, Columbus GA 31902
706-571-1200

Medical Center of Central Georgia
777 Hemlock St, Macon GA 31201-2155
478-633-1234

Medix School
2108 Cobb Pkwy SE, Smyrna GA 30080-7630
Berhan Bayleygn, Director of Admissions
770-980-0002
Website: www.medixschool.com

MIDDLE GEORGIA TECHNICAL COLLEGE
80 Cohen Walker Dr, Warner Robins GA 31088-2729
Dr. Ivan Allen, President
478-988-6800 Fax: 478-988-6835
Website: www.middlegatech.edu
E-mail: aparham@middlegatech.edu

Moultrie Technical College
222 Rock House Rd, Ashburn GA 31714

Moultrie Technical College
800 Veterans Pkwy N, Moultrie GA 31788
229-891-7000

Moultrie Technical College
52 Tech Dr, Tifton GA 31794
229-391-2600

North Georgia Technical College
434 Meeks Ave, Blairsville GA 30512-2983
Admissions
706-439-6300 Fax: 706-439-6301
Website: www.northgatech.edu
E-mail: info@northgatech.edu

North Georgia Technical College
8989 Highway 17, Toccoa GA 30577
706-779-8100 Fax: 706-779-8130
Website: www.northgatech.edu
E-mail: info@northgatech.edu

North Georgia Technical College
Clarkesville Campus
PO Box 65, Clarkesville GA 30523-0002
Admissions
706-754-7700 Fax: 706-754-7777
Website: www.northgatech.edu
E-mail: info@northgatech.edu

North Metro Technical College
5198 Ross Rd SE, Acworth GA 30102-3129
Missy Cusack, Director of Admissions
770-975-4000 Fax: 770-975-4142
Website: www.northmetrotech.edu
E-mail: info@northmetrotech.edu

Ogeechee Technical College
1 Joseph E Kennedy Blvd
Statesboro GA 30458-3199
912-681-5500

Okefenokee Technical College
1701 Carswell Ave, Waycross GA 31503-4016
912-287-6584

Omnitech Institute
4319 Covington Hwy Ste 202, Decatur GA 30035
404-284-8121

Portfolio Center
125 Bennett St NW, Atlanta GA 30309-1268
Catherine Menes, Admissions Department
404-351-5055 ext. 26 Fax: 404-355-8838
Website: www.portfoliocenter.com
E-mail: catherine@portfoliocenter.com

Powder Springs Beauty College
4114 Austell Powder Springs Rd
Powder Springs GA 30127
770-439-9432

Pro Way Hair School
5684 Memorial Dr, Stone Mountain GA 30083
770-879-6673

Rising Spirit Institute of Natural Health Excellence
4536 Chamblee Dunwoody Rd Ste 250
Atlanta GA 30338-6239
770-457-2021

Rivertown School of Beauty
4747 Hamilton Rd Ste B, Columbus GA 31904-6360
706-653-9223

Roffler Moler Hairstyling College
1311 Roswell Rd, Marietta GA 30062
770-565-3285

St. Joseph's Hospital
5665 Pchtree Dunwoody Rd NE
Atlanta GA 30342-1764
404-851-7120

Sandersville Technical College
1189 Deepstep Rd, Sandersville GA 31082
478-553-2060

Savannah River College
2528 Centerwest Pkwy Bldg A, Augusta GA 30909
Dawn McCraith, Director
706-738-5046

Savannah Technical College
5717 White Bluff Rd, Savannah GA 31405-5521
912-351-6362

Southeastern Beauty School
PO Box 12483, Columbus GA 31917-2483
706-687-1054

Southeastern Beauty School
PO Box 12483, Columbus GA 31917-2483
706-687-1054

Southeastern Technical College
3001 E 1st St, Vidalia GA 30474-8817
912-538-3100

South Georgia Technical College
900 S Georgia Tech Pkwy, Americus GA 31709
229-931-2004

South Georgia Technical College
402 N Midway Rd, Cordele GA 31015
229-271-4040

Southwest Georgia Technical College
15689 US Highway 19 N, Thomasville GA 31792
229-225-5096

Swainsboro Technical College
346 Kite Rd, Swainsboro GA 30401-5700
478-289-2200

TURNER JOB CORPS CENTER
2000 Schilling Ave, Albany GA 31705-1524
Yolande Haugabook, Career Development
229-883-8500 Fax: 229-434-0383
Website: www.jobcorpsworks.org
E-mail: haugabook.yolande@jobcorps.org

Ultrasound Diagnostic School
1140 Hammond Dr NE #8-1150
Atlanta GA 30328-5338
Dr. Richard C. Farmer, Executive Director
404-248-9070

Valdosta Technical College
1001 S Elm St, Sparks GA 31647
229-549-7368

Valdosta Technical College
4089 Val Tech Rd, Valdosta GA 31602-0928
Amanda Leavy, Admissions Coordinator
229-333-2100 Fax: 229-249-4980
Website: www.valdostatech.edu
E-mail: aleavy@valdostatech.edu

West Central Technical College
997 Newnan Rd, Carrollton GA 30116-6476
770-836-6800

West Central Technical College
4600 Timber Ridge Dr, Douglasville GA 30135-1225
770-947-7200

West Central Technical College
160 Martin Luther King Dr, Newnan GA 30263
678-423-2000

West Central Technical College
176 Murphy Campus Blvd, Waco GA 30182
770-537-6000

West Georgia Technical College
303 Fort Dr, La Grange GA 30240-5901
706-845-4323

Westwood College
1100 Spring St NW Ste 102, Atlanta GA 30309
404-745-9096

Westwood College
2220 Parklake Dr NE, Atlanta GA 30345
404-962-2999

HAWAII

GOLF ACADEMY OF HAWAII
46-001 Kamehameha Hwy, Kaneohe HI 96744
Paul Zagnoni, President
800-342-7342 Fax: 480-905-8705
Website: www.sdgagolf.com
E-mail: sdga@sdgagolf.com

Hawaii Business College
33 S King St 4th Floor, Honolulu HI 96813-4316
Roger Ramos, Director of Admissions
808-524-4014

Hawaii Institute of Hair Design
71 S Hotel St, Honolulu HI 96813
808-533-6596

Hawaii Technology Institute
629 Pohukaina St, Honolulu HI 96813-5021
808-522-2700

Heald College, Honolulu
1500 Kapiolani Blvd, Honolulu HI 96814-3732
Wendy N. Nishimura, Director of Admissions
808-955-1500 or 800-940-0530 Fax: 808-955-6964
Website: www.heald.edu
E-mail: wendy_nishimura@heald.edu

Medical Assisting School of Hawaii
33 S King St Ste 223, Honolulu HI 96813-4322
808-524-3363

NEW YORK TECHNICAL INSTITUTE OF HAWAII
1375 Dillingham Blvd, Honolulu HI 96817-4438
Brian Hamilton, Principal
808-841-5827 Fax: 808-841-5829
E-mail: nytihhawaii@hawaiiantel.net

Remington College
1111 Bishop St Ste 400, Honolulu HI 96813-2811
Del McCormick, Director of Admissions
808-942-1000

Travel Institute of the Pacific
1314 S King St Ste 1164, Honolulu HI 96814-1946
808-591-2708

IDAHO

Apollo College Boise
1200 N Liberty St, Boise ID 83704-8742
208-377-8080

Career Beauty College
57 College Ave, Rexburg ID 83440
208-356-0222

The Headmasters School of Hair Design
317 Coeur D Alene Lake Dr, Coeur d Alene ID 83814
208-664-0541

The Headmasters School of Hair Design
602 Main St, Lewiston ID 83501
208-743-1512

Milan Institute
8590 W Fairview Ave, Boise ID 83704
Barb DeHaan, Director
208-672-9500

Milan Institute
1021 W Hemingway, Nampa ID 83651
Barb DeHaan, Director
208-461-0616

Mr. Juan's College of Hair Design
586 Blue Lakes Blvd N, Twin Falls ID 83301-4033
208-733-7777

Mr. Leon's School of Hair Design
205 10th St, Lewiston ID 83501-1910
Lisa Salisbury, Owner
208-743-6822

Mr. Leon's School of Hair Design
618 S Main St, Moscow ID 83843
Lisa Salisbury, Owner
208-882-2923

NORTHWEST LINEMAN COLLEGE
7600 S Meridian Rd, Meridian ID 83642
Leann Day, Manager of Marketing & Communications
208-888-4817 Fax: 208-888-4275
Website: www.lineman.com
E-mail: nlc@lineman.com

Razzle Dazzle College of Hair Design
120 Holly St, Nampa ID 83686-5102
Christina Brown, President
208-465-7660

Sage Technical Services
2845 W Seltice Way, Coeur D Alene ID 83814-8901
208-765-6346

THE SCHOOL OF HAIRSTYLING
141 E Chubbuck Rd, Chubbuck ID 83202
Linda K. Mottishaw, Director of Education
208-232-9170 Fax: 208-232-9486
Website: www.theschoolofhairstyling.com
E-mail: lindamottishaw@msn.com

ILLINOIS

∴ **ADVOCATE ILLINOIS MASONIC**
School of Radiologic Technology
836 W Wellington Ave, Chicago IL 60657
Philis George, Director
773-296-8950 Fax: 773-296-8960
Website: www.advocatehealth.com
E-mail: IMMCSRT@advocatehealth.com

Advocate Trinity Hospital
2320 E 93rd St, Chicago IL 60617-3982
773-978-2000

Alvareita's College of Cosmetology
5400 W Main St, Belleville IL 62226
618-257-9193

Alvareita's College of Cosmetology
333 S Kansas St, Edwardsville IL 62025
618-656-2593

Alvareita's College of Cosmetology
3048 Godfrey Rd, Godfrey IL 62035
618-466-8952

AMERICAN FLORAL ART SCHOOL
634 S Wabash Ave #210, Chicago IL 60605-1808
James Moretz, Owner
312-922-9328 Fax: 312-922-9329

Blessing Hospital
PO Box 7005, Quincy IL 62305-7005
217-223-8400

Brown Mackie College - Moline
1527 47th Ave, Moline IL 61265-7062
309-762-2100

Cain's Barber College
365 E 51st St, Chicago IL 60615
773-536-4441

CALC Institute of Technology
235A E Center Dr, Alton IL 62002
618-474-0616

Cameo Beauty Academy
9714 S Cicero Ave, Oak Lawn IL 60453
708-636-4660

Cannella School of Hair Design
12840 Western Ave, Blue Island IL 60406
708-388-4949

Cannella School of Hair Design
9012 S Commercial Ave, Chicago IL 60617
773-221-4700

Cannella School of Hair Design
5912 W Roosevelt Rd, Chicago IL 60644-1471
773-287-3400

Cannella School of Hair Design
4269 S Archer Ave, Chicago IL 60632
773-890-0412

Cannella School of Hair Design
4217 W North Ave, Chicago IL 60639
773-278-4477

Cannella School of Hair Design
113 W Chicago St, Elgin IL 60123-5401
847-742-6611

Cannella School of Hair Design
191 N York St, Elmhurst IL 60126
630-833-6118

Capri Garfield Ridge School of Beauty College
2653 W 63rd St, Chicago IL 60629
773-778-8161

Capri Oak Forest College of Beauty Culture
15815 Rob Roy Dr, Oak Forest IL 60452
708-687-3020

CHICAGO SCHOOL OF MASSAGE THERAPY
17 N State St Fl 5, Chicago IL 60602-3047
Shaun McFarland, Director of Admissions
312-753-7900 Fax: 312-753-7901
Website: www.csmt.com
E-mail: pjb@csmt.com

Chubb Institute
25 E Washington St, Chicago IL 60602
800-248-2237

· College of Office Technology
1520 W Division St, Chicago IL 60622
Bill Bolton, Director of Admissions
773-278-0042 Fax: 773-278-0143
Website: www.cot.edu
E-mail: bbolton@cotedu.com

Computer Systems Institute
318 W Adams, 10th Floor, Chicago IL 60606
Charles Woods, Director of Admissions
312-346-6774

Computer Systems Institute
8930 Gross Point Rd, Skokie IL 60077-1854
Tony Jacobs, Career Advisor
847-967-5030

Concept College of Cosmetology
2500 Georgetown Rd, Danville IL 61832
217-442-9329

Concept College of Cosmetology
129 N Race St, Urbana IL 61801
217-344-7550

Cook County Hospital
1825 W Harrison St, Chicago IL 60612-3701
312-633-8533

· Cooking & Hospitality Institute of Chicago
361 W Chestnut St, Chicago IL 60610-3050
Catherine Brokenshire, Contact
312-944-0884

Cosmetology & Spa Institute
700 E Terra Cotta Ave, Crystal Lake IL 60014
815-385-9663

Coyne American Institute
330 N Green St, Chicago IL 60607
800-999-5220

DuQuoin Beauty College
212 S 20th St, Mount Vernon IL 62864
Carol Porterfield, Administrative Assistant
618-542-9777

Educators of Beauty
122 Wright St, La Salle IL 61301
800-610-2300

Educators of Beauty
128 S 5th St, Rockford IL 61104
815-969-7030

Educators of Beauty
211 E 3rd St, Sterling IL 61081
815-625-0247

Edward Hines Veterans Admin. Hospital
PO Box 5000, Hines IL 60141-1489
708-216-2153

Environmental Technical Institute
13010 Division St, Blue Island IL 60406-2607
708-385-0707

Environmental Technical Institute
1101 W Thorndale Ave, Itasca IL 60143-1334
630-285-9100

Fox College
4201 W 93rd St, Oak Lawn IL 60453-1999
Edward Kapelinski Jr., Director of Admissions
708-636-7700

∴ **GRAHAM HOSPITAL**
210 W Walnut St, Canton IL 61520-2497
Mary Kepple, Coordinator of Admissions, Recruitment
309-647-5240 ext. 2347 or 309-647-4086
Fax: 309-649-5127
Website: www.grahamschoolofnursing.org
E-mail: mkepple@grahamhospital.org

Greater West Town Woodworking & Shipping & Receiving School
2021 W Fulton St #204, Chicago IL 60612
Bob Fittin, Director of Training
312-563-9570

Hairmasters Institute of Cosmetology
506 S McClun St, Bloomington IL 61701
309-828-1884

Hair Professionals Academy of Cosmetology
825B Village Quarter Rd, West Dundee IL 60118
847-622-7871

Hair Professionals Academy of Cosmetology
1145 Butterfield Rd, Wheaton IL 60187
630-653-6630

HAIR PROFESSIONALS CAREER COLLEGE
10321 S Roberts Rd, Palos Hills IL 60465-1929
Linda Grant or Stephanie Marsala, Contacts
708-430-1755 Fax: 708-430-2282
Website: www.hairpros.edu
E-mail: hairprofessional@aol.com

HAIR PROFESSIONALS CAREER COLLEGE
2245 Gateway Dr, Sycamore IL 60178-3164
Linda Grant, Admissions
815-756-3596 Fax: 815-756-8983
Website: www.hairpros.edu
E-mail: sycamorehairpros@aol.com

HAIR PROFESSIONALS SCHOOL OF COSMETOLOGY
PO Box 40, Oswego IL 60543
Rosalie Clark, Contact
630-554-2266 Fax: 630-554-9574
Website: www.hairpros.edu
E-mail: oswegohairpros@aol.com

Hanover Park College of Beauty Culture
1166 E Lake St, Hanover Park IL 60133
630-830-6560

Illinois Center for Broadcasting
55 W 22nd St Ste 240, Lombard IL 60148-4888
Patrick Johnsen, Director
630-916-1700

Illinois Institute of Art, The
350 N Orleans St Lbby 136, Chicago IL 60654-1510
312-280-3500

ILLINOIS SCHOOL OF HEALTH CAREERS
11 E Adams St Ste 200, Chicago IL 60603
Jeffrey L. Jarmes, Executive Director
312-913-1230 Fax: 312-913-1113
Website: www.ishc.edu
E-mail: jjarmes@ishc.edu

Illinois Welding School
5901 Washington St, Bartonville IL 61607
309-633-0379

· ITT Technical Institute
7040 High Grove Blvd, Burr Ridge IL 60527-7595
Leo Rodriguez, Director of Recruitment
630-455-6470

· **ITT TECHNICAL INSTITUTE**
11551 184th Pl, Orland Park IL 60467-4900
Lillian McClain, Director
708-326-3200 Fax: 708-326-3250
Website: www.itt-tech.edu
E-mail: lcclain@itt-tech.edu

John Amico's School of Hair Design
15301 Cicero Ave, Oak Forest IL 60452
708-687-7800

La' James College of Hairstyling
485 Avenue of the Cities, East Moline IL 61244
309-755-1313

LaMonts International School of Cosmetology
60 E Elm St, Canton IL 61520
309-647-4224

· Lincoln Land Community College
5250 Shepherd Rd, Springfield IL 62703-5408
217-786-2200

Lincoln Technical Institute
8317 W North Ave, Melrose Park IL 60160-1605
708-344-4700

Loyola University Medical Center
2160 S 1st Ave, Maywood IL 60153-5590
708-216-9000

McDonough District Hospital
525 E Grant St, Macomb IL 61455-3318
309-833-4101

Medical Careers Institute
116 S Michigan Ave, Chicago IL 60603-6001
312-782-9804

∴ **METHODIST COLLEGE OF NURSING**
415 St Mark Ct, Peoria IL 61603
Mary Jane Dowling, Recruitment Coordinator
309-672-5566 Fax: 309-671-2752
Website: www.methodistcollegeofnursing.com
E-mail: mjdowling@mmci.org

Midwest Technical Institute
2731 N Farmers Market Rd
Springfield IL 62707-8805
800-504-8882

· Moraine Valley Community College
10900 S 88th Ave, Palos Hills IL 60465-0937
708-974-4300

· **MORRISON INSTITUTE OF TECHNOLOGY**
701 Portland Ave, Morrison IL 61270-2959
Richard C. Parkinson, Interim Director
815-772-7218 Fax: 815-772-7584
Website: www.morrisontech.edu
E-mail: admissions@morrison.tec.il.us

Private. Coed. Accreditation: ABET. Enrollment: 140. Student-faculty ratio: 13:1. Engineering Technology Associate of Applied Science degree in Architectural, Construction, Civil, Mechanical, Drafting & Design, and Surveying Technology. AAS degree in Systems & Network Administration.

Mr. John's School of Cosmetology
1745 E Eldorado St, Decatur IL 62521
217-423-8173

Mr. John's School of Cosmetology
300 S Broadway Ave Suite 111
Urbana IL 61801-3302
217-355-1466

Mr. John's School of Cosmetology & Nails
1429 S Main St, Jacksonville IL 62650
217-243-1744

Ms. Robert's Academy of Beauty Culture
17 E Park Blvd, Villa Park IL 60181
630-941-3880

Music Center of the North Shore
300 Green Bay Rd, Winnetka IL 60093-4088
847-446-3822

Niles School of Beauty Culture
8057 N Milwaukee Ave, Niles IL 60714
847-965-8061

Northwest Community Hospital
800 W Central Rd, Arlington Heights IL 60005-2392
847-618-1000

Northwestern Memorial Hospital
School of Nuclear Medicine Technology
251 E Huron St Galter 8-128, Chicago IL 60611
312-926-6609

Oehrlein School of Cosmetology
100 Meadow Ave, East Peoria IL 61611
309-699-1561

Olympia College
6880 N Frontage Rd, Burr Ridge IL 60527
630-920-1102

Olympia College
247 S State St Ste 400, Chicago IL 60604
312-913-1616

Olympia College
9811 Woods Dr #200, Skokie IL 60077
847-470-0277

Ort Technical Institute
5440 Fargo Ave, Skokie IL 60077
Arthur Eldar, Director
847-324-5588

Pivot Point Cosmetology Research Center
144 E Lake St Ste C, Bloomingdale IL 60108
847-985-5900

PIVOT POINT INTERNATIONAL
1560 Sherman Ave Ste 700, Evanston IL 60201-4813
Lars Juhl, Director of Admissions
847-866-0500 Ext. 7422 Fax: 847-866-7184
Website: www.pivot-point.com
E-mail: admissions@pivot-point.com

Professional Choice Hair Design Academy
2719 W Jefferson St, Joliet IL 60435
815-741-8224

Pyramid Career Institute
3057 N Lincoln Ave, Chicago IL 60657-4207
773-975-9898

ROCKFORD BUSINESS COLLEGE
730 N Church St, Rockford IL 61103
815-965-8616 Fax: 815-965-0360
Website: www.rockfordbusinesscollege.edu
E-mail: info@rbcsuccess.com
Established in 1862. Accredited by ACICS. Associate Degrees and Diplomas in Business Administration, Information Technology, Medical Assisting, Medical Office Assisting, Massage Therapy, Paralegal, Pharmacy Technician and Veterinary Technician.

Rosel School of Cosmetology
2444 W Devon Ave, Chicago IL 60659
773-508-5600

ST. ANTHONY COLLEGE OF NURSING
5658 E State St, Rockford IL 61108-2468
Cheryl Delgado, Admission Representative
815-227-2141 Fax: 815-395-2275
Website: sacn.edu
E-mail: cheryldelgado@sacn.edu

St. Elizabeth Hospital
211 S 3rd St, Belleville IL 62220-1998
618-234-2120

St. Francis Hospital
355 Ridge Ave, Evanston IL 60202-3399
847-492-4000

St. Francis Medical Center
530 NE Glen Oak Ave, Peoria IL 61603-3117
309-655-2020

SAINT FRANCIS MEDICAL CENTER COLLEGE OF NURSING
511 NE Greenleaf St, Peoria IL 61603-3744
Janice Farquharson, Director of Admissions/Registrar
309-655-2596 Fax: 309-624-8973
Website: www.sfmccon.edu
E-mail: janice.farquharson@osfhealthcare.org

Sanford-Brown College
1101 Eastport Plaza Dr, Collinsville IL 62234-6108
Connie Frazier, Director of Admissions
618-344-5600
Website: www.sanford-brown.edu
E-mail: cfrazier@sbc-collinsville.com

SER Business and Technical Institute
3948 W 26th St Ste 213, Chicago IL 60623-3705
773-227-3377

SPANISH COALITION FOR JOBS
2011 W Pershing Rd, Chicago IL 60609
Henrietta Barcelo, Recruitment & Publicity Coordinator
773-247-0707 Fax: 773-247-3924
Website: www.scj-usa.org
E-mail: hbarcelo@scj-usa.org

Sparks College
131 S Morgan St, Shelbyville IL 62565-2241
217-774-5112

STEVEN PAPAGEORGE HAIR ACADEMY
5230 N Clark St, Chicago IL 60640
Steven Papageorge, President
773-561-2376 Fax: 773-561-2377
Website: www.stevenpapageorgehairacademy.com
E-mail: papageorgehair@aol.com

Swedish-American Hospital
1401 E State St, Rockford IL 61104-2298
815-968-4400

Taylor Business Institute
318 W Adams St Fl 5, Chicago IL 60606-5751
312-658-5100

Trend Setters College of Cosmetology
605 E North St, Bradley IL 60915
815-932-5049

Trend Setters College of Cosmetology
19031 Old LaGrange Rd, Mokena IL 60448
708-478-6907

Tri-County Beauty Academy
219 N State St, Litchfield IL 62056
217-324-9062

Triton College
2000 5th Ave, River Grove IL 60171-1995
Jeffery Cooks, Director, Admission Services
708-456-0300 ext. 3130 Fax: 708-583-3147
Website: www.triton.edu
E-mail: triton@triton.edu
See listing under "Community and Junior Colleges"

Undergraduate School of Cosmetology
PO Box 195, Springfield IL 62705
217-753-8990

UNIVERSAL TECHNICAL INSTITUTE
601 Regency Dr, Glendale Heights IL 60139-2208
Karl Lewandowski, School Director
630-529-2662 Fax: 630-529-7567
Website: www.uticorp.com
E-mail: karllewandowski@uticorp.com

Vatterott College
3609 N Marx Dr, Quincy IL 62301-3318
217-224-0600

Vee's School of Beauty Culture
2701 State St, East Saint Louis IL 62205
618-274-1751

Westwood College
80 River Oaks Dr Ste D-49, Calumet City IL 60409
708-832-1988

Westwood College
8501 W Higgins Rd Ste 500, Chicago IL 60631
Tash Uray, Director of Admissions
773-380-6800 Fax: 773-714-0828
Website: www.westwood.edu
E-mail: turay@westwood.edu

Westwood College
17 N State St 3rd Floor, Chicago IL 60602
312-739-0850

Westwood College
7155 Janes Ave, Woodridge IL 60517
630-434-8244

Worsham College of Mortuary Science
495 Northgate Pkwy, Wheeling IL 60090-2646
Dede L. Frank, Director of Admissions
Stephanie J. Kann, Program Director
847-808-8444

INDIANA

A Cut Above Beauty College
3810 E Southport Rd, Indianapolis IN 46237
317-781-0959

Apex School of Beauty Culture
333 Jackson St, Anderson IN 46016
765-642-7560

Aviation Institute of Maintenance
7251 W McCarty St, Indianapolis IN 46241
317-243-4519

Ball Memorial Hospital
2401 W University Ave, Muncie IN 47303-3499
765-747-3393

BROWN MACKIE COLLEGE - FORT WAYNE
3000 E Coliseum Blvd, Fort Wayne IN 46805
Daniel Summer, Campus President
260-484-4400 Fax: 260-484-2678
Website: www.brownmackie.edu

Brown Mackie College - Merrillville
1000 E 80th Pl Ste 101N, Merrillville IN 46410-5644
219-769-3321

BROWN MACKIE COLLEGE - SOUTH BEND
1030 E Jefferson Blvd, South Bend IN 46617-3123
Connie Adelman, Campus President
574-237-0774 Fax: 574-237-3585
Website: www.brownmackie.edu

College of Court Reporting
111 W 10th St Ste 111, Hobart IN 46342-5969
219-942-1459

Community Hospital of Indianapolis
1500 N Ritter Ave, Indianapolis IN 46219-3027
317-355-5529

Creative Hair Styling Academy
2549 Highway Ave, Highland IN 46322
219-838-2004

David Demuth Institute of Cosmetology
2 SW 5th St, Richmond IN 47374
765-935-7964

Don Roberts Beauty Academy
152 E US Highway 30, Schererville IN 46375
219-864-1600

Don Roberts Beauty School
1354 Lincoln Way, Valparaiso IN 46383
219-462-5189

Evansville Tri-State Beauty College
4920 Tippecanoe Dr, Evansville IN 47715
812-479-6989

Good Samaritan Hospital
520 S 7th St, Vincennes IN 47591-1098
812-885-3195

Hair Arts Academy
933 N Walnut St, Bloomington IN 47404
812-339-1117

Indiana Business College
140 E 53rd St, Anderson IN 46013-1717
765-644-7514

Indiana Business College
2222 Poshard Rd, Columbus IN 47203-1843
812-379-9000

Indiana Business College
4601 Theatre Dr, Evansville IN 47715-3901
812-476-6000

Indiana Business College
6413 N Clinton St, Fort Wayne IN 46825
260-471-7667

Indiana Business College
550 E Washington St, Indianapolis IN 46204
317-264-5656

Indiana Business College
5460 Victory Dr Ste 100, Indianapolis IN 46203-5970
317-783-5100

Indiana Business College
2 Executive Dr, Lafayette IN 47905-4859
765-447-9550

Indiana Business College
830 N Miller Ave, Marion IN 46952-2338
765-662-7497

Indiana Business College
411 W Riggin Rd, Muncie IN 47303-6413
765-288-8681

Indiana Business College
3175 S 3rd Pl, Terre Haute IN 47802-3785
812-232-4458

Indiana University School of Allied Health Sciences
1140 W Michigan St, Indianapolis IN 46202-5119
317-274-4702

Indiana Vocational Technical College
PO Box 1763, Indianapolis IN 46206-1763
317-921-4882

International Business College
7205 Shadeland Station Way
Indianapolis IN 46256-3954
317-841-6400

ITT Technical Institute
9511 Angola Ct, Indianapolis IN 46268-1119
317-875-8640

IVY TECH COMMUNITY COLLEGE - BLOOMINGTON
200 Daniels Way, Bloomington IN 47404-1511
Neil Frederick, Contact
812-332-1559 Fax: 812-330-6106
Website: www.ivytech.edu
E-mail: nfrederi@ivytech.edu

Ivy Tech Community College - North Central
220 Dean Johnson Blvd, South Bend IN 46601-3415
Pam Decker, Director of Admissions
574-289-7001 Fax: 574-236-7177
Website: www.ivytech.edu
E-mail: pdecker@ivytech.edu

Ivy Tech Community College of Indiana - East Central
4301 S Cowan Rd, Muncie IN 47302-9448
765-289-2291

Ivy Tech Community College of Indiana - Kokomo
PO Box 1373, Kokomo IN 46903-1373
765-459-0561

Ivy Tech Community College of Indiana - Lafayette
PO Box 6299, Lafayette IN 47903-6299
765-772-9100

Ivy Tech Community College of Indiana - Northeast
3800 N Anthony Blvd, Fort Wayne IN 46805-1430
260-482-9171

Ivy Tech Community College of Indiana - Northwest
1440 E 35th Ave, Gary IN 46409-1401
219-981-1111

Ivy Tech Community College of Indiana - Richmond
2325 Chester Blvd, Richmond IN 47374-1220
765-966-2656

Ivy Tech Community College of Indiana - Southeast
590 Ivy Tech Dr, Madison IN 47250
812-265-2580

Ivy Tech Community College of Indiana - Southwest
3501 N 1st Ave, Evansville IN 47710-3319
812-426-2865

Ivy Tech Community College Wabash Valley
8000 S Education Dr, Terre Haute IN 47802
812-299-1121

Kaye Beauty College
6346 E 82nd St, Indianapolis IN 46250
317-576-8000

Kaye Beauty College
1111 S 10th St, Noblesville IN 46060
317-773-6189

LAFAYETTE BEAUTY ACADEMY
833 Ferry St, Lafayette IN 47901-1149
Anita Harbolt-Keim, Financial Aid Officer
765-742-0068 Fax: 765-420-0875
Website: www.lafayettebeautyacademy.com
E-mail: anita@lafayettebeautyacademy.com

Lakeshore Medical Laboratory Training Programs
402 Franklin St, Michigan City IN 46360-3327
Gina Watson, MT (ASCP), Program Director
219-872-7032

Lincoln Technical Institute
7225 Winton Dr Bldg 128
Indianapolis IN 46268-4198
Tony Rios, Executive Director
800-554-4465

The Masters of Cosmetology College
1732 Bluffton Rd, Fort Wayne IN 46809
260-747-6667

MedTech College
6612 E 75th St Ste 300, Indianapolis IN 46250
317-845-0100

Merrillville Beauty College
48 W 67th Pl, Merrillville IN 46410
219-769-2232

OLYMPIA COLLEGE
707 E 80th Pl Ste 200, Merrillville IN 46410
James Powell, President
219-756-6811 Fax: 219-756-6812
Website: www.cci.edu
E-mail: jpowell@cci.edu

PJ's College of Cosmetology
1414 Blackiston Mill Rd, Clarksville IN 47129
812-282-0459

PJ's College of Cosmetology
1400 W Main St, Greenfield IN 46140

PJ's College of Cosmetology
5539 Madison Ave, Indianapolis IN 46227

PJ's College of Cosmetology
2006 N Walnut St, Muncie IN 47303

PJ's College of Cosmetology
2026 Stafford Rd, Plainfield IN 46168

PJ's College of Cosmetology
115 N 9th St, Richmond IN 47374
765-962-3005

· Professional Careers Institute
7302 Woodland Dr, Indianapolis IN 46278-1736
317-299-6001

Ravenscroft Beauty College
6110 Stellhorn Rd, Fort Wayne IN 46815
260-486-8868

Reppert School of Auctioneering
PO Box 190, Auburn IN 46706-0190
Dennis Kruse, President
800-968-4444

Roger's Academy of Hair Design
2903 Mount Vernon Ave, Evansville IN 47712
812-428-4027

Rudae's School of Beauty Culture
5317 Coldwater Rd, Fort Wayne IN 46825
260-483-2466

Rudae's School of Beauty Culture
208 W Jefferson St, Kokomo IN 46901
765-459-4197

∴ St. Elizabeth School of Nursing
1508 Tippecanoe St, Lafayette IN 47904-2198
Anita K. Reed, Admissions Coordinator
765-423-6400

∴ St. Francis Hospital Center
1600 Albany St, Beech Grove IN 46107-1593
317-783-8220

· Sawyer College
7833 Indianapolis Blvd, Hammond IN 46324
Chris Artim, Director
219-844-0100

· Sawyer College
3803 E Lincoln Hwy, Merrillville IN 46410-5809
Linda Yednak, Interim Director
219-947-4555

Vincennes Beauty College
12 S 2nd St, Vincennes IN 47591
812-882-1086

IOWA

Allen College
1825 Logan Ave, Waterloo IA 50703-1999
319-226-2000

American College of Hairstyling
1531 1st Ave SE, Cedar Rapids IA 52402
319-362-1488

American College of Hairstyling
603 E 6th St, Des Moines IA 50309
515-244-0971

Bill Hill's College of Cosmetology
910 Avenue G, Fort Madison IA 52627
319-372-6248

Capri College
2945 Williams Pkwy SW
Cedar Rapids IA 52404-1475
319-364-1541

Capri College
425 E 59th St, Davenport IA 52807
563-388-6642

Capri College
PO Box 873, Dubuque IA 52004
563-588-2379

College of Hair Design
722 Water St Ste 201, Waterloo IA 50703
319-232-9995

Davenport Barber-Styling College
730 E Kimberly Rd, Davenport IA 52807
563-391-9950

Dayton's School of Hair Design
315 N Main St, Burlington IA 52601
319-752-3193

Dayton's School of Hair Design
23 S 2nd St, Keokuk IA 52632
319-524-6445

EQ School of Hair Design
536 W Broadway, Council Bluffs IA 51503
712-328-2613

The Faust Institute of Cosmetology
1543 18th St Ste 15, Spirit Lake IA 51360
712-336-3518

The Faust Institute of Cosmetology
1290 Lake Ave, Storm Lake IA 50588
712-732-6571

HAMILTON TECHNICAL COLLEGE

1011 E 53rd St, Davenport IA 52807-2653
Maryanne Hamilton, President
Mark Christy, Director
563-386-3570 Fax: 563-386-6756
Website: www.hamiltontechcollege.com
E-mail: mchristy@hamiltontechcollege.com

Established 1969. Coed. Accreditation: ACCSCT. Tuition: $6,300 per year. Enrollment: 350. Staff and faculty: 35. Degrees: Diploma, Associate and Bachelor areas of study include biomedical electronics, communication electronics, computer technology, industrial electronics, medical assisting technology, and Medical/Insurance coding. Suburban campus. Student services: employment service for undergraduates, placement service for graduates and facilities for handicapped.

· Hawkeye Community College
1501 E Orange Rd, Waterloo IA 50704
Molly Quinn, Director of Admissions
800-670-4769

Iowa School of Beauty
3305 70th St, Des Moines IA 50322
515-278-9939

Iowa School of Beauty
112 Nicholas Dr, Marshalltown IA 50158
641-752-4223

Iowa School of Beauty
609 W 2nd St, Ottumwa IA 52501
641-684-6504

Iowa School of Beauty
2524 Glenn Ave, Sioux City IA 51106
712-274-9733

· Iowa Western Community College
2700 College Rd, Council Bluffs IA 51503-0567
800-432-5852

La' James College of Hairstyling
6322 University Ave, Cedar Falls IA 50613
319-277-2150

La' James College of Hairstyling
3802 E 53rd St, Davenport IA 52807
563-441-7900

La' James College of Hairstyling
2604 1st Ave S, Fort Dodge IA 50501
515-576-3119

La' James College of Hairstyling
227 E Market St, Iowa City IA 52245-2164
319-337-2109

La' James College of Hairstyling
24 2nd St NE, Mason City IA 50401
641-424-2161

La' James International College
8805 Chambery Blvd, Johnston IA 50131
515-278-2208

Professional Cosmetology Institute
309 Kitty Hawk Dr, Ames IA 50010
515-232-7250

Total Look School of Cosmetology & Massage Therapy
806 3rd St W, Cresco IA 52136
563-547-3624

· Vatterott College
6100 Thornton Ave Ste 290
Des Moines IA 50321-2405
515-309-9000

WORLD WIDE COLLEGE OF AUCTIONEERING

(formerly Reisch)
PO Box 949, Mason City IA 50402-0949
Paul C. Behr, President
800-423-5242 Fax: 641-423-3067
Website: www.worldwidecollegeofauctioneering.com
E-mail: wwca@netconx.net

KANSAS

Academy of Hair Design
115 S 5th St, Salina KS 67401
785-825-8155

American Academy of Hair Design
901 SW 37th St, Topeka KS 66611
785-267-5800

AMERICAN INSTITUTE OF BAKING

PO Box 3999, Manhattan KS 66505-3999
Ken Embers, Admissions
800-633-5137 or 785-537-4750 Fax: 785-537-1493
Website: www.aibonline.org
E-mail: kembers@aibonline.org

Established 1919. Accredited by North Central Association of Colleges & Schools. Provides training for professional bakers for all industrial and retail levels and product types and for food plant maintenance engineers. Publishes specialized distance learning courses and training materials in several formats and languages, including print, video, on-line, and CD-ROMs in English, Spanish, French, and Chinese. Several types of certification awarded. Federal financial aid and scholarships available. Some dormitory housing by arrangement.

Bryan Career College
1527 SW Fairlawn Rd, Topeka KS 66604-2411
785-272-0889

Classic College of Hair Design
1675 S Rock Rd Ste 101, Wichita KS 67207
316-681-2288

College of Hair Design
10324 Mastin St, Overland Park KS 66212
913-492-4114

Community College of Cosmetology
3602 SW Topeka Blvd, Topeka KS 66611
785-267-7701

Crum's Beauty College
512 Poyntz Ave, Manhattan KS 66502
785-776-4794

Cutting Edge Hairstyling Academy
4327 State Ave, Kansas City KS 66102
913-321-0214

Cutting Edge Hairstyling Academy
7377 Quivira Rd, Shawnee KS 66216
913-962-0076

Hays Academy of Hair Design
1214 E 27th St, Hays KS 67601
785-628-3981

KAW Area Technical School
5724 Huntoon St, Topeka KS 66604
785-273-7140

LaBaron Hairdressing Academy
8119 Robinson St, Overland Park KS 66204
913-642-0077

· North Central Kansas Technical College
PO Box 507, Beloit KS 67420-0507
785-738-2276

Northeast Kansas Technical College
1501 W Riley St, Atchison KS 66002
913-367-6204

Northwest Kansas Technical College
1209 Harrison St, Goodland KS 67735
785-899-3641

Old Town Barber & Beauty College
1207 E Douglas Ave, Wichita KS 67211
316-264-4891

PINNACLE CAREER INSTITUTE

1601 W 23rd St Ste 200, Lawrence KS 66046-2703
Lisa Allen, Admissions Representative
785-841-9640 Fax: 785-841-4854
Website: www.pcitraining.edu
E-mail: lallen@pcitraining.edu

Salina Area Vocational Technical School
2562 Centennial Rd, Salina KS 67401
785-309-3100

Sidney's Hairdressing College
916 E 4th Ave, Hutchinson KS 67501
620-662-5481

SOUTHWEST KANSAS TECHNICAL SCHOOL

PO Box 1599, Liberal KS 67905-1599
Ed Poley, Director
620-604-2900 or 800-818-3819 Fax: 620-604-2901
Website: www.swkts.com
E-mail: epoley@usd480.net

Superior School of Hairdressing
1215 E Santa Fe St, Olathe KS 66061
Joe Hancock, Owner
913-782-4004

Vatterott College
3639 N Comotara St, Wichita KS 67226
Diana Otis, Co-Director
316-634-0066

Vernon's Kansas School of Cosmetology
2531 S Seneca St, Wichita KS 67217-2803
316-265-2629

Wichita Area Technical College
324 N Emporia St, Wichita KS 67202-2512
316-833-4664

Wichita Area Technical College
301 S Grove St, Wichita KS 67211
316-677-9282

Wichita Technical Institute
2051 S Meridian Ave, Wichita KS 67213-1927
316-943-2241

Wright Business School
10975 El Monte, Overland Park KS 66211
913-385-7700

WTI Topeka Campus
3712 SW Burlingame Cir, Topeka KS 66609
785-354-4568

XENON INTERNATIONAL ACADEMY

Hair, Skin, Nails
3804 W Douglas Ave, Wichita KS 67203
Kim McIntosh, Executive Director
316-943-5516 Fax: 316-943-7244
Website: www.xenonintl.com
E-mail: kmcintosh@xenonschool.com

KENTUCKY

Barrett & Company School of Hair Design
973 Kimberly Sq, Nicholasville KY 40356
859-885-9136

· BECKFIELD COLLEGE

16 Spiral Drive, Florence KY 41042
Leah Boerger, Contact
859-371-9393 Fax: 859-371-5096
Website: www.beckfield.edu
E-mail: lboerger@beckfield.edu

Bowling Green Technical College
1845 Loop Ave, Bowling Green KY 42101-3601
270-746-7461

Bowling Green Technical College
1127 Morgantown Rd, Bowling Green KY 42101-9202
270-746-7807

Bowling Green Technical College
129 State Ave, Glasgow KY 42141
270-651-5373

Brighton Center
601 Washington Ave, Newport KY 41071
859-491-8303

· Brown Mackie College - Hopkinsville
4001 Fort Campbell Blvd
Hopkinsville KY 42240-4948
270-886-1302

· Brown Mackie College - Louisville
3605 Fern Valley Rd, Louisville KY 40219-1916
Mark Donahue, Director of Admissions
502-968-7191 Fax: 502-357-9956
Website: www.brownmackie.edu
E-mail: mdonahue@brownmackie.edu

· BROWN MACKIE COLLEGE

Northern Kentucky Campus
309 Buttermilk Pike, Fort Mitchell KY 41017-2191
Joanne Dellefield, Director of Admissions
859-341-5627 Fax: 859-341-6483
Website: www.brownmackie.edu
E-mail: jdellefield@brownmackie.edu

Carl D. Perkins Job Corps Center
478 Meadows Br, Prestonsburg KY 41653-1519
Billie S. Gipson, Deputy Director Education & Training
606-886-1037

Central Kentucky Technical College
59 Corporate Dr, Danville KY 40422
859-239-7030

Central Kentucky Technical College
1500 Bypass N, Lawrenceburg KY 40342
502-839-8488

Central Kentucky Technical College
308 Vo Tech Rd, Lexington KY 40511-2626
Dr. Michael Krause, Dean of Student Affairs
859-246-2400

Collins School of Cosmetology
111 W Chester Ave, Middlesboro KY 40965-2809
606-248-3602

Cumberland Technical College Rockcastle County
PO Box 275, Mount Vernon KY 40456-0275
606-256-4346

Daymar College
4400 Breckenridge Ln #415, Louisville KY 40218
Shawn McDaniel, Director of Admissions
502-495-1040 Fax: 502-495-1518
Website: www.daymarcollege.com

Daymar College
3361 Buckland Sq, Owensboro KY 42301-5830
Vickie McDougal Director of Admissions
800-960-4090 Fax: 270-685-4090
Website: www.daymarcollege.com

Donta School of Beauty Culture
515 W Oak St, Louisville KY 40203
502-583-1018

Draughons Junior College
2421 Industrial Dr, Bowling Green KY 42101-4071
270-843-6750

EARLE C. CLEMENTS JOB CORPS CENTER
2302 US Highway 60 E, Morganfield KY 42437-6608
Academic Coordinator
270-389-5310 Fax: 270-389-5371
Website: www.clementsjobcorps.org
E-mail: lindsey.terry@jobcorps.org

East Kentucky Beauty College
5333 N Mayo Trl, Pikeville KY 41501
606-432-3627

Elizabethtown Beauty School
308 N Miles St, Elizabethtown KY 42701
270-765-2118

Elizabethtown Technical College
620 College Street Rd, Elizabethtown KY 42701
270-766-5133

Ezell's Cosmetology School
PO Box 1431, Murray KY 42071
270-753-4723

Gateway Community & Technical College
790 Thomas More Pkwy, Edgewood KY 41017
859-442-4150

Gateway Community & Technical College
90 Campbell Dr, Highland Heights KY 41076
859-442-4108

Gateway Community & Technical College
1025 Amsterdam Rd, Park Hills KY 41011-2031
859-292-3930

Hair Design School
7285 Turfway Rd, Florence KY 41042
859-283-2690

The Hair Design School
151 Chenoweth Ln, Louisville KY 40207
502-897-9401

Hair Design School
1049 Bardstown Rd, Louisville KY 40204
502-459-8150

Hair Design School
5314 Bardstown Rd, Louisville KY 40291
502-491-0070

Hazard Community and Technical College
One Community College Dr, Hazard KY 41701-2402
Germaine Shaffer, Director of Enrollment and Diversity Services
800-246-7521 ext. 73409

Interactive College of Technology
11 Spiral Dr Ste 8, Florence KY 41042
859-282-8989

ITT Technical Institute
10509 Timberwood Cir, Louisville KY 40223-5392
Alan S. Crews, Director
502-327-7424

J & M Academy of Cosmetology
110A Brighton Park Blvd, Frankfort KY 40601
502-695-8001

Jefferson Technical College
727 W Chestnut St, Louisville KY 40203-2036
502-213-4290

Jenny Lea Academy of Cosmetology
114 N Cumberland Ave, Harlan KY 40831
606-573-4276

Jenny Lea Academy of Cosmetology
74 Parkway Plaza Loop, Whitesburg KY 41858
606-573-4276

Kaufman Beauty School
701 E High St, Lexington KY 40502
859-266-2024

Lexington Beauty College
90 Southport Dr, Lexington KY 40503
859-278-7483

Louisville Technical Institute
3901 Atkinson Square Dr, Louisville KY 40218
Kevin Woods, Director of Admissions
800-844-6528 Fax: 502-456-2341
Website: www.louisvilletech.com
E-mail: kwoods@louisvilletech.com

Mayo Technical College
513 3rd St, Paintsville KY 41240-1032
606-789-5321

Motif Beauty Academy
23 W Lexington Ave, Winchester KY 40391
859-745-5886

Mr. Jim's Beauty College
1240 Carter Rd, Owensboro KY 42301
270-684-3505

Muhlenberg Job Corps Center
3875 Highway 181 N, Greenville KY 42345
270-338-5460

National College
115 E Lexington Ave, Danville KY 40422-1517
Gloria Walls, Director of Admissions
859-236-6991 Fax: 859-236-1063
Website: www.national-college.edu
E-mail: info@national-college.edu

National College
7627 Ewing Blvd, Florence KY 41042-1812
Doug Dedeker, Director of Admissions
859-525-6510 Fax: 859-525-8961
Website: www.national-college.edu
E-mail: info@national-college.edu

National College
2376 Sir Barton Way, Lexington KY 40509
Terry Fisher, Director of Admissions
859-253-0621 Fax: 859-254-7664
Website: www.national-college.edu
E-mail: info@national-college.edu

National College
4205 Dixie Hwy, Louisville KY 40216
Ted Scharre, Director of Admissions
502-447-7634 Fax: 502-447-7665
Website: www.national-college.edu
E-mail: info@national-college.edu

National College
50 National College Blvd, Pikeville KY 41501
Janet Head, Director of Admissions
606-478-7200 Fax: 606-478-7209
Website: www.national-college.edu
E-mail: info@national-college.edu

National College
125 S Killarney Ln, Richmond KY 40475
Keeley Gadd, Director of Admissions
859-623-8956 Fax: 859-623-8956
Website: www.national-college.edu
E-mail: info@national-college.edu

Nu-Tek Academy of Beauty
153 Evans Dr, Mount Sterling KY 40353
859-498-4460

Owensboro Community & Technical College
1501 Frederica St, Owensboro KY 42301-4806
270-687-7255

Paducah Technical College
509 S 30th St, Paducah KY 42001-4181
Arnold Harris, School Relations
800-995-4438

Pathology and Cytology Laboratories
290 Big Run Rd, Lexington KY 40503-2934
859-278-9513

Pat Wilson Beauty College
326 N Main St, Henderson KY 42420
270-826-5195

PJ's College of Cosmetology
1901 Russellville Rd Ste 10, Bowling Green KY 42101
270-846-6444

PJ's College of Cosmetology
124 S Public Sq, Glasgow KY 42141
270-651-6553

Rowan Technical College
609 Viking Dr, Morehead KY 40351-8320
606-783-1538

ST. ELIZABETH MEDICAL CENTER
School of Medical Technology
1 Medical Village Dr, Edgewood KY 41017-3441
Beth Warning, MS, MT(ASCP), Program Director
859-301-2170 Fax: 859-301-5560
Website: www.stelizabeth.com
E-mail: bwarning@stelizabeth.com

School of Hair Design
3968 Park Dr, Louisville KY 40216
502-447-0111

Southeast School of Cosmetology
PO Box 493, Manchester KY 40962
606-598-7901

Southwestern College of Business
8095 Connector Dr, Florence KY 41042
859-282-9999

Spencerian College
1575 Winchester Rd, Lexington KY 40505
Victor Lamoin Adcock II, Director of Admissions
800-456-3253
E-mail: ladcock@spencerian.edu

Spencerian College
4627 Dixie Hwy, Louisville KY 40216
Kathleen Belanger, Director of Admissions
502-447-1000 Fax: 502-447-4574
Website: www.spencerian.edu
E-mail: kbelanger@spencerian.edu

TREND SETTER'S ACADEMY OF BEAUTY CULTURE
6539 W Highway 22, Crestwood KY 40014
502-241-0565
E-mail: mbinghamtsa@aol.com

TREND SETTER'S ACADEMY OF BEAUTY CULTURE
622B Westport Rd, Elizabethtown KY 42701-2848
270-765-5243
E-mail: mbinghamtsa@aol.com

TREND SETTER'S ACADEMY OF BEAUTY CULTURE
7283 Dixie Hwy, Louisville KY 40258
502-937-6816
E-mail: mbinghamtsa@aol.com

TREND SETTERS' ACADEMY OF BEAUTY CULTURE
8111 Preston Hwy, Louisville KY 40219
502-962-7710
E-mail: mbinghamtsa@aol.com

LOUISIANA

Academy of Creative Hair Design
740 Oak Harbor Blvd, Slidell LA 70458-8823
985-643-2614

Alexandria Academy of Beauty
2305 Rapides Ave, Alexandria LA 71301
318-442-7715

American School of Business
702 Professional Dr N, Shreveport LA 71105-5646
318-798-3333

ASCENSION COLLEGE
320 E Ascension St, Gonzales LA 70737-2912
Dennis Kerr, President
225-647-6609 Fax: 225-647-4849
Website: www.ascensioncollege.org
E-mail: dkerrascen@eatel.net

Aveda Institute
1355 Polders Ln, Covington LA 70433-5638
985-892-9953

Ayers Institute
3010 Knight St Ste 300, Shreveport LA 71105-2577
318-868-3000

Bastrop Beauty School #1
117 S Vine St, Bastrop LA 71220
318-281-8652

Baton Rouge School of Computers
10425 Plaza Americana Dr
Baton Rouge LA 70816-8188
225-923-2525

Blue Cliff College
100 Asma Blvd Ste 350, Lafayette LA 70508
337-269-0620

Blue Cliff College
3200 Cleary Ave, Metairie LA 70002
504-456-3141

Blue Cliff College
200 N Thomas Dr #A, Shreveport LA 71107
318-425-7941

Camelot College
2618 Wooddale Blvd #A
Baton Rouge LA 70805-7539
225-928-3005

CAMERON COLLEGE
PO Box 19288, New Orleans LA 70179-0288
Eleanor Cameron Skov, President
504-821-5881 or 800-878-5881 Fax: 504-822-3467
Website: www.cameron.com
E-mail: cameroncollege@mindspring.com

CAREER TECHNICAL COLLEGE
2319 Louisville Ave, Monroe LA 71201
Rick Nail, Director
318-323-2889 Fax: 318-324-9883
Website: www.careertc.com
E-mail: rnail@careertc.com

Cloyd's Beauty School #1
603 Natchitoches St, West Monroe LA 71291
318-322-5314

Cloyd's Beauty School #2
1311 Winnsboro Rd, Monroe LA 71202
318-322-5314

Cloyd's Beauty School #3
2514 Ferrand St, Monroe LA 71201
Tina Mathieu, Contact
318-322-5314

Cosmetology Training Center
2516 Johnston St, Lafayette LA 70503
337-237-6868

Court Reporting Institute of Louisiana
12090 S Harrells Ferry Rd Ste A
Baton Rouge LA 70816
225-292-1950

Culinary Institute of New Orleans
2100 Saint Charles Ave, New Orleans LA 70130-7100
Robert Koehl, Director
504-525-2433

DELTA COLLEGE
19231 N 6th St, Covington LA 70433
Linda DeoGracias, Director
985-892-6651 Fax: 985-892-5332
E-mail: ldeogracias@deltacollege.com

Delta College of Arts & Technology
7380 Exchange Pl, Baton Rouge LA 70806-1529
225-928-7770

Delta School of Business and Technology
517 Broad St, Lake Charles LA 70601-4334
Gary Holt, President
337-439-5765

Demmon School of Beauty
1222 Ryan St, Lake Charles LA 70601
337-439-9265

Denham Springs Beauty College
923 Florida Ave SE, Denham Springs LA 70726
225-665-6188

Diesel Driving Academy
8067 Airline Hwy, Baton Rouge LA 70815-8108
225-929-9990

Diesel Driving Academy
PO Box 36949, Shreveport LA 71133-6949
318-636-6300

D-Jay's School of Beauty Arts & Sciences
5131 Government St, Baton Rouge LA 70806
225-926-2530

Domestic Health Care Institute
4826 Jamestown Ave, Baton Rouge LA 70808-3224
225-925-5312

Eastern College of Health Vocations
201 Evans Rd Ste 400, New Orleans LA 70123
504-885-3353

Gretna Career College Training Institute
1415 Whitney Ave, Gretna LA 70053-2436
Ava Himes, Director of Admissions
504-366-5409 Fax: 504-366-1294

Guy's Shreveport Academy of Cosmetology
1141 Shreveport Barksdale Hwy
Shreveport LA 71105
318-865-5591

HERZING COLLEGE
2400 Veterans Memorial Blvd #410
Kenner LA 70062-4715
Genny Bordelon, Director of Admissions
504-733-0074 Fax: 504-733-0020
Website: www.herzing.edu
E-mail: info@nor.herzing.edu

ITI Technical College
13944 Airline Hwy, Baton Rouge LA 70817-5927
225-752-4230

ITT Technical Institute
140 James Dr E, Saint Rose LA 70087-4005
Heidi J. Munoz, Director of Recruitment
504-463-0338

John Jay Kenner Academy
2844 Tennessee Ave, Kenner LA 70062
504-467-2951

L.E. Fletcher Technical Community College
PO Box 5033, Houma LA 70361-5033
985-857-3655

Lockworks Academie of Hairdressing
2834 S Sherwood Forest Blvd
Baton Rouge LA 70816
225-295-1435

Lockworks Academie of Hairdressing
2922 Johnston St, Lafayette LA 70503
337-233-0511

Louisiana Academy of Beauty
550 E Laurel Ave, Eunice LA 70535
337-457-7627

Louisiana Technical College
Acadian Campus
1933 W Hutchinson Ave, Crowley LA 70526-3215
337-788-7521

Louisiana Technical College
Alexandria Campus
PO Box 5698, Alexandria LA 71307-5698
318-487-5439

Louisiana Technical College
Ascension Campus
9697 Airline Hwy, Sorrento LA 70778-3007
225-675-5398

Louisiana Technical College
Avoyelles Campus
508 Choupique Ln, Cottonport LA 71327
318-876-2401

Louisiana Technical College
Bastrop Campus
PO Box 1120, Bastrop LA 71221-1120
Vettye Garrett, Asst. Dean
318-283-0836

Louisiana Technical College
Baton Rouge Campus
3250 N Acadian Thruway E
Baton Rouge LA 70805-6699
225-359-9204

Louisiana Technical College
Charles B. Coreil Campus
1124 Vocational Dr, Ville Platte LA 70586-2425
337-363-2197

Louisiana Technical College
Delta-Ouachita Technical Institute
609 Vocational Pkwy, West Monroe LA 71292-0127
318-397-6100

Louisiana Technical College
Evangeline Campus
PO Box 68, Saint Martinville LA 70582
337-394-6466

Louisiana Technical College
Florida Parishes Campus
PO Box 1300, Greensburg LA 70441
225-222-4251 Fax: 225-222-6064
Website: www.ltc.edu./region.html

Louisiana Technical College
Folkes Campus
PO Box 808, Jackson LA 70748-6240
225-634-2636

Louisiana Technical College
Gulf Area Campus
PO Box 878, Abbeville LA 70511-0878
Ray E. Lavergne, Director
337-893-4984

Louisiana Technical College
Hammond Area Campus
PO Box 489, Hammond LA 70404-0489
Dr Eddy Anne Ouder, Director of Admissions

Louisiana Technical College
Huey P. Long Campus
303 S Jones St, Winnfield LA 71483-3562
318-628-3815

Louisiana Technical College
Jefferson Campus
5200 Blair Rd, Metairie LA 70001-5605
Shannon Chaisson, Director of Admissions
504-736-7072

Louisiana Technical College
Jumonville Memorial Campus
605 Hospital Rd, New Roads LA 70760-2628
Clayton Chenevert, FAO
225-342-3768

Louisiana Technical College
Lafourche Campus
1425 Tiger Dr, Thibodaux LA 70301-4336
985-447-0924

Louisiana Technical College
Lamar Salter Campus
15014 Lake Charles Hwy, Leesville LA 71446-6511
Alan P. Dunbar, Coordinator Student Services
337-537-3135

Louisiana Technical College
Mansfield Campus
PO Box 1236, Mansfield LA 71052-1236
318-872-2243

Louisiana Technical College
Morgan Smith Campus
1230 N Main St, Jennings LA 70546-4110
337-824-4811

Louisiana Technical College
Natchitoches Campus
PO Box 657, Natchitoches LA 71458-0657
318-357-3162

Louisiana Technical College
North Central Campus
PO Box 548, Farmerville LA 71241-0548
318-368-3179

Louisiana Technical College
Northeast Louisiana Campus
1710 Warren St, Winnsboro LA 71295-2940
318-435-2163

Louisiana Technical College
Northwest Louisiana Campus
PO Box 835, Minden LA 71058-0835
Charles T. Strong, Director
318-371-3035

Louisiana Technical College
Oakdale Campus
PO Box EM, Oakdale LA 71463-1708
J. Darrell Rodriguez, Dean
318-335-3944

Louisiana Technical College
River Parishes Campus
PO Box AQ, Reserve LA 70084-0555
985-536-4418

Louisiana Technical College
Ruston Campus
PO Box 1070, Ruston LA 71273
318-251-4145

Louisiana Technical College
Sabine Valley Campus
PO Box 790, Many LA 71449-3839
318-256-4101

Louisiana Technical College
Shelby M. Jackson Campus
PO Box 1465, Ferriday LA 71334
318-757-6501

Louisiana Technical College
Shreveport-Bossier Campus
PO Box 78527, Shreveport LA 71137-8527
318-676-7811

Louisiana Technical College
Sullivan Campus
1710 Sullivan Dr, Bogalusa LA 70427-5866
Brenda Simon, Contact
985-732-6640

LOUISIANA TECHNICAL COLLEGE
Tallulah Campus
132 Old Highway 65, Tallulah LA 71284
Patrick T. Murphy, Dean
318-574-4820 Fax: 318-574-1868
Website: www.ltctallulah.com
E-mail: sccox@theltc.net

Louisiana Technical College
Tallulah Campus - Margaret Surles Extension
PO Box 368, Lake Providence LA 71254
318-559-0239

Louisiana Technical College
Teche Area Campus
PO Box 11057, New Iberia LA 70562-1057
337-373-0011

Louisiana Technical College
T. H. Harris Campus
332 E South St, Opelousas LA 70570-6113
Henrietta Brown, Student Personnel Services Officer
337-948-0239

Louisiana Technical College
West Jefferson Campus
475 Manhattan Blvd, Harvey LA 70058-4441
504-361-6464

Louisiana Technical College
Westside Campus
59125 Bayou Rd, Plaquemine LA 70764-2957
225-687-6392

Louisiana Technical College
Young Memorial Campus
PO Box 2148, Morgan City LA 70381-2148
985-380-2436

Medical Training College
10525 Plaza Americana Dr
Baton Rouge LA 70816-8190
225-926-5820

Moler Beauty College
1919 Veterans Blvd #100, Kenner LA 70062
504-467-1888

Moler Beauty College
3968 Old Gentilly Rd, New Orleans LA 70126-4859
504-282-2539

Neill Institute
1301A W Saint Peter St, New Iberia LA 70560
337-365-6570

New Orleans Job Corps Center
3052 General Collins Ave Ste 2
New Orleans LA 70114-6850
504-486-0641

Ochsner School of Allied Health Sciences
1516 Jefferson Hwy, New Orleans LA 70121-2429
504-842-3267

OMEGA INSTITUTE OF COSMETOLOGY
229 S Hollywood Rd, Houma LA 70360-2716
985-876-9334 Fax: 985-876-3612
Website: www.omegainstitutes.com
E-mail: pricilla@omegainstitutes.com

Opelousas School of Cosmetology
529 E Vine St, Opelousas LA 70570
337-942-6147

Our Lady of the Lake Medical Center
5000 Hennessy Blvd, Baton Rouge LA 70808-4350
225-769-7799

Pat Goins Beauty School
3138 Louisville Ave, Monroe LA 71201
318-322-0796

Pat Goins Benton Road Beauty School
1701 Old Minden Rd Ste 36, Bossier City LA 71111
318-746-7674

Pat Goins Ruston Beauty School
213 W Alabama Ave, Ruston LA 71270
318-255-2717

Pat Goins Shreveport Beauty School
6363 Hearne Ave Ste 106, Shreveport LA 71108
318-631-1833

Pineville Beauty School
1008 Main St, Pineville LA 71360
318-445-1040

Remington College
10551 Coursey Blvd, Baton Rouge LA 70816
225-922-3990

Remington College
303 Rue Louis XIV #8, Lafayette LA 70508-5760
337-981-4010

Remington College
321 Veterans Blvd, Metairie LA 70005
504-831-8889

Ronnie & Dorman's School of Hair Design
2002 Johnston St, Lafayette LA 70503
337-232-1806

Shreveport Job Corps Center
2815 Lillian St, Shreveport LA 71109-2899
318-227-9331

South Louisiana Beauty College
300 Howard Ave, Houma LA 70363
985-873-8978

Sowela Technical Community College
PO Box 16950, Lake Charles LA 70616
Susan Simmons, Dept. Head Student Services
337-491-2688

Stage One - The Hair School
209 W College St, Lake Charles LA 70605
337-474-0533

Unitech Training Academy
3605 Ambassador Caffery Pkwy, Lafayette LA 70503
337-988-6764

Vidalia Beauty School
208 Westside Dr, Vidalia LA 71373
318-336-2377

VORTEX HELICOPTERS
PO Box 9789, New Iberia LA 70562-9789
Mary Sheeran, Vice President
228-864-7357 Fax: 228-864-5850
Website: www.vortex-helicopters.com
E-mail: vortexheli@earthlink.net

MAINE

Headhunter Institute
1041 Brighton Ave, Portland ME 04102
207-772-2591

Kennebec Valley Community College
92 Western Ave, Fairfield ME 04937-1337
Kathy Moore, Director of Admissions
207-453-5035

Landing School of Boatbuilding, Design, Systems & Composites
PO Box 1490, Kennebunkport ME 04046-1490
Jade Elliott, Director of Student Services
207-985-7976 Fax: 207-985-7942
Website: www.landingschool.edu
E-mail: jadeelliott@landingschool.edu

Maine Medical Center
School of Surgical Technology
SMTC Fort Rd, South Portland ME 04106
Maureen Bien, RN, Program Director
207-767-9589

Mr. Bernard's School of Hair Fashion
PO Box 1163, Lewiston ME 04243
207-783-7765

New England School of Communications
One College Cir, Bangor ME 04401-2929
Nelson Jewell, Director of Admissions
888-877-1876

Northern Maine Community College
33 Edgemont Dr, Presque Isle ME 04769-2016
Bill Casavant, Director of Admissions
207-768-2700

Pierre's School of Cosmetology
635 Broadway, Bangor ME 04401-3363
207-942-0039

Pierre's School of Cosmetology
30 Skyway Dr, Caribou ME 04736
207-498-6067

Pierre's School of Cosmetology
319 Marginal Way, Portland ME 04101
207-774-9413

Pierre's School of Cosmetology
913 Main St, Sanford ME 04073
207-490-1274

Pierre's School of Cosmetology
251 Kennedy Memorial Dr, Waterville ME 04901
207-873-0682

Southern Maine Community College
2 Fort Rd, South Portland ME 04106-1698
Dr. James Ortiz, President
Scott MacDonald, Director of Financial Aid
207-741-5500 Fax: 207-741-5671
Website: www.smccme.edu
E-mail: oharmon@maine.rr.com

MARYLAND

Aaron's Academy of Beauty
340 Post Office Rd, Waldorf MD 20602
301-645-3681

ABI - AccuTech Business Institute
550 Highland St Ste 100, Frederick MD 21701-5775
301-694-0211

Aesthetics Institutes of Cosmetology
15958C Shady Grove Rd, Gaithersburg MD 20877
301-330-9252

All-State Career School
2200 Broening Hwy Ste 160
Baltimore MD 21224-6628
John McCullough, School Director/Director of Extension

Campuses
410-631-1818

American Beauty Academy
2518 University Blvd W, Wheaton MD 20902
301-949-3000

Award Beauty School
26 E Antietam St, Hagerstown MD 21740
301-733-4520

Baltimore School of Massage
6401 Dogwood Rd, Baltimore MD 21207-5225
Angela DenHerder, Campus Director
410-944-8855

BALTIMORE STUDIO OF HAIR DESIGN
318 N Howard St, Baltimore MD 21201
Maxine Sisserman, Administrator
410-539-1935 Fax: 410-539-2840
Website: www.baltimorestudio.net
E-mail: baltimorestudio@netscape.net

Blades School of Hair Design
PO Box 226, California MD 20619
301-862-9797

Broadcasting Institute of Maryland
7200 Harford Rd, Baltimore MD 21234-7765
410-254-2770

Del-Mar-Va Beauty Academy
111 Milford St, Salisbury MD 21804-6952
410-742-7929

Empire Beauty School
5633 Reisterstown Rd, Baltimore MD 21215
800-575-5983

Empire Beauty School
9616 Reistertown Rd Ste 105
Owings Mills MD 21117
800-575-5983

Everest Institute
8757 Georgia Ave Ste 650, Silver Spring MD 20910
301-495-4400

Hair Academy
8435 Annapolis Rd, New Carrollton MD 20784
301-459-2509

International Beauty School
227 Archer St, Bel Air MD 21014
410-838-0845

International Beauty School
119 N Centre St, Cumberland MD 21502
301-777-3020

Lincoln Technical Institute
9325 Snowden River Pkwy
Columbia MD 21046-1544
Paul McGuirk, Executive Director
410-290-7100

MARYLAND BEAUTY ACADEMY
152 Chartley Dr, Reisterstown MD 21136
Jaime Davidov, Director
410-517-0442 Fax: 410-517-2513
Website: www.baltimorestudio.net
E-mail: mdbeautyacademy@netscape.net

MARYLAND BEAUTY ACADEMY OF ESSEX
505 Eastern Blvd, Baltimore MD 21221
Justin Sisserman, Administrator
410-686-4477 Fax: 410-686-0786
Website: www.baltimorestudio.net
E-mail: mdbeautyacademy@netscape.net

MEDIX SCHOOL
700 York Rd, Towson MD 21204-2503
Lisa Harper, Director of Admissions
410-337-5155 Fax: 410-337-5104
Website: www.medixschooltowson.edu
E-mail: admissions@medixsch.com

Montgomery Beauty School
8736 Arliss St, Silver Spring MD 20901
301-459-2509

New Creation Academy of Hair Design
3930 Bexley Pl, Suitland MD 20746
Carla Robinson, President
Brandi Smith, Contact
301-899-9100

North American Trade Schools
6901 Security Blvd Ste 16, Baltimore MD 21244
Jerry Daly, Director
410-298-4844

Robert Paul Academy of Cosmetology Arts & Sciences
1811B York Rd Ste B, Timonium MD 21093
410-252-4481

TESST College of Technology
1520 S Caton Ave, Baltimore MD 21227-1063
H. V. Leslie, President
410-644-6400

TESST College of Technology
803 Glen Eagles Ct, Towson MD 21286-2201
Dianne McRae, President
410-296-5350

TESST Technology Institute
4600 Powder Mill Rd Ste 500
Beltsville MD 20705-2675
Tina Turk, Director of Admissions
301-937-8448

Ultrasound Diagnostic School
8401 Corporate Dr Ste 500
Landover MD 20785-2287
301-588-0786

Washington Conservatory of Music
One Westmoreland Cir, Bethesda MD 20816
202-320-2770

MASSACHUSETTS

Ailano School of Aesthetics
553 Forest Ave, Brockton MA 02301
Kera Arnone, Contact
508-587-3883

Ailano School of Cosmetology
PO Box 4740, Brockton MA 02303-4740
Karen Iolli, Owner/Adm
508-583-5433

BANCROFT SCHOOL OF MASSAGE THERAPY
333 Shrewsbury St, Worcester MA 01604-4614
Judie Morin, Admissions
508-757-7923 Fax: 508-791-5930
Website: bancroftsmt.com
E-mail: jmorin@bancroftsmt.com

Bay State School of Technology
225 Turnpike St, Canton MA 02021-2358
781-828-3434

Benjamin Franklin Institute of Technology
41 Berkeley St, Boston MA 02116-6307
Norman Kraft, Dean of Enrollment
617-423-4630 ext. 121 Fax: 617-482-3706
Website: www.bfit.edu
E-mail: admissions@bfit.edu

Blaine, The Beauty Career School
Boston Campus
30 West St, Boston MA 02111-1204
Wayne Fortes, Education Director
617-266-2661

Blaine, The Beauty Career School
Corporate Office
624 Worcester Rd, Framingham MA 01702
Teresa Ferent, Scholarship Director
580-370-7447

Blaine, The Beauty Career School
Framingham Campus
624 Worcester Rd, Framingham MA 01702
Gloria Weekes, Education Director
508-370-3700

Blaine, The Beauty Career School
Hyannis Campus
18 Center St, Hyannis MA 02601-5536
Ruthann Foss, Education Director
508-771-1680

Blaine, The Beauty Career School
Lowell Campus
231 Central St, Lowell MA 01852-2214
Annette Voss, Education Director
978-459-9959

Blaine, The Beauty Career School
Malden Campus
347 Pleasant St, Malden MA 02148-8121
David Maietta, Education Director
781-397-7400

Blaine, The Beauty Career School
Waltham Campus
314 Moody St, Waltham MA 02453-5202
Maryanne Crane, Education Director
781-899-1500

Bryman Institute
1505 Commonwealth Ave, Brighton MA 02135-3605
Kathleen Devine, Director of Admissions
617-783-9955

Butera School of Art
111 Beacon St, Boston MA 02116-1597
617-536-4623

Cambridge School of Culinary Arts
2020 Massachusetts Ave
Cambridge MA 02140-2104
Lillian Ascenzo, Contact
617-354-2020

Catherine E. Hinds Institute of Esthetics
300 Wildwood Ave, Woburn MA 01801-6815
Kim St. Cyr, Director of Admissions
781-935-3344

CENTER FOR DIGITAL IMAGING ARTS AT BOSTON UNIVERSITY
282 Moody St, Waltham MA 02453
800-808-2342

C.H. McCann Technical School
70 Hodges Cross Road, North Adams MA 01247
Patricia E. Durkee, Admissions
413-663-5383

Computer-Ed Business Institute
375 Westgate Dr, Brockton MA 02301-1818
508-941-0730

Computer-Ed Business Institute
5 Middlesex Ave, Somerville MA 02145
781-933-7681

East Coast Aero Tech School
150 Hanscom Dr, Bedford MA 01730-2630
Marty Goguen, Director of Admissions
781-274-8448

E.I.N.E. Inc. Electrology Institute of N.E.Sm
Esthetics Institute of N.E.sm
1501 Main St Suite 50, Tewksbury MA 01876
Mary Evangelista, Director
800-548-6339

The Elizabeth Grady School of Esthetics
222 Boston Ave, Medford MA 02155
781-391-9380

FINE MORTUARY COLLEGE
A Private Two Year College
150 Kerry Pl, Norwood MA 02062-4766
Lyn Prendergast, Ph.D., Executive Vice President
781-762-1211 Fax: 781-762-7177
Website: www.fine-ne.com
E-mail: fine@fine-ne.com

Gibbs College of Boston
a Private Two-Year College
126 Newbury St, Boston MA 02116-2904
Ida Zecco, Vice President of Admissions
617-578-7100

Hair in Motion Beauty Academy
73 Hamilton St, Worcester MA 01604
508-756-6060

HALLMARK INSTITUTE OF PHOTOGRAPHY
PO Box 308, Turners Falls MA 01376-0308
Shelley Nicholson, Director of Enrollment Services
413-863-2478 Fax: 413-863-4118
Website: hallmark.edu
E-mail: info@hallmark.edu

Henri's School of Hair Design
PO Box 2244, Fitchburg MA 01420
978-342-6061

ITT TECHNICAL INSTITUTE
333 Boston Providence Tpke
Norwood MA 02062-3932
Tom Ryan, Director of Recruiting
800-879-TECH (8324) Fax: 781-278-0766
Website: www.itt-tech.edu
E-mail: tryan@itt-tech.edu

Established 1990. Private. Coed. Accreditation: ACICS. Enrollment: 300. Student-faculty ratio: 11:1. Associate Degrees offered: Computer Drafting & Design, Computer Electronics Technology, Computer Network Systems, Multimedia.

ITT TECHNICAL INSTITUTE
10 Forbes Rd, Woburn MA 01801
Marilyn Lamont, Contact
781-937-8324 Fax: 781-937-3402
Website: www.itt-tech.edu
E-mail: mlamont@itt-tech.edu

Jolie Hair and Beauty Academy
44 Sewall St, Ludlow MA 01056
413-589-0747

Kay Harvey Hairdressing Academy
11 Central St, West Springfield MA 01089
413-732-7117

LaBaron Hairdressing Academy
240 Liberty St, Brockton MA 02301-5570
508-583-1700

LaBaron Hairdressing Academy
281 Union St, New Bedford MA 02740
508-996-6611

LAWRENCE MEMORIAL/REGIS COLLEGE NURSING AND RADIOGRAPHY PROGRAMS
170 Governors Ave, Medford MA 02155-1643
Admissions Coordinator
781-306-6600 Fax: 781-306-6142
Website: www.lmregis.org
E-mail: admissions@lmregis.org

Learning Institute for Beauty Sciences
867 Boylston St, Boston MA 02116
617-424-6565

Learning Institute for Beauty Sciences
384 Main St, Malden MA 02148
781-324-3400

Lowell Academy Hairstyling Institute
136 Central St, Lowell MA 01852
978-453-3235

Mansfield Beauty School
200 Parkingway St, Quincy MA 02169
617-479-1090

Mansfield Beauty School
266 Bridge St, Springfield MA 01103
413-788-7575

Massachusetts School of Barbering & Mens Hairstyling
1585 Hancock St, Quincy MA 02169
617-770-4444

Mildred Elley Business School
505 East St, Pittsfield MA 01201
413-499-8618

NEWBURY COLLEGE
129 Fisher Ave, Brookline MA 02445-5796
Salvadore Liberto, Vice President of Enrollment
617-730-7000 Fax: 617-731-9618
Website: www.newbury.edu
E-mail: info@newbury.edu

Private. Coed. Accreditation: NEASC, CIDA, NCAA, IACBE. Tuition: $18,900. Room & board: $10,100. Fees: $1,100. Enrollment: 925 full-time, 300 part-time. Faculty: 75. Student-faculty ratio: 15:1. Degrees: BA, BS, Associates. Library: access to 62,000,000 volumes. 7 buildings on 12 acres. 3 miles from downtown Boston, Free academic assistance, 6 varsity women's sports, 7 varsity men's sports. wireless campus.

New England Hair Academy
110 Florence St Suite 203, Malden MA 02148-3967
781-324-6799

New England Institute of Art
10 Brookline Place, Brookline MA 02445
Deborah Brent, Director of Admissions
800-903-4425

New England School of Art & Design at Suffolk University
75 Arlington St, Boston MA 02116
John Hamel, Director of Admissions
617-573-8785
Website: www.suffolk.edu/nesad

NEW ENGLAND SCHOOL OF PHOTOGRAPHY
537 Commonwealth Ave, Boston MA 02215-2005
Arthur Levi Rainville, Academic Director
800-676-3767 Fax: 617-437-0261
Website: www.nesop.com
E-mail: info@nesop.com

North Bennet Street School
39 N Bennet St, Boston MA 02113-1914
Cynthia Stone, Executive Director
617-227-0155

Porter and Chester Institute
134 Dulong Cir, Chicopee MA 01022-1153
413-593-3339

RETS Electronic School
570 Rutherford Ave, Charlestown MA 02129
800-739-8700

Rob Roy Academy
1872 Acushnet Ave, New Bedford MA 02746
508-995-8711

Rob Roy Academy
150 Pleasant St, Worcester MA 01609
508-799-2111

Rob Roy Academy Fall River Campus
260 S Main St, Fall River MA 02721
508-672-4751

Rob Roy Academy Taunton Campus
1 School St, Taunton MA 02780
508-822-1405

Salter School
184 W Boylston St Ste 1
West Boylston MA 01583-1700
508-853-1074

Southeastern Technical Institute
250 Foundry St, South Easton MA 02375-1780
Beverly A. Pusateri, Director
508-238-1860 Fax: 508-230-1558
Website: ti.sersd.org
E-mail: bpusateri@sersd.org

Ultrasound Diagnostic School
365 Cadwell Dr, Springfield MA 01104-1739
413-739-4700

Universal Technical Institute
1 Upland Rd, Norwood MA 02062
781-948-2030

MICHIGAN

Academy of Court Reporting
1330 W 14 Mile Rd, Clawson MI 48017-1495
248-353-4880

Bayshire Beauty Academy
917 Saginaw St, Bay City MI 48708-5614
Jim Goodrow, CEO
989-894-2431

Career Quest Learning Center
5000 Northwind Dr Ste 120, East Lansing MI 48823
517-318-3330

CARNEGIE INSTITUTE
550 Stephenson Hwy Ste 100, Troy MI 48083-1159
Gloria J. McEachern, President
248-589-1078 Fax: 248-589-1631
Website: www.carnegie-institute.edu
E-mail: info@carnegie-institute.edu

Chic University of Cosmetology
1735 4 Mile Rd NE, Grand Rapids MI 49525
616-363-9853

Chic University of Cosmetology
455 Standale Plaza NW, Grand Rapids MI 49534
616-735-9680

Chic University of Cosmetology
6091 Constitution Blvd, Portage MI 49024
269-329-3333

Davenport College of Business
200 Van Buren St W, Battle Creek MI 49017-3007
269-968-6105

Davenport College of Business
220 E Kalamazoo St, Lansing MI 48933-2110
517-484-2600

David Pressley School of Cosmetology
1127 S Washington Ave, Royal Oak MI 48067
Sally Pressley, Vice President
248-548-5090

Detroit Business Institute
23077 Greenfield Rd #LL28
Southfield MI 48075-3751
Greg Mitchell, Director of Admissions
248-552-6300 Fax: 248-552-7300
Website: www.dbisouthfield.com
E-mail: info@dbisouthfield.com

Detroit Business Institute - Downriver
19100 Fort St, Riverview MI 48193
Theresa Hernandez, Director of Admissions
734-479-0660 Fax: 734-479-0738
Website: www.dbidownriver.com
E-mail: info@dbidownriver.com

Dorsey Business School
30821 Barrington St, Madison Heights MI 48071-1871
248-588-9660

Dorsey Business School
31542 Gratiot Ave, Roseville MI 48066-4555
586-296-3225

Dorsey Business School
15755 Northline Rd, Southgate MI 48195-2334
734-285-5400

Dorsey Business School
34841 Veterans Plz, Wayne MI 48184-1733
734-595-1540

Douglas J Educational Center
333 Albert Ave Ste 110, East Lansing MI 48823
517-333-9656

Educational Institute of the American Hotel & Lodging Association
2113 N High St, Lansing MI 48906
800-344-4381 ext. PSC

Everest Institute
23400 Michigan Ave Ste 200, Dearborn MI 48124
313-562-4228

Everest Institute
300 River Place Dr Ste 1000, Detroit MI 48207
313-567-5350

Everest Institute
5177 W Main St, Kalamazoo MI 49009
Susan Smith, Director of Admission
269-381-9616 Fax: 269-381-2513
Website: www.everest-institute.com
E-mail: susans@cci.edu

Everest Institute
26111 Evergreen Rd Ste 201
Southfield MI 48076-4491
248-799-9933

Fiser's College of Cosmetology
329 1/2 E Maumee St, Adrian MI 49221-2907
Pam Fiser, Owner
517-264-2199

Flint Institute of Barbering
3214 Flushing Rd, Flint MI 48504
810-232-4711

Health Enrichment Center, Inc.
204 E Nepessing St, Lapeer MI 48446
Roxanne Sears, Business Manager
810-667-9453

Hillsdale Beauty College
64 Waldron St, Hillsdale MI 49242
517-437-4670

Houghton Lake Institute of Cosmetology
PO Box 669, Houghton Lake MI 48629

Howell College of Cosmetology
1800 Dorr Rd, Howell MI 48843-8801
517-546-4155

Kent Career/Technical Center
1655 E Beltline Ave NE
Grand Rapids MI 49525-4509
616-364-8421

Lawton School
20755 Greenfield Rd Ste 300
Southfield MI 48075-5406
248-569-7787

MACOMB COMMUNITY COLLEGE
44575 Garfield Rd, Clinton Township MI 48038-1139
Information Center
586-445-7999
Website: www.macomb.edu
E-mail: answer@macomb.edu

MACOMB COMMUNITY COLLEGE
14500 E 12 Mile Rd, Warren MI 48088-3896
Information Center
586-445-7999
Website: www.macomb.edu
E-mail: answer@macomb.edu

Michigan Barber School
8988-90 Grand River, Detroit MI 48204
313-894-2300

Michigan College of Beauty
15232 1/2 S Dixie Hwy, Monroe MI 48161
734-241-8877

Michigan College of Beauty
3498 Rochester Rd, Troy MI 48083
248-528-0303

MICHIGAN COLLEGE OF BEAUTY
5620 Dixie Hwy, Waterford MI 48329
Susan Pantello, CEO
Allison Murphy, Director of Admissions
248-623-9494 Fax: 248-623-6505
Website: www.michigancollegeofbeauty.com
E-mail: mcb1@myexcel.com

Michigan Institute of Aeronautics
47884 D St, Belleville MI 48111-1181
734-483-3758

M.J. Murphy Beauty College
201 W Broadway St, Mount Pleasant MI 48858
989-772-2339

Mr. David's School of Cosmetolgy
3600 S Dort Hwy, Flint MI 48507
810-742-9010

Northwestern Technological Institute
24567 Northwestern Hwy #200
Southfield MI 48075-2412
248-358-4006

OLYMPIA CAREER TRAINING INSTITUTE
1750 Woodworth St NE
Grand Rapids MI 49525-2301
Bobbi Blok, Director of Admissions
616-364-8464 Fax: 616-364-5454
Website: www.cci.edu
E-mail: rblok@cci.edu

Ross Medical Education Center
4741 Washtenaw Ave, Ann Arbor MI 48108
734-434-7320

Ross Medical Education Center
8110 Murphy Dr, Brighton MI 48116-7402
810-227-0160

Ross Medical Education Center
1036 Gilbert St, Flint MI 48532-3527
810-230-1100

Ross Medical Education Center
2035 28th St SE Ste O, Grand Rapids MI 49508-1539
616-243-3070

Ross Medical Education Center
913 W Holmes Rd Ste 260, Lansing MI 48910-4490
517-887-0180

Ross Medical Education Center
950 W Norton Ave, Muskegon MI 49441-4169
231-730-9531

Ross Medical Education Center
3568 Pine Grove Ave, Port Huron MI 48060-1958
810-982-0454

Ross Medical Education Center
9327 Telegraph Rd, Redford MI 48239-1260
313-794-6448

Ross Medical Education Center
4054 Bay Rd, Saginaw MI 48603-1201
989-793-9800

Ross Medical Education Center
27120 Dequindre Rd, Warren MI 48092-3537
586-574-0830

School of Creative Hair Design
470 Marshall St, Coldwater MI 49036-1139
517-279-2355

SER Business and Technical Institute
9301 Michigan Ave, Detroit MI 48210-2038
313-846-2240

Sharps Academy of Hairstyling
8166 Holly Rd, Grand Blanc MI 48439
810-695-6742

Specs Howard School of Broadcast Arts
19900 W 9 Mile Rd, Southfield MI 48075-3953
Nancy Shiner, Admissions Director
248-358-9000 Fax: 248-746-9772
Website: www.specshoward.edu
E-mail: info@specshoward.edu

Taratuta School of Truck Driving
2215 Oak Industrial Dr NE
Grand Rapids MI 49505-6037
John Taratuta, President
616-742-9000

TAYLORTOWN SCHOOL OF BEAUTY
23129 Ecorse Rd, Taylor MI 48180
Cynthia Stramecky, President
313-291-2177 Fax: 313-292-9754
Website: www.beautyschool.com
E-mail: cabtylady@aol.com

Twin City Beauty College
2600 Lincoln Ave, Saint Joseph MI 49085
269-428-2900

U.P. Academy of Hair Design
1625 Sheridan Rd, Escanaba MI 49829-1828
906-786-5750

Virginia Farrell Beauty School
22925 Woodward Ave, Ferndale MI 48220
248-398-4647

Virginia Farrell Beauty School
33425 5 Mile Rd, Livonia MI 48154
734-427-3970

Virginia Farrell Beauty School
23620 Harper Ave, Saint Clair Shores MI 48080-1448
586-775-6640

Virginia Farrell Beauty School
34580 Ford Rd, Westland MI 48185
734-729-9220

West Michigan College of Barbering & Beauty
3026 Lovers Ln, Kalamazoo MI 49001
269-381-4424

Wright Beauty Academy
492 Capital Ave SW, Battle Creek MI 49015
269-964-4016

Wright Beauty Academy
6666 Lovers Ln, Portage MI 49002
269-321-8708

MINNESOTA

Academy College
1101 E 78th St, Bloomington MN 55420-1402
Tracey Schantz, Director of Admissions
952-851-0066 Fax: 952-851-0094

Alexandria Technical College
1601 Jefferson St, Alexandria MN 56308-3707
320-762-0221

American Academy of Acupuncture & Oriental Medicine
1925 County Road B2 W, Roseville MN 55113
651-631-0204

Art Institutes International Minnesota
15 S 9th St, Minneapolis MN 55402-3137
612-332-3361

Aveda Institute
400 Central Ave SE, Minneapolis MN 55414
612-378-7404

Brown College
6860 Shingle Creek Pkwy, Brooklyn Center MN 55430
763-566-2279

Brown College
1440 Northland Dr, Mendota Heights MN 55120-1004
Dawn Bravo, VP Marketing
800-6-BROWN-6

Cosmetology Careers Unlimited - Duluth
121 W Superior St, Duluth MN 55802
218-722-7484

Cosmetology Careers Unlimited - Hibbing
110 E Howard St, Hibbing MN 55746
218-263-8354

Dakota County Technical College
1300 145th St E, Rosemount MN 55068-2999
800-548-5502

Duluth Business University
4724 Mike Colalillo Dr, Duluth MN 55807-2723
Bonnie Kupczynski, Director
800-777-8406 Fax: 218-628-2127
Website: www.dbumn.edu
E-mail: info@dbumn.edu

DUNWOODY COLLEGE OF TECHNOLOGY
818 Dunwoody Blvd, Minneapolis MN 55403-1192
Dr. C. Ben Wright, President
John Slama, Vice President Enrollment Management
612-374-5800 or 800-292-4625 Fax: 612-374-4128
Website: www.dunwoody.edu

Founded in 1914. Dunwoody is a private, non-profit, technical school offering AAS degrees or diplomas in 22 programs which can be completed in two years or less. Dunwoody College of Technology is accredited by the Commission on Institutions of Higher Education of the North Central Association of Colleges and Schools (NCA). Tuition: Approx. $3,100/Qtr. Enrollment: 1,300 full-time, 1,000 part-time. Faculty: 75. Student-faculty ratio: 12:1. Two buildings on a 12 acre campus. Programs include Architectural Drafting and Estimating, Automated Systems and Robotics, Automotive Collision and Refinishing, Automotive Collision Apprenticeship Cooperative, Automotive Service Technology, Automotive Technician Apprenticeship Cooperative, Computer Networking Systems, Construction Accounting, Electrical Construction Design & Management, Electrical Construction & Maintenance, Electronics Engineering Technology, Engineering Drafting and Design Technology, Food Technology, Graphic Design, Graphics & Printing Technologies, Heating & Cooling (HVAC), Home Appliance Technician, HVAC Systems Servicing, Interior Design, Land Surveying Educational Cooperative, Machining Technology, Mechanical/Architectural Design: Heating, Ventilation & Air Conditioning, Sound, Data and Alarms Systems Design, Welding, Information Professional.

Dunwoody offers scholarships for outstanding students, women, students in selected courses, plus comprehensive financial aid. For further information, call the Admissions Office at Dunwoody.

East Metro Opportunities Industrialization Center
1919 University Ave Ste 500, Saint Paul MN 55104
Norma Fuglie, Director of Training
651-291-5088

Globe College
7166 10th St N, Oakdale MN 55128
Mike Hughes, Campus Director
651-730-5100 Fax: 651-730-5151
Website: www.globecollege.edu
E-mail: admissions@globecollege.edu

Hennepin Technical College
9000 Brooklyn Blvd, Brooklyn Park MN 55445-2320
952-995-1300

Herzing College
5700 W Broadway Ave, Minneapolis MN 55428-3597
763-535-3000

Hibbing Community College
1515 E 25th St, Hibbing MN 55746-3300
Holly Bigelow, Director of Enrollment
800-224-4HCC or 218-262-7200 Fax: 218-262-6717
Website: www.hibbing.edu
E-mail: admissions@hibbing.edu

High-Tech Institute
5100 Gamble Dr Ste 200
Saint Louis Park MN 55416-1521
Jeri Prochaska, Director of Admissions
763-560-9700 Fax: 952-545-6149
Website: www.hightechinstitute.edu
E-mail: jprochaska@hightechinstitute.edu

Minneapolis Business College
1711 County Road B W, Roseville MN 55113-4036
651-636-7406

Minneapolis Community and Technical College
1501 Hennepin Ave, Minneapolis MN 55403-1779
Dena Russell, Director of Admissions
612-659-6282

Minnesota School of Business
5910 Shingle Creek Pkwy #200
Brooklyn Center MN 55430-2319
763-566-7777

Minnesota School of Business
1401 W 76th St Ste 500, Richfield MN 55423-3846
612-861-2000

Minnesota State College - Southeast Technical
Red Wing Campus
308 Pioneer Rd, Red Wing MN 55066
Al DuCett, Director of Admissions
877-853-8324 Fax: 507-453-2715
Website: www.southeastmn.edu
E-mail: aducett@southeastmn.edu
70+ degrees, diplomas & certificates (15+ online) in Business & Office Careers, Musical Instrument Repair, Physical Health, Transportation, Technology, and Trades.

Minnesota State College - Southeast Technical
Winona Campus
PO Box 409, 1250 Homer Rd, Winona MN 55987
Al DuCett, Director of Admissions
877-853-8324 Fax: 507-453-2715
Website: www.southeastmn.edu
E-mail: aducett@southeastmn.edu
70+ degrees, diplomas & certificates (15+ online) in Business & Office Careers, Musical Instrument Repair, Physical Health, Transportation, Technology, and Trades.

Minnesota State Community & Technical College
900 Highway 34 E, Detroit Lakes MN 56501-2698
Dale Westley, Director of Admissions
800-492-4836

Minnesota State Community & Technical College
PO Box 566, Wadena MN 56482-0566
Paul Drange, Director of Admissions
800-247-2007

Minnesota State Community and Technical College
1900 28th Ave S, Moorhead MN 56560-4899
Laurie McKeever, Director of Admissions
800-426-5603

Minnesota West Community and Technical College
Canby Campus
1011 1st St W, Canby MN 56220-9494
Jodi Weber, Contact
800-658-2535

Minnesota West Community and Technical College
Granite Falls Campus
1593 11th Ave, Granite Falls MN 56241-1061
Becky Weber, Contact
800-657-3247

Minnesota West Community and Technical College
Jackson Campus
PO Box 269, Jackson MN 56143-0269
Lynne Liepold, Contact
800-658-2522

Minnesota West Community and Technical College
Pipestone Campus
1314 N Hiawatha Ave, Pipestone MN 56164-2282
Laurel Berg, Contact
800-658-2330

Minnesota West Community and Technical College
Worthington Campus
1450 Collegeway, Worthington MN 56187-3024
Mitz Diemer, Contact
800-657-3966

Model College of Hair Design
201 8th Ave S, Saint Cloud MN 56301-4251
320-253-4222

NTI-School of CAD Technology
950 Blue Gentian Rd Ste 500, Saint Paul MN 55121
800-443-4223

Oliver Thein Beauty College
150 Cobblestone Ln, Burnsville MN 55337
612-435-3882

Rasmussen College
3500 Federal Dr, Eagan MN 55122-1346
651-687-9000

Rasmussen College
7905 Golden Triangle Dr Ste 100
Eden Prairie MN 55344-7220
952-545-2000

Rasmussen College
501 Holly Ln, Mankato MN 56001-6803
507-625-6556

RASMUSSEN COLLEGE - ST. CLOUD
226 Park Ave S, Saint Cloud MN 56301-3713
Admissions
320-251-5600 or 800-852-0460 Fax: 320-251-3702
Website: www.rasmussen.edu
E-mail: stcloud@rasmussen.edu

Regency Beauty Academy
40 County Road 10 NE, Blaine MN 55434
763-784-9102

Ridgewater College-Hutchinson Campus
2 Century Ave SE, Hutchinson MN 55350-3100
Dawn Bjork, Counselor
800-722-1151 Fax: 320-234-8506
Website: www.ridgewater.edu
E-mail: dawn.bjork@ridgewater.edu

Ridgewater College-Willmar Campus
PO Box 1097, Willmar MN 56201-1097
Sally Kerfeld, Director of Admissions
800-722-1151 Fax: 320-222-5212
Website: www.ridgewater.edu
E-mail: sally.kerfeld@ridgewater.edu

Rita's Moorhead Beauty College
1024 Center Ave, Moorhead MN 56560-2019
218-236-7201

Riverland Community College
1900 8th Ave NW, Austin MN 55912-1400
Dani Heiny, Director of Admissions
800-247-5039

Riverland Community College
Albert Lea Campus
2200 Riverland Dr, Albert Lea MN 56007
Dani Heiny, Director of Admissions
800-333-2584

Riverland Technical College
1225 3rd St SW, Faribault MN 55021-5720
800-422-0391

Rochester Community & Technical College
1926 Collegeview Rd E, Rochester MN 55904-8201
800-247-1296

St. Cloud Regency Beauty Academy
110 2nd St S, Waite Park MN 56387
320-251-0500

St. Cloud Technical College
1540 Northway Dr, Saint Cloud MN 56303-1240
Jodi Elness, Director of Enrollment Management
800-222-1009 Fax: 320-308-5981
Website: www.sctc.edu
E-mail: jelness@sctc.edu

Scot Lewis Beauty School
4124 Lancaster Ln N, Plymouth MN 55441
763-551-0562

Scot Lewis School
1905 Suburban Ave, Saint Paul MN 55119
651-209-6930

Scot Lewis School of Cosmetology
9749 Lyndale Ave S, Bloomington MN 55420
Carol Olinger, Director of Admissions
952-881-8662

Sr. Rosalind Gefre Schools of Massage
416 S Front St, Mankato MN 56001
Mary Pegram, Director of Admissions
507-344-0220 Fax: 507-344-0204
Website: www.sisterrosalind.org
E-mail: mankatocampus@sisterrosalind.org

Sr. Rosalind Gefre Schools of Massage
300 Elton Hills Dr NW, Rochester MN 55901
Steve King, Director of Admissions
507-286-8608 Fax: 507-282-2893
Website: www.sisterrosalind.org
E-mail: rochestercampus@sisterrosalind.org

Sr. Rosalind Gefre Schools of Massage
1007 Industrial Dr S, Sauk Rapids MN 56379
Anita Figallo, Director of Admissions
320-259-6185 Fax: 320-259-6173
Website: www.sisterrosalind.org
E-mail: saukrapidscampus@sisterrosalind.org

Sr. Rosalind Gefre Schools of Massage
149 Thompson Ave Ste 150
West Saint Paul MN 55118
Jen Maudel, Director of Admissions
651-554-3010 Fax: 651-554-7608
Website: www.sisterrosalind.org
E-mail: stpaulcampus@sisterrosalind.org

Summit Academy OIC
935 Olson Memorial Hwy
Minneapolis MN 55405-1359
612-377-0150

MISSISSIPPI

Academy of Hair Design #1
2003B Commerce St, Grenada MS 38901
662-226-2462

Academy of Hair Design #3
1815 Terry Rd, Jackson MS 39204
601-372-9800

Academy of Hair Design #4
3167 Highway 80 E, Pearl MS 39208-3503
601-939-4441

Academy of Hair Design #6
5912 US Highway 49, Hattiesburg MS 39401
601-583-1290

Academy of Hair Design #7
215 Highway 35 N, Carthage MS 39051
601-267-8031

Antonelli College
1500 N 31st Ave, Hattiesburg MS 39401-3056
601-583-4100

Antonelli College
2323 Lakeland Dr, Jackson MS 39232-9514
601-362-9991

Batesville Job Corps Center
821 Highway 51 S, Batesville MS 38606-2545
Fletcher Harris, Center Director
662-563-4656

Blue Cliff College
12251 Bernard Pkwy, Gulfport MS 39503
228-896-9727

Chris' Beauty College
1265 Pass Rd, Gulfport MS 39501
228-864-2920

Creations College of Cosmetology
PO Box 2635, Tupelo MS 38803-2635
662-844-9264

Day Spa Career College
3900 Bienville Blvd, Ocean Springs MS 39564
228-875-4809

Delta Beauty College
697 Delta Pl, Greenville MS 38701
662-332-0587

Final Touch Beauty School
5700 N Hills St, Meridian MS 39307
601-485-7733

Foster's Cosmetology College
PO Box 66, Ripley MS 38663
662-837-9334

Gibson's Barber & Beauty College
PO Box 990, West Point MS 39773
662-494-5444

Gulfport Job Corps Center
3300 20th St, Gulfport MS 39501-4311
Samuel Kolapo, Center Director
228-864-9691

ICS the Wright Beauty College
2077 Highway 72 E Annex, Corinth MS 38834
662-287-0944

J & J Hair Design College
116 E Franklin St, Carthage MS 39051-3716
601-267-3678

J & J Hair Design College
562 W Main St Ste B, Senatobia MS 38668
662-562-8010

Magnolia College of Cosmetology
4725 I-55 N, Jackson MS 39206
601-362-6940

Mississippi College of Beauty Culture
732 Sawmill Rd, Laurel MS 39440
601-428-7127

Mississippi Job Corps Center
PO Box 817, Crystal Springs MS 39059-0817
Rowan Torrey, Center Director
601-892-3348

Traxler School of Hair
2845 Suncrest Dr, Jackson MS 39212
601-371-3253

VIRGINIA COLLEGE
5360 I 55 N, Jackson MS 39211
601-977-0960 Fax: 601-956-4325

MISSOURI

Abbott Academy of Cosmetology Arts & Sciences
2101 Parkway Dr, Saint Peters MO 63376
636-447-0100

ALLIED COLLEGE - NORTH
13723 Riverport Dr Ste 103
Maryland Heights MO 63043
Heidi Wind, Campus President
866-501-1291 Fax: 314-739-5133
Website: www.alliedcollege.edu

Allied College - South
645 Gravois Bluffs Blvd, Fenton MO 63026
866-502-2627

American College of Hair Design
125 Duke Rd, Sedalia MO 65301
660-827-3295

Aviation Institute of Maintenance
3130 Terrace St, Kansas City MO 64111
816-753-9920

Bryan College
237 S Florence Ave, Springfield MO 65806
Jamie Carpenter, Executive Director
417-862-5700

Cape Girardeau Career & Technology Center
1080 S Silver Springs Rd
Cape Girardeau MO 63703-7511
573-334-0826

Central College of Cosmetology
PO Box 463, Waynesville MO 65583
573-336-3888

CHILLICOTHE BEAUTY ACADEMY
505 Elm St, Chillicothe MO 64601
Annette Robinson, Financial Aid Advisor
660-646-4198 Fax: 660-646-9983
Website: www.chillicothebeautyacademy.com
E-mail: cbainc@greenhills.net

Class Act I School of Cosmetology
512 Main St, Joplin MO 64801
417-781-7070

Columbia Beauty Academy
503 E Nifong Blvd, Columbia MO 65201
573-445-6611

Elaine Steven Beauty College
10420 W Florissant Ave, Saint Louis MO 63136
314-868-8196

EVEREST COLLEGE
1010 W Sunshine St, Springfield MO 65807-2446
Melanie Exter, Contact
417-864-7220 or 800-475-2699 Fax: 417-866-3335
Website: www.everest-college.com
E-mail: mexter@cci.edu

FRANKLIN TECHNOLOGY - MSSU
3950 Newman Rd, Joplin MO 64801
Dr. Richard Saporito, Director of Postsecondary Education
417-659-4400 Fax: 414-659-4408
Website: www.ftcjoplin.com
E-mail: saporito-r@mssu.edu

Grabber School of Hair Design
14557 Manchester Rd, Ballwin MO 63011-3960
636-227-4440

Hannibal Area Vocational Technical School
4550 McMasters Ave, Hannibal MO 63401-2285
Dr. Harold D. Ward, Director
573-221-4430

HERITAGE COLLEGE
1200 E 104th St Ste 300, Kansas City MO 64131
Larry Cartmill, Director
816-942-5474 Fax: 816-942-5405
Website: www.heritage-education.com
E-mail: info@heritage-education.com
Accredited Member School: ACCSCT. Providing quality education in Therapeutic Massage, Personal Training, X-Ray Medical Technician and Pharmacy Technician. Financial aid available to those who qualify.

Hickey College
940 Westport Plz, Saint Louis MO 63146-3127
Christopher A. Gearin, President
800-777-1544 or 314-434-2212 Fax: 314-434-1974
Website: www.hickeycollege.edu
E-mail: admin@hickeycollege.edu

High-Tech Institute - Kansas City
9001 State Line Rd, Kansas City MO 64114
816-444-4300

House of Heavilin Beauty College
2000 SW State Route 7, Blue Springs MO 64014
816-229-9000

House of Heavilin Beauty College
12020 Blue Ridge Ext, Grandview MO 64030
Amber Reed, Contact
816-767-8000

HOUSE OF HEAVILIN BEAUTY COLLEGE
5720 Troost Ave, Kansas City MO 64110-2826
Jerry Heavilin, President
816-523-2471 Fax: 816-523-6445
Website: www.kchair.edu
E-mail: sheavilin@kc-hair.com

IHM Health Studies Center
2500 Abbott Pl, Saint Louis MO 63143-2636
Taz A. Meyer, Director
314-768-1234

Independence College of Cosmetology
815 W 23rd St, Independence MO 64055
816-252-4247

Jerry's School of Hairstyling
1001 Royal Birkdale Dr, Columbia MO 65203
573-449-7527

Lewis & Clark Career Center
2400 Zumbehl Rd, Saint Charles MO 63301-1131
Midge Haas, Counselor
636-443-4950

Linn State Technical College
1 Technology Dr, Linn MO 65051-9606
Becky Dunn, Admissions
800-743-8324 Fax: 573-897-5026
Website: www.linnstate.edu
E-mail: admissions@linnstate.edu

Lutheran School of Nursing
3547 S Jefferson Ave, Saint Louis MO 63118-3909
Mary Debatin-Merod, Admissions Assistant
314-577-5850

Martinez School of Cosmetology
248 1/2 E Broadway St, Excelsior Springs MO 64024
816-630-3900

Merrell University of Beauty Arts & Science
1101R Southwest Boulevard
Jefferson City MO 65109
573-635-4433

Metro Business College
1732 N Kingshighway St
Cape Girardeau MO 63701-2122
573-334-9181

Metro Business College
1407 Southwest Blvd, Jefferson City MO 65109-5508
573-635-6600

Metro Business College
1202 E State Route 72, Rolla MO 65401-3938
800-978-7705

Midwest Institute for Medical Assistants
10910 Manchester Rd, Saint Louis MO 63122-1242
314-965-8363

Missouri Beauty Academy
222 E Columbia St, Farmington MO 63640
573-756-2730

Missouri College
10121 Manchester Rd, Saint Louis MO 63122-1525
Erin Cunningham, Director of Admissions
314-821-7700

Missouri College of Cosmetology North
2555 W Kearney St, Springfield MO 65803
417-866-2786

Missouri School of Barbering & Hairstyling
1125 N US Highway 67, Florissant MO 63031
314-839-0310

Missouri Tech
1167 Corporate Lake Dr, Saint Louis MO 63132
314-569-3600

NATIONAL ACADEMY OF BEAUTY ARTS
157 Concord Plz, Saint Louis MO 63128
Mary, Contact
314-842-3616 Fax: 314-842-9396
Website: www.nabacollege.com
E-mail: nationalacademy@sbcglobal.net

Neosho Beauty College
116 N Wood St, Neosho MO 64850
417-451-7216

New Dimensions School of Hair Design
705 Illinois Ave Ste 12, Joplin MO 64801
417-782-2875

Nichols Career Center
605 Union St, Jefferson City MO 65101-2814
573-659-3100

Paris II Educational Center
6840 N Oak Trafficway, Gladstone MO 64118
816-468-6666

Parks College of Engineering and Aviation of Saint Louis University
221 N Grand Blvd #119, Saint Louis MO 63103-2006
Edwin Harris, Ph.D., Dean of Admission
314-977-2500

Patricia Stevens College
330 N 4th St Ste 306, Saint Louis MO 63102-2008
Cynthia Musterman, J.D., President
800-871-0949

PATSY & ROB'S ACADEMY OF BEAUTY
18 Northwest Plz, Saint Ann MO 63074
Rob Bruner, President
314-298-8808 Fax: 314-298-3901
Website: www.praob.edu
E-mail: abeauty@praob.edu

Pinnacle Career Institute
1001 101st Ter Ste 325, Kansas City MO 64131-3367
800-614-0900

Professional Massage Training Center
229 E Commercial, Springfield MO 65803
417-863-7682

Ranken Technical College
4431 Finney Ave, Saint Louis MO 63113-2898
Admissions Office
314-371-0233 Fax: 314-371-0241
Website: www.ranken.edu
E-mail: admissions@ranken.edu

St. Louis College of Health Careers
1297 N Highway Dr, Fenton MO 63026-1909
636-529-0000

St. Louis College of Health Careers
909 S Taylor Ave, Saint Louis MO 63110-1511
314-652-0300

St. Louis Hair Academy
3701 Kossuth Ave, Saint Louis MO 63107
314-533-3125

Salem College of Hairstyling
1051 Kingshighway St Ste 1, Rolla MO 65401
573-368-3136

Sanford-Brown College
1345 Smizer Mill Rd, Fenton MO 63026
Kevin Frank, Director of HS Admissions
636-651-1600

Sanford-Brown College
75 Village Square Shop Ctr, Hazelwood MO 63042
314-731-1101

Sanford-Brown College
100 Richmond Center Blvd
Saint Peters MO 63376-5950
888-793-2433

Southeast Missouri Hospital
College of Nursing and Health Sciences
2001 William St #2, Cape Girardeau MO 63703-5815
Don Pugh, Registrar
573-334-6825

Stage One, The Hair Academy
547 County Highway, Benton MO 63736
573-335-5078

Vatterott College
809 Illinois Ave, Joplin MO 64801
417-781-5633

Vatterott College
8955 E 38th Terr, Kansas City MO 64129-1692
816-861-1000

Vatterott College
3925 Industrial Dr, Saint Ann MO 63074-1807
Shalisa Perry, Director of Admissions
800-345-6018

Vatterott College
3131 Frederick Ave, Saint Joseph MO 64506-2911
Sandra Wisdom, Director of Admissions
816-364-5399

Vatterott College
12970 Maurer Industrial Dr, Saint Louis MO 63127
Sherri Bremer, Director of Admissions
314-843-4200

Vatterott College
3850 S Campbell Ave, Springfield MO 65807-5340
417-831-8116

Wichita Technical Institute
1531 E 32nd St, Joplin MO 64804
417-206-9115

MONTANA

ACADEMY OF COSMETOLOGY, INC.
133 W Mendenhall St, Bozeman MT 59715
Verna Dupuis, Owner
406-587-1265 Fax: 406-585-7357
Website: www.academycosmetology.com
E-mail: vernadupuis@cs.com

Butte Academy of Beauty Culture
303 W Park St, Butte MT 59701
406-723-8565

College of Coiffure Art
1423 Wyoming Ave, Billings MT 59102
406-656-9114

Dahl's College of Beauty
718 Central Ave, Great Falls MT 59401
406-454-3453

Modern Beauty School
2700 Paxson St Ste G, Missoula MT 59801
406-721-1800

· Montana State University
Billings College of Technology
3803 Central Ave, Billings MT 59102-4307
R. J. Carr, Dean
406-656-4445

· Montana Tech College of Technology
25 Basin Creek Rd, Butte MT 59701-9704
406-496-3701

SAGE TECHNICAL COMMERICAL DRIVING SCHOOL
3044 Hesper Rd, Billings MT 59102-6732
Carmella or Lisa, Contacts
800-545-4546 Fax: 406-652-3129
Website: www.sageschools.com
E-mail: billings@sageschools.com

NEBRASKA

Bahner College of Hairstyling
1660 N Grant St, Fremont NE 68025
402-721-6500

∴ Bryan LGH College of Health Science School of Nursing
5035 Everett St, Lincoln NE 68506
Verla Youngquist, Recruiter
402-481-8697

Capitol School of Hairstyling - West
2819 S 125th Ave Ste 268, Omaha NE 68144
402-333-3329

College of Hair Design
304 S 11th St, Lincoln NE 68508
402-477-4040

· The Creative Center
10850 Emmet St, Omaha NE 68164-2911
Kim Guyer, Executive Director
402-898-1000

· Hamilton College - Lincoln Campus
PO Box 82826, Lincoln NE 68501-2826
Todd Lardenoit, Executive Director
402-474-5315

Joseph's College of Beauty
618 Court St, Beatrice NE 68310
402-223-3588

Joseph's College of Beauty
305 W 3rd St, Grand Island NE 68801
308-381-8848

Joseph's College of Beauty
828 W 2nd St, Hastings NE 68901
402-463-1357

Joseph's College of Beauty
2637 O St, Lincoln NE 68510
402-435-2333

Joseph's College of Beauty
202 W Madison Ave, Norfolk NE 68701
402-371-3358

Joseph's of Kearney School of Hair Design
2213 Central Ave, Kearney NE 68847
308-234-6594

· Myotherapy Institute
6020 S 58th St, Lincoln NE 68516
402-421-7410

North Platte Beauty Academy
107 W 6th St, North Platte NE 69101
308-532-4664

OMAHA SCHOOL OF MASSAGE THERAPY
9748 Park Dr, Omaha NE 68127-5002
Kym Kessler, Admission Advisor
402-331-3694 Fax: 402-331-0280
Website: www.osmt.com
E-mail: info@osmt.com

· Vatterott College
11818 I St, Omaha NE 68137
Todd S. Clark, Director
402-891-9411

Xenon International School of Hair Design
8516 Park Dr, Omaha NE 68127
402-393-2933

NEVADA

ACADEMY OF HAIR DESIGN
5191 W Charleston Blvd, Las Vegas NV 89102
Sandy Dunham, President
702-878-1185 Fax: 702-878-7289
Website: ahdvegas.com
E-mail: sdunham@ahd.lvcoxmail.com

Aces-Full Academy for Casino Dealers
557 E Sahara Ave Ste 220
Las Vegas NV 89104-2733
Douglas Mitchell, General Manager
702-369-1194

American Institute of Technology
4020 E Lone Mountain Rd
North Las Vegas NV 89081-2700
702-644-1234

· **CAREER COLLEGE OF NORTHERN NEVADA**
1195-A Corporate Blvd, Reno NV 89502-2331
Nathan Clark, Director
775-856-2266 Fax: 775-856-0935
Website: www.ccnn.edu
E-mail: lgoldhammer@ccnn4u.com
Established 1984. Private. Coed. Accreditation: Accrediting Commission of Career Schools and Colleges of Technology. Degrees offered: Electronic Engineering Technology, Computerized Business Management, Medical Assisting, Paralegal. Diploma programs available in Legal Office Administrator, Medical Assisting, Medical Insurance, Coding and Billing, Data Processing. Morning, afternoon, evening and weekend classes available. High school Diploma or GED required for admission.

Carson City Beauty Academy
2531 N Carson St, Carson City NV 89706
775-885-9853

· Heritage College
3315 Spring Mountain Rd, Las Vegas NV 89102
Mimi Ritenour, Director of Admissions
702-368-2338

· High-Tech Institute
2320 S Rancho Dr, Las Vegas NV 89102
702-385-6700

· ITT Technical Institute
168 Gibson Rd, Henderson NV 89014
702-558-5404

· Las Vegas College
170 N Stephanie St Ste 145
Henderson NV 89074-8811
888-741-4270

· **LE CORDON BLEU COLLEGE OF CULINARY ARTS**
1451 Center Crossing Rd, Las Vegas NV 89144
Admission Dept.
866-450-2433 or 702-365-7690 Fax: 702-365-7911
Website: www.VegasCulinary.com

Marinello School of Beauty
5001 E Bonanza Rd Ste 110, Las Vegas NV 89110
702-796-6200

Milan Institute
950 Industrial Way, Sparks NV 89431
Bob Leonard, Director
775-348-7200

Morrison University
10315 Professional Circle Suite 201
Reno NV 89521-4826
Charles Timinsky, Director of Enrollment
775-850-0700 Fax: 775-850-0711
Website: www.morrisonuniversity.com

PCI Dealers School
920 S Valley View Blvd, Las Vegas NV 89107-4416
Joel Lauer, Owner
702-877-4724

Pima Medical Institute
3333 E Flamingo Rd, Las Vegas NV 89121
702-458-7650

RENO TAHOE JOB TRAINING ACADEMY
3702 S Virginia St Ste H2, Reno NV 89502-6093
Kathleen Shupp, President/Director
775-329-5665 Fax: 775-324-1969
Website: www.renodealingschool.com

Southern Nevada University of Cosmetology
3430 E Tropicana Ave, Las Vegas NV 89121
702-458-6333

NEW HAMPSHIRE

Concord Academy of Hair Design
20 S Main St, Concord NH 03301
603-224-2211

CONTINENTAL ACADEMIE OF HAIR DESIGN
PO Box 370, Hudson NH 03051-0370
603-889-1614 Fax: 603-883-9546
Website: www.continentalacademie.net
E-mail: conacad1@aol.com

CONTINENTAL ACADEMIE OF HAIR DESIGN
228 Maple St, Manchester NH 03103
Sylvia Donah, Business Manager
603-622-5851 Fax: 603-883-9546
Website: www.continentalacademie.net
E-mail: conacad2@aol.com

Empire Beauty School
556 Main St, Laconia NH 03246
603-524-8777

Empire Beauty School #3
362 Route 108, Somersworth NH 03878
603-692-1515

KEENE BEAUTY ACADEMY
800 Park Ave, Keene NH 03431-1513
Melanie Chaloux, Admissions
603-357-3736 Fax: 603-355-8916
Website: www.keenebeautyacademy.com

· McIntosh College
23 Cataract Ave, Dover NH 03820-3990
Karen Arnold, Director of Admissions
888-876-3000

Michael's School of Hair Design
73 S River Rd Ste 26, Bedford NH 03110
603-668-4300

New England EMS Institute
1 Elliot Way, Manchester NH 03103-3502
603-628-2220

New England School of Hair Design
12 Interchange Dr, West Lebanon NH 03784
603-298-5199

· New Hampshire Community Technical College
505 Amherst St, Nashua NH 03063
Patricia Goodman, Director of Student Services
603-882-7022

· New Hampshire Community Technical College
277 Portsmouth Ave, Stratham NH 03885-2231
Laurilee A. Shennett, Admissions Recruiter
603-772-1194 ext. 317

Portsmouth Beauty School of Hair Design
140 Congress St, Portsmouth NH 03801
Mr. Fran Nardello, Administrator
603-436-7775

Upper Valley Teacher Institute
1 Court St Ste 210, Lebanon NH 03766
603-448-6507

NEW JERSEY

Academy of Massage Therapy
321 Main St, Hackensack NJ 07601
888-AMT-7898

American Business Academy
66 Moore St, Hackensack NJ 07601-7104
Kim Staudt, Director
201-488-9400

Artistic Academy of Hair Design
21 Broadway, Fair Lawn NJ 07410
201-794-3502

BERDAN INSTITUTE
201 Willowbrook Blvd, Wayne NJ 07470-7041
David Dahlke, Director of Admissions
973-837-1818 Fax: 973-837-1840
Website: www.berdaninstitute.com
E-mail: info@berdaninstitute.com

BEST CARE TRAINING INSTITUTE
68 S Harrison St, East Orange NJ 07017
Florence Brown, RN, MSN, APNC, Contact
973-673-3900 Fax: 973-673-0597
Website: www.bestcarehealth.com
E-mail: fbrown3260@aol.com

Burlington County Institute of Technology - Adult Education
695 Woodlane Rd, Mount Holly NJ 08060-3813
Dr. Fred Laier, Contact
609-267-4226

Cape May County Technical Institute
188 Crest Haven Rd
Cape May Court House NJ 08210
609-465-2161

Capri Institute of Hair Design
268 Brick Blvd, Brick NJ 08723
732-920-3600

Capri Institute of Hair Design
1595 Main Ave, Clifton NJ 07011
973-772-4610

Capri Institute of Hair Design
660 N Michigan Ave, Kenilworth NJ 07033
908-964-1330

Capri Institute of Hair Design
615 Winters Ave, Paramus NJ 07652
201-599-0880

Capri Institute of Hair Design
Roxbury Mall Route 10 E, Succasunna NJ 07876
973-584-9030

Central Career School
126 Corporate Blvd, South Plainfield NJ 07080-2408
908-412-8600

∴ Christ Hospital School of Nursing
176 Palisade Ave, Jersey City NJ 07306-1196
Lisa Cieckiewicz, Coordinator of Student Services
201-795-8360

Chubb Institute
2100 Route 38, Cherry Hill NJ 08002-2043
856-988-9880

THE CHUBB INSTITUTE
40 Journal Sq, Jersey City NJ 07306-4097
Valerie Yancey, Campus President
201-876-3800 Fax: 201-656-2091
Website: www.chubbinstitute.edu
E-mail: vyancey@chubbinstitute.edu

Chubb Institute
651 US Highway 1, North Brunswick NJ 08902
732-448-2600

Chubb Institute
8 Sylvan Way, Parsippany NJ 07054
973-682-4900

Cittone Institute
1697 Oak Tree Rd, Edison NJ 08820-2896
John Willie, Executive Director
732-548-8798

Cittone Institute
1000 Howard Blvd # 2, Mount Laurel NJ 08054-2355
Vivian Wagner, Executive Director
856-722-9333

Cittone Institute
160 E State Route 4, Paramus NJ 07652-5002
Laurie Brown, Executive Director
201-828-5911

Concorde School of Hair Design
9 Ward St, Bloomfield NJ 07003
973-680-0099

Concorde School of Hair Design
Route 35 & Sunset Ave, Ocean NJ 07712
732-918-0505

∴ Cooper Hospital/University Medical Center
1 Cooper Plz #217, Camden NJ 08103-1461
Joan D'Antonio, Director
856-342-2416

Cumberland County Technical Education Center
601 Bridgeton Ave, Bridgeton NJ 08302-4810
856-451-9000

DIVERS ACADEMY INTERNATIONAL
1500 Liberty Pl, Erial NJ 08081
Tamara M. Brown, Director
800-238-3483 Fax: 856-404-6104
Website: www.diversacademy.com
E-mail: cdiver@worldnet.att.net

Dover Business College
15 E Blackwell St, Dover NJ 07801-4643
973-285-8400

Dover Business College
East 81 Route 4 W, Paramus NJ 07652
201-843-8500

Drake College of Business
125 Broad St, Elizabeth NJ 07201-2334
908-352-5509

Du Cret School of the Arts
1030 Central Ave, Plainfield NJ 07060-2898
908-757-7171

Eastern School of Acupuncture & Traditional Medicine
427 Bloomfield Ave Ste 301, Montclair NJ 07042
973-746-8717

Empire Beauty School
2100 State Highway #38, Cherry Hill NJ 08002
800-575-5983

Empire Beauty School
1305 Blackwood Clementon Rd
Laurel Springs NJ 08021
800-575-5983

Empire Beauty School
1719 Brunswick Ave, Lawrenceville NJ 08648
800-575-5983

ENGINE CITY TECHNICAL INSTITUTE
DIESEL MECHANIC SCHOOL AND TRAINING CENTER
901 Hadley Rd, South Plainfield NJ 07080-2424
Robert N. Merkle, Jr., Director of Admissions
800-305-3487 Fax: 908-756-7156
Website: www.enginecitytech.com
E-mail: info@enginecitytech.com

European Academy of Cosmetology
1126 Morris Ave, Union NJ 07083
908-686-4422

Gloucester Township Technical School
343 Berlin Cross Keys Rd, Sicklerville NJ 08081-4000
Gayle Butler, Director of Admissions
856-767-7002

Harris School of Business
One Mall Dr Suite 700, Cherry Hill NJ 08002
Barbara Harris Miles, Contact
856-662-5300

Healthcare Training Institute
1969 Morris Ave, Union NJ 07083
908-851-7711

Helma Institute Massage Therapy
190 Midland Ave, Saddle Brook NJ 07663
201-226-0056

HoHoKus School of Business & Medical Sciences
10 S Franklin Tpke, Ramsey NJ 07446-2546
Thomas Eastwick, Director
201-327-8877 Fax: 201-327-9054
Website: www.hohokus.edu
E-mail: tomeastwick@aol.com

HOHOKUS SCHOOL OF TRADE AND TECHNICAL SCIENCES
634-638 Market St, Paterson NJ 07513-1402
Alan E. Concha, Vice President/Director
800-646-9353 Fax: 908-486-9321
Website: www.hohokustrades.com
E-mail: aconcha21@aol.com

Hohokus School - RETS Nutley
103 Park Ave, Nutley NJ 07110-3505
Thomas Eastwick, President
973-661-0600 Fax: 973-661-2954
Website: www.rets-institute.com
E-mail: admissions@rets-institute.com

∴ **HOLY NAME HOSPITAL SCHOOL OF NURSING**
690 Teaneck Rd, Teaneck NJ 07666-4254
Maureen Schmude, Registrar
201-833-3005 Fax: 201-833-7209
Website: www.schoolofnursing.info
E-mail: sr-tynan@mail.holyname.org

∴ **HUDSON AREA SCHOOL OF RADIOLOGIC TECHNOLOGY**
176 Palisade Ave, Jersey City NJ 07306
Kenneth Lee, D.H.S., R.T. (R)(M)
201-795-8246 Fax: 201-795-5818
Website: www.christhospital.org
E-mail: lleclaire@christhospital.org

The Institute for Health Education
7 Spielman Rd, Fairfield NJ 07004-3403
973-808-1666

Institute for Therapeutic Massage
125 Wanaque Ave, Pompton Lakes NJ 07442
973-839-6131

Joe Kubert School of Cartoon & Graphic Arts
37 Myrtle Ave, Dover NJ 07801-4028
973-361-1327

Joy's School of Hair Design
PO Box 2269, East Orange NJ 07019
973-673-4141

Katharine Gibbs School
180 Centennial Ave, Piscataway NJ 08854-3908
L. Terry Nighan, President
732-885-1580

KeySkills Learning
50 Mount Prospect Ave, Clifton NJ 07013
973-778-8136

Lincoln Technical Institute
1450 Clements Bridge Rd, Deptford NJ 08096
856-384-2888

Lincoln Technical Institute
70 McKee Dr, Mahwah NJ 07430-2106
Al Dobbs, Executive Director
201-529-1414

Lincoln Technical Institute
2299 Vauxhall Rd, Union NJ 07083-5032
Mark Dugan, Executive Director
908-964-7800

MCELLIS TRAINING INSTITUTE
800 Broad St, Newark NJ 07102
Sharon Bradbury, Assistant Director
973-643-6917 Fax: 973-643-6973
E-mail: mcellisinstitute@aol.com

Mercer County Vocational-Technical School
1085 Old Trenton Rd, Trenton NJ 08690
609-586-2129

Micropower Computer Institute
1203 W Saint Georges Ave, Linden NJ 07036
908-587-9070

Micro Tech Training Center
3000 Kennedy Blvd, Jersey City NJ 07306
201-216-9901

∴ Monmouth Medical Center
300 2nd Ave, Long Branch NJ 07740-6395
John A. Mihok, MT Program Director
732-222-5200

Natural Motion Institute of Hair Design
2800 John F Kennedy Blvd, Jersey City NJ 07306
201-659-0303

New Community Workforce Development Center
201 Bergen St, Newark NJ 07103
Karen Harrison-Bowers, Director
973-824-6484

New Horizons Beauty School
5518 Bergenline Ave, West New York NJ 07093
201-866-4000

New Jersey School of Locksmithing
392 Summit Ave, Jersey City NJ 07306
201-963-9688

Omega Institute
7050 Kaighns Ave, Pennsauken NJ 08109-4417
856-663-4299

Parisian Academy
Paul Mitchell Partner School
362 State St, Hackensack NJ 07601
201-487-2203

P.B. Cosmetology Education Centre
110 Monmouth St, Gloucester City NJ 08030
856-456-4927

Pennco Tech
99 Erial Rd, Blackwood NJ 08012-3964
856-232-0310

Performance Training
1012 Cox Cro Rd, Toms River NJ 08755-1344
732-505-9119

Raritan Valley Flying School
Route 206, Princeton NJ 08540
609-921-3100

Reignbow Beauty Academy
312 State St, Perth Amboy NJ 08861
732-442-6007

Reignbow Hair Fashion Institute
121 Watchung Ave, North Plainfield NJ 07060
908-754-4247

Rizzieri Aveda School for Beauty & Wellness
6001 W Lincoln Dr, Marlton NJ 08053
Meg Stezzi, Director of Recruiting
856-988-8600

Roman Academy of Beauty Culture
431 Lafayette Ave, Hawthorne NJ 07506
973-423-2223

Shore Beauty School
103 W Washington Ave, Pleasantville NJ 08232
609-645-3635

STAR TECHNICAL INSTITUTE
3003 English Creek Ave Suite 212
Egg Harbor Township NJ 08234-4880
George Z. Negrete, Director
609-407-2999 Fax: 609-646-9472
Website: www.startechnicalinstitute.com
E-mail: info@stareggharbor.com

Star Technical Institute
1255 Highway 70 Ste 12N, Lakewood NJ 08701-5900
732-901-9710

Star Technical Institute
43 S White Horse Pike, Stratford NJ 08084-1520
856-435-7827

StenoTech Career Institute
20 Just Rd, Fairfield NJ 07004-3490
Jean Melone, Director
973-882-4875

Stuart School of Business Administration
2400 Belmar Blvd, Wall NJ 07719-3970
732-681-7200

Teterboro School of Aeronautics
80 Moonachie Ave, Teterboro NJ 07608-1003
Richard Ciasulli, Director of Admissions
201-288-6300 Fax: 201-288-5609
Website: www.teterboroschool.com
E-mail: teterboroschool@nj.rr.com

Ultrasound Diagnostic School
675 US Highway 1 S 2nd Flr, Iselin NJ 08830
732-634-1131

NEW MEXICO

ALADDIN BEAUTY COLLEGE #22
108 S Union Ave, Roswell NM 88203
Peggy Richburg, Contact
505-623-6331 Fax: 505-622-2072
E-mail: abcinc2@qwest.net

Albuquerque Barber College
601 San Pedro Dr NE Ste 104
Albuquerque NM 87108
505-266-4900

Albuquerque TVI Community College
525 Buena Vista Dr SE, Albuquerque NM 87106-4096
Michael J. Glennon, President
Jane Campbell, Registrar
505-224-3061

Apollo College
1001 Menaul Blvd NE Ste C, Albuquerque NM 87107
800-368-7246 Fax: 505-254-1101

Business Skills Institute
Las Cruces Campus
1400 El Paseo St, Las Cruces NM 88001-6022
505-526-5579

DeWolff College of Hairstyling & Cosmetology
1500 Eubank Blvd NE, Albuquerque NM 87112
505-296-4100

Eddy County Beauty College
1115 W Mermod St, Carlsbad NM 88220
505-885-4545

International School
141 Quinella Rd, Sunland Park NM 88063
505-589-1414

New Mexico Aveda Institute de Bellas Artes
2614 Pennsylvania St NE, Albuquerque NM 87110
505-294-5333

Olympian University of Cosmetology
1810 10th St, Alamogordo NM 88310
505-437-2221

Olympian University of Cosmetology
6300 San Mateo Blvd NE Ste J
Albuquerque NM 87109-3564
Angela Lopez, Contact
505-765-1044

Olympian University of Cosmetology
1460 Missouri Ave # 5, Las Cruces NM 88001-5330
505-523-7181

Pima Medical Institute
2201 San Pedro Dr NE, Albuquerque NM 87110-4155
505-881-1234

Universal Therapeutic Massage Institute
3410 Aztec Rd NE, Albuquerque NM 87107-4403
Pamela Berben, School Director
505-888-0020

NEW YORK

Adirondack Beauty School
108 Dix Ave, Glens Falls NY 12801
518-745-1646

Advanced Software Analysis Institute of Business and Computer Technology
151 Lawrence St Ste 2, Brooklyn NY 11201-5208
718-522-9073

ALBANY COLLEGE OF PHARMACY
106 New Scotland Ave, Albany NY 12208-3492
Carly Connors, Director of Admissions
888-203-8010 Fax: 518-694-7322
Website: www.acp.edu
E-mail: admissions@acp.edu

Allen School
16318 Jamaica Ave, Jamaica NY 11432
718-291-2200

American Academy of Dramatic Arts - New York
120 Madison Ave, New York NY 10016-7089
Karen Higginbotham, Director of Admissions
800-463-8990 Fax: 212-685-8093
Website: www.aada.org
E-mail: admissions-ny@aada.org

American Barber Institute
252 W 29th St, New York NY 10001
212-290-2289

APEX TECHNICAL SCHOOL
635 Avenue of the Americas
New York NY 10011-2008
William Ott, Admissions Director
212-645-3300 Fax: 212-645-6984
Website: www.apextechnical.com

An Apex Tech education provides you with a foundation for achieving some of the things you want most in life: a challenging career opportunity and a promising future.

Licensed by the State of New York and accredited by The Accrediting Commission of Career Schools and Colleges of Technology, Apex Tech is a recognized leader in its field. We have provided companies in the New York metropolitan area with more than 15,000 skilled graduates since our founding in 1961.

We offer a choice of five certificate programs - which may be completed in as few as 5 to 7 months - in Automotive Mechanics (which is the only ASE (Automotive Service Excellence) certified program in NYC), Refrigeration & Air Conditioning, Welding Technology, Auto Body Repair and Automotive Service & Repair with ESL Spanish.

All of our programs have been evaluated by the New York Regents National Program on Non-collegiate Sponsored Instruction (PONSI) for college credit hour recommendations. As a result, you may be able to advance toward a degree through your studies at Apex.

Each are part of a focused hands-on training program designed to get you an entree in your field of choice in a minimum of time.

∴ **ARNOT OGDEN MEDICAL CENTER SCHOOL OF NURSING**
600 Roe Ave, Elmira NY 14905-1676
Linda MacAuslan, Director
607-737-4153 Fax: 607-737-4116
Website: www.arnothealth.org
E-mail: lmacauslan@aomc.org

∴ **ARNOT-OGDEN MEDICAL CENTER**
School of Radiologic Technology
600 Roe Ave, Elmira NY 14905-1629
Ellen Richards, BS RT (R) Director
607-737-4289 Fax: 607-737-4116
Website: www.arnotheath.org
E-mail: erichards@aomc.org

· The Art Institute of New York City
75 Varick St Fl 16, New York NY 10013-1917
Alfred W. Parcells, Jr., Director of Admissions
212-226-5500

Austin Beauty School
527 Central Ave, Albany NY 12206
518-438-7879

Beauty School of Middletown
RR 9, Hyde Park NY 12538
845-229-6541

Beauty School of Middletown
225 Dolson Ave Ste 100, Middletown NY 10940
845-343-2171

Berk Trade School
383 Pearl St, Brooklyn NY 11201
718-625-6037

· **BRAMSON O R T COLLEGE**
69-30 Austin St, Forest Hills NY 11375-4222
Aleksandra Kagan, Admissions Coordinator
718-261-5800 Fax: 718-575-5119
Website: www.bramsonort.edu
E-mail: akagan@bramsonort.edu

· Bryant & Stratton College
1259 Central Ave, Albany NY 12205
518-437-1802

· Bryant & Stratton College
40 Hazelwood Dr, Amherst NY 14228-2230
716-691-0012

· Bryant & Stratton College
8687 Carling Rd, Liverpool NY 13090
315-472-6603

· Bryant & Stratton College
200 Red Tail, Orchard Park NY 14127
716-677-9500

· Bryant & Stratton College
150 Bellwood Dr, Rochester NY 14606
585-720-0660

· Bryant & Stratton College
1225 Jeffson Rd, Rochester NY 14623
585-292-5627

· Bryant & Stratton College
953 James St, Syracuse NY 13203-2502
315-472-6603

Caliber Training Institute
500 Fashion Ave 2nd Floor, New York NY 10018
212-564-0500

Capri Cosmetology Learning Center
251 W Route 59, Nanuet NY 10954
845-623-6339

Career & Educational Consultants
270 Flatbush Ave Ext, Brooklyn NY 11201
718-858-8500

CAREER INSTITUTE OF HEALTH & TECHNOLOGY
340 Flatbush Avenue Ext, Brooklyn NY 11201
Mary Miller, Contact
718-422-1212 Fax: 718-422-1222
Website: www.careerinstitute.edu
E-mail: admissions@careerinstitute.edu

CAREER INSTITUTE OF HEALTH & TECHNOLOGY
200 Garden City Plz, Garden City NY 11530
Mary Miller, Contact
516-877-1225 Fax: 516-877-1959
Website: www.careerinstitute.edu
E-mail: admissions@careerinstitute.edu

CAREER INSTITUTE OF HEALTH & TECHNOLOGY
9525 Queens Blvd Ste 600, Rego Park NY 11374
Mary Miller, Contact
718-897-4868 Fax: 718-897-4863
Website: www.careerinstitute.edu
E-mail: admissions@careerinstitute.edu

Center for Natural Wellness School
3 Cerone Commercial Dr, Albany NY 12205
518-449-2737

Centurion Professional Training
2619 E 16th St, Brooklyn NY 11235
718-646-4507

Charles Stuart School of Locksmithing
1420 Kings Hwy, Brooklyn NY 11229-2004
Charles Wechsler, CEO
718-339-2640

Cheryl Fell's School of Business
2541 Military Rd, Niagara Falls NY 14304-1505
716-297-2750

THE CHUBB INSTITUTE
498 7th Ave, New York NY 10018
James Cruz, Director of Admissions
212-659-2116 Fax: 212-659-2175
Website: www.chubbinstitute.edu
E-mail: jamescruz@chubbinstitute.edu

· **COCHRAN SCHOOL OF NURSING**
967 N Broadway, Yonkers NY 10701-1301
Paulette McLean, Admissions Coordinator
914-964-4296 Fax: 914-964-4796
Website: www.cochranschoolofnursing.us
E-mail: admissions@cochranschoolofnursing.us

Columbia-Greene Beauty School
342 Main St, Catskill NY 12414
518-943-2224

Commercial Driver Training School
600 Patton Ave, West Babylon NY 11704-1421
631-249-1330

Continental School
633 Jefferson Rd, Rochester NY 14623-3231
585-272-8060

Continental School of Beauty Culture
215 Main St, Batavia NY 14020
585-344-0886

Continental School of Beauty Culture
326 Kenmore Ave, Buffalo NY 14223
716-833-5016

Continental School of Beauty Culture
515 N Union St, Olean NY 14760-2618
Rosemary Swick, Director
716-372-5095

Continental School of Beauty Culture
1050 Union Rd, West Seneca NY 14224
716-675-8205

Cope Institute
225 Broadway Fl 2, New York NY 10007
212-809-5935

CULINARY ACADEMY OF LONG ISLAND
125 Michael Dr, Syosset NY 11791
Michael Levitt, Director
516-364-4344 Fax: 516-364-1894
Website: www.culinaryacademy.edu
E-mail: admissions@culinaryacademy.edu

CULINARY ACADEMY OF NEW YORK
154 W 14th St, New York NY 10011-7307
Harold Kaplan, Contact
212-675-6655 Fax: 212-463-9194
Website: www.culinaryacademy.edu
E-mail: hkaplan@culinaryacademy.edu

David Hochstein Memorial Music School
50 Plymouth Ave N, Rochester NY 14614-1221
585-454-4596

· Ellis Hospital School of Nursing
1101 Nott St, Schenectady NY 12308-2425
518-243-4471

· Elmira Business Institute
303 N Main St, Elmira NY 14901
Lisa Roan, Admissions Director
607-733-7177

∴ **FAXTON-ST. LUKE'S HEALTHCARE SCHOOL OF MEDICAL RADIOGRAPHY**
PO Box 479, Utica NY 13503-0479
Rosemary Morin, MS, RTR, Director
315-624-6136 Fax: 315-624-4787
Website: mvnhealth.com
E-mail: valesand@mvnhealth.com

FEGS Trades & Business School
80 Vandam St, New York NY 10013
212-366-8466

Folk Art Institute
45 W 53rd St, New York NY 10022
212-977-7170

FRANKLIN CAREER INSTITUTE
5323 5th Ave, Brooklyn NY 11220
Richard C. Crance, Executive Director
718-535-3333 Fax: 718-535-3345
Website: www.franklincareer.edu
E-mail: rcrance@franklincareer.edu

FRANKLIN CAREER INSTITUTE
91 N Franklin St, Hempstead NY 11550
Richard C. Crance, Executive Director
516-481-4444 Fax: 516-481-8694
Website: www.franklincareer.edu
E-mail: rcrance@franklincareer.edu

THE FRENCH CULINARY INSTITUTE
462 Broadway, New York NY 10013-2618
Judy Currie-Hellmann, Director of Admission
212-219-8890 Fax: 212-431-3054
Website: www.frenchculinary.com
E-mail: jcurrie-hellmann@frenchculinary.com

Gemological Institute of America
580 5th Ave, New York NY 10036
212-944-5900

Global Business Institute
1931 Mott Ave, Far Rockaway NY 11691-4103
718-327-2220

Global Business Institute
209 W 125th St, New York NY 10027-4410
212-663-1500

Hair Design Institute at Fifth Avenue
6711 5th Ave, Brooklyn NY 11220
718-745-1000

Harlem School of Technology
215 W 125th St, New York NY 10027
212-932-2849

· Helene Fuld College of Nursing
1879 Madison Ave, New York NY 10035-2709
212-423-2700

Hunter Business School
3601 Hempstead Tpke, Levittown NY 11756-1375
516-796-1000

Institute of Allied Medical Professions
405 Park Ave, New York NY 10022-4405
212-758-1410

INSTITUTE OF AUDIO RESEARCH
64 University Pl, New York NY 10003-4595
Mark L. Kahn, Director of Admissions
800-544-2501 Fax: 212-677-6549
Website: www.audioschool.com
E-mail: contact@audioschool.com

Established 1969. Private. Coed. Accreditation: Accrediting Commission of Career Schools and Colleges of Technology (ACCSCT). Tuition: $14,150. Fees: $100. Faculty: 26. Student-faculty ratio: 15:1. Degrees: Diploma in Audio Recording and Production. 20,000 sq. ft. facility featuring a state-of-the-art all-digital recording studio and individual digital audio workstations for students. IAR offers 9-12 month career training in audio and recording arts. Program includes analog and digital audio technology with heavy emphasis on digital music production and audio post-production for film and video. Uniquely situated in the heart of NYC, the recording capital of the world and home of all major TV networks. IAR graduates find employment in recording studios, television stations, live concert sound, audio and video production houses, theater sound, radio, satellite and cable companies, jingle houses, post-production for film and television and more. In addition, IAR grads receive transfer credit towards a bachelors degree at various colleges nationwide. Financial aid available for eligible students.

THE INSTITUTE OF CULINARY EDUCATION
50 W 23rd St, New York NY 10010
Admissions Department
888-921-CHEF
Website: www.iceculinary.com/pattersons

· Institute of Design and Construction
141 Willoughby St, Brooklyn NY 11201
718-855-3661

· Interboro Institute
450 W 56th St, New York NY 10019
212-399-0091

· **ISLAND DRAFTING & TECHNICAL INSTITUTE**
128 Broadway (Route 110), Amityville NY 11701-2704
James G. DiLiberto, President
631-691-8733 Fax: 631-691-8738
Website: www.idti.edu
E-mail: info@idti.edu

· ITT Technical Institute
PO Box 327, Getzville NY 14068
716-689-2200

· Jamestown Business College
PO Box 429, Jamestown NY 14702
716-664-5100

Jon Louis School of Beauty
9114 Merrick Blvd, Jamaica NY 11432
718-658-6240

· **KATHARINE GIBBS SCHOOL**
320 S Service Rd, Melville NY 11747-3201
Derrick Ruffin, VP of Admissions
516-370-3510 Fax: 516-293-1763
Website: www.gibbslongisland.com
E-mail: druffin@gibbsmelville.com

· Katharine Gibbs School
50 W 40th St, New York NY 10018-2602
212-867-9300

Learning Institute for Beauty Sciences
3815 Broadway, Astoria NY 11103
718-726-8383

Learning Institute for Beauty Sciences
2384 86th St, Brooklyn NY 11214
718-373-2400

Learning Institute for Beauty Sciences
544 Route 111, Hauppauge NY 11788
631-724-0440

Learning Institute for Beauty Sciences
173A Fulton Ave, Hempstead NY 11550
516-483-6259

Learning Institute for Beauty Sciences
2981 Hempstead Tpke, Levittown NY 11756-1330
516-731-8300

Learning Institute for Beauty Sciences
22 W 34th St, New York NY 10001
212-695-4555

Leon Studio One School of Hair Design
5221 Main St, Williamsville NY 14221
716-631-3878

Lia Schorr Inst of Cosmetic Skin Care
686 Lexington Ave, New York NY 10022-2614
Lia Schorr, President
212-486-9541

· Long Island College Hospital School of Nursing
339 Hicks St, Brooklyn NY 11201
718-780-1000

Mandl School, The College of Allied Health
254 W 54th St, New York NY 10019-5516
Melvyn Weiner, President
212-247-3434

Manhattan School of Computer Technology
42 Broadway Fl 22, New York NY 10004-1638
212-349-9768

MarJon School of Beauty Culture
1154 Niagara Falls Blvd, Tonawanda NY 14150-9329
716-836-6240

Memorial Sloan Kettering Cancer Center
1275 York Ave, New York NY 10065
212-639-6561

Merkaz Bnos - Business School
2115 Benson Ave, Brooklyn NY 11214
718-234-4000

METROPOLITAN LEARNING INSTITUTE
9745 Queens Blvd Ste 401, Rego Park NY 11374
Boris Davydov, President
718-897-0482 Fax: 718-897-5667
Website: www.gettraining.org
E-mail: mli@gettraining.org

Midway Paris Beauty School
5440 Myrtle Ave, Ridgewood NY 11385
718-418-2790

Mildred Elley the College for Careers
800 New Loudon Rd Ste 5120
Latham NY 12110-3902
Jill Herrick, Enrollment Manager
800-622-6327

Modern Welding School
1842 State St, Schenectady NY 12304-2033
Pat Aucompaugh, Administrator
518-374-1216

Munson-Williams-Proctor Institute
310 Genesee St, Utica NY 13502-4799
Robert E. Baber, Dean
315-797-8260

Music Conservatory of Westchester
216 Central Ave, White Plains NY 10606-1102
914-761-3715

The Nail Academy
16204 Jamaica Ave, Jamaica NY 11432
718-297-6330

National Tractor Trailer School
175 Katherine St, Buffalo NY 14210-2007
716-849-6887

NATIONAL TRACTOR TRAILER SCHOOL
4650 Buckley Rd, Liverpool NY 13088
Kimberley Sather, Contact
315-451-2430 Fax: 315-453-7336
Website: www.ntts.edu
E-mail: ksather@ntts.edu

New York Automotive & Diesel Institute
17818 Liberty Ave, Jamaica NY 11433-1433
Mr. Dante Cicchetti, Director of Admissions
718-361-1300

NEW YORK CAREER INSTITUTE
11 Park Pl 4th Floor, New York NY 10007-2833
Cindy McMahon, Director of Admissions
212-962-0002 Fax: 212-385-7574
Website: www.nyci.edu
E-mail: info@nyci.edu

NEW YORK EYE & EAR INFIRMARY / ORTHOPTIC PROGRAM
310 E 14th St, New York NY 10003-4201
Sara Shippman, Chief Orthoptist
212-979-4375 Fax: 212-979-4564
Website: www.nyee.edu
E-mail: sshippman@nyee.edu

New York Institute of Business Technology
248 W 35th St, New York NY 10001-2505
Leith E. Yetman, Director of Admissions
212-725-9400

New York Institute of Massage
PO Box 645, Buffalo NY 14231
716-633-0355

New York International Beauty School
500 8th Ave Room 803, New York NY 10018-4133
212-868-7171

New York Methodist Hospital
Clinical Laboratory Science/School of Medical Technology
506 6th St, Brooklyn NY 11215-3609
Adrienne Arso-Paez, Program Director
718-780-3706

New York Paralegal School
299 Broadway Ste 200, New York NY 10007-1901
212-349-8800

NEW YORK SCHOOL FOR MEDICAL AND DENTAL ASSISTANTS
33-10 Queens Blvd, Long Island City NY 11101-2327
Donna Stirber-Gamelin, Executive Director of Admissions
718-793-2330 Fax: 718-793-0619
Website: www.nysmda.com
E-mail: info@nysmda.com

Northern Westchester School of Hairdressing
19 Bank St, Peekskill NY 10566
914-739-8400

Olean Business Institute
301 N Union St, Olean NY 14760-2691
Carl English, Director of Admissions
716-372-7978 Fax: 716-372-2120
Website: www.obi.edu
E-mail: cenglish@obi.edu

The Orlo School of Hair Design and Cosmetology
232 N Allen St, Albany NY 12206
518-459-7832

Phillips Beth Israel School of Nursing
776 Avenue of the Americas 4th Flr
New York NY 10001-6354
212-614-6110

Phillips Hairstyling Institute
709 E Genesee St, Syracuse NY 13210
315-422-9656

Plaza College
74-09 37th Ave, Jackson Heights NY 11372
Rose Ann Black, Dean of Administration
718-779-1430

Professional Business College
125 Canal St, New York NY 10002-5049
William Chong, Admissions Director
212-226-7300

Ridley-Lowell Business & Technical Institute
116 Front St, Binghamton NY 13905-3102
David Lounsbury, Executive Director
607-724-2941 Fax: 607-724-0799
Website: www.ridley.edu
E-mail: info@ridley.edu

Ridley-Lowell Business & Technical Institute
26 S Hamilton St, Poughkeepsie NY 12601-3328
E. Ann Bida, Director of Admissions
845-471-0330

Rochester Business Institute
1630 Portland Ave, Rochester NY 14621-3007
585-266-0430

St. Elizabeth College of Nursing
2215 Genesee St, Utica NY 13501-5930
315-798-8125

ST. JOSEPH'S COLLEGE OF NURSING AT SJHHC
206 Prospect Ave, Syracuse NY 13203-1806
Rhonda Reader, Assistant Dean for Admissions
315-448-5040 Fax: 315-448-5745
Website: www.sjhsyr.org/nursing
E-mail: collegeofnursing@sjhsyr.org

St. Vincent Catholic Medical Centers of New York
175-05 Horace Harding Expy
Flushing NY 11365-1535
718-357-0500

Samaritan Hospital
School of Nursing AD & LPN
2215 Burdett Ave, Troy NY 12180-2475
Mary Harknett-Martin, Director
518-271-3285

Sanford-Brown Institute
333 Westchester Ave, White Plains NY 10604
Director of Admissions
914-347-6817

SHEAR EGO INTERNATIONAL SCHOOL OF HAIR DESIGN
525 Titus Ave, Rochester NY 14617
Sharon Roemer, Director of Admissions
585-342-0070 Fax: 585-342-0863
Website: www.shearego.com
E-mail: sei@shearego.com

SIMMONS INSTITUTE OF FUNERAL SERVICE
1828 South Ave, Syracuse NY 13207-2005
Maurice C. Wightman, CEO
315-475-5142 Fax: 315-475-3817
Website: www.simmonsinstitute.com
E-mail: mcwightman20@aol.com

Sotheby's Institute of Art
1334 York Ave, New York NY 10021-4806
212-894-1111

Spanish-American Institute
215 W 43rd St, New York NY 10036-3967
212-840-7111

Spencer Business & Technical Institute
795 Pattersonville Rd, Pattersonville NY 12137-4329
518-374-7619

Studio Jewelers
32 E 31st St, New York NY 10016
212-686-1944

Suburban Technical School
175 Fulton Ave, Hempstead NY 11550-3771
516-481-6660

SUNY College of Agriculture & Technology
Morrisville NY 13408
Thomas Ver Dow, Dean of Enrollment Management
800-258-0111

SUNY College of Technology
Alfred NY 14802
Deborah J. Goodrich, Associate VP Enrollment Mgmt.
800-4AL-FRED Fax: 607-587-4299
Website: www.alfredstate.edu
E-mail: admissions@alfredstate.edu

SUNY Schenectady County Community College
78 Washington Ave, Schenectady NY 12305-2215
Robert Dinello, Director of Admissions
518-381-1366

SUNY Sullivan County Community College
112 College Rd, Loch Sheldrake NY 12759-5151
Sari Rosenheck, Director of Admissions
845-434-5750 Fax: 845-434-0923
Website: www.sullivan.suny.edu
E-mail: admissions@sullivan.suny.edu
Student Housing on Campus.

Troy School of Beauty Culture
15 Highland Ct, Troy NY 12180
518-273-7741

Ultrasound Diagnostic School
711 Stewart Ave Suite 200
Garden City NY 11530-4734
516-248-6060

Ultrasound Diagnostic School
120 E 16th St Fl 2, New York NY 10003-2103
212-645-9116

Utica School of Commerce
PO Box 462, Canastota NY 13032-0462
315-697-8200

VAUGHN COLLEGE OF AERONAUTICS AND TECHNOLOGY
8601 23rd Ave, Flushing NY 11369-1037
Vincent Papandrea, Director of Admissions
800-776-2376 Fax: 718-429-0671
Website: www.vaughn.edu
E-mail: admitme@vaughn.edu
Established 1932. Private. Coed. Accreditation: MSACS, ABET. Tuition: $13,400. Fees: $280. Enrollment: 842 full-time, 284 part-time. Faculty: 59. Student-faculty ratio: 11:1. Degrees: BS, AAS, AOS. Library: 62,000 vols. Offering bachelor and associate degrees in airport management, aviation maintenance, flight training, electronic technology, engineering, general management, mechatronic engineering, pre-engineering and computerized design/animated graphics. Hands-on training. Extensive career development services and financial aid available.

Westchester School of Beauty Culture
6 Gramatan Ave, Mount Vernon NY 10550
914-699-2344

NORTH CAROLINA

Anson College of Cosmetology
1217 E Caswell St, Wadesboro NC 28170
704-694-6677

ART INSTITUTE OF CHARLOTTE
2110 Water Ridge Pkwy, Charlotte NC 28217
Pamela Notemyer, Director of Admissions
800-872-4417 Fax: 704-357-1133
Website: www.artinstitutes.edu/charlotte
E-mail: admin@aii.edu
College of Applied Arts accredited by ACICS, providing career education in Culinary Arts Management, Fashion Marketing & Management, Graphic Design, Interactive Media Design, Interior Design, Financial aid available for those who qualify; Employment assistance program. Offering Associate's and Bachelor's degrees as well as certificate programs.

Brookstone College of Business
10125 Berkeley Place Dr, Charlotte NC 28262
704-547-8600

Brookstone College of Business
7815 National Service Rd
Greensboro NC 27409-9423
336-668-2627

Carolina Beauty College
5430 N Tryon St Ste O, Charlotte NC 28213
704-597-5503

Carolina Beauty College
5106 N Roxboro St, Durham NC 27704
919-477-1444

Carolina Beauty College
1917 E Wendover Ave, Greensboro NC 27405
336-886-4712

Carolina Beauty College
2001 E Wendover Ave, Greensboro NC 27405
336-272-2966

Carolina Beauty College
7736 N Point Blvd Ste C, Winston Salem NC 27106
336-759-7969

Carteret Community College
3505 Arendell St, Morehead City NC 28557-2989
Don Thompson, Director of Student Support
252-247-4142 ext. 149

Cheveux School Hair Design and Hairport
4781 Gum Branch Rd #1, Jacksonville NC 28540
910-455-5767

Cosmetology Institute of Beauty Arts & Science
807 Silas Creek Pkwy, Winston Salem NC 27127
336-773-1472

Dudley Beauty College
1950 John McDonald Ave, Charlotte NC 28216
704-392-2564

DUDLEY COSMETOLOGY UNIVERSITY
900 E Mountain St, Kernersville NC 27284
Eunice M. Dudley, President
336-996-2030 Fax: 336-996-9752
Website: www.dudleyq.com
E-mail: emdudley@dudleyq.com

ECPI College of Technology
4800 Airport Center Pkwy, Charlotte NC 28208-5886
704-399-1010

ECPI College of Technology
7802 Airport Center Dr, Greensboro NC 27409-9048
336-665-1400

ECPI College of Technology
4101 Doie Cope Rd, Raleigh NC 27613-7387
919-571-0057

Empire Beauty School
11032 E Independence Blvd, Matthews NC 28105
800-575-5983

Empire Beauty School
Shoppes at Kings Grant
10075 Weddington Road Ext, Concord NC 28027
800-575-5983

EnVisionary I-Care
133 Highway 70 W, Garner NC 27529
919-661-7773

Fayetteville Beauty College
3442 Bragg Blvd, Fayetteville NC 28303
910-487-0227

Hairstyling Institute of Charlotte
209B S Kings Dr, Charlotte NC 28204
704-334-5511

Haywood Community College
185 Freedlander Dr, Clyde NC 28721
Debbie Rowland, Coordinator of Admissions
828-627-4500 Fax: 828-627-4513
Website: www.haywood.edu
E-mail: drowland@haywood.edu

King's College
322 Lamar Ave, Charlotte NC 28204-2493
704-372-0266

Leon's Beauty School
1410 W Lee St, Greensboro NC 27403
336-274-4601

∴ **MERCY SCHOOL OF NURSING**
701 B Forest Point Cir, Charlotte NC 28273
Pamela Hatley, RN, MSN, Student Services
704-512-2010 Fax: 704-512-2050
Website:
www.carolinashealthcare.org\education\mercyson
E-mail: phatley@carolinas.org

· **MILLER-MOTTE TECHNICAL COLLEGE**
2205 Walnut St, Cary NC 27518
919-532-7171
Website: www.miller-motte.com

· Miller-Motte Technical College
5000 Market St, Wilmington NC 28405-3430
800-784-2110

Mitchell's Hairstyling Academy
222 Tallywood Shopping Ctr, Fayetteville NC 28303
910-485-6310

Mitchell's Hairstyling Academy
1021 N Spence Ave, Goldsboro NC 27534
919-778-8200

Mitchell's Hairstyling Academy
426 E Arlington Blvd, Greenville NC 27858
252-756-3050

Mitchell's Hairstyling Academy
2620 Forest Hills Rd #A, Wilson NC 27893
252-243-3158

Mr. David's School of Hair Design
4348 Market St #N-17, Wilmington NC 28403
910-763-4418

NASCAR Technical Institute
220 Byers Creek Rd, Mooresville NC 28117
704-658-1950

Oconaluftee Job Corps Center
502 Oconaluftee Job Corps Rd
Cherokee NC 28719-9203
Danny Muse, Education Supervisor
828-497-5411

Schenck Civilian Conservation Center
98 Schenck Dr, Pisgah Forest NC 28768-9718
828-862-6100

SCHOOL OF COMMUNICATION ARTS
3000 Wakefield Crossing Dr, Raleigh NC 27614-7076
Debra Ann Hooper, Director and VP
919-981-0972 Fax: 919-981-0946
Website: www.higherdigital.com
E-mail: school@higherdigital.com

Southeastern School of Neuromuscular
4 Woodlawn Green #200, Charlotte NC 28217
704-527-4979

Universal College of Beauty
1701 W Trade St, Charlotte NC 28216
704-333-6969

∴ Wilkes Regional Medical Center
School of Radiologic Technology
PO Box 609, North Wilkesboro NC 28659-0609
336-651-8431

Winston-Salem Barber School
1531 Silas Creek Pkwy, Winston Salem NC 27127
336-724-1459

NORTH DAKOTA

· **AAKERS COLLEGE**
4012 19th Ave S, Fargo ND 58103-7196
Elizabeth Largent, Director
701-277-3889 Fax: 701-277-5604
Website: www.aakers.edu
E-mail: blargent@aakers.edu

Headquarters Academy of Hair Design
108 Main St S, Minot ND 58701
701-852-8329

Josef's School of Hair Design
627 NP Ave N, Fargo ND 58102
701-235-0011

Josef's School of Hair Design
2011 S Washington St, Grand Forks ND 58201
701-772-2728

Moler Barber College of HairStyling
16 S 8th St, Fargo ND 58103
701-232-6773

R.D. Hairstyling College
124 N 4th St, Bismarck ND 58501
701-223-8804

Sr. Rosalind Gefre Schools of Massage
3101 39th St SW Ste E, Fargo ND 58104
Annie Thorseth, Director of Admissions
701-297-5993 Fax: 701-297-5994
Website: www.sisterrosalind.org
E-mail: fargocampus@sisterrosalind.org

OHIO

· **ACADEMY OF COURT REPORTING**
2044 Euclid Ave, Cleveland OH 44115-2282
Sheila Woods, Director of Admissions
216-861-3222 Fax: 216-861-4517
Website: www.acr.edu
E-mail: woods.sheila@acr.edu

· Academy of Court Reporting
630 E Broad St, Columbus OH 43215-3902
614-221-7770

· Academy of Court Reporting
2930 W Market St, Fairlawn OH 44333-3607
330-867-4030

Akron Institute
1600 S Arlington St Ste 100, Akron OH 44306
330-724-1600

Akron Machining Institute
2959 Barber Rd, Norton OH 44203-1005
330-745-1111

AMERICAN INSTITUTE OF ALTERNATIVE MEDICINE
Teaching Massage And Acupuncture
6685 Doubletree Ave, Columbus OH 43229-1113
Linda Fleming-Willis, Director of Administration
614-825-6278 Fax: 614-825-6279
Website: www.aiam.edu
E-mail: info@aiam.edu

American School of Technology
2100 Morse Rd #4599, Columbus OH 43229-6665
614-436-4820

· Antonelli College
124 E 7th St, Cincinnati OH 45202-2528
513-241-4338

· The Art Institute of Cincinnati
1171 E Kemper Rd, Cincinnati OH 45246
Marion Allman, President
513-751-1206 Fax: 513-751-1209
Website: www.theartinstituteofcincinnati.com
E-mail: aic@theartinstituteofcincinnati.com
See listing under "Art"

Ashland County - West Holmes Career Center
1783 State Route 60, Ashland OH 44805-9287
419-289-3313

· **ATS INSTITUTE OF TECHNOLOGY**
230 Alpha Park, Highland Heights OH 44143
Helen Bykov, Director of Education
440-449-1700 Fax: 440-449-1389
Website: www.atsinstitute.com
E-mail: info@atsinstitute.com

Beatrice Academy of Beauty
10500 Cedar Ave, Cleveland OH 44106
216-421-2313

· Bohecker College
653 Enterprise Pkwy, Ravenna OH 44266
800-794-2856

· Bradford School
2469 Stelzer Rd, Columbus OH 43219-3129
Raeann Lee, Director of Admissions
614-416-6200

Brown Aveda Institute
8816 Mentor Ave, Mentor OH 44060-6212
Susan Partin, Contact
440-255-9494

· Brown Mackie College - Cincinnati
1011 Glendale Milford Rd, Cincinnati OH 45215-1107
Robin Krout, President
513-771-2424 Fax: 513-771-3413
Website: www.brownmackie.edu
E-mail: rkrout@brownmackie.edu

· Brown Mackie College - Findlay
1700 Fostoria Ave Ste 100, Findlay OH 45840-6220
888-296-5059

· Bryant & Stratton College
1700 E 13th St, Cleveland OH 44114-3238
Shawn T. Kampa, Market Director of Admissions
216-771-1700 Fax: 216-771-7787
Website: www.bryantstratton.edu
E-mail: stkampa@bryantstratton.edu

· Bryant & Stratton College
27557 Chardon Rd, Willoughby Hills OH 44092-2794
Shawn Kampa, Director of Admissions
440-944-6800

Carousel Beauty College
125 E 2nd St, Dayton OH 45402
937-223-3572

Carousel Beauty College
3120 Woodman Dr, Kettering OH 45420
937-298-5752

Carousel Beauty College
633 S Breiel Blvd, Middletown OH 45044
513-422-2962

Carousel Beauty College
1475 Upper Valley Pike #956, Springfield OH 45504
937-323-0277

Carousel of Miami Valley Beauty College
7809 Waynetowne Blvd, Huber Heights OH 45424
937-233-8818

Century School of Cosmetology
434 Market St, Steubenville OH 43952
740-282-3312

Cleveland Clinic Foundation
9500 Euclid Ave, Cleveland OH 44195-0001
216-445-5719

Cleveland Institute of Dental and Medical Assistants
2450 Prospect Ave, Cleveland OH 44115
216-241-2930

Cleveland Institute of Dental and Medical Assistants
5564 Mayfield Rd, Lyndhurst OH 44124-2928
440-473-6273

Cleveland Institute of Dental and Medical Assistants
5733 Hopkins Rd, Mentor OH 44060-2035
440-946-9530

· Cleveland Institute of Electronics
1776 E 17th St, Cleveland OH 44114-3679
Scott Katzenmeyer, Director of Admissions
800-243-6446 Fax: 216-781-0331
Website: www.cie-wc.edu
E-mail: instruct@cie-wc.edu

Collins Career Center
11627 State Route 243, Chesapeake OH 45619-7962
740-867-6641

· Columbus State Community College
550 E Spring St, Columbus OH 43215-1786
Ken Conner, Director of Admissions
614-287-3669

∴ **COMMUNITY HOSPITAL SCHOOL OF NURSING**
2615 E High St, Springfield OH 45505-1494
Hedy Frick, Admissions
937-328-8905 Fax: 937-328-8668
Website: www.chsn.com
E-mail: succeed@chsn.com

∴ **COOPERATIVE MEDICAL TECHNOLOGY PROGRAM OF AKRON**
1 Perkins Sq, Akron OH 44308-1062
Sharon K. Shriber, MBA, Program Director
330-543-8720 Fax: 330-543-6303
Website: www.akronchildrens.org
E-mail: sshriber@chmca.org

Creative Images - A Certified Matrix Design Academy
1076 Kauffman Ave, Fairborn OH 45324
937-878-9555

Dayton Barber College
28 W 5th St, Dayton OH 45402
937-222-9101

ENGLISH NANNY AND GOVERNESS SCHOOL
30 S Franklin St, Chagrin Falls OH 44022-3213
Sheilagh Roth, Executive Director
800-733-1984 Fax: 440-247-0602
Website: www.nanny-governess.com
E-mail: admissions@nanny-governess.com

· ETI Technical College
2076 Youngstown Warren Rd, Niles OH 44446-4398
330-652-9919

Fairfield Career Center
4465 S Hamilton Rd, Groveport OH 43125-9333
614-836-5725

Fairview Academy
22610 Lorain Rd, Fairview Park OH 44126
440-734-5555

∴ **FIRELANDS REGIONAL MEDICAL CENTER SCHOOL OF NURSING**
1912 Hayes Ave, Sandusky OH 44870-4788
Holly J. Price, RN, Director
419-557-7111 Fax: 419-557-7116
Website: www.firelands.com
E-mail: priceh@firelands.com

· Gallipolis Career College
1176 Jackson Pike #312, Gallipolis OH 45631
740-446-4367

Gerber Akron Beauty School
33 Shiawassee Ave, Fairlawn OH 44333
330-867-6200

Hair Academy
6000 Mahoning Ave, Austintown OH 44515
330-792-6504

Hamrick Truck Driving School
1156 Medina Rd, Medina OH 44256-8121
330-239-2229

Hobart Institute of Welding Technology
400 Trade Sq E, Troy OH 45373-2463
Ron L. Scott, Vice President and General Manager
800-332-9448

Hocking College
3301 Hocking Pkwy, Nelsonville OH 45764-9704
Diane K. Wolf, Assistant Director of Admissions Information
800-282-4163

Hondros College
7410 South Ave, Boardman OH 44512-5719
Site Director
888-HONDROS

Hondros College
4675 Cornell Rd Suite 175
Cincinnati OH 45241-2495
Site Director
888-HONDROS

Hondros College
1810 Successful Dr, Fairborn OH 45324
Site Director
888-HONDROS

Hondros College
4100 Rockside Rd 2nd Floor
Independence OH 44131
Site Director
888-HONDROS

Hondros College
7350 Industrial Park Blvd, Mentor OH 44060
Site Director
888-HONDROS

Hondros College
1505 Corporate Woods Parkway #100
Uniontown OH 44685
Site Director
888-HONDROS

· Hondros College
4140 Executive Pkwy, Westerville OH 43081-3855
Andrea Nameche, V.P. Degree Division
888-HONDROS

Hondros College
The Trust Company Building
6135 Trust Dr Suite 110, Holland OH 43528-9358
Site Director
888-HONDROS

∴ **HURON SCHOOL OF NURSING**
Cleveland Clinic
13951 Terrace Rd, East Cleveland OH 44112-4308
Barbara Szigeti, MA, Coordinator of Student Services
216-761-7996 Fax: 216-761-7541
Website: www.cchseast.org/schools
E-mail: bszigeti@cchseast.org

Inner State Beauty School
5150 Mayfield Rd, Lyndhurst OH 44124
440-442-4500

Institute of Medical & Dental Technology
375 Glensprings Dr Ste 201
Cincinnati OH 45246-2396
513-851-8500

International Academy of Hair Design
8419 Colerain Ave, Cincinnati OH 45239
513-741-4777

International College of Broadcasting
6 S Smithville Rd, Dayton OH 45431-1833
J. Michael LeMaster, President
937-258-8251

ITT Technical Institute
4750 Wesley Ave, Cincinnati OH 45212-2244
Michael Thompson, Director
513-531-8300

ITT Technical Institute
14955 W Sprague Rd, Strongsville OH 44136-1758
440-234-9091

Kent State University
PO Box 5190, Kent OH 44242-0001
Paul Deutsch, Director of Admissions
330-672-2444

Kent State University-Ashtabula Campus
3325 W 13th St, Ashtabula OH 44004-2299
Kelly Sanford, Contact
440-964-3322

Kent State University-East Liverpool Campus
400 E 4th St, East Liverpool OH 43920-3497
Jamie Kenneally, Contact
330-385-3805

Kent State University-Geauga Campus
14111 Claridon Troy Rd, Burton OH 44021-9581
Dave Chappell, Contact
440-834-4187

Kent State University-Salem Campus
2491 State Route 45 S, Salem OH 44460-9412
Dennis Giacomino, Contact
330-332-0361

Kent State University-Stark Campus
6000 Frank Ave NW, North Canton OH 44720-7548
Jim Barrett, Contact
330-499-9600

Kent State University-Trumbull Campus
4314 Mahoning Ave NW, Warren OH 44483-1998
Linda Petrilla, Contact
330-678-4281

Kent State University - Tuscarawas Campus
330 University Dr NE, New Philadelphia OH 44663
Denise Testa, Contact
330-339-3391

Knox County Career Center
306 Martinsburg Rd, Mount Vernon OH 43050-4225
740-397-5820

Marinello-Eastern Hills Academy of Hair Design
7681 Beechmont Ave, Cincinnati OH 45255
513-231-8621

Marion Technical College
1467 Mount Vernon Ave, Marion OH 43302-5628
Joel Liles, Director of Admissions
740-389-4636

Medina County Career Center
1101 W Liberty St, Medina OH 44256-1346
330-725-8461

Moler-Hollywood Beauty College
130 E 6th St 2nd Floor, Cincinnati OH 45202-3210
513-621-5262

Moler-Pickens Beauty College
5951 Boymel Dr Ste S, Fairfield OH 45014-5548
513-874-5116

NATIONAL BEAUTY COLLEGE
4642 Cleveland Ave NW, Canton OH 44709-1837
Lori Campbell, Contact
330-499-9444 Fax: 330-499-2090
Website: www.nationalbc.com
E-mail: nationalbeauty@neo.rr.com

Nationwide Beauty Academy
5300 WestPointe Plaza Dr, Columbus OH 43228
614-921-9109

Northern Institute of Cosmetology
667 Broadway, Lorain OH 44052
440-244-4282

Ohio Business College
1907 N Ridge Rd E, Lorain OH 44055-3344
440-277-0021

Ohio Business College
5202 Timber Commons Dr
Sandusky OH 44870-8908
419-627-8345

Ohio Center for Broadcasting
6703 Madison Rd, Cincinnati OH 45227-2029
513-271-6060

OHIO CENTER FOR BROADCASTING
9000 Sweet Valley Dr, Valley View OH 44125-4220
Kathy Wenner, Admissions Director
216-447-9117 Fax: 216-642-9232
Website: www.beonair.com
E-mail: ocb@beonair.com

OHIO COLLEGE OF MASSOTHERAPY
225 Heritage Woods Dr, Copley OH 44321-1363
Erik Valiente, Admissions
330-665-1084 Fax: 330-665-5021
Website: www.ocm.edu
E-mail: erik.v@ocm.edu

Ohio Institute of Health Careers
1880 E Dublin Granville Rd, Columbus OH 43229
614-891-5030

OHIO INSTITUTE OF HEALTH CAREERS
631 Griswold Rd, Elyria OH 44035
866-636-4734
Website: www.ohioinstituteofhealthcareers.edu

Ohio Institute of Photography & Technology
2029 Edgefield Rd, Dayton OH 45439-1917
Robert A. Martin, Executive Director
937-294-6155

Ohio State Beauty Academy
57 Town Sq, Lima OH 45801
419-229-7896

Ohio State College of Barber Styling
4614 E Broad St, Columbus OH 43213
614-868-1015

Ohio State Cosmetology School
5970 Westerville Rd, Westerville OH 43081
614-890-3535

Ohio State Sch of Cosmetology Northland
4390 Karl Rd, Columbus OH 43224
614-263-1861

Ohio State School of Cosmetology
3717 S High St, Columbus OH 43207
614-491-0492

Ohio State School of Cosmetology East
6320 E Livingston Ave, Reynoldsburg OH 43068
614-868-1601

OHIO TECHNICAL COLLEGE
1374 E 51st St, Cleveland OH 44103-1228
Marc Brenner, President
216-881-1700 Fax: 216-881-9145
Website: www.ohiotechnicalcollege.com
E-mail: info@ohiotechnicalcollege.com

OHIO VALLEY COLLEGE OF TECHNOLOGY
16808 St. Clair Ave, PO Box 7000
East Liverpool OH 43920
Scott S. Rogers, Director
330-385-1070 Fax: 330-385-4606
Website: www.ovct.edu
E-mail: info@ovct.edu

Paramount Beauty Academy
1745 11th St, Portsmouth OH 45662
740-353-2436

PROFESSIONAL SKILLS INSTITUTE
20 Arco Dr, Toledo OH 43607-2901
Daniel A. Finch, Chairman/CEO
419-531-9610 Fax: 419-531-4732
Website: www.proskills.com
E-mail: admissions@proskills.com

Raphael's School of Beauty Culture
1324 Youngstown Warren Rd, Niles OH 44446
330-652-1559

Recording Workshop
455 Massieville Rd, Chillicothe OH 45601
740-663-1000

Remington College
14445 Broadway Ave, Cleveland OH 44125-1957
216-475-7520

REMINGTON COLLEGE - CLEVELAND WEST CAMPUS
26350 Brookpark Rd, North Olmsted OH 44070
Gary A. Azotea, Campus President
440-777-2560 Fax: 440-777-3238
Website: www.remingtoncollege.edu
E-mail: gary.azotea@remingtoncollege.edu

RETS Technical Center
555 E Alex Bell Rd, Centerville OH 45459-2712
Ken Miller, Director of Admissions
937-433-3410

Sanford-Brown College
17535 Rosbough Blvd, Cleveland OH 44130-8362
Christine Smith, Executive Director
440-239-9640

the school of advertising art
1725 E David Rd, Kettering OH 45440-1612
Jessica Kantner, Director of Admissions
877-300-9326 Fax: 937-294-5869
Website: www.saacollege.com
E-mail: jessica@saacollege.com

Southeastern Business College
1410 Industrial Dr, Chillicothe OH 45601-3977
Clark Derexson, Director
740-774-6300

Southeastern Business College
504 McCarty Ln, Jackson OH 45640
Connie Blackburn, Director
740-286-1554

Southeastern Business College
1522 Sheridan Dr, Lancaster OH 43130-1368
Katrina Sims, Director
740-687-6126

Southeastern Business College
3879 Rhodes Ave Ste A, New Boston OH 45662-4900
Janet Travis, Director
740-456-4124

Southwestern College of Business
111 W 1st St Ste 1140, Dayton OH 45402-1113
937-224-0061

Spa School
5050 N High St, Columbus OH 43214
614-888-1092

Stark State College of Technology
6200 Frank Ave NW, Canton OH 44720-7228
330-494-6170

Stautzenberger College
1796 Indian Wood Cir, Maumee OH 45337-4007
George Simon, President
800-552-5099

TDDS TECHNICAL INSTITUTE
1688 N Pricetown Rd - S.R. 534
Lake Milton OH 44429
Mike Rouzzo, Director of Admissions
330-538-2216 Fax: 330-538-0609
Website: www.tdds.edu
E-mail: info@tdds.edu

Technology Education College
2745 Winchester Pike, Columbus OH 43232-4827
Thomas Greenhouse, Director
614-759-7700

Tiffin Academy of Hair Design
104 E Market St, Tiffin OH 44883
419-447-3117

Toledo Academy of Beauty Culture - East
2592 Woodville Rd, Northwood OH 43619
419-693-7257

Toledo Academy of Beauty Culture - North
5020 Lewis Ave, Toledo OH 43612
419-478-5325

Toledo Academy of Beauty Culture - South
1554 S Byrne Rd, Toledo OH 43614
419-381-7218

Total Technical Institute
8720 Brookpark Rd, Cleveland OH 44129-6810
Dave Bryant, Director of Admissions
216-485-0900

Tri County Beauty College
111 W Kemper Rd, Cincinnati OH 45246
513-671-8340

Tri-State College of Massotherapy
9159 Market St #26, North Lima OH 44452
330-629-9998

Trumbull Business College
3200 Ridge Ave SE, Warren OH 44484-3200
330-369-3200

Valley Beauty School
1315 Cisler Dr, Marietta OH 45750-9452
740-373-3617

Valley Beauty School
627 Main St, Zanesville OH 43701
740-452-6821

Vatterott College - Cleveland
5025 E Royalton Rd, Broadview Heights OH 44147
440-526-1660

Virginia Marti College of Art & Design
11724 Detroit Ave, Lakewood OH 44107
Quinn Marti, Director of Admissions
216-221-8584 Fax: 216-221-2311
Website: www.vmcad.edu
E-mail: qmarti@vmcad.edu

Western Hills School of Beauty & Hair Design
6490 Glenway Ave, Cincinnati OH 45211
513-574-3818

YOUNGSTOWN COLLEGE OF MASSOTHERAPY
14 Highland Ave, Struthers OH 44471-2321
Angela Shodd, Student Relations
330-755-1406 Fax: 330-755-1605
Website: www.ycm.edu
E-mail: ycm@ycm.edu

OKLAHOMA

Academy of Cosmetology
607 W Grand Ave, Chickasha OK 73018
405-222-2323

ATI Career Training Center
2401 NW 23rd St Ste 14, Oklahoma City OK 73107
405-445-5740

Beauty Technical College
PO Box 1506, Tahlequah OK 74465
918-456-6360

Broken Arrow Beauty College
400 S Elm Pl, Broken Arrow OK 74012
918-251-9660

Canadian Valley Area Voc-Tech School
6505 E US Highway 66, El Reno OK 73036-9117
405-262-2629

CAREER POINT INSTITUTE
3138 S Garnett Rd, Tulsa OK 74146-1933
Brad Oakley, Director of Admissions
918-627-8074 Fax: 918-627-4007
E-mail: tadmdir@career-point.org

CC's Cosmetology College
4439 NW 50th St, Oklahoma City OK 73112
405-943-2300

CC's Cosmetology College
11630 E 21st St, Tulsa OK 74129
918-234-9444

Central State Beauty Academy
8494 NW Expressway St, Oklahoma City OK 73162
405-722-4499

Claremore Beauty College
200 N Cherokee Ave, Claremore OK 74017
918-341-4370

Enid Beauty College
1601 E Broadway Ave, Enid OK 73701
580-237-6677

Eve's College of Hairstyling
912 SW C Ave, Lawton OK 73501
580-355-6620

Great Plains Area Vocational Technical School
4500 SW Lee Blvd, Lawton OK 73505-8304
580-355-6371

HERITAGE COLLEGE
7100 S I-35 Service Rd Suite 7118
Oklahoma City OK 73149
Cheryl Morris, Director
405-631-3399 Fax: 405-631-6711
Website: www.heritage-education.com
E-mail: info@heritage-education.com
Accredited Member School: ACCSCT. Providing quality education in Esthetics, Therapeutic Massage, Personal Training, X-Ray Medical Technician and Surgical Technology. Financial aid available to those who qualify.

Hollywood Cosmetology Center
PO Box 890488, Oklahoma City OK 73189-0488
Janet Goble, Contact
405-364-3375

Indian Meridian Vocational Technical School
1312 S Sangre Rd, Stillwater OK 74074-1899
405-377-3333

Jenks Beauty College
535 W Main St, Jenks OK 74037
918-299-0901

Metro Area Vocational Technical School
1900 Springlake Dr, Oklahoma City OK 73111-5238
405-424-8324

Oklahoma Farriers College
PO Box 788, Sperry OK 74073-0788
Kathie R. Beaston, Director of Administration
918-288-7221

Oklahoma Health Academy
1939 N Moore Ave, Moore OK 73160
405-912-2777

OKLAHOMA HEALTH ACADEMY
2865 E Skelly Dr Ste 224, Tulsa OK 74105
Stephanie Holderman, Director of Admissions
918-748-9900 Fax: 918-748-9937
E-mail: stephanieh@oklahomahealthacademy.org

Oklahoma State Horseshoeing School
4802 Dogwood Rd, Ardmore OK 73401
Marcella Kester, Owner
800-634-2811

O. T. Autry Area Vocational Technical Center
1201 W Willow Rd, Enid OK 73703-2506
580-242-2750

Platt College
112 SW 11th St, Lawton OK 73501
580-355-4416

Platt College
309 S Ann Arbor Ave, Oklahoma City OK 73128-1112
405-946-7799

Platt College
2727 W Memorial Rd, Oklahoma City OK 73134
405-749-2433

Platt College
3801 S Sheridan Rd, Tulsa OK 74145-1111
Angie Morelock, Director of Admissions
918-663-9000 Fax: 918-622-1240
Website: www.plattcollege.org
E-mail: angiem@plattcollege.org

Ponca City Beauty College
122 N 1st St, Ponca City OK 74601
888-557-6709

Poteau Beauty College
301 Turman St, Poteau OK 74953-2343
918-647-4119

Pryor Beauty College
330 W Graham Ave, Pryor OK 74361
918-825-2795

Sand Springs Beauty College
28 E 2nd St, Sand Springs OK 74063
918-245-6627

School of Hair Design
116 W Jackson St, Hugo OK 74743
580-326-7338

School of Hair Design
1437 SE Washington St, Idabel OK 74745
580-286-7840

Shawnee Beauty College
410 E Main St, Shawnee OK 74801
405-275-3182

Southern School of Beauty
140 W Main St, Durant OK 74701
580-924-1049

SPARTAN COLLEGE OF AERONAUTICS AND TECHNOLOGY
8820 E Pine St, Tulsa OK 74115-5802
Director of Admissions
800-331-1204 Fax: 918-831-8609
Website: www.spartan.edu
E-mail: spartan@mail.spartan.edu
Established 1928. Coed. Accredited member school: ACCSCT. Providing Technical training and education in Avionics, Aviation Maintenance; Nondestructive Testing and Quality Control. Complete flight training program. Offering Diplomas, Associate of Applied Science and Bachelor of Science in Aviation Technology Management.

State Barber and Hair Design College
2514 S Agnew, Oklahoma City OK 73108
405-631-8621

Stillwater Beauty Academy
1684 Cimarron Plz, Stillwater OK 74075
405-377-4100

Technical Institute of Cosmetology Arts & Sciences
822 E 6th St, Tulsa OK 74120-3610
918-660-8828

Tulsa Community College Metro Campus
909 S Boston Ave, Tulsa OK 74119
918-595-7000

Tulsa Community College West Campus
7505 W 41st St, Tulsa OK 74107
918-595-7000

Tulsa County Area Vocational Technical District 18
3420 S Memorial Dr, Tulsa OK 74145-1340
918-627-7200

TULSA WELDING SCHOOL
2545 E 11th St, Tulsa OK 74104-3909
Mike Thurber, Director of Admissions
800-WELD-PRO Fax: 918-587-8170
Website: www.weldingschool.edu
E-mail: tws@ionet.net

Tuttle Vocational Technical Center
12777 N Rockwell Ave
Oklahoma City OK 73142-2710
405-722-7799

Vatterott College
4621 NW 23rd St, Oklahoma City OK 73127
405-945-0088

Vatterott College - Tulsa
4343 S 118th East Ave, Tulsa OK 74146
Tim Maloukis, Director of Admissions
918-835-8288 Fax: 918-836-9698
Website: www.vatterott-college.com
E-mail: tim.maloukis@vatterott-college.com

Virgil's Beauty College
111 S 9th St, Muskogee OK 74401
918-682-9429

Woodward Beauty College
502 Texas St, Woodward OK 73801
580-256-7520

Wright Business School
2219 SW 74th St Ste 122
Oklahoma City OK 73159-3931
800-645-9364

Yukon Beauty College
1231 Garth Brooks Blvd, Yukon OK 73099
405-354-3172

OREGON

Abdill Career College
843 E Main St Ste 203, Medford OR 97504
541-779-8384

Academy of Hair Design
305 Court St NE, Salem OR 97301
503-585-8122

Airman Proficiency Center
3565 NE Cornell Rd, Hillsboro OR 97124-6374
503-648-2831

Apollo College
2004 Lloyd Ctr Fl 3, Portland OR 97232-1309
503-761-6100 Fax: 503-761-3351

Astoria Beauty College
1180 Commercial St, Astoria OR 97103
503-325-3163

BEAU MONDE COLLEGE ACADEMY OF COSMETOLOGY
11131 NE Halsey St, Portland OR 97220
Dianna Peterson, Owner
503-252-7444 Fax: 503-252-7555
Website: www.beaumondecollege.com
E-mail: diannapeterson@cs.com

BEAU MONDE COLLEGE OF HAIR DESIGN
1221 SW 12th Ave, Portland OR 97205
Dianna Peterson, Owner
503-226-7355 Fax: 503-226-6512
Website: www.beaumondecollege.com
E-mail: diannapeterson@cs.com

Chemeketa Community College
PO Box 14007, Salem OR 97309-7070
Mike Morgan, Dean
503-399-5172

College of Cosmetology
357 E Main St, Klamath Falls OR 97601
541-882-6644

College of Hair Design Careers
1684 Clay St NE, Salem OR 97301-1952
503-588-5888

College of Legal Arts
8909 SW Barbur Blvd, Portland OR 97219
800-342-3465

Heald College, Portland
625 SW Broadway 4th Floor, Portland OR 97205-3408
Joan Hayward, Campus Director
503-229-0492

Magee Brothers Beaverton School of Beauty
18295A SW Tualatin Valley, Aloha OR 97007
503-649-1388

Northwest College of Hair Design
8307 SE Monterey Ave, Happy Valley OR 97086
503-659-2834

Northwest College of Hair Design
210 SE 4th Ave, Hillsboro OR 97123
503-844-7320

Phagans' Beauty College
142 SW 2nd St, Corvallis OR 97333
541-753-6466

Phagans' Central Oregon Beauty College
355 NE 2nd St, Bend OR 97701
541-382-6171

Phagans' Grants Pass College of Beauty
304 NE Agness Ave Ste F, Grants Pass OR 97526
541-479-6678

Phagans' Medford Beauty School
2320 Poplar Dr, Medford OR 97504-5273
541-772-6155

Phagans' Newport Academy of Cosmetology Careers
158 E Olive St, Newport OR 97365
541-265-3083

Phagans' School of Beauty
622 Lancaster Dr NE, Salem OR 97301
503-363-6800

Phagans' School of Hair Design
16550 SE McLoughlin Blvd, Milwaukie OR 97267
503-652-2668

Phagans' School of Hair Design
1542 NE Weidler St, Portland OR 97232-1411
503-239-0838

Phagans' Tigard Beauty School
8820 SW Center St, Tigard OR 97223
503-639-6107

PIONEER PACIFIC COLLEGE
27501 SW Parkway Ave, Wilsonville OR 97070-9296
Kristin Lynn, Director of Admissions
503-682-3903 Fax: 503-682-1514
Website: www.pioneerpacific.edu
E-mail: inquiries@pioneerpacific.edu

Pioneer Pacific College
Clackamas Learning Site
8800 SE Sunnyside Rd, Clackamas OR 97015
503-654-8000 Fax: 503-659-6107
Website: www.pioneerpacific.edu
E-mail: inquiries@pioneerpacific.edu

Pioneer Pacific College
Health Career Institute
27375 SW Parkway Ave, Wilsonville OR 97070
503-682-1862 Fax: 503-682-6801
Website: www.pioneerpacific.edu
E-mail: inquiries@pioneerpacific.edu

Pioneer Pacific College
Springfield Branch Campus
3800 Sports Way, Springfield OR 97477
Debra Marcus, Campus President
541-684-4644 Fax: 541-684-0665
Website: www.pioneerpacific.edu
E-mail: inquiries@pioneerpacific.edu

Roseburg Beauty College
700 SE Stephens St, Roseburg OR 97470
541-673-5533

Springfield College of Beauty
307 Q St, Springfield OR 97477
541-746-4473

Western Business College
425 SW Washington St, Portland OR 97204-2296
503-222-3225

WESTERN CULINARY INSTITUTE
921 SW Morrison St Suite 400, Portland OR 97205
Joanne Lazo, Director of Marketing
503-223-2245 or 888-848-3202 Fax: 503-223-5554
Website: www.wci.edu
E-mail: info@wci.edu

PENNSYLVANIA

Academy of Creative Hair Design
125 N Wilkes Barre Blvd, Wilkes Barre PA 18702
570-288-4574

Academy of Hair Design
1057 N Church St Suite A, Hazleton PA 18202-1465
570-784-1020

Allentown School of Cosmetology
1921 Union Blvd, Allentown PA 18109-1629
610-437-4626

Allied Medical & Technical Careers
517 Ash St, Scranton PA 18509-2903
Heather Petrochko, Director of Admissions
570-558-1818

All-State Career School
501 Seminole St, Lester PA 19029-1827
610-521-1818

All-State Career School
97 2nd St, N Versailles PA 15137
412-823-1818

Altoona Beauty School
1528 Valley View Blvd, Altoona PA 16602
814-942-3141

Ambler Beauty Academy
50 E Butler Ave, Ambler PA 19002
215-643-5994

American Beauty Academy
6912 Frankford Ave, Philadelphia PA 19135
215-331-1515

Antonelli Medical & Professional Institute
1700 Industrial Hwy, Pottstown PA 19464-9244
Randall Wampole, Director of Admissions
610-323-7270

THE ART INSTITUTE OF PITTSBURGH
The College for Creative Minds
420 Boulevard Of The Allies, Pittsburgh PA 15219
Jeffrey Bucklew, Director of Admissions
800-275-2470 or 412-263-6600 Fax: 412-263-6667
Website: www.aip.aii.edu
E-mail: pahughes@aii.edu
Established in 1921. Known as a leader in creative education. College is located in the heart of downtown, surrounded by limitless cultural, educational, and recreational opportunities. Licensed by the State of PA and accredited by Accrediting Council for Independent Colleges and Schools to confer Associate of Science and Bachelor of Science degrees. Approved for training of veterans and eligible veteran's dependents. Authorized by federal law to enroll non-immigrant alien students.
Enrollment: 2700+ students; Co-ed.
Financial Aid available to qualified students through various federal and state programs. Awards based on individual need and availability of funds. Other Institute scholarship programs are available. Information regard-

ing eligibility can be obtained by contacting an admissions representitive at 1-800-275-2470.

Student Housing: School sponsored housing available in the form of furnished apartments.

Bachelor degrees available in: Advertising, Culinary Management, Game Art and Design, Digital Media Production, Graphic Design, Industrial Design, Interactive Media Design, Interior Design, Media Arts and Animation, Photography, Visual Effects and Motion Graphics, Hotel and Restaurant Management, Fashion and Retail Management.

Associate Degrees available in: Culinary Arts, Graphic Design, Industrial Design, Interactive Media Design, Photography, Video Production, Restaurant and Catering Operations.

Diploma programs include: The Art of Cooking, Digital Design, Residential Planning, Web Design. Some classes available evenings, Saturdays, and online.

Admissions: Prospective students must be a high school graduate or hold a General Educational Development (GED) Certificate. High school students who have not yet graduated should submit a partial transcript that indicates their expected graduation date, SAT and ACT testing not required for admission, however, may be used to determine the student's preparedness for college-level course work in English and/or mathematics.

Faculty: 101 full-time and 37 part-time instructors.

Facilities: 10 floors of fully networked computer labs and specialty facilities such as editing suites, digital photography labs, a television production studio, an industrial design machine shop, fully equipped culinary kitchens and more.

AUTOMOTIVE TRAINING CENTER
114 Pickering Way, Exton PA 19341-1310
Don VanDemark, Vice President/Chief Operating Officer
610-363-6716 Fax: 610-363-8524
Website: www.autotraining.edu
E-mail: atc@autotraining.edu

Established 1917. Private. Coed. Accreditation: Accrediting Commission of Career Schools and Colleges of Technology. Fees: $150. Enrollment: 414 full-time, 34 part-time. Faculty: 65. Student-faculty ratio: 22:1. Diplomas in Automotive Technology, Collision Repair Technology, Diesel Technology. Library: 2,000 volumes. 2 buildings on 5 acres. Small, specialized classes in each aspect of Automotive, Diesel and Collision Repair Technology. High performance engine dynamometer. ASE/NATEF MASTER certified programs. Extensive hands-on training. Financial aid to those who qualify. No unrelated general academic course requirement. Experienced ASE certified instructors.

Automotive Training Center
900 Johnsville Blvd, Warminster PA 18974
Kimberly Ewing, Executive Director of Admissions
877-411-8041 Fax: 215-442-1030
Website: www.autotraining.edu
E-mail: kewing@autotraining.edu
See listing under "Career Schools"

Aviation Institute of Maintenance
3001 Grant Ave, Philadelphia PA 19114-1018
John Norton, School Director
215-676-7700

Baltimore School of Massage - York Campus
170 Red Rock Rd, York PA 17406-6046
Anita Perry-Strong, Campus Director
717-268-1881

Beaver Falls Beauty Academy
720 13th St, Beaver Falls PA 15010
724-843-7700

Berean Institute
1901 W Girard Ave, Philadelphia PA 19130
215-763-4833

Berks Technical Institute
2205 Ridgewood Rd, Wyomissing PA 19610-1168
Elizabeth Wade, Director of Admissions
610-372-1722 Fax: 610-376-4684
Website: www.berkstech.com

Bidwell Training Center
1815 Metropolitan St, Pittsburgh PA 15233-2233
412-323-4000

Bradford Regional Medical Center
School of Radiography
116 Interstate Pkwy, Bradford PA 16701-1036
S. Gregoire, Program Director
814-362-8292

Bradford School
125 W Station Square Dr, Pittsburgh PA 15219
Director of Admissions
412-391-6710

Bradley Academy for the Visual Arts
1409 Williams Rd, York PA 17402-9012
James T. Hannigan, Jr., Director of Admissions
800-864-7725

Bucks County School of Beauty Culture
1761 Bustleton Pike, Feasterville Trevose PA 19053
215-322-0666

BUSINESS INSTITUTE OF PENNSYLVANIA
632 Arch St, Meadville PA 16335-2720
800-289-2069 Fax: 814-724-2777
Website: www.biop.edu
E-mail: info@biop.edu

BUSINESS INSTITUTE OF PENNSYLVANIA
335 Boyd Dr, Sharon PA 16146-3843
800-289-2069 Fax: 724-983-8355
Website: www.biop.edu
E-mail: info@biop.edu

Butler Beauty School
233 S Main St, Butler PA 16001
724-287-0708

Cambria-Rowe Business College
422 S 13th St, Indiana PA 15701-2804
724-463-0222

Career Training Academy
4314 Old William Penn Highway Ste 103
Monroeville PA 15146
Gina Hudac, Admissions Representitive
412-372-3900 Fax: 412-373-4262
Website: www.careerta.edu
E-mail: admissions2@careerta.edu

CAREER TRAINING ACADEMY
950 5th Ave, New Kensington PA 15068-6308
John Reddy, Director
Tyna Putignano, Director of Admissions
724-337-1000 Fax: 724-335-7140
Website: www.careerta.edu
E-mail: admissions@careerta.edu

Branch campus in Monroeville, PA and in North Hills, PA. Accreditation: ACCSCT. Federal and state financial aid available for those who qualify.

Associate in Specialized Technology degrees available (15 to 19 months) for Advanced Bodyworker and Medical Assistant Comprehensive. Associate in Specialized Business degree available (17.5 months) for Advanced Medical Coder/Biller. Programs ranging from 6 to 10.5 months offer diplomas in Dental Assisting, Medical Assisting, Health Insurance Claims Examiner/Medical Biller, Therapeutic Massage Technician, Comprehensive Massage Therapist, Business Administration/Acct. Tech., and Business Administration/Hospitality and Tourism. Day & evening classes available for many of our programs. New class sessions begin often.

Student Massage Clinic available to the public most Saturdays throughout the year, which provides unique learning opportunity for students in any of our massage programs.

Admission requirements include application and $30.00 fee, high school transcripts and applicant must be a high school graduate or possess a GED diploma prior to beginning classes at Career Training Academy.

All locations offer free parking and small classes. Wide range of student participation in community service projects spearheaded by school.

Career Training Academy
1500 Northway Mall, Pittsburgh PA 15237
Anna Bartolini, Director North Hills Branch Campus
412-367-4000 Fax: 412-369-7223
Website: www.careerta.edu
E-mail: admissions3@careerta.edu

Center for Innovative Training & Education
714 Market St Ste 433, Philadelphia PA 19106
215-922-6555

Center for Innovative Training & Education
135 Franklin Ave, Scranton PA 18503-1935
570-922-6555

CHI Institute
520 Street Rd, Southampton PA 18966-3747
Mike Herbert, Director of Admissions
215-357-5100

CHI Institute/RETS Campus
1991 Sproul Rd Ste 42, Broomall PA 19008-3516
610-359-7630

Chubb Institute-Keystone School
400 S State Rd, Springfield PA 19064-1243
610-543-1747

Clearfield Beauty Academy
22 N 3rd St, Clearfield PA 16830
814-765-2022

Computer Learning Network
2900 Fairway Dr, Altoona PA 16602-4457
814-944-5643

Computer Learning Network
401 E Winding Hill Rd Ste 101
Mechanicsburg PA 17055-4989
Marlene Macauley, Director of Admissions
717-761-1481

Consolidated School of Business
2124 Ambassador Cir, Lancaster PA 17603-2389
Millie Liberatore, Director of Admissions
717-394-6211

Consolidated School of Business
1605 Clugston Rd, York PA 17404-1779
Robert Safran Jr., Vice President
717-764-9550

Dean Institute of Technology
1501 W Liberty Ave, Pittsburgh PA 15226-1103
412-531-4433

DELAWARE VALLEY ACADEMY OF MEDICAL & DENTAL ASSISTANTS
3330 Grant Ave, Philadelphia PA 19114-2600
Glenn Goldsmith, Director
215-676-1200
Website: delawarevalleyacademy.com
E-mail: delvalacad@aol.com

Douglas Education Center
130 7th St, Monessen PA 15062-1097
Sherry Lee Walters, Director of Enrollment Services
800-413-6013 Fax: 724-684-7463
Website: www.douglas-school.com
E-mail: swalters@douglas-school.com

DuBois Business College
1 Beaver Dr, Du Bois PA 15801-2490
Lisa J. Doty, Director of Admissions
814-371-6920

DuBois Business College
1001 Moore St, Huntingdon PA 16652-1846
Lisa J. Doty, Director of Admissions
814-641-0440

DuBois Business College
701 E 3rd St, Oil City PA 16301-2407
Lisa J. Doty, Director of Admissions
814-677-1322

Duffs Business Institute
100 Forbes Ave Ste 1200, Pittsburgh PA 15222-1320
412-261-4520

Empire Beauty School
1000 Carlisle St, Hanover PA 17331
800-575-5983

Empire Beauty School
3941 Jonestown Rd, Harrisburg PA 17109
800-575-5983

Empire Beauty School
1801 Columbia Ave, Lancaster PA 17603-4335
800-575-5983

Empire Beauty School
1776 Quentin Rd, Lebanon PA 17042
800-575-5983

Empire Beauty School
320 Mall Blvd The Plaza, Monroeville PA 15146
800-575-5983

Empire Beauty School
3370 S Birney Ave, Moosic PA 18507-1500
800-575-5893

Empire Beauty School
2632 S Broad St, Philadelphia PA 19145
800-575-5983

Empire Beauty School
4026 Woodhaven Rd, Philadelphia PA 19154
800-575-5983

Empire Beauty School
1522 Chestnut St, Philadelphia PA 19102
800-575-5983

Empire Beauty School
1000 McKnight Park Dr Ste 1006A
Pittsburgh PA 15237
800-575-5983

Empire Beauty School
141 E High St, Pottstown PA 19464
800-575-5983

Empire Beauty School
324 N Centre St, Pottsville PA 17901
800-575-5983

Empire Beauty School
2302 N 5th Street Hwy, Reading PA 19605
800-575-5983

Empire Beauty School
PO Box 397, Shamokin Dam PA 17876
800-575-5983

Empire Beauty School
206 W Hamilton Ave, State College PA 16801
800-575-5983

Empire Beauty School
435 York Rd, Warminster PA 18974
800-575-5983

Empire Beauty School
313 W Market St, West Chester PA 19382
800-575-5983

Empire Beauty School
2393 Mountain View Dr, West Mifflin PA 15122
800-575-5983

Empire Beauty School
1634 MacArthur Rd, Whitehall PA 18052
800-575-5983

Empire Beauty School
1808 E 3rd St, Williamsport PA 17701
800-575-5983

Empire Beauty School
2592 Eastern Blvd, York PA 17402
800-575-5983

Erie Business Center
246 W 9th St, Erie PA 16501-1392
Donna Perino, Director
814-456-7504 Fax: 814-456-6015
Website: www.eriebc.edu
E-mail: perinod@eriebc.edu

GECAC Training Institute
1006 W 10th St, Erie PA 16502
814-451-5610

Greater Johnstown Area Vocational Technical School
445 Schoolhouse Rd, Johnstown PA 15904-2927
814-266-6073

Great Lakes Institute of Technology
5100 Peach St, Erie PA 16509-2482
Barbara Bolt, Director of Admissions
800-394-4548

HUSSIAN SCHOOL OF ART
1118 Market St, Philadelphia PA 19107-3679
Lynne Wartman, Director of Admissions
215-981-0900 Fax: 215-864-9115
Website: www.hussianart.edu
E-mail: info@hussianart.edu

ICM School of Business and Medical Careers
10 Wood St, Pittsburgh PA 15222-1931
Maureen McBride, Assistant Director of Admissions
800-441-5222

INTERNATIONAL ACADEMY OF ADVANCED REFLEXOLOGY & MEDICAL REFLEXOLOGY CLINIC
1701 Snyder Rd, Green Lane PA 18054
Professor L.J. Telepo, President
215-234-0307 or 267-377-5128 Fax: 267-329-8008
Website: www.reflexology.net
E-mail: postsecondary@reflexology.net
See listing under "Allied Health Science"

INTERNATIONAL ACADEMY OF ADVANCED REFLEXOLOGY & MEDICAL REFLEXOLOGY CLINIC
1177 6th St, Whitehall PA 18052
Professor L.J. Telepo, President
215-234-0307 or 267-377-5128 Fax: 267-329-8008
Website: www.reflexology.net
E-mail: postsecondary@reflexology.net
See listing under "Allied Health Science"

International Academy of Design and Technology
555 Grant St, Pittsburgh PA 15219
Deborah L. Love, Director of Admissions
800-447-8324

ITT Technical Institute
3330 Tillman Dr, Bensalem PA 19020
215-244-8871

ITT Technical Institute
5020 Louise Dr, Mechanicsburg PA 17055-4899
Glen Feist, Director of Admissions
717-691-9263

ITT Technical Institute
105 Mall Blvd #200, Monroeville PA 15146-2230
412-856-5920

ITT TECHNICAL INSTITUTE
10 Parkway Ctr, Pittsburgh PA 15220-3805
Peggy Tiderman, Director of Recruitment
800-353-8324 Fax: 412-937-9425
Website: www.itt-tech.edu

Jean Madeline Education Center for Cosmetology
315A Bainbridge St, Philadelphia PA 19147
215-238-9998

JNA INSTITUTE OF CULINARY ARTS
1212 S Broad St, Philadelphia PA 19146-3119
Admissions Office
215-468-8800 Fax: 215-468-8838
Website: www.culinaryarts.com
E-mail: admissions@culinaryarts.com

Johnson College
3427 N Main Ave, Scranton PA 18508-1495
Dr. Ann L. Pipinski, President & CEO
Melissa Ide, Director of Enrollment Management
800-2WE-WORK or 570-342-6404 ext. 125
Fax: 570-348-2181
Website: www.johnson.edu
E-mail: admit@johnson.edu

Kaplan Career Institute
5650 Derry St, Harrisburg PA 17111-3571
Roy Hawkins, Director
717-564-4112

KEYSTONE TECHNICAL INSTITUTE
2301 Academy Dr, Harrisburg PA 17112-1012
Tom Bogush, Director of Admissions
717-545-4747 Fax: 717-901-9090
Website: www.acadcampus.com
E-mail: educdir@acadcampus.com

Established 1980. Private. Coed. Accreditation: ACCSCT. Enrollment: 210 full-time, 50 part-time. Faculty: 15. Student-faculty ratio: 20:1. Degrees offered: Occupational Associate Degrees (AST/ASB). Library: 2,000 volumes. 1 building on 8 acres. Combined classroom; real world lab experience and externships for career training in Medical Assistant, Dental Assistant, Massage Therapy, Paralegal, Culinary Arts, Child Care, Computers.

Kittanning Beauty School
120 Market St, Kittanning PA 16201
800-833-4247

Lancaster School of Cosmetology
50 Ranck Ave, Lancaster PA 17602-3222
Deborah A. Dunn, CEO
717-299-0200

Lansdale School of Cosmetology
215 W Main St, Lansdale PA 19446
215-362-2322

Laurel Business Institute
11-15 Penn St, Uniontown PA 15401
Lisa Tressler, Supervisor of Enrollment
724-439-4900

Lebanon County Career School
18 E Weidman St, Lebanon PA 17046
800-694-8804

Lehigh Valley College
2809 E Saucon Valley Rd
Center Valley PA 18034-8447
Sam Jarvis, Director of Marketing
800-227-9109 Fax: 610-791-7810
Website: www.lehighvalley.edu
E-mail: joshua.padron@lehighvalley.edu

Lehigh Valley Hospital & Health Network
Center for Education
PO Box 7017, Allentown PA 18105-7017
610-402-2556

LEVITTOWN BEAUTY ACADEMY LLC
Vermillion Square
8919 New Falls Rd, Levittown PA 19054
Cecelia Pine, Contact
866-820-0322 or 215-943-0298 Fax: 215-943-0966
Website: www.levittownbeautyacademy.com
E-mail: info@levittownbeautyacademy.com

Lincoln Technical Institute
5151 W Tilghman St, Allentown PA 18104-3212
Lisa Kuntz, Executive Director
610-398-5300

Lincoln Technical Institute
9191 Torresdale Ave, Philadelphia PA 19136-1595
Jim Kuntz, Executive Director
215-335-0800

LINCOLN TECHNICAL INSTITUTE
3600 Market St, Philadelphia PA 19104-2641
James Beatty, Director of Admissions
215-382-1553 Fax: 215-382-3875
Website: www.lincolntech.com
E-mail: jbeatty@lincolntech.com

L.T. International Beauty School
830 N Broad St, Philadelphia PA 19130
215-922-4478

McCann School of Business & Technology
1147 N 4th St, Sunbury PA 17801-1221
Lisa Davis, Director of Admissions
570-286-3058

MERCY HOSPITAL SCHOOL OF NURSING
1401 Boulevard of the Allies
Pittsburgh PA 15219-5107
Joanne Sperry, RN, MN Director
412-232-7940 Fax: 412-232-7951
Website: www.pmhs.org/son
E-mail: jsperry@mercy.pmhs.org

Metropolitan Career Center
162 W Chelten Ave, Philadelphia PA 19144-3359
215-843-7023

Metropolitan Career Center
Computer Technology Institute
100 S Broad St 8th Floor, Philadelphia PA 19110
215-568-9215

Mifflin-Juniata Career & Technology Center
700 Pitt St, Lewistown PA 17044
717-248-3933

NAWCC School of Horology
514 Poplar St, Columbia PA 17512
717-684-8261

New Castle School of Beauty Culture
314 E Washington St, New Castle PA 16101
724-654-6611

New Castle School of Trades
New Castle Youngstown Rd, Pulaski PA 16143
724-964-8811

North Central Industrial Technical Education Center
651 Montmorenci Rd, Ridgway PA 15853
814-772-1012

Northeastern Hospital School of Nursing
2301 E Allegheny Ave, Philadelphia PA 19134-4497
Pat Fleetwood, Recruiter
215-291-3145

North Hills Beauty Academy
813 W View Park Dr, Pittsburgh PA 15229
412-931-8563

Oakbridge Academy of Arts
1250 Greensburg Rd, Lower Burrell PA 15068
Admissions Department
724-335-5336

Orleans Technical Institute
1330 Rhawn St, Philadelphia PA 19111-2802
215-728-4450

Orleans Technical Institute
Center City Campus
1845 Walnut St 7th Fl, Philadelphia PA 19103-4709
215-854-1853

Pace Institute
606 Court St, Reading PA 19601-3542
610-375-7223

Penn Commercial Business/Technical School
242 Oak Spring Rd, Washington PA 15301-2871
Office of Admissions
888-309-784

Pennco Tech
3815 Otter St, Bristol PA 19007-3618
Glenn Slater, Director of Admissions
215-785-0111

Penn State Cosmetology Academy
2200 E State St, Hermitage PA 16148
724-347-4503

Pennsylvania Academy of Cosmetic Arts & Sciences
19 N Brady St, Du Bois PA 15801
814-371-4151

Pennsylvania Academy of Cosmetic Arts & Sciences
2445 Bedford St, Johnstown PA 15904
814-269-3444

Pennsylvania Academy of the Fine Arts
118 N Broad St, Philadelphia PA 19102-1598
Angela Smith, Director of Admissions
215-972-7625

PENNSYLVANIA GUNSMITH SCHOOL
812 Ohio River Blvd, Pittsburgh PA 15202-2699
George Thacker, Director
412-766-1812 Fax: 412-766-0855
Website: www.pagunsmith.com
E-mail: pgs@pagunsmith.edu

PENNSYLVANIA INSTITUTE OF TAXIDERMY
118 Industrial Park Rd, Ebensburg PA 15931
Ruthann Pinos, Director
814-472-4510 Fax: 814-472-4545
Website: www.studytaxidermy.com
E-mail: info@studytaxidermy.com

Pennsylvania Institute of Technology
800 Manchester Ave, Media PA 19063-4036
Dr. Paul N. Smith, President
Angela Cassetta, Dean of Enrollment Management
800-422-0025

PITTSBURGH INSTITUTE OF MORTUARY SCIENCE
5808 Baum Blvd, Pittsburgh PA 15206-3706
Karen Rocco, Registrar
412-362-8500 Fax: 412-362-1684
Website: www.pims.edu
E-mail: pims5808@aol.com

Pittsburgh Technical Institute
Cranberry Center at the Regional Learning Alliance
850 Cranberry Woods Dr
Cranberry Township PA 16066
866-233-5556

Pittsburgh Technical Institute
North Fayette Campus
1111 McKee Rd, Oakdale PA 15071
800-784-9675

PJA School
7900 W Chester Pike, Upper Darby PA 19082-1917
610-789-6700

POTTSVILLE HOSPITAL SCHOOL OF NURSING
420 S Jackson St, Pottsville PA 17901-3625
Angela Pasco, RN, MSN, Director
570-621-5027 Fax: 570-621-5113
Website: www.pottsvillehospitalschoolofnursing.com
E-mail: phson@pothosp.com

Princeton Information Technology Center
137 S Easton Rd, Glenside PA 19038
215-576-7377

Pruonto's Hair Design Institute
705 12th St, Altoona PA 16602
814-944-4494

Punxy Beauty School of Cosmetology Arts & Science
222 N Findley St, Punxsutawney PA 15767
814-938-8811

THE RESTAURANT SCHOOL AT WALNUT HILL COLLEGE
4207 Walnut St, Philadelphia PA 19104-5296
Karl D. Becker, Admissions Director
215-222-4200 ext. 3011 Fax: 215-222-4219
Website: www.walnuthillcollege.edu
E-mail: info@walnuthillcollege.edu

ROSEDALE TECHNICAL INSTITUTE
215 Beecham Dr Ste 2, Pittsburgh PA 15205
Kevin Auld, Contact
412-521-6200 Fax: 412-521-2520
Website: www.rosedaletech.org
E-mail: admissions@rosedaletech.org

Roxborough Memorial Hospital
5800 Ridge Ave, Philadelphia PA 19128-1737
Patricia E. Burke, R.N., Manager, Admissions & Recruitment
215-487-4459

ST. MARGARET SCHOOL OF NURSING
221 Seventh St Suite 100, Pittsburgh PA 15238
Ann D. Ciak, Director
412-784-4980 Fax: 412-784-4994
Website: www.upmc.edu/StMargaret/SchofNursing
E-mail: smhsonrninfo@upmc.edu

Schuylkill Institute of Business & Technology
118 S Centre St Ste 2, Pottsville PA 17901
570-622-4835

South Hills Beauty Academy
3269 W Liberty Ave, Pittsburgh PA 15216
412-561-3381

South Hills School of Business & Technology
508 58th St, Altoona PA 16602-1188
814-944-6134

South Hills School of Business & Technology
124 E Market St, Lewistown PA 17044-2125
Gloria Runk, Learning Site Director
717-248-8140

South Hills School of Business & Technology
200 Shady Lane, Philipsburg PA 16866-1900
Kris Matson, Learning Site Director
814-342-7427

South Hills School of Business & Technology
480 Waupelani Dr, State College PA 16801-4516
Maralyn Mazza, Director
888-282-7427

Star Technical Institute
9121 Roosevelt Blvd, Philadelphia PA 19114
215-969-5877

Star Technical Institute
1570 Garrett Rd, Upper Darby PA 19082-4500
Angela M. Toney, BS, CMA, EMT, Director
610-626-2700

Stroudsburg School of Cosmetology
100 N 8th St, Stroudsburg PA 18360
570-421-3387

Talent Academy
1345 W Chester Pike, Havertown PA 19083
610-352-1401

Thompson Institute
3010 Market St, Philadelphia PA 19104
Scott Dams, Director of Admissions
215-594-4000

Toni & Guy Hairdressing Academy
930 Peach St, Erie PA 16501
Barbara Bolt, Director of Admissions
800-775-4187

Triangle Tech
PO Box 551, Du Bois PA 15801-0551
Jason Vallozzi, Director of Admissions
814-371-2090

Triangle Tech
2000 Liberty St, Erie PA 16502-2594
814-453-6016

Triangle Tech
222 E Pittsburgh St #A, Greensburg PA 15601-3328
724-832-1050

Triangle Tech
1940 Perrysville Ave, Pittsburgh PA 15214-3897
412-359-1000

Triangle Tech
RR 1 Box 51, Sunbury PA 17801
570-988-0700

Tri-State Business Institute
5757 W Ridge Rd, Erie PA 16506-1013
814-838-7673

Ultrasound Diagnostic School
3600 Horizon Blvd, Trevose PA 19053-4900
215-244-4906

UNIVERSAL TECHNICAL INSTITUTE
750 Pennsylvania Dr, Exton PA 19341
Karen Hannigan-Robinson, Campus Admissions Director
877-884-3986 Fax: 610-646-8549
Website: www.uti-auto-tech.com
E-mail: khannigan@uticorp.com

UPMC SCHOOL OF MEDICAL IMAGING
3434 Forbes Ave Murdoch Bldg Ste 206
Pittsburgh PA 15213-2582
Denise Csonka Lake, Program Director
412-647-3528 Fax: 412-647-3713
Website: www.schoolofmedicalimaging.upmc.com
E-mail: laked@upmc.edu

Venus Beauty Academy
1033 Chester Pike, Sharon Hill PA 19079
610-586-2500

VET TECH INSTITUTE
125 7th St, Pittsburgh PA 15222-3410
Cheri Yaworski, Director of Admissions
800-570-0693 Fax: 412-232-4348
Website: www.vettechinstitute.com
E-mail: cyaworski@vettechinstitute.com

Welder Training & Testing Institute
729 E Highland St, Allentown PA 18109-3253
610-437-9720

WESTERN PENNSYLVANIA HOSPITAL SCHOOL OF NURSING
4900 Friendship Ave, Pittsburgh PA 15224-1724
Joan Brooks, Recruiter
412-578-5538 Fax: 412-578-1837
Website: www.wpahs.org/education
E-mail: sonadmissions@wpahs.org

Western School of Health & Business Careers
1 Monroeville Center, Monroeville PA 15146
412-373-6400

Western School of Health & Business Careers
421 7th Ave, Pittsburgh PA 15219-1907
Michael Joyce, Director of Admissions
800-333-6607

West Virginia Career Institute
PO Box 278, Mount Braddock PA 15465-0278
Sharron K. Stephens, Executive Director
724-437-4600

Williamson Free School of Mechanical Trades
106 S New Middletown Rd, Media PA 19063-5202
Ed Bailey, Director of Enrollment
610-566-1776

Winner Institute of Arts & Sciences
1 Winner Pl, Transfer PA 16154
724-646-2433

Wrightco Technologies Technical Training Institute
225 Sollenberger Rd, Chambersburg PA 17202
717-263-8142

Wrightco Technologies Technical Training Institute
728 Ben Franklin Hwy, Ebensburg PA 15931
814-472-5211

Wrightco Technologies Technical Training Institute
Route 422 W, Shelocta PA 15774
724-354-5162

Wrightco Technologies Technical Training Institute
2 W Main St Ste 200, Uniontown PA 15401
724-439-2080

WyoTech - Blairsville
500 Innovation Dr, Blairsville PA 15717
724-459-9500

York Technical Institute
1405 Williams Rd, York PA 17402
Cathi Killingsworth Bost, Vice President
800-227-9675

York Technical Institute
Lancaster Campus
3050 Hempland Rd, Lancaster PA 17601
Cathi Killingsworth Bost, Vice President
800-227-9675

Yorktowne Business Institute
W 7th Ave, York PA 17404-2099
Bonnie Gillespie, Admissions Director
800-840-1004

RHODE ISLAND

Arthur Angelo School of Cosmetology Hair Design
151 Broadway, Providence RI 02903
401-272-4300

Computer-Ed Business Institute
622 George Washington Hwy, Lincoln RI 02865
401-334-2430

International Yacht Restoration School
449 Thames St, Newport RI 02840
401-848-5777

Katharine Gibbs School
85 Garfield Ave, Cranston RI 02920-7807
Director of Admissions
401-861-1420

MTTI - MOTORING TECHNICAL TRAINING INSTITUTE
54 Water St, East Providence RI 02914-5022
Sharon Ring, Program Director
401-434-4840 or 866-454-6884 Fax: 401-434-9540
Website: www.mtti.edu
E-mail: info@mtti.edu

NEW ENGLAND TRACTOR TRAILER TRAINING
600 Moshassuck Valley Industrial Hwy
Pawtucket RI 02860-1752
Frederick Hazard, Director
401-725-1220 Fax: 401-724-1340
Website: www.nettts.com
E-mail: fhazard@nettts.com

Newport School of Hairdressing
226 Main St, Pawtucket RI 02860
401-725-6882

Sawyer School
101 Main St, Pawtucket RI 02860-4117
401-272-8400

Sawyer School
550 Hartford Ave, Providence RI 02909-5800
401-272-3280

Warwick Academy of Beauty Culture
1276 Bald Hill Rd Unit 100, Warwick RI 02886
401-737-4946

SOUTH CAROLINA

Academy of Cosmetology
5117 Dorchester Rd, Charleston SC 29418
843-552-3241

Academy of Hair Technology
3715 E North St Ste F, Greenville SC 29615
864-322-0300

BAMBERG JOB CORPS CENTER
PO Box 967, Bamberg SC 29003
Sam Kolapo, Center Director
803-245-5101 Fax: 803-245-5915
E-mail: kolapo.samuel@jobcorps.org

BETA TECH
7500 Two Notch Rd, Columbia SC 29223
803-754-7544 Fax: 803-714-6797
Website: www.betatech.edu

Beta Tech
8088 Rivers Ave, North Charleston SC 29406-9235
Katrina Varner, Director
843-569-0889

CHARLESTON COSMETOLOGY INSTITUTE
8484 Dorchester Rd, Charleston SC 29420-7319
Jerry R. Poer, Owner
843-552-3670 Fax: 843-760-0976
Website: www.charlestoncosmetology.com
E-mail: ccisc@aol.com

Columbia Beauty School
1824 Airport Blvd, Cayce SC 29033-1821
Gloria Smith, Assistant Director
803-796-5252

ECPI College of Technology
250 Berryhill Rd Ste 300, Columbia SC 29210
803-772-3333

ECPI College of Technology
1001 Keys Dr #100, Greenville SC 29615
864-288-2828

ECPI College of Technology
7410 Northside Dr Ste G101
North Charleston SC 29420
843-414-0350

GOLF ACADEMY OF THE CAROLINAS
3268 Waccamaw Blvd, Myrtle Beach SC 29579
Paul Zagnoni, President
800-342-7342 Fax: 480-905-8705
E-mail: sdga@sdgagolf.com

ITT Technical Institute
6 Independence Pointe, Greenville SC 29615-4506
Debbie Wiggins, Director
864-288-0777

Kenneth Shuler's School of Cosmetology
736 Martintown Rd, North Augusta SC 29841
803-278-1200

Kenneth Shuler's School of Cosmetology/Nail Design
449 Saint Andrews Rd, Columbia SC 29210
803-772-6042

Lacy Cosmetology School
3084 Whiskey Rd, Aiken SC 29803
803-648-6181

MILLER-MOTTE TECHNICAL COLLEGE
8085 Rivers Ave, North Charleston SC 29406-9239
James Weaver, Director
843-574-0101 Fax: 843-266-3424
Website: www.miller-motte.net

Plaza School of Beauty Culture
946 Oakland Ave, Rock Hill SC 29730
803-328-5166

South Carolina Criminal Justice Academy
PO Box 1993, Blythewood SC 29016
William R. Neill, Deputy Director
803-896-7779

Southeastern School of Neuromuscular & Massage Therapy
1420 Colonial Life Blvd W Ste 80
Columbia SC 29210
803-798-8800

Southeastern School of Neuromuscular Massage Therapy
4600 Goer Dr Ste 105, North Charleston SC 29406
Ronda Villa, Director
843-747-1279

Strand College of Hair Design
423 79th Ave N, Myrtle Beach SC 29572
843-449-1017

Sumter Beauty College
921 Carolina Ave, Sumter SC 29150
803-773-7311

Trident Technical College
1001 S Live Oak Dr, Moncks Corner SC 29461
843-899-8033

SOUTH DAKOTA

Black Hills Beauty College
623 Saint Joseph St, Rapid City SD 57701
605-342-0697

Lake Area Technical Institute
230 11th St NE, Watertown SD 57201
605-882-5284

Mitchell Technical Institute
821 N Capital St, Mitchell SD 57301-2002
Allen Dvorak, Director of Admissions
800-952-0042

Si Tanka University
PO Box 220, Eagle Butte SD 57625
605-964-6045

Southeast Technical Institute
2320 N Career Ave, Sioux Falls SD 57107
Tracy Noldner, Supervisor Student/Instructional Services
800-247-0789

Western Dakota Technical Institute
800 Mickelson Dr, Rapid City SD 57703-4018
Jill Elder, Admissions Coordinator
605-394-4034 Fax: 605-394-2204
Website: www.wdt.edu
E-mail: jill.elder@wdt.edu

TENNESSEE

Academy of Beauty Arts
633 Mimosa Dr NW, Cleveland TN 37312
423-476-3742

Arnold's Beauty School
1179 S 2nd St, Milan TN 38358
731-686-7351

The Beauty Institute
568 Colonial Rd, Memphis TN 38117
901-761-1888

Concorde Career College
5100 Poplar Ave Ste 132, Memphis TN 38137-0132
Tommy Stewart, Executive Campus Director
901-761-9494

Electronic Computer Programming College
3805 Brainerd Rd, Chattanooga TN 37411-3701
423-624-0077

Fayetteville Beauty School
201 Main Ave S, Fayetteville TN 37334
931-433-1305

Georgia Career Institute
755 N Chancery St, Mc Minnville TN 37110

High-Tech Institute
560 Royal Pkwy, Nashville TN 37214-3645
866-502-2627

HIGH-TECH INSTITUTE - MEMPHIS
5865 Shelby Oaks Cir, Memphis TN 38134
Tanya Legg, Director of Admissions
901-432-3800 Fax: 901-387-1181
Website: www.hightechinstitute.edu
E-mail: tlegg@hightechinstitute.edu

ITT Technical Institute
7260 Goodlett Farms Pkwy, Cordova TN 38016-4908
901-381-0200

Jacobs Creek Job Corps Civilian Conservation Center
984 Denton Valley Rd, Bristol TN 37620
Thomas J. Scott, Principal
423-878-4021

Jon Nave University of Cosmetology
5510 Crossings Cir, Antioch TN 37013

McCollum & Ross, The Hair School
1433 Hollywood Dr, Jackson TN 38301
731-427-6642

Middle Tennessee School of Cosmetology
880A E 10th St, Cookeville TN 38501
931-526-8735

Miller-Motte Technical College
6020 Shallowford Rd, Chattanooga TN 37421
423-510-9675

Miller-Motte Technical College
1820 Business Park Dr, Clarksville TN 37040-6023
Lisa Teague, Director of Admissions
931-553-0071 Fax: 931-552-2916
Website: www.miller-motte.com
E-mail: lteague@miller-motte.com

MILLER-MOTTE TECHNICAL COLLEGE
801 Space Park N, Goodlettsville TN 37072
Kevin Suhr, Campus Administrator
615-859-8090 Fax: 615-859-9634
Website: www.miller-motte.com
E-mail: ksuhr@miller-motte.com

Mister Wayne's School of Unisex Hair Design
170 S Willow Ave, Cookeville TN 38501
931-526-1478

NASHVILLE AUTO-DIESEL COLLEGE
1524 Gallatin Ave, Nashville TN 37206-3298
William Ormsby, Vice President of High School Admissions
800-228-6232 Fax: 615-262-8466
Website: www.nadcedu.com
E-mail: admissions@nadcedu.com

Established 1919. Private. Coed. Accreditation: ACCSCT. Enrollment: 2000+. Faculty: 71. Student-faculty ratio: 25:1. Diploma and academic associate degrees in auto-diesel, auto body repair, high performance and performance fabrication offered. 16 acre campus with on campus dormitories and cafeteria. Text books in technical courses included in tuition. Associate Degree general education classes may be taken on-line.

Nashville College
1556 Crestview Dr, Madison TN 37115-2120
615-868-2963

National College
1328 Highway 11W, Bristol TN 37620
Becky Wild, Director of Admissions
423-878-4440 Fax: 423-793-1060
Website: www.national-college.edu
E-mail: info@national-college.edu

National College of Business & Technology
3748 Nolensville Pike, Nashville TN 37211-3322
Lynda Dandridge, Director of Admissions
615-333-3344 Fax: 615-333-3429
Website: www.national-college.edu
E-mail: info@national-college.edu

New Directions Hair Academy
3744 Annex Ave #A-2, Nashville TN 37209
615-353-8333

New Wave Hair Academy
3250 Coleman Rd, Memphis TN 38128
901-323-6100

New Wave Hair Academy
804 S Highland St, Memphis TN 38111
901-320-9283

NORTH CENTRAL INSTITUTE
168 Jack Miller Blvd, Clarksville TN 37042-4810
Dr. John McCurdy, President
931-431-9700 Fax: 931-431-9771
Website: www.nci.edu
E-mail: admissions@nci.edu

Established 1988. Private. Coed. Accreditation: Accrediting Commission of the Council on Occupational Education. Student-faculty ratio: 20:1. Degrees: AAS in Aviation Technology - concentrations in Flight, Maintenance, or Operations/Air Traffic Control. FAA part 147 Aviation Maintenance Technician Program enables students to become FAA Certified Airframe/Powerplant Technicians. Our Credit Inventory Evaluation Service turns military training into college credit. Financial Aid and Veterans benefits to those who qualify.

Pellissippi State Technical Community College
PO Box 22990, Knoxville TN 37933-0990
Donna Mack, Contact
865-694-6568

Plaza Beauty School
4682 Spottswood Ave, Memphis TN 38117
901-761-4445

QUEEN CITY COLLEGE
1594 Fort Campbell Blvd, Clarksville TN 37042-3545
Laura Payne, Chief Administrator
931-645-2361 Fax: 931-551-4955
Website: www.queencitycollege.com
E-mail: qcc1594@aol.com

Remington College
Nashville Campus
441 Donelson Pike Ste 150, Nashville TN 37214
615-889-5520

Reuben Allen College
120 Center Park Dr, Knoxville TN 37922
865-966-0400

SAE Institute Nashville
7 Music Circle North, Nashville TN 37203
Mark Martin, Director
Cindy Cyrus, Admissions Manager
877-27-AUDIO

Southeastern Career College
2416 21st Ave S Ste 300, Nashville TN 37212-5318
Janice Miller, Director
800-336-4457

Southern Institute of Cosmetology
3099 S Perkins Rd, Memphis TN 38118
901-363-3553

Stylemasters Beauty Academy
223 N Cumberland St, Lebanon TN 37087
615-444-4908

Styles & Profiles Beauty College
119 S 2nd St, Selmer TN 38375
731-645-9728

Tennessee Academy of Cosmetology
7041 Stage Rd Ste 101, Memphis TN 38133
901-382-9085

Tennessee Academy of Cosmetology
7020 E Shelby Dr Ste 104, Memphis TN 38125
901-757-4166

Tennessee School of Beauty
4704 Western Ave, Knoxville TN 37921
865-588-7878

Tennessee Technology Center at Athens
PO Box 848, Athens TN 37371-0848
423-744-2814

Tennessee Technology Center at Covington
1600 Highway 51 S, Covington TN 38019
901-475-2526

Tennessee Technology Center at Crossville
PO Box 2959, Crossville TN 38557
931-484-7502

Tennessee Technology Center at Crump
PO Box 89, Crump TN 38327
731-632-3393

Tennessee Technology Center at Dickson
740 Highway 46 S, Dickson TN 37055-2556
615-441-6220

Tennessee Technology Center at Elizabethton
PO Box 789, Elizabethton TN 37644-0789
423-543-0070

Tennessee Technology Center at Harriman
PO Box 1109, Harriman TN 37748-1109
Amy Keeling, Coordinator Student Services
865-882-6703

Tennessee Technology Center at Hartsville
716 McMurry Blvd E, Hartsville TN 37074-2028
615-374-2147

Tennessee Technology Center at Hohenwald
813 W Main St, Hohenwald TN 38462-2206
931-796-5351

Tennessee Technology Center at Jacksboro
PO Box 419, Jacksboro TN 37757
423-566-9629

Tennessee Technology Center at Jackson
2468 Technology Center Dr, Jackson TN 38301
Jane Wicker, Coordinator of Student Services
731-424-0691

Tennessee Technology Center at Knoxville
1100 Liberty St, Knoxville TN 37919-2327
Marilyn Canady, Coordinator of Student Services
865-546-5567

Tennessee Technology Center at Livingston
740 Hi Tech Dr, Livingston TN 38570
931-823-5525

Tennessee Technology Center at McKenzie
PO Box 427, Mc Kenzie TN 38201-0427
Willie Huffman, Student Services
Carol Lynch, Student Services
731-352-5364

Tennessee Technology Center at Mc Minnville
241 Vo Tech Dr, Mc Minnville TN 37110-1322
931-473-5587

Tennessee Technology Center at Memphis
550 Alabama Ave, Memphis TN 38105-3604
901-543-6100

Tennessee Technology Center at Morristown
821 W Louise Ave, Morristown TN 37813-2094
423-586-5771

Tennessee Technology Center at Morristown
323 Phipps Bend Rd, Surgoinsville TN 37873
423-345-4130

Tennessee Technology Center at Murfreesboro
1303 Old Fort Pkwy, Murfreesboro TN 37129-3311
615-898-8010

Tennessee Technology Center at Nashville
100 White Bridge Rd, Nashville TN 37209-4515
615-741-1241

Tennessee Technology Center at Newbern
340 Washington St, Newbern TN 38059-1138
731-627-2511

Tennessee Technology Center at Oneida/Huntsville
355 Scott High Dr, Huntsville TN 37756-4149
423-663-4900

Tennessee Technology Center at Paris
312 S Wilson St, Paris TN 38242-5023
731-644-7365

Tennessee Technology Center at Pulaski
PO Box 614, Pulaski TN 38478-0614
931-424-4014

Tennessee Technology Center at Ripley
127 Industrial Dr, Ripley TN 38063-7360
731-635-3368

Tennessee Technology Center at Shelbyville
1405 Madison St, Shelbyville TN 37160-3629
931-685-5013

Tennessee Technology Center at Whiteville
PO Box 489, Whiteville TN 38075-0489
731-254-8521

University of Tennessee Medical Center
1924 Alcoa Hwy, Knoxville TN 37920
865-544-6404

Vatterott College - Memphis Campus
2655 Dividend Dr, Memphis TN 38132
Joe Lockwood, Director of Admissions
901-761-5730

Volunteer Beauty Academy
1791 Gallatin Pike N, Madison TN 37115
615-860-4200

Volunteer Beauty Academy
5666 Nolensville Pike, Nashville TN 37211
615-331-9111

West Tennessee Business College
1186 Highway 45 Bypass, Jackson TN 38301-3256
800-737-9822

William R. Moore College of Technology
1200 Poplar Ave, Memphis TN 38104-7240
Susan Smith, Admissions
901-726-1977

TEXAS

Academy of Hair Design
744 FM 1960 Rd W Ste G, Houston TX 77090
281-893-0980

Academy of Hair Design
512 S Chestnut St, Lufkin TX 75901
936-634-8440

Academy of Hair Design
3141 College St #A10, Port Arthur TX 77642
409-813-3100

Advanced Barber College and Hair Design
2818 S International, Weslaco TX 78596
956-969-0341

AIMS Academy
1106 N Highway 360 #305
Grand Prairie TX 75050-2511
972-988-3202

Alfred G. Glassell Jr. School of Art
PO Box 6826, Houston TX 77265-6826
713-639-7500

Allied Health Careers
5424 W Highway 290 Ste 105, Austin TX 78735-8828
Rebecca Serwatt, Director
512-892-5210

American Commercial College
402 Butternut St, Abilene TX 79602-1399
Tony Delgado, Director
325-672-8495

American Commercial College
2007 34th St, Lubbock TX 79411-1899
Michael Otto, Director
806-747-4339 Fax: 806-765-9838
Website: www.acc-careers.com
E-mail: mjotto@acc-careers.com

American Commercial College
5119 Twin Towers Blvd, Odessa TX 79762-5504
Donna Duree, Director
432-362-6768 Fax: 432-550-0556
Website: www.acc-careers.com
E-mail: americancc@acc-careers.com

American Commercial College
3177 Executive Dr, San Angelo TX 76904-6801
Nikki Lambert, Director of Admissions
325-942-6797

AMERICAN COMMERCIAL COLLEGE
4317 Barnett Rd, Wichita Falls TX 76310-2303
Don Dobbins, Director
940-691-0454 Fax: 940-691-0470
Website: www.acc-careers.com
E-mail: ddobbins@acc-careers.com

A New Beginning School of Massage
2525 Wallingwood Dr Ste 1501, Austin TX 78746
512-306-0975

Arlington Career Institute
901 E Avenue K, Grand Prairie TX 75050-2636
972-647-1607

Arlington Medical Institute
2301 N Collins St Ste 100, Arlington TX 76011-2645
817-265-0706

Art Institute of Dallas
8080 Park Ln Ste 100, Dallas TX 75231-5900
214-692-8080

Art Institute of Houston
1900 Yorktown St, Houston TX 77056
Brian A. Shumaker, Director of Admissions
800-275-4244

The Art Institute of Houston - Culinary
1900 Yorktown St, Houston TX 77056-4113
Director of Admissions
800-275-4244

Astrodome Dental Career Center
2646 S Loop W Ste 415, Houston TX 77054-2678
Martina Torres, Contact
713-664-5300

ATI Career Training Center
10003 Technology Blvd W, Dallas TX 75220-4316
Debra Chapman, Director of Admissions
214-902-8191

ATI Career Training Center
6351 Boulevard 26 Ste 100
North Richland Hills TX 76180
817-284-1141
Website: www.aticareertraining.edu

ATI Career Training Center
1100 E Campbell Rd Ste 250, Richardson TX 75081
214-646-8460

ATI Technical Training Center
6627 Maple Ave, Dallas TX 75235-4690
Rod Cass, Director of Admissions
214-352-2222

Austin Business College
2101 S IH-35 Ste 300, Austin TX 78741-3854
Lisa Ruszczuk, Contact
512-447-9415

Aveda Institute
19241 David Memorial Dr, Conroe TX 77385-8778
936-539-6770

AVIATION INSTITUTE OF MAINTENANCE
7555 Lemmon Ave, Dallas TX 75209-3017
James Cooper, School Director
214-333-9711 Fax: 214-333-9185
Website: www.aviationmaintenance.edu
E-mail: directoramd@aviationmaintenance.edu

Baldwin Beauty School #5
3005 S Lamar Blvd Ste 103, Austin TX 78704
512-441-6898

Baldwin Beauty School - North
8440 Burnet Rd, Austin TX 78758
512-458-4127

Behold! Beauty Academy
9937 Homestead Rd, Houston TX 77016
713-635-5252

Bill J. Priest Institute for Economic Development
1402 Corinth St, Dallas TX 75215
214-860-5900

Border Institute of Technology
9611 Acer Ave, El Paso TX 79925-6709
Miguel A. Gamino, Director of Admissions
915-593-7328

Bradford School of Business
4669 Southwest Freeway Ste 300, Houston TX 77027
713-629-1500

Business Skills Institute
El Paso Campus
7850 Paseo Del Norte #216, El Paso TX 79912-8001
915-845-7772

CANCER THERAPY & RESEARCH CENTER
School of Medical Dosimetry
7979 Wurzbach Rd, San Antonio TX 78229-4427
Melissa Blough, Ph.D., DABR, School Director
210-450-5669 Fax: 210-616-5682
Website: www.ctrc.net
E-mail: mblough@ctrc.net

Capitol City Careers
5424 W Highway 290 Ste 200, Austin TX 78735-8800
Richard S. Anthens, Director
512-892-2640

Capitol City Trade and Technical School
205 E Riverside Dr, Austin TX 78704-1281
Ray Perrilloux, Director
512-444-3257

Career Academy
32 Oaklawn Vlg, Texarkana TX 75501-4128
903-832-1021

Career Advancement & Applied Technology
9350 S Presa St, San Antonio TX 78223-4733
210-633-1000

Career Centers of Texas
1900 N Expressway, Brownsville TX 78521
956-547-8200

Career Centers of Texas
1620 S Padre Island Dr, Corpus Christi TX 78416
361-852-2900

Career Centers of Texas
2001 Beach St, Fort Worth TX 76103
817-688-1132

Career Centers of Texas - El Paso
8360 Burnham Rd Ste 100, El Paso TX 79907-1526
Barbara Martinez, Director of Admissions
915-595-1935 Fax: 915-595-6619
Website: www.careercenters.edu
E-mail: bmartinez@cct-ep.com

Career Point Institute
485 Spencer Ln, San Antonio TX 78201-2027
David Murguia III, VP of Marketing
Adrienne Divin, Director
210-732-3000

Career Quest
5430 Fredericksburg Rd #310, San Antonio TX 78229
Mike Maloto, Director of Admissions
210-366-2701

Careers Unlimited
335 S Bonner St, Tyler TX 75702
903-593-4424

CENTER FOR ADVANCED LEGAL STUDIES
3910 Kirby Dr Ste 200, Houston TX 77098-4151
Doyle Happa, Director
713-529-2778 Fax: 713-523-2715
Website: www.paralegal.edu
E-mail: info@paralegal.edu

Central Texas Beauty College
2010 S 57th St, Temple TX 76504-6948
254-773-9911

Central Texas Commercial College
PO Box 1324, Brownwood TX 76804-1324
325-646-0521

Central Texas Commercial College
9400 N Central Expy Ste 200, Dallas TX 75231-5034
214-368-3680

Charlie & Sue's School of Hair Design
1711 Briarcrest Dr, Bryan TX 77802
979-776-4375

Circle J Beauty School
1611 Spencer Hwy Ste E, South Houston TX 77587
713-946-5055

Compu Tech Consultants School
811 S Central Expy Ste 500, Richardson TX 75080
214-570-0404

COMPUTER CAREER CENTER
6101 Montana Ave, El Paso TX 79925-2021
Amber Borrego, Director
915-779-8031 Fax: 915-779-8097
Website: www.computercareercenter.edu
E-mail: aborrego@computercareercenter.com

Conlee's College of Cosmetology
402 Quinlan St, Kerrville TX 78028
830-896-2380

Coryell Cosmetology College
608 Leon, Gatesville TX 76528
254-248-1716

COURT REPORTING INSTITUTE OF DALLAS
1341 W Mockingbird Ln Ste 200 East
Dallas TX 75247
Cindy Smith, Director
214-350-9722 Fax: 214-631-0143
Website: www.crid.com
E-mail: csmith@crid.com

COURT REPORTING INSTITUTE OF HOUSTON
13101 Northwest Fwy Ste 100, Houston TX 77040
Cindy Smith, Director
713-996-8300 Fax: 713-996-8360
Website: www.crid.com
E-mail: csmith@crid.com

Culinary Academy of Austin
6020 Dillard Cir Ste B, Austin TX 78752
Steve Mannion, Director
512-451-5743

Culinary Institute
7070 Allensby St, Houston TX 77022-4322
Henry Cittone, Director of Admissions
713-692-0077

Dallas Barber and Stylist College
9357 Forest Ln, Dallas TX 75243-4205
214-360-9570

David L. Carrasco Job Corps Center
11155 Gateway Blvd W, El Paso TX 79935-5401
915-594-0022

Dolphin Technical Institute
4835 Concord Rd, Beaumont TX 77703
409-892-0677

Everest College
6060 N Central Expy Ste 101, Dallas TX 75206
214-234-4850

Everest Institute
9100 US Highway 290 E Ste 100, Austin TX 78754
512-928-1933

Everest Institute
9700 Bissonnet St Ste 1400, Houston TX 77036
713-772-4200

Everest Institute
255 Northpoint Dr #100, Houston TX 77060-3203
281-447-7037

Everest Institute
7151 Office City Dr, Houston TX 77087
713-645-7404

Everest Institute
6550 First Park Ten Blvd, San Antonio TX 78213-4302
210-732-7800

Exposito School of Hair Design
3710 Mockingbird Ln, Amarillo TX 79109
806-355-9111

Faris Computer School
1119 Kent Ave, Nederland TX 77627-3818
409-722-4072

Fort Worth Beauty School
6785 Camp Bowie Blvd Ste 100, Fort Worth TX 76116
817-924-4289

Franklin Beauty School #2
4965 Martin Luther King, Houston TX 77021
Ron Jemison, Vice President
713-645-9060

GARY JOB CORPS CENTER
PO Box 967, San Marcos TX 78667-0967
Dean Hoffman, Center Director
512-396-6561 Fax: 512-396-6666
Website: gary.jobcorps.gov
E-mail: garycenterdirector@jcdc.jobcorps.org

Gulf Coast Trades Center
PO Box 515, New Waverly TX 77358-0515
936-344-6677

Hallmark Institute of Aeronautics
Aeronautics Campus-Aviation Technology
8901 Wetmore Rd, San Antonio TX 78216-4229
Joe Fisher, President
210-826-1000 Fax: 210-826-3707
Website: www.hallmarkinstitute.edu
E-mail: sross@hallmarkinstitute.edu

Hallmark Institute of Technology - Technology Campus
10401 W IH 10, San Antonio TX 78230-1736
Joe Fisher, President
210-690-9000 Fax: 210-697-8225
Website: www.hallmarkinstitute.com
E-mail: sross@hallmarkinstitute.com
Electronics Engineering Technology, Business Office Administration, Computer Network Systems Technology, & Medical Assistant.

High-Tech Institute
4250 N Belt Line Rd, Irving TX 75038-4201
Tara Meredith, Office Manager
972-871-2824

Houstons Training and Education Center
7457 Harwin Dr Ste 190, Houston TX 77036
713-783-2221

Houston Training School
709 Shotwell St, Houston TX 77020-4801
713-675-4300

Houston Training School
6630 Gulf Freeway, Houston TX 77087

ICC Technical Institute
3333 Fannin St Ste 203, Houston TX 77004-2930
713-522-7799

Institute of Cosmetic Arts and Science
Massage Therapy
1105 Airline Rd, Corpus Christi TX 78412
Denise Miller, Director
361-991-8868

Institute of Cosmetology
7011 Harwin Dr Ste 100, Houston TX 77036
713-783-9988

Interactive Learning Systems
8585 N Stemmons Fwy Ste C15
Dallas TX 75247-3805
214-637-3377

Interactive Learning Systems
6200 Hillcroft St Ste 200, Houston TX 77081-3007
713-771-5336

Interactive Learning Systems
256 N Sam Houston Pkwy E, Houston TX 77060
281-931-7717

Interactive Learning Systems
1001 Southmore Ave, Pasadena TX 77502
713-920-1120

International Beauty College #3
1225 Belt Line Rd Ste 7, Garland TX 75040
972-530-1103

International Beauty College #4
2716 W Irving Blvd, Irving TX 75061
972-513-1176

International Business College
2006 W University Dr, Denton TX 76201-0644
940-380-0024

International Business College
5700 Cromo Dr, El Paso TX 79912-5538
915-842-0422

International Business College
1155 N Zaragoza Rd, El Paso TX 79907
915-859-3986

International Business School
1434 N Central Expressway Ste 116
Mc Kinney TX 75070
972-548-0774

International Business School
3305 Andrews Hwy, Midland TX 79703-5130
432-694-7584

ITT Technical Institute
15621 Blue Ash Dr Ste 160, Houston TX 77090-5819
281-873-0512

ITT TECHNICAL INSTITUTE
2950 S Gessner Rd Ste 100, Houston TX 77063-3751
Jennifer Gomez, Director of Recruitment
713-952-2294 Fax: 713-952-2393
Website: www.itt-tech.edu
E-mail: jgomez@itt-tech.edu

Jay's Technical Institute
9000 W Bellfort St Ste 110, Houston TX 77031
713-772-2410

Jones Beauty College
10909 Webbs Chapel Rd # 129, Dallas TX 75229
214-956-0088

Jones Beauty College #2
311A W Pioneer Pkwy, Grand Prairie TX 75051
214-956-0088

KD STUDIO - ACTORS CONSERVATORY
2600 N Stemmons Fwy Ste 117
Dallas TX 75207-2168
T. A. Taylor, Director of Education
877-278-2283 Fax: 214-630-5140
Website: www.kdstudio.com
E-mail: admissions@kdstudio.com

Established 1979. Private. Coed. Accreditation: TEA, NAST, Texas Higher Education Coordinating Board. Tuition: $11,000. Enrollment: 100 full-time. Faculty: 26. Student-faculty ratio: 18:1. Degrees: Applied Associates Degree. Private library Resource Center. This program is aimed at developing camera acting skills as well as stage acting. Faculty are involved as industry professionals. A showcase is performed upon graduation where agents, casting directors and local producers and directors attend. FA available. VA approved.

KINGS WAY MISSIONARY INSTITUTE
401 S 35th St, Mc Allen TX 78501
956-682-6187 Fax: 956-682-9030
Website: www.kingswaymissionary.com
E-mail: kingswaymissionary@aol.com

Kingwood College
20000 Kingwood Dr, Kingwood TX 77339-3801
Isaac Williams, Director of Enrollment Management
281-312-1600

Lincoln Technical Institute
2501 Arkansas Ln, Grand Prairie TX 75052-7206
Mike Ackerman, Executive Director
972-660-5701

Lubbock Hair Academy
2844 34th St, Lubbock TX 79410
806-795-0806

Metroplex Beauty School
519 N Galloway Ave, Mesquite TX 75149
972-288-5485

MID CITIES BARBER COLLEGE
2345 SW 3rd St Ste 101, Grand Prairie TX 75051
Nachita Cano, Director
972-642-1892 Fax: 972-642-8198
Website: www.midcitiesbarbercollege.com
E-mail: midcitiesbarber@earthlink.net

Milan Institute
7001 I-40 West, Amarillo TX 79106
Summer Smylie, Director
806-353-3500

Milan Institute
6151 NW Loop 410 Ste 210
San Antonio TX 78238-3327
Russell Schwarz, Director
210-647-5100

Milan Institute of Cosmetology
2400 SE 27th Ave, Amarillo TX 79103
Summer Smylie, Director
806-371-7600

Milan Institute of Cosmetology
5403 Walzem Rd, San Antonio TX 78218
Dee Harris, Director
210-656-1991

Milan Institute of Cosmetology
605 SW Military Dr, San Antonio TX 78221
Arlene Almaleh, Director
210-922-5900

Mims Classic Beauty College
5121 Blanco Rd, San Antonio TX 78216
210-344-2041

MJ's Beauty Academy
3939 S Polk St Ste 505, Dallas TX 75224
214-374-7500

MTI College of Business & Technology
7277 Regency Square Blvd, Houston TX 77036
713-974-7181

MTI College of Business & Technology
7333 Harwin Dr # 212, Houston TX 77036-2088
713-979-1800

National Beauty College
149 W Kingsley Rd Ste 230, Garland TX 75041
972-278-2020

Neilson Beauty College
416 W Jefferson Blvd, Dallas TX 75208
214-941-8756

North Central Texas College
1525 W California St, Gainesville TX 76240-4636
Michelle Winters, Registrar
940-668-3315

Northwest Educational Center
2910 Antoine Dr Ste B100, Houston TX 77092-7063
713-680-2929

Northwest Texas Healthcare System
PO Box 1110, Amarillo TX 79105
806-354-1110

THE OCEAN CORPORATION
10840 Rockley Rd, Houston TX 77099-3416
John Wood, President
281-530-0202 or 800-321-0298 Fax: 281-530-9143
Website: www.oceancorp.com
E-mail: admissions@oceancorp.com

Ogle School of Hair Design
6333 E Mockingbird Ln #201, Dallas TX 75214
214-821-0819

Ogle School of Hair Design
5063 Granbury Rd, Fort Worth TX 76133
817-294-2950

Ogle School of Hair Design
720 Arcadia St Apt B, Hurst TX 76053
817-284-9231

Ogle School of Hair Design
2200 W Park Row Dr Ste 106, Pantego TX 76013
817-277-6341

Page Parkes Center of Modeling and Acting
1535 West Loop S Ste 100, Houston TX 77027
Shannon Fergason, Director
713-807-8200

Pasadena Academy
2155 Red Bluff Rd, Pasadena TX 77506
713-473-1777

PCI Health Training Center
8101 John W Carpenter Fwy, Dallas TX 75247-4720
Mr. Kelly Drake, Director of Admissions
214-630-0568

PCI Health Training Center
1300 International Pkwy, Richardson TX 75081
214-630-0568

Pipo Academy of Hair Design
3000 Pershing Dr, El Paso TX 79903
915-565-3491

Remington College
1800 Eastgate Dr, Garland TX 75041-5513
972-686-7878

Remington College
3110 Hayes Rd, Houston TX 77082
281-899-1240

San Antonio Beauty College #3
4130 Naco Perrin Blvd, San Antonio TX 78217-2508
210-654-9734

San Antonio Beauty College #4
2423 Jamar St # 2, San Antonio TX 78226
210-433-7222

San Antonio College Medical Dental Assistants
1500 S Jackson Rd, Mc Allen TX 78503-9902
Gabe Garcia, Director of Admissions
956-630-1499

SAN ANTONIO COLLEGE OF MEDICAL AND DENTAL ASSISTANTS
7142 San Pedro Ave Ste 100, San Antonio TX 78216
Carig Czubati, Director of Admissions
210-733-0777 Fax: 210-735-2431
Website: www.sacmda.com
E-mail: cczubati@sac-mda.com

SCHOOL OF AUTOMOTIVE MACHINISTS
1911 Antoine Dr, Houston TX 77055-1803
Admissions
713-683-3817 Fax: 713-683-7077
Website: www.samracing.com
E-mail: admissions@samracing.com

Scott & White Memorial Hospital and Clinic
2401 S 31st St, Temple TX 76508-0002
Janet Duben-Engelkirk Ed.D., MT(ASCP), Program Director
254-724-5177

Sebring Career School
7060 Bissonnet St, Houston TX 77074
713-772-0702

Seguin Beauty College
102 E Court St, Seguin TX 78155
830-372-0935

SOUTHEASTERN CAREER INSTITUTE
12005 Ford Rd Suite 100, Dallas TX 75234-7288
972-385-1446 or 800-524-8800 Fax: 972-385-0641
Website: www.southeasterncareerinstitute.com

Southern Careers Institute
2301 S Congress Ave Ste 24A, Austin TX 78704-5298
512-448-4795

Southern Careers Institute
2422 Airline Rd, Corpus Christi TX 78414-2904
361-857-5700

Southern Careers Institute
4805 Maher Ave, Laredo TX 78041
956-723-2345

Southern Careers Institute
1414 N Jackson Rd, Pharr TX 78577
956-687-1415

Southern Careers Institute
1405 N Main Ste 100, San Antonio TX 78212
210-271-0096

SOUTH TEXAS BARBER COLLEGE
3917 Ayers St, Corpus Christi TX 78415
Juan A. Garcia, President
361-855-2297 Fax: 361-855-7212
E-mail: southtexasbarber@sbcglobal.net

South Texas Vocational-Technical Institute
2144 Central Blvd, Brownsville TX 78520
956-554-3515

South Texas Vocational - Technical Institute
2400 Daffodil Ave, Mc Allen TX 78501-6148
956-631-1107

South Texas Vocational-Technical Institute
2419 E Hagger Ave, Weslaco TX 78596
Mark S. Hudson, School Director
956-969-1564

Southwest Institute of Technology
5424 W Highway 290 Ste 200, Austin TX 78735-8800
Howard Roose, Director
512-892-2640

Southwest School of Business & Technical Careers
272 Commercial St, Eagle Pass TX 78852-4859
830-773-1373

Southwest School of Business & Technical Careers
602 W Southcross Blvd, San Antonio TX 78221-1038
210-921-0951

Southwest School of Business & Technical Careers
2402 San Pedro Ave, San Antonio TX 78212-2840
210-731-8449

Southwest School of Business & Technical Careers
122 W North St, Uvalde TX 78801

Star College of Cosmetology
700 E Whaley St, Longview TX 75601
903-758-8611

Star College of Cosmetology
705 N University Dr, Nacogdoches TX 75961
936-462-7232

Star College of Cosmetology
520 E Front St, Tyler TX 75702
903-596-7860

State Beauty Academy
663 Oriole Blvd, Duncanville TX 75116
972-298-0100

Stephenville Beauty College
951 S Lillian St, Stephenville TX 76401
254-968-2111

Sterling Health Center
15070 E Beltwood Pkwy, Addison TX 75001
Sterling Mansoori, Ph.D., Director
972-992-9293

Success Institute of Business
16120 Stuebner Airline Rd #104
Spring TX 77379-7321
713-682-2262

Sylvia's International School of Beauty
434 W Parker Rd, Houston TX 77091
713-697-1200

Texas Barber Colleges & Hairstyling School
5148 S Lancaster Rd Ste A, Dallas TX 75241
214-943-7255

Texas Barber Colleges & Hairstyling Schools
9275 Richmond Ave Ste 180, Houston TX 77063
713-953-0262

Texas Careers
194 Gateway St, Beaumont TX 77701
409-833-2722

Texas Careers
6410 McPherson Rd, Laredo TX 78041
956-717-5909

TEXAS CAREERS
1421 9th St, Lubbock TX 79401
Debra Sawyer, President
806-765-7051 Fax: 806-765-6980
Website: www.texascareers.com
E-mail: dsawyer@texascareers.com

TEXAS CAREERS
1015 Jackson-Keller Rd #102
San Antonio TX 78213-3752
Laura Bledsoe, Campus President
210-308-8584 Fax: 210-308-8985
Website: www.texascareers.com
E-mail: lbledsoe@texascareers.com

Texas College of Cosmetology
117 Sayles Blvd, Abilene TX 79605
325-677-0532

Texas College of Cosmetology
918 N Chadbourne St, San Angelo TX 76903
325-677-0532

Texas School of Business
3208 W Parkwood Ave, Friendswood TX 77546
281-648-0880

Texas School of Business
711 E Airtex Dr, Houston TX 77073-6032
281-443-8900

Texas School of Business Southwest
6363 Richmond Ave Ste 300
Houston TX 77057-5914
Diane Nguyen, Director of Admissions
713-975-7527

Texas Vocational School
1921 E Red River St, Victoria TX 77901-5625
361-575-4768

Toni & Guy Hairdressing Academy
2810 E Trinity Mills Rd, Carrollton TX 75006
972-416-8396

Trend Barber College
8250 W Bellfort St, Houston TX 77071-2202
Obinna Mbachu, President
713-721-0000

Tri-State Cosmetology Institute
3910 Doniphan Dr Ste C, El Paso TX 79922
915-585-8777

Tri-State Cosmetology Institute
6800 Gateway Blvd E Ste 4A, El Paso TX 79915
915-778-1741

Ultrasound Diagnostic School
2998 N Stemmons Fwy #B, Dallas TX 75247-6103
214-638-6400

Ultrasound Diagnostic School
10500 Forum Place Dr #200, Houston TX 77036-8507
713-664-9632

United Regional Health Care System
Medical Technology Program
1600 11th St, Wichita Falls TX 76301
Gwen Morman, MS, MT(ASCP), Program Director
940-764-3187

Universal Technical Institute
721 Lockhaven Dr, Houston TX 77073-5598
281-443-6262

University of Cosmetology Arts & Science
913 N 13th St, Harlingen TX 78550-5034
Lorena Salinas, Corp. Dir.
956-412-1212

University of Cosmetology Arts & Sciences
PO Box 720391, Mc Allen TX 78504-0391
956-687-9444

UNIVERSITY OF TEXAS M.D. ANDERSON CANCER CENTER
1515 Holcombe Blvd, Houston TX 77030-4009
Anne Bettinger, Academic Recruiter
713-745-1205 Fax: 713-792-0800
Website: www.mdanderson.org/healthsciences
E-mail: ambettin@mdanderson.org

Vanguard Institute of Technology
3017 S 10th St, Mc Allen TX 78503-3102
956-787-4388

Velma B's Beauty Academy
1511 S Ewing Ave, Dallas TX 75216
214-942-1541

Victoria Beauty College
1508 N Laurent St, Victoria TX 77901
361-575-4526

Western Technical College
9624 Plaza Cir, El Paso TX 79927-2105
Bill Terrell, Chief Administrative Officer
915-760-8123
Website: www.wtc-ep.edu
E-mail: bterrell@wtc-ep.edu

Western Technical College
9451 Diana Dr, El Paso TX 79924-6936
Bill Terrell, Chief Administrative Officer
915-566-9621 Fax: 915-565-9903
Website: www.wtc-ep.edu
E-mail: bterrell@wtc-ep.edu

Westwood Aviation Institute
8880 Telephone Rd, Houston TX 77061-5114
Glen Feist, Director of Admissions
800-776-7423

Westwood College
4232 North Fwy, Fort Worth TX 76137-5021
817-685-9994

Westwood College - Houston South
7322 Southwest Fwy Ste 1900, Houston TX 77074
713-777-4433

Westwood College of Technology
8390 Lyndon B Johnson Fwy, Dallas TX 75243
214-570-0100

UTAH

American Institute of Medical-Dental Technology
1675 N Freedom Blvd, Provo UT 84604-2540
801-377-2900

Ameritech College
12257 Business Park Dr Ste 108, Draper UT 84020
800-652-0907

Bridgerland Applied Technology Center
1301 N 600 W, Logan UT 84321
435-753-6780

Cameo College of Essential Beauty
124 E 5770 S, Murray UT 84107
801-484-6173

Careers Unlimited
University Mall #I-163, Orem UT 84097
801-687-1271

Certified Careers Institute
775 S 2000 E, Clearfield UT 84015
801-774-9900

Certified Careers Institute
1385 W 2200 S Ste 100
Salt Lake City UT 84119-7205
801-973-7008

Dallas Roberts Academy of Hair Design
1700 N State St Ste 18, Provo UT 84604
801-375-1501

DAVIS APPLIED TECHNOLOGY COLLEGE
550 E 300 S, Kaysville UT 84037
James Larson, Director of Marketing
801-593-2500 Fax: 801-593-7848
Website: www.datc.net
E-mail: james.larson@datc.net

Eagle Gate College
5588 S Green St, Murray UT 84123
801-268-9271

Evan's Hairstyling College
798 W 400 N, Orem UT 84057
801-224-6034

Evan's Hairstyling College
955 E Tabernacle St, Saint George UT 84770
435-673-6128

Fran Brown College of Beauty
521 W 600 N, Layton UT 84041
801-546-6166

Francois D. Hair Design Academy
111 W 9000 S, Sandy UT 84070
801-561-2244

Hairitage College of Beauty
5414 S 900 E, Salt Lake City UT 84117
801-266-4693

Hairitage Hair Academy
900 S Bluff St Ste 9, Saint George UT 84770
435-673-5233

ITT TECHNICAL INSTITUTE
920 Levoy Dr, Murray UT 84123-2500
Gary Wood, Director of Recruitment
801-263-3313 Fax: 801-263-3497
Website: www.itt-tech.edu
E-mail: gwood@itt-tech.edu

Kendall's Academy of Beauty Arts & Science
7353 S 900 E, Midvale UT 84047
801-561-5610

Kendall's Academy of Beauty Arts & Science
2230 S 700 E, Salt Lake City UT 84106
801-486-0101

L.D.S. BUSINESS COLLEGE
95 North 300 West, Salt Lake City UT 84101-3500
Kathleen Howe, Assistant Director of Admissions
801-524-8145 Fax: 801-524-1900
Website: www.ldsbc.edu
E-mail: admissions@ldsbc.edu

Established 1886. Owned by The Church of Jesus Christ of Latter-day Saints. Accredited by the Commission on Colleges and Universities of the Northwest Association of Schools, Colleges and Universities; Health programs accredited by Commission on Accreditation of Allied Health Programs.

Coed. Approximately 1,300 enrolled. 96% LDS. Students from every state and 50 foreign countries; 73% full time; average age 22.5 years.

2007-2008 Tuition: $1,300 for full-time, members of the LDS Church; $2,600 for others. Financial aid available: Federal Pell Grants; Federal Stafford Student Loans, Federal Subsidized and Unsubsidized Stafford Loans; Federal Parent Loans for Undergraduate Students; other campus loans. Application: complete financial aid information form, complete the Free Application for Federal Student Aid form; request that financial aid transcript be sent to the college.

On-campus residence halls for men and women. $4,160 to $4,580 per academic year including meal plans.

Two-year degrees in financial/managerial accounting; business; business information systems; interior design; executive medical assistant; medical administrative assistant; office technology with emphases in executive assistant and legal administrative assistant; associate of science in business; and general studies. One-year certificates in accounting; professional sales; IT support specialist; windows administration certificate; interior design sales associate; medical assistant; medical office assistant; transcription; coding; and office technology support. All students take courses offered by the College's LDS Institute of Religion.

Enrollment open to persons of any race, creed, gender, religion or national origin. Admission requirements include application (parts 1 through 7), $30 fee, and high school transcript or evidence of high school graduation. TOEFL and declaration of finances for international students.

Faculty: 15 full-time; 81 part-time. Student/faculty ratio: 20/1; Most faculty are practicing professionals with strong career-related skills.

Located in downtown Salt Lake City, close to world-class skiing, mountain sports, water sports. Wide range of on- and off-campus student activities. Two LDS wards. Devotional lectures featuring LDS general authorities; 90%+ placement rate; Career Services Center; Learning Assistance Lab. Library: 6,000 volumes, CD-ROM holdings.

Mountainland Applied Technology College
987 S Geneva Rd, Orem UT 84058
Mark Middlebrook, Director of Marketing/Development
801-863-7662

Mountain West College
3280 W 3500 S, West Valley City UT 84119
John Rios, Director of Admissions
801-840-4800

Myotherapy College of Utah
2120 South 1300 East Suite 102
Salt Lake City UT 84106
Vaughn L. Belnap, President/Director
801-484-7624

New Horizons Beauty College
550 N Main St Ste 115, Logan UT 84321
435-753-9779

Ogden-Weber Applied Technology College
200 N Washington Blvd, Ogden UT 84404
Elsa Zweifel, Student Recruitment
801-627-8300

Premier Hair Academy
4062 S 4000 W, West Valley UT 84120-4040
801-966-8414

Provo College
1450 W 820 N, Provo UT 84601-1305
801-375-1861

Skin Works School of Advanced Skin Care
2121 S 230 E, Salt Lake City UT 84115
801-530-0001

Southeast Applied Technology College
375 S Carbon Ave, Price UT 84501
435-613-1438

Southwest Applied Technology College
510 W 800 S, Cedar City UT 84720
435-586-2899

Stacey's Hands of Champions Beauty College
3721 S 250 W, Ogden UT 84405
801-394-5718

Stevens Henager College
755 Main St, Logan UT 84321
Josh Swayne, Executive Director
435-713-4777
Website: www.stevenshenager.edu

Tooele Applied Technology College
1655 E 3300 S, Salt Lake City UT 84106
801-493-8700

Uintah Basin Applied Technology College
1100 E Lagoon St, Roosevelt UT 84066
435-722-4523

Utah Career College
1902 W 7800 S, West Jordan UT 84088-4021
Denice Dunker, Director of Admissions
801-304-4224

Von Curtis Academy of Hair Design
480 N 900 E, Provo UT 84606
801-374-5111

VERMONT

Essex Technical Center
3 Educational Dr, Essex Junction VT 05452-3172

FLETCHER ALLEN HEALTH CARE SCHOOL OF CYTOTECHNOLOGY
111 Colchester Ave, Burlington VT 05401-1473
Sandra Giroux, Program Director
802-847-5133 Fax: 802-847-3632
Website: www.fahc.org/cytoschool
E-mail: sandra.giroux@vtmednet.org

NEW ENGLAND CULINARY INSTITUTE
56 College St, Montpelier VT 05602
Sherri Gilmore, Director of Admissions
877-223-6324 Fax: 802-225-3280
Website: www.neci.edu
E-mail: Admissions@neci.edu

Established in 1980. Private. Coed. Accreditation: ACCSCT, State of Vermont. Tuition: $9,940 - $23,835, depending on program - 2006. Room and board: $3,780 - $6,565, depending on program - 2006. Enrollment: 557. Faculty: 70. Programs have one of the lowest student-to-teacher ratios in culinary education, averaging 7 students with a maximum of 10 to each instructor in production classes. Degrees: Associate of Occupational Studies in Culinary Arts; Associate of Occupational Studies in Baking & Pastry Arts; Associate of Occupational Studies in Hospitality and Restaurant Management; Bachelor of Arts in Hospitality and Restaurant Management; Certificate program in Basic Cooking; Certificate program in Baking; Certificate program in Pastry. Paid internships. Intense, hands-on training in a variety of real foodservice operations on 2 campuses in scenic, safe Vermont. Advanced placement program for experienced students.

O'Briens Training Center
1475 Shelburne Rd, South Burlington VT 05403
802-658-9591

Vermont College of Cosmetology
400 Cornerstone Dr Ste 220, Williston VT 05495
802-863-4666

Woodbury College
660 Elm St, Montpelier VT 05602-4017
Denise MacMartin, Director of Admissions
800-639-6039 Fax: 802-229-2141
Website: www.woodbury-college.edu
E-mail: admiss@woodbury-college.edu

VIRGINIA

ACT COLLEGE
1100 Wilson Blvd Suite M780, Arlington VA 22209
Robert Boderman, EVP of Operations
703-527-6660 Fax: 703-527-6688
Website: www.actcollege.edu
E-mail: rboderman@actcollege.edu

Advanced Technology Institute
5700 Southern Blvd #100
Virginia Beach VA 23462-2409
757-490-1241

AKS Massage School
462 Herndon Pkwy Ste 208, Herndon VA 20170
703-464-0333

APPRENTICE SCHOOL - NORTHROP GRUMMAN NEWPORT NEWS
4101 Washington Ave
Newport News VA 23607-2704
Paul Hoffmann, Admissions Administrator
757-880-3717 Fax: 757-688-0305
Website: www.apprenticeschool.com
E-mail: paul.hoffmann@ngc.com

The Art Institute of Washington
1820 N Fort Myer Dr, Arlington VA 22209
Larry McHugh, Director of Admissions
703-358-9550

AUGUSTA MEDICAL CENTER
School of Clinical Laboratory Science
PO Box 1000, Fishersville VA 22939-1000
Bernadette Bekken, Program Director
540-332-4539 Fax: 540-332-4543
Website: www.augustamed.com/cls
E-mail: bbekken@augustamed.com

AVIATION INSTITUTE OF MAINTENANCE
1429 Miller Store Rd, Virginia Beach VA 23455-3324
Michael Huffman, Director
757-363-2121 Fax: 757-363-2044
Website: www.aviationmaintenance.edu
E-mail: directoramn@tidetech.com

BarPalma Beauty Careers Academy
3535 Franklin Rd SW Ste D, Roanoke VA 24014
540-343-0153

Beta Tech
7914 Midlothian Tpke, Richmond VA 23235-5230
Melissa Schick, Director
804-330-0111

Beta Tech West
7001 W Broad St, Richmond VA 23294-3701
804-672-2300

Blue Ridge Job Corps Center
245 W Main St, Marion VA 24354
276-783-7221

Braxton School
3600 W Broad St Ste 190, Richmond VA 23230-4939
804-353-4458

CAREER TRAINING SOLUTIONS
100 Riverside Pkwy Suite 123
Fredericksburg VA 22406
Christine Carroll, President
540-373-2200 Fax: 540-373-4465
Website: www.careertrainingsolutions.com
E-mail: christine.carroll@careertrainingsolutions.com

Carilion Health Systems
PO Box 13727, Roanoke VA 24036-3727
540-981-7347

Crescent Cosmetology University
34 Holloway Dr, Hampton VA 23666
757-826-4609

Danville Regional Medical Center
142 S Main St, Danville VA 24541-2987
Janet Nicol, Coordinator of Admissions
434-799-4510

ECPI College of Technology
10021 Balls Ford Rd #100, Manassas VA 20109-2666
703-330-5300

ECPI College of Technology
1001 Omni Blvd Ste 100
Newport News VA 23606-4215
757-838-9191

ECPI College of Technology
5555 Greenwich Rd Ste 300
Virginia Beach VA 23462-6542
757-671-7171 Fax: 757-671-8661
Website: www.ecpi.edu

ECPI Technical College
4305 Cox Rd, Glen Allen VA 23060-3359
804-934-0100

ECPI Technical College
800 Moorefield Park Dr, Richmond VA 23236-3686
804-330-5533

ECPI Technical College
5234 Airport Rd NW, Roanoke VA 24012-1603
540-563-8080

Empire Beauty School
10807 Hull Street Rd, Midlothian VA 23112
800-575-5983

Flatwoods Civilian Conservation Center
2803 Dungannon Rd, Coeburn VA 24230-5914
276-395-3384

Ghent Beauty Academy
2811 Lafayette Blvd, Norfolk VA 23509
757-855-2103

Graham Webb International Academy of Hair
1621 N Kent St #1617LL, Arlington VA 22209
703-243-9322

HERITAGE INSTITUTE
8255 Shoppers Square, Manassas VA 20111-2176
Tess Anderson, Director
703-361-7775 Fax: 703-335-9987
Website: www.heritage-education.com
E-mail: info@heritage-education.com

Accredited Member School: ACCSCT. Providing quality education in Therapeutic Massage, Personal Training, Cosmetology, and X-Ray Medical Technician. Financial aid available to those who qualify.

Hicks Academy of Beauty Culture
904 Loudoun Ave, Portsmouth VA 23707
757-399-2400

Jefferson College of Health Sciences
Formerly Community Hospital
PO Box 13186, Roanoke VA 24031-3186
Judith McKeon, Director of Admissions
540-985-8483

Kee Business College
803 Diligence Dr, Newport News VA 23606-4203
Sandi Bell, Director of Education
757-873-1111

Medical Careers Institute
1001 Omni Blvd Ste 200
Newport News VA 23606-4215
757-873-2423

Medical Careers Institute
800 Moorefield Park Dr #302, Richmond VA 23236
804-521-0400

Medical Careers Institute
5501 Greenwich Rd, Virginia Beach VA 23462-6540
757-497-8400

Miller-Motte Technical College
1011 Creekside Ln, Lynchburg VA 24502-4353
877-333-6622

National College
100 Logan St, Bluefield VA 24605
Tonya Elmore, Director of Admissions
276-326-3621 Fax: 276-322-5731
Website: www.national-college.edu
E-mail: info@national-college.edu

National College
1819 Emmet St N, Charlottesville VA 22901-2812
434-295-0136 Fax: 434-979-8061
Website: www.national-college.edu
E-mail: info@national-college.edu

National College
336 Old Riverside Dr, Danville VA 24541
Jeff Moore, Director of Admissions
434-793-6822 Fax: 434-793-3634
Website: www.national-college.edu
E-mail: info@national-college.edu

National College
1515 Country Club Rd, Harrisonburg VA 22802
Kathy Sours, Director of Admissions
540-432-0943 Fax: 540-432-1133
Website: www.national-college.edu
E-mail: info@national-college.edu

National College
104 Candlewood Ct, Lynchburg VA 24502-2653
Nancy Fortune, Director of Admissions
434-239-3500 Fax: 434-239-3948
Website: www.national-college.edu
E-mail: info@national-college.edu

National College
10 Church St, Martinsville VA 24114
Barbara Rakes, Director of Admissions
276-632-5621 Fax: 276-632-7915
Website: www.national-college.edu
E-mail: info@national-college.edu

National College
PO Box 6400, Roanoke VA 24017-0400
Ron Smith, Director of Admissions
540-986-1800 Fax: 540-444-4195
Website: www.national-college.edu
E-mail: info@national-college.edu

National College
1813 E Main St, Salem VA 24153-4598
Ron Smith, Director of Admissions
540-986-1800 Fax: 540-444-4195
Website: www.national-college.edu
E-mail: info@national-college.edu

Norfolk Skills Center
922 W 21st St, Norfolk VA 23517-1516
757-628-3300

Potomac Academy of Hair Design
350 S Washington St, Falls Church VA 22046
703-532-5050

Ralph's Virginia School of Cosmetology
3225 Old Forest Rd Ste 5, Lynchburg VA 24501
434-385-7722

Riverside School of Health Careers
316 Main St, Newport News VA 23601
Tracey Hiller, Recruitment Coordinator
757-240-2200 Fax: 757-240-2225
Website: www.riversideonline.com/rshc
E-mail: tracey.hiller@rivhs.com

Rockingham Memorial Hospital
School of Medical Technology
235 Cantrell Ave, Harrisonburg VA 22801-3293
Randall Vandevander, Program Director
540-564-5407

RSHT Training Center
702 Charlton Ave Ste A, Charlottesville VA 22903
434-245-0400

RSHT Training Center
1601 Willow Lawn Dr Ste 320, Richmond VA 23230
804-288-1000

Rudy & Kelly Academy of Hair & Nails
5606 Princess Anne Rd, Virginia Beach VA 23462
757-473-0994

Sentara School of Health Professions
1441 Crossways Blvd Suite 105
Chesapeake VA 23320
Shelly Vinson, Director
757-388-2900 Fax: 757-388-2905
Website: www.sentara.com/healthprofessions
E-mail: healthprofessions@sentara.com

Southside Virginia Community College
109 Campus Dr, Alberta VA 23821-2930
Ronald E. Mattox, Dean of Admissions
434-949-1014 Fax: 434-949-7863
Website: www.sv.vccs.edu
E-mail: ronald.mattox@sv.vccs.edu

Southside Virginia Community College
200 Daniel Rd, Keysville VA 23947
Ronald E. Mattox, Dean of Admissions
434-736-2018 Fax: 434-736-2082
Website: www.sv.vccs.edu
E-mail: ronald.mattox@sv.vccs.edu

Springfield Beauty Academy
4223 Annandale Rd, Annandale VA 22003
703-256-5662

Staunton School of Cosmetology
PO Box 2385, Staunton VA 24402-2385
540-885-0808

Stratford University
7777 Leesburg Pike #100 South
Falls Church VA 22043
Keith Evans, Contact
703-821-8570 Fax: 703-734-5335
Website: www.stratford.edu
E-mail: admissions@stratford.edu

Suffolk Beauty Academy
860 Portsmouth Blvd, Suffolk VA 23434
757-934-0656

TAP Center for Employment Training
108 N Jefferson St Suite 303, Roanoke VA 24016
Dr. Tom Bryant, Program Manager
540-767-6222

TESST Electronic School
6315 Bren Mar Dr, Alexandria VA 22312-3403
703-354-1005

Tidewater Tech
932 Ventures Way, Chesapeake VA 23320-2882
757-549-2121

Tidewater Tech
616 Denbigh Blvd, Newport News VA 23608-4416
757-874-2121

TIDEWATER TECH
7020 N Military Hwy, Norfolk VA 23518-4833
Laura Silva, Director of Admissions
757-853-2121 Fax: 757-852-9017
Website: www.tidewatertech.edu
E-mail: admdirttn@tidewatertech.edu

Tidewater Tech
2697 Dean Dr Ste 100
Virginia Beach VA 23452-7431
757-340-2121

VIRGINIA CAREER INSTITUTE
100 Constitution Dr Ste 101
Virginia Beach VA 23462-6758
Andy Tysinger, School Director
757-499-5447 Fax: 757-473-5735
Website: www.virginiacareerinstitute.edu
E-mail: atysinger@success.edu

Virginia School of Hair Design
101 W Queens Way, Hampton VA 23669
757-722-0211

VIRGINIA SCHOOL OF MASSAGE
2008 Morton Dr, Charlottesville VA 22903-6803
Admissions Department
434-293-4031 Fax: 434-293-4190
Website: www.steinered.com

Virginia School of Technology
9210 Arboretum Pkwy Suite 100
Richmond VA 23236-3472
804-323-1020

Wards Corner Beauty Academy
7525 Tidewater Dr Ste 45, Norfolk VA 23505
757-583-3300

Washington County Adult Skill Center
848 Thompson Dr, Abingdon VA 24210-2346
276-676-1948

Woodrow Wilson Rehabilitation Center
PO Box 1500, Fishersville VA 22939
540-332-7265

WASHINGTON

The Academy of Hair Design
208 S Wenatchee Ave, Wenatchee WA 98801-3062
509-662-9082

Apollo College
10102 E Knox Ave, Spokane WA 99206-4146
509-532-8888 Fax: 509-533-5983

The Art Institute of Seattle
2323 Elliott Ave, Seattle WA 98121-1642
206-448-0900

BATES TECHNICAL COLLEGE
1101 S Yakima Ave, Tacoma WA 98405-4895
David Borofsky, President
253-680-7000 Fax: 253-680-7101
Website: www.bates.ctc.edu
E-mail: info@bates.ctc.edu

Bellingham Beauty School
4192 Meridian St, Bellingham WA 98226
360-734-1090

Bellingham Technical College
3028 Lindbergh Ave, Bellingham WA 98225-1599
360-738-0221

Bellvue Beauty School
14045 NE 20th St, Bellevue WA 98007
425-643-0270

BJ's Beauty & Barber College
12020 Meridian E #K, Puyallup WA 98373
253-848-1595

BJ's Beauty & Barber College
5239 S Tacoma Way, Tacoma WA 98409
253-473-4320

Clare's Beauty College
104 N 4th Ave, Pasco WA 99301
509-547-8871

Clover Park Technical College
4500 Steilacoom Blvd SW
Lakewood WA 98499-4098
Dr. Sharon McGavick, President
253-589-5678

Columbia Basin College
2600 N 20th Ave, Pasco WA 99301-3379
509-547-0511

Divers Institute of Technology
PO Box 70667, Seattle WA 98107-0667
800-634-8377

Emil Fries School of Piano Tuning & Technology
2510 E Evergreen Blvd, Vancouver WA 98661-4323
Dr. Judy K. Dresser, President
360-693-1511

Everest College
155 Washington Ave Ste 200, Bremerton WA 98337
Rob Daniel, Director of Admissions
360-473-1120

Everest College
906 SE Everett Mall Way Ste 600, Everett WA 98208
425-789-7960

Everest College
981 Powell Ave SW, Renton WA 98057
Amanda Gaugler, Director of Education
425-255-3281

Gene Juarez Academy of Beauty
2222 S 314th St, Federal Way WA 98003
253-839-6483

Gene Juarez Academy of Beauty
10715 8th Ave NE, Seattle WA 98125
206-365-6900

Glen Dow Academy of Hair Design
309 W Riverside Ave, Spokane WA 99201
Laura Manson, Enrollments
509-624-3244

Greenwood Academy of Hair Design
8501 Greenwood Ave N, Seattle WA 98103
206-782-0220

Inland Northwest HVAC Training Center
811 E Sprague Ave Ste 6, Spokane WA 99202-2105
Tena Risley, Coordinator
509-747-8810

International Air and Hospitality Academy
2901 E Mill Plain Blvd, Vancouver WA 98661-4899
Lynn Rullman, School Director
800-868-1816

ITT Technical Institute
1615 75th St SW Ste 220, Everett WA 98203-6261
800-272-3791

ITT Technical Institute
13518 Indiana Ave, Spokane Valley WA 99216
Greg Alexander, Director of Admissions
509-926-2900

Kirkland Beauty School
17311 140th Ave NE, Woodinville WA 98072
425-487-0437

Lake Washington Technical College
11605 132nd Ave NE, Kirkland WA 98034-8505
James B. West, Director of Admissions
425-739-8100 Fax: 425-739-8110
Website: www.lwtc.ctc.edu

Milan Institute of Cosmetology
607 SE Everett Mall Way #5, Everett WA 98208
Amanda Gaughler, Director
425-353-8193

Mount Vernon Beauty School
615 S 1st St, Mount Vernon WA 98273
360-336-6553

Northwest Aviation College
506 23rd St NE, Auburn WA 98002-1609
Jamelle R. Garcia, President
253-854-4960

NORTHWEST SCHOOL OF WOODEN BOATBUILDING
42 N Water St, Port Hadlock WA 98339
Kendra Seaman, Contact Person
360-385-4948 Fax: 360-385-5089
Website: www.nwboatschool.org
E-mail: info@nwboatschool.org

Perry Technical Institute
2011 W Washington Ave, Yakima WA 98903-1296
509-453-0374

Phagans' Orchards Beauty School
10411 NE 4th Plain Blvd 109, Vancouver WA 98662
360-254-9519

Photographic Center Northwest
900 12th Ave, Seattle WA 98122-4412
206-720-7222

Pima Medical Institute
555 S Renton Village Pl Ste 400, Renton WA 98057
425-228-9600

PIMA MEDICAL INSTITUTE
9709 3rd Ave NE Ste 400, Seattle WA 98115
George Borchers, Campus Director
206-322-6100 Fax: 206-324-1985
Website: www.pmi.edu
E-mail: spima@pmi.edu

Pima Medical Institute
9709 3rd Ave NE Ste 400, Seattle WA 98115
206-322-6100

Professional Beauty School
214 S 6th St, Sunnyside WA 98944
509-837-4040

Professional Beauty School
PO Box 9243, Yakima WA 98909-0243
509-877-6443

Skagit Valley College
2405 E College Way, Mount Vernon WA 98273-5899
360-416-7600

SkillSource Office & Technology Center
234 N Mission St, Wenatchee WA 98801
509-665-0313

Stylemasters College of Hair Design
1224 Commerce Ave, Longview WA 98632
360-636-2720

WEST COAST TRAINING INC.
PO Box 970, Woodland WA 98674-1000
Eileen Kelgard, President
David Simpson, Director
800-755-5477 Fax: 360-225-6760
Website: www.heavyequipmenttraining.com
E-mail: wct@heavyequipmenttraining.com

WCT is a privately owned, co-ed institution established in 1959. Licensed with Oregon and Washington Dept. of Vocational Education. We are eligible to participate with the State of Alaska Student Loan Program, US Veterans Affairs Dept. and to provide training for various state Vocational Rehabilitation Departments, the Bureau of Indian Affairs, Native Tribal Corporations and other agencies such as Workmen's Compensation, Dept. of Labor and

Industries, W.I.N., W.I.A. and T.R.A., T.R.B., T.A.A and Dislocated Worker's Programs. This institution is an associate member of the Associated General Contractors and an honorary member of the Better Business Bureau.

HEAVY EQUIPMENT OPERATOR: Learn 6 pcs. of equipment: dozers, backhoes, trackhoes, graders, scrapers and loaders. Specialize on any 2 of your choice. Also learn basic surveying, grade checking, site preparation, and be a certified flagger. Classes start every month, year round. $6,247 tuition (includes registration fee, books and tools) plus $15.52 Wash. sales tax; 8 week training program. Includes job placement assistance.

CRANE & RIGGER'S COURSE: Learn track mounted, truck mounted and self-propelled cranes; lattice and hydraulic booms; practice with hook block, dragline and clamshell. Be certified up to 50 tons. 4 week program offered every month. $5,334 tuition (includes reg. fee, books and tools) plus $13.09 Wash. sales tax. Woodland, WA is located 30 miles north of Portland, Oregon. Housing referrals provided upon request. Includes Job Placement Assistance.

Western Business College
120 NE 136th Ave Ste 130
Vancouver WA 98684-6950
360-254-3282

Western Pacific Truck School
9901 Evergreen Way, Everett WA 98204-3831
Eric Wiltse, Campus Manager
800-333-1233

Western Pacific Truck School
11020 S Tacoma Way, Tacoma WA 98499-4687
Al Auge, Campus Manager
800-333-1233

WEST VIRGINIA

Beckley Beauty Academy
109 S Fayette St, Beckley WV 25801
304-253-8326

Boone County Career Center
3505 Daniel Boone Pkwy # B, Danville WV 25053
304-369-4585

Carver Career and Tech Education Center
4799 Midland Dr, Charleston WV 25306-6353
304-348-1965

Charleston School of Beauty Culture
210 Capitol St, Charleston WV 25301
304-346-9603

Clarksburg Beauty Academy
120 S 3rd St, Clarksburg WV 26301
304-624-6475

Garnet Career Center
422 Dickinson St, Charleston WV 25301-1787
304-348-6195

Harpers Ferry Job Corps Civilian Conservation Center
146 Buffalo Dr, Harpers Ferry WV 25425
304-728-5772

Huntington School of Beauty Culture
5185 US Route 60 Ste 115, Huntington WV 25705
304-736-6289

International Beauty School
201 W King St, Martinsburg WV 25401-3211
304-263-4929

Monongalia County Tech Education Center
1000 Mississippi St, Morgantown WV 26501-6841
304-291-9240

Morgantown Beauty College
276 Walnut St, Morgantown WV 26505
304-292-8475

Mountaineer Beauty College
PO Box 547, Saint Albans WV 25177
304-727-9999

MOUNTAIN STATE COLLEGE

1508 Spring St, Parkersburg WV 26101-3993
A. Michael McPeek, President
Judith Sutton, Director
304-485-5487 Fax: 304-485-3524
Website: www.mountainstate.org
E-mail: admin@mountainstate.org

Founded in 1888, devoted exclusively to training men and women for career employment and advancement. Accredited by the Accrediting Council for Independent Colleges and Schools (ACICS). The college operates on a quarter term calendar year. New students may begin the first week of each quarter or at the mid point of any quarter allowing for eight starting dates per year. Tuition is payable on a per term basis and books may be purchased from the book store located at the college. Federal Financial Aid programs are available to qualified students. Approved for Veterans Training, Vocational Rehabilitation Act, Trade Retraining Allowance. Associate Degrees: Medical Assistant, Medical Transcriptionist, Administrative Assistant, Computer Information Technology, Computer Information Technology with Diagnostic, Higher Accounting Management, Legal Office Technology, Dependency Disorders Technology. Diploma programs: Medical Secretarial, Legal Office. Small college, small classes, day & evening sessions. Free lifetime Career Services and Lifetime Refresher Privileges for graduates. "Friday Plus" non-instructional day allowing faculty to tutor students desiring additional assistance. Student Organizations & Academic recognitions include: Student Government, Golden Girl Honor Society, President's List, and Honor List. Admissions requirements include personal interview, application, High School Diploma or GED, attend the "Your Key to Success" seminar and satisfactory completion of the CPAt (Career Programs Assessment) developed by ACT. Friendly and caring faculty and staff dedicated to assisting student in achieving skills for employment requirements of industry, government, business, medical and legal offices, and community service agencies with promotable competence.

St. Mary's Medical Center
2900 1st Ave, Huntington WV 25702-1272
Dr. Sheila Kyle, VP Schools of Nursing & Health Professions
304-526-1270

Scott College of Cosmetology
1502 Market St, Wheeling WV 26003-3532
304-232-7798

Valley Beauty School
707 Market St, Parkersburg WV 26101
304-422-2226

Valley College of Technology
713 S Oakwood Ave, Beckley WV 25801-5968
304-252-9547

Valley College of Technology
287 Aikens Ctr, Martinsburg WV 25404
304-263-0979

West Virginia Business College
116 Pennsylvania Ave
Nutter Fort Stonewood WV 26301-4516
304-624-7695

West Virginia Business College
1052 Main St, Wheeling WV 26003-2702
304-232-0361

West Virginia Junior College
1000 Virginia St E, Charleston WV 25301-2817
Thomas A. Crouse, President
304-345-2820

West Virginia Junior College
148 Willey St, Morgantown WV 26505-5521
304-296-8282

WISCONSIN

Aurora Health Care
3000 W Montana St, Milwaukee WI 53215-3686
414-647-3000

BELLIN HOSPITAL

PO Box 23400, Green Bay WI 54305-3400
Randy Griswold, Program Director
920-433-3497 Fax: 920-433-5811
Website: www.bellin.org
E-mail: rcgris@bellin.org

Blackhawk Technical College
PO Box 5009, Janesville WI 53547-5009
Gregg Bosak, Administration, Community Information
608-757-7769 Fax: 608-757-7740
Website: www.blackhawk.edu
E-mail: gbosak@blackhawk.edu

Bryant & Stratton College
310 W Wisconsin Ave Suite 500, Milwaukee WI 53203
Kathryn Cotey, Director of Admissions
414-276-5200

Diesel Truck Driver Training School
7190 Elder Ln, Sun Prairie WI 53590
608-837-7800

Four Seasons Salon and Day Spa School
128 W 8th St Ste 8, Monroe WI 53566
608-325-4007

Gill-Tech Academy of Hair Design
230 S McCarthy Rd, Appleton WI 54914
Ann Everson, Director
920-739-8684

HERZING COLLEGE

5218 E Terrace Dr, Madison WI 53718-8340
Donald Madelung, President
Rebecca Abrams, Director of Admissions
800-582-1227 or 608-249-6611 Fax: 608-249-8593
Website: www.herzing.edu
E-mail: info@msn.herzing.edu

Established 1948. Private. Coed. Accreditation: NCA. Tuition: $8,000 - $9,000 (2 semesters). Fees: $75 - $600. Enrollment: 640. Faculty: 29. Student-Faculty ratio: 17:1.

Diplomas: Medical Billing, Medical Office, Bookkeeping & Payroll Accounting, Practical Nursing, Homeland Security Leadership. Associate Degrees: Computer, Electronics & Telecommunications Technology, Computer Network & Security Technology, Computer Information Systems, Interactive & Graphic Arts, Computer Aided Drafting, Business Administration, Legal Assisting/Paralegal, Nursing. Bachelor Degrees: Homeland Security & Public Safety, Interactive & Graphic Arts, Legal Studies, Healthcare Management, Accounting, Business Administration, Information Technology, Technology Management.

Founded in 1948 as one of the nation's first electronics schools. Certification preparation inbedded in curriculum: A+, Net+, MCSE, CCNA, Certified Electronics Technician and Associate. Three-year bachelor degree. Bachelor-completion program available online.

No dorms, but housing and job assistance to new and existing students.

Lakeshore Technical College
1290 North Ave, Cleveland WI 53015-1414
Information Fulfillment Specialist
888-GOTOLTC Fax: 920-693-3561
Website: www.gotoltc.edu
E-mail: info@gotoltc.edu

Lakeside School of Massage Therapy
1726 N 1st St, Milwaukee WI 53212
414-372-4345

Madison Cosmetology College
310 Westgate Mall, Madison WI 53711
608-271-4206

MADISON MEDIA INSTITUTE

College of Media Arts
2702 Agriculture Dr, Madison WI 53718-6787
Steve Hutchings, Director of Admissions
800-236-4997 or 608-663-2000 Fax: 608-442-0141
Website: www.madisonmedia.edu
E-mail: mmi@madisonmedia.com

MARSHFIELD CLINIC/ST. JOSEPH'S HOSPITAL

1000 N Oak Ave, Marshfield WI 54449
Julie J. Seehafer, MS, MT(ASCP)SH
Director, Laboratory Education
715-387-7440 Fax: 715-387-7121
Website: www.marshfieldlaboratories.org
E-mail: seehafer.julie@marshfieldclinic.org (Office)

Martin's College of Cosmetology
2575 W Mason St, Green Bay WI 54303
920-494-1430

Martin's College of Cosmetology
6414 Odana Rd, Madison WI 53719-1111
608-270-0188

Martin's College of Cosmetology
1034 S 18th St, Manitowoc WI 54220
920-684-3028

Professional Hair Design Academy
3408 Mall Dr, Eau Claire WI 54701
715-835-2345

Scientific College of Beauty/Barbering
326 Pearl St, La Crosse WI 54601
608-784-4702

Southwest Wisconsin Technical College
1800 Bronson Blvd, Fennimore WI 53809-9778
Student Services/Admissions
800-362-3322 ext. 2354

STATE COLLEGE OF BEAUTY CULTURE

1930 Grand Ave, Wausau WI 54403-6870
Andi Burns, Admissions Director
715-845-2888 Fax: 715-848-2121
Website: www.statecollegeofbeauty.com
E-mail: info@statecollegeofbeauty.com

Vici Beauty School
11010 W Hampton Ave, Milwaukee WI 53225-3859
Kyle Davis, Administrator
414-464-5002

Wisconsin College of Cosmetology
2960 Allied St, Green Bay WI 54304
920-336-8888

WISCONSIN CONSERVATORY OF MUSIC

1584 N Prospect Ave, Milwaukee WI 53202-6501
Sarah Wright, VP Business
414-276-5760 Fax: 414-276-6076
Website: www.wcmusic.org
E-mail: sarahwright@wcmusic.org

WYOMING

Cheeks Intl Academy of Beauty Culture
207 W 18th St, Cheyenne WY 82001
307-637-8700

Eastern Wyoming College
3200 W C St, Torrington WY 82240-1699
Dr. Jack Bottenfield, President
Tanya Howery, High School & College Relations
800-658-3195

Sage Technical School
2368 Oil Dr, Casper WY 82604-1505
Donald Washburn, Director
307-234-0242

Western Wyoming Community College
2500 College Dr, Rock Springs WY 82901-5802
Laurie Watkins, Director of Admissions
307-382-1600

PUERTO RICO

Academia Maison D'Esthetique
904 Ave Ponce de Leon, Santurce PR 00907
787-723-4672

ACADEMIA SERRANT

8180 Calle Concordia, Ponce PR 00717-1568
Yanira Pachecho Serrant, Administrative Director
787-259-4900 Fax: 787-842-4646
Website: www.serrant.com
E-mail: aserrant@tld.net

Academia Vocacional Del Turabo
41 Calle Campio Alonso, Caguas PR 00725-3657
Sr. Jaime Cruz, Contact
787-746-6634

Advance Tech College
PO Box 6602, Bayamón PR 00960
787-785-6841

Aguadilla Technical College
PO Box 988, Manatí PR 00674
787-891-6966

American Business College of Puerto Rico
2449 Ave Militar # 2 Road Km 113.9
Isabela PR 00662
787-830-4617

American Educational College
PO Box 62, Bayamon PR 00960-0062
787-798-1199

American Technological College
7310 Edif Embajador #3 Calle Ramon Powe
Ponce PR 00717
787-259-1341

American Technological College
Arzauga 112 Mendino Center 1105
Rio Piedras PR 00928
787-753-9118

Antilles School of Technical Careers
1851 Ave Fernandez Juncos
Santurce PR 00909-3006
787-764-7576

Bayamon Community College
PO Box 055176, Bayamon PR 00960
787-780-4370

Centro de Capacitacion y Asesoramiento
Ave Jose de Diego #159, Arecibo PR 00612
787-880-0146

Centro de Capacitacion y Asesoramiento
PMB Dept 484 HC 1 Box 29030, Caguas PR 00725
787-880-0146

Centro de Estudios Multidisciplinarios
6 Dr Vidal St, Humacao PR 00791
787-850-8333

Centro de Estudios Multidisciplinarios
1206 Calle 13, San Juan PR 00926
787-765-4210

Century College
Calle Progresso #125, Aguadilla PR 00603
787-882-5086

Colegio Educativo Tecnologico Industrial
Calle Eugenio Maria De Host, Arecibo PR 00613
Nilsa Lopez Rivera, Directora Ejecutiva
787-879-3300

Colegio Mayor de Technologia
PO Box 1490, Arroyo PR 00714
Julia Melendez, Director of Admissions
787-839-5266

Colegio Tecnico de Electricidad Galloza
HC 3 Box 32562, Aguada PR 00602
787-868-2974

Colegio Tecnico Metropolitano
1251 Franklin D Roosevelt Ave
Puerto Nuevo PR 00920
787-781-5140

Colegio Tecnologico y Comercial
165 Calle La Paz, Aguada PR 00602
Roberto Davila, Director
787-868-2688

Columbia Centro Universitario
PO Box 3062, Yauco PR 00698
787-856-0845

D'Mart Institute
Centro Comercial San Cristobal #215
Barranquitas PR 00794
787-857-6929

D'Mart Institute
Carreterra 159 KM 1.5 Desivo de Corozal
Corozal PR 00783
787-859-5391

EDIC College
PO Box 9120, Caguas PR 00726-9120
Virginia Cartagena, Director of Admissions
787-744-8519 Fax: 787-743-0855
Website: www.ediccollege.com
E-mail: edic@coqui.net

Educational Technical College
5 Calle Ramon Powell, Coamo PR 00769
787-825-0379

Educational Technical College
Segundo Nivel Ste 12
Carretera Num 2 Esquina #167, Bayamón PR 00959
787-780-8234

EMMAS BEAUTY ACADEMY
Carr 417 Bo Guanabano, Aguada PR 00602
Carlos Ramos Camara, CEO
787-868-4711 Fax: 787-252-0775
Website: www.emmasbeautyacademy.com
E-mail: emmasbeautyacademy@yahoo.com

Emmas Beauty Academy
Carr 149 Barrio Amuelas, Juana Díaz PR 00795
787-837-0303

EMMAS BEAUTY ACADEMY
9 Calle Munoz Rivera W, Mayaguez PR 00680
Carlos Ramos Camara, CEO
787-833-0980 Fax: 787-833-0613
Website: www.emmasbeautyacademy.com
E-mail: emmasbeautyacademy@yahoo.com

Escuela de Peritos Electricitas de Isabela, Inc.
PO Box 457, Isabela PR 00662-0457
Maria M. Santiago, Director
787-872-1747

Escuela Hotelera de San Juan
229 Calle Guayama, San Juan PR 00917
787-766-0606

Ferrer Zoraida Hispanic American College
52 Calle Ruiz Belvis #54, Caguas PR 00725-3586
787-734-4311

Globelle Technical Institute
114 Calle Marginal, Urb. Monte Carlo
Vega Baja PR 00693-4218
Gloria E. Cruz Lugo, President
787-858-0236

Guaynabo Technical College
71st Carazo St, Guaynabo PR 00969
787-644-0146

Humacao Community College
PO Box 9139, Humacao PR 00792
787-852-1430

Industrial Technical College
PO Box 8480, Humacao PR 00792
787-852-8806

Institucion Chaviano de Mayaguez
116 Calle Ramos Antonini E
Mayagüez PR 00680-5045
787-833-2474

Institute of Beauty Careers
1119 Ave Llorens Torres, Arecibo PR 00612
787-878-2880

Institute of Beauty Occupation
500 Calle Concepcion Vera, Moca PR 00676
787-818-4230

Instituto de Banca y Comercio
164 Ave Jose de Diego W, Cayey PR 00736
787-738-5555

Instituto de Banca y Comercio
250 Munoz Rivera, Fajardo PR 00738
787-860-6262

Instituto de Banca y Comercio
PO Box 6092, Guayama PR 00784
787-864-3220

Instituto de Banca y Comercio
61 Ponce De Leon Ave, Hato Rey PR 00919
Rafael Jimenez, Vice President
787-754-7120

Instituto de Banca y Comercio
56 Carr 2, Manati PR 00674
787-854-6709

Instituto de Banca y Comercio
155 E Mendez Vigo St, Mayaguez PR 00680
787-833-4647

Instituto de Educacion Tecnica Ocupacional La Reine
9 Calle Mercedes Moreno, Aguadilla PR 00603
787-819-0222

Instituto de Educacion Tecnica Ocupacional La Reine
A8 Avenida Colon, Manatí PR 00674
787-854-1119

Instituto de Educacion Vocacional
HC 3 Box 17272, Corozal PR 00783
787-859-6823

Instituto de Educacion Vocacional
Calle Comercio, Morovis PR 06578
787-862-1100

Instituto Irma Valentin
2018 Ave Borinquen, Santurce PR 00915
787-982-1716

Instituto Irma Valentin
137 Calle Dr Cueto, Utuado PR 00641
787-894-1395

Instituto Merlix
20 Calle Betances, Bayamon PR 00961
787-786-7035

Instituto Tecnico Del Futuro
PO Box 55016, Bayamon PR 00960
787-740-5030

Instituto Vocacional Aurea E Mendez
PO Box 8655, Caguas PR 00726
787-743-5327

International Junior College
1 Baldority St, Humacao PR 00791
787-786-2727

International Junior College
1315 Ave Ponce de Leon, San Juan PR 00907-3917
787-724-5858

International Technical College
104 Loaiza Cordero St, San Juan PR 00918
787-767-8389

John Dewey College
RD 2 Corujo Industrial Park, Bayamón PR 00959
787-648-4353

John Dewey College
Carr 3 KM 11 lote 7, Carolina PR 00986
787-769-1515

John Dewey College
PO Box 19538, San Juan PR 00910
787-753-0039

Leston College
Calle Dr Veve #52, Bayamón PR 00961
787-787-9661

Liceo de Arte Y Disenos
PO Box 1889, Caguas PR 00726-1889
Angel L. Garcia Viera, Presidente
787-743-7447

Liceo de Arte Y Tecnologia
PO Box 192346, San Juan PR 00919
787-754-8250

MBTI Business Training Institute
1256 Ave Ponce de Leon, Santurce PR 00907-3965
Miguel A. Fernandez, Contact
787-723-9403

Modern Hairstyling Institute
57 Calle Dr Veve, Bayamón PR 00961
787-778-0300

Modern Hairstyling Institute
60 Calle Fernandez Juncos N, Carolina PR 00985
787-752-8383

Modern Hairstyling Institute
51 Calle Celis Aguilera N, Fajardo PR 00738
787-863-9922

Montecarlo: Escuela de Hoteleria y Artes Servicios de Hospitalidad Monteclaro
PO Box 447, Palmer PR 00721
787-888-1135

National College of Business & Technology
PO Box 2036, Bayamon PR 00960-2036
787-780-5134

National College of Business and Technology
PO Box 4035, Arecibo PR 00614
787-879-5044

Politec Institute
78 Calle Guadalupe # 335577, Ponce PR 00730
787-843-0204

Ponce Paramedical College
PO Box 800106, Coto Laurel PR 00780
787-848-1589

PONCE PARAMEDICAL COLLEGE
1213 Calle Acacia Villa Flores, Ponce PR 00716-2901
Alberto Aristizabal, President
787-848-1589 Fax: 787-259-0169
Website: www.popac.edu
E-mail: ppcadmin@popac.edu

PROFESSIONAL ELECTRICAL SCHOOL
PO Box 1797, Manati PR 00674
Paulino Delgado Negron, Presidente
787-854-4776 Fax: 787-854-4776
E-mail: pes@libertypr.net

Professional Technical Institute
PO Box 607061, Bayamon PR 00960
787-740-6810

Puerto Rico Technical Jr College
703 Ave Ponce De Leon, Hato Rey PR 00917-5013
787-751-0133

Puerto Rico Technical Jr College
Calle Santiago R Palmer #15, Mayagüez PR 00680
787-832-2762

Ramirez College of Business Technology
PO Box 195460, San Juan PR 00919-5460
787-763-3120

Rogie's School of Beauty Culture
26 Res Gautier Benitez, Caguas PR 00725
787-746-3777

Rogie's School of Beauty Culture
PO Box 19828, San Juan PR 00910
787-722-2293

Serbia's Technical College
Calle Hostos 27 Esquina Vicente Pales
Guayama PR 00785
Merags Santos Arrida, Director
787-864-7254

Star Career College
19 Degerau St, Bayamón PR 00961
787-740-7490

TRINITY COLLEGE OF PUERTO RICO
PO Box 34360, Ponce PR 00734-4360
Ms. Maria I. Colon, Executive Director
787-842-0000 Fax: 787-284-2537
Website: www.csifpr.org/trinitycollege
E-mail: mcolon@csifpr.org

Universal Career Counseling
113 Paseo De La Atenas, Manatí PR 00674
787-728-7211

Universal Career Counseling Center
6 Calle Antonio Lopez N, Humacao PR 00791
787-728-7211

Universal Career Counseling Center
1902 Ave Fernandez Juncos, Santurce PR 00909
787-728-7268

Universal Technology College of Puerto Rico
Apartado 1955 Victoria Sta, Aguadilla PR 00605
787-882-2065

Universal Technology College of Puerto Rico
167 Ave Munoz Rivera Oeste Ste 2
Camuy PR 00627-2334
787-262-5786

Universidad del Este
PO Box 2010, Carolina PR 00984
787-257-7373

CHIROPRACTIC MEDICINE

CALIFORNIA

Cleveland Chiropractic College - Los Angeles Campus
590 N Vermont Ave, Los Angeles CA 90004-2196
Teresa Moore, Director of Admissions
800-466-CCLA (2252) or 323-906-2031
Fax: 323-906-2094
Website: www.cleveland.edu
E-mail: la.admissions@cleveland.edu

LIFE CHIROPRACTIC COLLEGE WEST
25001 Industrial Blvd, Hayward CA 94545-2801
Stephen D. Eckstone, Director of Admissions
800-788-4476 Fax: 510-780-4525
Website: www.lifewest.edu
E-mail: admissions@lifewest.edu

PALMER COLLEGE OF CHIROPRACTIC
West Campus
90 E Tasman Dr, San Jose CA 95134-1617
866-303-7939 or 408-944-6000 Fax: 408-944-6032
Website: www.palmer.edu
E-mail: pccw_admiss@palmer.edu

FLORIDA

PALMER COLLEGE OF CHIROPRACTIC
Florida Campus
4777 City Center Pkwy, Port Orange FL 32129-4153
866-585-9677 or 386-763-2709 Fax: 386-763-2620
Website: www.palmer.edu
E-mail: pccf_admiss@palmer.edu

GEORGIA

Life University
1269 Barclay Cir SE, Marietta GA 30060-2903
Dr. Deborah E. Heairlston, Director of New Student Development
770-426-2884 Fax: 770-426-2895
Website: www.life.edu
E-mail: admissions@life.edu

ILLINOIS

National University of Health Sciences
200 E Roosevelt Rd, Lombard IL 60148-4583
Dr. James Winterstein, President
800-826-6285 Fax: 630-889-6554
Website: www.nuhs.edu
E-mail: admissions@nuhs.edu

IOWA

Iowa Lakes Community College
300 S 18th St, Estherville IA 51334-2721
Anne Stansbury, Asst. Director of Admissions
712-362-7945 Fax: 712-362-8363
Website: www.iowalakes.edu
E-mail: info@iowalakes.edu

PALMER COLLEGE OF CHIROPRACTIC
Davenport Campus
1000 Brady St, Davenport IA 52803-5287
800-722-3648 or 563-884-5656 Fax: 563-884-5414
Website: www.palmer.edu
E-mail: pcadmit@palmer.edu

MINNESOTA

Northwestern Health Sciences University
Northwestern College of Chiropractic Admissions Office
2501 W 84th St, Minneapolis MN 55431
Dr. Mark Zeigler, President
Bill Kuehl, Director of Admissions
952-888-4777 ext. 409 Fax: 952-881-3028
Website: www.nwhealth.edu
E-mail: admit@nwhealth.edu

University of Minnesota
2900 University Ave, Crookston MN 56716-5001
218-281-6510 Fax: 218-281-8575
Website:
admissions.umcrookston.edu/requirements/apply.htm
E-mail: info@umcrookston.edu

MISSOURI

Cleveland Chiropractic College - Kansas City Campus
6401 Rockhill Rd, Kansas City MO 64131-1122
Melissa Denton, Director of Admissions
800-467-CCKC (2252) or 816-501-0100
Fax: 816-501-0205
Website: www.cleveland.edu
E-mail: kc.admissions@cleveland.edu

NEW YORK

NEW YORK CHIROPRACTIC COLLEGE
PO Box 800, Seneca Falls NY 13148-0800
Michael P. Lynch, Director of Admissions
800-234-6922 (NYCC) Fax: 315-568-3087
Website: www.nycc.edu
E-mail: enrolnow@nycc.edu

PENNSYLVANIA

INTERNATIONAL ACADEMY OF ADVANCED REFLEXOLOGY & MEDICAL REFLEXOLOGY CLINIC
1701 Snyder Rd, Green Lane PA 18054
Professor L.J. Telepo, President
215-234-0307 or 267-377-5128 Fax: 267-329-8008
Website: www.reflexology.net
E-mail: postsecondary@reflexology.net
See listing under "Allied Health Science"

INTERNATIONAL ACADEMY OF ADVANCED REFLEXOLOGY & MEDICAL REFLEXOLOGY CLINIC
1177 6th St, Whitehall PA 18052
Professor L.J. Telepo, President
215-234-0307 or 267-377-5128 Fax: 267-329-8008
Website: www.reflexology.net
E-mail: postsecondary@reflexology.net
See listing under "Allied Health Science"

Juniata College
1700 Moore St, Huntingdon PA 16652-2196
Michelle Bartol, Dean of Enrollment
877-JUNIATA Fax: 814-641-3100
Website: www.juniata.edu
E-mail: admissions@juniata.edu

SOUTH CAROLINA

SHERMAN COLLEGE OF STRAIGHT CHIROPRACTIC
PO Box 1452, Spartanburg SC 29304-1452
Lisa Hildebrand, Director of Admission
800-849-8771 or 864-578-8770 Fax: 864-599-4860
Website: www.sherman.edu
E-mail: admissions@sherman.edu

TEXAS

Parker College of Chiropractic
2500 Walnut Hill Ln, Dallas TX 75229-5609
Andrea Robles, Asst. Director of Admissions
972-438-6932 Fax: 214-902-2413
Website: www.parkercc.edu
E-mail: admissions@parkercc.edu

TEXAS CHIROPRACTIC COLLEGE
5912 Spencer Hwy, Pasadena TX 77505-1699
Sandra Hughes, D.C.; Director of Admission
281-487-1170 Fax: 281-991-4871
Website: www.txchiro.edu
E-mail: shughes@txchiro.edu

COMMUNICATIONS

ALABAMA

Judson College
302 Bibb St, Marion AL 36756
Michael Scotto, Director of Admissions
800-447-9472 Fax: 334-683-5147
Website: www.judson.edu
E-mail: admissions@judson.edu

University of Alabama in Huntsville
PO Box 1247, Huntsville AL 35899-0001
Nikki Willis, Assoc. Director for Recruiting Program and Events
1-800-UAH-CALL Fax: 256-824-6073
Website: www.uah.edu
E-mail: willisn@uah.edu

University of South Alabama
307 University Blvd N, Mobile AL 36688-3053
Melissa Haab, Director of Admissions
251-460-6141 Fax: 251-460-7876
Website: www.southalabama.edu
E-mail: admiss@usouthal.edu

ALASKA

University of Alaska Anchorage
PO Box 141629, Anchorage AK 99514-1629
Cecile Mitchell, Director of Enrollment Services
907-786-1480 Fax: 907-786-4888
Website: www.uaa.alaska.edu/
E-mail: enroll@uaa.alaska.edu

ARIZONA

Pima Community College
4905 E Broadway Blvd, Tucson AZ 85709-1010
Wendy Kilgore, Ph.D., Director of Admissions
520-206-4500 Fax: 520-206-4790
Website: www.pima.edu
E-mail: infocenter@pima.edu

CALIFORNIA

American Film Institute
AFI Conservatory
2021 N Western Ave, Los Angeles CA 90027
Danielle McVickers, Admissions Manager
323-856-7740 Fax: 323-856-7720
Website: www.afi.com
E-mail: dmcvickers@afi.com
Production Design.

Associated Technical College
1670 Wilshire Blvd, Los Angeles CA 90017-1690
Samuel Romano, Director of Admissions
213-353-1845 Fax: 213-413-4864
Website: www.associatedtechcollege.com
E-mail: decatc@earthlink.net

Butte College
3536 Butte Campus Dr, Oroville CA 95965-8399
Carole Gish, Director of Admissions
530-895-2511 Fax: 530-879-4313
Website: www.butte.edu
E-mail: admissions@butte.edu

California State University-San Bernadino
5500 University Pkwy
San Bernardino CA 92407-2393
Olivia Rosas, Director of Admissions
909-537-5188 Fax: 909-537-7034
Website: www.csusb.edu
E-mail: orosas@csusb.edu

Chapman University
One University Drive, Orange CA 92866-1099
Michael Drummy, Assistant Vice President for Enrollment
Services and Chief Admission Officer
714-997-6411 or 888-CUAPPLY Fax: 714-997-6713
Website: www.chapman.edu
E-mail: admit@chapman.edu

Columbia College Hollywood
18618 Oxnard St, Tarzana CA 91356-1411
Carmen Munoz & Jennifer Corinna, Admissions Coordinators
800-785-0585 Fax: 818-345-9053
Website: www.columbiacollege.edu
E-mail: admissions@columbiacollege.edu

Concordia University
1530 Concordia, Irvine CA 92612-3203
Lori McDonald, Executive Director of Enrollment Services
800-229-1200 or 949-854-8002 Fax: 949-854-6894
Website: www.cui.edu
E-mail: admission@cui.edu

Dominican University of California
50 Acacia Ave, San Rafael CA 94901-2298
Office of Admissions
888-323-6762 Fax: 415-485-3214
Website: www.dominican.edu
E-mail: enroll@dominican.edu

FRESNO CITY COLLEGE
1101 E University Ave, Fresno CA 93741-0002
Dayann Dietrich, Contact
559-442-8241 Fax: 559-237-4232
Website: www.fresnocitycollege.com
E-mail: fcc.admissions@scccd.com

Orange Coast College
PO Box 5005, Costa Mesa CA 92628-5005
Kristin Clark, Director of Admissions
714-432-5773 Fax: 714-432-5736
Website: www.orangecoastcollege.edu
E-mail: kclark@cccd.edu

PLATT (MEDIA ARTS) COLLEGE - SAN DIEGO
6250 El Cajon Blvd, San Diego CA 92115
Al Medro, Vice President
619-265-0107 or 866-752-8826 Fax: 619-308-0570
Website: www.platt.edu
E-mail: info@platt.edu

Point Loma Nazarene University
3900 Lomaland Dr, San Diego CA 92106-2810
Chip Killingsworth, Director of Undergraduate Admissions
800-733-7770 Fax: 619-849-2601
Website: www.pointloma.edu
E-mail: admissions@pointloma.edu

San Bernardino Valley College
701 S Mount Vernon Ave
San Bernardino CA 92410-2798
Kay Ragan, Ed.D., Director of Admissions
909-888-6511 Fax: 909-889-4988
Website: www.valleycollege.edu
E-mail: kragan@sbccd.cc.ca.us

San Diego Christian College
2100 Greenfield Dr, El Cajon CA 92019-1157
Rene Inman, Director of Admissions
800-676-2242 Fax: 619-590-1739
Website: www.sdcc.edu
E-mail: admissions@sdcc.edu

Simpson University
2211 College View Dr, Redding CA 96003-8606
Jim Herberger, Director of Admissions
888-9-SIMPSON Fax: 530-226-4861
Website: www.simpsonuniversity.edu
E-mail: admissions@simpsonuniversity.edu
See listing under "Universities"

COLORADO

Colorado Christian University
8787 W Alameda Ave, Lakewood CO 80226
Sean Kadel, Director of Admissions
800-44-FAITH Fax: 303-963-3201
Website: www.ccu.edu
E-mail: admissions@ccu.edu

San Juan Basin Technical College
PO Box 970, Cortez CO 81321-0970
Shannon South, Vice President
970-565-8457 Fax: 970-565-8450
Website: www.sjbtc.edu
E-mail: info@sjbtc.edu

UNIVERSITY OF DENVER UNIVERSITY COLLEGE
2211 S Josephine St, Denver CO 80208
Dr. Denise Pearson, Assistant Dean of Academics
303-871-3354 Fax: 303-871-4047
Website: www.universitycollege.du.edu
E-mail: ucolinfo@du.edu

CONNECTICUT

Albertus Magnus College
700 Prospect St, New Haven CT 06511-1189
Richard Lolatte, Dean of Admission
203-773-8501 or 800-578-9160 Fax: 203-773-5248
Website: www.albertus.edu
E-mail: admissions@albertus.edu

Middlesex Community College
100 Training Hill Rd, Middletown CT 06457-4889
Mensimah Shabazz, Director of Admissions
860-343-5800 Fax: 860-344-3055
Website: www.mxcc.commnet.edu
E-mail: mshabazz@mxcc.commnet.edu

DELAWARE

Wesley College
120 N State St, Dover DE 19901-3876
302-736-2300 Fax: 302-736-2301
Website: www.wesley.edu

DISTRICT OF COLUMBIA

Gallaudet University
800 Florida Ave NE, Washington DC 20002-3695
Charity Reedy Hines, Director of Admissions
202-651-5750 Fax: 202-651-5744
Website: www.gallaudet.edu
E-mail: admissions.office@gallaudet.edu

FLORIDA

City College
2000 W Commercial Blvd, Fort Lauderdale FL 33309
Mercedes Segal, Director of Admissions
954-492-5353 Fax: 954-491-1965
Website: www.citycollege.edu

Embry-Riddle Aeronautical University
Daytona Beach Campus
PO Box 11767, Daytona Beach FL 32120-1767
C. Richard Clarke, Director of Admissions
800-862-2416 Fax: 386-226-7070
Website: www.embryriddle.edu
E-mail: dbadmit@erau.edu

Florida State University
600 W College Ave, Tallahassee FL 32306-1096
Janice V. Finney, Director of Admissions
850-644-2525 Fax: 850-644-0197
Website: admissions.fsu.edu
E-mail: admissions@admin.fsu.edu

Lynn University
3601 N Military Trl, Boca Raton FL 33431-5598
Director of Admissions
561-237-7900 Fax: 561-237-7100
Website: www.lynn.edu
E-mail: admission@lynn.edu

Northwood University
2600 N Military Trl, West Palm Beach FL 33409-2999
Jack Letvinchuk, Director of Admissions
800-458-8325 Fax: 561-640-3328
Website: www.northwood.edu
E-mail: fladmit@northwood.edu

St. Thomas University
16401 NW 37th Ave, Miami Gardens FL 33054
Dr. Gloria Ruiz, Contact
800-367-9010 or 305-628-6546 Fax: 305-628-6591
Website: www.stu.edu
E-mail: signup@stu.edu

University of South Florida
4202 E Fowler Ave, Tampa FL 33620-6900
J. Robert Spatig, Director of Admissions
877-USF-BULL Fax: 813-974-9689
Website: www.usf.edu
E-mail: admissions@admin.usf.edu
See listing under "Universities"

GEORGIA

DeKalb Technical College
495 N Indian Creek Dr, Clarkston GA 30021-2397
Terry Richardson, Director of Admissions
404-297-9522 Fax: 404-294-6496
Website: www.dekalbtech.edu
E-mail: richardt@dekalbtech.edu

Kennesaw State University
1000 Chastain Rd NW, Kennesaw GA 30144-5591
Dr. Helen Ridley, Dean of Humanities and Social Science
770-423-6124
Website: www.kennesaw.edu

Portfolio Center
125 Bennett St NW, Atlanta GA 30309-1268
Catherine Menes, Admissions Department
404-351-5055 ext. 26 Fax: 404-355-8838
Website: www.portfoliocenter.com
E-mail: catherine@portfoliocenter.com

TOCCOA FALLS COLLEGE
PO Box 800899, Toccoa Falls GA 30598
888-785-5624 Fax: 706-282-6012
Website: www.tfc.edu
E-mail: admissions@tfc.edu

IDAHO

Brigham Young University - Idaho
120 Kimball Bldg, Rexburg ID 83460-1615
Rob Garrett, Director of Admissions
208-496-1020 Fax: 208-496-1220
Website: www.byui.edu
E-mail: admissions@byui.edu

Lewis-Clark State College
500 8th Ave, Lewiston ID 83501-2698
Diane Douglas, Ph.D., Registrar/Director of Admissions
800-933-5272 Fax: 208-792-2429
Website: www.lcsc.edu
E-mail: admissions@lcsc.edu

University of Idaho
Moscow ID 83844-4253
Lloyd Scott, Director of New Student Services
208-885-6163 Fax: 208-885-4477
Website: www.uidaho.edu
E-mail: nss@uidaho.edu

ILLINOIS

AMERICAN INTERCONTINENTAL UNIVERSITY ONLINE
5550 Prairie Stone Parkway Suite 400
Hoffman Estates IL 60192
Admissions Department
877-701-3800
Website: www.aiuonline.edu
E-mail: info@aiuonline.edu

Aurora University
347 S Gladstone Ave, Aurora IL 60506-4892
Carol R. Dunn, Ed.D., Vice President for Enrollment
800-742-5281 Fax: 630-844-5535
Website: www.aurora.edu
E-mail: admission@aurora.edu

Benedictine University
5700 College Rd, Lisle IL 60532-0900
630-829-6300 or 888-829-6363 Fax: 630-829-6301
Website: www.ben.edu
E-mail: admissions@ben.edu
See listing under "Universities"

Columbia College Chicago
600 S Michigan Ave, Chicago IL 60605-1996
Murphy Monroe, Executive Director of Admissions
312-344-7130 Fax: 312-344-8024
Website: www.colum.edu
E-mail: admissions@colum.edu

CONCORDIA UNIVERSITY
7400 Augusta St, River Forest IL 60305-1402
708-209-3100 Fax: 708-209-3176
Website: www.cuchicago.edu
E-mail: admission@cuchicago.edu

Roosevelt University
430 S Michigan Ave, Chicago IL 60605
Gwen E. Kanelos, Asst. Vice President for Enrollment Services
877-APPLY-RU Fax: 312-341-4216
Website: www.roosevelt.edu
E-mail: applyru@roosevelt.edu

Trinity International University
2065 Half Day Rd, Deerfield IL 60015-1241
847-945-8800 Fax: 847-317-8097
Website: www.tiu.edu
E-mail: tcadmissions@tiu.edu

INDIANA

Franklin College
101 Branigin Blvd, Franklin IN 46131
Jacqueline S. Acosta, Director of Admissions
800-852-0232 Fax: 317-738-8274
Website: www.franklincollege.edu
E-mail: admissions@franklincollege.edu

University of Evansville
1800 Lincoln Ave, Evansville IN 47722-0001
Don Vos, Dean of Admission
800-423-8633 Fax: 812-488-4076
Website: www.evansville.edu
E-mail: admission@evansville.edu

IOWA

Briar Cliff University
PO Box 2100, Sioux City IA 51104-0100
Sharisue Wilcoxon, VP for Enrollment Management
712-279-5200 Fax: 712-279-1632
Website: www.briarcliff.edu
E-mail: admissions@briarcliff.edu

Clarke College
1550 Clarke Dr, Dubuque IA 52001-3198
Andy Schroeder, Director of Admissions
800-383-2345 Fax: 563-584-8666
Website: www.clarke.edu
E-mail: andy.schroeder@clarke.edu

Graceland University
1 University Place, Lamoni IA 50140
Greg Sutherland, Interim Vice President for Enrollment and Dean of Admissions
641-784-5196 Fax: 641-784-5480
Website: www.admissions.graceland.edu
E-mail: admissions@graceland.edu

Iowa Lakes Community College
300 S 18th St, Estherville IA 51334-2721
Anne Stansbury, Asst. Director of Admissions
712-362-7945 Fax: 712-362-8363
Website: www.iowalakes.edu
E-mail: info@iowalakes.edu

Waldorf College
106 S 6th St, Forest City IA 50436-1713
Dr. Linda Hoopes, Vice President of Admission and Marketing
800-292-1903 or 641-585-8112 Fax: 641-585-8125
Website: www.waldorf.edu
E-mail: hoopesl@waldorf.edu
See listing under "Universities"

KANSAS

COLBY COMMUNITY COLLEGE
1255 S Range Ave, Colby KS 67701-4099
Director of Admissions
888-634-9350 or 785-460-4690 Fax: 785-460-4691
Website: www.colbycc.edu
E-mail: admissions@colbycc.edu

Independence Community College
PO Box 708, Independence KS 67301-0708
Dr. Terry Hetrick, President
800-842-6063 Fax: 620-331-5344
Website: www.indycc.edu
E-mail: admissions@indycc.edu

Tabor College
400 S Jefferson St, Hillsboro KS 67063-1758
Rusty Allen, Dean of Enrollment Management
800-822-6799 Fax: 620-947-6276
Website: www.tabor.edu
E-mail: admissions@tabor.edu
See listing under "Universities"

KENTUCKY

Bluegrass Community and Technical College
Oswald Building
470 Cooper Drive, Lexington KY 40506-0235
Shelbie Hugle, Director of Admissions
859-246-6200 Fax: 859-246-4664
Website: www.bluegrass.kctcs.edu
E-mail: bctc_info@kctcs.edu

Morehead State University
Morehead KY 40351-1689
Jeffrey Liles, Enrollment Services
800-585-6781 Fax: 606-783-5038
Website: www.moreheadstate.edu
E-mail: admissions@moreheadstate.edu

MAINE

HUSSON COLLEGE
One College Cir, Bangor ME 04401-2999
Jane Goodwin, Director of Admissions
800-4HU-SSON or 207-941-7100 Fax: 207-941-7935
Website: www.husson.edu
E-mail: admit@husson.edu
See listing under "Universities"

St. Joseph's College of Maine
278 Whites Bridge Rd, Standish ME 04084-5263
Vincent Kloskowski, Dean of Admissions
800-338-7057 Fax: 207-893-7862
Website: www.sjcme.edu
E-mail: admission@sjcme.edu

MARYLAND

Cecil College
One Seahawk Dr, North East MD 21901
Sandra S. Rajaski, Registrar & Director of Admissions
410-287-1000 Fax: 410-287-1001
Website: www.cecil.edu
E-mail: srajaski@cecil.edu

MASSACHUSETTS

Anna Maria College
50 Sunset Ln, Paxton MA 01612
Timothy M. Donahue, Director of Recruitment and Admissions
508-849-3360 Fax: 508-849-3362
Website: www.annamaria.edu
E-mail: admissions@annamaria.edu

Assumption College
500 Salisbury St, Worcester MA 01609-1294
Kathleen Murphy, Dean of Enrollment
508-767-7000 Fax: 508-799-4412
Website: www.assumption.edu
E-mail: admiss@assumption.edu

Boston University
121 Bay State Rd, Boston MA 02215
Kelly Walter, Executive Director of Admissions
617-353-2300 Fax: 617-353-9695
Website: web.bu.edu
E-mail: admissions@bu.edu

Bristol Community College
777 Elsbree St, Fall River MA 02720-7395
Rodney S. Clark, Director of Admissions
508-678-2811 ext. 2516, 2179 Fax: 508-730-3265
Website: www.bristol.mass.edu
E-mail: admissions@bristol.mass.edu

Emerson College
120 Boylston St, Boston MA 02116-4624
Sara S. Ramirez, Director of Undergraduate Admission
617-824-8600 Fax: 617-824-8609
Website: www.emerson.edu
E-mail: admission@emerson.edu

Gordon College
255 Grapevine Rd, Wenham MA 01984-1899
Barbara R. Layne, Associate Vice President, Enrollment
866-464-6736 Fax: 978-867-4682
Website: www.gordon.edu
E-mail: admissions@gordon.edu

Massachusetts Institute of Technology
77 Massachusetts Ave, Cambridge MA 02139-4307
617-253-1000 Fax: 617-253-4016
Website: my.mit.edu
E-mail: admissions@mit.edu

Newbury College
129 Fisher Ave, Brookline MA 02445-5796
Salvadore Liberto, Vice President of Enrollment
617-730-7000 Fax: 617-731-9618
Website: www.newbury.edu
E-mail: info@newbury.edu
See listing under "Universities"

University of Massachusetts Dartmouth
Old Westport Rd, North Dartmouth MA 02747-2300
Steven T. Briggs, Director of Admissions
508-999-8605 Fax: 508-999-8755
Website: explore.umassd.edu
E-mail: sbriggs@umassd.edu

MICHIGAN

Alma College
614 W Superior St, Alma MI 48801-1599
Evan Montague, Director of Admissions
800-321-ALMA Fax: 989-463-7057
Website: www.alma.edu
E-mail: admissions@alma.edu

Concordia University
4090 Geddes Rd, Ann Arbor MI 48105-2797
Gary Neumann, Director of Admissions
734-995-7300 Fax: 734-995-4610
Website: www.cuaa.edu
E-mail: admissions@cuaa.edu

Delta College
University Center MI 48710-0001
Duff Zube, Director of Admissions
989-686-9093 Fax: 989-667-2202
Website: www.delta.edu
E-mail: admit@delta.edu

Grand Valley State University
1 Campus Dr, Allendale MI 49401-9403
Jodi Chycinski, Director of Admissions
616-331-6611 Fax: 616-331-2000
Website: www.gvsu.edu
E-mail: go2gvsu@gvsu.edu

HILLSDALE COLLEGE
33 E College St, Hillsdale MI 49242-1298
Dr. Kirstin Kiledal, Director
517-607-2327 Fax: 517-607-2223
Website: www.hillsdale.edu
E-mail: kirstin.kiledal@hillsdale.edu

Lawrence Technological University
21000 W 10 Mile Rd, Southfield MI 48075-1058
Jane Rohrback, Director of Admissions
800-225-5588 Fax: 248-204-2228
Website: www.ltu.edu
E-mail: admissions@ltu.edu
See listing under "Universities"

MACOMB COMMUNITY COLLEGE
14500 E 12 Mile Rd, Warren MI 48088-3896
Information Center
586-445-7999
Website: www.macomb.edu
E-mail: answer@macomb.edu

Northwood University
4000 Whiting Dr, Midland MI 48640
Daniel F. Toland, Dean of Admissions
800-457-7878 Fax: 989-837-4490
Website: www.northwood.edu
E-mail: miadmit@northwood.edu

Oakland University
2200 N Squirrel Rd, Rochester MI 48309
Eleanor L. Reynolds, Assistant Vice President & Director of Admissions
248-370-2100
Website: www.oakland.edu
E-mail: ouinfo@oakland.edu

Specs Howard School of Broadcast Arts
19900 W 9 Mile Rd, Southfield MI 48075-3953
Nancy Shiner, Admissions Director
248-358-9000 Fax: 248-746-9772
Website: www.specshoward.edu
E-mail: info@specshoward.edu

MINNESOTA

Bethany Lutheran College
700 Luther Dr, Mankato MN 56001
Don Westphal, Dean of Admissions
507-344-7000 Fax: 507-344-7376
Website: www.blc.edu
E-mail: admiss@blc.edu

Crown College
8700 College View Dr, Saint Bonifacius MN 55375
Mitch Fisk, Director of Admissions
952-446-4142 Fax: 952-446-4149
Website: www.crown.edu
E-mail: johnsonj@crown.edu

Gustavus Adolphus College
800 W College Ave, Saint Peter MN 56082-1485
Mark H. Anderson, Dean of Admission
800-GUSTAVUS Fax: 507-933-7474
Website: www.gustavus.edu
E-mail: admission@gustavus.edu

Inver Hills Community College
2500 80th St E, Inver Grove Heights MN 55076
651-450-8500 Fax: 651-450-8679
Website: www.inverhills.edu

Minneapolis College of Art & Design
2501 Stevens Ave, Minneapolis MN 55404-4347
Admissions Office
800-874-6223 or 612-874-3760 Fax: 612-874-3701
Website: www.mcad.edu
E-mail: admissions@mcad.edu

Minnesota State University Moorhead
1104 7th Ave S, Moorhead MN 56563-0002
Regina Monson, Director of Admissions
218-477-2161 Fax: 218-477-4374
Website: go.mnstate.edu
E-mail: dragon@mnstate.edu

Pillsbury Baptist Bible College
315 S Grove Ave, Owatonna MN 55060-3097
Susanne Martin, Admissions Coordinator
507-451-2710 Fax: 507-451-0156
Website: www.pillsbury.edu
E-mail: admissions@pillsbury.edu

Ridgewater College-Hutchinson Campus
2 Century Ave SE, Hutchinson MN 55350-3100
Dawn Bjork, Counselor
800-722-1151 Fax: 320-234-8506
Website: www.ridgewater.edu
E-mail: dawn.bjork@ridgewater.edu

St. Cloud Technical College
1540 Northway Dr, Saint Cloud MN 56303-1240
Jodi Elness, Director of Enrollment Management
800-222-1009 Fax: 320-308-5981
Website: www.sctc.edu
E-mail: jelness@sctc.edu

University of Minnesota
2900 University Ave, Crookston MN 56716-5001
218-281-6510 Fax: 218-281-8575
Website: admissions.umcrookston.edu/requirements/apply.htm
E-mail: info@umcrookston.edu

MISSISSIPPI

Tougaloo College
500 W County Line Rd, Tougaloo MS 39174-9799
Juno Leggette Jacobs, Director of Admissions
601-977-7768 Fax: 601-977-4501
Website: www.tougaloo.edu
E-mail: jjacobs@tougaloo.edu

MISSOURI

Central Methodist University
411 Central Methodist Sq, Fayette MO 65248-1198
Larry Anderson, Director of Admissions
660-248-6247 Fax: 660-248-1872
Website: www.centralmethodist.edu
E-mail: landerso@centralmethodist.edu

East Central College
1964 Prairie Dell Rd, Union MO 63084
Karen Wieda, Registrar
636-583-5195 ext. 2220 Fax: 636-583-1897
Website: www.eastcentral.edu
E-mail: wiedaks@eastcentral.edu

Lindenwood University
209 S Kingshighway St
Saint Charles MO 63301-1695
Sheryl Guffey, Director of Admissions
636-949-2000 Fax: 636-949-4989
Website: www.lindenwood.edu

Northwest Missouri State University
800 University Dr, Maryville MO 64468-6001
Beverly Schenkel, Dean of Enrollment Management
660-562-1562 Fax: 660-562-1121
Website: www.nwmissouri.edu
E-mail: admissions@nwmissouri.edu

Stephens College
PO Box 2121, Columbia MO 65215-0001
David Adams, Dean of Enrollment Management
573-442-2211 Fax: 573-876-7237
Website: www.stephens.edu
E-mail: dadams@stephens.edu

Truman State University
100 E Normal, Kirksville MO 63501
Office of Admission
660-785-4114 Fax: 660-785-7456
Website: admissions.truman.edu
E-mail: admissions@truman.edu

University of Missouri
1 University Blvd, Saint Louis MO 63121-4499
Dr. John Hylton, Dean, Fine Arts & Communication
314-516-5458 Fax: 314-516-6759
Website: www.umsl.edu
E-mail: admissions@umsl.edu

WEBSTER UNIVERSITY
470 E Lockwood Ave, Saint Louis MO 63119-3194
Dr. Debra Carpenter, Dean, School of Communications
Website: www.webster.edu
E-mail: carpenda@webster.edu
800-753-6765 ext. 6924
314-968-7100 Fax: 314-968-7116 (graduate)
314-968-6991 Fax: 314-968-7115 (undergraduate)

Established 1915. Private. Coed. Accreditation: NCACS. Tuition: $18,240. Room and board: $7,500. Enrollment: 2,460 full-time, 1,153 part-time. Faculty: 160, Student-faculty ratio: 15:1. Degrees: BA, BFA, BM, BMEd, BS, BSN, MA, MBA, MAT, MSN, DMGT. Library: 400,000 volumes. 36 buildings on 45 acres. Nationally recognized program in communications including film, video and audio production as well as advertising and journalism. Students from 40 states and 30 countries. Beautiful suburban campus in a wooded community of 20,000. Average class size of 15. New 30,000 Sq. ft. library with 24 hour cyber cafe open in 2003. New Residence Halls for 320 additional students open in 2006. Campuses in four European countries, China and Thailand.

William Jewell College
500 College Hill, Liberty MO 64068-1896
Dr. Rick Winslow, VP Enrollment Management and Student Affairs
800-753-7009 Fax: 816-415-5040
Website: www.jewell.edu
E-mail: winslowr@william.jewell.edu

William Woods University
1 University Ave, Fulton MO 65251-1098
Jimmy Clay, Director of Admissions
573-642-2251 Fax: 573-592-1146
Website: www.williamwoods.edu
E-mail: admissions@williamwoods.edu
See listing under "Universities"

MONTANA

Carroll College
1601 N Benton Ave, Helena MT 59625-0002
Dr. Thomas J. Trebon, President
Cynthia Thornquist, Director of Admissions & Enrollment Operations
406-447-4384 Fax: 406-447-4533
Website: www.carroll.edu
E-mail: admission@carroll.edu

NEBRASKA

Midland Lutheran College
900 N Clarkson St, Fremont NE 68025-4200
Todd Hansen, Associate Director of Admissions
402-941-6501 Fax: 402-941-6513
Website: www.mlc.edu
E-mail: admissions@mlc.edu

Nebraska Wesleyan University
5000 Saint Paul Ave, Lincoln NE 68504-2794
Patricia Karthauser, V.P. for University Enrollment
402-466-2371 Fax: 402-465-2177
Website: www.nebrwesleyan.edu
E-mail: admissions@nebrwesleyan.edu

University of Nebraska at Kearney
905 W 25th St, Kearney NE 68849-0001
Dusty Newton, Director of Admissions
800-KEARNEY Fax: 308-865-8987
Website: www.unk.edu
E-mail: admissionsug@unk.edu

NEW HAMPSHIRE

Chester College of New England
40 Chester St, Chester NH 03036-4331
Pam Adie, Director of Admissions
603-887-4401 Fax: 603-887-1777
Website: www.chestercollege.edu
E-mail: padie@chestercollege.edu

Southern New Hampshire University
2500 N River Rd, Hooksett NH 03106-1045
Steve Soba, Director of Admissions
603-645-9611 Fax: 603-645-9693
Website: www.snhu.edu
E-mail: s.soba@snhu.edu

NEW JERSEY

Atlantic Cape Community College
5100 Black Horse Pike
Mays Landing NJ 08330-2699
Linda McLeod, Assistant Director of College Recruitment
609-343-5000 Fax: 609-343-4921
Website: www.atlantic.edu
E-mail: accadmit@atlantic.edu
See listing under "Community and Junior Colleges"

Bergen Community College
400 Paramus Rd, Paramus NJ 07652
Julian Gomez, Asst. Director of Admissions
201-447-7100 Fax: 201-444-7036
Website: www.bergen.edu
E-mail: jgomez@bergen.edu

New Jersey City University
2039 John F Kennedy Blvd
Jersey City NJ 07305-1588
Carmen Panlilio, Asst. V.P. for Admissions and Financial Aid
201-200-3234 Fax: 201-200-2044
Website: www.njcu.edu
E-mail: admissions@njcu.edu

Ramapo College of New Jersey
505 Ramapo Valley Rd, Mahwah NJ 07430-1623
Director of Admissions
201-684-7300 or 201-684-7301 Fax: 201-684-7964
Website: www.ramapo.edu
E-mail: admissions@ramapo.edu

RICHARD STOCKTON COLLEGE OF NEW JERSEY
PO Box 195, Pomona NJ 08240
John Iacovelli, Dean of Enrollment Management
866-RSC-2885 Fax: 609-626-5541
Website: www.stockton.edu
E-mail: admissions@stockton.edu
See listing under "Universities"

NEW YORK

Broome Community College
907 Upper Front St, Binghamton NY 13905
Anthony S. Fiorelli, Director of Admissions
607-778-5001 Fax: 607-778-5442
Website: www.sunybroome.edu
E-mail: fiorelli_a@sunybroome.edu

College of Saint Rose
432 Western Ave, Albany NY 12203-1419
Maryelizabeth Amico, Asst V.P. for Undergraduate Admissions
518-454-5150 Fax: 518-454-2013
Website: www.strose.edu
E-mail: admit@strose.edu

CUNY Hunter College
695 Park Ave, New York NY 10021
Aaron Gibbs, Assistant Director of Recruitment
212-650-3946 Fax: 212-650-3336
Website: www.hunter.cuny.edu
E-mail: aaron.gibbs@hunter.cuny.edu

Dowling College
150 Idle Hour Blvd, Oakdale NY 11769-1999
Diane Kazanecki-Kempter, Contact
631-244-3000 Fax: 631-244-1059
Website: www.dowling.edu
E-mail: admissions@dowling.edu

FIVE TOWNS COLLEGE
305 N Service Rd, Dix Hills NY 11746-5871
631-424-7000 ext. 2110 Fax: 631-656-2172
Website: www.fivetowns.edu
E-mail: admissions@ftc.edu
See listing under "Universities"

Hilbert College
5200 S Park Ave, Hamburg NY 14075-1597
Timothy Lee, Director of Admissions
716-649-7900 Fax: 716-649-0702
Website: www.hilbert.edu
E-mail: tlee@hilbert.edu

Institute of Audio Research
64 University Pl, New York NY 10003-4595
Mark L. Kahn, Director of Admissions
800-544-2501 or 212-777-8550 (NY, NJ, CT)
Fax: 212-677-6549
Website: www.audioschool.com
E-mail: contact@audioschool.com
See listing under "Career Schools"

Iona College
715 North Ave, New Rochelle NY 10801-1890
Kevin Cavanagh, Assistant V.P. for College Admissions
914-633-2502 Fax: 914-637-2778
Website: www.iona.edu

Long Island University-C. W. Post Campus
720 Northern Blvd, Brookville NY 11548-1300
Joanne Graziano, Executive Director of Admissions
516-299-2900 Fax: 516-299-2137
Website: www.liu.edu/cwpost
E-mail: enroll@cwpost.liu.edu

Marymount Manhattan College
221 E 71st St, New York NY 10021-4501
Jim Rogers, Dean of Admissions
800-MARYMOUNT Fax: 212-517-0448
Website: www.mmm.edu
E-mail: admissions@mmm.edu

Molloy College
1000 Hempstead Ave
Rockville Centre NY 11570-1100
Marguerite Lane, Director of Admissions
516-678-5000 ext. 6291 Fax: 516-256-2247
Website: www.molloy.edu
E-mail: admissions@molloy.edu
See listing under "Universities"

Pratt Institute
200 Willoughby Ave, Brooklyn NY 11205-3899
Heidi Metcalf, Director of Admissions
718-636-3600 Fax: 718-636-3670
Website: www.pratt.edu
E-mail: hmetcalf@pratt.edu
Advertising Art Direction
Graphic Design and Illustration

Roberts Wesleyan College
2301 Westside Dr, Rochester NY 14624-1997
Office of Admissions
585-594-6400 Fax: 585-594-6371
Website: www.roberts.edu
E-mail: admissions@roberts.edu

St. John's University
8000 Utopia Pkwy, Queens NY 11439
Office of Admission
877-STJ-5550 ext. 101 Fax: 718-990-2096
Website: www.stjohns.edu/learnmore
E-mail: admhelp@stjohns.edu
See listing under "Universities"

SUNY College at Brockport
350 New Campus Dr, Brockport NY 14420-2997
Bernard S. Valento, Director of Undergraduate Admissions
585-395-2751 Fax: 585-395-5452
Website: www.brockport.edu
E-mail: admit@brockport.edu

SUNY Niagara County Community College
3111 Saunders Settlement Rd
Sanborn NY 14132-9487
Kathleen Saunders, Director of Admissions
716-614-6200 Fax: 716-614-6820
Website: www.niagaracc.suny.edu
E-mail: admissions@niagaracc.suny.edu

SUNY Orange County Community College
115 South St, Middletown NY 10940-6437
Margot St. Lawrence, Director of Admissions
845-341-4030 Fax: 845-342-8662
Website: www.sunyorange.edu
E-mail: apply@sunyorange.edu
See listing under "Community and Junior Colleges"

SUNY Sullivan County Community College
112 College Rd, Loch Sheldrake NY 12759-5151
Sari Rosenheck, Director of Admissions
845-434-5750 Fax: 845-434-0923
Website: www.sullivan.suny.edu
E-mail: admissions@sullivan.suny.edu
Student Housing on Campus.

NORTH CAROLINA

Catawba College
2300 W Innes St, Salisbury NC 28144-2488
Dr. L. Russell Watjen, Ph.D., V.P. & Dean of Admissions
704-637-4402 Fax: 704-637-4222
Website: www.catawba.edu
E-mail: admission@catawba.edu

Chowan University
One University Pl, Murfreesboro NC 27855
Chad Holt, Dean of Admissions
800-488-4101 Fax: 252-398-1190
Website: www.chowan.edu
E-mail: holtc@chowan.edu

Haywood Community College
185 Freedlander Dr, Clyde NC 28721
Debbie Rowland, Coordinator of Admissions
828-627-4500 Fax: 828-627-4513
Website: www.haywood.edu
E-mail: drowland@haywood.edu

Peace College
15 E Peace St, Raleigh NC 27604-1194
Laura C. Bingham, President
800-PEACE-47 Fax: 919-508-2306
Website: www.peace.edu
E-mail: admissions@peace.edu

Salem College
Winston Salem NC 27108
Dana Evans, Dean of Admissions/Fin. Aid
800-32-SALEM Fax: 336-917-5572
Website: www.salem.edu
E-mail: admissions@salem.edu
See listing under "Women's Colleges"

NORTH DAKOTA

Dickinson State University
Dickinson ND 58601-4896
Steve Glasser, Director of Enrollment Services
800-279-4295 Fax: 701-483-2409
Website: www.dickinsonstate.edu
E-mail: dsu.hawks@dickinsonstate.edu

OHIO

Brown Mackie College - Cincinnati
1011 Glendale Milford Rd, Cincinnati OH 45215-1107
Robin Krout, President
513-771-2424 Fax: 513-771-3413
Website: www.brownmackie.edu
E-mail: rkrout@brownmackie.edu

Cincinnati Christian University
PO Box 4320, Cincinnati OH 45204
Erin Oppy, Executive Director of Undergraduate Admissions
513-244-8141 Fax: 513-244-8453
Website: www.ccuniversity.edu

Cleveland State University
2121 Euclid Ave RW 204, Cleveland OH 44115
Dr. Richard Arndt, Dean of Undergraduate Recruitment and College Partnerships
888-CSU-OHIO Fax: 216-687-9210
Website: www.csuohio.edu
E-mail: admissions@csuohio.edu

Franciscan University of Steubenville
University Blvd, Steubenville OH 43952
Margaret J. Weber, Director of Admissions
800-783-6220 or 740-283-6226 Fax: 740-284-5456
Website: www.admissions.edu
E-mail: mweber@franciscan.edu

OHIO CENTER FOR BROADCASTING
9000 Sweet Valley Dr, Valley View OH 44125-4220
Kathy Wenner, Admissions Director
216-447-9117 Fax: 216-642-9232
Website: www.beonair.com
E-mail: ocb@beonair.com

OHIO NORTHERN UNIVERSITY
525 S Main St, Ada OH 45810-1555
Nils Riess, Chair of the Communication Arts Dept.
419-772-2049
Website: www.onu.edu
E-mail: admissions-ug@onu.edu
See listing under "Universities"

The Ohio State University
School of Journalism and Communication
Derby Hall, 154 N Oval Mall, Columbus OH 43210
614-292-3400 Fax: 614-292-2055
Website: www.comm.ohio-state.edu
E-mail: krichbaum.19@osu.edu

Sinclair Community College
444 W 3rd St, Dayton OH 45402-1460
Director of Admissions
937-512-3000 Fax: 937-512-2393
Website: www.sinclair.edu
E-mail: admit@sinclair.edu

University of Dayton
300 College Park, Dayton OH 45469-1300
Robert F. Durkle, Director of Admission
800-837-7433 Fax: 937-229-4729
Website: admission.udayton.edu
E-mail: admission@udayton.edu

OKLAHOMA

Oklahoma State University
Stillwater OK 74078
Paul Smeyak, Department Head
405-744-6150
Website: www.okstate.edu
E-mail: paul.smeyak@okstate.edu

University of Tulsa
600 S College Ave, Tulsa OK 74104-3126
Earl Johnson, Dean of Admission
918-631-2307 Fax: 918-631-5003
Website: www.utulsa.edu
E-mail: admission@utulsa.edu

OREGON

Cascade College
9101 E Burnside St, Portland OR 97216-1599
Jim Murphy, Director of Enrollment Management
800-550-7678 Fax: 503-257-1222
Website: www.cascade.edu
E-mail: admissions@cascade.edu

Linn-Benton Community College
6500 Pacific Blvd SW, Albany OR 97321-3774
Christine Baker, Outreach Coordinator
541-917-4811 Fax: 541-917-4868
Website: www.linnbenton.edu
E-mail: admissions@linnbenton.edu

Marylhurst University
17600 Pacific Hwy (Hwy 43)
Marylhurst OR 97036-0261
Director of Admissions
800-634-9982 ext. 6268 Fax: 503-635-6585
Website: www.marylhurst.edu
E-mail: studentinfo@marylhurst.edu

PACIFIC UNIVERSITY
2043 College Way, Forest Grove OR 97116-1797
Karen M. Dunston, Executive Director of Admissions
800-677-6712 Fax: 503-352-2975
Website: www.pacific.edu
E-mail: admissions@pacific.edu

University of Portland
5000 N Willamette Blvd, Portland OR 97203-5798
Jason McDonald, Dean of Admissions
503-943-7911 Fax: 503-943-7315
Website: www.up.edu
E-mail: mcdonaja@up.edu

Warner Pacific College
2219 SE 68th Ave, Portland OR 97215-4026
Shannon Mackey, Director of Admissions
503-517-1000 Fax: 503-517-1352
Website: www.warnerpacific.edu
E-mail: admissions@warnerpacific.edu

PENNSYLVANIA

ART INSTITUTE OF PITTSBURGH
420 Boulevard Of The Allies, Pittsburgh PA 15219
Jeffrey Bucklew, Director of Admissions
800-275-2470 Fax: 412-263-6667
Website: www.aip.aii.edu
E-mail: pahughes@aii.edu
See listing under "Universities"

Central Pennsylvania College
College Hill & Valley Rds, Summerdale PA 17093
Katie Borrelli, Admissions Director
800-759-2727 Fax: 717-728-2505
Website: www.centralpenn.edu
E-mail: katie.borrelli@centralpenn.edu

Clarion University of Pennsylvania
840 Wood St, Clarion PA 16214-1232
William Bailey, Dean of Enrollment Management
814-393-2306 Fax: 814-393-2030
Website: www.clarion.edu
E-mail: admissions@clarion.edu

Community College of Allegheny County
Allegheny Campus: 808 Ridge Ave, Pittsburgh PA 15212 Admissions: 412.237.2700
Boyce Campus: 595 Beatty Rd, Monroeville PA 15146 Admissions: 724.325.6614
North Campus: 8701 Perry Highway, Pittsburgh PA 15237 Admissions: 412.369.3600
South Campus: 1750 Clairton Rd, West Mifflin PA 15122 Admissions: 412-469-4301
Website: www.ccac.edu

Community College of Beaver County
1 Campus Dr, Monaca PA 15061-2566
724-775-8561 Fax: 724-775-4687
Website: www.ccbc.edu
E-mail: admissions@ccbc.edu

Delaware Valley College
700 E Butler Ave, Doylestown PA 18901-2697
Stephen W. Zenko, Director of Admissions
800-2DE-LVAL Fax: 215-230-2968
Website: www.delval.edu
E-mail: stephenzenko@delval.edu

DeSales University
2755 Station Ave, Center Valley PA 18034-9565
610-282-1100 Fax: 610-282-2342
Website: www.desales.edu

Holy Family University
9801 Frankford Avenue, Philadelphia PA 19114
Lauren Campbell, Director of Admissions
215-637-3050 Fax: 215-281-1022
Website: www.holyfamily.edu
E-mail: admissions@holyfamily.edu

Juniata College
1700 Moore St, Huntingdon PA 16652-2196
Michelle Bartol, Dean of Enrollment
877-JUNIATA Fax: 814-641-3100
Website: www.juniata.edu
E-mail: admissions@juniata.edu

King's College
133 N River St, Wilkes Barre PA 18711-0801
Michelle Lawrence-Schmude, Dean of Admission
570-208-5900 Fax: 570-208-5971
Website: www.kings.edu
E-mail: admissions@kings.edu

Neumann College
1 Neumann Dr, Aston PA 19014-1298
Dennis Murphy, Director of Admissions
610-459-0905 Fax: 610-558-5652
Website: www.neumann.edu
E-mail: neumann@neumann.edu

Widener University
1 University Pl, Chester PA 19013-5792
Edwin Wright, Dean of Admissions
610-499-4000 Fax: 610-499-4676
Website: www.widener.edu
E-mail: admissions.office@widener.edu

RHODE ISLAND

New England Institute of Technology
2500 Post Rd, Warwick RI 02886-2244
Michael Kwiatkowski, Director of Admissions
401-739-5000 Fax: 401-738-5122
Website: www.neit.edu
E-mail: eflynn@neit.edu

SOUTH CAROLINA

Bob Jones University
1700 Wade Hampton Blvd
Greenville SC 29614-0001
David Christ, Director of Admissions
800-BJ-AND-ME Fax: 800-2-FAX-BJU
Website: www.bju.edu
E-mail: admissions@bju.edu
See listing under "Universities"

Columbia International University
PO Box 3122, Columbia SC 29230-3122
Michelle MacGregor, Director of University Admissions
800-777-2227 Fax: 803-786-4209
Website: www.ciu.edu
E-mail: yesciu@ciu.edu
See listing under "Theological Studies & Religious Vocations"

North Greenville University
PO Box 1892, Tigerville SC 29688-1892
Dr. Linwood Hagin, Dept. Chair
Website: www.ngu.edu
See listing under "Universities"

University of South Carolina - Upstate
800 University Way, Spartanburg SC 29303-4932
Donette Stewart, Assistant VC for Enrollment Services
864-503-5246 Fax: 864-503-5727
Website: www.uscupstate.edu
E-mail: dstewart@uscupstate.edu
See listing under "Universities"

TENNESSEE

Austin Peay State University
601 College St, Clarksville TN 37044-0002
931-221-7011 Fax: 931-221-6168
Website: www.apsu.edu
E-mail: admissions@apsu.edu

Lipscomb University
3901 Granny White Pike, Nashville TN 37204-3951
Ricky Holaway, Director of Admissions
800-333-4358 ext. 1776 Fax: 615-269-1804
Website: www.lipscomb.edu
E-mail: admissions@lipscomb.edu

Tennessee State University
3500 John A Merritt Blvd, Nashville TN 37209-1561
John Cade, Dean of Admissions & Records
615-963-5101 Fax: 615-963-2930
Website: www.tnstate.edu
E-mail: jcade@tnstate.edu

University of Tennessee
615 McCallie Ave, Chattanooga TN 37403-2504
Yancy Freeman, Director of Admissions
423-425-4111 Fax: 423-425-4157
Website: www.utc.edu
E-mail: Yancy-Freeman@utc.edu

TEXAS

Abilene Christian University
ACU Box 29000, Abilene TX 79699-0001
325-674-2000 Fax: 325-674-2202
Website: www.acu.edu
E-mail: info@admissions.acu.edu

Galveston College
4015 Avenue Q, Galveston TX 77550-7496
Brian Lowery, Registrar
409-763-6551 Fax: 409-944-1501
Website: www.gc.edu
E-mail: blowery@gc.edu

Lubbock Christian University
5601 19th St, Lubbock TX 79407-2099
Stan Scott, Director of Admissions
806-796-8800 Fax: 806-720-7162
Website: www.lcu.edu
E-mail: stan.scott@lcu.edu

Northwood University
1114 W FM 1382, Cedar Hill TX 75104-1204
Sylvia Correa, Director of Admissions
800-927-WOOD Fax: 972-291-3824
Website: www.northwood.edu
E-mail: ray@northwood.edu

Tyler Junior College
PO Box 9020, Tyler TX 75711-9020
Richard Minter, Dean
800-687-5680
Website: www.tjc.edu
E-mail: rmin@tjc.edu
See listing under "Community and Junior Colleges"

University of Houston
122 E Cullen Bldg, Houston TX 77204-2023
Office of Admission
713-743-9595
Website: www.uh.edu
E-mail: admissions@uh.edu

University of Texas at Arlington
Box 19111, Arlington TX 76019-0111
Hans Gatterdam, Director of Admission
817-272-6287 Fax: 817-272-3435
Website: www.uta.edu
E-mail: admissions@uta.edu

Weatherford College
225 College Park Dr, Weatherford TX 76086
Dr. Joe Birmingham, President
800-287-5471 Fax: 817-598-6205
Website: www.wc.edu
E-mail: willingham@wc.edu

VERMONT

NORWICH UNIVERSITY
158 Harmon Dr, Northfield VT 05663
Dr. Bill Estill, Department Head
800-468-6679 Fax: 802-485-2565
Website: www.norwich.edu
E-mail: westill@norwich.edu
See listing under "Universities"

Southern Vermont College
982 Mansion Dr, Bennington VT 05201-6002
Joel Wincowski, Director of Admissions
800-378-2782 Fax: 802-447-4695
Website: www.svc.edu
E-mail: admis@svc.edu

VIRGINIA

Radford University
PO Box 6903, Radford VA 24142
David W. Kraus, Director of Admissions
800-890-4265 Fax: 540-831-5038
Website: www.radford.edu
E-mail: ruadmiss@radford.edu

Randolph College
2500 Rivermont Ave, Lynchburg VA 24503
Patricia LeDonne, Director of Admissions
434-947-8100 Fax: 434-947-8996
Website: www.randolphcollege.edu
E-mail: admissions@randolphcollege.edu

WASHINGTON

SHORELINE COMMUNITY COLLEGE
16101 Greenwood Ave N, Shoreline WA 98133-5696
Chris Melton, Acting Registrar
206-546-4581 Fax: 206-546-5835
Website: www.shoreline.edu

WEST VIRGINIA

Davis & Elkins College
100 Campus Dr, Elkins WV 26241-3996
Renee Heckel, Director of Enrollment Management
800-624-3157 Fax: 304-637-1800
Website: www.davisandelkins.edu
E-mail: admiss@davisandelkins.edu

Fairmont State University
1201 Locust Ave, Fairmont WV 26554-2470
Steve Leadman, Director of Admissions
304-367-4219 or 800-641-5678 Fax: 304-367-4789
Website: www.fairmontstate.edu
E-mail: admit@fairmontstate.edu

WISCONSIN

Alverno College
PO Box 343922, Milwaukee WI 53234-3922
Dianna Gaebler, Director of Admissions
414-382-6100 Fax: 414-382-6354
Website: www.alverno.edu
E-mail: admissions@alverno.edu

Lakeland College
PO Box 359, Sheboygan WI 53082-0359
Nathan Dehne, Director of Admission
920-565-1100 Fax: 920-565-1215
Website: www.lakeland.edu
E-mail: admissions@lakeland.edu

MADISON MEDIA INSTITUTE
College of Media Arts
2702 Agriculture Dr, Madison WI 53718-6787
Steve Hutchings, Director of Admissions
800-236-4997 or 608-663-2000 Fax: 608-442-0141
Website: www.madisonmedia.edu
E-mail: mmi@madisonmedia.com

Marquette University
PO Box 1881, Milwaukee WI 53201-1881
Robert Blust, Director of Admissions
414-288-7302 Fax: 414-288-3764
Website: www.mu.edu
E-mail: admissions@marquette.edu

St. Norbert College
100 Grant St, De Pere WI 54115
Brian Studebaker, Director of Admission
800-236-4878 Fax: 920-403-4072
Website: www.snc.edu
E-mail: admit@snc.edu

WYOMING

Laramie County Community College
1400 E College Dr, Cheyenne WY 82007-3204
Jenny Hargett, Director of Admissions
307-778-5222 Fax: 307-778-1350
Website: www.lccc.wy.edu
E-mail: learnmore@lccc.wy.edu

University of Wyoming
Admissions Office
Dept 3435, Laramie WY 82071-3435
Brooke Culver, Contact
800-342-5996 Fax: 307-766-4042
Website: www.uwyo.edu
E-mail: why-wyo@uwyo.edu

GUAM

University of Guam
UOG Station, Mangilao GU 96923
Deborah Leon Guerrero, Registrar
671-735-2201 or 671-735-2208 Fax: 671-735-2203
Website: www.uog.edu
E-mail: admitme@uog9.uog.edu

·COMMUNITY AND JUNIOR COLLEGES

And Career Schools offering an Associate Degree

ALABAMA

Alabama Southern Community College
PO Box 2000, Monroeville AL 36461-2000
334-575-3156

Alabama Southern Community College
PO Box 2000, Thomasville AL 36784
334-636-4429

Bessemer State Technical College
PO Box 308, Bessemer AL 35021-0308
205-428-6391

Bevill State Community College
2631 Temple Ave N, Fayette AL 35555-1198
800-526-5755

Bevill State Community College
PO Box 9, Hamilton AL 35570-0009
205-921-3177

Bevill State Community College
1411 Indiana Ave, Jasper AL 35501-4962
800-777-0372

Bevill State Community College
PO Box 800, Sumiton AL 35148-0800
205-648-3271

Bishop State Community College
1365 Martin Luther King Ave, Mobile AL 36603
334-405-4400

BISHOP STATE COMMUNITY COLLEGE-MAIN
351 N Broad St, Mobile AL 36603-5898
Dr. Terry Hazzard, Dean of Students
251-690-6419 Fax: 251-690-6446
Website: www.bishop.edu
E-mail: thazzard@bishop.edu

Established 1927. Public. Coed. Accreditation: Commission on Colleges of the Southern Association of Colleges and Schools as well as program specific accrediting agencies. Tuition: $1,728. Fees: $432. Enrollment: 2,869 full-time, 2,353 part-time. Faculty: 208. Student-faculty ratio: 25:1. Degrees: Associate in Arts, Associate in Science, Associate in Applied Science, Associate in Occupational Technologies. Library: 63,304 volumes. 30 buildings. Four convenient locations; flexible class schedules; career opportunities; quality instructors; state-of-the-art facilities; small classes; online courses; off-campus locations; and adult education courses. Financial Aid and Scholarships are available.

CALHOUN COMMUNITY COLLEGE
PO Box 2216, Decatur AL 35609-2216
M. Wayne Tosh, Registrar
256-306-2500 Fax: 256-306-2941
Website: www.calhoun.edu
E-mail: pml@calhoun.edu

Established 1947. Coed. Accredited Member: SACS:CC. Offering AS and AAS degrees. As the largest of the 32 two-year institutions comprising The Alabama College System, Calhoun Community College is an open-admission, community based, state-supported, comprehensive community college dedicated to providing affordable, high-quality and accessible education to individuals in its service area.

Central Alabama Community College
PO Box 699, Alexander City AL 35011-0699
256-234-6346

Chattahoochee Valley Community College
2602 College Dr, Phenix City AL 36869-7960
334-291-4900

Community College of the Air Force
130 W Maxwell Blvd, Montgomery AL 36112
334-953-5033

Enterprise - Ozark Community College
PO Box 1300, Enterprise AL 36331-1300
334-347-2623

Gadsden State Community College
PO Box 227, Gadsden AL 35902-0227
256-549-8200

Gadsden State Community College
Harry M Ayers Campus
1801 Coleman Rd, Anniston AL 36207
256-835-5400

George C. Wallace Community College - Dothan
1141 Wallace Dr, Dothan AL 36303
334-983-3521

George C. Wallace State Community College
PO Box 2530, Selma AL 36702-2530
Mrs. Donitha J. Griffin, Dean of Students
334-876-9295 Fax: 334-876-9300
Website: www.wccs.edu
E-mail: dgriffin@wccs.edu

ITT Technical Institute
6270 Park South Dr, Bessmer AL 35022
205-497-5700

James H. Faulkner State Community College
1900 S US Highway 31, Bay Minette AL 36507-2619
334-580-2100

Jefferson Davis Community College
PO Box 958, Brewton AL 36427-0958
334-867-4832

Jefferson State Community College
2601 Carson Rd, Birmingham AL 35215-3098
205-853-1200

J. F. Drake State Technical College
3421 Meridian St N, Huntsville AL 35811
256-539-8161

J. F. Ingram State Technical College
PO Box 220350, Deatsville AL 36022-0350
334-285-7870

Lawson State Community College
3060 Wilson Rd SW, Birmingham AL 35221-1717
205-925-2515

LBW Community College
MacArthur Campus
PO Box 910, Opp AL 36467
334-493-3573

Lurleen B. Wallace Community College
PO Box 1418, Andalusia AL 36420-1418
Judy Hall, Director of Student Services
334-222-6591 ext. 2271

Marion Military Institute
1101 Washington St, Marion AL 36756
800-MMI-1842

Northeast Alabama Community College
PO Box 159, Rainsville AL 35986-0159
256-638-4418

Northwest-Shoals Community College
PO Box 2545, Muscle Shoals AL 35662-2545
256-331-5200

Prince Institute of Professional Studies
7735 Atlanta Hwy, Montgomery AL 36117-4231
334-271-1670

Reid State Technical College
PO Box 588, Evergreen AL 36401-0588
334-578-1313

Shelton State Community College
9500 Old Greensboro Rd
Tuscaloosa AL 35405-8522
205-759-1541

Snead State Community College
Walnut Rd, Boaz AL 35957
256-593-5120

Southern Community College
PO Box 830688, Tuskegee AL 36083-0688
334-727-5220

Southern Union State Community College
PO Box 1000, Wadley AL 36276-1000
256-395-2211

South University
5355 Vaughn Rd, Montgomery AL 36116-1120
334-395-8800

Trenholm State Technical College
Trenholm Campus
1225 Air Base Blvd, Montgomery AL 36108-3199
Dr. Anthony Molina, President
334-420-4200 Fax: 334-420-4206
Website: www.trenholmtech.cc.al.us
E-mail: molinaa@trenholmtech.cc.al.us

Wallace Community College Sparks Campus
PO Drawer 580, Eufaula AL 36072-0580
Jane Boyette, Coordinator Student Affairs
334-687-3543 ext. 4270

Wallace State Community College - Hanceville
PO Box 2000, Hanceville AL 35077-2000
256-352-8000

ALASKA

Ilisagvik College
PO Box 749, Barrow AK 99723
907-852-3333

Kenai Peninsula College
34820 College Dr, Soldotna AK 99669-9732
907-262-0300

Kodiak College
117 Benny Benson Dr, Kodiak AK 99615-6643
907-486-1235

Prince William Sound Community College
PO Box 97, Valdez AK 99686-0097
907-834-1600

University of Alaska Kuskokwim Campus
PO Box 368, Bethel AK 99559-0368
907-543-4500

University of Alaska Matanuska-Susitna
PO Box 2889, Palmer AK 99645-2889
907-745-9712

University of Alaska Northwest Campus
PO Box 400, Nome AK 99762-0400
907-443-2201

University of Alaska Sitka Campus
1332 Seward Ave, Sitka AK 99835-9418
907-747-6653

University of Alaska Southeast-Ketchikan
2600 7th Ave, Ketchikan AK 99901-5728
907-225-6177

ARIZONA

Apollo College
630 W Southern Ave, Mesa AZ 85210-5005
480-831-6585 Fax: 480-827-0022

Apollo College
8503 N 27th Ave, Phoenix AZ 85051-4063
602-864-1571 Fax: 602-864-8207

Apollo College
2701 W Bethany Home Rd, Phoenix AZ 85017-1705
602-433-1333 Fax: 602-433-1414

Apollo College
3550 N Oracle Rd, Tucson AZ 85705
520-888-5885 Fax: 520-887-3005

Arizona Western College
PO Box 929, Yuma AZ 85366-0929
Bryan Doak, Associate Dean for Enrollment Services
928-317-6000

Central Arizona College
273 E US Highway 60, Apache Junction AZ 85219
480-982-7261

Central Arizona College
8470 N Overfield Rd, Coolidge AZ 85228-9779
520-426-4444

Chandler-Gilbert Community College
2626 E Pecos Rd, Chandler AZ 85225-2499
480-732-7000

Cochise College
901 N Colombo Ave, Sierra Vista AZ 85635
Debbie Quick, Director of Admissions
520-515-5412

Coconino Community College
2800 S Lone Tree Rd, Flagstaff AZ 86001-2701
Steve Miller, Director of Admissions
520-527-1222 ext. 302

The Conservatory of Recording Arts & Sciences
2300 E Broadway Rd, Tempe AZ 85282-1707
Tonya Visconti, Director of Admissions
800-562-6383 or 480-858-9400 Fax: 480-829-1332
Website: cras.org
E-mail: info@cras.org
See listing under "Music"

Dinè College
Tsaile AZ 86556
520-724-3311

Eastern Arizona College
3714 W Church St, Thatcher AZ 85552
928-428-8233

Estrella Mountain Community College
3000 N Dysart Rd, Avondale AZ 85392
623-935-8015

Everest College
10400 N 25th Ave Suite 190, Phoenix AZ 85021-1610
Melissa Agee, Director of Admissions
602-942-4141

GateWay Community College
108 N 40th St, Phoenix AZ 85034-1795
Cathy Gibson, Director of Admissions & Records
602-286-8052

Glendale Community College
6000 W Olive Ave, Glendale AZ 85302-3090
Mary Lou Massal, Sr. Associate Dean, Enrollment Services
623-845-3000

High-Tech Institute
1515 E Indian School Rd, Phoenix AZ 85014-4973
602-279-9700

International Institute of the Americas
925 S Gilbert Rd Ste 201, Mesa AZ 85204-4440
Todd Olehausen, Director
480-545-8755 Fax: 480-926-1371
Website: www.iia.edu
E-mail: tolehausen@iia.edu

International Institute of the Americas
6049 N 43rd Ave, Phoenix AZ 85019-1600
John Pechota, Director of Admissions
602-242-6265 Fax: 602-589-1353
Website: www.iia.edu
E-mail: jpechota@iia.edu

International Institute of the Americas
5441 E 22nd St, Tucson AZ 85710
Leigh Anne Pechota, Director
520-748-9799 Fax: 520-748-9355
Website: www.iia.edu
E-mail: lpechota@iia.edu

Mesa Community College
1833 W Southern Ave, Mesa AZ 85202-4822
480-461-7000

Mohave Community College
1971 E Jagerson Ave, Kingman AZ 86409-1299
520-757-0879

Northland Pioneer College
PO Box 610, Holbrook AZ 86025-0610
520-524-7606

Paradise Valley Community College
18401 N 32nd St, Phoenix AZ 85032-1200
Dr. Shirley Green, Dean, Student Affairs
602-787-7020

Phoenix College
1202 W Thomas Rd, Phoenix AZ 85013-4234
602-264-2492

Pima Community College
4905 E Broadway Blvd, Tucson AZ 85709-1010
Wendy Kilgore, Ph.D., Director of Admissions
520-206-4500 Fax: 520-206-4790
Website: www.pima.edu
E-mail: infocenter@pima.edu

Rio Salado Community College
2323 W 14th St, Tempe AZ 85281-6950
480-517-8000

Scottsdale Community College
9000 E Chaparral Rd, Scottsdale AZ 85250-2699
480-423-6000

South Mountain Community College
7050 S 24th St, Phoenix AZ 85042-5898
602-243-8000

Tohono O'odham Community College
PO Box 3129, Sells AZ 85634
520-383-8401

Yavapai College
1100 E Sheldon St, Prescott AZ 86301-3297
928-445-7300

ARKANSAS

Arkansas Northeastern College
2501 S Division St, Blytheville AR 72315-5111
870-762-1020

Arkansas State University - Beebe
PO Box 1000, Beebe AR 72012-1000
501-882-6452

Arkansas State University - Newport
7648 Victory Blvd, Newport AR 72112
870-512-7800

Cossatot Community College of the University of Arkansas
PO Box 960, De Queen AR 71832-0960
Brenda Morris, Director of Admissions
870-584-4471

Crowley's Ridge College
100 College Dr, Paragould AR 72450-9775
Larry Bills, President
Nancy Joneshill, Director of Admissions
800-264-1096

East Arkansas Community College
1700 Newcastle Rd
Forrest City AR 72335
870-633-4480

Mid-South Community College
2000 W Broadway St, West Memphis AR 72301-3829
870-733-6722

National Park Community College
101 College Dr
Hot Springs National Park AR 71913-9173
501-760-4222

North Arkansas College
1515 Pioneer Ridge Dr, Harrison AR 72601
870-743-3000

Northwest Arkansas Community College
1 College Dr, Bentonville AR 72712-5091
479-636-9222

OUACHITA TECHNICAL COLLEGE

One College Cir, Malvern AR 72104
Linda Johnson, V.P. Student Affairs & Registrar
501-337-5000 ext. 1118 Fax: 501-337-9382
Website: www.otcweb.edu
E-mail: ljohnson@otcweb.edu

Phillips Community College of the University of Arkansas
PO Box 785, Helena AR 72342-0785
Dr. Steven Murray, Chancellor
Lynn Boone, Vice Chancellor for Student Services / Registrar
870-338-6474 Fax: 870-338-7542
Website: www.pccua.edu
E-mail: lboone@pccua.edu

Rich Mountain Community College
1100 College Dr, Mena AR 71953-2500
479-394-7622

South Arkansas Community College
PO Box 7010, El Dorado AR 71731-7010
870-862-8131

Southern Arkansas University Tech
100 Carr Rd, Camden AR 71701
870-574-4500

University of Arkansas at Fort Smith
PO Box 3649, Fort Smith AR 72913-3649
479-788-7000

University of Arkansas Community College at Batesville
PO Box 3350, Batesville AR 72503-3350
Andy Thomas, Director of Admissions
870-793-7581

University of Arkansas Community College at Hope
PO Box 140, Hope AR 71802-0140
Danita Ormand, Director of Enrollment Services
870-777-5722 Fax: 870-722-6630
Website: www.uacch.edu
E-mail: dormand@uacch.edu

University of Arkansas Community College at Morrilton
1537 University Blvd, Morrilton AR 72110
Susan Dewey, Admissions Counselor
800-264-1094

CALIFORNIA

Allan Hancock College
800 S College Dr, Santa Maria CA 93454-6399
805-922-6966

American River College
4700 College Oak Dr, Sacramento CA 95841-4286
916-484-8011

Antelope Valley College
3041 W Avenue K, Lancaster CA 93536-5426
661-722-6300

Bakersfield College
1801 Panorama Dr, Bakersfield CA 93305-1299
661-395-4301

Bakersfield College
1942 Randolph St, Delano CA 93215-1527
661-725-8020

Barstow Community College
2700 Barstow Rd, Barstow CA 92311-6608
760-252-2411

Berkeley City College
2020 Milvia St, Berkeley CA 94704-1111
510-981-2805

Brooks College
4825 E Pacific Coast Hwy
Long Beach CA 90804-3291
Chelena Adkins, Director of Admissions
562-597-6611

Brooks College
1120 Kifer Rd, Sunnyvale CA 94086-5303
408-328-5700

Butte College
3536 Butte Campus Dr, Oroville CA 95965-8399
Carole Gish, Director of Admissions
530-895-2511 Fax: 530-879-4313
Website: www.butte.edu
E-mail: admissions@butte.edu

Cabrillo College
6500 Soquel Dr, Aptos CA 95003-3194
831-479-6100

California Culinary Academy
625 Polk St, San Francisco CA 94102-3336
Nancy Seyfert, V.P. of Admissions
800-BAY-CHEF

Canada College
4200 Farm Hill Blvd, Redwood City CA 94061-1099
Michael McPartlin, Dean of Enrollment Services
650-306-3170

Cerritos College
11110 Alondra Blvd, Norwalk CA 90650-6296
562-860-2451

Cerro Coso Community College
3000 College Heights Blvd
Ridgecrest CA 93555-9571
Dr. Mitjl Capet, V.P. of Student Learning
760-384-6100

CHABOT COLLEGE

25555 Hesperian Blvd, Hayward CA 94545-2400
Judy Young, Director of Admissions
510-723-6600 Fax: 510-723-7510
Website: www.chabotcollege.edu
E-mail: ccarcom@clpccd.cc.ca.us

Chaffey College
5885 Haven Ave, Alta Loma CA 91737-9400
909-987-1737

Citrus College
1000 W Foothill Blvd, Glendora CA 91741-1885
626-963-0323

City College of San Francisco
50 Phelan Ave, San Francisco CA 94112-1821
415-239-3000

Coastline Community College
11460 Warner Ave, Fountain Valley CA 92708-2597
714-546-7600

College of Alameda
555 Atlantic Ave, Alameda CA 94501-2109
510-522-7221

College of Marin
835 College Ave, Kentfield CA 94904-2590
415-457-8811

College of Marin
1800 Ignacio Blvd, Novato CA 94949-4900
415-883-2211

College of San Mateo
1700 W Hillsdale Blvd, San Mateo CA 94402-3784
650-574-6161

College of the Canyons
26455 Rockwell Canyon Rd
Santa Clarita CA 91355-1899
661-259-7800

College of the Desert
43500 Monterey Ave, Palm Desert CA 92260-9399
760-346-8041

College of the Sequoias
915 S Mooney Blvd, Visalia CA 93277-2234
559-730-3700

College of the Siskiyous
800 College Ave, Weed CA 96094-2899
530-938-4461

Columbia College
11600 Columbia College Dr, Sonora CA 95370-8580
209-588-5100

Compton Community College
1111 E Artesia Blvd, Compton CA 90221-5393
310-900-1600

Consumnes River College-Eldorado Center
6699 Campus Dr, Placerville CA 95667-7744
530-642-5621

Contra Costa College
2600 Mission Bell Dr, San Pablo CA 94806-3195
510-235-7800

Copper Mountain College
PO Box 1398, Joshua Tree CA 92252-0879
760-366-3791

Cosumnes River College
8401 Center Pkwy, Sacramento CA 95823-5799
916-691-7344

Crafton Hills College
11711 Sand Canyon Rd, Yucaipa CA 92399-1799
Dr. Luis S. Gomez, President
909-389-3200

Cuesta College
PO Box 8106, San Luis Obispo CA 93403-8106
805-546-3100

Cuyamaca College
900 Rancho San Diego Pkwy
El Cajon CA 92019-4369
619-660-4000

Cypress College
9200 Valley View St, Cypress CA 90630-5897
714-484-7000

DeAnza College
21250 Stevens Creek Blvd
Cupertino CA 95014-5793
408-864-5678

Diablo Valley College
321 Golf Club Rd, Pleasant Hill CA 94523-1544
925-685-1230

D-Q University
PO Box 409, Davis CA 95617-0409
530-758-0470

East Los Angeles College
1301 Avenida Cesar Chavez
Monterey Park CA 91754-6001
323-265-8650

El Camino College
16007 Crenshaw Blvd, Torrance CA 90506-0002
310-660-3670

Evergreen Valley College
3095 Yerba Buena Rd, San Jose CA 95135-1598
Archie Sherman, Interim Director of Admissions & Records
408-274-7900 ext. 6423

Feather River Community College
570 Golden Eagle Ave, Quincy CA 95971-9124
530-283-0202

FIDM/The Fashion Institute of Design & Merchandising
17590 Gillette Ave, Irvine CA 92614
Director of Admissions
949-851-6200 or 888-974-3436 Fax: 949-851-6808
Website: www.fidm.edu
E-mail: info@fidm.com
See listing under "Community and Junior Colleges"

FIDM/THE FASHION INSTITUTE OF DESIGN & MERCHANDISING

919 S Grand Ave, Los Angeles CA 90015-1421
Tonian Hohberg, President
Website: www.fidm.edu
E-mail: info@fidm.com
Three other locations in California (see below)

Established 1969. Private. Coed. Admission open to high school graduates, GED, and some Ability-to-Benefit students. Accreditation: WASC and NASAD. Total enrollment 6,000 at four modern campuses located in cosmopolitan West Coast cities. Day, evening and weekend classes. Some courses are available online. State, Federal and institutional financial aid available. Scholarships.

The college offers Associate Degrees and AA Professional Designation programs in Fashion Design, Merchandise Marketing, Interior Design, Visual Communications, Graphic Design, Digital Media, Film & TV Costume Design, Merchandise Product Development, Footwear Design, Beauty Industry Merchandising & Marketing, Textile Design, Jewelry Design, Theatre Costume Design, International Manufacturing and Product Development, and Apparel Manufacturing Management. Collegiate level general studies and ESL access programs available.

Courses are taught by a faculty of over 200 industry professionals complemented by an active advisory board of internationally known executives. Unique features of the Institute include specialized libraries and workrooms, large costume and textile collections, tutoring centers and job placement assistance for part-time and graduate positions. Internships and complimentary portfolio evaluation are available.

The Student Housing Office provides resources and referrals for housing needs, roommate assistance, transportation and community resources. Student activities include clubs for each major, International Student Club and special parties, dances and social events.

New programs begin every 12 weeks. A Foreign Student Advisor is available. Admissions Advisors assist with required personal interviews (out-of-state by telephone) and requesting high school transcripts, college records (if applicable), entrance requirement project and references.

Tours/interviews:
Los Angeles:
213-624-1201 or 800-624-1200 Fax: 213-624-4799
San Francisco:
415-675-5200 or 800-422-3436 Fax: 415-296-7299
Irvine:
949-851-6200 or 888-974-3436 Fax: 949-851-6808
San Diego:
619-235-2049 or 800-243-3436 Fax: 619-232-4322

FIDM/The Fashion Institute of Design & Merchandising
1010 2nd Ave, San Diego CA 92101-4903
Director of Admissions
619-235-2049 or 800-243-3436 Fax: 619-232-4322
Website: www.fidm.edu
E-mail: info@fidm.com
See listing under "Community and Junior Colleges"

FIDM/The Fashion Institute of Design & Merchandising
55 Stockton St, San Francisco CA 94108-5829
Director of Admissions
415-675-5200 or 800-422-3436 Fax: 415-296-7299
Website: www.fidm.edu
E-mail: info@fidm.com
See listing under "Community and Junior Colleges"

Folsom Lake College
100 College Pkwy, Folsom CA 95630
916-608-6500

Foothill College
12345 S El Monte Rd, Los Altos Hills CA 94022-4597
650-949-7777

FRESNO CITY COLLEGE
1101 E University Ave, Fresno CA 93741-0002
Dayann Dietrich, Contact
559-442-8241 Fax: 559-237-4232
Website: www.fresnocitycollege.com
E-mail: fcc.admissions@scccd.com

Fullerton College
321 E Chapman Ave, Fullerton CA 92832-2011
714-992-7000

Gavilan Community College
5055 Santa Teresa Blvd, Gilroy CA 95020-9599
408-847-1400

Glendale Community College
1500 N Verdugo Rd, Glendale CA 91208-2894
818-240-1000

Golden West College
15744 Goldenwest St
Huntington Beach CA 92647-3197
714-892-7711

Grossmont College
8800 Grossmont College Dr, El Cajon CA 92020-1798
619-644-7000

Hartnell College
156 Homestead Ave, Salinas CA 93901-1697
831-755-6700

HEALD COLLEGE, MILPITAS
341 Great Mall Pkwy, Milpitas CA 95035-8008
Sharon Kitko, Director's Assistant
408-934-4900 Fax: 408-934-7777
Website: www.heald.edu

Imperial Valley College
PO Box 158, Imperial CA 92251-0158
760-352-8320

Irvine Valley College
5500 Irvine Center Dr, Irvine CA 92618-0300
949-451-5100

ITT Technical Institute
525 N Muller St, Anaheim CA 92801-5454
714-535-3700

ITT TECHNICAL INSTITUTE
2051 Solar Dr Ste 150, Oxnard CA 93030-0641
Milo Hegan, Director of Recruitment
805-988-0143 Fax: 805-988-1813
Website: www.itt-tech.edu
E-mail: mhegan@itt-tech.edu

ITT Technical Institute
10863 Gold Center Dr
Rancho Cordova CA 95670-6047
916-851-3900

ITT Technical Institute
670 Carnegie Dr, San Bernardino CA 92408-3519
909-889-4600

Lake Tahoe Community College
1 College Dr, South Lake Tahoe CA 96150-4500
530-541-4660

Laney College
900 Fallon St, Oakland CA 94607-4893
510-834-5740

Las Positas College
3033 Collier Canyon Rd, Livermore CA 94551-9797
925-373-5800

Lassen Community College
PO Box 3000, Susanville CA 96130-3000
530-257-6181

Long Beach City College
4901 E Carson St, Long Beach CA 90808-1780
562-938-4111

Los Angeles City College
855 N Vermont Ave, Los Angeles CA 90029-3588
323-953-4000

Los Angeles Harbor College
1111 Figueroa Pl, Wilmington CA 90744-2311
310-522-8200

Los Angeles Mission College
13356 Eldridge Ave, Sylmar CA 91342-3200
818-364-7600

Los Angeles Pierce College
6201 Winnetka Ave, Woodland Hills CA 91371-0001
818-347-0551

Los Angeles Southwest College
1600 W Imperial Hwy, Los Angeles CA 90047-4810
323-241-5225

Los Angeles Trade-Technical College
400 W Washington Blvd
Los Angeles CA 90015-4108
213-744-9058

Los Angeles Valley College
5800 Fulton Ave, Van Nuys CA 91401-4062
818-947-2600

Los Medanos College
2700 E Leland Rd, Pittsburg CA 94565-5197
925-439-2181

Marymount College
30800 Palos Verdes Dr E
Rancho Palos Verdes CA 90275-6299
310-377-5501

Mendocino College
1000 Hensley Creek Rd, Ukiah CA 95482
707-468-3000

Merced College
3600 M St, Merced CA 95348-2898
209-384-6000

Merced College-Los Banos Campus
16570 S Mercey Springs Rd
Los Banos CA 93635-9558

Merritt College
12500 Campus Dr, Oakland CA 94619-3196
510-531-4911

Mira Costa College
1 Barnard Dr, Oceanside CA 92056-3899
760-757-2121

Mission College
3000 Mission College Blvd
Santa Clara CA 95054-1897
408-988-2200

Modesto Junior College
435 College Ave, Modesto CA 95350-5800
209-575-6498

Monterey Peninsula College
980 Fremont Ave, Monterey CA 93940-4799
831-645-1376

Moorpark College
7075 Campus Rd, Moorpark CA 93021-1695
805-378-1400

Mt. San Antonio College
1100 N Grand Ave, Walnut CA 91789-1399
909-594-5611

Mt. San Jacinto College
1499 N State St, San Jacinto CA 92583-2399
951-487-6752

MTI College
5221 Madison Ave, Sacramento CA 95841-3003
Marije Miller, Director of Admissions
916-339-1500 Fax: 916-339-0305
Website: www.mticollege.edu
E-mail: mmiller@mticollege.edu

Napa Valley College
2277 Napa Vallejo Hwy, Napa CA 94558-6236
707-253-3076

Ohlone College
PO Box 3909, Fremont CA 94539-0390
510-659-6000

Orange Coast College
PO Box 5005, Costa Mesa CA 92628-5005
Kristin Clark, Director of Admissions
714-432-5773 Fax: 714-432-5736
Website: www.orangecoastcollege.edu
E-mail: kclark@cccd.edu

Oxnard College
4000 S Rose Ave, Oxnard CA 93033-6699
805-986-5800

Palomar College
1140 W Mission Rd, San Marcos CA 92069-1415
760-744-1150

Palo Verde College
1 College Dr, Blythe CA 92225-9561
760-921-5500

Pasadena City College
1570 E Colorado Blvd, Pasadena CA 91106-2041
626-585-7123

Porterville College
100 E College Ave, Porterville CA 93257-6058
559-791-2200

Queen of the Holy Rosary College
43326 Mission Blvd, Fremont CA 94539
510-657-2468

Redwoods Community College
7351 Tompkins Hill Rd, Eureka CA 95501-9300
707-476-4100

Reedley College
995 N Reed Ave, Reedley CA 93654-2099
Leticia Alvarez, Director of Admissions
559-638-3641

Rio Hondo College
3600 Workman Mill Rd, Whittier CA 90601-1699
562-692-0921

Riverside Community College
16130 Lasselle St, Moreno Valley CA 92551
951-571-6100

Riverside Community College
4800 Magnolia Ave, Riverside CA 92506-1293
951-222-8000

Sacramento City College
3835 Freeport Blvd, Sacramento CA 95822-1386
916-558-2111

Saddleback College
28000 Marguerite Pkwy
Mission Viejo CA 92692-3635
949-582-4500

San Bernardino Valley College
701 S Mount Vernon Ave
San Bernardino CA 92410-2798
Kay Ragan, Ed.D., Director of Admissions
909-888-6511 Fax: 909-889-4988
Website: www.valleycollege.edu
E-mail: kragan@sbccd.cc.ca.us

San Diego City College
1313 Park Blvd, San Diego CA 92101-4787
619-230-2400

San Diego Mesa College
7250 Mesa College Dr, San Diego CA 92111-4996
858-627-2600

San Diego Miramar College
10440 Black Mountain Rd, San Diego CA 92126-2999
619-388-7800

San Joaquin Delta College
5151 Pacific Ave, Stockton CA 95207-6370
209-954-5151

San Joaquin Valley College
201 New Stine Rd, Bakersfield CA 93309-2659
Jaime Delgado, Enrollment Services Director
661-834-1026 Fax: 559-651-4864
Website: www.sjvc.edu
E-mail: jaime.delgado@sjvc.edu

San Joaquin Valley College
295 E Sierra Ave, Fresno CA 93710-3616
Nora Twarynski, Enrollment Services Director
559-448-8282 Fax: 559-651-4864
Website: www.sjvc.edu
E-mail: nora.twarynski@sjvc.edu

San Joaquin Valley College
1700 McHenry Village Way Suite 6
Modesto CA 95350
Joseph Holt, Director of Admissions
209-527-7582 Fax: 559-651-4864
Website: www.sjvc.edu
E-mail: josephh@sjvc.edu

San Joaquin Valley College
11050 Olson Dr, Rancho Cordova CA 95670
Joseph Holt, Director of Admissions
559-651-2500 Fax: 559-651-4864
Website: www.sjvc.edu
E-mail: joseph.holt@sjvc.edu

San Joaquin Valley College
10641 Church St, Rancho Cucamonga CA 91730
Ramon Abreu, Enrollment Services Director
909-948-7582 Fax: 559-651-4864
Website: www.sjvc.edu
E-mail: ramon.abreu@sjvc.edu

San Joaquin Valley College
8400 W Mineral King Ave, Visalia CA 93291-9283
Susie Topjian, Enrollment Services Director
559-651-2500 Fax: 559-651-4864
Website: www.sjvc.edu
E-mail: susiet@sjvc.edu

San Joaquin Valley College
Fresno Aviation Campus
4985 E Anderson Ave, Fresno CA 93727-1501
Joseph Holt, Director of Admissions
559-453-0123 Fax: 559-651-4864
Website: www.sjvc.edu
E-mail: josephh@sjvc.edu

San Jose City College
2100 Moorpark Ave, San Jose CA 95128-2797
408-298-2181

Santa Ana College
1530 W 17th St, Santa Ana CA 92706-3398
714-564-6000

Santa Barbara Business College
211 S Real Rd, Bakersfield CA 93309-2139
661-835-1100

Santa Barbara City College
721 Cliff Dr, Santa Barbara CA 93109-2394
Patricia E. Canning, Coordinator, School Relations
805-965-0581 ext. 2201

Santa Monica College
1900 Pico Blvd, Santa Monica CA 90405-1644
310-434-4000

Santa Rosa Junior College
680 Sonoma Mountain Pkwy
Petaluma CA 94954-8553
707-778-2415

Santa Rosa Junior College
1501 Mendocino Ave, Santa Rosa CA 95401-4395
Renee LoPilato, Dean of Admissions
707-527-4011

Santiago Canyon College
8045 E Chapman Ave, Orange CA 92869
714-564-4000

Shasta College
PO Box 496006, Redding CA 96049-6006
530-225-4600

Sierra College
5000 Rocklin Rd, Rocklin CA 95677-3397
Gail Modder, A & R Program Manager
916-624-3333

Skyline College
3300 College Dr, San Bruno CA 94066-1698
650-738-4100

Solano Community College
4000 Suisun Valley Rd, Fairfield CA 94534-3197
707-864-7000

Southwestern College
900 Otay Lakes Rd, Chula Vista CA 91910-7297
619-421-6700

Taft College
29 Emmons Park Dr, Taft CA 93268-2317
661-763-7700

Ventura College
4667 Telegraph Rd, Ventura CA 93003-3899
805-654-6400

Victor Valley Community College
18422 Bear Valley Rd, Victorville CA 92395-5849
760-245-4271

West Hills Community College
300 W Cherry Ln, Coalinga CA 93210-1399
559-935-0801

West Los Angeles College
4800 Freshman Dr, Culver City CA 90230-3519
310-287-4200

West Valley College
14000 Fruitvale Ave, Saratoga CA 95070-5697
408-867-2200

Wyotech
980 Riverside Pkwy, West Sacramento CA 95605
916-376-8888

Yuba College
2088 N Beale Rd, Marysville CA 95901-7699
Connie Elder, Registrar
530-741-6989

COLORADO

Aims Community College
PO Box 69, Greeley CO 80632-0069
970-330-8008

Arapahoe Community College
5900 S Sante Fe Dr, Littleton CO 80160
303-797-4ACC (4222)

Blair College
1815 Jet Wing Dr, Colorado Springs CO 80916-2300
719-638-6580

Colorado Mountain College
PO Box 10001, Glenwood Springs CO 81602
800-621-8559

Colorado Mountain College
901 US Highway 24, Leadville CO 80461-9725
800-621-8559

Colorado Mountain College
PO Box 775288, Steamboat Springs CO 80477-5288
800-621-8559

Colorado Northwestern Community College
500 Kennedy Dr, Rangely CO 81648-3502
Tresa England, Director of Student Services
800-562-1105 Fax: 970-675-3343
Website: www.cncc.edu
E-mail: tresa.england@cncc.edu

Community College of Aurora
16000 E Centretech Pkwy, Aurora CO 80011-9036
Kristen Cusack, Director of Admissions and Records
303-360-4700 Fax: 303-361-7432
Website: www.ccaurora.edu
E-mail: enrollment@ccaurora.edu

Community College of Denver
PO Box 173363, Denver CO 80217-3363
303-556-2600

Denver Automotive & Diesel College
PO Box 9366, Denver CO 80209
Joseph R. Chalupa, College Director
800-347-3232

Front Range Community College
4616 S Shields St, Fort Collins CO 80526-3812
970-226-2500

Front Range Community College
3645 W 112th Ave, Westminster CO 80031-2105
303-466-8811

ITT Technical Institute
500 E 84th Ave, Thornton CO 80229-5328
Veronica Donahue, Director of Admissions
303-288-4488

Lamar Community College
2401 S Main St, Lamar CO 81052-3999
Bette Matkowski, President
719-336-2248

Morgan Community College
17800 County Road 20, Fort Morgan CO 80701
Judy Beckmann, Director of Student Support
800-622-0216

NORTHEASTERN JUNIOR COLLEGE
100 College Ave, Sterling CO 80751-2399
Dr. Lance Bolton, Chief Administrative Officer
Tina Joyce, Director of Admissions
970-521-7000 or 970-521-6752 Fax: 970-521-6801
Website: www.njc.edu
E-mail: tina.joyce@njc.edu

Otero Junior College
1802 Colorado Ave, La Junta CO 81050-3346
719-384-6831

Pikes Peak Community College
5675 S Academy Blvd
Colorado Springs CO 80906-5498
719-576-7711

Platt College
3100 S Parker Rd, Aurora CO 80014-3141
Jerald B. Sirbu, President
303-369-5151

Pueblo Community College
900 W Orman Ave, Pueblo CO 81004-1499
719-549-3200

Red Rocks Community College
13300 W 6th Ave, Lakewood CO 80228-1255
303-988-6160

Trinidad State Junior College
600 Prospect St, Trinidad CO 81082-2396
719-846-5621

CONNECTICUT

Asnuntuck Community College
170 Elm St, Enfield CT 06082-3873
Donna Shaw, Director of Admissions / Marketing
860-253-3010

Briarwood College
2279 Mount Vernon Rd, Southington CT 06489-1057
860-628-4751

Capital Community College
950 Main St, Hartford CT 06103-1211
860-906-5000

Gateway Community College
60 Sargent Dr, New Haven CT 06511-5918
203-789-7071

Gibbs College
10 Norden Pl, Norwalk CT 06855-1436
Anthony Reich, Director of Admissions
800-845-5333

Hartford College for Women
1265 Asylum Ave, Hartford CT 06105-2299
860-236-1215

Housatonic Community College
900 Lafayette Blvd, Bridgeport CT 06604
203-332-5000

Manchester Community College
PO Box 1046, Manchester CT 06045-1046
860-647-6000

Middlesex Community College
100 Training Hill Rd, Middletown CT 06457-4889
Mensimah Shabazz, Director of Admissions
860-343-5800 Fax: 860-344-3055
Website: www.mxcc.commnet.edu
E-mail: mshabazz@mxcc.commnet.edu

Mitchell College
437 Pequot Ave, New London CT 06320-4498
860-701-5000

Naugatuck Valley Community College
750 Chase Pkwy, Waterbury CT 06708-3089
203-575-8040

Northwestern Connecticut Community-Technical College
2 Park Pl, Winsted CT 06098-1706
860-738-6300

Norwalk Community College
188 Richards Ave, Norwalk CT 06854-1634
203-857-7000

Quinebaug Valley Community College
742 Upper Maple St, Danielson CT 06239-1440
860-774-1160

St. Vincent's College
2800 Main St, Bridgeport CT 06606-4292
Director of Admissions
203-576-5513

Three Rivers Community Technical College
574 New London Tpke, Norwich CT 06360-6500
860-823-2845

Three Rivers Community Technical College
Mahan Dr, Norwich CT 06360
860-886-0177

Tunxis Community College
271 Scott Swamp Rd, Farmington CT 06032-3187
860-677-7701

DELAWARE

Delaware Technical & Community College
100 Campus Dr, Dover DE 19904-1383
302-857-1000

Delaware Technical & Community College
PO Box 610, Georgetown DE 19947-0610
302-856-5400

Delaware Technical & Community College
400 Stanton Christiana Rd, Newark DE 19713-2197
302-454-3900

Delaware Technical & Community College
333 N Shipley St, Wilmington DE 19801-2499
302-571-5474

FLORIDA

ATI College of Health
1395 NW 167th St, Miami FL 33169
305-628-1000

Brevard Community College
1519 Clearlake Rd, Cocoa FL 32922-6597
321-632-1111

Broward Community College
225 E Las Olas Blvd, Fort Lauderdale FL 33301-2298
954-475-6500

Broward Community College-North Campus
1000 Coconut Creek Blvd
Coconut Creek FL 33066-1697
954-972-9100

Broward Community College-South Campus
7200 Pines Blvd, Pembroke Pines FL 33024-7299
954-963-8835

Central Florida Community College
PO Box 1388, Ocala FL 34478-1388
352-854-2322

Chipola College
3094 Indian Cir, Marianna FL 32446-3065
850-526-2761

City College
2400 SW 13th St, Gainesville FL 32608-2000
352-335-4000

City College
9300 S Dadeland Blvd Suite PH, Miami FL 33156
305-666-9242

Daytona Beach Community College
PO Box 2811, Daytona Beach FL 32120-2811
Tom LoBasso, Dean of Enrollment/Development
386-255-8131

Florida College
119 N Glen Arven Ave
Temple Terrace FL 33617-5578
813-988-5131

Florida Community College
Downtown Campus
101 W State St, Jacksonville FL 32202-3099
904-633-8100

Florida Community College
Kent Campus
3939 Roosevelt Blvd, Jacksonville FL 32205-8997
904-381-3400

Florida Community College
North Campus
4501 Capper Rd, Jacksonville FL 32218-4436
904-766-6500

Florida Community College
South Campus
11901 Beach Blvd, Jacksonville FL 32246-6624
904-646-2111

Florida Keys Community College
5901 College Rd, Key West FL 33040-4397
Cheryl Malsheimer, Director of Admissions & Records
305-296-9081 ext. 495

Florida Metropolitan University-Lakeland Campus
995 E Memorial Blvd Ste 110
Lakeland FL 33801-1973
Jodi De La Garza, Director of Admissions
863-686-1444

Florida National College
Hialeah Campus
4425 W 20th Ave, Hialeah FL 33012
Jorge Afonso, Campus Dean
305-821-3333 ext. 1022 Fax: 305-362-0595
Website: www.fnc.edu
E-mail: omarsnc@fnc.edu

Florida National College
South Campus
11865 SW 26th St, Miami FL 33175
Jon Beisenherz, Campus Dean
305-266-9999
Website: www.fnc.edu
E-mail: omarsnc@fnc.edu

Florida Technical College
1199 S Woodland Blvd, De Land FL 32720-7767
386-734-3303

Florida Technical College
12689 Challenger Pkwy # 130
Orlando FL 32826-2707
Timothy Vogeley, Dean
407-678-5600

Full Sail - Real World Education
3300 University Blvd, Winter Park FL 32792
407-679-0100

Gulf Coast Community College
5230 W Highway 98, Panama City FL 32401-1058
850-769-1551

Hillsborough Community College
1206 N Park Rd, Plant City FL 33563-1540
813-757-2100

Hillsborough Community College
1404 Tech Blvd, Tampa FL 33619-7865
813-253-7000

Hillsborough Community College
PO Box 30030, Tampa FL 33630-3030
813-253-7000

Hillsborough Community College
Ybor City Campus
PO Box 5096, Tampa FL 33675-5096
813-253-7601

Indian River Community College
3209 Virginia Ave, Fort Pierce FL 34981-5596
772-462-4700

ITT Technical Institute
3401 S University Dr, Davie FL 33328-2021
Darren Frost, Director of Recruitment
954-476-9300

ITT Technical Institute
7955 NW 12th St, Doral FL 33126-1823
305-477-3080

ITT Technical Institute
6600 Youngerman Cir Ste 10
Jacksonville FL 32244-6630
904-573-9100

ITT Technical Institute
1400 S International Pkwy, Lake Mary FL 32746-1607
407-660-2900

Keiser College
1800 Business Park Blvd, Daytona Beach FL 32114
Matt McEnany, Vice President
386-274-5060

Keiser College
2400 Interstate Dr, Lakeland FL 33805-2316
863-682-6020

Keiser College
900 S Babcock St, Melbourne FL 32901-1461
321-255-2255

Keiser College
5600 Lake Underhill Rd, Orlando FL 32807
Vicki Maurer, Director of Admissions
407-273-5800

Keiser College
6151 Lake Osprey Dr, Sarasota FL 34240-8441
Richard A. Rodman, Director of Admissions
941-907-3900

Keiser College
1700 Halstead Blvd, Tallahassee FL 32309-3489
James Wallis, Director of Admissions
850-906-9494

Keiser University
1500 NW 49th St, Fort Lauderdale FL 33309-3700
Anne O'Connell, Director Community Relations
954-776-4456

Lake City Community College
149 SE College Pl, Lake City FL 32025
386-752-1822

Lake-Sumter Community College
9501 US Highway 441, Leesburg FL 34788-8751
352-787-3747

Manatee Community College
5840 26th St W, Bradenton FL 34207-3596
941-752-5000

MedVance Institute
1630 S Congress Ave, Palm Springs FL 33461
561-304-3466

Miami-Dade College
300 NE 2nd Ave, Miami FL 33132-2296
305-237-3316

Miami-Dade Community College
11380 NW 27th Ave, Miami FL 33167-3495
305-237-1245

Miami-Dade Community College
11011 SW 104th St, Miami FL 33176-3393
305-237-2000

Miami-Dade Community College
Medical Center Campus
950 NW 20th St, Miami FL 33127-4693
305-347-4101

North Florida Community College
1000 Turner Davis Dr, Madison FL 32340-1602
850-973-2288

Okaloosa-Walton College
100 College Blvd E, Niceville FL 32578-1347
850-678-5111

Palm Beach Community College
4200 S Congress Ave, Lake Worth FL 33461-4796
561-868-3350

Pasco-Hernando Community College
11415 Ponce De Leon Blvd
Brooksville FL 34601-8698
352-796-6726

Pasco-Hernando Community College
34727 Blanton Rd, Dade City FL 33523-6283
352-567-6701

Pasco-Hernando Community College
10230 Ridge Rd, New Port Richey FL 34654-5129
727-847-2727

Pensacola Junior College
1000 College Blvd, Pensacola FL 32504-8998
850-484-1000

Polk Community College
999 Avenue H NE, Winter Haven FL 33881-4299
863-297-1000

St. John's River Community College
5001 Saint Johns Ave, Palatka FL 32177-3807
386-312-4200

St. Petersburg College
PO Box 13489, Saint Petersburg FL 33733-3489
727-341-3600

St. Petersburg College
600 Klosterman Rd, Tarpon Springs FL 34689-1299
727-791-2400

Santa Fe Community College
3000 NW 83rd St, Gainesville FL 32606-6200
Jackson N. Sasser, President
352-395-5787

Seminole Community College
100 Weldon Blvd, Sanford FL 32773-6199
407-328-4722

South Florida Community College
600 W College Dr, Avon Park FL 33825-9356
863-453-6661

SOUTHWEST FLORIDA COLLEGE
1685 Medical Ln, Fort Myers FL 33907-1157
866-SWFC-NOW or 239-939-4766 Fax: 239-936-4040
Website: www.swfc.edu
E-mail: studentinfo@swfc.edu

Tallahassee Community College
444 Appleyard Dr, Tallahassee FL 32304-2895
850-201-8595

Valencia Community College
PO Box 3028, Orlando FL 32802-3028
407-299-5000

Valencia Community College East Campus
701 N Econlockhatchee Trl, Orlando FL 32825-6404
407-299-5000

Webster College
2127 Grand Blvd, Holiday FL 34690-4554
727-942-0069

Webster College
2221 SW 19th Avenue Rd, Ocala FL 34471
Todd A. Matthews, Sr., Executive Director
352-629-1941

GEORGIA

Abraham Baldwin Agriculture College
2802 Moore Highway, Tifton GA 31793
229-391-5000

Andrew College
413 College St, Cuthbert GA 39840
E. Dean Sims, Director of Admissions
229-732-2171

Athens Technical College
800 Highway 29 N, Athens GA 30601-1546
706-355-5000

Atlanta Institute of Music
5985 Financial Dr #200, Norcross GA 30071-2950
770-242-7717

Atlanta Metro College
1630 Metropolitan Pkwy SW, Atlanta GA 30310-4498
404-756-4000

Augusta Technical College
3116 Deans Bridge Rd, Augusta GA 30906-3399
706-771-4000

Bainbridge College
2500 E Shotwell St, Bainbridge GA 39819-8409
229-248-2500

Bauder College
384 Northyards Blvd NW Ste 190
Atlanta GA 30313-2439
Terri A. Holte, Director of Admissions
404-237-7573

Brown Mackie College - Atlanta
6600 Peachtree Dunwoody NE, Atlanta GA 30328
770-638-0121

Chattahoochee Technical College
980 S Cobb Dr SE, Marietta GA 30060-3300
770-528-4465

Coastal Georgia Community College
3700 Altama Ave, Brunswick GA 31520-3632
912-264-7235

Columbus Technical College
928 Manchester Expressway
Columbus GA 31904-6577
706-649-1837

Dalton State College
650 College Dr, Dalton GA 30720
706-272-4436

Darton College
2400 Gillionville Rd, Albany GA 31707-3098
229-430-6000

DeKalb Technical College
495 N Indian Creek Dr, Clarkston GA 30021-2397
Terry Richardson, Director of Admissions
404-297-9522 Fax: 404-294-6496
Website: www.dekalbtech.edu
E-mail: richardt@dekalbtech.edu

East Georgia College
131 College Cir, Swainsboro GA 30401
478-289-2000

Gainesville College
PO Box 1358, Gainesville GA 30503-1358
770-718-3639

Georgia Highlands College
PO Box 1864, Rome GA 30162-1864
706-802-5000

Georgia Military College
201 E Greene St, Milledgeville GA 31061-3398
478-445-2700

Georgia Perimeter College
555 N Indian Creek Dr, Clarkston GA 30021-2396
404-299-4561

Georgia Perimeter College
3251 Panthersville Rd, Decatur GA 30034
404-244-5090

Gordon College
419 College Dr, Barnesville GA 30204-1762
Dr. Katrina Tobin, Director of Enrollment Services
770-358-5021

Gupton-Jones College of Funeral Service
5141 Snapfinger Woods Dr, Decatur GA 30035-4022
Patty S. Hutcheson, President
770-593-2257 Fax: 770-593-1891
Website: www.gupton-jones.edu
E-mail: gjcfs@mindspring.com

Gwinnett Technical College
5150 Sugarloaf Pkwy, Lawrenceville GA 30043-5702
770-962-7580

Lanier Technical College
2990 Landrum Education Dr
Oakwood GA 30566-3405
Michael C. Marlowe, Director of Admissions
770-531-6328

Middle Georgia College
1100 2nd St SE, Cochran GA 31014-1564
478-934-6221

Northwestern Technical College
265 Bicentennial Trl, Rock Spring GA 30739-2306
Dr. Ray Brooks, President
Greg Cross, Vice President for Student Services
706-764-3518

South Georgia College
100 College Park Dr W, Douglas GA 31533-5020
912-389-4231

Truett McConnell College
100 Alumni Dr, Cleveland GA 30528-1264
706-865-2134

Waycross College
2100 S Georgia Pkwy W, Waycross GA 31503-0154
912-285-6133

Young Harris College
PO Box 98, Young Harris GA 30582-0098
706-379-3111

HAWAII

Hawaii Community College
200 W Kawili St, Hilo HI 96720-4075
808-974-7311

HAWAII TOKAI INTERNATIONAL COLLEGE
2241 Kapiolani Blvd, Honolulu HI 96826-4310
Derrick Kerr, Director of Student Services
808-983-4187 Fax: 808-983-4107
Website: www.hawaiitokai.edu
E-mail: dkerr@tokai.edu

Heald College, Honolulu
1500 Kapiolani Blvd, Honolulu HI 96814-3732
Wendy N. Nishimura, Director of Admissions
808-955-1500 or 800-940-0530 Fax: 808-955-6964
Website: www.heald.edu
E-mail: wendy_nishimura@heald.edu

Honolulu Community College
874 Dillingham Blvd, Honolulu HI 96817-4598
808-845-9211

Kapiolani Community College
4303 Diamond Head Rd, Honolulu HI 96816-4496
808-734-9111

Kauai Community College
3-1901 Kaumualii Hwy, Lihue HI 96766-9500
808-245-8225 Fax: 808-245-8297
Website: kauai.hawaii.edu
E-mail: arkauai@hawaii.edu

Leeward Community College
96-045 Ala Ike St, Pearl City HI 96782-3393
808-455-0011

Maui Community College
310 W Kaahumanu Ave, Kahului HI 96732-1617
808-244-9181

TransPacific Hawaii College
5257 Kalanianaole Hwy, Honolulu HI 96821
John Norris, President
808-377-5402

Windward Community College
45-720 Keaahala Rd, Kaneohe HI 96744-3598
808-235-7400

IDAHO

College of Southern Idaho
PO Box 1238, Twin Falls ID 83303-1238
208-733-9554

Eastern Idaho Technical College
1600 S 25th E, Idaho Falls ID 83404
208-524-3000

ITT Technical Institute
12302 W Explorer Dr, Boise ID 83713-1569
208-322-8844

North Idaho College
1000 W Garden Ave, Coeur d Alene ID 83814-2199
208-769-3300

ILLINOIS

Black Hawk College
1501 State Highway 78, Kewanee IL 61443-8630
309-852-5671

Black Hawk College
6600 34th Ave, Moline IL 61265-5899
309-796-5000

Carl Sandburg College
2232 S Lake Storey Rd, Galesburg IL 61401-9576
309-344-2518

College of DuPage
425 Fawell Blvd, Glen Ellyn IL 60137-6708
630-942-2800

College of Lake County
19351 W Washington St, Grayslake IL 60030-1148
847-223-6601

Danville Area Community College
2000 E Main St, Danville IL 61832-5118
217-443-3222

Elgin Community College
1700 Spartan Dr, Elgin IL 60123-7193
847-214-7385

Frontier Community College
RR 1, Fairfield IL 62837-9801
618-842-3711

Gem City College
700 State St, Quincy IL 62301
217-222-0391

Harold S. Washington College
30 E Lake St, Chicago IL 60601-2403
312-553-5600

Harry S. Truman College
1145 W Wilson Ave, Chicago IL 60640-5691
773-878-1700

Heartland Community College
1500 W Raab Rd, Normal IL 61761-9446
309-827-0500

Highland Community College
2998 W Pearl City Rd, Freeport IL 61032-9341
815-235-6121

Illinois Central College
1 College Dr, Peoria IL 61635-0002
309-694-5011

Illinois Valley Community College
815 N Orlando Smith St, Oglesby IL 61348-9692
815-224-2720

ITT Technical Institute
1401 Feehanville Dr, Mount Prospect IL 60056-6005
847-375-8800

John A. Logan College
700 Logan College Rd, Carterville IL 62918
Terry Crain, Associate Dean Student Services
618-985-3741

John Wood Community College
150 S 48th St, Quincy IL 62305-0400
217-224-6500

Joliet Junior College
1216 Houbolt Rd, Joliet IL 60431-8311
815-729-9020

Kankakee Community College
100 College Dr, Kankakee IL 60901
815-802-8100

Kaskaskia College
27210 College Rd, Centralia IL 62801-7878
Tyra Taylor, Dean of Enrollment Management and Retention Services
618-545-3000 Fax: 618-532-1990
Website: www.kaskaskia.edu
E-mail: ttaylor@kaskaskia.edu

Kennedy-King College
6800 S Wentworth Ave, Chicago IL 60621-3798
773-602-5000

Kishwaukee College
21193 Malta Rd, Malta IL 60150-9699
815-825-2086

Lake Land College
5001 Lake Land Blvd, Mattoon IL 61938-9366
217-234-5253

Lewis & Clark Community College
5800 Godfrey Rd, Godfrey IL 62035-2426
618-466-3411

Lincoln College
300 Keokuk St, Lincoln IL 62656-1699
Stacy Rachel, Director of Enrollment Management
800-569-0556

Lincoln Land Community College
5250 Shepherd Rd, Springfield IL 62703-5408
217-786-2200

Lincoln Trail College
11220 State Highway 1, Robinson IL 62454
618-544-8657

MACCORMAC COLLEGE
29 E Madison St, Chicago IL 60602-4405
David F. Grassi, Associate Dean, Admissions
312-922-1884 ext. 101 Fax: 312-922-4328
Website: www.maccormac.edu
E-mail: dgrassi@maccormac.edu

Malcolm X College
1900 W Van Buren St, Chicago IL 60612-3197
312-850-7031

McHenry County College
8900 US Highway 14, Crystal Lake IL 60012-2761
815-455-3700

Moraine Valley Community College
10900 S 88th Ave, Palos Hills IL 60465-0937
708-974-4300

MORRISON INSTITUTE OF TECHNOLOGY
701 Portland Ave, Morrison IL 61270-2959
Richard C. Parkinson, Interim Director
815-772-7218 Fax: 815-772-7584
Website: www.morrisontech.edu
E-mail: admissions@morrison.tec.il.us

Private. Coed. Accreditation: ABET. Enrollment: 140. Student-faculty ratio: 13:1. Engineering Technology Associate of Applied Science degree in Architectural, Construction, Civil, Mechanical, Drafting & Design, and Surveying Technology. AAS degree in Systems & Network Administration.

Morton College
3801 S Central Ave, Cicero IL 60804-4398
708-656-8000

Northwestern Business College
7725 S Harlem Ave, Bridgeview IL 60455-1318
800-682-9113

Northwestern Business College
4829 N Lipps Ave, Chicago IL 60630-2298
Mark Sliz, Director of Admissions
773-777-4220

Oakton Community College
1600 E Golf Rd, Des Plaines IL 60016-1256
David Cole, Director of Enrollment Management
847-635-1600

Olive-Harvey College
10001 S Woodlawn Ave, Chicago IL 60628-1696
773-291-6100

Olney Central College
305 N West St, Olney IL 62450-1099
618-395-7777

Parkland College
2400 W Bradley Ave, Champaign IL 61821-1899
Mike Henry, Contact
217-351-2208

Prairie State College
202 S Halsted St, Chicago Heights IL 60411-8226
708-709-3500

Rend Lake College
RR 1, Ina IL 62846-9801
618-437-5321

Richard J. Daley College
7500 S Pulaski Rd, Chicago IL 60652-1299
773-838-7500

Richland Community College
1 College Park, Decatur IL 62521-8513
217-875-7200

Rock Valley College
3301 N Mulford Rd, Rockford IL 61114-5699
815-654-4250

St. Augustine College
1333 W Argyle St, Chicago IL 60640-3593
773-878-8756

Sauk Valley Community College
173 IL Route 2, Dixon IL 61021
815-288-5511

Shawnee Community College
8364 Shawnee College Rd, Ullin IL 62992
618-634-2242

Southeastern Illinois College
3575 College Rd, Harrisburg IL 62946-4925
618-252-6376

South Suburban College of Cook County
15800 State St, South Holland IL 60473
Jane Ellen Stocker, Dean of Enrollment Services
708-596-2000

Southwestern Illinois College
2500 Carlyle Ave, Belleville IL 62221-5899
618-235-2700

Spoon River College
23235 N County Road 22, Canton IL 61520
309-647-4645

Springfield College in Illinois
1500 N 5th St, Springfield IL 62702-2643
217-525-1420

TRITON COLLEGE
2000 5th Ave, River Grove IL 60171-1995
Jeffery Cooks, Director, Admission Services
708-456-0300 ext. 3130 Fax: 708-583-3147
Website: www.triton.edu
E-mail: triton@triton.edu

Established 1964. Coed. Tuition: $56.00 per semester hour. Est. total yearly exp.: $1,600 for in district students. Enrollment: 19,000. Faculty: 600. Degrees: AA, AAS, AES, AS, AFA. Library: 81,000 volumes. 18 buildings on 100+ acres. Training offered in over 84 career fields. University transfer program, pre-professional, liberal arts courses offered day, evening, and online. State and federal financial programs available. Strong athletic program with excellent facilities. Rolling admissions.

Wabash Valley College
2200 College Dr, Mount Carmel IL 62863-2657
618-262-8641

Waubonsee Community College
Route 47 at Waubonsee Dr, Sugar Grove IL 60554
630-466-7900

Wilbur Wright College North
4300 N Narragansett Ave, Chicago IL 60634-1591
773-777-7900

William Rainey Harper College
1200 W Algonquin Rd, Palatine IL 60067-7373
847-925-6000

INDIANA

Ancilla Domini College
Donaldson IN 46513
Erin Alonzo, Director of Admissions
574-936-8898 Fax: 574-935-1773
Website: www.ancilla.edu
E-mail: erin.alonzo@ancilla.edu

BROWN MACKIE COLLEGE - FORT WAYNE
3000 E Coliseum Blvd, Fort Wayne IN 46805
Daniel Summer, Campus President
260-484-4400 Fax: 260-484-2678
Website: www.brownmackie.edu

Brown Mackie College - Merrillville
1000 E 80th Pl Ste 101N, Merrillville IN 46410-5644
219-769-3321

Brown Mackie College - Michigan City
325 E US Highway 20, Michigan City IN 46360-7362
219-877-3100

BROWN MACKIE COLLEGE - SOUTH BEND
1030 E Jefferson Blvd, South Bend IN 46617-3123
Connie Adelman, Campus President
574-237-0774 Fax: 574-237-3585
Website: www.brownmackie.edu

Community College of Indiana - Valparaiso
3100 Ivy Tech Dr, Valparaiso IN 46383
219-464-8514

Davenport College of Business
7121 Grape Rd, Granger IN 46530-9069
574-277-8447

Indiana Business College Northwest
6300 Technology Dr, Indianapolis IN 46278
317-873-6500

International Business College
7205 Shadeland Station Way
Indianapolis IN 46256-3954
317-841-6400

ITT Technical Institute
12650 Hamilton Crossing, Carmel IN 46032
317-324-9706

ITT Technical Institute
2810 Dupont Commerce Ct, Fort Wayne IN 46825
260-497-6200

ITT Technical Institute
10999 Stahl Rd, Newburgh IN 47630-7430
Thomas G. Campbell Jr., Director of Admissions
812-858-1600

Ivy Tech Community College-Central Indiana
1 W 26th St, Indianapolis IN 46208-4777
317-921-4882

Ivy Tech Community College - North Central
220 Dean Johnson Blvd, South Bend IN 46601-3415
Pam Decker, Director of Admissions
574-289-7001 Fax: 574-236-7177
Website: www.ivytech.edu
E-mail: pdecker@ivytech.edu

Ivy Tech Community College of Indiana - Columbus
4475 Central Ave, Columbus IN 47203-1868
812-372-9925

Ivy Tech Community College of Indiana - Southern Indiana
8204 Highway 311, Sellersburg IN 47172-1829
812-246-3301

Ivy Tech State College
104 W 53rd St, Anderson IN 46013
765-643-7133

Mid-America College of Funeral Service
3111 Hamburg Pike, Jeffersonville IN 47130-9630
812-288-8878

Vincennes University
1002 N 1st St, Vincennes IN 47591-1504
Chris M. Crews, Director of Admission
812-888-4313

IOWA

AIB College of Business
2500 Fleur Dr, Des Moines IA 50321-1799
800-444-1921 Fax: 515-244-6773
Website: www.aib.edu
E-mail: admissions@aib.edu

Clinton Community College
1000 Lincoln Blvd, Clinton IA 52732-6299
563-244-7000

Des Moines Area Community College
600 N 2nd Ave W, Newton IA 50208-3049
641-791-3622

Des Moines Area Community College
Ankeny Campus
2006 S Ankeny Blvd, Ankeny IA 50023-8995
515-964-6200

Des Moines Area Community College
Boone Campus
1125 Hancock Dr, Boone IA 50036-5326
515-432-7203

Des Moines Area Community College
Carroll Campus
906 N Grant Rd, Carroll IA 51401-2525
712-792-1755

Des Moines Area Community College
Urban Campus
1100 7th St, Des Moines IA 50314-2503
515-244-4226

Ellsworth Community College
1100 College Ave, Iowa Falls IA 50126-1199
Annie Stelow, Admissions
800-322-9235

Hawkeye Community College
1501 E Orange Rd, Waterloo IA 50704
Molly Quinn, Director of Admissions
800-670-4769

Indian Hills Community College
721 N 1st St, Centerville IA 52544-1200
641-856-2143

Indian Hills Community College
525 Grandview Ave, Ottumwa IA 52501-1398
641-683-5111

Iowa Central Community College
316 NW 3rd St, Eagle Grove IA 50533-1399
515-448-4723

Iowa Central Community College
330 Avenue M, Fort Dodge IA 50501-5798
515-576-7201

Iowa Central Community College
916 Russell St, Storm Lake IA 50588-2018
712-732-2991

Iowa Central Community College
1725 Beach St, Webster City IA 50595-2699
515-832-1632

Iowa Lakes Community College
3200 College Dr, Emmetsburg IA 50536-1055
Anne Stansbury, Asst. Director of Admissions
712-852-5212 Fax: 712-362-8363
Website: www.iowalakes.edu
E-mail: info@iowalakes.edu

Iowa Lakes Community College
300 S 18th St, Estherville IA 51334-2721
Anne Stansbury, Asst. Director of Admissions
712-362-7945 Fax: 712-362-8363
Website: www.iowalakes.edu
E-mail: info@iowalakes.edu

Iowa Lakes Community College
1900 Grand Ave, Suite 8, Spencer IA 51301
Anne Stansbury, Assistant Director of Admissions
712-262-7141 Fax: 712-262-4047
Website: www.iowalakes.edu
E-mail: info@iowalakes.edu

Iowa Western Community College
923 E Washington St, Clarinda IA 51632-1958
712-542-5117

Iowa Western Community College
2700 College Rd, Council Bluffs IA 51503-0567
800-432-5852

Kirkwood Community College
PO Box 2068, Cedar Rapids IA 52406-2068
319-398-5411

Marshalltown Community College
3700 S Center St, Marshalltown IA 50158-4760
641-752-7106

Muscatine Community College
152 Colorado St, Muscatine IA 52761-5396
563-288-6001

Northeast Iowa Community College
PO Box 400, Calmar IA 52132-0400
563-562-3263

Northeast Iowa Community College
RR 1, Peosta IA 52068
563-556-5110

North Iowa Area Community College
500 College Dr, Mason City IA 50401-7213
641-423-1264

Northwest Iowa Community College
603 W Park St, Sheldon IA 51201-1046
Lisa Story, Director of Enrollment Management
712-324-5061 Fax: 712-324-4136
Website: www.nwicc.edu
E-mail: lstory@nwicc.edu

St. Luke's College
2720 Stone Park Blvd, Sioux City IA 51104-3734
712-279-3149

Scott Community College
500 Belmont Rd, Riverdale IA 52722-6804
563-441-4000

Southeastern Community College
PO Box 6007, Keokuk IA 52632
Kari Bevans, Director of Admissions
319-524-3221

Southeastern Community College
PO Box 180, West Burlington IA 52655
319-752-2731

SOUTHWESTERN COMMUNITY COLLEGE
1501 W Townline St, Creston IA 50801-1042
Lisa Carstens, Director of Admissions
641-782-7081 Fax: 641-782-3312
Website: www.swcciowa.edu
E-mail: carstens@swcciowa.edu

Western Iowa Tech Community College
200 Victory Dr, Cherokee IA 51012-2237
712-225-0238

Western Iowa Tech Community College
PO Box 5199, Sioux City IA 51102-5199
Dr. Carolyn Rants, Dean of Students
712-274-6400

KANSAS

Allen County Community College
1801 N Cottonwood St, Iola KS 66749-1607
John Masterson, President
Randy Weber, Director of Admissions
620-365-5116

Barton County Community College
245 NE 30th Rd, Great Bend KS 67530-9107
Dr. Veldon Law, President
800-748-7594

Barton County Community College
540 Grant Ave, Junction City KS 66441
785-238-8550

Brown Mackie College - Kansas City
9705 Lenexa Dr, Lenexa KS 66215
913-768-1900

Brown Mackie College - Salina
2106 S 9th St, Salina KS 67401-7307
785-825-5422

Butler Community College
901 S Haverhill Rd, El Dorado KS 67042-3225
316-321-2222

Cloud County Community College
PO Box 1002, Concordia KS 66901-1002
Heath Martin, Director of Admission
785-243-1435

Coffeyville Community College / Area Technical School
400 W 11th St, Coffeyville KS 67337-5065
620-251-7700

COLBY COMMUNITY COLLEGE
1255 S Range Ave, Colby KS 67701-4099
Director of Admissions
888-634-9350 or 785-460-4690 Fax: 785-460-4691
Website: www.colbycc.edu
E-mail: admissions@colbycc.edu

Cowley County Community College
PO Box 1147, Arkansas City KS 67005-1147
620-442-0430

Dodge City Community College
2501 N 14th Ave, Dodge City KS 67801-2399
620-225-1321

Donnelly College
608 N 18th St, Kansas City KS 66102-4298
Sr. Mary Agnes Patterson, Vice President
913-621-8724

Fort Scott Community College
2108 Horton St, Fort Scott KS 66701-3199
Mert Barrows, Director of Admissions
620-223-2700

Garden City Community College
801 N Campus Dr, Garden City KS 67846-6333
Nikki Geier, Director of Admissions
620-276-7611

Haskell Indian Nations University
155 Indian Ave Rm 1305, Lawrence KS 66046-4817
785-749-8404

Hesston College
PO Box 3000, Hesston KS 67062-2093
620-327-4221

Highland Community College
PO Box 68, Highland KS 66035-0068
785-442-6000

Hutchinson Community College
1300 N Plum St, Hutchinson KS 67501-5831
620-665-3500

Independence Community College
PO Box 708, Independence KS 67301-0708
Dr. Terry Hetrick, President
800-842-6063 Fax: 620-331-5344
Website: www.indycc.edu
E-mail: admissions@indycc.edu

Johnson County Community College
12345 College Blvd, Overland Park KS 66210-1299
913-469-3803 Fax: 913-469-2524
Website: www.jccc.edu
E-mail: jcccadmissions@jccc.edu

Kansas City Kansas Community College
7250 State Ave, Kansas City KS 66112-3003
913-596-9600

Labette Community College
200 S 14th St, Parsons KS 67357-9966
Tammy Fuentez, Director of Admissions
620-421-6700 Fax: 620-421-2309
Website: www.labette.edu
E-mail: tammyf@labette.edu

Neosho County Community College
800 W 14th St, Chanute KS 66720-2639
620-431-2820

Pratt Community College
Hwy 61, Pratt KS 67124
620-672-5641

Seward County Community College
PO Box 1137, Liberal KS 67905-1137
620-629-2710

KENTUCKY

Ashland Community and Technical College
1400 College Dr, Ashland KY 41101-3683
606-329-2999

Bluegrass Community and Technical College
Oswald Building
470 Cooper Drive, Lexington KY 40506-0235
Shelbie Hugle, Director of Admissions
859-246-6200 Fax: 859-246-4664
Website: www.bluegrass.kctcs.edu
E-mail: bctc_info@kctcs.edu

Daymar College
4400 Breckenridge Ln #415, Louisville KY 40218
Shawn McDaniel, Director of Admissions
502-495-1040 Fax: 502-495-1518
Website: www.daymarcollege.com

Daymar College
3361 Buckland Sq, Owensboro KY 42301-5830
Vickie McDougal Director of Admissions
800-960-4090 Fax: 270-685-4090
Website: www.daymarcollege.com

Daymar College - Northern Kentucky
76 Carothers Rd, Newport KY 41071
859-291-0800

Elizabethtown Community College
600 College St Rd, Elizabethtown KY 42701-3053
800-260-2ECC

Hazard Community and Technical College
One Community College Dr, Hazard KY 41701-2402
Germaine Shaffer, Director of Enrollment and Diversity Services
800-246-7521 ext. 73409

Henderson Community College
2660 S Green St, Henderson KY 42420-4699
270-827-1867

Hopkinsville Community College
PO Box 2100, Hopkinsville KY 42241-2100
270-886-3921

Jefferson Community & Technical College
109 E Broadway, Louisville KY 40202-2000
502-584-0181

Madisonville Community College
2000 College Dr, Madisonville KY 42431-9199
270-821-2250

Maysville Community & Technical College
1755 US Highway 68, Maysville KY 41056-8910
606-759-7141

Maysville Community College
1401 Dixie Hwy, Park Hills KY 41011-2816

National College
115 E Lexington Ave, Danville KY 40422-1517
Gloria Walls, Director of Admissions
859-236-6991 Fax: 859-236-1063
Website: www.national-college.edu
E-mail: info@national-college.edu

National College
7627 Ewing Blvd, Florence KY 41042-1812
Doug Dedeker, Director of Admissions
859-525-6510 Fax: 859-525-8961
Website: www.national-college.edu
E-mail: info@national-college.edu

National College
2376 Sir Barton Way, Lexington KY 40509
Terry Fisher, Director of Admissions
859-253-0621 Fax: 859-254-7664
Website: www.national-college.edu
E-mail: info@national-college.edu

National College
4205 Dixie Hwy, Louisville KY 40216
Ted Scharre, Director of Admissions
502-447-7634 Fax: 502-447-7665
Website: www.national-college.edu
E-mail: info@national-college.edu

National College
50 National College Blvd, Pikeville KY 41501
Janet Head, Director of Admissions
606-478-7200 Fax: 606-478-7209
Website: www.national-college.edu
E-mail: info@national-college.edu

National College
125 S Killarney Ln, Richmond KY 40475
Keeley Gadd, Director of Admissions
859-623-8956 Fax: 859-623-8956
Website: www.national-college.edu
E-mail: info@national-college.edu

Owensboro Community and Technical College
4800 New Hartford Rd, Owensboro KY 42303-1899
270-686-4400

Paducah Technical College
509 S 30th St, Paducah KY 42001-4181
Arnold Harris, School Relations
800-995-4438

Prestonsburg Community College
110 Bert T Combs Dr, Prestonsburg KY 41653-1815
606-886-3863

St. Catharine College
2375 Bardstown Rd, Saint Catharine KY 40061
800-599-2000

Somerset Community College
808 Monticello St, Somerset KY 42501-2936
606-679-8501

Southeast Kentucky Community and Technical College
300 College Rd, Cumberland KY 40823-1031
606-589-2145

West Kentucky Community and Technical College
PO Box 7380, Paducah KY 42002-7380
270-554-9200

LOUISIANA

Baton Rouge Community College
5310 Florida Blvd, Baton Rouge LA 70806
225-216-8040

Bossier Parish Community College
6220 E Texas St, Bossier City LA 71111
318-678-6000

Delgado Community College
615 City Park Ave, New Orleans LA 70119
Gwen A. Boutte, Director of Admissions
504-483-4410

Louisiana State University
1100 Florida Ave, New Orleans LA 70119-2714
504-948-8530

Louisiana State University at Eunice
PO Box 1129, Eunice LA 70535-1129
Ron Ryder, Registrar
337-457-7311 Fax: 337-550-1306
Website: www.lsue.edu
E-mail: rryder@lsue.edu

Louisiana Technical College
Lafayette Campus
1101 Bertrand Dr, Lafayette LA 70506-4909
Gen M. Bienvenu, Director of Admissions
337-262-5962

MedVance Institute
9255 Interline Ave, Baton Rouge LA 70809
225-248-1015

New Orleans School of Urban Missions
PO Box 53344, New Orleans LA 70153
800-385-6364

Nunez Community College
3700 LaFontaine St, Chalmette LA 70043
504-680-2240

River Parishes Community College
PO Box 310, Sorrento LA 70778
225-675-8270

School of Urban Missions
511 Westbank Expy, Gretna LA 70053
504-362-3634

Southern University at Shreveport
3050 M L King Dr, Shreveport LA 71107
318-674-3300

South Louisiana Community College
320 Devalcourt St, Lafayette LA 70506
337-521-8896

MAINE

Andover College
475 Lisbon St, Lewiston ME 04240
Wendy Burbank, Associate Director of Admissions
800-639-3110

Andover College
901 Washington Ave, Portland ME 04103-2791
Woody Burbank, Associate Director of Admissions
207-774-6126

Beal College
99 Farm Rd, Bangor ME 04401-6831
207-947-4591

Central Maine Community College
1250 Turner St, Auburn ME 04210-6498
Walter Clark, Director of Admissions
207-755-5100

Central Maine Medical Center
70 Middle St, Lewiston ME 04240
207-795-2840

Eastern Maine Community College
354 Hogan Rd, Bangor ME 04401-4206
207-974-4600

Kennebec Valley Community College
92 Western Ave, Fairfield ME 04937-1337
Kathy Moore, Director of Admissions
207-453-5035

Northern Maine Community College
33 Edgemont Dr, Presque Isle ME 04769-2016
Bill Casavant, Director of Admissions
207-768-2700

Southern Maine Community College
2 Fort Rd, South Portland ME 04106-1698
Dr. James Ortiz, President
Scott MacDonald, Director of Financial Aid
207-741-5500 Fax: 207-741-5671
Website: www.smccme.edu
E-mail: oharmon@maine.rr.com

Washington County Community College
RR 1 Box 22C, River Rd, Calais ME 04619
David R. Sousa, Dean of Students
207-454-1000

York County Community College
PO Box 529, Wells ME 04090-0529
207-646-9282

MARYLAND

Allegany College of Maryland
12401 Willowbrook Rd, Cumberland MD 21502-2596
301-784-5000

Anne Arundel Community College
101 College Pkwy, Arnold MD 21012-1857
410-647-7100

Baltimore City Community College
2901 Liberty Heights Ave, Baltimore MD 21215
Scheherazade Foreman, Director of Admissions
410-462-8000

BALTIMORE INTERNATIONAL COLLEGE
17 Commerce St, Baltimore MD 21202-3230
Kristin Ciarlo, Director of Admissions
410-752-4710 ext. 120 Fax: 410-752-3730
Website: www.bic.edu
E-mail: admissions@bic.edu

Founded in 1972, Baltimore International College is an independent college regionally accredited by the Commission on Higher Education, Middle States Association of Colleges and Schools. The college offers specialized masters, baccalaureate and associate's degrees, and a certificate program through its School of Culinary Arts, School of Hotel Restaurant and Catering Management, and School of Graduate Studies. The college's programs include a master of science in Hospitality Management degree, bachelor's degrees in Culinary Management, Hospitality Management, Hospitality Management with Marketing Concentration; associate's degrees in Professional Cooking, Professional Cooking and Baking and

Professional Baking and Pastry; and certificates in Professional Culinary Arts.

The college has a campus in Baltimore, MD., just two blocks from Baltimore's famous Inner Harbor and within easy walking distance of many of the city's major attractions. The college also has Virginia Park, a sprawling 100-acre preserve along the shore of Lough Ramor in Virginia, County Cavan, Ireland. The Virginia Park campus is home to the Park Hotel and a golf course, pleasure gardens, and 15 miles of walking paths. Students may take courses at the Virginia Park campus studying under European-educated chefs and hoteliers.

The mission of Baltimore International College is to provide qualified students with the education and experience they need to pursue progressive careers within the international foodservice and lodging industry.

Carroll Community College
1601 Washington Rd, Westminster MD 21157-6913
410-386-8000

Cecil College
One Seahawk Dr, North East MD 21901
Sandra S. Rajaski, Registrar & Director of Admissions
410-287-1000 Fax: 410-287-1001
Website: www.cecil.edu
E-mail: srajaski@cecil.edu

Chesapeake College
PO Box 8, Wye Mills MD 21679-0008
410-822-5400

College of Southern Maryland
PO Box 910, La Plata MD 20646-0910
301-934-2251

The Community College of Baltimore County
Catonsville Campus
800 S Rolling Rd, Catonsville MD 21228-5317
Diane Drake, Director of Admissions
410-455-4555

Community College of Baltimore County
Dundalk Campus
7200 Sollers Point Rd, Baltimore MD 21222-4692
Theresa Carr, Director of Admissions
410-285-9801

Community College of Baltimore County
Essex Campus
7201 Rossville Blvd, Baltimore MD 21237-3898
Marcia Amaimo, Director of Admissions
410-780-6363

Frederick Community College
7932 Opossumtown Pike, Frederick MD 21702-2097
Welcome and Registration Center
301-846-2430

Garrett College
PO Box 151, Mc Henry MD 21541
301-387-3000

Hagerstown Community College
11400 Robinwood Dr, Hagerstown MD 21742-6590
Dr. Daniel E. Bock, Assistant Director of Admissions
301-790-2800 Fax: 301-791-9165
Website: www.hagerstowncc.edu
E-mail: bockd@hagerstowncc.edu

Harford Community College
401 Thomas Run Rd, Bel Air MD 21015-1696
410-836-4000

Howard Community College
10901 Little Patuxent Pkwy
Columbia MD 21044-3197
Mary Ellen Duncan, President
410-772-4800

Kaplan College
Hagerstown Campus
18618 Crestwood Dr, Hagerstown MD 21742-2797
W. Christopher Motz, President
Steve Shinham, Director of Admissions
800-422-2670 Fax: 301-739-0474
Website: www.hagerstownbusinesscol.edu

Montgomery College
20200 Observation Dr, Germantown MD 20876-4098
Sherman Helberg, Contact
301-279-5036

Montgomery College
51 Mannakee St, Rockville MD 20850-1199
301-279-5000

Montgomery College
7600 Takoma Ave, Takoma Park MD 20912-4197
Sherman Helberg, Contact
301-279-5036

Prince George's Community College
301 Largo Rd, Largo MD 20774-2199
Vera L. Bagley, Director of Admissions and Records
301-322-0801 Fax: 301-322-0119
Website: www.pgcc.edu

School of Art & Design at Montgomery College
10500 Georgia Ave, Silver Spring MD 20902-4111
301-649-4454

Wor-Wic Community College
10452 Old Ocean City Blvd #7, Berlin MD 21811
410-641-4134

Wor-Wic Community College
32000 Campus Dr, Salisbury MD 21804-1485
410-334-2800

MASSACHUSETTS

Benjamin Franklin Institute of Technology
41 Berkeley St, Boston MA 02116-6307
Norman Kraft, Dean of Enrollment
617-423-4630 ext. 121 Fax: 617-482-3706
Website: www.bfit.edu
E-mail: admissions@bfit.edu

Berkshire Community College
1350 West St, Pittsfield MA 01201-5786
413-499-4660

BRISTOL COMMUNITY COLLEGE

777 Elsbree St, Fall River MA 02720
Rodney S. Clark, Director of Admissions
508-678-2811 ext. 2516, 2179 Fax: 508-730-3265
Website: www.bristol.mass.edu
E-mail: admissions@bristol.mass.edu

Established 1965. Public. Coed. Accreditation: New England Association of Schools and Colleges. Enrollment: 3,145 full-time, 3,782 part-time. Faculty: 345. Student-faculty ratio: 18:1. Degrees offered: Liberal Arts, Business Administration, Computer Information Systems, Engineering Technology, Health Sciences, Human Services & Public Safety, Office Administration. Library: 65,000 volumes. 9 buildings.

Bunker Hill Community College
250 Rutherford Ave, Boston MA 02129-2925
617-228-2000

Cape Cod Community College
2240 Iyannough Rd, West Barnstable MA 02668
508-362-2131

Caritas Laboure College
2120 Dorchester Ave, Dorchester MA 02124-5698
617-296-8300

Dean College
99 Main St, Franklin MA 02038-1994
508-541-1900

Endicott College
376 Hale St, Beverly MA 01915-2098
978-927-0585

Fisher College
118 Beacon St, Boston MA 02116-1501
Stephen Carter, Director of Admissions
800-446-1226

Greenfield Community College
1 College Dr, Greenfield MA 01301-9739
413-775-1000

Holyoke Community College
303 Homestead Ave, Holyoke MA 01040-1099
413-538-7000

Marian Court College
35 Littles Point Rd, Swampscott MA 01907-2840
781-595-6768

Massachusetts Bay Community College
50 Oakland St, Wellesley MA 02481-5307
781-239-3000

Massasoit Community College
1 Massasoit Blvd, Brockton MA 02302-3996
508-588-9100

Middlesex Community College
Springs Rd, Bedford MA 01730-1114
Darcy Orellana, Director of Admissions
800-818-3434

Middlesex Community College
33 Kearney Sq, Lowell MA 01852-1987
Darcy Orellana, Director of Admissions
800-818-3434

Mt. Wachusett Community College
444 Green St, Gardner MA 01440
Karin Schedin, Director of Admissions
978-632-6600 ext. 110

New England College of Finance
10 High St Ste 204, Boston MA 02110
617-951-2350

NORTHERN ESSEX COMMUNITY COLLEGE

100 Elliott St, Haverhill MA 01830
Nora B. Sheridan, Director of Admission
978-556-3700
Website: www.NECC.Mass.edu
E-mail: nsheridan@necc.mass.edu

North Shore Community College
1 Ferncroft Rd, Danvers MA 01923-4093
Jennifer Kirk, Director of Admissions & Recruitment Outreach
978-762-4000 Fax: 978-762-4015
Website: www.northshore.edu
E-mail: jkirk@northshore.edu

Quincy College
34 Coddington St, Quincy MA 02169-4501
617-984-1600

Quinsigamond Community College
670 W Boylston St, Worcester MA 01606-2092
508-853-2300

Roxbury Community College
1234 Columbus Ave, Boston MA 02120-3400
Dr. Rudolph Jones, Director of Admissions
617-541-5310

Springfield Technical Community College
1 Armory Sq, Springfield MA 01105-1296
Andrea Lucy-Allen, Director of Admissions
413-755-4202

URBAN COLLEGE OF BOSTON

178 Tremont St, Boston MA 02111-1006
Dr. Henry J. Johnson, Dean of Enrollment Services/Registrar
617-292-4723 ext. 6357 Fax: 617-423-4758
Website: www.urbancollege.edu
E-mail: johnson@urbancollege.edu

Chartered 1993. Private. Coed. Accreditation: Accredited by NEASC. Tuition: $125.00 per credit. Mission: To increase college access, retention, and degree completion among nontraditional students and adult learners from Boston's urban neighborhoods. Enrollment: 700 multicultural, and ethnically diverse students. The college provides a highly supportive environment that integrates a college education with career preparation, skill development and access to supportive services. Degrees: AA, Programs: Early Childhood Education, Human Services Administration, General Studies. Certificates: Early Childhood Education, Human Services Administration, General Studies, Direct Service Worker (Youth - Age 6-18) Family Services, Management, Personal Computer Applications, Youth Program Administration, Early Childhood Education in Spanish.

MICHIGAN

Alpena Community College
666 Johnson St, Alpena MI 49707-1495
989-356-9021

Bay de Noc Community College
2001 N Lincoln Rd, Escanaba MI 49829-2524
906-786-5802

Bay Mills Community College
12214 W Lakeshore Dr, Brimley MI 49715
906-248-3354

Charles S. Mott Community College
1401 E Court St, Flint MI 48503-6208
810-762-0200

Charles Stewart Mott Community College
2100 W Thompson Rd, Fenton MI 48430
810-762-0200

Delta College
University Center MI 48710-0001
Duff Zube, Director of Admissions
989-686-9093 Fax: 989-667-2202
Website: www.delta.edu
E-mail: admit@delta.edu

Finlandia University
601 Quincy St, Hancock MI 49930-1882
906-482-5300

Glen Oaks Community College
62249 Shimmel Rd, Centreville MI 49032-9784
269-467-9945

Gogebic Community College
E4946 Jackson Rd, Ironwood MI 49938-1366
906-932-4231

Grand Rapids Community College
143 Bostwick Ave NE, Grand Rapids MI 49503-3201
616-234-4000

Great Lakes College
150 Nugent Rd, Bad Axe MI 48413-8705
989-755-3444

Great Lakes College
3930 Traxler Ct, Bay City MI 48706-9286
989-686-1572

Great Lakes College
1231 Cleaver Rd, Caro MI 48723-9376
989-673-5857

Henry Ford Community College
5101 Evergreen Rd, Dearborn MI 48128-2407
313-845-9615

ITT TECHNICAL INSTITUTE

4020 Sparks Dr SE, Grand Rapids MI 49546-6192
Dennis Hormel, Director
616-956-1060 Fax: 616-956-5606
Website: www.itt-tech.edu
E-mail: dhormel@itt-tech.edu

ITT Technical Institute
1522 E Big Beaver Rd, Troy MI 48083-2008
Patricia Hyman, Director of Recruitment
248-524-1800

Jackson Community College
2111 Emmons Rd, Jackson MI 49201-8399
517-796-8425

Jackson Community College
at Lenawee Vo-Tech
1376 N Main St, Adrian MI 49221
517-265-5515

Jackson Community College
Hillsdale LeTarte Center
3120 W Carleton Rd PO Box 712, Hillsdale MI 49242
517-437-3343

Jackson Community College
JCC Flight Center Reynolds Municipal Airport
3610 Wildwood Ave, Jackson MI 49202
517-787-7012

Jackson Community College
JCC Lenawee Flight Center Lenawee County Airport
2651 Cadmus Rd, Adrian MI 49221
517-263-1351

Kalamazoo Valley Community College
PO Box 4070, Kalamazoo MI 49003-4070
Marilyn Schlack, President
269-372-5000

Kellogg Community College
450 North Ave, Battle Creek MI 49017-3397
269-965-3931

Kirtland Community College
10775 N Saint Helen Rd, Roscommon MI 48653-9699
989-275-5000

Lake Michigan College
2755 E Napier Ave, Benton Harbor MI 49022-1899
269-927-8100

Lansing Community College
419 N Capitol Ave, Lansing MI 48933-1293
517-483-1620

Lewis College of Business
17370 Meyers Rd, Detroit MI 48235-1423
313-862-6300

MACOMB COMMUNITY COLLEGE

44575 Garfield Rd, Clinton Township MI 48038-1139
Information Center
586-445-7999
Website: www.macomb.edu
E-mail: answer@macomb.edu

MACOMB COMMUNITY COLLEGE
14500 E 12 Mile Rd, Warren MI 48088-3896
Information Center
586-445-7999
Website: www.macomb.edu
E-mail: answer@macomb.edu

Mid-Michigan Community College
1375 S Clare Ave, Harrison MI 48625-9447
989-386-6622

Monroe County Community College
1555 S Raisinville Rd, Monroe MI 48161-9047
734-242-7300

Montcalm Community College
2800 College Dr, Sidney MI 48885-9723
989-328-2111

Muskegon Community College
221 S Quarterline Rd, Muskegon MI 49442-1493
231-773-9131

North Central Michigan College
1515 Howard St, Petoskey MI 49770-8740
Naomi DeWinter, Director Enrollment Management
888-298-6605

Northwestern Michigan College
1701 E Front St, Traverse City MI 49686-3061
Jim Bensley, Director of Admissions
800-748-0566 Fax: 231-995-1339
Website: www.nmc.edu
E-mail: jbensley@nmc.edu

Oakland Community College
2480 Opdyke Rd, Bloomfield Hills MI 48304
Dr. Maurice McCall, Director of Admissions
248-341-2000

Oakland Community College
27055 Orchard Lake Rd, Farmington Hills MI 48334
248-522-3400

Oakland Community College
739 S Washington, Royal Oak MI 48067
248-246-2400

Oakland Community College
22322 Rutland Dr, Southfield MI 48075
248-233-2700

Oakland Community College
7350 Cooley Lake Rd, Waterford MI 48327-4187
248-942-3100

Saginaw Chippewa Tribal College
2274 Enterprise Dr, Mount Pleasant MI 48858
989-775-4123

St. Clair County Community College
323 Erie St, Port Huron MI 48060-3812
810-984-3881

Schoolcraft College
18600 Haggerty Rd, Livonia MI 48152-2696
734-462-4400

Southwestern Michigan College
58900 Cherry Grove Rd, Dowagiac MI 49047-9726
Admissions Office
269-782-1000

Washtenaw Community College
PO Box D-1, Ann Arbor MI 48106-1610
734-973-3300

Wayne County Community College
801 W Fort St, Detroit MI 48226-3095
313-496-2500

West Shore Community College
PO Box 277, Scottville MI 49454-0277
231-845-6211

MINNESOTA

Academy College
1101 E 78th St, Bloomington MN 55420-1402
Tracey Schantz, Director of Admissions
952-851-0066 Fax: 952-851-0094

Alexandria Technical College
1601 Jefferson St, Alexandria MN 56308-3707
320-762-0221

Anoka-Ramsey Community College
Cambridge Campus
300 Polk Street South, Cambridge MN 55008
Charlotte Lindahl, Director of Admissions
763-689-7000

Anoka-Ramsey Community College
Coon Rapids Campus
11200 Mississippi Blvd NW
Coon Rapids MN 55433-3470
763-427-2600

Anoka Technical College
1355 Highway 10, Anoka MN 55303
763-576-4700

Art Institutes International Minnesota
15 S 9th St, Minneapolis MN 55402-3137
612-332-3361

Brown College
1440 Northland Dr, Mendota Heights MN 55120-1004
Dawn Bravo, VP Marketing
800-6-BROWN-6

Central Lakes College
501 W College Dr, Brainerd MN 56401-3900
218-855-8000

Central Lakes College
1830 Airport Rd, Staples MN 56479-3252
218-894-5100

Century College
3300 Century Ave N
White Bear Lake MN 55110-1842
651-779-3200

Dunwoody College of Technology
818 Dunwoody Blvd, Minneapolis MN 55403-1192
John Slama, Vice President Enrollment Management
800-292-4625 or 612-374-5800 Fax: 612-374-4128
Website: www.dunwoody.edu
E-mail: jslama@dunwoody.edu
See listing under "Career Schools"

Fond du Lac Tribal Community College
2101 14th St, Cloquet MN 55720
218-879-0800

HIBBING COMMUNITY COLLEGE
1515 E 25th St, Hibbing MN 55746-3300
Holly Bigelow, Director of Enrollment
800-224-4HCC or 218-262-7200 Fax: 218-262-6717
Website: www.hibbing.edu
E-mail: admissions@hibbing.edu

Inver Hills Community College
2500 80th St E, Inver Grove Heights MN 55076
651-450-8500 Fax: 651-450-8679
Website: www.inverhills.edu

ITASCA COMMUNITY COLLEGE
1851 E US Highway 169
Grand Rapids MN 55744-3397
Candace Perry, Director of Enrollment Services
218-327-4464 or 800-996-6422 Fax: 218-327-4350
Website: www.itascacc.edu
E-mail: iccinfo@itascacc.edu
Established 1922. Public. Coed. Accreditation: NCACS. Enrollment: 900 full-time, 250 part-time. Degrees: AA, AS, AAS, (start towards a bachelor's degree in any field) or a 2 year AAS degrees in Natural Res/Forestry or Accounting. Itasca offers specialty and transfer programs in American Indian Studies, Psychology, Engineering, Business, Education and Geography. Ten bldgs. on 25 acres. Located in scenic northern Minnesota. Itasca is the best place to start.

Lake Superior College
2101 Trinity Rd, Duluth MN 55811-3399
218-733-7600

LE CORDON BLEU COLLEGE OF CULINARY ARTS
1315 Mendota Heights Rd
Mendota Heights MN 55120
Kevin Sanderson, President
651-675-4700 Fax: 651-905-3550
Website: www.twincitiesculinary.com
E-mail: ksanderson@twincitiesculinary.com

Mesabi Range Community & Technical College
1100 Industrial Park, Eveleth MN 55734-8628
218-744-3302

Mesabi Range Community & Technical College
1001 Chestnut St W, Virginia MN 55792-3401
218-749-7700

Minneapolis Community and Technical College
1501 Hennepin Ave, Minneapolis MN 55403-1779
Dena Russell, Director of Admissions
612-659-6282

Minnesota State Community and Technical College
Fergus Falls
1414 College Way, Fergus Falls MN 56537-1009
218-739-7500

Minnesota West Community and Technical College
Canby Campus
1011 1st St W, Canby MN 56220-9494
Jodi Weber, Contact
800-658-2535

Minnesota West Community and Technical College
Granite Falls Campus
1593 11th Ave, Granite Falls MN 56241-1061
Becky Weber, Contact
800-657-3247

Minnesota West Community and Technical College
Jackson Campus
PO Box 269, Jackson MN 56143-0269
Lynne Liepold, Contact
800-658-2522

Minnesota West Community and Technical College
Pipestone Campus
1314 N Hiawatha Ave, Pipestone MN 56164-2282
Laurel Berg, Contact
800-658-2330

Minnesota West Community and Technical College
Worthington Campus
1450 Collegeway, Worthington MN 56187-3024
Mitz Diemer, Contact
800-657-3966

Normandale Community College
9700 France Ave S, Bloomington MN 55431-4399
Rick Smith, Director of Admissions
952-832-6000

North Hennepin Community College
7411 85th Ave N, Brooklyn Park MN 55445-2299
763-424-0702

Northland Community & Technical College
Highway 1 E, Thief River Falls MN 56701
Eugene Klinke, Director of Enrollment Management
800-959-6282

Northland Community and Technical College
2022 Central Ave NE
East Grand Forks MN 56721-2702
Mary Fontes, Dean of Students
800-451-3441 Fax: 218-773-4502
Website: www.northlandcollege.edu
E-mail: admissions@northlandcollege.edu

Pine Technical College
900 4th St SE, Pine City MN 55063-2198
320-629-5100

Rainy River Community College
1501 Highway 71, International Falls MN 56649-2187
Berta Hagen, Registrar
218-285-2207

Ridgewater College-Hutchinson Campus
2 Century Ave SE, Hutchinson MN 55350-3100
Dawn Bjork, Counselor
800-722-1151 Fax: 320-234-8506
Website: www.ridgewater.edu
E-mail: dawn.bjork@ridgewater.edu

Ridgewater College-Willmar Campus
PO Box 1097, Willmar MN 56201-1097
Sally Kerfeld, Director of Admissions
800-722-1151 Fax: 320-222-5212
Website: www.ridgewater.edu
E-mail: sally.kerfeld@ridgewater.edu

Riverland Community College
1900 8th Ave NW, Austin MN 55912-1400
Dani Heiny, Director of Admissions
800-247-5039

Rochester Community & Technical College
851 30th Ave SE, Rochester MN 55904-4999
507-285-7210

St. Cloud Technical College
1540 Northway Dr, Saint Cloud MN 56303-1240
Jodi Elness, Director of Enrollment Management
800-222-1009 Fax: 320-308-5981
Website: www.sctc.edu
E-mail: jelness@sctc.edu

St. Mary's Campus of the College of St. Catherine
2500 S 6th St, Minneapolis MN 55454-1401
612-332-5521

St. Paul College
A Community & Technical College
235 Marshall Ave, Saint Paul MN 55102-1800
651-221-1300

South Central College
1920 Lee Blvd, North Mankato MN 56003-2508
507-389-7200

Vermillion Community College
1900 E Camp St, Ely MN 55731-1996
800-475-6666

MISSISSIPPI

Coahoma Community College
3240 Friars Point Rd, Clarksdale MS 38614-9700
662-627-2571

Copiah-Lincoln Community College
11 Copiah Lincoln Circle, Natchez MS 39120
601-442-9111

Copiah-Lincoln Community College
PO Box 457, Wesson MS 39191-0457
601-643-5101

East Central Community College
PO Box 129, Decatur MS 39327-0129
601-635-2111

East Mississippi Community College
PO Box 158, Scooba MS 39358-0158
662-476-8442

Hinds Community College
1750 Chadwick Dr, Jackson MS 39204-3402
601-372-6507

Hinds Community College
PO Box 1100, Raymond MS 39154
601-857-5261

Hinds Community College
755 Highway 27, Vicksburg MS 39180-8699
601-638-0600

Holmes Community College
PO Box 369, Goodman MS 39079-0369
662-472-2312

Itawamba Community College
602 W Hill St, Fulton MS 38843
662-862-8000

Jones County Junior College
900 S Court St, Ellisville MS 39437-3999
601-477-4000

Meridian Community College
910 Highway 19 N, Meridian MS 39307-5801
601-483-8241

Mississippi Delta Community College
PO Box 668, Moorhead MS 38761-0668
662-246-6322

Mississippi Gulf Coast Community College
Gautier MS 39553
228-497-9602

Mississippi Gulf Coast Community College
Gulfport MS 39507
228-896-3355

Mississippi Gulf Coast Community College
PO Box 609, Perkinston MS 39573
601-928-5211

Northeast Mississippi Community College
101 Cunningham Blvd, Booneville MS 38829-1726
662-728-7751

Northwest Mississippi Community College
4975 Highway 51 N, Senatobia MS 38668
662-562-3200

Northwest Mississippi Community College
5197 W E Ross Pkwy, Southaven MS 38671
662-342-1570

Pearl River Community College
Station A, Poplarville MS 39470
601-795-6801

Southwest Mississippi Community College
Summit MS 39666
601-276-2001

MISSOURI

Crowder College
601 Laclede Ave, Neosho MO 64850-9165
Dr. Kent Farnsworth, President
Sonya Pearson, Dean of Students
1-866-238-7788

East Central College
1964 Prairie Dell Rd, Union MO 63084
Karen Wieda, Registrar
636-583-5195 ext. 2220 Fax: 636-583-1897
Website: www.eastcentral.edu
E-mail: wiedaks@eastcentral.edu

ITT Technical Institute
1930 Meyer Drury Dr, Arnold MO 63010
636-464-6600

ITT Technical Institute
9150 E 41st Ter, Kansas City MO 64133
816-276-1400

Jefferson College
1000 Viking Dr, Hillsboro MO 63050-2441
Amy Martin-Small, Director of Admissions and Financial Aid
636-797-3000

Longview Community College
500 SW Longview Rd, Lees Summit MO 64081-2105
Dr. Fred Grogan, President
816-672-2000

Maple Woods Community College
2601 NE Barry Rd, Kansas City MO 64156-1299
816-437-3000

METROPOLITAN COMMUNITY COLLEGE - BLUE RIVER

20301 E State Route 78
Independence MO 64057-2053
Renee Tolson, Contact
816-220-6577 Fax: 816-220-6511
Website: www.mcckc.edu/blueriver
E-mail: renee.tolson@mcckc.edu

Midwest Institute - Earth City
4260 Shoreline Dr, Earth City MO 63045
314-344-3334

Mineral Area College
PO Box 1000, Desloge MO 63601
573-431-4593

Moberly Area Community College
101 College Ave, Moberly MO 65270-1304
Dr. James Grant, Dean of Student Services
800-MACC-070

North Central Missouri College
1301 Main St, Trenton MO 64683-1824
Blaire Birdsong, Director of Admissions
660-359-3948

Ozarks Technical Community College
1001 E Chestnut Expressway
Springfield MO 65802-3625
Delvan Mitchell, Director of Admissions
417-447-7500 Fax: 417-447-6925
Website: www.otc.edu
E-mail: admissions@otc.edu

Penn Valley Community College
3201 SW Traffic Way, Kansas City MO 64111
816-759-4000

Ranken Technical College
4431 Finney Ave, Saint Louis MO 63113-2898
Admissions Office
314-371-0233 Fax: 314-371-0241
Website: www.ranken.edu
E-mail: admissions@ranken.edu

St. Charles Community College
4601 Mid Rivers Mall Dr, Cottleville MO 63376
Kathy Brockgreitens-Gober, Director of Admissions
636-922-8000 Fax: 636-922-8236
Website: www.stchas.edu
E-mail: adm-reg@stchas.edu

St. Louis Community College
11333 Big Bend Rd, Kirkwood MO 63122-5799
314-984-7500

St. Louis Community College
5600 Oakland Ave, Saint Louis MO 63110-1316
314-644-9100

St. Louis Community College at Florissant Valley
3400 Pershall Rd, Saint Louis MO 63135-1408
Janice Evans, Chair, Enrollment Management
314-595-4368

State Fair Community College
3201 W 16th St, Sedalia MO 65301-2199
Director of Admissions
660-530-5833 Fax: 660-596-7472
Website: www.sfccmo.edu
E-mail: mparris@sfccmo.edu

Three Rivers Community College
2080 Three Rivers Blvd, Poplar Bluff MO 63901
573-840-9605

WENTWORTH MILITARY ACADEMY & COLLEGE

1880 Washington Ave, Lexington MO 64067
MAJ Mike Herman, VP for Enrollment
800-962-7682 or 660-259-2221 Fax: 660-259-2677
Website: www.wma.edu
E-mail: admissions@wma.edu

College established 1923. Accreditation: The Higher Learning Commission of the NCA. Enrollment: 220 boarding students. 500 FTE non-boarding students. College has both military junior college (MJC) and civilian JC (CJC) divisions. MJC offers AA and AS degrees. Early Commissioning Program allows eligible ROTC cadets to earn Army commission in 2 years. Four-year ROTC scholarship also offered. CJC offers AA and AS degrees at Lexington campus and three satellites: Sheldon, Hermitage and Cameron. Affordable, quality education with small class sizes, individualized attention and outstanding faculty.

MONTANA

Blackfeet Community College
PO Box 819, Browning MT 59417
406-338-5441

Chief Dull Knife College
PO Box 98, Lame Deer MT 59043-0098
406-477-6215

Dawson Community College
PO Box 421, Glendive MT 59330-0421
Katherine Lee, Marketing Director
800-821-8320

Flathead Valley Community College
777 Grandview Dr, Kalispell MT 59901-2622
406-756-3846

Fort Belknap College
PO Box 159, Harlem MT 59526-0159
406-353-2607

Fort Peck Community College
PO Box 398, Poplar MT 59255
406-768-5551

Helena College of Technology of the Univ of Montana
1115 N Roberts St, Helena MT 59601-3054
406-444-6800

Little Big Horn College
Crow Agency MT 59022
406-638-3104

Miles Community College
2715 Dickinson St, Miles City MT 59301-4799
800-541-9281

Montana State University
Great Falls College of Technology
2100 16th Ave S, Great Falls MT 59405-4909
406-771-4300

Salish Kootenai College
PO Box 70, Pablo MT 59855
Jackie Moran, Admissions/Transfers
406-275-4866

Stone Child College
PO Box 1082, Box Elder MT 59521
406-395-4313

University of Montana
Missoula College of Technology
909 South Ave W, Missoula MT 59801-7910
406-243-7882

NEBRASKA

Central Community College-Columbus Campus
PO Box 1027, Columbus NE 68602-1027
Mary Young, Director of Admissions
402-564-7132 Fax: 402-562-1201
Website: www.cccneb.edu
E-mail: myoung@cccneb.edu

Central Community College-Grand Island Campus
PO Box 4903, Grand Island NE 68802-4903
Liz Kohaut, Director of Admissions
308-398-4222 Fax: 308-398-7398
Website: www.cccneb.edu
E-mail: lkohout@cccneb.edu

Central Community College-Hastings Campus
PO Box 1024, Hastings NE 68902-1024
Bob Glenn, Director of Admissions
402-463-9811 Fax: 402-562-1201
Website: www.cccneb.edu
E-mail: rglenn@cccneb.edu

Hamilton College
3350 N 90th St, Omaha NE 68134-4710
402-572-8500

ITT TECHNICAL INSTITUTE

9814 M St, Omaha NE 68127-2056
Frank de Monteur, Director
800-677-9260 Fax: 402-331-9495
Website: www.itt-tech.edu
E-mail: snielsen@itt-tech.edu

Little Priest Tribal College
PO Box 720, Winnebago NE 68071
402-878-2380

Metropolitan Community College
PO Box 3777, Omaha NE 68103-0777
Becky Nicks, Director of Admissions
402-449-8400 Fax: 402-457-2616
Website: www.mccnab.edu
E-mail: bnicks@mccnab.edu

Metropolitan Community College
30th & Fort Sts, Omaha NE 68111
402-449-8300

Metropolitan Community College
204th & Dodge St, Omaha NE 68103
402-457-2000

Mid-Plains Community College
McCook Community College Campus
1205 E 3rd St, Mc Cook NE 69001-2631
Kelly Rippen, Director of Recruitment
800-658-4348

Mid-Plains Community College
North Platte Community College - North Campus
1101 Halligan Dr, North Platte NE 69101-7659
Kelly Rippen, Director of Recruitment
800-658-4308 ext. 8107

Mid-Plains Community College
North Platte Community College - South Campus
601 W State Farm Rd, North Platte NE 69101
Kelly Rippen, Director of Recruitment
800-658-4308 ext. 8107

Nebraska College of Technical Agriculture
404 E 7th St, Curtis NE 69025
308-367-4124

Nebraska Indian Community College
PO Box 428, Macy NE 68039-0428
402-837-5078

Northeast Community College
PO Box 469, Norfolk NE 68702-0469
402-371-2020

Southeast Community College
4771 W Scott Rd, Beatrice NE 68310-7042
402-228-3468

Southeast Community College
8800 O St, Lincoln NE 68520-1299
402-437-2500

Southeast Community College
600 State St, Milford NE 68405
Larry Meyer, Director of Admissions
800-933-7223

Western Nebraska Community College
1601 E 27th St, Scottsbluff NE 69361-1815
308-635-3606

Western Nebraska Community College
Sidney NE 69162
800-221-9682

NEVADA

Career College of Northern Nevada
1195-A Corporate Blvd, Reno NV 89502-2331
Nathan Clark, Director
775-856-2266 Fax: 775-856-0935
Website: www.ccnn.edu
E-mail: lgoldhammer@ccnn4u.com
See listing under "Career Schools"

Community College of Southern Nevada
3200 E Cheyenne Ave
North Las Vegas NV 89030-4228
702-651-4536

Deep Springs College
Deep Springs, CA
HC 72 Box 45001, Dyer NV 89010-9712
760-872-2000

GREAT BASIN COLLEGE

1500 College Pkwy, Elko NV 89801-9930
Julie G. Byrnes, Director of Enrollment Management
775-753-2271 Fax: 775-753-2311
Website: www.gbcnv.edu
E-mail: julieb@gwmail.gbcnv.edu

Public. Coed. Accreditation: Northwest Association of Schools & Colleges. Tuition: $52.50-$79.00 per credit plus non-resident tuition of $2,481 per semester if applicable. Enrollment: 927 full-time, 2,188 part-time. Faculty: 125 full time and adjunct 232. Student-faculty ratio: 18:1. Degrees: Associate and some Baccalaureate. 12 buildings plus residence halls on 44 acres. GBC is the major provider of post-secondary education for rural Nevada.

Truckee Meadows Community College
7000 Dandini Blvd, Reno NV 89512-3999
Rita Huneycutt, Interim President
775-673-7000

Western Nevada Community College
2201 W College Pkwy, Carson City NV 89703-7316
775-445-3000

NEW HAMPSHIRE

New Hampshire Community Technical College
2020 Riverside Dr, Berlin NH 03570-3717
603-752-1113

New Hampshire Community Tech College
1 College Dr, Claremont NH 03743-9707
Charles Kusselow, Admissions Counselor
603-542-7744

New Hampshire Community Technical College
1066 Front St, Manchester NH 03102-8528
Jacquie Poirier, Director of Admissions
603-668-6706 Fax: 603-668-5354
Website: www.manchester.nhctc.edu
E-mail: jpoirier@nhctc.edu

New Hampshire Community Technical College
505 Amherst St, Nashua NH 03063
Patricia Goodman, Director of Student Services
603-882-7022

New Hampshire Community Technical College
277 Portsmouth Ave, Stratham NH 03885-2231
Laurilee A. Shennett, Admissions Recruiter
603-772-1194 ext. 317

New Hampshire Technical College
379 Belmont Rd, Laconia NH 03246
603-524-3207

New Hampshire Technical Institute
11 Institute Dr, Concord NH 03301-7400
603-271-6484

NEW JERSEY

Assumption College for Sisters
350 Bernardsville Rd, Mendham NJ 07945-2923
Sr. Mary Joseph Schultz, S.C.C., President
973-543-6528 Fax: 973-543-1738
Website: www.acs350.org
E-mail: acs@acs350.org

ATLANTIC CAPE COMMUNITY COLLEGE

5100 Black Horse Pike
Mays Landing NJ 08330-2699
Linda McLeod, Assistant Director of College Recruitment
609-343-5000 Fax: 609-343-4921
Website: www.atlantic.edu
E-mail: accadmit@atlantic.edu

Established 1964. Public. Coed. Accreditation: Middle States Association of Colleges and Secondary Schools. Tuition: $83.00 per credit. Fees: $18.00 per credit. Enrollment: 2,524 full-time, 3,339 part-time. Faculty: 70 full-time, 200 part-time. Degrees: AS, AA, AAS. Library: 78,000. 15 buildings on 537 acres. Home of New Jersey's largest cooking school. Leader in distance education. Casino Career Training. On-line degrees.

Bergen Community College
400 Paramus Rd, Paramus NJ 07652
Julian Gomez, Asst. Director of Admissions
201-447-7100 Fax: 201-444-7036
Website: www.bergen.edu
E-mail: jgomez@bergen.edu

Berkeley College
64 E Midland Ave, Paramus NJ 07652
800-446-5400

Berkeley College
430 Rahway Ave, Woodbridge NJ 07095-3305
800-446-5400

Brookdale Community College
765 Newman Springs Rd, Lincroft NJ 07738-1597
732-842-1900

Burlington County College
County Route 530, Pemberton NJ 08068
609-894-9311

Camden County College
PO Box 200, Blackwood NJ 08012-0200
856-227-7200

County College of Morris
214 Center Grove Rd, Randolph NJ 07869-2086
973-328-5000

Cumberland County College
PO Box 1500, Vineland NJ 08362-1500
856-691-8600

Essex County College
303 University Ave, Newark NJ 07102-1798
973-877-3000

Essex County College
West Essex Campus
730 Bloomfield Ave, West Caldwell NJ 07006-6783
Cheryl Newton-Banks, Assistant Director Enrollment Services
973-403-2560

Fairleigh Dickinson University
150 Kotte Pl, Hackensack NJ 07601-6112
201-692-2675

Gibbs College
630 W Mount Pleasant Ave
Livingston NJ 07039-1611
973-744-2010

Gloucester County College
1400 Tanyard Rd, Sewell NJ 08080
856-468-5000

Hudson County Community College
25 Journal Sq, Jersey City NJ 07306
201-656-2020

Mercer County Community College
James Kerney Campus
N Broad & Academy Sts, Trenton NJ 08608
609-586-0505

Mercer County Community College
West Windsor Campus
PO Box B, Trenton NJ 08690
Savita Bambhrolia, Director of Admissions
609-586-4800 Fax: 609-587-4666
Website: www.mccc.edu
E-mail: admiss@mccc.edu

Middlesex County College
2600 Woodbridge Ave, Edison NJ 08837-3675
732-548-6000

Ocean County College
College Dr, Toms River NJ 08754
732-255-0400

Passaic Co. Community College
1 College Blvd, Paterson NJ 07505
973-684-6800

Raritan Valley Community College
PO Box 3300, Somerville NJ 08876-1265
908-526-1200

Salem Community College
460 Hollywood Ave, Carneys Point NJ 08069-2799
856-299-2100

Sussex County Community College
1 College Hill, Newton NJ 07860
973-300-2100

Union County College
1033 Springfield Ave, Cranford NJ 07016-1528
908-709-7000

Union County College
12 W Jersey St, Elizabeth NJ 07201-2314
908-965-6000

Union County College
232 E 2nd St, Plainfield NJ 07060-1308
908-412-3559

Warren County Community College
475 State Route 57 W, Washington NJ 07882-4343
908-835-9222

NEW MEXICO

Albuquerque TVI Community College
525 Buena Vista Dr SE, Albuquerque NM 87106-4096
Jane Campbell, Registrar
505-224-3061

Apollo College
1001 Menaul Blvd NE Ste C, Albuquerque NM 87107
800-368-7246 Fax: 505-254-1101

Clovis Community College
417 Schepps Blvd, Clovis NM 88101-8381
505-769-2811

Eastern New Mexico University-Roswell
PO Box 6000, Roswell NM 88202-6000
505-624-7000

International Institute of the Americas
4201 Central Ave NW Suite J
Albuquerque NM 87105-1649
Ed Sigman, Director
505-880-2877 Fax: 505-352-0199
Website: www.iia.edu
E-mail: esigman@iia.edu

ITT Technical Institute
5100 Masthead St NE, Albuquerque NM 87109-4366
505-828-1114

Luna Community College
366 Luna Dr, Las Vegas NM 87701
Louella Marr-Montoya, Director of Admissions
505-454-2500

Mesalands Community College
911 S 10th St, Tucumcari NM 88401
505-461-4413

New Mexico Junior College
5317 N Lovington Hwy, Hobbs NM 88240-9123
505-392-4510

NEW MEXICO MILITARY INSTITUTE

101 W College Blvd, Roswell NM 88201-5173
Rear Admiral David R. Ellison, USN (Ret.), Superintendent
LTC. Steven D. Klein, VP, Enrollment & Marketing
800-421-5376 or 505-624-8050 Fax: 505-624-8058
Website: www.nmmi.edu
E-mail: admissions@nmmi.edu

Established 1891. State Supported. Coed. Accreditation: NCACS, New Mexico Department of Education. Estimated costs for 2004-2005 school year, out-of-state student: $10,166, in-state student: $7,670. Enrollment: 950. Faculty: 68. Student-faculty ratio: 18:1. Degree: AA. Library: 68,000 volumes. 19 buildings on 40 acre main campus. Additional acreage includes an 18-hole championship golf course. ROTC - offering an ARMY two year commissioning program. Prep school for all service academies. 90% of high school graduates receive their 4 year college degrees. 90% of junior college graduates receive their baccalaureate degrees. Quality education at a fair price.

New Mexico State University
2400 Scenic Dr, Alamogordo NM 88310-3722
505-439-3600

New Mexico State University
1500 University Dr, Carlsbad NM 88220-3509
505-234-9200

New Mexico State University
1500 N 3rd St, Grants NM 87020-2025
Irene Lutz, Director of Admissions
505-287-7981 Fax: 505-287-2329
Website: www.grants.nmsu.edu
E-mail: ilutz@nmsu.edu

New Mexico State University
Dona Ana Branch Community College
PO Box 30001, Las Cruces NM 88003-8001
505-527-7500

Northern New Mexico College
921 Paseo de Onate, Espanola NM 87532
505-747-2100

Northern New Mexico Community College
El Rito NM 87530
505-581-4501

San Juan College
4601 College Blvd, Farmington NM 87402-4699
505-326-3311

Santa Fe Community College
6401 S Richards Ave, Santa Fe NM 87508-4887
505-428-1000

Southwestern Indian Polytechnic Institute
PO Box 10146, Albuquerque NM 87184-0146
505-346-2347

University of New Mexico
200 College Rd, Gallup NM 87301-5603
505-863-7500

University of New Mexico
4000 University Dr, Los Alamos NM 87544-2233
505-662-5919

University of New Mexico
280 La Entrada Rd, Los Lunas NM 87031-7633
505-925-8500

UNIVERSITY OF NEW MEXICO

115 Civic Plaza Dr, Taos NM 87571-6401
Henry Trujillo, Senior Student Enrollment Associate
505-737-6200 Fax: 505-737-9317
Website: taos.unm.edu
E-mail: htrujil1@unm.edu

NEW YORK

AMERICAN ACADEMY MCALLISTER INSTITUTE OF FUNERAL SERVICE

619 W 54th St 6th Floor, New York NY 10019
Meg Dunn, President
212-757-1190 Fax: 212-765-5923
Website: www.funeraleducation.org
E-mail: info@funeraleducation.org

Briarcliffe College
1055 Stewart Ave, Bethpage NY 11714-3545
Theresa Donohue, Director of Admissions
516-918-3600 Fax: 516-470-6020
Website: www.briarcliffe.edu

Briarcliffe College
225 W Main St, Patchogue NY 11772-3019
888-756-9900

Broome Community College
907 Upper Front St, Binghamton NY 13905
Anthony S. Fiorelli, Director of Admissions
607-778-5001 Fax: 607-778-5442
Website: www.sunybroome.edu
E-mail: fiorelli_a@sunybroome.edu

Bryant & Stratton College
465 Main St Ste 400, Buffalo NY 14203-1713
716-884-9120

Business Informatics Center
134 S Central Ave, Valley Stream NY 11580-5431
516-561-0050

Clinton Community College
136 Clinton Point Dr, Plattsburgh NY 12901-6002
Robert C. Wood, Assoc. Dean for Enrollment
518-562-4200

The College of Westchester
PO Box 710, White Plains NY 10602
914-948-4442

Columbia-Greene Community College
4400 State Route 23, Hudson NY 12534-9543
518-828-4181

Corning Community College
1 Academic Dr, Corning NY 14830-3299
607-962-9011

Culinary Institute of America
1946 Campus Dr, Hyde Park NY 12538-1499
Dennis Craig, Director of Admissions
800-CULINARY (285-4627)

CUNY Borough of Manhattan Community College
199 Chambers St, New York NY 10007-1044
212-346-8800

CUNY Bronx Community College
W 181st and University Ave, Bronx NY 10453-2895
718-289-5100

CUNY Kingsborough Community College
2001 Oriental Blvd, Brooklyn NY 11235-2398
718-368-5000

CUNY Queensborough Community College
22205 56th Ave, Bayside NY 11364-1432
Winston Yarde, Director of Admissions
718-631-6262

Dutchess Community College
53 Pendell Rd, Poughkeepsie NY 12601-1512
845-431-8000

Erie Community College
City Campus
121 Ellicott St, Buffalo NY 14203-2698
716-842-2770

Erie Community College North
6205 Main St, Williamsville NY 14221-8402
716-634-0800

Erie Community College South
4041 Southwestern Blvd
Orchard Park NY 14127-2199
716-648-5400

Finger Lakes Community College
4355 Lakeshore Dr, Canandaigua NY 14424-8347
585-394-3500

Fulton-Montgomery Community College
2805 State Highway 67, Johnstown NY 12095
518-762-4651

Gamla College
1213 Elm Ave, Brooklyn NY 11230
718-339-4747

Genesee Community College
1 College Rd, Batavia NY 14020-9703
585-343-0055

Herkimer County Community College
100 Reservoir Rd, Herkimer NY 13350-1545
888-464-4222

Hostos Community College - CUNY
500 Grand Concourse, Bronx NY 10451-5323
Roland Velez, Director of Admissions
718-518-4406

ISLAND DRAFTING & TECHNICAL INSTITUTE

128 Broadway (Route 110), Amityville NY 11701-2704
James G. DiLiberto, President
631-691-8733 Fax: 631-691-8738
Website: www.idti.edu
E-mail: info@idti.edu

Jamestown Community College
PO Box 20, Jamestown NY 14702-0020
Nelson J. Garifi, Jr., Director of Marketing
800-388-8557

Jamestown Community College
Olean NY 14760
585-372-1661

Jefferson Community College
1220 Coffeen St, Watertown NY 13601-1897
315-786-2200

LaGuardia Community College / CUNY
31-10 Thompson Ave, Long Island City NY 11101
718-482-7200

LONG ISLAND BUSINESS INSTITUTE

6500 Jericho Tpke, Commack NY 11725-2907
Donna E. McCullough, President
631-499-7100 Fax: 631-499-7114
Website: www.libi.edu
E-mail: rnazar@libi.edu

Private. Coed. Accreditation: ACICS. Approvals: National Court Reporting Association, NY State Board of Regents. Tuition: $325.00 per credit hour. Fees: $50.00 application fee. Enrollment: 260. Faculty: 25. Student-faculty ratio: 12:1. Associate of Occupational Studies degree offered in Court Reporting. Diploma program in Court Reporting.

LONG ISLAND BUSINESS INSTITUTE

136-18 39 Ave, Flushing NY 11354
Donna E. McCullough, President
718-939-5100 Fax: 718-989-9235
Website: www.libi.edu
E-mail: dwang@libi.edu

Private. Coed. Accreditation: ACICS. Approvals. National Court Reporting Association, NY State Board of Regents. Tuition: $325.00 per credit hour. Fees: $50.00 application fee. Enrollment: 850. Faculty: 25. Student-faculty ratio: 12:1. Associate of Occupational Studies degree offered in Court Reporting, Office Technology with Medical Office, Business Management, Accounting. Diploma programs in Office Technology, Medical Insurance & Billing, Court Reporting.

Maria College of Albany
700 New Scotland Ave, Albany NY 12208-1715
518-438-3111

Mohawk Valley Community College
1101 Sherman Dr, Utica NY 13501-5394
315-792-5400

Monroe College
434 Main St, New Rochelle NY 10801-6410
914-632-5400

Monroe Community College
1000 E Henrietta Rd, Rochester NY 14623-5701
585-292-2000

Nassau Community College
1 Education Dr, Garden City NY 11530-6719
516-572-7501

North Country Community College
23 Santanoni, Saranac Lake NY 12983
Edwin Trathen, Assistant to the President for Enrollment Services
1-888-TRY-NCCC ext. 686

Onondaga Community College
4941 Onondaga Rd, Syracuse NY 13215-2001
315-498-2622

ROCHESTER INSTITUTE OF TECHNOLOGY NATIONAL TECHNICAL INSTITUTE FOR THE DEAF (NTID)

52 Lomb Memorial Dr, Rochester NY 14623-5604
Robert Borden, Director of NTID Admissions
585-475-6700 (v/TTY) or 866-644-6843 (v/TTY)
Fax: 585-475-2696
Website: www.rit.edu/ntid/getinfo
E-mail: NTIDAdmissions@rit.edu

Established 1965. Private. Coed. Tution $9,153 (NTID or NTID supported students only). Room & Board: $9,054. Fees: $669. Enrollment: 1,100. Faculty: 205. Degrees offered: MS, BS, AS, AAS, AOS. 238 buildings on 1,300 acres. Qualified deaf and hard-of-hearing students can earn bachelor's or master's degrees in more than 200 programs offered by RIT's seven other colleges - Applied Science and Technology, Business, Computing and Information Sciences, Engineering, Imaging Arts and Sciences, Liberal Arts, and Science. They also can earn associate degrees in more than 30 accredited NTID programs including: Accounting Technology, Administrative Support Technology, Applied Computer Technology, Applied Optical Technology, Arts and Imaging (pending state approval) Automation Technologies - Robotics, Business Technology, Computer Aided Drafting Technology, Computer Integrated Machining Technology, Laboratory Science Technology and Hospitality and Service Management. Additionally NTID offers degrees in American Sign Language-English Interpretation and a Master's of Science in Secondary Education of Students who are Deaf or Hard of Hearing.

Sage College of Albany
140 New Scotland Ave, Albany NY 12208-3425
518-292-1717

SUNY Adirondack Community College
640 Bay Rd, Queensbury NY 12804
Sarah Jane Linehan, Director of Enrollment Management
518-743-2264

SUNY Canton - College of Technology
34 Cornell Dr, Canton NY 13617-1037
315-386-7011

SUNY Cayuga County Community College
197 Franklin St, Auburn NY 13021-3011
Richard F. Landers, Director of Admissions
315-255-1743

SUNY College of Agriculture & Technology
Morrisville NY 13408
Thomas Ver Dow, Dean of Enrollment Management
800-258-0111

SUNY College of Technology
Alfred NY 14802
Deborah J. Goodrich, Associate VP Enrollment Mgmt.
800-4AL-FRED Fax: 607-587-4299
Website: www.alfredstate.edu
E-mail: admissions@alfredstate.edu

SUNY College of Technology
2 Main St, Delhi NY 13753-1110
Robert W. Mazzei, Director of Admissions
800-96-DELHI

SUNY Hudson Valley Community College
80 Vandenburgh Ave, Troy NY 12180-6025
Jack Mahoney, Director of Admissions
518-629-HVCC (629-4822)

SUNY Niagara County Community College
3111 Saunders Settlement Rd
Sanborn NY 14132-9487
Kathleen Saunders, Director of Admissions
716-614-6200 Fax: 716-614-6820
Website: www.niagaracc.suny.edu
E-mail: admissions@niagaracc.suny.edu

SUNY North Country Community College
PO Box 311, Ticonderoga NY 12883-0311
518-585-4454

SUNY ORANGE COUNTY COMMUNITY COLLEGE

115 South St, Middletown NY 10940-6437
Margot St. Lawrence, Director of Admissions
845-341-4030 Fax: 845-342-8662
Website: www.sunyorange.edu
E-mail: apply@sunyorange.edu

Established 1950. Public. Coed. Accreditation: Middle States Association of Colleges & Schools. Tuition: $2,900. Fees: $100 student activity/athletic fee, $200 technology fee, $18 insurance. Enrollment: 2,933 full-time, 3,118 part-time. Faculty: 175. Student-faculty ratio: 15:1. Library: 95,000 volumes, 33,000 microforms, 500 periodicals. 16 buildings on 32 acres. Also has an Extension Center in Newburgh servicing 1,000 students.

SUNY Rockland Community College
766 N Main St, Spring Valley NY 10977-1985
845-352-5535

SUNY Rockland Community College
185 N Main St, Spring Valley NY 10977-4105
845-352-5535

SUNY Rockland Community College
145 College Rd, Suffern NY 10901-3611
Charles Connolly, Coordinator of Admissions & Recruitment
845-574-4000

SUNY Schenectady County Community College
78 Washington Ave, Schenectady NY 12305-2215
Robert Dinello, Director of Admissions
518-381-1366

SUNY Suffolk County Community College
Crooked Hill Rd, Brentwood NY 11717-1017
631-851-6700

SUNY Suffolk County Community College
2 Speonk Riverhead Rd, Riverhead NY 11901-3433
631-548-2500

SUNY Suffolk County Community College
533 College Rd, Selden NY 11784-2851
631-451-4110

SUNY Sullivan County Community College
112 College Rd, Loch Sheldrake NY 12759-5151
Sari Rosenheck, Director of Admissions
845-434-5750 Fax: 845-434-0923
Website: www.sullivan.suny.edu
E-mail: admissions@sullivan.suny.edu
Student Housing on Campus.

T.C.I. Institute, The College of Technology
320 W 31st St, New York NY 10001-2789
Edward Gehrke, V.P. for Admissions
800-878-8246 Fax: 212-330-0891
Website: www.tcicollege.edu
E-mail: admissions@tcicollege.edu

Tompkins Cortland Community College
PO Box 139, Dryden NY 13053-0139
607-844-8211

Trocaire College
360 Choate Ave, Buffalo NY 14220-2094
Paul B. Hurley, Ph.D., President
Claudia M. Lesinski, Enrollment Management Officer
716-826-1200

Ulster County Community College
Stone Ridge NY 12484
845-687-5000

Utica School of Commerce
17 Elm St, Oneonta NY 13820-1828
Misty Davis, Admissions
607-432-7003

Villa Maria College of Buffalo
240 Pine Ridge Rd, Buffalo NY 14225-3913
Kevin Donovan, Director of Enrollment Management/Marketing
716-896-0700

Westchester Community College
75 Grasslands Rd, Valhalla NY 10595-1693
914-785-6600

Wood Tobe-Coburn School
8 E 40th St, New York NY 10016-0102
212-686-9040

NORTH CAROLINA

Alamance Community College
PO Box 8000, Graham NC 27253-8000
336-578-2002

Asheville Buncombe Technical Community College
340 Victoria Rd, Asheville NC 28801-4897
828-254-1921

Beaufort County Community College
PO Box 1069, Washington NC 27889
252-946-6194

Bladen Community College
PO Box 266, Dublin NC 28332-0266
910-862-2164

Blue Ridge Community College
College Dr, Flat Rock NC 28731
828-694-1700

Brunswick Community College
PO Box 30, Supply NC 28462-0030
910-755-7300

Caldwell Community College and Technical Institute
2855 Hickory Blvd, Hudson NC 28638
828-726-2200

Cape Fear Community College
411 N Front St, Wilmington NC 28401-3910
910-251-5100

Carolinas College of Health Sciences
PO Box 32861, Charlotte NC 28232-2861
Elizabeth West, Admissions Officer
704-355-5043

Carteret Community College
3505 Arendell St, Morehead City NC 28557-2989
Pamela Hilbert, V.P. for Instruction & Student Support
252-247-3058 ext. 144

Catawba Valley Community College
2550 US Highway 70 SE, Hickory NC 28602-8302
828-327-7000

Central Carolina Community College
1105 Kelly Dr, Sanford NC 27330-9000
Ron Miriello, Director of Admissions
919-775-5401

Central Piedmont Community College
PO Box 35009, Charlotte NC 28235-5009
704-330-2722

Cleveland Community College
137 S Post Rd, Shelby NC 28152-6205
704-484-4000

Coastal Carolina Community College
444 Western Blvd, Jacksonville NC 28546-6899
910-455-1221

College of the Albemarle
PO Box 2327, Elizabeth City NC 27906-2327
252-335-0821

Craven Community College
PO Box 885, New Bern NC 28563-0885
252-638-4131

Davidson County Community College
PO Box 1287, Lexington NC 27293-1287
336-249-8186

Durham Technical Community College
1637 E Lawson St, Durham NC 27703-5023
919-686-3333

ECPI College of Technology
4101 Doie Cope Rd, Raleigh NC 27613-7387
919-571-0057

Edgecombe Community College
2009 W Wilson St, Tarboro NC 27886-9361
Thomas B. Anderson, VP of Student Services
252-823-5166

Fayetteville Technical Community College
PO Box 35236, Fayetteville NC 28303-0236
910-678-8400

Forsyth Technical Community College
2100 Silas Creek Pkwy
Winston Salem NC 27103-5150
336-723-0371

Gaston College
201 Highway 321 S, Dallas NC 28034-1499
704-922-6200

Guilford Technical Community College
PO Box 309, Jamestown NC 27282-0309
336-334-4822

Halifax Community College
PO Box 809, Weldon NC 27890-0809
252-536-2551

Haywood Community College
185 Freedlander Dr, Clyde NC 28721
Debbie Rowland, Coordinator of Admissions
828-627-4500 Fax: 828-627-4513
Website: www.haywood.edu
E-mail: drowland@haywood.edu

Heritage Bible College
PO Box 1628, Dunn NC 28335
910-892-3178 Fax: 910-892-1809
Website: www.heritagebiblecollege.org
E-mail: generalinfo@heritagebiblecollege.org

Isothermal Community College
PO Box 804, Spindale NC 28160-0804
828-286-3636

James Sprunt Community College
PO Box 398, Kenansville NC 28349-0398
Lea Grady, Admissions
910-296-2500 Fax: 910-296-1636
Website: www.jamessprunt.edu

Johnston Community College
PO Box 2350, Smithfield NC 27577-2350
919-934-3051

King's College
322 Lamar Ave, Charlotte NC 28204-2493
704-372-0266

Lenoir Community College
PO Box 188, Kinston NC 28502-0188
252-527-6223

Louisburg College
501 N Main St, Louisburg NC 27549-2399
800-775-0208

Martin Community College
1161 Kehukee Park Rd, Williamston NC 27892-8307
252-792-1521

Mayland Community College
PO Box 547, Spruce Pine NC 28777-0547
Cathy B. Morrison, Director of Enrollment Management
828-765-7351 Fax: 828-765-0728
Website: www.mayland.edu
E-mail: cmorrison@mayland.edu

McDowell Technical Community College
54 College Dr, Marion NC 28752
Rick Wilson, Director of Admissions
828-652-6021

Mitchell Community College
500 W Broad St, Statesville NC 28677-5264
704-878-3200

Montgomery Community College
1011 Page St, Troy NC 27371-8387
910-576-6222

Nash Community College
PO Box 7488, Rocky Mount NC 27804-0488
252-443-4011

Pamlico Community College
PO Box 185, Grantsboro NC 28529-0185
252-249-1851

Piedmont Community College
PO Box 1197, Roxboro NC 27573-1197
336-599-1181

Pitt Community College
PO Box 7007, Greenville NC 27835-7007
252-321-4200

Randolph Community College
PO Box 1009, Asheboro NC 27204-1009
336-633-0200

Richmond Community College
PO Box 1189, Hamlet NC 28345-1189
910-582-7000

Roanoke-Chowan Community College
109 Community College Rd, Ahoskie NC 27910
252-862-1200

Robeson Community College
PO Box 1420, Lumberton NC 28359
Judith Revels, Director of Admissions
910-738-7101

Rockingham Community College
PO Box 38, Wentworth NC 27375-0038
336-342-4261

Rowan-Cabarrus Community College
PO Box 1595, Salisbury NC 28145-1595
704-637-0760

Sampson Community College
PO Box 318, Clinton NC 28329-0318
910-592-8081

Sandhills Community College
3395 Airport Rd, Pinehurst NC 28374
910-692-6185

South College
29 Turtle Creek Dr, Asheville NC 28803
Robert Davis, Dean of Academic Affairs
828-277-5521 Fax: 828-277-6151
Website: southcollegenc.com
E-mail: bdavis@southcollegenc.com

Southeastern Community College
PO Box 151, Whiteville NC 28472-0151
910-642-7141

South Piedmont Community College
PO Box 126, Polkton NC 28135-0126
John Curtis, Contact
704-272-5324 Fax: 704-272-8904
Website: www.spcc.edu
E-mail: jcurtis@spcc.edu

Southwestern Community College
447 College Dr, Sylva NC 28779-8581
828-586-4091

Stanly Community College
141 College Dr, Albemarle NC 28001-6418
704-982-0121

Surry Community College
630 S Main St, Dobson NC 27017-8432
336-386-8121

Tri-County Community College
2300 US Highway 64 E, Murphy NC 28906-7919
828-837-6810

Vance-Granville Community College
PO Box 917, Henderson NC 27536-0917
252-492-2061

Wake Technical Community College
9101 Fayetteville Rd, Raleigh NC 27603-5696
Dr. Robert E. Ireland, Director of Admissions
919-662-3357

Wayne Community College
PO Box 8002, Goldsboro NC 27533-8002
Kathy Garner, Public Information Officer
919-735-5151

Western Piedmont Community College
1001 Burkemont Ave, Morganton NC 28655-4511
828-438-6000

Wilkes Community College
PO Box 120, Wilkesboro NC 28697-0120
336-838-6100

Wilson Technical Community College
PO Box 4305, Wilson NC 27893-0305
252-291-1195

NORTH DAKOTA

Bismarck State College
PO Box 5587, Bismarck ND 58506
701-224-5400

Cankdeska Cikana Community College
PO Box 269, Fort Totten ND 58335-0269
701-766-4415

Fort Berthold Community College
PO Box 490, New Town ND 58763-0490
701-627-4738

Lake Region State College
1801 College Dr N, Devils Lake ND 58301
701-662-1600

Minot State University-Bottineau Campus
105 Simrall Blvd, Bottineau ND 58318-1159
Paula Berg, Associate Dean of Student Affairs
800-542-6866 Fax: 701-228-5499
Website: www.misu-b.nodak.edu
E-mail: paula.berg@misu.nodak.edu

North Dakota State College of Science
800 6th St N, Wahpeton ND 58076
701-671-1130

Sitting Bull College
1341 92nd St, Fort Yates ND 58538
Melody Azure, Director of Admissions / Registrar
701-854-3861

Turtle Mountain Community College
PO Box 340, Belcourt ND 58316-0340
701-477-7862

United Tribes Technical College
3315 University Dr, Bismarck ND 58504-7596
701-255-3285

Williston State College
PO Box 1326, Williston ND 58802-1326
Penny Soiseth, Associate Director Enrollment Services
701-774-4200 Fax: 701-774-4544
Website: www.wsc.nodak.edu
E-mail: penny.soiseth@wsc.nodak.edu

OHIO

The Art Institute of Cincinnati
1171 E Kemper Rd, Cincinnati OH 45246
Marion Allman, President
513-751-1206 Fax: 513-751-1209
Website: www.theartinstituteofcincinnati.com
E-mail: aic@theartinstituteofcincinnati.com
See listing under "Art"

Belmont Technical College
120 Fox Shannon Pl, Saint Clairsville OH 43950-8751
740-695-9500

Bowling Green State University - Firelands Campus
1 University Dr, Huron OH 44839
419-433-5560

Bradford School
2469 Stelzer Rd, Columbus OH 43219-3129
Raeann Lee, Director of Admissions
614-416-6200

Brown Mackie College - Akron
755 White Pond Dr Ste 101, Akron OH 44320-4221
330-733-8766

Brown Mackie College - Cincinnati
1011 Glendale Milford Rd, Cincinnati OH 45215-1107
Robin Krout, President
513-771-2424 Fax: 513-771-3413
Website: www.brownmackie.edu
E-mail: rkrout@brownmackie.edu

Brown Mackie College - North Canton
1320 W Maple St, North Canton OH 44720
330-494-1214

Bryant & Stratton College
12955 Snow Rd, Cleveland OH 44130-1013
Thomas M. Hartman, Director
216-265-3151

Central Ohio Technical College
1179 University Dr, Newark OH 43055-1767
740-366-9222

Chatfield College
20918 State Route 251, Saint Martin OH 45118-9059
513-875-3344

Cincinnati State Technical & Community College
3520 Central Pkwy, Cincinnati OH 45223-2612
513-569-1500

Clark State Community College
570 E Leffel Ln, Springfield OH 45505-4749
937-325-0691

Cleveland Institute of Electronics
1776 E 17th St, Cleveland OH 44114-3679
Scott Katzenmeyer, Director of Admissions
800-243-6446 Fax: 216-781-0331
Website: www.cie-wc.edu
E-mail: instruct@cie-wc.edu

Columbus State Community College
550 E Spring St, Columbus OH 43215-1786
Ken Conner, Director of Admissions
614-287-3669

Cuyahoga Community College
2900 Community College Ave
Cleveland OH 44115-3196
216-987-4000

Cuyahoga Community College
25444 Harvard Rd, Highland Hills OH 44122-6202
216-987-2019

Cuyahoga Community College
11000 W Pleasant Valley Rd
Parma Heights OH 44130-5199
440-842-7773

Edison State Community College
1973 Edison Dr, Piqua OH 45356-9239
937-778-8600

Hocking College
3301 Hocking Pkwy, Nelsonville OH 45764-9704
Diane K. Wolf, Assistant Director of Admissions Information
800-282-4163

ITT Technical Institute
3325 Stop 8 Rd, Dayton OH 45414-3425
Joe Graham, Director of Admissions
937-454-2267

ITT Technical Institute
4700 Richmond Rd, Warrensville Heights OH 44128
216-896-6500

ITT Technical Institute
1030 N Meridian Rd, Youngstown OH 44509-4098
Tom Flynn, Director of Admissions
800-832-5001

James A. Rhodes State College
4240 Campus Dr, Lima OH 45804-3597
419-995-8000

Jefferson Community College
4000 Sunset Blvd, Steubenville OH 43952-3598
740-264-5591

Kent State University-Ashtabula Campus
3325 W 13th St, Ashtabula OH 44004-2299
Kelly Sanford, Contact
440-964-3322

Kent State University-East Liverpool Campus
400 E 4th St, East Liverpool OH 43920-3497
Jamie Kenneally, Contact
330-385-3805

Kent State University-Geauga Campus
14111 Claridon Troy Rd, Burton OH 44021-9581
Dave Chappell, Contact
440-834-4187

Kent State University-Salem Campus
2491 State Route 45 S, Salem OH 44460-9412
Dennis Giacomino, Contact
330-332-0361

Kent State University-Stark Campus
6000 Frank Ave NW, North Canton OH 44720-7548
Jim Barrett, Contact
330-499-9600

Kent State University-Trumbull Campus
4314 Mahoning Ave NW, Warren OH 44483-1998
Linda Petrilla, Contact
330-678-4281

Kent State University - Tuscarawas Campus
330 University Dr NE, New Philadelphia OH 44663
Denise Testa, Contact
330-339-3391

Lakeland Community College
7700 Clocktower Dr, Kirtland OH 44094-5198
Tracey Cooper, Director of Admissions
440-953-7100

Lorain County Community College
1005 Abbe Rd N, Elyria OH 44035
Dione Somerville, Director of Admissions
440-365-5222

Marion Technical College
1467 Mount Vernon Ave, Marion OH 43302-5628
Joel Liles, Director of Admissions
740-389-4636

Mercy College of Northwest Ohio
2221 Madison Ave, Toledo OH 43604
419-251-1279

Miami-Jacobs Career College
110 N Patterson Blvd, Dayton OH 45402
Sean Kuhn, Regional Director of Admissions
937-222-7337

Miami University-Hamilton Campus
1601 University Blvd, Hamilton OH 45011-3399
513-785-3000

Miami University-Middletown Campus
4200 E University Blvd, Middletown OH 45042
513-727-3200

North Central State College
PO Box 698, Mansfield OH 44901-0698
Troy Shutler, Director of Admissions
419-755-4800

Northwest State Community College
22600 State Route 34, Archbold OH 43502-9542
Mark Thompson, Director of Admissions
419-267-5511 Fax: 419-267-5587
Website: www.northweststate.edu
E-mail: mthompson@northweststate.edu

Ohio Institute of Photography & Technology
2029 Edgefield Rd, Dayton OH 45439-1917
Robert A. Martin, Executive Director
937-294-6155

Ohio State University-A & T Institute
1328 Dover Rd, Wooster OH 44691-8905
330-264-3911

Owens Community College
3200 Bright Rd, Findlay OH 45840
William J. Ivoska PhD., Vice President of Student Services
567-429-3500 Fax: 567-423-0246
Website: www.owens.edu
E-mail: admissions@owens.edu

Owens Community College
PO Box 10000, Toledo OH 43699-1947
William J. Ivoska, Ph.D, Vice President of Student Services
567-661-7000 Fax: 567-661-7607
Website: www.owens.edu
E-mail: admissions@owens.edu

Sinclair Community College
444 W 3rd St, Dayton OH 45402-1460
Director of Admissions
937-512-3000 Fax: 937-512-2393
Website: www.sinclair.edu
E-mail: admit@sinclair.edu

Southern State Community College
100 Hobart Rd, Hillsboro OH 45133-9488
937-393-3431

Southern State Community College
12681 US Route 62, Sardinia OH 45171
937-695-0307

Southern State Community College
1850 Davids Dr, Wilmington OH 45177
937-382-6645

Southwestern College
201 E 2nd St, Franklin OH 45005-2267
937-746-6633

Southwestern College of Business
149 Northland Blvd, Cincinnati OH 45246
513-874-0432

Southwestern College of Business
630 Vine St Ste 200, Cincinnati OH 45202-2421
513-421-3212

Terra State Community College
2830 Napoleon Rd, Fremont OH 43420-9670
419-334-8400

University of Akron-Wayne College
1901 Smucker Rd, Orrville OH 44667-9192
330-683-2010

University of Cincinnati
Clermont College
4200 Clermont College Dr, Batavia OH 45103-1748
513-732-5200

University of Cincinnati
College of Allied Health Sciences
PO Box 670394, Cincinnati OH 45267-0394
Gilbert Hageman, Associate Dean
513-558-7495

University of Cincinnati
Raymond Walters College
9555 Plainfield Rd, Cincinnati OH 45236-1007
513-745-5700

Washington State Community College
710 Colegate Dr, Marietta OH 45750-9225
740-374-8716

Wright State University
7600 State Route 703, Celina OH 45822-2921
419-586-0300

Zane State College
1555 Newark Rd, Zanesville OH 43701-2694
740-454-2501

OKLAHOMA

Carl Albert State College
1507 S McKenna St, Poteau OK 74953-5207
918-647-1200

Connors State College
RR 1 Box 1000, Warner OK 74469-9700
918-463-2931

Eastern Oklahoma State College
1301 W Main St, Wilburton OK 74578-4901
918-465-2361

Murray State College
1 Murray Campus St, Tishomingo OK 73460-3137
580-371-2371

Northeastern Oklahoma A & M College
200 I St NE, Miami OK 74354-6434
Linda Oldham Barns, Director of Admissions
800-234-3409

Northern Oklahoma College
PO Box 310, Tonkawa OK 74653-0310
580-628-6200

Oklahoma City Community College
7777 S May Ave, Oklahoma City OK 73159-4419
405-682-1611

Oklahoma State University-Oklahoma City
900 N Portland Ave, Oklahoma City OK 73107-6120
405-947-4421

Oklahoma State University-Okmulgee
1801 E 4th St, Okmulgee OK 74447-3901
Cary Fox, Director of Admissions
800-722-4471

Redlands Community College
1300 S Country Club Rd, El Reno OK 73036-5300
Trish Hobson, Director of Admissions
405-262-2552

Rose State College
6420 SE 15th St, Midwest City OK 73110-2799
405-733-7300

Seminole State College
PO Box 351, Seminole OK 74818-0351
405-382-9950

Southwestern Oklahoma State University
409 E Mississippi Ave, Sayre OK 73662-1200
580-928-5533

SPARTAN COLLEGE OF AERONAUTICS AND TECHNOLOGY

8820 E Pine St, Tulsa OK 74115-5802
Director of Admissions
800-331-1204 Fax: 918-831-8609
Website: www.spartan.edu
E-mail: spartan@mail.spartan.edu

Established 1928. Coed. Accredited member school: ACCSCT. Providing Technical training and education in Avionics, Aviation Maintenance; Nondestructive Testing and Quality Control. Complete flight training program. Offering Diplomas, Associate of Applied Science and Bachelor of Science in Aviation Technology Management.

Tulsa Community College
3727 E Apache St, Tulsa OK 74115
918-595-7000

Tulsa Community College Southeast Campus
10300 E 81st St, Tulsa OK 74133
918-595-7000

Western Oklahoma State College
2801 N Main St, Altus OK 73521-1397
580-477-2000

OREGON

Apollo College
2004 Lloyd Ctr Fl 3, Portland OR 97232-1309
503-761-6100 Fax: 503-761-3351

Blue Mountain Community College
PO Box 100, Pendleton OR 97801-1000
541-276-1260

Central Oregon Community College
2600 NW College Way, Bend OR 97701-5933
Alicia Moore, Director of Admissions and Records
541-383-7500

Chemeketa Community College
PO Box 14007, Salem OR 97309-7070
Jeri Hunter, Director of Admissions
503-399-5106

Clackamas Community College
19600 S Molalla Ave, Oregon City OR 97045-7998
Cheryl Hollatz-Wisely, Director of Student Outreach
503-657-6958 ext. 2455

Clatsop Community College
1653 Jerome Ave, Astoria OR 97103-3698
503-325-0910

Klamath Community College
7390 S 6th St, Klamath Falls OR 97603
541-882-3521

Lane Community College
4000 E 30th Ave, Eugene OR 97405-0640
541-747-4501

Linn-Benton Community College
6500 Pacific Blvd SW, Albany OR 97321-3774
Christine Baker, Outreach Coordinator
541-917-4811 Fax: 541-917-4868
Website: www.linnbenton.edu
E-mail: admissions@linnbenton.edu

Mt. Hood Community College
26000 SE Stark St, Gresham OR 97030-3300
503-491-6422

Portland Community College
PO Box 19000, Portland OR 97280-0990
Dennis Bailey-Fougnier, Director of Admissions
503-977-4519

ROGUE COMMUNITY COLLEGE

3345 Redwood Hwy, Grants Pass OR 97527-9298
Peter Angstadt, President
Claudia Sullivan, Director of Enrollment Services
541-956-7500 Fax: 541-471-3585
Website: www.roguecc.edu
E-mail: csullivan@roguecc.edu

Established 1970. Public. Coed. Accreditation: NWASC. Tuition: $2,418. Enrollment: 10,000 full-time, 7,000 part-time. Faculty: 106 full-time, 372 part-time. Degrees offered: AA, AAS, AGS, AS. Programs in: Business technology, nursing, respiratory therapy, electronics, human services, fire science, automotive/diesel, computer science, criminal justice, construction technology, humanities, social science, and science/math.

Southwestern Oregon Community College
1988 Newmark Ave, Coos Bay OR 97420-2911
541-888-2525

Treasure Valley Community College
650 College Blvd, Ontario OR 97914-3423
541-889-6493

Umpqua Community College
PO Box 967, Roseburg OR 97470-0226
541-440-4600

PENNSYLVANIA

Allied Medical & Technical Institute
166 Slocum St, Forty Fort PA 18704-2936
570-288-8400

Antonelli Institute - Art & Photography
300 Montgomery Ave, Erdenheim PA 19038-8242
Dr. Thomas Treacy, President
215-836-2222 or 800-722-7871 Fax: 215-836-2794
Website: www.antonelli.edu
E-mail: admissions@antonelli.edu

Bradley Academy for the Visual Arts
1409 Williams Rd, York PA 17402-9012
James T. Hannigan, Jr., Director of Admissions
800-864-7725

Bucks County Community College
Swamp Rd, Newtown PA 18940
215-968-8000

Butler County Community College
PO Box 1203, Butler PA 16003-1203
724-287-8711

Cambria-Rowe Business College
221 Central Ave, Johnstown PA 15902-2406
814-536-5168

Commonwealth Technical Institute
Hiram G. Andrews Center
727 Goucher St, Johnstown PA 15905-3025
Joseph R. Rizzo, Sr., Contact
814-255-8200

Community College of Allegheny County
8701 Perry Hwy, Pittsburgh PA 15237-5353
412-366-7000

Community College of Allegheny County
Allegheny Campus: 808 Ridge Ave, Pittsburgh PA 15212 Admissions: 412.237.2700
Boyce Campus: 595 Beatty Rd, Monroeville PA 15146 Admissions: 724.325.6614
North Campus: 8701 Perry Highway, Pittsburgh PA 15237 Admissions: 412.369.3600
South Campus: 1750 Clairton Rd, West Mifflin PA 15122 Admissions: 412-469-4301
Website: www.ccac.edu

Community College of Allegheny County
Boyce Campus
595 Beatty Rd, Monroeville PA 15146-1348
724-325-1327

Community College of Allegheny County
South Campus
1750 Clairton Rd, West Mifflin PA 15122-3029
412-469-1100

Community College of Beaver County
1 Campus Dr, Monaca PA 15061-2566
724-775-8561 Fax: 724-775-4687
Website: www.ccbc.edu
E-mail: admissions@ccbc.edu

Community College of Philadelphia
1700 Spring Garden St, Philadelphia PA 19130-3936
215-751-8010

Delaware County Community College
901 Media Line Rd, Media PA 19063-1094
610-359-5000

Erie Business Center South
170 Cascade Galleria, New Castle PA 16101
724-658-9066

Erie Institute of Technology
940 Millcreek Mall, Erie PA 16565-1002
Barbara Bolt, Director of Admissions
814-868-9900

Harcum College
750 Montgomery Ave, Bryn Mawr PA 19010-3476
610-525-4100

Harrisburg Area Community College
1 HACC Dr, Harrisburg PA 17110-2999
717-780-2300

Johnson College
3427 N Main Ave, Scranton PA 18508-1495
Dr. Ann L. Pipinski, President & CEO
Melissa Ide, Director of Enrollment Management
800-2WE-WORK or 570-342-6404 ext. 125
Fax: 570-348-2181
Website: www.johnson.edu
E-mail: admit@johnson.edu

Keystone College
PO Box 50, La Plume PA 18440-0200
570-945-5141

Lackawanna College
501 Vine St, Scranton PA 18509-3251
570-961-7810

Lansdale School of Business
201 Church Rd, North Wales PA 19454-4148
215-699-5700

Lehigh Carbon Community College
4525 Education Park Dr
Schnecksville PA 18078-2502
610-799-1134

Lehigh Valley College
2809 E Saucon Valley Rd
Center Valley PA 18034-8447
Sam Jarvis, Director of Marketing
800-227-9109 Fax: 610-791-7810
Website: www.lehighvalley.edu
E-mail: joshua.padron@lehighvalley.edu

Lock Haven University-Clearfield Campus
PO Box 1410, Clearfield PA 16830-5410
James C. Reeser, Dean of Admissions
814-765-0559

Luzerne County Community College
1333 S Prospect St, Nanticoke PA 18634-3899
800-377-5222 ext. 337

Manor College
700 Fox Chase Rd, Jenkintown PA 19046-4118
215-885-2360

McCann School of Business & Technology
47 S Main St, Mahanoy City PA 17948-2698
570-773-1820

McCann School of Business & Technology
2650 Woodglen Rd, Pottsville PA 17901-1335
570-622-7622

Montgomery County Community College
340 DeKalb Pike, Blue Bell PA 19422-1400
215-641-6300

Newport Business Institute
945 Greensburg Rd, Lower Burrell PA 15068-3929
Admissions Department
800-752-7695

Newport Business Institute
941 W 3rd St, Williamsport PA 17701-5855
570-326-2869

Northampton Co. Area Community College
3835 Green Pond Rd, Bethlehem PA 18020-7599
610-861-5300

Peirce College
1420 Pine St, Philadelphia PA 19102-4603
215-545-6400

Penn State Fayette
The Eberly Campus
PO Box 519, Uniontown PA 15401-0519
724-430-4100

Pennsylvania College of Technology
Mansfield Rd, Wellsboro PA 16901
570-724-7703

Pennsylvania Culinary Institute
717 Liberty Ave, Pittsburgh PA 15222-3500
Jason Remaley, V.P. of Enrollment Management Office
800-432-2433

Pennsylvania Highlands Community College
PO Box 68, Johnstown PA 15907-0068
814-532-5300

Pennsylvania Institute of Technology
800 Manchester Ave, Media PA 19063-4036
Dr. Paul N. Smith, President
Angela Cassetta, Dean of Enrollment Management
800-422-0025

Pennsylvania School of Business
406 W Hamilton St, Allentown PA 18101-1604
610-264-8029

Pennsylvania State University
1600 Woodland Rd, Abington PA 19001-3918
215-881-7300

Pennsylvania State University
3000 Ivyside Park, Altoona PA 16601-3760
814-949-5000

Pennsylvania State University
College Place, Du Bois PA 15801
814-375-4700

Pennsylvania State University
120 Ridgeview Dr, Dunmore PA 18512-1602
570-963-4757

Pennsylvania State University
8380 Mohr Ln, Fogelsville PA 18051-1918
610-285-5000

Pennsylvania State University
Hazelton Campus, Hazleton PA 18201
570-450-3000

Pennsylvania State University
0 University Dr, Mc Keesport PA 15132-7647
412-675-9000

Pennsylvania State University
25 Yearsley Mill Rd, Media PA 19063-5522
610-892-1350

Pennsylvania State University
Mont Alto Campus, Mont Alto PA 17237
717-749-6000

Pennsylvania State University
PO Box 7009, Reading PA 19610-6009
610-320-4800

Pennsylvania State University
200 University Dr, Schuylkill Haven PA 17972-2202
570-385-6000

Pennsylvania State University
147 Shenango Ave, Sharon PA 16146-1537
724-983-5800

Pennsylvania State University
1031 Edgecomb Ave, York PA 17403-3326
717-771-4000

Pennsylvania State University - Wilkes Barre
PO Box PSU, Lehman PA 18627-0217
John S. Barnes, Admissions Officer
800-966-6613

PIA School of Specialized Technology
PO Box 10897, Pittsburgh PA 15236-0897
Vincent J. Mezza, Director of Admissions
800-444-1440 Fax: 412-466-0513
Website: www.pia.edu
E-mail: admissions@pia.edu
See listing under "Aeronautics, Aviation and Space"

PITTSBURGH INSTITUTE OF MORTUARY SCIENCE
5808 Baum Blvd, Pittsburgh PA 15206-3706
Karen Rocco, Registrar
412-362-8500 Fax: 412-362-1684
Website: www.pims.edu
E-mail: pims5808@aol.com

Reading Area Community College
PO Box 1706, Reading PA 19603-1706
David J. Adams, Director of Admissions
610-607-6224

Thaddeus Stevens College of Technology
750 E King St, Lancaster PA 17602-3113
717-299-7730

Westmoreland County Community College
145 Pavilion Ln, Youngwood PA 15697
724-925-4000

RHODE ISLAND

Community College of Rhode Island
Flanagan Campus
1762 Louisquisset Pike, Lincoln RI 02865-4513
Elizabeth A. Mancini, Assistant Dean of Enrollment Services
401-825-2003

Community College of Rhode Island
Knight Campus
400 East Ave, Warwick RI 02886-1805
Elizabeth A. Mancini, Assistant Dean of Enrollment Services
401-825-2003

Community College of Rhode Island
Providence Campus
1 Hilton St, Providence RI 02905-2313
Elizabeth A. Mancini, Assistant Dean of Enrollment Services
401-828-8146

SOUTH CAROLINA

Aiken Technical College
PO Box 696, Aiken SC 29802-0796
803-593-9231

Central Carolina Technical College
506 N Guignard Dr, Sumter SC 29150-2499
803-778-1961

Clinton Junior College
1029 Crawford Rd, Rock Hill SC 29730
803-327-7402

Denmark Technical College
PO Box 327, Denmark SC 29042-0327
803-793-5149

ECPI College of Technology
1001 Keys Dr #100, Greenville SC 29615
864-288-2828

Florence-Darlington Technical College
PO Box 100548, Florence SC 29501-0548
843-661-8324

FORREST JUNIOR COLLEGE
601 E River St, Anderson SC 29624-2405
Pamela Johnson, MBA, President
864-225-7653 Fax: 864-261-7471
Website: www.forrestcollege.edu
E-mail: info@forrestcollege.edu
Established 1946. Private. Coed. Accreditation: ACICS. Tuition: $110 per quarter hour. Fees: $250. Enrollment: 230 full-time, 10 part-time. Faculty: 38. Student-faculty ratio: 18:1. Degrees: Associate in Applied Science. Library: 5,000 volumes + online Learning Resource Network Library. 2 buildings on 3.5 acres. Small, personalized instruction. Career, Entrepreneurship oriented. Caters to working adults with children.

Greenville Technical College
PO Box 5616, Greenville SC 29606-5616
Carolyn Watkins, Dean of Admissions
800-723-0673 (US) or 800-922-1183 (SC)
Website: www.greenvilletech.com

Horry-Georgetown Technical College
PO Box 261966, Conway SC 29528-6066
843-349-5277

Horry-Georgetown Technical College
743 Hemlock Ave, Myrtle Beach SC 29577-5044
843-477-0808

Midlands Technical College
PO Box 2408, Columbia SC 29202-2408
803-738-8324

Northeastern Technical College
PO Box 1007, Cheraw SC 29520-1007
843-537-5286

Orangeburg-Calhoun Technical College
3250 Saint Matthews Rd NE
Orangeburg SC 29118-8299
803-536-0311

Piedmont Technical College
PO Box 1467, Greenwood SC 29648-1467
864-941-8324

Spartanburg Community College
PO Box 4386, Spartanburg SC 29305-4386
Nancy Garmroth, Dean of Admissions & Financial Aid
864-592-4810 Fax: 864-592-4945
Website: sccsc.edu

Spartanburg Methodist College
1200 Textile Rd, Spartanburg SC 29301-0009
800-772-7286

Technical College of the Lowcountry
PO Box 1288, Beaufort SC 29901
843-525-8324

Tri-County Tech College
PO Box 587, Pendleton SC 29670-0587
864-646-8361

Trident Technical College
PO Box 118067, Charleston SC 29423-8067
843-574-6111

University of South Carolina
PO Box 617, Allendale SC 29810-0617
Jane T. Brewer, Associate Dean for Student Services
803-584-6314

University of South Carolina
PO Box 889, Lancaster SC 29721-0889
803-285-7471

University of South Carolina
200 Miller Rd, Sumter SC 29150-2478
803-775-6341

University of South Carolina
PO Box 729, Union SC 29379-0729
864-429-8728

Williamsburg Technical College
601 Martin Luther King Ave
Kingstree SC 29556-4197
843-354-2021

York Technical College
452 Anderson Rd S, Rock Hill SC 29730-7318
803-327-8000

SOUTH DAKOTA

Colorado Technical University
3901 W 59th St, Sioux Falls SD 57108
605-361-0200

Kilian Community College
300 E 6th St, Sioux Falls SD 57103
Jacque Danielson, Director of Admissions
605-221-3100

Oglala Lakota Community College
PO Box 861, Pine Ridge SD 57770-0861
605-867-5857

Sisseton Wahpeton Community College
PO Box 689, Sisseton SD 57262-0689
605-698-3966

TENNESSEE

Chattanooga State Technical Community College
4501 Amnicola Hwy, Chattanooga TN 37406-1018
423-697-4400

Cleveland State Community College
PO Box 3570, Cleveland TN 37320-3570
423-472-7141

Columbia State Community College
PO Box 1315, Columbia TN 38402-1315
931-540-2722

Draughons Junior College
1860 Wilma Rudolph Blvd, Clarksville TN 37040-6718
Christi Nolder, Director of Admissions
931-552-7600

Draughons Junior College
340 Plus Park Blvd, Nashville TN 37217
615-361-7555

DRAUGHONS JUNIOR COLLEGE - MURFREESBORO
415 Golden Bear Ct, Murfreesboro TN 37128
615-217-9347 Fax: 615-217-9348
Website: www.draughons.org

Dyersburg State Community College
1516 Lake Rd, Dyersburg TN 38024-2411
731-286-3200

Hiwassee College
225 Hiwassee College Dr, Madisonville TN 37354
Jodie Moser, Director of Admissions
423-442-2001

ITT Technical Institute
10208 Technology Dr, Knoxville TN 37932-3343
865-671-2800

Jackson State Community College
2046 N Parkway, Jackson TN 38301-3797
731-424-3520

John A. Gupton College
1616 Church St, Nashville TN 37203-2934
615-327-3927

Martin Methodist College
433 W Madison St, Pulaski TN 38478-2716
800-727-1273

MEDVANCE INSTITUTE
1025 Highway 111, Cookeville TN 38501-4305
Shirley Cole, Campus Director
866-86-GO-MED or 931-526-3660 Fax: 931-372-2603
Website: www.medvance.edu

Motlow State Community College
PO Box 8500, Lynchburg TN 37352-8500
931-393-1500

Nashville State Technical Community College
120 White Bridge Pike, Nashville TN 37209-4515
615-353-3333

National College
1328 Highway 11W, Bristol TN 37620
Becky Wild, Director of Admissions
423-878-4440 Fax: 423-793-1060
Website: www.national-college.edu
E-mail: info@national-college.edu

National College of Business & Technology
3748 Nolensville Pike, Nashville TN 37211-3322
Lynda Dandridge, Director of Admissions
615-333-3344 Fax: 615-333-3429
Website: www.national-college.edu
E-mail: info@national-college.edu

Northeast State Technical Community College
PO Box 246, Blountville TN 37617-0246
423-323-3191

Nossi College of Art
907 Rivergate Pkwy Ste E6, Goodlettsville TN 37072
Cyrus Vatandoost, Executive Director
615-851-1088

Pellissippi State Technical Community College
PO Box 22990, Knoxville TN 37933-0990
Donna Mack, Contact
865-694-6568

Remington College
2731 Nonconnah Blvd #160
Memphis TN 38132-2131
901-345-1000

Roane State Community College
276 Patton Ln, Harriman TN 37748-8664
865-354-3000

Southwest Tennessee Community College
5983 Macon Cove, Memphis TN 38134
Vanessa R. Dowdy, Director of Admissions
901-333-5000 Fax: 901-333-4523
Website: www.southwest.tn.edu
E-mail: vdowdy@southwest.tn.edu

State Technical Institute
5983 Macon Cv, Memphis TN 38134-7642
901-377-4111

Volunteer State Community College
1480 Nashville Pike, Gallatin TN 37066-3188
615-452-8600

Walters State Community College
500 S Davy Crockett Pkwy
Morristown TN 37813-6899
423-585-2600

TEXAS

Alvin Community College
3110 Mustang Rd, Alvin TX 77511-4807
281-756-3531

Amarillo College
PO Box 447, Amarillo TX 79178-0001
806-371-5000

Angelina College
PO Box 1768, Lufkin TX 75902-1768
Dr. Larry M. Phillips, President
Judith M. Cutting, Director of Admissions/Registration
936-639-1301

Art Institute of Houston
1900 Yorktown St, Houston TX 77056
Brian A. Shumaker, Director of Admissions
800-275-4244

Austin Community College
5930 Middle Fiskville Rd, Austin TX 78752-4390
512-223-7598

Blinn College
902 College Ave, Brenham TX 77833-4098
Dennis K. Crowson, Registrar
979-830-4000

Blinn College
PO Box 6030, Bryan TX 77805-6030
Dennis K. Crowson, Registrar
979-209-7200

Blinn College
100 Ranger Dr, Schulenburg TX 78956-2247
Dennis K. Crowson, Registrar
979-743-5003

Blinn College
3701 Outlet Center Dr, Sealy TX 77474
Dennis K. Crowson, Registrar
979-627-7997

Brookhaven College
3939 Valley View Ln, Farmers Branch TX 75244-4997
972-860-4700

Cedar Valley College
3030 N Dallas Ave, Lancaster TX 75134-3799
972-860-8200

Central Texas College
PO Box 1800, Killeen TX 76540-1800
Lillian Kroeger, Director of Admissions
254-526-1104

Cisco Junior College
101 College Hts, Cisco TX 76437
254-442-2567

Clarendon College
PO Box 968, Clarendon TX 79226-0968
806-874-3571

Coastal Bend College
3800 Charco Rd, Beeville TX 78102-2197
361-358-2838

College of Biblical Studies
7000 Regency Square Blvd Ste 110
Houston TX 77036-3211
713-785-5995

College of the Mainland
1200 N Amburn Rd, Texas City TX 77591-2499
409-938-1211

Collin County Community College
4800 Preston Park Blvd, Plano TX 75093
972-881-5790

Commonwealth Institute of Funeral Service
415 Barren Springs Dr, Houston TX 77090-5918
281-873-0262

COVENANT SCHOOL OF NURSING AND ALLIED HEALTH

2002 W Loop 289 Ste 120, Lubbock TX 79407-7701
Admissions
806-797-0955 Fax: 806-793-0720
Website: www.covenantson.com
E-mail: admissionscsn@covhs.org

Del Mar College
101 Baldwin Blvd, Corpus Christi TX 78404-3894
361-698-1200

Eastfield College
3737 Motley Dr, Mesquite TX 75150-2099
214-860-7002

El Centro College
801 Main St, Dallas TX 75202-3698
214-860-2037

El Paso Community College
PO Box 20500, El Paso TX 79998-0500
915-831-2000

Frank Phillips College
PO Box 5118, Borger TX 79008-5118
806-274-5311

Galveston College
4015 Avenue Q, Galveston TX 77550-7496
Brian Lowery, Registrar
409-763-6551 Fax: 409-944-1501
Website: www.gc.edu
E-mail: blowery@gc.edu

Grayson County College
6101 Grayson Dr, Denison TX 75020
903-465-6030

Hill College - Hill County Campus
PO Box 619, Hillsboro TX 76645-0619
W. R. Auvenshine, President
254-582-2555

Hill College - Johnson County Campus
PO Box 1899, Cleburne TX 76033-1899
Pam Boehm, V.P. Student Services
817-641-9887

Houston Community College
PO Box 667517, Houston TX 77266-7517
713-718-2000

Howard College
1001 N Birdwell Ln, Big Spring TX 79720-0213
915-264-5022

Howard College
3200 Avenue C, Big Spring TX 79720
Brooke Everett, Contact
432-264-3700

Howard College
3197 Executive Dr, San Angelo TX 76904-6801
LeAnne Byrd, Contact
325-944-9585

ITT Technical Institute
551 Ryan Plaza Dr, Arlington TX 76011
817-794-5100

ITT Technical Institute
6330 E Highway 290 Ste 150, Austin TX 78723-1035
Willard Real, Director of Admissions
512-467-6800 Fax: 512-467-6677
Website: www.itt-tech.edu
E-mail: wreal@itt-tech.edu

ITT Technical Institute
2101 Waterview Pkwy, Richardson TX 75080-2208
972-279-0500

ITT Technical Institute
5700 Northwest Pkwy, San Antonio TX 78249-3303
Doug Howard, Director of Recruitment
210-694-4612

ITT TECHNICAL INSTITUTE

1001 Magnolia Ave, Webster TX 77598-2070
Roy Johnson, Registrar
281-316-4700 Fax: 281-316-4750
Website: www.itt.tech.edu

JACKSONVILLE COLLEGE

105 B J Albritton Dr, Jacksonville TX 75766-4759
Tam Clark, Academic Dean
903-586-2518 Fax: 903-586-0743
Website: www.jacksonville-college.edu
E-mail: acadean@jacksonville-college.edu

Established 1899. Private. Coed. Accreditation: SACS. Tuition: $5,600. Room and board: $2,746. Fees: $520. Enrollment: 220 full-time, 80 part-time. Faculty: 18. Student-faculty ratio: 15:1. Degrees: AA, AS, Junior College Diploma. Library: 23,000 volumes. 12 buildings on 18 acres. Quality education in a Christian environment. Outstanding music department with traveling choir, vocal and wind ensembles. International student office. NJCAA men's and women's basketball.

KD Studio - Actors Conservatory
2600 N Stemmons Fwy Ste 117
Dallas TX 75207-2168
T. A. Taylor, Director of Education
877-278-2283 Fax: 214-630-5140
Website: www.kdstudio.com
E-mail: admissions@kdstudio.com
See listing under "Career Schools"

Kilgore College
1100 Broadway Blvd, Kilgore TX 75662-3299
Ray McLeod, Director, Marketing & Enrollment
903-984-8531

LAMAR INSTITUTE OF TECHNOLOGY

855 E Lavaca St, Beaumont TX 77705
409-880-8321
Website: www.lit.edu
E-mail: comments@lit.edu

Lamar State College-Orange
410 W Front St, Orange TX 77630-5899
Rebecca Campbell, Registrar
409-883-7750

Lamar State College-Port Arthur
PO Box 310, Port Arthur TX 77641-0310
409-983-4921

Laredo Community College
1 W End Washington St, Laredo TX 78040-4348
956-722-0521

Lee College
PO Box 818, Baytown TX 77522-0818
Dr. Dennis Dressler, Director of Admissions
281-427-5611

Lon Morris College
800 College Ave, Jacksonville TX 75766
903-589-4000

McLennan Community College
1400 College Dr, Waco TX 76708-1498
Karen Clark, Coordinator, Student Admissions
254-299-8000 Fax: 254-299-8964
Website: www.mclennan.edu
E-mail: kclark@mclennan.edu

MedVance Institute
6220 W Park #180, Houston TX 77057
713-266-6594

Midland College
3600 N Garfield St, Midland TX 79705-6397
432-685-4500

Mountain View College
4849 W Illinois Ave, Dallas TX 75211-6599
214-860-8680

Navarro College
3200 W 7th Ave, Corsicana TX 75110-4899
903-874-6501

North Central Texas College
1525 W California St, Gainesville TX 76240-4636
Michelle Winters, Registrar
940-668-3315

Northeast Texas Community College
PO Box 1307, Mount Pleasant TX 75456-9991
903-572-1911

North Harris Montgomery Community College
250 N Sam Houston Parkway East, Houston TX 77060
281-260-3500

North Lake College
5001 N MacArthur Blvd, Irving TX 75038-3899
972-273-3000

Northwest Vista College
3535 N Ellison Dr, San Antonio TX 78251
210-348-2001

Odessa College
201 W University Blvd, Odessa TX 79764-7127
432-335-6400

Palo Alto College
1400 W Villaret Blvd, San Antonio TX 78224-2499
210-921-5000

Panola College
1109 W Panola St, Carthage TX 75633-2397
800-776-8153

Paris Junior College
2400 Clarksville St, Paris TX 75460-6298
903-785-7661

Ranger College
1100 College Cir, Ranger TX 76470-3298
254-647-3234

Remington College - Fort Worth Campus
300 E Loop 820, Fort Worth TX 76112-1280
Director of Recruitment
817-451-0017 Fax: 817-496-1257
Website: www.remingtoncollege.edu
E-mail: lynn.wey@remingtoncollege.edu

Richland College
12800 Abrams Rd, Dallas TX 75243-2199
972-238-6100

St. Phillip's College
1801 Martin Luther King Dr
San Antonio TX 78203-2098
210-531-3200

San Antonio College
1300 San Pedro Ave, San Antonio TX 78212-4299
210-733-2000

Sanford-Brown Institute Houston
10500 Forum Place Dr, Houston TX 77036
713-779-1110

San Jacinto College
5800 Uvalde Rd, Houston TX 77049-4513
281-458-4050

San Jacinto College
13735 Beamer Rd, Houston TX 77089-6099
281-484-1900

San Jacinto College
8060 Spencer Hwy, Pasadena TX 77505-5998
281-476-1501

South Plains College
1401 College Ave, Levelland TX 79336-6595
Kimbra Quinn, Director of Enrollment Management
806-894-9611 ext. 2113

South Plains College - Reese Campus
9730 Reese Blvd, Lubbock TX 79416
Kimbra Quinn, Director of New Student Relations
806-894-9611 ext. 2113

South Texas College
3201 Pecan Blvd, Mc Allen TX 78501-6661
956-631-4922

Southwest Texas Junior College
2401 Garner Field Rd, Uvalde TX 78801-6221
Joe C. Barker, Dean of Admissions
830-278-4401

Tarrant County Junior College
Northeast Campus
828 W Harwood Rd, Hurst TX 76054-3299
Cathie J. Jackson, Director of Admissions and Records
817-515-6100

Tarrant County Junior College
Northwest Campus
4801 Marine Creek Pkwy, Fort Worth TX 76179-3599
Cathie J. Jackson, Director of Admissions and Records
817-515-7100

Tarrant County Junior College
South Campus
5301 Campus Dr, Fort Worth TX 76119-5998
Cathie J. Jackson, Director of Admissions and Records
817-515-4100

Tarrant County Junior College
Southeast Campus
2100 Southeast Parkway, Arlington TX 76018
Cathie L. Jackson, Director of Admissions and Records
817-515-3100

Temple College
2600 S 1st St, Temple TX 76504-7435
Toni Borras, Director of Admissions & Records
254-298-8808 Fax: 254-298-8288
Website: www.templejc.edu
E-mail: admissionsrecords@templejc.edu

Texarkana Community College
2500 N Robison Rd, Texarkana TX 75501-3078
903-838-4541

Texas Culinary Academy
11400 Burnet Rd #2100, Austin TX 78758-3403
Paula M. Paulette, Vice President of Marketing & Admissions
512-837-2665

Texas Southmost College
80 Fort Brown St, Brownsville TX 78520-4993
956-544-3879

Texas State Technical College
1901 N Loop 499, Harlingen TX 78550
956-364-4001

Texas State Technical College Marshall
2650 E End Blvd S, Marshall TX 75672
903-935-1010

Texas State Technical College - Waco
3801 Campus Dr, Waco TX 76705-1696
Dawn Khoury, Director of Admissions
254-799-3611

Texas State Technical College
West Texas
300 Homer K Taylor Dr, Sweetwater TX 79556-4108
325-235-7300

Trinity Valley Community College
100 Cardinal St, Athens TX 75751
903-677-8822

Trinity Valley Community College
800 W Highway 243, Kaufman TX 75142-1899
972-932-4309

TYLER JUNIOR COLLEGE

PO Box 9020, Tyler TX 75711-9020
Joel Renaud, Director of Enrollment Management
903-510-2398 or 800-687-5680 ext. 2399
Fax: 903-510-2161
Website: www.tjc.edu
E-mail: jren@tjc.edu

Established 1926. Public. Coed. Accreditation: SACS. Tuition: $1,760. Room and board: $3,700. Enrollment: 9,000 full-time, 4,200 part-time. Faculty: 300. Student-faculty ratio: 20-25:1. Degrees offered: AA, AAS, Certificate. 30 buildings on 73 acres. Strong Liberal Arts - College Transfer. 35 Vocational Technical Programs. Strong Allied Health program. Outstanding Music-Drama department. Excellent Science, Mathematics program. Athletic programs: football, baseball, men's & women's basketball, men's & women's golf, women's volleyball, tennis, and soccer. Residential Life: 600 spaces available and Support Services available.

Vernon College
4400 College Dr, Vernon TX 76384-4092
940-552-6291

Victoria College
2200 E Red River St, Victoria TX 77901-4494
361-573-3291

WADE COLLEGE

Dallas Market Center, Suite 158
PO Box 421149, Dallas TX 75342
800-624-4850 or 214-637-3530 Fax: 214-637-0827
Harry Davros, President
Suzun Wade, Executive Director
Tanisha Shaw, Director of Academic Affairs
Website: www.wadecollege.edu

E-mail: admissions@wadecollege.edu
Established 1962. Coed. Private. Accreditation: SACS Commission on Colleges. Tuition: $9,300. Room: $3,600. Fees: $125. Enrollment: 250. Faculty: 20. Student - faculty ratio: 15:1. Degrees: AA in Merchandising and Design. Library: 5,000 volumes. Part of the world's largest wholesale merchandising complex - the Dallas Market Center.

Weatherford College
225 College Park Dr, Weatherford TX 76086
Dr. Joe Birmingham, President
800-287-5471 Fax: 817-598-6205
Website: www.wc.edu
E-mail: willingham@wc.edu

Western Texas College
6200 College Ave, Snyder TX 79549-6189
Deborah Baremore, Director of College Relations
888-GO-TO-WTC (468-6982)

Wharton County Junior College
911 E Boling Hwy, Wharton TX 77488-3298
979-532-4560

UTAH

College of Eastern Utah
451 E 400 N, Price UT 84501-2699
435-637-2120

Dixie State College of Utah
225 S 700 E, Saint George UT 84770-3876
435-652-7500

ITT TECHNICAL INSTITUTE
920 Levoy Dr, Murray UT 84123-2500
Gary Wood, Director of Recruitment
801-263-3313 Fax: 801-263-3497
Website: www.itt-tech.edu
E-mail: gwood@itt-tech.edu

L.D.S. BUSINESS COLLEGE
95 North 300 West, Salt Lake City UT 84101-3500
Kathleen Howe, Assistant Director of Admissions
801-524-8145 Fax: 801-524-1900
Website: www.ldsbc.edu
E-mail: admissions@ldsbc.edu
See listing under "Career Schools"

Mountain West College
3280 W 3500 S, West Valley City UT 84119
John Rios, Director of Admissions
801-840-4800

Salt Lake Community College
PO Box 30808, Salt Lake City UT 84130-0808
801-957-4111

Snow College
150 College Ave, Ephraim UT 84627-1299
435-283-7000

Stevens Henager College
755 Main St, Logan UT 84321
Josh Swayne, Executive Director
435-713-4777
Website: www.stevenshenager.edu

Stevens Henager College
1476 Sandhill Rd, Orem UT 84058-7310
801-375-5455

Stevens Henager College
383 W Vine St, Salt Lake City UT 84123
801-261-7600

Utah Valley State College
800 W University Pkwy, Orem UT 84058-0001
801-222-8000

VERMONT

Community College of Vermont
PO Box 120, Waterbury VT 05676-0120
802-241-3535

Landmark College
PO Box 820, River Rd S, Putney VT 05346-0820
Dale Herold, Dean of Admissions
802-387-6718

Sterling College
PO Box 72, Craftsbury Common VT 05827
802-586-7711

Vermont Technical College
PO Box 500, Randolph Center VT 05061
802-728-1000

VIRGINIA

Blue Ridge Community College
PO Box 80, Weyers Cave VA 24486-0080
540-234-9261

Bryant & Stratton College
8141 Hull St Rd, Richmond VA 23235-6411
David K. Mayle, Director of Admissions
804-745-2444 Fax: 804-745-6884
Website: www.bryantstratton.edu
E-mail: dkmayle@bryantstratton.edu

Bryant & Stratton College
301 Centre Pointe Dr, Virginia Beach VA 23462-4417
Tracy Nannery, Director
757-499-7900

Central Virginia Community College
3506 Wards Rd, Lynchburg VA 24502-2498
804-832-7600

Dabney S. Lancaster Community College
PO Box 1000, Clifton Forge VA 24422-1000
540-863-2800

Danville Community College
1008 S Main St, Danville VA 24541-4088
804-797-2222

Eastern Shore Community College
29300 Lankford Hwy, Melfa VA 23410-3000
757-787-5900

ECPI College of Technology
10021 Balls Ford Rd #100, Manassas VA 20109-2666
703-330-5300

ECPI College of Technology
1001 Omni Blvd Ste 100
Newport News VA 23606-4215
757-838-9191

ECPI College of Technology
5555 Greenwich Rd Ste 300
Virginia Beach VA 23462-6542
757-671-7171 Fax: 757-671-8661
Website: www.ecpi.edu

ECPI Technical College
800 Moorefield Park Dr, Richmond VA 23236-3686
804-330-5533

ECPI Technical College
5234 Airport Rd NW, Roanoke VA 24012-1603
540-563-8080

Germanna Community College
2130 Germanna Hwy, Locust Grove VA 22508
540-727-3000

ITT Technical Institute
500 Granby St # 3A, Norfolk VA 23510-1902
757-466-1260

ITT Technical Institute
300 Gateway Center Pkwy, Richmond VA 23235
804-330-4992

Jefferson College of Health Sciences
Formerly Community Hospital
PO Box 13186, Roanoke VA 24031-3186
Judith McKeon, Director of Admissions
540-985-8483

John Tyler Community College
13101 Jefferson Davis Hwy, Chester VA 23831-5316
800-522-3490

J. Sargeant Reynolds Community College
PO Box 85622, Richmond VA 23285-5622
804-371-3000

Lord Fairfax Community College
173 Skirmisher Ln, Middletown VA 22645-1745
800-906-5322

Mountain Empire Community College
3441 Mountain Empire Rd
Big Stone Gap VA 24219-0700
276-523-2400

National College
100 Logan St, Bluefield VA 24605
Tonya Elmore, Director of Admissions
276-326-3621 Fax: 276-322-5731
Website: www.national-college.edu
E-mail: info@national-college.edu

National College
1819 Emmet St N, Charlottesville VA 22901-2812
434-295-0136 Fax: 434-979-8061
Website: www.national-college.edu
E-mail: info@national-college.edu

National College
336 Old Riverside Dr, Danville VA 24541
Jeff Moore, Director of Admissions
434-793-6822 Fax: 434-793-3634
Website: www.national-college.edu
E-mail: info@national-college.edu

National College
1515 Country Club Rd, Harrisonburg VA 22802
Kathy Sours, Director of Admissions
540-432-0943 Fax: 540-432-1133
Website: www.national-college.edu
E-mail: info@national-college.edu

National College
104 Candlewood Ct, Lynchburg VA 24502-2653
Nancy Fortune, Director of Admissions
434-239-3500 Fax: 434-239-3948
Website: www.national-college.edu
E-mail: info@national-college.edu

National College
10 Church St, Martinsville VA 24114
Barbara Rakes, Director of Admissions
276-632-5621 Fax: 276-632-7915
Website: www.national-college.edu
E-mail: info@national-college.edu

New River Community College
PO Box 1127, Dublin VA 24084-1127
540-674-3600

Northern Virginia Community College
3001 N Beauregard St, Alexandria VA 22311-5065
703-845-6200

Northern Virginia Community College
4001 Wakefield Chapel Rd, Annandale VA 22003
703-323-3000

Northern Virginia Community College
6901 Sudley Rd, Manassas VA 20109-2305
703-368-0184

Northern Virginia Community College
1000 Harry Flood Byrd Hwy, Sterling VA 20164-8699
703-323-3000

Northern Virginia Community College
15200 Neabsco Mills Rd
Woodbridge VA 22191-4006
703-670-2191

Patrick Henry Community College
PO Box 5311, Martinsville VA 24115-5311
276-638-8777

Paul D. Camp Community College
100 N College Dr, Franklin VA 23851-2422
757-569-6700

Piedmont Virginia Community College
501 College Dr, Charlottesville VA 22902
804-977-3900

Rappahannock Community College
12745 College Dr, Saluda VA 23149
804-758-6700

Rappahannock Community College
52 Campus Dr, Warsaw VA 22572-4272
804-333-6700

Richard Bland College
11301 Johnson Rd, Petersburg VA 23805-7100
804-862-6100

Southside Virginia Community College
109 Campus Dr, Alberta VA 23821-2930
Ronald E. Mattox, Dean of Admissions
434-949-1014 Fax: 434-949-7863
Website: www.sv.vccs.edu
E-mail: ronald.mattox@sv.vccs.edu

Southside Virginia Community College
200 Daniel Rd, Keysville VA 23947
Ronald E. Mattox, Dean of Admissions
434-736-2018 Fax: 434-736-2082
Website: www.sv.vccs.edu
E-mail: ronald.mattox@sv.vccs.edu

Southwest Virginia Community College
PO Box SVCC, Richlands VA 24641-1101
276-964-2555

Thomas Nelson Community College
PO Box 9407, Hampton VA 23670-0407
757-825-2700

Tidewater Community College
1428 Cedar Rd, Chesapeake VA 23322-7199
757-547-9271

Tidewater Community College
121 College Pl, Norfolk VA 23510
757-822-1030

Tidewater Community College
State Route 135, Portsmouth VA 23703
757-484-2121

Tidewater Community College
1700 College Cres, Virginia Beach VA 23453-1999
757-468-6348

Virginia Highlands Community College
PO Box 828, Abingdon VA 24212-0828
276-676-5484

Virginia Western Community College
PO Box 14007, Roanoke VA 24038-4007
540-857-7311

Wytheville Community College
1000 E Main St, Wytheville VA 24382-3308
276-223-4700

WASHINGTON

Apollo College
10102 E Knox Ave, Spokane WA 99206-4146
509-532-8888 Fax: 509-533-5983

Bellevue Community College
3000 Landerholm Cir SE, Bellevue WA 98007-6484
425-564-1000

Big Bend Community College
7662 Chanute St NE, Moses Lake WA 98837-3299
509-762-5351

Centralia College
600 Centralia College Blvd, Centralia WA 98531
360-736-9391

Clark College
1800 E McLoughlin Blvd, Vancouver WA 98663-3598
360-992-2000

Columbia Basin College
2600 N 20th Ave, Pasco WA 99301-3379
509-547-0511

Edmonds Community College
20000 68th Ave W, Lynnwood WA 98036-5999
425-640-1500

Everest College
2156 Pacific Ave, Tacoma WA 98402
253-207-4000

Everett Community College
2000 Tower St, Everett WA 98201
Christine Kerlin, Associate Dean
425-388-9100 Fax: 425-388-9173
Website: www.everettcc.edu
E-mail: ckerlin@everettcc.edu

Grays Harbor College
1620 Edward P Smith Dr, Aberdeen WA 98520-7599
360-532-9020

Green River Community College
12401 SE 320th St, Auburn WA 98092-3622
253-833-9111

Highline Community College
PO Box 98000, Des Moines WA 98198-9800
206-878-3710

ITT Technical Institute
12720 Gateway Dr S Ste 100, Seattle WA 98168
Donna L. Green, Director
206-244-3300

ITT Technical Institute
13518 E Indiana Ave, Spokane Valley WA 99216
Greg Alexander, Director of Admissions
509-926-2900

Lower Columbia College
PO Box 3010, Longview WA 98632-0310
360-577-2300

North Seattle Community College
9600 College Way N, Seattle WA 98103-3599
206-527-3600
Website: www.northseattle.edu
E-mail: nsccinfo@sccd.ctc.edu

NORTHWEST INDIAN COLLEGE
2522 Kwina Rd, Bellingham WA 98226-9278
Crystal Bagby, Director of Admissions
360-676-2772 Fax: 360-392-4333
Website: www.nwic.edu/
E-mail: cbagby@nwic.edu

Olympic College
1600 Chester Ave, Bremerton WA 98337-1699
360-792-7479

Peninsula College
1502 E Lauridsen Blvd, Port Angeles WA 98362-6698
360-452-9277

Pierce College Fort Steilacoom
9401 Farwest Dr SW, Lakewood WA 98498-1999
Cherilyn Williams, Communications Coordinator
253-964-6435

Pierce College Puyallup
1601 39th Ave SE, Puyallup WA 98374-2210
Ruth Schindler, Admissions Coordinator
253-840-8470

RENTON TECHNICAL COLLEGE
3000 NE 4th St, Renton WA 98056-4195
Don Bressler, President
Becky Riverman, Registrar
425-235-2352 or 425-235-5840 Fax: 425-235-7832
Website: www.RTC.edu
E-mail: dgrant@RTC.edu
Established 1942. Coed. Accreditation: NASC. Enrollment: 3,356 (day). Faculty: 95. Degree: Associate's, Certificates of completion. 13 buildings on 30 acre main campus with many satellite locations. Day, evening and night training, retraining and upgrading in cooperation with industry for 16,000 total registrants.

Seattle Central Community College
1701 Broadway, Seattle WA 98122-2400
206-587-3800

SHORELINE COMMUNITY COLLEGE
16101 Greenwood Ave N, Shoreline WA 98133-5696
Chris Melton, Acting Registrar
206-546-4581 Fax: 206-546-5835
Website: www.shoreline.edu

Skagit Valley College
2405 E College Way, Mount Vernon WA 98273-5899
360-416-7600

South Puget Sound Community College
2011 Mottman Rd SW, Tumwater WA 98512-6292
360-754-7711

South Seattle Community College
6000 16th Ave SW, Seattle WA 98106-1499
206-764-5300

Spokane Community College
1810 N Greene St, Spokane WA 99217-5399
509-533-7000

Spokane Falls Community College
3410 W Fort George Wright Dr
Spokane WA 99224-5288
509-533-3500

Tacoma Community College
6501 S 19th St, Tacoma WA 98466
253-566-5000

WALLA WALLA COMMUNITY COLLEGE
500 Tausick Way, Walla Walla WA 99362-9270
Dr. Steven VanAusdle, President
509-527-4282 or 877-471-9292 Fax: 509-527-3661
Website: www.wwcc.edu
Established 1967. Public. State. Accreditation: NASC, SBCTC. Tuition: $2,048 resident, $2,407 non-resident. Faculty: 105. Library: over 36,000 volumes. Degree: AA or AS; Associate's degree for transfer & certified vocational programs such as enology & viticulture, farrier, cosmetology, business & commerce, culinary arts, mechanical & technical, and health science.

Wenatchee Valley College
PO Box 2058, Omak WA 98841
Alex Roberts, Director
509-422-7805

Wenatchee Valley College
1300 5th St, Wenatchee WA 98801-1799
Marco Azurdia, Dean, Student Development
509-682-6805

Whatcom Community College
237 W Kellogg Rd, Bellingham WA 98226-8003
360-676-2170

Yakima Valley Community College
PO Box 22520, Yakima WA 98907
509-574-4600

WEST VIRGINIA

Blue Ridge Community and Technical College
400 W Stephen St, Martinsburg WV 25401
Leslie See, Director of Enrollment
304-260-4380 Fax: 304-260-1752
Website: www.blueridgectc.edu
E-mail: lsee@blueridgectc.edu

Everest Institute
5514 Big Tyler Rd, Cross Lanes WV 25313-1304
304-776-6290

Huntington Junior College
900 5th Ave, Huntington WV 25701-2004
304-697-7550

New River Community & Technical College
167 Dye Dr, Beckley WV 25801
304-255-5812

Potomac State College of West Virginia University
101 Fort Ave Bldg 1, Keyser WV 26726-2694
304-788-6800

Southern West Virginia Community & Technical College
PO Box 2900, Mount Gay WV 25637
304-792-7160

Southern West Virginia Community & Technical College
Williamson WV 25661
304-235-2800

Valley College of Technology
616 Harrison St, Princeton WV 24740-3141
304-425-2323

West Virginia Junior College
176 Thompson Dr, Bridgeport WV 26330
Kathryn Stanley, Director of Admissions
304-842-4007 Fax: 304-842-8191
Website: www.wvjcinfo.net
E-mail: kstanley@wvjcinfo.net

West Virginia Northern Community College
150 Park Ave, Weirton WV 26062-3797
Frank Targoss, Counselor
304-723-2210

West Virginia Northern Community College
1704 Market St, Wheeling WV 26003-3643
304-233-5900

WV State Community & Technical College
PO Box 1000, Institute WV 25112
304-766-3118

WISCONSIN

Blackhawk Technical College
PO Box 5009, Janesville WI 53547-5009
Gregg Bosak, Administration, Community Information
608-757-7769 Fax: 608-757-7740
Website: www.blackhawk.edu
E-mail: gbosak@blackhawk.edu

Bryant & Stratton College
310 W Wisconsin Ave Suite 500, Milwaukee WI 53203
Kathryn Cotey, Director of Admissions
414-276-5200

Chippewa Valley Technical College
620 W Clairemont Ave, Eau Claire WI 54701-6162
Admissions Office
715-833-6246

College of Menominee Nation
PO Box 1179, Keshena WI 54135-1179
Cynthia Norton, Admissions Representative
715-799-5600

Fox Valley Technical College
PO Box 2277, Appleton WI 54912-2277
Bob Burdick, Registrar
920-735-5600

Fox Valley Technical College
150 N Campbell Rd, Oshkosh WI 54902-3498
920-735-5600

Gateway Technical College
400 County Road H, Elkhorn WI 53121-2046
Zina Haywood, Director of Admissions
262-741-8200

Gateway Technical College
3520 30th Ave, Kenosha WI 53144-1690
Zina Haywood, Director of Admissions
262-564-2200

Gateway Technical College
1001 S Main St, Racine WI 53403-1582
Zina Haywood, Director of Admissions
262-619-6200

Herzing College
5218 E Terrace Dr, Madison WI 53718-8340
Donald Madelung, President
800-582-1227 Fax: 608-249-8593
Website: www.herzing.edu
E-mail: info@msn.herzing.edu
See listing under "Universities"

ITT Technical Institute
6300 W Layton Ave, Milwaukee WI 53220-4612
414-282-9494

Lac Courte Oreilles Ojibwa Community College
13466 W Trepania Rd, Hayward WI 54843
715-634-4790

Madison Area Technical College
3550 Anderson St, Madison WI 53704-2599
608-246-6282

Madison Area Technical College
1300 W Main St, Watertown WI 53098-3526
920-261-3303

Mid-State Technical College
2600 W 5th St, Marshfield WI 54449-3209
715-387-2538

Mid-State Technical College
933 Michigan Ave, Stevens Point WI 54481-3195
715-344-3063

Mid-State Technical College
500 32nd St N, Wisconsin Rapids WI 54494-5512
715-423-5300

Milwaukee Area Technical College
5555 W Highland Rd, Mequon WI 53092-1143
262-238-2200

Milwaukee Area Technical College
700 W State St, Milwaukee WI 53233-1419
414-297-6600

Milwaukee Area Technical College
6665 S Howell Ave, Oak Creek WI 53154-1107
414-762-2500

Milwaukee Area Technical College
1200 S 71st St, West Allis WI 53214-3110
414-476-3040

Moraine Park Technical College
700 Gould St, Beaver Dam WI 53916-1994
920-887-1101

Moraine Park Technical College
235 N National Ave, Fond du Lac WI 54935
920-922-8611

Moraine Park Technical College
2151 N Main St, West Bend WI 53090-1598
262-334-3413

Nicolet Area Technical College
PO Box 518, Rhinelander WI 54501-0518
715-365-4410

Northcentral Technical College
1000 W Campus Dr, Wausau WI 54401-1880
Carolyn Michalski, Director of Admissions
715-675-3331

Northeast Wisconsin Technical College
PO Box 19042, Green Bay WI 54307-9042
800-422-NWTC

Northeast Wisconsin Technical College
1601 University Dr, Marinette WI 54143-4132
800-422-NWTC

Northeast Wisconsin Technical College
229 N 14th Ave, Sturgeon Bay WI 54235-1317
800-422-NWTC

Southwest Wisconsin Technical College
1800 Bronson Blvd, Fennimore WI 53809-9778
Student Services/Admissions
800-362-3322 ext. 2354

University of Wisconsin Barron County
1800 College Dr, Rice Lake WI 54868-2414
Dale Fenton, Director of Student Services
715-234-8024

University of Wisconsin Center
2909 Kellogg Ave, Janesville WI 53546-5606
608-755-2823

University of Wisconsin Center
705 Viebahn St, Manitowoc WI 54220-6601
920-683-4707

University of Wisconsin Center
1478 Midway Rd, Menasha WI 54952-1224
920-832-2620

University of Wisconsin Center
1200 US Hwy 14 W, Richland Center WI 53581-1316
608-647-6186

University of Wisconsin Center
1 University Dr, Sheboygan WI 53081-4760
920-459-3733

University of Wisconsin Center
400 S University Dr, West Bend WI 53095-3699
262-335-5201

University of Wisconsin Center-Fond du Lac
400 University Dr, Fond du Lac WI 54935
920-929-3606

University of Wisconsin Marathon County
518 S 7th Ave, Wausau WI 54401-5362
Nolan Beck, Director of Student Services
715-261-6239

University of Wisconsin-Marinette
750 W Bay Shore St, Marinette WI 54143-4253
Cynthia M. Bailey, Director Student Services
715-735-4301

University of Wisconsin - Marshfield/Wood County
2000 W 5th St, Marshfield WI 54449-3310
715-389-6530

University of Wisconsin Waukesha
1500 N University Dr, Waukesha WI 53188-2720
262-521-5200

Waukesha County Technical College
800 Main St, Pewaukee WI 53072-4601
262-691-5566

Western Wisconsin Technical College
PO Box 908, La Crosse WI 54602-0908
608-785-9200

Wisconsin Indianhead Technical College
1019 S Knowles Ave, New Richmond WI 54017-1738
715-246-6561

Wisconsin Indianhead Technical College
505 Pine Ridge Dr, Shell Lake WI 54871
Miriam Crandall, Registrar
800-243-9482 Fax: 715-468-2819
Website: www.witc.edu
E-mail: mimi.crandall@witc.edu
Campuses in Ashland, New Richmond, Rice Lake, Superior.

WYOMING

Casper College
125 College Dr, Casper WY 82601-4699
307-268-2110

Central Wyoming College
2660 Peck Ave, Riverton WY 82501-2273
Tami Shultz, Director of Admissions
307-855-2231

Eastern Wyoming College
3200 W C St, Torrington WY 82240-1699
Dr. Jack Bottenfield, President
Tanya Howery, High School & College Relations
800-658-3195

Laramie County Community College
1400 E College Dr, Cheyenne WY 82007-3204
Jenny Hargett, Director of Admissions
307-778-5222 Fax: 307-778-1350
Website: www.lccc.wy.edu
E-mail: learnmore@lccc.wy.edu

Northern Wyoming Community College
300 W Sinclair St, Gillette WY 82718-7834
307-686-0254

Northwest College
231 W 6th St, Powell WY 82435-1895
307-754-6000

Sheridan College
PO Box 1500, Sheridan WY 82801-1500
307-674-6446

Western Wyoming Community College
2500 College Dr, Rock Springs WY 82901-5802
Laurie Watkins, Director of Admissions
307-382-1600

Wyoming Technical Institute
4373 N 3rd St, Laramie WY 82072-9519
Glenn R. Halsey, Director of Admissions
307-742-3776

AMERICAN SAMOA

American Samoa Community College
PO Box 2609, Pago Pago AS 96799-2609
684-699-9155

GUAM

Guam Community College
PO Box 23069, G.M.F. GU 96921-0307
Virginia Charfauros Tudela, Ph.D., Registrar
671-735-5531

MARIANA ISLANDS

Northern Marianas College
PO Box 1250, Saipan MP 96950
670-234-5499

MARSHALL ISLANDS

College of the Marshall Islands
PO Box 1258, Majuro MH 96960-1258
692-625-5427

MICRONESIA

College of Micronesia
PO Box 159, Pohnpei FM 96941-0159
691-320-2480

PALAU

Palau Community College
PO Box 9, Palau PW 96940-0009
680-488-2470

PUERTO RICO

Columbia Centro Universitario
PO Box 8517, Caguas PR 00726-8517
787-743-4041

Electronic Data Processing College
PO Box 1674, San Sebastian PR 00685-1674
787-896-2137

Huertas Junior College
PO Box 8429, Caguas PR 00726-8429
787-746-1400

ICPR Junior College
558 Ave Munoz Rivera, San Juan PR 00918-3610
787-753-6335

Instituto de Banca y Comercio
61 Ponce De Leon Ave, Hato Rey PR 00919
Rafael Jimenez, Vice President
787-754-7120

University College of San Juan
180 Jose R. Oliver St, San Juan PR 00918
787-250-7111

University of Puerto Rico - Aguadilla
PO Box 160, Aguadilla PR 00604-0160
787-890-2681

University of Puerto Rico at Utuado
PO Box 2500, Utuado PR 00641-0500
787-894-2828

COMPUTER AND INFORMATION SCIENCE

ALABAMA

Bishop State Community College - Four Campuses
351 N Broad St, Mobile AL 36603-5898
Dr. Terry Hazzard, Dean of Students
251-690-6801 Fax: 251-690-6446
Website: www.bishop.edu
E-mail: thazzard@bishop.edu

CALHOUN COMMUNITY COLLEGE
PO Box 2216, Decatur AL 35609-2216
M. Wayne Tosh, Registrar
256-306-2500 Fax: 256-306-2941
Website: www.calhoun.edu
E-mail: sla@calhoun.edu

George C. Wallace State Community College
PO Box 2530, Selma AL 36702-2530
Mrs. Donitha J. Griffin, Dean of Students
334-876-9295 Fax: 334-876-9300
Website: www.wccs.edu
E-mail: dgriffin@wccs.edu

Herzing College
280 W Valley Ave, Homewood AL 35209-4816
Kim Conway, Director of Admissions
205-916-2800 Fax: 205-916-2807
Website: www.herzing.edu/birmingham
E-mail: info@bhm.herzing.edu

Trenholm State Technical College
Patterson Campus
3920 Troy Hwy, Montgomery AL 36116
Dr. Anthony Molina, President
334-420-4200 Fax: 334-420-4206
Website: www.trenholmtech.cc.al.us
E-mail: molinaa@trenholmtech.cc.al.us

University of Alabama in Huntsville
PO Box 1247, Huntsville AL 35899-0001
Nikki Willis, Assoc. Director for Recruiting Program and Events
1-800-UAH-CALL Fax: 256-824-6073
Website: www.uah.edu
E-mail: willisn@uah.edu

University of South Alabama
307 University Blvd N, Mobile AL 36688-3053
Melissa Haab, Director of Admissions
251-460-6141 Fax: 251-460-7876
Website: www.southalabama.edu
E-mail: admiss@usouthal.edu

ALASKA

University of Alaska Anchorage
PO Box 141629, Anchorage AK 99514-1629
Cecile Mitchell, Director of Enrollment Services
907-786-1480 Fax: 907-786-4888
Website: www.uaa.alaska.edu/
E-mail: enroll@uaa.alaska.edu

ARIZONA

Apollo College
2701 W Bethany Home Rd, Phoenix AZ 85017-1705
602-433-1333 Fax: 602-433-1414

Apollo College
3550 N Oracle Rd, Tucson AZ 85705
520-888-5885 Fax: 520-887-3005

Collins College: A School of Design and Technology
(Formerly Al Collins Graphic Design School)
1140 S Priest Dr, Tempe AZ 85281-5240
Toby Craver, Director of National Admissions
800-876-7070 Fax: 480-829-0183
Website: www.collinscollege.edu

Embry-Riddle Aeronautical University
Arizona Campus
3700 Willow Creek Rd, Prescott AZ 86301-3720
William Thompson, Director of Admissions
800-888-3728 Fax: 928-777-6613
Website: www.embryriddle.edu
E-mail: pradmit@erau.edu

International Institute of the Americas
925 S Gilbert Rd Ste 201, Mesa AZ 85204-4440
Todd Olehausen, Director
480-545-8755 Fax: 480-926-1371
Website: www.iia.edu
E-mail: tolehausen@iia.edu

International Institute of the Americas
6049 N 43rd Ave, Phoenix AZ 85019-1600
John Pechota, Director of Admissions
602-242-6265 Fax: 602-589-1353
Website: www.iia.edu
E-mail: jpechota@iia.edu

International Institute of the Americas
5441 E 22nd St, Tucson AZ 85710
Leigh Anne Pechota, Director
520-748-9799 Fax: 520-748-9355
Website: www.iia.edu
E-mail: lpechota@iia.edu

Pima Community College
4905 E Broadway Blvd, Tucson AZ 85709-1010
Wendy Kilgore, Ph.D., Director of Admissions
520-206-4500 Fax: 520-206-4790
Website: www.pima.edu
E-mail: infocenter@pima.edu

ARKANSAS

Northwest Technical Institute
709 S Old Missouri Rd, Springdale AR 72764
Charles L. Kelley, President
479-751-8824 Fax: 479-751-7780
Website: www.nti.tec.ar.us
E-mail: info@nit.tec.ar.us

Phillips Community College of the University of Arkansas
PO Box 785, Helena AR 72342-0785
Dr. Steven Murray, Chancellor
Lynn Boone, Vice Chancellor for Student Services / Registrar
870-338-6474 Fax: 870-338-7542
Website: www.pccua.edu
E-mail: lboone@pccua.edu

Williams Baptist College
PO Box 3737, Walnut Ridge AR 72476-3737
Angela Flippo, Vice President for Enrollment Management
800-722-4434 Fax: 870-759-4163
Website: www.williamsbaptistcollege.com
E-mail: admissions@wbcoll.edu

CALIFORNIA

BRYAN COLLEGE
2317 Gold Meadow Way, Gold River CA 95670-4443
Nora Wilkinson, Director of Admissions
866-649-2400 Fax: 916-641-8649
Website: www.ntcollege.com
E-mail: studentinfo@ntcollege.com

Butte College
3536 Butte Campus Dr, Oroville CA 95965-8399
Carole Gish, Director of Admissions
530-895-2511 Fax: 530-879-4313
Website: www.butte.edu
E-mail: admissions@butte.edu

California State University-San Bernadino
5500 University Pkwy
San Bernardino CA 92407-2393
Olivia Rosas, Director of Admissions
909-537-5188 Fax: 909-537-7034
Website: www.csusb.edu
E-mail: orosas@csusb.edu

Chabot College
25555 Hesperian Blvd, Hayward CA 94545-2400
Judy Young, Director of Admissions
510-723-6600 Fax: 510-723-7510
Website: www.chabotcollege.edu
E-mail: ccarcom@clpccd.cc.ca.us

Chapman University
One University Drive, Orange CA 92866-1099
Michael Drummy, Assistant Vice President for Enrollment
Services and Chief Admission Officer
714-997-6411 or 888-CUAPPLY Fax: 714-997-6713
Website: www.chapman.edu
E-mail: admit@chapman.edu

COLEMAN COLLEGE
8888 Balboa Ave, San Diego CA 92123-1506
Sheryl L. Ridens, Dean of Academics
858-499-0202 Fax: 858-499-0233
Website: www.coleman.edu
E-mail: admissions@coleman.edu

COLEMAN COLLEGE
1284 W San Marcos Blvd Suite 110
San Marcos CA 92069-4073
Darlene Ankton, Vice President
760-747-3990 Fax: 760-752-9808
Website: www.coleman.edu
E-mail: ncadmiss@coleman.edu

COLLEGE OF INFORMATION TECHNOLOGY
2701 E Chapman Ave Ste 101, Fullerton CA 92831
Mohammad Qamaruddin, Director
714-879-5100 Fax: 714-879-2272
Website: www.collegeofit.com
E-mail: mqamar@collegeofit.com

FRESNO CITY COLLEGE
1101 E University Ave, Fresno CA 93741-0002
Dayann Dietrich, Contact
559-442-8241 Fax: 559-237-4232
Website: www.fresnocitycollege.com
E-mail: fcc.admissions@scccd.com

ITT Technical Institute
12669 Encinitas Ave, Sylmar CA 91342-3664
Kelly Christensen, Director of Admissions
818-364-5151 Fax: 818-364-5150
Website: www.itt-tech.edu
E-mail: kchristensen@itt-tech.edu

MTI BUSINESS COLLEGE OF STOCKTON
6006 N El Dorado St, Stockton CA 95207-4349
Steven Brenner, Director
888-302-2009 Fax: 209-474-8705
Website: www.mtistockton.com
E-mail: mtistockton@comcast.net
Established 1968. Accredited: ACCSCT. Family owned/operated 36 years.

MTI College
5221 Madison Ave, Sacramento CA 95841-3003
Marije Miller, Director of Admissions
916-339-1500 Fax: 916-339-0305
Website: www.mticollege.edu
E-mail: mmiller@mticollege.edu

Northwestern Polytechnic University
47671 Westinghouse Dr, Fremont CA 94539
Dr. T. Hsu, Contact
510-657-5913 Fax: 510-657-8975
Website: www.npu.edu
E-mail: npuadm@npu.edu

Orange Coast College
PO Box 5005, Costa Mesa CA 92628-5005
Kristin Clark, Director of Admissions
714-432-5773 Fax: 714-432-5736
Website: www.orangecoastcollege.edu
E-mail: kclark@cccd.edu

Pacific States University
1516 S Western Ave, Los Angeles CA 90006
Dr. Brandon Kim, Associate University Dean
323-731-2383 Fax: 323-731-7276
Website: www.psuca.edu
E-mail: admissions@psuca.edu
See listing under "Universities"

Point Loma Nazarene University
3900 Lomaland Dr, San Diego CA 92106-2810
Chip Killingsworth, Director of Undergraduate Admissions
800-733-7770 Fax: 619-849-2601
Website: www.pointloma.edu
E-mail: admissions@pointloma.edu

San Bernardino Valley College
701 S Mount Vernon Ave
San Bernardino CA 92410-2798
Kay Ragan, Ed.D., Director of Admissions
909-888-6511 Fax: 909-889-4988
Website: www.valleycollege.edu
E-mail: kragan@sbccd.cc.ca.us

San Joaquin Valley College
8400 W Mineral King Ave, Visalia CA 93291-9283
Susie Topjian, Enrollment Services Director
559-651-2500 Fax: 559-651-4864
Website: www.sjvc.edu
E-mail: susiet@sjvc.edu

Simpson University
2211 College View Dr, Redding CA 96003-8606
Jim Herberger, Director of Admissions
888-9-SIMPSON Fax: 530-226-4861
Website: www.simpsonuniversity.edu
E-mail: admissions@simpsonuniversity.edu
See listing under "Universities"

COLORADO

Colorado Christian University
8787 W Alameda Ave, Lakewood CO 80226
Sean Kadel, Director of Admissions
800-44-FAITH Fax: 303-963-3201
Website: www.ccu.edu
E-mail: admissions@ccu.edu

Community College of Aurora
16000 E Centretech Pkwy, Aurora CO 80011-9036
Kristen Cusack, Director of Admissions and Records
303-360-4700 Fax: 303-361-7432
Website: www.ccaurora.edu
E-mail: enrollment@ccaurora.edu

IntelliTec College
2315 E Pikes Peak Ave
Colorado Springs CO 80909-6096
Michael Castellano, Contact
719-632-7626 Fax: 719-632-7451
Website: www.intelliteccollege.edu
E-mail: admcs@intelliteccollege.edu

NORTHEASTERN JUNIOR COLLEGE
100 College Ave, Sterling CO 80751-2399
Dr. Lance Bolton, Chief Administrative Officer
Tina Joyce, Director of Admissions
970-521-7000 or 970-521-6752 Fax: 970-521-6801
Website: www.njc.edu
E-mail: tina.joyce@njc.edu

San Juan Basin Technical College
PO Box 970, Cortez CO 81321-0970
Shannon South, Vice President
970-565-8457 Fax: 970-565-8450
Website: www.sjbtc.edu
E-mail: info@sjbtc.edu

UNIVERSITY OF DENVER UNIVERSITY COLLEGE
2211 S Josephine St, Denver CO 80208
Dr. Ernest Eugster, Academic Director
303-871-3354 Fax: 303-871-4047
Website: www.universitycollege.du.edu
E-mail: ucolinfo@du.edu

CONNECTICUT

Albertus Magnus College
700 Prospect St, New Haven CT 06511-1189
Richard Lolatte, Dean of Admission
203-773-8501 or 800-578-9160 Fax: 203-773-5248
Website: www.albertus.edu
E-mail: admissions@albertus.edu

Branford Hall Career Institute
1 Summit Pl, Branford CT 06405
800-959-7599
Website: www.branfordhall.com

Branford Hall Career Institute
35 N Main St, Southington CT 06489-2577
860-276-0600
Website: www.branfordhall.com

Branford Hall Career Institute
995 Day Hill Rd, Windsor CT 06095-1722
860-683-4900
Website: www.branfordhall.com

DELAWARE

Goldey-Beacom College
4701 Limestone Rd, Wilmington DE 19808-1993
Stacey Schwartz, Assistant Director of Admissions
302-998-8814 Fax: 302-996-5408
Website: www.gbc.edu
E-mail: admissions@gbc.edu

DISTRICT OF COLUMBIA

Gallaudet University
800 Florida Ave NE, Washington DC 20002-3695
Charity Reedy Hines, Director of Admissions
202-651-5750 Fax: 202-651-5744
Website: www.gallaudet.edu
E-mail: admissions.office@gallaudet.edu

Potomac College
4000 Chesapeake St NW, Washington DC 20016
Florence Tate, President
202-686-0876 Fax: 202-686-0818
Website: www.potomac.edu
E-mail: ftate@potomac.edu

FLORIDA

City College
2000 W Commercial Blvd, Fort Lauderdale FL 33309
Mercedes Segal, Director of Admissions
954-492-5353 Fax: 954-491-1965
Website: www.citycollege.edu

COLLEGE OF BUSINESS & TECHNOLOGY
8991 SW 107th Ave #200, Miami FL 33176-1412
Luis Llerena, Executive Director
305-273-4499 Fax: 305-596-3835
Website: www.cbt.edu
E-mail: admissions@cbt.edu

Embry-Riddle Aeronautical University
Daytona Beach Campus
PO Box 11767, Daytona Beach FL 32120-1767
C. Richard Clarke, Director of Admissions
800-862-2416 Fax: 386-226-7070
Website: www.embryriddle.edu
E-mail: dbadmit@erau.edu

Florida National College
Hialeah Campus
4425 W 20th Ave, Hialeah FL 33012
Jorge Afonso, Campus Dean
305-821-3333 ext. 1022 Fax: 305-362-0595
Website: www.fnc.edu
E-mail: omarsnc@fnc.edu

Florida National College
South Campus
11865 SW 26th St, Miami FL 33175
Jon Beisenherz, Campus Dean
305-266-9999
Website: www.fnc.edu
E-mail: omarsnc@fnc.edu

Florida State University
600 W College Ave, Tallahassee FL 32306-1096
Janice V. Finney, Director of Admissions
850-644-2525 Fax: 850-644-0197
Website: admissions.fsu.edu
E-mail: admissions@admin.fsu.edu

HERZING COLLEGE
1595 S Semoran Blvd #1501
Winter Park FL 32792-5509
Kathy Nagle, Director of Admissions
407-478-0500 Fax: 407-478-0501
Website: www.herzing.edu
E-mail: info@orl.herzing.edu

INTERNATIONAL ACADEMY OF DESIGN AND TECHNOLOGY
5959 Lake Ellenor Dr, Orlando FL 32809-4633
Dr. John Dietrich, VP of Admissions
877-753-0007 Fax: 407-888-4006
Website: www.iadt.edu
E-mail: info@iadt.edu

Jones College
5353 Arlington Expy, Jacksonville FL 32211-5588
Dorothy D. Jones, Chief Executive Officer
904-743-1122 Fax: 904-744-4446
Website: www.jones.edu
E-mail: fmccaffe@jones.edu

Jones College
11430 N Kendall Dr Ste 200, Miami FL 33176
Patricia Carbonell, Contact
305-275-9996 Fax: 305-743-4446
Website: www.jones.edu
E-mail: pcarbone@jones.edu

Key College
225 E Dania Beach Blvd #130
Dania Beach FL 33004
Ronald Dooley, President
954-923-4440 Fax: 954-923-9226
Website: www.keycollege.edu
E-mail: admissions@keycollege.edu

Lincoln College of Technology
2410 Metrocentre Blvd
West Palm Beach FL 33407-3105
Don Cunningham, Vice President of Admissions
561-688-2001 Fax: 561-842-9503
Website: www.lincolncollegeoftechnology.com
E-mail: dcunningham@lincolntech.com

Northwood University
2600 N Military Trl, West Palm Beach FL 33409-2999
Jack Letvinchuk, Director of Admissions
800-458-8325 Fax: 561-640-3328
Website: www.northwood.edu
E-mail: fladmit@northwood.edu

PC PROFESSOR
600 N Hiatus Rd Ste 105, Pembroke Pines FL 33026
954-704-4444 Fax: 954-704-2222
Website: www.pcprofessor.edu
E-mail: train@pcprofessor.com

St. Thomas University
16401 NW 37th Ave, Miami Gardens FL 33054
Dr. Edward Ajhar, Contact
800-367-9010 or 305-628-6546 Fax: 305-628-6591
Website: www.stu.edu
E-mail: signup@stu.edu

SOUTHWEST FLORIDA COLLEGE
1685 Medical Ln, Fort Myers FL 33907-1157
866-SWFC-NOW or 239-939-4766 Fax: 239-936-4040
Website: www.swfc.edu
E-mail: studentinfo@swfc.edu

University of South Florida
4202 E Fowler Ave, Tampa FL 33620-6900
J. Robert Spatig, Director of Admissions
877-USF-BULL Fax: 813-974-9689
Website: www.usf.edu
E-mail: admissions@admin.usf.edu
See listing under "Universities"

GEORGIA

Armstrong Atlantic State University
11935 Abercorn St, Savannah GA 31419-1997
Kim West, Asst. Dean and Registrar Enrollment Services
912-927-5277 Fax: 912-921-5462
Website: www.armstrong.edu
E-mail: admissions@mail.armstrong.edu

DeKalb Technical College
495 N Indian Creek Dr, Clarkston GA 30021-2397
Terry Richardson, Director of Admissions
404-297-9522 Fax: 404-294-6496
Website: www.dekalbtech.edu
E-mail: richardt@dekalbtech.edu

DeVry University - Decatur Campus
250 N Arcadia Ave, Decatur GA 30030
Eric Stafford, Director of Admissions
404-292-7900 Fax: 404-292-7011
Website: www.devry.edu
E-mail: estafford@admin.atl.devry.edu

Kennesaw State University
1000 Chastain Rd NW, Kennesaw GA 30144-5591
Laurence Peterson, Dean of College of Science and Mathematics
770-423-6160
Website: www.kennesaw.edu

MIDDLE GEORGIA TECHNICAL COLLEGE
80 Cohen Walker Dr, Warner Robins GA 31088-2729
Dr. Ivan Allen, President
478-988-6800 Fax: 478-988-6835
Website: www.middlegatech.edu
E-mail: aparham@middlegatech.edu

North Georgia Technical College
434 Meeks Ave, Blairsville GA 30512-2983
Admissions
706-439-6300 Fax: 706-439-6301
Website: www.northgatech.edu
E-mail: info@northgatech.edu

North Georgia Technical College
8989 Highway 17, Toccoa GA 30577
706-779-8100 Fax: 706-779-8130
Website: www.northgatech.edu
E-mail: info@northgatech.edu

North Georgia Technical College
Clarkesville Campus
PO Box 65, Clarkesville GA 30523-0002
Admissions
706-754-7700 Fax: 706-754-7777
Website: www.northgatech.edu
E-mail: info@northgatech.edu

North Metro Technical College
5198 Ross Rd SE, Acworth GA 30102-3129
Missy Cusack, Director of Admissions
770-975-4000 Fax: 770-975-4142
Website: www.northmetrotech.edu
E-mail: info@northmetrotech.edu

Valdosta Technical College
4089 Val Tech Rd, Valdosta GA 31602-0928
Amanda Leavy, Admissions Coordinator
229-333-2100 Fax: 229-249-4980
Website: www.valdostatech.edu
E-mail: aleavy@valdostatech.edu

HAWAII

Heald College, Honolulu
1500 Kapiolani Blvd, Honolulu HI 96814-3732
Wendy N. Nishimura, Director of Admissions
808-955-1500 or 800-940-0530 Fax: 808-955-6964
Website: www.heald.edu
E-mail: wendy_nishimura@heald.edu

IDAHO

Brigham Young University - Idaho
120 Kimball Bldg, Rexburg ID 83460-1615
Rob Garrett, Director of Admissions
208-496-1020 Fax: 208-496-1220
Website: www.byui.edu
E-mail: admissions@byui.edu

University of Idaho
Moscow ID 83844-4253
Lloyd Scott, Director of New Student Services
208-885-6163 Fax: 208-885-4477
Website: www.uidaho.edu
E-mail: nss@uidaho.edu

ILLINOIS

AMERICAN INTERCONTINENTAL UNIVERSITY ONLINE
5550 Prairie Stone Parkway Suite 400
Hoffman Estates IL 60192
Admissions Department
877-701-3800
Website: www.aiuonline.edu
E-mail: info@aiuonline.edu

Aurora University
347 S Gladstone Ave, Aurora IL 60506-4892
Carol R. Dunn, Ed.D., Vice President for Enrollment
800-742-5281 Fax: 630-844-5535
Website: www.aurora.edu
E-mail: admission@aurora.edu

Benedictine University
5700 College Rd, Lisle IL 60532-0900
630-829-6300 or 888-829-6363 Fax: 630-829-6301
Website: www.ben.edu
E-mail: admissions@ben.edu
See listing under "Universities"

College of Office Technology
1520 W Division St, Chicago IL 60622
Bill Bolton, Director of Admissions
773-278-0042 Fax: 773-278-0143
Website: www.cot.edu
E-mail: bbolton@cotedu.com

Columbia College Chicago
600 S Michigan Ave, Chicago IL 60605-1996
Murphy Monroe, Executive Director of Admissions
312-344-7130 Fax: 312-344-8024
Website: www.colum.edu
E-mail: admissions@colum.edu

CONCORDIA UNIVERSITY
7400 Augusta St, River Forest IL 60305-1402
708-209-3100 Fax: 708-209-3176
Website: www.cuchicago.edu
E-mail: admission@cuchicago.edu

International Academy of Design and Technology
1 N State St #500, Chicago IL 60602-3300
Cecily Arroyo, Director of Admissions
888-803-0111 Fax: 312-541-3929
Website: www.iadtchicago.edu
E-mail: carroyo@iadtchicago.com

ITT TECHNICAL INSTITUTE
11551 184th Pl, Orland Park IL 60467-4900
Lillian McClain, Director
708-326-3200 Fax: 708-326-3250
Website: www.itt-tech.edu
E-mail: lcclain@itt-tech.edu

Kaskaskia College
27210 College Rd, Centralia IL 62801-7878
Tyra Taylor, Dean of Enrollment Management and Retention Services
618-545-3000 Fax: 618-532-1990
Website: www.kaskaskia.edu
E-mail: ttaylor@kaskaskia.edu

MacCormac College
29 E Madison St, Chicago IL 60602-4405
David F. Grassi, Admissions Counselor
312-922-1884 ext. 101 Fax: 312-922-4328
Website: www.maccormac.edu
E-mail: dgrassi@maccormac.edu

MORRISON INSTITUTE OF TECHNOLOGY
701 Portland Ave, Morrison IL 61270-2959
Richard C. Parkinson, Interim Director
815-772-7218 Fax: 815-772-7584
Website: www.morrisontech.edu
E-mail: admissions@morrison.tec.il.us
Private. Coed. Accreditation: ABET. Enrollment: 140. Student-faculty ratio: 13:1. Engineering Technology Associate of Applied Science degree in Architectural, Construction, Civil, Mechanical, Drafting & Design, and Surveying Technology. AAS degree in Systems & Network Administration.

Roosevelt University
430 S Michigan Ave, Chicago IL 60605
Gwen E. Kanelos, Asst. Vice President for Enrollment Services
877-APPLY-RU Fax: 312-341-4216
Website: www.roosevelt.edu
E-mail: applyru@roosevelt.edu

Triton College
2000 5th Ave, River Grove IL 60171-1995
Jeffery Cooks, Director, Admission Services
708-456-0300 ext. 3130 Fax: 708-583-3147
Website: www.triton.edu
E-mail: triton@triton.edu
See listing under "Community and Junior Colleges"

Westwood College
8501 W Higgins Rd Ste 500, Chicago IL 60631
Tash Uray, Director of Admissions
773-380-6800 Fax: 773-714-0828
Website: www.westwood.edu
E-mail: turay@westwood.edu

INDIANA

BROWN MACKIE COLLEGE - FORT WAYNE
3000 E Coliseum Blvd, Fort Wayne IN 46805
Daniel Summer, Campus President
260-484-4400 Fax: 260-484-2678
Website: www.brownmackie.edu

BROWN MACKIE COLLEGE - SOUTH BEND
1030 E Jefferson Blvd, South Bend IN 46617-3123
Connie Adelman, Campus President
574-237-0774 Fax: 574-237-3585
Website: www.brownmackie.edu

Franklin College
101 Branigin Blvd, Franklin IN 46131
Jacqueline S. Acosta, Director of Admissions
800-852-0232 Fax: 317-738-8274
Website: www.franklincollege.edu
E-mail: admissions@franklincollege.edu

International Business College
5699 Coventry Ln, Fort Wayne IN 46804
260-459-4500 Fax: 260-436-1896
Website: www.ibcfortwayne.edu
E-mail: skinzer@ibcfortwayne.edu

Ivy Tech Community College - North Central
220 Dean Johnson Blvd, South Bend IN 46601-3415
Pam Decker, Director of Admissions
574-289-7001 Fax: 574-236-7177
Website: www.ivytech.edu
E-mail: pdecker@ivytech.edu

Rose-Hulman Institute of Technology
5500 Wabash Ave, Terre Haute IN 47803-3920
James A. Goecker, Dean of Admissions
812-877-8213 Fax: 812-877-8941
Website: www.rose-hulman.edu
E-mail: admissions@rose-hulman.edu

University of Evansville
1800 Lincoln Ave, Evansville IN 47722-0001
Don Vos, Dean of Admission
800-423-8633 Fax: 812-488-4076
Website: www.evansville.edu
E-mail: admission@evansville.edu

IOWA

AIB College of Business
2500 Fleur Dr, Des Moines IA 50321-1799
800-444-1921 Fax: 515-244-6773
Website: www.aib.edu
E-mail: admissions@aib.edu

Briar Cliff University
PO Box 2100, Sioux City IA 51104-0100
Sharisue Wilcoxon, VP for Enrollment Management
712-279-5200 Fax: 712-279-1632
Website: www.briarcliff.edu
E-mail: admissions@briarcliff.edu

Clarke College
1550 Clarke Dr, Dubuque IA 52001-3198
Andy Schroeder, Director of Admissions
800-383-2345 Fax: 563-584-8666
Website: www.clarke.edu
E-mail: andy.schroeder@clarke.edu

Graceland University
1 University Place, Lamoni IA 50140
Greg Sutherland, Interim Vice President for Enrollment and Dean of Admissions
641-784-5196 Fax: 641-784-5480
Website: www.admissions.graceland.edu
E-mail: admissions@graceland.edu

Hamilton College
7009 Nordic Dr, Cedar Falls IA 50613
Connie Reidy, Campus President
319-277-0220 Fax: 319-363-3812
Website: www.hamiltonia.edu
E-mail: coreidy@hamiltoncf.com

Hamilton College
3165 Edgewood Pkwy SW, Cedar Rapids IA 52404
Susan Spivey, Campus President
319-363-0481 Fax: 319-363-3812
Website: www.hamiltonia.edu
E-mail: sspivey@hamiltonia.edu

Hamilton College
1751 Madison Ave Ste 750, Council Bluffs IA 51503
Michael Zawisky, Executive Director
712-328-4212
Website: www.hamiltonia.edu
E-mail: mzawisky@hamiltonia.edu

Hamilton College
2570 4th St SW, Mason City IA 50401-4665
Joe Albers, Executive Director
641-423-2530 Fax: 641-423-7512
Website: www.hamiltonia.edu
E-mail: jalbers@hamiltonia.edu

Hamilton College
4655 121st St, Urbandale IA 50323-2311
Colleen McDermott, Campus President
515-727-2100 Fax: 515-727-2115
Website: www.hamiltonia.edu
E-mail: cmcdermott@hamiltonia.edu

Iowa Lakes Community College
3200 College Dr, Emmetsburg IA 50536-1055
Anne Stansbury, Asst. Director of Admissions
712-852-5212 Fax: 712-362-8363
Website: www.iowalakes.edu
E-mail: info@iowalakes.edu

Iowa Lakes Community College
300 S 18th St, Estherville IA 51334-2721
Anne Stansbury, Asst. Director of Admissions
712-362-7945 Fax: 712-362-8363
Website: www.iowalakes.edu
E-mail: info@iowalakes.edu

Northwest Iowa Community College
603 W Park St, Sheldon IA 51201-1046
Lisa Story, Director of Enrollment Management
712-324-5061 Fax: 712-324-4136
Website: www.nwicc.edu
E-mail: lstory@nwicc.edu

Waldorf College
106 S 6th St, Forest City IA 50436-1713
Dr. Linda Hoopes, Vice President of Admission and Marketing
800-292-1903 or 641-585-8112 Fax: 641-585-8125
Website: www.waldorf.edu
E-mail: hoopesl@waldorf.edu
See listing under "Universities"

KANSAS

COLBY COMMUNITY COLLEGE
1255 S Range Ave, Colby KS 67701-4099
Director of Admissions
888-634-9350 or 785-460-4690 Fax: 785-460-4691
Website: www.colbycc.edu
E-mail: admissions@colbycc.edu

Flint Hills Technical College
3301 W 18th Ave, Emporia KS 66801-5957
Lisa Kirmer, Dean of Student Services
620-343-4600 Fax: 620-343-4610
Website: www.fhtc.net
E-mail: lkirmer@fhtc.net

Independence Community College
PO Box 708, Independence KS 67301-0708
Dr. Terry Hetrick, President
800-842-6063 Fax: 620-331-5344
Website: www.indycc.edu
E-mail: admissions@indycc.edu

Tabor College
400 S Jefferson St, Hillsboro KS 67063-1758
Rusty Allen, Dean of Enrollment Management
800-822-6799 Fax: 620-947-6276
Website: www.tabor.edu
E-mail: admissions@tabor.edu
See listing under "Universities"

KENTUCKY

Bluegrass Community and Technical College
Oswald Building
470 Cooper Drive, Lexington KY 40506-0235
Shelbie Hugle, Director of Admissions
859-246-6200 Fax: 859-246-4664
Website: www.bluegrass.kctcs.edu
E-mail: bctc_info@kctcs.edu

Brown Mackie College - Louisville
3605 Fern Valley Rd, Louisville KY 40219-1916
Mark Donahue, Director of Admissions
502-968-7191 Fax: 502-357-9956
Website: www.brownmackie.edu
E-mail: mdonahue@brownmackie.edu

BROWN MACKIE COLLEGE
Northern Kentucky Campus
309 Buttermilk Pike, Fort Mitchell KY 41017-2191
Joanne Dellefield, Director of Admissions
859-341-5627 Fax: 859-341-6483
Website: www.brownmackie.edu
E-mail: jdellefield@brownmackie.edu

Daymar College
4400 Breckenridge Ln #415, Louisville KY 40218
Shawn McDaniel, Director of Admissions
502-495-1040 Fax: 502-495-1518
Website: www.daymarcollege.com

Daymar College
3361 Buckland Sq, Owensboro KY 42301-5830
Vickie McDougal Director of Admissions
800-960-4090 Fax: 270-685-4090
Website: www.daymarcollege.com

Louisville Technical Institute
3901 Atkinson Square Dr, Louisville KY 40218
Kevin Woods, Director of Admissions
800-844-6528 Fax: 502-456-2341
Website: www.louisvilletech.com
E-mail: kwoods@louisvilletech.com

Morehead State University
Morehead KY 40351-1689
Jeffrey Liles, Enrollment Services
800-585-6781 Fax: 606-783-5038
Website: www.moreheadstate.edu
E-mail: admissions@moreheadstate.edu

National College
115 E Lexington Ave, Danville KY 40422-1517
Gloria Walls, Director of Admissions
859-236-6991 Fax: 859-236-1063
Website: www.national-college.edu
E-mail: info@national-college.edu

National College
7627 Ewing Blvd, Florence KY 41042-1812
Doug Dedeker, Director of Admissions
859-525-6510 Fax: 859-525-8961
Website: www.national-college.edu
E-mail: info@national-college.edu

National College
2376 Sir Barton Way, Lexington KY 40509
Terry Fisher, Director of Admissions
859-253-0621 Fax: 859-254-7664
Website: www.national-college.edu
E-mail: info@national-college.edu

National College
4205 Dixie Hwy, Louisville KY 40216
Ted Scharre, Director of Admissions
502-447-7634 Fax: 502-447-7665
Website: www.national-college.edu
E-mail: info@national-college.edu

National College
50 National College Blvd, Pikeville KY 41501
Janet Head, Director of Admissions
606-478-7200 Fax: 606-478-7209
Website: www.national-college.edu
E-mail: info@national-college.edu

National College
125 S Killarney Ln, Richmond KY 40475
Keeley Gadd, Director of Admissions
859-623-8956 Fax: 859-623-8956
Website: www.national-college.edu
E-mail: info@national-college.edu

Spencerian College
1575 Winchester Rd, Lexington KY 40505
Victor Lamoin Adcock II, Director of Admissions
800-456-3253
E-mail: ladcock@spencerian.edu

Transylvania University
300 N Broadway, Lexington KY 40508-1776
859-233-8242 Fax: 859-233-8797
Website: www.transy.edu
E-mail: admissions@transy.edu

LOUISIANA

ASCENSION COLLEGE
320 E Ascension St, Gonzales LA 70737-2912
Dennis Kerr, President
225-647-6609 Fax: 225-647-4849
Website: www.ascensioncollege.org
E-mail: dkerrascen@eatel.net

CAMERON COLLEGE
PO Box 19288, New Orleans LA 70179-0288
Eleanor Cameron Skov, President
504-821-5881 or 800-878-5881 Fax: 504-822-3467
Website: www.cameron.com
E-mail: cameroncollege@mindspring.com

CAREER TECHNICAL COLLEGE
2319 Louisville Ave, Monroe LA 71201
Rick Nail, Director
318-323-2889 Fax: 318-324-9883
Website: www.careertc.com
E-mail: rnail@careertc.com

Louisiana State University at Eunice
PO Box 1129, Eunice LA 70535-1129
Ron Ryder, Registrar
337-457-7311 Fax: 337-550-1306
Website: www.lsue.edu
E-mail: rryder@lsue.edu

MAINE

HUSSON COLLEGE
One College Cir, Bangor ME 04401-2999
Jane Goodwin, Director of Admissions
800-4HU-SSON or 207-941-7100 Fax: 207-941-7935
Website: www.husson.edu
E-mail: admit@husson.edu
See listing under "Universities"

Southern Maine Community College
2 Fort Rd, South Portland ME 04106-1698
Dr. James Ortiz, President
Scott MacDonald, Director of Financial Aid
207-741-5500 Fax: 207-741-5671
Website: www.smccme.edu
E-mail: oharmon@maine.rr.com

MARYLAND

Cecil College
One Seahawk Dr, North East MD 21901
Sandra S. Rajaski, Registrar & Director of Admissions
410-287-1000 Fax: 410-287-1001
Website: www.cecil.edu
E-mail: srajaski@cecil.edu

Hagerstown Community College
11400 Robinwood Dr, Hagerstown MD 21742-6590
Dr. Daniel E. Bock, Assistant Director of Admissions
301-790-2800 Fax: 301-791-9165
Website: www.hagerstowncc.edu
E-mail: bockd@hagerstowncc.edu

Kaplan College
Hagerstown Campus
18618 Crestwood Dr, Hagerstown MD 21742-2797
W. Christopher Motz, President
Steve Shinham, Director of Admissions
800-422-2670 Fax: 301-739-0474
Website: www.hagerstownbusinesscol.edu

MASSACHUSETTS

Anna Maria College
50 Sunset Ln, Paxton MA 01612
Timothy M. Donahue, Director of Recruitment and Admissions
508-849-3360 Fax: 508-849-3362
Website: www.annamaria.edu
E-mail: admissions@annamaria.edu

Assumption College
500 Salisbury St, Worcester MA 01609-1294
Kathleen Murphy, Dean of Enrollment
508-767-7000 Fax: 508-799-4412
Website: www.assumption.edu
E-mail: admiss@assumption.edu

Becker College
Campuses in Worcester and Leicester, MA
61 Sever St, Worcester MA 01609-2165
Karen Schedin, Dean of Admissions
508-791-9241 Fax: 508-890-1500
Website: www.becker.edu
E-mail: admissions@becker.edu
See listing under "Universities"

Benjamin Franklin Institute of Technology
41 Berkeley St, Boston MA 02116-6307
Norman Kraft, Dean of Enrollment
617-423-4630 ext. 121 Fax: 617-482-3706
Website: www.bfit.edu
E-mail: admissions@bfit.edu

Boston University
121 Bay State Rd, Boston MA 02215
Kelly Walter, Executive Director of Admissions
617-353-2300 Fax: 617-353-9695
Website: web.bu.edu
E-mail: admissions@bu.edu

Bristol Community College
777 Elsbree St, Fall River MA 02720-7395
Rodney S. Clark, Director of Admissions
508-678-2811 ext. 2516, 2179 Fax: 508-730-3265
Website: www.bristol.mass.edu
E-mail: admissions@bristol.mass.edu

Gordon College
255 Grapevine Rd, Wenham MA 01984-1899
Barbara R. Layne, Associate Vice President, Enrollment
866-464-6736 Fax: 978-867-4682
Website: www.gordon.edu
E-mail: admissions@gordon.edu

ITT TECHNICAL INSTITUTE
333 Boston Providence Tpke
Norwood MA 02062-3932
Tom Ryan, Director of Recruiting
800-879-TECH (8324) Fax: 781-278-0766
Website: www.itt-tech.edu
E-mail: tryan@itt-tech.edu

Established 1990. Private. Coed. Accreditation: ACICS. Enrollment: 300. Student-faculty ratio: 11:1. Associate Degrees offered: Computer Drafting & Design, Computer Electronics Technology, Computer Network Systems, Multimedia.

Massachusetts Institute of Technology
77 Massachusetts Ave, Cambridge MA 02139-4307
617-253-1000 Fax: 617-253-4016
Website: my.mit.edu
E-mail: admissions@mit.edu

Newbury College
129 Fisher Ave, Brookline MA 02445-5796
Salvadore Liberto, Vice President of Enrollment
617-730-7000 Fax: 617-731-9618
Website: www.newbury.edu
E-mail: info@newbury.edu
See listing under "Universities"

North Shore Community College
1 Ferncroft Rd, Danvers MA 01923-4093
Jennifer Kirk, Director of Admissions & Recruitment Outreach
978-762-4000 Fax: 978-762-4015
Website: www.northshore.edu
E-mail: jkirk@northshore.edu

University of Massachusetts Dartmouth
Old Westport Rd, North Dartmouth MA 02747-2300
Steven T. Briggs, Director of Admissions
508-999-8605 Fax: 508-999-8755
Website: explore.umassd.edu
E-mail: sbriggs@umassd.edu

Worcester Polytechnic Institute
100 Institute Rd, Worcester MA 01609-2280
Edward J. Connor, Director of Admissions
508-831-5286 Fax: 508-831-5875
Website: admissions.wpi.edu
E-mail: admissions@wpi.edu

MICHIGAN

CARNEGIE INSTITUTE
550 Stephenson Hwy Ste 100, Troy MI 48083-1159
Gloria J. McEachern, President
248-589-1078 Fax: 248-589-1631
Website: www.carnegie-institute.edu
E-mail: info@carnegie-institute.edu

Davenport University
6191 Kraft Ave SE, Grand Rapids MI 49512
866-383-3548
Website: www.explore.davenport.edu

Delta College
University Center MI 48710-0001
Duff Zube, Director of Admissions
989-686-9093 Fax: 989-667-2202
Website: www.delta.edu
E-mail: admit@delta.edu

Grand Valley State University
1 Campus Dr, Allendale MI 49401-9403
Jodi Chycinski, Director of Admissions
616-331-6611 Fax: 616-331-2000
Website: www.gvsu.edu
E-mail: go2gvsu@gvsu.edu

ITT TECHNICAL INSTITUTE
4020 Sparks Dr SE, Grand Rapids MI 49546-6192
Dennis Hormel, Director
616-956-1060 Fax: 616-956-5606
Website: www.itt-tech.edu
E-mail: dhormel@itt-tech.edu

Lawrence Technological University
21000 W 10 Mile Rd, Southfield MI 48075-1058
Jane Rohrback, Director of Admissions
800-225-5588 Fax: 248-204-2228
Website: www.ltu.edu
E-mail: admissions@ltu.edu
See listing under "Universities"

MACOMB COMMUNITY COLLEGE
44575 Garfield Rd, Clinton Township MI 48038-1139
Information Center
586-445-7999
Website: www.macomb.edu
E-mail: answer@macomb.edu

MACOMB COMMUNITY COLLEGE
14500 E 12 Mile Rd, Warren MI 48088-3896
Information Center
586-445-7999
Website: www.macomb.edu
E-mail: answer@macomb.edu

Northwestern Michigan College
1701 E Front St, Traverse City MI 49686-3061
Jim Bensley, Director of Admissions
800-748-0566 Fax: 231-995-1339
Website: www.nmc.edu
E-mail: jbensley@nmc.edu

Northwood University
4000 Whiting Dr, Midland MI 48640
Daniel F. Toland, Dean of Admissions
800-457-7878 Fax: 989-837-4490
Website: www.northwood.edu
E-mail: miadmit@northwood.edu

Oakland University
2200 N Squirrel Rd, Rochester MI 48309
Eleanor L. Reynolds, Assistant Vice President & Director of Admissions
248-370-2100
Website: www.oakland.edu
E-mail: ouinfo@oakland.edu

MINNESOTA

Academy College
1101 E 78th St, Bloomington MN 55420-1402
Tracey Schantz, Director of Admissions
952-851-0066 Fax: 952-851-0094

Carleton College
1 N College St, Northfield MN 55057-4044
800-995-2275 or 507-646-4190 Fax: 507-646-4526
Website: www.carleton.edu
E-mail: admissions@acs.carleton.edu

Duluth Business University
4724 Mike Colalillo Dr, Duluth MN 55807-2723
Bonnie Kupczynski, Director
800-777-8406 Fax: 218-628-2127
Website: www.dbumn.edu
E-mail: info@dbumn.edu

Dunwoody College of Technology
818 Dunwoody Blvd, Minneapolis MN 55403-1192
John Slama, Vice President Enrollment Management
800-292-4625 or 612-374-5800 Fax: 612-374-4128
Website: www.dunwoody.edu
E-mail: jslama@dunwoody.edu
See listing under "Career Schools"

Globe College
7166 10th St N, Oakdale MN 55128
Mike Hughes, Campus Director
651-730-5100 Fax: 651-730-5151
Website: www.globecollege.edu
E-mail: admissions@globecollege.edu

Gustavus Adolphus College
800 W College Ave, Saint Peter MN 56082-1485
Mark H. Anderson, Dean of Admission
800-GUSTAVUS Fax: 507-933-7474
Website: www.gustavus.edu
E-mail: admission@gustavus.edu

Hibbing Community College
1515 E 25th St, Hibbing MN 55746-3300
Holly Bigelow, Director of Enrollment
800-224-4HCC or 218-262-7200 Fax: 218-262-6717
Website: www.hibbing.edu
E-mail: admissions@hibbing.edu

Minnesota State College - Southeast Technical
Red Wing Campus
308 Pioneer Rd, Red Wing MN 55066
Al DuCett, Director of Admissions
877-853-8324 Fax: 507-453-2715
Website: www.southeastmn.edu
E-mail: aducett@southeastmn.edu
70+ degrees, diplomas & certificates (15+ online) in Business & Office Careers, Musical Instrument Repair, Physical Health, Transportation, Technology, and Trades.

Minnesota State College - Southeast Technical
Winona Campus
PO Box 409, 1250 Homer Rd, Winona MN 55987
Al DuCett, Director of Admissions
877-853-8324 Fax: 507-453-2715
Website: www.southeastmn.edu
E-mail: aducett@southeastmn.edu
70+ degrees, diplomas & certificates (15+ online) in Business & Office Careers, Musical Instrument Repair, Physical Health, Transportation, Technology, and Trades.

Minnesota State University Moorhead
1104 7th Ave S, Moorhead MN 56563-0002
Regina Monson, Director of Admissions
218-477-2161 Fax: 218-477-4374
Website: go.mnstate.edu
E-mail: dragon@mnstate.edu

Northland Community and Technical College
2022 Central Ave NE
East Grand Forks MN 56721-2702
Deb Riely, Business Program Chair
800-451-3441 Fax: 218-773-4502
Website: www.northlandcollege.edu
E-mail: admissions@northlandcollege.edu

Pillsbury Baptist Bible College
315 S Grove Ave, Owatonna MN 55060-3097
Susanne Martin, Admissions Coordinator
507-451-2710 Fax: 507-451-0156
Website: www.pillsbury.edu
E-mail: admissions@pillsbury.edu

Ridgewater College-Hutchinson Campus
2 Century Ave SE, Hutchinson MN 55350-3100
Dawn Bjork, Counselor
800-722-1151 Fax: 320-234-8506
Website: www.ridgewater.edu
E-mail: dawn.bjork@ridgewater.edu

St. Cloud Technical College
1540 Northway Dr, Saint Cloud MN 56303-1240
Jodi Elness, Director of Enrollment Management
800-222-1009 Fax: 320-308-5981
Website: www.sctc.edu
E-mail: jelness@sctc.edu

University of Minnesota
2900 University Ave, Crookston MN 56716-5001
218-281-6510 Fax: 218-281-8575
Website:
admissions.umcrookston.edu/requirements/apply.htm
E-mail: info@umcrookston.edu

MISSOURI

Central Methodist University
411 Central Methodist Sq, Fayette MO 65248-1198
Larry Anderson, Director of Admissions
660-248-6247 Fax: 660-248-1872
Website: www.centralmethodist.edu
E-mail: landerso@centralmethodist.edu

Columbia College
1001 Rogers St, Columbia MO 65216-0001
Regina Morin, Director of Admissions
573-875-7352 Fax: 573-875-7506
Website: www.ccis.edu
E-mail: admissions@ccis.edu

East Central College
1964 Prairie Dell Rd, Union MO 63084
Karen Wieda, Registrar
636-583-5195 ext. 2220 Fax: 636-583-1897
Website: www.eastcentral.edu
E-mail: wiedaks@eastcentral.edu

EVEREST COLLEGE
1010 W Sunshine St, Springfield MO 65807-2446
Melanie Exter, Contact
417-864-7220 or 800-475-2699 Fax: 417-866-3335
Website: www.everest-college.com
E-mail: mexter@cci.edu

Harris-Stowe State University
3026 Laclede Ave, Saint Louis MO 63103-2199
LaShanda R. Boone, Director of Admissions
314-340-3300 Fax: 314-340-3555
Website: www.hssu.edu
E-mail: admissions@hssu.edu

Hickey College
940 Westport Plz, Saint Louis MO 63146-3127
Christopher A. Gearin, President
800-777-1544 or 314-434-2212 Fax: 314-434-1974
Website: www.hickeycollege.edu
E-mail: admin@hickeycollege.edu

Lindenwood University
209 S Kingshighway St
Saint Charles MO 63301-1695
Sheryl Guffey, Director of Admissions
636-949-2000 Fax: 636-949-4989
Website: www.lindenwood.edu

Northwest Missouri State University
800 University Dr, Maryville MO 64468-6001
Beverly Schenkel, Dean of Enrollment Management
660-562-1562 Fax: 660-562-1121
Website: www.nwmissouri.edu
E-mail: admissions@nwmissouri.edu

Ranken Technical College
4431 Finney Ave, Saint Louis MO 63113-2898
Admissions Office
314-371-0233 Fax: 314-371-0241
Website: www.ranken.edu
E-mail: admissions@ranken.edu

St. Charles Community College
4601 Mid Rivers Mall Dr, Cottleville MO 63376
Kathy Brockgreitens-Gober, Director of Admissions
636-922-8000 Fax: 636-922-8236
Website: www.stchas.edu
E-mail: adm-reg@stchas.edu

State Fair Community College
3201 W 16th St, Sedalia MO 65301-2199
Director of Admissions
660-530-5833 Fax: 660-596-7472
Website: www.sfccmo.edu
E-mail: mparris@sfccmo.edu

Truman State University
100 E Normal, Kirksville MO 63501
Office of Admission
660-785-4114 Fax: 660-785-7456
Website: admissions.truman.edu
E-mail: admissions@truman.edu

University of Missouri
1 University Blvd, Saint Louis MO 63121-4499
Dr. Mark Burkholder, Dean-College of Arts & Sciences
314-516-5501 Fax: 314-516-5415
Website: www.umsl.edu
E-mail: admissions@umsl.edu

Webster University
470 E Lockwood Ave, Saint Louis MO 63119-3194
Al Cawns, Chairman, Math & Computer Science
314-968-7023 Fax: 314-963-6050
Website: www.webster.edu
See listing under "Universities"

William Jewell College
500 College Hill, Liberty MO 64068-1896
Dr. Rick Winslow, VP Enrollment Management and Student Affairs
800-753-7009 Fax: 816-415-5040
Website: www.jewell.edu
E-mail: winslowr@william.jewell.edu

William Woods University
1 University Ave, Fulton MO 65251-1098
Jimmy Clay, Director of Admissions
573-642-2251 Fax: 573-592-1146
Website: www.williamwoods.edu
E-mail: admissions@williamwoods.edu
See listing under "Universities"

MONTANA

Carroll College
1601 N Benton Ave, Helena MT 59625-0002
Dr. Thomas J. Trebon, President
Cynthia Thornquist, Director of Admissions & Enrollment Operations
406-447-4384 Fax: 406-447-4533
Website: www.carroll.edu
E-mail: admission@carroll.edu

NEBRASKA

Midland Lutheran College
900 N Clarkson St, Fremont NE 68025-4200
Todd Hansen, Associate Director of Admissions
402-941-6501 Fax: 402-941-6513
Website: www.mlc.edu
E-mail: admissions@mlc.edu

Nebraska Wesleyan University
5000 Saint Paul Ave, Lincoln NE 68504-2794
Patricia Karthauser, V.P. for University Enrollment
402-466-2371 Fax: 402-465-2177
Website: www.nebrwesleyan.edu
E-mail: admissions@nebrwesleyan.edu

University of Nebraska at Kearney
905 W 25th St, Kearney NE 68849-0001
Dusty Newton, Director of Admissions
800-KEARNEY Fax: 308-865-8987
Website: www.unk.edu
E-mail: admissionsug@unk.edu

NEVADA

Career College of Northern Nevada
1195-A Corporate Blvd, Reno NV 89502-2331
Nathan Clark, Director
775-856-2266 Fax: 775-856-0935
Website: www.ccnn.edu
E-mail: lgoldhammer@ccnn4u.com
See listing under "Career Schools"

GREAT BASIN COLLEGE
1500 College Pkwy, Elko NV 89801-5032
Julie G. Byrnes, Director of Enrollment Management
775-753-2271 Fax: 775-753-2311
Website: www.gbcnv.edu
E-mail: julieb@gwmail.gbcnv.edu
See listing under "Universities"

Morrison University
10315 Professional Circle Suite 201
Reno NV 89521-4826
Charles Timinsky, Director of Enrollment
775-850-0700 Fax: 775-850-0711
Website: www.morrisonuniversity.com

NEW HAMPSHIRE

New Hampshire Community Technical College
1066 Front St, Manchester NH 03102-8528
Jacquie Poirier, Director of Admissions
603-668-6706 Fax: 603-668-5354
Website: www.manchester.nhctc.edu
E-mail: jpoirier@nhctc.edu

Southern New Hampshire University
2500 N River Rd, Hooksett NH 03106-1045
Steve Soba, Director of Admissions
603-645-9611 Fax: 603-645-9693
Website: www.snhu.edu
E-mail: s.soba@snhu.edu

NEW JERSEY

Atlantic Cape Community College
5100 Black Horse Pike
Mays Landing NJ 08330-2699
Linda McLeod, Assistant Director of College Recruitment
609-343-5000 Fax: 609-343-4921
Website: www.atlantic.edu
E-mail: accadmit@atlantic.edu
See listing under "Community and Junior Colleges"

Bergen Community College
400 Paramus Rd, Paramus NJ 07652
Julian Gomez, Asst. Director of Admissions
201-447-7100 Fax: 201-444-7036
Website: www.bergen.edu
E-mail: jgomez@bergen.edu

THE CHUBB INSTITUTE
40 Journal Sq, Jersey City NJ 07306-4097
Valerie Yancey, Campus President
201-876-3800 Fax: 201-656-2091
Website: www.chubbinstitute.edu
E-mail: vyancey@chubbinstitute.edu

HoHoKus School of Business & Medical Sciences
10 S Franklin Tpke, Ramsey NJ 07446-2546
Thomas Eastwick, Director
201-327-8877 Fax: 201-327-9054
Website: www.hohokus.edu
E-mail: tomeastwick@aol.com

New Jersey City University
2039 John F Kennedy Blvd
Jersey City NJ 07305-1588
Carmen Panlilio, Asst. V.P. for Admissions and Financial Aid
201-200-3234 Fax: 201-200-2044
Website: www.njcu.edu
E-mail: admissions@njcu.edu

Ramapo College of New Jersey
505 Ramapo Valley Rd, Mahwah NJ 07430-1623
Director of Admissions
201-684-7300 or 201-684-7301 Fax: 201-684-7964
Website: www.ramapo.edu
E-mail: admissions@ramapo.edu

RICHARD STOCKTON COLLEGE OF NEW JERSEY
PO Box 195, Pomona NJ 08240
John Iacovelli, Dean of Enrollment Management
866-RSC-2885 Fax: 609-626-5541
Website: www.stockton.edu
E-mail: admissions@stockton.edu
See listing under "Universities"

STAR TECHNICAL INSTITUTE
3003 English Creek Ave Suite 212
Egg Harbor Township NJ 08234-4880
George Z. Negrete, Director
609-407-2999 Fax: 609-646-9472
Website: www.startechnicalinstitute.com
E-mail: info@staregghharbor.com

NEW MEXICO

International Institute of the Americas
4201 Central Ave NW Suite J
Albuquerque NM 87105-1649
Ed Sigman, Director
505-880-2877 Fax: 505-352-0199
Website: www.iia.edu
E-mail: esigman@iia.edu

New Mexico State University
1500 N 3rd St, Grants NM 87020-2025
Irene Lutz, Director of Admissions
505-287-7981 Fax: 505-287-2329
Website: www.grants.nmsu.edu
E-mail: ilutz@nmsu.edu

NEW YORK

Briarcliffe College
1055 Stewart Ave, Bethpage NY 11714-3545
Theresa Donohue, Director of Admissions
516-918-3600 Fax: 516-470-6020
Website: www.briarcliffe.edu

Broome Community College
907 Upper Front St, Binghamton NY 13905
Anthony S. Fiorelli, Director of Admissions
607-778-5001 Fax: 607-778-5442
Website: www.sunybroome.edu
E-mail: fiorelli_a@sunybroome.edu

CAREER INSTITUTE OF HEALTH & TECHNOLOGY
340 Flatbush Avenue Ext, Brooklyn NY 11201
Mary Miller, Contact
718-422-1212 Fax: 718-422-1222
Website: www.careerinstitute.edu
E-mail: admissions@careerinstitute.edu

CAREER INSTITUTE OF HEALTH & TECHNOLOGY
200 Garden City Plz, Garden City NY 11530
Mary Miller, Contact
516-877-1225 Fax: 516-877-1959
Website: www.careerinstitute.edu
E-mail: admissions@careerinstitute.edu

CAREER INSTITUTE OF HEALTH & TECHNOLOGY
9525 Queens Blvd Ste 600, Rego Park NY 11374
Mary Miller, Contact
718-897-4868 Fax: 718-897-4863
Website: www.careerinstitute.edu
E-mail: admissions@careerinstitute.edu

THE CHUBB INSTITUTE
498 7th Ave, New York NY 10018
James Cruz, Director of Admissions
212-659-2116 Fax: 212-659-2175
Website: www.chubbinstitute.edu
E-mail: jamescruz@chubbinstitute.edu

College of Saint Rose
432 Western Ave, Albany NY 12203-1419
Maryelizabeth Amico, Asst V.P. for Undergraduate Admissions
518-454-5150 Fax: 518-454-2013
Website: www.strose.edu
E-mail: admit@strose.edu

CUNY Hunter College
695 Park Ave, New York NY 10021
Aaron Gibbs, Assistant Director of Recruitment
212-650-3946 Fax: 212-650-3336
Website: www.hunter.cuny.edu
E-mail: aaron.gibbs@hunter.cuny.edu

Dowling College
150 Idle Hour Blvd, Oakdale NY 11769-1999
Diane Kazanecki-Kempter, Contact
631-244-3000 Fax: 631-244-1059
Website: www.dowling.edu
E-mail: admissions@dowling.edu

Iona College
715 North Ave, New Rochelle NY 10801-1890
Kevin Cavanagh, Assistant V.P. for College Admissions
914-633-2502 Fax: 914-637-2778
Website: www.iona.edu

ISLAND DRAFTING & TECHNICAL INSTITUTE
128 Broadway (Route 110), Amityville NY 11701-2704
James G. DiLiberto, President
631-691-8733 Fax: 631-691-8738
Website: www.idti.edu
E-mail: info@idti.edu

Long Island University-C. W. Post Campus
720 Northern Blvd, Brookville NY 11548-1300
Joanne Graziano, Executive Director of Admissions
516-299-2900 Fax: 516-299-2137
Website: www.liu.edu/cwpost
E-mail: enroll@cwpost.liu.edu

Molloy College
1000 Hempstead Ave
Rockville Centre NY 11570-1100
Marguerite Lane, Director of Admissions
516-678-5000 ext. 6291 Fax: 516-256-2247
Website: www.molloy.edu
E-mail: admissions@molloy.edu
See listing under "Universities"

Monroe College
2501 Jerome Ave, Bronx NY 10468-4305
Evan Jerome, Director of Admissions
718-933-6700 Fax: 718-364-3552
Website: www.monroecollege.edu
E-mail: ejerome@monroecollege.edu

Olean Business Institute
301 N Union St, Olean NY 14760-2691
Carl English, Director of Admissions
716-372-7978 Fax: 716-372-2120
Website: www.obi.edu
E-mail: cenglish@obi.edu

Ridley-Lowell Business & Technical Institute
116 Front St, Binghamton NY 13905-3102
David Lounsbury, Executive Director
607-724-2941 Fax: 607-724-0799
Website: www.ridley.edu
E-mail: info@ridley.edu

Roberts Wesleyan College
2301 Westside Dr, Rochester NY 14624-1997
Office of Admissions
585-594-6400 Fax: 585-594-6371
Website: www.roberts.edu
E-mail: admissions@roberts.edu

St. John's University
8000 Utopia Pkwy, Queens NY 11439
Office of Admission
877-STJ-5550 ext. 101 Fax: 718-990-2096
Website: www.stjohns.edu/learnmore
E-mail: admhelp@stjohns.edu
See listing under "Universities"

St. Joseph's College
245 Clinton Ave, Brooklyn NY 11205-3688
Theresa LaRocca Meyer, V.P. for Enrollment Management
718-636-6800 Fax: 718-636-8303
Website: www.sjcny.edu
E-mail: tlaroccameyer@sjcny.edu

Siena College
515 Loudonville Rd, Loudonville NY 12211-1462
Heather Renault, Director of Admissions
518-783-2300 Fax: 518-783-2436
Website: www.siena.edu
E-mail: hrenault@siena.edu

SUNY College at Brockport
350 New Campus Dr, Brockport NY 14420-2997
Bernard S. Valento, Director of Undergraduate Admissions
585-395-2751 Fax: 585-395-5452
Website: www.brockport.edu
E-mail: admit@brockport.edu

SUNY College of Technology
Alfred NY 14802
Deborah J. Goodrich, Associate VP Enrollment Mgmt.
800-4AL-FRED Fax: 607-587-4299
Website: www.alfredstate.edu
E-mail: admissions@alfredstate.edu

SUNY Niagara County Community College
3111 Saunders Settlement Rd
Sanborn NY 14132-9487
Kathleen Saunders, Director of Admissions
716-614-6200 Fax: 716-614-6820
Website: www.niagaracc.suny.edu
E-mail: admissions@niagaracc.suny.edu

SUNY Orange County Community College
115 South St, Middletown NY 10940-6437
Margot St. Lawrence, Director of Admissions
845-341-4030 Fax: 845-342-8662
Website: www.sunyorange.edu
E-mail: apply@sunyorange.edu
See listing under "Community and Junior Colleges"

SUNY Sullivan County Community College
112 College Rd, Loch Sheldrake NY 12759-5151
Sari Rosenheck, Director of Admissions
845-434-5750 Fax: 845-434-0923
Website: www.sullivan.suny.edu
E-mail: admissions@sullivan.suny.edu
Student Housing on Campus.

United States Military Academy West Point
646 Swift Rd, West Point NY 10996-1905
Colonel Michael L. Jones, Director of Admissions
845-938-4041 Fax: 845-938-8121
Website: admissions.usma.edu
E-mail: admissions@usma.edu

Utica School of Commerce
201 Bleecker St, Utica NY 13501-2280
Bruce Davis, Director of Marketing
315-733-2307 Fax: 315-733-9281
Website: www.uscny.edu
E-mail: admissions@uscny.edu

Wells College
PO Box 500, Aurora NY 13026
Susan Sloan, Director of Admissions
800-952-9355 Fax: 315-364-3227
Website: www.wells.edu
E-mail: ssloan@wells.edu

NORTH CAROLINA

ART INSTITUTE OF CHARLOTTE
2110 Water Ridge Pkwy, Charlotte NC 28217
Pamela Notemyer, Director of Admissions
800-872-4417 Fax: 704-357-1133
Website: www.artinstitutes.edu/charlotte
E-mail: admin@aii.edu
See listing under "Career Schools"

Catawba College
2300 W Innes St, Salisbury NC 28144-2488
Dr. L. Russell Watjen, Ph.D., V.P. & Dean of Admissions
704-637-4402 Fax: 704-637-4222
Website: www.catawba.edu
E-mail: admission@catawba.edu

Haywood Community College
185 Freedlander Dr, Clyde NC 28721
Debbie Rowland, Coordinator of Admissions
828-627-4500 Fax: 828-627-4513
Website: www.haywood.edu
E-mail: drowland@haywood.edu

James Sprunt Community College
PO Box 398, Kenansville NC 28349-0398
Lea Grady, Admissions
910-296-2500 Fax: 910-296-1636
Website: www.jamessprunt.edu

Mayland Community College
PO Box 547, Spruce Pine NC 28777-0547
Cathy B. Morrison, Director of Enrollment Management
828-765-7351 Fax: 828-765-0728
Website: www.mayland.edu
E-mail: cmorrison@mayland.edu

South College
29 Turtle Creek Dr, Asheville NC 28803
Robert Davis, Dean of Academic Affairs
828-277-5521 Fax: 828-277-6151
Website: southcollegenc.com
E-mail: bdavis@southcollegenc.com

South Piedmont Community College
PO Box 126, Polkton NC 28135-0126
John Curtis, Contact
704-272-5324 Fax: 704-272-8904
Website: www.spcc.edu
E-mail: jcurtis@spcc.edu

NORTH DAKOTA

Dickinson State University
Dickinson ND 58601-4896
Steve Glasser, Director of Enrollment Services
800-279-4295 Fax: 701-483-2409
Website: www.dickinsonstate.edu
E-mail: dsu.hawks@dickinsonstate.edu

Mayville State University
330 3rd St NE, Mayville ND 58257-1299
Dr. Ray Gerszewski, Vice President Student Affairs
800-437-4104 Fax: 701-788-4748
Website: www.mayvillestate.edu
E-mail: admit@mayvillestate.edu

Minot State University-Bottineau Campus
105 Simrall Blvd, Bottineau ND 58318-1159
Paula Berg, Associate Dean of Student Affairs
800-542-6866 Fax: 701-228-5499
Website: www.misu-b.nodak.edu
E-mail: paula.berg@misu.nodak.edu

Valley City State University
101 College St SW, Valley City ND 58072-4024
Dan Klein, Director of Enrollment Services
800-532-8641 ext. 7101 Fax: 701-845-7299
Website: www.vcsu.edu
E-mail: enrollment.services@vcsu.edu
See listing under "Universities"

Williston State College
PO Box 1326, Williston ND 58802-1326
Penny Soiseth, Associate Director Enrollment Services
701-774-4200 Fax: 701-774-4544
Website: www.wsc.nodak.edu
E-mail: penny.soiseth@wsc.nodak.edu

OHIO

Brown Mackie College - Cincinnati
1011 Glendale Milford Rd, Cincinnati OH 45215-1107
Robin Krout, President
513-771-2424 Fax: 513-771-3413
Website: www.brownmackie.edu
E-mail: rkrout@brownmackie.edu

Bryant & Stratton College
1700 E 13th St, Cleveland OH 44114-3238
Shawn T. Kampa, Market Director of Admissions
216-771-1700 Fax: 216-771-7787
Website: www.bryantstratton.edu
E-mail: stkampa@bryantstratton.edu

Cincinnati Christian University
PO Box 4320, Cincinnati OH 45204
Erin Oppy, Executive Director of Undergraduate Admissions
513-244-8141 Fax: 513-244-8453
Website: www.ccuniversity.edu

Cleveland Institute of Electronics
1776 E 17th St, Cleveland OH 44114-3679
Scott Katzenmeyer, Director of Admissions
800-243-6446 Fax: 216-781-0331
Website: www.cie-wc.edu
E-mail: instruct@cie-wc.edu

Cleveland State University
2121 Euclid Ave RW 204, Cleveland OH 44115
Dr. Richard Arndt, Dean of Undergraduate Recruitment and College Partnerships
888-CSU-OHIO Fax: 216-687-9210
Website: www.csuohio.edu
E-mail: admissions@csuohio.edu

Davis College
4747 Monroe St, Toledo OH 43623-4389
Dana Stern, Admissions Director
419-473-2700 Fax: 419-473-2472
Website: www.daviscollege.edu
E-mail: learn@daviscollege.edu

Franciscan University of Steubenville
University Blvd, Steubenville OH 43952
Margaret J. Weber, Director of Admissions
800-783-6220 or 740-283-6226 Fax: 740-284-5456
Website: www.admissions.edu
E-mail: mweber@franciscan.edu

OHIO NORTHERN UNIVERSITY
525 S Main St, Ada OH 45810-1555
Robert A. Manzer, Dean
419-772-2130
Website: www.onu.edu
E-mail: admissions-ug@onu.edu
See listing under "Universities"

The Ohio State University
Department of Computer Science and Engineering
Dreese Laboratories, 2015 Neil Ave
Columbus OH 43210
614-292-5813 Fax: 614-292-2911
Website: cse.osu.edu
E-mail: webmaster@cse.ohio-state.edu

OHIO VALLEY COLLEGE OF TECHNOLOGY
16808 St. Clair Ave, PO Box 7000
East Liverpool OH 43920
Scott S. Rogers, Director
330-385-1070 Fax: 330-385-4606
Website: www.ovct.edu
E-mail: info@ovct.edu

Owens Community College
3200 Bright Rd, Findlay OH 45840
William J. Ivoska PhD., Vice President of Student Services
567-429-3500 Fax: 567-423-0246
Website: www.owens.edu
E-mail: admissions@owens.edu

Owens Community College
PO Box 10000, Toledo OH 43699-1947
William J. Ivoska, Ph.D, Vice President of Student Services
567-661-7000 Fax: 567-661-7607
Website: www.owens.edu
E-mail: admissions@owens.edu

REMINGTON COLLEGE - CLEVELAND WEST CAMPUS
26350 Brookpark Rd, North Olmsted OH 44070
Gary A. Azotea, Campus President
440-777-2560 Fax: 440-777-3238
Website: www.remingtoncollege.edu
E-mail: gary.azotea@remingtoncollege.edu

Sinclair Community College
444 W 3rd St, Dayton OH 45402-1460
Director of Admissions
937-512-3000 Fax: 937-512-2393
Website: www.sinclair.edu
E-mail: admit@sinclair.edu

University of Dayton
300 College Park, Dayton OH 45469-1300
Robert F. Durkle, Director of Admission
800-837-7433 Fax: 937-229-4729
Website: admission.udayton.edu
E-mail: admission@udayton.edu

Ursuline College
2550 Lander Rd, Cleveland OH 44124-4398
Sarah E. Sundermeier, Director of Admissions
888-URSULINE Toll Free Fax: 440-684-6138
Website: www.admission.ursuline.edu
E-mail: admission@ursuline.edu

Virginia Marti College of Art & Design
11724 Detroit Ave, Lakewood OH 44107
Quinn Marti, Director of Admissions
216-221-8584 Fax: 216-221-2311
Website: www.vmcad.edu
E-mail: qmarti@vmcad.edu

OKLAHOMA

Oklahoma State University
Stillwater OK 74078
G.E. Hedrick, Department Head
405-744-5668
Website: www.okstate.edu
E-mail: geh@a.cs.okstate.edu

University of Tulsa
600 S College Ave, Tulsa OK 74104-3126
Earl Johnson, Dean of Admission
918-631-2307 Fax: 918-631-5003
Website: www.utulsa.edu
E-mail: admission@utulsa.edu

Vatterott College - Tulsa
4343 S 118th East Ave, Tulsa OK 74146
Tim Maloukis, Director of Admissions
918-835-8288 Fax: 918-836-9698
Website: www.vatterott-college.com
E-mail: tim.maloukis@vatterott-college.com

OREGON

Linn-Benton Community College
6500 Pacific Blvd SW, Albany OR 97321-3774
Christine Baker, Outreach Coordinator
541-917-4811 Fax: 541-917-4868
Website: www.linnbenton.edu
E-mail: admissions@linnbenton.edu

PACIFIC UNIVERSITY
2043 College Way, Forest Grove OR 97116-1797
Karen M. Dunston, Executive Director of Admissions
800-677-6712 Fax: 503-352-2975
Website: www.pacific.edu
E-mail: admissions@pacific.edu

Rogue Community College
3345 Redwood Hwy, Grants Pass OR 97527-9298
Claudia Sullivan, Director of Enrollment Services
541-956-7500 Fax: 541-471-3585
Website: www.roguecc.edu
E-mail: csullivan@roguecc.edu
See listing under "Community and Junior Colleges"

University of Portland
5000 N Willamette Blvd, Portland OR 97203-5798
Jason McDonald, Dean of Admissions
503-943-7911 Fax: 503-943-7315
Website: www.up.edu
E-mail: mcdonaja@up.edu

PENNSYLVANIA

Berks Technical Institute
2205 Ridgewood Rd, Wyomissing PA 19610-1168
Elizabeth Wade, Director of Admissions
610-372-1722 Fax: 610-376-4684
Website: www.berkstech.com

Central Pennsylvania College
College Hill & Valley Rds, Summerdale PA 17093
Katie Borrelli, Admissions Director
800-759-2727 Fax: 717-728-2505
Website: www.centralpenn.edu
E-mail: katie.borrelli@centralpenn.edu

Clarion University of Pennsylvania
840 Wood St, Clarion PA 16214-1232
William Bailey, Dean of Enrollment Management
814-393-2306 Fax: 814-393-2030
Website: www.clarion.edu
E-mail: admissions@clarion.edu

Community College of Allegheny County
Allegheny Campus: 808 Ridge Ave, Pittsburgh PA 15212 Admissions: 412.237.2700
Boyce Campus: 595 Beatty Rd, Monroeville PA 15146 Admissions: 724.325.6614
North Campus: 8701 Perry Highway, Pittsburgh PA 15237 Admissions: 412.369.3600
South Campus: 1750 Clairton Rd, West Mifflin PA 15122 Admissions: 412-469-4301
Website: www.ccac.edu

Community College of Beaver County
1 Campus Dr, Monaca PA 15061-2566
724-775-8561 Fax: 724-775-4687
Website: www.ccbc.edu
E-mail: admissions@ccbc.edu

Delaware Valley College
700 E Butler Ave, Doylestown PA 18901-2697
Stephen W. Zenko, Director of Admissions
800-2DE-LVAL Fax: 215-230-2968
Website: www.delval.edu
E-mail: stephenzenko@delval.edu

DeSales University
2755 Station Ave, Center Valley PA 18034-9565
610-282-1100 Fax: 610-282-2342
Website: www.desales.edu

Erie Business Center
246 W 9th St, Erie PA 16501-1392
Donna Perino, Director
814-456-7504 Fax: 814-456-6015
Website: www.eriebc.edu
E-mail: perinod@eriebc.edu

Haverford College
370 Lancaster Ave, Haverford PA 19041-1392
Jess Lord, Dean of Admission
610-896-1350 Fax: 610-896-1338
Website: www.haverford.edu
E-mail: admission@haverford.edu

Holy Family University
9801 Frankford Avenue, Philadelphia PA 19114
Lauren Campbell, Director of Admissions
215-637-3050 Fax: 215-281-1022
Website: www.holyfamily.edu
E-mail: admissions@holyfamily.edu

Johnson College
3427 N Main Ave, Scranton PA 18508-1495
Dr. Ann L. Pipinski, President & CEO
Melissa Ide, Director of Enrollment Management
800-2WE-WORK or 570-342-6404 ext. 125
Fax: 570-348-2181
Website: www.johnson.edu
E-mail: admit@johnson.edu

Juniata College
1700 Moore St, Huntingdon PA 16652-2196
Michelle Bartol, Dean of Enrollment
877-JUNIATA Fax: 814-641-3100
Website: www.juniata.edu
E-mail: admissions@juniata.edu

KEYSTONE TECHNICAL INSTITUTE
2301 Academy Dr, Harrisburg PA 17112-1012
Tom Bogush, Director of Admissions
717-545-4747 Fax: 717-901-9090
Website: www.acadcampus.com
E-mail: educdir@acadcampus.com

Established 1980. Private. Coed. Accreditation: ACCSCT. Enrollment: 210 full-time, 50 part-time. Faculty: 15. Student-faculty ratio: 20:1. Degrees offered: Occupational Associate Degrees (AST/ASB). Library: 2,000 volumes. 1 building on 8 acres. Combined classroom; real world lab experience and externships for career training in Medical Assistant, Dental Assistant, Massage Therapy, Paralegal, Culinary Arts, Child Care, Computers.

King's College
133 N River St, Wilkes Barre PA 18711-0801
Michelle Lawrence-Schmude, Dean of Admission
570-208-5900 Fax: 570-208-5971
Website: www.kings.edu
E-mail: admissions@kings.edu

Lehigh Valley College
2809 E Saucon Valley Rd
Center Valley PA 18034-8447
Sam Jarvis, Director of Marketing
800-227-9109 Fax: 610-791-7810
Website: www.lehighvalley.edu
E-mail: joshua.padron@lehighvalley.edu

MOUNT ALOYSIUS COLLEGE
7373 Admiral Peary Hwy, Cresson PA 16630-1999
Frank C. Crouse Jr., Vice President for Enrollment Management
814-886-6383 or 888-823-2220 Fax: 814-886-6441
Website: www.mtaloy.edu
E-mail: admissions@mtaloy.edu

Neumann College
1 Neumann Dr, Aston PA 19014-1298
Dennis Murphy, Director of Admissions
610-459-0905 Fax: 610-558-5652
Website: www.neumann.edu
E-mail: neumann@neumann.edu

Washington & Jefferson College
60 S Lincoln St, Washington PA 15301-4801
Alton E. Newell, Vice President for Enrollment
724-223-6025 Fax: 724-223-6534
Website: www.washjeff.edu
E-mail: admission@washjeff.edu

Widener University
1 University Pl, Chester PA 19013-5792
Edwin Wright, Dean of Admissions
610-499-4000 Fax: 610-499-4676
Website: www.widener.edu
E-mail: admissions.office@widener.edu

RHODE ISLAND

MTTI - MOTORING TECHNICAL TRAINING INSTITUTE
54 Water St, East Providence RI 02914-5022
Sharon Ring, Program Director
401-434-4840 or 866-454-6884 Fax: 401-434-9540
Website: www.mtti.edu
E-mail: info@mtti.edu

New England Institute of Technology
2500 Post Rd, Warwick RI 02886-2244
Michael Kwiatkowski, Director of Admissions
401-739-5000 Fax: 401-738-5122
Website: www.neit.edu
E-mail: eflynn@neit.edu

SOUTH CAROLINA

Bob Jones University
1700 Wade Hampton Blvd
Greenville SC 29614-0001
David Christ, Director of Admissions
800-BJ-AND-ME Fax: 800-2-FAX-BJU
Website: www.bju.edu
E-mail: admissions@bju.edu
See listing under "Universities"

Forrest Junior College
601 E River St, Anderson SC 29624-2405
Pamela Johnson, MBA, President
864-225-7653 Fax: 864-261-7471
Website: www.forrestcollege.edu
E-mail: info@forrestcollege.edu
PC Repair, Networking, A+ Certification, N+ Certification.
See listing under "Community and Junior Colleges"

Greenville Technical College
PO Box 5616, Greenville SC 29606-5616
Carolyn Watkins, Dean of Admissions
800-723-0673 (US) or 800-922-1183 (SC)
Website: www.greenvilletech.com

Limestone College
1115 College Dr, Gaffney SC 29340-3799
Chris Phenicie, V.P. for Enrollment
864-489-7151 Fax: 864-488-8206
Website: www.limestone.edu
E-mail: cphenicie@limestone.edu

South University
9 Science Court, Columbia SC 29203
Trish Wade, Contact
803-799-9082 Fax: 803-799-9038
Website: www.southuniversity.edu
E-mail: twade@southuniversity.edu

Spartanburg Community College
PO Box 4386, Spartanburg SC 29305-4386
Nancy Garmroth, Dean of Admissions & Financial Aid
864-592-4810 Fax: 864-592-4945
Website: sccsc.edu

University of South Carolina - Upstate
800 University Way, Spartanburg SC 29303-4932
Donette Stewart, Assistant VC for Enrollment Services
864-503-5246 Fax: 864-503-5727
Website: www.uscupstate.edu
E-mail: dstewart@uscupstate.edu
See listing under "Universities"

SOUTH DAKOTA

NATIONAL AMERICAN UNIVERSITY
321 Kansas City St, Rapid City SD 57701-3692
Angela G. Beck, Director of Enrollment Management
605-394-4800 Fax: 605-394-4871
Website: www.rapid.national.edu
E-mail: rcadmissions@national.edu

Western Dakota Technical Institute
800 Mickelson Dr, Rapid City SD 57703-4018
Jill Elder, Admissions Coordinator
605-394-4034 Fax: 605-394-2204
Website: www.wdt.edu
E-mail: jill.elder@wdt.edu

TENNESSEE

Austin Peay State University
601 College St, Clarksville TN 37044-0002
931-221-7011 Fax: 931-221-6168
Website: www.apsu.edu
E-mail: admissions@apsu.edu

Lipscomb University
3901 Granny White Pike, Nashville TN 37204-3951
Ricky Holaway, Director of Admissions
800-333-4358 ext. 1776 Fax: 615-269-1804
Website: www.lipscomb.edu
E-mail: admissions@lipscomb.edu

Miller-Motte Technical College
1820 Business Park Dr, Clarksville TN 37040-6023
Lisa Teague, Director of Admissions
931-553-0071 Fax: 931-552-2916
Website: www.miller-motte.com
E-mail: lteague@miller-motte.com

National College
1328 Highway 11W, Bristol TN 37620
Becky Wild, Director of Admissions
423-878-4440 Fax: 423-793-1060
Website: www.national-college.edu
E-mail: info@national-college.edu

National College of Business & Technology
3748 Nolensville Pike, Nashville TN 37211-3322
Lynda Dandridge, Director of Admissions
615-333-3344 Fax: 615-333-3429
Website: www.national-college.edu
E-mail: info@national-college.edu

Tennessee State University
3500 John A Merritt Blvd, Nashville TN 37209-1561
John Cade, Dean of Admissions & Records
615-963-5101 Fax: 615-963-2930
Website: www.tnstate.edu
E-mail: jcade@tnstate.edu

University of Tennessee
615 McCallie Ave, Chattanooga TN 37403-2504
Yancy Freeman, Director of Admissions
423-425-4111 Fax: 423-425-4157
Website: www.utc.edu
E-mail: Yancy-Freeman@utc.edu

TEXAS

Abilene Christian University
ACU Box 29000, Abilene TX 79699-0001
325-674-2000 Fax: 325-674-2202
Website: www.acu.edu
E-mail: info@admissions.acu.edu

American Commercial College
2007 34th St, Lubbock TX 79411-1899
Michael Otto, Director
806-747-4339 Fax: 806-765-9838
Website: www.acc-careers.com
E-mail: mjotto@acc-careers.com

American Commercial College
5119 Twin Towers Blvd, Odessa TX 79762-5504
Donna Duree, Director
432-362-6768 Fax: 432-550-0556
Website: www.acc-careers.com
E-mail: americancc@acc-careers.com

COMPUTER CAREER CENTER
6101 Montana Ave, El Paso TX 79925-2021
Amber Borrego, Director
915-779-8031 Fax: 915-779-8097
Website: www.computercareercenter.edu
E-mail: aborrego@computercareercenter.com

Galveston College
4015 Avenue Q, Galveston TX 77550-7496
Brian Lowery, Registrar
409-763-6551 Fax: 409-944-1501
Website: www.gc.edu
E-mail: blowery@gc.edu

Hallmark Institute of Technology - Technology Campus
10401 W IH 10, San Antonio TX 78230-1736
Joe Fisher, President
210-690-9000 Fax: 210-697-8225
Website: www.hallmarkinstitute.com
E-mail: sross@hallmarkinstitute.com
Electronics Engineering Technology, Business Office Administration, Computer Network Systems Technology, & Medical Assistant.

ITT Technical Institute
6330 E Highway 290 Ste 150, Austin TX 78723-1035
Willard Real, Director of Admissions
512-467-6800 Fax: 512-467-6677
Website: www.itt-tech.edu
E-mail: wreal@itt-tech.edu

ITT TECHNICAL INSTITUTE
2950 S Gessner Rd Ste 100, Houston TX 77063-3751
Jennifer Gomez, Director of Recruitment
713-952-2294 Fax: 713-952-2393
Website: www.itt-tech.edu
E-mail: jgomez@itt-tech.edu

McLennan Community College
1400 College Dr, Waco TX 76708-1498
Fred Hills, Program Director, Computer Information Systems
254-299-8000 Fax: 254-299-8854
Website: www.mclennan.edu
E-mail: fhills@mclennan.edu

Northwood University
1114 W FM 1382, Cedar Hill TX 75104-1204
Sylvia Correa, Director of Admissions
800-927-WOOD Fax: 972-291-3824
Website: www.northwood.edu
E-mail: ray@northwood.edu

Remington College - Fort Worth Campus
300 E Loop 820, Fort Worth TX 76112-1280
Director of Recruitment
817-451-0017 Fax: 817-496-1257
Website: www.remingtoncollege.edu
E-mail: lynn.wey@remingtoncollege.edu

Temple College
2600 S 1st St, Temple TX 76504-7435
Toni Borras, Director of Admissions & Records
254-298-8808 Fax: 254-298-8288
Website: www.templejc.edu
E-mail: admissionsrecords@templejc.edu

Texas Woman's University
PO Box 425589, Denton TX 76204-5589
Erma Nieto-Brecht, Director of Admissions
866-809-6130 Fax: 940-898-3081
Website: www.twu.edu
E-mail: admissions@twu.edu

Tyler Junior College
PO Box 9020, Tyler TX 75711-9020
Joan Jones, Interim Dean
800-687-5680
Website: www.tjc.edu
E-mail: jjon@tjc.edu
See listing under "Community and Junior Colleges"

University of Houston
122 E Cullen Bldg, Houston TX 77204-2023
Office of Admission
713-743-9595
Website: www.uh.edu
E-mail: admissions@uh.edu

University of Texas at Arlington
Box 19111, Arlington TX 76019-0111
Hans Gatterdam, Director of Admission
817-272-6287 Fax: 817-272-3435
Website: www.uta.edu
E-mail: admissions@uta.edu

Weatherford College
225 College Park Dr, Weatherford TX 76086
Dr. Joe Birmingham, President
800-287-5471 Fax: 817-598-6205
Website: www.wc.edu
E-mail: willingham@wc.edu

UTAH

L.D.S. BUSINESS COLLEGE
95 North 300 West, Salt Lake City UT 84101-3500
Kathleen Howe, Assistant Director of Admissions
801-524-8145 Fax: 801-524-1900
Website: www.ldsbc.edu
E-mail: admissions@ldsbc.edu
See listing under "Career Schools"

Stevens Henager College
755 Main St, Logan UT 84321
Josh Swayne, Executive Director
435-713-4777
Website: www.stevenshenager.edu

Stevens Henager College
PO Box 9428, Ogden UT 84409-0428
Cindy Williams, Director of Admissions
801-394-7791 Fax: 801-621-0866
Website: www.stevenshenager.edu
E-mail: shcogden@yahoo.com

VERMONT

NORWICH UNIVERSITY
158 Harmon Dr, Northfield VT 05663
Dr. Frank Vanecek, Division Head
800-468-6679 Fax: 802-485-2087
Website: www.norwich.edu
E-mail: vanecek@norwich.edu
See listing under "Universities"

VIRGINIA

Bryant & Stratton College
8141 Hull St Rd, Richmond VA 23235-6411
David K. Mayle, Director of Admissions
804-745-2444 Fax: 804-745-6884
Website: www.bryantstratton.edu
E-mail: dkmayle@bryantstratton.edu

ECPI College of Technology
5555 Greenwich Rd Ste 300
Virginia Beach VA 23462-6542
757-671-7171 Fax: 757-671-8661
Website: www.ecpi.edu

Gibbs College - Northern Virginia
1980 Gallows Rd, Vienna VA 22182-3913
Everson Travers, Director of Admissions
703-556-8888 Fax: 703-556-0953
Website: www.gibbsva.edu
E-mail: etravers@gibbsva.edu

Marymount University
2807 N Glebe Rd, Arlington VA 22207-4299
Michael Canfield, Director of Admissions
800-548-7638 Fax: 703-522-0348
Website: www.marymount.edu
E-mail: admissions@marymount.edu

National College
100 Logan St, Bluefield VA 24605
Tonya Elmore, Director of Admissions
276-326-3621 Fax: 276-322-5731
Website: www.national-college.edu
E-mail: info@national-college.edu

National College
1819 Emmet St N, Charlottesville VA 22901-2812
434-295-0136 Fax: 434-979-8061
Website: www.national-college.edu
E-mail: info@national-college.edu

National College
336 Old Riverside Dr, Danville VA 24541
Jeff Moore, Director of Admissions
434-793-6822 Fax: 434-793-3634
Website: www.national-college.edu
E-mail: info@national-college.edu

National College
1515 Country Club Rd, Harrisonburg VA 22802
Kathy Sours, Director of Admissions
540-432-0943 Fax: 540-432-1133
Website: www.national-college.edu
E-mail: info@national-college.edu

National College
104 Candlewood Ct, Lynchburg VA 24502-2653
Nancy Fortune, Director of Admissions
434-239-3500 Fax: 434-239-3948
Website: www.national-college.edu
E-mail: info@national-college.edu

National College
10 Church St, Martinsville VA 24114
Barbara Rakes, Director of Admissions
276-632-5621 Fax: 276-632-7915
Website: www.national-college.edu
E-mail: info@national-college.edu

National College
1813 E Main St, Salem VA 24153-4598
Ron Smith, Director of Admissions
540-986-1800 Fax: 540-444-4195
Website: www.national-college.edu
E-mail: info@national-college.edu

Radford University
PO Box 6903, Radford VA 24142
David W. Kraus, Director of Admissions
800-890-4265 Fax: 540-831-5038
Website: www.radford.edu
E-mail: ruadmiss@radford.edu

Roanoke College
221 College Ln, Salem VA 24153-3794
James A. Pennix, Director of Admissions
540-375-2500 Fax: 540-375-2267
Website: www.roanoke.edu
E-mail: pennix@roanoke.edu

Southside Virginia Community College
109 Campus Dr, Alberta VA 23821-2930
Ronald E. Mattox, Dean of Admissions
434-949-1014 Fax: 434-949-7863
Website: www.sv.vccs.edu
E-mail: ronald.mattox@sv.vccs.edu

Southside Virginia Community College
200 Daniel Rd, Keysville VA 23947
Ronald E. Mattox, Dean of Admissions
434-736-2018 Fax: 434-736-2082
Website: www.sv.vccs.edu
E-mail: ronald.mattox@sv.vccs.edu

Stratford University
7777 Leesburg Pike #100 South
Falls Church VA 22043
Keith Evans, Contact
703-821-8570 Fax: 703-734-5335
Website: www.stratford.edu
E-mail: admissions@stratford.edu

UNIVERSITY OF MANAGEMENT AND TECHNOLOGY
1901 Fort Myer Dr Ste 700, Arlington VA 22209
703-516-0035 Fax: 703-516-0985
Website: www.umtweb.edu
E-mail: info@umtweb.edu

University of Mary Washington
1301 College Ave, Fredericksburg VA 22401-5300
Dr. Martin A. Wilder, Jr., Director of Admissions
540-654-2000 Fax: 540-654-1857
Website: www.umw.edu
E-mail: admit@umw.edu

WASHINGTON

BATES TECHNICAL COLLEGE
1101 S Yakima Ave, Tacoma WA 98405-4895
David Borofsky, President
253-680-7000 Fax: 253-680-7101
Website: www.bates.ctc.edu
E-mail: info@bates.ctc.edu

Everett Community College
2000 Tower St, Everett WA 98201
Christine Kerlin, Associate Dean
425-388-9100 Fax: 425-388-9173
Website: www.everettcc.edu
E-mail: ckerlin@everettcc.edu

Lake Washington Technical College
11605 132nd Ave NE, Kirkland WA 98034-8505
James B. West, Director of Admissions
425-739-8100 Fax: 425-739-8110
Website: www.lwtc.ctc.edu

North Seattle Community College
9600 College Way N, Seattle WA 98103-3599
206-527-3746
Website: www.northseattle.edu
E-mail: nsccinfo@sccd.ctc.edu

RENTON TECHNICAL COLLEGE
3000 NE 4th St, Renton WA 98056-4195
Becky Riverman, Registrar
425-235-2352 or 425-235-5840 Fax: 425-235-7832
Website: www.RTC.edu
E-mail: dgrant@RTC.edu

SHORELINE COMMUNITY COLLEGE
16101 Greenwood Ave N, Shoreline WA 98133-5696
Chris Melton, Acting Registrar
206-546-4581 Fax: 206-546-5835
Website: www.shoreline.edu

Walla Walla Community College
500 Tausick Way, Walla Walla WA 99362-9270
Susan Quinn, Director
509-527-4232 or 877-992-9922 Fax: 509-527-4232
Website: www.wwcc.edu
E-mail: susan.quinn@wwcc.edu
See listing under "Community and Junior Colleges"

WEST VIRGINIA

Blue Ridge Community and Technical College
400 W Stephen St, Martinsburg WV 25401
Leslie See, Director of Enrollment
304-260-4380 Fax: 304-260-1752
Website: www.blueridgectc.edu
E-mail: lsee@blueridgectc.edu

Davis & Elkins College
100 Campus Dr, Elkins WV 26241-3996
Renee Heckel, Director of Enrollment Management
800-624-3157 Fax: 304-637-1800
Website: www.davisandelkins.edu
E-mail: admiss@davisandelkins.edu

Fairmont State University
1201 Locust Ave, Fairmont WV 26554-2470
Steve Leadman, Director of Admissions
304-367-4892 or 800-641-5678 Fax: 304-367-4789
Website: www.fairmontstate.edu
E-mail: admit@fairmontstate.edu

Mountain State College
1508 Spring St, Parkersburg WV 26101-3993
Judith Sutton, Director
304-485-5487 Fax: 304-485-3524
Website: www.mountainstate.org
E-mail: admin@mountainstate.org
See listing under "Career Schools"

Mountain State University
Box 9003, Beckley WV 25802-9003
Tony England, Director of Admissions
866-FOR-MSU1 or 304-929-INFO Fax: 304-253-5072
Website: www.mountainstate.edu
E-mail: gomsu@mountainstate.edu
See listing under "Universities"

West Virginia Junior College
176 Thompson Dr, Bridgeport WV 26330
Kathryn Stanley, Director of Admissions
304-842-4007 Fax: 304-842-8191
Website: www.wvjcinfo.net
E-mail: kstanley@wvjcinfo.net

WISCONSIN

Alverno College
PO Box 343922, Milwaukee WI 53234-3922
Dianna Gaebler, Director of Admissions
414-382-6100 Fax: 414-382-6354
Website: www.alverno.edu
E-mail: admissions@alverno.edu

Blackhawk Technical College
PO Box 5009, Janesville WI 53547-5009
Gregg Bosak, Administration, Community Information
608-757-7769 Fax: 608-757-7740
Website: www.blackhawk.edu
E-mail: gbosak@blackhawk.edu

Herzing College
5218 E Terrace Dr, Madison WI 53718-8340
Donald Madelung, President
800-582-1227 Fax: 608-249-8593
Website: www.herzing.edu
E-mail: info@msn.herzing.edu
See listing under "Universities"

Lakeland College
PO Box 359, Sheboygan WI 53082-0359
Nathan Dehne, Director of Admission
920-565-1100 Fax: 920-565-1215
Website: www.lakeland.edu
E-mail: admissions@lakeland.edu

Marquette University
PO Box 1881, Milwaukee WI 53201-1881
Robert Blust, Director of Admissions
414-288-7302 Fax: 414-288-3764
Website: www.mu.edu
E-mail: admissions@marquette.edu

St. Norbert College
100 Grant St, De Pere WI 54115
Brian Studebaker, Director of Admission
800-236-4878 Fax: 920-403-4072
Website: www.snc.edu
E-mail: admit@snc.edu

Wisconsin Indianhead Technical College
505 Pine Ridge Dr, Shell Lake WI 54871
Laura Wassenaar, Dean
800-243-9482 Fax: 715-468-2819
Website: www.witc.edu
E-mail: laura.wassenaar@witc.edu

WYOMING

Laramie County Community College
1400 E College Dr, Cheyenne WY 82007-3204
Jenny Hargett, Director of Admissions
307-778-5222 Fax: 307-778-1350
Website: www.lccc.wy.edu
E-mail: learnmore@lccc.wy.edu

University of Wyoming
Admissions Office
Dept 3435, Laramie WY 82071-3435
Brooke Culver, Contact
800-342-5996 Fax: 307-766-4042
Website: www.uwyo.edu
E-mail: why-wyo@uwyo.edu

GUAM

University of Guam
UOG Station, Mangilao GU 96923
Deborah Leon Guerrero, Registrar
671-735-2201 or 671-735-2208 Fax: 671-735-2203
Website: www.uog.edu
E-mail: admitme@uog9.uog.edu

PUERTO RICO

TRINITY COLLEGE OF PUERTO RICO
PO Box 34360, Ponce PR 00734-4360
Ms. Maria I. Colon, Executive Director
787-842-0000 Fax: 787-284-2537
Website: www.csifpr.org/trinitycollege
E-mail: mcolon@csifpr.org

CONSERVATION/RENEWABLE NATURAL RESOURCES

ALASKA

University of Alaska Anchorage
PO Box 141629, Anchorage AK 99514-1629
Cecile Mitchell, Director of Enrollment Services
907-786-1480 Fax: 907-786-4888
Website: www.uaa.alaska.edu/
E-mail: enroll@uaa.alaska.edu

COLORADO

Colorado Northwestern Community College
500 Kennedy Dr, Rangely CO 81648-3502
Tresa England, Director of Student Services
800-562-1105 Fax: 970-675-3343
Website: www.cncc.edu
E-mail: tresa.england@cncc.edu

UNIVERSITY OF DENVER UNIVERSITY COLLEGE
2211 S Josephine St, Denver CO 80208
Dr. John Hill, Academic Director
303-871-3354 Fax: 303-871-4047
Website: www.universitycollege.du.edu
E-mail: ucolinfo@du.edu

FLORIDA

University of South Florida
4202 E Fowler Ave, Tampa FL 33620-6900
J. Robert Spatig, Director of Admissions
877-USF-BULL Fax: 813-974-9689
Website: www.usf.edu
E-mail: admissions@admin.usf.edu
See listing under "Universities"

GEORGIA

North Georgia Technical College
Clarkesville Campus
PO Box 65, Clarkesville GA 30523-0002
Admissions
706-754-7700 Fax: 706-754-7777
Website: www.northgatech.edu
E-mail: info@northgatech.edu

IDAHO

University of Idaho
Moscow ID 83844-4253
Lloyd Scott, Director of New Student Services
208-885-6163 Fax: 208-885-4477
Website: www.uidaho.edu
E-mail: nss@uidaho.edu

ILLINOIS

Roosevelt University
430 S Michigan Ave, Chicago IL 60605
Gwen E. Kanelos, Asst. Vice President for Enrollment Services
877-APPLY-RU Fax: 312-341-4216
Website: www.roosevelt.edu
E-mail: applyru@roosevelt.edu

INDIANA

University of Evansville
1800 Lincoln Ave, Evansville IN 47722-0001
Don Vos, Dean of Admission
800-423-8633 Fax: 812-488-4076
Website: www.evansville.edu
E-mail: admission@evansville.edu

IOWA

Iowa Lakes Community College
300 S 18th St, Estherville IA 51334-2721
Anne Stansbury, Asst. Director of Admissions
712-362-7945 Fax: 712-362-8363
Website: www.iowalakes.edu
E-mail: info@iowalakes.edu

MASSACHUSETTS

North Shore Community College
1 Ferncroft Rd, Danvers MA 01923-4093
Jennifer Kirk, Director of Admissions & Recruitment Outreach
978-762-4000 Fax: 978-762-4015
Website: www.northshore.edu
E-mail: jkirk@northshore.edu

MICHIGAN

Grand Valley State University
1 Campus Dr, Allendale MI 49401-9403
Jodi Chycinski, Director of Admissions
616-331-6611 Fax: 616-331-2000
Website: www.gvsu.edu
E-mail: go2gvsu@gvsu.edu

MINNESOTA

University of Minnesota
2900 University Ave, Crookston MN 56716-5001
218-281-6510 Fax: 218-281-8575
Website:
admissions.umcrookston.edu/requirements/apply.htm
E-mail: info@umcrookston.edu

MISSOURI

Northwest Missouri State University
800 University Dr, Maryville MO 64468-6001
Beverly Schenkel, Dean of Enrollment Management
660-562-1562 Fax: 660-562-1121
Website: www.nwmissouri.edu
E-mail: admissions@nwmissouri.edu

NEVADA

GREAT BASIN COLLEGE
1500 College Pkwy, Elko NV 89801-5032
Julie G. Byrnes, Director of Enrollment Management
775-753-2271 Fax: 775-753-2311
Website: www.gbcnv.edu
E-mail: julieb@gwmail.gbcnv.edu
See listing under "Universities"

NEW HAMPSHIRE

Antioch University New England
40 Avon St, Keene NH 03431-3516
David Caruso, President
Leatrice A. Oram, Director of Admissions
603-357-6265 Fax: 603-357-0718
Website: www.antiochne.edu
E-mail: admissions@antiochne.edu

NEW JERSEY

RICHARD STOCKTON COLLEGE OF NEW JERSEY
PO Box 195, Pomona NJ 08240
John Iacovelli, Dean of Enrollment Management
866-RSC-2885 Fax: 609-626-5541
Website: www.stockton.edu
E-mail: admissions@stockton.edu

Stockton College is a comprehensive liberal arts, co-ed institution founded in 1969. Advance Pre-Professional Degree Options: 7-yr BS/MD with UMDNJ; NJ Dental School; NJ Medical School, Robert Wood Johnson Medical, School of Osteopathic Medicine; NY College of Podiatric Medicine, Pennsylvania College of Podiatric Medicine, SUNY College of Optometry. Pharmacy doctorate program with Rutgers University. 5-yr Engineering with NJIT and Rutgers University. Dual BA/MA in Criminal Justice. 5-yr BS/MS in Computational Science. BS/MS in Nursing. Doctorate of Physical Therapy. Additional Programs: Forensic Science, Pre-Law, Pre-Occupational Therapy, and Pre-Veterinary.

NEW YORK

College of Saint Rose
432 Western Ave, Albany NY 12203-1419
Maryelizabeth Amico, Asst V.P. for Undergraduate Admissions
518-454-5150 Fax: 518-454-2013
Website: www.strose.edu
E-mail: admit@strose.edu

SUNY Sullivan County Community College
112 College Rd, Loch Sheldrake NY 12759-5151
Sari Rosenheck, Director of Admissions
845-434-5750 Fax: 845-434-0923
Website: www.sullivan.suny.edu
E-mail: admissions@sullivan.suny.edu
Student Housing on Campus.

NORTH CAROLINA

Catawba College
2300 W Innes St, Salisbury NC 28144-2488
Dr. L. Russell Watjen, Ph.D., V.P. & Dean of Admissions
704-637-4402 Fax: 704-637-4222
Website: www.catawba.edu
E-mail: admission@catawba.edu

Haywood Community College
185 Freedlander Dr, Clyde NC 28721
Debbie Rowland, Coordinator of Admissions
828-627-4500 Fax: 828-627-4513
Website: www.haywood.edu
E-mail: drowland@haywood.edu

NORTH DAKOTA

Minot State University-Bottineau Campus
105 Simrall Blvd, Bottineau ND 58318-1159
Paula Berg, Associate Dean of Student Affairs
800-542-6866 Fax: 701-228-5499
Website: www.misu-b.nodak.edu
E-mail: paula.berg@misu.nodak.edu

OHIO

Cleveland State University
2121 Euclid Ave RW 204, Cleveland OH 44115
Dr. Richard Arndt, Dean of Undergraduate Recruitment and College Partnerships
888-CSU-OHIO Fax: 216-687-9210
Website: www.csuohio.edu
E-mail: admissions@csuohio.edu

The Ohio State University
School of Natural Resources
Kottman Hall, 2021 Coffey Rd, Columbus OH 43210
614-292-2265 Fax: 614-292-7432
Website: snr.osu.edu
E-mail: burks.39@osu.edu

OKLAHOMA

Oklahoma State University
Stillwater OK 74078
Craig McKinley, Department Head
405-744-5438
Website: www.okstate.edu
E-mail: craig.mckinley@okstate.edu

PENNSYLVANIA

Juniata College
1700 Moore St, Huntingdon PA 16652-2196
Michelle Bartol, Dean of Enrollment
877-JUNIATA Fax: 814-641-3100
Website: www.juniata.edu
E-mail: admissions@juniata.edu

SOUTH DAKOTA

Western Dakota Technical Institute
800 Mickelson Dr, Rapid City SD 57703-4018
Jill Elder, Admissions Coordinator
605-394-4034 Fax: 605-394-2204
Website: www.wdt.edu
E-mail: jill.elder@wdt.edu

TEXAS

Abilene Christian University
ACU Box 29000, Abilene TX 79699-0001
325-674-2000 Fax: 325-674-2202
Website: www.acu.edu
E-mail: info@admissions.acu.edu

WASHINGTON

NORTHWEST INDIAN COLLEGE
2522 Kwina Rd, Bellingham WA 98226-9278
Crystal Bagby, Director of Admissions
360-676-2772 Fax: 360-392-4333
Website: www.nwic.edu/
E-mail: cbagby@nwic.edu

WYOMING

University of Wyoming
Admissions Office
Dept 3435, Laramie WY 82071-3435
Brooke Culver, Contact
800-342-5996 Fax: 307-766-4042
Website: www.uwyo.edu
E-mail: why-wyo@uwyo.edu

CONSTRUCTION TRADES

ALABAMA

George C. Wallace State Community College
PO Box 2530, Selma AL 36702-2530
Mrs. Donitha J. Griffin, Dean of Students
334-876-9295 Fax: 334-876-9300
Website: www.wccs.edu
E-mail: dgriffin@wccs.edu

Trenholm State Technical College
Patterson Campus
3920 Troy Hwy, Montgomery AL 36116
Dr. Anthony Molina, President
334-420-4200 Fax: 334-420-4206
Website: www.trenholmtech.cc.al.us
E-mail: molinaa@trenholmtech.cc.al.us

ARIZONA

Pima Community College
4905 E Broadway Blvd, Tucson AZ 85709-1010
Wendy Kilgore, Ph.D., Director of Admissions
520-206-4500 Fax: 520-206-4790
Website: www.pima.edu
E-mail: infocenter@pima.edu

Refrigeration School
4210 E Washington St, Phoenix AZ 85034-1894
Crystal Otts, Admissions Manager
602-275-7133 Fax: 602-267-4805
Website: www.refrigerationschool.com
E-mail: crystal@rsiaz.edu

ARKANSAS

Northwest Technical Institute
709 S Old Missouri Rd, Springdale AR 72764
Charles L. Kelley, President
479-751-8824 Fax: 479-751-7780
Website: www.nti.tec.ar.us
E-mail: info@nit.tec.ar.us

CALIFORNIA

Butte College
3536 Butte Campus Dr, Oroville CA 95965-8399
Carole Gish, Director of Admissions
530-895-2511 Fax: 530-879-4313
Website: www.butte.edu
E-mail: admissions@butte.edu

FRESNO CITY COLLEGE
1101 E University Ave, Fresno CA 93741-0002
Dayann Dietrich, Contact
559-442-8241 Fax: 559-237-4232
Website: www.fresnocitycollege.com
E-mail: fcc.admissions@scccd.com

ITT Technical Institute
12669 Encinitas Ave, Sylmar CA 91342-3664
Kelly Christensen, Director of Admissions
818-364-5151 Fax: 818-364-5150
Website: www.itt-tech.edu
E-mail: kchristensen@itt-tech.edu

Orange Coast College
PO Box 5005, Costa Mesa CA 92628-5005
Kristin Clark, Director of Admissions
714-432-5773 Fax: 714-432-5736
Website: www.orangecoastcollege.edu
E-mail: kclark@cccd.edu

San Joaquin Valley College
201 New Stine Rd, Bakersfield CA 93309-2659
Jaime Delgado, Enrollment Services Director
661-834-1026 Fax: 559-651-4864
Website: www.sjvc.edu
E-mail: jaime.delgado@sjvc.edu

San Joaquin Valley College
295 E Sierra Ave, Fresno CA 93710-3616
Nora Twarynski, Enrollment Services Director
559-448-8282 Fax: 559-651-4864
Website: www.sjvc.edu
E-mail: nora.twarynski@sjvc.edu

San Joaquin Valley College
10641 Church St, Rancho Cucamonga CA 91730
Ramon Abreu, Enrollment Services Director
909-948-7582 Fax: 559-651-4864
Website: www.sjvc.edu
E-mail: ramon.abreu@sjvc.edu

COLORADO

Colorado Northwestern Community College
500 Kennedy Dr, Rangely CO 81648-3502
Tresa England, Director of Student Services
800-562-1105 Fax: 970-675-3343
Website: www.cncc.edu
E-mail: tresa.england@cncc.edu

San Juan Basin Technical College
PO Box 970, Cortez CO 81321-0970
Shannon South, Vice President
970-565-8457 Fax: 970-565-8450
Website: www.sjbtc.edu
E-mail: info@sjbtc.edu

FLORIDA

EVERGLADES UNIVERSITY (MAIN CAMPUS)
5002 T-Rex Ave Suite 100, Boca Raton FL 33431
Kristi Mollis, President
888-772-6077 Fax: 561-912-1191
Website: www.evergladesuniversity.edu
E-mail: admissions-boca@evergladesuniversity.edu
See listing under "Universities"

EVERGLADES UNIVERSITY
Orlando Campus (Branch Campus)
887 E Altamonte Dr, Altamonte Springs FL 32701
Linda Volz, Vice President
866-289-1078 Fax: 407-482-9801
Website: www.evergladesuniversity.edu
E-mail: admissions-orl@evergladesuniversity.edu
See listing under "Universities"

EVERGLADES UNIVERSITY
Sarasota Campus (Branch Campus)
6001 Lake Osprey Dr, Suite 110, Sarasota FL 34240
Brad Brewer, Vice President
866-907-2262 Fax: 941-907-6634
Website: www.evergladesuniversity.edu
E-mail: admissions-sar@evergladesuniversity.edu
See listing under "Universities"

Lincoln College of Technology
2410 Metrocentre Blvd
West Palm Beach FL 33407-3105
Don Cunningham, Vice President of Admissions
561-688-2001 Fax: 561-842-9503
Website: www.lincolncollegeoftechnology.com
E-mail: dcunningham@lincolntech.com

GEORGIA

North Georgia Technical College
434 Meeks Ave, Blairsville GA 30512-2983
Admissions
706-439-6300 Fax: 706-439-6301
Website: www.northgatech.edu
E-mail: info@northgatech.edu

North Georgia Technical College
8989 Highway 17, Toccoa GA 30577
706-779-8100 Fax: 706-779-8130
Website: www.northgatech.edu
E-mail: info@northgatech.edu

North Georgia Technical College
Clarkesville Campus
PO Box 65, Clarkesville GA 30523-0002
Admissions
706-754-7700 Fax: 706-754-7777
Website: www.northgatech.edu
E-mail: info@northgatech.edu

IDAHO

Brigham Young University - Idaho
120 Kimball Bldg, Rexburg ID 83460-1615
Rob Garrett, Director of Admissions
208-496-1020 Fax: 208-496-1220
Website: www.byui.edu
E-mail: admissions@byui.edu

ILLINOIS

Kaskaskia College
27210 College Rd, Centralia IL 62801-7878
Tyra Taylor, Dean of Enrollment Management and Retention Services
618-545-3000 Fax: 618-532-1990
Website: www.kaskaskia.edu
E-mail: ttaylor@kaskaskia.edu

Triton College
2000 5th Ave, River Grove IL 60171-1995
Jeffery Cooks, Director, Admission Services
708-456-0300 ext. 3130 Fax: 708-583-3147
Website: www.triton.edu
E-mail: triton@triton.edu
See listing under "Community and Junior Colleges"

INDIANA

Ivy Tech Community College - North Central
220 Dean Johnson Blvd, South Bend IN 46601-3415
Pam Decker, Director of Admissions
574-289-7001 Fax: 574-236-7177
Website: www.ivytech.edu
E-mail: pdecker@ivytech.edu

IOWA

Iowa Lakes Community College
3200 College Dr, Emmetsburg IA 50536-1055
Anne Stansbury, Asst. Director of Admissions
712-852-5212 Fax: 712-362-8363
Website: www.iowalakes.edu
E-mail: info@iowalakes.edu

Northwest Iowa Community College
603 W Park St, Sheldon IA 51201-1046
Lisa Story, Director of Enrollment Management
712-324-5061 Fax: 712-324-4136
Website: www.nwicc.edu
E-mail: lstory@nwicc.edu

KANSAS

Flint Hills Technical College
3301 W 18th Ave, Emporia KS 66801-5957
Lisa Kirmer, Dean of Student Services
620-343-4600 Fax: 620-343-4610
Website: www.fhtc.net
E-mail: lkirmer@fhtc.net

SOUTHWEST KANSAS TECHNICAL SCHOOL
PO Box 1599, Liberal KS 67905-1599
Ed Poley, Director
620-604-2900 or 800-818-3819 Fax: 620-604-2901
Website: www.swkts.com
E-mail: epoley@usd480.net

KENTUCKY

Bluegrass Community and Technical College
Oswald Building
470 Cooper Drive, Lexington KY 40506-0235
Shelbie Hugle, Director of Admissions
859-246-6200 Fax: 859-246-4664
Website: www.bluegrass.kctcs.edu
E-mail: bctc_info@kctcs.edu

LOUISIANA

Louisiana Technical College
Florida Parishes Campus
PO Box 1300, Greensburg LA 70441
225-222-4251 Fax: 225-222-6064
Website: www.ltc.edu./region.html

MAINE

Landing School of Boatbuilding, Design, Systems & Composites
PO Box 1490, Kennebunkport ME 04046-1490
Jade Elliott, Director of Student Services
207-985-7976 Fax: 207-985-7942
Website: www.landingschool.edu
E-mail: jadeelliott@landingschool.edu

Southern Maine Community College
2 Fort Rd, South Portland ME 04106-1698
Dr. James Ortiz, President
Scott MacDonald, Director of Financial Aid
207-741-5500 Fax: 207-741-5671
Website: www.smccme.edu
E-mail: oharmon@maine.rr.com

MASSACHUSETTS

Benjamin Franklin Institute of Technology
41 Berkeley St, Boston MA 02116-6307
Norman Kraft, Dean of Enrollment
617-423-4630 ext. 121 Fax: 617-482-3706
Website: www.bfit.edu
E-mail: admissions@bfit.edu

MICHIGAN

Delta College
University Center MI 48710-0001
Duff Zube, Director of Admissions
989-686-9093 Fax: 989-667-2202
Website: www.delta.edu
E-mail: admit@delta.edu

MACOMB COMMUNITY COLLEGE
14500 E 12 Mile Rd, Warren MI 48088-3896
Information Center
586-445-7999
Website: www.macomb.edu
E-mail: answer@macomb.edu

MINNESOTA

Dunwoody College of Technology
818 Dunwoody Blvd, Minneapolis MN 55403-1192
John Slama, Vice President Enrollment Management
800-292-4625 or 612-374-5800 Fax: 612-374-4128
Website: www.dunwoody.edu
E-mail: jslama@dunwoody.edu
See listing under "Career Schools"

Hibbing Community College
1515 E 25th St, Hibbing MN 55746-3300
Holly Bigelow, Director of Enrollment
800-224-4HCC or 218-262-7200 Fax: 218-262-6717
Website: www.hibbing.edu
E-mail: admissions@hibbing.edu

Inver Hills Community College
2500 80th St E, Inver Grove Heights MN 55076
651-450-8500 Fax: 651-450-8679
Website: www.inverhills.edu

Minnesota State College - Southeast Technical
Red Wing Campus
308 Pioneer Rd, Red Wing MN 55066
Al DuCett, Director of Admissions
877-853-8324 Fax: 507-453-2715
Website: www.southeastmn.edu
E-mail: aducett@southeastmn.edu
70+ degrees, diplomas & certificates (15+ online) in Business & Office Careers, Musical Instrument Repair, Physical Health, Transportation, Technology, and Trades.

Minnesota State College - Southeast Technical
Winona Campus
PO Box 409, 1250 Homer Rd, Winona MN 55987
Al DuCett, Director of Admissions
877-853-8324 Fax: 507-453-2715
Website: www.southeastmn.edu
E-mail: aducett@southeastmn.edu
70+ degrees, diplomas & certificates (15+ online) in Business & Office Careers, Musical Instrument Repair, Physical Health, Transportation, Technology, and Trades.

Northland Community and Technical College
2022 Central Ave NE
East Grand Forks MN 56721-2702
Loren Abel, Carpentry Instructor
800-451-3441 Fax: 218-773-4502
Website: www.northlandcollege.edu
E-mail: admissions@northlandcollege.edu

Ridgewater College-Willmar Campus
PO Box 1097, Willmar MN 56201-1097
Sally Kerfeld, Director of Admissions
800-722-1151 Fax: 320-222-5212
Website: www.ridgewater.edu
E-mail: sally.kerfeld@ridgewater.edu

St. Cloud Technical College
1540 Northway Dr, Saint Cloud MN 56303-1240
Jodi Elness, Director of Enrollment Management
800-222-1009 Fax: 320-308-5981
Website: www.sctc.edu
E-mail: jelness@sctc.edu

MISSOURI

Linn State Technical College
1 Technology Dr, Linn MO 65051-9606
Becky Dunn, Admissions
800-743-8324 Fax: 573-897-5026
Website: www.linnstate.edu
E-mail: admissions@linnstate.edu

Ranken Technical College
4431 Finney Ave, Saint Louis MO 63113-2898
Admissions Office
314-371-0233 Fax: 314-371-0241
Website: www.ranken.edu
E-mail: admissions@ranken.edu

State Fair Community College
3201 W 16th St, Sedalia MO 65301-2199
Director of Admissions
660-530-5833 Fax: 660-596-7472
Website: www.sfccmo.edu
E-mail: mparris@sfccmo.edu

NEW HAMPSHIRE

New Hampshire Community Technical College
1066 Front St, Manchester NH 03102-8528
Jacquie Poirier, Director of Admissions
603-668-6706 Fax: 603-668-5354
Website: www.manchester.nhctc.edu
E-mail: jpoirier@nhctc.edu

NEW MEXICO

New Mexico State University
1500 N 3rd St, Grants NM 87020-2025
Irene Lutz, Director of Admissions
505-287-7981 Fax: 505-287-2329
Website: www.grants.nmsu.edu
E-mail: ilutz@nmsu.edu

NEW YORK

CAREER INSTITUTE OF HEALTH & TECHNOLOGY
340 Flatbush Avenue Ext, Brooklyn NY 11201
Mary Miller, Contact
718-422-1212 Fax: 718-422-1222
Website: www.careerinstitute.edu
E-mail: admissions@careerinstitute.edu

CAREER INSTITUTE OF HEALTH & TECHNOLOGY
200 Garden City Plz, Garden City NY 11530
Mary Miller, Contact
516-877-1225 Fax: 516-877-1959
Website: www.careerinstitute.edu
E-mail: admissions@careerinstitute.edu

CAREER INSTITUTE OF HEALTH & TECHNOLOGY
9525 Queens Blvd Ste 600, Rego Park NY 11374
Mary Miller, Contact
718-897-4868 Fax: 718-897-4863
Website: www.careerinstitute.edu
E-mail: admissions@careerinstitute.edu

ISLAND DRAFTING & TECHNICAL INSTITUTE
128 Broadway (Route 110), Amityville NY 11701-2704
James G. DiLiberto, President
631-691-8733 Fax: 631-691-8738
Website: www.idti.edu
E-mail: info@idti.edu

Pratt Institute
200 Willoughby Ave, Brooklyn NY 11205-3899
Heidi Metcalf, Director of Admissions
718-636-3600 Fax: 718-636-3670
Website: www.pratt.edu
E-mail: hmetcalf@pratt.edu
Construction Management

SUNY College of Technology
Alfred NY 14802
Deborah J. Goodrich, Associate VP Enrollment Mgmt.
800-4AL-FRED Fax: 607-587-4299
Website: www.alfredstate.edu
E-mail: admissions@alfredstate.edu

SUNY Orange County Community College
115 South St, Middletown NY 10940-6437
Margot St. Lawrence, Director of Admissions
845-341-4030 Fax: 845-342-8662
Website: www.sunyorange.edu
E-mail: apply@sunyorange.edu
See listing under "Community and Junior Colleges"

SUNY Sullivan County Community College
112 College Rd, Loch Sheldrake NY 12759-5151
Sari Rosenheck, Director of Admissions
845-434-5750 Fax: 845-434-0923
Website: www.sullivan.suny.edu
E-mail: admissions@sullivan.suny.edu
Student Housing on Campus.

NORTH CAROLINA

Haywood Community College
185 Freedlander Dr, Clyde NC 28721
Debbie Rowland, Coordinator of Admissions
828-627-4500 Fax: 828-627-4513
Website: www.haywood.edu
E-mail: drowland@haywood.edu

James Sprunt Community College
PO Box 398, Kenansville NC 28349-0398
Lea Grady, Admissions
910-296-2500 Fax: 910-296-1636
Website: www.jamessprunt.edu

Mayland Community College
PO Box 547, Spruce Pine NC 28777-0547
Cathy B. Morrison, Director of Enrollment Management
828-765-7351 Fax: 828-765-0728
Website: www.mayland.edu
E-mail: cmorrison@mayland.edu

South Piedmont Community College
PO Box 126, Polkton NC 28135-0126
John Curtis, Contact
704-272-5324 Fax: 704-272-8904
Website: www.spcc.edu
E-mail: jcurtis@spcc.edu

OHIO

Owens Community College
PO Box 10000, Toledo OH 43699-1947
William J. Ivoska, Ph.D, Vice President of Student Services
567-661-7000 Fax: 567-661-7607
Website: www.owens.edu
E-mail: admissions@owens.edu

OREGON

Rogue Community College
3345 Redwood Hwy, Grants Pass OR 97527-9298
Claudia Sullivan, Director of Enrollment Services
541-956-7500 Fax: 541-471-3585
Website: www.roguecc.edu
E-mail: csullivan@roguecc.edu
See listing under "Community and Junior Colleges"

PENNSYLVANIA

Community College of Allegheny County
Allegheny Campus: 808 Ridge Ave, Pittsburgh PA 15212 Admissions: 412.237.2700
Boyce Campus: 595 Beatty Rd, Monroeville PA 15146 Admissions: 724.325.6614
North Campus: 8701 Perry Highway, Pittsburgh PA 15237 Admissions: 412.369.3600
South Campus: 1750 Clairton Rd, West Mifflin PA 15122 Admissions: 412-469-4301
Website: www.ccac.edu

Johnson College
3427 N Main Ave, Scranton PA 18508-1495
Dr. Ann L. Pipinski, President & CEO
Melissa Ide, Director of Enrollment Management
800-2WE-WORK or 570-342-6404 ext. 125
Fax: 570-348-2181
Website: www.johnson.edu
E-mail: admit@johnson.edu

RHODE ISLAND

MTTI - MOTORING TECHNICAL TRAINING INSTITUTE
54 Water St, East Providence RI 02914-5022
Sharon Ring, Program Director
401-434-4840 or 866-454-6884 Fax: 401-434-9540
Website: www.mtti.edu
E-mail: info@mtti.edu

New England Institute of Technology
2500 Post Rd, Warwick RI 02886-2244
Michael Kwiatkowski, Director of Admissions
401-739-5000 Fax: 401-738-5122
Website: www.neit.edu
E-mail: eflynn@neit.edu

SOUTH CAROLINA

Bob Jones University
1700 Wade Hampton Blvd
Greenville SC 29614-0001
David Christ, Director of Admissions
800-BJ-AND-ME Fax: 800-2-FAX-BJU
Website: www.bju.edu
E-mail: admissions@bju.edu
See listing under "Universities"

SOUTH DAKOTA

Western Dakota Technical Institute
800 Mickelson Dr, Rapid City SD 57703-4018
Jill Elder, Admissions Coordinator
605-394-4034 Fax: 605-394-2204
Website: www.wdt.edu
E-mail: jill.elder@wdt.edu

TEXAS

Career Centers of Texas - El Paso
8360 Burnham Rd Ste 100, El Paso TX 79907-1526
Barbara Martinez, Director of Admissions
915-595-1935 Fax: 915-595-6619
Website: www.careercenters.edu
E-mail: bmartinez@cct-ep.com

McLennan Community College
1400 College Dr, Waco TX 76708-1498
Fred Quick, Coordinator, Building Construction Trade
254-753-6212 Fax: 254-299-8854
Website: www.mclennan.edu
E-mail: fquick@mclennan.edu

SAN ANTONIO COLLEGE OF MEDICAL AND DENTAL ASSISTANTS
7142 San Pedro Ave Ste 100, San Antonio TX 78216
Carig Czubati, Director of Admissions
210-733-0777 Fax: 210-735-2431
Website: www.sacmda.com
E-mail: cczubati@sac-mda.com

WASHINGTON

BATES TECHNICAL COLLEGE
1101 S Yakima Ave, Tacoma WA 98405-4895
David Borofsky, President
253-680-7000 Fax: 253-680-7101
Website: www.bates.ctc.edu
E-mail: info@bates.ctc.edu

RENTON TECHNICAL COLLEGE
3000 NE 4th St, Renton WA 98056-4195
Becky Riverman, Registrar
425-235-2352 or 425-235-5840 Fax: 425-235-7832
Website: www.RTC.edu
E-mail: dgrant@RTC.edu

Walla Walla Community College
500 Tausick Way, Walla Walla WA 99362-9270
Jerry Kjack, Director
509-527-4283 or 877-992-9922 Fax: 509-527-4572
Website: www.wwcc.edu
E-mail: jerry.kjack@wwcc.edu
See listing under "Community and Junior Colleges"

WEST COAST TRAINING INC.
PO Box 970, Woodland WA 98674-1000
Eileen Kelgard, President
David Simpson, Director
800-755-5477 Fax: 360-225-6760
Website: www.heavyequipmenttraining.com
E-mail: wct@heavyequipmenttraining.com
See listing under "Career Schools"

WISCONSIN

Wisconsin Indianhead Technical College
505 Pine Ridge Dr, Shell Lake WI 54871
Gene Rosburg, Dean
800-243-9482 Fax: 715-468-2819
Website: www.witc.edu
E-mail: eugene.rosburg@witc.edu

WYOMING

Laramie County Community College
1400 E College Dr, Cheyenne WY 82007-3204
Jenny Hargett, Director of Admissions
307-778-5222 Fax: 307-778-1350
Website: www.lccc.wy.edu
E-mail: learnmore@lccc.wy.edu

DENTISTRY

ALABAMA

Judson College
302 Bibb St, Marion AL 36756
Michael Scotto, Director of Admissions
800-447-9472 Fax: 334-683-5147
Website: www.judson.edu
E-mail: admissions@judson.edu

ALASKA

University of Alaska Anchorage
PO Box 141629, Anchorage AK 99514-1629
Cecile Mitchell, Director of Enrollment Services
907-786-1480 Fax: 907-786-4888
Website: www.uaa.alaska.edu/
E-mail: enroll@uaa.alaska.edu

ARIZONA

ARIZONA SCHOOL OF DENTISTRY AND ORAL HEALTH
A.T. STILL UNIVERSITY
5850 E Still Cir, Mesa AZ 85206
Admissions Counselor
866-626-2878 or 480-219-6000 Fax: 480-219-6100
Website: www.atsu.edu
E-mail: admissions@atsu.edu

CALIFORNIA

Chapman University
One University Drive, Orange CA 92866-1099
Michael Drummy, Assistant Vice President for Enrollment
Services and Chief Admission Officer
714-997-6411 or 888-CUAPPLY Fax: 714-997-6713
Website: www.chapman.edu
E-mail: admit@chapman.edu

Point Loma Nazarene University
3900 Lomaland Dr, San Diego CA 92106-2810
Chip Killingsworth, Director of Undergraduate Admissions
800-733-7770 Fax: 619-849-2601
Website: www.pointloma.edu
E-mail: admissions@pointloma.edu

UNIVERSITY OF THE PACIFIC
Arthur A. Dugoni School of Dentistry
2155 Webster St, San Francisco CA 94115-2333
Kathy Candito, Director of Admissions
415-929-6491 Fax: 415-749-3363
Website: www.dental.pacific.edu
E-mail: kcandito@pacific.edu

Western Career College
2157 Country Hills Dr, Antioch CA 94509-7435
Dr. Tim Gienapp, Executive Director
925-522-7777
Website: www.westerncollege.edu

Western Career College
7301 Greenback Ln Bldg A, Citrus Heights CA 95621
Jim Murphy, Executive Director
916-722-8200 Fax: 916-722-6883
Website: www.westerncollege.edu

Western Career College
380 Civic Dr Ste 300, Pleasant Hill CA 94523-1984
LaShawn Wells, Executive Director
925-609-6650 Fax: 926-609-6666
Website: www.westerncollege.edu

Western Career College
8909 Folsom Blvd, Sacramento CA 95826-3203
Sue Smith, Executive Director
916-361-5100 Fax: 916-361-6666
Website: www.westerncollege.edu

Western Career College
6201 San Ignacio Ave, San Jose CA 95119
Steve Ashab, Executive Director
408-360-0840 Fax: 408-360-0848
Website: www.westerncollege.edu

Western Career College
15555 E 14th St Ste 500, San Leandro CA 94578
Dawn Matthews, Executive Director
510-276-3888 Fax: 510-276-3653
Website: www.westerncollege.edu

COLORADO

IntelliTec College
772 Horizon Dr, Grand Junction CO 81506-3907
Jennifer Daniels, Contact
970-245-8101 Fax: 970-243-8074
Website: www.intelliteccollege.edu
E-mail: admgj@intelliteccollege.edu

ILLINOIS

Roosevelt University
430 S Michigan Ave, Chicago IL 60605
Gwen E. Kanelos, Asst. Vice President for Enrollment Services
877-APPLY-RU Fax: 312-341-4216
Website: www.roosevelt.edu
E-mail: applyru@roosevelt.edu

IOWA

Briar Cliff University
PO Box 2100, Sioux City IA 51104-0100
Sharisue Wilcoxon, VP for Enrollment Management
712-279-5200 Fax: 712-279-1632
Website: www.briarcliff.edu
E-mail: admissions@briarcliff.edu

Iowa Lakes Community College
300 S 18th St, Estherville IA 51334-2721
Anne Stansbury, Asst. Director of Admissions
712-362-7945 Fax: 712-362-8363
Website: www.iowalakes.edu
E-mail: info@iowalakes.edu

KANSAS

COLBY COMMUNITY COLLEGE
1255 S Range Ave, Colby KS 67701-4099
Director of Admissions
888-634-9350 or 785-460-4690 Fax: 785-460-4691
Website: www.colbycc.edu
E-mail: admissions@colbycc.edu

Flint Hills Technical College
3301 W 18th Ave, Emporia KS 66801-5957
Lisa Kirmer, Dean of Student Services
620-343-4600 Fax: 620-343-4610
Website: www.fhtc.net
E-mail: lkirmer@fhtc.net

NEW JERSEY

Bergen Community College
400 Paramus Rd, Paramus NJ 07652
Julian Gomez, Asst. Director of Admissions
201-447-7100 Fax: 201-444-7036
Website: www.bergen.edu
E-mail: jgomez@bergen.edu

RICHARD STOCKTON COLLEGE OF NEW JERSEY
PO Box 195, Pomona NJ 08240
John Iacovelli, Dean of Enrollment Management
866-RSC-2885 Fax: 609-626-5541
Website: www.stockton.edu
E-mail: admissions@stockton.edu

Stockton College is a comprehensive liberal arts, coed institution founded in 1969. Advance Pre-Professional Degree Options: 7-yr BS/MD with UMDNJ; NJ Dental School; NJ Medical School, Robert Wood Johnson Medical, School of Osteopathic Medicine; NY College of Podiatric Medicine, Pennsylvania College of Podiatric Medicine, SUNY College of Optometry. Pharmacy doctorate program with Rutgers University. 5-yr Engineering with NJIT and Rutgers University. Dual BA/MA in Criminal Justice. 5-yr BS/MS in Computational Science. BS/MS in Nursing. Doctorate of Physical Therapy. Additional Programs: Forensic Science, Pre-Law, Pre-Occupational Therapy, and Pre-Veterinary.

NEW YORK

Roberts Wesleyan College
2301 Westside Dr, Rochester NY 14624-1997
Office of Admissions
585-594-6400 Fax: 585-594-6371
Website: www.roberts.edu
E-mail: admissions@roberts.edu

OHIO

The Ohio State University
College of Dentistry
Postle Hall 305 W 12th Ave PO Box 182357
Columbus OH 43219
614-292-3361 Fax: 614-292-0813
Website: dent.osu.edu
E-mail: admissions@dentistry.dent.ohio-state.edu

PENNSYLVANIA

Juniata College
1700 Moore St, Huntingdon PA 16652-2196
Michelle Bartol, Dean of Enrollment
877-JUNIATA Fax: 814-641-3100
Website: www.juniata.edu
E-mail: admissions@juniata.edu

KEYSTONE TECHNICAL INSTITUTE
2301 Academy Dr, Harrisburg PA 17112-1012
Tom Bogush, Director of Admissions
717-545-4747 Fax: 717-901-9090
Website: www.acadcampus.com
E-mail: educdir@acadcampus.com

Established 1980. Private. Coed. Accreditation: ACCSCT. Enrollment: 210 full-time, 50 part-time. Faculty: 15. Student-faculty ratio: 20:1. Degrees offered: Occupational Associate Degrees (AST/ASB). Library: 2,000 volumes. 1 building on 8 acres. Combined classroom; real world lab experience and externships for career training in Medical Assistant, Dental Assistant, Massage Therapy, Paralegal, Culinary Arts, Child Care, Computers.

TEXAS

Abilene Christian University
ACU Box 29000, Abilene TX 79699-0001
325-674-2000 Fax: 325-674-2202
Website: www.acu.edu
E-mail: info@admissions.acu.edu

SAN ANTONIO COLLEGE OF MEDICAL AND DENTAL ASSISTANTS
7142 San Pedro Ave Ste 100, San Antonio TX 78216
Carig Czubati, Director of Admissions
210-733-0777 Fax: 210-735-2431
Website: www.sacmda.com
E-mail: cczubati@sac-mda.com

WEST VIRGINIA

West Virginia Junior College
176 Thompson Dr, Bridgeport WV 26330
Kathryn Stanley, Director of Admissions
304-842-4007 Fax: 304-842-8191
Website: www.wvjcinfo.net
E-mail: kstanley@wvjcinfo.net

WISCONSIN

Marquette University
PO Box 1881, Milwaukee WI 53201-1881
Robert Blust, Director of Admissions
414-288-7302 Fax: 414-288-3764
Website: www.mu.edu
E-mail: admissions@marquette.edu

St. Norbert College
100 Grant St, De Pere WI 54115
Brian Studebaker, Director of Admission
800-236-4878 Fax: 920-403-4072
Website: www.snc.edu
E-mail: admit@snc.edu

WYOMING

University of Wyoming
Admissions Office
Dept 3435, Laramie WY 82071-3435
Brooke Culver, Contact
800-342-5996 Fax: 307-766-4042
Website: www.uwyo.edu
E-mail: why-wyo@uwyo.edu

ENGINEERING

ALABAMA

University of Alabama in Huntsville
PO Box 1247, Huntsville AL 35899-0001
Nikki Willis, Assoc. Director for Recruiting Program and Events
1-800-UAH-CALL Fax: 256-824-6073
Website: www.uah.edu
E-mail: willisn@uah.edu

University of South Alabama
307 University Blvd N, Mobile AL 36688-3053
Melissa Haab, Director of Admissions
251-460-6141 Fax: 251-460-7876
Website: www.southalabama.edu
E-mail: admiss@usouthal.edu

ALASKA

University of Alaska Anchorage
PO Box 141629, Anchorage AK 99514-1629
Cecile Mitchell, Director of Enrollment Services
907-786-1480 Fax: 907-786-4888
Website: www.uaa.alaska.edu/
E-mail: enroll@uaa.alaska.edu

ARIZONA

Embry-Riddle Aeronautical University
Arizona Campus
3700 Willow Creek Rd, Prescott AZ 86301-3720
William Thompson, Director of Admissions
800-888-3728 Fax: 928-777-6613
Website: www.embryriddle.edu
E-mail: pradmit@erau.edu

Pima Community College
4905 E Broadway Blvd, Tucson AZ 85709-1010
Wendy Kilgore, Ph.D., Director of Admissions
520-206-4500 Fax: 520-206-4790
Website: www.pima.edu
E-mail: infocenter@pima.edu

CALIFORNIA

Butte College
3536 Butte Campus Dr, Oroville CA 95965-8399
Carole Gish, Director of Admissions
530-895-2511 Fax: 530-879-4313
Website: www.butte.edu
E-mail: admissions@butte.edu

Chapman University
One University Drive, Orange CA 92866-1099
Michael Drummy, Assistant Vice President for Enrollment
Services and Chief Admission Officer
714-997-6411 or 888-CUAPPLY Fax: 714-997-6713
Website: www.chapman.edu
E-mail: admit@chapman.edu

Cogswell College
1175 Bordeaux Dr, Sunnyvale CA 94089-1210
Dr. Vinh Phat, Engineering Contact
800-264-7955 or 408-541-0100 Fax: 408-747-0764
Website: www.cogswell.edu
E-mail: info@cogswell.edu

FRESNO CITY COLLEGE
1101 E University Ave, Fresno CA 93741-0002
Dayann Dietrich, Contact
559-442-8241 Fax: 559-237-4232
Website: www.fresnocitycollege.com
E-mail: fcc.admissions@scccd.com

Northwestern Polytechnic University
47671 Westinghouse Dr, Fremont CA 94539
Dr. J. Ghofvaniha, Contact
510-657-5913 Fax: 510-657-8975
Website: www.npu.edu
E-mail: npuadm@npu.edu

Orange Coast College
PO Box 5005, Costa Mesa CA 92628-5005
Kristin Clark, Director of Admissions
714-432-5773 Fax: 714-432-5736
Website: www.orangecoastcollege.edu
E-mail: kclark@cccd.edu

Point Loma Nazarene University
3900 Lomaland Dr, San Diego CA 92106-2810
Chip Killingsworth, Director of Undergraduate Admissions
800-733-7770 Fax: 619-849-2601
Website: www.pointloma.edu
E-mail: admissions@pointloma.edu

San Bernardino Valley College
701 S Mount Vernon Ave
San Bernardino CA 92410-2798
Kay Ragan, Ed.D., Director of Admissions
909-888-6511 Fax: 909-889-4988
Website: www.valleycollege.edu
E-mail: kragan@sbccd.cc.ca.us

Whittier College
PO Box 634, Whittier CA 90608-0634
Kieron Miller, Director of Admissions
562-907-4200 Fax: 562-907-4870
Website: www.whittier.edu
E-mail: kmiller@whittier.edu

CONNECTICUT

UNITED STATES COAST GUARD ACADEMY
15 Mohegan Ave, New London CT 06320-8131
Captain Susan D. Bibeau, Contact
800-883-8724 Fax: 860-701-6700
Website: www.uscga.edu
E-mail: admissions@uscga.edu

FLORIDA

Embry-Riddle Aeronautical University
Daytona Beach Campus
PO Box 11767, Daytona Beach FL 32120-1767
C. Richard Clarke, Director of Admissions
800-862-2416 Fax: 386-226-7070
Website: www.embryriddle.edu
E-mail: dbadmit@erau.edu

Florida State University
600 W College Ave, Tallahassee FL 32306-1096
Janice V. Finney, Director of Admissions
850-644-2525 Fax: 850-644-0197
Website: admissions.fsu.edu
E-mail: admissions@admin.fsu.edu

St. Thomas University
16401 NW 37th Ave, Miami Gardens FL 33054
Dr. Edward Ajhar, Contact
800-367-9010 or 305-628-6546 Fax: 305-628-6591
Website: www.stu.edu
E-mail: signup@stu.edu

University of South Florida
4202 E Fowler Ave, Tampa FL 33620-6900
J. Robert Spatig, Director of Admissions
877-USF-BULL Fax: 813-974-9689
Website: www.usf.edu
E-mail: admissions@admin.usf.edu
See listing under "Universities"

IDAHO

Brigham Young University - Idaho
120 Kimball Bldg, Rexburg ID 83460-1615
Rob Garrett, Director of Admissions
208-496-1020 Fax: 208-496-1220
Website: www.byui.edu
E-mail: admissions@byui.edu

University of Idaho
Moscow ID 83844-4253
Lloyd Scott, Director of New Student Services
208-885-6163 Fax: 208-885-4477
Website: www.uidaho.edu
E-mail: nss@uidaho.edu

ILLINOIS

Benedictine University
5700 College Rd, Lisle IL 60532-0900
630-829-6300 or 888-829-6363 Fax: 630-829-6301
Website: www.ben.edu
E-mail: admissions@ben.edu
See listing under "Universities"

Kaskaskia College
27210 College Rd, Centralia IL 62801-7878
Tyra Taylor, Dean of Enrollment Management and Retention Services
618-545-3000 Fax: 618-532-1990
Website: www.kaskaskia.edu
E-mail: ttaylor@kaskaskia.edu

INDIANA

Rose-Hulman Institute of Technology
5500 Wabash Ave, Terre Haute IN 47803-3920
James A. Goecker, Dean of Admissions
812-877-8213 Fax: 812-877-8941
Website: www.rose-hulman.edu
E-mail: admissions@rose-hulman.edu

University of Evansville
1800 Lincoln Ave, Evansville IN 47722-0001
Don Vos, Dean of Admission
800-423-8633 Fax: 812-488-4076
Website: www.evansville.edu
E-mail: admission@evansville.edu

IOWA

Briar Cliff University
PO Box 2100, Sioux City IA 51104-0100
Sharisue Wilcoxon, VP for Enrollment Management
712-279-5200 Fax: 712-279-1632
Website: www.briarcliff.edu
E-mail: admissions@briarcliff.edu

Hamilton College
4655 121st St, Urbandale IA 50323-2311
Colleen McDermott, Campus President
515-727-2100 Fax: 515-727-2115
Website: www.hamiltonia.edu
E-mail: cmcdermott@hamiltonia.edu

Iowa Lakes Community College
300 S 18th St, Estherville IA 51334-2721
Anne Stansbury, Asst. Director of Admissions
712-362-7945 Fax: 712-362-8363
Website: www.iowalakes.edu
E-mail: info@iowalakes.edu

Northwest Iowa Community College
603 W Park St, Sheldon IA 51201-1046
Lisa Story, Director of Enrollment Management
712-324-5061 Fax: 712-324-4136
Website: www.nwicc.edu
E-mail: lstory@nwicc.edu

KANSAS

COLBY COMMUNITY COLLEGE
1255 S Range Ave, Colby KS 67701-4099
Director of Admissions
888-634-9350 or 785-460-4690 Fax: 785-460-4691
Website: www.colbycc.edu
E-mail: admissions@colbycc.edu

KENTUCKY

Louisville Technical Institute
3901 Atkinson Square Dr, Louisville KY 40218
Kevin Woods, Director of Admissions
800-844-6528 Fax: 502-456-2341
Website: www.louisvilletech.com
E-mail: kwoods@louisvilletech.com

Transylvania University
300 N Broadway, Lexington KY 40508-1776
859-233-8242 Fax: 859-233-8797
Website: www.transy.edu
E-mail: admissions@transy.edu

MAINE

Landing School of Boatbuilding, Design, Systems & Composites
PO Box 1490, Kennebunkport ME 04046-1490
Jade Elliott, Director of Student Services
207-985-7976 Fax: 207-985-7942
Website: www.landingschool.edu
E-mail: jadeelliott@landingschool.edu

MARYLAND

Cecil College
One Seahawk Dr, North East MD 21901
Sandra S. Rajaski, Registrar & Director of Admissions
410-287-1000 Fax: 410-287-1001
Website: www.cecil.edu
E-mail: srajaski@cecil.edu

Hagerstown Community College
11400 Robinwood Dr, Hagerstown MD 21742-6590
Dr. Daniel E. Bock, Assistant Director of Admissions
301-790-2800 Fax: 301-791-9165
Website: www.hagerstowncc.edu
E-mail: bockd@hagerstowncc.edu

MASSACHUSETTS

Boston University
121 Bay State Rd, Boston MA 02215
Kelly Walter, Executive Director of Admissions
617-353-2300 Fax: 617-353-9695
Website: web.bu.edu
E-mail: admissions@bu.edu

Massachusetts Institute of Technology
77 Massachusetts Ave, Cambridge MA 02139-4307
617-253-1000 Fax: 617-253-4016
Website: my.mit.edu
E-mail: admissions@mit.edu

NORTHERN ESSEX COMMUNITY COLLEGE
100 Elliott St, Haverhill MA 01830
Nora B. Sheridan, Director of Admission
978-556-3700
Website: www.NECC.Mass.edu
E-mail: nsheridan@necc.mass.edu

North Shore Community College
1 Ferncroft Rd, Danvers MA 01923-4093
Jennifer Kirk, Director of Admissions & Recruitment Outreach
978-762-4000 Fax: 978-762-4015
Website: www.northshore.edu
E-mail: jkirk@northshore.edu

Smith College
Northampton MA 01063-0001
Debra Shaver, Director of Admissions
800-383-3232 Fax: 413-585-2527
Website: www.smith.edu
E-mail: admission@smith.edu

University of Massachusetts Dartmouth
Old Westport Rd, North Dartmouth MA 02747-2300
Steven T. Briggs, Director of Admissions
508-999-8605 Fax: 508-999-8755
Website: explore.umassd.edu
E-mail: sbriggs@umassd.edu

Worcester Polytechnic Institute
100 Institute Rd, Worcester MA 01609-2280
Edward J. Connor, Director of Admissions
508-831-5286 Fax: 508-831-5875
Website: admissions.wpi.edu
E-mail: admissions@wpi.edu

MICHIGAN

Delta College
University Center MI 48710-0001
Duff Zube, Director of Admissions
989-686-9093 Fax: 989-667-2202
Website: www.delta.edu
E-mail: admit@delta.edu

Grand Valley State University
1 Campus Dr, Allendale MI 49401-9403
Jodi Chycinski, Director of Admissions
616-331-6611 Fax: 616-331-2000
Website: www.gvsu.edu
E-mail: go2gvsu@gvsu.edu

Lake Superior State University
650 W Easterday Ave
Sault Sainte Marie MI 49783-1637
Susan Camp, Director of Admissions
888-800-LSSU Fax: 906-635-6696
Website: www.lssu.edu
E-mail: admissions@lssu.edu
See listing under "Universities"

Lawrence Technological University
21000 W 10 Mile Rd, Southfield MI 48075-1058
Jane Rohrback, Director of Admissions
800-225-5588 Fax: 248-204-2228
Website: www.ltu.edu
E-mail: admissions@ltu.edu
See listing under "Universities"

MACOMB COMMUNITY COLLEGE
44575 Garfield Rd, Clinton Township MI 48038-1139
Information Center
586-445-7999
Website: www.macomb.edu
E-mail: answer@macomb.edu

MACOMB COMMUNITY COLLEGE
14500 E 12 Mile Rd, Warren MI 48088-3896
Information Center
586-445-7999
Website: www.macomb.edu
E-mail: answer@macomb.edu

Northwestern Michigan College
1701 E Front St, Traverse City MI 49686-3061
Jim Bensley, Director of Admissions
800-748-0566 Fax: 231-995-1339
Website: www.nmc.edu
E-mail: jbensley@nmc.edu

Oakland University
2200 N Squirrel Rd, Rochester MI 48309
Eleanor L. Reynolds, Assistant Vice President & Director of Admissions
248-370-2100
Website: www.oakland.edu
E-mail: ouinfo@oakland.edu

MINNESOTA

Bethany Lutheran College
700 Luther Dr, Mankato MN 56001
Don Westphal, Dean of Admissions
507-344-7000 Fax: 507-344-7376
Website: www.blc.edu
E-mail: admiss@blc.edu

Dunwoody College of Technology
818 Dunwoody Blvd, Minneapolis MN 55403-1192
John Slama, Vice President Enrollment Management
800-292-4625 or 612-374-5800 Fax: 612-374-4128
Website: www.dunwoody.edu
E-mail: jslama@dunwoody.edu
See listing under "Career Schools"

Hibbing Community College
1515 E 25th St, Hibbing MN 55746-3300
Holly Bigelow, Director of Enrollment
800-224-4HCC or 218-262-7200 Fax: 218-262-6717
Website: www.hibbing.edu
E-mail: admissions@hibbing.edu

Inver Hills Community College
2500 80th St E, Inver Grove Heights MN 55076
651-450-8500 Fax: 651-450-8679
Website: www.inverhills.edu

MISSOURI

East Central College
1964 Prairie Dell Rd, Union MO 63084
Karen Wieda, Registrar
636-583-5195 ext. 2220 Fax: 636-583-1897
Website: www.eastcentral.edu
E-mail: wiedaks@eastcentral.edu

University of Missouri
1 University Blvd, Saint Louis MO 63121-4499
Dr. Bill Darby, Dean
314-516-6800 Fax: 314-516-6801
Website: www.umsl.edu
E-mail: admissions@umsl.edu

MONTANA

Carroll College
1601 N Benton Ave, Helena MT 59625-0002
Dr. Thomas J. Trebon, President
Cynthia Thornquist, Director of Admissions & Enrollment Operations
406-447-4384 Fax: 406-447-4533
Website: www.carroll.edu
E-mail: admission@carroll.edu

NEBRASKA

Metropolitan Community College
PO Box 3777, Omaha NE 68103-0777
Becky Nicks, Director of Admissions
402-449-8400 Fax: 402-457-2616
Website: www.mccnab.edu
E-mail: bnicks@mccnab.edu

NEW JERSEY

Bergen Community College
400 Paramus Rd, Paramus NJ 07652
Julian Gomez, Asst. Director of Admissions
201-447-7100 Fax: 201-444-7036
Website: www.bergen.edu
E-mail: jgomez@bergen.edu

RICHARD STOCKTON COLLEGE OF NEW JERSEY
PO Box 195, Pomona NJ 08240
John Iacovelli, Dean of Enrollment Management
866-RSC-2885 Fax: 609-626-5541
Website: www.stockton.edu
E-mail: admissions@stockton.edu
Stockton College is a comprehensive liberal arts, coed institution founded in 1969. Advance Pre-Professional Degree Options: 7-yr BS/MD with UMDNJ; NJ Dental School; NJ Medical School, Robert Wood Johnson Medical, School of Osteopathic Medicine; NY College of Podiatric Medicine, Pennsylvania College of Podiatric Medicine, SUNY College of Optometry. Pharmacy doctorate program with Rutgers University. 5-yr Engineering with NJIT and Rutgers University. Dual BA/MA in Criminal Justice. 5-yr BS/MS in Computational Science. BS/MS in Nursing. Doctorate of Physical Therapy. Additional Programs: Forensic Science, Pre-Law, Pre-Occupational Therapy, and Pre-Veterinary.

NEW MEXICO

New Mexico Military Institute
101 W College Blvd, Roswell NM 88201-5173
LTC. Steven D. Klein, VP, Enrollment & Marketing
800-421-5376 or 505-624-8050 Fax: 505-624-8058
Website: www.nmmi.edu
E-mail: admissions@nmmi.edu
See listing under "Community and Junior Colleges"

NEW YORK

Broome Community College
907 Upper Front St, Binghamton NY 13905
Anthony S. Fiorelli, Director of Admissions
607-778-5001 Fax: 607-778-5442
Website: www.sunybroome.edu
E-mail: fiorelli_a@sunybroome.edu

College of Saint Rose
432 Western Ave, Albany NY 12203-1419
Maryelizabeth Amico, Asst V.P. for Undergraduate Admissions
518-454-5150 Fax: 518-454-2013
Website: www.strose.edu
E-mail: admit@strose.edu

Institute of Audio Research
64 University Pl, New York NY 10003-4595
Mark L. Kahn, Director of Admissions
800-544-2501 or 212-777-8550 (NY, NJ, CT)
Fax: 212-677-6549
Website: www.audioschool.com
E-mail: contact@audioschool.com
See listing under "Career Schools"

Roberts Wesleyan College
2301 Westside Dr, Rochester NY 14624-1997
Office of Admissions
585-594-6400 Fax: 585-594-6371
Website: www.roberts.edu
E-mail: admissions@roberts.edu

SUNY College of Technology
Alfred NY 14802
Deborah J. Goodrich, Associate VP Enrollment Mgmt.
800-4AL-FRED Fax: 607-587-4299
Website: www.alfredstate.edu
E-mail: admissions@alfredstate.edu

SUNY Orange County Community College
115 South St, Middletown NY 10940-6437
Margot St. Lawrence, Director of Admissions
845-341-4030 Fax: 845-342-8662
Website: www.sunyorange.edu
E-mail: apply@sunyorange.edu
See listing under "Community and Junior Colleges"

United States Military Academy West Point
646 Swift Rd, West Point NY 10996-1905
Colonel Michael L. Jones, Director of Admissions
845-938-4041 Fax: 845-938-8121
Website: admissions.usma.edu
E-mail: admissions@usma.edu

VAUGHN COLLEGE OF AERONAUTICS AND TECHNOLOGY
8601 23rd Ave, Flushing NY 11369-1037
Vincent Papandrea, Director of Admissions
800-776-2376 Fax: 718-429-0671
Website: www.vaughn.edu
E-mail: admitme@vaughn.edu
Established 1932. Private. Coed. Accreditation: MSACS, ABET. Tuition: $13,400. Fees: $280. Enrollment: 842 full-time, 284 part-time. Faculty: 59. Student-faculty ratio: 11:1. Degrees: BS, AAS, AOS. Library: 62,000 vols. Offering bachelor and associate degrees in airport management, aviation maintenance, flight training, electronic technology, engineering, general management, mechatronic engineering, pre-engineering and computerized design/animated graphics. Hands-on training. Extensive career development services and financial aid available.

WEBB INSTITUTE
298 Crescent Beach Rd, Glen Cove NY 11542-1321
Stephen Ostendorff, Director of Admissions
516-671-2213 Fax: 516-674-9838
Website: www.webb-institute.edu
E-mail: admissions@webb-institute.edu

NORTH CAROLINA

Brevard College
One Brevard College Dr, Brevard NC 28712
Joretta Nelson, Vice President Enrollment Management
828-883-8292 Fax: 828-884-3790
Website: www.brevard.edu
E-mail: admissions@brevard.edu

Haywood Community College
185 Freedlander Dr, Clyde NC 28721
Debbie Rowland, Coordinator of Admissions
828-627-4500 Fax: 828-627-4513
Website: www.haywood.edu
E-mail: drowland@haywood.edu

OHIO

Cleveland Institute of Electronics
1776 E 17th St, Cleveland OH 44114-3679
Scott Katzenmeyer, Director of Admissions
800-243-6446 Fax: 216-781-0331
Website: www.cie-wc.edu
E-mail: instruct@cie-wc.edu

Cleveland State University
2121 Euclid Ave RW 204, Cleveland OH 44115
Dr. Richard Arndt, Dean of Undergraduate Recruitment and College Partnerships
888-CSU-OHIO Fax: 216-687-9210
Website: www.csuohio.edu
E-mail: admissions@csuohio.edu

OHIO NORTHERN UNIVERSITY
525 S Main St, Ada OH 45810-1555
419-772-2371
Website: www.onu.edu
E-mail: admissions-ug@onu.edu
See listing under "Universities"

The Ohio State University
College of Engineering
Hitchcock Hall, 2070 Neil Ave, Columbus OH 43210
614-292-2651 Fax: 614-688-3805
Website: engineering.osu.edu
E-mail: engosu@osu.edu

OHIO WESLEYAN UNIVERSITY
61 S Sandusky St, Delaware OH 43015-2398
Director of Admission
740-368-3020 Fax: 740-368-3314
Website: www.owu.edu
E-mail: owuadmit@owu.edu

Sinclair Community College
444 W 3rd St, Dayton OH 45402-1460
Director of Admissions
937-512-3000 Fax: 937-512-2393
Website: www.sinclair.edu
E-mail: admit@sinclair.edu

University of Dayton
300 College Park, Dayton OH 45469-1300
Robert F. Durkle, Director of Admission
800-837-7433 Fax: 937-229-4729
Website: admission.udayton.edu
E-mail: admission@udayton.edu

OKLAHOMA

Oklahoma State University
Stillwater OK 74078
David Thompson, Assoc. Dean
405-744-5140
Website: www.okstate.edu
E-mail: david.r.thompson@okstate.edu

University of Tulsa
600 S College Ave, Tulsa OK 74104-3126
Earl Johnson, Dean of Admission
918-631-2307 Fax: 918-631-5003
Website: www.utulsa.edu
E-mail: admission@utulsa.edu

OREGON

Linn-Benton Community College
6500 Pacific Blvd SW, Albany OR 97321-3774
Christine Baker, Outreach Coordinator
541-917-4811 Fax: 541-917-4868
Website: www.linnbenton.edu
E-mail: admissions@linnbenton.edu

University of Portland
5000 N Willamette Blvd, Portland OR 97203-5798
Jason McDonald, Dean of Admissions
503-943-7911 Fax: 503-943-7315
Website: www.up.edu
E-mail: mcdonaja@up.edu

PENNSYLVANIA

Community College of Allegheny County
Allegheny Campus: 808 Ridge Ave, Pittsburgh PA 15212 Admissions: 412.237.2700
Boyce Campus: 595 Beatty Rd, Monroeville PA 15146 Admissions: 724.325.6614
North Campus: 8701 Perry Highway, Pittsburgh PA 15237 Admissions: 412.369.3600
South Campus: 1750 Clairton Rd, West Mifflin PA 15122 Admissions: 412-469-4301
Website: www.ccac.edu

Community College of Beaver County
1 Campus Dr, Monaca PA 15061-2566
724-775-8561 Fax: 724-775-4687
Website: www.ccbc.edu
E-mail: admissions@ccbc.edu

Juniata College
1700 Moore St, Huntingdon PA 16652-2196
Michelle Bartol, Dean of Enrollment
877-JUNIATA Fax: 814-641-3100
Website: www.juniata.edu
E-mail: admissions@juniata.edu

Washington & Jefferson College
60 S Lincoln St, Washington PA 15301-4801
Alton E. Newell, Vice President for Enrollment
724-223-6025 Fax: 724-223-6534
Website: www.washjeff.edu
E-mail: admission@washjeff.edu

Widener University
1 University Pl, Chester PA 19013-5792
Edwin Wright, Dean of Admissions
610-499-4000 Fax: 610-499-4676
Website: www.widener.edu
E-mail: admissions.office@widener.edu

SOUTH CAROLINA

Bob Jones University
1700 Wade Hampton Blvd
Greenville SC 29614-0001
David Christ, Director of Admissions
800-BJ-AND-ME Fax: 800-2-FAX-BJU
Website: www.bju.edu
E-mail: admissions@bju.edu
See listing under "Universities"

TENNESSEE

Lipscomb University
3901 Granny White Pike, Nashville TN 37204-3951
Ricky Holaway, Director of Admissions
800-333-4358 ext. 1776 Fax: 615-269-1804
Website: www.lipscomb.edu
E-mail: admissions@lipscomb.edu

University of Tennessee
615 McCallie Ave, Chattanooga TN 37403-2504
Yancy Freeman, Director of Admissions
423-425-4111 Fax: 423-425-4157
Website: www.utc.edu
E-mail: Yancy-Freeman@utc.edu

TEXAS

Abilene Christian University
ACU Box 29000, Abilene TX 79699-0001
325-674-2000 Fax: 325-674-2202
Website: www.acu.edu
E-mail: info@admissions.acu.edu

Lubbock Christian University
5601 19th St, Lubbock TX 79407-2099
Stan Scott, Director of Admissions
806-796-8800 Fax: 806-720-7162
Website: www.lcu.edu
E-mail: stan.scott@lcu.edu

Tyler Junior College
PO Box 9020, Tyler TX 75711-9020
Richard Minter, Dean
800-687-5680
Website: www.tjc.edu
E-mail: rmin@tjc.edu
See listing under "Community and Junior Colleges"

University of Houston
122 E Cullen Bldg, Houston TX 77204-2023
Office of Admission
713-743-9595
Website: www.uh.edu
E-mail: admissions@uh.edu

University of Texas at Arlington
Box 19111, Arlington TX 76019-0111
Hans Gatterdam, Director of Admission
817-272-6287 Fax: 817-272-3435
Website: www.uta.edu
E-mail: admissions@uta.edu

Weatherford College
225 College Park Dr, Weatherford TX 76086
Dr. Joe Birmingham, President
800-287-5471 Fax: 817-598-6205
Website: www.wc.edu
E-mail: willingham@wc.edu

VERMONT

NORWICH UNIVERSITY
158 Harmon Dr, Northfield VT 05663
Dr. Dennis Tyner, Division Head
800-468-6679 Fax: 802-485-2260
Website: www.norwich.edu
E-mail: dtyner@norwich.edu
See listing under "Universities"

VIRGINIA

Randolph College
2500 Rivermont Ave, Lynchburg VA 24503
Patricia LeDonne, Director of Admissions
434-947-8100 Fax: 434-947-8996
Website: www.randolphcollege.edu
E-mail: admissions@randolphcollege.edu

WASHINGTON

Everett Community College
2000 Tower St, Everett WA 98201
Christine Kerlin, Associate Dean
425-388-9100 Fax: 425-388-9173
Website: www.everettcc.edu
E-mail: ckerlin@everettcc.edu

North Seattle Community College
9600 College Way N, Seattle WA 98103-3599
206-527-3746
Website: www.northseattle.edu
E-mail: nsccinfo@sccd.ctc.edu

SHORELINE COMMUNITY COLLEGE
16101 Greenwood Ave N, Shoreline WA 98133-5696
Chris Melton, Acting Registrar
206-546-4581 Fax: 206-546-5835
Website: www.shoreline.edu

WISCONSIN

Blackhawk Technical College
PO Box 5009, Janesville WI 53547-5009
Gregg Bosak, Administration, Community Information
608-757-7769 Fax: 608-757-7740
Website: www.blackhawk.edu
E-mail: gbosak@blackhawk.edu

Marquette University
PO Box 1881, Milwaukee WI 53201-1881
Robert Blust, Director of Admissions
414-288-7302 Fax: 414-288-3764
Website: www.mu.edu
E-mail: admissions@marquette.edu

WYOMING

Laramie County Community College
1400 E College Dr, Cheyenne WY 82007-3204
Jenny Hargett, Director of Admissions
307-778-5222 Fax: 307-778-1350
Website: www.lccc.wy.edu
E-mail: learnmore@lccc.wy.edu

University of Wyoming
Admissions Office
Dept 3435, Laramie WY 82071-3435
Brooke Culver, Contact
800-342-5996 Fax: 307-766-4042
Website: www.uwyo.edu
E-mail: why-wyo@uwyo.edu

ENGINEERING TECHNOLOGY

ALABAMA

George C. Wallace State Community College
PO Box 2530, Selma AL 36702-2530
Mrs. Donitha J. Griffin, Dean of Students
334-876-9295 Fax: 334-876-9300
Website: www.wccs.edu
E-mail: dgriffin@wccs.edu

Herzing College
280 W Valley Ave, Homewood AL 35209-4816
Kim Conway, Director of Admissions
205-916-2800 Fax: 205-916-2807
Website: www.herzing.edu/birmingham
E-mail: info@bhm.herzing.edu

ALASKA

University of Alaska Anchorage
PO Box 141629, Anchorage AK 99514-1629
Cecile Mitchell, Director of Enrollment Services
907-786-1480 Fax: 907-786-4888
Website: www.uaa.alaska.edu/
E-mail: enroll@uaa.alaska.edu

ARIZONA

Embry-Riddle Aeronautical University
Arizona Campus
3700 Willow Creek Rd, Prescott AZ 86301-3720
William Thompson, Director of Admissions
800-888-3728 Fax: 928-777-6613
Website: www.embryriddle.edu
E-mail: pradmit@erau.edu

Pima Community College
4905 E Broadway Blvd, Tucson AZ 85709-1010
Wendy Kilgore, Ph.D., Director of Admissions
520-206-4500 Fax: 520-206-4790
Website: www.pima.edu
E-mail: infocenter@pima.edu

Refrigeration School
4210 E Washington St, Phoenix AZ 85034-1894
Crystal Otts, Admissions Manager
602-275-7133 Fax: 602-267-4805
Website: www.refrigerationschool.com
E-mail: crystal@rsiaz.edu

CALIFORNIA

Butte College
3536 Butte Campus Dr, Oroville CA 95965-8399
Carole Gish, Director of Admissions
530-895-2511 Fax: 530-879-4313
Website: www.butte.edu
E-mail: admissions@butte.edu

California State University-San Bernadino
5500 University Pkwy
San Bernardino CA 92407-2393
Olivia Rosas, Director of Admissions
909-537-5188 Fax: 909-537-7034
Website: www.csusb.edu
E-mail: orosas@csusb.edu

FRESNO CITY COLLEGE
1101 E University Ave, Fresno CA 93741-0002
Dayann Dietrich, Contact
559-442-8241 Fax: 559-237-4232
Website: www.fresnocitycollege.com
E-mail: fcc.admissions@scccd.com

ITT Technical Institute
12669 Encinitas Ave, Sylmar CA 91342-3664
Kelly Christensen, Director of Admissions
818-364-5151 Fax: 818-364-5150
Website: www.itt-tech.edu
E-mail: kchristensen@itt-tech.edu

San Bernardino Valley College
701 S Mount Vernon Ave
San Bernardino CA 92410-2798
Kay Ragan, Ed.D., Director of Admissions
909-888-6511 Fax: 909-889-4988
Website: www.valleycollege.edu
E-mail: kragan@sbccd.cc.ca.us

COLORADO

Colorado Northwestern Community College
500 Kennedy Dr, Rangely CO 81648-3502
Tresa England, Director of Student Services
800-562-1105 Fax: 970-675-3343
Website: www.cncc.edu
E-mail: tresa.england@cncc.edu

CONNECTICUT

Middlesex Community College
100 Training Hill Rd, Middletown CT 06457-4889
Mensimah Shabazz, Director of Admissions
860-343-5800 Fax: 860-344-3055
Website: www.mxcc.commnet.edu
E-mail: mshabazz@mxcc.commnet.edu

FLORIDA

Embry-Riddle Aeronautical University
Daytona Beach Campus
PO Box 11767, Daytona Beach FL 32120-1767
C. Richard Clarke, Director of Admissions
800-862-2416 Fax: 386-226-7070
Website: www.embryriddle.edu
E-mail: dbadmit@erau.edu

Key College
225 E Dania Beach Blvd #130
Dania Beach FL 33004
Ronald Dooley, President
954-923-4440 Fax: 954-923-9226
Website: www.keycollege.edu
E-mail: admissions@keycollege.edu

University of South Florida
4202 E Fowler Ave, Tampa FL 33620-6900
J. Robert Spatig, Director of Admissions
877-USF-BULL Fax: 813-974-9689
Website: www.usf.edu
E-mail: admissions@admin.usf.edu
See listing under "Universities"

GEORGIA

DeKalb Technical College
495 N Indian Creek Dr, Clarkston GA 30021-2397
Terry Richardson, Director of Admissions
404-297-9522 Fax: 404-294-6496
Website: www.dekalbtech.edu
E-mail: richardt@dekalbtech.edu

HAWAII

Heald College, Honolulu
1500 Kapiolani Blvd, Honolulu HI 96814-3732
Wendy N. Nishimura, Director of Admissions
808-955-1500 or 800-940-0530 Fax: 808-955-6964
Website: www.heald.edu
E-mail: wendy_nishimura@heald.edu

IDAHO

Brigham Young University - Idaho
120 Kimball Bldg, Rexburg ID 83460-1615
Rob Garrett, Director of Admissions
208-496-1020 Fax: 208-496-1220
Website: www.byui.edu
E-mail: admissions@byui.edu

Lewis-Clark State College
500 8th Ave, Lewiston ID 83501-2698
Diane Douglas, Ph.D., Registrar/Director of Admissions
800-933-5272 Fax: 208-792-2429
Website: www.lcsc.edu
E-mail: admissions@lcsc.edu

ILLINOIS

Kaskaskia College
27210 College Rd, Centralia IL 62801-7878
Tyra Taylor, Dean of Enrollment Management and Retention Services
618-545-3000 Fax: 618-532-1990
Website: www.kaskaskia.edu
E-mail: ttaylor@kaskaskia.edu

MORRISON INSTITUTE OF TECHNOLOGY
701 Portland Ave, Morrison IL 61270-2959
Richard C. Parkinson, Interim Director
815-772-7218 Fax: 815-772-7584
Website: www.morrisontech.edu
E-mail: admissions@morrison.tec.il.us

Private. Coed. Accreditation: ABET. Enrollment: 140. Student-faculty ratio: 13:1. Engineering Technology Associate of Applied Science degree in Architectural, Construction, Civil, Mechanical, Drafting & Design, and Surveying Technology. AAS degree in Systems & Network Administration.

Roosevelt University
430 S Michigan Ave, Chicago IL 60605
Gwen E. Kanelos, Asst. Vice President for Enrollment Services
877-APPLY-RU Fax: 312-341-4216
Website: www.roosevelt.edu
E-mail: applyru@roosevelt.edu

Triton College
2000 5th Ave, River Grove IL 60171-1995
Jeffery Cooks, Director, Admission Services
708-456-0300 ext. 3130 Fax: 708-583-3147
Website: www.triton.edu
E-mail: triton@triton.edu
See listing under "Community and Junior Colleges"

INDIANA

Ivy Tech Community College - North Central
220 Dean Johnson Blvd, South Bend IN 46601-3415
Pam Decker, Director of Admissions
574-289-7001 Fax: 574-236-7177
Website: www.ivytech.edu
E-mail: pdecker@ivytech.edu

IOWA

Hamilton Technical College
1011 E 53rd St, Davenport IA 52807-2653
Mark Christy, Director
563-386-3570 Fax: 563-386-6756
Website: www.hamiltontechcollege.com
E-mail: mchristy@hamiltontechcollege.com
See listing under "Career Schools"

Northwest Iowa Community College
603 W Park St, Sheldon IA 51201-1046
Lisa Story, Director of Enrollment Management
712-324-5061 Fax: 712-324-4136
Website: www.nwicc.edu
E-mail: lstory@nwicc.edu

KANSAS

AIB International
1213 Bakers Way, Manhattan KS 66502-4576
Ken Embers, Admissions
800-633-5137 or 785-537-4750 Fax: 785-537-1493
Website: www.aibonline.org
E-mail: kembers@aibonline.org
See listing under "Career Schools"

KENTUCKY

Bluegrass Community and Technical College
Oswald Building
470 Cooper Drive, Lexington KY 40506-0235
Shelbie Hugle, Director of Admissions
859-246-6200 Fax: 859-246-4664
Website: www.bluegrass.kctcs.edu
E-mail: bctc_info@kctcs.edu

Louisville Technical Institute
3901 Atkinson Square Dr, Louisville KY 40218
Kevin Woods, Director of Admissions
800-844-6528 Fax: 502-456-2341
Website: www.louisvilletech.com
E-mail: kwoods@louisvilletech.com

Morehead State University
Morehead KY 40351-1689
Jeffrey Liles, Enrollment Services
800-585-6781 Fax: 606-783-5038
Website: www.moreheadstate.edu
E-mail: admissions@moreheadstate.edu

Spencerian College
1575 Winchester Rd, Lexington KY 40505
Victor Lamoin Adcock II, Director of Admissions
800-456-3253
E-mail: ladcock@spencerian.edu

MAINE

Landing School of Boatbuilding, Design, Systems & Composites
PO Box 1490, Kennebunkport ME 04046-1490
Jade Elliott, Director of Student Services
207-985-7976 Fax: 207-985-7942
Website: www.landingschool.edu
E-mail: jadeelliott@landingschool.edu

Southern Maine Community College
2 Fort Rd, South Portland ME 04106-1698
Dr. James Ortiz, President
Scott MacDonald, Director of Financial Aid
207-741-5500 Fax: 207-741-5671
Website: www.smccme.edu
E-mail: oharmon@maine.rr.com

MARYLAND

Hagerstown Community College
11400 Robinwood Dr, Hagerstown MD 21742-6590
Dr. Daniel E. Bock, Assistant Director of Admissions
301-790-2800 Fax: 301-791-9165
Website: www.hagerstowncc.edu
E-mail: bockd@hagerstowncc.edu

MASSACHUSETTS

Benjamin Franklin Institute of Technology
41 Berkeley St, Boston MA 02116-6307
Norman Kraft, Dean of Enrollment
617-423-4630 ext. 121 Fax: 617-482-3706
Website: www.bfit.edu
E-mail: admissions@bfit.edu

Bristol Community College
777 Elsbree St, Fall River MA 02720-7395
Rodney S. Clark, Director of Admissions
508-678-2811 ext. 2516, 2179 Fax: 508-730-3265
Website: www.bristol.mass.edu
E-mail: admissions@bristol.mass.edu

ITT TECHNICAL INSTITUTE
333 Boston Providence Tpke
Norwood MA 02062-3932
Tom Ryan, Director of Recruiting
800-879-TECH (8324) Fax: 781-278-0766
Website: www.itt-tech.edu
E-mail: tryan@itt-tech.edu

Established 1990. Private. Coed. Accreditation: ACICS. Enrollment: 300. Student-faculty ratio: 11:1. Associate Degrees offered: Computer Drafting & Design, Computer Electronics Technology, Computer Network Systems, Multimedia.

Massachusetts Institute of Technology
77 Massachusetts Ave, Cambridge MA 02139-4307
617-253-1000 Fax: 617-253-4016
Website: my.mit.edu
E-mail: admissions@mit.edu

North Shore Community College
1 Ferncroft Rd, Danvers MA 01923-4093
Jennifer Kirk, Director of Admissions & Recruitment Outreach
978-762-4000 Fax: 978-762-4015
Website: www.northshore.edu
E-mail: jkirk@northshore.edu

MICHIGAN

Delta College
University Center MI 48710-0001
Duff Zube, Director of Admissions
989-686-9093 Fax: 989-667-2202
Website: www.delta.edu
E-mail: admit@delta.edu

ITT TECHNICAL INSTITUTE
4020 Sparks Dr SE, Grand Rapids MI 49546-6192
Dennis Hormel, Director
616-956-1060 Fax: 616-956-5606
Website: www.itt-tech.edu
E-mail: dhormel@itt-tech.edu

Lake Superior State University
650 W Easterday Ave
Sault Sainte Marie MI 49783-1637
Susan Camp, Director of Admissions
888-800-LSSU Fax: 906-635-6696
Website: www.lssu.edu
E-mail: admissions@lssu.edu
See listing under "Universities"

Lawrence Technological University
21000 W 10 Mile Rd, Southfield MI 48075-1058
Jane Rohrback, Director of Admissions
800-225-5588 Fax: 248-204-2228
Website: www.ltu.edu
E-mail: admissions@ltu.edu
See listing under "Universities"

MACOMB COMMUNITY COLLEGE
14500 E 12 Mile Rd, Warren MI 48088-3896
Information Center
586-445-7999
Website: www.macomb.edu
E-mail: answer@macomb.edu

MINNESOTA

Dunwoody College of Technology
818 Dunwoody Blvd, Minneapolis MN 55403-1192
John Slama, Vice President Enrollment Management
800-292-4625 or 612-374-5800 Fax: 612-374-4128
Website: www.dunwoody.edu
E-mail: jslama@dunwoody.edu
See listing under "Career Schools"

Inver Hills Community College
2500 80th St E, Inver Grove Heights MN 55076
651-450-8500 Fax: 651-450-8679
Website: www.inverhills.edu

McNally Smith College of Music
19 Exchange St East, St. Paul MN 55101
Debbie Sandridge, Director of Admissions
800-594-9500 Fax: 651-291-0366
Website: www.mcnallysmith.edu
E-mail: dsandridge@mcnallysmith.edu
See listing under "Universities"

Minnesota State College - Southeast Technical
Red Wing Campus
308 Pioneer Rd, Red Wing MN 55066
Al DuCett, Director of Admissions
877-853-8324 Fax: 507-453-2715
Website: www.southeastmn.edu
E-mail: aducett@southeastmn.edu
70+ degrees, diplomas & certificates (15+ online) in Business & Office Careers, Musical Instrument Repair, Physical Health, Transportation, Technology, and Trades.

Minnesota State College - Southeast Technical
Winona Campus
PO Box 409, 1250 Homer Rd, Winona MN 55987
Al DuCett, Director of Admissions
877-853-8324 Fax: 507-453-2715
Website: www.southeastmn.edu
E-mail: aducett@southeastmn.edu
70+ degrees, diplomas & certificates (15+ online) in Business & Office Careers, Musical Instrument Repair, Physical Health, Transportation, Technology, and Trades.

Ridgewater College-Hutchinson Campus
2 Century Ave SE, Hutchinson MN 55350-3100
Dawn Bjork, Counselor
800-722-1151 Fax: 320-234-8506
Website: www.ridgewater.edu
E-mail: dawn.bjork@ridgewater.edu

St. Cloud Technical College
1540 Northway Dr, Saint Cloud MN 56303-1240
Jodi Elness, Director of Enrollment Management
800-222-1009 Fax: 320-308-5981
Website: www.sctc.edu
E-mail: jelness@sctc.edu

MISSOURI

East Central College
1964 Prairie Dell Rd, Union MO 63084
Karen Wieda, Registrar
636-583-5195 ext. 2220 Fax: 636-583-1897
Website: www.eastcentral.edu
E-mail: wiedaks@eastcentral.edu

Ozarks Technical Community College
1001 E Chestnut Expressway
Springfield MO 65802-3625
Delvan Mitchell, Director of Admissions
417-447-7500 Fax: 417-447-6925
Website: www.otc.edu
E-mail: admissions@otc.edu

State Fair Community College
3201 W 16th St, Sedalia MO 65301-2199
Director of Admissions
660-530-5833 Fax: 660-596-7472
Website: www.sfccmo.edu
E-mail: mparris@sfccmo.edu

NEBRASKA

Metropolitan Community College
PO Box 3777, Omaha NE 68103-0777
Becky Nicks, Director of Admissions
402-449-8400 Fax: 402-457-2616
Website: www.mccnab.edu
E-mail: bnicks@mccnab.edu

NEVADA

Career College of Northern Nevada
1195-A Corporate Blvd, Reno NV 89502-2331
Nathan Clark, Director
775-856-2266 Fax: 775-856-0935
Website: www.ccnn.edu
E-mail: lgoldhammer@ccnn4u.com
See listing under "Career Schools"

NEW JERSEY

Bergen Community College
400 Paramus Rd, Paramus NJ 07652
Julian Gomez, Asst. Director of Admissions
201-447-7100 Fax: 201-444-7036
Website: www.bergen.edu
E-mail: jgomez@bergen.edu

Hohokus School - RETS Nutley
103 Park Ave, Nutley NJ 07110-3505
Thomas Eastwick, President
973-661-0600 Fax: 973-661-2954
Website: www.rets-institute.com
E-mail: admissions@rets-institute.com

Mercer County Community College
West Windsor Campus
PO Box B, Trenton NJ 08690
Savita Bambhrolia, Director of Admissions
609-586-4800 Fax: 609-587-4666
Website: www.mccc.edu
E-mail: admiss@mccc.edu

NEW YORK

Broome Community College
907 Upper Front St, Binghamton NY 13905
Anthony S. Fiorelli, Director of Admissions
607-778-5001 Fax: 607-778-5442
Website: www.sunybroome.edu
E-mail: fiorelli_a@sunybroome.edu

College of Saint Rose
432 Western Ave, Albany NY 12203-1419
Maryelizabeth Amico, Asst V.P. for Undergraduate Admissions
518-454-5150 Fax: 518-454-2013
Website: www.strose.edu
E-mail: admit@strose.edu

Institute of Audio Research
64 University Pl, New York NY 10003-4595
Mark L. Kahn, Director of Admissions
800-544-2501 or 212-777-8550 (NY, NJ, CT)
Fax: 212-677-6549
Website: www.audioschool.com
E-mail: contact@audioschool.com
See listing under "Career Schools"

ISLAND DRAFTING & TECHNICAL INSTITUTE
128 Broadway (Route 110), Amityville NY 11701-2704
James G. DiLiberto, President
631-691-8733 Fax: 631-691-8738
Website: www.idti.edu
E-mail: info@idti.edu

SUNY College of Technology
Alfred NY 14802
Deborah J. Goodrich, Associate VP Enrollment Mgmt.
800-4AL-FRED Fax: 607-587-4299
Website: www.alfredstate.edu
E-mail: admissions@alfredstate.edu

SUNY Orange County Community College
115 South St, Middletown NY 10940-6437
Margot St. Lawrence, Director of Admissions
845-341-4030 Fax: 845-342-8662
Website: www.sunyorange.edu
E-mail: apply@sunyorange.edu
See listing under "Community and Junior Colleges"

T.C.I. Institute, The College of Technology
320 W 31st St, New York NY 10001-2789
Edward Gehrke, V.P. for Admissions
800-878-8246 Fax: 212-330-0891
Website: www.tcicollege.edu
E-mail: admissions@tcicollege.edu

VAUGHN COLLEGE OF AERONAUTICS AND TECHNOLOGY
8601 23rd Ave, Flushing NY 11369-1037
Vincent Papandrea, Director of Admissions
800-776-2376 Fax: 718-429-0671
Website: www.vaughn.edu
E-mail: admitme@vaughn.edu

Established 1932. Private. Coed. Accreditation: MSACS, ABET. Tuition: $13,400. Fees: $280. Enrollment: 842 full-time, 284 part-time. Faculty: 59. Student-faculty ratio: 11:1. Degrees: BS, AAS, AOS. Library: 62,000 vols. Offering bachelor and associate degrees in airport management, aviation maintenance, flight training, electronic technology, engineering, general management, mechatronic engineering, pre-engineering and computerized design/animated graphics. Hands-on training. Extensive career development services and financial aid available.

NORTH CAROLINA

Haywood Community College
185 Freedlander Dr, Clyde NC 28721
Debbie Rowland, Coordinator of Admissions
828-627-4500 Fax: 828-627-4513
Website: www.haywood.edu
E-mail: drowland@haywood.edu

Mayland Community College
PO Box 547, Spruce Pine NC 28777-0547
Cathy B. Morrison, Director of Enrollment Management
828-765-7351 Fax: 828-765-0728
Website: www.mayland.edu
E-mail: cmorrison@mayland.edu

South Piedmont Community College
PO Box 126, Polkton NC 28135-0126
John Curtis, Contact
704-272-5324 Fax: 704-272-8904
Website: www.spcc.edu
E-mail: jcurtis@spcc.edu

OHIO

Bryant & Stratton College
1700 E 13th St, Cleveland OH 44114-3238
Shawn T. Kampa, Market Director of Admissions
216-771-1700 Fax: 216-771-7787
Website: www.bryantstratton.edu
E-mail: stkampa@bryantstratton.edu

Cleveland Institute of Electronics
1776 E 17th St, Cleveland OH 44114-3679
Scott Katzenmeyer, Director of Admissions
800-243-6446 Fax: 216-781-0331
Website: www.cie-wc.edu
E-mail: instruct@cie-wc.edu

Cleveland State University
2121 Euclid Ave RW 204, Cleveland OH 44115
Dr. Richard Arndt, Dean of Undergraduate Recruitment and College Partnerships
888-CSU-OHIO Fax: 216-687-9210
Website: www.csuohio.edu
E-mail: admissions@csuohio.edu

Northwest State Community College
22600 State Route 34, Archbold OH 43502-9542
Mark Thompson, Director of Admissions
419-267-5511 Fax: 419-267-5587
Website: www.northweststate.edu
E-mail: mthompson@northweststate.edu

OHIO NORTHERN UNIVERSITY
525 S Main St, Ada OH 45810-1555
Dave Rouch, Chair of Technology Dept.
419-772-2168
Website: www.onu.edu
E-mail: admissions-ug@onu.edu
See listing under "Universities"

Owens Community College
3200 Bright Rd, Findlay OH 45840
William J. Ivoska PhD., Vice President of Student Services
567-429-3500 Fax: 567-423-0246
Website: www.owens.edu
E-mail: admissions@owens.edu

Owens Community College
PO Box 10000, Toledo OH 43699-1947
William J. Ivoska, Ph.D, Vice President of Student Services
567-661-7000 Fax: 567-661-7607
Website: www.owens.edu
E-mail: admissions@owens.edu

Sinclair Community College
444 W 3rd St, Dayton OH 45402-1460
Director of Admissions
937-512-3000 Fax: 937-512-2393
Website: www.sinclair.edu
E-mail: admit@sinclair.edu

University of Dayton
300 College Park, Dayton OH 45469-1300
Robert F. Durkle, Director of Admission
800-837-7433 Fax: 937-229-4729
Website: admission.udayton.edu
E-mail: admission@udayton.edu

OKLAHOMA

Oklahoma State University
Stillwater OK 74078
James Bose, Director
405-744-5638
Website: www.okstate.edu
E-mail: jim.bose@master.ceat.okstate.edu

OREGON

Linn-Benton Community College
6500 Pacific Blvd SW, Albany OR 97321-3774
Christine Baker, Outreach Coordinator
541-917-4811 Fax: 541-917-4868
Website: www.linnbenton.edu
E-mail: admissions@linnbenton.edu

Rogue Community College
3345 Redwood Hwy, Grants Pass OR 97527-9298
Claudia Sullivan, Director of Enrollment Services
541-956-7500 Fax: 541-471-3585
Website: www.roguecc.edu
E-mail: csullivan@roguecc.edu
See listing under "Community and Junior Colleges"

PENNSYLVANIA

Community College of Allegheny County
Allegheny Campus: 808 Ridge Ave, Pittsburgh PA 15212 Admissions: 412.237.2700
Boyce Campus: 595 Beatty Rd, Monroeville PA 15146 Admissions: 724.325.6614
North Campus: 8701 Perry Highway, Pittsburgh PA 15237 Admissions: 412.369.3600
South Campus: 1750 Clairton Rd, West Mifflin PA 15122 Admissions: 412-469-4301
Website: www.ccac.edu

Community College of Beaver County
1 Campus Dr, Monaca PA 15061-2566
724-775-8561 Fax: 724-775-4687
Website: www.ccbc.edu
E-mail: admissions@ccbc.edu

Johnson College
3427 N Main Ave, Scranton PA 18508-1495
Dr. Ann L. Pipinski, President & CEO
Melissa Ide, Director of Enrollment Management
800-2WE-WORK or 570-342-6404 ext. 125
Fax: 570-348-2181
Website: www.johnson.edu
E-mail: admit@johnson.edu

PIA School of Specialized Technology
PO Box 10897, Pittsburgh PA 15236-0897
Vincent J. Mezza, Director of Admissions
800-444-1440 Fax: 412-466-0513
Website: www.pia.edu
E-mail: admissions@pia.edu
See listing under "Aeronautics, Aviation and Space"

RHODE ISLAND

New England Institute of Technology
2500 Post Rd, Warwick RI 02886-2244
Michael Kwiatkowski, Director of Admissions
401-739-5000 Fax: 401-738-5122
Website: www.neit.edu
E-mail: eflynn@neit.edu

SOUTH CAROLINA

Greenville Technical College
PO Box 5616, Greenville SC 29606-5616
Carolyn Watkins, Dean of Admissions
800-723-0673 (US) or 800-922-1183 (SC)
Website: www.greenvilletech.com

Spartanburg Community College
PO Box 4386, Spartanburg SC 29305-4386
Nancy Garmroth, Dean of Admissions & Financial Aid
864-592-4810 Fax: 864-592-4945
Website: sccsc.edu

SOUTH DAKOTA

Western Dakota Technical Institute
800 Mickelson Dr, Rapid City SD 57703-4018
Jill Elder, Admissions Coordinator
605-394-4034 Fax: 605-394-2204
Website: www.wdt.edu
E-mail: jill.elder@wdt.edu

TENNESSEE

Austin Peay State University
601 College St, Clarksville TN 37044-0002
931-221-7011 Fax: 931-221-6168
Website: www.apsu.edu
E-mail: admissions@apsu.edu

Tennessee State University
3500 John A Merritt Blvd, Nashville TN 37209-1561
John Cade, Dean of Admissions & Records
615-963-5101 Fax: 615-963-2930
Website: www.tnstate.edu
E-mail: jcade@tnstate.edu

TEXAS

Abilene Christian University
ACU Box 29000, Abilene TX 79699-0001
325-674-2000 Fax: 325-674-2202
Website: www.acu.edu
E-mail: info@admissions.acu.edu

Hallmark Institute of Technology - Technology Campus
10401 W IH 10, San Antonio TX 78230-1736
Joe Fisher, President
210-690-9000 Fax: 210-697-8225
Website: www.hallmarkinstitute.com
E-mail: sross@hallmarkinstitute.com
Electronics Engineering Technology, Business Office Administration, Computer Network Systems Technology, & Medical Assistant.

ITT Technical Institute
6330 E Highway 290 Ste 150, Austin TX 78723-1035
Willard Real, Director of Admissions
512-467-6800 Fax: 512-467-6677
Website: www.itt-tech.edu
E-mail: wreal@itt-tech.edu

ITT TECHNICAL INSTITUTE
2950 S Gessner Rd Ste 100, Houston TX 77063-3751
Jennifer Gomez, Director of Recruitment
713-952-2294 Fax: 713-952-2393
Website: www.itt-tech.edu
E-mail: jgomez@itt-tech.edu

Lubbock Christian University
5601 19th St, Lubbock TX 79407-2099
Stan Scott, Director of Admissions
806-796-8800 Fax: 806-720-7162
Website: www.lcu.edu
E-mail: stan.scott@lcu.edu

Temple College
2600 S 1st St, Temple TX 76504-7435
Toni Borras, Director of Admissions & Records
254-298-8808 Fax: 254-298-8288
Website: www.templejc.edu
E-mail: admissionsrecords@templejc.edu

Tyler Junior College
PO Box 9020, Tyler TX 75711-9020
Joan Jones, Interim Dean
800-687-5680
Website: www.tjc.edu
E-mail: jjon@tjc.edu
See listing under "Community and Junior Colleges"

University of Houston
122 E Cullen Bldg, Houston TX 77204-2023
Office of Admission
713-743-9595
Website: www.uh.edu
E-mail: admissions@uh.edu

Western Technical College
9451 Diana Dr, El Paso TX 79924-6936
Bill Terrell, Chief Administrative Officer
915-566-9621 Fax: 915-565-9903
Website: www.wtc-ep.edu
E-mail: bterrell@wtc-ep.edu

UTAH

ITT TECHNICAL INSTITUTE
920 Levoy Dr, Murray UT 84123-2500
Gary Wood, Director of Recruitment
801-263-3313 Fax: 801-263-3497
Website: www.itt-tech.edu
E-mail: gwood@itt-tech.edu

VIRGINIA

ECPI College of Technology
5555 Greenwich Rd Ste 300
Virginia Beach VA 23462-6542
757-671-7171 Fax: 757-671-8661
Website: www.ecpi.edu

Southside Virginia Community College
109 Campus Dr, Alberta VA 23821-2930
Ronald E. Mattox, Dean of Admissions
434-949-1014 Fax: 434-949-7863
Website: www.sv.vccs.edu
E-mail: ronald.mattox@sv.vccs.edu

Southside Virginia Community College
200 Daniel Rd, Keysville VA 23947
Ronald E. Mattox, Dean of Admissions
434-736-2018 Fax: 434-736-2082
Website: www.sv.vccs.edu
E-mail: ronald.mattox@sv.vccs.edu

WASHINGTON

BATES TECHNICAL COLLEGE
1101 S Yakima Ave, Tacoma WA 98405-4895
David Borofsky, President
253-680-7000 Fax: 253-680-7101
Website: www.bates.ctc.edu
E-mail: info@bates.ctc.edu

Everett Community College
2000 Tower St, Everett WA 98201
Christine Kerlin, Associate Dean
425-388-9100 Fax: 425-388-9173
Website: www.everettcc.edu
E-mail: ckerlin@everettcc.edu

Lake Washington Technical College
11605 132nd Ave NE, Kirkland WA 98034-8505
James B. West, Director of Admissions
425-739-8100 Fax: 425-739-8110
Website: www.lwtc.ctc.edu

North Seattle Community College
9600 College Way N, Seattle WA 98103-3599
206-527-3730
Website: www.northseattle.edu
E-mail: nsccinfo@sccd.ctc.edu

SHORELINE COMMUNITY COLLEGE
16101 Greenwood Ave N, Shoreline WA 98133-5696
Chris Melton, Acting Registrar
206-546-4581 Fax: 206-546-5835
Website: www.shoreline.edu

Walla Walla Community College
500 Tausick Way, Walla Walla WA 99362-9270
Greg Farrens, Director
509-527-4684 or 877-992-9922 Fax: 509-527-4480
Website: www.wwcc.edu
E-mail: greg.farrens@wwcc.edu
See listing under "Community and Junior Colleges"

WEST VIRGINIA

Fairmont State University
1201 Locust Ave, Fairmont WV 26554-2470
Steve Leadman, Director of Admissions
304-367-4156 or 800-641-5678 Fax: 304-367-4789
Website: www.fairmontstate.edu
E-mail: admit@fairmontstate.edu

Mountain State University
Box 9003, Beckley WV 25802-9003
Tony England, Director of Admissions
866-FOR-MSU1 or 304-929-INFO Fax: 304-253-5072
Website: www.mountainstate.edu
E-mail: gomsu@mountainstate.edu
See listing under "Universities"

WISCONSIN

Herzing College
5218 E Terrace Dr, Madison WI 53718-8340
Donald Madelung, President
800-582-1227 Fax: 608-249-8593
Website: www.herzing.edu
E-mail: info@msn.herzing.edu
See listing under "Universities"

WYOMING

Laramie County Community College
1400 E College Dr, Cheyenne WY 82007-3204
Jenny Hargett, Director of Admissions
307-778-5222 Fax: 307-778-1350
Website: www.lccc.wy.edu
E-mail: learnmore@lccc.wy.edu

University of Wyoming
Admissions Office
Dept 3435, Laramie WY 82071-3435
Brooke Culver, Contact
800-342-5996 Fax: 307-766-4042
Website: www.uwyo.edu
E-mail: why-wyo@uwyo.edu

ETHNIC STUDIES

ALASKA

University of Alaska Anchorage
PO Box 141629, Anchorage AK 99514-1629
Cecile Mitchell, Director of Enrollment Services
907-786-1480 Fax: 907-786-4888
Website: www.uaa.alaska.edu/
E-mail: enroll@uaa.alaska.edu

CALIFORNIA

California State University-San Bernadino
5500 University Pkwy
San Bernardino CA 92407-2393
Olivia Rosas, Director of Admissions
909-537-5188 Fax: 909-537-7034
Website: www.csusb.edu
E-mail: orosas@csusb.edu

FLORIDA

University of South Florida
4202 E Fowler Ave, Tampa FL 33620-6900
J. Robert Spatig, Director of Admissions
877-USF-BULL Fax: 813-974-9689
Website: www.usf.edu
E-mail: admissions@admin.usf.edu
See listing under "Universities"

GEORGIA

Kennesaw State University
1000 Chastain Rd NW Box 115
Kennesaw GA 30144-5591
Website: www.kennesaw.edu

ILLINOIS

Columbia College Chicago
600 S Michigan Ave, Chicago IL 60605-1996
Murphy Monroe, Executive Director of Admissions
312-344-7130 Fax: 312-344-8024
Website: www.colum.edu
E-mail: admissions@colum.edu

Roosevelt University
430 S Michigan Ave, Chicago IL 60605
Gwen E. Kanelos, Asst. Vice President for Enrollment Services
877-APPLY-RU Fax: 312-341-4216
Website: www.roosevelt.edu
E-mail: applyru@roosevelt.edu

MASSACHUSETTS

Smith College
Northampton MA 01063-0001
Debra Shaver, Director of Admissions
800-383-3232 Fax: 413-585-2527
Website: www.smith.edu
E-mail: admission@smith.edu

MINNESOTA

Carleton College
1 N College St, Northfield MN 55057-4044
800-995-2275 or 507-646-4190 Fax: 507-646-4526
Website: www.carleton.edu
E-mail: admissions@acs.carleton.edu

MISSISSIPPI

Tougaloo College
500 W County Line Rd, Tougaloo MS 39174-9799
Juno Leggette Jacobs, Director of Admissions
601-977-7768 Fax: 601-977-4501
Website: www.tougaloo.edu
E-mail: jjacobs@tougaloo.edu

NEW JERSEY

New Jersey City University
2039 John F Kennedy Blvd
Jersey City NJ 07305-1588
Carmen Panlilio, Asst. V.P. for Admissions and Financial Aid
201-200-3234 Fax: 201-200-2044
Website: www.njcu.edu
E-mail: admissions@njcu.edu

RICHARD STOCKTON COLLEGE OF NEW JERSEY

PO Box 195, Pomona NJ 08240
John Iacovelli, Dean of Enrollment Management
866-RSC-2885 Fax: 609-626-5541
Website: www.stockton.edu
E-mail: admissions@stockton.edu
See listing under "Universities"

NEW MEXICO

Institute of American Indian Arts
83 A Van Nu Po, Santa Fe NM 87508-1300
John Gritts, Director of Admissions, Records & Enrollment
505-424-2330 Fax: 505-424-4500
Website: www.iaia.edu
E-mail: recruitment@iaia.edu

NEW YORK

College of Saint Rose
432 Western Ave, Albany NY 12203-1419
Maryelizabeth Amico, Asst V.P. for Undergraduate Admissions
518-454-5150 Fax: 518-454-2013
Website: www.strose.edu
E-mail: admit@strose.edu

CUNY Hunter College
695 Park Ave, New York NY 10021
Aaron Gibbs, Assistant Director of Recruitment
212-650-3946 Fax: 212-650-3336
Website: www.hunter.cuny.edu
E-mail: aaron.gibbs@hunter.cuny.edu

PENNSYLVANIA

Community College of Allegheny County
Allegheny Campus: 808 Ridge Ave, Pittsburgh PA 15212 Admissions: 412.237.2700
Boyce Campus: 595 Beatty Rd, Monroeville PA 15146 Admissions: 724.325.6614
North Campus: 8701 Perry Highway, Pittsburgh PA 15237 Admissions: 412.369.3600
South Campus: 1750 Clairton Rd, West Mifflin PA 15122 Admissions: 412-469-4301
Website: www.ccac.edu

TEXAS

University of Houston
122 E Cullen Bldg, Houston TX 77204-2023
Office of Admission
713-743-9595
Website: www.uh.edu
E-mail: admissions@uh.edu

WYOMING

University of Wyoming
Admissions Office
Dept 3435, Laramie WY 82071-3435
Brooke Culver, Contact
800-342-5996 Fax: 307-766-4042
Website: www.uwyo.edu
E-mail: why-wyo@uwyo.edu

GUAM

University of Guam
UOG Station, Mangilao GU 96923
Deborah Leon Guerrero, Registrar
671-735-2201 or 671-735-2208 Fax: 671-735-2203
Website: www.uog.edu
E-mail: admitme@uog9.uog.edu

FASHION ART

CALIFORNIA

California College of the Arts
1111 Eighth St, San Francisco CA 94107
Robynne Royster, Director of Admission
800-447-1-ART or 415-703-9523 Fax: 415-703-9539
Website: www.cca.edu
E-mail: enroll@cca.edu

CALIFORNIA DESIGN COLLEGE

3440 Wilshire Blvd 10th Floor
Los Angeles CA 90010-2102
Gregory J. Marick, President
213-251-3636 Fax: 213-385-3545
Website: www.aicdc.artinstitutes.edu

FASHION CAREERS COLLEGE

1923 Morena Blvd, San Diego CA 92110-3555
Silvana Carelli, Director of Enrollment
619-275-4700 Fax: 619-275-0635
Website: www.fashioncareerscollege.com
E-mail: info@fashioncareerscollege.com

Established 1979. Private. Coed. Accreditation: ACICS. Tuition: $16,900 per year for Fashion Business & Technology. $16,900 per year for Fashion Design & Technology program, day or evening program (tuition includes required books & certain supplies). Registration Fee: $25. Enrollment: 120 full-time. Faculty: 15. Student-faculty ratio: 10:1. Degree & Certificate programs. Library: 850 volumes. Theoretical and practical training gives students a relevant and comprehensive education in Fashion Business & Technology and Fashion Design & Technology. Placement assistance and internships available.

FIDM/The Fashion Institute of Design & Merchandising
17590 Gillette Ave, Irvine CA 92614
Director of Admissions
949-851-6200 or 888-974-3436 Fax: 949-851-6808
Website: www.fidm.edu
E-mail: info@fidm.com
See listing under "Community and Junior Colleges"

FIDM/THE FASHION INSTITUTE OF DESIGN & MERCHANDISING

919 S Grand Ave, Los Angeles CA 90015-1421
Director of Admissions
213-624-1201 or 800-624-1200 Fax: 213-624-4799
Website: www.fidm.edu
E-mail: info@fidm.com
See listing under "Community and Junior Colleges"

FIDM/The Fashion Institute of Design & Merchandising
1010 2nd Ave, San Diego CA 92101-4903
Director of Admissions
619-235-2049 or 800-243-3436 Fax: 619-232-4322
Website: www.fidm.edu
E-mail: info@fidm.com
See listing under "Community and Junior Colleges"

FIDM/The Fashion Institute of Design & Merchandising
55 Stockton St, San Francisco CA 94108-5829
Director of Admissions
415-675-5200 or 800-422-3436 Fax: 415-296-7299
Website: www.fidm.edu
E-mail: info@fidm.com
See listing under "Community and Junior Colleges"

GEMOLOGICAL INSTITUTE OF AMERICA

The Robert Mouawad Campus
5345 Armada Dr, Carlsbad CA 92008-4602
Jason Drake, Admissions Manager
800-421-7250 ext. 4001 or 760-603-4001
Fax: 760-603-4003
Website: www.gia.edu
E-mail: eduinfo@gia.edu

Established 1931. Nonprofit. Private. Coed. Accreditation: ACCSCT and DETC. Diplomas: Graduate Gemologist, Graduate Jeweler, Graduate Jeweler Gemologist, Jewelry Business Management, Applied Jewelry Arts. Degree: BBA (Bachelor of Business Administration). Financial aid. Classes begin year round.
See listing under "Home Study and Correspondence"

FLORIDA

INTERNATIONAL ACADEMY OF DESIGN AND TECHNOLOGY

5959 Lake Ellenor Dr, Orlando FL 32809-4633
Dr. John Dietrich, VP of Admissions
877-753-0007 Fax: 407-888-4006
Website: www.iadt.edu
E-mail: info@iadt.edu

Lynn University
3601 N Military Trl, Boca Raton FL 33431-5598
Director of Admissions
561-237-7900 Fax: 561-237-7100
Website: www.lynn.edu
E-mail: admission@lynn.edu

ILLINOIS

Columbia College Chicago
600 S Michigan Ave, Chicago IL 60605-1996
Murphy Monroe, Executive Director of Admissions
312-344-7130 Fax: 312-344-8024
Website: www.colum.edu
E-mail: admissions@colum.edu

International Academy of Design and Technology
1 N State St #500, Chicago IL 60602-3300
Cecily Arroyo, Director of Admissions
888-803-0111 Fax: 312-541-3929
Website: www.iadtchicago.edu
E-mail: carroyo@iadtchicago.com

MASSACHUSETTS

Bay State College
122 Commonwealth Ave, Boston MA 02116-2901
Craig Pfannenstiehl, President
617-217-9000 Fax: 617-536-1735

NEW JERSEY

New Jersey City University
2039 John F Kennedy Blvd
Jersey City NJ 07305-1588
Carmen Panlilio, Asst. V.P. for Admissions and Financial Aid
201-200-3234 Fax: 201-200-2044
Website: www.njcu.edu
E-mail: admissions@njcu.edu

NEW YORK

LABORATORY INSTITUTE OF MERCHANDISING

12 E 53rd St, New York NY 10022-5268
Kristina Gibson, Director of Admissions
800-677-1323 or 212-752-1530 Fax: 212-750-3432
Website: www.limcollege.edu
E-mail: admissions@limcollege.edu
See listing under "Universities"

Pratt Institute
200 Willoughby Ave, Brooklyn NY 11205-3899
Heidi Metcalf, Director of Admissions
718-636-3600 Fax: 718-636-3670
Website: www.pratt.edu
E-mail: hmetcalf@pratt.edu

NORTH CAROLINA

ART INSTITUTE OF CHARLOTTE

2110 Water Ridge Pkwy, Charlotte NC 28217
Pamela Notemyer, Director of Admissions
800-872-4417 Fax: 704-357-1133
Website: www.artinstitutes.edu/charlotte
E-mail: admin@aii.edu
See listing under "Career Schools"

OHIO

Davis College
4747 Monroe St, Toledo OH 43623-4389
Dana Stern, Admissions Director
419-473-2700 Fax: 419-473-2472
Website: www.daviscollege.edu
E-mail: learn@daviscollege.edu

The Ohio State University
Coll of Human Ecology, Dept of Consumer Sciences, Textiles
Campbell Hall, 1787 Neil Ave, Columbus OH 43210
614-292-6612 Fax: 614-688-3019
Website:
hec.osu.edu/cs/programs/tc/undergraduate.php
E-mail: mawhirter.1@osu.edu

Ursuline College
2550 Lander Rd, Cleveland OH 44124-4398
Sarah E. Sundermeier, Director of Admissions
888-URSULINE Toll Free Fax: 440-684-6138
Website: www.admission.ursuline.edu
E-mail: admission@ursuline.edu

PENNSYLVANIA

Art Institute of Philadelphia
1622 Chestnut St, Philadelphia PA 19103-5119
Larry McHugh, Director of Admissions
800-275-2474 Fax: 215-405-6399
Website: www.artinstitutes.edu/philadelphia
E-mail: aiphinfo@aii.edu

ART INSTITUTE OF PITTSBURGH
420 Boulevard Of The Allies, Pittsburgh PA 15219
Jeffrey Bucklew, Director of Admissions
800-275-2470 Fax: 412-263-6667
Website: www.aip.aii.edu
E-mail: pahughes@aii.edu
See listing under "Universities"

Lehigh Valley College
2809 E Saucon Valley Rd
Center Valley PA 18034-8447
Sam Jarvis, Director of Marketing
800-227-9109 Fax: 610-791-7810
Website: www.lehighvalley.edu
E-mail: joshua.padron@lehighvalley.edu

TENNESSEE

O'More College of Design
423 S Margin St, Franklin TN 37064-2816
Dr. K. Mark Hilliard, President
Chris Lee, Director of Enrollment Management
615-794-4254 Fax: 615-790-1662
Website: www.omorecollege.edu
E-mail: clee@omorecollege.edu

TEXAS

Texas Woman's University
PO Box 425589, Denton TX 76204-5589
Erma Nieto-Brecht, Director of Admissions
866-809-6130 Fax: 940-898-3081
Website: www.twu.edu
E-mail: admissions@twu.edu

Wade College
Dallas Market Center
PO Box 421149, Dallas TX 75342
Harry Davros, President
800-624-4850 or 214-637-3530 Fax: 214-637-0827
Website: www.wadecollege.edu
E-mail: admissions@wadecollege.edu
See listing under "Community and Junior Colleges"

VIRGINIA

Radford University
PO Box 6903, Radford VA 24142
David W. Kraus, Director of Admissions
800-890-4265 Fax: 540-831-5038
Website: www.radford.edu
E-mail: ruadmiss@radford.edu

GRADUATE SCHOOLS

ALABAMA

Faulkner University
5345 Atlanta Hwy, Montgomery AL 36109-3390
Mark Hunt, Director of Adult Enrollment
800-879-9816 ext. 7140

Samford University
800 Lakeshore Dr, Birmingham AL 35229-0002
205-726-3673

Troy University
Troy AL 36082-0001
Jim Hutto, Dean of Enrollment Management
334-670-3175

Troy University Dothan
PO Box 8368, Dothan AL 36304-0368
334-983-6556

United States Sports Academy
1 Academy Dr, Daphne AL 36526-7055
Charles Cornwall, Dean of Student Services
251-626-3303

University of Alabama
Box 870118, Tuscaloosa AL 35487
Dr. Lisa B. Harris, Director of Admissions
205-348-5666

University of Alabama in Huntsville
PO Box 1247, Huntsville AL 35899-0001
256-824-6199 Fax: 256-824-6405
Website: www.uah.edu
E-mail: admitme@email.uah.edu

ALASKA

University of Alaska Anchorage
PO Box 141629, Anchorage AK 99514-1629
Cecile Mitchell, Director of Enrollment Services
907-786-1480 Fax: 907-786-4888
Website: www.uaa.alaska.edu/
E-mail: enroll@uaa.alaska.edu

ARIZONA

Argosy University/Phoenix
2233 W Dunlap Ave, Phoenix AZ 85021-2859
Andy Hughes, Director of Admissions
866-216-2777 (toll Free)

ARIZONA SCHOOL OF HEALTH SCIENCES A.T. STILL UNIVERSITY
5850 E Still Circle, Mesa AZ 85206
Admissions Counselor
866-626-2878 or 480-219-6000 Fax: 480-219-6100
Website: www.atsu.edu
E-mail: info@ashs.edu

Asian Institute of Medical Studies
3131 N Country Club Rd #100, Tucson AZ 85716
520-322-6330

AZ School of Acupuncture & Oriental Medicine
4646 E Ft Lowell Rd Ste 105, Tucson AZ 85712
520-795-0787

Frank Lloyd Wright School of Architecture
Taliesin West, Scottsdale AZ 85261
Pamela S. Stefansson, Director of Admissions
480-860-2700

Phoenix Institute of Herbal Medicine & Acupuncture
301 E Bethany Home Rd #A100, Phoenix AZ 85012
602-274-1885

Southwest Coll of Naturopathic Medicine & Health Sciences
2140 E Broadway Rd, Tempe AZ 85282
480-858-9100

Thunderbird, The Garvin School of International Management
15249 N 59th Ave, Glendale AZ 85306-3236
Judy Johnson, Associate VP of Admissions & Financial Aid
800-848-9084 or 602-978-7100 Fax: 602-439-5432
Website: www.thunderbird.edu
E-mail: johnsonj@thunderbird.edu

University of Advancing Technology
2625 W Baseline Rd, Tempe AZ 85283
Lary Dougherty, Director of Admissions
800-658-5744

CALIFORNIA

Academy of Chinese Culture and Health Sciences
1601 Clay St, Oakland CA 94612-1531
Ruth Kierans, Director of Admission
510-763-7787

Acupuncture and Integrative Medicine College - Berkeley
2550 Shattuck Ave, Berkeley CA 94704
510-666-8248

Alliant International University
1000 S Fremont Ave, Alhambra CA 91803-4737
Stephanie Byers-Bell, Director of Admissions
626-284-2777

Alliant International University
5130 E Clinton Way, Fresno CA 93727-2014
Gregory Timberlake, Director of Admissions
559-456-2777

Alliant International University
2500 Michelson Dr Ste 250, Irvine CA 92612
949-833-2651

Alliant International University
425 University Ave Ste 211, Sacramento CA 95825
Gregory Timberlake, Director of Admissions
916-565-2955

Alliant International University - San Diego
10455 Pomerado Rd, San Diego CA 92131-1799
858-635-4772

AMERICAN BAPTIST SEMINARY OF THE WEST
2606 Dwight Way, Berkeley CA 94704-3029
510-841-1905 Fax: 510-841-2446
Website: www.absw.edu
E-mail: admissions@absw.edu

American College of Traditional Chinese Medicine
455 Arkansas St, San Francisco CA 94107-2813
JoAnn Vandenberg, Dean of Student Services
415-282-7600

American Conservatory Theater
30 Grant Ave, San Francisco CA 94108-5800
Melissa Smith, Conservatory Director
415-439-2350

AMERICAN FILM INSTITUTE
AFI Conservatory
2021 N Western Ave, Los Angeles CA 90027
Danielle McVickers, Admissions Manager
323-856-7740 Fax: 323-856-7720
Website: www.afi.com/education/conservatory
E-mail: dmcvickers@afi.com
Production Design.

American Graduate University
733 N Dodsworth Ave, Covina CA 91724-2408
Marie Sirney, V.P. Administration
626-966-4576

Antioch University
801 Garden St Ste 101
Santa Barbara CA 93101-1581
Ankara McPherson, Director of Admissions
805-962-8179

Argosy University / Orange County
3501 W Sunflower Ave, Santa Ana CA 92704
714-338-6200

Argosy University
San Francisco Bay Area Campus
999A Canal Blvd, Point Richmond CA 94804-3547
Cynthia Sirkin, Associate Director of Admissions
510-215-0277

Brooks Institute of Photography
801 Alston Rd, Santa Barbara CA 93108-2399
Inge B. Kautzmann, Director of Admissions
805-966-3888 ext. 217 or 218

California Baptist University
8432 Magnolia Ave, Riverside CA 92504-3297
951-689-5771

CALIFORNIA COAST UNIVERSITY
700 N Main St, Santa Ana CA 92701
Admissions Office: 888-CCU-UNIV or 714-547-9625
Fax: 714-547-5777
Dr. Thomas Neal, President
Dr. Cynthia Teeple, Academic Vice President
Website: www.calcoast.edu
E-mail: info@calcoast.edu

Established 1973. Proprietary. Coed. Accreditation: California Coast University holds accreditation through the Accrediting Commission of the Distance Education and Training Council (DETC). The DETC is an educational association located in Washington, D.C. Founded in 1926, it is the standard setting agency for distance education institutions. Approval: Bureau for Private Postsecondary and Vocational Education - State of California, charter member California Association of State Approved Colleges & Universities, member Association for Adult & Continuing Education, member The Alliance for Private Post Secondary Academic Institutions.

Tuition: $2,805-$12,070. California Coast University has selected the SLM Corporation, commonly known as Sallie Mae, to help the university provide financing for its students. Sallie Mae is the nation's leading provider of education funding. Sallie Mae also allows students to borrow additional loan amounts to cover additional expenses, such as textbooks, equipment, or living expenses.

Enrollment: 30,000. California Coast University is approved by the California State Approving Agency to enroll veterans or other eligible persons under Title 38, U.S. Code. California Coast University holds a Memorandum of Understanding with Defense Activity for Non-Traditional Education Support (DANTES) as an external degree provider.

A private college offering off-campus independent study programs in the traditional areas of business administration, management, psychology, education. Admissions: enroll year round, requires official transcripts, letters of recommendation, detailed curriculum vita or occupational history.

Process: evaluation of prior academic work followed by analysis of occupational history, including participation in workshops, seminars, training programs, specialized projects for credit. Credit is demonstrated by accelerated learning guides or study guides.

Residency: All course work may be completed off campus, utilizing correspondence methods. Interest free loans available to students.

California Institute of Integral Studies
1453 Mission St, San Francisco CA 94103
415-575-6150

California Institute of Technology
1200 E California Blvd, Pasadena CA 91106
626-395-6341

California Institute of the Arts
24700 McBean Pkwy, Valencia CA 91355-2397
Carol Kim, Director of Enrollment Services
800-545-ARTS

California National University for Advanced Studies
8550 Balboa Blvd Ste 210
Northridge CA 91325-3576
800-782-2422

California School of Podiatric Medicine
Samuel Merritt College
370 Hawthorne Ave, Oakland CA 94609
510-869-8727

California State University-Stanislaus
801 W Monte Vista Ave, Turlock CA 95382-0256
Lisa Bernardo, Director of Admissions
209-667-3129

California Western School of Law
225 Cedar St, San Diego CA 92101-3090
619-239-0391

Chapman University
One University Drive, Orange CA 92866-1099
Michael Drummy, Assistant Vice President for Enrollment
Services and Chief Admission Officer
714-997-6411 or 888-CUAPPLY Fax: 714-997-6713
Website: www.chapman.edu
E-mail: admit@chapman.edu

CHURCH DIVINITY SCHOOL OF THE PACIFIC
2451 Ridge Rd, Berkeley CA 94709-1217
Kathleen Crisp, Director of Admissions and Recruitment
510-204-0715 Fax: 510-204-0749
Website: www.cdsp.edu
E-mail: admissions@cdsp.edu

Claremont Graduate University
170 E 10th St, Claremont CA 91711-5909
Diane J. Guido, Associate Dean of Student Affairs
909-621-8069

CLAREMONT SCHOOL OF THEOLOGY
1325 N College Ave, Claremont CA 91711-3154
Sabrina Johnson, Director of Admission
909-447-2506 Fax: 909-447-6389
Website: www.cst.edu
E-mail: admission@cst.edu

Concordia University
1530 Concordia, Irvine CA 92612-3203
Lori McDonald, Executive Director of Enrollment Services
800-229-1200 or 949-854-8002 Fax: 949-854-6894
Website: www.cui.edu
E-mail: admission@cui.edu

DOMINICAN SCHOOL OF PHILOSOPHY & THEOLOGY
2301 Vine St, Berkeley CA 94708
John Knutsen, Director of Admissions
888-450-DSPT or 510-883-2073 Fax: 510-849-1372
Website: www.dspt.edu
E-mail: admissions@dspt.edu

Dongguk Royal University
440 Shatto Pl, Los Angeles CA 90020
213-487-0110

EMPEROR'S COLLEGE OF TRADITIONAL ORIENTAL MEDICINE
1807 Wilshire Blvd Ste B
Santa Monica CA 90403-5678
Mary Good, Director of Admissions
310-453-8300 Fax: 310-829-3838
Website: www.emperors.edu
E-mail: mary@emperors.edu

Fielding Graduate University
2112 Santa Barbara St
Santa Barbara CA 93105-3538
DeAnne Taylor, Director of Admissions
805-687-1099 Fax: 805-687-9793
Website: www.fielding.edu
E-mail: admission@fielding.edu

FIVE BRANCHES INSTITUTE
3031 Tisch Way Ste 605, San Jose CA 95128
Eleonor Mendelson, Director of Admissions
408-260-0208 Fax: 408-261-3166
Website: www.fivebranches.edu
E-mail: sicampus@fivebrances.edu

FIVE BRANCHES INSTITUTE
College of Traditional Chinese Medicine
200 7th Ave, Santa Cruz CA 95062-4668
Eleonor Mendelson, Admissions
831-476-9424 Fax: 831-476-8928
Website: www.fivebranches.edu
E-mail: tcm@fivebranches.edu

Franciscan School of Theology
1712 Euclid Ave, Berkeley CA 94709-1294
Registrar
510-848-5232

FULLER THEOLOGICAL SEMINARY
135 N Oakland Ave, Pasadena CA 91182-0002
Office of Admissions
800-2-FULLER Fax: 626-584-5449
Website: www.fuller.edu
E-mail: adm-email@dept.fuller.edu

Golden Gate Baptist Theological Seminary
201 Seminary Dr, Mill Valley CA 94941-3197
415-380-1300

GRADUATE THEOLOGICAL UNION
2400 Ridge Rd, Berkeley CA 94709-1212
Kathleen Kook, Assistant Dean for Admissions
800-826-4488 Fax: 510-649-1730
Website: www.gtu.edu
E-mail: gtuadm@gtu.edu

HEBREW UNION COLLEGE - JEWISH INSTITUTE OF RELIGION
3077 University Ave, Los Angeles CA 90007-3796
Dr. Matt Albert, Regional Director of Admissions and Recruitment
213-749-3424 Fax: 213-747-6128
Website: www.huc.edu
E-mail: malbert@huc.edu

Institute for Creation Research Graduate School
10946 Woodside Ave N, Santee CA 92071
619-448-0900

INSTITUTE OF TRANSPERSONAL PSYCHOLOGY
1069 E Meadow Cir, Palo Alto CA 94303-4231
Sydney J. Reuben, Director of Admissions
650-493-4430 Fax: 650-493-6835
Website: www.itp.edu
E-mail: itpinfo@itp.edu

Jesuit School of Theology at Berkeley
1735 LeRoy Ave, Berkeley CA 94709-1193
Patricia Abracia, Director of Admissions
800-824-0122

Keck Graduate Institute
535 Watson Dr, Claremont CA 91711
909-607-7855

La Sierra University
4500 Riverwalk Pkwy, Riverside CA 92505
Bobby Brown, Director of Admissions
800-874-5587

LIFE CHIROPRACTIC COLLEGE WEST
25001 Industrial Blvd, Hayward CA 94545-2801
Stephen D. Eckstone, Director of Admissions
800-788-4476 Fax: 510-780-4525
Website: www.lifewest.edu
E-mail: admissions@lifewest.edu

Logos Evangelical Seminary
9358 Telstar Ave, El Monte CA 91731-2816
626-571-5110

Loyola Marymount University
PO Box 15019, Los Angeles CA 90015-0019
213-736-1180

Mennonite Brethren Biblical Seminary
4824 E Butler Ave, Fresno CA 93727-5097
Chris Patton, Director of Admissions
559-251-8628

Monterey Institute of International Studies
460 Pierce St, Monterey CA 93940
Admissions Office
831-647-4100

National University School of Law
3580 Aero Ct, San Diego CA 92123-1711
619-563-7300

Newschool of Architecture and Design
1249 F St, San Diego CA 92101-6634
Gilbert D. Cooke, AIA, Dean
Barbara Wingate, Director of Admissions
619-235-4100 ext. 123

Northwestern Polytechnic University
47671 Westinghouse Dr, Fremont CA 94539
Dr. P. Hsu, Contact
510-657-5913 Fax: 510-657-8975
Website: www.npu.edu
E-mail: npuadm@npu.edu

Notre Dame de Namur University
1500 Ralston Ave, Belmont CA 94002-1997
Elaine Cohen, Graduate Dean
650-508-3527

Pacifica Graduate Institute
249 Lambert Rd, Carpinteria CA 93013-3019
Diane Huerta, Director of Admissions
805-969-3626 ext. 128

PACIFIC COLLEGE OF ORIENTAL MEDICINE
7445 Mission Valley Rd #105, San Diego CA 92108
619-574-6909 Fax: 619-574-6641
Website: www.pacificcollege.edu
E-mail: admissions-sd@pacificcollege.edu

Pacific Graduate School of Psychology
940 E Meadow Dr, Palo Alto CA 94303-4232
L. Barbara Bell, Director of Admissions
800-818-6136

Pacific Lutheran Theological Seminary
2770 Marin Ave, Berkeley CA 94708-1597
510-524-5264

Pacific Oaks College
5 Westmoreland Pl, Pasadena CA 91103-3592
800-684-0900

Pacific School of Religion
1798 Scenic Ave, Berkeley CA 94709-1323
Debra J. Mumford, Director of Recruitment and Admissions
800-999-0528

PALMER COLLEGE OF CHIROPRACTIC
West Campus
90 E Tasman Dr, San Jose CA 95134-1617
866-303-7939 or 408-944-6000 Fax: 408-944-6032
Website: www.palmer.edu
E-mail: pccw_admiss@palmer.edu

Pardee RAND Graduate School of Policy Studies
PO Box 2138, Santa Monica CA 90407-2138
310-393-0411

PHILLIPS GRADUATE INSTITUTE
5445 Balboa Blvd, Encino CA 91316-1509
Belinda Lombardo, Director of Admissions
818-386-5660 Fax: 818-386-5699
Website: www.pgi.edu
E-mail: info@pgi.edu

Point Loma Nazarene University
3900 Lomaland Dr, San Diego CA 92106-2810
Chip Killingsworth, Director of Undergraduate Admissions
800-733-7770 Fax: 619-849-2601
Website: www.pointloma.edu
E-mail: admissions@pointloma.edu

Remington College
123 Camino De La Reina #100N
San Diego CA 92108-3002
Christopher Tilley, Campus President
619-686-8600

St. Patrick's Seminary & University
320 Middlefield Rd, Menlo Park CA 94025-3563
Dr. Dorothy Tully, Contact
650-325-5621

SAMRA UNIVERSITY OF ORIENTAL MEDICINE
3000 S Robertson Blvd 4 Fl
Los Angeles CA 90034-3158
Simon Song, Director of Operations
310-202-6444 Fax: 310-202-6007
Website: www.samra.edu
E-mail: admissions@samra.edu

SAN FRANCISCO ART INSTITUTE
800 Chestnut St, San Francisco CA 94133
800-345-SFAI Fax: 415-749-4503
Website: www.sfai.edu
E-mail: admissions@sfai.edu

Founded in 1871, SFAI offers one of the most innovative and interdisciplinary environments in higher education. Offering accredited Master of Fine Arts, Summer Master of Fine Arts (MFA, SMFA), Post-Baccalaureate (PB), and Master of Arts (MA) programs, SFAI is committed to furthering the relationship between the practices and theories of contemporary art. SFAI's School of Studio Practice centers on the development of the artist's vision and MFA students work with faculty from each of the school's studio departments: Design+Technology, Film, New Genres, Painting, Photography, Printmaking, and Sculpture. SFAI's School of Interdisciplinary Studies is based on the premise that imagination combined with critical intelligence is essential for engaging and understanding contemporary art and global society, and offers three MA programs: History and Theory of Contemporary Art, Urban Studies, and Exhibition and Museum Studies. Together the two schools provide an inclusive model to address contemporary art and culture. The Summer MFA program has the same rigor as the Academic Year MFA program yet is designed for those who choose an alternate academic schedule. The Post-Baccalaureate program is an excellent way to prepare for entrance into an MFA program or to enhance skills and knowledge. SFAI's faculty is comprised of active artists, curators, writers, and scholars. Dean of Academic Affairs is renowned curator and critic Okwui Enwezor. Dean of Graduate Studies is artist and filmmaker Renee Green. Director of Exhibitions and Public Programs is curator Hou Hanru. Visiting artists and scholars play a significant role in education at SFAI, with recent visitors including Matthew Barney, William Kentridge, Raqs Media Collective, and others. SFAI's Graduate Center provides individual and group studios with 24-hour access. The 62,000 square-foot Graduate Center also includes a digital lab, film and sound studios, darkrooms, a woodshop, and a gallery for student work. Graduate students also take advantage of the resources at SFAI's main campus, which includes postproduction facilities and the first high-definition video research lab in the Bay Area. The Diego Rivera Gallery, and open-air amphitheater, and a 250-seat theater are also available to students for exhibiting and screening work. SFAI's Library collection includes more than 26,000 volumes with emphasis on modern and contemporary art, and over 200 current periodicals and an extensive image, video, and audio archive available only to students. SFAI has rolling application deadlines, and there is a fellowship program for students admitted into the graduate programs. Visit the SFAI website for application requirements.

SAN FRANCISCO THEOLOGICAL SEMINARY
105 Seminary Rd, San Anselmo CA 94960-2925
The Rev. Dr. Kyle Matsumoto Burch, Assoc. Dean of Enrollment
415-451-2831 or 800-447-8820 Fax: 415-451-2854
Website: www.sfts.edu
E-mail: admissions@sfts.edu

San Joaquin College of Law
901 5th St, Clovis CA 93612-1312
Joyce Morodomi, Director of Student Services
559-323-2100

Santa Barbara College of Oriental Medicine
1919 State St, Santa Barbara CA 93101
Laura Schlieske, Contact
800-549-6299

Saybrook Graduate School
747 Front St, 3rd Floor
San Francisco CA 94111-1920
Diana Hernandez, Dean of Admissions
800-825-4480

Scripps Research Institute
10550 N Torrey Pines Rd, La Jolla CA 92037
858-784-8469

Simpson University
2211 College View Dr, Redding CA 96003-8606
Jim Herberger, Director of Admissions
888-9-SIMPSON Fax: 530-226-4861
Website: www.simpsonuniversity.edu
E-mail: admissions@simpsonuniversity.edu
See listing under "Universities"

SOUTH BAYLO UNIVERSITY
School of Acupuncture & Oriental Medicine
1126 N Brookhurst St, Anaheim CA 92801
Seung W. Lee, Director of Admissions
714-533-1495 Fax: 714-533-6040
Website: www.southbaylo.edu
E-mail: swl@southbaylo.edu

Southern California College of Optometry
2575 Yorba Linda Blvd, Fullerton CA 92831-1615
714-449-7450

SOUTHERN CALIFORNIA INSTITUTE OF ARCHITECTURE
960 E 3rd St, Los Angeles CA 90013-1822
J.J. Jackman, Director of Admissions
213-613-2200 ext 321 Fax: 213-613-2260
Website: www.sciarc.edu
E-mail: admissions@sciarc.edu

Established 1972. Coed. Accreditation: NAAB, WASC. Tuition: $10,180/sem. Enrollment: 450. Faculty: 80. Student-faculty ratio: 15:1. Degrees offered: BArch, 3 yr MArch, 2 yr MArch, 2 Post-Grad degrees. Library: 30,000 volumes. Founded as a radical alternative to the conventional system of arch education; only architecture-focused academic library in Southern California; dark room; CNC facilities, print center, wood & metal shop all on premises; located in downtown LA.

Southern California University of Health Science
16200 Amber Valley Dr, Whittier CA 90604
Jan Price, Interim Admissions Director
877-434-7757

Southwestern University School of Law
675 S Westmoreland Ave
Los Angeles CA 90005-3905
213-738-6700

Starr King School for the Ministry
2441 Le Conte Ave, Berkeley CA 94709-1209
510-845-6232

Thomas Jefferson School of Law
2121 San Diego Ave, San Diego CA 92110-2928
Kenneth Vandevelde, Dean
619-297-9700 ext. 1600

TOURO UNIVERSITY COLLEGE OF OSTEOPATHIC MEDICINE - MARE ISLAND
1310 Johnson Ln, Vallejo CA 94592
Dr. Donald Haight, Director of Admissions
707-638-5270 Fax: 707-638-5250
Website: www.tu.edu
E-mail: haight@touro.edu

University of California
Parnassus and 3rd Ave
San Francisco CA 94143-0001
415-476-9000

University of California Hastings College of Law
200 McAllister St, San Francisco CA 94102
415-565-4600

University of East-West Medicine
970 W El Camino Real, Sunnyvale CA 94087
408-733-1878

University of Judaism
15600 Mulholland Dr, Los Angeles CA 90077-1519
Saul Korin, Director of Graduate Admissions
310-476-9777

University of La Verne
1950 3rd St, La Verne CA 91750-4443
800-876-4858

University of San Diego
5998 Alcala Park, San Diego CA 92110-2492
Admissions
619-260-4506

University of Southern California
Health Science Campus, Los Angeles CA 90033
323-226-6501

UNIVERSITY OF THE PACIFIC
Arthur A. Dugoni School of Dentistry
2155 Webster St, San Francisco CA 94115-2333
Kathy Candito, Director of Admissions
415-929-6491 Fax: 415-749-3363
Website: www.dental.pacific.edu
E-mail: kcandito@pacific.edu

University of the Pacific McGeorge School of Law
3200 5th Ave, Sacramento CA 95817-2799
Adam Barrett, Asst. Dean and Director of Admissions
916-739-7105

University of West Los Angeles
School of Law, School of Paralegal Studies
9920 S La Cienega Blvd, Inglewood CA 90301-4423
Lynda Freeman, Admissions Counselor
310-342-5254

University of West Los Angeles
School of Law, School of Paralegal Studies
6400 Canoga Ave Ste 271, Woodland Hills CA 91367
Lynda Freeman, Admissions Counselor
818-883-0529

Western State University College of Law
1111 N State College Blvd, Fullerton CA 92831-3014
Phyllis Hauptfeld, Assistant Dean of Admission
800-WSU-4LAW

Westminster Seminary California
1725 Bear Valley Pkwy, Escondido CA 92027-4128
760-480-8474

Whittier College
School of Law
3333 Harbor Blvd, Costa Mesa CA 92626-1501
Betty Vu, Director of Admissions
714-444-4141

Wright Institute
2728 Durant Ave, Berkeley CA 94704-1796
510-841-9230

Yo San University of Traditional Chinese Medicine
13315 Washington Blvd, Los Angeles CA 90066
310-577-3000

COLORADO

Adams State College
Alamosa CO 81102
Matt Gallegos, Director of Admissions
800-824-6494

Colorado School of Professional Psychology
555 E Pikes Peak Ave Ste 108
Colorado Springs CO 80903-3612
877-442-0505

Colorado State University - Pueblo
2200 Bonforte Blvd, Pueblo CO 81001-4990
719-549-2461

Colorado Technical University
4435 N Chestnut St
Colorado Springs CO 80907-3895
719-598-0200

Denver Seminary
6399 S Santa Fe Dr, Littleton CO 80120
Robert Jones, VP Student Services
303-762-6982 Fax: 303-783-3122
Website: denverseminary.edu
E-mail: robert.jones@denverseminary.edu

ILIFF SCHOOL OF THEOLOGY
2201 S University Blvd, Denver CO 80210-4798
Peggy Blocker, Director of Admissions
800-678-3360 or 303-765-3117 Fax: 303-777-0164
Website: www.iliff.edu
E-mail: admissions@iliff.edu

Naropa University
2130 Arapahoe Ave, Boulder CO 80302-6697
303-546-3572

National Theatre Conservatory
1050 13th St, Denver CO 80204-2157
Daniel Renner, Director of Education
303-446-4855

University of Colorado at Denver and Health Sciences Center
Downtown Denver Campus
PO Box 173364, Denver CO 80217-3364
303-556-2550

University of Colorado at Denver and Health Sciences Center
Health Sciences Program
4200 E 9th Ave Box C245, Denver CO 80262
Phoebe Lindsey Barton, Ph.D., Director

UNIVERSITY OF DENVER UNIVERSITY COLLEGE
2211 S Josephine St, Denver CO 80208
Dr. James R. Davis, Dean
303-871-3354 Fax: 303-871-4047
Website: www.universitycollege.du.edu
E-mail: ucolinfo@du.edu

University of Northern Colorado
Greeley CO 80639
Richard King, Interim Dean, Graduate School
970-351-2831

CONNECTICUT

Berkeley Divinity School at Yale
363 Saint Ronan St, New Haven CT 06511-2285
William Franklin, Dean
203-764-9300

HARTFORD SEMINARY
77 Sherman St, Hartford CT 06105-2260
Kelton Cobb, Seminary Academic Advisor
860-509-9513 Fax: 860-509-9509
Website: www.hartsem.edu
E-mail: info@hartsem.edu

Rensselaer at Hartford
275 Windsor St, Hartford CT 06120-2910
860-548-2400

St. Joseph College
1678 Asylum Ave, West Hartford CT 06117-2791
860-232-4571

University of Bridgeport
126 Park Ave, Bridgeport CT 06604-5620
Barbara L. Maryak, Dean of Admissions
203-576-4552

University of New Haven
300 Boston Post Rd, West Haven CT 06516
Director of Graduate Admissions
203-932-7133

DELAWARE

Widener University School of Law
PO Box 7474, Wilmington DE 19803-0474
Barbara Ayars, Assistant Dean of Admissions
302-477-2162

DISTRICT OF COLUMBIA

The Institute of World Politics
1521 16th St NW, Washington DC 20036
202-462-2101

Johns Hopkins University
1740 Massachusetts Ave NW
Washington DC 20036-1903
202-663-5600

University of the District of Columbia David A. Clarke School of Law
4200 Connecticut Ave NW, Washington DC 20008
Vivian W. Canty, Director of Admission
202-274-7341

Washington Theological Union
6896 Laurel St NW, Washington DC 20012-2016
202-726-8800

Wesley Theological Seminary
4500 Massachusetts Ave NW
Washington DC 20016-5690
The Rev. Chip Aldridge, Director of Admissions
800-882-4987

FLORIDA

Academy for Five Element Acupuncture
1170A E Hallendale Beach, Hallandale FL 33009
954-456-6336

ACUPUNCTURE & MASSAGE COLLEGE
10506 N Kendall Dr, Miami FL 33176
Joe Calareso, Admissions Director
305-595-9500 Fax: 305-595-2622
Website: www.amcollege.edu
E-mail: admissions@amcollege.edu

Argosy University / Tampa
4401 N Himes Ave Ste 150, Tampa FL 33614-7001
813-740-1108

ATLANTIC INSTITUTE OF ORIENTAL MEDICINE
100 E Broward Blvd Ste 100
Fort Lauderdale FL 33301-3510
Prof. Yan Cheng, Academic Dean
954-763-9840 Fax: 954-763-9844
Website: www.atom.edu
E-mail: dean@atom.edu

Barry University
11300 NE 2nd Ave, Miami Shores FL 33161-6695
800-695-2279

Bay Medical Center
615 N Bonita Ave, Panama City FL 32401
Sherry Tindall, Director of Education, Training, & Research
800-422-2418

CARLOS ALBIZU UNIVERSITY
2173 NW 99th Ave, Miami FL 33172-2209
Carlos Alicea, Director of Admissions, Recruitment & Outreach
305-593-1223 ext. 137 Fax: 305-593-1854
Website: www.mia.albizu.edu
E-mail: admissions@albizu.edu

Dragon Rises College Oriental Medicine
901 NW 8th Ave Ste B5, Gainesville FL 32601
352-371-2833

East West College of Natural Medicine
3808 N Tamiami Trail, Sarasota FL 34234
Meredith McKay, Chief Administrative Officer
941-355-9080

EVERGLADES UNIVERSITY (MAIN CAMPUS)
5002 T-Rex Ave Suite 100, Boca Raton FL 33431
Kristi Mollis, President
888-772-6077 Fax: 561-912-1191
Website: www.evergladesuniversity.edu
E-mail: admissions-boca@evergladesuniversity.edu
See listing under "Universities"

EVERGLADES UNIVERSITY
Orlando Campus (Branch Campus)
887 E Altamonte Dr, Altamonte Springs FL 32701
Linda Volz, Vice President
866-289-1078 Fax: 407-482-9801
Website: www.evergladesuniversity.edu
E-mail: admissions-orl@evergladesuniversity.edu
See listing under "Universities"

EVERGLADES UNIVERSITY
Sarasota Campus (Branch Campus)
6001 Lake Osprey Dr, Suite 110, Sarasota FL 34240
Brad Brewer, Vice President
866-907-2262 Fax: 941-907-6634
Website: www.evergladesuniversity.edu
E-mail: admissions-sar@evergladesuniversity.edu
See listing under "Universities"

Florida Atlantic University
PO Box 3091, Boca Raton FL 33431-0991
800-299-4328

Florida Coastal School of Law
8787 Baypine Rd, Jacksonville FL 32256
904-680-7700

Florida College of Integrative Medicine
7100 Lake Ellenor Dr, Orlando FL 32809
407-888-8689

Florida Metropolitan University
225 N Federal Hwy, Pompano Beach FL 33062
Fran Heaston, Director of Admissions
800-468-0168

Florida Metropolitan University-Brandon
3924 Coconut Palm Dr, Tampa FL 33619-1354
Marty Baca, Director of Admissions
877-338-0068

Florida Metropolitan University
Pinellas Campus
2471 N McMullen Booth Rd
Clearwater FL 33759-1359
Sandra Williams, Director of Admissions
800-353-3687

Knox Theological Seminary
5554 N Federal Hwy, Fort Lauderdale FL 33308
954-771-0376

Lynn University
3601 N Military Trl, Boca Raton FL 33431-5598
Director of Admissions
561-237-7900 Fax: 561-237-7100
Website: www.lynn.edu
E-mail: admission@lynn.edu

PALMER COLLEGE OF CHIROPRACTIC
Florida Campus
4777 City Center Pkwy, Port Orange FL 32129-4153
866-585-9677 or 386-763-2709 Fax: 386-763-2620
Website: www.palmer.edu
E-mail: pccf_admiss@palmer.edu

Reformed Theological Seminary
1231 Reformation Dr, Oviedo FL 32765
407-366-9493

ST. PETERSBURG THEOLOGICAL SEMINARY
10830 Navajo Dr, Saint Petersburg FL 33708
Angel Rosado, VP of Operations
727-399-0276 Fax: 727-399-1324
Website: www.sptseminary.edu
E-mail: sptsoffice@aol.com

St. Thomas University
16401 NW 37th Ave, Miami Gardens FL 33054
Marilyn Carballosa/Cristen Scolastico, Graduate Admissions
800-367-9010 or 305-628-6546 Fax: 305-628-6591
Website: www.stu.edu
E-mail: signup@stu.edu

Stetson University
1401 61st St S, Gulfport FL 33707-3299
727-345-1121

Trinity Baptist College
800-200 Hammond Blvd, Jacksonville FL 32221
R. Larry Appleby, Director of Admissions
904-596-2400

Trinity International University
South Florida Campus
111 NW 183rd St Ste 500, Miami FL 33169-4541
305-577-4600

GEORGIA

Argosy University/Atlanta
980 Hammond Dr NE Ste 100, Atlanta GA 30328
770-671-1200

Columbia Theological Seminary
701 S Columbia Dr, Decatur GA 30030-4118
Ann Clay Adams, Director of Admissions
404-378-8821

Emory University Hospital
1364 Clifton Rd NE, Atlanta GA 30322-1061
404-712-4881

Georgia State University
PO Box 4009, Atlanta GA 30302-4009
404-651-2365

INTERDENOMINATIONAL THEOLOGICAL CENTER

700 Martin Luther King Jr Dr SW
Atlanta GA 30314-4143
Walter Cabassa, Recruitment Coordinator
404-527-7792 Fax: 404-527-0901
Website: www.itc.edu
E-mail: wcabassa@itc.edu

Kennesaw State University
1000 Chastain Rd NW Box 0132
Kennesaw GA 30144-5591
David Baugher, Director of Graduate Admissions
770-420-4377 Fax: 770-423-6885
Website: www.kennesaw.edu

LaGrange College
601 Broad St, LaGrange GA 30240-2955
Andy Geeter, Director of Admission
800-593-2885

Mercer University in Macon
1400 Coleman Ave, Macon GA 31207-0003
John P. Cole, Sr. Assoc. V.P. for Admissions
478-301-2650

The Psychological Studies Institute
2055 Mount Paran Rd NW McCarty Building
Atlanta GA 30327
Robin Lay, Director of Recruiting
888-924-6774

University of Georgia
Athens GA 30602-0001
706-542-3000

HAWAII

Argosy University/Hawaii
1001 Bishop St Ste 400, Honolulu HI 96813-3403
808-536-5555

Chaminade University of Honolulu
3140 Waialae Ave, Honolulu HI 96816-1510
Joy Bouey, Dean of Enrollment Management
808-739-4619

Institute of Clinical Acupuncture and Oriental Medicine
100 N Beretania St Ste 203B, Honolulu HI 96817
808-521-2288

Traditional Chinese Medical College of Hawaii
65-1206 Mamalahoa Hwy, Kamuela HI 96743
808-885-9226

World Medicine Institute
1110 University Ave Ste 308, Honolulu HI 96826-1508
808-949-1050

ILLINOIS

ADLER SCHOOL OF PROFESSIONAL PSYCHOLOGY

65 E Wacker Pl, Chicago IL 60601-7296
Craig Hines, Director of Admissions
312-201-5900 Fax: 312-201-5917
Website: www.adler.edu
E-mail: admissions@adler.edu

AMERICAN INTERCONTINENTAL UNIVERSITY ONLINE

5550 Prairie Stone Parkway Suite 400
Hoffman Estates IL 60192
Admissions Department
877-701-3800
Website: www.aiuonline.edu
E-mail: info@aiuonline.edu

ARGOSY UNIVERSITY/CHICAGO

350 N Orleans St, Merchandise Mart
Chicago IL 60654
Jamal Scott, Director of Admissions
800-626-4123 Fax: 312-777-7750
Website: www.argosyu.edu
E-mail: jscott@argosyu.edu

Argosy University/Chicago Northwest
1000 N Plaza Dr Ste 100, Schaumburg IL 60173-4990
847-290-7400

Aurora University
347 S Gladstone Ave, Aurora IL 60506-4892
Carol R. Dunn, Ed.D., Vice President for Enrollment
800-742-5281 Fax: 630-844-5535
Website: www.aurora.edu
E-mail: admission@aurora.edu

Catholic Theological Union
5401 S Cornell Ave, Chicago IL 60615-5698
Kathy Van Duser, Director of Recruitment and Admissions
773-324-8000

Chicago School of Professional Psychology
325 N Wells St, Chicago IL 60610-4705
Office of Admission
312-329-6600

Chicago Theological Seminary
5757 S University Ave, Chicago IL 60637-1579
773-752-5757

De Paul University
2323 N Seminary Ave, Chicago IL 60614-3298
312-362-8000

Erikson Institute
420 N Wabash Ave, Chicago IL 60611
312-755-2250

Garrett Evangelical Theological Seminary
2121 Sheridan Rd, Evanston IL 60201-2926
847-866-3900

Illinois College of Optometry
3241 S Michigan Ave, Chicago IL 60616-3878
Lynn Petrica, Director of Recruitment
312-225-1700

INSTITUTE FOR CLINICAL SOCIAL WORK

200 N Michigan Ave Ste 407, Chicago IL 60601
Barbara Berger, Ph.D., Dean of Admissions
312-726-8480 Fax: 312-726-7216
Website: www.icsw.edu
E-mail: icsw@icsw.edu

John Marshall Law School
315 S Plymouth Ct, Chicago IL 60604-3907
William Powers, Assoc. Dean Admissions / Student Services
312-987-1406

Knowledge Systems Institute Graduate School
3420 Main St, Skokie IL 60076-2453
Judy Pan, Director of Admissions
847-679-3135

Lake Forest Graduate School of Management
230 S LaSalle St Ste 100, Chicago IL 60604
312-435-5330

Lake Forest Graduate School of Management
1905 W Field Ct, Lake Forest IL 60045
847-234-5080

Lake Forest Graduate School of Management
1295 E Algonquin Rd, Schaumburg IL 60196-4040
847-576-1212

LUTHERAN SCHOOL OF THEOLOGY AT CHICAGO

1100 E 55th St, Chicago IL 60615-5199
Dorothy C. Dominiak, Director of Admissions
800-635-1116 ext. 726 or 773-256-0726
Fax: 773-256-0782
Website: www.lstc.edu
E-mail: admissions@lstc.edu

MCCORMICK THEOLOGICAL SEMINARY

5460 S University Ave, Chicago IL 60615
Rev. Craig Howard, Director of Recruitment and Admissions
800-228-4687 Fax: 773-288-2612
Website: www.mccormick.edu
E-mail: admit@mccormick.edu

Meadville/Lombard Theological School
5701 S Woodlawn Ave, Chicago IL 60637-1602
773-753-3195

MIDWEST COLLEGE OF ORIENTAL MEDICINE

4334 N Hazel St Ste 206, Chicago IL 60613-1429
Kelly Westerlund, Contact
800-593-2320 Fax: 262-554-7475
Website: www.acupuncture.edu
E-mail: mwcadmissions@yahoo.com

National-Louis University
5202 Old Orchard Rd Ste 300, Skokie IL 60077-4409
224-233-2000

National University of Health Sciences
200 E Roosevelt Rd, Lombard IL 60148-4583
Dr. James Winterstein, President
800-826-6285 Fax: 630-889-6554
Website: www.nuhs.edu
E-mail: admissions@nuhs.edu

NORTHEASTERN ILLINOIS UNIVERSITY

5500 N Saint Louis Ave, Chicago IL 60625-4699
Janet Fredericks, Dean of Graduate College
773-442-6000 Fax: 773-442-6020
Website: www.neiu.edu
E-mail: j-fredericks@neiu.edu

NORTHERN BAPTIST THEOLOGICAL SEMINARY

660 E Butterfield Rd, Lombard IL 60148-5698
Charles Dresser, Executive Director of Enrollment Management
630-620-2180 Fax: 630-620-2190
Website: www.seminary.edu
E-mail: admissions@seminary.edu

Rockford College
5050 E State St, Rockford IL 61108-2393
William Laffey, Director of Admission
800-892-2984

Rosalind Franklin University of Medicine and Science
3333 Green Bay Rd, North Chicago IL 60064-3037
847-578-3000

School of the Art Institute of Chicago
37 S Wabash Ave, Chicago IL 60603-3002
Director of Admissions
800-232-7242

Seabury-Western Theological Seminary
2122 Sheridan Rd, Evanston IL 60201-2976
847-328-9300

Spertus College
618 S Michigan Ave, Chicago IL 60605-1901
312-922-9012 Fax: 312-922-6406
Website: www.spertus.edu
E-mail: college@spertus.edu

Trinity Evangelical Divinity School
2065 Half Day Rd, Deerfield IL 60015-1241
800-345-8337

University of Illinois
PO Box 1649, Peoria IL 61656-1649
309-438-2181

University of Illinois at Springfield
One University Plaza, Springfield IL 62794
217-206-4847

University of St. Mary of the Lake
1000 E Maple Ave, Mundelein IL 60060-1967
847-566-6401

VanderCook College of Music
3140 S Federal St, Chicago IL 60616-3704
Tamara V. Trutwin, Student Recruiter
Kelly Westergaard, Admissions Coordinator
800-448-2655 ext. 230

Wheaton College
501 College Ave, Wheaton IL 60187-5571
630-752-5000

INDIANA

ASSOCIATED MENNONITE BIBLICAL SEMINARIES

3003 Benham Ave, Elkhart IN 46517-1947
Regina Shands Stoltzfus, Director of Admissions
800-964-2627 Fax: 574-295-0092
Website: www.ambs.edu
E-mail: admissions@ambs.edu

BETHANY THEOLOGICAL SEMINARY

615 National Rd W, Richmond IN 47374-4019
Dr. Eugene F. Roop, President
800-287-8822 Fax: 765-983-1840
Website: www.brethren.org/bethany
E-mail: bethanysem@aol.com

Christian Theological Seminary
1000 W 42nd St, Indianapolis IN 46208-3301
Mary L. Harris, Associate Dean for Student Services
800-585-0508

Concordia Theological Seminary
6600 N Clinton St, Fort Wayne IN 46825-4996
Dr. Dean O. Wenthe, President
260-452-2100

Grace College and Theological Seminary
200 Seminary Dr, Winona Lake IN 46590-1224
800-54-GRACE

Indiana Wesleyan University
4201 S Washington St, Marion IN 46953-4974
765-674-6901

Oakland City University
138 N Lucretia St, Oakland City IN 47660
Brian J. Baker, Director of Admissions
800-737-5125 Fax: 812-749-1433
Website: www.oak.edu
E-mail: bbaker@oak.edu
See listing under "Universities"

Saint Meinrad School of Theology
200 Hill Dr, St Meinrad IN 47577
Rev. Jonathan Fassero, OSB, Director of Enrollment
800-634-6723

IOWA

Graceland University
1 University Place, Lamoni IA 50140
Greg Sutherland, Interim Vice President for Enrollment and Dean of Admissions
641-784-5196 Fax: 641-784-5480
Website: www.admissions.graceland.edu
E-mail: admissions@graceland.edu

Loras College
1450 Alta Vista St, Dubuque IA 52001-4399
Tim Hauber, Director of Admissions
800-245-6727

PALMER COLLEGE OF CHIROPRACTIC

Davenport Campus
1000 Brady St, Davenport IA 52803-5287
800-722-3648 or 563-884-5656 Fax: 563-884-5414
Website: www.palmer.edu
E-mail: pcadmit@palmer.edu

UNIVERSITY OF DUBUQUE THEOLOGICAL SEMINARY

2000 University Ave, Dubuque IA 52001-5050
800-369-8387 Fax: 563-589-3110
Website: udtseminary.net
E-mail: udtsadms@dbq.edu

WARTBURG THEOLOGICAL SEMINARY

PO Box 5004, Dubuque IA 52004-5004
Heather Devine, Director of Admissions
563-589-0200 Fax: 563-589-0333
Website: www.wartburgseminary.edu
E-mail: admissions@wartburgseminary.edu

KANSAS

Central Baptist Theological Seminary
6601 Monticello Rd, Shawnee KS 66226
800-677-2287

Fort Hays State University
600 Park St, Hays KS 67601-4099
785-628-4000

Southwestern College
100 College St, Winfield KS 67156-2499
620-229-6000

University of Kansas
Lawrence KS 66045-0001
Alan Cerveny, Director of Admissions

University of Kansas Medical Center
3901 Rainbow Blvd, Kansas City KS 66160-0001
913-588-5000

KENTUCKY

Asbury Theological Seminary
204 N Lexington Ave, Wilmore KY 40390-1199
Janelle Vernon, Director of Admissions
800-2-ASBURY

Brescia University
717 Frederica St, Owensboro KY 42301-3023
Sr. Mary Austin Blank, OSB, Director of Admissions
877-BRESCIA

LEXINGTON THEOLOGICAL SEMINARY
631 S Limestone, Lexington KY 40508-3288
Erika Smith, Director of Admissions
859-252-0361 Fax: 859-281-6042
Website: www.lextheo.edu
E-mail: esmith@lextheo.edu

Louisville Presbyterian Seminary
1044 Alta Vista Rd, Louisville KY 40205-1798
Kerry Rice, Director of Admissions
502-895-3411 or 800-264-1839 Fax: 502-992-9399
Website: www.lpts.edu
E-mail: admissions@lpts.edu
Degrees offered MDiv, MA, DMin, ThM

Southern Baptist Theological Seminary
2825 Lexington Rd, Louisville KY 40280-0004
502-897-4011

LOUISIANA

New Orleans Baptist Theological Seminary
3939 Gentilly Blvd, New Orleans LA 70126-4858
504-282-4455

MAINE

Bangor Theological Seminary
PO Box 411, Bangor ME 04402-0411
Michael K. Huddy Director of Admissions
800-287-6781

HUSSON COLLEGE
One College Cir, Bangor ME 04401-2999
800-477-4723 or 207-941-7100 Fax: 207-941-7935
Website: www.husson.edu
E-mail: springs@husson.edu
See listing under "Universities"

MARYLAND

Capital Bible Seminary
6511 Princess Garden Pkwy
Lanham Seabrook MD 20706-3538
301-552-1400

National Technological University
1001 Fleet St, Baltimore MD 21202-4346
410-843-6401

Peabody Institute of the Johns Hopkins University
1 E Mount Vernon Pl, Baltimore MD 21202-2397
410-659-8150

St. Mary's Seminary & University
5400 Roland Ave, Baltimore MD 21210-1929
410-864-4000

Tai Sophia Insitute
7750 Montpelier Rd, Laurel MD 20723-6010
800-735-2968

MASSACHUSETTS

Andover Newton Theological School
210 Herrick Rd, Newton Center MA 02459-2243
800-964-2687 ext. 272

Blessed John XXIII National Seminary
558 South Ave, Weston MA 02493-2618
781-899-5500

Boston College
885 Centre St, Newton MA 02459-1100
617-552-4350

Boston Graduate School for Psychoanalysis
1583 Beacon St, Brookline MA 02446-4602
617-277-3915

Cambridge College
1000 Massachusetts Ave
Cambridge MA 02138-5304
Joy King, Associate Director of Enrollment Services
800-877-GRAD

Conway School of Landscape Design
PO Box 179, Conway MA 01341
413-369-4044

Curry College
1071 Blue Hill Ave, Milton MA 02186-2395
Bruce Weckworth, Director of Admissions
617-333-2210

Elms College
291 Springfield St, Chicopee MA 01013-2839
800-255-3567

Episcopal Divinity School
99 Brattle St, Cambridge MA 02138-3494
Christopher J. Medeiros, Director of Admissions, Recruitment & Financial Aid
617-868-3450

Gordon-Conwell Theological Seminary
130 Essex St, South Hamilton MA 01982-2395
William B. Levin, Director of Admissions
978-468-7111

Hellenic College/Holy Cross Greek Orthodox School of Theology
50 Goddard Ave, Brookline MA 02445-7415
Sonia Belcher, Director
617-731-3500

Hult International Business School
1 Education St, Cambridge MA 02141
617-746-1990

Massachusetts College of Liberal Arts
375 Church St, North Adams MA 01247-4124
Monica Joslin, Dean of Academic Studies
413-662-5207

MASSACHUSETTS SCHOOL OF LAW AT ANDOVER
500 Federal St, Andover MA 01810
Paula Colby-Clements, Esq, Director of Admissions
978-681-0800 Fax: 978-681-6330
Website: www.mslaw.edu
E-mail: pcolby@mslaw.edu

Massachusetts School Professional Psychology
221 Rivermoor St, Boston MA 02132-4935
Mario Murga, Director of Admissions
617-327-6777

MGH Institute of Health Professions
36 1st Ave, Boston MA 02129-4557
Michael Bonanno, Manager of Admissions
617-726-3140

THE NATIONAL GRADUATE SCHOOL OF QUALITY SYSTEMS MANAGEMENT
186 Jones Rd, Falmouth MA 02540-2908
Virginia C. Petisce, VP Enrollment Management
508-457-1313 Fax: 508-457-5347
Website: www.ngs.edu
E-mail: vpetisce@ngs.edu

NEW ENGLAND COLLEGE OF OPTOMETRY
424 Beacon St, Boston MA 02115-1129
Taline Farra, O.D., Acting Director of Admissions
800-824-5526 Fax: 617-369-0162
Website: www.neco.edu
E-mail: admissions@neco.edu

New England School of Acupuncture
150 California St, Newton MA 02458
617-558-1788

Regis College
235 Wellesley St, Weston MA 02493-1571
781-768-2000

School of the Museum of Fine Arts, Boston
230 The Fenway, Boston MA 02115-5534
Office of Admissions
617-369-3626 or 800-643-6078 Fax: 617-369-4264
Website: www.smfa.edu
E-mail: admissions@smfa.edu
See listing under "Universities"

Simmons College
300 Fenway, Boston MA 02115-5898
617-521-2000

Southern New England School of Law
333 Faunce Corner Rd
North Dartmouth MA 02747-1252
508-998-9600

Springfield College
263 Alden St, Springfield MA 01109-3788
Donald Shaw, Director of Graduate Admissions
413-748-3684

Tufts University
136 Harrison Ave, Boston MA 02111-1800
617-636-7000

University of Massachusetts Boston
100 William T Morrissey Blvd, Boston MA 02125-3393
Liliana Mickle, Director of Undergraduate Admissions
617-287-6000

Western New England College
1215 Wilbraham Rd, Springfield MA 01119-2655
413-782-1321

Woods Hole Oceanographic Institution
86 Water St, Woods Hole MA 02543
508-289-2219

MICHIGAN

Andrews University
Berrien Springs MI 49104-0001
Randall Graves, Director of Recruitment Services
800-253-2874

CALVIN THEOLOGICAL SEMINARY
3233 Burton St SE, Grand Rapids MI 49546-4301
Greg Janke, Director of Admissions
616-957-6036 Fax: 616-957-8621
Website: www.calvinseminary.edu
E-mail: admissions@calvinseminary.edu

Kendall College of Art & Design
17 Fountain St NW, Grand Rapids MI 49503-3002
Dr. Oliver H. Evans, President
800-676-2787 or 616-451-2787 Fax: 616-831-9689
Website: www.kcad.edu
E-mail: brittons@ferris.edu

Kettering University
(formerly GMI Engineering & Management Institute)
1700 W 3rd Ave, Flint MI 48504-4898
Tony Hain, V.P., Graduate & Corporate Connections Program
800-955-4464

Michigan School of Professional Psychology
26811 Orchard Lake Rd
Farmington Hills MI 48334-4512
248-476-1122

MICHIGAN STATE UNIVERSITY COLLEGE OF LAW
230 Law College Bldg, East Lansing MI 48824
Cory Burke, Assistant Director of Admissions
517-432-0222 Fax: 517-432-0098
Website: www.law.msu.edu
E-mail: burkecor@msu.edu

Michigan Technological University
1400 Townsend Dr, Houghton MI 49931-1200
Dr. Sung M. Lee, Dean
906-487-2327

Michigan Theological Seminary
41550 E Ann Arbor Trl, Plymouth MI 48170
734-207-9581

Saints Cyril and Methodius Seminary
3535 Indian Trl, Orchard Lake MI 48324-1623
Karen Shirilla, Academic Dean
248-683-0312

Cooley Law School, Thomas M.
PO Box 13038, Lansing MI 48901-3038
517-371-5140

Western Michigan University
Kalamazoo MI 49008
269-387-1000

Western Theological Seminary
101 E 13th St, Holland MI 49423-3622
616-392-8555

MINNESOTA

Adler Graduate School
1550 E 78th St, Richfield MN 55423
Evelyn Haas, Director of Admissions
612-861-7554

Bethel Seminary
3949 Bethel Dr, Saint Paul MN 55112-6940
Joseph Dworak, Director of Admissions
651-638-6288

Capella University
225 S 6th St Fl 9, Minneapolis MN 55402-4652
Enrollment Services
888-CAPELLA (227-3552)

College of Saint Scholastica
1200 Kenwood Ave, Duluth MN 55811-4199
Brian Dalton, V.P. of Enrollment Management
800-447-5444

Crown College
8700 College View Dr, Saint Bonifacius MN 55375
Mitch Fisk, Director of Admissions
952-446-4142 Fax: 952-446-4149
Website: www.crown.edu
E-mail: johnsonj@crown.edu

Hazelden Graduate School
PO Box 11, Center City MN 55012
651-213-4175

LUTHER SEMINARY
2481 Como Ave, Saint Paul MN 55108-1496
Rev. Ronald Olson, Contact
800-588-4373 Fax: 651-641-3521
Website: www.luthersem.edu
E-mail: admissions@luthersem.edu

Mayo School of Health Sciences
200 1st Ave SW, Rochester MN 55905-0001
507-284-3678

Metropolitan State University
700 7th St E, Saint Paul MN 55106-5000
Monir Johnson, Director of Admissions
651-793-1300 Fax: 651-793-1546
Website: www.metrostate.edu
E-mail: monir.johnson@metrostate.edu

Northwestern Health Sciences University
Northwestern College of Chiropractic Admissions Office
2501 W 84th St, Minneapolis MN 55431
Dr. Mark Zeigler, President
Bill Kuehl, Director of Admissions
952-888-4777 ext. 409 Fax: 952-881-3028
Website: www.nwhealth.edu
E-mail: admit@nwhealth.edu

St. Mary's University of Minnesota
2500 Park Ave, Minneapolis MN 55404-4403
866-437-2788

UNITED THEOLOGICAL SEMINARY OF THE TWIN CITIES
3000 5th St NW, New Brighton MN 55112-2598
Admissions Office
651-255-6119 or 800-937-1316 Fax: 651-633-4315
Website: www.unitedseminary.edu
E-mail: admissions@unitedseminary.edu

Walden University
155 5th Ave S Ste 100, Minneapolis MN 55401-2511
Office of Student Enrollment
800-444-6795

William Mitchell College of Law
875 Summit Ave, Saint Paul MN 55105-3030
651-227-9171

MISSISSIPPI

Mississippi College
151 E Griffith St, Jackson MS 39201-1302
601-353-3907

Mississippi University for Women
Box W-280, Columbus MS 39701
Dr. Barbara Moore, Coordinator
877-GO-2-THEW

Reformed Theological Seminary
5422 Clinton Blvd, Jackson MS 39209-3099
601-923-1600

Wesley Biblical Seminary
PO Box 9938, Jackson MS 39286-0938
John Wilson, Vice President of Student Affairs & Admissions
601-957-1314

MISSOURI

Aquinas Institute of Theology
23 S Spring Ave, Saint Louis MO 63108-3323
Ron Knapp, M.Div., Director of Admissions
314-256-8800

ASSEMBLIES OF GOD THEOLOGICAL SEMINARY
1435 N Glenstone Ave, Springfield MO 65802-2131
Dr. Mario Guerreiro, Director of Enrollment Management
800-467-AGTS Fax: 417-268-1001
Website: www.agts.edu
E-mail: agts@agseminary.edu

Calvary Bible College & Theological Seminary
15800 Calvary Rd, Kansas City MO 64147-1341
Robert M. Reinsch, Director of Admissions
800-326-3960

Central Missouri State University
Warrensburg MO 64093-8888
Steve Wilson, Dean of Graduate Studies
800-956-0177

Columbia College
1001 Rogers St, Columbia MO 65216-0001
Regina Morin, Director of Admissions
573-875-7352 Fax: 573-875-7506
Website: www.ccis.edu
E-mail: gradadmissions@ccis.edu

Concordia Seminary
801 De Mun Ave, Saint Louis MO 63105-3199
314-721-5934

COVENANT THEOLOGICAL SEMINARY
12330 Conway Rd, Saint Louis MO 63141-8697
Dr. Bryan Chapell, President
800-264-8064 Fax: 314-434-4819
Website: www.covenantseminary.edu
E-mail: admissions@covenantseminary.edu

Eden Theological Seminary
475 E Lockwood Ave
Webster Groves MO 63119-3192
Diane Windler, Director of Admissions
800-969-3627

Forest Institute of Professional Psychology
1322 S Campbell Ave, Springfield MO 65807-1445
417-831-7902

KANSAS CITY UNIVERSITY OF MEDICINE AND BIOSCIENCES
College of Osteopathic Medicine
1750 Independence Ave
Kansas City MO 64106-1453
Phil Byrne, Director of Recruitment
800-234-4847 Fax: 816-283-2484
Website: www.kcumb.edu
E-mail: admissions@kcumb.edu

KENRICK SCHOOL OF THEOLOGY
5200 Glennon Dr, Saint Louis MO 63119-4330
Msgr. Ted L. Wojcicki, President-Rector
314-792-6100 Fax: 314-792-6500
Website: www.kenrick.edu
E-mail: registrar@kenrick.edu

KIRKSVILLE COLLEGE OF OSTEOPATHIC MEDICINE
A.T. STILL UNIVERSITY
800 W Jefferson St, Kirksville MO 63501-1443
Admissions Counselor
866-626-2878 or 660-626-2237 Fax: 660-626-2969
Website: www.atsu.edu
E-mail: admissions@atsu.edu

Logan College of Chiropractic
1851 Schoettler Rd, Chesterfield MO 63017-5529
Patrick Browne, VP of Enrollment Services
800-533-9210

MIDWESTERN BAPTIST THEOLOGICAL SEMINARY
5001 N Oak Trfy, Kansas City MO 64118-4697
816-414-3700 Fax: 816-414-3724
Website: www.mbts.edu

MIDWEST UNIVERSITY
851 Parr Rd, Wentzville MO 63385
Dr. James Song, President
636-327-4645 Fax: 636-327-4715
Website: www.midwest.edu
E-mail: inf@midwest.edu

NAZARENE THEOLOGICAL SEMINARY
1700 E Meyer Blvd, Kansas City MO 64131-1263
Roger L. Hahn, Dean of the Faculty
816-333-6254 Fax: 816-333-6271
Website: www.nts.edu
E-mail: rlhahn@nts.edu

Rockhurst University
1100 Rockhurst Rd, Kansas City MO 64110-2561
Mark Kopenski, VP of Enrollment Management
816-501-4000

Saint Paul School of Theology
5123 Truman Rd, Kansas City MO 64127
Alan D. Herndon, Director of Admissions
816-483-9600

SCHOOL OF HEALTH MANAGEMENT - ONLINE
A.T. STILL UNIVERSITY
800 W Jefferson St, Kirksville MO 63501-1443
Admissions Counselor
866-626-2878 or 660-626-2237 Fax: 660-626-2969
Website: www.atsu.edu
E-mail: admissions@atsu.edu

Truman State University
100 E Normal, Kirksville MO 63501
Office of Admission
660-785-4114 Fax: 660-785-7456
Website: admissions.truman.edu
E-mail: admissions@truman.edu

University of Missouri
102 Parker, Rolla MO 65409
Lynn Stichnote, Director of Admission
573-341-4164

University of Missouri
1 University Blvd, Saint Louis MO 63121-4499
Dr. Judith Walker de Felix, Dean of Graduate School
314-516-5458 Fax: 314-516-6759
Website: www.umsl.edu
E-mail: gradadm@umsl.edu

Webster University
470 E Lockwood Ave, Saint Louis MO 63119-3194
Matt Noland, Director
314-968-7100 Fax: 314-968-7116
Website: www.webster.edu
E-mail: nolan@webster.edu
See listing under "Universities"

MONTANA

Montana State University - Billings
1500 University Dr, Billings MT 59101-0252
Karen Everett, Director
800-565-MSUB

Montana Tech of the University of Montana
1300 W Park St, Butte MT 59701-8997
800-445-TECH

NEBRASKA

Chadron State College
1000 Main St, Chadron NE 69337-2690
308-432-6000

Clarkson College
101 S 42nd St, Omaha NE 68131-2715
Sara Bonney, Director of Admissions
800-647-5500 Fax: 402-552-6057
Website: www.clarksoncollege.edu
E-mail: admiss@clarksoncollege.edu

Peru State College
PO Box 10, Peru NE 68421-0010
402-872-2241

University of Nebraska Medical Center
987810 Nebraska Medical Center
Omaha NE 68198-7810
800-626-8431

NEVADA

Touro University College of Osteopathic Medicine
874 American Pacific Dr, Henderson NV 89014
702-856-3262

University of Nevada Las Vegas
4505 S Maryland Pkwy, Las Vegas NV 89154-9901
800-334-8658

NEW HAMPSHIRE

Antioch University New England
40 Avon St, Keene NH 03431-3516
David Caruso, President
Leatrice A. Oram, Director of Admissions
603-357-6265 Fax: 603-357-0718
Website: www.antiochne.edu
E-mail: admissions@antiochne.edu

Franklin Pierce Law Center
2 White St, Concord NH 03301-4176
603-228-9217

Rivier College
420 S Main St, Nashua NH 03060-5086
Ann McCormick, Director of Graduate Admissions
603-888-1311

NEW JERSEY

Immaculate Conception Seminary of Seton Hall University
400 S Orange Ave, South Orange NJ 07079-2646
973-761-9575

New Brunswick Theological Seminary
17 Seminary Pl, New Brunswick NJ 08901-1196
732-247-5241

New Jersey City University
2039 John F Kennedy Blvd, Jersey City NJ 07305
Carmen Panlilio, Asst. V.P. for Admissions and Financial Aid
201-200-3409 Fax: 201-200-3411
Website: www.njcu.edu
E-mail: admissions@njcu.edu

Princeton Theological Seminary
PO Box 821, Princeton NJ 08542-0803
609-921-8300

Rider University
2083 Lawrenceville Rd, Lawrenceville NJ 08648-3099
Dr. John Carpenter, Dean Graduate Studies
609-896-5033

Seton Hall University School of Law
1 Newark Center, Newark NJ 07102
973-642-8747

UMDNJ Graduate School of Biomedical Sciences
185 S Orange Ave, Newark NJ 07103
973-972-4511

UMDNJ-New Jersey Dental School
110 Bergen St, Newark NJ 07103-2400
973-972-4633

UMDNJ-New Jersey Medical School
185 S Orange Ave, Newark NJ 07103-2757
973-972-4539

UMDNJ-Robert Wood Johnson Medical School
671 Hoes Ln W, Piscataway NJ 08854
732-235-5600

UMDNJ School of Public Health
170 Frelinghuysen Rd Rm 236, Piscataway NJ 08854
732-445-0199

University of Medicine and Dentistry of New Jersey
School of Osteopathic Medicine
One Medical Center Dr Suite 210, Stratford NJ 08084
Paula F. Slade, M.A.S., Director of Enrollment Services
856-566-7050

Westminster Choir College of Rider University
101 Walnut Ln, Princeton NJ 08540-3819
Matthew T. Kadlubowski, Director of Admissions
609-921-7144

NEW MEXICO

Southwest Acupuncture College
1622 Galisteo St, Santa Fe NM 87505-4747
505-438-8884

NEW YORK

Adelphi University
Garden City NY 11530
516-877-3100

ALBANY LAW SCHOOL OF UNION UNIVERSITY
80 New Scotland Ave, Albany NY 12208-3494
Gail Bensen, Director of Admissions
518-445-2326 Fax: 518-445-2369
Website: www.albanylaw.edu
E-mail: admissions@albanylaw.edu

Bank Street College of Education
610 W 112th St, New York NY 10025-1898
212-875-4404

Bexley Hall Seminary
26 Broadway, Rochester NY 14607
585-546-2160

Brooklyn Law School
250 Joralemon St, Brooklyn NY 11201-3798
Henry W. Haverstick, III, Dean of Admissions & Financial Aid
718-780-7906

Christ the King Seminary
PO Box 607, East Aurora NY 14052-0607
585-652-8900

COLGATE ROCHESTER CROZER DIVINITY SCHOOL
1100 S Goodman St, Rochester NY 14620-2589
Robert Jones, V.P. of Enrollment Services
585-271-1320 or 888-937-3732 Fax: 585-271-8013
Website: www.crcds.edu
E-mail: admissions@crcds.edu

CUNY City College
Convent Ave at 138th St, New York NY 10031
Celia Lloyd, Interim Director of Admissions
212-650-6977

CUNY Graduate Center
365 5th Ave, New York NY 10016-4309
212-817-7000

FIVE TOWNS COLLEGE
305 N Service Rd, Dix Hills NY 11746-5871
631-424-7000 ext. 2110 Fax: 631-656-2172
Website: www.fivetowns.edu
E-mail: admissions@ftc.edu
See listing under "Universities"

Fordham University - Lincoln Center
113 W 60th St, New York NY 10023-7484
212-636-6000

General Theological Seminary
175 9th Ave, New York NY 10011-4983
212-243-5150

Hebrew Union College
Jewish Institute of Religion
1 W 4th St, New York NY 10012-1186
212-674-5300

Iona College
715 North Ave, New Rochelle NY 10801-1890
Kevin Cavanagh, Assistant V.P. for College Admissions
914-633-2502 Fax: 914-637-2778
Website: www.iona.edu

LAMONT-DOHERTY EARTH OBSERVATORY
of Columbia University
Palisades NY 10964
Mia Leo, Department Administrator
845-365-8550 Fax: 845-365-8163
Website: eesc.columbia.edu
E-mail: missy@ldeo.columbia.edu

Long Island University-C. W. Post Campus
720 Northern Blvd, Brookville NY 11548-1300
Beth Carson, Director of Graduate Admissions
516-299-2900 Fax: 516-299-2418
Website: www.liu.edu/cwpost
E-mail: enroll@cwpost.liu.edu

Long Island University
Rockland Graduate Campus
70 Route 340, Orangeburg NY 10962-2219
Kelly J. McCafferty, M.S., Director of Admissions
845-359-7200

Long Island University
Westchester Graduate Campus of Long Island University
735 Anderson Hill Rd, Purchase NY 10577
Ellen Brief, Admissions, Marketing and Student Services
800-472-3548

Manhattan College
4513 Manhattan College Pkwy
Riverdale NY 10471-4099
William J. Bisset Jr., Asst. V.P. for Enrollment Management
718-862-7200

Manhattan School of Music
120 Claremont Ave, New York NY 10027-4698
Amy A. Anderson, Director of Admission & Financial Aid
212-749-2802 ext. 2

Mannes College of Music
150 W 85th St, New York NY 10024-4499
Office of Admissions
800-292-3040

Mercy College
555 Broadway, Dobbs Ferry NY 10522-1189
Kathleen Jackson, Director of Admissions
800-MERCY-NY

Mid-America Baptist Theological Seminary
2810 Curry Rd, Schenectady NY 12303-3463
518-355-4000

Mount Sinai School of Medicine of New York University
Box 1022, 1 Gustave L Levy Place
New York NY 10029
212-241-6546

New York Academy of Art
111 Franklin St, New York NY 10013
212-966-0300

NEW YORK CHIROPRACTIC COLLEGE
PO Box 800, Seneca Falls NY 13148-0800
Michael P. Lynch, Director of Admissions
800-234-6922 (NYCC) Fax: 315-568-3087
Website: www.nycc.edu
E-mail: enrolnow@nycc.edu

New York College of Podiatric Medicine
1800 Park Ave, New York NY 10035-1940
Carlene Colston, Director of Admissions and Enrollment Management
800-526-6966

New York Law School
57 Worth St, New York NY 10013-2960
Tom Matos, Assistant Dean for Admissions
212-431-2888

New York Medical College
Valhalla NY 10595
914-594-4000

New York Theological Seminary
475 Riverside Suite Ste 500, New York NY 10115
Yon Su Kang, Contact
212-870-1211

Niagara University
PO Box 2011, Niagara University NY 14109-2011
George Pachter, Dean of Admissions & Records
800-462-2111

NY College of Traditional Chinese Medicine
155 1st St, Mineola NY 11501
516-739-1545

Ohr Somayach Tanenbaum Educational Center
PO Box 334, Monsey NY 10952-0334
845-425-1370

Pace University
1 Martine Ave, White Plains NY 10606
914-442-2000

Pacific College of Oriental Medicine - New York
915 Broadway 3rd Floor, New York NY 10010
212-982-3456

POLYTECHNIC UNIVERSITY
40 Saw Mill River Rd, Hawthorne NY 10532-1507
LaVerne Clark, Director of Campus Operations
914-323-2000 Fax: 914-323-2010
Website: www.poly.edu/west
E-mail: westinfo@west.poly.edu

PURCHASE COLLEGE STATE UNIVERSITY OF NEW YORK (SUNY)
735 Anderson Hill Rd, Purchase NY 10577-1400
Stephanie McCaine, Director of Admissions
914-251-6300 Fax: 914-251-6314
Website: www.purchase.edu
E-mail: admisn@purchase.edu
See listing under "Universities"

Rabbi Isaac Elchanan Theological Seminary
2495 Amsterdam Ave, New York NY 10033
212-960-5344

Roberts Wesleyan College
2301 Westside Dr, Rochester NY 14624-1997
Office of Admissions
585-594-6400 Fax: 585-594-6371
Website: www.roberts.edu
E-mail: admissions@roberts.edu

Rockefeller University
1230 York Ave, New York NY 10065
212-327-8000

Russell Sage Graduate School
45 Ferry St, Troy NY 12180-4115
518-244-2264

St. Bernard's School of Theology and Ministry
120 French Rd, Rochester NY 14618
585-271-3657

St. Joseph's Seminary
201 Seminary Ave, Yonkers NY 10704-1896
914-968-6200

St. Vladimir's Orthodox Theological Seminary
575 Scarsdale Rd, Tuckahoe NY 10707-1659
914-961-8313

Seminary of the Immaculate Conception
440 W Neck Rd, Huntington NY 11743-1626
631-423-0483

Sunbridge College
285 Hungry Hollow Rd, Spring Valley NY 10977
845-425-0055

SUNY at Albany
1400 Washington Ave, Albany NY 12222-1000
Jonathan Bartow, Director of Graduate Studies
518-442-3980

SUNY Health Science Center
450 Clarkson Ave, Brooklyn NY 11203-2056
718-270-1000

Teachers College of Columbia University
525 W 120th St, New York NY 10027-6625
212-678-3000

Touro College
225 Eastview Dr, Central Islip NY 11722
631-421-2244

Tri-State College of Acupuncture
265 W 14th St Ste 400, New York NY 10011
212-242-2255

Unification Theological Seminary
30 Seminary Dr, Barrytown NY 12507-5021
Tessa Thonett, Director of Admissions
845-752-3015

Union Theological Seminary
3041 Broadway, New York NY 10027-5792
Joseph C. Hough, Jr., President
212-662-7100

University at Buffalo SUNY
408 Capen Hall, Amherst NY 14260
716-645-2000

Weill Medical College of Cornell University
1300 York Ave, New York NY 10065
212-746-5454

Yeshiva University
Benjamin N. Cardozo School of Law
55 5th Ave, New York NY 10003-4301
Robert Schwartz, Assistant Dean for Admissions
212-790-0274

Yeshiva Zichron Aryeh
100 Cedarhurst Ave, Cedarhurst NY 11516
516-295-5700

NORTH CAROLINA

Atlantic University of Chinese Medicine
64 Westgate Pkwy, Asheville NC 28806
828-225-8550

East Carolina University
Ragsdale 113, Greenville NC 27858
Dr. Thomas Feldbush, Dean

HOOD THEOLOGICAL SEMINARY
1810 Lutheran Synod Dr, Salisbury NC 28144
Albert J. D. Aymer, President
704-636-6823 Fax: 704-636-7699
Website: www.hoodseminary.edu
E-mail: dmiller@hoodseminary.edu

Jung Tao School of Classical Chinese Medicine
207 Dale Adams Rd, Sugar Grove NC 28679
828-297-4181

NEW LIFE THEOLOGICAL SEMINARY
PO Box 790106, Charlotte NC 28206
Judith Main, Registrar
704-334-6882 Fax: 704-334-6885
Website: www.nlts.org
E-mail: jmain@nlts.org

Queens University of Charlotte
1900 Selwyn Ave, Charlotte NC 28274-0002
704-337-2212

Reformed Theological Seminary
2101 Carmel Rd, Charlotte NC 28226
704-366-5066

SOUTHEASTERN BAPTIST THEOLOGICAL SEMINARY
Southeastern College at Wake Forest
PO Box 1889, Wake Forest NC 27588-1889
Jerry L. Yandell, Director of Admissions
919-761-2280 or 800-284-6317 Fax: 919-556-0998
Website: www.sebts.edu
E-mail: admissions@sebts.edu

Southern Evangelical Seminary
3000 Tilley Morris Rd, Matthews NC 28105-8635
704-847-5600

University of North Carolina at Pembroke
PO Box 1510, Pembroke NC 28372-1510
910-521-6000

Wake Forest University
Medical Center Blvd, Winston Salem NC 27157-0001
336-748-4424

NORTH DAKOTA

Minot State University
500 University Ave W, Minot ND 58707-0002
Phyllis Butler, Contact
800-777-0750 ext. 3250

Tri-College University
Fargo ND 58105
701-231-8170

Valley City State University
101 College St SW, Valley City ND 58072-4024
School of Education - Graduate Studies
800-532-8641
Website: www.vcsu.edu/graduate
E-mail: graduate@vcsu.edu

OHIO

Ashland Theological Seminary
910 Center St, Ashland OH 44805-4007
Mario Guerreiro, Director of Admissions
419-289-5161

BEXLEY HALL SEMINARY
583 Sheridan Ave, Columbus OH 43209-2325
John Kevern, Dean & President
614-231-3095 Fax: 614-231-3236
Website: www.bexley.edu
E-mail: columbus@bexley.edu or rochester@bexley.edu

Capital University Law School
303 E Broad St, Columbus OH 43215-3200
Linda J. Mihely, Asst. Dean of Admission & Financial Aid
614-236-6310

Cleveland State University
2121 Euclid Ave RW 204, Cleveland OH 44115
Dr. William Bailey, Director of Graduate Admissions
888-CSU-OHIO Fax: 216-687-9210
Website: www.csuohio.edu
E-mail: admissions@csuohio.edu

Hebrew Union College - Jewish Institute of Religion
3101 Clifton Ave, Cincinnati OH 45220-2488
513-221-1875

Kent State University
PO Box 5190, Kent OH 44242-0001
330-672-2661

METHODIST THEOLOGICAL SCHOOL IN OHIO
3081 Columbus Pike, Delaware OH 43015-3211
Mary Kay Freshour, Director of Admissions and Financial Aid
800-333-6876 Fax: 740-362-3372
Website: www.mtso.edu
E-mail: admit@mtso.edu

Miami University
E High St, Oxford OH 45056
513-529-2531

Northeastern Ohio Univ Coll of Medicine
PO Box 95, Rootstown OH 44272-0095
330-325-2511

OHIO COLLEGE OF PODIATRIC MEDICINE
10515 Carnegie Ave, Cleveland OH 44106
Lois Lott, Dean of Student Affairs
216-231-3300 Fax: 216-231-1005
Website: www.ocpm.edu
E-mail: llott@ocpm.edu

Trinity Lutheran Seminary
2199 E Main St, Columbus OH 43209-2334
Karen S. White, Diaconal Minister, Director of Admissions
614-235-4136

United Theological Seminary
4501 Denlinger Rd, Trotwood OH 45426
Julie Hostetter, Director of Academic and Student Services
800-322-5817 Fax: 937-529-2292
Website: www.united.edu
E-mail: admissions@united.edu

University of Dayton
300 College Park, Dayton OH 45469-1300
Robert F. Durkle, Director of Admission
800-837-7433 Fax: 937-229-4729
Website: admission.udayton.edu
E-mail: admission@udayton.edu

University of Toledo
College of Graduate Studies
3000 Arlington Ave, Toledo OH 43614-2595
419-383-4000 Fax: 419-383-2800
Website: www.hsc.utoledo.edu
E-mail: admissions@meduohio.edu

Winebrenner Theological Seminary
950 N Main St, Findlay OH 45840
Dr. David Draper, President
800-992-4987

OKLAHOMA

Oklahoma City University
2501 N Blackwelder Ave
Oklahoma City OK 73106-1493
Shery Boyles, Director of Admissions
405-521-5050

Oklahoma State University
Stillwater OK 74078
Gordon Emslie, Dean
405-744-6368 Fax: 405-744-0355
Website: www.okstate.edu

Oklahoma State University Center of Health Sciences
College of Osteopathic Medicine
1111 W 17th St, Tulsa OK 74107-1898
918-582-1972

Oral Roberts University
Adult Learning Service Center
7777 S Lewis Ave, Tulsa OK 74171-0001
800-678-8876

Phillips Theological Seminary
901 N Mingo Rd, Tulsa OK 74116-5612
918-610-8303

OREGON

George Fox University
12753 SW 68th Ave, Portland OR 97223-8355
503-639-0559

Marylhurst University
17600 Pacific Hwy (Hwy 43)
Marylhurst OR 97036-0261
Director of Admissions
800-634-9982 ext. 6268 Fax: 503-635-6585
Website: www.marylhurst.edu
E-mail: studentinfo@marylhurst.edu

Mt. Angel Seminary
1 Abbey Dr, Saint Benedict OR 97373
503-845-3951

Multnomah Bible College and Biblical Seminary
8435 NE Glisan St, Portland OR 97220-5898
Daniel R. Lockwood, President
800-275-4672

National College of Naturopathic Medicine
049 SW Porter St, Portland OR 97201
503-499-4343

OREGON COLLEGE OF ORIENTAL MEDICINE
10525 SE Cherry Blossom Dr, Portland OR 97216
Nicola Moll, Admissions Coordinator
503-253-3443 Fax: 503-253-2701
Website: www.ocom.edu
E-mail: admissions@ocom.edu

Oregon Graduate Institute of Science & Technology
20000 NW Walker Rd, Beaverton OR 97006-8921
503-748-1121

Western Seminary
5511 SE Hawthorne Blvd, Portland OR 97215-3367
503-517-1800

Western States Chiropractic College
2900 NE 132nd Ave, Portland OR 97230-3014
Lee Smith, Director of Admissions
800-641-5641

PENNSYLVANIA

American College
270 S Bryn Mawr Ave, Bryn Mawr PA 19010-2105
610-526-1000

Arcadia University
450 S Easton Rd, Glenside PA 19038-3295
Dennis Nostrand, VP for Enrollment Management
877-ARCADIA (877-272-2342)

Bethel Seminary of the East
1605 Limekiln Pike, Dresher PA 19025-1007
215-641-4801

BIBLICAL THEOLOGICAL SEMINARY
200 N Main St, Hatfield PA 19440-2421
Pamela J. Smith, VP for Student Advancement
800-235-4021 Fax: 215-368-7002
Website: www.biblical.edu
E-mail: admissions@biblical.edu

Bryn Mawr College
101 N Merion Ave, Bryn Mawr PA 19010-2899
610-526-5000

Calvary Baptist Theological Seminary
1380 S Valley Forge Rd, Lansdale PA 19446
215-368-7538

Clarion University of Pennsylvania
840 Wood St, Clarion PA 16214-1232
William Bailey, Dean of Enrollment Management
814-393-2306 Fax: 814-393-2030
Website: www.clarion.edu
E-mail: admissions@clarion.edu

Duquesne University
600 Forbes Ave, Pittsburgh PA 15282-0001
Paul-James Cukanna, Director of Admissions
412-396-5000

Edinboro University of Pennsylvania
Edinboro PA 16444-0001
814-732-2000

EVANGELICAL SCHOOL OF THEOLOGY
121 S College St, Myerstown PA 17067-1299
Tom Maiello, Dean of Admissions
800-532-5775 Fax: 717-866-4667
Website: www.evangelical.edu
E-mail: admissions@evangelical.edu

Gannon University
109 University Sq, Erie PA 16541-0002
Debbie Meszaros, Director of Graduate Admissions
800-GANNON-U

Gwynedd-Mercy College
1325 Sumneytown Pike, Gwynedd Valley PA 19437
Dennis Murphy, V.P. Enrollment Management
800-DIAL-GMC

Holy Family University
9801 Frankford Avenue, Philadelphia PA 19114
Margaret Wendling, Director of Graduate Admissions
215-637-7203 Fax: 215-637-1478
Website: www.holyfamily.edu

Lancaster Theological Seminary of the United Church of Christ
555 W James St, Lancaster PA 17603-2830
Patricia Huffman Matz, Director of Admissions
800-393-0654 ext. 141

Lock Haven University
Lock Haven PA 17745
Enrollment Services
570-893-2006

LUTHERAN THEOLOGICAL SEMINARY
7301 Germantown Ave, Philadelphia PA 19119-1794
Louise Johnson, Director of Admissions
800-286-4616 Fax: 215-248-4577
Website: www.ltsp.edu
E-mail: admissions@ltsp.edu

Lutheran Theological Seminary at Gettysburg
61 Seminary Ridge, Gettysburg PA 17325-1795
Nancy E. Gable (Diaconal Minister), Assoc. Dean of Church Vocations
800-MLU-THER

MOUNT ALOYSIUS COLLEGE
7373 Admiral Peary Hwy, Cresson PA 16630-1999
Frank C. Crouse Jr., Vice President for Enrollment Management
814-886-6383 or 888-823-2220 Fax: 814-886-6441
Website: www.mtaloy.edu
E-mail: admissions@mtaloy.edu

Palmer Theological Seminary
6 E Lancaster Ave, Wynnewood PA 19096-3495
610-896-5000

Penn State Dickinson School of Law
150 S College St, Carlisle PA 17013-2861
717-240-5000

Penn State Great Valley School of Graduate Professional Studies
30 E Swedesford Rd, Malvern PA 19355-1488
610-648-3200

Pennsylvania Academy of the Fine Arts
118 N Broad St, Philadelphia PA 19102-1598
Angela Smith, Director of Admissions
215-972-7625

Pennsylvania College of Optometry
8360 Old York Rd, Elkins Park PA 19027-1598
Dr. James Caldwell, Director of Admissions
800-824-6262

Pennsylvania State Milton S Hershey Medical Center College of Medicine
500 University Dr Box 850, Hershey PA 17033
717-534-8521

Philadelphia College of Osteopathic Medicine
4170 City Ave, Philadelphia PA 19131-1610
Carol Fox, Associate Dean of Admissions
215-871-6700

Pittsburgh Theological Seminary
616 N Highland Ave, Pittsburgh PA 15206-2525
Rev. Sherry Sparks, Director of Admissions
800-451-4194 or 412-362-5610 ext. 2115
Fax: 412-363-3260
Website: www.pts.edu
E-mail: sparks@pts.edu
See listing under "Theological Studies & Religious Vocations"

Reformed Episcopal Seminary
826 2nd Ave, Blue Bell PA 19422-1257
Danae L. Smith, Contact
610-292-9852

Reformed Presbyterian Theological Seminary
7418 Penn Ave, Pittsburgh PA 15208-2594
Dr. Jerry O'Neill, President
412-731-8690

Robert Morris College
600 5th Ave, Pittsburgh PA 15219-3010
412-227-6800

Rosemont College
1400 Montgomery Ave, Rosemont PA 19010-1699
Richard Donagher, Director of Graduate Studies

ST. TIKHON'S ORTHODOX THEOLOGICAL SEMINARY
PO Box 130, South Canaan PA 18459-0130
Metropolitan Herman, President
Bishop Tikhon, Rector
Very Rev. Michael G. Dahulich, Ph.D., Dean
570-937-4411 Fax: 570-937-3100
Website: www.stots.edu
E-mail: stots@stots.edu

Seton Hill University
Greensburg PA 15601-1599
Jenell Krymowski, Program Advisor
800-826-6234

Temple University
3307 N Broad St, Philadelphia PA 19140-5101
215-787-7000

Temple University School of Podiatric Medicine
8th & Race St, Philadelphia PA 19107
215-629-0300

Temple University Tyler School of Art
Beech and Penrose Aves, Elkins Park PA 19027
215-782-2875

Trinity Episcopal School for Ministry
311 11th St, Ambridge PA 15003-2397
Shirley A. Bruce, Registrar/Financial Aid Director
724-266-3838

Westminster Theological Seminary
PO Box 27009, Philadelphia PA 19118-0009
Daniel A. Cason, Director of Admissions
800-373-0119

Widener University School of Law
PO Box 69380, Harrisburg PA 17106-9380
Eric Kniskern, Assistant Director of Admissions
717-541-3900

Won Institute of Graduate Studies
137 S Easton Rd, Glenside PA 19038
Director of Admissions
215-884-8942

SOUTH CAROLINA

Bob Jones University
1700 Wade Hampton Blvd
Greenville SC 29614-0001
David Christ, Director of Admissions
800-BJ-AND-ME Fax: 800-2-FAX-BJU
Website: www.bju.edu
E-mail: admissions@bju.edu
See listing under "Universities"

CIU Graduate School
PO Box 3122, Columbia SC 29230-3122
Michelle MacGregor, Director of University Admissions
800-777-2227 Fax: 803-333-0607
Website: www.ciu.edu
E-mail: yesgrad@ciu.edu
See listing under "Theological Studies & Religious Vocations"

Lutheran Theological Southern Seminary
4201 Main St, Columbia SC 29203-5863
803-786-5150

Medical University of South Carolina
PO Box 250402, Charleston SC 29425
843-792-2300

SHERMAN COLLEGE OF STRAIGHT CHIROPRACTIC
PO Box 1452, Spartanburg SC 29304-1452
Lisa Hildebrand, Director of Admission
800-849-8771 or 864-578-8770 Fax: 864-599-4860
Website: www.sherman.edu
E-mail: admissions@sherman.edu

South Carolina State University
PO Box 7127, Orangeburg SC 29117-0001
Lillian M. Adderson, Director of Admissions
803-536-7185

SOUTH DAKOTA

North American Baptist Seminary
1525 S Grange Ave, Sioux Falls SD 57105-1526
Melissa Hiatt, Director of Admissions
800-440-NABS (6227)

TENNESSEE

Church of God Theological Seminary
PO Box 3330, Cleveland TN 37320-3330
Dr. John T. Ramos, Registrar
423-478-1131

EMMANUEL SCHOOL OF RELIGION
One Walker Dr, Johnson City TN 37601-9438
David Fulks, Director of Admissions
423-461-1535 or 800-933-3771 Fax: 423-926-6198
Website: www.esr.edu
E-mail: admissions@esr.edu

Harding University Graduate School of Religion
1000 Cherry Rd, Memphis TN 38117-5424
Mark Parker, Director of Admissions
800-680-0809

Johnson Bible College
7900 Johnson Dr, Knoxville TN 37998-0001
Dr. John Ketchen, Director of Distance Learning
800-669-7889

Lipscomb University
3901 Granny White Pike, Nashville TN 37204-3951
Ricky Holaway, Director of Admissions
800-333-4358 ext. 1776 Fax: 615-269-1804
Website: www.lipscomb.edu
E-mail: admissions@lipscomb.edu

Meharry Medical College
1005 Dr DB Todd Jr Blvd, Nashville TN 37208-3599
615-327-6111

Memphis Theological Seminary
168 E Parkway S, Memphis TN 38104-4340
Barry Anderson, Director of Admissions
901-458-8232

Mid-America Baptist Theological Seminary
PO Box 2350, Cordova TN 38088
Duffy Guyton, Director of Admissions
901-751-8453

MIDDLE TENNESSEE SCHOOL OF ANESTHESIA
PO Box 417, Madison TN 37116-6414
Mary E. DeVasher, Dean
615-868-6503 Fax: 615-868-9885
Website: www.mtsa.edu
E-mail: ikey@mtsa.edu

Oxford Graduate School
500 Oxford Dr, Dayton TN 37321
423-775-6596

Peabody College of Vanderbilt University
Box 327, Nashville TN 37203
615-322-8410

Southern College of Optometry
1245 Madison Ave, Memphis TN 38104-2222
800-238-0180

Temple Baptist Seminary
1815 Union Ave, Chattanooga TN 37404
423-493-4221

TEXAS

ACADEMY OF ORIENTAL MEDICINE AT AUSTIN
2700 W Anderson Ln Ste 204, Austin TX 78757
Amy Scott, Admissions Director
512-492-3017 Fax: 512-454-7001
Website: www.aoma.edu
E-mail: info@aoma.edu

American College of Acupuncture
9100 Park West Dr, Houston TX 77063
John Paul Liang, Director
713-780-9777

Angelo State University
ASU Station 11025, San Angelo TX 76909
Dr. Carol Diminnie, Dean of Graduate School
325-942-2169

Austin Presbyterian Theological Seminary
100 E 27th St, Austin TX 78705-5711
Sam Riccobene, Director of Vocation & Admissions
512-472-6736

BAPTIST MISSIONARY ASSOCIATION THEOLOGICAL SEMINARY
1530 E Pine St, Jacksonville TX 75766-5407
Charley Holmes, President
903-586-2501 Fax: 903-586-0378
Website: www.bmats.edu
E-mail: bmatsem@bmats.edu

Baylor College of Medicine
1 Baylor Plz, Houston TX 77030-3498
713-798-4951

Baylor University Medical Center
3500 Gaston Ave, Dallas TX 75246-2088
214-820-2731

DALLAS THEOLOGICAL SEMINARY
3909 Swiss Ave, Dallas TX 75204-6411
Greg Hatteberg, Director of Admissions
214-841-3661 or 866-DTS-WORD Fax: 214-841-3664
Website: www.dts.edu
E-mail: admissions@dts.edu

Episcopal Theological Seminary of the Southwest
PO Box 2247, Austin TX 78768-2247
512-472-4133

Graduate Institute of Applied Linguistics
7500 W Camp Wisdom Rd, Dallas TX 75236
972-708-7340

Lamar University
PO Box 10009, Beaumont TX 77710-0009
409-880-8356

Oblate School of Theology
285 Oblate Dr, San Antonio TX 78216-6693
Dr. Marcella Hoesl, MM, Academic Dean
210-341-1366

South Texas College of Law
1303 San Jacinto St, Houston TX 77002-7000
Alicia Cramer, Director of Admissions
713-646-1510

Southwestern Assemblies of God University
1200 Sycamore St, Waxahachie TX 75165-2397
Pat Thompson, Admissions Counselor
972-937-4010

Texas A & M University System Health Science
Baylor College of Dentistry
3302 Gaston Ave, Dallas TX 75246-2013
214-828-8100

TEXAS COLLEGE OF TRADITIONAL CHINESE MEDICINE

4005 Manchaca Rd, Austin TX 78704
Admissions Coordinator
512-444-8082 Fax: 512-444-6345
Website: www.tctcm.edu
E-mail: info@texastcm.edu

TEXAS WOMAN'S UNIVERSITY

PO Box 425589, Denton TX 76204-5589
Erma Nieto-Brecht, Director of Admissions
866-809-6130 Fax: 940-898-3081
Website: www.twu.edu
E-mail: admissions@twu.edu

University of Houston
122 E Cullen Bldg, Houston TX 77204-2023
Office of Admission
713-743-9595
Website: www.uh.edu
E-mail: admissions@uh.edu

University of North Texas Health Science Center
3500 Camp Bowie Blvd, Fort Worth TX 76107-2690
Lynn Scott, Contact
817-735-2204

The University of Texas Medical Branch
301 University Blvd, Galveston TX 77555-0802
409-772-1215

UTAH

Southern Utah University
351 W Center St, Cedar City UT 84720-2470
Lou Workman, Dean, School of Continuing & Professional Studies
435-586-7850

University of Utah
1460 E 201 S, Salt Lake City UT 84112
801-581-7200

VERMONT

Bennington College
One College Drive, Bennington VT 05201
Ken Himmelman, Dean of Admissions & Financial Aid
800-833-6845

Saint Michael's College
One Winooski Park, Colchester VT 05439-0001
Jacqueline Murphy, Director
802-654-3000

School for International Training
World Learning
PO Box 676, Brattleboro VT 05302-0676
Meredith McDill, Contact
800-336-1616

Union Institute & University
Montpelier Campus
College St, Montpelier VT 05602
Dr. Brian Webb, Head
800-336-6794

Vermont Law School
PO Box 96, South Royalton VT 05068
802-763-8303

Woodbury College
660 Elm St, Montpelier VT 05602-4017
Denise MacMartin, Director of Admissions
800-639-6039 Fax: 802-229-2141
Website: www.woodbury-college.edu
E-mail: admiss@woodbury-college.edu

VIRGINIA

ARGOSY UNIVERSITY/WASHINGTON DC

1550 Wilson Blvd Ste 600, Arlington VA 22209
Emily Peck, Director of Admissions
703-526-5800 Fax: 703-243-8973
Website: www.argosyu.edu
E-mail: epeck@argosyu.edu

Atlantic University
215 67th St, Virginia Beach VA 23451-2061
Gregory Deming, Director of Admissions
800-428-1512

Baptist Theological Seminary at Richmond
3400 Brook Rd, Richmond VA 23227-4536
Director of Admissions
888-345-BTSR Fax: 804-355-8182
Website: www.btsr.edu
E-mail: admissions@btsr.edu

::: Catholic Distance University
120 E Colonial Hwy, Hamilton VA 20158-9012
Carol Ciullo, Graduate Registrar
888-254-4238 Fax: 540-338-4788
Website: www.cdu.edu
E-mail: cciullo@cdu.edu

Eastern Virginia Medical School
PO Box 1980, Norfolk VA 23501-1980
757-446-5600

Notre Dame Graduate School of Christendom College
134 Christendom Dr, Front Royal VA 22630
800-877-5456

Protestant Episcopal Theological Seminary
3737 Seminary Rd, Alexandria VA 22304-5202
Janice Sienkiewicz, Coordinator for Admissions and Community Life
703-370-6600

Radford University
PO Box 6928, Radford VA 24142
Dr. Carole Seyfrit, Director of Graduate Admissions
540-831-5431 Fax: 540-831-6061
Website: www.radford.edu
E-mail: gradcoll@radford.edu

Randolph College
2500 Rivermont Ave, Lynchburg VA 24503
Patricia LeDonne, Director of Admissions
434-947-8100 Fax: 434-947-8996
Website: www.randolphcollege.edu
E-mail: admissions@randolphcollege.edu

Reformed Theological Seminary
12500 Fair Lakes Cir Ste 325, Fairfax VA 22033
703-222-7871

Regent University
1000 Regent University Dr
Virginia Beach VA 23464-9800
757-226-4000

Stratford University
7777 Leesburg Pike #100 South
Falls Church VA 22043
Keith Evans, Contact
703-821-8570 Fax: 703-734-5335
Website: www.stratford.edu
E-mail: admissions@stratford.edu

UNION THEOLOGICAL SEMINARY AND PRESBYTERIAN SCHOOL OF CHRISTIAN EDUCATION

3401 Brook Rd, Richmond VA 23227-4597
Pat Morgan, Associate Director of Admissions
800-229-2990 Fax: 804-355-3919
Website: www.union-psce.edu
E-mail: admissn@union-psce.edu

UNIVERSITY OF NORTHERN VIRGINIA

10021 Balls Ford Rd, Manassas VA 20109
703-392-0771 Fax: 703-392-0756
Website: www.unva.edu

Virginia College of Osteopathic Medicine
2265 Kraft Dr, Blacksburg VA 24060
540-231-4000

WASHINGTON

Argosy University/Seattle
2601-A Elliott Ave, Seattle WA 98121-1318
206-283-4500

BAKKE GRADUATE UNIVERSITY OF MINISTRY

1013 8th Ave, Seattle WA 98104-1222
Judi Melton, Registrar
206-264-9100 Fax: 206-264-0613
Website: www.bgu.edu
E-mail: bgu@bgu.edu

Bastyr University
14500 Juanita Dr NE, Bothell WA 98028-4966
425-823-1300

Central Washington University
400 E University Way, Ellensburg WA 98926
Duncan Perry, Dean of Graduate Studies/Research

City University
11900 NE 1st St, Bellevue WA 98005-3030
800-426-5596

Faith Evangelical Lutheran Seminary
3504 N Pearl St, Tacoma WA 98407
253-752-2020

Gonzaga University
Spokane WA 99258-0029
Julie McCulloh, Dean of Admission
509-323-6572

Heritage University
3240 Fort Rd, Toppenish WA 98948-9599
509-865-8500

Mars Hill Graduate School
2525 220th St SE Ste 100, Bothell WA 98021
425-415-0505

Pacific Lutheran University
12180 Park Ave S, Tacoma WA 98447-0014
David E. Gunovich, Director of Admissions
253-535-7151

Seattle Institute of Oriental Medicine
916 NE 65th St #B, Seattle WA 98115
206-517-4541

Seattle University School of Law
901 12th Ave, Seattle WA 98122
Carol Cochran, Director of Admission
206-398-4200

WEST VIRGINIA

Alderson-Broaddus College
Philippi WV 26416
Eric A. Ruf, Director of Admissions
800-263-1549

Fairmont State University
1201 Locust Ave, Fairmont WV 26554-2470
Steve Leadman, Director of Admissions
304-367-4892 or 800-641-5678 Fax: 304-367-4789
Website: www.fairmontstate.edu
E-mail: admit@fairmontstate.edu

MOUNTAIN STATE UNIVERSITY

Box 9003, Beckley WV 25802-9003
866-FOR-MSU1 or 304-929-INFO Fax: 304-253-0789
Website: www.mountainstate.edu
E-mail: gomsu@mountainstate.edu

Master of Science in Nursing, Master of Health Science, Master of Arts or Master of Science in Interdisciplinary Studies, Master of Criminal Justice Administration, Master of Science in Physician Assistant, Master of Science in Strategic Leadership.

See listing under "Universities"

West Virginia School of Osteopathic Medicine
400 N Lee St, Lewisburg WV 24901-1196
304-645-6270

West Virginia Wesleyan College
59 College Ave, Buckhannon WV 26201-2699
Robert N. Skinner II, Director of Admission
800-722-9933

WISCONSIN

Medical College of Wisconsin
PO Box 26509, Milwaukee WI 53226-0509
Michael Istwan, Director of Admissions
414-456-8296

MIDWEST COLLEGE OF ORIENTAL MEDICINE

6232 Bankers Rd, Racine WI 53403-9747
Kelly Westerlund, Contact
800-593-2320 Fax: 262-554-7475
Website: www.acupuncture.edu
E-mail: mwcadmissions@yahoo.com

NASHOTAH HOUSE

2777 Mission Rd, Nashotah WI 53058-9793
The Very Rev. Robert S. Munday, Ph.D., Dean and President
262-646-6500 Fax: 262-646-6504
Website: www.nashotah.edu
E-mail: nashotah@nashotah.edu

Sacred Heart School of Theology
PO Box 429, Hales Corners WI 53130-0429
414-425-8300

Saint Francis Seminary
3257 S Lake Dr, Saint Francis WI 53235-3795
Registrar
414-747-6400

University of Wisconsin in La Crosse
115 Graff Main Hall, La Crosse WI 54601
Tim Lewis, Director of Admissions
608-785-8939

University of Wisconsin - Oshkosh
800 Algoma Blvd, Oshkosh WI 54901-8602
920-424-1223

WISCONSIN SCHOOL OF PROFESSIONAL PSYCHOLOGY

9120 W Hampton Ave Ste 212
Milwaukee WI 53225-4960
Howard Haven, Ph.D., Dean
414-464-9777 Fax: 414-358-5590
Website: www.wspp.edu
E-mail: admissions@wspp.edu

WYOMING

::: Columbia Commonwealth University
327 N St, Rock Springs WY 82901-5332
800-552-5522

GUAM

University of Guam
UOG Station, Mangilao GU 96923
Graduate Studies Office
671-735-2170
Website: www.uog.edu
E-mail: admitme@uog9.uog.edu

PUERTO RICO

CARLOS ALBIZU UNIVERSITY - SAN JUAN CAMPUS

PO Box 9023711, San Juan PR 00902-3711
Carlos Rodriguez, Director of Admissions
787-725-6500 Fax: 787-721-7187
Website: albizu.edu
E-mail: crodriguez@albizu.edu

Center for Advanced Studies on Puerto Rico and the Caribbean
PO Box 9023970, San Juan PR 00902-3970
787-723-4481

Evangelical Seminary of Puerto Rico
776 Ave Ponce de Leon, San Juan PR 00925-2207
Wilmarie Leduc Jorge, Registrar
787-763-6700 ext. 238

Inter American University of Puerto Rico
PO Box 70351, San Juan PR 00936
787-751-1912

Inter American University of Puerto Rico
School of Optometry
118 Calle Eleonor Roosevelt
San Juan PR 00918-3105
787-765-1915

Ponce School of Medicine
PO Box 7004, Ponce PR 00732
787-840-2575

HANDICAPPED, SCHOOLS FOR THE

ARIZONA

DEVEREUX-ARIZONA TREATMENT NETWORK
6436 E Sweetwater Ave, Scottsdale AZ 85254-4581
Admissions Office
480-998-2920 Fax: 480-443-1531
Website: www.devereuxaz.org

CALIFORNIA

DEVEREUX CALIFORNIA
PO Box 6784, Santa Barbara CA 93160
805-968-2525 Fax: 805-968-3247
Website: www.devereuxca.org

CONNECTICUT

DEVEREUX CENTER IN CONNECTICUT
81 Sabbaday Ln, Washington Depot CT 06793-1318
Admissions Office
860-868-7377 Fax: 860-868-7413
Website: www.devereuxct.org

FLORIDA

DEVEREUX-FLORIDA TREATMENT NETWORK
5850 T G Lee Blvd Ste 400, Orlando FL 32822
Linda Brooks, Director of Admissions
800-338-3738 or 407-812-4555 Fax: 407-816-6481
Website: www.devereuxfl.org
Locations throughout Florida

GEORGIA

ATLANTA AREA SCHOOL FOR THE DEAF
890 N Indian Creek Dr, Clarkston GA 30021-2228
Gail Allen, Professional Learning Coordinator
404-298-4874 Fax: 404-294-3521
Website: www.aasdweb.com
E-mail: gallen@doe.k12.ga.us

DEVEREUX-GEORGIA TREATMENT NETWORK
1291 Stanley Rd NW, Kennesaw GA 30152-4359
Admissions Office
800-342-3357 or 770-427-0147 Fax: 770-424-9408
Website: www.devereuxga.org

GEORGIA SCHOOL FOR THE DEAF
232 Perry Farm Rd SW, Cave Spring GA 30124-3018
Dr. Leah Shiver, School Director
800-497-3371 Fax: 706-777-2204
Website: www.gsdweb.org
E-mail: lshiver@doe.k12.ga.us

ILLINOIS

ILLINOIS SCHOOL FOR VISUALLY IMPAIRED
658 E State St, Jacksonville IL 62650-2183
Jan McGovern, Principal
217-479-4400 Fax: 217-479-4479
Website: www.isvi.net
E-mail: dhsvi38@dhs.state.il.us

MAINE

MAINE EDUCATIONAL CENTER FOR THE DEAF AND HARD OF HEARING
Governor Baxter School for the Deaf
Mackworth Island, Falmouth ME 04105
Larry S. Taub, Ed.D., Superintendent
207-781-3165 Fax: 207-781-6319
Website: www.gbsd.org
E-mail: larry.taub@gbsd.org

MASSACHUSETTS

DEVEREUX CENTER IN MASSACHUSETTS
60 Miles Rd, Rutland MA 01543-0197
Admissions Office
508-886-4746 Fax: 508-886-4773
Website: www.devereuxma.org

PERKINS SCHOOL FOR THE BLIND
175 N Beacon St, Watertown MA 02472
Christopher Underwood, Supervisor
617-972-7285 Fax: 617-972-7715
Website: www.perkins.org
E-mail: info@perkins.org

NEW YORK

DEVEREUX CENTER IN NEW YORK
40 Devereux Way, Red Hook NY 12571
Admissions Office
845-758-1899 Fax: 845-758-1817
Website: www.devereuxny.org

ROCHESTER INSTITUTE OF TECHNOLOGY NATIONAL TECHNICAL INSTITUTE FOR THE DEAF (NTID)
52 Lomb Memorial Dr, Rochester NY 14623-5604
Robert Borden, Director of NTID Admissions
585-475-6700 (v/TTY) or 866-644-6843 (v/TTY)
Fax: 585-475-2696
Website: www.rit.edu/ntid/getinfo
E-mail: NTIDAdmissions@rit.edu

Established 1965. Private. Coed. Tution $9,153 (NTID or NTID supported students only). Room & Board: $9,054. Fees: $669. Enrollment: 1,100. Faculty: 205. Degrees offered: MS, BS, AS, AAS, AOS. 238 buildings on 1,300 acres. Qualified deaf and hard-of-hearing students can earn bachelor's or master's degrees in more than 200 programs offered by RIT's seven other colleges - Applied Science and Technology, Business, Computing and Information Sciences, Engineering, Imaging Arts and Sciences, Liberal Arts, and Science. They also can earn associate degrees in more than 30 accredited NTID programs including: Accounting Technology, Administrative Support Technology, Applied Computer Technology, Applied Optical Technology, Arts and Imaging (pending state approval) Automation Technologies - Robotics, Business Technology, Computer Aided Drafting Technology, Computer Integrated Machining Technology, Laboratory Science Technology and Hospitality and Service Management. Additionally NTID offers degrees in American Sign Language-English Interpretation and a Master's of Science in Secondary Education of Students who are Deaf or Hard of Hearing.

ROCHESTER SCHOOL FOR THE DEAF
1545 Saint Paul St, Rochester NY 14621-3197
Harold Mowl Jr., Ph.D., Superintendent
585-544-1240 Fax: 585-544-0383
Website: www.rsdeaf.org

OHIO

ST. RITA SCHOOL FOR THE DEAF
1720 Glendale Milford Rd, Cincinnati OH 45215-1258
Gregory Ernst, Executive Director
513-771-7600 Fax: 513-326-8264
Website: www.srsdeaf.org
E-mail: gernst@srsdeaf.org

PENNSYLVANIA

DEVEREUX BENETO CENTER
655 Sugartown Rd Box 297, Malvern PA 19355
Admissions Office
800-935-6789 or 610-251-2407 Fax: 610-251-2415
Website: www.devereuxbeneto.org
LOCATIONS THROUGHOUT SOUTHEASTERN PENNSYLVANIA

THE DEVEREUX FOUNDATION
National Referral Office
444 Devereux Dr, Villanova PA 19085
Kimberleigh A. Nash
800-345-1292 or 610-542-3030 Fax: 610-542-3141
Website: www.devereux.org

DEVEREUX KANNER CENTER
390 E Boot Rd, West Chester PA 19380
Admissions Office
866-532-2212 Fax: 610-431-8191
Website: www.devereuxkanner.org

OVERBROOK SCHOOL FOR THE BLIND
6333 Malvern Ave, Philadelphia PA 19151
Bernadette M. Kappen, Director
215-877-0313 Fax: 215-877-2466
Website: www.obs.org
E-mail: bmk@obs.org

PATHWAY SCHOOL
162 Egypt Rd, Norristown PA 19403-3090
Louise Robertson, Director of Admissions
610-277-0660 Fax: 610-539-1493
Website: www.pathwayschool.org
E-mail: louiser@pathwayschool.org

WOODS SERVICES
PO Box 36, Langhorne PA 19047
Dan Shine, Director, Referral Development
800-782-3646 Fax: 215-750-4591
Website: www.woods.org
E-mail: dshine@woods.org

SOUTH CAROLINA

SOUTH CAROLINA SCHOOL FOR DEAF AND BLIND
355 Cedar Springs Rd, Spartanburg SC 29302
Barbara Bacon, Education Services Director
864-577-7557 Fax: 864-585-3555
Website: www.scsdb.org
E-mail: bbacon@scsdb.org

SOUTH DAKOTA

SOUTH DAKOTA SCHOOL FOR THE DEAF
2001 E 8th St, Sioux Falls SD 57103-1896
Dr. Maureen Schloss, Superintendent
605-367-5200 Fax: 605-367-5209
Website: www.sdsd.sdbor.edu
E-mail: sdsd@sdsd.sdbor.edu

TEXAS

DEVEREUX-TEXAS TREATMENT NETWORK-HOUSTON PROGRAM
1150 Devereux Dr, League City TX 77573-2043
Admissions Office
800-373-0011 or 281-335-1000 Fax: 281-332-2301
Website: www.devereuxtx.org

DEVEREUX-TEXAS TREATMENT NETWORK-VICTORIA PROGRAM
120 David Wade Dr, Victoria TX 77902-2666
Admissions Office
800-383-5000 or 361-575-8271 Fax: 361-575-6520
Website: www.devereuxtx.org

UTAH

UTAH SCHOOLS FOR THE DEAF AND THE BLIND
742 Harrison Blvd, Ogden UT 84404-5231
Timothy Smith, Superintendent
801-629-4700 Fax: 801-629-4896
Website: www.usdb.org
E-mail: lindar@usdb.org

VERMONT

AUSTINE SCHOOL FOR THE DEAF
60 Austine Dr, Brattleboro VT 05301
Cyndy Ward, Director of Related Services
802-258-9522 Voice/tty Fax: 802-258-9541
Website: www.vcdhh.org
E-mail: cward@vcdhh.org

BENNINGTON REGIONAL DAY PROGRAM
Bennington VT 05201
Brenda Seitz, Director of Special Education
802-258-9535 Fax: 802-258-9507
E-mail: bseitz@vcdhh.org

THE WILLIAM CENTER
60 Austine Dr, Brattleboro VT 05301
Dr. Ray Stevens, Director of the William Center
802-258-9537 Fax: 802-258-9593
Website: www.vcdhh.org - Education - William Center
E-mail: rstevens@vcdhh.org

WILLISTON REGIONAL DAY PROGRAM
195 Central School Dr, Williston VT 05495
Jennifer Bostwick, Director
802-879-4787 Fax: 802-879-5830
Website: www.vcdhh.org
E-mail: jbostwick@vcdhh.org

HOME ECONOMICS

CALIFORNIA

California State University-San Bernadino
5500 University Pkwy
San Bernardino CA 92407-2393
Olivia Rosas, Director of Admissions
909-537-5188 Fax: 909-537-7034
Website: www.csusb.edu
E-mail: orosas@csusb.edu

Orange Coast College
PO Box 5005, Costa Mesa CA 92628-5005
Kristin Clark, Director of Admissions
714-432-5773 Fax: 714-432-5736
Website: www.orangecoastcollege.edu
E-mail: kclark@cccd.edu

Point Loma Nazarene University
3900 Lomaland Dr, San Diego CA 92106-2810
Chip Killingsworth, Director of Undergraduate Admissions
800-733-7770 Fax: 619-849-2601
Website: www.pointloma.edu
E-mail: admissions@pointloma.edu

DISTRICT OF COLUMBIA

Gallaudet University
800 Florida Ave NE, Washington DC 20002-3695
Charity Reedy Hines, Director of Admissions
202-651-5750 Fax: 202-651-5744
Website: www.gallaudet.edu
E-mail: admissions.office@gallaudet.edu

FLORIDA

Florida State University
600 W College Ave, Tallahassee FL 32306-1096
Janice V. Finney, Director of Admissions
850-644-2525 Fax: 850-644-0197
Website: admissions.fsu.edu
E-mail: admissions@admin.fsu.edu

IDAHO

Brigham Young University - Idaho
120 Kimball Bldg, Rexburg ID 83460-1615
Rob Garrett, Director of Admissions
208-496-1020 Fax: 208-496-1220
Website: www.byui.edu
E-mail: admissions@byui.edu

University of Idaho
Moscow ID 83844-4253
Lloyd Scott, Director of New Student Services
208-885-6163 Fax: 208-885-4477
Website: www.uidaho.edu
E-mail: nss@uidaho.edu

IOWA

Iowa Lakes Community College
300 S 18th St, Estherville IA 51334-2721
Anne Stansbury, Asst. Director of Admissions
712-362-7945 Fax: 712-362-8363
Website: www.iowalakes.edu
E-mail: info@iowalakes.edu

MAINE

Southern Maine Community College
2 Fort Rd, South Portland ME 04106-1698
Dr. James Ortiz, President
Scott MacDonald, Director of Financial Aid
207-741-5500 Fax: 207-741-5671
Website: www.smccme.edu
E-mail: oharmon@maine.rr.com

MASSACHUSETTS

Boston University
121 Bay State Rd, Boston MA 02215
Kelly Walter, Executive Director of Admissions
617-353-2300 Fax: 617-353-9695
Website: web.bu.edu
E-mail: admissions@bu.edu

North Shore Community College
1 Ferncroft Rd, Danvers MA 01923-4093
Jennifer Kirk, Director of Admissions & Recruitment Outreach
978-762-4000 Fax: 978-762-4015
Website: www.northshore.edu
E-mail: jkirk@northshore.edu

MISSOURI

Northwest Missouri State University
800 University Dr, Maryville MO 64468-6001
Beverly Schenkel, Dean of Enrollment Management
660-562-1562 Fax: 660-562-1121
Website: www.nwmissouri.edu
E-mail: admissions@nwmissouri.edu

OHIO

ENGLISH NANNY AND GOVERNESS SCHOOL
30 S Franklin St, Chagrin Falls OH 44022-3213
Sheilagh Roth, Executive Director
800-733-1984 Fax: 440-247-0602
Website: www.nanny-governess.com
E-mail: admissions@nanny-governess.com

OKLAHOMA

Oklahoma State University
Stillwater OK 74078
Lona Robertson, Asst. Dean
405-744-5053
Website: www.okstate.edu
E-mail: lona.robertson@okstate.edu

OREGON

Linn-Benton Community College
6500 Pacific Blvd SW, Albany OR 97321-3774
Christine Baker, Outreach Coordinator
541-917-4811 Fax: 541-917-4868
Website: www.linnbenton.edu
E-mail: admissions@linnbenton.edu

PENNSYLVANIA

Community College of Allegheny County
Allegheny Campus: 808 Ridge Ave, Pittsburgh PA 15212 Admissions: 412.237.2700
Boyce Campus: 595 Beatty Rd, Monroeville PA 15146 Admissions: 724.325.6614
North Campus: 8701 Perry Highway, Pittsburgh PA 15237 Admissions: 412.369.3600
South Campus: 1750 Clairton Rd, West Mifflin PA 15122 Admissions: 412-469-4301
Website: www.ccac.edu

TENNESSEE

Lipscomb University
3901 Granny White Pike, Nashville TN 37204-3951
Ricky Holaway, Director of Admissions
800-333-4358 ext. 1776 Fax: 615-269-1804
Website: www.lipscomb.edu
E-mail: admissions@lipscomb.edu

Southwest Tennessee Community College
5983 Macon Cove, Memphis TN 38134
Vanessa R. Dowdy, Director of Admissions
901-333-5000 Fax: 901-333-4523
Website: www.southwest.tn.edu
E-mail: vdowdy@southwest.tn.edu

Tennessee State University
3500 John A Merritt Blvd, Nashville TN 37209-1561
John Cade, Dean of Admissions & Records
615-963-5101 Fax: 615-963-2930
Website: www.tnstate.edu
E-mail: jcade@tnstate.edu

University of Tennessee
615 McCallie Ave, Chattanooga TN 37403-2504
Yancy Freeman, Director of Admissions
423-425-4111 Fax: 423-425-4157
Website: www.utc.edu
E-mail: Yancy-Freeman@utc.edu

TEXAS

Abilene Christian University
ACU Box 29000, Abilene TX 79699-0001
325-674-2000 Fax: 325-674-2202
Website: www.acu.edu
E-mail: info@admissions.acu.edu

Texas Woman's University
PO Box 425589, Denton TX 76204-5589
Erma Nieto-Brecht, Director of Admissions
866-809-6130 Fax: 940-898-3081
Website: www.twu.edu
E-mail: admissions@twu.edu

University of Houston
122 E Cullen Bldg, Houston TX 77204-2023
Office of Admission
713-743-9595
Website: www.uh.edu
E-mail: admissions@uh.edu

VIRGINIA

Radford University
PO Box 6903, Radford VA 24142
David W. Kraus, Director of Admissions
800-890-4265 Fax: 540-831-5038
Website: www.radford.edu
E-mail: ruadmiss@radford.edu

WASHINGTON

SHORELINE COMMUNITY COLLEGE
16101 Greenwood Ave N, Shoreline WA 98133-5696
Chris Melton, Acting Registrar
206-546-4581 Fax: 206-546-5835
Website: www.shoreline.edu

WYOMING

University of Wyoming
Admissions Office
Dept 3435, Laramie WY 82071-3435
Brooke Culver, Contact
800-342-5996 Fax: 307-766-4042
Website: www.uwyo.edu
E-mail: why-wyo@uwyo.edu

GUAM

University of Guam
UOG Station, Mangilao GU 96923
Deborah Leon Guerrero, Registrar
671-735-2201 or 671-735-2208 Fax: 671-735-2203
Website: www.uog.edu
E-mail: admitme@uog9.uog.edu

: : :HOME STUDY AND CORRESPONDENCE

ALABAMA

American Sentinel University
2101 Magnolia Ave Ste 207, Birmingham AL 35205
205-323-6191

Andrew Jackson University
2919 John Hawkins Pkwy
Birmingham AL 35244-1095
800-429-9300

COLUMBIA SOUTHERN UNIVERSITY
25326 Canal Rd, Orange Beach AL 36561
251-981-3771 Fax: 251-981-3815
Website: www.columbiasouthern.edu
E-mail: admissions@columbiasouthern.edu

ARIZONA

COLLEGE OF THE HUMANITIES AND SCIENCES HARRISON MIDDLETON UNIVERSITY
1105 E Broadway Rd, Tempe AZ 85282
Kathleen Mirabile, Vice President
480-317-5955 Fax: 480-829-4999
Website: www.chumsci.edu
E-mail: kmirabile@chumsci.edu

International Import-Export Institute
11225 N 28th Dr Ste B201, Phoenix AZ 85029
602-648-5750

THE PARALEGAL INSTITUTE
PO Box 11408, Phoenix AZ 85061-1408
602-212-0501 Fax: 602-212-0502
Website: www.theparalegalinstitute.edu
E-mail: info@theparalegalinstitute.edu

SONORAN DESERT INSTITUTE
10245 E Via Linda Ste 102, Scottsdale AZ 85258
Ms. Toni Pino, Assistant Director
480-314-2102 Fax: 480-314-2138
Website: www.sonoranlearning.com
E-mail: info@sonoranlearning.com

ARKANSAS

Remington College Online
500 President Clinton Ave, Suite 305
Little Rock AR 72201
800-829-5488

CALIFORNIA

ALLIED BUSINESS SCHOOL
22952 Alcalde Dr, Laguna Hills CA 92653
949-598-0875 Fax: 949-461-9556
Website: www.alliedschools.com
E-mail: chislop@alliedschools.com

Applied Professional Training
PO Box 131717, Carlsbad CA 92013
800-431-8488

CALIFORNIA COAST UNIVERSITY
700 N Main St, Santa Ana CA 92701
Admissions Office: 888-CCU-UNIV or 714-547-9625
Fax: 714-547-5777
Dr. Thomas Neal, President
Dr. Cynthia Teeple, Academic Vice President
Website: www.calcoast.edu
E-mail: info@calcoast.edu

Established 1973. Proprietary. Coed. Accreditation: California Coast University holds accreditation through the Accrediting Commission of the Distance Education and Training Council (DETC). The DETC is an educational association located in Washington, D.C. Founded in 1926, it is the standard setting agency for distance education institutions. Approval: Bureau for Private Postsecondary and Vocational Education - State of California, charter member California Association of State Approved Colleges & Universities, member Association for Adult & Continuing Education, member The Alliance for Private Post Secondary Academic Institutions.

Tuition: $2,805-$12,070. California Coast University has selected the SLM Corporation, commonly known as Sallie Mae, to help the university provide financing for its students. Sallie Mae is the nation's leading provider of education funding. Sallie Mae also allows students to borrow additional loan amounts to cover additional expenses, such as textbooks, equipment, or living expenses.

Enrollment: 30,000. California Coast University is approved by the California State Approving Agency to enroll veterans or other eligible persons under Title 38, U.S. Code. California Coast University holds a Memorandum of Understanding with Defense Activity for Non-Traditional Education Support (DANTES) as an external degree provider.

A private college offering off-campus independent study programs in the traditional areas of business administration, management, psychology, education. Admissions: enroll year round, requires official transcripts, letters of recommendation, detailed curriculum vita or occupational history.

Process: evaluation of prior academic work followed by analysis of occupational history, including participation in workshops, seminars, training programs, specialized projects for credit. Credit is demonstrated by accelerated learning guides or study guides.

Residency: All course work may be completed off campus, utilizing correspondence methods. Interest free loans available to students.

Futures International High School
2204 El Camino Real #312, Oceanside CA 92054
760-721-0121

GEMOLOGICAL INSTITUTE OF AMERICA
The Robert Mouawad Campus
5345 Armada Dr, Carlsbad CA 92008-4602
Jason Drake, Admissions Manager
800-421-7250 ext. 4001 or 760-603-4001
Fax: 760-603-4003
Website: www.gia.edu
E-mail: eduinfo@gia.edu

Established 1931. Nonprofit. Private. Accreditation: Distance Education Training Council. Diploma: Gemologist, Graduate Gemologist, Accredited Jewelry Professional. Courses: Diamond Essentials, Diamonds & Diamond Grading, Colored Stone Essentials, Colored Stones, Gem Identification, Jewelry Essentials, Pearls, Pearl and Bead Stringing, Jewelry Business Management. Degree: BBA (Bachelor of Business Administration).

See listing under "Career Schools"

Holmes Institute
School of Consciousness Studies
2600 W Magnolia Blvd, Burbank CA 91505
818-556-7757

Hypnosis Motivation Institute
Extension School
18607 Ventura Blvd Ste 310, Tarzana CA 91356
800-479-9464

John Tracy Clinic
806 W Adams Blvd, Los Angeles CA 90007-2599
Gisele Ragusa, Ph.D., Program Director
Professional Distance Education
800-522-4582

Truck Marketing Institute
1090 Eugenia Pl Ste 101, Carpinteria CA 93013-2011
805-684-4558

William Howard Taft University
3700 S Susan St, Santa Ana CA 92704
714-850-4800

COLORADO

AMERICAN HEALTH SCIENCE UNIVERSITY
1010 S Joliet St #107, Aurora CO 80012-3150
Ann Peterson, Academic Dean
303-340-2054 Fax: 303-367-2577
Website: www.ahsu.edu
E-mail: cn@ahsu.edu

Aspen University
501 S Cherry St Ste 350, Denver CO 80246
800-441-4746

WESTON DISTANCE LEARNING
At-Home Professions - U.S. Career Institute
2001 Lowe St, Fort Collins CO 80525
Joyce Lindquist, Director of Student Services
800-347-7899 Fax: 970-223-1678
Website: www.uscareerinstitute.com
E-mail: enroll@uscareerinstitute.com

CONNECTICUT

Charter Oak State College
55 Paul Manafort Dr, New Britain CT 06053-2142
860-832-3800

Hanger Orthopedic Group
181 Patricia M Genova Dr, Newington CT 06111
860-667-5304

Westlawn Institute of Marine Technology
PO Box 6000, Mystic CT 06355
860-572-7900

FLORIDA

Citizen's High School
PO Box 66089, Orange Park FL 32065
904-276-1700

IMPAC University
900 W Marion Ave, Punta Gorda FL 33950
941-639-7512

National Training
PO Box 65789, Orange Park FL 32065
904-272-4000

Stenotype Institute Court Reporting School
3986 Boulevard Center Dr Bldg. 1200 #200
Jacksonville FL 32207-2819
904-246-7466

Universidad FLET
14540 SW 136th St Ste 202, Miami FL 33186
305-378-8700

University of St. Augustine for Health Sciences
1 University Blvd, Saint Augustine FL 32086
904-826-0084

GEORGIA

Ashworth College
430 Technology Pkwy, Norcross GA 30092
770-729-8400

James Madison High School
430 Technology Pkwy, Norcross GA 30092
770-729-8400

Professional Career Development Institute
430 Technology Pkwy, Norcross GA 30092
770-729-8400

HAWAII

Babel University Professional School of Translation
1720 Ala Moana Blvd Tradewinds Ste A5
Honolulu HI 96815
808-946-3773

ILLINOIS

American Health Information Management
233 N Michigan Ave Ste 2150, Chicago IL 60601
312-233-1184

AMERICAN INTERCONTINENTAL UNIVERSITY ONLINE
5550 Prairie Stone Parkway Suite 400
Hoffman Estates IL 60192
Admissions Department
877-701-3800
Website: www.aiuonline.edu
E-mail: info@aiuonline.edu

AMERICAN SCHOOL
2200 E 170th St, Lansing IL 60438-1002
Gary R. Masterton, President
708-418-2800
Website: www.americanschoolofcorr.org
E-mail: amschools@cs.com

Cardean University
111 N Canal St Ste 455, Chicago IL 60606
866-948-1289

KANSAS

Barclay College
607 N Kingman St, Haviland KS 67059
Herb Frazier, Director of Admissions
800-862-0226

LOUISIANA

SOUTHWEST UNIVERSITY
2200 Veterans Blvd, Kenner LA 70062
Dr. Grayce Lee, Director of Education
504-468-2900 Fax: 504-468-3213
Website: www.southwest.edu
E-mail: southwest@southwest.edu
Degree Granting Distance Education.

MARYLAND

GRIGGS INTERNATIONAL ACADEMY
PO Box 4437, Silver Spring MD 20914
Joan H. Wilson, Director of Admissions/Registrar
301-680-6570 Fax: 301-680-5157
Website: www.griggs.edu
E-mail: contact@griggs.edu

Griggs University
PO Box 4437, Silver Spring MD 20914-4437
Joan Wilson, Director of Admissions
301-680-6570 Fax: 301-680-6583
Website: www.griggs.edu
E-mail: registrar@griggs.edu

MASSACHUSETTS

RHODEC INTERNATIONAL
59 Coddington St Ste 104, Quincy MA 02169
Maureen Randall, Contact
617-472-4942 Fax: 617-472-3400
Website: www.rhodec.edu/us
E-mail: uscontact@rhodec.edu

MICHIGAN

Educational Institute of the American Hotel & Lodging Association
2113 N High St, Lansing MI 48906
800-344-4381 ext. PSC

MINNESOTA

ART INSTRUCTION SCHOOLS
3400 Technology Dr, Minneapolis MN 55418
612-362-5000 Fax: 612-362-5260
Website: www.artists-ais.edu
E-mail: info/edi@artists-ais.com

MISSOURI

Global University
1211 S Glenstone Ave, Springfield MO 65804-0315
417-862-9533

Grantham University
7200 NW 86th St Ste M, Kansas City MO 64153
800-955-2527

NEVADA

American Career Institute
2340 Paseo Del Prado Ste D-208
Las Vegas NV 89102
702-222-3522

NEW JERSEY

Institute of Logistical Management
PO Box 427, Burlington NJ 08016
Frank R. Breslin, Dean
609-747-1515

National Tax Training School
PO Box 767, Mahwah NJ 07430-0767
800-914-8138

NEW YORK

Sessions.edu Online School of Design
350 7th Ave Rm 1203, New York NY 10001-5013
Bob Timm, Director of Student Services & Office Infrastructure
212-239-3080

NORTH CAROLINA

AMERICAN INSTITUTE OF APPLIED SCIENCE
Criminal Investigation and Forensic Science
100 Hunter Pl, Youngsville NC 27596-9447
Marvin Joy, Director of Education
919-554-2500 Fax: 919-556-6784
Website: www.aiasinc.com
E-mail: aias@mindspring.com

OHIO

Brighton College
85 S Main St Ste G, Hudson OH 44236-3038
800-231-3803

Cleveland Institute of Electronics
1776 E 17th St, Cleveland OH 44114-3679
Scott Katzenmeyer, Director of Admissions
800-243-6446 Fax: 216-781-0331
Website: www.cie-wc.edu
E-mail: instruct@cie-wc.edu

HARDI Home Study Institute
1389 Dublin Rd, Columbus OH 43215-1084
614-488-1835

OKLAHOMA

Oral Roberts University
Adult Learning Service Center
7777 S Lewis Ave, Tulsa OK 74171-0001
888-900-4678

OREGON

Australasian College of Health Sciences
5940 SW Hood Ave, Portland OR 97239
503-244-0726

PENNSYLVANIA

Education Direct
925 Oak St, Scranton PA 18515-0999
570-342-7701

KEYSTONE NATIONAL HIGH SCHOOL
420 W 5th St, Bloomsburg PA 17815-1564
Vanessa Klingensmith, Manager, School Partnerships
866-730-5161 Fax: 570-784-2129
Website: www.onlineschoolsolutions.com
E-mail: info@onlineschoolsolutions.com

TENNESSEE

Diamond Council of America
3212 W End Ave Ste 202, Nashville TN 37203-5835
615-385-5301

Huntington College of Health Sciences
1204 Kenesaw Ave, Knoxville TN 37919
800-290-4226

Seminary Extension Independent Study Institute
901 Commerce St Ste 500, Nashville TN 37203-3631
Dr. Bill Vinson, Director
800-229-4612

UTAH

California College for Health Sciences
5295 Commerce Dr, Salt Lake City UT 84107
800-221-7374

Western Governors University
4001 S 700 E Suite 700, Salt Lake City UT 84107
801-274-3280

VERMONT

DLI Distance Learning International
PO Box 846, Saint Albans VT 05478-0846
Teresa Moore, Registrar
800-493-4114

VIRGINIA

Atlantic University
215 67th St, Virginia Beach VA 23451-2061
Gregory Deming, Director of Admissions
800-428-1512

Catholic Distance University
120 E Colonial Hwy, Hamilton VA 20158-9012
888-254-4238 Fax: 540-338-4788
Website: www.cdu.edu
E-mail: tcashen@cdu.edu

Richard Milburn High School
3421 Commission Ct Ste 201, Woodbridge VA 22192
703-494-0147

WORLD COLLEGE
5193 Shore Dr Ste 105, Virginia Beach VA 23455
John R. Drinko, Contact
757-464-4600 Fax: 757-464-3687
Website: www.worldcollege.edu
E-mail: instruct@cie-wc.edu

WASHINGTON

Skagit Valley College
2405 E College Way, Mount Vernon WA 98273-5899
Distance Education Officer
360-416-7600

WEST VIRGINIA

American Public University
111 W Congress St, Charles Town WV 25414
877-468-6268

MOUNTAIN STATE UNIVERSITY
Box 9003, Beckley WV 25802-9003
Tony England, Director of Admissions
866-FOR-MSU1 or 304-929-1433 Fax: 304-253-5072
Website: www.mountainstate.edu
E-mail: gomsu@mountainstate.edu

Established 1933. Private. Coed. Accreditation: The Higher Learning Commission of North Central Association of Colleges and Schools. 2006-07 Tuition & Fees: $7,800. Room & board: $5,058 - $7,026. Enrollment: 4,404. Faculty: 79 full-time, 237 part-time. Student-faculty ratio: 23:1. Degrees: AA, AS, BA, BS, BSN, BSW, MA, MCJA, MS, MHS, MSN, MSPA, MSSL. Library: 95,500 volumes. Largest private college in West Virginia; extensive financial aid package; same tuition for in-state or out-of-state students; extensive health science programs.

WYOMING

Columbia Commonwealth University
327 N St, Rock Springs WY 82901-5332
800-552-5522

INTERIOR DESIGN

ALABAMA

Judson College
302 Bibb St, Marion AL 36756
Michael Scotto, Director of Admissions
800-447-9472 Fax: 334-683-5147
Website: www.judson.edu
E-mail: admissions@judson.edu

Trenholm State Technical College
Patterson Campus
3920 Troy Hwy, Montgomery AL 36116
Dr. Anthony Molina, President
334-420-4200 Fax: 334-420-4206
Website: www.trenholmtech.cc.al.us
E-mail: molinaa@trenholmtech.cc.al.us

ARIZONA

Collins College: A School of Design and Technology
(Formerly Al Collins Graphic Design School)
1140 S Priest Dr, Tempe AZ 85281-5240
Toby Craver, Director of National Admissions
800-876-7070 Fax: 480-829-0183
Website: www.collinscollege.edu

CALIFORNIA

American Film Institute
AFI Conservatory
2021 N Western Ave, Los Angeles CA 90027
Danielle McVickers, Admissions Manager
323-856-7740 Fax: 323-856-7720
Website: www.afi.com
E-mail: dmcvickers@afi.com
Production Design.

Butte College
3536 Butte Campus Dr, Oroville CA 95965-8399
Carole Gish, Director of Admissions
530-895-2511 Fax: 530-879-4313
Website: www.butte.edu
E-mail: admissions@butte.edu

California College of the Arts
1111 Eighth St, San Francisco CA 94107
Robynne Royster, Director of Admission
800-447-1-ART or 415-703-9523 Fax: 415-703-9539
Website: www.cca.edu
E-mail: enroll@cca.edu

FIDM/THE FASHION INSTITUTE OF DESIGN & MERCHANDISING
919 S Grand Ave, Los Angeles CA 90015-1421
Director of Admissions
213-624-1201 or 800-624-1200 Fax: 213-624-4799
Website: www.fidm.edu
E-mail: info@fidm.com
See listing under "Community and Junior Colleges"

FIDM/The Fashion Institute of Design & Merchandising
55 Stockton St, San Francisco CA 94108-5829
Director of Admissions
415-675-5200 or 800-422-3436 Fax: 415-296-7299
Website: www.fidm.edu
E-mail: info@fidm.com
See listing under "Community and Junior Colleges"

Orange Coast College
PO Box 5005, Costa Mesa CA 92628-5005
Kristin Clark, Director of Admissions
714-432-5773 Fax: 714-432-5736
Website: www.orangecoastcollege.edu
E-mail: kclark@cccd.edu

Point Loma Nazarene University
3900 Lomaland Dr, San Diego CA 92106-2810
Chip Killingsworth, Director of Undergraduate Admissions
800-733-7770 Fax: 619-849-2601
Website: www.pointloma.edu
E-mail: admissions@pointloma.edu

COLORADO

ROCKY MOUNTAIN COLLEGE OF ART & DESIGN
1600 Pierce St, Denver CO 80214
Angela Carlson, Director of Admissions
800-888-2787 Fax: 303-759-4970
Website: www.rmcad.edu
E-mail: admissions@rmcad.edu

FLORIDA

Florida State University
600 W College Ave, Tallahassee FL 32306-1096
Janice V. Finney, Director of Admissions
850-644-2525 Fax: 850-644-0197
Website: admissions.fsu.edu
E-mail: admissions@admin.fsu.edu

INTERNATIONAL ACADEMY OF DESIGN AND TECHNOLOGY
5959 Lake Ellenor Dr, Orlando FL 32809-4633
Dr. John Dietrich, VP of Admissions
877-753-0007 Fax: 407-888-4006
Website: www.iadt.edu
E-mail: info@iadt.edu

IDAHO

Brigham Young University - Idaho
120 Kimball Bldg, Rexburg ID 83460-1615
Rob Garrett, Director of Admissions
208-496-1020 Fax: 208-496-1220
Website: www.byui.edu
E-mail: admissions@byui.edu

ILLINOIS

Columbia College Chicago
600 S Michigan Ave, Chicago IL 60605-1996
Murphy Monroe, Executive Director of Admissions
312-344-7130 Fax: 312-344-8024
Website: www.colum.edu
E-mail: admissions@colum.edu

HARRINGTON COLLEGE OF DESIGN
200 W Madison St, Chicago IL 60606-3433
Wendi Franczyk, VP of Admissions
877-939-4975 Fax: 312-697-8032
Website: www.harringtoncollege.com
E-mail: wfranczyk@harringtoncollege.com
See listing under "Universities"

International Academy of Design and Technology
1 N State St #500, Chicago IL 60602-3300
Cecily Arroyo, Director of Admissions
888-803-0111 Fax: 312-541-3929
Website: www.iadtchicago.edu
E-mail: carroyo@iadtchicago.com

Roosevelt University
430 S Michigan Ave, Chicago IL 60605
Gwen E. Kanelos, Asst. Vice President for Enrollment Services
877-APPLY-RU Fax: 312-341-4216
Website: www.roosevelt.edu
E-mail: applyru@roosevelt.edu

INDIANA

Ivy Tech Community College - North Central
220 Dean Johnson Blvd, South Bend IN 46601-3415
Pam Decker, Director of Admissions
574-289-7001 Fax: 574-236-7177
Website: www.ivytech.edu
E-mail: pdecker@ivytech.edu

KENTUCKY

Louisville Technical Institute
3901 Atkinson Square Dr, Louisville KY 40218
Kevin Woods, Director of Admissions
800-844-6528 Fax: 502-456-2341
Website: www.louisvilletech.com
E-mail: kwoods@louisvilletech.com

MASSACHUSETTS

Becker College
Campuses in Worcester and Leicester, MA
61 Sever St, Worcester MA 01609-2165
Karen Schedin, Dean of Admissions
508-791-9241 Fax: 508-890-1500
Website: www.becker.edu
E-mail: admissions@becker.edu
See listing under "Universities"

Newbury College
129 Fisher Ave, Brookline MA 02445-5796
Salvadore Liberto, Vice President of Enrollment
617-730-7000 Fax: 617-731-9618
Website: www.newbury.edu
E-mail: info@newbury.edu
See listing under "Universities"

New England School of Art & Design at Suffolk University
75 Arlington St, Boston MA 02116
John Hamel, Director of Admissions
617-573-8785
Website: www.suffolk.edu/nesad

MICHIGAN

College for Creative Studies
201 E Kirby St, Detroit MI 48202-4048
Julie Hingelberg, Dean of Enrollment Services
313-664-7425
Website: www.ccscad.edu

Delta College
University Center MI 48710-0001
Duff Zube, Director of Admissions
989-686-9093 Fax: 989-667-2202
Website: www.delta.edu
E-mail: admit@delta.edu

Kendall College of Art & Design
17 Fountain St NW, Grand Rapids MI 49503-3002
Dr. Oliver H. Evans, President
800-676-2787 or 616-451-2787 Fax: 616-831-9689
Website: www.kcad.edu
E-mail: brittons@ferris.edu

Lawrence Technological University
21000 W 10 Mile Rd, Southfield MI 48075-1058
Jane Rohrback, Director of Admissions
800-225-5588 Fax: 248-204-2228
Website: www.ltu.edu
E-mail: admissions@ltu.edu
See listing under "Universities"

MINNESOTA

Dunwoody College of Technology
818 Dunwoody Blvd, Minneapolis MN 55403-1192
John Slama, Vice President Enrollment Management
800-292-4625 or 612-374-5800 Fax: 612-374-4128
Website: www.dunwoody.edu
E-mail: jslama@dunwoody.edu
See listing under "Career Schools"

MISSOURI

Stephens College
PO Box 2121, Columbia MO 65215-0001
David Adams, Dean of Enrollment Management
573-442-2211 Fax: 573-876-7237
Website: www.stephens.edu
E-mail: dadams@stephens.edu

NEW YORK

NEW YORK SCHOOL OF INTERIOR DESIGN
170 E 70th St, New York NY 10021-5110
David Sprouls, Director of Admissions
800-33-NYSID or 212-472-1500 Fax: 212-472-1867
Website: www.nysid.edu
E-mail: admissions@nysid.edu
Established 1916. Private. Coed. College devoted to Interior Design education. Tuition: $21,450 per year. Fees: $145. Enrollment: 750. Faculty: 95. Accreditation: NASAD, FIDER. Four programs offered: Master of Fine Arts, 4-year Bachelor degree, 2-year Associate degree, 1-year non-degree Basic Interior Design. Located in Manhattan's historic Upper East Side near center of interior design industry. Faculty consists of Designers, Architects and Artists.

Pratt Institute
200 Willoughby Ave, Brooklyn NY 11205-3899
Heidi Metcalf, Director of Admissions
718-636-3600 Fax: 718-636-3670
Website: www.pratt.edu
E-mail: hmetcalf@pratt.edu

SUNY College of Technology
Alfred NY 14802
Deborah J. Goodrich, Associate VP Enrollment Mgmt.
800-4AL-FRED Fax: 607-587-4299
Website: www.alfredstate.edu
E-mail: admissions@alfredstate.edu

NORTH CAROLINA

ART INSTITUTE OF CHARLOTTE
2110 Water Ridge Pkwy, Charlotte NC 28217
Pamela Notemyer, Director of Admissions
800-872-4417 Fax: 704-357-1133
Website: www.artinstitutes.edu/charlotte
E-mail: admin@aii.edu
See listing under "Career Schools"

Salem College
Winston Salem NC 27108
Dana Evans, Dean of Admissions/Fin. Aid
800-32-SALEM Fax: 336-917-5572
Website: www.salem.edu
E-mail: admissions@salem.edu
See listing under "Women's Colleges"

OHIO

Davis College
4747 Monroe St, Toledo OH 43623-4389
Dana Stern, Admissions Director
419-473-2700 Fax: 419-473-2472
Website: www.daviscollege.edu
E-mail: learn@daviscollege.edu

The Ohio State University
Dept of Industrial, Interior, & Visual Communication Design
380 Hopkins Hall, 128 N Oval Mall
Columbus OH 43210
614-292-6746 Fax: 614-292-0217
Website: design.osu.edu
E-mail: design@osu.edu

Owens Community College
PO Box 10000, Toledo OH 43699-1947
William J. Ivoska, Ph.D, Vice President of Student Services
567-661-7000 Fax: 567-661-7607
Website: www.owens.edu
E-mail: admissions@owens.edu

OKLAHOMA

Oklahoma State University
Stillwater OK 74078
Donna Branson, Department Head
405-744-5049
Website: www.okstate.edu
E-mail: donna.branson@okstate.edu

OREGON

Marylhurst University
17600 Pacific Hwy (Hwy 43)
Marylhurst OR 97036-0261
Director of Admissions
800-634-9982 ext. 6268 Fax: 503-635-6585
Website: www.marylhurst.edu
E-mail: studentinfo@marylhurst.edu

PENNSYLVANIA

Art Institute of Philadelphia
1622 Chestnut St, Philadelphia PA 19103-5119
Larry McHugh, Director of Admissions
800-275-2474 Fax: 215-405-6399
Website: www.artinstitutes.edu/philadelphia
E-mail: aiphinfo@aii.edu

ART INSTITUTE OF PITTSBURGH
420 Boulevard Of The Allies, Pittsburgh PA 15219
Jeffrey Bucklew, Director of Admissions
800-275-2470 Fax: 412-263-6667
Website: www.aip.aii.edu
E-mail: pahughes@aii.edu
See listing under "Universities"

Community College of Allegheny County
Allegheny Campus: 808 Ridge Ave, Pittsburgh PA 15212 Admissions: 412.237.2700
Boyce Campus: 595 Beatty Rd, Monroeville PA 15146 Admissions: 724.325.6614
North Campus: 8701 Perry Highway, Pittsburgh PA 15237 Admissions: 412.369.3600
South Campus: 1750 Clairton Rd, West Mifflin PA 15122 Admissions: 412-469-4301
Website: www.ccac.edu

RHODE ISLAND

New England Institute of Technology
2500 Post Rd, Warwick RI 02886-2244
Michael Kwiatkowski, Director of Admissions
401-739-5000 Fax: 401-738-5122
Website: www.neit.edu
E-mail: eflynn@neit.edu

TENNESSEE

O'More College of Design
423 S Margin St, Franklin TN 37064-2816
Dr. K. Mark Hilliard, President
Chris Lee, Director of Enrollment Management
615-794-4254 Fax: 615-790-1662
Website: www.omorecollege.edu
E-mail: clee@omorecollege.edu

Watkins College of Art and Design and The Watkins Film School
2298 Metrocenter Blvd, Nashville TN 37228-1306
615-383-4848 or 866-887-6395 Fax: 615-383-4849
Website: www.watkins.edu
E-mail: admissions@watkins.edu

TEXAS

Abilene Christian University
ACU Box 29000, Abilene TX 79699-0001
325-674-2000 Fax: 325-674-2202
Website: www.acu.edu
E-mail: info@admissions.acu.edu

University of Texas at Arlington
Box 19111, Arlington TX 76019-0111
Hans Gatterdam, Director of Admission
817-272-6287 Fax: 817-272-3435
Website: www.uta.edu
E-mail: admissions@uta.edu

Wade College
Dallas Market Center
PO Box 421149, Dallas TX 75342
Harry Davros, President
800-624-4850 or 214-637-3530 Fax: 214-637-0827
Website: www.wadecollege.edu
E-mail: admissions@wadecollege.edu
See listing under "Community and Junior Colleges"

UTAH

L.D.S. BUSINESS COLLEGE
95 North 300 West, Salt Lake City UT 84101-3500
Kathleen Howe, Assistant Director of Admissions
801-524-8145 Fax: 801-524-1900
Website: www.ldsbc.edu
E-mail: admissions@ldsbc.edu
See listing under "Career Schools"

VIRGINIA

Marymount University
2807 N Glebe Rd, Arlington VA 22207-4299
Michael Canfield, Director of Admissions
800-548-7638 Fax: 703-522-0348
Website: www.marymount.edu
E-mail: admissions@marymount.edu

Radford University
PO Box 6903, Radford VA 24142
David W. Kraus, Director of Admissions
800-890-4265 Fax: 540-831-5038
Website: www.radford.edu
E-mail: ruadmiss@radford.edu

LANDSCAPE ARCHITECTURE

IDAHO

Brigham Young University - Idaho
120 Kimball Bldg, Rexburg ID 83460-1615
Rob Garrett, Director of Admissions
208-496-1020 Fax: 208-496-1220
Website: www.byui.edu
E-mail: admissions@byui.edu

University of Idaho
Moscow ID 83844-4253
Lloyd Scott, Director of New Student Services
208-885-6163 Fax: 208-885-4477
Website: www.uidaho.edu
E-mail: nss@uidaho.edu

MAINE

Southern Maine Community College
2 Fort Rd, South Portland ME 04106-1698
Dr. James Ortiz, President
Scott MacDonald, Director of Financial Aid
207-741-5500 Fax: 207-741-5671
Website: www.smccme.edu
E-mail: oharmon@maine.rr.com

MASSACHUSETTS

North Shore Community College
1 Ferncroft Rd, Danvers MA 01923-4093
Jennifer Kirk, Director of Admissions & Recruitment Outreach
978-762-4000 Fax: 978-762-4015
Website: www.northshore.edu
E-mail: jkirk@northshore.edu

NORTH CAROLINA

Haywood Community College
185 Freedlander Dr, Clyde NC 28721
Debbie Rowland, Coordinator of Admissions
828-627-4500 Fax: 828-627-4513
Website: www.haywood.edu
E-mail: drowland@haywood.edu

Mayland Community College
PO Box 547, Spruce Pine NC 28777-0547
Cathy B. Morrison, Director of Enrollment Management
828-765-7351 Fax: 828-765-0728
Website: www.mayland.edu
E-mail: cmorrison@mayland.edu

OHIO

The Ohio State University
Austin E. Knowlton School of Architecture
Knowlton Arch Bldg, 275 W Woodruff Ave
Columbus OH 43210
614-292-1012 Fax: 614-292-7106
Website: knowlton.osu.edu
E-mail: ugadvisor@knowlton.osu.edu

Owens Community College
PO Box 10000, Toledo OH 43699-1947
William J. Ivoska, Ph.D, Vice President of Student Services
567-661-7000 Fax: 567-661-7607
Website: www.owens.edu
E-mail: admissions@owens.edu

OKLAHOMA

Oklahoma State University
Stillwater OK 74078
Dale Maronek, Department Head
405-744-5414
Website: www.okstate.edu
E-mail: dale.maronek@okstate.edu

TEXAS

University of Houston
122 E Cullen Bldg, Houston TX 77204-2023
Office of Admission
713-743-9595
Website: www.uh.edu
E-mail: admissions@uh.edu

University of Texas at Arlington
Box 19111, Arlington TX 76019-0111
Hans Gatterdam, Director of Admission
817-272-6287 Fax: 817-272-3435
Website: www.uta.edu
E-mail: admissions@uta.edu

LAW

ALABAMA

Judson College
302 Bibb St, Marion AL 36756
Michael Scotto, Director of Admissions
800-447-9472 Fax: 334-683-5147
Website: www.judson.edu
E-mail: admissions@judson.edu

CALIFORNIA

Chapman University
One University Drive, Orange CA 92866-1099
Michael Drummy, Assistant Vice President for Enrollment
Services and Chief Admission Officer
714-997-6411 or 888-CUAPPLY Fax: 714-997-6713
Website: www.chapman.edu
E-mail: admit@chapman.edu

Fremont College
18000 Studebaker Rd Suite 900, Cerritos CA 90703
Mark Buch, President & COO
562-809-5100 Fax: 562-809-7100
Website: www.fremont.edu
E-mail: senon.lee@fremont.edu

John F. Kennedy University
100 Ellinwood Way, Pleasant Hill CA 94523-4817
800-696-5358
Website: www.jfku.edu

Point Loma Nazarene University
3900 Lomaland Dr, San Diego CA 92106-2810
Chip Killingsworth, Director of Undergraduate Admissions
800-733-7770 Fax: 619-849-2601
Website: www.pointloma.edu
E-mail: admissions@pointloma.edu

COLORADO

Everest College
Aurora Campus
14280 E Jewell Ave, Aurora CO 80012-5692
John Heckman, Director of Admissions
303-367-2757 Fax: 303-745-6245
Website: www.cci.edu

Kaplan College
500 E 84th Ave Suite W200
Thornton CO 80229-5316
Michael Como, Director of Admissions
800-848-0550 Fax: 303-295-0102
Website: www.kaplancollege.com
E-mail: admissions-045@kaplan.edu

CONNECTICUT

Branford Hall Career Institute
1 Summit Pl, Branford CT 06405
800-959-7599
Website: www.branfordhall.com

Branford Hall Career Institute
35 N Main St, Southington CT 06489-2577
860-276-0600
Website: www.branfordhall.com

Branford Hall Career Institute
995 Day Hill Rd, Windsor CT 06095-1722
860-683-4900
Website: www.branfordhall.com

DELAWARE

Wesley College
120 N State St, Dover DE 19901-3876
302-736-2300 Fax: 302-736-2301
Website: www.wesley.edu

FLORIDA

City College
2000 W Commercial Blvd, Fort Lauderdale FL 33309
Mercedes Segal, Director of Admissions
954-492-5353 Fax: 954-491-1965
Website: www.citycollege.edu

Florida State University
600 W College Ave, Tallahassee FL 32306-1096
Janice V. Finney, Director of Admissions
850-644-2525 Fax: 850-644-0197
Website: admissions.fsu.edu
E-mail: admissions@admin.fsu.edu

Key College
225 E Dania Beach Blvd #130
Dania Beach FL 33004
Ronald Dooley, President
954-923-4440 Fax: 954-923-9226
Website: www.keycollege.edu
E-mail: admissions@keycollege.edu

St. Thomas University
16401 NW 37th Ave, Miami Gardens FL 33054
Dr Gary Feinberg, Contact
800-367-9010 or 305-628-6546 Fax: 305-628-6591
Website: www.stu.edu
E-mail: signup@stu.edu

SOUTHWEST FLORIDA COLLEGE
1685 Medical Ln, Fort Myers FL 33907-1157
866-SWFC-NOW or 239-939-4766 Fax: 239-936-4040
Website: www.swfc.edu
E-mail: studentinfo@swfc.edu

IDAHO

University of Idaho
Moscow ID 83844-4253
Lloyd Scott, Director of New Student Services
208-885-6163 Fax: 208-885-4477
Website: www.uidaho.edu
E-mail: nss@uidaho.edu

ILLINOIS

Illinois Institute of Technology
Chicago-Kent College of Law
565 W Adams St, Chicago IL 60661-3601
Nicole Vilches, Assistant Dean for Admissions
312-906-5000 Fax: 312-906-5274
Website: www.kentlaw.edu
E-mail: admit@kentlaw.edu

Roosevelt University
430 S Michigan Ave, Chicago IL 60605
Gwen E. Kanelos, Asst. Vice President for Enrollment Services
877-APPLY-RU Fax: 312-341-4216
Website: www.roosevelt.edu
E-mail: applyru@roosevelt.edu

IOWA

Briar Cliff University
PO Box 2100, Sioux City IA 51104-0100
Sharisue Wilcoxon, VP for Enrollment Management
712-279-5200 Fax: 712-279-1632
Website: www.briarcliff.edu
E-mail: admissions@briarcliff.edu

Iowa Lakes Community College
300 S 18th St, Estherville IA 51334-2721
Anne Stansbury, Asst. Director of Admissions
712-362-7945 Fax: 712-362-8363
Website: www.iowalakes.edu
E-mail: info@iowalakes.edu

KENTUCKY

BROWN MACKIE COLLEGE
Northern Kentucky Campus
309 Buttermilk Pike, Fort Mitchell KY 41017-2191
Joanne Dellefield, Director of Admissions
859-341-5627 Fax: 859-341-6483
Website: www.brownmackie.edu
E-mail: jdellefield@brownmackie.edu

Daymar College
4400 Breckenridge Ln #415, Louisville KY 40218
Shawn McDaniel, Director of Admissions
502-495-1040 Fax: 502-495-1518
Website: www.daymarcollege.com

Daymar College
3361 Buckland Sq, Owensboro KY 42301-5830
Vickie McDougal Director of Admissions
800-960-4090 Fax: 270-685-4090
Website: www.daymarcollege.com

MARYLAND

Kaplan College
Hagerstown Campus
18618 Crestwood Dr, Hagerstown MD 21742-2797
W. Christopher Motz, President
Steve Shinham, Director of Admissions
800-422-2670 Fax: 301-739-0474
Website: www.hagerstownbusinesscol.edu

MASSACHUSETTS

Anna Maria College
50 Sunset Ln, Paxton MA 01612
Timothy M. Donahue, Director of Recruitment and Admissions
508-849-3360 Fax: 508-849-3362
Website: www.annamaria.edu
E-mail: admissions@annamaria.edu

Becker College
Campuses in Worcester and Leicester, MA
61 Sever St, Worcester MA 01609-2165
Karen Schedin, Dean of Admissions
508-791-9241 Fax: 508-890-1500
Website: www.becker.edu
E-mail: admissions@becker.edu
See listing under "Universities"

Boston University
121 Bay State Rd, Boston MA 02215
Kelly Walter, Executive Director of Admissions
617-353-2300 Fax: 617-353-9695
Website: web.bu.edu
E-mail: admissions@bu.edu

MASSACHUSETTS SCHOOL OF LAW AT ANDOVER
500 Federal St, Andover MA 01810
Paula Colby-Clements, Esq, Director of Admissions
978-681-0800 Fax: 978-681-6330
Website: www.mslaw.edu
E-mail: pcolby@mslaw.edu

NEW ENGLAND SCHOOL OF LAW
154 Stuart St, Boston MA 02116-5616
Michelle C. L'Etoile, Director of Admissions
617-422-7210 Fax: 617-457-3033
Website: www.nesl.edu
E-mail: admit@admin.nesl.edu

Worcester Polytechnic Institute
100 Institute Rd, Worcester MA 01609-2280
Edward J. Connor, Director of Admissions
508-831-5286 Fax: 508-831-5875
Website: admissions.wpi.edu
E-mail: admissions@wpi.edu

MICHIGAN

MACOMB COMMUNITY COLLEGE
44575 Garfield Rd, Clinton Township MI 48038-1139
Information Center
586-445-7999
Website: www.macomb.edu
E-mail: answer@macomb.edu

MICHIGAN STATE UNIVERSITY COLLEGE OF LAW
230 Law College Bldg, East Lansing MI 48824
Cory Burke, Assistant Director of Admissions
517-432-0222 Fax: 517-432-0098
Website: www.law.msu.edu
E-mail: burkecor@msu.edu

MISSOURI

Stephens College
PO Box 2121, Columbia MO 65215-0001
David Adams, Dean of Enrollment Management
573-442-2211 Fax: 573-876-7237
Website: www.stephens.edu
E-mail: dadams@stephens.edu

Truman State University
100 E Normal, Kirksville MO 63501
Office of Admission
660-785-4114 Fax: 660-785-7456
Website: admissions.truman.edu
E-mail: admissions@truman.edu

William Woods University
1 University Ave, Fulton MO 65251-1098
Jimmy Clay, Director of Admissions
573-642-2251 Fax: 573-592-1146
Website: www.williamwoods.edu
E-mail: admissions@williamwoods.edu
See listing under "Universities"

NEVADA

Career College of Northern Nevada
1195-A Corporate Blvd, Reno NV 89502-2331
Nathan Clark, Director
775-856-2266 Fax: 775-856-0935
Website: www.ccnn.edu
E-mail: lgoldhammer@ccnn4u.com
See listing under "Career Schools"

NEW JERSEY

New Jersey City University
2039 John F Kennedy Blvd
Jersey City NJ 07305-1588
Carmen Panlilio, Asst. V.P. for Admissions and Financial Aid
201-200-3234 Fax: 201-200-2044
Website: www.njcu.edu
E-mail: admissions@njcu.edu

RICHARD STOCKTON COLLEGE OF NEW JERSEY
PO Box 195, Pomona NJ 08240
John Iacovelli, Dean of Enrollment Management
866-RSC-2885 Fax: 609-626-5541
Website: www.stockton.edu
E-mail: admissions@stockton.edu

Stockton College is a comprehensive liberal arts, co-ed institution founded in 1969. Advance Pre-Professional Degree Options: 7-yr BS/MD with UMDNJ; NJ Dental School; NJ Medical School, Robert Wood Johnson Medical, School of Osteopathic Medicine; NY College of Podiatric Medicine, Pennsylvania College of Podiatric Medicine, SUNY College of Optometry. Pharmacy doctorate program with Rutgers University. 5-yr Engineering with NJIT and Rutgers University. Dual BA/MA in Criminal Justice. 5-yr BS/MS in Computational Science. BS/MS in Nursing. Doctorate of Physical Therapy. Additional Programs: Forensic Science, Pre-Law, Pre-Occupational Therapy, and Pre-Veterinary.

NEW YORK

ALBANY LAW SCHOOL OF UNION UNIVERSITY
80 New Scotland Ave, Albany NY 12208-3494
Gail Bensen, Director of Admissions
518-445-2326 Fax: 518-445-2369
Website: www.albanylaw.edu
E-mail: admissions@albanylaw.edu

College of Saint Rose
432 Western Ave, Albany NY 12203-1419
Maryelizabeth Amico, Asst V.P. for Undergraduate Admissions
518-454-5150 Fax: 518-454-2013
Website: www.strose.edu
E-mail: admit@strose.edu

Hilbert College
5200 S Park Ave, Hamburg NY 14075-1597
Timothy Lee, Director of Admissions
716-649-7900 Fax: 716-649-0702
Website: www.hilbert.edu
E-mail: tlee@hilbert.edu

Ridley-Lowell Business & Technical Institute
116 Front St, Binghamton NY 13905-3102
David Lounsbury, Executive Director
607-724-2941 Fax: 607-724-0799
Website: www.ridley.edu
E-mail: info@ridley.edu

Roberts Wesleyan College
2301 Westside Dr, Rochester NY 14624-1997
Office of Admissions
585-594-6400 Fax: 585-594-6371
Website: www.roberts.edu
E-mail: admissions@roberts.edu

St. John's University
8000 Utopia Pkwy, Queens NY 11439
Office of Admission
877-STJ-5550 ext. 101 Fax: 718-990-2096
Website: www.stjohns.edu/learnmore
E-mail: admhelp@stjohns.edu
See listing under "Universities"

NORTH CAROLINA

Salem College
Winston Salem NC 27108
Dana Evans, Dean of Admissions/Fin. Aid
800-32-SALEM Fax: 336-917-5572
Website: www.salem.edu
E-mail: admissions@salem.edu
See listing under "Women's Colleges"

South College
29 Turtle Creek Dr, Asheville NC 28803
Robert Davis, Dean of Academic Affairs
828-277-5521 Fax: 828-277-6151
Website: southcollegenc.com
E-mail: bdavis@southcollegenc.com

OHIO

Brown Mackie College - Cincinnati
1011 Glendale Milford Rd, Cincinnati OH 45215-1107
Robin Krout, President
513-771-2424 Fax: 513-771-3413
Website: www.brownmackie.edu
E-mail: rkrout@brownmackie.edu

Cleveland State University
2121 Euclid Ave RW 204, Cleveland OH 44115
Dr. Richard Arndt, Dean of Undergraduate Recruitment and College Partnerships
888-CSU-OHIO Fax: 216-687-9210
Website: www.csuohio.edu
E-mail: admissions@csuohio.edu

OHIO NORTHERN UNIVERSITY
525 S Main St, Ada OH 45810-1555
Dr. David Crago, Dean
419-772-2205
Website: www.onu.edu
See listing under "Universities"

The Ohio State University
Moritz College of Law
Drinko Hall, 55 W 12th Ave, Columbus OH 43210
614-292-8810 Fax: 614-292-1492
Website: moritzlaw.osu.edu
E-mail: lawadmit@osu.edu

University of Dayton
300 College Park, Dayton OH 45469-2760
Janet Hein, Assistant Dean and Director of Admission and Financial Aid
937-229-3555 Fax: 937-229-4194
Website: law.udayton.edu
E-mail: lawinfo@notes.udayton.edu

Ursuline College
2550 Lander Rd, Cleveland OH 44124-4398
Sarah E. Sundermeier, Director of Admissions
888-URSULINE Toll Free Fax: 440-684-6138
Website: www.admission.ursuline.edu
E-mail: admission@ursuline.edu

OKLAHOMA

University of Tulsa
600 S College Ave, Tulsa OK 74104-3126
Earl Johnson, Dean of Admission
918-631-2307 Fax: 918-631-5003
Website: www.utulsa.edu
E-mail: admission@utulsa.edu

PENNSYLVANIA

Berks Technical Institute
2205 Ridgewood Rd, Wyomissing PA 19610-1168
Elizabeth Wade, Director of Admissions
610-372-1722 Fax: 610-376-4684
Website: www.berkstech.com

Juniata College
1700 Moore St, Huntingdon PA 16652-2196
Michelle Bartol, Dean of Enrollment
877-JUNIATA Fax: 814-641-3100
Website: www.juniata.edu
E-mail: admissions@juniata.edu

KEYSTONE TECHNICAL INSTITUTE
2301 Academy Dr, Harrisburg PA 17112-1012
Tom Bogush, Director of Admissions
717-545-4747 Fax: 717-901-9090
Website: www.acadcampus.com
E-mail: educdir@acadcampus.com

Established 1980. Private. Coed. Accreditation: ACCSCT. Enrollment: 210 full-time, 50 part-time. Faculty: 15. Student-faculty ratio: 20:1. Degrees offered: Occupational Associate Degrees (AST/ASB). Library: 2,000 volumes. 1 building on 8 acres. Combined classroom; real world lab experience and externships for career training in Medical Assistant, Dental Assistant, Massage Therapy, Paralegal, Culinary Arts, Child Care, Computers.

MOUNT ALOYSIUS COLLEGE
7373 Admiral Peary Hwy, Cresson PA 16630-1999
Frank C. Crouse Jr., Vice President for Enrollment Management
814-886-6383 or 888-823-2220 Fax: 814-886-6441
Website: www.mtaloy.edu
E-mail: admissions@mtaloy.edu

Neumann College
1 Neumann Dr, Aston PA 19014-1298
Dennis Murphy, Director of Admissions
610-459-0905 Fax: 610-558-5652
Website: www.neumann.edu
E-mail: neumann@neumann.edu

Widener University
1 University Pl, Chester PA 19013-5792
Edwin Wright, Dean of Admissions
610-499-4000 Fax: 610-499-4676
Website: www.widener.edu
E-mail: admissions.office@widener.edu

SOUTH CAROLINA

Forrest Junior College
601 E River St, Anderson SC 29624-2405
Pamela Johnson, MBA, President
864-225-7653 Fax: 864-261-7471
Website: www.forrestcollege.edu
E-mail: info@forrestcollege.edu
Paralegal Studies.
See listing under "Community and Junior Colleges"

South University
9 Science Court, Columbia SC 29203
Trish Wade, Contact
803-799-9082 Fax: 803-799-9038
Website: www.southuniversity.edu
E-mail: twade@southuniversity.edu

SOUTH DAKOTA

NATIONAL AMERICAN UNIVERSITY
321 Kansas City St, Rapid City SD 57701-3692
Angela G. Beck, Director of Enrollment Management
605-394-4800 Fax: 605-394-4871
Website: www.rapid.national.edu
E-mail: rcadmissions@national.edu

Western Dakota Technical Institute
800 Mickelson Dr, Rapid City SD 57703-4018
Jill Elder, Admissions Coordinator
605-394-4034 Fax: 605-394-2204
Website: www.wdt.edu
E-mail: jill.elder@wdt.edu

TENNESSEE

Miller-Motte Technical College
1820 Business Park Dr, Clarksville TN 37040-6023
Lisa Teague, Director of Admissions
931-553-0071 Fax: 931-552-2916
Website: www.miller-motte.com
E-mail: lteague@miller-motte.com

TEXAS

Abilene Christian University
ACU Box 29000, Abilene TX 79699-0001
325-674-2000 Fax: 325-674-2202
Website: www.acu.edu
E-mail: info@admissions.acu.edu

CENTER FOR ADVANCED LEGAL STUDIES
3910 Kirby Dr Ste 200, Houston TX 77098-4151
Doyle Happa, Director
713-529-2778 Fax: 713-523-2715
Website: www.paralegal.edu
E-mail: info@paralegal.edu

SOUTHEASTERN CAREER INSTITUTE
12005 Ford Rd Suite 100, Dallas TX 75234-7288
972-385-1446 or 800-524-8800 Fax: 972-385-0641
Website: www.southeasterncareerinstitute.com

University of Houston
122 E Cullen Bldg, Houston TX 77204-2023
Office of Admission
713-743-9595
Website: www.uh.edu
E-mail: admissions@uh.edu

UTAH

ITT TECHNICAL INSTITUTE
920 Levoy Dr, Murray UT 84123-2500
Gary Wood, Director of Recruitment
801-263-3313 Fax: 801-263-3497
Website: www.itt-tech.edu
E-mail: gwood@itt-tech.edu

VERMONT

Green Mountain College
1 College Cir, Poultney VT 05764-1199
Sandra Bartholomew, Ph.D., Dean of Enrollment Management
802-287-8000 Fax: 802-287-8099
Website: www.greenmtn.edu
E-mail: bartholomews@greenmtn.edu

Woodbury College
660 Elm St, Montpelier VT 05602-4017
Denise MacMartin, Director of Admissions
800-639-6039 Fax: 802-229-2141
Website: www.woodbury-college.edu
E-mail: admiss@woodbury-college.edu

VIRGINIA

APPALACHIAN SCHOOL OF LAW
PO Box 2825, Grundy VA 24614-1825
Nancy Pruitt, Director of Student Services
800-895-7411 Fax: 276-935-8261
Website: www.asl.edu
E-mail: npruitt@asl.edu

Bryant & Stratton College
8141 Hull St Rd, Richmond VA 23235-6411
David K. Mayle, Director of Admissions
804-745-2444 Fax: 804-745-6884
Website: www.bryantstratton.edu
E-mail: dkmayle@bryantstratton.edu

WASHINGTON

CROWN COLLEGE
8739 S Hosmer St, Tacoma WA 98444-1836
John Wabel, CEO
253-531-3123 Fax: 253-531-3521
Website: www.crowncollege.edu
E-mail: jwabel@crowncollege.edu

WEST VIRGINIA

Mountain State College
1508 Spring St, Parkersburg WV 26101-3993
Judith Sutton, Director
304-485-5487 Fax: 304-485-3524
Website: www.mountainstate.org
E-mail: admin@mountainstate.org
See listing under "Career Schools"

WISCONSIN

Herzing College
5218 E Terrace Dr, Madison WI 53718-8340
Donald Madelung, President
800-582-1227 Fax: 608-249-8593
Website: www.herzing.edu
E-mail: info@msn.herzing.edu
See listing under "Universities"

Marquette University
PO Box 1881, Milwaukee WI 53201-1881
Robert Blust, Director of Admissions
414-288-7302 Fax: 414-288-3764
Website: www.mu.edu
E-mail: admissions@marquette.edu

St. Norbert College
100 Grant St, De Pere WI 54115
Brian Studebaker, Director of Admission
800-236-4878 Fax: 920-403-4072
Website: www.snc.edu
E-mail: admit@snc.edu

WYOMING

University of Wyoming
Admissions Office
Dept 3435, Laramie WY 82071-3435
Brooke Culver, Contact
800-342-5996 Fax: 307-766-4042
Website: www.uwyo.edu
E-mail: why-wyo@uwyo.edu

LETTERS

ALABAMA

Bishop State Community College - Four Campuses
351 N Broad St, Mobile AL 36603-5898
Dr. Terry Hazzard, Dean of Students
251-690-6801 Fax: 251-690-6446
Website: www.bishop.edu
E-mail: thazzard@bishop.edu

University of South Alabama
307 University Blvd N, Mobile AL 36688-3053
Melissa Haab, Director of Admissions
251-460-6141 Fax: 251-460-7876
Website: www.southalabama.edu
E-mail: admiss@usouthal.edu

ARIZONA

Pima Community College
4905 E Broadway Blvd, Tucson AZ 85709-1010
Wendy Kilgore, Ph.D., Director of Admissions
520-206-4500 Fax: 520-206-4790
Website: www.pima.edu
E-mail: infocenter@pima.edu

CALIFORNIA

Antioch University Southern California
400 Corporate Pointe, Culver City CA 90230-7615
Admissions Office
800-7-ANTIOCH Fax: 310-821-6032
E-mail: admissions@antiochla.edu
Master of Fine Arts in Creative Writing.

Butte College
3536 Butte Campus Dr, Oroville CA 95965-8399
Carole Gish, Director of Admissions
530-895-2511 Fax: 530-879-4313
Website: www.butte.edu
E-mail: admissions@butte.edu

California State University-San Bernadino
5500 University Pkwy
San Bernardino CA 92407-2393
Olivia Rosas, Director of Admissions
909-537-5188 Fax: 909-537-7034
Website: www.csusb.edu
E-mail: orosas@csusb.edu

Chapman University
One University Drive, Orange CA 92866-1099
Michael Drummy, Assistant Vice President for Enrollment
Services and Chief Admission Officer
714-997-6411 or 888-CUAPPLY Fax: 714-997-6713
Website: www.chapman.edu
E-mail: admit@chapman.edu

FRESNO CITY COLLEGE
1101 E University Ave, Fresno CA 93741-0002
Dayann Dietrich, Contact
559-442-8241 Fax: 559-237-4232
Website: www.fresnocitycollege.com
E-mail: fcc.admissions@scccd.com

New College School of Law
50 Fell St, San Francisco CA 94102-5206
Sharon Pittman, Dean of Admissions
415-241-1300 Fax: 415-241-9525
Website: www.newcollege.edu
E-mail: spittman@newcollege.edu or lawadmissions@newcollege.edu

San Diego Christian College
2100 Greenfield Dr, El Cajon CA 92019-1157
Rene Inman, Director of Admissions
800-676-2242 Fax: 619-590-1739
Website: www.sdcc.edu
E-mail: admissions@sdcc.edu

Whittier College
PO Box 634, Whittier CA 90608-0634
Kieron Miller, Director of Admissions
562-907-4200 Fax: 562-907-4870
Website: www.whittier.edu
E-mail: kmiller@whittier.edu

DELAWARE

Wesley College
120 N State St, Dover DE 19901-3876
302-736-2300 Fax: 302-736-2301
Website: www.wesley.edu

FLORIDA

Florida State University
600 W College Ave, Tallahassee FL 32306-1096
Janice V. Finney, Director of Admissions
850-644-2525 Fax: 850-644-0197
Website: admissions.fsu.edu
E-mail: admissions@admin.fsu.edu

St. Thomas University
16401 NW 37th Ave, Miami Gardens FL 33054
Andre Lightbourn, Director of Admissions
800-367-9010 or 305-628-6546 Fax: 305-628-6591
Website: www.stu.edu
E-mail: signup@stu.edu

University of South Florida
4202 E Fowler Ave, Tampa FL 33620-6900
J. Robert Spatig, Director of Admissions
877-USF-BULL Fax: 813-974-9689
Website: www.usf.edu
E-mail: admissions@admin.usf.edu
See listing under "Universities"

GEORGIA

Armstrong Atlantic State University
11935 Abercorn St, Savannah GA 31419-1997
Kim West, Asst. Dean and Registrar Enrollment Services
912-927-5277 Fax: 912-921-5462
Website: www.armstrong.edu
E-mail: admissions@mail.armstrong.edu

ILLINOIS

Columbia College Chicago
600 S Michigan Ave, Chicago IL 60605-1996
Murphy Monroe, Executive Director of Admissions
312-344-7130 Fax: 312-344-8024
Website: www.colum.edu
E-mail: admissions@colum.edu

Roosevelt University
430 S Michigan Ave, Chicago IL 60605
Gwen E. Kanelos, Asst. Vice President for Enrollment Services
877-APPLY-RU Fax: 312-341-4216
Website: www.roosevelt.edu
E-mail: applyru@roosevelt.edu

Trinity International University
2065 Half Day Rd, Deerfield IL 60015-1241
847-945-8800 Fax: 847-317-8097
Website: www.tiu.edu
E-mail: tcadmissions@tiu.edu

INDIANA

Franklin College
101 Branigin Blvd, Franklin IN 46131
Jacqueline S. Acosta, Director of Admissions
800-852-0232 Fax: 317-738-8274
Website: www.franklincollege.edu
E-mail: admissions@franklincollege.edu

Oakland City University
138 N Lucretia St, Oakland City IN 47660
Brian J. Baker, Director of Admissions
800-737-5125 Fax: 812-749-1433
Website: www.oak.edu
E-mail: bbaker@oak.edu
See listing under "Universities"

IOWA

Clarke College
1550 Clarke Dr, Dubuque IA 52001-3198
Andy Schroeder, Director of Admissions
800-383-2345 Fax: 563-584-8666
Website: www.clarke.edu
E-mail: andy.schroeder@clarke.edu

KANSAS

COLBY COMMUNITY COLLEGE
1255 S Range Ave, Colby KS 67701-4099
Director of Admissions
888-634-9350 or 785-460-4690 Fax: 785-460-4691
Website: www.colbycc.edu
E-mail: admissions@colbycc.edu

KENTUCKY

Morehead State University
Morehead KY 40351-1689
Jeffrey Liles, Enrollment Services
800-585-6781 Fax: 606-783-5038
Website: www.moreheadstate.edu
E-mail: admissions@moreheadstate.edu

Transylvania University
300 N Broadway, Lexington KY 40508-1776
859-233-8242 Fax: 859-233-8797
Website: www.transy.edu
E-mail: admissions@transy.edu

LOUISIANA

Our Lady of Holy Cross College
4123 Woodland Dr, New Orleans LA 70131-7399
Office of Enrollment Services
504-394-7744 Fax: 504-391-2421
Website: www.olhcc.edu

MASSACHUSETTS

Assumption College
500 Salisbury St, Worcester MA 01609-1294
Kathleen Murphy, Dean of Enrollment
508-767-7000 Fax: 508-799-4412
Website: www.assumption.edu
E-mail: admiss@assumption.edu

Boston University
121 Bay State Rd, Boston MA 02215
Kelly Walter, Executive Director of Admissions
617-353-2300 Fax: 617-353-9695
Website: web.bu.edu
E-mail: admissions@bu.edu

Emerson College
120 Boylston St, Boston MA 02116-4624
Sara S. Ramirez, Director of Undergraduate Admission
617-824-8600 Fax: 617-824-8609
Website: www.emerson.edu
E-mail: admission@emerson.edu

University of Massachusetts Dartmouth
Old Westport Rd, North Dartmouth MA 02747-2300
Steven T. Briggs, Director of Admissions
508-999-8605 Fax: 508-999-8755
Website: explore.umassd.edu
E-mail: sbriggs@umassd.edu

MICHIGAN

Alma College
614 W Superior St, Alma MI 48801-1599
Evan Montague, Director of Admissions
800-321-ALMA Fax: 989-463-7057
Website: www.alma.edu
E-mail: admissions@alma.edu

HILLSDALE COLLEGE
33 E College St, Hillsdale MI 49242-1298
Dr. Michael Jordan, Director
517-607-2445 Fax: 517-607-2208
Website: www.hillsdale.edu
E-mail: michael.jordan@hillsdale.edu

Lake Superior State University
650 W Easterday Ave
Sault Sainte Marie MI 49783-1637
Susan Camp, Director of Admissions
888-800-LSSU Fax: 906-635-6696
Website: www.lssu.edu
E-mail: admissions@lssu.edu
See listing under "Universities"

Oakland University
2200 N Squirrel Rd, Rochester MI 48309
Eleanor L. Reynolds, Assistant Vice President & Director of Admissions
248-370-2100
Website: www.oakland.edu
E-mail: ouinfo@oakland.edu

MINNESOTA

Bethany Lutheran College
700 Luther Dr, Mankato MN 56001
Don Westphal, Dean of Admissions
507-344-7000 Fax: 507-344-7376
Website: www.blc.edu
E-mail: admiss@blc.edu

Carleton College
1 N College St, Northfield MN 55057-4044
800-995-2275 or 507-646-4190 Fax: 507-646-4526
Website: www.carleton.edu
E-mail: admissions@acs.carleton.edu

Gustavus Adolphus College
800 W College Ave, Saint Peter MN 56082-1485
Mark H. Anderson, Dean of Admission
800-GUSTAVUS Fax: 507-933-7474
Website: www.gustavus.edu
E-mail: admission@gustavus.edu

Pillsbury Baptist Bible College
315 S Grove Ave, Owatonna MN 55060-3097
Susanne Martin, Admissions Coordinator
507-451-2710 Fax: 507-451-0156
Website: www.pillsbury.edu
E-mail: admissions@pillsbury.edu

MISSISSIPPI

Tougaloo College
500 W County Line Rd, Tougaloo MS 39174-9799
Juno Leggette Jacobs, Director of Admissions
601-977-7768 Fax: 601-977-4501
Website: www.tougaloo.edu
E-mail: jjacobs@tougaloo.edu

MISSOURI

East Central College
1964 Prairie Dell Rd, Union MO 63084
Karen Wieda, Registrar
636-583-5195 ext. 2220 Fax: 636-583-1897
Website: www.eastcentral.edu
E-mail: wiedaks@eastcentral.edu

Lindenwood University
209 S Kingshighway St
Saint Charles MO 63301-1695
Sheryl Guffey, Director of Admissions
636-949-2000 Fax: 636-949-4989
Website: www.lindenwood.edu

Northwest Missouri State University
800 University Dr, Maryville MO 64468-6001
Beverly Schenkel, Dean of Enrollment Management
660-562-1562 Fax: 660-562-1121
Website: www.nwmissouri.edu
E-mail: admissions@nwmissouri.edu

Stephens College
PO Box 2121, Columbia MO 65215-0001
David Adams, Dean of Enrollment Management
573-442-2211 Fax: 573-876-7237
Website: www.stephens.edu
E-mail: dadams@stephens.edu

Truman State University
100 E Normal, Kirksville MO 63501
Office of Admission
660-785-4114 Fax: 660-785-7456
Website: admissions.truman.edu
E-mail: admissions@truman.edu

Webster University
470 E Lockwood Ave, Saint Louis MO 63119-3194
Dr. David Wilson, Dean, College of Arts and Sciences
314-968-7160 Fax: 314-968-7173
Website: www.webster.edu
E-mail: clewelow@webster.edu
See listing under "Universities"

William Jewell College
500 College Hill, Liberty MO 64068-1896
Dr. Rick Winslow, VP Enrollment Management and Student Affairs
800-753-7009 Fax: 816-415-5040
Website: www.jewell.edu
E-mail: winslowr@william.jewell.edu

William Woods University
1 University Ave, Fulton MO 65251-1098
Jimmy Clay, Director of Admissions
573-642-2251 Fax: 573-592-1146
Website: www.williamwoods.edu
E-mail: admissions@williamwoods.edu
See listing under "Universities"

MONTANA

Carroll College
1601 N Benton Ave, Helena MT 59625-0002
Dr. Thomas J. Trebon, President
Cynthia Thornquist, Director of Admissions & Enrollment Operations
406-447-4384 Fax: 406-447-4533
Website: www.carroll.edu
E-mail: admission@carroll.edu

NEBRASKA

Midland Lutheran College
900 N Clarkson St, Fremont NE 68025-4200
Todd Hansen, Associate Director of Admissions
402-941-6501 Fax: 402-941-6513
Website: www.mlc.edu
E-mail: admissions@mlc.edu

Nebraska Wesleyan University
5000 Saint Paul Ave, Lincoln NE 68504-2794
Patricia Karthauser, V.P. for University Enrollment
402-466-2371 Fax: 402-465-2177
Website: www.nebrwesleyan.edu
E-mail: admissions@nebrwesleyan.edu

NEW JERSEY

Bergen Community College
400 Paramus Rd, Paramus NJ 07652
Julian Gomez, Asst. Director of Admissions
201-447-7100 Fax: 201-444-7036
Website: www.bergen.edu
E-mail: jgomez@bergen.edu

New Jersey City University
2039 John F Kennedy Blvd
Jersey City NJ 07305-1588
Carmen Panlilio, Asst. V.P. for Admissions and Financial Aid
201-200-3234 Fax: 201-200-2044
Website: www.njcu.edu
E-mail: admissions@njcu.edu

Ramapo College of New Jersey
505 Ramapo Valley Rd, Mahwah NJ 07430-1623
Director of Admissions
201-684-7300 or 201-684-7301 Fax: 201-684-7964
Website: www.ramapo.edu
E-mail: admissions@ramapo.edu

NEW YORK

College of Saint Rose
432 Western Ave, Albany NY 12203-1419
Maryelizabeth Amico, Asst V.P. for Undergraduate Admissions
518-454-5150 Fax: 518-454-2013
Website: www.strose.edu
E-mail: admit@strose.edu

Hilbert College
5200 S Park Ave, Hamburg NY 14075-1597
Timothy Lee, Director of Admissions
716-649-7900 Fax: 716-649-0702
Website: www.hilbert.edu
E-mail: tlee@hilbert.edu

Molloy College
1000 Hempstead Ave
Rockville Centre NY 11570-1100
Marguerite Lane, Director of Admissions
516-678-5000 ext. 6291 Fax: 516-256-2247
Website: www.molloy.edu
E-mail: admissions@molloy.edu
See listing under "Universities"

Roberts Wesleyan College
2301 Westside Dr, Rochester NY 14624-1997
Office of Admissions
585-594-6400 Fax: 585-594-6371
Website: www.roberts.edu
E-mail: admissions@roberts.edu

St. Joseph's College
245 Clinton Ave, Brooklyn NY 11205-3688
Theresa LaRocca Meyer, V.P. for Enrollment Management
718-636-6800 Fax: 718-636-8303
Website: www.sjcny.edu
E-mail: tlaroccameyer@sjcny.edu

Siena College
515 Loudonville Rd, Loudonville NY 12211-1462
Heather Renault, Director of Admissions
518-783-2300 Fax: 518-783-2436
Website: www.siena.edu
E-mail: hrenault@siena.edu

SUNY College at Brockport
350 New Campus Dr, Brockport NY 14420-2997
Bernard S. Valento, Director of Undergraduate Admissions
585-395-2751 Fax: 585-395-5452
Website: www.brockport.edu
E-mail: admit@brockport.edu

SUNY Sullivan County Community College
112 College Rd, Loch Sheldrake NY 12759-5151
Sari Rosenheck, Director of Admissions
845-434-5750 Fax: 845-434-0923
Website: www.sullivan.suny.edu
E-mail: admissions@sullivan.suny.edu
Student Housing on Campus.

United States Military Academy West Point
646 Swift Rd, West Point NY 10996-1905
Colonel Michael L. Jones, Director of Admissions
845-938-4041 Fax: 845-938-8121
Website: admissions.usma.edu
E-mail: admissions@usma.edu

NORTH CAROLINA

Brevard College
One Brevard College Dr, Brevard NC 28712
Joretta Nelson, Vice President Enrollment Management
828-883-8292 Fax: 828-884-3790
Website: www.brevard.edu
E-mail: admissions@brevard.edu

Catawba College
2300 W Innes St, Salisbury NC 28144-2488
Dr. L. Russell Watjen, Ph.D., V.P. & Dean of Admissions
704-637-4402 Fax: 704-637-4222
Website: www.catawba.edu
E-mail: admission@catawba.edu

Chowan University
One University Pl, Murfreesboro NC 27855
Chad Holt, Dean of Admissions
800-488-4101 Fax: 252-398-1190
Website: www.chowan.edu
E-mail: holtc@chowan.edu

OHIO

Cleveland State University
2121 Euclid Ave RW 204, Cleveland OH 44115
Dr. Richard Arndt, Dean of Undergraduate Recruitment and College Partnerships
888-CSU-OHIO Fax: 216-687-9210
Website: www.csuohio.edu
E-mail: admissions@csuohio.edu

OKLAHOMA

University of Tulsa
600 S College Ave, Tulsa OK 74104-3126
Earl Johnson, Dean of Admission
918-631-2307 Fax: 918-631-5003
Website: www.utulsa.edu
E-mail: admission@utulsa.edu

OREGON

PACIFIC UNIVERSITY
2043 College Way, Forest Grove OR 97116-1797
Karen M. Dunston, Executive Director of Admissions
800-677-6712 Fax: 503-352-2975
Website: www.pacific.edu
E-mail: admissions@pacific.edu

University of Portland
5000 N Willamette Blvd, Portland OR 97203-5798
Jason McDonald, Dean of Admissions
503-943-7911 Fax: 503-943-7315
Website: www.up.edu
E-mail: mcdonaja@up.edu

Warner Pacific College
2219 SE 68th Ave, Portland OR 97215-4026
Shannon Mackey, Director of Admissions
503-517-1000 Fax: 503-517-1352
Website: www.warnerpacific.edu
E-mail: admissions@warnerpacific.edu

PENNSYLVANIA

· Community College of Allegheny County
Allegheny Campus: 808 Ridge Ave, Pittsburgh PA 15212 Admissions: 412.237.2700
Boyce Campus: 595 Beatty Rd, Monroeville PA 15146 Admissions: 724.325.6614
North Campus: 8701 Perry Highway, Pittsburgh PA 15237 Admissions: 412.369.3600
South Campus: 1750 Clairton Rd, West Mifflin PA 15122 Admissions: 412-469-4301
Website: www.ccac.edu

Delaware Valley College
700 E Butler Ave, Doylestown PA 18901-2697
Stephen W. Zenko, Director of Admissions
800-2DE-LVAL Fax: 215-230-2968
Website: www.delval.edu
E-mail: stephenzenko@delval.edu

DeSales University
2755 Station Ave, Center Valley PA 18034-9565
610-282-1100 Fax: 610-282-2342
Website: www.desales.edu

Haverford College
370 Lancaster Ave, Haverford PA 19041-1392
Jess Lord, Dean of Admission
610-896-1350 Fax: 610-896-1338
Website: www.haverford.edu
E-mail: admission@haverford.edu

Juniata College
1700 Moore St, Huntingdon PA 16652-2196
Michelle Bartol, Dean of Enrollment
877-JUNIATA Fax: 814-641-3100
Website: www.juniata.edu
E-mail: admissions@juniata.edu

King's College
133 N River St, Wilkes Barre PA 18711-0801
Michelle Lawrence-Schmude, Dean of Admission
570-208-5900 Fax: 570-208-5971
Website: www.kings.edu
E-mail: admissions@kings.edu

MOUNT ALOYSIUS COLLEGE
7373 Admiral Peary Hwy, Cresson PA 16630-1999
Frank C. Crouse Jr., Vice President for Enrollment Management
814-886-6383 or 888-823-2220 Fax: 814-886-6441
Website: www.mtaloy.edu
E-mail: admissions@mtaloy.edu

Neumann College
1 Neumann Dr, Aston PA 19014-1298
Dennis Murphy, Director of Admissions
610-459-0905 Fax: 610-558-5652
Website: www.neumann.edu
E-mail: neumann@neumann.edu

Widener University
1 University Pl, Chester PA 19013-5792
Edwin Wright, Dean of Admissions
610-499-4000 Fax: 610-499-4676
Website: www.widener.edu
E-mail: admissions.office@widener.edu

SOUTH CAROLINA

University of South Carolina - Upstate
800 University Way, Spartanburg SC 29303-4932
Donette Stewart, Assistant VC for Enrollment Services
864-503-5246 Fax: 864-503-5727
Website: www.uscupstate.edu
E-mail: dstewart@uscupstate.edu
See listing under "Universities"

TENNESSEE

Austin Peay State University
601 College St, Clarksville TN 37044-0002
931-221-7011 Fax: 931-221-6168
Website: www.apsu.edu
E-mail: admissions@apsu.edu

Lipscomb University
3901 Granny White Pike, Nashville TN 37204-3951
Ricky Holaway, Director of Admissions
800-333-4358 ext. 1776 Fax: 615-269-1804
Website: www.lipscomb.edu
E-mail: admissions@lipscomb.edu

· Southwest Tennessee Community College
5983 Macon Cove, Memphis TN 38134
Vanessa R. Dowdy, Director of Admissions
901-333-5000 Fax: 901-333-4523
Website: www.southwest.tn.edu
E-mail: vdowdy@southwest.tn.edu

University of Tennessee
615 McCallie Ave, Chattanooga TN 37403-2504
Yancy Freeman, Director of Admissions
423-425-4111 Fax: 423-425-4157
Website: www.utc.edu
E-mail: Yancy-Freeman@utc.edu

TEXAS

· Galveston College
4015 Avenue Q, Galveston TX 77550-7496
Brian Lowery, Registrar
409-763-6551 Fax: 409-944-1501
Website: www.gc.edu
E-mail: blowery@gc.edu

· Temple College
2600 S 1st St, Temple TX 76504-7435
Toni Borras, Director of Admissions & Records
254-298-8808 Fax: 254-298-8288
Website: www.templejc.edu
E-mail: admissionsrecords@templejc.edu

· Tyler Junior College
PO Box 9020, Tyler TX 75711-9020
Joel Renaud, Director of Enrollment Management
800-687-5680
Website: www.tjc.edu
E-mail: jren@tjc.edu
See listing under "Community and Junior Colleges"

University of Dallas
1845 E Northgate Dr, Irving TX 75062-4736
Curt Eley, Dean
972-721-5000 Fax: 972-721-5017
Website: www.udallas.edu
E-mail: ugadmis@udallas.edu

· Weatherford College
225 College Park Dr, Weatherford TX 76086
Dr. Joe Birmingham, President
800-287-5471 Fax: 817-598-6205
Website: www.wc.edu
E-mail: willingham@wc.edu

VIRGINIA

Marymount University
2807 N Glebe Rd, Arlington VA 22207-4299
Michael Canfield, Director of Admissions
800-548-7638 Fax: 703-522-0348
Website: www.marymount.edu
E-mail: admissions@marymount.edu

Radford University
PO Box 6903, Radford VA 24142
David W. Kraus, Director of Admissions
800-890-4265 Fax: 540-831-5038
Website: www.radford.edu
E-mail: ruadmiss@radford.edu

Randolph College
2500 Rivermont Ave, Lynchburg VA 24503
Patricia LeDonne, Director of Admissions
434-947-8100 Fax: 434-947-8996
Website: www.randolphcollege.edu
E-mail: admissions@randolphcollege.edu

Roanoke College
221 College Ln, Salem VA 24153-3794
James A. Pennix, Director of Admissions
540-375-2500 Fax: 540-375-2267
Website: www.roanoke.edu
E-mail: pennix@roanoke.edu

WISCONSIN

Alverno College
PO Box 343922, Milwaukee WI 53234-3922
Dianna Gaebler, Director of Admissions
414-382-6100 Fax: 414-382-6354
Website: www.alverno.edu
E-mail: admissions@alverno.edu

Lakeland College
PO Box 359, Sheboygan WI 53082-0359
Nathan Dehne, Director of Admission
920-565-1100 Fax: 920-565-1215
Website: www.lakeland.edu
E-mail: admissions@lakeland.edu

Marquette University
PO Box 1881, Milwaukee WI 53201-1881
Robert Blust, Director of Admissions
414-288-7302 Fax: 414-288-3764
Website: www.mu.edu
E-mail: admissions@marquette.edu

St. Norbert College
100 Grant St, De Pere WI 54115
Brian Studebaker, Director of Admission
800-236-4878 Fax: 920-403-4072
Website: www.snc.edu
E-mail: admit@snc.edu

WYOMING

· Laramie County Community College
1400 E College Dr, Cheyenne WY 82007-3204
Jenny Hargett, Director of Admissions
307-778-5222 Fax: 307-778-1350
Website: www.lccc.wy.edu
E-mail: learnmore@lccc.wy.edu

LIBERAL ARTS AND SCIENCES

ALABAMA

Alabama A & M University
PO Box 908, Normal AL 35762
Antonio Boyle, Director of Admissions
256-372-5245

· Bishop State Community College - Four Campuses
351 N Broad St, Mobile AL 36603-5898
Dr. Terry Hazzard, Dean of Students
251-690-6801 Fax: 251-690-6446
Website: www.bishop.edu
E-mail: thazzard@bishop.edu

· **CALHOUN COMMUNITY COLLEGE**
PO Box 2216, Decatur AL 35609-2216
M. Wayne Tosh, Registrar
256-306-2500 Fax: 256-306-2941
Website: www.calhoun.edu
E-mail: rds@calhoun.edu

CONCORDIA COLLEGE
1804 Green St, Selma AL 36703
Evelyn Pickens, Director of Enrollment Management and Placement
334-874-5700 Fax: 334-874-3728
Website: www.cuis.edu/www/cus/cual.html
E-mail: epickens@concordiaselma.edu

Faulkner University
5345 Atlanta Hwy, Montgomery AL 36109-3398
Keith Mock, Director of Admissions
800-879-9816 ext. 7200

· George C. Wallace State Community College
PO Box 2530, Selma AL 36702-2530
Mrs. Donitha J. Griffin, Dean of Students
334-876-9295 Fax: 334-876-9300
Website: www.wccs.edu
E-mail: dgriffin@wccs.edu

Huntingdon College
1500 E Fairview Ave, Montgomery AL 36106-2148
334-833-4222

Judson College
302 Bibb St, Marion AL 36756
Michael Scotto, Director of Admissions
800-447-9472 Fax: 334-683-5147
Website: www.judson.edu
E-mail: admissions@judson.edu

Samford University
800 Lakeshore Dr, Birmingham AL 35229-0002
205-726-3673

Stillman College
PO Box 1430, Tuscaloosa AL 35403-1430
205-349-4240

Troy University
Troy AL 36082-0001
Jim Hutto, Dean of Enrollment Management
334-670-3175

Troy University Dothan
PO Box 8368, Dothan AL 36304-0368
334-983-6556

Troy University Montgomery
PO Box 4419, Montgomery AL 36103-4419
334-834-1400

University of Alabama
Box 870118, Tuscaloosa AL 35487
Dr. Lisa B. Harris, Director of Admissions
205-348-5666

University of Alabama in Huntsville
PO Box 1247, Huntsville AL 35899-0001
Nikki Willis, Assoc. Director for Recruiting Program and Events
1-800-UAH-CALL Fax: 256-824-6073
Website: www.uah.edu
E-mail: willisn@uah.edu

University of Mobile
5735 College Pkwy, Mobile AL 36613
800-946-7267

University of South Alabama
307 University Blvd N, Mobile AL 36688-3053
Melissa Haab, Director of Admissions
251-460-6141 Fax: 251-460-7876
Website: www.southalabama.edu
E-mail: admiss@usouthal.edu

University of West Alabama
Hwy 11, Livingston AL 35470
205-652-3400

ALASKA

Sheldon Jackson College
801 Lincoln St, Sitka AK 99835-7651
800-478-4556

University of Alaska Anchorage
PO Box 141629, Anchorage AK 99514-1629
Cecile Mitchell, Director of Enrollment Services
907-786-1480 Fax: 907-786-4888
Website: www.uaa.alaska.edu/
E-mail: enroll@uaa.alaska.edu

University of Alaska Southeast
11120 Glacier Hwy, Juneau AK 99801-8625
Paul Kraft, Dean of Students/Enrollment Management
907-796-6000

ARIZONA

Pima Community College
4905 E Broadway Blvd, Tucson AZ 85709-1010
Wendy Kilgore, Ph.D., Director of Admissions
520-206-4500 Fax: 520-206-4790
Website: www.pima.edu
E-mail: infocenter@pima.edu

Prescott College
220 Grove Ave, Prescott AZ 86301-2912
928-778-2090

University of Arizona
Tucson AZ 85721-0040
Paul Kohn, Director of Admissions
520-621-3237

ARKANSAS

Arkansas State University
PO Box 1630, State University AR 72467-1630
870-972-2100

Hendrix College
1600 Washington Ave, Conway AR 72032-3080
501-329-6811

John Brown University
2000 W University St, Siloam Springs AR 72761-2121
877-JBU-INFO

Lyon College
PO Box 2317, Batesville AR 72503-2317
Dan Rutledge, Director of Admissions
870-793-9813

Phillips Community College of the University of Arkansas
PO Box 785, Helena AR 72342-0785
Dr. Steven Murray, Chancellor
Lynn Boone, Vice Chancellor for Student Services / Registrar
870-338-6474 Fax: 870-338-7542
Website: www.pccua.edu
E-mail: lboone@pccua.edu

University of the Ozarks
415 N College Ave, Clarksville AR 72830-2880
Jim Decker, Director of Admissions
479-979-1000

Williams Baptist College
PO Box 3737, Walnut Ridge AR 72476-3737
Angela Flippo, Vice President for Enrollment Management
800-722-4434 Fax: 870-759-4163
Website: www.williamsbaptistcollege.com
E-mail: admissions@wbcoll.edu

CALIFORNIA

Antioch University
801 Garden St Ste 101
Santa Barbara CA 93101-1581
Ankara McPherson, Director of Admissions
805-962-8179

Antioch University Southern California
400 Corporate Pointe, Culver City CA 90230
Admissions Office
800-7-ANTIOCH Fax: 310-821-6032
Website: www.admissions@antiochla.edu
E-mail: admissions@antiochla.edu
Bachelor of Arts in Liberal Studies.

Biola University
13800 Biola Ave, La Mirada CA 90639-0001
562-903-4752

Butte College
3536 Butte Campus Dr, Oroville CA 95965-8399
Carole Gish, Director of Admissions
530-895-2511 Fax: 530-879-4313
Website: www.butte.edu
E-mail: admissions@butte.edu

California Baptist University
8432 Magnolia Ave, Riverside CA 92504-3297
951-689-5771

California State University-Chico
Chico CA 95929-0001
530-898-6116

California State University-San Bernadino
5500 University Pkwy
San Bernardino CA 92407-2393
Olivia Rosas, Director of Admissions
909-537-5188 Fax: 909-537-7034
Website: www.csusb.edu
E-mail: orosas@csusb.edu

California State University-Stanislaus
801 W Monte Vista Ave, Turlock CA 95382-0256
Lisa Bernardo, Director of Admissions
209-667-3749

Chapman University
One University Drive, Orange CA 92866-1099
Michael Drummy, Assistant Vice President for Enrollment
Services and Chief Admission Officer
714-997-6411 or 888-CUAPPLY Fax: 714-997-6713
Website: www.chapman.edu
E-mail: admit@chapman.edu

Claremont McKenna College
500 E 9th St, Claremont CA 91711-5903
909-621-8000

CONCORDIA UNIVERSITY
1530 Concordia, Irvine CA 92612-3203
Lori McDonald, Executive Director of Enrollment Services
800-229-1200 or 949-854-8002 Fax: 949-854-6894
Website: www.cui.edu
E-mail: admission@cui.edu

Dominican University of California
50 Acacia Ave, San Rafael CA 94901-2298
Office of Admissions
888-323-6762 Fax: 415-485-3214
Website: www.dominican.edu
E-mail: enroll@dominican.edu

FRESNO CITY COLLEGE
1101 E University Ave, Fresno CA 93741-0002
Dayann Dietrich, Contact
559-442-8241 Fax: 559-237-4232
Website: www.fresnocitycollege.com
E-mail: fcc.admissions@scccd.com

Fresno Pacific University
1717 S Chestnut Ave, Fresno CA 93702-4798
559-453-2000

Holy Names University
3500 Mountain Blvd, Oakland CA 94619-1699
Dr. Hoffman-Marr, Director of Admissions
510-436-1010

John F. Kennedy University
100 Ellinwood Way, Pleasant Hill CA 94523-4817
800-696-5358
Website: www.jfku.edu

La Sierra University
4500 Riverwalk Pkwy, Riverside CA 92505
Bobby Brown, Director of Admissions
800-874-5587

Mills College
5000 MacArthur Blvd, Oakland CA 94613-1000
510-430-2255

New College School of Law
50 Fell St, San Francisco CA 94102-5206
Sharon Pittman, Dean of Admissions
415-241-1300 Fax: 415-241-9525
Website: www.newcollege.edu
E-mail: spittman@newcollege.edu or lawadmissions@newcollege.edu

Notre Dame de Namur University
1500 Ralston Ave, Belmont CA 94002-1997
Martin Bednarek, Director of Admissions
800-263-0545

Orange Coast College
PO Box 5005, Costa Mesa CA 92628-5005
Kristin Clark, Director of Admissions
714-432-5773 Fax: 714-432-5736
Website: www.orangecoastcollege.edu
E-mail: kclark@cccd.edu

Point Loma Nazarene University
3900 Lomaland Dr, San Diego CA 92106-2810
Chip Killingsworth, Director of Undergraduate Admissions
800-733-7770 Fax: 619-849-2601
Website: www.pointloma.edu
E-mail: admissions@pointloma.edu

Pomona College
333 N College Way, Claremont CA 91711-4429
Peter W. Stanley, President

San Bernardino Valley College
701 S Mount Vernon Ave
San Bernardino CA 92410-2798
Kay Ragan, Ed.D., Director of Admissions
909-888-6511 Fax: 909-889-4988
Website: www.valleycollege.edu
E-mail: kragan@sbccd.cc.ca.us

SAN FRANCISCO ART INSTITUTE
800 Chestnut St, San Francisco CA 94133
800-345-SFAI Fax: 415-749-4503
Website: www.sfai.edu
E-mail: admissions@sfai.edu

Founded in 1871, SFAI offers one of the most innovative and interdisciplinary environments in higher education. Through its School of Interdisciplinary Studies, SFAI offers accredited Bachelor of Arts (BA) and Master of Arts (MA) programs. The School of Interdisciplinary Studies is based on the premise that imagination combined with critical intelligence is essential for engaging and understanding contemporary art and global society. The School of Interdisciplinary Studies offers three areas of study: History and Theory of Contemporary Art (BA, MA); Urban Studies (BA, MA); and Exhibition and Museum Studies (MA). The School for Interdisciplinary Studies also holds under its aegis SFAI's four centers for interdisciplinary study: Art+Science; Public Practice; Word, Text, and Image; and Media Culture. Each center sponsors symposia, seminars, research fellowships, and residencies. The School of Studio Practice is the complementary other half of SFAI, offering BFA, MFA, and Post-Baccalaureate programs, and consisting of the departments of: Design+Technology, Film, New Genres, Painting, Photography, Printmaking, and Sculpture. Together the two schools are committed to furthering the relationship between the practices and theories of contemporary art. The BA and MA programs are at their core interdisciplinary, and students can take courses in any department. SFAI's faculty is comprised of active writers, scholars, artists, and curators. Dean of Academic Affairs is renowned curator and critic Okwui Enwezor. Dean of Graduate Studies is artist and filmmaker Renee Green. Director of Exhibitions and Public Programs is curator Hou Hanru. Visiting artists and scholars play a significant role in education at SFAI, with recent visitors including Matthew Barney, William Kentridge, Raqs Media Collective, and others. All students have 24-hour access to the SFAI campus. SFAI's main campus includes studios, postproduction facilities, and the first high definition video research lab in the Bay Area. The Diego Rivera Gallery, an open-air amphitheater, and a 250-seat theater are also available to students for exhibiting and screening work. SFAI's library collection includes more than 26,000 volumes with emphasis on modern and contemporary art, over 200 current periodicals, and an extensive image, video, and audio archive available only to SFAI students. The 62,000 square-foot Graduate Center includes a digital lab, film and sound studios, darkrooms, a woodshop, and a gallery for student work. SFAI has rolling application deadlines, and there are competitive and need-based scholarships available to undergraduates, a fellowship program for graduate students, and community college scholarships for transfer students. Visit the SFAI website for specific application requirements.

Scripps College
1030 Columbia Ave, Claremont CA 91711-3948
909-621-8000

Simpson University
2211 College View Dr, Redding CA 96003-8606
Jim Herberger, Director of Admissions
888-9-SIMPSON Fax: 530-226-4861
Website: www.simpsonuniversity.edu
E-mail: admissions@simpsonuniversity.edu
See listing under "Universities"

Sonoma State University
1801 E Cotati Ave, Rohnert Park CA 94928-3609
Louis T. Levy, Senior Director Enrollment Services
707-664-2880

University of California-Santa Cruz
Santa Cruz CA 95064
831-459-0111

University of Judaism
15600 Mulholland Dr, Los Angeles CA 90077-1599
Bryan Pisetsky, Director of Undergraduate Admissions
310-476-9777

University of La Verne
1950 3rd St, La Verne CA 91750-4443
800-876-4858

University of San Diego
5998 Alcala Park, San Diego CA 92110-2492
Admissions
619-260-4506

Whittier College
PO Box 634, Whittier CA 90608-0634
Kieron Miller, Director of Admissions
562-907-4200 Fax: 562-907-4870
Website: www.whittier.edu
E-mail: kmiller@whittier.edu

WOODSIDE PRIORY SCHOOL
302 Portola Rd, Portola Valley CA 94028-7897
Al D. Zappelli, Director of Admissions
650-851-8223 Fax: 650-851-2839
Website: www.woodsidepriory.com
E-mail: azappelli@woodsidepriory.com
See listing under "Preparatory Schools - Coed"

COLORADO

Adams State College
Alamosa CO 81102
Matt Gallegos, Director of Admissions
800-824-6494

Colorado Christian University
8787 W Alameda Ave, Lakewood CO 80226
Sean Kadel, Director of Admissions
800-44-FAITH Fax: 303-963-3201
Website: www.ccu.edu
E-mail: admissions@ccu.edu

Colorado College
14 E Cache La Poudre St
Colorado Springs CO 80903-3243
719-389-6344

Colorado Northwestern Community College
500 Kennedy Dr, Rangely CO 81648-3502
Tresa England, Director of Student Services
800-562-1105 Fax: 970-675-3343
Website: www.cncc.edu
E-mail: tresa.england@cncc.edu

Colorado State University - Pueblo
2200 Bonforte Blvd, Pueblo CO 81001-4990
719-549-2461

Fort Lewis College
1000 Rim Dr, Durango CO 81301-3999
970-247-7010

Metropolitan State College
PO Box 173362, Campus Box 37
Denver CO 80217-3362
303-556-3215

NORTHEASTERN JUNIOR COLLEGE
100 College Ave, Sterling CO 80751-2399
Dr. Lance Bolton, Chief Administrative Officer
Tina Joyce, Director of Admissions
970-521-7000 or 970-521-6752 Fax: 970-521-6801
Website: www.njc.edu
E-mail: tina.joyce@njc.edu

Regis University
3333 Regis Blvd, Denver CO 80221-1099
303-458-4900

University of Colorado at Denver and Health Sciences Center
Downtown Denver Campus
PO Box 173364, Denver CO 80217-3364
303-556-2557

UNIVERSITY OF DENVER UNIVERSITY COLLEGE
2211 S Josephine St, Denver CO 80208
Tripp Baltz, Academic Director
303-871-3354 Fax: 303-871-4047
Website: www.universitycollege.du.edu
E-mail: ucolinfo@du.edu

University of Northern Colorado
Greeley CO 80639
Sandra Flake, Dean of Arts and Sciences
970-351-2707

Western State College of Colorado
Gunnison CO 81231-0001
Director of Admissions
800-876-5309

CONNECTICUT

Albertus Magnus College
700 Prospect St, New Haven CT 06511-1189
Richard Lolatte, Dean of Admission
203-773-8501 or 800-578-9160 Fax: 203-773-5248
Website: www.albertus.edu
E-mail: admissions@albertus.edu

Charter Oak State College
55 Paul Manafort Dr, New Britain CT 06053-2142
860-832-3800

Middlesex Community College
100 Training Hill Rd, Middletown CT 06457-4889
Mensimah Shabazz, Director of Admissions
860-343-5800 Fax: 860-344-3055
Website: www.mxcc.commnet.edu
E-mail: mshabazz@mxcc.commnet.edu

Post University
800 Country Club Rd, Waterbury CT 06708-3240
Sandra M. Fernandes, Associate Director of Admissions
Will Johnson, Associate Director of Admissions
203-596-4520

Quinnipiac University
275 Mount Carmel Ave, Hamden CT 06518-1905
Joan Isaac Mohr, VP & Dean of Admissions
203-582-8600

Trinity College
300 Summit St, Hartford CT 06106-3186
Larry Dow, Dean of Admissions & Financial Aid
860-297-2180

University of Bridgeport
126 Park Ave, Bridgeport CT 06604-5620
Barbara L. Maryak, Dean of Admissions
203-576-4552

University of Hartford
200 Bloomfield Ave, West Hartford CT 06117-1599
860-768-4100

University of New Haven
300 Boston Post Rd, West Haven CT 06516
Director of Undergraduate Admissions
203-932-7319

DELAWARE

Wesley College
120 N State St, Dover DE 19901-3876
302-736-2300 Fax: 302-736-2301
Website: www.wesley.edu

DISTRICT OF COLUMBIA

American University
4400 Massachusetts Ave NW
Washington DC 20016-8200
202-885-1000

Gallaudet University
800 Florida Ave NE, Washington DC 20002-3695
Charity Reedy Hines, Director of Admissions
202-651-5750 Fax: 202-651-5744
Website: www.gallaudet.edu
E-mail: admissions.office@gallaudet.edu

Trinity University
125 Michigan Ave NE, Washington DC 20017-1090
202-884-9000

University of the District of Columbia
4200 Connecticut Ave NW
Washington DC 20008-1174
LaVerne M. Hill-Flanagan, Director of Admissions
202-274-5100

FLORIDA

Barry University
11300 NE 2nd Ave, Miami Shores FL 33161-6695
800-695-2279

Bethune-Cookman College
640 Dr Mary McLeod Bethune Blvd
Daytona Beach FL 32114-3099
Edwin Coffie, Director of Admissions
800-448-0228

Clearwater Christian College
3400 Gulf To Bay Blvd, Clearwater FL 33759-4595
727-726-1153

Florida Atlantic University
PO Box 3091, Boca Raton FL 33431-0991
800-299-4328

Florida Southern College
111 Lake Hollingsworth Dr, Lakeland FL 33801-5607
Robert B. Palmer, V.P., Dean of Enrollment Management
863-680-4131

Florida State University
600 W College Ave, Tallahassee FL 32306-1096
Janice V. Finney, Director of Admissions
850-644-2525 Fax: 850-644-0197
Website: admissions.fsu.edu
E-mail: admissions@admin.fsu.edu

Lynn University
3601 N Military Trl, Boca Raton FL 33431-5598
Director of Admissions
561-237-7900 Fax: 561-237-7100
Website: www.lynn.edu
E-mail: admission@lynn.edu

Palm Beach Atlantic University
PO Box 24708, West Palm Beach FL 33416-4708
561-803-2000

Saint Leo University
PO Box 6665, Saint Leo FL 33574
Director of Admissions
800-334-5532

St. Thomas University
16401 NW 37th Ave, Miami Gardens FL 33054
Dr. Gloria Ruiz, Contact
800-367-9010 or 305-628-6546 Fax: 305-628-6591
Website: www.stu.edu
E-mail: signup@stu.edu

University of Central Florida
PO Box 160111, Orlando FL 32816
407-823-3000

University of South Florida
4202 E Fowler Ave, Tampa FL 33620-6900
J. Robert Spatig, Director of Admissions
877-USF-BULL Fax: 813-974-9689
Website: www.usf.edu
E-mail: admissions@admin.usf.edu
See listing under "Universities"

University of Tampa
401 W Kennedy Blvd, Tampa FL 33606-1490
813-253-3333

Warner Southern College
5301 US Highway 27 S, Lake Wales FL 33859-8725
863-638-1426

GEORGIA

Armstrong Atlantic State University
11935 Abercorn St, Savannah GA 31419-1997
Kim West, Asst. Dean and Registrar Enrollment Services
912-927-5277 Fax: 912-921-5462
Website: www.armstrong.edu
E-mail: admissions@mail.armstrong.edu

BEACON UNIVERSITY
6003 Veterans Pkwy, Columbus GA 31909
Admissions Department
706-323-5364 Fax: 706-323-3236
Website: www.beacon.edu
E-mail: beacon@beacon.edu

Brewton-Parker College
Highway 280, Mount Vernon GA 30445
800-342-1087

Clayton State University
5900 N Lee St, Morrow GA 30260
770-961-3500

DeKalb Technical College
495 N Indian Creek Dr, Clarkston GA 30021-2397
Terry Richardson, Director of Admissions
404-297-9522 Fax: 404-294-6496
Website: www.dekalbtech.edu
E-mail: richardt@dekalbtech.edu

Fort Valley State University
1005 State University Dr, Fort Valley GA 31030-3298
478-825-6307

Georgia Southern University
PO Box 8024, Statesboro GA 30460
Admissions Office
912-681-5532

Georgia Southwestern State University
800 Wheatley St, Americus GA 31709-4635
229-928-1279

Georgia State University
PO Box 4009, Atlanta GA 30302-4009
404-651-2365

Kennesaw State University
1000 Chastain Rd NW, Kennesaw GA 30144-5591
Dr. Helen Ridley, Dean of Humanities and Social Science
770-423-6124
Website: www.kennesaw.edu

LaGrange College
601 Broad St, LaGrange GA 30240-2955
Andy Geeter, Director of Admission
800-593-2885

Luther Rice University
3038 Evans Mill Rd, Lithonia GA 30038
Russ Sorrow, Director of Enrollment Management
770-484-1204 Fax: 770-484-1155
Website: www.lru.edu
E-mail: admissions@lru.edu

Mercer University in Macon
1400 Coleman Ave, Macon GA 31207-0003
John P. Cole, Sr. Assoc. V.P. for Admissions
478-301-2650

North Georgia College & State University
Dahlonega GA 30597-0001
706-864-1400

Oglethorpe University
4484 Peachtree Rd NE, Atlanta GA 30319-2797
Kelly Gosnell, Director of Admission
404-261-1441

Piedmont College
PO Box 10, Demorest GA 30535-0010
800-277-7020

Thomas University
1501 Millpond Rd, Thomasville GA 31792-7478
Darla M. Glass, Director of Student Affairs
229-226-1621

University of Georgia
Athens GA 30602-0001
706-542-3000

Valdosta State University
N Patterson St, Valdosta GA 31698-0001
229-333-5952

HAWAII

Brigham Young University
55-220 Kulanui St, Laie HI 96762-1293
808-293-3211

Kauai Community College
3-1901 Kaumualii Hwy, Lihue HI 96766-9500
808-245-8225 Fax: 808-245-8297
Website: kauai.hawaii.edu
E-mail: arkauai@hawaii.edu

IDAHO

Lewis-Clark State College
500 8th Ave, Lewiston ID 83501-2698
Diane Douglas, Ph.D., Registrar/Director of Admissions
800-933-5272 Fax: 208-792-2429
Website: www.lcsc.edu
E-mail: admissions@lcsc.edu

University of Idaho
Moscow ID 83844-4253
Lloyd Scott, Director of New Student Services
208-885-6163 Fax: 208-885-4477
Website: www.uidaho.edu
E-mail: nss@uidaho.edu

ILLINOIS

Augustana College
639 38th St, Rock Island IL 61201-2296
309-794-7000

Aurora University
347 S Gladstone Ave, Aurora IL 60506-4892
Carol R. Dunn, Ed.D., Vice President for Enrollment
800-742-5281 Fax: 630-844-5535
Website: www.aurora.edu
E-mail: admission@aurora.edu

Benedictine University
5700 College Rd, Lisle IL 60532-0900
630-829-6300 or 888-829-6363 Fax: 630-829-6301
Website: www.ben.edu
E-mail: admissions@ben.edu
See listing under "Universities"

Columbia College Chicago
600 S Michigan Ave, Chicago IL 60605-1996
Murphy Monroe, Executive Director of Admissions
312-344-7130 Fax: 312-344-8024
Website: www.colum.edu
E-mail: admissions@colum.edu

CONCORDIA UNIVERSITY
7400 Augusta St, River Forest IL 60305-1402
708-209-3100 Fax: 708-209-3176
Website: www.cuchicago.edu
E-mail: admission@cuchicago.edu

De Paul University
2323 N Seminary Ave, Chicago IL 60614-3298
312-362-8000

Illinois Wesleyan University
PO Box 2900, Bloomington IL 61702-2900
James R. Ruoti, Dean of Admissions
309-556-3031

Kaskaskia College
27210 College Rd, Centralia IL 62801-7878
Tyra Taylor, Dean of Enrollment Management and Retention Services
618-545-3000 Fax: 618-532-1990
Website: www.kaskaskia.edu
E-mail: ttaylor@kaskaskia.edu

Knox College
Galesburg IL 61401
309-341-7100

Lewis University
One University Parkway, Romeoville IL 60446
800-897-9000

MacMurray College
447 E College Ave, Jacksonville IL 62650-2590
217-479-7000

Millikin University
1184 W Main St, Decatur IL 62522-2084
Lin Stoner, Dean of Admission
800-373-7733

Monmouth College
700 E Broadway, Monmouth IL 61462-1963
309-457-2131

National-Louis University
5202 Old Orchard Rd Ste 300, Skokie IL 60077-4409
224-233-2000

North Central College
30 N Brainard St, Naperville IL 60540-4690
Martha Stolze, Director of Admissions
630-637-5800

NORTHEASTERN ILLINOIS UNIVERSITY
5500 N Saint Louis Ave, Chicago IL 60625-4699
Kate Forhan, Dean
773-442-4050 Fax: 773-442-4020
Website: www.neiu.edu
E-mail: k-forhan@neiu.edu

Olivet Nazarene University
1 University Ave
Bourbonnais IL 60914
815-939-5011

Principia College
Elsah IL 62028-9799
618-374-2131

Quincy University
1800 College Ave, Quincy IL 62301-2670
217-222-8020

Rockford College
5050 E State St, Rockford IL 61108-2393
William Laffey, Director of Admission
800-892-2984

Roosevelt University
430 S Michigan Ave, Chicago IL 60605
Gwen E. Kanelos, Asst. Vice President for Enrollment Services
877-APPLY-RU Fax: 312-341-4216
Website: www.roosevelt.edu
E-mail: applyru@roosevelt.edu

Spertus College
618 S Michigan Ave, Chicago IL 60605-1901
312-922-9012 Fax: 312-922-6406
Website: www.spertus.edu
E-mail: college@spertus.edu

Trinity Christian College
6601 W College Dr, Palos Heights IL 60463-0929
Joshua Lenarz, Director of Admissions
708-597-3000

Trinity International University
2065 Half Day Rd, Deerfield IL 60015-1241
847-945-8800 Fax: 847-317-8097
Website: www.tiu.edu
E-mail: tcadmissions@tiu.edu

Triton College
2000 5th Ave, River Grove IL 60171-1995
Jeffery Cooks, Director, Admission Services
708-456-0300 ext. 3130 Fax: 708-583-3147
Website: www.triton.edu
E-mail: triton@triton.edu
See listing under "Community and Junior Colleges"

University of Illinois at Springfield
One University Plaza, Springfield IL 62794
217-206-4847

University of St. Francis
500 Wilcox St, Joliet IL 60435
800-735-7500

Wheaton College
501 College Ave, Wheaton IL 60187-5571
630-752-5000

INDIANA

Ancilla Domini College
Donaldson IN 46513
Erin Alonzo, Director of Admissions
574-936-8898 Fax: 574-935-1773
Website: www.ancilla.edu
E-mail: erin.alonzo@ancilla.edu

Ball State University
2000 W University Ave, Muncie IN 47306-0002
765-285-5555

Bethel College
1001 W McKinley Ave, Mishawaka IN 46545-5591
Office of Admissions
574-257-3339

Franklin College
101 Branigin Blvd, Franklin IN 46131
Jacqueline S. Acosta, Director of Admissions
800-852-0232 Fax: 317-738-8274
Website: www.franklincollege.edu
E-mail: admissions@franklincollege.edu

Goshen College
1700 S Main St, Goshen IN 46526-4794
574-535-7000

Grace College
200 Seminary Dr, Winona Lake IN 46590-1224
800-54-GRACE

Hanover College
PO Box 108, Hanover IN 47243-0108
William D. Preble, Dean of Admission
800-213-2178

HOLY CROSS COLLEGE
PO Box 308, Notre Dame IN 46556-0308
Vincent M. Duke, Director of Admissions
574-239-8400 Fax: 574-239-8323
Website: www.hcc-nd.edu
E-mail: admissions@hcc-nd.edu

Indiana Wesleyan University
4201 S Washington St, Marion IN 46953-4974
765-674-6901

Ivy Tech Community College - North Central
220 Dean Johnson Blvd, South Bend IN 46601-3415
Pam Decker, Director of Admissions
574-289-7001 Fax: 574-236-7177
Website: www.ivytech.edu
E-mail: pdecker@ivytech.edu

Oakland City University
138 N Lucretia St, Oakland City IN 47660
Brian J. Baker, Director of Admissions
800-737-5125 Fax: 812-749-1433
Website: www.oak.edu
E-mail: bbaker@oak.edu
See listing under "Universities"

St. Mary-of-the-Woods College
Saint Mary of the Woods IN 47876
James P. Malley, Jr., Director of Admission
800-926-7692

University of Evansville
1800 Lincoln Ave, Evansville IN 47722-0001
Don Vos, Dean of Admission
800-423-8633 Fax: 812-488-4076
Website: www.evansville.edu
E-mail: admission@evansville.edu

Wabash College
301 W Wabash Ave, Crawfordsville IN 47933
David Collins, Sr. Assoc. Director of Admissions
800-345-5385

IOWA

Briar Cliff University
PO Box 2100, Sioux City IA 51104-0100
Sharisue Wilcoxon, VP for Enrollment Management
712-279-5200 Fax: 712-279-1632
Website: www.briarcliff.edu
E-mail: admissions@briarcliff.edu

Buena Vista University
610 W 4th St, Storm Lake IA 50588-1798
712-749-2235

Central College
812 University St, Pella IA 50219-1999
641-628-9000

DIVINE WORD COLLEGE SEMINARY
102 Jacoby Dr SW, Epworth IA 52045
Len Uhal, Director of Admissions
563-876-3332 Fax: 563-876-5515
Website: www.svdvocations.org
E-mail: dwm@mwci.net

Dordt College
498 4th Ave NE, Sioux Center IA 51250-1697
Quentin Van Essen, Executive Director of Admissions
800-343-6738

Graceland University
1 University Place, Lamoni IA 50140
Greg Sutherland, Interim Vice President for Enrollment and Dean of Admissions
641-784-5196 Fax: 641-784-5480
Website: www.admissions.graceland.edu
E-mail: admissions@graceland.edu

Grand View College
1200 Grandview Ave, Des Moines IA 50316-1599
515-263-2800

Grinnell College
PO Box 805, Grinnell IA 50112-0805
641-269-4000

Iowa Lakes Community College
3200 College Dr, Emmetsburg IA 50536-1055
Anne Stansbury, Asst. Director of Admissions
712-852-5212 Fax: 712-362-8363
Website: www.iowalakes.edu
E-mail: info@iowalakes.edu

Iowa Lakes Community College
300 S 18th St, Estherville IA 51334-2721
Anne Stansbury, Asst. Director of Admissions
712-362-7945 Fax: 712-362-8363
Website: www.iowalakes.edu
E-mail: info@iowalakes.edu

Iowa Lakes Community College
1900 Grand Ave, Suite 8, Spencer IA 51301
Anne Stansbury, Assistant Director of Admissions
712-262-7141 Fax: 712-262-4047
Website: www.iowalakes.edu
E-mail: info@iowalakes.edu

Loras College
1450 Alta Vista St, Dubuque IA 52001-4399
Tim Hauber, Director of Admissions
800-245-6727

Mount Mercy College
1330 Elmhurst Dr NE, Cedar Rapids IA 52402-4797
Jim Krystofiak, Dean of Admission
800-248-4504

Northwestern College
101 7th St SW, Orange City IA 51041-1996
712-737-7000

Northwest Iowa Community College
603 W Park St, Sheldon IA 51201-1046
Lisa Story, Director of Enrollment Management
712-324-5061 Fax: 712-324-4136
Website: www.nwicc.edu
E-mail: lstory@nwicc.edu

Wartburg College
PO Box 1003, Waverly IA 50677-0903
Brent Matthias, Interim Director of Admissions
319-352-8200

KANSAS

Baker University
PO Box 65, Baldwin City KS 66006-0065
785-594-6451

Bethel College
300 E 27th St, North Newton KS 67117-8061
316-283-2500

COLBY COMMUNITY COLLEGE
1255 S Range Ave, Colby KS 67701-4099
Director of Admissions
888-634-9350 or 785-460-4690 Fax: 785-460-4691
Website: www.colbycc.edu
E-mail: admissions@colbycc.edu

Fort Hays State University
600 Park St, Hays KS 67601-4099
785-628-4000

Friends University
2100 W University Ave, Wichita KS 67213-3397
316-261-5800

Independence Community College
PO Box 708, Independence KS 67301-0708
Dr. Terry Hetrick, President
800-842-6063 Fax: 620-331-5344
Website: www.indycc.edu
E-mail: admissions@indycc.edu

Mid-America Nazarene University
2030 E College Way, Olathe KS 66062-1851
913-782-3750

Newman University
3100 W McCormick St, Wichita KS 67213
Jann Reusser, Admissions Recruitment Coordinator
316-942-4291 ext. 2144

Ottawa University
1001 S Cedar St, Ottawa KS 66067-3399
785-242-5200

Southwestern College
100 College St, Winfield KS 67156-2499
620-229-6000

Tabor College
400 S Jefferson St, Hillsboro KS 67063-1758
Rusty Allen, Dean of Enrollment Management
800-822-6799 Fax: 620-947-6276
Website: www.tabor.edu
E-mail: admissions@tabor.edu
See listing under "Universities"

University of Kansas
Lawrence KS 66045-0001
Sally Frost-Mason, Dean

KENTUCKY

Alice Lloyd College
100 Purpose Rd, Pippa Passes KY 41844-9005
John Mills, Director of Admissions
888-280-4252

Bluegrass Community and Technical College
Oswald Building
470 Cooper Drive, Lexington KY 40506-0235
Shelbie Hugle, Director of Admissions
859-246-6200 Fax: 859-246-4664
Website: www.bluegrass.kctcs.edu
E-mail: bctc_info@kctcs.edu

Brescia University
717 Frederica St, Owensboro KY 42301-3023
Sr. Mary Austin Blank, OSB, Director of Admissions
877-BRESCIA

Campbellsville University
1 University Dr, Campbellsville KY 42718-2799
Scott Necessary, Coordinator of Undergraduate Admissions
270-789-5000

Morehead State University
Morehead KY 40351-1689
Jeffrey Liles, Enrollment Services
800-585-6781 Fax: 606-783-5038
Website: www.moreheadstate.edu
E-mail: admissions@moreheadstate.edu

Murray State University
Murray KY 42071
Phil Bryan, Director of Admissions
270-762-3011

Spalding University
851 S 4th St, Louisville KY 40203-2188
502-585-9911

Transylvania University
300 N Broadway, Lexington KY 40508-1776
859-233-8242 Fax: 859-233-8797
Website: www.transy.edu
E-mail: admissions@transy.edu

University of Kentucky
Lexington KY 40506-0001
Don Witt, Director of Admissions
859-257-9000

University of Louisville
2301 S 3rd St, Louisville KY 40292-2001
502-852-5555

LOUISIANA

Dillard University
2601 Gentilly Blvd, New Orleans LA 70122-3097
Linda G. Nash, Director of Admissions

Grambling State University
PO Box 864, Grambling LA 71245
318-274-3811

Louisiana College
PO Box 566, Pineville LA 71359-0001
318-487-7259

Louisiana State University at Alexandria
8100 Highway 71 S, Alexandria LA 71302-9121
Dr. Thomas Armstrong, Director of Admissions
318-445-3672 Fax: 318-473-6418
Website: www.lsua.edu

Louisiana State University at Eunice
PO Box 1129, Eunice LA 70535-1129
Ron Ryder, Registrar
337-457-7311 Fax: 337-550-1306
Website: www.lsue.edu
E-mail: rryder@lsue.edu

Northwestern State University
Natchitoches LA 71497-0001
Jana Lucky, Director of Enrollment Services
318-357-4503

Our Lady of Holy Cross College
4123 Woodland Dr, New Orleans LA 70131-7399
Office of Enrollment Services
504-394-7744 Fax: 504-391-2421
Website: www.olhcc.edu

ST. JOSEPH SEMINARY COLLEGE
Saint Benedict LA 70457
Dr. Russ Pottle, Director of Admissions
985-867-2225 Fax: 985-867-2270
Website: www.stjosephabbey.org
E-mail: acdean@stjosephabbey.org

MAINE

Bowdoin College
Brunswick ME 04011
207-725-3000

Colby College
150 Mayflower Hill Dr, Waterville ME 04901-4799
207-872-3000

St. Joseph's College of Maine
278 Whites Bridge Rd, Standish ME 04084-5263
Vincent Kloskowski, Dean of Admissions
800-338-7057 Fax: 207-893-7862
Website: www.sjcme.edu
E-mail: admission@sjcme.edu

Southern Maine Community College
2 Fort Rd, South Portland ME 04106-1698
Dr. James Ortiz, President
Scott MacDonald, Director of Financial Aid
207-741-5500 Fax: 207-741-5671
Website: www.smccme.edu
E-mail: oharmon@maine.rr.com

University of Maine
246 Main St, Farmington ME 04938
Sharon M. Oliver, Director of Admissions
207-778-7000

University of Maine
Orono ME 04469-0001
207-581-1110

University of Maine at Fort Kent
23 University Dr, Fort Kent ME 04743
888-TRY-UMFK

University of Southern Maine
PO Box 9300, Portland ME 04104-9300
207-780-4141

MARYLAND

Cecil College
One Seahawk Dr, North East MD 21901
Sandra S. Rajaski, Registrar & Director of Admissions
410-287-1000 Fax: 410-287-1001
Website: www.cecil.edu
E-mail: srajaski@cecil.edu

Goucher College
1021 Dulaney Valley Rd, Baltimore MD 21204-2780
410-337-6000

Griggs University
PO Box 4437, Silver Spring MD 20914-4437
Joan Wilson, Director of Admissions
301-680-6570 Fax: 301-680-6583
Website: www.griggs.edu
E-mail: registrar@griggs.edu

Hagerstown Community College
11400 Robinwood Dr, Hagerstown MD 21742-6590
Dr. Daniel E. Bock, Assistant Director of Admissions
301-790-2800 Fax: 301-791-9165
Website: www.hagerstowncc.edu
E-mail: bockd@hagerstowncc.edu

Johns Hopkins University
3400 N Charles St, Baltimore MD 21218-2680
410-516-8000

Morgan State University
1700 E Cold Spring Ln, Baltimore MD 21251-0002
443-885-3000

ST. JOHN'S COLLEGE
PO Box 2800, Annapolis MD 21404-2800
John Christensen, Director of Admissions
800-727-9238 Fax: 410-269-7916
Website: www.stjohnscollege.edu
E-mail: admissions@sjca.edu

University of Baltimore
1420 N Charles St, Baltimore MD 21201-5779
410-837-4200

University of Maryland Eastern Shore
Princess Anne MD 21853
Edwina Morse, Director of Admissions
410-651-6410

Villa Julie College
1525 Greenspring Valley Rd
Stevenson MD 21153-0641
Mark Hergan, V.P. Enrollment Services
410-486-7001

Washington College
300 Washington Ave, Chestertown MD 21620-1197
410-778-2800

MASSACHUSETTS

American International College
1000 State St, Springfield MA 01109-3155
Peter Miller, Dean of Admissions
413-737-7000

Anna Maria College
50 Sunset Ln, Paxton MA 01612
Timothy M. Donahue, Director of Recruitment and Admissions
508-849-3360 Fax: 508-849-3362
Website: www.annamaria.edu
E-mail: admissions@annamaria.edu

Assumption College
500 Salisbury St, Worcester MA 01609-1294
Kathleen Murphy, Dean of Enrollment
508-767-7000 Fax: 508-799-4412
Website: www.assumption.edu
E-mail: admiss@assumption.edu

Bay State College
122 Commonwealth Ave, Boston MA 02116-2901
Craig Pfannenstiehl, President
617-217-9000 Fax: 617-536-1735

Becker College
Campuses in Worcester and Leicester, MA
61 Sever St, Worcester MA 01609-2165
Karen Schedin, Dean of Admissions
508-791-9241 Fax: 508-890-1500
Website: www.becker.edu
E-mail: admissions@becker.edu
See listing under "Universities"

Boston University
121 Bay State Rd, Boston MA 02215
Kelly Walter, Executive Director of Admissions
617-353-2300 Fax: 617-353-9695
Website: web.bu.edu
E-mail: admissions@bu.edu

Bristol Community College
777 Elsbree St, Fall River MA 02720-7395
Rodney S. Clark, Director of Admissions
508-678-2811 ext. 2516, 2179 Fax: 508-730-3265
Website: www.bristol.mass.edu
E-mail: admissions@bristol.mass.edu

College of the Holy Cross
1 College St, Worcester MA 01610-2322
508-793-2011

Curry College
1071 Blue Hill Ave, Milton MA 02186-2395
Bruce Weckworth, Director of Admissions
617-333-2210

Elms College
291 Springfield St, Chicopee MA 01013-2839
800-255-3567

Emerson College
120 Boylston St, Boston MA 02116-4624
Sara S. Ramirez, Director of Undergraduate Admission
617-824-8600 Fax: 617-824-8609
Website: www.emerson.edu
E-mail: admission@emerson.edu

Fisher College
118 Beacon St, Boston MA 02116-1501
Stephen Carter, Director of Admissions
800-446-1226

Gordon College
255 Grapevine Rd, Wenham MA 01984-1899
Barbara R. Layne, Associate Vice President, Enrollment
866-464-6736 Fax: 978-867-4682
Website: www.gordon.edu
E-mail: admissions@gordon.edu

Hampshire College
Amherst MA 01002
Karen S. Parker, Director of Admissions
413-559-5471

Hellenic College/Holy Cross Greek Orthodox School of Theology
50 Goddard Ave, Brookline MA 02445-7415
Sonia Belcher, Director
617-731-3500

Lasell College
1844 Commonwealth Ave, Newton MA 02466-2716
617-243-2225

Lesley University
29 Everett St, Cambridge MA 02138-2790
Jane Raley, Director of Admissions
617-349-8800

Massachusetts College of Liberal Arts
375 Church St, North Adams MA 01247-4100
413-662-5000

Massachusetts Institute of Technology
77 Massachusetts Ave, Cambridge MA 02139-4307
617-253-1000 Fax: 617-253-4016
Website: my.mit.edu
E-mail: admissions@mit.edu

Mt. Ida College
777 Dedham St, Newton Center MA 02459-3323
617-969-7000

Nichols College
Dudley MA 01571-5000
Kimberly A. Kossuth, Director of Admissions
508-943-1560

NORTHERN ESSEX COMMUNITY COLLEGE
100 Elliott St, Haverhill MA 01830
Nora B. Sheridan, Director of Admission
978-556-3700
Website: www.NECC.Mass.edu
E-mail: nsheridan@necc.mass.edu

North Shore Community College
1 Ferncroft Rd, Danvers MA 01923-4093
Jennifer Kirk, Director of Admissions & Recruitment Outreach
978-762-4000 Fax: 978-762-4015
Website: www.northshore.edu
E-mail: jkirk@northshore.edu

Pine Manor College
400 Heath St, Chestnut Hill MA 02467-2332
Bill Nichols, Dean of Admission
617-731-7167

Regis College
235 Wellesley St, Weston MA 02493-1571
781-768-2000

Smith College
Northampton MA 01063-0001
Debra Shaver, Director of Admissions
800-383-3232 Fax: 413-585-2527
Website: www.smith.edu
E-mail: admission@smith.edu

Springfield College
263 Alden St, Springfield MA 01109-3788
Mary DeAngelo, Director of Admissions
800-343-1257

Suffolk University
8 Ashburton Pl, Boston MA 02108-2770
617-573-8460

University of Massachusetts Boston
100 William T Morrissey Blvd, Boston MA 02125-3393
Liliana Mickle, Director of Undergraduate Admissions
617-287-6000

University of Massachusetts Dartmouth
Old Westport Rd, North Dartmouth MA 02747-2300
Steven T. Briggs, Director of Admissions
508-999-8605 Fax: 508-999-8755
Website: explore.umassd.edu
E-mail: sbriggs@umassd.edu

Wellesley College
106 Central St, Wellesley MA 02481-8203
Board of Admission
781-283-2270

Western New England College
1215 Wilbraham Rd, Springfield MA 01119-2655
413-782-1321

Westfield State College
PO Box 1630, Westfield MA 01086
Michelle Mattie, Associate Dean, Admission and Enrollment Services
413-572-5300

Wheaton College
26 E Main St, Norton MA 02766-2322
Gail Berson, Dean of Admissions & Student Aid
800-394-6003

Worcester Polytechnic Institute
100 Institute Rd, Worcester MA 01609-2280
Edward J. Connor, Director of Admissions
508-831-5286 Fax: 508-831-5875
Website: admissions.wpi.edu
E-mail: admissions@wpi.edu

MICHIGAN

Albion College
611 E Porter St, Albion MI 49224-1831
800-858-6770

Alma College
614 W Superior St, Alma MI 48801-1599
Evan Montague, Director of Admissions
800-321-ALMA Fax: 989-463-7057
Website: www.alma.edu
E-mail: admissions@alma.edu

Andrews University
Berrien Springs MI 49104-0001
Randall Graves, Director of Recruitment Services
800-253-2874

Aquinas College
1607 Robinson Rd SE, Grand Rapids MI 49506-1799
Harry Knopke PhD, President
Paula Meehan, Dean of Admissions
800-678-9593

Ave Maria College
PO Box 373, Ypsilanti MI 48106-0373
866-866-3030

Concordia University
4090 Geddes Rd, Ann Arbor MI 48105-2797
Gary Neumann, Director of Admissions
734-995-7300 Fax: 734-995-4610
Website: www.cuaa.edu
E-mail: admissions@cuaa.edu

Delta College
University Center MI 48710-0001
Duff Zube, Director of Admissions
989-686-9093 Fax: 989-667-2202
Website: www.delta.edu
E-mail: admit@delta.edu

Eastern Michigan University
Ypsilanti MI 48197
800-GO-TO-EMU

Grand Valley State University
1 Campus Dr, Allendale MI 49401-9403
Jodi Chycinski, Director of Admissions
616-331-6611 Fax: 616-331-2000
Website: www.gvsu.edu
E-mail: go2gvsu@gvsu.edu

HILLSDALE COLLEGE
33 E College St, Hillsdale MI 49242-1298
Dr. Thomas Burke, Chairperson
517-607-2368 Fax: 517-607-2208
Website: www.hillsdale.edu
E-mail: tom.burke@hillsdale.edu

Hope College
PO Box 9000, Holland MI 49422-9000
616-395-7000

Lake Superior State University
650 W Easterday Ave
Sault Sainte Marie MI 49783-1637
Susan Camp, Director of Admissions
888-800-LSSU Fax: 906-635-6696
Website: www.lssu.edu
E-mail: admissions@lssu.edu
See listing under "Universities"

Lawrence Technological University
21000 W 10 Mile Rd, Southfield MI 48075-1058
Jane Rohrback, Director of Admissions
800-225-5588 Fax: 248-204-2228
Website: www.ltu.edu
E-mail: admissions@ltu.edu
See listing under "Universities"

MACOMB COMMUNITY COLLEGE
44575 Garfield Rd, Clinton Township MI 48038-1139
Information Center
586-445-7999
Website: www.macomb.edu
E-mail: answer@macomb.edu

MACOMB COMMUNITY COLLEGE
14500 E 12 Mile Rd, Warren MI 48088-3896
Information Center
586-445-7999
Website: www.macomb.edu
E-mail: answer@macomb.edu

Madonna University
36600 Schoolcraft Rd, Livonia MI 48150-1173
734-432-5300

Michigan Technological University
1400 Townsend Dr, Houghton MI 49931-1200
Nancy Rehling, Director of Admissions
906-487-2335

Northwestern Michigan College
1701 E Front St, Traverse City MI 49686-3061
Jim Bensley, Director of Admissions
800-748-0566 Fax: 231-995-1339
Website: www.nmc.edu
E-mail: jbensley@nmc.edu

Oakland University
2200 N Squirrel Rd, Rochester MI 48309
Eleanor L. Reynolds, Assistant Vice President & Director of Admissions
248-370-2100
Website: www.oakland.edu
E-mail: ouinfo@oakland.edu

Olivet College
300 S Main St, Olivet MI 49076-9724
269-749-7000

Siena Heights University
1247 E Siena Heights Dr, Adrian MI 49221-1796
517-263-0731

University of Detroit-Mercy
PO Box 19900, Detroit MI 48219-0900
313-993-1000

University of Michigan-Dearborn
4901 Evergreen Rd, Dearborn MI 48128-1491
The Office of Admissions & Orientation
313-593-5100

Western Michigan University
Kalamazoo MI 49008
269-387-1000

MINNESOTA

Augsburg College
2211 Riverside Ave, Minneapolis MN 55454-1350
612-330-1000

Bethany Lutheran College
700 Luther Dr, Mankato MN 56001
Don Westphal, Dean of Admissions
507-344-7000 Fax: 507-344-7376
Website: www.blc.edu
E-mail: admiss@blc.edu

Carleton College
1 N College St, Northfield MN 55057-4044
800-995-2275 or 507-646-4190 Fax: 507-646-4526
Website: www.carleton.edu
E-mail: admissions@acs.carleton.edu

College of Saint Scholastica
1200 Kenwood Ave, Duluth MN 55811-4199
Brian Dalton, V.P. of Enrollment Management
800-447-5444

Crown College
8700 College View Dr, Saint Bonifacius MN 55375
Mitch Fisk, Director of Admissions
952-446-4142 Fax: 952-446-4149
Website: www.crown.edu
E-mail: johnsonj@crown.edu

Gustavus Adolphus College
800 W College Ave, Saint Peter MN 56082-1485
Mark H. Anderson, Dean of Admission
800-GUSTAVUS Fax: 507-933-7474
Website: www.gustavus.edu
E-mail: admission@gustavus.edu

Hibbing Community College
1515 E 25th St, Hibbing MN 55746-3300
Holly Bigelow, Director of Enrollment
800-224-4HCC or 218-262-7200 Fax: 218-262-6717
Website: www.hibbing.edu
E-mail: admissions@hibbing.edu

Inver Hills Community College
2500 80th St E, Inver Grove Heights MN 55076
651-450-8500 Fax: 651-450-8679
Website: www.inverhills.edu

Macalester College
1600 Grand Ave, Saint Paul MN 55105-1899
651-696-6000

Minnesota State University Moorhead
1104 7th Ave S, Moorhead MN 56563-0002
Regina Monson, Director of Admissions
218-477-2161 Fax: 218-477-4374
Website: go.mnstate.edu
E-mail: dragon@mnstate.edu

Northland Community and Technical College
2022 Central Ave NE
East Grand Forks MN 56721-2702
Brian Huschle, Liberal Arts Chair
800-451-3441 Fax: 218-773-4502
Website: www.northlandcollege.edu
E-mail: admissions@northlandcollege.edu

Ridgewater College-Hutchinson Campus
2 Century Ave SE, Hutchinson MN 55350-3100
Dawn Bjork, Counselor
800-722-1151 Fax: 320-234-8506
Website: www.ridgewater.edu
E-mail: dawn.bjork@ridgewater.edu

Ridgewater College-Willmar Campus
PO Box 1097, Willmar MN 56201-1097
Sally Kerfeld, Director of Admissions
800-722-1151 Fax: 320-222-5212
Website: www.ridgewater.edu
E-mail: sally.kerfeld@ridgewater.edu

St. Cloud State University
720 4th Ave S, Saint Cloud MN 56301-4442
877-654-7278

St. Mary's University of Minnesota
700 Terrace Hts Ste 2, Winona MN 55987-1321
507-452-4430

University of Minnesota
2900 University Ave, Crookston MN 56716-5001
218-281-6510 Fax: 218-281-8575
Website:
admissions.umcrookston.edu/requirements/apply.htm
E-mail: info@umcrookston.edu

University of Minnesota
10 University Dr, Duluth MN 55812-2496
Beth Esselstrom, Director of Admissions
218-726-7171

University of Minnesota - Morris
600 E 4th St, Morris MN 56267-2132
Rodney Oto, Director
800-992-8863

MISSISSIPPI

Millsaps College
PO Box 15495, Jackson MS 39210
601-974-1000

Mississippi University for Women
1100 College St Unit W1613, Columbus MS 39701
Terri Heath, Director of Admissions
877-GO-2-THEW

Mississippi Valley State University
14000 Highway 82 W Box 7222
Itta Bena MS 38941-1401
Office of Admissions
662-254-3347

MISSOURI

Central Methodist University
411 Central Methodist Sq, Fayette MO 65248-1198
Larry Anderson, Director of Admissions
660-248-6247 Fax: 660-248-1872
Website: www.centralmethodist.edu
E-mail: landerso@centralmethodist.edu

Central Missouri State University
Warrensburg MO 64093-8888
Charles Petentler, Associate Director of Admissions
800-956-0177

Columbia College
1001 Rogers St, Columbia MO 65216-0001
Regina Morin, Director of Admissions
573-875-7352 Fax: 573-875-7506
Website: www.ccis.edu
E-mail: admissions@ccis.edu

Culver-Stockton College
1 College Hl, Canton MO 63435-1299
Betty Smith, Director of Enrollment Services
800-537-1883

Drury University
900 N Benton Ave, Springfield MO 65802-3791
417-873-7879

East Central College
1964 Prairie Dell Rd, Union MO 63084
Karen Wieda, Registrar
636-583-5195 ext. 2220 Fax: 636-583-1897
Website: www.eastcentral.edu
E-mail: wiedaks@eastcentral.edu

Lindenwood University
209 S Kingshighway St
Saint Charles MO 63301-1695
Sheryl Guffey, Director of Admissions
636-949-2000 Fax: 636-949-4989
Website: www.lindenwood.edu

Missouri Southern State University - Joplin
3950 Newman Rd, Joplin MO 64801-1512
417-625-9300

Missouri Valley College
500 E College St, Marshall MO 65340-3197
Dr. Lori Gates, Division Dean
660-831-4166

Rockhurst University
1100 Rockhurst Rd, Kansas City MO 64110-2561
Mark Kopenski, VP of Enrollment Management
816-501-4000

St. Charles Community College
4601 Mid Rivers Mall Dr, Cottleville MO 63376
Kathy Brockgreitens-Gober, Director of Admissions
636-922-8000 Fax: 636-922-8236
Website: www.stchas.edu
E-mail: adm-reg@stchas.edu

St. Louis University
221 N Grand Blvd, Saint Louis MO 63103-2097
314-977-2222

Southwest Baptist University
1600 University Ave, Bolivar MO 65613-2597
417-328-5281

State Fair Community College
3201 W 16th St, Sedalia MO 65301-2199
Director of Admissions
660-530-5833 Fax: 660-596-7472
Website: www.sfccmo.edu
E-mail: mparris@sfccmo.edu

Stephens College
PO Box 2121, Columbia MO 65215-0001
David Adams, Dean of Enrollment Management
573-442-2211 Fax: 573-876-7237
Website: www.stephens.edu
E-mail: dadams@stephens.edu

Truman State University
100 E Normal, Kirksville MO 63501
Office of Admission
660-785-4114 Fax: 660-785-7456
Website: admissions.truman.edu
E-mail: admissions@truman.edu

University of Missouri
102 Parker, Rolla MO 65409
Lynn Stichnote, Director of Admission
573-341-4164

University of Missouri
1 University Blvd, Saint Louis MO 63121-4499
Dr. Mark Burkholder, Dean-College of Arts & Sciences
314-516-5501 Fax: 314-516-5415
Website: www.umsl.edu
E-mail: admissions@umsl.edu

Webster University
470 E Lockwood Ave, Saint Louis MO 63119-3194
Dr. David Wilson, Dean, College of Arts and Sciences
314-968-7160 Fax: 314-968-7173
Website: www.webster.edu
E-mail: wilson@webster.edu
See listing under "Universities"

WENTWORTH MILITARY ACADEMY & COLLEGE
1880 Washington Ave, Lexington MO 64067
MAJ Mike Herman, VP for Enrollment
800-962-7682 or 660-259-2221 Fax: 660-259-2677
Website: www.wma.edu
E-mail: admissions@wma.edu

William Jewell College
500 College Hill, Liberty MO 64068-1896
Dr. Rick Winslow, VP Enrollment Management and Student Affairs
800-753-7009 Fax: 816-415-5040
Website: www.jewell.edu
E-mail: winslowr@william.jewell.edu

William Woods University
1 University Ave, Fulton MO 65251-1098
Jimmy Clay, Director of Admissions
573-642-2251 Fax: 573-592-1146
Website: www.williamwoods.edu
E-mail: admissions@williamwoods.edu
See listing under "Universities"

MONTANA

Carroll College
1601 N Benton Ave, Helena MT 59625-0002
Dr. Thomas J. Trebon, President
Cynthia Thornquist, Director of Admissions & Enrollment Operations
406-447-4384 Fax: 406-447-4533
Website: www.carroll.edu
E-mail: admission@carroll.edu

Montana State University - Billings
1500 University Dr, Billings MT 59101-0252
Karen Everett, Director
800-565-MSUB

Montana Tech of the University of Montana
1300 W Park St, Butte MT 59701-8997
800-445-TECH

Rocky Mountain College
1511 Poly Dr, Billings MT 59102-1796
Bonnie Knapp, Director of Admissions
800-877-6259

University of Montana - Western
710 S Atlantic St, Dillon MT 59725-3598
406-683-7011

NEBRASKA

Bellevue University
1000 Galvin Rd S, Bellevue NE 68005-3098
Joseph Wydeven, Dean, College of Arts & Sciences

Chadron State College
1000 Main St, Chadron NE 69337-2690
308-432-6000

College of Saint Mary
7000 Mercy Rd, Omaha NE 68106
Lorin Werth,V.P. for Enrollment
800-926-5534

Dana College
2848 College Dr, Blair NE 68008-1099
Duane A. Heffelfinger, Dean of Enrollment Management
800-444-3262

Doane College
1014 Boswell Ave, Crete NE 68333-2421
402-826-2161

Hastings College
PO Box 269, Hastings NE 68902-0269
402-463-2402

Metropolitan Community College
PO Box 3777, Omaha NE 68103-0777
Becky Nicks, Director of Admissions
402-449-8400 Fax: 402-457-2616
Website: www.mccnab.edu
E-mail: bnicks@mccnab.edu

Midland Lutheran College
900 N Clarkson St, Fremont NE 68025-4200
Todd Hansen, Associate Director of Admissions
402-941-6501 Fax: 402-941-6513
Website: www.mlc.edu
E-mail: admissions@mlc.edu

Nebraska Wesleyan University
5000 Saint Paul Ave, Lincoln NE 68504-2794
Patricia Karthauser, V.P. for University Enrollment
402-466-2371 Fax: 402-465-2177
Website: www.nebrwesleyan.edu
E-mail: admissions@nebrwesleyan.edu

Peru State College
PO Box 10, Peru NE 68421-0010
Office of Admissions
800-742-4412

Union College
3800 S 48th St, Lincoln NE 68506-4300
Buell Fogg, V.P. for Enrollment Services
800-228-4600

NEVADA

GREAT BASIN COLLEGE
1500 College Pkwy, Elko NV 89801-5032
Julie G. Byrnes, Director of Enrollment Management
775-753-2271 Fax: 775-753-2311
Website: www.gbcnv.edu
E-mail: julieb@gwmail.gbcnv.edu
See listing under "Universities"

University of Nevada Las Vegas
4505 S Maryland Pkwy, Las Vegas NV 89154-9901
800-334-8658

NEW HAMPSHIRE

Chester College of New England
40 Chester St, Chester NH 03036-4331
Pam Adie, Director of Admissions
603-887-4401 Fax: 603-887-1777
Website: www.chestercollege.edu
E-mail: padie@chestercollege.edu

Colby-Sawyer College
100 Main St, New London NH 03257-4648
603-526-3000

New Hampshire Community Technical College
1066 Front St, Manchester NH 03102-8528
Jacquie Poirier, Director of Admissions
603-668-6706 Fax: 603-668-5354
Website: www.manchester.nhctc.edu
E-mail: jpoirier@nhctc.edu

Rivier College
420 S Main St, Nashua NH 03060-5086
David Boisvert, Director of Undergraduate Admissions
603-897-8507

St. Anselm College
100 Saint Anselms Dr, Manchester NH 03102-1310
603-641-7000

Southern New Hampshire University
2500 N River Rd, Hooksett NH 03106-1045
Steve Soba, Director of Admissions
603-645-9611 Fax: 603-645-9693
Website: www.snhu.edu
E-mail: s.soba@snhu.edu

NEW JERSEY

Assumption College for Sisters
350 Bernardsville Rd, Mendham NJ 07945-2923
Sr. Mary Joseph Schultz, S.C.C., President
973-543-6528 Fax: 973-543-1738
Website: www.acs350.org
E-mail: acs@acs350.org

Atlantic Cape Community College
5100 Black Horse Pike
Mays Landing NJ 08330-2699
Linda McLeod, Assistant Director of College Recruitment
609-343-5000 Fax: 609-343-4921
Website: www.atlantic.edu
E-mail: accadmit@atlantic.edu
See listing under "Community and Junior Colleges"

Bergen Community College
400 Paramus Rd, Paramus NJ 07652
Julian Gomez, Asst. Director of Admissions
201-447-7100 Fax: 201-444-7036
Website: www.bergen.edu
E-mail: jgomez@bergen.edu

Bloomfield College
467 Franklin St, Bloomfield NJ 07003
973-748-9000

Caldwell College
9 Ryerson Ave, Caldwell NJ 07006-6195
973-618-3000

Centenary College
400 Jefferson St, Hackettstown NJ 07840-2100
Glenna Warren, Director of Admissions
908-852-1400

College of Saint Elizabeth
2 Convent Rd, Morristown NJ 07960-6923
973-292-4000

Fairleigh Dickinson University
285 Madison Ave, Madison NJ 07940-1099
800-338-8803

Felician College
262 S Main St, Lodi NJ 07644-2198
201-559-6000

Monmouth University
400 Cedar Ave, West Long Branch NJ 07764-1890
732-571-3400

New Jersey City University
2039 John F Kennedy Blvd
Jersey City NJ 07305-1588
Carmen Panlilio, Asst. V.P. for Admissions and Financial Aid
201-200-3234 Fax: 201-200-2044
Website: www.njcu.edu
E-mail: admissions@njcu.edu

Ramapo College of New Jersey
505 Ramapo Valley Rd, Mahwah NJ 07430-1623
Director of Admissions
201-684-7300 or 201-684-7301 Fax: 201-684-7964
Website: www.ramapo.edu
E-mail: admissions@ramapo.edu

RICHARD STOCKTON COLLEGE OF NEW JERSEY
PO Box 195, Pomona NJ 08240
John Iacovelli, Dean of Enrollment Management
866-RSC-2885 Fax: 609-626-5541
Website: www.stockton.edu
E-mail: admissions@stockton.edu
See listing under "Universities"

Rider University
2083 Lawrenceville Rd, Lawrenceville NJ 08648-3099
Susan Christian, Director of Admissions
609-896-5042

St. Peter's College
2627 John F Kennedy Blvd, Jersey City NJ 07306
888-SPC-9933

NEW MEXICO

College of the Southwest
6610 N Lovington Hwy, Hobbs NM 88240-9129
Dr. Steve Hill, Dean of Recuitment
505-392-6561 Fax: 505-392-6006
Website: www.csw.edu
E-mail: shill@csw.edu

Eastern New Mexico University
Portales NM 88130
800-367-3668

New Mexico Highlands University
PO Box 9000, Las Vegas NM 87701
Sara Harris, Contact
505-454-3388

New Mexico Military Institute
101 W College Blvd, Roswell NM 88201-5173
LTC. Steven D. Klein, VP, Enrollment & Marketing
800-421-5376 or 505-624-8050 Fax: 505-624-8058
Website: www.nmmi.edu
E-mail: admissions@nmmi.edu
See listing under "Community and Junior Colleges"

New Mexico State University
1500 N 3rd St, Grants NM 87020-2025
Irene Lutz, Director of Admissions
505-287-7981 Fax: 505-287-2329
Website: www.grants.nmsu.edu
E-mail: ilutz@nmsu.edu

St. John's College
1160 Camino Cruz Blanca, Santa Fe NM 87505-4599
L. Clendenin, Director of Admissions
800-331-5232 Fax: 505-984-6162
Website: www.stjohnscollege.edu
E-mail: admissions@sjcsf.edu

UNIVERSITY OF NEW MEXICO
115 Civic Plaza Dr, Taos NM 87571-6401
Henry Trujillo, Senior Student Enrollment Associate
505-737-6200 Fax: 505-737-9317
Website: taos.unm.edu
E-mail: htrujil1@unm.edu

NEW YORK

Adelphi University
Garden City NY 11530
516-877-3100

Alfred University
1 Saxson Dr, Alfred NY 14802
607-871-2111

Broome Community College
907 Upper Front St, Binghamton NY 13905
Anthony S. Fiorelli, Director of Admissions
607-778-5001 Fax: 607-778-5442
Website: www.sunybroome.edu
E-mail: fiorelli_a@sunybroome.edu

Cazenovia College
Cazenovia NY 13035-1084
Robert Croot, Dean of Admissions & Financial Aid
800-654-3210

Colgate University
13 Oak Dr, Hamilton NY 13346-1386
Gary Ross, Director of Admissions
315-228-7401

College of New Rochelle
29 Castle Pl, New Rochelle NY 10805-2339
914-654-5000

College of Saint Rose
432 Western Ave, Albany NY 12203-1419
Maryelizabeth Amico, Asst V.P. for Undergraduate Admissions
518-454-5150 Fax: 518-454-2013
Website: www.strose.edu
E-mail: admit@strose.edu

CUNY City College
Convent Ave at 138th St, New York NY 10031
Celia Lloyd, Interim Director of Admissions
212-650-6977

CUNY Hunter College
695 Park Ave, New York NY 10021
Aaron Gibbs, Assistant Director of Recruitment
212-650-3946 Fax: 212-650-3336
Website: www.hunter.cuny.edu
E-mail: aaron.gibbs@hunter.cuny.edu

Daemen College
4380 Main St, Amherst NY 14226-3592
Donna Shaffner, Director of Admissions
800-462-7652 Fax: 716-839-8229
Website: www.daemen.edu/admissions
E-mail: admissions@daemen.edu

Dowling College
150 Idle Hour Blvd, Oakdale NY 11769-1999
Diane Kazanecki-Kempter, Contact
631-244-3000 Fax: 631-244-1059
Website: www.dowling.edu
E-mail: admissions@dowling.edu

D'Youville College
320 Porter Ave, Buffalo NY 14201-1084
716-829-7600

Elmira College
One Park Pl, Elmira NY 14901-2099
Dr. Thomas Meier, President
Gary Fallis, Dean of Admissions
800-935-6472

Excelsior College
7 Columbia Cir, Albany NY 12203-5156
518-464-8500

Farmingdale SUNY
2350 Broadhollow Rd, Farmingdale NY 11735
631-420-2200

FIVE TOWNS COLLEGE
305 N Service Rd, Dix Hills NY 11746-5871
631-424-7000 ext. 2110 Fax: 631-656-2172
Website: www.fivetowns.edu
E-mail: admissions@ftc.edu
See listing under "Universities"

Fordham University
441 E Fordham Rd, Bronx NY 10458-9993
John W. Buckley, Dean of Admissions
718-817-4000

Fordham University - Lincoln Center
113 W 60th St, New York NY 10023-7484
212-636-6710

Hamilton College
198 College Hill Rd, Clinton NY 13323-1295
Richard Fuller, Dean of Admissions
315-859-4421

Hilbert College
5200 S Park Ave, Hamburg NY 14075-1597
Timothy Lee, Director of Admissions
716-649-7900 Fax: 716-649-0702
Website: www.hilbert.edu
E-mail: tlee@hilbert.edu

Hobart & William Smith Colleges
Pulteney St, Geneva NY 14456
John Young, Director of Admissions
315-789-5500

Houghton College
PO Box 128, Houghton NY 14744-0128
585-567-9200

Iona College
715 North Ave, New Rochelle NY 10801-1890
Kevin Cavanagh, Assistant V.P. for College Admissions
914-633-2502 Fax: 914-637-2778
Website: www.iona.edu

Le Moyne College
1419 Salt Springs Rd, Syracuse NY 13214-1301
800-333-4733

Long Island University
121 Speonk Riverhead Rd, Riverhead NY 11901
631-287-8010

Long Island University-C. W. Post Campus
720 Northern Blvd, Brookville NY 11548-1300
Joanne Graziano, Executive Director of Admissions
516-299-2900 Fax: 516-299-2137
Website: www.liu.edu/cwpost
E-mail: enroll@cwpost.liu.edu

Manhattan College
4513 Manhattan College Pkwy
Riverdale NY 10471-4099
Dr. Mary Ann O'Donnell, Dean of Arts
718-862-7200

Marist College
3399 North Rd, Poughkeepsie NY 12601
Jay E. Murray, Director of Admissions
845-575-3000

Marymount College at Fordham University
100 Marymount Ave, Tarrytown NY 10591-3796
914-631-3200

Marymount Manhattan College
221 E 71st St, New York NY 10021-4501
Jim Rogers, Dean of Admissions
800-MARYMOUNT Fax: 212-517-0448
Website: www.mmm.edu
E-mail: admissions@mmm.edu

Mercy College
555 Broadway, Dobbs Ferry NY 10522-1189
Kathleen Jackson, Director of Admissions
800-MERCY-NY

Molloy College
1000 Hempstead Ave
Rockville Centre NY 11570-1100
Marguerite Lane, Director of Admissions
516-678-5000 ext. 6291 Fax: 516-256-2247
Website: www.molloy.edu
E-mail: admissions@molloy.edu
See listing under "Universities"

Mt. St. Mary College
330 Powell Ave, Newburgh NY 12550-3494
845-561-0800

Nazareth College of Rochester
4245 East Ave, Rochester NY 14618-3790
585-389-2525

New York City College of Technology CUNY
300 Jay St, Brooklyn NY 11201-1909
Joe Lento, Director of Admissions
718-260-5000

New York Institute of Technology
PO Box 8000, Old Westbury NY 11568-8000
516-686-7516

Niagara University
PO Box 2011, Niagara University NY 14109-2011
George Pachter, Dean of Admissions & Records
800-462-2111

Nyack College
1 South Blvd
Nyack NY 10960-3698
845-358-1710

Pratt Institute
200 Willoughby Ave, Brooklyn NY 11205-3899
Heidi Metcalf, Director of Admissions
718-636-3600 Fax: 718-636-3670
Website: www.pratt.edu
E-mail: hmetcalf@pratt.edu
Critical and Visual Studies
Writing for Publication, Performance and Media

PURCHASE COLLEGE STATE UNIVERSITY OF NEW YORK (SUNY)
735 Anderson Hill Rd, Purchase NY 10577-1400
Stephanie McCaine, Director of Admissions
914-251-6300 Fax: 914-251-6314
Website: www.purchase.edu
E-mail: admisn@purchase.edu
See listing under "Universities"

Roberts Wesleyan College
2301 Westside Dr, Rochester NY 14624-1997
Office of Admissions
585-594-6400 Fax: 585-594-6371
Website: www.roberts.edu
E-mail: admissions@roberts.edu

Rochester Institute of Technology
1 Lomb Memorial Dr, Rochester NY 14623-5603
585-475-2411

St. John's University
8000 Utopia Pkwy, Queens NY 11439
Office of Admission
877-STJ-5550 ext. 101 Fax: 718-990-2096
Website: www.stjohns.edu/learnmore
E-mail: admhelp@stjohns.edu
See listing under "Universities"

St. John's University
300 Howard Ave, Staten Island NY 10301-4496
718-447-4343

St. Joseph's College
245 Clinton Ave, Brooklyn NY 11205-3688
Theresa LaRocca Meyer, V.P. for Enrollment Management
718-636-6800 Fax: 718-636-8303
Website: www.sjcny.edu
E-mail: tlaroccameyer@sjcny.edu

St. Joseph's College
155 W Roe Blvd, Patchogue NY 11772
631-447-3200

St. Lawrence University
2501 Saint Lawrence Univ, Canton NY 13617-1475
315-229-5011

Sarah Lawrence College
1 Meadway, Bronxville NY 10708
914-337-0700

SUNY at Albany
1400 Washington Ave, Albany NY 12222-1000
Thomas Flemming, Associate Director of Admissions
518-442-5435

SUNY at Stony Brook
Stony Brook NY 11794-0001
631-689-6000

SUNY College at Brockport
350 New Campus Dr, Brockport NY 14420-2997
Bernard S. Valento, Director of Undergraduate Admissions
585-395-2751 Fax: 585-395-5452
Website: www.brockport.edu
E-mail: admit@brockport.edu

SUNY College at Old Westbury
PO Box 210, Old Westbury NY 11568-0210
516-876-3000

SUNY College at Potsdam
Potsdam NY 13676
Thomas W. Nesbitt, Director of Admissions
315-267-2000

SUNY College of Agriculture & Technology
107 Schenectady Ave, Cobleskill NY 12043
Clayton A. Smith, Director of Admissions
800-295-8988

SUNY College of Technology
Alfred NY 14802
Deborah J. Goodrich, Associate VP Enrollment Mgmt.
800-4AL-FRED Fax: 607-587-4299
Website: www.alfredstate.edu
E-mail: admissions@alfredstate.edu

SUNY Institute of Technology Utica/Rome
PO Box 3050, Utica NY 13504-3050
315-792-7100

SUNY Niagara County Community College
3111 Saunders Settlement Rd
Sanborn NY 14132-9487
Kathleen Saunders, Director of Admissions
716-614-6200 Fax: 716-614-6820
Website: www.niagaracc.suny.edu
E-mail: admissions@niagaracc.suny.edu

SUNY Orange County Community College
115 South St, Middletown NY 10940-6437
Margot St. Lawrence, Director of Admissions
845-341-4030 Fax: 845-342-8662
Website: www.sunyorange.edu
E-mail: apply@sunyorange.edu
See listing under "Community and Junior Colleges"

SUNY Sullivan County Community College
112 College Rd, Loch Sheldrake NY 12759-5151
Sari Rosenheck, Director of Admissions
845-434-5750 Fax: 845-434-0923
Website: www.sullivan.suny.edu
E-mail: admissions@sullivan.suny.edu
Student Housing on Campus.

University at Buffalo, The State University of New York
15 Capen Hall, Buffalo NY 14260-1660
Patricia G. Armstrong, Director of Admissions
888-UB-ADMIT

University of Rochester
Wallis Hall, Rochester NY 14627
585-275-2121

Utica College
1600 Burrstone Rd, Utica NY 13502-4857
315-792-3111

Wagner College
One Campus Rd, Staten Island NY 10301
Leigh Ann DePascale, Director of Admissions
718-390-3411

Wells College
PO Box 500, Aurora NY 13026
Susan Sloan, Director of Admissions
800-952-9355 Fax: 315-364-3227
Website: www.wells.edu
E-mail: ssloan@wells.edu

NORTH CAROLINA

Barton College
PO Box 5000, Wilson NC 27893
252-399-6300

Belmont Abbey College
100 Belmont Mount Holly Rd
Belmont NC 28012-1802
888-222-0110

Brevard College
One Brevard College Dr, Brevard NC 28712
Joretta Nelson, Vice President Enrollment Management
828-883-8292 Fax: 828-884-3790
Website: www.brevard.edu
E-mail: admissions@brevard.edu

Catawba College
2300 W Innes St, Salisbury NC 28144-2488
Dr. L. Russell Watjen, Ph.D., V.P. & Dean of Admissions
704-637-4402 Fax: 704-637-4222
Website: www.catawba.edu
E-mail: admission@catawba.edu

Chowan University
One University Pl, Murfreesboro NC 27855
Chad Holt, Dean of Admissions
800-488-4101 Fax: 252-398-1190
Website: www.chowan.edu
E-mail: holtc@chowan.edu

Davidson College
PO Box 7156, Davidson NC 28035-7156
Chris Gruber, Acting Dean of Admission
800-768-0380

Greensboro College
815 W Market St, Greensboro NC 27401-1875
336-272-7102

Guilford College
5800 W Friendly Ave, Greensboro NC 27410-4173
Randy Doss, Dean of Enrollment
336-316-2100

Haywood Community College
185 Freedlander Dr, Clyde NC 28721
Debbie Rowland, Coordinator of Admissions
828-627-4500 Fax: 828-627-4513
Website: www.haywood.edu
E-mail: drowland@haywood.edu

Heritage Bible College
PO Box 1628, Dunn NC 28335
910-892-3178 Fax: 910-892-1809
Website: www.heritagebiblecollege.org
E-mail: generalinfo@heritagebiblecollege.org

James Sprunt Community College
PO Box 398, Kenansville NC 28349-0398
Lea Grady, Admissions
910-296-2500 Fax: 910-296-1636
Website: www.jamessprunt.edu

Lees-McRae College
PO Box 128, Banner Elk NC 28604-0128
Walt Crutchfield, Dean of Admissions
800-280-4562

Mars Hill College
Mars Hill NC 28754
Chad Holt, Dean of Enrollment
866-MHC-4-YOU

Mayland Community College
PO Box 547, Spruce Pine NC 28777-0547
Cathy B. Morrison, Director of Enrollment Management
828-765-7351 Fax: 828-765-0728
Website: www.mayland.edu
E-mail: cmorrison@mayland.edu

Meredith College
3800 Hillsborough St, Raleigh NC 27607-5298
Heidi L. Fletcher, Director of Admissions
919-760-8581

Montreat College
PO Box 1267, Montreat NC 28757-1267
800-622-6968

Mt. Olive College
634 Henderson St, Mount Olive NC 28365
Tim Woodard, Director of Admissions
919-658-2502

North Carolina State University
PO Box 7001, Raleigh NC 27695-0001
919-515-2011

Peace College
15 E Peace St, Raleigh NC 27604-1194
Laura C. Bingham, President
800-PEACE-47 Fax: 919-508-2306
Website: www.peace.edu
E-mail: admissions@peace.edu

Pfeiffer University
PO Box 960, Misenheimer NC 28109-0960
704-463-1360

Queens University of Charlotte
1900 Selwyn Ave, Charlotte NC 28274-0002
704-337-2212

St. Andrews Presbyterian College
1700 Dogwood Mile St, Laurinburg NC 28352-5521
Glenn Batten, Vice President for Enrollment
910-277-5554

Salem College
Winston Salem NC 27108
Dana Evans, Dean of Admissions/Fin. Aid
800-32-SALEM Fax: 336-917-5572
Website: www.salem.edu
E-mail: admissions@salem.edu
See listing under "Women's Colleges"

University of North Carolina at Greensboro
1000 Spring Garden St, Greensboro NC 27412-0001
336-334-5243

Warren Wilson College
PO Box 9000, Asheville NC 28815-9000
Richard Blomgren, Dean of Admissions
828-298-3325

Western Carolina University
University Dr, Cullowhee NC 28723-9646
828-227-7211

Wingate University
201 E Wilson St, Wingate NC 28174-9600
704-233-8000

Winston-Salem State University
601 S Mrtn Lther King Jr Dr
Winston Salem NC 27110-0003
336-750-2000

NORTH DAKOTA

Dickinson State University
Dickinson ND 58601-4896
Steve Glasser, Director of Enrollment Services
800-279-4295 Fax: 701-483-2409
Website: www.dickinsonstate.edu
E-mail: dsu.hawks@dickinsonstate.edu

Jamestown College
6000 College Ln, Jamestown ND 58405-0002
701-252-3467

Mayville State University
330 3rd St NE, Mayville ND 58257-1299
Dr. Ray Gerszewski, Vice President Student Affairs
800-437-4104 Fax: 701-788-4748
Website: www.mayvillestate.edu
E-mail: admit@mayvillestate.edu

Minot State University
500 University Ave W, Minot ND 58707-0002
Dennis Parisien, Enrollment Services Rep.
800-777-0750 ext. 3350

Minot State University-Bottineau Campus
105 Simrall Blvd, Bottineau ND 58318-1159
Paula Berg, Associate Dean of Student Affairs
800-542-6866 Fax: 701-228-5499
Website: www.misu-b.nodak.edu
E-mail: paula.berg@misu.nodak.edu

Valley City State University
101 College St SW, Valley City ND 58072-4024
Dan Klein, Director of Enrollment Services
800-532-8641 ext. 7101 Fax: 701-845-7299
Website: www.vcsu.edu
E-mail: enrollment.services@vcsu.edu
See listing under "Universities"

Williston State College
PO Box 1326, Williston ND 58802-1326
Penny Soiseth, Associate Director Enrollment Services
701-774-4200 Fax: 701-774-4544
Website: www.wsc.nodak.edu
E-mail: penny.soiseth@wsc.nodak.edu

OHIO

Baldwin-Wallace College
275 Eastland Rd, Berea OH 44017-2088
440-826-2900

Bowling Green State University
110 McFall Center, Bowling Green OH 43403-0001
866-CHOOSE-BGSU

Capital University
2199 E Main St, Columbus OH 43209-2394
614-236-6011

Cleveland State University
2121 Euclid Ave RW 204, Cleveland OH 44115
Dr. Richard Arndt, Dean of Undergraduate Recruitment and College Partnerships
888-CSU-OHIO Fax: 216-687-9210
Website: www.csuohio.edu
E-mail: admissions@csuohio.edu

College of Wooster
Wooster OH 44691-2363
Paul J. Deutsch, Dean of Admissions
800-877-9905

Defiance College
701 N Clinton St, Defiance OH 43512-1695
419-784-4010

Franciscan University of Steubenville
University Blvd, Steubenville OH 43952
Margaret J. Weber, Director of Admissions
800-783-6220 or 740-283-6226 Fax: 740-284-5456
Website: www.admissions.edu
E-mail: mweber@franciscan.edu

Heidelberg College
310 E Market St, Tiffin OH 44883-2462
418-448-2000

Kent State University
PO Box 5190, Kent OH 44242-0001
Paul Deutsch, Director of Admissions
330-672-2444

Lake Erie College
391 W Washington St, Painesville OH 44077-3389
440-352-3361

Malone College
515 25th St NW, Canton OH 44709-3897
John Chopka, Dean of Admissions
330-471-8100

Marietta College
215 5th St, Marietta OH 45750-4047
740-376-4600

Miami University
E High St, Oxford OH 45056
513-529-2531

Mt. Union College
1972 Clark Ave, Alliance OH 44601-3929
Vincent Heslop, Director of Admissions
800-334-6682

Mount Vernon Nazarene University
800 Martinsburg Rd, Mount Vernon OH 43050-9509
Timothy Eades, Director of Admissions
866-462-6868

Notre Dame College
4545 College Rd, Cleveland OH 44121-4293
216-381-1680

Oberlin College
Carnegie Bldg, Oberlin OH 44074
Debra Chermonte, Dean of Admissions & Financial Aid

Ohio Dominican University
1216 Sunbury Rd, Columbus OH 43219-2099
614-253-2741

OHIO NORTHERN UNIVERSITY
525 S Main St, Ada OH 45810-1555
Robert A. Manzer, Dean
419-772-2130
Website: www.onu.edu
E-mail: admissions-ug@onu.edu
See listing under "Universities"

The Ohio State University
Colleges of Arts and Sciences
Denny Hall, 164 W 17th Ave, Columbus OH 43210
614-292-6961 Fax: 614-292-6303
Website: artsandsciences.osu.edu

Ohio State University-Lima Campus
4240 Campus Dr, Lima OH 45804-3576
Garlene Smithson, Dir. Enrollment Services
419-995-8396

Ohio University
Chillicothe Campus
PO Box 629, Chillicothe OH 45601
Student Services
740-774-7200 Fax: 740-774-7295
Website: www.ohiou.edu/chillicothe/

Ohio University - Zanesville Branch
1425 Newark Rd, Zanesville OH 43701-2695
740-588-1439

OHIO WESLEYAN UNIVERSITY
61 S Sandusky St, Delaware OH 43015-2398
Director of Admission
740-368-3020 Fax: 740-368-3314
Website: www.owu.edu
E-mail: owuadmit@owu.edu

Owens Community College
3200 Bright Rd, Findlay OH 45840
William J. Ivoska PhD., Vice President of Student Services
567-429-3500 Fax: 567-423-0246
Website: www.owens.edu
E-mail: admissions@owens.edu

Owens Community College
PO Box 10000, Toledo OH 43699-1947
William J. Ivoska, Ph.D, Vice President of Student Services
567-661-7000 Fax: 567-661-7607
Website: www.owens.edu
E-mail: admissions@owens.edu

Sinclair Community College
444 W 3rd St, Dayton OH 45402-1460
Director of Admissions
937-512-3000 Fax: 937-512-2393
Website: www.sinclair.edu
E-mail: admit@sinclair.edu

University of Dayton
300 College Park, Dayton OH 45469-1300
Robert F. Durkle, Director of Admission
800-837-7433 Fax: 937-229-4729
Website: admission.udayton.edu
E-mail: admission@udayton.edu

University of Rio Grande
General Delivery, Rio Grande OH 45674-9999
Dr. Barry Thompson, Dean
740-245-5353 ext. 7254

Ursuline College
2550 Lander Rd, Cleveland OH 44124-4398
Sarah E. Sundermeier, Director of Admissions
888-URSULINE Toll Free Fax: 440-684-6138
Website: www.admission.ursuline.edu
E-mail: admission@ursuline.edu

Walsh University
2020 E Maple St, North Canton OH 44720
800-362-9846

Wilmington College
1870 Quaker Way, Wilmington OH 45177
937-382-6661

Youngstown State University
Sweeney Welcome Ctr, One University Plz
Youngstown OH 44555-0002
Sue Davis, Contact
877-GO-TO-YSU

OKLAHOMA

Bacone College
2299 Old Bacone Rd, Muskogee OK 74403-1568
Jerrett Phillips, Director of Admissions
918-781-7340

Oklahoma City University
2501 N Blackwelder Ave
Oklahoma City OK 73106-1493
Shery Boyles, Director of Admissions
405-521-5050

Oklahoma State University
Stillwater OK 74078
Bruce Crauder, Associate Dean
405-744-5663
Website: www.okstate.edu
E-mail: bruce.crauder@okstate.edu

Oklahoma Wesleyan University
2201 Silver Lake Rd, Bartlesville OK 74006-6299
918-333-6151

Oral Roberts University
7777 S Lewis Ave, Tulsa OK 74171-0001
Chris Belcher, Director of Undergraduate Admissions
800-678-8876

Rogers State University - Claremore Campus
1701 W Will Rogers Blvd, Claremore OK 74017-3259
Joe Wiley, President
918-343-7777

University of Tulsa
600 S College Ave, Tulsa OK 74104-3126
Earl Johnson, Dean of Admission
918-631-2307 Fax: 918-631-5003
Website: www.utulsa.edu
E-mail: admission@utulsa.edu

OREGON

Cascade College
9101 E Burnside St, Portland OR 97216-1599
Jim Murphy, Director of Enrollment Management
800-550-7678 Fax: 503-257-1222
Website: www.cascade.edu
E-mail: admissions@cascade.edu

Linfield College
900 SE Baker St, Mc Minnville OR 97128-6894
503-472-2200

Marylhurst University
17600 Pacific Hwy (Hwy 43)
Marylhurst OR 97036-0261
Director of Admissions
800-634-9982 ext. 6268 Fax: 503-635-6585
Website: www.marylhurst.edu
E-mail: studentinfo@marylhurst.edu

Oregon Institute of Technology
3201 Campus Dr, Klamath Falls OR 97601-8801
541-885-1000

PACIFIC UNIVERSITY
2043 College Way, Forest Grove OR 97116-1797
Karen M. Dunston, Executive Director of Admissions
800-677-6712 Fax: 503-352-2975
Website: www.pacific.edu
E-mail: admissions@pacific.edu

Reed College
3202 SE Woodstock Blvd, Portland OR 97202-8139
503-771-1112

Rogue Community College
3345 Redwood Hwy, Grants Pass OR 97527-9298
Claudia Sullivan, Director of Enrollment Services
541-956-7500 Fax: 541-471-3585
Website: www.roguecc.edu
E-mail: csullivan@roguecc.edu
See listing under "Community and Junior Colleges"

University of Portland
5000 N Willamette Blvd, Portland OR 97203-5798
Jason McDonald, Dean of Admissions
503-943-7911 Fax: 503-943-7315
Website: www.up.edu
E-mail: mcdonaja@up.edu

Warner Pacific College
2219 SE 68th Ave, Portland OR 97215-4026
Shannon Mackey, Director of Admissions
503-517-1000 Fax: 503-517-1352
Website: www.warnerpacific.edu
E-mail: admissions@warnerpacific.edu

Western Oregon University
345 Monmouth Ave N, Monmouth OR 97361-1314
David McDonald, Dean, Admission, Retention & Enrollment Management
877-877-1593

PENNSYLVANIA

Albright College
PO Box 15234, Reading PA 19612-5234
800-252-1856

Arcadia University
450 S Easton Rd, Glenside PA 19038-3295
Dennis Nostrand, VP for Enrollment Management
877-ARCADIA (877-272-2342)

Cabrini College
610 King of Prussia Rd, Radnor PA 19087-3698
Mark T. Osborn, VP for Enrollment Management
610-902-8100

California University of Pennsylvania
250 University Ave, California PA 15419-1394
724-938-4000

Carnegie Mellon University
5000 Forbes Ave, Pittsburgh PA 15213-3890
412-268-2000

Cedar Crest College
100 College Dr, Allentown PA 18104-6196
Judith A. Neyhart, Vice President Enrollment
800-360-1222

Chatham College
Woodland Rd, Pittsburgh PA 15232-2826
412-365-1100

Chestnut Hill College
9601 Germantown Ave, Philadelphia PA 19118-2693
Jodie King, Director of Admissions
215-248-7001

Clarion University of Pennsylvania
840 Wood St, Clarion PA 16214-1232
William Bailey, Dean of Enrollment Management
814-393-2306 Fax: 814-393-2030
Website: www.clarion.edu
E-mail: admissions@clarion.edu

College Misericordia
301 Lake St, Dallas PA 18612-1008
Admissions
570-674-6400

Community College of Allegheny County
Allegheny Campus: 808 Ridge Ave, Pittsburgh PA 15212 Admissions: 412.237.2700
Boyce Campus: 595 Beatty Rd, Monroeville PA 15146 Admissions: 724.325.6614
North Campus: 8701 Perry Highway, Pittsburgh PA 15237 Admissions: 412.369.3600
South Campus: 1750 Clairton Rd, West Mifflin PA 15122 Admissions: 412-469-4301
Website: www.ccac.edu

Community College of Beaver County
1 Campus Dr, Monaca PA 15061-2566
724-775-8561 Fax: 724-775-4687
Website: www.ccbc.edu
E-mail: admissions@ccbc.edu

DeSales University
2755 Station Ave, Center Valley PA 18034-9565
610-282-1100 Fax: 610-282-2342
Website: www.desales.edu

Duquesne University
600 Forbes Ave, Pittsburgh PA 15282-0001
Paul-James Cukanna, Director of Admissions
412-396-5000

Edinboro University of Pennsylvania
Edinboro PA 16444-0001
814-732-2000

Gannon University
109 University Sq, Erie PA 16541-0001
Christopher Tremblay, Director of Admissions
800-GANNON-U

Gettysburg College
300 N Washington St, Gettysburg PA 17325-1483
Gail Sweezey, Director of Admissions
717-337-6100

Gratz College
7605 Old York Rd, Melrose Park PA 19027
Jill Sigman, Director of Admissions
215-635-7300 Fax: 215-635-7320
Website: www.gratzcollege.edu
E-mail: admissions@gratz.edu

Gwynedd-Mercy College
1325 Sumneytown Pike, Gwynedd Valley PA 19437
Dennis Murphy, V.P. Enrollment Management
800-DIAL-GMC

Haverford College
370 Lancaster Ave, Haverford PA 19041-1392
Jess Lord, Dean of Admission
610-896-1350 Fax: 610-896-1338
Website: www.haverford.edu
E-mail: admission@haverford.edu

Holy Family University
9801 Frankford Avenue, Philadelphia PA 19114
Lauren Campbell, Director of Admissions
215-637-3050 Fax: 215-281-1022
Website: www.holyfamily.edu
E-mail: admissions@holyfamily.edu

Immaculata University
Immaculata PA 19345
Women's College Office of Admissions
610-647-4400

Juniata College
1700 Moore St, Huntingdon PA 16652-2196
Michelle Bartol, Dean of Enrollment
877-JUNIATA Fax: 814-641-3100
Website: www.juniata.edu
E-mail: admissions@juniata.edu

King's College
133 N River St, Wilkes Barre PA 18711-0801
Michelle Lawrence-Schmude, Dean of Admission
570-208-5900 Fax: 570-208-5971
Website: www.kings.edu
E-mail: admissions@kings.edu

Lafayette College
High St, Easton PA 18042
610-330-5000

La Roche College
9000 Babcock Blvd, Pittsburgh PA 15237-5898
Thomas Hassett, Director of Admissions
412-536-1272

La Salle University
1900 W Olney Ave, Philadelphia PA 19141-1199
Robert Voss, Dean of Admissions
215-951-1500

Lebanon Valley College
101 N College Ave, Annville PA 17003-1400
William Brown, Dean of Admissions & Financial Aid
866-LVC-4ADM

Lehigh University
27 Memorial Dr West, Bethlehem PA 18015-3094
Eric Kaplan, Dean of Admissions
610-758-3100

Lincoln University
Lincoln University PA 19352
Michael C. Taylor, Director of Admissions
800-790-0191

Lock Haven University
Lock Haven PA 17745
James C. Reeser, Dean of Admissions
570-893-2027

Mansfield University of Pennsylvania
Academy St, Mansfield PA 16933
570-662-4000

Mercyhurst College
501 E 38th St, Erie PA 16546-0001
800-825-1926

Messiah College
1 S College Ave, Grantham PA 17027
717-766-2511

MOUNT ALOYSIUS COLLEGE
7373 Admiral Peary Hwy, Cresson PA 16630-1999
Frank C. Crouse Jr., Vice President for Enrollment Management
814-886-6383 or 888-823-2220 Fax: 814-886-6441
Website: www.mtaloy.edu
E-mail: admissions@mtaloy.edu

Neumann College
1 Neumann Dr, Aston PA 19014-1298
Dennis Murphy, Director of Admissions
610-459-0905 Fax: 610-558-5652
Website: www.neumann.edu
E-mail: neumann@neumann.edu

Pennsylvania College of Technology
1 College Ave, Williamsport PA 17701
570-326-3761

Pennsylvania State University
Broadhead Rd, Monaca PA 15061
724-773-3500

Pennsylvania State University
3550 7th St Rd, New Kensington PA 15068-1765
Patricia K. Brady, Director of Admissions
724-334-5466

Point Park University
201 Wood St, Pittsburgh PA 15222-1984
Philip Clarke, Associate Director of Admissions
412-392-3430

Robert Morris College
600 5th Ave, Pittsburgh PA 15219-3010
412-227-6800

Robert Morris University
6001 University Blvd, Coraopolis PA 15108
412-262-8200

Rosemont College
1400 Montgomery Ave, Rosemont PA 19010-1699
Ms. Rennie Andrews, Director of Admissions
610-526-2966

Seton Hill University
Greensburg PA 15601-1599
Mary Kay Cooper, Director of Admissions and Adult Student Services
800-826-6234

Slippery Rock University
14 Maltby Dr, Slippery Rock PA 16057-1326
724-738-9000

Susquehanna University
514 University Ave, Selinsgrove PA 17870-1164
570-374-0101

Temple University
Broad St & Montgomery Ave, Philadelphia PA 19122
215-204-7000

Temple University Ambler
Ambler PA 19002
Michael Schlotterbeck, Contact
215-283-1252

Thiel College
75 College Ave, Greenville PA 16125-2181
724-589-2000

University of Pittsburgh
150 Finoli Dr, Greensburg PA 15601
Brandi S. Darr, Director of Admissions and Financial Aid
724-836-9880

University of Pittsburgh at Bradford
300 Campus Dr, Bradford PA 16701-2812
Alexander Nazemetz, Director of Admissions
814-362-7555

Washington & Jefferson College
60 S Lincoln St, Washington PA 15301-4801
Alton E. Newell, Vice President for Enrollment
724-223-6025 Fax: 724-223-6534
Website: www.washjeff.edu
E-mail: admission@washjeff.edu

Waynesburg College
51 W College St, Waynesburg PA 15370-1222
Robin L. Moore, Dean of Admissions
800-225-7393

Westminster College
New Wilmington PA 16172-0001
Doug Swartz, Director of Admissions
724-946-7100

Widener University
1 University Pl, Chester PA 19013-5792
Edwin Wright, Dean of Admissions
610-499-4000 Fax: 610-499-4676
Website: www.widener.edu
E-mail: admissions.office@widener.edu

Wilkes University
170 S Franklin St, Wilkes Barre PA 18766-0001
570-408-5000

RHODE ISLAND

Providence College
549 River Ave, Providence RI 02918-0002
401-865-1000

University of Rhode Island
Kingston RI 02881
401-874-1000

SOUTH CAROLINA

Benedict College
1600 Harden St, Columbia SC 29204-1086
Phyllis L. Thompson, Director of Admissions
803-253-5143

Charleston Southern University
PO Box 118087, Charleston SC 29423-8087
Cheryl Burton, Director of Admissions
800-947-7474

Clemson University
105 Sikes Hall, Clemson SC 29634
864-656-2287

College of Charleston
66 George St, Charleston SC 29424-1407
Suzette Stille, Admissions
843-953-5670

Columbia College
1301 Columbia College Dr, Columbia SC 29203-5998
Elizabeth G. Quackenbush, Director of Admissions
803-786-3871

Erskine College & Seminary
PO Box 176, Due West SC 29639
Bart Walker, Director of Admissions
864-379-8838 Fax: 864-379-3048
Website: www.erskine.edu
E-mail: admissions@erskine.edu

Greenville Technical College
PO Box 5616, Greenville SC 29606-5616
Carolyn Watkins, Dean of Admissions
800-723-0673 (US) or 800-922-1183 (SC)
Website: www.greenvilletech.com

Lander University
320 Stanley Ave, Greenwood SC 29649-2099
Jonathan Reece, Director of Admissions
888-4-LANDER

Limestone College
1115 College Dr, Gaffney SC 29340-3799
Chris Phenicie, V.P. for Enrollment
864-489-7151 Fax: 864-488-8206
Website: www.limestone.edu
E-mail: cphenicie@limestone.edu

North Greenville University
PO Box 1892, Tigerville SC 29688-1892
Dr. Tom Allen, Dean
Website: www.ngu.edu
See listing under "Universities"

South Carolina State University
PO Box 7127, Orangeburg SC 29117-0001
Lillian M. Adderson, Director of Admissions
803-536-7185

Spartanburg Community College
PO Box 4386, Spartanburg SC 29305-4386
Nancy Garmroth, Dean of Admissions & Financial Aid
864-592-4810 Fax: 864-592-4945
Website: sccsc.edu

University of South Carolina
Columbia SC 29208-0001
803-777-7700

University of South Carolina Beaufort
801 Carteret St, Beaufort SC 29902-4601
Anita M. Folsom, Director of Admissions
843-521-4101

University of South Carolina - Upstate
800 University Way, Spartanburg SC 29303-4932
Donette Stewart, Assistant VC for Enrollment Services
864-503-5246 Fax: 864-503-5727
Website: www.uscupstate.edu
E-mail: dstewart@uscupstate.edu
See listing under "Universities"

Winthrop University
701 W Oakland Ave, Rock Hill SC 29733-0001
803-323-2211

SOUTH DAKOTA

Black Hills State University
1200 University St, Spearfish SD 57799-0002
605-642-6011

Dakota State University
820 N Washington Ave, Madison SD 57042-1799
605-256-5112

TENNESSEE

Aquinas College
4210 Harding Rd, Nashville TN 37205
Diane C. LeJeune, Director of Admissions
615-297-7545 ext. 460 Fax: 615-279-3893
Website: www.aquinascollege.edu
E-mail: lejeuned@aquinascollege.edu

Austin Peay State University
601 College St, Clarksville TN 37044-0002
931-221-7011 Fax: 931-221-6168
Website: www.apsu.edu
E-mail: admissions@apsu.edu

Belmont University
1900 Belmont Blvd, Nashville TN 37212-3757
615-460-6000

Bryan College
PO Box 7000, Dayton TN 37321-7000
423-775-2041

Carson-Newman College
1646 Russell Ave, Jefferson City TN 37760
865-471-4000

Crichton College
255 N Highland St, Memphis TN 38111-4745
Shelly Luttrell, Dean of Admissions
901-320-9797 Fax: 901-320-9791
Website: www.crichton.edu
E-mail: admissions@crichton.edu

East Tennessee State University
PO Box 70730, Johnson City TN 37614
Dr. Don Johnson, Dean of Arts & Sciences
423-439-5671

Freed-Hardeman University
158 E Main St, Henderson TN 38340-2398
731-989-6000

INTERNATIONAL ACADEMY OF DESIGN & TECHNOLOGY
1 Bridgestone Park, Nashville TN 37214
Richard D. Wechner, President
615-232-7384 Fax: 615-391-0728
Website: www.iadtnashville.com
E-mail: rwechner@iadtnashville.com

King College
1350 King College Rd, Bristol TN 37620-2635
423-968-1187

Lee University
PO Box 3450, Cleveland TN 37320-3450
Dewayne Thompson, Dean of the College of Arts & Sciences
800-533-9930

Lipscomb University
3901 Granny White Pike, Nashville TN 37204-3951
Ricky Holaway, Director of Admissions
800-333-4358 ext. 1776 Fax: 615-269-1804
Website: www.lipscomb.edu
E-mail: admissions@lipscomb.edu

Southwest Tennessee Community College
5983 Macon Cove, Memphis TN 38134
Vanessa R. Dowdy, Director of Admissions
901-333-5000 Fax: 901-333-4523
Website: www.southwest.tn.edu
E-mail: vdowdy@southwest.tn.edu

Tennessee State University
3500 John A Merritt Blvd, Nashville TN 37209-1561
John Cade, Dean of Admissions & Records
615-963-5101 Fax: 615-963-2930
Website: www.tnstate.edu
E-mail: jcade@tnstate.edu

Tusculum College
PO Box 5051, Greeneville TN 37743
Melissa Ripley, Associate Director of Admissions
800-729-0256

Union University
1050 Union University Dr, Jackson TN 38305
731-668-1818

University of Memphis
Memphis TN 38152-0001
901-678-2000

University of Tennessee
615 McCallie Ave, Chattanooga TN 37403-2504
Yancy Freeman, Director of Admissions
423-425-4111 Fax: 423-425-4157
Website: www.utc.edu
E-mail: Yancy-Freeman@utc.edu

University of Tennessee
527 Andy Holt Tower, Knoxville TN 37996-0001
865-974-1000

University of Tennessee
Martin TN 38238-0001
731-587-7000

University of the South
735 University Ave, Sewanee TN 37383-1000
931-598-1000

TEXAS

Abilene Christian University
ACU Box 29000, Abilene TX 79699-0001
325-674-2000 Fax: 325-674-2202
Website: www.acu.edu
E-mail: info@admissions.acu.edu

ALLEN ACADEMY
3201 Boonville Rd, Bryan TX 77802
Camilla Viator, Director of Admissions
979-776-0731 Fax: 979-774-7769
Website: www.allenacademy.org
E-mail: cviator@allenacademy.org

Angelo State University
ASU Station 11014, San Angelo TX 76909
Bonnie Stennett, Coordinator of Recruiting
800-946-8627

Austin College
900 N Grand Ave, Sherman TX 75090-4400
903-813-2000

Galveston College
4015 Avenue Q, Galveston TX 77550-7496
Brian Lowery, Registrar
409-763-6551 Fax: 409-944-1501
Website: www.gc.edu
E-mail: blowery@gc.edu

Jacksonville College
105 B J Albritton Dr, Jacksonville TX 75766-4759
903-586-2518 Fax: 903-586-0743
Website: www.jacksonville-college.edu
E-mail: acadean@jacksonville-college.edu
See listing under "Community and Junior Colleges"

Lamar University
PO Box 10009, Beaumont TX 77710-0009
409-880-8508

McLennan Community College
1400 College Dr, Waco TX 76708-1498
Dr. Harry "Buddy" Powell, Dean, Arts and Sciences
254-299-8000 Fax: 254-299-8854
Website: www.mclennan.edu
E-mail: bpowell@mclennan.edu

Our Lady of the Lake University
411 SW 24th St, San Antonio TX 78207-4666
Mary Kay Cooper, Dean of Enrollment
210-434-6711

Prairie View A&M University
PO Box 519, Prairie View TX 77446
936-857-3311

Schreiner University
2100 Memorial Blvd, Kerrville TX 78028-5697
Todd D. Brown, Director of Admissions
800-343-4919

Southern Methodist University
PO Box 750181, Dallas TX 75275-0181
Ron Moss, Dean of Admission
214-768-2058

Temple College
2600 S 1st St, Temple TX 76504-7435
Toni Borras, Director of Admissions & Records
254-298-8808 Fax: 254-298-8288
Website: www.templejc.edu
E-mail: admissionsrecords@templejc.edu

Texas A&M International University
5201 University Blvd, Laredo TX 78041
956-326-2000

Texas A&M University
700 University Blvd, Kingsville TX 78363
361-593-2111

Texas Christian University
TCU Box 297013, Fort Worth TX 76129
817-257-7000

Texas Wesleyan University
1201 Wesleyan St, Fort Worth TX 76105-1536
Stephanie Boatner, Director of Freshman Admission
800-580-8980

Texas Woman's University
PO Box 425589, Denton TX 76204-5589
Erma Nieto-Brecht, Director of Admissions
866-809-6130 Fax: 940-898-3081
Website: www.twu.edu
E-mail: admissions@twu.edu

Tyler Junior College
PO Box 9020, Tyler TX 75711-9020
Richard Minter, Dean
800-687-5680
Website: www.tjc.edu
E-mail: rmin@tjc.edu
See listing under "Community and Junior Colleges"

University of Dallas
1845 E Northgate Dr, Irving TX 75062-4736
Curt Eley, Dean
972-721-5000 Fax: 972-721-5017
Website: www.udallas.edu
E-mail: ugadmis@udallas.edu

University of Houston
122 E Cullen Bldg, Houston TX 77204-2023
Office of Admission
713-743-9595
Website: www.uh.edu
E-mail: admissions@uh.edu

University of Houston-Clear Lake
2700 Bay Area Blvd, Houston TX 77058-1025
281-283-2500

University of Mary Hardin-Baylor
UMHB Station Box 8001, Belton TX 76513
254-295-8642

University of St. Thomas
3800 Montrose Blvd, Houston TX 77006-4626
Eduardo Prieto, Director of Admissions
713-522-7911

University of Texas at Arlington
Box 19111, Arlington TX 76019-0111
Hans Gatterdam, Director of Admission
817-272-6287 Fax: 817-272-3435
Website: www.uta.edu
E-mail: admissions@uta.edu

University of Texas at Tyler
3900 University Blvd, Tyler TX 75701-6622
Jim Hutto, Dean Enrollment Management
800-888-9537

University of the Incarnate Word
4301 Broadway St, San Antonio TX 78209-6318
210-829-6000

UTAH

Brigham Young University
Provo UT 84602-0001
801-378-5000

L.D.S. BUSINESS COLLEGE
95 North 300 West, Salt Lake City UT 84101-3500
Kathleen Howe, Assistant Director of Admissions
801-524-8145 Fax: 801-524-1900
Website: www.ldsbc.edu
E-mail: admissions@ldsbc.edu
See listing under "Career Schools"

Westminster College
1840 S 1300 E, Salt Lake City UT 84105-3617
801-832-2200

VERMONT

Bennington College
One College Drive, Bennington VT 05201
Ken Himmelman, Dean of Admissions & Financial Aid
800-833-6845

Castleton State College
Castleton VT 05735
William Allen Jr., Dean of Enrollment
800-639-8521

Goddard College
121 Pitkin Rd, Plainfield VT 05667
802-454-8311

Green Mountain College
1 College Cir, Poultney VT 05764-1199
Sandra Bartholomew, Ph.D., Dean of Enrollment Management
802-287-8000 Fax: 802-287-8099
Website: www.greenmtn.edu
E-mail: bartholomews@greenmtn.edu

Johnson State College
337 College Hill, Johnson VT 05656
802-635-2356

Lyndon State College
PO Box 919, Lyndonville VT 05851
802-626-6200

Saint Michael's College
One Winooski Park, Colchester VT 05439-0001
Jacqueline Murphy, Director
802-654-3000

Southern Vermont College
982 Mansion Dr, Bennington VT 05201-6002
Joel Wincowski, Director of Admissions
800-378-2782 Fax: 802-447-4695
Website: www.svc.edu
E-mail: admis@svc.edu

VIRGINIA

College of William and Mary
PO Box 8795, Williamsburg VA 23187-8795
757-221-4000

Ferrum College
PO Box 1000, Ferrum VA 24088-9001
Gilda Q. Woods, Director of Admissions
800-868-9797

George Mason University
4400 University Dr, Fairfax VA 22030-4444
Eddie Tallent, Director of Admissions
703-993-2400

Hampden-Sydney College
PO Box 667, Hampden Sydney VA 23943-0667
800-755-0733

James Madison University
800 S Main St, Harrisonburg VA 22807-0002
540-568-6211

Liberty University
PO Box 20000, Lynchburg VA 24506-8001
804-582-2000

Lynchburg College
1501 Lakeside Dr, Lynchburg VA 24501-3199
804-544-8100

Mary Baldwin College
Staunton VA 24401
Lisa A. Branson, Executive Director of Admissions and Financial Aid
800-468-2262 Fax: 540-887-7292
Website: www.mbc.edu
E-mail: admit@mbc.edu

Marymount University
2807 N Glebe Rd, Arlington VA 22207-4299
Michael Canfield, Director of Admissions
800-548-7638 Fax: 703-522-0348
Website: www.marymount.edu
E-mail: admissions@marymount.edu

Norfolk State University
700 Park Ave, Norfolk VA 23504
Michelle Marable, Director of Admissions
757-823-8600

PATRICK HENRY COLLEGE
1 Patrick Henry Cir, Purcellville VA 20132
Rebekah Knable, Director of Admissions
888-338-1776 Fax: 540-338-9808
Website: www.phc.edu
E-mail: admissions@phc.edu

Radford University
PO Box 6903, Radford VA 24142
David W. Kraus, Director of Admissions
800-890-4265 Fax: 540-831-5038
Website: www.radford.edu
E-mail: ruadmiss@radford.edu

Randolph College
2500 Rivermont Ave, Lynchburg VA 24503
Patricia LeDonne, Director of Admissions
434-947-8100 Fax: 434-947-8996
Website: www.randolphcollege.edu
E-mail: admissions@randolphcollege.edu

Randolph-Macon College
PO Box 5005, Ashland VA 23005-5505
804-752-7200

Roanoke College
221 College Ln, Salem VA 24153-3794
James A. Pennix, Director of Admissions
540-375-2500 Fax: 540-375-2267
Website: www.roanoke.edu
E-mail: pennix@roanoke.edu

St. Paul's College
406 Windsor Ave, Lawrenceville VA 23868-1202
804-848-3111

Shenandoah University
1460 University Dr, Winchester VA 22601-5195
Michael D. Carpenter, Director of Admissions
800-432-2266

Southside Virginia Community College
109 Campus Dr, Alberta VA 23821-2930
Ronald E. Mattox, Dean of Admissions
434-949-1014 Fax: 434-949-7863
Website: www.sv.vccs.edu
E-mail: ronald.mattox@sv.vccs.edu

Southside Virginia Community College
200 Daniel Rd, Keysville VA 23947
Ronald E. Mattox, Dean of Admissions
434-736-2018 Fax: 434-736-2082
Website: www.sv.vccs.edu
E-mail: ronald.mattox@sv.vccs.edu

University of Mary Washington
1301 College Ave, Fredericksburg VA 22401-5300
Dr. Martin A. Wilder, Jr., Director of Admissions
540-654-2000 Fax: 540-654-1857
Website: www.umw.edu
E-mail: admit@umw.edu

Virginia Polytechnic Institute & State University
Blacksburg VA 24061
540-231-6000

WASHINGTON

Antioch University
2326 6th Ave, Seattle WA 98121
Pam Smith Mentz, Director of Enrollment Services
888-268-4477

Central Washington University
400 E University Way, Ellensburg WA 98926
William Swain, Director of Admissions
509-963-3001

Eastern Washington University
Cheney WA 99004
509-359-6200

Everett Community College
2000 Tower St, Everett WA 98201
Christine Kerlin, Associate Dean
425-388-9100 Fax: 425-388-9173
Website: www.everettcc.edu
E-mail: ckerlin@everettcc.edu

Gonzaga University
502 E Boone Ave, Spokane WA 99258-0102
Julie McCulloh, Dean of Admission
800-322-2584

Heritage University
3240 Fort Rd, Toppenish WA 98948-9599
509-865-8500

North Seattle Community College
9600 College Way N, Seattle WA 98103-3599
206-527-3709
Website: www.northseattle.edu
E-mail: nsccinfo@sccd.ctc.edu

Pacific Lutheran University
12180 Park Ave S, Tacoma WA 98447-0014
David E. Gunovich, Director of Admissions
253-535-7151

Seattle Pacific University
3307 3rd Ave W, Seattle WA 98119-1997
206-281-2000

SHORELINE COMMUNITY COLLEGE
16101 Greenwood Ave N, Shoreline WA 98133-5696
Chris Melton, Acting Registrar
206-546-4581 Fax: 206-546-5835
Website: www.shoreline.edu

Walla Walla Community College
500 Tausick Way, Walla Walla WA 99362-9270
Dr. Sandra Blackaby, Vice President
509-527-4289 or 877-992-9922 Fax: 509-527-3661
Website: www.wwcc.edu
See listing under "Community and Junior Colleges"

Washington State University
1 SE Stadium Way, Pullman WA 99164-0001
509-335-3564

Whitworth College
300 W Hawthorne Rd, Spokane WA 99251-0001
Fred Pfursich, Dean of Admissions & Financial Aid
800-533-4668

WEST VIRGINIA

Alderson-Broaddus College
Philippi WV 26416
Eric A. Ruf, Director of Admissions
800-263-1549

Blue Ridge Community and Technical College
400 W Stephen St, Martinsburg WV 25401
Leslie See, Director of Enrollment
304-260-4380 Fax: 304-260-1752
Website: www.blueridgectc.edu
E-mail: lsee@blueridgectc.edu

Davis & Elkins College
100 Campus Dr, Elkins WV 26241-3996
Renee Heckel, Director of Enrollment Management
800-624-3157 Fax: 304-637-1800
Website: www.davisandelkins.edu
E-mail: admiss@davisandelkins.edu

Fairmont State University
1201 Locust Ave, Fairmont WV 26554-2470
Steve Leadman, Director of Admissions
304-367-4717 or 800-641-5678 Fax: 304-367-4789
Website: www.fairmontstate.edu
E-mail: admit@fairmontstate.edu

Glenville State College
200 High St, Glenville WV 26351-1200
304-462-4128

Mountain State University
Box 9003, Beckley WV 25802-9003
Tony England, Director of Admissions
866-FOR-MSU1 or 304-929-INFO Fax: 304-253-5072
Website: www.mountainstate.edu
E-mail: gomsu@mountainstate.edu
See listing under "Universities"

Shepherd University
PO Box 3210
Shepherdstown WV 25443
304-876-5000

West Virginia State University
PO Box 1000, Institute WV 25112-1000
304-766-3000

West Virginia Wesleyan College
59 College Ave, Buckhannon WV 26201-2699
Robert N. Skinner II, Director of Admission
800-722-9933

WISCONSIN

Alverno College
PO Box 343922, Milwaukee WI 53234-3922
Dianna Gaebler, Director of Admissions
414-382-6100 Fax: 414-382-6354
Website: www.alverno.edu
E-mail: admissions@alverno.edu

Beloit College
700 College St, Beloit WI 53511-5596
David Burrows, Dean
608-363-2668

Carroll College
100 N East Ave, Waukesha WI 53186-5593
James Wiseman, Dean of Admissions
800-CARROLL

Carthage College
2001 Alford Park Dr, Kenosha WI 53140-1994
262-551-6000

Concordia University
12800 N Lake Shore Dr, Mequon WI 53097-2402
262-243-5700

Lakeland College
PO Box 359, Sheboygan WI 53082-0359
Nathan Dehne, Director of Admission
920-565-1100 Fax: 920-565-1215
Website: www.lakeland.edu
E-mail: admissions@lakeland.edu

Lawrence University
PO Box 599, Appleton WI 54912-0599
920-832-7000

Marquette University
PO Box 1881, Milwaukee WI 53201-1881
Robert Blust, Director of Admissions
414-288-7302 Fax: 414-288-3764
Website: www.mu.edu
E-mail: admissions@marquette.edu

Mount Mary College
2900 N Menomonee River Pkwy
Milwaukee WI 53222-4597
414-256-1219

Northland College
1411 Ellis Ave, Ashland WI 54806-3999
800-753-1840

St. Norbert College
100 Grant St, De Pere WI 54115
Brian Studebaker, Director of Admission
800-236-4878 Fax: 920-403-4072
Website: www.snc.edu
E-mail: admit@snc.edu

University of Wisconsin
1 University Plz, Platteville WI 53818-3001
Angela Udelhofen, Recruitment Manager
608-342-1200

University of Wisconsin Green Bay
2420 Nicolet Dr, Green Bay WI 54311-7003
Pamela Harvey-Jacobs, Interim Director of Admissions
920-465-2111

University of Wisconsin in La Crosse
115 Graff Main Hall, La Crosse WI 54601
Tim Lewis, Director of Admissions
608-785-8939

University of Wisconsin - Oshkosh
800 Algoma Blvd, Oshkosh WI 54901-8602
920-424-0202

University of Wisconsin - Whitewater
800 W Main St, Whitewater WI 53190-1791
262-472-1234

Viterbo University
815 9th St S, La Crosse WI 54601-8802
608-796-3000

WYOMING

Laramie County Community College
1400 E College Dr, Cheyenne WY 82007-3204
Jenny Hargett, Director of Admissions
307-778-5222 Fax: 307-778-1350
Website: www.lccc.wy.edu
E-mail: learnmore@lccc.wy.edu

University of Wyoming
Admissions Office
Dept 3435, Laramie WY 82071-3435
Brooke Culver, Contact
800-342-5996 Fax: 307-766-4042
Website: www.uwyo.edu
E-mail: why-wyo@uwyo.edu

GUAM

University of Guam
UOG Station, Mangilao GU 96923
Deborah Leon Guerrero, Registrar
671-735-2201 or 671-735-2208 Fax: 671-735-2203
Website: www.uog.edu
E-mail: admitme@uog9.uog.edu

PUERTO RICO

Bayamon Central University
PO Box 1725, Bayamon PR 00960-1725
787-786-3030

Universidad Adventista de las Antillas
PO Box 118, Mayaguez PR 00681
Evelyn Del Valle Rivera, Director of Admissions
787-834-9595

University of Puerto Rico
R Ave Antonio R Barcelo, Cayey PR 00736-5534
787-738-2161

University of Puerto Rico
PO Box 9020, Mayaguez PR 00681
787-832-4040

University of Puerto Rico
PO Box 23303, Rio Piedras PR 00931-3303
787-764-0000

VIRGIN ISLANDS

University of the Virgin Islands
2 John Brewers Bay, Saint Thomas VI 00802
340-776-9200

LIBRARY SCIENCE

FLORIDA

Florida State University
600 W College Ave, Tallahassee FL 32306-1096
Janice V. Finney, Director of Admissions
850-644-2525 Fax: 850-644-0197
Website: admissions.fsu.edu
E-mail: admissions@admin.fsu.edu

University of South Florida
4202 E Fowler Ave, Tampa FL 33620-6900
J. Robert Spatig, Director of Admissions
877-USF-BULL Fax: 813-974-9689
Website: www.usf.edu
E-mail: admissions@admin.usf.edu
See listing under "Universities"

IOWA

Iowa Lakes Community College
3200 College Dr, Emmetsburg IA 50536-1055
Anne Stansbury, Asst. Director of Admissions
712-852-5212 Fax: 712-362-8363
Website: www.iowalakes.edu
E-mail: info@iowalakes.edu

Iowa Lakes Community College
300 S 18th St, Estherville IA 51334-2721
Anne Stansbury, Asst. Director of Admissions
712-362-7945 Fax: 712-362-8363
Website: www.iowalakes.edu
E-mail: info@iowalakes.edu

KENTUCKY

Bluegrass Community and Technical College
Oswald Building
470 Cooper Drive, Lexington KY 40506-0235
Shelbie Hugle, Director of Admissions
859-246-6200 Fax: 859-246-4664
Website: www.bluegrass.kctcs.edu
E-mail: bctc_info@kctcs.edu

MISSOURI

William Woods University
1 University Ave, Fulton MO 65251-1098
Jimmy Clay, Director of Admissions
573-642-2251 Fax: 573-592-1146
Website: www.williamwoods.edu
E-mail: admissions@williamwoods.edu
See listing under "Universities"

NEW YORK

Long Island University-C. W. Post Campus
720 Northern Blvd, Brookville NY 11548-1300
Beth Carson, Director of Graduate Admissions
516-299-2900 Fax: 516-299-2418
Website: www.liu.edu/cwpost
E-mail: enroll@cwpost.liu.edu

Pratt Institute
200 Willoughby Ave, Brooklyn NY 11205-3899
Heidi Metcalf, Director of Admissions
718-636-3600 Fax: 718-636-3670
Website: www.pratt.edu
E-mail: hmetcalf@pratt.edu

St. John's University
8000 Utopia Pkwy, Queens NY 11439
Office of Admission
877-STJ-5550 ext. 101 Fax: 718-990-2096
Website: www.stjohns.edu/learnmore
E-mail: admhelp@stjohns.edu
See listing under "Universities"

PENNSYLVANIA

Clarion University of Pennsylvania
840 Wood St, Clarion PA 16214-1232
William Bailey, Dean of Enrollment Management
814-393-2306 Fax: 814-393-2030
Website: www.clarion.edu
E-mail: admissions@clarion.edu

TEXAS

Texas Woman's University
PO Box 425589, Denton TX 76204-5589
Erma Nieto-Brecht, Director of Admissions
866-809-6130 Fax: 940-898-3081
Website: www.twu.edu
E-mail: admissions@twu.edu

MARKETING AND DISTRIBUTION

ALABAMA

Bishop State Community College - Four Campuses
351 N Broad St, Mobile AL 36603-5898
Dr. Terry Hazzard, Dean of Students
251-690-6801 Fax: 251-690-6446
Website: www.bishop.edu
E-mail: thazzard@bishop.edu

ALASKA

University of Alaska Anchorage
PO Box 141629, Anchorage AK 99514-1629
Cecile Mitchell, Director of Enrollment Services
907-786-1480 Fax: 907-786-4888
Website: www.uaa.alaska.edu/
E-mail: enroll@uaa.alaska.edu

ARIZONA

Pima Community College
4905 E Broadway Blvd, Tucson AZ 85709-1010
Wendy Kilgore, Ph.D., Director of Admissions
520-206-4500 Fax: 520-206-4790
Website: www.pima.edu
E-mail: infocenter@pima.edu

ARKANSAS

Phillips Community College of the University of Arkansas
PO Box 785, Helena AR 72342-0785
Dr. Steven Murray, Chancellor
Lynn Boone, Vice Chancellor for Student Services / Registrar
870-338-6474 Fax: 870-338-7542
Website: www.pccua.edu
E-mail: lboone@pccua.edu

CALIFORNIA

Butte College
3536 Butte Campus Dr, Oroville CA 95965-8399
Carole Gish, Director of Admissions
530-895-2511 Fax: 530-879-4313
Website: www.butte.edu
E-mail: admissions@butte.edu

Concordia University
1530 Concordia, Irvine CA 92612-3203
Lori McDonald, Executive Director of Enrollment Services
800-229-1200 or 949-854-8002 Fax: 949-854-6894
Website: www.cui.edu
E-mail: admission@cui.edu

Fashion Careers College
1923 Morena Blvd, San Diego CA 92110-3555
Silvana Carelli, Director of Enrollment
619-275-4700 Fax: 619-275-0635
Website: www.fashioncareerscollege.com
E-mail: info@fashioncareerscollege.com
See listing under "Fashion Art"

FIDM/The Fashion Institute of Design & Merchandising
17590 Gillette Ave, Irvine CA 92614
Director of Admissions
949-851-6200 or 888-974-3436 Fax: 949-851-6808
Website: www.fidm.edu
E-mail: info@fidm.com
See listing under "Community and Junior Colleges"

FIDM/THE FASHION INSTITUTE OF DESIGN & MERCHANDISING
919 S Grand Ave, Los Angeles CA 90015-1421
Director of Admissions
213-624-1201 or 800-624-1200 Fax: 213-624-4799
Website: www.fidm.edu
E-mail: info@fidm.com
See listing under "Community and Junior Colleges"

FIDM/The Fashion Institute of Design & Merchandising
1010 2nd Ave, San Diego CA 92101-4903
Director of Admissions
619-235-2049 or 800-243-3436 Fax: 619-232-4322
Website: www.fidm.edu
E-mail: info@fidm.com
See listing under "Community and Junior Colleges"

FIDM/The Fashion Institute of Design & Merchandising
55 Stockton St, San Francisco CA 94108-5829
Director of Admissions
415-675-5200 or 800-422-3436 Fax: 415-296-7299
Website: www.fidm.edu
E-mail: info@fidm.com
See listing under "Community and Junior Colleges"

FRESNO CITY COLLEGE
1101 E University Ave, Fresno CA 93741-0002
Dayann Dietrich, Contact
559-442-8241 Fax: 559-237-4232
Website: www.fresnocitycollege.com
E-mail: fcc.admissions@scccd.com

Orange Coast College
PO Box 5005, Costa Mesa CA 92628-5005
Kristin Clark, Director of Admissions
714-432-5773 Fax: 714-432-5736
Website: www.orangecoastcollege.edu
E-mail: kclark@cccd.edu

TRAVEL UNIVERSITY INTERNATIONAL
3870 Murphy Canyon Rd Suite #310
San Diego CA 92123-4403
Nancy Chappie, President
858-292-9755 Fax: 858-292-8008
Website: www.traveluniversity.edu
E-mail: travel@traveluniversity.edu

CONNECTICUT

Middlesex Community College
100 Training Hill Rd, Middletown CT 06457-4889
Mensimah Shabazz, Director of Admissions
860-343-5800 Fax: 860-344-3055
Website: www.mxcc.commnet.edu
E-mail: mshabazz@mxcc.commnet.edu

DELAWARE

Goldey-Beacom College
4701 Limestone Rd, Wilmington DE 19808-1993
Stacey Schwartz, Assistant Director of Admissions
302-998-8814 Fax: 302-996-5408
Website: www.gbc.edu
E-mail: admissions@gbc.edu

Wesley College
120 N State St, Dover DE 19901-3876
302-736-2300 Fax: 302-736-2301
Website: www.wesley.edu

DISTRICT OF COLUMBIA

Southeastern University
501 I St SW, Washington DC 20024-2788
Sean Jamieson, Director of Admissions
202-478-8210 Fax: 202-488-8093
Website: www.seu.edu
E-mail: admissions@admin.seu.edu

FLORIDA

City College
2000 W Commercial Blvd, Fort Lauderdale FL 33309
Mercedes Segal, Director of Admissions
954-492-5353 Fax: 954-491-1965
Website: www.citycollege.edu

INTERNATIONAL ACADEMY OF DESIGN AND TECHNOLOGY
5959 Lake Ellenor Dr, Orlando FL 32809-4633
Dr. John Dietrich, VP of Admissions
877-753-0007 Fax: 407-888-4006
Website: www.iadt.edu
E-mail: info@iadt.edu

Northwood University
2600 N Military Trl, West Palm Beach FL 33409-2999
Jack Letvinchuk, Director of Admissions
800-458-8325 Fax: 561-640-3328
Website: www.northwood.edu
E-mail: fladmit@northwood.edu

SOUTHWEST FLORIDA COLLEGE
1685 Medical Ln, Fort Myers FL 33907-1157
866-SWFC-NOW or 239-939-4766 Fax: 239-936-4040
Website: www.swfc.edu
E-mail: studentinfo@swfc.edu

University of South Florida
4202 E Fowler Ave, Tampa FL 33620-6900
J. Robert Spatig, Director of Admissions
877-USF-BULL Fax: 813-974-9689
Website: www.usf.edu
E-mail: admissions@admin.usf.edu
See listing under "Universities"

GEORGIA

DeKalb Technical College
495 N Indian Creek Dr, Clarkston GA 30021-2397
Terry Richardson, Director of Admissions
404-297-9522 Fax: 404-294-6496
Website: www.dekalbtech.edu
E-mail: richardt@dekalbtech.edu

Kennesaw State University
1000 Chastain Rd NW, Kennesaw GA 30144-5591
Timothy Mescon, Dean of College of Business
770-423-6425
Website: www.kennesaw.edu

IDAHO

University of Idaho
Moscow ID 83844-4253
Lloyd Scott, Director of New Student Services
208-885-6163 Fax: 208-885-4477
Website: www.uidaho.edu
E-mail: nss@uidaho.edu

ILLINOIS

AMERICAN INTERCONTINENTAL UNIVERSITY ONLINE
5550 Prairie Stone Parkway Suite 400
Hoffman Estates IL 60192
Admissions Department
877-701-3800
Website: www.aiuonline.edu
E-mail: info@aiuonline.edu

Aurora University
347 S Gladstone Ave, Aurora IL 60506-4892
Carol R. Dunn, Ed.D., Vice President for Enrollment
800-742-5281 Fax: 630-844-5535
Website: www.aurora.edu
E-mail: admission@aurora.edu

Columbia College Chicago
600 S Michigan Ave, Chicago IL 60605-1996
Murphy Monroe, Executive Director of Admissions
312-344-7130 Fax: 312-344-8024
Website: www.colum.edu
E-mail: admissions@colum.edu

International Academy of Design and Technology
1 N State St #500, Chicago IL 60602-3300
Cecily Arroyo, Director of Admissions
888-803-0111 Fax: 312-541-3929
Website: www.iadtchicago.edu
E-mail: carroyo@iadtchicago.com

Kaskaskia College
27210 College Rd, Centralia IL 62801-7878
Tyra Taylor, Dean of Enrollment Management and Retention Services
618-545-3000 Fax: 618-532-1990
Website: www.kaskaskia.edu
E-mail: ttaylor@kaskaskia.edu

MacCormac College
29 E Madison St, Chicago IL 60602-4405
David F. Grassi, Admissions Counselor
312-922-1884 ext. 101 Fax: 312-922-4328
Website: www.maccormac.edu
E-mail: dgrassi@maccormac.edu

Roosevelt University
430 S Michigan Ave, Chicago IL 60605
Gwen E. Kanelos, Asst. Vice President for Enrollment Services
877-APPLY-RU Fax: 312-341-4216
Website: www.roosevelt.edu
E-mail: applyru@roosevelt.edu

Trinity International University
2065 Half Day Rd, Deerfield IL 60015-1241
847-945-8800 Fax: 847-317-8097
Website: www.tiu.edu
E-mail: tcadmissions@tiu.edu

INDIANA

University of Evansville
1800 Lincoln Ave, Evansville IN 47722-0001
Don Vos, Dean of Admission
800-423-8633 Fax: 812-488-4076
Website: www.evansville.edu
E-mail: admission@evansville.edu

IOWA

AIB College of Business
2500 Fleur Dr, Des Moines IA 50321-1799
800-444-1921 Fax: 515-244-6773
Website: www.aib.edu
E-mail: admissions@aib.edu

Briar Cliff University
PO Box 2100, Sioux City IA 51104-0100
Sharisue Wilcoxon, VP for Enrollment Management
712-279-5200 Fax: 712-279-1632
Website: www.briarcliff.edu
E-mail: admissions@briarcliff.edu

Clarke College
1550 Clarke Dr, Dubuque IA 52001-3198
Andy Schroeder, Director of Admissions
800-383-2345 Fax: 563-584-8666
Website: www.clarke.edu
E-mail: andy.schroeder@clarke.edu

Graceland University
1 University Place, Lamoni IA 50140
Greg Sutherland, Interim Vice President for Enrollment and Dean of Admissions
641-784-5196 Fax: 641-784-5480
Website: www.admissions.graceland.edu
E-mail: admissions@graceland.edu

Hamilton College
7009 Nordic Dr, Cedar Falls IA 50613
Connie Reidy, Campus President
319-277-0220 Fax: 319-363-3812
Website: www.hamiltonia.edu
E-mail: coreidy@hamiltoncf.com

Hamilton College
3165 Edgewood Pkwy SW, Cedar Rapids IA 52404
Susan Spivey, Campus President
319-363-0481 Fax: 319-363-3812
Website: www.hamiltonia.edu
E-mail: sspivey@hamiltonia.edu

Hamilton College
1751 Madison Ave Ste 750, Council Bluffs IA 51503
Michael Zawisky, Executive Director
712-328-4212
Website: www.hamiltonia.edu
E-mail: mzawisky@hamiltonia.edu

Hamilton College
2570 4th St SW, Mason City IA 50401-4665
Joe Albers, Executive Director
641-423-2530 Fax: 641-423-7512
Website: www.hamiltonia.edu
E-mail: jalbers@hamiltonia.edu

Hamilton College
4655 121st St, Urbandale IA 50323-2311
Colleen McDermott, Campus President
515-727-2100 Fax: 515-727-2115
Website: www.hamiltonia.edu
E-mail: cmcdermott@hamiltonia.edu

Iowa Lakes Community College
3200 College Dr, Emmetsburg IA 50536-1055
Anne Stansbury, Asst. Director of Admissions
712-852-5212 Fax: 712-362-8363
Website: www.iowalakes.edu
E-mail: info@iowalakes.edu

Northwest Iowa Community College
603 W Park St, Sheldon IA 51201-1046
Lisa Story, Director of Enrollment Management
712-324-5061 Fax: 712-324-4136
Website: www.nwicc.edu
E-mail: lstory@nwicc.edu

KANSAS

COLBY COMMUNITY COLLEGE
1255 S Range Ave, Colby KS 67701-4099
Director of Admissions
888-634-9350 or 785-460-4690 Fax: 785-460-4691
Website: www.colbycc.edu
E-mail: admissions@colbycc.edu

KENTUCKY

Bluegrass Community and Technical College
Oswald Building
470 Cooper Drive, Lexington KY 40506-0235
Shelbie Hugle, Director of Admissions
859-246-6200 Fax: 859-246-4664
Website: www.bluegrass.kctcs.edu
E-mail: bctc_info@kctcs.edu

Morehead State University
Morehead KY 40351-1689
Jeffrey Liles, Enrollment Services
800-585-6781 Fax: 606-783-5038
Website: www.moreheadstate.edu
E-mail: admissions@moreheadstate.edu

LOUISIANA

Our Lady of Holy Cross College
4123 Woodland Dr, New Orleans LA 70131-7399
Office of Enrollment Services
504-394-7744 Fax: 504-391-2421
Website: www.olhcc.edu

MAINE

HUSSON COLLEGE
One College Cir, Bangor ME 04401-2999
Jane Goodwin, Director of Admissions
800-4HU-SSON or 207-941-7100 Fax: 207-941-7935
Website: www.husson.edu
E-mail: admit@husson.edu
See listing under "Universities"

St. Joseph's College of Maine
278 Whites Bridge Rd, Standish ME 04084-5263
Vincent Kloskowski, Dean of Admissions
800-338-7057 Fax: 207-893-7862
Website: www.sjcme.edu
E-mail: admission@sjcme.edu

MASSACHUSETTS

Assumption College
500 Salisbury St, Worcester MA 01609-1294
Kathleen Murphy, Dean of Enrollment
508-767-7000 Fax: 508-799-4412
Website: www.assumption.edu
E-mail: admiss@assumption.edu

Bay State College
122 Commonwealth Ave, Boston MA 02116-2901
Craig Pfannenstiehl, President
617-217-9000 Fax: 617-536-1735

Becker College
Campuses in Worcester and Leicester, MA
61 Sever St, Worcester MA 01609-2165
Karen Schedin, Dean of Admissions
508-791-9241 Fax: 508-890-1500
Website: www.becker.edu
E-mail: admissions@becker.edu
See listing under "Universities"

Boston University
121 Bay State Rd, Boston MA 02215
Kelly Walter, Executive Director of Admissions
617-353-2300 Fax: 617-353-9695
Website: web.bu.edu
E-mail: admissions@bu.edu

Emerson College
120 Boylston St, Boston MA 02116-4624
Sara S. Ramirez, Director of Undergraduate Admission
617-824-8600 Fax: 617-824-8609
Website: www.emerson.edu
E-mail: admission@emerson.edu

Newbury College
129 Fisher Ave, Brookline MA 02445-5796
Salvadore Liberto, Vice President of Enrollment
617-730-7000 Fax: 617-731-9618
Website: www.newbury.edu
E-mail: info@newbury.edu
See listing under "Universities"

North Shore Community College
1 Ferncroft Rd, Danvers MA 01923-4093
Jennifer Kirk, Director of Admissions & Recruitment Outreach
978-762-4000 Fax: 978-762-4015
Website: www.northshore.edu
E-mail: jkirk@northshore.edu

University of Massachusetts Dartmouth
Old Westport Rd, North Dartmouth MA 02747-2300
Steven T. Briggs, Director of Admissions
508-999-8605 Fax: 508-999-8755
Website: explore.umassd.edu
E-mail: sbriggs@umassd.edu

MICHIGAN

Delta College
University Center MI 48710-0001
Duff Zube, Director of Admissions
989-686-9093 Fax: 989-667-2202
Website: www.delta.edu
E-mail: admit@delta.edu

HILLSDALE COLLEGE
33 E College St, Hillsdale MI 49242-1298
Dr. Charles Davies, Director
517-607-2388 Fax: 517-607-2657
Website: www.hillsdale.edu
E-mail: charles.davies@hillsdale.edu

MACOMB COMMUNITY COLLEGE
44575 Garfield Rd, Clinton Township MI 48038-1139
Information Center
586-445-7999
Website: www.macomb.edu
E-mail: answer@macomb.edu

MACOMB COMMUNITY COLLEGE
14500 E 12 Mile Rd, Warren MI 48088-3896
Information Center
586-445-7999
Website: www.macomb.edu
E-mail: answer@macomb.edu

Northwood University
4000 Whiting Dr, Midland MI 48640
Daniel F. Toland, Dean of Admissions
800-457-7878 Fax: 989-837-4490
Website: www.northwood.edu
E-mail: miadmit@northwood.edu

MINNESOTA

Inver Hills Community College
2500 80th St E, Inver Grove Heights MN 55076
651-450-8500 Fax: 651-450-8679
Website: www.inverhills.edu

Minnesota State University Moorhead
1104 7th Ave S, Moorhead MN 56563-0002
Regina Monson, Director of Admissions
218-477-2161 Fax: 218-477-4374
Website: go.mnstate.edu
E-mail: dragon@mnstate.edu

Northland Community and Technical College
2022 Central Ave NE
East Grand Forks MN 56721-2702
Kit Brenan, Sales & Marketing Instructor
800-451-3441 Fax: 218-773-4502
Website: www.northlandcollege.edu
E-mail: admissions@northlandcollege.edu

Ridgewater College-Willmar Campus
PO Box 1097, Willmar MN 56201-1097
Sally Kerfeld, Director of Admissions
800-722-1151 Fax: 320-222-5212
Website: www.ridgewater.edu
E-mail: sally.kerfeld@ridgewater.edu

St. Cloud Technical College
1540 Northway Dr, Saint Cloud MN 56303-1240
Jodi Elness, Director of Enrollment Management
800-222-1009 Fax: 320-308-5981
Website: www.sctc.edu
E-mail: jelness@sctc.edu

University of Minnesota
2900 University Ave, Crookston MN 56716-5001
218-281-6510 Fax: 218-281-8575
Website: admissions.umcrookston.edu/requirements/apply.htm
E-mail: info@umcrookston.edu

MISSOURI

East Central College
1964 Prairie Dell Rd, Union MO 63084
Karen Wieda, Registrar
636-583-5195 ext. 2220 Fax: 636-583-1897
Website: www.eastcentral.edu
E-mail: wiedaks@eastcentral.edu

Lindenwood University
209 S Kingshighway St
Saint Charles MO 63301-1695
Sheryl Guffey, Director of Admissions
636-949-2000 Fax: 636-949-4989
Website: www.lindenwood.edu

Northwest Missouri State University
800 University Dr, Maryville MO 64468-6001
Beverly Schenkel, Dean of Enrollment Management
660-562-1562 Fax: 660-562-1121
Website: www.nwmissouri.edu
E-mail: admissions@nwmissouri.edu

Stephens College
PO Box 2121, Columbia MO 65215-0001
David Adams, Dean of Enrollment Management
573-442-2211 Fax: 573-876-7237
Website: www.stephens.edu
E-mail: dadams@stephens.edu

Truman State University
100 E Normal, Kirksville MO 63501
Office of Admission
660-785-4114 Fax: 660-785-7456
Website: admissions.truman.edu
E-mail: admissions@truman.edu

Webster University
470 E Lockwood Ave, Saint Louis MO 63119-3194
Dr. Benjamin Akande, Dean School of Business and Management
314-961-2660 ext. 5950 Fax: 314-968-7077
Website: www.webster.edu
E-mail: mtaylor@webster.edu
See listing under "Universities"

William Woods University
1 University Ave, Fulton MO 65251-1098
Jimmy Clay, Director of Admissions
573-642-2251 Fax: 573-592-1146
Website: www.williamwoods.edu
E-mail: admissions@williamwoods.edu
See listing under "Universities"

NEBRASKA

Metropolitan Community College
PO Box 3777, Omaha NE 68103-0777
Becky Nicks, Director of Admissions
402-449-8400 Fax: 402-457-2616
Website: www.mccnab.edu
E-mail: bnicks@mccnab.edu

University of Nebraska at Kearney
905 W 25th St, Kearney NE 68849-0001
Dusty Newton, Director of Admissions
800-KEARNEY Fax: 308-865-8987
Website: www.unk.edu
E-mail: admissionsug@unk.edu

NEVADA

Career College of Northern Nevada
1195-A Corporate Blvd, Reno NV 89502-2331
Nathan Clark, Director
775-856-2266 Fax: 775-856-0935
Website: www.ccnn.edu
E-mail: lgoldhammer@ccnn4u.com
See listing under "Career Schools"

NEW HAMPSHIRE

New Hampshire Community Technical College
1066 Front St, Manchester NH 03102-8528
Jacquie Poirier, Director of Admissions
603-668-6706 Fax: 603-668-5354
Website: www.manchester.nhctc.edu
E-mail: jpoirier@nhctc.edu

Southern New Hampshire University
2500 N River Rd, Hooksett NH 03106-1045
Steve Soba, Director of Admissions
603-645-9611 Fax: 603-645-9693
Website: www.snhu.edu
E-mail: s.soba@snhu.edu

NEW JERSEY

Bergen Community College
400 Paramus Rd, Paramus NJ 07652
Julian Gomez, Asst. Director of Admissions
201-447-7100 Fax: 201-444-7036
Website: www.bergen.edu
E-mail: jgomez@bergen.edu

New Jersey City University
2039 John F Kennedy Blvd
Jersey City NJ 07305-1588
Carmen Panlilio, Asst. V.P. for Admissions and Financial Aid
201-200-3234 Fax: 201-200-2044
Website: www.njcu.edu
E-mail: admissions@njcu.edu

Ramapo College of New Jersey
505 Ramapo Valley Rd, Mahwah NJ 07430-1623
Director of Admissions
201-684-7300 or 201-684-7301 Fax: 201-684-7964
Website: www.ramapo.edu
E-mail: admissions@ramapo.edu

RICHARD STOCKTON COLLEGE OF NEW JERSEY
PO Box 195, Pomona NJ 08240
John Iacovelli, Dean of Enrollment Management
866-RSC-2885 Fax: 609-626-5541
Website: www.stockton.edu
E-mail: admissions@stockton.edu
See listing under "Universities"

NEW YORK

Broome Community College
907 Upper Front St, Binghamton NY 13905
Anthony S. Fiorelli, Director of Admissions
607-778-5001 Fax: 607-778-5442
Website: www.sunybroome.edu
E-mail: fiorelli_a@sunybroome.edu

Dowling College
150 Idle Hour Blvd, Oakdale NY 11769-1999
Diane Kazanecki-Kempter, Contact
631-244-3000 Fax: 631-244-1059
Website: www.dowling.edu
E-mail: admissions@dowling.edu

Iona College
715 North Ave, New Rochelle NY 10801-1890
Kevin Cavanagh, Assistant V.P. for College Admissions
914-633-2502 Fax: 914-637-2778
Website: www.iona.edu

LABORATORY INSTITUTE OF MERCHANDISING
12 E 53rd St, New York NY 10022-5268
Kristina Gibson, Director of Admissions
800-677-1323 or 212-752-1530 Fax: 212-750-3432
Website: www.limcollege.edu
E-mail: admissions@limcollege.edu
See listing under "Universities"

Long Island University-C. W. Post Campus
720 Northern Blvd, Brookville NY 11548-1300
Joanne Graziano, Executive Director of Admissions
516-299-2900 Fax: 516-299-2137
Website: www.liu.edu/cwpost
E-mail: enroll@cwpost.liu.edu

Monroe College
2501 Jerome Ave, Bronx NY 10468-4305
Evan Jerome, Director of Admissions
718-933-6700 Fax: 718-364-3552
Website: www.monroecollege.edu
E-mail: ejerome@monroecollege.edu

Roberts Wesleyan College
2301 Westside Dr, Rochester NY 14624-1997
Office of Admissions
585-594-6400 Fax: 585-594-6371
Website: www.roberts.edu
E-mail: admissions@roberts.edu

SUNY College of Technology
Alfred NY 14802
Deborah J. Goodrich, Associate VP Enrollment Mgmt.
800-4AL-FRED Fax: 607-587-4299
Website: www.alfredstate.edu
E-mail: admissions@alfredstate.edu

SUNY Orange County Community College
115 South St, Middletown NY 10940-6437
Margot St. Lawrence, Director of Admissions
845-341-4030 Fax: 845-342-8662
Website: www.sunyorange.edu
E-mail: apply@sunyorange.edu
See listing under "Community and Junior Colleges"

SUNY Sullivan County Community College
112 College Rd, Loch Sheldrake NY 12759-5151
Sari Rosenheck, Director of Admissions
845-434-5750 Fax: 845-434-0923
Website: www.sullivan.suny.edu
E-mail: admissions@sullivan.suny.edu
Student Housing on Campus.

Utica School of Commerce
201 Bleecker St, Utica NY 13501-2280
Bruce Davis, Director of Marketing
315-733-2307 Fax: 315-733-9281
Website: www.uscny.edu
E-mail: admissions@uscny.edu

NORTH CAROLINA

ART INSTITUTE OF CHARLOTTE
2110 Water Ridge Pkwy, Charlotte NC 28217
Pamela Notemyer, Director of Admissions
800-872-4417 Fax: 704-357-1133
Website: www.artinstitutes.edu/charlotte
E-mail: admin@aii.edu
See listing under "Career Schools"

Catawba College
2300 W Innes St, Salisbury NC 28144-2488
Dr. L. Russell Watjen, Ph.D., V.P. & Dean of Admissions
704-637-4402 Fax: 704-637-4222
Website: www.catawba.edu
E-mail: admission@catawba.edu

NORTH DAKOTA

Dickinson State University
Dickinson ND 58601-4896
Steve Glasser, Director of Enrollment Services
800-279-4295 Fax: 701-483-2409
Website: www.dickinsonstate.edu
E-mail: dsu.hawks@dickinsonstate.edu

Williston State College
PO Box 1326, Williston ND 58802-1326
Penny Soiseth, Associate Director Enrollment Services
701-774-4200 Fax: 701-774-4544
Website: www.wsc.nodak.edu
E-mail: penny.soiseth@wsc.nodak.edu

OHIO

Brown Mackie College - Cincinnati
1011 Glendale Milford Rd, Cincinnati OH 45215-1107
Robin Krout, President
513-771-2424 Fax: 513-771-3413
Website: www.brownmackie.edu
E-mail: rkrout@brownmackie.edu

Davis College
4747 Monroe St, Toledo OH 43623-4389
Dana Stern, Admissions Director
419-473-2700 Fax: 419-473-2472
Website: www.daviscollege.edu
E-mail: learn@daviscollege.edu

The Ohio State University
Fisher College of Business, Marketing & Logistics
Schoenbaum Hall, 210 W Woodruff Ave
Columbus OH 43210
614-292-2715 Fax: 614-292-5735
Website: fisher.osu.edu
E-mail: fisherundergrad@cob.osu.edu

Ohio University
Chillicothe Campus
PO Box 629, Chillicothe OH 45601
Student Services
740-774-7200 Fax: 740-774-7295
Website: www.ohiou.edu/chillicothe/

Owens Community College
3200 Bright Rd, Findlay OH 45840
William J. Ivoska PhD., Vice President of Student Services
567-429-3500 Fax: 567-423-0246
Website: www.owens.edu
E-mail: admissions@owens.edu

Owens Community College
PO Box 10000, Toledo OH 43699-1947
William J. Ivoska, Ph.D, Vice President of Student Services
567-661-7000 Fax: 567-661-7607
Website: www.owens.edu
E-mail: admissions@owens.edu

University of Dayton
300 College Park, Dayton OH 45469-1300
Robert F. Durkle, Director of Admission
800-837-7433 Fax: 937-229-4729
Website: admission.udayton.edu
E-mail: admission@udayton.edu

Ursuline College
2550 Lander Rd, Cleveland OH 44124-4398
Sarah E. Sundermeier, Director of Admissions
888-URSULINE Toll Free Fax: 440-684-6138
Website: www.admission.ursuline.edu
E-mail: admission@ursuline.edu

OKLAHOMA

Oklahoma State University
Stillwater OK 74078
Joshua Wiener, Department Head
405-744-5192
Website: www.okstate.edu
E-mail: josh.wiener@okstate.edu

OREGON

Cascade College
9101 E Burnside St, Portland OR 97216-1599
Jim Murphy, Director of Enrollment Management
800-550-7678 Fax: 503-257-1222
Website: www.cascade.edu
E-mail: admissions@cascade.edu

Concordia University
2811 NE Holman St, Portland OR 97211-6099
Bobi Swan, Director of Admissions
503-288-9371 Fax: 503-280-8531
Website: www.cu-portland.edu
E-mail: cu-admissions@cu-portland.edu

PENNSYLVANIA

ART INSTITUTE OF PITTSBURGH
420 Boulevard Of The Allies, Pittsburgh PA 15219
Jeffrey Bucklew, Director of Admissions
800-275-2470 Fax: 412-263-6667
Website: www.aip.aii.edu
E-mail: pahughes@aii.edu
See listing under "Universities"

Central Pennsylvania College
College Hill & Valley Rds, Summerdale PA 17093
Katie Borrelli, Admissions Director
800-759-2727 Fax: 717-728-2505
Website: www.centralpenn.edu
E-mail: katie.borrelli@centralpenn.edu

Community College of Allegheny County
Allegheny Campus: 808 Ridge Ave, Pittsburgh PA 15212 Admissions: 412.237.2700
Boyce Campus: 595 Beatty Rd, Monroeville PA 15146 Admissions: 724.325.6614
North Campus: 8701 Perry Highway, Pittsburgh PA 15237 Admissions: 412.369.3600
South Campus: 1750 Clairton Rd, West Mifflin PA 15122 Admissions: 412-469-4301
Website: www.ccac.edu

DeSales University
2755 Station Ave, Center Valley PA 18034-9565
610-282-1100 Fax: 610-282-2342
Website: www.desales.edu

Erie Business Center
246 W 9th St, Erie PA 16501-1392
Donna Perino, Director
814-456-7504 Fax: 814-456-6015
Website: www.eriebc.edu
E-mail: perinod@eriebc.edu

Juniata College
1700 Moore St, Huntingdon PA 16652-2196
Michelle Bartol, Dean of Enrollment
877-JUNIATA Fax: 814-641-3100
Website: www.juniata.edu
E-mail: admissions@juniata.edu

King's College
133 N River St, Wilkes Barre PA 18711-0801
Michelle Lawrence-Schmude, Dean of Admission
570-208-5900 Fax: 570-208-5971
Website: www.kings.edu
E-mail: admissions@kings.edu

Lehigh Valley College
2809 E Saucon Valley Rd
Center Valley PA 18034-8447
Sam Jarvis, Director of Marketing
800-227-9109 Fax: 610-791-7810
Website: www.lehighvalley.edu
E-mail: joshua.padron@lehighvalley.edu

MOUNT ALOYSIUS COLLEGE
7373 Admiral Peary Hwy, Cresson PA 16630-1999
Frank C. Crouse Jr., Vice President for Enrollment Management
814-886-6383 or 888-823-2220 Fax: 814-886-6441
Website: www.mtaloy.edu
E-mail: admissions@mtaloy.edu

SOUTH CAROLINA

North Greenville University
PO Box 1892, Tigerville SC 29688-1892
Website: www.ngu.edu
See listing under "Universities"

University of South Carolina - Upstate
800 University Way, Spartanburg SC 29303-4932
Donette Stewart, Assistant VC for Enrollment Services
864-503-5246 Fax: 864-503-5727
Website: www.uscupstate.edu
E-mail: dstewart@uscupstate.edu
See listing under "Universities"

SOUTH DAKOTA

NATIONAL AMERICAN UNIVERSITY
321 Kansas City St, Rapid City SD 57701-3692
Angela G. Beck, Director of Enrollment Management
605-394-4800 Fax: 605-394-4871
Website: www.rapid.national.edu
E-mail: rcadmissions@national.edu

Western Dakota Technical Institute
800 Mickelson Dr, Rapid City SD 57703-4018
Jill Elder, Admissions Coordinator
605-394-4034 Fax: 605-394-2204
Website: www.wdt.edu
E-mail: jill.elder@wdt.edu

TENNESSEE

Lipscomb University
3901 Granny White Pike, Nashville TN 37204-3951
Ricky Holaway, Director of Admissions
800-333-4358 ext. 1776 Fax: 615-269-1804
Website: www.lipscomb.edu
E-mail: admissions@lipscomb.edu

TEXAS

Abilene Christian University
ACU Box 29000, Abilene TX 79699-0001
325-674-2000 Fax: 325-674-2202
Website: www.acu.edu
E-mail: info@admissions.acu.edu

Galveston College
4015 Avenue Q, Galveston TX 77550-7496
Brian Lowery, Registrar
409-763-6551 Fax: 409-944-1501
Website: www.gc.edu
E-mail: blowery@gc.edu

Northwood University
1114 W FM 1382, Cedar Hill TX 75104-1204
Sylvia Correa, Director of Admissions
800-927-WOOD Fax: 972-291-3824
Website: www.northwood.edu
E-mail: ray@northwood.edu

Temple College
2600 S 1st St, Temple TX 76504-7435
Toni Borras, Director of Admissions & Records
254-298-8808 Fax: 254-298-8288
Website: www.templejc.edu
E-mail: admissionsrecords@templejc.edu

University of Houston
122 E Cullen Bldg, Houston TX 77204-2023
Office of Admission
713-743-9595
Website: www.uh.edu
E-mail: admissions@uh.edu

University of Texas at Arlington
Box 19111, Arlington TX 76019-0111
Hans Gatterdam, Director of Admission
817-272-6287 Fax: 817-272-3435
Website: www.uta.edu
E-mail: admissions@uta.edu

UTAH

Stevens Henager College
PO Box 9428, Ogden UT 84409-0428
Cindy Williams, Director of Admissions
801-394-7791 Fax: 801-621-0866
Website: www.stevenshenager.edu
E-mail: shcogden@yahoo.com

VIRGINIA

Marymount University
2807 N Glebe Rd, Arlington VA 22207-4299
Michael Canfield, Director of Admissions
800-548-7638 Fax: 703-522-0348
Website: www.marymount.edu
E-mail: admissions@marymount.edu

Radford University
PO Box 6903, Radford VA 24142
David W. Kraus, Director of Admissions
800-890-4265 Fax: 540-831-5038
Website: www.radford.edu
E-mail: ruadmiss@radford.edu

WASHINGTON

Everett Community College
2000 Tower St, Everett WA 98201
Christine Kerlin, Associate Dean
425-388-9100 Fax: 425-388-9173
Website: www.everettcc.edu
E-mail: ckerlin@everettcc.edu

SHORELINE COMMUNITY COLLEGE
16101 Greenwood Ave N, Shoreline WA 98133-5696
Chris Melton, Acting Registrar
206-546-4581 Fax: 206-546-5835
Website: www.shoreline.edu

Walla Walla Community College
500 Tausick Way, Walla Walla WA 99362-9270
Dan Biagi, Director
509-527-4283 or 877-992-9922 Fax: 509-527-4480
Website: www.wwcc.edu
E-mail: dan.biagi@wwcc.edu
See listing under "Community and Junior Colleges"

WEST VIRGINIA

Davis & Elkins College
100 Campus Dr, Elkins WV 26241-3996
Renee Heckel, Director of Enrollment Management
800-624-3157 Fax: 304-637-1800
Website: www.davisandelkins.edu
E-mail: admiss@davisandelkins.edu

Fairmont State University
1201 Locust Ave, Fairmont WV 26554-2470
Steve Leadman, Director of Admissions
304-367-4892 or 800-641-5678 Fax: 304-367-4789
Website: www.fairmontstate.edu
E-mail: admit@fairmontstate.edu

Mountain State University
Box 9003, Beckley WV 25802-9003
Tony England, Director of Admissions
866-FOR-MSU1 or 304-929-INFO Fax: 304-253-5072
Website: www.mountainstate.edu
E-mail: gomsu@mountainstate.edu
See listing under "Universities"

WISCONSIN

Blackhawk Technical College
PO Box 5009, Janesville WI 53547-5009
Gregg Bosak, Administration, Community Information
608-757-7769 Fax: 608-757-7740
Website: www.blackhawk.edu
E-mail: gbosak@blackhawk.edu

Wisconsin Indianhead Technical College
505 Pine Ridge Dr, Shell Lake WI 54871
Laura Wassenaar, Dean
800-243-9482 Fax: 715-468-2819
Website: www.witc.edu
E-mail: laura.wassenaar@witc.edu

WYOMING

Laramie County Community College
1400 E College Dr, Cheyenne WY 82007-3204
Jenny Hargett, Director of Admissions
307-778-5222 Fax: 307-778-1350
Website: www.lccc.wy.edu
E-mail: learnmore@lccc.wy.edu

University of Wyoming
Admissions Office
Dept 3435, Laramie WY 82071-3435
Brooke Culver, Contact
800-342-5996 Fax: 307-766-4042
Website: www.uwyo.edu
E-mail: why-wyo@uwyo.edu

MASTER OF BUSINESS ADMINISTRATION

ALABAMA

University of South Alabama
307 University Blvd N, Mobile AL 36688-3053
Melissa Haab, Director of Admissions
251-460-6141 Fax: 251-460-7876
Website: www.southalabama.edu
E-mail: admiss@usouthal.edu

ALASKA

University of Alaska Anchorage
PO Box 141629, Anchorage AK 99514-1629
Cecile Mitchell, Director of Enrollment Services
907-786-1480 Fax: 907-786-4888
Website: www.uaa.alaska.edu/
E-mail: enroll@uaa.alaska.edu

ARIZONA

Thunderbird, The Garvin School of International Management
15249 N 59th Ave, Glendale AZ 85306-3236
Judy Johnson, Associate VP of Admissions & Financial Aid
800-848-9084 or 602-978-7100 Fax: 602-439-5432
Website: www.thunderbird.edu
E-mail: johnsonj@thunderbird.edu

CALIFORNIA

CALIFORNIA COAST UNIVERSITY
700 N Main St, Santa Ana CA 92701
Admissions Office: 888-CCU-UNIV or 714-547-9625
Fax: 714-547-5777
Dr. Thomas Neal, President
Dr. Cynthia Teeple, Academic Vice President
Website: www.calcoast.edu
E-mail: info@calcoast.edu

Established 1973. Proprietary. Coed. Accreditation: California Coast University holds accreditation through the Accrediting Commission of the Distance Education and Training Council (DETC). The DETC is an educational association located in Washington, D.C. Founded in 1926, it is the standard setting agency for distance education institutions. Approval: Bureau for Private Postsecondary and Vocational Education - State of California, charter member California Association of State Approved Colleges & Universities, member Association for Adult & Continuing Education, member The Alliance for Private Post Secondary Academic Institutions.

Tuition: $2,805-$12,070. California Coast University has selected the SLM Corporation, commonly known as Sallie Mae, to help the university provide financing for its students. Sallie Mae is the nation's leading provider of education funding. Sallie Mae also allows students to borrow additional loan amounts to cover additional expenses, such as textbooks, equipment, or living expenses.

Enrollment: 30,000. California Coast University is approved by the California State Approving Agency to enroll veterans or other eligible persons under Title 38, U.S. Code. California Coast University holds a Memorandum of Understanding with Defense Activity for Non-Traditional Education Support (DANTES) as an external degree provider.

A private college offering off-campus independent study programs in the traditional areas of business administration, management, psychology, education. Admissions: enroll year round, requires official transcripts, letters of recommendation, detailed curriculum vita or occupational history.

Process: evaluation of prior academic work followed by analysis of occupational history, including participation in workshops, seminars, training programs, specialized projects for credit. Credit is demonstrated by accelerated learning guides or study guides.

Residency: All course work may be completed off campus, utilizing correspondence methods. Interest free loans available to students.

Chapman University
One University Drive, Orange CA 92866-1099
Michael Drummy, Assistant Vice President for Enrollment
Services and Chief Admission Officer
714-997-6411 or 888-CUAPPLY Fax: 714-997-6713
Website: www.chapman.edu
E-mail: admit@chapman.edu

Concordia University
1530 Concordia, Irvine CA 92612-3203
Lori McDonald, Executive Director of Enrollment Services
800-229-1200 or 949-854-8002 Fax: 949-854-6894
Website: www.cui.edu
E-mail: admission@cui.edu

ITT Technical Institute
12669 Encinitas Ave, Sylmar CA 91342-3664
Kelly Christensen, Director of Admissions
818-364-5151 Fax: 818-364-5150
Website: www.itt-tech.edu
E-mail: kchristensen@itt-tech.edu

Point Loma Nazarene University
3900 Lomaland Dr, San Diego CA 92106-2810
Chip Killingsworth, Director of Undergraduate Admissions
800-733-7770 Fax: 619-849-2601
Website: www.pointloma.edu
E-mail: admissions@pointloma.edu

DELAWARE

Goldey-Beacom College
4701 Limestone Rd, Wilmington DE 19808-1993
Stacey Schwartz, Assistant Director of Admissions
302-998-8814 Fax: 302-996-5408
Website: www.gbc.edu
E-mail: admissions@gbc.edu

Wesley College
120 N State St, Dover DE 19901-3876
302-736-2300 Fax: 302-736-2301
Website: www.wesley.edu

FLORIDA

Embry-Riddle Aeronautical University
Daytona Beach Campus
PO Box 11767, Daytona Beach FL 32120-1767
C. Richard Clarke, Director of Admissions
800-862-2416 Fax: 386-226-7070
Website: www.embryriddle.edu
E-mail: dbadmit@erau.edu

EVERGLADES UNIVERSITY (MAIN CAMPUS)
5002 T-Rex Ave Suite 100, Boca Raton FL 33431
Kristi Mollis, President
888-772-6077 Fax: 561-912-1191
Website: www.evergladesuniversity.edu
E-mail: admissions-boca@evergladesuniversity.edu
See listing under "Universities"

EVERGLADES UNIVERSITY
Orlando Campus (Branch Campus)
887 E Altamonte Dr, Altamonte Springs FL 32701
Linda Volz, Vice President
866-289-1078 Fax: 407-482-9801
Website: www.evergladesuniversity.edu
E-mail: admissions-orl@evergladesuniversity.edu
See listing under "Universities"

EVERGLADES UNIVERSITY
Sarasota Campus (Branch Campus)
6001 Lake Osprey Dr, Suite 110, Sarasota FL 34240
Brad Brewer, Vice President
866-907-2262 Fax: 941-907-6634
Website: www.evergladesuniversity.edu
E-mail: admissions-sar@evergladesuniversity.edu
See listing under "Universities"

Lynn University
3601 N Military Trl, Boca Raton FL 33431-5598
Larissa R. Baia, Associate Director of Graduate Admissions
561-237-7900 Fax: 561-237-7100
Website: www.lynn.edu
E-mail: admission@lynn.edu

St. Thomas University
16401 NW 37th Ave, Miami Gardens FL 33054
Maria Espino, Graduate Admissions
800-367-9010 or 305-628-6546 Fax: 305-628-6591
Website: www.stu.edu
E-mail: signup@stu.edu

University of South Florida
4202 E Fowler Ave, Tampa FL 33620-6900
J. Robert Spatig, Director of Admissions
877-USF-BULL Fax: 813-974-9689
Website: www.usf.edu
E-mail: admissions@admin.usf.edu
See listing under "Universities"

GEORGIA

Keller Graduate School of Management of DeVry University
250 N Arcadia Ave, Decatur GA 30030
404-292-7900
Website: www.keller.edu

Kennesaw State University
1000 Chastain Rd NW, Kennesaw GA 30144-5591
Timothy Mescon, Dean of College of Business
770-423-6425
Website: www.kennesaw.edu

ILLINOIS

AMERICAN INTERCONTINENTAL UNIVERSITY ONLINE
5550 Prairie Stone Parkway Suite 400
Hoffman Estates IL 60192
Admissions Department
877-701-3800
Website: www.aiuonline.edu
E-mail: info@aiuonline.edu

Aurora University
347 S Gladstone Ave, Aurora IL 60506-4892
Carol R. Dunn, Ed.D., Vice President for Enrollment
800-742-5281 Fax: 630-844-5535
Website: www.aurora.edu
E-mail: admission@aurora.edu

Benedictine University
5700 College Rd, Lisle IL 60532-0900
630-829-6300 or 888-829-6363 Fax: 630-829-6301
Website: www.ben.edu
E-mail: admissions@ben.edu
See listing under "Universities"

Roosevelt University
430 S Michigan Ave, Chicago IL 60605
Gwen E. Kanelos, Asst. Vice President for Enrollment Services
877-APPLY-RU Fax: 312-341-4216
Website: www.roosevelt.edu
E-mail: applyru@roosevelt.edu

INDIANA

University of Evansville
1800 Lincoln Ave, Evansville IN 47722-0001
Don Vos, Dean of Admission
800-423-8633 Fax: 812-488-4076
Website: www.evansville.edu
E-mail: admission@evansville.edu

IOWA

Clarke College
1550 Clarke Dr, Dubuque IA 52001-3198
Andy Schroeder, Director of Admissions
800-383-2345 Fax: 563-584-8666
Website: www.clarke.edu
E-mail: andy.schroeder@clarke.edu

MASSACHUSETTS

Anna Maria College
50 Sunset Ln, Paxton MA 01612
Timothy M. Donahue, Director of Recruitment and Admissions
508-849-3360 Fax: 508-849-3362
Website: www.annamaria.edu
E-mail: admissions@annamaria.edu

University of Massachusetts Dartmouth
Old Westport Rd, North Dartmouth MA 02747-2300
Steven T. Briggs, Director of Admissions
508-999-8605 Fax: 508-999-8755
Website: explore.umassd.edu
E-mail: sbriggs@umassd.edu

Worcester Polytechnic Institute
100 Institute Rd, Worcester MA 01609-2280
Edward J. Connor, Director of Admissions
508-831-5286 Fax: 508-831-5875
Website: admissions.wpi.edu
E-mail: admissions@wpi.edu

MICHIGAN

Davenport University
6191 Kraft Ave SE, Grand Rapids MI 49512
866-383-3548
Website: www.explore.davenport.edu

Grand Valley State University
1 Campus Dr, Allendale MI 49401-9403
Jodi Chycinski, Director of Admissions
616-331-6611 Fax: 616-331-2000
Website: www.gvsu.edu
E-mail: go2gvsu@gvsu.edu

Lawrence Technological University
21000 W 10 Mile Rd, Southfield MI 48075-1058
Jane Rohrback, Director of Admissions
800-225-5588 Fax: 248-204-2228
Website: www.ltu.edu
E-mail: admissions@ltu.edu
See listing under "Universities"

MINNESOTA

Globe College
7166 10th St N, Oakdale MN 55128
Mike Hughes, Campus Director
651-730-5100 Fax: 651-730-5151
Website: www.globecollege.edu
E-mail: admissions@globecollege.edu

Minnesota State College - Southeast Technical
Red Wing Campus
308 Pioneer Rd, Red Wing MN 55066
Al DuCett, Director of Admissions
877-853-8324 Fax: 507-453-2715
Website: www.southeastmn.edu
E-mail: aducett@southeastmn.edu
70+ degrees, diplomas & certificates (15+ online) in Business & Office Careers, Musical Instrument Repair, Physical Health, Transportation, Technology, and Trades.

Minnesota State College - Southeast Technical
Winona Campus
PO Box 409, 1250 Homer Rd, Winona MN 55987
Al DuCett, Director of Admissions
877-853-8324 Fax: 507-453-2715
Website: www.southeastmn.edu
E-mail: aducett@southeastmn.edu
70+ degrees, diplomas & certificates (15+ online) in Business & Office Careers, Musical Instrument Repair, Physical Health, Transportation, Technology, and Trades.

MISSOURI

Columbia College
1001 Rogers St, Columbia MO 65216-0001
Regina Morin, Director of Admissions
573-875-7352 Fax: 573-875-7506
Website: www.ccis.edu
E-mail: admissions@ccis.edu

Stephens College
PO Box 2121, Columbia MO 65215-0001
David Adams, Dean of Enrollment Management
573-442-2211 Fax: 573-876-7237
Website: www.stephens.edu
E-mail: dadams@stephens.edu

University of Missouri
1 University Blvd, Saint Louis MO 63121-4499
Dr. Thomas Eyssell, Director-Graduate Studies
314-516-5885 Fax: 314-516-6420
Website: www.umsl.edu
E-mail: gradadm@umsl.edu

Webster University
470 E Lockwood Ave, Saint Louis MO 63119-3194
Dr. Benjamin Akande, Dean School of Business and Management
314-961-2660 ext. 5950 Fax: 314-968-7077
Website: www.webster.edu
E-mail: mtaylor@webster.edu
See listing under "Universities"

William Woods University
1 University Ave, Fulton MO 65251-1098
Jimmy Clay, Director of Admissions
573-642-2251 Fax: 573-592-1146
Website: www.williamwoods.edu
E-mail: admissions@williamwoods.edu
See listing under "Universities"

NEW HAMPSHIRE

Southern New Hampshire University
2500 N River Rd, Hooksett NH 03106-1045
Steve Soba, Director of Admissions
603-645-9611 Fax: 603-645-9693
Website: www.snhu.edu
E-mail: s.soba@snhu.edu

NEW JERSEY

RICHARD STOCKTON COLLEGE OF NEW JERSEY

PO Box 195, Pomona NJ 08240
John Iacovelli, Dean of Enrollment Management
866-RSC-2885 Fax: 609-626-5541
Website: www.stockton.edu
E-mail: admissions@stockton.edu
See listing under "Universities"

NEW YORK

College of Saint Rose
432 Western Ave, Albany NY 12203-1419
Maryelizabeth Amico, Asst V.P. for Undergraduate Admissions
518-454-5150 Fax: 518-454-2013
Website: www.strose.edu
E-mail: admit@strose.edu

Iona College
715 North Ave, New Rochelle NY 10801-1890
Kevin Cavanagh, Assistant V.P. for College Admissions
914-633-2502 Fax: 914-637-2778
Website: www.iona.edu

Long Island University-C. W. Post Campus
720 Northern Blvd, Brookville NY 11548-1300
Beth Carson, Director of Graduate Admissions
516-299-2900 Fax: 516-299-2418
Website: www.liu.edu/cwpost
E-mail: enroll@cwpost.liu.edu

Monroe College
2501 Jerome Ave, Bronx NY 10468-4305
Evan Jerome, Director of Admissions
718-933-6700 Fax: 718-364-3552
Website: www.monroecollege.edu
E-mail: ejerome@monroecollege.edu

St. John's University
Peter J. Tobin College of Business
8000 Utopia Pkwy, Queens NY 11439
Sheila Russell, Director of Graduate Admission
877-STJ-5550 ext. 101 Fax: 718-990-5242
Website: www.stjohns.edu/learnmore
E-mail: admhelp@stjohns.edu
See listing under "Universities"

OHIO

Cleveland State University
2121 Euclid Ave RW 204, Cleveland OH 44115
Dr. Richard Arndt, Dean of Undergraduate Recruitment and College Partnerships
888-CSU-OHIO Fax: 216-687-9210
Website: www.csuohio.edu
E-mail: admissions@csuohio.edu

University of Dayton
300 College Park, Dayton OH 45469-1300
Robert F. Durkle, Director of Admission
800-837-7433 Fax: 937-229-4729
Website: admission.udayton.edu
E-mail: admission@udayton.edu

OKLAHOMA

Oklahoma State University
Stillwater OK 74078
Ken Eastman, Program Director
405-744-2951
Website: www.okstate.edu
E-mail: ken.eastman@okstate.edu

OREGON

Marylhurst University
17600 Pacific Hwy (Hwy 43)
Marylhurst OR 97036-0261
Director of Admissions
800-634-9982 ext. 6268 Fax: 503-635-6585
Website: www.marylhurst.edu
E-mail: studentinfo@marylhurst.edu

PENNSYLVANIA

Holy Family University - Woodhaven
1311 Bristol Pike, Bensalem PA 19020
Honour Moore, Associate VP for Extended Learning
215-637-7700 ext. 5008 Fax: 215-633-0558
Website: www.holyfamily.edu
E-mail: hmoore@holyfamily.edu

MOUNT ALOYSIUS COLLEGE

7373 Admiral Peary Hwy, Cresson PA 16630-1999
Frank C. Crouse Jr., Vice President for Enrollment Management
814-886-6383 or 888-823-2220 Fax: 814-886-6441
Website: www.mtaloy.edu
E-mail: admissions@mtaloy.edu

SOUTH CAROLINA

North Greenville University
PO Box 1892, Tigerville SC 29688-1892
Dr. Sam Isgett, Exec. Vice President for Graduate Studies
Website: www.ngu.edu
See listing under "Universities"

SOUTH DAKOTA

NATIONAL AMERICAN UNIVERSITY

321 Kansas City St, Rapid City SD 57701-3692
Angela G. Beck, Director of Enrollment Management
605-394-4800 Fax: 605-394-4871
Website: www.rapid.national.edu
E-mail: rcadmissions@national.edu

TENNESSEE

Lipscomb University
3901 Granny White Pike, Nashville TN 37204-3951
Ricky Holaway, Director of Admissions
800-333-4358 ext. 1776 Fax: 615-269-1804
Website: www.lipscomb.edu
E-mail: admissions@lipscomb.edu

TEXAS

Texas Woman's University
PO Box 425589, Denton TX 76204-5589
Erma Nieto-Brecht, Director of Admissions
866-809-6130 Fax: 940-898-3081
Website: www.twu.edu
E-mail: admissions@twu.edu

University of Houston
122 E Cullen Bldg, Houston TX 77204-2023
Office of Admission
713-743-9595
Website: www.uh.edu
E-mail: admissions@uh.edu

UTAH

ITT TECHNICAL INSTITUTE

920 Levoy Dr, Murray UT 84123-2500
Gary Wood, Director of Recruitment
801-263-3313 Fax: 801-263-3497
Website: www.itt-tech.edu
E-mail: gwood@itt-tech.edu

VERMONT

Green Mountain College
1 College Cir, Poultney VT 05764-1199
Sandra Bartholomew, Ph.D., Dean of Enrollment Management
802-287-8000 Fax: 802-287-8099
Website: www.greenmtn.edu
E-mail: bartholomews@greenmtn.edu

NORWICH UNIVERSITY

158 Harmon Dr, Northfield VT 05663
Dr. Bill Clements, Program Director
800-686-6546
Website: www3.norwich.edu/mba
E-mail: mbainfo@norwich.edu
See listing under "Universities"

VIRGINIA

Radford University
PO Box 6903, Radford VA 24142
David W. Kraus, Director of Admissions
800-890-4265 Fax: 540-831-5038
Website: www.radford.edu
E-mail: ruadmiss@radford.edu

Stratford University
7777 Leesburg Pike #100 South
Falls Church VA 22043
Keith Evans, Contact
703-821-8570 Fax: 703-734-5335
Website: www.stratford.edu
E-mail: admissions@stratford.edu

UNIVERSITY OF MANAGEMENT AND TECHNOLOGY

1901 Fort Myer Dr Ste 700, Arlington VA 22209
703-516-0035 Fax: 703-516-0985
Website: www.umtweb.edu
E-mail: info@umtweb.edu

University of Mary Washington
1301 College Ave, Fredericksburg VA 22401-5300
Dr. Martin A. Wilder, Jr., Director of Admissions
540-654-2000 Fax: 540-654-1857
Website: www.umw.edu
E-mail: admit@umw.edu

WISCONSIN

Alverno College
PO Box 343922, Milwaukee WI 53234-3922
Dianna Gaebler, Director of Admissions
414-382-6100 Fax: 414-382-6354
Website: www.alverno.edu
E-mail: admissions@alverno.edu

WYOMING

University of Wyoming
Admissions Office
Dept 3435, Laramie WY 82071-3435
Brooke Culver, Contact
800-342-5996 Fax: 307-766-4042
Website: www.uwyo.edu
E-mail: why-wyo@uwyo.edu

GUAM

University of Guam
UOG Station, Mangilao GU 96923
Deborah Leon Guerrero, Registrar
671-735-2201 or 671-735-2208 Fax: 671-735-2203
Website: www.uog.edu
E-mail: admitme@uog9.uog.edu

ALABAMA

CALHOUN COMMUNITY COLLEGE
PO Box 2216, Decatur AL 35609-2216
M. Wayne Tosh, Registrar
256-306-2500 Fax: 256-306-2941
Website: www.calhoun.edu
E-mail: bsm@calhoun.edu

Judson College
302 Bibb St, Marion AL 36756
Michael Scotto, Director of Admissions
800-447-9472 Fax: 334-683-5147
Website: www.judson.edu
E-mail: admissions@judson.edu

University of Alabama in Huntsville
PO Box 1247, Huntsville AL 35899-0001
Nikki Willis, Assoc. Director for Recruiting Program and Events
1-800-UAH-CALL Fax: 256-824-6073
Website: www.uah.edu
E-mail: willisn@uah.edu

University of South Alabama
307 University Blvd N, Mobile AL 36688-3053
Melissa Haab, Director of Admissions
251-460-6141 Fax: 251-460-7876
Website: www.southalabama.edu
E-mail: admiss@usouthal.edu

ALASKA

University of Alaska Anchorage
PO Box 141629, Anchorage AK 99514-1629
Cecile Mitchell, Director of Enrollment Services
907-786-1480 Fax: 907-786-4888
Website: www.uaa.alaska.edu/
E-mail: enroll@uaa.alaska.edu

CALIFORNIA

California State University-San Bernadino
5500 University Pkwy
San Bernardino CA 92407-2393
Olivia Rosas, Director of Admissions
909-537-5188 Fax: 909-537-7034
Website: www.csusb.edu
E-mail: orosas@csusb.edu

Chapman University
One University Drive, Orange CA 92866-1099
Michael Drummy, Assistant Vice President for Enrollment
Services and Chief Admission Officer
714-997-6411 or 888-CUAPPLY Fax: 714-997-6713
Website: www.chapman.edu
E-mail: admit@chapman.edu

Concordia University
1530 Concordia, Irvine CA 92612-3203
Lori McDonald, Executive Director of Enrollment Services
800-229-1200 or 949-854-8002 Fax: 949-854-6894
Website: www.cui.edu
E-mail: admission@cui.edu

FRESNO CITY COLLEGE
1101 E University Ave, Fresno CA 93741-0002
Dayann Dietrich, Contact
559-442-8241 Fax: 559-237-4232
Website: www.fresnocitycollege.com
E-mail: fcc.admissions@scccd.com

Orange Coast College
PO Box 5005, Costa Mesa CA 92628-5005
Kristin Clark, Director of Admissions
714-432-5773 Fax: 714-432-5736
Website: www.orangecoastcollege.edu
E-mail: kclark@cccd.edu

Point Loma Nazarene University
3900 Lomaland Dr, San Diego CA 92106-2810
Chip Killingsworth, Director of Undergraduate Admissions
800-733-7770 Fax: 619-849-2601
Website: www.pointloma.edu
E-mail: admissions@pointloma.edu

San Bernardino Valley College
701 S Mount Vernon Ave
San Bernardino CA 92410-2798
Kay Ragan, Ed.D., Director of Admissions
909-888-6511 Fax: 909-889-4988
Website: www.valleycollege.edu
E-mail: kragan@sbccd.cc.ca.us

San Diego Christian College
2100 Greenfield Dr, El Cajon CA 92019-1157
Rene Inman, Director of Admissions
800-676-2242 Fax: 619-590-1739
Website: www.sdcc.edu
E-mail: admissions@sdcc.edu

Simpson University
2211 College View Dr, Redding CA 96003-8606
Jim Herberger, Director of Admissions
888-9-SIMPSON Fax: 530-226-4861
Website: www.simpsonuniversity.edu
E-mail: admissions@simpsonuniversity.edu
See listing under "Universities"

Whittier College
PO Box 634, Whittier CA 90608-0634
Kieron Miller, Director of Admissions
562-907-4200 Fax: 562-907-4870
Website: www.whittier.edu
E-mail: kmiller@whittier.edu

COLORADO

Colorado Christian University
8787 W Alameda Ave, Lakewood CO 80226
Sean Kadel, Director of Admissions
800-44-FAITH Fax: 303-963-3201
Website: www.ccu.edu
E-mail: admissions@ccu.edu

CONNECTICUT

Albertus Magnus College
700 Prospect St, New Haven CT 06511-1189
Richard Lolatte, Dean of Admission
203-773-8501 or 800-578-9160 Fax: 203-773-5248
Website: www.albertus.edu
E-mail: admissions@albertus.edu

UNITED STATES COAST GUARD ACADEMY
15 Mohegan Ave, New London CT 06320-8131
Captain Susan D. Bibeau, Contact
800-883-8724 Fax: 860-701-6700
Website: www.uscga.edu
E-mail: admissions@uscga.edu

DISTRICT OF COLUMBIA

Gallaudet University
800 Florida Ave NE, Washington DC 20002-3695
Charity Reedy Hines, Director of Admissions
202-651-5750 Fax: 202-651-5744
Website: www.gallaudet.edu
E-mail: admissions.office@gallaudet.edu

FLORIDA

Florida State University
600 W College Ave, Tallahassee FL 32306-1096
Janice V. Finney, Director of Admissions
850-644-2525 Fax: 850-644-0197
Website: admissions.fsu.edu
E-mail: admissions@admin.fsu.edu

University of South Florida
4202 E Fowler Ave, Tampa FL 33620-6900
J. Robert Spatig, Director of Admissions
877-USF-BULL Fax: 813-974-9689
Website: www.usf.edu
E-mail: admissions@admin.usf.edu
See listing under "Universities"

GEORGIA

Armstrong Atlantic State University
11935 Abercorn St, Savannah GA 31419-1997
Kim West, Asst. Dean and Registrar Enrollment Services
912-927-5277 Fax: 912-921-5462
Website: www.armstrong.edu
E-mail: admissions@mail.armstrong.edu

Kennesaw State University
1000 Chastain Rd NW, Kennesaw GA 30144-5591
Laurence Peterson, Dean of College of Science and Mathematics
770-423-6160
Website: www.kennesaw.edu

IDAHO

Brigham Young University - Idaho
120 Kimball Bldg, Rexburg ID 83460-1615
Rob Garrett, Director of Admissions
208-496-1020 Fax: 208-496-1220
Website: www.byui.edu
E-mail: admissions@byui.edu

Lewis-Clark State College
500 8th Ave, Lewiston ID 83501-2698
Diane Douglas, Ph.D., Registrar/Director of Admissions
800-933-5272 Fax: 208-792-2429
Website: www.lcsc.edu
E-mail: admissions@lcsc.edu

University of Idaho
Moscow ID 83844-4253
Lloyd Scott, Director of New Student Services
208-885-6163 Fax: 208-885-4477
Website: www.uidaho.edu
E-mail: nss@uidaho.edu

ILLINOIS

Aurora University
347 S Gladstone Ave, Aurora IL 60506-4892
Carol R. Dunn, Ed.D., Vice President for Enrollment
800-742-5281 Fax: 630-844-5535
Website: www.aurora.edu
E-mail: admission@aurora.edu

Benedictine University
5700 College Rd, Lisle IL 60532-0900
630-829-6300 or 888-829-6363 Fax: 630-829-6301
Website: www.ben.edu
E-mail: admissions@ben.edu
See listing under "Universities"

CONCORDIA UNIVERSITY
7400 Augusta St, River Forest IL 60305-1402
708-209-3100 Fax: 708-209-3176
Website: www.cuchicago.edu
E-mail: admission@cuchicago.edu

Roosevelt University
430 S Michigan Ave, Chicago IL 60605
Gwen E. Kanelos, Asst. Vice President for Enrollment Services
877-APPLY-RU Fax: 312-341-4216
Website: www.roosevelt.edu
E-mail: applyru@roosevelt.edu

Trinity International University
2065 Half Day Rd, Deerfield IL 60015-1241
847-945-8800 Fax: 847-317-8097
Website: www.tiu.edu
E-mail: tcadmissions@tiu.edu

INDIANA

Ancilla Domini College
Donaldson IN 46513
Erin Alonzo, Director of Admissions
574-936-8898 Fax: 574-935-1773
Website: www.ancilla.edu
E-mail: erin.alonzo@ancilla.edu

Franklin College
101 Branigin Blvd, Franklin IN 46131
Jacqueline S. Acosta, Director of Admissions
800-852-0232 Fax: 317-738-8274
Website: www.franklincollege.edu
E-mail: admissions@franklincollege.edu

Oakland City University
138 N Lucretia St, Oakland City IN 47660
Brian J. Baker, Director of Admissions
800-737-5125 Fax: 812-749-1433
Website: www.oak.edu
E-mail: bbaker@oak.edu
See listing under "Universities"

Rose-Hulman Institute of Technology
5500 Wabash Ave, Terre Haute IN 47803-3920
James A. Goecker, Dean of Admissions
812-877-8213 Fax: 812-877-8941
Website: www.rose-hulman.edu
E-mail: admissions@rose-hulman.edu

University of Evansville
1800 Lincoln Ave, Evansville IN 47722-0001
Don Vos, Dean of Admission
800-423-8633 Fax: 812-488-4076
Website: www.evansville.edu
E-mail: admission@evansville.edu

IOWA

Briar Cliff University
PO Box 2100, Sioux City IA 51104-0100
Sharisue Wilcoxon, VP for Enrollment Management
712-279-5200 Fax: 712-279-1632
Website: www.briarcliff.edu
E-mail: admissions@briarcliff.edu

Clarke College
1550 Clarke Dr, Dubuque IA 52001-3198
Andy Schroeder, Director of Admissions
800-383-2345 Fax: 563-584-8666
Website: www.clarke.edu
E-mail: andy.schroeder@clarke.edu

Graceland University
1 University Place, Lamoni IA 50140
Greg Sutherland, Interim Vice President for Enrollment and Dean of Admissions
641-784-5196 Fax: 641-784-5480
Website: www.admissions.graceland.edu
E-mail: admissions@graceland.edu

Iowa Lakes Community College
300 S 18th St, Estherville IA 51334-2721
Anne Stansbury, Asst. Director of Admissions
712-362-7945 Fax: 712-362-8363
Website: www.iowalakes.edu
E-mail: info@iowalakes.edu

KANSAS

Tabor College
400 S Jefferson St, Hillsboro KS 67063-1758
Rusty Allen, Dean of Enrollment Management
800-822-6799 Fax: 620-947-6276
Website: www.tabor.edu
E-mail: admissions@tabor.edu
See listing under "Universities"

KENTUCKY

Bluegrass Community and Technical College
Oswald Building
470 Cooper Drive, Lexington KY 40506-0235
Shelbie Hugle, Director of Admissions
859-246-6200 Fax: 859-246-4664
Website: www.bluegrass.kctcs.edu
E-mail: bctc_info@kctcs.edu

Morehead State University
Morehead KY 40351-1689
Jeffrey Liles, Enrollment Services
800-585-6781 Fax: 606-783-5038
Website: www.moreheadstate.edu
E-mail: admissions@moreheadstate.edu

LOUISIANA

Our Lady of Holy Cross College
4123 Woodland Dr, New Orleans LA 70131-7399
Office of Enrollment Services
504-394-7744 Fax: 504-391-2421
Website: www.olhcc.edu

MAINE

St. Joseph's College of Maine
278 Whites Bridge Rd, Standish ME 04084-5263
Vincent Kloskowski, Dean of Admissions
800-338-7057 Fax: 207-893-7862
Website: www.sjcme.edu
E-mail: admission@sjcme.edu

MARYLAND

Cecil College
One Seahawk Dr, North East MD 21901
Sandra S. Rajaski, Registrar & Director of Admissions
410-287-1000 Fax: 410-287-1001
Website: www.cecil.edu
E-mail: srajaski@cecil.edu

Hagerstown Community College
11400 Robinwood Dr, Hagerstown MD 21742-6590
Dr. Daniel E. Bock, Assistant Director of Admissions
301-790-2800 Fax: 301-791-9165
Website: www.hagerstowncc.edu
E-mail: bockd@hagerstowncc.edu

MASSACHUSETTS

Assumption College
500 Salisbury St, Worcester MA 01609-1294
Kathleen Murphy, Dean of Enrollment
508-767-7000 Fax: 508-799-4412
Website: www.assumption.edu
E-mail: admiss@assumption.edu

Boston University
121 Bay State Rd, Boston MA 02215
Kelly Walter, Executive Director of Admissions
617-353-2300 Fax: 617-353-9695
Website: web.bu.edu
E-mail: admissions@bu.edu

Gordon College
255 Grapevine Rd, Wenham MA 01984-1899
Barbara R. Layne, Associate Vice President, Enrollment
866-464-6736 Fax: 978-867-4682
Website: www.gordon.edu
E-mail: admissions@gordon.edu

Massachusetts Institute of Technology
77 Massachusetts Ave, Cambridge MA 02139-4307
617-253-1000 Fax: 617-253-4016
Website: my.mit.edu
E-mail: admissions@mit.edu

Smith College
Northampton MA 01063-0001
Debra Shaver, Director of Admissions
800-383-3232 Fax: 413-585-2527
Website: www.smith.edu
E-mail: admission@smith.edu

University of Massachusetts Dartmouth
Old Westport Rd, North Dartmouth MA 02747-2300
Steven T. Briggs, Director of Admissions
508-999-8605 Fax: 508-999-8755
Website: explore.umassd.edu
E-mail: sbriggs@umassd.edu

Worcester Polytechnic Institute
100 Institute Rd, Worcester MA 01609-2280
Edward J. Connor, Director of Admissions
508-831-5286 Fax: 508-831-5875
Website: admissions.wpi.edu
E-mail: admissions@wpi.edu

MICHIGAN

Alma College
614 W Superior St, Alma MI 48801-1599
Evan Montague, Director of Admissions
800-321-ALMA Fax: 989-463-7057
Website: www.alma.edu
E-mail: admissions@alma.edu

Delta College
University Center MI 48710-0001
Duff Zube, Director of Admissions
989-686-9093 Fax: 989-667-2202
Website: www.delta.edu
E-mail: admit@delta.edu

Grand Valley State University
1 Campus Dr, Allendale MI 49401-9403
Jodi Chycinski, Director of Admissions
616-331-6611 Fax: 616-331-2000
Website: www.gvsu.edu
E-mail: go2gvsu@gvsu.edu

HILLSDALE COLLEGE
33 E College St, Hillsdale MI 49242-1298
Professor Mark Watson, Director
517-607-2384 Fax: 517-607-2252
Website: www.hillsdale.edu
E-mail: mark.watson@hillsdale.edu

Lawrence Technological University
21000 W 10 Mile Rd, Southfield MI 48075-1058
Jane Rohrback, Director of Admissions
800-225-5588 Fax: 248-204-2228
Website: www.ltu.edu
E-mail: admissions@ltu.edu
See listing under "Universities"

MACOMB COMMUNITY COLLEGE
44575 Garfield Rd, Clinton Township MI 48038-1139
Information Center
586-445-7999
Website: www.macomb.edu
E-mail: answer@macomb.edu

MACOMB COMMUNITY COLLEGE
14500 E 12 Mile Rd, Warren MI 48088-3896
Information Center
586-445-7999
Website: www.macomb.edu
E-mail: answer@macomb.edu

Oakland University
2200 N Squirrel Rd, Rochester MI 48309
Eleanor L. Reynolds, Assistant Vice President & Director of Admissions
248-370-2100
Website: www.oakland.edu
E-mail: ouinfo@oakland.edu

MINNESOTA

Carleton College
1 N College St, Northfield MN 55057-4044
800-995-2275 or 507-646-4190 Fax: 507-646-4526
Website: www.carleton.edu
E-mail: admissions@acs.carleton.edu

Gustavus Adolphus College
800 W College Ave, Saint Peter MN 56082-1485
Mark H. Anderson, Dean of Admission
800-GUSTAVUS Fax: 507-933-7474
Website: www.gustavus.edu
E-mail: admission@gustavus.edu

Metropolitan State University
700 7th St E, Saint Paul MN 55106-5000
Monir Johnson, Director of Admissions
651-793-1300 Fax: 651-793-1546
Website: www.metrostate.edu
E-mail: monir.johnson@metrostate.edu

Minnesota State University Moorhead
1104 7th Ave S, Moorhead MN 56563-0002
Regina Monson, Director of Admissions
218-477-2161 Fax: 218-477-4374
Website: go.mnstate.edu
E-mail: dragon@mnstate.edu

Pillsbury Baptist Bible College
315 S Grove Ave, Owatonna MN 55060-3097
Susanne Martin, Admissions Coordinator
507-451-2710 Fax: 507-451-0156
Website: www.pillsbury.edu
E-mail: admissions@pillsbury.edu

MISSISSIPPI

Tougaloo College
500 W County Line Rd, Tougaloo MS 39174-9799
Juno Leggette Jacobs, Director of Admissions
601-977-7768 Fax: 601-977-4501
Website: www.tougaloo.edu
E-mail: jjacobs@tougaloo.edu

MISSOURI

Central Methodist University
411 Central Methodist Sq, Fayette MO 65248-1198
Larry Anderson, Director of Admissions
660-248-6247 Fax: 660-248-1872
Website: www.centralmethodist.edu
E-mail: landerso@centralmethodist.edu

Columbia College
1001 Rogers St, Columbia MO 65216-0001
Regina Morin, Director of Admissions
573-875-7352 Fax: 573-875-7506
Website: www.ccis.edu
E-mail: admissions@ccis.edu

Lindenwood University
209 S Kingshighway St
Saint Charles MO 63301-1695
Sheryl Guffey, Director of Admissions
636-949-2000 Fax: 636-949-4989
Website: www.lindenwood.edu

Northwest Missouri State University
800 University Dr, Maryville MO 64468-6001
Beverly Schenkel, Dean of Enrollment Management
660-562-1562 Fax: 660-562-1121
Website: www.nwmissouri.edu
E-mail: admissions@nwmissouri.edu

Stephens College
PO Box 2121, Columbia MO 65215-0001
David Adams, Dean of Enrollment Management
573-442-2211 Fax: 573-876-7237
Website: www.stephens.edu
E-mail: dadams@stephens.edu

Truman State University
100 E Normal, Kirksville MO 63501
Office of Admission
660-785-4114 Fax: 660-785-7456
Website: admissions.truman.edu
E-mail: admissions@truman.edu

University of Missouri
1 University Blvd, Saint Louis MO 63121-4499
Dr. Mark Burkholder, Dean-College of Arts & Sciences
314-516-5501 Fax: 314-516-5415
Website: www.umsl.edu
E-mail: admissions@umsl.edu

Webster University
470 E Lockwood Ave, Saint Louis MO 63119-3194
Dr. Ed Sakurai, Chairman, Math and Computer Science
314-968-7023 Fax: 314-963-6050
Website: www.webster.edu
E-mail: sakuraab@webster.edu
See listing under "Universities"

William Jewell College
500 College Hill, Liberty MO 64068-1896
Dr. Rick Winslow, VP Enrollment Management and Student Affairs
800-753-7009 Fax: 816-415-5040
Website: www.jewell.edu
E-mail: winslowr@william.jewell.edu

William Woods University
1 University Ave, Fulton MO 65251-1098
Jimmy Clay, Director of Admissions
573-642-2251 Fax: 573-592-1146
Website: www.williamwoods.edu
E-mail: admissions@williamwoods.edu
See listing under "Universities"

MONTANA

Carroll College
1601 N Benton Ave, Helena MT 59625-0002
Dr. Thomas J. Trebon, President
Cynthia Thornquist, Director of Admissions & Enrollment Operations
406-447-4384 Fax: 406-447-4533
Website: www.carroll.edu
E-mail: admission@carroll.edu

NEBRASKA

Midland Lutheran College
900 N Clarkson St, Fremont NE 68025-4200
Todd Hansen, Associate Director of Admissions
402-941-6501 Fax: 402-941-6513
Website: www.mlc.edu
E-mail: admissions@mlc.edu

Nebraska Wesleyan University
5000 Saint Paul Ave, Lincoln NE 68504-2794
Patricia Karthauser, V.P. for University Enrollment
402-466-2371 Fax: 402-465-2177
Website: www.nebrwesleyan.edu
E-mail: admissions@nebrwesleyan.edu

University of Nebraska at Kearney
905 W 25th St, Kearney NE 68849-0001
Dusty Newton, Director of Admissions
800-KEARNEY Fax: 308-865-8987
Website: www.unk.edu
E-mail: admissionsug@unk.edu

NEW JERSEY

New Jersey City University
2039 John F Kennedy Blvd
Jersey City NJ 07305-1588
Carmen Panlilio, Asst. V.P. for Admissions and Financial Aid
201-200-3234 Fax: 201-200-2044
Website: www.njcu.edu
E-mail: admissions@njcu.edu

Ramapo College of New Jersey
505 Ramapo Valley Rd, Mahwah NJ 07430-1623
Director of Admissions
201-684-7300 or 201-684-7301 Fax: 201-684-7964
Website: www.ramapo.edu
E-mail: admissions@ramapo.edu

RICHARD STOCKTON COLLEGE OF NEW JERSEY
PO Box 195, Pomona NJ 08240
John Iacovelli, Dean of Enrollment Management
866-RSC-2885 Fax: 609-626-5541
Website: www.stockton.edu
E-mail: admissions@stockton.edu

Stockton College is a comprehensive liberal arts, co-ed institution founded in 1969. Advance Pre-Professional Degree Options: 7-yr BS/MD with UMDNJ; NJ Dental School; NJ Medical School, Robert Wood Johnson Medical, School of Osteopathic Medicine; NY College of Podiatric Medicine, Pennsylvania College of Podiatric Medicine, SUNY College of Optometry. Pharmacy doctorate program with Rutgers University. 5-yr Engineering with NJIT and Rutgers University. Dual BA/MA in Criminal Justice. 5-yr BS/MS in Computational Science. BS/MS in Nursing. Doctorate of Physical Therapy. Additional Programs: Forensic Science, Pre-Law, Pre-Occupational Therapy, and Pre-Veterinary.

NEW YORK

College of Saint Rose
432 Western Ave, Albany NY 12203-1419
Maryelizabeth Amico, Asst V.P. for Undergraduate Admissions
518-454-5150 Fax: 518-454-2013
Website: www.strose.edu
E-mail: admit@strose.edu

CUNY Hunter College
695 Park Ave, New York NY 10021
Aaron Gibbs, Assistant Director of Recruitment
212-650-3946 Fax: 212-650-3336
Website: www.hunter.cuny.edu
E-mail: aaron.gibbs@hunter.cuny.edu

Daemen College
4380 Main St, Amherst NY 14226-3592
Donna Shaffner, Director of Admissions
800-462-7652 Fax: 716-839-8229
Website: www.daemen.edu/admissions
E-mail: admissions@daemen.edu

Dowling College
150 Idle Hour Blvd, Oakdale NY 11769-1999
Diane Kazanecki-Kempter, Contact
631-244-3000 Fax: 631-244-1059
Website: www.dowling.edu
E-mail: admissions@dowling.edu

Iona College
715 North Ave, New Rochelle NY 10801-1890
Kevin Cavanagh, Assistant V.P. for College Admissions
914-633-2502 Fax: 914-637-2778
Website: www.iona.edu

Long Island University-C. W. Post Campus
720 Northern Blvd, Brookville NY 11548-1300
Joanne Graziano, Executive Director of Admissions
516-299-2900 Fax: 516-299-2137
Website: www.liu.edu/cwpost
E-mail: enroll@cwpost.liu.edu

Molloy College
1000 Hempstead Ave
Rockville Centre NY 11570-1100
Marguerite Lane, Director of Admissions
516-678-5000 ext. 6291 Fax: 516-256-2247
Website: www.molloy.edu
E-mail: admissions@molloy.edu
See listing under "Universities"

PURCHASE COLLEGE STATE UNIVERSITY OF NEW YORK (SUNY)
735 Anderson Hill Rd, Purchase NY 10577-1400
Stephanie McCaine, Director of Admissions
914-251-6300 Fax: 914-251-6314
Website: www.purchase.edu
E-mail: admisn@purchase.edu
See listing under "Universities"

Roberts Wesleyan College
2301 Westside Dr, Rochester NY 14624-1997
Office of Admissions
585-594-6400 Fax: 585-594-6371
Website: www.roberts.edu
E-mail: admissions@roberts.edu

St. John's University
8000 Utopia Pkwy, Queens NY 11439
Office of Admission
877-STJ-5550 ext. 101 Fax: 718-990-2096
Website: www.stjohns.edu/learnmore
E-mail: admhelp@stjohns.edu
See listing under "Universities"

St. Joseph's College
245 Clinton Ave, Brooklyn NY 11205-3688
Theresa LaRocca Meyer, V.P. for Enrollment Management
718-636-6800 Fax: 718-636-8303
Website: www.sjcny.edu
E-mail: tlaroccameyer@sjcny.edu

Siena College
515 Loudonville Rd, Loudonville NY 12211-1462
Heather Renault, Director of Admissions
518-783-2300 Fax: 518-783-2436
Website: www.siena.edu
E-mail: hrenault@siena.edu

SUNY College at Brockport
350 New Campus Dr, Brockport NY 14420-2997
Bernard S. Valento, Director of Undergraduate Admissions
585-395-2751 Fax: 585-395-5452
Website: www.brockport.edu
E-mail: admit@brockport.edu

SUNY College of Technology
Alfred NY 14802
Deborah J. Goodrich, Associate VP Enrollment Mgmt.
800-4AL-FRED Fax: 607-587-4299
Website: www.alfredstate.edu
E-mail: admissions@alfredstate.edu

SUNY Orange County Community College
115 South St, Middletown NY 10940-6437
Margot St. Lawrence, Director of Admissions
845-341-4030 Fax: 845-342-8662
Website: www.sunyorange.edu
E-mail: apply@sunyorange.edu
See listing under "Community and Junior Colleges"

SUNY Sullivan County Community College
112 College Rd, Loch Sheldrake NY 12759-5151
Sari Rosenheck, Director of Admissions
845-434-5750 Fax: 845-434-0923
Website: www.sullivan.suny.edu
E-mail: admissions@sullivan.suny.edu
Student Housing on Campus.

United States Military Academy West Point
646 Swift Rd, West Point NY 10996-1905
Colonel Michael L. Jones, Director of Admissions
845-938-4041 Fax: 845-938-8121
Website: admissions.usma.edu
E-mail: admissions@usma.edu

Wells College
PO Box 500, Aurora NY 13026
Susan Sloan, Director of Admissions
800-952-9355 Fax: 315-364-3227
Website: www.wells.edu
E-mail: ssloan@wells.edu

NORTH CAROLINA

Catawba College
2300 W Innes St, Salisbury NC 28144-2488
Dr. L. Russell Watjen, Ph.D., V.P. & Dean of Admissions
704-637-4402 Fax: 704-637-4222
Website: www.catawba.edu
E-mail: admission@catawba.edu

Salem College
Winston Salem NC 27108
Dana Evans, Dean of Admissions/Fin. Aid
800-32-SALEM Fax: 336-917-5572
Website: www.salem.edu
E-mail: admissions@salem.edu
See listing under "Women's Colleges"

NORTH DAKOTA

Dickinson State University
Dickinson ND 58601-4896
Steve Glasser, Director of Enrollment Services
800-279-4295 Fax: 701-483-2409
Website: www.dickinsonstate.edu
E-mail: dsu.hawks@dickinsonstate.edu

OHIO

Cleveland State University
2121 Euclid Ave RW 204, Cleveland OH 44115
Dr. Richard Arndt, Dean of Undergraduate Recruitment and College Partnerships
888-CSU-OHIO Fax: 216-687-9210
Website: www.csuohio.edu
E-mail: admissions@csuohio.edu

Franciscan University of Steubenville
University Blvd, Steubenville OH 43952
Margaret J. Weber, Director of Admissions
800-783-6220 or 740-283-6226 Fax: 740-284-5456
Website: www.admissions.edu
E-mail: mweber@franciscan.edu

OHIO NORTHERN UNIVERSITY
525 S Main St, Ada OH 45810-1555
William Fuller, Chair of Mathematics & Statistics Dept.
419-772-2346
Website: www.onu.edu
E-mail: admissions-ug@onu.edu

The Ohio State University
College of Mathematical and Physical Sciences
Stillman Hall, 1947 College Rd, Columbus OH 43210
614-292-2874 Fax: 614-292-3639
Website: www.mps.ohio-state.edu
E-mail: handon.1@osu.edu

OHIO WESLEYAN UNIVERSITY
61 S Sandusky St, Delaware OH 43015-2398
Director of Admission
740-368-3020 Fax: 740-368-3314
Website: www.owu.edu
E-mail: owuadmit@owu.edu

University of Dayton
300 College Park, Dayton OH 45469-1300
Robert F. Durkle, Director of Admission
800-837-7433 Fax: 937-229-4729
Website: admission.udayton.edu
E-mail: admission@udayton.edu

Ursuline College
2550 Lander Rd, Cleveland OH 44124-4398
Sarah E. Sundermeier, Director of Admissions
888-URSULINE Toll Free Fax: 440-684-6138
Website: www.admission.ursuline.edu
E-mail: admission@ursuline.edu

OKLAHOMA

Oklahoma State University
Stillwater OK 74078
Alan Adolphson, Department Head
405-744-5688
Website: www.okstate.edu
E-mail: adolphs@okstate.edu

University of Tulsa
600 S College Ave, Tulsa OK 74104-3126
Earl Johnson, Dean of Admission
918-631-2307 Fax: 918-631-5003
Website: www.utulsa.edu
E-mail: admission@utulsa.edu

OREGON

Linn-Benton Community College
6500 Pacific Blvd SW, Albany OR 97321-3774
Christine Baker, Outreach Coordinator
541-917-4811 Fax: 541-917-4868
Website: www.linnbenton.edu
E-mail: admissions@linnbenton.edu

Warner Pacific College
2219 SE 68th Ave, Portland OR 97215-4026
Shannon Mackey, Director of Admissions
503-517-1000 Fax: 503-517-1352
Website: www.warnerpacific.edu
E-mail: admissions@warnerpacific.edu

PENNSYLVANIA

Clarion University of Pennsylvania
840 Wood St, Clarion PA 16214-1232
William Bailey, Dean of Enrollment Management
814-393-2306 Fax: 814-393-2030
Website: www.clarion.edu
E-mail: admissions@clarion.edu

Community College of Allegheny County
Allegheny Campus: 808 Ridge Ave, Pittsburgh PA 15212 Admissions: 412.237.2700
Boyce Campus: 595 Beatty Rd, Monroeville PA 15146 Admissions: 724.325.6614
North Campus: 8701 Perry Highway, Pittsburgh PA 15237 Admissions: 412.369.3600
South Campus: 1750 Clairton Rd, West Mifflin PA 15122 Admissions: 412-469-4301
Website: www.ccac.edu

DeSales University
2755 Station Ave, Center Valley PA 18034-9565
610-282-1100 Fax: 610-282-2342
Website: www.desales.edu

Holy Family University
9801 Frankford Avenue, Philadelphia PA 19114
Lauren Campbell, Director of Admissions
215-637-3050 Fax: 215-281-1022
Website: www.holyfamily.edu
E-mail: admissions@holyfamily.edu

Juniata College
1700 Moore St, Huntingdon PA 16652-2196
Michelle Bartol, Dean of Enrollment
877-JUNIATA Fax: 814-641-3100
Website: www.juniata.edu
E-mail: admissions@juniata.edu

King's College
133 N River St, Wilkes Barre PA 18711-0801
Michelle Lawrence-Schmude, Dean of Admission
570-208-5900 Fax: 570-208-5971
Website: www.kings.edu
E-mail: admissions@kings.edu

MOUNT ALOYSIUS COLLEGE
7373 Admiral Peary Hwy, Cresson PA 16630-1999
Frank C. Crouse Jr., Vice President for Enrollment Management
814-886-6383 or 888-823-2220 Fax: 814-886-6441
Website: www.mtaloy.edu
E-mail: admissions@mtaloy.edu

Washington & Jefferson College
60 S Lincoln St, Washington PA 15301-4801
Alton E. Newell, Vice President for Enrollment
724-223-6025 Fax: 724-223-6534
Website: www.washjeff.edu
E-mail: admission@washjeff.edu

Widener University
1 University Pl, Chester PA 19013-5792
Edwin Wright, Dean of Admissions
610-499-4000 Fax: 610-499-4676
Website: www.widener.edu
E-mail: admissions.office@widener.edu

SOUTH CAROLINA

Erskine College & Seminary
PO Box 176, Due West SC 29639
Bart Walker, Director of Admissions
864-379-8838 Fax: 864-379-3048
Website: www.erskine.edu
E-mail: admissions@erskine.edu

Limestone College
1115 College Dr, Gaffney SC 29340-3799
Chris Phenicie, V.P. for Enrollment
864-489-7151 Fax: 864-488-8206
Website: www.limestone.edu
E-mail: cphenicie@limestone.edu

North Greenville University
PO Box 1892, Tigerville SC 29688-1892
Website: www.ngu.edu
See listing under "Universities"

University of South Carolina - Upstate
800 University Way, Spartanburg SC 29303-4932
Donette Stewart, Assistant VC for Enrollment Services
864-503-5246 Fax: 864-503-5727
Website: www.uscupstate.edu
E-mail: dstewart@uscupstate.edu
See listing under "Universities"

TENNESSEE

Austin Peay State University
601 College St, Clarksville TN 37044-0002
931-221-7011 Fax: 931-221-6168
Website: www.apsu.edu
E-mail: admissions@apsu.edu

Lipscomb University
3901 Granny White Pike, Nashville TN 37204-3951
Ricky Holaway, Director of Admissions
800-333-4358 ext. 1776 Fax: 615-269-1804
Website: www.lipscomb.edu
E-mail: admissions@lipscomb.edu

Tennessee State University
3500 John A Merritt Blvd, Nashville TN 37209-1561
John Cade, Dean of Admissions & Records
615-963-5101 Fax: 615-963-2930
Website: www.tnstate.edu
E-mail: jcade@tnstate.edu

University of Tennessee
615 McCallie Ave, Chattanooga TN 37403-2504
Yancy Freeman, Director of Admissions
423-425-4111 Fax: 423-425-4157
Website: www.utc.edu
E-mail: Yancy-Freeman@utc.edu

TEXAS

Abilene Christian University
ACU Box 29000, Abilene TX 79699-0001
325-674-2000 Fax: 325-674-2202
Website: www.acu.edu
E-mail: info@admissions.acu.edu

Lubbock Christian University
5601 19th St, Lubbock TX 79407-2099
Stan Scott, Director of Admissions
806-796-8800 Fax: 806-720-7162
Website: www.lcu.edu
E-mail: stan.scott@lcu.edu

Texas Woman's University
PO Box 425589, Denton TX 76204-5589
Erma Nieto-Brecht, Director of Admissions
866-809-6130 Fax: 940-898-3081
Website: www.twu.edu
E-mail: admissions@twu.edu

Tyler Junior College
PO Box 9020, Tyler TX 75711-9020
Richard Minter, Dean
800-687-5680
Website: www.tjc.edu
E-mail: rmin@tjc.edu
See listing under "Community and Junior Colleges"

University of Dallas
1845 E Northgate Dr, Irving TX 75062-4736
Curt Eley, Dean
972-721-5000 Fax: 972-721-5017
Website: www.udallas.edu
E-mail: ugadmis@udallas.edu

University of Houston
122 E Cullen Bldg, Houston TX 77204-2023
Office of Admission
713-743-9595
Website: www.uh.edu
E-mail: admissions@uh.edu

University of Texas at Arlington
Box 19111, Arlington TX 76019-0111
Hans Gatterdam, Director of Admission
817-272-6287 Fax: 817-272-3435
Website: www.uta.edu
E-mail: admissions@uta.edu

VERMONT

NORWICH UNIVERSITY
158 Harmon Dr, Northfield VT 05663
Dr. Cathy Frey, Division Head
800-468-6679 Fax: 802-485-2333
Website: www.norwich.edu
E-mail: frey@norwich.edu
See listing under "Universities"

VIRGINIA

Radford University
PO Box 6903, Radford VA 24142
David W. Kraus, Director of Admissions
800-890-4265 Fax: 540-831-5038
Website: www.radford.edu
E-mail: ruadmiss@radford.edu

Randolph College
2500 Rivermont Ave, Lynchburg VA 24503
Patricia LeDonne, Director of Admissions
434-947-8100 Fax: 434-947-8996
Website: www.randolphcollege.edu
E-mail: admissions@randolphcollege.edu

Roanoke College
221 College Ln, Salem VA 24153-3794
James A. Pennix, Director of Admissions
540-375-2500 Fax: 540-375-2267
Website: www.roanoke.edu
E-mail: pennix@roanoke.edu

University of Mary Washington
1301 College Ave, Fredericksburg VA 22401-5300
Dr. Martin A. Wilder, Jr., Director of Admissions
540-654-2000 Fax: 540-654-1857
Website: www.umw.edu
E-mail: admit@umw.edu

WEST VIRGINIA

Davis & Elkins College
100 Campus Dr, Elkins WV 26241-3996
Renee Heckel, Director of Enrollment Management
800-624-3157 Fax: 304-637-1800
Website: www.davisandelkins.edu
E-mail: admiss@davisandelkins.edu

Fairmont State University
1201 Locust Ave, Fairmont WV 26554-2470
Steve Leadman, Director of Admissions
304-367-4642 or 800-641-5678 Fax: 304-367-4789
Website: www.fairmontstate.edu
E-mail: admit@fairmontstate.edu

WISCONSIN

Alverno College
PO Box 343922, Milwaukee WI 53234-3922
Dianna Gaebler, Director of Admissions
414-382-6100 Fax: 414-382-6354
Website: www.alverno.edu
E-mail: admissions@alverno.edu

Lakeland College
PO Box 359, Sheboygan WI 53082-0359
Nathan Dehne, Director of Admission
920-565-1100 Fax: 920-565-1215
Website: www.lakeland.edu
E-mail: admissions@lakeland.edu

Marquette University
PO Box 1881, Milwaukee WI 53201-1881
Robert Blust, Director of Admissions
414-288-7302 Fax: 414-288-3764
Website: www.mu.edu
E-mail: admissions@marquette.edu

St. Norbert College
100 Grant St, De Pere WI 54115
Brian Studebaker, Director of Admission
800-236-4878 Fax: 920-403-4072
Website: www.snc.edu
E-mail: admit@snc.edu

WYOMING

University of Wyoming
Admissions Office
Dept 3435, Laramie WY 82071-3435
Brooke Culver, Contact
800-342-5996 Fax: 307-766-4042
Website: www.uwyo.edu
E-mail: why-wyo@uwyo.edu

GUAM

University of Guam
UOG Station, Mangilao GU 96923
Deborah Leon Guerrero, Registrar
671-735-2201 or 671-735-2208 Fax: 671-735-2203
Website: www.uog.edu
E-mail: admitme@uog9.uog.edu

MECHANICS AND REPAIRERS

ALABAMA

Bishop State Community College - Four Campuses
351 N Broad St, Mobile AL 36603-5898
Dr. Terry Hazzard, Dean of Students
251-690-6801 Fax: 251-690-6446
Website: www.bishop.edu
E-mail: thazzard@bishop.edu

Trenholm State Technical College
Patterson Campus
3920 Troy Hwy, Montgomery AL 36116
Dr. Anthony Molina, President
334-420-4200 Fax: 334-420-4206
Website: www.trenholmtech.cc.al.us
E-mail: molinaa@trenholmtech.cc.al.us

ALASKA

University of Alaska Anchorage
PO Box 141629, Anchorage AK 99514-1629
Cecile Mitchell, Director of Enrollment Services
907-786-1480 Fax: 907-786-4888
Website: www.uaa.alaska.edu/
E-mail: enroll@uaa.alaska.edu

ARIZONA

Pima Community College
4905 E Broadway Blvd, Tucson AZ 85709-1010
Wendy Kilgore, Ph.D., Director of Admissions
520-206-4500 Fax: 520-206-4790
Website: www.pima.edu
E-mail: infocenter@pima.edu

Universal Technical Institute
10695 W Pierce St, Avondale AZ 85323-7946
John Palumbo, Director of Admissions
623-245-4600 Fax: 623-245-4603
Website: www.uticorp.com

ARKANSAS

Northwest Technical Institute
709 S Old Missouri Rd, Springdale AR 72764
Charles L. Kelley, President
479-751-8824 Fax: 479-751-7780
Website: www.nti.tec.ar.us
E-mail: info@nit.tec.ar.us

OUACHITA TECHNICAL COLLEGE
One College Cir, Malvern AR 72104
Adrian Ashley, Division Chair Applied Science
501-337-5000 ext. 1165 Fax: 501-337-9382
Website: www.otcweb.edu
E-mail: aashley@otcweb.edu

University of Arkansas Community College at Hope
PO Box 140, Hope AR 71802-0140
Ed Thaxton, Math Science & Technical Programs Division Chair
870-777-5722 Fax: 870-722-6630
Website: www.uacch.edu
E-mail: ethaxton@uacch.edu

CALIFORNIA

Chabot College
25555 Hesperian Blvd, Hayward CA 94545-2400
Judy Young, Director of Admissions
510-723-6600 Fax: 510-723-7510
Website: www.chabotcollege.edu
E-mail: ccarcom@clpccd.cc.ca.us

FRESNO CITY COLLEGE
1101 E University Ave, Fresno CA 93741-0002
Dayann Dietrich, Contact
559-442-8241 Fax: 559-237-4232
Website: www.fresnocitycollege.com
E-mail: fcc.admissions@scccd.com

Orange Coast College
PO Box 5005, Costa Mesa CA 92628-5005
Kristin Clark, Director of Admissions
714-432-5773 Fax: 714-432-5736
Website: www.orangecoastcollege.edu
E-mail: kclark@cccd.edu

San Bernardino Valley College
701 S Mount Vernon Ave
San Bernardino CA 92410-2798
Kay Ragan, Ed.D., Director of Admissions
909-888-6511 Fax: 909-889-4988
Website: www.valleycollege.edu
E-mail: kragan@sbccd.cc.ca.us

COLORADO

Colorado Northwestern Community College
500 Kennedy Dr, Rangely CO 81648-3502
Tresa England, Director of Student Services
800-562-1105 Fax: 970-675-3343
Website: www.cncc.edu
E-mail: tresa.england@cncc.edu

IntelliTec College
2315 E Pikes Peak Ave
Colorado Springs CO 80909-6096
Michael Castellano, Contact
719-632-7626 Fax: 719-632-7451
Website: www.intelliteccollege.edu
E-mail: admcs@intelliteccollege.edu

IntelliTec College
772 Horizon Dr, Grand Junction CO 81506-3907
Jennifer Daniels, Contact
970-245-8101 Fax: 970-243-8074
Website: www.intelliteccollege.edu
E-mail: admgj@intelliteccollege.edu

NORTHEASTERN JUNIOR COLLEGE
100 College Ave, Sterling CO 80751-2399
Dr. Lance Bolton, Chief Administrative Officer
Tina Joyce, Director of Admissions
970-521-7000 or 970-521-6752 Fax: 970-521-6801
Website: www.njc.edu
E-mail: tina.joyce@njc.edu

San Juan Basin Technical College
PO Box 970, Cortez CO 81321-0970
Shannon South, Vice President
970-565-8457 Fax: 970-565-8450
Website: www.sjbtc.edu
E-mail: info@sjbtc.edu

FLORIDA

Embry-Riddle Aeronautical University
Daytona Beach Campus
PO Box 11767, Daytona Beach FL 32120-1767
C. Richard Clarke, Director of Admissions
800-862-2416 Fax: 386-226-7070
Website: www.embryriddle.edu
E-mail: dbadmit@erau.edu

HENRY W. BREWSTER TECHNICAL CENTER
2222 N Tampa St, Tampa FL 33602-2196
William Cade, Department Head/Counselor
813-276-5464 Fax: 813-276-5756
Website: www.brewstertech.org

Lincoln College of Technology
2410 Metrocentre Blvd
West Palm Beach FL 33407-3105
Don Cunningham, Vice President of Admissions
561-688-2001 Fax: 561-842-9503
Website: www.lincolncollegeoftechnology.com
E-mail: dcunningham@lincolntech.com

NATIONAL AVIATION ACADEMY
6225 Ulmerton Rd, Clearwater FL 33760
Karen Acker, Registrar
727-531-2080 or 800-659-2080 Fax: 727-535-8727
Website: www.naa.edu
E-mail: admissions@naa.edu

GEORGIA

DeKalb Technical College
495 N Indian Creek Dr, Clarkston GA 30021-2397
Terry Richardson, Director of Admissions
404-297-9522 Fax: 404-294-6496
Website: www.dekalbtech.edu
E-mail: richardt@dekalbtech.edu

North Georgia Technical College
Clarkesville Campus
PO Box 65, Clarkesville GA 30523-0002
Admissions
706-754-7700 Fax: 706-754-7777
Website: www.northgatech.edu
E-mail: info@northgatech.edu

North Metro Technical College
5198 Ross Rd SE, Acworth GA 30102-3129
Missy Cusack, Director of Admissions
770-975-4000 Fax: 770-975-4142
Website: www.northmetrotech.edu
E-mail: info@northmetrotech.edu

Valdosta Technical College
4089 Val Tech Rd, Valdosta GA 31602-0928
Amanda Leavy, Admissions Coordinator
229-333-2100 Fax: 229-249-4980
Website: www.valdostatech.edu
E-mail: aleavy@valdostatech.edu

HAWAII

Kauai Community College
3-1901 Kaumualii Hwy, Lihue HI 96766-9500
808-245-8225 Fax: 808-245-8297
Website: kauai.hawaii.edu
E-mail: arkauai@hawaii.edu

NEW YORK TECHNICAL INSTITUTE OF HAWAII
1375 Dillingham Blvd, Honolulu HI 96817-4438
Brian Hamilton, Principal
808-841-5827 Fax: 808-841-5829
E-mail: nytihhawaii@hawaiiantel.net

IDAHO

Brigham Young University - Idaho
120 Kimball Bldg, Rexburg ID 83460-1615
Rob Garrett, Director of Admissions
208-496-1020 Fax: 208-496-1220
Website: www.byui.edu
E-mail: admissions@byui.edu

ILLINOIS

Kaskaskia College
27210 College Rd, Centralia IL 62801-7878
Tyra Taylor, Dean of Enrollment Management and Retention Services
618-545-3000 Fax: 618-532-1990
Website: www.kaskaskia.edu
E-mail: ttaylor@kaskaskia.edu

Triton College
2000 5th Ave, River Grove IL 60171-1995
Jeffery Cooks, Director, Admission Services
708-456-0300 ext. 3130 Fax: 708-583-3147
Website: www.triton.edu
E-mail: triton@triton.edu
See listing under "Community and Junior Colleges"

UNIVERSAL TECHNICAL INSTITUTE
601 Regency Dr, Glendale Heights IL 60139-2208
Karl Lewandowski, School Director
630-529-2662 Fax: 630-529-7567
Website: www.uticorp.com
E-mail: karllewandowski@uticorp.com

INDIANA

Ivy Tech Community College - North Central
220 Dean Johnson Blvd, South Bend IN 46601-3415
Pam Decker, Director of Admissions
574-289-7001 Fax: 574-236-7177
Website: www.ivytech.edu
E-mail: pdecker@ivytech.edu

IOWA

Iowa Lakes Community College
3200 College Dr, Emmetsburg IA 50536-1055
Anne Stansbury, Asst. Director of Admissions
712-852-5212 Fax: 712-362-8363
Website: www.iowalakes.edu
E-mail: info@iowalakes.edu

Northwest Iowa Community College
603 W Park St, Sheldon IA 51201-1046
Lisa Story, Director of Enrollment Management
712-324-5061 Fax: 712-324-4136
Website: www.nwicc.edu
E-mail: lstory@nwicc.edu

KANSAS

Flint Hills Technical College
3301 W 18th Ave, Emporia KS 66801-5957
Lisa Kirmer, Dean of Student Services
620-343-4600 Fax: 620-343-4610
Website: www.fhtc.net
E-mail: lkirmer@fhtc.net

KENTUCKY

Bluegrass Community and Technical College
Oswald Building
470 Cooper Drive, Lexington KY 40506-0235
Shelbie Hugle, Director of Admissions
859-246-6200 Fax: 859-246-4664
Website: www.bluegrass.kctcs.edu
E-mail: bctc_info@kctcs.edu

LOUISIANA

Louisiana Technical College
Florida Parishes Campus
PO Box 1300, Greensburg LA 70441
225-222-4251 Fax: 225-222-6064
Website: www.ltc.edu./region.html

LOUISIANA TECHNICAL COLLEGE
Tallulah Campus
132 Old Highway 65, Tallulah LA 71284
Patrick T. Murphy, Dean
318-574-4820 Fax: 318-574-1868
Website: www.ltctallulah.com
E-mail: sccox@theltc.net

MAINE

Southern Maine Community College
2 Fort Rd, South Portland ME 04106-1698
Dr. James Ortiz, President
Scott MacDonald, Director of Financial Aid
207-741-5500 Fax: 207-741-5671
Website: www.smccme.edu
E-mail: oharmon@maine.rr.com

MASSACHUSETTS

Benjamin Franklin Institute of Technology
41 Berkeley St, Boston MA 02116-6307
Norman Kraft, Dean of Enrollment
617-423-4630 ext. 121 Fax: 617-482-3706
Website: www.bfit.edu
E-mail: admissions@bfit.edu

MICHIGAN

Delta College
University Center MI 48710-0001
Duff Zube, Director of Admissions
989-686-9093 Fax: 989-667-2202
Website: www.delta.edu
E-mail: admit@delta.edu

MACOMB COMMUNITY COLLEGE
14500 E 12 Mile Rd, Warren MI 48088-3896
Information Center
586-445-7999
Website: www.macomb.edu
E-mail: answer@macomb.edu

MINNESOTA

Dunwoody College of Technology
818 Dunwoody Blvd, Minneapolis MN 55403-1192
John Slama, Vice President Enrollment Management
800-292-4625 or 612-374-5800 Fax: 612-374-4128
Website: www.dunwoody.edu
E-mail: jslama@dunwoody.edu
See listing under "Career Schools"

Hibbing Community College
1515 E 25th St, Hibbing MN 55746-3300
Holly Bigelow, Director of Enrollment
800-224-4HCC or 218-262-7200 Fax: 218-262-6717
Website: www.hibbing.edu
E-mail: admissions@hibbing.edu

Minnesota State College - Southeast Technical
Red Wing Campus
308 Pioneer Rd, Red Wing MN 55066
Al DuCett, Director of Admissions
877-853-8324 Fax: 507-453-2715
Website: www.southeastmn.edu
E-mail: aducett@southeastmn.edu
70+ degrees, diplomas & certificates (15+ online) in Business & Office Careers, Musical Instrument Repair, Physical Health, Transportation, Technology, and Trades.

Minnesota State College - Southeast Technical
Winona Campus
PO Box 409, 1250 Homer Rd, Winona MN 55987
Al DuCett, Director of Admissions
877-853-8324 Fax: 507-453-2715
Website: www.southeastmn.edu
E-mail: aducett@southeastmn.edu
70+ degrees, diplomas & certificates (15+ online) in Business & Office Careers, Musical Instrument Repair, Physical Health, Transportation, Technology, and Trades.

Northland Community and Technical College
2022 Central Ave NE
East Grand Forks MN 56721-2702
Dennis Wierma, Trades Division Chair
800-451-3441 Fax: 218-773-4502
Website: www.northlandcollege.edu
E-mail: admissions@northlandcollege.edu

Ridgewater College-Willmar Campus
PO Box 1097, Willmar MN 56201-1097
Sally Kerfeld, Director of Admissions
800-722-1151 Fax: 320-222-5212
Website: www.ridgewater.edu
E-mail: sally.kerfeld@ridgewater.edu

St. Cloud Technical College
1540 Northway Dr, Saint Cloud MN 56303-1240
Jodi Elness, Director of Enrollment Management
800-222-1009 Fax: 320-308-5981
Website: www.sctc.edu
E-mail: jelness@sctc.edu

MISSOURI

Linn State Technical College
1 Technology Dr, Linn MO 65051-9606
Becky Dunn, Admissions
800-743-8324 Fax: 573-897-5026
Website: www.linnstate.edu
E-mail: admissions@linnstate.edu

Ozarks Technical Community College
1001 E Chestnut Expressway
Springfield MO 65802-3625
Delvan Mitchell, Director of Admissions
417-447-7500 Fax: 417-447-6925
Website: www.otc.edu
E-mail: admissions@otc.edu

Ranken Technical College
4431 Finney Ave, Saint Louis MO 63113-2898
Admissions Office
314-371-0233 Fax: 314-371-0241
Website: www.ranken.edu
E-mail: admissions@ranken.edu

State Fair Community College
3201 W 16th St, Sedalia MO 65301-2199
Director of Admissions
660-530-5833 Fax: 660-596-7472
Website: www.sfccmo.edu
E-mail: mparris@sfccmo.edu

NEVADA

Career College of Northern Nevada
1195-A Corporate Blvd, Reno NV 89502-2331
Nathan Clark, Director
775-856-2266 Fax: 775-856-0935
Website: www.ccnn.edu
E-mail: lgoldhammer@ccnn4u.com
See listing under "Career Schools"

GREAT BASIN COLLEGE
1500 College Pkwy, Elko NV 89801-5032
Julie G. Byrnes, Director of Enrollment Management
775-753-2271 Fax: 775-753-2311
Website: www.gbcnv.edu
E-mail: julieb@gwmail.gbcnv.edu
See listing under "Universities"

NEW HAMPSHIRE

New Hampshire Community Technical College
1066 Front St, Manchester NH 03102-8528
Jacquie Poirier, Director of Admissions
603-668-6706 Fax: 603-668-5354
Website: www.manchester.nhctc.edu
E-mail: jpoirier@nhctc.edu

NEW JERSEY

ENGINE CITY TECHNICAL INSTITUTE
DIESEL MECHANIC SCHOOL AND TRAINING CENTER
901 Hadley Rd, South Plainfield NJ 07080-2424
Robert N. Merkle, Jr., Director of Admissions
800-305-3487 Fax: 908-756-7156
Website: www.enginecitytech.com
E-mail: info@enginecitytech.com

Teterboro School of Aeronautics
80 Moonachie Ave, Teterboro NJ 07608-1003
Richard Ciasulli, Director of Admissions
201-288-6300 Fax: 201-288-5609
Website: www.teterboroschool.com
E-mail: teterboroschool@nj.rr.com

NEW MEXICO

New Mexico State University
1500 N 3rd St, Grants NM 87020-2025
Irene Lutz, Director of Admissions
505-287-7981 Fax: 505-287-2329
Website: www.grants.nmsu.edu
E-mail: ilutz@nmsu.edu

NEW YORK

APEX TECHNICAL SCHOOL
635 Avenue of the Americas
New York NY 10011-2008
William Ott, Admissions Director
212-645-3300 Fax: 212-645-6984
Website: www.apextechnical.com
See listing under "Career Schools"

CAREER INSTITUTE OF HEALTH & TECHNOLOGY
340 Flatbush Avenue Ext, Brooklyn NY 11201
Mary Miller, Contact
718-422-1212 Fax: 718-422-1222
Website: www.careerinstitute.edu
E-mail: admissions@careerinstitute.edu

CAREER INSTITUTE OF HEALTH & TECHNOLOGY
200 Garden City Plz, Garden City NY 11530
Mary Miller, Contact
516-877-1225 Fax: 516-877-1959
Website: www.careerinstitute.edu
E-mail: admissions@careerinstitute.edu

CAREER INSTITUTE OF HEALTH & TECHNOLOGY
9525 Queens Blvd Ste 600, Rego Park NY 11374
Mary Miller, Contact
718-897-4868 Fax: 718-897-4863
Website: www.careerinstitute.edu
E-mail: admissions@careerinstitute.edu

SUNY College of Technology
Alfred NY 14802
Deborah J. Goodrich, Associate VP Enrollment Mgmt.
800-4AL-FRED Fax: 607-587-4299
Website: www.alfredstate.edu
E-mail: admissions@alfredstate.edu

NORTH CAROLINA

Haywood Community College
185 Freedlander Dr, Clyde NC 28721
Debbie Rowland, Coordinator of Admissions
828-627-4500 Fax: 828-627-4513
Website: www.haywood.edu
E-mail: drowland@haywood.edu

Mayland Community College
PO Box 547, Spruce Pine NC 28777-0547
Cathy B. Morrison, Director of Enrollment Management
828-765-7351 Fax: 828-765-0728
Website: www.mayland.edu
E-mail: cmorrison@mayland.edu

NORTH DAKOTA

Williston State College
PO Box 1326, Williston ND 58802-1326
Penny Soiseth, Associate Director Enrollment Services
701-774-4200 Fax: 701-774-4544
Website: www.wsc.nodak.edu
E-mail: penny.soiseth@wsc.nodak.edu

OHIO

OHIO TECHNICAL COLLEGE
1374 E 51st St, Cleveland OH 44103-1228
Marc Brenner, President
216-881-1700 Fax: 216-881-9145
Website: www.ohiotechnicalcollege.com
E-mail: info@ohiotechnicalcollege.com

Owens Community College
3200 Bright Rd, Findlay OH 45840
William J. Ivoska PhD., Vice President of Student Services
567-429-3500 Fax: 567-423-0246
Website: www.owens.edu
E-mail: admissions@owens.edu

Owens Community College
PO Box 10000, Toledo OH 43699-1947
William J. Ivoska, Ph.D, Vice President of Student Services
567-661-7000 Fax: 567-661-7607
Website: www.owens.edu
E-mail: admissions@owens.edu

OKLAHOMA

SPARTAN COLLEGE OF AERONAUTICS AND TECHNOLOGY
8820 E Pine St, Tulsa OK 74115-5802
Director of Admissions
800-331-1204 Fax: 918-831-8609
Website: www.spartan.edu
E-mail: spartan@mail.spartan.edu

Established 1928. Coed. Accredited member school: ACCSCT. Providing Technical training and education in Avionics, Aviation Maintenance; Nondestructive Testing and Quality Control. Complete flight training program. Offering Diplomas, Associate of Applied Science and Bachelor of Science in Aviation Technology Management.

Vatterott College - Tulsa
4343 S 118th East Ave, Tulsa OK 74146
Tim Maloukis, Director of Admissions
918-835-8288 Fax: 918-836-9698
Website: www.vatterott-college.com
E-mail: tim.maloukis@vatterott-college.com

OREGON

Linn-Benton Community College
6500 Pacific Blvd SW, Albany OR 97321-3774
Christine Baker, Outreach Coordinator
541-917-4811 Fax: 541-917-4868
Website: www.linnbenton.edu
E-mail: admissions@linnbenton.edu

Rogue Community College
3345 Redwood Hwy, Grants Pass OR 97527-9298
Claudia Sullivan, Director of Enrollment Services
541-956-7500 Fax: 541-471-3585
Website: www.roguecc.edu
E-mail: csullivan@roguecc.edu
See listing under "Community and Junior Colleges"

PENNSYLVANIA

AUTOMOTIVE TRAINING CENTER
114 Pickering Way, Exton PA 19341-1310
Don VanDemark, Vice President/Chief Operating Officer
610-363-6716 Fax: 610-363-8524
Website: www.autotraining.edu
E-mail: atc@autotraining.edu
See listing under "Career Schools"

Automotive Training Center
900 Johnsville Blvd, Warminster PA 18974
Kimberly Ewing, Executive Director of Admissions
877-411-8041 Fax: 215-442-1030
Website: www.autotraining.edu
E-mail: kewing@autotraining.edu
See listing under "Career Schools"

Community College of Allegheny County
Allegheny Campus: 808 Ridge Ave, Pittsburgh PA 15212 Admissions: 412.237.2700
Boyce Campus: 595 Beatty Rd, Monroeville PA 15146 Admissions: 724.325.6614
North Campus: 8701 Perry Highway, Pittsburgh PA 15237 Admissions: 412.369.3600
South Campus: 1750 Clairton Rd, West Mifflin PA 15122 Admissions: 412-469-4301
Website: www.ccac.edu

Johnson College
3427 N Main Ave, Scranton PA 18508-1495
Dr. Ann L. Pipinski, President & CEO
Melissa Ide, Director of Enrollment Management
800-2WE-WORK or 570-342-6404 ext. 125
Fax: 570-348-2181
Website: www.johnson.edu
E-mail: admit@johnson.edu

PENNSYLVANIA GUNSMITH SCHOOL
812 Ohio River Blvd, Pittsburgh PA 15202-2699
George Thacker, Director
412-766-1812 Fax: 412-766-0855
Website: www.pagunsmith.com
E-mail: pgs@pagunsmith.edu

PIA School of Specialized Technology
PO Box 10897, Pittsburgh PA 15236-0897
Vincent J. Mezza, Director of Admissions
800-444-1440 Fax: 412-466-0513
Website: www.pia.edu
E-mail: admissions@pia.edu
See listing under "Aeronautics, Aviation and Space"

ROSEDALE TECHNICAL INSTITUTE
215 Beecham Dr Ste 2, Pittsburgh PA 15205
Kevin Auld, Contact
412-521-6200 Fax: 412-521-2520
Website: www.rosedaletech.org
E-mail: admissions@rosedaletech.org

UNIVERSAL TECHNICAL INSTITUTE
750 Pennsylvania Dr, Exton PA 19341
Karen Hannigan-Robinson, Campus Admissions Director
877-884-3986 Fax: 610-646-8549
Website: www.uti-auto-tech.com
E-mail: khannigan@uticorp.com

RHODE ISLAND

MTTI - MOTORING TECHNICAL TRAINING INSTITUTE
54 Water St, East Providence RI 02914-5022
Sharon Ring, Program Director
401-434-4840 or 866-454-6884 Fax: 401-434-9540
Website: www.mtti.edu
E-mail: info@mtti.edu

New England Institute of Technology
2500 Post Rd, Warwick RI 02886-2244
Michael Kwiatkowski, Director of Admissions
401-739-5000 Fax: 401-738-5122
Website: www.neit.edu
E-mail: eflynn@neit.edu

NEW ENGLAND TRACTOR TRAILER TRAINING
600 Moshassuck Valley Industrial Hwy
Pawtucket RI 02860-1752
Frederick Hazard, Director
401-725-1220 Fax: 401-724-1340
Website: www.nettts.com
E-mail: fhazard@nettts.com

SOUTH CAROLINA

Spartanburg Community College
PO Box 4386, Spartanburg SC 29305-4386
Nancy Garmroth, Dean of Admissions & Financial Aid
864-592-4810 Fax: 864-592-4945
Website: sccsc.edu

SOUTH DAKOTA

Western Dakota Technical Institute
800 Mickelson Dr, Rapid City SD 57703-4018
Jill Elder, Admissions Coordinator
605-394-4034 Fax: 605-394-2204
Website: www.wdt.edu
E-mail: jill.elder@wdt.edu

TENNESSEE

NASHVILLE AUTO-DIESEL COLLEGE
1524 Gallatin Ave, Nashville TN 37206-3298
William Ormsby, Vice President of High School Admissions
800-228-6232 Fax: 615-262-8466
Website: www.nadcedu.com
E-mail: admissions@nadcedu.com
See listing under "Career Schools"

TEXAS

Hallmark Institute of Aeronautics
Aeronautics Campus-Aviation Technology
8901 Wetmore Rd, San Antonio TX 78216-4229
Joe Fisher, President
210-826-1000 Fax: 210-826-3707
Website: www.hallmarkinstitute.edu
E-mail: sross@hallmarkinstitute.edu

Tyler Junior College
PO Box 9020, Tyler TX 75711-9020
Joan Jones, Interim Dean
800-687-5680
Website: www.tjc.edu
E-mail: jjon@tjc.edu
See listing under "Community and Junior Colleges"

Western Technical College
9624 Plaza Cir, El Paso TX 79927-2105
Bill Terrell, Chief Administrative Officer
915-760-8123
Website: www.wtc-ep.edu
E-mail: bterrell@wtc-ep.edu

Western Technical College
9451 Diana Dr, El Paso TX 79924-6936
Bill Terrell, Chief Administrative Officer
915-566-9621 Fax: 915-565-9903
Website: www.wtc-ep.edu
E-mail: bterrell@wtc-ep.edu

VIRGINIA

Southside Virginia Community College
109 Campus Dr, Alberta VA 23821-2930
Ronald E. Mattox, Dean of Admissions
434-949-1014 Fax: 434-949-7863
Website: www.sv.vccs.edu
E-mail: ronald.mattox@sv.vccs.edu

Southside Virginia Community College
200 Daniel Rd, Keysville VA 23947
Ronald E. Mattox, Dean of Admissions
434-736-2018 Fax: 434-736-2082
Website: www.sv.vccs.edu
E-mail: ronald.mattox@sv.vccs.edu

WASHINGTON

BATES TECHNICAL COLLEGE
1101 S Yakima Ave, Tacoma WA 98405-4895
David Borofsky, President
253-680-7000 Fax: 253-680-7101
Website: www.bates.ctc.edu
E-mail: info@bates.ctc.edu

Everett Community College
2000 Tower St, Everett WA 98201
Christine Kerlin, Associate Dean
425-388-9100 Fax: 425-388-9173
Website: www.everettcc.edu
E-mail: ckerlin@everettcc.edu

Lake Washington Technical College
11605 132nd Ave NE, Kirkland WA 98034-8505
James B. West, Director of Admissions
425-739-8100 Fax: 425-739-8110
Website: www.lwtc.ctc.edu

SHORELINE COMMUNITY COLLEGE
16101 Greenwood Ave N, Shoreline WA 98133-5696
Chris Melton, Acting Registrar
206-546-4581 Fax: 206-546-5835
Website: www.shoreline.edu

Walla Walla Community College
500 Tausick Way, Walla Walla WA 99362-9270
Del Wilde, Director
509-527-4283 or 877-992-9922 Fax: 509-527-4572
Website: www.wwcc.edu
E-mail: del.wilde@wwcc.edu

WEST VIRGINIA

Blue Ridge Community and Technical College
400 W Stephen St, Martinsburg WV 25401
Leslie See, Director of Enrollment
304-260-4380 Fax: 304-260-1752
Website: www.blueridgectc.edu
E-mail: lsee@blueridgectc.edu

WISCONSIN

Blackhawk Technical College
PO Box 5009, Janesville WI 53547-5009
Gregg Bosak, Administration, Community Information
608-757-7769 Fax: 608-757-7740
Website: www.blackhawk.edu
E-mail: gbosak@blackhawk.edu

Wisconsin Indianhead Technical College
505 Pine Ridge Dr, Shell Lake WI 54871
Gene Rosburg, Dean
800-243-9482 Fax: 715-468-2819
Website: www.witc.edu
E-mail: eugene.rosburg@witc.edu

WYOMING

Laramie County Community College
1400 E College Dr, Cheyenne WY 82007-3204
Jenny Hargett, Director of Admissions
307-778-5222 Fax: 307-778-1350
Website: www.lccc.wy.edu
E-mail: learnmore@lccc.wy.edu

PUERTO RICO

PROFESSIONAL ELECTRICAL SCHOOL
PO Box 1797, Manati PR 00674
Paulino Delgado Negron, Presidente
787-854-4776 Fax: 787-854-4776
E-mail: pes@libertypr.net

MEDICINE

ALABAMA

Judson College
302 Bibb St, Marion AL 36756
Michael Scotto, Director of Admissions
800-447-9472 Fax: 334-683-5147
Website: www.judson.edu
E-mail: admissions@judson.edu

University of South Alabama
307 University Blvd N, Mobile AL 36688-3053
Melissa Haab, Director of Admissions
251-460-6141 Fax: 251-460-7876
Website: www.southalabama.edu
E-mail: admiss@usouthal.edu

CALIFORNIA

Chapman University
One University Drive, Orange CA 92866-1099
Michael Drummy, Assistant Vice President for Enrollment
Services and Chief Admission Officer
714-997-6411 or 888-CUAPPLY Fax: 714-997-6713
Website: www.chapman.edu
E-mail: admit@chapman.edu

Point Loma Nazarene University
3900 Lomaland Dr, San Diego CA 92106-2810
Chip Killingsworth, Director of Undergraduate Admissions
800-733-7770 Fax: 619-849-2601
Website: www.pointloma.edu
E-mail: admissions@pointloma.edu

FLORIDA

Florida National College
Hialeah Campus
4425 W 20th Ave, Hialeah FL 33012
Jorge Afonso, Campus Dean
305-821-3333 ext. 1022 Fax: 305-362-0595
Website: www.fnc.edu
E-mail: omarsnc@fnc.edu

Florida National College
South Campus
11865 SW 26th St, Miami FL 33175
Jon Beisenherz, Campus Dean
305-266-9999
Website: www.fnc.edu
E-mail: omarsnc@fnc.edu

Florida State University
600 W College Ave, Tallahassee FL 32306-1096
Janice V. Finney, Director of Admissions
850-644-2525 Fax: 850-644-0197
Website: admissions.fsu.edu
E-mail: admissions@admin.fsu.edu

University of South Florida
4202 E Fowler Ave, Tampa FL 33620-6900
J. Robert Spatig, Director of Admissions
877-USF-BULL Fax: 813-974-9689
Website: www.usf.edu
E-mail: admissions@admin.usf.edu
See listing under "Universities"

ILLINOIS

Roosevelt University
430 S Michigan Ave, Chicago IL 60605
Gwen E. Kanelos, Asst. Vice President for Enrollment Services
877-APPLY-RU Fax: 312-341-4216
Website: www.roosevelt.edu
E-mail: applyru@roosevelt.edu

IOWA

Briar Cliff University
PO Box 2100, Sioux City IA 51104-0100
Sharisue Wilcoxon, VP for Enrollment Management
712-279-5200 Fax: 712-279-1632
Website: www.briarcliff.edu
E-mail: admissions@briarcliff.edu

Iowa Lakes Community College
300 S 18th St, Estherville IA 51334-2721
Anne Stansbury, Asst. Director of Admissions
712-362-7945 Fax: 712-362-8363
Website: www.iowalakes.edu
E-mail: info@iowalakes.edu

MASSACHUSETTS

Worcester Polytechnic Institute
100 Institute Rd, Worcester MA 01609-2280
Edward J. Connor, Director of Admissions
508-831-5286 Fax: 508-831-5875
Website: admissions.wpi.edu
E-mail: admissions@wpi.edu

MINNESOTA

University of Minnesota
2900 University Ave, Crookston MN 56716-5001
218-281-6510 Fax: 218-281-8575
Website:
admissions.umcrookston.edu/requirements/apply.htm
E-mail: info@umcrookston.edu

MISSOURI

Truman State University
100 E Normal, Kirksville MO 63501
Office of Admission
660-785-4114 Fax: 660-785-7456
Website: admissions.truman.edu
E-mail: admissions@truman.edu

William Woods University
1 University Ave, Fulton MO 65251-1098
Jimmy Clay, Director of Admissions
573-642-2251 Fax: 573-592-1146
Website: www.williamwoods.edu
E-mail: admissions@williamwoods.edu
See listing under "Universities"

NEW JERSEY

Bergen Community College
400 Paramus Rd, Paramus NJ 07652
Julian Gomez, Asst. Director of Admissions
201-447-7100 Fax: 201-444-7036
Website: www.bergen.edu
E-mail: jgomez@bergen.edu

New Jersey City University
2039 John F Kennedy Blvd
Jersey City NJ 07305-1588
Carmen Panlilio, Asst. V.P. for Admissions and Financial Aid
201-200-3234 Fax: 201-200-2044
Website: www.njcu.edu
E-mail: admissions@njcu.edu

RICHARD STOCKTON COLLEGE OF NEW JERSEY
PO Box 195, Pomona NJ 08240
John Iacovelli, Dean of Enrollment Management
866-RSC-2885 Fax: 609-626-5541
Website: www.stockton.edu
E-mail: admissions@stockton.edu
Stockton College is a comprehensive liberal arts, co-ed institution founded in 1969. Advance Pre-Professional Degree Options: 7-yr BS/MD with UMDNJ; NJ Dental School; NJ Medical School, Robert Wood Johnson Medical, School of Osteopathic Medicine; NY College of Podiatric Medicine, Pennsylvania College of Podiatric Medicine, SUNY College of Optometry. Pharmacy doctorate program with Rutgers University. 5-yr Engineering with NJIT and Rutgers University. Dual BA/MA in Criminal Justice. 5-yr BS/MS in Computational Science. BS/MS in Nursing. Doctorate of Physical Therapy. Additional Programs: Forensic Science, Pre-Law, Pre-Occupational Therapy, and Pre-Veterinary.

NEW YORK

ALBANY COLLEGE OF PHARMACY
106 New Scotland Ave, Albany NY 12208-3492
Carly Connors, Director of Admissions
888-203-8010 Fax: 518-694-7322
Website: www.acp.edu
E-mail: admissions@acp.edu

College of Saint Rose
432 Western Ave, Albany NY 12203-1419
Maryelizabeth Amico, Asst V.P. for Undergraduate Admissions
518-454-5150 Fax: 518-454-2013
Website: www.strose.edu
E-mail: admit@strose.edu

Roberts Wesleyan College
2301 Westside Dr, Rochester NY 14624-1997
Office of Admissions
585-594-6400 Fax: 585-594-6371
Website: www.roberts.edu
E-mail: admissions@roberts.edu

OHIO

Brown Mackie College - Cincinnati
1011 Glendale Milford Rd, Cincinnati OH 45215-1107
Robin Krout, President
513-771-2424 Fax: 513-771-3413
Website: www.brownmackie.edu
E-mail: rkrout@brownmackie.edu

The Ohio State University
College of Medicine and Public Health
Meiling Hall, 370 W 9th Ave, Columbus OH 43210
Fred Sanfilippo, M.D., Ph.D., Dean
614-292-2220 Fax: 614-247-7959
Website: medicine.osu.edu
E-mail: medicine@osu.edu

OHIO WESLEYAN UNIVERSITY
61 S Sandusky St, Delaware OH 43015-2398
Director of Admission
740-368-3020 Fax: 740-368-3314
Website: www.owu.edu
E-mail: owuadmit@owu.edu

University of Toledo
College of Medicine
3000 Arlington Ave, Toledo OH 43614-2595
419-383-4000 Fax: 419-383-2800
Website: www.hsc.utoledo.edu
E-mail: admissions@meduohio.edu

Ursuline College
2550 Lander Rd, Cleveland OH 44124-4398
Sarah E. Sundermeier, Director of Admissions
888-URSULINE Toll Free Fax: 440-684-6138
Website: www.admission.ursuline.edu
E-mail: admission@ursuline.edu

PENNSYLVANIA

Juniata College
1700 Moore St, Huntingdon PA 16652-2196
Michelle Bartol, Dean of Enrollment
877-JUNIATA Fax: 814-641-3100
Website: www.juniata.edu
E-mail: admissions@juniata.edu

TEXAS

Abilene Christian University
ACU Box 29000, Abilene TX 79699-0001
325-674-2000 Fax: 325-674-2202
Website: www.acu.edu
E-mail: info@admissions.acu.edu

WISCONSIN

St. Norbert College
100 Grant St, De Pere WI 54115
Brian Studebaker, Director of Admission
800-236-4878 Fax: 920-403-4072
Website: www.snc.edu
E-mail: admit@snc.edu

PUERTO RICO

SAN JUAN BAUTISTA SCHOOL OF MEDICINE
PO Box 4968, Caguas PR 00726-4968
Lissette Torres Rodriguez, Registrar
787-743-3038 Fax: 787-746-3093
Website: www.sanjuanbautista.edu
E-mail: ltorres@sanjuanbautista.edu

MEN'S COLLEGES

CALIFORNIA

Don Bosco Technical Institute
1151 San Gabriel Blvd, Rosemead CA 91770-4251
626-307-6500

Yeshiva Ohr Elchonon Chabad
West Coast Talmudical Seminary
7215 Waring Ave, Los Angeles CA 90046
323-937-3763

DISTRICT OF COLUMBIA

Dominican House of Studies
487 Michigan Ave NE, Washington DC 20017-1585
202-529-5300

FLORIDA

St. John Vianney College Seminary
2900 SW 87th Ave, Miami FL 33165-3244
305-223-4561

St. Vincent DePaul Regional Seminary
10701 S Military Trl, Boynton Beach FL 33436-4899
Rev. Steven O'Hala, Academic Dean
561-732-4424 ext. 151 Fax: 561-732-8808
Website: www.svdp.edu
E-mail: sohala@svdp.edu
M.Div and M.A.

Talmudic College of Florida
1910 Alton Rd, Miami Beach FL 33139-1507
305-534-7050

GEORGIA

Morehouse College
830 Westview Dr SW, Atlanta GA 30314-3773
404-681-2800

ILLINOIS

Telshe Yeshiva-Chicago
3535 W Foster Ave, Chicago IL 60625-5526
773-463-7738

INDIANA

Wabash College
301 W Wabash Ave, Crawfordsville IN 47933
David Collins, Sr. Assoc. Director of Admissions
800-345-5385

LOUISIANA

Notre Dame Seminary
2901 S Carrollton Ave, New Orleans LA 70118-4391
504-866-7426

MARYLAND

Ner Israel Rabbinical College
400 Mount Wilson Ln, Baltimore MD 21208-1198
410-484-7200

Yeshiva College of the Nation's Capital
1216 Arcola Ave, Silver Spring MD 20902
301-593-2534

MICHIGAN

Sacred Heart Major Seminary
2701 W Chicago, Detroit MI 48206-1704
313-883-8500

MINNESOTA

St. John's University
PO Box 7155, Collegeville MN 56321-7155
320-363-2011

MISSOURI

Conception Seminary College
Conception MO 64433
Vincent Casper, Director of Admissions
660-944-2886

NEW JERSEY

Beth Medrash Govoha
617 6th St, Lakewood NJ 08701-2797
732-367-1060

Rabbinical College of America
226 Sussex Ave, Morristown NJ 07960-3632
973-267-9404

Talmudical Academy of New Jersey
Route 524, Adelphia NJ 07710
732-431-1600

NEW YORK

Beis Medrash Heichal Dovid
275 Beach 17th St, Far Rockaway NY 11691
718-868-2300

Beth HaMedrash Shaarei Yosher
4102 16th Ave #10, Brooklyn NY 11204-1052
718-854-2290

Beth HaTalmud Rabbinical College
2127 82nd St, Brooklyn NY 11214-2509
718-259-2525

Darkei Noam Rabbinical College
2822 Avenue J, Brooklyn NY 11210-3736
718-338-6464

Holy Trinity Orthodox Seminary
PO Box 36, Jordanville NY 13361
315-858-0945

Kehilath Yakov Rabbinical Seminary
206 Wilson St, Brooklyn NY 11211-7207
718-963-1212

Kol Yaakov Torah Center
29 W Maple Ave, Monsey NY 10952-2954
845-425-3863

Machzikei Hadath Rabbinical College
5407 16th Ave, Brooklyn NY 11204-1805
718-854-8777

Mesivta of Eastern Parkway Rabbinical Seminary
510 Dahill Rd, Brooklyn NY 11218-5559
718-438-1002

Mesivta Tifereth Jerusalem of America
145 E Broadway, New York NY 10002-6382
212-964-2830

Mesivta Torah Vodaath Seminary
425 E 9th St, Brooklyn NY 11218-5209
718-941-8000

Mirrer Yeshiva Central Institute
1795 Ocean Pkwy, Brooklyn NY 11223-2010
718-645-0536

Ohr HaMeir Theological Seminary
PO Box 2130, Peekskill NY 10566-0990
914-736-1500

Rabbinical Academy Mesivta Rabbi Chaim
1605 Coney Island Ave, Brooklyn NY 11230-4715
718-377-0777

Rabbinical College Beth Shraga
28 Saddle River Rd, Airmont NY 10952-3035
845-356-1980

Rabbinical College Bobover Yeshiva B'nei Zion
1577 48th St, Brooklyn NY 11219-3250
718-438-2018

Rabbinical College Ch' San Sofer of New York
1876 50th St, Brooklyn NY 11204-1252
718-236-1171

Rabbinical College of Long Island
205 W Beech St, Long Beach NY 11561-3244
516-255-4700

Rabbinical College of Ohr Shimon Yisroel
215 Hewes St, Brooklyn NY 11211-8102
718-855-4092

Rabbinical Seminary Adas Yereim
185 Wilson St, Brooklyn NY 11211-7206
718-388-1751

Rabbinical Seminary M'Kor Chaim
1571 55th St, Brooklyn NY 11219-4314
718-851-0183

Rabbinical Seminary of America
9215 69th Ave, Forest Hills NY 11375-5817
718-268-4700

Shor Yoshuv Institute
1 Cedarlawn Dr, Lawrence NY 11559-1714
516-239-9002

Talmudical Institute of Upstate New York
769 Park Ave, Rochester NY 14607-3046
585-473-2810

Talmudical Seminary Oholei Torah
667 Eastern Pkwy, Brooklyn NY 11213-3310
718-774-5050

Torah Temimah Talmudical Seminary
507 Ocean Pkwy, Brooklyn NY 11218-5913
718-853-8500

United Talmudical Seminary
82 Lee Ave, Brooklyn NY 11211-7900
718-963-9770

UTA Mesivta of Kiryas Joel
PO Box 2009, Monroe NY 10949
845-783-9901

Yeshiva and Kollel Harbotzas Torah
1049 E 15th St, Brooklyn NY 11230-4462
718-692-0208

Yeshiva D'Monsey Rabbinical College
2 Roman Blvd, Monsey NY 10952
845-426-3276

Yeshiva Karlin Stolin
1818 54th St, Brooklyn NY 11204-1545
718-232-7800

Yeshiva of Nitra Rabbinical College
194 Division Ave, Brooklyn NY 11211-7108
718-387-0422

Yeshiva of the Telshe Alumni
4904 Independence Ave, Bronx NY 10471
718-601-3523

Yeshiva Shaarei Torah of Rockland
91 W Carlton Rd, Suffern NY 10901
845-352-3431

Yeshiva Shaar HaTorah - Grodno
8396 117th St, Richmond Hill NY 11418-1469
718-846-1940

Yeshivath Viznitz
PO Box 446, Monsey NY 10952-0446
845-356-1010

Yeshivath Zichron Moshe
Laurel Park Rd, South Fallsburg NY 12779
845-434-5240

Yeshivat Mikdash Melech
1326 Ocean Pkwy, Brooklyn NY 11230-5601
718-339-1090

OHIO

Pontifical College Josephinum
7625 N High St, Columbus OH 43235-1499
614-885-5585

Rabbinical College of Telshe
28400 Euclid Ave, Wickliffe OH 44092-2523
440-943-5300

PENNSYLVANIA

St. Charles Borromeo Seminary
100 E Wynnewood Rd, Wynnewood PA 19096
610-667-3394

TALMUDICAL YESHIVA OF PHILADELPHIA
6063 Drexel Rd, Philadelphia PA 19131-1296
Rabbi Uri Mandelbaum, Director of Admissions
215-477-1000 Fax: 215-477-5065
E-mail: typ@attglobal.net

Valley Forge Military College
1001 Eagle Rd, Wayne PA 19087-3613
800-234-8362

Yeshiva Beth Moshe
930 Hickory St, Scranton PA 18505-2196
570-346-1747

SOUTH CAROLINA

The Citadel
171 Moultrie St, Charleston SC 29409-0002
843-953-5000

VIRGINIA

Hampden-Sydney College
PO Box 667, Hampden Sydney VA 23943-0667
800-755-0733

Virginia Military Institute
Lexington VA 24450
540-464-7000

MILITARY SCIENCE

ARIZONA

Embry-Riddle Aeronautical University
Arizona Campus
3700 Willow Creek Rd, Prescott AZ 86301-3720
William Thompson, Director of Admissions
800-888-3728 Fax: 928-777-6613
Website: www.embryriddle.edu
E-mail: pradmit@erau.edu

CALIFORNIA

ARMY AND NAVY ACADEMY
PO Box 3000, Carlsbad CA 92018-3000
Elizabeth Kalivas, Director of Admissions
760-729-2385 ext. 400 Fax: 760-434-5948
Website: www.armyandnavyacademy.org
E-mail: admissions@armyandnavyacademy.org

FLORIDA

Embry-Riddle Aeronautical University
Daytona Beach Campus
PO Box 11767, Daytona Beach FL 32120-1767
C. Richard Clarke, Director of Admissions
800-862-2416 Fax: 386-226-7070
Website: www.embryriddle.edu
E-mail: dbadmit@erau.edu

Florida Air Academy
1950 S Academy Dr, Melbourne FL 32901-4396
Colonel James Dwight, President
321-723-3211 ext. 30041 Fax: 321-676-0422
Website: www.flair.com
E-mail: tderegnaucourt@flair.com

IDAHO

Brigham Young University - Idaho
120 Kimball Bldg, Rexburg ID 83460-1615
Rob Garrett, Director of Admissions
208-496-1020 Fax: 208-496-1220
Website: www.byui.edu
E-mail: admissions@byui.edu

KANSAS

ST. JOHN'S MILITARY SCHOOL
PO Box 5020, Salina KS 67402
Jeff Coverdale, Director of Admissions
785-823-7231 Fax: 785-309-5489
Website: www.sjms.org
E-mail: jeffc@sjms.org

KENTUCKY

Morehead State University
Morehead KY 40351-1689
Jeffrey Liles, Enrollment Services
800-585-6781 Fax: 606-783-5038
Website: www.moreheadstate.edu
E-mail: admissions@moreheadstate.edu

MISSOURI

MISSOURI MILITARY ACADEMY
204 N Grand St, Mexico MO 65265
Maj. Dennis Diederich, Director of Admissions
888-564-6662 Fax: 573-581-0081
Website: www.mma-cadet.org
E-mail: info@mma.mexico.mo.us

WENTWORTH MILITARY ACADEMY & COLLEGE
1880 Washington Ave, Lexington MO 64067
MAJ Mike Herman, VP for Enrollment
800-962-7682 or 660-259-2221 Fax: 660-259-2677
Website: www.wma.edu
E-mail: admissions@wma.edu

NEW MEXICO

NEW MEXICO MILITARY INSTITUTE
101 W College Blvd, Roswell NM 88201-5173
Rear Admiral David R. Ellison, USN (Ret.), Superintendent
LTC. Steven D. Klein, VP, Enrollment & Marketing
800-421-5376 or 505-624-8050 Fax: 505-624-8058
Website: www.nmmi.edu
E-mail: admissions@nmmi.edu

Established 1891. State Supported. Coed. Accreditation: NCACS, New Mexico Department of Education. Estimated costs for 2004-2005 school year, out-of-state student: $10,166, in-state student: $7,670. Enrollment: 950. Faculty: 68. Student-faculty ratio: 18:1. Degree: AA. Library: 68,000 volumes. 19 buildings on 40 acre main campus. Additional acreage includes an 18-hole championship golf course. ROTC - offering an ARMY two year commissioning program. Prep school for all service academies. 90% of high school graduates receive their 4 year college degrees. 90% of junior college graduates receive their baccalaureate degrees. Quality education at a fair price.

NEW YORK

SUNY College at Brockport
350 New Campus Dr, Brockport NY 14420-2997
Bernard S. Valento, Director of Undergraduate Admissions
585-395-2751 Fax: 585-395-5452
Website: www.brockport.edu
E-mail: admit@brockport.edu

OHIO

University of Dayton
300 College Park, Dayton OH 45469-1300
Robert F. Durkle, Director of Admission
800-837-7433 Fax: 937-229-4729
Website: admission.udayton.edu
E-mail: admission@udayton.edu

OKLAHOMA

Oklahoma State University
Stillwater OK 74078
Jeffrey Hensley, Department Head
405-744-1775
Website: www.okstate.edu
E-mail: mnlinch@okstate.edu

PENNSYLVANIA

CARSON LONG MILITARY INSTITUTE
PO Box 98, New Bloomfield PA 17068-0098
Lieutenant Colonel David M. Comolli, Academic Dean
717-582-2121 Fax: 717-582-8763
Website: www.carsonlong.org
E-mail: carson6@pa.net

VERMONT

NORWICH UNIVERSITY
158 Harmon Dr, Northfield VT 05663
Col. Steven P. Carney, Professor of Military Science
800-468-6679
Website: www.norwich.edu/cadets/armyrotc.html
E-mail: nuadm@norwich.edu
See listing under "Universities"

VIRGINIA

Fishburne Military School
PO Box 988, Waynesboro VA 22980-0722
Brigadier General William Alexander, (VA), Superintendent
Major Scott Mangum, (VA), Director of Admissions
800-946-7773 Fax: 540-946-7738
Website: www.fishburne.org
E-mail: crichmond@fishburne.org

Hargrave Military Academy
200 Military Dr, Chatham VA 24531-4683
Frank Martin, Director of Admissions
800-432-2480 Fax: 434-432-3129
Website: www.hargrave.edu
E-mail: admissions@hargrave.edu
See listing under "Preparatory Schools for Boys"

MASSANUTTEN MILITARY ACADEMY
614 S Main St, Woodstock VA 22664-1205
Murali Sinnathamby, Director of Admissions
877-466-6222 or 540-459-2167 Fax: 540-459-5421
Website: www.militaryschool.com
E-mail: admissions@militaryschool.com

Radford University
PO Box 6903, Radford VA 24142
David W. Kraus, Director of Admissions
800-890-4265 Fax: 540-831-5038
Website: www.radford.edu
E-mail: ruadmiss@radford.edu

WISCONSIN

ST. JOHN'S NORTHWESTERN MILITARY ACADEMY
1101 N Genesee St, Delafield WI 53018-1498
Mr. Jack H. Albert, Jr., President
Maj. Duane Rutherford, Director of Enrollment Services
800-752-2338 or 262-646-7199 Fax: 262-646-7128
Website: www.sjnma.org
E-mail: admissions@sjnma.org

Established in 1884. Private. Boys grades 7-12. Accreditation: ISACS, NAIS, AMCSUS, TABS. Tuition, room & board: $29,750. Enrollment: 315 boarding; 9 day. Faculty: 39. Student-faculty ratio: 12:1. 10 buildings on 150 acres. Gym, pool, tennis courts, golf course. College preparatory boy's boarding school. Day program for grades 7-12 only. 30 minutes from Milwaukee and 90 minutes from Chicago. Extensive athletic and extracurricular offerings. JROTC honor school with distinction.

St. Norbert College
100 Grant St, De Pere WI 54115
Brian Studebaker, Director of Admission
800-236-4878 Fax: 920-403-4072
Website: www.snc.edu
E-mail: admit@snc.edu

GUAM

University of Guam
UOG Station, Mangilao GU 96923
Deborah Leon Guerrero, Registrar
671-735-2201 or 671-735-2208 Fax: 671-735-2203
Website: www.uog.edu
E-mail: admitme@uog9.uog.edu

ALABAMA

CALHOUN COMMUNITY COLLEGE
PO Box 2216, Decatur AL 35609-2216
M. Wayne Tosh, Registrar
256-306-2500 Fax: 256-306-2941
Website: www.calhoun.edu
E-mail: aprater@calhoun.edu

Judson College
302 Bibb St, Marion AL 36756
Michael Scotto, Director of Admissions
800-447-9472 Fax: 334-683-5147
Website: www.judson.edu
E-mail: admissions@judson.edu

University of Alabama in Huntsville
PO Box 1247, Huntsville AL 35899-0001
Nikki Willis, Assoc. Director for Recruiting Program and Events
1-800-UAH-CALL Fax: 256-824-6073
Website: www.uah.edu
E-mail: willisn@uah.edu

University of South Alabama
307 University Blvd N, Mobile AL 36688-3053
Melissa Haab, Director of Admissions
251-460-6141 Fax: 251-460-7876
Website: www.southalabama.edu
E-mail: admiss@usouthal.edu

ALASKA

University of Alaska Anchorage
PO Box 141629, Anchorage AK 99514-1629
Cecile Mitchell, Director of Enrollment Services
907-786-1480 Fax: 907-786-4888
Website: www.uaa.alaska.edu/
E-mail: enroll@uaa.alaska.edu

ARIZONA

THE CONSERVATORY OF RECORDING ARTS & SCIENCES
2300 E Broadway Rd, Tempe AZ 85282-1707
Tonya Visconti, Director of Admissions
800-562-6383 or 480-858-9400 Fax: 480-829-1332
Website: cras.org
E-mail: info@cras.org

Established 1987. Private. Coed. Accreditation: ACCSCT. Enrollment: 480. Faculty: 30. Student-faculty ratio: 12:1. Diploma: Master recording program. Certificate: Audio recording & production, music business, MIDI/computer/electronic music recording, sound reinforcement, concert sound, trouble shooting maintenance. Purpose is to train highly motivated students for entry level positions in the audio recording and music industries. Through extensive hands-on training with industry standard equipment and practice with current production techniques, students gain the confidence and expertise to enter the working world as Recording Engineers.

ARKANSAS

Williams Baptist College
PO Box 3737, Walnut Ridge AR 72476-3737
Angela Flippo, Vice President for Enrollment Management
800-722-4434 Fax: 870-759-4163
Website: www.williamsbaptistcollege.com
E-mail: admissions@wbcoll.edu

CALIFORNIA

Chapman University
One University Drive, Orange CA 92866-1099
Michael Drummy, Assistant Vice President for Enrollment
Services and Chief Admission Officer
714-997-6411 or 888-CUAPPLY Fax: 714-997-6713
Website: www.chapman.edu
E-mail: admit@chapman.edu

Cogswell College
1175 Bordeaux Dr, Sunnyvale CA 94089-1210
Dr. Tim Duncan, Dean of the College
800-264-7955 or 408-541-0100 Fax: 408-747-0764
Website: www.cogswell.edu
E-mail: info@cogswell.edu

COLBURN SCHOOL
200 S Grand Ave, Los Angeles CA 90012-3007
Kathleen Tesar, Director of Admissions and Student Affairs
213-621-2200 Fax: 213-621-2110
Website: www.colburnschool.edu
E-mail: admissions@colburnschool.edu

Concordia University
1530 Concordia, Irvine CA 92612-3203
Lori McDonald, Executive Director of Enrollment Services
800-229-1200 or 949-854-8002 Fax: 949-854-6894
Website: www.cui.edu
E-mail: admission@cui.edu

MUSICIANS INSTITUTE
1655 N McCadden Pl, Hollywood CA 90028
Steve Lunn, Director of Admissions
323-462-1384 Fax: 323-462-6978
Website: www.mi.edu
E-mail: admissions@mi.edu

Orange Coast College
PO Box 5005, Costa Mesa CA 92628-5005
Kristin Clark, Director of Admissions
714-432-5773 Fax: 714-432-5736
Website: www.orangecoastcollege.edu
E-mail: kclark@cccd.edu

Point Loma Nazarene University
3900 Lomaland Dr, San Diego CA 92106-2810
Chip Killingsworth, Director of Undergraduate Admissions
800-733-7770 Fax: 619-849-2601
Website: www.pointloma.edu
E-mail: admissions@pointloma.edu

San Bernardino Valley College
701 S Mount Vernon Ave
San Bernardino CA 92410-2798
Kay Ragan, Ed.D., Director of Admissions
909-888-6511 Fax: 909-889-4988
Website: www.valleycollege.edu
E-mail: kragan@sbccd.cc.ca.us

San Diego Christian College
2100 Greenfield Dr, El Cajon CA 92019-1157
Rene Inman, Director of Admissions
800-676-2242 Fax: 619-590-1739
Website: www.sdcc.edu
E-mail: admissions@sdcc.edu

SAN FRANCISCO CONSERVATORY OF MUSIC
50 Oak St, San Francisco CA 94102
Alexander Brose, Director of Admission
800-899-7326 Fax: 415-503-6299
Website: www.sfcm.edu
E-mail: admit@sfcm.edu

Simpson University
2211 College View Dr, Redding CA 96003-8606
Jim Herberger, Director of Admissions
888-9-SIMPSON Fax: 530-226-4861
Website: www.simpsonuniversity.edu
E-mail: admissions@simpsonuniversity.edu
See listing under "Universities"

Whittier College
PO Box 634, Whittier CA 90608-0634
Kieron Miller, Director of Admissions
562-907-4200 Fax: 562-907-4870
Website: www.whittier.edu
E-mail: kmiller@whittier.edu

COLORADO

Nazarene Bible College
1111 Academy Park Loop
Colorado Springs CO 80910-3717
Dr. Laurel Matson, VP for Enrollment & Student Development
719-596-5110 Fax: 719-884-5199
Website: www.nbc.edu
E-mail: admissions@nbc.edu

FLORIDA

THE BAPTIST COLLEGE OF FLORIDA
5400 College Dr, Graceville FL 32440-1831
Christopher M. Bishop, Director of Admissions
800-328-2660 Fax: 850-263-9026
Website: www.baptistcollege.edu
E-mail: admissions@baptistcollege.edu

Florida State University
600 W College Ave, Tallahassee FL 32306-1096
Janice V. Finney, Director of Admissions
850-644-2525 Fax: 850-644-0197
Website: admissions.fsu.edu
E-mail: admissions@admin.fsu.edu

HERZING COLLEGE
1595 S Semoran Blvd #1501
Winter Park FL 32792-5509
Kathy Nagle, Director of Admissions
407-478-0500 Fax: 407-478-0501
Website: www.herzing.edu
E-mail: info@orl.herzing.edu

Lynn University
3601 N Military Trl, Boca Raton FL 33431-5598
Lisa Leonard, Recruitment Coordinator
561-237-9014 Fax: 561-237-7100
Website: www.lynn.edu
E-mail: admission@lynn.edu

University of South Florida
4202 E Fowler Ave, Tampa FL 33620-6900
J. Robert Spatig, Director of Admissions
877-USF-BULL Fax: 813-974-9689
Website: www.usf.edu
E-mail: admissions@admin.usf.edu
See listing under "Universities"

GEORGIA

Armstrong Atlantic State University
11935 Abercorn St, Savannah GA 31419-1997
Kim West, Asst. Dean and Registrar Enrollment Services
912-927-5277 Fax: 912-921-5462
Website: www.armstrong.edu
E-mail: admissions@mail.armstrong.edu

Kennesaw State University
1000 Chastain Rd NW, Kennesaw GA 30144-5591
Joseph Meeks, Dean of the School of the Arts
770-423-6742
Website: www.kennesaw.edu

TOCCOA FALLS COLLEGE
PO Box 800899, Toccoa Falls GA 30598
888-785-5624 Fax: 706-282-6012
Website: www.tfc.edu
E-mail: admissions@tfc.edu

IDAHO

Brigham Young University - Idaho
120 Kimball Bldg, Rexburg ID 83460-1615
Rob Garrett, Director of Admissions
208-496-1020 Fax: 208-496-1220
Website: www.byui.edu
E-mail: admissions@byui.edu

University of Idaho
Moscow ID 83844-4253
Lloyd Scott, Director of New Student Services
208-885-6163 Fax: 208-885-4477
Website: www.uidaho.edu
E-mail: nss@uidaho.edu

ILLINOIS

Benedictine University
5700 College Rd, Lisle IL 60532-0900
630-829-6300 or 888-829-6363 Fax: 630-829-6301
Website: www.ben.edu
E-mail: admissions@ben.edu
See listing under "Universities"

Columbia College Chicago
600 S Michigan Ave, Chicago IL 60605-1996
Murphy Monroe, Executive Director of Admissions
312-344-7130 Fax: 312-344-8024
Website: www.colum.edu
E-mail: admissions@colum.edu

CONCORDIA UNIVERSITY
7400 Augusta St, River Forest IL 60305-1402
708-209-3100 Fax: 708-209-3176
Website: www.cuchicago.edu
E-mail: admission@cuchicago.edu

Roosevelt University
430 S Michigan Ave, Chicago IL 60605
Gwen E. Kanelos, Asst. Vice President for Enrollment Services
877-APPLY-RU Fax: 312-341-4216
Website: www.roosevelt.edu
E-mail: applyru@roosevelt.edu

INDIANA

Oakland City University
138 N Lucretia St, Oakland City IN 47660
Brian J. Baker, Director of Admissions
800-737-5125 Fax: 812-749-1433
Website: www.oak.edu
E-mail: bbaker@oak.edu
See listing under "Universities"

University of Evansville
1800 Lincoln Ave, Evansville IN 47722-0001
Don Vos, Dean of Admission
800-423-8633 Fax: 812-488-4076
Website: www.evansville.edu
E-mail: admission@evansville.edu

IOWA

Briar Cliff University
PO Box 2100, Sioux City IA 51104-0100
Sharisue Wilcoxon, VP for Enrollment Management
712-279-5200 Fax: 712-279-1632
Website: www.briarcliff.edu
E-mail: admissions@briarcliff.edu

Clarke College
1550 Clarke Dr, Dubuque IA 52001-3198
Andy Schroeder, Director of Admissions
800-383-2345 Fax: 563-584-8666
Website: www.clarke.edu
E-mail: andy.schroeder@clarke.edu

Graceland University
1 University Place, Lamoni IA 50140
Greg Sutherland, Interim Vice President for Enrollment and Dean of Admissions
641-784-5196 Fax: 641-784-5480
Website: www.admissions.graceland.edu
E-mail: admissions@graceland.edu

Iowa Lakes Community College
300 S 18th St, Estherville IA 51334-2721
Anne Stansbury, Asst. Director of Admissions
712-362-7945 Fax: 712-362-8363
Website: www.iowalakes.edu
E-mail: info@iowalakes.edu

Waldorf College
106 S 6th St, Forest City IA 50436-1713
Dr. Linda Hoopes, Vice President of Admission and Marketing
800-292-1903 or 641-585-8112 Fax: 641-585-8125
Website: www.waldorf.edu
E-mail: hoopesl@waldorf.edu
See listing under "Universities"

KANSAS

Tabor College
400 S Jefferson St, Hillsboro KS 67063-1758
Rusty Allen, Dean of Enrollment Management
800-822-6799 Fax: 620-947-6276
Website: www.tabor.edu
E-mail: admissions@tabor.edu
See listing under "Universities"

KENTUCKY

Morehead State University
Morehead KY 40351-1689
Jeffrey Liles, Enrollment Services
800-585-6781 Fax: 606-783-5038
Website: www.moreheadstate.edu
E-mail: admissions@moreheadstate.edu

MARYLAND

Cecil College
One Seahawk Dr, North East MD 21901
Sandra S. Rajaski, Registrar & Director of Admissions
410-287-1000 Fax: 410-287-1001
Website: www.cecil.edu
E-mail: srajaski@cecil.edu

Hagerstown Community College
11400 Robinwood Dr, Hagerstown MD 21742-6590
Dr. Daniel E. Bock, Assistant Director of Admissions
301-790-2800 Fax: 301-791-9165
Website: www.hagerstowncc.edu
E-mail: bockd@hagerstowncc.edu

MASSACHUSETTS

Anna Maria College
50 Sunset Ln, Paxton MA 01612
Timothy M. Donahue, Director of Recruitment and Admissions
508-849-3360 Fax: 508-849-3362
Website: www.annamaria.edu
E-mail: admissions@annamaria.edu

Assumption College
500 Salisbury St, Worcester MA 01609-1294
Kathleen Murphy, Dean of Enrollment
508-767-7000 Fax: 508-799-4412
Website: www.assumption.edu
E-mail: admiss@assumption.edu

Boston Conservatory
8 Fenway, Boston MA 02215-4099
Halley Shefler, Dean of Enrollment
617-912-9153 Fax: 617-247-3159
Website: www.bostonconservatory.edu
E-mail: admissions@bostonconservatory.edu

Boston University
121 Bay State Rd, Boston MA 02215
Kelly Walter, Executive Director of Admissions
617-353-2300 Fax: 617-353-9695
Website: web.bu.edu
E-mail: admissions@bu.edu

Gordon College
255 Grapevine Rd, Wenham MA 01984-1899
Barbara R. Layne, Associate Vice President, Enrollment
866-464-6736 Fax: 978-867-4682
Website: www.gordon.edu
E-mail: admissions@gordon.edu

LONGY SCHOOL OF MUSIC

1 Follen St, Cambridge MA 02138-3599
Admissions Office
617-876-0956 ext. 521 Fax: 617-876-9326
Website: www.longy.edu
E-mail: music@longy.edu

Established 1915. Private. Coed. Tuition: $15,620-$24,350. Enrollment (full-time & part-time): 50 undergraduate, 150 graduate, 300 non-degree. Faculty: 150, including members of the Boston Symphony Orchestra, Handel and Haydn Society, and international performers and teachers. Degrees: Undergraduate Diploma, Bachelor of Music (with Emerson College), Graduate Performance Diploma, Artist Diploma, Master of Music, Dalcroze Eurhythmics license and certificate. Two buildings in Harvard Square; acclaimed 300-seat concert hall is site of over 250 concerts yearly. Music Library. Degree or diploma programs in the following areas: chamber music, collaborative piano, composition, Dalcroze Eurhythmics, early music, modern American music, opera, organ, piano, strings, voice, woodwinds and brass.

Smith College
Northampton MA 01063-0001
Debra Shaver, Director of Admissions
800-383-3232 Fax: 413-585-2527
Website: www.smith.edu
E-mail: admission@smith.edu

University of Massachusetts Dartmouth
Old Westport Rd, North Dartmouth MA 02747-2300
Steven T. Briggs, Director of Admissions
508-999-8605 Fax: 508-999-8755
Website: explore.umassd.edu
E-mail: sbriggs@umassd.edu

Worcester Polytechnic Institute
100 Institute Rd, Worcester MA 01609-2280
Edward J. Connor, Director of Admissions
508-831-5286 Fax: 508-831-5875
Website: admissions.wpi.edu
E-mail: admissions@wpi.edu

MICHIGAN

Alma College
614 W Superior St, Alma MI 48801-1599
Evan Montague, Director of Admissions
800-321-ALMA Fax: 989-463-7057
Website: www.alma.edu
E-mail: admissions@alma.edu

Concordia University
4090 Geddes Rd, Ann Arbor MI 48105-2797
Gary Neumann, Director of Admissions
734-995-7300 Fax: 734-995-4610
Website: www.cuaa.edu
E-mail: admissions@cuaa.edu

Delta College
University Center MI 48710-0001
Duff Zube, Director of Admissions
989-686-9093 Fax: 989-667-2202
Website: www.delta.edu
E-mail: admit@delta.edu

Grand Valley State University
1 Campus Dr, Allendale MI 49401-9403
Jodi Chycinski, Director of Admissions
616-331-6611 Fax: 616-331-2000
Website: www.gvsu.edu
E-mail: go2gvsu@gvsu.edu

HILLSDALE COLLEGE

33 E College St, Hillsdale MI 49242-1298
Professor James Holleman, Director
517-607-2363 Fax: 517-607-2665
Website: www.hillsdale.edu
E-mail: james.holleman@hillsdale.edu

Interlochen Arts Academy
PO Box 199, Interlochen MI 49643-0199
231-276-7472
Website: www.interlochen.org
E-mail: admissions@interlochen.org

MACOMB COMMUNITY COLLEGE

44575 Garfield Rd, Clinton Township MI 48038-1139
Information Center
586-445-7999
Website: www.macomb.edu
E-mail: answer@macomb.edu

MINNESOTA

Bethany Lutheran College
700 Luther Dr, Mankato MN 56001
Don Westphal, Dean of Admissions
507-344-7000 Fax: 507-344-7376
Website: www.blc.edu
E-mail: admiss@blc.edu

Crown College
8700 College View Dr, Saint Bonifacius MN 55375
Mitch Fisk, Director of Admissions
952-446-4142 Fax: 952-446-4149
Website: www.crown.edu
E-mail: johnsonj@crown.edu

Gustavus Adolphus College
800 W College Ave, Saint Peter MN 56082-1485
Mark H. Anderson, Dean of Admission
800-GUSTAVUS Fax: 507-933-7474
Website: www.gustavus.edu
E-mail: admission@gustavus.edu

McNally Smith College of Music
19 Exchange St East, St. Paul MN 55101
Debbie Sandridge, Director of Admissions
800-594-9500 Fax: 651-291-0366
Website: www.mcnallysmith.edu
E-mail: dsandridge@mcnallysmith.edu
See listing under "Universities"

Minnesota State University Moorhead
1104 7th Ave S, Moorhead MN 56563-0002
Regina Monson, Director of Admissions
218-477-2161 Fax: 218-477-4374
Website: go.mnstate.edu
E-mail: dragon@mnstate.edu

Pillsbury Baptist Bible College
315 S Grove Ave, Owatonna MN 55060-3097
Susanne Martin, Admissions Coordinator
507-451-2710 Fax: 507-451-0156
Website: www.pillsbury.edu
E-mail: admissions@pillsbury.edu

SHATTUCK-ST. MARY'S SCHOOL

PO Box 218, Faribault MN 55021-0218
Amy D. Wolf, Director of Admissions
507-333-1618 Fax: 507-333-1661
Website: www.s-sm.org
E-mail: admissions@s-sm.org
See listing under "Preparatory Schools - Coed"

MISSISSIPPI

Tougaloo College
500 W County Line Rd, Tougaloo MS 39174-9799
Juno Leggette Jacobs, Director of Admissions
601-977-7768 Fax: 601-977-4501
Website: www.tougaloo.edu
E-mail: jjacobs@tougaloo.edu

MISSOURI

Central Methodist University
411 Central Methodist Sq, Fayette MO 65248-1198
Larry Anderson, Director of Admissions
660-248-6247 Fax: 660-248-1872
Website: www.centralmethodist.edu
E-mail: landerso@centralmethodist.edu

Northwest Missouri State University
800 University Dr, Maryville MO 64468-6001
Beverly Schenkel, Dean of Enrollment Management
660-562-1562 Fax: 660-562-1121
Website: www.nwmissouri.edu
E-mail: admissions@nwmissouri.edu

Stephens College
PO Box 2121, Columbia MO 65215-0001
David Adams, Dean of Enrollment Management
573-442-2211 Fax: 573-876-7237
Website: www.stephens.edu
E-mail: dadams@stephens.edu

Truman State University
100 E Normal, Kirksville MO 63501
Office of Admission
660-785-4114 Fax: 660-785-7456
Website: admissions.truman.edu
E-mail: admissions@truman.edu

University of Missouri
1 University Blvd, Saint Louis MO 63121-4499
Dr. James E. Richards, Jr., Department Chairperson
314-516-5980 Fax: 314-516-6593
Website: www.umsl.edu
E-mail: admissions@umsl.edu

WEBSTER UNIVERSITY

470 E Lockwood Ave, Saint Louis MO 63119-3194
Michael Parkinson, Department Chairman
800-752-6765 ext. 7032 Fax: 314-963-6048
Website: www.webster.edu
E-mail: parkinmi@webster.edu

Established 1915. Private. Coed. Accreditation: NCACS. Tuition: $18,240. Room and board: $7,300. Enrollment: 2,460 full-time, 1,153 part-time. Faculty: 160. Student-faculty ratio: 15:1. Degrees: BA, BFA, BM, BMEd, BS, BSN, MA, MBA, MAT, MSN, DMGT. Library: 400,000 volumes. 36 buildings on 45 acres. Nationally recognized programs in the performing arts and music including composition, jazz studies, vocal and instrumental performance, and music education. Students from 40 states and 30 countries. Beautiful suburban campus in a wooded community of 20,000. Average class size of 15. New Residence Halls for 320 additional students open in 2006. Campuses in four European countries, China and Thailand.

William Jewell College
500 College Hill, Liberty MO 64068-1896
Dr. Rick Winslow, VP Enrollment Management and Student Affairs
800-753-7009 Fax: 816-415-5040
Website: www.jewell.edu
E-mail: winslowr@william.jewell.edu

William Woods University
1 University Ave, Fulton MO 65251-1098
Jimmy Clay, Director of Admissions
573-642-2251 Fax: 573-592-1146
Website: www.williamwoods.edu
E-mail: admissions@williamwoods.edu
See listing under "Universities"

NEBRASKA

Nebraska Wesleyan University
5000 Saint Paul Ave, Lincoln NE 68504-2794
Patricia Karthauser, V.P. for University Enrollment
402-466-2371 Fax: 402-465-2177
Website: www.nebrwesleyan.edu
E-mail: admissions@nebrwesleyan.edu

University of Nebraska at Kearney
905 W 25th St, Kearney NE 68849-0001
Dusty Newton, Director of Admissions
800-KEARNEY Fax: 308-865-8987
Website: www.unk.edu
E-mail: admissionsug@unk.edu

NEW JERSEY

Bergen Community College
400 Paramus Rd, Paramus NJ 07652
Julian Gomez, Asst. Director of Admissions
201-447-7100 Fax: 201-444-7036
Website: www.bergen.edu
E-mail: jgomez@bergen.edu

New Jersey City University
2039 John F Kennedy Blvd
Jersey City NJ 07305-1588
Carmen Panlilio, Asst. V.P. for Admissions and Financial Aid
201-200-3234 Fax: 201-200-2044
Website: www.njcu.edu
E-mail: admissions@njcu.edu

Ramapo College of New Jersey
505 Ramapo Valley Rd, Mahwah NJ 07430-1623
Director of Admissions
201-684-7300 or 201-684-7301 Fax: 201-684-7964
Website: www.ramapo.edu
E-mail: admissions@ramapo.edu

RICHARD STOCKTON COLLEGE OF NEW JERSEY

PO Box 195, Pomona NJ 08240
John Iacovelli, Dean of Enrollment Management
866-RSC-2885 Fax: 609-626-5541
Website: www.stockton.edu
E-mail: admissions@stockton.edu
See listing under "Universities"

NEW YORK

College of Saint Rose
432 Western Ave, Albany NY 12203-1419
Maryelizabeth Amico, Asst V.P. for Undergraduate Admissions
518-454-5150 Fax: 518-454-2013
Website: www.strose.edu
E-mail: admit@strose.edu

CUNY Hunter College
695 Park Ave, New York NY 10021
Aaron Gibbs, Assistant Director of Recruitment
212-650-3946 Fax: 212-650-3336
Website: www.hunter.cuny.edu
E-mail: aaron.gibbs@hunter.cuny.edu

EASTMAN SCHOOL OF MUSIC OF THE UNIVERSITY OF ROCHESTER

26 Gibbs St, Rochester NY 14604-2599
Dr. Adrian Daly, Associate Dean for Admissions and Retention
585-274-1060 Fax: 585-232-8601
Website: www.esm.rochester.edu
E-mail: admissions@esm.rochester.edu

FIVE TOWNS COLLEGE

305 N Service Rd, Dix Hills NY 11746-5871
631-424-7000 ext. 2110 Fax: 631-656-2172
Website: www.fivetowns.edu
E-mail: admissions@ftc.edu
See listing under "Universities"

Institute of Audio Research
64 University Pl, New York NY 10003-4595
Mark L. Kahn, Director of Admissions
800-544-2501 or 212-777-8550 (NY, NJ, CT)
Fax: 212-677-6549
Website: www.audioschool.com
E-mail: contact@audioschool.com
See listing under "Career Schools"

Long Island University-C. W. Post Campus
720 Northern Blvd, Brookville NY 11548-1300
Joanne Graziano, Executive Director of Admissions
516-299-2900 Fax: 516-299-2137
Website: www.liu.edu/cwpost
E-mail: enroll@cwpost.liu.edu

Molloy College
1000 Hempstead Ave
Rockville Centre NY 11570-1100
Marguerite Lane, Director of Admissions
516-678-5000 ext. 6291 Fax: 516-256-2247
Website: www.molloy.edu
E-mail: admissions@molloy.edu
See listing under "Universities"

PURCHASE COLLEGE STATE UNIVERSITY OF NEW YORK (SUNY)
735 Anderson Hill Rd, Purchase NY 10577-1400
Stephanie McCaine, Director of Admissions
914-251-6300 Fax: 914-251-6314
Website: www.purchase.edu
E-mail: admisn@purchase.edu
See listing under "Universities"

Roberts Wesleyan College
2301 Westside Dr, Rochester NY 14624-1997
Office of Admissions
585-594-6400 Fax: 585-594-6371
Website: www.roberts.edu
E-mail: admissions@roberts.edu

SUNY Niagara County Community College
3111 Saunders Settlement Rd
Sanborn NY 14132-9487
Kathleen Saunders, Director of Admissions
716-614-6200 Fax: 716-614-6820
Website: www.niagaracc.suny.edu
E-mail: admissions@niagaracc.suny.edu

SUNY Orange County Community College
115 South St, Middletown NY 10940-6437
Margot St. Lawrence, Director of Admissions
845-341-4030 Fax: 845-342-8662
Website: www.sunyorange.edu
E-mail: apply@sunyorange.edu
See listing under "Community and Junior Colleges"

NORTH CAROLINA

Brevard College
One Brevard College Dr, Brevard NC 28712
Joretta Nelson, Vice President Enrollment Management
828-883-8292 Fax: 828-884-3790
Website: www.brevard.edu
E-mail: admissions@brevard.edu

Catawba College
2300 W Innes St, Salisbury NC 28144-2488
Dr. L. Russell Watjen, Ph.D., V.P. & Dean of Admissions
704-637-4402 Fax: 704-637-4222
Website: www.catawba.edu
E-mail: admission@catawba.edu

Peace College
15 E Peace St, Raleigh NC 27604-1194
Laura C. Bingham, President
800-PEACE-47 Fax: 919-508-2306
Website: www.peace.edu
E-mail: admissions@peace.edu

Salem College
Winston Salem NC 27108
Dana Evans, Dean of Admissions/Fin. Aid
800-32-SALEM Fax: 336-917-5572
Website: www.salem.edu
E-mail: admissions@salem.edu
See listing under "Women's Colleges"

NORTH DAKOTA

Dickinson State University
Dickinson ND 58601-4896
Steve Glasser, Director of Enrollment Services
800-279-4295 Fax: 701-483-2409
Website: www.dickinsonstate.edu
E-mail: dsu.hawks@dickinsonstate.edu

Oak Grove Lutheran School
124 N Terrace N, Fargo ND 58102-3899
Rachel Mathson, Director of Admissions
701-237-0212 Fax: 701-237-4217
Website: www.oakgrovelutheran.com
E-mail: oakgrove.lutheranschool@sendit.nodak.edu

Valley City State University
101 College St SW, Valley City ND 58072-4024
Dan Klein, Director of Enrollment Services
800-532-8641 ext. 7101 Fax: 701-845-7299
Website: www.vcsu.edu
E-mail: enrollment.services@vcsu.edu
See listing under "Universities"

OHIO

Cincinnati Christian University
PO Box 4320, Cincinnati OH 45204
Erin Oppy, Executive Director of Undergraduate Admissions
513-244-8141 Fax: 513-244-8453
Website: www.ccuniversity.edu

CLEVELAND INSTITUTE OF MUSIC
11021 East Blvd, Cleveland OH 44106
William Fay, Director of Admission
216-795-3107
Website: www.cim.edu/coladmission.php

Cleveland State University
2121 Euclid Ave RW 204, Cleveland OH 44115
Dr. Richard Arndt, Dean of Undergraduate Recruitment and College Partnerships
888-CSU-OHIO Fax: 216-687-9210
Website: www.csuohio.edu
E-mail: admissions@csuohio.edu

OHIO NORTHERN UNIVERSITY
525 S Main St, Ada OH 45810-1555
Nils Riess, Chair of Music Dept.
419-772-2150
Website: www.onu.edu
E-mail: admissions-ug@onu.edu
See listing under "Universities"

The Ohio State University
School of Music
Weigel Hall, 1866 College Rd, Columbus OH 43210
614-292-2870 Fax: 614-292-1102
Website: music.osu.edu
E-mail: music-ug@osu.edu

OHIO WESLEYAN UNIVERSITY
61 S Sandusky St, Delaware OH 43015-2398
Director of Admission
740-368-3020 Fax: 740-368-3314
Website: www.owu.edu
E-mail: owuadmit@owu.edu

Owens Community College
PO Box 10000, Toledo OH 43699-1947
William J. Ivoska, Ph.D, Vice President of Student Services
567-661-7000 Fax: 567-661-7607
Website: www.owens.edu
E-mail: admissions@owens.edu

University of Dayton
300 College Park, Dayton OH 45469-1300
Robert F. Durkle, Director of Admission
800-837-7433 Fax: 937-229-4729
Website: admission.udayton.edu
E-mail: admission@udayton.edu

OKLAHOMA

Mid-America Christian University
3500 SW 119th St, Oklahoma City OK 73170-4504
Haley Hope, Director of Admissions
405-691-3800 Fax: 405-692-3165
Website: www.macu.edu
E-mail: info@macu.edu

Oklahoma State University
Stillwater OK 74078
Brant Adams, Interim Department Head
405-744-6133
Website: www.okstate.edu
E-mail: brant.adams@okstate.edu

University of Tulsa
600 S College Ave, Tulsa OK 74104-3126
Earl Johnson, Dean of Admission
918-631-2307 Fax: 918-631-5003
Website: www.utulsa.edu
E-mail: admission@utulsa.edu

OREGON

Marylhurst University
17600 Pacific Hwy (Hwy 43)
Marylhurst OR 97036-0261
Director of Admissions
800-634-9982 ext. 6268 Fax: 503-635-6585
Website: www.marylhurst.edu
E-mail: studentinfo@marylhurst.edu

PACIFIC UNIVERSITY
2043 College Way, Forest Grove OR 97116-1797
Karen M. Dunston, Executive Director of Admissions
800-677-6712 Fax: 503-352-2975
Website: www.pacific.edu
E-mail: admissions@pacific.edu

University of Portland
5000 N Willamette Blvd, Portland OR 97203-5798
Jason McDonald, Dean of Admissions
503-943-7911 Fax: 503-943-7315
Website: www.up.edu
E-mail: mcdonaja@up.edu

Warner Pacific College
2219 SE 68th Ave, Portland OR 97215-4026
Shannon Mackey, Director of Admissions
503-517-1000 Fax: 503-517-1352
Website: www.warnerpacific.edu
E-mail: admissions@warnerpacific.edu

PENNSYLVANIA

Community College of Allegheny County
Allegheny Campus: 808 Ridge Ave, Pittsburgh PA 15212 Admissions: 412.237.2700
Boyce Campus: 595 Beatty Rd, Monroeville PA 15146 Admissions: 724.325.6614
North Campus: 8701 Perry Highway, Pittsburgh PA 15237 Admissions: 412.369.3600
South Campus: 1750 Clairton Rd, West Mifflin PA 15122 Admissions: 412-469-4301
Website: www.ccac.edu

Washington & Jefferson College
60 S Lincoln St, Washington PA 15301-4801
Alton E. Newell, Vice President for Enrollment
724-223-6025 Fax: 724-223-6534
Website: www.washjeff.edu
E-mail: admission@washjeff.edu

SOUTH CAROLINA

Columbia International University
PO Box 3122, Columbia SC 29230-3122
Michelle MacGregor, Director of University Admissions
800-777-2227 Fax: 803-786-4209
Website: www.ciu.edu
E-mail: yesciu@ciu.edu
See listing under "Theological Studies & Religious Vocations"

Erskine College & Seminary
PO Box 176, Due West SC 29639
Bart Walker, Director of Admissions
864-379-8838 Fax: 864-379-3048
Website: www.erskine.edu
E-mail: admissions@erskine.edu

Limestone College
1115 College Dr, Gaffney SC 29340-3799
Chris Phenicie, V.P. for Enrollment
864-489-7151 Fax: 864-488-8206
Website: www.limestone.edu
E-mail: cphenicie@limestone.edu

North Greenville University
PO Box 1892, Tigerville SC 29688-1892
Dr. Jacquelyn H. Griffin, Dean
Website: www.ngu.edu
See listing under "Universities"

TENNESSEE

Austin Peay State University
601 College St, Clarksville TN 37044-0002
931-221-7011 Fax: 931-221-6168
Website: www.apsu.edu
E-mail: admissions@apsu.edu

BLAIR SCHOOL OF MUSIC OF VANDERBILT UNIVERSITY
2400 Blakemore Ave, Nashville TN 37212-3406
Dwayne Sagen, Assistant Dean for Admissions
615-322-7679 Fax: 615-343-0324
Website: www.vanderbilt.edu
E-mail: dwayne.p.sagen@vanderbilt.edu

Lipscomb University
3901 Granny White Pike, Nashville TN 37204-3951
Ricky Holaway, Director of Admissions
800-333-4358 ext. 1776 Fax: 615-269-1804
Website: www.lipscomb.edu
E-mail: admissions@lipscomb.edu

Tennessee State University
3500 John A Merritt Blvd, Nashville TN 37209-1561
John Cade, Dean of Admissions & Records
615-963-5101 Fax: 615-963-2930
Website: www.tnstate.edu
E-mail: jcade@tnstate.edu

University of Tennessee
615 McCallie Ave, Chattanooga TN 37403-2504
Yancy Freeman, Director of Admissions
423-425-4111 Fax: 423-425-4157
Website: www.utc.edu
E-mail: Yancy-Freeman@utc.edu

TEXAS

Abilene Christian University
ACU Box 29000, Abilene TX 79699-0001
325-674-2000 Fax: 325-674-2202
Website: www.acu.edu
E-mail: info@admissions.acu.edu

Lubbock Christian University
5601 19th St, Lubbock TX 79407-2099
Stan Scott, Director of Admissions
806-796-8800 Fax: 806-720-7162
Website: www.lcu.edu
E-mail: stan.scott@lcu.edu

Texas Woman's University
PO Box 425589, Denton TX 76204-5589
Erma Nieto-Brecht, Director of Admissions
866-809-6130 Fax: 940-898-3081
Website: www.twu.edu
E-mail: admissions@twu.edu

University of Houston
122 E Cullen Bldg, Houston TX 77204-2023
Office of Admission
713-743-9595
Website: www.uh.edu
E-mail: admissions@uh.edu

University of Texas at Arlington
Box 19111, Arlington TX 76019-0111
Hans Gatterdam, Director of Admission
817-272-6287 Fax: 817-272-3435
Website: www.uta.edu
E-mail: admissions@uta.edu

Weatherford College
225 College Park Dr, Weatherford TX 76086
Dr. Joe Birmingham, President
800-287-5471 Fax: 817-598-6205
Website: www.wc.edu
E-mail: willingham@wc.edu

VIRGINIA

Mary Baldwin College
Staunton VA 24401
Lisa A. Branson, Executive Director of Admissions and Financial Aid
800-468-2262 Fax: 540-887-7292
Website: www.mbc.edu
E-mail: admit@mbc.edu

Radford University
PO Box 6903, Radford VA 24142
David W. Kraus, Director of Admissions
800-890-4265 Fax: 540-831-5038
Website: www.radford.edu
E-mail: ruadmiss@radford.edu

Randolph College
2500 Rivermont Ave, Lynchburg VA 24503
Patricia LeDonne, Director of Admissions
434-947-8100 Fax: 434-947-8996
Website: www.randolphcollege.edu
E-mail: admissions@randolphcollege.edu

University of Mary Washington
1301 College Ave, Fredericksburg VA 22401-5300
Dr. Martin A. Wilder, Jr., Director of Admissions
540-654-2000 Fax: 540-654-1857
Website: www.umw.edu
E-mail: admit@umw.edu

WASHINGTON

SHORELINE COMMUNITY COLLEGE
16101 Greenwood Ave N, Shoreline WA 98133-5696
Chris Melton, Acting Registrar
206-546-4581 Fax: 206-546-5835
Website: www.shoreline.edu

WEST VIRGINIA

Davis & Elkins College
100 Campus Dr, Elkins WV 26241-3996
Renee Heckel, Director of Enrollment Management
800-624-3157 Fax: 304-637-1800
Website: www.davisandelkins.edu
E-mail: admiss@davisandelkins.edu

WISCONSIN

Alverno College
PO Box 343922, Milwaukee WI 53234-3922
Dianna Gaebler, Director of Admissions
414-382-6100 Fax: 414-382-6354
Website: www.alverno.edu
E-mail: admissions@alverno.edu

MADISON MEDIA INSTITUTE
College of Media Arts
2702 Agriculture Dr, Madison WI 53718-6787
Steve Hutchings, Director of Admissions
800-236-4997 or 608-663-2000 Fax: 608-442-0141
Website: www.madisonmedia.edu
E-mail: mmi@madisonmedia.com

St. Norbert College
100 Grant St, De Pere WI 54115
Brian Studebaker, Director of Admission
800-236-4878 Fax: 920-403-4072
Website: www.snc.edu
E-mail: admit@snc.edu

WISCONSIN CONSERVATORY OF MUSIC
1584 N Prospect Ave, Milwaukee WI 53202-6501
Sarah Wright, VP Business
414-276-5760 Fax: 414-276-6076
Website: www.wcmusic.org
E-mail: sarahwright@wcmusic.org

WYOMING

University of Wyoming
Admissions Office
Dept 3435, Laramie WY 82071-3435
Brooke Culver, Contact
800-342-5996 Fax: 307-766-4042
Website: www.uwyo.edu
E-mail: why-wyo@uwyo.edu

PUERTO RICO

CONSERVATORY OF MUSIC
350 Calle Rafael Lamar, San Juan PR 00918
Eutimia Santiago, Director of Admissions
787-751-0160 ext. 275 Fax: 787-758-8268
Website: www.cmpr.edu
E-mail: admisiones@cmpr.edu

NURSING

ALABAMA

CALHOUN COMMUNITY COLLEGE
PO Box 2216, Decatur AL 35609-2216
M. Wayne Tosh, Registrar
256-306-2500 Fax: 256-306-2941
Website: www.calhoun.edu
E-mail: jog@calhoun.edu

George C. Wallace State Community College
PO Box 2530, Selma AL 36702-2530
Mrs. Donitha J. Griffin, Dean of Students
334-876-9295 Fax: 334-876-9300
Website: www.wccs.edu
E-mail: dgriffin@wccs.edu

Herzing College
280 W Valley Ave, Homewood AL 35209-4816
Kim Conway, Director of Admissions
205-916-2800 Fax: 205-916-2807
Website: www.herzing.edu/birmingham
E-mail: info@bhm.herzing.edu

Trenholm State Technical College
Trenholm Campus
1225 Air Base Blvd, Montgomery AL 36108-3199
Dr. Anthony Molina, President
334-420-4200 Fax: 334-420-4206
Website: www.trenholmtech.cc.al.us
E-mail: molinaa@trenholmtech.cc.al.us

University of Alabama in Huntsville
PO Box 1247, Huntsville AL 35899-0001
Nikki Willis, Assoc. Director for Recruiting Program and Events
1-800-UAH-CALL Fax: 256-824-6073
Website: www.uah.edu
E-mail: willisn@uah.edu

University of South Alabama
307 University Blvd N, Mobile AL 36688-3053
Melissa Haab, Director of Admissions
251-460-6141 Fax: 251-460-7876
Website: www.southalabama.edu
E-mail: admiss@usouthal.edu

ALASKA

University of Alaska Anchorage
PO Box 141629, Anchorage AK 99514-1629
Cecile Mitchell, Director of Enrollment Services
907-786-1480 Fax: 907-786-4888
Website: www.uaa.alaska.edu/
E-mail: enroll@uaa.alaska.edu

ARIZONA

Pima Community College
4905 E Broadway Blvd, Tucson AZ 85709-1010
Wendy Kilgore, Ph.D., Director of Admissions
520-206-4500 Fax: 520-206-4790
Website: www.pima.edu
E-mail: infocenter@pima.edu

ARKANSAS

Northwest Technical Institute
709 S Old Missouri Rd, Springdale AR 72764
Charles L. Kelley, President
479-751-8824 Fax: 479-751-7780
Website: www.nti.tec.ar.us
E-mail: info@nit.tec.ar.us

Phillips Community College of the University of Arkansas
PO Box 785, Helena AR 72342-0785
Dr. Steven Murray, Chancellor
Lynn Boone, Vice Chancellor for Student Services / Registrar
870-338-6474 Fax: 870-338-7542
Website: www.pccua.edu
E-mail: lboone@pccua.edu

University of Arkansas Community College at Hope
PO Box 140, Hope AR 71802-0140
Danita Ormand, Director of Enrollment Services
870-777-5722 Fax: 870-722-6630
Website: www.uacch.edu
E-mail: dormand@uacch.edu

CALIFORNIA

California State University-San Bernadino
5500 University Pkwy
San Bernardino CA 92407-2393
Olivia Rosas, Director of Admissions
909-537-5188 Fax: 909-537-7034
Website: www.csusb.edu
E-mail: orosas@csusb.edu

Chabot College
25555 Hesperian Blvd, Hayward CA 94545-2400
Judy Young, Director of Admissions
510-723-6600 Fax: 510-723-7510
Website: www.chabotcollege.edu
E-mail: ccarcom@clpccd.cc.ca.us

COLLEGE OF INFORMATION TECHNOLOGY
2701 E Chapman Ave Ste 101, Fullerton CA 92831
Mohammad Qamaruddin, Director
714-879-5100 Fax: 714-879-2272
Website: www.collegeofit.com
E-mail: mqamar@collegeofit.com

Concordia University
1530 Concordia, Irvine CA 92612-3203
Lori McDonald, Executive Director of Enrollment Services
800-229-1200 or 949-854-8002 Fax: 949-854-6894
Website: www.cui.edu
E-mail: admission@cui.edu

Dominican University of California
50 Acacia Ave, San Rafael CA 94901-2298
Office of Admissions
888-323-6762 Fax: 415-485-3214
Website: www.dominican.edu
E-mail: enroll@dominican.edu

Maric College
9055 Balboa Ave, San Diego CA 92123
Geraldine Rorrison, Director of Admissions
858-279-4500 Fax: 858-279-4885
Website: www.mariccollege.edu
E-mail: grorrison@mariccollege.edu

Orange Coast College
PO Box 5005, Costa Mesa CA 92628-5005
Kristin Clark, Director of Admissions
714-432-5773 Fax: 714-432-5736
Website: www.orangecoastcollege.edu
E-mail: kclark@cccd.edu

Point Loma Nazarene University
3900 Lomaland Dr, San Diego CA 92106-2810
Chip Killingsworth, Director of Undergraduate Admissions
800-733-7770 Fax: 619-849-2601
Website: www.pointloma.edu
E-mail: admissions@pointloma.edu

San Bernardino Valley College
701 S Mount Vernon Ave
San Bernardino CA 92410-2798
Kay Ragan, Ed.D., Director of Admissions
909-888-6511 Fax: 909-889-4988
Website: www.valleycollege.edu
E-mail: kragan@sbccd.cc.ca.us

San Joaquin Valley College
8400 W Mineral King Ave, Visalia CA 93291-9283
Susie Topjian, Enrollment Services Director
559-651-2500 Fax: 559-651-4864
Website: www.sjvc.edu
E-mail: susiet@sjvc.edu

Western Career College
2157 Country Hills Dr, Antioch CA 94509-7435
Dr. Tim Gienapp, Executive Director
925-522-7777
Website: www.westerncollege.edu

Western Career College
8909 Folsom Blvd, Sacramento CA 95826-3203
Sue Smith, Executive Director
916-361-5100 Fax: 916-361-6666
Website: www.westerncollege.edu

Western Career College
6201 San Ignacio Ave, San Jose CA 95119
Steve Ashab, Executive Director
408-360-0840 Fax: 408-360-0848
Website: www.westerncollege.edu

Western Career College
15555 E 14th St Ste 500, San Leandro CA 94578
Dawn Matthews, Executive Director
510-276-3888 Fax: 510-276-3653
Website: www.westerncollege.edu

COLORADO

Colorado Northwestern Community College
500 Kennedy Dr, Rangely CO 81648-3502
Tresa England, Director of Student Services
800-562-1105 Fax: 970-675-3343
Website: www.cncc.edu
E-mail: tresa.england@cncc.edu

San Juan Basin Technical College
PO Box 970, Cortez CO 81321-0970
Shannon South, Vice President
970-565-8457 Fax: 970-565-8450
Website: www.sjbtc.edu
E-mail: info@sjbtc.edu

DELAWARE

Wesley College
120 N State St, Dover DE 19901-3876
302-736-2300 Fax: 302-736-2301
Website: www.wesley.edu

FLORIDA

City College
2000 W Commercial Blvd, Fort Lauderdale FL 33309
Mercedes Segal, Director of Admissions
954-492-5353 Fax: 954-491-1965
Website: www.citycollege.edu

FLORIDA HOSPITAL COLLEGE OF HEALTH SCIENCES
671 Winyah Dr, Orlando FL 32803
Office of Enrollment Services
800-500-7747 or 407-303-8192 Fax: 407-303-5626
Website: www.fhchs.edu
E-mail: samantha.lopez@fhchs.edu or yvonne.l.williams@fhchs.edu

Established in 1992. Private. Coed. Accreditation. Commission on Colleges of the Southern Association of Colleges and Schools, 1866 Southern Lane, Decatur, GA 30033-4097. 404-679-4500. Tuition: $255 per credit hour (matriculation & program fees additional). Room only: $3,200 (2 trimesters). Enrollment: 635 full-time, 870 part-time. Faculty: 64. Degrees: BS, AS, and Certificates. Professional Programs: Diagnostic Medical Sonography, Health Sciences, Nuclear Medicine Technology, Nursing, Occupational Therapy Assistant, Pre-Professional Studies, Radiography. Professional programs are accredited by their respective accrediting bodies. The College provides state-of-the-art learning labs where students hone their skills before entering the clinical arena. Small class sizes allow instructors to know students on an individual basis. Graduates continue to outscore the national averages on licensure and credentialing examinations. Job outlook for careers in healthcare is excellent. College housing and financial aid is available for qualified students.

Florida State University
600 W College Ave, Tallahassee FL 32306-1096
Janice V. Finney, Director of Admissions
850-644-2525 Fax: 850-644-0197
Website: admissions.fsu.edu
E-mail: admissions@admin.fsu.edu

GALEN HEALTH INSTITUTES - SCHOOL OF NURSING
9549 Koger Boulevard North Suite 100
Saint Petersburg FL 33702-4372
727-577-1497 Fax: 727-576-4372
Website: www.galened.com
E-mail: dcole@galened.com

Galen Health Institute offers a full-time, two-year RN Program (one-year for licensed LPNs), a full-time, 12-month daytime LPN Program, and a part-time 18-month evening LPN Program. Programs are designed to prepare students to become registered nurses or licensed practical nurses who provide direct care to patients in a variety of settings. Programs include classroom lectures and activities, skills laboratory practice, and direct patient care experience in hospitals and other facilities (clinical rotations). For further information contact the Admissions Representative.

St. Thomas University
16401 NW 37th Ave, Miami Gardens FL 33054
Dr. John Abdirkin, Contact
800-367-9010 or 305-628-6546 Fax: 305-628-6591
Website: www.stu.edu
E-mail: signup@stu.edu

University of South Florida
4202 E Fowler Ave, Tampa FL 33620-6900
J. Robert Spatig, Director of Admissions
877-USF-BULL Fax: 813-974-9689
Website: www.usf.edu
E-mail: admissions@admin.usf.edu
See listing under "Universities"

GEORGIA

Armstrong Atlantic State University
11935 Abercorn St, Savannah GA 31419-1997
Kim West, Asst. Dean and Registrar Enrollment Services
912-927-5277 Fax: 912-921-5462
Website: www.armstrong.edu
E-mail: admissions@mail.armstrong.edu

Kennesaw State University
1000 Chastain Rd NW, Kennesaw GA 30144-5591
Richard Sowell, Dean of College of Health and Human Services
770-423-6565
Website: www.kennesaw.edu

North Georgia Technical College
434 Meeks Ave, Blairsville GA 30512-2983
Admissions
706-439-6300 Fax: 706-439-6301
Website: www.northgatech.edu
E-mail: info@northgatech.edu

North Georgia Technical College
Clarkesville Campus
PO Box 65, Clarkesville GA 30523-0002
Admissions
706-754-7700 Fax: 706-754-7777
Website: www.northgatech.edu
E-mail: info@northgatech.edu

North Metro Technical College
5198 Ross Rd SE, Acworth GA 30102-3129
Missy Cusack, Director of Admissions
770-975-4000 Fax: 770-975-4142
Website: www.northmetrotech.edu
E-mail: info@northmetrotech.edu

HAWAII

Kauai Community College
3-1901 Kaumualii Hwy, Lihue HI 96766-9500
808-245-8225 Fax: 808-245-8297
Website: kauai.hawaii.edu
E-mail: arkauai@hawaii.edu

IDAHO

Brigham Young University - Idaho
120 Kimball Bldg, Rexburg ID 83460-1615
Rob Garrett, Director of Admissions
208-496-1020 Fax: 208-496-1220
Website: www.byui.edu
E-mail: admissions@byui.edu

Lewis-Clark State College
500 8th Ave, Lewiston ID 83501-2698
Diane Douglas, Ph.D., Registrar/Director of Admissions
800-933-5272 Fax: 208-792-2429
Website: www.lcsc.edu
E-mail: admissions@lcsc.edu

ILLINOIS

Aurora University
347 S Gladstone Ave, Aurora IL 60506-4892
Carol R. Dunn, Ed.D., Vice President for Enrollment
800-742-5281 Fax: 630-844-5535
Website: www.aurora.edu
E-mail: admission@aurora.edu

Benedictine University
5700 College Rd, Lisle IL 60532-0900
630-829-6300 or 888-829-6363 Fax: 630-829-6301
Website: www.ben.edu
E-mail: admissions@ben.edu
See listing under "Universities"

BLESSING-RIEMAN COLLEGE OF NURSING
PO Box 7005, Quincy IL 62305-7005
Erin Flesner, Admission Counselor
Heather Mutter, Admission Counselor
217-228-5520 Fax: 217-223-4661
Website: www.brcn.edu
E-mail: admissions@brcn.edu

GRAHAM HOSPITAL
210 W Walnut St, Canton IL 61520-2497
Mary Kepple, Coordinator of Admissions, Recruitment
309-647-5240 ext. 2347 or 309-647-4086
Fax: 309-649-5127
Website: www.grahamschoolofnursing.org
E-mail: mkepple@grahamhospital.org

Kaskaskia College
27210 College Rd, Centralia IL 62801-7878
Tyra Taylor, Dean of Enrollment Management and Retention Services
618-545-3000 Fax: 618-532-1990
Website: www.kaskaskia.edu
E-mail: ttaylor@kaskaskia.edu

MENNONITE COLLEGE OF NURSING AT ILLINOIS STATE UNIVERSITY
PO Box 5810, Normal IL 61790-5810
Nancy Ridenour, Dean and Professor
309-438-7400 Fax: 309-438-2620
Website: www.mcn.ilstu.edu
E-mail: mcninfo@ilstu.edu

METHODIST COLLEGE OF NURSING
415 St Mark Ct, Peoria IL 61603
Mary Jane Dowling, Recruitment Coordinator
309-672-5566 Fax: 309-671-2752
Website: www.methodistcollegeofnursing.com
E-mail: mjdowling@mmci.org

ST. ANTHONY COLLEGE OF NURSING
5658 E State St, Rockford IL 61108-2468
Cheryl Delgado, Admission Representative
815-227-2141 Fax: 815-395-2275
Website: sacn.edu
E-mail: cheryldelgado@sacn.edu

SAINT FRANCIS MEDICAL CENTER COLLEGE OF NURSING
511 NE Greenleaf St, Peoria IL 61603-3744
Janice Farquharson, Director of Admissions/Registrar
309-655-2596 Fax: 309-624-8973
Website: www.sfmccon.edu
E-mail: janice.farquharson@osfhealthcare.org

Trinity College of Nursing & Health Sciences
2122 25th Ave, Rock Island IL 61201-5317
Joanne Cunningham, Director of Admissions
309-779-7700 Fax: 309-799-7748
Website: www.trinitycollegeqc.edu
E-mail: con@trinityqc.com

Triton College
2000 5th Ave, River Grove IL 60171-1995
Jeffery Cooks, Director, Admission Services
708-456-0300 ext. 3130 Fax: 708-583-3147
Website: www.triton.edu
E-mail: triton@triton.edu
See listing under "Community and Junior Colleges"

INDIANA

Ancilla Domini College
Donaldson IN 46513
Erin Alonzo, Director of Admissions
574-936-8898 Fax: 574-935-1773
Website: www.ancilla.edu
E-mail: erin.alonzo@ancilla.edu

BROWN MACKIE COLLEGE - FORT WAYNE
3000 E Coliseum Blvd, Fort Wayne IN 46805
Daniel Summer, Campus President
260-484-4400 Fax: 260-484-2678
Website: www.brownmackie.edu

BROWN MACKIE COLLEGE - SOUTH BEND
1030 E Jefferson Blvd, South Bend IN 46617-3123
Connie Adelman, Campus President
574-237-0774 Fax: 574-237-3585
Website: www.brownmackie.edu

Ivy Tech Community College - North Central
220 Dean Johnson Blvd, South Bend IN 46601-3415
Pam Decker, Director of Admissions
574-289-7001 Fax: 574-236-7177
Website: www.ivytech.edu
E-mail: pdecker@ivytech.edu

University of Evansville
1800 Lincoln Ave, Evansville IN 47722-0001
Don Vos, Dean of Admission
800-423-8633 Fax: 812-488-4076
Website: www.evansville.edu
E-mail: admission@evansville.edu

IOWA

Briar Cliff University
PO Box 2100, Sioux City IA 51104-0100
Sharisue Wilcoxon, VP for Enrollment Management
712-279-5200 Fax: 712-279-1632
Website: www.briarcliff.edu
E-mail: admissions@briarcliff.edu

Clarke College
1550 Clarke Dr, Dubuque IA 52001-3198
Andy Schroeder, Director of Admissions
800-383-2345 Fax: 563-584-8666
Website: www.clarke.edu
E-mail: andy.schroeder@clarke.edu

Graceland University
1 University Place, Lamoni IA 50140
Greg Sutherland, Interim Vice President for Enrollment and Dean of Admissions
641-784-5196 Fax: 641-784-5480
Website: www.admissions.graceland.edu
E-mail: admissions@graceland.edu

Hamilton College
7009 Nordic Dr, Cedar Falls IA 50613
Connie Reidy, Campus President
319-277-0220 Fax: 319-363-3812
Website: www.hamiltonia.edu
E-mail: coreidy@hamiltoncf.com

Hamilton College
3165 Edgewood Pkwy SW, Cedar Rapids IA 52404
Susan Spivey, Campus President
319-363-0481 Fax: 319-363-3812
Website: www.hamiltonia.edu
E-mail: sspivey@hamiltonia.edu

Hamilton College
2570 4th St SW, Mason City IA 50401-4665
Joe Albers, Executive Director
641-423-2530 Fax: 641-423-7512
Website: www.hamiltonia.edu
E-mail: jalbers@hamiltonia.edu

Hamilton College
4655 121st St, Urbandale IA 50323-2311
Colleen McDermott, Campus President
515-727-2100 Fax: 515-727-2115
Website: www.hamiltonia.edu
E-mail: cmcdermott@hamiltonia.edu

Iowa Lakes Community College
3200 College Dr, Emmetsburg IA 50536-1055
Anne Stansbury, Asst. Director of Admissions
712-852-5212 Fax: 712-362-8363
Website: www.iowalakes.edu
E-mail: info@iowalakes.edu

Iowa Lakes Community College
1900 Grand Ave, Suite 8, Spencer IA 51301
Anne Stansbury, Assistant Director of Admissions
712-262-7141 Fax: 712-262-4047
Website: www.iowalakes.edu
E-mail: info@iowalakes.edu

Northwest Iowa Community College
603 W Park St, Sheldon IA 51201-1046
Lisa Story, Director of Enrollment Management
712-324-5061 Fax: 712-324-4136
Website: www.nwicc.edu
E-mail: lstory@nwicc.edu

KANSAS

COLBY COMMUNITY COLLEGE
1255 S Range Ave, Colby KS 67701-4099
Director of Admissions
888-634-9350 or 785-460-4690 Fax: 785-460-4691
Website: www.colbycc.edu
E-mail: admissions@colbycc.edu

Flint Hills Technical College
3301 W 18th Ave, Emporia KS 66801-5957
Lisa Kirmer, Dean of Student Services
620-343-4600 Fax: 620-343-4610
Website: www.fhtc.net
E-mail: lkirmer@fhtc.net

Independence Community College
PO Box 708, Independence KS 67301-0708
Dr. Terry Hetrick, President
800-842-6063 Fax: 620-331-5344
Website: www.indycc.edu
E-mail: admissions@indycc.edu

Johnson County Community College
12345 College Blvd, Overland Park KS 66210-1299
913-469-3803 Fax: 913-469-2524
Website: www.jccc.edu
E-mail: jcccadmissions@jccc.edu

Labette Community College
200 S 14th St, Parsons KS 67357-9966
Tammy Fuentez, Director of Admissions
620-421-6700 Fax: 620-421-2309
Website: www.labette.edu
E-mail: tammyf@labette.edu

KENTUCKY

Bluegrass Community and Technical College
Oswald Building
470 Cooper Drive, Lexington KY 40506-0235
Shelbie Hugle, Director of Admissions
859-246-6200 Fax: 859-246-4664
Website: www.bluegrass.kctcs.edu
E-mail: bctc_info@kctcs.edu

BROWN MACKIE COLLEGE
Northern Kentucky Campus
309 Buttermilk Pike, Fort Mitchell KY 41017-2191
Joanne Dellefield, Director of Admissions
859-341-5627 Fax: 859-341-6483
Website: www.brownmackie.edu
E-mail: jdellefield@brownmackie.edu

FRONTIER SCHOOL OF MIDWIFERY & FAMILY NURSING
PO Box 528, Hyden KY 41749
Sherri Davis, Registrar
606-672-2312 Fax: 606-672-3776
Website: www.frontierschool.edu
E-mail: sherri.davis@midwives.org

GALEN COLLEGE OF NURSING
1031 Zorn Ave Ste 400, Louisville KY 40207
502-582-2305 Fax: 502-581-0425
Website: www.galencollege.edu
E-mail: mclaypoole@galened.com

Galen College of Nursing offers a full-time, two-year RN Program (one-year for licensed LPN's), a full-time, 12-month daytime LPN Program, and a part-time 18-month evening LPN Program. Programs are designed to prepare students to become registered nurses or licensed practical nurses who provide direct care to patients in a variety of settings. Programs include classroom lectures and activities, skills laboratory practice, and direct patient care experience in hospitals and other facilities (clinical rotations). For further information contact the Admissions Representative.

Morehead State University
Morehead KY 40351-1689
Jeffrey Liles, Enrollment Services
800-585-6781 Fax: 606-783-5038
Website: www.moreheadstate.edu
E-mail: admissions@moreheadstate.edu

LOUISIANA

Louisiana State University at Alexandria
8100 Highway 71 S, Alexandria LA 71302-9121
Dr. Thomas Armstrong, Director of Admissions
318-445-3672 Fax: 318-473-6418
Website: www.lsua.edu

Louisiana State University at Eunice
PO Box 1129, Eunice LA 70535-1129
Ron Ryder, Registrar
337-457-7311 Fax: 337-550-1306
Website: www.lsue.edu
E-mail: rryder@lsue.edu

Louisiana Technical College
Florida Parishes Campus
PO Box 1300, Greensburg LA 70441
225-222-4251 Fax: 225-222-6064
Website: www.ltc.edu./region.html

Our Lady of Holy Cross College
4123 Woodland Dr, New Orleans LA 70131-7399
Office of Enrollment Services
504-394-7744 Fax: 504-391-2421
Website: www.olhcc.edu

MAINE

HUSSON COLLEGE
Eastern Maine Medical Center
One College Cir, Bangor ME 04401-2999
Jane Goodwin, Director of Admissions
800-4HU-SSON or 207-941-7100 Fax: 207-941-7935
Website: www.husson.edu
E-mail: admit@husson.edu
See listing under "Universities"

St. Joseph's College of Maine
278 Whites Bridge Rd, Standish ME 04084-5263
Vincent Kloskowski, Dean of Admissions
800-338-7057 Fax: 207-893-7862
Website: www.sjcme.edu
E-mail: admission@sjcme.edu

Southern Maine Community College
2 Fort Rd, South Portland ME 04106-1698
Dr. James Ortiz, President
Scott MacDonald, Director of Financial Aid
207-741-5500 Fax: 207-741-5671
Website: www.smccme.edu
E-mail: oharmon@maine.rr.com

MARYLAND

Cecil College
One Seahawk Dr, North East MD 21901
Sandra S. Rajaski, Registrar & Director of Admissions
410-287-1000 Fax: 410-287-1001
Website: www.cecil.edu
E-mail: srajaski@cecil.edu

Hagerstown Community College
11400 Robinwood Dr, Hagerstown MD 21742-6590
Dr. Daniel E. Bock, Assistant Director of Admissions
301-790-2800 Fax: 301-791-9165
Website: www.hagerstowncc.edu
E-mail: bockd@hagerstowncc.edu

MASSACHUSETTS

Anna Maria College
50 Sunset Ln, Paxton MA 01612
Timothy M. Donahue, Director of Recruitment and Admissions
508-849-3360 Fax: 508-849-3362
Website: www.annamaria.edu
E-mail: admissions@annamaria.edu

Becker College
Campuses in Worcester and Leicester, MA
61 Sever St, Worcester MA 01609-2165
Karen Schedin, Dean of Admissions
508-791-9241 Fax: 508-890-1500
Website: www.becker.edu
E-mail: admissions@becker.edu
See listing under "Universities"

Bristol Community College
777 Elsbree St, Fall River MA 02720-7395
Rodney S. Clark, Director of Admissions
508-678-2811 ext. 2516, 2179 Fax: 508-730-3265
Website: www.bristol.mass.edu
E-mail: admissions@bristol.mass.edu

LAWRENCE MEMORIAL/REGIS COLLEGE NURSING AND RADIOGRAPHY PROGRAMS
170 Governors Ave, Medford MA 02155-1643
Admissions Coordinator
781-306-6600 Fax: 781-306-6142
Website: www.lmregis.org
E-mail: admissions@lmregis.org

North Shore Community College
1 Ferncroft Rd, Danvers MA 01923-4093
Jennifer Kirk, Director of Admissions & Recruitment Outreach
978-762-4000 Fax: 978-762-4015
Website: www.northshore.edu
E-mail: jkirk@northshore.edu

Southeastern Technical Institute
250 Foundry St, South Easton MA 02375-1780
Beverly A. Pusateri, Director
508-238-1860 Fax: 508-230-1558
Website: ti.sersd.org
E-mail: bpusateri@sersd.org

University of Massachusetts Dartmouth
Old Westport Rd, North Dartmouth MA 02747-2300
Steven T. Briggs, Director of Admissions
508-999-8605 Fax: 508-999-8755
Website: explore.umassd.edu
E-mail: sbriggs@umassd.edu

MICHIGAN

Delta College
University Center MI 48710-0001
Duff Zube, Director of Admissions
989-686-9093 Fax: 989-667-2202
Website: www.delta.edu
E-mail: admit@delta.edu

Grand Valley State University
1 Campus Dr, Allendale MI 49401-9403
Jodi Chycinski, Director of Admissions
616-331-6611 Fax: 616-331-2000
Website: www.gvsu.edu
E-mail: go2gvsu@gvsu.edu

Lake Superior State University
650 W Easterday Ave
Sault Sainte Marie MI 49783-1637
Susan Camp, Director of Admissions
888-800-LSSU Fax: 906-635-6696
Website: www.lssu.edu
E-mail: admissions@lssu.edu
See listing under "Universities"

MACOMB COMMUNITY COLLEGE
44575 Garfield Rd, Clinton Township MI 48038-1139
Information Center
586-445-7999
Website: www.macomb.edu
E-mail: answer@macomb.edu

Northwestern Michigan College
1701 E Front St, Traverse City MI 49686-3061
Jim Bensley, Director of Admissions
800-748-0566 Fax: 231-995-1339
Website: www.nmc.edu
E-mail: jbensley@nmc.edu

Oakland University
2200 N Squirrel Rd, Rochester MI 48309
Eleanor L. Reynolds, Assistant Vice President & Director of Admissions
248-370-2100
Website: www.oakland.edu
E-mail: ouinfo@oakland.edu

MINNESOTA

Crown College
8700 College View Dr, Saint Bonifacius MN 55375
Mitch Fisk, Director of Admissions
952-446-4142 Fax: 952-446-4149
Website: www.crown.edu
E-mail: johnsonj@crown.edu

Hibbing Community College
1515 E 25th St, Hibbing MN 55746-3300
Holly Bigelow, Director of Enrollment
800-224-4HCC or 218-262-7200 Fax: 218-262-6717
Website: www.hibbing.edu
E-mail: admissions@hibbing.edu

Inver Hills Community College
2500 80th St E, Inver Grove Heights MN 55076
651-450-8500 Fax: 651-450-8679
Website: www.inverhills.edu

Metropolitan State University
700 7th St E, Saint Paul MN 55106-5000
Monir Johnson, Director of Admissions
651-793-1300 Fax: 651-793-1546
Website: www.metrostate.edu
E-mail: monir.johnson@metrostate.edu

Minnesota State College - Southeast Technical
Red Wing Campus
308 Pioneer Rd, Red Wing MN 55066
Al DuCett, Director of Admissions
877-853-8324 Fax: 507-453-2715
Website: www.southeastmn.edu
E-mail: aducett@southeastmn.edu
70+ degrees, diplomas & certificates (15+ online) in Business & Office Careers, Musical Instrument Repair, Physical Health, Transportation, Technology, and Trades.

Minnesota State College - Southeast Technical
Winona Campus
PO Box 409, 1250 Homer Rd, Winona MN 55987
Al DuCett, Director of Admissions
877-853-8324 Fax: 507-453-2715
Website: www.southeastmn.edu
E-mail: aducett@southeastmn.edu
70+ degrees, diplomas & certificates (15+ online) in Business & Office Careers, Musical Instrument Repair, Physical Health, Transportation, Technology, and Trades.

Minnesota State University Moorhead
1104 7th Ave S, Moorhead MN 56563-0002
Regina Monson, Director of Admissions
218-477-2161 Fax: 218-477-4374
Website: go.mnstate.edu
E-mail: dragon@mnstate.edu

Northland Community and Technical College
2022 Central Ave NE
East Grand Forks MN 56721-2702
Barb Forrest, Nursing Program Director
800-451-3441 Fax: 218-773-4502
Website: www.northlandcollege.edu
E-mail: admissions@northlandcollege.edu

Ridgewater College-Hutchinson Campus
2 Century Ave SE, Hutchinson MN 55350-3100
Dawn Bjork, Counselor
800-722-1151 Fax: 320-234-8506
Website: www.ridgewater.edu
E-mail: dawn.bjork@ridgewater.edu

Ridgewater College-Willmar Campus
PO Box 1097, Willmar MN 56201-1097
Sally Kerfeld, Director of Admissions
800-722-1151 Fax: 320-222-5212
Website: www.ridgewater.edu
E-mail: sally.kerfeld@ridgewater.edu

St. Cloud Technical College
1540 Northway Dr, Saint Cloud MN 56303-1240
Jodi Elness, Director of Enrollment Management
800-222-1009 Fax: 320-308-5981
Website: www.sctc.edu
E-mail: jelness@sctc.edu

University of Minnesota
2900 University Ave, Crookston MN 56716-5001
218-281-6510 Fax: 218-281-8575
Website:
admissions.umcrookston.edu/requirements/apply.htm
E-mail: info@umcrookston.edu

MISSOURI

BARNES-JEWISH COLLEGE OF NURSING
306 S Kingshighway Blvd
Saint Louis MO 63110-1091
Karen Sartorius, Admissions
800-832-9009 Fax: 314-454-7057
Website: www.barnesjewishcollege.edu
E-mail: bjc-admissions@bjc.org

Central Methodist University
411 Central Methodist Sq, Fayette MO 65248-1198
Larry Anderson, Director of Admissions
660-248-6247 Fax: 660-248-1872
Website: www.centralmethodist.edu
E-mail: landerso@centralmethodist.edu

GRACELAND UNIVERSITY
1401 W Truman Rd, Independence MO 64050
Patricia K. Trachsel, Dean of Independence Campus
816-833-0524 Fax: 816-833-2990
Website: www.graceland.edu
E-mail: trachsel@graceland.edu

St. Charles Community College
4601 Mid Rivers Mall Dr, Cottleville MO 63376
Kathy Brockgreitens-Gober, Director of Admissions
636-922-8000 Fax: 636-922-8236
Website: www.stchas.edu
E-mail: adm-reg@stchas.edu

Truman State University
100 E Normal, Kirksville MO 63501
Office of Admission
660-785-4114 Fax: 660-785-7456
Website: admissions.truman.edu
E-mail: admissions@truman.edu

University of Missouri
1 University Blvd, Saint Louis MO 63121-4499
314-516-6066 Fax: 314-516-6730
Website: www.umsl.edu
E-mail: admissions@umsl.edu

Webster University
470 E Lockwood Ave, Saint Louis MO 63119-3194
Anne Schappe, Chairperson
314-968-7488 Fax: 314-963-6101
Website: www.webster.edu
E-mail: schappan@webster.edu
See listing under "Universities"

William Jewell College
500 College Hill, Liberty MO 64068-1896
Dr. Rick Winslow, VP Enrollment Management and Student Affairs
800-753-7009 Fax: 816-415-5040
Website: www.jewell.edu
E-mail: winslowr@william.jewell.edu

MONTANA

Carroll College
1601 N Benton Ave, Helena MT 59625-0002
Dr. Thomas J. Trebon, President
Cynthia Thornquist, Director of Admissions & Enrollment Operations
406-447-4384 Fax: 406-447-4533
Website: www.carroll.edu
E-mail: admission@carroll.edu

NEBRASKA

Central Community College-Grand Island Campus
PO Box 4903, Grand Island NE 68802-4903
Liz Kohaut, Director of Admissions
308-398-4222 Fax: 308-398-7398
Website: www.cccneb.edu
E-mail: lkohout@cccneb.edu

Clarkson College
101 S 42nd St, Omaha NE 68131-2715
Sara Bonney, Director of Admissions
800-647-5500 Fax: 402-552-6057
Website: www.clarksoncollege.edu
E-mail: admiss@clarksoncollege.edu

Metropolitan Community College
PO Box 3777, Omaha NE 68103-0777
Becky Nicks, Director of Admissions
402-449-8400 Fax: 402-457-2616
Website: www.mccnab.edu
E-mail: bnicks@mccnab.edu

Nebraska Wesleyan University
5000 Saint Paul Ave, Lincoln NE 68504-2794
Patricia Karthauser, V.P. for University Enrollment
402-466-2371 Fax: 402-465-2177
Website: www.nebrwesleyan.edu
E-mail: admissions@nebrwesleyan.edu

University of Nebraska at Kearney
905 W 25th St, Kearney NE 68849-0001
Dusty Newton, Director of Admissions
800-KEARNEY Fax: 308-865-8987
Website: www.unk.edu
E-mail: admissionsug@unk.edu

NEVADA

Career College of Northern Nevada
1195-A Corporate Blvd, Reno NV 89502-2331
Nathan Clark, Director
775-856-2266 Fax: 775-856-0935
Website: www.ccnn.edu
E-mail: lgoldhammer@ccnn4u.com
See listing under "Career Schools"

GREAT BASIN COLLEGE
1500 College Pkwy, Elko NV 89801-5032
Julie G. Byrnes, Director of Enrollment Management
775-753-2271 Fax: 775-753-2311
Website: www.gbcnv.edu
E-mail: julieb@gwmail.gbcnv.edu
See listing under "Universities"

NEW HAMPSHIRE

New Hampshire Community Technical College
1066 Front St, Manchester NH 03102-8528
Jacquie Poirier, Director of Admissions
603-668-6706 Fax: 603-668-5354
Website: www.manchester.nhctc.edu
E-mail: jpoirier@nhctc.edu

NEW JERSEY

Atlantic Cape Community College
5100 Black Horse Pike
Mays Landing NJ 08330-2699
Linda McLeod, Assistant Director of College Recruitment
609-343-5000 Fax: 609-343-4921
Website: www.atlantic.edu
E-mail: accadmit@atlantic.edu
See listing under "Community and Junior Colleges"

Bergen Community College
400 Paramus Rd, Paramus NJ 07652
Julian Gomez, Asst. Director of Admissions
201-447-7100 Fax: 201-444-7036
Website: www.bergen.edu
E-mail: jgomez@bergen.edu

HOLY NAME HOSPITAL SCHOOL OF NURSING
690 Teaneck Rd, Teaneck NJ 07666-4254
Maureen Schmude, Registrar
201-833-3005 Fax: 201-833-7209
Website: www.schoolofnursing.info
E-mail: sr-tynan@mail.holyname.org

Mercer County Community College
West Windsor Campus
PO Box B, Trenton NJ 08690
Savita Bambhrolia, Director of Admissions
609-586-4800 Fax: 609-587-4666
Website: www.mccc.edu
E-mail: admiss@mccc.edu

MUHLENBERG REGIONAL MEDICAL CENTER
Harold B. & Dorothy A. Snyder Schools of Nursing, Medical Imaging & Therapeutic Sciences
Plainfield, NJ 07061
Jane Vatsky, Director of Admissions
908-668-2400 Fax: 908-226-4640
Website: www.muhlenbergschools.org
E-mail: ssonmits@solarishs.org

Established 1894. Private. Coed. Accreditation: SON - N.J. Board of Nursing, NLN; SOR - JRCRT, NJDEP; SONMT - JRCNMT, NJDEP, SORT-JRCRT, NJRT Bd of Examiner, NJDEP, SODMS-CAAHEP. Total cost of entire program (average by school) SON - $26,004; SOR - $27,997; SONMT - $13,442; SORT - $12,308; SODMS - $18,929. Federal, state and institutional financial aid available. Residence $955/semester. Enrollment: 500. Student-faculty ratio: 10:1. Degrees: AS and Diploma. Cooperative program with Union County College, Cranford, N.J. Associate in Science degree awarded from UCC and diploma from Muhlenberg Harold B. & Dorothy A. Snyder Schools. Professional programs offered: Registered Nursing, Radiography, Nuclear Medicine Technology, Radiation Therapy, and Diagnostic Medical Sonography. Articulated with four year colleges and universities for baccalaureate degree.

New Jersey City University
2039 John F Kennedy Blvd
Jersey City NJ 07305-1588
Carmen Panlilio, Asst. V.P. for Admissions and Financial Aid
201-200-3234 Fax: 201-200-2044
Website: www.njcu.edu
E-mail: admissions@njcu.edu

OUR LADY OF LOURDES SCHOOL OF NURSING
1600 Haddon Ave, Camden NJ 08103
Marie Cebollero, Contact
856-757-3726 Fax: 856-757-3767
Website: www.ololnursing.com
E-mail: cebollerom@lourdesnet.org

Ramapo College of New Jersey
505 Ramapo Valley Rd, Mahwah NJ 07430-1623
Director of Admissions
201-684-7300 or 201-684-7301 Fax: 201-684-7964
Website: www.ramapo.edu
E-mail: admissions@ramapo.edu

RICHARD STOCKTON COLLEGE OF NEW JERSEY
PO Box 195, Pomona NJ 08240
John Iacovelli, Dean of Enrollment Management
866-RSC-2885 Fax: 609-626-5541
Website: www.stockton.edu
E-mail: admissions@stockton.edu

Stockton College is a comprehensive liberal arts, coed institution founded in 1969. Advance Pre-Professional Degree Options: 7-yr BS/MD with UMDNJ; NJ Dental School; NJ Medical School, Robert Wood Johnson Medical, School of Osteopathic Medicine; NY College of Podiatric Medicine, Pennsylvania College of Podiatric Medicine, SUNY College of Optometry. Pharmacy doctorate program with Rutgers University. 5-yr Engineering with NJIT and Rutgers University. Dual BA/MA in Criminal Justice. 5-yr BS/MS in Computational Science. BS/MS in Nursing. Doctorate of Physical Therapy. Additional Programs: Forensic Science, Pre-Law, Pre-Occupational Therapy, and Pre-Veterinary.

NEW YORK

ARNOT OGDEN MEDICAL CENTER SCHOOL OF NURSING
600 Roe Ave, Elmira NY 14905-1676
Linda MacAuslan, Director
607-737-4153 Fax: 607-737-4116
Website: www.arnothealth.org
E-mail: lmacauslan@aomc.org

Broome Community College
907 Upper Front St, Binghamton NY 13905
Anthony S. Fiorelli, Director of Admissions
607-778-5001 Fax: 607-778-5442
Website: www.sunybroome.edu
E-mail: fiorelli_a@sunybroome.edu

COCHRAN SCHOOL OF NURSING
967 N Broadway, Yonkers NY 10701-1301
Paulette McLean, Admissions Coordinator
914-964-4296 Fax: 914-964-4796
Website: www.cochranschoolofnursing.us
E-mail: admissions@cochranschoolofnursing.us

CROUSE HOSPITAL SCHOOL OF NURSING
736 Irving Ave, Syracuse NY 13210-1687
Amy Graham, Contact
315-470-7858 Fax: 315-470-5774
Website: www.crouse.org/nursing
E-mail: amygraham@crouse.org

Established 1913. Private, nonprofit. Coed. Accreditation (registration): National League for Nursing. Tuition: $7,352 per year. Room: $3,500. Enrollment: 290. Faculty: 30 full and part-time. Degrees: Accredited Associate degree program. Close to Syracuse University and SUNY Upstate Medical University. Students use facilities at SUNY Upstate Medical University for gym, pool, tennis & squash courts. NY State & Federal Financial Aid, Scholarships and Loans available for eligible students.

CUNY Hunter College
695 Park Ave, New York NY 10021
Aaron Gibbs, Assistant Director of Recruitment
212-650-3946 Fax: 212-650-3336
Website: www.hunter.cuny.edu
E-mail: aaron.gibbs@hunter.cuny.edu

Daemen College
4380 Main St, Amherst NY 14226-3592
Donna Shaffner, Director of Admissions
800-462-7652 Fax: 716-839-8229
Website: www.daemen.edu/admissions
E-mail: admissions@daemen.edu

Long Island University-C. W. Post Campus
720 Northern Blvd, Brookville NY 11548-1300
Joanne Graziano, Executive Director of Admissions
516-299-2900 Fax: 516-299-2137
Website: www.liu.edu/cwpost
E-mail: enroll@cwpost.liu.edu

Molloy College
1000 Hempstead Ave
Rockville Centre NY 11570-1100
Marguerite Lane, Director of Admissions
516-678-5000 ext. 6291 Fax: 516-256-2247
Website: www.molloy.edu
E-mail: admissions@molloy.edu
See listing under "Universities"

Monroe College
2501 Jerome Ave, Bronx NY 10468-4305
Evan Jerome, Director of Admissions
718-933-6700 Fax: 718-364-3552
Website: www.monroecollege.edu
E-mail: ejerome@monroecollege.edu

Roberts Wesleyan College
2301 Westside Dr, Rochester NY 14624-1997
Office of Admissions
585-594-6400 Fax: 585-594-6371
Website: www.roberts.edu
E-mail: admissions@roberts.edu

St. Joseph's College
245 Clinton Ave, Brooklyn NY 11205-3688
Theresa LaRocca Meyer, V.P. for Enrollment Management
718-636-6800 Fax: 718-636-8303
Website: www.sjcny.edu
E-mail: tlaroccameyer@sjcny.edu

ST. JOSEPH'S COLLEGE OF NURSING AT SJHHC
206 Prospect Ave, Syracuse NY 13203-1806
Rhonda Reader, Assistant Dean for Admissions
315-448-5040 Fax: 315-448-5745
Website: www.sjhsyr.org/nursing
E-mail: collegeofnursing@sjhsyr.org

SUNY College at Brockport
350 New Campus Dr, Brockport NY 14420-2997
Bernard S. Valento, Director of Undergraduate Admissions
585-395-2751 Fax: 585-395-5452
Website: www.brockport.edu
E-mail: admit@brockport.edu

SUNY College of Technology
Alfred NY 14802
Deborah J. Goodrich, Associate VP Enrollment Mgmt.
800-4AL-FRED Fax: 607-587-4299
Website: www.alfredstate.edu
E-mail: admissions@alfredstate.edu

SUNY Niagara County Community College
3111 Saunders Settlement Rd
Sanborn NY 14132-9487
Kathleen Saunders, Director of Admissions
716-614-6200 Fax: 716-614-6820
Website: www.niagaracc.suny.edu
E-mail: admissions@niagaracc.suny.edu

SUNY Orange County Community College
115 South St, Middletown NY 10940-6437
Margot St. Lawrence, Director of Admissions
845-341-4030 Fax: 845-342-8662
Website: www.sunyorange.edu
E-mail: apply@sunyorange.edu
See listing under "Community and Junior Colleges"

SUNY Sullivan County Community College
112 College Rd, Loch Sheldrake NY 12759-5151
Sari Rosenheck, Director of Admissions
845-434-5750 Fax: 845-434-0923
Website: www.sullivan.suny.edu
E-mail: admissions@sullivan.suny.edu
Student Housing on Campus.

NORTH CAROLINA

CABARRUS COLLEGE OF HEALTH SCIENCES
401 Medical Park Dr, Concord NC 28025
Mark Ellison, Director of Admissions
704-783-1556 Fax: 704-783-2077
Website: www.cabarruscollege.edu
E-mail: admissions@cabarruscollege.edu
See listing under "Universities"

Haywood Community College
185 Freedlander Dr, Clyde NC 28721
Debbie Rowland, Coordinator of Admissions
828-627-4500 Fax: 828-627-4513
Website: www.haywood.edu
E-mail: drowland@haywood.edu

James Sprunt Community College
PO Box 398, Kenansville NC 28349-0398
Lea Grady, Admissions
910-296-2500 Fax: 910-296-1636
Website: www.jamessprunt.edu

MERCY SCHOOL OF NURSING
701 B Forest Point Cir, Charlotte NC 28273
Pamela Hatley, RN, MSN, Student Services
704-512-2010 Fax: 704-512-2050
Website:
www.carolinashealthcare.org\education\mercyson
E-mail: phatley@carolinas.org

South Piedmont Community College
PO Box 126, Polkton NC 28135-0126
Joy Pope, Contact
704-272-5338
Website: www.spcc.edu
E-mail: jpope@spcc.edu

NORTH DAKOTA

Dickinson State University
Dickinson ND 58601-4896
Steve Glasser, Director of Enrollment Services
800-279-4295 Fax: 701-483-2409
Website: www.dickinsonstate.edu
E-mail: dsu.hawks@dickinsonstate.edu

Minot State University-Bottineau Campus
105 Simrall Blvd, Bottineau ND 58318-1159
Paula Berg, Associate Dean of Student Affairs
800-542-6866 Fax: 701-228-5499
Website: www.misu-b.nodak.edu
E-mail: paula.berg@misu.nodak.edu

Williston State College
PO Box 1326, Williston ND 58802-1326
Penny Soiseth, Associate Director Enrollment Services
701-774-4200 Fax: 701-774-4544
Website: www.wsc.nodak.edu
E-mail: penny.soiseth@wsc.nodak.edu

OHIO

Brown Mackie College - Cincinnati
1011 Glendale Milford Rd, Cincinnati OH 45215-1107
Robin Krout, President
513-771-2424 Fax: 513-771-3413
Website: www.brownmackie.edu
E-mail: rkrout@brownmackie.edu

Cleveland State University
2121 Euclid Ave RW 204, Cleveland OH 44115
Dr. Richard Arndt, Dean of Undergraduate Recruitment and College Partnerships
888-CSU-OHIO Fax: 216-687-9210
Website: www.csuohio.edu
E-mail: admissions@csuohio.edu

COMMUNITY HOSPITAL SCHOOL OF NURSING
2615 E High St, Springfield OH 45505-1494
Hedy Frick, Admissions
937-328-8905 Fax: 937-328-8668
Website: www.chsn.com
E-mail: succeed@chsn.com

FIRELANDS REGIONAL MEDICAL CENTER SCHOOL OF NURSING
1912 Hayes Ave, Sandusky OH 44870-4788
Holly J. Price, RN, Director
419-557-7111 Fax: 419-557-7116
Website: www.firelands.com
E-mail: priceh@firelands.com

Franciscan University of Steubenville
University Blvd, Steubenville OH 43952
Margaret J. Weber, Director of Admissions
800-783-6220 or 740-283-6226 Fax: 740-284-5456
Website: www.admissions.edu
E-mail: mweber@franciscan.edu

GALEN COLLEGE OF NURSING
100 E-Business Way Ste 200, Cincinnati OH 45241
513-475-3600 Fax: 513-475-3601
Website: www.galencollege.edu
E-mail: wcappelano@galencollege.edu
Galen College of Nursing offers a full-time, 21-month RN program (as little as one year for licensed LPNs) and a full-time, 12-month LPN program. Programs are designed to prepare students to become registered nurses or licensed practical nurses who provide direct care to patients in a variety of settings. Programs include classroom lectures and activities, clinical simulation laboratory practice and direct patient care experience in hospitals and other facilities (clinical rotations). For futher information, contact the admissions representative.

∴ **HURON SCHOOL OF NURSING**
Cleveland Clinic
13951 Terrace Rd, East Cleveland OH 44112-4308
Barbara Szigeti, MA, Coordinator of Student Services
216-761-7996 Fax: 216-761-7541
Website: www.cchseast.org/schools
E-mail: bszigeti@cchseast.org

· Northwest State Community College
22600 State Route 34, Archbold OH 43502-9542
Mark Thompson, Director of Admissions
419-267-5511 Fax: 419-267-5587
Website: www.northweststate.edu
E-mail: mthompson@northweststate.edu

The Ohio State University
College of Nursing
Newton Hall, 1585 Neil Ave, Columbus OH 43210
614-292-4041 Fax: 614-292-9399
Website: nursing.osu.edu
E-mail: nursing@osu.edu

· Owens Community College
3200 Bright Rd, Findlay OH 45840
William J. Ivoska PhD., Vice President of Student Services
567-429-3500 Fax: 567-423-0246
Website: www.owens.edu
E-mail: admissions@owens.edu

· Owens Community College
PO Box 10000, Toledo OH 43699-1947
William J. Ivoska, Ph.D, Vice President of Student Services
567-661-7000 Fax: 567-661-7607
Website: www.owens.edu
E-mail: admissions@owens.edu

· Sinclair Community College
444 W 3rd St, Dayton OH 45402-1460
Director of Admissions
937-512-3000 Fax: 937-512-2393
Website: www.sinclair.edu
E-mail: admit@sinclair.edu

University of Toledo
College of Nursing
3000 Arlington Ave, Toledo OH 43614-2595
419-383-4000 Fax: 419-383-2800
Website: www.hsc.utoledo.edu
E-mail: admissions@meduohio.edu

Ursuline College
2550 Lander Rd, Cleveland OH 44124-4398
Sarah E. Sundermeier, Director of Admissions
888-URSULINE Toll Free Fax: 440-684-6138
Website: www.admission.ursuline.edu
E-mail: admission@ursuline.edu

OKLAHOMA

University of Tulsa
600 S College Ave, Tulsa OK 74104-3126
Earl Johnson, Dean of Admission
918-631-2307 Fax: 918-631-5003
Website: www.utulsa.edu
E-mail: admission@utulsa.edu

OREGON

Concordia University
2811 NE Holman St, Portland OR 97211-6099
Bobi Swan, Director of Admissions
503-288-9371 Fax: 503-280-8531
Website: www.cu-portland.edu
E-mail: cu-admissions@cu-portland.edu

· Rogue Community College
3345 Redwood Hwy, Grants Pass OR 97527-9298
Claudia Sullivan, Director of Enrollment Services
541-956-7500 Fax: 541-471-3585
Website: www.roguecc.edu
E-mail: csullivan@roguecc.edu
See listing under "Community and Junior Colleges"

University of Portland
5000 N Willamette Blvd, Portland OR 97203-5798
Jason McDonald, Dean of Admissions
503-943-7911 Fax: 503-943-7315
Website: www.up.edu
E-mail: mcdonaja@up.edu

PENNSYLVANIA

· Community College of Allegheny County
Allegheny Campus: 808 Ridge Ave, Pittsburgh PA 15212 Admissions: 412.237.2700
Boyce Campus: 595 Beatty Rd, Monroeville PA 15146 Admissions: 724.325.6614
North Campus: 8701 Perry Highway, Pittsburgh PA 15237 Admissions: 412.369.3600
South Campus: 1750 Clairton Rd, West Mifflin PA 15122 Admissions: 412-469-4301
Website: www.ccac.edu

· Community College of Beaver County
1 Campus Dr, Monaca PA 15061-2566
724-775-8561 Fax: 724-775-4687
Website: www.ccbc.edu
E-mail: admissions@ccbc.edu

∴ **CONEMAUGH VALLEY MEMORIAL HOSPITAL**
School of Nursing
1086 Franklin St, Johnstown PA 15905-4398
Louise Pugliese, Director
814-534-9844 Fax: 814-534-3354
Website: www.conemaugh.org
E-mail: lpuglie@conemaugh.org
Two year program. Fully accredited. Excellent success of first time candidates taking licensure exam. Over 1,000 hours of clinical experience in a trauma medical center and community outreach services. Articulation agreement with University of Pittsburgh and Mount Aloysius College. BSN degree can be completed in 1-1/2 - 2 years. Approximately one-quarter of enrollment are men. Scholarship and financial aid available.

DeSales University
2755 Station Ave, Center Valley PA 18034-9565
610-282-1100 Fax: 610-282-2342
Website: www.desales.edu

Holy Family University
9801 Frankford Avenue, Philadelphia PA 19114
Lauren Campbell, Director of Admissions
215-637-3050 Fax: 215-281-1022
Website: www.holyfamily.edu
E-mail: admissions@holyfamily.edu

∴ **JAMESON MEMORIAL HOSPITAL SCHOOL OF NURSING**
1211 Wilmington Ave, New Castle PA 16105-2595
Jayne Sheehan, RN, MSN, CRNP, Director of Professional and Allied Health Education
724-656-4052 Fax: 724-656-4179
Website: www.jamesonhealthsystem.com
E-mail: lsoukovich@jamesonhealthsystem.com
Private. Coed. Accreditation: National League for Nursing Accrediting Commission, PA State Board of Nursing. Average tuition/year: $10,304. Average fees/year: $882 (PSU & JMH). Student-faculty ratio: 10-8:1. Diploma offered. Two year program with summers off. Clinical experience early in the program. Highly-skilled professional and caring faculty. Affiliated with Penn State University with college credits transferable to all colleges and universities. Most clinical experiences within Lawrence County. Approved for Veteran's Education.

Juniata College
1700 Moore St, Huntingdon PA 16652-2196
Michelle Bartol, Dean of Enrollment
877-JUNIATA Fax: 814-641-3100
Website: www.juniata.edu
E-mail: admissions@juniata.edu

∴ Lancaster General College of Nursing and Health Sciences
410 N Lime St, Lancaster PA 17602-2337
Elma Hess, Director of Admissions
717-544-4902 Fax: 717-544-5970
Website: www.lancastergeneralcollege.org
E-mail: elhess@lancastergeneral.org

∴ **MERCY HOSPITAL SCHOOL OF NURSING**
1401 Boulevard of the Allies
Pittsburgh PA 15219-5107
Joanne Sperry, RN, MN Director
412-232-7940 Fax: 412-232-7951
Website: www.pmhs.org/son
E-mail: jsperry@mercy.pmhs.org

MOUNT ALOYSIUS COLLEGE
7373 Admiral Peary Hwy, Cresson PA 16630-1999
Frank C. Crouse Jr., Vice President for Enrollment Management
814-886-6383 or 888-823-2220 Fax: 814-886-6441
Website: www.mtaloy.edu
E-mail: admissions@mtaloy.edu

Neumann College
1 Neumann Dr, Aston PA 19014-1298
Dennis Murphy, Director of Admissions
610-459-0905 Fax: 610-558-5652
Website: www.neumann.edu
E-mail: neumann@neumann.edu

∴ **POTTSVILLE HOSPITAL SCHOOL OF NURSING**
420 S Jackson St, Pottsville PA 17901-3625
Angela Pasco, RN, MSN, Director
570-621-5027 Fax: 570-621-5113
Website: www.pottsvillehospitalschoolofnursing.com
E-mail: phson@pothosp.com

∴ **ST. MARGARET SCHOOL OF NURSING**
221 Seventh St Suite 100, Pittsburgh PA 15238
Ann D. Ciak, Director
412-784-4980 Fax: 412-784-4994
Website: www.upmc.edu/StMargaret/SchofNursing
E-mail: smhsonrninfo@upmc.edu

∴ **WESTERN PENNSYLVANIA HOSPITAL SCHOOL OF NURSING**
4900 Friendship Ave, Pittsburgh PA 15224-1724
Joan Brooks, Recruiter
412-578-5538 Fax: 412-578-1837
Website: www.wpahs.org/education
E-mail: sonadmissions@wpahs.org

Widener University
1 University Pl, Chester PA 19013-5792
Edwin Wright, Dean of Admissions
610-499-4000 Fax: 610-499-4676
Website: www.widener.edu
E-mail: admissions.office@widener.edu

SOUTH CAROLINA

Bob Jones University
1700 Wade Hampton Blvd
Greenville SC 29614-0001
Kathleen Crispin, Director
800-BJ-AND-ME
Website: www.bju.edu
E-mail: admissions@bju.edu
See listing under "Universities"

Columbia International University
PO Box 3122, Columbia SC 29230-3122
Michelle MacGregor, Director of University Admissions
800-777-2227 Fax: 803-786-4209
Website: www.ciu.edu
E-mail: yesciu@ciu.edu
See listing under "Theological Studies & Religious Vocations"

· Greenville Technical College
PO Box 5616, Greenville SC 29606-5616
Carolyn Watkins, Dean of Admissions
800-723-0673 (US) or 800-922-1183 (SC)
Website: www.greenvilletech.com

University of South Carolina - Upstate
800 University Way, Spartanburg SC 29303-4932
Donette Stewart, Assistant VC for Enrollment Services
864-503-5246 Fax: 864-503-5727
Website: www.uscupstate.edu
E-mail: dstewart@uscupstate.edu
See listing under "Universities"

SOUTH DAKOTA

Presentation College
1500 N Main St, Aberdeen SD 57401-1280
JoEllen Lindner, VP for Enrollment
605-229-8492 Fax: 605-229-8425
Website: www.presentation.edu
E-mail: admit@presentation.edu

· Western Dakota Technical Institute
800 Mickelson Dr, Rapid City SD 57703-4018
Jill Elder, Admissions Coordinator
605-394-4034 Fax: 605-394-2204
Website: www.wdt.edu
E-mail: jill.elder@wdt.edu

TENNESSEE

Aquinas College
4210 Harding Rd, Nashville TN 37205
Diane C. LeJeune, Director of Admissions
615-297-7545 ext. 460 Fax: 615-279-3893
Website: www.aquinascollege.edu
E-mail: lejeuned@aquinascollege.edu

Austin Peay State University
601 College St, Clarksville TN 37044-0002
931-221-7011 Fax: 931-221-6168
Website: www.apsu.edu
E-mail: admissions@apsu.edu

Lipscomb University
3901 Granny White Pike, Nashville TN 37204-3951
Ricky Holaway, Director of Admissions
800-333-4358 ext. 1776 Fax: 615-269-1804
Website: www.lipscomb.edu
E-mail: admissions@lipscomb.edu

· Southwest Tennessee Community College
5983 Macon Cove, Memphis TN 38134
Vanessa R. Dowdy, Director of Admissions
901-333-5000 Fax: 901-333-4523
Website: www.southwest.tn.edu
E-mail: vdowdy@southwest.tn.edu

Tennessee State University
3500 John A Merritt Blvd, Nashville TN 37209-1561
John Cade, Dean of Admissions & Records
615-963-5101 Fax: 615-963-2930
Website: www.tnstate.edu
E-mail: jcade@tnstate.edu

University of Tennessee
615 McCallie Ave, Chattanooga TN 37403-2504
Yancy Freeman, Director of Admissions
423-425-4111 Fax: 423-425-4157
Website: www.utc.edu
E-mail: Yancy-Freeman@utc.edu

TEXAS

Abilene Christian University
ACU Box 29000, Abilene TX 79699-0001
325-674-2000 Fax: 325-674-2202
Website: www.acu.edu
E-mail: info@admissions.acu.edu

: American Commercial College
2007 34th St, Lubbock TX 79411-1899
Michael Otto, Director
806-747-4339 Fax: 806-765-9838
Website: www.acc-careers.com
E-mail: mjotto@acc-careers.com

: **GALEN HEALTH INSTITUTE SCHOOL OF NURSING**
4440 S Piedras Dr Suite 200, San Antonio TX 78228
210-733-3056 Fax: 210-733-5223
Website: www.galened.com
E-mail: emayo@galened.com
Galen Health Institute offers a full-time 12 month LVN Program. The program is designed to prepare students to become licensed vocational nurses who provide direct care to patients in a variety of settings. Programs include classroom lectures and activities, skills laboratory practice, and direct patient care experience in hospitals and other facilities (clinical rotations). For futher information contact the Admissions Representative.

· Galveston College
4015 Avenue Q, Galveston TX 77550-7496
Brian Lowery, Registrar
409-763-6551 Fax: 409-944-1501
Website: www.gc.edu
E-mail: blowery@gc.edu

Lubbock Christian University
5601 19th St, Lubbock TX 79407-2099
Stan Scott, Director of Admissions
806-796-8800 Fax: 806-720-7162
Website: www.lcu.edu
E-mail: stan.scott@lcu.edu

McLennan Community College
1400 College Dr, Waco TX 76708-1498
Dr. Cherry Beckworth, Program Director, Nursing
254-299-8000 Fax: 254-299-8854
Website: www.mclennan.edu
E-mail: cbeckworth@mclennan.edu

Prairie View A&M University
College of Nursing
6436 Fannin St, Houston TX 77030-1519
Veronica Anderson, Director of Admissions
713-797-7000 Fax: 713-797-7092
Website: www.pvamu.edu
E-mail: vfanderson@pvamu.edu

Temple College
2600 S 1st St, Temple TX 76504-7435
Toni Borras, Director of Admissions & Records
254-298-8808 Fax: 254-298-8288
Website: www.templejc.edu
E-mail: admissionsrecords@templejc.edu

Texas Woman's University
PO Box 425589, Denton TX 76204-5589
Erma Nieto-Brecht, Director of Admissions
866-809-6130 Fax: 940-898-3081
Website: www.twu.edu
E-mail: admissions@twu.edu

University of Texas at Arlington
Box 19111, Arlington TX 76019-0111
Hans Gatterdam, Director of Admission
817-272-6287 Fax: 817-272-3435
Website: www.uta.edu
E-mail: admissions@uta.edu

UNIVERSITY OF TEXAS-HOUSTON
6901 Bertner Ave, Houston TX 77030-3901
William D. Stewart, Coordinator of Admissions
713-500-2104 Fax: 713-500-2107
Website: http://son.uth.tmc.edu
E-mail: william.stewart@uth.tmc.edu

Weatherford College
225 College Park Dr, Weatherford TX 76086
Dr. Joe Birmingham, President
800-287-5471 Fax: 817-598-6205
Website: www.wc.edu
E-mail: willingham@wc.edu

VERMONT

NORWICH UNIVERSITY
158 Harmon Dr, Northfield VT 05663
Marilyn Rinker, Department Head
800-468-6679 Fax: 802-485-2607
Website: www.norwich.edu
E-mail: mrinker@norwich.edu

Southern Vermont College
982 Mansion Dr, Bennington VT 05201-6002
Joel Wincowski, Director of Admissions
800-378-2782 Fax: 802-447-4695
Website: www.svc.edu
E-mail: admis@svc.edu

VIRGINIA

Marymount University
2807 N Glebe Rd, Arlington VA 22207-4299
Michael Canfield, Director of Admissions
800-548-7638 Fax: 703-522-0348
Website: www.marymount.edu
E-mail: admissions@marymount.edu

Radford University
PO Box 6903, Radford VA 24142
David W. Kraus, Director of Admissions
800-890-4265 Fax: 540-831-5038
Website: www.radford.edu
E-mail: ruadmiss@radford.edu

Riverside School of Health Careers
316 Main St, Newport News VA 23601
Tracey Hiller, Recruitment Coordinator
757-240-2200 Fax: 757-240-2225
Website: www.riversideonline.com/rshc
E-mail: tracey.hiller@rivhs.com

Sentara School of Health Professions
1441 Crossways Blvd Suite 105
Chesapeake VA 23320
Shelly Vinson, Director
757-388-2900 Fax: 757-388-2905
Website: www.sentara.com/healthprofessions
E-mail: healthprofessions@sentara.com

Southside Regional Medical Center
801 S Adams St, Petersburg VA 23803-5133
Tonia Little, Director of Admissions
804-862-5800 Fax: 804-862-5937
Website: www.srmcnursing.org
E-mail: tlittle@chs.net

Southside Virginia Community College
109 Campus Dr, Alberta VA 23821-2930
Ronald E. Mattox, Dean of Admissions
434-949-1014 Fax: 434-949-7863
Website: www.sv.vccs.edu
E-mail: ronald.mattox@sv.vccs.edu

Southside Virginia Community College
200 Daniel Rd, Keysville VA 23947
Ronald E. Mattox, Dean of Admissions
434-736-2018 Fax: 434-736-2082
Website: www.sv.vccs.edu
E-mail: ronald.mattox@sv.vccs.edu

WASHINGTON

Everett Community College
2000 Tower St, Everett WA 98201
Christine Kerlin, Associate Dean
425-388-9100 Fax: 425-388-9173
Website: www.everettcc.edu
E-mail: ckerlin@everettcc.edu

North Seattle Community College
9600 College Way N, Seattle WA 98103-3599
206-527-3790
Website: www.northseattle.edu
E-mail: nsccinfo@sccd.ctc.edu

SHORELINE COMMUNITY COLLEGE
16101 Greenwood Ave N, Shoreline WA 98133-5696
Chris Melton, Acting Registrar
206-546-4581 Fax: 206-546-5835
Website: www.shoreline.edu

Walla Walla Community College
500 Tausick Way, Walla Walla WA 99362-9270
Marilyn Galusha, Director of Nursing
509-527-4240 or 877-992-9922 Fax: 509-527-3667
Website: www.wwcc.edu
E-mail: marilyn.galusha@wwcc.edu
See listing under "Community and Junior Colleges"

WEST VIRGINIA

Blue Ridge Community and Technical College
400 W Stephen St, Martinsburg WV 25401
Leslie See, Director of Enrollment
304-260-4380 Fax: 304-260-1752
Website: www.blueridgectc.edu
E-mail: lsee@blueridgectc.edu

Davis & Elkins College
100 Campus Dr, Elkins WV 26241-3996
Renee Heckel, Director of Enrollment Management
800-624-3157 Fax: 304-637-1800
Website: www.davisandelkins.edu
E-mail: admiss@davisandelkins.edu

Fairmont State University
1201 Locust Ave, Fairmont WV 26554-2470
Steve Leadman, Director of Admissions
304-367-4003 or 800-641-5678 Fax: 304-367-4789
Website: www.fairmontstate.edu
E-mail: admit@fairmontstate.edu

Mountain State University
Box 9003, Beckley WV 25802-9003
Tony England, Director of Admissions
866-FOR-MSU1 or 304-929-INFO Fax: 304-253-5072
Website: www.mountainstate.edu
E-mail: gomsu@mountainstate.edu
See listing under "Universities"

WISCONSIN

Alverno College
PO Box 343922, Milwaukee WI 53234-3922
Dianna Gaebler, Director of Admissions
414-382-6100 Fax: 414-382-6354
Website: www.alverno.edu
E-mail: admissions@alverno.edu

BELLIN COLLEGE OF NURSING
PO Box 23400, Green Bay WI 54305-3400
Penny Croghan, Director of Admissions
920-433-5803 Fax: 920-433-7416
Website: www.bcon.edu
E-mail: admissio@bcon.edu

Blackhawk Technical College
PO Box 5009, Janesville WI 53547-5009
Gregg Bosak, Administration, Community Information
608-757-7769 Fax: 608-757-7740
Website: www.blackhawk.edu
E-mail: gbosak@blackhawk.edu

Herzing College
5218 E Terrace Dr, Madison WI 53718-8340
Donald Madelung, President
800-582-1227 Fax: 608-249-8593
Website: www.herzing.edu
E-mail: info@msn.herzing.edu
See listing under "Universities"

Lakeshore Technical College
1290 North Ave, Cleveland WI 53015-1414
Information Fulfillment Specialist
888-GOTOLTC Fax: 920-693-3561
Website: www.gotoltc.edu
E-mail: info@gotoltc.edu

Marquette University
PO Box 1881, Milwaukee WI 53201-1881
Robert Blust, Director of Admissions
414-288-7302 Fax: 414-288-3764
Website: www.mu.edu
E-mail: admissions@marquette.edu

Wisconsin Indianhead Technical College
505 Pine Ridge Dr, Shell Lake WI 54871
Mary Ann Pebler, Dean
800-243-9482 Fax: 715-468-2819
Website: www.witc.edu
E-mail: maryann.pebler@witc.edu

WYOMING

Laramie County Community College
1400 E College Dr, Cheyenne WY 82007-3204
Jenny Hargett, Director of Admissions
307-778-5222 Fax: 307-778-1350
Website: www.lccc.wy.edu
E-mail: learnmore@lccc.wy.edu

University of Wyoming
Admissions Office
Dept 3435, Laramie WY 82071-3435
Brooke Culver, Contact
800-342-5996 Fax: 307-766-4042
Website: www.uwyo.edu
E-mail: why-wyo@uwyo.edu

GUAM

University of Guam
UOG Station, Mangilao GU 96923
Deborah Leon Guerrero, Registrar
671-735-2201 or 671-735-2208 Fax: 671-735-2203
Website: www.uog.edu
E-mail: admitme@uog9.uog.edu

OPTOMETRY

ALABAMA

Judson College
302 Bibb St, Marion AL 36756
Michael Scotto, Director of Admissions
800-447-9472 Fax: 334-683-5147
Website: www.judson.edu
E-mail: admissions@judson.edu

IOWA

Iowa Lakes Community College
300 S 18th St, Estherville IA 51334-2721
Anne Stansbury, Asst. Director of Admissions
712-362-7945 Fax: 712-362-8363
Website: www.iowalakes.edu
E-mail: info@iowalakes.edu

MASSACHUSETTS

Benjamin Franklin Institute of Technology
41 Berkeley St, Boston MA 02116-6307
Norman Kraft, Dean of Enrollment
617-423-4630 ext. 121 Fax: 617-482-3706
Website: www.bfit.edu
E-mail: admissions@bfit.edu

NEW ENGLAND COLLEGE OF OPTOMETRY
424 Beacon St, Boston MA 02115-1129
Taline Farra, O.D., Acting Director of Admissions
800-824-5526 Fax: 617-369-0162
Website: www.neco.edu
E-mail: admissions@neco.edu

MINNESOTA

University of Minnesota
2900 University Ave, Crookston MN 56716-5001
218-281-6510 Fax: 218-281-8575
Website:
admissions.umcrookston.edu/requirements/apply.htm
E-mail: info@umcrookston.edu

MISSOURI

University of Missouri
1 University Blvd, Saint Louis MO 63121-4499
Dr. Larry J. Davis, Dean
314-516-5606 Fax: 314-516-6708
Website: www.umsl.edu
E-mail: admissions@umsl.edu

NEW JERSEY

RICHARD STOCKTON COLLEGE OF NEW JERSEY
PO Box 195, Pomona NJ 08240
John Iacovelli, Dean of Enrollment Management
866-RSC-2885 Fax: 609-626-5541
Website: www.stockton.edu
E-mail: admissions@stockton.edu

Stockton College is a comprehensive liberal arts, co-ed institution founded in 1969. Advance Pre-Professional Degree Options: 7-yr BS/MD with UMDNJ; NJ Dental School; NJ Medical School, Robert Wood Johnson Medical, School of Osteopathic Medicine; NY College of Podiatric Medicine, Pennsylvania College of Podiatric Medicine, SUNY College of Optometry. Pharmacy doctorate program with Rutgers University. 5-yr Engineering with NJIT and Rutgers University. Dual BA/MA in Criminal Justice. 5-yr BS/MS in Computational Science. BS/MS in Nursing. Doctorate of Physical Therapy. Additional Programs: Forensic Science, Pre-Law, Pre-Occupational Therapy, and Pre-Veterinary.

NEW YORK

SUNY COLLEGE OF OPTOMETRY
33 W 42nd St, New York NY 10036-8003
Dr. Edward R. Johnston, VP Student Affairs
212-938-5500 or 800-291-3937 Fax: 212-938-5504
Website: www.sunyopt.edu
E-mail: admissions@sunyopt.edu

Established 1971. Public. Coed. Accreditation: Middle States Association of Colleges & Schools, Council on Optometric Education. Tuition: $13,620/$26,150. Enrollment: 285. Faculty: 134. Student-faculty ratio: 4:1. Degrees: O.D.; MS & PhD in Vision, Science. Library: 34,000 volumes.

OHIO

The Ohio State University
College of Optometry
Starling-Loving Hall, 320 W 10th Ave
Columbus OH 43210
614-292-2647 Fax: 614-292-7493
Website: optometry.osu.edu
E-mail: admissions@optometry.ohio-state.edu

Ursuline College
2550 Lander Rd, Cleveland OH 44124-4398
Sarah E. Sundermeier, Director of Admissions
888-URSULINE Toll Free Fax: 440-684-6138
Website: www.admission.ursuline.edu
E-mail: admission@ursuline.edu

OREGON

PACIFIC UNIVERSITY
2043 College Way, Forest Grove OR 97116-1797
Karen M. Dunston, Executive Director of Admissions
800-677-6712 Fax: 503-352-2975
Website: www.pacific.edu
E-mail: admissions@pacific.edu

PENNSYLVANIA

Juniata College
1700 Moore St, Huntingdon PA 16652-2196
Michelle Bartol, Dean of Enrollment
877-JUNIATA Fax: 814-641-3100
Website: www.juniata.edu
E-mail: admissions@juniata.edu

TEXAS

Abilene Christian University
ACU Box 29000, Abilene TX 79699-0001
325-674-2000 Fax: 325-674-2202
Website: www.acu.edu
E-mail: info@admissions.acu.edu

University of Houston
122 E Cullen Bldg, Houston TX 77204-2023
Office of Admission
713-743-9595
Website: www.uh.edu
E-mail: admissions@uh.edu

OSTEOPATHIC MEDICINE

ARIZONA

COLLEGE OF OSTEOPATHIC MEDICINE - MESA A.T. STILL UNIVERSITY
5850 E Still Circle, Mesa AZ 85206
866-626-2878 or 480-219-6000 Fax: 480-219-6100
Website: www.atsu.edu
E-mail: admissions@ashs.edu

CALIFORNIA

TOURO UNIVERSITY COLLEGE OF OSTEOPATHIC MEDICINE - MARE ISLAND
1310 Johnson Ln, Vallejo CA 94592
Dr. Donald Haight, Director of Admissions
707-638-5270 Fax: 707-638-5250
Website: www.tu.edu
E-mail: haight@touro.edu

FLORIDA

Lake Erie College of Osteopathic Medicine
5000 Lakewood Ranch Blvd, Bradenton FL 34211
June Flaim, Director of Student Affairs
941-756-0690 Fax: 941-782-5721
Website: www.lecom.edu
E-mail: bradenton@lecom.edu

IOWA

Des Moines University - Osteopathic Medical Center
3200 Grand Ave, Des Moines IA 50312-4198
Kendall Reed, D.O., F.A.C.O.S., Dean Osteopathic Medicine
515-271-1513 Fax: 515-271-7053
Website: www.dmu.edu
E-mail: dmuadmit@dmu.edu

MISSOURI

KANSAS CITY UNIVERSITY OF MEDICINE AND BIOSCIENCES
College of Osteopathic Medicine
1750 Independence Ave
Kansas City MO 64106-1453
Phil Byrne, Director of Recruitment
800-234-4847 Fax: 816-283-2484
Website: www.kcumb.edu
E-mail: admissions@kcumb.edu

KIRKSVILLE COLLEGE OF OSTEOPATHIC MEDICINE A.T. STILL UNIVERSITY
800 W Jefferson St, Kirksville MO 63501-1443
Admissions Counselor
866-626-2878 or 660-626-2237 Fax: 660-626-2969
Website: www.atsu.edu
E-mail: admissions@atsu.edu

NEW JERSEY

RICHARD STOCKTON COLLEGE OF NEW JERSEY
PO Box 195, Pomona NJ 08240
John Iacovelli, Dean of Enrollment Management
866-RSC-2885 Fax: 609-626-5541
Website: www.stockton.edu
E-mail: admissions@stockton.edu

Stockton College is a comprehensive liberal arts, coed institution founded in 1969. Advance Pre-Professional Degree Options: 7-yr BS/MD with UMDNJ; NJ Dental School; NJ Medical School, Robert Wood Johnson Medical, School of Osteopathic Medicine; NY College of Podiatric Medicine, Pennsylvania College of Podiatric Medicine, SUNY College of Optometry. Pharmacy doctorate program with Rutgers University. 5-yr Engineering with NJIT and Rutgers University. Dual BA/MA in Criminal Justice. 5-yr BS/MS in Computational Science. BS/MS in Nursing. Doctorate of Physical Therapy. Additional Programs: Forensic Science, Pre-Law, Pre-Occupational Therapy, and Pre-Veterinary.

PENNSYLVANIA

Juniata College
1700 Moore St, Huntingdon PA 16652-2196
Michelle Bartol, Dean of Enrollment
877-JUNIATA Fax: 814-641-3100
Website: www.juniata.edu
E-mail: admissions@juniata.edu

Lake Erie College of Osteopathic Medicine
1858 W Grandview Blvd, Erie PA 16509-1025
Amy Rowe, Admissions Coordinator
814-866-6641 Fax: 814-864-8123
Website: www.lecom.edu
E-mail: admissions@lecom.edu

PERSONAL AND MISCELLANEOUS SERVICES

ARIZONA

INTERNATIONAL ACADEMY OF BEAUTY
4812 S Mill Ave, Tempe AZ 85282-6730
480-964-8675 Fax: 480-964-5528
Website: www.intlacademy.biz
E-mail: intltempe@intlacademy.biz

INTERNATIONAL ACADEMY OF HAIR DESIGN
3350 N Arizona Ave Ste 4, Chandler AZ 85225
480-820-9422 Fax: 480-820-9348
Website: www.intlacademy.biz
E-mail: intlchandler@intlacademy.biz

SOUTHWEST INSTITUTE OF HEALING ARTS
1100 E Apache Blvd, Tempe AZ 85281
Admissions
480-994-9244 Fax: 480-994-3228
Website: www.swiha.org
E-mail: doyourdream@swiha.org

ARKANSAS

University of Arkansas Community College at Hope
PO Box 140, Hope AR 71802-0140
Bobby James, Vice Chancellor for Student Services
870-777-5722 Fax: 870-722-6630
Website: www.uacch.edu
E-mail: bjames@uacch.edu

CALIFORNIA

CALIFORNIA COSMETOLOGY COLLEGE
955 Monroe St, Santa Clara CA 95050-4808
408-247-2200 Fax: 408-247-9730
E-mail: admin@calcosmetcollege.com

CAREER ACADEMY OF BEAUTY
663 N Euclid St, Anaheim CA 92801
Dayna Pattison, Director
714-776-8400
Website: beautycareers.com
E-mail: info@beautycareers.com

COBA ACADEMY
102 N Glassell St, Orange CA 92866-1407
Roger N. Williams, Owner
714-633-5950 Fax: 714-633-5950
Website: www.coba.edu
E-mail: info@coba.edu

CULINARY INSTITUTE OF AMERICA AT GREYSTONE
2555 Main St, Saint Helena CA 94574-9504
800-888-7850 Fax: 845-451-1078
Website: www.ciaprochef.com
E-mail: ciaprochef@culinary.edu

MAKE-UP DESIGNORY
129 S San Fernando Blvd, Burbank CA 91502
Tate Holland, School Director
818-729-9420 Fax: 818-729-9971
Website: www.mud.edu
E-mail: tate@mud.edu

ROYALE COLLEGE OF BEAUTY
27485 Commerce Center Dr
Temecula CA 92590-2525
951-676-0833 Fax: 951-676-0653
Website: www.beautyschools.com
E-mail: roylcoll@aol.com

VICTOR VALLEY BEAUTY COLLEGE
16515 Mojave Dr, Victorville CA 92395-3821
Irma Silva, Director
760-245-2522 Fax: 760-245-5681
Website: www.victorvalleybeautycollege.com

COLORADO

TONI & GUY HAIRDRESSING ACADEMY
332 Main St, Colorado Springs CO 80911
Lynn Whitesides, Director
719-390-9898 Fax: 719-390-0977
Website: www.toniguyco.com
E-mail: whitesides@tigics.com

FLORIDA

ASM BEAUTY WORLD ACADEMY
6423 Stirling Rd, Davie FL 33314
Leticia Milazzo, Assistant School Director
877-678-9532 or 954-321-8411 Fax: 954-321-8683
Website: www.asmbeautyworld.com
E-mail: asm60@bellsouth.net

BENE'S INTERNATIONAL SCHOOL OF BEAUTY, BARBER, AND MASSAGE
7127 US Highway 19
New Port Richey FL 34652-1638
Patricia Martin, Contact
727-848-8415 Fax: 727-846-0269
Website: www.isbschool.com
E-mail: isbschool@aol.com

LORAINE'S ACADEMY
1012 58th St N, Saint Petersburg FL 33710-6391
Kathryn B. Alvarez, Vice President
727-347-4247 Fax: 727-347-6491
Website: www.lorainesacademy.edu

SUNSTATE ACADEMY OF HAIR DESIGN
2525 Drew St, Clearwater FL 33765-2818
727-538-3827 Fax: 727-539-6118
Website: www.sunstate.edu
E-mail: information@sunstate.edu

SUNSTATE ACADEMY OF HAIR DESIGN
2418 Colonial Blvd, Fort Myers FL 33907-1415
Debbie Rodriguez, Campus Director
239-278-1311 Fax: 239-278-1432
Website: www.sunstate.edu
E-mail: drodriguez@sunstate.edu

GEORGIA

GUPTON-JONES COLLEGE OF FUNERAL SERVICE
5141 Snapfinger Woods Dr, Decatur GA 30035-4022
Patty S. Hutcheson, President
770-593-2257 Fax: 770-593-1891
Website: www.gupton-jones.edu
E-mail: gjcfs@mindspring.com

INTERNATIONAL SCHOOL OF SKIN AND NAILCARE
5600 Roswell Rd NE, Atlanta GA 30342-1150
Alan R. Shinall, Operations Manager
404-843-1005 Fax: 404-843-1007
Website: www.skin-nails.com
E-mail: issn@skin-nails.com

IDAHO

THE SCHOOL OF HAIRSTYLING
141 E Chubbuck Rd, Chubbuck ID 83202
Linda K. Mottishaw, Director of Education
208-232-9170 Fax: 208-232-9486
Website: www.theschoolofhairstyling.com
E-mail: lindamottishaw@msn.com

ILLINOIS

HAIR PROFESSIONALS CAREER COLLEGE
10321 S Roberts Rd, Palos Hills IL 60465-1929
Linda Grant or Stephanie Marsala, Contacts
708-430-1755 Fax: 708-430-2282
Website: www.hairpros.edu
E-mail: hairprofessional@aol.com

HAIR PROFESSIONALS CAREER COLLEGE
2245 Gateway Dr, Sycamore IL 60178-3164
Linda Grant, Admissions
815-756-3596 Fax: 815-756-8983
Website: www.hairpros.edu
E-mail: sycamorehairpros@aol.com

HAIR PROFESSIONALS SCHOOL OF COSMETOLOGY
PO Box 40, Oswego IL 60543
Rosalie Clark, Contact
630-554-2266 Fax: 630-554-9574
Website: www.hairpros.edu
E-mail: oswegohairpros@aol.com

PIVOT POINT INTERNATIONAL
1560 Sherman Ave Ste 700, Evanston IL 60201-4813
Lars Juhl, Director of Admissions
847-866-0500 Ext. 7422 Fax: 847-866-7184
Website: www.pivot-point.com
E-mail: admissions@pivot-point.com

STEVEN PAPAGEORGE HAIR ACADEMY
5230 N Clark St, Chicago IL 60640
Steven Papageorge, President
773-561-2376 Fax: 773-561-2377
Website: www.stevenpapageorgehairacademy.com
E-mail: papageorgehair@aol.com

INDIANA

LAFAYETTE BEAUTY ACADEMY
833 Ferry St, Lafayette IN 47901-1149
Anita Harbolt-Keim, Financial Aid Officer
765-742-0068 Fax: 765-420-0875
Website: www.lafayettebeautyacademy.com
E-mail: anita@lafayettebeautyacademy.com

OLYMPIA COLLEGE
707 E 80th Pl Ste 200, Merrillville IN 46410
James Powell, President
219-756-6811 Fax: 219-756-6812
Website: www.cci.edu
E-mail: jpowell@cci.edu

KANSAS

XENON INTERNATIONAL ACADEMY
Hair, Skin, Nails
3804 W Douglas Ave, Wichita KS 67203
Kim McIntosh, Executive Director
316-943-5516 Fax: 316-943-7244
Website: www.xenonintl.com
E-mail: kmcintosh@xenonschool.com

KENTUCKY

TREND SETTER'S ACADEMY OF BEAUTY CULTURE
6539 W Highway 22, Crestwood KY 40014
502-241-0565
E-mail: mbinghamtsa@aol.com

TREND SETTER'S ACADEMY OF BEAUTY CULTURE
622B Westport Rd, Elizabethtown KY 42701-2848
270-765-5243
E-mail: mbinghamtsa@aol.com

TREND SETTER'S ACADEMY OF BEAUTY CULTURE
7283 Dixie Hwy, Louisville KY 40258
502-937-6816
E-mail: mbinghamtsa@aol.com

TREND SETTERS' ACADEMY OF BEAUTY CULTURE
8111 Preston Hwy, Louisville KY 40219
502-962-7710
E-mail: mbinghamtsa@aol.com

LOUISIANA

OMEGA INSTITUTE OF COSMETOLOGY
229 S Hollywood Rd, Houma LA 70360-2716
985-876-9334 Fax: 985-876-3612
Website: www.omegainstitutes.com
E-mail: pricilla@omegainstitutes.com

MAINE

Southern Maine Community College
2 Fort Rd, South Portland ME 04106-1698
Dr. James Ortiz, President
Scott MacDonald, Director of Financial Aid
207-741-5500 Fax: 207-741-5671
Website: www.smccme.edu
E-mail: oharmon@maine.rr.com

MARYLAND

BALTIMORE STUDIO OF HAIR DESIGN
318 N Howard St, Baltimore MD 21201
Maxine Sisserman, Administrator
410-539-1935 Fax: 410-539-2840
Website: www.baltimorestudio.net
E-mail: baltimorestudio@netscape.net

MARYLAND BEAUTY ACADEMY
152 Chartley Dr, Reisterstown MD 21136
Jaime Davidov, Director
410-517-0442 Fax: 410-517-2513
Website: www.baltimorestudio.net
E-mail: mdbeautyacademy@netscape.net

MARYLAND BEAUTY ACADEMY OF ESSEX
505 Eastern Blvd, Baltimore MD 21221
Justin Sisserman, Administrator
410-686-4477 Fax: 410-686-0786
Website: www.baltimorestudio.net
E-mail: mdbeautyacademy@netscape.net

MASSACHUSETTS

FINE MORTUARY COLLEGE
A Private Two Year College
150 Kerry Pl, Norwood MA 02062-4766
Lyn Prendergast, Ph.D., Executive Vice President
781-762-1211 Fax: 781-762-7177
Website: www.fine-ne.com
E-mail: fine@fine-ne.com

MICHIGAN

MICHIGAN COLLEGE OF BEAUTY
5620 Dixie Hwy, Waterford MI 48329
Susan Pantello, CEO
Allison Murphy, Director of Admissions
248-623-9494 Fax: 248-623-6505
Website: www.michigancollegeofbeauty.com
E-mail: mcb1@myexcel.com

TAYLORTOWN SCHOOL OF BEAUTY
23129 Ecorse Rd, Taylor MI 48180
Cynthia Stramecky, President
313-291-2177 Fax: 313-292-9754
Website: www.beautyschool.com
E-mail: cabtylady@aol.com

MINNESOTA

LE CORDON BLEU COLLEGE OF CULINARY ARTS
1315 Mendota Heights Rd
Mendota Heights MN 55120
Kevin Sanderson, President
651-675-4700 Fax: 651-905-3550
Website: www.twincitiesculinary.com
E-mail: ksanderson@twincitiesculinary.com

Minnesota State College - Southeast Technical
Red Wing Campus
308 Pioneer Rd, Red Wing MN 55066
Al DuCett, Director of Admissions
877-853-8324 Fax: 507-453-2715
Website: www.southeastmn.edu
E-mail: aducett@southeastmn.edu
70+ degrees, diplomas & certificates (15+ online) in Business & Office Careers, Musical Instrument Repair, Physical Health, Transportation, Technology, and Trades.

Minnesota State College - Southeast Technical
Winona Campus
PO Box 409, 1250 Homer Rd, Winona MN 55987
Al DuCett, Director of Admissions
877-853-8324 Fax: 507-453-2715
Website: www.southeastmn.edu
E-mail: aducett@southeastmn.edu
70+ degrees, diplomas & certificates (15+ online) in Business & Office Careers, Musical Instrument Repair, Physical Health, Transportation, Technology, and Trades.

MISSOURI

CHILLICOTHE BEAUTY ACADEMY
505 Elm St, Chillicothe MO 64601
Annette Robinson, Financial Aid Advisor
660-646-4198 Fax: 660-646-9983
Website: www.chillicothebeautyacademy.com
E-mail: cbainc@greenhills.net

HOUSE OF HEAVILIN BEAUTY COLLEGE
5720 Troost Ave, Kansas City MO 64110-2826
Jerry Heavilin, President
816-523-2471 Fax: 816-523-6445
Website: www.kchair.edu
E-mail: sheavilin@kc-hair.com

NATIONAL ACADEMY OF BEAUTY ARTS
157 Concord Plz, Saint Louis MO 63128
Mary, Contact
314-842-3616 Fax: 314-842-9396
Website: www.nabacollege.com
E-mail: nationalacademy@sbcglobal.net

PATSY & ROB'S ACADEMY OF BEAUTY
18 Northwest Plz, Saint Ann MO 63074
Rob Bruner, President
314-298-8808 Fax: 314-298-3901
Website: www.praob.edu
E-mail: abeauty@praob.edu

MONTANA

ACADEMY OF COSMETOLOGY, INC.
133 W Mendenhall St, Bozeman MT 59715
Verna Dupuis, Owner
406-587-1265 Fax: 406-585-7357
Website: www.academycosmetology.com
E-mail: vernadupuis@cs.com

NEVADA

ACADEMY OF HAIR DESIGN
5191 W Charleston Blvd, Las Vegas NV 89102
Sandy Dunham, President
702-878-1185 Fax: 702-878-7289
Website: ahdvegas.com
E-mail: sdunham@ahd.lvcoxmail.com

LE CORDON BLEU COLLEGE OF CULINARY ARTS
1451 Center Crossing Rd, Las Vegas NV 89144
Admission Dept.
866-450-2433 or 702-365-7690 Fax: 702-365-7911
Website: www.VegasCulinary.com

NEW HAMPSHIRE

CONTINENTAL ACADEMIE OF HAIR DESIGN
PO Box 370, Hudson NH 03051-0370
603-889-1614 Fax: 603-883-9546
Website: www.continentalacademie.net
E-mail: conacad1@aol.com

CONTINENTAL ACADEMIE OF HAIR DESIGN
228 Maple St, Manchester NH 03103
Sylvia Donah, Business Manager
603-622-5851 Fax: 603-883-9546
Website: www.continentalacademie.net
E-mail: conacad2@aol.com

KEENE BEAUTY ACADEMY
800 Park Ave, Keene NH 03431-1513
Melanie Chaloux, Admissions
603-357-3736 Fax: 603-355-8916
Website: www.keenebeautyacademy.com

NEW JERSEY

Mercer County Community College
West Windsor Campus
PO Box B, Trenton NJ 08690
Savita Bambhrolia, Director of Admissions
609-586-4800 Fax: 609-587-4666
Website: www.mccc.edu
E-mail: admiss@mccc.edu

NEW MEXICO

ALADDIN BEAUTY COLLEGE #22
108 S Union Ave, Roswell NM 88203
Peggy Richburg, Contact
505-623-6331 Fax: 505-622-2072
E-mail: abcinc2@qwest.net

NEW YORK

AMERICAN ACADEMY MCALLISTER INSTITUTE OF FUNERAL SERVICE
619 W 54th St 6th Floor, New York NY 10019
Meg Dunn, President
212-757-1190 Fax: 212-765-5923
Website: www.funeraleducation.org
E-mail: info@funeraleducation.org

CULINARY ACADEMY OF LONG ISLAND
125 Michael Dr, Syosset NY 11791
Michael Levitt, Director
516-364-4344 Fax: 516-364-1894
Website: www.culinaryacademy.edu
E-mail: admissions@culinaryacademy.edu

Hilbert College
5200 S Park Ave, Hamburg NY 14075-1597
Timothy Lee, Director of Admissions
716-649-7900 Fax: 716-649-0702
Website: www.hilbert.edu
E-mail: tlee@hilbert.edu

THE INSTITUTE OF CULINARY EDUCATION
50 W 23rd St, New York NY 10010
Admissions Department
888-921-CHEF
Website: www.iceculinary.com/pattersons

SHEAR EGO INTERNATIONAL SCHOOL OF HAIR DESIGN
525 Titus Ave, Rochester NY 14617
Sharon Roemer, Director of Admissions
585-342-0070 Fax: 585-342-0863
Website: www.shearego.com
E-mail: sei@shearego.com

SIMMONS INSTITUTE OF FUNERAL SERVICE
1828 South Ave, Syracuse NY 13207-2005
Maurice C. Wightman, CEO
315-475-5142 Fax: 315-475-3817
Website: www.simmonsinstitute.com
E-mail: mcwightman20@aol.com

NORTH CAROLINA

ART INSTITUTE OF CHARLOTTE
2110 Water Ridge Pkwy, Charlotte NC 28217
Pamela Notemyer, Director of Admissions
800-872-4417 Fax: 704-357-1133
Website: www.artinstitutes.edu/charlotte
E-mail: admin@aii.edu
See listing under "Career Schools"

DUDLEY COSMETOLOGY UNIVERSITY
900 E Mountain St, Kernersville NC 27284
Eunice M. Dudley, President
336-996-2030 Fax: 336-996-9752
Website: www.dudleyq.com
E-mail: emdudley@dudleyq.com

Mayland Community College
PO Box 547, Spruce Pine NC 28777-0547
Cathy B. Morrison, Director of Enrollment Management
828-765-7351 Fax: 828-765-0728
Website: www.mayland.edu
E-mail: cmorrison@mayland.edu

OHIO

AMERICAN INSTITUTE OF ALTERNATIVE MEDICINE
Teaching Massage And Acupuncture
6685 Doubletree Ave, Columbus OH 43229-1113
Linda Fleming-Willis, Director of Administration
614-825-6278 Fax: 614-825-6279
Website: www.aiam.edu
E-mail: info@aiam.edu

YOUNGSTOWN COLLEGE OF MASSOTHERAPY
14 Highland Ave, Struthers OH 44471-2321
Angela Shodd, Student Relations
330-755-1406 Fax: 330-755-1605
Website: www.ycm.edu
E-mail: ycm@ycm.edu

OREGON

BEAU MONDE COLLEGE ACADEMY OF COSMETOLOGY
11131 NE Halsey St, Portland OR 97220
Dianna Peterson, Owner
503-252-7444 Fax: 503-252-7555
Website: www.beaumondecollege.com
E-mail: diannapeterson@cs.com

BEAU MONDE COLLEGE OF HAIR DESIGN
1221 SW 12th Ave, Portland OR 97205
Dianna Peterson, Owner
503-226-7355 Fax: 503-226-6512
Website: www.beaumondecollege.com
E-mail: diannapeterson@cs.com

WESTERN CULINARY INSTITUTE
921 SW Morrison St Suite 400, Portland OR 97205
Joanne Lazo, Director of Marketing
503-223-2245 or 888-848-3202 Fax: 503-223-5554
Website: www.wci.edu
E-mail: info@wci.edu

PENNSYLVANIA

Career Training Academy
4314 Old William Penn Highway Ste 103
Monroeville PA 15146
Gina Hudac, Admissions Representitive
412-372-3900 Fax: 412-373-4262
Website: www.careerta.edu
E-mail: admissions2@careerta.edu

Career Training Academy
950 5th Ave, New Kensington PA 15068-6308
John Reddy, Director
Tyna Putignano, Director of Admissions
724-337-1000 Fax: 724-335-7140
Website: www.careerta.edu
E-mail: admissions@careerta.edu
See listing under "Career Schools"

Career Training Academy
1500 Northway Mall, Pittsburgh PA 15237
Anna Bartolini, Director North Hills Branch Campus
412-367-4000 Fax: 412-369-7223
Website: www.careerta.edu
E-mail: admissions3@careerta.edu

LEVITTOWN BEAUTY ACADEMY LLC
Vermillion Square
8919 New Falls Rd, Levittown PA 19054
Cecelia Pine, Contact
866-820-0322 or 215-943-0298 Fax: 215-943-0966
Website: www.levittownbeautyacademy.com
E-mail: info@levittownbeautyacademy.com

PITTSBURGH INSTITUTE OF MORTUARY SCIENCE
5808 Baum Blvd, Pittsburgh PA 15206-3706
Karen Rocco, Registrar
412-362-8500 Fax: 412-362-1684
Website: www.pims.edu
E-mail: pims5808@aol.com

SOUTH CAROLINA

CHARLESTON COSMETOLOGY INSTITUTE
8484 Dorchester Rd, Charleston SC 29420-7319
Jerry R. Poer, Owner
843-552-3670 Fax: 843-760-0976
Website: www.charlestoncosmetology.com
E-mail: ccisc@aol.com

SOUTH DAKOTA

Western Dakota Technical Institute
800 Mickelson Dr, Rapid City SD 57703-4018
Jill Elder, Admissions Coordinator
605-394-4034 Fax: 605-394-2204
Website: www.wdt.edu
E-mail: jill.elder@wdt.edu

TEXAS

DALLAS INSTITUTE OF FUNERAL SERVICE
3909 S Buckner Blvd, Dallas TX 75227-4314
Terry Parrish, Registrar/Admissions
800-235-5444 Fax: 214-388-0316
Website: dallasinstitute.edu
E-mail: difs@dallasinstitute.edu

MID CITIES BARBER COLLEGE
2345 SW 3rd St Ste 101, Grand Prairie TX 75051
Nachita Cano, Director
972-642-1892 Fax: 972-642-8198
Website: www.midcitiesbarbercollege.com
E-mail: midcitiesbarber@earthlink.net

SOUTH TEXAS BARBER COLLEGE
3917 Ayers St, Corpus Christi TX 78415
Juan A. Garcia, President
361-855-2297 Fax: 361-855-7212
E-mail: southtexasbarber@sbcglobal.net

VIRGINIA

VIRGINIA SCHOOL OF MASSAGE
2008 Morton Dr, Charlottesville VA 22903-6803
Admissions Department
434-293-4031 Fax: 434-293-4190
Website: www.steinered.com

WASHINGTON

BATES TECHNICAL COLLEGE
1101 S Yakima Ave, Tacoma WA 98405-4895
David Borofsky, President
253-680-7000 Fax: 253-680-7101
Website: www.bates.ctc.edu
E-mail: info@bates.ctc.edu

WISCONSIN

STATE COLLEGE OF BEAUTY CULTURE
1930 Grand Ave, Wausau WI 54403-6870
Andi Burns, Admissions Director
715-845-2888 Fax: 715-848-2121
Website: www.statecollegeofbeauty.com
E-mail: info@statecollegeofbeauty.com

Wisconsin Indianhead Technical College
505 Pine Ridge Dr, Shell Lake WI 54871
Miriam Crandall, Registrar
800-243-9482 Fax: 715-468-2819
Website: www.witc.edu
E-mail: mimi.crandall@witc.edu
Campuses in Ashland, New Richmond, Rice Lake, Superior.

PUERTO RICO

EMMAS BEAUTY ACADEMY
Carr 417 Bo Guanabano, Aguada PR 00602
Carlos Ramos Camara, CEO
787-868-4711 Fax: 787-252-0775
Website: www.emmasbeautyacademy.com
E-mail: emmasbeautyacademy@yahoo.com

EMMAS BEAUTY ACADEMY
9 Calle Munoz Rivera W, Mayaguez PR 00680
Carlos Ramos Camara, CEO
787-833-0980 Fax: 787-833-0613
Website: www.emmasbeautyacademy.com
E-mail: emmasbeautyacademy@yahoo.com

PHARMACY

ALABAMA

Judson College
302 Bibb St, Marion AL 36756
Michael Scotto, Director of Admissions
800-447-9472 Fax: 334-683-5147
Website: www.judson.edu
E-mail: admissions@judson.edu

University of South Alabama
307 University Blvd N, Mobile AL 36688-3053
Melissa Haab, Director of Admissions
251-460-6141 Fax: 251-460-7876
Website: www.southalabama.edu
E-mail: admiss@usouthal.edu

CALIFORNIA

San Joaquin Valley College
201 New Stine Rd, Bakersfield CA 93309-2659
Jaime Delgado, Enrollment Services Director
661-834-1026 Fax: 559-651-4864
Website: www.sjvc.edu
E-mail: jaime.delgado@sjvc.edu

San Joaquin Valley College
295 E Sierra Ave, Fresno CA 93710-3616
Nora Twarynski, Enrollment Services Director
559-448-8282 Fax: 559-651-4864
Website: www.sjvc.edu
E-mail: nora.twarynski@sjvc.edu

San Joaquin Valley College
1700 McHenry Village Way Suite 6
Modesto CA 95350
Joseph Holt, Director of Admissions
209-527-7582 Fax: 559-651-4864
Website: www.sjvc.edu
E-mail: josephh@sjvc.edu

San Joaquin Valley College
11050 Olson Dr, Rancho Cordova CA 95670
Joseph Holt, Director of Admissions
559-651-2500 Fax: 559-651-4864
Website: www.sjvc.edu
E-mail: joseph.holt@sjvc.edu

San Joaquin Valley College
10641 Church St, Rancho Cucamonga CA 91730
Ramon Abreu, Enrollment Services Director
909-948-7582 Fax: 559-651-4864
Website: www.sjvc.edu
E-mail: ramon.abreu@sjvc.edu

San Joaquin Valley College
8400 W Mineral King Ave, Visalia CA 93291-9283
Susie Topjian, Enrollment Services Director
559-651-2500 Fax: 559-651-4864
Website: www.sjvc.edu
E-mail: susiet@sjvc.edu

Western Career College
2157 Country Hills Dr, Antioch CA 94509-7435
Dr. Tim Gienapp, Executive Director
925-522-7777
Website: www.westerncollege.edu

Western Career College
7301 Greenback Ln Bldg A, Citrus Heights CA 95621
Jim Murphy, Executive Director
916-722-8200 Fax: 916-722-6883
Website: www.westerncollege.edu

Western Career College
6001 Shellmound St, Suite 145, Emeryville CA 94608
Dr. Paul Dancy, Contact
510-601-0133 Fax: 510-601-0793
Website: www.westerncollege.edu

Western Career College
380 Civic Dr Ste 300, Pleasant Hill CA 94523-1984
LaShawn Wells, Executive Director
925-609-6650 Fax: 926-609-6666
Website: www.westerncollege.edu

Western Career College
8909 Folsom Blvd, Sacramento CA 95826-3203
Sue Smith, Executive Director
916-361-5100 Fax: 916-361-6666
Website: www.westerncollege.edu

Western Career College
6201 San Ignacio Ave, San Jose CA 95119
Steve Ashab, Executive Director
408-360-0840 Fax: 408-360-0848
Website: www.westerncollege.edu

Western Career College
15555 E 14th St Ste 500, San Leandro CA 94578
Dawn Matthews, Executive Director
510-276-3888 Fax: 510-276-3653
Website: www.westerncollege.edu

Western Career College
1313 W Robinhood Dr Ste B, Stockton CA 95207
Dave Semrau, Executive Director
209-956-1240 Fax: 209-956-1244
Website: www.westerncollege.edu

COLORADO

San Juan Basin Technical College
PO Box 970, Cortez CO 81321-0970
Shannon South, Vice President
970-565-8457 Fax: 970-565-8450
Website: www.sjbtc.edu
E-mail: info@sjbtc.edu

FLORIDA

SOUTHWEST FLORIDA COLLEGE
1685 Medical Ln, Fort Myers FL 33907-1157
866-SWFC-NOW or 239-939-4766 Fax: 239-936-4040
Website: www.swfc.edu
E-mail: studentinfo@swfc.edu

ILLINOIS

Roosevelt University
430 S Michigan Ave, Chicago IL 60605
Gwen E. Kanelos, Asst. Vice President for Enrollment Services
877-APPLY-RU Fax: 312-341-4216
Website: www.roosevelt.edu
E-mail: applyru@roosevelt.edu

IOWA

Briar Cliff University
PO Box 2100, Sioux City IA 51104-0100
Sharisue Wilcoxon, VP for Enrollment Management
712-279-5200 Fax: 712-279-1632
Website: www.briarcliff.edu
E-mail: admissions@briarcliff.edu

Iowa Lakes Community College
300 S 18th St, Estherville IA 51334-2721
Anne Stansbury, Asst. Director of Admissions
712-362-7945 Fax: 712-362-8363
Website: www.iowalakes.edu
E-mail: info@iowalakes.edu

KENTUCKY

Brown Mackie College - Louisville
3605 Fern Valley Rd, Louisville KY 40219-1916
Mark Donahue, Director of Admissions
502-968-7191 Fax: 502-357-9956
Website: www.brownmackie.edu
E-mail: mdonahue@brownmackie.edu

National College
115 E Lexington Ave, Danville KY 40422-1517
Gloria Walls, Director of Admissions
859-236-6991 Fax: 859-236-1063
Website: www.national-college.edu
E-mail: info@national-college.edu

National College
7627 Ewing Blvd, Florence KY 41042-1812
Doug Dedeker, Director of Admissions
859-525-6510 Fax: 859-525-8961
Website: www.national-college.edu
E-mail: info@national-college.edu

National College
125 S Killarney Ln, Richmond KY 40475
Keeley Gadd, Director of Admissions
859-623-8956 Fax: 859-623-8956
Website: www.national-college.edu
E-mail: info@national-college.edu

MAINE

HUSSON COLLEGE
One College Cir, Bangor ME 04401-2999
Jane Goodwin, Director of Admissions
800-4HU-SSON or 207-941-7100 Fax: 207-941-7935
Website: www.husson.edu
E-mail: admit@husson.edu
See listing under "Universities"

MASSACHUSETTS

Benjamin Franklin Institute of Technology
41 Berkeley St, Boston MA 02116-6307
Norman Kraft, Dean of Enrollment
617-423-4630 ext. 121 Fax: 617-482-3706
Website: www.bfit.edu
E-mail: admissions@bfit.edu

MINNESOTA

University of Minnesota
2900 University Ave, Crookston MN 56716-5001
218-281-6510 Fax: 218-281-8575
Website: admissions.umcrookston.edu/requirements/apply.htm
E-mail: info@umcrookston.edu

MISSOURI

ST. LOUIS COLLEGE OF PHARMACY
4588 Parkview Pl, Saint Louis MO 63110-1088
Penny Bryant, Director of Admissions/Registrar
314-367-8700 Fax: 314-446-8310
Website: www.stlcop.edu

Truman State University
100 E Normal, Kirksville MO 63501
Office of Admission
660-785-4114 Fax: 660-785-7456
Website: admissions.truman.edu
E-mail: admissions@truman.edu

NEW JERSEY

RICHARD STOCKTON COLLEGE OF NEW JERSEY
PO Box 195, Pomona NJ 08240
John Iacovelli, Dean of Enrollment Management
866-RSC-2885 Fax: 609-626-5541
Website: www.stockton.edu
E-mail: admissions@stockton.edu

Stockton College is a comprehensive liberal arts, coed institution founded in 1969. Advance Pre-Professional Degree Options: 7-yr BS/MD with UMDNJ; NJ Dental School; NJ Medical School, Robert Wood Johnson Medical, School of Osteopathic Medicine; NY College of Podiatric Medicine, Pennsylvania College of Podiatric Medicine, SUNY College of Optometry. Pharmacy doctorate program with Rutgers University. 5-yr Engineering with NJIT and Rutgers University. Dual BA/MA in Criminal Justice. 5-yr BS/MS in Computational Science. BS/MS in Nursing. Doctorate of Physical Therapy. Additional Programs: Forensic Science, Pre-Law, Pre-Occupational Therapy, and Pre-Veterinary.

NEW YORK

ALBANY COLLEGE OF PHARMACY
106 New Scotland Ave, Albany NY 12208-3492
Carly Connors, Director of Admissions
888-203-8010 Fax: 518-694-7322
Website: www.acp.edu
E-mail: admissions@acp.edu

Roberts Wesleyan College
2301 Westside Dr, Rochester NY 14624-1997
Office of Admissions
585-594-6400 Fax: 585-594-6371
Website: www.roberts.edu
E-mail: admissions@roberts.edu

St. John's University
8000 Utopia Pkwy, Queens NY 11439
Office of Admission
877-STJ-5550 ext. 101 Fax: 718-990-2096
Website: www.stjohns.edu/learnmore
E-mail: admhelp@stjohns.edu
See listing under "Universities"

OHIO

Brown Mackie College - Cincinnati
1011 Glendale Milford Rd, Cincinnati OH 45215-1107
Robin Krout, President
513-771-2424 Fax: 513-771-3413
Website: www.brownmackie.edu
E-mail: rkrout@brownmackie.edu

OHIO NORTHERN UNIVERSITY
525 S Main St, Ada OH 45810-1555
Jon Sprague, Dean
419-772-2275
Website: www.onu.edu
E-mail: admissions-ug@onu.edu
See listing under "Universities"

Ohio State University
College of Pharmacy
150 Parks Hall, 500 W 12th Ave, Columbus OH 43210
614-292-5001 Fax: 614-292-6396
Website: www.pharmacy.ohio-state.edu
E-mail: agresta.6@osu.edu

Ursuline College
2550 Lander Rd, Cleveland OH 44124-4398
Sarah E. Sundermeier, Director of Admissions
888-URSULINE Toll Free Fax: 440-684-6138
Website: www.admission.ursuline.edu
E-mail: admission@ursuline.edu

PENNSYLVANIA

Community College of Beaver County
1 Campus Dr, Monaca PA 15061-2566
724-775-8561 Fax: 724-775-4687
Website: www.ccbc.edu
E-mail: admissions@ccbc.edu

Juniata College
1700 Moore St, Huntingdon PA 16652-2196
Michelle Bartol, Dean of Enrollment
877-JUNIATA Fax: 814-641-3100
Website: www.juniata.edu
E-mail: admissions@juniata.edu

SOUTH DAKOTA

Western Dakota Technical Institute
800 Mickelson Dr, Rapid City SD 57703-4018
Jill Elder, Admissions Coordinator
605-394-4034 Fax: 605-394-2204
Website: www.wdt.edu
E-mail: jill.elder@wdt.edu

TEXAS

Abilene Christian University
ACU Box 29000, Abilene TX 79699-0001
325-674-2000 Fax: 325-674-2202
Website: www.acu.edu
E-mail: info@admissions.acu.edu

Remington College - Fort Worth Campus
300 E Loop 820, Fort Worth TX 76112-1280
Director of Recruitment
817-451-0017 Fax: 817-496-1257
Website: www.remingtoncollege.edu
E-mail: lynn.wey@remingtoncollege.edu

SAN ANTONIO COLLEGE OF MEDICAL AND DENTAL ASSISTANTS
7142 San Pedro Ave Ste 100, San Antonio TX 78216
Carig Czubati, Director of Admissions
210-733-0777 Fax: 210-735-2431
Website: www.sacmda.com
E-mail: cczubati@sac-mda.com

University of Houston
122 E Cullen Bldg, Houston TX 77204-2023
Office of Admission
713-743-9595
Website: www.uh.edu
E-mail: admissions@uh.edu

UTAH

Stevens Henager College
PO Box 9428, Ogden UT 84409-0428
Cindy Williams, Director of Admissions
801-394-7791 Fax: 801-621-0866
Website: www.stevenshenager.edu
E-mail: shcogden@yahoo.com

VIRGINIA

National College
100 Logan St, Bluefield VA 24605
Tonya Elmore, Director of Admissions
276-326-3621 Fax: 276-322-5731
Website: www.national-college.edu
E-mail: info@national-college.edu

National College
336 Old Riverside Dr, Danville VA 24541
Jeff Moore, Director of Admissions
434-793-6822 Fax: 434-793-3634
Website: www.national-college.edu
E-mail: info@national-college.edu

National College
104 Candlewood Ct, Lynchburg VA 24502-2653
Nancy Fortune, Director of Admissions
434-239-3500 Fax: 434-239-3948
Website: www.national-college.edu
E-mail: info@national-college.edu

National College
1813 E Main St, Salem VA 24153-4598
Ron Smith, Director of Admissions
540-986-1800 Fax: 540-444-4195
Website: www.national-college.edu
E-mail: info@national-college.edu

WASHINGTON

North Seattle Community College
9600 College Way N, Seattle WA 98103-3599
206-527-3790
Website: www.northseattle.edu
E-mail: nsccinfo@sccd.ctc.edu

WYOMING

University of Wyoming
Admissions Office
Dept 3435, Laramie WY 82071-3435
Brooke Culver, Contact
800-342-5996 Fax: 307-766-4042
Website: www.uwyo.edu
E-mail: why-wyo@uwyo.edu

ALABAMA

CALHOUN COMMUNITY COLLEGE
PO Box 2216, Decatur AL 35609-2216
M. Wayne Tosh, Registrar
256-306-2500 Fax: 256-306-2941
Website: www.calhoun.edu
E-mail: aprater@calhoun.edu

CALIFORNIA

California College of the Arts
1111 Eighth St, San Francisco CA 94107
Robynne Royster, Director of Admission
800-447-1-ART or 415-703-9523 Fax: 415-703-9539
Website: www.cca.edu
E-mail: enroll@cca.edu

Orange Coast College
PO Box 5005, Costa Mesa CA 92628-5005
Kristin Clark, Director of Admissions
714-432-5773 Fax: 714-432-5736
Website: www.orangecoastcollege.edu
E-mail: kclark@cccd.edu

SAN FRANCISCO ART INSTITUTE
800 Chestnut St, San Francisco CA 94133
800-345-SFAI Fax: 415-749-4503
Website: www.sfai.edu
E-mail: admissions@sfai.edu

Founded in 1871, SFAI offers one of the most innovative and interdisciplinary environments in higher education. Through its School of Studio Practice, SFAI offers accredited Bachelor of Fine Arts (BFA), Master of Fine Arts (MFA), Summer Master of Fine Arts (SMFA), and Post-Baccalaureate (PB) programs. SFAI's School of Studio Practice centers on the development of the artist's vision and consists of the departments of: Design+Technology, Film, New Genres, Painting, Photography, Printmaking, and Sculpture. At SFAI students become part of an educational environment that sees experimentation as necessary for independent and collaborative invention. Founded in 1945 by Ansel Adams, SFAI's Photography Department was the first fine art photography program established in the United States, and faculty members have included Minor White, Imogen Cunningham, Lisette Model, Edward Weston, and Dorothea Lange. Today, the department functions as a fulcrum, balancing a legacy of import with a spirit of inquiry into the medium's future. Whether using a pinhole or pixels, students are challenged to experiment, take risks, and develop a unique visual voice. SFAI's faculty is comprised of active artists, scholars, writers, and curators. Dean of Academic Affairs is renowned curator and critic Okwui Enwezor. Dean of Graduate Studies is artist and filmmaker Renee Green. Director of Exhibitions and Public Programs is curator Hou Hanru. Visiting artists and scholars play a significant role in education at SFAI, with recent visitors including Matthew Barney, William Kentridge, Raqs Media Collective, and others. All students have 24-hour access to the SFAI campus. SFAI's main campus includes painting, photography, sculpture, and printmaking studios, postproduction facilities, and the first high-definition video research lab in the Bay Area. The Diego Rivera Gallery, an open-air amphitheater, and a 250-seat theater are also available to students for exhibiting and screening work. SFAI's library collection includes more than 26,000 volumes with emphasis on modern and contemporary art, over 200 current periodicals, and an extensive image, video, and audio archive available only to SFAI students. The 62,000 square-foot Graduate Center includes a digital lab, film and sound studios, darkrooms, a woodshop, and a gallery for student work. SFAI has rolling application deadlines, and there are competitive and need-based scholarships available to undergraduates, a fellowship program for graduate students, and community college scholarships for transfer students. Visit the SFAI website for specific application requirements.

CONNECTICUT

Albertus Magnus College
700 Prospect St, New Haven CT 06511-1189
Richard Lolatte, Dean of Admission
203-773-8501 or 800-578-9160 Fax: 203-773-5248
Website: www.albertus.edu
E-mail: admissions@albertus.edu

GEORGIA

North Georgia Technical College
Clarkesville Campus
PO Box 65, Clarkesville GA 30523-0002
Admissions
706-754-7700 Fax: 706-754-7777
Website: www.northgatech.edu
E-mail: info@northgatech.edu

Portfolio Center
125 Bennett St NW, Atlanta GA 30309-1268
Catherine Menes, Admissions Department
404-351-5055 ext. 26 Fax: 404-355-8838
Website: www.portfoliocenter.com
E-mail: catherine@portfoliocenter.com

IDAHO

Brigham Young University - Idaho
120 Kimball Bldg, Rexburg ID 83460-1615
Rob Garrett, Director of Admissions
208-496-1020 Fax: 208-496-1220
Website: www.byui.edu
E-mail: admissions@byui.edu

ILLINOIS

Columbia College Chicago
600 S Michigan Ave, Chicago IL 60605-1996
Murphy Monroe, Executive Director of Admissions
312-344-7130 Fax: 312-344-8024
Website: www.colum.edu
E-mail: admissions@colum.edu

HARRINGTON COLLEGE OF DESIGN
200 W Madison St, Chicago IL 60606-3433
Wendi Franczyk, VP of Admissions
877-939-4975 Fax: 312-697-8032
Website: www.harringtoncollege.com
E-mail: wfranczyk@harringtoncollege.com
See listing under "Universities"

INDIANA

Ivy Tech Community College - North Central
220 Dean Johnson Blvd, South Bend IN 46601-3415
Pam Decker, Director of Admissions
574-289-7001 Fax: 574-236-7177
Website: www.ivytech.edu
E-mail: pdecker@ivytech.edu

IOWA

Iowa Lakes Community College
300 S 18th St, Estherville IA 51334-2721
Anne Stansbury, Asst. Director of Admissions
712-362-7945 Fax: 712-362-8363
Website: www.iowalakes.edu
E-mail: info@iowalakes.edu

KENTUCKY

Morehead State University
Morehead KY 40351-1689
Jeffrey Liles, Enrollment Services
800-585-6781 Fax: 606-783-5038
Website: www.moreheadstate.edu
E-mail: admissions@moreheadstate.edu

MASSACHUSETTS

The Art Institute of Boston at Lesley University
700 Beacon St, Boston MA 02215-2598
Office of Admission
617-585-6710 Fax: 617-585-6720
Website: www.aiboston.edu
E-mail: admissions@aiboston.edu

HALLMARK INSTITUTE OF PHOTOGRAPHY
PO Box 308, Turners Falls MA 01376-0308
Shelley Nicholson, Director of Enrollment Services
413-863-2478 Fax: 413-863-4118
Website: hallmark.edu
E-mail: info@hallmark.edu

NEW ENGLAND SCHOOL OF PHOTOGRAPHY
537 Commonwealth Ave, Boston MA 02215-2005
Arthur Levi Rainville, Academic Director
800-676-3767 Fax: 617-437-0261
Website: www.nesop.com
E-mail: info@nesop.com

School of the Museum of Fine Arts, Boston
230 The Fenway, Boston MA 02115-5534
Office of Admissions
617-369-3626 or 800-643-6078 Fax: 617-369-4264
Website: www.smfa.edu
E-mail: admissions@smfa.edu
See listing under "Universities"

University of Massachusetts Dartmouth
Old Westport Rd, North Dartmouth MA 02747-2300
Steven T. Briggs, Director of Admissions
508-999-8605 Fax: 508-999-8755
Website: explore.umassd.edu
E-mail: sbriggs@umassd.edu

MICHIGAN

College for Creative Studies
201 E Kirby St, Detroit MI 48202-4048
Julie Hingelberg, Dean of Enrollment Services
313-664-7425
Website: www.ccscad.edu

Delta College
University Center MI 48710-0001
Duff Zube, Director of Admissions
989-686-9093 Fax: 989-667-2202
Website: www.delta.edu
E-mail: admit@delta.edu

Grand Valley State University
1 Campus Dr, Allendale MI 49401-9403
Jodi Chycinski, Director of Admissions
616-331-6611 Fax: 616-331-2000
Website: www.gvsu.edu
E-mail: go2gvsu@gvsu.edu

Kendall College of Art & Design
17 Fountain St NW, Grand Rapids MI 49503-3002
Dr. Oliver H. Evans, President
800-676-2787 or 616-451-2787 Fax: 616-831-9689
Website: www.kcad.edu
E-mail: brittons@ferris.edu

MACOMB COMMUNITY COLLEGE
14500 E 12 Mile Rd, Warren MI 48088-3896
Information Center
586-445-7999
Website: www.macomb.edu
E-mail: answer@macomb.edu

MINNESOTA

Minneapolis College of Art & Design
2501 Stevens Ave, Minneapolis MN 55404-4347
Admissions Office
800-874-6223 or 612-874-3760 Fax: 612-874-3701
Website: www.mcad.edu
E-mail: admissions@mcad.edu

Minnesota State University Moorhead
1104 7th Ave S, Moorhead MN 56563-0002
Regina Monson, Director of Admissions
218-477-2161 Fax: 218-477-4374
Website: go.mnstate.edu
E-mail: dragon@mnstate.edu

Pillsbury Baptist Bible College
315 S Grove Ave, Owatonna MN 55060-3097
Susanne Martin, Admissions Coordinator
507-451-2710 Fax: 507-451-0156
Website: www.pillsbury.edu
E-mail: admissions@pillsbury.edu

Ridgewater College-Willmar Campus
PO Box 1097, Willmar MN 56201-1097
Sally Kerfeld, Director of Admissions
800-722-1151 Fax: 320-222-5212
Website: www.ridgewater.edu
E-mail: sally.kerfeld@ridgewater.edu

MISSOURI

Columbia College
1001 Rogers St, Columbia MO 65216-0001
Regina Morin, Director of Admissions
573-875-7352 Fax: 573-875-7506
Website: www.ccis.edu
E-mail: admissions@ccis.edu

Webster University
470 E Lockwood Ave, Saint Louis MO 63119-3194
Debra Carpenter, Dean, School of Communications
314-968-6924 Fax: 314-963-6106
Website: www.webster.edu
E-mail: carpenda@webster.edu
See listing under "Universities"

NEW JERSEY

New Jersey City University
2039 John F Kennedy Blvd
Jersey City NJ 07305-1588
Carmen Panlilio, Asst. V.P. for Admissions and Financial Aid
201-200-3234 Fax: 201-200-2044
Website: www.njcu.edu
E-mail: admissions@njcu.edu

RICHARD STOCKTON COLLEGE OF NEW JERSEY
PO Box 195, Pomona NJ 08240
John Iacovelli, Dean of Enrollment Management
866-RSC-2885 Fax: 609-626-5541
Website: www.stockton.edu
E-mail: admissions@stockton.edu
See listing under "Universities"

NEW MEXICO

Institute of American Indian Arts
83 A Van Nu Po, Santa Fe NM 87508-1300
John Gritts, Director of Admissions, Records & Enrollment
505-424-2330 Fax: 505-424-4500
Website: www.iaia.edu
E-mail: recruitment@iaia.edu

NEW YORK

College of Saint Rose
432 Western Ave, Albany NY 12203-1419
Maryelizabeth Amico, Asst V.P. for Undergraduate Admissions
518-454-5150 Fax: 518-454-2013
Website: www.strose.edu
E-mail: admit@strose.edu

Long Island University-C. W. Post Campus
720 Northern Blvd, Brookville NY 11548-1300
Joanne Graziano, Executive Director of Admissions
516-299-2900 Fax: 516-299-2137
Website: www.liu.edu/cwpost
E-mail: enroll@cwpost.liu.edu

Marymount Manhattan College
221 E 71st St, New York NY 10021-4501
Jim Rogers, Dean of Admissions
800-MARYMOUNT Fax: 212-517-0448
Website: www.mmm.edu
E-mail: admissions@mmm.edu

Pratt Institute
200 Willoughby Ave, Brooklyn NY 11205-3899
Heidi Metcalf, Director of Admissions
718-636-3600 Fax: 718-636-3670
Website: www.pratt.edu
E-mail: hmetcalf@pratt.edu

SUNY Sullivan County Community College
112 College Rd, Loch Sheldrake NY 12759-5151
Sari Rosenheck, Director of Admissions
845-434-5750 Fax: 845-434-0923
Website: www.sullivan.suny.edu
E-mail: admissions@sullivan.suny.edu
Student Housing on Campus.

OHIO

Owens Community College
PO Box 10000, Toledo OH 43699-1947
William J. Ivoska, Ph.D, Vice President of Student Services
567-661-7000 Fax: 567-661-7607
Website: www.owens.edu
E-mail: admissions@owens.edu

University of Dayton
300 College Park, Dayton OH 45469-1300
Robert F. Durkle, Director of Admission
800-837-7433 Fax: 937-229-4729
Website: admission.udayton.edu
E-mail: admission@udayton.edu

OREGON

Marylhurst University
17600 Pacific Hwy (Hwy 43)
Marylhurst OR 97036-0261
Director of Admissions
800-634-9982 ext. 6268 Fax: 503-635-6585
Website: www.marylhurst.edu
E-mail: studentinfo@marylhurst.edu

PENNSYLVANIA

Antonelli Institute - Art & Photography
300 Montgomery Ave, Erdenheim PA 19038-8242
Dr. Thomas Treacy, President
215-836-2222 or 800-722-7871 Fax: 215-836-2794
Website: www.antonelli.edu
E-mail: admissions@antonelli.edu

Art Institute of Philadelphia
1622 Chestnut St, Philadelphia PA 19103-5119
Larry McHugh, Director of Admissions
800-275-2474 Fax: 215-405-6399
Website: www.artinstitutes.edu/philadelphia
E-mail: aiphinfo@aii.edu

ART INSTITUTE OF PITTSBURGH
420 Boulevard Of The Allies, Pittsburgh PA 15219
Jeffrey Bucklew, Director of Admissions
800-275-2470 Fax: 412-263-6667
Website: www.aip.aii.edu
E-mail: pahughes@aii.edu
See listing under "Universities"

TENNESSEE

Watkins College of Art and Design and The Watkins Film School
2298 Metrocenter Blvd, Nashville TN 37228-1306
615-383-4848 or 866-887-6395 Fax: 615-383-4849
Website: www.watkins.edu
E-mail: admissions@watkins.edu

TEXAS

University of Houston
122 E Cullen Bldg, Houston TX 77204-2023
Office of Admission
713-743-9595
Website: www.uh.edu
E-mail: admissions@uh.edu

WASHINGTON

SHORELINE COMMUNITY COLLEGE
16101 Greenwood Ave N, Shoreline WA 98133-5696
Chris Melton, Acting Registrar
206-546-4581 Fax: 206-546-5835
Website: www.shoreline.edu

PHYSICAL SCIENCE

ALABAMA

University of Alabama in Huntsville
PO Box 1247, Huntsville AL 35899-0001
Nikki Willis, Assoc. Director for Recruiting Program and Events
1-800-UAH-CALL Fax: 256-824-6073
Website: www.uah.edu
E-mail: willisn@uah.edu

ALASKA

University of Alaska Anchorage
PO Box 141629, Anchorage AK 99514-1629
Cecile Mitchell, Director of Enrollment Services
907-786-1480 Fax: 907-786-4888
Website: www.uaa.alaska.edu/
E-mail: enroll@uaa.alaska.edu

CALIFORNIA

Chapman University
One University Drive, Orange CA 92866-1099
Michael Drummy, Assistant Vice President for Enrollment
Services and Chief Admission Officer
714-997-6411 or 888-CUAPPLY Fax: 714-997-6713
Website: www.chapman.edu
E-mail: admit@chapman.edu

Concordia University
1530 Concordia, Irvine CA 92612-3203
Lori McDonald, Executive Director of Enrollment Services
800-229-1200 or 949-854-8002 Fax: 949-854-6894
Website: www.cui.edu
E-mail: admission@cui.edu

San Bernardino Valley College
701 S Mount Vernon Ave
San Bernardino CA 92410-2798
Kay Ragan, Ed.D., Director of Admissions
909-888-6511 Fax: 909-889-4988
Website: www.valleycollege.edu
E-mail: kragan@sbccd.cc.ca.us

DELAWARE

Wesley College
120 N State St, Dover DE 19901-3876
302-736-2300 Fax: 302-736-2301
Website: www.wesley.edu

FLORIDA

Florida State University
600 W College Ave, Tallahassee FL 32306-1096
Janice V. Finney, Director of Admissions
850-644-2525 Fax: 850-644-0197
Website: admissions.fsu.edu
E-mail: admissions@admin.fsu.edu

University of South Florida
4202 E Fowler Ave, Tampa FL 33620-6900
J. Robert Spatig, Director of Admissions
877-USF-BULL Fax: 813-974-9689
Website: www.usf.edu
E-mail: admissions@admin.usf.edu
See listing under "Universities"

IDAHO

University of Idaho
Moscow ID 83844-4253
Lloyd Scott, Director of New Student Services
208-885-6163 Fax: 208-885-4477
Website: www.uidaho.edu
E-mail: nss@uidaho.edu

ILLINOIS

Benedictine University
5700 College Rd, Lisle IL 60532-0900
630-829-6300 or 888-829-6363 Fax: 630-829-6301
Website: www.ben.edu
E-mail: admissions@ben.edu
See listing under "Universities"

CONCORDIA UNIVERSITY
7400 Augusta St, River Forest IL 60305-1402
708-209-3100 Fax: 708-209-3176
Website: www.cuchicago.edu
E-mail: admission@cuchicago.edu

Roosevelt University
430 S Michigan Ave, Chicago IL 60605
Gwen E. Kanelos, Asst. Vice President for Enrollment Services
877-APPLY-RU Fax: 312-341-4216
Website: www.roosevelt.edu
E-mail: applyru@roosevelt.edu

INDIANA

University of Evansville
1800 Lincoln Ave, Evansville IN 47722-0001
Don Vos, Dean of Admission
800-423-8633 Fax: 812-488-4076
Website: www.evansville.edu
E-mail: admission@evansville.edu

IOWA

Clarke College
1550 Clarke Dr, Dubuque IA 52001-3198
Andy Schroeder, Director of Admissions
800-383-2345 Fax: 563-584-8666
Website: www.clarke.edu
E-mail: andy.schroeder@clarke.edu

Graceland University
1 University Place, Lamoni IA 50140
Greg Sutherland, Interim Vice President for Enrollment and Dean of Admissions
641-784-5196 Fax: 641-784-5480
Website: www.admissions.graceland.edu
E-mail: admissions@graceland.edu

Iowa Lakes Community College
300 S 18th St, Estherville IA 51334-2721
Anne Stansbury, Asst. Director of Admissions
712-362-7945 Fax: 712-362-8363
Website: www.iowalakes.edu
E-mail: info@iowalakes.edu

KANSAS

Independence Community College
PO Box 708, Independence KS 67301-0708
Dr. Terry Hetrick, President
800-842-6063 Fax: 620-331-5344
Website: www.indycc.edu
E-mail: admissions@indycc.edu

KENTUCKY

Bluegrass Community and Technical College
Oswald Building
470 Cooper Drive, Lexington KY 40506-0235
Shelbie Hugle, Director of Admissions
859-246-6200 Fax: 859-246-4664
Website: www.bluegrass.kctcs.edu
E-mail: bctc_info@kctcs.edu

Morehead State University
Morehead KY 40351-1689
Jeffrey Liles, Enrollment Services
800-585-6781 Fax: 606-783-5038
Website: www.moreheadstate.edu
E-mail: admissions@moreheadstate.edu

MARYLAND

Cecil College
One Seahawk Dr, North East MD 21901
Sandra S. Rajaski, Registrar & Director of Admissions
410-287-1000 Fax: 410-287-1001
Website: www.cecil.edu
E-mail: srajaski@cecil.edu

MASSACHUSETTS

Boston University
121 Bay State Rd, Boston MA 02215
Kelly Walter, Executive Director of Admissions
617-353-2300 Fax: 617-353-9695
Website: web.bu.edu
E-mail: admissions@bu.edu

Massachusetts Institute of Technology
77 Massachusetts Ave, Cambridge MA 02139-4307
617-253-1000 Fax: 617-253-4016
Website: my.mit.edu
E-mail: admissions@mit.edu

Worcester Polytechnic Institute
100 Institute Rd, Worcester MA 01609-2280
Edward J. Connor, Director of Admissions
508-831-5286 Fax: 508-831-5875
Website: admissions.wpi.edu
E-mail: admissions@wpi.edu

MICHIGAN

Alma College
614 W Superior St, Alma MI 48801-1599
Evan Montague, Director of Admissions
800-321-ALMA Fax: 989-463-7057
Website: www.alma.edu
E-mail: admissions@alma.edu

HILLSDALE COLLEGE
33 E College St, Hillsdale MI 49242-1298
Dr. James Peters, Director
517-607-2388 Fax: 517-607-2657
Website: www.hillsdale.edu
E-mail: jim.peters@hillsdale.edu

MACOMB COMMUNITY COLLEGE
44575 Garfield Rd, Clinton Township MI 48038-1139
Information Center
586-445-7999
Website: www.macomb.edu
E-mail: answer@macomb.edu

MACOMB COMMUNITY COLLEGE
14500 E 12 Mile Rd, Warren MI 48088-3896
Information Center
586-445-7999
Website: www.macomb.edu
E-mail: answer@macomb.edu

MISSOURI

Truman State University
100 E Normal, Kirksville MO 63501
Office of Admission
660-785-4114 Fax: 660-785-7456
Website: admissions.truman.edu
E-mail: admissions@truman.edu

University of Missouri
1 University Blvd, Saint Louis MO 63121-4499
Dr. Mark Burkholder, Dean-College of Arts & Sciences
314-516-5501 Fax: 314-516-5415
Website: www.umsl.edu
E-mail: admissions@umsl.edu

NEW YORK

College of Saint Rose
432 Western Ave, Albany NY 12203-1419
Maryelizabeth Amico, Asst V.P. for Undergraduate Admissions
518-454-5150 Fax: 518-454-2013
Website: www.strose.edu
E-mail: admit@strose.edu

Iona College
715 North Ave, New Rochelle NY 10801-1890
Kevin Cavanagh, Assistant V.P. for College Admissions
914-633-2502 Fax: 914-637-2778
Website: www.iona.edu

Long Island University-C. W. Post Campus
720 Northern Blvd, Brookville NY 11548-1300
Joanne Graziano, Executive Director of Admissions
516-299-2900 Fax: 516-299-2137
Website: www.liu.edu/cwpost
E-mail: enroll@cwpost.liu.edu

Molloy College
1000 Hempstead Ave
Rockville Centre NY 11570-1100
Marguerite Lane, Director of Admissions
516-678-5000 ext. 6291 Fax: 516-256-2247
Website: www.molloy.edu
E-mail: admissions@molloy.edu
See listing under "Universities"

St. Joseph's College
245 Clinton Ave, Brooklyn NY 11205-3688
Theresa LaRocca Meyer, V.P. for Enrollment Management
718-636-6800 Fax: 718-636-8303
Website: www.sjcny.edu
E-mail: tlaroccameyer@sjcny.edu

SUNY College of Technology
Alfred NY 14802
Deborah J. Goodrich, Associate VP Enrollment Mgmt.
800-4AL-FRED Fax: 607-587-4299
Website: www.alfredstate.edu
E-mail: admissions@alfredstate.edu

SUNY Orange County Community College
115 South St, Middletown NY 10940-6437
Margot St. Lawrence, Director of Admissions
845-341-4030 Fax: 845-342-8662
Website: www.sunyorange.edu
E-mail: apply@sunyorange.edu
See listing under "Community and Junior Colleges"

SUNY Sullivan County Community College
112 College Rd, Loch Sheldrake NY 12759-5151
Sari Rosenheck, Director of Admissions
845-434-5750 Fax: 845-434-0923
Website: www.sullivan.suny.edu
E-mail: admissions@sullivan.suny.edu
Student Housing on Campus.

NORTH DAKOTA

Dickinson State University
Dickinson ND 58601-4896
Steve Glasser, Director of Enrollment Services
800-279-4295 Fax: 701-483-2409
Website: www.dickinsonstate.edu
E-mail: dsu.hawks@dickinsonstate.edu

OHIO

The Ohio State University
College of Mathematical and Physical Sciences
Stillman Hall, 1947 College Rd, Columbus OH 43210
614-292-2874 Fax: 614-292-3639
Website: www.mps.ohio-state.edu
E-mail: handon.1@osu.edu

University of Dayton
300 College Park, Dayton OH 45469-1300
Robert F. Durkle, Director of Admission
800-837-7433 Fax: 937-229-4729
Website: admission.udayton.edu
E-mail: admission@udayton.edu

OKLAHOMA

Oklahoma State University
Stillwater OK 74078
John Mintmire, Department Head
405-744-5796
Website: www.okstate.edu
E-mail: john.mintmire@okstate.edu

OREGON

Cascade College
9101 E Burnside St, Portland OR 97216-1599
Jim Murphy, Director of Enrollment Management
800-550-7678 Fax: 503-257-1222
Website: www.cascade.edu
E-mail: admissions@cascade.edu

PENNSYLVANIA

Community College of Allegheny County
Allegheny Campus: 808 Ridge Ave, Pittsburgh PA 15212 Admissions: 412.237.2700
Boyce Campus: 595 Beatty Rd, Monroeville PA 15146 Admissions: 724.325.6614
North Campus: 8701 Perry Highway, Pittsburgh PA 15237 Admissions: 412.369.3600
South Campus: 1750 Clairton Rd, West Mifflin PA 15122 Admissions: 412-469-4301
Website: www.ccac.edu

Juniata College
1700 Moore St, Huntingdon PA 16652-2196
Michelle Bartol, Dean of Enrollment
877-JUNIATA Fax: 814-641-3100
Website: www.juniata.edu
E-mail: admissions@juniata.edu

Washington & Jefferson College
60 S Lincoln St, Washington PA 15301-4801
Alton E. Newell, Vice President for Enrollment
724-223-6025 Fax: 724-223-6534
Website: www.washjeff.edu
E-mail: admission@washjeff.edu

TENNESSEE

Tennessee State University
3500 John A Merritt Blvd, Nashville TN 37209-1561
John Cade, Dean of Admissions & Records
615-963-5052 Fax: 615-963-2930
Website: www.tnstate.edu
E-mail: jcade@tnstate.edu

TEXAS

Abilene Christian University
ACU Box 29000, Abilene TX 79699-0001
325-674-2000 Fax: 325-674-2202
Website: www.acu.edu
E-mail: info@admissions.acu.edu

Texas Woman's University
PO Box 425589, Denton TX 76204-5589
Erma Nieto-Brecht, Director of Admissions
866-809-6130 Fax: 940-898-3081
Website: www.twu.edu
E-mail: admissions@twu.edu

University of Houston
122 E Cullen Bldg, Houston TX 77204-2023
Office of Admission
713-743-9595
Website: www.uh.edu
E-mail: admissions@uh.edu

University of Texas at Arlington
Box 19111, Arlington TX 76019-0111
Hans Gatterdam, Director of Admission
817-272-6287 Fax: 817-272-3435
Website: www.uta.edu
E-mail: admissions@uta.edu

VIRGINIA

Marymount University
2807 N Glebe Rd, Arlington VA 22207-4299
Michael Canfield, Director of Admissions
800-548-7638 Fax: 703-522-0348
Website: www.marymount.edu
E-mail: admissions@marymount.edu

Radford University
PO Box 6903, Radford VA 24142
David W. Kraus, Director of Admissions
800-890-4265 Fax: 540-831-5038
Website: www.radford.edu
E-mail: ruadmiss@radford.edu

Randolph College
2500 Rivermont Ave, Lynchburg VA 24503
Patricia LeDonne, Director of Admissions
434-947-8100 Fax: 434-947-8996
Website: www.randolphcollege.edu
E-mail: admissions@randolphcollege.edu

WYOMING

University of Wyoming
Admissions Office
Dept 3435, Laramie WY 82071-3435
Brooke Culver, Contact
800-342-5996 Fax: 307-766-4042
Website: www.uwyo.edu
E-mail: why-wyo@uwyo.edu

GUAM

University of Guam
UOG Station, Mangilao GU 96923
Deborah Leon Guerrero, Registrar
671-735-2201 or 671-735-2208 Fax: 671-735-2203
Website: www.uog.edu
E-mail: admitme@uog9.uog.edu

PODIATRIC MEDICINE

IOWA

Des Moines University - Osteopathic Medical Center
3200 Grand Ave, Des Moines IA 50312-4198
Robert M. Yoho, D.P.M., M.S., Dean, College of Podiatric Medicine & Surgery, Interim V.P. for Academic Administration
515-271-1464 Fax: 515-271-7017
Website: www.dmu.edu
E-mail: robert.yoho@dmu.edu

NEW JERSEY

New Jersey City University
2039 John F Kennedy Blvd
Jersey City NJ 07305-1588
Carmen Panlilio, Asst. V.P. for Admissions and Financial Aid
201-200-3234 Fax: 201-200-2044
Website: www.njcu.edu
E-mail: admissions@njcu.edu

RICHARD STOCKTON COLLEGE OF NEW JERSEY

PO Box 195, Pomona NJ 08240
John Iacovelli, Dean of Enrollment Management
866-RSC-2885 Fax: 609-626-5541
Website: www.stockton.edu
E-mail: admissions@stockton.edu

Stockton College is a comprehensive liberal arts, co-ed institution founded in 1969. Advance Pre-Professional Degree Options: 7-yr BS/MD with UMDNJ; NJ Dental School; NJ Medical School, Robert Wood Johnson Medical, School of Osteopathic Medicine; NY College of Podiatric Medicine, Pennsylvania College of Podiatric Medicine, SUNY College of Optometry. Pharmacy doctorate program with Rutgers University. 5-yr Engineering with NJIT and Rutgers University. Dual BA/MA in Criminal Justice. 5-yr BS/MS in Computational Science. BS/MS in Nursing. Doctorate of Physical Therapy. Additional Programs: Forensic Science, Pre-Law, Pre-Occupational Therapy, and Pre-Veterinary.

OHIO

OHIO COLLEGE OF PODIATRIC MEDICINE

10515 Carnegie Ave, Cleveland OH 44106
Lois Lott, Dean of Student Affairs
216-231-3300 Fax: 216-231-1005
Website: www.ocpm.edu
E-mail: llott@ocpm.edu

PENNSYLVANIA

Juniata College
1700 Moore St, Huntingdon PA 16652-2196
Michelle Bartol, Dean of Enrollment
877-JUNIATA Fax: 814-641-3100
Website: www.juniata.edu
E-mail: admissions@juniata.edu

PRECISION PRODUCTION TRADES

ALABAMA

- Bishop State Community College - Four Campuses
  351 N Broad St, Mobile AL 36603-5898
  Dr. Terry Hazzard, Dean of Students
  251-690-6801 Fax: 251-690-6446
  Website: www.bishop.edu
  E-mail: thazzard@bishop.edu
- **CALHOUN COMMUNITY COLLEGE**
  PO Box 2216, Decatur AL 35609-2216
  M. Wayne Tosh, Registrar
  256-306-2500 Fax: 256-306-2941
  Website: www.calhoun.edu
  E-mail: rls@calhoun.edu
  See listing under "Community and Junior Colleges"
- Trenholm State Technical College
  Patterson Campus
  3920 Troy Hwy, Montgomery AL 36116
  Dr. Anthony Molina, President
  334-420-4200 Fax: 334-420-4206
  Website: www.trenholmtech.cc.al.us
  E-mail: molinaa@trenholmtech.cc.al.us

ARIZONA

- Pima Community College
  4905 E Broadway Blvd, Tucson AZ 85709-1010
  Wendy Kilgore, Ph.D., Director of Admissions
  520-206-4500 Fax: 520-206-4790
  Website: www.pima.edu
  E-mail: infocenter@pima.edu
- Universal Technical Institute
  10695 W Pierce St, Avondale AZ 85323-7946
  John Palumbo, Director of Admissions
  623-245-4600 Fax: 623-245-4603
  Website: www.uticorp.com

ARKANSAS

- Northwest Technical Institute
  709 S Old Missouri Rd, Springdale AR 72764
  Charles L. Kelley, President
  479-751-8824 Fax: 479-751-7780
  Website: www.nti.tec.ar.us
  E-mail: info@nit.tec.ar.us
- **OUACHITA TECHNICAL COLLEGE**
  One College Cir, Malvern AR 72104
  Adrian Ashley, Division Chair Applied Science
  501-337-5000 ext. 1165 Fax: 501-337-9382
  Website: www.otcweb.edu
  E-mail: aashley@otcweb.edu
- Phillips Community College of the University of Arkansas
  PO Box 785, Helena AR 72342-0785
  Dr. Steven Murray, Chancellor
  Lynn Boone, Vice Chancellor for Student Services / Registrar
  870-338-6474 Fax: 870-338-7542
  Website: www.pccua.edu
  E-mail: lboone@pccua.edu
- University of Arkansas Community College at Hope
  PO Box 140, Hope AR 71802-0140
  Ed Thaxton, Math Science & Technical Programs Division Chair
  870-777-5722 Fax: 870-722-6630
  Website: www.uacch.edu
  E-mail: ethaxton@uacch.edu

CALIFORNIA

- Butte College
  3536 Butte Campus Dr, Oroville CA 95965-8399
  Carole Gish, Director of Admissions
  530-895-2511 Fax: 530-879-4313
  Website: www.butte.edu
  E-mail: admissions@butte.edu
- Chabot College
  25555 Hesperian Blvd, Hayward CA 94545-2400
  Judy Young, Director of Admissions
  510-723-6600 Fax: 510-723-7510
  Website: www.chabotcollege.edu
  E-mail: ccarcom@clpccd.cc.ca.us
- **FRESNO CITY COLLEGE**
  1101 E University Ave, Fresno CA 93741-0002
  Dayann Dietrich, Contact
  559-442-8241 Fax: 559-237-4232
  Website: www.fresnocitycollege.com
  E-mail: fcc.admissions@scccd.com
- **ITT TECHNICAL INSTITUTE**
  2051 Solar Dr Ste 150, Oxnard CA 93030-0641
  Milo Hegan, Director of Recruitment
  805-988-0143 Fax: 805-988-1813
  Website: www.itt-tech.edu
  E-mail: mhegan@itt-tech.edu
- Orange Coast College
  PO Box 5005, Costa Mesa CA 92628-5005
  Kristin Clark, Director of Admissions
  714-432-5773 Fax: 714-432-5736
  Website: www.orangecoastcollege.edu
  E-mail: kclark@cccd.edu

COLORADO

- IntelliTec College
  2315 E Pikes Peak Ave
  Colorado Springs CO 80909-6096
  Michael Castellano, Contact
  719-632-7626 Fax: 719-632-7451
  Website: www.intelliteccollege.edu
  E-mail: admcs@intelliteccollege.edu
- IntelliTec College
  772 Horizon Dr, Grand Junction CO 81506-3907
  Jennifer Daniels, Contact
  970-245-8101 Fax: 970-243-8074
  Website: www.intelliteccollege.edu
  E-mail: admgj@intelliteccollege.edu
- San Juan Basin Technical College
  PO Box 970, Cortez CO 81321-0970
  Shannon South, Vice President
  970-565-8457 Fax: 970-565-8450
  Website: www.sjbtc.edu
  E-mail: info@sjbtc.edu

FLORIDA

- **TULSA WELDING SCHOOL**
  3500 Southside Blvd, Jacksonville FL 32216-4634
  Roger Hess, President
  877-935-3529 Fax: 904-646-9956
  Website: www.weldingschool.com
  E-mail: tws@ionet.net

GEORGIA

- DeKalb Technical College
  495 N Indian Creek Dr, Clarkston GA 30021-2397
  Terry Richardson, Director of Admissions
  404-297-9522 Fax: 404-294-6496
  Website: www.dekalbtech.edu
  E-mail: richardt@dekalbtech.edu
- North Georgia Technical College
  Clarkesville Campus
  PO Box 65, Clarkesville GA 30523-0002
  Admissions
  706-754-7700 Fax: 706-754-7777
  Website: www.northgatech.edu
  E-mail: info@northgatech.edu
- North Metro Technical College
  5198 Ross Rd SE, Acworth GA 30102-3129
  Missy Cusack, Director of Admissions
  770-975-4000 Fax: 770-975-4142
  Website: www.northmetrotech.edu
  E-mail: info@northmetrotech.edu
- Valdosta Technical College
  4089 Val Tech Rd, Valdosta GA 31602-0928
  Amanda Leavy, Admissions Coordinator
  229-333-2100 Fax: 229-249-4980
  Website: www.valdostatech.edu
  E-mail: aleavy@valdostatech.edu

ILLINOIS

- Kaskaskia College
  27210 College Rd, Centralia IL 62801-7878
  Tyra Taylor, Dean of Enrollment Management and Retention Services
  618-545-3000 Fax: 618-532-1990
  Website: www.kaskaskia.edu
  E-mail: ttaylor@kaskaskia.edu
- Triton College
  2000 5th Ave, River Grove IL 60171-1995
  Jeffery Cooks, Director, Admission Services
  708-456-0300 ext. 3130 Fax: 708-583-3147
  Website: www.triton.edu
  E-mail: triton@triton.edu
  See listing under "Community and Junior Colleges"
- Westwood College
  8501 W Higgins Rd Ste 500, Chicago IL 60631
  Tash Uray, Director of Admissions
  773-380-6800 Fax: 773-714-0828
  Website: www.westwood.edu
  E-mail: turay@westwood.edu

INDIANA

- Ivy Tech Community College - North Central
  220 Dean Johnson Blvd, South Bend IN 46601-3415
  Pam Decker, Director of Admissions
  574-289-7001 Fax: 574-236-7177
  Website: www.ivytech.edu
  E-mail: pdecker@ivytech.edu

IOWA

- Northwest Iowa Community College
  603 W Park St, Sheldon IA 51201-1046
  Lisa Story, Director of Enrollment Management
  712-324-5061 Fax: 712-324-4136
  Website: www.nwicc.edu
  E-mail: lstory@nwicc.edu

KANSAS

- Flint Hills Technical College
  3301 W 18th Ave, Emporia KS 66801-5957
  Lisa Kirmer, Dean of Student Services
  620-343-4600 Fax: 620-343-4610
  Website: www.fhtc.net
  E-mail: lkirmer@fhtc.net

KENTUCKY

- Bluegrass Community and Technical College
  Oswald Building
  470 Cooper Drive, Lexington KY 40506-0235
  Shelbie Hugle, Director of Admissions
  859-246-6200 Fax: 859-246-4664
  Website: www.bluegrass.kctcs.edu
  E-mail: bctc_info@kctcs.edu

LOUISIANA

- Gretna Career College Training Institute
  1415 Whitney Ave, Gretna LA 70053-2436
  Ava Himes, Director of Admissions
  504-366-5409 Fax: 504-366-1294
- Louisiana Technical College
  Florida Parishes Campus
  PO Box 1300, Greensburg LA 70441
  225-222-4251 Fax: 225-222-6064
  Website: www.ltc.edu./region.html
- **LOUISIANA TECHNICAL COLLEGE**
  Tallulah Campus
  132 Old Highway 65, Tallulah LA 71284
  Patrick T. Murphy, Dean
  318-574-4820 Fax: 318-574-1868
  Website: www.ltctallulah.com
  E-mail: sccox@theltc.net

MAINE

- Landing School of Boatbuilding, Design, Systems & Composites
  PO Box 1490, Kennebunkport ME 04046-1490
  Jade Elliott, Director of Student Services
  207-985-7976 Fax: 207-985-7942
  Website: www.landingschool.edu
  E-mail: jadeelliott@landingschool.edu
- Southern Maine Community College
  2 Fort Rd, South Portland ME 04106-1698
  Dr. James Ortiz, President
  Scott MacDonald, Director of Financial Aid
  207-741-5500 Fax: 207-741-5671
  Website: www.smccme.edu
  E-mail: oharmon@maine.rr.com

MASSACHUSETTS

- North Shore Community College
  1 Ferncroft Rd, Danvers MA 01923-4093
  Jennifer Kirk, Director of Admissions & Recruitment Outreach
  978-762-4000 Fax: 978-762-4015
  Website: www.northshore.edu
  E-mail: jkirk@northshore.edu

MICHIGAN

- Delta College
  University Center MI 48710-0001
  Duff Zube, Director of Admissions
  989-686-9093 Fax: 989-667-2202
  Website: www.delta.edu
  E-mail: admit@delta.edu
- **MACOMB COMMUNITY COLLEGE**
  14500 E 12 Mile Rd, Warren MI 48088-3896
  Information Center
  586-445-7999
  Website: www.macomb.edu
  E-mail: answer@macomb.edu

MINNESOTA

- Dunwoody College of Technology
  818 Dunwoody Blvd, Minneapolis MN 55403-1192
  John Slama, Vice President Enrollment Management
  800-292-4625 or 612-374-5800 Fax: 612-374-4128
  Website: www.dunwoody.edu
  E-mail: jslama@dunwoody.edu
  See listing under "Career Schools"
- Minnesota State College - Southeast Technical
  Red Wing Campus
  308 Pioneer Rd, Red Wing MN 55066
  Al DuCett, Director of Admissions
  877-853-8324 Fax: 507-453-2715
  Website: www.southeastmn.edu
  E-mail: aducett@southeastmn.edu
  70+ degrees, diplomas & certificates (15+ online) in Business & Office Careers, Musical Instrument Repair, Physical Health, Transportation, Technology, and Trades.
- Minnesota State College - Southeast Technical
  Winona Campus
  PO Box 409, 1250 Homer Rd, Winona MN 55987
  Al DuCett, Director of Admissions
  877-853-8324 Fax: 507-453-2715
  Website: www.southeastmn.edu
  E-mail: aducett@southeastmn.edu
  70+ degrees, diplomas & certificates (15+ online) in Business & Office Careers, Musical Instrument Repair, Physical Health, Transportation, Technology, and Trades.
- Ridgewater College-Hutchinson Campus
  2 Century Ave SE, Hutchinson MN 55350-3100
  Dawn Bjork, Counselor
  800-722-1151 Fax: 320-234-8506
  Website: www.ridgewater.edu
  E-mail: dawn.bjork@ridgewater.edu
- St. Cloud Technical College
  1540 Northway Dr, Saint Cloud MN 56303-1240
  Jodi Elness, Director of Enrollment Management
  800-222-1009 Fax: 320-308-5981
  Website: www.sctc.edu
  E-mail: jelness@sctc.edu

MISSOURI

- East Central College
  1964 Prairie Dell Rd, Union MO 63084
  Karen Wieda, Registrar
  636-583-5195 ext. 2220 Fax: 636-583-1897
  Website: www.eastcentral.edu
  E-mail: wiedaks@eastcentral.edu
- Linn State Technical College
  1 Technology Dr, Linn MO 65051-9606
  Becky Dunn, Admissions
  800-743-8324 Fax: 573-897-5026
  Website: www.linnstate.edu
  E-mail: admissions@linnstate.edu

Ozarks Technical Community College
1001 E Chestnut Expressway
Springfield MO 65802-3625
Delvan Mitchell, Director of Admissions
417-447-7500 Fax: 417-447-6925
Website: www.otc.edu
E-mail: admissions@otc.edu

Ranken Technical College
4431 Finney Ave, Saint Louis MO 63113-2898
Admissions Office
314-371-0233 Fax: 314-371-0241
Website: www.ranken.edu
E-mail: admissions@ranken.edu

State Fair Community College
3201 W 16th St, Sedalia MO 65301-2199
Director of Admissions
660-530-5833 Fax: 660-596-7472
Website: www.sfccmo.edu
E-mail: mparris@sfccmo.edu

NEBRASKA

ITT TECHNICAL INSTITUTE
9814 M St, Omaha NE 68127-2056
Frank de Monteur, Director
800-677-9260 Fax: 402-331-9495
Website: www.itt-tech.edu
E-mail: snielsen@itt-tech.edu

NEVADA

GREAT BASIN COLLEGE
1500 College Pkwy, Elko NV 89801-5032
Julie G. Byrnes, Director of Enrollment Management
775-753-2271 Fax: 775-753-2311
Website: www.gbcnv.edu
E-mail: julieb@gwmail.gbcnv.edu
See listing under "Universities"

NEW HAMPSHIRE

New Hampshire Community Technical College
1066 Front St, Manchester NH 03102-8528
Jacquie Poirier, Director of Admissions
603-668-6706 Fax: 603-668-5354
Website: www.manchester.nhctc.edu
E-mail: jpoirier@nhctc.edu

NEW JERSEY

Bergen Community College
400 Paramus Rd, Paramus NJ 07652
Julian Gomez, Asst. Director of Admissions
201-447-7100 Fax: 201-444-7036
Website: www.bergen.edu
E-mail: jgomez@bergen.edu

HOHOKUS SCHOOL OF TRADE AND TECHNICAL SCIENCES
634-638 Market St, Paterson NJ 07513-1402
Alan E. Concha, Vice President/Director
800-646-9353 Fax: 908-486-9321
Website: www.hohokustrades.com
E-mail: aconcha21@aol.com

NEW YORK

APEX TECHNICAL SCHOOL
635 Avenue of the Americas
New York NY 10011-2008
William Ott, Admissions Director
212-645-3300 Fax: 212-645-6984
Website: www.apextechnical.com
See listing under "Career Schools"

ISLAND DRAFTING & TECHNICAL INSTITUTE
128 Broadway (Route 110), Amityville NY 11701-2704
James G. DiLiberto, President
631-691-8733 Fax: 631-691-8738
Website: www.idti.edu
E-mail: info@idti.edu

SUNY College of Technology
Alfred NY 14802
Deborah J. Goodrich, Associate VP Enrollment Mgmt.
800-4AL-FRED Fax: 607-587-4299
Website: www.alfredstate.edu
E-mail: admissions@alfredstate.edu

NORTH CAROLINA

AMERICAN INSTITUTE OF APPLIED SCIENCE
Criminal Investigation and Forensic Science
100 Hunter Pl, Youngsville NC 27596-9447
Marvin Joy, Director of Education
919-554-2500 Fax: 919-556-6784
Website: www.aiasinc.com
E-mail: aias@mindspring.com

Haywood Community College
185 Freedlander Dr, Clyde NC 28721
Debbie Rowland, Coordinator of Admissions
828-627-4500 Fax: 828-627-4513
Website: www.haywood.edu
E-mail: drowland@haywood.edu

James Sprunt Community College
PO Box 398, Kenansville NC 28349-0398
Lea Grady, Admissions
910-296-2500 Fax: 910-296-1636
Website: www.jamessprunt.edu

Mayland Community College
PO Box 547, Spruce Pine NC 28777-0547
Cathy B. Morrison, Director of Enrollment Management
828-765-7351 Fax: 828-765-0728
Website: www.mayland.edu
E-mail: cmorrison@mayland.edu

OHIO

Owens Community College
3200 Bright Rd, Findlay OH 45840
William J. Ivoska PhD., Vice President of Student Services
567-429-3500 Fax: 567-423-0246
Website: www.owens.edu
E-mail: admissions@owens.edu

Owens Community College
PO Box 10000, Toledo OH 43699-1947
William J. Ivoska, Ph.D, Vice President of Student Services
567-661-7000 Fax: 567-661-7607
Website: www.owens.edu
E-mail: admissions@owens.edu

OKLAHOMA

TULSA WELDING SCHOOL
2545 E 11th St, Tulsa OK 74104-3909
Mike Thurber, Director of Admissions
800-WELD-PRO Fax: 918-587-8170
Website: www.weldingschool.edu
E-mail: tws@ionet.net

OREGON

Linn-Benton Community College
6500 Pacific Blvd SW, Albany OR 97321-3774
Christine Baker, Outreach Coordinator
541-917-4811 Fax: 541-917-4868
Website: www.linnbenton.edu
E-mail: admissions@linnbenton.edu

Rogue Community College
3345 Redwood Hwy, Grants Pass OR 97527-9298
Claudia Sullivan, Director of Enrollment Services
541-956-7500 Fax: 541-471-3585
Website: www.roguecc.edu
E-mail: csullivan@roguecc.edu
See listing under "Community and Junior Colleges"

PENNSYLVANIA

Community College of Allegheny County
Allegheny Campus: 808 Ridge Ave, Pittsburgh PA 15212 Admissions: 412.237.2700
Boyce Campus: 595 Beatty Rd, Monroeville PA 15146 Admissions: 724.325.6614
North Campus: 8701 Perry Highway, Pittsburgh PA 15237 Admissions: 412.369.3600
South Campus: 1750 Clairton Rd, West Mifflin PA 15122 Admissions: 412-469-4301
Website: www.ccac.edu

Johnson College
3427 N Main Ave, Scranton PA 18508-1495
Dr. Ann L. Pipinski, President & CEO
Melissa Ide, Director of Enrollment Management
800-2WE-WORK or 570-342-6404 ext. 125
Fax: 570-348-2181
Website: www.johnson.edu
E-mail: admit@johnson.edu

SOUTH CAROLINA

Spartanburg Community College
PO Box 4386, Spartanburg SC 29305-4386
Nancy Garmroth, Dean of Admissions & Financial Aid
864-592-4810 Fax: 864-592-4945
Website: sccsc.edu

SOUTH DAKOTA

Western Dakota Technical Institute
800 Mickelson Dr, Rapid City SD 57703-4018
Jill Elder, Admissions Coordinator
605-394-4034 Fax: 605-394-2204
Website: www.wdt.edu
E-mail: jill.elder@wdt.edu

TEXAS

ATI Career Training Center
6351 Boulevard 26 Ste 100
North Richland Hills TX 76180
817-284-1141
Website: www.aticareertraining.edu

ITT TECHNICAL INSTITUTE
1001 Magnolia Ave, Webster TX 77598-2070
Roy Johnson, Registrar
281-316-4700 Fax: 281-316-4750
Website: www.itt.tech.edu

SCHOOL OF AUTOMOTIVE MACHINISTS
1911 Antoine Dr, Houston TX 77055-1803
Admissions
713-683-3817 Fax: 713-683-7077
Website: www.samracing.com
E-mail: admissions@samracing.com

Tyler Junior College
PO Box 9020, Tyler TX 75711-9020
Joan Jones, Interim Dean
800-687-5680
Website: www.tjc.edu
E-mail: jjon@tjc.edu
See listing under "Community and Junior Colleges"

Western Technical College
9624 Plaza Cir, El Paso TX 79927-2105
Bill Terrell, Chief Administrative Officer
915-760-8123
Website: www.wtc-ep.edu
E-mail: bterrell@wtc-ep.edu

UTAH

ITT TECHNICAL INSTITUTE
920 Levoy Dr, Murray UT 84123-2500
Gary Wood, Director of Recruitment
801-263-3313 Fax: 801-263-3497
Website: www.itt-tech.edu
E-mail: gwood@itt-tech.edu

WASHINGTON

BATES TECHNICAL COLLEGE
1101 S Yakima Ave, Tacoma WA 98405-4895
David Borofsky, President
253-680-7000 Fax: 253-680-7101
Website: www.bates.ctc.edu
E-mail: info@bates.ctc.edu

Everett Community College
2000 Tower St, Everett WA 98201
Christine Kerlin, Associate Dean
425-388-9100 Fax: 425-388-9173
Website: www.everettcc.edu
E-mail: ckerlin@everettcc.edu

Lake Washington Technical College
11605 132nd Ave NE, Kirkland WA 98034-8505
James B. West, Director of Admissions
425-739-8100 Fax: 425-739-8110
Website: www.lwtc.ctc.edu

SHORELINE COMMUNITY COLLEGE
16101 Greenwood Ave N, Shoreline WA 98133-5696
Chris Melton, Acting Registrar
206-546-4581 Fax: 206-546-5835
Website: www.shoreline.edu

Walla Walla Community College
500 Tausick Way, Walla Walla WA 99362-9270
Greg Farrens, Director
509-527-4684 or 877-992-9922 Fax: 509-527-4480
Website: www.wwcc.edu
E-mail: greg.farrens@wwcc.edu
See listing under "Community and Junior Colleges"

WISCONSIN

Wisconsin Indianhead Technical College
505 Pine Ridge Dr, Shell Lake WI 54871
Gene Rosburg, Dean
800-243-9482 Fax: 715-468-2819
Website: www.witc.edu
E-mail: eugene.rosburg@witc.edu

: :PREPARATORY SCHOOLS FOR BOYS

Primarily Boarding

ALABAMA

Lyman Ward Military Academy
PO Box 550, Camp Hill AL 36850-0550
Maj. Charles Livings, Director of Admissions
256-896-4127

ARKANSAS

Subiaco Academy
405 N Subiaco Ave, Subiaco AR 72865-9798
Fr. Aaron Pirrera, O.S.B., Headmaster
800-364-7824

CALIFORNIA

ARMY AND NAVY ACADEMY
PO Box 3000, Carlsbad CA 92018-3000
Elizabeth Kalivas, Director of Admissions
760-729-2385 ext. 400 Fax: 760-434-5948
Website: www.armyandnavyacademy.org
E-mail: admissions@armyandnavyacademy.org

ST. CATHERINES MILITARY ACADEMY
215 N Harbor Blvd, Anaheim CA 92805-2596
Angela Ippolito, Director of Admissions
714-772-1363 Fax: 714-772-3004
Website: www.stcatherinesmilitaryacademy.org
E-mail: admissions@stcatherinesmilitaryacademy.org

St. Michael's Preparatory School
19292 El Toro Rd, Silverado CA 92676-9710
949-858-0222

CONNECTICUT

Avon Old Farms School
500 Old Farms Rd, Avon CT 06001-2799
Kenneth H. LaRocque, Headmaster
800-464-2866

Oxford Academy
1393 Boston Post Rd, Westbrook CT 06498-1953
860-399-6247

The Rectory School
PO Box 68, Pomfret CT 06258
860-928-7759

ST. THOMAS MORE SCHOOL
45 Cottage Rd, Oakdale CT 06370-1051
Timothy Riordan, Director of Admissions
860-823-3861 Fax: 860-823-3863
Website: www.stthomasmoreschool.com
E-mail: stmadmit@stthomasmoreschool.com

SALISBURY SCHOOL
251 Canaan Rd, Salisbury CT 06068-1602
Peter B. Gilbert, Director of Admissions & Financial Aid
860-435-5700 Fax: 860-435-5750
Website: www.salisburyschool.org
E-mail: pgilbert@salisburyschool.org

South Kent School
40 Bulls Bridge Rd, South Kent CT 06785-1199
Richard A. Brande, Director of Admissions & Financial Aid
860-927-3539

WOODHALL SCHOOL
PO Box 550, Bethlehem CT 06751-0550
Matthew Woodhall, Contact
203-266-7788 Fax: 203-266-5896
Website: www.woodhallschool.org
E-mail: woodhallschool@woodhallschool.org

DISTRICT OF COLUMBIA

ST. ALBANS SCHOOL
Mount Saint Alban, Washington DC 20016
Mason Lecky, Director of Admissions and Financial Aid
202-537-6440 Fax: 202-537-2225
Website: www.stalbansschool.org
E-mail: sta_admission@cathedral.org

GEORGIA

Riverside Military Academy
2001 Riverside Dr, Gainesville GA 30501-1227
Jad Davis, Director of Admissions
800-GO-CADET (462-2338)

ILLINOIS

Marmion Academy
1000 Butterfield Rd, Aurora IL 60502
630-897-6936

INDIANA

Howe Military School
5755 N State Road 9, Howe IN 46746
260-562-2131 ext. 221

KANSAS

Maur Hill - Mount Academy
1000 Green St, Atchison KS 66002-3078
913-367-5482

ST. JOHN'S MILITARY SCHOOL
PO Box 5020, Salina KS 67402
Jeff Coverdale, Director of Admissions
785-823-7231 Fax: 785-309-5489
Website: www.sjms.org
E-mail: jeffc@sjms.org

MAINE

Bridgton Academy
PO Box 292, North Bridgton ME 04057-0292
Randall M. Greason, Headmaster
Lisa M. Antell, Director of Admissions
207-647-3322

MARYLAND

Georgetown Preparatory School
10900 Rockville Pike
North Bethesda MD 20852-3299
301-493-5000

MASSACHUSETTS

Belmont Hill School
350 Prospect St, Belmont MA 02478-2662
Michael R. Grant, Director of Admission
617-484-4410

Eaglebrook School
Pine Nook Rd, Deerfield MA 01342
413-774-7411

THE FESSENDEN SCHOOL
250 Waltham St, West Newton MA 02465-1750
Caleb W. Thomson '79, Director of Admissions
617-630-2300 Fax: 617-630-2303
Website: www.fessenden.org
E-mail: admissions@fessenden.org

HILLSIDE SCHOOL
404 Robin Hill St, Marlborough MA 01752
David Beecher, Headmaster
508-485-2824 Fax: 508-485-4420
Website: www.hillsideschool.net
E-mail: admissions@hillsideschool.net

ST. JOHN'S PREPARATORY SCHOOL
DAY SCHOOL ONLY
72 Spring St, Danvers MA 01923-1545
John A. Driscoll, Dean of Admissions and Freshman Academic Programs
978-774-1050 Fax: 978-774-5069
Website: www.stjohnsprep.org
E-mail: jdriscoll@stjohnsprep.org

MICHIGAN

ST. MARY'S PREPARATORY HIGH SCHOOL
3535 Indian Trl, Orchard Lake MI 48324-1601
Kevin Kosco, Dean of Admission
248-683-0531 Fax: 248-683-1740
Website: www.stmarysprep.com
E-mail: info@stmarysprep.com

MINNESOTA

Saint Thomas Academy
949 Mendota Heights Rd
Mendota Heights MN 55120-1496
John Kenney, Director of Admissions
651-454-4570

MISSISSIPPI

ST. STANISLAUS COLLEGE PREP
304 S Beach Blvd, Bay Saint Louis MS 39520-4301
Dolores Richmond, Director of Admissions
228-467-9057 Fax: 228-466-2972
Website: www.ststan.com
E-mail: admissions@ststan.com

MISSOURI

Chaminade College Preparatory School
425 S Lindbergh Blvd, Saint Louis MO 63131-2799
Matthew J. Saxer, Admissions Director
314-993-4400

MISSOURI MILITARY ACADEMY
204 N Grand St, Mexico MO 65265
Maj. Dennis Diederich, Director of Admissions
888-564-6662 Fax: 573-581-0081
Website: www.mma-cadet.org
E-mail: info@mma.mexico.mo.us

NEBRASKA

MOUNT MICHAEL BENEDICTINE SCHOOL
22520 Mount Michael Rd, Elkhorn NE 68022-3401
Director of Admissions
402-289-2541 Fax: 402-289-4539
Website: www.mountmichaelhs.com
E-mail: admissions@mountmichael.org

NEW HAMPSHIRE

CARDIGAN MOUNTAIN SCHOOL
62 Alumni Dr, Canaan NH 03741-7210
Marten J. Wennik, Interim Director of Admissions
603-523-3548 Fax: 603-523-3565
Website: www.cardigan.org
E-mail: mwennick@cardigan.org

Hampshire Country School
122 Hampshire Rd, Rindge NH 03461-3913
603-899-3325

NEW JERSEY

THE AMERICAN BOYCHOIR SCHOOL
19 Lambert Dr, Princeton NJ 08540-2304
Nathan Wadley, Associate Director of Admission
609-924-5858 Fax: 609-924-5812
Website: www.americanboychoir.org
E-mail: admissions@americanboychoir.org

NEW YORK

Gow School
PO Box 85, South Wales NY 14139
Robert Garcia, Director of Admissions
585-652-3450

MILFORD ACADEMY
PO Box 878, New Berlin NY 13411
Andrew Ruffino, Dean of Students
607-847-9280 Fax: 607-847-9250
Website: www.milfordacademy.org
E-mail: bc55@milfordacademy.org

SAINT THOMAS CHOIR SCHOOL
202 W 58th St, New York NY 10019-1406
Fr. Charles Wallace, Headmaster
Ruth Cobb, Director of Admissions
212-247-3311 Fax: 212-247-3393
Website: www.choirschool.org
E-mail: rcobb@choirschool.org

Trinity-Pawling School
700 State Route 22, Pawling NY 12564
845-855-3100

NORTH CAROLINA

CHRIST SCHOOL
500 Christ School Rd, Arden NC 28704-8405
Denis Stokes, Director of Admission
800-422-3212 or 828-684-6232 Fax: 828-684-4869
Website: www.christschool.org
E-mail: admission@christschool.org

Oak Ridge Military Academy
PO Box 498, Oak Ridge NC 27310-0498
Lieutenant Colonel Ray Wilson, Vice President for Admissions
336-643-4131 ext. 132

OHIO

Grand River Academy
PO Box 222, Austinburg OH 44010-0222
Sam Corabi, Director of Admission
440-275-2811

PENNSYLVANIA

Academy of the New Church Boys School
PO Box 707, Bryn Athyn PA 19009
215-947-4200

CARSON LONG MILITARY INSTITUTE
PO Box 98, New Bloomfield PA 17068-0098
Lieutenant Colonel David M. Comolli, Academic Dean
717-582-2121 Fax: 717-582-8763
Website: www.carsonlong.org
E-mail: carson6@pa.net

CFS The School at Church Farm
PO Box 2000, Paoli PA 19301-0319
Richard Lunardi, Director of Admissions
610-363-5347

THE KISKI SCHOOL
1888 Brett Ln, Saltsburg PA 15681-8951
Adam M. Schapiro, Associate Director of Admissions
877-547-5448 Fax: 724-639-8596
Website: www.kiski.org
E-mail: admissions@kiski.org

THE PHELPS SCHOOL
583 Sugartown Rd, Malvern PA 19355-2800
Michael J. Reardon, Director of Admissions
610-644-1754 Fax: 610-644-6679
Website: www.thephelpsschool.org
E-mail: admis@thephelpsschool.org

Saint Gregory's Academy
RR 8 Box 8214, Moscow PA 18444
Alan J. Hicks, Headmaster
570-842-8112

Valley Forge Military Academy
1001 Eagle Rd, Wayne PA 19087-3695
610-989-1200

SOUTH CAROLINA

Camden Military Academy
520 Highway 1 N, Camden SC 29020-2599
803-432-6001

TENNESSEE

McCallie School
500 Dodds Ave, Chattanooga TN 37404-3991
David Hughes, Director of Boarding Admission
423-624-8300

TEXAS

CENTRAL CATHOLIC HIGH SCHOOL
1403 N Saint Mary's St, San Antonio TX 78215-1785
Belia Gonzalez McDonald, Admissions Coordinator
210-225-6794 ext. 209 Fax: 210-227-9353
Website: www.cchs-satx.org
E-mail: admissions@cchs-satx.org

MARINE MILITARY ACADEMY
320 Iwo Jima Blvd, Harlingen TX 78550-3698
Admissions Department
956-423-6006 Fax: 956-421-9273
Website: www.marinemilitaryacademy.com
E-mail: admissions@mma-tx.org

VIRGINIA

BLUE RIDGE SCHOOL
273 Mayo Dr, Saint George VA 22935
William Darrin, III, Director of Admissions & Financial Aid
434-985-2811 Fax: 434-985-7215
Website: www.blueridgeschool.com
E-mail: admissions@blueridgeschool.com

CHRISTCHURCH SCHOOL
49 Seahorse Ln, Christchurch VA 23031
Nancy M. Nolan, Director of Admission
804-758-2306 or 800-296-2306 Fax: 804-758-0721
Website: www.christchurchschool.org
E-mail: admission@christchurchschool.org

Fishburne Military School
PO Box 988, Waynesboro VA 22980-0722
Brigadier General William Alexander, (VA), Superintendent
Major Scott Mangum, (VA), Director of Admissions
800-946-7773 Fax: 540-946-7738
Website: www.fishburne.org
E-mail: crichmond@fishburne.org

Fork Union Military Academy
PO Box 278, Fork Union VA 23055-0278
Lt. Gen. John E. Jackson Jr., USAF (Ret.), President
Lt. Col. Steve Macek, Director of Admissions
800-462-3862

HARGRAVE MILITARY ACADEMY
200 Military Dr, Chatham VA 24531-4683
Frank Martin, Director of Admissions
800-432-2480 Fax: 434-432-3129
Website: www.hargrave.edu
E-mail: admissions@hargrave.edu
Established 1909. Private. College Prep. Male Boarding 7th grade - post graduate. Accreditation: SACS, VAIS. Tuition: $26,500. Enrollment: 405. Faculty: 48. Student-faculty ratio: 11:1. Degrees: High School Diploma. Library: 6,000 volumes. 12 buildings on 214 acres. Wireless campus expands the classroom. Laptop computers issued to high school students. How to study course, indoor 50-meter pool, summer school, Judeo-Christian values, full athletic program.

Woodberry Forest School
Woodberry Forest VA 22989
Dennis M. Campbell, Headmaster
Joseph G. Coleman, Director of Admissions
540-672-3900

WISCONSIN

ST. JOHN'S NORTHWESTERN MILITARY ACADEMY
1101 N Genesee St, Delafield WI 53018-1498
Mr. Jack H. Albert, Jr., President
Maj. Duane Rutherford, Director of Enrollment Services
800-752-2338 or 262-646-7199 Fax: 262-646-7128
Website: www.sjnma.org
E-mail: admissions@sjnma.org
Established in 1884. Private. Boys grades 7-12. Accreditation: ISACS, NAIS, AMCSUS, TABS. Tuition, room & board: $29,750. Enrollment: 315 boarding; 9 day. Faculty: 39. Student-faculty ratio: 12:1. 10 buildings on 150 acres. Gym, pool, tennis courts, golf course. College preparatory boy's boarding school. Day program for grades 7-12 only. 30 minutes from Milwaukee and 90 minutes from Chicago. Extensive athletic and extracurricular offerings. JROTC honor school with distinction.

St. Lawrence Seminary High School
301 Church St, Mount Calvary WI 53057-9699
920-753-3911

: :PREPARATORY SCHOOLS - COEDUCATIONAL

Primarily Boarding

ALABAMA

Indian Springs School
190 Woodward Dr, Indian Springs AL 35124-3272
E.T. Brown III, Director of Admission
888-843-9493

Marion Military Institute
1101 Washington St, Marion AL 36756
800-MMI-1842

RANDOLPH SCHOOL
1005 Drake Ave SE, Huntsville AL 35802-1099
Nancy Hodges, Admissions Director
256-881-1701 Fax: 256-881-1784
Website: www.randolphschool.net
E-mail: admissions@randolphschool.net

ARIZONA

Fenster School of Southern Arizona
8500 E Ocotillo Dr, Tucson AZ 85750-9670
Michael Lyles, Director of Admissions
520-749-3340

HOLBROOK SDA INDIAN SCHOOL
PO Box 910, Holbrook AZ 86025
Mary June Bragg, Vice Principal
928-524-6845 Fax: 928-524-3190
Website: www.hissda.org
E-mail: hischool@cybertrails.com

Oak Creek Ranch School
PO Box 4329, Sedona AZ 86340-4329
David Wick Jr., Headmaster
928-634-5571

Orme School
HC 63 Box 3040, Mayer AZ 86333-9799
520-632-7601

Thunderbird Adventist Academy
7410 E Sutton Dr, Scottsdale AZ 85260-3915
480-948-3300

Verde Valley School
3511 Verde Valley School Rd
Sedona AZ 86351-9541
Donald W. Smith, Director of Admissions
928-284-2272

ARKANSAS

Harding Academy
PO Box 10775, Searcy AR 72149-0001
501-279-7200

CALIFORNIA

Athenian School
2100 Mount Diablo Scenic Blvd
Danville CA 94506-2002
925-837-5375

The Bishop's School
7607 La Jolla Blvd, La Jolla CA 92037-4703
Josie Alvarez, Director of Admissions
858-459-4021

Cate School
PO Box 5005, Carpinteria CA 93014-5005
Peter J. Mack, Director of Admission
805-684-4127

DUNN SCHOOL
PO Box 98, Los Olivos CA 93441-0098
Ann Greenough, Director of Admissions
805-688-6471 Fax: 805-686-2078
Website: www.dunnschool.org
E-mail: admissions@dunnschool.org

Happy Valley School
PO Box 850, Ojai CA 93024-0850
805-646-4343

HARKER SCHOOL
500 Saratoga Ave, San Jose CA 95129-1387
Nan Nielsen, Director of Admissions & Financial Aid
408-249-2510 Fax: 408-984-2325
Website: www.harker.org
E-mail: admissions@harker.org

IDYLLWILD ARTS ACADEMY
PO Box 38, Idyllwild CA 92549-0038
Karen Porter, Dean of Admission
951-659-2171 ext. 2223 Fax: 951-659-5463
Website: www.idyllwildarts.org
E-mail: admission@idyllwildarts.org

LINFIELD CHRISTIAN SCHOOL
31950 Pauba Rd, Temecula CA 92592-3523
Angelo Iacoboni, Director of Admissions
951-676-8111 Fax: 951-695-1291
Website: www.linfield.com
E-mail: info@linfield.com

LYCEE INTERNATIONAL DE LOS ANGELES
4155 Russell Ave, Los Angeles CA 90027-4509
Valerie Lesure, Director of Admissions
323-665-4526 Fax: 323-665-2607
Website: www.lilaschool.com
E-mail: valerie.lesure@lilaschool.com

Midland School
PO Box 8, Los Olivos CA 93441-0008
805-688-5114

MONTCLAIR COLLEGE PREPARATORY SCHOOL
8071 Sepulveda Blvd, Van Nuys CA 91402-4400
Dr. V.S. Simpson, Director
818-787-5290 Fax: 818-786-3382
Website: www.montclairprep.org

Monterey Bay Academy
783 San Andreas Rd
La Selva Beach CA 95076-1911
831-728-1481

Monte Vista Christian School
2 School Way, Watsonville CA 95076-9715
831-722-8178

OAK GROVE SCHOOL
220 W Lomita Ave, Ojai CA 93023-2298
Joy Maguire-Parsons, Admissions Director
805-646-8236 ext. 109 Fax: 805-646-6509
Website: www.oakgroveschool.com
E-mail: enroll@oakgroveschool.com

Ojai Valley School
723 El Paseo Rd, Ojai CA 93023-2498
805-646-1423

Robert Louis Stevenson High School
3152 Forest Lake Rd, Pebble Beach CA 93953-3200
831-626-5300

Sacred Heart Preparatory School
150 Valparaiso Ave, Atherton CA 94027-4402
Rick Diaz, Director of Admissions
650-322-1866

Southwestern Academy
2800 Monterey Rd, San Marino CA 91108-1798
626-799-5010

Squaw Valley Academy
PO Box 2667, Olympic Valley CA 96146-2667
Paul A. Jette, Head of School
530-583-1558

Thacher School
5025 Thacher Rd, Ojai CA 93023-9001
William P. McMahon, Director of Admission
805-646-4377

Villanova Prep School
12096 N Ventura Ave, Ojai CA 93023-3999
805-646-1464

The Webb Schools
1175 W Baseline Rd, Claremont CA 91711-2199
Leo G. Marshall, Director of Admission and Financial Aid
909-482-5214

WOODSIDE PRIORY SCHOOL
302 Portola Rd, Portola Valley CA 94028-7897
Al D. Zappelli, Director of Admissions
650-851-8223 Fax: 650-851-2839
Website: www.woodsidepriory.com
E-mail: azappelli@woodsidepriory.com
Located within 40 minutes of San Francisco, the Priory combines its rural 60-acre campus with a talented faculty, a 10:1 student/teacher ratio, a strong college and university preparatory curriculum, and a competitive athletic program. It seeks to embody the values at the heart of Benedictine education — belief in order and discipline in one's life, respect for learning, and an appreciation for the shared experience of community life. Priory students are challenged to develop their fullest potential in the classrooms, on the athletic fields and in their relationships with one another. The Boarding Program embodies a family model with professional residential advisors mentoring small groups of ten boarders each. International in scope, the program attracts students from all parts of the world and throughout the western United States. The goal of the Boarding Program is to develop individuals personally but to also be essential members of a community. Seamless interaction with the Priory's three hundred day students in the classrooms, sports, performing and visual arts, club and community service activities, as well as at Chapel and meals, provides for diversity and achievement of common goals. Come visit the Priory and see why it is the "Right Place at the Right Time" for you!

COLORADO

Accelerated Schools Foundation
2160 S Cook St, Denver CO 80210-4914
303-758-2003

Colorado Academy
3800 S Pierce St, Denver CO 80235-2404
303-986-1501

COLORADO ROCKY MOUNTAIN SCHOOL
1493 County Road 106, Carbondale CO 81623
Molly Hall, Director of Admission
970-963-2562 Fax: 970-963-9865
Website: www.crms.org
E-mail: mhall@crms.org

The Colorado Springs School
21 Broadmoor Ave
Colorado Springs CO 80906-3699
Amie Hilles, Director of Admissions
719-475-9747

Colorado Timberline Academy
35554 Highway 550, Durango CO 81301-8653
970-247-5898

Crested Butte Academy
PO Box 1180, Crested Butte CO 81224
888-633-0222

Denver Academy
4400 E Iliff Ave, Denver CO 80222
Dan Loan, Director of Admissions
303-777-5870

FOUNTAIN VALLEY SCHOOL OF COLORADO
6155 Fountain Valley School Rd
Colorado Springs CO 80911-2299
Randy Roach, Director of Admission and Financial Aid
719-390-7035 Fax: 719-390-7762
Website: www.fvs.edu
E-mail: admissions@fvs.edu

The Lowell Whiteman School
42605 County Road 36
Steamboat Springs CO 80487-9215
Deb Smith, Director of Admissions
970-879-1350

CONNECTICUT

CANTERBURY SCHOOL
101 Aspetuck Ave, New Milford CT 06776-1739
Thomas J. Sheehy III, Headmaster
Keith R. Holton, Director of Admission
860-210-3832 Fax: 860-350-1120
Website: www.cbury.org
E-mail: admissions@cbury.org

Founded in 1915 and still guided by lay Roman Catholics, Canterbury is a college preparatory coeducational boarding and day school for students in grades 9-12.

Our School

150-acre hilltop campus in New Milford, CT. Complete wireless campus network with internet access for all. Average class size: 12. Traditional two-semester school year. Numerous clubs and community service organizations. Library with 18,000 books, 36 computers, and access to major daily and weekly periodicals as well as 3,500 videos and DVDs.

Our Students

369 students (218 boarders, 151 day). 57% male, 43% female. Students from 17 states and 15 countries. SAT: the middle 50% of the class of 2004 scored in the 540-640 range (verbal) and 500-600 (math). Tuition: $38,000 (boarding), $29,000 (day). 38% receive financial aid.

The Faculty

75 members. 53% male, 47% female. 50 have advanced degrees. More than 50% of the faculty has been at Canterbury 5 years or more.

Academics

Canterbury offers a complete range of courses, including 15 A.P. courses. The fields of study include English, Mathematics, the Sciences, Languages, History, Computer Science, Fine Arts, Music, Theology, and Independent Study.

Arts

In the visual arts, Canterbury offers more than 15 courses from drawing to ceramics. For the music minded student, we have numerous instrumental offerings and 2 vocal groups.

Athletics

All 365 students participate in interscholastic sports each season. 52 teams participate in 19 sports, including water polo, cross country, soccer, field hockey, football, crew, basketball, hockey, wrestling, swimming, squash, volleyball, baseball, lacrosse, softball, golf, and tennis.

College

Our college placement office works with students during their entire time at Canterbury as they proceed through the selection, application, and acceptance processes. Here is a sample list of colleges and universities our students have attended in the past five years: Bates, Yale, Cornell, USMA (West Point), WPI, Bowdoin, Dartmouth, Brown, Bucknell, Colgate, Fairfield, Harvard, Holy Cross, Lehigh, Notre Dame, Northwestern, Providence, RPI, Tulane, Vanderbilt.

Cheshire Academy
10 Main St, Cheshire CT 06410-2496
203-272-5396

Choate Rosemary Hall School
333 Christian St, Wallingford CT 06492-3818
203-697-2000

FORMAN SCHOOL
PO Box 80, 12 Norfolk Rd, Litchfield CT 06759-0080
Beth Rainey, Director of Admissions
860-567-1802 Fax: 860-567-3501
Website: www.formanschool.org
E-mail: admissions@formanschool.org

THE GUNNERY
99 Green Hill Rd, Washington CT 06793-1200
Thomas W. Adams, Director of Admissions
860-868-7334 Fax: 860-868-1614
Website: www.gunnery.org
E-mail: admissions@gunnery.org.

THE HOTCHKISS SCHOOL
Lakeville CT 06039
Dr. Robert H. Mattoon Jr., Head of School
William D. Leahy, Dean of Admission
860-435-3102 Fax: 860-435-0042
Website: www.hotchkiss.org
E-mail: admission@hotchkiss.org

HYDE SCHOOL
PO Box 237, Woodstock CT 06281-0237
Holly E. Thompson, Director of Admissions
860-963-9096 Fax: 860-928-0612
Website: www.hyde.edu
E-mail: woodstock.admissions@hyde.edu

INDIAN MOUNTAIN SCHOOL
211 Indian Mountain Rd, Lakeville CT 06039-2029
Christopher C. Wilkes, Director Admission and Financial Aid
860-435-0871 Fax: 860-435-1380
Website: www.indianmountain.org
E-mail: admissions@indianmountain.org

Kent School
PO Box 2006, Kent CT 06757-0640
860-927-6000

LOOMIS CHAFFEE SCHOOL
4 Batchelder Rd, Windsor CT 06095-3031
Thomas D. Southworth, Director of Admissions
860-687-6000 Fax: 860-687-1100
Website: www.loomis.org
E-mail: admission@loomis.org

Marianapolis Preparatory School
PO Box 304, Thompson CT 06277
Daniel Harrop, Director of Admissions & Immigration Officer
860-923-9565

Marvelwood School
PO Box 3001, Kent CT 06757-3001
860-927-0047

POMFRET SCHOOL
398 Pomfret St, PO Box 128, Pomfret CT 06258
Erik Bertelsen, Assistant Head for Admissions and Enrollment
860-963-6120 Fax: 860-963-2042
Website: www.pomfretschool.org
E-mail: admission@pomfretschool.org

Rumsey Hall School
201 Romford Rd, Washington Depot CT 06794-1399
Matthew S. Hoeniger, Assistant Headmaster
860-868-0535

Suffield Academy
PO Box 999, Suffield CT 06078-0999
Charles Cahn III, Assistant Headmaster
800-668-7315

The Taft School
110 Woodbury Rd, Watertown CT 06795-2100
Frederick Wandelt, Director of Admissions
860-945-7777

WATKINSON SCHOOL
180 Bloomfield Ave, Hartford CT 06105-1096
John Crosson, Director of Admissions
860-236-5618 Fax: 860-233-8295
Website: www.watkinson.org
E-mail: john_crosson@watkinson.org

WESTMINSTER SCHOOL
995 Hopmeadow St, Simsbury CT 06070
Jon C. Deveaux, Director of Admissions
860-408-3000 Fax: 860-408-3001
Website: www.westminster-school.org
E-mail: admit@westminster-school.org

WOOSTER SCHOOL
91 Miry Brook Rd, Danbury CT 06810-7417
George N. King, Jr., Headmaster
Samuel Gaudet, Director of Admissions
203-830-3916 Fax: 203-790-7147
Website: www.woosterschool.org
E-mail: samuel.gaudet@woosterschool.org

DELAWARE

ARCHMERE ACADEMY
3600 Philadelphia Pike, Claymont DE 19703-3108
John J. Jordan, Director of Admissions
302-798-6632 or 610-485-0373 Fax: 302-798-7290
Website: www.archmereacademy.com
E-mail: jjordan@archmereacademy.com

Established 1932. Private. Coed. Accreditation: MSACS. Tuition: $17,100. Enrollment: 510. Faculty: 57. Student-faculty ratio: 9:1. Library: 14,000 volumes. 8 buildings on 38 acres, including Justin Diny Science Center and Performing Arts Center. Strong visual and performing arts programs. 18 Advanced Placement classes offered. Quiet, scenic, college-like campus in suburban setting. Multi-Media Center, Writing Center, Campus ministry, computerized library and science laboratories, extensive community service clubs, student publications, 26 sports teams. In 2007, a new student life center was constructed as part of a $16M campus renovation project.

ST. ANDREW'S SCHOOL
350 Noxontown Rd, Middletown DE 19709-1605
Daniel T. Roach, Headmaster
Louisa H. Zendt, Director of Admission
302-285-4231 Fax: 302-378-7120
Website: www.standrews-de.org
E-mail: admissions@standrews-de.org

FLORIDA

Admiral Farragut Academy
501 Park St N, Saint Petersburg FL 33710
David Graham, Director of Admissions
727-384-5500

Bolles School
7400 San Jose Blvd, Jacksonville FL 32217-3499
904-733-9292

Florida Air Academy
1950 S Academy Dr, Melbourne FL 32901-4396
Colonel James Dwight, President
321-723-3211 ext. 30041 Fax: 321-676-0422
Website: www.flair.com
E-mail: tderegnaucourt@flair.com

FOREST LAKE ACADEMY
3909 E Semoran Blvd, Apopka FL 32703-6199
Gloria Becker, Principal
407-862-8411 Fax: 407-862-7050
Website: www.forestlakeacademy.org
E-mail: beckerg@forestlake.org

Hobe Sound Christian Academy
PO Box 1065, Hobe Sound FL 33475-1065
800-881-5534

MONTVERDE ACADEMY
17235 7th St, Montverde FL 34756
Robin Revis-Pyke, Dean of Admission
407-469-2561 Fax: 407-469-3711
Website: www.montverde.org
E-mail: admissions@montverde.org

Pine Crest School
1501 NE 62nd St, Fort Lauderdale FL 33334-5199
954-492-4100

Saddlebrook Preparatory School
5700 Saddlebrook Way
Wesley Chapel FL 33543-4499
Michelle Axthelm, Admissions Coordinator
813-907-4300

Saint Andrew's School
3900 Jog Rd, Boca Raton FL 33434-4498
George E. Andrews II, Headmaster
561-210-2000

GEORGIA

DARLINGTON SCHOOL
1014 Cave Spring Rd SW, Rome GA 30161-4700
Casey Zimmer, Director of Admission & Financial Aid
706-235-6051 or 800-36-TIGER Fax: 706-232-3600
Website: www.darlingtonschool.org
E-mail: admission@darlingtonschool.org

Horizons School
1900 Dekalb Ave NE, Atlanta GA 30307-2300
Les Garber, Administrator
404-378-2219

Rabun Gap-Nacoochee School
339 Nacoochee Dr, Rabun Gap GA 30568-2200
Adele Yermack, Director of Admission
706-746-7467

St. Andrew's School
PO Box 30639, Savannah GA 31410-0639
Larry C. Berry, Headmaster
912-897-4941

TALLULAH FALLS SCHOOL
PO Box 249, Tallulah Falls GA 30573-0249
Susan M. Waldorf, Director of Admissions
706-754-0400 Fax: 706-754-5757
Website: tallulahfalls.org
E-mail: admissions@tallulahfalls.org

Woodward Academy
1662 Rugby Ave, College Park GA 30337
R.L. Slider, Vice-President\Dean of Admissions
404-765-4001

HAWAII

Hawaii Preparatory Academy
PO Box 428, Kamuela HI 96743-0428
808-885-7321

Mid-Pacific Institute
2445 Kaala St, Honolulu HI 96822-2299
808-973-5000

Seabury Hall
480 Olinda Rd, Makawao HI 96768-7352
Elaine Nelson, Director of Admissions
808-572-0807

IDAHO

Gem State Academy
16115 S Montana Ave, Caldwell ID 83607-8365
208-459-1627

ILLINOIS

Elgin Academy
350 Park St, Elgin IL 60120-4471
Dr. John W. Cooper, Head of School
Erik C. Calhoun, Director of Admission
847-695-0303

The Governor French Academy
219 W Main St, Belleville IL 62220-1537
Carol Wilson, Director of Admissions
618-233-7542

LAKE FOREST ACADEMY
1500 W Kennedy Rd, Lake Forest IL 60045-1099
Karen Cegelski, Dean of Admission
847-615-3267 Fax: 847-295-8149
Website: www.lfanet.org
E-mail: kcegelski@lfanet.org

The Latin School of Chicago
59 W North Blvd, Chicago IL 60610
Frank Hogan, Headmaster
312-582-6000

MORGAN PARK ACADEMY
2153 W 111th St, Chicago IL 60643-3917
J. William Adams, Headmaster
773-881-6700 Fax: 773-881-8409
Website: www.morganparkacademy.org

INDIANA

Brebeuf Jesuit Preparatory School
2801 W 86th St, Indianapolis IN 46268-1925
317-876-4726

CULVER ACADEMIES AND SUMMER CAMPS
1300 Academy Rd # 157, Culver IN 46511-1234
Mike Turnbull, Director of Admissions
574-842-7100 Fax: 574-842-8066
Website: www.culver.org
E-mail: admissions@culver.org

Howe Military School
5755 N State Road 9, Howe IN 46746
260-562-2131 ext. 221

La Lumiere School
PO Box 5005, La Porte IN 46352-5005
219-326-7450

IOWA

Scattergood Friends School
1951 Delta Ave, West Branch IA 52358-8507
Kenneth Hinshaw, Director
Sarah French, Admissions Director
319-643-7628

KANSAS

Thomas More Preparatory-Marian
1701 Hall St, Hays KS 67601-3145
785-625-6577

KENTUCKY

The June Buchanan School
100 Purpose Rd, Pippa Passes KY 41844-9701
Jeemes Akers, Director
606-368-6108

ONEIDA BAPTIST INSTITUTE

PO Box 67, Oneida KY 40972
606-847-4111 Fax: 606-847-4496
Website: www.oneidaschool.org
E-mail: admissions4obi@yahoo.com

MAINE

Carrabassett Valley Academy
3197 Carrabassett Dr
Carrabassett Valley ME 04947-5705
207-237-2250

Fryeburg Academy
745 Main St, Fryeburg ME 04037-1329
Stephanie S. Morin, Director of Admission
877-935-2013

Gould Academy
PO Box 860, Bethel ME 04217-0860
John A. Kerney, Director of Admissions & External Affairs
207-824-7777

Hebron Academy
PO Box 309, Hebron ME 04238-0309
Office of Admission
888-432-7664

HYDE SCHOOL

616 High St, Bath ME 04530-5002
Melissa Burroughs, Director of Admission
207-443-7101 Fax: 207-442-9346
Website: www.hyde.edu
E-mail: bath.admissions@hyde.edu

Kents Hill School
PO Box 257, Kents Hill ME 04349-0257
Loren B. Mitchell, Director of Admissions
207-685-4914

MAINE CENTRAL INSTITUTE

295 Main St, Pittsfield ME 04967
Clint Williams, Director of Admissions
207-487-2282 Fax: 207-487-3512
Website: www.mci-school.org
E-mail: cwilliams@mci-school.org

MARYLAND

Gunston Day School
PO Box 200, Centreville MD 21617-0200
Marc S. Buckley, Director of Admission
410-758-0620

McDonogh School
PO Box 380, Owings Mills MD 21117-0380
410-363-0600

Saint James School
College Rd, Saint James MD 21781-9999
Win Sherman, Director of Admissions
301-733-9330

SANDY SPRING FRIENDS SCHOOL

16923 Norwood Rd, Sandy Spring MD 20860-1199
Mecha Inman, Director of Admissions
301-774-7455 Fax: 301-924-1115
Website: www.ssfs.org
E-mail: admissions@ssfs.org

West Nottingham Academy
1079 Firetower Rd, Colora MD 21917-1599
Heidi K.L. Sprinkle, Director of Admission
410-658-5556

MASSACHUSETTS

Academy at Charlemont
Mohawk Trl, Charlemont MA 01339
413-339-4912

The Bement School
94 Main St, Deerfield MA 01342
Matthew Evans, Director of Admission
413-774-7061

BERKSHIRE SCHOOL

245 N Undermountain Rd, Sheffield MA 01257-9672
Andrew Bogardus, Director of Admission
413-229-1003 Fax: 413-229-1016
Website: www.berkshireschool.org
E-mail: admission@berkshireschool.org

BROOKS SCHOOL

1160 Great Pond Rd, North Andover MA 01845-1298
Kevin Breen, Interim Director of Admission
978-725-6272 Fax: 978-725-6298
Website: www.brooksschool.org
E-mail: admission@brooksschool.org

Buxton School
291 South St, Williamstown MA 01267
413-458-3919

THE CAMBRIDGE SCHOOL OF WESTON

Georgian Rd, Weston MA 02493-2198
Trish Saunders, Director of Admissions
781-642-8600 Fax: 781-398-8344
Website: www.csw.org
E-mail: admissions@csw.org

CHAPEL HILL-CHAUNCY HALL SCHOOL

785 Beaver St, Waltham MA 02452-5606
Lisa Zannella, Director of Admissions
781-314-0800 Fax: 781-894-5205
Website: www.chch.org
E-mail: admissions@chch.org

CONCORD ACADEMY

166 Main St, Concord MA 01742-2454
Pamela J. Safford, Associate Head for Enrollment and Planning
978-402-2250 Fax: 978-402-2345
Website: www.concordacademy.org
E-mail: admissions@concordacademy.org

CUSHING ACADEMY

PO Box 8000, Ashburnham MA 01430-8000
Deborah Gustafson, Interim Director of Admission
978-827-7300 Fax: 978-827-6253
Website: www.cushing.org
E-mail: admission@cushing.org

DEERFIELD ACADEMY

Deerfield MA 01342
Patricia L. Gimbel, Dean of Admission & Financial Aid
413-774-1400 Fax: 413-772-1100
Website: www.deerfield.edu
E-mail: admission@deerfield.edu

Desisto School
PO Box 369, Stockbridge MA 01262-0369
Ann Schulman, Director of Admissions
413-298-3776

Dewey Academy
389 Main St, Great Barrington MA 01230-1813
413-528-9800

Fay School
48 Main St, Southborough MA 01772-1595
508-485-0100

The Governors Academy
1 Elm St, Byfield MA 01922-2799
John Martin Doggett, Jr., Headmaster
978-499-3120

Groton School
PO Box 991, Groton MA 01450-0991
John M. Niles, Director of Admission
978-448-7510

LANDMARK SCHOOL

PO Box 227, Prides Crossing MA 01965-0227
Director of Admission
978-236-3000 Fax: 978-927-7268
Website: www.landmarkschool.org
E-mail: admission@landmarkschool.org

Enrollment High School: 315, Elementary/Middle School: 140. Landmark High School prepares students with language-based learning disabilities for college and beyond. The curriculum covers traditional secondary subjects as well as study skills and electives. Emphasis on skill acquisition and achievement help students become independent learners. Landmark offers individualized instruction and 1:1 tutorials to remediate learning differences. The program accepts students in grades 9-12, who possess average to superior intelligence and a history of healthy emotional development.

LAWRENCE ACADEMY

PO Box 992, Groton MA 01450-0992
Scott Wiggins, Head of School
Andi O'Hearn, Director of Admission
978-448-6535 Fax: 978-448-1519
Website: www.lacademy.edu
E-mail: admiss@lacademy.edu

Coeducational boarding and day school for grades 9-12. Enrollment: 394. Faculty 65. Tuition: $39,200 boarding, $29,900 day. Accreditation: NEASC.

Established in 1793, Lawrence Academy has occupied a small hill in rural New England for over 200 years. Boston, with its rich cultural and historical resources, active student life and a major international airport, is only one hour away. The school's setting, blends safe and quiet living with the advantages of a major cosmopolitan city. The warm community environment provides an ideal place to study and live.

Lawrence Academy offers a progressive student-centered curriculum. Traditional teaching is enhanced with seminars, group projects and independent study to train students' intellectual skills actively. More than seventy-five computers are distributed throughout the school to integrate technology into classes on a daily basis. A brand new academic center opened in 2005.

Two special programs complement classroom study: Winterim, a two week mini-term of special projects and trips, and the Independent Immersion Program (IIP), a program which qualifies students to design their own one or two year course of study.

A brand new Arts Center contains spacious studios for drawing, painting, ceramics, dance, music and computerized music. The recording studio allows students to mix and record their own CD's. The drama department produces three main stage productions per year and smaller productions in the black box theatre.

Athletic training is provided for all skill levels. Basic instruction is offered with some players progressing to division one, Olympic, and professional competition. A new sports complex, ice rink and 14 acres of playing fields support the schools athletic program.

THE MACDUFFIE SCHOOL

One Ames Hill Drive, Springfield MA 01105-1400
Linda Keating, Director of Admissions
413-734-4971 Fax: 413-734-6693
Website: www.macduffie.com
E-mail: admissions@macduffie.com

Established 1890. Private. Coed. College Preparatory, Grades 6 - 12. Accreditation: NEASC. Tuition: $17,995 - $18,995. Room and board: $13,905. Cultural Activities Fee: $850. Enrollment: 225. Faculty: 36. Student-Faculty Ratio: 6:1. Library: 8,000 volumes. Outstanding academic preparation, full arts program, competitive athletics. Ames Hill Boarding Program: small boarding component for grades 9-12. Students live with faculty families in stately homes on a 20-acre residential campus.

Middlesex School
PO Box 9122, Concord MA 01742-9122
978-369-2550

Milton Academy
170 Centre St, Milton MA 02186-3397
Paul Rebuck, Dean of Admission
617-898-2227

NOBLE AND GREENOUGH SCHOOL

10 Campus Dr, Dedham MA 02026-4099
Jennifer Hines, Dean of Enrollment Management
781-320-7100 Fax: 781-320-1329
Website: www.nobles.edu
E-mail: admission@nobles.edu

Northfield Mt. Hermon School
206 Main St, Northfield MA 01360-1089
Richard Mueller, Head
Pamela Safford, Director of Admissions
413-498-3227

PHILLIPS ACADEMY

180 Main St, Andover MA 01810-4161
Jane F. Fried, Dean of Admission
978-749-4050 Fax: 978-749-4068
Website: www.andover.edu
E-mail: admissions@andover.edu

ST. MARK'S SCHOOL

PO Box 9105, Southborough MA 01772-9105
Anne Behnke, Director of Admission
508-786-6000 Fax: 508-786-6120
Website: www.stmarksschool.org
E-mail: admission@stmarksschool.org

Tabor Academy
66 Spring St, Marion MA 02738-1581
508-748-2000

Walnut Hill School
12 Highland St, Natick MA 01760-2199
508-653-4312

Wilbraham & Monson Academy
423 Main St, Wilbraham MA 01095-1715
Christopher Moore, Director of Admission
John Boozang, Associate Director
413-596-6811

WILLISTON NORTHAMPTON SCHOOL

19 Payson Ave, Easthampton MA 01027-2246
Brian Wright, Headmaster
413-529-3241 Fax: 413-527-9494
Website: www.williston.com
E-mail: admission@williston.com

WINCHENDON SCHOOL

172 Ash St, Winchendon MA 01475-1700
J. William LaBelle, Headmaster
800-622-1119 Fax: 978-297-0911
Website: www.winchendon.org
E-mail: admissions@winchendon.org

WORCESTER ACADEMY

81 Providence St, Worcester MA 01604-4299
Jonathan G. Baker, Director of Admission & Financial Aid
508-754-5302 Fax: 508-752-2382
Website: www.worcesteracademy.org
E-mail: admission@worcesteracademy.org

MICHIGAN

Cranbrook Schools
PO Box 801, Bloomfield Hills MI 48303-0801
D. Scott Looney, Director of Admissions
248-645-3300

DETROIT COUNTRY DAY SCHOOL

22305 W 13 Mile Rd, Beverly Hills MI 48025-4435
Jorge Prosperi, Director of Admissions
248-646-7717 Fax: 248-646-2458
Website: www.dcds.edu
E-mail: jprosperi@dcds.edu

Interlochen Arts Academy
PO Box 199, Interlochen MI 49643-0199
231-276-7472
Website: www.interlochen.org
E-mail: admissions@interlochen.org

The Leelanau School
1 Old Homestead Rd, Glen Arbor MI 49636-9720
Heather M. Sack, Director of Admission
231-334-5800

MINNESOTA

St. Croix Lutheran High School
1200 Oakdale Ave, West Saint Paul MN 55118-2699
651-455-1521

St. John's Preparatory School
PO Box 4000, Collegeville MN 56321-4000
320-363-3315

SHATTUCK-ST. MARY'S SCHOOL

PO Box 218, Faribault MN 55021-0218
Amy D. Wolf, Director of Admissions
507-333-1618 Fax: 507-333-1661
Website: www.s-sm.org
E-mail: admissions@s-sm.org

Established 1858. Private. Coed. Accreditation: ISACS. Boarding tuition: $31,900, Day tuition: $19,600. Enrollment: 387. Faculty: 58. Average class size: 12 students. Degrees: High School Diploma. 250 acre campus, located 45 minutes south of Minneapolis/St. Paul. Grades 6-12. Students from 34 states and 20 countries. Advanced Placement courses in every discipline. Award winning choir, orchestra, dance, and drama programs. Campus facilities include 18 hole golf course, 2 ice arenas, indoor domed soccer field.

MISSISSIPPI

Bass Memorial Academy
6433 U S Highway 11, Lumberton MS 39455-7504
601-794-8561

Piney Woods School
5096 Highway 49 S, Piney Woods MS 39148
Dexter D. Whitley, Director of Student Support Services
601-845-2214

MISSOURI

Principia School
13201 Clayton Rd, Saint Louis MO 63131-1002
314-434-2100

Saint Paul Lutheran High School
PO Box 719, Concordia MO 64020-0719
Gloria Burrow, Director of Recruitment
660-463-2238

Thomas Jefferson School
4100 S Lindbergh Blvd, Saint Louis MO 63127-1698
Marie DeJesus, Director of Admissions
314-843-4151

WENTWORTH MILITARY ACADEMY & COLLEGE

1880 Washington Ave, Lexington MO 64067
MAJ Mike Herman, VP for Enrollment
800-962-7682 or 660-259-2221 Fax: 660-259-2677
Website: www.wma.edu
E-mail: admissions@wma.edu

Established 1880. Non-denominational. Accreditation: NCA, the Higher Learning Commission of the NCA and the State of Missouri. Enrollment: 200-250 boarding students, 500 FTE non-boarding students. Co-ed grades 9-14, student to teacher ratio 10:1, class size averages 8 students. Dorms are single gender by floor. Tuition, room, board and fees for boarding students for the 2007/2008 are $26,690-$27,490. Financial assistance is available. ROTC scholarships available for eligible college students.

Wentworth has three academic divisions: High School, military junior college (MJC) and civilian JC (CJC). HS provides college preparatory diploma requiring 26 credits in language arts, math, science, social studies and electives. The co-location of the college allows HS Students to dual enroll in college classes and receive joint credit for HS and College. Community service is a graduation requirement. MJC offers an AS/AA degree. Early Commissioning Program allows eligible ROTC cadets to earn Army commission in 2 years. Four-year ROTC scholarship also offered. CJC offers AA and AS degrees at Lexington campus and three satellites: Sheldon, Hermitage and Cameron.

Open enrollment in the HS allows students to enroll in fall and spring. The HS operates on a two-semester calendar, with grades reported every four weeks. A six-week summer academic session with college dual enrollment courses is also offered. The CJC operates on the semester system. Students may choose to enroll in either eight or sixteen-week classes during each semester.

The Academy prides itself on offering a quality education in a safe, structured small-town environment, with small class sizes and individualized attention. Organized competitive and intra-mural athletic program. Students must abide by an Honor Code. The historic 137-acre campus is 40 miles from Kansas City, allowing students access to big-city cultural and entertainment amenities.

MONTANA

Headwaters Academy
418 W Garfield St, Bozeman MT 59715-5545
406-585-9997

LUSTRE CHRISTIAN HIGH SCHOOL

HC 66 Box 57, Lustre MT 59225-9705
Al Leland, Supervising Teacher
406-392-5735 Fax: 406-392-5765
Website: www.lustrechristian.com
E-mail: lchs@nemont.net

Established 1928. Private. Coed. Accreditation: ACSI, Montana Office of Public Instruction. Tuition: $1,100. Room & board: $2,500. Fees: $185. Enrollment: 26. Faculty: 6. Student-faculty ratio: 5:1. High school diploma offered. 5 buildings on 37 acres. Specializing in college prep yet sucessfully works with struggling students. A modern dormitory houses out of state students. Offers a variety of extra curricular activities. Located in N.E. Montana in a rural setting. Evangelical Fundamental spiritual basis.

NEBRASKA

Platte Valley Academy
19338 W Campus Dr, Shelton NE 68876-9617
308-647-5151

NEW HAMPSHIRE

Brewster Academy
80 Academy Dr, Wolfeboro NH 03894-4128
603-569-1600

Dublin Christian Academy
PO Box 521, Dublin NH 03444-0521
603-563-8505

DUBLIN SCHOOL

PO Box 522, Dublin NH 03444-0522
Sheila Bogan, Director of Admission
603-563-1235 Fax: 603-563-8671
Website: www.dublinschool.org
E-mail: admission@dublinschool.org

HIGH MOWING SCHOOL-A WALDORF HIGH SCHOOL

222 Isaac Frye Hwy, Wilton NH 03086
Sam Rosario, Director of Admissions
603-654-2391 Fax: 603-654-6588
Website: www.highmowing.org
E-mail: admissions@highmowing.org

HOLDERNESS SCHOOL

PO Box 1879, Plymouth NH 03264-1879
Nancy Dalley, Admissions Administrator
603-536-1257 Fax: 603-536-1267
Website: www.holderness.org
E-mail: admissions@holderness.org

KIMBALL UNION ACADEMY

PO Box 188, Meriden NH 03770-0188
Rachel G. Tilney, Director of Admissions
603-469-2100 Fax: 603-469-2041
Website: www.kua.org
E-mail: admissions@kua.org

MEETING SCHOOL

120 Thomas Rd, Rindge NH 03461
Jacqueline Stillwell, Head of School
603-899-3366 Fax: 603-899-6216
Website: www.meetingschool.org
E-mail: office@meetingschool.org

NEW HAMPTON SCHOOL

PO Box 579, New Hampton NH 03256-0579
Dean of Admission
603-677-3401 Fax: 603-677-3481
Website: www.newhampton.org
E-mail: admissions@newhampton.org

Educating young people differently. Following a nationally acclaimed model for experience-based education, our students and adults work alongside each other to create a dynamic learning community marked by non-hierarchical relationships, mutual respect, and intentional responsibility. Our beautiful and well-equipped campus "village" is home to comprehensive, integrated- and life-changing-programs in academics, arts, athletics, adventure education, and community service/action. We care about college prep and campus life, a code of behavior rather than a code of dress. Come visit!

PHILLIPS EXETER ACADEMY

20 Main St, Exeter NH 03833-2460
Dr. Tyler C. Tingley, Principal
Michael Gary, Director of Admissions
603-777-3437 Fax: 603-777-4399
Website: www.exeter.edu
E-mail: admit@exeter.edu

Founded in 1781, Phillips Exeter Academy is well known for originating the Harkness teaching method whereby students and a teacher join in seminar style classes around an oval Harkness Table. Small classes and over 350 courses are offered to students who hail from 43 states and 28 foreign countries. Over $10 million in financial aid supports 39% of Exeter's students. A $806 million endowment supports Exeter's commitment to rigorous academics, an exceptional faculty, a diverse student body, a wide variety of co-curricular opportunities, and state-of-the-art resources.

Proctor Academy
PO Box 500, Andover NH 03216-0500
Michele E. Koenig, Director of Admission
603-735-6000

St. Paul's School
325 Pleasant St, Concord NH 03301-2591
Michael Hirschfeld, Director of Admissions
603-229-4700

TILTON SCHOOL

30 School St, Tilton NH 03276-5771
Katherine E. Saunders, Director of Admission
603-286-1733 Fax: 603-286-1705
Website: www.tiltonschool.org
E-mail: admissions@tiltonschool.org

Tilton School is an independent, coeducational, boarding and day school in Tilton, NH serving students in grades 9 through 12 and post-graduates. The school's curricular model stresses the acquisition of skills such as analytical thinking, problem solving, time management, collaboration, creativity, leadership, communication and adaptability. Tilton School challenges students to embrace and navigate a world marked by diversity and change. Through the quality of human relationships, Tilton School's faculty cultivates in its students the curiosity, the skills, the knowledge and understanding, the character and the integrity requisite for the passionate pursuit of lifelong personal success and service.

WHITE MOUNTAIN SCHOOL

371 W Farm Rd, Bethlehem NH 03574-5851
Amy Broberg, Director of Admission
603-444-2928 Fax: 603-444-5568
Website: www.whitemountain.org
E-mail: admissions@whitemountain.org

NEW JERSEY

BLAIR ACADEMY

PO Box 600, Blairstown NJ 07825-0600
T. Chandler Hardwick III, Headmaster
Barbara H. Haase, Dean of Admissions
800-462-5247 or 908-362-2024 Fax: 908-362-7975
Website: www.blair.edu
E-mail: admissions@blair.edu

Established 1848. Private. Coed. Accreditation: MSACS. Tuition, room & board: $36,900 (boarding)/$27,300 (day). Enrollment: 434. Faculty: 78. Student-faculty ratio: 6:1. Library: 22,000 volumes. 54 buildings on 315 acres. Blair's strong academic program offers Advanced Placement, Honors, and Independent Study courses. Other offerings of note: college level lecture series; dual student advisor system; SAT preparation. Blair has a competitive sports program and offers an extensive range of extracurricular activities.

THE HUN SCHOOL OF PRINCETON

176 Edgerstoune Rd, Princeton NJ 08540-6778
James M. Byer, Headmaster
609-921-7600 Fax: 609-279-9398
Website: www.hunschool.org
E-mail: admiss@hunschool.org

THE LAWRENCEVILLE SCHOOL

PO Box 6008, Lawrenceville NJ 08648-0008
Elizabeth A. Duffy, Head Master
Gregg Maloberti, Dean of Admissions
800-735-2030 or 609-895-2030 Fax: 609-895-2217
Website: www.lawrenceville.org
E-mail: admissions@lawrenceville.org

Established 1810. Coed. Accreditation: NAIS, NJAIS. Tuition: $39,397 boarding, $32,100 day. Est. extra expenses: $500. Enrollment: 551 boarding, 255 day. Faculty: 132. Degree: high school diploma. Library: 100,000 volumes. 31 major buildings on 700 acres. Gym. Pool. Hockey rink. Golf course. Rigorous academic. "English Plan" house system. Harkness Plan round-table teaching. Near Princeton.

PEDDIE SCHOOL

PO Box A, Hightstown NJ 08520-1010
John F. Green, Head
Raymond H. Cabot, Director of Admission
609-490-7501 Fax: 609-944-7901
Website: www.peddie.org
E-mail: admission@peddie.org

Established 1864. Coed. Accreditation: MSACS, NAIS, NJAIS. Tuition: $37,275 (boarding), $28,250 (day). Enrollment: 341 boarding, 198 day. Faculty: 91. 22 buildings on 230 acres surrounding Peddie Lake. Small classes. Laptop computers provided to all students. Outstanding faculty and diverse student body. Over $4.9 million in financial aid supports 42% of student body. Campus-wide computer network/internet. Art center. Theatre. Athletic center. Pool. 18 hole golf course. Rigorous academics. College counseling. Advanced placement. Near Princeton, NYC, and Philadelphia.

PENNINGTON SCHOOL

112 W Delaware Ave, Pennington NJ 08534-1616
Diane P. Monteleone, Director of Admission
609-737-6128 Fax: 609-730-1405
Website: www.pennington.org
E-mail: admiss@pennington.org

Founded in 1838, Co-ed, day and boarding, grades 6-12, boarding starts in 7th. Enrollment: 470. Tuition 2007-2008: $37,600 boarding, $25,200 day. The school intentionally seeks a diverse student population and proves a range of academic and extracurricular offerings to develop the gifts of each of its students. AP and Honors courses as well as academic support classes are available. A comprehensive ESL program is offered for international students, as is a Center for Learning for bright students with diagnosed language-based learning disabilities.

NEW MEXICO

Hammer United World College
PO Box 248, Montezuma NM 87731-0248
Tim Smith, Director of Admission
505-454-4200

The Menaul School
301 Menaul Blvd NE, Albuquerque NM 87107-1527
505-345-7727

NEW MEXICO MILITARY INSTITUTE

101 W College Ave, Roswell NM 88201-5173
Rear Admiral David R. Ellison, USN (Ret.), Superintendent
LTC. Steven D. Klein, VP, Enrollment & Marketing
800-421-5376 or 505-624-8050 Fax: 505-624-8058
Website: www.nmmi.edu
E-mail: admissions@nmmi.edu

Established 1891. Public. Coed. Accreditation: NCACS, New Mexico Department of Education. Estimated costs for 2004-2005 school year, out-of-state student: $10,166, in-state student: $7,670. Enrollment: 950. Faculty: 68. Student-faculty ratio: 18:1. Degree: AA. Library: 68,000 volumes. 19 buildings on 40 acre main campus. Additional acreage includes an 18-hole championship golf course. Challenging college preparatory high curriculum with 98% of our graduates continuing on to four-year colleges and universities. Modern campus with state of the art computer and athletic facilities. Modern rooms equipped with Internet, phones, and television. NMMI offers the best value in military boarding education in the country.

NEW YORK

Cascadilla Prep School
116 Summit Ave, Ithaca NY 14850-4734
John Kendall, Headmaster
607-272-3110

Darrow School
110 Darrow Rd, New Lebanon NY 12125-2608
518-794-6000

Hackley School
293 Benedict Ave, Tarrytown NY 10591-4395
914-631-0128

Harvey School
260 Jay St, Katonah NY 10536-3707
Ronald Romanowicz, Director of Admissions
914-232-3161

HOOSAC SCHOOL

PO Box 9, Hoosick NY 12089-0009
Dean S. Foster, Assistant Headmaster
800-822-0159 Fax: 518-686-3370
Website: www.hoosac.com
E-mail: info@hoosac.com

Houghton Academy
9790 Thayer St, Houghton NY 14744-8712
585-567-8115

Keio Academy of New York
3 College Rd, Purchase NY 10577-2108
914-694-4825

Kildonan School
425 Morse Hill Rd, Amenia NY 12501
845-373-8111

KNOX SCHOOL
541 Long Beach Rd, Saint James NY 11780-9735
Meredith Stanley, Director of Admissions
631-686-1600 Fax: 631-686-1650
Website: www.knoxschool.org
E-mail: mstanley@knoxschool.org

THE MASTERS SCHOOL
49 Clinton Ave, Dobbs Ferry NY 10522-2201
Lindsay C. Murphy, Director of Admission
914-479-6420 Fax: 914-693-7295
Website: www.themastersschool.com
E-mail: admission@themastersschool.com

MILLBROOK SCHOOL
131 School Rd, Millbrook NY 12545
Cynthia S. McWilliams, Director of Admissions
845-677-6873 Fax: 845-677-1265
Website: www.millbrook.org
E-mail: admissions@millbrook.org

National Sports Academy
821 Mirror Lake Dr, Lake Placid NY 12946
518-523-3460

NEW YORK MILITARY ACADEMY
78 Academy Ave
Cornwall on Hudson NY 12520-1325
CAPT Robert D. Watts, USN (Ret.), Superintendent
Maureen T. Kelly, Director of Admissions
888-ASK-NYMA (275-6962) Fax: 845-534-7699
Website: www.nyma.org
E-mail: admissions@nyma.ouboces.org

Day & Boarding grades: 7-12. Enrollment: 200 Boarding, 27 Day. Accredited MSACS. Expenses $28,900 (includes Tuition, Room, Board & Uniforms). Founded in 1889, the Academy is an independent, coeducational boarding and day school. A challenging college preparatory education in a structured environment is complemented by small classes, an accessible and caring faculty, daily tutorials, supervised study periods, interscholastic sports and leadership development through our Junior Army ROTC program. Each provides an opportunity for young men and women to realize their potential. English as a Second Language, SAT prep, college counseling/placement, mentoring program, marching band, drill team, honor guard and equitation. The campus-wide computer network provides cadets with individual dormitory room connections for Internet, e-mail and telephones with voicemail. Summer programs available.

North Country School
PO Box 187, Lake Placid NY 12946-0187
Christine LeFevre, Admissions Director
518-523-9329

NORTHWOOD SCHOOL
PO Box 1070, Lake Placid NY 12946-5070
Timothy Weaver, Director of Admissions
518-523-3382 Fax: 518-523-3405
Website: www.northwoodschool.com
E-mail: admissions@northwoodschool.com

Oakwood Friends School
22 Spackenkill Rd, Poughkeepsie NY 12603
845-462-4200

Redemption Christian Academy
Boarding and Post Graduate School
192 9th St, Troy NY 12180
Ms. Frances Grimes, Director of Admissions
518-272-6679

Stony Brook School
1 Chapman Pkwy, Stony Brook NY 11790-1704
631-751-1800

The Storm King School
314 Mountain Rd
Cornwall on Hudson NY 12520-1899
845-534-9860

Union Springs Academy
PO Box 524, Union Springs NY 13160-0524
Robert Raney, Admissions Director
315-889-7314

NORTH CAROLINA

Asheville School
360 Asheville School Rd, Asheville NC 28806-1571
Archibald R. Montgomery, Head of School
Andrew C. Hirt, Director of Admission
828-254-6345

Oak Ridge Military Academy
PO Box 498, Oak Ridge NC 27310-0498
Lieutenant Colonel Ray Wilson, Vice President for Admissions
336-643-4131 ext. 132

THE PATTERSON SCHOOL
PO Box 500, Patterson NC 28661-0500
Colin Stevens, Headmaster
828-758-2374 Fax: 828-758-9179
Website: www.pattersonschool.org
E-mail: admissions@pattersonschool.org

NORTH DAKOTA

Oak Grove Lutheran School
124 N Terrace N, Fargo ND 58102-3899
Rachel Mathson, Director of Admissions
701-237-0212 Fax: 701-237-4217
Website: www.oakgrovelutheran.com
E-mail: oakgrove.lutheranschool@sendit.nodak.edu

OHIO

Central Christian School
PO Box 9, Kidron OH 44636-0009
Barbara Reinford, Director of Development
330-857-7311

Gilmour Academy
34001 Cedar Rd, Gates Mills OH 44040-9356
440-473-8090

Notre Dame-Cathedral Latin School
13000 Auburn Rd, Chardon OH 44024-9330
440-286-6226

OLNEY FRIENDS SCHOOL
61830 Sandy Ridge Rd, Barnesville OH 43713-9404
Heidi Porter, Interim Director of Admissions
740-425-3655 Fax: 740-425-3202
Website: www.olneyfriends.org
E-mail: admissions@olneyfriends.org

WESTERN RESERVE ACADEMY
115 College St, Hudson OH 44236-2999
Barbara A. Flanagan, Dean of Admission
330-650-9717 Fax: 330-650-5858
Website: www.wra.net
E-mail: admission@wra.net

OREGON

The Delphian School
20950 SW Rock Creek Rd, Sheridan OR 97378-9740
Donetta Phelps, Director of Admissions
800-626-6610

Milo Adventist Academy
PO Box 278, Days Creek OR 97429-0278
Steve Rae, Admissions & Marketing
541-825-3200

OREGON EPISCOPAL SCHOOL
6300 SW Nicol Rd, Portland OR 97223-7599
Matthew Hanly, Head of School
503-246-7771 Fax: 503-293-1105
Website: www.oes.edu
E-mail: admit@mail.oes.edu

PENNSYLVANIA

GEORGE SCHOOL
PO Box 4460, Newtown PA 18940
Karen S. Hallowell, Contact
215-579-6547 Fax: 215-579-6549
Website: www.georgeschool.org
E-mail: admissions@georgeschool.org

Girard College School
2101 S College Ave, Philadelphia PA 19121
215-787-2600

The Hill School
717 E High St, Pottstown PA 19464-5791
Sally Keidel, Director of Admission & Enrollment Management
610-326-1000

MERCERSBURG ACADEMY
300 E Seminary St, Mercersburg PA 17236
Douglas Hale, Head of School
Christopher R. Tompkins, Asst. Head of School for Enrollment
717-328-6173 Fax: 717-328-6319
Website: www.mercersburg.edu
E-mail: admission@mercersburg.edu

Milton Hershey School
PO Box 830, Hershey PA 17033-0830
Dr. William L. Lepley, President & CEO
Dan Warner, Senior Officer, Admissions
800-322-3248

MMI PREPARATORY SCHOOL
154 Centre St, Freeland PA 18224
William A. Shergalis, Ph.D., President
570-636-1108 Fax: 570-636-0742
Website: www.mmiprep.org
E-mail: mmi@mmiprep.org

Moravian Academy
4313 Green Pond Rd, Bethlehem PA 18020-9770
610-691-1600

Perkiomen School
PO Box 130, Pennsburg PA 18073-0130
215-679-9511

Pine Forge Academy
PO Box 338, Pine Forge PA 19548-0338
610-326-5800

SHADY SIDE ACADEMY
423 Fox Chapel Rd, Pittsburgh PA 15238-2296
Katherine H. Mihm, Director of Admission
412-968-3180 Fax: 412-968-3213
Website: www.shadysideacademy.org
E-mail: kmihm@shadysideacademy.org

Shady Side Academy is Pittsburgh's largest, coeducational, college-preparatory independent school, serving 950 students. Young learners in grades Pre-K - 12 are offered enriching academic, athletic and arts opportunities at three age-specific campuses. Students work closely with experienced, caring teachers who encourage responsible development of mind and character. The Academy grounds feature a 650-seat theater, blackbox performance space, playing fields, and indoor swimming and hockey centers. Faculty members average 18 years of teaching experience and 66% hold advanced degrees. At the Academy's Junior School (grades Pre-K-5), located in Pittsburgh's East End, the curriculum offers broad themes to help children make meaningful connections between subject areas in a stimulating and structured but flexible environment. Children learn basic skills and concepts in an integrated approach. The Middle School (grades 6-8), located in the Pittsburgh suburb of Fox Chapel, is dedicated to the principle that 10- to 14-year-olds thrive in an environment that recognizes their uniqueness as a group and as individuals. With its own faculty and campus, the Middle School addresses students' readiness and needs in a supportive, student-centered environment. At the Senior School (grades 9-12), also located in Fox Chapel, students experience a traditional liberal arts program that helps deepen their understanding of the humanities, math and science, and the arts while they learn to think critically and creatively. In addition, a range of opportunities exists for students to discover talents and experience successes, including 40+ clubs, a strong service learning program, numerous visual and performing arts options, 26 different sports teams, international exchange partnerships, and independent study. A 5-Day boarding program is also available for grades 9-12, offering the best of home and school. Average SAT scores for the class of 2006 were 626 critical reading, 660- math and 630- writing. Shady Side Academy has traditionally enjoyed 100 percent college placement among its graduating seniors. The Academy's goal is the balanced development of students' analytical, artistic, and physical abilities; their ability to reason ethically and to listen carefully; and their ability to speak, write, and read with clarity and precision. www.shadysideacademy.org

Solebury School
6832 Phillips Mill Rd, New Hope PA 18938
215-862-5261

WESTTOWN SCHOOL
PO Box 1799, Westtown PA 19395-1799
Kate Holz, Director of Admissions
610-399-7900 Fax: 610-399-7909
Website: www.westtown.edu
E-mail: admissions@westtown.edu

WYOMING SEMINARY
201 N Sprague Ave, Kingston PA 18704-3593
Randolph I. Granger, Director of Admission
570-270-2160 Fax: 570-270-2191
Website: www.wyomingseminary.org
E-mail: admission@wyomingseminary.org

RHODE ISLAND

MOSES BROWN SCHOOL
250 Lloyd Ave, Providence RI 02906-2398
Evelyn Ranone, Dean of Upper & Middle School Admissions
401-831-7373 Fax: 401-455-0084
Website: www.mosesbrown.org
E-mail: admissions@mosesbrown.org

Portsmouth Abbey School
285 Corys Ln, Portsmouth RI 02871-1362
401-683-2005

ST. ANDREW'S SCHOOL
63 Federal Rd, Barrington RI 02806-2425
John D. Martin, Head Master
R. Scott Telford, Director of Admissions
401-246-1230 Fax: 401-246-0510
Website: www.standrews-ri.org
E-mail: inquiry@standrews-ri.org

Established 1893. Independent. Coed. Accreditation: NEASC, NAIS, State of Rhode Island. Tuition day students: $22,400. boarding students: $35,300. Enrollment 210. Faculty: 45. Student-faculty ratio: 5:1. High School diploma offered. Library: 10,700 volumes. 31 buildings on 100 acres. St. Andrew's School college prep program offers small classes (usually 8-12), a great deal of individual attention from teachers and advisors, and a structured environment for students with average to high average ability. In 2002, St. Andrew's was named an "Exemplary School" by learning expert Dr. Mel Levine, whose 25+ years research on learning and ground breaking program, Schools Attuned, are the backbone of our faculty's classroom methodology. Additionally, our programs for students with mild language-based learning disabilities and/or attentional issues are well regarded and successful. We search for students of good character who need academic attention, structure, and skill building.

St. George's School
372 Purgatory Rd, Middletown RI 02842
401-847-7565

SOUTH CAROLINA

Aiken Preparatory School
619 Barnwell Ave NW, Aiken SC 29801-6901
803-648-3223

Ben Lippen Schools
PO Box 3999, Columbia SC 29230-3999
Kay Perricelli, Admissions
803-786-7200

Bob Jones Academy
1700 Wade Hampton Blvd
Greenville SC 29614-1000
Stephen Jones III, President
David Christ, Director of Admissions
800-BJ-AND-ME Fax: 800-2FAX-BJU
Website: www.bju.edu
E-mail: admissions@bju.edu

SOUTH DAKOTA

Sunshine Bible Academy
400 Sunshine Dr, Miller SD 57362-6821
Gordon R. Werkema, Superintendent
605-853-3071

TENNESSEE

Baylor School
171 Baylor School Rd, Chattanooga TN 37405
423-267-8505

THE KING'S ACADEMY
202 Smothers Rd, Seymour TN 37865-5056
Janice Mink, Director of Admissions
865-573-8321 Fax: 865-573-8323
Website: www.thekingsacademy.net
E-mail: jmink@thekingsacademy.net

LAUSANNE COLLEGIATE SCHOOL
1381 W Massey Rd, Memphis TN 38120-3206
Molly B. Cook, Director of Admissions
901-474-1000 Fax: 901-474-1010
Website: www.lausanneschool.com
E-mail: mcook@lausanneschool.com

St. Andrew's-Sewanee School
290 Quintard Rd, Sewanee TN 37375-3000
931-598-5651

THE WEBB SCHOOL
PO Box 488, Bell Buckle TN 37020-0488
Matt Anderson, Director of Operations in Admissions
888-733-9322 Fax: 931-389-6657
Website: www.thewebbschool.com
E-mail: admissions@webbschool.com

TEXAS

ALLEN ACADEMY
3201 Boonville Rd, Bryan TX 77802
Camilla Viator, Director of Admissions
979-776-0731 Fax: 979-774-7769
Website: www.allenacademy.org
E-mail: cviator@allenacademy.org

Incarnate Word High School
727 E Hildebrand Ave, San Antonio TX 78212-2598
210-829-3100

MEMORIAL HALL SCHOOL
3721 Dacoma St, Houston TX 77092-8905
Rev. George Aurich, Headmaster
713-688-5566 Fax: 713-956-9751
Website: www.memorialhall.org
E-mail: memhallsch@aol.com

Presbyterian Pan American School
PO Box 1578, Kingsville TX 78364-1578
Barbara A. Chamness, Development Director
361-592-4307

SAINT MARY'S HALL
9401 Starcrest Dr, San Antonio TX 78217-4199
Elena D. Hicks, Director of Admission
210-483-9234 Fax: 210-655-5211
Website: www.smhall.org
E-mail: admissions@smhall.org

St. Stephen's Episcopal School
2900 Bunny Run, Austin TX 78746
Lawrence Sampleton, Director of Admission
512-327-1213

San Marcos Baptist Academy
2801 Ranch Road 12, San Marcos TX 78666-9406
Jeffrey D. Baergen, Director of Admissions
800-428-5120

TMI - The Episcopal School of Texas
20955 W Tejas Trl, San Antonio TX 78257-1604
Cindy Schneid, Director of Admission
210-698-7171

UTAH

WASATCH ACADEMY
120 S 100 W, Mount Pleasant UT 84647-1509
Kim Stephens, Director of Admissions
800-634-4690 Fax: 435-462-1450
Website: www.wacad.org
E-mail: admissions@wacad.org

VERMONT

Burke Mountain Academy
PO Box 78, East Burke VT 05832-0078
802-626-1516 ext. 1503

Burr and Burton Academy
PO Box 498, Manchester VT 05254-0498
802-362-1775

Green Mountain Valley School
271 Moulton Rd, Waitsfield VT 05673
802-496-2150

LONG TRAIL SCHOOL
1045 Kirby Hollow Rd, Dorset VT 05251-9776
Courtney M. Callo, Director of Admissions & Outreach
802-867-5717 Fax: 802-867-4525
Website: www.longtrailschool.org
E-mail: applylts@longtrailschool.org

LYNDON INSTITUTE
PO Box 127, Lyndon Center VT 05850-0127
Mary Thomas, Assistant Head for Admissions
802-626-5232 Fax: 802-626-6138
Website: www.lyndoninstitute.org
E-mail: mary.thomas@lyndoninstitute.org

Pine Ridge School
9505 Williston Rd, Williston VT 05495-9598
Joshua Doyle, Director of Admissions
802-434-2161

Putney School
418 Houghton Brook Rd, Putney VT 05346
802-387-5566

Rock Point School
1 Rock Point Rd, Burlington VT 05408-2736
802-863-1104

St. Johnsbury Academy
PO Box 906, Saint Johnsbury VT 05819
John J. Cummings, Director of Admissions
802-748-8171

Stratton Mountain School
7 World Cup Circle, Stratton Mountain VT 05155
802-297-1886

VERMONT ACADEMY
PO Box 500, Saxtons River VT 05154-0500
William Newman, Dean of Admissions
802-869-6229 Fax: 802-869-6242
Website: www.vermontacademy.org
E-mail: admissions@vermontacademy.org

VIRGINIA

Eastern Mennonite High School
801 Parkwood Dr, Harrisonburg VA 22802-2416
Jean S. Fisher, Admissions
540-432-4521

EPISCOPAL HIGH SCHOOL
1200 N Quaker Ln, Alexandria VA 22302-3000
Emily M. Atkinson, Director of Admissions
703-933-4062 Fax: 703-933-3016
Website: www.episcopalhighschool.org
E-mail: admissions@episcopalhighschool.org

MASSANUTTEN MILITARY ACADEMY
614 S Main St, Woodstock VA 22664-1205
Murali Sinnathamby, Director of Admissions
877-466-6222 or 540-459-2167 Fax: 540-459-5421
Website: www.militaryschool.com
E-mail: admissions@militaryschool.com

MILLER SCHOOL OF ALBEMARLE
1000 Samuel Miller Loop
Charlottesville VA 22903-7527
Jay Reeves, Director of Admissions
434-823-4805 Fax: 434-823-6617
Website: www.millerschool.org
E-mail: admissions@millerschool.org

NOTRE DAME ACADEMY
35321 Notre Dame Ln, Middleburg VA 20117-3621
Mrs. Cathy Struder, Director of Admission
540-687-5581 Fax: 540-687-3552
Website: www.notredameva.org
E-mail: cstruder@notredameva.org

OAK HILL ACADEMY
2635 Oak Hill Rd, Mouth of Wilson VA 24363-3004
Dr. Michael D. Groves, President
276-579-2619 Fax: 276-579-4722
Website: www.oak-hill.net
E-mail: info@oak-hill.net

Established 1878. Private. College Preparatory. Boarding for grades 8-12. Accreditation: VAIS. Tuition, room, board, and spending money: $21,350. Enrollment: 130. Faculty: 17. Student-teacher ratio: 10:1. Library: 6,000 volumes. Regular and advanced diplomas. Dual-credit courses. 12 buildings on over 400 acres. Athletics and arts. 95% of our graduates go on to college. Beautiful mountain setting.

Randolph-Macon Academy
200 Academy Dr, Front Royal VA 22630-2692
Pia G. Crandell, Ph.D., Director of Admissions
800-272-1172

St. Anne's-Belfield School
2132 Ivy Rd, Charlottesville VA 22903-1785
Jean Craig, Director of Admissions
434-296-5106

Shenandoah Valley Academy
234 W Lee Hwy, New Market VA 22844-9558
Brian or Joi Becker, Enrollment Management
540-740-2210

Stuart Hall
235 W Frederick St, Staunton VA 24401-3327
Stephanie Shafer, Dean of Admissions
888-306-8926

Tandem Friends School
279 Tandem Ln, Charlottesville VA 22902-7128
Tom O'Connor, Director of Admissions
434-296-1303

Virginia Episcopal School
PO Box 408, Lynchburg VA 24505-0408
Pamela Barile, Director of Admission
434-385-3607

WASHINGTON

AUBURN ADVENTIST ACADEMY
5000 Auburn Way S, Auburn WA 98092-7297
Jondelle McGhee, Public Relations/Recruiting
253-249-0105 or 253-939-5000 Fax: 253-351-9806
Website: www.auburn.org
E-mail: info@auburn.org

John F. Kennedy Memorial High School
140 S 140th St, Burien WA 98168
206-246-0500

Northwest School
1415 Summit Ave, Seattle WA 98122-3619
Anne Smith, Director of Admissions
206-682-7309

UPPER COLUMBIA ACADEMY
3025 E Spangle Waverly Rd
Spangle WA 99031-9799
Scott North, Recruiter
509-245-3600 Fax: 509-245-3643
Website: www.ucaa.org
E-mail: snorth@ucaa.org

WEST VIRGINIA

Linsly School
60 Knox Ln, Wheeling WV 26003-6489
304-233-3260

WISCONSIN

WAYLAND ACADEMY
101 N University Ave, Beaver Dam WI 53916-2253
Eric Peters, Dean of Admission and College Counseling
800-860-7725 Fax: 920-887-3373
Website: www.wayland.org
E-mail: admissions@wayland.org

GUAM

GUAM ADVENTIST ACADEMY
1200 Aguilar Rd, Yona GU 96915
John Youngberg, Principal
671-789-1515 Fax: 671-789-3547
Website: www.gaasda.org
E-mail: office@gaasda.org

PUERTO RICO

American Military Academy
PO Box 7884, Guaynabo PR 00970-7884
Vivian Simonet, Superintendent
787-720-6801

: :PREPARATORY SCHOOLS FOR GIRLS

Primarily Boarding

ARKANSAS

MOUNT ST. MARY ACADEMY
3224 Kavanaugh Blvd, Little Rock AR 72205-1899
Sr. Claudia S. Ward, RSM, Principal
501-664-8006 Fax: 501-666-4382
Website: www.mtstmary.edu
E-mail: srcward@mtstmary.edu

CALIFORNIA

Flintridge Sacred Heart Academy
440 Saint Katherine Dr
La Canada Flintridge CA 91011-4198
Jan Price, Director of Admissions
626-685-8333

SAN DOMENICO SCHOOL
1500 Butterfield Rd, San Anselmo CA 94960-1099
Risa Oganesoff Heersche, Director of Upper School Admissions
415-258-1905 Fax: 415-258-1906
Website: www.sandomenico.org
E-mail: rheersche@sandomenico.org

SANTA CATALINA SCHOOL
1500 Mark Thomas Dr, Monterey CA 93940-5291
Louise B. Douglas, Director of Admission
831-655-9356 Fax: 831-655-7535
Website: www.santacatalina.org
E-mail: admissions@santacatalina.org

CONNECTICUT

ACADEMY OF THE HOLY FAMILY
PO Box 691, Baltic CT 06330-0691
Sister Mary Loreto, SCMC, Principal
860-822-9272 Fax: 860-822-1318
Website: www.ahfbaltic.org
E-mail: principal@ahfbaltic.org

CONVENT OF THE SACRED HEART
1177 King St, Greenwich CT 06831-2998
Pamela McKenna, Director of Admissions
203-532-3534 Fax: 203-532-3301
Website: www.cshgreenwich.org
E-mail: admission@cshgreenwich.org

THE ETHEL WALKER SCHOOL
230 Bushy Hill Rd, Simsbury CT 06070-2698
Barbara Lundberg, Dean of Enrollment Management
860-408-4200 Fax: 860-408-4201
Website: www.ethelwalker.org
E-mail: admission_office@ethelwalker.org

Miss Porter's School
60 Main St, Farmington CT 06032-2288
860-409-3500

Westover School
PO Box 847, Middlebury CT 06762-0847
Ann S. Pollina, Head of School
203-758-2423

GEORGIA

Brenau Academy
500 Washington St SE, Gainesville GA 30501
Dr. Frank M. Booth, Headmaster
770-534-6140

HAWAII

St. Francis High School
2707 Pamoa Rd, Honolulu HI 96822-1886
808-988-4111

ILLINOIS

Woodlands Academy of the Sacred Heart
760 E Westleigh Rd, Lake Forest IL 60045-3263
Kathleen Creed, Director of Admissions
847-234-4300

INDIANA

Howe Military School
5755 N State Road 9, Howe IN 46746
260-562-2131 ext. 221

IOWA

Ideal Girls School
1661 Highway 1, Fairfield IA 52556
641-472-7224

KANSAS

Mt. St. Scholastica Academy
1000 Green St, Atchison KS 66002-3079
Amy DuLac, Director of Admissions
913-367-1334

LOUISIANA

ACADEMY OF THE SACRED HEART
PO Box 310, Grand Coteau LA 70541-0310
D'Lane Wimberley, Director of Admission
337-662-5275 Fax: 337-662-3011
Website: www.ashcoteau.org
E-mail: admission@ashcoteau.org

MARYLAND

BRYN MAWR SCHOOL
109 W Melrose Ave, Baltimore MD 21210-1397
Maureen Walsh, Headmistress
410-323-8800 ext. 248 Fax: 410-435-4678
Website: www.brynmawrschool.org
E-mail: admissions@brynmawrschool.org

Garrison Forest School
300 Garrison Forest Rd
Owings Mills MD 21117-4064
410-363-1500

OLDFIELDS SCHOOL
1500 Glencoe Rd, Glencoe MD 21152
Kimberly C. Loughlin, Director of Admission
410-472-4800 Fax: 410-472-6839
Website: www.oldfieldsschool.org
E-mail: admissions@oldfieldsschool.org

ST. TIMOTHY'S SCHOOL
8400 Greenspring Ave, Stevenson MD 21153-0644
Randy Stevens, Head of School
410-486-7401 Fax: 410-486-1167
Website: www.stt.org
E-mail: admis@stt.org

MASSACHUSETTS

DANA HALL SCHOOL
45 Dana Rd
PO Box 9010, Wellesley MA 02482-9010
Wendy Secor, Director of Admissions/Financial Aid
781-235-3010 Fax: 781-235-0577
Website: www.danahall.org
E-mail: admission@danahall.org

Miss Hall's School
492 Holmes Rd, Pittsfield MA 01201-7196
Kimberly Boland, Director of Admission
413-499-1300

STONELEIGH-BURNHAM SCHOOL
574 Bernardston Rd, Greenfield MA 01301-1100
Sharon L. Pleasant, Director of Admissions
413-774-2711 Fax: 413-772-2602
Website: www.sbschool.org
E-mail: admissions@sbschool.org

NEW JERSEY

MOUNT SAINT MARY ACADEMY
1645 US Highway 22, Watchung NJ 07069-6587
Donna Venezia Toryak, Director of Admissions
908-757-0108 ext. 4506 Fax: 908-756-8085
Website: www.mountsaintmary.org
E-mail: dtoryak@mountsaintmary.org

PURNELL SCHOOL
PO Box 500 - 51 Pottersville Rd, Pottersville NJ 07979
Nicole Moon, Director of Admission
908-439-2154 Fax: 908-439-4088
Website: www.purnell.org
E-mail: info@purnell.org

NEW YORK

EMMA WILLARD SCHOOL
285 Pawling Ave, Troy NY 12180-5294
Julie Bradley, Acting Director of Admissions
518-833-1320 Fax: 518-833-1805
Website: www.emmawillard.org
E-mail: admissions@emmawillard.org

NORTH CAROLINA

Oak Ridge Military Academy
PO Box 498, Oak Ridge NC 27310-0498
Lieutenant Colonel Ray Wilson, Vice President for Admissions
336-643-4131 ext. 132

SAINT MARY'S SCHOOL
900 Hillsborough St, Raleigh NC 27603-1689
Catherine C. Leary, Director of Admission and Financial Aid
919-424-4100 or 800-948-2557 Fax: 919-424-4122
Website: www.saint-marys.edu
E-mail: admissions@saint-marys.edu

SALEM ACADEMY
500 E Salem Ave, Winston Salem NC 27101
Gordon Bondurant, Head of School
336-721-2646 Fax: 336-917-5340
Website: www.salemacademy.com
E-mail: academy@salem.edu

OHIO

THE ANDREWS SCHOOL
38588 Mentor Ave, Willoughby OH 44094-7788
Kristina Dooley, Admission Director
440-942-3600 Fax: 440-954-5020
Website: www.andrews-school.org
E-mail: admissions@andrews-school.org

PENNSYLVANIA

Academy of the New Church Girls School
PO Box 707, Bryn Athyn PA 19009-0707
215-938-2595

GRIER SCHOOL
PO Box 308, Tyrone PA 16686-0308
Andrew Wilson, Headmaster
814-684-3000 Fax: 814-684-2177
Website: www.grier.org
E-mail: admissions@grier.org

LINDEN HALL
212 E Main St, Lititz PA 17543-2029
Kate R. Rill, Director of Admission
717-626-8512 Fax: 717-627-1384
Website: www.lindenhall.org
E-mail: admissions@lindenhall.org

TEXAS

Hockaday School
11600 Welch Rd, Dallas TX 75229-2999
214-363-6311

VIRGINIA

Chatham Hall
800 Chatham Hall Cir, Chatham VA 24531-3084
804-432-2941

FOXCROFT SCHOOL
PO Box 5555, Middleburg VA 20118-5555
Nicole Focareto, Director of Admission
540-687-4340 or 800-858-2364 Fax: 540-687-3627
Website: www.foxcroft.org
E-mail: admissions@foxcroft.org

MADEIRA SCHOOL
8328 Georgetown Pike, Mc Lean VA 22102-1200
Ann Miller, Director of Admissions
703-556-8200 Fax: 703-893-3289
Website: www.madeira.org
E-mail: admissions@madeira.org

St. Catherine's School
6001 Grove Ave, Richmond VA 23226-2600
Katherine S. Wallmeyer, Director of Admission
800-648-4982

St. Margaret's School
PO Box 158, Tappahannock VA 22560-0158
804-443-3357

WASHINGTON

Annie Wright School
827 Tacoma Ave N, Tacoma WA 98403-2899
Melinda Kinney, Director of Admission
253-272-2216

GUAM

ACADEMY OF OUR LADY OF GUAM
233 Archbishop Felixberto C Flores St
Hagatna GU 96910-5102
Sister Francis Jerome Cruz, RSM, President
671-477-8203 or 671-477-8725 Fax: 671-477-8555
Website: www.aolg.edu.gu
E-mail: acad@aolg.edu.gu

PROTECTIVE SERVICES

ALABAMA

Bishop State Community College - Four Campuses
351 N Broad St, Mobile AL 36603-5898
Dr. Terry Hazzard, Dean of Students
251-690-6801 Fax: 251-690-6446
Website: www.bishop.edu
E-mail: thazzard@bishop.edu

George C. Wallace State Community College
PO Box 2530, Selma AL 36702-2530
Mrs. Donitha J. Griffin, Dean of Students
334-876-9295 Fax: 334-876-9300
Website: www.wccs.edu
E-mail: dgriffin@wccs.edu

ARIZONA

Pima Community College
4905 E Broadway Blvd, Tucson AZ 85709-1010
Wendy Kilgore, Ph.D., Director of Admissions
520-206-4500 Fax: 520-206-4790
Website: www.pima.edu
E-mail: infocenter@pima.edu

CALIFORNIA

Butte College
3536 Butte Campus Dr, Oroville CA 95965-8399
Carole Gish, Director of Admissions
530-895-2511 Fax: 530-879-4313
Website: www.butte.edu
E-mail: admissions@butte.edu

California State University-San Bernadino
5500 University Pkwy
San Bernardino CA 92407-2393
Olivia Rosas, Director of Admissions
909-537-5188 Fax: 909-537-7034
Website: www.csusb.edu
E-mail: orosas@csusb.edu

Chabot College
25555 Hesperian Blvd, Hayward CA 94545-2400
Judy Young, Director of Admissions
510-723-6600 Fax: 510-723-7510
Website: www.chabotcollege.edu
E-mail: ccarcom@clpccd.cc.ca.us

San Joaquin Valley College
201 New Stine Rd, Bakersfield CA 93309-2659
Jaime Delgado, Enrollment Services Director
661-834-1026 Fax: 559-651-4864
Website: www.sjvc.edu
E-mail: jaime.delgado@sjvc.edu

San Joaquin Valley College
295 E Sierra Ave, Fresno CA 93710-3616
Nora Twarynski, Enrollment Services Director
559-448-8282 Fax: 559-651-4864
Website: www.sjvc.edu
E-mail: nora.twarynski@sjvc.edu

San Joaquin Valley College
1700 McHenry Village Way Suite 6
Modesto CA 95350
Joseph Holt, Director of Admissions
209-527-7582 Fax: 559-651-4864
Website: www.sjvc.edu
E-mail: josephh@sjvc.edu

San Joaquin Valley College
11050 Olson Dr, Rancho Cordova CA 95670
Joseph Holt, Director of Admissions
559-651-2500 Fax: 559-651-4864
Website: www.sjvc.edu
E-mail: joseph.holt@sjvc.edu

San Joaquin Valley College
10641 Church St, Rancho Cucamonga CA 91730
Ramon Abreu, Enrollment Services Director
909-948-7582 Fax: 559-651-4864
Website: www.sjvc.edu
E-mail: ramon.abreu@sjvc.edu

San Joaquin Valley College
8400 W Mineral King Ave, Visalia CA 93291-9283
Susie Topjian, Enrollment Services Director
559-651-2500 Fax: 559-651-4864
Website: www.sjvc.edu
E-mail: susiet@sjvc.edu

COLORADO

Colorado Northwestern Community College
500 Kennedy Dr, Rangely CO 81648-3502
Tresa England, Director of Student Services
800-562-1105 Fax: 970-675-3343
Website: www.cncc.edu
E-mail: tresa.england@cncc.edu

Everest College
Aurora Campus
14280 E Jewell Ave, Aurora CO 80012-5692
John Heckman, Director of Admissions
303-367-2757 Fax: 303-745-6245
Website: www.cci.edu

FLORIDA

City College
2000 W Commercial Blvd, Fort Lauderdale FL 33309
Mercedes Segal, Director of Admissions
954-492-5353 Fax: 954-491-1965
Website: www.citycollege.edu

GEORGIA

Armstrong Atlantic State University
11935 Abercorn St, Savannah GA 31419-1997
Ed Lyons, Director of Public Safety
Website: www.armstrong.edu

Kennesaw State University
1000 Chastain Rd NW Box 1402
Kennesaw GA 30144-5591
Ted Cochran, Director
770-423-6666
Website: www.kennesaw.edu

ILLINOIS

Kaskaskia College
27210 College Rd, Centralia IL 62801-7878
Tyra Taylor, Dean of Enrollment Management and Retention Services
618-545-3000 Fax: 618-532-1990
Website: www.kaskaskia.edu
E-mail: ttaylor@kaskaskia.edu

INDIANA

University of Evansville
1800 Lincoln Ave, Evansville IN 47722-0001
Don Vos, Dean of Admission
800-423-8633 Fax: 812-488-4076
Website: www.evansville.edu
E-mail: admission@evansville.edu

IOWA

Briar Cliff University
PO Box 2100, Sioux City IA 51104-0100
Sharisue Wilcoxon, VP for Enrollment Management
712-279-5200 Fax: 712-279-1632
Website: www.briarcliff.edu
E-mail: admissions@briarcliff.edu

Iowa Lakes Community College
300 S 18th St, Estherville IA 51334-2721
Anne Stansbury, Asst. Director of Admissions
712-362-7945 Fax: 712-362-8363
Website: www.iowalakes.edu
E-mail: info@iowalakes.edu

KANSAS

COLBY COMMUNITY COLLEGE
1255 S Range Ave, Colby KS 67701-4099
Director of Admissions
888-634-9350 or 785-460-4690 Fax: 785-460-4691
Website: www.colbycc.edu
E-mail: admissions@colbycc.edu

Labette Community College
200 S 14th St, Parsons KS 67357-9966
Tammy Fuentez, Director of Admissions
620-421-6700 Fax: 620-421-2309
Website: www.labette.edu
E-mail: tammyf@labette.edu

LOUISIANA

Louisiana State University at Eunice
PO Box 1129, Eunice LA 70535-1129
Ron Ryder, Registrar
337-457-7311 Fax: 337-550-1306
Website: www.lsue.edu
E-mail: rryder@lsue.edu

MAINE

HUSSON COLLEGE
One College Cir, Bangor ME 04401-2999
Jane Goodwin, Director of Admissions
800-4HU-SSON or 207-941-7100 Fax: 207-941-7935
Website: www.husson.edu
E-mail: admit@husson.edu
See listing under "Universities"

Southern Maine Community College
2 Fort Rd, South Portland ME 04106-1698
Dr. James Ortiz, President
Scott MacDonald, Director of Financial Aid
207-741-5500 Fax: 207-741-5671
Website: www.smccme.edu
E-mail: oharmon@maine.rr.com

MARYLAND

Cecil College
One Seahawk Dr, North East MD 21901
Sandra S. Rajaski, Registrar & Director of Admissions
410-287-1000 Fax: 410-287-1001
Website: www.cecil.edu
E-mail: srajaski@cecil.edu

Hagerstown Community College
11400 Robinwood Dr, Hagerstown MD 21742-6590
Dr. Daniel E. Bock, Assistant Director of Admissions
301-790-2800 Fax: 301-791-9165
Website: www.hagerstowncc.edu
E-mail: bockd@hagerstowncc.edu

MASSACHUSETTS

Anna Maria College
50 Sunset Ln, Paxton MA 01612
Timothy M. Donahue, Director of Recruitment and Admissions
508-849-3360 Fax: 508-849-3362
Website: www.annamaria.edu
E-mail: admissions@annamaria.edu

Becker College
Campuses in Worcester and Leicester, MA
61 Sever St, Worcester MA 01609-2165
Karen Schedin, Dean of Admissions
508-791-9241 Fax: 508-890-1500
Website: www.becker.edu
E-mail: admissions@becker.edu
See listing under "Universities"

Newbury College
129 Fisher Ave, Brookline MA 02445-5796
Salvadore Liberto, Vice President of Enrollment
617-730-7000 Fax: 617-731-9618
Website: www.newbury.edu
E-mail: info@newbury.edu
See listing under "Universities"

North Shore Community College
1 Ferncroft Rd, Danvers MA 01923-4093
Jennifer Kirk, Director of Admissions & Recruitment Outreach
978-762-4000 Fax: 978-762-4015
Website: www.northshore.edu
E-mail: jkirk@northshore.edu

MICHIGAN

Concordia University
4090 Geddes Rd, Ann Arbor MI 48105-2797
Gary Neumann, Director of Admissions
734-995-7300 Fax: 734-995-4610
Website: www.cuaa.edu
E-mail: admissions@cuaa.edu

Delta College
University Center MI 48710-0001
Duff Zube, Director of Admissions
989-686-9093 Fax: 989-667-2202
Website: www.delta.edu
E-mail: admit@delta.edu

Lake Superior State University
650 W Easterday Ave
Sault Sainte Marie MI 49783-1637
Susan Camp, Director of Admissions
888-800-LSSU Fax: 906-635-6696
Website: www.lssu.edu
E-mail: admissions@lssu.edu
See listing under "Universities"

MACOMB COMMUNITY COLLEGE
44575 Garfield Rd, Clinton Township MI 48038-1139
Information Center
586-445-7999
Website: www.macomb.edu
E-mail: answer@macomb.edu

Northwestern Michigan College
1701 E Front St, Traverse City MI 49686-3061
Jim Bensley, Director of Admissions
800-748-0566 Fax: 231-995-1339
Website: www.nmc.edu
E-mail: jbensley@nmc.edu

MINNESOTA

Hibbing Community College
1515 E 25th St, Hibbing MN 55746-3300
Holly Bigelow, Director of Enrollment
800-224-4HCC or 218-262-7200 Fax: 218-262-6717
Website: www.hibbing.edu
E-mail: admissions@hibbing.edu

Inver Hills Community College
2500 80th St E, Inver Grove Heights MN 55076
651-450-8500 Fax: 651-450-8679
Website: www.inverhills.edu

Ridgewater College-Willmar Campus
PO Box 1097, Willmar MN 56201-1097
Sally Kerfeld, Director of Admissions
800-722-1151 Fax: 320-222-5212
Website: www.ridgewater.edu
E-mail: sally.kerfeld@ridgewater.edu

MISSOURI

East Central College
1964 Prairie Dell Rd, Union MO 63084
Karen Wieda, Registrar
636-583-5195 ext. 2220 Fax: 636-583-1897
Website: www.eastcentral.edu
E-mail: wiedaks@eastcentral.edu

Lindenwood University
209 S Kingshighway St
Saint Charles MO 63301-1695
Sheryl Guffey, Director of Admissions
636-949-2000 Fax: 636-949-4989
Website: www.lindenwood.edu

State Fair Community College
3201 W 16th St, Sedalia MO 65301-2199
Director of Admissions
660-530-5833 Fax: 660-596-7472
Website: www.sfccmo.edu
E-mail: mparris@sfccmo.edu

Truman State University
100 E Normal, Kirksville MO 63501
Office of Admission
660-785-4114 Fax: 660-785-7456
Website: admissions.truman.edu
E-mail: admissions@truman.edu

University of Missouri
1 University Blvd, Saint Louis MO 63121-4499
Dr. Mark Burkholder, Dean-College of Arts & Sciences
314-516-5501 Fax: 314-516-5415
Website: www.umsl.edu
E-mail: admissions@umsl.edu

NEBRASKA

Metropolitan Community College
PO Box 3777, Omaha NE 68103-0777
Becky Nicks, Director of Admissions
402-449-8400 Fax: 402-457-2616
Website: www.mccnab.edu
E-mail: bnicks@mccnab.edu

Midland Lutheran College
900 N Clarkson St, Fremont NE 68025-4200
Todd Hansen, Associate Director of Admissions
402-941-6501 Fax: 402-941-6513
Website: www.mlc.edu
E-mail: admissions@mlc.edu

University of Nebraska at Kearney
905 W 25th St, Kearney NE 68849-0001
Dusty Newton, Director of Admissions
800-KEARNEY Fax: 308-865-8987
Website: www.unk.edu
E-mail: admissionsug@unk.edu

NEVADA

GREAT BASIN COLLEGE
1500 College Pkwy, Elko NV 89801-5032
Julie G. Byrnes, Director of Enrollment Management
775-753-2271 Fax: 775-753-2311
Website: www.gbcnv.edu
E-mail: julieb@gwmail.gbcnv.edu
See listing under "Universities"

NEW JERSEY

Bergen Community College
400 Paramus Rd, Paramus NJ 07652
Julian Gomez, Asst. Director of Admissions
201-447-7100 Fax: 201-444-7036
Website: www.bergen.edu
E-mail: jgomez@bergen.edu

New Jersey City University
2039 John F Kennedy Blvd
Jersey City NJ 07305-1588
Carmen Panlilio, Asst. V.P. for Admissions and Financial Aid
201-200-3234 Fax: 201-200-2044
Website: www.njcu.edu
E-mail: admissions@njcu.edu

RICHARD STOCKTON COLLEGE OF NEW JERSEY
PO Box 195, Pomona NJ 08240
John Iacovelli, Dean of Enrollment Management
866-RSC-2885 Fax: 609-626-5541
Website: www.stockton.edu
E-mail: admissions@stockton.edu

Stockton College is a comprehensive liberal arts, coed institution founded in 1969. Advance Pre-Professional Degree Options: 7-yr BS/MD with UMDNJ; NJ Dental School; NJ Medical School, Robert Wood Johnson Medical, School of Osteopathic Medicine; NY College of Podiatric Medicine, Pennsylvania College of Podiatric Medicine, SUNY College of Optometry. Pharmacy doctorate program with Rutgers University. 5-yr Engineering with NJIT and Rutgers University. Dual BA/MA in Criminal Justice. 5-yr BS/MS in Computational Science. BS/MS in Nursing. Doctorate of Physical Therapy. Additional Programs: Forensic Science, Pre-Law, Pre-Occupational Therapy, and Pre-Veterinary.

NEW MEXICO

New Mexico State University
1500 N 3rd St, Grants NM 87020-2025
Irene Lutz, Director of Admissions
505-287-7981 Fax: 505-287-2329
Website: www.grants.nmsu.edu
E-mail: ilutz@nmsu.edu

NEW YORK

Broome Community College
907 Upper Front St, Binghamton NY 13905
Anthony S. Fiorelli, Director of Admissions
607-778-5001 Fax: 607-778-5442
Website: www.sunybroome.edu
E-mail: fiorelli_a@sunybroome.edu

Hilbert College
5200 S Park Ave, Hamburg NY 14075-1597
Timothy Lee, Director of Admissions
716-649-7900 Fax: 716-649-0702
Website: www.hilbert.edu
E-mail: tlee@hilbert.edu

Iona College
715 North Ave, New Rochelle NY 10801-1890
Kevin Cavanagh, Assistant V.P. for College Admissions
914-633-2502 Fax: 914-637-2778
Website: www.iona.edu

Molloy College
1000 Hempstead Ave
Rockville Centre NY 11570-1100
Marguerite Lane, Director of Admissions
516-678-5000 ext. 6291 Fax: 516-256-2247
Website: www.molloy.edu
E-mail: admissions@molloy.edu
See listing under "Universities"

SUNY College at Brockport
350 New Campus Dr, Brockport NY 14420-2997
Bernard S. Valento, Director of Undergraduate Admissions
585-395-2751 Fax: 585-395-5452
Website: www.brockport.edu
E-mail: admit@brockport.edu

SUNY Sullivan County Community College
112 College Rd, Loch Sheldrake NY 12759-5151
Sari Rosenheck, Director of Admissions
845-434-5750 Fax: 845-434-0923
Website: www.sullivan.suny.edu
E-mail: admissions@sullivan.suny.edu
Student Housing on Campus.

NORTH CAROLINA

Haywood Community College
185 Freedlander Dr, Clyde NC 28721
Debbie Rowland, Coordinator of Admissions
828-627-4500 Fax: 828-627-4513
Website: www.haywood.edu
E-mail: drowland@haywood.edu

James Sprunt Community College
PO Box 398, Kenansville NC 28349-0398
Lea Grady, Admissions
910-296-2500 Fax: 910-296-1636
Website: www.jamessprunt.edu

Mayland Community College
PO Box 547, Spruce Pine NC 28777-0547
Cathy B. Morrison, Director of Enrollment Management
828-765-7351 Fax: 828-765-0728
Website: www.mayland.edu
E-mail: cmorrison@mayland.edu

OHIO

Cleveland State University
2121 Euclid Ave RW 204, Cleveland OH 44115
Dr. Richard Arndt, Dean of Undergraduate Recruitment and College Partnerships
888-CSU-OHIO Fax: 216-687-9210
Website: www.csuohio.edu
E-mail: admissions@csuohio.edu

Ohio University
Chillicothe Campus
PO Box 629, Chillicothe OH 45601
Student Services
740-774-7200 Fax: 740-774-7295
Website: www.ohiou.edu/chillicothe/

Owens Community College
3200 Bright Rd, Findlay OH 45840
William J. Ivoska PhD., Vice President of Student Services
567-429-3500 Fax: 567-423-0246
Website: www.owens.edu
E-mail: admissions@owens.edu

Owens Community College
PO Box 10000, Toledo OH 43699-1947
William J. Ivoska, Ph.D, Vice President of Student Services
567-661-7000 Fax: 567-661-7607
Website: www.owens.edu
E-mail: admissions@owens.edu

OKLAHOMA

University of Tulsa
600 S College Ave, Tulsa OK 74104-3126
Earl Johnson, Dean of Admission
918-631-2307 Fax: 918-631-5003
Website: www.utulsa.edu
E-mail: admission@utulsa.edu

OREGON

Linn-Benton Community College
6500 Pacific Blvd SW, Albany OR 97321-3774
Christine Baker, Outreach Coordinator
541-917-4811 Fax: 541-917-4868
Website: www.linnbenton.edu
E-mail: admissions@linnbenton.edu

Rogue Community College
3345 Redwood Hwy, Grants Pass OR 97527-9298
Claudia Sullivan, Director of Enrollment Services
541-956-7500 Fax: 541-471-3585
Website: www.roguecc.edu
E-mail: csullivan@roguecc.edu
See listing under "Community and Junior Colleges"

University of Portland
5000 N Willamette Blvd, Portland OR 97203-5798
Jason McDonald, Dean of Admissions
503-943-7911 Fax: 503-943-7315
Website: www.up.edu
E-mail: mcdonaja@up.edu

PENNSYLVANIA

Central Pennsylvania College
College Hill & Valley Rds, Summerdale PA 17093
Katie Borrelli, Admissions Director
800-759-2727 Fax: 717-728-2505
Website: www.centralpenn.edu
E-mail: katie.borrelli@centralpenn.edu

Community College of Allegheny County
Allegheny Campus: 808 Ridge Ave, Pittsburgh PA 15212 Admissions: 412.237.2700
Boyce Campus: 595 Beatty Rd, Monroeville PA 15146 Admissions: 724.325.6614
North Campus: 8701 Perry Highway, Pittsburgh PA 15237 Admissions: 412.369.3600
South Campus: 1750 Clairton Rd, West Mifflin PA 15122 Admissions: 412-469-4301
Website: www.ccac.edu

Community College of Beaver County
1 Campus Dr, Monaca PA 15061-2566
724-775-8561 Fax: 724-775-4687
Website: www.ccbc.edu
E-mail: admissions@ccbc.edu

Delaware Valley College
700 E Butler Ave, Doylestown PA 18901-2697
Stephen W. Zenko, Director of Admissions
800-2DE-LVAL Fax: 215-230-2968
Website: www.delval.edu
E-mail: stephenzenko@delval.edu

DeSales University
2755 Station Ave, Center Valley PA 18034-9565
610-282-1100 Fax: 610-282-2342
Website: www.desales.edu

Juniata College
1700 Moore St, Huntingdon PA 16652-2196
Michelle Bartol, Dean of Enrollment
877-JUNIATA Fax: 814-641-3100
Website: www.juniata.edu
E-mail: admissions@juniata.edu

King's College
133 N River St, Wilkes Barre PA 18711-0801
Michelle Lawrence-Schmude, Dean of Admission
570-208-5900 Fax: 570-208-5971
Website: www.kings.edu
E-mail: admissions@kings.edu

Lehigh Valley College
2809 E Saucon Valley Rd
Center Valley PA 18034-8447
Sam Jarvis, Director of Marketing
800-227-9109 Fax: 610-791-7810
Website: www.lehighvalley.edu
E-mail: joshua.padron@lehighvalley.edu

Widener University
1 University Pl, Chester PA 19013-5792
Edwin Wright, Dean of Admissions
610-499-4000 Fax: 610-499-4676
Website: www.widener.edu
E-mail: admissions.office@widener.edu

SOUTH DAKOTA

Western Dakota Technical Institute
800 Mickelson Dr, Rapid City SD 57703-4018
Jill Elder, Admissions Coordinator
605-394-4034 Fax: 605-394-2204
Website: www.wdt.edu
E-mail: jill.elder@wdt.edu

TENNESSEE

Austin Peay State University
601 College St, Clarksville TN 37044-0002
931-221-7011 Fax: 931-221-6168
Website: www.apsu.edu
E-mail: admissions@apsu.edu

Southwest Tennessee Community College
5983 Macon Cove, Memphis TN 38134
Vanessa R. Dowdy, Director of Admissions
901-333-5000 Fax: 901-333-4523
Website: www.southwest.tn.edu
E-mail: vdowdy@southwest.tn.edu

Tennessee State University
3500 John A Merritt Blvd, Nashville TN 37209-1561
John Cade, Dean of Admissions & Records
615-963-5101 Fax: 615-963-2930
Website: www.tnstate.edu
E-mail: jcade@tnstate.edu

University of Tennessee
615 McCallie Ave, Chattanooga TN 37403-2504
Yancy Freeman, Director of Admissions
423-425-4111 Fax: 423-425-4157
Website: www.utc.edu
E-mail: Yancy-Freeman@utc.edu

TEXAS

Abilene Christian University
ACU Box 29000, Abilene TX 79699-0001
325-674-2000 Fax: 325-674-2202
Website: www.acu.edu
E-mail: info@admissions.acu.edu

Galveston College
4015 Avenue Q, Galveston TX 77550-7496
Brian Lowery, Registrar
409-763-6551 Fax: 409-944-1501
Website: www.gc.edu
E-mail: blowery@gc.edu

McLennan Community College
1400 College Dr, Waco TX 76708-1498
Stephen Cook, Coordinator, Fire Fighters Academy
254-299-8000 Fax: 254-299-8854
Website: www.mclennan.edu
E-mail: scook@mclennan.edu

Temple College
2600 S 1st St, Temple TX 76504-7435
Toni Borras, Director of Admissions & Records
254-298-8808 Fax: 254-298-8288
Website: www.templejc.edu
E-mail: admissionsrecords@templejc.edu

Tyler Junior College
PO Box 9020, Tyler TX 75711-9020
Joan Jones, Interim Dean
800-687-5680
Website: www.tjc.edu
E-mail: jjon@tjc.edu
See listing under "Community and Junior Colleges"

Weatherford College
225 College Park Dr, Weatherford TX 76086
Dr. Joe Birmingham, President
800-287-5471 Fax: 817-598-6205
Website: www.wc.edu
E-mail: willingham@wc.edu

VIRGINIA

Marymount University
2807 N Glebe Rd, Arlington VA 22207-4299
Michael Canfield, Director of Admissions
800-548-7638 Fax: 703-522-0348
Website: www.marymount.edu
E-mail: admissions@marymount.edu

Radford University
PO Box 6903, Radford VA 24142
David W. Kraus, Director of Admissions
800-890-4265 Fax: 540-831-5038
Website: www.radford.edu
E-mail: ruadmiss@radford.edu

Roanoke College
221 College Ln, Salem VA 24153-3794
James A. Pennix, Director of Admissions
540-375-2500 Fax: 540-375-2267
Website: www.roanoke.edu
E-mail: pennix@roanoke.edu

Southside Virginia Community College
109 Campus Dr, Alberta VA 23821-2930
Ronald E. Mattox, Dean of Admissions
434-949-1014 Fax: 434-949-7863
Website: www.sv.vccs.edu
E-mail: ronald.mattox@sv.vccs.edu

Southside Virginia Community College
200 Daniel Rd, Keysville VA 23947
Ronald E. Mattox, Dean of Admissions
434-736-2018 Fax: 434-736-2082
Website: www.sv.vccs.edu
E-mail: ronald.mattox@sv.vccs.edu

WASHINGTON

CROWN COLLEGE
8739 S Hosmer St, Tacoma WA 98444-1836
John Wabel, CEO
253-531-3123 Fax: 253-531-3521
Website: www.crowncollege.edu
E-mail: jwabel@crowncollege.edu

Everett Community College
2000 Tower St, Everett WA 98201
Christine Kerlin, Associate Dean
425-388-9100 Fax: 425-388-9173
Website: www.everettcc.edu
E-mail: ckerlin@everettcc.edu

SHORELINE COMMUNITY COLLEGE
16101 Greenwood Ave N, Shoreline WA 98133-5696
Chris Melton, Acting Registrar
206-546-4581 Fax: 206-546-5835
Website: www.shoreline.edu

WEST VIRGINIA

Fairmont State University
1201 Locust Ave, Fairmont WV 26554-2470
Steve Leadman, Director of Admissions
304-367-4161 or 800-641-5678 Fax: 304-367-4789
Website: www.fairmontstate.edu
E-mail: admit@fairmontstate.edu

Mountain State University
Box 9003, Beckley WV 25802-9003
Tony England, Director of Admissions
866-FOR-MSU1 or 304-929-INFO Fax: 304-253-5072
Website: www.mountainstate.edu
E-mail: gomsu@mountainstate.edu
See listing under "Universities"

WISCONSIN

Blackhawk Technical College
PO Box 5009, Janesville WI 53547-5009
Gregg Bosak, Administration, Community Information
608-757-7769 Fax: 608-757-7740
Website: www.blackhawk.edu
E-mail: gbosak@blackhawk.edu

Herzing College
5218 E Terrace Dr, Madison WI 53718-8340
Donald Madelung, President
800-582-1227 Fax: 608-249-8593
Website: www.herzing.edu
E-mail: info@msn.herzing.edu
See listing under "Universities"

Wisconsin Indianhead Technical College
505 Pine Ridge Dr, Shell Lake WI 54871
Jeff Dodge, Public Safety Specialist
800-243-9482 Fax: 715-468-2819
Website: www.witc.edu
E-mail: jdodge@witc.edu

WYOMING

Laramie County Community College
1400 E College Dr, Cheyenne WY 82007-3204
Jenny Hargett, Director of Admissions
307-778-5222 Fax: 307-778-1350
Website: www.lccc.wy.edu
E-mail: learnmore@lccc.wy.edu

GUAM

University of Guam
UOG Station, Mangilao GU 96923
Deborah Leon Guerrero, Registrar
671-735-2201 or 671-735-2208 Fax: 671-735-2203
Website: www.uog.edu
E-mail: admitme@uog9.uog.edu

PSYCHOLOGY

ALABAMA

University of Alabama in Huntsville
PO Box 1247, Huntsville AL 35899-0001
Nikki Willis, Assoc. Director for Recruiting Program and Events
1-800-UAH-CALL Fax: 256-824-6073
Website: www.uah.edu
E-mail: willisn@uah.edu

University of South Alabama
307 University Blvd N, Mobile AL 36688-3053
Melissa Haab, Director of Admissions
251-460-6141 Fax: 251-460-7876
Website: www.southalabama.edu
E-mail: admiss@usouthal.edu

ALASKA

University of Alaska Anchorage
PO Box 141629, Anchorage AK 99514-1629
Cecile Mitchell, Director of Enrollment Services
907-786-1480 Fax: 907-786-4888
Website: www.uaa.alaska.edu/
E-mail: enroll@uaa.alaska.edu

ARKANSAS

Williams Baptist College
PO Box 3737, Walnut Ridge AR 72476-3737
Angela Flippo, Vice President for Enrollment Management
800-722-4434 Fax: 870-759-4163
Website: www.williamsbaptistcollege.com
E-mail: admissions@wbcoll.edu

CALIFORNIA

Antioch University Southern California
400 Corporate Pointe, Culver City CA 90230-7615
Admissions Office
800-7-ANTIOCH Fax: 310-821-6032
E-mail: admissions@antiochla.edu
Master of Arts in Psychology.

CALIFORNIA COAST UNIVERSITY

700 N Main St, Santa Ana CA 92701
Admissions Office: 888-CCU-UNIV or 714-547-9625
Fax: 714-547-5777
Dr. Thomas Neal, President
Dr. Cynthia Teeple, Academic Vice President
Website: www.calcoast.edu
E-mail: info@calcoast.edu

Established 1973. Proprietary. Coed. Accreditation: California Coast University holds accreditation through the Accrediting Commission of the Distance Education and Training Council (DETC). The DETC is an educational association located in Washington, D.C. Founded in 1926, it is the standard setting agency for distance education institutions. Approval: Bureau for Private Postsecondary and Vocational Education - State of California, charter member California Association of State Approved Colleges & Universities, member Association for Adult & Continuing Education, member The Alliance for Private Post Secondary Academic Institutions.

Tuition: $2,805-$12,070. California Coast University has selected the SLM Corporation, commonly known as Sallie Mae, to help the university provide financing for its students. Sallie Mae is the nation's leading provider of education funding. Sallie Mae also allows students to borrow additional loan amounts to cover additional expenses, such as textbooks, equipment, or living expenses.

Enrollment: 30,000. California Coast University is approved by the California State Approving Agency to enroll veterans or other eligible persons under Title 38, U.S. Code. California Coast University holds a Memorandum of Understanding with Defense Activity for Non-Traditional Education Support (DANTES) as an external degree provider.

A private college offering off-campus independent study programs in the traditional areas of business administration, management, psychology, education. Admissions: enroll year round, requires official transcripts, letters of recommendation, detailed curriculum vita or occupational history.

Process: evaluation of prior academic work followed by analysis of occupational history, including participation in workshops, seminars, training programs, specialized projects for credit. Credit is demonstrated by accelerated learning guides or study guides.

Residency: All course work may be completed off campus, utilizing correspondence methods. Interest free loans available to students.

Chapman University
One University Drive, Orange CA 92866-1099
Michael Drummy, Assistant Vice President for Enrollment
Services and Chief Admission Officer
714-997-6411 or 888-CUAPPLY Fax: 714-997-6713
Website: www.chapman.edu
E-mail: admit@chapman.edu

Concordia University
1530 Concordia, Irvine CA 92612-3203
Lori McDonald, Executive Director of Enrollment Services
800-229-1200 or 949-854-8002 Fax: 949-854-6894
Website: www.cui.edu
E-mail: admission@cui.edu

Fielding Graduate University
School of Psychology
2112 Santa Barbara St
Santa Barbara CA 93105-3538
DeAnne Taylor, Director of Admissions
805-687-1099 Fax: 805-687-9793
Website: www.fielding.edu
E-mail: admission@fielding.edu

FULLER THEOLOGICAL SEMINARY

135 N Oakland Ave, Pasadena CA 91182-0002
Office of Admissions
800-2-FULLER Fax: 626-584-5449
Website: www.fuller.edu
E-mail: adm-email@dept.fuller.edu

INSTITUTE OF TRANSPERSONAL PSYCHOLOGY

1069 E Meadow Cir, Palo Alto CA 94303-4231
Sydney J. Reuben, Director of Admissions
650-493-4430 Fax: 650-493-6835
Website: www.itp.edu
E-mail: itpinfo@itp.edu

John F. Kennedy University
100 Ellinwood Way, Pleasant Hill CA 94523-4817
800-696-5358
Website: www.jfku.edu

Orange Coast College
PO Box 5005, Costa Mesa CA 92628-5005
Kristin Clark, Director of Admissions
714-432-5773 Fax: 714-432-5736
Website: www.orangecoastcollege.edu
E-mail: kclark@cccd.edu

PEPPERDINE UNIVERSITY

Graduate School of Education and Pschology
6100 Center Dr, Los Angeles CA 90045
Fionnbarr Kelly, Director of Admissions
310-568-5744 Fax: 310-568-5755
Website: www.gsep.pepperdine.edu
E-mail: gsep@pepperdine.edu

The Graduate School of Education and Psychology of Pepperdine University offers two different master's degree programs and one doctoral degree program in psychology:
*Master of Arts in Psychology
*Master of Arts on Clinical Psychology with an emphasis in Marriage and Family Therapy
*Doctor of Psychology in Clinical Psychology
For more info visit: www.gsep.pepperdine.edu/psychology.

PHILLIPS GRADUATE INSTITUTE

5445 Balboa Blvd, Encino CA 91316-1509
Belinda Lombardo, Director of Admissions
818-386-5660 Fax: 818-386-5699
Website: www.pgi.edu
E-mail: info@pgi.edu

Point Loma Nazarene University
3900 Lomaland Dr, San Diego CA 92106-2810
Chip Killingsworth, Director of Undergraduate Admissions
800-733-7770 Fax: 619-849-2601
Website: www.pointloma.edu
E-mail: admissions@pointloma.edu

San Bernardino Valley College
701 S Mount Vernon Ave
San Bernardino CA 92410-2798
Kay Ragan, Ed.D., Director of Admissions
909-888-6511 Fax: 909-889-4988
Website: www.valleycollege.edu
E-mail: kragan@sbccd.cc.ca.us

San Diego Christian College
2100 Greenfield Dr, El Cajon CA 92019-1157
Rene Inman, Director of Admissions
800-676-2242 Fax: 619-590-1739
Website: www.sdcc.edu
E-mail: admissions@sdcc.edu

Simpson University
2211 College View Dr, Redding CA 96003-8606
Jim Herberger, Director of Admissions
888-9-SIMPSON Fax: 530-226-4861
Website: www.simpsonuniversity.edu
E-mail: admissions@simpsonuniversity.edu
See listing under "Universities"

Whittier College
PO Box 634, Whittier CA 90608-0634
Kieron Miller, Director of Admissions
562-907-4200 Fax: 562-907-4870
Website: www.whittier.edu
E-mail: kmiller@whittier.edu

COLORADO

Denver Seminary
6399 S Santa Fe Dr, Littleton CO 80120
Robert Jones, VP Student Services
303-762-6982 Fax: 303-783-3122
Website: denverseminary.edu
E-mail: robert.jones@denverseminary.edu

CONNECTICUT

Albertus Magnus College
700 Prospect St, New Haven CT 06511-1189
Richard Lolatte, Dean of Admission
203-773-8501 or 800-578-9160 Fax: 203-773-5248
Website: www.albertus.edu
E-mail: admissions@albertus.edu

DISTRICT OF COLUMBIA

Gallaudet University
800 Florida Ave NE, Washington DC 20002-3695
Charity Reedy Hines, Director of Admissions
202-651-5750 Fax: 202-651-5744
Website: www.gallaudet.edu
E-mail: admissions.office@gallaudet.edu

FLORIDA

CARLOS ALBIZU UNIVERSITY

2173 NW 99th Ave, Miami FL 33172-2209
Carlos Alicea, Director of Admissions, Recruitment & Outreach
305-593-1223 ext. 137 Fax: 305-593-1854
Website: www.mia.albizu.edu
E-mail: admissions@albizu.edu

Embry-Riddle Aeronautical University
Daytona Beach Campus
PO Box 11767, Daytona Beach FL 32120-1767
C. Richard Clarke, Director of Admissions
800-862-2416 Fax: 386-226-7070
Website: www.embryriddle.edu
E-mail: dbadmit@erau.edu

Florida State University
600 W College Ave, Tallahassee FL 32306-1096
Janice V. Finney, Director of Admissions
850-644-2525 Fax: 850-644-0197
Website: admissions.fsu.edu
E-mail: admissions@admin.fsu.edu

Lynn University
3601 N Military Trl, Boca Raton FL 33431-5598
Director of Admissions
561-237-7900 Fax: 561-237-7100
Website: www.lynn.edu
E-mail: admission@lynn.edu

St. Thomas University
16401 NW 37th Ave, Miami Gardens FL 33054
Dr. Gary Feinberg, Chair, Social Sciences
800-367-9010 or 305-628-6546 Fax: 305-628-6591
Website: www.stu.edu
E-mail: signup@stu.edu

University of South Florida
4202 E Fowler Ave, Tampa FL 33620-6900
J. Robert Spatig, Director of Admissions
877-USF-BULL Fax: 813-974-9689
Website: www.usf.edu
E-mail: admissions@admin.usf.edu
See listing under "Universities"

GEORGIA

Kennesaw State University
1000 Chastain Rd NW, Kennesaw GA 30144-5591
Dr. Helen Ridley, Dean of Humanities and Social Science
770-423-6124
Website: www.kennesaw.edu

Life University
1269 Barclay Cir SE, Marietta GA 30060-2903
Dr. Deborah E. Heairlston, Director of New Student Development
770-426-2884 Fax: 770-426-2895
Website: www.life.edu
E-mail: admissions@life.edu

TOCCOA FALLS COLLEGE

PO Box 800899, Toccoa Falls GA 30598
888-785-5624 Fax: 706-282-6012
Website: www.tfc.edu
E-mail: admissions@tfc.edu

IDAHO

Brigham Young University - Idaho
120 Kimball Bldg, Rexburg ID 83460-1615
Rob Garrett, Director of Admissions
208-496-1020 Fax: 208-496-1220
Website: www.byui.edu
E-mail: admissions@byui.edu

Lewis-Clark State College
500 8th Ave, Lewiston ID 83501-2698
Diane Douglas, Ph.D., Registrar/Director of Admissions
800-933-5272 Fax: 208-792-2429
Website: www.lcsc.edu
E-mail: admissions@lcsc.edu

University of Idaho
Moscow ID 83844-4253
Lloyd Scott, Director of New Student Services
208-885-6163 Fax: 208-885-4477
Website: www.uidaho.edu
E-mail: nss@uidaho.edu

ILLINOIS

ADLER SCHOOL OF PROFESSIONAL PSYCHOLOGY

65 E Wacker Pl, Chicago IL 60601-7296
Craig Hines, Director of Admissions
312-201-5900 Fax: 312-201-5917
Website: www.adler.edu
E-mail: admissions@adler.edu

AMERICAN INTERCONTINENTAL UNIVERSITY ONLINE

5550 Prairie Stone Parkway Suite 400
Hoffman Estates IL 60192
Admissions Department
877-701-3800
Website: www.aiuonline.edu
E-mail: info@aiuonline.edu

ARGOSY UNIVERSITY/CHICAGO
350 N Orleans St, Merchandise Mart
Chicago IL 60654
Jamal Scott, Director of Admissions
800-626-4123 Fax: 312-777-7750
Website: www.argosyu.edu
E-mail: jscott@argosyu.edu

Aurora University
347 S Gladstone Ave, Aurora IL 60506-4892
Carol R. Dunn, Ed.D., Vice President for Enrollment
800-742-5281 Fax: 630-844-5535
Website: www.aurora.edu
E-mail: admission@aurora.edu

Benedictine University
5700 College Rd, Lisle IL 60532-0900
630-829-6300 or 888-829-6363 Fax: 630-829-6301
Website: www.ben.edu
E-mail: admissions@ben.edu

CONCORDIA UNIVERSITY
7400 Augusta St, River Forest IL 60305-1402
708-209-3100 Fax: 708-209-3176
Website: www.cuchicago.edu
E-mail: admission@cuchicago.edu

Roosevelt University
430 S Michigan Ave, Chicago IL 60605
Gwen E. Kanelos, Asst. Vice President for Enrollment Services
877-APPLY-RU Fax: 312-341-4216
Website: www.roosevelt.edu
E-mail: applyru@roosevelt.edu

INDIANA

Oakland City University
138 N Lucretia St, Oakland City IN 47660
Brian J. Baker, Director of Admissions
800-737-5125 Fax: 812-749-1433
Website: www.oak.edu
E-mail: bbaker@oak.edu
See listing under "Universities"

University of Evansville
1800 Lincoln Ave, Evansville IN 47722-0001
Don Vos, Dean of Admission
800-423-8633 Fax: 812-488-4076
Website: www.evansville.edu
E-mail: admission@evansville.edu

IOWA

Briar Cliff University
PO Box 2100, Sioux City IA 51104-0100
Sharisue Wilcoxon, VP for Enrollment Management
712-279-5200 Fax: 712-279-1632
Website: www.briarcliff.edu
E-mail: admissions@briarcliff.edu

Clarke College
1550 Clarke Dr, Dubuque IA 52001-3198
Andy Schroeder, Director of Admissions
800-383-2345 Fax: 563-584-8666
Website: www.clarke.edu
E-mail: andy.schroeder@clarke.edu

Graceland University
1 University Place, Lamoni IA 50140
Greg Sutherland, Interim Vice President for Enrollment and Dean of Admissions
641-784-5196 Fax: 641-784-5480
Website: www.admissions.graceland.edu
E-mail: admissions@graceland.edu

Iowa Lakes Community College
300 S 18th St, Estherville IA 51334-2721
Anne Stansbury, Asst. Director of Admissions
712-362-7945 Fax: 712-362-8363
Website: www.iowalakes.edu
E-mail: info@iowalakes.edu

Waldorf College
106 S 6th St, Forest City IA 50436-1713
Dr. Linda Hoopes, Vice President of Admission and Marketing
800-292-1903 or 641-585-8112 Fax: 641-585-8125
Website: www.waldorf.edu
E-mail: hoopesl@waldorf.edu
See listing under "Universities"

KANSAS

Tabor College
400 S Jefferson St, Hillsboro KS 67063-1758
Rusty Allen, Dean of Enrollment Management
800-822-6799 Fax: 620-947-6276
Website: www.tabor.edu
E-mail: admissions@tabor.edu
See listing under "Universities"

KENTUCKY

Louisville Presbyterian Seminary
1044 Alta Vista Rd, Louisville KY 40205-1798
Kerry Rice, Director of Admissions
502-895-3411 or 800-264-1839 Fax: 502-992-9399
Website: www.lpts.edu
E-mail: admissions@lpts.edu
Degrees offered MDiv, MA, DMin, ThM
M. A. Marriage & Family Therapy (COAMFTE/AAMFT & AAPC Accred.)

Morehead State University
Morehead KY 40351-1689
Jeffrey Liles, Enrollment Services
800-585-6781 Fax: 606-783-5038
Website: www.moreheadstate.edu
E-mail: admissions@moreheadstate.edu

LOUISIANA

Louisiana State University at Alexandria
8100 Highway 71 S, Alexandria LA 71302-9121
Dr. Thomas Armstrong, Director of Admissions
318-445-3672 Fax: 318-473-6418
Website: www.lsua.edu

MAINE

HUSSON COLLEGE
One College Cir, Bangor ME 04401-2999
Jane Goodwin, Director of Admissions
800-4HU-SSON or 207-941-7100 Fax: 207-941-7935
Website: www.husson.edu
E-mail: admit@husson.edu
See listing under "Universities"

MARYLAND

Griggs University
PO Box 4437, Silver Spring MD 20914-4437
Joan Wilson, Director of Admissions
301-680-6570 Fax: 301-680-6583
Website: www.griggs.edu
E-mail: registrar@griggs.edu

Hagerstown Community College
11400 Robinwood Dr, Hagerstown MD 21742-6590
Dr. Daniel E. Bock, Assistant Director of Admissions
301-790-2800 Fax: 301-791-9165
Website: www.hagerstowncc.edu
E-mail: bockd@hagerstowncc.edu

MASSACHUSETTS

Anna Maria College
50 Sunset Ln, Paxton MA 01612
Timothy M. Donahue, Director of Recruitment and Admissions
508-849-3360 Fax: 508-849-3362
Website: www.annamaria.edu
E-mail: admissions@annamaria.edu

Assumption College
500 Salisbury St, Worcester MA 01609-1294
Kathleen Murphy, Dean of Enrollment
508-767-7000 Fax: 508-799-4412
Website: www.assumption.edu
E-mail: admiss@assumption.edu

Becker College
Campuses in Worcester and Leicester, MA
61 Sever St, Worcester MA 01609-2165
Karen Schedin, Dean of Admissions
508-791-9241 Fax: 508-890-1500
Website: www.becker.edu
E-mail: admissions@becker.edu
See listing under "Universities"

Boston University
121 Bay State Rd, Boston MA 02215
Kelly Walter, Executive Director of Admissions
617-353-2300 Fax: 617-353-9695
Website: web.bu.edu
E-mail: admissions@bu.edu

Gordon College
255 Grapevine Rd, Wenham MA 01984-1899
Barbara R. Layne, Associate Vice President, Enrollment
866-464-6736 Fax: 978-867-4682
Website: www.gordon.edu
E-mail: admissions@gordon.edu

Newbury College
129 Fisher Ave, Brookline MA 02445-5796
Salvadore Liberto, Vice President of Enrollment
617-730-7000 Fax: 617-731-9618
Website: www.newbury.edu
E-mail: info@newbury.edu
See listing under "Universities"

University of Massachusetts Dartmouth
Old Westport Rd, North Dartmouth MA 02747-2300
Steven T. Briggs, Director of Admissions
508-999-8605 Fax: 508-999-8755
Website: explore.umassd.edu
E-mail: sbriggs@umassd.edu

Worcester Polytechnic Institute
100 Institute Rd, Worcester MA 01609-2280
Edward J. Connor, Director of Admissions
508-831-5286 Fax: 508-831-5875
Website: admissions.wpi.edu
E-mail: admissions@wpi.edu

MICHIGAN

Alma College
614 W Superior St, Alma MI 48801-1599
Evan Montague, Director of Admissions
800-321-ALMA Fax: 989-463-7057
Website: www.alma.edu
E-mail: admissions@alma.edu

Delta College
University Center MI 48710-0001
Duff Zube, Director of Admissions
989-686-9093 Fax: 989-667-2202
Website: www.delta.edu
E-mail: admit@delta.edu

Grand Valley State University
1 Campus Dr, Allendale MI 49401-9403
616-331-2025 Fax: 616-331-2000
Website: www.gvsu.edu
E-mail: go2gvsu@gvsu.edu

HILLSDALE COLLEGE
33 E College St, Hillsdale MI 49242-1298
Dr. Fritz Tsao, Director
517-607-2473 Fax: 517-607-2208
Website: www.hillsdale.edu

MACOMB COMMUNITY COLLEGE
44575 Garfield Rd, Clinton Township MI 48038-1139
Information Center
586-445-7999
Website: www.macomb.edu
E-mail: answer@macomb.edu

MACOMB COMMUNITY COLLEGE
14500 E 12 Mile Rd, Warren MI 48088-3896
Information Center
586-445-7999
Website: www.macomb.edu
E-mail: answer@macomb.edu

MINNESOTA

ARGOSY UNIVERSITY / TWIN CITIES
(formerly Minnesota School of Professional Psychology)
1515 Central Pkwy, Eagan MN 55121-1756
O. Jeanne Stoneking, Director of Admissions
651-846-2882 Fax: 651-994-7956
Website: www.argosyu.edu
E-mail: tcadmissions@argosyu.edu

Bethany Lutheran College
700 Luther Dr, Mankato MN 56001
Don Westphal, Dean of Admissions
507-344-7000 Fax: 507-344-7376
Website: www.blc.edu
E-mail: admiss@blc.edu

Carleton College
1 N College St, Northfield MN 55057-4044
800-995-2275 or 507-646-4190 Fax: 507-646-4526
Website: www.carleton.edu
E-mail: admissions@acs.carleton.edu

Crown College
8700 College View Dr, Saint Bonifacius MN 55375
Mitch Fisk, Director of Admissions
952-446-4142 Fax: 952-446-4149
Website: www.crown.edu
E-mail: johnsonj@crown.edu

Gustavus Adolphus College
800 W College Ave, Saint Peter MN 56082-1485
Mark H. Anderson, Dean of Admission
800-GUSTAVUS Fax: 507-933-7474
Website: www.gustavus.edu
E-mail: admission@gustavus.edu

University of Minnesota
2900 University Ave, Crookston MN 56716-5001
218-281-6510 Fax: 218-281-8575
Website: admissions.umcrookston.edu/requirements/apply.htm
E-mail: info@umcrookston.edu

MISSISSIPPI

Tougaloo College
500 W County Line Rd, Tougaloo MS 39174-9799
Juno Leggette Jacobs, Director of Admissions
601-977-7768 Fax: 601-977-4501
Website: www.tougaloo.edu
E-mail: jjacobs@tougaloo.edu

MISSOURI

Central Methodist University
411 Central Methodist Sq, Fayette MO 65248-1198
Larry Anderson, Director of Admissions
660-248-6247 Fax: 660-248-1872
Website: www.centralmethodist.edu
E-mail: landerso@centralmethodist.edu

Columbia College
1001 Rogers St, Columbia MO 65216-0001
Regina Morin, Director of Admissions
573-875-7352 Fax: 573-875-7506
Website: www.ccis.edu
E-mail: admissions@ccis.edu

Northwest Missouri State University
800 University Dr, Maryville MO 64468-6001
Beverly Schenkel, Dean of Enrollment Management
660-562-1562 Fax: 660-562-1121
Website: www.nwmissouri.edu
E-mail: admissions@nwmissouri.edu

Stephens College
PO Box 2121, Columbia MO 65215-0001
David Adams, Dean of Enrollment Management
573-442-2211 Fax: 573-876-7237
Website: www.stephens.edu
E-mail: dadams@stephens.edu

Truman State University
100 E Normal, Kirksville MO 63501
Office of Admission
660-785-4114 Fax: 660-785-7456
Website: admissions.truman.edu
E-mail: admissions@truman.edu

University of Missouri
1 University Blvd, Saint Louis MO 63121-4499
Dr. Mark Burkholder, Dean-College of Arts & Sciences
314-516-5501 Fax: 314-516-5415
Website: www.umsl.edu
E-mail: admissions@umsl.edu

Webster University
470 E Lockwood Ave, Saint Louis MO 63119-3194
Bill Huddleston-Berry, Chairman, Behavioral Sciences
314-968-7160 Fax: 314-963-6094
Website: www.webster.edu
E-mail: huddlews@webster.edu
See listing under "Universities"

William Woods University
1 University Ave, Fulton MO 65251-1098
Jimmy Clay, Director of Admissions
573-642-2251 Fax: 573-592-1146
Website: www.williamwoods.edu
E-mail: admissions@williamwoods.edu
See listing under "Universities"

MONTANA

Carroll College
1601 N Benton Ave, Helena MT 59625-0002
Dr. Thomas J. Trebon, President
Cynthia Thornquist, Director of Admissions & Enrollment Operations
406-447-4384 Fax: 406-447-4533
Website: www.carroll.edu
E-mail: admission@carroll.edu

NEW HAMPSHIRE

Antioch University New England
40 Avon St, Keene NH 03431-3516
David Caruso, President
Leatrice A. Oram, Director of Admissions
603-357-6265 Fax: 603-357-0718
Website: www.antiochne.edu
E-mail: admissions@antiochne.edu

Southern New Hampshire University
2500 N River Rd, Hooksett NH 03106-1045
Steve Soba, Director of Admissions
603-645-9611 Fax: 603-645-9693
Website: www.snhu.edu
E-mail: s.soba@snhu.edu

NEW JERSEY

Bergen Community College
400 Paramus Rd, Paramus NJ 07652
Julian Gomez, Asst. Director of Admissions
201-447-7100 Fax: 201-444-7036
Website: www.bergen.edu
E-mail: jgomez@bergen.edu

New Jersey City University
2039 John F Kennedy Blvd
Jersey City NJ 07305-1588
Carmen Panlilio, Asst. V.P. for Admissions and Financial Aid
201-200-3234 Fax: 201-200-2044
Website: www.njcu.edu
E-mail: admissions@njcu.edu

Ramapo College of New Jersey
505 Ramapo Valley Rd, Mahwah NJ 07430-1623
Director of Admissions
201-684-7300 or 201-684-7301 Fax: 201-684-7964
Website: www.ramapo.edu
E-mail: admissions@ramapo.edu

RICHARD STOCKTON COLLEGE OF NEW JERSEY
PO Box 195, Pomona NJ 08240
John Iacovelli, Dean of Enrollment Management
866-RSC-2885 Fax: 609-626-5541
Website: www.stockton.edu
E-mail: admissions@stockton.edu
See listing under "Universities"

NEW YORK

College of Saint Rose
432 Western Ave, Albany NY 12203-1419
Maryelizabeth Amico, Asst V.P. for Undergraduate Admissions
518-454-5150 Fax: 518-454-2013
Website: www.strose.edu
E-mail: admit@strose.edu

CUNY Hunter College
695 Park Ave, New York NY 10021
Aaron Gibbs, Assistant Director of Recruitment
212-650-3946 Fax: 212-650-3336
Website: www.hunter.cuny.edu
E-mail: aaron.gibbs@hunter.cuny.edu

Daemen College
4380 Main St, Amherst NY 14226-3592
Donna Shaffner, Director of Admissions
800-462-7652 Fax: 716-839-8229
Website: www.daemen.edu/admissions
E-mail: admissions@daemen.edu

Hilbert College
5200 S Park Ave, Hamburg NY 14075-1597
Timothy Lee, Director of Admissions
716-649-7900 Fax: 716-649-0702
Website: www.hilbert.edu
E-mail: tlee@hilbert.edu

Iona College
715 North Ave, New Rochelle NY 10801-1890
Kevin Cavanagh, Assistant V.P. for College Admissions
914-633-2502 Fax: 914-637-2778
Website: www.iona.edu

Long Island University-C. W. Post Campus
720 Northern Blvd, Brookville NY 11548-1300
Joanne Graziano, Executive Director of Admissions
516-299-2900 Fax: 516-299-2137
Website: www.liu.edu/cwpost
E-mail: enroll@cwpost.liu.edu

Marymount Manhattan College
221 E 71st St, New York NY 10021-4501
Jim Rogers, Dean of Admissions
800-MARYMOUNT Fax: 212-517-0448
Website: www.mmm.edu
E-mail: admissions@mmm.edu

Molloy College
1000 Hempstead Ave
Rockville Centre NY 11570-1100
Marguerite Lane, Director of Admissions
516-678-5000 ext. 6291 Fax: 516-256-2247
Website: www.molloy.edu
E-mail: admissions@molloy.edu
See listing under "Universities"

PURCHASE COLLEGE STATE UNIVERSITY OF NEW YORK (SUNY)
735 Anderson Hill Rd, Purchase NY 10577-1400
Stephanie McCaine, Director of Admissions
914-251-6300 Fax: 914-251-6314
Website: www.purchase.edu
E-mail: admisn@purchase.edu
See listing under "Universities"

Roberts Wesleyan College
2301 Westside Dr, Rochester NY 14624-1997
Office of Admissions
585-594-6400 Fax: 585-594-6371
Website: www.roberts.edu
E-mail: admissions@roberts.edu

St. John's University
8000 Utopia Pkwy, Queens NY 11439
Office of Admission
877-STJ-5550 ext. 101 Fax: 718-990-2096
Website: www.stjohns.edu/learnmore
E-mail: admhelp@stjohns.edu
See listing under "Universities"

St. Joseph's College
245 Clinton Ave, Brooklyn NY 11205-3688
Theresa LaRocca Meyer, V.P. for Enrollment Management
718-636-6800 Fax: 718-636-8303
Website: www.sjcny.edu
E-mail: tlaroccameyer@sjcny.edu

SUNY College at Brockport
350 New Campus Dr, Brockport NY 14420-2997
Bernard S. Valento, Director of Undergraduate Admissions
585-395-2751 Fax: 585-395-5452
Website: www.brockport.edu
E-mail: admit@brockport.edu

SUNY College of Technology
Alfred NY 14802
Deborah J. Goodrich, Associate VP Enrollment Mgmt.
800-4AL-FRED Fax: 607-587-4299
Website: www.alfredstate.edu
E-mail: admissions@alfredstate.edu

SUNY Orange County Community College
115 South St, Middletown NY 10940-6437
Margot St. Lawrence, Director of Admissions
845-341-4030 Fax: 845-342-8662
Website: www.sunyorange.edu
E-mail: apply@sunyorange.edu
See listing under "Community and Junior Colleges"

SUNY Sullivan County Community College
112 College Rd, Loch Sheldrake NY 12759-5151
Sari Rosenheck, Director of Admissions
845-434-5750 Fax: 845-434-0923
Website: www.sullivan.suny.edu
E-mail: admissions@sullivan.suny.edu
Student Housing on Campus.

Wells College
PO Box 500, Aurora NY 13026
Susan Sloan, Director of Admissions
800-952-9355 Fax: 315-364-3227
Website: www.wells.edu
E-mail: ssloan@wells.edu

NORTH CAROLINA

Catawba College
2300 W Innes St, Salisbury NC 28144-2488
Dr. L. Russell Watjen, Ph.D., V.P. & Dean of Admissions
704-637-4402 Fax: 704-637-4222
Website: www.catawba.edu
E-mail: admission@catawba.edu

Peace College
15 E Peace St, Raleigh NC 27604-1194
Laura C. Bingham, President
800-PEACE-47 Fax: 919-508-2306
Website: www.peace.edu
E-mail: admissions@peace.edu

Salem College
Winston Salem NC 27108
Dana Evans, Dean of Admissions/Fin. Aid
800-32-SALEM Fax: 336-917-5572
Website: www.salem.edu
E-mail: admissions@salem.edu
See listing under "Women's Colleges"

NORTH DAKOTA

Dickinson State University
Dickinson ND 58601-4896
Steve Glasser, Director of Enrollment Services
800-279-4295 Fax: 701-483-2409
Website: www.dickinsonstate.edu
E-mail: dsu.hawks@dickinsonstate.edu

Valley City State University
101 College St SW, Valley City ND 58072-4024
Dan Klein, Director of Enrollment Services
800-532-8641 ext. 7101 Fax: 701-845-7299
Website: www.vcsu.edu
E-mail: enrollment.services@vcsu.edu
See listing under "Universities"

OHIO

Cincinnati Christian University
PO Box 4320, Cincinnati OH 45204
Erin Oppy, Executive Director of Undergraduate Admissions
513-244-8141 Fax: 513-244-8453
Website: www.ccuniversity.edu

Cleveland State University
2121 Euclid Ave RW 204, Cleveland OH 44115
Dr. Richard Arndt, Dean of Undergraduate Recruitment and College Partnerships
888-CSU-OHIO Fax: 216-687-9210
Website: www.csuohio.edu
E-mail: admissions@csuohio.edu

Franciscan University of Steubenville
University Blvd, Steubenville OH 43952
Margaret J. Weber, Director of Admissions
800-783-6220 or 740-283-6226 Fax: 740-284-5456
Website: www.admissions.edu
E-mail: mweber@franciscan.edu

The Ohio State University
Department of Psychology
Psychology Building, 1835 Neil Ave
Columbus OH 43210
614-292-8185 Fax: 614-292-4537
Website: www.psy.ohio-state.edu

University of Dayton
300 College Park, Dayton OH 45469-1300
Robert F. Durkle, Director of Admission
800-837-7433 Fax: 937-229-4729
Website: admission.udayton.edu
E-mail: admission@udayton.edu

Ursuline College
2550 Lander Rd, Cleveland OH 44124-4398
Sarah E. Sundermeier, Director of Admissions
888-URSULINE Toll Free Fax: 440-684-6138
Website: www.admission.ursuline.edu
E-mail: admission@ursuline.edu

OKLAHOMA

Mid-America Christian University
3500 SW 119th St, Oklahoma City OK 73170-4504
Haley Hope, Director of Admissions
405-691-3800 Fax: 405-692-3165
Website: www.macu.edu
E-mail: info@macu.edu

Oklahoma State University
Stillwater OK 74078
Maureen Sullivan, Department Head
405-744-7054
Website: www.okstate.edu
E-mail: maureen@okstate.edu

University of Tulsa
600 S College Ave, Tulsa OK 74104-3126
Earl Johnson, Dean of Admission
918-631-2307 Fax: 918-631-5003
Website: www.utulsa.edu
E-mail: admission@utulsa.edu

OREGON

Cascade College
9101 E Burnside St, Portland OR 97216-1599
Jim Murphy, Director of Enrollment Management
800-550-7678 Fax: 503-257-1222
Website: www.cascade.edu
E-mail: admissions@cascade.edu

Marylhurst University
17600 Pacific Hwy (Hwy 43)
Marylhurst OR 97036-0261
Director of Admissions
800-634-9982 ext. 6268 Fax: 503-635-6585
Website: www.marylhurst.edu
E-mail: studentinfo@marylhurst.edu

PACIFIC UNIVERSITY
2043 College Way, Forest Grove OR 97116-1797
Karen M. Dunston, Executive Director of Admissions
800-677-6712 Fax: 503-352-2975
Website: www.pacific.edu
E-mail: admissions@pacific.edu

Warner Pacific College
2219 SE 68th Ave, Portland OR 97215-4026
Shannon Mackey, Director of Admissions
503-517-1000 Fax: 503-517-1352
Website: www.warnerpacific.edu
E-mail: admissions@warnerpacific.edu

PENNSYLVANIA

Clarion University of Pennsylvania
840 Wood St, Clarion PA 16214-1232
William Bailey, Dean of Enrollment Management
814-393-2306 Fax: 814-393-2030
Website: www.clarion.edu
E-mail: admissions@clarion.edu

Community College of Allegheny County
Allegheny Campus: 808 Ridge Ave, Pittsburgh PA 15212 Admissions: 412.237.2700
Boyce Campus: 595 Beatty Rd, Monroeville PA 15146 Admissions: 724.325.6614
North Campus: 8701 Perry Highway, Pittsburgh PA 15237 Admissions: 412.369.3600
South Campus: 1750 Clairton Rd, West Mifflin PA 15122 Admissions: 412-469-4301
Website: www.ccac.edu

Delaware Valley College
700 E Butler Ave, Doylestown PA 18901-2697
Stephen W. Zenko, Director of Admissions
800-2DE-LVAL Fax: 215-230-2968
Website: www.delval.edu
E-mail: stephenzenko@delval.edu

Holy Family University
9801 Frankford Avenue, Philadelphia PA 19114
Lauren Campbell, Director of Admissions
215-637-3050 Fax: 215-281-1022
Website: www.holyfamily.edu
E-mail: admissions@holyfamily.edu

Juniata College
1700 Moore St, Huntingdon PA 16652-2196
Michelle Bartol, Dean of Enrollment
877-JUNIATA Fax: 814-641-3100
Website: www.juniata.edu
E-mail: admissions@juniata.edu

MOUNT ALOYSIUS COLLEGE
7373 Admiral Peary Hwy, Cresson PA 16630-1999
Frank C. Crouse Jr., Vice President for Enrollment Management
814-886-6383 or 888-823-2220 Fax: 814-886-6441
Website: www.mtaloy.edu
E-mail: admissions@mtaloy.edu

Washington & Jefferson College
60 S Lincoln St, Washington PA 15301-4801
Alton E. Newell, Vice President for Enrollment
724-223-6025 Fax: 724-223-6534
Website: www.washjeff.edu
E-mail: admission@washjeff.edu

Widener University
1 University Pl, Chester PA 19013-5792
Edwin Wright, Dean of Admissions
610-499-4000 Fax: 610-499-4676
Website: www.widener.edu
E-mail: admissions.office@widener.edu

SOUTH CAROLINA

Columbia International University
PO Box 3122, Columbia SC 29230-3122
Michelle MacGregor, Director of University Admissions
800-777-2227 Fax: 803-786-4209
Website: www.ciu.edu
E-mail: yesciu@ciu.edu
See listing under "Theological Studies & Religious Vocations"

Erskine College & Seminary
PO Box 176, Due West SC 29639
Bart Walker, Director of Admissions
864-379-8838 Fax: 864-379-3048
Website: www.erskine.edu
E-mail: admissions@erskine.edu

North Greenville University
PO Box 1892, Tigerville SC 29688-1892
Website: www.ngu.edu
See listing under "Universities"

South University
9 Science Court, Columbia SC 29203
Trish Wade, Contact
803-799-9082 Fax: 803-799-9038
Website: www.southuniversity.edu
E-mail: twade@southuniversity.edu

University of South Carolina - Upstate
800 University Way, Spartanburg SC 29303-4932
Donette Stewart, Assistant VC for Enrollment Services
864-503-5246 Fax: 864-503-5727
Website: www.uscupstate.edu
E-mail: dstewart@uscupstate.edu
See listing under "Universities"

TENNESSEE

Austin Peay State University
601 College St, Clarksville TN 37044-0002
931-221-7011 Fax: 931-221-6168
Website: www.apsu.edu
E-mail: admissions@apsu.edu

Crichton College
255 N Highland St, Memphis TN 38111-4745
Shelly Luttrell, Dean of Admissions
901-320-9797 Fax: 901-320-9791
Website: www.crichton.edu
E-mail: admissions@crichton.edu

Lipscomb University
3901 Granny White Pike, Nashville TN 37204-3951
Ricky Holaway, Director of Admissions
800-333-4358 ext. 1776 Fax: 615-269-1804
Website: www.lipscomb.edu
E-mail: admissions@lipscomb.edu

TEXAS

Abilene Christian University
ACU Box 29000, Abilene TX 79699-0001
325-674-2000 Fax: 325-674-2202
Website: www.acu.edu
E-mail: info@admissions.acu.edu

Lubbock Christian University
5601 19th St, Lubbock TX 79407-2099
Stan Scott, Director of Admissions
806-796-8800 Fax: 806-720-7162
Website: www.lcu.edu
E-mail: stan.scott@lcu.edu

Texas Woman's University
PO Box 425589, Denton TX 76204-5589
Erma Nieto-Brecht, Director of Admissions
866-809-6130 Fax: 940-898-3081
Website: www.twu.edu
E-mail: admissions@twu.edu

University of Houston
122 E Cullen Bldg, Houston TX 77204-2023
Office of Admission
713-743-9595
Website: www.uh.edu
E-mail: admissions@uh.edu

University of Texas at Arlington
Box 19111, Arlington TX 76019-0111
Hans Gatterdam, Director of Admission
817-272-6287 Fax: 817-272-3435
Website: www.uta.edu
E-mail: admissions@uta.edu

VERMONT

Green Mountain College
1 College Cir, Poultney VT 05764-1199
Sandra Bartholomew, Ph.D., Dean of Enrollment Management
802-287-8000 Fax: 802-287-8099
Website: www.greenmtn.edu
E-mail: bartholomews@greenmtn.edu

NORWICH UNIVERSITY
158 Harmon Dr, Northfield VT 05663
Dr. Johnnie Stones, Department Head
800-468-6679 Fax: 802-485-2252
Website: www.norwich.edu
E-mail: stones@norwich.edu
See listing under "Universities"

Southern Vermont College
982 Mansion Dr, Bennington VT 05201-6002
Joel Wincowski, Director of Admissions
800-378-2782 Fax: 802-447-4695
Website: www.svc.edu
E-mail: admis@svc.edu

VIRGINIA

ARGOSY UNIVERSITY/WASHINGTON DC
1550 Wilson Blvd Ste 600, Arlington VA 22209
Emily Peck, Director of Admissions
703-526-5800 Fax: 703-243-8973
Website: www.argosyu.edu
E-mail: epeck@argosyu.edu

Mary Baldwin College
Staunton VA 24401
Lisa A. Branson, Executive Director of Admissions and Financial Aid
800-468-2262 Fax: 540-887-7292
Website: www.mbc.edu
E-mail: admit@mbc.edu

Marymount University
2807 N Glebe Rd, Arlington VA 22207-4299
Michael Canfield, Director of Admissions
800-548-7638 Fax: 703-522-0348
Website: www.marymount.edu
E-mail: admissions@marymount.edu

Radford University
PO Box 6903, Radford VA 24142
David W. Kraus, Director of Admissions
800-890-4265 Fax: 540-831-5038
Website: www.radford.edu
E-mail: ruadmiss@radford.edu

Randolph College
2500 Rivermont Ave, Lynchburg VA 24503
Patricia LeDonne, Director of Admissions
434-947-8100 Fax: 434-947-8996
Website: www.randolphcollege.edu
E-mail: admissions@randolphcollege.edu

WEST VIRGINIA

Davis & Elkins College
100 Campus Dr, Elkins WV 26241-3996
Renee Heckel, Director of Enrollment Management
800-624-3157 Fax: 304-637-1800
Website: www.davisandelkins.edu
E-mail: admiss@davisandelkins.edu

Fairmont State University
1201 Locust Ave, Fairmont WV 26554-2470
Steve Leadman, Director of Admissions
304-367-4892 or 800-641-5678 Fax: 304-367-4789
Website: www.fairmontstate.edu
E-mail: admit@fairmontstate.edu

Mountain State College
1508 Spring St, Parkersburg WV 26101-3993
Judith Sutton, Director
304-485-5487 Fax: 304-485-3524
Website: www.mountainstate.org
E-mail: admin@mountainstate.org
See listing under "Career Schools"

Mountain State University
Box 9003, Beckley WV 25802-9003
Tony England, Director of Admissions
866-FOR-MSU1 or 304-929-INFO Fax: 304-253-5072
Website: www.mountainstate.edu
E-mail: gomsu@mountainstate.edu
See listing under "Universities"

WISCONSIN

Alverno College
PO Box 343922, Milwaukee WI 53234-3922
Dianna Gaebler, Director of Admissions
414-382-6100 Fax: 414-382-6354
Website: www.alverno.edu
E-mail: admissions@alverno.edu

St. Norbert College
100 Grant St, De Pere WI 54115
Brian Studebaker, Director of Admission
800-236-4878 Fax: 920-403-4072
Website: www.snc.edu
E-mail: admit@snc.edu

WISCONSIN SCHOOL OF PROFESSIONAL PSYCHOLOGY
9120 W Hampton Ave Ste 212
Milwaukee WI 53225-4960
Howard Haven, Ph.D., Dean
414-464-9777 Fax: 414-358-5590
Website: www.wspp.edu
E-mail: admissions@wspp.edu

WYOMING

University of Wyoming
Admissions Office
Dept 3435, Laramie WY 82071-3435
Brooke Culver, Contact
800-342-5996 Fax: 307-766-4042
Website: www.uwyo.edu
E-mail: why-wyo@uwyo.edu

GUAM

University of Guam
UOG Station, Mangilao GU 96923
Deborah Leon Guerrero, Registrar
671-735-2201 or 671-735-2208 Fax: 671-735-2203
Website: www.uog.edu
E-mail: admitme@uog9.uog.edu

PUERTO RICO

CARLOS ALBIZU UNIVERSITY - SAN JUAN CAMPUS
PO Box 9023711, San Juan PR 00902-3711
Carlos Rodriguez, Director of Admissions
787-725-6500 Fax: 787-721-7187
Website: albizu.edu
E-mail: crodriguez@albizu.edu

PUBLIC HEALTH

ALASKA

University of Alaska Anchorage
PO Box 141629, Anchorage AK 99514-1629
Cecile Mitchell, Director of Enrollment Services
907-786-1480 Fax: 907-786-4888
Website: www.uaa.alaska.edu/
E-mail: enroll@uaa.alaska.edu

CALIFORNIA

ITT Technical Institute
12669 Encinitas Ave, Sylmar CA 91342-3664
Kelly Christensen, Director of Admissions
818-364-5151 Fax: 818-364-5150
Website: www.itt-tech.edu
E-mail: kchristensen@itt-tech.edu

FLORIDA

University of South Florida
4202 E Fowler Ave, Tampa FL 33620-6900
J. Robert Spatig, Director of Admissions
877-USF-BULL Fax: 813-974-9689
Website: www.usf.edu
E-mail: admissions@admin.usf.edu
See listing under "Universities"

GEORGIA

North Georgia Technical College
434 Meeks Ave, Blairsville GA 30512-2983
Admissions
706-439-6300 Fax: 706-439-6301
Website: www.northgatech.edu
E-mail: info@northgatech.edu

North Georgia Technical College
Clarkesville Campus
PO Box 65, Clarkesville GA 30523-0002
Admissions
706-754-7700 Fax: 706-754-7777
Website: www.northgatech.edu
E-mail: info@northgatech.edu

ILLINOIS

Benedictine University
5700 College Rd, Lisle IL 60532-0900
630-829-6300 or 888-829-6363 Fax: 630-829-6301
Website: www.ben.edu
E-mail: admissions@ben.edu
See listing under "Universities"

MINNESOTA

Minnesota State University Moorhead
1104 7th Ave S, Moorhead MN 56563-0002
Regina Monson, Director of Admissions
218-477-2161 Fax: 218-477-4374
Website: go.mnstate.edu
E-mail: dragon@mnstate.edu

NEW JERSEY

RICHARD STOCKTON COLLEGE OF NEW JERSEY
PO Box 195, Pomona NJ 08240
John Iacovelli, Dean of Enrollment Management
866-RSC-2885 Fax: 609-626-5541
Website: www.stockton.edu
E-mail: admissions@stockton.edu

Stockton College is a comprehensive liberal arts, co-ed institution founded in 1969. Advance Pre-Professional Degree Options: 7-yr BS/MD with UMDNJ; NJ Dental School; NJ Medical School, Robert Wood Johnson Medical, School of Osteopathic Medicine; NY College of Podiatric Medicine, Pennsylvania College of Podiatric Medicine, SUNY College of Optometry. Pharmacy doctorate program with Rutgers University. 5-yr Engineering with NJIT and Rutgers University. Dual BA/MA in Criminal Justice. 5-yr BS/MS in Computational Science. BS/MS in Nursing. Doctorate of Physical Therapy. Additional Programs: Forensic Science, Pre-Law, Pre-Occupational Therapy, and Pre-Veterinary.

NEW YORK

CUNY Hunter College
695 Park Ave, New York NY 10021
Aaron Gibbs, Assistant Director of Recruitment
212-650-3946 Fax: 212-650-3336
Website: www.hunter.cuny.edu
E-mail: aaron.gibbs@hunter.cuny.edu

Long Island University-C. W. Post Campus
720 Northern Blvd, Brookville NY 11548-1300
Joanne Graziano, Executive Director of Admissions
516-299-2900 Fax: 516-299-2137
Website: www.liu.edu/cwpost
E-mail: enroll@cwpost.liu.edu

Monroe College
2501 Jerome Ave, Bronx NY 10468-4305
Evan Jerome, Director of Admissions
718-933-6700 Fax: 718-364-3552
Website: www.monroecollege.edu
E-mail: ejerome@monroecollege.edu

OHIO

The Ohio State University
School of Public Health
Starling-Loving Hall, 320 W 10th Ave
Columbus OH 43210
614-293-3907 Fax: 614-293-5412
Website: sph.osu.edu
E-mail: sph@osu.edu

PENNSYLVANIA

Community College of Allegheny County
Allegheny Campus: 808 Ridge Ave, Pittsburgh PA 15212 Admissions: 412.237.2700
Boyce Campus: 595 Beatty Rd, Monroeville PA 15146 Admissions: 724.325.6614
North Campus: 8701 Perry Highway, Pittsburgh PA 15237 Admissions: 412.369.3600
South Campus: 1750 Clairton Rd, West Mifflin PA 15122 Admissions: 412-469-4301
Website: www.ccac.edu

INTERNATIONAL ACADEMY OF ADVANCED REFLEXOLOGY & MEDICAL REFLEXOLOGY CLINIC
1701 Snyder Rd, Green Lane PA 18054
Professor L.J. Telepo, President
215-234-0307 or 267-377-5128 Fax: 267-329-8008
Website: www.reflexology.net
E-mail: postsecondary@reflexology.net
See listing under "Allied Health Science"

INTERNATIONAL ACADEMY OF ADVANCED REFLEXOLOGY & MEDICAL REFLEXOLOGY CLINIC
1177 6th St, Whitehall PA 18052
Professor L.J. Telepo, President
215-234-0307 or 267-377-5128 Fax: 267-329-8008
Website: www.reflexology.net
E-mail: postsecondary@reflexology.net
See listing under "Allied Health Science"

TEXAS

Texas Woman's University
PO Box 425589, Denton TX 76204-5589
Erma Nieto-Brecht, Director of Admissions
866-809-6130 Fax: 940-898-3081
Website: www.twu.edu
E-mail: admissions@twu.edu

VERMONT

Woodbury College
660 Elm St, Montpelier VT 05602-4017
Denise MacMartin, Director of Admissions
800-639-6039 Fax: 802-229-2141
Website: www.woodbury-college.edu
E-mail: admiss@woodbury-college.edu

SOCIAL SCIENCE

ALABAMA

Judson College
302 Bibb St, Marion AL 36756
Michael Scotto, Director of Admissions
800-447-9472 Fax: 334-683-5147
Website: www.judson.edu
E-mail: admissions@judson.edu

University of Alabama in Huntsville
PO Box 1247, Huntsville AL 35899-0001
Nikki Willis, Assoc. Director for Recruiting Program and Events
1-800-UAH-CALL Fax: 256-824-6073
Website: www.uah.edu
E-mail: willisn@uah.edu

University of South Alabama
307 University Blvd N, Mobile AL 36688-3053
Melissa Haab, Director of Admissions
251-460-6141 Fax: 251-460-7876
Website: www.southalabama.edu
E-mail: admiss@usouthal.edu

ALASKA

University of Alaska Anchorage
PO Box 141629, Anchorage AK 99514-1629
Cecile Mitchell, Director of Enrollment Services
907-786-1480 Fax: 907-786-4888
Website: www.uaa.alaska.edu/
E-mail: enroll@uaa.alaska.edu

CALIFORNIA

California State University-San Bernadino
5500 University Pkwy
San Bernardino CA 92407-2393
Olivia Rosas, Director of Admissions
909-537-5188 Fax: 909-537-7034
Website: www.csusb.edu
E-mail: orosas@csusb.edu

Chapman University
One University Drive, Orange CA 92866-1099
Michael Drummy, Assistant Vice President for Enrollment
Services and Chief Admission Officer
714-997-6411 or 888-CUAPPLY Fax: 714-997-6713
Website: www.chapman.edu
E-mail: admit@chapman.edu

Concordia University
1530 Concordia, Irvine CA 92612-3203
Lori McDonald, Executive Director of Enrollment Services
800-229-1200 or 949-854-8002 Fax: 949-854-6894
Website: www.cui.edu
E-mail: admission@cui.edu

Dominican University of California
50 Acacia Ave, San Rafael CA 94901-2298
Office of Admissions
888-323-6762 Fax: 415-485-3214
Website: www.dominican.edu
E-mail: enroll@dominican.edu

Fielding Graduate University
School of Human and Organization Development
2112 Santa Barbara St
Santa Barbara CA 93105-3538
DeAnne Taylor, Director of Admissions
805-687-1099 Fax: 805-687-9793
Website: www.fielding.edu
E-mail: admission@fielding.edu

FRESNO CITY COLLEGE
1101 E University Ave, Fresno CA 93741-0002
Dayann Dietrich, Contact
559-442-8241 Fax: 559-237-4232
Website: www.fresnocitycollege.com
E-mail: fcc.admissions@scccd.com

New College School of Law
50 Fell St, San Francisco CA 94102-5206
Sharon Pittman, Dean of Admissions
415-241-1300 Fax: 415-241-9525
Website: www.newcollege.edu
E-mail: spittman@newcollege.edu or lawadmissions@newcollege.edu

Orange Coast College
PO Box 5005, Costa Mesa CA 92628-5005
Kristin Clark, Director of Admissions
714-432-5773 Fax: 714-432-5736
Website: www.orangecoastcollege.edu
E-mail: kclark@cccd.edu

Point Loma Nazarene University
3900 Lomaland Dr, San Diego CA 92106-2810
Chip Killingsworth, Director of Undergraduate Admissions
800-733-7770 Fax: 619-849-2601
Website: www.pointloma.edu
E-mail: admissions@pointloma.edu

San Bernardino Valley College
701 S Mount Vernon Ave
San Bernardino CA 92410-2798
Kay Ragan, Ed.D., Director of Admissions
909-888-6511 Fax: 909-889-4988
Website: www.valleycollege.edu
E-mail: kragan@sbccd.cc.ca.us

San Diego Christian College
2100 Greenfield Dr, El Cajon CA 92019-1157
Rene Inman, Director of Admissions
800-676-2242 Fax: 619-590-1739
Website: www.sdcc.edu
E-mail: admissions@sdcc.edu

Whittier College
PO Box 634, Whittier CA 90608-0634
Kieron Miller, Director of Admissions
562-907-4200 Fax: 562-907-4870
Website: www.whittier.edu
E-mail: kmiller@whittier.edu

COLORADO

Colorado Christian University
8787 W Alameda Ave, Lakewood CO 80226
Sean Kadel, Director of Admissions
800-44-FAITH Fax: 303-963-3201
Website: www.ccu.edu
E-mail: admissions@ccu.edu

CONNECTICUT

Albertus Magnus College
700 Prospect St, New Haven CT 06511-1189
Richard Lolatte, Dean of Admission
203-773-8501 or 800-578-9160 Fax: 203-773-5248
Website: www.albertus.edu
E-mail: admissions@albertus.edu

DELAWARE

Wesley College
120 N State St, Dover DE 19901-3876
302-736-2300 Fax: 302-736-2301
Website: www.wesley.edu

DISTRICT OF COLUMBIA

Gallaudet University
800 Florida Ave NE, Washington DC 20002-3695
Charity Reedy Hines, Director of Admissions
202-651-5750 Fax: 202-651-5744
Website: www.gallaudet.edu
E-mail: admissions.office@gallaudet.edu

FLORIDA

Florida State University
600 W College Ave, Tallahassee FL 32306-1096
Janice V. Finney, Director of Admissions
850-644-2525 Fax: 850-644-0197
Website: admissions.fsu.edu
E-mail: admissions@admin.fsu.edu

Lynn University
3601 N Military Trl, Boca Raton FL 33431-5598
Director of Admissions
561-237-7900 Fax: 561-237-7100
Website: www.lynn.edu
E-mail: admission@lynn.edu

St. Thomas University
16401 NW 37th Ave, Miami Gardens FL 33054
Dr. Gary Feinberg, Chair, Social Sciences
800-367-9010 or 305-628-6546 Fax: 305-628-6591
Website: www.stu.edu
E-mail: signup@stu.edu

University of South Florida
4202 E Fowler Ave, Tampa FL 33620-6900
J. Robert Spatig, Director of Admissions
877-USF-BULL Fax: 813-974-9689
Website: www.usf.edu
E-mail: admissions@admin.usf.edu
See listing under "Universities"

GEORGIA

Armstrong Atlantic State University
11935 Abercorn St, Savannah GA 31419-1997
Kim West, Asst. Dean and Registrar Enrollment Services
912-927-5277 Fax: 912-921-5462
Website: www.armstrong.edu
E-mail: admissions@mail.armstrong.edu

Kennesaw State University
1000 Chastain Rd NW, Kennesaw GA 30144-5591
Dr. Helen Ridley, Dean of Humanities and Social Science
770-423-6124
Website: www.kennesaw.edu

IDAHO

Brigham Young University - Idaho
120 Kimball Bldg, Rexburg ID 83460-1615
Rob Garrett, Director of Admissions
208-496-1020 Fax: 208-496-1220
Website: www.byui.edu
E-mail: admissions@byui.edu

Lewis-Clark State College
500 8th Ave, Lewiston ID 83501-2698
Diane Douglas, Ph.D., Registrar/Director of Admissions
800-933-5272 Fax: 208-792-2429
Website: www.lcsc.edu
E-mail: admissions@lcsc.edu

University of Idaho
Moscow ID 83844-4253
Lloyd Scott, Director of New Student Services
208-885-6163 Fax: 208-885-4477
Website: www.uidaho.edu
E-mail: nss@uidaho.edu

ILLINOIS

Aurora University
347 S Gladstone Ave, Aurora IL 60506-4892
Carol R. Dunn, Ed.D., Vice President for Enrollment
800-742-5281 Fax: 630-844-5535
Website: www.aurora.edu
E-mail: admission@aurora.edu

Benedictine University
5700 College Rd, Lisle IL 60532-0900
630-829-6300 or 888-829-6363 Fax: 630-829-6301
Website: www.ben.edu
E-mail: admissions@ben.edu
See listing under "Universities"

CONCORDIA UNIVERSITY
7400 Augusta St, River Forest IL 60305-1402
708-209-3100 Fax: 708-209-3176
Website: www.cuchicago.edu
E-mail: admission@cuchicago.edu

INSTITUTE FOR CLINICAL SOCIAL WORK
200 N Michigan Ave Ste 407, Chicago IL 60601
Barbara Berger, Ph.D., Dean of Admissions
312-726-8480 Fax: 312-726-7216
Website: www.icsw.edu
E-mail: icsw@icsw.edu

Roosevelt University
430 S Michigan Ave, Chicago IL 60605
Gwen E. Kanelos, Asst. Vice President for Enrollment Services
877-APPLY-RU Fax: 312-341-4216
Website: www.roosevelt.edu
E-mail: applyru@roosevelt.edu

INDIANA

Ancilla Domini College
Donaldson IN 46513
Erin Alonzo, Director of Admissions
574-936-8898 Fax: 574-935-1773
Website: www.ancilla.edu
E-mail: erin.alonzo@ancilla.edu

Franklin College
101 Branigin Blvd, Franklin IN 46131
Jacqueline S. Acosta, Director of Admissions
800-852-0232 Fax: 317-738-8274
Website: www.franklincollege.edu
E-mail: admissions@franklincollege.edu

Oakland City University
138 N Lucretia St, Oakland City IN 47660
Brian J. Baker, Director of Admissions
800-737-5125 Fax: 812-749-1433
Website: www.oak.edu
E-mail: bbaker@oak.edu
See listing under "Universities"

University of Evansville
1800 Lincoln Ave, Evansville IN 47722-0001
Don Vos, Dean of Admission
800-423-8633 Fax: 812-488-4076
Website: www.evansville.edu
E-mail: admission@evansville.edu

IOWA

Briar Cliff University
PO Box 2100, Sioux City IA 51104-0100
Sharisue Wilcoxon, VP for Enrollment Management
712-279-5200 Fax: 712-279-1632
Website: www.briarcliff.edu
E-mail: admissions@briarcliff.edu

Clarke College
1550 Clarke Dr, Dubuque IA 52001-3198
Andy Schroeder, Director of Admissions
800-383-2345 Fax: 563-584-8666
Website: www.clarke.edu
E-mail: andy.schroeder@clarke.edu

Graceland University
1 University Place, Lamoni IA 50140
Greg Sutherland, Interim Vice President for Enrollment and Dean of Admissions
641-784-5196 Fax: 641-784-5480
Website: www.admissions.graceland.edu
E-mail: admissions@graceland.edu

Iowa Lakes Community College
3200 College Dr, Emmetsburg IA 50536-1055
Anne Stansbury, Asst. Director of Admissions
712-852-5212 Fax: 712-362-8363
Website: www.iowalakes.edu
E-mail: info@iowalakes.edu

Iowa Lakes Community College
300 S 18th St, Estherville IA 51334-2721
Anne Stansbury, Asst. Director of Admissions
712-362-7945 Fax: 712-362-8363
Website: www.iowalakes.edu
E-mail: info@iowalakes.edu

Iowa Lakes Community College
1900 Grand Ave, Suite 8, Spencer IA 51301
Anne Stansbury, Assistant Director of Admissions
712-262-7141 Fax: 712-262-4047
Website: www.iowalakes.edu
E-mail: info@iowalakes.edu

Waldorf College
106 S 6th St, Forest City IA 50436-1713
Dr. Linda Hoopes, Vice President of Admission and Marketing
800-292-1903 or 641-585-8112 Fax: 641-585-8125
Website: www.waldorf.edu
E-mail: hoopesl@waldorf.edu
See listing under "Universities"

KANSAS

COLBY COMMUNITY COLLEGE
1255 S Range Ave, Colby KS 67701-4099
Director of Admissions
888-634-9350 or 785-460-4690 Fax: 785-460-4691
Website: www.colbycc.edu
E-mail: admissions@colbycc.edu

Independence Community College
PO Box 708, Independence KS 67301-0708
Dr. Terry Hetrick, President
800-842-6063 Fax: 620-331-5344
Website: www.indycc.edu
E-mail: admissions@indycc.edu

Tabor College
400 S Jefferson St, Hillsboro KS 67063-1758
Rusty Allen, Dean of Enrollment Management
800-822-6799 Fax: 620-947-6276
Website: www.tabor.edu
E-mail: admissions@tabor.edu
See listing under "Universities"

KENTUCKY

Bluegrass Community and Technical College
Oswald Building
470 Cooper Drive, Lexington KY 40506-0235
Shelbie Hugle, Director of Admissions
859-246-6200 Fax: 859-246-4664
Website: www.bluegrass.kctcs.edu
E-mail: bctc_info@kctcs.edu

Morehead State University
Morehead KY 40351-1689
Jeffrey Liles, Enrollment Services
800-585-6781 Fax: 606-783-5038
Website: www.moreheadstate.edu
E-mail: admissions@moreheadstate.edu

Transylvania University
300 N Broadway, Lexington KY 40508-1776
859-233-8242 Fax: 859-233-8797
Website: www.transy.edu
E-mail: admissions@transy.edu

LOUISIANA

Louisiana State University at Alexandria
8100 Highway 71 S, Alexandria LA 71302-9121
Dr. Thomas Armstrong, Director of Admissions
318-445-3672 Fax: 318-473-6418
Website: www.lsua.edu

Our Lady of Holy Cross College
4123 Woodland Dr, New Orleans LA 70131-7399
Office of Enrollment Services
504-394-7744 Fax: 504-391-2421
Website: www.olhcc.edu

MARYLAND

Hagerstown Community College
11400 Robinwood Dr, Hagerstown MD 21742-6590
Dr. Daniel E. Bock, Assistant Director of Admissions
301-790-2800 Fax: 301-791-9165
Website: www.hagerstowncc.edu
E-mail: bockd@hagerstowncc.edu

MASSACHUSETTS

Anna Maria College
50 Sunset Ln, Paxton MA 01612
Timothy M. Donahue, Director of Recruitment and Admissions
508-849-3360 Fax: 508-849-3362
Website: www.annamaria.edu
E-mail: admissions@annamaria.edu

Assumption College
500 Salisbury St, Worcester MA 01609-1294
Kathleen Murphy, Dean of Enrollment
508-767-7000 Fax: 508-799-4412
Website: www.assumption.edu
E-mail: admiss@assumption.edu

Bay State College
122 Commonwealth Ave, Boston MA 02116-2901
Craig Pfannenstiehl, President
617-217-9000 Fax: 617-536-1735

Boston University
121 Bay State Rd, Boston MA 02215
Kelly Walter, Executive Director of Admissions
617-353-2300 Fax: 617-353-9695
Website: web.bu.edu
E-mail: admissions@bu.edu

Gordon College
255 Grapevine Rd, Wenham MA 01984-1899
Barbara R. Layne, Associate Vice President, Enrollment
866-464-6736 Fax: 978-867-4682
Website: www.gordon.edu
E-mail: admissions@gordon.edu

Massachusetts Institute of Technology
77 Massachusetts Ave, Cambridge MA 02139-4307
617-253-1000 Fax: 617-253-4016
Website: my.mit.edu
E-mail: admissions@mit.edu

Smith College
Northampton MA 01063-0001
Debra Shaver, Director of Admissions
800-383-3232 Fax: 413-585-2527
Website: www.smith.edu
E-mail: admission@smith.edu

University of Massachusetts Dartmouth
Old Westport Rd, North Dartmouth MA 02747-2300
Steven T. Briggs, Director of Admissions
508-999-8605 Fax: 508-999-8755
Website: explore.umassd.edu
E-mail: sbriggs@umassd.edu

Worcester Polytechnic Institute
100 Institute Rd, Worcester MA 01609-2280
Edward J. Connor, Director of Admissions
508-831-5286 Fax: 508-831-5875
Website: admissions.wpi.edu
E-mail: admissions@wpi.edu

MICHIGAN

Alma College
614 W Superior St, Alma MI 48801-1599
Evan Montague, Director of Admissions
800-321-ALMA Fax: 989-463-7057
Website: www.alma.edu
E-mail: admissions@alma.edu

Concordia University
4090 Geddes Rd, Ann Arbor MI 48105-2797
Gary Neumann, Director of Admissions
734-995-7300 Fax: 734-995-4610
Website: www.cuaa.edu
E-mail: admissions@cuaa.edu

Grand Valley State University
1 Campus Dr, Allendale MI 49401-9403
616-331-2025 Fax: 616-331-2000
Website: www.gvsu.edu
E-mail: go2gvsu@gvsu.edu

HILLSDALE COLLEGE
33 E College St, Hillsdale MI 49242-1298
Dr. Mickey Craig, Director
517-607-2473 Fax: 517-607-2208
Website: www.hillsdale.edu
E-mail: mickey.craig@hillsdale.edu

Lake Superior State University
650 W Easterday Ave
Sault Sainte Marie MI 49783-1637
Susan Camp, Director of Admissions
888-800-LSSU Fax: 906-635-6696
Website: www.lssu.edu
E-mail: admissions@lssu.edu
See listing under "Universities"

MACOMB COMMUNITY COLLEGE
44575 Garfield Rd, Clinton Township MI 48038-1139
Information Center
586-445-7999
Website: www.macomb.edu
E-mail: answer@macomb.edu

MACOMB COMMUNITY COLLEGE
14500 E 12 Mile Rd, Warren MI 48088-3896
Information Center
586-445-7999
Website: www.macomb.edu
E-mail: answer@macomb.edu

Oakland University
2200 N Squirrel Rd, Rochester MI 48309
Eleanor L. Reynolds, Assistant Vice President & Director of Admissions
248-370-2100
Website: www.oakland.edu
E-mail: ouinfo@oakland.edu

MINNESOTA

Bethany Lutheran College
700 Luther Dr, Mankato MN 56001
Don Westphal, Dean of Admissions
507-344-7000 Fax: 507-344-7376
Website: www.blc.edu
E-mail: admiss@blc.edu

Carleton College
1 N College St, Northfield MN 55057-4044
800-995-2275 or 507-646-4190 Fax: 507-646-4526
Website: www.carleton.edu
E-mail: admissions@acs.carleton.edu

Crown College
8700 College View Dr, Saint Bonifacius MN 55375
Mitch Fisk, Director of Admissions
952-446-4142 Fax: 952-446-4149
Website: www.crown.edu
E-mail: johnsonj@crown.edu

Gustavus Adolphus College
800 W College Ave, Saint Peter MN 56082-1485
Mark H. Anderson, Dean of Admission
800-GUSTAVUS Fax: 507-933-7474
Website: www.gustavus.edu
E-mail: admission@gustavus.edu

Minnesota State University Moorhead
1104 7th Ave S, Moorhead MN 56563-0002
Regina Monson, Director of Admissions
218-477-2161 Fax: 218-477-4374
Website: go.mnstate.edu
E-mail: dragon@mnstate.edu

Pillsbury Baptist Bible College
315 S Grove Ave, Owatonna MN 55060-3097
Susanne Martin, Admissions Coordinator
507-451-2710 Fax: 507-451-0156
Website: www.pillsbury.edu
E-mail: admissions@pillsbury.edu

MISSISSIPPI

Tougaloo College
500 W County Line Rd, Tougaloo MS 39174-9799
Juno Leggette Jacobs, Director of Admissions
601-977-7768 Fax: 601-977-4501
Website: www.tougaloo.edu
E-mail: jjacobs@tougaloo.edu

MISSOURI

Central Methodist University
411 Central Methodist Sq, Fayette MO 65248-1198
Larry Anderson, Director of Admissions
660-248-6247 Fax: 660-248-1872
Website: www.centralmethodist.edu
E-mail: landerso@centralmethodist.edu

Columbia College
1001 Rogers St, Columbia MO 65216-0001
Regina Morin, Director of Admissions
573-875-7352 Fax: 573-875-7506
Website: www.ccis.edu
E-mail: admissions@ccis.edu

Lindenwood University
209 S Kingshighway St
Saint Charles MO 63301-1695
Sheryl Guffey, Director of Admissions
636-949-2000 Fax: 636-949-4989
Website: www.lindenwood.edu

Northwest Missouri State University
800 University Dr, Maryville MO 64468-6001
Beverly Schenkel, Dean of Enrollment Management
660-562-1562 Fax: 660-562-1121
Website: www.nwmissouri.edu
E-mail: admissions@nwmissouri.edu

Stephens College
PO Box 2121, Columbia MO 65215-0001
David Adams, Dean of Enrollment Management
573-442-2211 Fax: 573-876-7237
Website: www.stephens.edu
E-mail: dadams@stephens.edu

Truman State University
100 E Normal, Kirksville MO 63501
Office of Admission
660-785-4114 Fax: 660-785-7456
Website: admissions.truman.edu
E-mail: admissions@truman.edu

University of Missouri
1 University Blvd, Saint Louis MO 63121-4499
Dr. Mark Burkholder, Dean-College of Arts & Sciences
314-516-5501 Fax: 314-516-5415
Website: www.umsl.edu
E-mail: admissions@umsl.edu

Webster University
470 E Lockwood Ave, Saint Louis MO 63119-3194
Bill Huddleston-Berry, Chairman, Behavioral Sciences
314-968-7160 Fax: 314-963-6094
Website: www.webster.edu
E-mail: huddlews@webster.edu
See listing under "Universities"

William Jewell College
500 College Hill, Liberty MO 64068-1896
Dr. Rick Winslow, VP Enrollment Management and Student Affairs
800-753-7009 Fax: 816-415-5040
Website: www.jewell.edu
E-mail: winslowr@william.jewell.edu

William Woods University
1 University Ave, Fulton MO 65251-1098
Jimmy Clay, Director of Admissions
573-642-2251 Fax: 573-592-1146
Website: www.williamwoods.edu
E-mail: admissions@williamwoods.edu
See listing under "Universities"

MONTANA

Carroll College
1601 N Benton Ave, Helena MT 59625-0002
Dr. Thomas J. Trebon, President
Cynthia Thornquist, Director of Admissions & Enrollment Operations
406-447-4384 Fax: 406-447-4533
Website: www.carroll.edu
E-mail: admission@carroll.edu

NEBRASKA

Midland Lutheran College
900 N Clarkson St, Fremont NE 68025-4200
Todd Hansen, Associate Director of Admissions
402-941-6501 Fax: 402-941-6513
Website: www.mlc.edu
E-mail: admissions@mlc.edu

Nebraska Wesleyan University
5000 Saint Paul Ave, Lincoln NE 68504-2794
Patricia Karthauser, V.P. for University Enrollment
402-466-2371 Fax: 402-465-2177
Website: www.nebrwesleyan.edu
E-mail: admissions@nebrwesleyan.edu

University of Nebraska at Kearney
905 W 25th St, Kearney NE 68849-0001
Dusty Newton, Director of Admissions
800-KEARNEY Fax: 308-865-8987
Website: www.unk.edu
E-mail: admissionsug@unk.edu

NEVADA

GREAT BASIN COLLEGE
1500 College Pkwy, Elko NV 89801-5032
Julie G. Byrnes, Director of Enrollment Management
775-753-2271 Fax: 775-753-2311
Website: www.gbcnv.edu
E-mail: julieb@gwmail.gbcnv.edu
See listing under "Universities"

NEW HAMPSHIRE

Antioch University New England
40 Avon St, Keene NH 03431-3516
David Caruso, President
Leatrice A. Oram, Director of Admissions
603-357-6265 Fax: 603-357-0718
Website: www.antiochne.edu
E-mail: admissions@antiochne.edu

Southern New Hampshire University
2500 N River Rd, Hooksett NH 03106-1045
Steve Soba, Director of Admissions
603-645-9611 Fax: 603-645-9693
Website: www.snhu.edu
E-mail: s.soba@snhu.edu

NEW JERSEY

Atlantic Cape Community College
5100 Black Horse Pike
Mays Landing NJ 08330-2699
Linda McLeod, Assistant Director of College Recruitment
609-343-5000 Fax: 609-343-4921
Website: www.atlantic.edu
E-mail: accadmit@atlantic.edu
See listing under "Community and Junior Colleges"

Bergen Community College
400 Paramus Rd, Paramus NJ 07652
Julian Gomez, Asst. Director of Admissions
201-447-7100 Fax: 201-444-7036
Website: www.bergen.edu
E-mail: jgomez@bergen.edu

New Jersey City University
2039 John F Kennedy Blvd
Jersey City NJ 07305-1588
Carmen Panlilio, Asst. V.P. for Admissions and Financial Aid
201-200-3234 Fax: 201-200-2044
Website: www.njcu.edu
E-mail: admissions@njcu.edu

Ramapo College of New Jersey
505 Ramapo Valley Rd, Mahwah NJ 07430-1623
Director of Admissions
201-684-7300 or 201-684-7301 Fax: 201-684-7964
Website: www.ramapo.edu
E-mail: admissions@ramapo.edu

RICHARD STOCKTON COLLEGE OF NEW JERSEY
PO Box 195, Pomona NJ 08240
John Iacovelli, Dean of Enrollment Management
866-RSC-2885 Fax: 609-626-5541
Website: www.stockton.edu
E-mail: admissions@stockton.edu
See listing under "Universities"

NEW MEXICO

College of the Southwest
6610 N Lovington Hwy, Hobbs NM 88240-9129
Dr. Steve Hill, Dean of Recuitment
505-392-6561 Fax: 505-392-6006
Website: www.csw.edu
E-mail: shill@csw.edu

New Mexico State University
1500 N 3rd St, Grants NM 87020-2025
Irene Lutz, Director of Admissions
505-287-7981 Fax: 505-287-2329
Website: www.grants.nmsu.edu
E-mail: ilutz@nmsu.edu

NEW YORK

College of Saint Rose
432 Western Ave, Albany NY 12203-1419
Maryelizabeth Amico, Asst V.P. for Undergraduate Admissions
518-454-5150 Fax: 518-454-2013
Website: www.strose.edu
E-mail: admit@strose.edu

CUNY Hunter College
695 Park Ave, New York NY 10021
Aaron Gibbs, Assistant Director of Recruitment
212-650-3946 Fax: 212-650-3336
Website: www.hunter.cuny.edu
E-mail: aaron.gibbs@hunter.cuny.edu

Daemen College
4380 Main St, Amherst NY 14226-3592
Donna Shaffner, Director of Admissions
800-462-7652 Fax: 716-839-8229
Website: www.daemen.edu/admissions
E-mail: admissions@daemen.edu

Dowling College
150 Idle Hour Blvd, Oakdale NY 11769-1999
Diane Kazanecki-Kempter, Contact
631-244-3000 Fax: 631-244-1059
Website: www.dowling.edu
E-mail: admissions@dowling.edu

Hilbert College
5200 S Park Ave, Hamburg NY 14075-1597
Timothy Lee, Director of Admissions
716-649-7900 Fax: 716-649-0702
Website: www.hilbert.edu
E-mail: tlee@hilbert.edu

Iona College
715 North Ave, New Rochelle NY 10801-1890
Kevin Cavanagh, Assistant V.P. for College Admissions
914-633-2502 Fax: 914-637-2778
Website: www.iona.edu

Long Island University-C. W. Post Campus
720 Northern Blvd, Brookville NY 11548-1300
Joanne Graziano, Executive Director of Admissions
516-299-2900 Fax: 516-299-2137
Website: www.liu.edu/cwpost
E-mail: enroll@cwpost.liu.edu

Marymount Manhattan College
221 E 71st St, New York NY 10021-4501
Jim Rogers, Dean of Admissions
800-MARYMOUNT Fax: 212-517-0448
Website: www.mmm.edu
E-mail: admissions@mmm.edu

Molloy College
1000 Hempstead Ave
Rockville Centre NY 11570-1100
Marguerite Lane, Director of Admissions
516-678-5000 ext. 6291 Fax: 516-256-2247
Website: www.molloy.edu
E-mail: admissions@molloy.edu
See listing under "Universities"

PURCHASE COLLEGE STATE UNIVERSITY OF NEW YORK (SUNY)
735 Anderson Hill Rd, Purchase NY 10577-1400
Stephanie McCaine, Director of Admissions
914-251-6300 Fax: 914-251-6314
Website: www.purchase.edu
E-mail: admisn@purchase.edu
See listing under "Universities"

Roberts Wesleyan College
2301 Westside Dr, Rochester NY 14624-1997
Office of Admissions
585-594-6400 Fax: 585-594-6371
Website: www.roberts.edu
E-mail: admissions@roberts.edu

St. John's University
8000 Utopia Pkwy, Queens NY 11439
Office of Admission
877-STJ-5550 ext. 101 Fax: 718-990-2096
Website: www.stjohns.edu/learnmore
E-mail: admhelp@stjohns.edu
See listing under "Universities"

St. Joseph's College
245 Clinton Ave, Brooklyn NY 11205-3688
Theresa LaRocca Meyer, V.P. for Enrollment Management
718-636-6800 Fax: 718-636-8303
Website: www.sjcny.edu
E-mail: tlaroccameyer@sjcny.edu

Siena College
515 Loudonville Rd, Loudonville NY 12211-1462
Heather Renault, Director of Admissions
518-783-2300 Fax: 518-783-2436
Website: www.siena.edu
E-mail: hrenault@siena.edu

SUNY College at Brockport
350 New Campus Dr, Brockport NY 14420-2997
Bernard S. Valento, Director of Undergraduate Admissions
585-395-2751 Fax: 585-395-5452
Website: www.brockport.edu
E-mail: admit@brockport.edu

SUNY College of Technology
Alfred NY 14802
Deborah J. Goodrich, Associate VP Enrollment Mgmt.
800-4AL-FRED Fax: 607-587-4299
Website: www.alfredstate.edu
E-mail: admissions@alfredstate.edu

SUNY Orange County Community College
115 South St, Middletown NY 10940-6437
Margot St. Lawrence, Director of Admissions
845-341-4030 Fax: 845-342-8662
Website: www.sunyorange.edu
E-mail: apply@sunyorange.edu
See listing under "Community and Junior Colleges"

SUNY Sullivan County Community College
112 College Rd, Loch Sheldrake NY 12759-5151
Sari Rosenheck, Director of Admissions
845-434-5750 Fax: 845-434-0923
Website: www.sullivan.suny.edu
E-mail: admissions@sullivan.suny.edu
Student Housing on Campus.

United States Military Academy West Point
646 Swift Rd, West Point NY 10996-1905
Colonel Michael L. Jones, Director of Admissions
845-938-4041 Fax: 845-938-8121
Website: admissions.usma.edu
E-mail: admissions@usma.edu

Wells College
PO Box 500, Aurora NY 13026
Susan Sloan, Director of Admissions
800-952-9355 Fax: 315-364-3227
Website: www.wells.edu
E-mail: ssloan@wells.edu

NORTH CAROLINA

Brevard College
One Brevard College Dr, Brevard NC 28712
Joretta Nelson, Vice President Enrollment Management
828-883-8292 Fax: 828-884-3790
Website: www.brevard.edu
E-mail: admissions@brevard.edu

Catawba College
2300 W Innes St, Salisbury NC 28144-2488
Dr. L. Russell Watjen, Ph.D., V.P. & Dean of Admissions
704-637-4402 Fax: 704-637-4222
Website: www.catawba.edu
E-mail: admission@catawba.edu

Mayland Community College
PO Box 547, Spruce Pine NC 28777-0547
Cathy B. Morrison, Director of Enrollment Management
828-765-7351 Fax: 828-765-0728
Website: www.mayland.edu
E-mail: cmorrison@mayland.edu

Salem College
Winston Salem NC 27108
Dana Evans, Dean of Admissions/Fin. Aid
800-32-SALEM Fax: 336-917-5572
Website: www.salem.edu
E-mail: admissions@salem.edu
See listing under "Women's Colleges"

NORTH DAKOTA

Dickinson State University
Dickinson ND 58601-4896
Steve Glasser, Director of Enrollment Services
800-279-4295 Fax: 701-483-2409
Website: www.dickinsonstate.edu
E-mail: dsu.hawks@dickinsonstate.edu

Valley City State University
101 College St SW, Valley City ND 58072-4024
Dan Klein, Director of Enrollment Services
800-532-8641 ext. 7101 Fax: 701-845-7299
Website: www.vcsu.edu
E-mail: enrollment.services@vcsu.edu
See listing under "Universities"

OHIO

Cleveland State University
2121 Euclid Ave RW 204, Cleveland OH 44115
Dr. Richard Arndt, Dean of Undergraduate Recruitment and College Partnerships
888-CSU-OHIO Fax: 216-687-9210
Website: www.csuohio.edu
E-mail: admissions@csuohio.edu

Franciscan University of Steubenville
University Blvd, Steubenville OH 43952
Margaret J. Weber, Director of Admissions
800-783-6220 or 740-283-6226 Fax: 740-284-5456
Website: www.admissions.edu
E-mail: mweber@franciscan.edu

OHIO NORTHERN UNIVERSITY
525 S Main St, Ada OH 45810-1555
Ellen Wilson, Chair of the Psychology & Sociology Dept.
419-772-2135
Website: www.onu.edu
E-mail: admissions-ug@onu.edu
See listing under "Universities"

The Ohio State University
School of Social and Behavioral Sciences
Derby Hall, 154 N Oval Mall, Columbus OH 43210
614-292-8448 Fax: 614-292-9530
Website: sbs.osu.edu

University of Dayton
300 College Park, Dayton OH 45469-1300
Robert F. Durkle, Director of Admission
800-837-7433 Fax: 937-229-4729
Website: admission.udayton.edu
E-mail: admission@udayton.edu

Ursuline College
2550 Lander Rd, Cleveland OH 44124-4398
Sarah E. Sundermeier, Director of Admissions
888-URSULINE Toll Free Fax: 440-684-6138
Website: www.admission.ursuline.edu
E-mail: admission@ursuline.edu

OKLAHOMA

Oklahoma State University
Stillwater OK 74078
Patricia Bell, Department Head
405-744-6104
Website: www.okstate.edu
E-mail: patricia.bell@okstate.edu

University of Tulsa
600 S College Ave, Tulsa OK 74104-3126
Earl Johnson, Dean of Admission
918-631-2307 Fax: 918-631-5003
Website: www.utulsa.edu
E-mail: admission@utulsa.edu

OREGON

Concordia University
2811 NE Holman St, Portland OR 97211-6099
Bobi Swan, Director of Admissions
503-288-9371 Fax: 503-280-8531
Website: www.cu-portland.edu
E-mail: cu-admissions@cu-portland.edu

Linn-Benton Community College
6500 Pacific Blvd SW, Albany OR 97321-3774
Christine Baker, Outreach Coordinator
541-917-4811 Fax: 541-917-4868
Website: www.linnbenton.edu
E-mail: admissions@linnbenton.edu

Marylhurst University
17600 Pacific Hwy (Hwy 43)
Marylhurst OR 97036-0261
Director of Admissions
800-634-9982 ext. 6268 Fax: 503-635-6585
Website: www.marylhurst.edu
E-mail: studentinfo@marylhurst.edu

PACIFIC UNIVERSITY
2043 College Way, Forest Grove OR 97116-1797
Karen M. Dunston, Executive Director of Admissions
800-677-6712 Fax: 503-352-2975
Website: www.pacific.edu
E-mail: admissions@pacific.edu

Rogue Community College
3345 Redwood Hwy, Grants Pass OR 97527-9298
Claudia Sullivan, Director of Enrollment Services
541-956-7500 Fax: 541-471-3585
Website: www.roguecc.edu
E-mail: csullivan@roguecc.edu
See listing under "Community and Junior Colleges"

University of Portland
5000 N Willamette Blvd, Portland OR 97203-5798
Jason McDonald, Dean of Admissions
503-943-7911 Fax: 503-943-7315
Website: www.up.edu
E-mail: mcdonaja@up.edu

Warner Pacific College
2219 SE 68th Ave, Portland OR 97215-4026
Shannon Mackey, Director of Admissions
503-517-1000 Fax: 503-517-1352
Website: www.warnerpacific.edu
E-mail: admissions@warnerpacific.edu

PENNSYLVANIA

Clarion University of Pennsylvania
840 Wood St, Clarion PA 16214-1232
William Bailey, Dean of Enrollment Management
814-393-2306 Fax: 814-393-2030
Website: www.clarion.edu
E-mail: admissions@clarion.edu

Community College of Allegheny County
Allegheny Campus: 808 Ridge Ave, Pittsburgh PA 15212 Admissions: 412.237.2700
Boyce Campus: 595 Beatty Rd, Monroeville PA 15146 Admissions: 724.325.6614
North Campus: 8701 Perry Highway, Pittsburgh PA 15237 Admissions: 412.369.3600
South Campus: 1750 Clairton Rd, West Mifflin PA 15122 Admissions: 412-469-4301
Website: www.ccac.edu

DeSales University
2755 Station Ave, Center Valley PA 18034-9565
610-282-1100 Fax: 610-282-2342
Website: www.desales.edu

Haverford College
370 Lancaster Ave, Haverford PA 19041-1392
Jess Lord, Dean of Admission
610-896-1350 Fax: 610-896-1338
Website: www.haverford.edu
E-mail: admission@haverford.edu

Holy Family University
9801 Frankford Avenue, Philadelphia PA 19114
Lauren Campbell, Director of Admissions
215-637-3050 Fax: 215-281-1022
Website: www.holyfamily.edu
E-mail: admissions@holyfamily.edu

Juniata College
1700 Moore St, Huntingdon PA 16652-2196
Michelle Bartol, Dean of Enrollment
877-JUNIATA Fax: 814-641-3100
Website: www.juniata.edu
E-mail: admissions@juniata.edu

King's College
133 N River St, Wilkes Barre PA 18711-0801
Michelle Lawrence-Schmude, Dean of Admission
570-208-5900 Fax: 570-208-5971
Website: www.kings.edu
E-mail: admissions@kings.edu

MOUNT ALOYSIUS COLLEGE
7373 Admiral Peary Hwy, Cresson PA 16630-1999
Frank C. Crouse Jr., Vice President for Enrollment Management
814-886-6383 or 888-823-2220 Fax: 814-886-6441
Website: www.mtaloy.edu
E-mail: admissions@mtaloy.edu

Washington & Jefferson College
60 S Lincoln St, Washington PA 15301-4801
Alton E. Newell, Vice President for Enrollment
724-223-6025 Fax: 724-223-6534
Website: www.washjeff.edu
E-mail: admission@washjeff.edu

Widener University
1 University Pl, Chester PA 19013-5792
Edwin Wright, Dean of Admissions
610-499-4000 Fax: 610-499-4676
Website: www.widener.edu
E-mail: admissions.office@widener.edu

SOUTH CAROLINA

Erskine College & Seminary
PO Box 176, Due West SC 29639
Bart Walker, Director of Admissions
864-379-8838 Fax: 864-379-3048
Website: www.erskine.edu
E-mail: admissions@erskine.edu

Limestone College
1115 College Dr, Gaffney SC 29340-3799
Chris Phenicie, V.P. for Enrollment
864-489-7151 Fax: 864-488-8206
Website: www.limestone.edu
E-mail: cphenicie@limestone.edu

University of South Carolina - Upstate
800 University Way, Spartanburg SC 29303-4932
Donette Stewart, Assistant VC for Enrollment Services
864-503-5246 Fax: 864-503-5727
Website: www.uscupstate.edu
E-mail: dstewart@uscupstate.edu
See listing under "Universities"

SOUTH DAKOTA

Presentation College
1500 N Main St, Aberdeen SD 57401-1280
JoEllen Lindner, VP for Enrollment
605-229-8492 Fax: 605-229-8425
Website: www.presentation.edu
E-mail: admit@presentation.edu

TENNESSEE

Austin Peay State University
601 College St, Clarksville TN 37044-0002
931-221-7011 Fax: 931-221-6168
Website: www.apsu.edu
E-mail: admissions@apsu.edu

Lipscomb University
3901 Granny White Pike, Nashville TN 37204-3951
Ricky Holaway, Director of Admissions
800-333-4358 ext. 1776 Fax: 615-269-1804
Website: www.lipscomb.edu
E-mail: admissions@lipscomb.edu

Tennessee State University
3500 John A Merritt Blvd, Nashville TN 37209-1561
John Cade, Dean of Admissions & Records
615-963-5101 Fax: 615-963-2930
Website: www.tnstate.edu
E-mail: jcade@tnstate.edu

University of Tennessee
615 McCallie Ave, Chattanooga TN 37403-2504
Yancy Freeman, Director of Admissions
423-425-4111 Fax: 423-425-4157
Website: www.utc.edu
E-mail: Yancy-Freeman@utc.edu

TEXAS

Abilene Christian University
ACU Box 29000, Abilene TX 79699-0001
325-674-2000 Fax: 325-674-2202
Website: www.acu.edu
E-mail: info@admissions.acu.edu

Texas Woman's University
PO Box 425589, Denton TX 76204-5589
Erma Nieto-Brecht, Director of Admissions
866-809-6130 Fax: 940-898-3081
Website: www.twu.edu
E-mail: admissions@twu.edu

Tyler Junior College
PO Box 9020, Tyler TX 75711-9020
Richard Minter, Dean
800-687-5680
Website: www.tjc.edu
E-mail: rmin@tjc.edu
See listing under "Community and Junior Colleges"

University of Dallas
1845 E Northgate Dr, Irving TX 75062-4736
Curt Eley, Dean
972-721-5000 Fax: 972-721-5017
Website: www.udallas.edu
E-mail: ugadmis@udallas.edu

University of Houston
122 E Cullen Bldg, Houston TX 77204-2023
Office of Admission
713-743-9595
Website: www.uh.edu
E-mail: admissions@uh.edu

VERMONT

NORWICH UNIVERSITY
158 Harmon Dr, Northfield VT 05663
Dr. Thomas Taylor, Division Head
800-468-6679 Fax: 802-485-2252
Website: www.norwich.edu
E-mail: ttaylor@norwich.edu

Southern Vermont College
982 Mansion Dr, Bennington VT 05201-6002
Joel Wincowski, Director of Admissions
800-378-2782 Fax: 802-447-4695
Website: www.svc.edu
E-mail: admis@svc.edu

Woodbury College
660 Elm St, Montpelier VT 05602-4017
Denise MacMartin, Director of Admissions
800-639-6039 Fax: 802-229-2141
Website: www.woodbury-college.edu
E-mail: admiss@woodbury-college.edu

VIRGINIA

Marymount University
2807 N Glebe Rd, Arlington VA 22207-4299
Michael Canfield, Director of Admissions
800-548-7638 Fax: 703-522-0348
Website: www.marymount.edu
E-mail: admissions@marymount.edu

Radford University
PO Box 6903, Radford VA 24142
David W. Kraus, Director of Admissions
800-890-4265 Fax: 540-831-5038
Website: www.radford.edu
E-mail: ruadmiss@radford.edu

Randolph College
2500 Rivermont Ave, Lynchburg VA 24503
Patricia LeDonne, Director of Admissions
434-947-8100 Fax: 434-947-8996
Website: www.randolphcollege.edu
E-mail: admissions@randolphcollege.edu

Roanoke College
221 College Ln, Salem VA 24153-3794
James A. Pennix, Director of Admissions
540-375-2500 Fax: 540-375-2267
Website: www.roanoke.edu
E-mail: pennix@roanoke.edu

University of Mary Washington
1301 College Ave, Fredericksburg VA 22401-5300
Dr. Martin A. Wilder, Jr., Director of Admissions
540-654-2000 Fax: 540-654-1857
Website: www.umw.edu
E-mail: admit@umw.edu

WASHINGTON

SHORELINE COMMUNITY COLLEGE
16101 Greenwood Ave N, Shoreline WA 98133-5696
Chris Melton, Acting Registrar
206-546-4581 Fax: 206-546-5835
Website: www.shoreline.edu

WEST VIRGINIA

Davis & Elkins College
100 Campus Dr, Elkins WV 26241-3996
Renee Heckel, Director of Enrollment Management
800-624-3157 Fax: 304-637-1800
Website: www.davisandelkins.edu
E-mail: admiss@davisandelkins.edu

Fairmont State University
1201 Locust Ave, Fairmont WV 26554-2470
Steve Leadman, Director of Admissions
304-367-4161 or 800-641-5678 Fax: 304-367-4789
Website: www.fairmontstate.edu
E-mail: admit@fairmontstate.edu

WISCONSIN

Alverno College
PO Box 343922, Milwaukee WI 53234-3922
Dianna Gaebler, Director of Admissions
414-382-6100 Fax: 414-382-6354
Website: www.alverno.edu
E-mail: admissions@alverno.edu

Lakeland College
PO Box 359, Sheboygan WI 53082-0359
Nathan Dehne, Director of Admission
920-565-1100 Fax: 920-565-1215
Website: www.lakeland.edu
E-mail: admissions@lakeland.edu

Marquette University
PO Box 1881, Milwaukee WI 53201-1881
Robert Blust, Director of Admissions
414-288-7302 Fax: 414-288-3764
Website: www.mu.edu
E-mail: admissions@marquette.edu

St. Norbert College
100 Grant St, De Pere WI 54115
Brian Studebaker, Director of Admission
800-236-4878 Fax: 920-403-4072
Website: www.snc.edu
E-mail: admit@snc.edu

WYOMING

University of Wyoming
Admissions Office
Dept 3435, Laramie WY 82071-3435
Brooke Culver, Contact
800-342-5996 Fax: 307-766-4042
Website: www.uwyo.edu
E-mail: why-wyo@uwyo.edu

GUAM

University of Guam
UOG Station, Mangilao GU 96923
Deborah Leon Guerrero, Registrar
671-735-2201 or 671-735-2208 Fax: 671-735-2203
Website: www.uog.edu
E-mail: admitme@uog9.uog.edu

SPEECH AND DRAMA

ALABAMA

CALHOUN COMMUNITY COLLEGE
PO Box 2216, Decatur AL 35609-2216
M. Wayne Tosh, Registrar
256-306-2500 Fax: 256-306-2941
Website: www.calhoun.edu
E-mail: rds@calhoun.edu

ALASKA

University of Alaska Anchorage
PO Box 141629, Anchorage AK 99514-1629
Cecile Mitchell, Director of Enrollment Services
907-786-1480 Fax: 907-786-4888
Website: www.uaa.alaska.edu/
E-mail: enroll@uaa.alaska.edu

CALIFORNIA

American Academy of Dramatic Arts - Los Angeles
1336 N LaBrea Ave, Hollywood CA 90028
Dan Justin, Director of Admissions
800-222-2867 Fax: 323-464-1250
Website: www.aada.org
E-mail: admissions-ca@aada.org

Chapman University
One University Drive, Orange CA 92866-1099
Michael Drummy, Assistant Vice President for Enrollment
Services and Chief Admission Officer
714-997-6411 or 888-CUAPPLY Fax: 714-997-6713
Website: www.chapman.edu
E-mail: admit@chapman.edu

Concordia University
1530 Concordia, Irvine CA 92612-3203
Lori McDonald, Executive Director of Enrollment Services
800-229-1200 or 949-854-8002 Fax: 949-854-6894
Website: www.cui.edu
E-mail: admission@cui.edu

Orange Coast College
PO Box 5005, Costa Mesa CA 92628-5005
Kristin Clark, Director of Admissions
714-432-5773 Fax: 714-432-5736
Website: www.orangecoastcollege.edu
E-mail: kclark@cccd.edu

Point Loma Nazarene University
3900 Lomaland Dr, San Diego CA 92106-2810
Chip Killingsworth, Director of Undergraduate Admissions
800-733-7770 Fax: 619-849-2601
Website: www.pointloma.edu
E-mail: admissions@pointloma.edu

San Bernardino Valley College
701 S Mount Vernon Ave
San Bernardino CA 92410-2798
Kay Ragan, Ed.D., Director of Admissions
909-888-6511 Fax: 909-889-4988
Website: www.valleycollege.edu
E-mail: kragan@sbccd.cc.ca.us

Whittier College
PO Box 634, Whittier CA 90608-0634
Kieron Miller, Director of Admissions
562-907-4200 Fax: 562-907-4870
Website: www.whittier.edu
E-mail: kmiller@whittier.edu

DISTRICT OF COLUMBIA

Gallaudet University
800 Florida Ave NE, Washington DC 20002-3695
Charity Reedy Hines, Director of Admissions
202-651-5750 Fax: 202-651-5744
Website: www.gallaudet.edu
E-mail: admissions.office@gallaudet.edu

NATIONAL CONSERVATORY OF DRAMATIC ARTS
1556 Wisconsin Ave NW
Washington DC 20007-2758
Nan Kyle Ficca, Vice President
202-333-2202 Fax: 202-333-1753
Website: theconservatory.org
E-mail: ncdadrama@aol.com

FLORIDA

Florida State University
600 W College Ave, Tallahassee FL 32306-1096
Janice V. Finney, Director of Admissions
850-644-2525 Fax: 850-644-0197
Website: admissions.fsu.edu
E-mail: admissions@admin.fsu.edu

Lynn University
3601 N Military Trl, Boca Raton FL 33431-5598
Director of Admissions
561-237-7900 Fax: 561-237-7100
Website: www.lynn.edu
E-mail: admission@lynn.edu

University of South Florida
4202 E Fowler Ave, Tampa FL 33620-6900
J. Robert Spatig, Director of Admissions
877-USF-BULL Fax: 813-974-9689
Website: www.usf.edu
E-mail: admissions@admin.usf.edu
See listing under "Universities"

IDAHO

Brigham Young University - Idaho
120 Kimball Bldg, Rexburg ID 83460-1615
Rob Garrett, Director of Admissions
208-496-1020 Fax: 208-496-1220
Website: www.byui.edu
E-mail: admissions@byui.edu

University of Idaho
Moscow ID 83844-4253
Lloyd Scott, Director of New Student Services
208-885-6163 Fax: 208-885-4477
Website: www.uidaho.edu
E-mail: nss@uidaho.edu

ILLINOIS

Columbia College Chicago
600 S Michigan Ave, Chicago IL 60605-1996
Murphy Monroe, Executive Director of Admissions
312-344-7130 Fax: 312-344-8024
Website: www.colum.edu
E-mail: admissions@colum.edu

Roosevelt University
430 S Michigan Ave, Chicago IL 60605
Gwen E. Kanelos, Asst. Vice President for Enrollment Services
877-APPLY-RU Fax: 312-341-4216
Website: www.roosevelt.edu
E-mail: applyru@roosevelt.edu

INDIANA

University of Evansville
1800 Lincoln Ave, Evansville IN 47722-0001
Don Vos, Dean of Admission
800-423-8633 Fax: 812-488-4076
Website: www.evansville.edu
E-mail: admission@evansville.edu

IOWA

Briar Cliff University
PO Box 2100, Sioux City IA 51104-0100
Sharisue Wilcoxon, VP for Enrollment Management
712-279-5200 Fax: 712-279-1632
Website: www.briarcliff.edu
E-mail: admissions@briarcliff.edu

Clarke College
1550 Clarke Dr, Dubuque IA 52001-3198
Andy Schroeder, Director of Admissions
800-383-2345 Fax: 563-584-8666
Website: www.clarke.edu
E-mail: andy.schroeder@clarke.edu

Graceland University
1 University Place, Lamoni IA 50140
Greg Sutherland, Interim Vice President for Enrollment and Dean of Admissions
641-784-5196 Fax: 641-784-5480
Website: www.admissions.graceland.edu
E-mail: admissions@graceland.edu

Iowa Lakes Community College
300 S 18th St, Estherville IA 51334-2721
Anne Stansbury, Asst. Director of Admissions
712-362-7945 Fax: 712-362-8363
Website: www.iowalakes.edu
E-mail: info@iowalakes.edu

Waldorf College
106 S 6th St, Forest City IA 50436-1713
Dr. Linda Hoopes, Vice President of Admission and Marketing
800-292-1903 or 641-585-8112 Fax: 641-585-8125
Website: www.waldorf.edu
E-mail: hoopesl@waldorf.edu
See listing under "Universities"

KANSAS

Independence Community College
PO Box 708, Independence KS 67301-0708
Dr. Terry Hetrick, President
800-842-6063 Fax: 620-331-5344
Website: www.indycc.edu
E-mail: admissions@indycc.edu

KENTUCKY

Bluegrass Community and Technical College
Oswald Building
470 Cooper Drive, Lexington KY 40506-0235
Shelbie Hugle, Director of Admissions
859-246-6200 Fax: 859-246-4664
Website: www.bluegrass.kctcs.edu
E-mail: bctc_info@kctcs.edu

Morehead State University
Morehead KY 40351-1689
Jeffrey Liles, Enrollment Services
800-585-6781 Fax: 606-783-5038
Website: www.moreheadstate.edu
E-mail: admissions@moreheadstate.edu

MARYLAND

Hagerstown Community College
11400 Robinwood Dr, Hagerstown MD 21742-6590
Dr. Daniel E. Bock, Assistant Director of Admissions
301-790-2800 Fax: 301-791-9165
Website: www.hagerstowncc.edu
E-mail: bockd@hagerstowncc.edu

MASSACHUSETTS

Boston University
121 Bay State Rd, Boston MA 02215
Kelly Walter, Executive Director of Admissions
617-353-2300 Fax: 617-353-9695
Website: web.bu.edu
E-mail: admissions@bu.edu

Emerson College
120 Boylston St, Boston MA 02116-4624
Sara S. Ramirez, Director of Undergraduate Admission
617-824-8600 Fax: 617-824-8609
Website: www.emerson.edu
E-mail: admission@emerson.edu

Worcester Polytechnic Institute
100 Institute Rd, Worcester MA 01609-2280
Edward J. Connor, Director of Admissions
508-831-5286 Fax: 508-831-5875
Website: admissions.wpi.edu
E-mail: admissions@wpi.edu

MICHIGAN

Alma College
614 W Superior St, Alma MI 48801-1599
Evan Montague, Director of Admissions
800-321-ALMA Fax: 989-463-7057
Website: www.alma.edu
E-mail: admissions@alma.edu

Delta College
University Center MI 48710-0001
Duff Zube, Director of Admissions
989-686-9093 Fax: 989-667-2202
Website: www.delta.edu
E-mail: admit@delta.edu

HILLSDALE COLLEGE
33 E College St, Hillsdale MI 49242-1298
Professor George Angell, Director
517-607-2377 Fax: 517-607-2665
Website: www.hillsdale.edu
E-mail: george.angell@hillsdale.edu

MACOMB COMMUNITY COLLEGE
44575 Garfield Rd, Clinton Township MI 48038-1139
Information Center
586-445-7999
Website: www.macomb.edu
E-mail: answer@macomb.edu

MACOMB COMMUNITY COLLEGE
14500 E 12 Mile Rd, Warren MI 48088-3896
Information Center
586-445-7999
Website: www.macomb.edu
E-mail: answer@macomb.edu

Specs Howard School of Broadcast Arts
19900 W 9 Mile Rd, Southfield MI 48075-3953
Nancy Shiner, Admissions Director
248-358-9000 Fax: 248-746-9772
Website: www.specshoward.edu
E-mail: info@specshoward.edu

MINNESOTA

Bethany Lutheran College
700 Luther Dr, Mankato MN 56001
Don Westphal, Dean of Admissions
507-344-7000 Fax: 507-344-7376
Website: www.blc.edu
E-mail: admiss@blc.edu

Minnesota State University Moorhead
1104 7th Ave S, Moorhead MN 56563-0002
Regina Monson, Director of Admissions
218-477-2161 Fax: 218-477-4374
Website: go.mnstate.edu
E-mail: dragon@mnstate.edu

Pillsbury Baptist Bible College
315 S Grove Ave, Owatonna MN 55060-3097
Susanne Martin, Admissions Coordinator
507-451-2710 Fax: 507-451-0156
Website: www.pillsbury.edu
E-mail: admissions@pillsbury.edu

SHATTUCK-ST. MARY'S SCHOOL
PO Box 218, Faribault MN 55021-0218
Amy D. Wolf, Director of Admissions
507-333-1618 Fax: 507-333-1661
Website: www.s-sm.org
E-mail: admissions@s-sm.org
See listing under "Preparatory Schools - Coed"

MISSOURI

Central Methodist University
411 Central Methodist Sq, Fayette MO 65248-1198
Larry Anderson, Director of Admissions
660-248-6247 Fax: 660-248-1872
Website: www.centralmethodist.edu
E-mail: landerso@centralmethodist.edu

Truman State University
100 E Normal, Kirksville MO 63501
Office of Admission
660-785-4114 Fax: 660-785-7456
Website: admissions.truman.edu
E-mail: admissions@truman.edu

Webster University
470 E Lockwood Ave, Saint Louis MO 63119-3194
Peter Sargent, Dean, College of Fine Arts
314-968-7006 Fax: 314-963-6102
Website: www.webster.edu
E-mail: sargenae@webster.edu
See listing under "Universities"

William Woods University
1 University Ave, Fulton MO 65251-1098
Jimmy Clay, Director of Admissions
573-642-2251 Fax: 573-592-1146
Website: www.williamwoods.edu
E-mail: admissions@williamwoods.edu
See listing under "Universities"

MONTANA

Carroll College
1601 N Benton Ave, Helena MT 59625-0002
Dr. Thomas J. Trebon, President
Cynthia Thornquist, Director of Admissions & Enrollment Operations
406-447-4384 Fax: 406-447-4533
Website: www.carroll.edu
E-mail: admission@carroll.edu

NEBRASKA

University of Nebraska at Kearney
905 W 25th St, Kearney NE 68849-0001
Dusty Newton, Director of Admissions
800-KEARNEY Fax: 308-865-8987
Website: www.unk.edu
E-mail: admissionsug@unk.edu

NEW JERSEY

Bergen Community College
400 Paramus Rd, Paramus NJ 07652
Julian Gomez, Asst. Director of Admissions
201-447-7100 Fax: 201-444-7036
Website: www.bergen.edu
E-mail: jgomez@bergen.edu

New Jersey City University
2039 John F Kennedy Blvd
Jersey City NJ 07305-1588
Carmen Panlilio, Asst. V.P. for Admissions and Financial Aid
201-200-3234 Fax: 201-200-2044
Website: www.njcu.edu
E-mail: admissions@njcu.edu

RICHARD STOCKTON COLLEGE OF NEW JERSEY
PO Box 195, Pomona NJ 08240
John Iacovelli, Dean of Enrollment Management
866-RSC-2885 Fax: 609-626-5541
Website: www.stockton.edu
E-mail: admissions@stockton.edu
See listing under "Universities"

NEW YORK

American Academy of Dramatic Arts - New York
120 Madison Ave, New York NY 10016-7089
Karen Higginbotham, Director of Admissions
800-463-8990 Fax: 212-685-8093
Website: www.aada.org
E-mail: admissions-ny@aada.org

College of Saint Rose
432 Western Ave, Albany NY 12203-1419
Maryelizabeth Amico, Asst V.P. for Undergraduate Admissions
518-454-5150 Fax: 518-454-2013
Website: www.strose.edu
E-mail: admit@strose.edu

Iona College
715 North Ave, New Rochelle NY 10801-1890
Kevin Cavanagh, Assistant V.P. for College Admissions
914-633-2502 Fax: 914-637-2778
Website: www.iona.edu

Long Island University-C. W. Post Campus
720 Northern Blvd, Brookville NY 11548-1300
Joanne Graziano, Executive Director of Admissions
516-299-2900 Fax: 516-299-2137
Website: www.liu.edu/cwpost
E-mail: enroll@cwpost.liu.edu

Molloy College
1000 Hempstead Ave
Rockville Centre NY 11570-1100
Marguerite Lane, Director of Admissions
516-678-5000 ext. 6291 Fax: 516-256-2247
Website: www.molloy.edu
E-mail: admissions@molloy.edu
See listing under "Universities"

St. Joseph's College
245 Clinton Ave, Brooklyn NY 11205-3688
Theresa LaRocca Meyer, V.P. for Enrollment Management
718-636-6800 Fax: 718-636-8303
Website: www.sjcny.edu
E-mail: tlaroccameyer@sjcny.edu

SUNY Niagara County Community College
3111 Saunders Settlement Rd
Sanborn NY 14132-9487
Kathleen Saunders, Director of Admissions
716-614-6200 Fax: 716-614-6820
Website: www.niagaracc.suny.edu
E-mail: admissions@niagaracc.suny.edu

SUNY Orange County Community College
115 South St, Middletown NY 10940-6437
Margot St. Lawrence, Director of Admissions
845-341-4030 Fax: 845-342-8662
Website: www.sunyorange.edu
E-mail: apply@sunyorange.edu
See listing under "Community and Junior Colleges"

NORTH CAROLINA

Catawba College
2300 W Innes St, Salisbury NC 28144-2488
Dr. L. Russell Watjen, Ph.D., V.P. & Dean of Admissions
704-637-4402 Fax: 704-637-4222
Website: www.catawba.edu
E-mail: admission@catawba.edu

NORTH DAKOTA

Dickinson State University
Dickinson ND 58601-4896
Steve Glasser, Director of Enrollment Services
800-279-4295 Fax: 701-483-2409
Website: www.dickinsonstate.edu
E-mail: dsu.hawks@dickinsonstate.edu

OHIO

Cleveland State University
2121 Euclid Ave RW 204, Cleveland OH 44115
Dr. Richard Arndt, Dean of Undergraduate Recruitment and College Partnerships
888-CSU-OHIO Fax: 216-687-9210
Website: www.csuohio.edu
E-mail: admissions@csuohio.edu

The Ohio State University, Department of Theatre
Drake Performance & Event Center
1849 Cannon Dr, Columbus OH 43210
614-292-5821 Fax: 614-292-3222
Website: theatre.osu.edu
E-mail: theatre-ugrad@osu.edu

University of Dayton
300 College Park, Dayton OH 45469-1300
Robert F. Durkle, Director of Admission
800-837-7433 Fax: 937-229-4729
Website: admission.udayton.edu
E-mail: admission@udayton.edu

OREGON

Cascade College
9101 E Burnside St, Portland OR 97216-1599
Jim Murphy, Director of Enrollment Management
800-550-7678 Fax: 503-257-1222
Website: www.cascade.edu
E-mail: admissions@cascade.edu

Warner Pacific College
2219 SE 68th Ave, Portland OR 97215-4026
Shannon Mackey, Director of Admissions
503-517-1000 Fax: 503-517-1352
Website: www.warnerpacific.edu
E-mail: admissions@warnerpacific.edu

PENNSYLVANIA

Community College of Allegheny County
Allegheny Campus: 808 Ridge Ave, Pittsburgh PA 15212 Admissions: 412.237.2700
Boyce Campus: 595 Beatty Rd, Monroeville PA 15146 Admissions: 724.325.6614
North Campus: 8701 Perry Highway, Pittsburgh PA 15237 Admissions: 412.369.3600
South Campus: 1750 Clairton Rd, West Mifflin PA 15122 Admissions: 412-469-4301
Website: www.ccac.edu

SOUTH CAROLINA

North Greenville University
PO Box 1892, Tigerville SC 29688-1892
Website: www.ngu.edu
See listing under "Universities"

University of South Carolina - Upstate
800 University Way, Spartanburg SC 29303-4932
Donette Stewart, Assistant VC for Enrollment Services
864-503-5246 Fax: 864-503-5727
Website: www.uscupstate.edu
E-mail: dstewart@uscupstate.edu
See listing under "Universities"

TENNESSEE

Austin Peay State University
601 College St, Clarksville TN 37044-0002
931-221-7011 Fax: 931-221-6168
Website: www.apsu.edu
E-mail: admissions@apsu.edu

Lipscomb University
3901 Granny White Pike, Nashville TN 37204-3951
Ricky Holaway, Director of Admissions
800-333-4358 ext. 1776 Fax: 615-269-1804
Website: www.lipscomb.edu
E-mail: admissions@lipscomb.edu

Tennessee State University
3500 John A Merritt Blvd, Nashville TN 37209-1561
John Cade, Dean of Admissions & Records
615-963-5101 Fax: 615-963-2930
Website: www.tnstate.edu
E-mail: jcade@tnstate.edu

TEXAS

Abilene Christian University
ACU Box 29000, Abilene TX 79699-0001
325-674-2000 Fax: 325-674-2202
Website: www.acu.edu
E-mail: info@admissions.acu.edu

KD STUDIO - ACTORS CONSERVATORY
2600 N Stemmons Fwy Ste 117
Dallas TX 75207-2168
T. A. Taylor, Director of Education
877-278-2283 Fax: 214-630-5140
Website: www.kdstudio.com
E-mail: admissions@kdstudio.com
Established 1979. Private. Coed. Accreditation: TEA, NAST, Texas Higher Education Coordinating Board. Tuition: $11,000. Enrollment: 100 full-time. Faculty: 26. Student-faculty ratio: 18:1. Degrees: Applied Associates Degree. Private library Resource Center. This program is aimed at developing camera acting skills as well as stage acting. Faculty are involved as industry professionals. A showcase is performed upon graduation where agents, casting directors and local producers and directors attend. FA available. VA approved.

Texas Woman's University
PO Box 425589, Denton TX 76204-5589
Erma Nieto-Brecht, Director of Admissions
866-809-6130 Fax: 940-898-3081
Website: www.twu.edu
E-mail: admissions@twu.edu

University of Houston
122 E Cullen Bldg, Houston TX 77204-2023
Office of Admission
713-743-9595
Website: www.uh.edu
E-mail: admissions@uh.edu

University of Texas at Arlington
Box 19111, Arlington TX 76019-0111
Hans Gatterdam, Director of Admission
817-272-6287 Fax: 817-272-3435
Website: www.uta.edu
E-mail: admissions@uta.edu

Weatherford College
225 College Park Dr, Weatherford TX 76086
Dr. Joe Birmingham, President
800-287-5471 Fax: 817-598-6205
Website: www.wc.edu
E-mail: willingham@wc.edu

VIRGINIA

Radford University
PO Box 6903, Radford VA 24142
David W. Kraus, Director of Admissions
800-890-4265 Fax: 540-831-5038
Website: www.radford.edu
E-mail: ruadmiss@radford.edu

Randolph College
2500 Rivermont Ave, Lynchburg VA 24503
Patricia LeDonne, Director of Admissions
434-947-8100 Fax: 434-947-8996
Website: www.randolphcollege.edu
E-mail: admissions@randolphcollege.edu

WEST VIRGINIA

Davis & Elkins College
100 Campus Dr, Elkins WV 26241-3996
Renee Heckel, Director of Enrollment Management
800-624-3157 Fax: 304-637-1800
Website: www.davisandelkins.edu
E-mail: admiss@davisandelkins.edu

Fairmont State University
1201 Locust Ave, Fairmont WV 26554-2470
Steve Leadman, Director of Admissions
304-367-4892 or 800-641-5678 Fax: 304-367-4789
Website: www.fairmontstate.edu
E-mail: admit@fairmontstate.edu

WISCONSIN

St. Norbert College
100 Grant St, De Pere WI 54115
Brian Studebaker, Director of Admission
800-236-4878 Fax: 920-403-4072
Website: www.snc.edu
E-mail: admit@snc.edu

STUDY ABROAD

ALASKA

University of Alaska Anchorage
PO Box 141629, Anchorage AK 99514-1629
Cecile Mitchell, Director of Enrollment Services
907-786-1480 Fax: 907-786-4888
Website: www.uaa.alaska.edu/
E-mail: enroll@uaa.alaska.edu

CALIFORNIA

Chapman University
One University Drive, Orange CA 92866-1099
Michael Drummy, Assistant Vice President for Enrollment
Services and Chief Admission Officer
714-997-6411 or 888-CUAPPLY Fax: 714-997-6713
Website: www.chapman.edu
E-mail: admit@chapman.edu

Concordia University
1530 Concordia, Irvine CA 92612-3203
Lori McDonald, Executive Director of Enrollment Services
800-229-1200 or 949-854-8002 Fax: 949-854-6894
Website: www.cui.edu
E-mail: admission@cui.edu

FIDM/The Fashion Institute of Design & Merchandising
919 S Grand Ave, Los Angeles CA 90015-1421
Director of Admissions
213-624-1201 or 800-624-1200 Fax: 213-624-4799
Website: www.fidm.edu
E-mail: info@fidm.com
See listing under "Community and Junior Colleges"

Orange Coast College
PO Box 5005, Costa Mesa CA 92628-5005
Kristin Clark, Director of Admissions
714-432-5773 Fax: 714-432-5736
Website: www.orangecoastcollege.edu
E-mail: kclark@cccd.edu

Point Loma Nazarene University
3900 Lomaland Dr, San Diego CA 92106-2810
Chip Killingsworth, Director of Undergraduate Admissions
800-733-7770 Fax: 619-849-2601
Website: www.pointloma.edu
E-mail: admissions@pointloma.edu

Whittier College
PO Box 634, Whittier CA 90608-0634
Kieron Miller, Director of Admissions
562-907-4200 Fax: 562-907-4870
Website: www.whittier.edu
E-mail: kmiller@whittier.edu

DELAWARE

Wesley College
120 N State St, Dover DE 19901-3876
302-736-2300 Fax: 302-736-2301
Website: www.wesley.edu

FLORIDA

Florida State University
600 W College Ave, Tallahassee FL 32306-1096
Janice V. Finney, Director of Admissions
850-644-2525 Fax: 850-644-0197
Website: admissions.fsu.edu
E-mail: admissions@admin.fsu.edu

Lynn University
3601 N Military Trl, Boca Raton FL 33431-5598
Nicolette Orezzoli, Director
561-237-7078 Fax: 561-237-7100
Website: www.lynn.edu
E-mail: admission@lynn.edu

University of South Florida
4202 E Fowler Ave, Tampa FL 33620-6900
J. Robert Spatig, Director of Admissions
877-USF-BULL Fax: 813-974-9689
Website: www.usf.edu
E-mail: admissions@admin.usf.edu
See listing under "Universities"

ILLINOIS

Benedictine University
5700 College Rd, Lisle IL 60532-0900
630-829-6300 or 888-829-6363 Fax: 630-829-6301
Website: www.ben.edu
E-mail: admissions@ben.edu
See listing under "Universities"

CONCORDIA UNIVERSITY
7400 Augusta St, River Forest IL 60305-1402
708-209-3100 Fax: 708-209-3176
Website: www.cuchicago.edu
E-mail: admission@cuchicago.edu

NORTHEASTERN ILLINOIS UNIVERSITY
5500 N Saint Louis Ave, Chicago IL 60625-4699
International Programs
773-442-4050 Fax: 773-442-4020
Website: www.neiu.edu

Roosevelt University
430 S Michigan Ave, Chicago IL 60605
Gwen E. Kanelos, Asst. Vice President for Enrollment Services
877-APPLY-RU Fax: 312-341-4216
Website: www.roosevelt.edu
E-mail: applyru@roosevelt.edu

INDIANA

University of Evansville
1800 Lincoln Ave, Evansville IN 47722-0001
Don Vos, Dean of Admission
800-423-8633 Fax: 812-488-4076
Website: www.evansville.edu
E-mail: admission@evansville.edu

IOWA

Briar Cliff University
PO Box 2100, Sioux City IA 51104-0100
Sharisue Wilcoxon, VP for Enrollment Management
712-279-5200 Fax: 712-279-1632
Website: www.briarcliff.edu
E-mail: admissions@briarcliff.edu

Clarke College
1550 Clarke Dr, Dubuque IA 52001-3198
Andy Schroeder, Director of Admissions
800-383-2345 Fax: 563-584-8666
Website: www.clarke.edu
E-mail: andy.schroeder@clarke.edu

Graceland University
1 University Place, Lamoni IA 50140
Greg Sutherland, Interim Vice President for Enrollment and Dean of Admissions
641-784-5196 Fax: 641-784-5480
Website: www.admissions.graceland.edu
E-mail: admissions@graceland.edu

Iowa Lakes Community College
3200 College Dr, Emmetsburg IA 50536-1055
Anne Stansbury, Asst. Director of Admissions
712-852-5212 Fax: 712-362-8363
Website: www.iowalakes.edu
E-mail: info@iowalakes.edu

Iowa Lakes Community College
300 S 18th St, Estherville IA 51334-2721
Anne Stansbury, Asst. Director of Admissions
712-362-7945 Fax: 712-362-8363
Website: www.iowalakes.edu
E-mail: info@iowalakes.edu

Iowa Lakes Community College
1900 Grand Ave, Suite 8, Spencer IA 51301
Anne Stansbury, Assistant Director of Admissions
712-262-7141 Fax: 712-262-4047
Website: www.iowalakes.edu
E-mail: info@iowalakes.edu

KENTUCKY

Bluegrass Community and Technical College
Oswald Building
470 Cooper Drive, Lexington KY 40506-0235
Shelbie Hugle, Director of Admissions
859-246-6200 Fax: 859-246-4664
Website: www.bluegrass.kctcs.edu
E-mail: bctc_info@kctcs.edu

MASSACHUSETTS

Anna Maria College
50 Sunset Ln, Paxton MA 01612
Timothy M. Donahue, Director of Recruitment and Admissions
508-849-3360 Fax: 508-849-3362
Website: www.annamaria.edu
E-mail: admissions@annamaria.edu

Boston University
121 Bay State Rd, Boston MA 02215
Kelly Walter, Executive Director of Admissions
617-353-2300 Fax: 617-353-9695
Website: web.bu.edu
E-mail: admissions@bu.edu

Gordon College
255 Grapevine Rd, Wenham MA 01984-1899
Barbara R. Layne, Associate Vice President, Enrollment
866-464-6736 Fax: 978-867-4682
Website: www.gordon.edu
E-mail: admissions@gordon.edu

Massachusetts Institute of Technology
77 Massachusetts Ave, Cambridge MA 02139-4307
617-253-1000 Fax: 617-253-4016
Website: my.mit.edu
E-mail: admissions@mit.edu

Newbury College
129 Fisher Ave, Brookline MA 02445-5796
Salvadore Liberto, Vice President of Enrollment
617-730-7000 Fax: 617-731-9618
Website: www.newbury.edu
E-mail: info@newbury.edu
See listing under "Universities"

New England School of Art & Design at Suffolk University
75 Arlington St, Boston MA 02116
John Hamel, Director of Admissions
617-573-8785
Website: www.suffolk.edu/nesad

University of Massachusetts Dartmouth
Old Westport Rd, North Dartmouth MA 02747-2300
Academic Advising
508-999-9299 Fax: 508-999-8850
Website: explore.umassd.edu

Worcester Polytechnic Institute
100 Institute Rd, Worcester MA 01609-2280
Edward J. Connor, Director of Admissions
508-831-5286 Fax: 508-831-5875
Website: admissions.wpi.edu
E-mail: admissions@wpi.edu

MICHIGAN

Alma College
614 W Superior St, Alma MI 48801-1599
Evan Montague, Director of Admissions
800-321-ALMA Fax: 989-463-7057
Website: www.alma.edu
E-mail: admissions@alma.edu

Grand Valley State University
1 Campus Dr, Allendale MI 49401-9403
616-331-2025 Fax: 616-331-2000
Website: www.gvsu.edu
E-mail: go2gvsu@gvsu.edu

HILLSDALE COLLEGE
33 E College St, Hillsdale MI 49242-1298
Dr. Ellen Justice-Templeton, Director
517-607-2442 Fax: 517-607-2208
Website: www.hillsdale.edu
E-mail: ellen.justicf@hillsdale.edu

MINNESOTA

Pillsbury Baptist Bible College
315 S Grove Ave, Owatonna MN 55060-3097
Susanne Martin, Admissions Coordinator
507-451-2710 Fax: 507-451-0156
Website: www.pillsbury.edu
E-mail: admissions@pillsbury.edu

University of Minnesota
2900 University Ave, Crookston MN 56716-5001
218-281-6510 Fax: 218-281-8575
Website: admissions.umcrookston.edu/requirements/apply.htm
E-mail: info@umcrookston.edu

MISSOURI

Columbia College
1001 Rogers St, Columbia MO 65216-0001
Regina Morin, Director of Admissions
573-875-7352 Fax: 573-875-7506
Website: www.ccis.edu
E-mail: admissions@ccis.edu

Stephens College
PO Box 2121, Columbia MO 65215-0001
David Adams, Dean of Enrollment Management
573-442-2211 Fax: 573-876-7237
Website: www.stephens.edu
E-mail: dadams@stephens.edu

Truman State University
100 E Normal, Kirksville MO 63501
Office of Admission
660-785-4114 Fax: 660-785-7456
Website: admissions.truman.edu
E-mail: admissions@truman.edu

University of Missouri
1 University Blvd, Saint Louis MO 63121-4499
Tracy Faschingbauer, Coordinator
314-516-5753 Fax: 314-516-6757
Website: www.umsl.edu
E-mail: admissions@umsl.edu

Webster University
470 E Lockwood Ave, Saint Louis MO 63119-3194
Mark Beirn, Study Abroad
314-968-7433 Fax: 314-968-7119
Website: www.webster.edu
E-mail: mbeirn@webster.edu
See listing under "Universities"

William Jewell College
500 College Hill, Liberty MO 64068-1896
Dr. Rick Winslow, VP Enrollment Management and Student Affairs
800-753-7009 Fax: 816-415-5040
Website: www.jewell.edu
E-mail: winslowr@william.jewell.edu

William Woods University
1 University Ave, Fulton MO 65251-1098
Jimmy Clay, Director of Admissions
573-642-2251 Fax: 573-592-1146
Website: www.williamwoods.edu
E-mail: admissions@williamwoods.edu
See listing under "Universities"

MONTANA

Carroll College
1601 N Benton Ave, Helena MT 59625-0002
Dr. Thomas J. Trebon, President
Cynthia Thornquist, Director of Admissions & Enrollment Operations
406-447-4384 Fax: 406-447-4533
Website: www.carroll.edu
E-mail: admission@carroll.edu

NEBRASKA

Nebraska Wesleyan University
5000 Saint Paul Ave, Lincoln NE 68504-2794
Patricia Karthauser, V.P. for University Enrollment
402-466-2371 Fax: 402-465-2177
Website: www.nebrwesleyan.edu
E-mail: admissions@nebrwesleyan.edu

NEW HAMPSHIRE

Southern New Hampshire University
2500 N River Rd, Hooksett NH 03106-1045
Steve Soba, Director of Admissions
603-645-9611 Fax: 603-645-9693
Website: www.snhu.edu
E-mail: s.soba@snhu.edu

NEW JERSEY

Bergen Community College
400 Paramus Rd, Paramus NJ 07652
Julian Gomez, Asst. Director of Admissions
201-447-7100 Fax: 201-444-7036
Website: www.bergen.edu
E-mail: jgomez@bergen.edu

New Jersey City University
2039 John F Kennedy Blvd
Jersey City NJ 07305-1588
Carmen Panlilio, Asst. V.P. for Admissions and Financial Aid
201-200-3234 Fax: 201-200-2044
Website: www.njcu.edu
E-mail: admissions@njcu.edu

Ramapo College of New Jersey
505 Ramapo Valley Rd, Mahwah NJ 07430-1623
Director of Admissions
201-684-7300 or 201-684-7301 Fax: 201-684-7964
Website: www.ramapo.edu
E-mail: admissions@ramapo.edu

RICHARD STOCKTON COLLEGE OF NEW JERSEY
PO Box 195, Pomona NJ 08240
John Iacovelli, Dean of Enrollment Management
866-RSC-2885 Fax: 609-626-5541
Website: www.stockton.edu
E-mail: admissions@stockton.edu
See listing under "Universities"

NEW YORK

AMERICAN UNIVERSITY IN CAIRO
420 5th Ave 3rd Floor, New York NY 10018
Student Affairs Office
212-730-8800 Fax: 212-730-1600
Website: www.aucegypt.edu
E-mail: aucegypt@aucnyo.edu

College of Saint Rose
432 Western Ave, Albany NY 12203-1419
Maryelizabeth Amico, Asst V.P. for Undergraduate Admissions
518-454-5150 Fax: 518-454-2013
Website: www.strose.edu
E-mail: admit@strose.edu

Hilbert College
5200 S Park Ave, Hamburg NY 14075-1597
Timothy Lee, Director of Admissions
716-649-7900 Fax: 716-649-0702
Website: www.hilbert.edu
E-mail: tlee@hilbert.edu

Iona College
715 North Ave, New Rochelle NY 10801-1890
Kevin Cavanagh, Assistant V.P. for College Admissions
914-633-2502 Fax: 914-637-2778
Website: www.iona.edu

Long Island University-C. W. Post Campus
720 Northern Blvd, Brookville NY 11548-1300
Joanne Graziano, Executive Director of Admissions
516-299-2900 Fax: 516-299-2137
Website: www.liu.edu/cwpost
E-mail: enroll@cwpost.liu.edu

Marymount Manhattan College
221 E 71st St, New York NY 10021-4501
Jim Rogers, Dean of Admissions
800-MARYMOUNT Fax: 212-517-0448
Website: www.mmm.edu
E-mail: admissions@mmm.edu

Molloy College
1000 Hempstead Ave
Rockville Centre NY 11570-1100
Marguerite Lane, Director of Admissions
516-678-5000 ext. 6291 Fax: 516-256-2247
Website: www.molloy.edu
E-mail: admissions@molloy.edu
See listing under "Universities"

Pratt Institute
200 Willoughby Ave, Brooklyn NY 11205-3899
Heidi Metcalf, Director of Admissions
718-636-3600 Fax: 718-636-3670
Website: www.pratt.edu
E-mail: hmetcalf@pratt.edu

Roberts Wesleyan College
2301 Westside Dr, Rochester NY 14624-1997
Office of Admissions
585-594-6400 Fax: 585-594-6371
Website: www.roberts.edu
E-mail: admissions@roberts.edu

SUNY College at Brockport
350 New Campus Dr, Brockport NY 14420-2997
Bernard S. Valento, Director of Undergraduate Admissions
585-395-2751 Fax: 585-395-5452
Website: www.brockport.edu
E-mail: admit@brockport.edu

Wells College
PO Box 500, Aurora NY 13026
Susan Sloan, Director of Admissions
800-952-9355 Fax: 315-364-3227
Website: www.wells.edu
E-mail: ssloan@wells.edu

NORTH CAROLINA

Salem College
Winston Salem NC 27108
Dana Evans, Dean of Admissions/Fin. Aid
800-32-SALEM Fax: 336-917-5572
Website: www.salem.edu
E-mail: admissions@salem.edu
See listing under "Women's Colleges"

OHIO

Franciscan University of Steubenville
University Blvd, Steubenville OH 43952
Margaret J. Weber, Director of Admissions
800-783-6220 or 740-283-6226 Fax: 740-284-5456
Website: www.admissions.edu
E-mail: mweber@franciscan.edu

University of Dayton
300 College Park, Dayton OH 45469-1300
Robert F. Durkle, Director of Admission
800-837-7433 Fax: 937-229-4729
Website: admission.udayton.edu
E-mail: admission@udayton.edu

Ursuline College
2550 Lander Rd, Cleveland OH 44124-4398
Sarah E. Sundermeier, Director of Admissions
888-URSULINE Toll Free Fax: 440-684-6138
Website: www.admission.ursuline.edu
E-mail: admission@ursuline.edu

OKLAHOMA

Oklahoma State University
Stillwater OK 74078
Gerry Auel, Program Director
405-744-8569
Website: www.okstate.edu
E-mail: gerry.auel@okstate.edu

OREGON

Cascade College
9101 E Burnside St, Portland OR 97216-1599
Jim Murphy, Director of Enrollment Management
800-550-7678 Fax: 503-257-1222
Website: www.cascade.edu
E-mail: admissions@cascade.edu

PENNSYLVANIA

Art Institute of Philadelphia
1622 Chestnut St, Philadelphia PA 19103-5119
Larry McHugh, Director of Admissions
800-275-2474 Fax: 215-405-6399
Website: www.artinstitutes.edu/philadelphia
E-mail: aiphinfo@aii.edu

Juniata College
1700 Moore St, Huntingdon PA 16652-2196
Michelle Bartol, Dean of Enrollment
877-JUNIATA Fax: 814-641-3100
Website: www.juniata.edu
E-mail: admissions@juniata.edu

MOUNT ALOYSIUS COLLEGE
7373 Admiral Peary Hwy, Cresson PA 16630-1999
Frank C. Crouse Jr., Vice President for Enrollment Management
814-886-6383 or 888-823-2220 Fax: 814-886-6441
Website: www.mtaloy.edu
E-mail: admissions@mtaloy.edu

SOUTH CAROLINA

Columbia International University
PO Box 3122, Columbia SC 29230-3122
Michelle MacGregor, Director of University Admissions
800-777-2227 Fax: 803-786-4209
Website: www.ciu.edu
E-mail: yesciu@ciu.edu
See listing under "Theological Studies & Religious Vocations"

TENNESSEE

Crichton College
255 N Highland St, Memphis TN 38111-4745
Shelly Luttrell, Dean of Admissions
901-320-9797 Fax: 901-320-9791
Website: www.crichton.edu
E-mail: admissions@crichton.edu

Lipscomb University
3901 Granny White Pike, Nashville TN 37204-3951
Ricky Holaway, Director of Admissions
800-333-4358 ext. 1776 Fax: 615-269-1804
Website: www.lipscomb.edu
E-mail: admissions@lipscomb.edu

TEXAS

Abilene Christian University
ACU Box 29000, Abilene TX 79699-0001
325-674-2000 Fax: 325-674-2202
Website: www.acu.edu
E-mail: info@admissions.acu.edu

University of Houston
122 E Cullen Bldg, Houston TX 77204-2023
Office of Admission
713-743-9595
Website: www.uh.edu
E-mail: admissions@uh.edu

VERMONT

NORWICH UNIVERSITY
158 Harmon Dr, Northfield VT 05663
Jennifer Hasenfus, International Programs
800-468-6679
Website: www.norwich.edu
E-mail: jhasenfu@norwich.edu

VIRGINIA

Marymount University
2807 N Glebe Rd, Arlington VA 22207-4299
Michael Canfield, Director of Admissions
800-548-7638 Fax: 703-522-0348
Website: www.marymount.edu
E-mail: admissions@marymount.edu

Radford University
PO Box 6903, Radford VA 24142
David W. Kraus, Director of Admissions
800-890-4265 Fax: 540-831-5038
Website: www.radford.edu
E-mail: ruadmiss@radford.edu

Randolph College
2500 Rivermont Ave, Lynchburg VA 24503
Patricia LeDonne, Director of Admissions
434-947-8100 Fax: 434-947-8996
Website: www.randolphcollege.edu
E-mail: admissions@randolphcollege.edu

WASHINGTON

SHORELINE COMMUNITY COLLEGE
16101 Greenwood Ave N, Shoreline WA 98133-5696
Chris Melton, Acting Registrar
206-546-4581 Fax: 206-546-5835
Website: www.shoreline.edu

WISCONSIN

Alverno College
PO Box 343922, Milwaukee WI 53234-3922
Dianna Gaebler, Director of Admissions
414-382-6100 Fax: 414-382-6354
Website: www.alverno.edu
E-mail: admissions@alverno.edu

St. Norbert College
100 Grant St, De Pere WI 54115
Brian Studebaker, Director of Admission
800-236-4878 Fax: 920-403-4072
Website: www.snc.edu
E-mail: admit@snc.edu

WYOMING

University of Wyoming
Admissions Office
Dept 3435, Laramie WY 82071-3435
Brooke Culver, Contact
800-342-5996 Fax: 307-766-4042
Website: www.uwyo.edu
E-mail: why-wyo@uwyo.edu

SUMMER SESSIONS

ALABAMA

CALHOUN COMMUNITY COLLEGE
PO Box 2216, Decatur AL 35609-2216
M. Wayne Tosh, Registrar
256-306-2500 Fax: 256-306-2941
Website: www.calhoun.edu
E-mail: pml@calhoun.edu
See listing under "Community and Junior Colleges"

ALASKA

University of Alaska Anchorage
PO Box 141629, Anchorage AK 99514-1629
Cecile Mitchell, Director of Enrollment Services
907-786-1480 Fax: 907-786-4888
Website: www.uaa.alaska.edu/
E-mail: enroll@uaa.alaska.edu

CALIFORNIA

Chapman University
One University Drive, Orange CA 92866-1099
Michael Drummy, Assistant Vice President for Enrollment
Services and Chief Admission Officer
714-997-6411 or 888-CUAPPLY Fax: 714-997-6713
Website: www.chapman.edu
E-mail: admit@chapman.edu

Orange Coast College
PO Box 5005, Costa Mesa CA 92628-5005
Kristin Clark, Director of Admissions
714-432-5773 Fax: 714-432-5736
Website: www.orangecoastcollege.edu
E-mail: kclark@cccd.edu

Point Loma Nazarene University
3900 Lomaland Dr, San Diego CA 92106-2810
Chip Killingsworth, Director of Undergraduate Admissions
800-733-7770 Fax: 619-849-2601
Website: www.pointloma.edu
E-mail: admissions@pointloma.edu

San Bernardino Valley College
701 S Mount Vernon Ave
San Bernardino CA 92410-2798
Kay Ragan, Ed.D., Director of Admissions
909-888-6511 Fax: 909-889-4988
Website: www.valleycollege.edu
E-mail: kragan@sbccd.cc.ca.us

San Diego Christian College
2100 Greenfield Dr, El Cajon CA 92019-1157
Rene Inman, Director of Admissions
800-676-2242 Fax: 619-590-1739
Website: www.sdcc.edu
E-mail: admissions@sdcc.edu

COLORADO

ILIFF SCHOOL OF THEOLOGY
2201 S University Blvd, Denver CO 80210-4798
Stephanie Yahas, Coordinator of Summer School
800-678-3360 or 303-765-3117 Fax: 303-777-0164
Website: www.iliff.edu
E-mail: admissions@iliff.edu

DELAWARE

Wesley College
120 N State St, Dover DE 19901-3876
302-736-2300 Fax: 302-736-2301
Website: www.wesley.edu

FLORIDA

Florida Air Academy
1950 S Academy Dr, Melbourne FL 32901-4396
Colonel James Dwight, President
321-723-3211 ext. 30041 Fax: 321-676-0422
Website: www.flair.com
E-mail: tderegnaucourt@flair.com

Jones College
5353 Arlington Expy, Jacksonville FL 32211-5588
Dorothy D. Jones, Chief Executive Officer
904-743-1122 Fax: 904-744-4446
Website: www.jones.edu
E-mail: fmccaffe@jones.edu

Jones College
11430 N Kendall Dr Ste 200, Miami FL 33176
Patricia Carbonell, Contact
305-275-9996 Fax: 305-743-4446
Website: www.jones.edu
E-mail: pcarbone@jones.edu

Lynn University
3601 N Military Trl, Boca Raton FL 33431-5598
Director of Admissions
561-237-7900 Fax: 561-237-7100
Website: www.lynn.edu
E-mail: admission@lynn.edu

SOUTHWEST FLORIDA COLLEGE
1685 Medical Ln, Fort Myers FL 33907-1157
866-SWFC-NOW or 239-939-4766 Fax: 239-936-4040
Website: www.swfc.edu
E-mail: studentinfo@swfc.edu

University of South Florida
4202 E Fowler Ave, Tampa FL 33620-6900
J. Robert Spatig, Director of Admissions
877-USF-BULL Fax: 813-974-9689
Website: www.usf.edu
E-mail: admissions@admin.usf.edu
See listing under "Universities"

GEORGIA

Kennesaw State University
1000 Chastain Rd NW, Kennesaw GA 30144-5591
Dr. Ralph Rascati, Dean
770-423-6000
Website: www.kennesaw.edu

North Georgia Technical College
434 Meeks Ave, Blairsville GA 30512-2983
Admissions
706-439-6300 Fax: 706-439-6301
Website: www.northgatech.edu
E-mail: info@northgatech.edu

North Georgia Technical College
8989 Highway 17, Toccoa GA 30577
706-779-8100 Fax: 706-779-8130
Website: www.northgatech.edu
E-mail: info@northgatech.edu

North Georgia Technical College
Clarkesville Campus
PO Box 65, Clarkesville GA 30523-0002
Admissions
706-754-7700 Fax: 706-754-7777
Website: www.northgatech.edu
E-mail: info@northgatech.edu

TOCCOA FALLS COLLEGE
PO Box 800899, Toccoa Falls GA 30598
888-785-5624 Fax: 706-282-6012
Website: www.tfc.edu
E-mail: admissions@tfc.edu

ILLINOIS

Benedictine University
5700 College Rd, Lisle IL 60532-0900
630-829-6300 or 888-829-6363 Fax: 630-829-6301
Website: www.ben.edu
E-mail: admissions@ben.edu
See listing under "Universities"

CONCORDIA UNIVERSITY
7400 Augusta St, River Forest IL 60305-1402
708-209-3100 Fax: 708-209-3176
Website: www.cuchicago.edu
E-mail: admission@cuchicago.edu

Roosevelt University
430 S Michigan Ave, Chicago IL 60605
Gwen E. Kanelos, Asst. Vice President for Enrollment Services
877-APPLY-RU Fax: 312-341-4216
Website: www.roosevelt.edu
E-mail: applyru@roosevelt.edu

INDIANA

Ancilla Domini College
Donaldson IN 46513
Erin Alonzo, Director of Admissions
574-936-8898 Fax: 574-935-1773
Website: www.ancilla.edu
E-mail: erin.alonzo@ancilla.edu

CULVER ACADEMIES AND SUMMER CAMPS
1300 Academy Rd # 157, Culver IN 46511-1234
Mike Turnbull, Director of Admissions
574-842-7100 Fax: 574-842-8066
Website: www.culver.org
E-mail: admissions@culver.org

IOWA

Briar Cliff University
PO Box 2100, Sioux City IA 51104-0100
Sharisue Wilcoxon, VP for Enrollment Management
712-279-5200 Fax: 712-279-1632
Website: www.briarcliff.edu
E-mail: admissions@briarcliff.edu

Graceland University
1 University Place, Lamoni IA 50140
Greg Sutherland, Interim Vice President for Enrollment and Dean of Admissions
641-784-5196 Fax: 641-784-5480
Website: www.admissions.graceland.edu
E-mail: admissions@graceland.edu

Iowa Lakes Community College
3200 College Dr, Emmetsburg IA 50536-1055
Anne Stansbury, Asst. Director of Admissions
712-852-5212 Fax: 712-362-8363
Website: www.iowalakes.edu
E-mail: info@iowalakes.edu

Iowa Lakes Community College
300 S 18th St, Estherville IA 51334-2721
Anne Stansbury, Asst. Director of Admissions
712-362-7945 Fax: 712-362-8363
Website: www.iowalakes.edu
E-mail: info@iowalakes.edu

Iowa Lakes Community College
1900 Grand Ave, Suite 8, Spencer IA 51301
Anne Stansbury, Assistant Director of Admissions
712-262-7141 Fax: 712-262-4047
Website: www.iowalakes.edu
E-mail: info@iowalakes.edu

KANSAS

Independence Community College
PO Box 708, Independence KS 67301-0708
Dr. Terry Hetrick, President
800-842-6063 Fax: 620-331-5344
Website: www.indycc.edu
E-mail: admissions@indycc.edu

KENTUCKY

National College
115 E Lexington Ave, Danville KY 40422-1517
Gloria Walls, Director of Admissions
859-236-6991 Fax: 859-236-1063
Website: www.national-college.edu
E-mail: info@national-college.edu

National College
7627 Ewing Blvd, Florence KY 41042-1812
Doug Dedeker, Director of Admissions
859-525-6510 Fax: 859-525-8961
Website: www.national-college.edu
E-mail: info@national-college.edu

National College
2376 Sir Barton Way, Lexington KY 40509
Terry Fisher, Director of Admissions
859-253-0621 Fax: 859-254-7664
Website: www.national-college.edu
E-mail: info@national-college.edu

National College
4205 Dixie Hwy, Louisville KY 40216
Ted Scharre, Director of Admissions
502-447-7634 Fax: 502-447-7665
Website: www.national-college.edu
E-mail: info@national-college.edu

National College
50 National College Blvd, Pikeville KY 41501
Janet Head, Director of Admissions
606-478-7200 Fax: 606-478-7209
Website: www.national-college.edu
E-mail: info@national-college.edu

National College
125 S Killarney Ln, Richmond KY 40475
Keeley Gadd, Director of Admissions
859-623-8956 Fax: 859-623-8956
Website: www.national-college.edu
E-mail: info@national-college.edu

LOUISIANA

Our Lady of Holy Cross College
4123 Woodland Dr, New Orleans LA 70131-7399
Office of Enrollment Services
504-394-7744 Fax: 504-391-2421
Website: www.olhcc.edu

MAINE

Southern Maine Community College
2 Fort Rd, South Portland ME 04106-1698
Dr. James Ortiz, President
Scott MacDonald, Director of Financial Aid
207-741-5500 Fax: 207-741-5671
Website: www.smccme.edu
E-mail: oharmon@maine.rr.com

MARYLAND

Hagerstown Community College
11400 Robinwood Dr, Hagerstown MD 21742-6590
Dr. Daniel E. Bock, Assistant Director of Admissions
301-790-2800 Fax: 301-791-9165
Website: www.hagerstowncc.edu
E-mail: bockd@hagerstowncc.edu

MASSACHUSETTS

The Art Institute of Boston at Lesley University
700 Beacon St, Boston MA 02215-2598
Office of Admission
617-585-6710 Fax: 617-585-6720
Website: www.aiboston.edu
E-mail: admissions@aiboston.edu

Bristol Community College
777 Elsbree St, Fall River MA 02720-7395
Rodney S. Clark, Director of Admissions
508-678-2811 ext. 2516, 2179 Fax: 508-730-3265
Website: www.bristol.mass.edu
E-mail: admissions@bristol.mass.edu

LANDMARK SCHOOL
PO Box 227, Prides Crossing MA 01965-0227
Director of Admission
978-236-3000 Fax: 978-927-7268
Website: www.landmarkschool.org
E-mail: admission@landmarkschool.org

Boarding and day tuition are based on six weeks, full and half-day options that combine academic skill development, 1:1 tutorials, and recreational activities. The Summer Program accepts students age 7-20, grades 1-12, of average to superior intelligence, with a history of healthy emotional development and a diagnosis of a language-based learning disability.

SCHOOL OF THE MUSEUM OF FINE ARTS, BOSTON
230 The Fenway, Boston MA 02115-5534
Office of Admissions
617-267-1219 Fax: 617-369-3679
Website: www.smfa.edu
E-mail: admissions@smfa.edu

The SMFA welcomes teens from a variety of backrounds to the pre-college summer studio in June and July. At the School you'll find an exciting community of artists and programs that will help you build skills, learn new forms of expression, and free yourself to see things, and do things, differently. The Pre-College Summer Studio for juniors and seniors in high school is a five-week intensive program that focuses on drawing, printmaking, painting, sculpture, ceramics, video, sound, and more while earning college credit. The Young Artists' Program is for ages 15-18.

University of Massachusetts Dartmouth
Old Westport Rd, North Dartmouth MA 02747-2300
Susan Lane, Associate Vice Chancellor
508-999-9202 Fax: 508-999-8621
Website: explore.umassd.edu
E-mail: slane@umassd.edu

WINCHENDON SCHOOL
172 Ash St, Winchendon MA 01475-1700
J. William LaBelle, Headmaster
800-622-1119 Fax: 978-297-0911
Website: www.winchendon.org
E-mail: admissions@winchendon.org

Worcester Polytechnic Institute
100 Institute Rd, Worcester MA 01609-2280
Edward J. Connor, Director of Admissions
508-831-5286 Fax: 508-831-5875
Website: admissions.wpi.edu
E-mail: admissions@wpi.edu

MICHIGAN

Delta College
University Center MI 48710-0001
Duff Zube, Director of Admissions
989-686-9093 Fax: 989-667-2202
Website: www.delta.edu
E-mail: admit@delta.edu

HILLSDALE COLLEGE
33 E College St, Hillsdale MI 49242-1298
Sam McArthur, Registrar
517-607-2360 Fax: 517-607-2657
Website: www.hillsdale.edu
E-mail: sam.mcarthur@hillsdale.edu

Lawrence Technological University
21000 W 10 Mile Rd, Southfield MI 48075-1058
Jane Rohrback, Director of Admissions
800-225-5588 Fax: 248-204-2228
Website: www.ltu.edu
E-mail: admissions@ltu.edu
See listing under "Universities"

MINNESOTA

Hibbing Community College
1515 E 25th St, Hibbing MN 55746-3300
Holly Bigelow, Director of Enrollment
800-224-4HCC or 218-262-7200 Fax: 218-262-6717
Website: www.hibbing.edu
E-mail: admissions@hibbing.edu

RASMUSSEN COLLEGE - ST. CLOUD
226 Park Ave S, Saint Cloud MN 56301-3713
Admissions
320-251-5600 or 800-852-0460 Fax: 320-251-3702
Website: www.rasmussen.edu
E-mail: stcloud@rasmussen.edu

Ridgewater College-Hutchinson Campus
2 Century Ave SE, Hutchinson MN 55350-3100
Dawn Bjork, Counselor
800-722-1151 Fax: 320-234-8506
Website: www.ridgewater.edu
E-mail: dawn.bjork@ridgewater.edu

Ridgewater College-Willmar Campus
PO Box 1097, Willmar MN 56201-1097
Sally Kerfeld, Director of Admissions
800-722-1151 Fax: 320-222-5212
Website: www.ridgewater.edu
E-mail: sally.kerfeld@ridgewater.edu

MISSISSIPPI

Tougaloo College
500 W County Line Rd, Tougaloo MS 39174-9799
Juno Leggette Jacobs, Director of Admissions
601-977-7768 Fax: 601-977-4501
Website: www.tougaloo.edu
E-mail: jjacobs@tougaloo.edu

MISSOURI

Central Methodist University
411 Central Methodist Sq, Fayette MO 65248-1198
Larry Anderson, Director of Admissions
660-248-6247 Fax: 660-248-1872
Website: www.centralmethodist.edu
E-mail: landerso@centralmethodist.edu

Ozark Christian College
1111 N Main St, Joplin MO 64801-4804
Troy Nelson, Director of Admissions
800-299-4622 Fax: 417-624-0090
Website: www.occ.edu
E-mail: occadmin@occ.edu
See listing under "Universities"

University of Missouri
1 University Blvd, Saint Louis MO 63121-4499
Ms. Linda Silman, Registrar
314-516-5545 Fax: 314-516-7096
Website: www.umsl.edu
E-mail: admissionsu@msx.umsl.edu

WENTWORTH MILITARY ACADEMY & COLLEGE
1880 Washington Ave, Lexington MO 64067
MAJ Mike Herman, VP for Enrollment
800-962-7682 or 660-259-2221 Fax: 660-259-2677
Website: www.wma.edu
E-mail: admissions@wma.edu

Coed. Grades 9-12. 6 weeks. Accredited by NCA and State of Missouri. Earn 15 high school credits in either core high school classes or dual enrollment college classes. Leadership instruction and application in classroom and outdoor activity. Co-ed, dorm by single gender. Leadership, enrichment, academics.

William Woods University
1 University Ave, Fulton MO 65251-1098
Jimmy Clay, Director of Admissions
573-642-2251 Fax: 573-592-1146
Website: www.williamwoods.edu
E-mail: admissions@williamwoods.edu
See listing under "Universities"

MONTANA

Carroll College
1601 N Benton Ave, Helena MT 59625-0002
Dr. Thomas J. Trebon, President
Cynthia Thornquist, Director of Admissions & Enrollment Operations
406-447-4384 Fax: 406-447-4533
Website: www.carroll.edu
E-mail: admission@carroll.edu

NEW HAMPSHIRE

Southern New Hampshire University
2500 N River Rd, Hooksett NH 03106-1045
Steve Soba, Director of Admissions
603-645-9611 Fax: 603-645-9693
Website: www.snhu.edu
E-mail: s.soba@snhu.edu

NEW JERSEY

New Jersey City University
2039 John F Kennedy Blvd
Jersey City NJ 07305-1588
Carmen Panlilio, Asst. V.P. for Admissions and Financial Aid
201-200-3234 Fax: 201-200-2044
Website: www.njcu.edu
E-mail: admissions@njcu.edu

Ramapo College of New Jersey
505 Ramapo Valley Rd, Mahwah NJ 07430-1623
Director of Admissions
201-684-7300 or 201-684-7301 Fax: 201-684-7964
Website: www.ramapo.edu
E-mail: admissions@ramapo.edu

RICHARD STOCKTON COLLEGE OF NEW JERSEY
PO Box 195, Pomona NJ 08240
John Iacovelli, Dean of Enrollment Management
866-RSC-2885 Fax: 609-626-5541
Website: www.stockton.edu
E-mail: admissions@stockton.edu
See listing under "Universities"

NEW YORK

Briarcliffe College
1055 Stewart Ave, Bethpage NY 11714-3545
Theresa Donohue, Director of Admissions
516-918-3600 Fax: 516-470-6020
Website: www.briarcliffe.edu

College of Saint Rose
432 Western Ave, Albany NY 12203-1419
Maryelizabeth Amico, Asst V.P. for Undergraduate Admissions
518-454-5150 Fax: 518-454-2013
Website: www.strose.edu
E-mail: admit@strose.edu

FIVE TOWNS COLLEGE
305 N Service Rd, Dix Hills NY 11746-5871
631-424-7000 ext. 2110 Fax: 631-656-2172
Website: www.fivetowns.edu
E-mail: admissions@ftc.edu
See listing under "Universities"

Hilbert College
5200 S Park Ave, Hamburg NY 14075-1597
Timothy Lee, Director of Admissions
716-649-7900 Fax: 716-649-0702
Website: www.hilbert.edu
E-mail: tlee@hilbert.edu

Iona College
715 North Ave, New Rochelle NY 10801-1890
Kevin Cavanagh, Assistant V.P. for College Admissions
914-633-2502 Fax: 914-637-2778
Website: www.iona.edu

LABORATORY INSTITUTE OF MERCHANDISING
12 E 53rd St, New York NY 10022-5268
Kristina Gibson, Director of Admissions
800-677-1323 or 212-752-1530 Fax: 212-750-3432
Website: www.limcollege.edu
E-mail: admissions@limcollege.edu
See listing under "Universities"

Long Island University-C. W. Post Campus
720 Northern Blvd, Brookville NY 11548-1300
Lee Kelly, Assistant Provost Enrollment Services
516-299-2431 Fax: 516-299-3939
Website: www.liu.edu/cwpost
E-mail: enroll@cwpost.liu.edu

Molloy College
1000 Hempstead Ave
Rockville Centre NY 11570-1100
Marguerite Lane, Director of Admissions
516-678-5000 ext. 6291 Fax: 516-256-2247
Website: www.molloy.edu
E-mail: admissions@molloy.edu
See listing under "Universities"

New York Military Academy
78 Academy Ave
Cornwall on Hudson NY 12520-1325
CAPT Robert D. Watts, USN (Ret.), Superintendent
Maureen T. Kelly, Director of Admissions
888-ASK-NYMA Fax: 845-534-7699
Website: www.nyma.org
E-mail: admissions@nyma.ouboces.org
See listing under "Preparatory Schools - Coed"

Pratt Institute
200 Willoughby Ave, Brooklyn NY 11205-3899
Heidi Metcalf, Director of Admissions
718-636-3600 Fax: 718-636-3670
Website: www.pratt.edu
E-mail: hmetcalf@pratt.edu

Roberts Wesleyan College
2301 Westside Dr, Rochester NY 14624-1997
Office of Admissions
585-594-6400 Fax: 585-594-6371
Website: www.roberts.edu
E-mail: admissions@roberts.edu

SUNY College at Brockport
350 New Campus Dr, Brockport NY 14420-2997
Bernard S. Valento, Director of Undergraduate Admissions
585-395-2751 Fax: 585-395-5452
Website: www.brockport.edu
E-mail: admit@brockport.edu

SUNY Sullivan County Community College
112 College Rd, Loch Sheldrake NY 12759-5151
Sari Rosenheck, Director of Admissions
845-434-5750 Fax: 845-434-0923
Website: www.sullivan.suny.edu
E-mail: admissions@sullivan.suny.edu
Student Housing on Campus.

NORTH DAKOTA

Williston State College
PO Box 1326, Williston ND 58802-1326
Penny Soiseth, Associate Director Enrollment Services
701-774-4200 Fax: 701-774-4544
Website: www.wsc.nodak.edu
E-mail: penny.soiseth@wsc.nodak.edu

OHIO

ART ACADEMY OF CINCINNATI
1212 Jackson St, Cincinnati OH 45202
Gregory Allgire Smith, President
513-562-6262 Fax: 513-562-8778
Website: www.artacademy.edu
E-mail: admissions@artacademy.edu
See listing under "Art"

Cleveland State University
2121 Euclid Ave RW 204, Cleveland OH 44115
Dr. Richard Arndt, Dean of Undergraduate Recruitment and College Partnerships
888-CSU-OHIO Fax: 216-687-9210
Website: www.csuohio.edu
E-mail: admissions@csuohio.edu

Owens Community College
3200 Bright Rd, Findlay OH 45840
William J. Ivoska PhD., Vice President of Student Services
567-429-3500 Fax: 567-423-0246
Website: www.owens.edu
E-mail: admissions@owens.edu

Owens Community College
PO Box 10000, Toledo OH 43699-1947
William J. Ivoska, Ph.D, Vice President of Student Services
567-661-7000 Fax: 567-661-7607
Website: www.owens.edu
E-mail: admissions@owens.edu

OKLAHOMA

Oklahoma State University
Stillwater OK 74078
Joan Payne, Associate Registrar
405-744-6876 Fax: 405-744-5285
Website: www.okstate.edu
E-mail: joan.payne@okstate.edu

OREGON

Cascade College
9101 E Burnside St, Portland OR 97216-1599
Jim Murphy, Director of Enrollment Management
800-550-7678 Fax: 503-257-1222
Website: www.cascade.edu
E-mail: admissions@cascade.edu

PENNSYLVANIA

Art Institute of Philadelphia
1622 Chestnut St, Philadelphia PA 19103-5119
Larry McHugh, Director of Admissions
800-275-2474 Fax: 215-405-6399
Website: www.artinstitutes.edu/philadelphia
E-mail: aiphinfo@aii.edu

Community College of Allegheny County
Allegheny Campus: 808 Ridge Ave, Pittsburgh PA 15212 Admissions: 412.237.2700
Boyce Campus: 595 Beatty Rd, Monroeville PA 15146 Admissions: 724.325.6614
North Campus: 8701 Perry Highway, Pittsburgh PA 15237 Admissions: 412.369.3600
South Campus: 1750 Clairton Rd, West Mifflin PA 15122 Admissions: 412-469-4301
Website: www.ccac.edu

Holy Family University
9801 Frankford Avenue, Philadelphia PA 19114
Lauren Campbell, Director of Admissions
215-637-3050 Fax: 215-281-1022
Website: www.holyfamily.edu
E-mail: admissions@holyfamily.edu

Juniata College
1700 Moore St, Huntingdon PA 16652-2196
Michelle Bartol, Dean of Enrollment
877-JUNIATA Fax: 814-641-3100
Website: www.juniata.edu
E-mail: admissions@juniata.edu

MOUNT ALOYSIUS COLLEGE
7373 Admiral Peary Hwy, Cresson PA 16630-1999
Frank C. Crouse Jr., Vice President for Enrollment Management
814-886-6383 or 888-823-2220 Fax: 814-886-6441
Website: www.mtaloy.edu
E-mail: admissions@mtaloy.edu

SOUTH CAROLINA

CIU Seminary & School of Missions
PO Box 3122, Columbia SC 29230-3122
Michelle MacGregor, Director of University Admissions
800-777-2227 Fax: 803-333-0607
Website: www.ciu.edu
E-mail: yessem@ciu.edu
See listing under "Theological Studies & Religious Vocations"

Columbia International University
PO Box 3122, Columbia SC 29230-3122
Michelle MacGregor, Director of University Admissions
800-777-2227 Fax: 803-786-4209
Website: www.ciu.edu
E-mail: yesciu@ciu.edu
See listing under "Theological Studies & Religious Vocations"

Spartanburg Community College
PO Box 4386, Spartanburg SC 29305-4386
Nancy Garmroth, Dean of Admissions & Financial Aid
864-592-4810 Fax: 864-592-4945
Website: sccsc.edu

SOUTH DAKOTA

NATIONAL AMERICAN UNIVERSITY
321 Kansas City St, Rapid City SD 57701-3692
Angela G. Beck, Director of Enrollment Management
605-394-4800 Fax: 605-394-4871
Website: www.rapid.national.edu
E-mail: rcadmissions@national.edu

Presentation College
1500 N Main St, Aberdeen SD 57401-1280
JoEllen Lindner, VP for Enrollment
605-229-8492 Fax: 605-229-8425
Website: www.presentation.edu
E-mail: admit@presentation.edu

TENNESSEE

Lipscomb University
3901 Granny White Pike, Nashville TN 37204-3951
Ricky Holaway, Director of Admissions
800-333-4358 ext. 1776 Fax: 615-269-1804
Website: www.lipscomb.edu
E-mail: admissions@lipscomb.edu

National College
1328 Highway 11W, Bristol TN 37620
Becky Wild, Director of Admissions
423-878-4440 Fax: 423-793-1060
Website: www.national-college.edu
E-mail: info@national-college.edu

National College of Business & Technology
3748 Nolensville Pike, Nashville TN 37211-3322
Lynda Dandridge, Director of Admissions
615-333-3344 Fax: 615-333-3429
Website: www.national-college.edu
E-mail: info@national-college.edu

THE WEBB SCHOOL
PO Box 488, Bell Buckle TN 37020-0488
Matt Anderson, Director of Operations in Admissions
888-733-9322 Fax: 931-389-6657
Website: www.thewebbschool.com
E-mail: admissions@webbschool.com

TEXAS

Abilene Christian University
ACU Box 29000, Abilene TX 79699-0001
325-674-2000 Fax: 325-674-2202
Website: www.acu.edu
E-mail: info@admissions.acu.edu

University of Houston
122 E Cullen Bldg, Houston TX 77204-2023
Office of Admission
713-743-9595
Website: www.uh.edu
E-mail: admissions@uh.edu

UTAH

WASATCH ACADEMY
120 S 100 W, Mount Pleasant UT 84647-1509
Kim Stephens, Director of Admissions
800-634-4690 Fax: 435-462-1450
Website: www.wacad.org
E-mail: admissions@wacad.org

VERMONT

NORWICH UNIVERSITY
158 Harmon Dr, Northfield VT 05663
Registrars Office
800-468-6679
Website: www.norwich.edu
E-mail: nuregstr@norwich.edu
See listing under "Universities"

Southern Vermont College
982 Mansion Dr, Bennington VT 05201-6002
Joel Wincowski, Director of Admissions
800-378-2782 Fax: 802-447-4695
Website: www.svc.edu
E-mail: admis@svc.edu

VIRGINIA

BLUE RIDGE SCHOOL
273 Mayo Dr, Saint George VA 22935
William Darrin, III, Director of Admissions & Financial Aid
434-985-2811 Fax: 434-985-7215
Website: www.blueridgeschool.com
E-mail: admissions@blueridgeschool.com

Fishburne Military School
PO Box 988, Waynesboro VA 22980-0722
Brigadier General William Alexander, (VA), Superintendent
Major Scott Mangum, (VA), Director of Admissions
800-946-7773 Fax: 540-946-7738
Website: www.fishburne.org
E-mail: crichmond@fishburne.org

Marymount University
2807 N Glebe Rd, Arlington VA 22207-4299
Michael Canfield, Director of Admissions
800-548-7638 Fax: 703-522-0348
Website: www.marymount.edu
E-mail: admissions@marymount.edu

MASSANUTTEN MILITARY ACADEMY
614 S Main St, Woodstock VA 22664-1205
Murali Sinnathamby, Director of Admissions
877-466-6222 or 540-459-2167 Fax: 540-459-5421
Website: www.militaryschool.com
E-mail: admissions@militaryschool.com

National College
100 Logan St, Bluefield VA 24605
Tonya Elmore, Director of Admissions
276-326-3621 Fax: 276-322-5731
Website: www.national-college.edu
E-mail: info@national-college.edu

National College
1819 Emmet St N, Charlottesville VA 22901-2812
434-295-0136 Fax: 434-979-8061
Website: www.national-college.edu
E-mail: info@national-college.edu

National College
336 Old Riverside Dr, Danville VA 24541
Jeff Moore, Director of Admissions
434-793-6822 Fax: 434-793-3634
Website: www.national-college.edu
E-mail: info@national-college.edu

National College
1515 Country Club Rd, Harrisonburg VA 22802
Kathy Sours, Director of Admissions
540-432-0943 Fax: 540-432-1133
Website: www.national-college.edu
E-mail: info@national-college.edu

National College
104 Candlewood Ct, Lynchburg VA 24502-2653
Nancy Fortune, Director of Admissions
434-239-3500 Fax: 434-239-3948
Website: www.national-college.edu
E-mail: info@national-college.edu

National College
10 Church St, Martinsville VA 24114
Barbara Rakes, Director of Admissions
276-632-5621 Fax: 276-632-7915
Website: www.national-college.edu
E-mail: info@national-college.edu

National College
1813 E Main St, Salem VA 24153-4598
Ron Smith, Director of Admissions
540-986-1800 Fax: 540-444-4195
Website: www.national-college.edu
E-mail: info@national-college.edu

Oak Hill Academy
2635 Oak Hill Rd, Mouth of Wilson VA 24363-3004
Dr. Michael D. Groves, President
276-579-2619 Fax: 276-579-4722
Website: www.oak-hill.net
E-mail: info@oak-hill.net
See listing under "Preparatory Schools - Coed"

Radford University
PO Box 6903, Radford VA 24142
David W. Kraus, Director of Admissions
800-890-4265 Fax: 540-831-5038
Website: www.radford.edu
E-mail: ruadmiss@radford.edu

Southside Virginia Community College
109 Campus Dr, Alberta VA 23821-2930
Ronald E. Mattox, Dean of Admissions
434-949-1014 Fax: 434-949-7863
Website: www.sv.vccs.edu
E-mail: ronald.mattox@sv.vccs.edu

Southside Virginia Community College
200 Daniel Rd, Keysville VA 23947
Ronald E. Mattox, Dean of Admissions
434-736-2018 Fax: 434-736-2082
Website: www.sv.vccs.edu
E-mail: ronald.mattox@sv.vccs.edu

WEST VIRGINIA

Davis & Elkins College
100 Campus Dr, Elkins WV 26241-3996
Renee Heckel, Director of Enrollment Management
800-624-3157 Fax: 304-637-1800
Website: www.davisandelkins.edu
E-mail: admiss@davisandelkins.edu

WISCONSIN

St. Norbert College
100 Grant St, De Pere WI 54115
Brian Studebaker, Director of Admission
800-236-4878 Fax: 920-403-4072
Website: www.snc.edu
E-mail: admit@snc.edu

WYOMING

University of Wyoming
Admissions Office
Dept 3435, Laramie WY 82071-3435
Brooke Culver, Contact
800-342-5996 Fax: 307-766-4042
Website: www.uwyo.edu
E-mail: why-wyo@uwyo.edu

GUAM

University of Guam
UOG Station, Mangilao GU 96923
Deborah Leon Guerrero, Registrar
671-735-2201 or 671-735-2208 Fax: 671-735-2203
Website: www.uog.edu
E-mail: admitme@uog9.uog.edu

TEACHER EDUCATION

ALABAMA

Alabama A & M University
PO Box 908, Normal AL 35762
Antonio Boyle, Director of Admissions
256-372-5245

Alabama State University
PO Box 271, Montgomery AL 36101-0271
334-229-4200

Auburn University
Auburn AL 36849
334-844-4000

Auburn University at Montgomery
PO Box 244023, Montgomery AL 36124
334-244-3000

Birmingham-Southern College
900 Arkadelphia Rd, Birmingham AL 35254-0002
800-523-5793

CALHOUN COMMUNITY COLLEGE
PO Box 2216, Decatur AL 35609-2216
M. Wayne Tosh, Registrar
256-306-2500 Fax: 256-306-2941
Website: www.calhoun.edu
E-mail: jfd@calhoun.edu

Faulkner University
5345 Atlanta Hwy, Montgomery AL 36109-3398
Keith Mock, Director of Admissions
800-879-9816 ext. 7200

Huntingdon College
1500 E Fairview Ave, Montgomery AL 36106-2148
334-833-4222

Jacksonville State University
700 Pelham Rd N, Jacksonville AL 36265-1602
256-782-5000

Judson College
302 Bibb St, Marion AL 36756
Michael Scotto, Director of Admissions
800-447-9472 Fax: 334-683-5147
Website: www.judson.edu
E-mail: admissions@judson.edu

Oakwood College
Oakwood Rd NW, Huntsville AL 35896-0001
256-726-7000

Samford University
800 Lakeshore Dr, Birmingham AL 35229-0002
205-726-3673

Spring Hill College
4000 Dauphin St, Mobile AL 36608-1791
334-460-4000

Stillman College
PO Box 1430, Tuscaloosa AL 35403-1430
205-349-4240

Troy University
Troy AL 36082-0001
Jim Hutto, Dean of Enrollment Management
334-670-3175

Troy University Dothan
PO Box 8368, Dothan AL 36304-0368
334-983-6556

Tuskegee University
Tuskegee Institute AL 36088
334-727-8011

University of Alabama
Box 870118, Tuscaloosa AL 35487
Dr. Lisa B. Harris, Director of Admissions
205-348-5666

University of Alabama at Birmingham
Univ Sta, Birmingham AL 35294-0001
205-934-4011

University of Alabama in Huntsville
PO Box 1247, Huntsville AL 35899-0001
Nikki Willis, Assoc. Director for Recruiting Program and Events
1-800-UAH-CALL Fax: 256-824-6073
Website: www.uah.edu
E-mail: willisn@uah.edu

University of Mobile
5735 College Pkwy, Mobile AL 36613
800-946-7267

University of Montevallo
Station 6030, Montevallo AL 35115
205-665-6030

University of North Alabama
Univ Sta, Florence AL 35632-0001
256-760-4100

University of South Alabama
307 University Blvd N, Mobile AL 36688-3053
Melissa Haab, Director of Admissions
251-460-6141 Fax: 251-460-7876
Website: www.southalabama.edu
E-mail: admiss@usouthal.edu

University of West Alabama
Hwy 11, Livingston AL 35470
205-652-3400

ALASKA

Sheldon Jackson College
801 Lincoln St, Sitka AK 99835-7651
800-478-4556

University of Alaska Anchorage
PO Box 141629, Anchorage AK 99514-1629
Cecile Mitchell, Director of Enrollment Services
907-786-1480 Fax: 907-786-4888
Website: www.uaa.alaska.edu/
E-mail: enroll@uaa.alaska.edu

University of Alaska Fairbanks
PO Box 757480, Fairbanks AK 99775
907-474-7581

University of Alaska Southeast
11120 Glacier Hwy, Juneau AK 99801-8625
Paul Kraft, Dean of Students/Enrollment Management
907-796-6000

ARIZONA

Arizona State University
PO Box 870112, Tempe AZ 85287-0112
480-965-9011

Southwestern College
2625 E Cactus Rd, Phoenix AZ 85032-7097
Admissions/Financial Aid Office
800-247-2697

University of Arizona
Tucson AZ 85721-0040
Paul Kohn, Director of Admissions
520-621-3237

ARKANSAS

Arkansas State University
PO Box 1630, State University AR 72467-1630
870-972-2100

Arkansas Tech University
215 W O St, Russellville AR 72801-2222
479-968-0389

Harding University
900 E Center Ave, Searcy AR 72149
501-279-4000

Henderson State University
1100 Henderson St, Arkadelphia AR 71999-0001
870-230-5000

Hendrix College
1600 Washington Ave, Conway AR 72032-3080
501-329-6811

John Brown University
2000 W University St, Siloam Springs AR 72761-2121
877-JBU-INFO

Lyon College
PO Box 2317, Batesville AR 72503-2317
Dan Rutledge, Director of Admissions
870-793-9813

Ouachita Baptist University
410 Ouachita St, Arkadelphia AR 71998-0001
David Goodman, Director of Admissions
870-245-5110

Philander Smith College
812 W 13th St, Little Rock AR 72202-3799
501-375-9845

Phillips Community College of the University of Arkansas
PO Box 785, Helena AR 72342-0785
Dr. Steven Murray, Chancellor
Lynn Boone, Vice Chancellor for Student Services / Registrar
870-338-6474 Fax: 870-338-7542
Website: www.pccua.edu
E-mail: lboone@pccua.edu

Southern Arkansas University
100 E University, Magnolia AR 71753
870-235-4000

University of Arkansas at Fayetteville
1 University of Arkansas, Fayetteville AR 72701-1201
479-575-2000

University of Arkansas at Little Rock
2801 S University Ave, Little Rock AR 72204-1000
501-569-3000

University of Arkansas at Monticello
PO Box 3600, Monticello AR 71656
870-367-6811

University of Arkansas at Pine Bluff
1200 University Dr, Pine Bluff AR 71601-2799
870-543-8000

University of Arkansas Community College at Hope
PO Box 140, Hope AR 71802-0140
Danita Ormand, Director of Enrollment Services
870-777-5722 Fax: 870-722-6630
Website: www.uacch.edu
E-mail: dormand@uacch.edu

University of Central Arkansas
201 Donaghey Ave, Conway AR 72035-5003
501-450-5000

University of the Ozarks
415 N College Ave, Clarksville AR 72830-2880
Jim Decker, Director of Admissions
479-979-1000

Williams Baptist College
PO Box 3737, Walnut Ridge AR 72476-3737
Angela Flippo, Vice President for Enrollment Management
800-722-4434 Fax: 870-759-4163
Website: www.williamsbaptistcollege.com
E-mail: admissions@wbcoll.edu

CALIFORNIA

Antioch University
801 Garden St Ste 101
Santa Barbara CA 93101-1581
Ankara McPherson, Director of Admissions
805-962-8179

Antioch University Southern California
400 Corporate Pointe, Culver City CA 90230-7615
Admissions Office
800-7-ANTIOCH Fax: 310-821-6032
E-mail: admissions@antiochla.edu
Master of Arts in Education and Teacher Credentialing Program.

Azusa Pacific University
901 E Alosta Ave, Azusa CA 91702
626-969-3434

Biola University
13800 Biola Ave, La Mirada CA 90639-0001
562-903-4752

California Baptist University
8432 Magnolia Ave, Riverside CA 92504-3297
951-689-5771

California State University-Bakersfield
9001 Stockdale Hwy, Bakersfield CA 93311-1022
661-664-2011

California State University-Chico
Chico CA 95929-0001
530-898-6116

California State University-Dominguez Hills
1000 E Victoria St, Carson CA 90747-0001
310-243-3300

California State University-East Bay
25800 Carlos Bee Blvd, Hayward CA 94542-3001
510-885-3000

California State University-Fresno
Fresno CA 93740-0001
559-278-4240

California State University-Fullerton
PO Box 34080
Fullerton CA 92634
714-278-2011

California State University-Los Angeles
5151 State University Dr, Los Angeles CA 90032
323-343-3000

California State University-Northridge
18111 Nordhoff St, Northridge CA 91330-0001
818-677-1200

California State University-San Bernadino
5500 University Pkwy
San Bernardino CA 92407-2393
Olivia Rosas, Director of Admissions
909-537-5188 Fax: 909-537-7034
Website: www.csusb.edu
E-mail: orosas@csusb.edu

California State University-San Marcos
San Marcos CA 92096-0001
760-750-4000

California State University-Stanislaus
801 W Monte Vista Ave, Turlock CA 95382-0256
Lisa Bernardo, Director of Admissions
209-667-3357

Chapman University
One University Drive, Orange CA 92866-1099
Michael Drummy, Assistant Vice President for Enrollment
Services and Chief Admission Officer
714-997-6411 or 888-CUAPPLY Fax: 714-997-6713
Website: www.chapman.edu
E-mail: admit@chapman.edu

CONCORDIA UNIVERSITY
1530 Concordia, Irvine CA 92612-3203
Lori McDonald, Executive Director of Enrollment Services
800-229-1200 or 949-854-8002 Fax: 949-854-6894
Website: www.cui.edu
E-mail: admission@cui.edu

Fielding Graduate University
School of Educational Leadership and Change
2112 Santa Barbara St
Santa Barbara CA 93105-3538
DeAnne Taylor, Director of Admissions
805-687-1099 Fax: 805-687-9793
Website: www.fielding.edu
E-mail: admission@fielding.edu

Fresno Pacific University
1717 S Chestnut Ave, Fresno CA 93702-4798
559-453-2000

HEBREW UNION COLLEGE - JEWISH INSTITUTE OF RELIGION
3077 University Ave, Los Angeles CA 90007-3796
Dr. Matt Albert, Regional Director of Admissions and Recruitment
213-749-3424 Fax: 213-747-6128
Website: www.huc.edu
E-mail: malbert@huc.edu

Holy Names University
3500 Mountain Blvd, Oakland CA 94619-1699
Dr. Hoffman-Marr, Director of Admissions
510-436-1010

Humboldt State University
1 Harpst St, Arcata CA 95521-8299
707-826-3011

INTERNATIONAL CHRISTIAN EDUCATION COLLEGE
Early Childhood Education
3807 Wilshire Blvd Ste 730
Los Angeles CA 90010-3108
Dr. Charles Chong Y. Lee, President
213-368-0316 Fax: 213-368-0318
E-mail: icec@sbcglobal.net

La Sierra University
4500 Riverwalk Pkwy, Riverside CA 92505
Bobby Brown, Director of Admissions
800-874-5587

Loyola Marymount University
7900 Loyola Blvd, Los Angeles CA 90045-2699
310-338-2700

Mills College
5000 MacArthur Blvd, Oakland CA 94613-1000
510-430-2255

Mt. St. Mary's College
12001 Chalon Rd, Los Angeles CA 90049-1599
310-954-4000

Notre Dame de Namur University
1500 Ralston Ave, Belmont CA 94002-1997
Martin Bednarek, Director of Admissions
800-263-0545

Orange Coast College
PO Box 5005, Costa Mesa CA 92628-5005
Kristin Clark, Director of Admissions
714-432-5773 Fax: 714-432-5736
Website: www.orangecoastcollege.edu
E-mail: kclark@cccd.edu

Pacific Union College
1 Angwin Ave, Angwin CA 94508-9797
707-965-6311

PEPPERDINE UNIVERSITY
Graduate School of Education and Psychology
6100 Center Dr, Los Angeles CA 90045
Fionnbarr Kelly, Director of Admissions
310-568-5744 Fax: 310-568-5755
Website: www.gsep.pepperdine.edu
E-mail: gsep@pepperdine.edu
*Master of Arts in Education and/or Teaching Credential
*Master of Arts in Educational Technology (Online)
*Master of Science in Administration and Preliminary Administrative Services Credential
*Master of Science in Workplace Learning and Performance
*Doctor of Education in Educational Leadership, Administration, and Policy
*Doctor of Education in Educational Technology
*Doctor of Education in Organization Change
*Doctor of Education in Organizational Leadership

Point Loma Nazarene University
3900 Lomaland Dr, San Diego CA 92106-2810
Chip Killingsworth, Director of Undergraduate Admissions
800-733-7770 Fax: 619-849-2601
Website: www.pointloma.edu
E-mail: admissions@pointloma.edu

San Bernardino Valley College
701 S Mount Vernon Ave
San Bernardino CA 92410-2798
Kay Ragan, Ed.D., Director of Admissions
909-888-6511 Fax: 909-889-4988
Website: www.valleycollege.edu
E-mail: kragan@sbccd.cc.ca.us

San Diego Christian College
2100 Greenfield Dr, El Cajon CA 92019-1157
Rene Inman, Director of Admissions
800-676-2242 Fax: 619-590-1739
Website: www.sdcc.edu
E-mail: admissions@sdcc.edu

San Diego State University
5500 Campanile Dr, San Diego CA 92182-0002
619-594-5200

San Francisco State University
1600 Holloway Ave, San Francisco CA 94132-1722
415-338-1111

San Jose State University
1 Washington Sq, San Jose CA 95192-0001
408-924-1000

Santa Clara University
500 El Camino Real, Santa Clara CA 95053-0001
408-554-4000

Simpson University
2211 College View Dr, Redding CA 96003-8606
Jim Herberger, Director of Admissions
888-9-SIMPSON Fax: 530-226-4861
Website: www.simpsonuniversity.edu
E-mail: admissions@simpsonuniversity.edu
See listing under "Universities"

Sonoma State University
1801 E Cotati Ave, Rohnert Park CA 94928-3609
Louis T. Levy, Senior Director Enrollment Services
707-664-2880

Stanford University
520 Lasuen Mall Union 232, Stanford CA 94305-3005
650-723-2300

University of California
Santa Barbara CA 93106
805-893-8000

University of Judaism
15600 Mulholland Dr, Los Angeles CA 90077-1599
Bryan Pisetsky, Director of Undergraduate Admissions
310-476-9777

University of La Verne
1950 3rd St, La Verne CA 91750-4443
800-876-4858

University of San Diego
5998 Alcala Park, San Diego CA 92110-2492
Admissions
619-260-4506

University of the Pacific
3601 Pacific Ave, Stockton CA 95211-0197
209-946-2011

Vanguard University of Southern California
55 Fair Dr, Costa Mesa CA 92626-6597
714-556-3610

COLORADO

Adams State College
Alamosa CO 81102
Matt Gallegos, Director of Admissions
800-824-6494

Colorado Christian University
8787 W Alameda Ave, Lakewood CO 80226
Sean Kadel, Director of Admissions
800-44-FAITH Fax: 303-963-3201
Website: www.ccu.edu
E-mail: admissions@ccu.edu

Colorado College
14 E Cache La Poudre St
Colorado Springs CO 80903-3243
719-389-6344

Colorado State University
1062 Campus Delivery, Fort Collins CO 80523
970-491-1101

Colorado State University - Pueblo
2200 Bonforte Blvd, Pueblo CO 81001-4990
719-549-2461

Mesa State College
1100 North Ave, Grand Junction CO 81501
970-248-1020

Metropolitan State College
PO Box 173362, Campus Box 21
Denver CO 80217-3362
303-556-6228

NORTHEASTERN JUNIOR COLLEGE
100 College Ave, Sterling CO 80751-2399
Dr. Lance Bolton, Chief Administrative Officer
Tina Joyce, Director of Admissions
970-521-7000 or 970-521-6752 Fax: 970-521-6801
Website: www.njc.edu
E-mail: tina.joyce@njc.edu

Regis University
3333 Regis Blvd, Denver CO 80221-1099
303-458-4900

University of Colorado
Boulder CO 80309-0001
303-492-1411

University of Colorado
1420 Austin Bluffs Pkwy
Colorado Springs CO 80918-3735
719-262-3000

University of Colorado at Denver and Health Sciences Center
Downtown Denver Campus
PO Box 173364, Denver CO 80217-3364
303-556-2717

University of Northern Colorado
Greeley CO 80639
Allen Huang, Interim Dean of Education
970-351-2817

Western State College of Colorado
Gunnison CO 81231-0001
Director of Admissions
800-876-5309

CONNECTICUT

Albertus Magnus College
700 Prospect St, New Haven CT 06511-1189
Richard Lolatte, Dean of Admission
203-773-8501 or 800-578-9160 Fax: 203-773-5248
Website: www.albertus.edu
E-mail: admissions@albertus.edu

Eastern Connecticut State University
83 Windham St, Willimantic CT 06226-2295
860-456-5000

Fairfield University
1073 N Benson Rd, Fairfield CT 06824-5171
203-254-4000

Quinnipiac University
275 Mount Carmel Ave, Hamden CT 06518-1905
Joan Isaac Mohr, VP & Dean of Admissions
203-582-8600

Sacred Heart University
5151 Park Ave, Fairfield CT 06825-1023
203-371-7999

St. Joseph College
1678 Asylum Ave, West Hartford CT 06117-2791
860-232-4571

Southern Connecticut State University
501 Crescent St, New Haven CT 06515-1355
203-392-5200

University of Bridgeport
126 Park Ave, Bridgeport CT 06604-5620
Barbara L. Maryak, Dean of Admissions
203-576-4552

University of Connecticut
Storrs CT 06269-0001
860-486-2000

University of Hartford
200 Bloomfield Ave, West Hartford CT 06117-1599
860-768-4100

University of New Haven
300 Boston Post Rd, West Haven CT 06516
Asst. Director of Undergraduate Admissions
203-932-7329

Western Connecticut State University
181 White St, Danbury CT 06810-6826
203-837-8200

DELAWARE

Delaware State University
1200 N DuPont Hwy, Dover DE 19901-2275
302-857-6060

University of Delaware
Newark DE 19711
302-831-2000

Wesley College
120 N State St, Dover DE 19901-3876
302-736-2300 Fax: 302-736-2301
Website: www.wesley.edu

DISTRICT OF COLUMBIA

Catholic University of America
620 Michigan Ave NE, Washington DC 20064-0001
202-319-5000

Gallaudet University
800 Florida Ave NE, Washington DC 20002-3695
Charity Reedy Hines, Director of Admissions
202-651-5750 Fax: 202-651-5744
Website: www.gallaudet.edu
E-mail: admissions.office@gallaudet.edu

George Washington University
2035 H St NW, Washington DC 20052-0002
202-994-1000

Trinity University
125 Michigan Ave NE, Washington DC 20017-1090
202-884-9000

University of the District of Columbia
4200 Connecticut Ave NW
Washington DC 20008-1174
LaVerne M. Hill-Flanagan, Director of Admissions
202-274-5100

FLORIDA

THE BAPTIST COLLEGE OF FLORIDA
5400 College Dr, Graceville FL 32440-1831
Christopher M. Bishop, Director of Admissions
800-328-2660 Fax: 850-263-9026
Website: www.baptistcollege.edu
E-mail: admissions@baptistcollege.edu

Barry University
11300 NE 2nd Ave, Miami Shores FL 33161-6695
800-695-2279

Bethune-Cookman College
640 Dr Mary McLeod Bethune Blvd
Daytona Beach FL 32114-3099
Edwin Coffie, Director of Admissions
800-448-0228

CARLOS ALBIZU UNIVERSITY
2173 NW 99th Ave, Miami FL 33172-2209
Carlos Alicea, Director of Admissions, Recruitment & Outreach
305-593-1223 ext. 137 Fax: 305-593-1854
Website: www.mia.albizu.edu
E-mail: admissions@albizu.edu

City College
2000 W Commercial Blvd, Fort Lauderdale FL 33309
Mercedes Segal, Director of Admissions
954-492-5353 Fax: 954-491-1965
Website: www.citycollege.edu

Clearwater Christian College
3400 Gulf To Bay Blvd, Clearwater FL 33759-4595
727-726-1153

Eckerd College
4200 54th Ave S, Saint Petersburg FL 33711
727-867-1166

Flagler College
PO Box 1027, Saint Augustine FL 32085-1027
904-829-6481

Florida A&M University
Tallahassee FL 32307
850-599-3000

Florida Atlantic University
PO Box 3091, Boca Raton FL 33431-0991
800-299-4328

Florida Southern College
111 Lake Hollingsworth Dr, Lakeland FL 33801-5607
Robert B. Palmer, V.P., Dean of Enrollment Management
863-680-4131

Florida State University
600 W College Ave, Tallahassee FL 32306-1096
Janice V. Finney, Director of Admissions
850-644-2525 Fax: 850-644-0197
Website: admissions.fsu.edu
E-mail: admissions@admin.fsu.edu

Jones College
5353 Arlington Expy, Jacksonville FL 32211-5588
Dorothy D. Jones, Chief Executive Officer
904-743-1122 Fax: 904-744-4446
Website: www.jones.edu
E-mail: fmccaffe@jones.edu

Jones College
11430 N Kendall Dr Ste 200, Miami FL 33176
Patricia Carbonell, Contact
305-275-9996 Fax: 305-743-4446
Website: www.jones.edu
E-mail: pcarbone@jones.edu

Lynn University
3601 N Military Trl, Boca Raton FL 33431-5598
Director of Admissions
561-237-7900 Fax: 561-237-7100
Website: www.lynn.edu
E-mail: admission@lynn.edu

Palm Beach Atlantic University
PO Box 24708, West Palm Beach FL 33416-4708
561-803-2000

Rollins College
1000 Holt Ave, Winter Park FL 32789
407-646-2000

Saint Leo University
PO Box 6665, Saint Leo FL 33574
Director of Admissions
800-334-5532

St. Thomas University
16401 NW 37th Ave, Miami Gardens FL 33054
Fr. Edward Blackwell, Contact
800-367-9010 or 305-628-6546 Fax: 305-628-6591
Website: www.stu.edu
E-mail: signup@stu.edu

Stetson University
421 N Woodland Boulevard, De Land FL 32720-3761
386-822-7000

University of Central Florida
PO Box 160111, Orlando FL 32816
407-823-3000

University of Florida
PO Box 114000, Gainesville FL 32611-4000
352-392-3261

University of Miami
PO Box 248006, Coral Gables FL 33124-8006
305-284-2211

University of North Florida
4567 Saint Johns Bluff Rd S
Jacksonville FL 32224-2645
904-620-1000

University of South Florida
4202 E Fowler Ave, Tampa FL 33620-6900
J. Robert Spatig, Director of Admissions
877-USF-BULL Fax: 813-974-9689
Website: www.usf.edu
E-mail: admissions@admin.usf.edu
See listing under "Universities"

University of Tampa
401 W Kennedy Blvd, Tampa FL 33606-1490
813-253-3333

University of West Florida
11000 University Pkwy, Pensacola FL 32514-5750
850-474-2000

Warner Southern College
5301 US Highway 27 S, Lake Wales FL 33859-8725
863-638-1426

GEORGIA

Albany State University
504 College Dr, Albany GA 31705-2796
229-430-4600

Armstrong Atlantic State University
11935 Abercorn St, Savannah GA 31419-1997
Kim West, Asst. Dean and Registrar Enrollment Services
912-927-5277 Fax: 912-921-5462
Website: www.armstrong.edu
E-mail: admissions@mail.armstrong.edu

Augusta State University
2500 Walton Way, Augusta GA 30904-4562
706-737-1400

Berry College
2277 Martha Berry Hwy NE
Mount Berry GA 30149-0149
706-232-5374

Brewton-Parker College
Highway 280, Mount Vernon GA 30445
800-342-1087

Clayton State University
5900 N Lee St, Morrow GA 30260
770-961-3500

Columbus State University
4225 University Ave, Columbus GA 31907-5645
706-568-2001

Emory University
200B Jones Center, Atlanta GA 30322
404-727-6123

Fort Valley State University
1005 State University Dr, Fort Valley GA 31030-3298
478-825-6307

Georgia College and State University
231 W Hancock St, Milledgeville GA 31061-3371
478-445-5350

Georgia Southern University
PO Box 8024, Statesboro GA 30460
Admissions Office
912-681-5532

Georgia Southwestern State University
800 Wheatley St, Americus GA 31709-4635
229-928-1279

Georgia State University
PO Box 4009, Atlanta GA 30302-4009
404-651-2365

Kennesaw State University
1000 Chastain Rd NW, Kennesaw GA 30144-5591
Yiping Wan, Dean of College of Education
770-423-6117
Website: www.kennesaw.edu

LaGrange College
601 Broad St, LaGrange GA 30240-2955
Andy Geeter, Director of Admission
800-593-2885

Mercer University in Macon
1400 Coleman Ave, Macon GA 31207-0003
John P. Cole, Sr. Assoc. V.P. for Admissions
478-301-2650

North Georgia College & State University
Dahlonega GA 30597-0001
706-864-1400

Oglethorpe University
4484 Peachtree Rd NE, Atlanta GA 30319-2797
Kelly Gosnell, Director of Admission
404-261-1441

Paine College
1235 15th St, Augusta GA 30901-3182
800-476-7703

Piedmont College
PO Box 10, Demorest GA 30535-0010
800-277-7020

Shorter College
315 Shorter Ave, Rome GA 30165-4267
800-868-6980

Spelman College
350 Spelman Ln SW, Atlanta GA 30314-4395
800-982-2411

Thomas University
1501 Millpond Rd, Thomasville GA 31792-7478
Darla M. Glass, Director of Student Affairs
229-226-1621

TOCCOA FALLS COLLEGE
PO Box 800899, Toccoa Falls GA 30598
888-785-5624 Fax: 706-282-6012
Website: www.tfc.edu
E-mail: admissions@tfc.edu

University of Georgia
Athens GA 30602-0001
706-542-3000

University of West Georgia
Carrollton GA 30118-0001
770-836-6500

Valdosta State University
N Patterson St, Valdosta GA 31698-0001
229-333-5952

Wesleyan College
4760 Forsyth Rd, Macon GA 31210-4462
800-447-6610

HAWAII

Brigham Young University
55-220 Kulanui St, Laie HI 96762-1293
808-293-3211

Chaminade University of Honolulu
3140 Waialae Ave, Honolulu HI 96816-1510
Joy Bouey, Dean of Enrollment Management
808-739-4619

Kauai Community College
3-1901 Kaumualii Hwy, Lihue HI 96766-9500
808-245-8225 Fax: 808-245-8297
Website: kauai.hawaii.edu
E-mail: arkauai@hawaii.edu

IDAHO

Boise State University
1910 University Dr, Boise ID 83725-0399
208-426-1011

Brigham Young University - Idaho
120 Kimball Bldg, Rexburg ID 83460-1615
Rob Garrett, Director of Admissions
208-496-1020 Fax: 208-496-1220
Website: www.byui.edu
E-mail: admissions@byui.edu

Idaho State University
PO Box 8270, Pocatello ID 83209-0001
208-282-0211

Lewis-Clark State College
500 8th Ave, Lewiston ID 83501-2698
Diane Douglas, Ph.D., Registrar/Director of Admissions
800-933-5272 Fax: 208-792-2429
Website: www.lcsc.edu
E-mail: admissions@lcsc.edu

Northwest Nazarene University
623 Holly St, Nampa ID 83686-5897
208-467-8011

University of Idaho
Moscow ID 83844-4253
Lloyd Scott, Director of New Student Services
208-885-6163 Fax: 208-885-4477
Website: www.uidaho.edu
E-mail: nss@uidaho.edu

ILLINOIS

AMERICAN INTERCONTINENTAL UNIVERSITY ONLINE
5550 Prairie Stone Parkway Suite 400
Hoffman Estates IL 60192
Admissions Department
877-701-3800
Website: www.aiuonline.edu
E-mail: info@aiuonline.edu

ARGOSY UNIVERSITY/CHICAGO
350 N Orleans St, Merchandise Mart
Chicago IL 60654
Jamal Scott, Director of Admissions
800-626-4123 Fax: 312-777-7750
Website: www.argosyu.edu
E-mail: jscott@argosyu.edu

Augustana College
639 38th St, Rock Island IL 61201-2296
309-794-7000

Aurora University
347 S Gladstone Ave, Aurora IL 60506-4892
Carol R. Dunn, Ed.D., Vice President for Enrollment
800-742-5281 Fax: 630-844-5535
Website: www.aurora.edu
E-mail: admission@aurora.edu

Benedictine University
5700 College Rd, Lisle IL 60532-0900
630-829-6300 or 888-829-6363 Fax: 630-829-6301
Website: www.ben.edu
E-mail: admissions@ben.edu

Bradley University
1501 W Bradley Ave, Peoria IL 61625-0002
800-447-6460

Chicago State University
9501 S King Dr, Chicago IL 60628-1598
773-995-2000

Columbia College Chicago
600 S Michigan Ave, Chicago IL 60605-1996
Murphy Monroe, Executive Director of Admissions
312-344-7130 Fax: 312-344-8024
Website: www.colum.edu
E-mail: admissions@colum.edu

CONCORDIA UNIVERSITY
7400 Augusta St, River Forest IL 60305-1402
708-209-3100 Fax: 708-209-3176
Website: www.cuchicago.edu
E-mail: admission@cuchicago.edu

De Paul University
1 E Jackson Blvd, Chicago IL 60604-2287
Carlene Klaas, Director of Admissions
312-362-8000

De Paul University
2323 N Seminary Ave, Chicago IL 60614-3298
312-362-8000

Eastern Illinois University
600 Lincoln Ave, Charleston IL 61920-3099
217-581-5000

Elmhurst College
190 S Prospect Ave, Elmhurst IL 60126-3296
630-279-4100

Eureka College
300 E College Ave, Eureka IL 61530-1500
309-467-3721

Illinois College
1101 W College Ave, Jacksonville IL 62650-2299
217-245-3000

Illinois State University
Normal IL 61790-0001
309-438-2111

Kendall College
900 N North Branch St, Chicago IL 60622
Office of Admissions
800-569-8179 Fax: 312-752-2021
Website: www.kendall.edu
E-mail: admissions@kendall.edu

Knox College
Galesburg IL 61401
309-341-7100

Lewis University
One University Parkway, Romeoville IL 60446
800-897-9000

Loyola University - Mundelein College
6525 N Sheridan Rd, Chicago IL 60626-5311
773-262-8100

Loyola University of Chicago
820 N Michigan Ave, Chicago IL 60611-2103
312-915-6000

MacMurray College
447 E College Ave, Jacksonville IL 62650-2590
217-479-7000

Millikin University
1184 W Main St, Decatur IL 62522-2084
Lin Stoner, Dean of Admission
800-373-7733

Monmouth College
700 E Broadway, Monmouth IL 61462-1963
309-457-2131

National-Louis University
5202 Old Orchard Rd Ste 300, Skokie IL 60077-4409
224-233-2000

North Central College
30 N Brainard St, Naperville IL 60540-4690
Martha Stolze, Director of Admissions
630-637-5800

NORTHEASTERN ILLINOIS UNIVERSITY
5500 N Saint Louis Ave, Chicago IL 60625-4699
Maureen Gillette, Dean
773-442-4050 Fax: 773-442-4020
Website: www.neiu.edu

Northern Illinois University
DeKalb IL 60115
815-753-1000

North Park College & Theological Seminary
3225 W Foster Ave, Chicago IL 60625-4810
773-244-6200

Olivet Nazarene University
1 University Ave
Bourbonnais IL 60914
815-939-5011

Principia College
Elsah IL 62028-9799
618-374-2131

Quincy University
1800 College Ave, Quincy IL 62301-2670
217-222-8020

Rockford College
5050 E State St, Rockford IL 61108-2393
William Laffey, Director of Admission
800-892-2984

Roosevelt University
430 S Michigan Ave, Chicago IL 60605
Gwen E. Kanelos, Asst. Vice President for Enrollment Services
877-APPLY-RU Fax: 312-341-4216
Website: www.roosevelt.edu
E-mail: applyru@roosevelt.edu

Southern Illinois University
Carbondale IL 62901-4400
618-453-2121

Southern Illinois University Edwardsville
Edwardsville IL 62026-0001
618-650-3705

Trinity Christian College
6601 W College Dr, Palos Heights IL 60463-0929
Joshua Lenarz, Director of Admissions
708-597-3000

Trinity International University
2065 Half Day Rd, Deerfield IL 60015-1241
847-945-8800 Fax: 847-317-8097
Website: www.tiu.edu
E-mail: tcadmissions@tiu.edu

University of Illinois at Springfield
One University Plaza, Springfield IL 62794
217-206-4847

University of St. Francis
500 Wilcox St, Joliet IL 60435
800-735-7500

Western Illinois University
1 University Cir, Macomb IL 61455-1390
309-295-1414

Wheaton College
501 College Ave, Wheaton IL 60187-5571
630-752-5000

INDIANA

Ancilla Domini College
Donaldson IN 46513
Erin Alonzo, Director of Admissions
574-936-8898 Fax: 574-935-1773
Website: www.ancilla.edu
E-mail: erin.alonzo@ancilla.edu

Anderson University
1100 E 5th St, Anderson IN 46012-3495
765-649-9071

Ball State University
2000 W University Ave, Muncie IN 47306-0002
765-285-5555

Bethel College
1001 W McKinley Ave, Mishawaka IN 46545-5591
Office of Admissions
574-257-3339

BROWN MACKIE COLLEGE - SOUTH BEND
1030 E Jefferson Blvd, South Bend IN 46617-3123
Connie Adelman, Campus President
574-237-0774 Fax: 574-237-3585
Website: www.brownmackie.edu

Butler University
4600 Sunset Ave, Indianapolis IN 46208-3443
317-940-8000

Calumet College of St. Joseph
2400 New York Ave, Whiting IN 46394-2195
219-473-7770

DePauw University
313 S Locust St, Greencastle IN 46135-1736
800-447-2495

Earlham College and Earlham School of Religion
801 National Rd W, Richmond IN 47374-4095
765-983-1200

Franklin College
101 Branigin Blvd, Franklin IN 46131
Jacqueline S. Acosta, Director of Admissions
800-852-0232 Fax: 317-738-8274
Website: www.franklincollege.edu
E-mail: admissions@franklincollege.edu

Goshen College
1700 S Main St, Goshen IN 46526-4794
574-535-7000

Grace College
200 Seminary Dr, Winona Lake IN 46590-1224
800-54-GRACE

Hanover College
PO Box 108, Hanover IN 47243-0108
William D. Preble, Dean of Admission
800-213-2178

Huntington College
2303 College Ave, Huntington IN 46750-1299
260-356-6000

Indiana State University
Terre Haute IN 47809-0001
Richard Toomey, Director of Admissions
812-237-6311

Indiana University
300 N Jordan Ave, Bloomington IN 47405-1106
812-855-4848

Indiana University at Kokomo
PO Box 9003, Kokomo IN 46904-9003
765-453-2000

Indiana University at South Bend
PO Box 7111, South Bend IN 46634-7111
574-237-4111

Indiana University East
2325 Chester Blvd, Richmond IN 47374-1289
765-973-8200

Indiana University Northwest
3400 Broadway, Gary IN 46408-1101
219-980-6500

Indiana University-Purdue University at Fort Wayne
2101 E Coliseum Blvd, Fort Wayne IN 46805-1445
260-481-6100

Indiana University Southeast
4201 Grant Line Rd, New Albany IN 47150-2158
812-941-2000

Indiana Wesleyan University
4201 S Washington St, Marion IN 46953-4974
765-674-6901

Manchester College
604 E College Ave, North Manchester IN 46962-1276
260-982-5000

Marian College
3200 Cold Spring Rd, Indianapolis IN 46222-1997
317-955-6000

Oakland City University
138 N Lucretia St, Oakland City IN 47660
Brian J. Baker, Director of Admissions
800-737-5125 Fax: 812-749-1433
Website: www.oak.edu
E-mail: bbaker@oak.edu
See listing under "Universities"

Purdue University
2200 169th St, Hammond IN 46323
219-989-2993

Purdue University
475 Stadium Mall Dr, West Lafayette IN 47907
765-494-4600

Purdue University
1401 S US Highway 421, Westville IN 46391-9542
219-785-5200

St. Joseph's College
PO Box 890, Rensselaer IN 47978-0890
219-866-6000

St. Mary-of-the-Woods College
Saint Mary of the Woods IN 47876
James P. Malley, Jr., Director of Admission
800-926-7692

St. Mary's College
46 Madeliva, Notre Dame IN 46556
574-284-4000

Taylor University
500 W Reade Ave, Upland IN 46989-1002
765-998-2751

University of Evansville
1800 Lincoln Ave, Evansville IN 47722-0001
Don Vos, Dean of Admission
800-423-8633 Fax: 812-488-4076
Website: www.evansville.edu
E-mail: admission@evansville.edu

University of Indianapolis
1400 E Hanna Ave, Indianapolis IN 46227-3697
317-788-3368

University of Southern Indiana
8600 University Blvd, Evansville IN 47712-3591
812-464-8600

Valparaiso University
Valparaiso IN 46383
219-464-5000

IOWA

Briar Cliff University
PO Box 2100, Sioux City IA 51104-0100
Sharisue Wilcoxon, VP for Enrollment Management
712-279-5200 Fax: 712-279-1632
Website: www.briarcliff.edu
E-mail: admissions@briarcliff.edu

Buena Vista University
610 W 4th St, Storm Lake IA 50588-1798
712-749-2235

Clarke College
1550 Clarke Dr, Dubuque IA 52001-3198
Andy Schroeder, Director of Admissions
800-383-2345 Fax: 563-584-8666
Website: www.clarke.edu
E-mail: andy.schroeder@clarke.edu

Coe College
1220 1st Ave NE, Cedar Rapids IA 52402-5092
319-399-8000

Cornell College
600 1st St SW, Mount Vernon IA 52314-1098
319-895-4000

Dordt College
498 4th Ave NE, Sioux Center IA 51250-1697
Quentin Van Essen, Executive Director of Admissions
800-343-6738

Graceland University
1 University Place, Lamoni IA 50140
Greg Sutherland, Interim Vice President for Enrollment and Dean of Admissions
641-784-5196 Fax: 641-784-5480
Website: www.admissions.graceland.edu
E-mail: admissions@graceland.edu

Grand View College
1200 Grandview Ave, Des Moines IA 50316-1599
515-263-2800

Grinnell College
PO Box 805, Grinnell IA 50112-0805
641-269-4000

Iowa Lakes Community College
3200 College Dr, Emmetsburg IA 50536-1055
Anne Stansbury, Asst. Director of Admissions
712-852-5212 Fax: 712-362-8363
Website: www.iowalakes.edu
E-mail: info@iowalakes.edu

Iowa Lakes Community College
300 S 18th St, Estherville IA 51334-2721
Anne Stansbury, Asst. Director of Admissions
712-362-7945 Fax: 712-362-8363
Website: www.iowalakes.edu
E-mail: info@iowalakes.edu

Iowa Lakes Community College
1900 Grand Ave, Suite 8, Spencer IA 51301
Anne Stansbury, Assistant Director of Admissions
712-262-7141 Fax: 712-262-4047
Website: www.iowalakes.edu
E-mail: info@iowalakes.edu

Loras College
1450 Alta Vista St, Dubuque IA 52001-4399
Tim Hauber, Director of Admissions
800-245-6727

Luther College
700 College Dr, Decorah IA 52101-1045
563-387-2000

Morningside College
1501 Morningside Ave, Sioux City IA 51106-1717
712-274-5000

Mount Mercy College
1330 Elmhurst Dr NE, Cedar Rapids IA 52402-4797
Jim Krystofiak, Dean of Admission
800-248-4504

Northwestern College
101 7th St SW, Orange City IA 51041-1996
712-737-7000

University of Dubuque
2000 University Ave, Dubuque IA 52001-5099
563-589-3000

Upper Iowa University
PO Box 1857, Fayette IA 52142-1857
563-425-5200

Waldorf College
106 S 6th St, Forest City IA 50436-1713
Dr. Linda Hoopes, Vice President of Admission and Marketing
800-292-1903 or 641-585-8112 Fax: 641-585-8125
Website: www.waldorf.edu
E-mail: hoopesl@waldorf.edu
See listing under "Universities"

Wartburg College
PO Box 1003, Waverly IA 50677-0903
Brent Matthias, Interim Director of Admissions
319-352-8200

KANSAS

Baker University
PO Box 65, Baldwin City KS 66006-0065
785-594-6451

Benedictine College
1020 N 2nd St, Atchison KS 66002-1499
913-367-5340

Bethany College
421 N 1st St, Lindsborg KS 67456-1897
785-227-3311

Bethel College
300 E 27th St, North Newton KS 67117-8061
316-283-2500

Emporia State University
1200 Commercial St, Emporia KS 66801-5087
620-343-1200

Fort Hays State University
600 Park St, Hays KS 67601-4099
785-628-4000

Friends University
2100 W University Ave, Wichita KS 67213-3397
316-261-5800

Independence Community College
PO Box 708, Independence KS 67301-0708
Dr. Terry Hetrick, President
800-842-6063 Fax: 620-331-5344
Website: www.indycc.edu
E-mail: admissions@indycc.edu

Kansas State University
Manhattan KS 66506
785-532-6250

McPherson College
PO Box 1402, Mc Pherson KS 67460-1402
620-241-0731

Newman University
3100 W McCormick St, Wichita KS 67213
Jann Reusser, Admissions Recruitment Coordinator
316-942-4291 ext. 2144

Ottawa University
1001 S Cedar St, Ottawa KS 66067-3399
785-242-5200

Pittsburg State University
1701 S Broadway St, Pittsburg KS 66762-7500
620-231-7000

Southwestern College
100 College St, Winfield KS 67156-2499
620-229-6000

Tabor College
400 S Jefferson St, Hillsboro KS 67063-1758
Rusty Allen, Dean of Enrollment Management
800-822-6799 Fax: 620-947-6276
Website: www.tabor.edu
E-mail: admissions@tabor.edu
See listing under "Universities"

University of Kansas
Lawrence KS 66045-0001
Karen Gallagher, Dean

University of Saint Mary
4100 S 4th St, Leavenworth KS 66048-5023
913-682-5151

Washburn University
1700 SW College Ave, Topeka KS 66621-0001
785-231-1010

Wichita State University
1845 N Fairmount St, Wichita KS 67260-0124
Gina Crabtree, Director of Admissions
316-978-3085

KENTUCKY

Alice Lloyd College
100 Purpose Rd, Pippa Passes KY 41844-9005
John Mills, Director of Admissions
888-280-4252

Asbury College
1 Macklem Dr, Wilmore KY 40390-1198
859-858-3511

Bellarmine University
2001 Newburg Rd, Louisville KY 40205-1877
502-452-8000

Berea College
Berea KY 40404-0001
859-985-3000

Campbellsville University
1 University Dr, Campbellsville KY 42718-2799
Scott Necessary, Coordinator of Undergraduate Admissions
270-789-5000

Eastern Kentucky University
521 Lancaster Ave, Richmond KY 40475-3102
859-622-1000

Kentucky State University
400 E Main St, Frankfort KY 40601-2334
502-597-6000

Kentucky Wesleyan College
3000 Frederica St, Owensboro KY 42301-6055
800-999-0592

Morehead State University
Morehead KY 40351-1689
Jeffrey Liles, Enrollment Services
800-585-6781 Fax: 606-783-5038
Website: www.moreheadstate.edu
E-mail: admissions@moreheadstate.edu

Murray State University
Murray KY 42071
Phil Bryan, Director of Admissions
270-762-3011

Northern Kentucky University
Newport KY 41099-0001
859-572-5100

Pikeville College
147 Sycamore St, Pikeville KY 41501
606-218-5250

Spalding University
851 S 4th St, Louisville KY 40203-2188
502-585-9911

Transylvania University
300 N Broadway, Lexington KY 40508-1776
859-233-8242 Fax: 859-233-8797
Website: www.transy.edu
E-mail: admissions@transy.edu

Union College
310 College St, Barbourville KY 40906-1499
Joretta Nelson, Vice President for Enrollment Management
800-489-8646

University of Kentucky
Lexington KY 40506-0001
Don Witt, Director of Admissions
859-257-9000

University of Louisville
2301 S 3rd St, Louisville KY 40292-2001
502-852-5555

Western Kentucky University
1 Big Red Way, Bowling Green KY 42101
270-745-0111

LOUISIANA

Centenary College of Louisiana
PO Box 41188, Shreveport LA 71134-1188
318-869-5011

Dillard University
2601 Gentilly Blvd, New Orleans LA 70122-3097
Linda G. Nash, Director of Admissions

Grambling State University
PO Box 864, Grambling LA 71245
318-274-3811

Louisiana College
PO Box 566, Pineville LA 71359-0001
318-487-7259

Louisiana State University
1 University Pl, Shreveport LA 71115-2301
318-797-5000

Louisiana State University and A & M College
Louisiana State Univ, Baton Rouge LA 70803-0001
225-578-3202

Louisiana State University at Alexandria
8100 Highway 71 S, Alexandria LA 71302-9121
Dr. Thomas Armstrong, Director of Admissions
318-445-3672 Fax: 318-473-6418
Website: www.lsua.edu

Louisiana Tech University
PO Box 3168, Ruston LA 71272-0001
318-257-0211

McNeese State University
4100 Ryan St, Lake Charles LA 70605-4510
337-475-5000

Nicholls State University
PO Box 2004, Thibodaux LA 70310-0001
985-446-8111

Northwestern State University
Natchitoches LA 71497-0001
Jana Lucky, Director of Enrollment Services
318-357-4503

Our Lady of Holy Cross College
4123 Woodland Dr, New Orleans LA 70131-7399
Office of Enrollment Services
504-394-7744 Fax: 504-391-2421
Website: www.olhcc.edu

Southeastern Louisiana University
PO Box 784, Hammond LA 70404-0784
985-549-2000

Southern University A&M College
Southern University, Baton Rouge LA 70813-0001
225-771-4500

University of Louisiana at Lafayette
PO Box 44672, Lafayette LA 70504
337-482-6678

University of Louisiana at Monroe
700 University Ave, Monroe LA 71209-9001
318-342-1000

University of New Orleans
New Orleans LA 70148-0001
504-280-6000

MAINE

Bowdoin College
Brunswick ME 04011
207-725-3000

HUSSON COLLEGE
One College Cir, Bangor ME 04401-2999
Jane Goodwin, Director of Admissions
800-4HU-SSON or 207-941-7100 Fax: 207-941-7935
Website: www.husson.edu
E-mail: admit@husson.edu
See listing under "Universities"

Southern Maine Community College
2 Fort Rd, South Portland ME 04106-1698
Dr. James Ortiz, President
Scott MacDonald, Director of Financial Aid
207-741-5500 Fax: 207-741-5671
Website: www.smccme.edu
E-mail: oharmon@maine.rr.com

Thomas College
180 W River Rd, Waterville ME 04901-5097
207-859-1111

University of Maine
246 Main St, Farmington ME 04938
Sharon M. Oliver, Director of Admissions
207-778-7000

University of Maine
9 OBrien Ave, Machias ME 04654-1321
207-255-1200

University of Maine
Orono ME 04469-0001
207-581-1110

University of Maine at Fort Kent
23 University Dr, Fort Kent ME 04743
888-TRY-UMFK

University of Maine at Presque Isle
181 Main St, Presque Isle ME 04769-2844
207-768-9532

University of Southern Maine
PO Box 9300, Portland ME 04104-9300
207-780-4141

MARYLAND

Bowie State University
14000 Jericho Park Rd, Bowie MD 20715-9465
301-464-3000

Coppin State University
2500 W North Ave, Baltimore MD 21216-3698
410-951-3000

Frostburg State University
Frostburg MD 21532-1001
301-687-4000

Goucher College
1021 Dulaney Valley Rd, Baltimore MD 21204-2780
410-337-6000

Griggs University
PO Box 4437, Silver Spring MD 20914-4437
Joan Wilson, Director of Admissions
301-680-6570 Fax: 301-680-6583
Website: www.griggs.edu
E-mail: registrar@griggs.edu

Hagerstown Community College
11400 Robinwood Dr, Hagerstown MD 21742-6590
Dr. Daniel E. Bock, Assistant Director of Admissions
301-790-2800 Fax: 301-791-9165
Website: www.hagerstowncc.edu
E-mail: bockd@hagerstowncc.edu

Hood College
401 Rosemont Ave, Frederick MD 21701
301-663-3131

Morgan State University
1700 E Cold Spring Ln, Baltimore MD 21251-0002
443-885-3000

Mt. St. Mary's University
16300 Old Emmitsburg Rd
Emmitsburg MD 21727-7799
301-447-6122

University of Maryland
College Park MD 20742-0001
301-405-1000

University of Maryland Eastern Shore
Princess Anne MD 21853
Edwina Morse, Director of Admissions
410-651-6410

Villa Julie College
1525 Greenspring Valley Rd
Stevenson MD 21153-0641
Mark Hergan, V.P. Enrollment Services
410-486-7001

Washington College
300 Washington Ave, Chestertown MD 21620-1197
410-778-2800

MASSACHUSETTS

Anna Maria College
50 Sunset Ln, Paxton MA 01612
Timothy M. Donahue, Director of Recruitment and Admissions
508-849-3360 Fax: 508-849-3362
Website: www.annamaria.edu
E-mail: admissions@annamaria.edu

Assumption College
500 Salisbury St, Worcester MA 01609-1294
Kathleen Murphy, Dean of Enrollment
508-767-7000 Fax: 508-799-4412
Website: www.assumption.edu
E-mail: admiss@assumption.edu

Atlantic Union College
PO Box 1000, South Lancaster MA 01561-1000
Office of Enrollment Services
800-282-2030

Bay State College
122 Commonwealth Ave, Boston MA 02116-2901
Craig Pfannenstiehl, President
617-217-9000 Fax: 617-536-1735

Becker College
Campuses in Worcester and Leicester, MA
61 Sever St, Worcester MA 01609-2165
Karen Schedin, Dean of Admissions
508-791-9241 Fax: 508-890-1500
Website: www.becker.edu
E-mail: admissions@becker.edu
See listing under "Universities"

Boston College
140 Commonwealth Ave
Chestnut Hill MA 02467-3800
617-552-8000

Boston University
121 Bay State Rd, Boston MA 02215
Kelly Walter, Executive Director of Admissions
617-353-2300 Fax: 617-353-9695
Website: web.bu.edu
E-mail: admissions@bu.edu

Bridgewater State College
Bridgewater MA 02325-0001
508-697-1237

Bristol Community College
777 Elsbree St, Fall River MA 02720-7395
Rodney S. Clark, Director of Admissions
508-678-2811 ext. 2516, 2179 Fax: 508-730-3265
Website: www.bristol.mass.edu
E-mail: admissions@bristol.mass.edu

Curry College
1071 Blue Hill Ave, Milton MA 02186-2395
Bruce Weckworth, Director of Admissions
617-333-2210

Eastern Nazarene College
23 E Elm Ave, Quincy MA 02170-2999
617-773-6350

Elms College
291 Springfield St, Chicopee MA 01013-2839
800-255-3567

Fisher College
118 Beacon St, Boston MA 02116-1501
Stephen Carter, Director of Admissions
800-446-1226

Gordon College
255 Grapevine Rd, Wenham MA 01984-1899
Barbara R. Layne, Associate Vice President, Enrollment
866-464-6736 Fax: 978-867-4682
Website: www.gordon.edu
E-mail: admissions@gordon.edu

Hampshire College
Amherst MA 01002
Karen S. Parker, Director of Admissions
413-559-5471

Harvard University
8 Garden St, Cambridge MA 02138-3630
617-495-1000

Lasell College
1844 Commonwealth Ave, Newton MA 02466-2716
617-243-2225

Lesley University
29 Everett St, Cambridge MA 02138-2790
Jane Raley, Director of Admissions
617-349-8800

Massachusetts College of Liberal Arts
375 Church St, North Adams MA 01247-4100
413-662-5381

Merrimack College
315 Turnpike St, North Andover MA 01845-5800
978-683-7111

Mt. Holyoke College
50 College St, South Hadley MA 01075-1424
413-538-2000

New England School of Art & Design at Suffolk University
75 Arlington St, Boston MA 02116
John Hamel, Director of Admissions
617-573-8785
Website: www.suffolk.edu/nesad

Northeastern University
360 Huntington Ave, Boston MA 02115-5000
617-373-2000

Pine Manor College
400 Heath St, Chestnut Hill MA 02467-2332
Bill Nichols, Dean of Admission
617-731-7167

Regis College
235 Wellesley St, Weston MA 02493-1571
781-768-2000

Salem State College
352 Lafayette St, Salem MA 01970-5353
978-741-6000

School of the Museum of Fine Arts, Boston
230 The Fenway, Boston MA 02115-5534
Office of Admissions
617-369-3626 or 800-643-6078 Fax: 617-369-4264
Website: www.smfa.edu
E-mail: admissions@smfa.edu
See listing under "Universities"

Springfield College
263 Alden St, Springfield MA 01109-3788
Mary DeAngelo, Director of Admissions
800-343-1257

Stonehill College
320 Washington St, Easton MA 02357-5610
508-565-1373

Suffolk University
8 Ashburton Pl, Boston MA 02108-2770
617-573-8460

Tufts University
520 Boston Ave, Medford MA 02155-5555
617-628-5000

University of Massachusetts
Amherst MA 01003
413-545-0111

University of Massachusetts Boston
100 William T Morrissey Blvd, Boston MA 02125-3393
Liliana Mickle, Director of Undergraduate Admissions
617-287-6000

University of Massachusetts Dartmouth
Old Westport Rd, North Dartmouth MA 02747-2300
Susan Lane, Associate Vice Chancellor
508-999-9202 Fax: 508-999-8621
Website: explore.umassd.edu
E-mail: slane@umassd.edu

University of Massachusetts Lowell
1 University Ave, Lowell MA 01854-2893
978-934-4000

Western New England College
1215 Wilbraham Rd, Springfield MA 01119-2655
413-782-1321

Westfield State College
PO Box 1630, Westfield MA 01086
Michelle Mattie, Associate Dean, Admission and Enrollment Services
413-572-5300

WHEELOCK COLLEGE
200 Riverway, Boston MA 02215-4104
Lisa Slavin, Dean of Enrollment
800-734-5212 Fax: 617-879-2449
Website: www.wheelock.edu
E-mail: undergrad@wheelock.edu

Worcester State College
486 Chandler St, Worcester MA 01602-2597
508-929-8000

MICHIGAN

Albion College
611 E Porter St, Albion MI 49224-1831
800-858-6770

Alma College
614 W Superior St, Alma MI 48801-1599
Evan Montague, Director of Admissions
800-321-ALMA Fax: 989-463-7057
Website: www.alma.edu
E-mail: admissions@alma.edu

Andrews University
Berrien Springs MI 49104-0001
Randall Graves, Director of Recruitment Services
800-253-2874

Aquinas College
1607 Robinson Rd SE, Grand Rapids MI 49506-1799
Paula Meehan, Dean of Admissions
616-732-4460

Baker College of Jackson
2800 Springport Rd, Jackson MI 49202-1230
Kelli Hoban, Director of Admissions
517-789-6123

Calvin College
3201 Burton St SE, Grand Rapids MI 49546-4388
800-688-0122

Central Michigan University
100 Warriner Hall, Mount Pleasant MI 48859-0001
989-774-4000

Concordia University
4090 Geddes Rd, Ann Arbor MI 48105-2797
Gary Neumann, Director of Admissions
734-995-7300 Fax: 734-995-4610
Website: www.cuaa.edu
E-mail: admissions@cuaa.edu

Delta College
University Center MI 48710-0001
Duff Zube, Director of Admissions
989-686-9093 Fax: 989-667-2202
Website: www.delta.edu
E-mail: admit@delta.edu

Eastern Michigan University
Ypsilanti MI 48197
800-GO-TO-EMU

Ferris State University
901 S State St, Big Rapids MI 49307-2295
231-591-2000

Grand Valley State University
1 Campus Dr, Allendale MI 49401-9403
616-331-2025 Fax: 616-331-2000
Website: www.gvsu.edu
E-mail: go2gvsu@gvsu.edu

HILLSDALE COLLEGE
33 E College St, Hillsdale MI 49242-1298
Dr. Kathy Connor, Chairperson
517-607-2424 Fax: 517-437-3923
Website: www.hillsdale.edu
E-mail: kathy.conner@hillsdale.edu

Hope College
PO Box 9000, Holland MI 49422-9000
616-395-7000

Lake Superior State University
650 W Easterday Ave
Sault Sainte Marie MI 49783-1637
Susan Camp, Director of Admissions
888-800-LSSU Fax: 906-635-6696
Website: www.lssu.edu
E-mail: admissions@lssu.edu
See listing under "Universities"

Lawrence Technological University
21000 W 10 Mile Rd, Southfield MI 48075-1058
Jane Rohrback, Director of Admissions
800-225-5588 Fax: 248-204-2228
Website: www.ltu.edu
E-mail: admissions@ltu.edu
See listing under "Universities"

Madonna University
36600 Schoolcraft Rd, Livonia MI 48150-1173
734-432-5300

Marygrove College
8425 W McNichols Rd, Detroit MI 48221-2599
313-927-1200

Michigan Technological University
1400 Townsend Dr, Houghton MI 49931-1200
Nancy Rehling, Director of Admissions
906-487-2335

Northern Michigan University
1401 Presque Isle Ave, Marquette MI 49855-5301
906-227-1000

Oakland University
2200 N Squirrel Rd, Rochester MI 48309
Eleanor L. Reynolds, Assistant Vice President & Director of Admissions
248-370-2100
Website: www.oakland.edu
E-mail: ouinfo@oakland.edu

Olivet College
300 S Main St, Olivet MI 49076-9724
269-749-7000

Saginaw Valley State University
7400 Bay Rd, University Center MI 48710-0001
989-790-4000

Siena Heights University
1247 E Siena Heights Dr, Adrian MI 49221-1796
517-263-0731

Spring Arbor University
106 E Main St, Spring Arbor MI 49283-9799
517-750-1200

University of Detroit-Mercy
PO Box 19900, Detroit MI 48219-0900
313-993-1000

University of Michigan-Dearborn
4901 Evergreen Rd, Dearborn MI 48128-1491
The Office of Admissions & Orientation
313-593-5100

Wayne State University
5980 Cass Ave, Detroit MI 48202-3489
313-577-2424

Western Michigan University
Kalamazoo MI 49008
269-387-1000

MINNESOTA

ARGOSY UNIVERSITY / TWIN CITIES
1515 Central Pkwy, Eagan MN 55121-1756
O. Jeanne Stoneking, Director of Admissions
651-846-2882 Fax: 651-994-7956
Website: www.argosyu.edu
E-mail: tcadmissions@argosyu.edu

Augsburg College
2211 Riverside Ave, Minneapolis MN 55454-1350
612-330-1000

Bemidji State University
1500 Birchmont Dr NE, Bemidji MN 56601-2699
877-236-4354

Bethany Lutheran College
700 Luther Dr, Mankato MN 56001
Don Westphal, Dean of Admissions
507-344-7000 Fax: 507-344-7376
Website: www.blc.edu
E-mail: admiss@blc.edu

Bethel College
3900 Bethel Dr, Saint Paul MN 55112-6999
651-638-6400

Carleton College
1 N College St, Northfield MN 55057-4044
800-995-2275 or 507-646-4190 Fax: 507-646-4526
Website: www.carleton.edu
E-mail: admissions@acs.carleton.edu

College of Saint Benedict
37 College Ave S, Saint Joseph MN 56374-2099
320-363-5011

College of St. Catherine
2004 Randolph Ave, Saint Paul MN 55105-1789
651-690-6000

College of Saint Scholastica
1200 Kenwood Ave, Duluth MN 55811-4199
Brian Dalton, V.P. of Enrollment Management
800-447-5444

Concordia College
901 8th St S, Moorhead MN 56562-0002
Dr. Marilyn Guy, Chairperson
218-299-3004

Concordia University-Saint Paul
275 Syndicate St N, Saint Paul MN 55104-5494
651-641-8278

Crown College
8700 College View Dr, Saint Bonifacius MN 55375
Mitch Fisk, Director of Admissions
952-446-4142 Fax: 952-446-4149
Website: www.crown.edu
E-mail: johnsonj@crown.edu

Gustavus Adolphus College
800 W College Ave, Saint Peter MN 56082-1485
Mark H. Anderson, Dean of Admission
800-GUSTAVUS Fax: 507-933-7474
Website: www.gustavus.edu
E-mail: admission@gustavus.edu

Hamline University
1536 Hewitt Ave, Saint Paul MN 55104-1284
651-523-2800

Macalester College
1600 Grand Ave, Saint Paul MN 55105-1899
651-696-6000

Minnesota State University Mankato
228 Wiecking Center, Mankato MN 56001
507-389-1866

Minnesota State University Moorhead
1104 7th Ave S, Moorhead MN 56563-0002
Regina Monson, Director of Admissions
218-477-2161 Fax: 218-477-4374
Website: go.mnstate.edu
E-mail: dragon@mnstate.edu

Pillsbury Baptist Bible College
315 S Grove Ave, Owatonna MN 55060-3097
Susanne Martin, Admissions Coordinator
507-451-2710 Fax: 507-451-0156
Website: www.pillsbury.edu
E-mail: admissions@pillsbury.edu

Ridgewater College-Willmar Campus
PO Box 1097, Willmar MN 56201-1097
Sally Kerfeld, Director of Admissions
800-722-1151 Fax: 320-222-5212
Website: www.ridgewater.edu
E-mail: sally.kerfeld@ridgewater.edu

St. Cloud State University
720 4th Ave S, Saint Cloud MN 56301-4442
877-654-7278

St. Mary's University of Minnesota
700 Terrace Hts Ste 2, Winona MN 55987-1321
507-452-4430

St. Olaf College
1500 Saint Olaf Ave, Northfield MN 55057-1001
507-646-2222

Southwest Minnesota State University
1501 State St, Marshall MN 56258-1598
507-537-7678

University of Minnesota
2900 University Ave, Crookston MN 56716-5001
218-281-6510 Fax: 218-281-8575
Website:
admissions.umcrookston.edu/requirements/apply.htm
E-mail: info@umcrookston.edu

University of Minnesota
10 University Dr, Duluth MN 55812-2496
Beth Esselstrom, Director of Admissions
218-726-7171

University of Minnesota
231 Pillsbury Dr SE, Minneapolis MN 55455-0230
612-625-2008

University of Minnesota - Morris
600 E 4th St, Morris MN 56267-2132
Rodney Oto, Director
800-992-8863

University of St. Thomas
2115 Summit Ave, Saint Paul MN 55105-1096
651-962-5000

Winona State University
PO Box 5838, Winona MN 55987-0838
507-457-5000

MISSISSIPPI

Alcorn State University
PO Box 359, Lorman MS 39096
601-877-6147

Belhaven College
1500 Peachtree St, Jackson MS 39202-1789
601-968-5927

Delta State University
Hwy 8 W, Cleveland MS 38733
662-846-3000

Jackson State University
1440 J.R. Lynch St, Jackson MS 39217
Stephanie Chatman, Director of Admissions
601-979-2100

Millsaps College
PO Box 15495, Jackson MS 39210
601-974-1000

Mississippi College
PO Box 4086, Clinton MS 39058-0001
601-925-3000

Mississippi State University
PO Box J, Mississippi State MS 39762-5509
662-325-2323

Mississippi University for Women
1100 College St Unit W1613, Columbus MS 39701
Terri Heath, Director of Admissions
877-GO-2-THEW

Mississippi Valley State University
14000 Highway 82 W Box 7222
Itta Bena MS 38941-1401
Office of Admissions
662-254-3347

Tougaloo College
500 W County Line Rd, Tougaloo MS 39174-9799
Juno Leggette Jacobs, Director of Admissions
601-977-7768 Fax: 601-977-4501
Website: www.tougaloo.edu
E-mail: jjacobs@tougaloo.edu

University of Mississippi
University MS 38677
662-232-7226

University of Southern Mississippi
PO Box 5165, Hattiesburg MS 39406-1000
601-266-5000

MISSOURI

Central Methodist University
411 Central Methodist Sq, Fayette MO 65248-1198
Larry Anderson, Director of Admissions
660-248-6247 Fax: 660-248-1872
Website: www.centralmethodist.edu
E-mail: landerso@centralmethodist.edu

Central Missouri State University
Warrensburg MO 64093-8888
Charles Petentler, Associate Director of Admissions
800-956-0177

Columbia College
1001 Rogers St, Columbia MO 65216-0001
Regina Morin, Director of Admissions
573-875-7352 Fax: 573-875-7506
Website: www.ccis.edu
E-mail: admissions@ccis.edu

Culver-Stockton College
1 College Hl, Canton MO 63435-1299
Betty Smith, Director of Enrollment Services
800-537-1883

Drury University
900 N Benton Ave, Springfield MO 65802-3791
417-873-7879

Harris-Stowe State University
3026 Laclede Ave, Saint Louis MO 63103-2199
LaShanda R. Boone, Director of Admissions
314-340-3300 Fax: 314-340-3555
Website: www.hssu.edu
E-mail: admissions@hssu.edu

Lincoln University
820 Chestnut St, Jefferson City MO 65101-3500
573-681-5000

Lindenwood University
209 S Kingshighway St
Saint Charles MO 63301-1695
Sheryl Guffey, Director of Admissions
636-949-2000 Fax: 636-949-4989
Website: www.lindenwood.edu

Maryville University of St. Louis
650 Maryville University Dr
Saint Louis MO 63141-7299
314-529-9300

Missouri Southern State University - Joplin
3950 Newman Rd, Joplin MO 64801-1512
417-625-9300

Missouri Valley College
500 E College St, Marshall MO 65340-3197
Dr. Dennis Ehlert, Division Dean
660-831-4170

Missouri Western State College
4525 Downs Dr, Saint Joseph MO 64507-2294
800-662-7041

Northwest Missouri State University
800 University Dr, Maryville MO 64468-6001
Beverly Schenkel, Dean of Enrollment Management
660-562-1562 Fax: 660-562-1121
Website: www.nwmissouri.edu
E-mail: admissions@nwmissouri.edu

Ozark Christian College
1111 N Main St, Joplin MO 64801-4804
Troy Nelson, Director of Admissions
800-299-4622 Fax: 417-624-0090
Website: www.occ.edu
E-mail: occadmin@occ.edu
See listing under "Universities"

Park University
8700 NW River Park Dr, Parkville MO 64152-3795
816-741-2000

Southeast Missouri State University
1 University Plz, Cape Girardeau MO 63701-4710
573-651-2000

Southwest Baptist University
1600 University Ave, Bolivar MO 65613-2597
417-328-5281

Stephens College
PO Box 2121, Columbia MO 65215-0001
David Adams, Dean of Enrollment Management
573-442-2211 Fax: 573-876-7237
Website: www.stephens.edu
E-mail: dadams@stephens.edu

Truman State University
100 E Normal, Kirksville MO 63501
Office of Admission
660-785-4114 Fax: 660-785-7456
Website: admissions.truman.edu
E-mail: admissions@truman.edu

University of Missouri
5100 Rockhill Rd, Kansas City MO 64110-2446
816-235-1000

University of Missouri
1 University Blvd, Saint Louis MO 63121-4499
Dr. Charles D. Schmitz, Dean College of Education
314-516-5109 Fax: 314-516-5227
Website: www.umsl.edu
E-mail: admissions@umsl.edu

Washington University in St. Louis
1 Brookings Dr, Saint Louis MO 63130-4899
314-935-5000

Webster University
470 E Lockwood Ave, Saint Louis MO 63119-3194
Dr. Brenda Fyfe, Dean, School of Education
314-968-7090 Fax: 314-968-7115
Website: www.webster.edu
E-mail: fyfebv@webster.edu
See listing under "Universities"

Westminister College
501 Westminster Ave, Fulton MO 65251-1299
573-642-3361

William Jewell College
500 College Hill, Liberty MO 64068-1896
Dr. Rick Winslow, VP Enrollment Management and Student Affairs
800-753-7009 Fax: 816-415-5040
Website: www.jewell.edu
E-mail: winslowr@william.jewell.edu

William Woods University
1 University Ave, Fulton MO 65251-1098
Jimmy Clay, Director of Admissions
573-642-2251 Fax: 573-592-1146
Website: www.williamwoods.edu
E-mail: admissions@williamwoods.edu
See listing under "Universities"

MONTANA

Carroll College
1601 N Benton Ave, Helena MT 59625-0002
Dr. Thomas J. Trebon, President
Cynthia Thornquist, Director of Admissions & Enrollment Operations
406-447-4384 Fax: 406-447-4533
Website: www.carroll.edu
E-mail: admission@carroll.edu

Montana State University - Billings
1500 University Dr, Billings MT 59101-0252
Karen Everett, Director
800-565-MSUB

Montana State University - Bozeman
103 Culbertson Hall, Bozeman MT 59715-5072
406-994-2452

Rocky Mountain College
1511 Poly Dr, Billings MT 59102-1796
Bonnie Knapp, Director of Admissions
800-877-6259

University of Montana
Missoula MT 59812-0001
406-243-0211

University of Montana - Western
710 S Atlantic St, Dillon MT 59725-3598
406-683-7011

NEBRASKA

Chadron State College
1000 Main St, Chadron NE 69337-2690
308-432-6000

College of Saint Mary
7000 Mercy Rd, Omaha NE 68106
Lorin Werth,V.P. for Enrollment
800-926-5534

Concordia University
800 N Columbia Ave, Seward NE 68434-1594
402-643-3651

Creighton University
2500 California Plz, Omaha NE 68178-0001
402-280-2700

Dana College
2848 College Dr, Blair NE 68008-1099
Duane A. Heffelfinger, Dean of Enrollment Management
800-444-3262

Doane College
1014 Boswell Ave, Crete NE 68333-2421
402-826-2161

Hastings College
PO Box 269, Hastings NE 68902-0269
402-463-2402

Nebraska Wesleyan University
5000 Saint Paul Ave, Lincoln NE 68504-2794
Patricia Karthauser, V.P. for University Enrollment
402-466-2371 Fax: 402-465-2177
Website: www.nebrwesleyan.edu
E-mail: admissions@nebrwesleyan.edu

Peru State College
PO Box 10, Peru NE 68421-0010
Office of Admissions
800-742-4412

Union College
3800 S 48th St, Lincoln NE 68506-4300
Buell Fogg, V.P. for Enrollment Services
800-228-4600

University of Nebraska
14th & R Sts, Lincoln NE 68588
402-472-7211

University of Nebraska at Kearney
905 W 25th St, Kearney NE 68849-0001
Dusty Newton, Director of Admissions
800-KEARNEY Fax: 308-865-8987
Website: www.unk.edu
E-mail: admissionsug@unk.edu

University of Nebraska at Omaha
60th and Dodge St, Omaha NE 68182-0001
402-554-2800

Wayne State College
1111 Main St, Wayne NE 68787-1172
402-375-7000

NEVADA

GREAT BASIN COLLEGE
1500 College Pkwy, Elko NV 89801-5032
Julie G. Byrnes, Director of Enrollment Management
775-753-2271 Fax: 775-753-2311
Website: www.gbcnv.edu
E-mail: julieb@gwmail.gbcnv.edu
See listing under "Universities"

University of Nevada
Reno NV 89557-0001
775-784-1110

University of Nevada Las Vegas
4505 S Maryland Pkwy, Las Vegas NV 89154-9901
800-334-8658

NEW HAMPSHIRE

Antioch University New England
40 Avon St, Keene NH 03431-3516
David Caruso, President
Leatrice A. Oram, Director of Admissions
603-357-6265 Fax: 603-357-0718
Website: www.antiochne.edu
E-mail: admissions@antiochne.edu

Colby-Sawyer College
100 Main St, New London NH 03257-4648
603-526-3000

Dartmouth College
Hanover NH 03755
603-646-1110

Franklin Pierce College
20 College Rd, Rindge NH 03461
800-437-0048

Keene State College
229 Main St, Keene NH 03435-0002
603-358-2276

New England College
98 Bridge St, Henniker NH 03242
603-428-2211

Plymouth State University
17 High St, MSC #44, Bagley House
Plymouth NH 03264-1595
603-535-5000

Rivier College
420 S Main St, Nashua NH 03060-5086
David Boisvert, Director of Undergraduate Admissions
603-897-8507

St. Anselm College
100 Saint Anselms Dr, Manchester NH 03102-1310
603-641-7000

Southern New Hampshire University
2500 N River Rd, Hooksett NH 03106-1045
Steve Soba, Director of Admissions
603-645-9611 Fax: 603-645-9693
Website: www.snhu.edu
E-mail: s.soba@snhu.edu

NEW JERSEY

Bergen Community College
400 Paramus Rd, Paramus NJ 07652
Julian Gomez, Asst. Director of Admissions
201-447-7100 Fax: 201-444-7036
Website: www.bergen.edu
E-mail: jgomez@bergen.edu

Caldwell College
9 Ryerson Ave, Caldwell NJ 07006-6195
973-618-3000

College of New Jersey
PO Box 7718, Ewing NJ 08628-0718
609-771-1855

College of Saint Elizabeth
2 Convent Rd, Morristown NJ 07960-6923
973-292-4000

Felician College
262 S Main St, Lodi NJ 07644-2198
201-559-6000

Kean University
1000 Morris Ave, Union NJ 07083-7133
908-527-2000

Monmouth University
400 Cedar Ave, West Long Branch NJ 07764-1890
732-571-3400

Montclair State University
Montclair State University, Montclair NJ 07043-1624
973-655-4000

New Jersey City University
2039 John F Kennedy Blvd
Jersey City NJ 07305-1588
Carmen Panlilio, Asst. V.P. for Admissions and Financial Aid
201-200-3234 Fax: 201-200-2044
Website: www.njcu.edu
E-mail: admissions@njcu.edu

Ramapo College of New Jersey
505 Ramapo Valley Rd, Mahwah NJ 07430-1623
Director of Admissions
201-684-7300 or 201-684-7301 Fax: 201-684-7964
Website: www.ramapo.edu
E-mail: admissions@ramapo.edu

RICHARD STOCKTON COLLEGE OF NEW JERSEY
PO Box 195, Pomona NJ 08240
John Iacovelli, Dean of Enrollment Management
866-RSC-2885 Fax: 609-626-5541
Website: www.stockton.edu
E-mail: admissions@stockton.edu
See listing under "Universities"

Rider University
2083 Lawrenceville Rd, Lawrenceville NJ 08648-3099
Susan Christian, Director of Admissions
609-896-5042

Rowan University
201 Mullica Hill Rd, Glassboro NJ 08028-1700
856-256-4000

St. Peter's College
2627 John F Kennedy Blvd, Jersey City NJ 07306
888-SPC-9933

Seton Hall University
400 S Orange Ave, South Orange NJ 07079-2697
973-761-9000

William Paterson University
300 Pompton Rd, Wayne NJ 07470-2103
973-720-2000

NEW MEXICO

New Mexico Highlands University
PO Box 9000, Las Vegas NM 87701
James Abreu, Contact
505-454-3357

New Mexico State University
1500 N 3rd St, Grants NM 87020-2025
Irene Lutz, Director of Admissions
505-287-7981 Fax: 505-287-2329
Website: www.grants.nmsu.edu
E-mail: ilutz@nmsu.edu

New Mexico State University
PO Box 30001, Las Cruces NM 88003-8001
505-646-0111

University of New Mexico
1 University Campus, Albuquerque NM 87131-0001
505-277-0111

NEW YORK

Adelphi University
Garden City NY 11530
516-877-3100

Alfred University
1 Saxson Dr, Alfred NY 14802
607-871-2111

Cazenovia College
Cazenovia NY 13035-1084
Robert Croot, Dean of Admissions & Financial Aid
800-654-3210

College of New Rochelle
29 Castle Pl, New Rochelle NY 10805-2339
914-654-5000

College of Saint Rose
432 Western Ave, Albany NY 12203-1419
Maryelizabeth Amico, Asst V.P. for Undergraduate Admissions
518-454-5150 Fax: 518-454-2013
Website: www.strose.edu
E-mail: admit@strose.edu

CUNY City College
Convent Ave at 138th St, New York NY 10031
Celia Lloyd, Interim Director of Admissions
212-650-6977

CUNY College of Staten Island
2800 Victory Blvd, Staten Island NY 10314-6600
718-982-2000

CUNY Hunter College
695 Park Ave, New York NY 10021
Aaron Gibbs, Assistant Director of Recruitment
212-650-3946 Fax: 212-650-3336
Website: www.hunter.cuny.edu
E-mail: aaron.gibbs@hunter.cuny.edu

CUNY York College
9420 Guy R Brewer Blvd, Jamaica NY 11451-0001
718-262-2000

Daemen College
4380 Main St, Amherst NY 14226-3592
Donna Shaffner, Director of Admissions
800-462-7652 Fax: 716-839-8229
Website: www.daemen.edu/admissions
E-mail: admissions@daemen.edu

Dominican College of Blauvelt
470 Western Hwy, Orangeburg NY 10962-1210
845-359-7800

Dowling College
150 Idle Hour Blvd, Oakdale NY 11769-1999
Diane Kazanecki-Kempter, Contact
631-244-3000 Fax: 631-244-1059
Website: www.dowling.edu
E-mail: admissions@dowling.edu

D'Youville College
320 Porter Ave, Buffalo NY 14201-1084
716-829-7600

Elmira College
1 Park Pl, Elmira NY 14901-2099
Gary Fallis, Dean of Admissions
607-735-1724

FIVE TOWNS COLLEGE
305 N Service Rd, Dix Hills NY 11746-5871
631-424-7000 ext. 2110 Fax: 631-656-2172
Website: www.fivetowns.edu
E-mail: admissions@ftc.edu
See listing under "Universities"

Fordham University
441 E Fordham Rd, Bronx NY 10458-9993
John W. Buckley, Dean of Admissions
718-817-4000

Fordham University - Lincoln Center
113 W 60th St, New York NY 10023-7484
Regis G. Bernhardt PhD, Dean
212-636-6000

Hofstra University
100 Hofstra University, Hempstead NY 11549-1000
516-463-6600

Houghton College
PO Box 128, Houghton NY 14744-0128
585-567-9200

Iona College
715 North Ave, New Rochelle NY 10801-1890
Kevin Cavanagh, Assistant V.P. for College Admissions
914-633-2502 Fax: 914-637-2778
Website: www.iona.edu

Ithaca College
953 Danby Rd, Ithaca NY 14850-7002
607-274-3011

Keuka College
PO Box 98, Keuka Park NY 14478-0098
315-536-4411

Le Moyne College
1419 Salt Springs Rd, Syracuse NY 13214-1301
800-333-4733

Long Island University
121 Speonk Riverhead Rd, Riverhead NY 11901
631-287-8010

Long Island University-C. W. Post Campus
720 Northern Blvd, Brookville NY 11548-1300
Joanne Graziano, Executive Director of Admissions
516-299-2900 Fax: 516-299-2137
Website: www.liu.edu/cwpost
E-mail: enroll@cwpost.liu.edu

Long Island University
Rockland Graduate Campus
70 Route 340, Orangeburg NY 10962-2219
Kelly J. McCafferty, M.S., Director of Admissions
845-359-7200

Manhattan College
4513 Manhattan College Pkwy
Riverdale NY 10471-4099
Dr. William Merriman, Dean of Education
718-862-7200

Manhattanville College
2900 Purchase St, Purchase NY 10577-2132
914-694-2200

Marymount College at Fordham University
100 Marymount Ave, Tarrytown NY 10591-3796
914-631-3200

Marymount Manhattan College
221 E 71st St, New York NY 10021-4501
Jim Rogers, Dean of Admissions
800-MARYMOUNT Fax: 212-517-0448
Website: www.mmm.edu
E-mail: admissions@mmm.edu

Medaille College
18 Agassiz Cir, Buffalo NY 14214-2695
716-884-3281

Mercy College
555 Broadway, Dobbs Ferry NY 10522-1189
Kathleen Jackson, Director of Admissions
800-MERCY-NY

Molloy College
1000 Hempstead Ave
Rockville Centre NY 11570-1100
Marguerite Lane, Director of Admissions
516-678-5000 ext. 6291 Fax: 516-256-2247
Website: www.molloy.edu
E-mail: admissions@molloy.edu
See listing under "Universities"

Mt. St. Mary College
330 Powell Ave, Newburgh NY 12550-3494
845-561-0800

Nazareth College of Rochester
4245 East Ave, Rochester NY 14618-3790
585-389-2525

New York Institute of Technology
PO Box 8000, Old Westbury NY 11568-8000
516-686-7516

Niagara University
PO Box 2011, Niagara University NY 14109-2011
George Pachter, Dean of Admissions & Records
800-462-2111

Nyack College
1 South Blvd
Nyack NY 10960-3698
845-358-1710

Pratt Institute
200 Willoughby Ave, Brooklyn NY 11205-3899
Heidi Metcalf, Director of Admissions
718-636-3600 Fax: 718-636-3670
Website: www.pratt.edu
E-mail: hmetcalf@pratt.edu
Art and Design Education

Roberts Wesleyan College
2301 Westside Dr, Rochester NY 14624-1997
Office of Admissions
585-594-6400 Fax: 585-594-6371
Website: www.roberts.edu
E-mail: admissions@roberts.edu

Russell Sage College
45 Ferry St, Troy NY 12180-4115
518-244-2000

St. Bonaventure University
Saint Bonaventure NY 14778-9999
585-375-2000

St. John Fisher College
3690 East Ave, Rochester NY 14618-3597
585-385-8000

St. John's University
8000 Utopia Pkwy, Queens NY 11439
Office of Admission
877-STJ-5550 ext. 101 Fax: 718-990-2096
Website: www.stjohns.edu/learnmore
E-mail: admhelp@stjohns.edu
See listing under "Universities"

St. Joseph's College
245 Clinton Ave, Brooklyn NY 11205-3688
Theresa LaRocca Meyer, V.P. for Enrollment Management
718-636-6800 Fax: 718-636-8303
Website: www.sjcny.edu
E-mail: tlaroccameyer@sjcny.edu

St. Joseph's College
155 W Roe Blvd, Patchogue NY 11772
631-447-3200

St. Lawrence University
2501 Saint Lawrence Univ, Canton NY 13617-1475
315-229-5011

Skidmore College
815 N Broadway, Saratoga Springs NY 12866-1698
518-580-5000

SUNY at Albany
1400 Washington Ave, Albany NY 12222-1000
Jonathan Bartow, Director of Graduate Studies
518-442-3980

SUNY College at Brockport
350 New Campus Dr, Brockport NY 14420-2997
Bernard S. Valento, Director of Undergraduate Admissions
585-395-2751 Fax: 585-395-5452
Website: www.brockport.edu
E-mail: admit@brockport.edu

SUNY College at Buffalo
1300 Elmwood Ave, Buffalo NY 14222-1004
716-878-4000

SUNY College at Old Westbury
PO Box 210, Old Westbury NY 11568-0210
516-876-3000

SUNY College at Potsdam
Potsdam NY 13676
Thomas W. Nesbitt, Director of Admissions
315-267-2000

SUNY Niagara County Community College
3111 Saunders Settlement Rd
Sanborn NY 14132-9487
Kathleen Saunders, Director of Admissions
716-614-6200 Fax: 716-614-6820
Website: www.niagaracc.suny.edu
E-mail: admissions@niagaracc.suny.edu

SUNY Orange County Community College
115 South St, Middletown NY 10940-6437
Margot St. Lawrence, Director of Admissions
845-341-4030 Fax: 845-342-8662
Website: www.sunyorange.edu
E-mail: apply@sunyorange.edu
See listing under "Community and Junior Colleges"

SUNY Sullivan County Community College
112 College Rd, Loch Sheldrake NY 12759-5151
Sari Rosenheck, Director of Admissions
845-434-5750 Fax: 845-434-0923
Website: www.sullivan.suny.edu
E-mail: admissions@sullivan.suny.edu
Student Housing on Campus.

Touro College
27 W 23rd St Ste 33, New York NY 10010-4202
212-463-0400

University at Buffalo, The State University of New York
15 Capen Hall, Buffalo NY 14260-1660
Patricia G. Armstrong, Director of Admissions
888-UB-ADMIT

University of Rochester
Wallis Hall, Rochester NY 14627
585-275-2121

Wagner College
One Campus Rd, Staten Island NY 10301
Leigh Ann DePascale, Director of Admissions
718-390-3411

NORTH CAROLINA

Appalachian State University
ASU Station, Boone NC 28608-0001
828-262-2000

Barton College
PO Box 5000, Wilson NC 27893
252-399-6300

Belmont Abbey College
100 Belmont Mount Holly Rd
Belmont NC 28012-1802
888-222-0110

Bennett College
900 E Washington St, Greensboro NC 27401-3298
336-273-4431

Campbell University
PO Box 546, Buies Creek NC 27506-0546
Herbert V. Kerner, Jr., Director of Admissions
800-334-4111

Catawba College
2300 W Innes St, Salisbury NC 28144-2488
Dr. L. Russell Watjen, Ph.D., V.P. & Dean of Admissions
704-637-4402 Fax: 704-637-4222
Website: www.catawba.edu
E-mail: admission@catawba.edu

Davidson College
PO Box 7156, Davidson NC 28035-7156
Chris Gruber, Acting Dean of Admission
800-768-0380

Duke University
Durham NC 27706-8001
919-684-8111

East Carolina University
Speight 154, Greenville NC 27858
Dr. Marilyn Sheerer, Dean

Elizabeth City State University
1704 Weeksville Rd, Elizabeth City NC 27909-7806
252-335-3400

Fayetteville State University
1200 Murchison Rd, Fayetteville NC 28301-4298
910-486-1111

Gardner-Webb University
PO Box 817, Boiling Springs NC 28017
704-406-2361

Greensboro College
815 W Market St, Greensboro NC 27401-1875
336-272-7102

Guilford College
5800 W Friendly Ave, Greensboro NC 27410-4173
Randy Doss, Dean of Enrollment
336-316-2100

Haywood Community College
185 Freedlander Dr, Clyde NC 28721
Debbie Rowland, Coordinator of Admissions
828-627-4500 Fax: 828-627-4513
Website: www.haywood.edu
E-mail: drowland@haywood.edu

High Point University
933 Montlieu Ave, High Point NC 27262-3598
336-841-9000

James Sprunt Community College
PO Box 398, Kenansville NC 28349-0398
Lea Grady, Admissions
910-296-2500 Fax: 910-296-1636
Website: www.jamessprunt.edu

Johnson C. Smith University
100 Beatties Ford Rd, Charlotte NC 28216-5302
704-378-1000

Lees-McRae College
PO Box 128, Banner Elk NC 28604-0128
Walt Crutchfield, Dean of Admissions
800-280-4562

Lenoir-Rhyne College
7th Ave and 8th St, Hickory NC 28603
828-328-1741

Livingstone College
701 W Monroe St, Salisbury NC 28144-5298
704-797-1000

Mars Hill College
Mars Hill NC 28754
Chad Holt, Dean of Enrollment
866-MHC-4-YOU

Meredith College
3800 Hillsborough St, Raleigh NC 27607-5298
Heidi L. Fletcher, Director of Admissions
919-760-8581

Methodist College
5400 Ramsey St, Fayetteville NC 28311-1498
910-630-7000

Montreat College
PO Box 1267, Montreat NC 28757-1267
800-622-6968

Mt. Olive College
634 Henderson St, Mount Olive NC 28365
Tim Woodard, Director of Admissions
919-658-2502

North Carolina A&T State University
1601 E Market St, Greensboro NC 27411
Lee Young, AVC Enrollment
336-334-7500

North Carolina Central University
PO Box 19617, Durham NC 27707-0022
919-560-6100

North Carolina State University
PO Box 7001, Raleigh NC 27695-0001
919-515-2011

North Carolina Wesleyan College
3400 N Wesleyan Blvd, Rocky Mount NC 27804-8677
252-985-5100

Peace College
15 E Peace St, Raleigh NC 27604-1194
Laura C. Bingham, President
800-PEACE-47 Fax: 919-508-2306
Website: www.peace.edu
E-mail: admissions@peace.edu

Pfeiffer University
PO Box 960, Misenheimer NC 28109-0960
704-463-1360

Queens University of Charlotte
1900 Selwyn Ave, Charlotte NC 28274-0002
704-337-2212

St. Andrews Presbyterian College
1700 Dogwood Mile St, Laurinburg NC 28352-5521
Glenn Batten, Vice President for Enrollment
910-277-5554

St. Augustine's College
1315 Oakwood Ave, Raleigh NC 27610-2298
919-516-4000

Salem College
Winston Salem NC 27108
Dana Evans, Dean of Admissions/Fin. Aid
800-32-SALEM Fax: 336-917-5572
Website: www.salem.edu
E-mail: admissions@salem.edu
See listing under "Women's Colleges"

Shaw University
118 E South St, Raleigh NC 27601-2399
919-546-8200

University of North Carolina
1 University Hts, Asheville NC 28804-3251
828-251-6600

University of North Carolina
Chapel Hill NC 27599-0001
919-962-2211

University of North Carolina
9201 University City Blvd, Charlotte NC 28223
704-547-2000

University of North Carolina
601 S College Rd, Wilmington NC 28403-3201
910-962-3000

University of North Carolina at Greensboro
1000 Spring Garden St, Greensboro NC 27412-0001
336-334-5243

University of North Carolina at Pembroke
PO Box 1510, Pembroke NC 28372-1510
910-521-6000

Wake Forest University
PO Box 7305, Winston Salem NC 27109-7305
336-759-5000

Warren Wilson College
PO Box 9000, Asheville NC 28815-9000
Richard Blomgren, Dean of Admissions
828-298-3325

Western Carolina University
University Dr, Cullowhee NC 28723-9646
828-227-7211

Wingate University
201 E Wilson St, Wingate NC 28174-9600
704-233-8000

Winston-Salem State University
601 S Mrtn Lther King Jr Dr
Winston Salem NC 27110-0003
336-750-2000

NORTH DAKOTA

Dickinson State University
Dickinson ND 58601-4896
Steve Glasser, Director of Enrollment Services
800-279-4295 Fax: 701-483-2409
Website: www.dickinsonstate.edu
E-mail: dsu.hawks@dickinsonstate.edu

Jamestown College
6000 College Ln, Jamestown ND 58405-0002
701-252-3467

Mayville State University
330 3rd St NE, Mayville ND 58257-1299
Dr. Ray Gerszewski, Vice President Student Affairs
800-437-4104 Fax: 701-788-4748
Website: www.mayvillestate.edu
E-mail: admit@mayvillestate.edu

Minot State University
500 University Ave W, Minot ND 58707-0002
Dennis Parisien, Enrollment Services Rep.
800-777-0750 ext. 3350

North Dakota State University
Fargo ND 58105
701-237-7211

University of Mary
7500 University Dr, Bismarck ND 58504-9652
701-255-7500

University of North Dakota
Box 8193 University Station, Grand Forks ND 58203
701-777-2011

Valley City State University
101 College St SW, Valley City ND 58072-4024
Dan Klein, Director of Enrollment Services
800-532-8641 ext. 7101 Fax: 701-845-7299
Website: www.vcsu.edu
E-mail: enrollment.services@vcsu.edu
See listing under "Universities"

OHIO

Ashland University
401 College Ave, Ashland OH 44805-3799
419-289-4142

Baldwin-Wallace College
275 Eastland Rd, Berea OH 44017-2088
440-826-2900

Bowling Green State University
110 McFall Center, Bowling Green OH 43403-0001
866-CHOOSE-BGSU

Capital University
2199 E Main St, Columbus OH 43209-2394
614-236-6011

Cedarville University
251 N Main St, Cedarville OH 45314
937-766-2211

Cincinnati Christian University
2700 Glenway, Cincinnati OH 45204
Erin Oppy, Executive Director of Undergraduate Admissions
513-244-8141 Fax: 513-244-8453
Website: www.ccuniversity.edu

Cleveland State University
2121 Euclid Ave RW 204, Cleveland OH 44115
Dr. Richard Arndt, Dean of Undergraduate Recruitment and College Partnerships
888-CSU-OHIO Fax: 216-687-9210
Website: www.csuohio.edu
E-mail: admissions@csuohio.edu

College of Wooster
Wooster OH 44691-2363
Paul J. Deutsch, Dean of Admissions
800-877-9905

Defiance College
701 N Clinton St, Defiance OH 43512-1695
419-784-4010

Denison University
PO Box B, Granville OH 43023-0603
740-587-0810

Franciscan University of Steubenville
University Blvd, Steubenville OH 43952
Margaret J. Weber, Director of Admissions
800-783-6220 or 740-283-6226 Fax: 740-284-5456
Website: www.admissions.edu
E-mail: mweber@franciscan.edu

Heidelberg College
310 E Market St, Tiffin OH 44883-2462
418-448-2000

John Carroll University
20700 N Park Blvd, Cleveland OH 44118-4581
216-397-1886

Kent State University
PO Box 5190, Kent OH 44242-0001
Paul Deutsch, Director of Admissions
330-672-2444

Lake Erie College
391 W Washington St, Painesville OH 44077-3389
440-352-3361

Malone College
515 25th St NW, Canton OH 44709-3897
John Chopka, Dean of Admissions
330-471-8100

Miami University
E High St, Oxford OH 45056
513-529-2531

Mt. Union College
1972 Clark Ave, Alliance OH 44601-3929
Vincent Heslop, Director of Admissions
800-334-6682

Mount Vernon Nazarene University
800 Martinsburg Rd, Mount Vernon OH 43050-9509
Timothy Eades, Director of Admissions
866-462-6868

Muskingum College
147 Center St, New Concord OH 43762-1193
740-826-8211

Ohio Dominican University
1216 Sunbury Rd, Columbus OH 43219-2099
614-253-2741

OHIO NORTHERN UNIVERSITY
525 S Main St, Ada OH 45810-1555
Tena Roepke, Director of the Center for Teacher Education
419-772-2118
Website: www.onu.edu
E-mail: admissions-ug@onu.edu
See listing under "Universities"

The Ohio State University
School of Teaching and Learning
Arps Hall, 1945 North High St, Columbus OH 43210
614-292-2581 Fax: 614-292-7695
Website: coe.ohio-state.edu
E-mail: edtl-oas@osu.edu

Ohio State University-Marion
1465 Mount Vernon Ave, Marion OH 43302-5695
740-389-6786

Ohio University - Zanesville Branch
1425 Newark Rd, Zanesville OH 43701-2695
740-588-1439

Otterbein College
78 W Home St, Westerville OH 43081-1489
614-890-3000

Owens Community College
3200 Bright Rd, Findlay OH 45840
William J. Ivoska PhD., Vice President of Student Services
567-429-3500 Fax: 567-423-0246
Website: www.owens.edu
E-mail: admissions@owens.edu

Owens Community College
PO Box 10000, Toledo OH 43699-1947
William J. Ivoska, Ph.D, Vice President of Student Services
567-661-7000 Fax: 567-661-7607
Website: www.owens.edu
E-mail: admissions@owens.edu

Shawnee State University
940 2nd St, Portsmouth OH 45662-4344
740-354-3205

University of Akron
381 Buchtel Mall, Akron OH 44304-1584
330-972-7111

University of Cincinnati
2700 Clifton Ave, Cincinnati OH 45220-2873
513-556-6000

University of Dayton
300 College Park, Dayton OH 45469-1300
Robert F. Durkle, Director of Admission
800-837-7433 Fax: 937-229-4729
Website: admission.udayton.edu
E-mail: admission@udayton.edu

University of Findlay
1000 N Main St, Findlay OH 45840-3695
419-422-8313

University of Rio Grande
General Delivery, Rio Grande OH 45674-9999
H. Paul Lloyd, Dean
740-245-5353 ext. 7328

University of Toledo
2801 W Bancroft St, Toledo OH 43606-3390
419-530-4636

Urbana University
579 College Way, Urbana OH 43078
937-484-1301

Ursuline College
2550 Lander Rd, Cleveland OH 44124-4398
Sarah E. Sundermeier, Director of Admissions
888-URSULINE Toll Free Fax: 440-684-6138
Website: www.admission.ursuline.edu
E-mail: admission@ursuline.edu

Walsh University
2020 E Maple St, North Canton OH 44720
800-362-9846

Wilmington College
1870 Quaker Way, Wilmington OH 45177
937-382-6661

Wittenberg University
PO Box 720, Springfield OH 45501-0720
937-327-6231

Wright State University
3640 Colonel Glenn Hwy, Dayton OH 45435-0002
937-775-3333

Youngstown State University
Sweeney Welcome Ctr, One University Plz
Youngstown OH 44555-0002
Sue Davis, Contact
877-GO-TO-YSU

OKLAHOMA

Bacone College
2299 Old Bacone Rd, Muskogee OK 74403-1568
Jerrett Phillips, Director of Admissions
918-781-7340

Cameron University
2800 W Gore Blvd, Lawton OK 73505-6377
580-581-2200

East Central University
1100 E 14th St
Ada OK 74820-6999
Pamla Armstrong, Director of Admissions
580-332-8000

Langston University
PO Box 907, Langston OK 73050-0907
405-466-2231

Mid-America Christian University
3500 SW 119th St, Oklahoma City OK 73170-4504
Haley Hope, Director of Admissions
405-691-3800 Fax: 405-692-3165
Website: www.macu.edu
E-mail: info@macu.edu

Northeastern State University
600 N Grand Ave, Tahlequah OK 74464-2301
918-456-5511

Northwestern Oklahoma State University
709 Oklahoma Blvd, Alva OK 73717
580-327-1700

Oklahoma Baptist University
500 W University St, Shawnee OK 74804-2590
405-275-2850

Oklahoma Christian University
PO Box 11000, Oklahoma City OK 73136-1100
405-425-5000

Oklahoma City University
2501 N Blackwelder Ave
Oklahoma City OK 73106-1493
Shery Boyles, Director of Admissions
405-521-5050

Oklahoma Panhandle State University
PO Box 430, Goodwell OK 73939-0430
580-349-2611

Oklahoma State University
Stillwater OK 74078
Kathy.Boyer, Coordinator
405-744-6350
Website: www.okstate.edu
E-mail: kathy.boyer@okstate.edu

Oklahoma Wesleyan University
2201 Silver Lake Rd, Bartlesville OK 74006-6299
918-333-6151

Oral Roberts University
7777 S Lewis Ave, Tulsa OK 74171-0001
Chris Belcher, Director of Undergraduate Admissions
800-678-8876

Southeastern Oklahoma State University
Station A, Durant OK 74701
580-924-0121

Southern Nazarene University
6729 NW 39th Expy, Bethany OK 73008-2694
405-789-6400

Southwestern Oklahoma State University
100 Campus Dr, Weatherford OK 73096-3098
580-772-6611

University of Central Oklahoma
100 N University Dr, Edmond OK 73034-5209
405-974-2000

University of Oklahoma at Norman
660 Parrington Oval, Norman OK 73019-3070
405-325-0311

University of Sciences & Arts of OK
PO Box 82345, Chickasha OK 73018
405-224-3140

University of Tulsa
600 S College Ave, Tulsa OK 74104-3126
Earl Johnson, Dean of Admission
918-631-2307 Fax: 918-631-5003
Website: www.utulsa.edu
E-mail: admission@utulsa.edu

OREGON

Cascade College
9101 E Burnside St, Portland OR 97216-1599
Jim Murphy, Director of Enrollment Management
800-550-7678 Fax: 503-257-1222
Website: www.cascade.edu
E-mail: admissions@cascade.edu

Corban College
5000 Deer Park Dr SE, Salem OR 97317-9330
503-581-8600

Lewis & Clark College
0615 SW Palatine Hill Rd, Portland OR 97219-7899
503-768-7000

Linfield College
900 SE Baker St, Mc Minnville OR 97128-6894
503-472-2200

Marylhurst University
17600 Pacific Hwy (Hwy 43)
Marylhurst OR 97036-0261
Director of Admissions
800-634-9982 ext. 6268 Fax: 503-635-6585
Website: www.marylhurst.edu
E-mail: studentinfo@marylhurst.edu

Oregon State University
Corvallis OR 97333-9800
541-737-0123

PACIFIC UNIVERSITY
2043 College Way, Forest Grove OR 97116-1797
Karen M. Dunston, Executive Director of Admissions
800-677-6712 Fax: 503-352-2975
Website: www.pacific.edu
E-mail: admissions@pacific.edu

Portland State University
PO Box 751, Portland OR 97207-0751
503-725-3000

Southern Oregon University
1250 Siskiyou Blvd, Ashland OR 97520-5010
541-552-7672

University of Portland
5000 N Willamette Blvd, Portland OR 97203-5798
Jason McDonald, Dean of Admissions
503-943-7911 Fax: 503-943-7315
Website: www.up.edu
E-mail: mcdonaja@up.edu

Warner Pacific College
2219 SE 68th Ave, Portland OR 97215-4026
Shannon Mackey, Director of Admissions
503-517-1000 Fax: 503-517-1352
Website: www.warnerpacific.edu
E-mail: admissions@warnerpacific.edu

Western Oregon University
345 Monmouth Ave N, Monmouth OR 97361-1314
David McDonald, Dean, Admission, Retention & Enrollment Management
877-877-1593

PENNSYLVANIA

Albright College
PO Box 15234, Reading PA 19612-5234
800-252-1856

Allegheny College
520 N Main St, Meadville PA 16335-3902
814-332-3100

Alvernia College
400 Saint Bernardine St, Reading PA 19607
610-796-8200

Arcadia University
450 S Easton Rd, Glenside PA 19038-3295
Dennis Nostrand, VP for Enrollment Management
877-ARCADIA (877-272-2342)

Bloomsburg University of Pennsylvania
400 E 2nd St, Bloomsburg PA 17815-1399
570-389-4000

California University of Pennsylvania
250 University Ave, California PA 15419-1394
724-938-4000

Carlow University
3333 5th Ave, Pittsburgh PA 15213-3165
412-578-6000

Cedar Crest College
100 College Dr, Allentown PA 18104-6196
Judith A. Neyhart, Vice President Enrollment
800-360-1222

Chatham College
Woodland Rd, Pittsburgh PA 15232-2826
412-365-1100

Chestnut Hill College
9601 Germantown Ave, Philadelphia PA 19118-2693
Jodie King, Director of Admissions
215-248-7001

Cheyney University of Pennsylvania
PO Box 200, Cheyney PA 19319-0200
610-399-2275

Clarion University of Pennsylvania
840 Wood St, Clarion PA 16214-1232
William Bailey, Dean of Enrollment Management
814-393-2306 Fax: 814-393-2030
Website: www.clarion.edu
E-mail: admissions@clarion.edu

College Misericordia
301 Lake St, Dallas PA 18612-1008
Admissions
570-674-6400

Community College of Allegheny County
Allegheny Campus: 808 Ridge Ave, Pittsburgh PA 15212 Admissions: 412.237.2700
Boyce Campus: 595 Beatty Rd, Monroeville PA 15146 Admissions: 724.325.6614
North Campus: 8701 Perry Highway, Pittsburgh PA 15237 Admissions: 412.369.3600
South Campus: 1750 Clairton Rd, West Mifflin PA 15122 Admissions: 412-469-4301
Website: www.ccac.edu

Drexel University
3141 Chestnut St, Philadelphia PA 19104-2875
Dana R. Davies, Director of Undergraduate Enrollment
800-2-DREXEL

Duquesne University
600 Forbes Ave, Pittsburgh PA 15282-0001
Paul-James Cukanna, Director of Admissions
412-396-5000

Eastern University
1300 Eagle Rd, Saint Davids PA 19087-3696
610-341-5800

East Stroudsburg University of PA
200 Prospect St
East Stroudsburg PA 18301
570-424-3211

Edinboro University of Pennsylvania
Edinboro PA 16444-0001
814-732-2000

Elizabethtown College
1 Alpha Dr, Elizabethtown PA 17022-2298
717-361-1000

Gannon University
109 University Sq, Erie PA 16541-0001
Christopher Tremblay, Director of Admissions
800-GANNON-U

Geneva College
3200 College Ave, Beaver Falls PA 15010-3599
724-846-5100

Gratz College
7605 Old York Rd, Melrose Park PA 19027
Jill Sigman, Director of Admissions
215-635-7300 Fax: 215-635-7320
Website: www.gratzcollege.edu
E-mail: admissions@gratz.edu

Gwynedd-Mercy College
1325 Sumneytown Pike, Gwynedd Valley PA 19437
Dennis Murphy, V.P. Enrollment Management
800-DIAL-GMC

Holy Family University
9801 Frankford Avenue, Philadelphia PA 19114
Lauren Campbell, Director of Admissions
215-637-3050 Fax: 215-281-1022
Website: www.holyfamily.edu
E-mail: admissions@holyfamily.edu

Immaculata University
Immaculata PA 19345
Women's College Office of Admissions
610-647-4400

Indiana University of Pennsylvania
Indiana PA 15705-0001
724-357-2100

Juniata College
1700 Moore St, Huntingdon PA 16652-2196
Michelle Bartol, Dean of Enrollment
877-JUNIATA Fax: 814-641-3100
Website: www.juniata.edu
E-mail: admissions@juniata.edu

King's College
133 N River St, Wilkes Barre PA 18711-0801
Michelle Lawrence-Schmude, Dean of Admission
570-208-5900 Fax: 570-208-5971
Website: www.kings.edu
E-mail: admissions@kings.edu

Kutztown University of Pennsylvania
Kutztown PA 19530
610-683-4000

Lancaster Bible College
901 Eden Rd, Lancaster PA 17601-5036
Joanne M. Roper, Associate VP for Admissions
866-LBC-4YOU or 717-560-8271 Fax: 717-560-8213
Website: www.lbc.edu
E-mail: admissions@lbc.edu
See listing under "Theological Studies & Religious Vocations"

La Roche College
9000 Babcock Blvd, Pittsburgh PA 15237-5898
Thomas Hassett, Director of Admissions
412-536-1272

La Salle University
1900 W Olney Ave, Philadelphia PA 19141-1199
Robert Voss, Dean of Admissions
215-951-1500

Lebanon Valley College
101 N College Ave, Annville PA 17003-1400
William Brown, Dean of Admissions & Financial Aid
866-LVC-4ADM

Lock Haven University
Lock Haven PA 17745
James C. Reeser, Dean of Admissions
570-893-2027

Lycoming College
700 College Pl, Williamsport PA 17701-5192
570-321-4000

Mansfield University of Pennsylvania
Academy St, Mansfield PA 16933
570-662-4000

Marywood University
2300 Adams Ave, Scranton PA 18509-1598
570-348-6211

Mercyhurst College
501 E 38th St, Erie PA 16546-0001
800-825-1926

Millersville University of Pennsylvania
PO Box 1002, Millersville PA 17551-0302
717-872-3024

MOUNT ALOYSIUS COLLEGE
7373 Admiral Peary Hwy, Cresson PA 16630-1999
Frank C. Crouse Jr., Vice President for Enrollment Management
814-886-6383 or 888-823-2220 Fax: 814-886-6441
Website: www.mtaloy.edu
E-mail: admissions@mtaloy.edu

Muhlenberg College
2400 W Chew St, Allentown PA 18104-5586
610-821-3100

Neumann College
1 Neumann Dr, Aston PA 19014-1298
Dennis Murphy, Director of Admissions
610-459-0905 Fax: 610-558-5652
Website: www.neumann.edu
E-mail: neumann@neumann.edu

Pennsylvania State University
Broadhead Rd, Monaca PA 15061
724-773-3500

Pennsylvania State University
201 Shields Bldg PO Box 300
University Park PA 16802-3000
814-865-4700

Point Park University
201 Wood St, Pittsburgh PA 15222-1984
Philip Clarke, Associate Director of Admissions
412-392-3430

Robert Morris College
600 5th Ave, Pittsburgh PA 15219-3010
412-227-6800

Robert Morris University
6001 University Blvd, Coraopolis PA 15108
412-262-8200

Rosemont College
1400 Montgomery Ave, Rosemont PA 19010-1699
Ms. Rennie Andrews, Director of Admissions
610-526-2966

St. Francis University
PO Box 600, Loretto PA 15940-0600
814-472-3000

St. Vincent College
300 Fraser Purchase Rd, Latrobe PA 15650-2690
724-539-9761

Seton Hill University
Greensburg PA 15601-1599
Mary Kay Cooper, Director of Admissions and Adult Student Services
800-826-6234

Shippensburg University
1871 Old Main Dr, Shippensburg PA 17257-2299
717-477-7447

Slippery Rock University
14 Maltby Dr, Slippery Rock PA 16057-1326
724-738-9000

Susquehanna University
514 University Ave, Selinsgrove PA 17870-1164
570-374-0101

Temple University
Broad St & Montgomery Ave, Philadelphia PA 19122
215-204-7000

Thiel College
75 College Ave, Greenville PA 16125-2181
724-589-2000

University of Pennsylvania
3400 Spruce St, Philadelphia PA 19104-4274
215-898-5000

University of Pittsburgh
150 Finoli Dr, Greensburg PA 15601
Brandi S. Darr, Director of Admissions and Financial Aid
724-836-9880

University of Pittsburgh at Bradford
300 Campus Dr, Bradford PA 16701-2812
Alexander Nazemetz, Director of Admissions
814-362-7555

University of Scranton
800 Linden St, Scranton PA 18510-4501
570-941-7400

Villanova University
800 E Lancaster Ave, Villanova PA 19085
610-519-4500

Washington & Jefferson College
60 S Lincoln St, Washington PA 15301-4801
Alton E. Newell, Vice President for Enrollment
724-223-6025 Fax: 724-223-6534
Website: www.washjeff.edu
E-mail: admission@washjeff.edu

Waynesburg College
51 W College St, Waynesburg PA 15370-1222
Robin L. Moore, Dean of Admissions
800-225-7393

West Chester University of Pennsylvania
S High St, West Chester PA 19383-0001
610-436-1000

Widener University
1 University Pl, Chester PA 19013-5792
Edwin Wright, Dean of Admissions
610-499-4000 Fax: 610-499-4676
Website: www.widener.edu
E-mail: admissions.office@widener.edu

Wilkes University
170 S Franklin St, Wilkes Barre PA 18766-0001
570-408-5000

York College of Pennsylvania
PO Box 15199, York PA 17405-7199
717-846-7788

RHODE ISLAND

Providence College
549 River Ave, Providence RI 02918-0002
401-865-1000

Rhode Island College
600 Mount Pleasant Ave, Providence RI 02908-1924
401-456-8000

Salve Regina University
100 Ochre Point Ave, Newport RI 02840-4192
401-847-6650

University of Rhode Island
Kingston RI 02881
401-874-1000

SOUTH CAROLINA

Benedict College
1600 Harden St, Columbia SC 29204-1086
Phyllis L. Thompson, Director of Admissions
803-253-5143

Charleston Southern University
PO Box 118087, Charleston SC 29423-8087
Cheryl Burton, Director of Admissions
800-947-7474

The Citadel
171 Moultrie St, Charleston SC 29409-0002
843-953-5000

Clemson University
105 Sikes Hall, Clemson SC 29634
864-656-2287

Coastal Carolina University
PO Box 261954, Conway SC 29528-6054
Office of Admissions
800-277-7000 Fax: 843-349-2127
Website: www.coastal.edu
E-mail: admissions@coastal.edu

College of Charleston
66 George St, Charleston SC 29424-1407
Suzette Stille, Admissions
843-953-5670

Columbia College
1301 Columbia College Dr, Columbia SC 29203-5998
Elizabeth G. Quackenbush, Director of Admissions
803-786-3871

Columbia International University
PO Box 3122, Columbia SC 29230-3122
Michelle MacGregor, Director of University Admissions
800-777-2227 Fax: 803-786-4209
Website: www.ciu.edu
E-mail: yesciu@ciu.edu
See listing under "Theological Studies & Religious Vocations"

Converse College
580 E Main St, Spartanburg SC 29302-0006
864-596-9000

Erskine College & Seminary
PO Box 176, Due West SC 29639
Bart Walker, Director of Admissions
864-379-8838 Fax: 864-379-3048
Website: www.erskine.edu
E-mail: admissions@erskine.edu

Francis Marion University
PO Box 100547, Florence SC 29501-0547
843-661-1362

Furman University
3300 Poinsett Hwy, Greenville SC 29613-0002
864-294-2000

Lander University
320 Stanley Ave, Greenwood SC 29649-2099
Jonathan Reece, Director of Admissions
888-4-LANDER

Limestone College
1115 College Dr, Gaffney SC 29340-3799
Chris Phenicie, V.P. for Enrollment
864-489-7151 Fax: 864-488-8206
Website: www.limestone.edu
E-mail: cphenicie@limestone.edu

Morris College
100 W College St, Sumter SC 29150-3599
803-934-3200

Newberry College
2100 College St, Newberry SC 29108-2197
800-845-4955

North Greenville University
PO Box 1892, Tigerville SC 29688-1892
Dr. Richard Nesmith, Dean
Website: www.ngu.edu
See listing under "Universities"

Presbyterian College
503 S Broad St, Clinton SC 29325
Richard Dana Paul, Dean of Admissions
800-476-7272

South Carolina State University
PO Box 7127, Orangeburg SC 29117-0001
Lillian M. Adderson, Director of Admissions
803-536-7185

Southern Wesleyan University
PO Box 1020, Central SC 29630-1020
864-644-5000

University of South Carolina
Columbia SC 29208-0001
803-777-7700

University of South Carolina - Upstate
800 University Way, Spartanburg SC 29303-4932
Donette Stewart, Assistant VC for Enrollment Services
864-503-5246 Fax: 864-503-5727
Website: www.uscupstate.edu
E-mail: dstewart@uscupstate.edu
See listing under "Universities"

Winthrop University
701 W Oakland Ave, Rock Hill SC 29733-0001
803-323-2211

Wofford College
429 N Church St, Spartanburg SC 29303-3663
864-597-4000

SOUTH DAKOTA

Augustana College
29th and South Smt, Sioux Falls SD 57197-0001
605-274-0770

Black Hills State University
1200 University St, Spearfish SD 57799-0002
605-642-6011

Dakota State University
820 N Washington Ave, Madison SD 57042-1799
605-256-5112

Dakota Wesleyan University
1200 W University Ave, Mitchell SD 57301
605-995-2600

Mt. Marty College
1105 W 8th St, Yankton SD 57078-3724
605-668-1514

South Dakota State University
PO Box 2201, Brookings SD 57007-0001
605-688-4151

University of Sioux Falls
1101 W 22nd St, Sioux Falls SD 57105-1699
605-331-5000

University of South Dakota
414 E Clark St, Vermillion SD 57069-2307
605-677-5011

TENNESSEE

Aquinas College
4210 Harding Rd, Nashville TN 37205
Diane C. LeJeune, Director of Admissions
615-297-7545 ext. 460 Fax: 615-279-3893
Website: www.aquinascollege.edu
E-mail: lejeuned@aquinascollege.edu

Austin Peay State University
601 College St, Clarksville TN 37044-0002
931-221-7011 Fax: 931-221-6168
Website: www.apsu.edu
E-mail: admissions@apsu.edu

Belmont University
1900 Belmont Blvd, Nashville TN 37212-3757
615-460-6000

Bryan College
PO Box 7000, Dayton TN 37321-7000
423-775-2041

Carson-Newman College
1646 Russell Ave, Jefferson City TN 37760
865-471-4000

Christian Brothers University
650 E Parkway S, Memphis TN 38104-5568
901-321-3000

Crichton College
255 N Highland St, Memphis TN 38111-4745
Shelly Luttrell, Dean of Admissions
901-320-9797 Fax: 901-320-9791
Website: www.crichton.edu
E-mail: admissions@crichton.edu

East Tennessee State University
PO Box 70685, Johnson City TN 37614
Dr. Martha Collins, Dean of Education
423-439-7626

Freed-Hardeman University
158 E Main St, Henderson TN 38340-2398
731-989-6000

King College
1350 King College Rd, Bristol TN 37620-2635
423-968-1187

Lee University
PO Box 3450, Cleveland TN 37320-3450
Debbie Murray, Dean of the College of Education
800-533-9930

Le Moyne-Owen College
807 Walker Ave, Memphis TN 38126-6595
901-774-9090

Lincoln Memorial University
PO Box 2012, Harrogate TN 37752
423-869-3611

Lipscomb University
3901 Granny White Pike, Nashville TN 37204-3951
Ricky Holaway, Director of Admissions
800-333-4358 ext. 1776 Fax: 615-269-1804
Website: www.lipscomb.edu
E-mail: admissions@lipscomb.edu

Maryville College
502 E Lamar Alexander Pkwy
Maryville TN 37804-5919
865-981-8000

Middle Tennessee State University
1301 E Main St, Murfreesboro TN 37132-0001
615-898-2300

Milligan College
1 Milligan College, Milligan College TN 37682
423-461-8700

Peabody College of Vanderbilt University
Box 327, Nashville TN 37203
615-322-8410

Tennessee State University
3500 John A Merritt Blvd, Nashville TN 37209-1561
John Cade, Dean of Admissions & Records
615-963-5101 Fax: 615-963-2930
Website: www.tnstate.edu
E-mail: jcade@tnstate.edu

Tennessee Technological University
PO Box 5006, Cookeville TN 38505-0001
931-372-3101

Tennessee Temple University
1815 Union Ave, Chattanooga TN 37404-3587
423-493-4100

Trevecca Nazarene University
333 Murfreesboro Rd, Nashville TN 37210-2834
615-248-1200

Tusculum College
PO Box 5051, Greeneville TN 37743
Melissa Ripley, Associate Director of Admissions
800-729-0256

Union University
1050 Union University Dr, Jackson TN 38305
731-668-1818

University of Memphis
Memphis TN 38152-0001
901-678-2000

University of Tennessee
615 McCallie Ave, Chattanooga TN 37403-2504
Yancy Freeman, Director of Admissions
423-425-4111 Fax: 423-425-4157
Website: www.utc.edu
E-mail: Yancy-Freeman@utc.edu

University of Tennessee
527 Andy Holt Tower, Knoxville TN 37996-0001
865-974-1000

University of Tennessee
Martin TN 38238-0001
731-587-7000

TEXAS

Abilene Christian University
ACU Box 29000, Abilene TX 79699-0001
325-674-2000 Fax: 325-674-2202
Website: www.acu.edu
E-mail: info@admissions.acu.edu

Angelo State University
ASU Station 11014, San Angelo TX 76909
Bonnie Stennett, Coordinator of Recruiting
800-946-8627

Arlington Baptist College
3001 W Division St, Arlington TX 76012-3425
Janie Taylor, Director of Admissions
817-461-8741 Fax: 817-274-1138
Website: www.abconline.edu
E-mail: jhall@abconline.org

Austin College
900 N Grand Ave, Sherman TX 75090-4400
903-813-2000

Baylor University
Po Box 97008, Waco TX 76798-7008
254-710-1011

Concordia University
3400 N I H 35, Austin TX 78705-2702
512-486-2000

Dallas Baptist University
3000 Mountain Creek Pkwy, Dallas TX 75211-9209
214-333-7100

East Texas Baptist University
1209 N Grove St, Marshall TX 75670-1498
903-935-7963

Lamar University
PO Box 10009, Beaumont TX 77710-0009
409-880-8661

Midwestern State University
3410 Taft Blvd, Wichita Falls TX 76308-2096
940-397-4000

Our Lady of the Lake University
411 SW 24th St, San Antonio TX 78207-4666
Mary Kay Cooper, Dean of Enrollment
210-434-6711

Prairie View A&M University
PO Box 519, Prairie View TX 77446
936-857-3311

St. Edward's University
3001 S Congress Ave, Austin TX 78704-6489
512-448-8400

St. Mary's University of San Antonio
1 Camino Santa Maria St
San Antonio TX 78228-8500
210-436-3011

Sam Houston State University
PO Box 2026, Huntsville TX 77341
936-294-1111

Schreiner University
2100 Memorial Blvd, Kerrville TX 78028-5697
Todd D. Brown, Director of Admissions
800-343-4919

Southern Methodist University
PO Box 750181, Dallas TX 75275-0181
Ron Moss, Dean of Admission
214-768-2058

Stephen F. Austin State University
PO Box 6078, Nacogdoches TX 75962-0001
936-468-2011

Texas A&M University
College Station TX 77843-0001
979-845-3211

Texas A&M University
700 University Blvd, Kingsville TX 78363
361-593-2111

Texas A&M University - Corpus Christi
6300 Ocean Dr, Corpus Christi TX 78412-5503
361-825-5700

Texas Christian University
TCU Box 297013, Fort Worth TX 76129
817-257-7000

Texas Lutheran University
1000 W Court St, Seguin TX 78155-5978
830-372-8000

Texas Southern University
3100 Cleburne St, Houston TX 77004-4583
713-313-7011

Texas Tech University
1 Texas Tech University, Lubbock TX 79409-0001
806-742-2011

Texas Wesleyan University
1201 Wesleyan St, Fort Worth TX 76105-1536
Stephanie Boatner, Director of Freshman Admission
800-580-8980

Texas Woman's University
PO Box 425589, Denton TX 76204-5589
Erma Nieto-Brecht, Director of Admissions
866-809-6130 Fax: 940-898-3081
Website: www.twu.edu
E-mail: admissions@twu.edu

Trinity University
715 Stadium Dr, San Antonio TX 78212-7200
210-999-7011

University of Dallas
1845 E Northgate Dr, Irving TX 75062-4736
Curt Eley, Dean
972-721-5000 Fax: 972-721-5017
Website: www.udallas.edu
E-mail: ugadmis@udallas.edu

University of Houston
122 E Cullen Bldg, Houston TX 77204-2023
Office of Admission
713-743-9595
Website: www.uh.edu
E-mail: admissions@uh.edu

University of Houston-Clear Lake
2700 Bay Area Blvd, Houston TX 77058-1025
281-283-2500

University of Mary Hardin-Baylor
UMHB Station Box 8001, Belton TX 76513
254-295-8642

University of St. Thomas
3800 Montrose Blvd, Houston TX 77006-4626
Eduardo Prieto, Director of Admissions
713-522-7911

University of Texas at Arlington
Box 19111, Arlington TX 76019-0111
Hans Gatterdam, Director of Admission
817-272-6287 Fax: 817-272-3435
Website: www.uta.edu
E-mail: admissions@uta.edu

University of Texas at Austin
0 the Univ of Texas, Austin TX 78712
512-471-3434

University of Texas at San Antonio
6900 N Loop 1604 W, San Antonio TX 78249-1130
210-458-4011

University of Texas at Tyler
3900 University Blvd, Tyler TX 75701-6622
Jim Hutto, Dean Enrollment Management
800-888-9537

University of the Incarnate Word
4301 Broadway St, San Antonio TX 78209-6318
210-829-6000

Wayland Baptist University
1900 W 7th St, Plainview TX 79072-6998
806-296-5521

West Texas A & M University
WTAMU Box 907, Canyon TX 79016-0001
806-651-2000

UTAH

Brigham Young University
Provo UT 84602-0001
801-378-5000

Southern Utah University
351 W Center St, Cedar City UT 84720-2470
Prent Klag, Dept. Chair
435-586-7803

University of Utah
1460 E 201 S, Salt Lake City UT 84112
801-581-7200

Utah State University
Logan UT 84322-0001
435-797-1000

Westminster College
1840 S 1300 E, Salt Lake City UT 84105-3617
801-832-2200

VERMONT

Bennington College
One College Drive, Bennington VT 05201
Ken Himmelman, Dean of Admissions & Financial Aid
800-833-6845

Castleton State College
Castleton VT 05735
William Allen Jr., Dean of Enrollment
800-639-8521

College of St. Joseph
71 Clement Rd, Rutland VT 05701-3899
802-773-5900

Goddard College
121 Pitkin Rd, Plainfield VT 05667
802-454-8311

Green Mountain College
1 College Cir, Poultney VT 05764-1199
Sandra Bartholomew, Ph.D., Dean of Enrollment Management
802-287-8000 Fax: 802-287-8099
Website: www.greenmtn.edu
E-mail: bartholomews@greenmtn.edu

Johnson State College
337 College Hill, Johnson VT 05656
802-635-2356

Lyndon State College
PO Box 919, Lyndonville VT 05851
802-626-6200

NORWICH UNIVERSITY
158 Harmon Dr, Northfield VT 05663
Dr. Diane Byrne, Program Director
800-468-6679 Fax: 802-485-2364
Website: www.norwich.edu
E-mail: dbryne@norwich.edu

Saint Michael's College
One Winooski Park, Colchester VT 05439-0001
Jacqueline Murphy, Director
802-654-3000

University of Vermont
194 S Prospect St, Burlington VT 05401-3518
802-656-3131

VIRGINIA

Averett University
420 W Main St, Danville VA 24541-3692
434-791-5600

Bluefield College
3000 College Dr, Bluefield VA 24605-1799
276-326-3682

Bridgewater College
402 E College St, Bridgewater VA 22812-1599
540-828-8000

Christopher Newport University
1 University Pl, Newport News VA 23606
757-594-7000

College of William and Mary
PO Box 8795, Williamsburg VA 23187-8795
757-221-4000

Eastern Mennonite University
1200 Park Rd, Harrisonburg VA 22802-2404
540-432-4000

Emory & Henry College
PO Box 947, Emory VA 24327-0947
276-944-4121

Ferrum College
PO Box 1000, Ferrum VA 24088-9001
Gilda Q. Woods, Director of Admissions
800-868-9797

George Mason University
4400 University Dr, Fairfax VA 22030-4444
Dr. Jack Levy, Chairperson
703-993-2144

Hampton University
Hampton VA 23669
757-727-5000

James Madison University
800 S Main St, Harrisonburg VA 22807-0002
540-568-6211

Liberty University
PO Box 20000, Lynchburg VA 24506-8001
804-582-2000

Longwood University
201 High St, Farmville VA 23909-1801
804-395-2000

Lynchburg College
1501 Lakeside Dr, Lynchburg VA 24501-3199
804-544-8100

Mary Baldwin College
Staunton VA 24401
Lisa A. Branson, Executive Director of Admissions and Financial Aid
800-468-2262 Fax: 540-887-7292
Website: www.mbc.edu
E-mail: admit@mbc.edu

Marymount University
2807 N Glebe Rd, Arlington VA 22207-4299
Michael Canfield, Director of Admissions
800-548-7638 Fax: 703-522-0348
Website: www.marymount.edu
E-mail: admissions@marymount.edu

Norfolk State University
700 Park Ave, Norfolk VA 23504
Michelle Marable, Director of Admissions
757-823-8600

Old Dominion University
1 Old Dominion University, Norfolk VA 23529-1000
757-683-3000

Radford University
PO Box 6903, Radford VA 24142
David W. Kraus, Director of Admissions
800-890-4265 Fax: 540-831-5038
Website: www.radford.edu
E-mail: ruadmiss@radford.edu

Randolph College
2500 Rivermont Ave, Lynchburg VA 24503
Patricia LeDonne, Director of Admissions
434-947-8100 Fax: 434-947-8996
Website: www.randolphcollege.edu
E-mail: admissions@randolphcollege.edu

Randolph-Macon College
PO Box 5005, Ashland VA 23005-5505
804-752-7200

Roanoke College
221 College Ln, Salem VA 24153-3794
James A. Pennix, Director of Admissions
540-375-2500 Fax: 540-375-2267
Website: www.roanoke.edu
E-mail: pennix@roanoke.edu

St. Paul's College
406 Windsor Ave, Lawrenceville VA 23868-1202
804-848-3111

Shenandoah University
1460 University Dr, Winchester VA 22601-5195
Michael D. Carpenter, Director of Admissions
800-432-2266

Southside Virginia Community College
109 Campus Dr, Alberta VA 23821-2930
Ronald E. Mattox, Dean of Admissions
434-949-1014 Fax: 434-949-7863
Website: www.sv.vccs.edu
E-mail: ronald.mattox@sv.vccs.edu

Southside Virginia Community College
200 Daniel Rd, Keysville VA 23947
Ronald E. Mattox, Dean of Admissions
434-736-2018 Fax: 434-736-2082
Website: www.sv.vccs.edu
E-mail: ronald.mattox@sv.vccs.edu

University of Richmond
Richmond VA 23173
804-289-8000

University of Virginia
PO Box 400160, Charlottesville VA 22904
804-924-0311

University of Virginia College at Wise
1 College Ave, Wise VA 24293
276-328-0100

Virginia Commonwealth University
901 W Franklin St, Richmond VA 23284
804-828-0100

Virginia Intermont College
1013 Moore St, Bristol VA 24201-4225
540-669-6101

Virginia Polytechnic Institute & State University
Blacksburg VA 24061
540-231-6000

Virginia State University
1 Hayden Dr, Petersburg VA 23806-0001
804-524-5000

Virginia Wesleyan College
1584 Wesleyan Dr, Norfolk VA 23502-5599
757-455-3200

WASHINGTON

Antioch University
2326 6th Ave, Seattle WA 98121
Pam Smith Mentz, Director of Enrollment Services
888-268-4477

BATES TECHNICAL COLLEGE
1101 S Yakima Ave, Tacoma WA 98405-4895
David Borofsky, President
253-680-7000 Fax: 253-680-7101
Website: www.bates.ctc.edu
E-mail: info@bates.ctc.edu

Central Washington University
400 E University Way, Ellensburg WA 98926
William Swain, Director of Admissions
509-963-3001

City University
11900 NE 1st St, Bellevue WA 98005-3030
800-426-5596

Eastern Washington University
Cheney WA 99004
509-359-6200

Gonzaga University
502 E Boone Ave, Spokane WA 99258-0102
Julie McCulloh, Dean of Admission
800-322-2584

Pacific Lutheran University
12180 Park Ave S, Tacoma WA 98447-0014
David E. Gunovich, Director of Admissions
253-535-7151

St. Martin's University
5300 Pacific Ave SE, Lacey WA 98503-1297
360-491-4700

Seattle Pacific University
3307 3rd Ave W, Seattle WA 98119-1997
206-281-2000

Seattle University
901 12th Ave, Seattle WA 98122
206-296-6000

SHORELINE COMMUNITY COLLEGE
16101 Greenwood Ave N, Shoreline WA 98133-5696
Chris Melton, Acting Registrar
206-546-4581 Fax: 206-546-5835
Website: www.shoreline.edu

University of Puget Sound
1500 N Warner St, Tacoma WA 98416-0005
253-879-3100

Walla Walla College
204 S College Ave, College Place WA 99324-1198
509-527-2615

Washington State University
1 SE Stadium Way, Pullman WA 99164-0001
509-335-3564

Western Washington University
516 High St, Bellingham WA 98225-5996
360-650-3000

Whitworth College
300 W Hawthorne Rd, Spokane WA 99251-0001
Fred Pfursich, Dean of Admissions & Financial Aid
800-533-4668

WEST VIRGINIA

Alderson-Broaddus College
Philippi WV 26416
Eric A. Ruf, Director of Admissions
800-263-1549

Bethany College
Bethany WV 26032
304-829-7000

Bluefield State College
219 Rock St, Bluefield WV 24701-2198
304-327-4000

Concord University
Athens WV 24712
Michael Curry, Vice President of Financial Aid & Admissions
888-384-5249

Davis & Elkins College
100 Campus Dr, Elkins WV 26241-3996
Renee Heckel, Director of Enrollment Management
800-624-3157 Fax: 304-637-1800
Website: www.davisandelkins.edu
E-mail: admiss@davisandelkins.edu

Fairmont State University
1201 Locust Ave, Fairmont WV 26554-2470
Steve Leadman, Director of Admissions
304-367-4241 or 800-641-5678 Fax: 304-367-4789
Website: www.fairmontstate.edu
E-mail: admit@fairmontstate.edu

Glenville State College
200 High St, Glenville WV 26351-1200
304-462-4128

Marshall University
400 Hal Greer Blvd, Huntington WV 25755-0003
304-696-3170

Salem International University
PO Box 500, Salem WV 26426-0500
304-782-5011

University of Charleston
2300 MacCorkle Ave SE, Charleston WV 25304-1099
304-357-4800

West Liberty State College
PO Box 295, West Liberty WV 26074
304-336-5000

West Virginia State University
PO Box 1000, Institute WV 25112-1000
304-766-3000

West Virginia University
PO Box 6001, Morgantown WV 26506-6001
304-293-0111

West Virginia Wesleyan College
59 College Ave, Buckhannon WV 26201-2699
Robert N. Skinner II, Director of Admission
800-722-9933

WISCONSIN

Alverno College
PO Box 343922, Milwaukee WI 53234-3922
Dianna Gaebler, Director of Admissions
414-382-6100 Fax: 414-382-6354
Website: www.alverno.edu
E-mail: admissions@alverno.edu

Beloit College
700 College St, Beloit WI 53511-5596
Thomas Warren, Chairperson
608-363-2336

Cardinal Stritch University
6801 N Yates Rd, Milwaukee WI 53217-3985
414-410-4000

Carroll College
100 N East Ave, Waukesha WI 53186-5593
James Wiseman, Dean of Admissions
800-CARROLL

Carthage College
2001 Alford Park Dr, Kenosha WI 53140-1994
262-551-6000

Concordia University
12800 N Lake Shore Dr, Mequon WI 53097-2402
262-243-5700

Edgewood College
1000 Edgewood College Dr, Madison WI 53711
608-663-4861

Lakeland College
PO Box 359, Sheboygan WI 53082-0359
Nathan Dehne, Director of Admission
920-565-1100 Fax: 920-565-1215
Website: www.lakeland.edu
E-mail: admissions@lakeland.edu

Marian College of Fond du Lac
45 S National Ave, Fond du Lac WI 54935-4621
Eric Peterson, Dean of Admission
800-262-7426 ext. 7650

Marquette University
PO Box 1881, Milwaukee WI 53201-1881
Robert Blust, Director of Admissions
414-288-7302 Fax: 414-288-3764
Website: www.mu.edu
E-mail: admissions@marquette.edu

Mount Mary College
2900 N Menomonee River Pkwy
Milwaukee WI 53222-4597
414-256-1219

Northland College
1411 Ellis Ave, Ashland WI 54806-3999
800-753-1840

Ripon College
PO Box 248, Ripon WI 54971-0248
920-748-8115

St. Norbert College
100 Grant St, De Pere WI 54115
Brian Studebaker, Director of Admission
800-236-4878 Fax: 920-403-4072
Website: www.snc.edu
E-mail: admit@snc.edu

Silver Lake College
2406 S Alverno Rd, Manitowoc WI 54220-9319
920-684-6691

University of Wisconsin
PO Box 4004, Eau Claire WI 54702
715-836-2637

University of Wisconsin
PO Box 2000, Kenosha WI 53141-2000
262-595-2345

University of Wisconsin
1 University Plz, Platteville WI 53818-3001
Angela Udelhofen, Recruitment Manager
608-342-1200

University of Wisconsin
410 S 3rd St, River Falls WI 54022
715-425-3911

University of Wisconsin
PO Box 2000, Superior WI 54880
715-394-8101

University of Wisconsin Green Bay
2420 Nicolet Dr, Green Bay WI 54311-7003
Pamela Harvey-Jacobs, Interim Director of Admissions
920-465-2111

University of Wisconsin in La Crosse
115 Graff Main Hall, La Crosse WI 54601
Tim Lewis, Director of Admissions
608-785-8939

University of Wisconsin - Oshkosh
800 Algoma Blvd, Oshkosh WI 54901-8602
920-424-0202

University of Wisconsin-Stout
124 Bowman Hall, Menomonie WI 54751-2662
715-232-1123

University of Wisconsin - Whitewater
800 W Main St, Whitewater WI 53190-1791
262-472-1234

Viterbo University
815 9th St S, La Crosse WI 54601-8802
608-796-3000

WYOMING

University of Wyoming
Admissions Office
Dept 3435, Laramie WY 82071-3435
Brooke Culver, Contact
800-342-5996 Fax: 307-766-4042
Website: www.uwyo.edu
E-mail: why-wyo@uwyo.edu

GUAM

University of Guam
UOG Station, Mangilao GU 96923
Deborah Leon Guerrero, Registrar
671-735-2201 or 671-735-2208 Fax: 671-735-2203
Website: www.uog.edu
E-mail: admitme@uog9.uog.edu

PUERTO RICO

Bayamon Central University
PO Box 1725, Bayamon PR 00960-1725
787-786-3030

Pontifical Catholic University of Puerto Rico
2250 Ave Las Americas, Ponce PR 00717-0777
787-841-2000

Universidad Adventista de las Antillas
PO Box 118, Mayaguez PR 00681
Evelyn Del Valle Rivera, Director of Admissions
787-834-9595

University of Puerto Rico
R Ave Antonio R Barcelo, Cayey PR 00736-5534
787-738-2161

University of Puerto Rico
CUH Station Rd 908 Bo Tejas, Humacao PR 00791
787-850-0000

University of Puerto Rico
PO Box 23303, Rio Piedras PR 00931-3303
787-764-0000

University of Puerto Rico at Arecibo
PO Box 4010, Arecibo PR 00614
787-815-0000

University of Puerto Rico at Ponce
PO Box 7186, Ponce PR 00732-7186
787-844-8181

University of Puerto Rico
Bayamón University College
Carretera 174, Km 2.8, Bayamón PR 00959
787-786-2885

THEOLOGICAL STUDIES & RELIGIOUS VOCATIONS

ALABAMA

HUNTSVILLE BIBLE COLLEGE
904 Oakwood Ave NW, Huntsville AL 35811
John Clay, Contact
256-539-0834 Fax: 256-539-0854
Website: www.huntsvillebiblecollege.com
E-mail: hbc@huntsvillebiblecollege.com

Judson College
302 Bibb St, Marion AL 36756
Michael Scotto, Director of Admissions
800-447-9472 Fax: 334-683-5147
Website: www.judson.edu
E-mail: admissions@judson.edu

Southeastern Bible College
2545 Valleydale Rd, Birmingham AL 35244
Lynn Gannett-Malick, Director of Enrollment Management
800-749-8878 Fax: 205-970-9207
Website: www.sebc.edu
E-mail: admissions@sebc.edu

ALASKA

ALASKA BIBLE COLLEGE
PO Box 289, Glennallen AK 99588-0289
907-822-3201 Fax: 907-822-5027
Website: www.akbible.edu
E-mail: info@akbible.edu

ARKANSAS

Williams Baptist College
PO Box 3737, Walnut Ridge AR 72476-3737
Angela Flippo, Vice President for Enrollment Management
800-722-4434 Fax: 870-759-4163
Website: www.williamsbaptistcollege.com
E-mail: admissions@wbcoll.edu

CALIFORNIA

AMERICAN BAPTIST SEMINARY OF THE WEST
2606 Dwight Way, Berkeley CA 94704-3029
510-841-1905 Fax: 510-841-2446
Website: www.absw.edu
E-mail: admissions@absw.edu

Chapman University
One University Drive, Orange CA 92866-1099
Michael Drummy, Assistant Vice President for Enrollment
Services and Chief Admission Officer
714-997-6411 or 888-CUAPPLY Fax: 714-997-6713
Website: www.chapman.edu
E-mail: admit@chapman.edu

CHURCH DIVINITY SCHOOL OF THE PACIFIC
2451 Ridge Rd, Berkeley CA 94709-1217
Kathleen Crisp, Director of Admissions and Recruitment
510-204-0715 Fax: 510-204-0749
Website: www.cdsp.edu
E-mail: admissions@cdsp.edu

CLAREMONT SCHOOL OF THEOLOGY
1325 N College Ave, Claremont CA 91711-3154
Sabrina Johnson, Director of Admission
909-447-2506 Fax: 909-447-6389
Website: www.cst.edu
E-mail: admission@cst.edu

COMMUNITY CHRISTIAN COLLEGE
251 Tennessee St, Redlands CA 92373
909-335-8863 Fax: 909-335-9101
Website: www.cccollege.net
E-mail: admin@cccollege.net

Concordia University
1530 Concordia, Irvine CA 92612-3203
Lori McDonald, Executive Director of Enrollment Services
800-229-1200 or 949-854-8002 Fax: 949-854-6894
Website: www.cui.edu
E-mail: admission@cui.edu

DOMINICAN SCHOOL OF PHILOSOPHY & THEOLOGY
2301 Vine St, Berkeley CA 94708
John Knutsen, Director of Admissions
888-450-DSPT or 510-883-2073 Fax: 510-849-1372
Website: www.dspt.edu
E-mail: admissions@dspt.edu

FULLER THEOLOGICAL SEMINARY
135 N Oakland Ave, Pasadena CA 91182-0002
Office of Admissions
800-2-FULLER Fax: 626-584-5449
Website: www.fuller.edu
E-mail: adm-email@dept.fuller.edu

GRADUATE THEOLOGICAL UNION
2400 Ridge Rd, Berkeley CA 94709-1212
Kathleen Kook, Assistant Dean for Admissions
800-826-4488 Fax: 510-649-1730
Website: www.gtu.edu
E-mail: gtuadm@gtu.edu

HEBREW UNION COLLEGE - JEWISH INSTITUTE OF RELIGION
3077 University Ave, Los Angeles CA 90007-3796
Dr. Matt Albert, Regional Director of Admissions and Recruitment
213-749-3424 Fax: 213-747-6128
Website: www.huc.edu
E-mail: malbert@huc.edu

Point Loma Nazarene University
3900 Lomaland Dr, San Diego CA 92106-2810
Chip Killingsworth, Director of Undergraduate Admissions
800-733-7770 Fax: 619-849-2601
Website: www.pointloma.edu
E-mail: admissions@pointloma.edu

San Diego Christian College
2100 Greenfield Dr, El Cajon CA 92019-1157
Rene Inman, Director of Admissions
800-676-2242 Fax: 619-590-1739
Website: www.sdcc.edu
E-mail: admissions@sdcc.edu

SAN FRANCISCO THEOLOGICAL SEMINARY
105 Seminary Rd, San Anselmo CA 94960-2925
The Rev. Dr. Kyle Matsumoto Burch, Assoc. Dean of Enrollment
415-451-2831 or 800-447-8820 Fax: 415-451-2854
Website: www.sfts.edu
E-mail: admissions@sfts.edu

Simpson University
2211 College View Dr, Redding CA 96003-8606
Jim Herberger, Director of Admissions
888-9-SIMPSON Fax: 530-226-4861
Website: www.simpsonuniversity.edu
E-mail: admissions@simpsonuniversity.edu
See listing under "Universities"

SOUTHERN CALIFORNIA SEMINARY
2075 E Madison Ave, El Cajon CA 92019
Steve Perdue, Admissions Director
888-389-7244 Fax: 619-442-4510
Website: www.socalsem.edu
E-mail: sperdue@socalsem.edu

COLORADO

Colorado Christian University
8787 W Alameda Ave, Lakewood CO 80226
Sean Kadel, Director of Admissions
800-44-FAITH Fax: 303-963-3201
Website: www.ccu.edu
E-mail: admissions@ccu.edu

Denver Seminary
6399 S Santa Fe Dr, Littleton CO 80120
Robert Jones, VP Student Services
303-762-6982 Fax: 303-783-3122
Website: denverseminary.edu
E-mail: robert.jones@denverseminary.edu

ILIFF SCHOOL OF THEOLOGY
2201 S University Blvd, Denver CO 80210-4798
Peggy Blocker, Director of Admissions
800-678-3360 or 303-765-3117 Fax: 303-777-0164
Website: www.iliff.edu
E-mail: admissions@iliff.edu

Nazarene Bible College
1111 Academy Park Loop
Colorado Springs CO 80910-3717
Dr. Laurel Matson, VP for Enrollment & Student Development
719-596-5110 Fax: 719-884-5199
Website: www.nbc.edu
E-mail: admissions@nbc.edu

CONNECTICUT

HARTFORD SEMINARY
77 Sherman St, Hartford CT 06105-2260
Kelton Cobb, Seminary Academic Advisor
860-509-9513 Fax: 860-509-9509
Website: www.hartsem.edu
E-mail: info@hartsem.edu

FLORIDA

THE BAPTIST COLLEGE OF FLORIDA
5400 College Dr, Graceville FL 32440-1831
Christopher M. Bishop, Director of Admissions
800-328-2660 Fax: 850-263-9026
Website: www.baptistcollege.edu
E-mail: admissions@baptistcollege.edu

ST. PETERSBURG THEOLOGICAL SEMINARY
10830 Navajo Dr, Saint Petersburg FL 33708
Angel Rosado, VP of Operations
727-399-0276 Fax: 727-399-1324
Website: www.sptseminary.edu
E-mail: sptsoffice@aol.com

St. Thomas University
16401 NW 37th Ave, Miami Gardens FL 33054
Dr. Thomas Ryan, Department Chair
800-367-9010 or 305-628-6546 Fax: 305-628-6591
Website: www.stu.edu
E-mail: signup@stu.edu

St. Vincent DePaul Regional Seminary
10701 S Military Trl, Boynton Beach FL 33436-4899
Rev. Steven O'Hala, Academic Dean
561-732-4424 ext. 151 Fax: 561-732-8808
Website: www.svdp.edu
E-mail: sohala@svdp.edu
M.Div and M.A.

GEORGIA

BEULAH HEIGHTS UNIVERSITY
PO Box 18145, Atlanta GA 30316-0145
Dr. James B. Keiller, V.P. & Dean for Academic Affairs
404-627-2681 Fax: 404-627-0702
Website: www.beulah.org
E-mail: bhu@beulah.org

INTERDENOMINATIONAL THEOLOGICAL CENTER
700 Martin Luther King Jr Dr SW
Atlanta GA 30314-4143
Walter Cabassa, Recruitment Coordinator
404-527-7792 Fax: 404-527-0901
Website: www.itc.edu
E-mail: wcabassa@itc.edu

Luther Rice University
3038 Evans Mill Rd, Lithonia GA 30038
Russ Sorrow, Director of Enrollment Management
770-484-1204 Fax: 770-484-1155
Website: www.lru.edu
E-mail: admissions@lru.edu

TOCCOA FALLS COLLEGE
PO Box 800899, Toccoa Falls GA 30598
888-785-5624 Fax: 706-282-6012
Website: www.tfc.edu
E-mail: admissions@tfc.edu

HAWAII

HAWAII THEOLOGICAL SEMINARY
PO Box 861754, Wahiawa HI 96786
Kevin Gilbert, President
808-622-4487 Fax: 808-595-4779
Website: www.hits.edu
E-mail: info@hits.edu

IDAHO

Brigham Young University - Idaho
120 Kimball Bldg, Rexburg ID 83460-1615
Rob Garrett, Director of Admissions
208-496-1020 Fax: 208-496-1220
Website: www.byui.edu
E-mail: admissions@byui.edu

ILLINOIS

CONCORDIA UNIVERSITY
7400 Augusta St, River Forest IL 60305-1402
708-209-3100 Fax: 708-209-3176
Website: www.cuchicago.edu
E-mail: admission@cuchicago.edu

LUTHERAN SCHOOL OF THEOLOGY AT CHICAGO
1100 E 55th St, Chicago IL 60615-5199
Dorothy C. Dominiak, Director of Admissions
800-635-1116 ext. 726 or 773-256-0726
Fax: 773-256-0782
Website: www.lstc.edu
E-mail: admissions@lstc.edu

MCCORMICK THEOLOGICAL SEMINARY
5460 S University Ave, Chicago IL 60615
Rev. Craig Howard, Director of Recruitment and Admissions
800-228-4687 Fax: 773-288-2612
Website: www.mccormick.edu
E-mail: admit@mccormick.edu

NORTHERN BAPTIST THEOLOGICAL SEMINARY
660 E Butterfield Rd, Lombard IL 60148-5698
Charles Dresser, Executive Director of Enrollment Management
630-620-2180 Fax: 630-620-2190
Website: www.seminary.edu
E-mail: admissions@seminary.edu

Spertus College
618 S Michigan Ave, Chicago IL 60605-1901
312-922-9012 Fax: 312-922-6406
Website: www.spertus.edu
E-mail: college@spertus.edu

Trinity International University
2065 Half Day Rd, Deerfield IL 60015-1241
847-945-8800 Fax: 847-317-8097
Website: www.tiu.edu
E-mail: tcadmissions@tiu.edu

INDIANA

ASSOCIATED MENNONITE BIBLICAL SEMINARIES
3003 Benham Ave, Elkhart IN 46517-1947
Regina Shands Stoltzfus, Director of Admissions
800-964-2627 Fax: 574-295-0092
Website: www.ambs.edu
E-mail: admissions@ambs.edu

BETHANY THEOLOGICAL SEMINARY
615 National Rd W, Richmond IN 47374-4019
Dr. Eugene F. Roop, President
800-287-8822 Fax: 765-983-1840
Website: www.brethren.org/bethany
E-mail: bethanysem@aol.com

CROSSROADS BIBLE COLLEGE
601 N Shortridge Rd, Indianapolis IN 46219-4912
Tiffany Powell, Director of Enrollment Management
317-352-8736 ext. 230 or 800-822-3119 ext. 230
Fax: 317-352-9145
Website: www.crossroads.edu
E-mail: tpowell@crossroads.edu

Oakland City University
138 N Lucretia St, Oakland City IN 47660
Brian J. Baker, Director of Admissions
800-737-5125 Fax: 812-749-1433
Website: www.oak.edu
E-mail: bbaker@oak.edu
ATS Accredited.
See listing under "Universities"

University of Evansville
1800 Lincoln Ave, Evansville IN 47722-0001
Don Vos, Dean of Admission
800-423-8633 Fax: 812-488-4076
Website: www.evansville.edu
E-mail: admission@evansville.edu

IOWA

Briar Cliff University
PO Box 2100, Sioux City IA 51104-0100
Sharisue Wilcoxon, VP for Enrollment Management
712-279-5200 Fax: 712-279-1632
Website: www.briarcliff.edu
E-mail: admissions@briarcliff.edu

Graceland University
1 University Place, Lamoni IA 50140
Greg Sutherland, Interim Vice President for Enrollment and Dean of Admissions
641-784-5196 Fax: 641-784-5480
Website: www.admissions.graceland.edu
E-mail: admissions@graceland.edu

UNIVERSITY OF DUBUQUE THEOLOGICAL SEMINARY
2000 University Ave, Dubuque IA 52001-5050
800-369-8387 Fax: 563-589-3110
Website: udtseminary.net
E-mail: udtsadms@dbq.edu

Waldorf College
106 S 6th St, Forest City IA 50436-1713
Dr. Linda Hoopes, Vice President of Admission and Marketing
800-292-1903 or 641-585-8112 Fax: 641-585-8125
Website: www.waldorf.edu
E-mail: hoopesl@waldorf.edu
See listing under "Universities"

WARTBURG THEOLOGICAL SEMINARY
PO Box 5004, Dubuque IA 52004-5004
Heather Devine, Director of Admissions
563-589-0200 Fax: 563-589-0333
Website: www.wartburgseminary.edu
E-mail: admissions@wartburgseminary.edu

KANSAS

Tabor College
400 S Jefferson St, Hillsboro KS 67063-1758
Rusty Allen, Dean of Enrollment Management
800-822-6799 Fax: 620-947-6276
Website: www.tabor.edu
E-mail: admissions@tabor.edu
See listing under "Universities"

KENTUCKY

LEXINGTON THEOLOGICAL SEMINARY
631 S Limestone, Lexington KY 40508-3288
Erika Smith, Director of Admissions
859-252-0361 Fax: 859-281-6042
Website: www.lextheo.edu
E-mail: esmith@lextheo.edu

Louisville Presbyterian Seminary
1044 Alta Vista Rd, Louisville KY 40205-1798
Kerry Rice, Director of Admissions
502-895-3411 or 800-264-1839 Fax: 502-992-9399
Website: www.lpts.edu
E-mail: admissions@lpts.edu
Degrees offered MDiv, MA, DMin, ThM

Transylvania University
300 N Broadway, Lexington KY 40508-1776
859-233-8242 Fax: 859-233-8797
Website: www.transy.edu
E-mail: admissions@transy.edu

MARYLAND

Griggs University
PO Box 4437, Silver Spring MD 20914-4437
Joan Wilson, Director of Admissions
301-680-6570 Fax: 301-680-6583
Website: www.griggs.edu
E-mail: registrar@griggs.edu

MAPLE SPRINGS BAPTIST BIBLE COLLEGE & SEMINARY
4130 Belt Rd, Capitol Heights MD 20743-5711
Rev. Percy V. Coker, Registrar
301-736-3631 Fax: 301-735-6507
Website: www.msbbcs.edu

MASSACHUSETTS

Anna Maria College
50 Sunset Ln, Paxton MA 01612
Timothy M. Donahue, Director of Recruitment and Admissions
508-849-3360 Fax: 508-849-3362
Website: www.annamaria.edu
E-mail: admissions@annamaria.edu

Assumption College
500 Salisbury St, Worcester MA 01609-1294
Kathleen Murphy, Dean of Enrollment
508-767-7000 Fax: 508-799-4412
Website: www.assumption.edu
E-mail: admiss@assumption.edu

Boston University
121 Bay State Rd, Boston MA 02215
Kelly Walter, Executive Director of Admissions
617-353-2300 Fax: 617-353-9695
Website: web.bu.edu
E-mail: admissions@bu.edu

Gordon College
255 Grapevine Rd, Wenham MA 01984-1899
Barbara R. Layne, Associate Vice President, Enrollment
866-464-6736 Fax: 978-867-4682
Website: www.gordon.edu
E-mail: admissions@gordon.edu

MICHIGAN

Alma College
614 W Superior St, Alma MI 48801-1599
Evan Montague, Director of Admissions
800-321-ALMA Fax: 989-463-7057
Website: www.alma.edu
E-mail: admissions@alma.edu

CALVIN THEOLOGICAL SEMINARY
3233 Burton St SE, Grand Rapids MI 49546-4301
Greg Janke, Director of Admissions
616-957-6036 Fax: 616-957-8621
Website: www.calvinseminary.edu
E-mail: admissions@calvinseminary.edu

Concordia University
4090 Geddes Rd, Ann Arbor MI 48105-2797
Gary Neumann, Director of Admissions
734-995-7300 Fax: 734-995-4610
Website: www.cuaa.edu
E-mail: admissions@cuaa.edu

MINNESOTA

Crown College
8700 College View Dr, Saint Bonifacius MN 55375
Mitch Fisk, Director of Admissions
952-446-4142 Fax: 952-446-4149
Website: www.crown.edu
E-mail: johnsonj@crown.edu

LUTHER SEMINARY
2481 Como Ave, Saint Paul MN 55108-1496
Rev. Ronald Olson, Contact
800-588-4373 Fax: 651-641-3521
Website: www.luthersem.edu
E-mail: admissions@luthersem.edu

Pillsbury Baptist Bible College
315 S Grove Ave, Owatonna MN 55060-3097
Susanne Martin, Admissions Coordinator
507-451-2710 Fax: 507-451-0156
Website: www.pillsbury.edu
E-mail: admissions@pillsbury.edu

UNITED THEOLOGICAL SEMINARY OF THE TWIN CITIES
3000 5th St NW, New Brighton MN 55112-2598
Admissions Office
651-255-6119 or 800-937-1316 Fax: 651-633-4315
Website: www.unitedseminary.edu
E-mail: admissions@unitedseminary.edu

MISSISSIPPI

MAGNOLIA BIBLE COLLEGE
PO Box 1109, Kosciusko MS 39090-1109
Garvis Semore, President
800-748-8655 Fax: 662-289-1850
Website: www.magnolia.edu
E-mail: gsemore@magnolia.edu

Tougaloo College
500 W County Line Rd, Tougaloo MS 39174-9799
Juno Leggette Jacobs, Director of Admissions
601-977-7768 Fax: 601-977-4501
Website: www.tougaloo.edu
E-mail: jjacobs@tougaloo.edu

WESLEY COLLEGE
PO Box 1070, Florence MS 39073-1070
Charles M. Elliott, V.P. for Academic Affairs
601-845-2265 Fax: 601-845-2266
Website: www.wesleycollege.edu
E-mail: admissions@wesleycollege.edu

MISSOURI

ASSEMBLIES OF GOD THEOLOGICAL SEMINARY
1435 N Glenstone Ave, Springfield MO 65802-2131
Dr. Mario Guerreiro, Director of Enrollment Management
800-467-AGTS Fax: 417-268-1001
Website: www.agts.edu
E-mail: agts@agseminary.edu

CENTRAL BIBLE COLLEGE
3000 N Grant Ave, Springfield MO 65803-1096
Jamie Bell, Executive Director of Enrollment Services
800-831-4222 ext. 1290 Fax: 417-833-5141
Website: www.cbcag.edu
E-mail: cbcinfo@cbcag.edu

Central Methodist University
411 Central Methodist Sq, Fayette MO 65248-1198
Larry Anderson, Director of Admissions
660-248-6247 Fax: 660-248-1872
Website: www.centralmethodist.edu
E-mail: landerso@centralmethodist.edu

COVENANT THEOLOGICAL SEMINARY
12330 Conway Rd, Saint Louis MO 63141-8697
Dr. Bryan Chapell, President
800-264-8064 Fax: 314-434-4819
Website: www.covenantseminary.edu
E-mail: admissions@covenantseminary.edu

Evangel University
1111 N Glenstone Ave, Springfield MO 65802-2191
Cheri Meyer, Director of Undergraduate Admissions
417-865-2811 Fax: 417-865-9599
Website: www.evangel.edu
E-mail: meyerc@evangel.edu

KENRICK SCHOOL OF THEOLOGY
5200 Glennon Dr, Saint Louis MO 63119-4330
Msgr. Ted L. Wojcicki, President-Rector
314-792-6100 Fax: 314-792-6500
Website: www.kenrick.edu
E-mail: registrar@kenrick.edu

MIDWESTERN BAPTIST THEOLOGICAL SEMINARY
5001 N Oak Trfy, Kansas City MO 64118-4697
816-414-3700 Fax: 816-414-3724
Website: www.mbts.edu

MIDWEST UNIVERSITY
851 Parr Rd, Wentzville MO 63385
Dr. James Song, President
636-327-4645 Fax: 636-327-4715
Website: www.midwest.edu
E-mail: inf@midwest.edu

NAZARENE THEOLOGICAL SEMINARY
1700 E Meyer Blvd, Kansas City MO 64131-1263
Roger L. Hahn, Dean of the Faculty
816-333-6254 Fax: 816-333-6271
Website: www.nts.edu
E-mail: rlhahn@nts.edu

OZARK CHRISTIAN COLLEGE
1111 N Main St, Joplin MO 64801-4804
Troy Nelson, Director of Admissions
800-299-4622 Fax: 417-624-0090
Website: www.occ.edu
E-mail: occadmin@occ.edu
See listing under "Universities"

William Jewell College
500 College Hill, Liberty MO 64068-1896
Dr. Rick Winslow, VP Enrollment Management and Student Affairs
800-753-7009 Fax: 816-415-5040
Website: www.jewell.edu
E-mail: winslowr@william.jewell.edu

William Woods University
1 University Ave, Fulton MO 65251-1098
Jimmy Clay, Director of Admissions
573-642-2251 Fax: 573-592-1146
Website: www.williamwoods.edu
E-mail: admissions@williamwoods.edu
See listing under "Universities"

MONTANA

Carroll College
1601 N Benton Ave, Helena MT 59625-0002
Dr. Thomas J. Trebon, President
Cynthia Thornquist, Director of Admissions & Enrollment Operations
406-447-4384 Fax: 406-447-4533
Website: www.carroll.edu
E-mail: admission@carroll.edu

LUSTRE CHRISTIAN HIGH SCHOOL
HC 66 Box 57, Lustre MT 59225-9705
Al Leland, Supervising Teacher
406-392-5735 Fax: 406-392-5765
Website: www.lustrechristian.com
E-mail: lchs@nemont.net
See listing under "Preparatory Schools - Coed"

NEBRASKA

Midland Lutheran College
900 N Clarkson St, Fremont NE 68025-4200
Todd Hansen, Associate Director of Admissions
402-941-6501 Fax: 402-941-6513
Website: www.mlc.edu
E-mail: admissions@mlc.edu

NEW JERSEY

Assumption College for Sisters
350 Bernardsville Rd, Mendham NJ 07945-2923
Sr. Mary Joseph Schultz, S.C.C., President
973-543-6528 Fax: 973-543-1738
Website: www.acs350.org
E-mail: acs@acs350.org

RICHARD STOCKTON COLLEGE OF NEW JERSEY
PO Box 195, Pomona NJ 08240
John Iacovelli, Dean of Enrollment Management
866-RSC-2885 Fax: 609-626-5541
Website: www.stockton.edu
E-mail: admissions@stockton.edu
See listing under "Universities"

NEW YORK

COLGATE ROCHESTER CROZER DIVINITY SCHOOL
1100 S Goodman St, Rochester NY 14620-2589
Robert Jones, V.P. of Enrollment Services
585-271-1320 or 888-937-3732 Fax: 585-271-8013
Website: www.crcds.edu
E-mail: admissions@crcds.edu

College of Saint Rose
432 Western Ave, Albany NY 12203-1419
Maryelizabeth Amico, Asst V.P. for Undergraduate Admissions
518-454-5150 Fax: 518-454-2013
Website: www.strose.edu
E-mail: admit@strose.edu

Iona College
715 North Ave, New Rochelle NY 10801-1890
Kevin Cavanagh, Assistant V.P. for College Admissions
914-633-2502 Fax: 914-637-2778
Website: www.iona.edu

Molloy College
1000 Hempstead Ave
Rockville Centre NY 11570-1100
Marguerite Lane, Director of Admissions
516-678-5000 ext. 6291 Fax: 516-256-2247
Website: www.molloy.edu
E-mail: admissions@molloy.edu
See listing under "Universities"

Roberts Wesleyan College
2301 Westside Dr, Rochester NY 14624-1997
Office of Admissions
585-594-6400 Fax: 585-594-6371
Website: www.roberts.edu
E-mail: admissions@roberts.edu

St. John's University
8000 Utopia Pkwy, Queens NY 11439
Office of Admission
877-STJ-5550 ext. 101 Fax: 718-990-2096
Website: www.stjohns.edu/learnmore
E-mail: admhelp@stjohns.edu
See listing under "Universities"

NORTH CAROLINA

Apex School of Theology
2945 S Miami Blvd Ste 114, Durham NC 27703
Dr. J.E. Perkins, President
919-572-1625 Fax: 919-572-1762
Website: www.apexsot.edu
E-mail: info@apexsot.edu

Brevard College
One Brevard College Dr, Brevard NC 28712
Joretta Nelson, Vice President Enrollment Management
828-883-8292 Fax: 828-884-3790
Website: www.brevard.edu
E-mail: admissions@brevard.edu

Chowan University
One University Pl, Murfreesboro NC 27855
Chad Holt, Dean of Admissions
800-488-4101 Fax: 252-398-1190
Website: www.chowan.edu
E-mail: holtc@chowan.edu

Heritage Bible College
PO Box 1628, Dunn NC 28335
910-892-3178 Fax: 910-892-1809
Website: www.heritagebiblecollege.org
E-mail: generalinfo@heritagebiblecollege.org

HOOD THEOLOGICAL SEMINARY
1810 Lutheran Synod Dr, Salisbury NC 28144
Albert J. D. Aymer, President
704-636-6823 Fax: 704-636-7699
Website: www.hoodseminary.edu
E-mail: dmiller@hoodseminary.edu

JOHN WESLEY COLLEGE
2314 N Centennial St, High Point NC 27265-3197
Dr. Brian Donley, President
Greg Workman, Admissions Officer
336-889-2262 ext. 127 Fax: 336-889-2261
Website: www.johnwesley.edu
E-mail: admissions@johnwesley.edu

Established 1932. Private. Coed. Accreditation: ABHE. Tuition: $9,280. Room and board: $2,190. Enrollment: 150. Student-faculty ratio: 12:1. Degrees: AA, BA, Bth. Library: 47,000 volumes. 2 buildings on 25 acres. John Wesley College offers specialized studies in the area of Christian ministries; pastoral, Bible/theology, counseling (psychology), elementary christian school teacher education, youth & childrens ministry, missions, music, management and ethics, and pre-seminary. Distance education is offered. A christian college with a distinctly personal and practical approach to Bible based education, located in the center of the fast growing Piedmont area of North Carolina.

LEE UNIVERSITY CHARLOTTE CENTER
1209 Little Rock Rd, Charlotte NC 28214-2310
Thomas Tatum, Center Director
704-394-2307 Fax: 704-393-3689
Website: http://caps.leeuniversity.edu/charlotte-center/
E-mail: ttatum@carolina.rr.com

NEW LIFE THEOLOGICAL SEMINARY
PO Box 790106, Charlotte NC 28206
Judith Main, Registrar
704-334-6882 Fax: 704-334-6885
Website: www.nlts.org
E-mail: jmain@nlts.org

SOUTHEASTERN BAPTIST THEOLOGICAL SEMINARY
Southeastern College at Wake Forest
PO Box 1889, Wake Forest NC 27588-1889
Jerry L. Yandell, Director of Admissions
919-761-2280 or 800-284-6317 Fax: 919-556-0998
Website: www.sebts.edu
E-mail: admissions@sebts.edu

NORTH DAKOTA

Oak Grove Lutheran School
124 N Terrace N, Fargo ND 58102-3899
Rachel Mathson, Director of Admissions
701-237-0212 Fax: 701-237-4217
Website: www.oakgrovelutheran.com
E-mail: oakgrove.lutheranschool@sendit.nodak.edu

OHIO

BEXLEY HALL SEMINARY
583 Sheridan Ave, Columbus OH 43209-2325
John Kevern, Dean & President
614-231-3095 Fax: 614-231-3236
Website: www.bexley.edu
E-mail: columbus@bexley.edu or rochester@bexley.edu

Cincinnati Christian University
PO Box 4320, Cincinnati OH 45204
Erin Oppy, Executive Director of Undergraduate Admissions
513-244-8141 Fax: 513-244-8453
Website: www.ccuniversity.edu

Franciscan University of Steubenville
University Blvd, Steubenville OH 43952
Margaret J. Weber, Director of Admissions
800-783-6220 or 740-283-6226 Fax: 740-284-5456
Website: www.admissions.edu
E-mail: mweber@franciscan.edu

METHODIST THEOLOGICAL SCHOOL IN OHIO
3081 Columbus Pike, Delaware OH 43015-3211
Mary Kay Freshour, Director of Admissions and Financial Aid
800-333-6876 Fax: 740-362-3372
Website: www.mtso.edu
E-mail: admit@mtso.edu

PAYNE THEOLOGICAL SEMINARY
PO Box 474, Wilberforce OH 45384-0474
Dr. Leah Gaskin Fitchue, Contact
937-376-2946 Fax: 937-376-3330
Website: www.payne.edu
E-mail: lfitchue@payne.edu

United Theological Seminary
4501 Denlinger Rd, Trotwood OH 45426
Julie Hostetter, Director of Academic and Student Services
800-322-5817 Fax: 937-529-2292
Website: www.united.edu
E-mail: admissions@united.edu

University of Dayton
300 College Park, Dayton OH 45469-1300
Robert F. Durkle, Director of Admission
800-837-7433 Fax: 937-229-4729
Website: admission.udayton.edu
E-mail: admission@udayton.edu

Ursuline College
2550 Lander Rd, Cleveland OH 44124-4398
Sarah E. Sundermeier, Director of Admissions
888-URSULINE Toll Free Fax: 440-684-6138
Website: www.admission.ursuline.edu
E-mail: admission@ursuline.edu

OKLAHOMA

Mid-America Christian University
3500 SW 119th St, Oklahoma City OK 73170-4504
Haley Hope, Director of Admissions
405-691-3800 Fax: 405-692-3165
Website: www.macu.edu
E-mail: info@macu.edu

OREGON

Cascade College
9101 E Burnside St, Portland OR 97216-1599
Jim Murphy, Director of Enrollment Management
800-550-7678 Fax: 503-257-1222
Website: www.cascade.edu
E-mail: admissions@cascade.edu

Concordia University
2811 NE Holman St, Portland OR 97211-6099
Bobi Swan, Director of Admissions
503-288-9371 Fax: 503-280-8531
Website: www.cu-portland.edu
E-mail: cu-admissions@cu-portland.edu

Marylhurst University
17600 Pacific Hwy (Hwy 43)
Marylhurst OR 97036-0261
Director of Admissions
800-634-9982 ext. 6268 Fax: 503-635-6585
Website: www.marylhurst.edu
E-mail: studentinfo@marylhurst.edu

Warner Pacific College
2219 SE 68th Ave, Portland OR 97215-4026
Shannon Mackey, Director of Admissions
503-517-1000 Fax: 503-517-1352
Website: www.warnerpacific.edu
E-mail: admissions@warnerpacific.edu

PENNSYLVANIA

BIBLICAL THEOLOGICAL SEMINARY
200 N Main St, Hatfield PA 19440-2421
Pamela J. Smith, VP for Student Advancement
800-235-4021 Fax: 215-368-7002
Website: www.biblical.edu
E-mail: admissions@biblical.edu

DeSales University
2755 Station Ave, Center Valley PA 18034-9565
610-282-1100 Fax: 610-282-2342
Website: www.desales.edu

EVANGELICAL SCHOOL OF THEOLOGY
121 S College St, Myerstown PA 17067-1299
Tom Maiello, Dean of Admissions
800-532-5775 Fax: 717-866-4667
Website: www.evangelical.edu
E-mail: admissions@evangelical.edu

Gratz College
7605 Old York Rd, Melrose Park PA 19027
Jill Sigman, Director of Admissions
215-635-7300 Fax: 215-635-7320
Website: www.gratzcollege.edu
E-mail: admissions@gratz.edu

Juniata College
1700 Moore St, Huntingdon PA 16652-2196
Michelle Bartol, Dean of Enrollment
877-JUNIATA Fax: 814-641-3100
Website: www.juniata.edu
E-mail: admissions@juniata.edu

King's College
133 N River St, Wilkes Barre PA 18711-0801
Michelle Lawrence-Schmude, Dean of Admission
570-208-5900 Fax: 570-208-5971
Website: www.kings.edu
E-mail: admissions@kings.edu

LANCASTER BIBLE COLLEGE
901 Eden Rd, Lancaster PA 17601-5036
Dr. Peter W. Teague, President
Joanne M. Roper, Associate VP for Admissions
866-LBC-4YOU or 717-560-8271 Fax: 717-560-8213
Website: www.lbc.edu
E-mail: admissions@lbc.edu

Established 1933. Private. Coed. Accreditation: MSA, AABC, ACSI approval. Tuition $13,200. Room and board: $5,980. Fees: $600. Enrollment: 564 full-time, 226 part-time. Faculty: 86. Student-faculty ratio: 18:1. Degrees: AS in Bible, BS in Bible, BS in Education. Library: 176,566 volumes. 16 buildings on 100 acres. Departments: Biblical Counseling, Church & Ministry Leadership, Christian Education, Health, Physical Ed & Athletics, Intercultural Studies, Music, Office Administration, Teacher Education.

LUTHERAN THEOLOGICAL SEMINARY
7301 Germantown Ave, Philadelphia PA 19119-1794
Louise Johnson, Director of Admissions
800-286-4616 Fax: 215-248-4577
Website: www.ltsp.edu
E-mail: admissions@ltsp.edu

MORAVIAN THEOLOGICAL SEMINARY
1200 Main St, Bethlehem PA 18018
Rev. Melissa Johnson, Director of Admissions
610-861-1516 Fax: 610-861-1569
Website: www.moravianseminary.edu
E-mail: seminary@moravian.edu

Neumann College
1 Neumann Dr, Aston PA 19014-1298
Dennis Murphy, Director of Admissions
610-459-0905 Fax: 610-558-5652
Website: www.neumann.edu
E-mail: neumann@neumann.edu

PITTSBURGH THEOLOGICAL SEMINARY

616 N Highland Ave, Pittsburgh PA 15206-2525
Rev. Sherry Sparks, Director of Admissions
412-362-5610 ext. 2115 or 800-451-4194 Admissions only
Fax: 412-363-3260
Website: www.pts.edu
E-mail: sparks@pts.edu

Established 1794. PTS is affiliated with the Presbyterian Church, U.S.A. and serves students of any denomination. Our primary mission is to train lay and ordained leaders for the Church through rigorous academic and practical experience. Special emphases are urban, educational and counseling ministries. Degrees offered: Master of Divinity, MA, Master of Sacred Theology, Doctor of Ministry and three dual degrees in social work, law, and public policy. Part-time and evening programs, child care and financial aid available. We are located on a 13 acre park-like campus in an urban setting between the Highland Park and East Liberty area of Pittsburgh.

ST. TIKHON'S ORTHODOX THEOLOGICAL SEMINARY

PO Box 130, South Canaan PA 18459-0130
Metropolitan Herman, President
Bishop Tikhon, Rector
Very Rev. Michael G. Dahulich, Ph.D., Dean
570-937-4411 Fax: 570-937-3100
Website: www.stots.edu
E-mail: stots@stots.edu

TALMUDICAL YESHIVA OF PHILADELPHIA

6063 Drexel Rd, Philadelphia PA 19131-1296
Rabbi Uri Mandelbaum, Director of Admissions
215-477-1000 Fax: 215-477-5065
E-mail: typ@attglobal.net

RHODE ISLAND

ZION BIBLE COLLEGE

27 Middle Hwy, Barrington RI 02806-1296
Director of Recruiting
401-246-0900 Fax: 401-246-0906
Website: www.zbc.edu
E-mail: recruiting@zbc.edu

SOUTH CAROLINA

Bob Jones University
1700 Wade Hampton Blvd
Greenville SC 29614-0001
David Christ, Director of Admissions
800-BJ-AND-ME Fax: 800-2-FAX-BJU
Website: www.bju.edu
E-mail: admissions@bju.edu
See listing under "Universities"

CIU Seminary & School of Missions
PO Box 3122, Columbia SC 29230-3122
Michelle MacGregor, Director of University Admissions
800-777-2227 Fax: 803-333-0607
Website: www.ciu.edu
E-mail: yessem@ciu.edu
See listing under "Theological Studies & Religious Vocations"

COLUMBIA INTERNATIONAL UNIVERSITY

PO Box 3122, Columbia SC 29230-3122
Phone 800-777-2227, Fax: 803-786-4209
Dr. William H. Jones, President
Michelle MacGregor, Director of University Admissions
Website: www.ciu.edu
E-mail: yesciu@ciu.edu

Established 1923. Multidenominational. Coed. Privately supported, nonprofit. Accredited by The Commission on Colleges of the Southern Association of Colleges and Schools (SACS). Bible College accredited by the Accrediting Association of Bible Colleges (AABC) and Seminary by the Association of Theological Schools (ATS). Graduate School is approved for Teacher Education programs by the South Carolina Department of Education, Division of Teacher Education and Certification, which is affiliated with the National Association of State Directors of Teacher Education and Certification (NASDTEC) and by the Association of Christian Schools International (ACSI).

CIU Graduate School: Enrollment (Fall 2006) 135 students. Tuition: $425 full time, $450 part time per credit hour for semesters and summer and winter short terms. Curriculum: Master of Education, Curriculum and Instruction (Generalist, School Technology, Learning Disabilities, Christian School Guidance, ESL); Master of Education, Educational Administration; Master of Arts in Bible Teaching; Master of Arts in Teaching for State Certification; Master of Arts in Counseling; Master of Arts in Teaching English as a Foreign Language; Ed.D. programs: Doctor of Education in Educational Leadership (Christian School Education, Christian Higher Education). Admissions: Christian testimony, baccalaureate degree, transcripts with 3.0 GPA for MA in Counseling or upper 50% GRE score, PPST (MAT only), essay, and references.

Bible College: Enrollment (Fall 2006) 471 students. Tuition: $7,600 for each semester (two). Curriculum: one year Bible Certificate, AA, BS, BA. Bible major combines with one of the following: Applied English, Bible Teaching, Biblical Languages, Business and Organizational Leadership, Communication, Deaf Ministry, Family & Church Education, General Studies, Humanities, Intercultural Studies (Missions), Middle Eastern Studies, Music, Nursing (cooperative program through General Studies), Outdoor Leadership, Pastoral Ministries, Psychology, Radio Broadcasting, Teacher Education, Teaching English as a Foreign Language (TEFL), Video Production, Youth Ministry. Admission: Christian testimony, SAT or ACT and HS transcripts or GED required, references, essay.

CIU Seminary & School of Missions: Enrollment (Fall 2006) 356 students. Tuition: $400 full time, $425 part time per credit hour for semesters and short terms. Curriculum: Biblical Ministry Certificate; Master of Arts (General); Master of Arts in Bible Exposition; Master of Arts in Educational Ministries; Master of Arts in Pastoral Counseling and Spiritual Formation; Master of Arts in Leadership for Evangelism and Mobilization; Master of Arts in Intercultural Studies; Master of Divinity with the following tracks: Intercultural Studies, Academic Ministries, Bible Exposition, Educational Ministries, Pastoral Counseling and Spiritual Formation; Doctor of Ministry with concentrations in Pastoral Leadership, Missions, Member Care, and Preaching. Flexible training for college graduates, with or without Bible training, and for pastors or missionaries. Admission: Christian testimony, baccalaureate degree transcripts with 2.5 GPA, 3.0 GPA for MA Pastoral Counseling & Spiritual Formation, essay, references. Separate housing for single graduate students, on campus mobile home park for some married students. Faculty to student ratio: 1:18. Admissions deadline: August 1 - fall; January 1 - spring. Located on scenic 400 acre campus, seven miles from state capital.

CIU serves Christ and His church by inspiring, developing and equipping people for lifelong pursuit of God and servant leadership in His global cause.

Erskine College & Seminary
PO Box 176, Due West SC 29639
Bart Walker, Director of Admissions
864-379-8838 Fax: 864-379-3048
Website: www.erskine.edu
E-mail: admissions@erskine.edu

North Greenville University
PO Box 1892, Tigerville SC 29688-1892
Dr. Walter Johnson, Dept. Chair
Website: www.ngu.edu
See listing under "Universities"

SOUTHERN METHODIST COLLEGE

PO Box 1027, Orangeburg SC 29116-1027
Gary Briden, President
803-534-7826 Fax: 803-534-7827
Website: www.smcollege.edu
E-mail: smcinfo@smcollege.edu

TENNESSEE

Crichton College
255 N Highland St, Memphis TN 38111-4745
Shelly Luttrell, Dean of Admissions
901-320-9797 Fax: 901-320-9791
Website: www.crichton.edu
E-mail: admissions@crichton.edu

EMMANUEL SCHOOL OF RELIGION

One Walker Dr, Johnson City TN 37601-9438
David Fulks, Director of Admissions
423-461-1535 or 800-933-3771 Fax: 423-926-6198
Website: www.esr.edu
E-mail: admissions@esr.edu

Free Will Baptist Bible College
3606 W End Ave, Nashville TN 37205
Ryan Lewis, Director of Recruitment
800-76-FWBBC Fax: 615-269-6028
Website: www.fwbbc.edu
E-mail: recruit@fwbbc.edu

Lipscomb University
3901 Granny White Pike, Nashville TN 37204-3951
Ricky Holaway, Director of Admissions
800-333-4358 ext. 1776 Fax: 615-269-1804
Website: www.lipscomb.edu
E-mail: admissions@lipscomb.edu

NORTH TENNESSEE BIBLE INSTITUTE AND SEMINARY

PO Box 3797, Clarksville TN 37043-3797
Dr. William Corley, Chancellor
931-552-1510 Fax: 931-552-1464
Website: www.ntbis.com
E-mail: drwhc@ntbis.com

TEXAS

Abilene Christian University
ACU Box 29000, Abilene TX 79699-0001
325-674-2000 Fax: 325-674-2202
Website: www.acu.edu
E-mail: info@admissions.acu.edu

Arlington Baptist College
3001 W Division St, Arlington TX 76012-3425
Janie Taylor, Director of Admissions
817-461-8741 Fax: 817-274-1138
Website: www.abconline.edu
E-mail: jhall@abconline.org

BAPTIST MISSIONARY ASSOCIATION THEOLOGICAL SEMINARY

1530 E Pine St, Jacksonville TX 75766-5407
Charley Holmes, President
903-586-2501 Fax: 903-586-0378
Website: www.bmats.edu
E-mail: bmatsem@bmats.edu

BAPTIST UNIVERSITY OF THE AMERICAS

8019 S Panam Expy, San Antonio TX 78224-1336
Mary Ranjel, Director of Admissions
800-721-1396 Fax: 210-924-2701
Website: www.bua.edu
E-mail: mranjel@bua.edu

DALLAS THEOLOGICAL SEMINARY

3909 Swiss Ave, Dallas TX 75204-6411
Greg Hatteberg, Director of Admissions
214-841-3661 or 866-DTS-WORD Fax: 214-841-3664
Website: www.dts.edu
E-mail: admissions@dts.edu

HOUSTON GRADUATE SCHOOL OF THEOLOGY

2501 Central Parkway Suite A19, Houston TX 77092
Keith A. Jenkins, Ph.D., President
Daniel K. Dunlap, Ph.D., Dean of the Faculty
713-942-9505 or 877-TRY-HGST Fax: 713-942-9506
Website: www.hgst.edu
E-mail: mevans@hgst.edu

Established 1983. Private. Coed. Evangelical, Multicultural and Ecumenical. Accreditation: ATS (Association of Theological Schools in the US & Canada).

Degrees offered: MA, MA in Counseling (LPC & LMFT), M Div, D Min, and D Min for Military Chaplains (approved by all military branches); Certificate Program in Spiritual Formation; DMin also offered in Korean language. Undergraduate Degree Required.

Full-time 2007-08 Tuition: $8,190. Fees: $300. Rolling Application Deadlines - Fee: $50. Federal & Private financial aid available. Institutional Application & FAFSA required. Approved by Veterans Administration. Approximately 240 students. Faculty: 10 full-time, 21 part-time (90% with terminal degrees).

Fall, Bridge, Spring, May, and Summer I & II Terms. Classes taught day & evening, seven days a week. Campus conveniently located near center of 4th largest metropolitan area in the U.S.

KINGS WAY MISSIONARY INSTITUTE

401 S 35th St, Mc Allen TX 78501
956-682-6187 Fax: 956-682-9030
Website: www.kingswaymissionary.com
E-mail: kingswaymissionary@aol.com

Lubbock Christian University
5601 19th St, Lubbock TX 79407-2099
Stan Scott, Director of Admissions
806-796-8800 Fax: 806-720-7162
Website: www.lcu.edu
E-mail: stan.scott@lcu.edu

University of Dallas
1845 E Northgate Dr, Irving TX 75062-4736
Curt Eley, Dean
972-721-5000 Fax: 972-721-5017
Website: www.udallas.edu
E-mail: ugadmis@udallas.edu

VIRGINIA

Baptist Theological Seminary at Richmond
3400 Brook Rd, Richmond VA 23227-4536
Director of Admissions
888-345-BTSR Fax: 804-355-8182
Website: www.btsr.edu
E-mail: admissions@btsr.edu

Catholic Distance University
120 E Colonial Hwy, Hamilton VA 20158-9012
Marianne Evans Mount, Executive VP
888-254-4238 Fax: 540-338-4788
Website: www.cdu.edu
E-mail: tcashen@cdu.edu

UNION THEOLOGICAL SEMINARY AND PRESBYTERIAN SCHOOL OF CHRISTIAN EDUCATION

3401 Brook Rd, Richmond VA 23227-4597
Pat Morgan, Associate Director of Admissions
800-229-2990 Fax: 804-355-3919
Website: www.union-psce.edu
E-mail: admissn@union-psce.edu

WASHINGTON

BAKKE GRADUATE UNIVERSITY OF MINISTRY

1013 8th Ave, Seattle WA 98104-1222
Judi Melton, Registrar
206-264-9100 Fax: 206-264-0613
Website: www.bgu.edu
E-mail: bgu@bgu.edu

TRINITY LUTHERAN COLLEGE

4221 228th Ave SE, Issaquah WA 98029-9264
Jon Olson, VP of College Advancement
425-392-0400 Fax: 425-392-0404
Website: www.tlc.edu
E-mail: admission@tlc.edu

WEST VIRGINIA

Davis & Elkins College
100 Campus Dr, Elkins WV 26241-3996
Renee Heckel, Director of Enrollment Management
800-624-3157 Fax: 304-637-1800
Website: www.davisandelkins.edu
E-mail: admiss@davisandelkins.edu

Mountain State University
Box 9003, Beckley WV 25802-9003
Tony England, Director of Admissions
866-FOR-MSU1 or 304-929-INFO Fax: 304-253-5072
Website: www.mountainstate.edu
E-mail: gomsu@mountainstate.edu
See listing under "Universities"

WISCONSIN

Lakeland College
PO Box 359, Sheboygan WI 53082-0359
Nathan Dehne, Director of Admission
920-565-1100 Fax: 920-565-1215
Website: www.lakeland.edu
E-mail: admissions@lakeland.edu

Marquette University
PO Box 1881, Milwaukee WI 53201-1881
Robert Blust, Director of Admissions
414-288-7302 Fax: 414-288-3764
Website: www.mu.edu
E-mail: admissions@marquette.edu

NASHOTAH HOUSE
2777 Mission Rd, Nashotah WI 53058-9793
The Very Rev. Robert S. Munday, Ph.D., Dean and President
262-646-6500 Fax: 262-646-6504
Website: www.nashotah.edu
E-mail: nashotah@nashotah.edu

St. Norbert College
100 Grant St, De Pere WI 54115
Brian Studebaker, Director of Admission
800-236-4878 Fax: 920-403-4072
Website: www.snc.edu
E-mail: admit@snc.edu

WYOMING

University of Wyoming
Admissions Office
Dept 3435, Laramie WY 82071-3435
Brooke Culver, Contact
800-342-5996 Fax: 307-766-4042
Website: www.uwyo.edu
E-mail: why-wyo@uwyo.edu

PUERTO RICO

COLEGIO PENTECOSTAL MIZPA
PO Box 20966, San Juan PR 00928-0966
Rev. Daniel Cruz, President
787-720-4476 Fax: 787-720-2012
Website: www.colmizpa.edu
E-mail: presidente@colmizpa.edu

UNIVERSITIES AND COLLEGES

ALABAMA

Alabama A & M University
PO Box 908, Normal AL 35762
Antonio Boyle, Director of Admissions
256-372-5245

Alabama State University
PO Box 271, Montgomery AL 36101-0271
334-229-4200

Athens State University
300 N Beaty St, Athens AL 35611-1902
256-233-8100

Auburn University
Auburn AL 36849
334-844-4000

Auburn University at Montgomery
PO Box 244023, Montgomery AL 36124
334-244-3000

Birmingham-Southern College
900 Arkadelphia Rd, Birmingham AL 35254-0002
800-523-5793

CONCORDIA COLLEGE
1804 Green St, Selma AL 36703
Evelyn Pickens, Director of Enrollment Management and Placement
334-874-5700 Fax: 334-874-3728
Website: www.cuis.edu/www/cus/cual.html
E-mail: epickens@concordiaselma.edu

Faulkner University
5345 Atlanta Hwy, Montgomery AL 36109-3398
Keith Mock, Director of Admissions
800-879-9816 ext. 7200

Herzing College
280 W Valley Ave, Homewood AL 35209-4816
Kim Conway, Director of Admissions
205-916-2800 Fax: 205-916-2807
Website: www.herzing.edu/birmingham
E-mail: info@bhm.herzing.edu

Huntingdon College
1500 E Fairview Ave, Montgomery AL 36106-2148
334-833-4222

HUNTSVILLE BIBLE COLLEGE
904 Oakwood Ave NW, Huntsville AL 35811
John Clay, Contact
256-539-0834 Fax: 256-539-0854
Website: www.huntsvillebiblecollege.com
E-mail: hbc@huntsvillebiblecollege.com

Jacksonville State University
700 Pelham Rd N, Jacksonville AL 36265-1602
256-782-5000

Judson College
302 Bibb St, Marion AL 36756
Michael Scotto, Director of Admissions
800-447-9472 Fax: 334-683-5147
Website: www.judson.edu
E-mail: admissions@judson.edu

Miles College
PO Box 3800, Birmingham AL 35208
205-929-1654

Oakwood College
Oakwood Rd NW, Huntsville AL 35896-0001
256-726-7000

Samford University
800 Lakeshore Dr, Birmingham AL 35229-0002
205-726-3673

Selma University
1501 Lapsley St, Selma AL 36701
334-872-2533

Southern Christian University
1200 Taylor Rd, Montgomery AL 36117
800-351-4040

Spring Hill College
4000 Dauphin St, Mobile AL 36608-1791
334-460-4000

Stillman College
PO Box 1430, Tuscaloosa AL 35403-1430
205-349-4240

Strayer University
3570 Grandview Pkwy, Birmingham AL 35243
205-453-6300

Talladega College
627 Battle St W, Talladega AL 35160-2354
256-362-0206

Troy University
Troy AL 36082-0001
Jim Hutto, Dean of Enrollment Management
334-670-3175

Troy University Dothan
PO Box 8368, Dothan AL 36304-0368
334-983-6556

Troy University Montgomery
PO Box 4419, Montgomery AL 36103-4419
334-834-1400

Troy University - Phenix City
1 University Pl, Phenix City AL 36869
334-297-1007

Tuskegee University
Tuskegee Institute AL 36088
334-727-8011

University of Alabama
Box 870118, Tuscaloosa AL 35487
Dr. Lisa B. Harris, Director of Admissions
205-348-5666

University of Alabama at Birmingham
Univ Sta, Birmingham AL 35294-0001
205-934-4011

University of Alabama in Huntsville
PO Box 1247, Huntsville AL 35899-0001
Nikki Willis, Assoc. Director for Recruiting Program and Events
1-800-UAH-CALL Fax: 256-824-6073
Website: www.uah.edu
E-mail: willisn@uah.edu

University of Mobile
5735 College Pkwy, Mobile AL 36613
800-946-7267

University of Montevallo
Station 6030, Montevallo AL 35115
205-665-6030

University of North Alabama
Univ Sta, Florence AL 35632-0001
256-760-4100

University of South Alabama
307 University Blvd N, Mobile AL 36688-3053
Melissa Haab, Director of Admissions
251-460-6141 Fax: 251-460-7876
Website: www.southalabama.edu
E-mail: admiss@usouthal.edu

University of West Alabama
Hwy 11, Livingston AL 35470
205-652-3400

Virginia College
65 Bagby Dr, Birmingham AL 35209
205-802-1200

ALASKA

ALASKA BIBLE COLLEGE
PO Box 289, Glennallen AK 99588-0289
907-822-3201 Fax: 907-822-5027
Website: www.akbible.edu
E-mail: info@akbible.edu

Alaska Pacific University
4101 University Dr, Anchorage AK 99508-4672
Ernie Norton, Director of Admissions
800-252-7528

Charter College
2221 E Northern Lights Blvd Ste 120
Anchorage AK 99508-4157
907-276-7712

Sheldon Jackson College
801 Lincoln St, Sitka AK 99835-7651
800-478-4556

University of Alaska Anchorage
PO Box 141629, Anchorage AK 99514-1629
Cecile Mitchell, Director of Enrollment Services
907-786-1480 Fax: 907-786-4888
Website: www.uaa.alaska.edu/
E-mail: enroll@uaa.alaska.edu

University of Alaska
Bristol Bay Campus
PO Box 1070, Dillingham AK 99576-1070
907-842-5109

University of Alaska
Chuchi Campus
PO Box 297, Kotzebue AK 99752-0297
907-442-3400

University of Alaska Fairbanks
PO Box 757480, Fairbanks AK 99775
907-474-7581

University of Alaska Interior Campus
PO Box 756720, Fairbanks AK 99775-6720
907-474-7211

University of Alaska Matanuska-Susitna
PO Box 2889, Palmer AK 99645-2889
907-745-9712

University of Alaska Southeast
11120 Glacier Hwy, Juneau AK 99801-8625
Paul Kraft, Dean of Students/Enrollment Management
907-796-6000

University of Alaska Southeast-Ketchikan
2600 7th Ave, Ketchikan AK 99901-5728
907-225-6177

University of Alaska
Tanana Valley Campus
PO Box 758000, Fairbanks AK 99775-8000
907-474-7400

ARIZONA

American Indian College of the Assemblies of God
10020 N 15th Ave, Phoenix AZ 85021-2199
Steve Clindaniel, Director of Admissions
602-944-3335

Apollo College
630 W Southern Ave, Mesa AZ 85210-5005
480-831-6585 Fax: 480-827-0022

Apollo College
8503 N 27th Ave, Phoenix AZ 85051-4063
602-864-1571 Fax: 602-864-8207

Apollo College
2701 W Bethany Home Rd, Phoenix AZ 85017-1705
602-433-1333 Fax: 602-433-1414

Apollo College
3550 N Oracle Rd, Tucson AZ 85705
520-888-5885 Fax: 520-887-3005

Arizona State University
PO Box 870112, Tempe AZ 85287-0112
480-965-9011

Arizona State University Polytechnic
7001 E Williams Field Rd, Mesa AZ 85212
480-727-3278

Arizona State University West
PO Box 37110, Phoenix AZ 85069-7110
602-543-5500

Collins College: A School of Design and Technology
(Formerly Al Collins Graphic Design School)
1140 S Priest Dr, Tempe AZ 85281-5240
Toby Craver, Director of National Admissions
800-876-7070 Fax: 480-829-0183
Website: www.collinscollege.edu

The Conservatory of Recording Arts & Sciences
2300 E Broadway Rd, Tempe AZ 85282-1707
Tonya Visconti, Director of Admissions
800-562-6383 or 480-858-9400 Fax: 480-829-1332
Website: cras.org
E-mail: info@cras.org
See listing under "Music"

Grand Canyon University
3300 W Camelback Rd, Phoenix AZ 85017-1097
602-249-3300

International Baptist College
2150 E Southern Ave, Tempe AZ 85282
480-838-7070

International Institute of the Americas
925 S Gilbert Rd Ste 201, Mesa AZ 85204-4440
Todd Olehausen, Director
480-545-8755 Fax: 480-926-1371
Website: www.iia.edu
E-mail: tolehausen@iia.edu

International Institute of the Americas
6049 N 43rd Ave, Phoenix AZ 85019-1600
John Pechota, Director of Admissions
602-242-6265 Fax: 602-589-1353
Website: www.iia.edu
E-mail: jpechota@iia.edu

International Institute of the Americas
5441 E 22nd St, Tucson AZ 85710
Leigh Anne Pechota, Director
520-748-9799 Fax: 520-748-9355
Website: www.iia.edu
E-mail: lpechota@iia.edu

Midwestern University
19555 N 59th Ave, Glendale AZ 85308-6814
James Walter, Director of Admissions
623-572-3275

Northcentral University
505 W Whipple St, Prescott AZ 86301
928-541-7777

Northern Arizona University
PO Box 4084, Flagstaff AZ 86011-0001
520-523-9011

Phoenix First Pastors College
1220 E Rosemonte Dr, Phoenix AZ 85024-2921
602-867-4587

Phoenix Seminary
4222 E Thomas Rd Ste 400, Phoenix AZ 85018
602-850-8000

Prescott College
220 Grove Ave, Prescott AZ 86301-2912
928-778-2090

Remington College
875 W Elliot Rd #126, Tempe AZ 85284-1133
Joe Drennen, President
800-395-4322

Southwestern College
2625 E Cactus Rd, Phoenix AZ 85032-7097
Admissions/Financial Aid Office
800-247-2697

University of Advancing Technology
2625 W Baseline Rd, Tempe AZ 85283
Lary Dougherty, Director of Admissions
800-658-5744

University of Arizona
Tucson AZ 85721-0040
Paul Kohn, Director of Admissions
520-621-3237

University of Phoenix
4615 E Elwood St, Phoenix AZ 85040-1908
480-966-9577

Western International University
9215 N Black Canyon Hwy, Phoenix AZ 85021-2718
602-943-2311

ARKANSAS

Arkansas Baptist College
1621 Martin Luther King Dr, Little Rock AR 72202
501-370-4000

Arkansas State University
PO Box 1630, State University AR 72467-1630
870-972-2100

Arkansas State University Mountain Home
1600 S College St, Mountain Home AR 72653
Tonya Sexton, Director of Marketing & Public Relations
870-508-6109

Arkansas Tech University
215 W O St, Russellville AR 72801-2222
479-968-0389

Central Baptist College
1501 College Ave, Conway AR 72032
501-329-6872

Ecclesia College
9653 Nations Dr, Springdale AR 72762
800-735-9926

Harding University
900 E Center Ave, Searcy AR 72149
501-279-4000

Henderson State University
1100 Henderson St, Arkadelphia AR 71999-0001
870-230-5000

Hendrix College
1600 Washington Ave, Conway AR 72032-3080
501-329-6811

John Brown University
2000 W University St, Siloam Springs AR 72761-2121
877-JBU-INFO

Lyon College
PO Box 2317, Batesville AR 72503-2317
Dan Rutledge, Director of Admissions
870-793-9813

Ouachita Baptist University
410 Ouachita St, Arkadelphia AR 71998-0001
David Goodman, Director of Admissions
870-245-5110

Philander Smith College
812 W 13th St, Little Rock AR 72202-3799
501-375-9845

Southern Arkansas University
100 E University, Magnolia AR 71753
870-235-4000

University of Arkansas at Fayetteville
1 University of Arkansas, Fayetteville AR 72701-1201
479-575-2000

University of Arkansas at Little Rock
2801 S University Ave, Little Rock AR 72204-1000
501-569-3000

University of Arkansas at Monticello
PO Box 3600, Monticello AR 71656
870-367-6811

University of Arkansas at Pine Bluff
1200 University Dr, Pine Bluff AR 71601-2799
870-543-8000

University of Arkansas for Medical Sciences
4301 W Markham St, Little Rock AR 72205-7101
501-686-5000

University of Central Arkansas
201 Donaghey Ave, Conway AR 72035-5003
501-450-5000

University of the Ozarks
415 N College Ave, Clarksville AR 72830-2880
Jim Decker, Director of Admissions
479-979-1000

Williams Baptist College
PO Box 3737, Walnut Ridge AR 72476-3737
Angela Flippo, Vice President for Enrollment Management
800-722-4434 Fax: 870-759-4163
Website: www.williamsbaptistcollege.com
E-mail: admissions@wbcoll.edu

CALIFORNIA

American Institute of Health Science
3501 Atlantic Ave, Long Beach CA 90807
562-988-2278

American InterContinental University
12655 W Jefferson Blvd, Los Angeles CA 90066
310-302-2000

Antioch University
801 Garden St Ste 101
Santa Barbara CA 93101-1581
Ankara McPherson, Director of Admissions
805-962-8179

Antioch University Southern California
400 Corporate Pointe, Culver City CA 90230-7615
Admissions Office
800-7-ANTIOCH Fax: 310-821-6032
E-mail: admissions@antiochla.edu

Argosy University
San Francisco Bay Area Campus
999A Canal Blvd, Point Richmond CA 94804-3547
Cynthia Sirkin, Associate Director of Admissions
510-215-0277

Armstrong University
1301 Marina Village Pkwy Suite 340
Alameda CA 94601-1084
510-865-1336

Art Institute of California - Inland Empire
630 E Brier Dr, San Bernardino CA 92408
909-915-2100

The Art Institute of California - San Francisco
1170 Market St, San Francisco CA 94102-4908
Director of Admissions
888-493-3261

Azusa Pacific University
901 E Alosta Ave, Azusa CA 91702
626-969-3434

Bethany University
800 Bethany Dr, Scotts Valley CA 95066-2896
831-438-3800

Bethesda Christian University
730 N Euclid St, Anaheim CA 92801-4132
Dr. Grace Sung Cho, D.D., Chancellor
714-517-1945

Biola University
13800 Biola Ave, La Mirada CA 90639-0001
562-903-4752

Brooks Institute of Photography
801 Alston Rd, Santa Barbara CA 93108-2399
Inge B. Kautzmann, Director of Admissions
805-966-3888 ext. 217 or 218

California Baptist University
8432 Magnolia Ave, Riverside CA 92504-3297
951-689-5771

California Christian College
4881 E University Ave, Fresno CA 93703-3599
559-251-4215

CALIFORNIA COAST UNIVERSITY

700 N Main St, Santa Ana CA 92701
Admissions Office: 888-CCU-UNIV or 714-547-9625
Fax: 714-547-5777
Dr. Thomas Neal, President
Dr. Cynthia Teeple, Academic Vice President
Website: www.calcoast.edu
E-mail: info@calcoast.edu

Established 1973. Proprietary. Coed. Accreditation: California Coast University holds accreditation through the Accrediting Commission of the Distance Education and Training Council (DETC). The DETC is an educational association located in Washington, D.C. Founded in 1926, it is the standard setting agency for distance education institutions. Approval: Bureau for Private Postsecondary and Vocational Education - State of California, charter member California Association of State Approved Colleges & Universities, member Association for Adult & Continuing Education, member The Alliance for Private Post Secondary Academic Institutions.

Tuition: $2,805-$12,070. California Coast University has selected the SLM Corporation, commonly known as Sallie Mae, to help the university provide financing for its students. Sallie Mae is the nation's leading provider of education funding. Sallie Mae also allows students to borrow additional loan amounts to cover additional expenses, such as textbooks, equipment, or living expenses.

Enrollment: 30,000. California Coast University is approved by the California State Approving Agency to enroll veterans or other eligible persons under Title 38, U.S. Code. California Coast University holds a Memorandum of Understanding with Defense Activity for Non-Traditional Education Support (DANTES) as an external degree provider.

A private college offering off-campus independent study programs in the traditional areas of business administration, management, psychology, education. Admissions: enroll year round, requires official transcripts, letters of recommendation, detailed curriculum vita or occupational history.

Process: evaluation of prior academic work followed by analysis of occupational history, including participation in workshops, seminars, training programs, specialized projects for credit. Credit is demonstrated by accelerated learning guides or study guides.

Residency: All course work may be completed off campus, utilizing correspondence methods. Interest free loans available to students.

California College of the Arts
1111 Eighth St, San Francisco CA 94107
Robynne Royster, Director of Admission
800-447-1-ART or 415-703-9523 Fax: 415-703-9539
Website: www.cca.edu
E-mail: enroll@cca.edu

California College of the Arts
Oakland Campus
5212 Broadway, Oakland CA 94618-1487
Robynne Royster, Director of Admission
800-447-1-ART Fax: 415-703-9539
Website: www.cca.edu
E-mail: enroll@cca.edu

California Institute of Technology
1200 E California Blvd, Pasadena CA 91106
626-395-6341

California Lutheran University
60 W Olsen Rd, Thousand Oaks CA 91360-2787
805-492-2411

California Polytechnic State University
San Luis Obispo CA 93407
805-756-1111

California State Polytechnic University
3801 W Temple Ave, Pomona CA 91768-2557
909-869-2000

California State University-Bakersfield
9001 Stockdale Hwy, Bakersfield CA 93311-1022
661-664-2011

California State University Channel Isle
1 University Dr, Camarillo CA 93012
805-437-8400

California State University-Chico
Chico CA 95929-0001
530-898-6116

California State University-Dominguez Hills
1000 E Victoria St, Carson CA 90747-0001
310-243-3300

California State University-East Bay
25800 Carlos Bee Blvd, Hayward CA 94542-3001
510-885-3000

California State University-Fresno
Fresno CA 93740-0001
559-278-4240

California State University-Fullerton
PO Box 34080
Fullerton CA 92634
714-278-2011

California State University-Long Beach
1250 N Bellflower Blvd, Long Beach CA 90840-0006
562-985-4111

California State University-Los Angeles
5151 State University Dr, Los Angeles CA 90032
323-343-3000

California State University-Monterey Bay
100 Campus Center, Seaside CA 93955-8000
831-582-3000

California State University-Northridge
18111 Nordhoff St, Northridge CA 91330-0001
818-677-1200

California State University-Sacramento
6000 J St, Sacramento CA 95819-2605
916-278-6011

California State University-San Bernadino
5500 University Pkwy
San Bernardino CA 92407-2393
Olivia Rosas, Director of Admissions
909-537-5188 Fax: 909-537-7034
Website: www.csusb.edu
E-mail: orosas@csusb.edu

California State University-San Marcos
San Marcos CA 92096-0001
760-750-4000

California State University-Stanislaus
801 W Monte Vista Ave, Turlock CA 95382-0256
Lisa Bernardo, Director of Admissions
209-667-3070

Chapman University
One University Drive, Orange CA 92866-1099
Michael Drummy, Assistant Vice President for Enrollment
Services and Chief Admission Officer
714-997-6411 or 888-CUAPPLY Fax: 714-997-6713
Website: www.chapman.edu
E-mail: admit@chapman.edu

Charles R. Drew University of Medicine & Science
1621 E 120th St, Los Angeles CA 90059
323-563-4800

Claremont McKenna College
500 E 9th St, Claremont CA 91711-5903
909-621-8000

COGSWELL COLLEGE

1175 Bordeaux Dr, Sunnyvale CA 94089-1210
Patricia Del Rio, Director of Admissions
800-264-7955 or 408-541-0100 Fax: 408-747-0764
Website: www.cogswell.edu
E-mail: info@cogswell.edu

Established in 1907. Private. Nonprofit. Coed. WASC accredited. Fusion of Art and Engineering. Bachelor of Arts Degrees: Digital Art and Animation (DAA), Digital Motion Picture (DMP). Bachelor of Science Degrees: Digital Audio Technology (DAT), Digital Arts Engineering (DAE), Electrical Engineering (EE), Software Engineering (SE), Fire Science (distance learning). Hands-on creative environment. Student-teacher ratio 12:1. Professional-quality software programs. Internships. Portfolio required for DAA, DAT and DMP majors.

COLEMAN COLLEGE
8888 Balboa Ave, San Diego CA 92123-1506
Sheryl L. Ridens, Dean of Academics
858-499-0202 Fax: 858-499-0233
Website: www.coleman.edu
E-mail: admissions@coleman.edu

COLEMAN COLLEGE
1284 W San Marcos Blvd Suite 110
San Marcos CA 92069-4073
Darlene Ankton, Vice President
760-747-3990 Fax: 760-752-9808
Website: www.coleman.edu
E-mail: ncadmiss@coleman.edu

COMMUNITY CHRISTIAN COLLEGE
251 Tennessee St, Redlands CA 92373
909-335-8863 Fax: 909-335-9101
Website: www.cccollege.net
E-mail: admin@cccollege.net

Concordia University
1530 Concordia, Irvine CA 92612-3203
Lori McDonald, Executive Director of Enrollment Services
800-229-1200 or 949-854-8002 Fax: 949-854-6894
Website: www.cui.edu
E-mail: admission@cui.edu

Concord Law School
10866 Wilshire Blvd Ste 1200, Los Angeles CA 90024
800-439-4794

Design Institute of San Diego
8555 Commerce Ave, San Diego CA 92121-2610
Paula Parrish, Director of Admissions
858-566-1200

Dominican University of California
50 Acacia Ave, San Rafael CA 94901-2298
Office of Admissions
888-323-6762 Fax: 415-485-3214
Website: www.dominican.edu
E-mail: enroll@dominican.edu

Emmanuel Bible College
1605 E Elizabeth St, Pasadena CA 91104
626-791-2575

Expression College for Digital Arts
6601 Shellmound St, Emeryville CA 94608
510-654-2934

Fashion Careers College
1923 Morena Blvd, San Diego CA 92110-3555
Silvana Carelli, Director of Enrollment
619-275-4700 Fax: 619-275-0635
Website: www.fashioncareerscollege.com
E-mail: info@fashioncareerscollege.com
See listing under "Fashion Art"

FIDM/The Fashion Institute of Design & Merchandising
17590 Gillette Ave, Irvine CA 92614
Director of Admissions
949-851-6200 or 888-974-3436 Fax: 949-851-6808
Website: www.fidm.edu
E-mail: info@fidm.com
See listing under "Community and Junior Colleges"

FIDM/The Fashion Institute of Design & Merchandising
919 S Grand Ave, Los Angeles CA 90015-1421
Director of Admissions
213-624-1201 or 800-624-1200 Fax: 213-624-4799
Website: www.fidm.edu
E-mail: info@fidm.com
See listing under "Community and Junior Colleges"

FIDM/The Fashion Institute of Design & Merchandising
1010 2nd Ave, San Diego CA 92101-4903
Director of Admissions
619-235-2049 or 800-243-3436 Fax: 619-232-4322
Website: www.fidm.edu
E-mail: info@fidm.com
See listing under "Community and Junior Colleges"

FIDM/The Fashion Institute of Design & Merchandising
55 Stockton St, San Francisco CA 94108-5829
Director of Admissions
415-675-5200 or 800-422-3436 Fax: 415-296-7299
Website: www.fidm.edu
E-mail: info@fidm.com
See listing under "Community and Junior Colleges"

Fresno Pacific University
1717 S Chestnut Ave, Fresno CA 93702-4798
559-453-2000

Golden Gate University
536 Mission St, San Francisco CA 94105-2967
415-442-7000

Harvey Mudd College
Claremont CA 91711-3104
Peter Osgood, Contact
909-621-8011

Holy Names University
3500 Mountain Blvd, Oakland CA 94619-1699
Dr. Hoffman-Marr, Director of Admissions
510-436-1010

Hope International University
2500 Nutwood Ave, Fullerton CA 92831-3104
714-879-3901

Humboldt State University
1 Harpst St, Arcata CA 95521-8299
707-826-3011

Humphreys College
6650 Inglewood Ave, Stockton CA 95207-3896
209-478-0800

Institute of Computer Technology
3200 Wilshire Blvd, Los Angeles CA 90010-1308
Director of Admissions
213-381-3333

Interior Designers Institute
1061 Camelback St, Newport Beach CA 92660-3228
949-675-4451

ITT Technical Institute
9680 Granite Ridge Dr, San Diego CA 92123-2657
858-571-8500

John F. Kennedy University
100 Ellinwood Way, Pleasant Hill CA 94523-4817
800-696-5358
Website: www.jfku.edu

The Kings College and Seminary
14800 Sherman Way, Van Nuys CA 91405
818-779-8040

Laguna College of Art and Design
2222 Laguna Canyon Rd
Laguna Beach CA 92651-1136
Anthony Padilla, V.P. of Enrollment
800-255-0762

La Sierra University
4500 Riverwalk Pkwy, Riverside CA 92505
Bobby Brown, Director of Admissions
800-874-5587

Life Pacific College
1100 W Covina Blvd, San Dimas CA 91773-3298
800-356-0001

Lincoln University
401 15th St, Oakland CA 94612-2801
510-628-8010

Loma Linda University
Loma Linda CA 92350-0001
Richard Weismeyer, Director
800-422-4558

Loyola Marymount University
7900 Loyola Blvd, Los Angeles CA 90045-2699
310-338-2700

Master's College and Seminary
21726 Placerita Canyon Rd, Newhall CA 91321-1235
661-259-3540

Menlo College
1000 El Camino Real, Atherton CA 94027-4300
650-688-3753

Mt. St. Mary's College
12001 Chalon Rd, Los Angeles CA 90049-1599
310-954-4000

National Hispanic University
14271 Story Rd, San Jose CA 95127-3889
Outreach & Recruitment
408-273-2680

National University
11255 N Torrey Pines Rd, La Jolla CA 92037-1011
858-642-8000

New College School of Law
50 Fell St, San Francisco CA 94102-5206
Sharon Pittman, Dean of Admissions
415-241-1300 Fax: 415-241-9525
Website: www.newcollege.edu
E-mail: spittman@newcollege.edu or lawadmissions@newcollege.edu

Newschool of Architecture and Design
1249 F St, San Diego CA 92101-6634
Gilbert D. Cooke, AIA, Dean
Barbara Wingate, Director of Admissions
619-235-4100 ext. 123

Northwestern Polytechnic University
47671 Westinghouse Dr, Fremont CA 94539
Dr. P. Hsu, Contact
510-657-5913 Fax: 510-657-8975
Website: www.npu.edu
E-mail: npuadm@npu.edu

Notre Dame de Namur University
1500 Ralston Ave, Belmont CA 94002-1997
Martin Bednarek, Director of Admissions
800-263-0545

Occidental College
1600 Campus Rd, Los Angeles CA 90041-3314
323-259-2500

Otis College of Art and Design
9045 Lincoln Blvd, Los Angeles CA 90045-3505
Samuel Hoi, President
310-665-6800

PACIFIC STATES UNIVERSITY
1516 S Western Ave, Los Angeles CA 90006-4299
Dr. Brandon Kim, Associate University Dean
323-731-2383 Fax: 323-731-7276
Website: www.psuca.edu
E-mail: admissions@psuca.edu

Established 1928. Private. Coed. Accreditation: Accrediting Council for Independent Colleges & Schools (ACICS). Tuition: BBA - $7,920, MBA - $8,400. Fees: $1,910. Enrollment: 300. Faculty: 22. Student-faculty ratio: 8:1. Degrees: BBA, MBA, BSCIS, MSCS, MSIS. Library: 15,000 volumes. 7 buildings. International student body & faculty. Located in the great metropolitan city of Los Angeles. Financial aid and scholarships are available. Limited on campus housing.

Pacific Union College
1 Angwin Ave, Angwin CA 94508-9797
707-965-6311

Patten University
2433 Coolidge Ave, Oakland CA 94601-2699
Dr. Gary Moncher, President
Inez Bailey, Director of Admissions
510-261-8500

Pepperdine University
24255 Pacific Coast Hwy, Malibu CA 90263-0002
310-456-4000

Pitzer College
1050 N Mills Ave, Claremont CA 91711-6101
909-621-8219

PLATT (MEDIA ARTS) COLLEGE - SAN DIEGO
6250 El Cajon Blvd, San Diego CA 92115
Al Medro, Vice President
619-265-0107 or 866-752-8826 Fax: 619-308-0570
Website: www.platt.edu
E-mail: info@platt.edu

Point Loma Nazarene University
3900 Lomaland Dr, San Diego CA 92106-2810
Chip Killingsworth, Director of Undergraduate Admissions
800-733-7770 Fax: 619-849-2601
Website: www.pointloma.edu
E-mail: admissions@pointloma.edu

Pomona College
333 N College Way, Claremont CA 91711-4429
Peter W. Stanley, President

Remington College
123 Camino De La Reina #100N
San Diego CA 92108-3002
Christopher Tilley, Campus President
619-686-8600

St. Mary's College
1928 Saint Marys Rd, Moraga CA 94556-2744
925-631-4000

Samuel Merritt College
370 Hawthorne Ave, Oakland CA 94609-3108
Anne Seed, Assoc. Director of Admission
510-869-6610

San Diego Christian College
2100 Greenfield Dr, El Cajon CA 92019-1157
Rene Inman, Director of Admissions
800-676-2242 Fax: 619-590-1739
Website: www.sdcc.edu
E-mail: admissions@sdcc.edu

San Diego State University
5500 Campanile Dr, San Diego CA 92182-0002
619-594-5200

SAN FRANCISCO ART INSTITUTE
800 Chestnut St, San Francisco CA 94133
800-345-SFAI Fax: 415-749-4503
Website: www.sfai.edu
E-mail: admissions@sfai.edu

Founded in 1871, SFAI offers one of the most innovative and interdisciplinary environments in higher education. Offering accredited Bachelor of Fine Arts (BFA), Bachelor of Arts (BA), Master of Fine Arts (MFA), Summer Master of Fine Arts (SMFA), Post-Baccalaureate (PB), and Master of Arts (MA) programs, SFAI is committed to furthering the relationship between the practices and theories of contemporary art. SFAI's School of Studio Practice centers on the development of the artist's vision and consists of the departments of: Design+Technology, Film, New Genres, Painting, Photography, Printmaking, and Sculpture. SFAI's School of Interdisciplinary Studies offers BA and MA programs in History and Theory of Contemporary Art, Urban Studies, and Exhibition and Museum Studies (MA only). Together the two schools provide an inclusive model to address contemporary art and culture, and the programs prepare students to be creative practitioners in a variety of professional fields. The Summer MFA program has the same rigor as the Academic Year MFA, yet is designed for those who choose an alternate academic schedule. The Post-Baccalaureate program is an excellent way to prepare for entrance into an MFA program or to enhance skills and knowledge. SFAI's faculty is comprised of active artists, curators, writers, and scholars. Dean of Academic Affairs is renowned curator and critic Okwui Enwezor. Dean of Graduate Studies is artist and filmmaker Renee Green. Director of Exhibitions and Public Programs is curator Hou Hanru. Visiting artists and scholars play a significant role in education at SFAI, with recent visitors including Matthew Barney, William Kentridge, Raqs Media Collective, and others. All students have 24-hour access to the SFAI campus. SFAI's main campus includes painting, photography, sculpture, and printmaking studios, post-production facilities, and the first high-definition video research lab in the Bay Area. The Diego Rivera Gallery, an open-air amphitheater, and a 250-seat theater are also available to students for exhibiting and screening work. SFAI's library collection includes more than 26,000 volumes with emphasis on modern and contemporary art, over 200 current periodicals, and an extensive image, video, and audio archive available only to SFAI students. The 62,000 square-foot Graduate Center includes a digital lab, film and sound studios, darkrooms, a woodshop, and a gallery for student work. SFAI has rolling application deadlines, and there are competitive and need-based scholarships available to undergraduates, a fellowship program for graduate students, and community college scholarships for transfer students. Visit the SFAI website for specific application requirements.

SAN FRANCISCO CONSERVATORY OF MUSIC
50 Oak St, San Francisco CA 94102
Alexander Brose, Director of Admission
800-899-7326 Fax: 415-503-6299
Website: www.sfcm.edu
E-mail: admit@sfcm.edu

San Francisco State University
1600 Holloway Ave, San Francisco CA 94132-1722
415-338-1111

San Jose State University
1 Washington Sq, San Jose CA 95192-0001
408-924-1000

Santa Clara University
500 El Camino Real, Santa Clara CA 95053-0001
408-554-4000

Shasta Bible College & Graduate School
2951 Goodwater Ave, Redding CA 96002
530-221-4275

SIMPSON UNIVERSITY
2211 College View Dr, Redding CA 96003-8606
Jim Herberger, Director of Admissions
888-9-SIMPSON Fax: 530-226-4861
Website: www.simpsonuniversity.edu
E-mail: admissions@simpsonuniversity.edu

Established 1921. Private. Coeducational. Accreditation: WASC. Tuition: $18,600. Room and board: $6,400. Fees: Internet: $72; Parking: $80; Deposit: $10; Application fee: $25; Music Lessons: $250 per credit. Enrollment: 1,000 full-time, 100 part-time. Faculty: 60. Student-faculty ratio: 18:1.

Degrees offered: Bible and Theology, Business Administration, Communication, Cross-Cultural Studies, Discipleship and Education Ministries, Elementary Education, English, English for Teachers, General Ministries, History, Liberal Studies, Management Information Systems (MIS), Mathematics, Math for Teachers, Music Education, Music With Emphasis in Applied Piano, Music With Emphasis in Applied Voice, Music With Emphasis in Applied Instruments, Worship Ministries, Music Composition, Music with Liberal Arts Emphasis, Pastoral Studies, Psychology, Social Science, Social Science for teachers, World Missions, Youth Ministries, Biology, Outdoor Leadership, Pre-Nursing Certificate.

Library: 100,000 volumes. 15 buildings on 85 acres. First school to have a Vice President for Spiritual Formation, Student led chapel, Professor translated the book of Obadiah for the NKJV of the Bible, Hebrew Professor is third most sought after Hebrew Scholar in the world, 85% of undergrads live on campus, fifty countries represented by our student body and faculty past and present.

SOKA UNIVERSITY OF AMERICA
1 University Dr, Aliso Viejo CA 92656
Eric Hauber, Ph.D., Special Assistant to the President
949-480-4150 Fax: 949-480-4151
Website: www.soka.edu
E-mail: hauber@soka.edu

Sonoma State University
1801 E Cotati Ave, Rohnert Park CA 94928-3609
Louis T. Levy, Senior Director Enrollment Services
707-664-2880

SOUTHERN CALIFORNIA INSTITUTE OF ARCHITECTURE
960 E 3rd St, Los Angeles CA 90013-1822
J.J. Jackman, Director of Admissions
213-613-2200 ext 321 Fax: 213-613-2260
Website: www.sciarc.edu
E-mail: admissions@sciarc.edu

Established 1972. Coed. Accreditation: NAAB, WASC. Tuition: $10,180/sem. Enrollment: 450. Faculty: 80. Student-faculty ratio: 15:1. Degrees offered: BArch, 3 yr MArch, 2 yr MArch, 2 Post-Grad degrees. Library: 30,000 volumes. Founded as a radical alternative to the conventional system of arch education; only architecture-focused academic library in Southern California; dark room; CNC facilities, print center, wood & metal shop all on premises; located in downtown LA.

SOUTHERN CALIFORNIA SEMINARY
2075 E Madison Ave, El Cajon CA 92019
Steve Perdue, Admissions Director
888-389-7244 Fax: 619-442-4510
Website: www.socalsem.edu
E-mail: sperdue@socalsem.edu

Stanford University
Hopkins Marine Station, Pacific Grove CA 93950
831-373-0464

Stanford University
520 Lasuen Mall Union 232, Stanford CA 94305-3005
650-723-2300

Thomas Aquinas College
10000 Ojai Rd, Santa Paula CA 93060-9621
800-634-9797

Touro University International
5665 Plaza Dr 3rd Floor, Cypress CA 90630
714-816-0366

Trinity Life Bible College
5225 Hillsdale Blvd, Sacramento CA 95842
916-348-4689

University of California
110 Sproul Hall, Berkeley CA 94720-5804
510-642-6000

University of California
1 Shields Ave, Davis CA 95616
530-752-1011

University of California
Irvine CA 92697-0001
949-824-5011

University of California
9500 Gilman Dr, La Jolla CA 92093
858-534-2230

University of California
Los Angeles CA 90095-0001
310-825-4321

University of California
900 University Ave, Riverside CA 92521-0001
951-827-1012

University of California
Santa Barbara CA 93106
805-893-8000

University of California-Davis
2315 Stockton Blvd, Sacramento CA 95817-2201
916-453-3096

University of California-Irvine Med. Ctr
101 The City Dr S, Orange CA 92868-3201
714-456-5678

University of California Los Angeles
Center for the Health Sciences
10833 Le Conte Ave, Los Angeles CA 90095-3075
310-825-5654

University of California Medical Center
200 W Arbor Dr #H-910C, San Diego CA 92103-1911
619-543-6654

University of California-Santa Cruz
Santa Cruz CA 95064
831-459-0111

University of Judaism
15600 Mulholland Dr, Los Angeles CA 90077-1599
Bryan Pisetsky, Director of Undergraduate Admissions
310-476-9777

University of La Verne
1950 3rd St, La Verne CA 91750-4443
800-876-4858

University of Redlands
PO Box 3080, Redlands CA 92373-0999
909-793-2121

University of San Diego
5998 Alcala Park, San Diego CA 92110-2492
Admissions
619-260-4506

University of San Francisco
2130 Fulton St, San Francisco CA 94117-1050
415-422-5555

University of Southern California
Univ Park, Los Angeles CA 90089-0001
213-740-2311

University of the Pacific
3601 Pacific Ave, Stockton CA 95211-0197
209-946-2011

UNIVERSITY OF THE WEST
1409 N Walnut Grove Ave, Rosemead CA 91770
Grace Hsiao, Registrar & Admissions Officer
626-571-8811 Fax: 626-571-1413
Website: www.uwest.edu
E-mail: graceh@uwest.edu

Vanguard University of Southern California
55 Fair Dr, Costa Mesa CA 92626-6597
714-556-3610

Westmont College
955 La Paz Rd, Santa Barbara CA 93108-1099
Joyce Luy, Director of Admissions
805-565-6200

Westwood College
3250 Wilshire Blvd Fl 4, Los Angeles CA 90010
213-739-9999

Whittier College
PO Box 634, Whittier CA 90608-0634
Kieron Miller, Director of Admissions
562-907-4200 Fax: 562-907-4870
Website: www.whittier.edu
E-mail: kmiller@whittier.edu

William Jessup University
1190 Saratoga Ave Ste 210, San Jose CA 95129
408-278-4343

Woodbury University
7500 N Glenoaks Blvd, Burbank CA 91504-1099
818-767-0888

World Mission University
500 Shatto Pl Ste 600, Los Angeles CA 90020
213-385-2322

COLORADO

Adams State College
Alamosa CO 81102
Matt Gallegos, Director of Admissions
800-824-6494

American University of Paris
950 S Cherry St Ste 240, Denver CO 80246
303-757-6333

Art Institute of Colorado
1200 Lincoln St, Denver CO 80203-2172
David Zorn, President
Brian A. Parker, Director of Admissions
800-275-2420

CollegeAmerica - Colorado
Main Campus
1385 S Colorado Blvd 5th Floor
Denver CO 80222-3304
Barbara Thomas, President
303-691-9756

CollegeAmerica - Colorado Springs
3645 Citadel Dr S, Colorado Springs CO 80909
719-637-0600

CollegeAmerica - Fort Collins
4601 S Mason St, Fort Collins CO 80525-3740
Anna DiTorrice-Mull, Director of Admissions
970-223-6060

College for Financial Planning
8000 E Maplewood Ave, Greenwood Vlg CO 80111
303-220-1200

Colorado Christian University
8787 W Alameda Ave, Lakewood CO 80226
Sean Kadel, Director of Admissions
800-44-FAITH Fax: 303-963-3201
Website: www.ccu.edu
E-mail: admissions@ccu.edu

Colorado College
14 E Cache La Poudre St
Colorado Springs CO 80903-3243
719-389-6344

Colorado School of Mines
1500 Illinois St, Golden CO 80401
Bill Young, Director of Enrollment Management
303-273-3220

COLORADO SCHOOL OF TRADITIONAL CHINESE MEDICINE
1441 York St Ste 202, Denver CO 80206
David DiBrigida, Administrative Director
303-329-6355 Fax: 303-388-8165
Website: www.cstcm.edu
E-mail: admin@cstcm.edu

Colorado State University
1062 Campus Delivery, Fort Collins CO 80523
970-491-1101

Colorado State University - Pueblo
2200 Bonforte Blvd, Pueblo CO 81001-4990
719-549-2461

Colorado Technical University
4435 N Chestnut St
Colorado Springs CO 80907-3895
719-598-0200

DeVry Institute of Technology
5775 DTC Blvd, Greenwood Village CO 80111
303-694-6600

Fort Lewis College
1000 Rim Dr, Durango CO 81301-3999
970-247-7010

Jones International University
9697 E Mineral Ave, Centennial CO 80112-3446
Education Center
800-811-5663

Mesa State College
1100 North Ave, Grand Junction CO 81501
970-248-1020

Metropolitan State College
PO Box 173362, Campus Box 16
Denver CO 80217-3362
William S. Hathaway-Clark, Director of Admissions
303-556-3058

Naropa University
2130 Arapahoe Ave, Boulder CO 80302-6697
303-546-3572

National American University
5125 N Academy Blvd
Colorado Springs CO 80918-4001
Jeanne Liepe, Campus Director
719-277-0588

National American University
1325 S Colorado Blvd #100, Denver CO 80222-3308
Nathan Larson, Regional President
303-758-6700

Nazarene Bible College
1111 Academy Park Loop
Colorado Springs CO 80910-3717
Dr. Laurel Matson, VP for Enrollment & Student Development
719-596-5110 Fax: 719-884-5199
Website: www.nbc.edu
E-mail: admissions@nbc.edu

Regis University
3333 Regis Blvd, Denver CO 80221-1099
303-458-4900

ROCKY MOUNTAIN COLLEGE OF ART & DESIGN
1600 Pierce St, Denver CO 80214
Angela Carlson, Director of Admissions
800-888-2787 Fax: 303-759-4970
Website: www.rmcad.edu
E-mail: admissions@rmcad.edu

Teikyo Loretto Heights University
3001 S Federal Blvd, Denver CO 80236-2711
303-936-8441

United States Air Force Academy
USAF Academy CO 80840
719-333-1110

University of Colorado
Boulder CO 80309-0001
303-492-1411

University of Colorado
1420 Austin Bluffs Pkwy
Colorado Springs CO 80918-3735
719-262-3000

University of Colorado at Denver and Health Sciences Center
Downtown Denver Campus
PO Box 173364, Denver CO 80217-3364
303-556-5600

University of Colorado at Denver and Health Sciences Center
Health Sciences Program
4200 E 9th Ave Box C245, Denver CO 80262
Phoebe Lindsey Barton, Ph.D., Director

University of Denver
2199 S University Blvd, Denver CO 80208-0001
303-871-2000

UNIVERSITY OF DENVER UNIVERSITY COLLEGE
2211 S Josephine St, Denver CO 80208
Dr. James R. Davis, Dean
303-871-3354 Fax: 303-871-4047
Website: www.universitycollege.du.edu
E-mail: ucolinfo@du.edu

University of Northern Colorado
Greeley CO 80639
Gary Gullickson, Director of Admissions
970-351-2881

University of Phoenix
Colorado Division
10004 Park Meadows Dr, Lonetree CO 80124-5453
303-755-9090

Western State College of Colorado
Gunnison CO 81231-0001
Director of Admissions
800-876-5309

Yeshiva Toras Chaim Talmudic Seminary
1555 Stuart St, Denver CO 80204
303-629-8200

CONNECTICUT

Albertus Magnus College
700 Prospect St, New Haven CT 06511-1189
Richard Lolatte, Dean of Admission
203-773-8501 or 800-578-9160 Fax: 203-773-5248
Website: www.albertus.edu
E-mail: admissions@albertus.edu

ALLEN INSTITUTE CENTER FOR INNOVATIVE LEARNING
PO Box 100, Hebron CT 06248
Dan Spada, Director of Marketing and Communication
866-666-6910 Fax: 860-859-4159
Website: www.theallen institute.org
E-mail: dspada@eastersealsct.org

Beth Benjamin Academy of Connecticut
132 Prospect St, Stamford CT 06901-1284
203-325-4351

Central Connecticut State University
1615 Stanley St, New Britain CT 06053-2439
860-832-3200

Connecticut College
270 Mohegan Ave, New London CT 06320-4150
860-447-1911

Eastern Connecticut State University
83 Windham St, Willimantic CT 06226-2295
860-456-5000

Fairfield University
1073 N Benson Rd, Fairfield CT 06824-5171
203-254-4000

HARTT COMMUNITY DIVISION
200 Bloomfield Ave, West Hartford CT 06117
Alana Seddon, Interim Director
860-768-7768 Fax: 860-768-4777
Website: www.hartford.edu/hartt/community
E-mail: harttcomm@hartford.edu

Holy Apostles College and Seminary
33 Prospect Hill Rd, Cromwell CT 06416-2027
860-632-3000

Paier College of Art
20 Gorham Ave, Hamden CT 06514-3902
203-287-3032

Post University
800 Country Club Rd, Waterbury CT 06708-3240
Sandra M. Fernandes, Associate Director of Admissions
Will Johnson, Associate Director of Admissions
203-596-4520

Quinnipiac University
275 Mount Carmel Ave, Hamden CT 06518-1905
Joan Isaac Mohr, VP & Dean of Admissions
203-582-8600

Sacred Heart University
5151 Park Ave, Fairfield CT 06825-1023
203-371-7999

Southern Connecticut State University
501 Crescent St, New Haven CT 06515-1355
203-392-5200

Trinity College
300 Summit St, Hartford CT 06106-3186
Larry Dow, Dean of Admissions & Financial Aid
860-297-2180

UNITED STATES COAST GUARD ACADEMY
15 Mohegan Ave, New London CT 06320-8131
Captain Susan D. Bibeau, Contact
800-883-8724 Fax: 860-701-6700
Website: www.uscga.edu
E-mail: admissions@uscga.edu

University of Bridgeport
126 Park Ave, Bridgeport CT 06604-5620
Barbara L. Maryak, Dean of Admissions
203-576-4552

University of Connecticut
1084 Shennecossett Rd, Groton CT 06340-6048
860-486-4444

University of Connecticut
Storrs CT 06269-0001
860-486-2000

University of Connecticut
32 Hillside Ave, Waterbury CT 06710-2217
203-757-1231

University of Connecticut
1800 Asylum Ave, West Hartford CT 06117-2699
860-241-4700

University of Connecticut Health Center
263 Farmington Ave, Farmington CT 06032-1956
860-679-2000

University of Hartford
200 Bloomfield Ave, West Hartford CT 06117-1599
860-768-4100

University of New Haven
300 Boston Post Rd, West Haven CT 06516
Director of Undergraduate Admissions
203-932-7319

Wesleyan University
Middletown CT 06459-0001
860-685-2000

Western Connecticut State University
181 White St, Danbury CT 06810-6826
203-837-8200

Yale University
38 Hillhouse Ave, New Haven CT 06511
203-432-4771

DELAWARE

Delaware State University
1200 N DuPont Hwy, Dover DE 19901-2275
302-857-6060

Goldey-Beacom College
4701 Limestone Rd, Wilmington DE 19808-1993
Stacey Schwartz, Assistant Director of Admissions
302-998-8814 Fax: 302-996-5408
Website: www.gbc.edu
E-mail: admissions@gbc.edu

University of Delaware
Newark DE 19711
302-831-2000

Wesley College
120 N State St, Dover DE 19901-3876
302-736-2300 Fax: 302-736-2301
Website: www.wesley.edu

Wilmington College
320 N DuPont Hwy, New Castle DE 19720-6491
302-328-9401

DISTRICT OF COLUMBIA

American University
4400 Massachusetts Ave NW
Washington DC 20016-8200
202-885-1000

Catholic University of America
620 Michigan Ave NE, Washington DC 20064-0001
202-319-5000

CORCORAN COLLEGE OF ART AND DESIGN
500 17th St NW, Washington DC 20006-4804
Elizabeth Paladino, Director of Admission
202-639-1814 or 888-CORCORAN Fax: 202-639-1830
Website: www.corcoran.edu
E-mail: admissions@corcoran.org

Gallaudet University
800 Florida Ave NE, Washington DC 20002-3695
Charity Reedy Hines, Director of Admissions
202-651-5750 Fax: 202-651-5744
Website: www.gallaudet.edu
E-mail: admissions.office@gallaudet.edu

Georgetown University
37th and O St NW, Washington DC 20057-0001
202-687-0100

George Washington University
2035 H St NW, Washington DC 20052-0002
202-994-1000

Howard University
2400 6th St NW, Washington DC 20059-0002
202-806-6100

Potomac College
4000 Chesapeake St NW, Washington DC 20016
Florence Tate, President
202-686-0876 Fax: 202-686-0818
Website: www.potomac.edu
E-mail: ftate@potomac.edu

Southeastern University
501 I St SW, Washington DC 20024-2788
Sean Jamieson, Director of Admissions
202-478-8210 Fax: 202-488-8093
Website: www.seu.edu
E-mail: admissions@admin.seu.edu

Strayer University
1133 15th St NW, Washington DC 20005
202-419-0400

University of the District of Columbia
4200 Connecticut Ave NW
Washington DC 20008-1174
LaVerne M. Hill-Flanagan, Director of Admissions
202-274-5100

FLORIDA

American InterContinental University
2250 N Commerce Pkwy, Weston FL 33326
888-603-4888

Argosy University/Sarasota
5250 17th St, Sarasota FL 34235-8242
800-331-5995

Art Institute of Tampa
4401 N Himes Ave Ste 150, Tampa FL 33614
813-873-2112

Asbury Theological Seminary
Florida Campus
8401 Valencia College Ln, Orlando FL 32825
Rev. Eric Currie, Assistant Director of Admissions
407-482-7500

Ave Maria University
1025 Commons Cir, Naples FL 34119
877-283-8648

THE BAPTIST COLLEGE OF FLORIDA
5400 College Dr, Graceville FL 32440-1831
Christopher M. Bishop, Director of Admissions
800-328-2660 Fax: 850-263-9026
Website: www.baptistcollege.edu
E-mail: admissions@baptistcollege.edu

Barry University
11300 NE 2nd Ave, Miami Shores FL 33161-6695
800-695-2279

Beacon College
105 E Main St, Leesburg FL 34748-5162
Carolyn Scott, Director of Admissions
352-787-7660

Bethune-Cookman College
640 Dr Mary McLeod Bethune Blvd
Daytona Beach FL 32114-3099
Edwin Coffie, Director of Admissions
800-448-0228

CARLOS ALBIZU UNIVERSITY
2173 NW 99th Ave, Miami FL 33172-2209
Carlos Alicea, Director of Admissions, Recruitment & Outreach
305-593-1223 ext. 137 Fax: 305-593-1854
Website: www.mia.albizu.edu
E-mail: admissions@albizu.edu

City College
2000 W Commercial Blvd, Fort Lauderdale FL 33309
Mercedes Segal, Director of Admissions
954-492-5353 Fax: 954-491-1965
Website: www.citycollege.edu

Clearwater Christian College
3400 Gulf To Bay Blvd, Clearwater FL 33759-4595
727-726-1153

Eckerd College
4200 54th Ave S, Saint Petersburg FL 33711
727-867-1166

Edison College
PO Box 60210, Fort Myers FL 33906-6210
Billee Silva, Director Student Development
239-489-9054

Edward Waters College
1658 Kings Rd, Jacksonville FL 32209-6199
904-355-3030

EVERGLADES UNIVERSITY (MAIN CAMPUS)
5002 T-Rex Ave Suite 100, Boca Raton FL 33431
Kristi Mollis, President
888-772-6077 Fax: 561-912-1191
Website: www.evergladesuniversity.edu
E-mail: admissions-boca@evergladesuniversity.edu

Private. Coed. Accreditation: ACCSCT. Tuition: $450 per credit. Enrollment: 740. Faculty: 118. Classes are offered on campus and online, small student-faculty ratio, courses are taught one subject per month, monthly start dates. Financial aid to those who qualify, placement assistance available upon graduation.

EVERGLADES UNIVERSITY
Orlando Campus (Branch Campus)
887 E Altamonte Dr, Altamonte Springs FL 32701
Linda Volz, Vice President
866-289-1078 Fax: 407-482-9801
Website: www.evergladesuniversity.edu
E-mail: admissions-orl@evergladesuniversity.edu

Private. Coed. Accreditation: ACCSCT. Tuition: $450 per credit. Enrollment: 740. Faculty: 118. Student-faculty ratio: 8:1. Classes are offered on campus, small student-faculty ratio, courses are taught one subject per month, monthly start dates. Financial aid to those who qualify, placement assistance available upon graduation.

EVERGLADES UNIVERSITY
Sarasota Campus (Branch Campus)
6001 Lake Osprey Dr, Suite 110, Sarasota FL 34240
Brad Brewer, Vice President
866-907-2262 Fax: 941-907-6634
Website: www.evergladesuniversity.edu
E-mail: admissions-sar@evergladesuniversity.edu

Private. Coed. Accreditation: ACCSCT. Tuition: $450 per credit. Enrollment: 740. Faculty: 118. Student-faculty ratio: 8:1. Classes are offered on campus and on-line, small student-faculty ratio, courses are taught one subject per month, monthly start dates. Financial aid to those who qualify, placement assistance available upon graduation.

Flagler College
PO Box 1027, Saint Augustine FL 32085-1027
904-829-6481

Florida A&M University
Tallahassee FL 32307
850-599-3000

Florida Atlantic University
PO Box 3091, Boca Raton FL 33431-0991
800-299-4328

Florida Gulf Coast University
10501 FGCU Blvd, Fort Myers FL 33965-0001
239-590-1000

Florida Institute of Technology
150 W University Blvd, Melbourne FL 32901-6975
Judi Marino, Director of Admissions
800-888-4348

Florida International University
Tamiami Trl, Miami FL 33199-0001
305-348-2000

Florida International University
Biscayne Blvd and 151st St, North Miami FL 33181
305-940-5625

Florida Memorial University
15800 NW 42nd Ave, Opa Locka FL 33054-6199
305-626-3600

Florida Metropolitan University
225 N Federal Hwy, Pompano Beach FL 33062
Fran Heaston, Director of Admissions
800-468-0168

Florida Metropolitan University-Brandon
3924 Coconut Palm Dr, Tampa FL 33619-1354
Marty Baca, Director of Admissions
877-338-0068 (Toll Free)

Florida Metropolitan University-Lakeland Campus
995 E Memorial Blvd Ste 110
Lakeland FL 33801-1973
Jodi De La Garza, Director of Admissions
863-686-1444

Florida Metropolitan University
Melbourne Campus
2401 N Harbor City Blvd, Melbourne FL 32935
321-253-2929

Florida Metropolitan University
Orlando College - North
5421 Diplomat Cir, Orlando FL 32810-5601
Charlene Donnelly, Director of Admissions
800-628-5870

Florida Metropolitan University
Orlando South
9200 Southpark Center Loop, Orlando FL 32819
Annette Cloin, Contact
407-851-2525

Florida Metropolitan University
Pinellas Campus
2471 N McMullen Booth Rd
Clearwater FL 33759-1359
Sandra Williams, Director of Admissions
800-353-3687

Florida Metropolitan University
Tampa Campus
3319 W Hillsborough Ave, Tampa FL 33614-5801
Donnie Broughton, Director of Admissions
813-879-6000

Florida Southern College
111 Lake Hollingsworth Dr, Lakeland FL 33801-5607
Robert B. Palmer, V.P., Dean of Enrollment Management
863-680-4131

Florida State University
600 W College Ave, Tallahassee FL 32306-1096
Janice V. Finney, Director of Admissions
850-644-2525 Fax: 850-644-0197
Website: admissions.fsu.edu
E-mail: admissions@admin.fsu.edu

HERZING COLLEGE
1595 S Semoran Blvd #1501
Winter Park FL 32792-5509
Kathy Nagle, Director of Admissions
407-478-0500 Fax: 407-478-0501
Website: www.herzing.edu
E-mail: info@orl.herzing.edu

Hobe Sound Bible College
PO Box 1065, Hobe Sound FL 33475-1065
772-546-5534

HODGES UNIVERSITY
4501 Colonial Blvd, Fort Myers FL 33966
Rita Lampus, Vice President of Enrollment Management
800-466-0019 or 239-482-0019 Fax: 239-938-7891
Website: www.hodges.edu
E-mail: admit@hodges.edu

HODGES UNIVERSITY
2655 Northbrooke Dr, Naples FL 34119
Rita Lampus, Vice President of Enrollment Management
800-466-8017 or 239-513-1122 Fax: 239-598-6253
Website: www.hodges.edu
E-mail: admit@hodges.edu

Established 1990. Private. Coed. Accreditation: SACS. Tuition: $15,300 (3 semesters). Fees: $190/semester. Enrollment: 1316 full-time, 515 part-time. Faculty: 103. Student-faculty ratio: 15:1. Degrees: AS, BS, MS, MBA, MPA, MIS, MPS. 2 buildings. Changed name in May 2007 from International College to Hodges University.

International Academy of Design & Technology
5104 Eisenhower Blvd, Tampa FL 33634-6313
Richard Costa, V.P. of Admissions and Marketing
813-880-8092

INTERNATIONAL ACADEMY OF DESIGN AND TECHNOLOGY
5959 Lake Ellenor Dr, Orlando FL 32809-4633
Dr. John Dietrich, VP of Admissions
877-753-0007 Fax: 407-888-4006
Website: www.iadt.edu
E-mail: info@iadt.edu

Jacksonville University
2800 University Blvd N, Jacksonville FL 32211-3394
904-744-3950

Johnson & Wales University
1701 NE 127th St, North Miami FL 33181-2518
Jeff Greenip, Director of Admissions
305-892-7000

Jones College
5353 Arlington Expy, Jacksonville FL 32211-5588
Dorothy D. Jones, Chief Executive Officer
904-743-1122 Fax: 904-744-4446
Website: www.jones.edu
E-mail: fmccaffe@jones.edu

Jones College
11430 N Kendall Dr Ste 200, Miami FL 33176
Patricia Carbonell, Contact
305-275-9996 Fax: 305-743-4446
Website: www.jones.edu
E-mail: pcarbone@jones.edu

Lake Erie College of Osteopathic Medicine
5000 Lakewood Ranch Blvd, Bradenton FL 34211
June Flaim, Director of Student Affairs
941-756-0690 Fax: 941-782-5721
Website: www.lecom.edu
E-mail: bradenton@lecom.edu

Lynn University
3601 N Military Trl, Boca Raton FL 33431-5598
Director of Admissions
561-237-7900 Fax: 561-237-7100
Website: www.lynn.edu
E-mail: admission@lynn.edu

Miami International University of Art & Design
1501 Biscayne Blvd, Miami FL 33132
Elsia Suarez, Director of Admissions
800-225-9023

New College of Florida
5700 N Tamiami Trl, Sarasota FL 34243-2146
941-359-4310

North Tennessee Bible Institute and Seminary
556 W Bayshore Dr, Eastpoint FL 32328
Dr. Celeste Wall, President
850-927-4711

Northwood University
2600 N Military Trl, West Palm Beach FL 33409-2999
Jack Letvinchuk, Director of Admissions
800-458-8325 Fax: 561-640-3328
Website: www.northwood.edu
E-mail: fladmit@northwood.edu

Nova Southeastern University
3301 College Ave, Davie FL 33314-7796
954-262-7300

Nova Southeastern University Health Profession
3200 S University Dr, Davie FL 33328-2018
Marla Frohlinger, Director of Admissions
954-262-1101

Palm Beach Atlantic University
PO Box 24708, West Palm Beach FL 33416-4708
561-803-2000

Pensacola Christian College
PO Box 18000, Pensacola FL 32523-9160
850-478-8496

Polytechnic University of the Americas
8180 NW 36th St, Doral FL 33166
305-418-4220

Ringling School of Art & Design
2700 N Tamiami Trl, Sarasota FL 34234-5812
James H. Dean, Dean of Admissions
941-351-5100

Rollins College
1000 Holt Ave, Winter Park FL 32789
407-646-2000

Saint Leo University
PO Box 6665, Saint Leo FL 33574
Director of Admissions
800-334-5532

St. Thomas University
16401 NW 37th Ave, Miami Gardens FL 33054
Andre Lightbourn, Director of Admissions
800-367-9010 or 305-628-6546 Fax: 305-628-6591
Website: www.stu.edu
E-mail: signup@stu.edu

Schiller International University
300 E Bay Dr, Largo FL 33770
Markus Leibrecht, Director of Admissions
727-736-5082

Southeastern University
1000 Longfellow Blvd, Lakeland FL 33801-6099
863-667-5000

South University
1760 N Congress Ave
West Palm Beach FL 33409-5178
Steven A. Schwab, President
561-697-9200

Stetson University
421 N Woodland Boulevard, De Land FL 32720-3761
386-822-7000

Strayer University
2200 N Alafaya Trl Ste 500, Orlando FL 32826
407-926-2000

Strayer University
6302 E Martin Luther King Blvd Ste 450
Tampa FL 33619
813-663-0100

Strayer University
4902 Eisenhower Blvd Ste 100, Tampa FL 33634
813-882-0100

Trinity Baptist College
800-200 Hammond Blvd, Jacksonville FL 32221
R. Larry Appleby, Director of Admissions
904-596-2400

Trinity College of Florida
2430 Welbilt Blvd, Trinity FL 34655-4401
Dr. David Colburn, VP of Enrollment & Adult Education
800-388-0869

University of Central Florida
PO Box 160111, Orlando FL 32816
407-823-3000

University of Florida
PO Box 114000, Gainesville FL 32611-4000
352-392-3261

University of Miami
PO Box 248006, Coral Gables FL 33124-8006
305-284-2211

University of Miami
4600 Rickenbacker Cswy, Miami FL 33149-1031
305-361-4000

University of North Florida
4567 Saint Johns Bluff Rd S
Jacksonville FL 32224-2645
904-620-1000

University of South Florida
140 7th Ave S, Saint Petersburg FL 33701-5001
727-893-9536

UNIVERSITY OF SOUTH FLORIDA
4202 E Fowler Ave, Tampa FL 33620-8001
J. Robert Spatig, Director of Admissions
877-USF-BULL Fax: 813-974-9689
Website: www.usf.edu
E-mail: admissions@admin.usf.edu

Public. Coed. Accreditation: Southern Association of Colleges and Schools. Tuition: $3,340 - Florida Residents, $16,040 - out of state. Room & board: $7,590. Enrollment: 44,038 total, 34,077 undergraduate. Student-faculty ratio: 18:1. Degrees: 87 undergraduate majors across 13 schools and colleges. Library: 2,000,000 volumes. 1,700 acre campus.

The University of South Florida is one of the nation's top 63 public research universities and one of 76 community engaged universities as designated by the Carnegie Foundation for the Advancement of Teaching. It is one of only ten universities in the nation and is the only Florida university - public or private - to receive both designations. With more than 200 majors and degree programs, USF offers world-class academic programs in virtually every field. As a metropolitan university, USF offers students easy access to the wide range of employment, cultural and recreational opportunities afforded by the Tampa Bay region, as well as access to Florida's finest beaches, Busch Gardens and historic Ybor City.

University of Tampa
401 W Kennedy Blvd, Tampa FL 33606-1490
813-253-3333

University of West Florida
11000 University Pkwy, Pensacola FL 32514-5750
850-474-2000

Warner Southern College
5301 US Highway 27 S, Lake Wales FL 33859-8725
863-638-1426

Webber International University
PO Box 96, Babson Park FL 33827-0096
863-638-1431

Yeshiva Gedolah Rabbinical College
1140 Alton Rd, Miami Beach FL 33139
305-673-5664

GEORGIA

Albany State University
504 College Dr, Albany GA 31705-2796
229-430-4600

American InterContinental University
3330 Peachtree Rd NE, Atlanta GA 30326-1016
404-965-5700

American InterContinental University
6600 Peachtree Dunwoody Rd
500 Embassy Row, Atlanta GA 30328
404-965-6500

Armstrong Atlantic State University
11935 Abercorn St, Savannah GA 31419-1997
Kim West, Asst. Dean and Registrar Enrollment Services
912-927-5277 Fax: 912-921-5462
Website: www.armstrong.edu
E-mail: admissions@mail.armstrong.edu

Art Institute of Atlanta
6600 Peachtree Dunwoody Rd
100 Embassy Row, Atlanta GA 30328-1649
Donna Scott, Director of Admissions
800-275-4242

Atlanta Christian College
2605 Ben Hill Rd, East Point GA 30344-1999
404-761-8861

Augusta State University
2500 Walton Way, Augusta GA 30904-4562
706-737-1400

BEACON UNIVERSITY
6003 Veterans Pkwy, Columbus GA 31909
Admissions Department
706-323-5364 Fax: 706-323-3236
Website: www.beacon.edu
E-mail: beacon@beacon.edu

Berry College
2277 Martha Berry Hwy NE
Mount Berry GA 30149-0149
706-232-5374

BEULAH HEIGHTS UNIVERSITY
PO Box 18145, Atlanta GA 30316-0145
Dr. James B. Keiller, V.P. & Dean for Academic Affairs
404-627-2681 Fax: 404-627-0702
Website: www.beulah.org
E-mail: bhu@beulah.org

Brewton-Parker College
Highway 280, Mount Vernon GA 30445
800-342-1087

Carver Bible College
3870 Cascade Rd SW, Atlanta GA 30331-2184
404-527-4520

Clark Atlanta University
223 James Brawley Dr SW, Atlanta GA 30314
404-880-8000

Clayton State University
5900 N Lee St, Morrow GA 30260
770-961-3500

Columbus State University
4225 University Ave, Columbus GA 31907-5645
706-568-2001

Covenant College
14049 Scenic Hwy, Lookout Mountain GA 30750
706-820-1560

Emmanuel College
PO Box 129, Franklin Springs GA 30639-0129
800-860-8800

Emory University
200B Jones Center, Atlanta GA 30322
404-727-6123

Fort Valley State University
1005 State University Dr, Fort Valley GA 31030-3298
Gerri McCord, Dean of Admissions & Enrollment
478-825-6307

Georgia College and State University
231 W Hancock St, Milledgeville GA 31061-3371
478-445-5350

Georgia Institute of Technology
225 North Ave NW, Atlanta GA 30332-0002
404-894-2000

Georgia Southern University
PO Box 8024, Statesboro GA 30460
Admissions Office
912-681-5532

Georgia Southwestern State University
800 Wheatley St, Americus GA 31709-4635
229-928-1279

Georgia State University
PO Box 4009, Atlanta GA 30302-4009
404-651-2365

Herzing College
3393 Peachtree Rd NE, Atlanta GA 30326
Richard Hinton, Director of Admissions
404-816-4533

ITT Technical Institute
1000 Cobb Place Blvd NW, Kennesaw GA 30144
770-426-3000

Kennesaw State University
1000 Chastain Rd NW, Kennesaw GA 30144-5591
Dr. Ralph Rascati, Dean
770-423-6000
Website: www.kennesaw.edu

LaGrange College
601 Broad St, LaGrange GA 30240-2955
Andy Geeter, Director of Admission
800-593-2885

Life University
1269 Barclay Cir SE, Marietta GA 30060-2903
Dr. Deborah E. Heairlston, Director of New Student Development
770-426-2884 Fax: 770-426-2895
Website: www.life.edu
E-mail: admissions@life.edu

Luther Rice University
3038 Evans Mill Rd, Lithonia GA 30038
Russ Sorrow, Director of Enrollment Management
770-484-1204 Fax: 770-484-1155
Website: www.lru.edu
E-mail: admissions@lru.edu

Macon State College
100 College Station Dr, Macon GA 31206-5145
478-471-2800

Medical College of Georgia
1120 15th St, Augusta GA 30912-0004
706-721-2725

Mercer University in Atlanta
3001 Mercer University Dr, Atlanta GA 30341-4155
678-547-6000

Mercer University in Macon
1400 Coleman Ave, Macon GA 31207-0003
John P. Cole, Sr. Assoc. V.P. for Admissions
478-301-2650

Morehouse School of Medicine
720 Westview Dr SW, Atlanta GA 30310-1495
404-752-1500

North Georgia College & State University
Dahlonega GA 30597-0001
706-864-1400

North Metro Technical College
5198 Ross Rd SE, Acworth GA 30102-3129
Missy Cusack, Director of Admissions
770-975-4000 Fax: 770-975-4142
Website: www.northmetrotech.edu
E-mail: info@northmetrotech.edu

Oglethorpe University
4484 Peachtree Rd NE, Atlanta GA 30319-2797
Kelly Gosnell, Director of Admission
404-261-1441

Oxford College of Emory University
100 Hamill St
Oxford GA 30054-2291
Jennifer B. Taylor, Director of Admissions
770-784-8888

Paine College
1235 15th St, Augusta GA 30901-3182
800-476-7703

Piedmont College
PO Box 10, Demorest GA 30535-0010
800-277-7020

Reinhardt College
7300 Reinhardt College Cir, Waleska GA 30183-2981
770-720-5600

Savannah College of Art & Design
PO Box 2072, Savannah GA 31402-2072
800-869-7223

Savannah College of Art and Design
PO Box 77300, Atlanta GA 30357
877-722-3285

Savannah State University
3219 College St, Savannah GA 31404-5255
912-356-2187

Shorter College
315 Shorter Ave, Rome GA 30165-4267
800-868-6980

Southern Polytech State University
1100 S Marietta Pkwy SE, Marietta GA 30060-2855
770-528-7200

South University
709 Mall Blvd, Savannah GA 31406-4881
912-201-8000

Strayer University
3101 TowerCreek Pkwy SE Ste 700
Atlanta GA 30339
770-612-2170

Thomas University
1501 Millpond Rd, Thomasville GA 31792-7478
Darla M. Glass, Director of Student Affairs
229-226-1621

TOCCOA FALLS COLLEGE
PO Box 800899, Toccoa Falls GA 30598
888-785-5624 Fax: 706-282-6012
Website: www.tfc.edu
E-mail: admissions@tfc.edu

University of Georgia
Athens GA 30602-0001
706-542-3000

University of West Georgia
Carrollton GA 30118-0001
770-836-6500

Valdosta State University
N Patterson St, Valdosta GA 31698-0001
229-333-5952

HAWAII

Brigham Young University
55-220 Kulanui St, Laie HI 96762-1293
808-293-3211

Chaminade University of Honolulu
3140 Waialae Ave, Honolulu HI 96816-1510
Eric Nemoto, Director Financial Aid
800-735-3733

Hawaii Business College
33 S King St 4th Floor, Honolulu HI 96813-4316
Roger Ramos, Director of Admissions
808-524-4014

Hawaii Pacific University
1164 Bishop St, Honolulu HI 96813
808-544-0200

Hawaii Pacific University
45-045 Kamehameha Hwy, Kaneohe HI 96744-5297
808-235-3641

HAWAII THEOLOGICAL SEMINARY
PO Box 861754, Wahiawa HI 96786
Kevin Gilbert, President
808-622-4487 Fax: 808-595-4779
Website: www.hits.edu
E-mail: info@hits.edu

University of Hawaii at Hilo
200 W Kawili St, Hilo HI 96720-4075
808-933-3301

University of Hawaii at Manoa
2444 Dole St, Honolulu HI 96822-2302
808-956-5280

University of Hawaii - West Oahu
96-129 Ala Ike St, Pearl City HI 96782
808-454-4700

IDAHO

Albertson College of Idaho
2112 Cleveland Blvd, Caldwell ID 83605-4432
208-459-5000

Boise Bible College
8695 W Marigold St, Boise ID 83714-1220
800-893-7755

Boise State University
1910 University Dr, Boise ID 83725-0399
208-426-1011

Brigham Young University - Idaho
120 Kimball Bldg, Rexburg ID 83460-1615
Rob Garrett, Director of Admissions
208-496-1020 Fax: 208-496-1220
Website: www.byui.edu
E-mail: admissions@byui.edu

Idaho State University
PO Box 8270, Pocatello ID 83209-0001
208-282-0211

Lewis-Clark State College
500 8th Ave, Lewiston ID 83501-2698
Diane Douglas, Ph.D., Registrar/Director of Admissions
800-933-5272 Fax: 208-792-2429
Website: www.lcsc.edu
E-mail: admissions@lcsc.edu

New Saint Andrews College
PO Box 9025, Moscow ID 83843
208-882-1566

Northwest Nazarene University
623 Holly St, Nampa ID 83686-5897
208-467-8011

University of Idaho
Moscow ID 83844-4253
Lloyd Scott, Director of New Student Services
208-885-6163 Fax: 208-885-4477
Website: www.uidaho.edu
E-mail: nss@uidaho.edu

ILLINOIS

AMERICAN INTERCONTINENTAL UNIVERSITY ONLINE
5550 Prairie Stone Parkway Suite 400
Hoffman Estates IL 60192
Admissions Department
877-701-3800
Website: www.aiuonline.edu
E-mail: info@aiuonline.edu

Augustana College
639 38th St, Rock Island IL 61201-2296
309-794-7000

Aurora University
347 S Gladstone Ave, Aurora IL 60506-4892
Carol R. Dunn, Ed.D., Vice President for Enrollment
800-742-5281 Fax: 630-844-5535
Website: www.aurora.edu
E-mail: admission@aurora.edu

BENEDICTINE UNIVERSITY
5700 College Rd, Lisle IL 60532-0900
Kari Gibbons, Dean of Enrollment
630-829-6300 or 888-829-6363 Fax: 630-829-6301
Website: www.ben.edu
E-mail: admissions@ben.edu

Established 1887. Private. Coed. Accreditation: North Central Association of Colleges & Schools. Tuition: $19,800. Room & board: $6,773. Fees: $510. Enrollment: 1,967 full-time, 1,957 part-time. Faculty: 142. Student-faculty ratio: 13:1. Degrees: AA, BA, BBA, BS, MAEd, MBA, MEd, MPH, MS, PhD, EdD. Library: 162,000 volumes. 10 buildings on 108 acres plus a Sports Complex. Located 25 miles west of Chicago in the heart of the DuPage County Research and Development Corridor. Recreational, educational and cultural facilities of the city are easily accessible.

Blackburn College
700 College Ave, Carlinville IL 62626-1498
217-854-3231

BLESSING-RIEMAN COLLEGE OF NURSING
PO Box 7005, Quincy IL 62305-7005
Erin Flesner, Admission Counselor
Heather Mutter, Admission Counselor
217-228-5520 Fax: 217-223-4661
Website: www.brcn.edu
E-mail: admissions@brcn.edu

Bradley University
1501 W Bradley Ave, Peoria IL 61625-0002
800-447-6460

Chicago State University
9501 S King Dr, Chicago IL 60628-1598
773-995-2000

Christian Life College
400 E Gregory St, Mount Prospect IL 60056
847-259-1840

COLUMBIA COLLEGE CHICAGO
600 S Michigan Ave, Chicago IL 60605-1900
Murphy Monroe, Executive Director of Admissions
312-344-7130 Fax: 312-344-8024
Website: www.colum.edu
E-mail: admissions@colum.edu

CONCORDIA UNIVERSITY
7400 Augusta St, River Forest IL 60305-1402
708-209-3100 Fax: 708-209-3176
Website: www.cuchicago.edu
E-mail: admission@cuchicago.edu

De Paul University
1 E Jackson Blvd, Chicago IL 60604-2287
Carlene Klaas, Director of Admissions
312-362-8000

De Paul University
2323 N Seminary Ave, Chicago IL 60614-3298
312-362-8000

Dominican University
7900 Division St, River Forest IL 60305-1066
708-366-2490

Eastern Illinois University
600 Lincoln Ave, Charleston IL 61920-3099
217-581-5000

East-West University
816 S Michigan Ave, Chicago IL 60605-2103
312-939-0111

Elmhurst College
190 S Prospect Ave, Elmhurst IL 60126-3296
630-279-4100

Eureka College
300 E College Ave, Eureka IL 61530-1500
309-467-3721

Governors State University
1 University Pkwy, University Park IL 60466-0975
708-534-5000

Greenville College
315 E College Ave, Greenville IL 62246-1199
618-664-1840

HARRINGTON COLLEGE OF DESIGN
200 W Madison St, Chicago IL 60606-3433
Wendi Franczyk, VP of Admissions
312-939-4975 Fax: 312-697-8032
Website: www.harringtoncollege.com
E-mail: wfranczyk@harringtoncollege.com

Harrington College of Design is a specialized college that focuses on the creative fields of interior design, commercial digital photography and communication design. That means - even right out of high school - you have the option to pursue programs that make the most of your creative side. At Harrington, you can pursue a Bachelor of Fine Arts Degree in Interior Design, Bachelor of Fine Arts Degree in Communication Design, an Associate of Applied Science Degree in Interior Design or Associate of Applied Science Degree in Digital Photography. Harrington is accredited by the Accrediting Council for Independent Colleges and Schools to award associate degrees and bachelor's degrees. Harrington is also an accredited institutional member of the National Association of Schools of Art and Design. The Bachelor of Fine Arts Degree in Interior Design is accredited by the Council for Interior Design Accreditation (formerly FIDER). Harrington's campus is located in the heart of Chicago, one of the most visually inspiring, action-packed cities. Plus, classes are taught by instructors who are still practicing in their field - so you can get the book smarts and the real-world learning opportunities they bring into the classroom. Programs are built on learning in a variety of formats - lectures, studio, small group collaboration and independent study. Our Career Services Department is dedicated to helping students find jobs, internships and employment during school and after graduation. Financial aid is available for those who qualify.

Hebrew Theological College
7135 Carpenter Rd, Skokie IL 60077-3263
Schmuel Schuman, Registrar
847-982-2500

Illinois College
1101 W College Ave, Jacksonville IL 62650-2299
217-245-3000

The Illinois Institute of Art
1000 N Plaza Dr, Schaumburg IL 60173-4942
847-619-3450

Illinois Institute of Art, The
350 N Orleans St Lbby 136, Chicago IL 60654-1510
312-280-3500

Illinois Institute of Technology
3300 S Federal St, Chicago IL 60616-3793
Brent Benner, Director of Admissions
312-567-3000

Illinois State University
Normal IL 61790-0001
309-438-2111

Illinois Wesleyan University
PO Box 2900, Bloomington IL 61702-2900
James R. Ruoti, Dean of Admissions
309-556-3031

International Academy of Design and Technology
1 N State St #500, Chicago IL 60602-3300
Cecily Arroyo, Director of Admissions
888-803-0111 Fax: 312-541-3929
Website: www.iadtchicago.edu
E-mail: carroyo@iadtchicago.com

Judson College
1151 N State St, Elgin IL 60123-1498
847-695-2500

Kendall College
900 N North Branch St, Chicago IL 60622
Office of Admissions
800-569-8179 Fax: 312-752-2021
Website: www.kendall.edu
E-mail: admissions@kendall.edu

Knox College
Galesburg IL 61401
309-341-7100

Lake Forest College
555 N Sheridan Rd, Lake Forest IL 60045-2399
847-234-3100

Lakeview College of Nursing
903 N Logan Ave, Danville IL 61832-3731
217-443-5238

Lewis University
One University Parkway, Romeoville IL 60446
800-897-9000

LEXINGTON COLLEGE
310 S Peoria St, Chicago IL 60607-3534
Jennifer Reiff, Admissions Counselor
312-226-6294 Fax: 312-226-6405
Website: www.lexingtoncollege.edu
E-mail: admissions@lexingtoncollege.edu

Lincoln Christian College
100 Campus View Dr, Lincoln IL 62656-2167
217-732-3168

Loyola University
6525 N Sheridan Rd, Chicago IL 60626-5385
773-508-2320

Loyola University
2160 S 1st Ave, Maywood IL 60153-3304
708-216-3229

Loyola University of Chicago
820 N Michigan Ave, Chicago IL 60611-2103
312-915-6000

MacMurray College
447 E College Ave, Jacksonville IL 62650-2590
217-479-7000

McKendree College
701 College Rd, Lebanon IL 62254-1299
618-537-6830

MENNONITE COLLEGE OF NURSING AT ILLINOIS STATE UNIVERSITY
PO Box 5810, Normal IL 61790-5810
Nancy Ridenour, Dean and Professor
309-438-7400 Fax: 309-438-2620
Website: www.mcn.ilstu.edu
E-mail: mcninfo@ilstu.edu

Midstate College
411 W Northmoor Rd, Peoria IL 61614-3595
309-692-4092

Midwestern University
555 31st St, Downers Grove IL 60515-1235
Raelene Brower, Director of Admissions
630-969-4400

Millikin University
1184 W Main St, Decatur IL 62522-2084
Lin Stoner, Dean of Admission
800-373-7733

Monmouth College
700 E Broadway, Monmouth IL 61462-1963
309-457-2131

Moody Bible Institute
820 N La Salle Dr, Chicago IL 60610-3263
800-967-4624

National-Louis University
5202 Old Orchard Rd Ste 300, Skokie IL 60077-4409
224-233-2000

North Central College
30 N Brainard St, Naperville IL 60540-4690
Martha Stolze, Director of Admissions
630-637-5800

NORTHEASTERN ILLINOIS UNIVERSITY
5500 N Saint Louis Ave, Chicago IL 60625-4699
Janice Harring-Hendon, Executive Director of Enrollment Services
773-442-4050 Fax: 773-442-4020
Website: www.neiu.edu
E-mail: jharringhendon@neiu.edu

Northern Illinois University
DeKalb IL 60115
815-753-1000

North Park College & Theological Seminary
3225 W Foster Ave, Chicago IL 60625-4810
773-244-6200

Northwestern University
303 E Chicago Ave, Chicago IL 60611-3008
312-503-6950

Northwestern University
1801 Hinman Ave, Evanston IL 60208-1260
847-491-3741

Olivet Nazarene University
1 University Ave
Bourbonnais IL 60914
815-939-5011

Principia College
Elsah IL 62028-9799
618-374-2131

Quincy University
1800 College Ave, Quincy IL 62301-2670
217-222-8020

Robert Morris College
905 Meridian Lake Dr, Aurora IL 60504-4904
630-375-8000

Robert Morris College
1000 Tower Ln #200, Bensenville IL 60106-1040
630-787-7800

Robert Morris College
401 S State St, Chicago IL 60605-1229
312-935-6800

Robert Morris College
43 Orland Square Dr, Orland Park IL 60462-3206
708-226-3800

Robert Morris College
3101 Montvale Dr, Springfield IL 62704-4260
217-793-2500

Rockford College
5050 E State St, Rockford IL 61108-2393
William Laffey, Director of Admission
800-892-2984

Roosevelt University
430 S Michigan Ave, Chicago IL 60605
Gwen E. Kanelos, Asst. Vice President for Enrollment Services
877-APPLY-RU Fax: 312-341-4216
Website: www.roosevelt.edu
E-mail: applyru@roosevelt.edu

Roosevelt University
1400 N Roosevelt Blvd, Schaumburg IL 60173
847-619-8600

Rush University
College Admission Services
600 S Paulina St #440, Chicago IL 60612-3806
Hicela Castruita, Director
312-942-7100

Saint John's College
Department of Nursing
421 N 9th St, Springfield IL 62702
217-525-5628

St. Xavier University
3700 W 103rd St, Chicago IL 60655-3199
773-298-3000

Shimer College
3424 S State St, Chicago IL 60616-3893
312-235-3500

Southern Illinois University
Carbondale IL 62901-4400
618-453-2121

Southern Illinois University
PO Box 19621, Springfield IL 62794
217-545-8000

Southern Illinois University Edwardsville
Edwardsville IL 62026-0001
618-650-3705

Trinity Christian College
6601 W College Dr, Palos Heights IL 60463-0929
Joshua Lenarz, Director of Admissions
708-597-3000

Trinity College of Nursing & Health Sciences
2122 25th Ave, Rock Island IL 61201-5317
Joanne Cunningham, Director of Admissions
309-779-7700 Fax: 309-799-7748
Website: www.trinitycollegeqc.edu
E-mail: con@trinityqc.com

Trinity International University
2065 Half Day Rd, Deerfield IL 60015-1241
847-945-8800 Fax: 847-317-8097
Website: www.tiu.edu
E-mail: tcadmissions@tiu.edu

University of Chicago
5801 S Ellis Ave, Chicago IL 60637-1476
773-702-1234

University of Illinois
901 W Illinois St, Urbana IL 61801
217-333-1000

University of Illinois at Chicago
PO Box 5220, Chicago IL 60680-5220
312-996-3000

University of Illinois at Springfield
One University Plaza, Springfield IL 62794
217-206-4847

University of St. Francis
500 Wilcox St, Joliet IL 60435
800-735-7500

VanderCook College of Music
3140 S Federal St, Chicago IL 60616-3704
Tamara V. Trutwin, Student Recruiter
Kelly Westergaard, Admissions Coordinator
800-448-2655 ext. 230

Western Illinois University
1 University Cir, Macomb IL 61455-1390
309-295-1414

West Suburban College of Nursing
3 Erie Ct, Oak Park IL 60302
Admissions
708-763-6530

Wheaton College
501 College Ave, Wheaton IL 60187-5571
630-752-5000

INDIANA

Anderson University
1100 E 5th St, Anderson IN 46012-3495
765-649-9071

Art Institute of Indianapolis
3500 Depauw Blvd, Indianapolis IN 46268
317-613-4800

Ball State University
2000 W University Ave, Muncie IN 47306-0002
765-285-5555

Bethel College
1001 W McKinley Ave, Mishawaka IN 46545-5591
Office of Admissions
574-257-3339

Butler University
4600 Sunset Ave, Indianapolis IN 46208-3443
317-940-8000

Calumet College of St. Joseph
2400 New York Ave, Whiting IN 46394-2195
219-473-7770

CROSSROADS BIBLE COLLEGE
601 N Shortridge Rd, Indianapolis IN 46219-4912
Tiffany Powell, Director of Enrollment Management
317-352-8736 ext. 230 or 800-822-3119 ext. 230
Fax: 317-352-9145
Website: www.crossroads.edu
E-mail: tpowell@crossroads.edu

Davenport University
8200 Georgia St, Merrillville IN 46410-6128
800-748-7880

DePauw University
313 S Locust St, Greencastle IN 46135-1736
800-447-2495

Earlham College and Earlham School of Religion
801 National Rd W, Richmond IN 47374-4095
765-983-1200

Franklin College
101 Branigin Blvd, Franklin IN 46131
Jacqueline S. Acosta, Director of Admissions
800-852-0232 Fax: 317-738-8274
Website: www.franklincollege.edu
E-mail: admissions@franklincollege.edu

Goshen College
1700 S Main St, Goshen IN 46526-4794
574-535-7000

Grace College
200 Seminary Dr, Winona Lake IN 46590-1224
800-54-GRACE

Hanover College
PO Box 108, Hanover IN 47243-0108
William D. Preble, Dean of Admission
800-213-2178

HOLY CROSS COLLEGE
PO Box 308, Notre Dame IN 46556-0308
Vincent M. Duke, Director of Admissions
574-239-8400 Fax: 574-239-8323
Website: www.hcc-nd.edu
E-mail: admissions@hcc-nd.edu

Huntington College
2303 College Ave, Huntington IN 46750-1299
260-356-6000

Indiana Institute of Technology
1600 E Washington Blvd, Fort Wayne IN 46803-1297
260-422-5561

Indiana State University
Terre Haute IN 47809-0001
Richard Toomey, Director of Admissions
812-237-6311

Indiana University
300 N Jordan Ave, Bloomington IN 47405-1106
812-855-4848

Indiana University at Kokomo
PO Box 9003, Kokomo IN 46904-9003
765-453-2000

Indiana University at South Bend
PO Box 7111, South Bend IN 46634-7111
574-237-4111

Indiana University East
2325 Chester Blvd, Richmond IN 47374-1289
765-973-8200

Indiana University Northwest
3400 Broadway, Gary IN 46408-1101
219-980-6500

Indiana University-Purdue University at Fort Wayne
2101 E Coliseum Blvd, Fort Wayne IN 46805-1445
260-481-6100

Indiana University-Purdue University at Indianapolis
355 Lansing St, Indianapolis IN 46202-2815
317-274-5555

Indiana University Southeast
4201 Grant Line Rd, New Albany IN 47150-2158
812-941-2000

Indiana Wesleyan University
4201 S Washington St, Marion IN 46953-4974
765-674-6901

International Business College
5699 Coventry Ln, Fort Wayne IN 46804
260-459-4500 Fax: 260-436-1896
Website: www.ibcfortwayne.edu
E-mail: skinzer@ibcfortwayne.edu

Manchester College
604 E College Ave, North Manchester IN 46962-1276
260-982-5000

Marian College
3200 Cold Spring Rd, Indianapolis IN 46222-1997
317-955-6000

Martin University
PO Box 18567, Indianapolis IN 46218-0567
317-543-3235

Mid-America Reformed Seminary
229 Seminary Dr, Dyer IN 46311
219-864-2400

OAKLAND CITY UNIVERSITY
138 N Lucretia St, Oakland City IN 47660
Brian J. Baker, Director of Admissions
800-737-5125 Fax: 812-749-1433
Website: www.oak.edu
E-mail: bbaker@oak.edu
Established 1865. Private. Coed. Accreditation: North Central Association of Colleges and Schools, NCATE, Association of Theological Schools (ATS), JACBE. Tuition: $13,860. Room & board: $5,400. Fees: $460. Enrollment: 600 full-time, 54 part-time. Faculty: 51. Student-faculty ratio: 17:1. Degrees in: Business, Education, Music, Art, Religious Studies, Criminal Justice, Biology, Psychology, Graphic Design, Applied Mathematics, English, Humanities, Social Sciences. Library: 83,000 volumes. 15 buildings on 16 acres.

Purdue University
2200 169th St, Hammond IN 46323
219-989-2993

Purdue University
475 Stadium Mall Dr, West Lafayette IN 47907
765-494-4600

Purdue University
1401 S US Highway 421, Westville IN 46391-9542
219-785-5200

Rose-Hulman Institute of Technology
5500 Wabash Ave, Terre Haute IN 47803-3920
James A. Goecker, Dean of Admissions
812-877-8213 Fax: 812-877-8941
Website: www.rose-hulman.edu
E-mail: admissions@rose-hulman.edu

St. Joseph's College
PO Box 890, Rensselaer IN 47978-0890
219-866-6000

Taylor University
1025 W Rudisill Blvd, Fort Wayne IN 46807-2197
260-744-8600

Taylor University
500 W Reade Ave, Upland IN 46989-1002
765-998-2751

Tri-State University
Angola IN 46703
260-665-4100

University of Evansville
1800 Lincoln Ave, Evansville IN 47722-0001
Don Vos, Dean of Admission
800-423-8633 Fax: 812-488-4076
Website: www.evansville.edu
E-mail: admission@evansville.edu

University of Indianapolis
1400 E Hanna Ave, Indianapolis IN 46227-3697
317-788-3368

University of Notre Dame
220 Main Building, Notre Dame IN 46556
574-631-5000

University of St. Francis
2701 Spring St, Fort Wayne IN 46808-3994
Matthew P. Nettleton, Director of Admissions
260-434-3279

University of Southern Indiana
8600 University Blvd, Evansville IN 47712-3591
812-464-8600

Valparaiso University
Valparaiso IN 46383
219-464-5000

IOWA

Ashford University
400 N Bluff Blvd, Clinton IA 52732-3910
866-711-1700

Briar Cliff University
PO Box 2100, Sioux City IA 51104-0100
Sharisue Wilcoxon, VP for Enrollment Management
712-279-5200 Fax: 712-279-1632
Website: www.briarcliff.edu
E-mail: admissions@briarcliff.edu

Buena Vista University
610 W 4th St, Storm Lake IA 50588-1798
712-749-2235

Central College
812 University St, Pella IA 50219-1999
641-628-9000

Clarke College
1550 Clarke Dr, Dubuque IA 52001-3198
Andy Schroeder, Director of Admissions
800-383-2345 Fax: 563-584-8666
Website: www.clarke.edu
E-mail: andy.schroeder@clarke.edu

Coe College
1220 1st Ave NE, Cedar Rapids IA 52402-5092
319-399-8000

Cornell College
600 1st St SW, Mount Vernon IA 52314-1098
319-895-4000

DIVINE WORD COLLEGE SEMINARY
102 Jacoby Dr SW, Epworth IA 52045
Len Uhal, Director of Admissions
563-876-3332 Fax: 563-876-5515
Website: www.svdvocations.org
E-mail: dwm@mwci.net

Dordt College
498 4th Ave NE, Sioux Center IA 51250-1697
Quentin Van Essen, Executive Director of Admissions
800-343-6738

Drake University
2507 University Ave, Des Moines IA 50311-4505
Laura Linn, Director of Admissions
515-271-2011

Emmaus Bible College
2570 Asbury Rd, Dubuque IA 52001-3096
563-588-8000

Faith Baptist Bible College
1900 NW 4th St, Ankeny IA 50023-2192
515-964-0601

Graceland University
1 University Place, Lamoni IA 50140
Greg Sutherland, Interim Vice President for Enrollment and Dean of Admissions
641-784-5196 Fax: 641-784-5480
Website: www.admissions.graceland.edu
E-mail: admissions@graceland.edu

Grand View College
1200 Grandview Ave, Des Moines IA 50316-1599
515-263-2800

Grinnell College
PO Box 805, Grinnell IA 50112-0805
641-269-4000

Hamilton College
7009 Nordic Dr, Cedar Falls IA 50613
Connie Reidy, Campus President
319-277-0220 Fax: 319-363-3812
Website: www.hamiltonia.edu
E-mail: coreidy@hamiltoncf.com

Hamilton College
3165 Edgewood Pkwy SW, Cedar Rapids IA 52404
Susan Spivey, Campus President
319-363-0481 Fax: 319-363-3812
Website: www.hamiltonia.edu
E-mail: sspivey@hamiltonia.edu

Hamilton College
1751 Madison Ave Ste 750, Council Bluffs IA 51503
Michael Zawisky, Executive Director
712-328-4212
Website: www.hamiltonia.edu
E-mail: mzawisky@hamiltonia.edu

Hamilton College
2570 4th St SW, Mason City IA 50401-4665
Joe Albers, Executive Director
641-423-2530 Fax: 641-423-7512
Website: www.hamiltonia.edu
E-mail: jalbers@hamiltonia.edu

Hamilton College
4655 121st St, Urbandale IA 50323-2311
Colleen McDermott, Campus President
515-727-2100 Fax: 515-727-2115
Website: www.hamiltonia.edu
E-mail: cmcdermott@hamiltonia.edu

Hamilton Technical College
1011 E 53rd St, Davenport IA 52807-2653
Mark Christy, Director
563-386-3570 Fax: 563-386-6756
Website: www.hamiltontechcollege.com
E-mail: mchristy@hamiltontechcollege.com
See listing under "Career Schools"

Iowa State University
Ames IA 50011-0001
515-294-4111

Iowa Wesleyan College
601 N Main St, Mount Pleasant IA 52641-1398
Donald G. Hapward, Director of Admissions
319-385-8021

Kaplan University
1801 E Kimberly Rd #1, Davenport IA 52807-2095
563-355-3500

Loras College
1450 Alta Vista St, Dubuque IA 52001-4399
Tim Hauber, Director of Admissions
800-245-6727

Luther College
700 College Dr, Decorah IA 52101-1045
563-387-2000

Maharishi University of Management
1000 N 4th St, Fairfield IA 52557-0002
641-472-7000

MERCY COLLEGE OF HEALTH SCIENCES
928 6th Ave, Des Moines IA 50309-1225
Susan Rhoades, Dean Enrollment & Student Services
515-643-3180 Fax: 515-643-6698
Website: www.mchs.edu
E-mail: srhoades@mercydesmoines.org

Morningside College
1501 Morningside Ave, Sioux City IA 51106-1717
712-274-5000

Mount Mercy College
1330 Elmhurst Dr NE, Cedar Rapids IA 52402-4797
Jim Krystofiak, Dean of Admission
800-248-4504

Northwestern College
101 7th St SW, Orange City IA 51041-1996
712-737-7000

St. Ambrose University
518 W Locust St, Davenport IA 52803-2898
563-333-6000

Simpson College
701 N C St, Indianola IA 50125-1297
515-961-6251

University of Dubuque
2000 University Ave, Dubuque IA 52001-5099
563-589-3000

University of Iowa
107 Calvin Hall, Iowa City IA 52242-1315
319-335-3500

University of Northern Iowa
Cedar Falls IA 50614-0001
319-273-2311

Upper Iowa University
PO Box 1857, Fayette IA 52142-1857
563-425-5200

Vennard College
PO Box 29, University Park IA 52595-0029
800-686-8391

WALDORF COLLEGE
106 S 6th St, Forest City IA 50436-1713
Dr. Linda Hoopes, Vice President of Admission and Marketing
800-292-1903 or 641-585-8112 Fax: 641-585-8125
Website: www.waldorf.edu
E-mail: hoopesl@waldorf.edu
Established 1903. Private. Coed. Accreditation: North Central Association of Colleges and Schools. Tuition: $17,791. Fees: $785. Room & board: $5,534. Enrollment: 650 full-time, 90 part-time. Faculty: 70 full and part-time. Student-faculty ratio: 15:1. Degrees: BA/BS in Biology, Business, Communications, Elementary Education K-6, Secondary Education, Music Education, Foundation of Education, English, History, Humanities, Computer Information Systems, Music, Psychology, Physical Science (also will receive BS in Chemical Engineering from Iowa State University in this dual degree), Theatre Arts, and Wellness. Library: 55,000 volumes, 5,863 bound periodicals. 13 buildings on 40+ acres. All incoming students receive a laptop computer to use for the 4 years they are here.

Wartburg College
PO Box 1003, Waverly IA 50677-0903
Brent Matthias, Interim Director of Admissions
319-352-8200

William Penn University
201 Trueblood Ave, Oskaloosa IA 52577-1757
641-673-1012

KANSAS

Baker University
PO Box 65, Baldwin City KS 66006-0065
785-594-6451

Baker University School of Nursing
1500 SW 10th Ave, Topeka KS 66604-1301
888-866-4242

Barclay College
607 N Kingman St, Haviland KS 67059
Herb Frazier, Director of Admissions
800-862-0226

Benedictine College
1020 N 2nd St, Atchison KS 66002-1499
913-367-5340

Bethany College
421 N 1st St, Lindsborg KS 67456-1897
785-227-3311

Bethel College
300 E 27th St, North Newton KS 67117-8061
316-283-2500

Central Christian College of Kansas
PO Box 1403, Mc Pherson KS 67460-1403
Dr. David Ferrell, Director of Admissions
800-835-0078

Emporia State University
1200 Commercial St, Emporia KS 66801-5087
620-343-1200

Fort Hays State University
600 Park St, Hays KS 67601-4099
785-628-4000

Friends University
2100 W University Ave, Wichita KS 67213-3397
316-261-5800

Kansas State University
Manhattan KS 66506
785-532-6250

Kansas State University - Salina
College of Technology & Aviation
2310 Centennial Rd, Salina KS 67401-8058
785-826-2640

Kansas Wesleyan University
100 E Claflin Ave, Salina KS 67401-6196
785-827-5541

Manhattan Christian College
1415 Anderson Ave, Manhattan KS 66502-4081
785-539-3571

McPherson College
PO Box 1402, Mc Pherson KS 67460-1402
620-241-0731

Mid-America Nazarene University
2030 E College Way, Olathe KS 66062-1851
913-782-3750

Newman University
3100 W McCormick St, Wichita KS 67213
Jann Reusser, Admissions Recruitment Coordinator
316-942-4291 ext. 2144

Ottawa University
1001 S Cedar St, Ottawa KS 66067-3399
785-242-5200

Pittsburg State University
1701 S Broadway St, Pittsburg KS 66762-7500
620-231-7000

Southwestern College
100 College St, Winfield KS 67156-2499
620-229-6000

Sterling College
125 W Cooper St, Sterling KS 67579
Cal White, V.P. Enrollment Services
800-346-1017

TABOR COLLEGE
400 S Jefferson St, Hillsboro KS 67063
Rusty Allen, Dean of Enrollment Management
800-822-6799 Fax: 620-947-6276
Website: www.tabor.edu
E-mail: admissions@tabor.edu

Established 1908. Mennonite Brethren. Coed. 500 Students. On-campus housing. Offers students a decidedly Christian education. Degrees offered in health and biological science, business, communications, mathematical and computer sciences, liberal arts, music, psychology, social science, teacher education, theological studies and religious vocations. Financial aid available.

University of Kansas
Lawrence KS 66045-0001
Alan Cerveny, Director of Admissions

University of Kansas Medical Center
3901 Rainbow Blvd, Kansas City KS 66160-0001
913-588-5000

University of Saint Mary
4100 S 4th St, Leavenworth KS 66048-5023
913-682-5151

Washburn University
1700 SW College Ave, Topeka KS 66621-0001
785-231-1010

Wichita State University
1845 N Fairmount St, Wichita KS 67260-0124
Gina Crabtree, Director of Admissions
316-978-3085

KENTUCKY

Alice Lloyd College
100 Purpose Rd, Pippa Passes KY 41844-9005
John Mills, Director of Admissions
888-280-4252

Asbury College
1 Macklem Dr, Wilmore KY 40390-1198
859-858-3511

Bellarmine University
2001 Newburg Rd, Louisville KY 40205-1877
502-452-8000

Berea College
Berea KY 40404-0001
859-985-3000

Brescia University
717 Frederica St, Owensboro KY 42301-3023
Sr. Mary Austin Blank, OSB, Director of Admissions
877-BRESCIA

Campbellsville University
1 University Dr, Campbellsville KY 42718-2799
Scott Necessary, Coordinator of Undergraduate Admissions
270-789-5000

Centre College
600 W Walnut St, Danville KY 40422-1394
859-238-5200

Clear Creek Baptist Bible College
300 Clear Creek Rd, Pineville KY 40977-9752
606-337-3196

Eastern Kentucky University
521 Lancaster Ave, Richmond KY 40475-3102
859-622-1000

Embry-Riddle Aeronautical University
300 High Rise Dr Suite 392, Louisville KY 40213-3253
J. Michael Novak, Director of Enrollment Management
888-409-3728

FRONTIER SCHOOL OF MIDWIFERY & FAMILY NURSING
PO Box 528, Hyden KY 41749
Sherri Davis, Registrar
606-672-2312 Fax: 606-672-3776
Website: www.frontierschool.edu
E-mail: sherri.davis@midwives.org

Georgetown College
400 E College St, Georgetown KY 40324-1696
502-863-8011

Kentucky Christian University
100 Academic Pkwy, Grayson KY 41143-2205
606-474-3000

Kentucky Mountain Bible College
PO Box 10, Vancleve KY 41385-0010
800-879-5622

Kentucky State University
400 E Main St, Frankfort KY 40601-2334
502-597-6000

Kentucky Wesleyan College
3000 Frederica St, Owensboro KY 42301-6055
800-999-0592

Lindsey Wilson College
210 Lindsey Wilson St, Columbia KY 42728-1223
270-384-8100

Mid-Continent University
99 E Powell Rd, Mayfield KY 42066-9007
Butch Booth, Director of Admissions
800-894-8878

Morehead State University
Morehead KY 40351-1689
Jeffrey Liles, Enrollment Services
800-585-6781 Fax: 606-783-5038
Website: www.moreheadstate.edu
E-mail: admissions@moreheadstate.edu

Murray State University
Murray KY 42071
Phil Bryan, Director of Admissions
270-762-3011

Northern Kentucky University
Newport KY 41099-0001
859-572-5100

Pikeville College
147 Sycamore St, Pikeville KY 41501
606-218-5250

Spalding University
851 S 4th St, Louisville KY 40203-2188
502-585-9911

Strayer University
220 Lexington Green Cir Ste 550
Lexington KY 40503
859-971-4400

Sullivan University
PO Box 998, Fort Knox KY 40121-0998
502-942-8500

Sullivan University
2355 Harrodsburg Rd, Lexington KY 40504-3307
800-467-6281

Sullivan University
3101 Bardstown Rd, Louisville KY 40205-3000
800-844-1354

Thomas More College
333 Thomas More Pkwy, Crestview Hills KY 41017
859-341-5800

Transylvania University
300 N Broadway, Lexington KY 40508-1776
859-233-8242 Fax: 859-233-8797
Website: www.transy.edu
E-mail: admissions@transy.edu

Union College
310 College St, Barbourville KY 40906-1499
Joretta Nelson, Vice President for Enrollment Management
800-489-8646

University of Kentucky
Lexington KY 40506-0001
Don Witt, Director of Admissions
859-257-9000

University of Louisville
2301 S 3rd St, Louisville KY 40292-2001
502-852-5555

University of the Cumberlands
6178 College Station Dr
Williamsburg KY 40769-1372
606-549-2200

Western Kentucky University
1 Big Red Way, Bowling Green KY 42101
270-745-0111

LOUISIANA

Centenary College of Louisiana
PO Box 41188, Shreveport LA 71134-1188
318-869-5011

Dillard University
2601 Gentilly Blvd, New Orleans LA 70122-3097
Linda G. Nash, Director of Admissions

Grambling State University
PO Box 864, Grambling LA 71245
318-274-3811

Louisiana College
PO Box 566, Pineville LA 71359-0001
318-487-7259

Louisiana State University
1 University Pl, Shreveport LA 71115-2301
318-797-5000

Louisiana State University and A & M College
Louisiana State Univ, Baton Rouge LA 70803-0001
225-578-3202

Louisiana State University at Alexandria
8100 Highway 71 S, Alexandria LA 71302-9121
Dr. Thomas Armstrong, Director of Admissions
318-445-3672 Fax: 318-473-6418
Website: www.lsua.edu

Louisiana State University Health Sciences Center
433 Bolivar St, New Orleans LA 70112-2223
504-568-4808

Louisiana Tech University
PO Box 3168, Ruston LA 71272-0001
318-257-0211

Loyola University New Orleans
6363 Saint Charles Ave, New Orleans LA 70118-6143
504-865-2011

McNeese State University
4100 Ryan St, Lake Charles LA 70605-4510
337-475-5000

Newcomb College of Tulane University
1229 Broadway St, New Orleans LA 70118-5210
504-865-5594

Nicholls State University
PO Box 2004, Thibodaux LA 70310-0001
985-446-8111

Northwestern State University
Natchitoches LA 71497-0001
Jana Lucky, Director of Enrollment Services
318-357-4503

Northwestern State University
1800 Line Ave, Shreveport LA 71101-4653
Norann Planchock, Director
318-677-3100

Our Lady of the Lake College
7434 Perkins Rd, Baton Rouge LA 70808
Marvell Nesmith, Director of Admissions
225-768-1700

ST. JOSEPH SEMINARY COLLEGE
Saint Benedict LA 70457
Dr. Russ Pottle, Director of Admissions
985-867-2225 Fax: 985-867-2270
Website: www.stjosephabbey.org
E-mail: acdean@stjosephabbey.org

Southeastern Louisiana University
PO Box 784, Hammond LA 70404-0784
985-549-2000

Southern University A&M College
Southern University, Baton Rouge LA 70813-0001
225-771-4500

Southern University in New Orleans
6400 Press Dr, New Orleans LA 70126-1009
504-286-5000

Tulane University
6823 Saint Charles Ave, New Orleans LA 70118-5698
504-865-4000

University of Louisiana at Lafayette
PO Box 43370, Lafayette LA 70504
337-482-6729

University of Louisiana at Monroe
700 University Ave, Monroe LA 71209-9001
318-342-1000

University of New Orleans
New Orleans LA 70148-0001
504-280-6000

William Carey College
3939 Gentilly Blvd Box 309, New Orleans LA 70126
Tom Huebner, Director of Admissions
504-865-1502

Xavier University
1 Drexel Dr, New Orleans LA 70125-1098
504-486-7411

MAINE

Bates College
1 Bates College, Lewiston ME 04240
207-786-6000

Bowdoin College
Brunswick ME 04011
207-725-3000

Colby College
150 Mayflower Hill Dr, Waterville ME 04901-4799
207-872-3000

College of the Atlantic
105 Eden St, Bar Harbor ME 04609-1198
207-288-5015

HUSSON COLLEGE
One College Cir, Bangor ME 04401-2999
William Beardsley, President
Jane Goodwin, Director of Admissions
800-4-HUSSON or 207-941-7100 Fax: 207-941-7935
Website: www.husson.edu
E-mail: admit@husson.edu

Established 1898. Private. Coed. Accreditation: NEASC, NLN. Tuition: $11,970. Room and board: $6,500. Fees: $280. Enrollment: 1,531 full-time, 721 part-time. Faculty: 100. Student-faculty ratio: 21:1. Degrees: associate's, bachelor's, doctorate's, master's. Library: 39,020 volumes. 8 buildings on 200 acres, new Center for Family Business building. New Clara L. Swan Fitness Center. Furman Student Center. Gym. Pool. International Center for Language Studies (ICLS). The Commons. Programs include accounting, business administration, chemistry/pre-pharmacy, computer information systems, english, nursing and physical therapy, occupational therapy, physical education, secondary education, master of science in business, health care management and nurse practitioner, science and humanities, biology, elementary education, hospitality management, paralegal studies, psychology, criminal justice.

Maine College of Art
97 Spring St, Portland ME 04101-3987
Jodie Lane, Director of Admissions
800-639-4808

Maine Maritime Academy
Battle Ave, Castine ME 04420-0001
Jeff Wright, Director of Admissions
207-326-2206

St. Joseph's College of Maine
278 Whites Bridge Rd, Standish ME 04084-5263
Vincent Kloskowski, Dean of Admissions
800-338-7057 Fax: 207-893-7862
Website: www.sjcme.edu
E-mail: admission@sjcme.edu

Thomas College
180 W River Rd, Waterville ME 04901-5097
207-859-1111

Unity College
90 Quaker Hill Rd, Unity ME 04988-3712
207-948-3131

University of Maine
46 University Dr, Augusta ME 04330
207-621-3000

University of Maine
246 Main St, Farmington ME 04938
Sharon M. Oliver, Director of Admissions
207-778-7000

University of Maine
9 OBrien Ave, Machias ME 04654-1321
207-255-1200

University of Maine
Orono ME 04469-0001
207-581-1110

University of Maine at Fort Kent
23 University Dr, Fort Kent ME 04743
888-TRY-UMFK

University of Maine at Presque Isle
181 Main St, Presque Isle ME 04769-2844
207-768-9532

University of New England
11 Hills Beach Rd, Biddeford ME 04005-9526
207-283-0171

University of Southern Maine
PO Box 9300, Portland ME 04104-9300
207-780-4141

Westbrook College
716 Stevens Ave, Portland ME 04103-2693
207-797-7261

MARYLAND

Baltimore Hebrew University
5800 Park Heights Ave, Baltimore MD 21215-3996
410-578-6900

BALTIMORE INTERNATIONAL COLLEGE

17 Commerce St, Baltimore MD 21202-3230
Kristin Ciarlo, Director of Admissions
410-752-4710 ext. 120 Fax: 410-752-3730
Website: www.bic.edu
E-mail: admissions@bic.edu

Founded in 1972, Baltimore International College is an independent college regionally accredited by the Commission on Higher Education, Middle States Association of Colleges and Schools. The college offers specialized masters, baccalaureate and associate's degrees, and a certificate program through its School of Culinary Arts, School of Hotel Restaurant and Catering Management, and School of Graduate Studies. The college's programs include a master of science in Hospitality Management degree, bachelor's degrees in Culinary Management, Hospitality Management, Hospitality Management with Marketing Concentration; associate's degrees in Professional Cooking, Professional Cooking and Baking and Professional Baking and Pastry; and certificates in Professional Culinary Arts.

The college has a campus in Baltimore, MD., just two blocks from Baltimore's famous Inner Harbor and within easy walking distance of many of the city's major attractions. The college also has Virginia Park, a sprawling 100-acre preserve along the shore of Lough Ramor in Virginia, County Cavan, Ireland. The Virginia Park campus is home to the Park Hotel and a golf course, pleasure gardens, and 15 miles of walking paths. Students may take courses at the Virginia Park campus studying under European-educated chefs and hoteliers.

The mission of Baltimore International College is to provide qualified students with the education and experience they need to pursue progressive careers within the international foodservice and lodging industry.

Bowie State University
14000 Jericho Park Rd, Bowie MD 20715-9465
301-464-3000

Capitol College
11301 Springfield Rd, Laurel MD 20708-9759
800-950-1992

Columbia Center
6740 Alexander Bell Dr, Columbia MD 21046-2100
410-290-1777

Columbia Union College
7600 Flower Ave, Takoma Park MD 20912-7794
301-891-4000

Coppin State University
2500 W North Ave, Baltimore MD 21216-3698
410-951-3000

Frostburg State University
Frostburg MD 21532-1001
301-687-4000

Goucher College
1021 Dulaney Valley Rd, Baltimore MD 21204-2780
410-337-6000

ITT Technical Institute
11301 Red Run Blvd, Owings Mills MD 21117
443-394-7115

Johns Hopkins University
600 N Wolfe St, Baltimore MD 21287-0005
410-955-3182

Johns Hopkins University
3400 N Charles St, Baltimore MD 21218-2680
410-516-8000

Loyola College
4501 N Charles St, Baltimore MD 21210-2694
410-617-2000

MAPLE SPRINGS BAPTIST BIBLE COLLEGE & SEMINARY

4130 Belt Rd, Capitol Heights MD 20743-5711
Rev. Percy V. Coker, Registrar
301-736-3631 Fax: 301-735-6507
Website: www.msbbcs.edu

Maryland Institute College of Art
1300 W Mount Royal Ave, Baltimore MD 21217-4191
Theresa Lynch Bedoya, VP, Dean of Admissions & Financial Aid
410-225-2222

McDaniel College
2 College Hl, Westminster MD 21157-4303
410-848-7000

Morgan State University
1700 E Cold Spring Ln, Baltimore MD 21251-0002
443-885-3000

Mt. St. Mary's University
16300 Old Emmitsburg Rd
Emmitsburg MD 21727-7799
301-447-6122

National Labor College
1000 New Hampshire Ave, Silver Spring MD 20903
301-431-6400

ST. JOHN'S COLLEGE

PO Box 2800, Annapolis MD 21404-2800
John Christensen, Director of Admissions
800-727-9238 Fax: 410-269-7916
Website: www.stjohnscollege.edu
E-mail: admissions@sjca.edu

St. Mary's College of Maryland
18952 E Fisher Rd, Saint Marys City MD 20686
301-862-0200

Salisbury University
1101 Camden Ave, Salisbury MD 21801-6837
410-543-6000

Sojourner-Douglass College
500 N Caroline St, Baltimore MD 21205-1898
410-276-0306

Strayer University
1520 Jabez Run Ste 100, Millersville MD 21108
410-923-4500

Strayer University
4 Research Pl Ste 100, Rockville MD 20850
301-548-5500

Towson State University
8000 York Rd, Towson MD 21252-0002
410-830-2000

United States Naval Academy
121 Blake Rd, Annapolis MD 21402
410-293-1000

University of Baltimore
1420 N Charles St, Baltimore MD 21201-5779
410-837-4200

University of Maryland
520 W Lombard St, Baltimore MD 21201
410-706-3100

University of Maryland
1000 Hilltop Cir, Baltimore MD 21250-0001
410-455-1000

University of Maryland
College Park MD 20742-0001
301-405-1000

University of Maryland
Univ Blvd And Adelphi Rd
College Park MD 20742-0001
301-985-7000

University of Maryland Eastern Shore
Princess Anne MD 21853
Edwina Morse, Director of Admissions
410-651-6410

Villa Julie College
1525 Greenspring Valley Rd
Stevenson MD 21153-0641
Mark Hergan, V.P. Enrollment Services
410-486-7001

Washington College
300 Washington Ave, Chestertown MD 21620-1197
410-778-2800

MASSACHUSETTS

American International College
1000 State St, Springfield MA 01109-3155
Peter Miller, Dean of Admissions
413-737-7000

Amherst College
PO Box 5000, Amherst MA 01002
413-542-2000

Anna Maria College
50 Sunset Ln, Paxton MA 01612
Timothy M. Donahue, Director of Recruitment and Admissions
508-849-3360 Fax: 508-849-3362
Website: www.annamaria.edu
E-mail: admissions@annamaria.edu

The Art Institute of Boston at Lesley University
700 Beacon St, Boston MA 02215-2598
Office of Admission
617-585-6710 Fax: 617-585-6720
Website: www.aiboston.edu
E-mail: admissions@aiboston.edu

Assumption College
500 Salisbury St, Worcester MA 01609-1294
Kathleen Murphy, Dean of Enrollment
508-767-7000 Fax: 508-799-4412
Website: www.assumption.edu
E-mail: admiss@assumption.edu

Atlantic Union College
PO Box 1000, South Lancaster MA 01561-1000
Office of Enrollment Services
800-282-2030

Babson College
PO Box 57310, Babson Park MA 02457-0310
781-235-1200

Bay State College
122 Commonwealth Ave, Boston MA 02116-2901
Craig Pfannenstiehl, President
617-217-9000 Fax: 617-536-1735

BECKER COLLEGE

Campuses in Worcester and Leicester, MA
61 Sever St, Worcester MA 01609-2165
Karen Schedin, Dean of Admissions
508-791-9241 Fax: 508-890-1500
Website: www.becker.edu
E-mail: admissions@becker.edu

Established 1887. Private. Coed. Accreditation: New England Association of Schools and Colleges, Inc. Tuition: $20,500. Room & board: $8,500. Fees: $610. Enrollment: 843 full-time, 171 part-time. Student-faculty ratio: 15:1. Degrees: AS, BA, BS. Library: 65,000 volumes. 47 buildings on 100 acres. One campus in Worcester (city) and one campus in Leicester (rural). On-site Preschool, Veterinary Clinic, and Equestrian facility adjacent to campus. State-of-the-art Health Sciences facilities. Joint BS/JD program. Army ROTC program. NCAA Division III Athletics. Financial aid for those who qualify. Member of the Colleges of the Worcester Consortium.

Benjamin Franklin Institute of Technology
41 Berkeley St, Boston MA 02116-6307
Norman Kraft, Dean of Enrollment
617-423-4630 ext. 121 Fax: 617-482-3706
Website: www.bfit.edu
E-mail: admissions@bfit.edu

Bentley College
175 Forest St, Waltham MA 02452-4705
781-891-2000

Berklee College of Music
1140 Boylston St, Boston MA 02215-3693
Damien S. Bracken, Director of Admissions
800-BERKLEE

Boston Architectural Center
320 Newbury St, Boston MA 02115-2795
617-262-5000

Boston Baptist College
950 Metropolitan Ave, Boston MA 02136
617-364-3510

Boston College
140 Commonwealth Ave
Chestnut Hill MA 02467-3800
617-552-8000

Boston Conservatory
8 Fenway, Boston MA 02215-4099
Halley Shefler, Dean of Enrollment
617-912-9153 Fax: 617-247-3159
Website: www.bostonconservatory.edu
E-mail: admissions@bostonconservatory.edu

Boston University
121 Bay State Rd, Boston MA 02215
Kelly Walter, Executive Director of Admissions
617-353-2300 Fax: 617-353-9695
Website: web.bu.edu
E-mail: admissions@bu.edu

Boston University Medical Center
100 E Newton St, Boston MA 02118-2308
617-638-5300

Brandeis University
415 South St, Waltham MA 02453-2700
781-736-3500

Bridgewater State College
Bridgewater MA 02325-0001
508-697-1237

Clark University
950 Main St, Worcester MA 01610-1473
508-793-7711

College of the Holy Cross
1 College St, Worcester MA 01610-2322
508-793-2011

Curry College
1071 Blue Hill Ave, Milton MA 02186-2395
Bruce Weckworth, Director of Admissions
617-333-2210

Eastern Nazarene College
23 E Elm Ave, Quincy MA 02170-2999
617-773-6350

Elms College
291 Springfield St, Chicopee MA 01013-2839
800-255-3567

Emerson College
120 Boylston St, Boston MA 02116-4624
Sara S. Ramirez, Director of Undergraduate Admission
617-824-8600 Fax: 617-824-8609
Website: www.emerson.edu
E-mail: admission@emerson.edu

Emmanuel College
400 The Fenway, Boston MA 02115-5798
617-735-9715

Fisher College
118 Beacon St, Boston MA 02116-1501
Stephen Carter, Director of Admissions
800-446-1226

Fitchburg State College
160 Pearl St, Fitchburg MA 01420-2697
978-345-2151

Framingham State College
PO Box 9101, Framingham MA 01704-0101
508-620-1220

Franklin W. Olin College of Engineering
Olin Way, Needham MA 02492
781-292-2300

Gordon College
255 Grapevine Rd, Wenham MA 01984-1899
Barbara R. Layne, Associate Vice President, Enrollment
866-464-6736 Fax: 978-867-4682
Website: www.gordon.edu
E-mail: admissions@gordon.edu

Hampshire College
Amherst MA 01002
Karen S. Parker, Director of Admissions
413-559-5471

Harvard University
8 Garden St, Cambridge MA 02138-3630
617-495-1000

Hebrew College
160 Herrick Rd, Newton Centre MA 02459-2237
Kate A. Nachman, Director of Admissions
617-559-8610

Hellenic College/Holy Cross Greek Orthodox School of Theology
50 Goddard Ave, Brookline MA 02445-7415
Sonia Belcher, Director
617-731-3500

ITT TECHNICAL INSTITUTE
333 Boston Providence Tpke
Norwood MA 02062-3932
Tom Ryan, Director of Recruiting
800-879-TECH (8324) Fax: 781-278-0766
Website: www.itt-tech.edu
E-mail: tryan@itt-tech.edu

Established 1990. Private. Coed. Accreditation: ACICS. Enrollment: 300. Student-faculty ratio: 11:1. Associate Degrees offered: Computer Drafting & Design, Computer Electronics Technology, Computer Network Systems, Multimedia.

Lasell College
1844 Commonwealth Ave, Newton MA 02466-2716
617-243-2225

Massachusetts College of Art
621 Huntington Ave, Boston MA 02115-5801
617-232-1555

Massachusetts College of Liberal Arts
375 Church St, North Adams MA 01247-4100
Denise Richardello, Vice President for Enrollment and External Relations
413-662-5410

Massachusetts Institute of Technology
77 Massachusetts Ave, Cambridge MA 02139-4307
617-253-1000 Fax: 617-253-4016
Website: my.mit.edu
E-mail: admissions@mit.edu

Massachusetts Maritime Academy
Cape Cod
101 Academy Dr, Buzzards Bay MA 02532-3400
CDR. Keith D. Rabine, Dean of Enrollment Services
800-544-3411

Merrimack College
315 Turnpike St, North Andover MA 01845-5800
978-683-7111

Mt. Ida College
777 Dedham St, Newton Center MA 02459-3323
617-969-7000

NEWBURY COLLEGE
129 Fisher Ave, Brookline MA 02445-5796
Salvadore Liberto, Vice President of Enrollment
617-730-7000 Fax: 617-731-9618
Website: www.newbury.edu
E-mail: info@newbury.edu

Private. Coed. Accreditation: NEASC, CIDA, NCAA, IACBE. Tuition: $18,900. Room & board: $10,100. Fees: $1,100. Enrollment: 925 full-time, 300 part-time. Faculty: 75. Student-faculty ratio: 15:1. Degrees: BA, BS, Associates. Library: access to 62,000,000 volumes. 7 buildings on 12 acres. 3 miles from downtown Boston, Free academic assistance, 6 varsity women's sports, 7 varsity men's sports. wireless campus.

Nichols College
Dudley MA 01571-5000
Kimberly A. Kossuth, Director of Admissions
508-943-1560

Northeastern University
360 Huntington Ave, Boston MA 02115-5000
617-373-2000

Pine Manor College
400 Heath St, Chestnut Hill MA 02467-2332
Bill Nichols, Dean of Admission
617-731-7167

Regis College
235 Wellesley St, Weston MA 02493-1571
781-768-2000

Richmond University, London, England
343 Congress St Ste 3100, Boston MA 02210-1214
617-450-5617

Salem State College
352 Lafayette St, Salem MA 01970-5353
978-741-6000

SCHOOL OF THE MUSEUM OF FINE ARTS, BOSTON
230 The Fenway, Boston MA 02115-5534
Office of Admissions
617-369-3626 or 800-643-6078 Fax: 617-369-4264
Website: www.smfa.edu
E-mail: admissions@smfa.edu

The School of the Museum of Fine Arts, Boston (SMFA), is a fine arts college that offers students the opportunity to design their own individualized course of study and tailor a program that best suits their needs and goals. Similar to an artists' colony, the Museum School's focus is on creative investigation, risk-taking, and exploration of individual vision.

A division of the Museum of Fine Arts, Boston, and in partnership with Tufts and Northeastern Universities, the SMFA, or Museum School, offers a diverse curriculum with a full range of studio and academic resources. The School's extensive interdisciplinary studio curriculum is developed continually in order to incorporate new media and new approaches, concepts, and theories. A large faculty of working artists and an intimate student-faculty ratio of 9:1 provide each student extensive opportunities for individual consultation and dialogue.

Program options include the all-studio Diploma, Bachelor of Fine Arts, Bachelor of Fine Arts in Art Education, five-year combined degree program (BFA and BS or BA), Master of Fine Arts, Master of Arts in Teaching in Art Education, and the Post-Baccalaureate certificate program. All students in degree programs are jointly enrolled at the Museum School and Tufts University and receive a Tufts or Northeastern degree.

Students at the Museum School have the city of Boston as their campus, where a short walk can span many different landscapes, including Copley Square, Fenway Park, Newbury Street, and Chinatown. The more than 60 major universities and colleges in the Boston area make this coastal city a mecca for students. The city is devoted to the arts. Along with the Museum of Fine Arts (which is adjacent to the School) are the Isabella Stewart Gardner Museum, the Institute of Contemporary Art, and the Photographic Resource Center. Across the Charles River in Cambridge are the List Center, associated with the Massachusetts Institute of Technology, and the many museums associated with Harvard University, including the Fogg Museum, the Busch-Reisinger Museum, the Sackler Museum, the Carpenter Center, and the Harvard University Museum. Boston also has a lively gallery scene, with spaces ranging from the traditional to the most avant-garde.

Simon's Rock College of Bard
80 Alford Rd, Great Barrington MA 01230-1559
413-528-0771

Springfield College
263 Alden St, Springfield MA 01109-3788
Mary DeAngelo, Director of Admissions
800-343-1257

Stonehill College
320 Washington St, Easton MA 02357-5610
508-565-1373

Suffolk University
8 Ashburton Pl, Boston MA 02108-2770
617-573-8460

Tufts University
520 Boston Ave, Medford MA 02155-5555
617-628-5000

University of Massachusetts
Amherst MA 01003
413-545-0111

University of Massachusetts at Worcester
55 Lake Ave N, Worcester MA 01655-0001
508-856-8989

University of Massachusetts Boston
100 William T Morrissey Blvd, Boston MA 02125-3393
Liliana Mickle, Director of Undergraduate Admissions
617-287-6000

University of Massachusetts Dartmouth
Old Westport Rd, North Dartmouth MA 02747-2300
Steven T. Briggs, Director of Admissions
508-999-8605 Fax: 508-999-8755
Website: explore.umassd.edu
E-mail: sbriggs@umassd.edu

University of Massachusetts Lowell
1 University Ave, Lowell MA 01854-2893
978-934-4000

Wentworth Institute of Technology
550 Huntington Ave, Boston MA 02115-5998
David C. Planchard, Director of Admissions
617-442-9010

Western New England College
1215 Wilbraham Rd, Springfield MA 01119-2655
413-782-1321

Westfield State College
PO Box 1630, Westfield MA 01086
Michelle Mattie, Associate Dean, Admission and Enrollment Services
413-572-5300

Wheaton College
26 E Main St, Norton MA 02766-2322
Gail Berson, Dean of Admissions & Student Aid
800-394-6003

WHEELOCK COLLEGE
200 Riverway, Boston MA 02215-4104
Lisa Slavin, Dean of Enrollment
800-734-5212 Fax: 617-879-2449
Website: www.wheelock.edu
E-mail: undergrad@wheelock.edu

Williams College
Williamstown MA 01267
413-597-3131

Worcester Polytechnic Institute
100 Institute Rd, Worcester MA 01609-2280
Edward J. Connor, Director of Admissions
508-831-5286 Fax: 508-831-5875
Website: admissions.wpi.edu
E-mail: admissions@wpi.edu

Worcester State College
486 Chandler St, Worcester MA 01602-2597
508-929-8000

MICHIGAN

Adrian College
110 S Madison St, Adrian MI 49221-2575
517-265-5161

Albion College
611 E Porter St, Albion MI 49224-1831
800-858-6770

ALMA COLLEGE
614 W Superior St, Alma MI 48801-1599
Evan Montague, Director of Admissions
800-321-ALMA Fax: 989-463-7057
Website: www.alma.edu
E-mail: admissions@alma.edu

Andrews University
Berrien Springs MI 49104-0001
Randall Graves, Director of Recruitment Services
800-253-2874

Aquinas College
1607 Robinson Rd SE, Grand Rapids MI 49506-1799
Paula Meehan, Dean of Admissions
616-732-4460

Ave Maria College
PO Box 373, Ypsilanti MI 48106-0373
866-866-3030

Baker College of Auburn Hills
1500 University Dr, Auburn Hills MI 48326-2642
248-340-0600

Baker College of Cadillac
9600 E 13th St, Cadillac MI 49601-9574
Mike Tisdale, Director of Admissions
231-876-3100

Baker College of Clinton Township
34950 Little Mack Ave
Clinton Township MI 48035-4701
586-791-6610

Baker College of Flint
1050 W Bristol Rd, Flint MI 48507-5508
810-767-4000

Baker College of Jackson
2800 Springport Rd, Jackson MI 49202-1230
Kelli Hoban, Director of Admissions
517-789-6123

Baker College of Muskegon
1903 Marquette Ave, Muskegon MI 49442-1453
231-726-4904

Baker College of Owosso
1020 S Washington St, Owosso MI 48867-4400
989-729-3300

Baker College of Port Huron
3403 Lapeer Rd, Port Huron MI 48060-2597
Dan Kenny, Director of Admissions
888-262-2442

Calvin College
3201 Burton St SE, Grand Rapids MI 49546-4388
800-688-0122

Central Michigan University
100 Warriner Hall, Mount Pleasant MI 48859-0001
989-774-4000

Cleary University - Livingston Campus
3750 Cleary Dr, Howell MI 48843
517-548-3670

Cleary University - Washtenaw Campus
3601 Plymouth Rd, Ann Arbor MI 48105-2659
734-332-4477

College for Creative Studies
201 E Kirby St, Detroit MI 48202-4048
Julie Hingelberg, Dean of Enrollment Services
313-664-7425
Website: www.ccscad.edu

Concordia University
4090 Geddes Rd, Ann Arbor MI 48105-2797
Gary Neumann, Director of Admissions
734-995-7300 Fax: 734-995-4610
Website: www.cuaa.edu
E-mail: admissions@cuaa.edu

Cornerstone University
1001 E Beltline Ave NE
Grand Rapids MI 49525-5897
616-949-5300

Davenport University
6191 Kraft Ave SE, Grand Rapids MI 49512
866-383-3548
Website: www.explore.davenport.edu

Davenport University
5300 Bay Rd, Saginaw MI 48604
989-799-7800

Davenport University - Central Region
3555 E Patrick Rd, Midland MI 48642-5891
989-835-5588

Davenport University - Eastern Region
4801 Oakman Blvd, Dearborn MI 48126-3799
313-581-4400

Davenport University - Warren
27650 Dequindre Rd, Warren MI 48092
Tracey Schaffer, Director of Enrollment Services
586-558-8700

Eastern Michigan University
Ypsilanti MI 48197
800-GO-TO-EMU

Ferris State University
901 S State St, Big Rapids MI 49307-2295
231-591-2000

Grace Bible College
PO Box 910, Grand Rapids MI 49509-0910
800-968-1887

Grand Valley State University
1 Campus Dr, Allendale MI 49401-9403
Jodi Chycinski, Director of Admissions
616-331-6611 Fax: 616-331-2000
Website: www.gvsu.edu
E-mail: go2gvsu@gvsu.edu

Great Lakes Christian College
6211 W Willow Hwy, Lansing MI 48917-1231
517-321-0242

HILLSDALE COLLEGE
33 E College St, Hillsdale MI 49242-1298
Jeffrey S. Lantis, Director of Admissions
517-607-2327 Fax: 517-607-2223
Website: www.hillsdale.edu
E-mail: admissions@hillsdale.edu

Hope College
PO Box 9000, Holland MI 49422-9000
616-395-7000

Kalamazoo College
1200 Academy St, Kalamazoo MI 49006-3295
269-337-7000

Kendall College of Art & Design
17 Fountain St NW, Grand Rapids MI 49503-3002
Dr. Oliver H. Evans, President
800-676-2787 or 616-451-2787 Fax: 616-831-9689
Website: www.kcad.edu
E-mail: brittons@ferris.edu

LAKE SUPERIOR STATE UNIVERSITY

650 W Easterday Ave, Sault Sainte Marie MI 49783
Susan Camp, Director of Admissions
888-800-LSSU (5778) Fax: 906-635-6696
Website: www.lssu.edu
E-mail: admissions@lssu.edu

Accreditation: North Central Association of Colleges and Schools. Lake Superior State University is known for strong and distinctive academic programs taught by faculty who take an interest in student success. Our students are afforded many opportunities to actively engage with faculty members on research projects and experiential learning. LSSU is Michigan's smallest public university providing a personal approach to education. We're located in the beautiful Upper Peninsula of Michigan forty-five minutes north of the Mackinac Bridge, in an international setting bordering Canada and North America's largest fresh water inland lake, Lake Superior.

LAWRENCE TECHNOLOGICAL UNIVERSITY

21000 W 10 Mile Rd, Southfield MI 48075-1058
Jane Rohrback, Director of Admissions
800-225-5588 Fax: 248-204-2228
Website: www.ltu.edu
E-mail: admissions@ltu.edu

Established 1932. Private. Coed. Accreditation: North Central Association plus all professional programs hold additional accreditation. Undergraduate Tuition: $17,000 - $21,000. Graduate Tuition: $7,000 - $10,000. Room & board: $7,227. UG Fees: $250 - $280; Grad Fees: $200. Enrollment: 1,625 full-time, 2,523 part-time. Faculty: 415. Student-faculty ratio: 12:1. Degrees offered: DBA, DMIT, DEMS, MS, MSEd, ME, MBA, BS, BFA, AS. Library: 126,000 volumes plus numerous CD-ROM and Internet database search systems. 10 buildings on 125 acres. Over 60 degree programs are offered. "Real world" student projects augment most of Lawrence Tech's programs, contributing to a remarkable 90% placement rate. Lawrence Tech is Michigan's first wireless laptop campus. High end Laptops are provided to all undergraduates and included in tuition. A Standard & Poors survey ranks LTU in the top third of U.S. colleges which supply the leaders of America's most successful corporations.

Madonna University
36600 Schoolcraft Rd, Livonia MI 48150-1173
734-432-5300

Marygrove College
8425 W McNichols Rd, Detroit MI 48221-2599
313-927-1200

Michigan Jewish Institute
25401 Coolidge Hwy, Oak Park MI 48237
248-414-6900

Michigan State University
250 Administration Bldg, East Lansing MI 48824
517-355-1855

Michigan Technological University
1400 Townsend Dr, Houghton MI 49931-1200
Nancy Rehling, Director of Admissions
906-487-2335

Northern Michigan University
1401 Presque Isle Ave, Marquette MI 49855-5301
906-227-1000

Northwood University
4000 Whiting Dr, Midland MI 48640
Daniel F. Toland, Dean of Admissions
800-457-7878 Fax: 989-837-4490
Website: www.northwood.edu
E-mail: miadmit@northwood.edu

Oakland University
2200 N Squirrel Rd, Rochester MI 48309
Eleanor L. Reynolds, Assistant Vice President & Director of Admissions
248-370-2100
Website: www.oakland.edu
E-mail: ouinfo@oakland.edu

Olivet College
300 S Main St, Olivet MI 49076-9724
269-749-7000

Reformed Bible College
3333 E Beltline Ave NE
Grand Rapids MI 49525-9749
Nate Vander Stelt, Director of Enrollment Management
616-988-3621

Rochester College
800 W Avon Rd, Rochester Hills MI 48307-2764
248-218-2000

Saginaw Valley State University
7400 Bay Rd, University Center MI 48710-0001
989-790-4000

Siena Heights University
1247 E Siena Heights Dr, Adrian MI 49221-1796
517-263-0731

Spring Arbor University
106 E Main St, Spring Arbor MI 49283-9799
517-750-1200

University of Detroit-Mercy
PO Box 19900, Detroit MI 48219-0900
313-993-1000

University of Michigan-Ann Arbor
1220 Student Activities Bldg, Ann Arbor MI 48109
734-764-1817

University of Michigan-Ann Arbor
400 N Ingalls St, Ann Arbor MI 48109-2029
Elaine Cosme-Petersen, Marketing, Recruiting Coordinator
734-764-7188

University of Michigan-Dearborn
4901 Evergreen Rd, Dearborn MI 48128-1491
The Office of Admissions & Orientation
313-593-5100

University of Michigan-Flint
303 E Kearsley St, Flint MI 48502-1950
810-762-3000

Walsh College of Accountancy & Business Administration
PO Box 7006, Troy MI 48007-7006
Diane Zalapi, Asst. V.P., Student Services
248-823-1610

Wayne State University
5980 Cass Ave, Detroit MI 48202-3489
313-577-2424

Western Michigan University
Kalamazoo MI 49008
269-387-1000

MINNESOTA

ARGOSY UNIVERSITY / TWIN CITIES

(formerly Minnesota School of Professional Psychology and Medical Institute of Minnesota)
1515 Central Pkwy, Eagan MN 55121-1756
O. Jeanne Stoneking, Director of Admissions
651-846-2882 Fax: 651-994-7956
Website: www.argosyu.edu
E-mail: tcadmissions@argosyu.edu

Augsburg College
2211 Riverside Ave, Minneapolis MN 55454-1350
612-330-1000

Bemidji State University
1500 Birchmont Dr NE, Bemidji MN 56601-2699
877-236-4354

Bethany Lutheran College
700 Luther Dr, Mankato MN 56001
Don Westphal, Dean of Admissions
507-344-7000 Fax: 507-344-7376
Website: www.blc.edu
E-mail: admiss@blc.edu

Bethel College
3900 Bethel Dr, Saint Paul MN 55112-6999
651-638-6400

Carleton College
1 N College St, Northfield MN 55057-4044
800-995-2275 or 507-646-4190 Fax: 507-646-4526
Website: www.carleton.edu
E-mail: admissions@acs.carleton.edu

College of Saint Scholastica
1200 Kenwood Ave, Duluth MN 55811-4199
Brian Dalton, V.P. of Enrollment Management
800-447-5444

College of Saint Scholastica
340 Cedar St, Saint Paul MN 55101
651-298-1015

College of Visual Arts
344 Summit Ave, Saint Paul MN 55102-2124
L. Tanaka, Director of Student Affairs
651-224-3416

Concordia College
901 8th St S, Moorhead MN 56562-0002
Thomas Thomsen, President
Scott Ellingson, Director of Admissions
218-299-3004

Concordia University-Saint Paul
275 Syndicate St N, Saint Paul MN 55104-5494
651-641-8278

Crossroads College
920 Mayowood Rd SW, Rochester MN 55902-2382
Ralph Anderson, Director of Admissions
800-456-7651

Crown College
8700 College View Dr, Saint Bonifacius MN 55375
Mitch Fisk, Director of Admissions
952-446-4142 Fax: 952-446-4149
Website: www.crown.edu
E-mail: johnsonj@crown.edu

Gustavus Adolphus College
800 W College Ave, Saint Peter MN 56082-1485
Mark H. Anderson, Dean of Admission
800-GUSTAVUS Fax: 507-933-7474
Website: www.gustavus.edu
E-mail: admission@gustavus.edu

Hamline University
1536 Hewitt Ave, Saint Paul MN 55104-1284
651-523-2800

Macalester College
1600 Grand Ave, Saint Paul MN 55105-1899
651-696-6000

Martin Luther College
1995 Luther Ct, New Ulm MN 56073-3300
507-354-8221

MCNALLY SMITH COLLEGE OF MUSIC

19 Exchange St East, St. Paul MN 55101
Debbie Sandridge, Director of Admissions
800-594-9500 or 651-291-0177 Fax: 651-291-0366
Website: www.mcnallysmith.edu
E-mail: dsandridge@mcnallysmith.edu

Established 1985. Private. Coed. Accreditation: National Association of Schools of Music. Tuition: $13,920 per year. Fees: vary. Faculty: 50. Student-faculty ratio: 8:1. Bachelor of Music Degree in Music Performance (emphasis in Guitar, Bass, Drums, Keyboard, Voice, or Brass & Woodwinds). Bachelor of Arts Degree in Music (Business). AAS Degrees in Recording Technology, Music Production, Music Business, and Music Performance. Diploma programs available. Campus located in downtown St. Paul, in the heart of the Twin Cities music scene. State of the art studios, concert stage and theater, music library, and rehearsal rooms. World class faculty.

Metropolitan State University
700 7th St E, Saint Paul MN 55106-5000
Monir Johnson, Director of Admissions
651-793-1300 Fax: 651-793-1546
Website: www.metrostate.edu
E-mail: monir.johnson@metrostate.edu

Minnesota State University Mankato
228 Wiecking Center, Mankato MN 56001
507-389-1866

Minnesota State University Moorhead
1104 7th Ave S, Moorhead MN 56563-0002
Regina Monson, Director of Admissions
218-477-2161 Fax: 218-477-4374
Website: go.mnstate.edu
E-mail: dragon@mnstate.edu

National American University
112 W Market, Bloomington MN 55425-5521
Seamus White, Director of Admissions
952-883-0439

National American University
6120 Earle Brown Dr Suite 100
Brooklyn Center MN 55430
Jeffrey Allen, PhD, Campus Vice President
763-560-8377

National American University
1550 W Highway 36, Roseville MN 55113
Matthew Mottl, Director of Admissions
651-644-1265

North Central University
910 Elliot Ave, Minneapolis MN 55404-1391
612-343-4779

Northwestern College
3003 Snelling Ave N, Saint Paul MN 55113-1598
Dr. Douglas Huffman, Dean of Admissions
651-631-5111

Northwest Technical College
905 Grant Ave SE, Bemidji MN 56601
Richard Lehmann, Admissions
800-942-8324

Oak Hills Christian College
1600 Oak Hills Rd SW, Bemidji MN 56601-8826
Dan Hovestol, Admissions Director
218-751-8670

Pillsbury Baptist Bible College
315 S Grove Ave, Owatonna MN 55060-3097
Susanne Martin, Admissions Coordinator
507-451-2710 Fax: 507-451-0156
Website: www.pillsbury.edu
E-mail: admissions@pillsbury.edu

St. Cloud State University
720 4th Ave S, Saint Cloud MN 56301-4442
877-654-7278

St. Mary's University of Minnesota
700 Terrace Hts Ste 2, Winona MN 55987-1321
507-452-4430

St. Olaf College
1500 Saint Olaf Ave, Northfield MN 55057-1001
507-646-2222

Southwest Minnesota State University
1501 State St, Marshall MN 56258-1598
507-537-7678

University of Minnesota
2900 University Ave, Crookston MN 56716-5001
218-281-6510 Fax: 218-281-8575
Website:
admissions.umcrookston.edu/requirements/apply.htm
E-mail: info@umcrookston.edu

University of Minnesota
10 University Dr, Duluth MN 55812-2496
Beth Esselstrom, Director of Admissions
218-726-7171

University of Minnesota
231 Pillsbury Dr SE, Minneapolis MN 55455-0230
612-625-2008

University of Minnesota - Morris
600 E 4th St, Morris MN 56267-2132
Rodney Oto, Director
800-992-8863

University of Minnesota Rochester
855 30th Ave SE, Rochester MN 55904-4945
Dick Westerlund, Program Director
507-280-2838

University of St. Thomas
2115 Summit Ave, Saint Paul MN 55105-1096
651-962-5000

Winona State University
PO Box 5838, Winona MN 55987-0838
507-457-5000

MISSISSIPPI

Alcorn State University
PO Box 359, Lorman MS 39096
601-877-6147

Belhaven College
1500 Peachtree St, Jackson MS 39202-1789
601-968-5927

Blue Mountain College
PO Box 160, Blue Mountain MS 38610
800-235-0136

Delta State University
Hwy 8 W, Cleveland MS 38733
662-846-3000

Jackson State University
1440 J.R. Lynch St, Jackson MS 39217
Stephanie Chatman, Director of Admissions
601-979-2100

MAGNOLIA BIBLE COLLEGE
PO Box 1109, Kosciusko MS 39090-1109
Garvis Semore, President
800-748-8655 Fax: 662-289-1850
Website: www.magnolia.edu
E-mail: gsemore@magnolia.edu

Millsaps College
PO Box 15495, Jackson MS 39210
601-974-1000

Mississippi College
PO Box 4086, Clinton MS 39058-0001
601-925-3000

Mississippi State University
PO Box J, Mississippi State MS 39762-5509
662-325-2323

Mississippi University for Women
1100 College St Unit W1613, Columbus MS 39701
Terri Heath, Director of Admissions
877-GO-2-THEW

Mississippi University for Women-Tupelo
1918 Briar Ridge Rd, Tupelo MS 38804-5904
Kay Brown, Contact
662-844-0284

Mississippi Valley State University
14000 Highway 82 W Box 7222
Itta Bena MS 38941-1401
Office of Admissions
662-254-3347

Rust College
150 Rust Ave, Holly Springs MS 38635-2330
662-252-8000

Southeastern Baptist College
4229 Highway 15 N, Laurel MS 39440-1096
601-426-6346

Tougaloo College
500 W County Line Rd, Tougaloo MS 39174-9799
Juno Leggette Jacobs, Director of Admissions
601-977-7768 Fax: 601-977-4501
Website: www.tougaloo.edu
E-mail: jjacobs@tougaloo.edu

University of Mississippi
University MS 38677
662-232-7226

University of Mississippi Medical Center
2500 N State St, Jackson MS 39216-4500
601-984-1010

University of Southern Mississippi
PO Box 5165, Hattiesburg MS 39406-1000
601-266-5000

University of Southern Mississippi
730 E Beach Blvd, Long Beach MS 39560
228-865-4500

WESLEY COLLEGE
PO Box 1070, Florence MS 39073-1070
Charles M. Elliott, V.P. for Academic Affairs
601-845-2265 Fax: 601-845-2266
Website: www.wesleycollege.edu
E-mail: admissions@wesleycollege.edu

William Carey College
1856 Beach Dr, Gulfport MS 39507-1508
228-867-9201

William Carey College
498 Tuscan Ave, Hattiesburg MS 39401-5461
800-962-5991

MISSOURI

Avila University
11901 Wornall Rd, Kansas City MO 64145-1698
Patricia Harper, Director of Admissions
816-942-8400

Baptist Bible College
628 E Kearney St, Springfield MO 65803-3498
800-228-5754

BARNES-JEWISH COLLEGE OF NURSING
306 S Kingshighway Blvd
Saint Louis MO 63110-1091
Karen Sartorius, Admissions
800-832-9009 Fax: 314-454-7057
Website: www.barnesjewishcollege.edu
E-mail: bjc-admissions@bjc.org

Calvary Bible College & Theological Seminary
15800 Calvary Rd, Kansas City MO 64147-1341
Robert M. Reinsch, Director of Admissions
800-326-3960

CENTRAL BIBLE COLLEGE
3000 N Grant Ave, Springfield MO 65803-1096
Jamie Bell, Executive Director of Enrollment Services
800-831-4222 ext. 1290 Fax: 417-833-5141
Website: www.cbcag.edu
E-mail: cbcinfo@cbcag.edu

Central Christian College of the Bible
911 E Urbandale Dr, Moberly MO 65270-1923
Troy Titus, Director of Admissions
888-263-3900

Central Methodist University
411 Central Methodist Sq, Fayette MO 65248-1198
Larry Anderson, Director of Admissions
660-248-6247 Fax: 660-248-1872
Website: www.centralmethodist.edu
E-mail: landerso@centralmethodist.edu

Central Missouri State University
Warrensburg MO 64093-8888
Charles Petentler, Associate Director of Admissions
800-956-0177

Clayton University
11939 Manchester Road #123, Saint Louis MO 63131

College of the Ozarks
Point Lookout MO 65726
417-334-6411

Colorado Technical University
520 E 19th Ave, North Kansas City MO 64116-3614
Michael Murdie, Director of Admissions
816-472-7400

Columbia College
1001 Rogers St, Columbia MO 65216-0001
Regina Morin, Director of Admissions
573-875-7352 Fax: 573-875-7506
Website: www.ccis.edu
E-mail: admissions@ccis.edu

Cox College of Nursing & Health Sciences
1423 N Jefferson Ave, Springfield MO 65802-1917
417-269-3401

Culver-Stockton College
1 College Hl, Canton MO 63435-1299
Betty Smith, Director of Enrollment Services
800-537-1883

Deaconess College of Nursing
6150 Oakland Ave, Saint Louis MO 63139-3215
Michelle McGrail, Dean of Enrollment and Student Affairs
314-768-3044

DeVry University
1801 Park 270 Dr Suite 260, Saint Louis MO 63146
Amy Moebes, Assistant Director of Admissions
314-542-4222

Drury University
900 N Benton Ave, Springfield MO 65802-3791
417-873-7879

Evangel University
1111 N Glenstone Ave, Springfield MO 65802-2191
Cheri Meyer, Director of Undergraduate Admissions
417-865-2811 Fax: 417-865-9599
Website: www.evangel.edu
E-mail: meyerc@evangel.edu

EVEREST COLLEGE
1010 W Sunshine St, Springfield MO 65807-2446
Melanie Exter, Contact
417-864-7220 or 800-475-2699 Fax: 417-866-3335
Website: www.everest-college.com
E-mail: mexter@cci.edu

Fontbonne University
6800 Wydown Blvd, Saint Louis MO 63105-3098
314-889-1419

GRACELAND UNIVERSITY
1401 W Truman Rd, Independence MO 64050
Patricia K. Trachsel, Dean of Independence Campus
816-833-0524 Fax: 816-833-2990
Website: www.graceland.edu
E-mail: trachsel@graceland.edu

Hannibal-LaGrange College
2800 Palmyra Rd, Hannibal MO 63401-1999
573-221-3675

Harris-Stowe State University
3026 Laclede Ave, Saint Louis MO 63103-2199
LaShanda R. Boone, Director of Admissions
314-340-3300 Fax: 314-340-3555
Website: www.hssu.edu
E-mail: admissions@hssu.edu

Kansas City Art Institute
4415 Warwick Blvd, Kansas City MO 64111-1820
800-522-5224

Lincoln University
Truman Educ Center Bldg 499
Fort Leonard Wood MO 65473
573-681-5421

Lincoln University
820 Chestnut St, Jefferson City MO 65101-3500
573-681-5000

Lindenwood University
209 S Kingshighway St
Saint Charles MO 63301-1695
Sheryl Guffey, Director of Admissions
636-949-2000 Fax: 636-949-4989
Website: www.lindenwood.edu

Maryville University of St. Louis
650 Maryville University Dr
Saint Louis MO 63141-7299
314-529-9300

Messenger College
300 E 50th St, Joplin MO 64804-4909
417-624-7070

Missouri Baptist University
1 College Park Dr, Saint Louis MO 63141-8698
314-434-1115

Missouri Southern State University - Joplin
3950 Newman Rd, Joplin MO 64801-1512
417-625-9300

Missouri State University
901 S National Ave, Springfield MO 65897
417-836-5000

Missouri State University - West Plains
128 Garfield, West Plains MO 65775
417-255-7255

Missouri Tech
1167 Corporate Lake Dr, Saint Louis MO 63132
314-569-3600

Missouri Valley College
500 E College St, Marshall MO 65340-3197
J. Kenneth Bryant, President
660-831-4108

Missouri Western State College
4525 Downs Dr, Saint Joseph MO 64507-2294
800-662-7041

National American University
3620 Arrowhead Ave, Independence MO 64057-1791
Janet Miller, Director of Admission
816-353-4554

Northwest Missouri State University
800 University Dr, Maryville MO 64468-6001
Beverly Schenkel, Dean of Enrollment Management
660-562-1562 Fax: 660-562-1121
Website: www.nwmissouri.edu
E-mail: admissions@nwmissouri.edu

OZARK CHRISTIAN COLLEGE
1111 N Main St, Joplin MO 64801-4804
Troy Nelson, Director of Admissions
800-299-4622 or 417-624-2518 Fax: 417-624-0090
Website: www.occ.edu
E-mail: occadmin@occ.edu

Established 1942. Private. Coed. Accreditation: ABHE. Tuition: $7,840. Room & board: $2,025. Fees: $480. Enrollment: 712 full-time, 135 part-time. Faculty: 43. Student-faculty ratio: 20:1. Degrees: Bachelors Degrees in Theology; Biblical Literature with majors in Bible and Psychology, Bible and Deaf Ministry; Christian Education; Bible and Ministry; Bible and Missions; Music Ministry and Music and Worship. Associate degrees in Bible, Elementary, Middle School, Secondary Education, or Nursing. Coop degree programs with Missouri Southern State College in Joplin, Mo., Pittsburg State University in Pittsburg, KS., and Fort Hays State University, Hays, KS. 96% of graduates enter degree-related fields.

Park University
8700 NW River Park Dr, Parkville MO 64152-3795
816-741-2000

Ranken Technical College
4431 Finney Ave, Saint Louis MO 63113-2898
Admissions Office
314-371-0233 Fax: 314-371-0241
Website: www.ranken.edu
E-mail: admissions@ranken.edu

Research College of Nursing
2525 E Meyer Blvd, Kansas City MO 64132
816-995-2800

Rockhurst University
1100 Rockhurst Rd, Kansas City MO 64110-2561
Mark Kopenski, VP of Enrollment Management
816-501-4000

St. Louis Christian College
1360 Grandview Dr, Florissant MO 63033-6499
Dr. Ronald L. Oakes, Academic Dean
Rick Fordyce, Registrar
314-837-6777

ST. LOUIS COLLEGE OF PHARMACY
4588 Parkview Pl, Saint Louis MO 63110-1088
Penny Bryant, Director of Admissions/Registrar
314-367-8700 Fax: 314-446-8310
Website: www.stlcop.edu

St. Louis University
221 N Grand Blvd, Saint Louis MO 63103-2097
314-977-2222

Saint Luke's College
8320 Ward Parkway Suite 300
Kansas City MO 64114
Josh Richards Asst. Director of Admissions
816-932-2367

Southeast Missouri State University
1 University Plz, Cape Girardeau MO 63701-4710
573-651-2000

Southwest Baptist University
1600 University Ave, Bolivar MO 65613-2597
417-328-5281

Southwest Baptist University
4431 S Fremont Ave, Springfield MO 65804-7307
417-841-5046

Truman State University
100 E Normal, Kirksville MO 63501
Office of Admission
660-785-4114 Fax: 660-785-7456
Website: admissions.truman.edu
E-mail: admissions@truman.edu

University of Missouri
228 Jesse Hall, Columbia MO 65211-0001
573-882-2121

University of Missouri
5100 Rockhill Rd, Kansas City MO 64110-2446
816-235-1000

University of Missouri
102 Parker, Rolla MO 65409
Lynn Stichnote, Director of Admission
573-341-4164

University of Missouri
1 University Blvd, Saint Louis MO 63121-4499
John Kundel, Director of Admissions
314-516-5451 Fax: 314-516-5310
Website: www.umsl.edu
E-mail: admissions@umsl.edu

Washington University in St. Louis
1 Brookings Dr, Saint Louis MO 63130-4899
314-935-5000

WEBSTER UNIVERSITY
470 E Lockwood Ave, Saint Louis MO 63119-3194
Niel DeVasto, Director of Admissions
Website: www.webster.edu
E-mail: admit@webster.edu
800-753-6765
314-968-7100 Fax: 314-968-7116 (graduate)
314-968-6991 Fax: 314-968-7115 (undergraduate)

Established 1915. Private. Coed. Accreditation: NCACS. Tuition: $18,240. Room and board: $7,300. Enrollment: 2,460 full-time, 1,153 part-time. Faculty: 160, Student-faculty ratio: 15:1. Degrees: BA, BFA, BM, BMEd, BS, BSN, MA, MBA, MAT, MSN, DMGT. Library: 400,000 volumes. 36 buildings on 45 acres. Nationally recognized programs in the performing arts and communications. Regionally recognized programs in education and business. Students from 40 states and 30 countries. Beautiful suburban campus in a wooded community of

20,000. Average class size of 15. New Residence Halls for 320 additional students open in 2006. Campuses in four European countries, China and Thailand.

Westminister College
501 Westminster Ave, Fulton MO 65251-1299
573-642-3361

William Jewell College
500 College Hill, Liberty MO 64068-1896
Dr. Rick Winslow, VP Enrollment Management and Student Affairs
800-753-7009 Fax: 816-415-5040
Website: www.jewell.edu
E-mail: winslowr@william.jewell.edu

WILLIAM WOODS UNIVERSITY
1 University Ave, Fulton MO 65251-2388
Jimmy Clay, Director of Admissions
573-592-4296 Fax: 573-592-1146
Website: www.williamwoods.edu
E-mail: admission@williamwoods.edu
Established 1892. Private. Coed. Accreditation: North Central Association of Colleges & Schools, Higher Learning Commission. Tuition: $14,300. Room & board: $2,625 room, $2,625 board. Enrollment: 1,025. Student-faculty ratio: 14:1. Degrees: BA, BS, BSW, AA Paralegal, MED, MBA. Equestrian Science, Equine Administration, Interpreting and Sign Language, Sports Management, Human Administration.

MONTANA

Carroll College
1601 N Benton Ave, Helena MT 59625-0002
Dr. Thomas J. Trebon, President
Cynthia Thornquist, Director of Admissions & Enrollment Operations
406-447-4384 Fax: 406-447-4533
Website: www.carroll.edu
E-mail: admission@carroll.edu

Montana State University - Billings
1500 University Dr, Billings MT 59101-0252
Karen Everett, Director
800-565-MSUB

Montana State University - Bozeman
103 Culbertson Hall, Bozeman MT 59715-5072
406-994-2452

Montana State University Northern
PO Box 7751, Havre MT 59501-7751
406-265-3700

Montana Tech of the University of Montana
1300 W Park St, Butte MT 59701-8997
800-445-TECH

Rocky Mountain College
1511 Poly Dr, Billings MT 59102-1796
Bonnie Knapp, Director of Admissions
800-877-6259

University of Great Falls
1301 20th St S, Great Falls MT 59405-4996
Cathy Day, Director of Admissions
406-791-5200

University of Montana
Missoula MT 59812-0001
406-243-0211

University of Montana - Western
710 S Atlantic St, Dillon MT 59725-3598
406-683-7011

NEBRASKA

Bellevue University
1000 Galvin Rd S, Bellevue NE 68005-3098
Mary Hawkins, V.P. of Enrollment
800-756-7920

Chadron State College
1000 Main St, Chadron NE 69337-2690
308-432-6000

Clarkson College
101 S 42nd St, Omaha NE 68131-2715
Sara Bonney, Director of Admissions
800-647-5500 Fax: 402-552-6057
Website: www.clarksoncollege.edu
E-mail: admiss@clarksoncollege.edu

Concordia University
800 N Columbia Ave, Seward NE 68434-1594
402-643-3651

Creighton University
2500 California Plz, Omaha NE 68178-0001
402-280-2700

Dana College
2848 College Dr, Blair NE 68008-1099
Duane A. Heffelfinger, Dean of Enrollment Management
800-444-3262

Doane College
1014 Boswell Ave, Crete NE 68333-2421
402-826-2161

Grace University
1311 S 9th St, Omaha NE 68108-3629
402-449-2800

Hastings College
PO Box 269, Hastings NE 68902-0269
402-463-2402

Midland Lutheran College
900 N Clarkson St, Fremont NE 68025-4200
Todd Hansen, Associate Director of Admissions
402-941-6501 Fax: 402-941-6513
Website: www.mlc.edu
E-mail: admissions@mlc.edu

Nebraska Christian College
12550 S 114th St, Papillion NE 68046-4256
402-935-9400

Nebraska Wesleyan University
5000 Saint Paul Ave, Lincoln NE 68504-2794
Patricia Karthauser, V.P. for University Enrollment
402-466-2371 Fax: 402-465-2177
Website: www.nebrwesleyan.edu
E-mail: admissions@nebrwesleyan.edu

Peru State College
PO Box 10, Peru NE 68421-0010
Office of Admissions
800-742-4412

Union College
3800 S 48th St, Lincoln NE 68506-4300
Buell Fogg, V.P. for Enrollment Services
800-228-4600

University of Nebraska
14th & R Sts, Lincoln NE 68588
402-472-7211

University of Nebraska at Kearney
905 W 25th St, Kearney NE 68849-0001
Dusty Newton, Director of Admissions
800-KEARNEY Fax: 308-865-8987
Website: www.unk.edu
E-mail: admissionsug@unk.edu

University of Nebraska at Omaha
60th and Dodge St, Omaha NE 68182-0001
402-554-2800

Wayne State College
1111 Main St, Wayne NE 68787-1172
402-375-7000

York College
912 Kiplinger Ave, York NE 68467-2631
402-363-5600

NEVADA

Art Institute of Las Vegas
2350 Corporate Cir, Henderson NV 89074-7737
702-369-9944

GREAT BASIN COLLEGE
1500 College Pkwy, Elko NV 89801-9930
Julie G. Byrnes, Director of Enrollment Management
775-753-2271 Fax: 775-753-2311
Website: www.gbcnv.edu
E-mail: julieb@gwmail.gbcnv.edu
Public. Coed. Accreditation: Northwest Association of Schools & Colleges. Tuition: $52.50-$79.00 per credit plus non-resident tuition of $2,481 per semester if applicable. Enrollment: 927 full-time, 2,188 part-time. Faculty: 125 full time and adjunct 232. Student-faculty ratio: 18:1. Degrees: Associate and some Baccalaureate. 12 buildings plus residence halls on 44 acres. GBC is the major provider of post-secondary education for rural Nevada.

Morrison University
10315 Professional Circle Suite 201
Reno NV 89521-4826
Charles Timinsky, Director of Enrollment
775-850-0700 Fax: 775-850-0711
Website: www.morrisonuniversity.com

Sierra Nevada College-Lake Tahoe
999 Tahoe Boulevard, Incline Village NV 89451
Dr. Ben Solomon, President
800-332-8666

University of Nevada
Reno NV 89557-0001
775-784-1110

University of Nevada Las Vegas
4505 S Maryland Pkwy, Las Vegas NV 89154-9901
800-334-8658

NEW HAMPSHIRE

Chester College of New England
40 Chester St, Chester NH 03036-4331
Pam Adie, Director of Admissions
603-887-4401 Fax: 603-887-1777
Website: www.chestercollege.edu
E-mail: padie@chestercollege.edu

Colby-Sawyer College
100 Main St, New London NH 03257-4648
603-526-3000

Daniel Webster College
20 University Dr, Nashua NH 03063-1323
Paul LaBarre, Director of Enrollment Services
603-577-6600

Dartmouth College
Hanover NH 03755
603-646-1110

Franklin Pierce College
5 Chenell Dr, Concord NH 03301-8540
603-228-1155

Franklin Pierce College
17 Bradco Rd, Keene NH 03431-3900
603-357-0079

Franklin Pierce College
670 N Commercial St Ste 206, Manchester NH 03101

Franklin Pierce College
73 Corporate Dr, Portsmouth NH 03801-2847
603-433-2000

Franklin Pierce College
20 College Rd, Rindge NH 03461
800-437-0048

Granite State College
8 Old Suncook Rd, Concord NH 03301-6400
603-228-3000

Hesser College
25 Hall St, Concord NH 03301-3471
603-225-9200

Hesser College
3 Sundial Ave, Manchester NH 03103-7230
603-668-6660

Hesser College
410 Amherst St, Nashua NH 03063-1222
603-883-0404

Hesser College
170 Commerce Way, Portsmouth NH 03801-3226
603-436-5300

Hesser College
11 Manor Pkwy, Salem NH 03079
603-898-3480

Keene State College
229 Main St, Keene NH 03435-0002
603-358-2276

Magdalen College
511 Kearsarge Mountain Rd, Warner NH 03278
603-456-2656

New England College
98 Bridge St, Henniker NH 03242
603-428-2211

Plymouth State University
17 High St, MSC #44, Bagley House
Plymouth NH 03264-1595
603-535-5000

Rivier College
420 S Main St, Nashua NH 03060-5086
David Boisvert, Director of Undergraduate Admissions
603-897-8507

St. Anselm College
100 Saint Anselms Dr, Manchester NH 03102-1310
603-641-7000

Southern New Hampshire University
2500 N River Rd, Hooksett NH 03106-1045
Steve Soba, Director of Admissions
603-645-9611 Fax: 603-645-9693
Website: www.snhu.edu
E-mail: s.soba@snhu.edu

Thomas More College of Liberal Arts
6 Manchester St, Merrimack NH 03054-4855
603-880-8308

University of New Hampshire
Durham NH 03824
603-862-1234

University of New Hampshire
400 Commercial St, Manchester NH 03101-1113
603-668-0700

NEW JERSEY

Berkeley College
44 Rifle Camp Rd, West Paterson NJ 07424-3367
800-446-5400

Bloomfield College
467 Franklin St, Bloomfield NJ 07003
973-748-9000

Caldwell College
9 Ryerson Ave, Caldwell NJ 07006-6195
973-618-3000

Centenary College
400 Jefferson St, Hackettstown NJ 07840-2100
Glenna Warren, Director of Admissions
908-852-1400

College of New Jersey
PO Box 7718, Ewing NJ 08628-0718
609-771-1855

Drew University
36 Madison Ave, Madison NJ 07940-1493
973-408-3000

Fairleigh Dickinson University
285 Madison Ave, Madison NJ 07940-1099
800-338-8803

Fairleigh Dickinson University
1000 River Rd, Teaneck NJ 07666-1996
201-692-2000

Felician College
262 S Main St, Lodi NJ 07644-2198
201-559-6000

Georgian Court University
900 Lakewood Ave, Lakewood NJ 08701-2697
732-364-2200

Kean University
1000 Morris Ave, Union NJ 07083-7133
908-527-2000

Monmouth University
400 Cedar Ave, West Long Branch NJ 07764-1890
732-571-3400

Montclair State University
Montclair State University, Montclair NJ 07043-1624
973-655-4000

New Jersey City University
2039 John F Kennedy Blvd
Jersey City NJ 07305-1588
Carmen Panlilio, Asst. V.P. for Admissions and Financial Aid
201-200-3234 Fax: 201-200-2044
Website: www.njcu.edu
E-mail: admissions@njcu.edu

New Jersey Institute of Technology
University Heights, Newark NJ 07102
973-596-3000

Princeton University
Princeton NJ 08544-0001
609-258-3000

Rabbi Jacob Joseph School
1 Plainfield Ave, Edison NJ 08817-4476
732-985-6533

Ramapo College of New Jersey
505 Ramapo Valley Rd, Mahwah NJ 07430-1623
Director of Admissions
201-684-7300 or 201-684-7301 Fax: 201-684-7964
Website: www.ramapo.edu
E-mail: admissions@ramapo.edu

RICHARD STOCKTON COLLEGE OF NEW JERSEY

PO Box 195, Pomona NJ 08240
John Iacovelli, Dean of Enrollment Management
866-RSC-2885 Fax: 609-626-5541
Website: www.stockton.edu
E-mail: admissions@stockton.edu

Stockton College is a comprehensive liberal arts, coed institution founded in 1969. The suburban campus is on 1,600 acres located at the tip of the Pine Barrens. Stockton College offers a superior environment for highly motivated students to prosper. Opportunities for self-directed degree programs and innovative flexibility in curriculum balance with a traditional Liberal Arts approach to learning.

Enrollment: 7,213 full and part-time students, Males 47%, Females 53%. Resident students: approx. 31%. Average Class Size: 22. Undergraduate Tuition and Fees: $9,058. Room and Board: $8,502. Housing: Stockton offers a wide variety of on-campus housing options, from traditional residence hall to new townhouse-style apartments. Areas of Study: Biochemistry / Molecular Biology, Biological Sciences, Business Studies, Chemistry, Communication Studies, Computational Sciences, Computer and Information Sciences, Criminal Justice, Economics, Environmental Studies, Forensic Science, Geology, Historical Studies, Languages and Cultural Studies, Liberal Arts Studies, Literatures, Marine Science, Mathematics, Philosophy and Religion, Physics, Political Science, Psychology, Public Health, Social Work, Sociology and Anthropology, Speech Pathology and Audiology, Teacher Education, Visual and Performing Arts. Advance Pre-Professional Degrees: 7-year BS/MD with University of Medicine and Dentistry of New Jersey; New Jersey Dental School, New Jersey Medical School, Robert Wood Johnson Medical, School of Osteopathic Medicine; New York College of Podiatric Medicine, Pennsylvania College of Podiatric Medicine, State University of New York College of Optometry. Pharmacy doctorate program with the Ernest Mario School of Pharmacy at Rutgers University. 5-year "3+2" Engineering with New Jersey Institute of Technology and Rutgers, The State University of New Jersey. Dual BA/MA in Criminal Justice. 5-year BS/MS in Computational Science. BS/MS in Nursing. Doctorate of Physical Therapy. Additional Programs: Pre-Law, Pre-Occupational Therapy, and Pre-Veterinary. Graduate Degrees: Education, Holocaust and Genocide Studies, Instructional Technology, Business Administration. Honors Program: Available to qualified incoming freshman. Special Academic Options: College credit for AP, distance learning, self-designed majors, study abroad programs, summer session, and a variety of internship programs.

Admissions Requirements: Applicants must submit an admissions application and a $50 application fee. Freshman are required to submit: an essay, official high school transcript, SAT I or ACT, TOEFL for international students. Transfer must submit official transcripts from all colleges. Application Deadline: May 1. Rolling application. Financial Aid: Each year millions of dollars are allotted from federal, state, and college sources to fill this need. FAFSA form is required. Faculty Profile: All courses are taught by professors with 94% of them holding terminal degrees and 49% are full-time. Special Facilities: Bacharach Institute for Rehabilitation and AtlantiCare Regional Medical Center located on campus. Nacote Creek Biological/Environmental Field Station.

Rider University
2083 Lawrenceville Rd, Lawrenceville NJ 08648-3099
Susan Christian, Director of Admissions
609-896-5042

Rowan University
200 N Broadway, Camden NJ 08102-1102
856-757-2857

Rowan University
201 Mullica Hill Rd, Glassboro NJ 08028-1700
856-256-4000

Rutgers-The State University of New Jersey
Camden Campus
311 N 5th St, Camden NJ 08102-1405
856-225-6026

Rutgers-The State University of New Jersey
Newark Campus
Newark NJ 07102
973-353-5568

Rutgers-The State University of New Jersey
New Brunswick Campus
35 College Ave, New Brunswick NJ 08901
732-932-4636

St. Peter's College
Hudson Terrace, Englewood Cliffs NJ 07632
201-568-7730

St. Peter's College
2627 John F Kennedy Blvd, Jersey City NJ 07306
888-SPC-9933

Seton Hall University
400 S Orange Ave, South Orange NJ 07079-2697
973-761-9000

SOMERSET CHRISTIAN COLLEGE

PO Box 9035, Zarephath NJ 08890
Anthony Viscioni, VP of Enrollment Management & Communications
800-234-9305 Fax: 732-356-4846
Website: www.somerset.edu
E-mail: info@somerset.edu

Stevens Institute of Technology
Castle Point on Hudson, Hoboken NJ 07030
201-216-5100

Thomas Edison State College
101 W State St, Trenton NJ 08608-1101
609-984-1100

UMDNJ-School of Health Related Professions
65 Bergen St, Newark NJ 07107-3001
973-972-5453

UMDNJ-School of Nursing
30 Bergen St, Newark NJ 07107
973-972-4322

UMDNJ-University of Medicine and Dentistry of New Jersey
65 Bergen St, Newark NJ 07107-3001
973-972-4300

Westminster Choir College of Rider University
101 Walnut Ln, Princeton NJ 08540-3819
Matthew T. Kadlubowski, Director of Admissions
609-921-7144

William Paterson University
300 Pompton Rd, Wayne NJ 07470-2103
973-720-2000

NEW MEXICO

Apollo College
1001 Menaul Blvd NE Ste C, Albuquerque NM 87107
800-368-7246 Fax: 505-254-1101

College of Santa Fe
1600 Saint Michaels Dr, Santa Fe NM 87505-7634
505-473-6011

College of the Southwest
6610 N Lovington Hwy, Hobbs NM 88240-9129
Dr. Steve Hill, Dean of Recuitment
505-392-6561 Fax: 505-392-6006
Website: www.csw.edu
E-mail: shill@csw.edu

Eastern New Mexico University
Portales NM 88130
800-367-3668

Institute of American Indian Arts
83 A Van Nu Po, Santa Fe NM 87508-1300
John Gritts, Director of Admissions, Records & Enrollment
505-424-2330 Fax: 505-424-4500
Website: www.iaia.edu
E-mail: recruitment@iaia.edu

International Institute of the Americas
4201 Central Ave NW Suite J
Albuquerque NM 87105-1649
Ed Sigman, Director
505-880-2877 Fax: 505-352-0199
Website: www.iia.edu
E-mail: esigman@iia.edu

National American University
4775 Indian Sch Rd NE #200
Albuquerque NM 87110-3976
505-265-7517

National American University
1601 Rio Rancho Dr SE #200
Rio Rancho NM 87124-1093
505-891-1111

National College of Midwifery
209 State Road 240, Taos NM 87571
505-758-8914

New Mexico Highlands University
PO Box 9000, Las Vegas NM 87701
Director of Student Recruitment
800-338-NMHU

New Mexico Institute of Mining & Technology
801 Leroy Pl, Socorro NM 87801-4750
505-835-5011

New Mexico State University
PO Box 30001, Las Cruces NM 88003-8001
505-646-0111

St. John's College
1160 Camino Cruz Blanca, Santa Fe NM 87505-4599
L. Clendenin, Director of Admissions
800-331-5232 Fax: 505-984-6162
Website: www.stjohnscollege.edu
E-mail: admissions@sjcsf.edu

Southwestern College
PO Box 4788, Santa Fe NM 87502-4788
Kristine Schmidt BA, Director of Admissions
877-471-5756 ext. 26

University of New Mexico
1 University Campus, Albuquerque NM 87131-0001
505-277-0111

University of Phoenix
New Mexico Division
7471 Pan Amrcan West Fwy NE
Albuquerque NM 87109-4645
505-821-4800

Western New Mexico University
PO Box 680, Silver City NM 88062-0680
505-538-6011

NEW YORK

Adelphi University
Garden City NY 11530
516-877-3100

ALBANY COLLEGE OF PHARMACY

106 New Scotland Ave, Albany NY 12208-3492
Carly Connors, Director of Admissions
888-203-8010 Fax: 518-694-7322
Website: www.acp.edu
E-mail: admissions@acp.edu

Alfred University
1 Saxson Dr, Alfred NY 14802
607-871-2111

Alfred University - New York State College of Ceramics
2 Pine St, Alfred NY 14802-1214
607-871-2411

AMERICAN UNIVERSITY IN CAIRO

420 5th Ave 3rd Floor, New York NY 10018
Student Affairs Office
212-730-8800 Fax: 212-730-1600
Website: www.aucegypt.edu
E-mail: aucegypt@aucnyo.edu

Bard College
Annandale on Hudson NY 12504
845-758-6822

Berkeley College - Westchester Campus
99 Church St, White Plains NY 10601-1505
800-446-5400

Boricua College
186 N 6th St, Brooklyn NY 11211-3209
718-782-2200

Boricua College
3755 Broadway, New York NY 10032-1599
212-694-1000

Briarcliffe College
1055 Stewart Ave, Bethpage NY 11714-3545
Theresa Donohue, Director of Admissions
516-918-3600 Fax: 516-470-6020
Website: www.briarcliffe.edu

Canisius College
2001 Main St, Buffalo NY 14208-1098
716-883-7000

Cazenovia College
Cazenovia NY 13035-1084
Robert Croot, Dean of Admissions & Financial Aid
800-654-3210

Central Yeshiva Tomchei Tmimim Lubavitz
841 Ocean Pkwy, Brooklyn NY 11230-2700
Joseph Wilmowsky, Registrar
718-434-0784

Clarkson University
PO Box 5500, Potsdam NY 13699
315-268-6400

Colgate University
13 Oak Dr, Hamilton NY 13346-1386
Gary Ross, Director of Admissions
315-228-7401

College of Mount Saint Vincent
6301 Riverdale Ave, Riverdale NY 10471-1093
718-405-3200

College of New Rochelle
755 Co Op City Blvd, Bronx NY 10475-1601
718-320-0300

College of New Rochelle
332 E 149th St, Bronx NY 10451-5606
718-665-1310

College of New Rochelle
1368 Fulton St, Brooklyn NY 11216-2600
718-638-2500

College of New Rochelle
29 Castle Pl, New Rochelle NY 10805-2339
914-654-5000

College of New Rochelle
125 Barclay St, New York NY 10007-2199
212-815-1710

College of New Rochelle
144 W 125th St, New York NY 10027-4423
212-662-7500

College of Saint Rose
432 Western Ave, Albany NY 12203-1419
Maryelizabeth Amico, Asst V.P. for Undergraduate Admissions
518-454-5150 Fax: 518-454-2013
Website: www.strose.edu
E-mail: admit@strose.edu

Columbia University
2960 Broadway, New York NY 10027-6900
212-854-1754

Columbia University
168th & Broadway, New York NY 10032
212-305-5756

Concordia College
171 White Plains Rd, Bronxville NY 10708-1998
914-337-9300

Cooper Union
30 Cooper Sq, New York NY 10003
212-353-4100

Cornell University
410 Thurston Ave, Ithaca NY 14850-2432
607-255-2000

CUNY Bernard M. Baruch College
17 Lexington Ave, New York NY 10010-5518
212-802-2000

CUNY Brooklyn College
2900 Bedford Ave, Brooklyn NY 11210-2814
718-951-5000

CUNY City College
Convent Ave at 138th St, New York NY 10031
Celia Lloyd, Interim Director of Admissions
212-650-6977

CUNY College of Staten Island
2800 Victory Blvd, Staten Island NY 10314-6600
718-982-2000

CUNY Hunter College
695 Park Ave, New York NY 10021
Aaron Gibbs, Assistant Director of Recruitment
212-650-3946 Fax: 212-650-3336
Website: www.hunter.cuny.edu
E-mail: aaron.gibbs@hunter.cuny.edu

CUNY John Jay College of Criminal Justice
899 10th Ave, New York NY 10019-1029
212-237-8000

CUNY Lehman College
250 Bedford Park Blvd W, Bronx NY 10468-1527
718-960-8000

CUNY Medgar Evers College
1650 Bedford Ave, Brooklyn NY 11225-2010
718-270-4900

CUNY Queens College
6530 Kissena Blvd, Flushing NY 11367-1575
718-997-5000

CUNY York College
9420 Guy R Brewer Blvd, Jamaica NY 11451-0001
718-262-2000

Daemen College
4380 Main St, Amherst NY 14226-3592
Donna Shaffner, Director of Admissions
800-462-7652 Fax: 716-839-8229
Website: www.daemen.edu/admissions
E-mail: admissions@daemen.edu

Davis College
400 Riverside Dr, Johnson City NY 13790
Brian Murphy, VP of Enrollment Management
607-729-1581

Dominican College of Blauvelt
470 Western Hwy, Orangeburg NY 10962-1210
845-359-7800

Dowling College
150 Idle Hour Blvd, Oakdale NY 11769-1999
Diane Kazanecki-Kempter, Contact
631-244-3000 Fax: 631-244-1059
Website: www.dowling.edu
E-mail: admissions@dowling.edu

D'Youville College
320 Porter Ave, Buffalo NY 14201-1084
716-829-7600

Elmira College
1 Park Pl, Elmira NY 14901-2099
Gary Fallis, Dean of Admissions
607-735-1724

Excelsior College
7 Columbia Cir, Albany NY 12203-5156
518-464-8500

Farmingdale SUNY
2350 Broadhollow Rd, Farmingdale NY 11735
631-420-2200

Fashion Institute of Technology
227 W 27th St, New York NY 10001-5992
212-217-7999

FIVE TOWNS COLLEGE

305 N Service Rd, Dix Hills NY 11746-5871
631-424-7000 ext. 2110 Fax: 631-656-2172
Website: www.fivetowns.edu
E-mail: admissions@ftc.edu

Founded in 1972. Private, co-ed college offering 2-year, 4-year and graduate degree programs. Accreditation: MSACS and NYS Board of Regents. Tuition: $15,200 per year ($635 per credit, plus fees). Enrollment: 1,000 students. Faculty: 85. Degrees: AA, AS, AAS, BFA, BMus, BPS, BS, MusM, MS in Education, DMA. Rolling admissions. 5 buildings on 40 wooded acres. Library: 35,000 volumes and music archives. Majors: Accounting, Audio Recording Technology, Broadcasting and Journalism, Business Management, Childhood Education, Communications, Mass Communication, Jazz/Commercial Music, Liberal Arts, Music Business, Music Composition/Songwriting, Music Education, Music Performance, Musical Theatre, Theatre Arts, and Film/Video Production. Financial aid, Internships program and Career Services available.

Fordham University
441 E Fordham Rd, Bronx NY 10458-9993
John W. Buckley, Dean of Admissions
718-817-4000

Fordham University - Lincoln Center
113 W 60th St, New York NY 10023-7484
Robert Grimes, S.J., Ph.D., Dean
212-636-6000

Globe Institute of Technology
291 Broadway Fl 2, New York NY 10007-1814
212-349-4330

Hamilton College
198 College Hill Rd, Clinton NY 13323-1295
Richard Fuller, Dean of Admissions
315-859-4421

Hartwick College
West St
Oneonta NY 13820
607-431-4000

Hilbert College
5200 S Park Ave, Hamburg NY 14075-1597
Timothy Lee, Director of Admissions
716-649-7900 Fax: 716-649-0702
Website: www.hilbert.edu
E-mail: tlee@hilbert.edu

Hobart & William Smith Colleges
Pulteney St, Geneva NY 14456
John Young, Director of Admissions
315-789-5500

Hofstra University
100 Hofstra University, Hempstead NY 11549-1000
516-463-6600

Houghton College
PO Box 128, Houghton NY 14744-0128
585-567-9200

Houghton College
910 Union Rd, West Seneca NY 14224-3499
716-674-6363

Iona College
715 North Ave, New Rochelle NY 10801-1890
Kevin Cavanagh, Assistant V.P. for College Admissions
914-633-2502 Fax: 914-637-2778
Website: www.iona.edu

Iona College
PO Box 1522, Pearl River NY 10965-8522
845-620-1350

Ithaca College
953 Danby Rd, Ithaca NY 14850-7002
607-274-3011

Jewish Theological Seminary of America
3080 Broadway, New York NY 10027-4650
Jan Michael Skidds, Associate Director of Admissions
212-678-8000

Juilliard School
60 Lincoln Center Plz, New York NY 10023-6588
Lee Cioppa, Associate Dean for Admissions
212-799-5000

Keller Graduate School of DeVry University
120 W 45th St Ste 200, New York NY 10036
Jennifer Blumberg, Admissions Representative
212-556-0002

Keuka College
PO Box 98, Keuka Park NY 14478-0098
315-536-4411

LABORATORY INSTITUTE OF MERCHANDISING

12 E 53rd St, New York NY 10022-5268
Kristina Gibson, Director of Admissions
800-677-1323 or 212-752-1530 Fax: 212-750-3432
Website: www.limcollege.edu
E-mail: admissions@limcollege.edu

Established 1939. Private. Coed. Accreditation: Middle States Association of Schools & Colleges. Tuition: $17,250. Fees: $450. Enrollment: 1,000. Faculty: 115. Student-faculty ratio: 9:1. Degrees offered: BBA, BPS, AAS. Library: 12,000 volumes. 2 five week internships, full semester work co-op, weekly fashion industry field trips, weekly fashion industry guest lectures, over 90% career placement within 90 days of graduation.

Le Moyne College
1419 Salt Springs Rd, Syracuse NY 13214-1301
800-333-4733

Long Island University
2nd Ave, Brentwood NY 11717
Marlyne Hynds, Asst. Provost
631-273-5112

Long Island University
555 Broadway, Dobbs Ferry NY 10522-1134
914-693-4500

Long Island University
121 Speonk Riverhead Rd, Riverhead NY 11901
631-287-8010

Long Island University-Brooklyn Campus
1 University Plz, Brooklyn NY 11201-5372
718-488-1000

Long Island University-C. W. Post Campus
720 Northern Blvd, Brookville NY 11548-1300
Joanne Graziano, Executive Director of Admissions
516-299-2900 Fax: 516-299-2137
Website: www.liu.edu/cwpost
E-mail: enroll@cwpost.liu.edu

Long Island University
Rockland Graduate Campus
70 Route 340, Orangeburg NY 10962-2219
Kelly J. McCafferty, M.S., Director of Admissions
845-359-7200

Manhattan College
4513 Manhattan College Pkwy
Riverdale NY 10471-4099
William J. Bisset Jr., Asst. V.P. for Enrollment Management
718-862-7200

Manhattan School of Music
120 Claremont Ave, New York NY 10027-4698
Amy A. Anderson, Director of Admission & Financial Aid
212-749-2802 ext. 2

Manhattanville College
2900 Purchase St, Purchase NY 10577-2132
914-694-2200

Marist College
3399 North Rd, Poughkeepsie NY 12601
Jay E. Murray, Director of Admissions
845-575-3000

Marymount Manhattan College
221 E 71st St, New York NY 10021-4501
Jim Rogers, Dean of Admissions
800-MARYMOUNT Fax: 212-517-0448
Website: www.mmm.edu
E-mail: admissions@mmm.edu

Medaille College
18 Agassiz Cir, Buffalo NY 14214-2695
716-884-3281

Mercy College
1200 Waters Pl, Bronx NY 10461-2704
718-798-8952

Mercy College
555 Broadway, Dobbs Ferry NY 10522-1189
Kathleen Jackson, Director of Admissions
800-MERCY-NY

Mercy College
277 Martine Ave, White Plains NY 10601
914-948-3666

Mercy College
2651 Strang Blvd, Yorktown Heights NY 10598-2997
914-245-6100

Mercy College - Manhattan Campus
66 W 35th St, New York NY 10001
212-615-3351

Metropolitan College of New York
75 Varick St, New York NY 10013-1919
212-343-1234

MOLLOY COLLEGE

1000 Hempstead Ave
Rockville Centre NY 11570-1100
Marguerite Lane, Director of Admissions
516-678-5000 ext. 6291 Fax: 516-256-2247
Website: www.molloy.edu
E-mail: admissions@molloy.edu

Established 1955. Private. Coed. Accreditation: MSACS, NLN, Board of Regents of New York, CSWE, NCATE. Tuition: $15,560. Fees: $500. Enrollment: 1,990 full-time, 844 part-time, 840 graduate. Faculty: 303. Student-faculty ratio: 11:1. Degrees: AA, AAS, BA, BFA, BS, MBA in Accounting and Business, MS in Education, Nursing. Library: 133,500 volumes. 4 buildings on 30 acres.

Monroe College
2501 Jerome Ave, Bronx NY 10468-4305
Evan Jerome, Director of Admissions
718-933-6700 Fax: 718-364-3552
Website: www.monroecollege.edu
E-mail: ejerome@monroecollege.edu

Mt. St. Mary College
330 Powell Ave, Newburgh NY 12550-3494
845-561-0800

Nazareth College of Rochester
4245 East Ave, Rochester NY 14618-3790
585-389-2525

New School University
66 W 12th St, New York NY 10011-8603
212-229-5600

New York City College of Technology CUNY
300 Jay St, Brooklyn NY 11201-1909
Joe Lento, Director of Admissions
718-260-5000

NEW YORK COLLEGE OF HEALTH PROFESSIONS

6801 Jericho Tpke, Syosset NY 11791
Mary Rodas, Associate Director of Admissions
800-9-CAREER Fax: 516-364-0989
Website: www.nycollege.edu
E-mail: admissions@nycollege.edu

New York Institute of Technology
PO Box 8000, Old Westbury NY 11568-8000
516-686-7520

New York Institute of Technology
PO Box 8000, Old Westbury NY 11568-8000
516-686-7516

New York Institute of Technology
Central Islip Campus
211 Carleton Ave, Central Islip NY 11722
631-348-3000

New York Institute of Technology
Manhattan Campus
1855 Broadway, New York NY 10023-7602
212-261-1508

NEW YORK SCHOOL OF INTERIOR DESIGN

170 E 70th St, New York NY 10021-5110
David Sprouls, Director of Admissions
800-33-NYSID or 212-472-1500 Fax: 212-472-1867
Website: www.nysid.edu
E-mail: admissions@nysid.edu

Established 1916. Private. Coed. College devoted to Interior Design education. Tuition: $21,450 per year. Fees: $145. Enrollment: 750. Faculty: 95. Accreditation: NASAD, FIDER. Four programs offered: Master of Fine Arts, 4-year Bachelor degree, 2-year Associate degree, 1-year non-degree Basic Interior Design. Located in Manhattan's historic Upper East Side near center of interior design industry. Faculty consists of Designers, Architects and Artists.

New York University
70 Washington Sq S, New York NY 10012-1019
212-998-1212

New York University Medical Center
550 1st Ave, New York NY 10016-6481
212-263-5111

Niagara University
PO Box 2011, Niagara University NY 14109-2011
George Pachter, Dean of Admissions & Records
800-462-2111

Nyack College
1 South Blvd
Nyack NY 10960-3698
845-358-1710

Pace University
1 Pace Plz, New York NY 10038-1502
212-346-1200

Pace University
861 Bedford Rd, Pleasantville NY 10570-2799
914-773-3200

Pace University
White Plains Campus
78 N Broadway, White Plains NY 10603
914-442-4000

Parsons School of Design
66 5th Ave, New York NY 10011-8802
212-229-8953

Paul Smith's College
Paul Smiths NY 12970
Amber DeBeer, Assistant Director of Admissions
800-421-2605

Polytechnic University
6 Metrotech Ctr, Brooklyn NY 11201-3840
718-260-3600

Polytechnic University
105 Maxess Rd Suite 201N, Melville NY 11747-3857
631-755-4300

Pratt Institute
200 Willoughby Ave, Brooklyn NY 11205-3899
Heidi Metcalf, Director of Admissions
718-636-3600 Fax: 718-636-3670
Website: www.pratt.edu
E-mail: hmetcalf@pratt.edu

PURCHASE COLLEGE STATE UNIVERSITY OF NEW YORK (SUNY)

735 Anderson Hill Rd, Purchase NY 10577-1400
Thomas Schwarz, President
Stephanie McCaine, Director of Admissions
914-251-6300 Fax: 914-251-6314
Website: www.purchase.edu
E-mail: admisn@purchase.edu

Established in 1967. Public. Coed. Accreditation: MSACS, NY State Board of Regents. Tuition: $4,350 for NYS residents, $10,610 for non-residents. Room and board: $7,310. Fees: $1,091.50. Enrollment: 3,302 full-time, 518 part-time, with 65% of total living on campus. Faculty: 341. Student-faculty ratio: 13.8:1. 36 buildings designed by celebrated architects. Located on 550 acres in a semi-rural setting less than an hour from New York City.

Curriculum: The Liberal Arts and Sciences divisions offer a traditional Liberal Arts program leading to BA and BS (within Natural Sciences) degrees in Humanities (Art History, Cinema Studies, Creative Writing, Drama Studies, History, Journalism, Language and Culture, Literature, and Philosophy), Natural Sciences (Biology, Chemistry, Environmental Science, Mathematics-with a concentration in Computer Science, New Media, and Psychology-with a concentration in Psychobiology), Social Sciences (Anthropology, Economics-with a concentration in Business Economics, Political Science, and Sociology), and Interdisciplinary programs (Asian Studies, Liberal Arts - with concentrations in lesbian/gay studies, liberal studies, and media, society, and the arts, Media Studies, and Women's Studies). Nationally ranked conservatories of Dance, Music, Theater Arts and Film, and The School of Art+ Design offer professional training programs with BFA degrees in Acting, Arts Management, Dance, Dramatic Writing, Film, Theatre Design/Technology, Visual Arts, and a Mus.B in Music. The Conservatories also offer MFA degrees in Dance, Theatre Design/Tech. and Visual Arts, an MM in Music, and an MA degree in Art History. The BFA, Mus.B, MM and MFA programs are only offered to full-time, daytime students. The Music Conservatory also offers a two-year Artist's Diploma, and a one-year Performer's Certificate. Continuing Education offers certificate programs in Arts Management, Child Care, Early Childhood Development, Computer Languages with Business Applications, Computer Science, Data Processing, Economics, Environmental Management, and General Business.

Purchase College is unique in that it has the largest Visual Arts facility in the U.S., the only dance building in the country designed specifically for the training and performance of dance, and a large science research center. In addition, Purchase has a Performing Arts Center which houses four theatres, ranging from a 1,400 seat concert hall to an experimental black box theatre; and the Neuberger Museum, the sixth largest university museum in the U.S. with a permanent collection that exceeds 14,000 works.

The Library holds 273,483 volumes, 1,975 subscriptions, 14,375 records and CD's and 237,277 microforms. It has a computerized card catalog which can access an inter-library loan system, with local institutions and other SUNY colleges; and a microcomputer lab.

For more information please call, or make a reservation for our information sessions - most Mondays and Fridays at 9:30 A.M or 2:00 PM.

Rensselaer Polytechnic Institute
110 8th St, Troy NY 12180-3590
518-276-6000

Roberts Wesleyan College
2301 Westside Dr, Rochester NY 14624-1997
Office of Admissions
585-594-6400 Fax: 585-594-6371
Website: www.roberts.edu
E-mail: admissions@roberts.edu

Rochester Institute of Technology
1 Lomb Memorial Dr, Rochester NY 14623-5603
585-475-2411

ROCHESTER INSTITUTE OF TECHNOLOGY NATIONAL TECHNICAL INSTITUTE FOR THE DEAF (NTID)

52 Lomb Memorial Dr, Rochester NY 14623-5604
Robert Borden, Director of NTID Admissions
585-475-6700 (v/TTY) or 866-644-6843 (v/TTY)
Fax: 585-475-2696
Website: www.rit.edu/ntid/getinfo
E-mail: NTIDAdmissions@rit.edu

Established 1965. Private. Coed. Tution $9,153 (NTID or NTID supported students only). Room & Board: $9,054. Fees: $669. Enrollment: 1,100. Faculty: 205. Degrees offered: MS, BS, AS, AAS, AOS. 238 buildings on 1,300 acres. Qualified deaf and hard-of-hearing students can earn bachelor's or master's degrees in more than 200 programs offered by RIT's seven other colleges - Applied Science and Technology, Business, Computing and Information Sciences, Engineering, Imaging Arts and Sciences, Liberal Arts, and Science. They also can earn associate degrees in more than 30 accredited NTID programs including: Accounting Technology, Administrative Support Technology, Applied Computer Technology, Applied Optical Technology, Arts and Imaging (pending state approval) Automation Technologies - Robotics, Business Technology, Computer Aided Drafting Technology, Computer Integrated Machining Technology, Laboratory Science Technology and Hospitality and Service Management. Additionally NTID offers degrees in American Sign Language-English Interpretation and a Master's of Science in Secondary Education of Students who are Deaf or Hard of Hearing.

St. Bonaventure University
Saint Bonaventure NY 14778-9999
585-375-2000

St. Francis College
180 Remsen St, Brooklyn NY 11201-4398
718-522-2300

St. John Fisher College
3690 East Ave, Rochester NY 14618-3597
585-385-8000

St. John's University
101 Murray St, New York NY 10007-2165
212-962-4111

ST. JOHN'S UNIVERSITY

8000 Utopia Pkwy, Queens NY 11439
Beth Evans, Associate VP & Executive Director Enrollment Management
877-STJ-5550 ext.101 Fax: 718-990-2096
Website: www.stjohns.edu/learnmore/
E-mail: admhelp@stjohns.edu

Established 1870 by the Vincentian Community. Roman Catholic. Campuses in Queens, Staten Island, and Manhattan, NY. Additional locations in Oakdale, NY, and Rome, Italy. Accreditation: Middle States Association of Colleges and Schools; AACSB International - The Association to Advance Collegiate Schools of Business; American Association for the Accreditation of Laboratory Animal Care; American Bar Association; American Chemical Society; American Council on Pharmaceutical Education; American Library Association; American Psychological Association; American Speech-Language-Hearing Association; Association of American Law Schools; CACREP: Council for Accreditation of Counseling and related education programs; NASAD: National Association of Schools of Art and Design; TEAC: Teacher Education Accreditation Council.

Tuition: $24,400. Room and board: $11,470. Full-time Undergraduate Enrollment: 14,983. Total University Enrollment: 20,069. Male: 41%, Female: 59%. More than 90% of students receive financial aid.

Modern, on-campus housing is available at St. John's 105-acre campus in Queens, NY, and its 16.5 acre campus on Staten Island, NY. The Manhattan campus offers limited housing. Resident students: 2,965. Library: 1.7 million volumes. Academic facilities include microcomputer laboratories, 17 microcomputer classrooms, 104 multimedia classrooms, and a television and radio production center. Big East athletic facilities include lacrosse and baseball fields, tennis courts, basketball courts, weight rooms, a cardiovascular fitness center, a new soccer stadium, and a new University field house. More than 180 academic clubs, fraternities, and sororities.

Faculty: 648 full-time faculty, 86% with Ph.D. or other terminal degree. Student-faculty ratio: 17:1.

Undergraduates earn B.A., B.S., or B.F.A. degrees in nearly 100 majors, including arts and sciences, business, education, and fine arts. Also offered: six-year Pharm.D. program, B.A./M.A. and B.S./M.A. in selected areas. Pre-professional programs: administrative studies, advertising communications, communication arts, computer science, criminal justice, cytotechnology, funeral service administration, health services administration, hospitality management, journalism, legal studies, medical technology, physician assistant, sport management, telecommunications, television and film, toxicology. Army ROTC is available. Graduate degrees: M.A., M.S., M.B.A., J.D., Ph.D., Ed.D.

Admission requirements: institutional application and $30 processing fee (fee is waived for those who apply on-line at www.stjohns.edu/apply), FAFSA, high school transcript (college transcript for transfers), and official scores on SAT or ACT, TOEFL and declaration of finances for foreign students. Rolling Admission policy except for Pharm.D. program, which has a February 1st deadline for Fall admission.

The Queens and Staten Island campuses are in residential areas a short distance from New York City's cultural, financial, and entertainment centers. Beaches, parks, and other recreational sites are nearby.

St. John's University
300 Howard Ave, Staten Island NY 10301-4496
718-447-4343

St. Joseph's College
245 Clinton Ave, Brooklyn NY 11205-3688
Theresa LaRocca Meyer, V.P. for Enrollment Management
718-636-6800 Fax: 718-636-8303
Website: www.sjcny.edu
E-mail: tlaroccameyer@sjcny.edu

St. Joseph's College
155 W Roe Blvd, Patchogue NY 11772
631-447-3200

St. Lawrence University
2501 Saint Lawrence Univ, Canton NY 13617-1475
315-229-5011

St. Thomas Aquinas College
125 Route 340, Sparkill NY 10976-1050
845-398-4000

Sarah Lawrence College
1 Meadway, Bronxville NY 10708
914-337-0700

School of Visual Arts
209 E 23rd St, New York NY 10010-3994
212-592-2000

Siena College
515 Loudonville Rd, Loudonville NY 12211-1462
Heather Renault, Director of Admissions
518-783-2300 Fax: 518-783-2436
Website: www.siena.edu
E-mail: hrenault@siena.edu

Skidmore College
815 N Broadway, Saratoga Springs NY 12866-1698
518-580-5000

SUNY at Albany
1400 Washington Ave, Albany NY 12222-1000
Thomas Flemming, Associate Director of Admissions
518-442-5435

SUNY at Binghamton
PO Box 6001, Binghamton NY 13902-6001
607-777-2000

SUNY at Stony Brook
Stony Brook NY 11794-0001
631-689-6000

SUNY College at Brockport
350 New Campus Dr, Brockport NY 14420-2997
Bernard S. Valento, Director of Undergraduate Admissions
585-395-2751 Fax: 585-395-5452
Website: www.brockport.edu
E-mail: admit@brockport.edu

SUNY College at Buffalo
1300 Elmwood Ave, Buffalo NY 14222-1004
716-878-4000

SUNY College at Cortland
PO Box 2000, Cortland NY 13045-0900
Mark Yacavone, Assistant Director
607-753-4711

SUNY College at Fredonia
Fredonia NY 14063
716-673-3111

SUNY College at Geneseo
1 College Cir, Geneseo NY 14454-1401
585-245-5211

SUNY College at New Paltz
1 Hawk Dr, New Paltz NY 12561
845-257-2121

SUNY College at Old Westbury
PO Box 210, Old Westbury NY 11568-0210
516-876-3000

SUNY College at Oneonta
Oneonta NY 13820
607-436-3500

SUNY College at Oswego
Oswego NY 13126
315-312-2500

SUNY College at Plattsburgh
Plattsburgh NY 12901
518-564-2000

SUNY College at Potsdam
Potsdam NY 13676
Thomas W. Nesbitt, Director of Admissions
315-267-2000

SUNY College of Agriculture & Technology
107 Schenectady Ave, Cobleskill NY 12043
Clayton A. Smith, Director of Admissions
800-295-8988

SUNY College of Agriculture & Technology
Morrisville NY 13408
Thomas Ver Dow, Dean of Enrollment Management
800-258-0111

SUNY College of Environmental Science & Forestry
1 Forestry Dr, Syracuse NY 13210-2712
315-470-6500

SUNY College of Technology
Alfred NY 14802
Deborah J. Goodrich, Associate VP Enrollment Mgmt.
800-4AL-FRED Fax: 607-587-4299
Website: www.alfredstate.edu
E-mail: admissions@alfredstate.edu

SUNY EMPIRE STATE COLLEGE

2875 Union Rd Ste 34, Cheektowaga NY 14227-1461
Jennifer Riley, Asst. Director of Admissions
716-853-7700 Fax: 518-587-9759
Website: www.esc.edu
E-mail: admissions@esc.edu

SUNY Empire State College
200 N Central Ave, Hartsdale NY 10530-1925
914-948-6206

SUNY Empire State College
21 British American Blvd, Latham NY 12110-1405
518-783-6203

SUNY Empire State College
325 Hudson St Flr 5, New York NY 10013-1005
212-647-7800

SUNY Empire State College
PO Box 130, Old Westbury NY 11568-0130
516-997-4700

SUNY Empire State College
1475 Winton Rd N, Rochester NY 14609-5803
585-244-3884

SUNY EMPIRE STATE COLLEGE

1 Union Ave, Saratoga Springs NY 12866-4309
Jennifer Riley, Assistant Director of Admissions
800-847-3000 Fax: 518-587-9759
Website: www.esc.edu
E-mail: admissions@esc.edu

SUNY Empire State College
219 Walton St Fl 1, Syracuse NY 13202-1226
315-472-5799

SUNY Institute of Technology Utica/Rome
PO Box 3050, Utica NY 13504-3050
315-792-7100

SUNY Maritime College
6 Pennyfield Ave, Bronx NY 10465-4127
718-409-7200

SUNY Upstate Medical University
750 E Adams St, Syracuse NY 13210
315-464-5540

SWEDISH INSTITUTE
College of Health Sciences
226 W 26th St, New York NY 10001-6700
Tamica Ward, Director of Admissions
212-924-5900 ext. 125 Fax: 212-924-7600
Website: www.swedishinstitute.edu
E-mail: admissions@swedishinstitute.edu
Established 1916. Private. Coed. Degrees: Associate in Occupational Studies in Massage Therapy. Master of Science in Acupuncture. Focused program in massage therapy features Western & Eastern approaches. Can be completed in 16 months full-time. The Master of Science in Acupuncture focuses on classical Chinese Acupuncture. Full time students can complete the degree in three years.

Syracuse University
Syracuse NY 13244-0001
315-443-1870

Touro College
27 W 23rd St Ste 33, New York NY 10010-4202
212-463-0400

Touro College
240 E 123rd St, New York NY 10035-2038
212-722-1575

Union College
Schenectady NY 12308
518-388-6000

United States Merchant Marine Academy
300 Steamboat Rd, Kings Point NY 11024-1699
516-773-5000

United States Military Academy West Point
646 Swift Rd, West Point NY 10996-1905
Colonel Michael L. Jones, Director of Admissions
845-938-4041 Fax: 845-938-8121
Website: admissions.usma.edu
E-mail: admissions@usma.edu

University at Buffalo, The State University of New York
15 Capen Hall, Buffalo NY 14260-1660
Patricia G. Armstrong, Director of Admissions
888-UB-ADMIT

University of Rochester
Wallis Hall, Rochester NY 14627
585-275-2121

Utica College
1600 Burrstone Rd, Utica NY 13502-4857
315-792-3111

Utica School of Commerce
201 Bleecker St, Utica NY 13501-2280
Bruce Davis, Director of Marketing
315-733-2307 Fax: 315-733-9281
Website: www.uscny.edu
E-mail: admissions@uscny.edu

Vassar College
124 Raymond Ave, Poughkeepsie NY 12604-0002
845-437-7000

VAUGHN COLLEGE OF AERONAUTICS AND TECHNOLOGY
8601 23rd Ave, Flushing NY 11369-1037
Vincent Papandrea, Director of Admissions
800-776-2376 Fax: 718-429-0671
Website: www.vaughn.edu
E-mail: admitme@vaughn.edu
Established 1932. Private. Coed. Accreditation: MSACS, ABET. Tuition: $13,400. Fees: $280. Enrollment: 842 full-time, 284 part-time. Faculty: 59. Student-faculty ratio: 11:1. Degrees: BS, AAS, AOS. Library: 62,000 vols. Offering bachelor and associate degrees in airport management, aviation maintenance, flight training, electronic technology, engineering, general management, mechatronic engineering, pre-engineering and computerized design/animated graphics. Hands-on training. Extensive career development services and financial aid available.

Wagner College
One Campus Rd, Staten Island NY 10301
Leigh Ann DePascale, Director of Admissions
718-390-3411

WEBB INSTITUTE
298 Crescent Beach Rd, Glen Cove NY 11542-1321
Stephen Ostendorff, Director of Admissions
516-671-2213 Fax: 516-674-9838
Website: www.webb-institute.edu
E-mail: admissions@webb-institute.edu

Wells College
PO Box 500, Aurora NY 13026
Susan Sloan, Director of Admissions
800-952-9355 Fax: 315-364-3227
Website: www.wells.edu
E-mail: ssloan@wells.edu

Word of Life Bible Institute
PO Box 129, Pottersville NY 12860-0129
518-494-4723

Yeshiva and Kolel Bais Medrash Elyon
73 Main St, Monsey NY 10952-3013
845-356-7064

Yeshiva Derech Chaim
1573 39th St, Brooklyn NY 11218-4413
718-438-5476

Yeshiva Gedolah Bais Yisroel
2002 Avenue J, Brooklyn NY 11210-3645
718-258-7400

Yeshiva Gedolah Imrei Yosef D'Spinka
1460 56th St, Brooklyn NY 11219-4617
718-972-1989

Yeshiva Novominsk
1569 47th St, Brooklyn NY 11219-2742
718-438-2727

Yeshiva University
500 W 185th St, New York NY 10033-3299
212-960-5400

NORTH CAROLINA

Apex School of Theology
2945 S Miami Blvd Ste 114, Durham NC 27703
Dr. J.E. Perkins, President
919-572-1625 Fax: 919-572-1762
Website: www.apexsot.edu
E-mail: info@apexsot.edu

Appalachian State University
ASU Station, Boone NC 28608-0001
828-262-2000

Barton College
PO Box 5000, Wilson NC 27893
252-399-6300

Belmont Abbey College
100 Belmont Mount Holly Rd
Belmont NC 28012-1802
888-222-0110

Brevard College
One Brevard College Dr, Brevard NC 28712
Joretta Nelson, Vice President Enrollment Management
828-883-8292 Fax: 828-884-3790
Website: www.brevard.edu
E-mail: admissions@brevard.edu

CABARRUS COLLEGE OF HEALTH SCIENCES
401 Medical Park Dr, Concord NC 28025
Mark Ellison, Director of Admissions
704-783-1556 Fax: 704-783-2077
Website: www.cabarruscollege.edu
E-mail: admissions@cabarruscollege.edu
Established: 1942. Private. Coed. Accreditation: Southern Association of Colleges & Schools. Tuition: $7,800. Enrollment: 410. Degrees Offered: Baccalaureate in Health Services Management, Medical Imaging, Nursing. Associates in Medical Assistant, Nursing, Occupational Therapy Assistant, Science, Surgical Technology. Affiliated with Northeast Medical Center, a magnet hospital.

Campbell University
PO Box 546, Buies Creek NC 27506-0546
Herbert V. Kerner, Jr., Director of Admissions
800-334-4111

Carolinas College of Health Sciences
PO Box 32861, Charlotte NC 28232-2861
Elizabeth West, Admissions Officer
704-355-5043

Catawba College
2300 W Innes St, Salisbury NC 28144-2488
Dr. L. Russell Watjen, Ph.D., V.P. & Dean of Admissions
704-637-4402 Fax: 704-637-4222
Website: www.catawba.edu
E-mail: admission@catawba.edu

Chowan University
One University Pl, Murfreesboro NC 27855
Chad Holt, Dean of Admissions
800-488-4101 Fax: 252-398-1190
Website: www.chowan.edu
E-mail: holtc@chowan.edu

Davidson College
PO Box 7156, Davidson NC 28035-7156
Chris Gruber, Acting Dean of Admission
800-768-0380

Duke University
Durham NC 27706-8001
919-684-8111

East Carolina University
1000 E 5th St, Greenville NC 27858

Elizabeth City State University
1704 Weeksville Rd, Elizabeth City NC 27909-7806
252-335-3400

Elon University
2700 Campus Box, Elon NC 27244
Susan C. Klopman, Dean of Admissions
800-334-8448

Fayetteville State University
1200 Murchison Rd, Fayetteville NC 28301-4298
910-486-1111

Gardner-Webb University
PO Box 817, Boiling Springs NC 28017
704-406-2361

Gardner-Webb University
PO Box 908, Statesville NC 28687-0908
704-872-3664

Greensboro College
815 W Market St, Greensboro NC 27401-1875
336-272-7102

Guilford College
5800 W Friendly Ave, Greensboro NC 27410-4173
Randy Doss, Dean of Enrollment
336-316-2100

High Point University
933 Montlieu Ave, High Point NC 27262-3598
336-841-9000

Johnson & Wales University
801 W Trade St, Charlotte NC 28202
980-598-1000

Johnson C. Smith University
100 Beatties Ford Rd, Charlotte NC 28216-5302
704-378-1000

JOHN WESLEY COLLEGE
2314 N Centennial St, High Point NC 27265-3197
Greg Workman, Admissions Officer
336-889-2262 ext. 127 Fax: 336-889-2261
Website: www.johnwesley.edu
E-mail: admissions@johnwesley.edu
See listing under "Theological Studies & Religious Vocations"

Lees-McRae College
PO Box 128, Banner Elk NC 28604-0128
Walt Crutchfield, Dean of Admissions
800-280-4562

LEE UNIVERSITY CHARLOTTE CENTER
1209 Little Rock Rd, Charlotte NC 28214-2310
Thomas Tatum, Center Director
704-394-2307 Fax: 704-393-3689
Website: http://caps.leeuniversity.edu/charlotte-center/
E-mail: ttatum@carolina.rr.com

Lenoir-Rhyne College
7th Ave and 8th St, Hickory NC 28603
828-328-1741

Livingstone College
701 W Monroe St, Salisbury NC 28144-5298
704-797-1000

Mars Hill College
Mars Hill NC 28754
Chad Holt, Dean of Enrollment
866-MHC-4-YOU

Meredith College
3800 Hillsborough St, Raleigh NC 27607-5298
Heidi L. Fletcher, Director of Admissions
919-760-8581

Methodist College
5400 Ramsey St, Fayetteville NC 28311-1498
910-630-7000

Montreat College
PO Box 1267, Montreat NC 28757-1267
800-622-6968

Mt. Olive College
634 Henderson St, Mount Olive NC 28365-1299
Tim Woodard, Director of Admissions
919-658-2502

North Carolina A&T State University
1601 E Market St, Greensboro NC 27411
Lee Young, AVC Enrollment
336-334-7500

North Carolina Central University
PO Box 19617, Durham NC 27707-0022
919-560-6100

North Carolina School of the Arts
1533 S Main St, Winston Salem NC 27127
Sheeler Lawson, Director of Admissions
336-770-3290

North Carolina State University
PO Box 7001, Raleigh NC 27695-0001
919-515-2011

North Carolina Wesleyan College
3400 N Wesleyan Blvd, Rocky Mount NC 27804-8677
252-985-5100

Peace College
15 E Peace St, Raleigh NC 27604-1194
Laura C. Bingham, President
800-PEACE-47 Fax: 919-508-2306
Website: www.peace.edu
E-mail: admissions@peace.edu

Pfeiffer University
PO Box 960, Misenheimer NC 28109-0960
704-463-1360

Piedmont Baptist College
716 Franklin St, Winston Salem NC 27101-5197
800-937-5097

Queens University of Charlotte
1900 Selwyn Ave, Charlotte NC 28274-0002
704-337-2212

Roanoke Bible College
715 N Poindexter St, Elizabeth City NC 27909-4054
252-334-2070

St. Andrews Presbyterian College
1700 Dogwood Mile St, Laurinburg NC 28352-5521
Glenn Batten, Vice President for Enrollment
910-277-5554

St. Augustine's College
1315 Oakwood Ave, Raleigh NC 27610-2298
919-516-4000

Shaw University
118 E South St, Raleigh NC 27601-2399
919-546-8200

Strayer University
3200 Spring Forest Rd, Raleigh NC 27616
919-878-9900

University of North Carolina
1 University Hts, Asheville NC 28804-3251
828-251-6600

University of North Carolina
Chapel Hill NC 27599-0001
919-962-2211

University of North Carolina
9201 University City Blvd, Charlotte NC 28223
704-547-2000

University of North Carolina
601 S College Rd, Wilmington NC 28403-3201
910-962-3000

University of North Carolina at Greensboro
1000 Spring Garden St, Greensboro NC 27412-0001
336-334-5243

University of North Carolina at Pembroke
PO Box 1510, Pembroke NC 28372-1510
910-521-6000

Wake Forest University
PO Box 7305, Winston Salem NC 27109-7305
336-759-5000

Warren Wilson College
PO Box 9000, Asheville NC 28815-9000
Richard Blomgren, Dean of Admissions
828-298-3325

Western Carolina University
University Dr, Cullowhee NC 28723-9646
828-227-7211

Wingate University
201 E Wilson St, Wingate NC 28174-9600
704-233-8000

Winston-Salem Bible College
PO Box 777, Winston Salem NC 27102-0777
336-774-0900

Winston-Salem State University
601 S Mrtn Lther King Jr Dr
Winston Salem NC 27110-0003
336-750-2000

NORTH DAKOTA

Dickinson State University
Dickinson ND 58601-4896
Steve Glasser, Director of Enrollment Services
800-279-4295 Fax: 701-483-2409
Website: www.dickinsonstate.edu
E-mail: dsu.hawks@dickinsonstate.edu

Jamestown College
6000 College Ln, Jamestown ND 58405-0002
701-252-3467

Mayville State University
330 3rd St NE, Mayville ND 58257-1299
Dr. Ray Gerszewski, Vice President Student Affairs
800-437-4104 Fax: 701-788-4748
Website: www.mayvillestate.edu
E-mail: admit@mayvillestate.edu

Medcenter One College of Nursing
512 N 7th St, Bismarck ND 58501-4425
Mary Smith, Director of Student Services
701-323-6271

Minot State University
500 University Ave W, Minot ND 58707-0002
Dennis Parisien, Enrollment Services Rep.
800-777-0750 ext. 3350

North Dakota State University
Fargo ND 58105
701-237-7211

Trinity Bible College
50 6th Ave S, Ellendale ND 58436-7150
Jerry A. Grimshaw, Enrollment Manager
701-349-3621

University of Mary
7500 University Dr, Bismarck ND 58504-9652
701-255-7500

University of North Dakota
Box 8193 University Station, Grand Forks ND 58203
701-777-2011

VALLEY CITY STATE UNIVERSITY

101 College St SW, Valley City ND 58072-4024
Dan Klein, Director of Enrollment Services
800-532-8641 ext. 7101 Fax: 701-845-7299
Website: www.vcsu.edu
E-mail: enrollment.services@vcsu.edu

Established 1890. Public. Coed. 563 women, 474 men; 34% live on campus. Accreditation: NCACS, NCATE, NASM. 69% of students received financial assistance in 2005-2006. Tuition: $131.36/credit in-state, $139.84/credit MN; $164.19/credit SD, MT, KS, MI, MO, NE, Manitoba, Saskatchewan; $197.04/credit WUE States; $350.72/credit other out of state and international. Room and Board: $3,414. Four residence halls. Each room individually wired for internet and TV cable. Family student housing also available. Numerous student organizations, some academic based, a fraternity and a sorority. BS, BA in 35 areas spanning Business Administration, Computer Information Systems, Communication Arts, Social Science, Education (including M.Ed.), Psychology, Fine Arts, Health and Physical Education, Mathematics, and Science. VCSU first in North Dakota, second in the US to provide a laptop computer to each student and faculty. Student model is Dell D630 laptop computer; software and hardware updates on regular basis. Unlimited access to information 24 hours a day seven days a week. Student to faculty ratio is 13:1. Campus has 29 historic and modern buildings on 64 acres. High-speed wired and wireless internet access throughout campus. Rhoades Science Center has science labs throughout, a planetarium, photo lab, and greenhouse. Athletic facilities include a swimming pool in Student Center, a physical ed building, a 2,500 seat fieldhouse with a new wood floor, synthetic 400 meter outdoor track surrounding the football field with bench seating in the stadium, tennis courts, racquetball courts, a baseball and softball fields. Two nine-hole golf courses offering student discounts. Fine arts facilities include a ceramics building, a 220 seat performance auditorium in the music building, an historic 850 seat Vangstad auditorium, and a theatre in the round for more intimate settings. The four-level library has 91,346 volumes, 59,400 microfilms, 15,624 aud/vid, records, and CDs, 1,937 periodical subscriptions, over 1,500 of these on-line. Campus is in a rural town of about 7,000 with a wooded hill to the south and a meandering river on the north side of the campus. A historic footbridge connects the campus to Valley City, ND which is located about 50 minutes west of Fargo, ND. The climate consists of warm to hot summers and cold winters. To be admitted, students must have completed four units of high school English and three units in each subject of Math, Lab Science, and Social Science. International students must complete the TOEFL and declare financial ability. A $35 application fee, high school transcript, college transcripts, proof of immunization are also required of all applicants.

OHIO

Allegheny Wesleyan College
2161 Woodsdale Rd, Salem OH 44460
800-292-3153

Antioch University McGregor
800 Livermore St, Yellow Springs OH 45387
937-767-6321

Art Institute of Ohio - Cincinnati
1011 Glendale Milford Rd, Cincinnati OH 45215
513-771-2829

Ashland University
401 College Ave, Ashland OH 44805-3799
419-289-4142

Athenaeum of Ohio
6616 Beechmont Ave, Cincinnati OH 45230-2000
513-231-2223

Baldwin-Wallace College
275 Eastland Rd, Berea OH 44017-2088
440-826-2900

Bluffton University
1 University Dr, Bluffton OH 45817
419-358-3000

Bowling Green State University
110 McFall Center, Bowling Green OH 43403-0001
866-CHOOSE-BGSU

Capital University
2199 E Main St, Columbus OH 43209-2394
614-236-6011

Case Western Reserve University
10900 Euclid Ave, Cleveland OH 44106
216-368-2000

Cedarville University
251 N Main St, Cedarville OH 45314
937-766-2211

Central State University
PO Box 1004, Wilberforce OH 45384-1004
937-376-6011

Cincinnati Christian University
PO Box 4320, Cincinnati OH 45204
Erin Oppy, Executive Director of Undergraduate Admissions
513-244-8141 Fax: 513-244-8453
Website: www.ccuniversity.edu

Cincinnati College of Mortuary Science
645 W North Bend Rd, Cincinnati OH 45224-1428
Dr. Dan Flory, President
513-761-2020

Circleville Bible College
PO Box 458, Circleville OH 43113-0458
800-701-0222

Cleveland Institute of Art
11141 East Blvd, Cleveland OH 44106-1700
216-421-7000

CLEVELAND INSTITUTE OF MUSIC

11021 East Blvd, Cleveland OH 44106
William Fay, Director of Admission
216-795-3107
Website: www.cim.edu/coladmission.php

Cleveland State University
2121 Euclid Ave RW 204, Cleveland OH 44115
Dr. Richard Arndt, Dean of Undergraduate Recruitment and College Partnerships
888-CSU-OHIO Fax: 216-687-9210
Website: www.csuohio.edu
E-mail: admissions@csuohio.edu

College of Mount Saint Joseph
5701 Delhi Rd, Cincinnati OH 45233-1669
513-244-4200

College of Wooster
Wooster OH 44691-2363
Paul J. Deutsch, Dean of Admissions
800-877-9905

Columbus College of Art & Design
107 N 9th St, Columbus OH 43215-1700
877-997-CCAD

Davis College
4747 Monroe St, Toledo OH 43623-4389
Dana Stern, Admissions Director
419-473-2700 Fax: 419-473-2472
Website: www.daviscollege.edu
E-mail: learn@daviscollege.edu

Defiance College
701 N Clinton St, Defiance OH 43512-1695
419-784-4010

Denison University
PO Box B, Granville OH 43023-0603
740-587-0810

Franciscan University of Steubenville
University Blvd, Steubenville OH 43952
Margaret J. Weber, Director of Admissions
800-783-6220 or 740-283-6226 Fax: 740-284-5456
Website: www.admissions.edu
E-mail: mweber@franciscan.edu

Franklin University
201 S Grant Ave, Columbus OH 43215-5399
614-341-6300

God's Bible School and College
1810 Young St, Cincinnati OH 45202-6838
Aaron Profitt, Director of Admissions
513-721-7944

Heidelberg College
310 E Market St, Tiffin OH 44883-2462
418-448-2000

Hiram College
PO Box 96, Hiram OH 44234-0096
800-362-5280

Hocking College
3301 Hocking Pkwy, Nelsonville OH 45764-9704
Diane K. Wolf, Assistant Director of Admissions Information
800-282-4163

John Carroll University
20700 N Park Blvd, Cleveland OH 44118-4581
216-397-1886

Kent State University
PO Box 5190, Kent OH 44242-0001
Paul Deutsch, Director of Admissions
330-672-2444

Kenyon College
1 Kenyon College, Gambier OH 43022-9623
740-427-5000

Kettering College of Medical Arts
3737 Southern Blvd, Kettering OH 45429-1299
David Lofthouse, Director of Enrollment Services
800-433-5262

Lake Erie College
391 W Washington St, Painesville OH 44077-3389
440-352-3361

Laura & Alvin Siegal College of Judaic Studies
26500 Shaker Blvd, Cleveland OH 44122-7116
216-464-4050

Lourdes College
6832 Convent Blvd, Sylvania OH 43560-2898
800-878-3210

Malone College
515 25th St NW, Canton OH 44709-3897
John Chopka, Dean of Admissions
330-471-8100

Marietta College
215 5th St, Marietta OH 45750-4047
740-376-4600

MedCentral College of Nursing
335 Glessner Ave, Mansfield OH 44903-2265
Christopher M. Harris, Director for Enrollment Management
419-520-2600

Miami University
E High St, Oxford OH 45056
513-529-2531

Mount Carmel College of Nursing
127 S Davis Ave, Columbus OH 43222-1504
800-556-6972

Mt. Union College
1972 Clark Ave, Alliance OH 44601-3929
Vincent Heslop, Director of Admissions
800-334-6682

Mount Vernon Nazarene University
800 Martinsburg Rd, Mount Vernon OH 43050-9509
Timothy Eades, Director of Admissions
866-462-6868

Muskingum College
147 Center St, New Concord OH 43762-1193
740-826-8211

MYERS UNIVERSITY

3921 Chester Ave, Cleveland OH 44114-4624
Ronald G. Brown, Vice President for Enrollment Management
216-432-8992 Fax: 216-361-9274
Website: www.myers.edu
E-mail: rgbrown@myers.edu

Oberlin College
Carnegie Bldg, Oberlin OH 44074
Debra Chermonte, Dean of Admissions & Financial Aid

Ohio Dominican University
1216 Sunbury Rd, Columbus OH 43219-2099
614-253-2741

OHIO NORTHERN UNIVERSITY

525 S Main St, Ada OH 45810-1555
Karen P. Condeni, V.P. & Dean of Admissions & Financial Aid
888-408-4668 Fax: 419-772-2313
Website: www.onu.edu
E-mail: admissions-ug@onu.edu

Established 1871. Private. Coed. Accreditation: Higher Learning Commission & Member of NCA, ACS, CAAHEP, NASM, EAC of ABET, ACPE, AALS, ABA, AACSB International, NCATE, Ohio Dept. of Education. 2006-07 Tuition: $28,260 - $31,755. Room & board: $7,080. Fees: $210. Enrollment: 3,442 full-time, 84 part-time. Faculty: 321. Student-faculty ratio: 14:1. Degrees offered: BA, BFA, BM, BS, BSCLS, BSBA, BSCE, BSCPE, BSEE, BSN, BSME, PharmD, MET, LLM, JD. Over 45 buildings on 285 acres. Colleges of: Arts & Sciences, Business Administration, Engineering, Pharmacy & Law; Direct Entry Pharmacy Program.

The Ohio State University
Enarson Hall, 154 W 12th Ave
Columbus OH 43210-1390
Dr. Mabel Freeman, Asst. V.P., Undergraduate Admissions and First Year Experience
614-292-3980 Fax: 614-292-4818
Website: www.osu.edu
E-mail: freeman.9@osu.edu

Ohio State University-Lima Campus
4240 Campus Dr, Lima OH 45804-3576
Garlene Smithson, Dir. Enrollment Services
419-995-8396

Ohio State University-Mansfield Campus
1680 University Dr, Mansfield OH 44906-1547
419-755-4011

Ohio State University-Marion
1465 Mount Vernon Ave, Marion OH 43302-5695
740-389-6786

Ohio State University-Newark
1179 University Dr, Newark OH 43055-1797
740-366-3321

Ohio University
PO Box 640, Athens OH 45701-0640
740-593-1000

Ohio University
Chillicothe Campus
PO Box 629, Chillicothe OH 45601
Student Services
740-774-7200 Fax: 740-774-7295
Website: www.ohiou.edu/chillicothe/

Ohio University
Eastern Campus
45425 National Rd W
Saint Clairsville OH 43950-9724
740-695-1720

Ohio University
Lancaster Campus
1570 Granville Pike, Lancaster OH 43130-1097
740-654-6711

Ohio University
Southern Campus
1804 Liberty Ave, Ironton OH 45638-2279
740-533-4600

Ohio University - Zanesville Branch
1425 Newark Rd, Zanesville OH 43701-2695
740-588-1439

OHIO WESLEYAN UNIVERSITY
61 S Sandusky St, Delaware OH 43015-2398
Director of Admission
740-368-3020 Fax: 740-368-3314
Website: www.owu.edu
E-mail: owuadmit@owu.edu

Otterbein College
78 W Home St, Westerville OH 43081-1489
614-890-3000

PAYNE THEOLOGICAL SEMINARY
PO Box 474, Wilberforce OH 45384-0474
Dr. Leah Gaskin Fitchue, Contact
937-376-2946 Fax: 937-376-3330
Website: www.payne.edu
E-mail: lfitchue@payne.edu

Rosedale Bible College
2270 Rosedale Rd, Irwin OH 43029
740-857-1311

Shawnee State University
940 2nd St, Portsmouth OH 45662-4344
740-354-3205

Temple Baptist College
11965 Kenn Rd, Cincinnati OH 45240
Dr. Tanmay Pramanik, Dean of Student Affairs
513-851-3800

Union Institute & University
440 E McMillan St, Cincinnati OH 45206-1925
513-861-6400

University of Akron
381 Buchtel Mall, Akron OH 44304-1584
330-972-7111

University of Cincinnati
2700 Clifton Ave, Cincinnati OH 45220-2873
513-556-6000

University of Cincinnati
OMI College of Applied Science
2220 Victory Pkwy, Cincinnati OH 45206-2839
Rita K. Hessley, PhD, Dean
513-556-6567

University of Dayton
300 College Park, Dayton OH 45469-1300
Robert F. Durkle, Director of Admission
800-837-7433 Fax: 937-229-4729
Website: admission.udayton.edu
E-mail: admission@udayton.edu

University of Findlay
1000 N Main St, Findlay OH 45840-3695
419-422-8313

University of Northwestern Ohio
1441 N Cable Rd, Lima OH 45805-1498
Rick Morrison, Director of Admissions
419-998-3120

University of Rio Grande
General Delivery, Rio Grande OH 45674-9999
Dr. Chris Pines, Dean
740-245-5353 ext. 7426

University of Toledo
2801 W Bancroft St, Toledo OH 43606-3390
419-530-4636

Urbana University
579 College Way, Urbana OH 43078
937-484-1301

Ursuline College
2550 Lander Rd, Cleveland OH 44124-4398
Sarah E. Sundermeier, Director of Admissions
888-URSULINE Toll Free Fax: 440-684-6138
Website: www.admission.ursuline.edu
E-mail: admission@ursuline.edu

Walsh University
2020 E Maple St, North Canton OH 44720
800-362-9846

Wilberforce University
PO Box 1001, Wilberforce OH 45384-1001
937-376-2911

Wilmington College
1870 Quaker Way, Wilmington OH 45177
937-382-6661

Wittenberg University
PO Box 720, Springfield OH 45501-0720
937-327-6231

Wright State University
3640 Colonel Glenn Hwy, Dayton OH 45435-0002
937-775-3333

Xavier University
3800 Victory Pkwy, Cincinnati OH 45207-1092
513-745-3000

Youngstown State University
Sweeney Welcome Ctr, One University Plz
Youngstown OH 44555-0002
Sue Davis, Contact
877-GO-TO-YSU

OKLAHOMA

Bacone College
2299 Old Bacone Rd, Muskogee OK 74403-1568
Jerrett Phillips, Director of Admissions
918-781-7340

Cameron University
2800 W Gore Blvd, Lawton OK 73505-6377
580-581-2200

East Central University
1100 E 14th St
Ada OK 74820-6999
Pamla Armstrong, Director of Admissions
580-332-8000

Family of Faith College
PO Box 1805, Shawnee OK 74802
405-273-5331

Hillsdale Free Will Baptist College
PO Box 7208, Moore OK 73153
405-912-9000

ITT Technical Institute
1900 NW Expressway St #305R
Oklahoma City OK 73118
405-810-4100

Langston University
PO Box 907, Langston OK 73050-0907
405-466-2231

Mid-America Christian University
3500 SW 119th St, Oklahoma City OK 73170-4504
Haley Hope, Director of Admissions
405-691-3800 Fax: 405-692-3165
Website: www.macu.edu
E-mail: info@macu.edu

Northeastern State University
600 N Grand Ave, Tahlequah OK 74464-2301
918-456-5511

Northwestern Oklahoma State University
709 Oklahoma Blvd, Alva OK 73717
580-327-1700

Oklahoma Baptist University
500 W University St, Shawnee OK 74804-2590
405-275-2850

Oklahoma Christian University
PO Box 11000, Oklahoma City OK 73136-1100
405-425-5000

Oklahoma City University
2501 N Blackwelder Ave
Oklahoma City OK 73106-1493
Shery Boyles, Director of Admissions
405-521-5050

Oklahoma Panhandle State University
PO Box 430, Goodwell OK 73939-0430
580-349-2611

Oklahoma State University
Stillwater OK 74078
Paul Carney, Director of Undergraduate Admissions
405-744-7275 Fax: 405-744-7092
Website: www.okstate.edu
E-mail: admit@okstate.edu

Oklahoma Wesleyan University
2201 Silver Lake Rd, Bartlesville OK 74006-6299
918-333-6151

Oral Roberts University
7777 S Lewis Ave, Tulsa OK 74171-0001
Chris Belcher, Director of Undergraduate Admissions
800-678-8876

Rogers State University - Claremore Campus
1701 W Will Rogers Blvd, Claremore OK 74017-3259
Joe Wiley, President
918-343-7777

St. Gregory's University
1900 W MacArthur St, Shawnee OK 74804-2499
405-878-5100

Southeastern Oklahoma State University
Station A, Durant OK 74701
580-924-0121

Southern Nazarene University
6729 NW 39th Expy, Bethany OK 73008-2694
405-789-6400

Southwestern Christian University
PO Box 340, Bethany OK 73008-0340
Megan Miles, Director of Admissions
405-789-7661

Southwestern Oklahoma State University
100 Campus Dr, Weatherford OK 73096-3098
580-772-6611

SPARTAN COLLEGE OF AERONAUTICS AND TECHNOLOGY
8820 E Pine St, Tulsa OK 74115-5802
Director of Admissions
800-331-1204 Fax: 918-831-8609
Website: www.spartan.edu
E-mail: spartan@mail.spartan.edu

Established 1928. Coed. Accredited member school: ACCSCT. Providing Technical training and education in Avionics, Aviation Maintenance; Nondestructive Testing and Quality Control. Complete flight training program. Offering Diplomas, Associate of Applied Science and Bachelor of Science in Aviation Technology Management.

University of Central Oklahoma
100 N University Dr, Edmond OK 73034-5209
405-974-2000

University of Oklahoma at Norman
660 Parrington Oval, Norman OK 73019-3070
405-325-0311

University of Oklahoma Health Sciences
1000 Stanton L Young Blvd
Oklahoma City OK 73190
405-271-4000

University of Sciences & Arts of OK
PO Box 82345, Chickasha OK 73018
405-224-3140

University of Tulsa
600 S College Ave, Tulsa OK 74104-3126
Earl Johnson, Dean of Admission
918-631-2307 Fax: 918-631-5003
Website: www.utulsa.edu
E-mail: admission@utulsa.edu

OREGON

Apollo College
2004 Lloyd Ctr Fl 3, Portland OR 97232-1309
503-761-6100 Fax: 503-761-3351

The Art Institute of Portland
1122 NW Davis St, Portland OR 97209-2911
503-228-6528

Birthingway College of Midwifery
12113 SE Foster Rd, Portland OR 97266
503-760-3131

Cascade College
9101 E Burnside St, Portland OR 97216-1599
Jim Murphy, Director of Enrollment Management
800-550-7678 Fax: 503-257-1222
Website: www.cascade.edu
E-mail: admissions@cascade.edu

Concordia University
2811 NE Holman St, Portland OR 97211-6099
Bobi Swan, Director of Admissions
503-288-9371 Fax: 503-280-8531
Website: www.cu-portland.edu
E-mail: cu-admissions@cu-portland.edu

Corban College
5000 Deer Park Dr SE, Salem OR 97317-9330
503-581-8600

Eastern Oregon University
One University Blvd, La Grande OR 97850
Sherri Edualson, Director of Admissions
800-452-8639

George Fox University
414 N Meridian St, Newberg OR 97132-2625
503-538-8383

Gutenberg College
1883 University St, Eugene OR 97403
541-683-5141

ITT Technical Institute
6035 NE 78th Ct, Portland OR 97218-2852
503-255-6500

Lewis & Clark College
0615 SW Palatine Hill Rd, Portland OR 97219-7899
503-768-7000

Linfield College
900 SE Baker St, Mc Minnville OR 97128-6894
503-472-2200

Linfield College
2215 NW Northrup St, Portland OR 97210-2982
503-229-7161

Marylhurst University
17600 Pacific Hwy (Hwy 43)
Marylhurst OR 97036-0261
Director of Admissions
800-634-9982 ext. 6268 Fax: 503-635-6585
Website: www.marylhurst.edu
E-mail: studentinfo@marylhurst.edu

Multnomah Bible College and Biblical Seminary
8435 NE Glisan St, Portland OR 97220-5898
Daniel R. Lockwood, President
800-275-4672

Northwest Christian College
828 E 11th Ave, Eugene OR 97401-3745
541-343-1641

OREGON COLLEGE OF ART & CRAFT
8245 SW Barnes Rd, Portland OR 97225-6399
Debrah Spencer, Interim Director of Admissions
503-297-5544 or 800-390-0632 Fax: 503-297-9651
Website: www.ocac.edu
E-mail: admissions@ocac.edu

Oregon Institute of Technology
3201 Campus Dr, Klamath Falls OR 97601-8801
541-885-1000

Oregon State University
Corvallis OR 97333-9800
541-737-0123

PACIFIC NORTHWEST COLLEGE OF ART
1241 NW Johnson St, Portland OR 97209-3023
Chris Sweet, Director of Admissions
503-821-8972 Fax: 503-821-8978
Website: www.pnca.edu
E-mail: admissions@pnca.edu

PACIFIC UNIVERSITY
2043 College Way, Forest Grove OR 97116-1797
Karen M. Dunston, Executive Director of Admissions
800-677-6712 Fax: 503-352-2975
Website: www.pacific.edu
E-mail: admissions@pacific.edu

Portland State University
PO Box 751, Portland OR 97207-0751
503-725-3000

Reed College
3202 SE Woodstock Blvd, Portland OR 97202-8139
503-771-1112

Southern Oregon University
1250 Siskiyou Blvd, Ashland OR 97520-5010
541-552-7672

University of Oregon
1217 University of Oregon, Eugene OR 97403
541-346-1000

University of Portland
5000 N Willamette Blvd, Portland OR 97203-5798
Jason McDonald, Dean of Admissions
503-943-7911 Fax: 503-943-7315
Website: www.up.edu
E-mail: mcdonaja@up.edu

Walla Walla University School of Nursing
10345 SE Market St, Portland OR 97216
503-251-6115

Warner Pacific College
2219 SE 68th Ave, Portland OR 97215-4026
Shannon Mackey, Director of Admissions
503-517-1000 Fax: 503-517-1352
Website: www.warnerpacific.edu
E-mail: admissions@warnerpacific.edu

Western Oregon University
345 Monmouth Ave N, Monmouth OR 97361-1314
David McDonald, Dean, Admission, Retention & Enrollment Management
877-877-1593

Willamette University
900 State St, Salem OR 97301-3931
503-370-6300

PENNSYLVANIA

Albright College
PO Box 15234, Reading PA 19612-5234
800-252-1856

Allegheny College
520 N Main St, Meadville PA 16335-3902
814-332-3100

Alvernia College
400 Saint Bernardine St, Reading PA 19607
610-796-8200

Arcadia University
450 S Easton Rd, Glenside PA 19038-3295
Dr. Jerry M. Greiner, President
Dennis Nostrand, VP for Enrollment Management
877-ARCADIA (877-272-2342)

Art Institute of Philadelphia
1622 Chestnut St, Philadelphia PA 19103-5119
Larry McHugh, Director of Admissions
800-275-2474 Fax: 215-405-6399
Website: www.artinstitutes.edu/philadelphia
E-mail: aiphinfo@aii.edu

THE ART INSTITUTE OF PITTSBURGH

The College for Creative Minds
420 Boulevard Of The Allies, Pittsburgh PA 15219
Jeffrey Bucklew, Director of Admissions
800-275-2470 or 412-263-6600 Fax: 412-263-6667
Website: www.aip.aii.edu
E-mail: pahughes@aii.edu

Established in 1921. Known as a leader in creative education. College is located in the heart of downtown, surrounded by limitless cultural, educational, and recreational opportunities. Licensed by the State of PA and accredited by Accrediting Council for Independent Colleges and Schools to confer Associate of Science and Bachelor of Science degrees. Approved for training of veterans and eligible veteran's dependents. Authorized by federal law to enroll non-immigrant alien students.

Enrollment: 2700+ students; Co-ed.

Financial Aid available to qualified students through various federal and state programs. Awards based on individual need and availability of funds. Other Institute scholarship programs are available. Information regarding eligibility can be obtained by contacting an admissions representitive at 1-800-275-2470.

Student Housing: School sponsored housing available in the form of furnished apartments.

Bachelor degrees available in: Advertising, Culinary Management, Game Art and Design, Digital Media Production, Graphic Design, Industrial Design, Interactive Media Design, Interior Design, Media Arts and Animation, Photography, Visual Effects and Motion Graphics, Hotel and Restaurant Management, Fashion and Retail Management.

Associate Degrees available in: Culinary Arts, Graphic Design, Industrial Design, Interactive Media Design, Photography, Video Production, Restaurant and Catering Operations.

Diploma programs include: The Art of Cooking, Digital Design, Residential Planning, Web Design. Some classes available evenings, Saturdays, and online.

Admissions: Prospective students must be a high school graduate or hold a General Educational Development (GED) Certificate. High school students who have not yet graduated should submit a partial transcript that indicates their expected graduation date, SAT and ACT testing not required for admission, however, may be used to determine the student's preparedness for college-level course work in English and/or mathematics.

Faculty: 101 full-time and 37 part-time instructors.

Facilities: 10 floors of fully networked computer labs and specialty facilities such as editing suites, digital photography labs, a television production studio, an industrial design machine shop, fully equipped culinary kitchens and more.

Baptist Bible College and Seminary
538 Venard Rd, Clarks Summit PA 18411-1297
Glen Amos, Director of Admissions
570-586-2400

Bloomsburg University of Pennsylvania
400 E 2nd St, Bloomsburg PA 17815-1399
570-389-4000

Bryn Athyn College of the New Church
PO Box 717, Bryn Athyn PA 19009
215-938-2543

Bucknell University
Lewisburg PA 17837
570-577-2000

Cabrini College
610 King of Prussia Rd, Radnor PA 19087-3698
Mark T. Osborn, VP for Enrollment Management
610-902-8100

California University of Pennsylvania
250 University Ave, California PA 15419-1394
724-938-4000

Carnegie Mellon University
5000 Forbes Ave, Pittsburgh PA 15213-3890
412-268-2000

Central Pennsylvania College
College Hill & Valley Rds, Summerdale PA 17093
Katie Borrelli, Admissions Director
800-759-2727 Fax: 717-728-2505
Website: www.centralpenn.edu
E-mail: katie.borrelli@centralpenn.edu

Chestnut Hill College
9601 Germantown Ave, Philadelphia PA 19118-2693
Jodie King, Director of Admissions
215-248-7001

Cheyney University of Pennsylvania
PO Box 200, Cheyney PA 19319-0200
610-399-2275

Clarion University of Pennsylvania
840 Wood St, Clarion PA 16214-1232
William Bailey, Dean of Enrollment Management
814-393-2306 Fax: 814-393-2030
Website: www.clarion.edu
E-mail: admissions@clarion.edu

Clarion University - Venango Campus
1801 W 1st St, Oil City PA 16301
814-676-6591

College Misericordia
301 Lake St, Dallas PA 18612-1008
Admissions
570-674-6400

Curtis Institute of Music
1726 Locust St, Philadelphia PA 19103-6187
215-893-5252

Delaware Valley College
700 E Butler Ave, Doylestown PA 18901-2697
Stephen W. Zenko, Director of Admissions
800-2DE-LVAL Fax: 215-230-2968
Website: www.delval.edu
E-mail: stephenzenko@delval.edu

DeSales University
2755 Station Ave, Center Valley PA 18034-9565
610-282-1100 Fax: 610-282-2342
Website: www.desales.edu

Dickinson College
PO Box 1773, Carlisle PA 17013-2896
717-243-5121

Drexel University
3141 Chestnut St, Philadelphia PA 19104-2875
Dana R. Davies, Director of Undergraduate Enrollment
800-2-DREXEL

Duquesne University
600 Forbes Ave, Pittsburgh PA 15282-0001
Paul-James Cukanna, Director of Admissions
412-396-5000

Eastern University
1300 Eagle Rd, Saint Davids PA 19087-3696
610-341-5800

East Stroudsburg University of PA
200 Prospect St
East Stroudsburg PA 18301
570-424-3211

Edinboro University of Pennsylvania
Edinboro PA 16444-0001
814-732-2000

Elizabethtown College
1 Alpha Dr, Elizabethtown PA 17022-2298
717-361-1000

Franklin and Marshall College
PO Box 3003, Lancaster PA 17604-3003
717-291-3911

Gannon University
109 University Sq, Erie PA 16541-0001
Christopher Tremblay, Director of Admissions
800-GANNON-U

Geneva College
3200 College Ave, Beaver Falls PA 15010-3599
724-846-5100

Gettysburg College
300 N Washington St, Gettysburg PA 17325-1483
Gail Sweezey, Director of Admissions
717-337-6100

Gratz College
7605 Old York Rd, Melrose Park PA 19027
Jill Sigman, Director of Admissions
215-635-7300 Fax: 215-635-7320
Website: www.gratzcollege.edu
E-mail: admissions@gratz.edu

Grove City College
100 Campus Dr, Grove City PA 16127-2104
Jeffrey C. Mincey, Director of Admissions
724-458-2100

Gwynedd-Mercy College
1325 Sumneytown Pike, Gwynedd Valley PA 19437
Dennis Murphy, V.P. Enrollment Management
800-DIAL-GMC

Haverford College
370 Lancaster Ave, Haverford PA 19041-1392
Jess Lord, Dean of Admission
610-896-1350 Fax: 610-896-1338
Website: www.haverford.edu
E-mail: admission@haverford.edu

Holy Family University
9801 Frankford Avenue, Philadelphia PA 19114
Lauren Campbell, Director of Admissions
215-637-3050 Fax: 215-281-1022
Website: www.holyfamily.edu
E-mail: admissions@holyfamily.edu

Holy Family University - Newtown
Newtown PA 18940
Karen Galardi, Executive Director
215-504-2000 Fax: 215-504-2050
Website: www.holyfamily.edu
E-mail: kgalardi@holyfamily.edu

Holy Family University - Woodhaven
1311 Bristol Pike, Bensalem PA 19020
Honour Moore, Associate VP for Extended Learning
215-637-7700 ext. 5008 Fax: 215-633-0558
Website: www.holyfamily.edu
E-mail: hmoore@holyfamily.edu

Immaculata University
Immaculata PA 19345
Women's College Office of Admissions
610-647-4400

Indiana University of Pennsylvania
Indiana PA 15705-0001
724-357-2100

ITT Technical Institute
760 Moore Rd, King of Prussia PA 19406
610-491-8004

Juniata College
1700 Moore St, Huntingdon PA 16652-2196
Michelle Bartol, Dean of Enrollment
877-JUNIATA Fax: 814-641-3100
Website: www.juniata.edu
E-mail: admissions@juniata.edu

King's College
133 N River St, Wilkes Barre PA 18711-0801
Michelle Lawrence-Schmude, Dean of Admission
570-208-5900 Fax: 570-208-5971
Website: www.kings.edu
E-mail: admissions@kings.edu

Kutztown University of Pennsylvania
Kutztown PA 19530
610-683-4000

Lafayette College
High St, Easton PA 18042
610-330-5000

Lake Erie College of Osteopathic Medicine
1858 W Grandview Blvd, Erie PA 16509-1025
Amy Rowe, Admissions Coordinator
814-866-6641 Fax: 814-864-8123
Website: www.lecom.edu
E-mail: admissions@lecom.edu

La Roche College
9000 Babcock Blvd, Pittsburgh PA 15237-5898
Thomas Hassett, Director of Admissions
412-536-1272

La Salle University
33 University Dr, Newtown PA 18940
215-579-7335

La Salle University
1900 W Olney Ave, Philadelphia PA 19141-1199
Robert Voss, Dean of Admissions
215-951-1500

Lebanon Valley College
101 N College Ave, Annville PA 17003-1400
William Brown, Dean of Admissions & Financial Aid
866-LVC-4ADM

Lehigh University
27 Memorial Dr West, Bethlehem PA 18015-3094
Eric Kaplan, Dean of Admissions
610-758-3100

Lincoln University
Lincoln University PA 19352
Michael C. Taylor, Director of Admissions
800-790-0191

Lock Haven University
Lock Haven PA 17745
James C. Reeser, Dean of Admissions
570-893-2027

Lycoming College
700 College Pl, Williamsport PA 17701-5192
570-321-4000

Mansfield University of Pennsylvania
Academy St, Mansfield PA 16933
570-662-4000

Marywood University
2300 Adams Ave, Scranton PA 18509-1598
570-348-6211

Mercyhurst College
501 E 38th St, Erie PA 16546-0001
800-825-1926

Messiah College
1 S College Ave, Grantham PA 17027
717-766-2511

Messiah College
2026 N Broad St, Philadelphia PA 19121-2305
215-769-2526

Millersville University of Pennsylvania
PO Box 1002, Millersville PA 17551-0302
717-872-3024

Moravian College
1200 Main St, Bethlehem PA 18018-6650
610-861-1300

MORAVIAN THEOLOGICAL SEMINARY

1200 Main St, Bethlehem PA 18018
Rev. Melissa Johnson, Director of Admissions
610-861-1516 Fax: 610-861-1569
Website: www.moravianseminary.edu
E-mail: seminary@moravian.edu

MOUNT ALOYSIUS COLLEGE
7373 Admiral Peary Hwy, Cresson PA 16630-1999
Frank C. Crouse Jr., Vice President for Enrollment Management
814-886-6383 or 888-823-2220 Fax: 814-886-6441
Website: www.mtaloy.edu
E-mail: admissions@mtaloy.edu

Muhlenberg College
2400 W Chew St, Allentown PA 18104-5586
610-821-3100

Neumann College
1 Neumann Dr, Aston PA 19014-1298
Dennis Murphy, Director of Admissions
610-459-0905 Fax: 610-558-5652
Website: www.neumann.edu
E-mail: neumann@neumann.edu

PENNSYLVANIA COLLEGE OF ART AND DESIGN
PO Box 59, Lancaster PA 17608-0059
Susan Matson, Director of Enrollment Management
717-396-7833 Fax: 717-396-1339
Website: www.pcad.edu
E-mail: admissions@pcad.edu

Pennsylvania College of Technology
1 College Ave, Williamsport PA 17701
570-326-3761

Pennsylvania State University
777 W Harrisburg Pike, Middletown PA 17057
717-948-6000

Pennsylvania State University
Broadhead Rd, Monaca PA 15061
724-773-3500

Pennsylvania State University
3550 7th St Rd, New Kensington PA 15068-1765
Patricia K. Brady, Director of Admissions
724-334-5466

Pennsylvania State University
201 Shields Bldg PO Box 300
University Park PA 16802-3000
814-865-4700

Pennsylvania State University
The Behrend College
5091 Station Rd, Erie PA 16563-0002
814-898-6000

Philadelphia Biblical University
200 Manor Ave, Langhorne PA 19047-2943
Josh Edwards, Contact
800-366-0049

Philadelphia University
4201 Henry Ave, Philadelphia PA 19144-5409
215-951-2700

Point Park University
201 Wood St, Pittsburgh PA 15222-1984
Philip Clarke, Associate Director of Admissions
412-392-3430

Reconstructionist Rabbinical College
1299 Church Rd, Wyncote PA 19095-1898
Rabbi Daniel Aronson, Dean of Admissions
215-576-0800

THE RESTAURANT SCHOOL AT WALNUT HILL COLLEGE
4207 Walnut St, Philadelphia PA 19104-5296
Karl D. Becker, Admissions Director
215-222-4200 ext. 3011 Fax: 215-222-4219
Website: www.walnuthillcollege.edu
E-mail: info@walnuthillcollege.edu

Robert Morris College
600 5th Ave, Pittsburgh PA 15219-3010
412-227-6800

Robert Morris University
6001 University Blvd, Coraopolis PA 15108
412-262-8200

Rosemont College
1400 Montgomery Ave, Rosemont PA 19010-1699
Ms. Rennie Andrews, Director of Admissions
610-526-2966

St. Francis University
PO Box 600, Loretto PA 15940-0600
814-472-3000

St. Joseph's University
5600 City Ave, Philadelphia PA 19131-1376
610-660-1000

St. Vincent College
300 Fraser Purchase Rd, Latrobe PA 15650-2690
724-539-9761

St. Vincent Seminary
300 Fraser Purchase Rd, Latrobe PA 15650
724-537-4592

Seton Hill University
Greensburg PA 15601-1599
Mary Kay Cooper, Director of Admissions and Adult Student Services
800-826-6234

Shippensburg University
1871 Old Main Dr, Shippensburg PA 17257-2299
717-477-7447

Slippery Rock University
14 Maltby Dr, Slippery Rock PA 16057-1326
724-738-9000

Strayer University
3600 Horizon Blvd Ste 100, Trevose PA 19053
215-953-5999

Susquehanna University
514 University Ave, Selinsgrove PA 17870-1164
570-374-0101

Swarthmore College
500 College Ave, Swarthmore PA 19081-1390
610-328-8000

Temple University
Broad St & Montgomery Ave, Philadelphia PA 19122
215-204-7000

Temple University
3307 N Broad St, Philadelphia PA 19140-5101
215-787-7000

Temple University Ambler
Ambler PA 19002
Michael Schlotterbeck, Contact
215-283-1252

Temple University Center City
1515 Market St, Philadelphia PA 19102
215-204-8822

Temple University Tyler School of Art
Beech and Penrose Aves, Elkins Park PA 19027
215-782-2875

Thiel College
75 College Ave, Greenville PA 16125-2181
724-589-2000

Thomas Jefferson University
111 S 11th St, Philadelphia PA 19107-4824
215-955-6000

University of Pennsylvania
3400 Spruce St, Philadelphia PA 19104-4274
215-898-5000

University of Pittsburgh
150 Finoli Dr, Greensburg PA 15601
Brandi S. Darr, Director of Admissions and Financial Aid
724-836-9880

University of Pittsburgh
4200 5th Ave, Pittsburgh PA 15260-3583
412-624-4141

University of Pittsburgh at Bradford
300 Campus Dr, Bradford PA 16701-2812
Alexander Nazemetz, Director of Admissions
814-362-7555

University of Pittsburgh at Johnstown
450 Schoolhouse Rd, Johnstown PA 15904-2990
814-269-7000

University of Pittsburgh at Titusville
504 E Main St #287, Titusville PA 16354-2010
814-827-4400

University of Scranton
800 Linden St, Scranton PA 18510-4501
570-941-7400

University of the Arts
320 S Broad St, Philadelphia PA 19102-4994
Susan Gandy, Director of Admissions
800-616-2787

University of the Sciences in Philadelphia
600 S 43rd St, Philadelphia PA 19104-4418
215-596-8800

Ursinus College
PO Box 1000, Collegeville PA 19426-1000
610-409-3000

Villanova University
800 E Lancaster Ave, Villanova PA 19085
610-519-4500

Washington & Jefferson College
60 S Lincoln St, Washington PA 15301-4801
Alton E. Newell, Vice President for Enrollment
724-223-6025 Fax: 724-223-6534
Website: www.washjeff.edu
E-mail: admission@washjeff.edu

Waynesburg College
51 W College St, Waynesburg PA 15370-1222
Robin L. Moore, Dean of Admissions
800-225-7393

West Chester University of Pennsylvania
S High St, West Chester PA 19383-0001
610-436-1000

Westminster College
New Wilmington PA 16172-0001
Doug Swartz, Director of Admissions
724-946-7100

Widener University
1 University Pl, Chester PA 19013-5792
Edwin Wright, Dean of Admissions
610-499-4000 Fax: 610-499-4676
Website: www.widener.edu
E-mail: admissions.office@widener.edu

Wilkes University
170 S Franklin St, Wilkes Barre PA 18766-0001
570-408-5000

York College of Pennsylvania
PO Box 15199, York PA 17405-7199
717-846-7788

RHODE ISLAND

Brown University
1 Prospect St, Providence RI 02912
401-863-1000

Bryant University
1150 Douglas Pike, Smithfield RI 02917-1287
401-232-6000

Johnson & Wales University
8 Abbott Park Pl, Providence RI 02903-3775
401-598-1000

New England Institute of Technology
2500 Post Rd, Warwick RI 02886-2244
Michael Kwiatkowski, Director of Admissions
401-739-5000 Fax: 401-738-5122
Website: www.neit.edu
E-mail: eflynn@neit.edu

Providence College
549 River Ave, Providence RI 02918-0002
401-865-1000

Rhode Island College
600 Mount Pleasant Ave, Providence RI 02908-1924
401-456-8000

Rhode Island School of Design
2 College St, Providence RI 02903-2717
401-454-6100

Roger Williams University
1 Old Ferry Rd, Bristol RI 02809-2921
Michelle Beauregard, Director of Freshman Admission
800-458-7144 ext. 3500

Roger Williams University
150 Washington St, Providence RI 02903-3300
401-274-2200

Salve Regina University
100 Ochre Point Ave, Newport RI 02840-4192
401-847-6650

University of Rhode Island
Kingston RI 02881
401-874-1000

ZION BIBLE COLLEGE
27 Middle Hwy, Barrington RI 02806-1296
Director of Recruiting
401-246-0900 Fax: 401-246-0906
Website: www.zbc.edu
E-mail: recruiting@zbc.edu

SOUTH CAROLINA

Allen University
1530 Harden St, Columbia SC 29204-1085
803-376-5701

Anderson College
316 Boulevard, Anderson SC 29621-4035
864-231-2000

Benedict College
1600 Harden St, Columbia SC 29204-1086
Phyllis L. Thompson, Director of Admissions
803-253-5143

BOB JONES UNIVERSITY
1700 Wade Hampton Blvd
Greenville SC 29614-0001
Stephen Jones, President
David Christ, Director of Admissions
800-BJ-AND-ME Fax: 800-2-FAX-BJU
Website: www.bju.edu
E-mail: admissions@bju.edu

Established 1927. Private. Coed. Tuition: $9,180. Room and board: $4,980. Enrollment: 2,806 boarding, 1,472 day. Faculty: 242 full-time, 148 part-time. Degrees: AAA, AAS, BA, BFA, BMus, BS, BSN, EdS, MA, MAT, MBA, MDiv, MEd, MME, MMin, MMus, MS, DMin, SMin, DpasTh, PhD, EdD. Library: 303,400 volumes. 73 buildings on 225 acres. Gym. Pool. 2 & 3 year trade programs available. Unusual Films produces outstanding Christian films. University Press produces Christian and educational texts.

Charleston Southern University
PO Box 118087, Charleston SC 29423-8087
Cheryl Burton, Director of Admissions
800-947-7474

Claflin University
700 College Ave, Orangeburg SC 29115-4477
803-535-5000

Clemson University
105 Sikes Hall, Clemson SC 29634
864-656-2287

Coastal Carolina University
PO Box 261954, Conway SC 29528-6054
Office of Admissions
800-277-7000 Fax: 843-349-2127
Website: www.coastal.edu
E-mail: admissions@coastal.edu

Coker College
300 E College Ave, Hartsville SC 29550-3797
843-383-8000

College of Charleston
66 George St, Charleston SC 29424-1407
Suzette Stille, Admissions
843-953-5670

Columbia International University
PO Box 3122, Columbia SC 29230-3122
Michelle MacGregor, Director of University Admissions
800-777-2227 Fax: 803-786-4209
Website: www.ciu.edu
E-mail: yesciu@ciu.edu
See listing under "Theological Studies & Religious Vocations"

Erskine College & Seminary
PO Box 176, Due West SC 29639
Bart Walker, Director of Admissions
864-379-8838 Fax: 864-379-3048
Website: www.erskine.edu
E-mail: admissions@erskine.edu

Francis Marion University
PO Box 100547, Florence SC 29501-0547
843-661-1362

Furman University
3300 Poinsett Hwy, Greenville SC 29613-0002
864-294-2000

Greenville Technical College
PO Box 5616, Greenville SC 29606-5616
Carolyn Watkins, Dean of Admissions
800-723-0673 (US) or 800-922-1183 (SC)
Website: www.greenvilletech.com

Lander University
320 Stanley Ave, Greenwood SC 29649-2099
Jonathan Reece, Director of Admissions
888-4-LANDER

Limestone College
1115 College Dr, Gaffney SC 29340-3799
Chris Phenicie, V.P. for Enrollment
864-489-7151 Fax: 864-488-8206
Website: www.limestone.edu
E-mail: cphenicie@limestone.edu

Morris College
100 W College St, Sumter SC 29150-3599
803-934-3200

Newberry College
2100 College St, Newberry SC 29108-2197
800-845-4955

NORTH GREENVILLE UNIVERSITY
PO Box 1892, Tigerville SC 29688-1892
Charles "Buddy" Freeman, Exec Vice President for Admissions & Financial Planning
864-977-7001 Fax: 864-977-7177
Website: www.ngu.edu
E-mail: bfreeman@ngu.edu

Established 1892. Private. Coed. Accreditation: SACS. Tuition: $11,180. Room and Board: $6,420. Fees: $200. Enrollment: 1,649 full-time, 195 part-time. Faculty: 73 full-time, 74 part-time. Student-faculty ratio: 18:1. Majors: Accounting, Biology, Business Administration, Christian Studies, Church Music, Elementary/Early Childhood Education, Elementary Education, English, History/Political Science, Intercultural Studies (Missions), Interdisciplinary Studies, International Business, Mass Communications, Mathematics, Music Composition, Music Education, Music Performance, Outdoor Leadership, Psychology, Social Studies, Sports Management, Youth Ministry. Minors: Accounting, American Studies, Art, Biology, Broadcasting, Business Administration, Christian Studies, Computer Science, Counseling/Psychology, Economics, Education, English, History, International Business, Journalism, Management, Marketing, Mass Communications, Music, Natural Science, Spanish, Sport Management, Theatre, Visual Arts, Youth Ministry. Associates Degrees: Arts, Fine Arts, Science.

Presbyterian College
503 S Broad St, Clinton SC 29325
Richard Dana Paul, Dean of Admissions
800-476-7272

South Carolina State University
PO Box 7127, Orangeburg SC 29117-0001
Lillian M. Adderson, Director of Admissions
803-536-7185

SOUTHERN METHODIST COLLEGE
PO Box 1027, Orangeburg SC 29116-1027
Gary Briden, President
803-534-7826 Fax: 803-534-7827
Website: www.smcollege.edu
E-mail: smcinfo@smcollege.edu

Southern Wesleyan University
PO Box 1020, Central SC 29630-1020
864-644-5000

South University
9 Science Court, Columbia SC 29203
Trish Wade, Contact
803-799-9082 Fax: 803-799-9038
Website: www.southuniversity.edu
E-mail: twade@southuniversity.edu

Strayer University
200 Center Point Cir # 300, Columbia SC 29210
803-750-2500

University of South Carolina
471 University Pkwy, Aiken SC 29801
803-648-6851

University of South Carolina
Columbia SC 29208-0001
803-777-7700

University of South Carolina Beaufort
801 Carteret St, Beaufort SC 29902-4601
Anita M. Folsom, Director of Admissions
843-521-4101

UNIVERSITY OF SOUTH CAROLINA - UPSTATE
800 University Way, Spartanburg SC 29303-4932
Donette Stewart, Assistant VC for Enrollment Services
864-503-5246 Fax: 864-503-5727
Website: www.uscupstate.edu
E-mail: dstewart@uscupstate.edu

Public. Coed. Accredited by the Commission on Colleges of the Southern Association of Colleges and Schools. Tuition: $7,437. Room & board: $3,200 - $4,500. Fees: $175. Enrollment: 4,600 full-time, 681 part-time. Faculty: 336. Student-faculty ratio: 18:1. Degrees offered: Bachelor of Arts, Bachelor of Sciences, Master's of Education. Library: 215,000+ volumes. 12 buildings on 300 acres. Small class size, Metropolitan mission, all professional schools are Nationally Accredited, Scholarships available, Modern expanding campus facilities, NCAA Division I Athletics.

Voorhees College
Voorhees Rd, Denmark SC 29042
803-793-3351

Winthrop University
701 W Oakland Ave, Rock Hill SC 29733-0001
803-323-2211

W.L. Bonner Bible College
4430 Argent Ct, Columbia SC 29203
803-754-3950

Wofford College
429 N Church St, Spartanburg SC 29303-3663
864-597-4000

SOUTH DAKOTA

Augustana College
29th and South Smt, Sioux Falls SD 57197-0001
605-274-0770

Black Hills State University
1200 University St, Spearfish SD 57799-0002
605-642-6011

Dakota State University
820 N Washington Ave, Madison SD 57042-1799
605-256-5112

Dakota Wesleyan University
1200 W University Ave, Mitchell SD 57301
605-995-2600

Mt. Marty College
1105 W 8th St, Yankton SD 57078-3724
605-668-1514

National American University
1270 Ryan St - 28 MSS/DPE, Ellsworth AFB SD 57706
605-923-5856

NATIONAL AMERICAN UNIVERSITY
321 Kansas City St, Rapid City SD 57701-3692
Angela G. Beck, Director of Enrollment Management
605-394-4800 Fax: 605-394-4871
Website: www.rapid.national.edu
E-mail: rcadmissions@national.edu

National American University
2801 S Kiwanis Ave Ste 100
Sioux Falls SD 57105-4293
605-334-5430

Northern State University
1200 S Jay St, Aberdeen SD 57401-7198
605-626-3011

Oglala Lakota College
PO Box 490, Kyle SD 57752-0490
605-455-2321

Presentation College
1500 N Main St, Aberdeen SD 57401-1280
JoEllen Lindner, VP for Enrollment
605-229-8492 Fax: 605-229-8425
Website: www.presentation.edu
E-mail: admit@presentation.edu

Sinte Gleska University
PO Box 105, Mission SD 57555-0105
605-856-5880

South Dakota School of Mines and Technology
501 E Saint Joseph St, Rapid City SD 57701-3901
605-394-2511

South Dakota State University
PO Box 2201, Brookings SD 57007-0001
605-688-4151

University of Sioux Falls
1101 W 22nd St, Sioux Falls SD 57105-1699
605-331-5000

University of South Dakota
414 E Clark St, Vermillion SD 57069-2307
605-677-5011

TENNESSEE

American Baptist College
1800 Baptist World Center Dr
Nashville TN 37207-4994
Marcella Lockhart, Executive Asst. for Administration
615-256-1463

AQUINAS COLLEGE
4210 Harding Rd, Nashville TN 37205
Diane C. LeJeune, Director of Admissions
615-297-7545 ext. 460 Fax: 615-279-3893
Website: www.aquinascollege.edu
E-mail: lejeuned@aquinascollege.edu

Austin Peay State University
601 College St, Clarksville TN 37044-0002
931-221-7011 Fax: 931-221-6168
Website: www.apsu.edu
E-mail: admissions@apsu.edu

Baptist Memorial College of Health Science
1003 Monroe Ave, Memphis TN 38104-3104
Office of Admissions
866-575-2247

Belmont University
1900 Belmont Blvd, Nashville TN 37212-3757
615-460-6000

Bethel College
325 Cherry Ave, McKenzie TN 38201-1735
Tina L. Hodges, Director of Admissions
731-352-4030

BLAIR SCHOOL OF MUSIC OF VANDERBILT UNIVERSITY
2400 Blakemore Ave, Nashville TN 37212-3406
Dwayne Sagen, Assistant Dean for Admissions
615-322-7679 Fax: 615-343-0324
Website: www.vanderbilt.edu
E-mail: dwayne.p.sagen@vanderbilt.edu

Bryan College
PO Box 7000, Dayton TN 37321-7000
423-775-2041

Carson-Newman College
1646 Russell Ave, Jefferson City TN 37760
865-471-4000

Christian Brothers University
650 E Parkway S, Memphis TN 38104-5568
901-321-3000

CRICHTON COLLEGE
255 N Highland St, Memphis TN 38111-4745
Shelly Luttrell, Dean of Admissions
901-320-9797 Fax: 901-320-9791
Website: www.crichton.edu
E-mail: admissions@crichton.edu

Accreditation: SACS. Tuition: $9,960. Room & board: $5,380.20. Fees: $18 per credit hour. Enrollment: 1,080. Student-faculty ratio: 13:1. Degrees: Pre-Med, Pre-Law, Pre-Nursing, Sciences, Psychology, Business, Bible & Theology. Nondenominational, Christ centered education in urban setting.

Cumberland University
1 Cumberland Sq, Lebanon TN 37087-3408
Jason Brewer, Director of Admissions
615-444-2562

East Tennessee State University
PO Box 70731, Johnson City TN 37614-1326
Dr. Linda Doran, Vice Provost

Fisk University
1000 17th Ave N, Nashville TN 37208-3051
William Carter, Director of Admissions
615-329-8766

Freed-Hardeman University
158 E Main St, Henderson TN 38340-2398
731-989-6000

Free Will Baptist Bible College
3606 W End Ave, Nashville TN 37205
Ryan Lewis, Director of Recruitment
800-76-FWBBC Fax: 615-269-6028
Website: www.fwbbc.edu
E-mail: recruit@fwbbc.edu

INTERNATIONAL ACADEMY OF DESIGN & TECHNOLOGY
1 Bridgestone Park, Nashville TN 37214
Richard D. Wechner, President
615-232-7384 Fax: 615-391-0728
Website: www.iadtnashville.com
E-mail: rwechner@iadtnashville.com

ITT Technical Institute
2845 Elm Hill Pike, Nashville TN 37214-3717
James Royster, Director of Recruitment
615-889-8700

King College
1350 King College Rd, Bristol TN 37620-2635
423-968-1187

Lambuth University
705 Lambuth Blvd, Jackson TN 38301-5296
731-425-2500

Lane College
545 Lane Ave, Jackson TN 38301-4598
731-426-7500

Lee University
PO Box 3450, Cleveland TN 37320-3450
Dale W. Goff, V.P. Institutional Advancement
800-533-9930

Le Moyne-Owen College
807 Walker Ave, Memphis TN 38126-6595
901-774-9090

Lincoln Memorial University
PO Box 2012, Harrogate TN 37752
423-869-3611

Lipscomb University
3901 Granny White Pike, Nashville TN 37204-3951
Ricky Holaway, Director of Admissions
800-333-4358 ext. 1776 Fax: 615-269-1804
Website: www.lipscomb.edu
E-mail: admissions@lipscomb.edu

Maryville College
502 E Lamar Alexander Pkwy
Maryville TN 37804-5919
865-981-8000

Memphis College of Art
1930 Poplar Ave, Memphis TN 38104-2764
901-272-5100

Middle Tennessee State University
1301 E Main St, Murfreesboro TN 37132-0001
615-898-2300

Milligan College
1 Milligan College, Milligan College TN 37682
423-461-8700

NORTH TENNESSEE BIBLE INSTITUTE AND SEMINARY
PO Box 3797, Clarksville TN 37043-3797
Dr. William Corley, Chancellor
931-552-1510 Fax: 931-552-1464
Website: www.ntbis.com
E-mail: drwhc@ntbis.com

O'More College of Design
423 S Margin St, Franklin TN 37064-2816
Dr. K. Mark Hilliard, President
Chris Lee, Director of Enrollment Management
615-794-4254 Fax: 615-790-1662
Website: www.omorecollege.edu
E-mail: clee@omorecollege.edu

Peabody College of Vanderbilt University
Box 327, Nashville TN 37203
615-322-8410

Rhodes College
2000 N Parkway, Memphis TN 38112-1624
901-843-3000

South College
3904 Lonas Dr, Knoxville TN 37909
Walter Hosea, Director of Admissions
865-251-1800

Southern Adventist University
PO Box 370, Collegedale TN 37315-0370
423-238-2111

Strayer University
2620 Thousand Oaks Blvd, Memphis TN 38118-2427
901-369-0835

Strayer University
6211 Shelby Oaks Dr, Memphis TN 38134
901-383-6750

Strayer University
30 Rachel Dr Ste 200, Nashville TN 37214
615-871-2260

Tennessee State University
3500 John A Merritt Blvd, Nashville TN 37209-1561
John Cade, Dean of Admissions & Records
615-963-5101 Fax: 615-963-2930
Website: www.tnstate.edu
E-mail: jcade@tnstate.edu

Tennessee Technological University
PO Box 5006, Cookeville TN 38505-0001
931-372-3101

Tennessee Temple University
1815 Union Ave, Chattanooga TN 37404-3587
423-493-4100

Tennessee Wesleyan College
PO Box 40, Athens TN 37371-0040
423-745-7504

Trevecca Nazarene University
333 Murfreesboro Rd, Nashville TN 37210-2834
615-248-1200

Tusculum College
PO Box 5051, Greeneville TN 37743
Melissa Ripley, Associate Director of Admissions
800-729-0256

Union University
1050 Union University Dr, Jackson TN 38305
731-668-1818

University of Memphis
Memphis TN 38152-0001
901-678-2000

University of Tennessee
615 McCallie Ave, Chattanooga TN 37403-2504
Yancy Freeman, Director of Admissions
423-425-4111 Fax: 423-425-4157
Website: www.utc.edu
E-mail: Yancy-Freeman@utc.edu

University of Tennessee
527 Andy Holt Tower, Knoxville TN 37996-0001
865-974-1000

University of Tennessee
Martin TN 38238-0001
731-587-7000

University of Tennessee Health Science Center
800 Madison Ave, Memphis TN 38163-0002
901-448-5500

University of the South
735 University Ave, Sewanee TN 37383-1000
931-598-1000

Vanderbilt University
W End Ave, Nashville TN 37240-0001
615-322-7311

Watkins College of Art and Design
and The Watkins Film School
2298 Metrocenter Blvd, Nashville TN 37228-1306
615-383-4848 or 866-887-6395 Fax: 615-383-4849
Website: www.watkins.edu
E-mail: admissions@watkins.edu

Williamson Christian College
200 Seaboard Ln, Franklin TN 37067
615-771-7066

TEXAS

Abilene Christian University
ACU Box 29000, Abilene TX 79699-0001
325-674-2000 Fax: 325-674-2202
Website: www.acu.edu
E-mail: info@admissions.acu.edu

Amberton University
1700 Eastgate Dr, Garland TX 75041-5511
972-279-6511

Angelo State University
ASU Station 11014, San Angelo TX 76909
Bonnie Stennett, Coordinator of Recruiting
800-946-8627

Argosy University/Dallas
8080 Park Ln Ste 400, Dallas TX 75231
214-890-9900

Arlington Baptist College
3001 W Division St, Arlington TX 76012-3425
Janie Taylor, Director of Admissions
817-461-8741 Fax: 817-274-1138
Website: www.abconline.edu
E-mail: jhall@abconline.org

Austin College
900 N Grand Ave, Sherman TX 75090-4400
903-813-2000

Austin Graduate School of Theology
1909 University Ave, Austin TX 78705-5610
Mark Martin, Registrar
512-476-2772

BAPTIST UNIVERSITY OF THE AMERICAS
8019 S Panam Expy, San Antonio TX 78224-1336
Mary Ranjel, Director of Admissions
800-721-1396 Fax: 210-924-2701
Website: www.bua.edu
E-mail: mranjel@bua.edu

Baylor University
Po Box 97008, Waco TX 76798-7008
254-710-1011

Brazosport College
500 College Dr, Lake Jackson TX 77566-3199
979-230-3000

COLLEGE OF SAINT THOMAS MORE
3020 Lubbock Ave, Fort Worth TX 76109
Maria Stromberg, Registrar
817-923-8459 Fax: 817-924-3206
Website: www.cstm.edu
E-mail: pflores@cstm.edu

Concordia University
3400 N I H 35, Austin TX 78705-2702
512-486-2000

The Criswell College
4010 Gaston Ave, Dallas TX 75246-1537
Tommy Weir, VP Institutional Advancement
800-899-0012

Dallas Baptist University
3000 Mountain Creek Pkwy, Dallas TX 75211-9209
214-333-7100

Dallas Christian College
2700 Christian Pkwy, Dallas TX 75234-7299
800-688-1029

East Texas Baptist University
1209 N Grove St, Marshall TX 75670-1498
903-935-7963

Hardin-Simmons University
2200 Hickory St, Abilene TX 79601-2345
325-670-1000

Houston Baptist University
7502 Fondren Rd, Houston TX 77074-3298
David Melton, Director of Admissions
281-649-3000

Howard Payne University
1000 Fisk Ave, Brownwood TX 76801-2715
325-646-2502

Huston-Tillotson University
900 Chicon St, Austin TX 78702-9997
512-505-3000

Jarvis Christian College
PO Box 1470, Hawkins TX 75765-1470
903-769-5700

Lamar University
PO Box 10009, Beaumont TX 77710-0009
409-880-8888

Le Tourneau University
PO Box 7001, Longview TX 75607-7001
903-233-3000

Lubbock Christian University
5601 19th St, Lubbock TX 79407-2099
Stan Scott, Director of Admissions
806-796-8800 Fax: 806-720-7162
Website: www.lcu.edu
E-mail: stan.scott@lcu.edu

McMurry University
14th and Sayles, Abilene TX 79697-0001
325-793-3800

Midwestern State University
3410 Taft Blvd, Wichita Falls TX 76308-2096
940-397-4000

Northwood University
1114 W FM 1382, Cedar Hill TX 75104-1204
Sylvia Correa, Director of Admissions
800-927-WOOD Fax: 972-291-3824
Website: www.northwood.edu
E-mail: ray@northwood.edu

Our Lady of the Lake University
411 SW 24th St, San Antonio TX 78207-4666
Mary Kay Cooper, Dean of Enrollment
210-434-6711

Paul Quinn College
3837 Simpson Stuart Rd, Dallas TX 75241-4398
214-376-1000

Prairie View A&M University
PO Box 519, Prairie View TX 77446
936-857-3311

Rice University
6100 Main St, Houston TX 77005-1892
800-527-6957

Rio Grande Bible Institute
4300 S US Highway 281, Edinburg TX 78539-9699
956-380-8100

St. Edward's University
3001 S Congress Ave, Austin TX 78704-6489
512-448-8400

St. Mary's University of San Antonio
1 Camino Santa Maria St
San Antonio TX 78228-8500
210-436-3011

Sam Houston State University
PO Box 2026, Huntsville TX 77341
936-294-1111

Schreiner University
2100 Memorial Blvd, Kerrville TX 78028-5697
Todd D. Brown, Director of Admissions
800-343-4919

Southern Methodist University
PO Box 750181, Dallas TX 75275-0181
Ron Moss, Dean of Admission
214-768-2058

Southwestern Adventist University
PO Box 567, Keene TX 76059-0567
800-433-2240

Southwestern Assemblies of God University
1200 Sycamore St, Waxahachie TX 75165-2397
Pat Thompson, Admissions Counselor
972-937-4010

Southwestern Baptist Theological Seminary
PO Box 22000, Fort Worth TX 76122
817-923-1921

Southwestern Christian College
PO Box 10, Terrell TX 75160-9002
972-524-3341

Southwestern University
PO Box 740, Georgetown TX 78627
512-863-6511

Stephen F. Austin State University
PO Box 6078, Nacogdoches TX 75962-0001
936-468-2011

Sul Ross State University
Alpine TX 79832-0001
432-837-8032

Tarleton State University
PO Box T0030, Stephenville TX 76402
254-968-9000

Texas A&M at Galveston
PO Box 1675, Galveston TX 77553-1675
409-740-4400

Texas A&M International University
5201 University Blvd, Laredo TX 78041
956-326-2000

Texas A&M University
College Station TX 77843-0001
979-845-3211

Texas A&M University
700 University Blvd, Kingsville TX 78363
361-593-2111

Texas A&M University - Commerce
PO Box 3011, Commerce TX 75429
903-886-5102

Texas A&M University - Corpus Christi
6300 Ocean Dr, Corpus Christi TX 78412-5503
361-825-5700

Texas A&M University - Texarkana
PO Box 5518, Texarkana TX 75505-5518
903-223-3000

TEXAS CHIROPRACTIC COLLEGE
5912 Spencer Hwy, Pasadena TX 77505-1699
Sandra Hughes, D.C.; Director of Admission
281-487-1170 Fax: 281-991-4871
Website: www.txchiro.edu
E-mail: shughes@txchiro.edu

Texas Christian University
TCU Box 297013, Fort Worth TX 76129
817-257-7000

Texas College
2404 N Grand Ave, Tyler TX 75702
903-593-8311

Texas Lutheran University
1000 W Court St, Seguin TX 78155-5978
830-372-8000

Texas Southern University
3100 Cleburne St, Houston TX 77004-4583
713-313-7011

Texas State University - San Marcos
601 University Dr, San Marcos TX 78666-4685
512-245-2111

Texas Tech University
1 Texas Tech University, Lubbock TX 79409-0001
806-742-2011

Texas Tech University Health Science Center
Lubbock TX 79430
806-743-3111

Texas Wesleyan University
1201 Wesleyan St, Fort Worth TX 76105-1536
Stephanie Boatner, Director of Freshman Admission
800-580-8980

Trinity University
715 Stadium Dr, San Antonio TX 78212-7200
210-999-7011

University of Dallas
1845 E Northgate Dr, Irving TX 75062-4736
Curt Eley, Dean
972-721-5000 Fax: 972-721-5017
Website: www.udallas.edu
E-mail: ugadmis@udallas.edu

University of Houston
122 E Cullen Bldg, Houston TX 77204-2023
Office of Admission
713-743-9595
Website: www.uh.edu
E-mail: admissions@uh.edu

University of Houston-Clear Lake
2700 Bay Area Blvd, Houston TX 77058-1025
281-283-2500

University of Houston-Downtown
1 Main St, Houston TX 77002-1014
713-221-8000

University of Houston-Victoria
3007 N Ben Wilson St, Victoria TX 77901
361-570-4848

University of Mary Hardin-Baylor
UMHB Station Box 8001, Belton TX 76513
254-295-8642

University of North Texas
PO Box 305309, Denton TX 76203-5309
940-565-2000

University of St. Thomas
3800 Montrose Blvd, Houston TX 77006-4626
Eduardo Prieto, Director of Admissions
713-522-7911

University of Texas at Arlington
Box 19111, Arlington TX 76019-0111
Hans Gatterdam, Director of Admission
817-272-6287 Fax: 817-272-3435
Website: www.uta.edu
E-mail: admissions@uta.edu

University of Texas at Austin
0 the Univ of Texas, Austin TX 78712
512-471-3434

University of Texas at Brownsville
80 Fort Brown, Brownsville TX 78520
956-544-8200

University of Texas at Dallas
PO Box 830688, Richardson TX 75083-0688
972-690-2111

University of Texas at El Paso
500 W University Ave, El Paso TX 79968-8900
915-747-5000

University of Texas at San Antonio
6900 N Loop 1604 W, San Antonio TX 78249-1130
210-458-4011

University of Texas at Tyler
3900 University Blvd, Tyler TX 75701-6622
Jim Hutto, Dean Enrollment Management
800-888-9537

University of Texas Health Science Center
PO Box 20036, Houston TX 77225-0036
713-500-4472

University of Texas Health Science Center
7703 Floyd Curl Dr, San Antonio TX 78229
210-567-7000

UNIVERSITY OF TEXAS-HOUSTON
6901 Bertner Ave, Houston TX 77030-3901
William D. Stewart, Coordinator of Admissions
713-500-2104 Fax: 713-500-2107
Website: http://son.uth.tmc.edu
E-mail: william.stewart@uth.tmc.edu

University of Texas of the Permian Basin
4901 E University Blvd, Odessa TX 79762-8122
432-552-2020

University of Texas-Pan American
1201 W University Dr, Edinburg TX 78539-2909
956-381-2011

University of Texas Southwestern Medical Center
5323 Harry Hines Blvd, Dallas TX 75390-7208
214-648-3111

University of the Incarnate Word
4301 Broadway St, San Antonio TX 78209-6318
210-829-6000

Wayland Baptist University
1900 W 7th St, Plainview TX 79072-6998
806-296-5521

West Texas A & M University
WTAMU Box 907, Canyon TX 79016-0001
806-651-2000

Wiley College
711 Wiley Ave, Marshall TX 75670-5199
903-927-3300

UTAH

Brigham Young University
Provo UT 84602-0001
801-378-5000

ITT TECHNICAL INSTITUTE
920 Levoy Dr, Murray UT 84123-2500
Gary Wood, Director of Recruitment
801-263-3313 Fax: 801-263-3497
Website: www.itt-tech.edu
E-mail: gwood@itt-tech.edu

Southern Utah University
351 W Center St, Cedar City UT 84720-2470
D. Mark Barton, Asst. VP Student Services
435-586-7715

Stevens Henager College
PO Box 9428, Ogden UT 84409-0428
Cindy Williams, Director of Admissions
801-394-7791 Fax: 801-621-0866
Website: www.stevenshenager.edu
E-mail: shcogden@yahoo.com

University of Utah
1460 E 201 S, Salt Lake City UT 84112
801-581-7200

Utah State University
Logan UT 84322-0001
435-797-1000

Weber State University
1001 University Cir, Ogden UT 84408
801-626-6000

Westminster College
1840 S 1300 E, Salt Lake City UT 84105-3617
801-832-2200

VERMONT

Bennington College
One College Drive, Bennington VT 05201
Ken Himmelman, Dean of Admissions & Financial Aid
800-833-6845

Castleton State College
Castleton VT 05735
William Allen Jr., Dean of Enrollment
800-639-8521

Champlain College
PO Box 670, Burlington VT 05402-0670
802-860-2727

College of St. Joseph
71 Clement Rd, Rutland VT 05701-3899
802-773-5900

Goddard College
121 Pitkin Rd, Plainfield VT 05667
802-454-8311

Green Mountain College
1 College Cir, Poultney VT 05764-1199
Sandra Bartholomew, Ph.D., Dean of Enrollment Management
802-287-8000 Fax: 802-287-8099
Website: www.greenmtn.edu
E-mail: bartholomews@greenmtn.edu

Johnson State College
337 College Hill, Johnson VT 05656
802-635-2356

Lyndon State College
PO Box 919, Lyndonville VT 05851
802-626-6200

Marlboro College
PO Box A, Marlboro VT 05344
802-257-4333

Middlebury College
Middlebury VT 05753-6200
802-443-5000

New England Culinary Institute
5 Franklin St, Essex VT 05452
Sherri Gilmore, Director of Admissions
877-223-6324 Fax: 802-225-3280
Website: www.neci.edu
E-mail: Admissions@neci.edu
See listing under "Career Schools"

New England Culinary Institute
56 College St, Montpelier VT 05602
Sherri Gilmore, Director of Admissions
877-223-6324 Fax: 802-225-3280
Website: www.neci.edu
E-mail: Admissions@neci.edu
See listing under "Career Schools"

NORWICH UNIVERSITY
158 Harmon Dr, Northfield VT 05663
Shelby Wallace, Director of Admissions
LTC Skip Davison, Director of Recuitment
800-468-6679 Fax: 802-485-2032
Website: www.norwich.edu
E-mail: nuadm@norwich.edu

Established 1819. Nations first private Military College. Accreditation: NEASC.

Student Body: Coed. 1,100 Cadets, 450 residential students, 375 commuter day students.

Tuition: $21,696. Exceptional opportunities for academic, leadership and merit scholarships.

Student Housing: Room and board: $7,964. Nine on-campus dormitories with off-campus housing available in the local community.

Curriculum: 30 Academic majors with specialized programs in Architecture, Business, Computer Science, Information Assurance, Engineering, Nursing, Math and Science. Online Masters programs offered in Business Administration, Civil Engineering, Diplomacy, Electrical Engineering, Justice Administration, Information Assurance, Military History, Nursing, Public Administration, Organizational Leadership, and Education.

Admission requirements include application, $35 fee, academic record, SAT/ACT scores, personal essay, letters of recommendation and extracurricular activities. Those applying for the Corps of Cadets must meet physical standards. TOEFL and declaration of finances for international students required. Rolling admissions.

Faculty: 144 full-time, 104 part-time. ROTC: Army, Navy, Air Force and Marine Corps.

Facilities: 42 buildings on 1,200 acres. Library: 300,000+ volumes. 4 athletic facilities. Ice Hockey Arena, Student Lounge, Nautilus and Weight Rooms, Indoor Swimming Pool, and Computer Labs in all teaching facilities, dorms are wired.

Environment: Norwich is located in the middle of ski-country in Vermont. Stowe, Sugarbush and Killington ski resorts are located within an hour's drive. Northfield is 10-miles south of the state capital of Montpelier. Burlington International Airport is an hour drive. Boston and Montreal are a 3-hour drive from campus.

Saint Michael's College
One Winooski Park, Colchester VT 05439-0001
Jacqueline Murphy, Director
802-654-3000

Southern Vermont College
982 Mansion Dr, Bennington VT 05201-6002
Joel Wincowski, Director of Admissions
800-378-2782 Fax: 802-447-4695
Website: www.svc.edu
E-mail: admis@svc.edu

University of Vermont
194 S Prospect St, Burlington VT 05401-3518
802-656-3131

Woodbury College
660 Elm St, Montpelier VT 05602-4017
Denise MacMartin, Director of Admissions
800-639-6039 Fax: 802-229-2141
Website: www.woodbury-college.edu
E-mail: admiss@woodbury-college.edu

VIRGINIA

American Military University
10110 Battleview Pkwy Ste 200, Manassas VA 20109
703-330-5398

APPALACHIAN SCHOOL OF LAW
PO Box 2825, Grundy VA 24614-1825
Nancy Pruitt, Director of Student Services
800-895-7411 Fax: 276-935-8261
Website: www.asl.edu
E-mail: npruitt@asl.edu

The Art Institute of Washington
1820 N Fort Myer Dr, Arlington VA 22209
Larry McHugh, Director of Admissions
703-358-9550

Averett University
420 W Main St, Danville VA 24541-3692
434-791-5600

Bluefield College
3000 College Dr, Bluefield VA 24605-1799
276-326-3682

Bridgewater College
402 E College St, Bridgewater VA 22812-1599
540-828-8000

Catholic Distance University
120 E Colonial Hwy, Hamilton VA 20158-9012
Marianne Evans Mount, Executive VP
888-254-4238 Fax: 540-338-4788
Website: www.cdu.edu
E-mail: tcashen@cdu.edu

Christendom College
134 Christendom Dr, Front Royal VA 22630
540-636-2900

Christopher Newport University
1 University Pl, Newport News VA 23606
757-594-7000

College of William and Mary
PO Box 1346, Gloucester Point VA 23062
804-642-7000

College of William and Mary
PO Box 8795, Williamsburg VA 23187-8795
757-221-4000

Eastern Mennonite University
1200 Park Rd, Harrisonburg VA 22802-2404
540-432-4000

Emory & Henry College
PO Box 947, Emory VA 24327-0947
276-944-4121

Ferrum College
PO Box 1000, Ferrum VA 24088-9001
Gilda Q. Woods, Director of Admissions
800-868-9797

George Mason University
4400 University Dr, Fairfax VA 22030-4444
Eddie Tallent, Director of Admissions
703-993-2400

Gibbs College - Northern Virginia
1980 Gallows Rd, Vienna VA 22182-3913
Everson Travers, Director of Admissions
703-556-8888 Fax: 703-556-0953
Website: www.gibbsva.edu
E-mail: etravers@gibbsva.edu

Graham Bible College
PO Box 1630, Bristol VA 24203-1630
Dr. Philip R. Blevins, President
423-968-4201

Hampton University
Hampton VA 23669
757-727-5000

James Madison University
800 S Main St, Harrisonburg VA 22807-0002
540-568-6211

Jefferson College of Health Sciences
Formerly Community Hospital
PO Box 13186, Roanoke VA 24031-3186
Judith McKeon, Director of Admissions
540-985-8483

Liberty University
PO Box 20000, Lynchburg VA 24506-8001
804-582-2000

Longwood University
201 High St, Farmville VA 23909-1801
804-395-2000

Lynchburg College
1501 Lakeside Dr, Lynchburg VA 24501-3199
804-544-8100

Marymount University
2807 N Glebe Rd, Arlington VA 22207-4299
Michael Canfield, Director of Admissions
800-548-7638 Fax: 703-522-0348
Website: www.marymount.edu
E-mail: admissions@marymount.edu

Norfolk State University
700 Park Ave, Norfolk VA 23504
Michelle Marable, Director of Admissions
757-823-8600

Old Dominion University
1 Old Dominion University, Norfolk VA 23529-1000
757-683-3000

PATRICK HENRY COLLEGE
1 Patrick Henry Cir, Purcellville VA 20132
Rebekah Knable, Director of Admissions
888-338-1776 Fax: 540-338-9808
Website: www.phc.edu
E-mail: admissions@phc.edu

Radford University
PO Box 6903, Radford VA 24142
David W. Kraus, Director of Admissions
800-890-4265 Fax: 540-831-5038
Website: www.radford.edu
E-mail: ruadmiss@radford.edu

Randolph College
2500 Rivermont Ave, Lynchburg VA 24503
Patricia LeDonne, Director of Admissions
434-947-8100 Fax: 434-947-8996
Website: www.randolphcollege.edu
E-mail: admissions@randolphcollege.edu

Randolph-Macon College
PO Box 5005, Ashland VA 23005-5505
804-752-7200

Roanoke College
221 College Ln, Salem VA 24153-3794
James A. Pennix, Director of Admissions
540-375-2500 Fax: 540-375-2267
Website: www.roanoke.edu
E-mail: pennix@roanoke.edu

St. Paul's College
406 Windsor Ave, Lawrenceville VA 23868-1202
804-848-3111

Shenandoah University
1460 University Dr, Winchester VA 22601-5195
540-665-4500

Southern Virginia University
1 University Hill Dr, Buena Vista VA 24416
540-261-8400

Stratford University
7777 Leesburg Pike #100 South
Falls Church VA 22043
Keith Evans, Contact
703-821-8570 Fax: 703-734-5335
Website: www.stratford.edu
E-mail: admissions@stratford.edu

Strayer University
45150 Russell Branch Pkwy, Ashburn VA 20147
703-729-8800

Strayer University
700 Independence Pkwy Ste 400
Chesapeake VA 23320
757-382-9900

Strayer University
9990 Battleview Pkwy, Manassas VA 20109-2368
703-330-8400

Strayer University
PO Box 487, Newington VA 22122
703-339-1850

UNIVERSITY OF MANAGEMENT AND TECHNOLOGY

1901 Fort Myer Dr Ste 700, Arlington VA 22209
703-516-0035 Fax: 703-516-0985
Website: www.umtweb.edu
E-mail: info@umtweb.edu

University of Mary Washington
1301 College Ave, Fredericksburg VA 22401-5300
Dr. Martin A. Wilder, Jr., Director of Admissions
540-654-2000 Fax: 540-654-1857
Website: www.umw.edu
E-mail: admit@umw.edu

UNIVERSITY OF NORTHERN VIRGINIA

10021 Balls Ford Rd, Manassas VA 20109
703-392-0771 Fax: 703-392-0756
Website: www.unva.edu

University of Richmond
Richmond VA 23173
804-289-8000

University of Virginia
PO Box 400160, Charlottesville VA 22904
804-924-0311

University of Virginia College at Wise
1 College Ave, Wise VA 24293
276-328-0100

Virginia Commonwealth University
901 W Franklin St, Richmond VA 23284
804-828-0100

Virginia Intermont College
1013 Moore St, Bristol VA 24201-4225
540-669-6101

Virginia Polytechnic Institute & State University
Blacksburg VA 24061
540-231-6000

Virginia State University
1 Hayden Dr, Petersburg VA 23806-0001
804-524-5000

Virginia Union University
1500 N Lombardy St, Richmond VA 23220-1711
804-257-5600

Virginia University of Lynchburg
2058 Garfield Ave, Lynchburg VA 24501
434-528-5276

Virginia Wesleyan College
1584 Wesleyan Dr, Norfolk VA 23502-5599
757-455-3200

Washington & Lee University
Lexington VA 24450
540-463-8400

WASHINGTON

Antioch University
2326 6th Ave, Seattle WA 98121
Pam Smith Mentz, Director of Enrollment Services
888-268-4477

Apollo College
10102 E Knox Ave, Spokane WA 99206-4146
509-532-8888 Fax: 509-533-5983

Central Washington University
400 E University Way, Ellensburg WA 98926
William Swain, Director of Admissions
509-963-3001

City University
11900 NE 1st St, Bellevue WA 98005-3030
800-426-5596

Cornish College of the Arts
1000 Lenora St, Seattle WA 98121
Eric Pedersen, Director of Admission
800-726-ARTS (2787)

CROWN COLLEGE

8739 S Hosmer St, Tacoma WA 98444-1836
John Wabel, CEO
253-531-3123 Fax: 253-531-3521
Website: www.crowncollege.edu
E-mail: jwabel@crowncollege.edu

DIGIPEN INSTITUTE OF TECHNOLOGY

5001 150th Ave NE, Redmond WA 98052
Admissions
425-558-0299 Fax: 425-558-0378
Website: www.digipen.edu
E-mail: admissions@digipen.edu

Eastern Washington University
Cheney WA 99004
509-359-6200

Evergreen State College
2700 Evergreen Pkwy NW, Olympia WA 98505-0005
360-866-6000

Gonzaga University
502 E Boone Ave, Spokane WA 99258-0102
Julie McCulloh, Dean of Admission
800-322-2584

Heritage University
3240 Fort Rd, Toppenish WA 98948-9599
509-865-8500

Intercollegiate Center for Nursing Education
2917 W Fort Gorge Wright Dr, Spokane WA 99204
509-324-7360

Northwest Baptist Seminary
4301 N Stevens St, Tacoma WA 98407-6699
253-759-6104

Northwest College of Art
16301 Creative Dr NE, Poulsbo WA 98370
Craig Freeman, President
360-779-9993

Northwest University
PO Box 579, Kirkland WA 98083-0579
Myles Corrigan, Associate V.P. - Enrollment
425-889-5209

Pacific Lutheran University
12180 Park Ave S, Tacoma WA 98447-0014
David E. Gunovich, Director of Admissions
253-535-7151

Puget Sound Christian College
PO Box 13108, Everett WA 98206-3108
425-257-3090

St. Martin's University
5300 Pacific Ave SE, Lacey WA 98503-1297
360-491-4700

Seattle Pacific University
3307 3rd Ave W, Seattle WA 98119-1997
206-281-2000

Seattle University
901 12th Ave, Seattle WA 98122
206-296-6000

TRINITY LUTHERAN COLLEGE

4221 228th Ave SE, Issaquah WA 98029-9264
Jon Olson, VP of College Advancement
425-392-0400 Fax: 425-392-0404
Website: www.tlc.edu
E-mail: admission@tlc.edu

University of Puget Sound
1500 N Warner St, Tacoma WA 98416-0005
253-879-3100

University of Washington
Seattle WA 98195-0001
206-543-2100

Walla Walla College
204 S College Ave, College Place WA 99324-1198
509-527-2615

Washington State University
1 SE Stadium Way, Pullman WA 99164-0001
509-335-3564

Western Washington University
516 High St, Bellingham WA 98225-5996
360-650-3000

Whitman College
345 Boyer Ave, Walla Walla WA 99362-2083
509-527-5111

Whitworth College
300 W Hawthorne Rd, Spokane WA 99251-0001
Fred Pfursich, Dean of Admissions & Financial Aid
800-533-4668

WEST VIRGINIA

Alderson-Broaddus College
Philippi WV 26416
Eric A. Ruf, Director of Admissions
800-263-1549

Appalachian Bible College
PO Box ABC, Bradley WV 25818-1353
Rita K. Pritt, Director of Admissions
800-678-9222

Bethany College
Bethany WV 26032
304-829-7000

Bluefield State College
219 Rock St, Bluefield WV 24701-2198
304-327-4000

Concord University
Athens WV 24712
Michael Curry, Vice President of Financial Aid & Admissions
888-384-5249

Davis & Elkins College
100 Campus Dr, Elkins WV 26241-3996
Renee Heckel, Director of Enrollment Management
800-624-3157 Fax: 304-637-1800
Website: www.davisandelkins.edu
E-mail: admiss@davisandelkins.edu

Fairmont State University
1201 Locust Ave, Fairmont WV 26554-2470
Steve Leadman, Director of Admissions
304-367-4892 or 800-641-5678 Fax: 304-367-4789
Website: www.fairmontstate.edu
E-mail: admit@fairmontstate.edu

Glenville State College
200 High St, Glenville WV 26351-1200
304-462-4128

Marshall University
400 Hal Greer Blvd, Huntington WV 25755-0003
304-696-3170

MOUNTAIN STATE UNIVERSITY

Box 9003, Beckley WV 25802-9003
Tony England, Director of Admissions
866-FOR-MSU1 or 304-929-1433 Fax: 304-253-5072
Website: www.mountainstate.edu
E-mail: gomsu@mountainstate.edu

Established 1933. Private. Coed. Accreditation: The Higher Learning Commission of North Central Association of Colleges and Schools. 2006-07 Tuition & Fees: $7,800. Room & board: $5,058 - $7,026. Enrollment: 4,404. Faculty: 79 full-time, 237 part-time. Student-faculty ratio: 23:1. Degrees: AA, AS, BA, BS, BSN, BSW, MA, MCJA, MS, MHS, MSN, MSPA, MSSL. Library: 95,500 volumes. Largest private college in West Virginia; extensive financial aid package; same tuition for in-state or out-of-state students; extensive health science programs.

Ohio Valley University
1 Campus View Dr, Vienna WV 26105
800-678-6780

Salem International University
PO Box 500, Salem WV 26426-0500
304-782-5011

Shepherd University
PO Box 3210
Shepherdstown WV 25443
304-876-5000

University of Charleston
2300 MacCorkle Ave SE, Charleston WV 25304-1099
304-357-4800

West Liberty State College
PO Box 295, West Liberty WV 26074
304-336-5000

West Virginia State University
PO Box 1000, Institute WV 25112-1000
304-766-3000

West Virginia University
PO Box 6001, Morgantown WV 26506-6001
304-293-0111

West Virginia University at Parkersburg
300 Campus Dr, Parkersburg WV 26101
304-424-8220

West Virginia University Institute of Technology
405 Fayette Pike, Montgomery WV 25136-2436
304-442-3071

West Virginia Wesleyan College
59 College Ave, Buckhannon WV 26201-2699
Robert N. Skinner II, Director of Admission
800-722-9933

Wheeling Jesuit University
316 Washington Ave, Wheeling WV 26003-6295
304-243-2000

WISCONSIN

Alverno College
PO Box 343922, Milwaukee WI 53234-3922
Dianna Gaebler, Director of Admissions
414-382-6100 Fax: 414-382-6354
Website: www.alverno.edu
E-mail: admissions@alverno.edu

BELLIN COLLEGE OF NURSING

PO Box 23400, Green Bay WI 54305-3400
Penny Croghan, Director of Admissions
920-433-5803 Fax: 920-433-7416
Website: www.bcon.edu
E-mail: admissio@bcon.edu

Beloit College
700 College St, Beloit WI 53511-5596
James Zielinski, Director of Admissions
608-363-2500

Cardinal Stritch University
6801 N Yates Rd, Milwaukee WI 53217-3985
414-410-4000

Carroll College
100 N East Ave, Waukesha WI 53186-5593
James Wiseman, Dean of Admissions
800-CARROLL

Carthage College
2001 Alford Park Dr, Kenosha WI 53140-1994
262-551-6000

Columbia College of Nursing
2121 E Newport Ave, Milwaukee WI 53211-2952
414-961-3530

Concordia University
12800 N Lake Shore Dr, Mequon WI 53097-2402
262-243-5700

Edgewood College
1000 Edgewood College Dr, Madison WI 53711
608-663-4861

HERZING COLLEGE

5218 E Terrace Dr, Madison WI 53718-8340
Donald Madelung, President
Rebecca Abrams, Director of Admissions
800-582-1227 or 608-249-6611 Fax: 608-249-8593
Website: www.herzing.edu
E-mail: info@msn.herzing.edu

Established 1948. Private. Coed. Accreditation: NCA. Tuition: $8,000 - $9,000 (2 semesters). Fees: $75 - $600. Enrollment: 640. Faculty: 29. Student-Faculty ratio: 17:1.

Diplomas: Medical Billing, Medical Office, Bookkeeping & Payroll Accounting, Practical Nursing, Homeland Security Leadership. Associate Degrees: Computer, Electronics & Telecommunications Technology, Computer Network & Security Technology, Computer Information Systems, Interactive & Graphic Arts, Computer Aided Drafting, Business Administration, Legal Assisting/Paralegal, Nursing. Bachelor Degrees: Homeland Security & Public Safety, Interactive & Graphic Arts, Legal Studies, Healthcare Management, Accounting, Business Administration, Information Technology, Technology Management.

Founded in 1948 as one of the nation's first electronics schools. Certification preparation inbedded in curriculum: A+, Net+, MCSE, CCNA, Certified Electronics Technician and Associate. Three-year bachelor degree. Bachelor-completion program available online.

No dorms, but housing and job assistance to new and existing students.

Lakeland College
PO Box 359, Sheboygan WI 53082-0359
Nathan Dehne, Director of Admission
920-565-1100 Fax: 920-565-1215
Website: www.lakeland.edu
E-mail: admissions@lakeland.edu

Lawrence University
PO Box 599, Appleton WI 54912-0599
920-832-7000

Maranatha Baptist Bible College
745 W Main St, Watertown WI 53094-7638
920-261-9300

Marian College of Fond du Lac
45 S National Ave, Fond du Lac WI 54935-4621
Eric Peterson, Dean of Admission
800-262-7426 ext. 7650

Marquette University
PO Box 1881, Milwaukee WI 53201-1881
Robert Blust, Director of Admissions
414-288-7302 Fax: 414-288-3764
Website: www.mu.edu
E-mail: admissions@marquette.edu

Milwaukee Institute of Art & Design
273 E Erie St, Milwaukee WI 53202-6003
Mark Fetherston, Director of Admissions
414-291-8070

Milwaukee School of Engineering
1025 N Broadway, Milwaukee WI 53202-3109
414-277-7300

Northland Baptist Bible College
W10085 Pike Plains Rd, Dunbar WI 54119
715-324-6900

Northland College
1411 Ellis Ave, Ashland WI 54806-3999
800-753-1840

Ottawa University
245 S Executive Dr Ste 110
Brookfield WI 53005-4204
262-879-0200

Ripon College
PO Box 248, Ripon WI 54971-0248
920-748-8115

St. Norbert College
100 Grant St, De Pere WI 54115
Brian Studebaker, Director of Admission
800-236-4878 Fax: 920-403-4072
Website: www.snc.edu
E-mail: admit@snc.edu

Silver Lake College
2406 S Alverno Rd, Manitowoc WI 54220-9319
920-684-6691

University of Wisconsin
PO Box 4004, Eau Claire WI 54702
715-836-2637

University of Wisconsin
PO Box 2000, Kenosha WI 53141-2000
262-595-2345

University of Wisconsin
716 Langdon St, Madison WI 53706-1481
608-262-1234

University of Wisconsin
PO Box 413, Milwaukee WI 53201-0413
414-229-1122

University of Wisconsin
1 University Plz, Platteville WI 53818-3001
Angela Udelhofen, Recruitment Manager
608-342-1200

University of Wisconsin
410 S 3rd St, River Falls WI 54022
715-425-3911

University of Wisconsin
2100 Main St, Stevens Point WI 54481-3871
715-346-0123

University of Wisconsin
PO Box 2000, Superior WI 54880
715-394-8101

UNIVERSITY OF WISCONSIN BARABOO/SAUK CO.
1006 Connie Rd, Baraboo WI 53913-1015
Ruth Joyce, Asst. Dean for Student Services
608-355-5230 Fax: 608-355-5289
Website: www.baraboo.uwc.edu
E-mail: boouinfo@uwc.edu

University of Wisconsin Green Bay
2420 Nicolet Dr, Green Bay WI 54311-7003
Pamela Harvey-Jacobs, Interim Director of Admissions
920-465-2111

University of Wisconsin in La Crosse
115 Graff Main Hall, La Crosse WI 54601
Tim Lewis, Director of Admissions
608-785-8939

University of Wisconsin - Oshkosh
800 Algoma Blvd, Oshkosh WI 54901-8602
920-424-0202

University of Wisconsin-Stout
124 Bowman Hall, Menomonie WI 54751-2662
715-232-1123

University of Wisconsin - Whitewater
800 W Main St, Whitewater WI 53190-1791
262-472-1234

Viterbo University
815 9th St S, La Crosse WI 54601-8802
608-796-3000

Wisconsin Indianhead Technical College
505 Pine Ridge Dr, Shell Lake WI 54871
Miriam Crandall, Registrar
800-243-9482 Fax: 715-468-2819
Website: www.witc.edu
E-mail: mimi.crandall@witc.edu
Campuses in Ashland, New Richmond, Rice Lake, Superior.

Wisconsin Lutheran College
8800 W Bluemound Rd, Milwaukee WI 53226-4626
414-443-8800

WSLH SCHOOL OF CYTOTECHNOLOGY
465 Henry Mall, Madison WI 53706
Michele Smith, Education Coordinator
608-262-3524 Fax: 608-265-6294
Website: www.slh.wisc.edu/cytology/index.html
E-mail: msmith27@wisc.edu

WYOMING

University of Wyoming
Admissions Office
Dept 3435, Laramie WY 82071-3435
Brooke Culver, Contact
800-342-5996 Fax: 307-766-4042
Website: www.uwyo.edu
E-mail: why-wyo@uwyo.edu

GUAM

Pacific Islands Bible College
PO Box 22619, Barrigada GU 96921
671-472-8716

University of Guam
UOG Station, Mangilao GU 96923
Deborah Leon Guerrero, Registrar
671-735-2201 or 671-735-2208 Fax: 671-735-2203
Website: www.uog.edu
E-mail: admitme@uog9.uog.edu

PUERTO RICO

American University of Puerto Rico
PO Box 2037, Bayamon PR 00960-2037
787-798-2040

Atlantic College
PO Box 1774, Guaynabo PR 00970-1774
Zaida Perez, Director of Admissions
787-720-1022

Bayamon Central University
PO Box 1725, Bayamon PR 00960-1725
787-786-3030

Caribbean University
PO Box 493, Bayamon PR 00960-0493
787-780-0070

Colegio Biblico Pentecostal de Puerto Rico
PO Box 901, Saint Just PR 00978-0901
787-761-0640

COLEGIO PENTECOSTAL MIZPA
PO Box 20966, San Juan PR 00928-0966
Rev. Daniel Cruz, President
787-720-4476 Fax: 787-720-2012
Website: www.colmizpa.edu
E-mail: presidente@colmizpa.edu

CONSERVATORY OF MUSIC
350 Calle Rafael Lamar, San Juan PR 00918
Eutimia Santiago, Director of Admissions
787-751-0160 ext. 275 Fax: 787-758-8268
Website: www.cmpr.edu
E-mail: admisiones@cmpr.edu

Electronic Data Processing College
PO Box 192303, Hato Rey PR 00919-2303
787-765-3560

ESCUELA DE ARTES PLASTICAS PUERTO RICO
PO Box 9021112, San Juan PR 00902-1112
Marine's Lopez-Lopez, Dean Student Affairs
Juan Negroni, Admissions Officer
787-729-0007 Fax: 787-721-3798
Website: www.eap.edu.pr
E-mail: eap@coqui.net

Inter American University
Call Box 20000, Aguadilla PR 00605
787-891-0925

Inter American University of Puerto Rico
PO Box 4050, Arecibo PR 00614
787-878-5475

Inter American University of Puerto Rico
PO Box 517, Barranquitas PR 00794-0517
787-857-3600

Inter American University of Puerto Rico
500 Road 830, Bayamon PR 00957
787-279-1912

Inter American University of Puerto Rico
PO Box 70003, Fajardo PR 00738
787-863-2390

Inter American University of Puerto Rico
PO Box 10004, Guayama PR 00785
787-864-2222

Inter American University of Puerto Rico
PO Box 191293, Hato Rey PR 00919
787-250-1912

Inter American University of Puerto Rico
104 Turpo Industrial Park Rd #1, Mercedita PR 00715
787-284-1912

Inter American University of Puerto Rico
PO Box 5100, San German PR 00683
787-264-1912

Pontifical Catholic University of Puerto Rico
PO Box 144045, Arecibo PR 00614
787-881-1212

Pontifical Catholic University of Puerto Rico
5 Calle Santiago Palmer S, Guayama PR 00784-4965
787-864-0550

Pontifical Catholic University of Puerto Rico
PO Box 1326, Mayagüez PR 00681
787-834-5151

Pontifical Catholic University of Puerto Rico
2250 Ave Las Americas, Ponce PR 00717-0777
787-841-2000

SAN JUAN BAUTISTA SCHOOL OF MEDICINE
PO Box 4968, Caguas PR 00726-4968
Lissette Torres Rodriguez, Registrar
787-743-3038 Fax: 787-746-3093
Website: www.sanjuanbautista.edu
E-mail: ltorres@sanjuanbautista.edu

Universidad Adventista de las Antillas
PO Box 118, Mayaguez PR 00681
Evelyn Del Valle Rivera, Director of Admissions
787-834-9595

Universidad Central Del Caribe
PO Box 60327, Bayamon PR 00960-6032
787-798-3001

Universidad Del Turabo
PO Box 3030, Gurabo PR 00778
787-743-7979

Universidad Metropolitana
PO Box 21150, San Juan PR 00928-1150
787-766-1717

Universidad Politecnica de Puerto Rico
PO Box 192017, San Juan PR 00919-2017
787-754-8000

University of Puerto Rico
PO Box 4800, Carolina PR 00984-4800
787-257-0000

University of Puerto Rico
R Ave Antonio R Barcelo, Cayey PR 00736-5534
787-738-2161

University of Puerto Rico
CUH Station Rd 908 Bo Tejas, Humacao PR 00791
787-850-0000

University of Puerto Rico
PO Box 9020, Mayaguez PR 00681
787-832-4040

University of Puerto Rico
PO Box 23303, Rio Piedras PR 00931-3303
787-764-0000

University of Puerto Rico
PO Box 365067, San Juan PR 00936-5067
787-758-2525

University of Puerto Rico at Arecibo
PO Box 4010, Arecibo PR 00614
787-815-0000

University of Puerto Rico at Ponce
PO Box 7186, Ponce PR 00732-7186
787-844-8181

University of Puerto Rico
Bayamón University College
Carretera 174, Km 2.8, Bayamón PR 00959
787-786-2885

University of the Sacred Heart
PO Box 12383, Santurce PR 00914
787-728-1515

VIRGIN ISLANDS

University of the Virgin Islands
2 John Brewers Bay, Saint Thomas VI 00802
340-776-9200

University of the Virgin Islands
RR 2 Box 10000
Kingshill VI 00850
340-776-9200

VETERINARY MEDICINE

ALABAMA

Judson College
302 Bibb St, Marion AL 36756
Michael Scotto, Director of Admissions
800-447-9472 Fax: 334-683-5147
Website: www.judson.edu
E-mail: admissions@judson.edu

ARIZONA

Apollo College
8503 N 27th Ave, Phoenix AZ 85051-4063
602-864-1571 Fax: 602-864-8207

Apollo College
2701 W Bethany Home Rd, Phoenix AZ 85017-1705
602-433-1333 Fax: 602-433-1414

CALIFORNIA

Chapman University
One University Drive, Orange CA 92866-1099
Michael Drummy, Assistant Vice President for Enrollment
Services and Chief Admission Officer
714-997-6411 or 888-CUAPPLY Fax: 714-997-6713
Website: www.chapman.edu
E-mail: admit@chapman.edu

Western Career College
7301 Greenback Ln Bldg A, Citrus Heights CA 95621
Jim Murphy, Executive Director
916-722-8200 Fax: 916-722-6883
Website: www.westerncollege.edu

Western Career College
380 Civic Dr Ste 300, Pleasant Hill CA 94523-1984
LaShawn Wells, Executive Director
925-609-6650 Fax: 926-609-6666
Website: www.westerncollege.edu

Western Career College
8909 Folsom Blvd, Sacramento CA 95826-3203
Sue Smith, Executive Director
916-361-5100 Fax: 916-361-6666
Website: www.westerncollege.edu

Western Career College
6201 San Ignacio Ave, San Jose CA 95119
Steve Ashab, Executive Director
408-360-0840 Fax: 408-360-0848
Website: www.westerncollege.edu

Western Career College
15555 E 14th St Ste 500, San Leandro CA 94578
Dawn Matthews, Executive Director
510-276-3888 Fax: 510-276-3653
Website: www.westerncollege.edu

Western Career College
1313 W Robinhood Dr Ste B, Stockton CA 95207
Dave Semrau, Executive Director
209-956-1240 Fax: 209-956-1244
Website: www.westerncollege.edu

COLORADO

Bel-Rea Institute of Animal Technology
1681 S Dayton St, Denver CO 80247-3048
Paulette Kaufman, Administrator
303-751-8700 Fax: 303-751-9969
Website: www.bel-rea.com
E-mail: admissions@bel-rea.com

NORTHEASTERN JUNIOR COLLEGE
100 College Ave, Sterling CO 80751-2399
Dr. Lance Bolton, Chief Administrative Officer
Tina Joyce, Director of Admissions
970-521-7000 or 970-521-6752 Fax: 970-521-6801
Website: www.njc.edu
E-mail: tina.joyce@njc.edu

INDIANA

BROWN MACKIE COLLEGE - SOUTH BEND
1030 E Jefferson Blvd, South Bend IN 46617-3123
Connie Adelman, Campus President
574-237-0774 Fax: 574-237-3585
Website: www.brownmackie.edu

IOWA

Briar Cliff University
PO Box 2100, Sioux City IA 51104-0100
Sharisue Wilcoxon, VP for Enrollment Management
712-279-5200 Fax: 712-279-1632
Website: www.briarcliff.edu
E-mail: admissions@briarcliff.edu

KENTUCKY

Brown Mackie College - Louisville
3605 Fern Valley Rd, Louisville KY 40219-1916
Mark Donahue, Director of Admissions
502-968-7191 Fax: 502-357-9956
Website: www.brownmackie.edu
E-mail: mdonahue@brownmackie.edu

MASSACHUSETTS

Becker College
Campuses in Worcester and Leicester, MA
61 Sever St, Worcester MA 01609-2165
Karen Schedin, Dean of Admissions
508-791-9241 Fax: 508-890-1500
Website: www.becker.edu
E-mail: admissions@becker.edu
See listing under "Universities"

North Shore Community College
1 Ferncroft Rd, Danvers MA 01923-4093
Jennifer Kirk, Director of Admissions & Recruitment Outreach
978-762-4000 Fax: 978-762-4015
Website: www.northshore.edu
E-mail: jkirk@northshore.edu

Worcester Polytechnic Institute
100 Institute Rd, Worcester MA 01609-2280
Edward J. Connor, Director of Admissions
508-831-5286 Fax: 508-831-5875
Website: admissions.wpi.edu
E-mail: admissions@wpi.edu

MICHIGAN

MACOMB COMMUNITY COLLEGE
44575 Garfield Rd, Clinton Township MI 48038-1139
Information Center
586-445-7999
Website: www.macomb.edu
E-mail: answer@macomb.edu

MINNESOTA

Duluth Business University
4724 Mike Colalillo Dr, Duluth MN 55807-2723
Bonnie Kupczynski, Director
800-777-8406 Fax: 218-628-2127
Website: www.dbumn.edu
E-mail: info@dbumn.edu

University of Minnesota
2900 University Ave, Crookston MN 56716-5001
218-281-6510 Fax: 218-281-8575
Website:
admissions.umcrookston.edu/requirements/apply.htm
E-mail: info@umcrookston.edu

MISSOURI

Truman State University
100 E Normal, Kirksville MO 63501
Office of Admission
660-785-4114 Fax: 660-785-7456
Website: admissions.truman.edu
E-mail: admissions@truman.edu

William Woods University
1 University Ave, Fulton MO 65251-1098
Jimmy Clay, Director of Admissions
573-642-2251 Fax: 573-592-1146
Website: www.williamwoods.edu
E-mail: admissions@williamwoods.edu
See listing under "Universities"

NEW JERSEY

RICHARD STOCKTON COLLEGE OF NEW JERSEY
PO Box 195, Pomona NJ 08240
John Iacovelli, Dean of Enrollment Management
866-RSC-2885 Fax: 609-626-5541
Website: www.stockton.edu
E-mail: admissions@stockton.edu

Stockton College is a comprehensive liberal arts, coed institution founded in 1969. Advance Pre-Professional Degree Options: 7-yr BS/MD with UMDNJ; NJ Dental School; NJ Medical School, Robert Wood Johnson Medical, School of Osteopathic Medicine; NY College of Podiatric Medicine, Pennsylvania College of Podiatric Medicine, SUNY College of Optometry. Pharmacy doctorate program with Rutgers University. 5-yr Engineering with NJIT and Rutgers University. Dual BA/MA in Criminal Justice. 5-yr BS/MS in Computational Science. BS/MS in Nursing. Doctorate of Physical Therapy. Additional Programs: Forensic Science, Pre-Law, Pre-Occupational Therapy, and Pre-Veterinary.

NEW MEXICO

Apollo College
1001 Menaul Blvd NE Ste C, Albuquerque NM 87107
800-368-7246 Fax: 505-254-1101

NEW YORK

College of Saint Rose
432 Western Ave, Albany NY 12203-1419
Maryelizabeth Amico, Asst V.P. for Undergraduate Admissions
518-454-5150 Fax: 518-454-2013
Website: www.strose.edu
E-mail: admit@strose.edu

Roberts Wesleyan College
2301 Westside Dr, Rochester NY 14624-1997
Office of Admissions
585-594-6400 Fax: 585-594-6371
Website: www.roberts.edu
E-mail: admissions@roberts.edu

SUNY College of Technology
Alfred NY 14802
Deborah J. Goodrich, Associate VP Enrollment Mgmt.
800-4AL-FRED Fax: 607-587-4299
Website: www.alfredstate.edu
E-mail: admissions@alfredstate.edu

OHIO

Brown Mackie College - Cincinnati
1011 Glendale Milford Rd, Cincinnati OH 45215-1107
Robin Krout, President
513-771-2424 Fax: 513-771-3413
Website: www.brownmackie.edu
E-mail: rkrout@brownmackie.edu

The Ohio State University
College of Veterinary Medicine
127 Vet Med Acad Bldg, 1900 Coffey Rd
Columbus OH 43210
614-292-8831 Fax: 614-292-6989
Website: vet.osu.edu
E-mail: graham.194@osu.edu

OHIO WESLEYAN UNIVERSITY
61 S Sandusky St, Delaware OH 43015-2398
Director of Admission
740-368-3020 Fax: 740-368-3314
Website: www.owu.edu
E-mail: owuadmit@owu.edu

Ursuline College
2550 Lander Rd, Cleveland OH 44124-4398
Sarah E. Sundermeier, Director of Admissions
888-URSULINE Toll Free Fax: 440-684-6138
Website: www.admission.ursuline.edu
E-mail: admission@ursuline.edu

OKLAHOMA

Oklahoma State University
Stillwater OK 74078
Michael Lorenz, Dean
405-744-6651
Website: www.okstate.edu
E-mail: michael.lorenz@okstate.edu

PENNSYLVANIA

Johnson College
3427 N Main Ave, Scranton PA 18508-1495
Dr. Ann L. Pipinski, President & CEO
Melissa Ide, Director of Enrollment Management
800-2WE-WORK or 570-342-6404 ext. 125
Fax: 570-348-2181
Website: www.johnson.edu
E-mail: admit@johnson.edu

Juniata College
1700 Moore St, Huntingdon PA 16652-2196
Michelle Bartol, Dean of Enrollment
877-JUNIATA Fax: 814-641-3100
Website: www.juniata.edu
E-mail: admissions@juniata.edu

VET TECH INSTITUTE
125 7th St, Pittsburgh PA 15222-3410
Cheri Yaworski, Director of Admissions
800-570-0693 Fax: 412-232-4348
Website: www.vettechinstitute.com
E-mail: cyaworski@vettechinstitute.com

SOUTH DAKOTA

NATIONAL AMERICAN UNIVERSITY
321 Kansas City St, Rapid City SD 57701-3692
Angela G. Beck, Director of Enrollment Management
605-394-4800 Fax: 605-394-4871
Website: www.rapid.national.edu
E-mail: rcadmissions@national.edu

TEXAS

Abilene Christian University
ACU Box 29000, Abilene TX 79699-0001
325-674-2000 Fax: 325-674-2202
Website: www.acu.edu
E-mail: info@admissions.acu.edu

WISCONSIN

St. Norbert College
100 Grant St, De Pere WI 54115
Brian Studebaker, Director of Admission
800-236-4878 Fax: 920-403-4072
Website: www.snc.edu
E-mail: admit@snc.edu

WYOMING

University of Wyoming
Admissions Office
Dept 3435, Laramie WY 82071-3435
Brooke Culver, Contact
800-342-5996 Fax: 307-766-4042
Website: www.uwyo.edu
E-mail: why-wyo@uwyo.edu

WOMEN'S COLLEGES

ALABAMA

Judson College
302 Bibb St, Marion AL 36756
Michael Scotto, Director of Admissions
800-447-9472 Fax: 334-683-5147
Website: www.judson.edu
E-mail: admissions@judson.edu

CALIFORNIA

Mills College
5000 MacArthur Blvd, Oakland CA 94613-1000
510-430-2255

Mt. St. Mary's College
12001 Chalon Rd, Los Angeles CA 90049-1599
310-954-4000

Mt. St. Mary's College - Doheny Campus
10 Chester Pl, Los Angeles CA 90007-2518
213-746-0450

Scripps College
1030 Columbia Ave, Claremont CA 91711-3948
909-621-8000

CONNECTICUT

Hartford College for Women
1265 Asylum Ave, Hartford CT 06105-2299
860-236-1215

St. Joseph College
1678 Asylum Ave, West Hartford CT 06117-2791
860-232-4571

DISTRICT OF COLUMBIA

Trinity University
125 Michigan Ave NE, Washington DC 20017-1090
202-884-9000

GEORGIA

Agnes Scott College
141 E College Ave, Decatur GA 30030-3770
404-471-6000

Brenau University
500 Washington St SE, Gainesville GA 30501
800-252-5119

Spelman College
350 Spelman Ln SW, Atlanta GA 30314-4395
800-982-2411

Strayer University
3355 Northeast Expy NE Ste 100, Atlanta GA 30341
770-454-9270

Wesleyan College
4760 Forsyth Rd, Macon GA 31210-4462
800-447-6610

ILLINOIS

Loyola University - Mundelein College
6525 N Sheridan Rd, Chicago IL 60626-5311
773-262-8100

INDIANA

St. Mary-of-the-Woods College
Saint Mary of the Woods IN 47876
James P. Malley, Jr., Director of Admission
800-926-7692

St. Mary's College
46 Madeliva, Notre Dame IN 46556
574-284-4000

KENTUCKY

Midway College
512 E Stephens St, Midway KY 40347-1120
800-755-0031

MARYLAND

College of Notre Dame of Maryland
4701 N Charles St, Baltimore MD 21210-2404
410-435-0100

Hood College
401 Rosemont Ave, Frederick MD 21701
301-663-3131

MASSACHUSETTS

Bay Path College
588 Longmeadow St, Longmeadow MA 01106-2292
Lisa Casassa, Director of Admissions
413-565-1331

Lesley University
29 Everett St, Cambridge MA 02138-2790
Jane Raley, Director of Admissions
617-349-8800

Mt. Holyoke College
50 College St, South Hadley MA 01075-1424
413-538-2000

Pine Manor College
400 Heath St, Chestnut Hill MA 02467-2332
Bill Nichols, Dean of Admission
617-731-7167

Regis College
235 Wellesley St, Weston MA 02493-1571
781-768-2000

Simmons College
300 Fenway, Boston MA 02115-5898
617-521-2000

Smith College
Northampton MA 01063-0001
Debra Shaver, Director of Admissions
800-383-3232 Fax: 413-585-2527
Website: www.smith.edu
E-mail: admission@smith.edu

Wellesley College
106 Central St, Wellesley MA 02481-8203
Board of Admission
781-283-2270

MINNESOTA

College of Saint Benedict
37 College Ave S, Saint Joseph MN 56374-2099
320-363-5011

College of St. Catherine
2004 Randolph Ave, Saint Paul MN 55105-1789
651-690-6000

MISSISSIPPI

Mississippi University for Women
1100 College St Unit W1613, Columbus MS 39701
Terri Heath, Director of Admissions
877-GO-2-THEW

Mississippi University for Women-Tupelo
1918 Briar Ridge Rd, Tupelo MS 38804-5904
Kay Brown, Contact
662-844-0284

MISSOURI

Cottey College
1000 W Austin Blvd, Nevada MO 64772-2790
417-667-8181

Stephens College
PO Box 2121, Columbia MO 65215-0001
David Adams, Dean of Enrollment Management
573-442-2211 Fax: 573-876-7237
Website: www.stephens.edu
E-mail: dadams@stephens.edu

NEBRASKA

College of Saint Mary
7000 Mercy Rd, Omaha NE 68106
Lorin Werth,V.P. for Enrollment
800-926-5534

NEW JERSEY

Assumption College for Sisters
350 Bernardsville Rd, Mendham NJ 07945-2923
Sr. Mary Joseph Schultz, S.C.C., President
973-543-6528 Fax: 973-543-1738
Website: www.acs350.org
E-mail: acs@acs350.org

College of Saint Elizabeth
2 Convent Rd, Morristown NJ 07960-6923
973-292-4000

NEW YORK

Barnard College
3009 Broadway, New York NY 10027-6598
212-854-5262

Marymount College at Fordham University
100 Marymount Ave, Tarrytown NY 10591-3796
Gerard Reedy, S.J., Ph.D., Dean
914-631-3200

Russell Sage College
45 Ferry St, Troy NY 12180-4115
518-244-2000

NORTH CAROLINA

Bennett College
900 E Washington St, Greensboro NC 27401-3298
336-273-4431

Meredith College
3800 Hillsborough St, Raleigh NC 27607-5298
Heidi L. Fletcher, Director of Admissions
919-760-8581

Peace College
15 E Peace St, Raleigh NC 27604-1194
Laura C. Bingham, President
800-PEACE-47 Fax: 919-508-2306
Website: www.peace.edu
E-mail: admissions@peace.edu

SALEM COLLEGE
Winston Salem NC 27108-0548
Dana Evans, Dean of Admissions/Fin. Aid
800-32-SALEM Fax: 336-917-5572
Website: www.salem.edu
E-mail: admissions@salem.edu

Established 1772. Moravian. Enrollment: 1,000. Comprehensive fee for boarding students: $27,500, day students: $17,949, plus $215 Student Government Association fee for boarding and day students. Four year, liberal arts, residential college for women conferring Bachelor of Arts, Bachelor of Science and Bachelor of Music degrees with majors in American studies, accounting, art, arts management, biology, business administration, chemistry, communication, creative writing, economics, English, French, German, history, interior design, international business, international relations, mathematics, medical technology, music, music education, not-for-profit management, philosophy, psychology, religion, sociology, and Spanish. Teacher certification is offered in early childhood, ESL, middle grades, secondary and learning disabilities.

Admissions: College recognizes that variations in school curricula, methods of teaching, and aptitudes of students make it difficult for any one pattern of entrance standards to be required. It is recommended that candidates present 16 academic units which include 4 in English, 2 in a foreign language, 2 in history, 3 in math, and 3 in science. SAT and/or ACT are required. Transfer students must have a 2.0 GPA. Committee on Admissions considers each application individually and bases its decision on the general excellence of the candidate's school record, test scores, extracurricular activities, and personal qualifications of the applicants. The College welcomes students of different racial, ethnic, religious, and geographic backgrounds.

Financial Aid: Salem offers both need-based financial assistance and competitive, no-need scholarships. Every effort is made to assist as many students as funds will permit. Approximately 70% receive financial aid, which consists of a combination of grant, loan and/or work. The competitive scholarships range from $5,000-$16,975 per year.

Accreditation: Southern Association of Colleges and Secondary Schools, National Association of Schools of Music, National Council for the Accreditation of Teacher Education; course in medical technology recognized by the American Medical Association and the American Society of Clinical Pathologists.

OHIO

Ursuline College
2550 Lander Rd, Cleveland OH 44124-4398
Sarah E. Sundermeier, Director of Admissions
888-URSULINE Toll Free Fax: 440-684-6138
Website: www.admission.ursuline.edu
E-mail: admission@ursuline.edu

PENNSYLVANIA

Bryn Mawr College
101 N Merion Ave, Bryn Mawr PA 19010-2899
610-526-5000

Carlow University
3333 5th Ave, Pittsburgh PA 15213-3165
412-578-6000

Cedar Crest College
100 College Dr, Allentown PA 18104-6196
Judith A. Neyhart, Vice President Enrollment
800-360-1222

Chatham College
Woodland Rd, Pittsburgh PA 15232-2826
412-365-1100

Moore College of Art and Design
20th & Race St, Philadelphia PA 19103-1178
215-568-4000

Rosemont College
1400 Montgomery Ave, Rosemont PA 19010-1699
Ms. Rennie Andrews, Director of Admissions
610-526-2966

Wilson College
1015 Philadelphia Ave
Chambersburg PA 17201-1285
717-264-4141

SOUTH CAROLINA

Columbia College
1301 Columbia College Dr, Columbia SC 29203-5998
Elizabeth G. Quackenbush, Director of Admissions
803-786-3871

Converse College
580 E Main St, Spartanburg SC 29302-0006
864-596-9000

TEXAS

Texas Woman's University
PO Box 425589, Denton TX 76204-5589
Erma Nieto-Brecht, Director of Admissions
866-809-6130 Fax: 940-898-3081
Website: www.twu.edu
E-mail: admissions@twu.edu

VIRGINIA

Hollins University
PO Box 9707, Roanoke VA 24020
800-456-9595

Mary Baldwin College
Staunton VA 24401
Lisa A. Branson, Executive Director of Admissions and Financial Aid
800-468-2262 Fax: 540-887-7292
Website: www.mbc.edu
E-mail: admit@mbc.edu

Sweet Briar College
Sweet Briar VA 24595
804-381-6100

WISCONSIN

Alverno College
PO Box 343922, Milwaukee WI 53234-3922
Dianna Gaebler, Director of Admissions
414-382-6100 Fax: 414-382-6354
Website: www.alverno.edu
E-mail: admissions@alverno.edu

Mount Mary College
2900 N Menomonee River Pkwy
Milwaukee WI 53222-4597
414-256-1219

WOMEN'S STUDIES

ALABAMA

University of Alabama in Huntsville
PO Box 1247, Huntsville AL 35899-0001
Nikki Willis, Assoc. Director for Recruiting Program and Events
1-800-UAH-CALL Fax: 256-824-6073
Website: www.uah.edu
E-mail: willisn@uah.edu

ALASKA

University of Alaska Anchorage
PO Box 141629, Anchorage AK 99514-1629
Cecile Mitchell, Director of Enrollment Services
907-786-1480 Fax: 907-786-4888
Website: www.uaa.alaska.edu/
E-mail: enroll@uaa.alaska.edu

CALIFORNIA

Point Loma Nazarene University
3900 Lomaland Dr, San Diego CA 92106-2810
Chip Killingsworth, Director of Undergraduate Admissions
800-733-7770 Fax: 619-849-2601
Website: www.pointloma.edu
E-mail: admissions@pointloma.edu

FLORIDA

Florida State University
600 W College Ave, Tallahassee FL 32306-1096
Janice V. Finney, Director of Admissions
850-644-2525 Fax: 850-644-0197
Website: admissions.fsu.edu
E-mail: admissions@admin.fsu.edu

University of South Florida
4202 E Fowler Ave, Tampa FL 33620-6900
J. Robert Spatig, Director of Admissions
877-USF-BULL Fax: 813-974-9689
Website: www.usf.edu
E-mail: admissions@admin.usf.edu
See listing under "Universities"

ILLINOIS

Roosevelt University
430 S Michigan Ave, Chicago IL 60605
Gwen E. Kanelos, Asst. Vice President for Enrollment Services
877-APPLY-RU Fax: 312-341-4216
Website: www.roosevelt.edu
E-mail: applyru@roosevelt.edu

KENTUCKY

Bluegrass Community and Technical College
Oswald Building
470 Cooper Drive, Lexington KY 40506-0235
Shelbie Hugle, Director of Admissions
859-246-6200 Fax: 859-246-4664
Website: www.bluegrass.kctcs.edu
E-mail: bctc_info@kctcs.edu

MASSACHUSETTS

Boston University
121 Bay State Rd, Boston MA 02215
Kelly Walter, Executive Director of Admissions
617-353-2300 Fax: 617-353-9695
Website: web.bu.edu
E-mail: admissions@bu.edu

University of Massachusetts Dartmouth
Old Westport Rd, North Dartmouth MA 02747-2300
Jeanette Riley, Assistant Professor
508-999-8279 Fax: 508-999-8621
Website: explore.umassd.edu
E-mail: jlriley@umassd.edu

MINNESOTA

Carleton College
1 N College St, Northfield MN 55057-4044
800-995-2275 or 507-646-4190 Fax: 507-646-4526
Website: www.carleton.edu
E-mail: admissions@acs.carleton.edu

Pillsbury Baptist Bible College
315 S Grove Ave, Owatonna MN 55060-3097
Susanne Martin, Admissions Coordinator
507-451-2710 Fax: 507-451-0156
Website: www.pillsbury.edu
E-mail: admissions@pillsbury.edu

MISSOURI

Columbia College
1001 Rogers St, Columbia MO 65216-0001
Regina Morin, Director of Admissions
573-875-7352 Fax: 573-875-7506
Website: www.ccis.edu
E-mail: admissions@ccis.edu

University of Missouri
1 University Blvd, Saint Louis MO 63121-4499
Dr. Mark Burkholder, Dean-College of Arts & Sciences
314-516-5501 Fax: 314-516-5415
Website: www.umsl.edu
E-mail: admissions@umsl.edu

NEBRASKA

Nebraska Wesleyan University
5000 Saint Paul Ave, Lincoln NE 68504-2794
Patricia Karthauser, V.P. for University Enrollment
402-466-2371 Fax: 402-465-2177
Website: www.nebrwesleyan.edu
E-mail: admissions@nebrwesleyan.edu

NEW JERSEY

New Jersey City University
2039 John F Kennedy Blvd
Jersey City NJ 07305-1588
Carmen Panlilio, Asst. V.P. for Admissions and Financial Aid
201-200-3234 Fax: 201-200-2044
Website: www.njcu.edu
E-mail: admissions@njcu.edu

RICHARD STOCKTON COLLEGE OF NEW JERSEY
PO Box 195, Pomona NJ 08240
John Iacovelli, Dean of Enrollment Management
866-RSC-2885 Fax: 609-626-5541
Website: www.stockton.edu
E-mail: admissions@stockton.edu
See listing under "Universities"

NEW YORK

College of Saint Rose
432 Western Ave, Albany NY 12203-1419
Maryelizabeth Amico, Asst V.P. for Undergraduate Admissions
518-454-5150 Fax: 518-454-2013
Website: www.strose.edu
E-mail: admit@strose.edu

CUNY Hunter College
695 Park Ave, New York NY 10021
Aaron Gibbs, Assistant Director of Recruitment
212-650-3946 Fax: 212-650-3336
Website: www.hunter.cuny.edu
E-mail: aaron.gibbs@hunter.cuny.edu

PURCHASE COLLEGE STATE UNIVERSITY OF NEW YORK (SUNY)
735 Anderson Hill Rd, Purchase NY 10577-1400
Stephanie McCaine, Director of Admissions
914-251-6300 Fax: 914-251-6314
Website: www.purchase.edu
E-mail: admisn@purchase.edu
See listing under "Universities"

SUNY College at Brockport
350 New Campus Dr, Brockport NY 14420-2997
Bernard S. Valento, Director of Undergraduate Admissions
585-395-2751 Fax: 585-395-5452
Website: www.brockport.edu
E-mail: admit@brockport.edu

Wells College
PO Box 500, Aurora NY 13026
Susan Sloan, Director of Admissions
800-952-9355 Fax: 315-364-3227
Website: www.wells.edu
E-mail: ssloan@wells.edu

NORTH CAROLINA

Salem College
Winston Salem NC 27108
Dana Evans, Dean of Admissions/Fin. Aid
800-32-SALEM Fax: 336-917-5572
Website: www.salem.edu
E-mail: admissions@salem.edu
See listing under "Women's Colleges"

OHIO

The Ohio State University
Department of Women's Studies
286 University Hall, 230 N Oval Mall
Columbus OH 43210
614-292-1021 Fax: 614-292-0276
Website: womens-studies.osu.edu
E-mail: womstd.info@osu.edu

University of Dayton
300 College Park, Dayton OH 45469-1300
Robert F. Durkle, Director of Admission
800-837-7433 Fax: 937-229-4729
Website: admission.udayton.edu
E-mail: admission@udayton.edu

PENNSYLVANIA

Community College of Allegheny County
Allegheny Campus: 808 Ridge Ave, Pittsburgh PA 15212 Admissions: 412.237.2700
Boyce Campus: 595 Beatty Rd, Monroeville PA 15146 Admissions: 724.325.6614
North Campus: 8701 Perry Highway, Pittsburgh PA 15237 Admissions: 412.369.3600
South Campus: 1750 Clairton Rd, West Mifflin PA 15122 Admissions: 412-469-4301
Website: www.ccac.edu

INTERNATIONAL ACADEMY OF ADVANCED REFLEXOLOGY & MEDICAL REFLEXOLOGY CLINIC
1701 Snyder Rd, Green Lane PA 18054
Professor L.J. Telepo, President
215-234-0307 or 267-377-5128 Fax: 267-329-8008
Website: www.reflexology.net
E-mail: postsecondary@reflexology.net
See listing under "Allied Health Science"

INTERNATIONAL ACADEMY OF ADVANCED REFLEXOLOGY & MEDICAL REFLEXOLOGY CLINIC
1177 6th St, Whitehall PA 18052
Professor L.J. Telepo, President
215-234-0307 or 267-377-5128 Fax: 267-329-8008
Website: www.reflexology.net
E-mail: postsecondary@reflexology.net
See listing under "Allied Health Science"

MOUNT ALOYSIUS COLLEGE
7373 Admiral Peary Hwy, Cresson PA 16630-1999
Frank C. Crouse Jr., Vice President for Enrollment Management
814-886-6383 or 888-823-2220 Fax: 814-886-6441
Website: www.mtaloy.edu
E-mail: admissions@mtaloy.edu

TEXAS

Texas Woman's University
PO Box 425589, Denton TX 76204-5589
Erma Nieto-Brecht, Director of Admissions
866-809-6130 Fax: 940-898-3081
Website: www.twu.edu
E-mail: admissions@twu.edu

University of Houston
122 E Cullen Bldg, Houston TX 77204-2023
Office of Admission
713-743-9595
Website: www.uh.edu
E-mail: admissions@uh.edu

VIRGINIA

Radford University
PO Box 6903, Radford VA 24142
David W. Kraus, Director of Admissions
800-890-4265 Fax: 540-831-5038
Website: www.radford.edu
E-mail: ruadmiss@radford.edu

WASHINGTON

SHORELINE COMMUNITY COLLEGE
16101 Greenwood Ave N, Shoreline WA 98133-5696
Chris Melton, Acting Registrar
206-546-4581 Fax: 206-546-5835
Website: www.shoreline.edu

WYOMING

University of Wyoming
Admissions Office
Dept 3435, Laramie WY 82071-3435
Brooke Culver, Contact
800-342-5996 Fax: 307-766-4042
Website: www.uwyo.edu
E-mail: why-wyo@uwyo.edu

INDEX

Explanation

Schools are listed alphabetically. Each entry has the school name, state abbreviation and a three letter classification code. For example Aaker's Business College, ND (TCT) is found in the **Career Schools** "(TCT)" classification in the state of North Dakota "ND".

Classification codes and their corresponding classifications:

(AAT) Aeronautics, Aviation and Space
(AGR) Agriculture
(AHS) Allied Health Science
(ARC) Architecture
(ART) Art
(BIO) Biological Science
(BKS) Ethnic Studies
(BUS) Business and Management
(CPC) Chiropractic Medicine
(CTS) Construction Trades
(DNT) Dentistry
(EGN) Engineering
(EGT) Engineering Technology
(EMB) Personal and Miscellaneous Services
(FRS) Conservation/Renewable Natural Resources
(FSA) Fashion Art
(GRD) Graduate Schools
(HME) Home Economics
(HMS) Home Study and Correspondence
(HND) Handicapped, Schools for the
(IFS) Computer and Information Science
(INT) Interior Design
(JRC) Community and Junior Colleges
(JRN) Communications
(LAS) Liberal Arts and Sciences
(LAW) Law
(LBS) Library Science
(LND) Landscape Architecture
(LTR) Letters
(MBA) Master of Business Administration
(MCR) Mechanics and Repairers
(MED) Medicine
(MIL) Military Science
(MKD) Marketing and Distribution
(MNC) Men's Colleges
(MTH) Mathematics
(MUS) Music
(NRS) Nursing
(OPT) Optometry
(OST) Osteopathic Medicine
(PBH) Public Health
(PHR) Pharmacy
(PHS) Physical Science
(PHT) Photography
(POD) Podiatric Medicine
(PPT) Precision Production Trades
(PRB) Preparatory Schools for Boys
(PRC) Preparatory Schools Coeducational
(PRG) Preparatory Schools for Girls
(PSY) Psychology
(PTS) Protective Services
(SCT) Business - Administrative Support
(SCW) Social Science
(SPD) Speech and Drama
(SSS) Summer Sessions
(STA) Study Abroad
(TCT) Career Schools
(TED) Teacher Education
(TSR) Theological & Religious Vocations
(UNC) Universities and Colleges
(VET) Veterinary Medicine
(WMC) Women's Colleges
(WMS) Women's Studies

A

Aakers College, ND (TCT)
Aaron's Academy of Beauty, MD (TCT)
Abbott Acad of Cosmetology Arts/Sciences, MO (TCT)
Abdill Career College, OR (TCT)
ABI - AccuTech Business Institute, MD (TCT)
Abilene Christian University, TX (UNC)
Abington Memorial Hospital, PA (AHS)
Abraham Baldwin Agriculture College, GA (JRC)
Academia Maison D'Esthetique, PR (TCT)
Academia Serrant, PR (TCT)
Academia Vocacional Del Turabo, PR (TCT)
Academy at Charlemont, MA (PRC)
Academy College, MN (JRC)
Academy Education Services, CA (TCT)
Academy for Five Element Acupuncture, FL (GRD)
Academy for Practical Nursing/Health Occ, FL (TCT)
Academy of Art University, CA (ARC)
Academy of Beauty Arts, TN (TCT)
Academy of Beauty Culture, CO (TCT)
Academy of Chinese Culture & Health Sci., CA (GRD)
Academy of Cosmetology, MT (TCT)
Academy of Cosmetology, OK (TCT)
Academy of Cosmetology, SC (TCT)
Academy of Court Reporting, MI (TCT)
Academy of Court Reporting, OH (TCT)
Academy of Creative Hair Design, LA (TCT)
Academy of Creative Hair Design, PA (TCT)
Academy of Hair Design, KS (TCT)
Academy of Hair Design, NV (TCT)
Academy of Hair Design, OR (TCT)
Academy of Hair Design, PA (TCT)
Academy of Hair Design, TX (TCT)
Academy of Hair Design, WA (TCT)
Academy of Hair Design #1, MS (TCT)
Academy of Hair Design #3, MS (TCT)
Academy of Hair Design #4, MS (TCT)
Academy of Hair Design #6, MS (TCT)
Academy of Hair Design #7, MS (TCT)
Academy of Hair Technology, SC (TCT)
Academy of Healing Arts Massage, FL (TCT)
Academy of Massage Therapy, NJ (TCT)
Academy of Oriental Medicine at Austin, TX (GRD)
Academy of Our Lady of Guam, GU (PRG)
Academy of the Holy Family, CT (PRG)
Academy of the New Church Boys School, PA (PRB)
Academy of the New Church Girls School, PA (PRG)
Academy of the Sacred Heart, LA (PRG)
Academy Pacific Travel College, CA (TCT)
Accelerated Schools Foundation, CO (PRC)
Accotink Academy, VA (HND)
Aces-Full Academy for Casino Dealers, NV (TCT)
ACT College, VA (TCT)
Acupuncture & Massage College, FL (GRD)
Acupuncture & Integrative Medicine Coll., CA (GRD)
A Cut Above Beauty College, IN (TCT)
Adams State College, CO (UNC)
Adcon Technical Institute, CA (TCT)
Adelphi University, NY (UNC)
Adirondack Beauty School, NY (TCT)
Adler Graduate School, MN (GRD)
Adler School of Professional Psychology, IL (GRD)
Admiral Farragut Academy, FL (PRC)
Adrian College, MI (UNC)
Adrian's Beauty College of Turlock, CA (TCT)
Advanced/Basic Hair Design Training Ctr, FL (TCT)
Advanced Barber College and Hair Design, TX (TCT)
Advanced College, CA (TCT)
Advanced Software Analysis, NY (TCT)
Advanced Technology Institute, VA (TCT)
Advanced Training Associates, CA (TCT)
Advance Science Institute, FL (TCT)
Advance Tech College, PR (TCT)
Advocate Illinois Masonic, IL (TCT)
Advocate Trinity Hospital, IL (TCT)
Aesthetics Institutes of Cosmetology, MD (TCT)
Agnes Scott College, GA (WMC)
Aguadilla Technical College, PR (TCT)
AIB College of Business, IA (JRC)
Aiken Preparatory School, SC (PRC)
Aiken Technical College, SC (JRC)
Ailano School of Aesthetics, MA (TCT)
Ailano School of Cosmetology, MA (TCT)
AIMS Academy, TX (TCT)
Aims Community College, CO (JRC)
Airman Proficiency Center, OR (TCT)
Akron General Medical Center, OH (AHS)
Akron Institute, OH (TCT)
Akron Machining Institute, OH (TCT)
AKS Massage School, VA (TCT)
Alabama A & M University, AL (UNC)
Alabama Institute for the Deaf and Blind, AL (HND)
Alabama Southern Community College, AL (JRC)
Alabama State College of Barber Styling, AL (TCT)
Alabama State University, AL (UNC)
Aladdin Beauty College, NM (TCT)
Alamance Community College, NC (JRC)
Alameda Beauty College, CA (TCT)
Alaska Bible College, AK (UNC)
Alaska Pacific University, AK (UNC)
Alaska Vocational Technical School, AK (TCT)
Albany College of Pharmacy, NY (UNC)
Albany Law School of Union University, NY (GRD)
Albany State University, GA (UNC)
Albany Technical College, GA (TCT)
Albert Einstein Medical Center, PA (AHS)
Albertson College of Idaho, ID (UNC)
Albertus Magnus College, CT (UNC)
Albion College, MI (UNC)
Albright College, PA (UNC)
Albuquerque Barber College, NM (TCT)
Albuquerque TVI Community College, NM (TCT)
Alcorn State University, MS (UNC)
Alderson-Broaddus College, WV (UNC)
Alexandria Academy of Beauty, LA (TCT)
Alexandria Technical College, MN (JRC)
Alfred G. Glassell School of Art, TX (TCT)
Alfred University, NY (UNC)
Alfred Univ.-NY State Coll. of Ceramics, NY (UNC)
Alhambra Beauty College, CA (TCT)
Alice Lloyd College, KY (UNC)
Allan Hancock College, CA (JRC)
Allegany College of Maryland, MD (JRC)
Allegheny College, PA (UNC)
Allegheny Valley Hospital, PA (AHS)
Allegheny Wesleyan College, OH (UNC)
Allen Academy, TX (PRC)
Allen College, IA (TCT)
Allen County Community College, KS (JRC)
Allen Inst. Ctr. for Innovative Learning, CT (UNC)
Allen School, NY (TCT)
Allentown School of Cosmetology, PA (TCT)
Allen University, SC (UNC)
Alliance Theological Seminary, NY (TSR)
Alliant International University, CA (GRD)
Allied Business School, CA (HMS)
Allied College - North, MO (TCT)
Allied College - South, MO (TCT)
Allied Health Careers, TX (TCT)
Allied Medical & Technical Careers, PA (TCT)
Allied Medical & Technical Institute, PA (JRC)
All Saints Healthcare System, WI (AHS)
All-State Career School, MD (TCT)
All-State Career School, PA (TCT)
Alma College, MI (UNC)
Alpena Community College, MI (JRC)
Altamaha Technical College, GA (TCT)
Altoona Beauty School, PA (TCT)
Altoona Hospital, PA (AHS)
Alvareita's College of Cosmetology, IL (TCT)
Alvernia College, PA (UNC)
Alverno College, WI (UNC)
Alvin Community College, TX (JRC)
Amarillo College, TX (JRC)
Amberton University, TX (UNC)
Ambler Beauty Academy, PA (TCT)
American Academy McAllister Institute, NY (JRC)
American Academy of Acupuncture, MN (TCT)
American Academy of Art, IL (ART)
American Academy of Cosmetology, CT (TCT)
American Academy of Dramatic Arts, CA (TCT)
American Academy of Dramatic Arts, NY (TCT)
American Academy of Hair Design, KS (TCT)
American Baptist College, TN (UNC)
American Baptist Seminary of the West, CA (GRD)
American Barber Institute, NY (TCT)
American Beauty Academy, MD (TCT)
American Beauty Academy, PA (TCT)
American Beauty College, CA (TCT)
The American Boychoir School, NJ (PRB)
American Business Academy, NJ (TCT)
American Business College of Puerto Rico, PR (TCT)
American Career College, CA (TCT)
American Career Institute, NV (HMS)
American College, PA (GRD)
American College of Acupuncture, TX (GRD)
American College of California, CA (TCT)
American College of Hair Design, MO (TCT)
American College of Hairstyling, IA (TCT)
American College of Health Professions, CA (TCT)
American College of Medical Technology, CA (TCT)
American Coll of Traditional Chinese Med, CA (GRD)
American Commercial College, TX (TCT)
American Conservatory Theater, CA (GRD)
American Educational College, PR (TCT)
American Film Institute, CA (GRD)
American Floral Art School, IL (TCT)
American Graduate University, CA (GRD)
American Health Information Management, IL (HMS)
American Health Science University, CO (HMS)
American Indian Coll of Assemblies/God, AZ (UNC)
American Inst. of Alternative Medicine, OH (TCT)
American Institute of Applied Science, NC (HMS)
American Institute of Baking, KS (TCT)
American Institute of Health Science, CA (UNC)
American Inst. of Medical-Dental Tech., UT (TCT)
American Institute of Technology, AZ (TCT)
American Institute of Technology, NV (TCT)
American InterContinental University, CA (UNC)
American InterContinental University, FL (UNC)
American InterContinental University, GA (UNC)
American Intercontinental Univ Online, IL (UNC)
American International College, MA (UNC)
American Military Academy, PR (PRC)
American Military University, VA (UNC)
American Professional Institute, AR (TCT)
American Professional Institute, GA (TCT)
American Public University, WV (HMS)
American River College, CA (JRC)
American Samoa Community College, AS (JRC)
American School, IL (HMS)
American School for the Deaf, CT (HND)
American School of Business, LA (TCT)
American School of Technology, OH (TCT)
American Sentinel University, AL (HMS)
American Technological College, PR (TCT)
American University, DC (UNC)
American University in Cairo, NY (UNC)
American University of Paris, CO (UNC)
American University of Puerto Rico, PR (UNC)
Americare School of Nursing, FL (TCT)
Ameritech College, UT (TCT)
Amherst College, MA (UNC)
Ancilla Domini College, IN (JRC)
Anderson College, SC (UNC)
Anderson Memorial Hospital, SC (AHS)
Anderson University, IN (UNC)
Andover College, ME (JRC)
Andover Newton Theological School, MA (GRD)
Andrew College, GA (JRC)
Andrew Jackson University, AL (HMS)
Andrews School, OH (PRG)
Andrews University, MI (UNC)
A New Beginning School of Massage, TX (TCT)
Angelina College, TX (JRC)
Angelo State University, TX (UNC)
Anna Maria College, MA (UNC)
Anne Arundel Community College, MD (JRC)
Annie Wright School, WA (PRG)
Anoka-Ramsey Community College, MN (JRC)
Anoka Technical College, MN (JRC)
Anson College of Cosmetology, NC (TCT)
Antelope Valley College, CA (JRC)
Antilles School of Technical Careers, PR (TCT)
Antioch University, CA (UNC)
Antioch University, WA (UNC)
Antioch University McGregor, OH (UNC)
Antioch University New England, NH (GRD)
Antioch University Southern California, CA (UNC)
Antonelli College, MS (TCT)
Antonelli College, OH (TCT)
Antonelli Institute - Art & Photography, PA (JRC)
Antonelli Medical & Professional Inst, PA (TCT)
Apex School of Beauty Culture, IN (TCT)
Apex School of Theology, NC (UNC)
Apex Technical School, NY (TCT)
Apollo College, AZ (UNC)
Apollo College, NM (UNC)
Apollo College, OR (UNC)
Apollo College, WA (UNC)
Apollo College Boise, ID (TCT)
Appalachian Bible College, WV (UNC)
Appalachian School of Law, VA (UNC)
Appalachian State University, NC (UNC)
Appalachian Technical College, GA (TCT)
Applied Professional Training, CA (HMS)
Apprentice Sch. - Northrop Grumman, VA (TCT)
Aquinas College, MI (UNC)
Aquinas College, TN (UNC)
Aquinas Institute of Theology, MO (GRD)
ARAMARK Healthcare Support Services, PA (AHS)
ARAMARK Healthcare Support Services SW, MO (AHS)
Arapahoe Community College, CO (JRC)
Arcadia University, PA (UNC)
Archmere Academy, DE (PRC)
Argosy University/Atlanta, GA (GRD)
Argosy University/Chicago, IL (GRD)
Argosy University/Chicago Northwest, IL (GRD)
Argosy University/Dallas, TX (UNC)
Argosy University/Hawaii, HI (GRD)
Argosy University/Orange County, CA (GRD)
Argosy University/Phoenix, AZ (GRD)
Argosy University/Sarasota, FL (UNC)
Argosy University/Seattle, WA (GRD)
Argosy University/Tampa, FL (GRD)
Argosy University/Twin Cities, MN (UNC)
Argosy University/Washington DC, VA (GRD)
Argosy University/San Francisco Campus, CA (UNC)
Ari Ben Aviator, FL (TCT)
Arizona Academy of Beauty, AZ (TCT)
Arizona Academy of Beauty - North, AZ (TCT)
Arizona Automotive Institute, AZ (TCT)
Arizona College of Allied Health, AZ (TCT)
Arizona Sch of Dentistry & Oral Health, AZ (DNT)
Arizona School of Health Sciences, AZ (GRD)
AZ State School for the Deaf & Blind, AZ (HND)
Arizona State University, AZ (UNC)
Arizona State University Polytechnic, AZ (UNC)
Arizona State University West, AZ (UNC)
Arizona Western College, AZ (JRC)
Arkadelphia Beauty College, AR (TCT)
Arkansas Aviation Technologies Center, AR (TCT)
Arkansas Baptist College, AR (UNC)
Arkansas Beauty School, AR (TCT)
Arkansas Beauty School - Conway, AR (TCT)
Arkansas Career Training Institute, AR (TCT)
AR College of Barbering & Hair Design, AR (TCT)
Arkansas Northeastern College, AR (JRC)
Arkansas School for the Blind, AR (HND)
Arkansas School for the Deaf, AR (HND)
Arkansas State University, AR (UNC)
Arkansas State University - Beebe, AR (JRC)
Arkansas State University Mountain Home, AR (UNC)
Arkansas State University - Newport, AR (JRC)
Arkansas State University Searcy Campus, AR (TCT)
Arkansas Tech University, AR (UNC)
Arkansas Valley Technical Institute, AR (TCT)
Arlington Baptist College, TX (UNC)
Arlington Career Institute, TX (TCT)
Arlington Medical Institute, TX (TCT)
Armstrong Atlantic State University, GA (UNC)
Armstrong County Memorial Hospital, PA (AHS)
Armstrong University, CA (UNC)
Army and Navy Academy, CA (PRB)
Arnold/Padrick's Univ of Cosmetology, GA (TCT)
Arnold's Beauty School, TN (TCT)
Arnot-Ogden Medical Center, NY (TCT)
Arrowhead Regional Medical Center, CA (TCT)
Art Academy of Cincinnati, OH (ART)
Art Center College of Design, CA (ART)
The Art Center Design College, AZ (ART)
The Art Center Design College, NM (ART)
Angelo School of Cosmetology Hair Design, RI (TCT)
Arthur James Cancer Hospital, OH (AHS)
Arthur's Beauty College, AR (TCT)
Art Institute of Atlanta, GA (UNC)
The Art Inst. of Boston at Lesley Univ., MA (UNC)
Art Institute of California, CA (TCT)
Art Institute of CA Inland Empire, CA (UNC)
Art Institute of California, CA (ART)
Art Institute of California, CA (TCT)
Art Institute of California - San Fran, CA (UNC)
Art Institute of Charlotte, NC (TCT)
Art Institute of Cincinnati, OH (ART)
Art Institute of Colorado, CO (UNC)
Art Institute of Dallas, TX (TCT)
Art Institute of Fort Lauderdale, FL (TCT)
Art Institute of Houston, TX (JRC)
Art Institute of Houston - Culinary, TX (TCT)
Art Institute of Indianapolis, IN (UNC)
Art Institute of Las Vegas, NV (UNC)
Art Institute of New York City, NY (TCT)

Art Institute of Ohio - Cincinnati, OH (UNC)
Art Institute of Philadelphia, PA (UNC)
Art Institute of Phoenix, AZ (TCT)
Art Institute of Pittsburgh, PA (UNC)
Art Institute of Portland, OR (UNC)
Art Institute of Seattle, WA (TCT)
Art Institute of Tampa, FL (UNC)
Art Institute of Washington, VA (UNC)
Art Institutes International Minnesota, MN (JRC)
Art Instruction Schools, MN (HMS)
Artistic Academy of Hair Design, NJ (TCT)
Artistic Beauty College, AZ (TCT)
Artistic Beauty College, CO (TCT)
Asbury College, KY (UNC)
Asbury Theological Seminary, FL (UNC)
Asbury Theological Seminary, KY (GRD)
Ascension College, LA (TCT)
Asheville Buncombe Technical Comm. Coll., NC (JRC)
Asheville School, NC (PRC)
Ashford University, IA (UNC)
Ashland Community and Technical College, KY (JRC)
Ashland County-West Holmes Career Center, OH (TCT)
Ashland Theological Seminary, OH (GRD)
Ashland University, OH (UNC)
Ashworth College, GA (HMS)
Asian American Intl Beauty College, CA (TCT)
Asian Institute of Medical Studies, AZ (GRD)
ASM Beauty World Academy, FL (TCT)
Asnuntuck Community College, CT (JRC)
Aspen University, CO (HMS)
Assemblies of God Theological Seminary, MO (GRD)
Associated Mennonite Biblical Seminaries, IN (GRD)
Associated Pathologist Laboratories, NV (AHS)
Associated Technical College, CA (TCT)
Assumption College, MA (UNC)
Assumption College for Sisters, NJ (JRC)
Astoria Beauty College, OR (TCT)
Astrodome Dental Career Center, TX (TCT)
Athenaeum of Ohio, OH (UNC)
Athenian School, CA (PRC)
Athens State University, AL (UNC)
Athens Technical College, GA (JRC)
ATI Career Training Center, FL (TCT)
ATI Career Training Center, OK (TCT)
ATI Career Training Center, TX (TCT)
ATI College of Health, FL (JRC)
ATI Technical Training Center, TX (TCT)
Atlanta Area School for the Deaf, GA (HND)
Atlanta Christian College, GA (UNC)
Atlanta Institute of Music, GA (JRC)
Atlanta Job Corps Center, GA (TCT)
Atlanta Medical Center, GA (TCT)
Atlanta Metro College, GA (JRC)
Atlanta School of Massage, GA (TCT)
Atlanta Technical College, GA (TCT)
Atlantic Cape Community College, NJ (JRC)
Atlantic College, PR (UNC)
Atlantic Co. Vocational Technical School, NJ (AHS)
Atlantic Institute of Oriental Medicine, FL (GRD)
Atlantic Technical Center, FL (TCT)
Atlantic Union College, MA (UNC)
Atlantic University, VA (HMS)
Atlantic University of Chinese Medicine, NC (GRD)
ATS Institute of Technology, OH (TCT)
Auburn Adventist Academy, WA (PRC)
Auburn University, AL (UNC)
Auburn University at Montgomery, AL (UNC)
Audio Recording Technology Institute, FL (TCT)
Augsburg College, MN (UNC)
Augusta Medical Center, VA (TCT)
Augustana College, IL (UNC)
Augustana College, SD (UNC)
Augusta State University, GA (UNC)
Augusta Technical College, GA (JRC)
Aultman Hospital, OH (AHS)
Aurora Health Care, WI (TCT)
Aurora University, IL (UNC)
Austin Beauty School, NY (TCT)
Austin Business College, TX (TCT)
Austin College, TX (UNC)
Austin Community College, TX (JRC)
Austine School for the Deaf, VT (HND)
Austin Graduate School of Theology, TX (UNC)
Austin Peay State University, TN (UNC)
Austin Presbyterian Theological Seminary, TX (GRD)
Australasian College of Health Sciences, OR (HMS)
Automotive Training Center, PA (TCT)
Avalon Beauty College, CA (TCT)
Avance Beauty College, CA (TCT)
Aveda Institute, LA (TCT)
Aveda Institute, MN (TCT)
Aveda Institute, TX (TCT)
Ave Maria College, MI (UNC)
Ave Maria University, FL (UNC)
Averett University, VA (UNC)
Aviation & Electronic School of America, CA (TCT)
Aviation Institute of Maintenance, GA (TCT)
Aviation Institute of Maintenance, IN (TCT)
Aviation Institute of Maintenance, MO (TCT)
Aviation Institute of Maintenance, PA (TCT)
Aviation Institute of Maintenance, TX (TCT)
Aviation Institute of Maintenance, VA (TCT)
Avila University, MO (UNC)
Avon Old Farms School, CT (PRB)
Award Beauty School, MD (TCT)
Ayers Institute, LA (TCT)
AZ School of Acupuncture & Oriental Med, AZ (GRD)
Azusa Pacific University, CA (UNC)

B

Babel University Professional School, HI (HMS)
Babson College, MA (UNC)
Bacone College, OK (UNC)
Bahner College of Hairstyling, NE (TCT)
Bainbridge College, GA (JRC)
Baker College of Auburn Hills, MI (UNC)
Baker College of Cadillac, MI (UNC)
Baker College of Clinton Township, MI (UNC)
Baker College of Flint, MI (UNC)
Baker College of Jackson, MI (UNC)
Baker College of Muskegon, MI (UNC)
Baker College of Owosso, MI (UNC)
Baker College of Port Huron, MI (UNC)
Bakersfield College, CA (JRC)
Baker University, KS (UNC)
Baker University School of Nursing, KS (UNC)
Bakke Graduate University of Ministry, WA (GRD)
Baldwin Beauty School #5, TX (TCT)
Baldwin Beauty School - North, TX (TCT)
Baldwin-Wallace College, OH (UNC)
Ball Memorial Hospital, IN (TCT)
Ball State University, IN (UNC)
Baltimore City Community College, MD (JRC)
Baltimore Hebrew University, MD (UNC)
Baltimore International College, MD (UNC)
Baltimore School of Massage, MD (TCT)
Baltimore School of Massage-York Campus, PA (TCT)
Baltimore Studio of Hair Design, MD (TCT)
Bamberg Job Corps Center, SC (TCT)
Bancroft School of Massage Therapy, MA (TCT)
Bangor Theological Seminary, ME (GRD)
Bank Street College of Education, NY (GRD)
Baptist/St. Vincent's Health System, FL (TCT)
Baptist Bible College, MO (UNC)
Baptist Bible College and Seminary, PA (UNC)
The Baptist College of Florida, FL (UNC)
Baptist Health System, TX (AHS)
Baptist Hospital, TX (AHS)
Baptist Hospital of Southeast Texas, TX (AHS)
Baptist Medical Center, AL (TCT)
Baptist Medical Center, SC (AHS)
Baptist Medical Centers, FL (TCT)
Baptist Memorial Coll. of Health Science, TN (UNC)
Baptist Memorial Hospital, TN (AHS)
Baptist Missionary Theological Seminary, TX (GRD)
Baptist School of Nursing-NW, AR (NRS)
Baptist School of Nursing-SE, AR (NRS)
Baptist Schools of Allied Health, AR (TCT)
Baptist Theological Seminary, VA (GRD)
Baptist University of the Americas, TX (UNC)
Baran Institute of Technology, CT (TCT)
Barclay College, KS (UNC)
Bard College, NY (UNC)
Barnard College, NY (WMC)
Barnes-Jewish College of Nursing, MO (UNC)
BarPalma Beauty Careers Academy, VA (TCT)
Barrett & Company School of Hair Design, KY (TCT)
Barry University, FL (UNC)
Barstow Community College, CA (JRC)
Barton College, NC (UNC)
Barton County Community College, KS (JRC)
Bass Memorial Academy, MS (PRC)
Bastrop Beauty School #1, LA (TCT)
Bastyr University, WA (GRD)
Bates College, ME (UNC)
Bates Technical College, WA (TCT)
Batesville Job Corps Center, MS (TCT)
Baton Rouge Community College, LA (JRC)
Baton Rouge General Medical Center, LA (AHS)
Baton Rouge School of Computers, LA (TCT)
Bauder College, GA (JRC)
Bayamon Central University, PR (UNC)
Bayamon Community College, PR (TCT)
Bay de Noc Community College, MI (JRC)
Bayfront Medical Center, FL (TCT)
Bayhealth Medical Center, DE (AHS)
Baylor College of Medicine, TX (GRD)
Baylor School, TN (PRC)
Baylor University, TX (UNC)
Baylor University Medical Center, TX (GRD)
Bay Medical Center, FL (GRD)
Bay Mills Community College, MI (JRC)
Bayonne Hospital School of Nursing, NJ (NRS)
Bay Path College, MA (WMC)
Bayshire Beauty Academy, MI (TCT)
Bay State College, MA (AHS)
Bay State College, MA (UNC)
Bay State School of Technology, MA (TCT)
Bay Vista College of Beauty, CA (TCT)
Beacon College, FL (UNC)
Beacon University, GA (UNC)
Beal College, ME (JRC)
Beatrice Academy of Beauty, OH (TCT)
Beaufort County Community College, NC (JRC)
Beau Monde College Acad of Cosmetology, OR (TCT)
Beau Monde College of Hair Design, OR (TCT)
Beauty and Barber Academy, FL (TCT)
Beauty College of America, GA (TCT)
The Beauty Institute, TN (TCT)
Beauty School of Middletown, NY (TCT)
Beauty Schools of America, FL (TCT)
Beauty Technical College, OK (TCT)
Beaver Falls Beauty Academy, PA (TCT)
Becker College, MA (UNC)
Beckfield College, KY (TCT)
Beckley Beauty Academy, WV (TCT)
Beebe Medical Center School of Nursing, DE (TCT)
Bee-Jay's Hairstyling Academy, AR (TCT)
Behold! Beauty Academy, TX (TCT)
Beis Medrash Heichal Dovid, NY (MNC)
Belhaven College, MS (UNC)
Bellarmine University, KY (UNC)
Bellevue Community College, WA (JRC)
Bellevue Hospital Center, NY (AHS)
Bellevue University, NE (UNC)
Bellin College of Nursing, WI (UNC)
Bellingham Beauty School, WA (TCT)
Bellingham Technical College, WA (TCT)
Bellin Hospital, WI (TCT)
Bellvue Beauty School, WA (TCT)
Belmont Abbey College, NC (UNC)
Belmont Hill School, MA (PRB)
Belmont Technical College, OH (JRC)
Belmont University, TN (UNC)
Beloit College, WI (UNC)
Bel-Rea Institute of Animal Technology, CO (TCT)
The Bement School, MA (PRC)
Bemidji State University, MN (UNC)
Benedict College, SC (UNC)
Benedictine College, KS (UNC)
Benedictine University, IL (UNC)
Benefits Health Care-West Campus, MT (AHS)
Benes International School of Beauty, FL (TCT)
Benjamin Franklin Inst. of Technology, MA (JRC)
Ben Lippen School, SC (PRC)
Bennett Beauty Institute, DC (TCT)
Bennett College, NC (WMC)
Bennington College, VT (UNC)
Bennington Regional Day Program, VT (HND)
Ben Taub Hospital, TX (AHS)
Bentley College, MA (UNC)
Berdan Institute, NJ (TCT)
Berea College, KY (UNC)
Berean Institute, PA (TCT)
Bergen Community College, NJ (JRC)
Berkeley City College, CA (JRC)
Berkeley College, NJ (JRC)
Berkeley College, NJ (UNC)
Berkeley College - Westchester Campus, NY (UNC)
Berkeley Divinity School, CT (GRD)
Berklee College of Music, MA (UNC)
Berkshire Community College, MA (JRC)
Berkshire Medical Center, MA (AHS)
Berkshire School, MA (PRC)
Berks Technical Institute, PA (TCT)
Berk Trade School, NY (TCT)
Berry College, GA (UNC)
Bessemer State Technical College, AL (JRC)
Best Care Training Institute, NJ (TCT)
Beta Tech, SC (TCT)
Beta Tech, VA (TCT)
Beta Tech West, VA (TCT)
Bethany College, KS (UNC)
Bethany College, WV (UNC)
Bethany Lutheran College, MN (UNC)
Bethany Theological Seminary, IN (GRD)
Bethany University, CA (UNC)
Beth Benjamin Academy of Connecticut, CT (UNC)
Bethel College, IN (UNC)
Bethel College, KS (UNC)
Bethel College, MN (UNC)
Bethel College, TN (UNC)
Bethel Seminary, MN (GRD)
Bethel Seminary of the East, PA (GRD)
Bethesda Christian University, CA (UNC)
Bethesda Memorial Hospital, FL (TCT)
Beth HaMedrash Shaarei Yosher, NY (MNC)
Beth HaTalmud Rabbinical College, NY (MNC)
Beth Israel Healthcare, MA (AHS)
Beth Medrash Govoha, NJ (MNC)
Bethune-Cookman College, FL (UNC)
Beulah Heights University, GA (UNC)
Bevill State Community College, AL (JRC)
Bexley Hall Seminary, NY (GRD)
Bexley Hall Seminary, OH (GRD)
Biblical Theological Seminary, PA (GRD)
Bidwell Training Center, PA (TCT)
Big Bend Community College, WA (JRC)
Bill Hill's College of Cosmetology, IA (TCT)
Bill Priest Inst. Economic Development, TX (TCT)
Biola University, CA (UNC)
Birmingham-Southern College, AL (UNC)
Birthingway College of Midwifery, OR (UNC)
Bishop Clarkson Memorial Hospital, NE (AHS)
The Bishop's School, CA (PRC)
Bishop State Community College-Central, AL (JRC)
Bishop State Community College-Carver, AL (TCT)
Bishop State Community College-Main, AL (JRC)
Bishop State Community College, AL (TCT)
Bismarck State College, ND (JRC)
BJ's Beauty & Barber College, WA (TCT)
Blackburn College, IL (UNC)
Blackfeet Community College, MT (JRC)
Black Hawk College, IL (JRC)
Blackhawk Technical College, WI (JRC)
Black Hills Beauty College, SD (TCT)
Black Hills State University, SD (UNC)
Black River Technical College, AR (TCT)
Bladen Community College, NC (JRC)
Blades School of Hair Design, MD (TCT)
Blaine The Beauty Career School, MA (TCT)
Blair Academy, NJ (PRC)
Blair College, CO (JRC)
Blair School of Music of Vanderbilt U., TN (UNC)
Blessed John XXIII National Seminary, MA (GRD)
Blessing Hospital, IL (TCT)
Blessing-Rieman College of Nursing, IL (UNC)
Blinn College, TX (JRC)
Blood Center of SE Wisconsin, WI (AHS)
Bloomfield College, NJ (UNC)
Bloomington Hospital, IN (AHS)
Bloomington-Normal School of Radiography, IL (AHS)
Bloomsburg University of Pennsylvania, PA (UNC)
Blue Cliff College, LA (TCT)
Blue Cliff College, MS (TCT)
Blue Cliff School of Therapeutic Massage, AL (TCT)
Bluefield College, VA (UNC)
Bluefield Regional Medical Center, WV (AHS)
Bluefield State College, WV (UNC)
Bluegrass Community & Technical College, KY (JRC)
Blue Mountain College, MS (UNC)
Blue Mountain Community College, OR (JRC)
Blue Ridge Community & Technical College, WV (JRC)
Blue Ridge Community College, NC (JRC)
Blue Ridge Community College, VA (JRC)
Blue Ridge Job Corps Center, VA (TCT)
Blue Ridge School, VA (PRB)
Bluffton University, OH (UNC)
Blytheville Academy of Cosmetology, AR (TCT)
Bob Jones Academy, SC (PRC)
Bob Jones University, SC (UNC)
Bohecker's Business College, OH (TCT)
Boise Bible College, ID (UNC)

C

Central Michigan University, MI (UNC)
Central Missouri State University, MO (UNC)
Central Ohio Technical College, OH (JRC)
Central Oregon Community College, OR (JRC)
Central Pennsylvania College, PA (UNC)
Central Piedmont Community College, NC (JRC)
Central State Beauty Academy, OK (TCT)
Central State University, OH (UNC)
Central Suffolk Hospital, NY (AHS)
Central Texas Beauty College, TX (TCT)
Central Texas College, TX (JRC)
Central Texas Commercial College, TX (TCT)
Central Virginia Community College, VA (JRC)
Central Washington University, WA (UNC)
Central Wyoming College, WY (JRC)
Central Yeshiva Tomchei Tmimim Lubavitz, NY (UNC)
Centre College, KY (UNC)
Centro de Capacitacion y Asesoramiento, PR (TCT)
Centro de Estudios Multidisciplinarios, PR (TCT)
Centura-St. Anthony Hospital, CO (TCT)
Centurion Professional Training, NY (TCT)
Century College, MN (JRC)
Century College, PR (TCT)
Century School of Cosmetology, OH (TCT)
Cerritos College, CA (JRC)
Cerro Coso Community College, CA (JRC)
Certified Careers Institute, UT (TCT)
CFS The School at Church Farm, PA (PRB)
Chabot College, CA (JRC)
Chadron State College, NE (UNC)
Chaffey College, CA (JRC)
Chaminade College Preparatory School, MO (PRB)
Chaminade University of Honolulu, HI (UNC)
Champlain College, VT (UNC)
Champlain Valley Physicians Hospital, NY (AHS)
Chandler-Gilbert Community College, AZ (JRC)
Chaparral College, AZ (TCT)
Chapel Hill-Chauncy Hall School, MA (PRC)
Chapman School of Seamanship, FL (TCT)
Chapman University, CA (UNC)
Charity-Delgado School of Nursing, LA (HME)
Charles of Italy Beauty College, AZ (TCT)
Charles R. Drew Univ. of Med. & Science, CA (UNC)
Charles Stewart Mott Community College, MI (JRC)
Charles Stuart School of Locksmithing, NY (TCT)
Charleston Cosmetology Institute, SC (TCT)
Charleston School of Beauty Culture, WV (TCT)
Charleston Southern University, SC (UNC)
Charlie & Sue's School of Hair Design, TX (TCT)
Charlotte Technical Center, FL (TCT)
Charter College, AK (UNC)
Charter Oak State College, CT (HMS)
Chase College, CA (TCT)
Chatfield College, OH (JRC)
Chatham College, PA (WMC)
Chatham Hall, VA (PRG)
Chattahoochee Technical College, GA (JRC)
Chattahoochee Valley Community College, AL (JRC)
Chattanooga State Tech. Comm. College, TN (JRC)
Cheeks Intl Academy of Beauty Culture, CO (TCT)
Cheeks Intl Academy of Beauty Culture, WY (TCT)
Chemeketa Community College, OR (JRC)
Cheryl Fell's School of Business, NY (TCT)
Chesapeake College, MD (JRC)
Cheshire Academy, CT (PRC)
Chester College of New England, NH (UNC)
Chestnut Hill College, PA (UNC)
Cheveux School Hair Design and Hairport, NC (TCT)
Cheyney University of Pennsylvania, PA (UNC)
Chicago School of Massage Therapy, IL (TCT)
Chicago Sch. of Professional Psychology, IL (GRD)
Chicago State University, IL (UNC)
Chicago Theological Seminary, IL (GRD)
Chic University of Cosmetology, MI (TCT)
Chief Dull Knife College, MT (JRC)
CHI Institute, PA (TCT)
CHI Institute/RETS Campus, PA (TCT)
Child Development Ctr. of Northern VA, VA (HND)
Children's Hospital, MA (AHS)
Children's Hospital & Medical Center, OH (AHS)
Children's Hospital of Los Angeles, CA (TCT)
Chillicothe Beauty Academy, MO (TCT)
Chipola College, FL (JRC)
Chippewa Valley Technical College, WI (JRC)
C.H. McCann Technical School, MA (TCT)
Choate Rosemary Hall School, CT (PRC)
Chowan University, NC (UNC)
Chris' Beauty College, MS (TCT)
Christchurch School, VA (PRB)
Christendom College, VA (UNC)
Christ Hospital, OH (AHS)
Christ Hospital School of Nursing, NJ (TCT)
Christiana Care Health Services, DE (AHS)
Christian Brothers University, TN (UNC)
Christian Life College, IL (UNC)
Christian Theological Seminary, IN (TSR)
Christopher Newport University, VA (UNC)
Christ School, NC (PRB)
Christ the King Seminary, NY (GRD)
Chubb Institute, IL (TCT)
Chubb Institute, NJ (TCT)
Chubb Institute, NY (TCT)
Chubb Institute-Keystone School, PA (TCT)
Church Divinity School of the Pacific, CA (GRD)
Church of God Theological Seminary, TN (GRD)
Cincinnati Christian University, OH (UNC)
Cincinnati College of Mortuary Science, OH (UNC)
Cincinnati State Technical & Comm Coll, OH (JRC)
Circle J Beauty School, TX (TCT)
Circleville Bible College, OH (UNC)
Cisco Junior College, TX (JRC)
The Citadel, SC (MNC)
Citizens General Hospital, PA (NRS)
Citizen's High School, FL (HMS)
Citizens Medical Center, TX (AHS)
Citrus College, CA (JRC)
Cittone Institute, NJ (TCT)
City College, FL (JRC)
City College, FL (TCT)
City College, FL (UNC)
City College of San Francisco, CA (JRC)
City of Hope Medical Center, CA (TCT)
City University, WA (UNC)
Columbia Biblical Seminary, SC (GRD)
Clackamas Community College, OR (JRC)
Claflin University, SC (UNC)
Claremont Graduate University, CA (GRD)
Claremont McKenna College, CA (UNC)
Claremont School of Theology, CA (GRD)
Claremore Beauty College, OK (TCT)
Clarendon College, TX (JRC)
Clare's Beauty College, WA (TCT)
Clarion University of Pennsylvania, PA (UNC)
Clarion University - Venango Campus, PA (UNC)
Clarita Career College, CA (TCT)
Clark Atlanta University, GA (UNC)
Clark College, WA (JRC)
Clarke College, IA (UNC)
Clarksburg Beauty Academy, WV (TCT)
Clarkson College, NE (UNC)
Clarkson University, NY (UNC)
Clark State Community College, OH (JRC)
Clark University, MA (UNC)
Class Act I School of Cosmetology, MO (TCT)
Classic College of Hair Design, KS (TCT)
Clatsop Community College, OR (JRC)
Clayton State University, GA (UNC)
Clayton University, MO (UNC)
Clear Creek Baptist Bible College, KY (UNC)
Clearfield Beauty Academy, PA (TCT)
Clearfield Hospital, PA (AHS)
Clearwater Christian College, FL (UNC)
Cleary University - Livingston Campus, MI (UNC)
Cleary University - Washtenaw Campus, MI (UNC)
Clemson University, SC (UNC)
Cleveland Chiropractic College, MO (BIO)
Cleveland Chiropractic College of LA, CA (BIO)
Cleveland Clinic Foundation, OH (TCT)
Cleveland Community College, NC (JRC)
Cleveland Institute of Art, OH (UNC)
Cleveland Institute Dental Medical Asst., OH (TCT)
Cleveland Institute of Electronics, OH (JRC)
Cleveland Institute of Music, OH (UNC)
Cleveland State Community College, TN (JRC)
Cleveland State University, OH (UNC)
Cleveland Veterans Affairs Medical Ctr, OH (AHS)
Clinton Community College, IA (JRC)
Clinton Community College, NY (JRC)
Clinton Junior College, SC (JRC)
Cloud County Community College, KS (JRC)
Clover Park Technical College, WA (TCT)
Clovis Community College, NM (JRC)
Cloyd's Beauty School #1, LA (TCT)
Cloyd's Beauty School #2, LA (TCT)
Cloyd's Beauty School #3, LA (TCT)
Coachella Valley Technical Skills Center, CA (TCT)
Coahoma Community College, MS (JRC)
Coastal Bend College, TX (JRC)
Coastal Carolina Community College, NC (JRC)
Coastal Carolina University, SC (UNC)
Coastal Georgia Community College, GA (JRC)
Coastline Community College, CA (JRC)
COBA Academy, CA (TCT)
Cobb Beauty College, GA (TCT)
Cochise College, AZ (JRC)
Cochran School of Nursing, NY (TCT)
Coconino Community College, AZ (JRC)
Coe College, IA (UNC)
Coffeyville Community College, KS (JRC)
Cogswell College, CA (UNC)
Coker College, SC (UNC)
Colburn School, CA (TCT)
Colby College, ME (UNC)
Colby Community College, KS (JRC)
Colby-Sawyer College, NH (UNC)
Colegio Biblico Pentecostal De PR, PR (UNC)
Colegio Educativo Tecnologico Industrial, PR (TCT)
Colegio Mayor de Technologia, PR (TCT)
Colegio Pentecostal Mizpa, PR (UNC)
Colegio Tecnico de Electricidad Galloza, PR (TCT)
Colegio Tecnico Metropolitano, PR (TCT)
Colegio Tecnologico y Comercial, PR (TCT)
Coleman College, CA (UNC)
Colgate Rochester Crozer Divinity School, NY (GRD)
Colgate University, NY (UNC)
Colleen O'Hara's Beauty Academy, CA (TCT)
CollegeAmerica, AZ (TCT)
CollegeAmerica - Colorado, CO (UNC)
CollegeAmerica - Colorado Springs, CO (UNC)
CollegeAmerica - Fort Collins, CO (UNC)
College for Creative Studies, MI (UNC)
College for Financial Planning, CO (UNC)
College Misericordia, PA (UNC)
College of Alameda, CA (JRC)
College of Automotive Management, CA (TCT)
College of Biblical Studies, TX (JRC)
College of Business & Technology, FL (TCT)
College of Career Training, CA (TCT)
College of Charleston, SC (UNC)
College of Coiffure Art, MT (TCT)
College of Cosmetology, OR (TCT)
College of Court Reporting, IN (TCT)
College of DuPage, IL (JRC)
College of Eastern Utah, UT (JRC)
College of Hair Design, IA (TCT)
College of Hair Design, KS (TCT)
College of Hair Design, NE (TCT)
College of Hair Design Careers, OR (TCT)
College of Information Technology, CA (TCT)
College of Lake County, IL (JRC)
College of Legal Arts, OR (TCT)
College of Marin, CA (JRC)
College of Menominee Nation, WI (JRC)
College of Micronesia, FM (JRC)
College of Mount Saint Joseph, OH (UNC)
College of Mount Saint Vincent, NY (UNC)
College of New Jersey, NJ (UNC)
College of New Rochelle, NY (UNC)
College of Notre Dame of Maryland, MD (WMC)
College of Office Technology, IL (TCT)
College of Saint Benedict, MN (WMC)
College of Saint Catherine, MN (WMC)
College of Saint Elizabeth, NJ (WMC)
College of Saint Joseph, VT (UNC)
College of Saint Mary, NE (WMC)
College of Saint Rose, NY (UNC)
College of Saint Scholastica, MN (UNC)
College of Saint Thomas More, TX (UNC)
College of San Mateo, CA (JRC)
College of Santa Fe, NM (UNC)
College of Southern Idaho, ID (JRC)
College of Southern Maryland, MD (JRC)
College of the Albemarle, NC (JRC)
College of the Atlantic, ME (UNC)
College of the Canyons, CA (JRC)
College of the Desert, CA (JRC)
College of the Holy Cross, MA (UNC)
College of the Humanities and Sciences, AZ (HMS)
College of the Mainland, TX (JRC)
College of the Marshall Islands, MH (JRC)
College of the Ozarks, MO (UNC)
College of the Sequoias, CA (JRC)
College of the Siskiyous, CA (JRC)
College of the Southwest, NM (UNC)
College of Visual Arts, MN (UNC)
The College of Westchester, NY (JRC)
College of William and Mary, VA (UNC)
College of Wooster, OH (UNC)
Collin County Community College, TX (JRC)
Collins Career Center, OH (TCT)
Collins College School of Design & Tech., AZ (UNC)
Collins School of Cosmetology, KY (TCT)
Colorado Academy, CO (PRC)
Colorado Ctr for Medical Laboratory Sci., CO (TCT)
Colorado Christian University, CO (UNC)
Colorado College, CO (UNC)
Colorado Institute of Taxidermy, CO (TCT)
Colorado Mountain College, CO (JRC)
Colorado Northwestern Community College, CO (JRC)
Colorado Rocky Mountain School, CO (PRC)
Colorado School for the Deaf and Blind, CO (HND)
Colorado School of Healing Arts, CO (TCT)
Colorado School of Mines, CO (UNC)
Colorado Sch. of Professional Psychology, CO (GRD)
Colorado School of Trades, CO (TCT)
CO Sch of Traditional Chinese Medicine, CO (UNC)
The Colorado Springs School, CO (PRC)
Colorado State University, CO (UNC)
Colorado State University - Pueblo, CO (UNC)
Colorado Technical University, CO (UNC)
Colorado Technical University, MO (UNC)
Colorado Technical University, SD (JRC)
Colorado Timberline Academy, CO (PRC)
Columbia Basin College, WA (JRC)
Columbia Beauty Academy, MO (TCT)
Columbia Beauty School, SC (TCT)
Columbia Center, MD (UNC)
Columbia Centro Universitario, PR (JRC)
Columbia Centro Universitario, PR (TCT)
Columbia College, CA (JRC)
Columbia College, IL (UNC)
Columbia College, MO (UNC)
Columbia College, SC (WMC)
Columbia College Hollywood, CA (TCT)
Columbia College of Nursing, WI (UNC)
Columbia Commonwealth University, WY (HMS)
Columbia-Greene Beauty School, NY (TCT)
Columbia-Greene Community College, NY (JRC)
Columbia HealthOne, CO (AHS)
Columbia Hospital, WI (AHS)
Columbia International University, SC (TSR)
Columbia Southern University, AL (HMS)
Columbia State Community College, TN (JRC)
Columbia Theological Seminary, GA (GRD)
Columbia Union College, MD (UNC)
Columbia University, NY (UNC)
Columbus College of Art & Design, OH (UNC)
Columbus Regional Hospital, IN (AHS)
Columbus State Community College, OH (JRC)
Columbus State University, GA (UNC)
Columbus Technical College, GA (JRC)
Comanche Co. Memorial Hospital, OK (AHS)
Commercial Driver Training School, NY (TCT)
Commonwealth Institute / Funeral Service, TX (JRC)
Commonwealth Technical Institute, PA (JRC)
Community Business College, CA (TCT)
Community Christian College, CA (UNC)
Community College of Allegheny County, PA (JRC)
Community College of Aurora, CO (JRC)
Community College of Baltimore County, MD (JRC)
Community College of Beaver County, PA (JRC)
Community College of Cosmetology, KS (TCT)
Community College of Denver, CO (JRC)
Community College of Indiana-Valparaiso, IN (JRC)
Community College of Philadelphia, PA (JRC)
Community College of Rhode Island, RI (JRC)
Community College of Southern Nevada, NV (JRC)
Community College of the Air Force, AL (JRC)
Community College of Vermont, VT (JRC)
Community Hospital of Indianapolis, IN (TCT)
Community Hospital School of Nursing, OH (TCT)
Compton Community College, CA (JRC)
Compu-Med Vocational Careers, FL (TCT)
Compu Tech Consultants School, TX (TCT)
Computer Career Center, TX (TCT)
Computer-Ed Business Institute, MA (TCT)
Computer-Ed Business Institute, RI (TCT)
Computer Learning Network, PA (TCT)
Computer Systems Institute, IL (TCT)
Computer Tutor Business & Technical Inst, CA (TCT)
Concept College of Cosmetology, IL (TCT)
Conception Seminary College, MO (MNC)
Concord Academy, MA (PRC)
Concord Academy of Hair Design, NH (TCT)

Concorde Career College, CA (AHS)
Concorde Career College, CO (AHS)
Concorde Career College, MO (AHS)
Concorde Career College, TN (TCT)
Concorde Career Institute, CA (AHS)
Concorde Career Institute, CA (TCT)
Concorde Career Institute, FL (AHS)
Concorde Career Institute, OR (AHS)
Concorde Career Institute, TX (AHS)
Concorde School of Hair Design, NJ (TCT)
Concordia College, AL (UNC)
Concordia College, MN (UNC)
Concordia College, NY (UNC)
Concordia Seminary, MO (GRD)
Concordia Theological Seminary, IN (GRD)
Concordia University, CA (BUS)
Concordia University, IL (UNC)
Concordia University, MI (UNC)
Concordia University, NE (UNC)
Concordia University, OR (UNC)
Concordia University, TX (UNC)
Concordia University, WI (UNC)
Concordia University-St. Paul, MN (UNC)
Concord Law School, CA (UNC)
Concord University, WV (UNC)
Conemaugh Valley Memorial Hospital, PA (AHS)
Conlee's College of Cosmetology, TX (TCT)
Connecticut Center for Massage Therapy, CT (TCT)
Connecticut Childrens Medical Center, CT (AHS)
Connecticut Childrens Medical Center, CT (TCT)
Connecticut College, CT (UNC)
Connecticut Culinary Institute, CT (TCT)
Connecticut Institute for the Blind, CT (HND)
Connecticut Institute of Hair Design, CT (TCT)
Connecticut Junior Republic, CT (HND)
Connors State College, OK (JRC)
Conservatory of Music, PR (UNC)
Conservatory of Recording Arts/Sciences, AZ (MUS)
Conservatory of Recording Arts/Sciences, AZ (TCT)
Consolidated School of Business, PA (TCT)
Consumnes River College-Eldorado Center, CA (JRC)
Continental Academie of Hair Design, NH (TCT)
Continental School, NY (TCT)
Continental School of Beauty Culture, NY (TCT)
Contra Costa College, CA (JRC)
Convent of the Sacred Heart, CT (PRG)
Converse College, SC (WMC)
Conway School of Landscape Design, MA (GRD)
Cook County Hospital, IL (TCT)
Cooking & Hospitality Inst. of Chicago, IL (TCT)
Cooperative Medical Technology Program, OH (TCT)
Cooper Hospital/Univ Medical Center, NJ (TCT)
Cooper Union, NY (UNC)
Coosa Valley Technical College, GA (TCT)
Coosa Valley Technical Institute, GA (TCT)
Cope Institute, NY (TCT)
Copiah-Lincoln Community College, MS (JRC)
Copper Mountain College, CA (JRC)
Coppin State University, MD (UNC)
Coral Ridge Nurse's Asst Training School, FL (TCT)
Corban College, OR (UNC)
Corcoran College of Art & Design, DC (UNC)
Core Institute, FL (TCT)
Cornell College, IA (UNC)
Cornell University, NY (UNC)
Cornerstone University, MI (UNC)
Corning Community College, NY (JRC)
Cornish College of the Arts, WA (UNC)
Cortiva Institute - Colorado, CO (TCT)
Coryell Cosmetology College, TX (TCT)
Cosmetology & Spa Institute, IL (TCT)
Cosmetology Careers Unlimited - Duluth, MN (TCT)
Cosmetology Careers Unlimited - Hibbing, MN (TCT)
Cosmetology Inst of Beauty Arts & Sci., NC (TCT)
Cosmetology Training Center, LA (TCT)
Cossatot Community College Univ. of AR, AR (JRC)
Cosumnes River College, CA (JRC)
Cottey College, MO (WMC)
Cotton Boll Technical Institute, AR (TCT)
County College of Morris, NJ (JRC)
County Univ. Sch. of Dental & Oral Surg., NY (AHS)
Court Reporting Institute of Dallas, TX (TCT)
Court Reporting Institute of Houston, TX (TCT)
Court Reporting Institute of Louisiana, LA (TCT)
Covenant College, GA (UNC)
Covenant Medical Center, IA (AHS)
Covenant Sch. of Nursing & Allied Health, TX (JRC)
Covenant Theological Seminary, MO (GRD)
Cowley County Community College, KS (JRC)
Cox College of Nursing & Health Sciences, MO (UNC)
Coyne American Institute, IL (TCT)
Crafton Hills College, CA (JRC)
Cranbrook Academy of Art, MI (ART)
Cranbrook Schools, MI (PRC)
Craven Community College, NC (JRC)
Creations College of Cosmetology, MS (TCT)
The Creative Center, NE (TCT)
Creative Circus, GA (TCT)
Creative Hair Styling Academy, IN (TCT)
Creative Images-Matrix Design Academy, OH (TCT)
Creighton University, NE (UNC)
Crescent Cosmetology University, VA (TCT)
Crested Butte Academy, CO (PRC)
Crichton College, TN (UNC)
The Criswell College, TX (UNC)
Crossroads Bible College, IN (UNC)
Crossroads College, MN (UNC)
Crouse Hospital School of Nursing, NY (NRS)
Crowder College, MO (JRC)
Crowley's Ridge College, AR (JRC)
Crowley's Ridge Technical Institute, AR (TCT)
Crown College, MN (UNC)
Crown College, WA (UNC)
Crum's Beauty College, KS (TCT)
Cuesta College, CA (JRC)
Culinary Academy of Austin, TX (TCT)
Culinary Academy of Long Island, NY (TCT)
Culinary Academy of New York, NY (TCT)
Culinary Institute, TX (TCT)
Culinary Institute of America, NY (JRC)
Culinary Institute of America Greystone, CA (TCT)
Culinary Institute of New Orleans, LA (TCT)
Culver Academies & Summer Camps, IN (PRC)
Culver-Stockton College, MO (UNC)
Cumberland County College, NJ (JRC)
Cumberland Co. Tech. Education Center, NJ (TCT)
Cumberland Technical College, KY (TCT)
Cumberland University, TN (UNC)
CUNY Bernard M. Baruch College, NY (UNC)
CUNY Borough/Manhattan Comm. College, NY (JRC)
CUNY Bronx Community College, NY (JRC)
CUNY Brooklyn College, NY (UNC)
CUNY City College, NY (UNC)
CUNY College of Staten Island, NY (UNC)
CUNY Graduate Center, NY (GRD)
CUNY Hunter College, NY (UNC)
CUNY John Jay College Criminal Justice, NY (UNC)
CUNY Kingsborough Community College, NY (JRC)
CUNY Lehman College, NY (UNC)
CUNY Medgar Evers College, NY (UNC)
CUNY Queensborough Community College, NY (JRC)
CUNY Queens College, NY (UNC)
CUNY York College, NY (UNC)
Curry College, MA (UNC)
Curtis Institute of Music, PA (UNC)
Cushing Academy, MA (PRC)
Cutting Edge Hairstyling Academy, KS (TCT)
Cuyahoga Community College, OH (JRC)
Cuyamaca College, CA (JRC)
Cynthia's Beauty Academy, CA (TCT)
Cypress College, CA (JRC)

D

Dabney S. Lancaster Community College, VA (JRC)
Daemen College, NY (UNC)
Dahl's College of Beauty, MT (TCT)
Dakota Co. Technical College, MN (TCT)
Dakota State University, SD (UNC)
Dakota Wesleyan University, SD (UNC)
Dallas Baptist University, TX (UNC)
Dallas Barber and Stylist College, TX (TCT)
Dallas Christian College, TX (UNC)
Dallas Institute of Funeral Service, TX (EMB)
Dallas Roberts Academy of Hair Design, UT (TCT)
Dallas Theological Seminary, TX (GRD)
Dalton State College, GA (JRC)
Dana College, NE (UNC)
Dana Hall School, MA (PRG)
Danbury Hospital, CT (TCT)
Daniel Freeman Mem. Hospital, CA (TCT)
Daniel Webster College, NH (UNC)
Danville Area Community College, IL (JRC)
Danville Community College, VA (JRC)
Danville Regional Medical Center, VA (TCT)
Darkei Noam Rabbinical College, NY (MNC)
Darlington School, GA (PRC)
Darlyne McGee's Academy of Cosmetology, FL (TCT)
Darrow School, NY (PRC)
Dartmouth College, NH (UNC)
Darton College, GA (JRC)
Davenport Barber-Styling College, IA (TCT)
Davenport College of Business, IN (JRC)
Davenport College of Business, MI (TCT)
Davenport University, IN (UNC)
Davenport University, MI (AHS)
Davenport University, MI (UNC)
Davenport University - Central Region, MI (UNC)
Davenport University - Eastern Region, MI (UNC)
Davenport University - Warren, MI (UNC)
David Demuth Institute of Cosmetology, IN (TCT)
David Hochstein Memorial Music School, NY (TCT)
David L. Carrasco Job Corps Center, TX (TCT)
David Pressley School of Cosmetology, MI (TCT)
Davidson College, NC (UNC)
Davidson County Community College, NC (JRC)
Davis & Elkins College, WV (UNC)
Davis Applied Technology College, UT (TCT)
Davis College, NY (UNC)
Davis College, OH (UNC)
Dawn Training Centre, DE (TCT)
Dawson Community College, MT (JRC)
Daymar College, KY (JRC)
Daymar College - Northern Kentucky, KY (JRC)
Day Spa Career College, MS (TCT)
Daytona Beach Community College, FL (JRC)
Dayton Barber College, OH (TCT)
Dayton's School of Hair Design, IA (TCT)
DCH Regional Medical Center, AL (TCT)
Deaconess College of Nursing, MO (UNC)
Dean College, MA (JRC)
Dean Institute of Technology, PA (TCT)
DeAnza College, CA (JRC)
Deep Muscle Therapy School, DE (TCT)
Deep Springs College, NV (JRC)
Deerfield Academy, MA (PRC)
Defiance College, OH (UNC)
DeKalb Medical Center, GA (TCT)
DeKalb Technical College, GA (JRC)
Delaware County Community College, PA (JRC)
Delaware State University, DE (UNC)
Delaware Technical & Community College, DE (JRC)
Delaware Valley Academy-Medical & Dental, PA (TCT)
Delaware Valley College, PA (UNC)
Delgado Community College, LA (JRC)
Del Mar College, TX (JRC)
Del-Mar-Va Beauty Academy, MD (TCT)
Delphian School, OR (PRC)
Delta Beauty College, MS (TCT)
Delta College, LA (TCT)
Delta College, MI (JRC)
Delta College of Arts & Technology, LA (TCT)
Delta Connection Academy, FL (TCT)
Delta School of Business and Technology, LA (TCT)
Delta State University, MS (UNC)
Delta Technical Institute, AR (TCT)
Demmon School of Beauty, LA (TCT)
Denham Springs Beauty College, LA (TCT)
Denison University, OH (UNC)
Denmark Technical College, SC (JRC)
Denver Academy, CO (PRC)
Denver Academy of Court Reporting, CO (TCT)
Denver Automotive & Diesel College, CO (TCT)
Denver Health Medical Center, CO (TCT)
Denver Seminary, CO (GRD)
De Paul Medical Center, VA (AHS)
De Paul University, IL (UNC)
DePauw University, IN (UNC)
DeSales University, PA (UNC)
Desert Career College, CA (TCT)
Desert Institute of the Healing Arts, AZ (TCT)
Design Institute of San Diego, CA (UNC)
Design School of Cosemetology, CA (TCT)
Desisto School, MA (PRC)
Des Moines Area Community College, IA (JRC)
Des Moines Univ. Osteopathic Medical Ctr, IA (AHS)
Detroit Business Institute, MI (TCT)
Detroit Country Day School, MI (PRC)
Detroit Health Department, MI (AHS)
Devereux-Arizona Treatment Network, AZ (HND)
Devereux Beneto Center, PA (HND)
Devereux California, CA (HND)
Devereux Center in Connecticut, CT (HND)
Devereux Center in Massachusetts, MA (HND)
Devereux Center in New York, NY (HND)
Devereux-Florida Treatment Network, FL (HND)
Devereux Foundation in Pennsylvania, PA (HND)
Devereux-Georgia Treatment Network, GA (HND)
Devereux Kanner Center, PA (HND)
Devereux-Texas Treatment Network, TX (HND)
DeVoe College of Beauty, AZ (TCT)
DeVry College of Technology, NJ (BUS)
DeVry Institute of Technology, CO (UNC)
DeVry Institute of Technology, NY (BUS)
DeVry University, AZ (BUS)
DeVry University, CA (BUS)
DeVry University, CO (BUS)
DeVry University, FL (BUS)
DeVry University, FL (MBA)
DeVry University, GA (BUS)
DeVry University, IL (BUS)
DeVry University, IL (MBA)
DeVry University, IN (BUS)
DeVry University, MD (MBA)
DeVry University, MO (BUS)
DeVry University, MO (UNC)
DeVry University, NC (MBA)
DeVry University, NV (BUS)
DeVry University, OH (BUS)
DeVry University, OR (BUS)
DeVry University, PA (BUS)
DeVry University, TX (BUS)
DeVry University, TX (MBA)
DeVry University, VA (BUS)
DeVry University, VA (MBA)
DeVry University, WA (BUS)
DeVry University, WI (BUS)
Dewey Academy, MA (PRC)
DeWolff Coll of Hairstyling\Cosmetology, NM (TCT)
D.G. Erwin Technical Center, FL (TCT)
Diablo Valley College, CA (JRC)
Diamond Council of America, TN (HMS)
Dickinson College, PA (UNC)
Dickinson State University, ND (UNC)
Diesel Driving Academy, LA (TCT)
Diesel Truck Driver Training School, WI (TCT)
DigiPen Institute of Technology, WA (UNC)
Dillard University, LA (UNC)
Dinè College, AZ (JRC)
Divers Academy International, NJ (TCT)
Divers Institute of Technology, WA (TCT)
Divine Providence Hospital, PA (AHS)
Divine Word College Seminary, IA (UNC)
Dixie State College of Utah, UT (JRC)
D-Jay's School of Beauty Arts & Sciences, LA (TCT)
DLI Distance Learning International, VT (HMS)
D'Mart Institute, PR (TCT)
DMC University Laboratories, MI (AHS)
Doane College, NE (UNC)
Dodge City Community College, KS (JRC)
Dolphin Technical Institute, TX (TCT)
Domestic Health Care Institute, LA (TCT)
Dominican College of Blauvelt, NY (UNC)
Dominican House of Studies, DC (MNC)
Dominican School of Philosophy/Theology, CA (GRD)
Dominican University, IL (UNC)
Dominican University of California, CA (UNC)
Don Bosco Technical Institute, CA (MNC)
Dongguk Royal University, CA (GRD)
Donnelly College, KS (JRC)
Don Roberts Beauty Academy, IN (TCT)
Don Roberts Beauty School, IN (TCT)
Donta School of Beauty Culture, KY (TCT)
Dordt College, IA (UNC)
Dorsey Business School, MI (TCT)
Douglas Education Center, PA (TCT)
Douglas J Educational Center, MI (TCT)
Dover Business College, NJ (TCT)
Dowling College, NY (UNC)
D-Q University, CA (JRC)
Dragon Rises College Oriental Medicine, FL (GRD)
Drake College of Business, NJ (TCT)
Drake University, IA (UNC)
Draughons Junior College, KY (TCT)
Draughons Junior College, TN (JRC)
Draughons Junior College - Murfreesboro, TN (JRC)
Drew University, NJ (UNC)
Drexel University, PA (UNC)
Drury University, MO (UNC)
Dublin Christian Academy, NH (PRC)
Dublin School, NH (PRC)
DuBois Business College, PA (TCT)
Du Cret School of the Arts, NJ (TCT)
Dudley Beauty College, DC (TCT)

G

H

Hebrew Union College, CA (GRD)
Hebrew Union College, NY (GRD)
Hebrew Union College, OH (GRD)
Hebron Academy, ME (PRC)
Heidelberg College, OH (UNC)
Helena College of Tech of the Univ of MT, MT (JRC)
Helene Fuld College of Nursing, NY (TCT)
Helene Fuld Medical Center, NJ (AHS)
Helene Fuld School of Nursing, NJ (NRS)
Helicopter Adventures, FL (TCT)
Hellenic College/Holy Cross Sch Theology, MA (UNC)
Helma Institute Massage Therapy, NJ (TCT)
Henderson Community College, KY (JRC)
Henderson State University, AR (UNC)
Hendrick Medical Center, TX (AHS)
Hendrix College, AR (UNC)
Hennepin County Medical Center, MN (AHS)
Hennepin Technical College, MN (TCT)
Henri's School of Hair Design, MA (TCT)
Henry Ford Community College, MI (JRC)
Henry Ford Hospital, MI (AHS)
Henry W. Brewster Technical Center, FL (TCT)
Heritage Bible College, NC (JRC)
Heritage Christian University, AL (TSR)
Heritage College, CO (TCT)
Heritage College, MO (TCT)
Heritage College, NV (TCT)
Heritage College, OK (TCT)
Heritage Institute, FL (TCT)
Heritage Institute, VA (TCT)
Heritage University, WA (UNC)
Herkimer County Community College, NY (JRC)
Herzing College, AL (UNC)
Herzing College, FL (UNC)
Herzing College, GA (UNC)
Herzing College, LA (TCT)
Herzing College, MN (TCT)
Herzing College, WI (UNC)
Hesser College, NH (UNC)
Hesston College, KS (JRC)
Hibbing Community College, MN (JRC)
Hickey College, MO (TCT)
Hicks Academy of Beauty Culture, VA (TCT)
Highland Community College, IL (JRC)
Highland Community College, KS (JRC)
Highline Community College, WA (JRC)
High Mowing School-A Waldorf High School, NH (PRC)
High Point University, NC (UNC)
High-Tech Institute, AZ (JRC)
High-Tech Institute, CA (TCT)
High-Tech Institute, FL (TCT)
High-Tech Institute, GA (TCT)
High-Tech Institute, MN (TCT)
High-Tech Institute, MO (TCT)
High-Tech Institute, NV (TCT)
High-Tech Institute, TN (TCT)
High-Tech Institute, TX (TCT)
Hilbert College, NY (UNC)
Hill College, TX (JRC)
Hillcrest Baptist Medical Center, TX (AHS)
Hillsborough Community College, FL (JRC)
Hillsborough Community College Ybor Camp, FL (JRC)
Hill School, PA (PRC)
Hillsdale Beauty College, MI (TCT)
Hillsdale College, MI (UNC)
Hillsdale Free Will Baptist College, OK (UNC)
Hillside School, MA (PRB)
Hilltop Beauty School, CA (TCT)
Hinds Community College, MS (JRC)
Hiram College, OH (UNC)
Hiwassee College, TN (JRC)
Hobart & William Smith Colleges, NY (UNC)
Hobart Institute of Welding Technology, OH (TCT)
Hobe Sound Bible College, FL (UNC)
Hobe Sound Christian Academy, FL (PRC)
Hochstim School of Radiography, NY (AHS)
Hockaday School, TX (PRG)
Hocking College, OH (UNC)
Hodges University, FL (UNC)
Hofstra University, NY (UNC)
HoHoKus School, NJ (TCT)
HoHoKus Sch of Trade/Technical Sciences, NJ (TCT)
Hohokus School - RETS Nutley, NJ (TCT)
Holbrook SDA Indian School, AZ (PRC)
Holderness School, NH (PRC)
Hollins University, VA (WMC)
Hollywood Cosmetology Center, OK (TCT)
Holmes Community College, MS (JRC)
Holmes Institute, CA (HMS)
Holy Apostles College and Seminary, CT (UNC)
Holy Cross College, IN (UNC)
Holy Cross Hospital, MD (AHS)
Holy Family Hospital, WA (AHS)
Holy Family University, PA (UNC)
Holy Name Hospital School of Nursing, NJ (TCT)
Holy Names University, CA (UNC)
Holyoke Community College, MA (JRC)
Holy Spirit Hospital, PA (AHS)
Holy Trinity Orthodox Seminary, NY (MNC)
Home for Crippled Children, PA (HND)
Hondros College, OH (TCT)
Honolulu Community College, HI (JRC)
Hood College, MD (WMC)
Hood Theological Seminary, NC (GRD)
Hoosac School, NY (PRC)
Hope Career Institute, FL (TCT)
Hope Center, FL (HND)
Hope College, MI (UNC)
Hope International University, CA (UNC)
Hopfer School of Nursing, NY (NRS)
Hopkinsville Community College, KY (JRC)
Horizons School, GA (PRC)
Horry-Georgetown Technical College, SC (JRC)
Hostos Community College - CUNY, NY (JRC)
The Hotchkiss School, CT (PRC)
Hot Springs Beauty College, AR (TCT)
Houghton Academy, NY (PRC)
Houghton College, NY (UNC)
Houghton Lake Institute of Cosmetology, MI (TCT)
Housatonic Community College, CT (JRC)
House of Heavilin Beauty College, MO (TCT)
Houston Baptist University, TX (UNC)
Houston Community College, TX (JRC)
Houston Graduate School of Theology, TX (TSR)
Houstons Training and Education Center, TX (TCT)
Houston Training School, TX (TCT)
Howard College, TX (JRC)
Howard Community College, MD (JRC)
Howard Payne University, TX (UNC)
Howard University, DC (UNC)
Howard University School of Divinity, DC (TSR)
Howell College of Cosmetology, MI (TCT)
Howe Military School, IN (PRC)
Hudson Area School of Radiologic Tech., NJ (TCT)
Hudson County Community College, NJ (JRC)
Huertas Junior College, PR (JRC)
Hult International Business School, MA (GRD)
Humacao Community College, PR (TCT)
Humanities Center Inst. of Allied Health, FL (TCT)
Humboldt State University, CA (UNC)
Humphreys College, CA (UNC)
The Hun School of Princeton, NJ (PRC)
Hunter Business School, NY (TCT)
Huntingdon College, AL (UNC)
Huntington College, IN (UNC)
Huntington College of Dental Technology, CA (TCT)
Huntington College of Health Sciences, TN (HMS)
Huntington Junior College, WV (JRC)
Huntington Memorial Hospital, CA (TCT)
Huntington School of Beauty Culture, WV (TCT)
Huntsville Bible College, AL (UNC)
Huntsville Hospital, AL (TCT)
Hurley Medical Center, MI (AHS)
Huron School of Nursing, OH (TCT)
Hussian School of Art, PA (TCT)
Husson College, ME (UNC)
Huston-Tillotson University, TX (UNC)
Hutchinson Community College, KS (JRC)
Hyde School, CT (PRC)
Hyde School, ME (PRC)
Hypnosis Motivation Institute, CA (HMS)

I

ICC Technical Institute, TX (TCT)
ICDC College, CA (TCT)
ICM School of Business & Medical Careers, PA (TCT)
ICPR Junior College, PR (JRC)
ICS The Wright Beauty College, MS (TCT)
Idaho State School for the Deaf/Blind, ID (HND)
Idaho State University, ID (UNC)
Ideal Girls School, IA (PRG)
Idyllwild Arts Academy, CA (PRC)
IHM Health Studies Center, MO (AHS)
IHM Health Studies Center, MO (TCT)
Iliff School of Theology, CO (GRD)
Ilisagvik College, AK (JRC)
Illinois Center for Broadcasting, IL (TCT)
Illinois Central College, IL (JRC)
Illinois College, IL (UNC)
Illinois College of Optometry, IL (GRD)
The Illinois Institute of Art, IL (UNC)
The Illinois Institute of Art, IL (UNC)
Illinois Institute of Technology, IL (UNC)
IIT Chicago-Kent College of Law, IL (BUS)
Illinois School for the Deaf, IL (HND)
Illinois School for Visually Impaired, IL (HND)
Illinois School of Health Careers, IL (TCT)
Illinois State University, IL (UNC)
Illinois Valley Community College, IL (JRC)
Illinois Welding School, IL (TCT)
Illinois Wesleyan University, IL (UNC)
Image School of Cosmetology, CA (TCT)
Immaculata University, PA (UNC)
Immaculate Conception Seminary, NJ (GRD)
Immanuel Medical Center, NE (AHS)
IMPAC University, FL (HMS)
Imperial Valley College, CA (JRC)
Incarnate Word High School, TX (PRC)
Independence College of Cosmetology, MO (TCT)
Independence Community College, KS (JRC)
Indiana Business College, IN (TCT)
Indiana Business College Northwest, IN (JRC)
Indiana Institute of Technology, IN (UNC)
Indiana School for the Deaf, IN (HND)
Indiana State School for the Blind, IN (HND)
Indiana State University, IN (UNC)
Indiana University, IN (UNC)
Indiana University at Kokomo, IN (UNC)
Indiana University at South Bend, IN (UNC)
Indiana University East, IN (UNC)
Indiana University Northwest, IN (UNC)
Indiana University of Pennsylvania, PA (UNC)
Indiana Univ-Purdue Univ at Fort Wayne, IN (UNC)
Indiana Univ-Purdue Univ at Indianapolis, IN (UNC)
Indiana University School of Allied Hlth, IN (TCT)
Indiana University Southeast, IN (UNC)
Indiana Vocational Technical College, IN (TCT)
Indiana Wesleyan University, IN (UNC)
Indian Hills Community College, IA (JRC)
Indian Meridian Vocational Tech School, OK (TCT)
Indian Mountain School, CT (PRC)
Indian River Community College, FL (JRC)
Indian Springs School, AL (PRC)
Industrial Management and Training, CT (TCT)
Industrial Technical College, PR (TCT)
Ingalls Memorial Hospital, IL (AHS)
Inland Northwest HVAC Training Center, WA (TCT)
Inland Technical Skills Center, CA (TCT)
Inner State Beauty School, OH (TCT)
Institucion Chaviano de Mayaguez, PR (TCT)
Institute for Business and Technology, CA (TCT)
Institute for Clinical Social Work, IL (GRD)
Institute for Creation Research Grad Sch, CA (GRD)
The Institute for Health Education, NJ (TCT)
Institute for Therapeutic Massage, NJ (TCT)
Institute of Allied Medical Professions, NY (TCT)
Institute of American Indian Arts, NM (UNC)
Institute of Audio Research, NY (TCT)
Institute of Beauty Careers, PR (TCT)
Institute of Beauty Occupation, PR (TCT)
Institute of Business & Medical Careers, CO (TCT)
Institute of Clinical Acupuncture, HI (GRD)
Institute of Computer Technology, CA (UNC)
Institute of Cosmetic Arts and Science, TX (TCT)
Institute of Cosmetology, TX (TCT)
The Institute of Culinary Education, NY (TCT)
Institute of Design and Construction, NY (TCT)
Institute of Living Schools, CT (HND)
Institute of Logistical Management, NJ (HMS)
Institute of Medical & Dental Technology, OH (TCT)
Institute of Network Technology, CA (TCT)
Institute of Technology - Clovis Campus, CA (TCT)
Institute of Technology - Modesto Campus, CA (TCT)
Institute of Technology - Sacramento, CA (TCT)
Institute of Transpersonal Psychology, CA (GRD)
The Institute of World Politics, DC (GRD)
Instituto de Banca y Comercio, PR (JRC)
Instituto de Banca y Comercio, PR (TCT)
Instituto de Educacion Tecnica, PR (TCT)
Instituto de Educacion Vocacional, PR (TCT)
Instituto Irma Valentin, PR (TCT)
Instituto Merlix, PR (TCT)
Instituto Tecnico Del Futuro, PR (TCT)
Instituto Vocacional Aurea E Mendez, PR (TCT)
Integrated Digital Technologies, CA (TCT)
IntelliTec College, CO (TCT)
Interactive College of Technology, GA (TCT)
Interactive College of Technology, KY (TCT)
Interactive Learning Systems, TX (TCT)
Inter American University, PR (UNC)
Inter American University of Puerto Rico, PR (GRD)
Inter American University of Puerto Rico, PR (UNC)
Interboro Institute, NY (TCT)
Intercoast Colleges, CA (TCT)
Intercollegiate Center/Nursing Education, WA (UNC)
Interdenominational Theological Center, GA (GRD)
Interior Designers Institute, CA (UNC)
Interlochen Arts Academy, MI (PRC)
International Academy, FL (TCT)
Intl Academy of Advanced Reflexology, PA (AHS)
Intl Academy of Advanced Reflexology, PA (TCT)
International Academy of Beauty, AZ (TCT)
International Academy of Design & Tech, FL (UNC)
International Academy of Design & Tech, IL (UNC)
International Academy of Design & Tech, PA (TCT)
International Academy of Design & Tech, TN (UNC)
International Academy of Hair Design, AZ (TCT)
International Academy of Hair Design, OH (TCT)
International Air & Hospitality Academy, WA (TCT)
International Baptist College, AZ (UNC)
International Beauty Academy, CO (TCT)
International Beauty College #3, TX (TCT)
International Beauty College #4, TX (TCT)
International Beauty School, MD (TCT)
International Beauty School, WV (TCT)
International Bible Center, TX (TSR)
International Business College, IN (JRC)
International Business College, IN (UNC)
International Business College, TX (TCT)
International Business School, TX (TCT)
International Christian Education Coll., CA (TCT)
International City Beauty College, GA (TCT)
International College of Broadcasting, OH (TCT)
International Coll. of Hospitality Mgmt., CT (TCT)
International Import-Export Institute, AZ (HMS)
International Institute of the Americas, AZ (JRC)
International Institute of the Americas, AZ (UNC)
International Institute of the Americas, NM (JRC)
International Junior College, PR (TCT)
International Prof School of Body Work, CA (TCT)
International School, NM (TCT)
International School of Cosmetology, CA (TCT)
International School of Skin/Nailcare, GA (TCT)
International Technical College, PR (TCT)
International Theological Seminary, CA (TSR)
International Training Careers, FL (TCT)
International Yacht Restoration School, RI (TCT)
Inver Hills Community College, MN (JRC)
Iona College, NY (UNC)
Iona College at Blue Hill, NY (UNC)
Iowa Braille and Sight Saving School, IA (HND)
Iowa Central Community College, IA (JRC)
Iowa Lakes Community College, IA (JRC)
Iowa Methodist Medical Center, IA (AHS)
Iowa School for the Deaf, IA (HND)
Iowa School of Beauty, IA (TCT)
Iowa State University, IA (UNC)
Iowa Wesleyan College, IA (UNC)
Iowa Western Community College, IA (JRC)
Irvine Valley College, CA (JRC)
Island Drafting & Technical Institute, NY (JRC)
Isothermal Community College, NC (JRC)
Itasca Community College, MN (JRC)
Itawamba Community College, MS (JRC)
Ithaca College, NY (UNC)
ITI Technical College, LA (TCT)
ITT Technical Institute, AL (JRC)
ITT Technical Institute, AR (TCT)
ITT Technical Institute, AZ (TCT)
ITT Technical Institute, CA (JRC)
ITT Technical Institute, CA (TCT)
ITT Technical Institute, CA (UNC)
ITT Technical Institute, CO (JRC)
ITT Technical Institute, FL (JRC)
ITT Technical Institute, FL (TCT)
ITT Technical Institute, GA (UNC)
ITT Technical Institute, ID (JRC)
ITT Technical Institute, IL (JRC)
ITT Technical Institute, IL (TCT)
ITT Technical Institute, IN (JRC)
ITT Technical Institute, IN (TCT)
ITT Technical Institute, KY (TCT)
ITT Technical Institute, LA (TCT)

ITT Technical Institute, MA (TCT)
ITT Technical Institute, MA (UNC)
ITT Technical Institute, MD (UNC)
ITT Technical Institute, MI (JRC)
ITT Technical Institute, MO (BUS)
ITT Technical Institute, MO (JRC)
ITT Technical Institute, NE (JRC)
ITT Technical Institute, NM (JRC)
ITT Technical Institute, NV (TCT)
ITT Technical Institute, NY (TCT)
ITT Technical Institute, OH (JRC)
ITT Technical Institute, OH (TCT)
ITT Technical Institute, OK (UNC)
ITT Technical Institute, OR (UNC)
ITT Technical Institute, PA (TCT)
ITT Technical Institute, PA (UNC)
ITT Technical Institute, SC (TCT)
ITT Technical Institute, TN (JRC)
ITT Technical Institute, TN (TCT)
ITT Technical Institute, TN (UNC)
ITT Technical Institute, TX (JRC)
ITT Technical Institute, TX (TCT)
ITT Technical Institute, UT (UNC)
ITT Technical Institute, VA (JRC)
ITT Technical Institute, WA (JRC)
ITT Technical Institute, WA (TCT)
ITT Technical Institute, WI (JRC)
Iverson Business School, GA (TCT)
Ivory Dental Technology College, CA (TCT)
Ivy Tech Community College - Bloomington, IN (TCT)
Ivy Tech Community College Central IN, IN (JRC)
Ivy Tech Community College North Central, IN (JRC)
Ivy Tech Community College - Columbus, IN (JRC)
Ivy Tech Community College East Central, IN (TCT)
Ivy Tech Community College - Kokomo, IN (TCT)
Ivy Tech Community College - Lafayette, IN (TCT)
Ivy Tech Community College - Northeast, IN (TCT)
Ivy Tech Community College - Northwest, IN (TCT)
Ivy Tech Community College - Richmond, IN (TCT)
Ivy Tech Community College - Southeast, IN (TCT)
Ivy Tech Community College - Southern, IN (JRC)
Ivy Tech Community College - Southwest, IN (TCT)
Ivy Tech Community College Wabash Valley, IN (TCT)
Ivy Tech State College, IN (JRC)

J

J & J Hair Design College, MS (TCT)
J & M Academy of Cosmetology, KY (TCT)
Jack Mabley Development Center, IL (HND)
Jackson Community College, MI (JRC)
Jackson Memorial Medical Center, FL (TCT)
Jackson State Community College, TN (JRC)
Jackson State University, MS (UNC)
Jacksonville College, TX (JRC)
Jacksonville State University, AL (UNC)
Jacksonville University, FL (UNC)
Jacobs Creek Job Corps Civilian Center, TN (TCT)
James Albert School of Cosmetology, CA (TCT)
James A. Rhodes State Coll, OH (JRC)
James Haley Veteran's Hospital, FL (AHS)
James H. Faulkner State Comm. College, AL (JRC)
James Madison High School, GA (HMS)
James Madison University, VA (UNC)
Jameson Memorial Hosp School of Nursing, PA (NRS)
James Sprunt Community College, NC (JRC)
Jamestown Business College, NY (TCT)
Jamestown College, ND (UNC)
Jamestown Community College, NY (JRC)
Jarvis Christian College, TX (UNC)
Javelin Technical Training Center, GA (TCT)
Jay's Technical Institute, TX (TCT)
Jean Madeline Educ. Ctr. for Cosmetology, PA (TCT)
Je Boutique College of Beauty, CA (TCT)
Jefferson College, MO (JRC)
Jefferson College of Health Sciences, VA (UNC)
Jefferson Community & Technical College, KY (JRC)
Jefferson Community College, NY (JRC)
Jefferson Community College, OH (JRC)
Jefferson Davis Community College, AL (JRC)
Jefferson Davis Community College, AL (TCT)
Jefferson Regional Medical Center, AR (TCT)
Jefferson State Community College, AL (JRC)
Jefferson Technical College, KY (TCT)
Jenks Beauty College, OK (TCT)
Jennie Edmundson Memorial Hospital, IA (AHS)
Jenny Lea Academy of Cosmetology, KY (TCT)
Jerry's School of Hairstyling, MO (TCT)
Jersey Shore Medical Center, NJ (AHS)
Jesuit School of Theology at Berkeley, CA (GRD)
Jewish Theological Seminary of America, NY (UNC)
J. F. Drake State Technical College, AL (JRC)
J. F. Ingram State Technical College, AL (JRC)
JNA Institute of Culinary Arts, PA (TCT)
Joe Kubert Sch of Cartoon & Graphic Arts, NJ (TCT)
John A. Gupton College, TN (JRC)
John A. Logan College, IL (JRC)
John Amico's School of Hair Design, IL (TCT)
John Brown University, AR (UNC)
John Carroll University, OH (UNC)
John Dewey College, PR (TCT)
John F. Kennedy Memorial High School, WA (PRC)
John F. Kennedy University, CA (UNC)
John Jay Kenner Academy, LA (TCT)
John Marshall Law School, IL (GRD)
Johns Hopkins University, DC (GRD)
Johns Hopkins University, MD (UNC)
Johnson & Wales University, CO (TCT)
Johnson & Wales University, FL (UNC)
Johnson & Wales University, NC (UNC)
Johnson & Wales University, RI (UNC)
Johnson Bible College, TN (GRD)
Johnson College, PA (JRC)
Johnson County Community College, KS (JRC)
Johnson C. Smith University, NC (UNC)
Johnson State College, VT (UNC)
Johnston Community College, NC (JRC)
John Tracy Clinic, CA (HMS)
John Tyler Community College, VA (JRC)
John Wesley College, NC (TSR)
John Wesley Intl. Barber/Beauty Coll, CA (TCT)
John Wood Community College, IL (JRC)
Jolie Hair and Beauty Academy, MA (TCT)
Joliet Junior College, IL (JRC)
Jones Beauty College, TX (TCT)
Jones Beauty College #2, TX (TCT)
Jones College, FL (UNC)
Jones County Junior College, MS (JRC)
Jones International University, CO (UNC)
Jon Louis School of Beauty, NY (TCT)
Jon Nave University of Cosmetology, TN (TCT)
Josef's School of Hair Design, ND (TCT)
Joseph's College of Beauty, NE (TCT)
Joseph's of Kearney Sch of Hair Design, NE (TCT)
Joy's School of Hair Design, NJ (TCT)
JPS Inst. for Health Career Development, TX (AHS)
J. Sargeant Reynolds Community College, VA (JRC)
Judson College, AL (UNC)
Judson College, IL (UNC)
Juilliard School, NY (UNC)
June Buchanan School, KY (PRC)
Jung Tao School of Chinese Medicine, NC (GRD)
Juniata College, PA (UNC)

K

Kaiser Permanente Medical Center, CA (TCT)
Kalamazoo College, MI (UNC)
Kalamazoo Valley Community College, MI (JRC)
Kambly School/Developmentally Impaired, MI (HND)
Kankakee Community College, IL (JRC)
Kansas City Art Institute, MO (UNC)
Kansas City Kansas Community College, KS (JRC)
KC Univ. of Medicine and Biosciences, MO (GRD)
Kansas School for the Deaf, KS (HND)
Kansas State School for the Blind, KS (HND)
Kansas State University, KS (UNC)
Kansas Wesleyan University, KS (UNC)
Kapiolani Community College, HI (JRC)
Kaplan Career Institute, PA (TCT)
Kaplan College, CO (TCT)
Kaplan College - Hagerstown Campus, MD (JRC)
Kaplan University, IA (UNC)
Kaskaskia College, IL (JRC)
Katharine Gibbs School, NJ (TCT)
Katharine Gibbs School, NY (TCT)
Katharine Gibbs School, RI (TCT)
Kauai Community College, HI (JRC)
Kaufman Beauty School, KY (TCT)
KAW Area Technical School, KS (TCT)
Kaye Beauty College, IN (TCT)
Kay Harvey Hairdressing Academy, MA (TCT)
KD Studio - Actors Conservatory, TX (TCT)
Kean University, NJ (UNC)
Keck Graduate Institute, CA (GRD)
Kee Business College, VA (TCT)
Keene Beauty Academy, NH (TCT)
Keene State College, NH (UNC)
Kehilath Yakov Rabbinical Seminary, NY (MNC)
Keio Academy of New York, NY (PRC)
Keiser Career College, FL (TCT)
Keiser College, FL (JRC)
Keiser University, FL (JRC)
Keller Graduate School of Management, CA (BUS)
Keller Graduate School, IL (BUS)
Keller Graduate School of DeVry Univ., IL (MBA)
Keller Graduate School, IL (BUS)
Keller Graduate School, IL (MBA)
Keller Graduate School, MO (MBA)
Keller Graduate School, NY (UNC)
Keller Graduate School, OH (BUS)
Keller Graduate School, VA (MBA)
Keller Graduate School, WI (MBA)
Keller Graduate School of Management, AZ (BUS)
Keller Graduate School of Management, AZ (MBA)
Keller Graduate School of Management, CA (BUS)
Kellogg Community College, MI (JRC)
Kenai Peninsula College, AK (JRC)
Kendall College, IL (UNC)
Kendall College of Art & Design, MI (UNC)
Kendall's Academy of Beauty Arts/Science, UT (TCT)
Kennebec Valley Community College, ME (JRC)
Kennedy-King College, IL (JRC)
Kennesaw State University, GA (UNC)
Kenneth Shuler's School of Cosmetology, SC (TCT)
Kenrick School of Theology, MO (GRD)
Kensington College, CA (TCT)
Kent Career/Technical Center, MI (TCT)
Kent School, CT (PRC)
Kents Hill School, ME (PRC)
Kent State University, OH (UNC)
Kent State University-Ashtabula Campus, OH (JRC)
Kent State University-East Liverpool, OH (JRC)
Kent State University-Geauga Campus, OH (JRC)
Kent State University-Salem Campus, OH (JRC)
Kent State University-Stark Campus, OH (JRC)
Kent State University-Trumbull Campus, OH (JRC)
Kent State University, OH (JRC)
Kentucky Christian University, KY (UNC)
Kentucky Mountain Bible College, KY (UNC)
Kentucky School for the Blind, KY (HND)
Kentucky School for the Deaf, KY (HND)
Kentucky State University, KY (UNC)
Kentucky Wesleyan College, KY (UNC)
Kenyon College, OH (UNC)
Kettering College of Medical Arts, OH (UNC)
Kettering University, MI (EGN)
Keuka College, NY (UNC)
Key College, FL (TCT)
KeySkills Learning, NJ (TCT)
Keystone College, PA (JRC)
Keystone National High School, PA (HMS)
Keystone Technical Institute, PA (TCT)
Kildonan School, NY (PRC)
Kilgore College, TX (JRC)
Kilian Community College, SD (JRC)
Kim Anh Academy of Beauty, CA (TCT)
Kimball Union Academy, NH (PRC)
King College, TN (UNC)
The Kings Academy, TN (PRC)
King's College, NC (JRC)
King's College, PA (UNC)
The Kings College and Seminary, CA (UNC)
King's Daughter's Hospital, IN (AHS)
Kings Way Missionary Institute, TX (TCT)
Kingwood College, TX (TCT)
Kirkland Beauty School, WA (TCT)
Kirksville Coll. of Osteopathic Medicine, MO (GRD)
Kirkwood Community College, IA (JRC)
Kirtland Community College, MI (JRC)
Kishwaukee College, IL (JRC)
The Kiski School, PA (PRB)
Kittanning Beauty School, PA (TCT)
Klamath Community College, OR (JRC)
Knowledge Systems Institute, IL (IFS)
Knox College, IL (UNC)
Knox County Career Center, OH (TCT)
Knox School, NY (PRC)
Knox Theological Seminary, FL (GRD)
Kodiak College, AK (JRC)
Kol Yaakov Torah Center, NY (MNC)
Kutztown University of Pennsylvania, PA (UNC)

L

LaBaron Hairdressing Academy, KS (TCT)
LaBaron Hairdressing Academy, MA (TCT)
La Belle Beauty Academy, FL (TCT)
La Belle Beauty School, FL (TCT)
Labette Community College, KS (JRC)
Laboratory Institute of Merchandising, NY (UNC)
Lac Courte Oreilles Ojibwa Comm College, WI (JRC)
Lackawanna College, PA (JRC)
Lacy Cosmetology School, SC (TCT)
Lafayette Beauty Academy, IN (TCT)
Lafayette College, PA (UNC)
Lafayette General Medical Center, LA (AHS)
La Grange College, GA (UNC)
LaGuardia Community College / CUNY, NY (JRC)
Laguna College of Art and Design, CA (UNC)
La' James College of Hairstyling, IA (TCT)
La' James College of Hairstyling, IL (TCT)
Lake Area Technical Institute, SD (TCT)
Lake Charles Memorial Hospital, LA (AHS)
Lake City Community College, FL (JRC)
Lake College, CA (TCT)
Lake Erie College, OH (UNC)
Lake Erie College\Osteopathic Medicine, FL (UNC)
Lake Erie College\Osteopathic Medicine, PA (UNC)
Lake Forest Academy, IL (PRC)
Lake Forest Beauty College, CA (TCT)
Lake Forest College, IL (UNC)
Lake Forest Graduate Sch. of Management, IL (GRD)
Lake Grove School-Maple Valley, MA (HND)
Lake Grove School, NY (HND)
Lake Grove School at Durham, CT (HND)
Lake Land College, IL (JRC)
Lakeland College, WI (UNC)
Lakeland Community College, OH (JRC)
Lakeland Regional Medical Center, FL (TCT)
Lakeland Village School, WA (HND)
Lake Michigan College, MI (JRC)
Lake Region State College, ND (JRC)
Lakeshore Medical Lab Training Programs, IN (TCT)
Lakeshore Technical College, WI (TCT)
Lakeside School of Massage Therapy, WI (TCT)
Lake-Sumter Community College, FL (JRC)
Lake Superior College, MN (JRC)
Lake Superior State University, MI (UNC)
Lake Tahoe Community College, CA (JRC)
Lake Technical Center, FL (TCT)
Lakeview College of Nursing, IL (UNC)
Lake Washington Technical College, WA (TCT)
La Lumiere School, IN (PRC)
Lamar Community College, CO (JRC)
Lamar Institute of Technology, TX (JRC)
Lamar State College-Orange, TX (JRC)
Lamar State College-Port Arthur, TX (JRC)
Lamar University, TX (UNC)
Lambuth University, TN (UNC)
Lamont-Doherty Earth Observatory, NY (GRD)
LaMonts Intl School of Cosmetology, IL (TCT)
Lamson College, AZ (TCT)
Lancaster Beauty School, CA (TCT)
Lancaster Bible College, PA (TSR)
Lancaster General College of Nursing, PA (AHS)
Lancaster School of Cosmetology, PA (TCT)
Lancaster Theological Seminary, PA (GRD)
Lander University, SC (UNC)
Landing School of Boatbuilding & Design, ME (TCT)
Landmark College, VT (JRC)
Landmark School, MA (PRC)
Lane College, TN (UNC)
Lane Community College, OR (JRC)
Laney College, CA (JRC)
Langston University, OK (UNC)
Lanier Technical College, GA (JRC)
Lanier Technical College, GA (TCT)
Lankenau Hospital, PA (AHS)
Lansdale School of Business, PA (JRC)
Lansdale School of Cosmetology, PA (TCT)
Lansing Community College, MI (JRC)
Laramie County Community College, WY (JRC)
Laredo Community College, TX (JRC)
La Roche College, PA (UNC)
La Salle University, PA (UNC)
Lasell College, MA (UNC)
La Sierra University, CA (UNC)
Las Positas College, CA (JRC)
Lassen Community College, CA (JRC)
Las Vegas College, NV (TCT)
Latin School of Chicago, IL (PRC)
Latrobe Area Hospital, PA (AHS)
Laura/Alvin Siegal Coll Judaic Studies, OH (UNC)

Laura Baker School, MN (HND)
Laurel Business Institute, PA (TCT)
Lausanne Collegiate School, TN (PRC)
Lavelle School/Blind-Visually Impaired, NY (HND)
Lawrence Academy, MA (PRC)
Lawrence Memorial/Regis College, MA (TCT)
Lawrence Technological University, MI (UNC)
Lawrence University, WI (UNC)
Lawrenceville School, NJ (PRC)
Lawson State Community College, AL (JRC)
Lawton School, MI (TCT)
LBW Community College, AL (JRC)
L.D.S. Business College, UT (TCT)
Learning Institute for Beauty Sciences, MA (TCT)
Learning Institute for Beauty Sciences, NY (TCT)
Lebanon County Career School, PA (TCT)
Lebanon Valley College, PA (UNC)
Le Cordon Bleu College of Culinary Arts, FL (TCT)
Le Cordon Bleu College of Culinary Arts, GA (TCT)
Le Cordon Bleu College of Culinary Arts, MN (JRC)
Le Cordon Bleu College of Culinary Arts, NV (TCT)
Lee College, TX (JRC)
Lee County High Tech Center North, FL (TCT)
Lee County High Tech Center Central, FL (TCT)
The Leelanau School, MI (PRC)
Lees-McRae College, NC (UNC)
Lee's School of Cosmetology, AR (TCT)
Lee University, TN (UNC)
Lee University Charlotte Center, NC (UNC)
Leeward Community College, HI (JRC)
L.E. Fletcher Technical Community Coll., LA (TCT)
Lehigh Carbon Community College, PA (JRC)
Lehigh University, PA (UNC)
Lehigh Valley College, PA (JRC)
Lehigh Valley Hospital & Health Network, PA (TCT)
Le Moyne College, NY (UNC)
Le Moyne-Owen College, TN (UNC)
Lenoir Community College, NC (JRC)
Lenoir Memorial Hospital, NC (AHS)
Lenoir-Rhyne College, NC (UNC)
Leon Institute of Hair Design, CT (TCT)
Leon's Beauty School, NC (TCT)
Leon's Hair Training Academy, AR (TCT)
Leon Studio One School of Hair Design, NY (TCT)
Lesley University, MA (WMC)
Leston College, PR (TCT)
Le Tourneau University, TX (UNC)
Levine School of Music, DC (TCT)
Levittown Beauty Academy, PA (TCT)
Lewis & Clark Career Center, MO (TCT)
Lewis & Clark College, OR (UNC)
Lewis & Clark Community College, IL (JRC)
Lewis-Clark State College, ID (UNC)
Lewis College of Business, MI (JRC)
Lewis University, IL (UNC)
Lexington Beauty College, KY (TCT)
Lexington College, IL (UNC)
Lexington Theological Seminary, KY (GRD)
Lia Schorr Inst of Cosmetic Skin Care, NY (TCT)
Liberty Training Institute, CA (TCT)
Liberty University, VA (UNC)
Liceo de Arte Y Disenos, PR (TCT)
Liceo de Arte Y Tecnologia, PR (TCT)
Life Chiropractic College West, CA (GRD)
Life Pacific College, CA (UNC)
Life University, GA (UNC)
Limestone College, SC (UNC)
Lincoln Christian College, IL (UNC)
Lincoln College, IL (JRC)
Lincoln College of Technology, FL (TCT)
Lincoln Land Community College, IL (JRC)
Lincoln Memorial University, TN (UNC)
Lincoln Technical Institute, IL (TCT)
Lincoln Technical Institute, IN (TCT)
Lincoln Technical Institute, MD (TCT)
Lincoln Technical Institute, NJ (TCT)
Lincoln Technical Institute, PA (TCT)
Lincoln Technical Institute, TX (TCT)
Lincoln Trail College, IL (JRC)
Lincoln University, CA (UNC)
Lincoln University, MO (UNC)
Lincoln University, PA (UNC)
Linden Hall, PA (PRG)
Lindenwood University, MO (UNC)
Lindsey Hopkins Technical Education Ctr, FL (TCT)
Lindsey Wilson College, KY (UNC)
Linfield Christian School, CA (PRC)
Linfield College, OR (UNC)
Linn-Benton Community College, OR (JRC)
Linn State Technical College, MO (TCT)
Linsly Institute, WV (PRC)
Lipscomb University, TN (UNC)
Little Big Horn College, MT (JRC)
Little Priest Tribal College, NE (JRC)
Lively Area Vocational Technical Center, FL (TCT)
Lively Area Vocational Technical School, FL (TCT)
Livingstone College, NC (UNC)
Lock Haven University, PA (UNC)
Lock Haven University-Clearfield Campus, PA (JRC)
Lockworks Academie of Hairdressing, LA (TCT)
Logan College of Chiropractic, MO (GRD)
Logos Evangelical Seminary, CA (GRD)
Lola Beauty College, CA (TCT)
Loma Linda University, CA (UNC)
Long Beach City College, CA (JRC)
Long Island Business Institute, NY (JRC)
Long Island College Hospital, NY (TCT)
Long Island University, NY (UNC)
Long Island University-Brooklyn Campus, NY (UNC)
Long Island University-C. W. Post Campus, NY (UNC)
Long Island University-Rockland Campus, NY (UNC)
Long Island University-Westchester, NY (GRD)
Long Technical College, AZ (TCT)
Long Trail School, VT (PRC)
Longview Community College, MO (JRC)
Longwood University, VA (UNC)
Longy School of Music, MA (MUS)
Lon Morris College, TX (JRC)

Loomis Chaffee School, CT (PRC)
Lorain County Community College, OH (JRC)
Loraine's Academy, FL (TCT)
Loras College, IA (UNC)
Lord Fairfax Community College, VA (JRC)
Lorenzo Walker Institute of Technology, FL (TCT)
Los Amigos Research & Education Inst., CA (TCT)
Los Angeles City College, CA (JRC)
Los Angeles Co. Coll. Nursing/Alld Hlth, CA (TCT)
Los Angeles Co. Harbor UCLA Medical Ctr., CA (TCT)
Los Angeles Harbor College, CA (JRC)
Los Angeles Mission College, CA (JRC)
Los Angeles Pierce College, CA (JRC)
Los Angeles Southwest College, CA (JRC)
Los Angeles Trade-Technical College, CA (JRC)
Los Angeles Valley College, CA (JRC)
Los Medanos College, CA (JRC)
Louisburg College, NC (JRC)
Louisiana Academy of Beauty, LA (TCT)
Louisiana College, LA (UNC)
Louisiana School/Visually Impaired, LA (HND)
Louisiana State School for the Deaf, LA (HND)
Louisiana State University, LA (JRC)
Louisiana State University, LA (UNC)
Louisiana State University & A & M Coll., LA (UNC)
Louisiana State University at Alexandria, LA (UNC)
Louisiana State University at Eunice, LA (JRC)
Louisiana State Univ. Health Sci. Center, LA (UNC)
Louisiana Technical College - Acadian, LA (TCT)
Louisiana Technical College - Alexandria, LA (TCT)
Louisiana Technical College - Ascension, LA (TCT)
Louisiana Technical College - Avoyelles, LA (TCT)
Louisiana Technical College - Bastrop, LA (TCT)
Louisiana Technical College-Baton Rouge, LA (TCT)
Louisiana Tech. Coll.-Charles B Coreil, LA (TCT)
Louisiana Tech. Coll. Delta-Ouachita, LA (TCT)
Louisiana Technical College - Evangeline, LA (TCT)
Louisiana Tech. Coll. - Florida Parishes, LA (TCT)
Louisiana Technical College - Folkes, LA (TCT)
Louisiana Technical College - Gulf Area, LA (TCT)
Louisiana Technical College - Hammond, LA (TCT)
Louisiana Technical College - Huey Long, LA (TCT)
Louisiana Technical College - Jefferson, LA (TCT)
Louisiana Technical College - Jumonville, LA (TCT)
Louisiana Technical College - Lafayette, LA (JRC)
Louisiana Technical College - LaFourche, LA (TCT)
Louisiana Technical College-Lamar Salter, LA (TCT)
Louisiana Technical College - Mansfield, LA (TCT)
Louisiana Technical College - M. Smith, LA (TCT)
Louisiana Technical College-Natchitoches, LA (TCT)
Louisiana Tech. Coll. - North Central, LA (TCT)
Louisiana Technical College-NE Louisiana, LA (TCT)
Louisiana Technical Coll. - NW Louisiana, LA (TCT)
Louisiana Technical College - Oakdale, LA (TCT)
Louisiana Tech. Coll. - River Parishes, LA (TCT)
Louisiana Technical College - Ruston, LA (TCT)
Louisiana Technical Coll.-Sabine Valley, LA (TCT)
Louisiana Tech. College - Shelby Jackson, LA (TCT)
Louisiana Tech. Coll.-Shreveport-Bossier, LA (TCT)
Louisiana Technical College - Sullivan, LA (TCT)
Louisiana Technical College - Tallulah, LA (TCT)
Louisiana Technical College - Teche Area, LA (TCT)
Louisiana Technical College - T H Harris, LA (TCT)
Louisiana Tech. Coll. - West Jefferson, LA (TCT)
Louisiana Technical College - Westside, LA (TCT)
Louisiana Tech. Coll. - Young Memorial, LA (TCT)
Louisiana Tech University, LA (UNC)
Louisville Presbyterian Seminary, KY (GRD)
Louisville Technical Institute, KY (TCT)
Lourdes College, OH (UNC)
Lowell Academy Hairstyling Institute, MA (TCT)
Lowell Whiteman School, CO (PRC)
Lower Columbia College, WA (JRC)
Loyola College, MD (UNC)
Loyola Marymount University, CA (GRD)
Loyola Marymount University, CA (UNC)
Loyola University, IL (UNC)
Loyola University Medical Center, IL (TCT)
Loyola University - Mundelein College, IL (WMC)
Loyola University New Orleans, LA (UNC)
Loyola University of Chicago, IL (UNC)
L.T. International Beauty School, PA (TCT)
Lubbock Christian University, TX (UNC)
Lubbock Hair Academy, TX (TCT)
Luna Community College, NM (JRC)
Lurleen B. Wallace Community College, AL (JRC)
Lustre Christian High School, MT (PRC)
Lutheran School of Nursing, MO (TCT)
Lutheran School of Theology at Chicago, IL (GRD)
Lutheran Theological Seminary, PA (GRD)
Lutheran Theological Southern Seminary, SC (GRD)
Luther College, IA (UNC)
Luther Rice University, GA (UNC)
Luther Seminary, MN (GRD)
Luzerne County Community College, PA (JRC)
Lycee International De Los Angeles, CA (PRC)
Lycoming College, PA (UNC)
Lyle's Bakersfield College of Beauty, CA (TCT)
Lyle's College of Beauty, CA (TCT)
Lyle's Fresno College of Beauty, CA (TCT)
Lyman Ward Military Academy, AL (PRB)
Lyme Academy College of Fine Arts, CT (ART)
Lynchburg College, VA (UNC)
Lynchburg General Hosp School of Nursing, VA (NRS)
Lyndon Institute, VT (PRC)
Lyndon State College, VT (UNC)
Lynn University, FL (UNC)
Lynn University Conservatory of Music, FL (MUS)
Lyon College, AR (UNC)
Lytle's Redwood Empire Beauty College, CA (TCT)

M

Macalester College, MN (UNC)
MacCormac College, IL (JRC)
MacDuffie School, MA (PRC)
Machzikei Hadath Rabbinical College, NY (MNC)
MacMurray College, IL (UNC)
Macomb Community College, MI (JRC)
Macon State College, GA (UNC)
Madeira School, VA (PRG)
Madera Beauty College, CA (TCT)
Madison Area Technical College, WI (JRC)
Madison Cosmetology College, WI (TCT)
Madison Media Institute, WI (TCT)
Madisonville Community College, KY (JRC)
Madonna University, MI (UNC)
Magdalen College, NH (UNC)
Magee Brothers Beaverton Sch of Beauty, OR (TCT)
Magnolia Bible College, MS (UNC)
Magnolia College of Cosmetology, MS (TCT)
Maharishi University of Management, IA (UNC)
Maine Central Institute, ME (PRC)
Maine College of Art, ME (UNC)
Maine Educational Center for the Deaf, ME (HND)
Maine Maritime Academy, ME (UNC)
Maine Medical Center, ME (TCT)
Make-up Designory, CA (TCT)
Malcolm X College, IL (JRC)
Malone College, OH (UNC)
Manatee Community College, FL (JRC)
Manatee Technical Institute, FL (TCT)
Manatee Technical Institute East Campus, FL (TCT)
Manchester Beauty College, CA (TCT)
Manchester College, IN (UNC)
Manchester Community College, CT (JRC)
Mandl School College of Allied Health, NY (TCT)
Manhattan Beauty School, FL (TCT)
Manhattan Christian College, KS (UNC)
Manhattan College, NY (UNC)
Manhattan Hairstyling Academy, FL (TCT)
Manhattan School of Computer Technology, NY (TCT)
Manhattan School of Music, NY (UNC)
Manhattanville College, NY (UNC)
Mannes College of Music, NY (GRD)
Manor College, PA (JRC)
Mansfield Beauty School, MA (TCT)
Mansfield University of Pennsylvania, PA (UNC)
Maple Springs Baptist Bible Coll. & Sem., MD (UNC)
Maple Woods Community College, MO (JRC)
Maranatha Baptist Bible College, WI (UNC)
Margate School of Beauty, FL (TCT)
Maria College of Albany, NY (JRC)
Marianapolis Preparatory School, CT (PRC)
Marian College, IN (UNC)
Marian College of Fond du Lac, WI (UNC)
Marian Court College, MA (JRC)
Maria Parham Hospital, NC (AHS)
Maric College, CA (TCT)
Maric College East County, CA (TCT)
Maric College - Sacremento Campus, CA (TCT)
Maricopa Beauty College, AZ (TCT)
Marie Katzenbach School for the Deaf, NJ (HND)
Marietta College, OH (UNC)
Marinello-Eastern Hills Academy, OH (TCT)
Marinello School of Beauty, CA (TCT)
Marinello School of Beauty, NV (TCT)
Marine Military Academy, TX (PRB)
Marion Co. School Radiologic Technology, FL (TCT)
Marion General Hospital, OH (AHS)
Marion Military Institute, AL (JRC)
Marion Military Institute, AL (PRC)
Marion Technical College, OH (JRC)
Marist College, NY (UNC)
MarJon School of Beauty Culture, NY (TCT)
Marlboro College, VT (UNC)
Marmion Academy, IL (PRB)
Marquette General Hospital, MI (AHS)
Marquette University, WI (UNC)
Marsha Kay Beauty College, AR (TCT)
Marshalltown Community College, IA (JRC)
Marshall University, WV (UNC)
Marshfield Clinic/St. Josephs Hospital, WI (TCT)
Mars Hill College, NC (UNC)
Mars Hill Graduate School, WA (GRD)
Martha Lloyd School, PA (HND)
Martin Community College, NC (JRC)
Martinez Adult Education, CA (TCT)
Martinez School of Cosmetology, MO (TCT)
Martin Luther College, MN (UNC)
Martin Methodist College, TN (JRC)
Martin's College of Cosmetology, WI (TCT)
Martin University, IN (UNC)
Marvelwood School, CT (PRC)
Mary Baldwin College, VA (WMC)
Marygrove College, MI (UNC)
Maryland Beauty Academy, MD (TCT)
Maryland Beauty Academy of Essex, MD (TCT)
Maryland General Hospital, MD (AHS)
Maryland Institute College of Art, MD (UNC)
Maryland School for the Blind, MD (HND)
Maryland School for the Deaf, MD (HND)
Mary Lanning Memorial Hospital, NE (AHS)
Marylhurst University, OR (UNC)
Marymount College, CA (JRC)
Marymount College, NY (WMC)
Marymount Manhattan College, NY (UNC)
Marymount University, VA (UNC)
Maryville College, TN (UNC)
Maryville University of St. Louis, MO (UNC)
Mary Washington Hospital, VA (AHS)
Marywood University, PA (UNC)
Massachusetts Bay Community College, MA (JRC)
Massachusetts College of Art, MA (UNC)
Massachusetts College of Liberal Arts, MA (UNC)
MA College of Pharmacy & Health Sciences, MA (AHS)
Massachusetts Institute of Technology, MA (UNC)
Massachusetts Maritime Academy, MA (UNC)
MA Sch. of Barbering & Mens Hairstyling, MA (TCT)
Massachusetts School of Law at Andover, MA (GRD)
Massachusetts School Professional Psych., MA (PSY)
Massanutten Military Academy, VA (PRC)
Massasoit Community College, MA (JRC)
Master's College and Seminary, CA (UNC)
The Masters of Cosmetology College, IN (TCT)
The Masters School, NY (PRC)

Maui Community College, HI (JRC)
Maur Hill - Mount Academy, KS (PRB)
Mayland Community College, NC (JRC)
Mayo School of Health Sciences, MN (GRD)
Mayo Technical College, KY (TCT)
Maysville Community & Technical College, KY (JRC)
Maysville Community College, KY (JRC)
Mayville State University, ND (UNC)
MBTI Business Training Institute, PR (TCT)
McCallie School, TN (PRB)
McCann School of Business & Technology, PA (JRC)
McCann School of Business & Technology, PA (TCT)
McCollum & Ross The Hair School, TN (TCT)
McCormick Theological Seminary, IL (GRD)
McDaniel College, MD (UNC)
McDonogh School, MD (PRC)
McDonough District Hospital, IL (TCT)
McDowell Technical Community College, NC (JRC)
MCed Career College, CA (TCT)
McEllis Training Institute, NJ (TCT)
McHenry County College, IL (JRC)
McIntosh College, NH (TCT)
McKendree College, IL (UNC)
McKennan Hospital, SD (AHS)
McLennan Community College, TX (JRC)
McLeod Regional Medical Center, SC (AHS)
McMurry University, TX (UNC)
McNally Smith College of Music, MN (UNC)
McNeese State University, LA (UNC)
McPherson College, KS (UNC)
Meadville/Lombard Theological School, IL (GRD)
Medaille College, NY (UNC)
Medcenter One College of Nursing, ND (UNC)
Medcenter One Health System, ND (AHS)
MedCentral College of Nursing, OH (UNC)
Medical Assisting School of Hawaii, HI (TCT)
Medical Career Center, FL (TCT)
Medical Career Institute South Florida, FL (TCT)
Medical Careers Institute, IL (TCT)
Medical Careers Institute, VA (TCT)
Medical Center, GA (TCT)
Medical Center of Beaver County, PA (AHS)
Medical Center of Central Georgia, GA (TCT)
Medical Center of Louisiana/Charity Cmps, LA (AHS)
Medical College Hospitals, PA (AHS)
Medical College of Georgia, GA (UNC)
Medical College of Wisconsin, WI (GRD)
Medical Institute, CA (TCT)
Medical Training College, LA (TCT)
Medical University of South Carolina, SC (GRD)
Medina County Career Center, OH (TCT)
Medix School, GA (TCT)
Medix School, MD (TCT)
MedTech College, IN (TCT)
MedVance Institute, FL (JRC)
MedVance Institute, LA (JRC)
MedVance Institute, TN (JRC)
MedVance Institute, TX (JRC)
Meeting School, NH (PRC)
Meharry Medical College, TN (GRD)
Melbourne Beauty School, FL (TCT)
Mellie's Beauty College, AR (TCT)
Memorial Hall School, TX (PRC)
Memorial Hospital, CO (TCT)
Memorial Hospital, OH (AHS)
Memorial Hospital School of Nursing, NY (NRS)
Memorial Hospital System, TX (AHS)
Memorial Sloan Kettering Cancer Center, NY (TCT)
Memphis College of Art, TN (UNC)
Memphis Theological Seminary, TN (GRD)
The Menaul School, NM (PRC)
Mendocino College, CA (JRC)
Menlo College, CA (UNC)
Mennonite Brethren Biblical Seminary, CA (GRD)
Mennonite College of Nursing, IL (UNC)
Merced College, CA (JRC)
Merced College-Los Banos Campus, CA (JRC)
Mercer County Community College, NJ (JRC)
Mercer County Vocational-Tech. School, NJ (TCT)
Mercer Medical Center, NJ (NRS)
Mercersburg Academy, PA (PRC)
Mercer University in Atlanta, GA (UNC)
Mercer University in Macon, GA (UNC)
Mercy College, NY (UNC)
Mercy College - Manhattan Campus, NY (UNC)
Mercy College of Health Sciences, IA (UNC)
Mercy College of Northwest Ohio, OH (JRC)
Mercy Hospital, MD (AHS)
Mercy Hospital, ME (AHS)
Mercy Hospital School of Nursing, PA (TCT)
Mercyhurst College, PA (UNC)
Mercy Medical Center, NY (AHS)
Mercy Medical Center, WI (AHS)
Mercy Medical Center - Sioux City, IA (AHS)
Mercy School of Nursing, NC (TCT)
Mercy-St. Luke's Hospital, IA (AHS)
Meredith College, NC (WMC)
Meridia Health System, OH (AHS)
Meridian Community College, MS (JRC)
Merkaz Bnos - Business School, NY (TCT)
Merrell Univ of Beauty Arts & Science, MO (TCT)
Merrillville Beauty College, IN (TCT)
Merrimack College, MA (UNC)
Merritt College, CA (JRC)
Mesabi Range Community & Technical Coll., MN (JRC)
Mesa Community College, AZ (JRC)
Mesalands Community College, NM (JRC)
Mesa State College, CO (UNC)
Mesivta Eastern Parkway Rabbinical Sem., NY (MNC)
Mesivta Tifereth Jerusalem of America, NY (MNC)
Mesivta Torah Vodaath Seminary, NY (MNC)
Messenger College, MO (UNC)
Messiah College, PA (UNC)
Methodist College, NC (UNC)
Methodist College of Nursing, IL (TCT)
Methodist Hospital, PA (NRS)
Methodist Hospital, TN (AHS)
Methodist Hospital, TX (AHS)
Methodist Hosp/Clarian Health Partners, IN (AHS)
Methodist Theological School in Ohio, OH (GRD)
Metro Area Vocational Technical School, OK (TCT)
Metro Business College, MO (TCT)
MetroHealth Medical Center, OH (AHS)
Metroplex Beauty School, TX (TCT)
Metropolitan Career Center, PA (TCT)
Metropolitan College of New York, NY (UNC)
Metropolitan Community College, MO (JRC)
Metropolitan Community College, NE (JRC)
Metropolitan Learning Institute, NY (TCT)
Metropolitan State College, CO (UNC)
Metropolitan State University, MN (UNC)
MGH Institute of Health Professions, MA (GRD)
Miami Ad School, FL (TCT)
Miami-Dade College, FL (JRC)
Miami-Dade Community College, FL (JRC)
Miami-Dade Community College-Medical Ctr, FL (JRC)
Miami International Univ of Art & Design, FL (UNC)
Miami-Jacobs College, OH (JRC)
Miami Job Corps Center, FL (TCT)
Miami Lakes Educational Center, FL (TCT)
Miami University, OH (UNC)
Miami University-Hamilton Campus, OH (JRC)
Miami University-Middletown Campus, OH (JRC)
Miami Valley Hospital, OH (AHS)
Michael's School of Hair Design, NH (TCT)
Michigan Barber School, MI (TCT)
Michigan College of Beauty, MI (TCT)
Michigan Institute of Aeronautics, MI (TCT)
Michigan Jewish Institute, MI (UNC)
Michigan School for the Blind, MI (HND)
Michigan Sch of Professional Psychology, MI (GRD)
Michigan State University, MI (UNC)
MI State Univ. - Detroit College of Law, MI (GRD)
Michigan Technological University, MI (UNC)
Michigan Theological Seminary, MI (GRD)
Micropower Computer Institute, NJ (TCT)
Micro Tech Training Center, NJ (TCT)
Mid-America Baptist Theological Seminary, NY (GRD)
Mid-America Baptist Theological Seminary, TN (GRD)
Mid-America Christian University, OK (UNC)
Mid-America College of Funeral Service, IN (JRC)
Mid-America Nazarene University, KS (UNC)
Mid-America Reformed Seminary, IN (UNC)
Mid Cities Barber College, TX (TCT)
Mid-Continent University, KY (UNC)
Middlebury College, VT (UNC)
Middle Georgia College, GA (JRC)
Middle Georgia Technical College, GA (TCT)
Middlesex Community College, CT (JRC)
Middlesex Community College, MA (JRC)
Middlesex County College, NJ (JRC)
Middlesex School, MA (PRC)
Middle Tennessee School of Anesthesia, TN (GRD)
Middle Tennessee School of Cosmetology, TN (TCT)
Middle Tennessee State University, TN (UNC)
Middletown Regional Hospital, OH (AHS)
Midland College, TX (JRC)
Midland Lutheran College, NE (UNC)
Midland School, CA (PRC)
Midlands Technical College, SC (JRC)
Mid-Michigan Community College, MI (JRC)
Mid-Pacific Institute, HI (PRC)
Mid-Plains Community College, NE (JRC)
Mid-South Community College, AR (JRC)
Midstate College, IL (UNC)
Mid-State Technical College, WI (JRC)
Midway College, KY (WMC)
Midway Paris Beauty School, NY (TCT)
Midwest College of Oriental Medicine, IL (GRD)
Midwest College of Oriental Medicine, WI (GRD)
Midwestern Baptist Theological Seminary, MO (GRD)
Midwestern State University, TX (UNC)
Midwestern University, AZ (UNC)
Midwestern University, IL (UNC)
Midwest Institute - Earth City, MO (JRC)
Midwest Institute for Medical Assistants, MO (TCT)
Midwest Technical Institute, IL (TCT)
Midwest University, MO (GRD)
Mifflin-Juniata Career & Technology Ctr, PA (TCT)
Milan Institute, CA (AHS)
Milan Institute, CA (TCT)
Milan Institute, ID (TCT)
Milan Institute, NV (TCT)
Milan Institute, TX (TCT)
Milan Institute of Cosmetology, CA (TCT)
Milan Institute of Cosmetology, TX (TCT)
Milan Institute of Cosmetology, WA (TCT)
Milburn School for Hearing Handicapped, NJ (HND)
Mildred Elley Business School, MA (TCT)
Mildred Elley the College for Careers, NY (TCT)
Miles College, AL (UNC)
Miles Community College, MT (JRC)
Milford Academy, NY (PRB)
Millbrook School, NY (PRC)
Miller-Motte Technical College, NC (TCT)
Miller-Motte Technical College, SC (TCT)
Miller-Motte Technical College, TN (TCT)
Miller-Motte Technical College, VA (TCT)
Miller School of Albemarle, VA (PRC)
Millersville University of Pennsylvania, PA (UNC)
Milligan College, TN (UNC)
Millikin University, IL (UNC)
Mill Neck Lutheran School, NY (HND)
Millsaps College, MS (UNC)
Mills College, CA (WMC)
Mills Peninsula Health Services, CA (TCT)
Milo Adventist Academy, OR (PRC)
Milton Academy, MA (PRC)
Milton Hershey School, PA (PRC)
Milton S. Hershey Medical Center Hosp., PA (AHS)
Milwaukee Area Technical College, WI (JRC)
Milwaukee Institute of Art & Design, WI (UNC)
Milwaukee School of Engineering, WI (UNC)
Mims Classic Beauty College, TX (TCT)
Mineral Area College, MO (JRC)
Mineral Area Regional Medical Center, MO (AHS)
Minneapolis Business College, MN (TCT)
Minneapolis College of Art & Design, MN (ART)
Minneapolis Community and Tech College, MN (JRC)
Minneapolis VA Medical Center, MN (AHS)
Minnesota School for the Deaf, MN (HND)
Minnesota School of Business, MN (TCT)
Minnesota State College Southeast Tech., MN (TCT)
MN State Community & Technical College, MN (JRC)
MN State Community & Technical College, MN (TCT)
Minnesota State University Mankato, MN (UNC)
Minnesota State University Moorhead, MN (UNC)
Minnesota West Community & Tech College, MN (JRC)
Minot State University, ND (UNC)
Minot State University-Bottineau Campus, ND (JRC)
Mira Costa College, CA (JRC)
Mirrer Yeshiva Central Institute, NY (MNC)
Misers Inspection and Training, CO (TCT)
Miss Hall's School, MA (PRG)
Mission College, CA (JRC)
Mississippi Baptist Medical Center, MS (AHS)
Mississippi College, MS (GRD)
Mississippi College, MS (UNC)
Mississippi College of Beauty Culture, MS (TCT)
Mississippi Delta Community College, MS (JRC)
Mississippi Gulf Coast Community College, MS (JRC)
Mississippi Job Corps Center, MS (TCT)
Mississippi School for the Blind, MS (HND)
Mississippi School for the Deaf, MS (HND)
Mississippi State University, MS (UNC)
Mississippi University for Women, MS (UNC)
Mississippi University for Women-Tupelo, MS (UNC)
Mississippi Valley State University, MS (UNC)
Miss Marty's Sch. Beauty & Hairstyling, CA (TCT)
Missouri Baptist University, MO (UNC)
Missouri Beauty Academy, MO (TCT)
Missouri College, MO (TCT)
Missouri College of Cosmetology North, MO (TCT)
Missouri Military Academy, MO (PRB)
Missouri School for the Blind, MO (HND)
Missouri School for the Deaf, MO (HND)
Missouri Sch. of Barbering & Hairstyling, MO (TCT)
Missouri Southern State University, MO (UNC)
Missouri State University, MO (UNC)
Missouri State University - West Plains, MO (UNC)
Missouri Tech, MO (UNC)
Missouri Valley College, MO (UNC)
Missouri Western State College, MO (UNC)
Miss Porter's School, CT (PRG)
Mister Wayne's Sch of Unisex Hair Design, TN (TCT)
Mitchell College, CT (JRC)
Mitchell Community College, NC (JRC)
Mitchell's Hairstyling Academy, NC (TCT)
Mitchell Technical Institute, SD (TCT)
MJM Institute of Cosmetology, CO (TCT)
M.J. Murphy Beauty College, MI (TCT)
MJ's Beauty Academy, TX (TCT)
MMI Preparatory School, PA (PRC)
Moberly Area Community College, MO (JRC)
Model College of Hair Design, MN (TCT)
Model Secondary School for the Deaf, DC (HND)
Modern Beauty Academy, CA (TCT)
Modern Beauty School, MT (TCT)
Modern Hairstyling Institute, PR (TCT)
Modern Technology School, CA (TCT)
Modern Welding School, NY (TCT)
Modesto Junior College, CA (JRC)
Mohave Community College, AZ (JRC)
Mohawk Valley Community College, NY (JRC)
Moler Barber College, CA (TCT)
Moler Barber College of HairStyling, ND (TCT)
Moler Beauty College, LA (TCT)
Moler-Hollywood Beauty College, OH (TCT)
Moler-Pickens Beauty College, OH (TCT)
Molloy College, NY (UNC)
Monmouth College, IL (UNC)
Monmouth Medical Center, NJ (TCT)
Monmouth University, NJ (UNC)
Monongalia County Tech Education Center, WV (TCT)
Monroe College, NY (JRC)
Monroe College, NY (UNC)
Monroe Community College, NY (JRC)
Monroe County Community College, MI (JRC)
Monsour Medical Center, PA (AHS)
Montana School for the Deaf and Blind, MT (HND)
Montana State University - Billings, MT (UNC)
MSU Billings College of Technology, MT (TCT)
Montana State University - Bozeman, MT (UNC)
Montana State Univ Great Falls College, MT (JRC)
Montana State University Northern, MT (UNC)
Montana Tech College of Technology, MT (TCT)
Montana Tech of the University of MT, MT (EGN)
Montcalm Community College, MI (JRC)
Montclair College Preparatory School, CA (PRC)
Montclair State University, NJ (UNC)
Montebello Beauty College, CA (TCT)
Montecarlo: Escuela de Hoteleria y Artes, PR (TCT)
Montefiore Medical Center, NY (AHS)
Monterey Bay Academy, CA (PRC)
Monterey Institute of Intl. Studies, CA (GRD)
Monterey Peninsula College, CA (JRC)
Monte Vista Christian School, CA (PRC)
Montgomery Beauty School, MD (TCT)
Montgomery College, MD (JRC)
Montgomery Community College, NC (JRC)
Montgomery County Community College, PA (JRC)
Montgomery Job Corps Center, AL (TCT)
Montreat College, NC (UNC)
Montserrat College of Art, MA (ART)
Montverde Academy, FL (PRC)
Moody Bible Institute, IL (UNC)
Moore College of Art and Design, PA (WMC)
Moorpark College, CA (JRC)
Moraine Park Technical College, WI (JRC)
Moraine Valley Community College, IL (JRC)
Moravian Academy, PA (PRC)
Moravian College, PA (UNC)
Moravian Theological Seminary, PA (UNC)
Morehead State University, KY (UNC)

Morehouse College, GA (MNC)
Morehouse School of Medicine, GA (UNC)
Morgan Community College, CO (JRC)
Morgan Park Academy, IL (PRC)
Morgan State University, MD (UNC)
Morgantown Beauty College, WV (TCT)
Morningside College, IA (UNC)
Morning Sky Residential School, CA (HND)
Moro Beauty College, CA (TCT)
Morris College, SC (UNC)
Morrison Institute of Technology, IL (JRC)
Morrison University, NV (UNC)
Morristown Memorial Hospital, NJ (AHS)
Morton College, IL (JRC)
Moses Brown School, RI (PRC)
Moses H. Cone Memorial Hospital, NC (AHS)
Motif Beauty Academy, KY (TCT)
Motlow State Community College, TN (JRC)
Motorcycle Mechanics Institute, AZ (TCT)
Motorcycle Mechanics Institute, FL (TCT)
Moultrie Technical College, GA (TCT)
Mountaineer Beauty College, WV (TCT)
Mountain Empire Community College, VA (JRC)
Mountain Lake Children's Residence, NY (HND)
Mountainland Applied Technology College, UT (TCT)
Mountainside Hospital, NJ (AHS)
Mountain State College, WV (TCT)
Mountain State University, WV (UNC)
Mountain View College, TX (JRC)
Mountain West College, UT (JRC)
Mount Aloysius College, PA (UNC)
Mt. Angel Seminary, OR (GRD)
Mt. Carmel College of Nursing, OH (UNC)
Mt. Holyoke College, MA (WMC)
Mt. Hood Community College, OR (JRC)
Mt. Ida College, MA (UNC)
Mt. Marty College, SD (UNC)
Mt. Mary College, WI (WMC)
Mt. Mercy College, IA (UNC)
Mt. Michael Benedictine School, NE (PRB)
Mt. Olive College, NC (UNC)
Mt. St. Mary Academy, AR (PRG)
Mt. St. Mary Academy, NJ (PRG)
Mt. St. Mary College, NY (UNC)
Mt. St. Mary's College, CA (UNC)
Mt. St. Mary's College - Doheny Campus, CA (WMC)
Mt. St. Mary's University, MD (UNC)
Mt. St. Scholastica Academy, KS (PRG)
Mt. San Antonio College, CA (JRC)
Mt. San Jacinto College, CA (JRC)
Mt. Sierra College, CA (TCT)
Mt. Sinai Medical Center, FL (TCT)
Mt. Sinai School of Medicine, NY (GRD)
Mt. Union College, OH (UNC)
Mt. Vernon Beauty School, WA (TCT)
Mt. Vernon Nazarene University, OH (UNC)
Mt. Wachusett Community College, MA (JRC)
Mr. Bernard's School of Hair Fashion, ME (TCT)
Mr. David's School of Cosmetolgy, MI (TCT)
Mr. David's School of Hair Design, NC (TCT)
Mr. Jim's Beauty College, KY (TCT)
Mr. John's School of Cosmetology, IL (TCT)
Mr. John's School of Cosmetology & Nails, IL (TCT)
Mr. Juan's College of Hair Design, ID (TCT)
Mr. Leon's School of Hair Design, ID (TCT)
Ms. Robert's Academy of Beauty Culture, IL (TCT)
MTI Business College of Stockton, CA (TCT)
MTI College, CA (JRC)
MTI College of Business & Technology, TX (TCT)
MTTI - MotoRing Technical Training Inst., RI (TCT)
Mueller College of Holistic Studies, CA (TCT)
Muhlenberg College, PA (UNC)
Muhlenberg Job Corps Center, KY (TCT)
Muhlenberg Regional Medical Center, NJ (NRS)
Multnomah Bible Coll. & Biblical Sem., OR (UNC)
Munson Medical Center, MI (AHS)
Munson-Williams-Proctor Institute, NY (TCT)
Murray State College, OK (JRC)
Murray State University, KY (UNC)
Muscatine Community College, IA (JRC)
Music Center of the North Shore, IL (TCT)
Music Conservatory of Westchester, NY (TCT)
Musicians Institute, CA (TCT)
Muskegon Community College, MI (JRC)
Muskingum College, OH (UNC)
Muskogee General Hospital, OK (AHS)
Myers University, OH (UNC)
My-Le's Beauty College, CA (TCT)
Myotherapy College of Utah, UT (TCT)
Myotherapy Institute, NE (TCT)

N

Nail Academy, NY (TCT)
Napa State Hospital, CA (AHS)
Napa Valley College, CA (JRC)
Naropa University, CO (UNC)
NASCAR Technical Institute, NC (TCT)
Nash Community College, NC (JRC)
Nashotah House, WI (GRD)
Nashville Auto-Diesel College, TN (TCT)
Nashville College, TN (TCT)
Nashville State Technical Community Coll, TN (JRC)
Nassau Community College, NY (JRC)
National Academy of Beauty Arts, MO (TCT)
National American University, CO (UNC)
National American University, MN (UNC)
National American University, MO (UNC)
National American University, NM (UNC)
National American University, SD (UNC)
National Aviation Academy, FL (TCT)
National Beauty College, OH (TCT)
National Beauty College, TX (TCT)
National Career Education, CA (TCT)
National College, KY (JRC)
National College, TN (JRC)
National College, VA (JRC)
National College, VA (TCT)
National College of Business & Tech., PR (TCT)
National College of Business & Tech., TN (JRC)
National College of Midwifery, NM (UNC)
National Coll. of Naturopathic Medicine, OR (GRD)
National Conservatory of Dramatic Arts, DC (TCT)
National Grad. Sch. Quality Systems Mgmt, MA (GRD)
National Heavy Equipment Operator School, FL (TCT)
National Hispanic University, CA (UNC)
National Institute of Technology, CA (TCT)
National Labor College, MD (UNC)
National-Louis University, IL (UNC)
National Massage Therapy Institute, DE (TCT)
National Park Community College, AR (JRC)
National Polytechnic College, CA (TCT)
National School of Technology, FL (TCT)
National Sports Academy, NY (PRC)
National Tax Training School, NJ (HMS)
National Technological University, MD (GRD)
National Theatre Conservatory, CO (GRD)
National Tractor Trailer School, NY (TCT)
National Training, FL (HMS)
National University, CA (UNC)
National University of Health Sciences, IL (GRD)
National University School of Law, CA (GRD)
Nationwide Beauty Academy, OH (TCT)
Natural Motion Institute of Hair Design, NJ (TCT)
Naugatuck Valley Community College, CT (JRC)
Navarro College, TX (JRC)
NAWCC School of Horology, PA (TCT)
Nazarene Bible College, CO (UNC)
Nazarene Theological Seminary, MO (GRD)
Nazareth College of Rochester, NY (UNC)
Nazareth Hospital, PA (AHS)
Nebraska Christian College, NE (UNC)
Nebraska Coll of Technical Agriculture, NE (JRC)
Nebraska Indian Community College, NE (JRC)
Nebraska Methodist College, NE (AHS)
Nebraska School for Visually Handicapped, NE (HND)
Nebraska Wesleyan University, NE (UNC)
Neill Institute, LA (TCT)
Neilson Beauty College, TX (TCT)
Neosho Beauty College, MO (TCT)
Neosho County Community College, KS (JRC)
Ner Israel Rabbinical College, MD (MNC)
Neumann College, PA (UNC)
Newberry College, SC (UNC)
Newberry School of Beauty, CA (TCT)
Newbridge College, CA (TCT)
New Brunswick Theological Seminary, NJ (GRD)
Newbury College, MA (UNC)
New Castle School of Beauty Culture, PA (TCT)
New Castle School of Trades, PA (TCT)
New College of Florida, FL (UNC)
New College School of Law, CA (UNC)
Newcomb College of Tulane University, LA (UNC)
New Community Workforce Development Ctr., NJ (TCT)
New Concept Massage & Beauty School, FL (TCT)
New Creation Academy of Hair Design, MD (TCT)
New Dimensions School of Hair Design, MO (TCT)
New Directions Hair Academy, TN (TCT)
New England College, NH (UNC)
New England College of Finance, MA (JRC)
New England College of Optometry, MA (GRD)
New England Conservatory of Music, MA (MUS)
New England Culinary Institute, VT (TCT)
New England Culinary Institute, VT (UNC)
New England EMS Institute, NH (TCT)
New England Hair Academy, MA (TCT)
New England Institute of Art, MA (TCT)
New England Institute of Technology, RI (UNC)
New England School of Acupuncture, MA (GRD)
New England School of Art & Design, MA (TCT)
New England School of Communications, ME (TCT)
New England School of Hair Design, NH (TCT)
New England School of Law, MA (LAW)
New England School of Photography, MA (TCT)
New England Technical Institute, CT (TCT)
New England Tractor Trailer Training, CT (TCT)
New England Tractor Trailer Training, RI (TCT)
New Hampshire Community Tech College, NH (JRC)
New Hampshire Technical College, NH (JRC)
New Hampshire Technical Institute, NH (JRC)
New Hampton School, NH (PRC)
New Hanover Regional Medical Center, NC (AHS)
New Horizons Beauty College, UT (TCT)
New Horizons Beauty School, NJ (TCT)
New Jersey City University, NJ (UNC)
New Jersey Institute of Technology, NJ (UNC)
New Jersey School of Locksmithing, NJ (TCT)
New Life Theological Seminary, NC (GRD)
Newman University, KS (UNC)
New Mexico Aveda Inst de Bellas Artes, NM (TCT)
New Mexico Highlands University, NM (UNC)
New Mexico Institute Mining & Technology, NM (UNC)
New Mexico Junior College, NM (JRC)
New Mexico Military Institute, NM (JRC)
New Mexico Military Institute, NM (PRC)
New Mexico School for the Deaf, NM (HND)
New Mexico School Visually Handicapped, NM (HND)
New Mexico State University, NM (JRC)
New Mexico State University, NM (UNC)
New Mexico State Univ. Dona Ana Branch, NM (JRC)
New Orleans Baptist Theological Seminary, LA (GRD)
New Orleans Job Corps Center, LA (TCT)
New Orleans School of Urban Missions, LA (JRC)
Newport Business Institute, PA (JRC)
Newport School of Hairdressing, RI (TCT)
New Professions Technical Institute, FL (TCT)
New River Community & Technical College, WV (JRC)
New River Community College, VA (JRC)
New Saint Andrews College, ID (UNC)
Newschool of Architecture & Design, CA (UNC)
New School University, NY (UNC)
New Tyler Barber College, AR (TCT)
New Wave Hair Academy, TN (TCT)
New World School of the Arts, FL (ART)
New York Academy of Art, NY (GRD)
New York Automotive & Diesel Institute, NY (TCT)
New York Career Institute, NY (TCT)
New York Chiropractic College, NY (GRD)
New York City College of Technology CUNY, NY (UNC)
New York College of Health Professions, NY (UNC)
New York College of Podiatric Medicine, NY (GRD)
New York Eye & Ear Infirmary, NY (TCT)
New York Institute for Special Education, NY (HND)
New York Inst. of Business Technology, NY (TCT)
New York Institute of Massage, NY (TCT)
New York Institute of Technology, NY (UNC)
New York International Beauty School, NY (TCT)
New York Law School, NY (GRD)
New York Medical College, NY (GRD)
New York Methodist Hospital, NY (TCT)
New York Military Academy, NY (PRC)
New York Paralegal School, NY (TCT)
New York Presbyterian Hospital, NY (AHS)
New York School for Medical Dental Asst., NY (TCT)
New York School for the Deaf, NY (HND)
New York School of Interior Design, NY (UNC)
New York State School for the Blind, NY (HND)
New York State School for the Deaf, NY (HND)
New York Technical Institute of Hawaii, HI (TCT)
New York Theological Seminary, NY (GRD)
New York University, NY (UNC)
New York University Medical Center, NY (UNC)
Niagara University, NY (UNC)
Nicholls State University, LA (UNC)
Nichols Career Center, MO (TCT)
Nichols College, MA (UNC)
Nick Harris Detective Academy, CA (TCT)
Nicolet Area Technical College, WI (JRC)
Niles School of Beauty Culture, IL (TCT)
Noble and Greenough School, MA (PRC)
Norfolk Skills Center, VA (TCT)
Norfolk State University, VA (UNC)
Normandale Community College, MN (JRC)
Normandy Beauty School of Jacksonville, FL (TCT)
North Adrian's Beauty College, CA (TCT)
North American Baptist Seminary, SD (GRD)
North American Computer Consultants, CA (TCT)
North American Trade Schools, MD (TCT)
Northampton Co. Area Community College, PA (JRC)
North Arkansas College, AR (JRC)
North Bennet Street School, MA (TCT)
North Carolina A&T State University, NC (UNC)
North Carolina Central University, NC (UNC)
North Carolina School for the Deaf, NC (HND)
North Carolina School of the Arts, NC (UNC)
North Carolina State University, NC (UNC)
North Carolina Wesleyan College, NC (UNC)
North Central College, IL (UNC)
North Central Industrial Tech. Ed. Ctr., PA (TCT)
North Central Institute, TN (TCT)
North Central Kansas Technical College, KS (TCT)
North Central Michigan College, MI (JRC)
North Central Missouri College, MO (JRC)
North Central State College, OH (JRC)
Northcentral Technical College, WI (JRC)
North Central Texas College, TX (JRC)
Northcentral University, AZ (UNC)
North Central University, MN (UNC)
North Country Community College, NY (JRC)
North Country School, NY (PRC)
North Dakota School for the Blind, ND (HND)
North Dakota State College of Science, ND (JRC)
North Dakota State University, ND (UNC)
Northeast Alabama Community College, AL (JRC)
Northeast Community College, NE (JRC)
Northeastern Hospital School of Nursing, PA (TCT)
Northeastern Illinois University, IL (UNC)
Northeastern Junior College, CO (JRC)
Northeastern Ohio Univ Coll of Medicine, OH (GRD)
Northeastern Oklahoma A&M College, OK (JRC)
Northeastern State University, OK (UNC)
Northeastern Technical College, SC (JRC)
Northeastern University, MA (UNC)
Northeast Iowa Community College, IA (JRC)
Northeast Kansas Technical College, KS (TCT)
Northeast Mississippi Community College, MS (JRC)
Northeast State Tech Community College, TN (JRC)
Northeast Texas Community College, TX (JRC)
Northeast Wisconsin Technical College, WI (JRC)
Northern Arizona University, AZ (UNC)
Northern Baptist Theological Seminary, IL (GRD)
Northern Essex Community College, MA (JRC)
Northern Hospital of Surry County, NC (AHS)
Northern Illinois University, IL (UNC)
Northern Institute of Cosmetology, OH (TCT)
Northern Kentucky University, KY (UNC)
Northern Maine Community College, ME (JRC)
Northern Marianas College, MP (JRC)
Northern Michigan University, MI (UNC)
Northern New Mexico College, NM (JRC)
Northern New Mexico Community College, NM (JRC)
Northern Oklahoma College, OK (JRC)
Northern State University, SD (UNC)
Northern Virginia Community College, VA (JRC)
Northern Westchester Sch of Hairdressing, NY (TCT)
Northern Wyoming Community College, WY (JRC)
Northfield Mt. Hermon School, MA (STA)
North Florida Community College, FL (JRC)
North Florida Cosmetology Institute, FL (TCT)
North Florida Institute, FL (TCT)
North Georgia College & State University, GA (UNC)
North Georgia Technical College, GA (TCT)
North Greenville University, SC (UNC)
North Harris Montgomery Comm. College, TX (JRC)
North Hennepin Community College, MN (JRC)
North Hills Beauty Academy, PA (TCT)
North Idaho College, ID (JRC)
North Iowa Area Community College, IA (JRC)
North Iowa Mercy Health Center, IA (AHS)
North Kansas City Hospital, MO (AHS)
North Lake College, TX (JRC)
Northland Baptist Bible College, WI (UNC)
Northland College, WI (UNC)
Northland Community & Technical College, MN (JRC)

Northland Pioneer College, AZ (JRC)
North Memorial Medical Center, MN (AHS)
North Metro Technical College, GA (UNC)
North Mississippi Medical Center, MS (AHS)
North Oaks Medical Center, LA (AHS)
North Park Coll. & Theological Seminary, IL (UNC)
North Platte Beauty Academy, NE (TCT)
Northport VA Medical Center, NY (AHS)
North Seattle Community College, WA (JRC)
North Shore Community College, MA (JRC)
North Technical Education Center, FL (TCT)
North Tennessee Bible Inst. & Seminary, FL (UNC)
North Tennessee Bible Inst. & Seminary, TN (UNC)
Northwest Arkansas Community College, AR (JRC)
Northwest Aviation College, WA (TCT)
Northwest Baptist Seminary, WA (UNC)
Northwest Christian College, OR (UNC)
Northwest College, WY (JRC)
Northwest College of Art, WA (ART)
Northwest College of Hair Design, OR (TCT)
Northwest College Medical Dental Assts., CA (TCT)
Northwest Community Hospital, IL (TCT)
Northwest Educational Center, TX (TCT)
Northwestern Business College, IL (JRC)
Northwestern College, IA (UNC)
Northwestern College, MN (UNC)
Northwestern CT Comm. Technical College, CT (JRC)
Northwestern Health Sciences University, MN (GRD)
Northwestern Memorial Hospital, IL (TCT)
Northwestern Michigan College, MI (JRC)
Northwestern Oklahoma State University, OK (UNC)
Northwestern Polytechnic University, CA (UNC)
Northwestern State University, LA (UNC)
Northwestern Technical College, GA (JRC)
Northwestern Technological Institute, MI (TCT)
Northwestern University, IL (UNC)
Northwest Indian College, WA (JRC)
Northwest Iowa Community College, IA (JRC)
Northwest Kansas Technical College, KS (TCT)
Northwest Lineman College, CA (TCT)
Northwest Lineman College, ID (TCT)
Northwest Medical Center, PA (AHS)
Northwest Mississippi Community College, MS (JRC)
Northwest Missouri State University, MO (UNC)
Northwest Nazarene University, ID (UNC)
Northwest School, WA (PRC)
Northwest School of Wooden Boatbuilding, WA (TCT)
Northwest-Shoals Community College, AL (JRC)
Northwest State Community College, OH (JRC)
Northwest Technical College, MN (UNC)
Northwest Technical Institute, AR (TCT)
Northwest Texas Healthcare System, TX (TCT)
Northwest University, WA (UNC)
Northwest Vista College, TX (JRC)
Northwood School, NY (PRC)
Northwood University, FL (UNC)
Northwood University, MI (UNC)
Northwood University, TX (UNC)
Norwalk Community College, CT (JRC)
Norwalk Hospital, CT (TCT)
Norwich University, VT (UNC)
Nossi College of Art, TN (JRC)
Notre Dame Academy, VA (PRC)
Notre Dame-Cathedral Latin School, OH (PRC)
Notre Dame College, OH (AHS)
Notre Dame de Namur University, CA (UNC)
Notre Dame Grad Sch of Christendom Coll., VA (GRD)
Notre Dame Seminary, LA (MNC)
Nouvelle Institute, FL (TCT)
Nova Southeastern University, FL (UNC)
Nova Southeastern Univ Health Profession, FL (UNC)
NTI-School of CAD Technology, MN (TCT)
NTMA Training Center of Southern CA, CA (TCT)
Nunez Community College, LA (JRC)
Nu-Tek Academy of Beauty, KY (TCT)
Nyack College, NY (UNC)
NY College Traditional Chinese Medicine, NY (GRD)

O

Oakbridge Academy of Arts, PA (TCT)
Oak Creek Ranch School, AZ (PRC)
Oak Grove Lutheran High School, ND (PRC)
Oak Grove School, CA (PRC)
Oak Hill Academy, VA (PRC)
Oak Hills Christian College, MN (UNC)
Oakland City University, IN (UNC)
Oakland Community College, MI (JRC)
Oakland County Health Division, MI (AHS)
Oakland University, MI (UNC)
Oak Ridge Military Academy, NC (PRC)
Oakton Community College, IL (JRC)
Oakwood College, AL (UNC)
Oakwood Friends School, NY (PRC)
Oakwood - Hospital Annapolis Center, MI (AHS)
Oberlin College, OH (UNC)
Oblate School of Theology, TX (GRD)
O'Briens Training Center, VT (TCT)
Occidental College, CA (UNC)
Occupational Training Services, CA (TCT)
The Ocean Corporation, TX (TCT)
Ocean County College, NJ (JRC)
Oceanside College of Beauty, CA (TCT)
Ochsner School of Allied Health Sciences, LA (TCT)
Oconaluftee Job Corps Center, NC (TCT)
Odessa College, TX (JRC)
Oehrlein School of Cosmetology, IL (TCT)
Ogden-Weber Applied Technology College, UT (TCT)
Ogeechee Technical College, GA (TCT)
Oglala Lakota College, SD (UNC)
Oglala Lakota Community College, SD (JRC)
Ogle School of Hair Design, TX (TCT)
Oglethorpe University, GA (UNC)
Ohio Business College, OH (TCT)
Ohio Center for Broadcasting, OH (TCT)
Ohio Center for Broadcasting - Colorado, CO (TCT)
Ohio College of Massotherapy, OH (TCT)
Ohio College of Podiatric Medicine, OH (GRD)
Ohio Dominican University, OH (UNC)
Ohio Institute of Health Careers, OH (TCT)
Ohio Institute of Photography & Tech, OH (JRC)
Ohio Northern University, OH (UNC)
Ohio School for the Deaf, OH (HND)
Ohio State Beauty Academy, OH (TCT)
Ohio State College of Barber Styling, OH (TCT)
Ohio State Cosmetology School, OH (TCT)
Ohio State Sch of Cosmetology Northland, OH (TCT)
Ohio State School for the Blind, OH (HND)
Ohio State School of Cosmetology, OH (TCT)
Ohio State School of Cosmetology East, OH (TCT)
Ohio State University, OH (UNC)
Ohio State University-A & T Institute, OH (JRC)
Ohio State University Hospitals, OH (AHS)
Ohio State University-Lima Campus, OH (UNC)
Ohio State University-Mansfield Campus, OH (UNC)
Ohio State University-Marion, OH (UNC)
Ohio State University-Newark, OH (UNC)
Ohio Technical College, OH (TCT)
Ohio University, OH (UNC)
Ohio University Southern Campus, OH (UNC)
Ohio University, OH (UNC)
Ohio Valley College of Technology, OH (TCT)
Ohio Valley General Hospital, PA (NRS)
Ohio Valley Hospital, OH (NRS)
Ohio Valley Medical Center, WV (AHS)
Ohio Valley University, WV (UNC)
Ohio Wesleyan University, OH (UNC)
Ohlone College, CA (JRC)
Ohr HaMeir Theological Seminary, NY (MNC)
Ohr Somayach Tanenbaum Educational Ctr., NY (GRD)
Ojai Valley School, CA (PRC)
Okaloosa Applied Technical Center, FL (TCT)
Okaloosa-Walton College, FL (JRC)
Okefenokee Technical College, GA (TCT)
Oklahoma Baptist University, OK (UNC)
Oklahoma Christian University, OK (UNC)
Oklahoma City Community College, OK (JRC)
Oklahoma City University, OK (UNC)
Oklahoma Farriers College, OK (TCT)
Oklahoma Health Academy, OK (TCT)
Oklahoma Panhandle State University, OK (UNC)
Oklahoma School for the Deaf, OK (HND)
Oklahoma State Horseshoeing School, OK (TCT)
Oklahoma State University, OK (UNC)
OSU College of Osteopathic Medicine, OK (GRD)
Oklahoma State University-Oklahoma City, OK (JRC)
Oklahoma State University-Okmulgee, OK (JRC)
Oklahoma Wesleyan University, OK (UNC)
Old Dominion University, VA (UNC)
Oldfields School, MD (PRG)
Old Town Barber & Beauty College, KS (TCT)
Olean Business Institute, NY (TCT)
Olive-Harvey College, IL (JRC)
Oliver Thein Beauty College, MN (TCT)
Olivet College, MI (UNC)
Olivet Nazarene University, IL (UNC)
Olive View/UCLA Medical Centers, CA (AHS)
Olney Central College, IL (JRC)
Olney Friends School, OH (PRC)
Olympia Career Training Institute, MI (TCT)
Olympia College, IL (TCT)
Olympia College, IN (TCT)
Olympian University of Cosmetology, NM (TCT)
Olympic College, WA (JRC)
Omaha School of Massage Therapy, NE (TCT)
Omega Institute, NJ (TCT)
Omega Institute of Cosmetology, LA (TCT)
Omnitech Institute, GA (TCT)
O'More College of Design, TN (UNC)
Oneida Baptist Institute, KY (PRC)
Onondaga Community College, NY (JRC)
Opelousas School of Cosmetology, LA (TCT)
Oral Roberts University, OK (UNC)
Orangeburg-Calhoun Technical College, SC (JRC)
Orange Coast College, CA (JRC)
Orange Technical Educ. Center-Mid FL, FL (TCT)
Orange Technical Educ. Center-Orlando, FL (TCT)
Orange Technical Educ. Ctr.-Winter Park, FL (TCT)
Orange Technical Educ. Center-Westside, FL (TCT)
Oregon College of Art & Craft, OR (UNC)
Oregon College of Oriental Medicine, OR (GRD)
Oregon Episcopal School, OR (PRC)
Oregon Graduate Institute/Science & Tech, OR (GRD)
Oregon Health & Science University, OR (AHS)
Oregon Institute of Technology, OR (UNC)
Oregon State School for the Blind, OR (HND)
Oregon State School for the Deaf, OR (HND)
Oregon State University, OR (UNC)
Orleans Technical Institute, PA (TCT)
Orleans Technical Institute Center City, PA (TCT)
Orlo School of Hair Design & Cosmetology, NY (TCT)
Orme School, AZ (PRC)
Ort Technical Institute, IL (TCT)
O T Autry Area Vocational Tech Center, OK (TCT)
Otero Junior College, CO (JRC)
Otis College of Art and Design, CA (ART)
Ottawa University, KS (UNC)
Ottawa University, WI (UNC)
Otterbein College, OH (UNC)
Ouachita Baptist University, AR (UNC)
Ouachita Technical College, AR (JRC)
Our Lady of Holy Cross College, LA (AHS)
Our Lady of Lourdes School of Nursing, NJ (NRS)
Our Lady of the Lake College, LA (UNC)
Our Lady of the Lake Medical Center, LA (TCT)
Our Lady of the Lake University, TX (UNC)
Overbrook School for the Blind, PA (HND)
Overton Brooks VA Medical Center, LA (AHS)
Owensboro Community & Technical College, KY (JRC)
Owensboro Community & Technical College, KY (TCT)
Owensboro Mercy Health System, KY (AHS)
Owens Community College, OH (JRC)
Oxford Academy, CT (PRB)
Oxford College of Emory University, GA (UNC)
Oxford Graduate School, TN (GRD)
Oxman College, CA (TCT)
Oxnard College, CA (JRC)
Ozarka College, AR (TCT)
Ozark Christian College, MO (UNC)
Ozarks Technical Community College, MO (JRC)

P

Pace Institute, PA (TCT)
Pace University, NY (GRD)
Pace University, NY (UNC)
Pacifica Graduate Institute, CA (GRD)
Pacific College, CA (TCT)
Pacific College of Oriental Medicine, CA (GRD)
Pacific College of Oriental Medicine, NY (GRD)
Pacific Graduate School of Psychology, CA (GRD)
Pacific Islands Bible College, GU (UNC)
Pacific Lutheran Theological Seminary, CA (GRD)
Pacific Lutheran University, WA (UNC)
Pacific Northwest College of Art, OR (UNC)
Pacific Oaks College, CA (GRD)
Pacific School of Religion, CA (GRD)
Pacific States University, CA (UNC)
Pacific Union College, CA (NRS)
Pacific Union College, CA (UNC)
Pacific University, OR (UNC)
Paducah Technical College, KY (JRC)
Page Parkes Center of Modeling & Acting, TX (TCT)
Paier College of Art, CT (UNC)
Paine College, GA (UNC)
Palau Community College, PW (JRC)
Palladium Technical Academy, CA (TCT)
Palm Beach Atlantic University, FL (UNC)
Palm Beach Community College, FL (JRC)
Palmer College of Chiropractic, IA (GRD)
Palmer College of Chiropractic Florida, FL (GRD)
Palmer College of Chiropractic West, CA (GRD)
Palmer Theological Seminary, PA (GRD)
Palo Alto College, TX (JRC)
Palomar College, CA (JRC)
Palomar Institute of Cosmetology, CA (TCT)
Palo Verde College, CA (JRC)
Pamlico Community College, NC (JRC)
Panola College, TX (JRC)
Paradise Valley Community College, AZ (JRC)
The Paralegal Institute, AZ (HMS)
Paramount Beauty Academy, OH (TCT)
Paramount School of Beauty, CA (TCT)
Pardee RAND Grad Sch of Policy Studies, CA (GRD)
Paris Beauty College, CA (TCT)
Parisian Academy, NJ (TCT)
Paris II Educational Center, MO (TCT)
Paris Junior College, TX (JRC)
Parker College of Chiropractic, TX (BIO)
Parkland College, IL (JRC)
Parks College, CO (TCT)
Parks College of St. Louis University, MO (TCT)
Park University, MO (UNC)
Parkview Medical Center, CO (TCT)
Parkview School OK School for the Blind, OK (HND)
Parma Community General Hospital, OH (AHS)
Parsons School of Design, NY (UNC)
Pasadena Academy, TX (TCT)
Pasadena City College, CA (JRC)
Pascack Valley Hospital, NJ (AHS)
Pasco-Hernando Community College, FL (JRC)
Passaic Co. Community College, NJ (JRC)
Pat Goins Beauty School, LA (TCT)
Pat Goins Benton Road Beauty School, LA (TCT)
Pat Goins Ruston Beauty School, LA (TCT)
Pat Goins Shreveport Beauty School, LA (TCT)
Pathology and Cytology Laboratories, KY (TCT)
Pathway School, PA (HND)
Patricia Stevens College, MO (TCT)
Patrick Henry College, VA (UNC)
Patrick Henry Community College, VA (JRC)
Patsy & Rob's Academy of Beauty, MO (TCT)
Patten University, CA (UNC)
The Patterson School, NC (PRC)
Patton State Hospital, CA (AHS)
Pat Wilson Beauty College, KY (TCT)
Paul D. Camp Community College, VA (JRC)
Paul Mitchell The School, CA (TCT)
Paul Quinn College, TX (UNC)
Paul Smith's College, NY (UNC)
Payne Theological Seminary, OH (UNC)
P.B. Cosmetology Education Centre, NJ (TCT)
PCI Dealers School, NV (TCT)
PCI Health Training Center, TX (TCT)
PC Professor, FL (TCT)
Peabody College of Vanderbilt University, TN (UNC)
Peabody Institute Johns Hopkins Univ., MD (GRD)
Peace College, NC (UNC)
Pearl River Community College, MS (JRC)
Peddie School, NJ (PRC)
Peirce College, PA (JRC)
Pelican Flight Training Center, FL (TCT)
Pellissippi State Technical Comm. Coll., TN (JRC)
Peninsula College, WA (JRC)
Penn Commercial Business/Technical Sch., PA (TCT)
Pennco Tech, NJ (TCT)
Pennco Tech, PA (TCT)
Pennington School, NJ (PRC)
Penn State Cosmetology Academy, PA (TCT)
Penn State Dickinson School of Law, PA (GRD)
Penn State Fayette Eberly Campus, PA (JRC)
Penn State Great Valley School, PA (GRD)
PA Academy of Cosmetic Arts & Sciences, PA (TCT)
Pennsylvania Academy of the Fine Arts, PA (TCT)
Pennsylvania College of Art and Design, PA (UNC)
Pennsylvania College of Optometry, PA (GRD)
Pennsylvania College of Technology, PA (JRC)
Pennsylvania College of Technology, PA (UNC)
Pennsylvania Culinary Institute, PA (JRC)
Pennsylvania Gunsmith School, PA (TCT)
Pennsylvania Highlands Community College, PA (JRC)
Pennsylvania Hospital, PA (AHS)
Pennsylvania Institute of Taxidermy, PA (TCT)
Pennsylvania Institute of Technology, PA (JRC)

Pennsylvania School for the Deaf, PA (HND)
Pennsylvania School of Business, PA (JRC)
Penn State Hershey College of Medicine, PA (GRD)
Pennsylvania State University, PA (JRC)
Pennsylvania State University, PA (UNC)
Penn Valley Community College, MO (JRC)
Penrose-St. Francis Health System, CO (TCT)
Pensacola Christian College, FL (UNC)
Pensacola Junior College, FL (JRC)
Pepperdine University, CA (PSY)
Pepperdine University, CA (UNC)
Performance Training, NJ (TCT)
Perkins School for the Blind, MA (HND)
Perkiomen School, PA (PRC)
Perry Technical Institute, WA (TCT)
Peru State College, NE (UNC)
Pfeiffer University, NC (UNC)
Phagans' Beauty College, OR (TCT)
Phagans' Central Oregon Beauty College, OR (TCT)
Phagans' Grants Pass College of Beauty, OR (TCT)
Phagans' Medford Beauty School, OR (TCT)
Phagans' Newport Academy of Cosmetology, OR (TCT)
Phagans' Orchards Beauty School, WA (TCT)
Phagans' School of Beauty, OR (TCT)
Phagans' School of Hair Design, OR (TCT)
Phagans' Tigard Beauty School, OR (TCT)
The Phelps School, PA (PRB)
Philadelphia Biblical University, PA (UNC)
Philadelphia Coll. Osteopathic Medicine, PA (GRD)
Philadelphia University, PA (UNC)
Philander Smith College, AR (UNC)
Phillips Academy, MA (PRC)
Phillips Beth Israel School of Nursing, NY (TCT)
Phillips Comm. Coll. of the Univ. of AR, AR (JRC)
Phillips Exeter Academy, NH (PRC)
Phillips Graduate Institute, CA (GRD)
Phillips Hairstyling Institute, NY (TCT)
Phillips Theological Seminary, OK (GRD)
Phlebotomy Learning Center, CO (TCT)
Phoenix College, AZ (JRC)
Phoenix East Aviation, FL (TCT)
Phoenix First Pastors College, AZ (UNC)
Phoenix Institute of Herbal Medicine, AZ (GRD)
Phoenix Seminary, AZ (UNC)
Photographic Center Northwest, WA (TCT)
PIA School of Specialized Technology, PA (AAT)
Pickens Technical Center, CO (TCT)
Piedmont Baptist College, NC (UNC)
Piedmont College, GA (UNC)
Piedmont Community College, NC (JRC)
Piedmont Technical College, SC (JRC)
Piedmont Virginia Community College, VA (JRC)
Pierce College, WA (JRC)
Pierre's School of Cosmetology, ME (TCT)
Pikes Peak Community College, CO (JRC)
Pikeville College, KY (UNC)
Pikeville Medical Center, KY (AHS)
Pillsbury Baptist Bible College, MN (UNC)
Pima Community College, AZ (JRC)
Pima Medical Institute, AZ (TCT)
Pima Medical Institute, CA (TCT)
Pima Medical Institute, CO (TCT)
Pima Medical Institute, NM (TCT)
Pima Medical Institute, NV (TCT)
Pima Medical Institute, WA (TCT)
Pine Crest School, FL (PRC)
Pine Forge Academy, PA (PRC)
Pinellas Technical Education Center, FL (TCT)
Pine Manor College, MA (UNC)
Pine Ridge School, VT (PRC)
Pine Technical College, MN (JRC)
Pineville Beauty School, LA (TCT)
Piney Woods School, MS (PRC)
Pinnacle Career Institute, KS (TCT)
Pinnacle Career Institute, MO (TCT)
Pioneer Pacific College, OR (TCT)
Pipo Academy of Hair Design, TX (TCT)
Pitt Community College, NC (JRC)
Pittsburgh Institute of Mortuary Science, PA (JRC)
Pittsburgh Technical Institute, PA (TCT)
Pittsburgh Theological Seminary, PA (TSR)
Pittsburg State University, KS (UNC)
Pitzer College, CA (UNC)
Pivot Point Cosmetology Research Center, IL (TCT)
Pivot Point International, IL (TCT)
PJA School, PA (TCT)
PJ's College of Cosmetology, IN (TCT)
PJs College of Cosmetology, KY (TCT)
Platt College, CA (TCT)
Platt College, CA (UNC)
Platt College, CO (JRC)
Platt College, OK (TCT)
Platte Valley Academy, NE (PRC)
Plaza Beauty School, TN (TCT)
Plaza College, NY (TCT)
Plaza School of Beauty Culture, SC (TCT)
Plymouth State University, NH (UNC)
Point Loma Nazarene University, CA (UNC)
Point Park University, PA (UNC)
Point Park Univ.-St. Francis Med. Ctr., PA (AHS)
Politec Institute, PR (TCT)
Polk Community College, FL (JRC)
Polytechnic University, NY (GRD)
Polytechnic University, NY (UNC)
Polytechnic University of the Americas, FL (UNC)
Pomfret School, CT (PRC)
Pomona College, CA (UNC)
Ponca City Beauty College, OK (TCT)
Ponce Paramedical College, PR (TCT)
Ponce School of Medicine, PR (GRD)
Pontifical Catholic Univ. of Puerto Rico, PR (UNC)
Pontifical College Josephinum, OH (MNC)
Porter and Chester Institute, CT (TCT)
Porter and Chester Institute, MA (TCT)
Porter and Chester Institute of Branford, CT (TCT)
Porter Memorial Hospital, IN (AHS)
Porterville College, CA (JRC)
Porterville Development Center, CA (TCT)
Portfolio Center, GA (TCT)
Port Huron Hospital, MI (AHS)
Portland Community College, OR (JRC)
Portland State University, OR (UNC)
Port St. Lucie Beauty Academy, FL (TCT)
Portsmouth Abbey School, RI (PRC)
Portsmouth Beauty School of Hair Design, NH (TCT)
Post University, CT (UNC)
Poteau Beauty College, OK (TCT)
Potomac Academy of Hair Design, VA (TCT)
Potomac College, DC (UNC)
Potomac State College of West Virginia U, WV (JRC)
Pottsville Hospital School of Nursing, PA (TCT)
Poway Academy of Hair Design, CA (TCT)
Powder Springs Beauty College, GA (TCT)
Poynter Institute for Media Studies, FL (TCT)
Prairie State College, IL (JRC)
Prairie View A&M University, TX (NRS)
Prairie View A&M University, TX (UNC)
Pratt Community College, KS (JRC)
Pratt Institute, NY (UNC)
The Praxis Institute, FL (TCT)
The Praxis Institute, FL (TCT)
Precision Technical Institute, CA (TCT)
Premiere Career College, CA (TCT)
Premier Hair Academy, UT (TCT)
Presbyterian College, SC (UNC)
Presbyterian Hospital, NC (AHS)
Presbyterian Hospital, TX (AHS)
Presbyterian Pan American School, TX (PRC)
Prescott College, AZ (UNC)
Presentation College, SD (UNC)
Pressley Ridge School, PA (HND)
Prestonsburg Community College, KY (JRC)
Prince George's Community College, MD (JRC)
Prince Institute of Professional Studies, AL (JRC)
Prince Regional Vocational Tech School, CT (TCT)
Princeton Information Technology Center, PA (TCT)
Princeton Theological Seminary, NJ (GRD)
Princeton University, NJ (UNC)
Prince William Sound Community College, AK (JRC)
Principia College, IL (UNC)
Principia School, MO (PRC)
Proctor Academy, NH (PRC)
Professional Beauty School, WA (TCT)
Professional Business College, NY (TCT)
Professional Career Development Inst, GA (HMS)
Professional Career Institute, CA (TCT)
Professional Careers Institute, IN (TCT)
Professional Choice Hair Design Academy, IL (TCT)
Professional Cosmetology Education Ctr, AR (TCT)
Professional Cosmetology Institute, IA (TCT)
Professional Electrical School, PR (TCT)
Professional Golfers Career College, CA (TCT)
Professional Hair Design Academy, WI (TCT)
Professional Institute of Beauty, CA (TCT)
Professional Massage Training Center, MO (TCT)
Professional Skills Institute, OH (TCT)
Professional Technical Institute, PR (TCT)
Professional Training Center, FL (TCT)
Protestant Episcopal Theologcl. Seminary, VA (GRD)
Providence College, RI (UNC)
Providence Hospital, MI (AHS)
Provo College, UT (TCT)
Pro Way Hair School, GA (TCT)
Pruonto's Hair Design Institute, PA (TCT)
Pryor Beauty College, OK (TCT)
The Psychological Studies Institute, GA (GRD)
Public Health Foundation Enterprises, CA (TCT)
Pueblo Community College, CO (JRC)
Puerto Rico Technical Jr College, PR (TCT)
Puget Sound Christian College, WA (TSR)
Pulaski Technical College, AR (TCT)
Punxy Beauty School of Cosmetology Arts, PA (TCT)
Purchase College SUNY, NY (UNC)
Purdue University, IN (UNC)
Purnell School, NJ (PRG)
Putney School, VT (PRC)
Pyramid Career Institute, IL (TCT)

Q

Quantum Helicopters, AZ (TCT)
Queen City College, TN (TCT)
Queen of Peace Hospital, SD (AHS)
Queen of the Holy Rosary College, CA (JRC)
Queens University of Charlotte, NC (UNC)
Quincy College, MA (JRC)
Quincy University, IL (UNC)
Quinebaug Valley Community College, CT (JRC)
Quinnipiac University, CT (UNC)
Quinsigamond Community College, MA (JRC)

R

Rabbi Isaac Elchanan Theological Sem., NY (GRD)
Rabbi Jacob Joseph School, NJ (UNC)
Rabbinical Academy Mesivta Rabbi Chaim, NY (MNC)
Rabbinical College Beth Shraga, NY (MNC)
Rabbinical Coll. Bobovr Yeshiva Bnei Zn., NY (MNC)
Rabbinical Coll. Ch' San Sofer of NY, NY (MNC)
Rabbinical College of America, NJ (MNC)
Rabbinical College of Long Island, NY (MNC)
Rabbinical College of Ohr Shimon Yisroel, NY (MNC)
Rabbinical College of Telshe, OH (MNC)
Rabbinical Seminary Adas Yereim, NY (MNC)
Rabbinical Seminary M'Kor Chaim, NY (MNC)
Rabbinical Seminary of America, NY (MNC)
Rabun Gap-Nacoochee School, GA (PRC)
Radford M. Locklin Technical Center, FL (TCT)
Radford University, VA (UNC)
Radiation Therapy Services, FL (TCT)
Rainier School, WA (HND)
RainStar University, AZ (TCT)
Rainy River Community College, MN (JRC)
Ralph's Virginia School of Cosmetology, VA (TCT)
Ramapo College of New Jersey, NJ (UNC)
Ramirez College of Business Technology, PR (TCT)
Randolph College, VA (UNC)
Randolph Community College, NC (JRC)
Randolph-Macon Academy, VA (PRC)
Randolph-Macon College, VA (UNC)
Randolph School, AL (PRC)
Ranger College, TX (JRC)
Ranken Technical College, MO (JRC)
Raphael's School of Beauty Culture, OH (TCT)
Rapid City Regional Hospital, SD (AHS)
Rapides Regional Medical Center, LA (AHS)
Rappahannock Community College, VA (JRC)
Raritan Bay Medical Center, NJ (NRS)
Raritan Valley Community College, NJ (JRC)
Raritan Valley Flying School, NJ (TCT)
Rasmussen College, MN (TCT)
Ravenscroft Beauty College, IN (TCT)
Razzle Dazzle College of Hair Design, ID (TCT)
R.D. Hairstyling College, ND (TCT)
Reading Area Community College, PA (JRC)
Reading Hospital & Medical Center, PA (AHS)
Reconstructionist Rabbinical College, PA (UNC)
Recording Workshop, OH (TCT)
The Rectory School, CT (PRB)
Redemption Christian Academy, NY (PRC)
Redlands Community College, OK (JRC)
Red Rocks Community College, CO (JRC)
Redwoods Community College, CA (JRC)
Reed College, OR (UNC)
Reedley College, CA (JRC)
Reformed Bible College, MI (UNC)
Reformed Episcopal Seminary, PA (GRD)
Reformed Presbyterian Theological Sem., PA (GRD)
Reformed Theological Seminary, FL (GRD)
Reformed Theological Seminary, MS (GRD)
Reformed Theological Seminary, NC (GRD)
Reformed Theological Seminary, VA (GRD)
Refrigeration School, AZ (TCT)
Regency Beauty Academy, MN (TCT)
Regent University, VA (GRD)
Regional West Medical Center, NE (AHS)
Regis College, MA (UNC)
Regis University, CO (UNC)
Reid Hospital & Health Care Services, IN (AHS)
Reid State Technical College, AL (JRC)
Reignbow Beauty Academy, NJ (TCT)
Reignbow Hair Fashion Institute, NJ (TCT)
Reinhardt College, GA (UNC)
Remington College, AL (TCT)
Remington College, AR (HMS)
Remington College, AR (TCT)
Remington College, AZ (UNC)
Remington College, CA (UNC)
Remington College, CO (TCT)
Remington College, FL (TCT)
Remington College, HI (TCT)
Remington College, LA (TCT)
Remington College, OH (TCT)
Remington College, TN (JRC)
Remington College, TN (TCT)
Remington College, TX (JRC)
Remington College, TX (TCT)
Rend Lake College, IL (JRC)
Reno Tahoe Job Training Academy, NV (TCT)
Rensselaer at Hartford, CT (GRD)
Rensselaer Polytechnic Institute, NY (UNC)
Renton Technical College, WA (JRC)
Reppert School of Auctioneering, IN (TCT)
Research College of Nursing, MO (UNC)
Research Medical Center, MO (AHS)
Restaurant School at Walnut Hill College, PA (UNC)
RETS Electronic School, MA (TCT)
RETS Technical Center, OH (TCT)
Reuben Allen College, TN (TCT)
Rhodec International, MA (HMS)
Rhode Island College, RI (UNC)
Rhode Island Hospital, RI (AHS)
Rhode Island School of Design, RI (UNC)
Rhodes College, TN (UNC)
Rice Memorial Hospital, MN (AHS)
Rice University, TX (UNC)
Richard Bland College, VA (JRC)
Richard J. Daley College, IL (JRC)
Richard Milburn High School, VA (HMS)
Richard's Beauty College, CA (TCT)
Richard Stockton College of New Jersey, NJ (UNC)
Richland College, TX (JRC)
Richland Community College, IL (JRC)
Richmond Community College, NC (JRC)
Richmond University London England, MA (UNC)
Rich Mountain Community College, AR (JRC)
Rider University, NJ (UNC)
Ridge Vocational-Technical Center, FL (TCT)
Ridgewater College-Hutchinson Campus, MN (JRC)
Ridgewater College-Willmar Campus, MN (JRC)
Ridley-Lowell Business & Technical Inst., CT (TCT)
Ridley-Lowell Business & Technical Inst., NY (TCT)
Ringling School of Art & Design, FL (UNC)
Rio Grande Bible Institute, TX (UNC)
Rio Hondo College, CA (JRC)
Rio Salado Community College, AZ (JRC)
Ripon College, WI (UNC)
Rising Spirit Inst. of Natural Health, GA (TCT)
Rita's Moorhead Beauty College, MN (TCT)
Riverland Community College, MN (AHS)
Riverland Community College, MN (TCT)
Riverland Technical College, MN (TCT)
River Parishes Community College, LA (JRC)
Riverside Academy, VA (HND)
Riverside Community College, CA (JRC)
Riverside Hairstyling Academy, FL (TCT)
Riverside Hospital, OH (AHS)
Riverside Military Academy, GA (PRB)
Riverside School of Health Careers, VA (TCT)
Rivertown School of Beauty, GA (TCT)
Rivier College, NH (UNC)
Rizzieri Aveda School, NJ (TCT)
Roane State Community College, TN (JRC)
Roanoke Bible College, NC (UNC)
Roanoke-Chowan Community College, NC (JRC)

Roanoke College, VA (UNC)
The Robert B. Adams/LabCorp CLS Program, AL (AHS)
Robert Louis Stevenson High School, CA (PRC)
Robert Morgan Educational Center, FL (TCT)
Robert Morris College, IL (UNC)
Robert Morris College, PA (UNC)
Robert Morris University, PA (UNC)
Roberto-Venn Guitar Making School, AZ (TCT)
Robert Packer Hospital, PA (AHS)
R. Paul Academy of Cosmetology Arts/Sci, MD (TCT)
Roberts Wesleyan College, NY (UNC)
Robeson Community College, NC (JRC)
Rob Roy Academy, MA (TCT)
Rob Roy Academy Fall River Campus, MA (TCT)
Rob Roy Academy Taunton Campus, MA (TCT)
Rochester Business Institute, NY (TCT)
Rochester College, MI (UNC)
Rochester Community & Technical College, MN (JRC)
Rochester Community & Technical College, MN (TCT)
Rochester General Hospital, NY (AHS)
Rochester Institute of Technology, NY (UNC)
Rochester Institute of Technology (NTID), NY (JRC)
Rochester School for the Deaf, NY (HND)
Rockefeller University, NY (GRD)
Rockford Business College, IL (TCT)
Rockford College, IL (UNC)
Rockford Memorial Hospital, IL (AHS)
Rockhurst University, MO (UNC)
Rockingham Community College, NC (JRC)
Rockingham Memorial Hospital, VA (TCT)
Rock Point School, VT (PRC)
Rock Valley College, IL (JRC)
Rocky Mountain College, MT (UNC)
Rocky Mountain College of Art & Design, CO (UNC)
Roffler Moler Hairstyling College, GA (TCT)
Roger's Academy of Hair Design, IN (TCT)
Rogers State University, OK (UNC)
Roger Williams University, RI (UNC)
Rogie's School of Beauty Culture, PR (TCT)
Rogue Community College, OR (JRC)
Rolf Institute of Structural Integration, CO (TCT)
Rollins College, FL (UNC)
Roman Academy of Beauty Culture, NJ (TCT)
Ronnie & Dorman's School of Hair Design, LA (TCT)
Roosevelt University, IL (UNC)
R. Franklin University of Medicine, IL (GRD)
Roseburg Beauty College, OR (TCT)
Rosedale Bible College, OH (UNC)
Rosedale Technical Institute, PA (TCT)
Rose-Hulman Institute of Technology, IN (UNC)
Rosel School of Cosmetology, IL (TCT)
Rosemead Beauty School, CA (TCT)
Rosemont College, PA (WMC)
Rose State College, OK (JRC)
Ross Medical Education Center, FL (TCT)
Ross Medical Education Center, MI (TCT)
Rowan-Cabarrus Community College, NC (JRC)
Rowan Technical College, KY (TCT)
Rowan University, NJ (UNC)
Roxborough Memorial Hospital, PA (TCT)
Roxbury Community College, MA (JRC)
Royale College of Beauty, CA (TCT)
Royer-Greaves School for Blind, PA (HND)
RSHT Training Center, VA (TCT)
Rudae's School of Beauty Culture, IN (TCT)
Rudy & Kelly Academy of Hair & Nails, VA (TCT)
Rumsey Hall School, CT (PRC)
Rush University, IL (UNC)
Russell Sage College, NY (WMC)
Russell Sage Graduate School, NY (GRD)
Rust College, MS (UNC)
Rutgers-The State University of N.J., NJ (UNC)
Rutland Regional Medical Center, VT (AHS)

S

Sacramento City College, CA (JRC)
Sacramento Medical Foundation Blood Bank, CA (AHS)
Sacred Heart Hospital, PA (AHS)
Sacred Heart Hospital, SD (AHS)
Sacred Heart Hospital, WI (AHS)
Sacred Heart Major Seminary, MI (MNC)
Sacred Heart Medical Center, WA (AHS)
Sacred Heart Preparatory School, CA (PRC)
Sacred Heart School of Theology, WI (GRD)
Sacred Heart University, CT (UNC)
Saddleback College, CA (JRC)
Saddlebrook Preparatory School, FL (PRC)
SAE Institute Nashville, TN (TCT)
Safford College of Beauty Culture, AZ (TCT)
Sage College, CA (TCT)
Sage College of Albany, NY (JRC)
Sage Technical Commerical Driving School, MT (TCT)
Sage Technical School, WY (TCT)
Sage Technical Services, ID (TCT)
Saginaw Chippewa Tribal College, MI (JRC)
Saginaw Valley State University, MI (UNC)
St. Albans School, DC (PRB)
St. Alexius Medical Center, ND (AHS)
St. Alphonsus Regional Medical Center, ID (AHS)
St. Ambrose University, IA (UNC)
St. Andrews Presbyterian College, NC (UNC)
St. Andrew's School, DE (PRC)
St. Andrew's School, FL (PRC)
St. Andrew's School, GA (PRC)
St. Andrew's School, RI (PRC)
St. Andrew's-Sewanee School, TN (PRC)
St. Anne's-Belfield School, VA (PRC)
St. Anselm College, NH (UNC)
St. Anthony College of Nursing, IL (TCT)
St. Anthony Medical Center, IL (AHS)
St. Augustine College, IL (JRC)
St. Augustine's College, NC (UNC)
St. Barnabas Medical Center, NJ (AHS)
St. Bernard's Sch of Theology & Ministry, NY (GRD)
St. Bonaventure University, NY (UNC)
St. Catharine College, KY (JRC)
St. Catherines Military Academy, CA (PRB)
St. Catherine's School, VA (PRG)
St. Charles Borromeo Seminary, PA (MNC)
St. Charles Community College, MO (JRC)
St. Charles Hospital, OH (AHS)
St. Clair County Community College, MI (JRC)
St. Cloud Hospital, MN (AHS)
St. Cloud Regency Beauty Academy, MN (TCT)
St. Cloud State University, MN (UNC)
St. Cloud Technical College, MN (JRC)
St. Coletta School, WI (HND)
St. Croix Lutheran High School, MN (PRC)
St. Dominic-Jackson Memorial Hospital, MS (AHS)
St. Edward's University, TX (UNC)
St. Elizabeth College of Nursing, NY (TCT)
St. Elizabeth Hospital, IL (TCT)
St. Elizabeth Hospital, OH (AHS)
St. Elizabeth Hospital, TX (AHS)
St. Elizabeth Hospital, WI (AHS)
St. Elizabeth Medical Center, KY (TCT)
St. Elizabeth School of Nursing, IN (TCT)
St. Francis Career College, CA (TCT)
St. Francis College, NY (UNC)
St. Francis High School, HI (PRG)
St. Francis Hospital, IL (TCT)
St. Francis Hospital, NJ (NRS)
St. Francis Hospital, OK (AHS)
St. Francis Hospital, WI (AHS)
St. Francis Hospital Center, IN (TCT)
St. Francis Medical Center, IL (TCT)
St. Francis Medical Center, LA (AHS)
St. Francis Medical Center, NJ (AHS)
St. Francis Medical Ctr. Coll./Nursing, IL (TCT)
St. Francis Seminary, WI (GRD)
St. Francis University, PA (UNC)
St. George's School, RI (PRC)
St. Gregory's Academy, PA (PRB)
St. Gregory's University, OK (UNC)
St. James Mercy Hospital, NY (AHS)
St. James School, MD (PRC)
St. John Fisher College, NY (UNC)
St. John of God Community Services, NJ (HND)
St. Johnsbury Academy, VT (PRC)
St. John's College, IL (UNC)
St. John's College, MD (UNC)
St. John's College, NM (UNC)
St. John's Hospital, IL (AHS)
St. John's Hospital, MI (AHS)
St. John's Mercy Medical Center, MO (AHS)
St. John's Military School, KS (PRB)
St. John's Northwestern Military Academy, WI (PRB)
St. John's Preparatory School, MA (PRB)
St. John's Preparatory School, MN (PRC)
St. John's Regional Health Center, MO (AHS)
St. John's Regional Medical Center, CA (TCT)
St. John's Regional Medical Center, MO (AHS)
St. John's River Community College, FL (JRC)
St. John's School of Nursing, MO (NRS)
St. John's University, MN (MNC)
St. John's University, NY (UNC)
St. John Vianney College Seminary, FL (MNC)
St. Joseph College, CT (WMC)
St. Joseph Hospital, CA (AHS)
St. Joseph Hospital & Health Center, IN (AHS)
St. Joseph Hospital/Marshfield Clinic, WI (AHS)
St. Joseph's College, IN (UNC)
St. Joseph's College, NY (UNC)
St. Joseph's College of Maine, ME (UNC)
St. Joseph's Hospital College of Nursing, NY (TCT)
St. Joseph Seminary College, LA (UNC)
St. Joseph's Hospital, GA (TCT)
St. Joseph's Hospital, KY (AHS)
St. Joseph's Hospital, PA (AHS)
St. Joseph's Hospital, RI (AHS)
St. Joseph's Institute for the Deaf, MO (HND)
St. Joseph's Seminary, NY (GRD)
St. Joseph's University, PA (UNC)
St. Lawrence Seminary High School, WI (PRB)
St. Lawrence University, NY (UNC)
St. Leo University, FL (UNC)
St. Louis Christian College, MO (UNC)
St. Louis College of Health Careers, MO (TCT)
St. Louis College of Pharmacy, MO (UNC)
St. Louis Community College, MO (JRC)
St. Louis Hair Academy, MO (TCT)
St. Louis University, MO (UNC)
St. Luke's College, IA (JRC)
St. Luke's College, MO (UNC)
St. Luke's Hospital, MA (AHS)
St. Luke's Hospital, PA (NRS)
St. Luke's Hospital/Mayo Clinic, FL (AHS)
St. Luke's Medical Center, OH (AHS)
St. Luke's Medical Center, WI (AHS)
St. Luke's Midland Regional Medical Ctr., SD (AHS)
St. Margaret Hospital, IN (AHS)
St. Margaret School of Nursing, PA (TCT)
St. Margaret's School, VA (PRG)
St. Mark's School, MA (PRC)
St. Martin's University, WA (UNC)
St. Mary of Providence School, IL (HND)
St. Mary-of-the-Woods College, IN (WMC)
St. Mary's Campus Coll. of St. Catherine, MN (JRC)
St. Mary's College, CA (UNC)
St. Mary's College, IN (WMC)
St. Mary's College of Maryland, MD (UNC)
St. Mary Seminary/Graduate Sch. Theology, OH (TSR)
St. Mary's Hall, TX (PRC)
St. Mary's Hospital, CT (AHS)
St. Mary's Hospital, OK (AHS)
St. Mary's Hospital, VA (AHS)
St. Mary's Hospital/Mayo Medical Center, MN (AHS)
St. Mary's Medical Center, MI (AHS)
St. Mary's Medical Center, WV (TCT)
St. Mary's Preparatory High School, MI (PRB)
St. Mary's School, NC (PRG)
St. Mary's School for the Deaf, NY (HND)
St. Mary's Seminary & University, MD (GRD)
St. Mary's University of Minnesota, MN (GRD)
St. Mary's University of Minnesota, MN (UNC)
St. Mary's University of San Antonio, TX (UNC)
St. Meinrad School of Theology, IN (GRD)
St. Michael's College, VT (UNC)
St. Michael's Preparatory School, CA (PRB)
St. Norbert College, WI (UNC)
St. Olaf College, MN (UNC)
St. Patrick Hospital, MT (AHS)
St. Patrick's Hospital, LA (AHS)
St. Patrick's Seminary & University, CA (GRD)
St. Paul College, MN (JRC)
St. Paul Lutheran High School, MO (PRC)
St. Paul School of Theology, MO (GRD)
St. Paul's College, VA (UNC)
St. Paul's School, NH (PRC)
St. Petersburg College, FL (JRC)
St. Petersburg Theological Seminary, FL (GRD)
St. Peter's College, NJ (UNC)
St. Phillip's College, TX (JRC)
St. Rita School for the Deaf, OH (HND)
SS. Cyril and Methodius Seminary, MI (GRD)
St. Stanislaus College Prep, MS (PRB)
St. Stephen's Episcopal School, TX (PRC)
St. Thomas Academy, MN (PRB)
St. Thomas Aquinas College, NY (UNC)
St. Thomas Choir School, NY (PRB)
St. Thomas Hospital, TN (AHS)
St. Thomas More School, CT (PRB)
St. Thomas University, FL (UNC)
St. Tikhon's Orthodox Theological Sem., PA (GRD)
St. Timothy's School, MD (PRG)
St. Vincent Catholic Medical Center, NY (TCT)
St. Vincent College, PA (UNC)
St. Vincent DePaul Regional Seminary, FL (MNC)
St. Vincent Hospital, WI (AHS)
St. Vincent Hospital & Medical Center, OR (AHS)
St. Vincent Infirmary Medical Center, AR (AHS)
St. Vincent's College, CT (JRC)
St. Vincent Seminary, PA (UNC)
St. Vincent's Hospital & Health Center, MT (AHS)
St. Vincent's Hospital & Medical Center, NY (AHS)
St. Vincent's Medical Center, NY (AHS)
St. Vladimir's Orthodox Theological Sem., NY (GRD)
St. Xavier University, IL (UNC)
Salem Academy, NC (PRG)
Salem College, NC (WMC)
Salem College of Hairstyling, MO (TCT)
Salem Community College, NJ (JRC)
Salem International University, WV (UNC)
Salem State College, MA (UNC)
Salina Area Vocational Technical School, KS (TCT)
Salisbury School, CT (PRB)
Salisbury University, MD (UNC)
Salish Kootenai College, MT (JRC)
Salter School, MA (TCT)
Salt Lake Community College, UT (JRC)
Salve Regina University, RI (UNC)
Samaritan Hospital School of Nursing, NY (TCT)
Samaritan Medical Center, NY (AHS)
Samford University, AL (UNC)
Sam Houston State University, TX (UNC)
Sampson Community College, NC (JRC)
Samra University of Oriental Medicine, CA (GRD)
Samuel Merritt College, CA (UNC)
San Antonio Beauty College #3, TX (TCT)
San Antonio Beauty College #4, TX (TCT)
San Antonio College, TX (JRC)
San Antonio College Medical Dental Asst., TX (TCT)
San Bernardino Valley College, CA (JRC)
Sandersville Technical College, GA (TCT)
Sandhills Community College, NC (JRC)
San Diego Christian College, CA (UNC)
San Diego City College, CA (JRC)
San Diego Mesa College, CA (JRC)
San Diego Miramar College, CA (JRC)
San Diego State University, CA (UNC)
San Domenico School, CA (PRG)
Sand Springs Beauty College, OK (TCT)
Sandy Spring Friends School, MD (PRC)
San Fernando Beauty Academy, CA (TCT)
Sanford-Brown College, IL (TCT)
Sanford-Brown College, MO (TCT)
Sanford-Brown College, OH (TCT)
Sanford-Brown Institute, FL (TCT)
Sanford Brown Institute, FL (TCT)
Sanford-Brown Institute, NY (TCT)
Sanford-Brown Institute Houston, TX (JRC)
San Francisco Art Institute, CA (UNC)
San Francisco Conservatory of Music, CA (UNC)
San Francisco State University, CA (UNC)
San Francisco Theological Seminary, CA (GRD)
San Jacinto College, TX (JRC)
San Joaquin College of Law, CA (GRD)
San Joaquin Delta College, CA (JRC)
San Joaquin General Hospital, CA (TCT)
San Joaquin Valley College, CA (JRC)
San Jose City College, CA (JRC)
San Jose State University, CA (UNC)
San Juan Basin Technical College, CO (TCT)
San Juan Bautista School of Medicine, PR (UNC)
San Juan College, NM (JRC)
San Marcos Baptist Academy, TX (PRC)
Santa Ana College, CA (JRC)
Santa Barbara Business College, CA (JRC)
Santa Barbara Business College, CA (TCT)
Santa Barbara City College, CA (JRC)
Santa Barbara Coll. of Oriental Medicine, CA (GRD)
Santa Barbara Cottage & Gen. Hosp., CA (TCT)
Santa Catalina School, CA (PRG)
Santa Clara University, CA (UNC)
Santa Fe Community College, FL (JRC)
Santa Fe Community College, NM (JRC)
Santa Monica College, CA (JRC)
Santa Rosa Junior College, CA (JRC)
Santiago Canyon College, CA (JRC)
Sarah Lawrence College, NY (UNC)
Sarasota County Technical Institute, FL (TCT)
Sarasota Memorial Hospital, FL (AHS)
Sarasota School of Massage Therapy, FL (TCT)

Sauk Valley Community College, IL (JRC)
Savannah College of Art & Design, GA (UNC)
Savannah College of Art and Design, GA (UNC)
Savannah River College, GA (TCT)
Savannah State University, GA (UNC)
Savannah Technical College, GA (TCT)
Sawyer College, IN (TCT)
Sawyer School, CT (TCT)
Sawyer School, RI (TCT)
Saybrook Graduate School, CA (GRD)
Scattergood Friends School, IA (PRC)
Scenic Mountain Medical Center, TX (AHS)
Schenck Civilian Conservation Center, NC (TCT)
Schiller International University, FL (UNC)
Schilling-Douglas School of Hair Design, DE (TCT)
Schoolcraft College, MI (JRC)
School for International Training, VT (GRD)
School for the Deaf, NY (HND)
School of Advertising Art, OH (TCT)
School of Art & Design @ Montgomery Coll, MD (JRC)
School of Automotive Machinists, TX (TCT)
School of Communication Arts, NC (TCT)
School of Creative Hair Design, MI (TCT)
School of Hair Design, KY (TCT)
School of Hair Design, OK (TCT)
The School of Hairstyling, ID (TCT)
The School of Health Careers, FL (TCT)
School of Health Management, MO (GRD)
School of the Art Institute of Chicago, IL (GRD)
School of the Museum of Fine Arts, MA (UNC)
School of Urban Missions, LA (JRC)
School of Visual Arts, NY (UNC)
Schreiner University, TX (UNC)
Schuylkill Institute of Business & Tech., PA (TCT)
Scientific College of Beauty/Barbering, WI (TCT)
Scot Lewis Beauty School, MN (TCT)
Scot Lewis School, MN (TCT)
Scot Lewis School of Cosmetology, MN (TCT)
Scott & White Memorial Hospital & Clinic, TX (TCT)
Scott Cole Academy, AZ (TCT)
Scott College of Cosmetology, WV (TCT)
Scott Community College, IA (JRC)
Scottsdale Community College, AZ (JRC)
Scottsdale Culinary Institute, AZ (TCT)
Scranton State School for the Deaf, PA (HND)
Scripps College, CA (WMC)
Scripps Memorial Hospital, CA (TCT)
Scripps Research Institute, CA (GRD)
Seabury Hall, HI (PRC)
Seabury-Western Theological Seminary, IL (TSR)
Searcy Beauty College, AR (TCT)
Seattle Central Community College, WA (JRC)
Seattle Institute of Oriental Medicine, WA (GRD)
Seattle Pacific University, WA (UNC)
Seattle University, WA (UNC)
Seattle University School of Law, WA (GRD)
Sebring Career School, TX (TCT)
Seguin Beauty College, TX (TCT)
Selma University, AL (UNC)
Seminary Ext. Independent Study Inst., TN (HMS)
Seminary of the Immaculate Conception, NY (GRD)
Seminole Community College, FL (JRC)
Seminole State College, OK (JRC)
Sentara School of Health Professions, VA (TCT)
Sequoia Institute, CA (TCT)
Serbia's Technical College, PR (TCT)
SER Business and Technical Institute, IL (TCT)
SER Business and Technical Institute, MI (TCT)
Sessions.edu Online School of Design, NY (HMS)
Seton Hall University, NJ (UNC)
Seton Hall University School of Law, NJ (GRD)
Seton Hill University, PA (UNC)
Settlement Music School, PA (MUS)
Seward County Community College, KS (JRC)
Sewickley Valley Hospital, PA (AHS)
Shady Side Academy, PA (PRC)
Shadyside Hospital, PA (AHS)
Shands Jacksonville Medical Center, FL (TCT)
Shannon West Texas Memorial Hospital, TX (AHS)
Sharon Regional Health System, PA (AHS)
Sharps Academy of Hairstyling, MI (TCT)
Shasta Bible College & Graduate School, CA (UNC)
Shasta College, CA (JRC)
Shattuck-St. Mary's School, MN (PRC)
Shawnee Beauty College, OK (TCT)
Shawnee Community College, IL (JRC)
Shawnee State University, OH (UNC)
Shaw University, NC (UNC)
Shear Ego Intl School of Hair Design, NY (TCT)
Sheldon Jackson College, AK (UNC)
Shelton State Community College, AL (JRC)
Shenandoah University, VA (UNC)
Shenandoah Valley Academy, VA (PRC)
Shepherd University, WV (UNC)
Sheridan College, WY (JRC)
Sheridan Technical Center, FL (TCT)
Sherman College of Straight Chiropractic, SC (GRD)
Shimer College, IL (UNC)
Shippensburg University, PA (UNC)
Shore Beauty School, NJ (TCT)
Shoreline Community College, WA (JRC)
Shore Memorial Hospital, NJ (AHS)
Shorter College, GA (UNC)
Shor Yoshuv Institute, NY (MNC)
Shreveport Job Corps Center, LA (TCT)
Sidney's Hairdressing College, KS (TCT)
Siena College, NY (UNC)
Siena Heights University, MI (UNC)
Sierra Academy of Aeronautics, CA (TCT)
Sierra College, CA (JRC)
Sierra College of Beauty, CA (TCT)
Sierra Nevada College-Lake Tahoe, NV (UNC)
Sierra Valley Business College, CA (TCT)
Silver Lake College, WI (UNC)
Simi Valley Adult Education, CA (TCT)
Simmons College, MA (WMC)
Simmons Institute of Funeral Service, NY (TCT)
Simon's Rock College of Bard, MA (UNC)

Simpson College, IA (UNC)
Simpson University, CA (UNC)
Sinclair Community College, OH (JRC)
Sinte Gleska University, SD (UNC)
Sioux Valley Hospital, SD (AHS)
Sisseton Wahpeton Community College, SD (JRC)
Sisters of Charity Medical Center, NY (AHS)
Si Tanka University, SD (TCT)
Sitting Bull College, ND (JRC)
Skagit Valley College, WA (JRC)
Skidmore College, NY (UNC)
SkillSource Office & Technology Center, WA (TCT)
Skin Works School of Advanced Skin Care, UT (TCT)
Skyline College, CA (JRC)
Slippery Rock University, PA (UNC)
Smith College, MA (WMC)
Snead State Community College, AL (JRC)
Snow College, UT (JRC)
Sodexho Marriott Healthcare Mid-Atlantic, MD (AHS)
Sodexho Marriott Services, MA (AHS)
Sojourner-Douglass College, MD (UNC)
Soka University of America, CA (UNC)
Solano Community College, CA (JRC)
Solebury School, PA (PRC)
Somerset Christian College, NJ (UNC)
Somerset Community College, KY (JRC)
Somerset Community Hospital, PA (AHS)
Sonoma College, CA (TCT)
Sonoma College - San Francisco, CA (TCT)
Sonoma State University, CA (UNC)
Sonoran Desert Institute, AZ (HMS)
Sotheby's Institute of Art, NY (TCT)
South Arkansas Community College, AR (JRC)
South Baylo University, CA (GRD)
South Carolina Criminal Justice Academy, SC (TCT)
South Carolina School for Deaf and Blind, SC (HND)
South Carolina State University, SC (UNC)
South Central College, MN (JRC)
South Coast College, CA (TCT)
South College, NC (JRC)
South College, TN (UNC)
South Dakota School for the Deaf, SD (HND)
South Dakota School Visually Handicapped, SD (HND)
South Dakota School Mines and Technology, SD (UNC)
South Dakota State University, SD (UNC)
Southeast Alabama Medical Center, AL (TCT)
Southeast Applied Technology College, UT (TCT)
Southeast Arkansas College, AR (TCT)
Southeast Community College, NE (JRC)
Southeastern Baptist College, MS (UNC)
Southeastern Baptist Theological Sem., NC (GRD)
Southeastern Beauty School, GA (TCT)
Southeastern Bible College, AL (TSR)
Southeastern Business College, OH (TCT)
Southeastern Career College, TN (TCT)
Southeastern Career Institute, TX (TCT)
Southeastern Community College, IA (JRC)
Southeastern Community College, NC (JRC)
Southeastern Illinois College, IL (JRC)
Southeastern Louisiana University, LA (UNC)
Southeastern Oklahoma State University, OK (UNC)
Southeastern School of Cosmetology, AL (TCT)
Southeastern School of Neuromuscular, FL (TCT)
Southeastern School of Neuromuscular, NC (TCT)
Southeastern School of Neuromuscular, SC (TCT)
Southeastern Technical College, GA (TCT)
Southeastern Technical Institute, MA (TCT)
Southeastern University, DC (BUS)
Southeastern University, FL (UNC)
Southeast Kentucky Community/Tech Coll, KY (JRC)
Southeast MO Hospital College of Nursing, MO (TCT)
Southeast Missouri State University, MO (UNC)
Southeast School of Cosmetology, KY (TCT)
Southeast Technical Institute, SD (TCT)
Southern Adventist University, TN (UNC)
Southern Arkansas University, AR (UNC)
Southern Arkansas University Tech, AR (JRC)
Southern Baptist Theological Seminary, KY (GRD)
Southern California College of Optometry, CA (GRD)
Southern California Inst. Architecture, CA (UNC)
Southern California Institute of Tech, CA (TCT)
Southern CA Regional Occupational Center, CA (TCT)
Southern California Seminary, CA (UNC)
Southern CA University of Health Science, CA (GRD)
Southern Careers Institute, TX (TCT)
Southern Christian University, AL (UNC)
Southern College of Optometry, TN (GRD)
Southern Community College, AL (JRC)
Southern Connecticut State University, CT (UNC)
Southern Evangelical Seminary, NC (GRD)
Southern Illinois University, IL (UNC)
Southern Illinois Univ. Edwardsville, IL (UNC)
Southern Institute of Cosmetology, AR (TCT)
Southern Institute of Cosmetology, TN (TCT)
Southern Maine Community College, ME (JRC)
Southern Methodist College, SC (UNC)
Southern Methodist University, TX (UNC)
Southern Nazarene University, OK (UNC)
Southern Nevada Univ of Cosmetology, NV (TCT)
Southern New England School of Law, MA (GRD)
Southern New Hampshire University, NH (UNC)
Southern Oregon University, OR (UNC)
Southern Polytech State University, GA (UNC)
Southern Regional Medical Center, GA (AHS)
Southern School of Beauty, OK (TCT)
Southern State Community College, OH (JRC)
Southern Union State Community College, AL (AHS)
Southern Union State Community College, AL (JRC)
Southern University A&M College, LA (UNC)
Southern University at Shreveport, LA (JRC)
Southern University in New Orleans, LA (UNC)
Southern Utah University, UT (UNC)
Southern Vermont College, VT (UNC)
Southern Virginia University, VA (UNC)
Southern Wesleyan University, SC (UNC)
Southern WV Community & Technical Coll., WV (JRC)
South Florida Community College, FL (JRC)
South Florida Institute of Technology, FL (TCT)

South Georgia College, GA (JRC)
South Georgia Technical College, GA (TCT)
South Hills Beauty Academy, PA (TCT)
South Hills School of Business & Tech., PA (TCT)
South Kent School, CT (PRB)
South Louisiana Beauty College, LA (TCT)
South Louisiana Community College, LA (JRC)
South Mountain Community College, AZ (JRC)
South Piedmont Community College, NC (JRC)
South Plains College, TX (JRC)
South Puget Sound Community College, WA (JRC)
South Seattle Community College, WA (JRC)
Southside Regional Medical Center, VA (AHS)
Southside Virginia Community College, VA (JRC)
South Suburban College of Cook County, IL (JRC)
South Texas Barber College, TX (TCT)
South Texas College, TX (JRC)
South Texas College of Law, TX (GRD)
South Texas Vocational-Technical Inst., TX (TCT)
South University, AL (JRC)
South University, FL (UNC)
South University, GA (UNC)
South University, SC (UNC)
Southwest Acupuncture College, NM (GRD)
Southwest Applied Technology College, UT (TCT)
Southwest Baptist University, MO (UNC)
Southwest Coll of Naturopathic Medicine, AZ (GRD)
Southwestern Academy, CA (PRC)
Southwestern Adventist University, TX (UNC)
Southwestern Assemblies of God Univ., TX (UNC)
Southwestern Baptist Theological Sem., TX (UNC)
Southwestern Christian College, TX (UNC)
Southwestern Christian University, OK (UNC)
Southwestern College, AZ (UNC)
Southwestern College, CA (JRC)
Southwestern College, KS (UNC)
Southwestern College, NM (UNC)
Southwestern College, OH (JRC)
Southwestern College of Business, KY (TCT)
Southwestern College of Business, OH (JRC)
Southwestern College of Business, OH (TCT)
Southwestern Community College, IA (JRC)
Southwestern Community College, NC (JRC)
Southwestern Illinois College, IL (JRC)
Southwestern Indian Polytechnic Inst., NM (JRC)
Southwestern Michigan College, MI (JRC)
Southwestern Oklahoma State University, OK (JRC)
Southwestern Oklahoma State University, OK (UNC)
Southwestern Oregon Community College, OR (JRC)
Southwestern University, TX (UNC)
Southwestern University School of Law, CA (GRD)
Southwest Florida College, FL (JRC)
Southwest General Hospital, OH (AHS)
Southwest Georgia Technical College, GA (TCT)
Southwest Institute of Healing Arts, AZ (TCT)
Southwest Institute of Technology, TX (TCT)
Southwest Kansas Technical School, KS (TCT)
Southwest Minnesota State University, MN (UNC)
Southwest Mississippi Community College, MS (JRC)
SW Mississippi Regional Medical Center, MS (AHS)
SW School of Business & Tech Careers, TX (TCT)
Southwest Tennessee Community College, TN (JRC)
Southwest Texas Junior College, TX (JRC)
Southwest University, LA (HMS)
Southwest Virginia Community College, VA (JRC)
Southwest Wisconsin Technical College, WI (JRC)
Sowela Technical Community College, LA (TCT)
Space Coast Health Institute, FL (TCT)
Spalding University, KY (UNC)
Spanish-American Institute, NY (TCT)
Spanish Coalition for Jobs, IL (TCT)
Sparks College, IL (TCT)
Spartanburg Community College, SC (JRC)
Spartanburg Methodist College, SC (JRC)
Spartan Coll of Aeronautics & Technology, OK (UNC)
Spa School, OH (TCT)
Specs Howard School of Broadcast Arts, MI (TCT)
Spectrum Health, MI (AHS)
Spelman College, GA (WMC)
Spencer Business & Technical Institute, NY (TCT)
Spencerian College, KY (TCT)
Spertus College, IL (GRD)
Spokane Community College, WA (JRC)
Spokane Falls Community College, WA (JRC)
Spoon River College, IL (JRC)
Spring Arbor University, MI (UNC)
Springfield Beauty Academy, VA (TCT)
Springfield College, MA (UNC)
Springfield College in Illinois, IL (JRC)
Springfield College of Beauty, OR (TCT)
Springfield Technical Community College, MA (JRC)
Spring Hill College, AL (UNC)
Squaw Valley Academy, CA (PRC)
Sr. Rosalind Gefre School of Massage, MN (TCT)
Sr. Rosalind Gefre School of Massage, ND (TCT)
Stacey's Hands of Champions Beauty Coll, UT (TCT)
Stage One The Hair Academy, MO (TCT)
Stage One - The Hair School, LA (TCT)
Stamford Hospital, CT (TCT)
Stanford University, CA (UNC)
Stanly Community College, NC (JRC)
Star Academy for Pet Stylists, FL (TCT)
Star Career College, PR (TCT)
Star College of Cosmetology, TX (TCT)
Stark State College of Technology, OH (TCT)
Starr King School for the Ministry, CA (GRD)
Star Technical Institute, DE (TCT)
Star Technical Institute, NJ (TCT)
Star Technical Institute, PA (TCT)
State Barber and Hair Design College, OK (TCT)
State Beauty Academy, TX (TCT)
State College of Beauty Culture, WI (TCT)
State Fair Community College, MO (JRC)
State Technical Institute, TN (JRC)
Staunton School of Cosmetology, VA (TCT)
Stautzenberger College, OH (TCT)
StenoTech Career Institute, NJ (TCT)
Stenotype Inst. Court Reporting School, FL (TCT)

Stephen F. Austin State University, TX (UNC)
Stephens College, MO (WMC)
Stephenville Beauty College, TX (TCT)
Sterling College, KS (UNC)
Sterling College, VT (JRC)
Sterling Health Center, TX (TCT)
Stetson University, FL (GRD)
Stetson University, FL (UNC)
Steven Papageorge Hair Academy, IL (TCT)
Stevens Henager College, UT (JRC)
Stevens Henager College, UT (UNC)
Stevens Institute of Technology, NJ (UNC)
Stillman College, AL (UNC)
Stillwater Beauty Academy, OK (TCT)
Stone Academy, CT (TCT)
Stone Child College, MT (JRC)
Stonehill College, MA (UNC)
Stoneleigh-Burnham School, MA (PRG)
Stony Brook School, NY (PRC)
The Storm King School, NY (PRC)
Strand College of Hair Design, SC (TCT)
Stratford University, VA (UNC)
Stratton Mountain School, VT (PRC)
Strayer University, AL (UNC)
Strayer University, DC (UNC)
Strayer University, FL (UNC)
Strayer University, GA (UNC)
Strayer University, GA (WMC)
Strayer University, KY (UNC)
Strayer University, MD (UNC)
Strayer University, NC (UNC)
Strayer University, PA (UNC)
Strayer University, SC (UNC)
Strayer University, TN (UNC)
Strayer University, VA (UNC)
Stroudsburg School of Cosmetology, PA (TCT)
Stuart Hall, VA (PRC)
Stuart School of Business Administration, NJ (TCT)
Studio Jewelers, NY (TCT)
Stylemasters Beauty Academy, TN (TCT)
Stylemasters College of Hair Design, WA (TCT)
Styles & Profiles Beauty College, TN (TCT)
Subiaco Academy, AR (PRB)
Suburban Technical School, NY (TCT)
Success Institute of Business, TX (TCT)
Suffield Academy, CT (PRC)
Suffolk Beauty Academy, VA (TCT)
Suffolk University, MA (UNC)
Sullivan University, KY (UNC)
Sul Ross State University, TX (UNC)
Summit Academy OIC, MN (TCT)
Sumter Beauty College, SC (TCT)
Sunbridge College, NY (GRD)
Suncoast Center for Natural Health, FL (TCT)
Sunshine Bible Academy, SD (PRC)
Sunstate Academy of Hair Design, FL (TCT)
SUNY Adirondack Community College, NY (JRC)
SUNY at Albany, NY (UNC)
SUNY at Binghamton, NY (UNC)
SUNY at Stony Brook, NY (UNC)
SUNY Canton - College of Technology, NY (JRC)
SUNY Cayuga County Community College, NY (JRC)
SUNY College at Brockport, NY (UNC)
SUNY College at Buffalo, NY (UNC)
SUNY College at Cortland, NY (UNC)
SUNY College at Fredonia, NY (UNC)
SUNY College at Geneseo, NY (UNC)
SUNY College at New Paltz, NY (UNC)
SUNY College at Old Westbury, NY (UNC)
SUNY College at Oneonta, NY (UNC)
SUNY College at Oswego, NY (UNC)
SUNY College at Plattsburgh, NY (UNC)
SUNY College at Potsdam, NY (UNC)
SUNY College of Agriculture & Technology, NY (UNC)
SUNY College Environ. Science - Forestry, NY (UNC)
SUNY College of Optometry, NY (OPT)
SUNY College of Technology, NY (JRC)
SUNY Educational Opportunity Center, NY (AHS)
SUNY Empire State College, NY (UNC)
SUNY Health Science Center, NY (GRD)
SUNY Hudson Valley Community College, NY (JRC)
SUNY Institute of Technology Utica/Rome, NY (UNC)
SUNY Maritime College, NY (UNC)
SUNY Niagara County Community College, NY (JRC)
SUNY North Country Community College, NY (JRC)
SUNY Orange County Community College, NY (JRC)
SUNY Rockland Community College, NY (JRC)
SUNY Schenectady County Community Coll., NY (JRC)
SUNY Suffolk County Community College, NY (JRC)
SUNY Sullivan County Community College, NY (JRC)
SUNY Upstate Medical University, NY (UNC)
Superior School of Hairdressing, KS (TCT)
Surry Community College, NC (JRC)
Susquehanna University, PA (UNC)
Sussex County Community College, NJ (JRC)
SUTECH School of Voc/Tech Training, CA (TCT)
Suwannee-Hamilton Technical Center, FL (TCT)
Swainsboro Technical College, GA (TCT)
Swarthmore College, PA (UNC)
Swedish-American Hospital, IL (TCT)
Swedish Institute, NY (UNC)
Sweet Briar College, VA (WMC)
Sylvia's International School of Beauty, TX (TCT)
Syracuse University, NY (UNC)

T

Tabor Academy, MA (PRC)
Tabor College, KS (UNC)
Tacoma Community College, WA (JRC)
Taft College, CA (JRC)
The Taft School, CT (PRC)
Tai Sophia Insitute, MD (GRD)
Talent Academy, PA (TCT)
Talladega College, AL (UNC)
Tallahassee Community College, FL (JRC)
Tallahassee Memorial Hospital, FL (TCT)
Tallulah Falls School, GA (PRC)
Talmudical Academy of New Jersey, NJ (MNC)
Talmudical Institute of Upstate New York, NY (MNC)
Talmudical Seminary Oholei Torah, NY (MNC)
Talmudical Yeshiva of Philadelphia, PA (MNC)
Talmudic College of Florida, FL (MNC)
Tampa General Hospital, FL (TCT)
Tandem Friends School, VA (PRC)
TAP Center for Employment Training, VA (TCT)
Taratuta School of Truck Driving, MI (TCT)
Tarleton State University, TX (UNC)
Tarrant County Junior College, TX (JRC)
Taylor Business Institute, IL (TCT)
Taylor Technical Institute, FL (TCT)
Taylortown School of Beauty, MI (TCT)
Taylor University, IN (UNC)
TCI Institute The College of Technology, NY (JRC)
TDDS Technical Institute, OH (TCT)
Teachers College of Columbia University, NY (GRD)
Technical Career Institute, FL (TCT)
Technical College of the Lowcountry, SC (JRC)
Technical Education Center - Osceola, FL (TCT)
Technical Institute of Cosmetology Arts, OK (TCT)
Technology Education College, OH (TCT)
Teikyo Loretto Heights University, CO (UNC)
Telshe Yeshiva-Chicago, IL (MNC)
Temple Baptist College, OH (UNC)
Temple Baptist Seminary, TN (GRD)
Temple College, TX (JRC)
Temple University, PA (UNC)
Temple University Center City, PA (UNC)
Temple Univ School of Podiatric Medicine, PA (GRD)
Temple University Tyler School of Art, PA (UNC)
Tennessee Academy of Cosmetology, TN (TCT)
Tennessee School for the Blind, TN (HND)
Tennessee School for the Deaf, TN (HND)
Tennessee School of Beauty, TN (TCT)
Tennessee State University, TN (UNC)
Tennessee Technological University, TN (UNC)
Tennessee Technology Center at Athens, TN (TCT)
Tennessee Technology Center at Covington, TN (TCT)
Tennessee Technology Center Crossville, TN (TCT)
Tennessee Technology Center at Crump, TN (TCT)
Tennessee Technology Center at Dickson, TN (TCT)
Tennessee Technology Center Elizabethton, TN (TCT)
Tennessee Technology Center at Harriman, TN (TCT)
Tennessee Technology Center Hartsville, TN (TCT)
Tennessee Technology Center at Hohenwald, TN (TCT)
Tennessee Technology Center at Jacksboro, TN (TCT)
Tennessee Technology Center at Jackson, TN (TCT)
Tennessee Technology Center at Knoxville, TN (TCT)
Tennessee Technology Center Livingston, TN (TCT)
Tennessee Technology Center at Mc Kenzie, TN (TCT)
Tennessee Technology Center Mc Minnville, TN (TCT)
Tennessee Technology Center at Memphis, TN (TCT)
Tennessee Technology Center Morristown, TN (TCT)
Tennessee Technology Center Murfreesboro, TN (TCT)
Tennessee Technology Center at Nashville, TN (TCT)
Tennessee Technology Center at Newbern, TN (TCT)
Tennessee Technology Center Oneida/Hunts, TN (TCT)
Tennessee Technology Center at Paris, TN (TCT)
Tennessee Technology Center at Pulaski, TN (TCT)
Tennessee Technology Center at Ripley, TN (TCT)
Tennessee Technology Center Shelbyville, TN (TCT)
Tennessee Technology Center Whiteville, TN (TCT)
Tennessee Temple University, TN (UNC)
Tennessee Wesleyan College, TN (UNC)
Terra State Community College, OH (JRC)
TESST College of Technology, MD (TCT)
TESST Electronic School, VA (TCT)
TESST Technology Institute, MD (TCT)
Teterboro School of Aeronautics, NJ (TCT)
Texarkana College, TX (JRC)
Texas A&M at Galveston, TX (UNC)
Texas A&M International University, TX (UNC)
Texas A&M University, TX (UNC)
Texas A&M University - Commerce, TX (UNC)
Texas A&M University - Corpus Christi, TX (UNC)
Texas A&M Univ.-Baylor Coll. Dentistry, TX (GRD)
Texas A&M University - Texarkana, TX (UNC)
Texas Barber Colleges & Hairstyling Sch, TX (TCT)
Texas Careers, TX (TCT)
Texas Chiropractic College, TX (UNC)
Texas Christian University, TX (UNC)
Texas College, TX (UNC)
Texas College of Cosmetology, TX (TCT)
Texas College of Traditional Chinese Med, TX (GRD)
Texas Culinary Academy, TX (JRC)
Texas Heart Institute, TX (AHS)
Texas Lutheran University, TX (UNC)
Texas School of Business, TX (TCT)
Texas School of Business Southwest, TX (TCT)
Texas Southern University, TX (UNC)
Texas Southmost College, TX (JRC)
Texas State Technical College, TX (JRC)
Texas State University - San Marcos, TX (UNC)
Texas Tech University, TX (UNC)
Texas Tech University Health Science Ctr, TX (UNC)
Texas Vocational School, TX (TCT)
Texas Wesleyan University, TX (UNC)
Texas Woman's University, TX (AHS)
Texas Woman's University, TX (GRD)
Thacher School, CA (PRC)
Thaddeus Stevens College of Technology, PA (JRC)
Thanh Le College School of Cosmetology, CA (TCT)
Theda Clark Regional Medical Center, WI (AHS)
Thiel College, PA (UNC)
Thomas Aquinas College, CA (UNC)
Thomas College, ME (UNC)
Thomas Edison State College, NJ (UNC)
Thomas Jefferson School, MO (PRC)
Thomas Jefferson School of Law, CA (GRD)
Thomas Jefferson University, PA (UNC)
Thomas M. Cooley Law School, MI (LAW)
Thomas More College, KY (UNC)
Thomas More College of Liberal Arts, NH (UNC)
Thomas More Preparatory-Marian, KS (PRC)
Thomas Nelson Community College, VA (JRC)
Thomas University, GA (UNC)
Thompson Institute, PA (TCT)
Three Rivers Community College, MO (JRC)
Three Rivers Community Technical College, CT (JRC)
Thunderbird Adventist Academy, AZ (PRC)
Thunderbird The Garvin School, AZ (GRD)
Tidewater Community College, VA (JRC)
Tidewater Tech, VA (TCT)
Tiffin Academy of Hair Design, OH (TCT)
Tiffin University, OH (SCT)
Tilton School, NH (PRC)
Timken Mercy Medical Center, OH (AHS)
TMI - The Episcopal School of Texas, TX (PRC)
Toccoa Falls College, GA (UNC)
Tohono O'odham Community College, AZ (JRC)
Toledo Academy of Beauty Culture - East, OH (TCT)
Toledo Academy of Beauty Culture - North, OH (TCT)
Toledo Academy of Beauty Culture - South, OH (TCT)
Tom P. Haney Technical Center, FL (TCT)
Tompkins Cortland Community College, NY (JRC)
Toni & Guy Hairdressing Academy, CO (TCT)
Toni & Guy Hairdressing Academy, PA (TCT)
Toni & Guy Hairdressing Academy, TX (TCT)
Tooele Applied Technology College, UT (TCT)
Torah Temimah Talmudical Seminary, NY (MNC)
Total Look Sch of Cosmetology & Massage, IA (TCT)
Total Technical Institute, OH (TCT)
Tougaloo College, MS (UNC)
Touro College, NY (GRD)
Touro College, NY (UNC)
Touro Infirmary, LA (AHS)
Touro Univ. Coll. / Osteopathic Medicine, CA (GRD)
Touro Univ. Coll. / Osteopathic Medicine, NV (GRD)
Touro University International, CA (UNC)
Towson State University, MD (UNC)
Traditional Chinese Medical College HI, HI (GRD)
TransPacific Hawaii College, HI (JRC)
Transylvania University, KY (UNC)
Travel Institute of the Pacific, HI (TCT)
Travel University International, CA (TCT)
Traviss Technical Center, FL (TCT)
Traxler School of Hair, MS (TCT)
Treasure Valley Community College, OR (JRC)
Trend Barber College, TX (TCT)
Trend Setter's Academy of Beauty Culture, KY (TCT)
Trend Setters' Academy of Beauty Culture, KY (TCT)
Trend Setters College of Cosmetology, IL (TCT)
Trenholm State Technical College, AL (IFS)
Trenholm State Technical College, AL (JRC)
Trevecca Nazarene University, TN (UNC)
Triangle Tech, PA (TCT)
Tri-College University, ND (GRD)
Tri-County Beauty Academy, IL (TCT)
Tri County Beauty College, OH (TCT)
Tri-County Community College, NC (JRC)
Tri-County Health Nutrition Services, CO (AHS)
Tri-County Tech College, SC (JRC)
Trident Technical College, SC (JRC)
Trident Technical College, SC (TCT)
Trinidad State Junior College, CO (JRC)
Trinity Baptist College, FL (UNC)
Trinity Bible College, ND (UNC)
Trinity Christian College, IL (UNC)
Trinity College, CT (UNC)
Trinity College of Florida, FL (UNC)
Trinity College of Nursing, IL (UNC)
Trinity College of Puerto Rico, PR (TCT)
Trinity Episcopal School for Ministry, PA (GRD)
Trinity Evangelical Divinity School, IL (GRD)
Trinity International University, FL (GRD)
Trinity International University, IL (UNC)
Trinity Life Bible College, CA (UNC)
Trinity Lutheran College, WA (UNC)
Trinity Lutheran Seminary, OH (GRD)
Trinity Medical Center, ND (AHS)
Trinity Medical Center East, OH (NRS)
Trinity-Pawling School, NY (PRB)
Trinity University, DC (WMC)
Trinity University, TX (UNC)
Trinity Valley Community College, TX (JRC)
Tri-State Business Institute, PA (TCT)
Tri-State College of Acupuncture, NY (GRD)
Tri-State College of Massotherapy, OH (TCT)
Tri-State Cosmetology Institute, TX (TCT)
Tri-State University, IN (UNC)
Triton College, IL (JRC)
Trocaire College, NY (JRC)
Troy School of Beauty Culture, NY (TCT)
Troy University, AL (UNC)
Troy University Montgomery, AL (UNC)
Troy University - Phenix City, AL (UNC)
Truck Driving Academy, CA (TCT)
Truckee Meadows Community College, NV (JRC)
Truck Marketing Institute, CA (HMS)
Truett McConnell College, GA (JRC)
Truman Medical Center, MO (AHS)
Truman State University, MO (UNC)
Trumbull Business College, OH (TCT)
Tucson College, AZ (TCT)
Tufts University, MA (GRD)
Tufts University, MA (UNC)
Tulane University, LA (UNC)
Tulare Beauty College, CA (TCT)
Tulsa Community College, OK (JRC)
Tulsa Community College Metro Campus, OK (TCT)
Tulsa Community College Southeast Campus, OK (JRC)
Tulsa Community College West Campus, OK (TCT)
Tulsa County Area Voc Tech District 18, OK (TCT)
Tulsa Welding School, FL (TCT)
Tulsa Welding School, OK (TCT)
Tunxis Community College, CT (JRC)
Turner Job Corps Center, GA (TCT)
Turtle Mountain Community College, ND (JRC)
Tusculum College, TN (UNC)
Tuskegee University, AL (UNC)
Tuttle Vocational Technical Center, OK (TCT)
Twin City Beauty College, MI (TCT)
Tyler Junior College, TX (JRC)

U

Uintah Basin Applied Technology College, UT (TCT)
Ulster County Community College, NY (JRC)
Ultrasound Diagnostic School, GA (TCT)
Ultrasound Diagnostic School, MA (TCT)
Ultrasound Diagnostic School, MD (TCT)
Ultrasound Diagnostic School, NJ (TCT)
Ultrasound Diagnostic School, NY (TCT)
Ultrasound Diagnostic School, PA (TCT)
Ultrasound Diagnostic School, TX (TCT)
UMDNJ Grad. Sch. of Biomedical Sciences, NJ (GRD)
UMDNJ-New Jersey Dental School, NJ (GRD)
UMDNJ-New Jersey Medical School, NJ (GRD)
UMDNJ-Robert Wood Johnson Medical School, NJ (GRD)
UMDNJ-Sch. of Health Related Professions, NJ (UNC)
UMDNJ-School of Nursing, NJ (UNC)
UMDNJ School of Public Health, NJ (GRD)
UMDNJ-University of Medicine & Dentistry, NJ (UNC)
Umpqua Community College, OR (JRC)
Undergraduate School of Cosmetology, IL (TCT)
Unification Theological Seminary, NY (GRD)
Uni Health America/Glendale Mem Hospital, CA (AHS)
Union College, KY (UNC)
Union College, NE (UNC)
Union College, NY (UNC)
Union County College, NJ (JRC)
Union Institute & University, OH (UNC)
Union Institute & University, VT (GRD)
Union Memorial Hospital, MD (NRS)
Union Springs Academy, NY (PRC)
Union Theological Seminary, NY (GRD)
Union Theological Sem. & Presbyterian, VA (GRD)
Union University, TN (UNC)
Unitech Training Academy, LA (TCT)
United Beauty College, CA (TCT)
United Health Services Hospital, NY (AHS)
United Hospital Center, WV (AHS)
United Regional Health Care System, TX (TCT)
United States Air Force Academy, CO (UNC)
United States Coast Guard Academy, CT (UNC)
United States Merchant Marine Academy, NY (UNC)
United States Military Academy, NY (UNC)
United States Naval Academy, MD (UNC)
United States Sports Academy, AL (GRD)
United Talmudical Seminary, NY (MNC)
United Theological Seminary, OH (GRD)
United Theological Seminary/Twin Cities, MN (GRD)
United Tribes Technical College, ND (JRC)
United Truck & Car Driving School, CA (TCT)
Unity College, ME (UNC)
Universal Career Counseling, PR (TCT)
Universal Career Counseling Center, PR (TCT)
Universal College of Beauty, CA (TCT)
Universal College of Beauty, NC (TCT)
Universal Technical Institute, AZ (TCT)
Universal Technical Institute, CA (TCT)
Universal Technical Institute, FL (TCT)
Universal Technical Institute, IL (TCT)
Universal Technical Institute, MA (TCT)
Universal Technical Institute, PA (TCT)
Universal Technical Institute, TX (TCT)
Universal Technology College, PR (TCT)
Universal Therapeutic Massage Institute, NM (TCT)
Universal Training Center, CA (TCT)
Universidad Adventista de las Antillas, PR (UNC)
Universidad Central Del Caribe, PR (UNC)
Universidad del Este, PR (TCT)
Universidad Del Turabo, PR (UNC)
Universidad FLET, FL (HMS)
Universidad Metropolitana, PR (UNC)
Universidad Politecnica de Puerto Rico, PR (UNC)
University at Buffalo SUNY, NY (GRD)
University at Buffalo SUNY, NY (UNC)
University College of San Juan, PR (JRC)
University Health Center, PA (AHS)
University Hospital, TX (AHS)
University Hospital Health System, GA (AHS)
University Hospital of Cleveland, OH (AHS)
University Hospital of Oklahoma City, OK (AHS)
University Medical Center, LA (AHS)
University of Advancing Technology, AZ (UNC)
University of Akron, OH (UNC)
University of Akron-Wayne College, OH (JRC)
University of Alabama, AL (UNC)
University of Alabama at Birmingham, AL (UNC)
University of Alabama Hospital, AL (AHS)
University of Alabama in Huntsville, AL (UNC)
University of Alaska Anchorage, AK (UNC)
University of Alaska Bristol Bay Campus, AK (UNC)
University of Alaska Chuchi Campus, AK (UNC)
University of Alaska Fairbanks, AK (UNC)
University of Alaska Interior Campus, AK (UNC)
University of Alaska Kuskokwim Campus, AK (JRC)
University of Alaska Matanuska-Susitna, AK (JRC)
University of Alaska Northwest Campus, AK (JRC)
University of Alaska Sitka Campus, AK (JRC)
University of Alaska Southeast, AK (UNC)
University of Alaska Southeast-Ketchikan, AK (JRC)
University of Alaska Tanana Valley Cmps, AK (UNC)
University of Arizona, AZ (UNC)
University of Arizona Medical Center, AZ (MED)
University of Arkansas at Fayetteville, AR (UNC)
University of Arkansas at Fort Smith, AR (JRC)
University of Arkansas at Little Rock, AR (UNC)
University of Arkansas at Monticello, AR (UNC)
University of Arkansas at Pine Bluff, AR (UNC)
University of Arkansas Community College, AR (JRC)
University of Arkansas/Medical Sciences, AR (UNC)
University of Arkansas - Monticello, AR (TCT)
University of Baltimore, MD (UNC)
University of Bridgeport, CT (UNC)
University of California, CA (GRD)
University of California, CA (UNC)
University of California-Davis, CA (UNC)
University of CA Hastings College of Law, CA (GRD)
University of California-Irvine Med. Ctr, CA (UNC)
UCLA Center for the Health Sciences, CA (UNC)
University of California Medical Center, CA (UNC)
University of California-Santa Cruz, CA (UNC)
University of Central Arkansas, AR (UNC)
University of Central Florida, FL (UNC)
University of Central Oklahoma, OK (UNC)
University of Charleston, WV (UNC)
University of Chicago, IL (UNC)
Univ. of Chicago Hospital/Roosevelt U., IL (AHS)
University of Cincinnati, OH (JRC)
University of Cincinnati, OH (UNC)
Univ. of Cincinnati Coll. Allied Health, OH (JRC)
University of Cincinnati/OMI College, OH (UNC)
University of Cincinnati, OH (JRC)
University of Colorado, CO (UNC)
University of Colorado at Denver, CO (UNC)
University of Colorado Health Sciences, CO (UNC)
University of Connecticut, CT (UNC)
University of Connecticut Health Center, CT (UNC)
University of Cosmetology Arts & Science, TX (TCT)
University of Dallas, TX (UNC)
University of Dayton, OH (UNC)
University of Delaware, DE (UNC)
University of Denver, CO (UNC)
University of Denver University College, CO (UNC)
University of Detroit-Mercy, MI (UNC)
University of Dubuque, IA (UNC)
University of Dubuque Theological Sem., IA (GRD)
University of East West Medicine, CA (GRD)
University of Evansville, IN (UNC)
University of Findlay, OH (UNC)
University of Florida, FL (UNC)
University of Georgia, GA (UNC)
University of Great Falls, MT (UNC)
University of Guam, GU (UNC)
University of Hartford, CT (UNC)
University of Hawaii at Hilo, HI (UNC)
University of Hawaii at Manoa, HI (UNC)
University of Hawaii - West Oahu, HI (UNC)
University of Houston, TX (UNC)
University of Houston-Clear Lake, TX (UNC)
University of Houston-Downtown, TX (UNC)
University of Houston-Victoria, TX (UNC)
University of Idaho, ID (UNC)
University of Illinois, IL (GRD)
University of Illinois, IL (UNC)
University of Illinois at Chicago, IL (UNC)
University of Illinois at Springfield, IL (UNC)
University of Indianapolis, IN (UNC)
University of Iowa, IA (UNC)
University of Judaism, CA (UNC)
University of Kansas, KS (UNC)
University of Kansas Medical Center, KS (UNC)
University of Kentucky, KY (UNC)
Univ. of Kentucky Chandler Medical Ctr., KY (AHS)
University of La Verne, CA (UNC)
University of Louisiana at Lafayette, LA (UNC)
University of Louisiana at Monroe, LA (UNC)
University of Louisville, KY (UNC)
University of Maine, ME (UNC)
University of Maine at Presque Isle, ME (UNC)
University of Management and Technology, VA (UNC)
University of Mary, ND (UNC)
University of Mary Hardin-Baylor, TX (UNC)
University of Maryland, MD (UNC)
University of Maryland Eastern Shore, MD (UNC)
University of Mary Washington, VA (UNC)
University of Massachusetts, MA (UNC)
University of Massachusetts at Worcester, MA (UNC)
University of Massachusetts Boston, MA (UNC)
University of Massachusetts Dartmouth, MA (UNC)
University of Massachusetts Lowell, MA (UNC)
UMDNJ-School of Osteopathic Medicine, NJ (GRD)
University of Memphis, TN (UNC)
University of Miami, FL (UNC)
University of Michigan-Ann Arbor, MI (UNC)
University of Michigan-Dearborn, MI (UNC)
University of Michigan-Flint, MI (UNC)
University of Minnesota, MN (UNC)
University of Minnesota Rochester, MN (UNC)
University of Mississippi, MS (UNC)
University of Mississippi Medical Center, MS (UNC)
University of Missouri, MO (UNC)
University of Mobile, AL (UNC)
University of Montana, MT (UNC)
Univ of Montana Missoula College of Tech, MT (JRC)
University of Montana - Western, MT (UNC)
University of Montevallo, AL (UNC)
University of Nebraska, NE (UNC)
University of Nebraska at Kearney, NE (UNC)
University of Nebraska at Omaha, NE (UNC)
University of Nebraska Medical Center, NE (GRD)
University of Nevada, NV (UNC)
University of Nevada Las Vegas, NV (UNC)
University of New England, ME (UNC)
University of New Hampshire, NH (UNC)
University of New Haven, CT (UNC)
University of New Mexico, NM (JRC)
University of New Mexico, NM (UNC)
University of New Orleans, LA (UNC)
University of North Alabama, AL (UNC)
University of North Carolina, NC (UNC)
University of North Carolina at Pembroke, NC (UNC)
University of North Carolina Hospitals, NC (AHS)
University of North Dakota, ND (UNC)
University of Northern Colorado, CO (UNC)
University of Northern Iowa, IA (UNC)
University of Northern Virginia, VA (UNC)
University of North Florida, FL (UNC)
University of North Texas, TX (UNC)
University of N Texas Health Science Ctr, TX (GRD)
University of Northwestern Ohio, OH (UNC)
University of Notre Dame, IN (UNC)
University of Oklahoma at Norman, OK (UNC)
University of Oklahoma Health Sciences, OK (UNC)
University of Oregon, OR (UNC)
University of Pennsylvania, PA (UNC)
University of Phoenix, AZ (UNC)
University of Phoenix, CO (UNC)
University of Phoenix-NM Division, NM (UNC)
University of Pittsburgh, PA (UNC)
University of Pittsburgh at Bradford, PA (UNC)
University of Pittsburgh at Johnstown, PA (UNC)
University of Pittsburgh at Titusville, PA (UNC)
University of Portland, OR (UNC)
University of Puerto Rico, PR (UNC)
University of Puerto Rico - Aguadilla, PR (JRC)
University of Puerto Rico at Arecibo, PR (UNC)
University of Puerto Rico at Ponce, PR (UNC)
University of Puerto Rico at Utuado, PR (JRC)
Univ. of Puerto Rico/Bayamon Univ. Coll., PR (UNC)
University of Puget Sound, WA (UNC)
University of Redlands, CA (UNC)
University of Rhode Island, RI (UNC)
University of Richmond, VA (UNC)
University of Rio Grande, OH (UNC)
University of Rochester, NY (UNC)
University of Rochester Medical Center, NY (MED)
Univ. of St. Augustine for Health Sci., FL (HMS)
University of St. Francis, IL (UNC)
University of St. Francis, IN (UNC)
University of Saint Mary, KS (UNC)
University of St. Mary of the Lake, IL (GRD)
University of St. Thomas, MN (UNC)
University of St. Thomas, TX (UNC)
University of San Diego, CA (UNC)
University of San Francisco, CA (UNC)
University of Sciences & Arts of OK, OK (UNC)
University of Scranton, PA (UNC)
University of Sioux Falls, SD (UNC)
University of South Alabama, AL (UNC)
University of South Carolina, SC (JRC)
University of South Carolina, SC (UNC)
University of South Dakota, SD (UNC)
University of Southern California, CA (GRD)
University of Southern California, CA (UNC)
University of Southern Indiana, IN (UNC)
University of Southern Maine, ME (UNC)
University of Southern Mississippi, MS (UNC)
University of South Florida, FL (UNC)
University of Tampa, FL (UNC)
University of Tennessee, TN (UNC)
Univ. of Tennessee Health Science Center, TN (UNC)
University of Tennessee Medical Center, TN (TCT)
University of Texas, TX (UNC)
University of Texas at Austin, TX (UNC)
University of Texas at Brownsville, TX (UNC)
University of Texas at Dallas, TX (UNC)
University of Texas at El Paso, TX (UNC)
University of Texas at San Antonio, TX (UNC)
University of Texas at Tyler, TX (UNC)
University of TX Health Science Center, TX (UNC)
University of Texas Health Science Ctr., TX (UNC)
University of Texas-Houston, TX (UNC)
University of Texas Anderson Cancer Ctr., TX (TCT)
University of Texas Medical Branch, TX (GRD)
University of Texas of the Permian Basin, TX (UNC)
University of Texas-Pan American, TX (UNC)
University of Texas S.W. Medical Center, TX (UNC)
University of the Arts, PA (UNC)
University of the Cumberlands, KY (UNC)
University of the District of Columbia, DC (UNC)
University of the D.C. School of Law, DC (GRD)
University of the Incarnate Word, TX (UNC)
University of the Ozarks, AR (UNC)
University of the Pacific, CA (GRD)
University of the Pacific, CA (UNC)
University of the Sacred Heart, PR (UNC)
University of the Sciences Philadelphia, PA (UNC)
University of the South, TN (UNC)
University of the Virgin Islands, VI (UNC)
University of the West, CA (UNC)
University of Toledo, OH (GRD)
University of Toledo, OH (UNC)
University of Tulsa, OK (UNC)
University of Utah, UT (UNC)
University of Vermont, VT (UNC)
University of Virginia, VA (UNC)
University of Virginia College at Wise, VA (UNC)
University of Washington, WA (UNC)
University of West Alabama, AL (UNC)
University of West Florida, FL (UNC)
University of West Georgia, GA (UNC)
University of West Los Angeles, CA (GRD)
University of Wisconsin, WI (UNC)
University of Wisconsin Baraboo/Sauk Co., WI (UNC)
Univ. of Wisconsin Center-Barron County, WI (JRC)
University of Wisconsin Center, WI (JRC)
University of Wisconsin, WI (UNC)
University of Wisconsin - LaCrosse, WI (UNC)
University of Wisconsin Marathon County, WI (JRC)
University of Wisconsin-Marinette, WI (JRC)
Univ. of Wisconsin - Marshfield/Wood Co., WI (JRC)
University of Wisconsin, WI (UNC)
University of Wisconsin Waukesha, WI (JRC)
University of Wisconsin, WI (UNC)
University of Wyoming, WY (UNC)
U.P. Academy of Hair Design, MI (TCT)
UPMC School of Medical Imaging, PA (TCT)
Upper Columbia Academy, WA (PRC)
Upper Iowa University, IA (UNC)
Upper Valley Teacher Institute, NH (TCT)
Urbana University, OH (UNC)
Urban College of Boston, MA (JRC)
Ursinus College, PA (UNC)
Ursuline College, OH (UNC)
Utah Career College, UT (TCT)
Utah Schools for the Deaf and the Blind, UT (HND)
Utah State University, UT (UNC)
Utah Valley Regional Medical Center, UT (AHS)
Utah Valley State College, UT (JRC)
UTA Mesivta of Kiryas Joel, NY (MNC)
Utica College, NY (UNC)
Utica School of Commerce, NY (JRC)
Utica School of Commerce, NY (TCT)

Utica School of Commerce, NY (UNC)

V

Valdosta State University, GA (UNC)
Valdosta Technical College, GA (TCT)
Valencia Community College, FL (JRC)
Valencia Community College East Campus, FL (JRC)
Valley Beauty School, OH (TCT)
Valley Beauty School, WV (TCT)
Valley City State University, ND (UNC)
Valley College of Technology, WV (JRC)
Valley College of Technology, WV (TCT)
Valley Forge Christian College, PA (BUS)
Valley Forge Military Academy, PA (PRB)
Valley Forge Military College, PA (MNC)
Valley Hospital, NJ (AHS)
Valley View Regional Hospital, OK (AHS)
Valparaiso University, IN (UNC)
Vance-Granville Community College, NC (JRC)
Vanderbilt University, TN (UNC)
VanderCook College of Music, IL (UNC)
Vanguard Institute of Technology, TX (TCT)
Vanguard University of Southern CA, CA (UNC)
Vassar College, NY (UNC)
Vatterott College, IA (TCT)
Vatterott College, IL (TCT)
Vatterott College, KS (TCT)
Vatterott College, MO (TCT)
Vatterott College, NE (TCT)
Vatterott College, OH (TCT)
Vatterott College, OK (TCT)
Vatterott College, TN (TCT)
Vaughn College of Aeronautics and Tech, NY (UNC)
Vee's School of Beauty Culture, IL (TCT)
Velma B's Beauty Academy, TX (TCT)
Velvatex College of Beauty Culture, AR (TCT)
Vennard College, IA (UNC)
Ventura College, CA (JRC)
Venus Beauty Academy, PA (TCT)
Verde Valley School, AZ (PRC)
Vermillion Community College, MN (JRC)
Vermont Academy, VT (PRC)
Vermont College of Cosmetology, VT (TCT)
Vermont Law School, VT (GRD)
Vermont Technical College, VT (JRC)
Vernon College, TX (JRC)
Vernon's Kansas School of Cosmetology, KS (TCT)
Veterans Administration Hospital, WV (AHS)
Veterans Administration Medical Center, MA (AHS)
Veterans Administration Medical Center, OR (AHS)
Veterans Affairs Medical Center, CA (AHS)
Veterans Affairs Medical Center, NY (AHS)
Veterans Affairs Medical Center, TX (AHS)
Veterans Affairs Medical Center, UT (AHS)
Vet Tech Institute, PA (TCT)
Vici Beauty School, WI (TCT)
Victoria Beauty College, TX (TCT)
Victoria College, TX (JRC)
Victor Valley Beauty College, CA (TCT)
Victor Valley Community College, CA (JRC)
Vidalia Beauty School, LA (TCT)
Villa Julie College, MD (UNC)
Villa Maria College of Buffalo, NY (JRC)
Villanova Prep School, CA (PRC)
Villanova University, PA (UNC)
Vincennes Beauty College, IN (TCT)
Vincennes University, IN (JRC)
Virgil's Beauty College, OK (TCT)
Virginia Career Institute, VA (TCT)
Virginia College, AL (TCT)
Virginia College, AL (UNC)
Virginia College, MS (TCT)
Virginia College of Osteopathic Medicine, VA (GRD)
Virginia Commonwealth University, VA (UNC)
Virginia Episcopal School, VA (PRC)
Virginia Farrell Beauty School, MI (TCT)
Virginia Highlands Community College, VA (JRC)
Virginia Home for Boys, VA (HND)
Virginia Intermont College, VA (UNC)
Virginia Marti College of Art & Design, OH (TCT)
Virginia Military Institute, VA (MNC)
Virginia Polytechnic Inst. & State Univ., VA (UNC)
Virginia School Center, CA (TCT)
Virginia School for the Deaf and Blind, VA (HND)
Virginia School of Hair Design, VA (TCT)
Virginia School of Massage, VA (TCT)
Virginia School of Technology, VA (TCT)
Virginia State University, VA (UNC)
Virginia Union University, VA (UNC)
Virginia University of Lynchburg, VA (UNC)
Virginia Wesleyan College, VA (UNC)
Virginia Western Community College, VA (JRC)
Viterbo University, WI (UNC)
Volunteer Beauty Academy, TN (TCT)
Volunteer State Community College, TN (JRC)
Von Curtis Academy of Hair Design, UT (TCT)
Voorhees College, SC (UNC)
Vortex Helicopters, LA (TCT)

W

Wabash College, IN (MNC)
Wabash Valley College, IL (JRC)
Wade College Dallas Market Center, TX (JRC)
Wadley Regional Medical Center, TX (AHS)
Wagner College, NY (UNC)
Wake Forest University, NC (GRD)
Wake Forest University, NC (UNC)
Wake Technical Community College, NC (JRC)
Walden University, MN (GRD)
Waldorf College, IA (UNC)
Wallace Community College Sparks Campus, AL (JRC)
Wallace State Community College, AL (JRC)
Walla Walla College, WA (UNC)
Walla Walla Community College, WA (JRC)
Walla Walla University School of Nursing, OR (UNC)
Walnut Hill School, MA (PRC)
Walsh Coll. Accountancy & Bus. Admin., MI (UNC)
Walsh University, OH (UNC)
Walter Boswell Memorial Hospital, AZ (AHS)
Walter Reed Medical Center, DC (TCT)
Walters State Community College, TN (JRC)
Wards Corner Beauty Academy, VA (TCT)
Warner Pacific College, OR (UNC)
Warner Southern College, FL (UNC)
Warren County Community College, NJ (JRC)
Warren Wilson College, NC (UNC)
Wartburg College, IA (UNC)
Wartburg Theological Seminary, IA (GRD)
Warwick Academy of Beauty Culture, RI (TCT)
Wasatch Academy, UT (PRC)
Washburn University, KS (UNC)
Washington & Jefferson College, PA (UNC)
Washington & Lee University, VA (UNC)
Washington Adventist Hospital, MD (AHS)
Washington Bible College, MD (MUS)
Washington College, MD (UNC)
Washington Conservatory of Music, MD (TCT)
Washington County Adult Skill Center, VA (TCT)
Washington County Community College, ME (JRC)
Washington Holmes Technical Center, FL (TCT)
Washington Hospital, PA (NRS)
Washington Hospital Center, DC (TCT)
Washington State Community College, OH (JRC)
Washington State School for the Blind, WA (HND)
Washington State School for the Deaf, WA (HND)
Washington State University, WA (UNC)
Washington Theological Union, DC (GRD)
Washington University in St. Louis, MO (UNC)
Washtenaw Community College, MI (JRC)
Watkins Institute-College of Art/Design, TN (UNC)
Watkinson School, CT (PRC)
Waubonsee Community College, IL (JRC)
Waukesha County Technical College, WI (JRC)
Wausau Hospital Center, WI (AHS)
Waycross College, GA (JRC)
Wayland Academy, WI (PRC)
Wayland Baptist University, TX (UNC)
Wayne Community College, NC (JRC)
Wayne County Community College, MI (JRC)
Waynesburg College, PA (UNC)
Wayne State College, NE (UNC)
Wayne State University, MI (UNC)
Weatherford College, TX (JRC)
Webber International University, FL (UNC)
Webb Institute, NY (UNC)
The Webb School, TN (PRC)
The Webb Schools, CA (PRC)
Weber State University, UT (UNC)
Webster College, FL (JRC)
Webster University, MO (UNC)
Weill Medical College of Cornell Univ, NY (GRD)
Welborn Baptist Hospital, IN (AHS)
Welder Training & Testing Institute, PA (TCT)
Wellesley College, MA (WMC)
Wells College, NY (UNC)
Wenatchee Valley College, WA (JRC)
Wentworth Institute of Technology, MA (UNC)
Wentworth Military Academy, MO (JRC)
Wentworth Military Academy, MO (PRC)
Wesleyan College, GA (WMC)
Wesleyan University, CT (UNC)
Wesley Biblical Seminary, MS (GRD)
Wesley College, DE (UNC)
Wesley College, MS (UNC)
Wesley Theological Seminary, DC (GRD)
West Boca Medical Center, FL (AHS)
Westbrook College, ME (UNC)
West Central Technical College, GA (TCT)
Westchester Community College, NY (JRC)
Westchester County Medical Center, NY (AHS)
Westchester School of Beauty Culture, NY (TCT)
West Chester University of Pennsylvania, PA (UNC)
West Coast Training, WA (TCT)
West Coast Ultrasound Institute, CA (TCT)
Westech College, CA (TCT)
Western Business College, OR (TCT)
Western Business College, WA (TCT)
Western Career College, CA (TCT)
Western Carolina University, NC (UNC)
Western Connecticut State University, CT (UNC)
Western Culinary Institute, OR (TCT)
Western Dakota Technical Institute, SD (TCT)
Western Governors University, UT (HMS)
Western Hills Sch of Beauty & Hair Dsgn., OH (TCT)
Western Illinois University, IL (UNC)
Western International University, AZ (UNC)
Western Iowa Tech Community College, IA (JRC)
Western Kentucky University, KY (UNC)
Western Michigan University, MI (UNC)
Western Nebraska Community College, NE (JRC)
Western Nevada Community College, NV (JRC)
Western New England College, MA (UNC)
Western New Mexico University, NM (UNC)
Western Oklahoma State College, OK (JRC)
Western Oregon University, OR (UNC)
Western Pacific Truck School, CA (TCT)
Western Pacific Truck School, WA (TCT)
Western Pennsylvania Hospital, PA (TCT)
Western Pennsylvania School for Blind, PA (HND)
Western Pennsylvania School for the Deaf, PA (HND)
Western Piedmont Community College, NC (JRC)
Western Reserve Academy, OH (PRC)
Western Reserve Care System, OH (AHS)
Western School of Health & Bus. Careers, PA (TCT)
Western Seminary, OR (GRD)
Western State College of Colorado, CO (UNC)
Western States Chiropractic College, OR (GRD)
Western State University College of Law, CA (GRD)
Western Technical College, TX (TCT)
Western Texas College, TX (JRC)
Western Theological Seminary, MI (GRD)
Western University of Health Sciences, CA (AHS)
Western Washington University, WA (UNC)
Western Wisconsin Technical College, WI (JRC)
Western Wyoming Community College, WY (JRC)
Westfield State College, MA (UNC)
West Georgia Technical College, GA (TCT)
West Hills Community College, CA (JRC)
West Jersey Health System, NJ (AHS)
West Kentucky Comm. & Technical College, KY (JRC)
Westlawn Institute of Marine Technology, CT (HMS)
West Liberty State College, WV (UNC)
West Los Angeles College, CA (JRC)
West Los Angeles VA Medical Center, CA (AHS)
West Michigan Coll of Barbering & Beauty, MI (TCT)
Westminister College, MO (UNC)
Westminster Choir College of Rider Univ., NJ (UNC)
Westminster College, PA (UNC)
Westminster College, UT (UNC)
Westminster School, CT (PRC)
Westminster Seminary California, CA (GRD)
Westminster Theological Seminary, PA (GRD)
Westmont College, CA (UNC)
Westmoreland County Community College, PA (JRC)
West Nottingham Academy, MD (PRC)
Weston Distance Learning, CO (HMS)
Weston Jesuit School of Theology, MA (TSR)
Westover School, CT (PRG)
West Park Hospital, WY (AHS)
West Shore Community College, MI (JRC)
West Suburban College of Nursing, IL (UNC)
West Tennessee Business College, TN (TCT)
West Texas A & M University, TX (UNC)
Westtown School, PA (PRC)
West Valley College, CA (JRC)
West Virginia Business College, WV (TCT)
West Virginia Career Institute, PA (TCT)
West Virginia Junior College, WV (JRC)
West Virginia Junior College, WV (TCT)
West Virginia Northern Community College, WV (JRC)
West Virginia Sch./Osteopathic Medicine, WV (GRD)
West Virginia Schools/Deaf and Blind, WV (HND)
West Virginia State University, WV (UNC)
West Virginia University, WV (UNC)
West Virginia University at Parkersburg, WV (UNC)
West Virginia University Hospital, WV (AHS)
West Virginia University Inst of Tech., WV (UNC)
West Virginia Wesleyan College, WV (UNC)
Westwood Aviation Institute, TX (TCT)
Westwood College, CA (TCT)
Westwood College, CA (UNC)
Westwood College, GA (TCT)
Westwood College, IL (TCT)
Westwood College, TX (TCT)
Westwood College - Denver North, CO (TCT)
Westwood College - Denver South, CO (TCT)
Westwood College - Houston South, TX (TCT)
Westwood College - Inland Empire, CA (TCT)
Westwood College of Aviation Technology, CA (TCT)
Westwood College of Aviation Technology, CO (TCT)
Westwood College of Technology, TX (TCT)
Westwood College - South Bay Campus, CA (TCT)
Wharton County Junior College, TX (JRC)
Whatcom Community College, WA (JRC)
Wheaton College, IL (UNC)
Wheaton College, MA (UNC)
Wheeling Hospital, WV (AHS)
Wheeling Jesuit University, WV (UNC)
Wheelock College, MA (UNC)
White Mountain School, NH (PRC)
Whitman College, WA (UNC)
Whittier College, CA (UNC)
Whittier College School of Law, CA (GRD)
Whitworth College, WA (UNC)
Wichita Area Technical College, KS (AAT)
Wichita Area Technical College, KS (TCT)
Wichita State University, KS (UNC)
Wichita Technical Institute, KS (TCT)
Wichita Technical Institute, MO (TCT)
Widener University, PA (UNC)
Widener University School of Law, DE (GRD)
Widener University School of Law, PA (GRD)
Wilberforce University, OH (UNC)
Wilbraham & Monson Academy, MA (PRC)
Wilbur Wright College North, IL (JRC)
Wiley College, TX (UNC)
Wilkes Barre General Hospital, PA (AHS)
Wilkes Community College, NC (JRC)
Wilkes Regional Medical Center, NC (TCT)
Wilkes University, PA (UNC)
Willamette University, OR (UNC)
William Beaumont Hospital, MI (AHS)
William Carey College, LA (UNC)
William Carey College, MS (UNC)
The William Center, VT (HND)
William Howard Taft University, CA (HMS)
William Jessup University, CA (UNC)
William Jewell College, MO (UNC)
William Mitchell College of Law, MN (GRD)
William Paterson University, NJ (UNC)
William Penn University, IA (UNC)
William Rainey Harper College, IL (JRC)
William Moore College of Technology, TN (TCT)
Williams Baptist College, AR (UNC)
Williamsburg Technical College, SC (JRC)
Williams College, MA (UNC)
Williamson Christian College, TN (UNC)
Williamson Free School of Mech. Trades, PA (TCT)
Williamsport Hospital, PA (AHS)
William T. McFatter Technical Center, FL (TCT)
William Woods University, MO (UNC)
Williston Northampton School, MA (PRC)
Williston Regional Day Program, VT (HND)
Williston State College, ND (JRC)
Wilmington College, DE (UNC)
Wilmington College, OH (UNC)
Wilson College, PA (WMC)
Wilson Technical Community College, NC (JRC)
Winchendon School, MA (PRC)
Winchester Memorial Hospital, VA (AHS)
Windham Community Memorial Hospital, CT (TCT)
Windham Regional Vocational Tech School, CT (TCT)
Windward Community College, HI (JRC)

X

Y

Z